W9-ABM-120

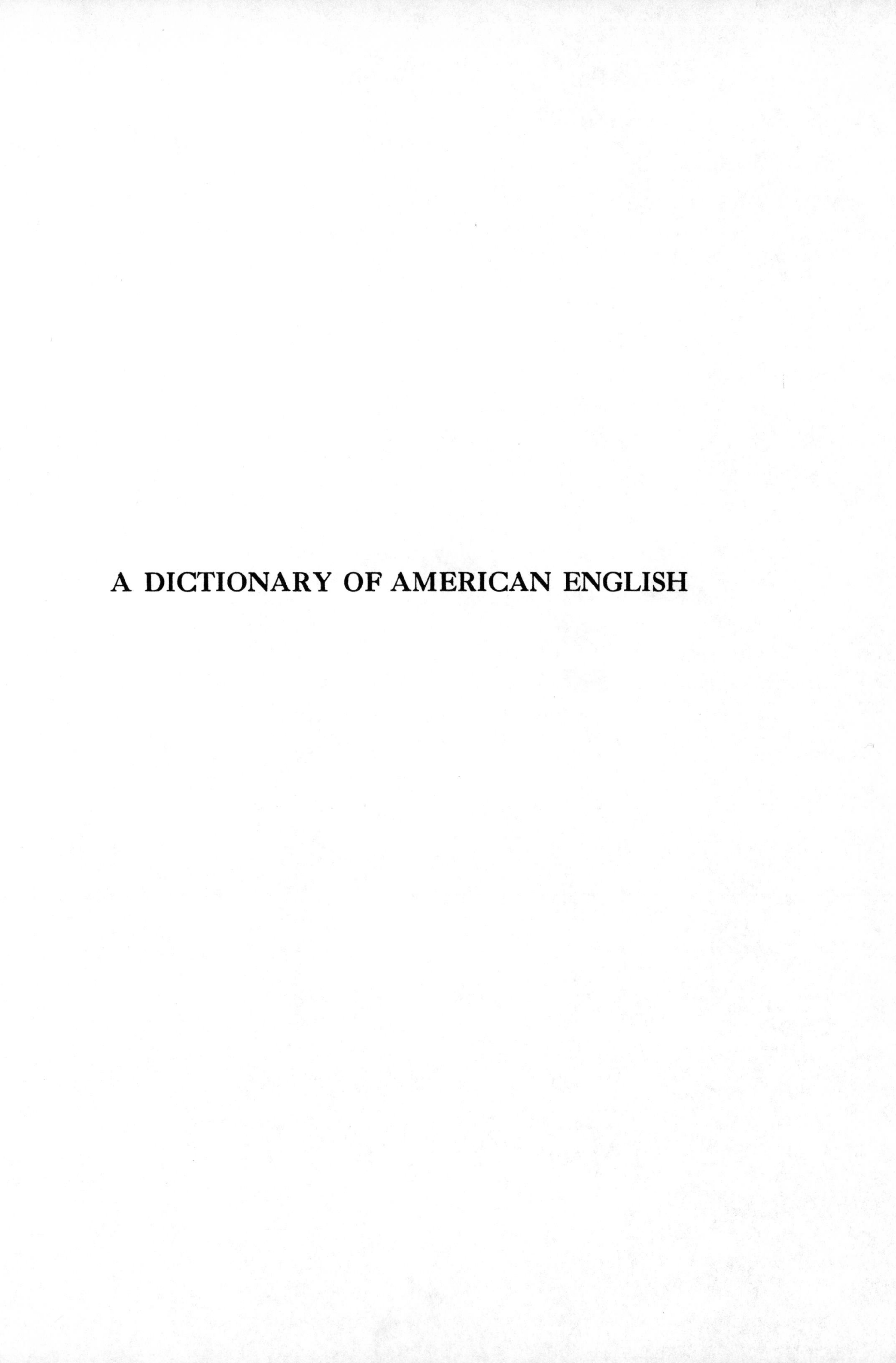

A DICTIONARY OF AMERICAN ENGLISH

A DICTIONARY OF AMERICAN ENGLISH

ON HISTORICAL PRINCIPLES

Compiled at
THE UNIVERSITY OF CHICAGO

under the editorship of
SIR WILLIAM A. CRAIGIE
Co-editor of the Oxford English Dictionary

and

JAMES R. HULBERT
Professor of English, the University of Chicago

VOLUME I, A—CORN PATCH

THE UNIVERSITY OF CHICAGO PRESS · CHICAGO · ILLINOIS

THE UNIVERSITY OF CHICAGO PRESS, CHICAGO 37
Oxford University Press, London, England
The University of Toronto Press, Toronto 5, Canada

 Published 1938. Fourth Impression 1960. Printed in the U.S.A.

PREFACE

A COMPLETE historical dictionary of American English would include and illustrate by dated quotations every word which has been current in the spoken or written language from the time when the first English-speaking colonists settled on these shores. Such a dictionary could be compiled, but only after very many years spent in collecting, and many more in digesting, the material collected. Not only is it impracticable at the present time, but its very comprehensiveness would render it ineffective in exhibiting clearly those features by which the English of the American colonies and the United States is distinguished from that of England and the rest of the English-speaking world. To do this as fully as possible is one of the chief aims of the present less ambitious work, which includes, however, not only words and phrases which are clearly or apparently of American origin, or have greater currency here than elsewhere, but also every word denoting something which has a real connection with the development of the country and the history of its people. Without going outside of these two principles of selection, it has been found necessary to collect and present a mass of evidence far surpassing in quantity what anyone would naturally anticipate.

Even on this basis some restrictions have been found advisable or necessary. The end of the nineteenth century has been selected as a fitting point at which to terminate the admission of new words, however common some of these may have become in recent use. The illustration of those already current before that date, however, is frequently carried into the first quarter of the present century. It has also been found necessary to restrict the inclusion of slang and dialect words to those which are of early date or special prominence, as those sections of the vocabulary can be treated with proper fulness only in separate dictionaries after special collections of material have been made for that purpose.

The different types of words and phrases which with these limitations properly find a place in the dictionary can be more readily ascertained by inspection than by any attempt at classification, although some idea of their number, variety, and interest will be obtained from the general survey given in the prefatory note to this volume. Whatever their nature may be, it is always a matter of interest to know in what relationship they stand to earlier or later English usage in Britain or the British colonies. To indicate this in a concise manner, certain symbols are used, the meanings of which are explained on another page. By observing these, and the appended dates when given, the reader will learn at a glance some of the essential facts regarding the history of each word or sense here recorded.

By far the greater part of the material on which the dictionary is based has been collected at the University of Chicago, from 1925 onward, by the editors and special staff engaged on the work, and by a considerable number of graduate and other students working under their direction. Useful contributions have also been made by students in other universities, especially those of Missouri and Kansas, thanks to the interest taken in the work by Professors Robert Lee Ramsay and Josephine May Burnham respectively. The Delegates of the Oxford University Press generously granted the free use of the American material collected for the *New English Dictionary*, in which up to the present time American usage has been more fully represented than in any other work. Full use has naturally been made of the successive collections of Americanisms by Pickering, Bartlett, Schele de Vere, Farmer, Clapin, and Thornton, as well as of the special works by Mr. Mencken and Professor Krapp. To Thornton in particular the dictionary is frequently indebted for its earliest instances, as well as the illustration of many colloquialisms and rarer uses. Through the courtesy of Harvard College it has been possible for the dictionary to utilize the twenty volumes of manuscript notes, many of them dealing with American English, made by the late C. W. Ernst, of Boston, and now deposited in the Treasure Room of Widener library.

When the dictionary is nearer completion it will be possible to publish a list of all the more important works cited in it, and to show what editions of these have been used. In the meantime every effort has been made to combine clearness with conciseness, so that the reader may readily be able to identify the work or edition referred to.

In a work of this nature, which primarily treats of words in their historical aspect and in relation to the thing or concept denoted by them, it is not necessary to deal, otherwise than exceptionally, with pronunciation and etymology, two of the features to which the usual dictionaries devote special attention and for which they are commonly consulted. The great majority of the words included here are of such a nature that their normal pronunciation is familiar to every educated person, and special comment is required only in rare instances. In these the appended note is as a rule of a historical nature rather than a statement of present-day forms or variants, such as are exhibited in the ordinary dictionaries or will be brought out by the linguistic survey now in progress. For a large proportion of the words, also, the ultimate etymology has only a remote interest, and has been indicated only when the word has come directly into American use or without having clearly passed through English before its adoption here.

The cost of the ten years' work spent in collecting the material for the dictionary, and in preparing it up to this point, has been mainly borne by research funds provided by the General Education Board of New York, with further contributions from the University of Chicago and the American Council of Learned Societies. The last-mentioned organization has also generously underwritten the cost of the printing of the first two parts. To these bodies, as well as to all those who have assisted in the collecting itself, the credit of having made the dictionary possible is justly due.

November 19, 1938

PREFATORY NOTE TO VOLUME I

THIS first volume of the dictionary contains the whole of the letters A and B, and about three-quarters of C. In each of these the character of the vocabulary varies to some extent, as will appear from the following brief classification of the more important words.

In A, the largest group of words denoting actual things consists of the names of plants or trees and animals. Of the former there are at least fifty requiring special notice, without reckoning more than forty which have *American* as a specific addition to the name (as in *American aloe*). These range from common words like *alder*, *almond*, *apple*, *artichoke*, *ash*, *aspen*, and *aster*, through those less familiar, as *absinthe*, *agrimony*, *amaranth*, *arrow-grass*, *avens*, up to the purely botanical names *ailanthus*, *althea*, *andromeda*, *arbor vitae*, etc. Some of the genera, and many of the species, are purely American, and have their history exhibited here for the first time; but even those familiar in English use, as *apple* or *ash*, have an American record which possesses points of interest. The list of animal names (including birds and insects) is smaller, but extends to more than fifty if those with the addition *American* are also reckoned. The most interesting of this group are the puzzling *alewife*, the *alligator* and *alligator gar*, the *American eagle* (both real and symbolic) and *American horse*. Of these *alewife* is purely American, as also are *ancon* (*sheep*) and *angleworm*.

Natural or artificial products, and some domestic or other articles, also provide a number of names of things. Among these, special interest attaches to *alkali* and *anthracite*, the *argand* and *astral* lamps, the *air-tight* stove and *andirons*, the *ash-hopper*, and the *axe* wielded by the *axeman*, together with *ambrotype*, *arctics*, and *artificials*. The importance of the apple in American life is illustrated by *apple brandy*, *-butter*, *-jack*, *pie*, *-sauce*, *-toddy*, etc., as well as by *apple-corer* and *-parer*, while the *ash-cake* and *ash-pone* are reminders of pioneer days. From these times also the *ark* or *accommodation boat* on the rivers, with the *accommodation car*, *coach*, *stage* or *train* and the *ambulance* on land, lead up to the *automobile* and *auto*, etc., of modern days.

Relating also to the world of tangible things are the words denoting buildings or parts of these, several of which have acquired special American senses, as *aisle*, *annex*, *apartment* (also with *building* or *hotel* added), *arcade*, *attic*, and *auditorium*. Noteworthy too are the special uses of *addition*, *alley* and *alleyway*, *area-way*, and *avenue*. To these may be added various topographical terms, as *air-line*, *alkali desert* (or *flat* or *plain*), *alluvion*, *arm* (of a stream, etc.), and *artery*. *Alder swamp* and *ash swamp* are examples of a large type of compounds in which the prevailing tree is used to distinguish the nature of the ground. Farming words (such as *acre* or *arpent*) are but slightly represented, but progress in this occupation can be clearly traced under *agricultural*, *agriculture*, and *agricultur(al)ist*.

Wider areas are represented by various proper names as *Alabama*, *Alaska*, *Albany*, *Alleghany*, *Arizona*, *Arkansas*. These, together with the adjectives derived from them, as *Alabamian*, etc., are frequently used as specific designations for a large variety of things. Great interest naturally attaches to the history of *America* and *American*, and the numerous special applications of the latter. Other names connecting places with persons, or designating particular races, are *Acadian*, *African* (as a synonym of *Negro*), *Algerine*, *Algonkin*, the invented *Amerind* or *Amerindian*, and *Apache*. The original connection with England survives in the compounds *Anglo-American*, *-Canadian*, and *-Indian*. The modern extended use of *Anglo-Saxon* also appears to owe much of its currency to American influence, while *aborigines* and *aboriginal* were, for natural reasons, largely used by American writers before they became common in England.

The military and naval terms naturally in the main designate things or places, as *abatis*, *accoutrement*, *ammunition*, *armament*, *armory*, *arsenal*, *artillery*, etc., or persons, as *adjutant*, *admiral*, *aid(e)-de-camp*, *artillerist*, but also include some that are more abstract, as *admiralty*, *alarm*, *ambuscade*, *ambush*, *armistice*, or *army*. The history of these is frequently made interesting by the natural difference between the colonial days and the new régime after 1774. The direct influence of French is sometimes apparent, as in *ambersear* and its variants for 'embrasure.'

The legal vocabulary presents few novelties (such as *affiant*) in the words themselves, but some show slight changes in meaning or have come into more familiar use than in England. At least forty are of some importance, including designations of persons, as *administrator*, *advocate*, *appellant*, *appraiser*, *attorney*, and *auditor;* legal proceedings or documents, as *affidavit*, *alienation*, *appeal* (with the *Court of appeals*), *appraisal*, *assignment*, and *assizes;* and offenses such as *arson* or *assault*.

Administration and politics, on the other hand, provide a large number of new terms in addition to fresh uses of the old. The richness of the vocabulary in this respect is a clear indication of the intense interest generally taken in public affairs, especially after 1774. It is only necessary to mention *abolition*, *admission* (of states), *Africanize*, *alien*, *ambassador*, *amendment*, *annexation*, *assembly*, and their derivatives or attributive uses, to indicate the historical importance of this class of words. An interesting group within it consists of those formed with the prefix *Anti-*, the number of which indicates the extent to which public opinion was liable to be divided on any subject, and some of which were of serious import, as *anti-abolition*, *-Catholic*, *-federal*, *-mason*, etc. In not a few cases the word acquires its special sense by being limited to particular circumstances, as *addresser*, (Indian) *agency* and *agent*, *American system* (of protective tariffs), *annexationist*, (Indian) *annuity*, *answer* (of Congress to the President), *apportionment* (of representatives), *assumption* (of state debts), *available* (as a candidate). In the quotations illustrating such words much interesting historical material will be found.

Society and social life are also well represented by a number of miscellaneous terms, the diversity of which can be inferred from such examples as *actor*, *actress*, *aid society*, *almshouse*, *amalgamation* (of the white and black races), *apple-bee*, *aristocrat*, *art-union*, *Athenaeum*, etc. Glimpses of history lie behind *ante-bellum*, *ante-revolutionary*, *anti-rent*, *anti-saloon*, *anti-slavery*, and *argonaut*.

Religious interests and movements account for a limited number of words, partly of older origin, as *Anabaptist*, *Antinomian* or *Arminian*, and partly new, either in actual formation, as *Adventist*, or in application, as *altar* (at open-air meetings), *apostle* (among the Mormons), *association*, and *awakening*. To the last group also belong the distinctive *amen corner* and *anxious bench* or *seat*.

Education too has its special vocabulary, chiefly in its higher branches, although it also includes *abecedarian*. The number of important terms is not great, but the articles on *academic(al)*, *academy*, *admittatur*, *advanced standing*, *alma mater*, *alumna* and *alumnus*, help to illustrate the progress of education during the centuries.

Commerce, industry, and finance play a smaller part in A than in various other letters, but are represented by some important words, as to *accommodate* (with a loan), *accommodation* (=loan), *advertisement*, *appreciate* (in value), *appreciation*, *appropriation*, *assay*, and *auction* (with *auction-block*, etc.). Among occupational names may be noted *accountant*, *adventurer*, *agent*, *apprentice*, *artist* (in its older senses), *assayer*, and *auctioneer*.

A different phase of the vocabulary is presented by the numerous entries of colloquial words and phrases, many of which are distinctively American either in origin or in their present-day currency. A number of these will be found recorded under the monosyllables or minor parts of speech, as *about*, *all*, *along*, *any*, *as*, *at*, and *away*. Others of a more definite type occur under *aboard*, *account*, *ahead*, *alive*, *almighty*, *ambition*, *A No. 1*, *a-plenty*, *apt*, *aside*, *awful*, and *awfully* (these last being recognized as Americanisms by English writers of a century ago). The colloquial *ain't* and *an't* are also illustrated, and a few dialectal forms, as *acrost*, *amost*, *ary*, *attackt*.

Some of these colloquialisms are survivals from older English, such as the frequent use of *a-* with verbal nouns illustrated under A *prep.*[1] 3, 4. A number of the more permanent examples of this are significant of special interests, as *a-fishing*, *a-fowling*, *a-gunning*, *a-hunting*, *a-shooting*, *a-sleighing*, and *a-whaling*. Other survivals of various types are *abovestairs*, *acold*, *acclimate*, *acclimation*, *accommodations*, *admire* or *aim* (to do a thing), *allow*, *ambition* (as a verb), *ancient* (=long-lived), *angle-rod*, *arrearage*, and *avails*.

Among miscellaneous Americanisms not mentioned above may be noted *absquatulate*, *affiliate* and *affiliation*, *amendatory*, *Americanism* itself, *Americanize* (and *-ization*), *Anglify*, and *appearing* (as in *fine-appearing*).

Only one foreign language, Spanish, has made direct contributions of any note, to the number of some twenty words, including *acequia*, *adobe*, *alameda* and *alamo*, *alcaide*, *alcalde*, *alfalfa*, *aparejo*, *arriero*, and *arroyo*. The Indian tongues (apart from proper names) are represented only by *apishemore* and *atamasco lily*.

The words beginning with B differ considerably in character from those in A, as the greater number of them designate things rather than ideas, so that the abstract element is less prominent than in the preceding letter. In other respects also the distribution is different. Names of trees and plants, for instance, are not quite so numerous as in A, although a fair number appear with the adjectives *black* and *blue*, as *black alder* and *blue ash*. Other tree names of some importance are *basswood*, *beech*, *big tree*, *birch*, *buckeye*, *and butternut*. Among plants and their produce are the *bayberry*, *bean*, *benne* (now proved to be of West African origin), *blueberry*, *blue grass*, *broomcorn*, and *buckwheat*. Animal life is represented by groups including the *badger*, *bear* (with the colloquial variant *bar*), *beaver*, *beef*, *bighorn*, *bison* or *buffalo*, and *bronco;* the *bald eagle*, *bluebird*, *bobolink*, *bobwhite*, and *buzzard;* the *bass* and *bullfrog;* the *bee*, the *boll weevil*, and the generic *bug*.

Articles of various kinds, implements, etc., include *bacon*, *bagasse*, *baggage* (yielding many compounds), *bagging*, *bale*, *banjo*, *bead*, *blanket*, *bowie knife*, *brogan*, *brownstone*, *buckshot*, *buckskin*, and *bull tongue* (plow). Travel by land or water is represented by *bobsled* and *buggy*, the *bark canoe*, *bat(t)eau* or *battoe*, and the *broadhorn*. Among terms of building are *balcony*, *barn*, *block*, and *blockhouse*, to which may be appended *barn-yard* and *boardfence*.

There are various distinctive topographical terms, as *backbone*, *bald*, *barren*, *bay*, *bayou*, *bench*, *bluff*, *bottom*, *branch*, and *butte*. Of special interest is the set of words formed by the extensive use of the adjective *back* to designate any part of the country lying behind the early settlements on the coast, as *back country, county, lands, parts, settlement,* and the better-known *backwoods* (now traced back to 1742), which has long passed into general English use. Similar terms are also used to designate the inhabitants of those areas, as *back farmer, inhabitant, settler,* and *backwoodsman* (from 1784). The names of localities occurring here are *Badger State, Bad Lands, Baltimore, Bay State, Bloody Ground* (Kentucky), *Border, Boston, Bourbon, Bowery,* and *Buckeye State.* Some of these have attributive uses or derivatives presenting points of interest, as *Border ruffian, Bostonese, Bostonian, Bourbon whisky,* and *Bowery boy.*

The administrative and political vocabulary is small compared to that found in A, but includes such varied types as *bailiff, bailiwick, barony, ballot* and *ballot-box, bureau, blue laws, blue lights, barn-burner, bloody shirt, bucktail, bulldoze,* and the verb and noun *bolt* expressing desertion of party.

Social activities or fashions are represented by a few such terms as *baseball, basket-ball, bee* (as in *apple-bee,* etc.), *bloomer(s), bundle* and *bundling.* The distinction of race denoted by the noun and adjective *black* may also be noted. Business, education, and religion are scantily represented by *bank* (with *bank bill,* etc.), *bakery, bar, bar-room, bachelor* (of arts), and *Baptists.*

The number of miscellaneous terms which either in themselves or in their special application can be classed as Americanisms is fairly large and characteristic. It includes *banner* (with *state,* etc.), *beat* (n. and v.), *begin, belittle, big bug, big knife, blaze* (n. and v.), *bleacher, blizzard, boatable, bogus, boodle, boom* (n. and v.), *boost, bootlegger, boss* (n. and v.), *brand* (n. and v.), *Britisher, Brother Jonathan, buck* (v.), *bullwhacker, bully* (adj.), *bum, bummer, bunco, buncombe* or *bunkum, burg, bushwhacking, bust* (=burst), *buster,* and *byme-by.* For most of these the dictionary presents fuller evidence than has hitherto been available, thus making clearer their origin, history, or place in the language.

The proportion of foreign words, not previously adopted or known in English, is remarkably small and unimportant. The Spanish *vaquero* appears disguised as *buckayro* and *buckaroo,* while *buckra* is one of the few Negro words of African origin which have become generally known.

A survey of the portion of C included in this volume shows that it contains a larger proportion of the abstract element than B, but it is also rich in concrete terms, some of which are of considerable importance. Among the names of trees and plants are *cactus, cane, cedar, cereals, checkerberry, cherry, chestnut, chokeberry, chokecherry, clover,* and *corn* in its specific American sense, along with the native *camas, cassine, catalpa, chinquapin, cohosh* and *coontie.* The animals, in addition to the important *cattle* with its compounds, include the *carcajou, caribou, catamount, cayuse, chickaree, chipmunk, cinnamon bear,* and *coon.* The birds supply the *canvas duck, chickadee,* and *chuck-will's-widow,* as well as the domestic *chicken.* The water yields the *catfish, cisco, clam,* and *cod,* and other forms include the *chigoe, chinch, chinch bug, cicada,* and *copperhead.*

Articles and substances of various kinds include the *canoe, car,* and *carryall; calico* and *carpetbag, cinch,* and *coonskin; clapboard, coal, copper,* and *copperas; chewing gum, chowder, cider,* and (corn) *cob.* Money is represented by the officially-named *cent.* In the matter of housing or building the more important words are *cabin, caboose, capitol,* and *chamber.*

A number of the topographical terms are noteworthy, as *campus, canal, canebrake, cañon* or *canyon, cape, chute, city, claybank, clearing, coast, common, continent* (with its adj. *continental*), *cooley,* and *corduroy* (*road,* etc.). Place names also are frequent and important, as *California* (which is not of American origin), *Canada, Cape Cod, Cape May, Carolina, Chautauqua, Chinatown, Colo-*

rado, *Columbia*, *Concord*, *Conestoga*, and *Connecticut*. The adjectives formed from these, as *Californian*, *Canadian*, and the attributive uses, as *Concord grape*, *Conestoga wagon*, add many distinctive terms to the vocabulary.

Administration, law and politics bulk largely here, as in A, because of the number of abstract terms beginning with *com-* and *con-*. Among the more important words are *cabinet*, *campaign*, *carpetbagger*, *caucus*, *census*, *chief magistrate*, *circuit court*, *circuit judge*, *collector*, *colony* (with *colonial*, *colonist*, *colonize*, etc.), *commission*, *commissioner*, *committee*, *committeeman*, *compromise*, *comptroller*, *confederacy*, *confederate*, *conferee*, *conference*, *congress* and *congressional*, *conservative*, *constable*, *constitution* with its derivatives, *convention*, and *copperhead*. In the material presented under these and other headings connected with them much information on many points of American history will be found.

Religion and ecclesiastical matters are represented by *Campbellite*, *camp meeting*, *Christian Science*, *church*, *circuit* (with *c. preacher* and *c. rider*), *congregation* with its derivatives, *consociate* and *consociation*. Under the head of education the more notable terms are *class*, *class day*, *classmate*, *coeducation*, *college*, *collegiate*, *commence*, *commencement*, and *common school*. Business or commercial interests account for special senses of *claim*, *clerk*, *company*, and *corner*.

Among the miscellaneous words which are either purely American in origin or have acquired a special American sense or currency are *cahoot(s)*, *cakewalk*, *calculate*, *calumet*, *camp*, *can* (n. and v.) and *canning*, *cave* (v.), *cavort*, *chance*, *chestnut*, *chink*, *chirk*, *chore*, *chunk*, *chunky*, *cinch*, *cloudburst*, *coast* (v.) and *coasting*, *cocktail*, *color* and *colored*, *come-back*, *commute* and *commuter*, *complected*, *conniption (fit)*, *considerable*, and *contraption*.

Words adopted from other languages are fairly numerous, as the Spanish *caballada* (with its colloquial forms *cavy-yard*, etc.), *caballero*, *cafeteria*, *calaboose*, *chaparral*, *chaparreras*, and the French *cache*. Various Indian languages are represented by the tribal names *Catawba*, *Cherokee*, *Cheyenne*, *Chickasaw*, *Chinook*, *Chippeway*, and *Choctaw*.

This survey of the more prominent words covered by the present volume will serve to indicate the extensive and varied character of its contents. A brief study of these alone will be sufficient to show that a historical dictionary of American English must be much more than a collection of Americanisms,—that it must illustrate fully the manifold ways in which the language has been adapted to the country and its inhabitants, and has thus constantly added new shades of meaning to ordinary words, given them a wider currency, or brought them into connection with new conditions and circumstances.

It is only by close comparison with the English record that it is possible to decide how much is really new in the American vocabulary. The requisite evidence for this is not always readily available, and special investigation may be necessary to obtain it. In the later portion of this volume various English datings, i.e. those enclosed within { }, can now be more correctly stated, and others can be added where no date has been given. The words in question, with the dates as now ascertained, are these: Bobtail, 5. a, 1605, 1829. Burning mountain, *c*1650. Californian, *a.*, 1759. Cardinal grosbeak, 1783. Cardroom, 1788. Carriage-builder, 1852. Carriageway, 1800. Carrion flower, 1842. Carrot seed, 1791. Cashmere, 2., 1839. Caspian tern, 1784. Casting, 2., 1851; 3., 1847. Castor-oil plant, 1809. Cast steel, 1791. Catch, *v.* 2., 1744 (in cricket). Catesby's lily, 1798, Cat ham (cat-hammed, 1844). Cat show, 1876. Cattle show, 1851. Cherry pie, 1747. Chunk, *n.* 1., 1672. Church session, 1646–85. Circular saw, 1825. City charter, 1766. Civil service, 1829. Class leader, 1815. Class meeting, 2., 1815. Clubhouse, 1818. Cochin China, 1848. Cod-fishing, 1734. Commercial traveller, 1841. Communication, 1. b., 1740. Compting room, 1684. Compulsory (education), 1861. Consulate, 1601. Corn country, 1734. Corner cupboard, 1838.

Of the staff which has been engaged in the preparation of the first volume of the Dictionary the more permanent and important members, whose efficient co-operation has been an important factor in the success of the undertaking, have been the following: Mr. George Watson, who did much valuable work as research associate and assistant editor, and had the charge of putting A and B through the Press; Dr. M. M. Mathews, who has all along been connected with the work in various ways, and has acted as assistant editor from the beginning of C; Mr. A. W. Read, who has also as assistant editor prepared a portion of the copy for C; Dr. Catherine Sturtevant, who after previously assisting in bibliographical work, in checking quotations, and in editing, has since 1937 supervised the preparation of copy and the correction of proof; Mrs. Tessa C. Bell, who from the beginning acted as secretary, helped to organize the collecting, and kept the steadily growing register of readers and books read; and Mrs. George D. Brodsky, whose careful copying and arranging of material has been of steady service for a number of years. More recently Mr. Woodford A. Heflin and Mr. Robert W. Wadsworth have joined the staff, and have worked on the last half of the volume.

The editors also desire to record their appreciation of the help given by Mr. Albert Matthews of Boston, who read the proofs of the first part (pp. 1–116), improved their contents by his criticisms, and generously furnished many additional illustrations from his own extensive collections.

And do not thou contemn this swelling tide,
  And stream of words, that now doth rise so high
Above the usual banks, and spreads so wide
  Over the borders of antiquity:
Which, I confess, comes ever amplify'd
  With th' abounding humours that do multiply.

. . . .

And who (in time) knows whither we may vent
  The treasure of our tongue? To what strange shores
This gain of our best glory shall be sent,
  T' enrich unknowing nations with our stores?
What worlds in th' yet unformed occident,
  May come refin'd with th' accents that are ours?

Or who can tell for what great work in hand
  The greatness of our style is now ordain'd?
What pow'rs it shall bring in, what spir'ts command?
  What thoughts let out; what humours keep restrain'd?
What mischief it may pow'rfully withstand;
  And what fair ends may thereby be attain'd?

1599, S. DANIEL, *Musophilus*, ad fin.

EXPLANATION OF SPECIAL LETTERING AND SYMBOLS

The size of the (boldface) type used for the heading of each entry indicates the relative importance of words with respect to their history or present currency.

The date of the quotation is usually followed by the author's name in capitals, or in small letters when he is quoting a source or when the name is that of the editor of the work.

* indicates that the word or sense is found in English before 1600.

+ indicates that the word or sense clearly or to all appearance originated within the present limits of the United States.

|| indicates that the term or sense is known only from the passage cited and may be an individualism.

{ } encloses the earliest, latest, or inclusive dates (so far as known) for the occurrence of the word or sense in England (or in other than American English), or a statement relative to this. When a definition is not preceded by a + mark but is followed by a date in braces later than that of the earliest quotation, it has been assumed that the sense is not (or is not with certainty) of American origin.

When none of these symbols is used, the inference is that the word or sense is to all appearance part of the common stock of English, although lexicographical evidence for deciding its precise origin is lacking.

† before a form in boldface type denotes that that spelling is obsolete.

[ ] frequently contains the etymology.

Editorial additions briefly elucidating some matter in a quotation are also given within brackets.

When enclosing quotations, brackets denote that such illustrations are inserted with a qualification, being sometimes anticipative of more definite American usage or illustrative of historical use and being sometimes the work of a non-American writer or of an American in a foreign environment.

' ' in the reference encloses the pseudonym under which the author produced the work quoted.

In references, large capitals indicate volumes, small capitals parts or sections, and lower-case letters chapters or prefatory pages, e.g. III., II., xxi.

When a subordinate sense marked **b** follows a sense which is not marked **a,** this signifies that the subordinate sense is derived from (i.e. is not collateral with) this antecedent sense.

Numbered paragraphs, (1), (2), etc., are used to illustrate different contexts in which the word occurs.

Paragraphs preceded by (*a*), (*b*), etc., exhibit different forms or spellings of the word.

The printing of a word in small capitals signifies that further information will be found under that word.

LIST OF ABBREVIATIONS

(In addition to many others that are obvious)

a (before a date)	= *ante*, before
a., *adj.*, adj.	= adjective
abbrev.	= abbreviation
absol., absol.	= absolute, -ly
ad. (in etymologies)	= adaptation of
adv., adv.	= adverb
app.	= apparently
attrib.	= attributive, -ly
B. '48 (etc.)	= Bartlett, 1848 (1859, 1877)
B. and L.	= Barrère and Leland (1889)
c (before a date)	= *circa*, about
Cent.	= Century Dictionary (1889–91)
Cf., cf.	= compare
Cl.	= Clapin (1902)
colloq.	= colloquial, -ly
colloq.[2]	= a lower grade of colloquialism
comb.	= combination
dial., dial.	= dialect
Dict.	= Dictionary
E.	= East
E.	= English
ellipt., ellipt.	= elliptical, -ly
Eng.	= England
esp.	= especially
F.	= Farmer (1889)
F., Fr.	= French
f. (in etymologies)	= formed on
F. and H.	= Farmer and Henley (1890–1904)
fem.	= feminine
fig., fig.	= figurative, -ly
freq.	= frequent, -ly
intr.	= intransitive
It.	= Italian
L.	= Latin
masc.	= masculine
mod.	= modern
Mex.	= Mexican
n., n.	= noun
Obs., obs.	= obsolete
occas.	= occasional, -ly
O.E.D.	= Oxford English Dictionary
Pg.	= Portuguese
Pick.	= Pickering (1816)
p.p.	= past participle
ppl. a., ppl. a.	= participial adjective
pple.	= participle
prep., prep.	= preposition
pron.	= pronoun
pronunc.	= pronunciation
Prov.	= Provencal
pr. pple.	= present participle
p.t.	= past tense
q.v.	= *quod vide*, which see
refl., refl.	= reflexive
S.	= South
Sc., Sc.	= Scotch
sc.	= *scilicet*, namely
S.E.	= South-East
Sp.	= Spanish
spec., spec.	= specifically
Stand.	= Standard Dictionary (1893–95)
s.v.	= *sub voce*, under the word
S.W.	= South-West
Th.	= Thornton *Glossary*
Th. S.	= Thornton *Supplement*
tr.	= transitive
transf., transf.	= transferred sense
v., vb.	= verb
var.	= variant of
vbl. n.	= verbal noun
W.	= West
W. '06 (etc.)	= Webster, 1806 (1828, etc.)
Worc.	= Worcester (1846, 1860)

A

***A,** *letter.* Also † **ay.** First letter of the alphabet.

I. 1. As a brand or mark.

+In quots. used as the initial letter of *Adulterer* or *Adulteress:* cf. AD.

1651 *Maine Province & Ct. Rec.* (1928) I. 164 Its ordered that mis Batcheller for her adultery shall . . . be branded with the letter A. **1694** *Mass. Acts & Resolves* (1869) I. 171 Every person and persons so offending shall for ever after wear a capital A. **1784** *Conn. Acts & Laws* 8 Both of them shall be . . . burnt on the Forehead with the Letter A, on a hot Iron. **1837** HAWTHORNE in *Salem Gazette* 14 Nov. 1/3 A young woman . . . whose doom it was to wear the letter A on the breast of her gown, . . . so that the capital A might have been thought to mean Admirable, or any thing rather than Adulteress. **1850** — *Scarlet Letter* 37 This rag of scarlet cloth . . . assumed the shape of a letter. It was the capital letter A.

+2. The highest mark for university, college, or school class-work. *Straight A's*, a continuous series of such marks.

The system of grading by means of the letters A, B, C, etc., has been used in various institutions (e.g. Augustana College, Rock Island, Ill.) since 1883.

1897 FLANDRAU *Harvard Episodes* 57 'College life,' mutters the father of the man who got sixteen A's and brain fever.

3. Denoting a superior or the best grade of a commodity.

1886 *Harper's Mag.* June 93/1 'A' sugar is simply a term to designate the higher grades. . . . 'B' sugar is more brown.

II. 4. *From A to izzard* (*zee*, or *zed*): **a.** From beginning to end of the alphabet. *colloq.* or *dial.* {1799}

1830 in *Mass. Spy* 28 July, I will teach you your alphabet from A to Zed and from Zed back again to A. [Given as a Southernism (Th.).] **1839** BRIGGS *H. Franco* I. 4 She read the dictionary through from *A* to *izzard.* **1846** *Spirit of Times* (N.Y.) 25 April 108/1 The names of the numerous beauties, from A to Izzard, well 'asterisked.'

+b. Thoroughly; completely.

1864 A. J. DICKSON *Across Plains* (1929) 134, I immediately went into conference with my neighbor, . . . who knows wagons from "a to izzard." **1910** C. HARRIS *Eve's Husband* 127, I ransacked my incompetency from A to izzard.

+5. *A and izzard*, the beginning and end.

1835 [P. H. NICKLIN] *Virginia Springs* 19 That celebrated spot which is . . . the Ay and Izzard of a tour to the Virginia Springs.

***A,** *prep.*[1] Now *colloq.* or *dial.* [Reduced form of *o'*, *on.*]

I. *1. Of location: On, upon. {-1645, 1861, now *dial.*}

1622 'MOURT' *Relation* 64 That night we returned againe a ship board. **1674** *Brookhaven Rec.* 34 Whosoever shall run . . . a hors back in the streetes . . . shall forfet 10s. **1669** *Md. Archives* II. 159 Sett a Beggar a horse back & he will ride. **1909** WASON *Happy Hawkins* 18, I then noticed two fellers a hoss back. **1910** J. HART *Vigilante Girl* xxii. 315 The rogue who was a-ship had divided the swag with the rogue who was ashore.

***b.** To or at (one side). {-1684}

1823 COOPER *Pioneers* xxxiv, Knocking that carpenter's face a-one-side, as you call it. **1845** SIMMS *Wigwam & Cabin* 46 And there, a little a-one side, . . . was a woman.

***2.** Of time: On, at. {-1721; now in archaic phrases.}

1686 SEWALL *Diary* I. 134 Seeing the warrants to arrive a Thorsday night. **1707** *Virginia State P.* I. 117 We had taken five more of them a Monday. **1775** *Essex Inst. Coll.* XIII. 162 After I got here a Friday. **1849** *Knickerb.* XXXIV. 151/1 This lady read a play to Bunkum a-Monday week. **1871** EGGLESTON *Hoosier Schoolm.* xii. 108 We'll tend to his case a Christmas. **1891** R. T. COOKE *Huckleberries* 143 Ef we have the chintz by sundown a Saturday.

II. With gerund (and frequently hyphened).

Much more freq. used colloq. in U.S. than in England. 'In literary Eng. the *a* is [now] omitted. . . . But most of the southern [English] dialects, and the vulgar speech both in England and America, retain the earlier usage' (O.E.D.).

***3.** In the action of (doing something). Cf. A-FISHING, A-GUNNING, A-HUNTING, etc. {1523-1769; in later use *colloq.* and *dial.*}

1637 *Essex Inst. Coll.* IX. 49 Giles . . . said I was the strangest troublesome man a falling out and quarrelling. **1638** UNDERHILL *Newes from America* 18 Thinking his own vessel to be there a trading with them. **1654** JOHNSON *Wonder-W. Prov.* 171 When any Vessel was a coming in. **1674** *Conn. Public Rec.* II. 237 His mercy . . . in so signally a freeing us from those eminent dangers of warr. **1681** *Huntington Rec.* I. 317 [Indians] ware seen the next morning . . . a drinking the Rum. **1684** Q. STOCKWELL in I. Mather *Providences* (1684) 33 We went over a mighty mountain; we were eight dayes a going over it. **1684** *Portsmouth Rec.* 222 If any Swine be seen a killing of a lamb. **1692** *Md. Hist. Mag.* XIII. 208 His store . . . [was] full of Indians a dealing with him for goods. **1726** FRANKLIN *Journal* Wks. 1905 II. 58 The oyster-merchants . . . lay them upon certain beds in the river . . . a-fattening. **1760** *Essex Inst. Coll.* XX. 205 The men kept continually a grinding there Axes. **1770** *Carroll P.* in *Md. Hist. Mag.* XIII. 59 We are busy a housing, ploughing, in our wheat. **1772** *Ib.* XIV. 287 The Smiths being out a Coaling. **1832** PAULDING *Westward Ho* I. 121 The bear I shot . . . while we were a-wooding. *c***1845** W. I. PAULDING *Madmen All* 190 Like a real Kaintucky porker a-rootin' in the woods. **1846** *Knickerb.* XXVII. 276, I was in the woods a-chopping. **1863** 'GAIL HAMILTON' *Gala-Days* 36, I stop for the night a-cousining. **1871** STOWE *Sam Lawson* 10 He'd spent days in the woods a-loggin' and . . . a-lumberin'. **1893** CRITTENDEN *Ranch Verses* 12 The cattle are 'a-browzin'.'

***4.** With verbs of motion in similar use.

*a***1649** WINTHROP *Hist.* 346 The Welcome, of Boston, about 300 tons. . . . fell a rolling. **1704** *Boston News-Letter* 22 May 2/2 Peter Lawrence is going a Privateering from Rhode Island in a good Sloop. **1757** *Lett. to Washington* II. 62 Order them out in Parties with some of Your Men a Scalping. **1760** R. ROGERS *Journals* 161 Capt. James Tute . . . went out a scouting. **1771** WASHINGTON *Diaries* II. 42 Went a driving in his Neck after breakfast. **1828** *Yankee* July 227/1 It is new for city girls to go a black-berrying. **1845** COOPER *Chainbearer* xxiii, I went a berryin' this forenoon. **1848** *Knickerb.* XVIII. 224 He only came 'to go a-crabbing, or may-be a-eeling in Swan Creek.' **1854** THOREAU *Walden* 222 If he and his family would live simply, they might all go a-huckle-berrying. **1855** [PRAY] *Mem. J. G. Bennet* 155 Come, my love, let's a shopping in this classic town. **1858** THOREAU *Maine Woods* 86 Joe had conducted two white men a-moose-hunting in the same direction the year before. **1909** STRATTON-PORTER *Girl of Limberlost* xxi. 390 When he's afraid he just goes a-humping for Aunt Margaret.

***A,** *prep.*[2] Now *colloq.* or *dial.* [Reduced form of *o'*, *of.*] Of. {-1673; now *dial.*}

1622-1772 [see A CLOCK]. **1662** *R. I. Court Rec.* II. 21 William Marble of Boston being . . . found guilty a riott. **1672** *Brookhaven Rec.* 43 A pound a butter. **1676** *New Castle Court Rec.* 39 The tyme a yeare nott admitting my doing what [etc.]. **1775** *Essex Inst. Coll.* XLVIII. 61 Our men com of [=off] a Cobil hil jest at the don [=dawn] of the day. **1843** 'CARLTON' *New Purchase* I. xii. 92 After that the path's a sort a blind. **1898** WESTCOTT *D. Harum* 345 What do you say? . . . 'll you make it a couple a hunderd?

***A,** *v.* Now *colloq.* or *dial.* Also **'a, 'a'.** Reduced form of 'have.' Followed by p.p., with which it is occas. hyphened. {Now *colloq.* or *dial.*}

1658 *Southold Rec.* I. 472 Beefe and pork . . . would a bin as good as beaver to him. **1692** *Essex Inst. Coll.* XLV. 142 His wife would a done with it in tyme. **1697** *Ib.* XI. 79 Attwood should a bin bound to William Baker. **1777** *Ib.* XLV. 208 Mr. Brown . . . had like to a been lost. **1777** *Md. Hist. Mag.* VI. 144 You would not a thought of Billy Ogg's house. **1840** COOPER *Pathfinder* ii, The lad would have dashed into a Mingo camp single-handed, rather than not a-come. **1854** M. J. HOLMES *Tempest & Sunshine* xv. 212 Yes, it *is* Bill, and no mistake, but who'd a thought it. **1859** STOWE *Minister's Wooing* xvi, You ought to 'a' heard her talk. **1878** BEADLE *Western Wilds* 186 They might a got it stopped then. **1898** PAGE *Red Rock* 483 If Delia Dove had been where I was, she'd never 'a surrendered.

***A,** *prefix.* With past pples. {-1684; now *dial.*}

1759 *Essex Inst. Coll.* XIX. 65, I . . . found that we was abelated out at 4 pence per Day. **1788** WASHINGTON *Diaries* III. 295 The house [was] a good deal a dangered.

A 1, *phrase.* Also **A-1.** [In E. orig. the highest classification of a vessel and stores on Lloyd's list. Cf. A No. 1.] First-class. {1837-}

1846 HOLMES *Berkshire Festival* 44 He . . . murmurs unconscious of space and of time, 'A 1. Extra-super.' **1857** CONGDON *Tribune Essays* (1869) 10 The agonies of the A1 carpenters and the griefs of the superior blacksmiths. **1875** 'MARK TWAIN' *Sk., Some Learned Fables,* The A1 Barber Shop. **1887** TOURGEE *Button's Inn* 125 She's A-1, all wool, . . . and a yard wide! **1897** R. M. STUART *Simpkinsville* 13 Proph' was a capital A-1 hunter. **1902** 'MARK TWAIN' in *Harper's Mag.* Jan. 267 When it comes to A1 right-down solid mysteriousness.

Aaron's rod. *local.* [Cf. Numbers xvii. 8.] {1834-, of other plants.} +The common orpine, *Sedum telephium.* — **1891** *Cent., Sedum Telephium,* . . . known as Aaron's-rod because sometimes growing when pressed and apparently dried. **1891** *Amer. Folk-Lore* IV. 148 *Sedum telephium* . . . : in New Hampshire I have found it called Blow-leaf, also Aaron's Rod. **1892** *Ib.* V. 96.

A.B. [Abbreviation.]

1. An abbrev. of med. and mod. L. *Artium baccalaureus* 'Bachelor of Arts' (see BACHELOR). {In E. more usu. B.A.}

1773 *Boston News Letter* 29 April 2/2 Last Friday departed this life, after a lingering illness, John Alden, A.B., aged 22. **1798** O. THOMPSON (*title*), An Oration, Urging the Necessity of Religion, . . . By Otis Thompson, A.B. **1827** *Harvard Reg.* Dec. 194 A piece of parchment . . . certifying that I am admitted to be by all A. B.! **1840** DANA *Two Years* xxviii. 320 Then I could see them receiving their A.B.s from the dignified, feudal-looking President [of Harvard]. **1842** *Knickerb.* XIX. 429 A man may go through college and write A.B. after his name, and even A.M., and be no great things either. **1853** *Songs of Yale* Preface 4 Presentation Day . . . , when the graduating Class . . . are presented to the President as qualified for the first degree, or the A.B. **1871** [L. H. BAGG] *At Yale* 549 One [graduate] . . . came up to New Haven at the close of senior year, passed the term and annual examinations of the four years' course, and so secured his A.B. degree. **1893** POST *Harvard Stories* 274 Jack . . . lost a *cum laude* and had to 'take his A.B. straight.' **1895** *Rep. to Harvard Club of Chicago* 2 Such graduates as had educational qualifications equivalent to the Harvard A.B.

2. *Naut.* An abbrev. (esp. in ships' papers) of 'able-bodied.'

1847 *Knickerb.* XXIX. 151 Observe this group of sailors; real A.B. sailors.

***Aback,** *adv.* +*Aback of,* back from. *Obs.* or *dial.* (Cf. BACK *of.*) — **1783** W. FLEMING in *Travels Amer. Col.* 663 Fern Creek is lost in ponds and low flat land a back of the Falls. **1836** EDWARD *Hist. Texas* v. 79 Those districts . . . aback of the older settled ones.

+**Abalone.** *Calif.* Also **abelone.** [Mexican-Sp. Cf. AVALONE.] A univalve mollusc of the genus *Haliotis;* a sea-ear or ear-shell. Also attrib., esp. with *shell.*

1870 *Amer. Naturalist* III. 250 These shells are popularly called Sea-ears. . . . In California the people call them *Abalones. Ib.* 256 The exports of Haliotis or Abalone shells from San Francisco . . . in the year 1866. **1883** GOODE *Fishery Industr. U.S.* (1887) II. 622 The Abalone Fishery. *Ib.*, In California these mollusks are all known as "abalone," which is said to be a corruption of Spanish *aulon* or *aulone.* **1887** JACKSON *Between Whiles* ii. 172 A bit of carved abalone shell Alf had got from a Nez Percé Indian. **1889** *Cent., Abalone-meat,* the dried animal of the abalone. It is exported from California in large quantities. **1902** BRET HARTE in *Harper's Mag.* April 735/1 A small tanklike sitting-room, whose chief decorations consisted of large *abelone* shells, dried marine algæ, coral.

***Abate,** *v.* +*tr.* To refrain from exacting (customs); to remit. — **1715** *Mass. H. Repr. Journals* I. 48 Praying that the Duty upon Eleven Negro Women and Children by him Imported, may be abated. **1718** *Ib.* II. 67 Praying that the Duty of Four Pounds on a Negro Boy he lately imported, may be abated. **1806** WEBSTER, *Abate,* v., to . . . remit as a tax (Con.).

||**Abatied,** *pp.* Also †**abbatied.** [ABATIS. Cf. later E. *abatised.*] Furnished with an abatis. — **1781** WASHINGTON *Diaries* II. 239 The Batteries . . . appeared to be well friezed, ditched and abbatied. *Ib.*, Fort N. 8 is also abatied and friezed at the top.

Abatis. Also **abattis, abbatis;** † **abbate, abbette, -ee, abbertee.** [F. *abatis.*]

1. *Mil.* A defence or obstruction formed of felled trees piled lengthwise with the sharpened ends of boughs and branches pointing in the direction of the expected assault. {1766-}

1775 SCHUYLER in Sparks *Corr. Rev.* (1853) I. 6 He has picketed the ditch, and secured it with an abatis. **1777** *Md. Hist. Mag.* V. 227 They have strengthen'd the first work . . . with Pickquets & Abbateis. **1779** *Mass. H. S. Coll.* 2 Ser. II. 470 The troops . . . had made an Abbertee fort for their Security against the enemy. **1809** IRVING *Knickerb.* III. ix, He forthwith proceeded to . . . fortify his position with a double row of abbatis. **1849** PARKMAN *Oregon Trail* 11 Dead and broken trees, thick-set as a military abattis. **1862** McClellan *Own Story* 272 Every kind of obstruction which the country affords, such as abattis, marsh, inundation, etc., was skilfully used. **1892** JACKSON *Memoirs* xxii. 439 An abatis . . . felled to protect the approach to some woods. **1907** C. C. ANDREWS *Recoll.* 195 My skirmish line . . . pressed on . . . over fallen trees, and two lines of abbatis.

transf. **1888** E. B. CUSTER *Tenting on Plains* vii. 212 In a land of venomous serpents, it behooved a man to carry his own abatis everywhere.

||**2.** *transf.* An array of fallen trees.

1902 WHITE *Blazed Trail* xx. 152 There had interposed in his trail abattises [*sic*] of down timber a quarter of a mile wide.

Abattoir. Also **abbatoir.** [F. *abattoir.*] A public slaughter-house. {1840-}

[**1847** WEBSTER.] **1867-8** *Ill. Agric. Soc. Trans.* VII. 466 Number of Hogs Slaughtered at the Communipaw Abbatoirs, N. Y., **1889** *Cent.* s.v., In . . . the United States abattoirs of great size have been erected . . . for the humane and rapid slaughter of large numbers of animals. **1893** POST *Harvard Stories* 49 He was in a four-oar above the Brighton abattoir.

A, B, C. Also **A, B, and C.**

1. In allusive or fig. use. {1879-}

1802 *Ann. 7th Congress* 1 Sess. 1173 The operation is as plain as A, B, C. **1845** JUDD *Margaret* I. ii. 6 We must get the master to learn you your a, b, c's in this matter. **1868** MRS. WHITNEY *P. Strong* 201 Not by any means with A, B, and C regularity either. **1877** *Vermont Bd. Agric. Rep.* IV. 33 It is believed that we of this nineteenth century . . . are yet in our *a, b, c* of a complete and perfected agriculture. **1887** N. PERRY *Flock of Girls* 128 Marigold was stupid on . . . some points that to the keen, practical girl . . . seem like A, B, C.

+**2.** *Gaming.* (See quotation.)

1841 *Laws Ala.* 145 If any person shall hereafter be guilty of keeping . . . any gaming table, called A B C or E O, or roulette, or rowley powley.

Abecedarian. Also **abcdarian.** [med. L. *abecedarius,* adj.] One who is learning the alphabet; one of a school-class acquiring rudiments. {1603}

1668 F. Drake *Roxbury* (1878) 195 [John Prudden promised] to instruct . . . the children, . . . all A. B. C. Darians excepted. **1845** JUDD *Margaret* II. i. 195 The goal of every breathless, whip-fearing, abcdarian's valorous strife, the high-sounding Amperzand, no letter! **1857** M. J. HOLMES *Meadow-Brook* vi, At a quarter of four, I called up my class of Abecedarians to read. **1856** GOODRICH *Recoll.* I. 39 The little brood which gathered under the wing of Aunt Delight, when I was an a-b-c-darian. **1880** *New Eng. Journal of Educ.* 20 May 325/1, [Timetable] 9.00 to 9.15 Opening Exercise; 9.15 to 9.25 Abecedarians; [etc.]. . . . Abecedarians should have at least four recitations per day.

Abele. [Du. *abeel.*] The white or silver poplar tree, *Populus alba.* Also attrib. with *tree.* {1681-}

1828 WEBSTER (citing *Encyc.*) s. v. *Poplar,* The abele, the white poplar, the black poplar. **1847** WOOD *Botany* 507 Abele or Silver-leaf Poplar, . . . a highly ornamental tree, native of Europe. **1852** *Horticulturist* VII. 347 If the nurserymen *will* raise Ailanthus and Abeles by the thousands, . . . and tell us nothing about pestilential odors and suckers. **1892** APGAR *Trees Northern U.S.* 168 White Poplar or Abele Tree. Branches very white with down when young.

+**Aberginian, -ean.** *Hist.* Also **Abarginian, Abergenian.** (See quotations and cf. next.)

App. a native name and not an early formation from L. *aborigines.*

1634 WOOD *New Eng. Prospect* II. i. 57 Our Indians that live to the North-ward of them be called Abarginians. *Ib.* 49 The very name of a Mowhack would strike the heart of a poore Abergenian dead. **1687** R. BLOME *Isles & Terr. in Amer.* 232 To the North [are the] Aberginians. **1701** C. W[OLLEY] *Journal N. Y.* (1902) 34 The Aberginians or Northern Indians in New-England. **1764** HUTCHINSON *Hist. Mass.* I. 456 There was great enmity between the Tarrenteens and Aberginians, or Indians of Massachusets bay. *a***1817** DWIGHT *Travels* III. 39 The two last of these [Indian] nations I suppose to have been comprehended under the common name of Aberginians. **1832** WILLIAMSON *Maine* I. 459 The clans between the Pawkunawkutts and the Piscataqua . . . have been called the 'Abergineans,' or Northern Indians.

+**Aberginny,** *a.* Also **Abergeny, -ieney.** [See prec.] Belonging to the 'Aberginians.' — **1628** LEVETT in *Mass. H. S. Coll.* 3 Ser. VIII. 174 Two sagamores . . . [said] that I had the right fashion of the aberieney sagamores. **1643** WILLIAMS *Key* 21 Natives, Salvages, . . . Abergeny men, Pagans, Barbarians, Heathen. **1654** JOHNSON *Wonder-W. Prov.* 16 The Abarginny-men consisting of Mattachusets, Wippanaps and Tarratines.

+**Abert's finch, pipilo, towhee.** [J. J. *Abert,* 1820-97.] The gray towhee, *Pipilo aberti.* — **1869** *Amer. Naturalist* III. 472, I was struck with surprise at the great numbers of Abert's Finch . . . frequenting the grove. *Ib.* 476 [I] obtained the first eggs of . . . Abert's Pipilo. **1890** *Cent.* 4506, In the southwest, and thence into Mexico, is another set of species, of plain grayish coloration in both sexes, as . . . Abert's towhee, *P. aberti.*

+**Abisselfa.** *S.* Also **abbiselfa.** [Lit. '*a* by itself *a.*'] (See quot. 1848.) — **1835** [LONGSTREET] *Georgia Scenes* 76 In the good old days of fescues, abisselfas, and anpersants. **1848** BARTLETT 1 In the olden time, the first letter of the alphabet was denominated 'abisselfa' when it formed a syllable by itself, as in the word *able.*

||**Abluvion.** [med. L. *abluvion-em.*] The action or process of washing away. — *a***1817** DWIGHT *Travels* II. 57 Several considerable lots have been washed away from the Hadley shore. . . . It cannot be wondered at, that this process of alluvion, and abluvion, which has gone on ever since the deluge, . . . should produce even greater changes than these.

***Aboard,** *adv.*

+**1.** *All aboard,* the call of a conductor directing passengers to enter a train, street-car, etc. that is about to start.

Originally an announcement that all the passengers were on board a vessel or vehicle. 'Many even of the coach-phrases in America are derived from a seafaring life; as, for instance, . . . "Are ye all aboard?"' (1841 Buckingham *America* II. 127).

1837 J. C. NEAL *Charcoal Sk.* (1838) 76 He . . . gave himself a gentle impulse, crying 'All aboard!' and slid slowly but majestically down. **1853** B. F. TAYLOR *Jan. & June* 57 The shrill whistle of the iron boatswain [of a train] as he pipes 'all aboard.' **1865** TROWBRIDGE *Three Scouts* xix. 189 The signal-bell was ringing. . . . 'All aboard!' cried the conductor, waving his hand at the engineer. **1873** BEADLE *Undevel. West* 251 All aboard for Yosemite and the Big Trees. **1887** GEORGE *40 Yrs. on Rail* 37 Wright . . . waved his hand to the engineer and shouted 'All aboard.' **1902** MCFAUL *Ike Glidden* xxxi. 297 He and his bride boarded the train, and the conductor announced 'All aboard.'

transf. **1878** I. L. BIRD *Rocky Mts.* 148 'Head them [=cattle] off, boys!' our leader shouted; 'all aboard! hark away!' and . . . away we all went at a hand-gallop. **1907** C. C. ANDREWS *Recoll.* 169 At dusk a non-commissioned officer of the guard would call out 'All aboard,' and upstairs we promptly would go.

+**2.** On, or into, a railroad train.

1856 M. J. HOLMES *L. Rivers* iv. 33 She . . . told him that 'the trunks . . . were every one on 'em left!' 'No, they are not. . . . I saw them aboard myself.' **1887** GEORGE *40 Years on Rail* iv. 55 They jumped aboard while the engineer got out to investigate into the cause of our delay. **1901** MERWIN & WEBSTER *Calumet K* xv. 297, I . . . jumped for the lever and hollered for him to get aboard.

+**b.** On horseback. *humorous.*

1884 SWEET & KNOX *Through Texas* v. 63 At one o'clock we were all aboard.

+**3.** *colloq.* or *slang.* Within one.

1851 A. T. JACKSON *Forty-niner* (1920) 47 But towards morning some of the men got too much gin aboard and a quarrel started.

* **Aboard,** *prep.* +On or into (a train, street-car, etc.).

1855 *Knickerb.* XLV. 561, I . . . put myself 'a-board' the six-o'clock Train. **1874** B. F. TAYLOR *World on Wheels* I. xvi. 121 Climb aboard the train and be a passenger. **1883** DE VERE in *Encycl. Brit.* Suppl. I. 201/2 Travellers by rail are urged to 'go aboard the cars,' as coaches are called. **1884** *Harper's Mag.* Aug. 465/1 In ten minutes more they were aboard the train. **1901** MCCUTCHEON *Graustark* 26 You might have climbed aboard the train.

+**Abogado.** *S.E. & S.W.* [Sp.] An advocate or counselor-at-law. — **1803** *Ann. 8th Congress* 2 Sess. 1517 The fees of the Abogado, or person consulted by the judges on law points, are twelve and a half cents for every leaf of which the process consists. **1884** BRET HARTE *On Frontier* 199 Why did you send for the abogado Poindexter when my brother called? **1889** *Cent., Abogado* . . . [is thus] used in parts of the United States settled by Spaniards.

* **Abolish,** *v. tr.* To put an end to (slavery and the slave-trade); to suppress. {1728-}

1773 FRANKLIN *Writings* (1906) VI. 39, I have since had the Satisfaction to learn that a Disposition to abolish Slavery prevails in North America. **1790** *Ann. 1st Congress* I. 1241 Did it not desire Congress to interfere and abolish the slave trade? **1840** CHANNING *Works* 589/1 The Free States cannot rightfully use the power of their own legislatures or of Congress to abolish slavery in the States where it is established. **1862** EMERSON *Misc.* (1892) 285 Congress can, by edict, . . . abolish slavery, and pay for such slaves as we ought to pay for. **1879** TOURGEE *Fool's Errand* xxi. 128 It has always been claimed that slavery was abolished as a military necessity.

* **ABOLITION.** Now *Hist.*

1. The suppression *of* the slave-trade or *of* slavery, esp. by legislative action; the legal extinction *of* slavery. {1788-}

1787 *Synod of N. Y. & Phila. Minutes* 539-40 The Synod . . . recommend . . . to every member of their body . . . to do every thing in their power . . . to promote the abolition of slavery. **1789** FRANKLIN *Writings* X. 61, I wish success to your endeavours for obtaining an abolition of the Slave trade. **1790** *Ann. 1st Congress* I. 1239 The following memorial of the Pennsylvania Society for promoting the Abolition of Slavery. **1822** *Ann. 17th Congress* 1 Sess. I. 137 The memorial of the Pennsylvania Society for promoting the abolition of slavery and the slave trade. **1833** P. HONE *Diary* I. 79 The friends of immediate abolition of slavery in the United States. **1863** W. PHILLIPS *Speeches* v. 78 That great issue, the abolition of slavery. **1881** *Harper's Mag.* Jan. 258/1 Indubitably the abolition of African slavery . . . is the most important event since the discovery of America.

b. In elliptical use. Also comb. (quot. 1854).

1790 WASHINGTON *Diaries* IV. 104 He used arguments to show the . . . impolicy of keeping these people in a state of Slavery; with declarations, however, that he did not wish for more than a gradual abolition. **1834** *S. Lit. Messenger* I. 87 Abolition if not dead here, is in a state too desperately feeble to give us an hour's uneasiness. **1838** *Corr. R. W. Griswold* (1898) 22 Our friends here [Herkimer, N. Y.] . . . are shocked to death if you name the name of Abolition—the fools! . . . Curse this miserable, this shameful fear of the topic of Abolition. **1842** J. STURGE *Visit U. S.* 23 Under cover of abolition, lurked a design of assailing institutions and opinions justly held in regard throughout the Christian world. **1849** F. DOUGLASS *Life* 41 If a slave . . . did anything very wrong in the mind of a slaveholder, it was spoken of as the fruit of abolition. **1854** *State Register* 4 Sept., In the order-loving, law-abiding, abolition-ridden city of Chicago. **1910** O. G. VILLARD *John Brown* 586 When Brown assailed slavery in Virginia, the outlook for Abolition was never so hopeful.

2. *attrib.* **a.** Supporting or advocating the abolishment of slavery and the slave-trade.

1837 P. HONE *Diary* I. 278 An abolition paper was established . . . which, becoming obnoxious to the slave holders, was assailed. **1843** *Nile's Nat. Reg.* 13 May 175 That Great Britain would rather assist the country [=Texas] as an independent abolition state than purchase it. **1852** BRISTED *Upper Ten Th.* iii. 63 One of our Abolition members at Washington. **1856** HAMBLETON *Biog. H. A. Wise* 189 This American party as the deadly enemy of the abolition party. **1866** RICHARDSON *Secret Service* xv. 197 The people were greatly incensed at the 'Abolition Soldiery.' **1867** EDWARDS *Shelby* xxv. 448 Shelby . . . dragged the Abolition priests from their pulpits. **1898** PAGE *Red Rock* 20 One of those abolition chaps who was making a speech.

b. Of or pertaining to the suppression of slavery.

1833 in *Century Mag.* Sept. (1885) 785 The enemies of the abolition cause had formed a conspiracy. **1835** P. HONE *Diary* I. 156 The abolition question continues to agitate the public mind. **1835** FINN *Comic Almanac* Dec., The abolition riots in New York. **1837** *S. Lit. Messenger* III. 644 The absolute abolition strength in the House of Representatives. **1848** W. E. BURTON *Waggeries* 65 It's raything too far south for you to go the abolition ticket. **1854** H. H. RILEY *Puddleford* 175 We had an 'abolition meeting' about these days. **1862** S. COX *In Congress* (1865) 239 Events, says Phillips, are grinding out the freedom of the negro; and these abolition bills are events. **1881-5** MCCLELLAN *Own Story* 152 During the autumn of 1861 Secretary Cameron made quite an abolition speech.

+**Abolitional,** *a.* [ABOLITION.] Pertaining or relating to the abolition of slavery. — **1846** S. SMITH *Theatrical Apprent.* ii. 30 Of course we could not encourage him in such abolitional ideas.

+**Abolitionary,** *a.* [ABOLITION.] Advocating the abolition of the slave trade. {1868} — **1859** J. REDPATH *Roving Editor* 118 If slavery had no other evils, the fact that it separates families, forever, . . . would make me an abolitionary insurrectionist.

+**Abolitiondom.** *Obs.* [ABOLITION.] The Northern or Federal States, as advocating the abolition of negro slavery. — **1857** *Lawrence* (Kansas) *Republican* 28 May 4 Brown the official . . . cursing . . . all abolitiondom for having stolen that precious four quires of paper. **1861** *Knoxville* (Tenn.) *Reg.* in *N.Y. Times* 27 Dec., They [=people in Tenn.] cannot be sold to Abolitiondom. **1877** BARTLETT 2 *Abolitiondom,* said in the Confederate States, during the late civil war, of the loyal States.

+**Abolitioner.** =ABOLITIONIST. — **1855** *Herald of Freedom* 8 Sept. 2/4 Jist then, the man on my right whispered, 'that's an abolitioner.' **1859** J. REDPATH *Roving Editor* 227 One of them put me in jail once, and he was a great big abolitioner, too, when he come here.

Abolitionism. Now *Hist.* The principles, measures, or practices of the abolitionists (see next); advocacy of the abolition of negro slavery. {1808-}

1834 *S. Lit. Messenger* I. 87 In two years abolitionism will be as prostrate as anti-masonry is now. **1849** F. DOUGLASS *Life* 237 The slightest manifestation of humanity towards a colored person was denounced as abolitionism. **1860** PIERCE in Logan *Great Conspiracy* 261 If, through the madness of Northern Abolitionism, that dire calamity must come, the fighting will . . . be within our own borders. **1875** *N. Amer. Rev.* CXX. 73 [To] exterminate every scoundrel . . . tainted with Freesoilism or Abolitionism.

Abolitionist. Now *Hist.* [Cf. prec.] An advocate or supporter of the abolition of negro slavery in the U.S. instead of its gradual extinction. {1790-}

In very frequent use *c* 1836-*c* 1870.

1834 CARRUTHERS *Kentuckian in N. Y.* I. 77 I am no abolitionist, in the incendiary meaning of the term. **1836** *Diplom. Corr. Texas* (1908) I. 152 The abolitionists everywhere oppose it on the old grounds of an opposition to the extension of slavery. **1838** P. HONE *Diary* I. 320 The two curses of our country . . . are the fanaticism of the abolitionists of the North, and the violence of the nullifiers of the South. **1844** *McDonogh Papers* 80 Permit me to ask you why the abolitionists oppose . . . a removal of the colored people of our country to Africa. **1854** M. J. HOLMES *Tempest & Sunshine* xxvi. 379 I s'pose you're too good abolitionists to own niggers. **1862** NORTON *Army Lett.* 125 Uncle Joseph's folks . . . are strong abolitionists. **1866** *Congress. Globe* 24 Feb. 1014/2 Abolitionists, Black Republicans, fanatics, disunionists, amalgamationists, woolly heads, nigger worshipers were the gentlest terms employed. **1886** POORE *Reminisc.* I. 209 He . . . was taking especial pains not to say anything that could offend the Abolitionists, who were beginning to throw a large vote. **1898** HARPER *S. B. Anthony* I. 180 That little band of Abolitionists who never had wavered in their belief that slavery must ultimately disrupt the Union.

b. Attrib. with *party, speaker, view,* etc.

1838-9 KEMBLE *Residence in Georgia* (1863) 90 Of a decidedly abolitionist tendency. **1844** J. R. GODLEY *Letters from A.* II. 67 A New York gentleman . . . who is considered as the leader of the Abolitionist party. **1852** STOWE *Uncle Tom* xv, The minister . . . inclined strongly to Abolitionist views. **1857** GUNN *N. Y. Boarding-Houses* 182 He had been . . . tarred and feathered, as an Abolitionist-lecturer, down South. **1886** A. JOHNSTON *Hist. U. S.* 236 In 1840 . . . the Abolitionist speakers were mobbed. *Ib.*, An Abolitionist meeting.

+**Abolitionize,** *v.* [ABOLITION.]

1. *tr.* To imbue with the principles or views of the abolitionists; to make averse to negro slavery.

1854 C. Robinson *Kansas Conflict* (1892) 94 So it is with the colonizationist societies and their dupes they send to abolitionize Kansas. **1855** HAMBLETON *Biog. Sk. H. A. Wise* (1856) 252 The Know Nothings have Abolitionized Pennsylvania. **1860** HELPER *Impending Crisis* 258 All of which [religious bodies] are destined at no distant day to become thoroughly abolitionized. **1860** *Congress. Globe* 4 Jan. 334/2 Some of them then declared that they came into the American party to abolitionize it.

1866 Richardson *Secret Service* v. 88 They fear . . . that the border will gradually become Abolitionized, and extend free territory to the Gulf itself.

2. To remodel on abolition principles.

1860 *Richmond Enquirer* 1 June 2/4 (Th. S.), The Methodist General Conference have defeated the Anti-slavery resolution, which proposed to abolitionize the general discipline.

+**Abolition party.** A political group seeking the abolition of negro slavery.

1852 J. B. Jones *Col. Vanderbomb* 133 [This] has been acknowledged by . . . the abolition party. 1856 Douglas in *34 Congress* (1 Sess.) *Rep. Committees* 10 The votes of men . . . opposed to placing the political destinies of the Territory in the keeping of the Abolition party of the northern States. 1863 W. Phillips *Speeches* vi. 132 Dr. Channing has thanked the Abolition party.

+**Abolition Society.** A society for effecting the abolition of slavery.

1790 Maclay *Deb. Senate* 169 Our President produced the petitions and memorials of the Abolition Society. 1794 *U. S. Reg.* (Phila.) 158 The Abolition Society was instituted in 1774. 1797 *Ann. 5th Congress* I. 664 This memorial . . . had been treated as coming from an Abolition Society —it was a memorial of the General Meeting of the people called Quakers. 1817 *Ann. 15th Congress* 1 Sess. I. 517 A petition of the Abolition Society of Kentucky, praying that the plan . . . for colonizing the free people of color, may be carried into effect. 1818 *Niles' Reg.* XIV. 176/1 Are abolition societies daily established in the different sections of our republic in mere mockery? 1852 Stowe *Uncle Tom* xix, Your father . . . becomes a regular church-member and deacon, and in due time joins an Abolition society. 1858 Douglas in Logan *Great Conspiracy* 68 The moment the Abolition Societies were organized throughout the North.

+**Aboriginal,** *n.* [See next.] One of the original or native inhabitants of North America; an American Indian. {1845–}

*a*1752 W. Douglass *Summary* I. 157 Notwithstanding of the unpoliteness and want of fire-arms amongst the American aboriginals. 1767 Hutchinson *Hist. Mass. Bay* iii. 269 A good friend to the aboriginals of every tribe. 1789 Morse *Univ. Geog.* (1796) I. 467 The confederation of the New England colonies . . . were of great utility . . . for defence against the aboriginals. 1792 *Mass. H. S. Coll.* I. 273 It is so long since the Aboriginals quitted these grounds, that their monuments are almost effaced. 1805 *Ann. 9th Congress* 2 Sess. 1028 When the American comes into contact with the aboriginal. 1843 'Carlton' *New Purchase* I. xvi. 117 On such gigantic flooring do primitive Buckeyes . . . sleep, after the departure of the red aboriginals. 1848 *Ladies' Repository* VIII. 290 How rapidly the aboriginals of America are wasting before the march of civilization!

Aboriginal, *a.* {1788–}

+**1.** Originally belonging to or living in North America; American Indian.

1698 Sewall *Letter-book* 192 A small desquisition relating to the aboriginal natives of America. 1751 Eliot *Field-Husb.* iii. 49 The aboriginal-natives, the Indian inhabitants of this country. *a*1752 W. Douglass *Summary* I. 155 The aboriginal Americans have no honesty, no honour. 1789 Morse *Univ. Geog.* (1796) I. 86 We shall . . . confine ourselves to the proper aboriginal Americans, or Indians. 1835 Jackson *Message to Congress* 7 Dec., The plan of removing the Aboriginal people . . . to the country west of the Mississippi river. 1838 *S. Lit. Messenger* IV. 533 In his draughts of the aboriginal warrior, he is only second to Cooper. 1841 Cooper *Deerslayer* x, Beauty among the women of the aboriginal Americans . . . is by no means uncommon. 1869 Browne *Adv. Apache Country* 238 The treachery of the aboriginal race . . . in the southern part of California. 1877 Allen *American Bison* 473 The bison, . . . the most important animal to the aboriginal tribes of this continent.

+**2.** Pertaining or relating to the native American Indians.

1775 Adair *Indians* 52, I shall now shew a farther parity, between the Hebrew language, and the Aboriginal American dialects. 1823 Cooper *Pioneers* xxv, Elizabeth . . . evidently put little faith in his aboriginal descent. 1834 Peck *Gaz. Illinois* p. vii, Many aboriginal names in the west were first written in French. 1834 *Mass. H. S. Coll.* 3 Ser. VI. 152 There was an aboriginal town of considerable magnitude at this place. 1854 Bartlett *Mex. Boundary* I. p. vi, Vocabularies of more than twenty aboriginal languages. 1871 *Rep. Indian Affairs* (1872) 556 All of whom wear the badges of aboriginal royalty in the shape of medals.

Aborigine. [Aborigine-s. Cf. Abrigoin.] One of the aborigines; an American Indian. — 1858 Vielé *Following Drum* 216 The aborigine was inclined to dispute the point. 1876 Burroughs *Winter Sunshine* vi. 133 If the red aborigine ever had his summer of fulness and contentment.

Aborigines, *n. pl.* {1593–} +The earliest known inhabitants of the country or their descendants; the native peoples or Red Indians.

'Not an English word. It may be well to let it pass into disuse' (W.'28).

1724 Sewall *Letter-book* II. 177, I subscribe the Company's opinion as to educating some of the Aborigines so as to fit them for the work of the ministry. 1724 *Mass. H. S. Coll.* IV. 159 The right the aborigines of this country . . . had, or have, to lands in it. 1775 Ramsey *Tennessee* (1853) 119 The whole nation, being the aborigines and sole owners by occupancy. 1793 B. Lincoln in *Mass. H. S. Coll.* 3 Ser. V. 123 There were a number present whose mothers sprang from the aborigines of the country. 1813 *Niles' Reg.* V. 77/2 What is it to her, that humanity must lament the destruction of these *Aborigines?* 1820 Irving *Sketch Book* II. 214 It has been the lot of the unfortunate aborigines of America . . . to be doubly wronged by the white men. 1830 *Collegian* 153 Our aborigines have been endowed by them [*sc.* English writers] with marvellous sagacities. 1883 Zeigler & Grosscup *Alleghanies* 288 The other aborigines . . . were, with moccasined feet, threading their ways through the crowds. 1902 White *Conjuror's House* ix. 107 We have in our weekly congregational singing over forty regular attendants from the aborigines.

***About,** *adv.* (In colloq. uses.)

1. Almost; nearly. {1614–; now *colloq.*}

1848 Whipple *Ess. & Rev.* (1850) I. 300 The difference between duty and conduct . . . about measures the difference between the real and the actual. 1871 Townsend *Mormon Trials* 8 About everybody of ecclesiastical prominence in the Church has several wives. 1902 Clapin 3, I reckon the local election about pleased you.

2. Out of bed, afoot, esp. as attending to one's duties; astir, in evidence. {1815–}

1745 *Essex Inst. Coll.* XLVIII. 299, [May] 9. A little better this morning. . . . 10. I was still out of case but keept about. 1839 *Lexington Observer & Rep.* 10 April, Why, they're all up and about, particularly Sal. 1853 *Knickerb.* XLII. 653 [During] the State-Election . . . 'Woolly-Heads' were 'about,' and 'far-off the coming shone' of dignified 'Silver-Grays.' 1858 Vielé *Following Drum* 172 General Harney . . . had come down . . . to administer 'jesse' . . . and let the community . . . feel that he was 'about.'

+**3.** *About right,* pretty well or effectively; thoroughly. *colloq.*

*a*1859 *New Eng. Stories* (B.), I fell foul of the old mare; and if I didn't give it to her about right, then there's none o' me, that's all. 1859 Bartlett 2 To do a thing *about right* is to do it well.

b. *About East:* see East *adv.*

+**4.** *About and about,* pretty much alike or the same.

1867 *Congress. Globe* 8 Jan. 331/2 Men were created equal. That is, at the very outstart the cytoblast, the primal cell, . . . was about and about.

***Above,** *adv.* +To or in the upper reaches of a river.

1671 *N.Y. State Col. Hist.* XII. 480 For what before war had to be brought here [=the town of Newcastle in Delaware] is delivered above and what debts is due us can not be receaved for that they come not below. 1807 *Ann. 10th Congress* 1 Sess. I. 636 Some one . . . said they must return to Colonel Burr, who would stay in the bend, above, all night. 1816 Brackenridge *Jrnl. Voy. Missouri* 197 Certainly as it respects the margin of [the stream], . . . there must consequently be a hiatus between the settlements which may hereafter be made above, and those below. 1821 Cooper *Spy* xxvi, I have never known whether he belonged above or below. *Ib.* note, The American party was called the party belonging 'above' and the British that of 'below.' The terms had reference to the course of the Hudson.

***Above,** *prep.* Used in various phrases: see Bend, Huckleberry, Par, Snake, etc.

Abovestairs, Above stairs, *adv.* Upstairs. {1758; now *obs.*}

1677 *New Castle Court Rec.* 131 Captain Billop come downe from abovestairs. 1688–9 Sewall *Diary* I. 295 The hall . . . is above stairs. 1851 *Harper's Mag.* April 662/2 Their ears are often startled with a cry from above-stairs. 1854 M. J. Holmes *Tempest & Sunshine* xviii. 253 His mother . . . was obliged to remain above stairs for a time. 1893 M. Howe *Honor* 182 The mourner whose all lies cold . . . in a darkened chamber above-stairs.

+**Abri-, Abrogoin** (also **abbregyne, abrogan, abergoin**), colloquial forms of Aborigine(s.

1830 *Western Monthly Rev.* III. 357 The inmates, as the Kentucky orator said, 'in this sublime state of retiracy among the abrogoines' had their skins [etc.]. 1837 Bird *Nick of Woods* I. 120 Thar's always abbregynes in the cover. *Ib.* 229 The abbregynes ar' making a rush for the cabin. 1840 *S. Lit. Messenger* VI. 416/1 My fixed determination to retire . . . among the abrigoins. 1841 *Ib.* VII. 54/1 Observed a mangled abrogoin . . . when Long forgot to peel his tarnal skelp off. 1859 Bartlett 1 The term 'aborigines' is corrupted by some of the illiterate people of the West into *Abergoins* or *Abrogans.*

***Abroad,** *adv.*

+**1.** Out of the Colonies or United States; in or to a foreign country; *esp.* in or to Europe. Also *from abroad.*

1704 *Boston News-Letter* 4 Dec. 2/2 Ships . . . bound for . . . any other of Her Majesties Plantations abroad. 1768 Franklin *Ess.* Wks. 1840 II. 371 If our manufactures are too dear they will not vend abroad. 1775 *Journals Cont. Congress* III. 477 Our bills will not pass abroad. 1838 P. Hone *Diary* 12 Dec., That distinguished class of learned pundits who had been 'abroad,' as the term then was. 1850 Mitchell *Lorgnette* II, 34 Jokes, which make the lady . . . blush to her eyes, unless indeed, she is lately returned from 'abroad.' 1869 'Mark Twain' (*title*), The Innocents Abroad; or, The New Pilgrim's Progress. 1869 *Causes Reduct. Tonnage* (1870) 62 During the war . . . a large number of ships . . . were sold abroad. 1891 Stockton (*title*), The Rudder Grangers Abroad and Other Stories.

+2. *To be all abroad*, 'to be at a loss; be puzzled, perplexed, bewildered, nonplussed; be all or quite at sea' (*Cent.*). *colloq.*

1860 HOLMES *Professor* i. 6 The female boarder in black attire looked so puzzled, and, in fact, 'all abroad,' ... that I left her to recover her wits.

* **Absent**, *a.* +Of lots: Assigned to one who has remained absent. *Obs.* — **1643** *New Haven Col. Rec.* I. 95 The committee appointed to dispose of the absent lott mett. **1649** *Ib.* 425 All that have a desire to have any of the absent lotts. **1651** *New Haven Town Rec.* 74 [That] the land the Towne gave to Joseph Pecke out of the absent lotts, be disposed of.

* **Absentee.**

+**1.** A loyalist who absented himself from his residence during the American Revolution.

1777 *Mass. Acts & Resolves* 9 April V. 630 The said agent ... shall return an inventory ... of such absentee's estate that has come to his hands, to the said judge of probate. **1779** *N. H. Comm. Safety Rec.* 203 The farm ... lately own'd by John Vance, an absentee. **1832** WILLIAMSON *Maine* II. 466 Copies of the confiscation or 'absentees act,' were transmitted [*c* 1778] to every legislative assembly in the Union.

+**2.** *Law.* 'One who is without the jurisdiction of a particular court or judge' (*Cent.*)

+**3.** *attrib.* Belonging to an owner who lives away.

1868 *Indian Laws & Tr.* III. 710 The sale of both the absentee and other lands.

Absenteeism. [E., f. ABSENTEE.] **a.** The practice of absenting oneself from landed property. {1829-} +**b.** (See quot. 1888.) — **1849** T. T. JOHNSON *Sights Gold Region* xxvii. 276 The extensive system of absenteeism of the landed proprietors. **1888** M. LANE *Pol. Catch-Words* 13 Sept. 15 *Absenteeism* ... does duty in defining the position of congressmen, like the late Senator Nye, whose constituency is in one state and their residence in another.

+**Absent treatment.** Mental treatment of a patient who is not present. — **1887** *Century Mag.* July 431 'Absent treatments' ... are based on the theory that to think of another entirely and abstractedly occasions a spiritual presence of that other.

Absinthe. Also †**absanth.** [F. *absinthe* wormwood.]

+**1.** The sagebrush or prairie sage, a species of artemisia.

1843 FREMONT *Exped.* 14 The *artemesia*, absinthe, or prairie sage, as it is variously called. **1843** T. TALBOT *Journals* 36 Country affording nothing but sage or wormwood or more properly absinthe. **1846** SAGE *Scenes Rocky Mts.* xv, On the right lay a broad expanse of undulating prairie, covered with stately clusters of *absinthe*. **1848** PARKMAN *Oregon Trail* x. 146 Multitudes of strange medicinal herbs, more especially the absanth, which covered every declivity.

+**2.** Attrib. with *bush.*

1843 FREMONT *Exped.* 56 *Absinthe* bushes, which grew in many thick patches.

+**Absquatalize, Absquatiate, Absquattle,** obsolete variants of next. — **1839** MARRYAT *Diary* II. 34 The editor of the *Philadelphia Gazette* is wrong in calling *absquatiated* a Kentucky phrase. *Ib.*, By the way, there is a little corruption in the word as the *Gazette* uses it; *absquatalized* is the true reading. **1840** *Cambridge Journal* 4 Nov, Some ... wretch ... did recently ... abstract our overcoat and absquatalize therewith. **1848** W. E. BURTON *Waggeries* 17 Let's licker one more round and then absquattle.

+**Absquatulate,** *v. colloq.* or *slang.* Also **-elate, -ilate, absquotulate, -ilate.** [Of fanciful origin: cf. *abscond* and *squat* v.]

1. *intr.* To depart or go away, esp. in a clandestine, surreptitious, or hurried manner; to abscond, decamp.

Freq. *c*1835-*c*1855; now rare. Illustrated by Thornton from 1837 to 1862.

Termed 'a western phrase' (1838 *Knickerb.* XII. 230). 'Used only in familiar language' (B. '48). 'A factitious vulgarism' (B. '59). 'It is now less often heard than formerly, having been replaced in some degree by the word *skedaddle*' (F. '89). 'In the 40's to absquatulate was in good usage, but it has since disappeared' (Mencken).

1833 BERNARD *Kentuckian* (De Vere, 577). **1834** 'DOWNING' *A. Jackson* 36 If you absquotulate, you are ded before you can say Jack Robinson. **1837** BIRD *Nick of Woods* II. 83 Your blooded brown horse has absquotulated. **1840** KENNEDY *Quodlibet* 183 We may ... hear of many more Whigs following the example of our absquatulating cashier. **1843** 'CARLTON' *New Purchase* I. xiv. 100 They become indignant at the legal invasion of their domain, and hastily—absquatulate; that is, translated—they go and squat in another place. **1847** *Knickerb.* XXIX. 370 Had a thunderbolt ... fallen among the ... darkies, they could not have absquatulated with greater velocity. **1861** J. LAMONT *Sea-horses* xi. 179 [An old bull-walrus] heard us, and lazily awaking, raised his head and prepared to absquatulate. **1864** T. L. NICHOLS *Amer. Life* I. 388 When a squatter removes, he absquatulates. **1868** H. M. FLINT *Railroads* 250 He had committed some offence ... and at the morning recess he 'absquatulated.' **1890** *Buckskin Mose* i. 18 The vagabond had 'absquatulated' with the whole of the joint-stock funds.

2. Of things: To part, separate, fall away.

1842 *Spirit of Times* 29 June (Th.), When Mr. F. again called, the shingle had absquatulated from the shutter. *Ib.* 7 Nov. (Th.), A Wharf Absquatulated. [Heading of a description of an accident.]

+**Absquatulation.** **a.** An absconding. **b.** A disappearance or defalcation. — **1849** *Knickerb.* XXXIV. 407/1 I'l risk my pile that his mammy aint aprised of his absquatilation. **1854** 'O. OPTIC' *In Doors & Out* (1876) 48 The general discovered an 'absquatulation' of some fifteen hundred dollars—just enough to keep the dapper little bookkeeper in opera tickets and 2:40's.

+**Absquatulator.** An absconder. — **1842** *Spirit of Times* 20 June (Th.), [Sketch of] the career of a foreign absquatulator.

* **Abstract.** An epitome or summary of the evidences of ownership of real estate. {1858} Also attrib. with *office*, etc.

1820 *Ann. 16th Congress* 1 Sess. I. 692 An act to authorize the Governor of Illinois to obtain certain abstracts of land from certain public offices. *Ib.* 696. **1874** *Ill. Revised Statutes* (1883) 910 An abstract book ... shall be so kept as to show a true chain of title to each tract and the incumbrances thereon. **1880** *Harper's Mag.* Oct. 718/2 The books containing what are technically called 'abstracts' of Chicago titles. **1880** *Hist. Columbia Co., Wis.* 495 Abstract offices ... contain a complete and perfect history ... of every piece of land in the county. *Ib.*, The abstract office ... was started ... in 1859. **1889** *Kansas City Times & Star* 1 July, The Kansas City Abstract Company ... owns all the abstracts of Kansas City and Jackson County completed in 1868.

+**Abstractionist.** One who is given to abstractions or ideals; an idealist.

1844 EMERSON *Ess.* II. viii, Nature ... punishes abstractionists and will only forgive an induction which is rare and casual. **1856** P. CARTWRIGHT *Autobiog.* xxviii. 437, I have indulged in the fond hope that these Northern abstractionists would ... go and set up for themselves. **1863** B. TAYLOR *H. Thurston* I. 37 Your fanatical abstractionists never look at anything in a practical way. **1864** E. SARGENT *Peculiar* II. 100 The man who tries to undo a wrong is an abstractionist, is he?

* **Abut,** *v.* +*tr.* To define (a piece of land) by stating the bounds. *Obs.* — **1651** *Dedham Rec.* 186 Eleazer Lusher is requested to refer those grants in the Record that ar entered unbutteled to those enteries that ar abutted to prevent questions & mistakes. **1663** *Groton Rec.* 10 Every man ... shall bring a note of all his lands ... bounded & abutted unto the Towne-Clark.

Abutment. Also †**abuttment.** {1644-}

+**1.** *pl.* Bounds; limits; confines. *Obs.*

1665 *Hartford Land Distrib.* 405 All that land within these after abutments on the great river west. **1666** *Ib.* 121 All that percell within these abutments. **1669** *Dedham Rec.* IV. 187 To bring the returne of grants to the Recorder both in respect of quantitie, qualitie, and abuttments. **1693** *Providence Rec.* IV. 244 A certaine tract of land & swampe ... the bounds & abuttments whereof shall more amply appeare.

2. The masonry or rock supporting either end of the arch of a bridge. {1823-}

1773 *Md. Hist. Mag.* XV. 195 The water went about a foot over Ellicotts bridge; ... it washed a good deal of dirt from the abutments. **1789** MORSE *Amer. Geog.* 180 The abuttment at Charlestown, from the old landing, is 100 feet. **1813** *Niles' Reg.* III. 322/2 The bridge consists of two abutments, and one arch. **1855** GLISAN *Jrnl. Army Life* 169 Two immense stone towers ... form abutments for the bridge. **1882** WORTHEN *Econ. Geol. Ill.* II. 70 The St. Louis limestone also affords good building stone, especially for ... abutments and culverts.

Abuttal, *n.* [f. *abut* v.] *pl.* Bounds; =ABUTMENT 1. {1630, 1780-} — **1638** *Dedham Rec.* 40 To make vp the valewe of 12 acres according to their seuerall wants, as by the abuttalls & bownds marked out appereth. **1639** *Cambridge Prop. Rec.* 47 The abuttals of this land [enumerated].

+**Abuttal,** *v.* [f. prec.] **1.** *tr.* To define (a tract of land) by specifying its boundaries; to bound. **2.** *intr.* To border *on* a property. — **(1) 1636** *Dedham Rec.* 20 Set out ... by Thomas Bartlet lotts for seuerall men as followeth, viz[t] ... all these confirmed at this meeting & are abuttalled as by the particulers in foll: appeareth. — **(2) 1641** *Cambridge Prop. Rec.* 71 A small garden on the otherside the highway abuttalinge on John Trumbull.

+**Abuttalment, -elment.** [Cf. ABUTMENT, ABUTTAL.] *pl.* Bounds of land; =ABUTMENT. — **1700** *Dedham Rec.* V. 274 Any one of them with the Survaier shall have power to ... make return ... of the qvantity bounds and abuttelments to be entered in the Booke of grants.

+**Abutter.** Also †**abuttar, -or.** [f. *abut* v.] An owner of contiguous property or land.

1673 *Boston Rec.* 82 Such of the present abutters or borderers on the said flatts as shall come in undertakes of the aforesaid wall or wharfe. **1722** *Ib.* 171 Voted that part of the said money be improved for paveing, ... provided the abutters doe their parts. **1725** *Ib.* 191 That the abuttars rake the same together to be left or taken away at the descresion of the scavengers. **1807** *Boston Selectmen* 3 June 344 The abuttors ... having regulated the side walk & paved the same with stone & brick. **1874** *Fitchburg City Docum.* 220 The concrete walks ... have been wholly paid for by the abutters. **1877** *Congress. Rec.* 9 Nov. 303/1 The boundaries of the land will become the property of the United States, and the abutters will be defined in the records. **1896** *Ib.* 14 Dec. 154/1 The consent of abutters certainly should be had yearly before a renewal of license [of a saloon].

* **Acacia.** Also †**acassia, accacia; acasee, -ce.**

+**1.** The North American locust tree (*Robinia pseudacacia*), sometimes called false or bastard acacia.

1640 PARKINSON *Theater of Plants* 1550 Robinus his false Acacia of America. I have given it a place with another *Virginia* like it, but not with the true ones as is most fit. *c***1728** CATESBY *Carolina* I. 43 Acacia. This tree I never saw but at the plantation of Mr. Waring on Ashley River, growing in shallow water. **1775** BURNABY *Travels* 12 The woods [of Virginia] . . . adorned and beautified with red-flowering maples, sassafras-trees, dog-woods, acacias, red-buds. **1785** WASHINGTON *Diaries* II. 383, 3 rows of a species of the acacia (or acasee), used in the West Indias for incircling their gardens. **1797** IMLAY *Western Territory* (ed. 3) 269 The acacia is the same in Louisiana as in France, much more common, and less straight. The natives . . . make their bows of it. **1817** S. BROWN *Western Gaz.* 96 The accacia, grape vine, and rich pastures disappear. **1841** L. M. CHILD *Lett. N. Y.* ix. 65, I begged of the gardener a single sprig of acacia.

2. Popularly applied to other species of this genus or to similar plants of other genera.

1640 [see 1]. **1785** MARSHALL *Amer. Grove* 53 *Gleditsia.* Triple-Thorned Acacia, or Honey Locust. **1813** MUHLENBERG *Cat. Plants* 96 Glandulous acacia. *Ib.*, Short-lobed acacia. *Ib.*, Weak acacia. **1850** [S. F. COOPER] *Rural Hours* 413 The pods of the Acacia, frequently called the Honey-locust, are handsome and very large. **1854** BARTLETT *Narr.* II. 563 The mezquit or acacia, the tornilla, the fouquiera, . . . all armed with the most terrific spikes or thorns. **1857** GRAY *Botany* 109 *Gymnocladus triacanthos.* Three-thorned Acacia, or Honey-Locust. **1869** FULLER *Flower Gatherers* 50 Alice Palmer thought it might be some kind of Acacia. **1880** CABLE *Grandissimes* vii. 49 By and by the way led through a broad, grassy lane . . . among some wild acacias. **1889** *Cent.* s.v., The green-barked acacia of Arizona is *Parkinsonia Torreyana*. . . . The rose or bristly acacia is *Robinia hispida.*

* **Academic,** *a.* and *n.*

+**1.** *adj.* Pertaining or belonging to that department of a university or college which deals with classical, mathematical, and general literary studies, as distinguished from those that are technical or professional.

1856 *S. Lit. Messenger* XXII. 244/1 In the academic department of the University. *Ib.* 245/2 A student . . . may graduate in the six Academic schools in a single session. *Ib.* 247/1 Out of about 375 students in all—professional and Academic. **1879** J. McCOSH in *Princeton Book* 132 The Academic Department has a close connection with the Scientific. **1892** *Nation* 22 Sept. 216/2 There is also a cross-line of cleavage between the sophomore and junior years of each of these colleges [of the University of Chicago]; the two lower years being termed the 'academic college' and the two higher years the 'university college.' We have thus six 'colleges,' three 'academic' and three 'university.'

+**2.** *n.* An academic student.

1856 *S. Lit. Messenger* XXII. 248/1 If we compare these with our Masters of Arts, it seems in strong contrast with one out of every 43 (7 out of 304 Academics).

* **Academical,** *a.* + = ACADEMIC *a.*

1813 *Yale Coll. Catalogue of Officers*, etc., Nov. 5 List of the Students in the academical Institution of Yale college. **1822** *Yale Coll. Catalogue* 24 The Academical Faculty. *Ib.* 28 The medical students . . . are subject to the same moral and religious restraints as those of the Academical College. **1837** PECK *New Guide* 347 Augusta College . . . [has] collegiate, academical, and primary departments. **1856** *S. Lit. Messenger* XXII. 250/2 Of these, 177 were professional students; there were some 268 Academical students. **1871** [L. H. BAGG] *At Yale* 682 In regard to the terms of admission, courses of study, etc., the college, or 'academical department' is first treated of. **1884** *Science* 425/4 The American use of 'academical' as applying to an undergraduate classical college, in distinction from a scientific or professional school.

* **ACADEMY.**

* **1.** A school, seminary, or other institution, having a status between an elementary school and a college or university.

Now only *Hist.*, except in the names of existing institutions.

1640 E. WINSLOW in *Winthrop P.* 169 Mr. Paddy . . . purposeth there to lay the foundacon of an Academy, & reade the arts to some that are fitt for that purpose. **1722** *New-Eng. Courant* 5–12 Nov. 2/1 To restrain young Students from publishing in print those things which . . . are a disgrace to the Academy. **1749** (*title*), Constitution of the Publick Academy in the City of Philadelphia. **1758** *N. H. Hist. Soc. Coll.* IX. 37 To raise a Sufficient Fund for erecting & carrying on an Academy or College. **1773** ADAMS *Works* (1850) II. 321 Their academy [*sc.* Philadelphia] emits from nine to fourteen graduates annually. **1794** *Mass. H. S. Coll.* III. 146 The general court . . . established an academy at Machias, by the name of Washington Academy, . . . and gave for its support a township of land. **1806** FESSENDEN *Poems* 141 *note*, It is fashionable in New England for the middling class of society . . . to send their sons to some one of their academies. **1831** PECK *Guide* 246 Belleville Academy . . . is a select boarding school for boys. **1834** — *Gaz. Illinois* 88 An academy has been established in Chicago, that bids fair to become an important institution. **1856** GOODRICH *Recoll.* I. 150 A man . . . was employed to keep a high-school, or, as it was then [*c.* 1805] called, an Academy. **1865** MRS. WHITNEY *Gayworthys* xi. 99 When he gets through at Winthorpe Academy . . . he will have a little time to spare between that and college. **1885** *Rep. Indian Affairs* 105 Chickasaw nation have three large academies. **1904** 'O. HENRY' *Heart of West* 234 Uncle Cal . . . sent her to the academy over at Birdstail for two years.

b. Grandiloquently: A school.

'The simple, unassuming appellation of "school" was the universal name till about the year 1795; after that time "academies," "seminaries," "lyceums," "institutes," &c. were perpetually springing up in every quarter among us' (1830 Watson *Philadelphia* 248).

1807 IRVING, etc. *Salmagundi* xiii. 299 The academies with which every lane and alley of our cities abounds. **1809** KENDALL *Travels* III. 197 The other grammar-schools, called academies, . . . established in different parts of the country. **1817** PAULDING *Lett. from South* I. 249 Schools, where A, B, C, is taught, have become Academies and Seminaries. **1829** SHERWOOD *Gaz. Georgia* (ed. 2) 141 Many of these, however, are misnamed; for an academy supposes instruction in the higher branches of education; but some are no better than 'old field schools.' **1852** *S. Lit. Messenger* XVIII. 753/1 The corps of pedagogues of country schools—academies, I beg pardon for not saying. **1889** FARMER 4 A writer in *Putnam's Magazine* sarcastically remarks that 'schools no longer exist in the towns and villages; academies and colleges supplant them.'

2. An institution where pupils are trained in a special science or art. {1734–}

See also DANCING, MILITARY, NAVAL ACADEMY.

1788 H. M. Brooks *Gleanings* 18 Dancing Academy [at] Concert Hall. **1808** *Ann. 10th Congress* 1 Sess. II. 2809 The major, . . . and two captains, took charge of the Academy, the students of which were the cadets belonging to the regiment of artillery. **1812** *Ann. 12th Congress* 1 Sess. 1328 It is improper, therefore, even to vest the President with a discretionary power to remove the Academy [i.e. West Point] elsewhere.

3. A society or association for the promotion of literature, art, or science. {1691–}

1780 ADAMS *Let.* Wks. 1852 VII. 250 A [proposed] society under the name of 'the American Academy for refining, improving, and ascertaining the English Language.' **1781** FRANKLIN *Writings* VIII. 257 The honour done me by the American Academy of Arts and Sciences. **1807** IRVING, etc. *Salmagundi* xii. 268 The pictures belonging to the Academy of Arts. **1810** (*title*), Memoirs of the Connecticut Academy of Arts and Sciences, incorporated A.D. 1799. **1865** *Illinois Private Laws* II. 14 An association, . . . formed in the city of Chicago, called 'The Chicago Academy of Sciences.' **1884** *Century Mag.* March 678/2 No sooner is the 'Interocean City' of some farthest Western frontier of civilization out of the log-cabin period, than it has at once a Broadway, a Fifth Avenue, and an Academy of Music. **1890** (*title*), Annals of the American Academy of Political and Social Science, Philadelphia.

4. A building or set of buildings occupied by one or other kind of academy.

1765 R. ROGERS *Acc. N. America* 82 The houses in general are well built, . . . especially some of the public buildings; . . . such, in particular, is the academy. **1805** H. M. BROOKS *Gleanings* 60 The Female Apartment in Bradford Academy. **1814** *Western Gleaner* (Pittsburgh) I. 108 The visitors of the academy are obliged to pay 25 cents for the right of admission. **1835** [LONGSTREET] *Georgia Scenes* 81 'Open the door of the Academy' (Michael would allow no body to call it a school-house). **1865** *Atlantic Mo.* XV. 148 In its shadow [is] the town academy.

+**5.** (See quotation.)

1859 *Harper's Mag.* Aug. 428/1 Among preachers of the Holston Conference this [Jefferson] Circuit was familiarly known as the 'Academy,' from a secret suspicion that 'the appointing power' was wont to send to it, for *schooling*, such cases among the young itinerants as were supposed to need a severe régime.

6. Attrib. with *ball, building, gate, house, teacher,* etc.

1803 *Ann. 7th Congress* 2 Sess. 1330 No grant or promise of an academy or college township was inserted. **1829** SHERWOOD *Gaz. Georgia* (ed. 2) 51 The poor school and Academy Funds drawn by this county are amalgamated. **1837** PECK *Gaz. Illinois* 162 Bloomington . . . has . . . a handsome academy building. **1850** FOOTE *Sketches Va.* 395 The Presbytery . . . agree to build an academy-house. *a***1852** A. LAWRENCE *Diary & Corr.* 26 My academy lessons, little academy balls. **1869** STOWE *Oldtown Folks* 459 Excited theological arguments . . . to which the academy boys sometimes listened. **1878** — *Poganuc People* vii. 77 The wilderness of learning grew so wild . . . that only the Academy teacher seemed able to follow it through. **1905** A. H. RICE *Sandy* 116 At the academy gate he met Mr. Moseley.

Acadian, *n.* and *a.* [*Acadia*, Latinized form of F. *Acadie*, = Nova Scotia and New Brunswick. Cf. CADIAN.]

1. *n.* A native or inhabitant of Acadia; one of the French settlers of Acadia, or of the descendants of these in Louisiana.

In 1713 a large part of Acadia, subsequently named Nova Scotia, was ceded to Great Britain. As a military measure, its French inhabitants were expelled by the British in 1755, and distributed among the colonies. Many eventually went to Louisiana, when still a French colony.

1705 *Boston News-Letter* 14 May, At break of day . . . our harbour was beset with . . . some Accadians at Pessemequady and Port Royall, and Cannadians. **1758** *Memoirs of the Last War* 17 The French inhabitants (whom for distinction-sake I shall call Acadians) . . . were allowed by the treaty their option either to retire . . . or to remain there. **1766** H. GORDON in *Travels Amer. Col.* 482 The upper settlers of the Colony are just planted, consisting of poor Acadians for the most part. **1798** G. MINOT *Contin. Hist. Mass. Bay* I. 223 An ungenerous cunning, and subtle kind of severity, calculated to render the Acadians subservient to the English interests to the latest hour. **1803** *Ann. 8th Congress* 2 Sess. 1506 The three succeeding settlements, up to Baton Rouge, contain mostly Acadians. *Ib.* 1524 The Acadians manufacture a little cotton into quilts and cottonades. **1832** WILLIAMSON *Maine* II. 264 The energetic exertions of its government [in 1749] to bring the Acadians or French Neutrals, into obedience. **1876** BANCROFT *Hist.* III. ii. 30 The gentle and unsuspecting character of the Acadians. **1878** *Hallberger's Illus. Mag.* 577 (F.), The Native Louisianian, . . . and the Acadian, more universally known . . . as the Cajen.

+**b.** A French Louisianian of humble station.

1880 *Scribner's Mo.* Jan. 383/1 The term 'Acadian' . . . may frequently be heard applied to all the humbler classes of French origin throughout the state.

2. *a.* Of or belonging to Acadia; originating from Acadia.

1826 FLINT *Recoll.* 322 The inhabitants [of La.] are principally French . . . and the very Arcadian [*sic*] race, about which so much has been said and sung. **1847** LONGFELLOW *Evangeline* I. i In the Acadian land, on the shores of the Basin of Minas. *Ib.* 33 Thus dwelt together in love, these simple Acadian farmers. **1862** *Rep. Comm. Patents: Agric.* 233 The Arcadian [*sic*] settlement in Canada. **1865** *Atlantic Mo.* XV. 1 Her mother having been of Acadian kin. **1876** BANCROFT *Hist.* III. x. 417 He sent De Pontleroy . . . to travel through America . . . in the guise of an Acadian wanderer.

+**b.** In names of birds: (see quotations).

1839 AUDUBON *Synopsis Birds* 24 *Ulula Acadica*, . . . Acadian Night-Owl. . . . Saw-whet. **1839** PEABODY *Mass. Birds* 275 The Acadian or Little Owl, *Strix acadia*, . . . is a beautiful and animated bird. **1872** COUES *Key* 206 *Nyctale acadica*. . . . Acadian Owl. Saw-whet Owl. **1874** — *Birds N.W.* 249 *Empidonax Acadicus*, . . . Acadian, or small Green-crested Flycatcher. *Ib.* 315 *Nyctale Acadica*, . . . Acadian or Saw-whet Owl. **1890** *Cent.* s.v. *Empidonax*, Four species are very common woodland migratory insectivorous birds of the eastern United States: the Acadian flycatcher, *E. acadicus* [etc.].

* **Accepted,** *ppl. a.* (See quotation.) — **1798** *Doc. Hist. N.Y. State* (1849) I. 675 Those who were received by the original settlers as 'accepted inhabitants,' might have been born in America.

* **Accession,** *n.*

+**1.** The joining of a State with the Union.

1781 HAMILTON *Works* (1886) VIII. 34 The accession of Maryland to the Confederacy will be a happy event. **1790** WASHINGTON in *State P.* (1819) I. 13 The recent accession of . . . North Carolina to the constitution of the United States.

+**2.** A book or the like added to a library. Also attrib. with *book, catalogue*, etc.

1877 *Library Journal* May 316/1 The first of all records to be filled, and by no means the last in importance to the faithful librarian, is the book of accessions. *Ib.*, The luxury of a good accession-catalogue written up to date. *Ib.*, The accession-book properly kept up is the librarian's official indicator for his whole collection. *Ib.* 317/2 In many libraries it is customary in replacing a lost book to give it the same accession-number as the original. **1881** *Mass. H. S. Proc.* XIX. 146 The Librarian's accession book.

+**Accession,** *v.* [See prec. 2.] *tr.* To enter in a book or list of additions to a library. — **1892** G. M. JONES *Salem* (Mass.) *Public Library Rep.* 9 The new books have been promptly accessioned. **1896** *Library Journal* Dec. 129/2 Accessioning, classifying, and cataloging.

+**Accidental insurance.** (See quot. and next.) — **1865** *Boston Directory* 526/2 New York Accidental Insurance Company, . . . for insuring against accidents of all kinds. **1867** *N.Y. State Business Directory* 965/2 Insurance Companies, Life: . . . New York Accidental, 141 Broadway.

Accident insurance. Insurance against accident. Also attrib. with *company*, etc.

1866 *Boston Directory* 565/2 Travelers' Insurance Company, of Hartford, Conn. [is] the Pioneer Accident Insurance Company in America. **1871** HOWELLS *Wedding Journey* i. 6 So Basil . . . bought an accident-insurance ticket. **1875** 'MARK TWAIN' *Sk., Sp. Accident Insurance*, Ever since I have been a director in an accident-insurance company. **1880** *Harper's Mag.* July 193/1 We buy a new revolver and take out an accident-insurance policy. **1906** L. BELL *C. Lee* 221 Once when he was going on a journey she asked him to take out an accident insurance policy.

Accidently, *adv.* Accidentally; by chance. {1611, 1782; now *Obs.*}— **1712** *Portsmouth Rec.* 313 He was accidently drownded. **1797** B. HAWKINS *Letters* 136 Any person who should kill another accidently. **1864** *Ill. Agric. Soc. Trans.* V. 906, I once accidently put corn stalks around a tree.

+**Accident-ticket.** An accident-insurance ticket. — **1889** 'MARK TWAIN' *Conn. Yankee* xxx. 382 You couldn't clean up a tournament and pile the result without finding one of my accident-tickets in every helmet.

Acclimate, *v.* [Fr. *acclimater.*]

1. *tr.* To habituate, inure, or accustom (a person) to a new or strange climate. Chiefly *p.p.* Also *refl.*

Orig. E. {1792–1859}, but superseded by *acclimatize* {1836–}, which also has been used by some Amer. writers.

1800 [see ACCLIMATED *ppl. a.*]. **1827** COOPER *Prairie* vi, A companion who would be so serviceable in their new abode, . . . until the family were thoroughly 'acclimated.' **1835** [INGRAHAM] *South-West* II. 245 Born and raised in this climate (acclimated as they are termed). **1857** BRAMAN *Inf. Texas* i. 15, I do not make all these recommendations because I think there is any critical period or season here, called the acclimating, but I know [etc.]. **1860** HOLMES *Professor* iv. 104 These races dying out, the white man has to acclimate himself. **1880** CABLE *Grandissimes* ii. 14 You're not 'acclimated,' as they call it, . . . and the city is full of the fever. *c***1900** M. J. HOLMES *Aikenside* i. 12 Miss Atherstone's health is far too delicate for her to incur the risk of a climate like ours. If she were well acclimated, I should be glad. **1908** 'YESLAH' *Tenderfoot S. Calif.* xv. 131 The natives tell you it takes a year to get acclimated.

+**b.** To inure (plants) to new climatic conditions.

1872 *Vermont Bd. Agric. Rep.* 85 Your trees will be already acclimated, and allowed to feed on their own natural element.

+**2.** To adapt (a person) to unaccustomed conditions. Chiefly in *p.p.*

1836 *Jrnl. Southern Hist.* (1935) I. 360, I think I should be unable to stand up under the fine dinners of New Orleans, until I had been acclimated to their rich soups and their many flavoured wines. **1850** MRS. HAWTHORNE in *N. Hawthorne & Wife* (1885) I. 369 You cannot think how pretty the room looks, though with such a low stud that I have to get acclimated to it. **1857** EMERSON *Poems, Art*, 'Tis the privilege of Art Thus to play its cheerful part, Man on earth to acclimate. **1872** HOLMES *Poet* iii. 75, I have not been long enough at this table to get well acclimated.

transf. **1890** *Harper's Mag.* March 519/2 Certain details of touch and flavor, acclimated and naturalized to the American kitchen.

3. *intr.* To become habituated or accustomed *to* some new condition.

1861 WINTHROP *C. Dreeme* 174 Until I acclimate to the atmosphere of work.

Acclimated, *ppl. a.* Inured or adapted to a new or strange climate. {1856–}

1800 Commons, etc. *Doc. Hist.* I. 253 The proprietor of several thousand arpents of land . . . is desirous to dispose of 45 acclimated negroes. **1852** *Knickerb.* XL. 199 My chaperon was an acclimated northerner. **1873** 'MARK TWAIN' & WARNER *Gilded Age* xvi. 153 The fever . . . left him, very thin, a little sallow but an 'acclimated' man.

+**Acclimation.** [ACCLIMATE *v.*] The process of acclimating or of becoming accustomed to a different or less natural climate. Also attrib. {1859}

1826 FLINT *Recoll.* 132 Emigrants generally suffer some kind of sickness, which is called 'seasoning,' implying that it is the summit of the gradual process of *acclimation.* **1832** *Deb. Congress* 15 June 3596 The culture of the cane . . . had been introduced by the Jesuits; and by the gradual acclimation of the cane, it had become firmly established. **1853** KANE *Grinnell Exped.* iii. 26, [I] could temper down at pleasure the abruptness of my acclimation. **1864** G. P. MARSH *Man & Nature* 19 *note*, The laws of acclimation of plants. **1873** 'MARK TWAIN' & WARNER *Gilded Age* xvi. 154 Taking every morning before breakfast a dose of bitters . . . out of the acclimation jug.

‖ **Acclimator.** [ACCLIMATE *v.*] One who inures others to a new climate. — **1827** COOPER *Prairie* xxxi, He an acclimator! I will engage to get the brats acclimated to a fever-and-agy bottom in a week.

+**Acclimature.** [ACCLIMATE *v.*] 'State of being inured to a climate' (Worc. '46, citing Caldwell).

* **Accommodate,** *v.*

+**1.** *tr.* To provide or supply (a person) with (a loan of) money. 'A commercial sense' (W. '28).

1811 *Ann. 11th Congress* 3 Sess. 610 [Because] the Bank of the United States . . . has committed the fault of not accommodating everybody, it must now cease to accommodate anybody. **1846** S. SMITH *Theatr. Apprent.* 68, I asked him for a loan of fifty cents, but he had not the money to accommodate me! **1880** BARNETT *Commercial Dict.* 10 Bills of exchange made . . . by a party . . . for the purpose of benefiting or accommodating some other party.

+**2.** *intr.* To provide or furnish visitors with accommodation. *local.*

1870 *Putnam's Mag.* Jan. 79/1 The question (where is the hotel?) invariably called forth the response, 'Thar' ain't nun'; but Farmer Smoot accommodates.'

Accommodation. Also † **accomodation, -idation, -adation (accomandation), acomodation, -adation.**

+**1.** Land conferred upon a colonist; a grant of land or real estate. Also fully *accommodation of land*, etc. *Obs.*

1636 *Essex Inst. Coll.* IV. 94/1 The town promised first acomodations vnto them. **1654** JOHNSON *Wonder-W. Prov.* 11 Others eying the best Grasse-platts and best Situation for Farmes and large Accommodations. **1659** *Hempstead Town Rec.* I. 33 One halfe of my Accomodations of Land. **1660** *New Haven Rec.* 465 [He] doth alienate for ever . . . his whole accomodation, both upland & meadow. **1666** *Groton Rec.* 17 A five acre acomadation of vpland. **1679** *Conn. Public Rec.* III. 42 Such persons as have propriety there and doe not com and build upon their accomadations. **1684** *Maine Doc. Hist.* XXIV. 230 They will afford each of said Families equall accommodation of Lands with himself.

2. Room and provision for one's needs, convenience, or

comfort; lodgings, entertainment. {1604–} Now chiefly *pl.* {1722–1803}

(*a*) **1704** S. KNIGHT *Journal* 25 Where alliting, in full assurance of good accomodation, wee were going in. **1797** *Ann. 4th Congress* 2 Sess. 2314 A committee was appointed to inquire into the state of the President's household, and to report ... what farther accommodation was necessary. **1821** COOPER *Spy* ii, A residence ... was kept furnished, and ready for his accommodation. **1840** KENNEDY *Quodlibet* 64 If our worthy representative would lay out some of his 'accommodation' in a more solid manner.

(*b*) **1704** *Boston News-Letter* 16 Oct. 2/2 A convenient back-dwelling House, with other Accommodations in Pudding-Lane ... to be lett. **1719** *Md. Hist. Mag.* XVIII. 9 There are not sufficient accommodations in the way of lodging &c. at the Court House. **1776** *Journals Cont. Congress* V. 422 Board and accommodations for prisoners at Trenton. **1804** *Md. Hist. Mag.* IV. 3 We rode to the house of ... a neighbouring farmer, where we found good accommodations. **1821** COOPER *Spy* i, The door was too nearly closed to admit of a minute scrutiny of the accommodations within. **1853** BALDWIN *Flush Times Alab.* 50 The 'accommodations' at the 'American Hotel' were not such as were calculated to beguile a spiritual mind. **1865** *Atlantic Mo.* XV. 346 Two very small closets afforded a little additional space; but the accommodations were certainly far from brilliant. **1869** BRACE *New West* i. 20 The run up the coast was ... delightful. ... The accommodations were luxurious **1880** 'MARK TWAIN' *Tramp Abroad* xxxii. 353 Other people ... drift around to two or three hotels, in the rain, before they find accommodations. **1901** MCCUTCHEON *Graustark* 15 He telegraphed ahead for accommodations.

+**3.** Financial or pecuniary aid in an emergency; a loan of money. {1824–}

1790 HAMILTON in *Ann. 1st Congress* II. 2058 The accommodations which they might derive in the way of their business, at a low rate. **1811** *Ann. 11th Congress* 3 Sess. 602 With a capital of ten millions, it [the Bank of the U.S.] has furnished accommodations of fifteen millions a year. **1837** *Democratic Rev.* I. 112 They stood in the perpetual relation of applicants for, and dispensers of, 'accommodation,'—of the means of conducting their daily business. **1865** PHILLIPS *Paper Currency* II. 15 Individuals when pressed obtain a temporary accommodation by issuing and having discounted their promissory notes.

4. Short for: Accommodation stage or train.

1829 A. ROYALL *Penna.* II. 9, I ... intended to take the Accommodation in the morning. **1877** 'Martin' *Hist. Great Riots* 117 The Sharpsville 'accommodation,' which had been lying for two hours without an engine, was supplied and departed. **1909** WHITE *Rules of Game* I. vii, They tramped to the station and boarded the single passenger car of the accommodation.

‖**Accommodational,** *a. local.* Offering accommodations; accommodative. — **1829** *Virginia Lit. Museum* 16 Dec. 418 A short time ago, we saw a tavern, recommended in a printed handbill as the most *accommodational* on the road.

+**Accommodation boat, car, coach,** one making local calls or stops to serve passengers. — **1838** *Boston Almanac* 49 Accommodation boats. — **1836** *Merchants' & Taylors' Guide* (Boston) 65 The price of the tickets is $2.00—accommodation cars $1.50. **1892** *Harper's Mag.* Feb. 426/1 What may be called accommodation cars [of an elevator] halt at the lower floors. — **1830** *Collegian* 125 One of these vehicular conveniences that, by the association of contrast, are styled 'Accommodation Coaches.' **1840** *S. Lit. Messenger* VI. 224/2 My appointed seat in the old lumbering vehicle, honored with the name of an 'Accommodation Coach.'

+**Accommodation fare.** The fare on an accommodation stage. — **1811** *Daily Advertiser* (Phila.) 11 July, From Philadelphia to New York. The Accommodation-fare through 3 dollars.

+**Accommodation house.** A house for accommodating travelers. — **1878** I. L. BIRD *Rocky Mts.* 165 Though the hosts kept 'an accommodation house for travellers,' they would take nothing for my entertainment!

+**Accommodation land.** 'Land acquired for the purpose of being added to other land for its improvement' (*Cent.* citing Rapalje & Lawrence.)

+**Accommodation line.** A line of 'accommodation stages.' — **1834** [R. BAIRD] *Valley Mississippi* xiii. 147 There are two lines daily called the mail and Accommodation Lines.

+**Accommodation note.** 'One drawn and offered for discount, for the purpose of borrowing its amount' (W. '28). — **1797** *Ann. 5th Congress* I. 395 Many of such notes were what was called 'accommodation notes'; all were acknowledgments of debt, and therefore no proof of wealth. *Ib.* 401 Accommodation notes ... were often renewed.

+**Accommodation paper.** Notes, or bills of exchange, made, indorsed, or accepted by a person to accommodate or favor another in the course of business.

1829 SHERWOOD *Gaz. Georgia* (ed. 2) 75 The Bank to collect the debts due the State, and debtors to be allowed to renew their notes, ... as persons borrowing money on accommodation paper. **1833** *Deb. Congress* 1 March 1900 Whether any considerable portion of it consists of what is called accommodation paper, regularly renewed. **1852** *Knickerb.* XXXIX. 54 He ... only ventures upon decided approval of 'accommodation paper' when he is very sure of his man.

+**Accommodation stage** (or **stagecoach**). =ACCOMMODATION COACH.

1811 *Columbian Sentinel (Boston)* 25 Sept. 3/1. **1826** *Amer. Traveller* 14 March 2/5 The new lines of stages from Boston to Albany, called the Express and Citizens' lines of stages; or otherwise denominated 'Accommodation Stages.' **1829** A. ROYALL *Penna.* II. 49 He ... has the impudence to mention 'mail stages and accommodation stages'—very accommodating stages indeed! **1843** 'CARLTON' *New Purchase* I. iii. 17 So remarkably accommodating were the old-fashioned accommodation stages and stage owners! **1860** WORC., *Accommodation stage-coach,* ... a stage-coach ... designed to accommodate passengers, as to time, in distinction from the mail-stage.

+**Accommodation train.** A train that stops at local stations, in distinction from an express or 'fast' train; a 'mixed train.'

In some States now also applied to 'a freight train with a passenger coach.'

1838 *Boston Almanac* 49 Depots on the Providence Rail Road. Accommodation Train. **1856** *Mich. Agric. Soc. Trans.* VII. 333 They run four passenger trains ... and one accommodation train from Detroit to Kalamazoo. **1869** HALE *Sybaris* 96 People did not choose to churn along in snuffy old accommodation trains. **1891** ELLIS *Check No. 2134* iv. 28 To board the accommodation train, it was necessary for the agent to display the red light or flag. **1911** *Southern Reporter* LV. 595 A 'mixed or accommodation train.'

* **Account.**

1. *By all accounts,* according to every report. *colloq.* {Also E.}

1825 NEAL *Bro. Jonathan* I. 10 [She was] the prettiest one though, 'by all accounts,' there was 'a-goin,' as everybody 'allowed.'

2. *Of no account,* of no good or consequence; of no value or use; worthless. Cf. 'COUNT *n.* {1767–}

'An expression of utter contempt, ... much used in the South and South-West' (Clapin).

1853 F. W. THOMAS *Randolph* 119 It is no matter where old Nat dies; he's old, now, and of no account nohow to nobody. **1859** BARTLETT 2 These hogs are of no account. **1871** BARNUM *Struggles & Triumphs* 669 What the *Herald* said, good or bad, was, like the editor himself, literally of 'no account.' **1888** P. H. SHERIDAN *Memoirs* I. 47 As the 'regular troops up there were of no account, the citizens ... intended cleaning up the hostiles.'

b. Ellipt. *No account,* =prec. (Cf. NO-ACCOUNT *a.*)

1850 GARRARD *Wah-To-Yah* i. 2 Your money's no account. **1852** STOWE *Uncle Tom* xi, 'Then it's no account talking,' said the woman. **1878** BEADLE *Western Wilds* 187 Little Si Duvall, a splintery feller with no legs to speak of, and every body said no account.

+**3.** *To hand in one's accounts,* to die. *colloq.*

1873 ALDRICH *Marj. Daw* 150 The hotel remains to-day pretty much the same as when Jonathan Bayley handed in his accounts in 1840.

***Accountant.** A professional keeper or inspector of accounts; 'an officer in a public office who has charge of the accounts' (W. '28).

*a*1656 BRADFORD *Hist.* 349 This year also Mr. Sherley would needs send them over a new accountante. **1798** *Ann. 5th Congress* I. 562 An act allowing an additional compensation to the Accountant of the War Department. **1802** *Ann. 7th Congress* App. 1305 The Accountant of the Navy Department. **1893** 'MARK TWAIN' *P. Wilson* ii, He ... offered his services now in the humble capacities of land surveyor and expert accountant. **1909** *Indian Laws & Tr.* III. 422 To employ in the Office of Indian Affairs an expert accountant.

+**Accounting office.** An office appropriated to the keeping of accounts. — **1804** *Ann. 8th Congress* 1 Sess. 266 The organization of the accounting offices of the Treasury, War, and Navy Department.

+**Accounting officer.** An officer who keeps or checks accounts. — **1802** *Ann. 7th Congress* App. 1304 That the accounting officers of the Treasury Department be ... authorized ... to make ... allowances for clerk hire. **1823** *Ann. 18th Congress* 1 Sess. I. 825 The settlement which had been made by the accounting officer. **1841** TRUMBULL *Autobiog.* 96 In May, 1777, ... my military accounts were audited and settled at Albany, by the proper accounting officer, John Carter.

***Accoutrement, Accouterment.** Also †**acuttrement, accoutriment, accotroment.** *pl.* The equipment or outfit of a soldier other than arms and dress. {18th c.} Cf. COUTREMENT.

(*a*) **1704** SEWALL *Diary* II. 93 [The Indians] left many of their own accoutrements, for haste, and carried nothing away of ours. **1745** *Georgia Col. Rec.* VI. 144 Others ... are charged with feloniously stealing the King's arms, ammunitions and accoutrements. **1778** *Journals Cont. Congress* X. 30 The cartouch boxes, and several other articles of military accoutrements. **1807** *Ann. 10th Congress* 1 Sess. I. 422 Colonel Burr made many inquiries of me, relative ... to the state of its militia; the discipline, arms, accoutrements [etc.]. **1858** VIELÉ *Following Drum* 117 His military coat, hat and accoutrements taken from him.

(*b*) **1787** T. Speed *Danville Polit. Club, Ky.* (1894) 128 Ought the inhabitants ... submit to the impressment of their arms and accouterments? **1867** EDWARDS *Shelby* 499 Splendid arms, magnificent accouterments, silver spurs, ... and all the pomp of war.

***Ace.** +A point scored in baseball; a run. — **1845** in *Appleton's Ann. Cycl.* (1886) 77/2 The game [in baseball] to consist of twenty-one counts or aces. *Ib.*, No ace or base can be made on a foul strike.

+**Acequia.** *S.W.* Also †**acecquia.** [Sp.] An irrigating ditch or channel. (Cf. SEQUIA.)

1844 GREGG *Commerce* I. 152 All the *acequias* for the valley of the Rio del Norte are conveyed from the main stream, except where a tributary of more convenient waters happens to join it. **1847** RUXTON *Adv. Rocky Mts.* (1848) 186 His only care being, that the river rise high enough to fill his *acequia*, or irrigating ditch. **1869** BROWNE *Adv. Apache Country* 48 A proposition has been entertained by Congress to reclaim this vast tract of country . . . by means of a grand canal from the Colorado, with a connected system of acequias. **1873** BEADLE *Undevel. West* 486 An *acecquia*, taken out of the river above, runs along the bluffs. **1887** *Outing* X. 12/1 Back of its hacienda is a fine orchard and vegetable garden, watered by an acequia.

***Acknowledge,** *v.* +**1.** *intr.* To own *to* something; to admit or confess having. — **1857** HAMMOND *Northern Scenes* 127 Smith blazed away at him, . . . but the deer dashed forward. . . . Smith acknowledged to a severe attack of the Buck fever. — +**2.** *To acknowledge the corn:* see CORN *n.*

***A clock,** *prep. phr. Obs.* Of the clock; o'clock {-1741}

1622 'MOURT' *Relation* 28 About 11. a clocke our Shallop came to us. **1634** *Essex Inst. Coll.* IV. 89/2 The market . . . to continew from 9 a'clock in the morning to 4 of the clock after noone. **1675** *Md. Archives* II. 422 The house is adjourned till one a clock. **1702** C. MATHER *Magnalia* (1853) I. v. 382 Two a clock in the morning. **1741** *Amer. Mag.* I. 116 About one a clock the flakes [of snow] grew larger. **1772** *Md. Hist. Mag.* XIV. 138 It began to snow . . . between 4 & 5 a clock, I measured it at 9 a clock.

***Acold,** *a.* Cold; chilled. {*c* 1314-1608; 1821-70 *arch.*; 1881- *dial.*}

1676 TOMPSON *Poet. Works* 50 An honest grace would hold Till an hot puddin grew at heart a cold. **1744** FRANKLIN *Acc. Fire-places* 6 To make a fire . . . by which they might warm themselves when acold. **1825** NEAL *Bro. Jonathan* III. 165 His blood was a-cold with it. **1845** *Knickerb.* XXVI. 471 He must be a-cold. Make him a good warm toddy.

+**Acold** (in *death a-cold*), =of cold. — **1825** NEAL *Bro. Jonathan* I. 357 What could possess you, to run out . . . barefooted—enough to get your death a-cold. **1869** ALCOTT *Little Women* II. 225 Here he is . . . getting his death a-cold pattering over that canvas.

***Acorn,** *n.* Also † **acorne, akorne, acchorn, acron.**

***1.** The fruit of the oak-tree.

1612 SMITH *Virginia* 10 The acornes of one kind [of oak are] . . . somewhat sweetish. **1634** A. WHITE *Brief Rel. Md.* (1910) 45 The soyle . . . is excellent so that we cannot sett downe a foot, but tread on . . . acchorns, walnutts, saxafras, etc. *a***1649** WINTHROP *Hist.* I. 128 There was great scarcity of corn, by reason of the spoil our hogs had made at harvest . . . (there being no acorns). **1654** JOHNSON *Wonder-W. Prov.* ix. 20 The poore Indians . . . were forced to lengthen out their owne food with acorns. **1690** *Maine Doc. Hist.* V. 146 Our provetions was very shorte, Indian corn & acorens. **1709** LAWSON *Carolina* 67 Oaks of four or five sorts, . . . each bearing very good acorns. **1797** TRUMBULL *Hist. Conn.* (1898) I. 8 Such were the necessities of the people [i.e. first settlers] that they fed on clams, muscles, ground-nuts, and acorns. **1806** *Ann. 9th Congress* 2 Sess. 1114 A species of white oak . . . produces a large acorn in great abundance, upon which the bears feed; and which is very fattening to hogs. **1819** SCHOOLCRAFT *Journal* 29 [We had] acorns for supper. **1834** PECK *Gaz. Illinois* 9 The acorns and other fruits from the trees . . . accelerate the growth of swine. **1848** E. BRYANT *California* 268 The acorn, mush or atole, . . . constitutes the principal food of these Indians in their wild state. **1881** *Rep. Indian Affairs* 12 Native flour is composed of . . . the acorn. **1891** RYAN *Pagan* 179 A big drove of hogs on a white-oak flat, when the acorns are a good crop.

||**2.** *To come to the acorns*, to experience adversity.

1835 BIRD *Hawks of Hawk-h.* I. xix. 256 You're no Johnny Raw, I see; but you'll come to the acorns yet!

+**3.** Attrib. with *bread, meal, oil, year.*

1687 *Huntington Rec.* I. 490 Butt if it bee a great acorne year people may have libertie to turne them [*sc.* hogs] out to the common after Indian corn is all gathered in. **1709** LAWSON *Carolina* 178 As to the Indians food, it is . . . fowl of all sorts . . ., acorns and acorn oil [etc.]. **1848** E. BRYANT *California* xxviii. 345 Their breakfast . . . consisted of . . . a kettle of *atole* made of acorn-meal. **1882** J. HAWTHORNE *Fortune's Fool* I. xxiii, What I need now is a bellyful of venison and acorn-bread. *a* **1918** G. STUART *On Frontier* I. 65 These little cakes of acorn bread were bitter to taste but highly nutritious.

||**Acorn,** *v.* [ACORN *n.*] *intr.* To search for acorns. — *a* **1841** [W. HAWES] *Sporting Scenes* I. 152 It might be an unmanageable colt, . . . or a stray porker acorn-ing.

***ACRE.** Also † **acrre; ackre, acker, accer, acher, -or; acer, acor, aker, akar, akor.**

***1.** A measure of land, comprising 4840 square yards; a piece or plot of land of this area.

(*a*) **1622** 'MOURT' *Relation* 132 We set . . . some twentie acres of Indian corne. **1631** *Mass. Bay Rec.* I. 91 There is graunted to Mr. Gouernor 600 ac[res] of land. **1636** *Dedham Rec.* 20 Set out and measured for Abraham Shawe 12 acres. **1693** *Providence Rec.* V. 37 Thirty acres of land by the eighteene foote pole. **1708** *Ib.* XI. 124 The piece of land . . . to be a quarter of one acre & tenn poles. **1788** WASHINGTON *Diaries* III. 330 The first acre . . . was also sown with . . . white clover. **1820** *Ann. 16th Congress* 1 Sess. I. 891 The number of acres of land sold at the several land offices. **1843** *Diplom. Corr. Texas* (1911) III. 870 She possesses at least fifty million of acres river bottom land. **1896** WILKINS *Madelon* 286 The Gordon acres . . . had been lying fallow for the last ten years.

(*b*) **1635** *Cambridge Prop. Rec.* 3 Five ackers moore or les. **1649** *Boston Rec.* 95 Paine . . . hath let to him 500 accers of land, . . . painge forty shillings per annum. **1697** *N. H. Probate Rec.* I. 423 My lands in the great bay being thirty fiouer ackers.

(*c*) **1634** *Maine Doc. Hist.* III. 32 A pece of ground . . . about 4 or 5 akers. **1639** *Boston Rec.* 39 An hundred akers of upland ground. **1656** *Springfield Rec.* I. 157 Aker for aker of house lotts and aker for aker of meddowe. **1672** *Derby* (Conn.) *Rec.* 21 His first devision . . . containing five akers more or les. **1702** *Waterbury Prop. Rec.* 56 Five acers for a paustor [=pasture]. **1821** J. FOWLER *Journal* 41 The brush in which we camped contained from 10 to 20 acors.

2. As a measure of coal: (see quotation).

1880 *Harper's Mag.* Dec. 55 An acre of coal . . . means 120,000 bushels . . . in a 'seam' four feet eight inches thick.

+**3.** Attrib. with *lot.*

1869 HALE *Sybaris* 130 This, if you chose to divide it so, would be a freehold acre-lot for so many families.

Across lots: see LOT *n.*

+**Acrost,** *adv. colloq.* or *dial.* [f. *across* + *-t.*] From side to side; through, across.

1779 *Mass. Hist. Soc.* 2 Ser. II. 467 The Lake . . . is . . . about 8 miles acrost. *Ib.*, The outlet of this Lake . . . was two rods acrost. **1846** WHITCHER *Bedott P.* vii. 77 Kier said he heered her stretch her neck acrost and whisper. **1908** *Dial. Notes* III. 285.

+**Acrost,** *prep. colloq.* or *dial.* [See prec.]

1. From one side to another of; across.

1759 *Essex Inst. Coll.* XIX. 145 The enemy fired at our men a crost the river. **1777** *Ib.* XLV. 210 The poor fellow attempted . . . to come in a canoe a crost the river. **1779** *Mass. H. S. Coll.* 2 Ser. II. 469 A tree that was fell acrost the same [outlet]. **1849** LOWELL *Two Gunners* iii, Acrost lots in a pond . . . twenty rod beyond [was] a goose. **1852** STOWE *Uncle Tom* xxii, A good, round, school-boy hand, that Tom said might be read 'most acrost the room.' **1898** CANFIELD *Maid of Frontier* 182, I wheeled my horse acrost the road. **1906** F. LYNDE *Quickening* 2 A-smashin' the whisky jug acrost the wagon tire.

2. *To come acrost*, to come upon, fall in with.

1831 *Louisville* (Ky.) *Advertiser* 17 Oct., I came acrost a feller . . . fast asleep. **1848** LOWELL *Biglow P.* I. ix, I come acrost a kin' o' hut. **1875** 'MARK TWAIN' *Sk., Jumping Frog*, One day a feller . . . come acrost him with his box.

***ACT,** *n.*

***1.** A decision or decree of a legislative body, council, or court of justice; a legislative enactment.

1620 '*Mayflower*' *Compact*, [We] frame such . . . ordinances, acts, constitutions . . . as shall be thought most meet . . . for the general good of the colony. **1630** *Mass. Bay Rec.* I. 82 Contrary to an act of Court formerly made. **1646** *Springfield Rec.* I. 187 Whatsoever they shall soe order . . . shall stand in force as the Act of the towne. **1666** *Maryland Archives* II. 101 Thomas Brooke . . . ordered to present those two Acts passed this howse, to the Upper howse. **1716** *Mass. H. Repr. Journals* I. 111 An Act relating to Sureties . . . in Civil Actions. **1759** (*title*), Acts and Laws of His Majesty's Province of the Massachusetts-Bay in New-England. **1787** *Constitution* iv. §1 Full faith . . . shall be given in each state to the public acts . . . of every other state. **1823** THACHER *Military Journal* 427 The resolutions of Congress . . . are as . . . binding on the United States, as the most solemn acts of confederation or legislation.

b. A decree, edict, or order of Congress.

1779 *Secret Journal of Congress* 16 Oct. 1 A certified copy of an act of Congress of the 4th instant. **1789** *Ann, 1st Congress* I. 44 That six hundred copies of the acts of Congress . . . be printed. **1796** *Ann. 4th Congress* 2 Sess. 1687 Certain claims . . . excepted from the act of limitation. **1806** *Ann. 9th Congress* 1 Sess. 1238 From and after the passing of this act. **1825** *Austin Papers* (1924) II. 1077 A list of the Acts passed the last session of Congress. **1855** GLISAN *Jrnl. Army Life* 182 An act of congress permitting officers of the navy to command mail steamers. **1881-5** MCCLELLAN *Own Story* 114, I procured the passage of an act authorizing the appointment of additional aides-de-camp to general officers.

***2.** A formal record of a legislative decree or resolve.

1634 *Watertown Rec.* 1 One of them . . . shall keep the Records and Acts of the towne. **1789** *Ann. 1st Congress* I. 77 The bill to provide for the safe-keeping of the acts, records, and seal of the United States.

b. An official or legal document.

1788 JEFFERSON *Writings* (1855) II. 501 These captains and masters shall lodge in the chancery . . . the acts which they may have made in other ports.

3. A college exercise. *Obs.* {1641-}

1643 *New Eng. First-Fruits* I. §4 The students of the first classis . . . as they have kept their publick Acts in former yeares, ourselves being present at them; so have they lately kept two solemn Acts for their Commencement.

+**4.** *To do the . . act,* to act in a manner characteristic of a specified person or type. *colloq.*

1887 *Harper's Mag.* May 990/2 He at once began . . . to abuse the negro, accusing him of . . . doing the dude act in charcoal. **1904** W. H. Smith *Promoters* iii. 72 They did the hospitality act up in great shape. **1907** M. C. Harris *Tents of Wickedness* 41 She thought she was going to do the Melburn act and ride roughshod over prejudices.

***Act,** *v.* **1.** *intr.* To carry out military movements; to operate. {1684} **2.** To seem to be. *colloq.* {*dial.* 1886–} — **(1) 1780** *Heath P.* 96 About three thousand militia shall act upon the island, about 1,500 near Quaker Hill. — **(2) 1891** Freeman *New Eng. Nun* 153, I gave Sarah Rogers one of them nice printed ones, an' she acted glad enough to have it.

+**Actional,** *a. Obs.* Of the nature of a legal action; involving an action or actions. — **1662** *R. I. Col. Rec.* I. 497 It shall be alowed on the actionall case aforesayd. **1664** *Ib.* II. 31 That two Courts of Triall in the yeare be held . . . for the triall of any actionall matter.

Actionist. +One who advocates or favors separate State action. — **1851** *Harper's Mag.* III. 557/2 A letter from Hon. J. L. Orr . . ., reflecting . . . upon the spirit manifested by the 'actionists' toward the 'cooperationists.'

***Actor.** A stage-player or dramatic performer.

'There is a contract . . . dated July 11, 1716, by which . . . Charles and Mary Stagg, his wife, "actors," [agree] to build a theatre in Williamsburg, and to provide actors, scenery, and music out of England' (1907 Tyler *Williamsburg* 224).

1760 Seilhamer *Hist. Amer. Theatre* (1888) I. 115 The principal characters . . . were performed with great justice, and the applause . . . did less honor to the abilities of the actors than to the taste of their auditors. **1762** *Ib.* 127 The inhabitants [of Providence] . . . did . . . pass a vote that no stage-plays be acted in said town; yet the actors thereof . . . are now daily continuing to exhibit stage-plays. **1794** Hodgkinson *Lett. Emigration* 41 The general mediocrity of talents in the New York actors. **1832** Dunlap *Hist. Amer. Theater* 173 The person . . . will long be entitled to the character of the most perfect actor America has seen. **1846** S. Smith *Theatr. Apprent.* 21 My landlord hinted . . . that he had lost a good deal by the actor-folks. **1852** *Harper's Mag.* V. 409/1 A favorite actor may now and then be toasted at a public dinner. **1886** B. Matthews & Hutton *Actors & Actresses* IV. 37 The future master of the American stage, . . . surrounded by a group of veteran actors, began a career.

***Actress.** A female stage-actor. {1666–}

1806 Webster. **1832** Dunlap *Hist. Amer. Theater* 105 An involuntary laugh from the audience had nearly destroyed . . . the hopes of the actress [=Mrs. Melmoth]. **1855** Thompson *Doesticks* xxvi. 231 An actress, to be popular at this theatre, must be willing to play any part. **1884** *N.Y. Times & Express* June, An engraver . . . made a couple of dozen such buttons for a leading actress.

***Actuary. a.** (See quot. 1847.) **b.** An officer, as of an insurance company, who computes premiums, compiles tables of mortality, etc.; one expert in the application of the law of chances to financial risks, as in life, fire, or accident insurance. {1842 Brande; 1849–}

1847 Webster, *Actuary,* . . . in America, . . . is chiefly applied to the manager of a life insurance company. **1851** Cist *Cincinnati* 95 New York Life Insurance Co. . . . Pliny Freeman, Actuary. **1881** *Harper's Mag.* Jan. 275/2 Another [insurance] company . . . bought up, according to its actuary's testimony, a large number [of policies] 'simply as a gratuity.'

+**AD,** *abbrev.* (See quotations and cf. A, 1.) — **1641** *Plymouth Col. Rec.* II. 28 The Court doth censure them as followeth: That . . . They shall weare . . . two letters, viz., AD, for adulterers, daly, vpon the outeside of their vppermost garment. **1658** *Plymouth Laws* 113 Whosoever shall comitt adultery shalbee severely punished by . . . [being made] to weare two capitall letters viz. A D. cut out in cloth and sowed on theire uper most garments on theire arme or backe.

+**Ad.** *colloq.* [Abbreviation.] An advertisement. (Cf. Want-ad.)

'Another Americanism . . . which has been generally adopted on both sides of the Atlantic' (Farmer). 'A printer's usual abbreviation . . . now generally adopted . . . in the whole advertising business of the country' (Clapin).

1868 *Putnam's Mag.* Aug. 215/2 In the newspaper offices and the advertising business they say 'ad.' **1884** Nye *Baled Hay* 202 He wouldn't run any of his ads. **1888** *Century Mag.* Dec. 299/1 The astute Mr. Cummiskey booked a ten-dollar 'ad' on the spot. **1909** 'O. Henry' *Options* 6, I know every end of the business from editing to setting up the classified ads.

***Adam.** [Biblical name of the first man.]

+**1.** In humorous uses: *Outward Adam,* one's body. *Adam's leather,* the human skin.

1835 Bird *Hawks of Hawk-h.* II. i. 17 Never show an inch of Adam's leather to an Indian. **1836** Crockett *Adventures* 56, I had no sooner elongated my outward Adam, than they at it again, with renewed vigour. *Ib.* 91 Having the gentility of his outward Adam thus endorsed by his tailor.

2. *Adam and Eve.* [Gen. ii. 21–24.] Popular name of the putty root (a species of orchis), *Aplectrum hiemale.* Also locally applied to other plants (see quotations).

'So called from the bulb of the preceding year being always connected with the new one' (B. '59). The name is similarly used in E. dialects of other plants: see Britten & Holland *Plant-names* and *Eng. Dial. Dict.*

1821 *Mass. H. S. Coll.* 2 Ser. IX. 149 Plants, which are indigenous in the township of Middlebury, [Vermont, include] . . . *Cymbidium hyemale,* Adam and Eve. **1843** Torrey *Flora N.Y.* II. 270 Adam & Eve . . . [grows in] woods, in rich vegetable mould: rare. **1847** Wood *Botany* 531 Adam-and-Eve; Putty-root. . . . A fine plant, in woods, Can., Ohio to N. Eng. (rare) and Flor. . . . May, Jn. **1893** *Amer. Folk-Lore* VI. 136 *Aconitum napellus,* Adam and Eve. Washington Co., Me.

***Adamantine,** *a.* and *n.*

+**1.** *Adamantine candle,* a candle made of hard wax.

1851 Cist *Cincinnati* 223 Thomas Emery . . . manufactures . . . adamantine candles. **1860** *Texas Almanac* 248 Lard Oil, Sperm, Star, and Adamantine Candles. **1861** *Army Regulations* 243 One pound of sperm candles, or one and one-fourth pound of adamantine candles. **1882** *Rep. Indian Affairs* 432 Candles, adamantine: . . . 8,450 awarded.

+**2.** A member of the extreme faction of the 'Hardshells' (q.v.). Also *Adamantine Hard.*

1854 A. M. Murray *Lett. from U.S.* (1856) I. 197 Party terms . . . such as Adamantines, Hard-shells, Soft-shells, Loco-focos, Rick-burners, and Pollywogs. It seems these names . . . have originated in casual expressions made use of by public speakers which have happened to hit the fancy of the hearers, so that they became cant terms. **1889** *Cent.* s.v. *Hard,* Of the more conservative of the two factions . . . the extreme members were called the Adamantine Hards.

Adamite.[1] *Obs.* [Adam] One of a sect whose members claimed to have attained the innocence of Adam, and hence dispensed with clothing and marriage. {1621–}— **1656** *Conn. Public Rec.* I. 283 It is ordered . . . that no towne within this jurisdiction shall entertaine any Quakers, Ranters, Adamites, or such like notorious heritiques. **1668** *Ib.* II. 87 Heretical books . . . such . . . as contayne the errors of Quakers, Ranters, Adamites or such like notorious heretiques.

+**Adamite.**[2] [*Adam-s:* see def.] An adherent or supporter of John Adams, second President of the U.S. (1797–1801), or of his son John Quincy Adams, sixth President (1825–9).

'A current appellation, from 1821 to 1832, for the adherents of John Quincy Adams' (Clapin).

1800 *Aurora* (Phila.) 16 May (Th.) The three parties are now known by the designation of the Republicans, the Adamites, the Pickeronians.

+**Adam's cup.** (See quot.) — **1836** Lincoln *Botany* 169 Side-saddle flower . . . is sometimes called Adam's cup, in reference also to the shape of the leaf.

+**Adamsism.** [See Adamite 2.] Support of John Quincy Adams or advocacy of his political principles or policy. — **1824** W. L. Marcy in Mackenzie *Van Buren* (1846) 199 The attack upon Mr. Mallory is by every body regarded as cruel and savage. . . . I hope this proceeding will cure him of his Adamsism.

+**Adam's needle.** [With allusion to Gen. iii. 7.] Popular name of one or other species of yucca, esp. *Yucca gloriosa* or *filamentosa.*

1791 Bartram *Travels* 71 Betwixt them, the water and marshes, is a barricade of Palmetto royal (*Yucca gloriosa*) or Adam's needle. **1843** T. Talbot *Journals* 14 'The Adam's needle' . . . has a tall stalk covered with white flowers shaded in crimson. **1846** *Congress. Exec. Doc. No. 41* 405 A plant which is extremely useful to the Mexicans as a substitute for soap . . . by us [called] Adams needle, or Spanish bayonet; its botanical name is *Yucca angustifolia.* **1858** Warder *Hedges & Evergr.* II. 282 *Yucca gloriosa.*—This kind of Adam's needle is native of the Southern States. **1891** *Cent.* s.v. *Yucca,* From their sharp-pointed leaves with threads hanging from their edges, *Y. filamentosa* and *Y. aloifolia* are known as Adam's needle and thread and as Eve's thread.

***Adder.**[1] Loosely applied to various snakes more or less resembling the viper.

'Applied to . . . various spotted serpents, venomous or harmless, as species of *Toxicophis, Heterodon,* etc.' (Cent.).

1832 Williamson *Maine* I. 170 Eight species of Serpents have been seen among us; viz. 1. the Rattlesnake; . . . 6. the Adder. **1839** Storer *Mass. Reptiles* 227 *Coluber Eximius,* the Chicken Snake, . . . is [also] known by the names of . . . milk snake, and chequered adder. **1853** Hawthorne *Note-books* II. 228 She called it an adder, but it appears to have been a striped snake. **1875** *Amer. Naturalist* IX. 10 The Flat-head Adder or Blowing Viper, *Heterodon platyrhinos.*

***Adder.**[2] +'An instrument for performing addition' (*Cent.*); an adding-machine. — [**1864** Webster, *Adder,* one who, or that which, adds.] **1890** *N.Y. Herald* Jan. (Advt.), The Adder is so called because really too simple to be styled a 'machine.'

***Adderbolt.** ?*Obs.* The dragon-fly {1703; now *dial.*} — **1743** Catesby *Carolina* II. p. xxxvii, I observed in Carolina . . . the Adder-bolt, the Cicada. **1789** Morse *Amer. Geog.* (1792) 62 Of the astonishing variety of insects found in America, we will mention the Glow worm, . . . Adder bolt. **1828** Webster s.v. *Adder-fly.*

+**Adder's-mouth.** A species of terrestrial orchid of the genus *Microstylis,* esp. *M. ophioglossoides;* a plant of this genus.

1840 Dewey *Mass. Flowering Plants* 202 *M. ophioglossoides.* Nutt.

Adder-mouth [*sic*] . . . : root bulbous; roots of trees; June. **1843** TORREY *Flora N.Y.* II. 268 *Microstylis monophylles*, . . . Short-stalked Adder's-mouth, . . . [grows in] deep shady swamps. **1857** GRAY *Botany* 451 *Microstylis*, Nutt. Adder's-Mouth. . . . Little herbs from solid bulbs, . . . [with] a raceme of minute greenish flowers. **1889** *Cent.* s.v., Adder's-mouth . . . [is] found in cool damp woods in North America, with . . . a single leaf shaped somewhat like the head of a snake.

∗ **Adder's-tongue.**

∗**1.** A species of fern, *Ophioglossum vulgatum;* so called from the shape of the spore-bearing branches.

1832 WILLIAMSON *Maine* I. 120 Adder's-tongue grows two feet high, in running water, and is said to be a remedy for the hydrophobia. **1853** *Knickerb.* XLII. 172 We brought in our aprons . . . spotted adders' tongues, and dandelions. **1869** FULLER *Flower Gatherers* 48 On account of its narrow spotted leaves, it is often called 'Adder's Tongue' by country people. **1878** STOWE *Poganuc People* xvii. 182 The spotted adder's tongue, with its waving yellow bells of blossom.

+**2.** (See quotations.) *Obs.*

1784 CUTLER in *Mem. Academy* I. 434 *Convallaria*, . . . Harewort, . . . is called Adder's Tongue, and mistaken for one of the ferns, which is known by that name in England. **1795** WINTERBOTHAM *Hist. View* III. 397 Among the . . . plants of New-England, the following have been employed for medicinal purposes: . . . Adder's tongue, *Convallaria bifolia.* Unicorn, *Aletris farinosa.*

+**3.** The dogtooth violet, *Erythronium Americanum.*

1821 *Mass. H. S. Coll.* 2 Ser. IX. 150 Plants, which are indigenous in the town of Middlebury, [Vermont, include] . . . *Erythronium lanceolatum*, (Pursh.) Adder's tongue. **1835** HOFFMAN *Winter in West* I. 145, I could fancy . . . the lilac-tinted adder's-tongue, and straw-coloured arrow-head, shooting through the long grass between. **1857** GRAY *Botany* 471 Yellow Adder's-tongue. . . . Low copses, &c.; common. May. **1882** *Century Mag.* Sept. 778/1 Flowers grew in abundance among the snow-banks—adder's-tongue, bluebells, . . . and half a dozen other species.

+**Adder-tongue fern.** =ADDER'S-TONGUE 1. — **1845** LINCOLN *Botany* App. 133/2.

+**Adding-machine.** A calculating machine designed to perform arithmetical addition; =ADDER *n.*[2] — **1874** KNIGHT 12/2. **1911** HARRISON *Queed* viii. 102 He was as definite as an adding-machine, as practical as a cash register.

∗ **ADDITION.** Also † **adition, adittion.**

+**1.** An added lot, plot, or extent of land; a piece *of* land added to existing holdings.

Freq. in place-names, esp. with early owner's name prefixed: see *Md. Hist. Mag.* XXI. pp. 24–361 (1667, etc.)

1636 *Springfield Rec.* I. 159 [A lot with] an adition . . . of as much marish as makes the whole twenty fouer acres. **1646** *Ib.* 187 They shall have power to give an addition of meddow to them. **1654** JOHNSON *Wonder-W. Prov.* 129 They purchased some addition of the Town of Newbery. **1654** *Portsmouth Rec.* 65 To lay out the adition of land granted to Mr. Almy. **1721** *Mass. H. Repr. Journals* III. 12 A Petition . . . praying for an addition of 3700 acres of land, to be added to their former grant.

+**2.** An area near a city, town, or village, more recently laid out into lots, streets, etc., as an extension of the residential section.

1786 *Md. Journal* 6 Jan. (Th.) Found, in Howard's new Addition to Baltimore-Town, 127 panes of glass. **1788** *Ib.* 19 Feb. (Th.) About 500 lots in Rogers's Addition to Baltimore-Town. **1813** *Ann. 12th Congress* 2 Sess. 100 Proprietors . . . of the property contained in 'Deakins, Lee, and Casanave's' addition to Georgetown. **1885** *Harper's Mag.* April 694/2 The centre of an important new quarter of the town, or 'addition,' as the trans-Mississippi word is. **1896** *Dialect Notes* I. 384 Knox's addition to the city of —. Used in legal papers, etc. North Mississippi Valley. **1923** R. HERRICK *Lilla* 24 The new Addition . . . was a new strip of prairie [near Chicago] which the Porter Realty Company was preparing to put on the market.

+**3.** A part added to a building.

c **1638** *Harvard Rec.* I. 172 For unloading the lumber prepard for the Addition: [£]3 10[*s*.]. **1660** *Plymouth Laws* 127 An adition shalbee erected of fourteen foot longe of equall hight with the prison att the one end therof. **1693** *Boston Rec.* 216 Edward Peggy desired liberty to make an addition to the westwardly end of his hous. **1850** G. HINES *Voyage* 15 It [was] necessary . . . for the missionaries to build an addition to their house. **1861** *Army Regulations* 163 The quartermaster shall make . . . reports . . . of the additions, alterations, and repairs that are needed. **1887** WILKINS *Humble Romance* 120 Hiram Arms never ought to have put on them additions.

+**4.** *Addition, division, and silence*, 'a Philadelphia expression, which, for a time, had a vogue as a catch phrase' (F.).

1867 W. H. KEMBLE *Let. to T. J. Coffey* March (Cl.) Evans . . . has a claim of some magnitude that he wishes you to help him in. Put him through as you would me. He understands addition, division and silence.

∗ **ADDRESS,** *n.*

1. 'A message of respect, congratulation, thanks, petition, &c.' (W. '28); an expression of views or sentiments transmitted in writing to an authority. {1751–}

In the Colonial period esp. one presented to the King, the Governor, or the Supreme Court.

1660 *Mass. Col. Rec.* IV. 1. 449 Ordered, that our addresses be made to the kings most excellent majesty, as also to the high Court of Parliament. **1685** SEWALL *Diary* I. 71 Magistrates vote an Address to be sent by the ship now ready to sail. **1692** BULKELEY *Will & Doom* 163 They prepar'd an address to be sent to his majesty. **1705** *Boston News-Letter* 29 Oct. 2/2 The Quakers have . . . endeavored by their false addresses at home in England, to misrepresent the Government of this Province. **1724** *Harvard Coll. Rec.* II. 508 The following address was voted to be presented to the Gen[era]ll Court. **1774** *Journals Cont. Congress* I. 53 The Congress . . . resolved unanimously, that a loyal address to his majesty be prepared. *Ib.* 62 An address to the people of Great Britain. **1776** TRUMBULL *M'Fingal* I. 21 Addresses signed, then chose Committees To stop all drinking of Bohea-teas. **1796** *Ann. 4th Congress* 2 Sess. 1522 The Senate waited on the President of the United States, and the Vice President . . . presented the Address then agreed to. **1823** *Amer. Baptist Mag.* IV. 164 Address of the General Convention of the Baptist Denomination to their Constituents.

+**2.** A formal statement of opinion or policy made by the President to Congress.

1791 *Amer. Daily Advertiser* 26 Oct. 3/3 After the delivery of the above address [by Washington], Mr. Speaker and the members returned to the house. **1796** WASHINGTON (*title*), Farewell Address. **1797** *Ann. 5th Congress* I. 630 The President . . . being seated, rose and delivered the following Address. **1825** (*title*), The Speeches, Addresses, and Messages of the several Presidents of the United States at the opening of Congress. **1862** LINCOLN in Logan *Great Conspiracy* 445 In the Inaugural Address I briefly pointed out the total inadequacy of Disunion, as a remedy for the differences. **1923** R. HERRICK *Lilla* 224 Lilla . . . read the newspapers to him with the President's last address to the Congress.

+**3.** A formal request, directed to the executive by one or both branches of a legislature, requesting the removal of a judge.

1822 *Missouri Intell.* 2 July 3/2 If any of the judges . . . must be removed, even without cause, still let it be done by address. **1863** W. PHILLIPS *Speeches* 161 The power of address, whenever it has been used in this Commonwealth, has been used to remove judges who had not violated any law. **1872** *Congress. Globe* 17 April 2500/2 'Cannot you remove him by "address"?' 'No; you cannot remove him by "address" under the Constitution.' **1882** H. ADAMS *J. Randolph* 132 The Constitutions of England, of Massachusetts, of Pennsylvania, authorized the removal of an obnoxious judge on a mere address of the legislature.

∗ **Address,** *v.*

+**1.** *tr.* To force (a judge) *out* (*of* office) by a petition to the executive.

1822 *Missouri Intell.* 2 July 3/2 If any of the judges have corruptly discharged their duties, impeach them. If they are incompetent, address them out. **1872** *Congress. Globe* 17 April 2500/2 I ask the Senator from Pennsylvania if he would 'address' a man out of office, because he is stricken down by sickness and unable to hold court? Would that be a reason for 'addressing' him out? *Ib.*, The Constitution does not provide for addressing a judge out of office. It can only be done by impeachment. **1874** R. H. COLLINS *Kentucky* I. 27 David Ballengall, an assistant judge, . . . [was] 'addressed' out of office, because a Scotchman unnaturalized.

2. To court as a lover.

1859 ELWYN *Glossary* 13 To 'keep company,' is the phrase in New England, among a certain class, for what is called *courting*, or, among the very refined, *addressing.*

+**Addressee.** A person to whom a letter, document, paper, or other article of mail is addressed. {*a*1858–}

1810 R. PETERS in *Life Jay* II. 332 Nothing must go with a pamphlet but the mere direction, under the pains and penalties of sousing the correspondent or addressee in all costs of enormous postage. **1879** *Reg. U.S. P.O. Dept.* 280 The postmaster shall also, at the time of its arrival, notify the addressee or addressees thereof that such letter or package has been received. **1889** FARMER 6 This new word, *addressee*, has been popularised in the post office department. The post office clerks . . . coined the word *addressee.* It is such a convenient word, that it is coming into general use.

Addresser. One who joins in signing an address. {1681–}

Freq. applied to the colonists, chiefly Loyalists, who in 1774–5 signed addresses presented to T. Hutchinson, Governor of Massachusetts, and his successor T. Gage.

1705 Perry *Hist. Coll. Col. Church* I. 175 If by my Lord Bp. of London's Letter, we, the addressers & subscribers to that Paper, must stand debarr'd from drawing up papers or making subscriptions. **1773** TRUMBULL *M'Fingal* II. (1785) 32 Shame with pointing gestures, Marks out th' Addressers and Protesters. **1774** J. ANDREWS *Letters* 18 The just resentment of the Addressers. **1779** JEFFERSON *Writings* (1854) IV. 179 The address of the Senate was soon after that. . . . The addressers had not yet their strength around them. **1813** ADAMS *Works* X. 38, I read, within a few days, an address to General and Governor Gage, from the bar, and the name of Caleb Strong among the addressers. **1847** L. SABINE *Amer. Loyalists* 291 James Forrest, Merchant, of Boston, an Addresser of Hutchinson in 1774. *Ib.* 630 One of the eighteen country gentlemen who were Addressers of Gage. **1876** BANCROFT *Hist.* IV. 347 One hundred and twenty-nine, chiefly the addressers to Hutchinson, . . . ostentatiously set their names to a protest.

Addressor. ?*Obs.* =ADDRESSER. {1691, 1806}

1774 J. ANDREWS *Letters* (1866) 60 They proceeded to make all the addressors and protestors there make a publick recantation. **1775** *Essex Inst. Coll.* XIII. 176 There is now a resident Addressor in Marblehead. **1853** SIMMS *Sword & Distaff* 33 You were one of the addressors of Sir Henry [Clinton]—an unforgivable offence.

+**Adios,** *interj. S.W.* [Sp. *adios, a dios*, lit. 'to God.'] Good-bye; farewell; adieu. Hence as *n.*, a farewell.

1846–7 MAGOFFIN *Santa Fe Trail* (1926) 130 On receiving her pay she bowed most politely, shook hands with a kind '*adios*.' **1850** GARRARD *Wah-To-Yah* xiii. 167 With an adios to the Mexican . . . , we mounted. **1853** BREWERTON *With Kit Carson* (1930) 34 Our host and his family had turned out . . . to make their adios and see us off. **1870** 'MARK TWAIN' *Screamers* (1871) x. 58 'You are the loser by the rupture, not me. Adios.' I then left. **1895** REMINGTON *Pony Tracks* 24 Bidding *adios* to the First Infantry . . . we trot off down the road.

Adit. A horizontal or nearly horizontal opening or passage by which a mine is either entered or drained. {1602–}

'In the United States an adit is usually called a *tunnel*, though the latter, strictly speaking, passes entirely through a hill, and is open at both ends' (1881 Raymond *Mining Gloss.* s.v.).

1758 FRANKLIN *Works* (1840) VI. 537 An adit carried . . . into the hill horizontally, till it meet with a perpendicular shaft sunk from its top. **1818** *Jrnl. Science* I. 136 Account of the Strata perforated by . . . the great adit to the Southampton Lead Mine. **1853** *Harper's Mag.* VI. 447 Another adit, as the drift is generally termed in this case, is then opened lower down on the declivity. **1860** GREELEY *Overland Journey* 290 The average yield of gold by quartz vein stone . . . will not pay the average cost of sinking shafts, running drifts or adits. **1870** *Scribner's Mo.* I. 154 A narrow drift or adit was pushed through from the west shaft . . . permitting the water to escape.

+**Adjourn,** *n.* (See quotation.) — **1851** HALL *College Words* 3 At Bowdoin College, *adjourns* are the occasional holidays given when a Professor unexpectedly absents himself from recitation.

***Adjourn,** *v.* + (See quotation.) — **1856** HALL *College Words* (ed. 2) 4 At the University of Vermont, . . . the students *adjourn* a recitation, when they leave the recitation-room *en masse*, despite the Professor.

***Adjunct,** *a.* and *n.*

+**1.** *Adjunct professor*, a member of the faculty of a university or college ranking immediately below a professor.

1826 *Catalogue of Univ. at Cambridge* 6 John W. Webster, M.D., Adjunct Erving Professor of Chemistry. **1840** J. QUINCY *Harvard Univ.* II. 305 In 1808, John Collins Warren, M.D., and in 1809, John Gorham, M.D., were appointed Adjunct Professors. **1846** N. F. MOORE *Hist. Sk. Columbia Coll.* 101 Mr. Henry Drisler, jun., . . . received a temporary appointment, as classical instructor of the Freshman Class, and was afterwards retained in office, with the title of Adjunct Professor. **1851** CIST *Cincinnati* 69 The Classes . . . are divided among the Adjunct Professors of Mathematics and Languages and the Professor of Modern Languages. **1851–2** *Catalogue Va. University* 27 The Board of Visitors . . . have appointed an Adjunct Professor of Law. **1904** *N.Y. Tribune* 8 Nov. 5 A. D. F. Hamlin, now adjunct professor of architecture.

+**2.** *ellipt.* as *n.* An adjunct professor.

1876 D. C. GILMAN *University Probl.* (1898) 29 Promoting them because of their merit to successive posts, as scholars, fellows, assistants, adjuncts, professors, and university professors.

Adjutancy. The office or rank of an adjutant. {1820.} — **1775** R. ALDEN in *Biogr. N. Hale* 157, I would accept of a lieutenancy but should prefer an adjutancy.

***Adjutant.** A staff officer who assists the commanding officer. {1600–}

'The title is also given to officers having similar functions attached to larger or smaller divisions of troops, to garrisons, and to the War Department of the United States government' (*Cent.*).

1757 *General Orders* 93 Adj[utan]t for the Ragulars [*sic*] the 17th Regt.; Adj[utant] for the Provencials the N. York Regt. **1776** *Journals Cont. Congress* IV. 14 The Congress proceeded to the election of an Adjutant for the batallion. **1802** *Ann. 7th Congress* App. 1306 That the regiment of artillerists shall consist of . . . four majors, one adjutant [etc.]. **1865** BOUDRYE *Fifth N.Y. Cavalry* 89 The Adjutant's quarters are crowded with work. **1891** A. BIERCE *Soldiers & Civilians* 113 The adjutant saluted and retired. The colonel . . . turned to look again at the enemy's guns.

Adjutant-General. [See prec. and GENERAL *n.*] A staff-officer who is the principal assistant of the commanding officer of a corps area, a division, or other unit in the discharge of his duties, as in publishing orders, conducting correspondence, regulating details of the service, etc.; also, the military officer having charge of the militia of a State or Territory. {1645–}

1757 *General Orders* 126 Each corp is to have an Orderly Searg[ean]t for . . . the Adjt. Gen[era]ll when ever sent for. **1777** *N. J. Archives* 2 Ser. I. 525 Adjutants General, Aids de Camp, and Majors of Brigade, may properly be called the *military staff*. **1780** *Heath Papers* 105 The returns which are made to the Adjutant Gen[era]l of the army. **1790** *Ann. 1st Congress* II. 1816 The adjutant general should have the rank of brigadier. **1811** *Ann. 12th Congress* 1 Sess. 1883 William Paulding, jun., Adjutant General of the State of New York. **1846** POLK *Diary* (1929) 82 General R. Jones, the Adjutant-General of the army, called and handed me despatches. **1861** *Army Regulations* 520 One assistant adjutant-general with the rank of major. **1885** *Century Mag.* XXX. 306/1 Chestney, then adjutant-general of Elzey's brigade.

b. *U.S. Army.* (See quotations.)

1847 *Army Regulations* 165 The Adjutant-General of the army is charged with the record of all military appointments, promotions, resignations, deaths, and other casualties; with the registry of all commissioned officers, the filling up of their commissions, and with their distribution. **1861** *Army Regulations* 128 The recruiting service will be conducted by the Adjutant-General, under the direction of the Secretary of War. *Ib.*, The Adjutant-General will select the field officers, and announce in orders the number of Captains and Lieutenants to be selected for this duty from each regiment by the Colonel. **1889** *Cent.* s.v., By law there is but one adjutant-general of the United States army. He is a principal officer of the War Department of the United States government.

***Admeasure,** *v. Obs.* +*tr.* To mete or measure out (land). — **1672** YEAMANS in Poyas *Peep into Past* (1853) 40 You are forthwith to admeasure and lay out for a town . . . all that point of land there. **1709** *N. C. Col. Rec.* I. 705 You are to direct and order colonel Broughton our Surveyor General to admeasure and set out 5000 acres of land. **1769** [see next].

***Admeasurement.** *Obs.* The measurement of land. {*a*1626} — **1769** *N. H. Prov. Papers* (1873) VII. 222, I directed the Surveyor General of Lands . . . to renew the line . . . surveyed, admeasured, and marked by Walter Bryant, Esq., . . . also to extend by actual admeasurement and plainly to mark the remaining part of the said line.

+**Administrador.** *La. & S.W.* [Sp., ='administrator'] A manager or overseer; a steward. — **1803** *Ann. 8th Congress* 2 Sess. 1521 (Descr. Louisiana) The administrador is also subordinate to the Intendant, and . . . manages everything respecting the custom-house. **1838** BROOKS *Idomen* (1843) 40 My white 'administrador' reported the amount of labor. **1865** *Atlantic Mo.* XV. 60 Then the Administrador woke us all up. **1895** REMINGTON *Pony Tracks* 66 The *administrador* . . . moves about in the discharge of his responsibilities, and they are universal; . . . from the negotiation for the sale of five thousand head of cattle to the 'busting' of a bronco which no one else can 'crawl.'

***Administration.**

1. The persons who collectively compose the government or its executive department; +the President and his cabinet. {1731–}

1716 SEWALL *Diary* III. 104 Pray'd for the Lt. Govr. who was at the head of the Administration, and for his family. **1806** FESSENDEN *Democracy Unveiled* I. 179 The faction, which has built itself up on the ruins of the Washington and Adams administrations. **1808** *Ann. 10th Congress* 2 Sess. 825 The Administration have committed greater errors. **1829** JACKSON *Annual Message*, A negotiation commenced and nearly completed . . . by the late Administration. **1871** *Scribner's Mo.* I. 298 The action of the United States . . . had alienated many of the supporters of the Administration. **1885** MCCLELLAN *Own Story* 242 The administration, and especially the Secretary of War, were inimical to me. **1905** *N. Y. Ev. Post* 3 Aug. 6 Despite the domestication of the term 'administration' in our political vocabulary, the word commonly connotes the personnel of the executive department, and not the art of conducting governmental business.

+**b.** The term or terms during which a President holds office.

1796 WASHINGTON *Farewell Address* §49 In reviewing the incidents of my administration, I am unconscious of intentional error. **1808** JEFFERSON in *Messages & P.* (1896) I. 436 In the first or second year of the Administration of President Adams. **1830** JACKSON *Messages & P.* (1896) II. 485 In the administration of Mr. Jefferson we have two examples of the exercise of the right of appropriation. **1839** J. WOODBERRY *Ann. Rep. Treasurer* 15 Losses appear to have occurred from defaults among officers in every 'administration' or presidential term.

+**2.** Attrib., esp. in the sense: Supporting the existing administration.

1808 *Ann. 10th Congress* 2 Sess. 198 What he calls our own Administration paper [*sc.* the *National Intelligencer*]. **1810** *Steele Papers* II. 644 The administration men . . . speak confidently as to the arrangement with France. **1827** *Mass. Spy* 12 Sept. (Th.) The pertinacity of one of the Administration Candidates in this district. **1837** *Diplom. Corr. Texas* (1908) I. 171 Many of the administration party forbore acting for fear of its being considered . . . as an attack on the administration. *Ib.* 263 The administration Editor, of this place, . . . is decidedly in favor of annexation. **1840** *Congress. Globe* 10 April 319/3 The abuse which was daily heaped on the Administration party. **1841** *Ib.* 16 Jan., App. 367/3 If that agent, the agent of an Administration State, . . . has expressed opinions. **1855** *Harper's Mag.* X. 829/1 At the last election, the Administration candidate had a clear majority. **1869** *Congress. Globe* 18 March 137/3 No measure could pass here unless it was an administration measure. **1870** *Ib.* 21 Dec. 243/2, I am an administration man, and whatever you do will always find in me the most careful and candid consideration.

+**Administrationist.** A supporter or member of the administration. — **1899** *Boston Globe* 21 July 7/4 Gen. Alger has finally been forced by . . . certain administrationists at Washington to tender his resignation.

* **Administrator.** A person appointed by a court to manage or dispose of the estate of a deceased person.

The corresponding verb *administer*, and the noun *administration*, have also been in use from early in the 17th century.

1634 *Plymouth Col. Rec.* I. 25 William Bradford, gent., the deputed administrator of Godbert Godbertson, hath sold . . . the late dwelling house. **1638** *R. I. Col. Rec.* I. 24, I do ffurthere . . . binde . . . my executors, my administrators and assignes. **1674** *Conn. Public Rec.* II. 239 The administrators of the sayd Henry Greye's estate. **1715** *Boston News-Letter* 14 March 2/2 To pay in their respective Debts to Mr. Timothy Prout, Administrator to the said Estate. **1731** *Md. Hist. Mag.* XIX. 287 The former sume . . . will onely pass through my hands as Administrator. **1786** *Ib.* 287, I am . . . Administrator of the aforesaid Wm. Poutney. **1809** *Ann. 10th Congress* 2 Sess. 337 Robert B. Sellers, administrator on the estate of William Sellers, deceased. **1861** *Army Regulations* 273 The said heirs, executors, and administrators. **1869** TOURGEE *Toinette* x. (1881) 120 The administrator of the elder Lovett's estate.

Administratrix. A female administrator. {1626–}

1639 *Conn. Public Rec.* I. 40 The Court admitteth the relict . . . to be Administratrix for the use of her and her children. **1674** *Ib.* II. 230 This Court grants the administratrix . . . to sell the land of her late husband. **1694** *Essex Inst. Coll.* XII. 299 My said grandmother was made adminestratrex [*sic*]. **1704** *N. C. Col. Rec.* I. 613 Mary Swann administratrix [of] dec[ease]d's estate. **1714** *Duxbury Rec.* 98 Grace Sprague, widdow of William Sprague . . . and administratrix of the estate. **1822** *Ann. 17th Congress* 1 Sess. I. 178 Charlotte J. Bullus, widow and administratrix of John Bullus. **1871** *Rep. Indian Affairs* (1872) 202 The mother-in-law of Joel W. Garrett was administratrix.

* **Admiral.**

* **1.** A naval officer of the highest rank; the commander-in-chief of a fleet or squadron.

The title was not official until 1866 (see quotation). Cf. HIGH-, REAR-, VICE-ADMIRAL.

1616 (*title*), A Description of New England: or the Observations, and Discoueries, of Captain Iohn Smith (Admirall of that Country) in the North of America. **1641** *Mass. Liberties* 227 By generall officers we meane, our Governor, Deputy Governor, Assistants, Treasurer, Generall of our warres, and our Admirall at sea. *a* **1656** BRADFORD *Hist.* 169 Captaine Francis West, who [in 1623] had a commission to be admirall of New-England.

1776 *Corr. Esek Hopkins* 38 [A letter of 15 April] To the Honble. Esek Hopkins, Esqr., Admiral of the Continental Fleet on Board the Ship Alfred. **1776** *Journal Cont. Congress* VI. 954 Resolved, . . . that the rank of the naval officers be to the rank of officers in the land service as follows: Admiral as a General, Vice Admiral as a Lieutenant General, Rear Admiral as a Major General. **1800** *Ann. 6th Congress* 676 A bill for the appointment of Admirals for the Navy. **1814** *Ann. 13th Congress* II. 1502 The expediency of providing by law for the appointment of Admirals in the Navy of the United States. **1840** *Niles' Nat. Reg.* 11 April 92/2 The expediency of giving a more perfect organization to the navy by creating the rank of admiral. **1841** UPSHUR in Force *State P. Class VI., Naval Affairs* I. 325 It is now expedient to establish the grade of rear admiral, without any distinction of flags, leaving the promotions to vice admiral and admiral for future services, and an enlarged establishment. **1864** KINNEY *Battles Civil War* IV. 397 It was thought that we must sink, and the cry rang out over the ship, 'Save the admiral! Save the admiral [=Rear Admiral Farragut]!' **1866** *Army & Navy Journal* 28 July 781 The bill . . . creating that [grade] of Admiral in the Navy, has become law. . . . Vice Admiral Farragut [was nominated] for promotion to the rank of Admiral. **1899** *Ib.* 4 March 2/1 For the third time in the history of the country there is now a full Admiral of the Navy. . . . It is Admiral Dewey. **1915** *Naval Appropriation Bill, Ib.* 6 March 859 Hereafter the commander-in-chief of the U. S. Atlantic Fleet, . . . the U. S. Pacific Fleet, . . . the Asiatic Fleet, respectively, shall each . . . have the rank and pay of an admiral.

+**2.** A State officer of Maine (see quotation). *Obs.*

1658 GORGES *Briefe Narrat.* II. iv. 46 To these I appointed an Admirall with his Lievetenant or Judge, for the ordering and determining of Maritine Causes.

* **Admiralty.**

* **1.** That branch of the administration of justice that takes cognizance of maritime cases or questions.

[**1650** *Md. Council Proc.* 254 That it be recommended to the Committee for the Admiralty to affixe a day to the Lord Baltamore for his comeing.] **1699** SEWALL *Diary* I. 498 Capt. Natha. Byfield is sworn Judge of the Admiralty. **1715** *Boston News-Letter* 17 Jan. 2/2 Robert Mompesson Esq., Barrister at Law, . . . Chief Justice, and Judge of the Admiralty of this Province. **1779** *Penna. Col. Rec.* XI. 713 Resolved, that the Hon'ble George Ross, Esq'r, be commissioned Judge of the Admiralty of this State. **1822** *Ann. 17th Congress* 1 Sess. I. 198 Thus Judge Story expressly confined the jurisdiction in civil cases of admiralty, to the ebb and flow of the tide—and the Supreme Court in criminal cases, to the high seas. **1865** *Atlantic Mo.* XV. 159 Chief Justice Taney['s] . . . acquaintance with . . . equity and admiralty; his opinions on corporate and municipal powers.

* **2.** *Court of admiralty*, =ADMIRALTY COURT. ?*Obs.*

1678 *Doc. Hist. N. Y. State* (1849) I. 89 The Court of Admiralty hath been by speciall comission or by the Court of Mayor & Aldermen att New Yorke. **1684** *Plymouth Laws* 205 The Gov[erno]r . . . and . . . other substantiall persons . . . of this Collonie shall have full power to acte as a Court of Admirallity. **1692** BULKELEY *Will & Doom* 103 By their act . . . the court of assistants is made a court of admiralty. **1714** *Boston News-Letter* 2–9 Aug. 2/2 A Parcel of Tobacca and Painters Colours, condemn'd at the Court of Admiralty, to be sold. **1785** in *S. Lit. Messenger* XXVIII. 38/2 The sanction of that law was no doubt a forfeiture of vessel and cargo, recoverable in a Court of Admiralty. **1789** *Ann. 1st Congress* I. 813 For the sake of forming a Court of Admiralty in each, authorized not only to take cognizance of all marine concerns, but also of all seizures. **1811** MEASE *Philadelphia* 97 Admiralty. This court has original and exclusive cognizance, with a few recent exceptions, of all revenue cases. It has also cognizance original and exclusive of all admiralty cases.

3. Attrib. with *case, libel, proceedings*, etc.

1686 SEWALL *Diary* I. 135 Court makes a Decree in the Admiralty Case. **1712** *Ib.* II. 335, I went to the Chief Justice, and there . . . Mr. Weaver [signed] an Admiralty Warrant. **1717** *Ib.* III. 118 The afternoon was taken up with the Admiralty Cause. **1782** TRUMBULL *M'Fingal* IV. (1785) 76 Our or'tors . . . , loud as admiralty-libel, Read awful chapters from the Bible. **1789** MACLAY *Deb. Senate* 86 The effect of the motion [brought forward by Mr. Lee of Va.] was to exclude the Federal jurisdiction from each of the States, except in admiralty and maritime cases. **1792** *Ann. 2nd Congress* 624 An act to ascertain the fees in Admiralty proceedings in the District Courts of the United States. **1822** *Ann. 17th Congress* 1 Sess. I. 47 To define more particularly the admiralty jurisdiction of the district courts. **1869** *Causes Reduction of Tonnage* (1870) 71 Anchors and chains according to Lloyds' and underwriters' rules, and admiralty test.

Admiralty court. A tribunal having jurisdiction over maritime cases. *Obs.* (Cf. ADMIRALTY 2.)

'In the United States, there is no admiralty court, distinct from others; but the district courts, established in the several states by Congress, are invested with admiralty powers' (W. '28).

[*a***1649** WINTHROP *Hist.* I. 102 We bound over Capt. Stone . . . to appear in the admiralty court in England. **1653** *Suffolk Deeds* II. 53 Securitie being given in the Admiraltie Court, that such goods . . . shall be imported into this Comon Wealth.] **1774** J. ANDREWS *Letters* 73 The action of the Portsmouth pleasure boat or gondalo so long depending before the Admiralty Court. **1778** *Journals Cont. Congress* X. 114 All prizes libelled in the admiralty court in the State of South Carolina. **1789** *Ann. 1st Congress* I. 783 Mr. Tucker said, he did not move to strike out the district to prevent the establishment of Admiralty Courts; he approved of such courts.

***Admiration.** +A word game designed to test the players' vocabulary. — **1828** *Yankee* Sept. 288/1 While the girls are at work [=quilting], they amuse themselves with . . . some sort of a play . . . ; one that we call admiration, is a very good one.

* **Admire,** *v.*

1. *intr.* To marvel or wonder *at* some thing or person. {1600–1865; now *dial.*}

'To wonder at; to be affected with slight surprise.—*Ray*. In New England, particularly in Maine, this word is used in this sense' (B. '48).

1638 HOOKER *Works* I. 8 Thus the people admired at Gods great goodnesse. **1674** Jillson *Dark & Bl. Ground* 18 They made very much of him and admire att his knife, gunn and hatchett. **1692** *Witchcraft Cases* 172 At him . . . I do most admire. **1735** *Letter Book J. Browne* (1929) 16 Besides I can but admire at your cutting any this fall. **1774** J. ANDREWS *Letters* 31 Aug., I . . . could not but admire at the subservient honors paid his Excellency. **1837** BIRD *Nick of Woods* II. 220 Roland did not admire long at the unlooked for resurrection of his old ally of the ruin. **1859** ELWYN *Glossary* 13, I admire at you. **1865** 'GAIL HAMILTON' *Skirmishes* 437 Sound Orthodox piety . . . is a thing to be admired (at).

2. To be desirous or pleased, to like, *to* do something. Now *dial.* or *colloq.* {1645–76; now *dial.*}

'This verb is much used in New England' (Pickering s.v.). 'Much and very absurdly used in New England' (B. '48). 'It is an error to follow this verb with an infinitive' (W. '47).

c **1770** *Lett. to B. Franklin* (Duane, 1859) 194, I should admire to come and see and hear all about every thing there once a year. **1801** MRS. BOWNE *Life* 71, I admire to see a boat rowed. **1833** NEAL *Down-Easters* I. 56, I can't say't I admire to see peeked-toed shoes. **1850** *Knickerb.* XXXVI. 487 Wouldn't you 'admire' to see a man sent ashore at Jersey City with a line from one of our steamers. **1864** 'MARK TWAIN' *Sketches* (1926) 128 My comrade said he did not admire to smell a whale; and I adopt his sentiments while I scorn his language. **1887** WILKINS *Humble Romance* 149, I s'pose Mis' Stevens would admire to have an egg for supper. **1905** A. ADAMS *Outlet* 202, I'll be all ready to start . . . in fifteen minutes, and I'd admire to have you all go along.

* **Admission.**

1. The action of admitting or the fact of being admitted as a student to a college or university.

1655 *Harvard Coll. Rec.* III. 329 Every schollar shall procure for himselfe a true coppy of the lawes which being signed with the Presidents and one of the Fellows hands shall be a testimony of his admission into the

Colledge. **1767** *Harvard Coll. Rec.* III. 347 Upon the receipt of which [certificate] the President shall sign an order for the admission of such persons. **1790** E. STILES *Lit. Diary* 7 Sept., Tutors began Exam[ination] of Freshmen for admission. **1837–8** *Yale Catalogue* 5 The regular examination for admission into College, commences on the Monday preceding the public commencement. **1871** [L. H. BAGG] *At Yale* 543 At nine o'clock of a summer's morning, the 'candidate for admission to Yale College' presents himself, with fear and trembling, at the door of Alumni Hall. **1872** *Bowdoin Catalogue* 31 Applicants for admission should produce testimonials of good moral character.

+**b.** =ADMITTATUR.

1697 SEWALL *Diary* I. 456 Willard . . . went to Cambridge and was admitted and then went into the River, and was drowned with his admission in his pocket. **1734** *Harvard Coll. Rec.* I. 134 A true coppy of the College Laws . . . signed by the President, & major part of the tutors, shall be his admission into the College.

+**2.** *Admission to the bar*, the granting of authority to practice as an attorney-at-law (†or as a barrister).

1766 ADAMS *Works* II. 197 A meeting of the bar at the Coffee House, for the admission of three young gentlemen. **1798** in *Mass. H. S. Proc.* XIX. 171 It will be proper, at the expiration of that period [three years], if he continues the assiduity and attention which he has hitherto manifested, to allow of his admission to the bar. **1881** *Mass. H. S. Proc.* XIX. 143 There seems to have been [in the eighteenth century] no regular time of study prescribed as requisite for admission to the bar.

b. (See first quotation and ADMIT *v.* 2, quotation 1768.)

1824 *Ohio Revised Statutes* (1860) I. 92 The judges of the said court . . . shall direct their clerk to administer an oath of office, and to record the admission of such applicant. **1874** *Colo. Gen. Laws* (1877) 94 Persons producing . . . evidence of their admission as attorneys at law in other states.

+**3.** The formal admittance of a state *into* the Union.

1777 *Journals Cont. Congress* IX. 924/2 No other colony shall be admitted into the same [confederation of states] unless such admission be agreed to by nine states. **1788** Marshall *Kentucky* (1812) 334 The admission of the said district [of Kentucky] into the federal union as a separate member thereof. **1791** *Ann. 1st Congress* II. 1783 The act for the admission of the State of Vermont into this Union. **1837** *Democratic Rev.* I. 83 The formal admission of that State into the Union by Congress. **1876** *General Laws, Colorado* (1877) 84 The admission of the State of Colorado into the Union is now complete.

4. An admission fee. {Also E.}

1861 *Chicago Tribune* 19 July 1/8 Fare from Chicago . . . $2.50. Admission to the Great Eastern, 50 cts. **1889** *Cent.* s.v., The admission was one dollar.

+**5.** *Admission day*, in certain Western States, a legal holiday commemorating the admission of the state into the Union.

1896 *Chicago Daily News Almanac* 233 The Legal Holidays: . . . Sept. 9 —Admission Day. In California. **1904** *Los Angeles Express* 9 Sept. 5 Admission day this year was not celebrated by any street parade.

+**6.** *Admission fee*, a charge or fee for admittance.

1842 *Knickerb.* XX. 498 Certain persons under the title of 'Professors' being stationed at the gates to exact considerable admission fees. **1848** ARMSTRONG *Stocks* 8 The admission fee is $400. **1876** INGRAM *Centennial Expos.* 708 Visitors who came to the Exhibition without first providing themselves with the proper admission fee.

* **Admit,** *v.*

+**1.** *tr.* To receive (a state) *into* the Union; to invest with the rank of a state.

1777 *Journals Cont. Congress* IX. 924/2 Canada acceding to this confederation . . . shall be admitted into and entitled to all the advantages of this Union. **1786** Marshall *Kentucky* (1812) 265 Provided . . . that the proposed state shall . . . be admitted into the Federal Union. **1787** *Constitution* iv. §3 New States may be admitted by the Congress into this Union. **1791** *Ann. 1st Congress* II. 2311 The State of Vermont having petitioned the Congress to be admitted a member of the United States. **1815** *Niles' Reg.* VIII. 67/2 Five new states have been admitted into the union. **1849** *Knickerb.* XXXIII. 92 Ever since Texas has been admitted into the Union. **1886** A. JOHNSTON *Hist. U.S.* 218 Arkansas was admitted to the Union in 1836. **1904** *Los Angeles Express* 9 Sept. 5 September 9 is the day that California was admitted to statehood.

+**2.** *To admit to the bar*, or *as barrister* or *attorney*, etc., to give authority to practice law.

In England, 'a barrister is never admitted to the bar, but is always *called*' (Mencken).

1768 in *Mass. H. S. Proc.* XIX. 149 We will not recommend any persons to be admitted to the Inferior Court, as attorneys, who have not studied with some barrister three years at least. **1817** ADAMS *Works* X. 245 Samuel Quincy and John Adams had been admitted barristers at that term [Nov. 1758]. **1835** HOFFMAN *Winter in West* I. 113 A graduate of Williams College had been recently admitted to the bar. **1846** MANSFIELD *Winfield Scott* 21 In 1806, Scott was admitted to the bar. **1882** THAYER *From Log Cabin* xxii. 342 Garfield . . . was admitted to the bar before he exchanged the quiet of teaching for the roar of battle. **1900** C. C. MANSFIELD *Uncle Terry* 55, I tutored some, read law, and was admitted to the bar.

* **Admittance.**

+**1.** An admission fee.

1798 H. M. Brooks *Gleanings* 87 Admittance, for grown persons, one Quarter of a Dollar.—Children half price. **1805** *Columbian Centinel* 29 June, Admittance to the Museum, 25 cents. *Ib.*, The Invisible Lady . . . continues to be exhibited among the other curiosities, at 25 cents admittance. **1841** BUCKINGHAM *Amer., N. States* II. 446 Admittance 50 cents. Tickets may be procured at the principal hotels.

+**b.** Attrib. with *fee.*

1838 *S. Lit. Messenger* IV. 61/1 Each auditor paid an admittance fee.

|| **2.** Permission; leave.

1806 LEWIS & ORDWAY *Journals* (1916) 355 Informed us that the most of our horses . . . were safe, but some . . . had been [made] use of by the admittance of the head chief.

+**Admittatur.** [L. 'let be admitted.'] A student's certificate of admission to a college, signed by the president and other members of the faculty. *Obs.*

1683 SEWALL *Let.* in *Mass. H. S. Coll.* 4 Ser. VIII. 516 What if I should print the Colledge-Laws? that so every student admitted may have a fair *Admittatur* to keep per him. . . . They are without both Laws and *Admittatur.* **1828** *Harvard Reg.* Feb. 377 The Freshman . . . travels wearily over in visions the term he is to wait for his initiation into college ways and his *Admittatur.* **1832** *New Eng. Mag.* III. 238, I received my *admittatur* and returned home, to pass the vacation and procure the college uniform. **1850** WOOLSEY *Hist. Disc. Yale* 45 Every Freshman, on his admission, was required to write off a copy of them [College laws] for himself, to which the admittatur of the officers was subscribed.

***Admonition.** Formal admonishment for the infraction of a rule or regulation of a college, etc. — **1646** *Harvard Rec.* I. 26 Any scholar . . . absent from prayer or lectures . . . shall bee liable to admonition. **1667** *Ib.* 203 If . . . continually, they shall so dare to offend [*sc.* by entering the kitchen], they shall be lyable to an admonition. **1734** *Ib.* 142 If any undergraduate shall play at cards or dice, he shall be punished by fine . . . , with admonition. **1790** *Harvard Laws* 8 Any undergraduate . . . guilty of indecent or irreverent behaviour at prayer . . . shall be liable to admonition. **1848** *Laws Univ. at Camb.* 21 (Hall, '56).

+**ADOBE.** *S.W. & W.* [Sp. Cf. ADOBEY, DOBE, DOBIE.]

1. A sun-dried or sun-baked brick

[**1834** J. L. STEPHENS *Centr. Amer.* (1854) 224 The houses in Costa Rica are . . . built of adobes or undried bricks two feet long and one broad, made of clay mixed with straw to give adhesion. **1838** 'TEXIAN' *Mexico v. Texas* 250 It was a little *Jacal*, or cabin, built with large unburnt bricks, called *adobes*, in the language of the country.] **1843** T. TALBOT *Journals* 23 The Fort is built on an elevated level near the river. It is built of 'Adobes.' **1846** *Life & Corr. Quitman* I. 279 The more common houses are of sun-dried brick . . . called *adobes*. The whole country being a sort of mixture of brick-kiln and cement, they are made without trouble. *a***1861** WINTHROP *J. Brent* 182 The tender hues of morning glorified the blue adobes of Bridger's shabby fort. **1873** MILLER *Amongst Modocs* xv. 185 Had it been a dry autumn the ground would have been hard as an adobe. **1907** HODGE *Handbook* I. 15 Houses constructed of adobes are very comfortable, being warm in winter and cool in summer.

fig. **1856** [G. H. DERBY] *Phoenixiana* viii. 83 Captain George P. Jambs, of the U.S. Artillery, a thorough-going *adobe*, as the Spaniard had it.

b. Sun-baked mud or clay used as a building material.

1844 GREGG *Commerce of Prairies* II. 81 Some inferior houses of *adobe* were so much soaked by the rains, that they tumbled to the ground. **1854** BARTLETT *Narr.* I. 188 The houses at El Paso are . . . built of *adobe*, i.e. the mud of the valley formed into bricks. **1865** NORTON *Army Lett.* 272 The houses in town [Brownsville, Texas] are adobe (mud brick) or 'jacal,' mud and sticks. **1881** *Amer. Naturalist* XV. 978 All of the houses are built of 'adobe.' **1889** E. B. CUSTER *Tenting on Plains* v. 175 A post where the quarters were old and of adobe.

c. A simple make of concrete.

1869 BROWNE *Adv. Apache Country* 118 The walls . . . are composed of a concrete of mud and gravel, very hard. . . . This concrete, or adobe, was cast in large blocks, several feet square.

2. Clay or soil used or suitable for making such bricks.

1856 [G. H. DERBY] *Phoenixiana* xix. 133 We have . . . Indians employed . . . in mixing adobe for the type moulds. **1881** RAYMOND *Mining Gloss.*, *Adobe*, Sp., clay suitable for . . . sun-dried bricks.

3. *ellipt.* =ADOBE HOUSE.

1821 DEWEES *Lett. from Texas* 21 The remainder of the buildings are adobes, except a few which are made of wood. **1850** J. L. TYSON *Diary in Calif.* 83 We came opposite the old mission of Santa Barbara. It consists of a small collection of *adobes*. **1873** BEADLE *Undevel. West* 686 A two-story *adobe*, plastered and dun-colored. **1883** *Harper's Mag.* March 491/1 The town is a collection of inferior adobes. **1897** *Outing* XXX. 74/2 In the old adobe . . . Resánoff dined with the comandante.

4. In attributive use. **a.** In sense: Built or constructed of adobe or sun-dried bricks, as *adobe dwelling*. See also ADOBE BUILDING, etc.

1847 Ruxton *Adv. Rocky Mts.* (1848) 190 The adobe residence of the Governor. **1866** *Rep. Indian Affairs* 119 An adobe stable. **1869** Browne *Adv. Apache Country* 272 The ruins of . . . the adobe store-houses and offices. **1876** Bret Harte *G. Conroy* xvii, The courtyard of the first large *adobe* dwelling. **1881** *Amer. Naturalist* XV. 25, I detected the shape of an adobe hut upon the tremendous horizon. **1907** White *Arizona Nights* 280 The adobe corrals of the home ranch.

b. In sense: Suitable for making sun-dried bricks, as *adobe clay.*

a1861 Winthrop *Canoe & Saddle* xi. 225 The mission was a hut-like structure of adobe clay, plastered upon a frame of sticks. **1869** Brace *New West* xviii. 236 The low lands along the river-bottoms (not the adobe soils) . . . are the best land for it. **1872** C. King *Sierra Nevada* xiii. 267 Plodding until evening through sand . . . , at last crossing adobe meadows. **1882** *Rep. Indian Affairs* 1 Sept. 1 Large tracts of adobe land.

c. In sense: Of sun-dried clay or soil, as *adobe brick, dust.*

1857 *Lawrence* (Kansas) *Republican* 2 July 1 The large and economical *adobe* brick . . . supersedes other material for walls and fences. **1869** Browne *Adv. Apache Country* 402 Stone, wood, scraps of sheet-iron, adobe-bricks, mud, . . . and even canvas, are the component parts [of chimneys]. **1917** Sinclair *King Coal* 29 The law required sprinkling the mines with 'adobe-dust.'

d. *Adobe yard*, one for making or storing adobe bricks.

1867 J. Meline *Santa Fé & Back* 36 Julesburg has six houses, including a store, adobe-yard, blacksmith shop and—billiard saloon!

+**Adobe building, house, wall.** *S.W. & W.* One built of adobe or sun-dried bricks.

1854 Bartlett *Narr.* I. 255 San Bernardino is a collection of adobe buildings. **1869** Browne *Adv. Apache Country* 32 An ancient adobe building, in which Mr. Banning carried on his staging and teaming operations. **1910** J. Hart *Vigilante Girl* 153 The low adobe buildings of their Mexican forerunners were the . . . safest for an earthquake country. — **1843** Fremont *Exped.* 182 The missionary establishment of Dr. Whitman, which consisted, at this time, of one *adobe* house. **1853** Brewerton *With Kit Carson* (1930) 32 San Francisco, with its sandy streets and low adobe houses. **1869** Browne *Adv. Apache Country* 52 Here, in a good adobe house, with such comforts as this wild region affords, dwell Mr. Hamblin and his wife. **1907** White *Arizona Nights* 4 We came upon an adobe house, a fruit tree, and a round corral. — **1847** Ruxton *Adv. Rocky Mts.* (1848) 185 Quaint little buildings, looking, with their adobe walls, like turf stacks. **1881** *Amer. Naturalist* XV. 25 No one ever built an adobe wall in this wilderness without first having found water. **1910** Hart *Vigilante Girl* 152 Around the mound there ran a rectangle of adobe walls.

+**Adobey, Adobie, Adoby,** varr. Adobe. Also attrib.

1844 Lee & Frost *Oregon* 210 Fort Boisais . . . is a parallelogram . . . , with adobic [*sic*] walls. **1845** Green *Texian Exped.* viii. 91 The guard . . . occupied a small adoby house. **1846** Sage *Scenes Rocky Mts.* xxi. 174 Rude hovels . . . one story high and built of *adobies.* **1850** G. Hines *Voyage* 188 Two or three small buildings [of Fort Walla-Walla] are enclosed in an adobey wall.

***Adopted,** *ppl. a.* +**1.** Of citizens: Admitted to the rights and privileges of a native. **2.** Chosen as one's abode or field of activity. — **(1) 1805** *Ann. 9th Congress* 1 Sess. 784 Some of our honest adopted citizens from Great Britain. **1808** *Ann. 10th Congress* 2 Sess. 586 At this very moment our native citizens and adopted brethren . . . are doomed to the most intolerable thraldom in the British navy. **1859** L. Wilmer *Press Gang* 109 On the score of natural equity, a free negro, born in the United States, has a much better right to vote than any 'adopted citizen.' — **(2) 1830** *Deb. Congress* 9 Dec. 2 [Hon. R. H. Adams] was called by the Legislature of his adopted State to a seat in the councils of the nation.

Adopting Act. An act requiring the acceptance in the main of the Westminster Confession and Catechisms by ministers and ministerial candidates. — **1735** Baird *Acts of Presbyterian Ch.* (1856) 6 Ordered, That each Presbytery have the whole Adopting Act inserted in their Presbytery book. **1844** Rupp *Relig. Denominations* 579 The 'Adopting Act' . . . was a very important measure in its subsequent application to the authorized theological and practical system of the American Presbyterian Churches. **1895** Thompson *Hist. Presbyterian Churches* 26 The Adopting Act of 1729, by which its ministers and licentiates . . . were required to subscribe to the Westminster Confession and Catechisms.

***A-ducking,** *vbl. n.* [See A *prep.*[1] 4 and cf. Ducking.] Duck-shooting. — **1768** Washington *Diaries* I. 253 Went a ducking . . . and killd 2 mallards and 5 bald faces. **1771** *Ib.* II. 8 They went a ducking and I again rid to my mill. **1863** 'Gail Hamilton' *Gala-Days* 97 We went a-ducking once down in Swamp-shire.

***Advance,** *n.*

+**1.** A body of troops forming the forward part of a column or army; an advanced guard.

1780 *Heath Papers* 96 The 1500 (the advance of the militia) will be supported by 1,500 more. **1826** Cooper *Mohicans* xiv, [The enemy] met us hard by, in our outward march to ambush his advance, and scattered us, like driven deer, through the defile to the shores of Horicon. **1861** *Chicago Tribune* 19 July 1/5 The advance of Burnside's Brigade reached the fortification in time to take one prisoner. **1865** Boudrye *Fifth N. Y. Cavalry* 37 Without opposition the advance entered the town. **1866** 'F. Kirkland' *Bk. Anecdotes* 309 The advance dashed around the camp, a group looking on in wonder.

+**2.** A student's preparatory lesson. *Obs.*

1848 [N. Ames] *Childe Harvard* 13 Even to save him from perdition He cannot get 'the advance,' forgets 'the review.' **1851** Hall *College Words* 6 The lesson which a student prepares for the first time is called *the advance,* in contradistinction to *the review.*

+**3.** *Advance agent*, an agent who goes before in order to make business or other arrangements, as for traveling lecturers, theatrical companies, circuses, etc. Also *fig.*

1882 Sweet & Knox *Texas Siftings* 38 Do you think I am the advance agent of a variety show? **1891** *Century Mag.* Jan. 427 He was the advance agent of that mysterious combination known as an English syndicate. **1897** *Congress. Rec.* March 177/1 That great priest and apostle of protection, and that grand advance agent of prosperity, William McKinley.

+**4.** *Advance bill:* (see quotation).

1889 *Cent., Advance-note,* . . . a draft on the owner or agent of a vessel, generally for one month's wages, given by the master to the sailors on their signing the articles of agreement. Known in the United States as an *advance-bill.* The practice was abolished in the United States by act of Congress in 1884.

+**5.** *Advance corps*, an advance guard.

1780 *Heath Papers* III. 33 An action . . . between the advance corps under . . . Lt. Colo. Thompson . . . and a body of the enemy.

***Advanced,** *ppl. a.*

+**1.** *Advanced standing*, the status of being allowed credit toward a degree for courses pursued at another college.

Provision for 'admitting a scholar, who comes recommended from another College, into the same standing as he had there' was made at Harvard in 1767 (*Harvard Coll. Rec.* III. 348).

1790 *Laws of Harvard College* 7 No person shall be admitted to an advanced standing, unless, upon examination by the President, Professors and Tutors, he shall be found qualified. **1818** *Circular Letter* in *N. Amer. Rev.* March 422 Persons may be admitted to advanced standing at any part of the College course [in Harvard Univ.]. **1871** [L. H. Bagg] *At Yale* 548 'Candidates for advanced standing' . . . are obliged to pass both the regular freshman entrance examination, and an examination on all the studies pursued up to that time by the class they propose to join. **1900** *Dialect Notes* II. 21 *Advanced standing, admission to,* admission to a higher than the freshmen, or lowest class, on proof of proficiency in the work already done by the class.

+**b.** *Advanced student*, one admitted to 'advanced standing.'

1871 [L. H. Bagg] *At Yale* 689 Whether an 'advanced student' comes from a private tutor, or from another college, or drops from a higher class at Yale, makes little difference.

+**2.** *Advanced female*, one who agitates for women's rights.

'A sarcastic allusion to the "women's righters," as they are slangily called' (F.).

1871 *N. Y. Tribune* 2 Feb. (De Vere) The short-sightedness of the advanced female to the interest of her own cause. **1895** S. Hale *Letters* 288 She is a lion-hunter *enragée,* advanced female, views, everything.

+**Advance guard.** [For *advanced guard.*] A body of troops before or in front of the main army, esp. to guard against surprise.

1758 *Essex Inst. Coll.* XVIII. 113 The Advance Guard . . . have cleared off the Trees and built Breastworks. *Ib.* 343 They met an Indian within ¼ of a Mile of the Advance-Guard. **1856** Glisan *Jrnl. Army Life* 300 The advance guard of the regulars met with a few Indians. **1861** *Chicago Tribune* 19 July 1/1 Fighting had taken place between the advance guard of the Federal army, and the rebel forces. **1865** Boudrye *Fifth N. Y. Cavalry* 139 An advance guard was pushed to Allen's Mill. **1885** *Outing* Oct. 17/1 A note . . . stating that the advance-guard had run across the Chiricahuas . . . in a cañon.

+**Advent Christian.** One of a division of the Adventists. — **1884** *Schaff's Relig. Encycl.* III. 2581/2 The most numerous branch [of Adventists] is the Advent Christians. . . . They have two or three weekly papers. **1904** [see Adventist].

+**Adventism.** [See next.] The doctrine that Christ is coming again to establish a personal reign on earth, esp. as preached by William Miller (from 1831) and his followers, who predicted an immediate coming; the tenets of the Adventists; Millerism.

1874 Wellcome *Hist. Second Advent Message* 592 Judaism is being taught. If brethren do not mean to teach it let them tell us so and not teach this under the cloak of Adventism. **1885** McClintock & Strong *Cycl. Suppl.* I. 52/2 The Modern Phase of Adventism . . . began in America about the close of the last century. **1902** Clapin 7 The chief tenet of Adventism was a belief in the physical second advent of Jesus-Christ, which event Miller affirmed would take place on the 23rd of October 1844.

+**Adventist.** [f. *Advent* (second) coming of Christ.] One of a religious denomination, comprising several branches, who believe in or look for the early second coming of Christ to reign personally on earth; a Millerite. More fully *Second Adventist.* (Cf. *Seventh-day Adventist.*) Also attrib.

1844 Cist *Cincinnati Misc.* 29 As the day approaches . . . the faithful adventists continue nearly the whole time, day and night at the Tabernacle. **1874** Wellcome *Hist. Second Advent Message* 227 Those who have attempted to edit papers for the Adventists, and have led parties into strange and speculative vagaries. **1879** B. F. Taylor *Summer-Savory* xvii. 141 An Adventist, a Soul-Sleeper, and a Baptist march in doctrinal procession . . . , preaching 'each after his kind.' **1880** *Harper's Mag.* Aug. 346 The concerns of the meeting-houses—Seventh-day, Close-communion Baptist, and Adventist, by preference—were amongst their strongest pre-occupations [i.e. in islands of Maine]. **1881** *Amer. Cycl.* XIV. 745 Second Adventists, or Adventists, . . . believe in the speedy second advent of Christ and the end of the world. **1904** *Amer. Almanac* 173 Adventists [include] 1. Evangelical. 2. Advent Christians. 3. Seventh Day. 4. Church of God. 5. Life and Advent Union. 6. Churches of God in Jesus Christ.

* **Adventure.** +Used as a name for some localities occupied by early settlers in Maryland. — **1700** *Md. Hist. Mag.* XX. 292 (1644) Browns Adventure. *Ib.* 353 (1678) Goodmans Adventure. *Ib.* 365 (1695) Gilbert Adventure.

* **Adventurer.** One who engages or shares in commercial enterprises or business activities; a speculator in trade or real estate. Cf. *merchant adventurer.*

[**1608** Smith *Newes from Va.* Wks. 1884 I. 40 Not willing to trifle away more time . . . , we thought good, for the better content of the aduenturers, . . . to fraight home Maister Nelson, with cedar wood.] **1627** *Plymouth Laws* 30 Such planters as are heirs to such as dyed before the right of the land was yielded to the adventurers. **1636** *Springfield Rec.* I. 160 We . . . being al of the first adventurers & subscribers for this plantation. **1649** *Md. Council Proc.* 229 Divers Adventurers or Planters haue for a long time . . . refused to take grants for his Lo[rdshi]pp. **1661** *R. I. Col. Rec.* I. 449 Which tracke of land is faierly promised or ingaged to a sartaine number of adventurers vpon the designe of purches of it; which adventurers are members of this collony. **1735** *Boston Rec.* 121 It's much to be feared the generous Adventurers will soon be obliged to lay aside their Trade and Navigation. **1778** *Journals Cont. Congress* XI. 416 That loan office certificates . . . bearing an interest of four per cent . . . be issued to such fortunate adventurers in the first class. **1779** Durrett *Louisville* (1893) 137 The new adventurers may be tempted to run too great risques in making new settlements. **1802** *Ann. 7th Congress* App. 1371 The Postmaster General . . . is authorized . . . to contract with private companies, or adventurers for carrying the mail. **1802** Ellicott *Journal* 135 A large proportion . . . are descended from the original French settlers and adventurers. **1865** *Atlantic Mo.* XV. 392 Many of them . . . sold out at moderate prices to shrewd adventurers, who made themselves rich men.

* **Advertisement.** Also † **advertizment.**

1. A public notice or announcement, as in a newspaper or periodical, or less usually by handbill, placard, etc. {1692–} Abbrev. *ad* (q.v.).

'The words *advertisement* and *chastisement* are differently accented by the standard authors, and by people on both sides of the Atlantic' (1789 Webster *Dissertation* 137). While in 1806 Webster stresses this word on the third syllable, in edd. 1828, 1847 the stress is placed on the second. Worc. '46, '60, W. '64, and *Cent.* '89 give both stressings, with preference for the latter; but *Stand.* '93 reverses this. The meter requires *adverti'sement* in quots. 1784, 1903, and 1904.

1704 *Boston News-Letter* 8 May 2/2 All such Advertisements are to be brought in Writing to said Post-Masters. **1713** *Boston Rec.* 185 Ordered. That an Advertizm[en]t be printed. **1740** Stephens *Proc. Georgia* 538 The Carolina printed News-Papers coming with them, I could not but observe an Advertisement in one of them. **1784** *Mass. Centinel* 24 March If any gentleman wants a wife, . . . An Advertisement does the thing. **1816** *Niles' Reg.* IX. 428/1 The *Niagara Journal* . . . contains 70 advertisements, some of them very extensive. **1865** *Atlantic Mo.* XV. 170, I have seen the most heartless advertisements in the newspapers. **1903** Sheldon in *N. Y. Sun* 15 Nov., Tempting advertisement Catching every eye. **1904** *Critic* May 433 Can authors' booms collapse and die? . . . Do advertisements ever lie?

+2. *Advertisement board*, a bill-board.

1880 *Harper's Mag.* Dec. 72 The advertisement boards were freshly covered with clean notices.

* **Advertiser.** +An advertising agent. — **1871** Barnum *Struggles & Triumphs* 93 While traveling . . . [in] Georgia, our advertiser, who was in advance of our party, . . . arranged with a poor widow woman named Hayes, to . . . let us lodge in her hut.

Advertising, *ppl. a.* or *vbl. n.* Connected with, engaged in, advertising. {1807–}

1828 *Yankee* April 145/2 If a man pay for an advertising-sheet, in our country, the fault is his own. **1878** *Harper's Mag.* Jan. 234/2 On the ground-floor a paler beam shows the advertising-rooms, where a few sleepy clerks await the last advertisements. **1884** H. S. Cummings *Sk. Class 1862 Dartmouth Coll.* 45 In November, 1871, he was made the advertising agent of the Pennsylvania Railroad Company. **1912** W. Irwin *Red Button* 260 Her radiance fills and illuminates the office of the Thomas W. North Advertising Agency.

+**Advice-book.** *Obs.* A book for recording information or intelligence. — **1726** Penhallow *Indian Wars* (1824) 35 If any enterprise was on foot, he should (in his advice book) join L.A. the two first letters of his name.

* **Advisement.**

+1. *Under advisement*, under consideration or combined deliberation. Also *in advisement*, in deliberation.

'*To have under advisement*, i.e., under consideration, [is] rarely heard in England, but common in the States' (F.).

1735 *Penna. Col. Rec.* IV. 23 Till the Bill for establishing Courts of Equity comes under advisement. **1880** Wallace *Ben-Hur* v. xv, The matter is still in advisement. **1888** *Phila. Ev. Bulletin* 23 Feb. (F.) Judge Miles Beach has under advisement a demurrer in a most remarkable case. **1898** Page *Red Rock* 320 As he made Major Welch . . . a very reasonable proposal . . . [as to] the Red Rock land adjoining, the Major agreed to take it under advisement.

* **2.** Notification, intimation. {–1654}

1841 *Knickerb.* XVII. 344 Our advisement of the public opening of this fine collection came at so late an hour.

* **Adviser.** +At some Universities: A member of the faculty appointed or selected to advise students with respect to studies or other matters. — **1887** *Lippincott's Mag.* Sept. 453 One great power of appeal . . . playing between teachers and students [at Harvard Univ.] is exercised through the 'advisers.' Each matriculate is expected to designate one of his professors whom he will consider his adviser while at the university. The professor is to be consulted by the student as a personal friend and guide. **1888–9** C. W. Eliot *Report Harvard Coll.* 64 A committee of 13 members of the Faculty, each of whom should act as adviser to about 25 Freshmen. **1914** V. L. Collins *Princeton* 376 Each [first-year man] has an 'adviser' among the younger members of the faculty to whom he is encouraged to go with all or any of his perplexities.

Advisory, *a.*

1. Pertaining or relating to the giving of advice. {1862–}

1787 Adams *Works* IV. 356 The powers of both these bodies are merely advisory. **1789** Morse *Amer. Geog.* 170 The churches claim no jurisdiction over each other, and the power of ecclesiastical councils is only advisory. **1809** Ramsay *Hist. S. Car.* II. 20 Churches, as corporations, can enforce their by-laws, but their powers as spiritual courts are merely advisary [*sic*]. **1865** Stowe *Little Foxes* (1866) 114 Parents would do well to . . . use with a wise moderation those advisory and admonitory powers with which they guided their [children's] earlier days.

b. Containing or consisting of advice.

1806 Webster. **1828** *Ib.* s.v., Their opinion is merely advisory.

2. Having the function of advising. {1882}

1778 *Result of Convention at Ipswich, Essex* 45 We think therefore that the members of that court ought never to be advisory to any officer in the state. **1879** *Washington cable* in *Daily Chron.* (London) 2 June, The Advisory Committees of the Democratic Caucuses of the House of Representatives and the Senate. **1882** Thayer *From Log-Cabin* xxiii. 378 [In 1863–4 Garfield's] name appeared on the Catalogue of Hiram Institute as 'Advisory Principal and Lecturer.'

* **Advocate.** One whose profession is to plead causes in a court of justice or law; a counselor, attorney.

1788 Franklin *Autobiog.* 416 Being bred a lawyer, he might consider us both as merely advocates for contending clients in a suit, he for the proprietaries and I for the Assembly. **1815** Ticknor in *Life* I. 33 Mr. Wirt . . . is undoubtedly a powerful advocate and a thorough lawyer, by general consent. **1836** *S. Lit. Messenger* II. 434 We have seen advocates whittling during a defence, and judges whittling on the bench.

Advocate-General. {1679} An attorney-general. *Obs.*

1724 *New-Eng. Courant* 1 June 1/2 As to the apprehensions which the Judge, the Advocate General, and other Officers of the Court, had. **1761** J. Otis *Sp.* in Minot *Mass. Bay* (1803) II. 92, I was solicited to argue this cause as Advocate-General.

* **Adz, Adze.** Also † **ads, adse, adds, addes.** The carpenter's and cooper's tool of that name.

1622 'Mourt' *Relation* 141 You shall need an Ads or Hatchet. **1635** *Maine Doc. Hist.* III. 67, 2 old square Addes. **1638** *Md. Archives* IV. 74 An old adze, an old broad-axe. **1646** *Essex Probate Rec.* I. 90, 2 adds, 2 hand sawes. **1661** *N. H. Probate Rec.* I. 51, I give him . . . an Axe, handsaw, Adze, Augre. **1702** *Essex Inst. Coll.* XLII. 160 Inventory of ship . . . [includes] a small Hamer and Adz. **1796** Barton *Disappointment* III. iv, Mr. Trushoop, where's your adz? open the chest. **1791** Jillson *Dark & Bl. Ground* 111 Floor boards are hewn with ax and adz. **1794** Humphreys *Industry* 20 Let the keen adze the stubborn live-oak wound. **1843** 'Carlton' *New Purchase* I. xvi. 117 The trees whence they are severally hewed by the means of axe and adze. **1867** Edwards *Shelby* 477 As well give a carpenter an adze and a jack plane to make a watch. **1900** Stockton *Afield & Afloat* 161 That's the cheapest way of makin' a step. . . . I've just been up to Mr. Kefford's to borrow his adze.

Aeronaut. {1784–} A balloonist or (more recently) aviator. — **1846** Corcoran *Pickings* 66 Like Clayton's the aeronaut's balloon when inflated with gas. **1859** *Harper's Weekly* 1 June 392/1 Mr. Wise . . . the veteran aeronaut. **1862** *Amer. Ann. Cycl.* II. 185/1 The aeronauts kept up their observations until dark of Saturday, pointing out the position of the batteries [during the battle of Seven Pines].

+**Affiant.** [Fr.] One who makes an affidavit.

1807 *Ann. 10th Congress* 1 Sess. I. 476 The affidavit of David Fisk, . . . that . . . a certain David Floyd . . . came to this affiant [etc.]. *Ib.* 477 This affiant asked what other object they had. **1868** *Congress. Globe* 19 Oct. 452/2 In nearly all cases where this affiant challenged persons [as not being lawful voters] no attention was paid to the challenges, but on the contrary this affiant was told . . . that this affiant must leave the window; that they were going to let them vote. **1871** *Rep. Indian Affairs* (1872) 218 For which affiant raised, boarded, clothed, and schooled said ward. **1878** *Congress Rec.* 16 June (1879) 2041/1 Said deputy marshal denied affiant the right to make a bond . . . and carried affiant to the city of Montgomery.

Affidavit.

1. 'A declaration upon oath; in the United States, more generally, a declaration in writing, signed by the party, and sworn to, before an authorized magistrate' (W. '28). {1622–}

'Also applied to statements made on affirmation' (W. '64).

1639 *Mass. H. S. Coll.* 4 Ser. VI. 54 The noate that Edward Dillingham gave you, I never saw yt. I pray therefore take his affidavit. **1707** SEWALL *Diary* II. 200 Some began to be hot to send for the book wherein the affidavits are, . . . and to burn it. **1745** *Georgia Col. Rec.* VI. 145 The President communicated your Letter . . . to the Magistrates, together with an Affidavit relating to Mr. John Terry. **1775** *Journals Cont. Congress* III. 435 Sundry affidavits from Wyoming, relative to disturbances there, . . . were read. **1775** SCHUYLER in Sparks *Corr. Rev.* (1853) I. 9, I inclose . . . copies of two affidavits made by persons from Canada. **1816** *Ann. 14th Congress* 2 Sess. 274 The deposition of witnesses taken before a justice of the peace, or other person authorized to take affidavits . . . may be read in evidence. **1839** *S. Lit. Messenger* V. 99/2 Requiring him to make affidavit that his defence was just. **1853** SIMMS *Sword & Distaff* 490, I can take your lieutenant's affidavit and yours, embodying your suspicions, and issue the warrants. **1880** *Harper's Mag.* July 214/2 The proper affidavits were made and Mr. Poacher saw trouble ahead. **1901** CHURCHILL *Crisis* 328 The Commissioner thereupon attested the affidavit to Colonel Carvel.

2. Attrib. with *commissioner, man.*

1778 *Md. Journal* 24 Nov. (Th.) This affidavit-man is a Dutchman, with whom I was obliged to converse by an interpreter. **1821** W. L. Mackenzie *Van Buren* (1846) 190 Cornelius Hogeboom . . . is an affidavit commissioner.

Affiliate, *v.* {1761–}

+**1.** *intr.* To associate or co-operate *with* another or others, esp. in a common policy.

1852 *Congress. Globe* 18 March, App. 322/1 Can we affiliate with the Whigs? Never! **1868** *Ib.* 13 July 4016/2, I was fearful that he had been affiliating with the party that nominated Seymour at the New York convention. **1879** TOURGEE *Fool's Errand* xxi. 125 The instincts of what was termed 'Unionism' . . . led them to affiliate somewhat coolly with the party of reconstruction. **1891** HARBEN *Almost Persuaded* 27 Our nearest neighbors live several miles away, and we don't affiliate with them much. **1907** *Springfield W. Republican* 7 Nov. 15 Payments in cash are scarce, thousands of workingmen have affiliated with banks, and the necessities of life are being bought with scrip.

+**2.** To combine *with* something. Also ellipt.

1877 RAYMOND *Mines & Mining* 98 Platinum . . . , though it does not amalgamate, . . . affiliates with the gold amalgam. **1884** E. LAZARUS in *Century Mag.* Dec. 217 It was impossible that the inharmonious elements . . . should ever affiliate and result in a sound, systematic whole. **1887** *Ib.* July 431/2 Here they [=phenomena] affiliate with the whole mass of superstitions which accumulated in the early history of the human race.

+**3.** To associate or fraternize.

1843 T. WEED *Letters* (1866) 9 Our cabin passengers . . . are as diverse in characters and pursuit, as in birth and language. But we all affiliate and harmonize wonderfully.

Affiliation. {1751–}

+**1.** Relationship or association, as in politics or (more recently) church fellowship, etc.; freq. *pl.*, connections, relations.

1852 *Congress. Globe* App., 15 March 323/3 Certain merchants with whom he has affiliations in New Mexico. **1862** *Ib.* Jan. 589/2, I am here almost without any affiliation in political sentiment. **1888** *Congress. Rec.* May 3853/1 These workmen have no affiliation with gentlemen of infinite leisure. **1890** *Ib.* 2 July 6927/2 One . . . should be the clerk of the court, the other a citizen appointed, of opposite political affiliations. **1904** ROOSEVELT in *N. Y. Times* 23 March 2, I have not the slightest idea what your political affiliations are.

+**2.** Confederation; combination; union.

1904 *Atlantic Mo.* March 293 The affiliation of local billboard interests into a national body, for the purpose of more successfully opposing adverse public action.

Afghan, *n.* [Short for *Afghan shawl* {1833}.] A kind of blanket or coverlet of knitted or crocheted wool, esp. used as a covering for a sofa or as a carriage robe.

1863 MRS. WHITNEY *F. Gartney* xiii, Mr. Gartney . . . springing . . . to a sitting position, throwing off as he did so, the afghan Faith had laid over his feet. **1870** 'M. HARLAND' *For Better, for Worse* 282 She wrapped the child's afghan about her feet. **1878** COOKE *Happy Dodd* 324 A small afghan . . . as bright in its tints . . . as the gayest of autumnal foliage. **1893** KATE WIGGIN *P. Oliver* ii. 17 Margery was crocheting a baby's afghan.

***A-fishing:** see A *prep.*[1] 3 and FISH *v.* {Now *dial.* or *arch.*, esp. echoing the Biblical use in John xxi. 3.}

1624 WINSLOW *Good Newes* 35 He intended to goe to Munhiggen . . . to buy bread from the ships that came thither a fishing. **1674** SEWALL *Diary* I. 4 Mr. Gookin, Jr. was gone a fishing. **1726** PENHALLOW *Indian Wars* (1824) 91 Capt. Samuel . . . boarded Lieut. Tilton, as he lay at anchor a fishing. **1759** *Essex Inst. Coll.* XIX. 188 Leut. Shepord went up the Lake a fishing. **1785** *Md. Hist. Mag.* XX. 45 He did . . . pass down and up Jones's falls in canoes which went a fishing. **1840** DANA *Two Years* xxii. 166 The officer . . . went off beyond the point a fishing. **1856** [GOODRICH] *G. Go-Ahead* 84 Mother, may I go a-fishing with Ben Hooker this afternoon? **1876** 'MARK TWAIN' *Tom Sawyer* vi. 53 To stay home from school and go a-fishing.

+**Afoul,** *adv.* and *a.*

1. *Naut.* In collision or entanglement; foul.

1809 BARLOW *Columbiad* VII. 521 Above, with shrouds afoul and gunwales mann'd, Thick halberds clash. **1840** DANA *Two Years* XV. 137 After paying out chain, we swung clear, but our anchors were no doubt afoul of hers. **1841** TOTTEN *Naval Text-bk.* 328 A vessel ran a-foul of us.

2. In violent or hostile contact. With verbs, as *fall, run, set.*

1833 S. SMITH *Major Downing* 107 He fell afoul of him with a great club, and knocked him down. **1839** BRIGGS *H. Franco* I. 180 With one accord they all fell afoul of him and beat him. **1854** M. J. HOLMES *Tempest & Sunshine* XV. 202 Now be keerful and not run afoul of the plaguy lye leech. **1870** 'F. FERN' *Ginger-Snaps* 10 The hostess . . . [may] set some maiden a-foul of the piano! **1892** *Harper's Mag.* Aug. 377/1 The ice crystals cannot grow out into the water very far without running afoul of other crystals.

A-fowling: see A *prep.*[1] 4 and FOWL *v.* ?*Obs.*

1622 'MOURT' *Relation* 79 This afternoone one of our people being a fouling . . . there came by him twelve Indians. **1636** *Mass. H. S. Coll.* 4 Ser. VII. 55 William Quick stayd there behind, & we fear went ashore a fowling. **1686** SEWALL *Diary* I. 124 He was going a fowling. **1723** *New-Eng. Courant* 12–19 Aug. 2/1 Mr. Willard, Minister of the Town, who went a Fowling the same Day, was missing. **1760** S. NILES in *Mass. H. S. Coll.* 3 Ser. VI. 243 Lieutenant Fletcher and his two sons . . . went a fowling.

***Africa.** *S. Obs. slang.* [From the place-name, with allusion to negro temperament.] +Temper; anger. — **1838** *S. Lit. Messenger* IV. 162/1 Well, it sort o' raised his Africky, at first.

***African,** *n.*

***1.** A member of the negroid African race; a Negro (spec., one actually brought from Africa).

1700 SEWALL *Selling of Joseph* in *Mass. H. S. Proc.* VII. 163 It might not be unreasonable to enquire whether we are not culpable in forcing the Africans to become slaves amongst our selves. **1721** *New-Eng. Courant* 18–25 Dec. 1/1 On Thursday last was solemnized here the Wedding of two Africans . . .: One of the Negroes is said to belong to a certain famous Lawyer in this Town. **1770** *Broadside Verse* (1930) 49/2 Take him ye Africans, he longs for you. **1788** *Mass. Convention on U. S. Const.* 222 The article which respected the Africans. **1800** *Boston Selectmen* 3 Sept., All Africans and Negroes resident in this town. **1809** *Ann. 10th Congress* 2 Sess. 1451 The American Convention for promoting the abolition of slavery and improving the condition of the Africans. **1840** *S. Lit. Messenger* VI. 192/2 For the Africans of Virginia never spoke their native dialects, at least to any extent, in Virginia. **1859** *Harper's Mag.* Oct. 695 Reports . . . that large numbers of Africans have been recently landed on the coast of Florida. **1865** BOUDRYE *Fifth N. Y. Cavalry* 157 Opening the low door, I invited a pure African out, and learned there were none but slaves present.

+**2.** =NIGGER (in the woodpile).

1879 *Congress. Rec.* 11 June 1931/1 There is a gigantic African here [i.e. in the Army Appropriation Bill] . . . I want the African taken out of the bill. **1892** *Ib.* 19 Jan. 431/1 It is indeed difficult to know just how many Africans are hid away in this wood pile [=the bill with reference to public printing].

***African,** *a.*

1. Belonging to the negroid stock of Africa; of Negro race or origin. {1646–}

1722 C. MATHER *Diary* II. 672 My African servant must be præpared for the baptism, which he has been long seeking for. **1773** *Forensic Dispatch* (Boston) 8 African slaves. **1779** Ramsey *Tennessee* (1853) 201 They . . . found an African negro . . . asleep by one of the fires. **1789** *Boston Selectmen* 11 Feb. 161 Application . . . by a number of Blacks . . . [for] the use of Faneuil Hall for once, to accommodate them in hearing an African preacher. **1790** *Ann. 1st Congress* I. 1239 The improvement of the condition of the African race. **1812** J. BREVARD *MS. Let.* 4 Dec. in *Brevard P.* I. (N.C.H.C.), You spoke . . . of giving me one of those African boys. **1828** PAULDING *New Mirror* 39 The African negro adores a painted gourd. **1845** *Knickerb.* XXVI. 334 Concert this evening, by the

African Melodists. **1865** *Atlantic Mo.* XV. 119 Northern Senators and Representatives have presented the claims of the African race.

b. Of animals, plants, etc.: Originating (or regarded as originating) in Africa. {1706–}

(*a*) **1819** *Plough Boy* I. 69 The sow was of the African or Guinea breed. **1854** *Penna. Agric. Rep.* 73 For two pair African bantums, $2.00. **1884** *Amer. Naturalist* XVIII. 949 The dealer . . . permitted me to separate a male 'African cut-throat finch' from his mate.

(*b*) **1836** LINCOLN *Botany* App. 103 *Hibiscus vesicarius*, African Hibiscus. *Ib.* 143 *Tagetes erecta*, African Marygold. **1840** DEWEY *Mass. Flowering Plants* 129 African Marygold is from Mexico; . . . yellow flowers. **1845** LINCOLN *Botany* App. 129/1 *Millium nigricans*, African millet. . . . Exotic. **1892** APGAR *Trees Northern U. S.* 190 *Cedrus Atlantica*, Mt. Atlas, Silver, or African Cedar, . . . has been considered a silvery variety of *Cedrus Libani*. . . . From Africa.

+2. Of or pertaining to the Negro in America.

1789 MORSE *Amer. Gaz.* (1797) s.v. *Philadelphia*, The African church is a large, neat building. It is supplied with a negro clergyman. **1795** J. SCOTT *Gaz.* s.v. *Philadelphia*, African schools . . . have also been established. **1805** JAY *Corr.* IV. 302 African free school in the city of New York. **1818** FEARON *Sketches* 168 The three 'African Churches' as they are called are for all those native Americans who are black, or have any shade of colour darker than white. **1828** [H. FINN, etc.] *Whimwhams* 58 The old negro-dame . . . could spell, though African seminaries, colonization societies, and emancipation tracts were not in fashion. **1835** ABDY *Journal* I. 7 This ceremony was omitted at the *African* schools, as they are called. **1854** *Ann. 15th Congress* 1 Sess. I. 1771 [Proposals for] African Colonization. **1881** *Harper's Mag.* April 738/2 Dulcie . . . rushed forward with an African yell.

+3. Connected with the importation of Negroes from Africa into America.

1790 *Ann. 1st Congress* I. 1224 The licentious wickedness of the African trade for slaves. **1795** *Mass. H. S. Coll.* IV. 196 The African trade never was prosecuted in any great degree by the merchants of Massachusetts. **1818** *Ann. 15th Congress* 1 Sess. I. 71 The expediency of . . . amending the laws of the United States, on the subject of the African slave trade. **1886** LOGAN *Great Conspiracy* 2 As far back as 1699, a controversy sprang up between the Colonies and the Home Government, upon the African Slavery question.

+b. *African fever*, slavery.

1859 L. WILMER *Press Gang* 112 The 'African Fever' which afflicts poor Columbia might have proved a comparatively harmless disease if it had been judiciously treated.

African-born, *a.* Of Negroes: Born in Africa. — **1766** *Rind's Va. Gazette* 8 Aug. 3 Run away . . . , a tall black Negro Man named Jack . . . [who] speaks plain for an African born. **1789** *Fayetteville* (N.C.) *Gazette* 12 Oct., A negro fellow, by the name of London, . . . African born.

+Africanian. [f. AFRICAN *n.*] A Negro born in Africa. — **1845** LYELL *Second Visit* (1849) I. 267 The native-born colored race . . . speak of these 'Africanians' with much of the contempt with which Europeans talk of negroes.

Africanism. {1641–} A mannerism or peculiarity of Negro speech. — **1788** *Mass. Centinel* 30 July 155/3 *Africanisms.* To the many *bon mots*, bulls, and blunders which are fathered upon the unfortunate natives of Africa, the following may be added. **1884** CABLE *Creoles* 260 The rich Creole . . . dropped the West Indian softness that had crept into his pronunciation, and the Africanisms of his black nurse.

+Africanization. [f. next.] The action or fact of bringing under Negro supremacy; 'the act of placing under Negro domination' (B. '59).

'This and the preceding [*Africanize*] are words of recent introduction by Southern political writers' (B. '59).

1856 S. CARTWRIGHT in *Life of Quitman* (1860) II. 230 The Clayton-Bulwer Treaty, the preposterous claims . . . , and the Africanization of tropical America. **1890** *Congress. Rec.* 23 Jan. 806/2, I said I was not in favor of the africanization of this continent or of any part of it.

+Africanize, *v.* [f. AFRICAN.]

1. *tr.* To bring under the supremacy of an African populace; 'to place under Negro domination' (B. '59). Also transf. (quot. 1855).

'A cant term which has of late acquired very general and very melancholy currency' (De Vere). 'Originated to describe a tendency, but has become a reality, since in several Southern states the colored population is in the majority' (M. Lane *Pol. Catch-Words*).

1853 LD. CLARENDON in J. F. Rhodes *Hist. U. S.* (1893) II. 26 A violent and wholly unfounded article in the Washington *Union* charging them with an intrigue with Spain to 'Africanize' Cuba. **1855** *Herald of Freedom* 3 March 1/1 To determine whether the incubus of slavery . . . shall be fastened upon us, and the Territory [of Kansas] be Africanized. **1871** DE VERE 577 Of late . . . several of the Southern States have been literally Africanized. **1884** *N. Amer. Rev.* Oct. 429 This is a white man's country; and a white man's government; and the white race will never allow a section of it to be Africanized.

2. To impart a Negro character to.

1889 *Cent.* **1890** *Harper's Mag.* Jan. 224/1 Her recitals first developed in the white child . . . the power of fancy,—Africanizing it, perhaps, to a degree that after-education could not totally remove.

+Africo-American, *a.* and *n.* = AFRO-AMERICAN.

1835 ABDY *Journal* I. 8 The first Africo-American free school was established at New York in 1787. **1844** 'UNCLE SAM' *Peculiarities* II. 181 The Declaration of Independence is celebrated . . . on the *fifth* [of July] . . . by the black natives, or Africo-Americans. **1881** TOURGEE *'Zouri's Christmas* iv, Three healthier . . . young Africo-Americans never rollicked about a cabin.

+Afro-American, *a.* and *n.*

1. *a.* Of or pertaining to, representing or designating, the Negro population of America.

1890 *Advance* 23 Jan. 80/1 The Afro-American Convention in Chicago. *Ib.* 61/2 The Afro-American League is now a fact. **1891** I. G. PENN (*title*), The Afro-American Press, and its Editors.

2. *n.* An American of African lineage or descent; an American Negro.

1890 *Advance* 23 Jan. 61/2 To encourage all State and local leagues . . . in obtaining for the Afro-American an equal chance. **1891** I. G. PENN *Afro-American Press* 524 The condition of the Afro-American in the Union, particularly in the South.

***After,** *prep.*

1. Past or later than (a specified hour). {1812; also *dial.*}

1732 B. LYNDE *Diary* (1880) 24 A.M. ½ after 5 I went with son's horse . . . and at 10 was in the Council. **1751** MACSPARRAN *Diary* (1899) 62 We crossed Bristol Ferry and got to Newport abt. 1-2 an Hour after 12. **1770** FITHIAN *Princetoniana* (1900) 7 Every Student must rise by half an hour after five. **1789** MACLAY *Deb. Senate* 67 Speaker, Wynkoop, and myself called on Mrs. Morris half after ten. **1899** QUINN *Penna. Stories* 134 Mrs. De Lancey's dinner party . . . had reached the lower right-hand box by a quarter after eight. **1908** F. B. CALHOUN *Miss Minerva* 18 Miss Minerva's bedtime was half after nine o'clock, summer or winter.

2. Engaged or involved in, bent on (doing something). {Anglo-Irish}

1792 BRACKENRIDGE *Adv. Capt. Farrago* xiii. 59 The Irishman . . . utterly refused to be *after* fighting in any such manner. **1800** WEEMS *Letters* II. 137, I fear you'll be after printing too many.

3. For; in order to have.

1796 MORSE *Amer. Geog.* I. 301 A prevailing desire after a peaceable accommodation. **1856** M. J. HOLMES *L. Rivers* xv. 192 That's a plaguy smart feller, and I kinder think he's got a notion after 'Leny.

***Afterclap.**

***1.** An unexpected subsequent stroke or event; a surprising (and esp. disagreeable) sequel. {Now rare except *dial.*}

'It is now seldom heard except in familiar conversation' (B. '48). 'Once current in England, but very rarely heard now, if at all' (F.).

1654 JOHNSON *Wonder-W. Prov.* 139 But let N. England beware of an after-clap, & provoke the Lord no longer. **1845** HOOPER *Simon Sugg's Adv.* iv. 48 So he isn't taken red-handed, after-claps may go to the devil! **1851** MELVILLE *Moby-Dick* xviii, He got so frightened about his plaguy soul, that he shrinked and sheered away from whales, for fear of the after-clap. **1872** W. J. FLAGG *Good Investment* xiii, I don't want any such infernal after-clap as that, you know.

2. An unjust or additional demand beyond the terms of a bargain, agreement, or stipulation. {1755; 1888 *s.w. dial.*}

'Current in Pennsylvania and the Western States' (F.).

1835 LONGSTREET *Georgia Scenes* 28, I'm a man that, when he makes a bad trade, makes the most of it until he can make a better. I'm for no rues and after-claps. **1880** *Overland Mo.* (F.) His blamed afterclaps raised my rile. . . . I was na' goin' to stan' that rush anyhow, as I had agreed afore to pay fifty dollars for the trade.

After-feed. Grass that grows after a crop has been mown or cut. {1847 (Halliwell); 1863} — **1714** *Boston News-Letter* 30 Aug. 1/1 A sore scorching Drought . . . threatening a great Diminution of the Ungathered Corn and Fruits, and total Deprivation of the After-Feed. **1803** *Lit. Mag.* (Phila.) Dec. 210 The after-feed has been generally cut off, which is much against the farmers; as the crop of hay was short. **1831** *Mass. Laws* 19 March 687 The number of acres of pasture land . . . with the after-feed of the whole farm.

***Aftermath.** A second crop or growth of grass in a season.

1786 WASHINGTON *Diaries* III. 96 The aftermath is more valuable, and the second growth quicker. **1814** J. TAYLOR *Arator* 176 The grazing of the after math of the meadows. **1858** FLINT *Milch Cows* 180 The tall Oat Grass . . . after being mown . . . shoots up a very thick aftermath.

+Afternoons, *adv.* During the afternoon; on afternoons. — **1896** *Vermont Agric. Rep.* XV. 36, I prefer to gather sap afternoons.

+After-ripening. (See quotations.) — **1867** *Iowa Agric. Soc. Rep.* (1868) 188 To make the wine: gather the fruit with the stems on. . . . Leave for three or four days in a cellar, . . . thus causing after-ripening. **1872** *Vermont Bd. Agric. Rep.* 72 Shortly after begins after-ripening, a chemical change, whereby the starch, abundant in the unripe or green fruit, is transformed into sugar.

***Agate.**

***1.** A semipellucid variegated chalcedony; a precious stone cut from this.

1818 *Jrnl. Science* I. 236 Agate. Rolled mass occurred near Powles

Hook, New Jersey. **1831** PECK *Guide* 45 Talc [and] agate . . . are found in this Territory north of the Arkansas river. **1846** WEBB *Altowan* I. 223 A few arrows formed of grease-wood . . . and a few splinters of agate, from which she had probably selected their heads. **1881** *Harper's Mag.* Jan. 234/2 Around this fire-place were set . . . agates, and fragments of fossils.

+**b.** 'A child's playing-marble made of agate, or of glass in imitation of agate' (*Cent.*).

+**2.** A size of type (approximately 5½ point) between nonpareil and pearl. {=Eng. *ruby*}

1838 *Democratic Rev.* I. 61 Light faced Book and Job Printing Types, . . . [including] Diamond, Pearl, . . . Agate. **1871** RINGWALT *Encycl. Printing* 24/2 Agate . . . is chiefly used in newspaper work, and . . . for pocket editions of the Bible and Prayer Books.

Agave. [mod. L.] A plant or species of the genus *Agave;* esp. the century-plant or American aloe, *A. Americana,* native to the south-west. {1830–}

1838 'TEXIAN' *Mexico* v. *Texas* 10 Hardly can one find . . . a sturdy *agave*, or a half withered *opuntia* sadly vegetating in the rocky crevices. **1845** GREEN *Texian Exped.* xv. 260 While the juice of the agave inspired the soul, the ass's milk filled the stomach. **1854** BARTLETT *Narr.* I. 254 The agave . . . , with its brilliant yellow blossoms, completed the floral array. **1865** *Atlantic Mo.* XV. 424 The deserted house was embowered in . . . Mexican agaves and English ivies. **1910** J. HART *Vigilante Girl* xiv. 189 That agave . . . 's just about to burst into blossoms.

***Age.** +**1.** The right to make the final bet in a game of poker. **2.** The player having this right. — (1) **1844** Shields *S. S. Prentiss* (1883) 334 You can't expect me to take a hand in this game when he . . . has the age of me to boot. **1882** *Poker: how to play it* 10 The player entitled to bet first may withhold his bet until the others have bet round to him, which is called 'holding the age.' **1907** 'MARK TWAIN' *Autobiog.* in *N. Amer. Rev.* CIV. 569. How could I talk when he was talking? He 'held the age,' as the poker-clergy say. — (2) **187.** in *Poker: how to play it* (1882) 47 Before the dealer begins, . . . the player next to his left, who is called the *ante-man*, or *age*, must deposit in the pool an *ante.* **1887** KELLER *Draw Poker* 21 The ante must be placed on the table by the age before any cards are dealt.

+**Ageable,** *a. S.* Advanced in age; aged, old.

1845 HOOPER *Taking Census* i. 153 Judy Tompkins, ageable woman, and four children. **1887** *Harper's Mag.* April 732/1 Cynthy Stubblefield ain't the ageable person Mapp make out. **1899** GREEN *Virginia Word-Bk.* 39 They are right ageable people.

Agency. {1658–}

I. +**1.** The position or function of a Colonial agent (see AGENT 1).

1762 *Mass. House Jrnl.* 19 April, [Voted] that William Bollan . . . be dismissed from his Agency for this Province. **1769** D. DE BERDT in *Mass. Col. Soc. Publ.* XIII. 383 In obedience to your Lordships commands I here inclose you my original appointment to the Agency for the Lower Counties on Delaware. **1770** *Mass. Col. Soc. Publ.* XIII. 299 I don't imagine the agency of the Colonies . . . can come into worse [hands], as he was a man of no influence.

II. +**2.** The office or function of an Indian agent.

1707 *S. Car. Statutes at Large* (1837) II. 314, I will neither directly nor indirectly trade with any Indian . . . during the time of my agency. **1784** JEFFERSON *Works* (1894) III. 495 It would be our interest to have an agency kept up with the Overhill Cherokees, & Martin the agent. If S. Carol[in]a & Georgia would then be contented with one other agency, . . . it would be well.

+**3.** The area in the charge of an Indian agent.

1796 B. HAWKINS *Letters* 32, I do hereby authorize Stephen Hawkins . . . to pursue and apprehend the said offenders, wherever to be found within the agency South of the Ohio. **1812** *Niles' Reg.* III. 205/2 Travelling through the agency seems to be perfectly safe. **1856** WHIPPLE *Explor. Ry. Route* Extracts 8 From Ring's plantation to Choctaw agency . . . the road led us over hilly ground.

+**4.** A fort or station in an Indian territory or reservation, where the agent of the government has his office or headquarters; more fully *Indian agency* (q.v.).

1824 *Statutes at Large* (1856) IV. 25 It shall be the duty of each Indian agent to reside and keep his agency within, or near the territory claimed by the tribe or tribes of Indians for which he may be agent. **1853** GLISAN *Jrnl. Army Life* 107 Major Sibley met with a small band of these Indians at the agency. **1877** *Rep. Indian Affairs* 46 No clothing, blanket, tent, implement, or utensil of any kind has been issued at this agency for nearly two years. **1885** E. B. CUSTER *Boots & Saddles* vii. 85 Tin cans, spoons, and forks, that they had bought at the Agency . . . were left there as offerings to an unseen God. **1890** *Harper's Mag.* April 734/1 A force of cavalry and infantry to protect the agency and its white inhabitants from the Indians they were there to feed and instruct. **1909** *Indian Laws & Tr.* III. 387 The Secretary of the Interior . . . is . . . directed to restore to the rolls of the Klamath Agency . . . those Modoc Indians now enrolled at the Quapaw Agency.

+**5.** Attrib. with *barn, building, clerk, farm, farmer, house,* etc.

1852 MRS. ELLET *Pioneer Women* 286 The 'agency house,' a log building standing a few rods from the fort. **1866** *Rep. Indian Affairs* 90 A person to reside on the agency farm to attend to the cultivation of the crop. **1868** *Indian Laws & Tr.* III. 714 Stipulations . . . for the location of said Crow Indians on a reservation adjoining that of the Gros Ventres, . . . occupying and using in common all agency buildings. **1873** BEADLE *Undevel. West* 526 The party, consisting of Agent Miller, B. M. Thomas, Agency Farmer, . . . left Defiance. *Ib.* 527 The last grain in the Agency storehouse was issued to them on the 14th. **1878** — *Western Wilds* 249 The band have recognized their friends coming . . . and soon they unite in the quadrangle inclosed by the Agency buildings. *Ib.* 252 Mr. Thomas V. Keams, Agency Clerk, was acting in place of Miller. **1883** *Rep. Indian Affairs* 78 A jail and barracks . . . have been constructed and the agency barn finished.

+**b.** *Agency Indian*, one under the supervision or authority of an Indian agent.

1891 *Boston* (Mass.) *Jrnl.* 1 Jan. 2/3 Does not our Government undertake to clothe and feed the agency Indians? **1901** WHITE *Westerners* viii. 57 Rain-in-the-Face was at once an agency Indian and a reckless man.

* **Agent.**

+**1.** A person appointed to represent in London the interests of an American colony or of some division of it.

1646 *Mass. Col. Rec.* II. 161 The Courte hath found it necessary to send an agent into England to negotiate for this colony with the Parliament. **1650** *Ib.* III. 200 Mr. Edward Winslow, agent for this country in England. **1681** *Ib.* V. 304 Wm. Staughton, Esqr., and Samuel Nowell, Esqr., were the persons so chosen to be our agents. **1728** *Duxbury Rec.* 240 The Town . . . voted that sixteen pounds should be paid out of their treasury towards the support of our Agent in England. **1748** *N. J. Archives* VII. 120 New York has been without an Agent for a dozen years past, but now this spring they have appointed Robert Charles for their Agent. **1762** *Mass. H. S. Coll.* LXXIV. 57 A letter from the several Agents for the Colonies in North America. **1768** *Boston Chronicle* 14 Nov. 434 The assembly of the three lower counties of this province [Penna.], have appointed Dennys De Berdt, Esq. [an Englishman], their agent, in England. **1774** (*title*), The Petitions of Mr. Bollan, Agent for the Council of the Province of Massachusetts Bay, . . . to the Two Houses of Parliament.

+**2.** =INDIAN AGENT.

1707 *S. Car. Statutes at Large* (1837) II. 311 For the further preventing abuses . . . Thomas Nairne . . . is . . . appointed the agent to reside among the Indians, subject to the Government of South Carolina. **1754** *Mass. H. S. Coll.* 3 Ser. V. 19 He would direct the Secretary or Agent for Indian affairs to attend them with the records of that office. **1796** B. HAWKINS *Letters* 32 The agent of the Cherokees, his assistants and all others in authority. **1800** — *Sk. Creek Country* 56 Here is the public establishment for the Lower Creeks; and here the agent resides. **1818** *Ann. 15th Congress* 1 Sess. I. 84 The expediency of requiring by law the nomination of agents to Indian tribes, to be submitted to the Senate. **1834** *Statutes at Large* (1856) IV. 729 That any superintendent or agent may refuse an application for a license to trade, if [etc.]. **1873** BEADLE *Undevel. West* 586 The Orbayes refuse to receive an agent or make any treaty. **1890** *Harper's Mag.* April 734/2 The Indians had grown restless under the efforts of the agent to teach them farming and the other industries of the whites.

3. One employed to direct or manage a commercial undertaking or some department of this.

1706 *Duxbury Rec.* 202 The said town voted to choose two Agents . . . to agree and bargain with . . . workmen to build the said Meeting house. **1796** *Essex Inst. Coll.* LIV. 106 The Directors shall appoint an Agent who shall personally . . . direct the whole business of said Company. **1843** *Lowell Offering* III. 192 Do the superintendents, agents, etc., 'the powers that be' over us, . . . do all in their power to make us healthy?

b. One who sells or takes orders on behalf of a producer or employer.

1872 *Atlantic Mo.* March 314 It was no very uncommon thing . . . for the planter to receive from his agent in London . . . a bill of charges which the price of the tobacco had not covered. **1877** PHELPS *Story of Avis* 295 Word was brought . . . that a book-agent had called. . . . The woman wore gray clothes and carried a little agent's bag.

+**c.** A station-agent or ticket-agent.

1835 *Boston Mercantile Journal* 25 June, Tickets may be had at the Depot . . . Price $1. George M. Dexter, Agent. **1852** *N. Y. Common Plea Rep.* 523 Ann Kelly . . . delivered her trunk to the agent, . . . receiving from him a check therefor.

+**4.** *ellipt.* A 'road-agent'; a highwayman.

1881 HAYES *New Colorado* 154 We reached it before long, and concluded the 'agents,' or robbers, had an excellent eye for position. **1904** WHITE *Blazed Trail Stories* 152 Nex' time I drives stage some of these yere agents massacrees me from behind a bush.

+**5.** *Agent of truancy*, in the State of New York, an officer who enforces attendance at school.

1877 *N. Y. City Bd. Education Rep.* 41 To carry out the provisions of the law relating to the inspection of . . . establishments where children are employed, it was found necessary to appoint an agent of truancy. **1884** *Encycl. Brit.* XVII. 461/2 The law [of compulsory education] is enforced in the city [of New York] by the city superintendent, who has twelve assistants known as 'agents of truancy.'

6. *Agent victualler*, an officer stationed at a port to supervise the victualing of naval vessels. *Obs.* {1769, 1834}

1777 *N. H. Comm. Safety* 105 Supply Clapp Agent Victualler with [rice]. *Ib.* 118 Ordered the R. G. to let Col. Clapp have one hundred & fifty pounds, to be accounted for as Agent Victualler.

+**Age-to-come Adventist:** see quotation and ADVENTIST. — **1884** *Schaff's Relig. Encycl.* III. 2581/2 The Age-to-come Adventists believe that the Jews are to be re-established in Jerusalem.... They are not numerous.

***Aggrievance.** *Obs.* A grievance. {-1664}

1677 *Plymouth Rec.* 152 A draught of the particulars of theire agrievantes [*sic*] respecting the premises. **1692** BULKELEY *Will & Doom* 103 Reviews upon aggrievance by the judicatory for small causes. **1718** *Mass. H. Repr. Journals* II. 11 That addition may be made to the Act . . . that may relieve them under an aggrievance, which the present law will not reach. **1753** *Md. Hist. Mag.* III. 368 The Articles . . . which had been agitated in the Committee of Agrievances.

Agitator. An apparatus for shaking or stirring a substance. {1871}

1847 *Rep. Comm. Patents* (1848) 26 A patent . . . granted for an improvement in the distillation of crude turpentine, consisting merely of an agitator or stirring apparatus. **1861** GESNER *Coal, Petroleum & Oils* 45 Agitators or stirrers in retorts have been introduced. **1874** RAYMOND *6th Rep. Mines* 413 All drains should lead into the agitators; and the quicksilver floor . . . should be washed with a hose every day. *Ib.*, The precious metal left in the tailings is very difficult to concentrate after leaving the agitators. **1875** KNIGHT 1625/1 Vertical agitators . . . are provided at each end of the tank [used in paper-making].

Agrarian, *n.*

1. a. One who favors a redistribution or equal division of landed property, or a change in the tenure of land. {1818, 1882}. **b.** A member or adherent of certain political parties.

' "Agrarians" is the name here given to people who meet to recommend the Government to keep the revenues in safe custody, in treasuries of their own, instead of intrusting it to speculating banks' (1841 Buckingham *America* I. 124). 'Sometimes applied to agitators accused of leveling tendencies or of hostile designs against the holders of property, as to certain political parties at different times' (*Cent.*).

1832 FERRALL *Ramble* 327 There are those of them called 'agrarians' who contend that there should be a law passed to prohibit individuals holding beyond a certain quantity of ground. **1838** COOPER *Home as Found* xxiii, The reader is not to suppose . . . that Mr. Dodge was an agrarian, or that he looked forward to a division of property. **1838** Buckingham *America* I. 176, 2000 radicals, agrarians, Fanny-Wright men, and Locofocos . . . who . . . have thrown themselves on the bounty of the Van Buren party. **1879** J. LALOR tr. *Von Holst's Const. Hist.* II. 397 'Agrarians' was the accursed name to be fastened on them [=the Equal Rights Party, 1835], and to make them an abomination in the eyes of all those who took any interest in law or social order.

||**2.** The land itself; landed property. *Obs.*

1778 ADAMS *Works* (1851) IV. 359 The agrarian in America is divided among the common people in every state.

Agrarianism. The principle or theory of a redistribution or equal division of lands, or of a change in land-tenure. {1808}

1830 S. BRECK in *Recoll.* (1877) iii. 118 A pupil of Robert Owen, a female named Fanny Wright, has been lecturing . . . upon agrarianism and infidelity. **1836** *Knickerb.* VII. 43, I care not whether the Fanny Wright doctrines or Agrarianism prevails. **1838** *Democratic Rev.* I. 258 The absurd cry of 'Agrarianism' was raised . . . by a large majority of the press. **1855** Hambleton *H. A. Wise* 355 [The Republican party] will defend the State against agrarianism, freesoilism and abolitionism.

***Agreeable,** *a.* (as *n.*). *To do the agreeable*, to act in an agreeable or courteous manner. *colloq.*

1839 TOWNSEND *Narr.* i. 127, I endeavored to do the agreeable to the fair ones. **1852** *Harper's Mag.* V. 419/2 A gentleman-visitor was 'doing the agreeable' to one of the ladies. **1875** STOWE *We & Neighbors* iv. 51 Harry has such boundless confidence in my powers of doing the agreeable.

Agricultural, *a.* {1776-}

1. Of, pertaining to, or concerned with agriculture.

1794 WASHINGTON in *Sinclair's Corr.* (1831) II. 18 An attempt . . . is making to establish a state society in Pennsylvania for agricultural improvements. **1808** *Ann. 10th Congress* 2 Sess. 157 We, the merchants, ought, therefore, to be cautious how we charge agricultural men with hostility to commerce. **1831** PECK *Guide* 300 Morgan County is destined to become one of the richest agricultural counties of the State. **1839** *Indiana H. Rep.* J. 599 Their object of permanently establishing, at the seat of government of this state, . . . an agricultural and horticultural wareroom and general seed store. **1847** *Revised Stat. Ohio* (1860) I. 64 There shall be created . . . a fund, which shall be known as the 'state agricultural fund.' **1865** *Atlantic Mo.* XV. 83 Mr. Solon Robinson, agricultural editor of the 'New York Tribune.'

b. Used or employed in husbandry.

1825 *Austin Papers* (1924) II. 1028 Are you not in want of many kinds of agricultural Implements? **1850** *New Eng. Farmer* II. 331 Agricultural furnace. This furnace is adapted to boiling vegetables, and cooking food generally for stock. **1865** *Atlantic Mo.* XV. 694 [In] Illinois . . . farmers . . . by use of agricultural machinery are able to produce a very large amount of grain. **1883** *Rep. Indian Affairs* p. xlvi, A judicious distribution of agricultural implements among these Indians.

2. Founded or conducted to promote the interests or study of agriculture.

1785 in *Trans. Amer. Inst. N. Y.* (1855) 389 It was proposed to form a society in Philadelphia for the promotion of agriculture, and accordingly, Messrs. George Morgan, George Clymer, [etc.] . . . agreed to create an agricultural society. **1794** WASHINGTON in *Sinclair's Corr.* (1831) II. 18 It will be some time, I fear, before an agricultural society, with congressional aids, will be established in this country. **1797** *S. Car. Statutes at Large* (1839) V. 318 An act . . . to convey two squares of land to the Agricultural Society of South Carolina. **1819** *Amer. Farmer* I. 83, I beg leave . . . to tender to the 'Agricultural Society of Virginia,' my thanks. **1839** BUEL *Farmer's Companion* 281 The Agricultural periodicals of our country. **1849** *New England Farmer* I. 234 An agricultural school does not convey an idea of what we want; nor does an agricultural college convey any more definitely the true object to be gained. **1850** *Ib.* II. 42 Agricultural seminaries should be commenced on a moderate scale. **1855** *Trans. Amer. Inst. N. Y.* 270 Judge Van Wyck made several observations on the subject of agricultural colleges, expressing doubts of any utility equal to the experiment of such system. **1857-8** *Ill. Agric. Soc. Trans.* III. 563 But the great want . . . is an Agricultural University. **1873** *Newton* (Kansas) *Kansan* 13 Feb. 3/5 An agricultural association is about to be formed for Sedgwick county. **1887** *Ill. Dept. Agric. Trans.* (1889) 9 To bring the Board into more intimate relations with the agricultural and industrial associations of the State. **1894** *Vermont Agric. Rep.* XIV. 107 The weekly agricultural newspaper . . . is . . . necessary for the salvation of the farmer.

b. Held for the joint exhibition and sale of agricultural produce, farm stock, etc.

1819 *Plough Boy* I. 149 The approaching Agricultural Fairs . . . will be held at the times and places following. **1820** E. WATSON *Hist. Canals N. Y.*, etc. 211 First Agricultural exhibition, 1807. **1854** *Penna. Agric. Rep.* 229 The enclosure of an Agricultural Fair and Cattle Show. **1893** HOWELLS *Coast of Bohemia* 9 He spent a very miserable time in the Fine Arts Department of the Pymantoning County Agricultural Fair.

+**3.** *Agricultural ant*, a species of ant, as the *Pogonomyrmex barbatus* of Texas, that clears the vicinity of its nest of verdure or herbage.

1868 *Amer. Naturalist* II. 157 Such structures are remarkable . . . , reminding us of the intelligence shown by the Agricultural Ant of Texas. **1879** McCOOK (*title*), The Natural History of the Agricultural Ant of Texas.

+**Agriculturalist,** *n.* An agriculturist. {1819 (Rees' Cycl.), 1854-}

1805-9 HENRY *Campaign agst. Quebec* (1812) 93 He was an agriculturalist, which in the vagueness and uncertainty of our country is called a farmer. **1808** *Ann. 10th Congress* 2 Sess. 157 What have the agriculturalists to do with your neutral commerce? **1840** *Diplom. Corr. Texas* (1908) I. 453 As a draughtsman, civil engineer, and agriculturalist I believe he is unsurpassed. **1849** WHIPPLE *Lit. & Life* vi. 194 Every truly practical man, whether he be merchant, mechanic, or agriculturalist.

Agriculture. The cultivation of the soil; the science or art of husbandry; farming, tillage. {1603-}

1743 CATESBY *Carolina* II. p. xvi, [Account] of the Agriculture of Carolina. **1767** *Doc. Hist. N. Y. State* (1849) I. 733 There is a small manufactory of Linen in this City [=New York], . . . supported chiefly by . . . a set of men who call themselves the Society of Arts and Agriculture. **1776** *Journals Cont. Congress* IV. 224 Resolved, that it be recommended to the said assemblies . . . that they take the earliest measures for erecting and establishing in each and every colony a society for the improvement of agriculture, arts, manufactures, and commerce. **1778** ADAMS *Works* (1852) IV. 47 Agriculture is the most essential interest of America, and even of the Massachusetts Bay. **1839** *Indiana H. Rep.* 599 The committee on agriculture, to which was referred the memorial . . . praying for a loan to aid Osborn and Willets [etc.]. **1862** *Congress. Globe* 13 May 2098/2 The amendments of the House bill No. 269, to establish a Department of Agriculture. **1894** *Rep. Secy. Agric. 1893* 450 Statistics of the Colleges having Courses in Agriculture.

b. *Board of Agriculture*, a Federal or State board for the promotion of agricultural interests.

'In my correspondence with General Washington, I strongly inculcated the establishment of "a Board of Agriculture," and I understand that he recommended that measure to the attention of Congress' (1831 Sir J. Sinclair *Corr.* II. 53).

1796 WASHINGTON in *Ann. 4th Congress* 2 Sess. II. 1594 It will not be doubted that . . . agriculture is of primary importance. . . . Among the means which have been employed to this end . . . [is] the establishment of Boards . . . charged with collecting and diffusing information. **1797** SWIFT in *Ann. 4th Congress* 1835 A Board, to consist of not more than thirty persons, which shall be called 'A Board of Agriculture.' **1820** *Plough Boy* I. 294, I could wish . . . that the Board of Agriculture . . . would recommend to scientific gentlemen . . . to examine the Spire Grass in their respective vicinities. **1846** in *Revised Statutes of Ohio* (1860) I. 61 The Ohio state board of agriculture, hereinafter created. **1894** *Vermont Agric. Rep.* XIV. 109 The chief reason why the State, through the Board of Agriculture, should require a different system.

Agriculturist. One engaged or skilled in agriculture; a farmer, husbandman; =AGRICULTURALIST. {1760–}

1798 I. ALLEN *Hist. Vermont* 263 You ask me if the Vermontese are good agriculturists? I answer that putting everything together they have made a rapid progress in that useful branch of science. **1823** COOPER *Pioneers* xxix, He who changes ... his farm every six months ... ! an agriculturist yesterday, a shoemaker to-day! **1824** *Ann. 18th Congress* 1 Sess. I. 1662 To inquire if an increase of the duty ... on any article of foreign growth ... will be for the interest of the agriculturist. **1840** BUEL *Farmer's Companion* 280 Our Agriculturists are our privileged class, if we have such. They are our sovereigns. **1865** *Atlantic Mo.* XV. 661 The agriculturist says that women take care of young chickens much better than men. **1881** *Rep. Indian Affairs* 46 Hardly the land which we should select to try the experiment of making men self-supporting as agriculturists.

* **Agrimony.** A plant or species of the genus *Agrimonia* of the rose-family; esp. the common agrimony, *A. Eupatoria*, formerly valued in medicine.

[1670 D. DENTON *Brief Desc. N.Y.* (1845) 4 The herbs which the countrey naturally afford are purslain, white orage, egrimony, ... and many more.]

1784 CUTLER in *Mem. Academy* I. 448 Agrimony ... [grows] by fences. July. *Ib.* 478 Honesty. Hemp Agrimony. ... In moist places, by brooks and rivers. **1795** WINTERBOTHAM *Hist. View* III. 398 Among the native and uncultivated plants of New-England, the following have been employed for medical purposes: ... Wild hyssop ... Agrimony. **1818** *Mass. H. S. Coll.* 2 Ser. VIII. 170 In July the lover of plants is gratified with ... the white spirea, agrimony, the common iris. **1832** WILLIAMSON *Maine* I. 119 Agrimony (*Agrimonia Eupatoria*) has yellow blossoms; ... its root is used by the natives in fevers, and its leaves for diet-drink and the jaundice. **1843** TORREY *Flora N. Y.* I. 206 Common Agrimony ... [grows in] borders of woods, fields, etc. ... The root ... is sweet-scented [and] was formerly in repute as a tonic. **1881** *Harper's Mag.* Oct. 645/2 The agrimony and enchanter's nightshade are sly and cautious.

+**Agrippina.** Some article of ship's furniture. — **1830** COOPER *Water Witch* II. ii. 39 Against the bulkhead of each state room stood an agrippina of mahogany. *Ib.* 40 The outer portion of the cabin ... had its agrippina, its piles of cushions, its chairs.

+**Aguardiente.** *S.W.* Also **-dienta, aguadiente.** [Sp., ='brandy.' Cf. AQUARDIENTE.] 'A kind of brandy distilled from red wine' (B. '59); 'any distilled liquor, whether rum, brandy, or whiskey' (B. '77).

1834 A. PIKE *Sketches* 103 The first glass of the aguadiente, or white brandy, ... generally touched her lips. *Ib.* 112 A cuartillo of aguardiente, or grape whiskey, was ... placed upon the table. **1836** EDWARD *Hist. Texas* 117 Those ... exceed them in their thirst for pulque and *aguardiente.* **1844** GREGG *Commerce of Prairies* II. 77 There is very little wine or legitimate *aguardiente* manufactured in New Mexico. **1878** BEADLE *Western Wilds* 190 The priest ... stood ready to grant extreme unction if *aguardiente* and gambling resulted in fatal 'accidents.' **1886** BRET HARTE *Snow-bound* 38, I really cannot undertake to ... keep him from drinking *aguardiente* with suspicious characters at the bar.

* **AGUE.**

The unusual form has led to several popular variations of pronunciation: (1) *ager* (also *aguer, agir, agur*), recorded as early as 1818; (2) *agy* (*aguy*), *agee*, from at least 1840; and (3) *ague* rhyming with *plague*, from 1859 or earlier.

* **1.** Fever of a malarial character, attended by periodically recurring paroxysms, characterized by chill, fever, and sweating; intermittent fever; also, a fit or spell of this.

1650 BRADSTREET *Poems* (1897) 54 Diseases not declined as you, Nor cold nor hot, ague nor pleurisy, ... nor quinsy. **1685** [see FEVER]. **1693** C. MATHER *Wonders Invis. World* 74 Wasting Sicknesses, especially burning and mortal Agues, have shot the Arrows of Death in at our Windows. **1706** *Boston News-Letter* 14 Jan. 2 South-Carolina. Nov. 11. We have had here for a considerable time, a Feaver attended with an unusual Ague; ... while it was warm weather 'twas not mortal. **1712** J. HEMPSTEAD *Diary* 10 My wife hath got the ague in her Breast bad. **1739** STEPHENS *Proc. Georgia* 481 The soldiers were addicted to Agues. **1786** WASHINGTON *Diaries* III. 109 Taken with an Ague ... which ... confined me to the House till evening. **1817** J. BRADBURY *Travels* 328 Agues were very prevalent, and it will perhaps be found, that all countries in a state of nature are liable to this disease in the proportion of their fertility. **1825** NEAL *Bro. Jonathan* I. 262 He ... shook violently, as with an ague, all over. **1834** [BAIRD] *Valley Mississippi* viii. 85 These maladies are intermitting and remitting bilious fevers, ... which have received the names of 'ague', 'dumb ague' and 'chill and fever.' **1844** LEE & FROST *Oregon* ix. 108 The epidemic ague ... commenced, according to the best authorities, in 1830. **1871** De Vere 432 The ague ... comes creeping up a fellow's back like a ton of wild cats, goes crawling through his joints like iron spikes.

b. Occas. in *ague and fever.* (Cf. FEVER *and ague.*)

1699 E. WARD *Trip New-Eng.* 48 The Country, by its Climate, is always troubled with an Ague and Fever. **1707** ARCHDALE *Descr. Carolina* 9 What may properly belong to the Country, is to have some gentle Touches of Agues and Feavers, ... especially to New-comers. **1713** *Mass. H. S. Coll.* 6 Ser. V. 269 Your mother has had the ague and fever every other day. **1817** E. P. FORDHAM *Narr.* 57 The Ague and Fever are very common here. **1844** LEE & FROST *Oregon* xxi. 250 During this visit he had a violent attack of the ague and fever. **1848** E. BRYANT *California* ii. 30 The prevailing diseases of this country—the ague and bilious fevers. **1850** G. HINES *Voyage* 336 The ague and fever ... attacks many of the whites who come to settle in the Wallamette valley.

2. Attrib. with *charmer, chill, fit, pill,* etc.

1775 ADAIR *Indians* 87 Our ague-charmers, and water-casters, ... like birds of night keep where the Indians frequently haunt. **1787** FRENEAU *Misc. Works* 419 You ague-cheek'd, cream-colour'd son of a bitch. **1835** [Longstreet] *Georgia Scenes* 191 The chills ran from my head to my toes, like ague fits. **c1835** CATLIN *Indians* II. 89 The grim shaking and chattering of an ague chill. **1851** *Polly Peablossom* 157 The Doctor immediately had any quantity of patients—all of whom ... would come in person ... for a few 'agur pills.' **1859** *Harper's Mag.* Sept. 574/1 You go ahead, and make your Indian vegetable ager pills. **1859** M. J. HOLMES *Rosamond* vii, Have you an ague chill, really? or what makes your teeth chatter so? **1901** CHURCHILL *Crisis* 153 Fakirs ... selling pain-killers and ague-cures.

+**Ague-and-feverish,** *a.* [See prec. 1 b.] Subject to, suffering from, ague. — **1832** [KENNEDY] *Swallow Barn* I. vii. 80 Bulrush, a spare, ague-and-feverish husbandman, ... occupies a muddy slip of marsh land.

Ague-cake. Swelling due to enlargement of the spleen or liver resulting from ague. {1641, 1801}

1775 ROMANS *Florida* 242 Jaundice, the ague cake, and other inveterate chronical disorders. **1832** FERRALL *Ramble thro' U. S.* 216, I have seen many, particularly females, who had immense swellings or protuberances on their stomachs, which they denominate 'ague-cakes.' **1841** STEELE *Summer Journey* 156 Their boy ... was afflicted with an ague cake, which they wished me to feel in his side.

+**Ague-grass, -root.** The star-grass, *Aletris farinosa.* — **1687** CLAYTON *Virginia* in *Phil. Trans.* XLI. 158 There is another Root of the Species of Hyacinths, the Leaves whereof are grass-like ... and spread like a Star upon the Ground. ... Some call it ague-grass, others ague-root, others Star-grass.

+**Ague-weed. a.** The boneset, *Eupatorium perfoliatum.* **b.** The five-flowered gentian, *G. quinqueflora.* (Cent.)

Aguish, *a.* Of places or conditions: Productive of, tending to produce or induce, ague. {1627–}

1738 BYRD *Dividing Line* (1929) 70 Not so much as a Zealand Frog cou'd endure so aguish a Situation. **1843** 'CARLTON' *New Purchase* I. xxxi. 295 Having been with missionaries in aguish districts and having had a comfortable night's repose amid the aguish household. **1854** THOREAU *Walden* i. (1863) 48 A dirt floor for the most part, dank, clammy, and aguish.

A-gunning: see A *prep.*[1] 3, 4 and GUN *v.*, GUNNING *vbl. n.* (Freq. with *go.*) {1689–; now rare.}

1700 SEWALL *Diary* II. 9 Three young men ... went in a canoo a gunning before day-light, and were drowned. **1734** *Harvard Rec.* I. 154 No Undergraduates shall ... go a guning [*sic*], fishing, or scating over deep waters. **1744** *New Eng. Hist. Register* (1859) XIII. 111 Daniel Preston, ... being in a canoe ... a gunning for wild-Fowl. **1769** WASHINGTON *Diaries* I. 312 Went a Gunning up the Creek. Killd 7 Ducks. **1783** J. MAY *Jrnl. & Lett.* (1873) 32 Went a gunning this afternoon, and killed some gray and black squirrels. **1839** *S. Lit. Messenger* V. 377/1, I'll go a gunning ... and see if I can't get a chance at some of these bears. **c1849** [PAIGE] *Dow's Sermons* I. 25 They go out a-gunning for the barbarous purpose. **1904** 'O. HENRY' *Heart of West* 119 Thinkin' it was ... one of the Mayfield girls comin' a-gunnin'.

+**A harrow.** A harrow having the form of an A.

1867 *Iowa Agric. Soc. Rep.* (1868) 169 As soon as the corn appears in the row, drag with an A harrow. **1874** *Vermont B. Agric. Rep.* II. 662 A snowplow shaped like an A harrow, for clearing winter roads. **1875** KNIGHT 1068/1 The letter 'A' harrow ... is very handy in ground from which stumps have not been eradicated. It is easily lifted by the corner or by the bow.

* **Ahead,** *adv.*

+**1.** Forward in respect of action, or with the matter in hand; onward without hesitation or delay. Usu. with *go.* {1840–}

'A seaman's phrase in very common use' (B. '48). In very freq. currency from c1835. In early use freq. ascribed to Crockett, to whom De Vere (p. 605) attributes the origin of the phrase. '*Go ahead.* ... This idiomatic phrase ... is very characteristic of the restless and energetic progress of the American people' (Clapin).

1833 *Niles' Reg.* XLIV. 145/1 Our pen got 'a running,' and it did not seem easy to stop it. So we 'let it go a-head.' **1833** S. BRECK in *Recoll.* (1877) 277 The modern fashion in all things is 'to go ahead,' push on, keep moving, and the faster, the better. **1834** CROCKETT *Narr. Life* i. 1, I throw aside all ... fawning apologies, and, according to my own maxim, just 'go ahead.' **1835** *Knickerb.* V. 54 They stimulate in the bosoms of all the desire to advance,—or, 'go ahead.' **1845** *N. Y. Comm. Adv.* 29 Nov. (B.) Our banks ... are probably right to drive ahead, regardless of consequences. **1852** STOWE *Uncle Tom* xii, Well, then, we'll all go ahead and buy up niggers. **1853** *Harper's Mag.* VI. 703/1 Society is tumbling 'ahead' neck and heels. **1857** *Mich. Agric. Soc. Trans.* VIII. 589 We hope that we shall still be able to 'go ahead' without calling for the tax. **1873** *Newton* (Kansas) *Kansan* 2 Jan. 2/2 They went ahead with it.

+**2.** In advance *of* another in respect of progress, prosperity, success, etc. {1876}

'To "get ahead of," to outwit or outdo, by superior sagacity or activity' (B. '77, p. 775).

1825 NEAL *Bro. Jonathan* I. 385, I was working, all the time, to get ahead of Edith. **1863** S. C. MASSETT *Drifting About* 125 Montgomery had got 'ahead of me' in the sale of 'Brannan's store.' **1863** [HOLLAND] *Letters Joneses* 68 All European countries are ahead of us in this matter. **1883** DE VERE in *Ency. Brit. Suppl.* I. 201/2 One school-boy is . . . *ahead* of another; American churches are *ahead* of English churches; and the press is *ahead* of all others in the world. **1920** BOK *Americanization of E. Bok* 165 He always kept 'a huckleberry or two' ahead of his readers.

+**b.** *ellipt.* In an advanced, leading, or successful position or state.

1828 *Free Press* (Tarboro, N. C.) 14 Nov., In Virginia the Jackson Ticket is far a-head. **1834** CARRUTHERS *Kentuckian* I. 26 When the feller had got considerable ahead, the word came out that he was studyin to be a doctor. **1838** *Knickerb.* XII. 317 This, then, is the reason why Blueville never got ahead. **1878** *Ill. Dep. Agric. Trans.* XIV. 284 The Jersey was much ahead; had large cream globules which rise easy. **1882** BEADLE *Western Wilds* 615 My sheep had done well, and that was all I was ahead. **1886** P. STAPLETON *Major's Christmas* 194 Your grandfather said you'd come out ahead, True, but this is so grand, so like the story. **1904** W. H. SMITH *Promotors* i. 21 We can go on and finish our plant, and be ahead every dollar that they've blown in!

+**3.** In advance; beforehand.

1900 DRANNAN *Plains & Mts.* 132 Johnnie West and I having enough meat ahead to last several days, we pulled out for Taos. **1905** A. H. RICE *Sandy* 164, I don't think you can g-get a dance there. . . . She is always engaged ahead.

+**A-here,** in *look a-here* "look ye ('ee) here," =Look here! Pay attention. *colloq.* or *dial.*

1843 [STEPHENS] *High Life N. Y.* I. xi. 173 Look a here, cousin John, why don't you ask if he ever plays all fours. **1869** BROWNE *Adv. Apache Country* 184 'Look-a-here!' said she, . . . hauling out a couple of grinning skulls . . . ; 'that's what we're all coming to.' **1875** HOLLAND *Sevenoaks* 54 Now ye look a here! Don't you say nothing about this. **1898** CANFIELD *Maid of Frontier* 178 'Look ahere,' says he, 'you folks . . . has been tryin' to lay me out.'

+**A-hold.** Also **a-holt.** [The *a* is probably the indefinite article confused with A *prep.*[2]] With a grip, tight grasp, or firm hold (*of* or *on* something). *colloq.* or *dial.*

1872 EGGLESTON *End of World* xi. 77 You gripped a-holt of the truth that air time. **1878** LANIER *Marshes of Glynn* 76, I will heartily lay me a-hold on the greatness of God. **1879** *Scribner's Mo.* May 17 With one bee a-hold of your collar . . . , and another a-hold of each arm, . . . the odds are greatly against you. **1884** 'MARK TWAIN' *H. Finn* vi. 43 [To] take a-hold of a prowling, thieving, . . . free nigger.

+**Ahsahta.** [Mandan-Indian name.] The mountain sheep or bighorn, *Ovis montana.* — **1805** LEWIS & CLARK *Journal* (1904) I. 239–40 The Mandan Indians call this sheep Ar-Sar-ta. **1814** BIDDLE *Hist. Exped. Lewis & Clark* I. 202 [renders above word as] ahsahta. **1836** IRVING *Astoria* xxxix. 455 The principal quadrupeds . . . were the stag, fallow deer, . . . ahsahta, bighorn. **1837** — *Bonneville* I. 230 Numerous gangs of elk, large flocks of the ahsahta or bighorn.

+**A-huckleberrying:** see A *prep.*[1] 4 and HUCKLEBERRYING *vbl. n.* — **1854** THOREAU *Walden* 222 If he and his family would live simply, they might all go a-huckleberrying . . . for their amusement. **1867** 'T. LACKLAND' *Homespun* I. 70 It is as much an art to go a-huckleberrying. **1878** STOWE *Poganuc People* xix. 210 We'll take Saturday afternoon to go a-huckleberrying.

A-hunting: see A *prep.*[1] 3, 4, and HUNTING *vbl. n.*

1624 WINSLOW *Good Newes* 43 All the men [=Indians] . . . tooke their bowes and arrowes and went forth, telling them [=the Englishmen] they went a hunting. **1642** *Md. Archives* IV. 167 They were 3. daies out a hunting. **1677** *N. H. Hist. Soc. Coll.* III. 100 His son being on the outher sid of Meremack River a hunting. **1721** *Essex Inst. Coll.* XXXV. 143 A young pretty fellow, who went a hunting. **1750** WALKER *Journal* 15–16 June, We went a hunting & killed 3 Turkeys. Hunted & killed 3 Bears & some Turkeys. **1847** C. LANMAN *Summer in Wild* 191, I must go a-hunting for my sporting friend. **1874** GLISAN *Jrnl. Army Life* 454 When off duty they can . . . go a-hunting or fishing.

A-husking: see A *prep.*[1] 3 and HUSKING *vbl. n.* — **1737** J. EDWARDS *Faithful Narrative* 119 She and some others of the Children were in a Room by themselves, a husking Indian corn. **1743** MACSPARRAN *Diary* 13 My men stayed out long a husking.

***Aid,** *n.* Also † **ayde.**

***1.** A helper or assistant.

1664 *R. I. Hist. Soc.* X. 69 [He] saide to the Constable & his ayde, Stand off at your perell. **1782** FRENEAU *Poems* (1786) 244 Then turning about, to the printer he said, 'Who late was my servant shall now be my Aid.' **1883** *Wheelman* I. 397 The 'American boss' is described with effective touches, and his aids and henchmen figure no less actively in the story. **1884** CABLE *Dr. Sevier* xxxii, Nobody's seen that picture but you and one 'aid,' and just as soon as he saw it he said, [etc.].

+**2.** An aide-de-camp; =AIDE.

1780 S. HOLTEN in *Essex Inst. Coll.* LVI. 94 One of Gen. Lincoln's aids is arrived with the accounts of the surrender of Charlestown. **1825** NEAL *Bro. Jonathan* III. 45 He wanted several major-generals;—a number of 'aids.' **1832** [KENNEDY] *Swallow Barn* I. 190 Ned and myself formed a part of his retinue, like a pair of aids somewhat behind the commander-in-chief. **1866** 'F. KIRKLAND' *Bk. Anecdotes* 222/2 An aid rode up with an order . . . [to] the General. **1880** *Scribner's Mo.* Feb. 484 Five aids were appointed, . . . our Highland Laddie to ride at the front with the captain. **1907** *Chicago Tribune* 8 May 2 Gen. A. W. Greely . . . arrived with his chief of staff . . . and his aids.

Aid-de-camp. (Also unhyphened, and † **aid-du-camp, adecamp.**) Pl. **aids-de-camp, aid-de-camps.** Variant of AIDE-DE-CAMP. {1732}

In very freq. use from *c*1777 to *c*1870, in preference to *aide-de-camp*. In Webster, 1806–1864, as the only form, and 1890–1909 as the preferred form.

1726 PENHALLOW *Indian Wars* (1824) 65 Several compliments passed on each side, which were sent by major Handy the Aid-de-Camp. **1755** *Broadside Verse* (1930) 121/2 Their Chief we have a Prisoner made . . . ; The Aid Decamp resign'd himself. **1776** *Journals Cont. Congress* V. 418 Resolved, That the aids de camp of the commander in chief rank as lieutenant colonels. **1802** *Ann. 7th Congress* App. 1306 There shall be one brigadier-general, with one aid-de-camp. **1850** GLISAN *Jrnl. Army Life* 7 Not fully appreciating all the duties of an aid-de-camp, I was at first a little disconcerted. **1878** BEADLE *Western Wilds* 532 Custer . . . was made full captain and aid-de-camp of General McClellan.

+**Aide.** Also † **ade.** Short for AIDE-DE-CAMP. (Cf. AID 2.)

1777 J. M. LINCOLN *Papers R. Lincoln* (1904) 11 They . . . fired on the flag and killed an ade. **1826** COOPER *Mohicans* xxxiii, Attended by the aide of Montcalm with his guard, all the white men . . . passed from before the eyes of the Delawares. **1862** NORTON *Army Lett.* 91 Those in the rear of us received the order, but the aide sent to us was shot. **1886** LOGAN *Great Conspiracy* 306 McDowell . . . sends back an aide with orders to the regimental commanders. **1901** CHURCHILL *Crisis* 261 Bright aides dashing hither and thither on spirited chargers.

Aide-de-camp. An officer who assists a general by receiving and transmitting his orders and performing other confidential duties. (Plural: *aides-de-camp.*) {1670–}

Agreeing with British use and gradually taking the place of AID-DE-CAMP. In Worc. 1846–60, *Cent.* 1889, etc., given as the preferred form.

1761 NILES *Indian Wars* II. 322 Several compliments passed on each side, which were sent by Major Hardy, the aide-de-camp. **1821** COOPER *Spy* vii, Captain Wharton, I claim your assistance as an aide-de-camp. **1847** *Army Regulations* 7 Brevet Generals . . . will be entitled to aides-de-camp. **1866** MCCLELLAN in *Own Story* 219 The staff for each [army] being distinct, except with regard to my personal aides-de-camp. **1892** M. A. Jackson *Memoirs* 391 General Jackson . . . asked me to accept the position of aide-de-camp on his staff.

|| **Aide-ship.** [AIDE.] An appointment as an aide-de-camp. — **1862** JACKSON in M. A. Jackson *Life* 305, I will give him [Captain Morrison] an aide-ship.

+**Aid Society.** An organization or society whose object it is to assist the indigent, needy, or helpless; esp. an organization of ladies which holds meetings or work-parties to promote charity and other church work.

1853 BRACE in *Dangerous Classes* (1872) 90 P.S.—I forgot to tell you the name we have chosen—'Children's Aid Society.' **1857** *Lawrence* (Kansas) *Republican* 4 June 2 The emigrant aid society held its annual meeting in this city [Boston] today. **1862** G. W. WILDER *MS Diary* 29 Jan., After noon I took the ladies to the Aid Society. **1866** 'F. KIRKLAND' *Bk. Anecdotes* 615 Have you a Soldiers' Aid Society in your neighborhood? **1867** F. MOORE *Women of the War* 214 Mrs. Wittenmeyer, as president of the Ladies' Aid Society of Iowa. **1882** E. K. GODFREY *Nantucket* 292 [The] Children's Aid Society; . . . its object is to provide a home for young girls who have no parents. **1898** PAGE *Red Rock* 265 The steps Mrs. Welch and her Aid Society had been taking in their philanthropic efforts on behalf of the freedmen. **1908** F. B. CALHOUN *Miss Minerva* 77 'Aunt Minerva's gone to the Aid Society,' remarked the host.

Ailanthus, Ailantus. [f. *aylanto*, the Molucca name, whence mod. L. *Ailantus*, more usu. *Ailanthus*, by influence of Gr. ἄνθος 'flower.']

1. The tree of heaven or Chinese sumach, *Ailanthus glandulosa*, of rapid growth, and freq. raised as a shade-tree. {1861–} Also attrib.

1845 HIRST *Poems* 158 O'er me let a green Ailanthus grow, . . . the Tree of Heaven. **1852** *Horticulturist* VII. 345 'Down with the Ailanthus!' is the cry we hear on all sides, . . . now that this 'tree of heaven' . . . has penetrated all parts of the union. **1858** WARDER *Hedges & Evergreens* 20 Trees of the hardiest drought-enduring kinds—such as Ailanthus. **1860** *Darlington's Weeds & Plants* 76 Perhaps no tree has been the subject of as much newspaper discussion as the Ailanthus, and there is much to be said for and against its cultivation as a shade tree. **1897** SUDWORTH *Arborescent Flora* 268 Ailanthus; . . . native of China, but thoroughly naturalized by cultivation in this country; in many localities, especially in Central and Southern States, escaped and forming dense thickets. **1904** GLASGOW *Deliverance* 81 A clump of riotous ailanthus shoots.

2. *Ailanthus silkworm,* or *worm,* a silkworm, *Bombyx (Philosania) cynthia,* which feeds on the leaves of the ailanthus.

1868 *Rep. Comm. Agric.* (1869) 284 The ailanthus silk-worm . . . is indigenous to the temperate regions of China. **1876** *Field & Forest* I. 77 The material [used for fishing tackle] is generally obtained from the silk-worm proper, . . . the ailanthus-worm, . . . and one or two allied species.

3. *Ailanthus-* or *ailantus-tree* = sense 1.

1853 *Harper's Mag.* VI. 848/2 The poor Ailanthus-tree has, we observe, been outlawed by Congress. **1861** WINTHROP *Open Air* 309 Brightley's bedroom . . . looked down upon a snowy ravine, planted alternately with lamp-posts and ailanthus-trees. **1880** H. JAMES in *Harper's Mag.* July 292/2 The ailantus-trees . . . diffused an aroma that you were not yet critical enough to dislike as it deserved.

* **Aim,** *v. intr.* To have an aim, purpose, or intention *to* do something; to endeavor, purpose, or intend. Now chiefly *colloq.* or *dial.* {1649; now *dial.*}

1650 BRADSTREET *Works* (1867) 193 Belosus . . . , Not so content but aiming to be great. **1665** *R. I. Col. Rec.* II. 120 This the Court hath done, aimeing alsoe therein to save the towne. **1789** *Ann. 1st Congress* I. 898 Mr. Hartley . . . conceived gentlemen were aiming to throw embarrassments in the way of the bill. **1847** L. COLLINS *Kentucky* 220 He was aiming to reach Bullick's lick. **1851** CIST *Cincinnati* 312 Each city is aiming to extend the circle of its business and influence. **1874** LONG *Wild-Fowl* 15, I have aimed to instruct rather than to amuse. **1901** WHITE *Westerners* i. 7 We aims to pull through, but we don't aim to take no lumber with us. **1908** C. H. PARKHURST *Lower than Angels* 25 The fringe of green, that borders every flowing brook, pictures . . . the thought that the prophet here aims to tell.

Ain't, *v. colloq.* or *dial.* Also **aint, eint.** Contracted form of *air n't* 'are not' (see AIR *v.*); hence by extension used for *is not* and *am not.* Cf. AN'T *v.* {1778–, *dial.*}

1779 *Essex Inst. Coll.* XLIV. 321 Please to inquire for him, if the tryal aint over. **1795** B. DEARBORN *Columbian Grammar* 133 Improprieties, commonly called Vulgarisms, . . . [include] Aint for Are not. **1825** NEAL *Bro. Jonathan* I. 317 You ain't afeard o' nothing. **1837** SHERWOOD *Georgia* 69 *Aint,* for is not, and am not. **1840** THOMPSON *Green Mt. Boys* I. i. 15 What in the world can have got the Captain, that he aint in? **1841** GREELEY in *Corr. R. W. Griswold* (1898) 53 The Biographical Annual . . . is not well designed or got up. . . . It ain't in good keeping. **1867** S. HALE *Letters* 31 Ain't it fun to be Consuls? **1886** STOCKTON *Mrs. Lecks* 27 Cold baked beans . . . ain't exactly company vittles. **1901** CHURCHILL *Crisis* 76 A low breed that ain't fit for freedom.

Ain't, reduced form of HAIN'T (='have not'). {1875–, *dial.*} — **1845** SIMMS *Wigwam & Cabin* Ser. I. 7 But you ain't said . . . who was your Carolina gineral. **1852** J. WEIR *S. Kenton* 107, I s'pose you ain't had your ears bored for the hollow horn lately? **1871** HAY *Pike Co. Ballads* 13, I don't go much on religion, I never ain't had no show.

Air, *v.* Dialect variant of *are,* pres. pl. of BE *v.* (Cf. AIN'T *v.*) — **1777** *Md. Hist. Mag.* VI. 144 You must divide this . . . , as I think it may serve you both if you air moderate. **1863** S. C. MASSETT *Drifting About* 236 If thar air any parsons here who knew. **1884** CABLE *Dr. Sevier* xxxiv, Oh, yes! ye *air* too busy—a-courtin' thim I-talian froot gerls.

Air-balloon. *Obs.* [Fr. *balon aërostatique.*] A balloon. {1753–1829.} — **1784** *Mass. Centinel* 14 July, The taste for Air Balloon matters has grown to such an extraordinary pitch, that nothing can pretend to have any intrinsic value in it, unless it has this name as an appendage. **1795** ASBURY *Journal* II. 256, I rode out to take the air; and saw the wandering air-balloon. **1818** FESSENDEN *Ladies Monitor* 33 With head as empty as an air-balloon.

+**Air-brake.** One of a system of continuous brakes on railway-cars, that are operated by means of compressed air.

1871 *Rep. Comm. Patents* (1872) I. 253 Westinghouse, George, jr., . . . Valve device for steam-power air-brake couplings, July 4, 1871. **1873** BEADLE *Undevel. West* 235 The air-brake, which was a novelty to me, and a perfect success. **1881** J. BUEL *Border Outlaws* 197 The vigilant engineer . . . applying the air-brakes brought the locomotive to a stand-still. **1887** GEORGE *40 Yrs. on Rail* 178 The introduction of the Westinghouse air-brake has greatly decreased the duties of the brakemen.

+**Air-foundry.** *Obs.* A foundry provided with an air-furnace or -furnaces.

1815 *Niles' Reg.* VIII. 141/1 There are in Pittsburgh, three large and extensive air-founderies, where are cast all kinds of hollow-ware. **1819** DANA *Geog. Sketches* 76 There are [in Steubenville, O.] a printing office . . . and an air foundry. **1837** JENKINS *Ohio Gaz.* 370 Portsmouth . . . contained . . . one air foundery, with a cupola and brass foundery.

Air-furnace.

1. A furnace having a natural draft, as distinguished from a *blast-furnace. Obs.* {1784}

1780 *R. I. Commerce* II. 96 The Air Furnace for casting Iron Cannon in this Town [=Providence]. **1796** *Ann. 4th Congress* 2 Sess. 2571 The works consist of a fort, . . . a guard House, an air furnace for heating shot. **1814** BRACKENRIDGE *Views La.* 150 The three modes of smelting, to wit, the open furnace, the ash furnace, and the air furnace, . . . have all been introduced since the Americans took possession of the country. **1816** *Mass. H. S. Coll.* 2 Ser. VII. 118 An air furnace, now extinct, was erected many years since, by the late Aaron Hobart, Esq. who . . . furnished the publick with cannon and shot. **1816** *Niles' Reg.* IX. Suppl. 183/2 Fuel necessary for the air furnace, . . . 1 cord per week.

2. 'An air-heating furnace for warming apartments' (*Cent.*)

Air-hole. A hole or natural opening in ice covering rivers or ponds, esp. one caused by the current or by springs. {1766}

1847 RUXTON *Adv. Rocky Mts.* xxv. (1848) 210 An air-hole in the ice where the animals could drink. **1864** T. L. NICHOLS *Amer. Life* I. 18, I used to skate miles up and down the Connecticut river, and when thirsty, creep carefully to the edges of the air-holes, or 'glades,' in the ice, and drink. **1868** CHANNING *Recoll. Newport* 30 The pond . . . presented an unbroken surface of crystal; and no one dreamt of an air-hole. **1874** LONG *Wild-Fowl* 51 Great quantities of ducks are often killed in the air-holes about freezing-up time.

Airish, *a.* Cool; fresh; chilly. *colloq.* or *dial.* {n.E. (1641–) and Sc.}

1882 BEADLE *Western Wilds* 613 Going westward on any line one will find the winters growing dryer, also more 'airish.' **1885** 'CRADDOCK' *Prophet* 267 It air toler'ble airish in the fog. **1889** — *Despot* 479 Kem up close by the fire, gentlemen. . . . Airish out'n doors, ain't it?

+**AIR-LINE.** Also **air line.**

1. A direct (or nearly direct) line between two points on the earth's surface; a bee-line. {1852}

1813 J. QUINCY in *Ann. 12th Congress* 2 Sess. 544 They will not rigidly observe any air-lines or water-lines in enforcing their necessary levies. **1829** COOPER *Wish-ton-wish* ii. 27 This clearing, which by an air line might have been half a mile from the place where his horse had stopped. **1840** *Congress. Globe* 12 June 459/3 The bill of the House supposed that they must travel through the air, for they were to charge for their mileage by an air line. **1848** COOPER *Oak Openings* I. 20 This insect rose and . . . darted away towards its hive, in an air-line. **1860** HELPER *Impending Crisis* 353 Take any common map . . . and rule an air line across it from Baltimore to St. Louis. **1865–6** *Ill. Agric. Soc. Trans.* VI. 316 A tract of 345 acres of swampy land, . . . which tract is about four miles from the court house, in a direct air-line. **1883** *Harper's Mag.* May 928/1 Three points in the air line of the bridge are also determined. **1889** *Century Mag.* Feb. 631/2 It was 'some two miles, by the road.' Of course, in an air line it is much less. **1912** H. CROLY *M. A. Hanna* 30 As an air line the distance . . . was some forty miles, but this stretch was increased to sixty by the necessity of following the watercourses and dodging hills.

fig. **1904** *N. Y. Tribune* 7 Nov. 2 The President . . . has marched straight up to his great fame by the air line, and not . . . by compromise with wrong.

2. A direct railroad route.

'In the Western States, with their level surface and vast unbroken prairies, railroads could often be built in straight lines; . . . for a few years a tendency to build such air-lines has agitated Legislatures, from whom help was asked' (De Vere 361). 'An air-line is now often extended to mean the most direct road from one point to another' (Clapin).

1853 *Congress. Globe* 18 Feb. 674/2 This 'air line' runs its whole length . . . through a country . . . eminently adapted for the construction . . . of a railroad. **1864** *Ib.* March 1264/2, I invite any gentleman who supposes that by voting for this bill he is voting for an air-line, to look . . . and see the kind of air-line it is proposed to establish. **1875** HOLLAND *Sevenoaks* 359 A grand combination had been made . . . for working up a 'corner' in the Muscogee Air Line. **1903** *N. Y. Ev. Post* 17 Aug., The public regards the purchase of the Seaboard air line as another serious step in the direction of railroad consolidation.

fig. **1888** *St. Louis Globe Democrat* 24 Jan. (F.) An author must take the air-line or we will not travel.

3. *attrib.* Straight (as may be), direct.

1866 S. ANDREWS *South since War* 214 The air-line distance between the two points. **1895** *Outing* Dec. 214/2 Pursuing an even air-line route across the roughest country.

+**b.** *Air-line railroad, railway, road,* a direct railroad line or route.

1863 *Congress. Globe* Feb. 813/1 A proposition to construct an air-line railroad between Washington and New York. **1870** *Congress. Globe* 10 March 1846/3 Suppose you charter the so-called 'air-line' road contemplated by this bill. **1883** P. M. HALE *Woods & Timbers N. C.* 270 The Raleigh and Augusta Air-Line Railroad, 99 miles in length. **1884** R. GRANT *Average Man* xiii, He was . . . a director in the Selma & Peatville Air-line Railway.

+**Air-slack,** *v.* (See quotation.) — **1846** EMMONS *Agric. N. Y.* I. 228 Lime has a strong attraction for carbonic acid and water; hence, when exposed, it absorbs both, or, as the phrase is, air-slacks.

Air-tight, *a.* and *n.*

+**1.** Of stoves: Made of sheet iron, and so constructed that the draft can be almost entirely cut off.

1844 EMERSON *Young America* Misc. (1856) 376 In America, out of doors all seems a market; in doors, an air-tight stove of conventionalism. **1857** YOUMANS *Household Science* 68 The so-called air-tight stoves are very common. **1882** FOOTE *Led-Horse Claim* v. 68 He found the Doctor asleep in his arm-chair before an air-tight stove. **1904** M. E. WALLER *Wood-carver* 32 Uncle Shim took down the air-tight stove and the fire-board, and cleaned up the fire-place.

+**b.** *ellipt.* An air-tight stove.

1843 [STEPHENS] *High Life N. Y.* II. xxxi. 227 Speakin' of stoves, Par, I got . . . what they call an air tight, and a little teenty tointy handful of wood keeps 'em warm as blazes a hull day and night tu [=too]. **1850** JUDD *R. Edney* vi. 87, I want you to kindle a fire in the air-tight in the parlor. **1861** STOWE *Pearl Orr's Island* I. viii. 56 The advent of those sullen gnomes the air-tights, or . . . the cooking stoves. **1886** P. STAPLETON *Major's Christmas* 119 She . . . ran up stairs to build a fire in the little airtight.

+**2.** *pl.* Canned tomatoes. *S.W. colloq.*

1907 WHITE *Arizona Nights* I. xvi. 219 On top of a few incidental pounds of *chile con*, baked beans, soda biscuits, 'air tights', and other delicacies.

+**Air town.** A town which is still 'in the air.' — **1880** *Harper's Mag.* Oct. 729/1 The tent and 'dug out' can not long satisfy the men who see future Chicagoes in even the 'air towns' found at the termini of constructed track on the railroads.

∗**AISLE.**

1. A passage between the rows of seats or benches in a church, school, theater, etc. {1731–} (Cf. BROAD AISLE.)

1806 WEBSTER, *Aisle*, . . . a walk in a church. **1817** PAULDING *Lett. from South* II. 83 Nothing was heard but . . . the cautious footsteps of the villagers, creeping up the aisle. **1833** *Niles' Reg.* XLIV. 326/2 We do not allow strangers, with ladies, to stand in the aisles more than ten minutes. **1843** *Knickerb.* XXI. 120 He once walked up the aisle of the church on Sunday, wearing a pair of breeches of a peculiar fashion in front. **1865** *Atlantic Mo.* XV. 168, I have been content to admire them as they . . . swept up the aisles of our church on Sunday. **1874** EGGLESTON *Circuit Rider* 219 It was too late to withdraw, the aisle beyond her was already full of standing people. **1903** I. BACHELLER *Darrel of Blessed Isles* xiv. 152 The [school-] teacher . . . dragged him roughly to the aisle and over the floor space. **1904** *Mobile W. Register* 28 May 4 She sailed down the aisle on Wednesday just before the curtain rose for the matinee.

attrib. **1870** F. FERN *Ginger-Snaps* 26 The sexton . . . doubling up with a dexterous twist any aisle-chairs which have done duty *pro tem.* **1879** B. F. TAYLOR *Summer-Savory* xxi. 169 Suppose Dorcas should . . . have a fair, and . . . have the profits besides, for the aisle carpet, the pulpit cushion [etc.].

+**2.** A passageway or gangway in a building, store, etc.

1827 *Western Monthly Rev.* I. 73 The long aisles of all the stories [of a factory] to the fourth loft. **1851** HOOPER *Widow Rugby's Husband* 108, I have seen him . . . charge up to the steps and into one door of the Court-house, dash furiously along the aisle [etc.]. **1869** TOURGEE *Toinette* xxxvii. (1881) 382 Geoffrey remembered the cheery tones of Toinette as she came down the aisle [of the hospital]. **1904** *N. Y. Sun* 9 Aug. 8 They move steadily along the aisles [of St. Louis Fair]. **1911** FERBER *Dawn O'Hara* viii. 108 The single narrow aisle of the front shop was crowded. It was not easy to elbow one's way through the packed little space.

+**3.** A passage in a railway or street car.

1842 FANNY BUTLER in *Bentley's Misc.* XII. 2 The seats . . . are placed down the whole length of the vehicle, one behind the other, leaving a species of aisle in the middle for the uneasy . . . to fidget up and down. **1849** A. MACKAY *Western World* I. 100 A small compartment, with no vacant space but the narrow aisle in the centre, with nine-and-fifty distillers of tobacco-juice around you! **1856** *Knickerb.* XLVII. 278 Now the aisle [of a street car] is full, and short men are hanging upon the leather straps. **1873** in *Sat. Rev.* (London) 22 Nov. 662/2 The Deputy-Sheriff placed his prisoners in the smoking-car of the train. . . . Men were standing on the seats, and the aisle was packed. **1889** *Harper's Mag.* Oct. 736/2 He . . . collected the price of three hours reading . . . and went on down the aisle. **1905** G. ATHERTON *Travelling Thirds* 14 They were in a large, open car furnished with wooden seats and a door for each aisle. **1906** *Harper's Mag.* April 746 The man . . . stood, with feet far apart, in the aisle of the swaying sleeper. **1911** LINCOLN *Cap'n Warren's Wards* i. 4 Conversation across the aisle was brisk.

+**4.** A main garden walk.

1840 DEWEY *Mass. Flowering Plants* 38 Candy-tuft. A species with whitish flowers has been long cultivated as edging for aisles in gardens and walks.

+**5.** An aisle-like space or passage in a wood or forest.

1855 J. ABBOTT *Napoleon* II. 385 Through the deep aisles of the forest. **1858** HAWTHORNE *Fr. & It. Journals* I. 211 An aisle of over-shadowing trees. **1861–2** *Ill. Agric. Soc. Trans.* V. 209 Its massive aisles of towering oak and maple. **1882** J. HAWTHORNE *Fortune's Fool* xxxviii, She moved slowly and saunteringly along the vistaed aisle. **1911** L. J. VANCE *Cynthia* 336 The aisles and vistas of the cedar-clad slopes.

+**Aitch.** [Abbrev.] An aitch-bone. — **1885** *Boston Sunday Herald* 18 Oct. 9 The dealer hangs up in his stall . . . the richest of flanks, juicy and inviting aitches.

+**Alabama.**

1. Name of a southern state, used attrib.

1808 JEFFERSON *Writings* III. 486 A small tribe of Alabama Indians, on the western side of the Mississippi. **1832** *Louisville Public Advt.* 8 March, 25 bales Alabama cotton for sale. **1866** 'F. KIRKLAND' *Bk. Anecdotes* 37/1 John G. Whittier . . . met with an Alabama planter in Boston. **1872** *Alabama Journal of Senate* 26 Feb. 543 To confer certain authority upon the 'Alabama detectives.' **1889** VASEY *Agric. Grasses* 36 *Sorghum halepense* (Johnson Grass; Mean's Grass) . . . has been called Egyptian Grass . . . [and] Alabama Guinea grass. **1901** MOHR *Plant Life Ala.* 319 Alabama Bristle Fern. *Ib.* 552 *Prunus alabamensis*, Alabama Cherry, [is] a tree below medium size. *Ib.* 848/2 Alabama flora, relation to tropical American. **1905** N. DAVIS *Northerner* 253 This is quite respectable weather—for an Alabama winter.

b. *Alabama screamer*, a rowdy. *Obs. slang.*

1822 *Amer. Beacon* (Norfolk, Va.) 6 Sept. 4/1 (Th. S.) The bargemen . . . are divided into classes, such as Tuscaloosa Roarers, Alabama Screamers, Cahawba Scrougers, and the like gentle names.

2. The name of a Confederate privateer (1862–4), British-built and largely British-manned, which committed serious depredations on Northern shipping during the Civil War; used in *Alabama claims, question*, etc.

1867 SEWARD *Let. to C. F. Adams* 29 Nov., A letter which Lord Stanley wrote . . . concerning the question of arbitration upon the so-called Alabama claims. **1871** GRANT in *Messages & P.* (1898) VII. 122 The acts committed by the vessels which have given rise to the claims known as the 'Alabama Claims.' **1886** A. JOHNSTON *Hist.* 376 The Alabama Arbitrators met at Geneva, in Switzerland, in 1872. **1889** FARMER 9 The political incident known as the 'Alabama Question.'

+**Alabamian,** *n.* and *a.*

1. *n.* A native or resident of Alabama.

1832 *Deb. Congress* 15 June 3570, I will not even discuss this great question of Southern wrongs as an Alabamian, but as a Southern man. **1847** *Knickerb.* XXIX. 539 You will find yourself participating as deeply in the ardor . . . of the deer-chase as if you were a native Alabamian. **1852** *Democratic Rev.* XXX. 85 A tall, lanky Alabamian. **1862** POLLARD *First Year of War* 307 At Shiloh, the troops engaged were principally Tennesseeans, Mississippians, Alabamians, [etc.]. **1869** TOURGEE *Toinette* xxi. (1881) 228 An Alabamian . . . would have said 'pack' instead of 'tote.' **1886** LOGAN *Great Conspiracy* 196 He told the Alabamians how their State . . . was kept in the Confederacy.

2. *adj.* Of or belonging to Alabama.

1850 NORTHALL *Yankee Hill* 105 There were quite a number of passengers, and among them a very corpulent Alabamian planter.

+**Alacran.** *S.W.* [Sp.] A scorpion. — **1844** KENDALL *Santa Fé Exped.* II. iv. 105 We had been led to suppose that we were to be taken through Durango, the city of pretty women and *alicrans* [*sic*]. **1848** HUGHES *Doniphan's Exped.* 356 The soldiers [while in Chihuahua] would sometimes shake their blankets, toss the . . . lizards, and alacrans, . . . exclaiming angrily, 'd—n the scorpion family.' **1891** *Dialect Notes* I. 243 (Texas words) *Alacran*, a scorpion. Different species of the genus *scorpio*, common in Texas and Mexico.

Alameda. *S.W.* [Sp., f. ALAMO.] A public promenade, walk, or road with a row of trees (esp. poplars) on each side. {1843–}

1831 PATTIE *Personal Narr.* 242 Upon the Alameda, a promenade north of the city. **1846–7** MAGOFFIN *Santa Fe Trail* (1926) 243 The tall shady poplars of the *alameda.* **1848** E. BRYANT *California* xxiv. 317 A broad *alameda*, shaded by stately trees, . . . forming a most beautiful drive or walk. **1854** BARTLETT *Narr.* II. 488 Two fine Alamedas, the fashionable promenades of the town. **1869** BROWNE *Adv. Apache Country* 246 There is a beautiful Alameda at the northern end of the city. **1890** BRET HARTE *Waif of Plains* 214 Then, you could ride up and down the Alameda when we are going by. **1911** *N. Y. Ev. Post* 7 Jan. Suppl. 2 When Frederick Law Olmsted planned Franklin Park in the Roxbury section of Boston . . . there was to be a wide avenue, or alameda.

+**Alamo.** *S.W.* [Sp. ='poplar'.] One or other species of cottonwood, esp. the common species *Populus monilifera.* — [**1846** EMORY *Reconnoissance* 100 We reached the Alamo or cotton wood. *Ib.*, Neither was there any cotton wood at the Alamo, as its name would signify.] **1854** *H. Rep. Executive Doc. No. 91*, IV. (1856) 11 The alamos grow to a good large size and are quite abundant. **1856** WHIPPLE *Explor. Ry. Route* Extracts 10 A beautiful stream . . . finely timbered with post oak, alamo, and elm.

Alamode. Also †**a la mode, allamod.** [Fr. *à la mode* in the manner or fashion.] A light, glossy, black silk fabric for hoods, handkerchiefs, etc. More fully *silk alamode. Obs.* {1676–1702}

c1686 in Hutchinson *Diary & Lett.* I. 37, 63 yds. allamods. **1691** SEWALL *Letter-Book* 116 Send . . . the rest in alamode narrow and broad. **1711** *Springfield Rec.* II. 39 Silke alamode; 13 yards & an halfe. **1727** *Boston News-Letter* 7–14 Dec. 2/2 Persons may be supplyed with . . . muslins, lute-strings, alamodes, gloves. **1751** MACSPARRAN *Diary* 19 Nov., Pd. Mr. Mumford . . . and 15[*s.*] towards a yard & half a la mode. **1764** *Essex Inst. Coll.* XLIX. 281 Just imported from London, . . . alamode for black handkerchiefs.

*Alarm. Also †al(l)arum, allaroome, alerum.

*1. A call to arms; a sound or signal giving notice of danger.

1622 'MOURT' *Relation* 80 He went home & gave the alarm, so the people ... armed themselves. **1636** *Plymouth Laws* 56 The Court [decided] that three pieces shott of distinctly one after another shalbe an allarum. **1642** *Md. Council Proc.* 103 Upon the hearing of an alarum every housekeeper to answer and continue it soe far as he may. **1657** *Southampton Rec.* I. 153 The letting off of one gun shall bee sufficient allarum in the night, and ... then all Inhabitants from the North end of the towne to Tho. Sayres shall repaire to about Mr. Gosmer's. **1705** *Boston News-Letter* 17 Sept. 2/2 On Wednesday ... there was here a very great appearance of men in the train-Bands: occasioned by the Castle's giving of the alarm at the sight of 5 vessels seen coming in. **1775** *Essex Inst. Coll.* XLVIII. 46 We herd that they had alerum from Salem. **1777** *Ib.* XIII. 121 That all ... Officers and Matrosses uppon hearing an alarm beat round the town shall immediately repair to the parade. **1855** THOMPSON *Doesticks* 95 First night, went to bed with my boots on, ready for an alarm [=fire alarm]. **1865** BOUDRYE *Fifth N. Y. Cavalry* 96 Only two shots were fired, and no alarm raised. **1889** BRAYLEY *Boston Fire Dept.* 220 The first regular alarm given by the telegraphic system was sounded for a fire in the building of John Ward.

*2. A state of general apprehension or excitement; an attack, etc., causing this.

1622 'MOURT' *Relation* 66 A cry of some savages ... caused an alarm. **1690** SEWALL *Diary* I. 330 But I did not observe a continual beat of the drum, so caus'd not an alarm. **1705** *Boston News-Letter* 11 June 2/2 On Wednesday night ... three ships coming from Lisbon ... occasioned an alarm in the town. **1711** *N. C. Col. Rec.* I. 814, I have carried on the abovementioned works during the late alarm. **1777** *Md. Hist. Mag.* V. 223 For some time past there has not been one night without one or two allarms. **1829** COOPER *Wish-ton-Wish* i. 23 Indian alarms, as they were termed, were not unfrequent. **1837** IRVING *Bonneville* III. 258 There was a second alarm, and it was discovered that several horses were missing. **1856** GLISAN *Jrnl. Army Life* 286 False alarms are the order of the night down in the village.

+3. Apprehension; anxiety; uneasiness.

1833 *Deb. Congress* 26 Feb. 1781 This General Assembly views with alarm ... the proposition ... for abandoning ... the principle of protection. **1834** *Ib.* 18 Feb. 604 They regard with alarm the late measures of the President. **1834** Commons, etc. *Doc. Hist.* VI. 208 This committee views with serious alarm the deplorable condition of the ... children employed in the cotton and woollen manufactories in this country.

4. *attrib.* Serving as an alarm; by which an alarm is given.

1825 NEAL *Bro. Jonathan* II. 396 Two or three alarm shots were fired. **1837** IRVING *Bonneville* III. 67 Alarm signals, to arouse the country and collect the scattered bands for vengeance. **1872** EGGLESTON *End of World* v. 40 In behind the donjon chimney he pulled an alarm cord. **1876** BANCROFT *Hist.* V. 592 A man-of-war in New York Bay fired alarm-cannon. **1884** CABLE *Sevier* lv, All the alarm signals were for fire except this one.

+b. *Alarm duty*, the 'duty' of being prepared or ready to respond to an alarm.

1837 *S. Lit. Messenger* III. 644 There is a detachment of citizen soldiery ... always on what is called alarm duty.

Alarm-bell. A bell rung to give notice of danger, as from hostile attack, fire, etc. {1641–}

1801 *Essex Inst. Coll.* LIII. 206 The Free School ... has a spire, and here the alarm bell is hung, also the school bell. **1833** *Niles' Reg.* XLIV. 331/1 There are no public alarm bells for fires in Boston. **1844** A. LAWRENCE *Diary & Corr.* 184 The alarm-bell rang, calling all soldiers to their posts. **1872** ROE *Barriers Burned Away* xli, In the southwest he saw a brilliant light. He heard the alarm-bells, and knew there was a fire.

Alarm clock. A clock with a bell which automatically rings at any time for which it is set, esp. in order to arouse sleepers. {Also Eng. Cf. the earlier *larum clock* (1697), *alarm-watch* (1678)}

1751 *Boston News-Letter* 10 Oct., To be sold ... eight day and small alarm clocks. **1835** J. TODD *Student's Manual* 69 The students in Yale and Amherst Colleges have generally the alarm-clock. **1852** MITCHELL *Dream Life* 122 It is nothing for him to quit sleep at the first tinkling of the alarm clock. **1873** BAILEY *Life in Danbury* 80 He has a vigorous old alarm clock ... that when it goes off makes a noise somewhat like a boiler explosion. **1902** LORIMER *Lett. from Merchant* 212 There's no alarm clock for the sleepy man like an early rising manager.

Alarm gun. A gun fired to give an alarm.

[**1757** *General Orders* 53 After the larem gun is fired.] **1761** S. NILES *Indian Wars* II. 433 Alarm-guns were fired at George's Fort. **1776** FITHIAN *Journal* II. 215 The alarm guns were fired a little before twelve o'clock. **1798** A. HOLMES *E. Stiles* 261 A British fleet ... anchored off West-Haven. Alarm guns were fired. **1823** THACHER *Military Journal* 239 The alarm guns were fired, and the drums throughout our camp beat to arms.

+**Alarm list.** *Obs.* A number of men required to serve only during an alarm. — *a*1752 W. DOUGLASS *Summary* II. 363 The alarum list, and the training militia [of Md.], are ... under the same regulations as in the colonies already mentioned. **1792** BELKNAP *Hist. N. H.* III. 286 Men capable of bearing arms, from forty to sixty years of age, and who are exempted from the training band, are called the *alarm list.* **1835** *Biogr. Isaac Hill* 6 Her father ... commanded a company of alarmlist at the battle of Lexington.

Alarm-post. *Mil.* An appointed position to which troops resort in the event of an alarm. {1721–}

1758 *Lett. to Washington* II. 380, I did not loose a moment in ... appointing alarum posts. **1775** *Essex Inst. Coll.* LIII. 82 He marched off ... and chose another alarm post. **1780** *Heath Papers* 138 A third [regiment] to Constitution Island as their alarm post. [**1841** TRUMBULL *Autobiog.* 18 The parade and alarm post was a field ... in full view of the enemy's lines at the entrance of Boston.]

Alaska. [Name of a territory in the north-west of N. America, acquired by the United States in 1867.] +Used attrib. in specific names of various commodities found in or obtained from Alaska (cf. next).

1884 SARGENT *Rep. Forests* 7 The most valuable species of the northern Coast Forest [is] ... the Alaska cedar (*Chamaecyparis* [*nootkatensis*]). **1897** SUDWORTH *Arborescent Flora* 45 *Tsuga mertensiana* ... Alaska Pine [of] Northwestern lumbermen. *Ib.* 79 *Chamaecyparis nootkatensis* ... Alaska Ground Cypress. ... Alaska Cypress. **1897** *Boston Transcript* 11 Sept. 24/3 Skunk skins are one of the biggest items in the fur market. They go under the attractive name of 'Alaska sable.'

+**Alaskan,** *n.* and *a.* [See prec.]

1. *n.* A native or inhabitant of Alaska.

1881 WILLARD *Life in Alaska* (1884) 16 It is the custom of the Alaskans to compel the murderer to stay beside the corpse. **1883** JULIA M. WRIGHT (*title*), Among the Alaskans.

2. *adj.* Native or indigenous to Alaska; found, living, or growing in Alaska.

1884 *Science* Nov. 475/2 The wood is chiefly spruce (*Abies*) and yellow Alaskan cedar (*Chamaecyparis*). **1890** *Cent.* s.v. *Grayling*, The American or Alaskan grayling, *Thymallus signifer.*

Albacore.* Also **alber-, albicore. [Pg. *albacor, -core.*] One or other fish of the tunny kind, as the germon or long-finned tunny, *Orcynus germo* or *O. alalonga*, found in the Atlantic, esp. near the West Indies.

1775 A. BURNABY *Travels through Middle Settlements* 3 We saw several bonetas, grampuses, albicores, and fish of different kinds. **1818** *Niles' Reg.* XV. 43/1 One of the 'expeditions' ... has succeeded in catching ... what is called an albicore; or Horse Mackarel! **1839** STORER *Mass. Fishes* 48 On the coast of New England, this fish [i.e. tunny] is called 'horse-mackerel' and 'albicore.' **1887** GOODE *Fisheries & Fishery Indust.* II. 600 The fish caught by trolling in summer [in S. Calif.] are chiefly barracuda, bonito, albicore, yellow-tail. **1897** *Outing* June 258 'Albacore!' ... There they were, hundreds of them; the water alive with the jumping school, dead ahead.

attrib. **1897** *Outing* June 258 His tail immediately began the curious 'albacore tattoo.' *Ib.* 260 We ... saw numbers of large yellowtail, but they refused our albacore baits.

+**Albanian.** [See next.] A native or inhabitant of Albany, N. Y.

1710 Sheldon *Deerfield* (1895) I. 375 You may adjust the Post as is proposed, ... but the Albanians must not think to make a purse from us [Mass.], and to exact more than it would be done for by our people. **1794** *Mass. H. S. Coll.* IV. 54 The Albanians and people of Skenectady were Hollanders. **1807** IRVING, etc. *Salmagundi* x. 218 Albanians cutting up sturgeon; air, 'O the roast beef of Albany.' **1822** J. YATES in Mackenzie *Van Buren* 188 To find an Albanian after so short a residence in the metropolis of our state, rising into notice, ... is no small proof of merit. **1849** *Knickerb.* XXXIII. 431 Have the old ladies' gone into training in preparation of doing battle ... with those obdurate Albanians? **1866** RICHARDSON *Secret Service* ii. 33 The Albanian was an advocate of Slavery. **1896** A. M. EARLE *Colonial Days N. Y.* 26 He lay drunk for a month at a time, and was incorrigibly lazy,—so aggravated Albanians wrote of him.

Albany. +Name of the capital of New York, used in: *A. ale*, a kind of ale brewed at Albany. *A. beech-drops*, the pine-drops, *Pterospora andromedea. A. beef*, 'sturgeon; a fish which abounds in the Hudson river' (B. '48). *A. beer* (see quotation). *A. hemp*, the wood nettle. *A. pea*, a variety of edible pea. *A. slip*, a potters' clay. *A. strawberry* (see quot.)

1821 W. DALTON *Travels U. S.* 74 Albany ale is almost as much famed in this country as London porter is throughout England. **1845** S. SMITH *Theatr. Apprent.* i. 21 My landlord hinted that I was in debt for ... sundry pots of porter and Albany ale. — **1836** LINCOLN *Botany* App. 130 Albany beech-drops ... [are] very tall, bearing a many-flowered raceme. **1847** WOOD *Botany* 380 Albany Beech-drops [are found] in various parts of N.Y. and Vt.; rare. First discovered by Dr. D. S. C. H. Smith, near Niagara Falls, 1816. **1869** FULLER *Flower Gatherers* 190 The other flower he mentioned was the 'Albany Beech-drops,' or 'Fall-Bird's Nest.' **1891** *Cent.*, *Pterospora andromedea*, known as 'pine drops,' ... from its early discovery near Albany and its resemblance to beech-drops, is also known as 'Albany beech-drops.' — **1791** J. LONG *Voyages* 118 This fish [sturgeon] is very common in Albany, and is sold at 1d. per lb. York currency. The flesh is called Albany beef. **1793** P. CAMPBELL *Travels* 170 They [=sturgeon] are so numerous in Hudson's River in the State of New York, that they are called in derision, Albany beef. **1800** J. MAUDE *Niagara* 25 No fish, save sturgeon, vulgarly called Albany beef, and that soon bought up. **1857** *Harper's Mag.* Oct. 711/1 The boys were evidently full of Albany beef, as sturgeon was and is now called. *c***1866** LOSSING *Hudson* 145 The Sturgeon . . . are sold in such quantities in Albany, that they have been called, in derision, 'Albany beef.' *a***1870** CHIPMAN *Notes on Bartlett* 4 *Albany Beef*, sturgeon; so called because a part of the sturgeon's flesh 'has much the look, and not a little of the taste, as well as texture, of ox' muscle. — **1829** *Free Press* (Tarboro, N. C.) 23 Jan., Albany beer, best northern cider. — **1859** BARTLETT 5 Albany hemp (*Urtica canadensis*), Canada nettle, so called from the use made of its fibrous bark. — **1785** WASHINGTON *Diaries* II. 363 Sowed one Bushel and three Pecks of the Albany or field Pea. **1786** *Ib.* III. 42, I sowed two rows of the Albany Peas in Drills 10 feet asunder. **1825** LORAIN *Pract. Husbandry* 513 The Albany and lady pea are lenient plants. — **1909** *Cent. Suppl.*, *Albany slip*, a clay dug from the shore of the Hudson river at Albany, New York, used extensively . . . by American potters. — **1862** *Rep. Comm. Patents: Agric.* 186 Wilson's Albany is certainly a very valuable variety, although our Boston friends condemn it. **1863** *Horticulturist* XVIII. 122/1 The Wilson's Albany . . . is by far the most productive of all strawberries.

+**Albany plan.** A plan suggested by B. Franklin at a convention in Albany in 1754, for 'establishing one general government over all the colonies, based upon the consent of the governed' (1891 Ordronaux *Const. Leg.* 83). — **1754** FRANKLIN *Writings* III. 235 The powers proposed by the Albany Plan of Union. *Ib.* 237 The proposed alteration of the Albany plan. **1789** *Ib.* 227 You may follow the Albany Plan with the enclosed remark.

+**Albany regency.** A group of politicians meeting at Albany, N. Y., who controlled Democratic nominations and exercised great influence in national affairs, 1820–54. (Cf. REGENCY.)

1832 J. Q. ADAMS *Mem.* VIII. 489 The proceedings of what are called the Albany Regency—the predominant party in the State of New York. **1833** *Niles' Register* 28 Dec. 294/2 You . . . can measure the strength of the Albany regency in Pennsylvania. It is down—down forever. **1882** *Congress. Rec.* 14 Dec. 282/1 The Albany regency . . . was a body of able and astute politicians of the Democratic party who . . . undertook to control all the patronage of the party. **1884** BARNES *Mem. T. Weed* 36 In Mr. Edwin Croswell, the Albany Regency, so first called [*c.* 1830] by Mr. Weed, had an adviser . . . of rare ability.

Albatross. [The name of the sea-bird.] +'A thin untwilled woolen material used for women's dresses.' (*Cent.* '89).

Albert tie. A former fashion of bow or neck-tie. — **1855** THOMPSON *Doesticks* xxxii. 289, I now discovered that he had stolen . . . an 'Albert tie' and a false collar from my neck.

+**Albright.** [Jacob *Albright* (1759–1808), Methodist clergyman of Penna.] One of a religious denomination formerly also called *Albright's children, people*, or *brethren*, and now named the 'Evangelical Association.'

1815 Stapleton *Evangelical Hist.* (1908) 8 This indenture . . . between Andrew Mowrer . . . [and the] trustees of the Evangelist Concretion and Albright's Children, or Albright's people, as they call themselves. **1847** HOWE *Ohio* 371 There are 15 churches, of which the . . . Albrights, Dunkers and African Baptists have each one. **1883** SCHAFF *Relig. Encycl.* I. 776/1 Several years after his [=Albright's] death . . . his followers, who had been known as 'Albright People,' adopted for their organization the name of . . . 'Evangelical Association of North America.' *Ib.* II. 1493/1 The Evangelical Association, or 'Albrights,' is the outgrowth of the labors of the Rev. Jacob Albright, a local preacher. **1917** A. STAPLETON *Wonderful Story* 93 The first regular conference of 'The Albright Brethren,' as they were then called, was held . . . [in] Lebanon County, November 13–15, 1807.

Album. {1651–} A blank book for the insertion of autographs, verses, etc.; 'also, a book at public places in which visitors enter their names' (W. '47).

The latter 'in England is called a *Visitors' Book*' (O.E.D.).

1820 FLINT *Lett. from Amer.* 294 There is a large tavern on each side of the [Niagara] river, and in the *album* kept at one of these, . . . upwards of a hundred folio pages had been written with names within five months. **1830** *Collegian* 177 In the Album, at the top of the Mount, I found . . . the following effusion of some admirer of nature. *c***1881** J. S. OGILVIE *Album-Writer's Friend* Pref., Who . . . has not been invited to write a few words of sentiment in the album of a friend?

+**Alcabala.** [Sp.] A tax on sales of real estate or merchandise. — **1836** HOLLEY *Texas* xi. 213 All the produce of agriculture or industry of the new settlers, shall be free from excise duty, Alcabala, or other duties.

+**Alcade, †Alcaide.** [Fr. *alcade*, Sp. *alcaide.*] **a.** The governor of a fort or castle. **b.** An alcalde.

1809 F. CUMING *Western Tour* 308 Mr. Pierre . . . now possesses a hundred negroes, and is alcade of the quarter. **1827** *Western M. Rev.* I. 70 Mr. Chaplin . . . was elected by the people, chiefly Americans, *Alcaide*, and commandant of Nacogdoches. **1831** PATTIE *Personal Narr.* 41 The alcaide asked us for the invoice of our goods. **1836** QUITMAN in *Life & Corr.* 147 Sent Parker with a note to the commandant, or alcade. **1850** COLTON *Three Years* i. 17 Stockton informed me to-day that I had been appointed Alcade of Monterey and its jurisdiction. **1853** 'P. PAXTON' *Yankee in Texas* 122 If any of the neighborhood had a difficulty, they never thought of goin' to the Alcade, but jest left it out to Old Charley. **1854** BARTLETT *Narr.* I. 276, I inquired for the alcade, and . . . exhibited my letters. **1873** BEADLE *Undevel. West* 746 Edwin M. Bryant—first American Alcade of San Francisco.

Alcalde. Also † **alcalda.** [Sp. Cf. ALCADE.] In regions under Spanish influence, an official of a town, with powers of magistrate or justice of the peace; a magistrate in a mining camp. {1666}

1803 *Ann. 8th Congress* 2 Sess. 1516 There are two Alcaldes [in Louisiana], whose jurisdiction, civil and criminal, extends through the city of New Orleans. **1808** JEFFERSON *Writings* XII. 114 Ought we not immediately to suppress this new appointment of a Spanish Alcalde at Bayou Pierre? **1834** A. PIKE *Prose Sk.* 107 He had even been an Alcalde, which title generally implies a greater knave with a better opportunity, and a wider flight for his genius. **1836** EDWARD *Hist. Texas* 119 Every village has an Indian *alcalde* or chief, now elected every two years. **1839** LEONARD *Adventures* (1904) 198 A passport . . . must be renewed by the Alcalde or Squire in each district. **1845** GREEN *Texian Exped.* vi. 56, I . . . crossed the river to a small town of Galveston, . . . demanded of the alcalde five good mules. **1848** *Californian* (San Fr.) 15 March 3/2 The only public journals we have in California are entirely filled with bickerings and complaints at the Governor, the Alcaldes and the town Councils. **1854** BARTLETT *Narr.* I. 158 The alcalde . . . was invested with the powers of a justice of the peace. **1863** *Rio Abajo Press* 28 April 2 Texas papers publish . . . that several Alcaldas had been killed in the Territory, while endeavoring to enforce the draft. **1873** MILLER *Amongst Modocs* x. 129 This Alcalde was appointed by the new commissioners of the new county. **1880** P. H. BURNETT *Recoll.* 342 In most mining camps they had an alcalde, whose decisions were prompt. **1889** K. MUNROE *Golden Days* iv. 34 The office of the alcalde, or chief magistrate, . . . was the bar-room.

attrib. **1885** C. H. SHINN *Mining Camps* 104 The various functions of government were performed without clashing, by this happily invented alcalde-system.

+**Alcaldeship.** The position or office of an alcalde. — **1885** C. H. SHINN *Mining Camps* 97 The most important alcaldeship in California . . . was that of San Francisco.

***Alchemy.** Also † **accumy, alcumy, alcamy, alchimy, alchymy.** A mixed metal resembling brass. Usually attrib. with *spoon*. *Obs.* {–1695}

1638 *Newhaven Col. Rec.* 4 Twelve alcumy spoones. **1645** *Essex Inst. Coll.* L. 336 Dozen alcamy spoones, 3s. 4d. **1651** *Mayflower Descendants* X. 39, I give my daughter Jane . . . two alchymy spoones. **1680** *Maine H. S. Coll.* III. 230 Sealed & delivered with one bason of alchimy. **1689** *Conn. Probate Rec.* I. 469 The inventory of William Hooker [included] . . . ½ doz. accumy spoons. **1714** SEWALL *Diary* II. 419, I presented my son and daughter with . . . 6 alchimy spoons.

+**Alchy,** colloquial or facetious reduction of *alcohol.* — **1846** *Knickerb.* XXVIII. 40 Fifteen young ladies under the age of ten had signed the pledge against 'King Alchy.' **1854** LEONARD & YOUNG *Nat. Temp. Songster* 110 A glorious victory we'll obtain, When Alchy is no more.

+**Alcoholist.** One who indulges in intoxicating liquor. — **1888** *Forum* Sept. 103 Of 250 chronic alcoholists nearly 90% had fatty degeneration of the liver. **1894** *Pop. Sci. Monthly* Nov. 99 Man may be a moderate alcoholist.

+**Alcohol stove.** A stove using alcohol as fuel. — **1879** BISHOP *4 Months in Sneak-box* 41 Alcohol stoves are small, and the fuel used too expensive.

***Alder.**

***1.** A tree or shrub of the genus *Alnus;* in America commonly the black alder (q.v.).

1637 MORTON *New Canaan* 65 Alder; of this sorte there is plenty by rivers sides. **1684** *Manchester Town Rec.* 19 Bounded . . . on the . . . west at a bunch of alders with a stake in them. **1709** LAWSON *Carolina* 67 The timber that the woods afford . . . consists of . . . bay, willow, alder, and holly. **1754** ELIOT *Field-Husb.* v. 123 The destruction . . . among alders and other sorts of growth. **1785** MARSHALL *Amer. Grove* 20 The species are . . . silver-leaved alder, . . . sea-side alder, . . . common alder. This grows very common in most parts of Pennsylvania. **1813** MUHLENBERG *Cat. Plants* 84 *Alnus glutosa*, clammy alder. **1832** BROWNE *Sylva Amer.* 115 *Alnus serrulata* . . . is found in the Northern, Middle and Western States, and it is every where designated by the name of common Alder. **1848** E. BRYANT *California* vii. 124 Surrounded by clumps of witch-hazel and alders. **1857** GRAY *Botany* 412 *Alnus incana*, Willd. (Speckled or Hoary Alder). . . . *A. serrulata*, Ait. (Smooth Alder). . . . *Alnaster viridis*, D. C. (Green or Mountain Alder). **1864** LOWELL *Fireside Travels* 153 He laid the bags upon a platform of alders, which he bent down. **1875** *Amer. Naturalist* IX. 201 Along the borders of all the numerous mountain streams [in Utah] the common alder . . . is abundant. **1889** P. BUTLER *Recoll.* 7 In the middle of Long Swamp . . . the alders were so thick that there was scarcely room . . . to get through. *a***1918** G. STUART *On Frontier* II. 97 The willows, alders, and tall rye grass along the streams.

+**2.** (See quotation.) *Obs.*

1819 *Western Rev.* I. 229 *Betula rupestris*, Rock Birch, . . . has more the habit and appearance of an Alder than of a Birch, and is accordingly called *Alder* by the countrymen.

3. Attrib. with *bark, bough, brush, clump, flower, marsh, scrub, spout, stake, thicket.*

1663 *Plymouth Rec.* 65 Bounded with a burch tree and alder stake. **1845** JUDD *Margaret* II. i. 185 She carries to the maples the alder-spouts which Chilion makes. **1857** S. H. HAMMOND *Northern Scenes* 205 This stream, with the broad alder marsh that stretches away on either side. **1867** 'T. LACKLAND' *Homespun* I. 32 The drops of rain fringe the . . . alder boughs. **1876** BURROUGHS *Winter Sunshine* vii. 165, I have learned to look . . . in the very midst of an alder-clump. **1880** *Harper's Mag.* June 69 The alder thickets are hanging full with drooping catkins. **1880** *Ib.* Oct. 651/2 Further up we passed through thick alder scrub. **1889** *Ib.* Jan. 230/2 Alder brush seems to be the favorite building material. **1896** WILKINS *Madelon* 268 The alder-flower shook out sweetness. **1901** MOHR *Plant Life Ala.* 467 The bark, known as 'alder bark,' is used as a dye-stuff, and in domestic medicine.

Alderberry, error for ELDERBERRY. — **1854** *Penna. Agric. Rep.* 176 There were . . . other good wines exhibited, made from the blackberry, alderberry and tomato. **1862-3** HALE *If, Yes, & Perhaps* (1868) 22 At sunrise I always made a cruise inland and collected the gentians and black alder-berries.

Alder bush. A bush of the alder.

1837 HAWTHORNE *Note-books* I. 40 The bank was . . . fringed with alder-bushes, bending and dipping into the stream. **1867** 'T. LACKLAND' *Homespun* I. 99 A . . . black snake uncoiled himself from the fork of an alder-bush. **1880** *Harper's Mag.* June 71 The restless starling . . . keeps a sharp look-out for his enemy . . . from the high alder bush. **1890** BRET HARTE *Waif of Plains* 98 Pursuer and pursued presently found themselves safely beyond the half-dry stream and fringe of alder bushes.

*** Alderman.** A member of the legislative branch of a town or city government; the title of such an official.

He is elected by the popular vote of a ward or of the city at large.

1641 GORGES *Charter to Acomenticus,* [I] doe establishe the . . . inhabitants of Acomenticus . . . into one bodie . . . corporate . . . hereafter to continue by the name of the Maior, Aldermen. *Ib.,* The Maior and Aldermen of Acomenticus . . . shall keep Sessions of the Peace. **1665** *Doc. Hist. N. Y. State* (1849) I. 603 Such persons . . . shall bee knowne and call'd by the name & style of Mayor, Aldermen & Sherriffe. **1665** in *N. Y. Lib. Bulletin, Hist.* No. 2, May (1899) 173 All such warrants . . . as shall bee made by the said Mayor and Aldermen. **1686** *Charter* in Munsell *Ann. Albany* II. 68 There shall be forever hereafter . . . a mayor, . . . six aldermen, and six assistants. **1705** *Boston News-Letter* 11 June 2/2 On Thursday last dyed Mr. Jer. Tothil, one of our Aldermen. **1724** JONES *Virginia* 32 Williamburgh is . . . governed by a Mayor and Aldermen. **1789** *Penna. Archives* XVI. 53 The following gentlemen . . . elected Aldermen [of Phila.] . . . took their oaths . . . for the exercise of their office of Aldermen. **1812** *Ann. 12th Congress* 1 Sess. 2284 The corporation of the City of Washington shall be composed of a mayor, a board of aldermen, and a board of common council. **1830** COOPER *Water Witch* i, They see in Alderman Van Beverout a well employed man. **1833** *Niles' Reg.* XLIV. 183/2 A candidate for the office of alderman at the late election in that city [*sc.* New York]. **1851** J. H. ROSS *In New York* 27 The City is at present divided into nineteen Wards, each of which elects one Alderman. **1865** *Atlantic Mo.* XV. 22 Though the mayor, and common council and board of aldermen, . . . should march daily through it [=a business street]. **1895** *Denver Times* 5 March 1/5 The Republicans elect seven of the eight aldermen.

Aldermanic, *a.* Pertaining to an alderman {1770-} — **1865** *Nation* I. 814 There are newspapers in this city which constantly use the word 'aldermanic.' **1901** *Daily News* (Chicago) 27 Dec. 2/4 The suspicious activity of known gangsters at the aldermanic primaries.

Alderney. [Name of one of the Channel Islands.] A breed of cattle; one (esp. a cow) of this breed.

1818 in *Mass. Bd. Agric., 1st Rep.* (1854) II. 272 With this [letter] you will receive a pound of butter, made from the Alderney cow, imported in 1815, and now in my possession. **1826** *Ib.* II. 274 Mr. Parsons . . . thinks the Alderney a very valuable breed. **1856** *Ib., 3rd Rep.* II. 190 The Alderneys are famous only as milchers. They are a small and ill-formed race. **1856** *Rep. Comm. Patents: Agric.* 24 The Short-horns, Ayrshires, and Alderneys are considered the best for dairy purposes. **1884** ROE *Nature's Story* 184 A fawn-colored Alderney, the favorite of the barn-yard.

+Alder swamp. Wet ground in which alder brush grows.

[**1640** *Md. Hist. Mag.* VI. 67 Unto a swamp called Alder Swamp.] **1775** *R. I. Hist. Soc.* VI. 14 [We] got into an alder swamp. **1849** CHAMBERLAIN *Indiana Gaz.* 11 White maple, tamarack and alder swamps; beautiful small lakes and iron ore . . . are scattered promiscuously together. **1889** *Harper's Mag.* Jan. 231/1 Where beavers inhabit an alder swamp. **1900** C. C. MUNN *Uncle Terry* 89 The morning sun . . . changed . . . an alder swamp to a fantastic fairyland.

Alder tree. The alder bush. — **1785** MARSHALL *Amer. Grove* 19 *Betula-Alnus.* The alder tree. The species with us are [three in number]. **1865** *Atlantic Mo.* XV. 183 He heard low voices in the alder-trees, voices he knew.

Alderwoman. +A woman who holds an aldermanic office. {In a casual Eng. instance (1640) used for 'the wife of an alderman.'} — **1888** *Daily Inter-Ocean* 14 Feb. (F.) The new alderwomen are now figuring on an appropriation for tidies to cover the backs of the benches. **1895** *N. Amer. Rev.* Sept. 267 When women shall have become, not only votresses, but . . . alderwomen.

*** Ale.** Also † **aile.**

*** 1.** A malted liquor, commonly distinguished from other kinds by its light color.

1666 *Boston Rec.* 33 Robert Coxe hath lyberty graunted to sell scuruy grasse aile. **1676** *Ib.* 102 Mrs. Rolfe is aproued of to sell bottle ale out of dore. **1707** *Ib.* 65 Her petition for lycence to sell or bottle ale by retaile disallowed. **1727** *Boston Selectmen* 166 Sundry pet[it]ions for retailing beer, ale, cyder and perry without dores approved. **1779** WARNER in Jesse *Selwyn* (1844) IV. 254 An untapped barrel of ale. **1818** DARBY *Emigrant's Guide* 258 The objects of human wants [in Pittsburgh include] . . . three breweries, in which are made an immense quantity of beer, porter, and ale. **1847** LONGFELLOW *Evangeline* I. 51 Flagons of home-brewed ale. **1878** *Amer. Home Cook Book* 12 Put in the water and ale. **1897** *P. B. Book* 55 The principal difference between ale and porter is, that in brewing porter the malt used is browned until it is 'carameled.'

+2. *Ale-cocktail:* (see quotation).

1838 'UNCLE SAM' in *Bentley's Misc.* IV. 47 The other passengers having all retired . . . to the bar-room, where ale-cocktail (ale with ginger and pepper in it) . . . and Monongahela (whiskey-punch) were in great demand.

*** Ale-house.** A house for the retailing of ale.

1638 *Plymouth Laws* 62 Greate inconveniences . . . occationed by yeong men and other labourers that have dyeted in inns and ale-houses. **1658** *Suffolk Deeds* III. 131 Tavernes or alehowses of custome he shall not haunt or frequent. **1669** *Md. Archives* II. 187 The People being mett at an ale House said to him they would have but one burgess. **1718** *Boston Selectmen* 41 Henry Bridgham haveing formerly a grant to keep an ale house, asks that his lycence may be in full to sell strong drink as an inholder. **1771** FRANKLIN *Autobiog.* 304 Meredith . . . was often seen drunk in the streets and playing at low games in ale-houses. **1807** *Ann. 10th Congress* 1 Sess. I. 1021 Was there no difference between freemen . . . and wretches . . . educated in ale-houses, such as composed their standing army? **1845** *Lowell Offering* V. 127 One of your companions at the ale house. **1868** *Putnam's Mag.* Feb. 240/2 Many years ago . . ., on the corner of Thames and Temple streets, . . . New York, stood an ancient wooden ale-house.

b. Attrib. with *keeper.*

1647 *R. I. Col. Rec.* I. 185 The head officer . . . shall binde by Recognizance every such Taverne, Alehouse keeper and Victualler . . . not to vse such games as are judged by the Lawes of England to be vnlawfull.

Alepine. *Obs.* Also **alapine, alla-, allopeen.** [Obs. E. *alapeen* (1739), *alepine* (1757), F. *alépine,* f. *Alep* Aleppo.] A dress stuff of wool and silk or mohair and cotton.

1745 in J. F. Watson *Philadelphia* (1830) 179 Single allopeens, children's stays, jumps and bodice. **1754** *S. C. Gazette* 22 Jan. 3/1 [They] have imported . . . ginghams, bombazines, alapines. **1762** H. M. Brooks *Gleanings* 37 Bombazeen, allopeen, . . . Hungarians, dimothy. **1845** *Transcript & Chron.* (Providence, R. I.) 8 Jan. 3 Bombazines, alepines, . . . and all other articles for mourning, will be marked at low prices.

+Alewife. Also † **ail-, aylwife, alewive.** Pl. **-wives.**

1. A fish (*Pomolobus pseudoharengus*) found in great numbers along the Atlantic coast; the branch herring.

Possibly adopted from an Indian name, but the form *aloofe,* sometimes cited in support of this, appears in only one source (quot. 1679), and is probably a misprint. Cf. ALLIZE.

'Alewife [is called] Alewhap, pl. alewhaps,—Conn.' (Chipman, *a* 1870). 'In Maryland and Virginia they are called "old wives" ' (B. '77).

1633 *Plymouth Col. Rec.* XI. 14 Whereas God . . . hath cast the ffish (called) alewiues or herringes in the middest of the towne. **1634** WOOD *New Eng. Prospect* I. ix. 34 Alewives be a kind of fish which is much like a herring, which in the latter end of Aprill come up to the fresh rivers to spawne, in such multitudes as is allmost incredible. **1634** *Mass. Bay Rec.* I. 114 Mr. Israell Stoughton hath liberty . . . to sell the alewyves hee takes there att 5s the thousand. **1646** *Suffolk Deeds* I. 71 To allow sufficient water in the ould river for the alewives to come to the wyres before the Grantors house. **1654** JOHNSON *Wonder-w. Prov.* 83 The Lord is pleased to provide for them great store of fish in the spring time, and especially alewives about the bignesse of a herring. **1663** *Maine Hist. Soc. Coll.* III. 92 The alewives come in the end of April. **1675** JOSSELYN *Two Voyages* 107 The alewife is like a herrin, but has a bigger bellie, therefore called an alewife. **1679** WINTHROP in *Phil. Trans.* XII. 1066 Where the ground is bad or worn out, the Indians used to put two or three of the forementioned fishes, under or adjacent to each corn-hill. . . . The English have learned the like husbandry, where these aloofes come up in great plenty. **1734** *Jrnls. Mass. Ho. Repr.* 50 A Bill entitled an Act to prevent the destruction of the fish commonly called alewives. **1747** *Duxbury Rec.* 277 All obstructions shall forthwith be removed on Southworth's Mill river, . . . so that alewives may run into the Mill pond. **1765** R. ROGERS *Concise Acc.* 67 In the before-mentioned rivers is great plenty of fish, such as shad, ail-wives, sturgeon. **1788** J. MAY *Jour. & Lett.* 23 The people came on shore with the seine, and as many as a 100,000 alewives. **1824** *Mass. Spy* 19 May (Th.) It is calculated that 40,000 alewives were taken in Plymouth at one haul last week. **1838** *Mass. Zool. Survey Rep.* 42 The *Clupea vernalis*—alewife—is taken in immense quantities still, . . . although in several places . . .the various encroachments of man have sensibly diminished them. **1880** *Harper's Mag.* Aug. 350/1 He must . . . set weirs for herring, menhaden, alewives and mackerel.

b. (See quotations.)

1839 STORER *Mass. Fishes* 112 *Clupea fasciata* [Le Sueur] (fasciated Herring) is known under the name of alewive by the fishermen of Sandwich, and appears only in the spring. **1842** *Nat. Hist. N. Y., Zoology* IV. 258 The American Alewive. *Alosa tyrannus*. ... In our waters, they appear with the Shad about the first of April, but are never sufficiently numerous to form a separate fishery. **1884** ROE *Nature's Story* 197 These half-grown fish [=shad] are ... sold as herrings or 'alewives.'

2. Attrib., esp. with *fishery*.

1634 WOOD *New Eng. Prospect* I. x. 43 This town [of Salem] wants an alewife river, which is a great inconvenience; it hath two good harbours. **1635** *Cambridge Prop. Rec.* 36 That is to say in Aylwife Meaddow twelve ackers and halfe. **1755** *Ib.* 352 The regulation of the alewive fishery. **1793** *Mass. H. S. Coll.* III. 2 The alewife-fish come into Snipatuct pond. **1794** *Ib.* 145 A small settlement was made ... at the last falls, on account of the alewive fishery. **1801** *Mass. Acts & Laws* 13 June iii, An act to regulate the alewive fishery in the brook ... in the County of Barnstable. **1832** WILLIAMSON *Maine* I. 52 Here is one of the best alewive-fisheries in the State. **1883** GOODE *Fishery Indust.* (1887) 8 The shad and alewife and the oyster fisheries.

***Alexanders.** +The meadow parsnip (*Thaspium aureum*), or other plant similar to this.

1637 MORTON *New Canaan* II. iii, The country there naturally affordeth very good pot-herbes and sallet herbes, ... as potmarioram, tyme, alexander [*sic*], angellica, ... in very great abundance. **1791** MUHLENBERG *Index Florae* 166 *Smyrnium*, Alexanders. **1813** — *Cat. Plants* 31 Alexanders: ... Pens. fl. Maio, Virg., Car. **1821** *Mass. H. S. Coll.* 2 Ser. IX. 156 Plants, which are indigenous in the township of Middlebury, [Vermont, include] ... Alexanders. **1843** TORREY *Flora N. Y.* I. 270 *Zizia cordata*. ... Heart-leaved Alexanders. ... Borders of woods, and thickets on hill-sides. *Ib.* 272 *Thaspium atropurpureum*. Purple Alexanders. **1847** WOOD *Botany* 287 *Zizia aurea*, ... Golden Alexanders, ... [grow on] hills and meadows, U. S. and Canada.

Alfalfa. [Sp.] A variety of lucern (*Medicago sativa*), much grown in the West, esp. in arid regions, for pasture and forage. {1845-}

1855 BROWNE in *Trans. Amer. Inst. N. Y.* 618 Chilian Clover, or alfalfa ..., from Chili, a perennial variety of lucerne, which succeeds well in our middle and southern States. **1879** *Webster's Suppl.* s.v., Alfalfa ... is cultivated in California and Texas for fodder. **1882** *Harper's Mag.* April 690/2 Hay and its substitutes, alfalfa and lucern, take high rank in the list of crops. **1885** *Rep. Indian Affairs* 144 Walker River Reserve has 12 acres under cultivation, sown in alfalfa. **1887** *Scribner's Mag.* Oct. 509/2 He ... gazes over his fields of *alfalfa*, which is excellent Spanish for lucern. **1905** *Springfield W. Republican* 15 Dec. 15 Alfalfa, a grass introduced from Asia into California, ... now is the mainstay of the sheep and cattle in all of the Rocky Mountain States.

b. Attrib. with *clover, fever, seed*.

1856 *Rep. Comm. Patents: Agric.* 254 About two years since, I obtained from the Patent Office a small parcel of 'Alfalfa' seed, the lucerne grass of the Andes. **1863** *Ill. Agric. Soc. Trans.* V. 869 Alfalfa clover has been used for soiling. **1872** *Trinity Journal* (Weaverville) 6 April (F.) Earl, of Douglas City, has been ... plowing up the ground, and seeding it with alfalfa. Everybody in that section has had the alfalfa fever.

+**Alfilaria, -eria.** [Mexican-Sp. Cf. next.] =next. — **1889** VASEY *Agric. Grasses* 102 Alfilaria. This annual, supposed to have been introduced from Europe, does not seem to be mentioned in any work on forage plants. [**1897** B. HARRADEN *H. Strafford* 115 Carpets of the little pink blossom of the alfilaria, the first spring flower.]

+**Alfilerilla.** [Amer.-Sp. *alfilerillo*, f. Sp. *alfiler* a pin.] The pin-grass or pin-clover (*Erodium cicutarium*) of the Southwest. — **1889** *Cent.* s.v., Alfilerilla ... is a low herb, but a valuable forage-plant. **1897** *Outing* March 551/2 The sleek Herefords lifted their white faces from the ferny circlets of alfilerilla. **1908** D. A. MACDOUGAL *Bot. Features N. A. Deserts* 70 Finding its way about, across the mesas and over the hill-slopes, is the alfilerilla, ... a relative of the geranium.

+**Alforja.** *S.W.* [Mexican-Sp. Cf. next.] A saddlebag. — **1847** RUXTON *Adv. Rocky Mts.* 77 To it flock venders of saddles, bridles, bits, spurs, whips, alforjas. **1848** E. BRYANT *California* App. 466 Parties of men ... carrying with them pack-saddles and *alforjases* [*sic*] or large saddle-bags, adapted to the pack-saddle. **1922** P. A. ROLLINS *Cowboy* 155 All or a part of the parcels might have been stuffed into 'alforjas,' which were wide, leathern or canvas bags ... hanging from the crosses on the saddle's top.

Alforge. *Obs.* [Pg. Cf. prec.] The pouches of the cheek. {*a*1704, 1748} — **1704** S. KNIGHT *Journal* 43 In comes a tall country fellow, with his alfogeos [*sic*] full of tobacco.

Algerian, *a.* Originating, or regarded as originating, from Algeria. **1856** *Rep. Comm. Patents: Agric.* 199, I received from the Patent Office, last spring, a small package of 'Algerian' wheat, which I sowed ... ; it produced well, having a large berry.

Algerine, *n.*

1. An inhabitant or native of Algeria; an Algerian. {1669-}

1678 J. HULL *Diary* 163 James Elson was taken by the Algerines, where I lost only my eighth part of the ship. **1785** JEFFERSON *Writings* IV. 25 The Algerines ... have taken two of our vessels, and I fear will ask ... a tribute for the forbearance of their piracies. **1790** WASHINGTON *Diaries* IV. 107 The Algerines demanding a much larger sum, it was conceived that acceding to it might establish a precedent. **1813** *Niles' Reg.* III. 285/2 Thus is a 'triple alliance' formed against the United States—Savages, Britons and Algerines. **1827** COOPER *Red Rover* I. vii. 205 This vessel was ... intended as a present or a scourge to the Algerines; but —but she has changed owners.

fig. **1841** FOOTE *Texas & Texans* 83 A transaction which doubtless will ... call down retributive vengeance upon these American Algerines. *a***1861** WINTHROP *J. Brent* vii. 71 He's one er them Algerines what don't know a dark hint, till it begins to make motions.

+**2.** *transf.* In *pl.*, the colloquial name of a faction in Rhode Island politics in the middle of the 19th cent.

1844 *Congress. Globe* 11 Mar. 360/1 The gentleman from Rhode Island had talked of 'ruffianism' in that State, and of 'Algerines'; but if the proposition he made to this House was not a specimen of 'Algerineism,' he apprehended it was not to be found in Rhode Island. **1885** *Congress. Rec.* 21 Jan. 912/1 Bitterly as the conflict was waged between the 'Dorrites' and the 'Algerines,' as the contending parties were called.

Algerine, *a.*

1. Belonging or pertaining to Algiers; characteristic of Algerian pirates. {1682-}

1715 SEWALL *Diary* III. 34 [The dinner] was in remembrance of his landing ... at Boston after his Algerin captivity. **1723** *Weekly Mercury* 21-28 Nov. 2/1 Capt. John Parker in the Snow Henry of Philadelphia ... was met by an Algerine Rover who plundered him of several trifles. **1790** MACLAY *Deb. Senate* 277 The committee on the Algerine business. **1795** HAMILTON in *Ann. 3rd Congress* 1336 Computing the Army and Navy Establishments on the scale of an Indian and Algerine war. **1818** FEARON *Sketches* 150 An American, tall, determined, and with an eye that flashes with Algerine cruelty. **1846** *Knickerb.* XXVIII. 69 We believe that ... a legal stop might be put to the Algerine practices of our book-printers.

2. *transf.* (Cf. ALGERINE *n.* 2.)

1845 GREELEY in Mackenzie *Van Buren* 299 Our paragon of Democrats [=Ritchie] ... can sympathize with the victims of 'Algerine' tyranny in Rhode Island.

+**Algerineism.** The practice of terrorism. — **1844** (see ALGERINE *n.* 2).

+**Algic,** *a.* and *n.* (See quot. 1839.) — **1834** SCHOOLCRAFT in *Hist. & Scientific Sk. Mich.* 92 The ... plan of a society of Inquiry respecting the Indians, was adopted ... at Detroit in 1832, under the title of the Algic Society. **1839** — *Algic Researches* I. 12 The term Algic is introduced, in a generic sense, for all that family of tribes who, about A.D. 1600, were found spread out ... along the Atlantic, ... extending ... west to the Mississippi. [The word is] derived from the words Alleghany and Atlantic. **1839** — *Knickerb.* XIII. 214 The Algics, if they were not the primitive explorers, were the Argonauts here.

+**Algodon.** [Sp.] The cottonwood. — **1878** BEADLE *Western Wilds* 76 A little grove of algodones beyond the hacienda.

+**Algonkin, Algonquin,** *n.* and *a.* [Amer. Indian.]

1. *n.* A member of an important widespread family of American Indian tribes, formerly inhabiting various eastern and middle States, and parts of Canada.

1667 TRACY in Fernow *N. Y. Documents* (1853) III. 151 By our authority wee haue hindred the Algonquins from making warre upon them [=the Dutch]. **1721** *Mass. H. Repr. Journal* III. 111 [A letter bearing] the Signature of the ... Abnaquoise, and of ... the Algonquins, the Hurons [etc.]. **1760** JEFFERYS *Hist. French Dominions* 78 These last [the Iroquois] give a different origin to mankind from the Algonkins. **1765** CROGHAN *Journals* 26 Sept., Alagonkins [*sic*] ... settled near Trois Rivers. **1770** *Doc. rel. Hist. N. Y.* VIII. 228 In the evening 16 Algonkins ettc. arrived. **1812** STODDARD *Sk. Louisiana* 433 The ... language ... of the Algonquins [is said] to have sweetness and elegance. **1892** A. E. LEE *Hist. Columbus* (O.) I. 67 The Lenapes ... paternally styled the other Algonquins as children or grandchildren.

b. Their language.

1869 PARKMAN *Discov. Great West* iv. 39 He spoke Algonquin fluently.

2. *a.* Designating or pertaining to this family of Indians or their language.

1705 BEVERLEY *Virginia* III. 24 [Va. Indians] have a sort of general Language, like what Lahontan calls the Algonkine. **1760** JEFFERYS *Hist. French Dominions* 47 The Christinax, a nation ... speaking the Algonkin tongue. *Ib.* 71 The Indians, ... amongst several of the Algonkin nations, allow of a plurality of wives. **1841** COOPER *Deerslayer* xv, Hurry, who had some knowledge of the Algonquin language. **1875** WHITNEY *Life of Language* 220 An Algonkin verb makes a host of distinctions. **1876** BANCROFT *Hist.* I. 15 The natives, Indians of Algonkin descent, received them with unsuspecting hospitality. **1919** *Maine my State* 25 Canada, the original home of the great Algonkin family.

***Alguazil.** [Sp.] In regions under Spanish influence, an officer of the law; a sheriff.

1803 *Ann. 8th Congress* 2 Sess. 1520 (Descr. La.) This council distributes among its members several important offices, such as Alguazil Mayor or High Sheriff. **1836** HOLLEY *Texas* xii. 243 Each municipality ... continues to elect an alguazil or sheriff. **1858** *Texas Almanac* 162 The *Alguazil*, or Sheriff of the Colony, was appointed by the Supreme Judge.

***Alien,** *n.* and *a.*

1. *n.* One who is not a native or citizen of the United States.

1781-2 JEFFERSON *Notes Va.* (1787) 259 By our laws . . . no alien can hold lands. **1790** *Ann. 1st Congress* I. 1109 The policy of admitting aliens to the rights of citizenship. **1798** [C. WILLIAMSON] *Descr. Genesee* vi, The law . . . by which foreigners, though aliens, are enabled to hold real property within the State of New-York. **1802** *Ann. 7th Congress* App. 1329 Any alien, being a free white person, may be admitted to become a citizen of the United States. **1832** CLAY *Speeches* (1842) 169 He has filled . . . some of the highest offices under this government, . . . and he is still at heart an alien. **1837** *S. Lit. Messenger* III. 673 A summary of the laws relating to Aliens in the United States. **1841** *Niles' Nat. Reg.* 20 Feb. 390/3 The supreme court of Illinois . . . decided that aliens, under the laws of the state, have a right to vote. **1874** *Colo. Gen. Laws* (1877) 90 The personal estate of an alien, dying intestate, . . . shall be distributed in the same manner as the estate of natural born citizens.

+b. (See quotation.)

1882 *Nation* 19 Oct. 331/1 The State of Arkansas . . . certainly could not have supposed that capitalists at home and the aliens (as they were wont to call all Northern bondholders) had forgotten . . . the special acts of her Legislature.

2. Attrib. with *bill*, etc. *Alien and Sedition Act* or *Laws*, measures enacted by the Federalists in 1798 to suppress undue opposition to the government.

1798 *Virginia Resolution* 21 Dec., The General Assembly doth particularly protest against the palpable and alarming infractions of the Constitution, in the two late cases of the 'Alien and Sedition Acts.' **1798** WASHINGTON *Letter* Writings XIV. 132 The Alien and Sedition Laws are now the desiderata of the Opposition. **1798** JEFFERSON *Writings* X. 61 The X. Y. Z. fever has considerably abated . . . and the alien and sedition laws are working hard. **1837** *Democratic Rev.* I. 21 The new government, which bade fair, by its alien and sedition laws, to strangle the infant genius of American liberty. **1865** *Atlantic Mo.* XV. 191 Matthew Lyon, . . . once famous for . . . his trial under the Alien and Sedition Act. — **1798** JEFFERSON *Writings* (1854) IV. 249 Our alien bill struggles hard for a passage. It has been considerably mollified. — **1856** HAMBLETON *Biog. Wise* 55 The men who shaped and penned the odious alien law.

3. *adj.* That owes allegiance to a foreign country. Esp. in *alien enemy*.

1798 *Ann. 5th Congress* II. 1974 The question is . . . whether this Government has any power, under the Constitution, to remove alien friends out of the United States. *Ib.*, If Congress has any power which they can exercise on the persons of alien merchants. **1812** *Ann. 12th Congress* I. 314 An act respecting alien enemies. **1851** *Ann. 5th Congress* II. 2009 *headline*, [Bill on] Alien Enemies. **1862** KETTELL *Hist. Rebellion* I. 231 A bill was also passed sequestrating the property of alien enemies, and 'alien enemies' were defined to be all those who did not take the oath of allegiance to the Confederacy.

***Alien,** *v.* =ALIENATE *v.*

1638 *Newhaven Rec.* 1 That he . . . hath an absolute . . . power to give, alien, dispose or sell, all or any part of the lands. **1657** *Charleston Land Rec.* 148, I . . . grant, alien, enfeoff, and confirm unto the sayd Job Lane . . . a certain parcell of arrable land. **1682** *Penna. Archives* I. 53 The premises . . . intended to be hereby aliened, enfeoffed, and confirmed. **1900** DIX *Deacon Bradbury* 8 But I . . . have . . . bargained, sold, aliened, remised, released, enfeoffed [etc.].

Alienage. The state or condition of being an alien. {1809} — **a1828** JUDGE STORY (W.), Why restore estates, forfeitable on account of alienage? **1863** LINCOLN in *Messages & P.* VI. 181 Such an amendment . . . as will make . . . voting an estoppel against any plea of exemption from military service . . . on the ground of alienage.

***Alienate,** *v. tr.* To transfer the ownership of (land) to another.

1636 *Dedham Rec.* 24 Noe person . . . shall at any tyme heerafter alienate, bargen, sell, set over or assigne the sayd lott. **1653** *Charlestown Land Rec.* 129, I . . . have alinated, sould, asseighned and sett over and doe by these presents alienate . . . fiftenne accers of land. **1793** JEFFERSON *Anas* (1903) 110 It had no right to dismember or alienate any portion of territory once ultimately consolidated with us. **c1820** ADAMS *Works* (1851) VI. 508 If John Randolph should manumit one of his negroes and alienate to him his plantation. **1832** CLAY *Speeches* (1842) 221 It is manifest that neither the present generation nor posterity can derive much advantage from this mode of alienating public lands. **1836** EDWARD *Hist. Texas* vii. 145 The proprietors of said lands . . . must alienate two-thirds of the same by sale. **1874** *Colo. Gen. Laws* (1877) 90 All aliens may . . . alienate, sell, assign and transmit the same [lands and tenements] to their heirs.

***Alienation.** The action of transferring ownership.

1637 *Dedham Rec.* 29 That the sayd grownd . . . shalbe at his owne disposeing in case of sale or other alienacion at his pleasure. **1666** *Conn. Public Rec.* II. 39 Such as may be appointed to administer to the estate may . . . make alienation of such lands. **c1820** ADAMS *Works* (1851) VI. 509 The right, power, and authority of alienation are essential to property. **1877** *Colo. Civil Procedure Code* 95 An action for the recovery of real property against a person in possession, cannot be prejudiced by any alienation made by such person. **1881** *Rep. Indian Affairs* p. xlix, The title to be acquired by the Poncas shall not be subject to alienation.

***Alienee.** A person to whom the title of property is transferred. — **1790** *Ann. 1st Congress* II. 1213 The alienee . . . would hereafter have a just demand against the public for four shillings. **c1792** HAMILTON *Works* (1885) II. 292 A saving . . . might have been made by providing for it [=a debt] in the hands of alienees.

+Alienism. *rare.* =ALIENAGE. {1854-} — **1808** JOHNSON *Rep. Cases Supreme Ct. N. Y.* II. 381 The prisoner was convicted of murder. On his arraignment, he suggested his *alienism*, which was admitted.

Alimony. *Law.* An allowance for maintenance given to one of the parties, usu. the wife, upon the legal separation or divorce of a married couple. {1655-} — **1814** Johnson *N.Y. Cases in Chancery* I. 110 If no divorce can or ought to be decreed, perhaps the bill may be sustained for alimony. **1846** *Ill. Supreme Court Rep.* VIII. 436 Bill in Chancery for an increase of alimony, the custody of two infant children, [etc.]. **1906** *Kansas City Times* 7 July 4/2 Goulds Willing to Give Their Count Alimony. **1925** *N.Y. Times* 1 Feb. 22/2 Mrs. Strasburger is asking for $500 a week alimony.

***Alive,** *a.* In special uses: (see quotations).

1845 JUDD *Margaret* II. i. 186 Her mother 'stirs it off' and a due quantity of the 'quick' and 'alive' crystal sweet is the result. **1892** GUNTER *Miss Dividends* xvi. 234 The locomotives . . . are moving about slowly, with a view to keeping themselves what is technically called 'alive'—that is, their steam up, sufficient to give them power of motion.

***Alkali.**

+1. Any of various chemical salts commonly found in the soil of western states.

1848 E. BRYANT *California* viii. 124, I found the liquid bitter with salt and alkali. **1853** HANDSAKER *Pioneer Life* (1908) 61 We have seen plenty of water today but it would be death to use it, as it contains so much alkali. **1869** BOWLES *New West* xiv. 278 In looking out . . . on the starry heavens, . . . one almost forgets alkali. **1878** BEADLE *Western Wilds* 124 The land . . . is a complete desert, generally whitened by alkali. **1889** E. B. CUSTER *Tenting on Plains* xx. 585 Even then, they look from the windows of the Pullman car on to the desert, white with alkali. **1902** WISTER *Virginian* xxvi. 298 Thick heat rose . . . from the caked alkali.

+2. Land, or a region, excessively impregnated with alkali.

1870 'MARK TWAIN' *Sk., Petrified Man*, That awful five days journey, through alkali, sagebrush, peril of body, and imminent starvation. **1873** BEADLE *Undevel. West* 247 Farther west comes the alkali, or in places the chemical springs. **1878** — *Western Wilds* 139 A region . . . where even the high plains are dotted by tracts of alkali. **1902** WISTER *Virginian* ix. 101 Sunrise found the white stage lurching eternally on across the alkali. **1904** WHITE *Blazed Trail Stories* x. 182 Tom, and Alfred, and the ponies . . . had done the alkali for three days. **1910** J. HART *Vigilante Girl* xxv. 351 The whitish stretches of alkali which lay like leprous patches on the desert's bosom.

+3. An inhabitant of an alkali region.

1907 WHITE *Arizona Nights* I. ii. 31 A white-faced woman who looked mighty good to us alkalis opened the flaps.

4. Attrib. with *bed, bottom, cloud, marsh, spring, swamp*.

1850 SAWYER *Way Sketches* 40 The water of all Alkali swamps and springs should be carefully avoided by emigrants. *Ib.* 41 Thence six miles to the Alkali lakes and marshes. There are several of these marshes. *Ib.* 73 We now drove nine miles . . . over a sage country, occasionally striking the alkali bottoms. **1869** BROWNE *Adv. Apache Country* 476 It is always a source of happiness to think . . . that there are no more gnats and alkali-clouds to swallow. **1913** J. B. ELLIS *Lahoma* 128, I'm just so . . . dead killed by all these sand-hills and alkali beds.

+Alkali desert. In the Southwest, 'wide districts of land . . . more appropriately called a desert, covered with an efflorescence of alkali' (B. '77).

1870 PINE *Beyond the West* 214 This road often led them . . . over alkali deserts. **1872** 'MARK TWAIN' *Roughing It* xviii. 142 That species of deserts whose concentrated hideousness shames the diffused and diluted horrors of Sahara—an 'alkali' desert. **1878** BEADLE *Western Wilds* 390 The red hills and alkali deserts of Wyoming. **1893** M. HOWE *Honor* 268 Stuart . . . had lived for months in the alkali desert of Arizona, enduring the terrible climate.

+Alkali dust. Dust of alkali land.

1869 BROWNE *Adv. Apache Country* 476 Breathing clouds of alkali-dust. **1872** 'MARK TWAIN' *Roughing It* 144 The alkali dust cut through our lips, . . . and made our noses bleed and kept them bleeding. **1883** BEADLE *Western Wilds* 589 His hair and whiskers are turned to a creamy white by the villainous powder known as alkali dust. **1889** E. B. CUSTER *Tenting on Plains* xii. 358 It soon became gray with layer upon layer of alkali dust. **1907** WHITE *Arizona Nights* III. xiv. 348 The sparse vegetation was grey with the alkali dust.

+Alkalied, *a.* Affected by living in an alkali region; impregnated with alkali.

1864 A. J. DICKSON *Across Plains* (1929) 119 They made a business of buying alkalied or sore footed stock. **1870** BEADLE *Utah* 444 It is only where small streams have run some distance across the plain that they are, in local phrase, 'alkalied.' **1907** WHITE *Arizona Nights* I. vii. 126 The trouble with you fellows . . . is that you're so plumb alkalied you don't know the real thing when you see it.

+Alkali flat. A stretch of land impregnated with alkali.

1871 DE VERE 177 The Alkali Flats are now crossed by the Pacific

Railroad. **1878** BEADLE *Western Wilds* 388, I am convinced there is little to see but rolling plains, . . . alkali flats and sand-hills. **1881** *Amer. Naturalist* XV. 25 The grease wood of the alkali flats. **1884** NYE *Baled Hay* 153 We . . . worry along with polygamy and the odor of the alkali flat. **1902** 'MARK TWAIN' in *Harper's Mag.* Jan. 269 In a slick alkali flat which was surfaced like steel.

+**Alkali grass.** A grass of several varieties, esp. *Distichlis*, growing in the western States, and well adapted to alkaline soil. — **1870** PINE *Beyond the West* 376 Our horses [were] recruited with a few blades of alkali grass about the spring. **1894** *Amer. Folk-Lore* VII. 102 *Zygadenus elegans*, . . . alkali-grass; Minn.

+**Alkali lake.** A lake whose water is impregnated with alkali. — **1850** L. SAWYER *Way Sketches* 41 Thence six miles to the Alkali lakes and marshes. **1869** BROWNE *Adv. Apache Country* 528 Twenty-five town-sites agreeably situated in the middle of an alkali lake! **a1918** G. STUART *On Frontier* I. 111 This lonely creek . . . then sinks into the bare white bed of a dry alkali lake.

+**Alkali land.** A region whose soil is excessively impregnated with alkali. — **1872** C. NORDHOFF *California* 144 Frequently a farm would extend into the midst of this alkali land. **1913** BARNES *Western Grazing Grounds* 54 There are great areas . . . in the alkali lands which grow a fine crop of sacaton.

Alkaline, *a.* {1677-}

+**1.** Of water, soil, etc.: Impregnated with alkali.

1854 MARCY *Expl. Red River* i. 8 The water in the creek is alkaline, but quite palatable. **1869** BOWLES *New West* xiv. 277 These alkaline valleys of the Great Interior Basin. **1870** *Amer. Naturalist* IV. 33 Occasionally the plain is marked by a tract of white alkaline salts. **1873** BEADLE *Undevel. West* 57 This penetrating alkaline dust sifts in at the smallest crevice. **1878** — *Western Wilds* 105 Salt lakes, alkaline 'sinks' and mud flats alone relieve the dreary monotony. **1885** *Rep. Indian Affairs* 23 The lands, too, are none of the best, 'Gumbo' or alkaline soil prevailing to a large extent. **1902** WISTER *Virginian* xxvi. 299 The horses drank . . . from the sluggish yellow water, and its alkaline taste and warmth were equally welcome to the men.

+**2.** *Alkaline grass:* (see quotation and ALKALI GRASS).

1889 VASEY *Agric. Grasses* 61 *Distichlis maritima* (Salt grass; Alkaline Grass) . . . is a perennial grass, growing . . . abundantly in alkaline soil throughout the arid districts of the Rocky Mountains.

+**Alkali plain.** A level stretch of land abounding in alkali.

1869 BROWNE *Adv. Apache Country* 513 In the alkali plains and sage-deserts and rugged mountain ranges of Nevada, you find him with his pick and shovel. **1870** PINE *Beyond the West* 215 There are [in Oregon] many . . . alkali plains, that would make better soap than wheat. **1878** BEADLE *Western Wilds* 125 The hot sun, . . . gravel beds, and alkali plains would absorb it all. **1890** *Harper's Mag.* Oct. 807/1 The writer met recently, in the Colorado desert of Arizona, a forlorn census-taker . . . roaming over the alkali-plains. **1897** *Boston Transcript* 23 Dec. 8/2 He rode across the alkali plains when they were covered with mud.

+**Alkali sink.** A cavity (or 'sink-hole') filled with a mixture of water and alkali soil. — **1886** *Boston Herald* 16 July, It is only an 'alkali sink' —a natural well, filled with a paste as yielding as water.

***All,** *n. colloq.* The sum of the matter. — **1861** LOWELL *Biglow P.* II. p. lxxviii, All is, he couldn't love em. **1869** STOWE *Oldtown Folks* 239 All is, when I begin a thing I like to go through with it.

***All,** *a.* and *adv.*

+**1.** With various nouns in colloquial phrases, usually of comparison, as (*like*) *all creation, fury, nature, out-doors, possessed, wrath:* see these words.

+**2.** *All the way from . . . to . . .*, denoting limits in numbers, etc.

1878 BEADLE *Western Wilds* 493 The value of the booty taken has been estimated all the way from $150,000 to $300,000. **1904** *N. Y. Ev. Post* 7 Oct. 7 The organized labor vote of the State is variously estimated all the way from 22,000 up to 40,000. **1905** *Atlantic Mo.* Nov. 580 The periodicals pay all the way from half a cent to fifteen cents a word.

3. With a qualifying adverb: (see quotation).

1781 WITHERSPOON *Druid P.* No. 6, It is *partly all* gone, it is *mostly all* gone. This is an absurdity or barbarism, as well as a vulgarism.

4. *All but*, almost. +In elliptic use.

1810 WEEMS *Letters* III. 14 Doctor Fendall . . . sold 60 doll[ar]s all but. **1825** NEAL *Bro. Jonathan* I. 10 It was her pride . . . to keep the hearth stone . . . 'as beautiful' as the red brick hearth of neighbour Nathan Libbey, 'all but.'

5. In various phrases, as *all of a heap, all to pieces, for all it is worth;* see these words. Also ALL OF.

Allahabad. Also **Alle-, Aleabad.** A variety of cotton goods imported from India. — **1811** H. M. Brooks *Gleanings* 101 One bale . . . Aleabad [*sic*] Mowsannas. **c1811** *Ib.*, Guzzenahs, Allebad [*sic*], Emerty.

+**All around,** *adv.* and *a.*

1. *adv.* On all sides; in all quarters; completely.

1856 M. J. HOLMES *Homestead on Hillside* ii, Stepchildren, half-sisters, and double connections all around. **1878** BEADLE *Western Wilds* 538 The trail shows that twelve American horses, shod all around, have passed at a walk.

2. Through the circuit of a number of persons.

1871 DE VERE 315 If a man . . . runs for an office, . . . he has only to take them [=voters] to a saloon, and order some complicated beverage *all around*, to secure their good-will for the day. **1900** DIX *Deacon Bradbury* 194 Emmie doesn't say anything at all about being generous all around.

3. *a.* Completely surrounding or radiating.

1886 DORSEY *Midshipman Bob* 72 The streets running out like spokes, and a big 'all-around' street like a tire. **1886** *Harper's Mag.* June 18/2 This arrangement gives a clear sweep . . . enabling the forward gun to cover an all-around fire.

4. *fig.* Good for all purposes or in all respects.

1883 *Harper's Mag.* Aug. 453/1 It is not the best all-around boat. **1890** *Ib.* Sept. 593/2 For all-around pleasure the usual small boat is no better than a harness cask. **1904** *Forum* Oct. 257 The most comprehensive and in many ways the best all-around American city school exhibit. **1906** *Atlantic Mo.* Jan. 43 The president of an American university is bound to be . . . one of the very great, all-around men of his generation.

+**All-aroundness.** The state of being developed in all ways. — **1888** *Voice* (N.Y.) 6 Sept., Let all good people note the all-aroundness of our chieftain's character.

+**All-createdly,** *adv. colloq.* [Cf. CREATION.] Excessively. — **1856** G. D. BREWERTON *War in Kansas* 317 So as I wor all-createdly riled, I jest up an' let 'em hev it.

+**All day.** *colloq.* Used to denote that all is over for or with a person (or thing).

1836 *Knickerb.* VIII. 205 Marlinspike now swore that it was all day with him; and . . . he might as well content himself. **1846** *Spirit of Times* (N.Y.) 6 June 170/2, I came to the conclusion that it was 'all day' with my 'tile.' **1860** HOLLAND *Miss Gilbert* xiii. 231 Then she lifted up her face and I knew it was all day with me. **1865** *Atlantic Mo.* XV. 396 It ud be all day wid us 'fore we'd time. **1889** MUNROE *Golden Days* xiv. 153 If you hadn't toed the mark, good and square . . . , 'twould have been all day with me.

All-day, *a.* Continuing for a whole day; capable of working throughout a whole day.

a1870 CHIPMAN *Notes on Bartlett* 5 An all-day horse, etc.—*Ct.* **1877** *Rep. Indian Affairs* 14 On June 17th engaged in an all-day fight with the hostiles.

+**Alleghanian,** *n.* An inhabitant of the region of the Alleghany Mts. or of 'Alleghania,' a name suggested in 1845 by Hoffman and others as a substitute for 'United States.'

Also in the name of a newspaper, the *Cumberland Alleghanian* (1820).

1844 J. P. DURBIN *Observations* (1846) II. 216 There is nothing in Ireland to which a Switzer or an Alleghanian would give the name [of mountain]. **c1847** HOFFMAN in Barnes *Hoffman* 281 A play to be called The First Alleghanian—or three years in the life of Washington, etc.

+**Alleghanian,** *a.* Also **-anean, -enian.** Pertaining to the Alleghany mountains or to 'Alleghania' (cf. prec.).

1828 WEBSTER s.v. *Alleghanean.* **1839** *S. Lit. Messenger* V. 477/1, I shall begin with a general sketch of the Alleghanian region of Virginia. **c1847** HOFFMAN in Barnes *Hoffman* 281 The Alleghenian General [=Washington]. **1901** MOHR *Plant Life Ala.* 674 Butterfly Weed . . . [grows in the] Alleghenian, Carolinian, and Louisianian areas.

+**Alleghany.** [Name of a mountain system of the S.E. and a river of Pa.]. *Alleghany hell-bender, plum:* (see quotations). *A. skiff*, a make of skiff designed for navigating the Alleghany river. *A. sloe:* (see quotation). *A. vine*, the climbing fumitory, *Adlumia cirrhosa*, native to the Alleghany region. (See also ALLIGATOR FISH, quot. 1807.)

1842 *Nat. Hist. N. Y., Zoology* III. 89 The Allegany Hell-bender . . . feeds on worms, crayfish, fishes, and aquatic reptiles. — **1892** APGAR *Trees Northern U.S.* 98 *Prunus Alleghaniensis*, Porter. (Alleghany Plum.) A low, straggling bush. . . . Mountains of Pennsylvania. — **1826** FLINT *Recoll.* 14 What the people call 'covered sleds,' or ferry-flats, and Alleghany-skiffs, carrying from eight to twelve tons. — **1897** SUDWORTH *Arborescent Flora* 238 *Prunus alleghaniensis*, Porter: Alleghany Sloe. — **1850** [S. F. COOPER] *Rural Hours* 169 Landed and gathered wild flowers . . . and Alleghany vine. *Ib.* 170 The Alleghany vine, with its pale pink clusters and very delicate foliage, is very common in some places. **1863** *Rep. Comm. Agric.* 158 There is a pretty climbing plant, known in cultivation as the Alleghany vine. **1892** *Amer. Folk-Lore* V. 92 Alleghany vine [grows in] N. Ohio.

+**Alleghany,** *v. tr.* (See quotation.) — **1895** J. WINSOR *Mississippi Basin* 176 This 'trusting' process was so common hereabouts that, according to a memorial of some traders who had suffered by French blandishments interfering with the spring payments, it was termed 'Alleghanying' the poor Indians.

Allemande. {1685-} +A figure in a play-party dance, in which the gentleman swings the lady to the right or left; hence, a call to execute such a figure. — **1883** C. PHELPS in *Harper's Mag.* Jan. 284/1 What pressure of hands was exchanged when Sandy authorized 'alamande left'!

Alleviator. {1811-} +'A contrivance for raising sick and wounded persons from bed, in order to change the linen, &c.' (Th.). — **1824** *Mass. Spy* 15 Dec., Jenks's Alleviator.

***ALLEY.**[1]

***1.** A lane or narrow passageway in a town.

1640 *Conn. H. S. Coll.* XIV. 66 Abuttinge ... on the ally leadinge to the meetinge house. **1650** *Harvard Rec.* I. 34 To the cook [belongs] ... the way leader to the hatch door the turret & the north alley unto the walk. **1701** *Boston Rec.* 11 In any of the streets, highwayes, lanes or alleyes within this Neck of Boston. **1717** *Boston Selectmen* 15 The sd. Sel. M. resolved upon & actually layd out a six foot alley thro' John Jepsons land. **1742** *N. H. Probate Rec.* III. 97 All that part of said dwelling house which is on the eastward side of the alley or entry going into said house. **1794** *Mass. H. S. Coll.* III. 248 The following enumeration at this period (1794) is the most accurate that can be obtained, viz. ninety-seven streets, thirty-six lanes, twenty-six alleys, eighteen courts, a few squares. **1812** *Ann. 12th Congress* 1 Sess. 2289 To cause the avenues, streets, lanes, and alleys, to be kept clean, and to appoint officers for that purpose. **1828** A. SHERBURNE *Mem.* (1831) x. 212 The alley or gate-way which led from the street to Mr. Baldwin's meeting-house. **1833** *Niles' Reg.* XLIV. 162/1 This ground has been closely built upon, having one narrow street ... and many narrow lanes and alleys from thence to the wharves. **1875** STOWE *We & Our Neighbors* 174 He started out on his usual afternoon tour of ... ministration in one of the poorest alleys of his neighborhood. **1891** J. A. RIIS *How Other Half Lives* 21 Once I asked the agent of a notorious Fourth Ward alley how many people might be living in it.

+**b.** A narrow roadway laid out at a more or less regular interval between streets; a lane cutting directly across a block or square in the rear of the houses or other buildings and serving as a means of access to these for various purposes.

1729 *Baltimore Town Rec.* 10 The commissioners ... shall cause the same sixty acres to be ... divided into convenient streets, lanes, and allies, as near as may be into sixty equal lots. **1747** *Ib.* 22 To survey the same and lay it out into lotts with convenient streets and alleys. **1809** *Ann. 10th Congress* 2 Sess. 1805 Whenever the proprietor ... shall ... subdivide such square or lot into convenient building lots ... and alleys for their accommodation. **1817** S. BROWN *Western Gaz.* 101 Each block of lots has the advantage of two 16 feet alleys. **1835** J. MARTIN *Descr. Virginia* 139 Fire plugs are connected with the distributing pipes at every intersection of the alleys with 2nd. and 3rd. streets. **1844** *Indiana Senate J.* 63 An act to vacate a certain alley in the town of West Logan. **1865** MRS. WHITNEY *Gayworthys* xli. 378 She entered by the brick alley that tunnelled the block half a dozen doors below. **1880** *Harper's Mag.* July 261/1 It was a house standing a little back from the street; and an alley ran along one side of the lot. **1893** 'MARK TWAIN' *P. Wilson* Introd., William Hicks ... is still helping ... in Macaroni Vermicelli's horse-feed shed which is up the back alley as you turn around the corner.

+**2.** An open passage left in a field to facilitate cultivation or harvesting; a space between the rows of a standing crop.

1833 SILLIMAN *Man. Sugar Cane* 17 There is great danger of disturbing the roots, which ... extend far into the alleys. **1856** *Rep. Comm. Patents: Agric.* p. xl, Run a single-horse plough through the alleys several times to keep the earth mellow and clean. **1862** *Ib.* 471 Alleys are needed in a large vineyard to facilitate getting about when harvesting.

***3.** A narrow enclosure used for playing bowls, nine-pins, ten-pins, &c.

1825- [see BOWLING ALLEY]. **1835-** [see TEN-PIN]. **1895** *Outing* Aug. 444/1 Like a ten-pin ball sent spinning down its alley.

***4.** An aisle or passageway between pews in a church. {-1776} See also BROAD ALLEY.

1646 *Dedham Rec.* 115 To make the seats in the meeting house ... on the east side of the middle alley in the old house. **1688** SEWALL *Diary* I. 203 [The corpse was] carried in at the western dore, and set in the alley before the pulpit. **1697** *Braintree Rec.* 36 Uniting the mens seats with the womens in the present alley [of the meeting-house]. **1737** E. PARKMAN *Diary* 27 After the blessing and when I was down in the alley going out. **1742** *Md. Hist. Mag.* VIII. 361 To enlarge the pew ... from the outermost angle of the pulpet to the alley.

b. A passage between stalls, etc.

1901 *Vermont Dairymen's Assoc. Rep.* 66 A file of a dozen milkers marched down one of the long alleys [in a dairy].

Alley.[2] [Abbr. of *alabaster.*] A marble or taw; orig. one made of alabaster or real marble. {1720-}

1848 BARTLETT 7 [An] alley ... is often made of white marble or of painted clay. **1859** ELWYN *Glossary* 15 'A white alley,' may be heard from every school-boy in the marble season. **1876** 'MARK TWAIN' *Tom Sawyer* ii. 27 I'll give you a marvel. I'll give you a white alley ... White alley, Jim; and it's a bully taw.

Alley-pin. [ALLEY *n.*[1] 3.] A ten-pin. — **1856** *Knickerb.* XLVII. 278 Occasionally the car is brought to a full stop, and the 'standees' are thrown against each other like alley-pins by a 'ten-strike.'

+**Alleyway.** [ALLEY *n.*[1] 1, 4.]

1. A narrow lane in a town; an alley.

1788 FRENEAU *Misc. Works* 223 The article stipulated expressly, that the alley-way should be sufficient for the passing and repassing of the plaintiff. **1841** *Knickerb.* XVII. 286 There's another one playin' out in the alley-vay [*sic*]. **1850** C. MATHEWS *Moneypenny* 100 A very mean and low account of a writer who ... lived in an alley-way. **1882** *Harper's Mag.* June 81 Substantial walls of adobe, with narrow alleyways running between. **1895** G. KING *New Orleans* 128 Lepers, who ... infested the alleyways and corners.

2. A narrow passageway, as in a barn, a steamship, or a house.

1854 *Harper's Mag.* IX. 849/2, I was taken to the Auburn state-prison. And as I walked along the concealed alley-ways, ... I bethought me of my theft of fruit. **1903** C. MOFFETT *Careers of Danger* 382 Our side of the cab is quite cut off from the fireman's side by a swelling girth of boiler, which leaves an alleyway at right or left wide enough for a man's body and no wider. **1904** *N. Y. Tribune* 31 July, [The cattleman on a boat] shakes the hay loose, and carries it along the alleyways in front of the cattle. **1911** J. VANCE *Cynthia* 171 Cynthia entered the other stateroom and shut the door to the alleyway.

+**All-fired,** *a. colloq.* Extreme, excessive, 'terrible.' Also in superl. *allfiredest.*

'Probably a puritanical corruption of *hell-fired*' (B. '59).

(1)1835 *Boston Pearl* 28 Nov. (Th.) His boss gin him a most all-fired cut with a horsewhip. **1842** 'UNCLE SAM' *Peculiarities* I. 217 In our all-fired haste in going a-head. *Ib.* II. 19, I'd get all fired applause for it. **1845** *Knickerb.* XXVI. 182 The doctor 'll charge an all-fired price. **1853** KENNEDY *Backwater Chron.* viii. 104 You have fairly run away from me up this infernal all-fired hill. **1854** M. J. HOLMES *Tempest & Sunshine* xv. 205, I hate dreams mightily, for it takes me an allfired while to get to sleep all over. **a1861** WINTHROP *J. Brent* xxvi. 279 Fourteen hundred dollars—an all-fired price. **1888** *Cincinnati Enquirer* (F.) One morning I heard an all-fired screaming and yelling down below my hut in a deep hollow. **1902** BANKS *Newspaper Girl* 17 It's an all-fired shame for girls to be working in newspaper offices at night.

(2)1851 *Polly Peablossom* 52, I hearn the alfiredest crackin' in the cane. **1854** M. J. HOLMES *Tempest & Sunshine* xxii. 303 If this isn't a leetle the allfiredest muss a feller ever got into, Josh ain't no judge. **1864** LOWELL *Fireside Travels* 192 This 'ere's the allfiredest, powerfullest moon 't ever you did see. **1885** D. PORTER *Incidents of Civil War* (1886) 187, I reckon you'd think so ef you seen it [a Confederate ram]; it's the allfiredest strong thing ever I seen. **1898** WESTCOTT *D. Harum* 182, I had the all-firedist lickin' ahead of me 't I'd ever got.

+**All-fired,** *adv. colloq.* [Cf. prec.] Extremely, exceedingly, inordinately.

1837 *Yale Lit. Mag.* II. 149 Star's an all-fired good ox. **1843** *Ib.* IX. 73 Won't it make Mister Hugh all-fired mad though, when he hears on't. **1847** *Great Kalamazoo Hunt* 50, I was so all-fired blowed that I hadn't wind enough left to laugh. **1853** 'P. PAXTON' *Yankee in Texas* 121, I rode an all fired smart chunk of a pony. **1857** *Knickerb.* XLIX. 41 And this was little Sam, whom I remembered as an 'all-fired' cute youngster. **1865** *Atlantic Mo.* XV. 671, I didn't feel so all-fired cold as I hev sometimes. **1874** *Vermont Bd. Agric. Rep.* 662 Another gentleman thought it would take an all-fired smart man to steer the roller. **1884** NYE *Baled Hay* 89, I ... go up under the trees ... and think how all-fired pleasant ... them little, short lives was. **1915** D. R. CAMPBELL *Proving Virginia* 69 But the money come all-fired slow.

+**All-firedly,** *adv. colloq.* [f. ALL-FIRED *a.*] Exceedingly; inordinately.

1833 GREENE *Dod. Duckworth* II. 176 He was seldom downright drunk; but was often all-firedly sprung. **1850** JUDD *R. Edney* vii. 108 You will get all-firedly licked. **1854** MILNE *Farm Fence* 8 (B.) Wonder if it is rum that makes potatoes rot so all-firedly.

All-fours. A game at cards, now known as 'seven-up.' {1707-1851}

'So named from the four particulars by which it is reckoned, and which, joined in the hand of either of the parties, are said to make all-fours. The *all four* are *high, low, Jack* and *the game*' (Johnson).

1732 *S. C. Gazette* 26/2 The widow ... had determined the event of a short courtship between a certain gentleman and herself, by a game at all-fours. **1774** FITHIAN *Journal* I. 163, I am ashamed that I may record here what does no honour to my old aunt. I saw her with three partners round a table playing cards at that vulgar game fit only for the meanest gamblers 'all fours.' **1805-9** HENRY *Camp. Quebec* 141 The play was for biscuit, and most usually at a game called 'all-fours.' **1818** WEEMS *Lett.* III. 225 He was easily over-persuaded ... to try his luck at All Fours. **1832** KENNEDY *Swallow Barn* I. 59, I ... carefully paid off sundry small debts of honour, contracted at the forbidden game of all fours. **1837** *Knickerb.* X. 379 Put him down to 'all fours,' and he will play game. **1857** [D. H. STROTHER] *Virginia* 41 The parties [=disappointed fishers] ... betook themselves to 'all-fours' for the remainder of the day. **1859** HALE *If, Yes, & Perhaps* (1868) 187 Dennis could see into the card-room, and came to Polly to ask if he might not go and play allfours.

+**All-hands,** *a. Naut.* Engaging the whole crew. Also ellipt. — **1840** DANA *Two Years* xxxiii. 424 The first day of 'all hands,' one of those little incidents occurred. *Ib.* 431 Under the 'all hands' system, out of every other thirty-six hours, we had only four below. **1841** — *Seaman's Man.* 167 The cook ... is also expected to pull and haul about decks in all-hands work.

***All-heal.** {1597-1725} +(See quotations) — **1737** BRICKELL *N. Carolina* 22 Stargrass ... is used with good Success in most Fevers in this Country; Rushes of several sorts; the Herb Mastick, Indian-all-heal. **1784** CUTLER in *Mem. Academy* I. 461 *Galeopsis* ... Allheal. Hemp-leaved Dead-Nettle. Blossoms purple. By the roadside. Gloucester. August.

All hollow: see HOLLOW *adv.*

+**All horse.** Completely developed as, or like, a horse. — **1860** HOLMES *Professor* vii. 197 It is a common saying of a jockey that he is 'all horse.' **1868** WOODRUFF *Trotting Horse* 50 At ten, you have probably got no horse at all worth mentioning: while mine is now 'all horse,' and in his true prime.

* **Alligator.**

* **1.** A lizard-like reptile resembling the crocodile; also, the true crocodile, found in Florida. (Cf. 'GATOR.)

1682 ASH *Carolina* 32 There is in the mouth of their rivers, or in lakes near the sea, a creature . . . call'd the alligator or crocodile, whose scaly back is impenitrable. **1709** LAWSON *Carolina* 126 The allegator. . . . They frequent the sides of the rivers, in the banks of which they make their dwellings. **1738** STEPHENS *Proc. Georgia* 165 An alligator snapped one, and carried him quite off. **c1740** CATESBY *Carolina* II. 63 The alligator. . . . In Carolina they lie torpid, from about October to March, in caverns and hollows in the banks of rivers; and at their coming out in the spring, make an hideous bellowing noise. **1781–2** JEFFERSON *Notes Va.* (1787) 6 Alligators . . . have been seen as high up as the Acansas [*sic*]. **1782** ST. JOHN *Lett.* 236 The southern provinces are the countries where nature has formed the greatest variety of alligators, snakes, serpents. **1791** BARTRAM *Travels* 90, I have made use of the terms alligator and crocodile indiscriminately for this animal, alligator being the country name. **1806** *Ann. 9th Congress* 2 Sess. 1117 Notwithstanding . . . the northern latitude . . . , they [=Lewis and Clark expedition] this day met with an alligator. **1812** STODDARD *Sk. Louisiana* 163 Alligators of various sizes are numerous in all the waters of the low country. **1819** E. DANA *Geog. Sketches* 51 The Alligator, too well known to require description, is not now dreaded by the inhabitants, though it formerly was considered ferocious and dangerous. **1834** [R. BAIRD] *Valley Mississippi* v. 44 The alligator abounds in the rivers and marshes as far north as 34°. **1850** [LEWIS] *La. Swamp Doctor* 197 The unmelodious bellow of the alligator . . . arose from a lake. **1882** *Amer. Naturalist* XVI. 533 The hunting of alligators in Florida is carried on to such an extent as to threaten the extirpation of the species there.

fig. **1883** SHIELDS *S. S. Prentiss* 399 In his argument of the cause he was unusually severe upon the opposite party. The papers had announced that there was to be 'a skinning of the alligator,' and many were present to enjoy the fun and excitement.

+**2. a.** The 'hellbender' or 'mud-devil,' *Menopoma alleghe-niensis.*

'[Used] in the Western States' (B. '59).

+**b.** *local.* 'The little brown fence-lizard, *Sceloporus undulatus*, common in many parts of the United States' (*Cent.*).

+**c.** *Conn.* The larva of the hellgrammite (*Corydalus cornutus*), a favorite bait for the bass.

c1893 *Dialect Notes* I. 339.

+**3. a.** Nickname for a Mississippi keelboatman, rough-and-ready frontiersman or Indian fighter. (Cf. *half-horse, half-alligator.*)

1808 SCHULTZ *Travels* (1810) II. 145 One said, 'I am a man; I am a horse; I am a team. . . . The other replied, 'I am an alligator, half man, half horse; can whip any on the Mississippi by G-d.' [**1814** *Analectic Mag.* IV. 63 The Mississippi navigator, who affirmed himself to be 'all alligator but his head, which was of aqua-fortis.'] **1837** BIRD *Nick of Woods* II. 246 He . . . launched his broad-horn on the narrow bosom of the Salt, and was soon afterwards transformed into a Mississippi alligator. **1850** [LEWIS] *La. Swamp Doctor* 82 The Kentuckian . . . disclosed a set of teeth that clearly showed that his half of the alligator lay above.

+**b.** *colloq.* A member of the Virginia House of Delegates. *Obs.*

c1870 BAGBY *Old Va. Gentleman* 290 This bell . . . called the truant 'Alligators' from their haunts in the barrooms and faro-banks when there was a close vote in the General Assembly. *Ib.* 291.

+**4.** A hog of an inferior breed; a razor-back.

1841 *Cultivator* VIII. 152, I am anxious that he should soon get rid of his land-pikes and alligators at such prices as will enable him to buy a better breed. **1852** *Mich. Agric. Soc. Trans.* III. 332 Swine variously known as narragansetts, alligators, land sharks and flea breeders.

+**5.** Attrib. with *hunt, season, shooting, steak, tribe,* etc.

1825 NEAL *Bro. Jonathan* II. 438 Somewhat o' the alligator tribe. **1836** *Knickerb.* VIII. 153, [I] was out . . . in a canoe near this place, on an alligator hunt. **1846** THORPE *Myst. Backwoods* 142 Certainty of aim, therefore, tells in alligator shooting, as it does in every thing else connected with sporting. **1852** *Knickerb.* XL. 52 Taking up my rifle, (which I always carry in alligator-season,) I jumped ashore. **1856** W. A. PHILLIPS *Conquest of Kansas* 285 Queer-looking, alligator guns these were, for we recaptured some of them when the war broke out. **1868** *Putnam's Mag.* I. 592/2 La Salle and his companions existed . . . on alligator-steaks.

b. In sense 3 a, with *breed, dialect.*

1835 *Cincinnati Mirror* in *Niles' Reg.* XLIX. 116/2 These Yankees . . . soon . . . pick up our odd bits of snapping turtle and alligator dialect, and put on our habits. **1838** *Bentley's Miscel.* IV. 590 We [Kentuckians] are the critturs, the real ky-an alligator breed, strong as a steam-enjine.

c. In the sense: Made of alligator skin.

1869 W. MURRAY *Adventures* 26 A pair of huge alligator-leather boots. **1892** *Harper's Mag.* Feb. 486/2 'Are you the man who invented paper soles for shoes?' . . . 'Yes, sir; also . . . paper alligator bags.' **1907** W. LILLIBRIDGE *Trail* 173 A dapper commercial salesman with an imitation alligator grip.

+**Alligator boat. a.** Apparently: A boat towed by an alligator or alligators. *Humorous.* **b.** A boat facetiously alleged to be used for dredging alligators out of the Mississippi. — **1844** *Spirit of Times* (Phila.) 10 Sept. (Th.) It takes a man . . . to ride one of these here alligator boats head on to a sawyer. **1883** 'MARK TWAIN' *Life Mississippi* xxiv. 230 He . . . observed that it was an 'alligator boat.' 'An alligator boat? What's it for?'

+**Alligator fish.** (See quotations.)

1772 ROMANS in Phillips *Notes* (1924) 124 There is also a fish called the gar fish or allegator fish from the shape of its head and teeth. **1807** C. SCHULTZ *Travels* I. 123, I have been well assured that this river produces a fish which, from its resemblance to the alligator, is called the Alleghany alligator fish. — **1889** *Cent., Alligator fish,* an agonoid fish, *Podothecus acipenserinus*, . . . common from Puget Sound northward.

+**Alligator gar.** [Cf. GAR.] The gar-pike (*Lepidosteus tristoechus*), found in southern waters.

1832 *Amer. Naturalist* XVI. 383 The Alligator Gar . . . [is] often seen in the waters of the Mississippi, twelve or fourteen feet long. **1841** W. KENNEDY *Texas* 132 The alligator gar . . . is armed with almost impenetrable scales, and, from its strength and voracity, may be termed the river-shark. **1846** THORPE *Myst. Backwoods* 38 The alligator gar grows to the enormous length of fifteen feet; its head resembles the alligator's; within its wide-extended jaws glisten innumerable rows of teeth. **1851** *Polly Peablossom* 129, I was nearly thrown into the lake by the plunge of a monster alligator gar. **1871** DE VERE 383 His name of Alligator Gar refers less to these hostile meetings than to his resemblance to the reptile.

+**Alligator hide.** =ALLIGATOR SKIN. — **1883** 'MARK TWAIN' *Life Mississippi* xxiv. 268 All the government shoes are made of alligator-hide. **1894** 'O. HENRY' *Cabbages & Kings* xii. 217 Even old Doc. Gregg wants three pairs of alligator-hide slippers.

+**Alligator hole.** A nest or hibernating place of alligators.

1797 B. HAWKINS *Letters* 85 It was then difficult to find water anywhere; . . . he had often been under the necessity of hunting for alligator holes to get some. **1842** BUCKINGHAM *Slave States* I. 155 In their retreats, or nests, called alligator-holes, as large a brood as a hundred are seen at a time. **1853** SIMMS *Sword & Distaff* 171 He raised himself out of the alligator hole which had harbored him.

+**Alligatorism.** [ALLIGATOR 3.] Roughness of character. — **1830** Perrin *Ky. Pioneer Press* (1888) 77 Each party kept half a dozen bullies under pay, genuine specimens of Kentucky alligatorism, to flog every poor fellow who should attempt to vote illegally.

Alligator pear. The tree *Persea persea* or *gratissima* of the southern States, or its fruit; the avocado. {1763–}

1766 STORK *E. Florida* 61 The plantane-tree and allegator pear, the tenderest of the tropical plants, are in full perfection at Augustine. **1806** WEBSTER, *Avocado,* the alligator pear. **1813** MUHLENBERG *Cat. Plants* 41 *Laurus . . . persea,* alligator pear. Louisiana. **1869** J. G. FULLER *Flower Gatherers* 140 There is another small laurel . . . which produces a fine fruit called the Alligator Pear. **1870** *Amer. Naturalist* III. 401 The *Persea Carolinensis*, or Alligator pear, sometimes called the Red Bay.

+**Alligator skin.** The dressed skin of the alligator.

1820 *Boston Daily Advertiser* 3 July 2/5 Alligator and seal skins. **1838** C. GILMAN *Recoll.* xix. 132 Coarse oak chairs, seated with hickory shavings, or deer or alligator skins. **1884** SWEET & KNOX *Through Texas* i. 19 His long boots of alligator-skin reached to his knees. **1886** P. STAPLETON *Major's Christmas* 70 Giddy mashers with their alligater skin carpet bags. **1890** *Harper's Mag.* May 916/2 She could have left . . . his masks in her alligator-skin bag.

+**Alligator snapper.** =ALLIGATOR TURTLE 2. — **1884** GOODE *Nat. Hist. Aquat. Animals* 153, I have myself seen an 'Alligator Snapper,' of perhaps forty pounds weight.

+**Alligator tail.** The tail of an alligator, used in making soup. — **1844** *Knickerb.* XXIII. 365 The soup from alligator-tail being very palatable and delicate, a speculation was afoot contemplating the supply of the northern market with that article. **1855** SIMMS *Forayers* 510 Gi' me two young alligator tail, . . . and I gi' you fus' rate tuttle soup.

+**Alligator terrapin.** The snapping turtle, *Chelydra serpentina,* found east of the Rocky Mts. — **1835** SIMMS *Partisan* 317 Three enormous terrapins of that doubtful brood which the vulgar in the southern country describe as the alligator terrapin. **1855** — *Forayers* 545 What we call the alligator terrapin is the best of the tribe—the fattest, richest, best flavored. **1891** *Cent.* s.v. *Snapping-turtle,* The alligator-terrapin or alligator-tortoise . . . is common in the rivers and streams of North America, and attains a large size.

+**Alligator tooth.** A special form of tine for a harrow or similar implement. — **1856** *Mich. Agric. Soc. Trans.* VII. 629 Alligator tooth, by S. B. Scranton. This tooth was one of a number designed to be used on marshes for tearing down the bogs and making them smooth.

+**Alligator tortoise.** The alligator terrapin. — **1839** STORER *Mass. Reptiles* 212 The snake tortoise . . . Its crested tail . . . gives it the distinction at the South, of 'alligator tortoise.' **1891** [see ALLIGATOR TERRAPIN].

+**Alligator tree.** 'The sweet-gum tree, *Liquidambar styraciflua*, of the southern United States' (*Cent.*); so called from the ridges on its branches.

+**Alligator turtle. 1.** The alligator terrapin. **2.** A large snapping-turtle (*Macrochelys lacertina*) of the Southern United States (*Cent.*). — (1)**1842** *Nat. Hist. N. Y., Zoology* III. 8 The Snapping Turtle . . . is one of our largest turtles. . . . In other sections, it is known under the names of Logger-head, Alligator Turtle and Couta. **1885** *Stand. Nat. Hist.* (1888) III. 452 The elongated tail of the animal . . . has . . . given rise to the popular name, 'alligator-turtle.'

+**Allize.** *Obs.* The alewife. — **1637** MORTON *New Canaan* 89 There is a fish, (by some called shadds, by some allizes,) that at the spring of the yeare passe up the rivers to spaune in the ponds.

+**All man.** *colloq.* A man through and through. — **1895** REMINGTON *Pony Tracks* 77 If a man is to 'hold down' a big ranch in Northern Mexico he has got to be 'all man,' because it is 'a man's job.'

+**All-nation,** *adv. colloq.* [Cf. TARNATION.] Exceedingly. — **1847** *Knickerb.* XXX. 14 With the remark, that it was 'all-nation hot inside the clap-boards.'

Allodial, *a.* Involving or held in full ownership. {1656-} **1796** *Ann. 4th Congress* 2 Sess. 2708 In this country, where lands are generally held and cultivated under allodial tenures, the sums of money for which lands are commonly sold afford a more correct standard. **1818** DARBY *Emigrant's Guide* 5 When the papers containing the whole of these preliminary proceedings were returned to the land office in New Orleans, the final patent issued, granting the land in (Franc-alleu,) allodial tenure. **1828** WEBSTER s.v. *Allodium*, In the United States, most lands are allodial.

All of.

+**1.** As much as; no less than; quite; at least.

1829 SANDS *Writings* II. 57 They actually appointed a sub-committee, consisting of Miss Cross, who was all of six feet high. **1856** *Mich. Agric. Soc. Trans.* VII. 317 He puts down the average price per bbl. at $11, which is all of $2 per bbl. too high. **1862** LOWELL *Biglow P.* II. ii, 'Twould put the clock back all o' fifty years. **1883** 'MARK TWAIN' *Life Mississippi* xviii. 220 It must have been all of fifteen minutes . . . of dull, homesick silence. **1898** A. NICHOLAS *Idyl of Wabash* 20 There was Mr. Littledale, all of thirty-one. **1902** WISTER *Virginian* v. 63 It must have been all of ten miles that we had driven when he spoke. **1902** 'MARK TWAIN' in *Harper's Mag.* Feb. 433 'About how far might it be to the scene of the explosion?' 'All of a mile!'

+**2.** *For all of me (him, etc.)*, as far as I care.

1854 M. J. HOLMES *Tempest & Sunshine* xix. 267 No;—he may have her and go to the old boy for all of Josh. **1889** 'MARK TWAIN' *Conn. Yankee* xxii. 143 So I got his bandana, he could keep his hardware for all of me. **1903** K. D. WIGGIN *Rebecca* xxii. 241 She can sit where she likes for all of me. **1911** HARRISON *Queed* xvii. 209 Thus they parted, almost precipitately, and, for all of him, might never have met again in this world.

Allopeen, obs. variant of ALEPINE.

* **Allot,** *v.*

* **1.** *tr.* To apportion or assign (land) to a person. (Cf. LOT *v.*)

1622 'MOURT' *Relation* 68 To greater families we allotted larger plots, to every person halfe a pole in breadth, and three in length. **1632** *Plymouth Col. Rec.* I. 5 An acre of land was allowed and allotted to each person. **1642** *Springfield Rec.* I. 170 To lay out the lands, . . . allotinge to every present inhabitant his proportion. **1719** *Mass. H. Repr. Journals* II. 208 A committee fully empowered by this court to allott out the lands. **1835** *Govt. Contract* in Thoburn *Hist. Oklahoma* (1916) 74 To remove the Creek Indians . . . to a point in the new country allotted to the Creeks west of the territory of Arkansas. **1885** *Rep. Indian Affairs* 7 Nothing has been done . . . towards completing the work . . . of allotting lands in severalty to Indians. **1908** *Indian Laws & Tr.* III. 383 To enable the Secretary of the Interior to survey, allot, classify, and appraise the lands in said reservation.

+**2.** *intr.* To determine *upon*, to intend. *colloq.* or *dial.*

1816 PICKERING 31 To *Allot* (with the preposition *upon*). Ex. I allot upon going to such a place. This verb is used only in conversation, and that, chiefly in the interior of New England. **1829** *Va. Lit. Museum* 30 Dec. 459 To lot or allot . . . upon going thither. New England [use]. **1888** *Banner of Light* (F.), Senator W. seems to have allotted upon a course that is hardly to be commended.

* **Allotment.** A portion of land specially assigned to a person. Also attrib. with *certificate.*

1635 [see ALLOTTER]. **1636** *Springfield Rec.* I. 157 Which said 40 acres is not disposed to them as any alotments of towne lands. **1639** *R. I. Col. Rec.* I. 89 The home allottments shall be foure acres a piece. **1657** *New Haven Town Rec.* 81 Which meddow was his first alotment from the towne. **1664** *Groton Rec.* 11 The towne has granted vnto Shadock an alotment containing a single mans proportion. **1681** *Early Conn. Prob. Rec.* 291 They agree, by casting lotts, which allottment shall belong to each of them. **1723** *Waterbury Prop. Rec.* 120 He that neglects to take up his alottment in his proper day . . . shall loose his turn. **1741** *Brookhaven Rec.* 150 The said several tracts, parcels and allotments of land and meadow. **1861** *N. Y. Tribune* 30 Dec., President Lincoln had appointed the following persons to provide for allotment certificates among the volunteers from New York State. **1871** *Scribner's Mo.* I. 533 Allotments of land were let at an annual rental. **1883** *Rep. Indian Affairs* 86 Many of them have taken allotments. **1903** *Indian Laws & Tr.* III. 5 Nothing herein contained shall be construed to prevent allottees from disposing of timber and stone on their allotments.

Allottee. One who receives an allotment or to whom an allotment is due. Also *attrib.* {1846-}

1866 *Rep. Indian Affairs* 264 A limited number of allottees, under the treaty of 1861, heads of families, have . . . received patents for their land. **1885** *Ib.* 112 The majority of the allottee class have squandered their property. **1909** *Indian Laws & Tr.* III. 385 The allotment of any Indian . . . held in trust by the U. S. for the use and benefit of the allottee.

+**Allotter.** One who makes allotments. {1862} — **1635** *Boston Rec.* 5 That none shall sell their houses or allotments to any new comers, but with the consent and allowance of those that are appointed allotters. *Ib.* 7 Four of them shall, by the assignments of the Allotters, lay out their proportion of allotments for farmes att Rumley Marsh.

* **All over.**

+**1.** Throughout, in all respects, consistently.

1834 DAVIS *Lett. J. Downing* 41 Now this is the Gineral all over; and I am off to-morrow to Philadelphia. *c***1846** *Southern Standard* (B.), We have read this work so far with great interest; it is Dickens all over. **1880** 'MARK TWAIN' *Tramp Abroad* xxxix. 456 That is European management, all over! An inch a day—think of that!

+**2.** Everywhere; all places.

1904 *Rochester Post Express* 12 Sept. 3 News Flashes from All Over. **1906** *Harper's Mag.* Oct. 764 They'd been hunting all over for her. **1911** *N. Y. Evening Post* 12 Jan. 16 They came from all over, and showed it. They were . . . from every section of the country.

+**All-overish,** *a.* [f. prec. Cf. 'an all-over sort of feeling' {1851}.] Generally indisposed or out of sorts.

1833 *Sketches Crockett* 52, I wish I may be shot if I know how I felt; but I tell you what, it made me feel quite all-overish. **1843** [STEPHENS] *High Life in N. Y.* I. 168 There is a terrible all-overish sort of a feeling in a young feller when he's been a cruising among the gals all day. **1855** *Putnam's Mag.* Dec. 575/1, I felt the satire to its full extent. I grew —all-over-ish, no other phrase expresses it. **1899** GREEN *Va. Word-Book* 33 To feel all-overish.

+**All-overishness.** [f. prec.] A feeling of general indisposition.

1845 S. SMITH *Theatr. Apprent.* 216 A feeling of all-over-ish-ness, like that experienced by a timid child while enjoying (?) the luxury of a cold shower-bath. **1874** EGGLESTON *Circuit Rider* vi. 61, I feel a kind of all-overishness myself.

* **Allow,** *v.*

* **1.** *intr.* To approve or accept *of;* to permit or sanction. {-1748}

1638 *Springfield Rec.* I. 165 It shall be esteemed that the Plantation doth allowe of the said purchase. *a***1656** BRADFORD *Hist.* 307 [They] so farr proceeded in as they were constrained to allow therof. *Ib.* 325 They would not alow of what Mr. Allerton did alone, except they liked it. **1660** *Springfield Rec.* I. 202 Before . . . the Select Townsmen . . . allow of his admission. **1691** *Witchcraft Cases* 179 Spiritual teachers, who . . . do yet allow of, encourage, yea, and practise this very abomination. **1721** *Mass. H. Repr. Journals* III. 16 An Account of Mr. John Dyer . . . read and allowed of. **1819** WALSH *Appeal from Judgements Gt. Brit.* 5 To allow of no printing press. **1855** ABBOTT *Napoleon* II. 322 They would allow of no neutrality.

2. To declare, to maintain; to think or believe. *colloq.* or *dial.* {1875- *dial.*}

1825 NEAL *Bro. Jonathan* I. 28 Her large eyes would sparkle—so the men 'allowed'—like the mischief. **1835** HOFFMAN *Winter in West* II. 125 He was very glad I was going his way, as 'he allowed the gentleman to be right good company, and he did not mistrust but that we'd have a tip-top time of it.' **1847** PARKMAN in *Knickerb.* XXX. 22 If they couldn't, why he allowed he'd find out how to make 'em! **1849** N. KINGSLEY *Diary* 66 He allowed he never enjoyed an evening so well in his life. **1853** 'P. PAXTON' *Yankee in Texas* 114 'I allow,' meaning 'I think,' 'I consider,' is, I believe, of Alabama origin. **1856** E. W. FARNHAM *California* 207 In those days they 'allowed' that California was no better than other countries. **1864** NORTON *Army Lett.* 216 He 'allowed it was all up with him,' and I allowed ditto. **1866** C. H. SMITH *Bill Arp* 22 Where is Hamlin? I allow that he is dead, or I would ask him too. **1871** G. A. TOWNSEND *Mormon Trials* 13 Well, in the first place, he allowed he was doing his religious duties, and he allowed that he had got to live with some one else. **1876** BRET HARTE *G. Conroy* xxxvii, I allows one thing, he allows another, and this yer man gives me the lie and I stabs him! **1891** RYAN *Told in Hills* 91, I allow we'd better freeze to it. **1898** WESTCOTT *D. Harum* 138 He'll allow that if he gits in the fust word, he'll take the pole.

+**3.** To purpose or intend (to do something). *colloq.* or *dial.*

1875 BRET HARTE *Tales Argonauts* 11, I allowed to go to bed. **1890** RYAN *Told in Hills* 199, I didn't allow to come to the house myself. **1891** — *Pagan* 235 Now what you allow to do about it?

+**All-possessed,** *adv.* [See POSSESSED *a.*] Extremely, desperately. — **1881** *Harper's Mag.* Oct. 750/2 You needn't be so all-possessed poor that you can't pay an honest woman for . . . cooking your venison.

+**All-rail,** *a.* Wholly by rail. — **1879** *Lumberman's Gaz.* 3 Dec. This is probably the first all-rail shipment of lumber from the interior of Michigan to a far western State.

All-round, *a.* and *n.* **a.** Extending completely around; fitting closely all the way round. **b.** A collar of this kind. — **1860** HOLMES *Professor* vi. 134 If any of my young friends should be tempted to waste their substance on white kids and 'all-rounds' . . . by anything I have said. **1866** MRS. WHITNEY *L. Goldthwaite* xvi. 226 A cane, an all-round white collar, and a natty little tie.

Alls, *n. pl. S.* {1721–63; now *dial.*} One's belongings. — **1830** A. ROYALL *Southern Tour* I. 153, I shall not go without you, so pack up your alls and be ready.

+**All sorts of,** *adj. phr.* Of a comprehensive character. (Used esp. to express commendation.)

1841 *Corr. R. W. Griswold* 93, I wish you to write 'all sorts' of an article for the Messenger. **1844** POE *Thingum Bob* Wks. 1914 IV. 179 To pen an Ode upon the 'Oil-of-Bob' Is all sorts of a job. **1847** [ROBB] *Squatter Life* 133 She was all sorts of a gal—thar warn't a sprinklin' too much of her. **1852** [HALIBURTON] *Traits Amer. Humor* I. 229 If you can only get Kit rid of them little failings, you'll find him all sorts of a horse.

Allspice.

1. The West Indian spice also known as 'pimenta,' from the berries of the tree *Eugenia pimenta.* {1621–}

1707 *Boston News-Letter* 27 Jan. 2/2 To be sold on reasonable terms . . ., Jamaica & Leeward-Islands fine sugar, pemento or all spice. **1711** *Ib.* 12 March 2/2 Alspice, pepper, and ginger . . . to be sold by Zabdiel Boylston, at his shop . . . in Boston. **1759** *Newport* (R.I.) *Mercury* 26 June 4/3 Imported . . . and to be sold by Jacob Richardson, . . . pepper, allspice, tea, coffee. **1806** *Austin Papers* (1924) I. 105, 100 lb. allspice. **1878** *Amer. Home Cook Book* 104 Add half an ounce of allspice.

+**2.** One or other of certain aromatic shrubs native to the U. S., as the Carolina and the wild allspice (see quots.).

1768 MILLER *Gard. Dict.* (ed. 8) I. 3 The bark . . . has a very strong aromatic scent; from whence the inhabitants of Carolina gave it the title of Allspice. **1785** MARSHALL *Amer. Grove* 24 *Calycanthus floridus.* Carolinian Allspice. **1802** J. DRAYTON *S. Carolina* 72 Sweet scented shrub, or Carolina alspice, (*Calycanthus Floridus,*) grows abundantly in the middle and upper country, near low lands. **1813** MUHLENBERG *Cat. Plants* 41 *Laurus . . . benzoin* (allspice, feverbush). Pens. fl. Apr. Car. *Ib.* 51 *Calycanthus.* Allspice, shrub . . . ; downy. Car. Pens. H. fl. Apr. **1847** DARLINGTON *Weeds & Plants* 286 Wild Allspice. Fever-bush. . . . An infusion of the brittle spicy twigs . . . is now chiefly prescribed as a diet-drink for sickly cows, in the spring of the year. **1859** BARTLETT 434 Wild Allspice . . . [was] formerly used as a substitute for allspice.

3. Attrib. (in sense 1) with *tree.*

1709 LAWSON *Carolina* 104 In the same [low] ground commonly grows the Piemento, or All-spice tree.

All-standing, *adv.* [Of nautical origin {1824–}.]

1. Without warning or preparation; suddenly.

1837 *S. Lit. Messenger* III. 178 This reflection brought me up, as the sailors say, 'all standing.' **1844** KENDALL *Narr.* I. 60, I walked directly off the giddy height—to use a common expression, went over all-standing. *a***1846** *Quarter Race Kentucky,* etc. 63 A woman . . . sprung at his head . . . and caught him by the wool, bringing him up 'all standing.'

+**2.** (See quot. 1846.)

1840 DANA *Two Years* xxxi. 373 The mate . . . turned in 'all standing,' and was always on deck the moment he was called. **1846** LEVINGE *Echoes fr. Backwoods* I. 235 He had turned in with all his clothes on, as he had done during the three nights on board the schooner, what the Yankees term 'all standing,' viz., in boots, great coat, &c.

||**All-to-pieces,** *a.* [See PIECE *n.*] Thorough-going; excessive. — **1846–51** [WHITCHER] *Bedott P.* xi. 123 She was an all-to-pieces snuff-taker, ye know.

+**Alluviation.** The process of depositing alluvium. — **1847** C. LANMAN *Summer in Wild.* 132 They have been striped with various colors by mineral alluviations. **1877** GILBERT *Geol. Henry Mts.* 139 The same may be said of the changes by planation and alluviation. In each case . . . the watershed makes a leap.

***Alluvion.** Matter gradually deposited by a river or by floods; alluvium; land formed by such deposits. {1731–}

1812 JEFFERSON *Writings* XVIII. 65 If the right of alluvion is not given to urban proprietors [of N.O.], much less would it to a mere holder of the bed of a road. **1814** BRACKENRIDGE *Views* 127 In the rich alluvia, it is thought that wheat sowed in the spring is best. **1815** DRAKE *Cincinnati* ii. 69 The older alluvions are composed chiefly of sand, gravel and water worn pebbles. **1827** COOPER *Prairie* xxxii, A solitary willow had taken root in the alluvion. **1831** M. A. HOLLEY *Texas* (1833) 56 Forest trees and undergrowth common in the rich alluvions of the Mississippi. **1838** H. COLMAN *Mass. Agric. Rep.* (1839) 9 There are extended alluvions or intervales, which furnish a productive soil. **1843** N. BOONE *Journal* (1917) 203 The latter part of the day we came to a yellowish alluvion on the red. **1888** *Harper's Mag.* June 41/1 Cutting deep its own alluvion across the magnificent plain of Saline County.

attrib. **1814** BRACKENRIDGE *Views* 159 The alluvion lands constitute the third division. **1832** S. G. GOODRICH *System of Univ. Geog.* 31 There is a remarkable alluvion formation through which the Merrimack passes. **1837** PECK *New Guide* 202 Immediately on the banks of the Ohio, and other large rivers, are strips of rich alluvion soil.

+**All-wheat,** *a.* Wholly of wheat. — **1884** *Rep. Comm. Agric.* 460 The districts where all-wheat farming is practiced.

All wool, All-wool, *a.* {1882} +*fig.* Thoroughly genuine. *colloq.* Usu. with addition of 'and a yard wide.'

1882 PECK *Sunshine* 85 You want to pick out [as the 'boss combination girl' of Rock Co.] a thoroughbred, that is, all wool, a yard wide. **1884** NYE *Baled Hay* 147 The only all-wool, yard-wide bald head we remember on the American stage is . . . worn by . . . Couldock. **1892** *Congress. Rec.* 10 Feb. 1038/1 The people of the State of Ohio are 'all wool and a yard wide' on the subject of sustaining this Government. **1902** HARBEN *A. Daniel* 312 'She's all right,' said Abner Daniel. . . . 'She's all wool an' a yard wide.' **1904** 'O. HENRY' *Heart of West* 239 Standing by it was the good, fine, all-wool girl that never let him know it.

||**Alma.** [L.] Short for 'alma mater' (q. v.). — **1841** TRUMBULL *Autobiog.* 288, I then thought of Yale—although not my alma, yet she was within my native state, and poor.

***Alma mater.** [L., 'fostering mother.'] A metaphorical term for the college or university which one has attended. {1710–}

1696 SEWALL *Diary* I. 435 Lt. Govr. complemented the Pressedent [of Harvard] &c., . . . and promis'd his Interposition for them, as become such an Alumnus to such an Alma Mater. **1725** *Mass. Col. Soc. Publ.* VI. 201, I think they were drawn up in a true Roman diction, & both for language & sentiments exceed anything I ever yet saw from my own Alma Mater. *a***1790** BOWDOIN in Quincy *Hist. Harvard* II. 539, I give to my Alma Mater, the University of Cambridge, . . . four hundred pounds. **1827** *Harvard Reg.* Aug. 161 The time has almost arrived when another brood of our Alma Mater, having been thoroughly instructed, are about to fly of themselves. **1838** *S. Lit. Messenger* IV. 576/1 It was truly delightful to witness the proofs of attachment . . . to the prosperity of their *Alma Mater.* **1842** *Yale Lit. Mag.* VIII. 47 With a spirit worthy of the alma mater, our friends have come forward to our aid. **1860** HOLLAND *Miss Gilbert* xxiii. 400 He had never visited his alma mater with such anticipations of pleasure. **1866** 'F. KIRKLAND' *Bk. Anecdotes* 198 Whatever sums . . . were placed to his credit at his *alma mater.*

***Almanac.** Also † **almanack, -ick.** A pamphlet or book containing a calendar and astronomical data, usually with a variety of other information.

1646 DANFORTH (*title*), An Almanack for the year of our Lord 1646. *a***1649** WINTHROP *Hist.* I. 348 The next [thing printed] was an almanac [for 1639] made for New England by Mr. William Peirce, mariner. **1654** JOHNSON *Wonder-W. Prov.* 165 Mr. Sam. Danforth . . . put forth many Almanacks. **1674** SEWALL *Diary* I. 6 Copys of letters in Almanack, 1672. **1695** *Maine Doc. Hist.* V. 429 [The Indians] left behind them . . . a small bag in which was his beads, crusefix, almanick, & som other tromperey. **1724** *New-Eng. Courant* 16–23 Nov. 2/2 There is just publish'd . . . The New England Diary, or Almanack for the Year of our Lord 1725. **1743** FRANKLIN *Poor Richard 1744* 1 I leave him to settle the affair with the buyers of his almanack. **1768** Chalkley *Scotch-Irish Settlement Va.* I. 462 To . . . 2 alminicks, 1 alminick. **1807** IRVING, etc. *Salmagundi* xiii, I put as implicit faith in poetry as I do in the almanac or the newspaper. **1865** MRS. WHITNEY *Gayworthys* xx. 194 You find from the almanac that the moon, on that night, rose at ten o'clock. **1917** MATHEWSON *Sec. Base Sloan* 91 If they were to believe the almanac, spring had really been there some time.

attrib. **1807** IRVING, etc. *Salmagundi* viii. 164 This is the universal remark among the almanac quidnuncs, and weather-wiseacres of the day.

Almanac-maker. The compiler of an almanac. {1611–}

1705 *Boston News-Letter* 8 Oct. 2/2 There is now published an almanack for 1706 by N.W. with a short Answer to some Reflections cast on him last year by the then Almanack-makers. **1736** FRANKLIN *Poor Richard 1737* 1 However we almanack-makers may miss it in other things . . . we always hit the day of the month. **1788** FRENEAU *Misc. Works* 150 [Poem on] the almanac maker. **1807** IRVING, etc. *Salmagundi* xiii. 283, I have seen many wise men in my time, . . . philosophers, editors, and almanac-makers. **1836** *Quarter Race Kentucky* (1846) 18 Beginning to doubt . . . whether my friend Dave had been regularly appointed almanac-maker for this year, I hedged a five. **1862** *N. Am. Rev.* XCV. 217 Judge Phelps . . . is the almanac-maker of the [Latter-Day] Saints, and has put forth some . . . remarkable predictions.

***Almighty,** *a.* +Unusually great. *colloq.*

1836 CROCKETT *Exploits* 15 He is on the Eve of an almighty thrashing. **1838** DE QUINCEY *Writings* (1897) XIV. 137 Such rubbish, such 'almighty' nonsense (to speak *transatlanticè*), no eye has ever beheld. **1846** CORCORAN *Pickings* 47 You see, the fact is, Squire, they had an almighty deal to say up in our parts about Orleans. **1890** *Congress. Rec.* 23 June 6393/1, I think every man in this House whose olfactory nerves are in a healthy condition can smell an almighty lot of 'smoke' in this bill.

b. In the superlative.

1845 GREEN *Texian Exped.* 91 Yonder is the almightiest fight you ever did see. *a***1846** *Quarter Race Kentucky,* etc. 123–4, I chased that d—d fire a mile and a half, the almightiest hardest race you ever heer'd tell on.

Almighty, *adv.* Exceedingly; monstrously. *colloq.* {1833}

1833 J. JONES *Green Mt. Boy* I. iii, I shall look almighty fierce. **1838** *Lexington Observer & Rep.* 2 June, I ain't so almighty taken with her. *a***1846** *Quarter Race Kentucky,* etc. 156, I have secured Granger, and an almighty tough job I had of it. **1848** DURIVAGE & BURNHAM *Stray Subjects* 109, I felt almighty blue. **1854** M. J. HOLMES *Tempest & Sunshine* v. 69 That's almighty queer stuff to make soup on. **1873** 'MARK

TWAIN' & WARNER *Gilded Age* xxxi. 284 He talked freely with Philip about Ruth, an almighty fine girl, he said. **1878** STOWE *Poganuc People* iii. 35 'Yis,' said Hiel, 'but Sim's almighty plucky.' **1888** *N. Y. Mercury* 21 July (F.) Another passenger to the 'Rookery.' I wonder whether the other boys gits as many customers to that place as Luke Hyatt? If they do it must be almighty full sometimes.

+**Almighty dollar.** The dollar conceived as all powerful.

In the 1855 issue of the *Creole Village* (as a part of *Wolfert's Roost*), Irving claimed that the phrase was 'used for the first time in this sketch.'

1836 *Public Ledger* (Phila.) 2 Dec. (Th.) 'The Almighty Dollar' is the only object of worship. **1837** IRVING *Creole Village* in *The Magnolia* 317 The almighty dollar, that great object of universal devotion throughout our land. *Ib.* 325, I . . . prayed that the inhabitants might long retain their happy ignorance . . . and their contempt for the almighty dollar. **1838** *Knickerb.* XII. 375 A grassy corner, . . . where, for one 'almighty dollar,' a shallow grave may be purchased. **1850** *Congress. Globe* 12 March, App. 306 That class of people, sneered at by the gentleman from North Carolina, but most invaluable, who seek the 'almighty dollar,' and the comforts and education it furnishes. **1857** J. D. BORTHWICK *California* 165 The almighty dollar exerted a still more powerful influence [in Calif.] than in the old States. **1902** *Outing* June 345/2 No sooner does a first class specimen [of a bulldog] make his début on the English benches than we hear . . . that the owner has fallen a victim to the Almighty Dollar. **1905** G. W. WISHARD *(title)* How to Get the Almighty Dollar behind Spelling Reform. **1910** *N. Y. Ev. Post* 9 Dec. 1 It looks to me as if the . . . Company is running the present subway for the almighty dollar alone.

***Almond.**

1. The almond tree, *Prunus Amygdalus* (*A. communis*), or related species. {1697–}

1682 ASH *Carolina* 6 Fruit trees there are in abundance of various and excellent kinds, the Orange, Lemon, Pomegranate, Fig and Almond. **1813** MUHLENBERG *Cat. Plants* 48 *Amygdalus.* Almond . . . Pens.; fl. April. **1836** LINCOLN *Botany* App. 74 *Amygdalus nana*, flowering almond. **1847** WOOD *Botany* 242 *A. communis*, Almond. . . . Scarcely cultivated in this country for the fruit, which we receive mostly from Europe. *Ib.* 243 *A. pumila*, Dwarf double-flowering Almond. **1856** *Rep. Comm. Patents: Agric.* p. xvii, The Almond . . . is cultivated for ornament or its fruit in the central and southern portions of the United States. **1892** SARGENT *Silva N. A.* IV. 9 In California, . . . the cultivation of the Almond has recently assumed importance.

***2.** The fruit of this tree or a related species.

1650 BRADSTREET *Poems* (1897) 84 Of almonds, quinces, wardens, and the peach The season's now at hand of all and each. **1699** SEWALL *Diary* I. 492 Betty came in afterward, and serv'd almonds and raisins. **1761** [see ALLSPICE 1]. **1781–2** JEFFERSON *Notes Va.* (1787) 40 The orchards produce apples, pears, . . . almonds, and plumbs. **1851** P. BARRY *Fruit Garden* 351 Soft Sweet Shell, Ladies' Thin Shell, etc.—This is the almond of the shops, of which such immense quantities are annually imported from abroad. **1882** 'M. HARLAND' *Eve's Daughters* 443 A lady . . . ate a few sweet almonds chewed very fine when thus troubled, and always found relief. **1902** L. RICHARDS *Mrs. Tree* 218 Sit down! There are burnt almonds in the ivory box.

b. Attrib. in sense 'made with almonds.'

1828 E. LESLIE *Receipts* 18 Almond Pudding. *Ib.* 46 Almond cakes should be baked in pans that are as thin as possible. **1882** MRS. OWENS *Cook Book* 188 [Recipe for] Layer Cake, Almond Nagout. *Ib.* 225 Almond Blanc Mange.

+**Almond pine.** *Obs.* (See quotations.) — **1709** LAWSON *Carolina* 89 The smaller almond-pine . . . bears kernels in the apple, tasting much like an almond. *Ib.* 98 The almond-pine serves for masts very well.

***Almond tree.** =ALMOND 1. — **1846** BROWNE *Trees Amer.* 224 The common Almond-tree . . . is neither a handsome-shaped tree, nor of long duration. *Ib.* 225 An avenue of almond-trees . . . will often retain its beauty for more than a month. **1859** ELLIOTT *Western Fruit Book* 42 The almond tree is . . . easily grown from seed. **1900** WICKSON *Calif. Fruits* (ed. 3) 406 The barren almond trees were largely grafted into prunes or made into firewood.

***Almshouse.** A house in which the indigent are cared for; a poorhouse.

1662 *Boston Rec.* 7 Itt is ordered . . . to receiue Mr Webbs legacie . . . for the erecting of an allmehouse [*sic*]. **1664** *Ib.* 24 Mrs. Jane Woodcock widdow hath liberty of admittance into the allme house. **1685** SEWALL *Diary* I. 72 Walk with the honored Governour up Hoar's Lane, so to the alms house. **1704** *Boston Rec.* 29 That the overseers of the Poor have liberty to procure some meet person . . . to preach a sermon to the persons in the Almes-House once every Saboth day. **1725** *New-Eng. Courant* 26 April 2/2 Any persons that want ockam, may be supplyed at any time at the Alms-House in Boston. **1772** A. G. WINSLOW *Diary* 66 There were 10 corn baskets of the feast . . . sent to the prison & almshouse. **1799** in Willis *Convalescent* 453 The procession will move by the left, in front of the Alms-house. **1813** *Niles' Reg.* IV. 76/1 Ten cart-loads of provisions . . . were conveyed to the Alms-house. **1840** *Knickerb.* XVI. 54 The almshouse has also afforded them an asylum in cases of emergency. **1865** *Atlantic Mo.* XV. 753 In the outskirts of the city . . . was the almshouse, filled with the lame, the blind, the halt . . . and the poor. **1891** FREEMAN *New-Eng. Nun* 81 The almshouse . . . stood in its bare, sandy lot, and there were no leaves or branches to cast shadows on its walls.

b. Attrib. with *ground, lot, office*, etc.

1701 SEWALL *Diary* II. 29 The new burying place, close to the Almshouse ground. **1808** *Ann. 10th Congress* 1 Sess. II. 2857 In a straight line to the northeastern corner of the alms-house lot [in Alexandria, Va.]. **1836** *Niles' Nat. Reg.* 3 Sept. 16/2 The alms house office is continually thronged with application for admissions by foreign paupers. **1856** D. MACLEOD *F. Wood* 184 The constantly increasing expenses of the Almshouse Department.

+**Almud.** [Sp.] A Spanish and Portuguese measure of varying quantity, used in Texas for about a peck. — **1849** AUDUBON *Western Journal* (1906) 113 Beans are seventy-five cents an 'Almud.' **1900** SMITHWICK *Evol. State* 42 Any one person was prohibited from planting more than an *almud* of tobacco seed.

***Aloe. a.** The American aloe (q.v.). **b.** The false aloe, *Agave Virginica.*

1775 BURNABY *Travels* 99 In the gardens is a very large collection of . . . balsams of Peru, aloes, pomegranates, and other tropical plants. **1841** W. KENNEDY *Texas* 180 The valuable Mexican aloe, the Spanish palmetto . . . lend an attraction to this almost uninhabited region. **1849** AUDUBON *Western Journal* (1906) 72 Roma, named after General Roman of Texan celebrity, . . . [is] only an interminable chaparral of musquit, cactus (of three species), an occasional aloe, maguay and wild sage.

***Along,** *adv.*

+**1. a.** *To get along*, to manage, particularly under hardship or difficulty. {1868–}

Noted by British travellers, 1831–c1850, as an Americanism.

1830 S. SMITH *Lett. J. Downing* (1834) 34, I wish you'd write me . . . whether you think I could get along with the business [of Governorship]. **1831** MRS. TROLLOPE *Domestic Manners* (1832) I. iii. 32 The house was . . . in what appeared to me a very comfortless condition, but I was then new to Western America, and unaccustomed to their mode of 'getting along,' as they term it. **1837** *S. Lit. Messenger* III. 196 It also enables the opera to 'get along' with much less expense and difficulty. **1849** WILLIS *Rural Lett.* ii. 320 It looks like a town where everybody 'gets along,' where there are six or seven rather rich people, and no such thing as a pauper. **1852** STOWE *Uncle Tom* xvi, She'll get along in heaven better than you or I. **1863** MRS. WHITNEY *F. Gartney* xiv, It is everybody's business . . . to know just how everybody is 'getting along.' **1896** J. C. HARRIS *Sister Jane* 5 She expressed supreme contempt for men who had no knack of getting along in the world.

+**b.** *To be along*, to come to a place; to call.

1831 M. A. HOLLEY *Texas* (1833) 21 The captain . . . sent word that he would be along for us about sun-set. **1892** 'MARK TWAIN' *Amer. Claimant* xvi. 162 They'll be along as soon as it's done. **1903** 'O. HENRY' *Roads of Destiny* 107 'It 'll be along,' said this queer Mr. Kearny; 'it 'll be along on the beams of my bright but not very particular star.'

+**2.** *Right along*, continuously; without interruption.

1856 *Mich. Agric. Soc. Trans.* VII. 806 The result was, his corn grew right along, for it could not help it. **1885** *Lisbon* (Dakota) *Star* 2 Jan. 8/2 The Lisbon mills have no trouble, and are running to their full capacity right along. **1906** *Springfield W. Republican* 25 Jan. 1 Public interest in the automobile is increasing right along.

b. Throughout a certain time. {1888–9, *dial.*}

1857 *Lawrence* (Kansas) *Republican* 28 May 3 Nobody would pay the freight on them. . . . They were kept along until the other day, when they were sold.

+**c.** *Along back*, for some time in the (recent) past.

1851 N. KINGSLEY *Diary* 165 Worked as usual to day, took out 50 ounces and 4 dollars, which gains on our days along back. **1880** *Harper's Mag.* Dec. 85/1 She's had an easy time along back, but she's seen the last on't. **1894** WILKINS *Pembroke* iii. 51, I've made up my mind that I've made a mistake along back.

+**3.** Of time: Advanced in its course.

1883 'MARK TWAIN' *Life on Miss.* xxviii, Far along in the day, we saw one steamboat. **1902** *N. Y. Tribune* (Weekly Rev.) 26 April 8 The afternoon was well along by this time.

+**b.** Denoting approximation to a time, age, number, etc.

*c***1870** 'MARK TWAIN' *Sk., To Raise Poultry*, In the one case you start out with a friend along about eleven o'clock. **1886** *Harper's Mag.* Oct. 808/1 He come to the house 'long in the fust part of the evenin'. **1897** 'MARK TWAIN' *Following Equator* xxi. 290 He was along toward fifty.

+**c.** Advanced (in years).

1899 'MARK TWAIN' *Man that corrupted Hadleyberg*, etc. (1900) 159, I am well along, and my memory is not as good as it was.

+**4.** In company with another or others; accompanying.

'Often used absolutely in common speech in the United States: as, I was not along' (*Cent.*).

1773 FITHIAN *Journal* I. 53 Rode home about nine o-clock, he along. **1852** STOWE *Uncle Tom* i, A little humanity, thrown in along, goes a heap further than all your jawin'. **1857** M. J. HOLMES *Meadow-Brook* iii, Charlie muttered something about 'not wanting a *gal* stuck along.' **1882** HOWELLS *Lady of Aroostook* 137 'Our captain's wife . . . was not along.' 'Not along?' repeated Mrs. Erwin. . . . 'Who were the other passengers?' **1888** ROOSEVELT in *Century Mag.* April 856 The last spring I was out, there were half a dozen wagons along. **1900** DRANNAN *Plains & Mts.* 241 Having plenty of horses along we could change when we liked.

Along of, *prep. colloq.* or *dial.* [Cf. Long *adv.*] Because of; on account of. {1767–, *dial.*}

a1861 Winthrop *J. Brent* xvi. 190 We was a little late one morning along of our horses havin' strayed off from camp. **1865** Mrs. Whitney *Gayworthys* xxxiii. 327, I'm bound to say I've been put to great inconveniences along of you. **1870** W. Thornbury *Old Stories* 25 Turning to Mr. Hawkins furiously, he said, 'This is all along of you.' **1878** Beadle *Western Wilds* ii. 27 It happened along o' family matters and the war. **1903** K. Wiggin *Rebecca* vi. 70 Rebecca never'll come to grief along of her beauty, that's certain.

Aloofe: See Alewife.

Alpaca. {1811–}

1. A cloth made of alpaca wool. {1838–}

1860 Worc. **1865** *Chicago Tribune* 10 April 1 Fine Lustre Alpaca . . . $1, with the Best Assortment of Plain Alpacas ever shown in this City. **1866** *Maine Agric. Soc. Ret.* 87 We are paying Great Britain an enormous sum of money every year for this class of goods, to say nothing about alpacas, fine worsteds and fine woollens. **1870** 'M. Harland' *For Better, for Worse* 279 She wore a dress of white alpaca, with a very full and long skirt.

b. *attrib.* Made of alpaca cloth.

1860 M. J. Holmes *Maude* v. 53 A little, dumpy figure in black was alighting, carefully holding up her alpaca dress. **1863** Mrs. Whitney *F. Gartney* vi. 63 Her plain gray merino dress over a quilted black alpaca petticoat. **1882** E. K. Godfrey *Nantucket* 71 With the exception of the manufacture of a few linen or alpaca coats, there is no industry . . . here in the winter. **1904** Glasgow *Deliverance* 109 She wore a severe black alpaca dress, made from a cast-off one of her mother's. **1910** C. Harris *Eve's Husband* 68 The colonel wore a thin black alpaca coat.

2. A dress or other garment made of alpaca cloth.

1868 Mrs. Whitney *P. Strong* 187 A merino gown, or a poplin alpaca, isn't much; but [etc.]. **1891** Freeman *New Eng. Nun* 43 I've been thinkin' of fixin' over my old alpaca a little.

Alphabet, *v.* {c1700–} *tr.* To arrange alphabetically; to alphabetize.

1884 *Oxford Eng. Dict., Alphabet*, v. . . .; in regular use with Librarians, etc., in U. S. **1887** Edmands in *Library Journal* XII. 327 In this alfabeting work I hav [*sic*] been much helped by this motto. *Ib.*, In alfabeting we hav to deal with letters, with words, and with groups of words. **1889** Cutter *Rules for Dict. Catalogue* (ed. 2) 103 The order of alphabeting is to be that of the English alphabet. *Ib.* 116 Mr. Edmands correctly states as the principle of alphabeting 'Something follows nothing.'

Alpine, *a.* {1607–} Of plants: Growing on high grounds. (Freq. in specific names.)

1843 Torrey *Flora N. Y.* I. 232 *Epilobium Alpinum* . . . Alpine Willow-herb. . . . High mountains of Essex county. *Ib.* 240 *Circaea Alpina*, . . . Alpine Enchanter's Nightshade. *Ib.* 251 Purple Alpine Hair-grass. *Ib.* 456 Few-flowered Alpine Meadow-grass. **1845** Lincoln *Botany* App. 163/1 *Saxifraga nivalis*, alpine saxifrage. **1857** Gray *Botany* 258 Alpine Azalea. . . . *Loiseleuria procumbens*, Desv. . . . [Grows on] Alpine summits of the White Mountains, New Hampshire, on rocks. June. **1863** *Ib.* p. xlvii, The Alpine Strawberry . . . with small, very fragrant fruit.

Alsike. [The place-name *Alsike*, near Upsala in Sweden] The distinctive name of a species of clover, *Trifolium hybridum.* {1852–}

1855 Browne in *Trans. Amer. Inst. N. Y.* 619 Alsyke or Swedish clover, (*Trifolium hybridum*,) [recently introduced] from England, believed to have originated in the south of Sweden. . . . may be sown with autumn or spring grain. **1866** *Rep. Comm. Agric.* 352 Alsike clover . . . is a pale red perennial species of clover. . . . [It] thrives best on marly clay. **1872** *Vermont Bd. Agric. Rep.* I. 127 It is only a few years since the Alsike clover has been employed as a forage plant in this country. **1878** *25th Rep. Mass. Board Agric.* I. 130 You can depend upon a good return from the alsike for four or five years at least. **1889** Vasey *Agric. Grasses* 81 Alsike Clover . . . differs from common red clover in being later, taller, more tender and succulent.

* **Altar.** +An enclosed space in a church or at an open-air meeting.

1820 J. Flint *Lett. from Amer.* 236 The little inclosure [at a camp-meeting in the woods] . . . is by the religious called *Altar*, and some scoffers are wicked enough to call it *Pen.* **1846** *Knickerb.* XXVIII. 302 Directly in front of it was a large inclosure . . . called the altar, where the converts were expected to appear. **1856** P. Cartwright *Autobiog.* 388 Mourners, in crowds, came to the altar for the prayers of the Church. **1877** Habberton *Jericho Road* 130 A tin-shop apprentice . . . hurried forward to the altar, and dropped at the bench with a groan.

attrib. **1877** Habberton *Jericho Road* 127 In response to an exhortation, several persons had knelt at wooden benches inside the altar-rail. *Ib.* 128 There, on the altar-steps stood a man.

***Alter,** *v.* + *tr.* To geld or castrate; also (*Cent.*) to spay. — **1852** *Florida Plant Rec.* 62, I have sheared the sheep and altered the lambs.

Alternate. {1718} +One chosen to act in place of a delegate at a political convention, etc., in case of the absence of the other. — **1860** Halstead *Nat. Political Conventions* 155 The Trustees of the National Democratic Hall of the State of New York . . . recommended . . . the following names as delegates and alternates to represent them at the Richmond Convention. **1884** *Nat. Dem. Convention Proc.* 18 A Delegate: 'Is the gentleman a Delegate?' Mr. Cochran: 'Yes; I am the alternate of Joseph J. O'Donohue.' **1888** Bryce *Amer. Commonw.* II. lxix. 542 If the delegate is present to vote the alternate is silent; if from any cause the delegate is absent, the alternate steps into his shoes.

Althea, Althæa. {1785–} +A species of hibiscus; the Rose of Sharon. Also attrib. with *bush, tree.*

1785 Washington *Diaries* II. 347 The Althea trees were also planted. **1808** T. Ashe *Travels* xxvi. 228 Among the shrubs are seen, the althea, arbutus. **1827** *Western Monthly Rev.* I. 323 Althea grows in great beauty in all parts of the [Mississippi] valley. **1838** [Ingraham] *Burton* II. viii. 118 They descended into the secluded walk, overhung with the laurel, althea, and arborvitae. **1857** Gray *Botany* 69 *Hibiscus Syriacus*, the Shrubby Althæa of the old gardeners, is cultivated about houses. **1883** *Harper's Mag.* April 727/1 Near it is the striking foliage of the variegated-leaved althea. **1884** Craddock *Tennessee Mts.* i. 17 The chickens were going to roost in an althea bush beside the porch.

* **Altitude.** *In* (one's) *altitudes*, drunk. *Obs.* — **1722** Franklin *Dogood P.* Wks. II. 43 [Intemperate drinkers] are seldom known to be drunk, tho they are very often boozey, . . . in their Altitudes [etc.].

* **Alum.** Also † **allom(e, allum.**

1. The mineral salt of that name.

1639 *Maryland Archives* IV. 83 A box of twine, allome, and other goods. **1651** *Conn. Public Rec.* I. 223 If the said John Wenthrop Esqr. shall discouer . . . mynes of . . . black lead, allom, stone salt, salt springs, or any other the like. **1750** Walker *Journal* 12 May, Under the Rock is a soft Kind of Stone almost like Allum in taste. **1815** Drake *Cincinnati* ii. 72 In the bottoms of Paint-creek . . . large quantities of bog ore can be obtained—coperas, alum and ochre abound in the same places. **1834** Peck *Gaz. Illinois* 237 Native alum is said to be found in considerable quantities near this site [=Fort Edwards]. **1846** Sage *Scenes Rocky Mts.* xv, Among the mineral productions incident to this region are . . . nitre, alum, coal. **1883** [see Alum basket].

2. Attrib. with *bank, earth, hill, mine, ore, rock*, etc.

1765 Croghan *Journal* 9 Set off and sailed to a place, called the Alum Hill, so called from the great quantity of that mineral found there. **1775** Cresswell *Journal* 96 Saw an Alum mine near to Mr. Shepperd's W. Va. **1784** Filson *Kentucke* 32 There is an allum bank on the south side of Cumberland River. **1795** Winterbotham *Hist. View* II. 90 Allum ore has been found at Barrington [N. H.]. **1817** S. Brown *Western Gaz.* 26 Travellers speak of an allum hill a considerable distance up Mine river. **1827** Drake & Mansf. *Cincinnati* viii. 62 The alum-earth is obtained from the hills of the Ohio river, near the mouth of the Scioto, where there are vast beds of it. **1847** L. Collins *Kentucky* 401 Vanceburg, where there is also a large quarry of alum rock. **1904** *McClure's Mag.* April 593 Thus was begun the 'Alum War,' famous in chemistry, journalism, and legislation.

+**b.** *Alum basket:* (see quotation).

1883 'Mark Twain' *Life on Miss.* xxxviii. 404 Three 'alum' baskets of various colors—being skeleton-frame of wire, clothed-on with cubes of crystallized alum in the rock-candy style.

Aluminum. A tin-white, tenacious metal that takes a brilliant polish, and is now extensively used for making utensils, instruments, etc. {1812–}

This form is in common use in mining, manufacturing, and the trade in the U. S.; the form *aluminium* is used with practical uniformity in Great Britain and generally by chemists in the U. S. (W. 1909).

1836 T. P. Jones *Conversations on Chemistry* 180 The aluminum obtained from it [=alumine] exhibited some of the metallic characteristics. **1855** *Proc. Amer. Phil. Soc.* VI. 142 A light substitute for the copper cent in currency . . . eventually . . . will be found in aluminum. **1889** *Smithsonian Inst. Rep.* 723 Aluminum . . . takes a brilliant polish, and may be rolled or forged as easily as gold or silver. **1889** *Scientific Amer.* 14 Sept. 167/3 Aluminum . . . is used largely in making watch cases and chains. **1916** *Instructions to 'Wear-Ever' Salesmen* 20 The most important service of aluminum, however, is rendered in the manufacture of cooking utensils. For this service it is preeminently fitted.

+**Alumna.** Pl. **alumnae.** [L., fem. of *alumnus.*] A woman graduate of a particular college or university. Also attrib.

1882 'M. Harland' *Eve's Daughters* 177 The statistics of the comparative death-rates of the Alumnæ and Alumni of Oberlin. **1885** A. G. Howes *Health Statistics* 20 The alma mater of each alumna. **1892** *Wellesley College Pres. Rep.* 17 The Alumnæ have special qualifications for this form of work. **1896** *Century Mag.* March 798/1 The average salary of the alumna teacher would be below rather than above $1000 a year. **1910** *Catalogue Vassar College* 3 The editors . . . have tried to obtain the information necessary for a complete record of the alumnæ.

+**Alumnus.** Pl. **alumni.** [L.]

1. One who has been educated at, or graduated by, a particular college or university. {1846–}

More frequently used in the plural than the singular.

sing. **1696** Sewall *Diary* I. 435 Lt. Govr. . . . promised his Interposition for them, as become such an Alumnus to such an Alma Mater. **1815** *Mass. H. S. Proc.* 2 Ser. V. 180 The oldest alumnus at Com[mencement] of whom I heard was Mr. Henry Hill (1756). **1832** R. C. Sands *Writings* II. 293, I am no alumnus of the college. **1838** *S. Lit. Messenger* IV. 576/2

Alexander Dimitry, . . . a distinguished alumnus of the college. **1843** *Yale Lit. Mag.* VIII. 436 Is there one alumnus of Yale, be he graduate or undergraduate, who feels no concern for the reputation of our common alma mater? **1850** *Knickerb.* XXXVI. 525 The Governor of the State, Hamilton Fish, an *alumnus* of the college, had come from Albany in order to be present. **1855** *Harvard Mag.* I. 413 Speculations too abstruse for an Undergraduate to write or an Alumnus to understand.

pl. **1823** J. & R. C. MORSE *Pocket Gaz.* 320 The number of *alumni*, that is, the number who have been educated at each college since its establishment. **1827** *Harvard Reg.* Oct. 234 Inquir'st thou, stranger, what are the pursuits Of our alumni? **1832** HONE *Diary* I. 52 Ogden Hoffman made the annual address before the alumni of Columbia College. **1838** *S. Lit. Messenger* IV. 576/1 It was truly delightful to witness the proofs of attachment and devotedness to the prosperity of their *alma mater* evinced by several of the alumni. **1843** HOPKINS in Hall *College Words* (1851) 7 So far as I know, the Society of the Alumni of Williams College was the first association of the kind in this country. . . . It was formed September 5th, 1821. **1846** *Knickerb.* XXVIII. 278 We have to return our thanks to the Associated Alumni of Middlebury College. **1851** *Harper's Mag.* Sept. 561/1 At the meeting of the Alumni [of Yale] it was announced that [etc.]. **1874** *Rep. U. S. Commiss. Educ. 1873*, 181 Williams College. . . . The trustees and alumni have built and furnished a new boarding-hall. **1890** *Harper's Mag.* Sept. 618/1 The alumni had taken a new interest in the college.

2. Appos. or attrib., usu. in plural, with *association*, *banquet*, *day*, *dinner*, *meeting*, *orator*, *professor* (supported by the alumni), *society*, *song*, *weekly*, etc.

1843 HOPKINS in Hall *College Words* (1851) 8 Last year, for the first time, the voice of an Alumnus orator was heard at Harvard and at Yale. **1851** HALL *Ib.* 8 An Alumni Society was formed at Columbia College in the year 1829. **1860** *Songs of Yale* p. iv, Alumni Songs. These were written to be sung at the annual meetings of the Society of Alumni. **1871** [L. H. BAGG] *At Yale* 24 In the main hall, . . . examinations, alumni meetings, etc., are held. **1890** S. W. NORTON in McLaughlin *Higher Educ. Mich.* (1891) 131 The faculty [of Hillsdale College] at present . . . consists of . . . Samuel Wilber Norton, acting alumni professor of rhetoric. **1894** *Educator* (Phila.) Feb. 268/1 His interest in the deaf . . . extends influentially to . . . their religious assemblies, and *alumni* gatherings. **1895** *Century Mag.* Sept. 794/2 How often at an alumni banquet is intellectual supremacy in college life praised? **1896** *Cosmopolitan* XX. 440/2 At the alumni dinners of colleges . . . he found himself an honored guest. **1899** QUINN *Pennsylv. Stories* 177 He could come back at any time . . . to his Chapter-house, to the Alumni meetings. **1906** *Springfield Weekly Republ.* 28 June 10 Tuesday was alumni day at Yale, when hundreds of old graduates . . . gathered in alumni hall.

+**Alum root.** One or other of various plants with astringent roots, as *Heuchera Americana* or *Geranium maculatum;* the root of this.

1813 MUHLENBERG *Cat. Plants* 29 American Heuchera (alum root) . . . Pens. fl. Maio. **1818** NUTTALL *N. Amer. Plants* I. 174 Allum-root [is found] on the mountains of North Carolina, Virginia, and Tennessee. **1847** WOOD *Botany* 280 Alum-root. . . . A neat plant, rare in the southern parts of N. Eng. and N. Y., frequent at the W. and S. **1901** MOHR *Plant Life Ala.* 534 Alum Root . . . [grows in the] Alleghenian and Carolinian areas. *Ib.*, The root, called 'alum root,' is used medicinally.

+**Alum salt.** Alum. ?*Obs.*

1781 *Virginia State P.* I. 610 Small vessels with . . . a cargoe of Alum Salt, brown sugar, etc., with which they run up the different Rivers & trade as friends. **1824** DODDRIDGE *Notes* 121 The common price of a bushel of allum salt, at an early period was a good cow and calf. **1831** *Deb. Congress* 8 Feb. 120 A bill to repeal the duty on alum salt. **1856** *Rep. Comm. Patents: Agric.* 311 A strong brine . . . made from good rock or alum salt.

Alum slate. Rock in thin layers that yields alum. {1805-} — **1789** MORSE *Amer. Geog.* 183 Allum slate, or stone, has been found in some parts [of Mass.]. **1821** *Jrnl. Science* III. 28 Alum Slate. . . . On its banks [*sc.* of the Saline River] there is an acclivity . . . composed of a black slate (aluminous shistus).

+**Alum spring.** A spring whose water is impregnated with alum. — **1835** in *S. Lit. Messenger* IV. 517/1 The place selected is famous as the site of an alum spring of great power.

Alum stone. Stone yielding alum; also alunite. {1833-} — **1789** MORSE *Amer. Geog.* 183 Allum slate, or stone, has been found in some parts. **1821** *Jrnl. Science* III. 245 In Ohio . . . Alum-stone is frequently found one, two and three feet in thickness, remarkably rich.

A.M. Abbrev. of *artium magister*, Master of Arts, the academic degree next above the A.B.

Retained longer in this form in America than in England (where 'M.A.' is the more common), and still to some extent in use.

1717 (*title*), The Character and Blessedness of the Upright. A sermon occasion'd by the death of . . . Wait Winthrop esq.; . . . by Joseph Sewall, A.M. **1747** (*title*), The Life and Character of . . . Benjamin Colman . . . By Ebenezer Turell, A.M. **1766** (*title*), The Annals or History of Yale-College . . . By Thomas Clap, A.M. **1842** *Knickerb.* XIX. 429 A man may go through college and write A.B. after his name, and even A.M., and be no great things either. **1870** [R. TOMES] *Decorum* 246 The titles of A.B. and A.M. are never added to the superscription of an ordinary letter. **1884** ROE *Nature's Story* 101 He had never received any degree except his simple A.M.

Amalgamate, *v.* {1797-, in general sense.} Of persons: **a.** To combine or coalesce, esp. by intermarriage. +**b.** (See quot. 1859 and next.) — **1811** J. Q. ADAMS *Diary* (1928) 90 The Emperor [of Russia] . . . said, . . . Do they [=immigrants to U. S.] all amalgamate well together? **1850** G. HINES *Voyage* 412 From continual intermarriages . . . an amalgamated population has been produced [in Oregon]. **1859** BARTLETT 8 *Amalgamate* . . . is universally applied, in the United States, to the mixing of the black and white races.

Amalgamation. {1775- in general sense.} +The fusion of the white and black races by intermarriage.

1837 *Baltimore Com. Transcript* 8 June 2/1 (Th. S.) *Amalgamation.* A black man and a white woman were lately brought before the Police Court in Boston charged with unlawfully marrying. *c***1838** CHANNING *Works* 559 The spirit of caste . . . will certainly postpone amalgamation long enough to give the world opportunity to . . . manage the subject much better than ourselves. **1840** *Congress. Globe* 28 Jan. 150 Mr. Johnson of Maryland . . . considered the question of Abolition was but one degree in the rear of amalgamation. **1865** *Atlantic Mo.* XV. 507 The author of the pamphlet which last spring advocated amalgamation. **1867** L. M. CHILD *Romance of Republic* xxxiv. 390 You may be an advocate for amalgamation, but I am not. **1905** *N.Y. Ev. Post* 11 Oct. 4 If the white race are permeated with race consciousness, there is no danger of amalgamation.

+**Amalgamationist.** One who favors amalgamation, or the union of the black and white races.

1838 HAR. MARTINEAU *Western Travel* I. 229 You are an amalgamationist! cried she. I told her that the party term was new to me. *Ib.*, He had heard . . . that I was an amalgamationist. **1838** I. A. JEWETT *Passages in Travel* I. 45, I am an American, and not an abolitionist, or an amalgamationist. **1863** B. TAYLOR *H. Thurston* i. 11 The epithets 'Infidel!' 'Fanatic!' and 'Amalgamationist!' had been hurled at them. **1892** J. D. COX in *Atlantic Mo.* March 386/1 The charge that abolitionists were incendiaries and amalgamationists.

Amalgamator. {1838}

1. An apparatus for extracting metals by combining them with mercury. {1875-}

1869 BROWNE *Adv. Apache Country* 475 Two heavy men, one of whom persists in telling you all about a patent amalgamator. **1874** *Vermont Bd. Agric. Rep.* II. 757 This composition of gold and black sand is next put into an amalgamator, in which the gold deposits itself. **1876** INGRAM *Centennial Exp.* 194 A small stream of water that ran through a trough into the amalgamator.

+**2.** One who operates an amalgamating machine.

1882 *Rep. Precious Metals* 529 Mill: General foreman, . . . Wood helpers, Amalgamators.

+**3.** An amalgamationist.

1865 *Atlantic Mo.* XV. 508 A lank Virginian . . . began pitching into me on the subject of 'Northern amalgamators.'

***Amaranth.** One or other of various plants of the genus *Amarantus.* Also attrib.

1813 MUHLENBERG *Cat. Plants* 86 Amaranth . . . , white. Pens.; fl. Aug. **1819** M'MURTRIE *Sk. Louisville* 211 Pellitory leaved Amaranth. . . . White do. . . . Clustered do. **1821** *Mass. H. S. Coll.* 2 Ser. IX. 146 *Amaranthus oleraceus*, Pot amaranth. **1835** HOFFMAN *Winter in West* I. 144 The deep-hued lichnidia and gorgeous golden rod, which, with jonquils and amaranth, the purple foxglove and saffron-coloured silk-weed, paint the surface of the soil. **1840** DEWEY *Mass. Flowering Plants* 95 *Amaranthus blitum.* L. Low Amaranth. Smaller than the others, . . . supposed to be introduced. *Ib.*, *A. oleraceus.* L. Pot Amaranth. **1847** WOOD *Botany* 471 *A. hybridus*, Hybrid Amaranth. *A. pumilus*, Dwarf Amaranth. *A. spinosus*, Spiny Amaranth. **1847** DARLINGTON *Weeds & Plants* (1860) 275 *A. hybridus.* . . . Hybrid Amarantus. Green Amaranth. Pigweed. **1857** GRAY *Botany* 368 *A. panicularus*, Prince's Feather. Red Amaranth. *A. spinosus*, Thorny Amaranth. *Ib.* 369 *Euxolus.* False Amaranth. **1872** *Vermont Bd. Agric. Rep.* I. 268 The green amaranth or red root, when it springs up after cultivation is over, near the end of the summer, will in the few weeks . . . fully perfect its seeds. **1891** FREEMAN *New Eng. Nun* 167 She carried them in the little basket which had held the little bunches of life-everlasting and amaranth flowers and dried grasses.

+**Amargosa bush.** *S.W.* [See next.] The goatbush, *Castela erecta* or *texana.* — **1878** *Proc. U.S. Nat. Museum* I. 122 This little bird [was] perched upon the topmost twig of an amargosa bush.

+**Amargoso-bark.** *S.W.* [Sp. *amargoso* bitter.] 'The bark of the goatbush, *Castela erecta*, a simarubaceous shrub of the lower Rio Grande valley in Texas and of northern Mexico' (*Cent.*).

+**Amazing,** *adv. colloq.* or *dial.* Wonderfully; marvelously. (Cf. 'MAZING.)

1824 IRVING *Tales Trav.* I. 54 All of whom laughed, and took it in amazing good spirit. **1845** S. SMITH *J. Downing's Lett.* 43 Everything here [=N.Y.] on a Mayday looks amazin' different, and smells amazin' different. **1846** WHITCHER *Bedott P.* i. 24 The snow is amazin' deep in that section. **1847** [ROBB] *Squatter Life* 42 You don't look amazin' like a mud moulder, hoss! *Ib.* 145 A small mite of courtin' would spur me up amazin'. **1859** STOWE *Minister's Wooing* iv, Her mother was a most amazin' smart woman. **1878** *Harper's Mag.* Sept. 574 Parson he reckoned he'd be amazin' forehanded this year.

Amazingly, *adv. colloq.* or *dial.* Wonderfully; exceedingly; vastly. {1673–}

'Used only in colloquial language and applied to trifling things' (B. '48). **1834** DAVIS *Lett. J. Downing* 17 The Gineral is amazingly tickled with the Yankees. *c***1850** WHITCHER *Bedott P.* xxii. 242 Mr. Bedott wants to see you amazinly. **1891** RYAN *Pagan* 113 The young olive-branches . . . leaned to her amazingly.

* **Amazon.** +Designating a fashion of woman's 'bonnet.'—**1843** *Niles' Nat. Reg.* 6 May 160/1 Amazone bonnets; . . . this new article . . . is superseding as it surpasses every thing of the season from abroad. They are altogether American, really beautiful and becoming.

* **Ambassador.**

1. A messenger sent to conduct negotiations.

1638 UNDERHILL *Newes from America* 8 [The Indians] sent early aboard an ambassador, a grave senior. *a***1649** WINTHROP *Hist.* I. 178 The two ambassadors set to their marks—one a bow with an arrow in it, and the other a hand. **1841** COOPER *Deerslayer* xiii, Deerslayer seated himself on a stool, and watched the progress of the ambassador.

2. A minister (now usually a resident minister) who represents his government in diplomatic relations with another country. {1603–}

'The United States sends and receives . . . only ministers of the second rank, who are often popularly called ambassadors' (*Cent.*).

1776 ADAMS *Works* IX. 421 Your motion . . . for sending ambassadors to France with conditional instructions, was murdered. **1787** *Constitution* ii. §2 The President . . . shall nominate and . . . appoint Ambassadors, other public Ministers and Consuls. **1794** *Ann. 3d Congress* 690 A negotiation was to commence under an Ambassador Extraordinary. **1893** COX *Congress. Directory* 281 France: James B. Eustis, Ambassador Extraordinary and Plenipotentiary, Paris. . . . Great Britain: Thomas F. Bayard, Ambassador Extraordinary and Plenipotentiary, London. **1904** *McClure's Mag.* April 598 In Paris the American Ambassador is negotiating a treaty for the extradition of bribers.

Ambeer. Also **ambier, ambia, amber.** Tobacco-juice. {1763–}

1848 BARTLETT *Americanisms* 391 *Ambia* [is] used in the South and West for tobacco juice. It is a euphemism for the spittle produced by this voluntary ptyalism. **1851** *Polly Peablossom* 115 You'll see . . . the infernal Chawbacks . . . a chawin' what is cured, and squirtin' ambeer all over the country. **1871** MILLER *Songs of Sierras* 52 The bronzed mate . . . Spirted a stream of amber wide Across and over the ship side. **1878** BEADLE *Western Wilds* xxii. 353 Beatty . . . everted his leathery lips, and . . . ejected a gill or so of ambeer into the water-seck. **1899** GREEN *Va. Word-Book* 42 *Ambeer,* tobacco juice; the spittle produced by chewing tobacco.

+**Amber-fish.** A fish of the genus *Seriola* (esp. *S. dorsalis*), found on the coasts of the U.S.

1675 JOSSELYN *New England* 107 The Sea-bream, Dorado, or Amber-fish; they follow ships as doth the Dolphing, and are good meat. **1775** ROMANS *Florida* App. 19 A little to the north hereof is a small reef . . . where vast quantities of groopers, snappers, amber-fish, porgys [etc.] . . . may be taken. **1802** ELLICOTT *Journal* 255 Along the Florida Reef, and among the Keys, a great abundance and variety of fish may be taken: such as . . . amber-fish. **1881** *Bulletin U. S. Fish Commission* 42 The Amber-fish is quite common off the West Florida coast. . . . It is a good food-fish. **1897** [see AMBERJACK 2].

+**Amberjack.**

1. A variety of blende or sphalerite.

1888 *Harper's Mag.* June 48/1 Along the line of Spring River, lead, . . . galena, and zinc, as blende or black-jack and amber-jack, are abundant.

2. A species of amber-fish, *Seriola dumerili.*

1893– in Dicts. **1897** *Outing* Jan. 330/2 Not inferior to the kingfish for sport is the amber fish, or amberjack. *Ib.*, The amberjack . . . loves warm water, and . . . swarms in the neighborhood of Palm Beach. **1904** *N. Y. Times* 4 March 9 August Belmont made a big catch of amberjacks.

Amber plum. A variety of yellow plum. {1718}—**1786** WASHINGTON *Diaries* III. 24 Three Amber Plumbs next the cross walk.

+**Ambersear.** Also **ambozear, -zeur, ambusier, -ser.** [F. *embrasure.*] An embrasure.

The forms are based upon the French pronunciation of the word. Some English dictionaries (1780–1835) agree in stressing the last syllable.

1755 R. Rogers *Jrnls.* (1883) 34 *note,* Observed Ambussers built upon the mount, about thirty rods to the south-west of Crown Point post. **1758** *Lett. to Washington* II. 268 The Parapet on the last Curtain is up, the last Bastion is layd over with logs and two of the amburiers [*sic*] done. **1776** *Essex Inst. Coll.* XLIII. 187 There are two Forts. . . . No. 1 contains 10 ambozeurs. *Ib.* 188 They have erected a Sand Bank Battery laid out for five Ambozears.

+**Amber Stream.** (See quotation.)—**1841** CIST *Cincinnati* 66 This amber-colored loam imparts its tinge to the waters of the Ohio during its floods, and has given origin to the poetical name of the 'Amber Stream.'

* **Ambition,** *n.* +Spite; petty malice; grudge. *dial.*

1829 *Va. Lit. Museum* 16 Dec. 418 *Ambition,* 'spite,' a Virginianism. 'He brought the action against me, for *ambition.*' **1836** *Quarter Race Kentucky* (1846) 16 We have no ambition against you, so draw the bet to one hundred dollars. **1848** BARTLETT 9 In North Carolina this word is used instead of the word *grudge,* as, 'I had an ambition against that man.' I am credibly informed that it is even used in this manner by educated men. **1901** *Scribner's Mag.* April 395/1 His friends . . . kept urging him to revenge. A woman wanted them to stop. 'Hit jes' raises the ambition in him and don't do no good nohow.'

Ambition, *v.*

1. *tr.* To have as an object of ambition; to aim at; to desire. {1664–}

1788 FRANKLIN *Works* (1888) IX. 471, I [am] determined to quit all public business with my present employment [President of the State of Penna.] At eighty-three one certainly has a right to *ambition* repose. **1807** JEFFERSON *Writings* XI. 182 This is what I ambition for my own country. **1813** *Ib.* XIII. 208, I value your opinion too highly not to ambition its concurrence with my own. **1838** COOPER *Homeward B.* xvii, We have tongues and sounds in plenty, Captain Truck, and no gentleman that has such diet, need ambition a stock-fish! **1857** *Knickerb.* XLIX. 39 The idea of sparking every pretty girl I met was rather above my bend then, and I didn't ambition it.

b. *intr.* To have an ambition *to* be something. {1688–}

1818 JEFFERSON *Anas* (1903) 40 A malignant neighbor of mine, who ambitioned to be his correspondent. **1869** MRS. WHITNEY *Hitherto* xviii. 249 There were those who were, and those who only ambitioned to be.

2. To move with ambition. {*a* 1628}

1906 'MARK TWAIN' *What is Man?* vi. 105 These [qualities] have exalted him, enthused him, ambitioned him to higher and higher flights.

+**3.** *dial.* To be of opinion (*that* . . .).

1898 WESTCOTT *D. Harum* 153 He ambitioned that if his mother'd raise a thousan' dollars on her place he'd be sure to take care of the int'rist.

* **Ambitious,** *a.* ||Vicious. (Cf. AMBITION *n.*)—**1837** BIRD *Nick of Woods* I. 26 The fight had made him as ambitious as a wild-cat. *Ib.* 86 He's never ambitious, except among Injuns and horses.

Ambozear, -zeur: see AMBERSEAR.

* **Ambrosia.** A coarse annual weed also known as ragweed or bitterweed.

1821 NUTTALL *Trav. Arkansa* 204 The *Ambrosias* or bitter weeds were higher than my head on horseback. **1831** S. J. HALE *Flora* 19 Ambrosia . . . [is] found in Upper Louisiana. **1847** WOOD *Botany* 353 *A[mbrosia] trifida,* Tall Ambrosia. . . . A very tall, herbaceous plant, not very common in N. E. . . . In the W. States it is abundant.

+**Ambrotype.** A kind of photograph on glass in which the dark background shows through. Also attrib.

[**1855** *Notes & Q.* 7 April 270 Ambrotype Likenesses.—The Boston Atlas states that a most valuable improvement in the art of producing likenesses [etc.].] **1857** *Texas Almanac* Advt., Ambrotype and Photographic Galleries. **1863** NORTON *Army Lett.* 136, I . . . did it up in a little box like an ambrotype. **1864** M. A. ROOT *Camera & Pencil* 373 Isaac Rehn, . . . in company with Cutting of Boston, perfected . . . the 'Ambrotype,' or positive on glass. **1871** *Scribner's Mo.* II. 631 The picture flatters her,—ambrotypes always do. **1884** CABLE *Dr. Sevier* lvii, The sick man drew from his breast a small ambrotype, pressed it to his lips. **1904** WALLER *Wood-Carver* 133, I wished I'd hed one er them new-fangled ambrotype boxes.

+**Ambrotypic,** *a.* [f. prec.] Suggestive after the manner of an ambrotype.—**1861** *Ill. Agric. Soc.* IV. 264, I give a voice to a few thoughts ambrotypic of what the workingman is, and what he ought to be.

Ambulance.

1. A vehicle for carrying the injured or sick. {1854–}

'An ambulance is a light wagon, and generally has two springs behind, and one transverse one in front. The seats can be so arranged that two or even three persons may lie at full length' (1864 Fremantle *3 Months in S. States* 10).

1854 BARTLETT *Narr.* II. 114 Having made ambulances for our wounded and interred the dead, we proceeded on our march. **1861** *Army Regulations* 106 The active ambulances follow the troops engaged to succor the wounded and remove them to the depôts. **1865** KELLOGG *Rebel Prisons* 276 An ambulance would hold four, and from this number I have often seen two taken out dead. **1873** ALDRICH *Marj. Daw,* etc. 108 The melancholy line of ambulances bearing our wounded to Washington. **1889** E. B. CUSTER *Tenting on Plains* iii. 119 The General had an ambulance fitted up as a traveling-wagon for me.

+**2.** A vehicle resembling a hospital ambulance, used in the West as a touring caravan.

1860 GREELEY *Overland Journey* 160 The ox-wagons were held to the bottom by the weight of their loads, while our 'ambulance' was light, and likely to be swept down stream. **1869** BROWNE *Adv. Apache Country* 39 Our little ambulance and four mules groaned under their precious loads. **1873** BEADLE *Undevel. West* iv. 83 A private party in prairie ambulances. **1881** *Rep. Indian Affairs* 333 Our outfit was a four-mule ambulance and driver, tent and fly. **1890** *Century Mag.* Dec. 173 Governor Micheltorena . . . brought with him an ambulance, not much better than a common spring wagon. **1899** T. HALL *Tales* 95 Once in a while she caught sight of a muffled figure in an ambulance that stopped for water for its thirsty mules.

3. Attrib. with *boy, corps, depot, train,* etc.

1861 *Md. Hist. Mag.* V. 304, [I] was enjoying a hickory crib which proves the good taste and . . . skill of my ambulance boys. **1861** *Army Regulations* 106 The service of the ambulance wagons and other means of removing the wounded. *Ib.*, The ambulance depôt is generally established at the most convenient building nearest the field of battle. **1866** 'F. KIRKLAND' *Bk. Anecdotes* 283 The First Brigade . . . to be left . . . as a guard for an ambulance train. **1868** BEECHER *Norwood* 488 Directing some of the ambulance men to remove the body. **1886** BRET HARTE *Snow-bound* 49 They've stopped the bleeding with John's ambulance things. **1897** *Outing* May 183/1 A new organization known as the ambulance corps was added to the militia this year.

+**b.** *Ambulance-chaser*, a lawyer who incites persons to sue for damages because of accident. *slang.*

1897 *Congress. Rec.* 24 July 2961/1 In New York City there is a style of lawyers known to the profession as 'ambulance chasers,' because they are on hand wherever there is a railway wreck, or a street-car collision, or a gasoline explosion, with . . . their offers of professional service. **1909** *Springfield W. Repub.* 28 Jan. 6 The so-called 'ambulance chasers,' or lawyers who make a business of promoting damage suits against railroads and street railways on the basis of contingent fees which run from 20 to 50 per cent of the amount of damages sought to be recovered.

***Ambuscade,** *n.* An ambush (esp. of Indians).

1666 *Doc. Hist. N. Y. State* (1849) I. 72 That small party drew the French into an ambuscade of neare 200 Mohaukes planted behind trees. **1675** EASTON *Indian War* 25 The Indians by Ambuscade treacherously killed 8 that wear going to treat with them. **1709** LAWSON *Carolina* 199 Their Field Counsellors . . . are accustomed to Ambuscades, and Surprizes, which Methods are commonly used by the Savages. **1788** FRANKLIN *Autobiog.* 401 The only danger I apprehend of obstruction to your [=Braddock's] march is from ambuscades of Indians. **1792** *Ann. 2nd Congress* 1134 He gained permission to leave them some distance on the road, where he formed an ambuscade. **1837** IRVING *Bonneville* I. i. 20 The mountain tribes . . . laid ambuscades in their path, or attacked them in their night encampments. **1838** DRAKE *Tales & Sk.* 104 The more experienced of the garrison felt satisfied that a powerful party was in ambuscade, near the spring. **1843** 'CARLTON' *New Purchase* I. xvii. 128 In this way Indians and woodsmen often lie in ambuscade for deer at the licks, or enemies in war. **1853** RAMSEY *Tennessee* 112 While passing a narrow defile . . . they were startled by the terrific yell of Indians, in ambuscade. **1879** *Harper's Mag.* Aug. 324 The ambuscade in which Colonel Williams fell occurred near a small lake. **1923** J. H. COOK *On Old Frontier* 171 In the art of concealment and ambuscade they were as expert, I think, as any savages on the American continent.

***Ambuscade,** *v.* [f. prec.] *tr.* To attack or beset by ambush.

1676 *Maine Doc. Hist.* VI. 123 Going ouer a River wee were ambuscaded. **1754** *Lett. to Washington* I. 26 Such Stratagems of War as to ambuscade, decoy, and circumvent the subtil French. **1761** J. ROWE *Letters* 408 He has recover'd his Spirits & declares he'll never couch to a disorderly Peasantry unless they ambuscade him. **1853** RAMSEY *Tennessee* 591 A party of Indians . . . ambuscaded a path near Calvin's Blockhouse . . . and fired upon Samuel Wear. **1856** GLISAN *Jrnl. Army Life* 322 [From] Smith's valley . . . they returned to Pistol River to ambuscade the train.

+**Ambuscader.** [f. prec.] One who lays an ambuscade. {1825-} — **1676** *Maine Doc. Hist.* VI. 152 There wilbe more danger of ambushcaders [*sic*]. **1775** ADAIR *Indians* 258 Perhaps, they are the most artful ambuscaders, and wolfish savages, in America.

***Ambuscado.** *Obs.* =AMBUSCADE *n.* {-1819}

1676 *Maine Doc. Hist.* VI. 110 The men [=Narragansett Indians] . . . by ambuscadoes & secret skulkinge soe infests the passages and highwayes that many teamsters hath thereby been cutt of. **1677** HUBBARD *Narr.* 19 They set out with a Troop of Horse in each wing, to prevent the danger of the Enemies Ambuscadoes. **1704** *Boston News-Letter* 14 Aug. 2/1 Allin & his Company, in passing from Northampton to Wakefield, . . . the Enemy from an Ambuscado fired upon their Scouts. **1708** *Ib.* 4 Oct. 4/2 They only design'd to draw our Boats after them towards an Ambuscado which we judged to be under the Bank out of our sight. **1716** CHURCH *Philip's War* 5 This party . . . were fired on by an Ambuscado of about a dozen Indians.

***Ambush,** *n.* A concealed position taken up in order to attack by surprise; a party hidden to make such an attack.

1622 'MOURT' *Relation* 15 Least other of the Indians should lie in Ambush. **a1649** WINTHROP *Hist.* I. 253 They started three Indians, whom they pursued till they were brought into an ambush of fifty. **1676** *Conn. Public Rec.* II. 471 Capt. Samfort . . . by his [i.e. an Indian's] direccion laid some English and Indians in ambush at the passage out. **1704** *Boston News-Letter* 7 June 2/2 Some of the sculking Enemy lay in Ambush for people at Cochecho. **1776** MCINTOSH in Sparks *Corr. Rev.* (1853) I. 168 After examining very particularly . . . around the town, I placed . . . ambushes in the different roads leading to it. **1812** MARSHALL *Kentucky* 142 James M'Afee was fired on by five Indians lying in ambush. **1821** COOPER *Spy* vi, He particularly disliked the ambush of the detachment under Lawton. **1854** BARTLETT *Narr.* I. 295 A party of ten Americans . . . was fired upon by a band of Apaches lying in ambush. **1867** EDWARDS *Shelby* xx. 341 Colonel Williams reached his place of ambush in time.

Ambush, *v.*

1. *tr.* To surround or waylay for a surprise attack. {1631-}

1716 CHURCH *Philip's War* (1865) I. 126 Some brisk Bridgwater lads, had ambush'd them, fired upon them, and killed the old man. **1780** CLINTON in Sparks *Corr. Rev.* (1853) I. 135 A report prevails, that this party were ambushed by the enemy, and defeated. **1826** COOPER *Mohicans* xiv, In our outward march to ambush his advance. **1840** — *Pathfinder* vi, Was it well done . . . to ambush a dozen Mingoes alone! **1853** SIMMS *Sword & Distaff* 67 We can ambush them, as they ambushed us. **1880** *Scribner's Mo.* Feb. 504 From behind the log and brush fences the prowling Indian ambushed the backwoodsman as he tilled his field. **1923** J. H. COOK *On Old Frontier* 30 These visits were generally made in the full moon, the especial object being to ambush a few white men or Mexicans and secure more guns, pistols, and knives.

***2.** To place (men) in ambush.

1755 R. Rogers *Jrnls.* (1883) 32 *note*, They came . . . within seventy rods of the point where we were well ambushed for them. **1860** CLAIBORNE *Sam. Dale* vii. 127 He . . . ambushed his force in a cane-brake. **1867** EDWARDS *Shelby* viii. 139 Shelby had anticipated this and ambushed Captain John Jarrett.

3. *intr.* To form an ambush. {1626-} Also *fig.*

1755 R. Rogers *Jrnls.* (1883) 34 *note*, Found a good place to ambush within sixty rods of the fort, and immediately went back and took our partners and ambushed. **1765** R. ROGERS *Ib.* 80 My Lord How did us the honour to accompany us, being fond, as he expressed himself, to learn our method of marching, ambushing, retreating, &c. **1856** *Kansas Hist. Coll.* II. 232 Two nights we ambushed in the woods, about 100 in number. **a1861** WINTHROP *J. Brent* viii. 86 Ef they can serve you a mean trick they'll do it; and they're ambushin' now to . . . see what it is.

***Ambushment.** An ambuscade or ambush.

1638 UNDERHILL *Newes from America* 11 Pursuing them, a hundred more [Indians] started out of the ambushments, and almost surrounded him and his company. **1716** CHURCH *Philip's War* 70 Prevent the Ambushments of the Enemy on your main body. **1725** KIDDER *Exped. Lovewell* (1865) 85 The Indians fired upon them (from an Ambushment) both in front & Rear. **1827** COOPER *Prairie* iii, If there were just six of us, lad, what a beautiful ambushment we might make upon them. **1847** RUXTON *Adv. Rocky Mts.* xxvii. (1848) 236 He approaches his ambushment within a few feet, whiz flies the home-drawn arrow. **1867** EDWARDS *Shelby* viii. 33 In a sudden surprise or ambushment it is vitally necessary that the main body shall have time to form and prepare for action.

+**Amen corner.** That part of a church where those sit whose habit is to offer expressions of assent during the service.

1860 *Harper's Mag.* Jan. 279/2 The Rev. Judson Noth, a local Methodist preacher, . . . was one of the best 'scotchers' that occupied the 'Amen Corner.' **1871** EGGLESTON *Duffels* viii. (1893) 163 The cross seats near the pulpit . . . were . . . said by scoffers to be the 'Amen Corners.' **1880** *Harper's Mag.* Dec. 160 It was a grand occasion for Brother J—, with a crowded house, and Father P. in the Amen corner. **1904** HARBEN *Georgians* vii. 67 Carden and Leftwich had arrived and were in their places in the 'amen corner,' at the right of the crude pulpit.

transf. **1884** *Congress. Rec.* 24 April 3207/1 When commiserated upon the fact that he was compelled to go to what is commonly known here as the amen corner, [he] frankly said that any seat in the Senate was better than none. **1894** *Ib.* Jan. 1502/2 One of those saintly Republican monopolists who sit in the 'Amen corner' of protected privilege.

***Amend,** *v.* +*tr.* To alter (the Constitution) by the addition of a new article.

1794 *Ann. 3rd Congress* 23 The following motion, . . . to wit: That the Constitution be amended by adding . . . the following clause. **1842** *Niles' Nat. Reg.* 5 March 14 The Senate then took up . . . the resolution to amend the constitution. **1884** BLAINE *20 Years of Congress* I. 54 The whole number of States was thirty-six. The assent of three-fourths of that number was required to amend the Constitution.

+**Amendatory,** *a.* In the nature of an amendment.

1790 MACLAY *Deb. Senate* 285 The message accompanying the proclamation calls for an amendatory law. **1798** *Filson Club* (Ky.) *Publ. No. 31* 128 In which light they appear to have been considered by the amendatory act passed on this subject. **1803** *Ann. 7th Congress* 2 Sess. 603 Mr. Bayard . . . reported an amendatory bill; which was read twice. **1862** LINCOLN *Messages & P.* VI. 136, I recommend the adoption of the following resolution and articles amendatory to the Constitution of the United States. **1876** BANCROFT *Hist. U. S.* VI. xlvi. 304 It is the testimony of Jefferson that an amendatory bill was prepared. **1882** *National Bank Act* 77 That Congress may at any time amend, alter, or repeal this act and the acts of which this is amendatory.

***Amendment.**

1. An alteration intended to improve or modify an actual or proposed measure, enactment, etc.; the clause or paragraph embodying this; +*spec.* a new article added to the Constitution. {1696-}

1699 Quincy *Hist. Harvard* (1840) I. 605 July 13th, 1699. Amendments to the College Bill proposed and agreed to by a Committee of the whole Board. **1738** *Penna. Col. Rec.* IV. 324 They hope the Governour would recede from this part of the Amendment. **1787** *Constitution* v, The Congress, whenever two thirds of both Houses shall deem it necessary, shall propose Amendments to this Constitution, or . . . shall call a Convention for proposing Amendments. **1789** MACLAY *Deb. Senate* 30 The dignity and preëminence of the Senate was the object aimed at by the amendment. **1790** *Ann. 1st Congress* II. 1481 The proceedings of a Convention of that State [=N. Car.], recommending certain amendments to the Constitution of the United States. **1814** *Ann. 13th Congress* 1 Sess. I. 843 The adoption of this amendment by the States. **a1817** DWIGHT *Travels* IV. 499 Money-bills are originated in the House of Representatives, but the Senate may propose amendments. **1838** *Diplom. Corr. Texas* (1908) I. 333 This amendment is now before the House and Mr. Adams has been occupying the morning hour upon it for several days. **1861** Logan *Great Conspiracy* 155, I believe, Mr. President, that . . . it must be by Legislation; which is more ready, more certain, and more likely to be satisfactory, than Constitutional Amendment. **1865** *Nation* I. 35 It is instructive, too, to read arguments for the Amendment. **1874** *Congress. Rec.* 6 Jan. 429/1 For nearly a decade you have been legislating for the negro by amendments to the Constitution and by acts of Congress. **1917** *Statutes at Large* XL. 1. 1050 Resolved . . . That the following amendment to the Constitution be . . . proposed . . . : The manufacture, sale, or transportation of intoxicating liquors . . . is hereby prohibited.

+**2.** An additional piece of land; an addition.

1738 *Southampton Rec.* III. 125 The amendment . . . begins at the above sd. pine tree. *Ib.*, Two little hommocks . . . of segg at the S end of the amendment. *Ib.* 127 We proseded to lay out the Seder swamps for amendments to several of the poor lots.

+**Amen seat.** [Cf. AMEN CORNER.] A seat in a church frequented by those who are moved to say 'Amen' during the service. — **1876** HABBERTON *Jericho Road* xiv. 128 In an 'amen' seat sat an old half-breed.

‖ **Americ,** *a. Obs.* =AMERICAN *a.* 1. — **1708** TOMPSON *Poet. Works* 148 Winthrop the first Lord of the Americk coast.

* **America.**

1. In limited sense, the early British colonies or the later United States.

1650 Bradstreet *Tenth Muse* (1678) p. x., In praise of the author, Mistris Anne Bradstreet, . . . at present residing . . . in America, alias Nov-Anglia. **1654** JOHNSON *Wonder-W. Prov.* 9 When your feete are once safely set on the shores of America, you shall . . . establish civill government. **1764** *Providence Gaz.* 18 Aug. (Th.) America can answer all expenses of government. **1781** WITHERSPOON *Druid P.* No. v, Some observations upon the present state of the English language in America. *Ib.*, Vulgarisms in England and America. **1791** *Gazette U. S.* (Phila.) 16 Feb. 3/1 *America* is used very generally both by writers and public speakers, when they only intend the territory of the United States. . . . It may have first come into use as being much shorter to say *Americans*, than citizens of the United States: Some use Atlantic America for the United States—others United America—the last is the most proper. **1807** *Ann. 10th Congress* 1 Sess. I. 13 We can calculate . . . that a five years' state of non-intercourse with Great Britain will establish the manufacturers of America. **1837** BIRD *Nick of Woods* I. i. 13 The Exiles of America, who first forsook their homes on the borders of the Atlantic. **1852** STOWE *Uncle Tom* xvii, A youth of African descent, defending the retreat of fugitives through America into Canada. **1861** [NEWELL] *Orpheus C. Kerr* I. 117 The women of America, my boy, are a credit to the America eagle.

b. *West.* The eastern States, or those east of the Mississippi or Missouri.

1857 S. Oregon writer in *N. Y. Tribune* (Th.), [Some people here] are talking of going back to America. **1860** *Rocky M. News* (Denver) 11 April, We'll go back to America, Dressed-up so slick and fine. **1867** DIXON *New America* I. 3 The current jest, everywhere to be heard from Atchison to Salt Lake, runs, that a man who means to cross the Missouri is going on a trip to America.

2. *Young America*: see YOUNG *a.*

* **AMERICAN,** *n.*

***1.** A member of an aboriginal race of the North American continent; an American Indian. {1578–}

In later use only with defining adj., *aboriginal* or *native*.

1641 W. CASTELL *Petition to Parlt.*, Those who . . . shall religiously endeavour to make millions of those silly seduced Americans, to heare . . . the mysterie of godlinesse. *Ib.*, What those blind and spirituall distressed Americans are, we were. **1686** SEWALL *Letter-book* I. 23 The Americans wellfare here, in New-Spain and elsewhere, . . . may be much forwarded by the ministers and Christians in England helping together. **a1752** W. DOUGLASS *Summary* I. 155 The aboriginal Americans have no honesty, no honour. **1794** S. WILLIAMS *Vermont* 188 If we have seen one American, we may be said to have seen them all, their colour and make are so nearly the same. **1841** COOPER *Deerslayer* x, Beauty among the women of the aboriginal Americans . . . is by no means uncommon. *Ib.* xvi, The native Americans are habitually cautious.

2. A native or citizen of the United States, or the earlier British colonies included in these, not belonging to one of the aboriginal races.

?**1697** MATHER *Magnalia* Introd. (1855) I. 33 One poor feeble American, . . . capable of touching this work no otherwise than in a digression. **1708** TOMPSON *Poet. Works* 147 The Illustrious . . . Winthrop . . . Being the third of a renowned line Which wee Americans deemed next divine. **1759** FRANKLIN *Ess.* Wks. 1840 III. 283 The Americans were in a sort of disgrace at court for not having broken through all the cautions laid upon them. **1768** *Let.* in Tudor *Otis* (1823) 300 As Americans, they . . . beseech you to represent their grievances to the king, our sovereign. **1785** Ramsey *Tennessee* (1853) 315 Had they been possessed of that manly and soldierly spirit that becomes an American, they must have acted like Hubbard. **1796** WASHINGTON *Farewell Address*, The name of American, which belongs to you in your national capacity, must always exalt the just pride of patriotism, more than appellatives derived from local discriminations. **1799** *Mass. H. S. Coll.* VI. 149 If an inhabitant of New-York was asked by a foreigner, to what country he belonged, his reply would be, that he was an American. **1803** *Ann. 7th Congress* 2 Sess. 115 When our wealth, our power, and our resources, are the boast of every American. **1819** E. EVANS *Pedestrious Tour* 358 The Americans are a mixed people, but the institutions of the country direct their affections to one common centre. **1825** NEAL *Bro. Jonathan* I. 12 Jonathan Peters, in the first place, was an American; one of that singular people, who know a little, and but a little, of everything. **1838** COOPER *Home as Found* iii. 45 Indeed the American has a better gentility than common, as, besides his own, he may take root in that of Europe. **1864** LOWELL *Fireside Travels* 97 The American is nomadic in religion, in ideas, in morals. **1873** W. MATHEWS *Getting on in World* xix. 308 Americans must be Americans, and blow up as a necessity of their existence. **1887** DEPEW *Orations & Sp.* (1890) 85 The uprising which followed the guns of Sumter . . . expressed the value placed by Americans upon their institutions, their Constitution, and their liberty.

b. A person from the earlier United States in southern or western areas not yet included in these.

1807 *Ann. 10th Congress* 1 Sess. I. 591 He had been informed the Territory was divided by parties (I mean Upper Louisiana), which he attributed to the Americans. **1814** BRACKENRIDGE *Views* 113 The small number of Americans settled here, is also owing to the tide of emigration having set in for the western states. **1819** E. DANA *Geographical Sk.* 225 The population consists of French and Americans (as people from the United States are there commonly called). **1834** *Visit to Texas* xxi. 199 The common saying is, that five Indians will chase twenty Mexicans, but five Americans (that is from the United States of the North) will chase the Indians. **1840** DANA *Two Years* xxi. 215 The Americans (as those from the United States are called) . . . are indeed more industrious and effective than the Spaniards. **1854** BARTLETT *Narr.* I. 295 A party of Americans bound for California had been attacked. **1873** BEADLE *Undevel. West* 448 The Exchange, the only hotel in the city for white men, or rather Americans, the other distinction, though perfectly accurate, not being well relished here.

3. *pl.* **a.** The special designation of a regiment. More fully *Royal Americans. Obs.*

1747 NEWCASTLE in *Penna. Col. Rec.* V. 129 You will also endeavor to have his [Gen. Phillip's] Regiment compleated out of the Americans. **1757** DINWIDDIE in *Lett. to Washington* II. 84, I think it was your Duty . . . to conform your Regiment to the Allowances given the Americans. **1757** *Army Orders* 52 The artilery is to send . . . two [12-pounders] to the head of the Royal Americans. **1760** CROGHAN *Journal* 25 Oct., A Detachment of the Royal Americans. **1826** COOPER *Mohicans* vi, This is not such a supper as a major of the Royal Americans has a right to expect. *Ib.* xxxii, A company of the Royal Americans.

+**b.** A member or supporter of the American party (q.v.).

1855 *Harper's Mag.* XI. 544/1 In Tennessee, Andrew Johnson, the Democratic candidate, is re-elected Governor over M. P. Gentry, who was supported by the Whigs and Americans. **1856** *Ib.* XIII. 839/1 In Massachusetts and Rhode Island the Republicans and Americans have united upon tickets for Presidential electors. **1857** *Ib.* XIV. 550 A committee . . . consisting of two Democrats, two Republicans, and one American.

4. The English language as spoken in the United States.

1802 *Port Folio* 28 Aug. 266/2 [A Latin verse] which my schoolmaster has translated into American. **1834** *Knickerb.* IV. 17 Acting as no American ever acts, and talking a language which on the other side of the water may pass for American simply because it is not English. **1857** CHANDLESS *Visit Salt Lake* I. ii. 8 The Missourian . . . expressed his astonishment that I could speak such good 'American,' having been so short a time in the country. **1881** *Harper's Mag.* April 682/1 The *padrona* . . . supposed in good broad American . . . it 'would be put in the papers like it was before.' **1886** HOWELLS *Ib.* Jan. 325/1 When their [*sc.* novelists'] characters speak, we should like to hear them speak true American, with all the varying Tennesseean, Philadelphian, Bostonian, and New York accents. **1902** *Nation* 11 Dec. 468/1 Is it good American to write, 'Mr. Bispham absurded'? **1919** MENCKEN *American Language* 26 American thus shows its character in a constant experimentation, . . . a steady reaching out for new and vivid forms.

* **AMERICAN,** *a.*

1. Pertaining to those parts of North America occupied by, or adjacent to, the early British colonies. {1647–1775}

(1)**1654** JOHNSON *Wonder-W. Prov.* 74 Wilson, who this yeare landed the third time upon this American shore from his Native Country. **1666** *Md. Archives* II. 109 Whither it bee probable that the American Plantations should leaue of planting these staple, valuable, & imperishable comodities. **1690** *Mass. H. S. Coll.* 4 Ser. V. 239 The safety and defence of their majesties' Colonies and subjects in these American parts. **1693** C. MATHER *Wond. Invis. World* 11 The first planters of these Colonies were . . . so peaceable, that they embraced a voluntary exile in a squalid, horrid, American desart. **1740** *Georgia Col. Rec.* IV. 664 Ships . . . come up to the Town [Savannah], where the Worm (which is the plague of the American seas) does not eat. **1755** *State Col. N. Amer.* 37 If . . . we would secure our American dominions against the French. **1774** *Journals Cont. Congress* I. 15 The unhappy differences which have long subsisted and are encreasing between Great Britain and the American Colonies.

(2)**1648** SHEPARD *Clear Sunshine* 51 My prayer . . . is, that the fall of the churches . . . may not bee the rising of these American Gentiles. *Ib.* 55 I confesse it passeth my skill to tell how the Gospel should be generally received by these American natives. **1666** TOMPSON *Poet. Wks.* 105 Remarks on the bright, and dark side of that American pillar Mr. William Tompson. **1732** FRANKLIN *Poor Richard 1733* 23 Poor Richard, an American prince, without subjects. **1767** *Doc. Hist. N. Y. State* (1849) I. 734 Those, who were desirous of distinguishing themselves as American patriots. **1775** ADAIR *Indians* 13 The American Indians neither vary from the rest of mankind, in their internal construction, nor external appearance, except in colour. **1776** TRUMBULL *M'Fingal* II. 35 Has not Gage . . . made the Amer'can bishop's see grow, By many a new-converted Negro?

(3)**1647** WARD *Simple Cobler* 24 Divers make it an article of our American creed. **1670** *N. Car. Col. Rec.* I. 209, I shall endeavour by the next to send your honour some of our American raritys. **1719** (*title*), American Weekly Mercury. **1738** STEPHENS *Proc. Georgia* 80 We were catch'd in a heavy American rain. **1747** FRANKLIN *Electrical Exper.* (1751) 16 An account of American Electricity. **1764** J. OTIS *Rights British Col.* 54 American manufactures could have been brought to such perfection. **1774** *Boston Gazette* 10 Jan., Romans . . . has come here to procure . . . the assistance of some gentlemen (lovers and encouragers of American literature). **1776** HUTCHINSON *Diary & Lett.* II. 68 The American wool, even in the northern parts of the Continent, is of a coarse staple.

+**2.** Pertaining to the United States.

This continuation of the earlier use is the natural result of the lack of an adjective form corresponding to 'United States.' — For examples of the use of the adj. in the specific names of plants, trees, birds, etc., see the separate entries below.

(1) **1776** *Penna. Ev. Post* 28 May 266/2 The Union Flag of the American States waved upon the Capitol. **1807** *Ann. 10th Congress* 1 Sess. I. 14 The next town within the American limits. **1809** FRENEAU *Poems* I. Adv. 3 Whether the following verses have any real claim to the attention of the citizens of the American United States. **1815** *Niles' Reg.* VIII. 67/1 New states can be hereafter formed only of American territory and American population. **1827** DRAKE & MANSF. *Cincinnati* i. 23 The state of Ohio is destined . . . to attain a degree of power and prosperity, . . . giving her a pre-eminent rank in the American Confederacy. **1837** *S. Lit. Messenger* III. 663, I took occasion to cross the ferry, which starts from a point near the base of the American falls. **1847** LANMAN *Summer in Wild.* xxii. 132 The American coast of Lake Superior extends to about twice the length of that which belongs to Canada. **1848** E. BRYANT *California* 244 Here . . . we found ourselves under American authority, and about to be 'annexed' to the American Union. **1856** STOWE *Dred* II. 91 The cholera, which was then making fearful havoc on our American shore.

(2) **1777** *Journals Cont. Congress* IX. 797 The enemy have frequently obliged the American soldiers in their possession as prisoners of war to labour in erecting works or fortifications. **1796** *Ann. 4th Congress* 2 Sess. 1691 Two clauses had been omitted in the bill for the protection and relief of American seamen. **1808** *Ann. 10th Congress* 2 Sess. 536 Napoleon tells the American Minister, virtually, that we are very good Americans. **1837** PECK *New Guide* 278 Some of the early American settlers provided orchards [in Illinois]. **1856** STOWE *Dred* I. 248 He conceived the hopeless project of imitating the example set by the American race. **1880** ADAMS *Democracy* ii. 31 An American Senator represents a sovereign state. **1881** *Harper's Mag.* May 803/1 With the exception of psalmodists and tune and ballad writers, American composers were unhonored and unknown. **1909** G. F. PARKER *G. Cleveland* 84 Demands for the protection of American citizens came from Mexico, England, and Turkey.

(3) **1777** *Journals Cont. Congress* IX. 769 A reward for his merit and services in the American army. **1789** *Ann. 1st Congress* I. 112 It is obvious that such policy would go to exclude American shipping altogether from foreign ports. *Ib.* 178 He believed no ship paid a clear profit of five per cent. to the owner at this time; such was the embarrassed state of American commerce. **1818** *Ann. 15th Congress* 1 Sess. I. 175 The memorial of the Philadelphia Society for the promotion of American manufactures. **1836** *Diplom. Corr. Texas* (1908) I. 116 Altho' sailing under the American flag, the vessell will not be American property. **1839** *S. Lit. Messenger* V. 5/2 He was proscribed for his long and faithful services in the American consulate. **1846** *Knickerb.* XXVII. 412 A wagon was approaching, . . . over which waved the American flag with its stars and stripes. **1880** *Harper's Mag.* July 270/1 While he was concerned in the management of the American Post-office. **1881** *Ib.* Jan. 320/1 There is some 'honest hilarity' still left among the grave judges of our highest American tribunal.

(4) **1791** *Ann. 2nd Congress* 20 The design . . . of a monument for perpetuating the memory of the American Revolution. **1799** WELD *Travels* 156 Our landlord . . . came to us, to request that we would excuse the confused state in which his house was, as this was the anniversary day of 'American Independence.' **1824** CLAY in *House Repr.* 30 March, We must speedily adopt a genuine American policy. **1837** *S. Lit. Messenger* III. 643 On the subject of American slavery, her detestation is avowed as being entertained long before entering the slave states. **1856** HAMBLETON *Biog. H. A. Wise* 243 The 'American Reformation' now in progress, is sustained by men of all the various political complexions. **1866** RICHARDSON *Secret Service* iii. 52 It first proved what has since been abundantly demonstrated in the Crimean War, and the American Rebellion—the superiority of earthworks over brick and stone. **1881** *Harper's Mag.* Jan. 274/1 The average duration of an American policy is only about seven years.

(5) **1802** *Ann. 7th Congress* 2 Sess. 288 He had seen many pieces of American [gold] coin. **1837** *S. Lit. Messenger* III. 760 This is truly an 'American Book.' **1865** *Atlantic Mo.* XV. 76 There is no need of referring to the rapid advance of American literature. **1881** *Harper's Mag.* Jan. 191/1 The romance of the earlier days of the city of New York . . . is precisely the material for a stirring chapter of American folk-lore. **1886** HOWELLS *Ib.* Jan. 324/1 We shall probably never have a great American novel as fancied by the fondness of critics.

(6) **1821** COOPER *Spy* xiii, The board now fairly groaned with American profusion. *Ib.* xv, The weather . . . now changed with the suddenness of the American climate. **1837** *S. Lit. Messenger* III. 569 The table did not indeed display the abundant luxuries of an American or Scotch breakfast. **1851** *N. Amer. Misc.* I. 47/2 That of Mr. Webster possesses a Republican fervor, an American grandiloquence. **1864** GRAY *War Lett.* 359 The table [on the steamboat] is pretty good, though I never saw the American system of numerous little dishes ever carried to such an extent.

b. In the names of societies, publications, etc.

1780 [see ACADEMY 4]. **1810** *Ann. Repts. Amer. Bd. Comm.* (1834) 11 The Board shall be known by the name . . . of the American Board of Commissioners for Foreign Missions. **1813** *Western Gleaner* (Pittsburgh) I. 31 The attempts, however, made by the American Vineyard Society near Philadelphia . . . deserve the greatest praise. **1818** *Ann. 15th Congress* 1 Sess. II. 528 The most obvious interest of the States who have . . . recognised the existence of the American Colonization Society. **1836** (*title*), The American Expositor, or Intellectual Definer. . . . By R. Claggett, A. M. **1838** *Democratic Rev.* I. 241 The name of the writer of the letter was withheld when it was published in the American Citizen. **1842** *McDonogh Papers* 70 On Saturday morning . . . the agent of the American Colonization Society . . . crossed the river to . . . see them take their departure. **1864** C. VAUX *Villas* (ed. 2) p. xvi, An American Institute of Architects has been formally organized. **1881** *Harper's Mag.* April 662/1 Scholarships are given by the American Missionary Association of New York.

c. In restricted sense. (Cf. AMERICAN *n.* 2 b. and AMERICAN HORSE.)

1823 JAMES *Exped.* I. 243 They [=the Pawneemahas] have always demeaned themselves well toward the American whites. **1837** *S. Lit. Messenger* III. 60 As to the 'American adventurers' along the coast he spoke of them as entitled to but little consideration. **1841** FOOTE *Texas & Texans* II. 83 A transaction . . . which will . . . call down retributive vengeance upon these American Algerines. **1869** BROWNE *Adv. Apache Country* 61 Tebarro, the next great [Indian] chief, wrapped himself in an American blanket, and dyed his face a gloomy black. **1891** *Harper's Mag.* June 4/2 His horse is an American, i.e. one which comes from the States, and is in no wise allied to the bronco.

3. Used to designate English as spoken or written in the United States.

1740 *Georgia Col. Rec.* IV. 670 The American Dialect distinguishes Land into Pine, Oak and Hickory. **1789** WEBSTER *Diss. Eng. Lang.* 19 Nothing but the establishment of schools and some uniformity in the use of books, can annihilate differences in speaking and preserve the purity of the American tongue. **1802** *Ann. 7th Congress* 1 Sess. 687 To express my idea still more clearly, and in American language. **1806** WEBSTER *Dict.* Pref. (ad fin.), In fifty years from this time, the American-English will be spoken by more people, than all the other dialects of the language. **1815** *N. Amer. Rev.* I. 310 To his transatlantic brethren, how little would there be in his labours to admire, but the American language, and the American literature? **1822** *Missionary Herald* XVIII. 148 The father told the Osages how well his children were fed and clothed, and how fast they learned to speak the American language. **1872** EGGLESTON *Hoosier Schoolm.* Pref. 4 Mr. Lowell . . . has given careful attention to American dialects. **1894** HEMPL in *Dialect Notes* I. 315 The systematic study of American speech. **1919** MENCKEN (*title*), The American Language.

American aloe. The century plant (*Agave americana*), frequently cultivated for ornament, and flowering only after a long period. †Also, the false aloe, *A. Virginica.* {1731–}

[**1731** MILLER *Gard. Dict.* s.v. *Aloe*, A vulgar Error . . . relating to the large American Aloe, which is, that it never flowers until it is an hundred Years old.] **1781–2** JEFFERSON *Notes Va.* (1787) 38 American aloe. *Agave Virginica.* **1814** RICH *Amer. Plants* 38 American Aloe. Corol superior, funnel form. **1848** E. BRYANT *California* xxxiii. 391 Among the plants I noticed the American aloe, (*Agave americana*) which is otherwise called maguey. **1856** *Rep. Comm. Patents: Agric.* 243 The 'Great American aloes,' or 'Century plant,' . . . the fibre of which is manufactured into cordage and various other articles of use. **1858** WARDER *Hedges & Evergreens* 284 American Aloe is native of the tropical parts of South America . . . . The Aloe develops itself grandly in the Southern States; but in the Northern, must be kept in a conservatory. **1870** *Amer. Naturalist* III. 399 A large specimen of the American aloe (*Agave Americana*) standing in the Post Office yard perished from the same cause.

+**American antelope.** [tr. *Antilope americana* (Ord, 1815).] The pronghorn or cabrit (*Antilocapra americana*), a ruminant of the Western

U. S. — **1868** *Amer. Naturalist* Dec. 537 American Antelope (*Antilocapra americana*) [are] very abundant along the upper Missouri, and to the Rocky Mountains.

+American arbor-vitae. An evergreen shrub (*Thuja occidentalis*), often planted for ornament.

1785 MARSHALL *Amer. Grove* 152 *Thuja odorata.* American sweet-scented Arbor Vitæ. **1815** DRAKE *Cincinnati* ii. 80 A catalogue of the forest trees [of Miami Co. includes] Hazle nut, . . . American arbor vitae. **1832** BROWNE *Sylva Amer.* 302 American Arbor Vitæ . . . [grows] on the banks of . . . the Hudson amidst the highlands, along the Erie canal from Rome to Montezuma, and near the rapids of the Potomac in Virginia. **1856** *Rep. Comm. Patents: Agric.* 316 The 'American arbor-vitæ' . . . makes the finest ornamental hedge known to this climate. **1892** APGAR *Trees Northern U. S.* 194 American Arbor-Vitæ. . . . Wild north, and extensively cultivated throughout under more than a score of named varieties.

+American ash. The white ash, *Fraxinus americana.*

1744 F. MOORE *Voy. Georgia* 98 The trees in the grove are mostly bay, . . . hickory, American ash. **1785** MARSHALL *Amer. Grove* 51 *Fraxinus alba,* American White Ash. **1820** T. GREEN *Univ. Herbal* II. 856/2 *Fraxinus americana,* American Ash-tree.—There are several varieties of this, White Ash, Red Ash, Black Ash, &c. **1846** BROWNE *Trees Amer.* 395 We have considered all the alleged species of the American ash, only as varieties. **1897** SUDWORTH *Arborescent Flora* 327 *Fraxinus americana,* White Ash. . . . Common names [include] . . . American Ash (Iowa).

+American aspen. A variety of poplar tree, *Populus tremuloides.* Also attrib. with *tree.*

1785 MARSHALL *Amer. Grove* 107 American Aspen-tree. **1810** MICHAUX *Arbres* I. 39 American aspen (Trémble d'Amérique) . . . dans les États du milieu et du nord. **1832** BROWNE *Sylva Amer.* 257 The American aspen is ordinarily about 30 feet in height and five or six inches in diameter. **1847** DARLINGTON *Weeds & Plants* 330 American aspen . . . is occasionally planted about houses and lawns, for shade and ornament. **1850** *New Eng. Farmer* II. 411 The American Aspen is a small, graceful tree. **1892** APGAR *Trees Northern U. S.* 168 American Aspen . . . [is] common both in forests and in cultivation.

+American avoset. =AVOSET.

1785 PENNANT *Arctic Zoology* II. 502 Avoset, . . . American, . . . with a slender black bill. **1813** WILSON *Ornithology* VII. 126 American Avoset. *Recurvirostra Americana.* . . . In describing the long-legged Avoset of this volume, the similarity between that and the present was taken notice of. **1844** *Nat. Hist. N. Y., Zoology* II. 267 The American Avoset, or Blue-stocking as it is called in New Jersey, is a scarce bird on the shores of this State. **1858** BAIRD *Birds Pacific R. R.* 703 American Avosit . . . appears to inhabit the whole of North America to the Arctic regions.

+American badger. (See quots.) — **1826** GODMAN *Nat. Hist.* I. 179 The American Badger has been . . . but recently established as a species distinct from the badger of Europe. *Ib.* 181 The American badger is a pretty little animal, and its aspect is not unlike that of some small pug-faced dogs. **1889** *Cent.* 417/3 The American badger, *Taxidea americana,* resembles the foregoing [=European species], but differs in the dental formula.

+American barn owl. (See quots.) — **1844** *Nat. Hist N. Y., Zoology* II. 31 The American Barn Owl, *Strix Pratincola,* . . . is nocturnal, feeding on field mice, shrew moles, etc. **1874** COUES *Birds N. W.* 298 *Strix Flammea* var. *Americana,* (Aud.) Schl. . . . The American Barn Owl . . . appears of rather delicate and sensitive organization.

+American bear. A bear (*Ursus americana*) found in the western U.S. — **1826** GODMAN *Nat. Hist.* I. 114 American, or Black Bear . . . is found throughout North America, from the shores of the Arctic Sea, to its southern extremity. *Ib.* 130 The yellow bear of Carolina is also a variety of the black or American bear. **1832** *N. H. Hist. Soc. Coll.* III. 197 The American Bear has a long pointed nose, and is generally smaller than most other kinds.

+American Beauty.

1. A variety of apple.

1859 ELLIOTT *Western Fruit Book* 122 American Beauty, [also called] Sterling Beauty. . . . Flesh white, crisp, and juicy, with a sweet, rich, vinous flavor.

2. A hybrid variety of cultivated rose with deep-pink to crimson flowers. Also attrib. with *rose.*

1887 *Columbus* (O.) *Hort. Soc. Journal* II. 43 The American Beauty is one of the finest introductions of late years, popular as a winter bloomer. **1889** *Garden & Forest* 16 Oct. 588/1 Flowers were in great demand in New York. . . . Fine American Beauty Roses retailed for a dollar each. **1905** N. DAVIS *Northerner* 212 'You have dropped your rose,' he said to Joan, as the American Beauty in her hair tumbled to the floor. **1911** LINCOLN *Cap'n Warren* xiii. 208 Then came, by messenger, a dozen American Beauty roses.

+American beech. A variety of beech tree, *Fagus americana* (*F. ferruginea*).

1785 MARSHALL *Amer. Grove* 46 American Beech Tree. . . . The nuts are eaten by swine. **1847** DARLINGTON *Weeds & Plants* (1860) 319 American Beech . . . [grows in] low moist woodlands. **1857** GRAY *Botany* 408 American Beech. . . . Woods; common, especially northward, and along the Alleghanies southward. **1892** APGAR *Trees Northern U. S.* 161 American Beech . . . [is a] large tree, 60 to 100 ft. high, with . . . firm, light-colored, close-grained wood.

+American bison. =BUFFALO *n.* — **1890** E. B. CUSTER *Following Guidon* 180 All of the wide plains about us for hundreds of miles . . . were stamped with the presence of the American bison.

+American bittern. A wading bird (*Botaurus mugitans* or *B. lentiginosus*) allied to the heron.

1813 WILSON *Ornithology* VIII. 35 American Bittern, *Ardea Minor,* . . . is another nocturnal species, common to all our sea and river marshes. **1844** *Nat. Hist. N. Y., Zoology* II. 226 The American Bittern . . . is a shy and solitary bird, preferring the depths of swamps and marshes. **1870** *Amer. Naturalist* III. 178, I have never seen more beautiful feathers than those of the American Bittern. **1874** COUES *Birds N.W.* 523 [The] American Bittern . . . is migratory, and its movements are regular.

+American black poplar. A variety of poplar (*Populus hudsonica*) found in New York state and Canada. — **1810** MICHAUX *Arbres* I. 40 American black poplar, nom donné par moi. **1832** BROWNE *Sylva Amer.* 256 The wood of the American black poplar is inferior to that of the Virginian and Lombardy poplars. **1859** HILLHOUSE tr. *Michaux's Sylva* II. 167 Several large trees . . . are seen growing in New York, near the Park, which are called American Black Poplars.

+American blight. (See quotation.) — **1851** BARRY *Fruit Garden* 366 The Woolly Aphis or American Blight . . . is a small insect, covered with a white woolly substance that conceals its body. They infest the apple tree in particular.

+American-born, *a.* Born in America.

1779 *N. J. Archives* 2 Ser. III. 530 Ran away from the subscriber, . . . a likely, stout Mulatto lad, . . . American born. **1781** S. PETERS *Hist. Conn.* (1829) 270 Those American born Spaniards, I say, were yet, after all, excluded from royal honors and trust. **1860** HOLMES *E. Venner* xii, Every American-born husband is a possible President of these United States. **1884** *Century Mag.* XXVII. 517/1 American born rams of the breed were sold for enormous prices. **1923** R. HERRICK *Lilla* 226 He thinks the Reibens should be interned, although both of them are American born.

+American Bottom. A stretch of level ground in southwestern Illinois, extending along the east bank of the Mississippi from Alton to Chester.

1807 C. SCHULTZ *Travels* II. 38 You next ride fifteen miles over one of the richest and most beautiful tracts I have ever seen. It is called the American Bottom, and is a prairie of such extent as to weary the eye in tracing its boundaries. **1824** [W. N. BLANE] *Excursion U. S.* 190 Eight miles before coming to the Mississippi I passed a sudden declivity, and found myself upon a large plain, extending to the river, and called the 'American Bottom.' **1835** C. J. LATROBE *Rambler in N. A.* II. 237 That proverbially fertile plain, stretching along the eastern banks of the Mississippi for nearly eighty miles, above and below St. Louis, and called the 'American Bottom.' **1845** *Knickerb.* XXV. 189 About six miles from the Mississippi river . . . is situated a remarkable group of mounds, which rise out of the level prairie of the American Bottom. **1857–8** *Ill. Agric. Soc. Trans.* III. 411 He settled first in the American Bottom, and then in the prairie at New Design.

+American buffalo. =BUFFALO *n.* — **1890** E. B. CUSTER *Following Guidon* 201 These great black blotches against the faultless sky were my introduction to the American buffalo.

+American-built, *a.* Of ships: Built in America.

1790 *Ann. 1st Congress* II. 1560 Because owning American built ships should be an object to foreigners who traded with the United States. **1866** 'F. KIRKLAND' *Bk. Anecdotes* 373/1 The stranger looked like an American-built vessel, having long mast-heads and a sharp overhanging bow. **1878** A. L. PERRY *Pol. Econ.* 556 Tonnage dues were . . . thirty cents per ton on American-built but foreign-owned ships.

+American carp. (See quotation.) — **1860** *Harper's Mag.* March 488/2 The sun-fish . . . is sometimes called the 'American carp,' and has, for a scientific name, that of *Pomotis vulgaris.*

+American ceanothus. A shrub (*Ceanothus americanus*) also known as redroot or New Jersey tea. — **1785** MARSHALL *Amer. Grove* 27 American Ceanothus, or New-Jersey Tea-Tree. This is a low shrub, growing common in most parts of North America.

+American centaury. A genus of plants (*Sabbatia*) native to America.

1836 LINCOLN *Botany* App. 135 *Sabbatia angularis,* American centaury. **1843** TORREY *Flora N. Y.* II. 113 American Centaury . . . is very bitter, and is used in domestic practice as a tonic. **1857** GRAY *Botany* 342 American Centaury . . . [has] handsome (white or rose-purple) flowers. **1869** FULLER *Flower Gatherers* 288 Uncle John described the *Sabbatia* or American Centaury, and told the boys where they would be likely to find one species at least, the *stellaris.* **1901** MOHR *Plant-life Ala.* 670 The herb, 'American centaury,' . . . is an obsolete medicine.

+American chameleon. (See quotation.) — **1881** *Amer. Naturalist* XV. 96 The green lizard . . . of the Southern United States is sometimes called the American chameleon, but it is not related to the chameleon of the Old World.

+American cherry. *Obs.* One or other of the wild cherries of the Southern states. Also attrib. with *tree.*

1741 *Georgia Hist. Soc. Coll.* II. 250 In the choicest part of this land grow persimmon trees, and a few black mulberry and American cherry trees, and hickory. **1763** *S. Car. Hist. Coll.* II. 468 A few black mulberry and American cherry trees . . . grow on this land. **1765** R. ROGERS *Concise Acc.* 138 On these lands [N. & S. Car.] are found the black mulberry, the American cherry, fox and cluster grapes, as they are called by the inhabitants, the former about the size of a small cherry, the latter of a white currant.

+**American chestnut.** The ordinary chestnut (*Castanea dentata*) of the United States. Also attrib. with *tree.*

1785 MARSHALL *Amer. Grove* 46 American Chesnut Tree. . . . The timber is used much for rails, splitting free and out-lasting most of our Oaks. **1832** BROWNE *Sylva Amer.* 131 The American chesnut sometimes attains the height of 70 or 80 feet with a circumference of 15 or 16 feet. **1859** HILLHOUSE tr. *Michaux's Sylva* III. 12 Though the American Chestnut nearly resembles that of Europe in its general appearance, its foliage, its fruit, & the properties of its wood, it is treated by botanists as a distinct species. **1901** MOHR *Plant-life Ala.* 468 American Chestnut . . . Important timber and nut tree.

+**American columbo.** The plant *Frasera carolinensis.* Also, the root of this, used medicinally.

1836 LINCOLN *Botany* App. 98 *Frasera verticillata,* American columbo. . . . Medicinal. [Grows in] swamps. **1843** TORREY *Flora N. Y.* II. 109 American Columbo. . . . The root . . . is esteemed a good bitter tonic. **1857** GRAY *Botany* 344 American Columbo. . . . Tall and showy herbs. **1901** MOHR *Plant-life Ala.* 672 The root, known as 'American colombo,' is used in medicine.

+**American coot.** The common coot or 'shuffler,' *Fulica americana.*

1835 AUDUBON *Ornith. Biog.* III. 291 The American Coot . . . [is] extremely numerous in the southern parts of the Floridas, and the lower portions of Louisiana. **1844** *Nat. Hist. N. Y., Zoology* II. 272 The American Coot . . . frequents low marshy spots near the coast. **1869** *Amer. Naturalist* III. 231 In the marshes and low swampy islands near the coast, occur . . . the American Coot and the Florida Gallinule.

+**American cowslip.** A flower (*Dodecatheon Meadia*) found in the central U.S.; also called 'shooting star.'

1787 *Fam. Plants* I. 107 *Dodecatheon,* . . . American Cowslip. **1813** MUHLENBERG *Cat. Plants* 19 American cowslip. . . . Pens. fl. Maio. **1828** BECK in *Trans. Albany Inst.* I. 16 American cowslip . . . has an extensive range from east to west. **1847** WOOD *Botany* 385 American cowslip, or Mead's cowslip. **1863** *Rep. Comm. Agric.* 159 The American cowslip . . . is a native of the western States.

+**American creeper.** (See quotations.) — **1858** BAIRD *Birds Pacific R.R.* 372 *Certhia Americana,* . . . American Creeper, . . . [inhabits] North America generally. **1874** COUES *Birds N. W.* 751 (Index), American Creeper, 26. [*Ib.* 27 I am unable to perceive any difference between American and European examples.]

+**American crossbill.** The red crossbill, *Loxia curvirostra.* — **1811** WILSON *Ornithology* IV. 44 American Crossbill. *Curvirostra Americana.* . . . This species is a regular inhabitant of almost all our pine forests situated north of 40°. **1844** *Nat. Hist. N. Y., Zoology* II. 182 The American Crossbill . . . may be considered as a northern species, breeding in this State and as far South as Pennsylvania.

+**American crow.** The common American species of crow, *Corvus americanus.*

1834 AUDUBON *Ornith. Biog.* II. 317 The American Crow . . . is an extremely shy bird, having found familiarity with man no way to his advantage. **1857** *Rep. Comm. Patents: Agric.* 135 The American crow . . . congregates in immense numbers in the Southern and Western States during winter. **1870** *Amer. Naturalist* III. 384 Winter Birds . . . seen in the vicinity of Utica, N.Y. [include] . . . American Crow.

+**American cypress.** A variety of tree (*Taxodium distichum*) allied to the cypress; better known as 'bald cypress.' — **1775** ROMANS *Nat. Hist. Florida* 25 If these swamps are not altogether sand, but mixed with clay, and other earth, their produce is in general . . . American deciduous cypress. **1813** MUHLENBERG *Cat. Plants* 89 Bald cypress, deciduous cypress, or American cypress. **1876** *Field & Forest* I. 36 Of the American Cypress . . . there are some noble specimens in several of the parks [at Washington].

+**American desert. a.** An indefinite area to the east of the Rio Grande and the Rocky Mountains, at one time regarded as a desert. Freq. with the adj. *Great.* **b.** A tract of country lying south and west of Great Salt Lake.

1834 PIKE *Sketches* 10 It is into this great American desert that I wish to conduct my readers. **1836** IRVING *Astoria* II. 114 The Great American Desert . . . is a region that almost discourages all hope of cultivation. **1844** LEE & FROST *Oregon* xix. 207 These two ladies are the first white females who came to Oregon, and the first who adventured across the American desert. **1873** BEADLE *Undevel. West* 626 Leaving the Rio Grande, we enter the 'American Desert,' which continues with but bare oases all the way to and beyond the Colorado. **1887** C. B. GEORGE *40 Years on Rail* vii. 130 The engineer suffers . . . when he crosses the long, treeless tracts of prairie land, or the arid plains of our American desert. **1891** *Century Mag.* March 643 The young Western communities that are rising into vigorous health upon this same 'American Desert.' **1904** W. H. SMITH *Promoters* xxi. 307, I can't afford to pay that price, even for a friend who can wet up the American Desert.

+**American dipper.** The water-ouzel, *Cinclus mexicanus.* — **1828** BONAPARTE *Ornithology* III. 5 Having seen nothing but the dried skin of the American Dipper, . . . we [etc.]. **1849** AUDUBON *Ornith. Biog.* V. 303 The present bird is merely an immature individual of the American Dipper. **1858** BAIRD *Birds Pacific R. R.* 229 American Dipper . . . [inhabits the] Rocky mountains from British America to Mexico. **1874** COUES *Birds N.W.* 10 American Dipper [or] Water Ouzel.

+**American eagle.**

1. The bald eagle (*Haliaëtus leucocephalus*), a large bird of prey.

1786 in *Amer. Museum* (1789) II. 182 Gold coins . . . stamped with the impression of the American eagle. **1817** PAULDING *Lett. from South* II. 254 On the summit of the cliff, resides the American eagle, emblem of our freedom. **1849** *Knickerb.* XXXIV. 150/2 While he was a-talking about the American eagle, a tolerable-sized bird of that specie come and lit onto his crown. **1884** ROE *Nature's Story* 50 We have only two species of the genuine eagle in this country, the bald, or American, and the golden, or ring-tailed. **1892** BENDIRE *N. A. Birds* 274 The Bald or American Eagle, our national emblem, is pretty generally distributed over the entire United States.

2. A conventional representation of the bald eagle used to symbolize the United States.

1782 *Journals of Congress* (1823) IV. 39 The escutcheon on the breast of the American eagle displayed proper. **1789** WASHINGTON *Diaries* IV. 34 Over the center of it [=an arch] a canopy was erected 20 feet high, with the American eagle perched on the top. **1813** *Niles' Reg.* V. 147/1 The theatre presented a transparent painting, exhibiting the American eagle spreading over a considerable portion of the globe. **1819** *Ib.* XVI. 240/2 The cause which has driven into the woods at the approach of the American eagle, the same people who had quit the forest [etc.]. **1833** H. BARNARD in *Md. Hist. Mag.* XIII. 356 The Union badge is an American Eagle, mounted upon black with a small tassell. **1897** FLANDRAU *Harvard Episodes* 299 If his father had seen fit to send him to a business college to learn how to audit accounts, and make an American eagle with a fist full of thunderbolts in two penstrokes. **1906** PITTMAN *Belle of Blue Grass C.* xvi. 248 The rostrum, where the politicians were flying the American Eagle, for this was the opening of the campaign season.

+**American elk. 1.** The moose. **2.** The wapiti.

(1) **1771** PENNANT *Synopsis* 40 The two pair of American Elk or Moose [which] I have examined. **1775** ROMANS *Nat. Hist. Florida* 174 The Moose, or American Elk, found in the higher latitudes on the river, naturally leads a life . . . approaching to a state of domestication.

(2) **1858** THOREAU *Letters* (1865) 170 The American elk of American authors (*Cervus Canadensis*) is a distinct animal from the moose (*Cervus alces*). **1890** *Cent.* s.v. *Moose,* The American elk or wapiti, *Elephas (Cervus) canadensis.*

+**American elm.** The white elm (*Ulmus americana*), a species common in the United States, or a variety of this.

1785 MARSHALL *Amer. Grove* 156 American rough leaved Elm-tree . . . rises to the height of about thirty feet, with a pretty strong trunk. *Ib.,* *Ulmus mollifolia,* American Soft-leaved Elm. **1813** MUHLENBERG *Cat. Plants* 29 American elm, (white elm) (weeping elm) . . . Pens. fl. Apr. **1815** *N. Amer. Rev.* II. 59 Not a single American elm was started, though many of their branches were twisted off. **1843** T. TALBOT *Journals* 29 The Indians in addition use many roots. . . . The following are external applications: sassafras, American Elm. **1851** E. S. WORTLEY *Travels U. S.* x. 54 It is deliciously cool, protected from the sun by the overshadowing masses of foliage of the most magnificent weeping (American) elms. **1857** GRAY *First Lessons* 28 Figure 54 represents a spreading-topped tree (American Elm). **1868** BEECHER *Norwood* 4 Of all trees, no other unites, in the same degree, majesty and beauty, grace and grandeur, as the American Elm! **1897** SUDWORTH *Arborescent Flora* 181 Weeping American Elm.

+**Americaness.** A female American; a woman of American birth.

1838 COOPER *Home as Found* I. vi. 93 Every true American and Americaness was expected to be at his or her post, for the solemn occasion. **1844** 'UNCLE SAM' *Peculiarities* II. 273 He approached the fountain with his companion, after admiring a very beautiful Americaness. *a***1888** *Hallberger's Illus. Mag.* (F.) This lady is like most Americanesses—she hates walking.

+**American goldfinch.** The thistle-bird, *Chrysomitris* or *Spinus tristis.*

*c***1730** CATESBY *Carolina* I. 43 *Carduelis Americanus:* The American Goldfinch . . . agrees, in size and Shape, with our Goldfinch . . . In Virginia they are most frequent. **1783** LATHAM *Synopsis* III. 288 American Goldfinch. . . . These inhabit North America, particularly about New York, where they are summer birds. **1831** AUDUBON *Ornith. Biog.* I. 172 The American Goldfinch . . . passes over the State of Louisiana in the beginning of January. **1844** *Nat. Hist. N. Y., Zoology* II. 166 The Yellow-Bird, or American Goldfinch, . . . is often kept in cages for its song. **1884** ROE *Nature's Story* 114 A fit associate for the song sparrow is the American goldfinch, or yellowbird.

+**American goshawk.** A species of hawk, *Astur atricapillus;* the chicken-hawk. — **1839** PEABODY *Mass. Birds* 266 The American Goshawk . . . will dash down at the farmer's door and carry off chickens so rapidly that it is hardly possible to shoot the robber. **1844** *Nat. Hist. N. Y., Zoology* II. 19 The American Goshawk . . . preys on ducks, pigeons, hares, etc. **1874** COUES *Birds N. W.* 338 The American Goshawk . . . [is] one of the handsomest birds of the family when in perfect plumage.

+**American hazel(nut).** The species of hazel (*Corylus americana*) common in the United States.

1785 MARSHALL *Amer. Grove* 37 American Hazelnut . . . grows very common in a rich, loose, moist soil. **1813** MUHLENBERG *Cat. Plants* 88 *Corylus Americana:* American hazle. . . . Pens.: fl. April. **1843** TORREY *Flora N. Y.* II. 186 American Hazel-nut. Wild Filbert. . . . [The nuts] are frequently seen in our markets and fruit stores. **1890** *Cent.* s.v. *Hazel*, The American hazel . . . is a bush, usually growing in dense thickets from which it excludes nearly all other vegetation. **1901** MOHR *Plant-life Ala.* 61 The American hazelnut . . . in the forests of mountains in Clay and Cleburne counties frequently forms the dense brushy undergrowth.

+**American hellebore.** Swamp or green hellebore, *Veratrum viride.* — **1820** *U. S. Pharmacopœia* 257 [Recipe for] Ointment of American Hellebore. Take of American hellebore in powder, two ounces [etc.]. **1832** WILLIAMSON *Maine* I. 124 The American Hellebore and the Poke have some resemblance. **1857** GRAY *Botany* 476 American White Hellebore. Indian Poke. . . . [Grows in] swamps and low grounds. **1880** GARROD & BAXTER *Materia Med.* 382 American or Green Hellebore; called also Swamp Hellebore and Indian Poke; growing in the marshy and swampy districts of the United States and Canada.

+**American hemp.** The century plant. — **1855** *Trans. Amer. Inst. N. Y.* 333 *Agave Americana*, . . . the Admirable American Hemp.

+**American holly.** An evergreen tree (*Ilex opaca*) used for ornamental and commercial purposes.

1785 MARSHALL *Amer. Grove* 63 *Ilex aquifolium*, American Common Holly, . . . grows in Maryland, New Jersey, &c., generally in moist ground. **1810** MICHAUX *Arbres* I. 27 American Holly (Houx d'Amérique), dans toutes les parties. **1832** BROWNE *Sylva Amer.* 169 The American Holly is first met with in Connecticut and is common in all the more Southern States. **1846** — *Trees Amer.* 167 The American Holly . . . is a beautiful evergreen tree. . . . Its principal use is for inlaying mahogany furniture. **1847** DARLINGTON *Weeds & Plants* 216 American Holly . . . becomes a handsome little tree under cultivation. **1876** *Field & Forest* I. 34 The American Holly . . . is in cultivation in several of the public and private grounds [at Washington]. **1897** SUDWORTH *Arborescent Flora* 277–278.

+**American hornbeam.** The blue beech (*Carpinus americana* or *caroliniana*), a small tree indigenous to America.

1785 MARSHALL *Amer. Grove* 25 American Hornbeam. This grows common by most of our river and creek sides. **1810** MICHAUX *Arbres* I. 32 American horn-beam, (Charme d'Amérique), . . . seul nom. **1832** BROWNE *Sylva Amer.* 127 The American Hornbeam is found as far north as Nova Scotia, New Brunswick and Lower Canada. **1850** *New Eng. Farmer* II. 411 The American Hornbeam is a small, round-headed tree. **1857** GRAY *Botany* 409 American Hornbeam, Blue or Water Beech, . . . [grows] along streams. **1859** HILLHOUSE tr. *Michaux's Sylva* III. 26 The trunk of the American Hornbeam . . . is obliquely and irregularly fluted, frequently through all its length. **1894** COULTER *Bot. W. Texas* III. 413 American hornbeam, Blue or Water beech, . . . [grows] along streams.

+**American horse.** *S.W.* and *W.* [AMERICAN *a.* 2 c.] A horse from the East, distinguished by its large size from the breeds common in the southwest or California.

1837 *Diplom. Corr. Texas* (1908) I. 187 A large number of fine American horses have lately been seen tied out, which there is no doubt had been stolen from citizens of Texas. **1843** T. TALBOT *Journals* 20 Towards dusk, each man mounted his fine American or Spanish horse, . . . shaggy pony or worse mule as the case might be. **1848** E. BRYANT *California* iv. 52 Such [Indians] as rode ponies were desirous of *swapping* them for the American horses of the emigrants. **1855** F. S. MARRYAT *Mtns. & Molehills* xiv. 256 We had now six horses, all American, good sound cattle, that had come to California across the plains. **1869** BROWNE *Adv. Apache Country* 460 We encountered during the day several large bands of American horses, which had been recruiting . . . after their dreary journey across the plains. **1873** BEADLE *Undevel. West* 617 Their band contained several American horses of superior breed. **1883** *Rep. Indian Affairs* 107, I have quite recently issued 220 head of American horses to them that were purchased for them.

+**American horse-chestnut.** The buckeye, *Æsculus flava, glabra*, and *Californica.* — **1832** BROWNE *Sylva Amer.* 227 We have denominated it Ohio Buckeye, . . . and have prefixed the synonyme of American Horse Chestnut, [etc.]. **1897** SUDWORTH *Arborescent Flora* 293 *Æscula glabra*, Ohio Buckeye. . . . Common names [include] . . . American Horse Chestnut (Pa.).

+**AMERICANISM.**

1. A word, phrase, or idiom peculiar to American usage in speech or writing, as contrasted with that of England or other English-speaking countries. {1826–}

1781 WITHERSPOON *Druid P.* No. 5, The first class I call Americanisms, by which I understand an use of phrases or terms, or a construction of sentences, even among persons of rank and education, different from the use of the same terms or phrases, or the construction of similar sentences, in Great Britain. *Ib.*, The word Americanism, which I have coined for the purpose, is exactly similar in its formation and signification to the word Scotticism. **1809** WEBSTER in *Monthly Anthology* VII. 209, I am accused of introducing into my Dictionary Americanism [*sic*] and vulgarisms. *Ib.* 264 'Lengthy, *a.*, . . . ' is the worst of the whole catalogue of Americanisms. **1816** PICKERING p. iii, I first began the practice of occasionally noting Americanisms . . . during my residence in London. **1836** *S. Lit. Messenger* II. 257 The Americanisms of our language have been a prolific source of ridicule and reproach for the British critics. **1846** COOPER *Redskins* xx, It wanted about an hour to sunset—or sun-down to use our common Americanism. **1847** GOODRICH *Webster's Dictionary* p. vii, With regard to Americanisms, properly so called, . . . they are less numerous than has generally been supposed. **1848** BARTLETT (*title*), Dictionary of Americanisms. A Glossary of Words and Phrases, colloquially used in the United States. **1855** *Georgetown* (Ky.) *Herald* 14 June, It is obviously a good old English word of classical usage, and no Americanism at all. **1875** WHITNEY *Life & Growth Lang.* 156 No small number of what the English stigmatize as Americanisms are cases of survival from former good usage. **1884** NYE *Baled Hay* 56 That is where we get left, if I may be allowed an Americanism, or whatever it is. **1891** *Harper's Mag.* July 215 Briticisms and Americanisms, by Brander Matthews. *Ib.* 216/1 In America there is no necessity to plead for the right of the Americanism to exist. The cause is won.

2. Adherence or attachment to America, esp. the United States; love of America; preference for American institutions, customs, etc. {1853–}

'A love of America and preference of her interest' (W. '06).

1797 JEFFERSON *Let. to E. Rutledge* 24 June, The parties have in debate mutually charged each other . . . with being governed by an attachment to this or that of the belligerent nations, rather than the dictates of reason and pure Americanism. **1807** *N. Y. Herald* 29 Sept. 2/4 Americanism and our country forever. **1834** SIMMS *Guy Rivers* 115 A well-smoked picture of the Washington family in a tarnished gilt frame—asserting the Americanism of the proprietor and place. **1838** *Democratic Rev.* I. 151 He was a calm but powerful debater in Congress, remarkable abroad for unadulterated 'Americanism.' *c*1856 T. FLOURNOY in Claiborne *Sam. Dale* v. 87 Governor Claiborne—who was almost enthusiastic in his Americanism—advised me to declare martial law. **1884** *Century Mag.* March 678/1 Those living Americans, whose Americanism did not begin within the last half century.

3. Adoption or display of American ideas, habits, etc.; an American peculiarity of views or conduct.

1857 *Harper's Mag.* May 845/1 It would be interesting to note the class of 'Americanisms' that are the growth of our religion, and appear especially in our pulpits and conference meetings. **1858** WILLIS *Convalescent* 376 He would have been still more curiously interested . . . in the utter Americanism of his driver! **1864** LOWELL *Study Windows, Lincoln*, The earnest simplicity and unaffected Americanism of his own character. **1868** HAWTHORNE *Note-Books* I. 160 Here is an Englishman . . . upholding everything English . . . and . . . expressing his dislike of all Americanisms. **1870** EMERSON *Soc. & Solitude* ii. 232, I hate this shallow Americanism which hopes to get rich by credit, to get knowledge by raps on midnight tables [etc.]. **1887** LOWELL *Addresses* (1914) 184 By Americanism I mean that which we cannot help, . . . that way of looking at things and of treating men which we derive from the soil that holds our fathers. **1893** *Nation* 2 Feb. 75/1 The spread of American influence and domination abroad, known as 'Americanism.'

Americanist. [Fr. *Américaniste.*] A student of subjects pertaining to America, particularly its antiquities or ethnology. {1876–}

1881 *Nation* 21 April 277/2 The programme . . . of the International Congress of Americanists to be held at Madrid, Sept. 18–22. **1882** *Harper's Mag.* Aug. 351/1 Amid the general excitement of 'Americanists,' Brasseur de Bourbourg tried his skill upon one of the few Maya manuscripts. **1890** *Critic* (N.Y.) 14 June, 'Americanist' is an expressive neologism, which we owe to the scholars of France. **1900** *Amer. Anthropologist* Oct.–Dec. 749 Prof. John Comfort Fillmore, . . . whose untimely loss all Americanists so deeply mourn.

+**American ivy.** The Virginia creeper, *Ampelopsis quinquefolia.*

1785 MARSHALL *Amer. Grove* 59 *Hedera quinquefolia*, American Ivy, or Virginian Creeper. This hath a climing stem, attaching itself to any neighbouring support. **1843** TORREY *Flora N. Y.* I. 148 American Ivy . . . [grows in] borders of woods, copses, etc.; common. **1847** DARLINGTON *Weeds & Plants* 84 American Ivy . . . is one of the most ornamental of the climbers and is much cultivated . . . for covering walls and buildings. **1884** ROE *Nature's Story* 356 He now has . . . a rustic porch covered with American ivy.

+**Americanization.** The process of rendering American, or the state of being Americanized.

'The act of rendering American, or of subjection to the laws and usages of the United States' (B. '59).

1858 *Brownson's Q. Rev.* April 190 All the Americanization I insist on is, that our Catholic population shall feel and believe that a man may be a true American, and a good Catholic. **1866** LOWELL *Seward-Johnson Reaction* Prose Wks. 1890 V. 313 They are fully resolved to have the great stake they played for and won, and that stake was the Americanization of all America, nothing more and nothing less. **1880** CABLE *Grandissimes* xxxix. 309 Louisiana, no longer incredulous of her Americanization, had laid hold of her new liberties. **1884** *Century Mag.* Sept. 768 This territory [Arizona] presents a serious social problem; a considerable population here of European origin would be a welcome adjunct in the 'Americanization' of the territory. **1902** *Nation* 16 Oct. 296/1 The Sultan of Bacolod ... actually prefers death to the kind of Americanization which has been going on in Luzon, and Samar, and elsewhere these last four years. **1920** BOK *Americanization of E. Bok* 1 A family of four from the Netherlands who were to make an experiment of Americanization.

+Americanize, *v.*

1. *tr.* To render American in character; to make similar to the people, customs, or institutions of the United States.

Earliest, and most frequently, in the past pple. *Americanized.*

(1) **1797** J. JAY *Corr. & P.* (1893) IV. 232, I wish to see our people more Americanized, if I may use that expression; until we feel and act as an independent nation, we shall always suffer from foreign intrigue. **1801** JEFFERSON *Writings* VIII. 96 We return like foreigners, and, like them, require a considerable residence here to become Americanized. **1802** *Ib.* 150, I do not think you can do better than to fix here for a while, until you become Americanized and understand the map of the country. **1819** RAMSAY (*title*), Universal History Americanised; or an Historical View of the World. **1824** JACKSON *Let.* in Parton *Life* III. 36 It is time we should become a little more Americanized, and instead of feeding the paupers and laborers of Europe, feed our own. **1853** BALDWIN *Flush Times Ala.* 6 He was built after the model and structure of Bolingbroke in his youth, *Americanized* and *Hoosierized* a little. **1858** *Brownson's Q. Rev.* April 190, I want the Church Americanized no more than I want her Irishized. *a***1861** WINTHROP *J. Brent* iii. 25 He represented the same period of history modernized, and the same type of man Americanized. **1871** J. L. BOWEN in *Scribner's Mo.* I. 556 Can these men be Americanized? **1884** SWEET & KNOX *Through Texas* xxx. 397 By degrees he becomes Americanized. **1891** *Harper's Mag.* June 3/1 To see their countries become Americanized was the nightmare of rulers. **1904** *N. Y. Ev. Post* 25 May 14 The younger one is already Americanized, but one can see at a glance that the other will never take root in the alien soil in which she has been transplanted.

(2) **1806** WEBSTER, *Americanize*, v.t., to render American. **1841** FOOTE *Texas & Texans* II. 199 The great importance of Americanizing Texas by filling it with a population from this country. **1854** BARTLETT *Narr.* II. 502 A large commerce has now grown up between Monterey and the United States, which will tend to Americanize the place. **1856** *Harper's Mag.* XII. 858/1 Captain de Lacy ... inquired of passed midshipman Brook, 'How they Americanized Irishmen so rapidly?' **1866** *Congress. Globe* 31 Jan. 559/1 If she [=the South] would prosper, she must Americanize her system of life. **1898** *Library Journal* June 229/2 The library should be wholly American, and its influence tend wholly toward Americanizing the foreign-born. **1899** *Boston Herald* 4 July 4/7 We must Americanize and shorten the word.

2. *intr.* To become assimilated to the ways of the United States; to become American in character, etc.

1875 HOWELLS *Foregone Conclusion* 77 He was Americanizing in that good lady's hands as fast as she could transform him. **1882** — *Three Villages* (1884) 15 The Irish ... have Americanized in such degree that it is hard to know some of them from ourselves in their slouching and nasal speech. **1904** *Rochester Post-Express* 4 Oct. 4 The popular delusion that the Italian does not Americanize as do immigrants of other nationalities. **1905** *N. Y. Ev. Post* 19 Oct. 5, I fancy Asia will not Americanize very fast.

+Americanized, *ppl. a.* Made American in character. — **1881** *Nation* 30 June 463/2 Powers's 'Handy Book about Books' had not got out of print when Sabin prepared a new and Americanized edition.

+Americanizing, *vbl. n.* The act of rendering or becoming American or like America; the using of Americanisms.

1858 *Brownson's Q. Rev.* April 190 The Americanizing of the Catholic body does and will go on of itself. **1865** *Nation* I. 108 National safety calls for the 'Americanizing' of Europe. **1895** F. HALL in *Academy* 30 March 279/1 Such persons, if corrected, one by another, for Americanizing unnecessarily, are always very thankful.

+American joy. App. (by misreading) for: American ivy (q.v.). — **1813** MUHLENBERG *Cat. Plants* 26 American joy ..., heart-leaved: Illini. Georg. Pens. **1893** *Amer. Folk-Lore* VI. 139 *Ampelopsis quinquefolia*, five-fingered ivy; American joy. N.Y.

+American jute. The Indian mallow or velvet-leaf (*Abutilon avicennæ*), whose fiber is useful, but which is usually considered a weed. — **1863** *Rep. Comm. Agric.* 158 In the swamp ... the surface is beautiful in August with the yellow flowers of the *Hibiscus palustris*, or American 'Jute'. **1893** *Amer. Folk-Lore* VI. 139 *Abutilon avicennæ*, American jute. West Va.

+American knights. [See KNIGHT.] — **1888** LANE *Pol. Catch-Words* 13 Sept. 15 *American Knights*, Knights of the Golden Circle.

+American larch (tree).

1. The tamarack or hackmatack (*Larix americana* or *laricina*).

1785 MARSHALL *Amer. Grove* 104 *Pinus-Larix nigra.* Black American Larch-Tree. **1810** MICHAUX *Arbres* I. 31 American larch. ... Dénomination générale. **1832** BROWNE *Sylva Amer.* 193 In the north of the United States this tree is commonly designated by the name of Hackmatack, but we have preferred that of American Larch. *Ib.* 194 The American larch is a magnificent vegetable with a straight, slender trunk 80 or 100 feet in height. **1850** *New Eng. Farmer* II. 411 The American Larch ... is occasionally cultivated as an ornamental tree. **1851** SPRINGER *Forest Life* 33 The American Larch ... is sometimes known to attain an elevation of seventy feet. **1876** *Field & Forest* I. 36 The American Larch seems to have had but few admirers [at Washington], its place being mostly usurped by its English relative. **1892** APGAR *Trees Northern U. S.* 188 American Larch. ... A tree of large size ... growing wild in all the northern portion of our region.

2. (See quotations.)

1785 MARSHALL *Amer. Grove* 103 *Pinus-Larix rubea.* Red American Larch-Tree. The cones are of a fine red colour at their first appearance. *Ib.* 104 *Pinus-Larix alba.* White American Larch-Tree.

+American laurel. The mountain laurel or calico bush, *Kalmia latifolia.*

1785 MARSHALL *Amer. Grove* 71 *Kalmia.* Kalmia, or American Laurel. **1842** *Lowell Offering* II. 83 The slight fragrance of kalmia, or American Laurel, which flourishes here in much profusion, is borne upon the morning breeze. **1850** *Knickerb.* XXXVI. 291 Kalm, the Swedish botanist, who first carried the American laurel to Europe. **1857** GRAY *Botany* 255 American Laurel ... [grows on] rocky hills and damp soil, rather common from Maine to Ohio and Kentucky.

+American lime (-tree). =next.

1785, 1818 [see next]. **1832** BROWNE *Sylva Amer.* 305 American Lime or Bass Wood, *Tilia Americana.* **1846** — *Trees Amer.* 47 The American Lime-tree ..., when cultivated, proves highly ornamental. **1859** HILLHOUSE tr. *Michaux's Sylvia* III. 81 The American Lime Tree has been long cultivated in Europe.

+American linden. The basswood, *Tilia americana.*

1785 MARSHALL *Amer. Grove* 153 *Tilia americana*, American black Lime, or Linden-Tree ... often becomes a tree of a large size. **1818** *Jrnl. Science* I. 371, June 28 American lime or linden-tree ... in flower. **1850** *New Eng. Farmer* II. 142 The American Lime, Linden, or Basswood is sometimes found cultivated as an ornamental tree. **1884** SARGENT *Rep. Forests* 27 Lime Tree ... Bass Wood ... American Linden. **1889** *Cent.*, *Basswood*, ... the common name of the American linden or lime-tree.

+American linn. =prec. — **1876** *Field & Forest* I. 17 The European Linden ... as a shade tree is superior to our American Lin. **1883** P. M. HALE *Woods & Timbers N. C.* 130 American Linn ... is found from Canada to Georgia.

+Americanly, *adv.* In a manner characteristic of America. — **1832** F. A. BUTLER *Jrnl.* (1835) II. 64 Miss — ... sings very well, but pronounces Italian very Americanly, which is a pity. **1886** HOWELLS in *Harper's Mag.* Jan. 325/1 For our novelists to try to write Americanly, from any motive, would be a dismal error.

+American merino. A variety of merino sheep, bred in America.

1857–8 *Ill. Agric. Soc. Trans.* III. 458 There are three classes of Merino, the French, Spanish, and what is termed of late years, the American. The latter is a stock of sheep which have been bred from our earliest importation by Messrs. Humphrey and Jarvis, as far back as 1802. **1863** RANDALL *Pract. Shepherd* iii. 29 This great breeder has effected quite as marked an improvement in the American Merino, as Mr. Bakewell effected among the long-wooled sheep of England. **1884** *Century Mag.* Feb. 513/1 They carry their finely clothed blue-blooded bodies on four legs, for they are the famous American Merino sheep.

+American mezereon. The leatherwood, *Dirca palustris.* — **1784** CUTLER in *Mem. Academy* I. 421 American Mezerion. ... Blossoms greenish white. Berry pale red. In hedges and woodland. **1795** WINTERBOTHAM *Hist. View* III. 397 Among the native and uncultivated plants of New-England, the following have been employed for medical purposes: Tivertwig, or Amer. mazerion. **1821** *Mass. H. S. Coll.* 2 Ser. IX. 149 Plants, which are indigenous in the township of Middlebury, [Vermont, include] ... American mezereon.

+American mistletoe. A parasitic plant (*Phoradendron flavescens*) found on the red maple and other trees. — **1857** GRAY *Botany* 383 American Mistletoe. ... New Jersey to Illinois and southward, preferring elms and hickories. April. **1876** *Field & Forest* I. 66 The American Mistletoe. ... This parasitic shrub has been found growing on several Pepperidge or Sour-gum trees ... in this district. **1901** MOHR *Plant Life Ala.* 52 The ... shrubby parasites of trees are represented by a single species, the American mistletoe.

+American mountain-ash. A native species of mountain-ash, *Pyrus (Sorbus) americana.* — **1847** DARLINGTON *Weeds & Plants* 134 *Pyrus Americana.* DC. ... American Pyrus. American Mountain Ash. ... This elegant tree is often seen in cultivation. *a***1862** THOREAU *Maine Woods* 310 The prevailing shrubs and small trees along the shore were ... American mountain-ash, ... chokeberry [etc.].

+American nettle-tree. The hackberry, *Celtis occidentalis.* — **1785** MARSHALL *Amer. Grove* 29 American Yellow-Fruited Nettle-tree. ... The juice of the fruit is said to be astringent. **1810** MICHAUX *Arbres* I. 37 American nettle-tree ..., dans tous les Etats-Unis. **1846** BROWNE *Trees Amer.* 517 The American Nettle-Tree ... is ... appropriate for many purposes, but from its comparative scarcity ... it never has been applied to many uses in the arts.

+American olive (-tree). The devil-wood, *Asmanthus americanus.*

1785 MARSHALL *Amer. Grove* 98 American Olive tree ... grows naturally in Carolina and Florida, and is a beautiful ever-green tree. **1813** MUHLENBERG *Cat. Plants* 2 American olive (purple-berried bay). **1836** LINCOLN *Botany* App. 128 *Olea americana* (American olive), ... [flowers in] September. **1866** *Land We Love* (Charlotte, N. C.) May 78 American Olive . . . is a very fine evergreen, producing clusters of small white flowers. **1901** Mohr *Plant Life Ala.* 14 Their banks adorned with evergreen andromedas, American olive, . . . sweet bay, and azaleas.

+**American osprey.** (See quotation.) — **1858** Baird *Birds Pacific R. R.* 44 *Pandion Carolinensis*, Gmelin, the Fish Hawk; the American Osprey, [is found] throughout temperate North America.

+**American panther.** The catamount. — **1888** Warner *On Horseback* 100 The scene of a desperate encounter between Big Tom and a catamount, or American panther.

+**American partridge.** The bob-white or quail, *Ortyx virginianus.*

1743 Catesby *Carolina* II. p. xliv, The American Partridge . . . is little more than half the size of the *Perdix Cinerea*, or common Partridge. **1781–2** Jefferson *Notes Va.* (1788) 74 Birds of Virginia [include] . . . American partridge, American quail. **1809** F. Cuming *Western Tour* 255 Notes resembling . . . the call of the quail, or American partridge. **1839** Peabody *Mass. Birds* 353 The American Quail, or Partridge, . . . is a gentle bird, and fond of associating with its own race. **1844** *Nat. Hist. N. Y., Zoology* II. 202 The common American Quail, or Partridge, as it is indifferently called in various sections of the country, occurs in every part of the State. **1874** Coues *Birds N.W.* 430 The American Partridges have been separated as a subfamily from those of the Old World.

+**American party.** A political party supporting American interests; *spec.* one active in national affairs from 1853 to 1859, antagonistic to the influence of the foreign-born; colloq. called *Know-nothing party* (q.v.).

'A party organization that first became active in New York in 1844. It accomplished very little until about 1853, when it appeared as a political secret society' (Lane). — Cf. *Native American Party.*

1835 *Louisville Public Advt.* 24 June, An 'American party' might have a good run. **1855** *Harper's Mag.* X. 829/1 The candidates presented by the 'Know Nothing' or 'American' party have to a great extent formed a centre around which all the elements of opposition to the Administration have gathered. **1864** *Congress. Globe* 7 March 979/2 The American party had men up for office and I supported them not because they were pro-slavery or anti-slavery, but because they were the choice of the American party. It was well known that the American party was neutral upon that subject.

+**American pestilence.** = American plague. — **1811** Mease *Philadelphia* 37 Philadelphia has suffered severely by the American pestilence, commonly called yellow fever.

+**American pipit.** The common titlark or pipit, *Anthus ludovicianus* or *pennsylvanicus.* — **1876** Burroughs *Winter Sunshine* viii. 171 The third day . . . the American pipit or titlark, from the far North, a brown bird about the size of a sparrow, dropped upon the deck of the ship.

+**American plague.** (See quotation.) — **1830** J. F. Watson *Philadelphia* 600 Noah Webster, speaking of this sickness, says, after the severe winter the city was severely visited with 'the American plague.' The same disease Doctor Bond has said was yellow fever, supposed to have been introduced by a load of sick people from Dublin.

+**American plan.** The system of charging an inclusive price for room and board in a hotel.

This distinctive system was noted by early English travelers, e.g.: **1805** Parkinson *Tour* 566 It is customary when you put your horse up and lodge in a tavern to pay a regular price, dine or not, for every meal, which is called boarding in the house. **1833** T. Hamilton *Men & Manners* II. 158 It is the invariable custom in the United States to charge by the day or week; and travellers are thus obliged to pay for meals whether they eat them or not.

[**1856** Murray *Letters from U.S.* 56, I like one American plan, of paying for inn accommodations; no bill of items is ever given. The payment is at the rate of three or four dollars a-day, and there is an end of it.] **1879** *Appleton's Guide to U.S. & Canada* 1 The [N.Y.] hotels conducted on the regular or American plan. **1886** *Appleton's Hand Bk. Summer Resorts* 201 Earle's Hotel: . . . American plan, room and board, $2.00 per day. **1899** *Baedeker's U.S.* p. xxvi, A distinction is made between Hotels on the American Plan . . . and Hotels on the European Plan. **1906** 'O. Henry' *Rolling Stones* (1912) 14 The Hotel Ingles, a beanery run on the American plan.

+**American plane (-tree).** The buttonwood, *Platanus occidentalis.*

1785 Marshall *Amer. Grove* 105 American Plane-Tree, or large Button Wood, . . . is sometimes sawed into boards. **1836** Lincoln *Botany* App. 126 Buttonwood, American plane-tree, false sycamore. **1857** Gray *Botany* 401 American Plane or Sycamore.

+**American pride.** *Obs.* A species of lobelia. — **1784** Cutler in *Mem. Academy* I. 484 *Lobelia.* . . . American Pride. Blossoms scarlet. Borders of brooks and rivers.

+**American quail.** (See American partridge, quots. 1781, 1839–44.)

+**American raspberry.** The black raspberry or blackcap, *Rubus occidentalis.* — **1785** Marshall *Amer. Grove* 138 American Raspberry. . . . The flowers are . . . succeeded by small fruit of a reddish black colour when ripe. **1821** Nuttall *Trav. Arkansa* 168 Near the Arkansa, we meet with the hazel . . . and the American raspberry.

+**American redstart.** A species of flycatching warbler, *Setophaga (Muscicapa) ruticilla.*

1808 Wilson *Ornithology* I. 103 American Redstart . . . makes its appearance in Pennsylvania, from the south, late in April; and leaves us again about the beginning of September. *Ib.* 105 The American Redstart builds frequently in low bushes. **1831** Audubon *Ornith. Biog.* I. 202 The American Redstart . . . is one of the most lively, as well as one of the handsomest, of our Fly-catchers. **1844** *Nat. Hist. N. Y., Zoology* II. 111 The American Redstart . . . is found during the summer throughout the Union. . . . It is shy and solitary. **1890** *Cent.* s.v. *Redstart*, American Redstart. . . . This beautiful bird abounds in woodland in eastern North America.

+**American rose-bay.** The great laurel or rhododendron, *Rhododendron maximum.*

1832 Williamson *Hist. Maine* I. 119 We begin with . . . the 'American Rose-bay.' . . . It is large, straggling, and quite irregular in its manner of growth. **1846** Browne *Trees Amer.* 361 The wood of the American rose bay is hard, compact, and fine-grained. **1847** Wood *Botany* 376 American Rose Bay . . . [is] a splendid flowering shrub . . . most abundant in the Middle States.

+**American scoter.** The common scoter, *Œdemia americana.*

1838 Eyton *Monograph on Anatidæ* 144 *Melanitta Americana*, . . . American Scoter, . . . [was] brought home by Dr. Richardson from the neighbourhood of Hudson's Bay. **1839** Peabody *Mass. Birds* 391 The American Scoter Duck. . . . Early in November, it is found in Boston market, and the flesh of the young is considered good. **1849** Audubon *Ornith. Biog.* V. 117 The American Scoter ranges along the whole coast of our Atlantic States. **1858** Baird *Birds Pacific R. R.* 807 According to Degland . . . the American scoter differs from the European in having the bill broader. **1875** *Fur, Fin, & Feather* 119 Of the various fowl called vulgarly coot, are the pied-duck, . . . the surf-duck . . . and the American scoter.

+**American senna.** The wild senna, *Cassia marilandica*, the leaves of which are medicinal (quot. 1901).

1784 Cutler in *Mem. Academy* I. 441 American Senna, . . . a small shrub, . . . makes an elegant appearance amongst flowering shrubs in gardens. **1843** Torrey *Flora N.Y.* I. 189 American or Wild Senna . . . [has] medicinal qualities. **1847** Wood *Botany* 236 American Senna. . . . This beautiful plant is frequently met with in alluvial soils. **1847** Darlington *Weeds & Plants* 109 American Senna . . . [is a] very showy species. **1901** Mohr *Plant Life Ala.* 555 *Cassia marilandica*, Wild Senna. . . . The leaves, 'American Senna,' are used medicinally.

+**American swan.** The whistling swan, *Cygnus (Olor) americanus.*

1844 *Nat. Hist. N. Y., Zoology* II. 353 The American Swan . . . is very common on the Chesapeake bay during the winter. Abundant also on the Pacific Coast of America. **1849** Audubon *Ornith. Biog.* V. 134 The nest of the Common American Swan . . . [is] built of moss-peat, nearly six feet long. **1858** Baird *Birds Pacific R. R.* 758 The common American swan is equally abundant on both sides of the continent, as well as throughout the interior. **1874** Coues *Birds N.W.* 545 American or Whistling Swan . . . is only seen in the United States during the migrations, and in winter.

+**American sycamore.** = American plane. — **1850** *New Eng. Farmer* II. 142 The Buttonwood, or American Sycamore, is every where well known in New England. **1892** Apgar *Trees Northern U.S.* 139 American Sycamore . . . [is] found on river-banks throughout; also cultivated.

+**American system.** The policy of fostering American industries by means of high tariff duties and of encouraging internal development.

1824 Clay in *Ann. 18th Congress* 1 Sess. II. 1978 That remedy consists in modifying our foreign policy, and in adopting a genuine American system. *Ib.* 1985 The American system, with its increase of the national wealth. **1829** Sands *Writings* II. 120, I believe most attorneys think the encouragement a part of the great American System. **1833** T. Hamilton *Men & Manners* I. 192 'The American system,' as it is called, was strenuously supported by the rich northern merchants, who expected to find in manufactures a new and profitable investment for their capital. **1838** *Democratic Rev.* I. 291 The consummation . . . will be realized by . . . the final extinction of the last vestige of the American System policy. **1846** Colton *Clay* I. 428 Internal improvement, and protection of American interests, labor industry and arts, are commonly understood to be the leading measures which constitute the American system. **1852** *Harper's Mag.* V. 856/2 'The Courier,' a daily paper, . . . was intended to be the especial advocate of the 'American System.' **1886** Logan *Great Conspiracy* 15 The institution of the now fully established American System of Protection.

+**American thorn.** The cockspur thorn, *Cratægus Crus-galli.* — **1809** Breck *Recoll.* (1877) App. 265 The exteriors of some of the fields offer well-plashed hedges of the American thorn.

+**American torpedo.** *Obs.* = next. — **1823** J. Thacher *Military Jrnl.* 146 The American Torpedo, and other ingenious submarine machinery, invented by Mr. David Bushnell, for the purpose of destroying shipping while at anchor.

+**American turtle.** *Obs.* (See quot. and preceding.) — **1788** Humphreys *Life Putnam* (1794) 114 A Machine . . . had been invented by Mr. David Bushnell [of Saybrook], for submarine navigation. . . . To this Magazine [*sic*] (called the American Turtle) was attached a Magazine of

Powder, which it was intended to be fastened under the bottom of a ship with a driving screw.

+**American water-cress.** A plant of the same genus as the bitter-cress. — **1836** LINCOLN *Botany* App. 84 *Cardamine pennsylvanica*, American water-cress. **1857** GRAY *Botany* 32 *C. rotundifolia.* American Water-Cress. . . . Leaves with just the taste of the English Water-Cress. . . . Flowers white.

+**American widgeon.** The baldpate or widgeon, *Mareca americana.*

1813 WILSON *Ornithology* VIII. 86 American Widgeon, *Anas Americana*, . . . is a handsomely marked and sprightly species, very common in winter along our whole coast, from Florida to Rhode Island. **1844** *Nat. Hist. N. Y., Zoology* II. 345 The American Widgeon, or Bald-pate, appears in this State in the spring, and late in the autumn. **1858** BAIRD *Birds Pacific R. R.* 783 American Widgeon . . . [inhabits the] continent of North America. Accidental in Europe. **1874** LONG *Wild-Fowl* 206 American widgeon (*Anas Americana*). Local name . . . [is] Bald-pate. *Ib.* 209 American widgeon. . . . Their flesh is excellent eating, but they soon spoil in warm weather if the entrails are not drawn.

+**American wistaria.** The North American species *Wistaria* (or *Kraunhia*) *pubescens.* — **1891** *Cent.* s.v. *Wistaria*, The American wistaria . . . is a native of swamp margins from Virginia to Illinois and southward. **1901** MOHR *Plant Life Ala.* 122 The American wistaria (*Kraunhia pubescens*), with its compound racemes of sky-blue flowers, adorns the lower border of the hammocks.

+**American woodcock.** The common woodcock, *Philohela minor.*

1812 WILSON *Ornithology* VI. 40 American woodcock . . . is universally known to our sportsmen. It arrives in Pennsylvania early in March. **1835** AUDUBON *Ornith. Biog.* III. 475 The American Woodcock . . . is found dispersed in abundance during winter, over the southern parts of the Union. **1839** PEABODY *Mass. Birds* 373 The American Woodcock. . . . From August till their departure, they are in good order for the table. **1858** BAIRD *Birds Pacific R. R.* 709 American Woodcock . . . [inhabits] eastern North America. **1874** COUES *Birds N.W.* 472 American Woodcock . . . frequently visits corn-fields and other cultivated tracts in the vicinity of swampy grounds. **1891** *Cent.* 6965/2 [The] American Woodcock . . . abounds in most of its range, and is one of the leading game-birds of America.

+**American yew.** The Pacific yew, *Taxus baccata*, var. *Canadensis.*

1843 TORREY *Flora N. Y.* II. 236 American Yew. Ground Hemlock. . . . Rocky banks, and in woods. **1852** *Horticulturist* VII. 392 The American Yew . . . is . . . a spreading shrub, about 3 or four feet high. **1869** *Amer. Naturalist* III. 130 The Hemlock . . . is early in flower, as also the American Yew. **1891** *Cent.* 7020/1 American yew . . . [is] a prostrate shrub with straggling branches, common in dark woods.

+**Americo-Indian,** *a.* American-Indian. — **1844** GREGG *Commerce of Prairies* II. 235 All the Americo-Indian tribes have . . . preserved their traditions on this subject [=cosmogony].

+**Americo-Saxon,** *a.* Combining Saxon and American characteristics. — **1848** COOPER *Oak Openings* I. iv. 62 It was not so much Anglo-Saxon as Americo-Saxon, that was to be seen in the physical outlines and hues of this nearly self-destroyed being.

+**Amerind.** [f. *American* + *Indian.* Introduced by Dr. C. P. G. Scott.] An American Indian. Also attrib. — **1897-8** POWELL *Ann. Rep. Bureau Amer. Ethnol.* I. p. xlviii, The brilliant work of Miss Alice Fletcher . . . [on] the tribal fraternities of the Amerinds. **1900** A. E. JENKS in *Amer. Anthropologist* Dec. 677 The social philosophy of the Amerind. **1901** W. J. MCGEE *Ib.* March 10 Many Amerind tribes denote themselves by a term connoting animals. **1901** *Nation* 19 Sept. 226/2 On every page of this handsome and sober volume [=Dellenbaugh's *North Americans*] one's teeth are set on edge by the unspeakable word 'Amerind.'

+**Amerindian,** *a.* [Cf. prec.] Pertaining to the American Indians. — **1897-8** *Ann. Rep. Bureau Amer. Ethnol.* II. 835 The four worlds of wide-spread Amerindian mythology. **1900** A. E. JENKS in *Amer. Anthropologist* Dec. 677 Such beliefs occur constantly in Amerindian mythology. **1910** H. H. JOHNSTON *Negro in New World* vi, The Spaniards did not exterminate the Amerindian peoples of tropical America.

***Amiable,** *a.* ‖Favorably disposed (*to* a thing). — **1875** HOWELLS *Foregone Conclusion* v. 72 A phase of that foreign eccentricity to which their nation [*sc.* Italians] is so amiable.

+**Amish,** *a.* Designating a strict and ascetic sect of Mennonites who follow the teaching of Jacob Amman. Also ellipt. — **1844** RUPP *Relig. Denom.* 560 [Account of the] Omish or Amish Church. **1872** *Amer. Cycl.* XI. 383/2 Another body of rigid Mennonites are called the Omish or Amish church, after Jacob Amen, a Mennonite preacher of Switzerland in the 17th century. **1880** *Libr. Univ. Knowl.* IX. 700 The Amish Mennonites . . . are sometimes called Hookers, because they substitute hooks for buttons on their clothes. **1883** *Schaff's Relig. Encycl.* (1884) III. 2404/1 The Mennonites and the Amish baptize by pouring. **1903** *N. Y. Times* 9 Sept., A young farmer . . . [who] was a member of the Amish sect, commonly known as the Hook and Eye Dutch. **1904** *Columbus Dispatch* 25 Sept. 3 The Amish settlement, comprising one-half the people of Troy, Geauga county, believe that the world is flat.

Ammunition. {*a*1626–}

1. Military supplies, formerly of all kinds; in later usage material used in the discharge of firearms.

1642 *Md. Council Proc.* 104 We authorize you . . . to muster all men able to bear arms . . . and provide all arms and amunition. *a***1649** WINTHROP *Hist.* I. 117 The fort and all the ammunition were delivered to them. **1668** *Maine Doc. Hist.* VI. 25 Every souldier is to bring in to the feild such ammunition as is allowable by law. **1685** SEWALL *Diary* I. 96 Generall Court . . . voted that care be taken to see that all persons are furnisht with arms and ammunition according to law. **1713** *Maine Wills* 166, I will and bequeath to Mr. Phillip Hubbard all my worldly goods . . . [including my] gunn and ammunition. **1745** *Penna. Col. Rec.* V. 5 Supplying those nations with arms, ammunition, & other necessaries for acting offensively against the French. **1765** TIMBERLAKE *Mem.* 25, I took what salt and ammunition we had left, and carried it along the shore. **1806** *Ann. 9th Congress* 1 Sess. 1244 Any non-commissioned officer or soldier who shall be convicted . . . of having . . . wasted the ammunition delivered out to him. **1850** GARRARD *Wah-To-Yah* ii. 32 St. Vrain made the party, through the chiefs, a present of tobacco and ammunition. **1874** KNIGHT 91/1 Ammunition . . . for artillery, when the projectiles, their cartridges, primers, etc., are packed in the same box, . . . is designated in the United States service as 'fixed ammunition'; this is the description furnished for field and rifled siege artillery. **1925** TILGHMAN *Dugout* 4 [They] spent what money they had on ammunition and supplies and set up as buffalo hunters.

2. Attrib., in sense of 'containing ammunition,' with *box, house, place.*

1635 *Mass. Bay Rec.* I. 138 The order for building an ammunicion howse att Newe Towne is repeated. **1637** *Essex Inst. Coll.* IX. 57 An ammunition house . . . to be made. **1653** *Dedham Rec.* 217 A bill given to Eleazer Dwight . . . for worke about the ammunition place. **1874** LONG *Wild-Fowl* 20, I usually made a practice of reloading as fast as possible between shots, carrying an ammunition-box and loading-tools with me. **1916** W. A. DUPUY *Uncle Sam* 59 He was to remain with the ammunition cargo.

b. +*Ammunition boat*, a boat for conveying ammunition. *A. bread*, bread supplied to soldiers. {1663} +*A. cart*, a cart for carrying ammunition. +*A. chest*, a box in which the ammunition of the field-cannon is packed. +*A. pouch*, a leather bag for carrying cartridges. +*A. shoe, stocking* (see quot.). *A. wagon*, a vehicle for carrying ammunition. {1858}

1760 CROGHAN *Journal* 107 About 10 came on a great squawl, . . . the flower [was] wet and the Ammunition Boat allmost staved to Pieces. **1867** F. MOORE *Women of War* 262 Solid shot, directed at the ammunition boat, . . . would pass over our heads. — **1699** J. DICKENSON *God's Protecting Providence* 79 We had five Roves of Ammonition Bread. **1835** [see *Ammunition shoe* (below)]. — **1776** *S. C. Hist. Soc. Coll.* III. 260 Resolved, That Capt. Benjamin Huger, be authorized . . . to provide a proper baggage-waggon and ammunition-cart. **1841** FOOTE *Texas & Texans* II. 232 Our ammunition-cart broke down. — **1807** IRVING, etc. *Salmagundi* xv. 362 A mighty force of trunks and bandboxes, like so many ammunition chests. **1861** *Army Regulations* 407 Keys for ammunition chests. *Ib.* 411 Ends for ammunition chests. — **1837** BIRD *Nick of Woods* I. vi. 92 Horses were caught . . . , ammunition pouches and provender-bags filled. **1857** OLMSTED *Journey thro' Texas* 53 Both pommel and cantle were hung with blankets, overcoats, ammunition-pouches, lunch-bags, et cetera. — **1835** *Encycl. Amer.* I. 216/2 Ammunition Bread, Shoes, Stockings, &c.; such as are contracted for by government, and served out to private soldiers. — **1861** *Army Regulations* 110 If a wagon takes fire in the park, remove it if possible; if not, remove first the ammunition wagons, then those to leeward of the fire. **1862** NORTON *Army Lett.* 106 With their tents and all the baggage wagons . . . and ammunition wagons, this field is pretty well filled up.

***Amnesty.** +Attrib. with *act, bill, oath, proclamation* (see quotations).

Proclamations 'offering amnesty and pardon to certain persons who had . . . participated in the said rebellion' were issued on 8 Dec. 1863 and 26 March 1864.

1867 RICHARDSON *Beyond Mississippi* 148 The legislature [of Kansas in 1859] also passed an 'amnesty act' directing that all persons charged with crimes arising from political disturbances . . . should be set at liberty. — **1867** *Congress. Globe* XXXVII. p. iii, Amnesty bill, [many references]. — **1871** DE VERE 287 To secure the loyalty of conquered Southerners, a multitude of oaths were exacted of them . . . : the Amnesty Oath . . . secured pardon according to the terms of an amnesty granted by the President. — **1865** *Annual Cycl. 1864* 778/1 The benefits of the amnesty proclamation issued by President Lincoln on December 8th, 1863, were sought by a large number of persons.

+**Amole.** *S.W.* [Mexican-Sp., from Nahuatl *atl* water, *molli* stew, substitute for soap.] The soap-plant, *Chlorogalum pomeridianum* or similar species. — **1843** FREMONT *Exped.* 249 Near the river . . . are great quantities of *ammole*, (soap plant), the leaves of which are used in California for making . . . mats for saddle-cloths. **1844** GREGG *Commerce of Prairies* I. 160 Among the wild productions of New Mexico is the *palmilla*—a species of palmetto . . . whose roots, . . . when bruised, form a saponaceous pulp called *amole*, much used by the natives for washing clothes. **1849** *Harper's Mag.* Jan. (1878) 274 Their [S. Calif. Indians] only method of washing was to put the clothes in a brook, . . . using as soap a native bulb called amole. **1885** HAVARD *Flora W. & S. Texas* 518 Lechuguilla is the most important of the soap or 'amole' plants of Southwestern Texas and Northern Mexico.

Amorpha. [mod. L.] The false indigo or lead plant, *Amorpha fruticosa, canescens*, or related species. — **1843** FREMONT *Exped.* 14 Along our route the *amorpha* has been in very abundant but variable bloom. **1847** LONGFELLOW *Evangeline* II. iv. 13 Prairies . . . bright with luxuriant clusters of roses and purple amorphas. **1901** MOHR *Plant Life Ala.* 563 *Amorpha glabra.* Smooth Amorpha. . . . Flowers blue. May, June. Infrequent.

Amost, A'most, *adv. dial.* [Reduced form of *almost.*] Very nearly. {1710; now *dial.*}

1758 *Essex Inst. Coll.* XVIII. 105 The Regulars . . . were a most all swept off by grape shot. **1760** *Ib.* XX. 198 This day we came from our lodging and there staid till amost knitt [*sic*]. **1783** *Ib.* XLV. 291 Brother John told her the war was a most over and then you would come home. **1834** CARRUTHERS *Kentuckian* I. 36 The . . . old gentleman sometimes gives her a talk in the carriage that throws her a'most into a faintin spell. **1865** TROWBRIDGE *Three Scouts* 64, I might have married a'most any man I pleased. **1878** COOKE *Happy Dodd* vii. 69, I call that a most an excellent sermon. **1899** GREEN *Va. Word-Book* 42. **1908** *Dialect Notes* III. 286. **1914** *Ib.* IV. 68.

||**Amovability.** Power to remove or dismiss from an office. — **1816** JEFFERSON *Writings* XV. 37 Let us retain amovability on the concurrence of the executive and legislative branches.

Ampersand, -zand, -sant. Also † **anpersant.** [Corruption of 'and, per se, and.'] The symbol '&,' meaning 'and.' {1859–}

1835 LONGSTREET *Georgia Scenes* 94 In the good old days of fescues, abisselfas, and anpersants, terms which used to be familiar in this country during the Revolutionary War. **1845** JUDD *Margaret* II. i. 195 Webster, moreover, advertises us that & is no letter. . . . The high-sounding Amperzand, no letter! **1854** SHILLABER *Mrs. Partington* 295 Does she yet stand, like the ampersand on the sign, beckoning some other Jones to write his name on the blank space in her heart?

***Amphitheatre.**

+**1.** A large building in which circus acts as well as dramatic performances are given. *Obs.*

1797 MORSE *Amer. Gaz.* I Philadelphia . . . [has] a medical theatre, a laboratory, an amphitheatre. **1845** S. SMITH *Theatr. Apprent.* 71, I visited the Broadway amphitheatre and witnessed the representation of 'Lock and Key.' **1858** *Chicago Daily Press* 19 Feb., The play of the 'Fall of Delhi' is taking a most successful run at North's Amphitheater.

+**2.** A room in a medical college or a hospital where operations are performed in the presence of students.

1851 CIST *Cincinnati* 112 Medical College of Ohio . . . contains large lecture rooms and an amphitheatre, together with apartments for the library. **1883** TALMAGE in *Chr. Herald* 9 May 256/1 The students gathered in the amphitheatre to see a painful operation.

Amusette. *Obs.* [F.] **a.** A light field cannon (invented by Marshal Saxe) in former use. {1761–1816} **b.** (See quot. 1776.) — **1775** J. ADAMS in *Warren-Adams Lett.* I. 54 They are casting Pateraras and making Amuzettes. **1776** C. LEE in Sparks *Corr. Rev.* (1853) I. 202, I am furnishing myself with four-ounced rifle-amusettes, which will carry an infernal distance.

+**Amy Dardin.** A widow of Mecklenburg County, Va., whose claim to be compensated for a horse came before Congress at intervals from 1796 to 1815. 'Amy's case came to be a proverb for procrastination' (Th.). — **1817** PAULDING *Lett. from South* I. 189 An old man, who . . . had a claim of some kind or other, with which he went to Washington . . . and took the field against Amy Dardin's horse. *Ib.* 190 He and Amy Dardin's horse alike have run their race, and their claims have survived them.

Anabaptism.** The doctrine of the Anabaptists. — *a1649** WINTHROP *Hist.* I. 322 [Some] were of the rigid separation, and [others] savored anabaptism. **1702** C. MATHER *Magnalia* (1853) I. i. 114 He was an irrefragable disputant against the errors, especially those of Anabaptism, which with trouble he saw rising in his colony.

***Anabaptist.** A member of a religious sect which rejects infant baptism and requires the rebaptism of adults joining its communion. Also attrib.

*a***1649** WINTHROP *Hist.* II. 39 Divers of them turned professed anabaptists, and would not wear any arms. **1663** *Ass. of Burgesses* in Neill *Virginia Carolorum* 298 John Porter . . . was so far an ana-baptist as to be against the baptizing of children. **1676** SEWALL *Diary* I. 30 Mr. Shepard . . . discoursed of reformation, especially the disorderly meetings of Quakers and Anabaptists. **1680** *Ib.* II. 14 John Russell the Anabaptist minister is buried. **1740** STEPHENS *Proc. Georgia* 632 One of them being an Anabaptist teacher. **1784** FILSON *Kentucke* 29 The Anabaptists were the first that promoted public worship in Kentucke. **1790** *Ann. 1st Congress* II. 1416 Mr. Jackson . . . introduced an account of the mischief which had resulted from the interference of a sect called Anabaptists in the State of Georgia. *c***1808** ADAMS *Works* (1851) VI. 549 All the religious sects,—the Catholics, . . . the Anabaptists, . . . and even the Quaker meetings,—may interest themselves in the choice [of a commander-in-chief of the army]. **1821** A. WELBY *Visit N. Amer.* 177 We have lately attended services at the churches of the Anabaptists, the Swedenborgians, &c.

***Anabaptistical,** *a.* Pertaining to the Anabaptists. — **1653** *Boston Rec.* I Renowncing all manner of knowne errors, . . . all Anabaptisticall inthusiasmes and Familisticall delusions. **1702** SEWALL *Diary* III. 398 That some short Treatise be drawn up and translated into Indian to prevent the spreading of the Anabaptistical Notions.

Anabaptistry.** *Obs.* The beliefs and practices of the Anabaptists. — **1642** Bradford *Hist.* 461 Their underworkers . . . have lately come amongst us. . . . secretly also sowing the seeds of Familisme, and Anabaptistrie. **1643** *Mass. H. S. Coll.* 4 Ser. VI. 178 Mr. Freeman, whom I suppose the countrey left out in regard to his professed Anabaptistry & separacon from the Churches. *a1649** WINTHROP *Hist.* II. 177 Anabaptistry . . . spread in the country, which occasioned the magistrates, at the last court, to draw an order for banishing such as continued obstinate.

||**Anachorism.** A thing out of place in a (certain) country. — **1862** LOWELL *Biglow P.* II. 79 Opinions [that are] anachronisms at once and anachorisms, foreign both to the age and the country.

||**Anachronize,** *v. tr.* To put (a person or thing) into a wrong chronological position. — **1870** LOWELL *Among my Books* Ser. I. 198 One of his contemporaries who endeavored to anachronize himself, so to speak.

Anaconda. {1768–} +*fig.* The Union army of General McClellan, which was expected to 'crush the rebellion.'

1861 [NEWELL] *Orpheus C. Kerr* I. 205 [McClellan's] great anaconda has gathered itself in a circle around the doomed rabbit of rebellion. **1862** Cox in *Congress. Globe* 30 Jan. 569/2 My colleague wound up his speech by the figure of the anaconda, in which he tried to be humorous at the expense of General Scott, who originated the trope. **1862** GURLEY *Ib.* 29 Jan. 554/1 A hundred thousand soldiers would have leaped for joy at the order to go; but no, this most likely would have . . . stirred up the great anaconda too soon! **1866** *Congress. Globe* 17 July 3857/2 When he [Grant] assumed supreme command . . . the anaconda of which so much had been said early in the war was no longer a myth. **1879** *Southern Hist. Soc. P.* XI. 119 Our turn had come for a little squeeze in the folds of the traditional 'Anaconda,' that the New York *Herald* had so graphically depicted as encircling the South.

Anæsthesia, Anesthesia. {1721–} +A state of insensibility to pain, induced by a gas or drug; entire or partial loss of sensation by means of ether, chloroform, cocaine, etc. {1848–}

1846 HOLMES *Letter to W. T. G. Morton* 21 Nov., The state produced . . . should, I think, be called *anæsthesia*. This signifies insensibility. . . . The adjective will be *anæsthetic*. Thus we might say, the 'state of anæsthesia,' or the 'anæsthetic state.' **1865** *Harper's Mag.* Sept. 457/1 A meeting of Boston dentists was called, and a committee of twelve appointed to make a formal protest against anæsthesia. **1876** BARTHOLOW *Materia Med.* (1879) 360 The term *anæsthetic* . . . means an agent capable of producing anæsthesia, or insensibility to pain.

+**Anæsthetic, Anesthetic,** *a.* and *n.*

1. *a.* Of the nature of, pertaining or belonging to, anæsthesia; inducing anæsthesia. {1847–}

1846 [see ANÆSTHESIA]. **1846** HOLMES *Letter to W. T. G. Morton* 21 Nov., The means employed would be properly called the 'anti-æsthetic agent.' Perhaps it might be allowable to say 'anæsthetic agent;' but this admits of question. *c***1865** *Harper's Mag.* Sept. 460/1 The comfort of anæsthetic agents to the soldier does not stop here [with the operation]. **1866** *Nation* 26 June 812/1 The anæsthetic value of nitrous oxide.

2. *n.* An anæsthetic agent. {1848–}

1854 DUNGLISON *Dict. Med. Science* (ed. 11) 69/2 Different agents have been used as anæsthetics,—sulphuric ether, compound ether [etc.]. **1865** *Harper's Mag.* Sept. 459/2 Dr. Morton has attended the principal battlefields, administering anæsthetics with his own hands. *Ib.* 453/1 Dr. Morton . . . is the man who first introduced ether as an anæsthetic. **1890** *Cent.* 971/3 Chloroform, . . . when skilfully administered, in proper cases, . . . is a safe anæsthetic.

+**Anagreeta.** (See quotation.) — **1775** ROMANS *Florida* 122 Anagreeta is the corn gathered before maturity, and dried in an oven or the hot sun . . . , [making] a fine mixture in puddings especially with pease, but this is only practised in the provinces of New York and New Jersey.

Analyse, *v.* {1601–} +*intr.* To perform an academic exercise in analysis. — **1701** *Mass. Acts & Resolves* VII. 312 Resolved, that . . . Samuel Willard . . . be desired to take the care and over sight of the Colledge and students there . . . and to bring forward the exercises of analisyng. **1734** *Harvard Rec.* I. 139 If any Resident Bachelour, Senior or Junior Sophis[ter] shall neglect to analyse, in his course according to the direction of the President, . . . he shall be punish[ed] by the President.

***Analysis.** +(See quotation and preceding.) — **1734** *Harvard Coll. Rec.* I. 140 No Undergraduate . . . shall have leave to be Absent, so as to omitt his declamation, or Analysis.

***Anan,** *adv. dial.* An interrogative used when one has not understood another person; 'what?' {Now *dial.*}

1789 WEBSTER *Diss. Eng. Lang.* 188 A word derived from the same root, is still retained . . . which is sometimes pronounced *nan* and sometimes *anan.* It is used for *what,* or *what do you say.* **1826** COOPER *Mohicans* vi, 'I am an unworthy instructor in the art of psalmody.' 'Anan!' **1859** ELWYN *Glossary* 16 *Anan,* . . . only occasionally heard, so far as my experience goes. . . . I have heard it in Chester County, Pennsylvania. **1870** *Nation* July 56/2 (Penna. words), In 'strict' families the younger folks must not use the brusque 'what?' in addressing their elders and betters, but the word 'nan?' ('anan').

Anarchist. One who believes in the political doctrine that society should not be governed by any constituted authority. Also attrib. {1791–}

1861 *N. Y. Tribune* 9 Nov. 4/5 By what law . . . do these libelers couple the names of the sound and the rotten, of the patriot and the anarchist? **1886** *Harper's Mag.* Nov. 959/1 There has been in Chicago an organization of anarchists. *Ib.* 960/1 The whole country rose in a cry of consternation and indignation at the crime of European anarchists upon American soil. **1891** *Congress. Rec.* 2 March 3777/1 If I had my say, I would stop the immigration of Mormons, communists, anarchists, nihilists [etc.].

Anatta, Anatto. Also **anata, annatto, arnotto.** An orange-red dye or coloring matter made from a tropical plant (*Bixa orellana*). {a1682–}

1792 J. Pope *Tour S. & W.* 98 Anata is a Shrub . . . bearing a red Flower, which the Creeks infuse in Water or decoct. With this Infusion or Decoction, they dye their Leggens, Moccasons [etc.]. **1804** Roberts *Penna. Farmer* 164 Arnotta; used for colouring cheese. **1838** *S. Lit. Messenger* IV. 232 He wore a hunting shirt dyed with arnotto according to the fashion of the country. **1858** Flint *Milch Cows*, etc. 250 The use of annatto to color the cheese artificially is somewhat common in this country. **1861** *Ill. Agric. Soc. Trans.* IV. 101 They are basted with a preparation made of melted butter, of the best kind, colored with anotta. **1873–4** *Vermont Board Agric. Rep.* II. 92 In reply to a question, Mr. D. said he had used carrots for coloring. . . . Preferred carrots to annatto, or its preparations.

+**Anchorage-ground.** A place for anchoring; an anchoring ground. — **1824** Irving *Tales Trav.* I. 272, I had no longer an anchorage-ground for my heart. **1833** H. Barnard in *Md. Hist. Mag.* XIII. 370 We again dropped into this . . . anchorage ground. **1840** Cooper *Pathfinder* xxv, There ought to have been signals concerted, and an anchorage-ground buoyed out.

Anchor button. A metal button bearing the figure of an anchor. — **1827** *Harvard Reg.* 214 The groups of young fishermen in their short jackets, with anchor buttons.

Anchor ice. Ice that forms on the bottom of lakes and streams. {1877–} — **1815** *Niles' Reg.* IX. 201/1 On the same day the anchor-ice began to run a little. **1851** Springer *Forest Life* 86 Our oxen are often very reluctant to enter the water while the anchor ice runs.

Anchor-maker. {1598, 1831} — **1833** *Niles' Reg.* XLIV. 366/2, [I have] never finished or made an anchor, but sold a great quantity of anchor iron to merchants, who sell to the anchor maker.

Anchor-making. — **1781** Peters *Hist. Conn.* (1829) 199 Anchor making is done by water and trip hammers.

Anchor smith. A maker of anchors. {1662–1703}

1667 *Suffolk Deeds* V. 210 The some of thirty Pounds starling . . . well & truly paid by Henery Kemble, . . . Anchor Smith. **1696** *York Deeds* IV. 96 Henry Kemble, . . . Ancor Smith. **1708** *Boston News-Letter* 31 May 2/2 Sold by Nathaniel Wheeler, Anchor Smith near the South Battery. **1795** *Mass. H. S. Coll.* IV. 199 Excepting such tradesmen as rope-makers, anchor-smiths, and ship-carpenters, . . . scarcely any family had more than two [blacks]. **1876** Bancroft *Hist.* IV. 544 The father of Greene . . . was at once an anchor-smith, a miller, a farmer, and . . . a preacher.

Anchor watch. A watch set while a ship lies at single anchor. — **1840** Dana *Two Years* ix. 75 Carrying hides . . . until eight bells, when all hands were called aft, and the 'anchor watch' set. **1851** Melville *Moby Dick* lxvi. 336 Upon Stubb setting the anchor-watch after his supper was concluded. **1876** Davis *Polaris Exp.* viii. 219 The tidal observations were made by . . . the anchor-watch during the remaining nine hours.

Anchor works. An establishment for making anchors. — **1795** *Essex Inst. Coll.* LIV. 103 To the anchor works may be annexed with very little experience, a suitable apparatus for making shovels, scythes, hoes, axes, etc. **1815** *Mass. H. S. Coll.* 2 Ser. III. 171 On the Town Brook . . . are . . . one Cotton Factory, (brick); Shovel Factory; Anchor works; Slitting Mill; . . . two Grist Mills.

***Anchovy.**

***1.** The small European fish *Engraulis encrasicholus*, extensively used as a savory or flavoring ingredient.

1705 *Boston News-Letter* 20 Aug. 2/1 The loading on board the Prize is said to consist of . . . 400 Baskets of Rezins, some Currants, Anchoves and Olives. **1715** *Ib.* 16 May 2/2 At the Store-House No. 28 . . . are to be sold by Capt. William Tudor fine Gorgona Anchovis. **1761** E. Singleton *Social N. Y.* 364 Pickles of all sorts in small quantities, very fit for the Army, such as . . . Peppers, Capers, Anchovies, etc. **1845** J. W. Norris *Chicago Directory* 98 Exchange Coffee House. . . . Clams, Sardines, Anchovies. **1848** W. E. Burton *Waggeries* 121 Four large lobsters, pots of anchovies, . . . salad and other vegetables. **1884** Goode *Aquatic Animals* 550 'Small Herring,' 'Anchovies', 'Skarp Herring,' 'Spiced Herring.'

+**2.** (See quotations.)

1839 Storer *Mass. Fishes* 62 The several species of foreign Atherinæ, are known by the names 'Atherine,' 'Sand Smelts,' and 'Anchovies,' and are much valued as articles of food. **1842** *Nat. Hist. N. Y., Zoology* IV. 142 The Dotted Silverside, *Atherina notata*. . . . They are known under the names of Anchovies and Sand Smelts. They are esteemed a savory food.

***Ancient,** *n. Obs.*

***1.** An ensign or banner.

a1649 Winthrop *Hist.* I. 14 Our captain put forth his ancient in the poop, and heaved out his skiff. **1686** Sewall *Diary* I. 140 Ships with their Ancients out, and Forts their Flaggs. **1704** *Boston News-Letter* 22 May 2/1 He took the Canoo in the night, . . . took the Ancient for a Sayl, and sails to the Man of War.

***2.** An ensign-bearer.

1631 *Mass. Bay Rec.* I. 91 Mr. William Gennison is chosent anchient to Capt[ain] Pattricke. **1633** *Ib.* 103 Serieant Morris is chosen ancient to Capt[ain] Underhill.

***Ancient,** *a.*

***1.** Belonging to past (but not remote) time; earlier, former. Now *Obs.* exc. *arch.*

1640 *Plymouth Col. Rec.* II. 4 An auncient act doth restraine all persons . . . to trade or traffic with the Indians or natiues. **a1656** Bradford *Hist.* 440 Though this patente and plantation were much the ancienter, yet this inlargemente of the same (in which Sityate stood) was granted after theirs. **1698** *Boston Rec.* 230 To renew the antiant bounds of the high way leading from the Black horse Lane to the mill. **1703** *Cambridge Prop. Rec.* 220 It is mutually agreed . . . that he . . . shall have the ancient high way layd through his land. **1712** *Boston Rec.* 158 Voted . . . the said lane be nine feet wide according to the antient deeds. **1733** *Ib.* 49 Voted, to chuse a committe to take effectual care to open the antient natural water-course in Water Street. **1792** Jefferson *Letter* 9 April, in *Writings* (1854) III. 347 It is rather probable that . . . Congress would take it off your hands, in compliance with an ancient vote of that body. **1793** *Ib.* IV. 54 Profound arguments . . . entitle him really to his ancient signature. **1819** *Ann. 16th Congress* 1 Sess. I. 740 The expediency of providing, by law, for the final adjustment of the ancient titles to land within the Territory of Michigan. **1826** Cooper *Mohicans* xvii, Magua . . . uttered a yell of pleasure when he beheld his ancient prisoners again at his mercy. **1831** Holley *Texas Lett.* (1833) 55 A number of the ancient inhabitants, also, returned to their former possessions, and thus the town has been gradually re-peopled.

+**2.** *The Ancient Dominion*, the state of Virginia. (Cf. *Old Dominion* s.v. Old *a.*)

1699 *Virginia State P.* I. 63 A Generall Assembly of this his Majesties most ancient Colloney and Dominion of Virginia. **1705** Makemie *Persuasive* Dedication, To His Excellency Major Edward Nott, Her Majestys Governor of the Ancient Dominion of Virginia. **1789** Maclay *Deb. Senate* 14 The member from the ancient dominion . . . is said to be a notorious anti-Federalist. **1795** Winterbotham *Hist. View* III. 109 Virginia prides itself in being 'The Ancient Dominion.' **1803** *Ann. 7th Congress* 2 Sess. 469 The sovereign and despotic sway of the 'Ancient Dominion' over most of the other states in the Union. **1824** 'A. Singleton' *Lett. from S. & West* 69 The chief sickness, in this 'ancientest dominion,' is in the autumn. **1827** [G. Mellen] *Chronicle of '26* 14 The good bold 'ancient dominion' never . . . long forgets her self-respect. **1850** Foote *Sk. Virginia* 393 The Smiths came to Virginia to commence log colleges in the 'Ancient Dominion.'

+**3.** *Ancient order society*, a religious sect following certain teachings of Rev. Alexander Campbell (1788–1866).

1837 Jenkins *Ohio Gaz.* 130 Of this number . . . 725 are episcopal methodists; about 300 are supposed to belong to the ancient order society; 200 to the presbyterians.

+**4.** *Ancient diggings*, mining excavations made by a prehistoric race.

1865 *Atlantic Mo.* XV. 308 This was the first instance where 'ancient diggings'—as they are familiarly called in the Lake Superior region—were ever recognized as such.

Ancon. *Obs.* {1706–} +A former breed of sheep having a long body and short, crooked legs. — **a1811** Shattuck in *Phil. Trans.* CIII. 93 Its forelegs . . . appear like elbows, while the animal is walking. I have taken the liberty to call them *ancon*, from the Greek word. **1811** D. Humphreys *Ib.* 92 The breed of ancons . . . being less able than others to get over fences. *Ib.* 93 Since the introduction of Merinos, . . . more highly recommended by their fleeces, the ancon breed seems in danger of becoming almost extinct. **1852** T. Ross *Humboldt's Trav.* I. ix. 342 The sheep . . . called ancon sheep in Connecticut. **1871** *18th Rep. Mass. Bd. Agric.* I. 115 [Control of breeding] took place in Massachusetts, in 1791, in relation to the 'Ancon' or 'Otter' sheep. **1873** *Amer. Naturalist* VII. 742 Ancon or Otter Sheep . . . were raised till within a few years on the farm of Hon. William Hale of Barrington, N.H.

+**Andes grass.** A species of grass, *Arrhenatherum arenacium*. — **1835** P. Shirreff *Tour* 26, I saw [near Phila.] several fields of a newly introduced grass, called Andes grass, said to have been lately brought from the range of hills in South America bearing that name.

***Andiron.** (See also Handiron.) 'An iron utensil used, in Great Britain, where coal is the common fuel, to support the ends of a spit; but in America, used to support the wood in fire places' (W. '28).

'It was originally designed, as it still is in America, to prop up the extremities of logs of wood whilst they were being burnt' (*Encyclop. Dict.*, '79).

1640 *Essex Probate Rec.* I. 12, I give unto Elezabeth Nicksone my payer of Anderens. **1649** *Conn. Public Rec.* I. 501 Andirons and doggs &c. in the chimny. **1655** *Essex Probate Rec.* I. 224 A p[air] of Endirons, firepan & toungs. **1698** *Essex Inst. Coll.* III. 157 To my daughter . . . the brase heads of a pair of andirons. **1711** *Ib.* IV. 187/1 A pair of andirons with double brasses. **1744** *N. H. Probate Rec.* III. 210, I give to my Son . . . a trammel and a pair of andirons. **1761** *Essex Inst. Coll.* XLVIII. 96 To be sold by George Deblois . . . frying pans, andirons, shovel and tongs. **1791** Jillson *Dark & Bl. Ground* 107 Sections of logs that are hauled in and fit over the andirons. **1813** *Niles' Reg.* V. 190/1 Copper and brass wares, particularly utensils for distillers, sugar-refiners and brewers, andirons and other articles for household use. **1845** *Knickerb.* XV. 444 The andirons, with lions-heads for tops, still rested in the old fire-place. **1852** *Harper's Mag.* March 446/2 A great log was lying across the andirons, behind and beneath which there was a blazing and glowing fire. **1874** B. F. TAYLOR *World on Wheels* II. iii. 208 There are andirons, too—the old andirons, with rings in the top, whereon many temples of flame have been builded. **1891** EGGLESTON in *Century Mag.* Feb. 547 A chimney that had a pair of andirons and three logs of wood in it.

+**Andrew's cross.** *Bot.* The St. Andrew's cross. — **1813** MUHLENBERG *Cat. Plants* 68 Andrew's cross, Peter's wort: . . . dwarf. Car., Georg.

Andromeda. A genus of shrubs, some varieties of which are native to America; a species or plant of this genus. {1794-}

1765 BARTRAM *Journal* (1766) 15 Dissolved rotton leaves of the kalmia, vaccinium, dwarf-myrtle, andromeda, . . . and other evergreens. **1785** MARSHALL *Amer. Grove* 7 *Andromeda calyculata.* Ever-green Dwarf Andromeda. This is a low shrub, growing on mossy land. . . . *Andromeda paniculata.* Panicled Andromeda. This shrub grows in boggy wet ground. . . . *Andromeda racemosa.* Pennsylvanian Red-bud Andromeda. **1818** *Mass. H. S. Coll.* 2 Ser. VIII. 171 Among the plants in the neighbouring towns . . . are rosemary-leaved andromeda [etc.]. **1832** BROWNE *Sylva Amer.* 116 This is the only species of Andromeda which rises to a sufficient height to be ranked among forest trees. **1837** WILLIAMS *Florida* 89 These galls are usually covered with titi and other andromedas. **1847** DARLINGTON *Weeds & Plants* 213 *A. Mariana.* . . . Maryland Andromeda. Stagger-bush. . . . New England to Florida. **1901** MOHR *Plant Life Ala.* 47 A host of evergreen shrubs, . . . azaleas and andromedas of the heather family . . . form the dense undergrowth.

***Anemone.** The wind-flower; a plant or flower of the genus *Anemone*, of which many species are native to North America.

1784 CUTLER in *Mem. Academy* I. 458 White anemone . . . [grows] amongst bushes and in shady places. May. **1821** *Mass. H. S. Coll.* 2 Ser. IX. 146 Plants, which are indigenous in the township of Middlebury, [Vt., include] . . . *Anemone nemorosa*, Low anemone. **1836** LINCOLN *Botany* App. 75 Low anemone; . . . rue anemone; . . . garden anemone. **1843** T. TALBOT *Journals* 14 The prairie is covered with the greatest profusion of flowers. The rose, daisy, anemone, lupine. **1847** WOOD *Botany* 140 Wood Anemone, . . . Virginian anemone, . . . Poppy-leaved anemone, . . . Star anemone. **1852** MITCHELL *Dream Life* 35, I love to search out the sunny slopes . . . where the frail anemone . . . will touch your heart. **1855** *Harvard Mag.* I. 236 Two very beautiful species of the Anemone grow wild with us in the woods. **1858** VIELÉ *Following Drum* 254 At the root, through lush green grasses, burned the red anemone. **1880** *Harper's Mag.* June 72 Some trembling cluster of anemone, nodding from its velvety bed of moss.

***Angel.** A former English coin of the value of ten shillings (Phillips, 1706); its equivalent in a bill or bills. — **1713** SEWALL *Diary* II. 413, [I] gave him an Angel . . . to buy him and Madam Brattle a pair of gloves. **1717** *Ib.* III. 129 Give Mr. Little the Funeral Sermons . . . with an Angel Bill of Credit. **1724** *Ib.* 331 Mr. Barth. Green had an angel sent to him to insert it [=a notice] in his News-Letter of Feb. 13, which he did.

+**Angel-cake.** [Cf. ANGEL'S FOOD.] A kind of white sponge cake. — **1897** *Amer. Dainties* 44 [Recipe for] Angel Cake. **1904** *N. Y. Times* 13 June 8 To have angel cake would be sacrilegious. **1905** *N. Y. Ev. Post* 4 Aug. 7 Angel cake, sponge cake, and ice-cream cake have conspired to relegate the seed cake to practical oblivion.

Angel-fish. {1668-} (See quots.) — **1709** LAWSON *N. Carolina* 156 The Angel-Fish is shaped like an English Bream. He is so call'd from his golden colour, which shines all about his head and belly. *Ib.*, The Sheeps-Head . . . is much of the bigness of the Angel-Fish, and flat as he is. *c*1733 CATESBY *Carolina* II. 31 The Angel-Fish . . . are esteemed in Carolina an excellent eating Fish. **1842** *Nat. Hist. N.Y., Zoology* IV. 98 The Banded Ephippus, *Ephippus faber.* Schoepff states that it is called angel-fish in Carolina. *Ib.* 363 The American Angel-fish, *Squatina dumerili.* . . . This is a very rare species.

***Angelica.** A plant belonging to the genus *Angelica* and others resembling it.

1637 MORTON *New Canaan* II. iii, The country there naturally affordeth . . Angellica, Pursland, Violets, and Anniseeds, in very great abundance. **1687** CLAYTON *Virginia* in *Phil. Trans.* XLI. 155 The herb called there Angelica, . . . which I take to be *Libanotis vera latifolia Dodonæi*, . . . stops the flux and cures it to a wonder. **1699** *Mass. H. S. Coll.* 4 Ser. V. 306 Angelica, that we brought over with us, is grown out five or six inches long already. **1709** LAWSON *Carolina* 77 Our pot-herbs and others . . . are angelica wild and tame, balm, buglos. **1723** *Weekly Mercury* 9-16 May 4/2 He will truck for . . . sweet finnel, angelica, green licorice, lavender tops, and rosemary in flowers. **1778** CARVER *Travels* 100 The ground is stored with useful roots, with angelica, spikenard, and groundnuts as large as hens eggs. **1784** CUTLER in *Mem. Academy* I. 431 *Aralia*, . . . berry-bearing angelica, shot bush. **1792** IMLAY *Western Territory* 207 Of herbs, &c. we have of the wild sort . . . angelica, fennel, lovage. **1807** GASS *Journal* xii. 132 There are a great quantity of sweet roots and herbs, such as sweet myrrh, angelica and several other. **1817** *Niles' Reg.* XII. 224/1 Some school boys belonging to Hillsboro', N. C. stopping at a spring, met with what they thought was angelico, but which was hemlock. **1836** EDWARD *Hist. Texas* ii. 43 Let us look at some of the roots and plants below, such as . . . the angelica, the sarsaparilla. **1847** WOOD *Botany* 291 Garden Angelica. . . . Cultivated in gardens occasionally for the sake of the stalks, which are to be blanched and eaten as celery. **1857** GRAY *Botany* 153 Angelica, . . . *A. Curtisii*, Buckley; nearly glabrous. [Grows on] Cheat Mountain, Virginia, and southward in the Alleghanies. **1889** *Cent.* s.v., The great angelica of the United States is *Archangelica atropurpurea.*

+**Angelica tree.** A shrub (*Aralia spinosa*) in appearance resembling the palm.

1785 MARSHALL *Amer. Grove* 11 Virginian Angelica Tree. . . . rises with a thick woody stem to the height of ten or twelve feet. **1806** SHECUT *Flora Carolin.* I. 168 Angelica tree, called also prickly-ash, tooth-ache tree, wild liquorice, &c., the English names of the genus *Aralia.* **1847** WOOD *Botany* 295 Angelica Tree. . . . [Grows in] damp woods, Penn. to Flor. and La. **1857** GRAY *Botany* 159 Angelica-tree, Hercules' Club, [grows on] river-banks, Pennsylvania to Kentucky and southward. **1892** APGAR *Trees Northern U. S.* 109 Angelica-tree . . . usually dies to the ground after flowering. **1901** MOHR *Plant Life Ala.* 640 Angelica Tree. . . . Arborescent, clear trunk 30 feet high.

+**Angel's food.** (See quots. and ANGEL CAKE.) — **1881** MRS. OWENS *Cook Bk.* 161 Angel's food. In other words, White Sponge Cake. **1883** *Practical Housekeeping* 65 Angel's Food. Use the whites of eleven eggs [etc.].

+**Angel sleeve.** (See quotation.) — **1889** E. B. CUSTER *Tenting on Plains* v. 174 The sting was inflicted before the war, and in the far back days of 'angel sleeves,' which fell away from the arm to the shoulder.

***Angle,** *n.* An angular piece (*of* land). {-1656} — **1664** *Groton Rec.* 149 At Vnquetenorset four acres, more or lesse, lying in severall spongs or angles. **1671** *Rowley Rec.* I. 212 A small angle of land . . . lieth betwene the path and the pond.

***Angle,** *v.* {Rare.}

+**1.** *intr.* To lie in an oblique direction.

1741 *Boston Rec.* 274 They have computed the charge of fixing piers . . . set angling cross the channel.

+**2.** To obtain an angle by which to discover the location of a hive of wild bees. (Cf. ANGLING *vbl. n.*)

1848 COOPER *Oak Openings* I. i. 21, I must 'angle' for them chaps. . . . Many a man who can 'line' a bee, can do nothing at an 'angle.'

3. *tr.* To turn or twist. Also *refl.*

1872 *Harper's Mag.* Oct. 781/2 The more I 'angled' the paddle and sculled, the worse it was. **1876** MRS. WHITNEY *Sights & Insights* xx, Back and forth, making sharp turns, the road angles itself up the precipitous hillside.

+**4.** *intr.* To move at an angle; to sidle.

1890 *Congress. Rec.* 18 Feb. 1464/1 Mr. MacBride then angled up to me and . . . said to me: Mr. Clayton, do not get excited. **1903** A. ADAMS *Log Cowboy* ix. 127 The old man started for him, angling across the street in disregard of sidewalks. *Ib.* xvii. 262 As we angled across it [*i. e.* the valley], the town seemed as dead as those that slept in the graveyard.

Angle-dog. An angle-worm. {1889 *dial.*} — **1867** 'T. LACKLAND' *Homespun* 96 We pocketed the well-scoured angle-dogs, shouldered our birch fishing-rod, and sallied forth.

***Angle-rod.** {-1711} =ANGLING-ROD. — **1836** EDWARD *Hist. Texas* 67 To pass through one of these cane-brakes, or properly speaking Angle-rod Brakes, . . . is a novelty.

+**Angleworm.** The common earthworm, *Lumbricus terrestris* and allied species, used extensively as bait in fishing. {s.w. dial. *angle*, 1888-}

1832 WILLIAMSON *Hist. Maine* I. 168 We have among us, in summer, a variety of native worms, . . . the Earthworm, the Brandling, the Angle-worm. **1874** B. F. TAYLOR *World on Wheels* II. vi. 235 Flax seed was expressed and impressed in an oleaginous bag, whose slippery contents wriggled about on the tremulous lid like a packet of angle-worms. **1884** ROE *Nature's Story* 196 Angle-worms and other bait are employed in the Delaware and Southern rivers. **1897** FLANDRAU *Harvard Episodes* 112 The industrious robins rip elastic angle-worms from the sod. **1900** *Everybody's Mag.* III. 521/2 He collected a small gourdful of angle-worms. *a*1918 G. STUART *On Frontier* I. 65 Having no shortening they dug angle-worms and crushed them up with the acorns.

Anglican, *n.* {*a*1797} +(See quotation.) — **1836** EDWARD *Hist. Texas* 125 Thus the Creole party is divided into several factions. First, the Aristocratic. . . . They are also called Yorkinos and Anglicans, because under English influence, and leaning towards European connections.

Anglican, *a.* {1635-} (See quotation.) — **1796** JEFFERSON *Writings* IX. 335 An Anglican monarchical aristocratical party has sprung up, whose avowed object is to draw over us the substance . . . of the British government.

Anglicanism. {1846–} + =ANGLICISM. — **1900** *Kansas Hist. Coll.* VI. 217 He resembled the best English pattern rather than our more acute American model. Of his unconscious Anglicanism, the most elaborate picture of Kansas that he ever drew in a sentence is an example.

Anglicism. {1642–} Inclination towards England or English views. — **1810** JEFFERSON *Writings* XII. 373 The Anglicism of 1808, against which we are now struggling, . . . is a longing for a King, and an English King rather than any other.

Anglicization. The process of making English in character. {1878} — **1883** *American* VII. 51 Then the Anglicization of Boston has reached a point which is calamitous.

Anglicize, *v.* {1748–} *tr.* To make English in customs or character. — **1710** SEWALL *Letter-book* I. 401 The best thing we can do for our Indians is to Anglicize them. . . . Though some of their aged men are tenacious enough of Indianisme, . . . others . . . wish that their people may be made English as fast as they can. **1876** J. BURROUGHS *Winter Sunshine* I. 23 The negro is . . . thoroughly anglicised.

+**Anglicizer.** One who assumes English manners or speech. — **1886** *American* XII. 181 A sense which our Anglicisers entirely ignore.

+**Anglify,** *v. tr.* To anglicize. Also *anglified* ppl. a. {1816–}

1751 FRANKLIN *Ess.* Wks. 1840 II. 320 Why should Pennsylvania, founded by the English, become a colony of aliens, who will shortly be so numerous as to Germanize us instead of our Anglifying them. **1778** ADAMS *Fam. Lett.* (1876) 346, I can only say that we have many . . . difficulties . . . to give satisfaction to certain half-anglified Americans. **1805** WEEMS *Lett.* II. 318 As I shall have a good deal of trouble in Anglifying, modernizing, &c. &c. I thought 5 pr. cent ought to be allowed me. **1890** H. C. BUNNER *Short Sixes* (1891) 217 They had two English servants and some other American 'help'; but they called the Americans by their last names, which anglified them to some extent.

***Angling,** *vbl. n.* +The process of obtaining an angle in tracing wild bees. (See ANGLE *v.* 2.) — **1848** COOPER *Oak Openings* II. iii. 36 Indians are not expert, . . . on account of the 'angle-ing' part of the process, which much exceeds their skill in mathematics.

***Angling-rod.** A fishing pole.

1689 SEWALL *Diary* I. 288 Cous. Samuel Sewall hath aboard the America . . . one Angling Rod: 1 Hat in a Paper. **1793** *Mass. H. S. Coll.* III. 7 In the summer, one may . . . catch them [i.e. fish] in the sea . . . with an angling rod, and a fathom or two of line. **1827** *Western Mo. Rev.* I. 210 Everyone has seen the larger reed cane in the form in which it is used for angling rods. **1847** DARLINGTON *Weeds & Plants* 388 The culms of this species [of cane] are well known from their common use as angling rods.

+**Anglo-African,** *a.* Having a mixed character of English and African. — **1866** RICHARDSON *Secret Service* vi. 85 He speaks fluently, and with grammatical correctness, but in the Anglo-African dialect.

+**Anglo-America.** Those parts of the American continent under the influence of English culture; the United States and Canada. — **1846** BROWNE *Trees Amer.* 1 Genus *Magnolia* . . . [grows in] Spain, Italy, Britain, and Anglo-America. *Ib.* 109 Horse-chesnut . . . [grows in] Britain and Anglo-America.

+**Anglo-American,** *n.*

1. An American of English descent.

[**1738** *Remarks on Trial of J. P. Zenger* i. 16 (Signature of letter:) I am yours, &c. Anglo-Americanus.] **1787** S. S. SMITH *Ess. Complexion* (1788) 194 The Anglo-Americans on the frontiers of the states, who acquire their sustenance principally by hunting. **1788** *Mass. H. S. Coll.* 2 Ser. X. 86 They, as well as the tribe at New London, are by the Anglo-Americans, called Mohegans. **1789** MORSE *Amer. Geog.* 63 The greater part are descended from the English, and, for the sake of distinction, are called Anglo-Americans. **1795** WINTERBOTHAM *Hist. View* III. 237 The Chicasaws . . . glory in saying, that they never shed the blood of an Anglo-American. **1809** TYLER *Yankey in London* 28 There is an undescribable something clinging to the heart of every Anglo-American which sensibly associates us with the glory of old England. **1823** COOPER *Pioneers* vii, The former were generally called, by the Anglo-Americans, Iroquois, or the Six Nations. **1834** PIKE *Sketches* 9 The world of prairie . . . has been rarely, and parts of it never, trodden by the foot or beheld by the eye of an Anglo-American. **1846** *S. Lit. Messenger* XII. 19/2 The middle and northern parts [of St. Louis] are most rapidly progressing, under the conjoint enterprise of the German and that unequalled being, the Anglo-American. **1856** SIMMS *Charlemont* 19 That sleepless discontent of temper, which, perhaps, . . . is the moral failing in the character of the Anglo-American. **1891** SWASEY *Early Days Calif.* 49 Sutter's Fort at that time was at once the ark of refuge, safety, and supply to the early Anglo-American immigrants.

b. In special contrast to the non-English races on the borders of the United States.

1834 BRACKENRIDGE *Recoll.* ii. 27 When sent for occasionally to act as interpreter to some stray Anglo-American, the little English boy . . . could not comprehend a single word. **1835** [INGRAHAM] *South-West* I. ix. 101 A clothing or hat store, kept by Americans, that is to say, Anglo Americans as distinguished from the Louisianian French. **1841** FOOTE *Texas & Texans* I. 95 Certain chivalrous Anglo-Americans . . . will be introduced. **1842** *McDonogh Papers* 64 The Anglo-Americans, a term by which all Americans and strangers generally are called by the natives of Louisiana of French descent. **1858** *Texas Almanac* 114 The Anglo-Americans of Texas were threatened with subjection to military despotism.

2. A Canadian, because of the continued adherence of Canada to Great Britain.

1781–2 JEFFERSON *Notes Va.* (1787) 15 In case of war with our neighbours, the Anglo-Americans or the Indians, the route to New-York becomes a frontier through almost its whole length. **1786** — *Writings* V. 402 We can no longer be called Anglo-Americans. That appellation now describes only the inhabitants of Nova Scotia, Canada, &c.

+**Anglo-American,** *a.* [Cf. F. *anglo-américain* (1784).]

1. Combining American situation, character, etc. with English origin.

1809 F. CUMING *Western Tour* 219 At the conflux of the rivers Allegheny and Monongahela, the French . . . had the principal of a line of posts . . . to prevent the spreading of Anglo-American colonization. **1837** *S. Lit. Messenger* III. 464 The Anglo-American colonies were distracted by war and internal confusion. **1841** FOOTE *Texas & Texans* I. 91 The heroic achievements of these three hundred Anglo-American soldiers. **1845** Cist *Cincinnati Misc.* 258 With all the advance in civilization and improvement which characterizes the Anglo-american race, it may be well doubted if we have not left . . . habits and customs which we ought to have carried with us. **1851** CIST *Cincinnati* 34 Destined to render the Anglo-American race paramount throughout this great continent. **1858** *Texas Almanac* 145 Sudden changes produced by the transfer of Texas from Spanish rule to Anglo-American dominion. **1869** BRACE *New West* xvi. 209 He . . . falls, to a degree, into the current of Anglo-American civilization. **1870** *Amer. Naturalist* III. 57 When the first Anglo-American pioneers . . . explored the country east and north of the Tennessee River. **1880** CABLE *Grandissimes* liii. 402 It is not certain that they entered deeper . . . than a comparison of . . . Anglo-American and Franco-American conventionalities.

2. Pertaining to both England and America.

1812 MARSHALL *Kentucky* 81 The Anglo-American army, then on its march to attack the French and Indians, posted in Fort Duquesne. **1843** *Knickerb.* XXII. 90 The 'American Book Circular' recently put forth by Mr. Geo. P. Putnam, of the Anglo-American House of Wiley and Putnam. **1872** *Amer. Ann. Cycl.* XI. 717 A large amount of cable was manufactured for the Anglo-American and Falmouth and Malta Telegraph Companies for repairs.

Anglo-Americanism. =AMERICANISM 2. {*c*1803 (*Christian Observer* II. 554)} — **1841** FOOTE *Texas & Texans* I. 110 In the land [England] whence what we now call Anglo-Americanism has derived its origin.

Anglo-Canadian, *a.* and *n.* (One) combining English and Canadian origin or qualities. {1839} — **1876** BANCROFT *Hist.* V. 130 He found himself supported by more than . . . three hundred and thirty Anglo-Canadian militia.

+**Anglo-confederate,** *a.* Pertaining to the English and the Confederate forces during the Civil War, which were said to be in alliance. — **1864** *National Almanac* (Phila.) 505/1 The Anglo-Confederate blockade-running steamer Chatham is captured. **1870** *Causes Reduct. Tonnage* p. ix, Of this amount [of shipping], 110,163 tons were destroyed by anglo-confederate pirates.

+**Anglo-federal,** *a.* Pertaining to the Federalists who were accused of having leanings toward England. Also *Anglo-federalism, -ist.* — **1800** *Aurora* (Phila.) 8 Jan. (Th.) The nicknames Anglo-federal, Anglo-federalism, &c., were also current. **1817** FEARON *Sketches* (1818) 145 It is an unholy league between apostates . . . on the one part, and on the other the anglo-federalists, the monarchists.

Anglo-Indian. +An American Indian under English influence. — **1845** DE SMET *Oregon Missions* (1847) 162 The worthy Bishop . . . has established his See on the Red River, a tributary of the Winnipeg, amidst the possessions of the Anglo-Indians.

Anglo-Indian, *a.* +Pertaining to those American Indians who allied themselves with the English.

1812 *Niles' Reg.* II. 6/2 We close this article by annexing the following Anglo-Indian account of the battle. **1840** *S. Lit. Messenger* VI. 335/2 The Anglo-Indian forces . . . were more numerous and powerful than had ever before been collected. **1845** DE SMET *Oregon Missions* (1847) 164 The great Indian district of the United States . . . is bounded on the north-west by the Anglo-Indian possessions.

+**Angloman.** An admirer or partisan of England. {anglomane, 1860; angloman, 1880} — **1787** JEFFERSON *Writings* (1905) VI. 370 It will be of great consequence to France and England, to have America governed by a Galloman or Angloman. **1791** *Ib.* V. 329, I learn that some Anglo men [*sic*] have censured it [=a note to a reprint of a pamphlet by Paine]. **1812** *Ib.* IX. 354 The triangular war must be the idea of the Anglo men [*sic*] and malcontents, in other words, the federalists and quids.

+**Anglomania.** An excessive fondness for that which is English. {1809–}

1787 JEFFERSON *Writings* VI. 145, I know your taste for the works of art gives you a little disposition to Anglomania. **1860** CLAIBORNE *Life & Corr. Quitman* 315 The head of a great republic, elected, too, by a party never accused of Anglo-mania. **1883** *Wheelman* May 150/2, I begin to fear that the epidemic of Anglo-mania is spreading.

Anglomaniac. One who has an excessive regard for England and its culture. {1837–} Also attrib. or as adj.

1880 *Scribner's Mo.* Oct. 855/1 No one will remember, next year, . . . when the aristocratic anglo-maniac's dog-cart has replaced the rag-picker's. **1884** *Boston Jrnl.* 30 Dec. 2/4 New York has shopkeepers whose chief business is to cater to the tastes of the Anglomaniacs. **1886** *Harper's Mag.* Aug. 474 A dude of Anglomaniac tendencies. **1895** CHAMBLISS *Diary* 55 It is no wonder that some of our officers are regular Anglomaniacs. **1899** HALE *Lowell & Friends* 275 When Lowell came home he would take pleasure in snubbing the Anglomaniacs who are sometimes found in New England, who want to show by their pronunciation or the choice of their words that they have crossed the ocean.

+**Anglomany.** Anglomania. — **1793** JEFFERSON *Writings* (1895) VI. 237 If the author of 'Plain truth' was now to be charged with that pamphlet, this put along side of his present Anglomany would decide the voice of the yeomanry of the country on the subject. **1805** — *Writings* (1905) XI. 68 Delaware [is] on a poise, as she has been since 1775, and will be till Anglomany with her yields to Americanism.

+**Anglophobia.** Fear or dread of England. {1816-} — **1793** JEFFERSON *Writings* VI. 250 We are going on here in the same spirit still. The Anglophobia has seized violently on three members of our council. *Ib.* 251 Anglophobia, secret Antigallomany, . . . have decided the complexion of our dispositions.

+**Anglophobiac,** *a.* and *n.* (One) having an intense dread or dislike of England. — **1893** *N. Amer. Rev.* Aug. 170 The work of an anglophobiac who labors . . . to widen and prolong the schism. **1894** *Pop. Sci. Monthly* XLV. 476 The Anglophobiac American who proposed cutting a canal through Yucatan.

+**Anglo-rebel,** *a.* Pertaining to the forces of England and the Confederacy, said to be in alliance during the Civil War. — **1863** *Boston Sunday Herald* 26 April 1/3 The Anglo-Rebel navy that was fitting out in England. **1864** *N. Y. Herald* 6 July 1/1 They have sunk the Anglo-Rebel Pirate Alabama.

Anglo-Saxon, *n.* {1610-} One who is of English descent or stock, whether in Great Britain, the United States, or other parts of the world. {1853-}

1846 *Spirit of Times* (N.Y.) 6 June 177/3 The Anglo-Saxon 'never can acknowledge the corn' to the cross of negro and Indian. **1859** STOWE *Minister's Wooing* xxvi, As compared with the Anglo-Saxon, the French appear to be gifted with a *naïve* childhood of nature. **1865** *Atlantic Mo.* XV. 19 For whether the visitor be an Ostiak . . . or an Anglo-Saxon from either side of the Atlantic, he meets his fellow-visitors to the Great Fair on the common ground . . . of human appetite. **1886** *Andover Rev.* Dec. 598 The tendency of the German is to think before he acts, while the tendency of the Anglo-Saxon is to act before he thinks.

Anglo-Saxon, *a.* {1726-} Pertaining to the English people or culture in Great Britain, its colonies and dominions, the United States, etc. {1840-}

Used in place of 'English,' because that term may be taken as applying to England alone.

1832 R. CHOATE in *Deb. Congress* 13 June 3515 The whole circle of the . . . arts, trades, and branches of manufacture, which characterize the . . . industry of the Anglo-Saxon race of men. **1832** D. H. LEWIS *Ib.* 15 June 3579 Our ancestors believed they had embodied this fine conception of Anglo-Saxon liberty in our constitution. **1838** in Buckingham *America* (1841) II. 205 The Anglo-Saxon race have invariably been the most cruel of all Europeans to foreign enemies or subjects. **1850** W. COLTON *Deck & Port* xiv. 389 They had the Anglo-Saxon blood in them, and decided that a man has a right to live where he pleases on this green earth of God's. **1865** *Atlantic Mo.* XV. 9 These people drink beverages of a temperature which would take the skin off Anglo-Saxon mouths. *Ib.* 500 Two causes in our Anglo-Saxon nature prevent this easy faculty and flow of expression. **1869** TOURGEE *Toinette* xxix. (1881) 312 That cream of the Caucasian—the Anglo-Saxon-American of the XIXth century.

Anglo-Saxondom. The realm or domain under the influence of those of English descent or culture. {1850-}

1848 LOWELL *Biglow P.* I. ii. 25 Caleb sez . . . Thet Anglo Saxondom's idee 's abreakin' 'em [=the Mexicans] to pieces. **1872** C. KING *Sierra Nevada* xiv. 282 There were no precedents for the acting. . . . 'Anglo-Saxondom's idea' reigned supreme, developing a plot of riotous situation, and inconceivably sudden change. **1893** STRONG *New Era* 75 The overwhelming numbers and the amazing wealth of the future . . . will make this continent the great centre of Anglo-Saxondom.

Anglo-Saxonize, *v. tr.* To imbue with English character or culture. — **1893** STRONG *New Era* iv. 80 This race is destined to dispossess many weaker ones, assimilate others, & mould the remainder, until . . . it has Anglo-Saxonized mankind.

+**Anglo-Yankee,** *a.* Pertaining to New Englanders, who were conceived as being under English influence. — **1846** EMORY *Military Reconn.* 96 They all spoke exultingly of having thrown off 'the detestable Anglo-Yankee yoke.'

+**Angola pea.** (See quotation.) — **1856** *Rep. Comm. Patents: Agric.* 257 The celebrated 'Oregon pea' . . . has been cultivated . . . by my father about fifty years. He obtained the seed from the captain of a slaver, from the coast of Angola, a year or two after the cession of Louisiana; and it has been known and cultivated here ever since that period as the 'Angola pea.'

Angora cloth. A fabric of silk-like wool. {1867-} — **1884** NYE *Baled Hay* 152 Angora cloth is a Parisian novelty. *Ib.*, This Angora cloth is a perfect type of shaggy materials.

+**Anguilla seed.** The seed of sea-island cotton. — **1828** Commons, etc. *Doc. Hist.* I. 268 The seed, as I have been informed by respectable gentlemen from the Bahamas, was in the first instance produced from a small island in the West Indies, celebrated for its cotton, called Anguilla. It was therefore long after its introduction into this country called Anguilla seed.

Anigh, *adv.* and *prep. dial.* or *arch.*

1. *adv.* Near, at a short distance. {1868-; also *dial.*}

1856 A. CARY *Married* 63 There ain't a brute beast in Woodside that don't foller after him if he goes a nigh. **1869** MRS. WHITNEY *Hitherto* xxxviii. 420 If, haply, I might be worthy yet to dwell anigh.

2. *prep.* Near to; close to. {1773-}

1856 M. J. HOLMES *L. Rivers* vi. 61 While I think on't, I charge you never to go a nigh 'em. **1891** M. E. RYAN *Pagan of Alleghanies* 271 Him up there on the mountain, and not a-nigh her. **1906** F. LYNDE *Quickening* 159 Don't you nev' come anigh me again.

***A-nights,** *adv.* By or at night. (Latterly conceived of as a plural.) {Now *arch.*}

1663 *East-Hampton Rec.* I. 205 To make a yard to put up the drie Cattell a nights. **1705** BEVERLY *Virginia* IV. 66 Chinches are a sort of flat Bug, which lurks in the Bedsteads and Bedding, and disturbs People's Rest a-nights. **1744** FRANKLIN *Acc. Fire-places* 16 It is us'd . . . to shut up and secure it a nights. **1759** *Essex Inst. Coll.* XIX. 150 Our duty very heard at work a days and on gaurd a nights. **1889** *Cent.* s.v. A.[3], To stay out a nights.

***Anise.** =next. — **1709** LAWSON *Carolina* 78 The more physical [herbs] are . . . Tobacco, . . . Anise, Coriander.

***Aniseed (-tree).** +The Florida star anise, *Illicium floridanum.*

[**1637**: see ANGELICA]. **1813** MUHLENBERG *Cat. Plants* 53 Aniseed tree . . . . ; small-flowered. . . . Flor. **1818** NUTTALL *N. Amer. Plants* II. 17 Aniseed tree (*Illicium*). . . . Small trees having the aspect of Laurus.

Anker. Also † **ankor, ancor, anchor, ancher.** A liquid measure usually reckoned at ten gallons; a cask or keg holding this quantity. {1750-1816}

(*a*) **1654** *Conn. Public Rec.* 255 It is . . . ordred, that every ancor of liquors that is landed in any place . . . shall pay to the publique treasury 10 ss. **1600** *Ib.* 353 Noe person . . . shal sell wine vnder a quarter cask, nor liquors vnder an ankor. **1661** *Boston Rec.* 3 The said water bayliffes shall haue ½ of the said anchor if nott owned. **1687** *Maine Doc. Hist.* VI. 266 You are . . . [to] giue to the sachem a blankett, and an anchor of rhum. **1694** *Conn. Probate Rec.* I. 414, I give to my son . . . a chest & a anchor or small cask. **1723** *New-Eng. Courant* 2-9 Sept. 2/2 Five quarter-casks and an anchor of French brandy, two hogsheads of clarret. **1855** SIMMS *Forayers* 534 An anchor of Geneva, and a box of cocoa, and a bag of coffee.

(*b*) **1654** *R. I. Col. Rec.* I. 274 That we brought eighteen ankers of liquers the first voyage, and six the last. **1659** *R. I. Court Rec.* 52 He tooke out an Ancker of liquors out of William Cadmans cellar in the night time. **1678** *New Castle Court Rec.* 351, 3 ankers and a ½ of Rom. **1682** *Penna. Archives* Ser. I. I. 47 Two anchers of beere. **1761** *Penna. Gazette* 15 Oct. 1/3 To be sold, . . . choice old brandy in anchors and quarter-casks. **1830** COOPER *Water Witch* II. ii. 57, I have known him throw in fifty ankers of gin, without a farthing for freight.

+**Ankle-boot.** A shoe which covers the ankle. — **1861** *Army Regulations* 482 Boots: . . . For all Officers—ankle or Jefferson.

Ankle-jack. An ankle-boot. {1848} — **1825** *Missouri Intell.* 4 Nov. 1/4 Wear those shoes facetiously yclept ancle jacks; they are not very elegant—not very romantic; but take my word for it: they are very comfortable.

Annex. [Apparently reintroduced from Fr. *annexe*, and not a continuation of the older English use {1541-1686}.]

1. An additional part of a building; a supplementary building added to, or adjoining, the original or main one. {1863-}

1876 INGRAM *Centennia Exp.* 80 The North annex to the main building. **1886** POORE *Reminisc.* II. 398 The supper was served in a emporarily constructed 'annex,' where preparations were made for seating five hundred persons at a time. **1887** GEORGE *40 Years on Rai* ix. 176 They al marched to the annex of the exposition building to see the 'John Bull.' **1897** MARK TWAIN *Following Equator* l. 477 We liked its annex better, and went thither. **1905** *N. Y. Ev. Post* 16 Aug. 1 Mr. Witte and Baron Rosen appeared on the veranda of the hotel annex.

+**2.** An organization established at Harvard University in 1879 for giving 'private collegiate instruction to women.' Also attrib.

1880 *Harper's Mag.* Dec. 103 Of the success of the Annex in its first year there is only one opinion. **1881** W. H. HILLS *Students' Songs* (1885) 34 'Where are you going, my pretty maid?' . . . 'I'm going to the Annex, sir,' she said. . . . 'I'm going to be cultured, sir,' she said. **1884** *Century Mag.* Aug. 640/1 Well! he secured an Annex girl, And she beguiled a Yale professor. **1888** *Nation* 26 Jan. 69 The Harvard Annex has been established for about eight years. . . . The students of the Harvard Annex are no tpermitted to gain a degree, but are obliged to content themselves with certificates. **1893** D. C. GILMAN *University Probl.* (1898) 304 The remarkable success which has attended what is called the Annex[1] of Harvard University. [*Footnote* [1]Now Radcliffe College.]

3. Humorously: An appendage or addition.
1887 *Harper's Mag.* Oct. 658/1 There arrived a dog, with a man annex. from the City of Brotherly Love. The way that dog went about ... followed by his annex [etc.]. **1888** BILLINGS *Hardtack* 85 It would indeed have been a most admirable arrangement in many respects ... could each man have been provided with an excellent Magee Range with copper-boiler annex.

Annexation. {1611–}

+1. The adding of further territory to the United States.
1820 CLAY *Speeches* (1860) I. p. xiv, The difference between those who may be disinclined to its annexation to our confederacy, and me, is, that their system begins where mine may ... terminate **1836** *Diplom. Corr. Texas* (1908) I. 122 As I have said before, there is n my mind no doubt that the present Administration can carry the measure of Annexation. **1844** P. HONE *Diary* II. 209 The annexation of Texas to the United States ... seems now likely to take place. **1846** CORCORAN *Pickings* 193 He was ... 'a-talkin' about Annexation and Oregon, and all that.' **1852** *Harper's Mag.* V. 695/2 Fresh movements were on foot for the conquest and annexation of Southern California. **1856** HAMBLETON *Biog. H. A. Wise* 296 The annexa ion of Texas and the acquisition of California. **1872** *Atlantic Mo.* Feb. 253 The President's ... scheme for the annexation of San Domingo. **1892** M. A. JACKSON *Gen. Jackson* 29 After the close of the Mexican war and the annexation of California.

+2. An annex or addition.
1848 *Knickerb.* XXXII. 179 Let him step into the St. Charles [hotel], with its spacious free-stone 'annexation,' and observe the new parlors and rooms which have come in with that accession. **1890** RYAN *Told in Hills* 183 One can be an M.D., an L.S.D., or any of the annexations, without ... people considering his education finished.

+Annexationist. One who favors the annexation of territory. Also attrib.
1852 LUDLOW *Hist. U. S.* 209 The great annexationist majority were almost all pro-slavery men. **1883** *Phila. Ev. Telegraph* XL. No. 128, The speaker announced himsel no annexationist. **1888** LANE *Pol. Catch-Words* 13 Sept. 15 *Annexationist,* one who advocates the annexation of outside territory to the United States. The word came prominently into use in the course of the discussions preceding the annexation of Texas.

+Anniversarian. One who commemorates an anniversary by making an address or composing a poem. — **1898** *Official Congress Directory* 31 William Henry Fleming ... was chosen private anniversarian of the Phi Beta Kappa Society in 1873.

***Anniversary,** *a.* and *n.*

***1.** *a.* Celebrated or observed at the same date in successive years; held annually at or about the same time.
+*Anniversary week,* that week of the year during which religious and benevolent societies hold their annual meetings. 'Eastern U.S.' (W. '79).
1686 SEWALL *Diary* I. 124 Monday, March 8th, 1685–6. Anniversary Town-Meeting. **1704** *Boston News-Letter* 7 June 2/2 The anniversary Election Sermon was preached by the Rd. Mr. Jon. Russel. **1715** *Ib.* 9 May 2/2 Rhode-Island May 6th. Wednesday last being the Anniversary Day for chusing our Governour. **1724** C. MATHER *Let.* in *Diary* II. 791 The religion of this country also not encouraging the anniversary celebration of any stated and certain days, anything that look'd that way openly done might be misinterpreted. **1725** *New-Eng. Courant* 15–22 Feb. 1/1 The anniversary meeting of the freeholders and other inhabitants of this town ... at which the most important affairs are consulted and transacted. **1751** *N. H. Hist. Soc. Coll.* IX. 15 The anniversary convention of ministers in this province which was first formed in the year 1747. **1856** *Harper's Mag.* XIII. 124/1, Imagine the thoughts of some well-educated but impoverished country minister as he looks upon our city during Anniversary Week. **1860** *Agric. Convention, Chicago* 3 The anniversary week ... opened Tuesday, June 26th, with the annual meeting of the Illinois Natural History Society. **1873** BEADLE *Undevel. West* 338 The Mormons celebrate the 24th of July—'Anniversary Day.'

+2. *n. pl.* The meetings in Anniversary Week.
1856 *Harper's Mag.* July 269/1 The Anniversaries are long since over. **1857** *Ib.* May 842/2 A year ago we took occasion of the occurrence of the May Anniversaries to plead for a more just ... remuneration of our ministers.

***Annoy,** *v. tr.* To obstruct (a thing); to interfere with the proper function of (a thing). *Obs.* {–1721}
1637 *Boston Rec.* 18 Digging holes and annoying the high Way with stinking fish. **1651** *Dedham Rec.* 183 An order to be drawen to restrayne anoying high wayes ... in the Towne or in the woodes. **1672** *Springfield Rec.* II. 112 The causey over ag[ains]t Thomas Dayes is much annoyed by waters that come from the springs in the hills. **1710** *Boston Rec.* 107 To set up posts ... so as to stop carts from anoying the pavement.

***Annoyance.** A source of damage, obstruction, or inconvenience; (a) nuisance. *Obs.* {–1754}
1634 *Boston Rec.* 1 It is ... ordered that no person shall leave any fish or garbage neere the said Bridge ... whereby any anoyance may come to the people. **1660** *Ib.* 154 Instructions were given to the water bayliffes to cleare the flatts of all matters of anoyance. **1672** *Springfield Rec.* II. 112 It is hereby ordered that all such annoyances by ditches, banks, or any other Stops of the water ... shalbe removed. **1687** *Ib.* 190 So they are to secure the causey from al annoyances. **1713** *Boston Rec.* 102 An order to prevent annoyance by gutters conveying water from off from houses.

***Annual,** *n.* +An examination held every year. Also attrib. — **1871** [L. H. BAGG] *At Yale* 277 On the morning of Presentation Day the Freshmen now assume their Annual hats. *Ib.* 278 The members of the committee ... wear ... tiny forks of gold, inscribed 'Annual.' ... The last session of freshman 'Annual' closes at noon of the Thursday before Commencement. *Ib.* 281 Each of the two factions also adopted its own style of Annual cap. **1895** W. S. TYLER *Amherst College* 175 In 1859–60, 'annuals' ... [had] taken the place of the 'senior examination' on the whole course.

***Annual,** *a.*

1. In specific names: Growing anew from seed each year. {*a* 1626–}
1740 *Georgia Col. Rec.* IV. 664 So does the Annual Cotton, whereof large quantities have been raised. **1843** TORREY *Flora N. Y.* II. 455 *Poa annua,* ... Annual Meadow-grass. ... Cultivated grounds, garden paths, roadsides, etc. **1901** MOHR *Plant Life Ala.* 757 *Iva ciliata,* Annual Marsh Elder, ... [grows] in cultivated fields. Adventive with grain seed from the West.

***2.** Recurring each year.
+*Annual message,* the 'message' which the President of the U.S. sends to Congress every year, or that of a Governor to a State legislature. — +*Annual conference,* in the Methodist Episcopal Church of America, an assembly, meeting every year, which has jurisdiction over certain ecclesiastical matters and sends delegates to the 'general conference.'
1806 *Ann. 9th Congress* 2 Sess. 11 Annual Message. The following Message was received [by Congress] from the President of the United States. **1854** BENTON *30 Years' View* I. 684 President Jackson delivered his last Annual Message ... under circumstances to be grateful to his heart. **1890** *Congress. Rec.* 1 Dec. 2/2 The Chair lays before the Senate the annual message of the President of the United States, which the Secretary will read. — **1837** *Wisconsin Ho. Repr. Journal* 440 Annual Message of Governor [=Henry Dodge]. **1906** *N.Y. Ev. Post* 3 Jan. 1 The annual message of Gov. Higgins was transmitted to the Legislature to-day — **1832** WILLIAMSON *Maine* II. 697 There are seven Annual Conferences, composed only of those who are in full 'connexion,' that is, those who are in Elders' or Deacons' orders. **1844** Rupp *Relig. Denominations* 448 An annual conference is composed of all the travelling preachers, deacons, and elders within a specified district of country. **1851** *Polly Peablossom* 80 At the next annual conference ... this one made his appearance.

Annualist. {1829} +In Ohio, one who advocated that the legislature should meet annually (instead of biennially). — **1894** *Columbus* (Ohio) *Dispatch* 7 Mar., He was interrupted again and again by the annualists, who asked him innumerable questions.

***Annuity.**

+1. A yearly payment (often in goods and provisions) made by the United States government to Indians or an Indian tribe.
1797 B. HAWKINS *Letters* 91, I shall not give drafts for the Creek annuity until I have a meeting of the chiefs. **1812** *Niles' Reg.* II. 295/1 That the Indian tribes should put to hazard the large annuities which they have been so long in the habit of receiving from the United States. **1820** *Ann. 16th Congress* 1 Sess. II. 616 A statement of all annuities payable by the United States to Indians or Indian tribes. **1839** *Knickerb.* XIII. 25 They [Indians] assemble here to receive their annuities. **1846** M'KENNEY *Memoirs* I. 26 The sums due to the various Indian tribes, on account of the annuities due them. **1849** *Pres. Mess. Congress* II. 1016 Game is fast disappearing ... and the Indian thinks only of annuities and goods, instead of war and plunder. **1857** *Harper's Mag.* Oct. 638/2 To this was added the suspicion of the red men ... that they were to be cheated of their annuities. **1873** BEADLE *Undevel. West* 586 They now receive regular annuities of Government goods. **1885** *Century Mag.* April 833 These [Puyallup] Indians are self-supporting, their annuities having long ago expired. **1905** *Indian Laws & Tr.* III. 131 For permanent annuity, in lieu of interest on stock, ... six thousand dollars.

+2. Attrib. with *article, fund, Indian, money,* etc.
1849 *Pres. Mess. Congress* II. 1015 Besides this annuity-money, the band receives every year ten thousand dollars in goods. **1850** GARRARD *Wah-To-Yah* i. 4 The unsophisticated Indian ... soon barters away his ... annuity money. **1866** *Rep. Indian Affairs* 83 With the balance of the annuity fund ... I purchased provisions and issued them to the Indians. **1870** KEIM *Sheridan's Troopers* (1885) 31 The treaty defined the annuity articles to be annually distributed as follows. **1870** *Congress. Globe* 30 June 5010/2 [This amendment] is changing the law in existence almost from time immemorial, that when a tribe of annuity Indians take a frontierman's cattle ..., a deduction shall be made from the next annuity to be paid to those Indians.

+Annuity goods. Supplies and provisions annually given by the United States government to Indians and Indian tribes.
1868 *Indian Laws & Tr.* III. 716 The half-breeds of said tribe shall share equally ... in the distribution of annuity goods. **1871** *Rep. Indian Affairs* (1872) 540 The Bannacks heretofore under the chieftain Tyg-gee, have been in, received their annuity-goods, and again departed. **1873** BEADLE *Undevel. West* 530 The annuity goods and provisions of that year were soon exhausted. **1878** — *Western Wilds* 357 A Southern Ute ... tricked out in all the gaudy finery which they affect when annuity goods are plenty. **1883** *Rep. Indian Affairs* 15 To regulate issues of 'annuity

goods' proportionately to the amount of work an Indian has done for himself or the number of days he has worked for the reservation.

Annunciator. {1753–} +A signalling apparatus, as at a hotel desk or for an elevator, usually run by electricity. Also attrib. {1879–}

1853 A. Bunn *Old Eng. & New Eng.* 39 There is an appendage to this office of a remarkable character called an 'Annunciator,' invented, we believe, by Jackson, of New York city, whereby all the bell-pulls of the house are brought within one focus. **1876** Ingram *Centennial Exp.* 297 There was a fine display of electric burglar alarms, hotel and house annunciators [etc.]. **1878** *Harper's Mag.* Jan. 199 'The Big Iron Bath-House' [is] supplied . . . with all the modern conveniences, including speaking-tubes and electrical annunciators. **1884** Howells *Silas Lapham* xxv. 459 'Ring that bell, Mr. Rogers,' said the Englishman . . . , glancing at the annunciator button in the wall. **1889** *Harper's Mag.* Oct. 737/2 That's our new phonographic annunciator. **1900** *Engineering Mag.* XIX. 705 There should be push-buttons at each window with an annunciator at the store-keeper's desk.

+A No. 1, A number 1.

1. As a rating of vessels. Cf. A 1.

1838 Cooper *Homeward B.* xii, A No. 1, as Mr. Leash calls his ship. **1846** *Spirit of Times* (N.Y.) 6 June 171/1 She . . . was set down as a 'fast running' vessel, being rated at our insurance offices A No. 1. **1857** Butler *Goodrich's Fifth School Reader* 55 Vessels are classified according to their age, strength, and other qualities. The best class is called A, and No. 1 implies that the Swiftsure stands at the head of the best class of vessels. **1857** *Harper's Mag.* Feb. 348/2 An A No. 1 clipper going before the wind under full sail.

2. *fig.* Of the first or very best class or grade. Cf. A. 1.

The original application to vessels is indicated in some of the quotations.

(*a*) **1838** Cooper *Homeward B.* xii, I set all the Effinghams down as tip-tops, or A No. 1, as Mr. Leash calls his ship. **1845** *Knickerb.* XXV. 105 But she was the first girl of his acquaintance, and he determined to commence at 'A No. 1,' and try down to 'etc.,' with no number. **1846** *Spirit of Times* (N.Y.) 4 July 218/1 New Orleans stands A No. 1, in the United States, in the way of magnificent hotels. **1857** *Knickerb.* XLIX. 42 A man can always afford to run on the straight-out moral figure, which you know is the shortest way to an A No. 1 credit. **1863** [Newell] *O. C. Kerr* 1st Ser. 237, I'd rather ride in it than in Queen Victoria's bang-up, A, No. 1, stage coach. **1872** *Vermont Bd. Agric. Rep.* 220, I have earnestly endeavored to . . . hold my position in the market as a maker of an 'A No. 1' article. **1881** *Harper's Mag.* Aug. 478/2 From his youth up he has been as you now find him—A No. 1, extra inspected, scaled and screened, [etc.]. **1900** Stockton *Afield & Afloat* 405 He told . . . how he had always longed for first-class A-No. 1, copper-fastened literature. **1906** H. Fitzgerald *Sam Steele's Adv.* 60 Ned Britton . . . 'll sign with us, Cap'n Gay, and I guess you'll find him A No. 1.

(*b*) **1856** Stowe *Dred* I. 324, [I have] got . . . an a number one cook, and no mistake! **1876** C. Hindley *Life Cheap Jack* 229 She is a prime girl, she is; she is A. Number one, copper-bottomed, and can sail as well in her stays as out of her stays.

***Another,** *a.* +*Another sort*, differently. — **1871** *Ill. Agric. Soc. Trans.* VIII. 229 His calves and his pigs would thrive another sort.

* **Answer.** A formal reply to a speech, +*spec.* that formerly made by Congress to the President's speech.

'The change from the address delivered in person, with its answer, to the message sent by the private secretary, and no answer, was introduced by Mr. Jefferson, and considered a reform' (1856 Benton *30 Years* II. 32).

1721 *Mass. H. Repr. Journals* III. 17 The committee appointed to prepare an answer . . . on the 10th currant, made report as follows. **1789** *Ann. 1st Congress* II. 32 The committee appointed to prepare an answer to the President's speech, delivered to the Senate and House of Representatives of the United States. **1816** Pickering 32 *Answer* . . . is always used by us to signify the Reply of the Senate or House of Representatives to the *Speech* of the President (or of the Governor of a state) at the opening of a session of the Legislature.

* **Ant. a.** The well-known insect noted for its social organization and industry. Also attrib. **b.** A termite.

1676 Tompson *Poet. Works* 59 Busie like the ants or nimble bees. **1737** Brickell *N. Carolina* 158 The Pismire or Ant, is a . . . wise insect. . . . [They] gather Corn for their Winter provisions. **1790** Deane *New-Eng. Farmer* 11, *Ants*, an insect which sometimes annoys fields. **1823** James *Exped.* I. 195 A singular description of food is made use of by some tribes of Snake Indians, consisting . . . of a species of ant. **1865** *Atlantic Mo.* XV. 734/1 Flies never infest her kitchen, cockroaches and red ants never invade her premises. **1888** *Ill. Dept. Agric. Trans.* XXVI. II. p. xiii, Our common white ant (*Termes flavipes*) has been . . . reported to me for its injuries to buildings and other woodwork.

attrib. **1853** 'P. Paxton' *Yankee in Texas* 163 Texas, in fact, may be entomologically divided into . . . the ant country and the roach and flea country.

An't, A'n't, *v.*[1] *colloq.* or *dial.*

1. Contraction of 'are not'; also used for 'am not' and 'is not.' (Cf. Ain't *v.*) {1706–}

(1) **1723** *New-Eng. Courant* 16–23 Sept. 1/1 An't you an impudent, saucy, sorry Fellow. **1779** *Broadside Verse* (1930) 190/2 Some say they [=there] an't victuals nor drink. **1830** Sands *Writings* II. 164 Why, canvas-back ducks a'n't over plenty in this house, ma'am. **1840** Bird *Robin Day* v. 13 They a'n't kings, but presidents. **1845** Kirkland *Western Clearings* 11 An't my victuals good enough for you? **1856** Stowe *Dred* I. 57 Lord's marcy that we an't 'sumed. **1872** Eggleston *Hoosier Schoolm.* i. 12 We a'n't none of your saft sort in these diggings. *Ib.* 18, I guess you're a little skeered, . . . a'n't you?

(2) *c*1790 Witherspoon *Lect. M. Philos. & Eloquence* (1810) 172 The mere vulgarisms of discourse in the pulpit, or at the bar, such as, I an't, I can't, I shan't. **1793** *Md. Hist. Mag.* VI. 356, I ant against baring a part of the burthen. **1818** Fessenden *Ladies Monitor* 171 Provincial words [include] . . . *ant*, for am not. **1834** Simms *G. Rivers* I. 66 But I an't scrupulous. **1872** Eggleston *End of World* xv. 103, I a'n't out of my head.

(3) **1777** *Essex Inst. Coll.* XLII. 326 Please to let me know how I shall dirict a letter to you if this ant right. **1806** Fessenden *Democracy Unveiled* II. 175 Satan an't so easy shammed. **1827** Cooper *Prairie* xvii, As you think the object an't a man, you shall see his whole formation. **1845** Judd *Margaret* I. xv. 134 He'll have to lose his oxen if it an't paid durn soon. **1854** Shillaber *Mrs. Partington* 279 What is a man without credit? He a'n't nothing—he a'n't nowhere. **1874** Long *Wild-Fowl* 144 Oh! he's going; he a'n't coming this way.

||**2.** *A'n't I?*, used in place of 'do I?'

1815 Humphreys *Yankey in Eng.* 22, I'm rather in a strait, jest now, and don't want to stan chaffering and stickling, ant I. *Ib.* 70, I don't want to be twitted, hectored, and plagued, ant I?

A'n't, *v.*[2] *dial.* Var. of *ha'n't* 'have not.' — **1838** C. Gilman *Recoll.* vi. 52 They began to twit me, and I a'nt hearn the last of it yit. **1848** *S. Lit. Messenger* XIV. 474/2 Miss Fanny, a'nt you never missed one of them old China dishes? **1863** 'G. Hamilton' *Gala-Days* 42 No, I 'a'n't seen nothin' of it. *Ib.*, *I* 'a'n't took it.

+Ant-catcher. The rock wren, *Salpinctes obsoletus.* — **1825** Bonaparte *Ornithology* I. 6 [The] Rocky Mountain Antcatcher, *Myiothera obsoleta*, . . . is one of those beings which seem created to puzzle the naturalist. *Ib.* 9 The antcatchers are never found in settled districts, where their favorite insects are . . . less abundant. *Ib.* 8 The Antcatchers . . . dwell in regions where the ants are so numerous . . . that without their agency . . . the produce of the soil would inevitably be destroyed.

+Ante, *n.* The preliminary stake in poker, or one put up in the course of the game.

'*Ante*, the poker term, . . . probably came into American from the Spanish' (Mencken).

'The *ante* is the stake first put up, before the cards are dealt or betting on the hands begins. Each player puts his *ante* in the pool, before (*ante*) beginning the game or hand' (B. '77). See also Penny ante.

1838 *Victims of Gambling* 86 The one next to the dealer [at brag] puts up into the pool . . . any sum he may choose, unless the amount has been . . . fixed by the company. This sum is called the ante. *a*1846 *Quarter Race Kentucky*, etc. 200 The strongest cards which fell to his hand yielded but the bare *ante*, whilst no brag of his remained uncoiled when his opponent was superior. **1852** Baldwin in *S. Lit. Messenger* XVIII. 435/2 A negro *ante* and twenty on the call, was moderate playing. **1876** Bret Harte *G. Conroy* xxxvi, That a rational human being who held such a hand should be content with a small *ante*, without 'raising the other players.' **1883** Shields *S. S. Prentiss* 23 No matter how small the amount of the 'ante,' . . . yet thousands may be won and lost at a single sitting. **1909** Wason *Happy Hawkins* 261, I had seen the ol' man sit in a game where steers was the ante an' car loads the limit.

+Ante, *v.* [See also Anti *v.*]

1. *tr.* In poker and other games of chance, to place money or its equivalent (usually chips) in the pool before all the cards are drawn. Also with *up.*

(*a*) **1854** *San Diego Herald* in *Thornton* (1912) 971 Playin' at billiards an' monte Till they've nary red cent to ante. **1876** Miller *First Families* xi. 93, I raise you five ounces and ante the dust [=gold]. **1900** Smithwick *Evol. State* 79 He anteed his dollar and raised his gun.

(*b*) **1861** *Congress. Globe* Dec. 126/1 [Senator Polk] is not familiar with scenes where hundreds of dollars are 'anted up.' *c*1865 'Mark Twain' *Sk., Jumping Frog*, When it come to that, Smiley would ante up money on him as long as he had a red. **1888** *N. Y. Mercury* 21 July (F.) You can ante up your fifty cents. **1903** A. Adams *Log Cowboy* xii. 184 Flood, who had anteed up his last bean and joined us

b. *absol.* To make an 'ante.' Also *fig.*

1845 Hooper *S. Sugg's Adv.* x. 129 'Yes!' . . . it's a game that all can win at! Ante up! Ante up, boys—friends I mean—don't back out. **1851** — *Widow Rugby's Husb.* 75 The town-boys began to 'hustle' their victims closer together; 'Ante up, Jim!' shouted the ardent friends of that individual. **1870** Nowland *Indianapolis* 163 Often the passer by . . . would hear his sonorous voice demanding 'Tom' to ante, as he had put up last. **1872** 'Mark Twain' *Roughing It* xlvii, You ruther hold over me, pard. I reckon I can't call that hand. Ante and pass the buck.

2. To pay *up;* to come out *with.*

1861 T. Polk in *N. Y. Tribune* 10 Aug., You have heard of the difficulty that *The Bulletin* has fallen into. I have had to 'ante up' there at the rate of $200. **1873** Miller *Amongst Modocs* iv. 43 If I don't make the sports *ante*, my name ain't Boston. **1889** K. Munroe *Golden Days* v. 48 All hands has anted up handsome. **1891** Ryan *Told in Hills* 331 The fellows that stripped this boy will be good enough to ante up with everything they've got of his.

3. To work *off*, dispose of.

1845 HOOPER *Simon Sugg's Adv.* xii. 144 Exsept $500 dollers I anteed off amongst the boys of a night, I couldn't git off a sent. **1857** *Knickerb.* XLIX. 43, I *did* hear that you anted off a thousand shares of Yonkville on Kimball . . . in trade for Texas lands.

4. To push (one's way) *into* a place.

1873 'MARK TWAIN' & WARNER *Gilded Age* xiii. 124, I'd bet a hundred dollars he will ante his way right into the United States Senate when his territory comes in.

+**Ante-bellum,** *attrib. phr.* Before the war; *spec.*, pertaining to the time before the Civil War, 1861–1865.

1870 MEDBERY *Men of Wall St.* 112 State bonds . . . in ante-bellum times furnished the ground work of our entire banking system. **1871** *Rep. Indian Affairs* (1872) 564 The large stock-raisers who number their cattle by the thousand, after the *ante bellum* style. **1881** *Boston Commonwealth* March 5 In *ante-bellum* times, the editor was a bitter denunciator of abolition. **1883** E. A. SMITH *Geol. Survey Ala.* 355 The handsome residences of the prosperous planters of *ante-bellum* days. **1894** *Congress. Rec.* June 5765/2 Sugar production in Louisiana steadily increased from the time when sugar-making first began, away back in antebellum times, until 1861. **1901** B. T. WASHINGTON *Up from Slavery* 140 An old, antebellum coloured man came a distance of twelve miles. **1909** *Springfield W. Repub.* 25 Feb. 14 An ante-bellum minister read the scripture; another led in prayer.

* **Antelope.**

+**1.** The pronghorn or cabrit (*Antilocapra americana*) of the western U. S.

1804 LEWIS & CLARK *Exped.* (1893) I. 120 Of all the animals we had seen the antelope seems to possess the most wonderful fleetness. **1805** LEWIS in *Ann. 9th Congress* 2 Sess. 1048 Skins of beaver, small and large foxes, wolves, antelopes and elk. **1807** GASS *Journal* 36 On the hills above this creek we saw some goats or antelopes, which the French call cabres. **1823** JAMES *Exped.* I. 171 Although they saw a few bisons, and antelopes, and elks, they were not so fortunate as to kill any game for subsistence. **1838** COOPER *Homeward B.* ix, I take over lots of cockney hunters every summer, who just get a shot at a grizzly bear or two, or at an antelope. **1846** SAGE *Scenes Rocky Mts.* iv, The antelope of the grand prairies differs but little in size and shape from the common sheep. **1859** MARCY *Prairie Trav.* vii. 243 The antelope . . . frequents the most elevated, bleak and naked prairies in all latitudes from Mexico to Oregon. **1868** *Amer. Naturalist* Dec. 537 There seems to be some foundation for the belief that the horns of these Antelopes are deciduous. **1877** CATON (*title*), The Antelope and Deer of America. **1890** E. B. CUSTER *Following Guidon* 9 They are the fleetest animals we have, except the antelope. **1901** MCCUTCHEON *Graustark* 9 There was a pretty look of fear in her eyes as she surveyed the massive bears and the stark, stiff antelopes.

+**b.** In collective use. Also =antelope meat.

1847 RUXTON *Adv. Rocky Mts.* (1848) 205 The fare in Laforey's house was what might be expected in a hunter's establishment; venison, antelope, [etc.]. **1870** KEIM *Sheridan's Troopers* (1885) 207 Venison, antelope, elk, or bear, is never used except in times of great scarcity. **1881** *Rep. Indian Affairs* 122, I estimate 7,000 deer and antelope were killed during February and March. **1895** *Outing* Aug. 402 The antelope were standing well bunched together. **1902** WISTER *Virginian* iv. 49 In a moment we were in the clean plains, with the prairie-dogs and the pale herds of antelope.

+**2.** The mountain sheep. *Obs.*

1812 STODDARD *Sk. Louisiana* 358 Among other animals incident to the country may be noticed the Ibex, or Antelope of California, called by the Spaniards mountain sheep.

3. Attrib. with *meat, skin, steak*, etc.

1846 SAGE *Scenes Rocky Mts.* iv, We reached the antelope range, and saw four or five of these animals scouring the boundless expanse. **1847** RUXTON *Adv. Rocky Mts.* (1848) 241 At night I . . . made a fire, and cooked an appola of antelope-meat. **1848** PARKMAN in *Knickerb.* XXXII. 45 He would be kneeling by Delorier, instructing him in the true method of frying antelope-steaks. **1849** AUDUBON *Western Journal* (1906) 148, I have seen some elk and antelope skins dressed and terrapin shells are everywhere. **1860** GREELEY *Overland Journey* 175 We obtained a generous supply of fresh bread and another antelope ham. **1872** 'MARK TWAIN' *Roughing It* xii. 105 At the Green River station we had breakfast —hot biscuits, fresh antelope steaks, and coffee.

+**Antelope-goat.** The Rocky Mountain goat, *Haplocerus montanus.* — **1884** *Century Mag.* Dec. 193 Professor Spencer F. Baird . . . places this animal among the antelopes with the distinctive generic name of *Aplocerus montanus.* . . . As a popular name mountain antelope or antelope-goat might be suggested. **1888** ROOSEVELT in *Century Mag.* XXXVI. 202/2, [I] devoted my entire energies to the chase of but one animal, the white antelope-goat, at present the least known and rarest of all American game.

+**Ante-man.** [ANTE *n.*] The player who puts up the 'ante.' — **1887** KELLER *Draw Poker* 68 If a number of players have gone in, it is best generally for the ante-man to make good and go in.

+**Ante-revolutionary,** *a.* Pertaining to the time before the American (or French) Revolution. {1860}

1837 *S. Lit. Messenger* III. 464 These towns . . . still exist and are the only means we now have of becoming acquainted with the ante-revolutionary Frenchmen. **1851** HAWTHORNE *Twice-told Tales* II. 26 The black, lowering sky . . . wore . . . the same visage as when it frowned upon the ante-Revolutionary New-Englanders. **1856** SIMMS *Charlemont* 256 The very pistols that he wields, those clumsy . . . ante-revolutionary machines, which his stout grandsire carried at Camden and Eutaw. **1860** HOLMES *E. Venner* ii, A family without ante-Revolutionary recollections. **1869** TOURGEE *Toinette* i. (1881) 7 It was a rambling town of the olden time, with a history that went back into the ante-revolutionary days.

+**Ante-war,** *attrib. phr.* =ANTE-BELLUM. — **1878** *N. Amer. Rev.* 123 To go back to ante-war money, ante-war wages, and ante-war prices, might be tolerable if at the same time we could go back to ante-war freedom from debt and ante-war lightness of national taxation. **1879** TOURGEE *Fool's Errand* xxii. 130 Some tale of heroic endurance by which his companion had . . . avoided prosecution in the ante-war era.

Antherine. *Obs.* An obsolete variety of poplin. {1710–39} — **1712** *Boston News-Letter* 9–16 June 2/2 The ladies may have their choice of silks, . . . poplins, antherines, &c. **1714** *Essex Inst. Coll.* XLIII. 51, 1 pc. [=piece] anterine, 40 yds. at 2s.

Anthony over: see ANTONY OVER.

+**Anthony rule.** In the U. S. Senate, an order of business devised by Henry B. Anthony, senator from Rhode Island (1859–1884), and submitted on April 19–21, 1870.

1870 *Congress. Globe* 17 June 4541/3 The Chair will state the distinction between this and what was popularly known in the Senate as the 'Anthony rule,' under which the Calendar was gone over subject to objection. **1879** *Congress. Rec.* 5 Feb. 995/1 What is known as the Anthony rule can only be suspended on one day's notice given, or by unanimous consent. **1882** *Ib.* 3 Feb. 872/1 The great advantage we have . . . received from the . . . Anthony rule.

Anthracite. A variety of coal, hard and almost purely carbon. {1812–}

1821 *Jrnl. Science* III. 41 Anthracite.—On the north bank . . . there is a large quantity of blind coal. **1832** WILLIAMSON *Maine* I. 181 Anthracite . . . burns slowly without flame, smoke or odour. **1833** E. T. COKE *Subaltern's Furlough* I. 67 That which is termed 'anthracite' will not blaze or burn easily, unless English coal is mixed with it. **1839** *S. Lit. Messenger* V. 837/2 The hickory blazing (confound your scorching anthracite). **1841** BUCKINGHAM *America* I. 164 There is a description of coal burned here, called anthracite, which is very hard, scarcely at all bituminous. . . . We preferred discontinuing the use of it in our apartment altogether, and substituting English coal, called here Liverpool coal. **1853** Marcy *Explor. Red River* (1854) 153 He calls this coal 'anthracite, the same, to all appearances, as he had seen in the coal basins of Pennsylvania.' **1882** HOWELLS *Modern Instance* xiii, He had pulled up two armchairs in front of the glowing grate of anthracite.

b. Attrib. with *iron, land, stove*, etc.

1840 *Niles' Nat. Reg.* 20 June 256/1 Anthracite iron. Malleable iron has been made from pigs formed at the anthracite furnace at Roaring Creek, Pa. **1853** KANE *Grinnell Exp.* ii. 21 Three anthracite stoves. **1877** Raymond *Mines & Mining* 363 The development of the vast anthracite-iron industry, which has contributed so much to the prosperity of Pennsylvania. *Ib.* 371 The anthracite lands of Pennsylvania.

c. *Anthracite nail:* (see quotation and prec., quot. 1840).

1840 *Niles' Nat. Reg.* 1 Aug. 352/1 Anthracite nails are made from the ore at the works of Messrs. Reeve & Whitaker, Phoenixville, Pa. in the short space of twenty-four hours.

Anthracite coal. =ANTHRACITE. {1837–}

1830 J. F. WATSON *Philadelphia* 707 When the anthracite coal up the Schuylkill, at Mount Carbon, &c. was first effectively discovered, since the year 1800, it was deemed of little value, because they could devise no way to ignite it. . . . It was in the year 1808, that Judge Fell, at Wyoming, made the first experiment to use that coal in a grate of his own construction. **1833** *Niles' Reg.* XLIV. 4/2 A mine of anthracite coal is said to have been discovered on the Potomac. **1836** P. HONE *Diary* I. 213 This was the first voyage ever made from New York to Albany by a steamboat propelled by anthracite coal. **1840** *Knickerb.* XV. 102 It is remarkable, that notwithstanding the vast quantities of anthracite coal which are used in our cities, there should be so little curiosity manifested to know its origin. **1866** GREGG *Life in Army* i. 21 [My father] invented the first furnace ever used for smelting ore by the use of Anthracite coal.

b. Attrib. with *basin, bed, company, formation.*

1835 *Encycl. Amer.* I. 274 In Pennsylvania, the anthracite coal formation is known to cover a tract of country many miles in width. **1856** J. P. LESLEY *Manual of Coal* 86 The anthracite coal-beds . . . from Soloman's Gap to Scranton. *Ib.* 217 The long, narrow anthracite coal basin. **1877** Raymond *Mines & Mining* 375 The foundation on the part of the great anthracite-coal companies of a new department in their administration for the . . . improvement of the workingmen.

Anthrax. A bacterial disease of animals, particularly cattle and sheep; splenic fever. {1876–}

1878 *Rep. Comm. Agric.* 455 The doctor . . . found that the cattle had been dying of 'malignant anthrax,' or 'black-leg.' **1880** *Ib.* 494 Six cattle . . . promptly perished by anthrax. **1884** *Ib.* 256 Similar facts have long been noticed with other diseases, and particularly with anthrax.

+Anti, *n.*[1]

1. Abbrev. of ANTI-FEDERALIST. *Obs.*

1788 H. KNOX in *Life & Corr. R. King* (1894) I. 335 The majority of the Antis is so great at Poughkeepsie, that I ask no questions. **1789** FISHER AMES *Letter* Wks. (1854) I. 33 The *antis* will laugh at their own fears. **1792** *Md. Hist. Mag.* XII. 315 Should I be so happy as to be the object of your choice, I promise to have all Tories and Anti's turned out of office. **1801** *Spirit of Farmers' Museum* 56 There Feds shall cease to charge the Antis With making Frenchmen rule brave yankees. **1807** IRVING, etc. *Salmagundi* (1824) 188 One old tenant, who always, just before the election, became a violent anti.

2. Abbrev. of other compounds of ANTI-, as *Anti-mormon.*

a **1850** FORD *Hist. Illinois* (1854) 419 But soon after the anties had arrived with their force near Nauvoo . . . Mr. Brayman came to Springfield. *Ib.* 417 This treaty was agreed to by Gen. Singleton . . . and others, on the side of the anties, and by Major Parker and some leading Mormons on the other side. **1890** NORTON *Polit. Americanisms* 5 *Anties*, or *Antys*, a faction of Democrats who in 1849–50 voted with the Whigs.

Anti, *n.*[2] and *v.* =ANTE.

1844 J. COWELL *Thirty Years* 94 The dealer makes the game, or value of the beginning bet, and called the anti. **1853** 'P. PAXTON' *Yankee in Texas* 121, I win a quarter race with him, four bales anti, just afore I took sick. *Ib.* 97 Anti ten cows and calves on ither the stranger er me. **1859** BARTLETT 9 *To anti*, to risk; to venture a bet; as, 'I'll *anti* all I'm worth on that.' This term is derived from the game of poker—the amount placed in the pool by each player being called the *anti.* South-western. **1871** DE VERE 579 What will you anti he won't be re-elected.

Anti-, *prefix*, denoting opposition or hostility to the thing or idea expressed by the second part of the compound.

Common in English use from the seventeenth century. The American examples of historical interest are separately illustrated under ANTI-ABOLITION, etc.

1. With nouns, usually abstract, to denote opposition to some principle or thing.

1783 J. KENT in *Life & Lett. Simeon Baldwin* (1918) 165 I pray God to forgive the Wickedness & Antipatriotism of the times. *c***1808** ADAMS *Works* (1851) VI. 535 Mr. Hillhouse has known favoritisms and anti-favoritisms enough in both houses. **1821** JEFFERSON *Writings* XV. 311 How many of our youths she [=Harvard] now has, learning the lessons of anti-Missourianism, I know not. **1833** *Niles' Reg.* XLIV. 1/1 National republicans or Clay men—anti-masons—proclamation-men or anti proclamation-men—nullifiers or anti-nullifiers . . . have been so jostled that no party knows exactly where is its own present location. **1855** Hambleton *Biog. H. A. Wise* 303 Anti-naturalization . . . is a plank of the black cockade federalism of the days of the elder Adams. **1857** WILLIS *Convalescent* 241 This open and flagrant anti-Puritanism was so wholly unlike all we had heard of the tone and temper of Nantucket. **1871** STOWE *Pink & White Tyranny* iv. 46 She doesn't know anything about ritualism and anti-ritualism.

2. In compounds denoting persons opposed to the thing, etc., designated by the second element.

1721 J. T. Buckingham *Newspaper Lit.* I. 56 Above forty persons have subscribed for the *Courant* since the first of January. . . . And, by one Advertisement more, the Anti-Couranters will be in great danger of adding forty more . . . before the first of March. **1759** *Boston Gazette* 11 June [Letter addressed] to the Trading and Farming People of New England . . . [by] an Anti-Canadian. **1770** ADAMS *Works* (1850) II. 243 We met to return thanks to the ninety-two anti-rescinders. **1809** IRVING *Knickerb.* v. iv, The sergeant-at-arms . . . declared that it was just . . . to declare instant war against these unchristian anti-pumpkinites. **1825** *Catawba Journal* 26 July, The anti-conventionists in this state . . . have unwarily got into bad company. **1841** *Congress. Globe* Jan., App. 153/1 The high tariffite, and the anti-tariffite—the distributionist, and the anti-distributionist—the assumptionist, and the anti-assumptionist. **1849** *Life & Corr. Quitman* 210 Any other view of the subject, whether by bond-payer or anti-bonder, would . . . be opposed to the principles of our government. **1850** JUDD *R. Edney* xx. 261 'You belong to the anti-dogs?' asked the landlord. **1856** HAMBLETON *Biog. H. A. Wise* 300 These are generally known as the anti-Know Nothing resolutions. **1861** *N. Y. Tribune* 9 Nov. 4/5 An 'Abolitionist' is also . . . a Woman's-Rights-Man, an Anti-Sabbatarian. **1870** F. FERN *Ginger-Snaps* 131 Till all you anti-Sabbatarians are mad to abolish Sunday. **1894** 'MARK TWAIN' *Those Twins* iv, The teetotalers, and the anti-teetotalers. **1899** *Review of Reviews* March p. xiv, In the States the Anti-Expansionists and Anti all other movements have been christened 'Aunties.' **1909** 'O. HENRY' *Options* 123 Keep telling 'em . . . to let the gold-dust family do their work. Talk to 'em like a born anti-Bryanite.

3. In attributive (or predicative) compounds with a noun as the second element, as *anti-assessment act.*

1824 *Catawba Journal* 9 Nov., The anti-caucus ticket will be supported . . . by all who are . . . opposed to caucus nominations. **1837** *S. Lit. Messenger* III. 473 'Tis not alone in . . . playing the part of corresponding secretary to some Anti-Tobacco-chewing . . . Society. **1844** *N. Y. Evening Post* 20 Dec. 2/4 An Anti-Tax Meeting was held in Lancaster County on Saturday last, by landholders opposed to the present tax law. **1846** MACKENZIE *Van Buren* 189 Mr. Russel H. Nevins was one of the Vice Presidents of the great Anti-Texas-annexation meeting. **1847** L. COLLINS *Kentucky* 208 The intensely exciting contest of three years duration [*c*1825], between the 'Relief' or 'New Court,' and the 'Anti-Relief' or 'Old Court' parties. *a***1848** *N.Y. Express* (B., p. 240), The Anti-Sabbath meeting . . . has at length taken place in Boston. About 300 females were on hand. **1852** BRISTED *Upper Ten Th.* i. 34, I consider the Anti-Capital-punishment agitators . . . directly responsible for half the rascality in this city and this state. **1852** *Harper's Mag.* V. 334/1 If there have been any little anti-Maine-Law episodes in my life, they have been my occasional weeks at the Watering-Places. **1856** GREELEY in Harper *S. B. Anthony* (1898) 147 My political antagonists take advantage of such publications to make the Tribune responsible for the Anti-Bible, Anti-Union etc. doctrines. **1857** *Harper's Mag.* Jan. 284/1 This story is no doubt made up by some of the Anti-Maine law people, who are always trying to throw suspicion on the temperance men. *Ib.* March 550/2 The election of Mr. Green, 'Anti-Benton Democrat.' **1859** *Tribune Almanac* 63/2 The candidates of the Anti-Lecompton or Broderick Democracy. **1859** L. WILMER *Press Gang* 144 They long to have a socialistic, anti-marrying, anti-Sabbath-keeping, anti-Bible-reading policy, in America. **1865** *Atlantic Mo.* XV. 745 The convention, when elected on the 4th of February preceding, was largely Anti-Secession. **1872** *Ib.* May 644 General Butler with his . . . anti-repudiation party. **1880** 'MARK TWAIN' in *Atl. Mo.* XLVI. 227 Edward, as a boy, had interested himself in . . . penny missionary affairs, anti-tobacco organizations, anti-profanity associations. **1882** *Nation* Aug. 106/3 The term 'officers' used in the Anti-Assessment Act. *Ib.* 186/1 The Stalwart portion of the majority which voted for the Anti-Chinese Bill. *Ib.* Sept. 212/2 The election of four Anti-Stalwart delegates. **1884** *Century Mag.* July 409/2 Tennessee was the first State to pass an anti-Ku Klux statute. **1885** *Ib.* April 827 A faction-fight . . . between the Tammany and anti-Tammany members. **1894** 'MARK TWAIN' *P. Wilson* xi, There was a strong rum party and a strong anti-rum party. **1895** *Chicago Tribune* 6 April 1 Anti-Silver Democrats to be kept out.

4. With adjectives.

1812 *Steele Papers* II. 688 You will bear in mind that there are anti-electoral democrats, who have come in thro' federal aid. **1822** *Ann. 17th Congress* 1 Sess. I. 264 An argument so sectional and anti-national in its character, surely comes with bad grace. **1834** Edward *Hist. Texas* (1836) 217, I do not wish to believe there is any anti-Mexican party in Texas. **1841** FOOTE *Texas & Texans* II. 388 The avowed object of these enkindlers of an Anti-Texan feeling is to prevent the future annexation of Texas to the United States. **1846** CORCORAN *Pickings* 9 Ah, Jim! you must be elected president of the Unreformed Drunkards;—you can go the Anti-Washingtonian ticket strong! **1873** BEADLE *Undevel. West* 319 All the anti-Chinese orators regularly employed a house full of Chinese servants. **1882** *Advance* (Chicago) 27 April (Washington corr.), The anti-British, pro-Irish, and generally discontented element.

+Anti-abolition. [ANTI- 1, 3.] Opposition to the abolition of slavery. Also attrib.

1842 BUCKINGHAM *Slave States* II. 76 Both are Anti-abolition papers. **1854** M. J. HOLMES *Tempest & Sunshine* viii. 117 His attempts at anti-abolition had not succeeded as well as he anticipated. **1857** OLMSTED *Journey thro' Texas* p. xxv, Out of a few localities . . . there is no society in which an avowal of positive anti-abolition opinion would not be considered eccentric.

+Anti-abolitionist. [ANTI- 2.] One who opposed the abolition of slavery. {1862}

1835 *S. Lit. Messenger* I. 772, I am both from conviction and expediency, a decided anti-abolitionist. **1836** *Ib.* II. 665 A tit-bit for the anti-abolitionists. **1840** HONE *Diary* II. 6 He is a fine fellow and a true Whig, but an out-and-out anti-abolitionist. **1841** BUCKINGHAM *America* I. v. 93 Dr. Hawkes is himself an openly avowed anti-abolitionist. **1862** 'E. KIRKE' *Among Pines* 57 Anti-Abolitionist and Southern-sympathizer though I was.

+Anti-administration. [ANTI- 3.] *attrib.* and *pred.* Opposed or acting in opposition to the President and his party.

1834 *Deb. Congress* 19 March 1007 That meeting [in New Orleans] was composed of every description of persons, . . . administration and anti-administration men. **1855** *Harper's Mag.* X. 829/1 The Legislature, in both branches, is Anti-Administration by very large majorities. **1860** MORDECAI *Virginia* xxi. 232 He became the anti-administration combatant, and opened on Mr. Jefferson in a series of . . . articles against him and his principles. **1872** *Atlantic Mo.* May 642 Mr. Nast . . . in his new character as caricaturist of the anti-administration senators.

+Anti-affirmant. [ANTI- 2.] One opposed to the acceptance of an affirmation in place of an oath. — **1789** MACLAY *Deb. Senate* 89 [We] now took up the judiciary, and the affair of the affirmations. Ran Ellsworth so hard, and the other anti-affirmants, on the anti-constitutionalism of the clause, that they at last consented to have a question taken.

+Anti-American, *n.* and *a.* [ANTI- 2, 4.]

1. *n.* An opponent of America or the American Party.

[**1788** W. GORDON *History* (1789) I. 158 The Massachusetts and New-York assemblies . . . also encouraged the Anti-Americans to resume the plan of taxing the colonies.] **1855** HAMBLETON *Biog. H. A. Wise* 340 Influence as many of the Anti-Americans to vote with us as possible.

2. *adj.* Opposed to America or that which is American. or to the American Party in politics.

1838 Buckingham *America* (1841) I. 173 Our young men are returned rogues and fops, with extravagant anti-American notions. **1855** HAMBLETON *H. A. Wise* 340 A perfect list . . . of every man who will vote the Anti-American ticket. **1859** L. WILMER *Press Gang* 51 Many of our most influential public journals are Anti-American in feeling and sentiment.

+**Anti-Americanism.** [ANTI- 1.] Opposition to what is distinctively American. — **1844** HONE *Diary* II. 238 Most of them seem to have escaped the foppery of foreign manners and the bad taste of anti-Americanism.

+**Anti-Anglican,** *a.* [ANTI- 4.] Opposed to England or the English. {1809} — **1775** ADAIR *Indians* 255 The aforesaid chieftain . . . had a French commission. . . . A flourishing flag . . . was displayed day and night, in the middle of their anti-anglican theatre.

+**Anti-assumptionist.** [ANTI- 1.] One opposed to the assumption of the State debts by the Federal government. — **1841** *Congress. Globe* Jan., App. 1531 The assumptionist and the anti-assumptionist . . . were united against the Democracy. **1883** MACMASTER *Hist.* I. 580 The Anti-assumptionists hoped to win through a bargain they had just completed with one of the Middle States.

+**Anti-bank.** [ANTI- 3.] *attrib.* Opposed to the establishment or continuance of a United States bank.

1837 MACKENZIE *Van Buren* (1846) 177 The final vote will not shew the full anti-bank strength. **1837** CALHOUN *Wks.* III. 79, I am neither a bank man nor an anti-bank man. **1841** *Congress. Globe* Jan., App. 153/1 The Abolitionist and the slave holder, the bank man and the anti-bank man . . . were united against the Democracy. **1862** *N. Y. Tribune* 23 June, Had this Constitution been submitted whole, with all its anti-Bank, anti-Negro imperfections on its head, it would have stood a better chance.

+**Anti-bankism.** [ANTI- 1.] Opposition to the establishment or continuance of a bank of the United States. — **1855** [PRAY] *Mem. J. G. Bennet* 358 Anti-bankism and anti-rentism . . . were prominent ones [*sc.* doctrines] upon which the leaders of this movement proposed to act.

+**Anti-bankite.** [ANTI- 2.] One who opposed the establishment or continuance of a bank of the United States. — **1844** 'UNCLE SAM' *Peculiarities* II. 46, I'm in for pulling an anti-bankite's nose.

Anti-Catholic, *a.* Opposed to the Catholics or to the Catholic faith. {1819–}

1844 HOFFMAN in *Corr. Griswold* (1898) 153 To devote himself to an anti-Catholic Review. **1859** L. WILMER *Press Gang* 363 His newspaper organs produced that agitation which led to all the Anti-Catholic riots in America. **1894** *Century Mag.* March 791/1 This document has been published in many of the anti-Catholic newspapers; in some of them it has been standing week by week.

+**Anti-cholera.** [ANTI- 1.] (See quotation.) — **1833** E. T. COKE *Subaltern's Furlough* ix. I. 146 Others . . . would only take 'anti-cholera,' as they termed brandy and port wine.

+**Anti-Clintonian.** [ANTI- 2.] One opposed to De Witt Clinton (1769–1825), candidate for the presidency in 1812; a 'Bucktail.' — **1818** *Niles' Reg.* XIV. 192/1 The anti-Clintonians have succeeded in electing their whole ticket, for congress and corporation officers. **1819** *Ib.* XVI. 224/1 The Clintonians and the anti-Clintonians each claim . . . the exclusive designation of 'republicans.' **1885** SCHOULER *Hist. U. S.* III. 227 Better success in constitutional reform was attained in New York, in spite of an incessant turmoil between Clintonians and the anti-Clintonians.

Anti-commercial, *a.* [ANTI- 4.] Opposed to the development of commerce. {1797}

1811 *Steele Papers* II. 650 The accompanying paper contains the anti commercial Bill just reported by the committee on Foreign relations. **1814** *Niles' Reg.* VI. 1/1 We shall shew . . . that the 'commerce,' about which some persons clamor so much, must needs be an insignificant thing, without an intercourse with those states, they (the foolish men of the east) are pleased to call *anti-commercial.*

Anti-constitutional, *a.* [ANTI- 4.] Opposed to the Constitution. {1735 (*Cent. D.*)}

1764 Wirt *P. Henry* (1818) App. p. v, It is hoped that . . . British patriots will never consent to the exercise of any anticonstitutional power. **1781** PETERS *Hist. Conn.* (1829) 179 They discovered that subjection to be anti-constitutional and oppressive.

+**Anti-constitutionalism.** [ANTI- 1.] The quality or character of being contrary to the Constitution. — **1789** [see ANTI-AFFIRMANT].

+**Anti-coolie.** [ANTI- 3.] *attrib.* Opposed to Chinese labor or the use of this.

1869 BRACE *New West* xvi. 210 Employers found him too useful to permit him to be driven off by 'anti-coolie' vagabonds. **1878** B. F. TAYLOR *Between Gates* 87 Americans . . . would organize him [=the Chinaman] out of existence with the Anti-Coolie Societies, and the Caucasian Orders, and the White League. **1888** *Congress. Rec.* App. 18 Aug. 439/2 The anti-cooly act became a law on the 9th of February, 1869.

+**Anti-Democrat.** [ANTI- 2.] One that is opposed to the Democratic party and its principles.

1802 (*title*), The Republican; or, Anti-Democrat. **1855** BRISTED in *Fraser's Mag.* LII. 521 Many of the Southern anti-Democrats in Jackson's and Van Buren's time (under the name of *State-rights Whigs*) carried them [*sc.* doctrines] to greater lengths than the Democrats themselves.

+**Anti-democratic,** *a.* [ANTI- 4.] Opposed to democracy or the principles of the Democratic party. — **1837** *Democratic Review* Oct. 10 That extensive anti-democratic corruption of sentiment in some portions of our people. **1842** F. WOOD in MacLeod *Biog.* 98 We question that the policy of high duties is beneficial to us; but we know, if it were so, that it is iniquitous, anti-democratic, and unequal.

+**Anti-effort Baptist.** [ANTI- 3.] A Baptist who is opposed to missions. — **1867** W. H. DIXON *New America* II. 308 In a very short time this body was divided into Old School Baptists (called by their enemies Anti-effort Baptists), Sabbatarians [etc.].

+**Anti-embargo.** [ANTI- 3.] *attrib.* Opposed to the prohibition of imports and exports, specifically to the Embargo Acts in the United States, 1807 ff. — **1808** *Ann. 10th Congress* 2 Sess. 607 The anti-embargo men of Massachusetts. *Ib.* 924 The language of the anti-embargo men.

+**Anti-embargoist.** [ANTI- 1.] One who opposes the prohibition of imports and exports. — **1808** *Ann. 10th Congress* 2 Sess. 779 We anti-embargoists show that things would not have been thus, had our advice been taken.

Anti-Episcopalian. [ANTI- 2.] One who opposes the Episcopal denomination. — **1769** FRANKLIN *Letter* 23 Feb. (MS.), I do not conceive that Bishops residing in America would either be of such Advantage to Episcopalians, or such Disadvantage to Anti-episcopalians, as either seems to imagine.

+**Anti-fed.** Abbrev. of ANTI-FEDERALIST. *Obs.*

1788 *Maryland Jrnl.* 3 June (Th.) The famous Dr. Spring asked a lady on which side she was, fed. or antifed. **1798** FESSENDEN in *Sp. Farmers' Museum* (1801) 43 These fine fellows should be led By Lyon, sturdy Antifed, Who ought to howl with broken head. **1803** *Steele Papers* I. 415 [Those] who have observed the progress of the American Government have marked the period when Fed and Antifed ceased to [design]ate the real character of parties. **1806** FESSENDEN *Democracy Unveiled* II. 83 Ye Tories, Demos, Antifeds, Of hollow hearts, and wooden heads.

+**Anti-federal,** *a.* and *n.* [ANTI- 2 and 4.]

1. *a.* Opposed to the extension of much power to the federal government; pertaining to a political party which supported states' rights, called so until *c.* 1800.

1788 KING in *Life* (1894) I. 327 Of three thousand [N.Y.] votes given . . . not more than two hundred were in favor of the antifederal Ticket. **1789** JEFFERSON *Writings* VII. 286 The Virginia Assembly met October 23. . . . They are furiously antifederal. **1798** FESSENDEN in *Sp. Farmers' Museum* (1801) 42 For scarce an Antifederal noddy, Has half a soul to bless his body! **1810** F. CUMING *Western Tour* 56 A party which attempted to prevent the concurrence of the states to the present constitution . . . and was called Antifederal. **1838** *Democratic Rev.* I. 226 The anti-federal, since Democratic, party were far from being opposed to that great instrument, as a whole. **1865** *Atlantic Mo.* XV. 191 Other leaders of the Anti-Federal party fare no better.

2. *n.* =ANTI-FEDERALIST.

1806 FESSENDEN *Democracy Unveiled* I. 13 As Tories many of you vex'd us; As Antifederals then perplex'd us.

+**Anti-federalism.** [ANTI- 1.] The principles or doctrines of the opponents of federalism.

1788 C. GORE in *Life & Corr. R. King* (1894) I. 348 Non-residence in one candidate . . . who was abhorred for his antifederalism. **1789** *Boston Centinel* Feb., On Wednesday last, finished its wicked career The genius of Antifederalism. It was born in August, 1787. **1793** JEFFERSON *Anas* (1903) 118 They raised the cry of anti-federalism against those who censured the mode of administration. **1824** MARSHALL *Kentucky* I. 303 The community was deeply affected with anti-federalism, and the mania of national dissolution. **1840** HONE *Diary* II. 35, I was brought up after the manner of Virginian anti-Federalism.

+**Anti-federalist.** [ANTI- 2.] One opposed to the delegation of power to the federal government; particularly, a member of a political party in the early years of the U. S. government.

'This word was formed about the year 1788. . . . The word is not now [1815] much used; having been superseded by various other names, which have been successively given to the same party' (P.).

1787 *Independent Gazetter* (Phila.) 28 Sept. This antifederalist should reflect that his name may yet be known and himself branded with infamy as an enemy to the happiness of the United States. **1788** *Penna. Gazette* 9 Jan. 3/2 It is the duty of the antifœderalists, in a particular manner in Pennsylvania, to learn wisdom from the conduct of the republican party. **1789** MACLAY *Deb. Senate* 14 The member from the ancient dominion . . . is said to be a notorious anti-Federalist. **1793** STEELE *Papers* I. 99 Mr. Steele while at Congress wrote as many letters to the Antifederalists as to the Federalists. **1799** *Ann. 7th Congress* 2 Sess. 1402 This was conformably to agreement, two Federalists and two anti-Federalists. **1808** *Ann. 10th Congress* 1 Sess. I. 334 Those who opposed those [*sc.* the two first] Administrations, . . . disliking the name of Anti-Federalists, . . . assumed the more popular name of *Republicans.* **1835** *Knickerb.* V. 217 This was strenuously opposed by the anti-federalists.

+**Antifogmatic.** [ANTI- 1: a jocular formation on *fog,* n.] An alcoholic beverage (rum, whisky, etc.) taken on the pretext of counteracting the effects of fog. *Obs.*

1789 *Mass. Spy* 12 Nov. 4/2 Rum. Its great utility in preserving the planters from the effects of the damp and unwholesome air of the morning has given it the medical name of an Antifogmatick. **1809** WEEMS

Marion ix. (1833) 77 And now suppose you take a glass of peach; . . . they say it is good of a rainy morning. . . . O, yes, famous of a rainy morning, a mighty antifogmatic. **1813** PAULDING *J. Bull & Br. Jonathan* xviii. 92 They were also wonderful boys for what they called antifogmatics. **a1827** J. BERNARD *Retrosp.* 206 For mint-sling, . . . as you proceeded southwardly, obtained the medicinal name of an 'antifogmatic.' **1834** *S. Lit. Messenger* I. 182, I had no doubt of the virtues of his medicine, but as I was quite well, I would rather try the anti-fogmatic. **1840** SIMMS *Border Beagles* 99, I had just risen to take my antifogmatic. **1852** *As Good as a Comedy* 134 (Th.) Tom Nettles [was] mixing a couple of rosy anti-fogmatics. **a1877** *Baltimore Gazette* (B.), The typical Richmond man takes an 'eye-opener,' then . . . an 'anti-fog-matic,' then . . . his regular 'bitters.'

‖**Antifogmatical,** *a.* [f. prec.] Given to the use of 'antifogmatics.'— **1845** *Nauvoo Neighbor* 26 Feb. (Th.), We wish the present generation was a little more antifogmatical.

+**Anti-Freemason.** =ANTI-MASON. — **1838** *Knickerb.* XII. 173 The fort where Morgan, the Anti-Freemason, was confined.

Anti-gambling. [ANTI- 3.] *attrib.* Directed against gambling. — **1840** *Niles' Nat. Reg.* 28 March 52/3 The revenue arising from convictions for violations of the anti-gambling law. **1855** *Harper's Mag.* XI. 258/1 Among the more prominent measures passed, we notice the law for the reduction of fees in office, the anti-gambling bill . . . and the Maine Liquor Law.

+**Anti-imperialist.** [ANTI- 2.] One opposed to an imperialistic policy, esp. to the acquisition of territory beyond sea. Also attrib.

'In use especially since the Spanish-American war of 1898' (*Cent. Suppl.*). **1899** (*title*) The Anti-Imperialist. Brookline, Mass. **1900** *Chicago Daily News Almanac* 123/1 The Anti-Imperialist League . . . [was called] to order . . . in the city of Chicago. **1903** TRENT *Hist. Amer. Lit.* 55 The crusading fervour of the abolitionists and the latter-day zeal of the 'anti-imperialists.' **1910** L. F. ABBOTT in *Outlook* 25 June 371 The extreme wing of the Liberal party, whom we should call Anti-Imperialists.

‖**Anti-inoculator.** [ANTI-] One opposed to inoculation for smallpox. — **1721** *New-Eng. Courant* 13–20 Nov. 1/2 We have receiv'd the following Letter from an unknown Hand, in favour of Inoculation, which we hope our Readers (Anti-Inoculators) will bear with.

+**Anti-Jackson.** [ANTI- 3.] *attrib.* Opposed to Andrew Jackson as President of the United States (1829–37).

1833 *Niles' Reg.* XLIV. 337/2 The Jackson and anti-Jackson parties have united, to put down the anti-masonic. *Ib.* 354/1 Mr. Seymour . . . has been nominated, in several of the anti-Jackson papers, for the office of governor. **1834** *Deb. Congress* 19 March 1007 That meeting [in New Orleans] was composed of every description of persons, . . . Jackson men and anti-Jackson men [etc.]. **1834** *Boston Ev. Transcript* 10 April 2/2 The Anti-Jackson men, or Whigs, as they are now called.

+**Anti-liquor.** [ANTI- 3.] *attrib.* Opposed to the liquor trade.

1852 (*title*), Massachusetts Anti-Liquor Law. Boston. **1855** HAMBLETON *Biog. Sk. H. A. Wise* (1856) 68 A combination of Abolitionists, Whigs, Know Nothings and anti-Liquor men, against the great Nebraska principle. **1884** *N. Y. Times* 5/5 How the stringent anti-liquor laws of Iowa are evaded. **1910** C. HARRIS *Eve's Husband* 138, I have determined to run on the anti-liquor ticket.

+**Anti-machine.** [ANTI- 3.] *attrib.* Opposed to the domination of politics by a group of self-organized (and frequently corrupt) politicians. Also *ellipt.* — **1881** *Nation* 6 Jan. 1/2 In the contest for the Speakership of the Assembly, the Conklingite Machine [was] . . . represented by General Sharpe and the 'Anti-Machine' by Mr. Skinner. **1882** *Ib.* 21 Dec. 519/2 With a Democrat who is a thorough partisan, a Republican Machine man can strike hands; . . . with an anti-Machine man never. **1913** LA FOLLETTE *Autobiog.* 128, I had been elected as an anti-machine member.

+**Anti-machinist.** [See prec.] One belonging to the anti-machine party. — **1881** *Nation* 6 Jan. 1/2 The anti-Machinists tend to settle on Mr. Chauncey Depew.

+**Anti-mason.** [ANTI- 2.] An opponent of Freemasonry.

1828 Barnes *Life Th. Weed* (1884) I. 307 If under these multiplied difficulties the Anti-Masons incline to bestow their votes upon Mr. Southwick. *Ib.* We, too, shall vote for an Anti-Mason, according to the 'strictest order of the sect.' **1832** *Louisville Public Advt.* 17 Oct., Claymen, antimasons, and bankites, where are you? **1833** *Niles' Reg.* XLIV. 268/2 He was supported by the anti-masons. **1838** *Congress. Globe* Apr., App. 275/2 Counterfeit Democrats, National Republicans, Antimasons, and Abolitionists. **c1845** W. J. PAULDING *Madmen All* 192 Waal, we've got some o' most all kinds [of people]: . . . Masons, Anti-Masons, Mormons. **1865** *Atlantic Mo.* XV. 596 The shoemaker . . . coming thither to have an evening's chat about . . . William Wirt and the Anti-Masons. **1878** BEADLE *Western Wilds* 186 They forted and held their own, and they daresn't an anti-mason show hisself.

+**Anti-masonic,** *a.* [ANTI- 4.] Pertaining to the sentiment and agitation against Freemasons.

1826 (*newspaper title*), Anti-Masonic Enquirer. **1828–30** H. D. WARD (*title*), The Anti-Masonic Review and Magazine. **1830** (*title*), The Proceedings of the United States Anti-Masonic Convention, held at Philadelphia, September 11. **1833** *Niles' Reg.* XLIV. 223/2 The votes given to Mr. Odiorne, the anti-masonic candidate for congress. **1834** *S. Lit. Messenger* I. 73 The rising importance of the Anti-Masonic party. **1841** *Niles' Nat. Reg.* 20 Feb. 400/1 A democratic anti-masonic convention is to be held in May next at Harrisburg. **1855** [PRAY] *Mem. J. G. Bennet* 121 The political fanaticism which was connected with the Anti-Masonic cause endured for several years. **1899** QUINN *Penna. Stories* 59 His grandfather . . . had been one of the local leaders of the Anti-Masonic party.

+**Anti-masonry.** [ANTI- 1.] Opposition to the Order of Freemasons; spec. that which in 1826 and following years crystallized into a political party, wielding national influence.

1827 Barnes *Mem. Th. Weed* (1884) 31 The subject of my communication was anti-masonry. **1830** *Deb. Congress* 2 Feb. 108/2 Now, I can have . . . a banner with inscriptions upon it: . . . Anti-Sunday Mails, Anti-Masonry. **1831** HOLLEY *Texas Lett.* (1833) 128 There is neither masonry, anti-masonry, nullification nor court intrigues. **1832** BARNES *Mem. Th. Weed* (1884) 47 The principle of anti-masonry is an honest principle. **1834** *S. Lit. Messenger* I. 87 In two years abolitionism will be as prostrate as anti-masonry is now. **1837** *Ib.* III. 463 Anti-masonry maintained its ground in the western parts of New York. **1841** EMERSON *Misc.* 219 Anti-masonry had a deep right and wrong, which gradually emerged to sight out of the turbid controversy. **1854** BENTON *30 Years' View* I. 283/1 Anti-masonry soon ceased to have a distinctive existence, [and] died out. **1879** H. O'REILLY (*title*), American Political-Antimasonry.

+**Anti-means Baptist.** [ANTI- 3.] (See quotation.) — **1872** EGGLESTON *Hoosier Schoolm.* xii. 102 They call themselves 'Anti-means Baptists' from their Antinomian tenets.

+**Anti-mission.** [ANTI- 3.] *attrib.* =next. — **1883** *Schaff's Relig. Encycl.* I. 212/1 Anti-Mission Baptists, with 40,000 members. **1910** *U. S. Census, Religious Bodies* (1919) II. 136 The antimission movement.

+**Anti-missionary,** *a.* [ANTI- 3.] Opposed to the sending of missionaries; applied particularly to a sect of Baptists.

1847 L. COLLINS *Kentucky* 112 To these add 7,085 anti-missionary Baptists, many of whom claim to be United Baptists. **1853** BALDWIN *Flush Times Ala.* 122 His grandfather . . . was a noted divine of the Anti-Missionary or Hard-shell Baptist persuasion in Georgia.

+**Anti-monopolist.** [ANTI- 2.] An opponent of monopolies. Also attrib.

1850 *Corr. R. W. Griswold* (1898) 261, I was to be put in nomination by the anti-monopolists in the Legislature. **1881** *Nation* 9 June 397/2 We are greatly afraid the Anti-Monopolist movement is going to produce worse cases of demagogy than even the Granger movement. **1886** *N. Amer. Review* July 87 Anti-monopolists have no war with honest corporations. **1888** LANE *Pol. Catch-Words* 13 Sept. 15 *Anti-Monopolists*, those who are opposed to the creation of corporations that have the control of any article of common use. They would have the government foster competition even to the extent of offering bounties and granting exceptional privileges.

+**Anti-monopoly.** [ANTI- 3.] *attrib.* Opposed to the power and influence of large corporations, whose monopolies tended to be corrupt.

1881 *Nation* 10 March 160/2 The 'Anti-Monopoly League' meeting, held two or three weeks ago. **1883** *Facts for People* (N.Y.: Anti-Monopoly League) 33 The gentlemen at the head of the Anti-Monopoly party. **1884** CUMMINGS *Sk. Class of 1862 Dartmouth Coll.* 39 He claims to be an anti-monopoly Republican, and approximating Universalism in creed. **1884** *Chicago Tribune* 15 May 7/1 The Anti-Monopoly organization of the United States. **1886** *N. Amer. Review* July 87 The main purpose of the anti-monopoly movement is to resist public corruption and corporate aggression.

***Antimony.** The elementary mineral body of that name.

c1612 STRACHEY *Virginia Brit.* 39 Here Captain Argoll found a myne of antimonye. **1651** *Conn. Public Rec.* I. 223 If the said John Wenthrop Esqr shall discouer . . . any mineralls, as antimony, vitriall, black lead, . . . the said John Wenthrop Esqr . . . shall injoye foreuer the said mynes. **1709** LAWSON *Carolina* 82 Lead and copper has been found, so has antimony heretofore. **1804** BURK *Hist. Virginia* 121 They saw a mine of antimony, which the Indians made use of to ornament themselves, and the faces of their idols. **1808** ASHE *Travels* vii. 63 Besides the minerals I have mentioned, I have seen specimens of tin, antimony, . . . and many others. **1873** RAYMOND *Silver & Gold* 214 Thus producing, in one operation, from crude ore, metallic antimony, several tons of which were shipped to New York.

+**Anti-Mormon.** [ANTI- 2.] One opposed to the Mormons. (See also ANTI *n.*[1] 2.) — **1833** *Louisville Daily Herald* 22 Nov. (title of article) The Mormons and the Anti-Mormons. **1848** *S. Lit. Messenger* XIV. 647/1 But one resource now remained to the anti-Mormons and of this also they were soon bereft—to wit: the administration of Justice in the Courts of the State. **a1850** FORD *Hist. Illinois* (1854) 404 The anti-Mormons complained of a large number of larcenies and robberies.

attrib. **a1850** *Ib.* 404 The Mormon press . . . and the anti-Mormon papers . . . kept up a continual fire at each other. **1870** BEADLE *Utah* 88 The anti-Mormon excitement . . . ceased not till their . . . expulsion from the State [Ill.].

+**Anti-Nebraska.** [ANTI- 3.] *attrib.* Opposed to an act of 1854 by which the territory of Nebraska was organized, free from slavery.

1854 *N. Y. Tribune* 19 Aug. 4/5 The Anti-Nebraska Convention was no more Whig than the Temperance Convention was. **1855** *Harper's Mag.* X. 542/2 In Illinois, Lyman Trumbull, 'Anti-Nebraska Democrat,' succeeds James Shields. **1903** W. E. CURTIS *The True A. Lincoln* 146 With his usual candor, he had addressed letters to the Whigs and Anti-Nebraska men who had been elected to the Legislature, asking their support.

+**Anti-Negro.** [ANTI- 3.] *attrib.* Hostile to the Negro, particularly to his influence in politics. — **1862** GREELEY in Logan *Great Conspiracy* 432 The Rebels are everywhere using the late Anti-Negro riots in the North . . . to convince the Slaves that they have nothing to hope from a Union success. **1862** [see ANTI-BANK].

Antinomian, *n.* and *a.* {1645-}

1. *n.* An adherent of the Antinomian sect or a believer in Antinomian principles.

1654 JOHNSON *Wonder-W. Prov.* 8 Antinomians . . . deny the Morall Law to be the Rule of Christ. **1747** D. NEAL *Hist. New-Eng.* (ed. 2) I. 162 They burst out into a flame, one party branding the other as Antinomians and Familists; the other reproaching their opponents with being Legalists. **1764** HUTCHINSON *Hist. Mass* (1795) I. i. 75 Their letters and private papers shew that they were pious and devout, and with the name of antinomians paid the strictest regard to moral virtue. **1850** HAWTHORNE *Scarlet Letter* ii. 58 It might be, that an Antinomian, a Quaker, or other heterodox religionist, was to be scourged out of the town.

2. *adj.* Opposed to recognition of the moral law as binding upon Christians under the 'law of grace.'

1669 MORTON *New-Eng. Mem.* 106 There arose great troubles . . . at Boston, by the broaching of Antinomian and Familistical Opinions. **1702** C. MATHER *Magnalia* (1853) I. iv. 124 There was a time when the suppression of an antinomian and familistical faction, which extreamly threatned the ruin of the country, was generally thought much owing unto this renowned man. **1720** D. NEAL *Hist. New-Eng.* I. 289 The Government was disturbed by persons of Antinomian and Familistical principles. **1748** *N. H. Hist. Soc. Coll.* IX. 9 Four members dissenting from the paragraph which contains an enumeration of Antinomian errors. **1823** *Baptist Mag.* IV. 104 In the early stages of that revival of religion, a kind of antinomian spirit prevailed to a great extent. **1872** [see ANTI-MEANS].

Antinomianism. [Cf. prec.] Antinomian tenets. {1643-} — *a***1649** WINTHROP *Hist.* II. 260 There came hither [in 1645] to Boston . . . out of England one Captain Partridge, who had served the parliament, but in the ship he broached and zealously maintained divers points of antinomianism and familism.

+**Anti-nullification.** [ANTI- 3.] *attrib.* Opposed to the principle that a state of the Union can nullify legislation of the federal government. — **1831** J. Q. ADAMS in *C. Miner* (1916) 141 My Anti-Nullification 4th of July discourse. **1833** 'ELMWOOD' *Yankee among Nullifiers* 60 Notwithstanding my anti-nullification principles, my practice was daily increasing. **1846** MANSFIELD *Winfield Scott* 234 The legislature of Georgia, also a strong anti-tariff state, passed anti-nullification resolutions, by strong majorities.

+**Anti-nullifier.** [ANTI- 2.] One who opposes the principle of nullification.

1830 *Mass. Spy* 27 Oct. (Th.) In Columbia [S. C.], the seat of Government, and the very focus of Nullification, two Nullifiers, and two anti-Nullifiers are chosen to the Assembly. **1833** *Niles' Reg.* XLIV. 1/1 Nullifiers or anti-nullifiers—state-rights men or constitutionalists . . . have been so *jostled* that no party knows exactly where is its own present location. **1860** KENNEDY *Wirt* II. 346 All the loyal who enjoyed the favor or confidence of the great Anti-Nullifier.

Antipædobaptist. [ANTI- 2.] One opposed to the baptism of infants. Also attrib. {1651-}

1648 *Platform Church-Discipline* Pref. (1772) 11 That which we are wont to answer the antipaedo-baptists, may suffice here. **1693** C. MATHER *Wond. Invis. World* 10 The Names of Congregational, Presbyterian, Episcopalian, or Antipædobaptist, are swallowed up in that of Christian. **1769** HUTCHINSON *Coll. Orig. P.* 399 Antipædobaptists in New-England had equal reason to complain of the same spirit. **1774** ADAMS *Works* (1850) II. 397 Mr. Backus is come . . . with a design to apply to the Congress for a redress of grievances of the anti-pedobaptists in our Province. **1821** *Western Carolinian* 24 April, Mr. Love belonged to that denomination of Christians called Anti-pedo-Baptists. **1844** 'UNCLE SAM' *Peculiarities* II. 165 The river Schuylkill, near Philadelphia, is much used by the anti-paedo-Baptist niggers, for *total* immersion, in their 'baptisms for riper years.'

Antipædobaptistical, *a.* [ANTI- 4.] Opposed to infant baptism. — **1769** HUTCHINSON *Coll. Orig. P.* 382, I suppose this to be the same Person who was sentenced to be fined or whipped for his antipædobaptistical tenets.

+**Anti-polygamy.** [ANTI- 3.] *attrib.* Opposed to, directed against, or counteracting polygamy.

1873 BEADLE *Undevel. West* 675 The Ninety-per-cent. Spring, which Gentiles call the Anti-polygamy Spring, is some two miles west of Hooper's. **1884** *Century Mag.* May 121/2 The passage of the Edmunds Anti-Polygamy Bill, disfranchising all persons living in polygamy. *Ib.* 122/1 It is entirely within the power of the Mormon women to turn any anti-polygamy bill into a farce, if they choose.

+**Anti-Populist.** [ANTI- 3.] *attrib.* Opposed to the People's Party, a political organization active in the U. S. in the 1890's. — **1895** *Denver Times* 5 March 5/2 A citizens' caucus has been called . . . to place an anti-Populist ticket in the field for city offices in the near election.

+**Anti-Prohibition.** [ANTI- 1, 3.] Opposition to Prohibition. Also *attrib.* — **1895** *Voice* 28 March 4/2 Appointing anti-Prohibition police commissioners in the different cities [in Kansas]. **1909** 'MARK TWAIN' *Is Shakespeare Dead?* xi. 128 High tariff and low tariff, and prohibition and anti-prohibition.

+**Anti-Prohibitionist.** [ANTI- 2.] An opponent of Prohibition. — **1890** *Voice* 17 July, The 'bootlegger' is a grim spectre to the anti-Prohibitionist.

+**Anti-protection.** [ANTI- 3.] *attrib.* Opposed to the levying of a protective tariff. — **1832** *Deb. Congress* 16 June 3636 The new race of statesmen in the anti-protection States regard the United States as . . . a quasi community not endowed with power to make the terms [etc.].

+**Anti-rent.** [ANTI- 1, 3.] =ANTI-RENTISM. Also attrib. {1879}

1844 *N.Y. W. Tribune* 20 July 1/6 Anti-Rent Difficulties.—We understand . . . that the Sheriff of Rensselaer County . . . while attempting to serve a process upon some of the Manor tenants in Stephentown . . . met with forcible resistance. **1845** *Ib.* 16 Aug. 5/2 Here is Anti-Rent, as vigorous as in 1839 and far more formidable. **1846** COOPER *Redskins* iv, She is anti-rent, while she wishes to keep on good terms with her landlord. **1852** *Harper's Mag.* V. 834/1 Another Anti-Rent outrage occurred at Berlin, Rensselaer County, in this State, on the 4th September. Several persons, disguised as Indians, went to the home of a Mr. Shaw. **1855** [PRAY] *Mem. J. G. Bennet* 357 The origin of the Anti-rent war may be traced to the lectures of Frances Wright, in 1828 and 1829. **1883** *Amer. Cycl.* I. 570/2 In 1839 associations were formed . . . and soon became known as anti-rent associations. . . . The anti-rent associations determined to form a political party.

+**Anti-renter.** [ANTI- 2.] One who is opposed to the paying of rent, particularly during the agitation in New York, 1839–1850, in which the tenants on the estates of the patroons broke away from the paying of feudal fees and services.

1845 *N. Y. W. Tribune* 16 Aug. 5/2 A leaseholder in . . . Andes, having fallen in arrears with his rent (being probably an active Anti-Renter). *Ib.*, The Anti-Renters are not all ignorant, depraved and characterless persons. **1846** COOPER *Redskins* Preface, Last, though not least in this catalogue of marauders, the anti-renter. **1848** W. ARMSTRONG *Stocks* 29 The matter is not benefited any by the property being located among the sons of liberty—the anti-renters. **1852** BRISTED *Upper Ten Th.* i. 34 It has been the great abettor of the Anti-Renters throughout. **1864** T. L. NICHOLS *Amer. Life* I. 330 The *Tribune* has been the organ of Socialism, especially in the form of Fourierism, of Free Soil, of the anti-Renters, of Woman's Rights, [etc.].

+**Anti-rentism.** [ANTI- 1. Cf. prec.] The policy or practice of refusal to pay rent on the manorial lands of New York. — **1845** COOPER *Chainbearer* xxii, Doctrines . . . published in journals devoted to anti-rentism in the State of New York. **1847** *Knickerb.* XXIX. 330 Neither Millerism, Mormonism, . . . to say nothing of Fourierism and Anti-Rentism have existed at the South. **1855** [PRAY] *Mem. J. G. Bennet* 357 Anti-rentism was rampart in this year [1845].

+**Anti-republican,** *n.* [ANTI- 2.] A member of a group or party opposing the Republicans. — **1795** JEFFERSON *Writings* (1896) VII. 46 Hence the anti-republicans appeared a considerable majority in both houses of Congress. *Ib.* 47 The Anti-republicans consist of . . . tories [etc.]

+**Anti-Republican,** *a.* [ANTI- 4.] Opposed or contrary to the rule of representatives elected by the people; aristocratic in sympathy or tendencies.

1790 MACLAY *Deb. Senate* 267 The practice [of dressing for levee day], however, considered as a feature of royalty, is certainly anti-republican. **1795** *Ann. 3rd Congress* 1069 Mr. Sedgwick said, that it had always appeared to him anti-Republican to attempt to narrow the powers of this Government over the militia. **1808** D. HITCHCOCK *Poet. Dict.* 102 He set up an anti-republican school. **1829** CHANNING *Works* (1884) 458/2 The taint of anti-Republican tendencies was fastened upon them [=the Federalists] by their opponents, and this reproach no party could survive. **1845** COOPER *Chainbearer* ix, The government of churches by means of a presbytery is anti-republican, opposed to our glorious institutions. **1886** LOGAN *Great Conspiracy* 668 For the very purpose of nipping in the bud any anti-republican conspiracy likely to germinate from Slavery.

+**Anti-restraint.** [ANTI- 3.] *attrib.* Opposed to the 'restraining law' on banking. — **1837** MACKENZIE *Van Buren* (1846) 176 The anti-restraint committee met this evening and our chairman (Maison) submitted his bill.

+**Anti-revolutionism.** [ANTI- 1.] Opposition to the American Revolution. — **1789** MACLAY *Deb. Senate* 74 Yesterday was the anniversary of his Britannic Majesty's birth. . . . The old leaven of anti-revolutionism has leavened the whole lump; nor can we keep the Congress free from the influence of it.

+**Anti-revolutionist.** [ANTI- 2. {1837}] An opponent of the American Revolution. — **1790** MACLAY *Deb. Senate* 300 We have thousands and tens of thousands of anti-revolutionists ready to blow the coals of contention.

+Anti-saloon. [ANTI- 3.] *attrib.* Opposed to the liquor trade. Freq. in *Anti-Saloon League.*

(1) **1888** *N. Amer. Rev.* Aug. 148 In the latter convention good men . . . wanted an anti-saloon plank put in the platform. **1891** *Cycl. Temperance Prohib.* 29/2 The Anti-Saloon Republicans . . . [were] never a strong factor in the Prohibition work. **1893** *Voice* (N.Y.) 24 Aug., The People's Party . . . had a very hard time . . . swallowing a very mild dose of anti-saloon medicine.

(2) **1892** (*title*), Documents . . . upon Law Enforcement. [Lowell, published by] The Anti-saloon League. **1894** *Arena* May 828 They organize leagues of various sorts, 'Anti-Saloon Republican Leagues,' . . . and the like. **1900** J. ROWNTREE & A. SHERWELL *Temperance Problem* (ed. 7) 282 The list was furnished by the State Superintendent of the Minnesota Anti-Saloon League. **1909** *Nation* 29 April 427/2 Brewers and distillers, who . . . have joined with the reform clubs and Anti-Saloon League in securing the passage of a drastic excise law.

+Anti-scalping. [ANTI- 4.] *attrib.* (See SCALP *v.*, SCALPING *vbl. n.*) — **1897** *Congress. Rec.* 19 Feb. 1989/1 A petition of sundry citizens of Massachusetts, praying for the passage of the antiscalping railroad ticket bill.

+Anti-slavery. [ANTI- 1, 3.]

1. Opposition to, agitation against, slavery.

1820 *Relf's Philadelphia Gazette* 19 Oct., Anti-Slavery. . . . The Citizens of the city and county of Philadelphia . . . who are opposed to the extension of slavery . . . are invited to assemble [etc.]. **1830** *Deb. Congress* 2 Feb. 108/2 Missouri Question, Colonization Society, Anti-Slavery, . . . Anti-Sunday Mails, Anti-Masonry. **1853** *S. Lit. Messenger* XIX. 315/1 The fury of Anti-Slavery is now at its height. **1878** *Harper's Mag.* April 683 [Poem] To a pioneer of antislavery.

2. *attrib.* **a.** Applied to societies, parties, or persons opposed to slavery.

'[Of] Anti-Slavery Societies . . . the first was formed in Philadelphia on April 14, 1775, with Dr. Franklin as President' (1881 Lossing *Cycl. U.S. Hist.* I. 52).

(1) **1833** in *Century Mag.* Sept. (1885) 785 Garrison . . . has been engaged in forming what they call 'The New England Anti-Slavery Society.' **1840** CHANNING *Works* (1884) 585/2 The power of the Anti-Slavery Association is not a little broken by internal divisions. **1840** *Niles' Reg.* 9 May 145/2 The Massachusetts Anti-Slavery Society have chosen 23 gentlemen . . . as their representatives. **1861** [H. JACOBS] *Life Slave Girl* 245 The Anti-Slavery Society agreed to pay her expenses to New York.

(2) **1856** *Harper's Mag.* XII. 404/1 To such an extremity have the differences between the pro-slavery and anti-slavery parties been carried, that an actual appeal to arms was at one time considered most imminent. **1857** GLISAN *Jrnl. Army Life* 388 A renewal of the excitement there [*sc.* Kansas] between the slavery and anti-slavery party. **1878** J. B. FREMONT in *Harper's Mag.* Jan. 275/2 In short, my pretty rooms were the headquarters of the antislavery party.

(3) **1856** HAMBLETON *Biog. H. A. Wise* 240 Buffington . . . and Morris [of Mass.] . . . are reliable anti-slavery whigs. **1859** STOWE *Minister's Wooing* ix, She was not a thoroughly indoctrinated anti-slavery woman. **1862** LINCOLN in Logan *Great Conspiracy* 435 You know also that the last Session of Congress had a decided majority of Anti-Slavery men. **1865** *Nation* I. 99 Mr. Van Buren was one of the ablest and most effective of the anti-slavery 'agitators' of 1848. **1881** *Harper's Mag.* Jan. 258/2 The sincerity and the unflinching zeal of the antislavery leaders [*c*1846] are not to be questioned.

b. With miscellaneous nouns.

1820 *Niles' Reg.* XIX. 127 An attempt is making in Philadelphia to get up, what its projectors call, an 'anti-slavery' ticket, for electors of president and vice-president of the United States. **1835** *S. Lit. Messenger* (1838) IV. 197/2 He talked of . . . the Anti-Slavery movements at the North. **1837** *Ib.* III. 649/1 The politicians of Carolina . . . bow ready assent to her anti-slavery propositions. **1841** HONE *Diary* II. 79 Mr. Adams brings forward 'in season and out of season' his anti-slavery opposition. **1849** F. DOUGLASS *Life* 117, I got a pretty correct idea of the principles, measures and spirit of the anti-slavery reform. **1851** *Harper's Mag.* Jan. 268/2 Resolutions expressive . . . of disapprobation of anti-slavery agitation . . . were adopted with much applause. **1861** Logan *Great Conspiracy* 221 An anti-Slavery speech of Mr. Slade, of Vermont, which Mr. Rhett violently denounced. **1865** *Atlantic Mo.* XV. 71 No anti-slavery novel has described a man of such marked ability. **1881** *Harper's Mag.* Jan. 259/1 The antislavery music was in the air and everybody had to hear it.

3. In predicative use as an adj.

1851 CIST *Cincinnati* 81 The first Wesleyan Church is Anti-Slavery. **1864** TROWBRIDGE *Cudjo's Cave* iii. 36, I never suspected he was anti-slavery till I talked with him. **1864** LINCOLN in Logan *Great Conspiracy* 544, I am naturally anti-Slavery. If Slavery is not wrong, nothing is wrong. **1878** *Harper's Mag.* Jan. 276/1 He was thoroughly English, thoroughly antislavery.

+Anti-slaveryist. [ANTI- 2.] One who is opposed to slavery. — **1862** WADSWORTH in *N.Y. Herald* 13 March, He [=Lincoln] had been teased and pressed by radical anti-slaveryists until he was compelled to offer a compromise.

+Anti-Southern, *a.* [ANTI- 4.] Opposed to the interests of the Southern States.

1852 BRISTED *Upper Ten Th.* 177 He knew Benson's anti-Southern feelings. **1861** W. S. SPEER *Let.* in *N.Y. Tribune* 8 Nov., I was stigmatized as an Abolitionist, or Black Republican, an anti-Southern man.

+Anti-suffrage. [ANTI- 3.] *attrib.* Opposed to the extension of the right to vote; specialized in the latter part of the 19th century to the question of woman's suffrage. — **1886** HOWELLS in *Harper's Mag.* Dec. 66/2, I signed the anti-suffrage petition.

+Anti-suffragist. [ANTI- 2.] One who is opposed to the extension of the right to vote, particularly to women. — **1886** HOWELLS in *Harper's Mag.* Dec. 64/2, I acknowledge that I made a speech . . . on behalf of the anti-suffragists.

+Anti-tariff. [ANTI- 3.] *attrib.* Opposed to the levying of (protective) tariffs.

1820 *Niles' Reg.* XIX. 235 Report on the Anti-Tariff Petitions. **1830** PAULDING *Chron. Gotham* 67 'Let us alone,' as the anti-tariff folks say. **1830** R. Y. HAYNE in *Deb. Congress* 27 Jan. 85/1 These anti-tariff resolutions were unanimously adopted. **1833** H. BARNARD in *Md. Hist. Mag.* XIII. 272 In comes J. C. Calhoun at the head of the anti Tariff and the State Sovereignty parties. **1846** [see ANTI-NULLIFICATION].

+Anti-tariff, *v.* [f. prec.] *tr.* To represent as an anti-tariffite. — **1855** [PRAY] *Mem. J. G. Bennet* 104 'Well, then,' says Clay, 'anti-tariff him in the *Journal.*'

+Anti-tariffite. [ANTI- 2.] One opposed to (protective) tariffs. — **1833** *Niles Reg.* XLIV. 1/1 Tariffites or anti-tariffites, etc. etc. have been so *jostled* that no party knows exactly where is its own present location. **1841** *Congress. Globe* Jan., App. 153/1 The high tariffite and the anti-tariffite . . . were united against the Democracy.

Anti-temperance. [ANTI- 1, 3.] **1.** *attrib.* Opposed to temperance. **2.** Opposition to temperance. — **(1)** [**1842** DICKENS *Amer. Notes* II. 34 The usual anti-temperance recipe for keeping out the cold.] **1882** 'MARK TWAIN' *White Elephant* i. 23 The anti-temperance mass meeting was in session. — **(2) 1843** 'CARLTON' *New Purchase* I. xvii. 134 Carlton, . . . the stingo is safe—anti-temperance beats!

Anti-tobacco. [ANTI- 3.] *attrib.* Opposed to the (sale and) use of tobacco. {1864} — **1869** *Overland Mo.* III. 441 The Anti-Tobacco Society of Massachusetts will rejoice in this partial confirmation of their theory. **1880** 'MARK TWAIN' in *Atl. Mo.* XLVI. 227 Edward, as a boy, had interested himself in . . . anti-tobacco organizations.

Anti-tobacconist. [ANTI- 2.] One opposed to the use of tobacco. — **1865** *Nation* I. 330 There have been conventions of . . . teetotallers and of anti-tobacconists.

+Anti-trust. [ANTI- 3.] *attrib.* Opposed to large monopolistic combinations in trade and industry. — **1890** *Congress. Rec.* 21 March 2465/2 Will the Senator inform me upon what ground the Missouri anti-trust bill was declared unconstitutional in his own State? **1903** E. JOHNSON *Railway Transportation* 387 The interpretation thus put upon the 'anti-trust' law by the Supreme Court. **1908** *Ann. Amer. Acad. Pol. & Social Sci.* July 45 Effects of anti-trust legislation on business.

+Anti-union. [ANTI- 3.] *attrib.*

1. Opposed to a federal government, particularly to that of the United States. During the Civil War, opposed to the Northern side as distinct from the Confederacy.

1813 *Niles' Reg.* V. 3/2 They may expose the British anti-union demagogues. **1856** GREELEY in I. H. Harper *Anthony* (1898) I. 147 To make the Tribune responsible for the Anti-Bible, Anti-Union, etc. doctrines, which your convention generally put forth. **1862** *N.Y. Herald* 27 March Other anti-Union writers endeavor to draw some gratification from the State paper, but they evidently fail.

2. Opposed to trade-unionism.

1878 PINKERTON *Strikers* 206 The officers of the road secured a volunteer anti-union engineer and fireman to move the cars.

+Anti-Unionist. [ANTI- 2.] One opposed to having a federal government. — **1800** JEFFERSON *Writings* (1896) VII. 447 However, as it has been made it shews who are the Anti-Unionists in principle.

Anti-war. [ANTI- 3.] *attrib.* Opposed to war or to some particular war.

1857 GOODRICH *Recoll.* II. 51 The democrats were overjoyed that Colonel S. took pains to show his hatred and contempt for the anti-war party. **1866** 'F. KIRKLAND' *Bk. Anecdotes* 116 During the gubernatorial canvass between Vallandigham the anti-war candidate, and Brough the Union Republican candidate. **1898** PAGE *Red Rock* 43 As for Blair, she had long deserted the anti-war side.

+Anti-Yazoo. [ANTI- 3.] *attrib.* Opposed to the land speculations in the Yazoo region. — **1796** *Aurora* (Phila.) 5 Dec. (Th.), [I was informed] that the Yazoo-men (as they are called in this place) were making every exertion to prevent General Jackson from being elected a Representative. . . . The people appeared to be the anti-Yazoo party.

Antony over. Also **Anthony, Ant'ny, Anty.** A ball-game played by boys (see quotation 1871). {Scots dial.} — **1871** DE VERE 579 *Antony Over*, a game of ball played by two parties of boys, on opposite sides of a schoolhouse, over which the ball is thrown. Used in Pennsylvania. **1883** EGGLESTON *Hoosier School-Boy* vii. 48 Play Anthony-over? The little boys can play that. I suppose there are boys in these days who do not know what 'Anthony-over' is. **1899** ADE *Doc. Horne* xi. 118 Why he and the alligator moved the dresser out from the wall and began to play 'ant'ny over' with my eye.

Antwerp. [The Belgian city of that name.]

1. A variety of raspberry. Usu. *Red Antwerp.*

1847 DARLINGTON *Weeds & Plants* 126 *Ida Rubus,* Antwerp Raspberry, Garden Raspberry, . . . is much cultivated for its favorite fruit. **1851** CIST *Cincinnati* 296 Of these, the red Antwerp is the general favorite. **1859** ELLIOTT *Western Fruit Book* 466 It is rare that the true Red Antwerp raspberry is found West of the State of New York. It is a Dutch sort, originally from Antwerp city. **1862** *Rep Comm. Patents: Agric.* 167 We are told that on the Hudson river fields are planted with a variety of the Red Antwerp, which has received its American cognomen from that stream, the Hudson River Red Antwerp. **1884** ROE *Nature's Story* 258 Webb, carrying a little basket lined with grapevine leaves, gleaned the long row of Antwerp raspberries.

2. A variety of homing pigeon originally bred in Antwerp, Belgium. {1839–}

1890 *Cent.* s.v. *Pigeon,* Some of these names [of fancy pigeons] are from localities, actual or alleged, as Antwerps [etc.]. **1905** *Encycl. Amer.* XIV. 341 Two main types of the Belgian homer have been distinguished as the Antwerp and the Liège varieties, the former being larger but less graceful in form than the latter. **1918** *U.S. Statutes* 19 April, An Antwerp, or homing pigeon, commonly called carrier pigeon.

* **Anvil.**

* **1.** The block (usually of iron or steel) on which metal is shaped by hammering.

*a***1649** WINTHROP *Hist.* I. 469 Here was an anvil, with a beak horn at the end of it, which I think was carried to Con. **1669** *York Deeds* II. 69 The Smyths shopp with bellows, anvell, beckorne, vice, sledg hammer & some ould irons. **1678** *New Castle Court Rec.* 267 Smiths Tooles: one pr. of bellowes, one anvill. **1738** *N.H. Hist. Soc. Coll.* II. 80 [A committee was appointed] to procure an anvil . . . fit for the work of a blacksmith. **1792** *Ann. 2nd Congress* 1109 Two complete traveling forges were sent forward, and upon examination both of them were found to be without an anvil. **1829** WEEMS *Franklin* i. 6 Those better ensigns of American wisdom—the Sledge Hammer and Anvil. **1847** L. COLLINS *Kentucky* 540 A rock . . . which closely resembles a blacksmith's anvil. **1881** W. O. STODDARD *E. Hardery* 2 With that the blacksmith pulled a glowing bar of iron from the coals to the anvil.

2. An object resembling an anvil in use or shape.

1872 *Amer. Naturalist* April 228 Large stones [among N.J. prehistoric relics] that appear to have been utilized by the Redman, and are called 'anvils' for want of a more correct designation. **1874** LONG *Wild-Fowl* 35 From its construction, the anvil and ejector remaining in the shell, the extra tool for punching off caps needed with all other shells is dispensed with.

+**3.** *Anvil-rock sandstone:* (see quotations).

1862 DANA *Manual of Geology* 330 Above the twelfth [coal bed in Ky.] there is the massive Sandstone . . . called the Anvil Rock, from the form of two masses of it in South-western Kentucky. **1869** *Amer. Naturalist* III. 44 The 'Anvil-rock Sandstones,' and the 'Mahoning Sandstone,' in the Kentucky section, are identical.

‖ **Anxietude.** Anxiety. — **1816** PICKERING 34 *Anxietude:* I never saw this word but once in any of our publications; and that was only in a newspaper.

+**Anxious bench.**

1. =ANXIOUS SEAT.

1832 MRS. TROLLOPE *Domestic Manners* I. 111 As the poor creatures approached the rail their sobs and groans became audible. They seated themselves in the 'anxious benches'; the hymn ceased, and two or three priests walked down from the tribune [etc.]. **1839** BRIGGS *H. Franco* II. 135, I persisted in my refusal, and he left me, and commenced operations upon a little boy who was soon prevailed upon to take a seat upon the anxious bench. **1839** H. CASWALL *America* 324 Persons under excitement are called forward to the 'anxious benches' to make confession. **1871** DE VERE 234 Thus, persons who are peculiarly excited to a consciousness of their sinfulness, and the necessity of seeking salvation, are called *anxious mourners,* and are led by the ministers or deacons to the *anxious bench* or *seat,* a bench near the altar, there to receive aid and comfort.

2. *On the anxious bench,* uneasy, anxious.

1906 *N.Y. Ev. Post* 23 Nov. 1 The entire diplomatic corps at Havana is . . . on the 'anxious bench.'

+**Anxious meeting.** 'A religious meeting consequent on a revival' (B. '59).

+**Anxious seat.**

1. A seat near the preacher in an evangelistic service, on which sit those who are strongly influenced by the preaching.

1835 A. REED & J. MATHESON *Visit* I. 13, I was speedily led to conclude that . . . [the preacher] was about to try the anxious seat. *Ib.* II. 35 The other measure, . . . which is, I believe, altogether new, has received the somewhat barbarous and canting denomination of 'Anxious Seat.' **1837** *Knickerb.* X. 141 Both [forms of revivals] . . . were new, and both prescribed one . . . principle, 'the anxious seat.' **1839** MARRYAT *Diary Amer.* II. 184 In front of the pulpit there was a space railed off, and strewed with straw, which I was told was the *Anxious seat,* and on which sat those who were touched by their consciences or the discourse of the preacher. **1847** *Knickerb.* XXIX. 481 Burchard . . . asked him . . . if he would not go forward into the anxious-seat. **1850** *Ib.* XXXV. 366 His face wore the expression of a sinner on the 'anxious seat.' **1851** *Ib.* XXXVIII. 184 They have built a kind of calf-pen for smokers, at the foot of Boston Common, with seats like the anxious-seats at a camp-meeting. **1865** MRS. WHITNEY *Gayworthys* v. 52 We're in for a revival. . . . You'll see 'em in the anxious-seats, before long. **1888** J. KIRKLAND *McVeys* 19 'Seekers' were sought for and urged forward to the 'anxious seat' or 'mourners bench' by zealous friends. **1890** *Century Mag.* Dec. 306 Never mind the anxious seat. I've sat on it long enough for one night.

fig. **1856** GOODRICH *Recoll.* 65 [The dye-tub] frequently became the anxious seat of the lover, who was permitted to carry on his courtship, the object of his addresses sitting demurely in the opposite corner.

2. *On the anxious seat,* in a state of uneasiness; troubled.

1839 *Knickerb.* XIII. 345 He did look as if he had been on 'the anxious seat,' as he used to say, when things puzzled him. **1862** STOWE *Pearl Orr's Island* II. i. 1 What a life you did lead me in them days! I think you kep' me on the anxious seats a pretty middlin' spell. **1865** *Atlantic Mo.* XV. 454 Almira . . . had long been upon the anxious-seat as regarded matrimony. **1884** NYE *Baled Hay* 17 By telling . . . lies about both I managed to keep the two elements on the anxious seat. **1887** FRANCIS *Saddle & Moccasin* 226 Oh, the boys kept him on the 'anxious seat' for two or three days, and that cured him [of card-playing]. **1894** *Congress. Rec.* Feb. 2382/1, I am glad to see so many gentlemen 'on the anxious seat.' **1906** *N.Y. Ev. Post* 4 Jan. 4 All the men present were on the anxious seat, seeking to learn whether their new judge was 'easy' or 'tough.'

* **Any,** *a.* A large or considerable (number or quantity). {Also E. *colloq.*}

1861 NORTON *Army Lett.* 26 In the woods near us we found any quantity of grapes and chinquapins. **1862** *Ib.* 50 We cut down any number of the poles.

* **Any,** *adv.* To any extent; at all. {1834–, *dial.*}

1780 S. HOLTEN in *Essex Inst. Coll.* LVI. 96, I have not traveled any this day on account of my horses. **1817** *Analectic Mag.* May 437 If our readers are any like ourselves, we think they cannot help laughing. **1830** S. SMITH *Lett. J. Downing* (1834) 6 It is not likely Mr. Ruggles will be Speaker any this winter. **1850** WATSON *Camp-Fires Revol.* 139 We hadn't slept any for two nights. **1864** 'MARK TWAIN' *Sk. Sixties* (1926) 126 They keep a field-glass there, . . . but it did not help the matter any to speak of. **1869** — *Innocents* xlviii. 504 Palestine has not changed any since those days, in manners, customs, architecture or people. **1880** P. H. BURNETT *Recoll. Old Pioneer* 12, I had never danced any, and . . . I determined I would break the ice. **1894** *Outing* May 144/1 His anger was not diminished any when she asked him if he wasn't glad that his wish came true. **1897** — May 130/1 The fox is not helping to reduce this distance any. **1905** *Springfield W. Repub.* 17 Nov. 8 It is not likely that a wholesale recount would have reduced Gov. Russell's plurality much, or any. **1911** H. P. FAIRCHILD *Greek Immigration* 101 Costa was not used to springs, and he did not mind this any.

* **Anybody,** *pron.* +*Anybody's race* or *game,* one in which the participants are so evenly matched that any one of them may win. — **1898** *Forum* Jan. 576 In Greater New York it was what is called 'anybody's race,' till close upon the day of election.

Anyhow, *adv.*

1. In any manner or way. {1740–}

1773 FITHIAN *Journal* I. 77 There are two negroes, . . . who are constantly, when the weather will any how permit, working in it [=a garden]. **1837** *S. Lit. Messenger* III. 105 Yet my education has been picked up . . . in all manner of ways helter-skelter, higgledy-piggledy; or, as they say in the West, 'any how.' **1848** BARTLETT 12 *Anyhow you can fix it,* at any rate whatever. **1899** GREEN *Va. Word-book* 43 *Anyhow and everywhere,* by any means and every means.

2. In spite of conditions or what might be said; anyway, in any case. {1842–}

1825 NEAL *Bro. Jonathan* I. 381, I was ready to go abroad, any how, then. **1836** *S. Lit. Messenger* II. 554 [We have] returned from a visit to what one of the men who accompanied us called, 'The last postoffice I ever did see, anyhow!' **1856** STOWE *Dred* I. 208 'Who is God, mammy,' says I, 'any how?' **1892** *Harper's Mag.* Feb. 486/1 What do you want, anyhow? **1904** W. H. SMITH *Promoters* ii. 41 Say, how is that for a scheme, anyhow?

+**Anything else.** 'A hyperbolical phrase, denoting a strong affirmation, which has recently sprung up and become quite common' (B. '59). *a***1859** *Newspaper* (B.), *Loco Foco.* Didn't Gen. Cass get mad at Hull's cowardice, and break his sword? *Whig.* He didn't do anything else.

* **Anyways,** *adv. colloq.*

* **1.** In any way; to any extent. {–1834}

1638 *Springfield Rec.* I. 164 It is ordered . . . not to sell or any ways pass away any cannoe . . . untill it be five years old. **1842** MRS. KIRKLAND *Forest Life* xi. 94 We can't make them any ways comfortable here. *c* **1849** [PAIGE] *Dow's Sermons* I. 82, I can't crowd it into my narrow belief that Paul's mental machinery was any ways out of kilter. **1863** MRS. WHITNEY *F. Gartney* xix, It's kinder handy, . . . havin' a minister round the house, sayin' she should be took anyways sudden! **1875** BRET HARTE *Tales Argonauts* 71, I've been out a dozen times with Jack Oakhurst . . . and I never saw him anyways cut before.

2. In any case; at any rate. {1865}

1865 'Mark Twain' *Sk., Jumping Frog,* Anyways, I've got *my* opinion. **1876** — *Tom Sawyer* ii. 13 Talk don't hurt—anyways it don't if she don't cry. **1899** S. O. Jewett *Queen's Twin,* etc. 129 Her bonnet was made at home annyways.

Anywhere, adv.* +*Anywhere from . . . to,* anything between . . . and. — **1897 *Outing* XXIV. 471/1 The tarpon will be anywhere from fifty to three hundred feet away when the boat is ready to follow him. **1909** 'O. Henry' *Options* 6, I'll guarantee an increase of anywhere from ten thousand to a hundred thousand a year.

Anywheres, *adv. dial.* In any place; anywhere. {*dial.*}

1775 *Essex Inst. Coll.* XIII. 171 Your house will be as safe as anywheres to put the candles in. **1815** Humphreys *Yankey in England* 49 Seems to me, I can git my living easier by my wits, a-most ennywheres. **1829** *Virginia Lit. Museum* 214 *No hows, . . . anywheres* are very common in the state of New York. **1856** *Knickerb.* XLVII. 45 Have you seen him anywheres about? **1858** *Ib.* LII. 534 The company was mostly white, and as select as could be picked up 'any wheres.' **1864** Trowbridge *Cudjo's Cave* 96, I've got as right smart a little nigger boy as there is anywheres in Tennessee. **1884** 'Mark Twain' *H. Finn* ii. 6 If you are anywheres where it won't do for you to scratch. **1891** Wilkins *New Eng. Nun* 145, I've got to get a pin. . . . I can't keep it anywheres. *Ib.* 302 You ain't goin' anywheres to-morrow night.

+**A.P.** Abbrev. of 'Advance Paid.' — **1817** M. Birkbeck *Journey in A.* 71 The sections thus sold are marked immediately on the general plan . . . with the letters A.P. 'advance paid.'

+**A.P.A.** Abbrev. of 'American Protective Association': a secret society founded in Iowa in 1887, to oppose unrestricted immigration and the influence of Roman Catholics in education and politics. — **1893** J. P. Altgeld *Live Questions* (1899) 408 Do you think the A.P.A. sentiment is strongly diffused among Protestants? **1896** *Congress. Rec.* 4 Feb. 1309/1 There have been men making A.P.A. capital on your side. **1900** *Ib.* 7 April 3887/1 Action on the part of Senators . . . because of intimidation from a certain organization known as the A.P.A.

+**Apache.** [Mex.-Sp., of uncertain origin.]

1. An Indian belonging to a group of warlike, and originally nomadic, tribes inhabiting Arizona and New Mexico. Also attrib.

1745 *H. Moll's Atlas Minor* Plate 46, Apaches. **1779** Jefferys *Amer. Atlas* Map 5, Apaches nation. **1808** Pike *Exped.* App. iii. 10 The Appaches are a nation of Indians who extend from the black mountains in New Mexico to the frontiers of Cogquilla, keeping the frontiers of three provinces in a continual state of alarm. **1834** A. Pike *Prose Sk.* 126 He immediately mounted his mare, and . . . overtook four Apaches, very leisurely driving his cattle before them. *Ib.* 138 Here, a filthy, ragged fellow with half a shirt, . . . long, dirty woolen stockings, and Apache moccasins. **1854** Bartlett *Narr.* I. 256 The frequent attacks of the Apaches led to the abandonment of the place. **1855** Glisan *Jrnl. Army Life* 227 Our troops in New Mexico are kept constantly in active service —the Apache Indian being very troublesome. **1869** Browne *Adv. Apache Country* 146 Bill Rhodes's Apache fight is now one of the standard incidents in the history of Arizona. **1892** *Congress. Rec.* App. 6 June 444/2 This is like giving an Apache a bottle of tangle-foot whisky to fit him for a race.

2. *Apache plume,* a rosaceous shrub (*Fallucia paradoxa*) of New Mexico (*Cent.* '89).

A-packing. [A *prep.*] *To send a-packing,* to send off. {'send packing,' 1594} — **1753** *Md. Hist. Mag.* III. 367 Did he not say he wou'd . . . send them a packing to their own Parishes if he were Governor? **1856** Simms *Charlemont* 372 Is it ever too late to send such a rascal a-packing?

+**Aparejo.** Also **aparajo, apparejo, -ajo, -aho.** [Sp. Cf. Arapajo.] A kind of saddle used in the Southwest, made of a joined pair of leather cushions stuffed with hay.

1844 J. Gregg *Commerce Prairies* I. 180 It is necessary too for the *aparejo* to be firmly bound on to prevent its slipping and chafing the mule's back. **1847** Ruxton *Adv. Rocky Mts.* (1848) 76 It is no uncommon thing to see mules so lacerated by the chafings of the aparejos, that the rib-bones are plainly discernible. **1850** B. Taylor *Eldorado* vii. (1856) 63 Shouldering our packs until we should be able to purchase an *aparĕjo,* or pack-saddle. **1859** G. A. Jackson *MS. Diary* 6 Will start for trappers camp in a few days to bring up my mule and apparaho. **1869** Browne *Adv. Apache Country* 39 A few extra mules and jacks to lend to intimate friends going on prospecting tours, some spare saddles and *apparejos, . . .* would also be advisable. **1873** Miller *Amongst Modocs* i. 3 A narrow little pack trail, . . . barely wide enough to admit of . . . little Mexican mules with their apparajos, to pass in single file. **1895** Remington *Pony Tracks* 175 Along came the superintendent, with . . . nine pack-mules with their creaking *aparejos.* **1904** *Omaha Daily Bee* 6 July 4 The aparejo . . . as a valuable method of holding the cargo and protecting the animal's body from injuries, has never been improved upon.

Apartment.

1. A room or portion of a house. {1641-}

1704 S. Knight *Journal* 22, I then betook me to my Apartment, which was a little Room parted from the Kitchen by a single bord partition. **1773** H. Finlay *Journal* 30 There's no apartment appropriated for the rece't and delivery of letters. **1807** Irving, etc. *Salmagundi* v. 116 The music struck up from an adjoining apartment and summoned the company to a dance. **1822** *Missionary Herald* XVIII. 81 They had nearly completed a large dwelling house, divided into five apartments. **1865** *Atlantic Mo.* XV. 112 He . . . bought . . . a large building that had been used as barracks for the soldiers, and, fitting it up in plain, commodious apartments, formed there a great family-establishment. **1880** Cable *Grandissimes* xiii, There is . . . directly behind it, a sleeping apartment.

+**2.** A set of rooms, among other sets in one building, designed for a single household; a flat.

1876 *N.Y. Herald* 16 Aug. 2/2 To let . . . Nice apartments—from two to eight rooms. **1882** *Harper's Mag.* Nov. 919/1 There is no prospect, in fact, of desirable flats—that is, apartments of any size, convenient, light, and airy—being other than expensive in New York. **1883** 'S. Bonner' *Dialect Tales* 67 They hed three rooms leadin' out of the photograph gallery—an apartment, they called it. **1884** *N.Y. Herald* 27 Oct. 2/2 [Adv.] Elegant apartment in the finest home club apartment house in New York; nine rooms. **1890** *Harper's Mag.* Jan. 327/1 Mr. and Mrs. Delancy Robinson reside in a cozy flat, or 'apartment,' as they prefer to call it, in New York city. **1903** *N.Y. Ev. Post* 12 Sept., The chief distinction between a flat and an apartment, according to the accepted definition, is that the apartment has an elevator.

3. +*Apartment building,* an apartment house. +*Apartment hotel,* a hotel letting rooms or suites of rooms by the month, etc.; a residential hotel. +*Apartment house,* a house containing a number of suites of rooms, suitable for housekeeping.

1883 *Chicago Tribune* 4 May 9/3 To Rent . . . Flat in elegant apartment building, 7 rooms. — **1902** *N.Y. Herald* 14 Oct. 19/4 The Arlington . . . High Class Apartment Hotel. Just completed. . . . An apartment hotel centrally located, with every new device . . . for the comfort . . . of its guests. **1904** *N.Y. Ev. Post* 10 Sept. 6 There are thousands of wealthy New Yorkers . . . who wish a permanent city habitation, the maintenance of which will give them no annoyance. For these the apartment hotel seems divinely ordained. **1911** Lincoln *Cap'n Warren's Wards* 33 It was a large room, in spite of the fact that it was one of a suite in an apartment hotel. — **1876** *N.Y. Herald* 5 Oct. 2/3 A home . . . in the elegant new apartment house Osborne, No. 661 5th av. A whole house on each floor. **1882** *Harper's Mag.* Nov. 919/1 It is twelve years since the first apartment-houses were built. **1886** Stockton *Hundredth Man* ii, Those large apartment-houses, so popular in New York. **1895** *Outing* XXVI. 395/2 Will you be glad to get home, Meg—back to your paved streets and apartment house? **1902** *Chicago Record-Herald* 6 July, The apartment-house property at the . . . corner of Jackson avenue.

+**Apee.** (See quotation.) — **1830** J. F. Watson *Philadelphia* 716 Philadelphia has long enjoyed the reputation of a peculiar cake called the *apee.* . . . Ann Page, still alive, . . . first made them, many years ago, under the common name of cakes. . . . On her cakes she impressed the letters A.P., the letters of her name, and from this cause, even since the initials have been disused on them, the cakes have continued to be called *apees.*

Apex. {1637-} +In mining, 'the end or edge of a vein nearest the surface' (Raymond *Gloss.,* 1881).

+**Apex-right.** A mining right based on the ownership of land at the apex of a vein. — **1898** *Engineering Mag.* XVI. 121/1 Besides, of such productive work No 'apex-right' or legal quirk Could thwart the rich requital.

+**Apishamore.** Also **apishemeau, appichimoe.** [Algonkin (Chippewa form) *apishimon,* anything to lie down upon.] A mat or animal skin used as a covering; in later use restricted to a saddle-blanket of buffalo hide.

1839 Townsend *Narr.* 145 We remained in camp, trading buffalo robes, apishemeaus, etc., of the Indians. **1846** Webb *Altowan* I. 36 The fire was extinguished, and the saddles and appichimoes laid down for a bed. **1848** Ruxton *Far West* iii. 101 Thus La Bonté picked up three excellent mules for a mere song, with their accompanying pack-saddles, *apishamores,* and lariats. **1850** Garrard *Wah-To-Yah* i. 12 Each pair taking an *apishamore* (saddle blanket), [they] would collect our blankets full of the fuel.

+**A-plenty,** *a.* and *adv.* [In origin, *a,* article +*plenty* n. {1627-}; in later use the *a* is regarded as a prep.] In abundance; plentiful.

1830 Cooper *Water Witch* III. ii. 68 A sailor's blessing on you—fair winds and a plenty. **1832** Catlin *Indians* I. 25 M'Kenzie . . . said . . . 'There are cattle a plenty on that spot.' **1846** *Knickerb.* XXVII. 412 Form a line, my christian friends! Look a-plenty, but when you have got enough . . . give others an opportunity. **1876** 'Mark Twain' *Tom Sawyer* vi. 59 Sho, there's ticks a-plenty. **1891** B. Matthews *Americanisms & Briticisms* 14 There are Briticisms a-plenty in the talk of the Londoner. **1892** *Harper's Mag.* April 694/2 At present there are trout a-plenty in the streams.

+**Apollino.** (See quotations.) — **1819** *Plough Boy* I. 131/3 The Apollino combines the music of a Church Organ, a Grand Orchestra, a Martial Band, and a Harp. *Ib.* 147/1 The Apollino, a musical instrument, invented by Mr. Job Plimpton, of this city. **1821** J. Howison *Recoll.* 322 The museum is also enriched with that astonishing piece of musical mechanism called the Apollino.

***Apostle.**

***1.** One who carries a belief in religion or in social reform into fresh territory, or is a prominent advocate of some new principle.

a1649 SHEPHERD in *Unpubl. Corr. Baxter & J. Eliot* (1931) 8 The name of the Apostle to the Indians must always stand in distinguished brightness on that roll of the servants . . . whom New England delights . . . to honour. **a1817** DWIGHT *Travels* III. 126 The celebrated John Elliot, commonly styled the 'Apostle Elliot,' and the 'Apostle of the Indians.' **1850** FOOTE *Sk. Virginia* 391 From his school came out the man that had been truly styled the Apostle of Virginia. **1866** 'F. KIRKLAND' *Bk. Anecdotes* 23 Mr. Jefferson, the great Apostle of Democracy in America. *Ib.* 151 Standing at the grave of the great Apostle of Slavery and Secession, John C. Calhoun.

+2. An official of high rank in the Mormon Church. (Also as a term of distinction or address.)

1842 E. E. Folk *Mormon Monster* (1900) 52 My father's family received frequent visits from Apostles Brigham Young and Heber C. Kimball. **1862** *N. Amer. Review* July 222 The quorum of the 'Twelve Apostles,' a travelling council, who go where the President bids. **1882** C. V. WAITE *Adv. in Far West* 91 In Salt Lake City . . . I had met most of the principal Apostles and High Dignitaries. **1902** W. A. LINN *Story of Mormons* 101 An apostle was an elder, and it was his calling to baptize, ordain, administer the sacrament, confirm, preach, and take the lead in all meetings. **1906** *Congress. Rec.* Dec. 241/1 We protest that Apostle Reed Smoot ought not to be permitted to qualify . . . as a member of the United States Senate.

***Apothecary.**

***1.** One who prepares and sells drugs. {-1812; now *arch.*}

1647 *Boston Rec.* 89 Wm. Davice, the apotecary, shall have leave to sett up a payll afor his . . . window 3 foot from his howse. **a1649** WINTHROP *Hist.* I. 136 Mr. Firmin, an apothecary, was chosen deacon. **1707** *Boston News-Letter* 21 July 2/1 The Pinnacle on the Gable end of Mr. Creese Apothecary his House. **1727** *Boston Selectmen* 165 Liberty granted to Thomas Folker Apothacary to open a shop. **1794** *Ann. 3rd Congress* 1456 Nothing herein contained shall be construed to extend . . . to physicians, apothecaries, surgeons, or chemists. **1809** [cf. sense 2]. **1826** COOPER *Mohicans* xii, The richest shop of apothecary's ware in all the colonies. **1851** GLISAN *Jrnl. Army Life* 83, I shall have to undertake the tedious duty of educating another person into the profession of apothecary. **1867** EDWARDS *Shelby* 234 He was an apothecary, a farrier, a horse-trader [etc.]; . . . there was no trade or calling which he couldn't assume or personate to perfection. **1887** N. PERRY *Flock of Girls* 100 You might go with this prescription to the apothecary.

attrib. **1854** *Penna. Agric. Rep.* 395 Best pair of Apothecary Scales.

2. *Apothecary('s) shop, + store,* an establishment for the retailing or dispensing of drugs. {1601}

1777 *Journals Cont. Congress* VII. 162 There [shall] be an Inspector General of the Army . . . whose business it shall be to visit the Military hospitals and Apothecaries Shops in every part of the Continent. **1809** KENDALL *Travels* III. 128 There does not appear to be any vocation known by the name of *apothecary;* but a druggist's shop is sometimes called an *apothecary's store.* **1837** PECK *Gaz. Illinois* 302 Tremont . . . now contains six stores, . . . one apothecary's shop. **1850** [H. C. LEWIS] *La. Swamp Doctor* 114 We had all assembled in the apothecary's shop of the establishment [=hospital].

(*b*) **1721** *Mass. H. S. Coll.* 4 Ser. II. 164 We have fourteen apothecary shops in Boston. **1773** J. ROWE *Diary* 241, I still continue in great pain. The doctor has made an apothecary shop in my stomach. **1844** *Knickerb.* XXIII. 72 Sundry jars and bottles filled with fancy-colored powders and liquids, for an apothecary shop.

+Appalachian, *a.* Also †**Apalachian, -atchian, -atean, -atæan.** [f. *Apalachi, -ache,* etc., native name of a tribe of Indians (see sense 1).]

1. Designating or pertaining to a range of mountains in the eastern United States or to the region occupied by them; also, designating a tribe of Indians formerly holding a part of north-west Florida.

1672 TALBOT tr. Lederer *Three Marches from Va.* (1902) 6 The Apalatæan mountains . . . are barren rocks, . . . deserted by all living creatures but bears. **1682** ASH *Carolina* 34 It's supposed . . . that the Apalatean Mountains . . . yields [*sic*] ore both of gold and silver. **1743** CATESBY *Carolina* I. p. v, The Apalatchian Mountains have their southern Beginning near the Bay of Mexico. **1797** MORSE *Amer. Gaz., Apalachy* . . . is by some writers, applied to a town and harbour in Florida, 90 miles E. of Pensacola. . . . The tribes of the Apalachian Indians lie around it. **1820** IRVING *Sketch Bk.* I. 57 They are a dismembered branch of the great Appalachian family. **1853** SIMMS *Sword & Distaff* 47 The mountain rangers from that section of the Apalachian slopes, which divides, or rather unites, the states of North and South Carolina and Georgia. **1857** *Harper's Mag.* Nov. 723/2 We might . . . have given a lengthy account of the Apalachian system through all its ups and downs. **1886** WINCHELL *Walks & Talks* 267 In the Appalachian region, however, a similar seesaw occurred. The loaded Appalachian belt came up in a series of mountain folds fifteen thousand feet high.

2. *Appalachian bean:* (see quotation).

1797 IMLAY *Western Territory* (ed. 3) 239 The apallachian beans are so called because they were obtained from a nation of the natives of that name. . . . These beans boil tender, are tolerably well tasted, but are sweetish, and rather insipid.

***Apparel.**

***1.** Clothing; attire.

1619 *Va. House Burg. Jrnl.* 10 Against excesse of apparell, that every man be cessed in the Churche for all publique contributions. **1639** J. ENDECOTT in *Winthrop P.* 139 Vnnecessarie brauerie in apparell . . . tends to the scandall of religion. **1648** SHEPARD *Clear Sunshine* 15, I marvailed to see so many Indian men, women, and children in English apparell. **1695** *Maine Doc. Hist.* V. 420 Tis also evident they have been Frenchified both in spirit & apparell sence their former treaty with us. **1707** *Boston News-Letter* 24 Feb. 2/2 An Indian Girl . . . had on English Apparrel. **1805** *Salem Gazette* 11 Oct., Samuel Mylod . . . colours all kinds of wearing apparel. **1855** GLISAN *Jrnl. Army Life* 184 Everybody is coming out in summer apparel. **1875** KNIGHT 2822/1 The ordinary wringing injures fine apparel.

***2.** The rigging of a ship. {Now *arch.*}

1653 *Va. House Burg. Jrnl.* 92 Whereas the ship Leopoldus of Dunkirk . . . has been adjudged fforfeited, with her tackle, apparel, and ffurniture to this country. **1692** *Maine Doc. Hist.* V. 366 We . . . have had an Inuentory of the Tackell and Apparill & Stores belonging to said Slope. **1721** *New-Eng. Courant* 7-14 Aug. 2/2 The abovesaid Pirate . . . cut down her Mainmast, with all the Tackle and Apparel belon[g]ing thereunto, and cast them into the Sea. **1794** *Ann. 3rd Congress* 1448 In case the value thereof shall amount to four hundred dollars, the vessel on board of which the same shall be seized, together with her tackle, apparel, and furniture, shall also be forfeited. **1817** *Ann. 14th Congress* 2 Sess. 841 The ship or vessel . . . together with her cargo, tackle, apparel, and furniture, shall be forfeited to the United States.

***Appeal,** *n.*

***1.** Transfer of a case at law from an inferior court to a higher.

1645 *Plymouth Laws* 79 It is enacted that in case of appeale from one court to another that upon the second verdict order or decree execucon shalbe presently made forth. **1672** *Mass. Colony General Laws* 3 It shall be in the liberty of every man cast, condemned or sentenced in any Inferiour Court, to make his Appeal to the Court of Assistants. **1777** *Journals Cont. Congress* VIII. 467 That . . . a new hearing [be] awarded on the appeal brought against the judgment of the Court of admiralty. **1803** *Ann. 8th Congress* 2 Sess. 1577 The expediency of allowing writs of error and appeals from the judgments and decrees of said judges to the Supreme Court. **1812** *Ann. 12th Congress* 1 Sess. 1276 An appeal may be taken from a Judge sitting in the District Court to the same Judge sitting in the Circuit Court. **1836** EDWARD *Hist. Texas* vii. 174 The law concerning this appeal in the trial of Civil Plenario. **1877** *Colorado Gen. Laws* 255 No appeal shall be dismissed on account of a defect, or informality in the appeal bond . . . , if the appellant or appellants shall . . . file a good and sufficient bond. **1910** *Indian Laws & Tr.* III. 441 For payment of costs, witness fees, charges in appeals, and other expenses incident to suits brought in the courts.

+2. *Court of Appeals,* a court to which cases from inferior courts are taken.

{In English use, *Court of Appeal.*}

1777 *Journals Cont. Congress* VIII. 607 Resolved, That Thursday next be assigned to take into consideration the propriety of establishing a court of appeals. **1792** BELKNAP *Hist. N.H.* III. 256 The dernier resort was to a court of appeals, consisting of the Governor and Council. **1792** IMLAY *Western Territory* 175 There is also [in Ky.] a supreme court called the Court of Appeals, composed of the judges of the two superior courts, which assembles twice a year. **1825** DOUGHERTY *Light to People of Ky.* 1 The old court of appeals has decided in favor of your occupant laws. **1835** in *S. Lit. Messenger* IV. 303/1 Arrived at Lewisburg, I went over to the Court House, where the court of appeals was in session. **1852** *Harper's Mag.* V. 256/1 In the State of New York, the Court of Appeals has decided against the constitutionality of the law of 1851. **1855** F. WOOD in MacLeod *Biog.*, There is . . . a Court of Appeals, to which to apply against the subjection.

***Appeal,** *v.*

***1.** *intr.* To apply to a higher tribunal in an effort to have a decision reversed.

a1649 WINTHROP *Hist.* II. 8 He appealed unto England, but Mr. Gorge would not admit his appeal, but seized some of his cattle. **1686** SEWALL *Diary* I. 121 He [having been fined] appeals: Mr. Shrimpton and Luscombe his sureties. **1721** *Mass. Bay Acts & Resolves* (1902) X. 106 From which judgment he appealed to the Superiour Court next ensuing. **1827** *Ill. Revised Laws* (1833) 62 Either party may appeal or prosecute a writ of error. **1828** WEBSTER s.v., By special statute or agreement, a party may appeal before trial, upon a fictitious issue and judgment. **1851** *Iowa Code* 26 He will pay all costs and sums of money which may be adjudged against him in the court appealed to. **1910** *Mass. Acts & Resolves* 484 A party who is aggrieved by the judgment of a police, district or municipal court . . . may . . . appeal therefrom to the superior court.

∗2. *tr.* To take (a case) to a higher court. {–1590}
1828 WEBSTER s.v., We say the cause was appealed before or after trial. **1862** *Mass. Gen. Statutes Suppl.* (1867) 171 Any action or prosecution so appealed or removed. **1903** A. B. HART *Actual Government* 154 Small cases usually fall first to a lower court; then, if appealed, to the middle jurisdiction. **1905** *N.Y. Ev. Post* 30 May 4 It was appealed to the Supreme Court of the United States.

∗Appealant. *Obs.* =APPELLANT. — **1669** *R.I. Col. Rec.* II. 258 The said apealant or apealants giving in bond or security. **1670** *Plymouth Laws* 161 It is enacted by the Court that incase of appeale the appealant shall sumons the defendant to answare.

+Appeal bond. [APPEAL *n.* 1.] A bond given by one who appeals a case to a higher court. — **1826** *Ill. Revised Laws* 404 The court shall render judgment against the party who removed the said case into the circuit court, and his security in the appeal bond, for all costs. **1852** *Ohio Revised Statutes* (1860) II. 1165 Each appeal bond shall be payable to the adverse party, or otherwise, as may be directed by the court. **1877** *Ill. Revised Statutes* (1883) 841 Any informality or insufficiency of the appeal bond. **1877** [see APPEAL *n.* 1].

∗Appearance. The amount of attendance at a gathering. *Obs.* {–1704} — **1705** *Boston News-Letter* 17 Sept. 2/2 There was here a very great appearance of Men in the Train-Bands. **1716** *Boston Rec.* 121 In as much as . . . there is now too slender appearance of the inhabit[an]ts at present. **1747** *Penna. Col. Rec.* V. 153 Finding so thin an appearance of the Representatives and most of the principal members absent.

+Appearance docket. (See quotation.) — **1853** *Ohio Revised Statutes* (1860) II. 1034 On the appearance docket he [=clerk of the court of common pleas] shall enter all actions in the order in which they were brought, the date of the summons, . . . the time of filing the petition, and all subsequent pleadings.

Appearer. {1608–} One who appears before a court. {1863–} — **1793** *State P.* (1819) I. 118 These appearers, with the said privateer, arrived at this port . . . at about four o'clock in the morning.

∗Appearing, *ppl. a.* +With a defining adjective preceding, often with hyphen: In appearance; -looking.
1839 *Mass. H. S. Coll.* 3 Ser. IX. 95 All these, with his beauties of person, rendered him the best appearing Indian ever seen in this quarter. **1851** A. O. HALL *Manhattaner* 4 On my left, Algiers, a very fitting cognomen for an uncivilized appearing strip of land. **1857–8** *Ill. Agric. Soc. Trans.* III. 343 We found here several varieties [of apples] which we were not able to identify—fine appearing fruits, probably of Southern origin. **1879** HOWELLS *Lady of Aroostook* xviii. 215 'She is very fine-appearing,' said Lydia. Staniford smiled at the countrified phrase. **1897** *Outing* March 564/1 Never was any ancient thing so new-appearing . . . as these old ramparts of Avignon. *Ib.* July 351/1 First prize for best-appearing [cycling] club at Long Branch. **1903** C. T. BRADY *Bishop* i. 2 One rather hard-featured, rude-appearing woman.

∗Appellant. One who appeals from a lower to a higher court.
1706 *Mass. H.S. Coll.* 2 Ser. VIII. 241 Your appellants stand committed by virtue of a warrant or commitment. **1771** *Mass. Col. Soc. Publ.* VI. 16 John Randal, . . . appellant vs. Thomas Bodkin. **1777** *Journals Cont. Congress* VIII. 467 Resolved, That the prayer of the petition be granted . . . unless the appellants can shew that notice was duly given of their appeal. **1832** WILLIAMSON *Maine* II. 16 Appeals were allowed from this tribunal to the Superior Court—the appellant being put under recognizance to prosecute the cause. **1877** [see APPEAL *n.* 1].

Appellate, *a.* Of a nature to deal with appeals. {1768–}
The word was erroneously attacked as an Americanism during the early 19th c.: see Pickering.
1787 *Constitution* iii. § 2 In all the other cases . . . the supreme court shall have appellate jurisdiction, both as to law and fact. **1822** *Ann. 17th Congress* 1 Sess. I. 92 The argument runs thus: that, although they could not exercise appellate jurisdiction where a State is a party, . . . yet, when the controversy arises under the Constitution, laws or treaties, . . . they may assume appellate jurisdiction. **1843** G. Hines *Voyage* (1850) 428 The jurisdiction of the Supreme Court shall be both appellate and original. **1877** *Colorado Gen. Laws* 254 In all appeals . . . the proceedings in the appellate court shall be in all respects, *de novo*. **1896** *Columbus* (Ohio) *Dispatch* 18 July 1/4 Secretary Olney . . . shows that the awards, if unanimous, should be final equally with those of the appellate tribunal. **1904** *N.Y. Ev. Post* 3 May 2 Justices Freidman and MacLean of the Appellate Term had decided that Moulton had a right to bring such suit.

∗Appellee. + The defendant in a case that is appealed. — **1771** *Mass. Col. Soc. Publ.* VI. 16 John Randal of Bristol . . . appellant vs. Thomas Bodkin of Boston . . . appellee, from the Judgment of an Inferior Court . . . when and where the appellee was Plt. [=plaintiff] and the appellant was Def. [=defendant]. **1827** *Ill. Revised Laws* (1833) 395 If . . . the appellee is not found in the county, the court shall continue the case until the next term. **1851** *Iowa Code* 27 The matter shall stand for hearing at that time if required by the appellee.

+Appendicitis. Inflammation of the vermiform appendix.
1886 FITZ in *Amer. Jour. Med. Sciences* Oct. 323 As a circumscribed peritonitis is simply one event . . . in the history of inflammation of the appendix, it seems preferable to use the term appendicitis. **1906** GOULD *Biographic Clinics* IV. 22 A patient . . . suffering from abdominal cramps supposed to indicate appendicitis.

Appertainment. {1606} =APPURTENANCE. *Obs.* — **1660** *Oyster Bay Rec.* I. 1 Two lotts with the midows and all other apertanments there unto belonging are John Richbells.

∗Appertenance. *Obs.* =APPURTENANCE. — **1638** *Charlestown Land Rec.* 2 One roode of grounde . . . with a dwelling-house, Brew house and other apertinances. **1653** *Suffolk Deeds* II. 68, I . . . doe heereby couenant . . . to warrant . . . the said bargayned premises with their Appertenances.

∗APPLE.

∗1. The fruit of the common orchard tree *Pyrus malus*, or the tree itself.
1641 *Suffolk Deeds* I. 25 [They] reserve vnto themselves . . . one third part of all such apples . . . as shalbe yearly growinge vpon the sayd iland. **1647** ELIOT *Day Breaking* 387 Having given the children some apples, . . . we departed. **1681** *Penna. Mag.* VI. 175 Here are abundance of good Fruits: all sorts of Apples, Cherries [etc.]. **1698** G. THOMAS *Acc. Pensilvania* 18 The common Planting Fruit-Trees, are Apples, . . . Pears, Peaches, &c. **1719** J. HEMPSTEAD *Diary* 92, I was about home gathering Winter aples. **1745** *N.H. Probate Rec.* III. 283, I give & bequeath to my well beloved son . . . one third of the aples that shall grow in my orchards. **1781–2** JEFFERSON *Notes Va.* (1787) 40 The orchards produce apples, pears [etc.]. *c*1790 T. COXE *View U.S.* 63 The produce, manufactures, and exports of Pennsylvania are very many and various, viz. . . . apples, peaches, plumbs. **1816** W. DARBY *Geogr. Descr.* 150 The apple, though cultivated, . . . seems to be an exotic in southern Louisiana. **1831** PECK *Guide* 140 Of domestic fruits, the apple and peach are chiefly cultivated [in Ill.]. **1855** GLISAN *Jrnl. Army Life* 208 A gentleman of veracity has just assured me that, feeling a desire for an apple, he asked [at Benicia, Calif.] the price of same the other day, and was told two dollars and a half each. **1888** C. D. WARNER *On Horseback* 23 The pie of the country,—two thick slabs of dough, with a squeezing of apple between.

2. Attrib. with *blossom, bough, chest, harvest, juice, room, scion, seed, year.*
1699 *Mass. H.S. Coll.* 4 Ser. V. 306 Apple-seeds, sown by us since we came, came up in January. **1708** E. COOK *Sot-weed Factor* 19 There with good punch and apple juice We spent our hours without abuse. **1764** WASHINGTON *Diaries* I. 200 From hence to the end of the Row are apple Scions to graft upon. **1775** *Essex Inst. Coll.* XLVIII. 57 This day I made a apel Chest for granfarther. **1825** NEAL *Bro. Jonathan* I. 128 The ground [was] white with apple-blossoms. **1828** WEBSTER, *Apple-harvest*, the gathering of apples, or the time of gathering. **1853** FOWLER *Home for All* 120 A small closet off the apple-room. **1857** GRAY *First Lessons* 10 Take next the seed of a Plum or Peach, or an Almond, or an Apple-seed. **1859** STOWE *Minister's Wooing* xi, Great sailing islands of cloud . . . looked in and out through the . . . blossoming apple-boughs. **1886** *Century Mag.* Feb. 507/2 He said he really forgot whether it was an apple year.

b. In the sense: Made of or with apples. {1606–}
Freq. in combination with names of foods.
1807 IRVING, etc. *Salmagundi* vi. 127 A present of a pot of apple sweetmeats. **1809** IRVING *Knickerb.* v. i, Some buxom country heiress . . . deeply skilled in the mystery of making apple-sweetmeats. **1831** PECK *Guide* 235 A dose of calomel is taken at night, in a little apple honey. **1832** L. CHILD *Frugal Housewife* 118 [Recipe for] Apple Marmalade. **1846** E. FARNHAM *Prairie Land* 134 Sidney . . . had been initiated into the mysteries of pound-cake, jumbles, and apple-tarts. **1859** BARTLETT 90 Cobbler, . . . a sort of pie; . . . according to its fruit, it is an apple or a peach cobbler. Western. *c*1865 BAGBY *Old Va. Gentleman* 48 A true Virginian . . . must have . . . persimmon beer, apple-bread, milk and peaches, mutton stew, dewberries. **1865** *Chicago Tribune* 10 April 1 Pure Ohio Apple Cider . . . for sale. **1878** *Amer. Home Cook Book* 182 [Recipe for making] Apple Snow. **1881** 'M. HARLAND' *Common Sense* 249 Apple Omelette. **1891** *Harper's Mag.* Oct. 822/1 The apple cider flowed.

3. Comb. with *-holder, -monger, -pedlar, -picker; -cutting, -gathering, -roasting.*
1725 *New-Eng. Courant* 4 Jan. 2/1 Where Apple-mongers sit, your Stocks were shown. **1848** *Knickerb.* XVIII. 217 The apple-gatherings . . . furnish sources of enjoyment. **1849** *Rep. Comm. Patents* (1850) 333, I lay no claim to the invention of the combination of a rotating apple holder or shaft. **1851** ROSS *In New York* 47 The seat . . . was thereafter occupied by an apple-pedlar. **1862** 'GAIL HAMILTON' *Country Living* 70 A few dismal little apples escaped the common fate. . . . No apple-roasting in winter evenings. **1869** ALCOTT *Little Women* II. 354 At four o'clock a lull took place, . . . while the apple-pickers rested. **1878** STOWE *Poganuc People* xxii. 247 Long before the evening was through, the task of apple-cutting was accomplished.

+Apple-bee. [APPLE 2.] A social gathering, or 'bee,' held for the purpose of preparing apples for drying.
1827 *Harvard Reg.* Nov. 273 Once Ebenezer Hodge invited me To help his Dolly at an apple bee. **1828** *Yankee* April 131/2, I was invited to an apple-bee; a party assembled to assist a certain young widow in paring and cutting apples. **1836** R. WESTON *Visit* 196 One evening I was invited to an 'apple-bee' at the house of Mrs M'Queen. **1866** WHITTIER *Snow-bound* 361 The huskings and the apple-bees, The sleigh-rides and the summer sails. **1878** STOWE *Poganuc People* xxii. 242 Young men, maids, and matrons were taking their places to assist in the apple-bee. **1882** *Maine Bd. Agric. Rep.* XXVI. 405 The primitive way of preserving apples by paring, coring and stringing, and hanging on long poles in the

spacious kitchen, inaugurated the apple bee. **1889** R. T. COOKE *Steadfast* 25 'It's everlastin' hard,' she confided to a neighbor at an apple-bee.

+**Apple-beetle.** [APPLE 2.] — **1832** WILLIAMSON *Maine* I. 171 Of the Beetle class: . . . 4. Apple.

+**Apple-bin.** [APPLE 2.] A receptacle for apples. — **1854** SHILLABER *Mrs. Partington* 16 What they suppose must have been a cellar, was in reality an apple-bin. **1863** MITCHELL *My Farm* 145 The native tree . . . retains a stock of reserved vitality, which . . . will carry a good tale to the apple bin.

+**Apple borer.** [APPLE 3.] The apple-tree borer. — **1858** *Ill. Agric. Soc. Trans.* III. 344 The most destructive of these, . . . and the only one mentioned in fruit books, is that known as the apple borer. *Ib.* 498 This practice . . . will more effectually ward off the apple borer than any other method we have yet tried.

+**Apple-boy.** [APPLE 2.] A boy who sells apples. — **1858** *N.Y. Tribune* 14 Jan., I got the cars . . . after . . . flattening out an apple-boy and pop-corn vendor.

+**Apple brandy.** [APPLE 2 b.] A liquor distilled from apple cider.

*c***1780** *Md. Hist. Mag.* II. 256, [I] accepted 13 gals. of peach brandy in satisfaction of the damage. . . . He cheated me with apple brandy. **1785** Ramsey *Tennessee* (1853) 297 It shall and may be lawful for the aforesaid land tax, and all free polls, to be paid in the following manner: . . . good peach or apple brandy, at three shillings per gallon. **1807** C. JANSON *Stranger in A.* 397 My friend and myself, after supper, were very moderately indulging ourselves with a glass of apple brandy. . . . This is the common drink of the country. **1811** *Agric. Museum* I. 92, I find it best to put into the cask a pint or pint and half of French or good apple brandy. **1813** PAULDING *J. Bull & Br. Jon.* xix. 102 Preferring . . . apple-brandy, tea, cucumbers. **1847** *Rep. Comm. Patents* (1848) 380 No county in the state exceeded this in the production of apples and apple brandy. **1865** *Nation* I. 268/1 At the store or tavern of every village . . . apple brandy is always for sale by the glass. **1868** *Congress. Globe* 6 July 3741/3 In the . . . Alleganies . . . there are . . . a very large amount of apple orchards, and the fruit is mostly applied to the distillation of apple brandy.

+**Apple-bud moth.** =APPLE MOTH. — **1869** *Mass. Board Agric. 17th Rep.* I. 235 The Apple-Bud Moth, the most injurious enemy of the apple-tree, next to the canker-worm, . . . in this state, is a small, reddish-brown larva.

+**Apple-bug.** [APPLE 2.] **1.** A species of water-beetle. **2.** The plum weevil, *Conotrachelus nenuphar.* — (1) **1832** KENNEDY *Swallow Barn* I. 129 The apple-bugs (as schoolboys call that glossy black insect which frequents the summer pools, and is distinguished for the perfume of the apple) danced in myriads over the surface of the still water. **1868** *Rep. Comm. Agric.* (1869) 80 The fifth family, *Gyrinidæ*, comprises those oval water-beetles usually known by the name of 'whirligigs' or apple-bugs. — (2) **1889** FARMER 19/2 [The] Apple bug . . . deposits its eggs by puncturing the fruit, causing premature decay.

+**Apple-butter.** [APPLE 2 b.]

1. A preserve made of apple juice and pulp, usually spiced, and stewed down to a butter-like consistency.

1819 NOAH *She would be a Soldier* I. i, Can she milk—knit garters—make apple butter and maple sugar—dance a reel after midnight? **1832** *Mirror of Lit.*, etc. 20 May 323/2 Apple butter . . . is made by stewing apples in new cider, after it has been boiled down to one-third of its bulk. **1854** [W. BROMWELL] *Locomotive Sk.* 35 In Pennsylvania, among the Germans, particularly, there is a description of sauce called *apple butter*, and it is principally in the manufacture of this article that the cider and apples are consumed. **1857** [STROTHER] *Virginia* 202 Helping to stir apple-butter at a boiling frolic. **1862** GRAY *War Letters* 15 The woman fed us on pies, 'apple and quince butter'—she said she had no 'cow butter'—and coffee. **1866** GREGG *Life in Army* i. 19, I took my lessons in . . . manufacturing sugar, cider, apple butter and sour krout. **1870** *Congress. Globe* April 2685/1 Apple-butter is a substitute for butter; it is spread upon bread and eaten in like manner. **1880** *Congress. Rec.* March 1534/2 If I draw my finger across the page, the ink comes off as though it were printed with apple-butter. **1887** *Scribner's Mag.* I. 628/2 Eunice [is] parin' apples for apple-butter. **1889** *Century Mag.* Jan. 409/2 Hot meats were surrounded by pickles, both sweet and sour; and over all predominated the conventional apple-butter.

2. Attrib. and comb. with *kettle, maker, pot, stirring.*

1851 CIST *Cincinnati* ii. 49 Apple-butter makers. **1856** *Harper's Mag.* Jan. 163/1 She looked mournfully around at each familiar object . . . the churn, the apple-butter pot, the venerable quilting frame. *Ib.*, She mounted the reversed apple-butter kettle. **1880** *Ib.* Aug. 354/2 There is church twice a month, sewing bees, and apple-butter stirrings.

Apple-cart. [APPLE 2.] A cart used by a vendor to hold apples. Chiefly fig., esp. in *to upset the apple-cart*, to impair plans or to ruin an undertaking. {1796–, largely *dial.*}

*c***1799** FESSENDEN *Poems* (1806) 100 Spunkey . . . talketh big words to congress, and threateneth to overturn their apple-cart, and set his foot in it! **1825** NEAL *Bro. Jonathan* II. 388 'Where is he?' 'There; there! down with his apple-cart.' **1829** SANDS *Writings* II. 199 It is like an apple cart with two wheels, extremely liable to be upset. **1834** CARRUTHERS *Kentuckian* I. 101 Smash my apple-cart, if there wasn't more cryin and snifflin than I've seen at many an honest man's funeral. **1837** J. C. NEAL *Charcoal Sk.* (1838) 37, I only want to caution you, or I'll upset your apple cart, and spill your peaches. **1857** H. RILEY *Puddleford P.* (1875) 252 He demolished an apple-cart, and absolutely turned everything topsy-turvy. *a***1909** 'O. HENRY' *Roads of Destiny* viii. 141, I can upset your apple-cart any day I want to.

+**Apple-codling.** [APPLE 2.] The codling-moth. — **1871** *Ill. Agric. Soc. Trans.* VIII. 158 Grapeberry moth, called also Grape-codling, for the reason that its destructive work in the vineyard is . . . similar to that of the Apple-codling in the orchard.

Apple-corer. [APPLE 3.] An implement for removing cores from apples. {1747–}

1862 LOWELL *Biglow P.* II. iii, A Baldin hain't no more 'f a chance with them new apple-corers Than [etc.]. **1875** HOWELLS *Foregone Conclusion* xiv. 199 When he has made his fortune with a patent back-action apple-corer. **1878** STOWE *Poganuc People* xxii. 244 A new patent apple-peeler and corer, warranted to take the skin from an apple with a quickness and completeness hitherto unimaginable. **1883** *Practical Housekeeping* 490 Apple Corers . . . are simply tin tubes made of different sizes for large or small apples.

+**Apple-cut.** [APPLE 2.] An apple-bee or apple-cutting. — **1845** *Lowell Offering* V. 87 My mind involuntarily reverted to . . . the apple-cut frolics, and kindred associations. **1873** HOLLEY *Betsy Bobbet* 290, I have seen enough boldness used by a passel of girls at one huskin' bee, or apple-cut, to supply 4 presedential elections. **1876** BURROUGHS *Winter Sunshine* VII. 159 Then those rural gatherings that enlivened the autumn in the country, known as 'apple-cuts,' now alas! nearly obsolete.

Apple-cutting. [APPLE 3.]

1. A scion of an apple-tree.

1826 JEFFERSON *Writings* XVIII. 352 As the season for engrafting is passing rapidly by I will not detain the apple-cuttings.

+**2.** An apple-bee.

1850 T. D. PRICE *MS. Diary* 16 Sept., We had an apple cutting at D. E. Davis' home. **1859** A. CARY *Country Life* 246 He had called to ask her to come to an 'apple cutting' at his mother's house. **1878** STOWE *Poganuc People* xxi. 238 Mis' Hawkins . . . says they're goin' to hev an apple-cuttin' there tomorrow night.

Apple-dumpling. [APPLE 2 b.] A pastry consisting of an apple or apples baked in an envelope of dough. {1721–}

1817 J. GALLATIN *Diary* 115, I cannot see my right eye and my cheek is like an apple-dumpling. **1826** Commons, etc. *Doc. Hist.* I. 299 Apple-dumplings and apple-pies . . . have presented themselves to our delightful palates. **1836** DUNLAP *Mem. Water Drinker* (1837) I. 116 Yes, and chickens and greens, and a good apple dumpling, with a hearty welcome. **1843** *Knickerb.* XXI. 281 Poor 'Trip' dropped upon the ground with the emphasis of a squashed apple-dumpling. **1851** MELVILLE *Moby Dick* xvii. 94 Hell is an idea first born of an undigested apple-dumpling. **1880** *Harper's Mag.* Oct. 687/2, I wish he had seen her eating apple-dumplings for dinner.

* **Apple-fritter.** [APPLE 2 b.] A fritter made with a center of apple.

1811 IRVING in Warner *Life* (1882) 87 Stand by a frying pan for an hour and listen to the cooking of apple-fritters. **1881** 'M. HARLAND' *Common Sense* 405 [For] Apple Fritters [make] a batter according to the preceding receipt. **1891** *Amer. N. & Q.* VI. 179 There are few persons who are not familiar with 'apple-fritters' and 'oyster-fritters.' **1896** E. HIGGINSON *Tales* 239, I want that you should hold this candle while I fry the apple-fritters.

+**Apple-haw.** [APPLE 2.] The may or summer haw. — **1861** WOOD *Botany* 331 *Cratægus æstivalis.* Apple Haw. [Grows] in the edges of ponds and rivers, S. Car. to Fla. and La. **1901** MOHR *Plant Life Ala.* 125 The smaller trees, of which the most conspicuous are planer tree, red maple, . . . and the apple haw.

+**Apple-hole.** [APPLE 2.] (See quotation.) — **1876** BURROUGHS *Winter Sunshine* VII. 154 Do you remember the apple hole in the garden? . . . In the fall we excavated a circular pit in the warm mellow earth, and covering the bottom with clean rye straw, emptied in basketful after basketful of hardy choice varieties.

Apple-jack. [APPLE 2 b.]

1. A pastry made of apples baked in a crust. {*a*1825– *dial.*}

1835 KENNEDY *Horse Shoe Robinson* I. 22 Besides these, I can throw in two apple-jacks, a half dozen of rolls.

+**2.** An alcoholic beverage distilled from apple juice; apple brandy.

1816 'SCENE PAINTER' *Emigrant's Guide* 30 A partial distillation is also made from apples, . . . called Apple-Jack. **1838** 'UNCLE SAM' in *Bentley's Misc.* IV. 134 There was nothing to be had that day but potatoes, bread, and applejack, . . . a description of brandy made from apples. *c***1845** *Big Bear Arkansas* 51, I'll give you a pint of apple-jack. **1865** BOUDRYE *Fifth N.Y. Cavalry* 174 They were all loud in their denunciations of Gen. Early, the 'apple-jack bibber,' as many of them called him. **1867** 'P. NASBY' *Swingin round the Cirkle* 171 He drinks apple-jack instead of corn whiskey. **1885** *Southern Hist. Soc. P.* XIII. 142 If there was a barrel . . . or a runlet of 'apple jack' or 'peach brandy,' . . . they [Federal cavalry-men] would find it. **1890** *Congress. Rec.* 21 April 3636/2, I had had some experience with Kentucky apple-jack, which it was popularly believed among the boys would dissolve a piece of the fattest pork thrown into it.

1895 M. A. Jackson *Memoirs* 531 His medical director and I 'sampled' some very new and very fiery apple-jack. **1903** A. B. HART *Actual Government* 401 Peach brandy, apple-jack, and rough corn whiskey may easily be manufactured by farmers.

attrib. **1857** *Harper's Mag.* Nov. 731/2 An apple-jack distillery, where the best may be obtained for twelve and a half cents a quart.

+**Apple-leather.** [APPLE 2 b.] *Penna. & Md.* 'Apples parboiled and stirred into a paste of considerable consistency; then rolled out and dried in the sun. When dry, it is about as tough as leather, and comes away in sheets of the thickness of tanned cowhide,—whence its name' (B. '77).

+**Apple maggot.** A species of maggot which especially feeds on crab-apples and haws. — **1867** *Amer. Jrnl. Horticulture* Dec. II. 338 The apple maggot . . . breeds naturally in our wild haws and crabs, but . . . has been noticed to attack the cultivated apple. **1882** *Rep. Comm. Agric.* 195 The Apple Maggot (*Trypeta pomonella* Walsh.) . . . is becoming quite common in certain parts of New York and New England. *Ib.* 196 The Apple Maggot is much more apt to infest early apples than the winter varieties.

+**Apple-mill.** [APPLE 2.] A cider-mill. — **1829** SHERWOOD *Gaz. Georgia* (ed. 2) 253 A grinding mill, for breaking the canes and extracting the juice, may be of a very simple construction, having three upright rollers, on the plan of an apple-mill.

Apple-moth. [APPLE 2.] The codling moth. — **1851** BARRY *Fruit Garden* 368 The Apple Worm.—The apple moth deposits its eggs in the eye or calyx of the young fruit. **1863** MITCHELL *My Farm* 142 But there is not a specimen of it that is not bored through and through by the inevitable grub of the apple-moth.

Apple of Peru. a. =APPLE-PERU. **b.** (See quots. 1847, 1901.)

1705 BEVERLY *Virginia* II. 24 The James-Town Weed . . . resembles the thorny Apple of Peru. **1828** WEBSTER, *Thorn-apple*, . . . a popular name of the *Datura Stramonium*, or apple of Peru. **1847** WOOD *Botany* 446 *Nicandra physaloides.* Apple of Peru. . . . Native of Peru, cultivated in gardens, from whence it has in a few instances strayed into the neighboring fields. **1901** MOHR *Plant Life Ala.* 708 *Physalodes physalodes.* Apple of Peru. . . . Adventive and naturalized from southern Ontario to Pennsylvania, Ohio, and Missouri, and along the mountains to North Carolina.

Apple orchard. An orchard in which apples are grown. {1807–}

1721 *New-Eng. Courant* 14–21 Aug. 2/2 There was a larger Apple Orchard at that Place, than on any other Part of the Province. **1760** WASHINGTON *Diaries* I. 130 Laid the Worm round my Apple Orchard and made the Fence. **1767** Commons, etc. *Doc. Hist.* I. 245 The one on which the subscriber lives has . . . a large apple orchard. **1794** T. COOPER *America* 51 Every farm-house in the middle and southern states has its peach orchard, and its apple orchard. **1833** HALL *Harpe's Head* 17 An apple-orchard had been planted. **1835** REED & MATHESON *Visit* I. 44 Apple-orchards prevail greatly about here [in N.J.]. **1859** STOWE *Minister's Wooing* iii. 28 The window looked out under the overarching boughs of a thick apple-orchard. **1896** WILKINS *Madelon* xxii. 264 An old apple orchard, the trees thereof bent to the ground like distorted old men. **1900** DIX *Deacon Bradbury* 163 He was . . . never angrily quick to chase an occasional pair of school-boys from his apple-orchard.

+**Apple-parer.** [APPLE 3.] A device for paring apples.

1833 S. SMITH *Major Downing* 162 Peleg, who is all the while whitlin, and sawin, and makin clocks, and apple parers, and churns. **1856** *Mich. Agric. Soc. Trans.* VII. 53 D. O. & W. S. Penfield, Detroit, [exhibited] twelve nonpareil apple parers, iron. **1857** *Knickerb.* XLIX. 168 They had been in everything, from an apple-parer to a steam-engine. **1860** HOLMES *Professor* x. 310 A poet . . . can dispense with an apple-parer and a reaping-machine. **1872** FLAGG *Good Investment* xii. 547/2 The household labor was further alleviated by introducing the latest-contrived . . . apple-parer. **1876** INGRAM *Centennial Exp.* 328 The improved Turn-table apple parer is . . . arranged so as to loosen the apple on the fork after the paring is finished.

Apple-paring. [APPLE 3.]

+**1.** =APPLE-BEE.

1819 NOAH *She would be a Soldier* I. i, I'm the boy for a race, for an apple-paring or quilting frolic—fight a cock . . . with any one. **1857** H. RILEY *Puddleford P.* (1875) 109 In the winter, husking-bees, apple-parings, and house-warmings were held every week at some of the farm-houses. **1868** BEECHER *Norwood* 464 They didn't have an apple-parin' at our town to make apple-sarse for Lee's army, I guess! **1879** D. J. HILL *Bryant* 39 Huskings and apple-parings had not gone out of fashion.

2. Attrib. with *bee, frolic* (=sense 1), *machine.*

(1) **1851** BUSHNELL *Work & Play* (1864) 380 The apple-paring and quilting frolics, you may set down, if you will, as the polka-dances and masquerades of homespun. **1864** T. L. NICHOLS *Amer. Life* I. 27 Then come the 'apple-paring bees.'

(2) **1852** *Mich. Agric. Soc. Trans.* III. 445, 1 Apple-paring machine. **1876** INGRAM *Centennial Exp.* 328 'The Bay State Apple Paring and Slicing Machine' . . . pares and slices the apple in one operation.

+**Apple-peeler.** [APPLE 3.] A device or implement for peeling apples; an apple-parer. — **1858** *Harper's Mag.* May 731/2 The president and some of his adherents whipped out their apple-peelers [=pocket-knives], and threatening death to all who approached, heroically stood their ground. **1878** [see APPLE-CORER].

Apple-peeling. [APPLE 3.] +=APPLE-BEE. — **1871** EGGLESTON *Hoosier Schoolm.* iv. 46 One night at a apple-peelin' I tuck a sheet . . . to splice out the table-cloth. **1887** — *The Graysons* ix, '[I am] only peeling some apples to dry.' 'Let me help you; we'll have an apple-peeling all to ourselves.'

+**Apple-peru.** (Cf. APPLE OF PERU.) The thorn-apple or jimson-weed, *Datura stramonium.*

1784 CUTLER in *Mem. Academy* I. 419 Appleperu. . . . Common by the waysides. August. **1795** WINTERBOTHAM *Hist. View* III. 397 Among the . . . plants of New-England, the following have been employed for medical purposes: . . . Appleperu [etc.]. **1813** *Henderson's N.C. Almanack* 23 Strammonium is known in some parts of the country by the name of Apple peru and in others by that of James-Town weed. **1850** HAWTHORNE *Scarlet L.* i. 56 A grass-plot, much overgrown with burdock, pig-weed, apple-peru, and such unsightly vegetation. *a***1870** CHIPMAN *Notes on Bartlett* 219 Jamestown Weed . . . Apple Peru,—at Salem, Mass.

***Apple pie.** [APPLE 1.]

***1.** A pie variously made of apples and pastry.

In England now usually called 'apple-tart.'

1697 SEWALL *Diary* I. 460 For Dinner, very good Rost Lamb, Turkey, Fowls, Aplepy. **1742** Woolsey *Hist. Disc. Yale* (1850) 71 For supper for four [students], . . . apple-pie, which shall be made of one and three fourth pounds dough, one quarter pound hog's fat, two ounces sugar and half a peck apples. **1805** *Pocumtuc Housewife* (1906) 24 Squash Pie with Raisins, . . . Apple Pies. **1828** *Yankee* May 147/1 A husking supper [concluded with] a dessert of apple-pie and cheese. **1832** KENNEDY *Swallow Barn* I. 67 A troop . . . are seen . . . armed with tin kettles, in which are deposited their leather-coated apple-pies. **1835** HOFFMAN *Winter in West* I. 80 The huge piles of buckwheat cakes . . . flanked each by a cold apple pie. **1850** [S. F. COOPER] *Rural Hours* 299 The apple-pie they are now eating, will no more compare with the puddings, and tarts, and pies eaten every day in past times at their good mother's table. **1871** A. C. DAY *Knickerb. Life* (1897) 213 The Yankee Thanksgiving, with its turkey, cranberry sauce, mince, pumpkin, apple pie, and cider. **1886** Z. F. SMITH *Kentucky* 388 [They] occupied it [=the time] by dividing among them an apple pie, which quickly vanished. **1888** C. D. FERGUSON *Exper. Forty-niner* x. 148 Mrs. Phelps commenced making dried apple pies which sold readily at one dollar a pie.

2. *Apple-pie order*, trim or neat order or condition. {1813–}

1823 G. MCCALL *Lett. from Frontiers* (1868) 134 He was . . . told to have his boat and boat's crew in apple-pie order in half an hour. *a***1848** *N.Y. Tribune* (B.) The ferry-boats are kept running in apple-pie order under the vigilant superintendence of Capt. Woolsey. **1859** ELWYN *Glossary* 16 It is common in New England [to say] 'Things are in apple-pie order,' meaning neatly arranged. **1860** *Let.* in *Wisconsin Alumni Mag.* (1929) 226 He is very gentlemanly and precise and dignified—everything in 'apple pie order.' **1886** *Boston Herald* 28 Nov. 12/8 The fashionable woman, whose coiffure is always in apple-pie order, and who rides in her carriage. **1897** *Outing* XXX. 464/1 There were both a turf and a dirt court, and each was kept in apple-pie order the whole time.

‖**b.** Hence (as nonce-word) *apple-pie orderliness.*

1881 *Scribner's Mo.* XXI. 890/1 The purpose of the admonition is fulfilled in an apple-pie orderliness.

+**Apple pine.** [APPLE 2.] The white pine, *Pinus strobus.* — **1832** BROWNE *Sylva Amer.* 242 This species . . . is known . . . in New Hampshire and Maine by the secondary denominations of Pumpkin Pine, Apple Pine.

Apple pomace. [APPLE 2.] The residue of apple-pulp after the juice has been expressed. {1664} — **1768** WASHINGTON *Diaries* I. 297 Sowed Apple Pummice in the New Garden—from Crab Apples. **1846** EMMONS *Agric. N.Y.* I. 360 All manufacturing establishments have various kinds of wastes, such as . . . apple pumice, in which, during decomposition, much ammonia and the phosphates exist.

Apple-pudding. [APPLE 2 b.] A pudding made with apples. {1807}

*c***1788** Buckingham *Newspaper Lit.* I. 323 How to make an Apple Pudding, being a . . . sublime Dissertation . . . by Yankee Doodle, Esq. **1807** IRVING, etc. *Salmagundi* v. 117 She was a young lady of most voluminous proportions . . . and . . . looked like an apple-pudding tied in the middle. **1832** L. M. CHILD *Frugal Housewife* 63 A plain, unexpensive apple pudding may be made by rolling out a bit of common pie-crust [etc.]. **1843** *Knickerb.* XXII. 40 The signs of the zodiac, . . . and the way to make an apple-pudding, these had a fresh interest. **1881** 'M. HARLAND' *Common Sense* 372 [Receipt for] Baked Apple Pudding.

Apple pulp. [APPLE 2.] Apple pomace. — **1804** J. ROBERTS *Penna. Farmer* 18 Sawdust, tanners bark, and rotten leaves, are best for the compost dunghil; as well as the apple pulp, after being pressed for cyder.

+**Apple-roaster.** [APPLE 3.] A container for roasting apples. — **1642** *Md. Archives* IV. 97 An apple-roster, & a meat-heater. **1717** *Mass. H.S. Coll.* 6 Ser. V. 365 One apple roaster, 2 brass skimmers.

+**Apple-sarse.** (See APPLE-PARING 1, quot. 1868, and cf. next.)

+**Apple-sass,** colloq. or dial. pron. of next.

[**1801** (cf. the rhyme words s.v. APPLE-SAUCE).] **1833** S. SMITH *Major Downing* 117 A load of apples and apple-sass, and a few sassages. **1862** NORTON *Army Lett.* 115 Pancakes and hoecakes and apple sass. **1878** *Ill. Dep. Agric. Trans.* XIV. 146 The lack of 'apple-sass' in that far-off clime hardly compensate[s] for a change from . . . Illinois. **1888** *Mo. Re-*

publican 5 March (F.), There is enough . . . of the golden fruit to make any amount of apple sass, apple jack, cider. **1890** BRET HARTE *Waif of Plains* 11, I'm goin' to . . . have things giv' to me. Baby clothes, and apples, and apple sass.

Apple-sauce. [APPLE 2 b.] 'A sauce made of stewed apples' (W. '28). {1824}

1801 *Sp. Farmers' Museum* 235 Set the cups, and beaker glass, The pumpkin, and the apple sauce. **1830** S. SMITH *Lett. J. Downing* (1834) 21 Uncle Joshua tackled up, and started off to Boston with a load of turkeys and apple-sauce. **1854** SHILLABER *Mrs. Partington* 271 Buckets and apple-sauce, in which subscribers generally paid, had ceased to be negotiable articles. **1863** 'GAIL HAMILTON' *Gala-Days* 225 A land flowing with maple-molasses and sugar, and cider apple-sauce. **1888** C. D. WARNER *On Horseback* 145 We noted at the tables in this region a singular use of the word fruit. When we were asked, 'Will you have some of the fruit?' and said Yes, we always got apple-sauce. **1897** W. E. BARTON *Hero in Homespun* 229 Jennie brought out . . . a high pie, . . . made of several layers of biscuit dough alternating with apple sauce.

+**Apple-slump.** [APPLE 2 b.] A dish consisting of apples and molasses baked on a layer of dough in a pot.

1831 *Finn's Comic Annual* 140 The pumpkin pies and apple slump . . . were smoking on the table. **1848** BARTLETT 311 A favorite dish in New England, called an apple slump. **1884** E. E. HALE *Christmas in Narragansett* 11 They had done justice to Ingham's ducks and Polly's apple-slump.

+**Apple smeller.** A species of water-beetle, *Gyrinus natator.* — *c***1830** GODMAN in *Waldie's Library* II. 85/1 Their distant relatives, called by the boys the water-witches and apple smellers, . . . [have] a delightful smell, exactly similar to that of the richest, mellowest apple.

+**Apple-stand.** [APPLE 2.] A stall or booth at which apples are sold.

1845 *Corr. R. W. Griswold* (1898) 201 Where Nassau street right-angles Ann, . . . apple stands are near. **1863** MRS. WHITNEY *F. Gartney* v, Bridget Foye sat at her apple-stand in the cheery morning sunlight. **1878** H. H. JACKSON *Travel at Home* 144 This [was] within stone's throw of an apple-stand and a meeting-house. **1884** *Century Mag.* July 480/2 [Poem] At an Apple-stand.

+**Apple-toddy.** [APPLE 2 b.] A whisky or brandy punch flavored with roasted apples.

1809 IRVING *Knickerb.* v. ii, The inhabitants . . . were prone to . . . get fuddled with . . . apple-toddy. *a***1821** C. BIDDLE *Autobiog.* iii. 165 He frequently drank too much apple toddy. **1834** H. BRACKENRIDGE *Recoll.* xvii. 195 Almost the only social people were a few who met now and then to drink apple toddy and sing songs. **1839** F. J. GRUND *Aristocracy in A.* II. 264 In the middle of the room stood a large basin, which . . . I, . . . on drawing near, discovered to be full of that exquisite beverage called 'apple toddy.' **1852** HAWTHORNE *Note-books* II. 197 Anon . . . came the apple-toddy, a very rich and spicy compound. **1857** *Knickerb.* XLIX. 186 Mrs. Van brought out a great bowl, and made some apple-toddy. **1885** *Century Mag.* XXX. 607/1 Welcoming the Christmas in with goblets of egg-nog and apple-toddy. **1904** GLASGOW *Deliverance* 155 Why, they use to say that you couldn't get to the Hall unless you swam your way through apple toddy.

***Apple-tree.**

***1.** A tree which bears apples.

*c***1638** *Harvard Rec.* I. 172 For thirty Apple-trees & setting them, [£]6. **1648** *Suffolk Deeds* II. 121 Edward Bendall hath liberty . . . to plant & transplant Apple or fruite trees for his benyfitt. **1675** JOSSELYN *Two Voyages* 29 There being not one Apple-tree, nor Pear planted yet [in 1638] in no part of the Country, but upon that Island [*sc.* the Governor's Island]. **1680** *Oyster Bay Rec.* I. 128 All my young aplle treese lately planted . . . and my nussery of aple treese and peach treese. **1724** H. JONES *Virginia* 41 At the Plantations are . . . Apple-Trees, planted out in Orchards, on purpose almost for the Hogs. **1748** *N.H. Probate Rec.* III. 534, I give and bequeath to my mother . . . the fruit that shall grow upon sixteen appletrees. **1789** J. MAY *Jrnl. & Lett.* (1873) 127 The apple-trees are now in blow; the oaks and chestnuts but just leaved out. **1835** HOFFMAN *Winter in West* I. 115 Here, too, are apple trees . . . brought by the French to this country in 1731. **1855** *Ill. Agric. Soc. Trans.* I. 276 Mr. C. Bryant does not think that cutting the apple tree is beneficial in the least. **1865** D. G. MITCHELL *Doctor Johns* ix, The parson . . . paced back and forth under the apple-trees. **1904** GLASGOW *Deliverance* 432 From the bough of an old apple-tree . . . he heard . . . a solitary thrush.

‖**2.** *Within two rows of apple-trees,* within a fair distance.

1869 CONKLING in *Congress. Globe* 2 March 1793/2 It does not come, if I may use the expression, within two rows of apple-trees of the point here at all.

+**3.** *Apple-tree borer,* an insect which infests apple-trees, either round-headed (*Saperda candida*) or flat-headed (*Chrysobothris femorata*).

1838 *Mass. Zool. Survey Rep.* 90 The most notoriously noxious insect of this genus, is the *Saperda bivittata*, the parent of the apple-tree borer. **1851** BARRY *Fruit Garden* 367 The Apple Tree Borer is a very troublesome insect in some sections of the country. **1852** *Horticulturist* VII. 238/2 The Apple Tree Borer in some parts . . . has destroyed whole orchards. **1862** *Rep. Comm. Patents: Agric.* 617 Probably the *most* widespread and universally destructive insect to *fruit* trees is the 'apple tree borer,' . . . which has hitherto almost defied all the efforts resorted to for its extermination. **1872** *Ill. Agric. Trans.* 70 Washes of various kinds tend to . . . prevent the attacks of the apple-tree borer.

+**4.** *Apple-twig borer,* a small beetle that infests the twigs of apple-trees.

1856 A. FITCH *Noxious Insects* (3rd Rep. N.Y. Agric. Soc.) 330 Apple twig borer, *Bostrichus bicaudatus*, . . . has been common of late years in the orchards of Michigan and Illinois. **1868** *Rep. Comm. Agric.* 99 The larvæ of *Amphicerus* (*Apate*) *bicaudatus* . . . or apple-twig borer . . . perforate the twigs at the buds, . . . thus causing the twigs to wither and die.

Apple-water. [APPLE 2 b.] Juice from apples diluted with water. — **1832** L. M. CHILD *Frugal Housewife* 32 Apple water. This [is] given as sustenance when the stomach is too weak to bear broth.

+**Apple-whisky.** [APPLE 2 b.] Liquor distilled from apples. — **1837** J. C. NEAL *Charcoal Sk.* (1838) 160 Pumpkins, cabbages, and apple whiskey is always good for a weakly constitution. **1865** *N.Y. Tribune* in *Morn. Star* 20 April (Th. S.), The genuine Virginia stimulant known as apple-jack, or apple whisky. **1886** S. W. MITCHELL *R. Blake* 3 [He] filled the air with ingenious blasphemy, to which the swearing of all other lands is as milk to apple-whiskey.

Apple-woman. [APPLE 2.] A woman who sells apples. {*c*1714–}

1807 IRVING, etc. *Salmagundi* v. 111 Some ambitious heroes who . . . hector every old apple-woman in the [theatre] lobbies. **1852** MITCHELL *Dream Life* 192 The old apple-women, with their noses frost-bitten, look cheerful, and blue. **1873** HOLLAND *A. Bonnicastle* xxii, The sailors were singing, . . . apple-women were chaffing, but nothing could divert me. **1898** PAGE *Red Rock* p. ix, When they . . . greet the apple-woman on the corner, or the wagoner on the road.

+**Applewood.** [APPLE 2.] The wood of the apple-tree. — **1805** *Pocumtuc Housewife* (1906) 29 Thrifty housekeepers are wont to gather the whitest and lightest of applewood ashes as they fall in the fireplace.

+**Apple-worm.** [APPLE 2.]

1. A larva of the codling moth, *Carpocapsa pomonella.*

1850 *New Eng. Farmer* II. 252 The others were bored by the common apple-worm. **1853** *Mich. Agric. Soc. Trans.* V. 135 The apple worm has for two seasons past, destroyed or greatly injured all my apples and pears. **1855** *Ib.* VI. 160 The apple worm first made its appearance in the fruit here, one year ago. **1872** *Vermont Bd. Agric. Rep.* 56 The codling moth, which lays the egg that produces the apple worm, is a great injury to us. **1882** *Rep. Comm. Agric.* 195 Without doubt the most important insect enemy of the apple is the codlin-moth or Apple-worm, as it is often called.

+**2.** *Apple-worm moth,* a codling moth.

1869 *Amer. Entomologist* Feb. 112/1 This moth is variously known as the Apple-worm Moth, or the Codling-worm Moth.

***Apple-yard.** [APPLE 2.] 'An orchard; an inclosure for apples' (W. '28).

Applicant. {1764} +A student who applies himself diligently. *Obs.* — **1809** *Monthly Anthology* VII. 263 'Applicant,' *n.*, one who makes request. This is a mean word, and by Mr. Webster is not explained in the most common sense, a hard student. **1829** *Va. Lit. Museum* 16 Dec. 418 *Applicant,* 'a diligent student'—not uncommon. [**1851** HALL *College Words* 10 At present the word *applicant* is never used in the sense of a diligent student.]

Appointee. {1727–}

1. One who is appointed to an office or an honor. {1768–}

1768 *Circular of Mass. Representatives* (W. '28) The commission authorizes them to make appointments, and pay the appointees. **1880** CABLE *Grandissimes* ix. 57 Men who . . . came forward and gave in their allegiance to the President's appointee.

+**2.** At Yale, 'one who receives an appointment at a college exhibition or commencement' (Hall).

1847 [J. MITCHELL] *Scenes & Characters* 194 To the gratified appointee, —if his ambition for the honor has the intensity it has in some bosoms,— the day is the proudest he will ever see. **1852** BRISTED *Five Years Eng. Univ.* (ed. 2) 382, I suspect that a man in the first class of the 'Poll' has usually read mathematics to more profit than many of the 'appointees,' even of the 'oration men' at Yale.

***Appointer.** +(See quotation.) *Obs.* — **1640** *Dedham Rec.* III. 66 It is nowe ordered that [three men named] . . . shall heerafter set out & appoynt such tymber trees vnto such of our towne as shall haue neede thereof, . . . and that one of the sayd appoynters doth mark every one of the sayd trees.

+**Appointive,** *a.* [f. *appoint* v.] Of a nature to be filled by appointment.

1881 TOURGEE in *N. Amer. Rev.* CXXXII. 314 If the system is right why not apply it to every appointive place in the Government except the cabinet. **1882** *American* IV. 85 They demand that as to the minor appointive places there shall be a system. **1903** *Cosmopolitan Mag.* June 159 High appointive posts under the federal government. **1913** LA FOLLETTE *Autobiog.* 115 We were then in the midst of the Wisconsin fight, and besides I did not desire an appointive office.

***Appointment.**

+1. (See quot. 1851 and cf. APPOINTEE.)

1847 [J. MITCHELL] *Scenes & Characters* 69 The object of appointments is to incite to study, and promote good scholarship. **1850** *Yale Lit. Mag.* XV. 210 If e'er ye would take an 'appointment,' young man, Beware o' the 'blade' and 'fine fellow,' young man! **1851** HALL *College Words* 10 In many American colleges, students to whom are assigned a part in the exercises of an exhibition or commencement, are said to receive an *appointment.* Appointments are given as a reward for superiority in scholarship. **1854** *Presentation Day Songs* (Yale) 14 June, Some have crammed for appointments, and some for degrees. **1871** [L. H. BAGG] *At Yale* 590 The 'honors' which are held out as an inducement for scholastic effort are chiefly in the form of appointments for Junior Exhibition and Commencement.

+2. a. *Appointment office:* (see quot. 1843).

1843 *P. O. Laws & Reg.* II. 2 Appointment Office. To this office are assigned all questions which relate to the establishment and discontinuance of post offices, . . . appointment and removal of deputy postmasters [etc.]. **1880** LAMPHERE *U.S. Govt.* 52/1 The reception-room of the Appointment Office is always open to the public.

+b. *Appointments office,* a placement bureau.

1904–5 *Harvard Univ. Catalogue* p. xiii, The Appointments Office carries on the work hitherto in charge of the Appointment Committee, namely, that of procuring positions for undergraduates, graduates, and all past members of the University seeking employment.

+c. *Appointment committee:* (see quotation).

1897–8 *Harvard Univ. Cat.* 488 Appointment Committee. The Committee . . . recommends for positions of various kinds men who are studying or who have studied under this Faculty, whether or not holders of degrees. **1904–5** [see b].

+Appola (apolla). [Of obscure origin.] A cut or steak *of* venison. (Fremont and Sage also use the phrase *en appolas* to describe meat roasted 'on sticks around the fire.') — **1843** FREMONT *Exped.* 113 To-night the camp fires, girdled with *appolas* of fine venison, looked cheerful in spite of the stormy weather. **1847** RUXTON *Adv. Rocky Mts.* (1848) 241 At night I returned to camp, made a fire, and cooked an appola of antelope-meat. **1848** — *Far West* iv. 158 As he turned his apolla [*sic*] of tender loin, he sighed.

Apportionment. {1628–}

+1. The assignment of the number of representatives that each state may send to the House of Representatives, or that each district may send to the state legislature, on the basis of the distribution of population.

1791 *Ann. 2nd Congress* 119 An act for an apportionment of Representatives among the several States according to the first enumeration. **1792** *Ib.* 415 Apportionment Bill . . . for an Apportionment of Representatives among the several States. **1792** JEFFERSON *Let.* Writings V. 493 The bill for apportioning representatives among the several States, without explaining any principle at all . . . to guide future apportionments. **1801** *Ann. 7th Congress* 1 Sess. 326 The apportionment of Representatives amongst the several States, according to the second enumeration of the people, ought to be in the ratio of one Representative for every thirty-three thousand persons in each State. **1851** *Ohio Constitution* xi, The apportionment of this State for members of the General Assembly shall be made every ten years. **1882** *Ill. Revised Statutes* (1883) 522 Until the taking and return of the next federal census, and the apportionment thereunder, as provided in the constitution.

attrib. **1842** *Niles' Nat. Reg.* 2 July 287/3 Mr. Adams called for . . . the message of the president in relation to the apportionment bill. **1852** *Harper's Mag.* V. 116/2 An amendment to the apportionment bill, fixing the number of members of the House of Representatives at 234 . . . , was adopted.

+2. The assignment of direct taxes on the basis of population.

1778 *Journals Cont. Congress* XI. 638 The Delegates [moved], . . . so far as relates to the criterion fixed on for settling the proportion of taxes to be paid by each State, that an amendment may be made, so that the rule of apportionment may be varied. **1840** *Niles' Nat. Reg.* 28 March 52/2 An apportionment of $600,000, among the counties of Maryland, in the ratio of their property values. **1889** *Cent.* s.v., Apportionment . . . of direct taxes . . . [is] a Congressional power rarely exercised.

Appraisal. {1817} +The setting of a price on property; valuation. Cf. APPRAISEMENT. — **1863** B. TAYLOR *H. Thurston* iii, After arranging for an inventory and appraisal of the live stock, . . . Mr. Hammond took his departure. **1882** *National Bank Act* 72 The shares so surrendered . . . shall . . . be sold at public sale, within thirty days after the final appraisal provided in this section. **1904** F. LYNDE *Grafters* 236 They drove to the Building and Loan office where the joint letter of appraisal was written and signed.

***Appraise,** *v. tr.* To set a price upon; esp. to estimate the value of (property) for legal purposes.

1636 *Conn. Public Rec.* 1 The saide plantacions . . . where such swine are may appraise them att a value. **1776** *Journals Cont. Congress* V. 425 Resolved, That the governor of the colony of Connecticut be requested to appoint judicious and indifferent persons to appraise the vessel. **1787** WASHINGTON *Diaries* III. 155 Went to the plantation of Jno. Robinson to have his stock of horses and cattle appraised to me. **1819** *Missouri Intell.* 12 Nov. 1/4 Taken up by John Sneathton, . . . a sorrel horse . . . appraised to eighty dollars. **1846** D. WELLS *Our Strength* 17 A discrepancy between the real and appraised value of property. **1876** T. D. PRICE *MS. Diary* 7 March, Went to help appraise old Mrs. Thomas' farm.

Appraisement. {1642–1745} =APPRAISAL.

1676 *N.Y. State Col. Hist.* XII. 555 As to the appraisment off Daniel Makeey Estate . . . I can not tell, and must bee informed by better lawyers. **1677** *New Castle Court Rec.* 139 The appraizers . . . makeing returne of their appraizement of the cattle of John Heyland. **1694** *N. Car. Col. Rec.* I. 393 A petition exhibited by Elizabeth Arnord praying an apprasem[en]te. Ordered that William John Godfrey be appraisors of the estate. **1746** *N. J. Archives* 1 Ser. VI. 200 Provided that no tools or instruments impress'd be made use of . . . till appraisement be made by two lawful men upon oath. **1792** *Ann. 2nd Congress* 1136 It appeared to him [=Ensign Shamburgh] as if they were parties concerned, and glad to lose their horses, because they had a very great appraisement for the same. **1814** *Ann. 13th Congress* 1 Sess. I. 624 After appraisement, they gave bond for the amount, which they paid upon the vessel and cargo being decreed forfeited. **1846** COOPER *Redskins* vii, If land is wanted for a road, or a fort, or a canal, it must be taken, under a law, by appraisement. **1882** *Harper's Mag.* April 691/1 Farm property in the Animas Valley has doubled in appraisement during the past twelve months, and is now worth $100 an acre. **1913** *Statutes at Large* XXXVIII. 95 The same [Act of Congress] is hereby amended to provide that the classification and appraisement of such lands shall be completed.

***Appraiser.** A person appointed to appraise property.

1677 [see APPRAISEMENT]. **1694** *N. Car. Col. Rec.* I. 393 That Mr. George Muschamp . . . and Mr. John West be appraisers of the said estate. **1715** *Ib.* II. 206 The consideration money by the said Appraisers appointed. **1812** *Ann. 12th Congress* 1 Sess. 2288 To provide for the appointment of appraisers and measurers of builders' work and materials. **1868** *Colorado Gen. Laws* 585 The appraisers . . . shall return their appraisement . . . within ten days. **1880** *Harper's Mag.* May 901/1 The position of examiner in the Appraiser's department. **1908** *Indian Laws & Tr.* III. 382 It shall be the duty of the appraisers to ascertain the names of the . . . occupants of any such lots.

Appraisor. *Obs.* =APPRAISER. — **1676** *N.Y. St. Col. Hist.* XII. 555 As to the appraisment off Daniel Makeey Estate, whether ye can make the appraizors take the things, I can not tell. **1694** [see APPRAISEMENT].

Appreciate, *v.*

+1. *tr.* To raise (currency, property, etc.) in value. {1880–}

1778 J. PENN in *N.E. Hist. Reg.* XXX. 320, I expect Congress will in a few days agree on some plan for appreciating the currency. **1779** *Braintree Town Rec.* 502 Voted, the Town will come into measures to appreciate our Currancy. **1779** P. WEBSTER *Pol. Ess.* (1791) 33 Any probable attempt to raise or appreciate the value of the money, would hoard it immediately. **1780** J. JONES *Letters* 16 That resolution has already appreciated the money. **1787** *Ib.* 153, I am told it has had the effect to appreciate the warrants 2½ per cent. **1789** D. RAMSAY *Hist. Rev.* II. 135 The whole sum in circulation would be appreciated by a reduction of its quantity. **1857** *Lawrence* (Kansas) *Republican* 4 June 4, I see . . . our farms teeming with abundant products, and greatly appreciated in value. **1865** *Congress. Globe* 7 Feb. 639/1 A Federal victory appreciates our currency, . . . but a Federal disaster depreciates the currency. **1874** *Congress. Rec.* 2 April 2725/2 Without any hardship you gradually appreciate the value of greenbacks and bring them up to gold. **a1889** *Rural Register* (F.), These improvements will appreciate the farm immensely.

+b. To raise in respect of character, etc.

1864 *Congress. Globe* 8 June 2796/2 The terms of the letter certainly appreciate General Butler in my estimation.

+2. *intr.* To rise in value.

1779 *Lett. to Franklin* 110, I trust our money will appreciate by just degrees. **1780** J. REED *Life & Corr.* (1847) II. 200 The Continental money has evidently appreciated and still goes on, though slowly. **1809** *Monthly Anthology* Oct. 263 Mr. Webster . . . gives 'Appreciate, *v.* to value, estimate, rise in value,' yet this third signification, being neuter or intransitive, is not, we believe, found in a single English author, and in the United States is only admitted into genteel company by inadvertence. **1869** [see APPRECIATION]. **1878** *Congress. Rec.* 13 Feb. 980/2 If silver has depreciated gold has correspondingly appreciated. **1883** *N.Y. paper* in *Pall Mall Gazette* 9 July, Prior to his death values appreciated so considerably that he became the richest man in the city. **1888** *Baltimore American* (F.), His Pennsylvania lands have not appreciated as he had hoped, and when he left the Cabinet he was a poor man.

***Appreciation.** +An increase in value or amount.

1777 ADAMS *Works* (1854) IX. 470 An act is necessary for allowing a depreciation or an appreciation . . . upon specialties. **1779** *Journals Cont. Congress* XV. 1261 Resolved, That . . . salaries . . . be annually . . . altered according to the appreciation of the continental currency. **1789** MORSE *Amer. Geog.* 120 This difference may be considered rather as an appreciation of gold and silver, than a depreciation of paper. **1792** HAMILTON *Works* (Lodge) II. 314 The rapid appreciation of the debt. **1869** *Congress. Globe* 27 Feb. 1669/1, I was glad to see our bonds appreciate in the market, and that the holders should get the benefit of that appreciation. **1883** *N.Y. paper* in *Pall Mall Gazette* 9 July, John Jacob [Astor] has become, chiefly by the appreciation of the values of the property purchased by his father and grandfather, one of the three phenomenally rich men of Gotham. **1888** J. S. NICHOLSON *Treat. Money* 61 When we speak of the appreciation of gold, what we mean is, that in the countries using gold as the standard money, the general level of prices has become lower. **1896** *Boston Journal* 8 July 5/6 The act of 1873, demonetizing silver, . . . has resulted in the appreciation of gold.

***Apprentice.**

***1.** One who is bound by an agreement to give services in return for instruction in the trade or occupation of a master.

1631 *Mass. Bay Rec.* I. 90 Lucy Smith is bound as an apprentice with Mr. Roger Ludlowe for 7 yeares. **1657** *Suffolk Deeds* III. 68 The master shall sufficiently maintaine the said John Judson his apprentice, with meate, drinke, cloathing and all necessaryes meete for an apprentise to haue. **1674** SEWALL *Diary* I. 7 My Brother Stephen was bound Apprentice to Mr. Edmund Batter, Merch[ant]. **1714** *Maine Wills* 189 Untill they [= my children] shall be of suitable age to be put apprentise. **1723** *New-Eng. Courant* 23–30 Sept. 2/2 James Franklin, printer in Queen-Street, wants a likely lad for an apprentice. **1795** *Columbian Centinel* 4 March, Mr. Erving proposes to receive as apprentices to the Cotton & Woolen Manufactory . . . any number of boys or girls, from the age of ten to fourteen. **1807** *Ann. 10th Congress* 1 Sess. II. 2307 This indenture . . . witnesseth that John Strawhan . . . hath . . . placed and bound himself apprentice unto Greenbury Griffin, . . . waterman, to learn the said trade. **1817** H. M. Brooks *Gleanings* 137 Ran away from the subscriber, an indented apprentice, of the name of James Bails. **1841** A. LAWRENCE *Diary & Corr.* 159 An apprentice on board the United States ship 'Columbus,' in this harbor, thirteen years old, . . . came to-day. **1881** *Rep. Indian Affairs* p. xxxiv, The . . . job work done by apprentices in the harness, shoe, tin, and blacksmith shops. **1890** FIELD *Bright Skies* 123 The black man was no longer a slave, but an 'apprentice,' who could be 'bound out' to hard labor under conditions.

2. Attrib. with *blacksmith, boy, girl*, etc.

1723 *New-Eng. Courant* 18–25 Nov. 1/2 The young girls spend the evening and half the night in search after, or in company with apprentice boys, young merchants, &c. **1856** M. J. HOLMES *Gable-roofed House* i, Something in the face and appearance of the apprentice girl deeply interested Anna. **1883** 'MARK TWAIN' *Life Miss.* li. 503 He was an apprentice-blacksmith in our village.

Apprenticeship. The position of an apprentice. {1612–}

1644 *Southampton Rec.* I. 35 The sayd child shall be of the age of thirty years before he shall be released of his aforesayd apprenticeshippe. **1665** *Boston Rec.* 28 Robert Walker acknowledgd Thomas Jeffery his saruant hath serued his time of aprentiship. **1692** BULKELEY *Will & Doom* 250 Any man that had served . . . an apprenticeship of seven years may set up his trade without leave of any. **1737** BRICKELL *N. Carolina* 267 Neither can any Servant give a second Indenture on himself before he is out of his Apprentiship. **1855** *A. Lawrence's Diary & Corr.* 28 On the 22d of April, 1807, Mr. Lawrence became of age; and his apprenticeship, which had lasted seven years, was terminated. **1856** M. J. HOLMES *Gable-roofed House* i, Mrs. Lamport . . . refused to release Josephine until the term of her apprenticeship should have expired. **1888** *Cent. Mag.* Dec. 278/1 By the first [bill in 1861], all negroes . . . born after its passage should remain free; and all others, after suitable apprenticeship for children, should become free in the year 1893.

+Apprizal. *Obs.* Also **ap-, apprisall.** [f. APPRIZE *v.* Cf. E. *prizal* (1610).] Appraisal.

1641 *Mass. Bay Rec.* I. 319 It is ordered, that the treasurer shall pay the debts of the country at a dew apprisall. **1654** *Watertown Rec.* 46 Delivered to John Studly, in goods apon aprisall w[hi]ch goods weare a p[ar]t of Mary Danises, in some fower pownds. **1705** *Boston News-Letter* 16 April 2/1 The Receiver may cause an Apprizal of the Goods outward bound in said Ships if he pleases. **1730** SEWALL *Letter-book* II. 281 As for the charge and cost of the apprizal, . . . I will see them paid.

***Apprize,** *v. Obs.* Also **ap(p)rise.** *tr.* To appraise, value. {–1754; chiefly *Sc.*}

1638 *Springfield Rec.* I. 164 The plantation shall bye the said lotts as indifferent men shall apprise them. **1678** *Boston Rec.* 123 Wee beinge called . . . to apprise a p[ar]cell of Beau[e]r . . . doe value 13 skins . . . to be worth in mony 10 ld. **1702** *Topsfield Rec.* I. 124 Wee being sworn to aprise a Hors taken up by John Borman . . . doe aprise him at thirty Shillings. **1720** *Boston Rec.* 146 Such a sume as it shall be valued at by indifferent men chosen to apprize the same. **1730** SEWALL *Letter-book* II. 281 The Gentlemen who are to apprize the Lands at Boston. **1828** WEBSTER s.v., To apprize the goods and estate of a deceased person.

Apprizement. *Obs.* Appraisement. {1605}

1676 *Conn. Public Rec.* II. 313 The overpluss of the apprizment is not returnable to the debtor. **1679** *Ib.* III. 43 Judgments and apprizements shall be duely made. **1684** *Hempstead Town Rec.* I. 432 An aprizement of the estate. **1701** *Boston Rec.* 16 [He] shall make application to one of His Maj[es]ties justices of the peace within this town, to order an apprizement, award and give judgment. **1720** *Mass. H. Repr. Journals* II. 311 The Commissioners . . . are directed and required to accept no apprizement of lands . . . unless they are duly certified. **1730** SEWALL *Letter-book* II. 283, [I] desire you to be . . . speedy with the Apprizement of the Shrewsbury and Ruttland Farms. **1828** WEBSTER s.v., He purchased the article at the apprizement.

Apprizer. *Obs.* Also **-ser, -sor.** One who appraises. {1609–1815, *Sc.*}

1654 *Maine H. S. Coll.* 2 Ser. IV. 107 That the apprizers had gon contrary to theire oaths. **1673** *Plymouth Laws* 168 That two meet men of good judgment be chosen apprisers. **1676** *Conn. Probate Rec.* I. 309 She made a true presentment of the Estate . . . to the apprisers. **1694** *N. Car. Col. Rec.* I. 421 Two of the apprisors appointed to apprise the estate . . . are by departure or sickness disabled. **1710** *Boston Rec.* 109 They do nominate Capt. Timo. Clark to be one of the apprizers there of. **1730** SEWALL *Letter-book* II. 281 To put down . . . the sum each piece is apprized at, with the Names of the apprizers at the Bottom signed by them. **1828** WEBSTER s.v., When apprizers act under the authority of law, they must be sworn. **1857** H. RILEY *Puddleford P.* (1875) 179 Now, Mr. Sheriff, . . . bring on your ap*prizers*; a thousand dollars' worth of property to pay a little over three hundred.

***Approach,** *n.* **1.** =APPROACHING *vbl. n.* **+2.** The making of secret overtures for the purpose of influencing a person's actions. — **(1) 1850** GARRARD *Wah-To-Yah* i. 21 St. Vrain, dismounting, took his rifle, and soon was on the 'approach,' leaving us . . . to await the gun report. — **(2) 1893** *Congress. Rec.* 28 Sept. 1874/1 The idea that he [Samuel Hooper] was subject to approach is . . . ridiculous.

***Approach,** *v.*

+1. *tr.* In hunting: To steal up on (an animal or herd). Cf. APPROACHING.

1833 CATLIN *Indians* I. 219 We saw immense herds of buffaloes; and although we had no horses to run them, we successfully approached them on foot. **1846** SAGE *Scenes Rocky Mts.* v, Thus early, I had learned, that to approach buffalo with success, the hunter should carefully maintain the leeward. **1850** GARRARD *Wah-To-Yah* i. 13 Branson and I . . . 'approached' a band of bulls. **1872** EGGLESTON *Hoosier Schoolm.* iv. 49 He approached a word as Bull approached the raccoon. *transf.* **1847** PARKMAN in *Knickerb.* XXX. 129 'What do you mean to do?' 'I shall "approach,"' replied the Captain. 'You don't mean to "approach" with your pistols, do you?'

+2. To make overtures to (a person) in order to influence his actions.

1857 *Lawrence* (Kansas) *Republican* 30 July 2 An editor of this place had approached him, saying, they were about to start a Walker party in the Territory, and offering inducements to him to become an organ under it. **1893** *Congress. Rec.* Sept. 1874/1 Nearly every bit of everything that is said about public men being corrupted or approached is false.

***Approaching,** *vbl. n.* **+**In hunting: The action of stealing up on an animal or herd.

1839 TOWNSEND *Narrative of a Journey* iii. 158 They have listened to the garrulous hunter's details of 'approaching,' and 'running,' and 'quartering.' **1847** PARKMAN in *Knickerb.* XXX. 129 Pistols, rifles, 'running' and 'approaching' were mingled in an inextricable medley in his brain. **1849** — *Oregon Trail* 91 *note*, In 'approaching' the hunter conceals himself, and crawls on the ground towards the game, or lies in wait to kill them.

Approbamus. [L., 'we approve.'] A certificate of approbation given to a student. — **1774** BELKNAP in *Life* (1847) 71 (Hall), [The Indian] appeared to be an ingenious, sensible, serious young man; and we gave him an *approbamus*, of which there is a copy on the next page.

***Approbate,** *v.* {–1623}

***1.** *tr.* To approve or sanction legally or formally. {After 1600 only in Sc. law (1836–80).}

1716 *Narrag. Hist. Reg.* III. 278 Every innholder who shall be approbated by the Selectmen. **1761** *Boston Selectmen* 21 Oct. 165 Mrs. Simpson apply'd to the Select men for their approbation as an inholder . . . and was approbated accordingly. **1782** I. PUTNAM in Lossing *Encycl. U.S. Hist.* II. 1163/1 The authority of this town [Brookline] . . . have run into a great error in approbating an additional number of public houses. **1798** Hall *Coll. Words* (1856) 13 By the twelfth statute, a student [of Harvard] incurs . . . no penalty by declaiming . . . without having his piece previously approbated. **1812** *Advt.* in *Boston Gazette* 25 June (Th.), Diplomas for Physicians and Graduates engrossed according to the latest form approbated by the President of Harvard University. **1832** WILLIAMSON *Maine* II. 698 At the monthly meetings, they [Friends] record births and deaths, . . . [and] approbate marriages. **1842** *Mass. Acts & Resolves* 623 The agent . . . pressed me, in an urgent manner, to approbate the proposed measure. **1847** [J. MITCHELL] *Scenes & Characters* 195 How often does the professor whose duty it is to criticise and approbate the pieces for this exhibition wish they were better!

+b. In ecclesiastical use: To certify that (a person) is qualified to preach.

1779 E. PARKMAN *Diary* 113 He was graduated at Yale College, [and] approbated by the Association at New London. **1816** PICKERING 36 *To Approbate* . . . is now in common use with our clergy as a sort of technical term, to denote a person who is licensed to preach. **a1852** J. S. POPKIN in *Mem.* p. lxxxv, I was approbated by the Boston Association. **1853** [see APPROBATION]. **1882** *Schaff's Relig. Encycl.* I. 720/2 In 1769 he [Nathanael Emmons] was approbated as a preacher.

2. To approve of; to regard with favor. {1623}

'We sometimes see *approbate, belittle, jeopardize, engagedness, grade*, and *lengthy* in books. . . . But none of these I presume can be said to have the stamp of good use among us' (1836 L. Matthews *Lectures* 130).

1802 *Balance* (Hudson, N.Y.) 26 Jan. 27 (Th.), A Boston Editor, in a rage for approbating Mr. Jefferson's mode of addressing Congress. **1802** *Mass. Spy* 31 March (Th.), The administration of Governor Strong is generally and thoroughly approbated. **1811** WEEMS *Letters* III. 47 Let me know whether you approbate my advice in a former letter. **1845** JUDD *Margaret* I. vi. 28, I approbated the girl . . . that she manifests such improvement in speech. **1859** O. PRATT in *Journal of Discourses* VI. 352–3 (Th.), If the Lord did not intend to approbate a crime, he would have reproved him. **1861** O. J. VICTOR *Hist. Rebellion* I. 192/1 While they [=Mississippi delegates] regret the necessity for this action, they approbate it. **1870** *Congress Globe* 17 Feb. 1373/2 In no single instance does Holy Writ approbate it.

* **Approbation.** Formal authorization or approval. {–1839}

*a***1649** WINTHROP *Hist.* I. 66 The matter was debated . . . and, by the approbation of all the assembly, except three, was concluded an error. **1653** *Portsmouth Rec.* 61 To forfeit 5 pound for euery month that he . . . shall stay longer . . . without the aprobation of the Towne. **1692** *Boston Rec.* 212 It is orderd that . . . no parson put any cow into the comon . . . without the approbation and a note to the cow keepers. **1718** *H. Repr. Mass. Journals* II. 90 A plot of 200 acres of land, laid out by Jonas Haughton, Surveyor, . . . presented to the House for Approbation. **1730** J. COMER *Diary* (1923) 108 [They] declined to stand on the stool of approbation at Newport. **1776** *Journals Cont. Congress* V. 425 Resolved, . . . That a plan of confederation be prepared and transmitted to the respective Colonies for their consideration and approbation. **1853** M. BLAKE *Mendon Association* 76 List of persons approbated to preach the Gospel, with the date of their approbation.

* **Appropriation.**

+**1.** The setting apart of a sum of money for a special purpose; the sum so assigned. {1858–}

1761 *Descr. S. Carolina* 35 The after mentioned heads of appropriation will best shew in what manner those public revenues are applied. **1787** *Constitution* i. § 9 No money shall be drawn from the treasury but in consequence of appropriations made by law. **1789** *Ann. 1st Congress* I. 91 The bill making appropriations for the service of the present year. **1812** *Niles' Reg.* II. 350/2 The appropriation for 1813 . . . will probably be more than two millions. **1827** [G. MELLEN] *Chronicle of '26* 33, I think the House should make appropriation. **1835** [INGRAHAM] *South-West* I. 234 Appropriations have been made for public schools. **1841** *S. Lit. Messenger* VII. 17/2 The work upon it has been suspended for the want of an appropriation. **1861** *Army Regulations* 161 The commutation shall be charged to the appropriation for the work. **1874** *Vermont Bd. Agric. Rep.* II. 768 As there is an appropriation to pay express charges, such charges need not be prepaid. **1887** GEORGE *40 Years on Rail* 253 As no appropriation was made by Congress to defray the cost, Mr. Armstrong . . . fitted up a car at his own expense. **1894** *Dept. Agric. Yearbook* 39 Out of this appropriation money will be used to make analyses of food materials not heretofore analyzed. **1903** *Profitable Advertising* Nov. 474 For a nominal appropriation we shall be pleased to submit preliminary sketches.

2. Attrib. with *act, law.*

1812 *Niles' Reg.* II. 131/1 The appropriation laws of the United States for the year 1812, were passed about the 21st and 24th of February last. **1894** *Dept. Agric. Yearbook* 37 The terms of the appropriation act.

+**Appropriation bill.** A legislative bill proposing or authorizing an appropriation of money.

1789 *Ann. 1st Congress* I. 928 A message was received from the Senate, with the Invalids, and the Appropriation bills, to which sundry amendments were proposed. **1802** *Steele Papers* (1924) I. 262 The house have passed a partial appropriation bill for the civil list. **1820** *Niles' Reg.* XVIII. 33/1 The time spent in debating on the Missouri bill, has delayed the passage of the annual appropriation bills by congress. **1853** *Mich. Agric. Soc. Trans.* IV. 387 Our law makers find plenty of time to pass appropriation bills to pay their own expenses. **1861** *Chicago Tribune* 19 July 1/6 The House concurred in the Senate's amendment to the navy Appropriation bill. **1873** BEADLE *Undevel. West* 528 Congress did not adjourn without passing the Indian Appropriation Bill. **1897** *Boston Journal* 27 Jan. 10/2 The Committee . . . reported an appropriation bill of $150,000 for the extermination of the gypsy moth.

* **Approved,** *ppl. a.* +(See quotation.) — **1809** KENDALL *Travels* I. 17 There is a distinction [in Conn.] between *settled, approved* and *lawful inhabitants,* and the contrary.

* **Appurtenance.** A minor property, right or privilege, attached to another.

1639 T. Lechford *Note-Book* (1885) 157 One little house and one frame with all the timbers and appurtenances thereto belonging. **1640** *Suffolk Deeds* I. 15 A messuage called Winesemet with the apurtainances. **1688** SEWALL *Diary* I. 221 The said Hogg-Island, with the members and appurtenances thereof. **1724** *Maine Wills* 265, I give & bequeath unto my beloved son . . . the houses, buildings & appurtenances thereto belonging. **1789** MORSE *Amer. Geog.* 176 Ebenezer Crafts and Jacob Davis . . . gave a . . . mansion house, lands and appurtenances, in Leicester [Mass.], for that use. **1837** PECK *Gaz. Illinois* 131 Comfortable dwellings, fine barns and all appurtenances. **1846** DUNHAM *Legal Forms* 21 To have and to hold the same premises, with all the privileges and appurtenances thereto belonging. **1880** BARNET *Dict. Commercial Use* 24 Appurtenances of a ship include whatever is on board a ship for the objects of the voyage and adventure in which she is engaged, belonging to the owner. **1889** F. B. CLARK *Form Book* (ed. 2) 221 The following described real estate . . . with the appurtenances thereunto belonging.

* **Apricot.** Also †**apricock.** The plum-like fruit of the apricot-tree; the tree itself (cf. next).

1676 GLOVER *Acc. Va.* in *Phil. Trans.* XI. 628 Here are likewise Apricocks, and some sorts of English Plums. **1743** CATESBY *Carolina* II. p. xx, *Malus Armeniaca.* The Apricock-Tree. Apricocks no more than peaches agree well with this climate; though both these trees arrive to a large stature. **1771** FRENEAU *Poems* (1786) 51 Orchards . . . Laden with apples red, sweet scented peach, Pear, cherry, apricot, or spungy plumb. **1792** IMLAY *Western Territory* 92 Kentucky produces . . . all the fruits, with the addition of apricots and nectarines. **1815** DRAKE *Cincinnati* 55 Some finer varieties [of cherries and plums] . . . as well as the apricot and nectarine, have not yet been successfully cultivated. **1838** C. NEWELL *Revol. Texas* 169 The Apricot is adapted to the climate of Texas. **1847** WOOD *Botany* 242 *Prunus Armeniaca,* Willd. Common Apricot . . . Fruit . . . ripe July, Aug. *Ib.,* Black Apricot; . . . flowers white . . . ; fruit dark purple when mature. **1862** *Rep. Comm. Patents: Agric.* 163 Apricots and Figs of native varieties are produced, but none of any varieties having repute. **1881** *Rep. Indian Affairs* 140 The Indians produce corn, . . . peaches, plums, apricots, and grapes.

* **Apricot-tree.** The tree (*Prunus Armeniaca,* or a variety of this) which bears the apricot.

1709 LAWSON *Carolina* 110 The biggest apricock-tree I ever saw, as they told me, was grafted on a peach-stock, in the ground. **1737** BRICKELL *N. Carolina* 102 The apricock-tree grows to be very large, exceeding most apple trees. **1743** [see prec.]. **1846** BROWNE *Trees Amer.* 243 *P. A. Ovalifolia.* Oval-leaved Apricot-tree, the leaves of which are oval, and the fruit small. . . . *P. A. Cordifolia.* Heart-shaped-leaved Apricot-tree, with broad, heart-shaped leaves, and large fruit.

+**April-currant.** *Obs.* (See quotation.) — **1737** BRICKELL *N. Carolina* 89 April-Currans [*sic*] so call'd, from their being ripe in that month, grow on the banks of the rivers, or where clay has been thrown up; the fruit when ripe is red, and very soon gone.

* **Apron.**

+**1.** A covering or flap (in a vehicle, canoe, etc.) which protects like an apron. {1879} Also attrib.

1790 *Penna. Packet* 22 April 2/1 For Sale, . . . a new Sulkey, with a top and apron, and harness compleat. **1805** LEWIS & CLARK *Orig. Journals* (1904) III. II. 168 Their canoes are . . . very light, wide in the middle and tapers at each end, with aperns, and heads of animals carved on the bow. **1869** ALCOTT *Little Women* II. 112 When we were shut in by the wooden apron, the man drove so fast that Flo was frightened. **1880** *Harper's Mag.* Aug. 398 This canoe, with the paddle, apron, and rigging, weighs eighty-five pounds. **1893** K. SANBORN *S. California* 177 The corners of the aprons [on a saddle] are tipped with silver. **1910** J. HART *Vigilante Girl* 137 The express messenger . . . had hitched the apron-strap around his leg.

+**2.** (See quotations.)

1814 BRACKENRIDGE *Views of La.* 187 On the south side there is a broad apron or step, about half way down. *Ib.* 188 The step, or apron, has been used as a kitchen garden, by the monks of La Trappe. — **1863** RANDALL *Pract. Shepherd* vii. 71 The cross extended into a pendulous 'apron' —a short fold or two on and immediately back of each elbow. — **1876** *Field & Forest* II. 73 This mass is very conspicuous even in the rapidly swimming crab, and causes the abdominal flap (called apron by fishermen) to be opened almost to its fullest extent.

+**3.** A piece of canvas, leather, or other material forming part of some apparatus or machine.

1833 SILLIMAN *Man. Sugar Cane* 59 Although the apron gave way when the pan was first put in operation, . . . encouraging results have been obtained. **1846** *Rep. Comm. Patents* (1847) 285 What I claim is the confining apron in combination with the main cylinder. **1849** *Ib.* (1850) 226, I do not claim an endless web or apron made of metal. **1887** *Harper's Mag.* June 121/2 The fluid pulp is spread over this 'wire' from the breast board of the strainers by an 'apron' or fan-shaped rubber or oilskin cloth. **1899** *Sat. Ev. Post* 10 June 795 Eight hundred thousand yards of cotton duck . . . are used annually in making 'aprons' for the harvesters.

4. A structure in connection with a dam or sluiceway to prevent the washing away of the bottom or the banks, or to direct the course of floating objects. {1721–}

1847 *Knickerb.* XXIX. 64 The freshet has carried away the apron of our dam. **1857** HAMMOND *Northern Scenes* 131 A few rods above the place . . . was an old dam, the apron of which remained. **1871** *N.Y. Game Laws* in *Fur, Fin & Feather* (1872) 23 Which sluice-way shall be protected on each side by an apron at least one foot in height. **1902** WHITE *Blazed Trail* xlviii. 337 Shearer and Thorpe had often discussed the advisability of constructing an artificial apron of logs to receive the impact.

+**Apron-cloth.** [APRON 1.] A cloth to be drawn over the lap in an open carriage. — **1857** [D. H. STROTHER] *Virginia* 139 The apron-cloth was drawn up over their legs, and with a brisk chirrup and a crack of the whip they started into the storm.

∗ Apt, *a.* Likely. {*dial.*}

1716 SEWALL *Diary* III. 71 Am apt to think the snowy morning hindred many. **1810** M. DWIGHT *Journey to Ohio* (1912) 39, I would be *apt* to think it was a *terrible* parcel, to use the language of the people round me. **1851** *S. Lit. Messenger* XVII. 294/2 Suppose we should run agin another boat to-night, we'd be apt to go down ourselves, wouldn't we? **1864** NORTON *Army Lett.* 215 One hundred days of a summer's campaign will be apt to knock some of the romance out of him. **1904** 'O. HENRY' *Cabbages & Kings* iii. 52 'You will be apt to find Dr. Gregg at the hotel,' said the consul. **1904** *Churchman* 13 Aug. 269 The situation in France is not apt to change greatly before the meeting of the French Chambers in the autumn.

A-purpose. [A *prep.*[1]] *dial.* or *colloq.* On purpose; intentionally. {*dial.*}

1835 BIRD *Hawks of Hawk-h.* I. x. 130 We're all keeping awake, just a-purpose to be ready and handy. **1853** SIMMS *Sword & Distaff* 266 He forgot a-purpose! **1861** STOWE *Pearl Orr's Isl.* I. v. 35 Stay a bit, I'll make ye a few a-purpose. **1871** EGGLESTON in *Scribner's Mo.* II. 73, I believe the wicked minx dropped it over a purpose. **1880** 'MARK TWAIN' *Tramp Abroad* xxiii. 226 Well, if he done it a-purpose, I reckon he wouldn't stand no chance.

+Aqua(r)diente, -dente, variants of AGUARDIENTE.

1839 BRIGGS *H. Franco* I. 253 Ruffally . . . contrived to have a whole bladder of Aquadente to himself. **1845** GREEN *Texian Exped.* x. 134 Her caballero . . . serves her with either coffee, chocolate, or aquardiente and a cigarrito. **1850** GARRARD *Wah-To-Yah* xiii. 174 The room filled with gay ladies, . . . partaking of the favorite *aquardiente*, by way of support, against the fatigues of the *fandango*. **1889** MUNROE *Golden Days* iii. 22 Moore drank liberally of aquadiente, a fiery native liquor.

∗ Aqueduct.

∗1. A conduit or artificial channel for bringing water from a source; an elevated structure carrying a canal over a river or valley.

1798 *Essex Inst. Coll.* VI. 44/1 That Capt. Daniel Frye pay . . . two dollars per annum for the priviledge of the aqueduct. *Ib.* 44/2 A certain aqueduct called 'Frye's Aqueduct.' **1800** *Mass. H. S. Coll.* VI. 215 From this pond proceeds a brook, which . . . receives the springs, which supply the aqueduct of the town. **1818** *Niles' Reg.* XV. 16/2 Three aqueducts have been thrown across valleys intervening in the course of the canal. **1837** PECK *New Guide* 179 The aqueduct of the Pennsylvania canal, across the Alleghany river. *a***1864** BUSHNELL *Work & Play* 290 Mr. Madison, for example, had an aqueduct of logs. **1889** BRAYLEY *Boston Fire Dept.* 201 Forty-nine reservoirs . . . were placed in convenient parts of the city. . . . Besides the above, there were thirty-three fire-plugs in the aqueducts. **1890** *Century Mag.* Dec. 188 My father . . . about fifty years ago made a stone aqueduct.

2. Attrib. with *bridge*, *company*, *corporation*, etc.

1796 *Mass. Statute* 10 June 5 The Corporation . . . for bringing fresh water into Boston by subterraneous Pipes, shall be empower'd to assume the appellation of 'The Aqueduct Corporation.' **1798** *Ib.* 21 June 14 A Corporation by the name of 'The first Aqueduct Company in Wrentham.' **1821** *Jrnl. Science* III. 161 Aqueduct bridges of wood or iron. **1856** D. MACLEOD *F. Wood* 170 The Croton Aqueduct Department attends to the sewerage. **1878** *Harper's Mag.* Mar. 483/1 The aqueduct pipes form an arch two hundred feet clear span, supporting a roadway.

∗ Arable, *a.* Also †**arabell, arrable, aurable.** Capable of being plowed; suitable for tillage or cultivation.

In freq. use from *c*1820, esp. with *land*.

1655 *Essex Probate Rec.* I. 208 Arrable ground at home. **1662** *Brookhaven Rec.* 7 With all the meadow, and pasture, arable land, . . . within the limits. **1664** *Rowley Rec.* 152 Two hundred acres of pasture land . . . within which is included . . . his plowing or aurable land. **1672** *Derby* (Conn.) *Rec.* 49 One lott of arable land containing seven acers. **1708** *Providence Rec.* XVII. 243 It being upland, low Land, arabell Land, meadow & Orchard. **1789** MORSE *Amer. Geog.* 50 Numerous tracts of fine arable and grazing land intervene between the ridges. **1796** *Ann. 4th Congress* 2 Sess. 2648 Arable land, . . . at one shilling per acre. **1840** *Michigan Agric. Soc. Trans.* (1853) 315 While the Peninsula of Michigan has been most liberally supplied with an uncommonly deep and arable soil, . . . the States of Ohio and Indiana . . . are in great part destitute. **1854** BARTLETT *Narr.* II. 97 Without wood, water, or arable land, this place can never rise to importance. **1883** *Rep. Indian Affairs* 139 This reservation consists of a table-land . . . of which over 300,000 [acres] is arable.

+Arancel, -sel. *S.W.* [Sp. *arancil* tariff.] A tariff or import duty. — **1836** HOLLEY *Texas* xi. 214 In conformity with the last fee bill, Arancel, of notary public's of the ancient audience of Mexico. **1844** GREGG *Commerce of Prairies* I. 114 All the coarser cotton goods . . . were prohibited by the *Arancel* of 1837; and still continue to be, with some modifications. **1888** J. WEBB *Adventures* 12 (MS.), One third 'Aransel' or import duties on all goods sold in each state.

+Arapajo, -aho, variants of APAREJO. — **1854** DELANO *Life on Plains* 334 We purchased 12 beautiful Peruvian mules, with necessary arapahoes (Mexican pack saddles). **1903** WHITE *Forest* iii. 24 One hears strange, suggestive words and phrases—arapajo, capote, . . . and a dozen others coined into the tender of daily use.

+Arbor Day. [L. *arbor* tree.] A day of each year legally set apart for the planting of trees wherever required. {1897–} Also attrib.

Introduced in Nebraska in 1872, and afterwards adopted by certain other states.

1872 Eggleston *Arbor Day* (1896) 14 Resolved, That Wednesday, the 10th day of April, 1872, be . . . consecrated for tree planting in the State of Nebraska, and the state board of agriculture hereby name it Arbor Day. **1873** *Nebraska Bd. of Agric. Rep.* 333 To become a competitor, and entitled to the 'Arbor Day' premiums, the planting may be done on any day in the month of April. **1886** *Pop. Sci. Monthly* March 691 The Arbor-day idea . . . has been formally adopted already by seventeen of our States. **1889** *Harper's Mag.* July 312/1 Arbor Day . . . reminds us of the indirect ministry of trees as guardians of the sources of rivers. *Ib.* 313 Arbor Day will make the country visibly more beautiful every year. **1892** *Congress. Rec.* June 5404/2 In every quarter of the country 'arbor days' are days named by law, and also by custom, for planting forest trees to make lumber for the generations yet to come. **1903** *Nation* 29 Oct. 340 Miss Jarvis seems to think that on 'Arbor Day' every American is moved by an irresistible impulse to plant a tree.

Arboretum. [L.] A botanical tree-garden. {1838–} — **1852** *Harper's Mag.* Dec. 6 An *arboretum*, or scientific collection of trees, forming a kind of boundary plantation to the whole area. *c***1881** *King's Handbook Boston* (ed. 4) 125 An arboretum [i.e. Arnold's] which will ultimately contain all trees, shrubs, and herbaceous plants that can grow there in the open air.

Arbor vitae. [L., 'tree of life.']

1. One or other species of evergreen shrubs or trees belonging to the genus *Thuya* or *Thuja*, esp. the white cedar, *T. occidentalis*, of the northern states. {1664–}

1781–2 JEFFERSON *Notes Va.* (1787) 39 Arbor vitae, *Thuya occidentalis.* **1785** MARSHALL *Amer. Grove* 151 Arbor Vitae, or Tree of Life. *Ib.* 152 Striped leaved Arbor Vitæ. **1785–** [see AMERICAN ARBOR-VITAE]. **1815** DRAKE *Cincinnati* ii. 83 The arbor vitae, hemlock, yew, . . . I have only found at the falls of the Little Miami. **1832** BROWNE *Sylva Amer.* 303 The arbor vitæ is 45 or 50 feet in height. **1847** WOOD *Botany* 517 Arbor Vitæ . . . abounds in . . . the northern parts of the U.S. on the rocky borders of streams and lakes. . . . The wood is very light, soft and durable. Its most important use is for fences. **1848** E. BRYANT *California* 225 Among the varieties of trees I noticed . . . the Chinese *arbor vitae.* *a***1861** T. WINTHROP *Open Air* 25 As soon as through the riverside belt of gnarled arbor-vitae sunbeams flickered. **1863** B. TAYLOR *H. Thurston* ii. 35 Mrs. Babb . . . had gathered . . . chrysanthemums, with some sprigs of arbor-vitæ, and stuck them into an old glass flower-jar. **1878** STOWE *Poganuc People* iii. 28 The arbor vitæ, the spruce, the cedar and juniper, with their balsamic breath, filled the aisles with a spicy fragrance. **1892** APGAR *Trees Northern U.S.* 194 *Thuya orientalis*, L. (Eastern or Chinese Arbor-Vitæ) . . . is not so good a species for general cultivation. *Ib.*, *Thuya gigantea*, Nutt. (Giant Arbor-Vitæ) . . . [is] a very large and graceful tree . . . from the Pacific coast.

2. Attrib. with *tree*.

1839 *S. Lit. Messenger* V. 475/1 Arbor-vitæ trees that love . . . limestone cliffs. **1863** 'GAIL HAMILTON' *Gala-Days* 70 The arbor-vitæ trees growing wild along the river banks. **1910** C. HARRIS *Eve's Husband* 31 An arbor-vitæ tree in our family plot.

∗ Arbutus. A shrub or tree of the genus *Arbutus* belonging to the heath family; esp. the strawberry-tree, *A. Unedo*, characterized by bright scarlet berries, and freq. cultivated for ornamental purposes. Also attrib.

1785 MARSHALL *Amer. Grove* 42 *Epigæa repens.* Trailing Arbutus. This grows naturally upon northern hills, or mountains, with trailing shrubby stalks. **1808** ASHE *Travels* xiii. 119 The shrubs distinguishing the Reach, are the arbutus and the honey locust. **1846** WEBB *Altowan* I. iv. 142 Dwarf arbutus . . . forms the principal ingredient of Indian fumigation. **1866** MRS. WHITNEY *L. Goldthwaite* viii, Tiny trails of wintergreen and arbutus, filled . . . a china dish upon her bureau top. **1880** *Harper's Mag.* June 72 There was the shy Arbutus too. And where in all New England does that darling show so full and sweet a face as in its home upon that sunny slope. **1884** ROE *Nature's Story* 175 In the twilight the explorers returned with handfuls of hepatica and arbutus buds.

Arcade. [Fr.] A long arched or roofed passageway; any covered avenue, esp. one that has a row of shops, stalls, etc., on one or both sides. {1731–}

1834 *Phila. As It Is* 14 The Arcade stands on Chesnut street, west of Sixth street. . . . The first story is occupied as stores and shops. **1849** WILLIS *Rural Lett.* xiv. 126 Wherever there is a butcher's shop and a post-office, . . . an 'Arcade' and a milliner. **1851** CIST *Cincinnati* 167 The Metropolitan Bath House . . . consist[s] of an arcade of 130 feet in length. **1865** *Atlantic Mo.* XV. 718 The large hotel, to which the cottage was attached by a long arcade or covered gallery. **1884** CABLE *Dr. Sevier* xl. 300 The quaint gas-lit arcades of any of the market-houses.

∗ Arch. **+1.** A small storage vault cut through the lower wall of a cellar. **+2.** An arched structure in a boiling house for maple sugar. — **(1)** **1845** *Lowell Offering* V. 256 We . . . descend into her cellar. . . . Here is a nice arch for potatoes and all other freeze-able commodities. **(2)**

1874 *Vermont Bd. Agric. Rep.* II. 729 The sugar house . . . should be large enough to accommodate the arches for boiling and sugaring off. *Ib.*, A separate arch for sugaring off should not be dispensed with. **1878** *Ib.* V. 110 Almost any intelligent farmer knows how to build an arch. *Ib.*, The whole length flue [should be] the whole width of the arch.

+**Archee.** A chief official in the Mormon Church. — **1882** MRS. WAITE *Adv. Far West* 250 Brigham Young and his two Counselors form the First Presidency, under the title of the Gods, or Grand Archees. . . . A few, also, of the Apostles, hold the rank of Grand Archees. . . . Next in importance, is a body of men called Archees. *Ib.* 251 The Archees have discretionary and independent power over the lives of all gentiles and 'apostates.'

* **Archery.** The art or practice of shooting with bow and arrow. Also attrib.

1647 *R.I. Col. Rec.* I. 160 That such Lawes be made . . . to propagate Archerie, which is both man-like and profitable. *Ib.* 186 To the end also that we may come to outshoot these natives in their own bow; Be it enacted . . . that that statute touching Archerie, shall be revived and propagated throwout the whole Colonie. **1828** WEBSTER s.v. *Bow*, The use of the bow is called archery. **1881** [M. SHERWOOD] *Home Amusements* 124 Indeed, it looks as if Archery were to prove a very formidable rival to Lawn Tennis. **1882** *Harper's Mag.* Dec. 58/2 Arlington rejoices . . . in an archery club and a 'German.' **1886** *Outing* VII. 377/2 It is well known that here in the United States archery is but little practiced. **1894** T. C. KNAUFF *Athletics* 306 Why such a noble and interesting sport as archery has been suffered to decline, . . . it is hard to explain.

* **Architect.**

* **1. a.** A master builder. **b.** One who professionally prepares the plans or designs of houses or other buildings, and superintends their erection.

1771 JEFFERSON *Let. to T. Adams* 1 June, I desired the favor of you to procure me an architect. I . . . request . . . that you will send him in as soon as you can. **1788** FRENEAU *Misc. Works* 399 Of such a structure that it is possible the architect might have been inwardly composing soliloquies . . . at the time he was employed in constructing it. **1801** PERRY *Royal Dict.*, *Architect*, a chief builder, designer, and surveyor of buildings. **1822** *Ann. 17th Congress* 1 Sess. I. 387 That the Architect of the Public Buildings be in future appointed by the President . . . with the advice and consent of the Senate. **1840** COOPER *Deerslayer* xi, Opening for himself doors in spots where the architects had neglected to place them. **1871** [L. H. BAGG] *At Yale* 126 David R. Brown was the architect; the masonry was superintended by Lyman Treat. **1897** MOORE *How To Build* i. 2 Select an honest architect, one who will not accept a commission from contractors or dealers in materials.

+**2.** *Architect's linen* (see quotations).

1880 *Harper's Mag.* Oct. 659/2 In modern work what is called 'architect's linen' is used instead of parchment,—a transparent linen on which the pattern can be easily traced.

* **Architecture.** The art or science of building or constructing; a particular method or style of this.

1781-2 JEFFERSON *Notes Va.* (1788) 163 The genius of architecture seems to have shed its maledictions over this land. **1812** CLAY *Speeches* (1860) I. 30 Nor . . . could we derive any apology . . . from the want of materials for naval architecture. **1823** COOPER *Pioneers* iii, The village . . . consisted of some fifty buildings, . . . which, in their architecture, bore no great marks of taste. **1825** NEAL *Bro. Jonathan* III. 382 Here was a cluster of one story houses, . . . a sort of rubble architecture. **1844** S. M. FULLER *Summer on Lakes* 47 Sometimes they looked attractive,—the little brown houses, the natural architecture of the country.

Archives. Records of historical value or importance; public documents. {1638-}

1783 R. R. LIVINGSTON in Sparks *Corr. Rev.* IV. 2 That the troops be withdrawn, without carrying off any property; . . . that records and archives shall be restored. **1821** *Ann. 17th Congress* 1 Sess. II. 2519 You will . . . demand and receive . . . all the remaining archives and documents which ought to have been transferred to the United States on the cession of this province [of Florida]. **1838** *Diplom. Corr. Texas* (1908) I. 330 You will on your arrival there take possession of the archives of the Texian Legation. **1865** *Chicago Tribune* 10 April 1 Five hundred barrels government archives, to be shipped in four lots. **1881-5** MCCLELLAN *Own Story* 93 The defence of the capital, containing, as it did, the executive and legislative, the archives of the government . . . was a matter of vital importance.

+**Arch kettle.** [ARCH.] A kettle for boiling maple sap. — **1898** I. H. HARPER *S. B. Anthony* I. 7 Opening out of the kitchen was a room containing the cheese press, and the big arch kettle.

+**Arch-stone State.** Occasional for: The 'Keystone State,' Pennsylvania. — **1840** *Congress. Globe* 25 Jan., App. 263 In this severance and sectioning, what would Pennsylvania, that 'arch-stone' State, say?

+**Arc lamp.** 'A lamp in which the light is given out by an electric arc' (*Cent.*) — **1883** H. GREER *Dict. Electricity* 181 There are several forms of Weston arc lamps. *Ib.* 183 Mr. Weston has devised several forms of automatic cut-outs for use in his arc lamps. **1901** MERWIN & WEBSTER *Calumet K* xvi. 307 She disappeared in the shadow of an arc lamp.

+**Arc light.** An electric light produced by the voltaic arc. — **1885** BROCKETT *Our Country's Progress* 653/2 The arc light is no longer an experiment, either as regards its practicability or economy. *Ib.* 654/1 For small rooms, offices, and dwellings the arc light is utterly unsuited. **1905** N. DAVIS *Northerner* 229 Under the arc-light . . . the whole scene was illumined as if by a noonday sun. *Ib.* 243 The steady glare of the arc-light beyond. **1906** F. LYNDE *Quickening* 220 Tom was under the arc-light at the gates.

* **Arctic,** *n.* +A warm, frequently fur-lined, waterproof overshoe, suitable for cold or stormy weather. Usu. *pl.*

1878 'MARK TWAIN' in *Atl. Mo.* XLI. 327 He shook the snow of his native city from his arctics, and went forth into the world. **1884** NYE *Baled Hay* 66 My arctics stand where I can reach them in case it [=the weather] should change its mind. **1886** *Leslie's Mo.* April 391/2 A pair of lumberman's boots, . . . protected below [the knee] by a stout pair of arctics. **1891** S. M. WELCH *Recoll. 1830-40* 173 India rubbers, arctics or 'gums,' were not then invented. **1895** KING *Fort Frayne* xii. 162 Seven soldiers in their fur caps . . . and arctics. **1911** *Springfield W. Republican* 9 Feb. 16 A new pair of arctics, the single buckle kind.

attrib. **1890** *Harper's Mag.* June 69/2 To see Mr. Fox pacing the platform . . . with mittens and arctic overshoes.

* **Arctic,** *a.* In specific names of birds (see quotations). {c1780-}

1839 PEABODY *Mass. Birds* 276 The Arctic, or White-Horned Owl, *Strix arctica*, is a rare and beautiful bird. *Ib.* 382 The Arctic Jager, *Lestris parasiticus*, . . . by means of its long tail, . . . can suddenly check its flight or change its direction. **1844** *Nat. Hist. N.Y., Zoology* II. 190 The Arctic Woodpecker, *Picus arcticus*, . . . has been seen in Pennsylvania. . . . Geographic range from New-York to the Arctic regions. *Ib.* 282 The Arctic Puffin, *Mormon arcticus*, . . . visits the coast of this State almost every winter. *Ib.* 302 The Arctic Tern, *Sterna arctica*, . . . is not rare in the autumn on the seacoast . . . of New-Jersey. **1869** *Amer. Naturalist* III. 32 Arctic Bluebird (*Sialia arctica*) . . . is more shy and silent than either of the other species. *Ib.* 78 Arctic Ground-Finch (*Pipilo arcticus*). **1874** COUES *Birds N.W.* 686 Arctic Tern. . . . North America generally, south to the Middle States, and on the Pacific side to California.

* **Ardent,** *a.* and *n.*

* **1.** *Ardent spirits*, distilled alcoholic liquors, such as rum, brandy, whisky, or gin.

1790 S. DEANE *New-Eng. Farmer* 21/2 The use of ardent spirits, which are more costly, and less wholesome than beer, might thus be lessened. **1792** *Ann. 2nd Congress* 1023 Ardent spirits and malt liquors are . . . the two principal manufactures of grain. **1811** *Ann. 12th Congress* 1 Sess. 2073 While the consumption of ardent spirits continues to form so common a drink, . . . it will operate against the use of malt liquors. **1821** SCOTT in *National Gazette* 22 Dec., Scheme for restricting the Use of Ardent Spirits in the United States. **1837** PECK *New Guide* 153 The introduction of ardent spirits, and of several diseases, are the evils furnished the Indian race, by contact with the whites. **1851** *Harper's Mag.* Aug. 413/2 The article prohibiting licenses for the sale of ardent spirits . . . was also adopted. **1874** GLISAN *Jrnl. Army Life* 456 The use of ardent spirits . . . is very common in the service. **1881** *Rep. Indian Affairs* p. xxx, Existing statutes prohibit the introduction of ardent spirits into the Indian country under any pretense.

+**2.** *The ardent(s)*, ardent spirits; alcoholic liquor.

1835 MCCALL *Lett. from Frontiers* (1868) 286 They were, as ever, quiet and well-behaved, although they indulged freely in the *ardents*. **1836** CROCKETT *Exploits* 170 The water [was] delightful, especially when mixed with a little of the ardent. **1860** *Harper's Mag.* July 277/1 A man who was termed 'a first-rate fellow,' excepting his fondness for the 'ardent.' **1902** MCFAUL *Ike Glidden* xiv. 108 He knew Ben had a likin' fer a taste o' the ardent, and he took a bottle o' sp'rits with him.

+**Are,** *adv. dial.* Also **air, 'air, ar.** [E. (colloq.) *'ere* reduced from *there.*] There, redundantly after *that* or *them.*

1825 NEAL *Bro. Jonathan* I. 244 Is that 'air fellow gone yet? **1834** DAVIS *Lett. J. Downing* 15 If you can't get them are pantaloons mended. **a1845** S. Smith *Theatr. Apprent.* 214 If you serve me that ar kind of a trick! **1878** STOWE *Poganuc People* i. 11 Your papa . . . don't believe in keeping none of them air prayer-book days. **1903** I. BACHELLER *Darrel* ix. 92 That air girl had a mighty power in her eye.

* **Area.**

+**1.** *The Area of Freedom*, the United States, as contrasted with neighboring subject countries.

'A phrase which came into use in connection with the annexation of Texas' (Th.).

1845 *Congress. Globe* 8 Jan., App. 79/1 Is our aid invoked to relieve her [=Texas] from a condition of servitude and extend 'the area of freedom'? Why, sir, in the same breath in which we are called upon to extend 'the area of freedom,' we are assured [etc.]. *Ib.* 25 Jan. 188, 190. **1848** LOWELL *Biglow P.* I. v, Thet's the reason I want to spread Freedom's aree.

2. A sunken space or court before the windows and door of a basement story, usu. fenced off from the street by railings. {1694-}

1864 T. L. NICHOLS *Amer. Life* II. 159 He . . . was found dead one day from having staggered into an area. **1897** MOORE *How to Build* ii. 9 In city houses 'areas' should be constructed to secure light for cellar windows.

b. Attrib. with *fence, rail, railing.*

1847 *Knickerb.* XXX. 220 He leaped the area-rail and dashed the frail support away. **1856** D. MACLEOD *F. Wood* 205 You saw some of them lounging about upon drinking-house steps, over area-railings, looking on, as calm, uninterested judges of a street-fight. **1862** *Trial C. M. Jefferds* 8 The prisoner fled into Sixteenth street, . . . sprang over an area fence, and hid himself under a stoop.

+**3.** *Area-way*, an area (in sense 2) serving as a passage.

1903 *N.Y. Times* 30 Oct. 1 The body was concealed in the home until Monday night, when it was placed in the areaway. **1907** *Chicago Ev. Post* 4 May 3 The building is connected with the main hospital by a covered areaway. **1916** W. A. DU PUY *Uncle Sam* 52 The areaway upon which its single window looked.

***Arethusa.**

+**1.** A small swamp-plant, *A. bulbosa*, bearing a handsome rose-colored flower.

1819 M'MURTRIE *Sk. Louisville* 212 Bulbous Arethusa. . . . Drooping d[itt]o. **1843** HAWTHORNE *Note-books* II. 132 The appearance of the . . . Arethusa, one of the . . . sweetest of the whole race of flowers. **1847** WOOD *Botany* 535 *A. bulbosa.* Bulbous Arethusa. . . . This beautiful and interesting plant is found only in wet meadows and swamps, Can. to Va. **1887** BURROUGHS in *Century Mag.* July 324 Still another pretty flower that perpetuates the name of a Grecian nymph . . . is the Arethusa. **1896** S. HALE *Letters* 298 We started off on a great walk after arethusa.

+**2.** A species of orchis (*Pogonia*).

1836 LINCOLN *Botany* App. 126 *Pogonia ophioglossoides* (snake-mouth arethusa). **1840** DEWEY *Mass. Flowering Plants* 199 *Pogonia verticillata.* Nutt. Whorled Arethusa . . . [Grows in] swamps; June. *Ib., Pogonia ophioglossoides.* R. Br. Snake-mouthed Arethusa. . . . The flower resembles a snake's head.

Argali. Also **argalia, argolia, agolia.** [E. (*a*1779), from Mongolian or Tungusian.] +The mountain sheep or big-horn, *Ovis montana.* Also *attrib.* — **1805** LEWIS & CLARK *Exped.* (1893) I. 333 There was a great abundance of the argali or big-horned animal in the high country through which it [=Judith's river] passes. *Ib.* II. 623 The women . . . [wore] a long skirt of argalia or ibex skin, reaching down to the ankles. **1836** EDWARD *Texas* 111 The wolverine, when it has seized the harmless argali of the mountains. **1837** IRVING *Bonneville* I. iii. 48 The ahsahta, argali, or big-horn . . . has the head and horns of a sheep, and its flesh is said to be delicious mutton. **1874** COUES *Birds N.W.* 537 At the foot of some cliffs near by lay whitening the heads and horns of the argali . . . shot by previous travelers.

Argand. *attrib.* Applied to the burner and lamp invented by Aimé Argand about 1782. {1790-}

1830 WATSON *Philadelphia* 184 They had then no argand or other lamps in parlours, but dipt candles. **1839** *S. Lit. Messenger* V. 753/2 She had contrived to ascertain, that a mat was wanting for the argean [*sic*] lamp. **1846** *Rep. Comm. Patents* (1847) 276, I claim the cup . . . for heating or supplying air to the outside of the flame of an argand lamp. **1857** YOUMANS *Household Science* 112 An important advantage gained by the Argand burner is the great steadiness of light caused by the chimney. **1881** HOWELLS *Modern Instance* xxviii. 349 He was again drinking in its prettiness in the subdued light of the shaded argand burner.

+**Argee.** Corn whiskey. — *a***1861** WINTHROP *J. Brent* ii. 22 Some likes it . . . but taint like good old Argee to me. *Ib.* 288 We could qualify it [water] with argee from our flasks. **1861** — *Open Air* 147 What a hard lot we were all round, livin' on nothing but argee whiskey.

***Argonaut.**

***1.** An adventurer who sails to a foreign country in quest of fortune, discovery, etc.

1807 IRVING, etc. *Salmagundi* (1824) 85 A celebrated Roman Knight . . . became a great favourite of Prince Madoc, and accompanied that famous argonaut in the voyage which ended in the discovery of this Continent. **1817** PAULDING *Lett. from South* I. 16 There is something in the fire-side simplicity and minuteness of these early historians that is inexpressibly interesting to the descendants and countrymen of the first old argonauts of this western world. **1839** *Knickerb.* XIII. 214 The Algics, if they were not the primitive explorers, were the Argonauts here.

+**2.** One who ventured to California in search of gold soon after its discovery there in 1848. (Cf. *forty-niner.*)

1873 *Overland Mo.* (San Fr.) X. 434 Argonauts of '49. **1875** BRET HARTE (*title*), Tales of the Argonauts, and Other Sketches. **1883** *Harper's Mag.* May 822/1 The wild life of the Argonauts of '49. **1890** HASKINS (*title*), Argonauts of California. **1892** *Congress. Rec.* 25 March 2565/1 [The leader of the western pioneers] must have had the mental power and balance which 'the Argonauts' termed 'a level head.'

transf. **1877**- (*title*), The Argonaut [San Fr. newspaper]. **1893** K. SANBORN *S. California* 1 The *fin-de-siècle* Argonaut, in Pullman train, flees the cold and grip.

Argufier. *colloq.* One who argues. {*colloq.*} — **1806** FESSENDEN *Democracy Unveiled* II. 204 His honour might have pass'd . . . For quite a decent country Squire, And no bad Jury-argufier.

Argufy, *v. colloq.* and *dial.* Also †**arguefy, argefy, argyfy.** [Irreg. f. *argue* v. and *-fy.*]

'This vile word . . . in this country . . . is only heard among the most illiterate' (B. '48).

1. *tr.* To be evidence of (something); to signify. {*c*1800}

1789 S. LOW *Politician Outwitted* I. ii, What argufies your signifies, or your magnifies?

2. *intr.* To argue; to wrangle. {1751-; now *colloq.* and *dial.*}

1813 PAULDING *J. Bull & Br. Jon.* xxiii. 122 They stopt in the fields from their work to arguefy. *a***1849** HOFFMAN in Pritts *Border Life* 689 So they argufied and they counted. **1862** NORTON *Army Lett.* 111, I can dispute and 'argufy' with a man, . . . but I never quarrelled with a woman yet but I got the worst of it. **1879** TOURGEE *Fool's Errand* xv. 79 A couple of Northern ministers . . . were a-spoutin' an' argyfyin' around here. **1917** WILKINS & KINGSLEY *Alabaster Box* xxvi. 280 You got him kind of het up with argufying.

3. *tr.* To dispute or debate (a topic, etc.). {*colloq.* and *dial.*}

1812 *Niles' Reg.* III. 206/1 But general Armstrong is well prepared to 'argufy' this point. **1817** *N. Amer. Rev.* IV. 183 After dinner [we] smoked a dirty pipe, 'argufied the topick,' whether the crops were likely to be spoilt. **1843** 'CARLTON' *New Purchase* I. xix. 157 So I argefied the pint agin this way.

4. To persuade (a person) by argument.

1853 SIMMS *Sword & Distaff* 417 We must, both on us, argufy him into the sense of this needcessity.

+**Arid belt.** A tract of country extending from Canada to Mexico, through the middle of the United States, in which stock-raising is a chief industry. — **1888** ROOSEVELT in *Century Mag.* Feb. 495/1 The great grazing lands of the West lie in what is known as the arid belt. **1894** *Congress. Rec.* 11 Aug. 8430/1 In this entire arid belt nature has provided in one way or another a sufficient amount of water, and all the necessary material for the construction of dams, basins, and reservoirs.

***Aristocracy.** A class superior to the rest of the community in respect of birth, wealth, or other advantages.

Cf. also *Bacon-and-rice* and *Codfish aristocracy.*

1654 JOHNSON *Wonder-W. Prov.* lv. 107 The chiefe court . . . consists of a mixt company, part aristocracy, and part democracy of magistrates. **1794** J. T. Buckingham *Newspaper Lit.* II. 121 The present Editor . . . neither devoting it [=*Salem Gazette*] to the cause of unfeeling Aristocracy, or [*sic*] employing it in kindling the vindictive rage of Democracy. *c***1808** ADAMS *Works* (1851) VI. 530 Connecticut has always been governed by an aristocracy. **1830** *Deb. Congress* 29 Dec. 386 This controversy concerning the tariff . . . between the aristocracy and the people. **1832** CLAY *Speeches* (1842) 182, I allude to the charge brought against the manufacturing system, as favoring the growth of aristocracy. **1834** *Deb. Congress* 25 Feb. 680 The Executive denunciation includes . . . that portion of society which, if there be such a thing as an aristocracy of wealth in this country, can be classed most properly under that designation. **1837** *S. Lit. Messenger* III. 178 The way I looked down upon the 'aristocracy of wealth' . . . was truly a sin. **1865** MRS. WHITNEY *Gayworthys* xxiii. 218 She had here the very thing that gave tone to . . . those 'born to it' in the metropolitan aristocracy. **1897** *Outing* XXX. 346/2 The New York Athletic Club . . . might satisfy the needs of the metropolitan cyclers representing the business aristocracy. **1903** *McClure's Mag.* Nov. 24/1 The good old days before great wealth formed aristocracy.

Aristocrat. [F. *aristocrate.*] A member of the aristocracy; one with aristocratic traits or principles. {1790-}

'"Aristocrat" means, in the parlance of the country, . . . a man of gentleman-like tastes, habits, opinions, and associations' (1846 Cooper *Redskins* xii.).

1776 in *S. Lit. Messenger* XXVII. 325/2 That a certain set of Aristocrats . . . have to this time kept us at Bay on the first line, which declares all men to be born equally free and independent. **1798** WASHINGTON *Writings* XIV. 123 The friends of government . . . are charged by them as being monarchists, aristocrats, and infractors of the constitution. **1809** F. CUMING *Western Tour* 56 There are two ruling or prevailing parties: . . . Federal . . . and . . . Antifederal. They nickname each other Aristocrats and Democrats, and it is astonishing to what a height their mutual animosity is carried. *c***1820** ADAMS *Works* (1851) VI. 506 Could not Mr. Hancock command . . . one vote, besides his own? If he could, he was an aristocrat. **1867** EDWARDS *Shelby* 13 The children of Virginia, Kentucky, Tennessee and the Carolinas—aristocrats to the core—would . . . shed blood like water rather than yield an inch. **1869** TOURGEE *Toinette* xxxiv. (1881) 349 Two days before, . . . the hoof strokes of the flying Aristocrat had awakened the wondering echoes of the almost deserted streets. **1871** [L. H. BAGG] *At Yale* 298 Denizens of the new Farnam College, who . . . are chaffed at as 'aristocrats' . . . by those who prefer to put up with the inconveniences of the old buildings. **1889** *Century Mag.* Nov. 153/2 The inhabitants of the Blue Ridge . . . look with jealousy upon the planters in the valley as 'restercrats.'

Aristocratic, *a.* {1602-} +(See quotations.) — **1846** COOPER *Redskins* x, Ravensnest [was] termed an 'aristocratic residence.' The word 'aristocratic,' I find since my return home, has got to be a term of expansive signification, its meaning depending on the particular habits and opinions of the person who happens to use it. **1859** BARTLETT 12 *Aristocratic*, strangely misapplied in those parts of the country where the population is not dense. The city, in the surrounding country towns, is deemed 'aristocratic.' The people in the villages consider the inhabitants of the towns 'aristocratic,' and so on. The term is . . . very common in small country newspapers and in political speeches in out of the way places.

+**Arizona.** [The name of the southwestern State.]

1. Attrib. in names of birds, etc. (see quotations).

(1) **1869** *Amer. Naturalist* III. 474 The resident species not found westward of this valley were . . . the Arizona song-sparrow (*Melospiza fallax*), the lead-colored Gnatcatcher. **1881** *Ib.* XV. 214 Later, in Arizona, I noticed . . . the Arizona or lead-colored gnat-catcher (*Polioptila plumbea*). **1891** *Cent.* s.v. *Woodpecker*, Arizona woodpecker, *Picus* (*Dendrocopus*) *arizonae*, [is] a bird lately discovered in Arizona.

(2) **1891** *Garden & Forest* 317 *Arbutus Arizonica*, The Arizona Arbutus . . . is apparently confined to the mountain ranges of southern Arizona. **1897** SUDWORTH *Arborescent Flora* 17 *Pinus strobiformis*, . . . Arizona White Pine. *Ib.* 19 *Pinus arizonica*, . . . Arizona Yellow Pine (Cal.), Arizona Pine. *Ib.* 76 *Cupressus guadalupensis*, . . . Arizona Cypress. **1897** SUDWORTH *Arborescent Flora* 356 *Abies arizonica* Merriam. Arizona Cork Fir.

2. *Arizona fever*, great desire to migrate to Arizona.

1873 BEADLE *Undevel. West* 669 All my friends who were 'footloose' had the 'Arizona fever.'

+**Arizonian,** *a.* and *n.* **1.** Pertaining to Arizona or its inhabitants. **2.** A native or resident of Arizona. — (1) *c***1857** WHITMAN *Amer. Primer* (1904) 35 Arizonian names have the sense of the ecstatic monk. (2) **1883** *Harper's Mag.* March 502/1 The bluff Arizonians themselves are apt to indulge in a derisive way of speaking of the army and its relation to the savages.

* **Ark.**

+**1.** A large, rectangular, flat-bottomed boat, esp. used on larger rivers to transport produce, stock, etc., to market.

Very frequent *c*1800–*c*1815; now (since *c*1860) *Hist.* 'Before the use of steamboats, they were employed on the Ohio and Mississippi rivers' (B. '48). Defined as 'a lumber vessel or ship' (W. '06).

Current in the 'Southern and Western States' (Pickering). 'On the western rivers, they were denominated Kentucky boats' (Howe *Hist. Coll. Ohio* 207).

1759 *New Amer. Mag.* August 627/2 Our great boat called the ark, being near 80 foot long and 30 wide, landed this day . . . 76 horses. **1759** *Essex Inst. Coll.* XIX. 143 An ark that was built within about 12 days was launched into the lake. **1791** E. Watson *Western Canals* (1820) 62 The batteauxmen, who ply between Newtown and Middletown, in Pennsylvania, carry from six to eight hundred bushels. Their boats, or arks, require from four to seven men to serve them. **1798** [C. WILLIAMSON] *Descr. Genesee* vii, A Mr. Kryder, a farmer on the Juniata River, . . . has made so considerable improvement on this sort of boat, that arks are now used which carry five hundred barrels. **1803** T. HARRIS *Journal of Tour* (1805) 139 This led to the building of those large flat-bottomed boats called arks. They are made with plank, fastened upon ribs, or knees, by wooden bolts. Their form is that of a parallelogram. **1811** R. SUTCLIFFE *Travels* (1815) vii. 118 The boats, which are called arks, and have frequently a kind of cottage upon them, in which several persons are accommodated. **1823** JAMES *Exped.* I. 15 From Olean downward, the Alleghany and Ohio bear along with their current fleets of rude arks laden with cattle, horses, household furniture [etc.]. **1829** J. MACAULEY *Hist. N. Y.* I. 76 Arks and Durham boats are the only vessels used [on the Susquehanna River]; the former carry from twenty to seventy tons, and draw from one foot eight inches, to two feet of water; the latter carry from 20 to 40 tons, and draw from 1 to 2 feet. **1833** J. FINCH *Travels* 311 In the year 1825, more than eight hundred and forty large arks, and nine hundred rafts of timber, besides smaller boats, passed down the [Susquehanna] river. **1836** W. O'BRYAN *Travels* 94 When they get to Philadelphia they sell the ark to be ripped up for fire wood, or any coarse work; return, and build another. **1843** 'CARLTON' *New Purchase* I. viii. 43 The usual mode then of going down [the Ohio River] . . . was in arks, broad-horns, keel-boats, batteaux, canoes and rafts. **1849** WILLIS *Rural Lett.* xiv. 127 The arks are built and the materials of the rafts collected, ready to launch with the first thaw. **1855** *Knickerb.* XLVI. 271 The ark, the broad-horn, and the flat-boat have almost vanished from our inland rivers.

+**b.** (See quotations.)

1893 *Stand. Dict., Ark,* (Eastern United States,) a moored scow covered by a house in which a business is done, as in oysters, etc. **1905** *Forestry Bureau, Bull. 61 Ark*, see Wanigan. . . . *Wanigan*, a houseboat used as sleeping quarters or as kitchen and dining room by river drivers. (N.W., L.S.)

+**c.** Comb. with *builder, like, roofed.*

1808 *Ann. 10th Congress* 2 Sess. 52 Our dismantled, ark-roofed vessels . . . are indeed decaying in safety at our wharves. **1833** C. MINER in *Life* (1916) 62 The situation . . . rendered it necessary to obtain provisions, teams, miners, ark-builders, and other laborers. **1843** FREMONT *Exped.* 188 The emigrants . . . making ark-like rafts, on which they had embarked their families and household.

+**2.** A large wagon for conveying farm-produce, etc.

1838 *Knickerb.* XII. 191 They drove their long 'arks,' or market-wagons, filled with blaäing calves. **1843** *Ib.* XXII. 6 Through the mountain passes . . . there flowed a stream of pedlers' carts, wagons, carry-alls, and arks, which inundated the land. **1844** *Ib.* XXIII. 155 The tilted wheel of the huge grim'd ark. **1891** S. M. WELCH *Recoll. 1830–40* 66 This tavern was so known by its patronage, the teamsters and freight handlers of the broad tire wheels; enormous arks of the so-called 'Pennsylvania wagons,' driven with four to ten horses.

3. A large trunk, chest, or box. {*arch.* or *dial.*}

1863 'GAIL HAMILTON' *Gala-Days* i. 3 The old ark . . . pitched headforemost into the wall. **1866** MRS. WHITNEY *L. Goldthwaite* iii. 47 The 'ark,' as they called Mrs. Linceford's huge light French box.

+**Ark,** *v.* [f. ARK *n.* 1.] *tr.* To load (animals, etc.) on an ark or flat-boat. — **1845** *St. Louis Reveille* 4 Aug. (Th.), I stood by while all the animals were arked, each one more obstinate than the former.

+**Arkansan.** A native or inhabitant of Arkansas.

1861 *Chicago Tribune* 19 July 1/4 The Missourians claimed it was the Arkansans who wished to kill the prisoners. **1866** RICHARDSON *Secret Service* xxii. 268 A party of native Arkansans . . . coming up the Mississippi in an open skiff. **1884** CABLE *Dr. Sevier* xv, A tall Arkansan, with high-combed hair.

+**Arkansas,** *n.* and *a.* Also †**Arkansaw, Arkansa.** [Native name (*Ac-, Akansa, -sas, -sea, -seas, Arkansea, -sa, Arkansaw, -sas,* etc.).]

1. *n.* (See quotation.)

1772 D. TAITT in *Travels Amer. Col.* 520 The Quarpas . . . or Arkansaws (a small nation on the west side of Mississippi).

2. *To go to Arkansas:* (see quotation).

*a***1850** FORD *Hist. Ill.* 444 They wrote [in 1846] that several of them 'had gone to Arkansas,' by which was understood that they had drowned their prisoners in the Ohio river, and left their bodies to float with the current in the direction to Arkansas.

3. Short for 'Arkansas stone' (see 7).

1869 G. A. ROGERS in *Eng. Mechanic* 22 Oct. 125 A sharp-edged Arkansas can be rubbed on the outside. *Ib.*, To sharpen them on the oilstone—slips of Turkey stone, Arkansas, or Washington being used with sweet oil.

4. *adj.* Of or belonging to Arkansas.

1819 *Ann. 15th Congress* 2 Sess. I. 911 A petition of sundry inhabitants of the Arkansaw country, praying that a separate territorial government may be established for the said country. **1819** *Statutes at Large* III. 494 The Arkansaw Territory. **1856** *Rep. Comm. Patents: Agric.* 256 The soil was a rich, sandy loam, in the Arkansas 'bottom.' **1861** [NEWELL] *Orpheus C. Kerr* I. 294 A moral work issued by the Arkansaw Tract Society. **1878** B. F. TAYLOR *Between Gates* 121 Sometimes the tune seemed to be 'The Arkansas Traveler.'

5. In specific names (see quotations).

1845 LINCOLN *Botany* App. 174/1 *Streptanthus ovalifolius*, (Arkansas cabbage,) leaves oval. Grows in Arkansas. — **1833** S. J. HALE *Flora* 40 Arkansa Coreopsis, *Coreopsis tinctoria*, . . . flowers in June. — **1858** BAIRD *Birds Pacific R.R.* 422 *Chrysomitris Psaltria*, Bonap.; Arkansas-Finch . . . [inhabits the] southern Rocky mountains to the coast of California. **1881** *Amer. Naturalist* XV. 213 In some willow trees . . . I found several nests of the Arkansas finch. — **1825** BONAPARTE *Ornithology* I. 19 The Arkansaw Flycatcher appears to inhabit all the region extending west of the Missouri river. **1869** *Amer. Naturalist* III. 309, I had a pet bird of the species known as the Arkansas Flycatcher (*Tyrannus verticalis*). — **1874** COUES *Birds N.W.* 116 *Chrysomitris Psaltria*. Arkansaw Goldfinch. Mexican Siskin. *Ib.* 117 The Arkansas Goldfinch is only known to occur along the southern border of the Missouri region. — **1870** *Amer. Naturalist* III. 477 McGillivray's Warbler . . . , Arkansas Kingbird (*Tyrannus verticalis*). — **1825** BONAPARTE *Ornithology* I. 54 The Arkansaw Siskin inhabits the country near the base of the Rocky mountains, south of the river Platte. **1849** AUDUBON *Ornith. Biog.* V. 85 Arkansaw Siskin . . . visits the lower parts of Louisiana at irregular periods, although always during winter.

6. *Arkansas toothpick*, 'a bowie knife of a peculiar kind, the blade of which shuts up into the handle' (B. '59).

1837 *Alabama Acts* 30 June 7 If any person carrying any knife or weapon, known as Bowie Knives or Arkansaw Tooth-picks . . . shall cut or stab another. **1840** *Daily Pennant* (St. Louis) 20 July (Th.), The young gentleman who borrowed a brace of duelling pistols, and an 'Arkansas toothpick,' from our office. **1849** A. MACKAY *Western World* I. 16 He used to walk the deck with an 'Arkansas toothpick' in his hand, a frightful looking knife, with a pointed blade seven inches long, with which he occasionally whittled. **1869** A. K. MCCLURE *Rocky Mts.* 377 A brace of faithful pistols in his belt, and a huge 'Arkansas toothpick,' or bowie knife, in a leather sheath. **1881** A. B. GREENLEAF *Ten Years in Texas* 27 All these . . . could be seen with a Navy six-shooter and an Arkansas toothpick suspended to a raw-hide belt buckled around their waists. **1888** BILLINGS *Hardtack* 274 A dirk knife—a real 'Arkansas toothpick'—was no unusual sight.

7. *Arkansas stone*, 'a fine-grain whetstone found in Arkansas, and used to sharpen surgical and dental instruments' (*Cent.*). [Cf. sense 3.]

+**Arkansian.** =ARKANSAN.

1862 POLLARD *First Year of War* 307 At Shiloh, the troops engaged were principally Tennesseeans, . . . Texans, Arkansians, and Kentuckians. **1882** BAILLIE-GROHMAN *Camps in Rockies* 91 The leader, or 'waggon-boss,' a lanky Arkansian, came strolling down to our camp. **1890** F.

HEMPSTEAD *Hist. Arkansas* 85 Rust commanded a brigade of Texans, but with some Arkansians in it.

Ark-shell. A small bivalve mollusk of the genus *Arca;* esp. Noah's ark, *A. Noae;* the shell of this. {1854-} — **1870** *Amer. Naturalist* III. 286 At the edge of the beach, . . . a large fleet of Ark shells is coming ashore. *Ib.* 467 The queen Ark-shell (*Arca Noae* Linn.), called Noah's Ark.

+Arlington. [Name of the estate of G. W. P. Custis on the Potomac R.] *Arlington meal, sheep:* (see quotations).

1809 LIVINGSTON *Sheep* (1810) 50 From these sheep I turn . . . to the Arlington long-woolled sheep. These . . . were derived from the stock of that distinguished farmer, soldier, statesman, and patriot, Washington. *Ib.* 59 The Arlington long-woolled breed. **1884** *Century Mag.* XXVII. 516/1 The Arlington sheep . . . seem to have been a valuable breed of long-wooled sheep, but are now unknown. — **1879** MRS. WHITNEY *Just How* 41 Two heaping cups of 'Arlington meal,' or graham flour, unsifted, in bread-bowl.

***Arm,** *n.*[1]

***1.** A branch of a river, stream, etc.

1622 'MOURT' *Relation* 22 A river . . . deviding it selfe into two armes by an high banke. **a1656** BRADFORD *Hist.* 99 They . . . found it [=the river] to open it selfe into 2. armes with a high cliffe of sand in the enterance. **1813** *Ann. 13th Congress* 1 Sess. I. 49 Elk river—an arm of the Chesapeake. **1826** COOPER *Mohicans* viii, A ragged oak . . . [whose] upper branches overhung that arm of the stream. **1860** ABBOTT *South & North* 63 At the entrance of one of the four arms of the river. **1867** RICHARDSON *Beyond Mississippi* 142 He would swim the narrow arm of the stream.

***2. a.** An inlet (*of* the sea).

1635 *Maine Doc. Hist.* III. 64 That arme of the Bay of Casko. **1789** MORSE *Amer. Gaz.* (1797) 81/1 The waters of Casco extend several arms or creeks of salt water into the country. **1817** *Ann. 14th Congress* 2 Sess. 1007 North river . . . is rather a creek or arm of Currituck sound. **1837** WILLIAMS *Florida* 19 The western arm is called Escambia Bay. **1837** COOPER *Recoll. Europe* I. 32 The anchorage in the arm of the sea off this little haven.

***b.** A portion or extent *of* land, prairie, swamp, etc., projecting from the main body. Now *local.*

1654 JOHNSON *Wonder-W. Prov.* 19 The place picked out by this people to settle themselves, was in the bosome of the out-stretched arme of Cape Cod, now called Gloster. **1669** *Portsmouth Rec.* 415 On the westermost part of my lands at the place commonly called the westermost Arme. **1671** *Providence Rec.* III. 188 The uper end of an arme of the great swampe. **1685** *Ib.* XIV. 115 That arme of the great swampe which butteth westward. **1712** *Ib.* XI. 159 That arme of the s[ai]d swampe sometimes called Hearndens Arme. **1834** PECK *Gaz. Illinois* 246 Long arms of prairie extending between the creeks and smaller streams. **1840** *Cultivator* VIII. 19 When I first entered this arm of the Grand Prairie. **1843** N. BOONE *Journal* (1917) 230 This timber . . . runs . . . across to the Arkansas, arms of it extending north of the Arkansas. **1902** CLAPIN 24 In Western Florida, an arm of the prairie extending into and partly surrounded by woods.

***Arm,** *n.*[2] (See also ARMS *n. pl.*) A branch of the military service, as cavalry, infantry, or artillery. {1798-}

1846 WORCESTER. **1855** SIMMS *Forayers* 521 To such a force of mounted men, the foe can oppose nothing. With this particular arm, . . . you may surprise all his outposts. **1861** *Army Regulations* 72 Volunteers and militia take the left of regular troops of the same arm. **1865** BOUDRYE *Fifth N.Y. Cavalry* 17 The first battle of Bull Run clearly demonstrated the importance of the cavalry arm of the service. **1881-5** MCCLELLAN *Own Story* 373 Another column of all arms, under Col. Warren, was sent on the same day . . . to Ashland.

***Arm,** *v. tr.* To furnish or equip with arms or weapons.

1622 'MOURT' *Relation* 51 About midnight we heard a great and hideous cry, and our Sentinell called, *Arme, Arme.* **1654** JOHNSON *Wonder-W. Prov.* 15 Being armed with bow and arrowes, they approached within shot of the ship. **1666** *Md. Archives* II. 326 The Governour can neyther arme soldiers to fight for you, nor send commis[sione]rs . . . without hazarding his hono[u]r. **1777** *Journals Cont. Congress* IX. 912 Every state shall always keep up a well regulated and disciplined militia, sufficiently armed and accoutred. *Ib.* 921 The officers and men so cloathed, armed and equipped. **1797** *Ann. 5th Congress* I. 25 The bill to prevent the arming of private ships. **1797** J. T. Buckingham *Newspaper Lit.* II. 69 The Jacobins . . . are opposed to arming our vessels, or fitting out a single ship of war. **1815** *Md. Hist. Mag.* I. 231 Under the impression that she was a Runner . . . weakly arm'd and mann'd. **1881-5** MCCLELLAN *Own Story* 53 The objects I had in view were . . . to rally the Union men of the mountain region, to arm and embody them.

***Armadillo.** *S.W. & W.* + The peba, *Tatusia novemcincta* or *Dasypus novemcinctus*, found esp. in Texas.

1763 W. ROBINSON in W. Roberts *Nat. Hist. Florida* 100 The animals are the same as in Old Mexico, *viz.* the armidillo, flying squirrel, [etc.]. **1838** 'TEXIAN' *Mexico* v. *Texas* 94, I am horribly cramped by the wild *armadillo* of the rocks. **1845** DE SMET *Oregon Missions* (1847) 104 Salamanders swarm in sandy places, and armadilloes are not rare in the vicinity of the great Dalles. **1890** *Cent.* s.v. *Peba,* The true peba is South American, but the name has also been given to the Texan armadillo. **1891** *Ib.* s.v. *Tatusia,* The peba . . . [is] notable as the only armadillo of the United States.

Armament.

1. *Naval armament,* 'a naval force, including ships, men, and all the necessary furniture' (W. '28). {1699-}

1780 *Heath P.* III. 61 Our naval armament has fallen into their hands. **1794** *Ann. 3rd Congress* 459 For the purpose of defraying the cost of a naval armament, . . . there shall be levied . . . an additional duty of one per cent. **1798** *Ann. 5th Congress* I. 579 An act providing a naval armament. **1812** P. HAMILTON in *Amer. State P.* Class VI. I. 276 But in providing a naval armament there are other considerations, of the highest importance. **1814** T. J. Stevens *American Record* 388 A few heavy guns will be sufficient to afford complete protection against any naval armament whatever.

2. Military or naval equipment, esp. cannons or guns. {1721-}

1847 *Army Regulations* 13 Preservation of armaments and ammunition. 1. Guns and carriages. **1861** G. WELLES in Baxter *Ironclad Warship* 246 Construction of . . . ironclad vessels of war . . . to carry an armament of from 80 to 120 tons in weight. **1881-5** MCCLELLAN *Own Story* 46 Until I commenced sending troops to West Virginia, my time was fully occupied . . . in endeavoring to provide for their food, armament, and equipment.

+Arm-band. A band for wearing about the arm, esp. as an ornament.

1797 B. HAWKINS *Letters* 253 The goods he wants are . . . 3 pair arm bands, 3 pair wrist bands. **1823** E. JAMES *Exped.* I. 43 The squaws wore . . . silver arm-bands and large ear-rings. **1846** M'KENNEY *Memoirs* I. 178, I opened a box . . . and took out a pair of silver arm-bands and a silver gorget.

Arm-chair. Also **arm chair.** A chair having arms or side-supports for resting the elbows. {1633-} Cf. ARMED *a.*

1727 *Md. Hist. Mag.* XVIII. 226 Send me . . . a strong couch and two arm chairs to match. **1834** *Harvardiana* I. 29, I reposed myself in my arm-chair. **1851** HAWTHORNE *Ho. Seven Gables* xviii, [To] sit awhile in one of their leathern-cushioned arm-chairs, listening to the gossip of the day. **1875** STOWE *We & Our Neighbors* 88 When she had made Eva sit down in an old-fashioned claw-footed arm-chair in the warmest corner. **1885** 'CRADDOCK' *Prophet* iv. 85 There were cushions in their rude arm-chairs. **1886** B. P. POORE *Reminisc.* II. 233 The Senators retained their comfortable arm-chairs.

Arm-chest. [ARMS *n. pl.*] A box or chest in which arms are kept. {1823}

1828 SHERBURNE *Mem.* iii. (1831) 66 The arm chest on the weather side of the quarter deck. **1830** COOPER *Water Witch* III. vii, An arm-chest, which had been emptied of its contents. **1861** *Army Regulations* 390 Arm-chests are to be preserved and accounted for as other ordnance stores.

Armed, *a.* [ARM *n.*[1]] *Armed chair*=ARM-CHAIR. {1693, 1795} — **1713** SEWALL *Diary* II. 403 When Gen[era]l Nicholson staid not . . . [the chairs] were remov'd, and the Governour's Arm'd Chair took place again. **1798** I. ALLEN *Hist. Vermont* 47 [The] committee . . . ordered him to be tied in an armed chair. **1844** Cist *Cincinnati Misc.* 95 The cabin seats are armed chairs. **1853** *Knickerb.* XLII. 171 That great armed-chair with the blue and buff cushion.

***Armed,** *ppl. a.*

***1.** Furnished with arms or weapons; bearing arms.

1638 UNDERHILL *Newes from America* 12 The governor and council sent forth myself, with twenty armed soldiers, . . . to take the government of that place for . . . three months. **1675** ANDROS in Easton *Indian War* 78 There shall continue an armed sloope to ply in the sound. **1704** S. KNIGHT *Journal* 17 Every lifeless trunk, with its shatter'd limbs, appear'd an armed enymie. **1775** *Journals Cont. Congress* III. 316 The resolves of Congress, for fitting out four armed vessels. **1788** FRANKLIN *Autobiog.* 408 The armed brethren, too, kept watch, and reliev'd as methodically as in any garrison town. **1798** *Ann. 5th Congress* II. 1797 The commanders of our public and private armed vessels. **1813** *Ann. 12th Congress* 2 Sess. 84 The destruction of armed vessels of the enemy . . . of the United States. **1840** COOPER *Pathfinder* xix, A capture on the high seas is piracy, unless your boat is regularly commissioned either as a public or a private armed cruiser. **1854** BARTLETT *Narr.* II. 496 About forty long-bearded men, armed to the teeth. **1895** M. A. JACKSON *Memoirs* 642 The armed infantry fired volleys.

2. *Armed neutrality,* a neutrality in which the participating nations maintain their establishments on a war footing. {*c*1803-}

1780 ADAMS in *Revol. Diplom. Corr.* III. (1889) 646 The invitation of the Empress of Russia to accede to an armed neutrality. **1790** JEFFERSON *Writings* V. 197 If we can but establish the principles of the armed neutrality for ourselves, we must become the carriers for all parties as far as we can raise vessels. **1797** *Ann. 5th Congress* I. 82 The armed neutrality was confined to the then existing war.

Arm-glove. A glove extending over the arm. {1740} — **1805-9** HENRY *Camp. Quebec* 105 We supplied ourselves with arm-gloves, and renewed our mockasins.

+**Arm-in-arm Convention.** A Republican convention held at Philadelphia in 1866 (see quotation). — **1892** BROWN & STRAUSS *Dict. Politics* (1907) 29 Arm-in-arm convention [was] a name given to a convention of Republicans that supported President Johnson's policy of reconstruction. Its name arose from the fact that the members from Massachusetts and from South Carolina entered the convention together at the head of the delegates.

Arminian, *n.* and *a.*

1. *n.* A member of the Protestant sect founded by the Dutch theologian Arminius (1560–1609); a believer in the doctrines of Arminius. {1618–}

1654 JOHNSON *Wonder-W. Prov.* 24 Arminians, who attribute Gods election or reprobation to the will of man. **1682** SEWALL *Diary* II. 20* Zadori, the Hungarian, whom I find to be an Arminian. **1794** Buckingham *Newspaper Lit.* II. 232 Not damning a man for a different opinion, I'd mix with the Calvinist, Baptist, Arminian, Treat each like a man. **1848** DRAKE *Pioneer Life Ky.* viii. 195 The 'Church of England' ... was regarded [as] ... an organized body of Arminians enlisted in the service of despotism. **1859** STOWE *Minister's Wooing* iv, Can't Arminians have anything right about them? **1883** *Schaff's Relig. Encycl.* I. 145/2 The Wesleyans throughout the British Empire, and the Methodists in America, are universally Arminians.

transf. **1835** [TODD] *Notes* 57 A Dutchman on horseback is easily recognised, for if the animal offend him, he, in a great passion, calls him an Arminian.

2. *adj.* Pertaining to, advocating, or following the doctrines of Arminius. {1618–}

1748 *New Hampshire Hist. Soc. Collections* IX. 9 In their opinion Armenian & other pernicious errors prevailed as much as Antinomian. **1781** PETERS *Hist. Conn.* (1829) 254 Preaching against ... Arminian governors, and false-hearted counsellors, and episcopizing curates. **1869** STOWE *Oldtown Folks* 5 Parson Lothrop belonged to a numerous class in the third generation of Massachusetts clergy, commonly called Arminian. *Ib.* 53 The conjugal relation, ... often, like everything else, had its Calvinistic and its Arminian side.

Arminianism. {1618–} The doctrines or tenets of the Arminians (see prec.). — **1713** C. MATHER *Diary* II. 207 To warn them ... against three Systems of Error ... ; the false Thoughts of Popery, and of Quakerism, and of Arminianism. **1713** SEWALL *Diary* II. 400 Mr. Jno Barnard preaches a Sermon too much savoring of Arminianisme. **1739** Temple & Sheldon *Hist. Northfield, Mass.* 230 We judge it highly reasonable we should be heard upon the objections we have to make against some of the doctrines you have delivered as aforesaid, which doctrines we judge to be Arminianism.

‖**Armist.** (See quotation). — **1856** C. Robinson *Kansas Conflict* (1892) 397 One of them asked my husband, 'Are you a Northern armist,' He said, 'I am.' I understood the answer to mean that my husband was opposed to the Northern or free-soil party. I cannot say that I understood the question.

Armistice. A cessation of hostilities by agreement of the opposing forces; a short truce. {1707–}

1813 CLAY *Speeches* (1860) I. 52 The Secretary of State writes to Mr. Russell, authorizing him to agree to an armistice. **1843** *Diplom. Corr. Texas* (1911) III. 1463 The news of some recent success of our soldiers ... as it reached here after armistice, was on that account to be regretted. **1862** NORTON *Army Lett.* 121 The enemy took advantage of an armistice granted them to bury the dead. **1867** EDWARDS *Shelby* 129 General Blunt attempted no pursuit; ... the terms of the Armistice forbade it.

***Armlet.**

***1.** A broad band of metal or other material worn to protect or adorn the arm.

1826 COOPER *Mohicans* xxviii, This patriarch ... also wore armlets, and cinctures above the ankles, of the latter precious metal [=silver]. **1835** HOFFMAN *Winter in West* I. 292 Broad plates suspended over their chests, with armlets of the same metal, made quite a rich display. **1856** WHIPPLE, etc. *Indian Tribes* 52 (H. R. 33 Congr. Ex. Doc. No. 91 III.), Mojave armlets of thick leather. **1870** KEIM *Sheridan's Troopers* (1885) 198 Silver armlets, six or eight brass wire bracelets on each arm.

+**2.** 'A clasp or loop for confining the sleeve to the upper portion of the arm. Used to loop up the short sleeve of children's dresses' (Knight).

Armoire. *S.W.* An ambry or cupboard. {1823–36} — **1834** BRACKENRIDGE *Recoll.* ii. 24 The furniture ... was of the most common kind, consisting of an armoire, a rough table or two, and some coarse chairs. **1860** *Texas Almanac* 242 Chairs, bureaus, tables, ... armoires.

+**Armonica.** [Ital., fem. of *armonico* harmonious.] The 'musical glasses' invented by Franklin. (See also HARMONICA.) — **1762** FRANKLIN *Let.* Wks. 1887 III. 204 In honor of your musical language, I have borrowed from it the name of this instrument, calling it the Armonica. **1764** *Ib.* 255 The case of the Armonica came home to-night. **1766** *Ib.* 463 The Armonica for cousin Josiah. *c*1775 CARTER in Fithian *Journal* I. 59 *note,* An armonica, being the musical glasses without water, framed into a complete instrument.

***Armor, Armour,** *n.*

***1.** Outfit worn to protect the body from offensive weapons; defensive covering.

1622 'MOURT' *Relation* 17 We marched thorow boughes and bushes, ... which tore our very armour in peeces. **1637** *Conn. Public Rec.* I. 12 If there be any arm[ou]r, gones, swordes, ... that were lost, landed or leafte in any plantacons, they are to be delivered into the handes of the saide constables. *a***1649** WINTHROP *Hist.* I. 194 We could not follow them [=Indians] in our armour. **1692** BULKELEY *Will & Doom* 123 It shall be lawful for the chief commanders ... to take ... every such person and persons, with their ships, armor, ammunition and other goods. [**1858** LONGFELLOW *Courtship M. Standish* IV. 71 The Captain ... stamped on the floor, till his armor Clanged on the wall, where it hung.]

+**2.** The steel plating or other protective covering of a warship, fortification, etc. {1870–}

1838 *Knickerb.* XII. 373 One of the most interesting practical exhibitions ... was that of the 'marine armor' off the battery. **1855** W. M. GWIN (*title*), Report [of] the Committee on Naval Affairs, who were instructed to inquire into the expediency of using submarine armors in the United States navy. **1861** *Naval War Records* 1 Ser. IV. 222 This addition would nearly treble the strength of the armor and make it impervious to balls from Paixhans guns at ... half a mile. **1874** KNIGHT 150/2 Iron armor [for war-vessels] was suggested in the United States in 1812. **1886** *Harper's Mag.* June 18/1 There is protection obtained by constructing a vessel of steel, but not such as is provided by armor.

***Armor,** *v.* +*tr.* To furnish or cover (a warship) with armor-plating. {1864–}

1861 J. A. DAHLGREN *Let.* 15 Feb. in M. Dahlgren *Memoir* 249 So little having been determined with regard to the preferable mode of armoring ships. **1861** *Boston Commercial Bulletin* 16 March, The times of line-of-battleships are over; ... they will be no match for a heavily armored, fast, iron-cased frigate. **1861** Baxter *Ironclad Warship* (1933) 246 To provide armored batteries ... for the defence of the various harbors along our sea-coast. **1886** *Harper's Mag.* June 13/2 These vessels ... will be armored with steel or compound armor.

Armor-clad, *a.* Clad in armor; protected by armor-plating. {1869} **1887** *Nation* 15 Dec. 470/2 The Secretary recommends the construction of ... two armor-clad vessels to cost ... not more than $6,000,000. **1905** *N.Y. Herald* 7 July 4/6 A twelve inch shell loaded with only a small charge of dunnite ... will crumple in the side of the heaviest armorclad vessel.

***Armorer.** Also **armourer.**

***1.** One who makes or repairs arms († or armour).

1689 *Maine Doc. Hist.* IX. 66 Wee ... are under great disadvantage by reason of ... the want of a chyrurgeon & an armorer. **1701** *Ib.* X. 91 The government has thought good to settle with you [=Indians] an armourer who ... shall repair ... all of your guns that may prove defective. **1726** PENHALLOW *Indian Wars* (1824) 93 The hiring an armourer at the publick charge, was also engaged, but nothing done therein. **1776** *Journals Cont. Congress* V. 558 Resolved ... That Col. Biddle be directed to employ an armourer or armourers for the army in New Jersey. **1795** *Ann. 4th Congress* 2 Sess. 2577 The caboose with a forge, hearth, armorer's tools, spare coppers, boilers, &c. are all complete. **1812** *Ann. 12th Congress* 1 Sess. 1242 Orders have recently been given to increase the number of armorers. **1825** JEFFERSON *Autobiog.* Wks. 1854 I. 98 The people now armed themselves with such weapons as they could find in armorer's shops. **1861** *Army Regulations* 248 Armorers, carriage-makers, and blacksmiths, of the Ordnance Department.

2. One (usu. an officer) who has charge or supervision of the arms of a ship, regiment, etc. {1753–} Also *master-armorer.*

1775 *N.H. Comm. Safety* 6 Ordered that Nathaniel Perkins ... shall be armourer of Col. Poor's regiment & be allowed the same wages ... as is allowed armourers in the Massachusetts service. **1828** WEBSTER s.v., The armorer of a ship has the charge of the arms, to see that they are in a condition fit for service. **1852** *Harper's Mag.* V. 161/1 Ask the master-armorer any questions whatever about the workings of the establishment. **1861** *Army Regulations* 391 At an armory, all articles purchased, fabricated, or repaired are to be inspected by the master armorer before being paid for, or turned into store.

Armor-plate. A plate of steel to afford protection against gun-fire. {1874} — **1863** *Rep. Comm. Patents* I. 299 Edward Brady: ... Improved means of affixing defensive armor plates. **1866** J. ERICSSON in Church *Life* II. 116 The sides of steam-frigates, ... covered with armor-plates of sufficient thickness to resist heavy projectiles.

Armor-plating. The protective steel plating of a war-vessel. {1864–} — **1863** BABBITT in *Rep. Comm. Patents* I. 222 The invention consists in a peculiar dovetailed construction of the parts forming the armor plating. **1865** H. A. WISE in M. Dahlgren *Memoir* (1882) 302 The practice at the test battery against armor plating. **1875** KNIGHT 1202 The thickness of armor-plating has been greatly increased since its first introduction.

***Armory.** Also **armoury.**

***1.** A building or room in which arms are stored.

1653 *Boston Rec.* 6 If a convenient fayre roome ... be sequestered & set apart for an armory & the meeting of the artillery. **1656** R. KEAYNE *Will* in *Mass. H. S. Coll.* 5 Ser. V. 160 [Money bequeathed for building a hall] with rooms for ... a library, also an armory. **1789** MORSE *Amer. Geog.* 427 The public buildings [of Charleston, S.C.] are an ... armoury, poor house. **1846** *Niles' Nat. Reg.* 20 June 256/2 There are a million and a half muskets in the various armories of the U. States. **1852** *Harper's Mag.* V. 146 The visitor finds ... in the centre [of the plain] a vast public square occupied and surrounded by the buildings of the

Armory. **1889** *Cent.* s.v., The State militia are usually provided with armories, which include offices, drill-rooms, etc.

+2. A place or building where arms are made; a factory for arms.

1794 *Ann. 3rd Congress* 1428 There shall be established, at each of the aforesaid arsenals, a national armory. **1799** *Ann. 6th Congress* 247 The national armory at Springfield. **1812** *Ann. 12th Congress* 1 Sess. 1242 The public armories at Springfield and Harper's Ferry are in operation and well conducted. *Ib.*, A site was purchased and buildings erected for an armory at Rocky Mount (South Carolina). **1851** CIST *Cincinnati* 331 That the west has a just claim to the next armory that may be established, the other great sections of the United States each possessing one. **1865** *Atlantic Mo.* XV. 711/1 A strike among the workmen at the armory . . . at Harper's Ferry. **1883** 'MARK TWAIN' *Life on Miss.* lviii. 567 The Rock Island establishment is a national armory and arsenal.

3. Attrib. with *officer, workshop,* etc.

*a***1861** WINTHROP *C. Dreeme* 19 He left the armory-door of the Seventh, with his hand upon a howitzer. **1861** *Army Regulations* 392 A return of armory officers and men. **1865** *Atlantic Mo.* XV. 711 There would be time enough to see all the armory workshops [at Harper's Ferry].

* **Armpit.** +*Up to the armpits*, completely, totally, utterly. *colloq.*

1869 *Congress. Globe* April 549/1 The company is steeped in fraud to the very armpits. **1871** *Ib.* 17 Feb. 1343/1 A poor mistaken man, who had been steeped in this rebellion to his armpits for years, accepted this pardon. **1878** *Congress. Rec.* Feb. 713/1 There certainly has been purgatory in the vicinity of his chamber, and I know that Colonel Polk has been in it up to his armpits.

* **Arms,** *n. pl.*

* **1.** Weapons of offense or defense.

1622 'MOURT' *Relation* 133 Amongst other recreations, we exercised our armes. **1631** *Mass. Bay Rec.* I. 84 It is ordered, that euery town . . . take especial care that euery person . . . [be] furnished with . . . armes allowable by the captain. **1637** *Plymouth Col. Rec.* I. 54 To agree with Leiftennante Holmes to exercise the inhabitantes of the colony in the use of armes. **1645** *Southampton Rec.* I. 38 From [Nov. 1 to March 1] . . . there shall be a cessation of bearing of armes vnto the meeting howse vpon the Lord's daye. **1689** *Maine Doc. Hist.* V. 5 The spare armes belonging to the publique stores that are left in the magazine. **1705** *Boston News-Letter* 23 April 2/2 He found on shore one of their arms, and supposes that he either kill'd or wounded the owner. **1776** *Declar. Independence,* The present King of Great Britain . . . has constrained our fellow citizens . . . to bear arms against their country. **1798** *Ann. 5th Congress* II. 1927 The bill providing arms for the militia throughout the United States. **1840** COOPER *Pathfinder* xi, Although the regular arms of the regiment were muskets, some fifty rifles were produced on the present occasion. **1861** *Army Regulations* 61 The two sentinels will, with arms at port, then approach each other. *Ib.*, The new guard standing at presented arms. **1881–5** MCCLELLAN *Own Story* 379 Orders were sent to Gen. Sumner to get his command under arms.

* **2.** *pl.* Heraldic bearings or devices. Also *transf.*

1651 *Suffolk Deeds* I. 136 The dwelling house commonly knowne by the signe of the Kings armes in Boston. **1694** *Harvard Rec.* I. 347 Mr. Newman's proposal about procuring the colledge-armes in Bilboa. **1751** GIST *Journals* 61 Their captain's name or title was the Crane, as I knew by his picture or arms [=totem] painted on a tree. **1783** J. T. Buckingham *Newspaper Lit.* I. 255 The device for the arms of the Commonwealth of Massachusetts. **1847** *Army Regulations* 155 Arms of the United States, as established by an Act of Congress. **1876** INGRAM *Centennial Expos.* 608 Connecticut State building: . . .Over this porch were the State arms.

||**Arm-shop.** A gunsmith's shop. — **1871** 'MARK TWAIN' *Screamers* (F.), 'I want to know where I can find an arm-shop,' replied McCracken, mildly.

* **Army.**

* **1.** A body of armed troops; a (or the) military land-force.

1655 L. STRONG *Babylon's Fall* in *Narr. Early Md.* (1910) 242 That night Captain Stone and his army appeared in the river . . . with eleven or twelve vessels, . . . some of which had plundred by the way, in which their whole army were wafted. **1692** BULKELEY *Will & Doom* 205, 2 sh. a week shall be allowed for every horse employ'd for the army's use. **1707** [?C. MATHER] *Mem. Deplorable State* 4 The country are at a vast charge in maintaining an army yearly. **1775** *Journals Cont. Congress* II. 77 We are now compelled to raise an Army, which . . . we hope . . . will be able to defend us and all America. *Ib.* 84 To convey . . . to Providence . . . five thousand barrels of flour for the use of the Continental Army. *Ib.* 85 That they immediately furnish the American army before Boston with . . . powder. **1798** *Ann. 5th Congress* I. 531 Resolved, that it is expedient to raise a provisional army, to be employed, when necessary, for internal security and defence. **1806** *Ann. 9th Congress* 1 Sess. 1238 Every officer now in the army of the United States. **1861** *Army Regulations* 3 It has been found expedient to revise the Regulations for the Army. **1862** KEYES in McClellan *Own Story* 268 Four divisions . . . withdrawn altogether from . . . the Army of the Potomac. **1884** *Century Mag.* XXVII. 498/1 The Second Cavalry Brigade of the Army of the Mississippi. **1904** *Amer. Almanac & Year-book* 450 The United States Army . . . is organized under the act of Congress of February 2, 1901. . . . By act of 1901, the army shall at no time exceed 100,000 men.

2. A vast horde of worms. (Cf. ARMY WORM.)

1654 JOHNSON *Wonder-w. Prov.* 214 The Lord was pleased to awaken us with an army of caterpillers. **1841** G. POWERS *Hist. Sk. Coös Co.* 105 An army of worms . . . began to appear the latter part of July, 1770, and continued their ravages until September. The inhabitants denominated them the 'Northern Army,' as they seemed to advance from the north or north-west. *Ib.* 107 In ten days from the first appearing of the Northern Army, nothing remained of this corn but the bare stalks! **1865** FITCH *Rep. Insects N. Y.* 117 The colonies or armies of these worms are usually discovered when the worms are a third grown and about half an inch long.

3. In attributive use. {1674–} **a.** In sense: Of, belonging to, or connected with the army.

1777 *Journals Cont. Congress* VII. 341 Their pay as commissioners for settling the army accounts. **1795** HAMILTON in *Ann. 3rd Congress* 1336 The army and navy establishments. **1810** *Ann. 12th Congress* 1 Sess. 1604 You have six thousand men now on your army rolls. **1812** *Niles' Reg.* II. 131/1 The army quota of this state [is] twenty nine companies. **1814** *Ann. 13th Congress* II. 1503 A few remarks, made on the Army bill. **1817** *Yankee Traveller* 77 Extravagant and libertine officers and army contractors. **1844** S. M. FULLER *Summer on Lakes* 22 He passed from one army station to another. **1844** EMERSON *Ess.* II. viii, Why should we refuse to eat bread, until we have found his regiment and section in our army-files? **1850** GLISAN *Jrnl. Army Life* 5 However much I may like army-life. **1861** *Army Regulations* 11 Meritorious non-commissioned officers, examined by an Army Board. **1862** LINCOLN in McClellan *Own Story* 483 Try just now to save the army material and *personnel.* **1865** TROWBRIDGE *Three Scouts* xxxvi. 377 A carriage . . . brought his mother and father to the army police-office. **1874** BUSHNELL *Forgiveness* 125 We meet another strangely impressive example in the army discipline. **1892** M. A. JACKSON *Gen. Jackson* 55 He handed an Army Catalogue to his visitor, and asked him to suggest a suitable officer to fill the chair. **1903** *Boston Ev. Transcript* 24 Aug., The environment of the Charleston Navy Yard is duplicated wherever there is an army post.

b. In sense: Worn or used in the army.

1813 *Niles' Reg.* III. 295/2 Feathers for the army uniforms. **1861** WINTHROP *Open Air* 270 Kitchens, armed with Captain Vielé's capital army cooking-stoves. **1861** [NEWELL] *Orpheus C. Kerr* I. 131, I espied Great Britain seated by the roadside, contemplating an army biscuit. **1864** 'PENNIMAN' *Tanner-Boy* 260 His [=an army officer's] patent-leather army boots were unsoiled by a single . . . flake of mud. **1865** *Atlantic Mo.* XV. 278 An old army-blanket. *Ib.* 673 All this . . . was to be made up into tents, accoutrements, and army-clothing. **1867** CRAWFORD *Mosby* 182 Men in ambush opened on them with Colt's army-pistols. **1872** ROE *Barriers Burned Away* xlvii, Christine and Dennis at last received an army biscuit (hard-tack in the soldier's vernacular). **1885** *Texas Siftings*, 'It's not too late to have a funeral . . . ,' replied Dr. Blister, drawing an army-size revolver. **1898** PAGE *Red Rock* 231 The bands appeared . . . equipped with new army muskets and ammunition. *Ib.* 291 An old army haversack over his shoulder. **1901** CHURCHILL *Crisis* 21 [Lincoln] wore an old blue army overcoat.

c. In sense: Serving in or with the army.

1853 SIMMS *Sword & Distaff* 416 He sought the sheriff, who was a well-known army man. **1854** *Ann. 13th Congress* I. 27 Memorial of army officers. **1862** NORTON *Army Lett.* 110 It seems just about like throwing it [=money] away to . . . give it to those army sharks, the sutlers. **1886** POORE *Reminisc.* II. 126 With the war came the army correspondents. **1916** EASTMAN *From Deep Woods* 78 He was one of the first army scouts. *Ib.* 122 The kindness of several army surgeons.

+**Army blue. a.** The blue uniform formerly worn by the U.S. (or the Federal) army. **b.** Blue cloth for making this.

1881 *Harper's Mag.* April 716/1 The inmates all wear the army blue. **1885** E. B. CUSTER *Boots & Saddles* xxvii. 248 He found his way to many a heart that beat under the army blue. **1890** RYAN *Told in Hills* 209 Petticoats . . . were of regular army blue, their only trimming belt and bands of the 'yaller.' **1895** KING *Fort Frayne* 290 Farrar was . . . just about the happiest fellow that wore the army blue. **1907** W. LILLIBRIDGE *Trail* 286 Outside was an old army-blue greatcoat.

+**Army-cloth.** 'Cloth from which soldiers' uniforms are made' (*Cent.*) — **1877** *Rep. Indian Affairs* 5 We should have a uniform material, made of wool—like army-cloth—for Indian clothing.

Army corps. A unit of an army consisting of several divisions, and embracing each arm of the service. {Also E.}

1847 *Army Regulations* 118 A suitable staff . . . will be attached to each brigade, division, and army-corps. **1862** KEYS in McClellan *Own Story* 268 The distinct understanding that four army corps should be employed. **1866** 'F. KIRKLAND' *Bk. Anecdotes* 626 One of the skirmishes between the Fourteenth Army Corps . . . and the Confederate forces. **1901** CHURCHILL *Crisis* 417 A political general came . . . from Washington, . . . [and] took possession of three army corps and their chief.

+**Army Register.** A periodical official list of all the commissioned officers in the army. {=E. 'Army List'}

1815 (*title*), Army Register, Adjutant and Inspector General's Office, May 17, 1815. **1820** *Ann. 16th Congress* 1 Sess. II. 68 The President communicated a letter from the Secretary of War, transmitting a copy of the Army Register, for each member of the Senate. **1861** (*title*), Official Army Register. **1865** (*title*), Official Army Register of the Volunteer Force of the United States Army.

+Army Regulations. A book issued by the government, containing the acts of Congress and the rules of the War Department for the management of the army.

1847 *Gen. Regulations for Army* (binder's title), Army Regulations, 1847. **1861** (*binder's title*), Revised U.S. Army Regulations. **1862** *Regulations for Army Confed. States* (binder's title), Army Regulations. **1865** *Atlantic Mo.* XV. 626 They study the 'Army Regulations' to make sure that they concede no more.

+Army wagon.

1. A wagon for transporting army stores or ammunition.

1865 KELLOGG *Rebel Prisons* 276 They had two ambulances and an army wagon, in which they always carried the patients. **1865** TROWBRIDGE *Three Scouts* xvi. 166 Amid clouds of dust raised by army wagons and troops passing to the front. **1883** *Century Mag.* XXVII. 138/2 Three or four army wagons, each with a team of four good mules. **1888** *Ib.* XXXVII. 159/1 The army wagon, the big blue wagon, ... was blessed or was cursed.

2. 'A wagon designed for the use of foot-soldiers on the plains, and so constructed that the men can quickly jump off the seats when attacked, and spring back again at once' (Knight).

+Army worm. [ARMY 2.] The larva of the cotton-moth (*Leucania unipuncta*), a caterpillar very destructive to grass, grain, etc.

Also applied, with distinguishing terms (q.v.), to related species.

1840 *Niles' Nat. Reg.* 4 July 279/2 The insect has destroyed the entire wheat crop on Sturge's prairie.... This insect is known as the army worm, and has never appeared here [Michigan] before. **1842** BUCKINGHAM *E. & W. States* II. 209 In the spring [of c1820], the rich meadows [of Indiana] were infested with small worms on the high grass, in such quantities that they were called the 'army worms.' **1849** *Rep. Comm. Patents: Agric.* (1850) 9 Such insects as ... army and boll worms, annually destroy crops to the amount of twenty millions of dollars. **1854** *Harper's Mag.* VIII. 455/1 The moth that indicates the advent of the army-worm has a Quaker-like simplicity in its light, chocolate-colored body and wings. **1866** C. H. SMITH *Bill Arp* 95 In a week more the army worm had come along and devoured every pea vine on the plantation. **1881** *Amer. Naturalist* XV. 750 The true army worm has ... appeared in force in Central Illinois and ... Indiana, doing much injury ..., especially to oats. **1890** *Congress. Rec.* 21 April 3643 The crops are poor and every cotton-field destroyed by the 'army worm.' **1906** *Springfield W. Repub.* 19 July 15 The army worm has attacked the cranberry bogs of the Cape, after an absence of several years.

+Arocoun (aroughcun), etc. *Obs.* [Native name.] The raccoon. — **1610** *Estate of Virginia* 29 There are Arocouns, and Apossouns, in shape like to pigges. **c1615** STRACHEY *Virginia* (1849) I. x. 122 There is a beast they call arocoune, much like a badger, ... which useth to live on trees, as squirrells doe. **1616** SMITH *New England* 17 Beuers, wolues, foxes, both blacke and other; aroughconds, wild-cats, beares. **1624** — *Virginia* II. 27 A beast they call Aroughcun [etc., following Strachey].

***Around,** *adv.*

Frequently employed, chiefly in colloquial phrases, in place of Eng. *round* or *about*. Cf. ALL-AROUND *a.*

+1. Here and there at random; at, in, or to diverse places round about or in turn. *To board around* (cf. BOARD *v.*).

1776 A. R. ROBBINS *Journal* (1850) 6 Exercised and walked around with the officers in A.M. **1828** WEBSTER, *Around* ... [is] used in a looser sense, ... as, to travel around from town to town. **1834** *Deb. Congress* 6 Feb. 492 In looking around, the President had a right to select an officer who would honestly ... discharge his duty. **1869** BOWLES *New West* 170 We generally 'boarded around,' that is, ate at the mess which happened to have the most inviting meal. **1873** BEADLE *Undeveloped West* 651 It is told around for a fact that I could tell great confessions. **1890** *Harper's Mag.* Feb. 444/2 The introduction of homœopathy ... forced the old-school doctor to stir around and learn something ... about his business. **1898** A. NICHOLAS *Idyl of Wabash* 188 Teachers boarded around in those days.

+b. To some place, etc., expressed or implied; to a thing needing to be dealt with.

1857 *Lawrence* (Kansas) *Republican* 11 June 3 Persons wishing an outfit ... will do well to call around. **1887** WILKINS *Humble Romance* 35 There has been a good many things I haven't got around to. **1909** WHITE *Rules of Game* II. i, Come around some time.

+c. Through the round or circuit of a number of persons.

1834 *Deb. Congress* 6 Feb. 492 In looking around, the President had a right to select an officer who [etc.]. **1845** *N.Y. Commercial Advertiser* 13 Dec. (B.), The Senator was shinning around, to get gold for the rascally bank-rags which he was obliged to take. **1883** *Harper's Mag.* Feb. 446/1 The apples and nuts are just enough to go around. **1891** *Fur, Fin, & Feather* March 184 The sportsman will not find wolf-hunting very profitable in Taney county; there is not enough to [go] around. **1894** 'MARK TWAIN' *Letters* (1917) II. xxxiv. 614 It was around, this long time, that the concern was tottering. **a1906** 'O. HENRY' *Trimmed Lamp*, etc. 3 They came to the big city to find work because there was not enough to eat at their homes to go around.

+2. Moving or going about, esp. near by; astir.

1849 N. KINGSLEY *Diary* 58 Our captain is out around to day as it is so pleasant. **1864** NORTON *Army Lett.* 242 My health continues so-so, able to be around all the time. **1884** *Lisbon* (Dakota) *Star* 18 July, He is now able to be around, but has not yet fully recovered. **1887** F. FRANCIS *Saddle & Moccasin* 61 Mr. Maroney ain't long gone to bed.... I guess he'll be around at midday.

+3. Somewhere near; close by; about; present.

1848 BARTLETT 170 *To hang around*, to loiter about. **1856** M. J. HOLMES *Gilberts* iv, 'Anyway, Adeline likes him,' said she, 'and oh, she's so nice and good when he's around.' **a1859** *Police Gazette* (B.), I was standing around when the fight took place. **1865** 'GAIL HAMILTON' *Skirmishes* 220 He likes much to be 'around' when anything is going on. **1887** F. FRANCIS *Saddle & Moccasin* 56 He said ... he had promised his parents ... to sit around and reflect on Sunday mornings. **1902** WISTER in *Harper's Mag.* Feb. 464, I was not sure how much I really wanted to 'keep around.'

+4. *To come around*, to revive, come round.

1890 *Cent.* 1120/3 *To come round* or *around*, ... to recover; revive, as after fainting; regain one's former state of health. **1906** H. FITZGERALD *Sam Steele's Adv.* 71 By Jinks, Sam, he come around all right, and is alive an' kickin' today.

***Around,** *prep.* (Cf. note to AROUND *adv.*)

+1. From place to place over; about.

1828 WEBSTER. **1864** *Ib.* s.v., To travel around the country.

+2. About (a place, etc.); near by. *colloq.* {Also E.}

1848 BARTLETT 170 To 'hang around' a person, is to hang about him, to seek to be intimate with him. **1859** — 12 A friend assures me he has heard a clergyman in his sermon say of one of the disciples, that 'he stood around the cross.' **1888** *Missouri Repub.* 24 Feb. (F.), The people who hung around the hall in which the committee was in session.

+3. Past by making a circuit or turn. Also fig., esp. *to get* or *come around*, to cajole, deceive.

a1859 *Wedding at Nutmegville* (B.), I can tell you how it's all been brought about; they've come around that young man, they've come around him. **1859** BARTLETT 92 To get around [a person]. **1875** 'MARK TWAIN' *Old Times on Miss.* viii. (1876) 44 This has got to be learned; there isn't any getting around it. **1875** STOWE *We & Our Neighbors* iii. 38 Eva is my girl; I sha'n't let anyone get around her. **1887** *Atlantic Mo.* Feb. 279/2 Girls appear to know by intuition how to circumvent (which is, being translated, come around) the male dwellers in the abode. **1904** WALLER *Wood-carver* 282 Twiddie came singing around the corner of the house.

+4. Some time near (a specified hour); about.

1888 *N.Y. Mercury* (F.), Presuming he was born around three o'clock in the afternoon, he is under Leo and the Sun.

Arpen, variant (cf. Prov. *arpen*) of ARPENT. {1601}

1808 *Ann. 10th Congress* 1 Sess. II. 2875 A tract of land bordering on the river Detroit, and not exceeding in depth forty arpens, French measure. **1819** *Missouri Intell.* 23 April 3/2 Lands at public auction 7056 arpens on the Missouri. **1830** S. GIRARD *Will* 9 Real estate ... consisting of upwards of two hundred and eighty thousand *arpens*, or acres of land. **1852** REYNOLDS *Hist. Illinois* 31 The grants were generally made by so many *arpens* in front.

***Arpent.** {-1727}

+1. A French measure of land, of about an acre, used in Louisiana and some other states.

'A French acre, or 100 square rods' (W. '06). 'Parisian arpent, of one hundred and eighty feet square' (*Ann. Congress*, 1803). 'It is generally, even at this time, by the arpent, and not by the acre, that transfers of land are made in Louisiana' (1818 Darby *Emigrant's Guide* 6). 'A French acre, or *arpent*, is eleven rods and sixty-seven hundredths of a rod' (1852 Reynolds *Hist. Illinois* 31).

1800 Commons, etc. *Doc. Hist.* I. 253 The proprietor of several thousand arpents of land. **1803** *Ann. 8th Congress* 2 Sess. 1515 One Parisian arpent ... may be expected to produce ... twelve hundred weight of sugar. **1812** *McDonogh Papers* 10 They were sold at a price ... as high as 30, 35, and 40 cents per French arpent. **1816** *Niles' Reg.* X. 202/1 His experiments in the cultivation of the sugar cane have produced him at the rate of 2500 lbs of sugar ... per arpent. **1847** *Rep. Comm. Patents* (1848) 194 A bushel of seed weighing about twenty pounds, is enough for an arpent. **1883** CABLE in *Century Mag.* June 219 Truck-gardens covered the fertile arpents between and beyond.

+b. Attrib. with *land, lot.*

1837 WILLIAMS *Florida* 123 The gardens in the suburbs were sold ... in arpent lots. **1852** REYNOLDS *Hist. Illinois* 48 The arpent lands of this common field extended ... to the Mississippi.

+2. As a measure of length (see first quotation).

1818 DARBY *Emigrant's Guide* 6 The arpent is used also as a measure of length, being 180 feet, or 30 toises French, equal to 192 feet English or American feet, nearly. **1821** NUTTALL *Trav. Arkansa* xvi. 313 As the settlements are chiefly in single lines along the bank of the river, the land is commonly sold by the measurement in front, running back about 40 arpents, and has been disposed of at as much as 3000 dollars per arpent in front. **1822** *Ann. 17th Congress* 1 Sess. I. 127 A tract of land ... containing forty arpents on the Mississippi river and forty arpents back.

1833 SILLIMAN *Man. Sugar Cane* 18 Forty-two arpents of the permanent rail were in operation the last season. **1888** CABLE *Bonaventure* 68 For 'Thanase there was . . . the five-arpent pony-race.

+**Arrastre.** *W.* Also incorrectly **ar(r)astra.** [Mexican-Sp. (in Sp. = a dragging or leading).] A contrivance for grinding and mixing ores, consisting of a heavy stone dragged around on a circular bed of flat stones; a drag-mill.

(*a*) **1844** GREGG *Commerce of Prairies* II. 109 Crushing-mills (*arrastres*, as called at some mines) . . . are somewhat singular machines. **1881** RAYMOND *Mining Gloss.* s.v., The arrastre is chiefly used for ores containing free gold, and amalgamation is combined with the grinding. **1901** *Munsey's Mag.* XXV. 662/1 Then he begins sluicing, or builds an arrastre—the arrastre is the embryonic stamp mill.

(*b*) **1869** BROWNE *Adv. Apache Country* 266 Remains of arastras and 'whims' [in a deserted mine] . . . showed to some extent the large amount of labor expended upon these works. **1874** RAYMOND *6th Rep. Mines* 341 In the arrastra process nothing under $200-ore will pay working. **1876** — *8th Rep. Mines* 235 Retort gold from arrastras and some stamp-mills. **1882** *Rep. Precious Metals* 279 Four new steam arrastras, to replace others, worn out, have just been completed. **1909** 'MARK TWAIN' *Is Shakespeare Dead?* vii. 74, I know all about . . . arastras and how to charge them with quicksilver and sulphate of copper.

* **Arrearage.** Also †**arrerage, arearage.**

* **1.** The condition of being in arrears. {-*a*1637}

1699 *Virginia State P.* I. 63 The pay due to the rangers and their officers, we find to be thirteene mounth in arre[r]age.

* **2.** *pl.* Moneys outstanding or overdue; debts; arrears. {-1691}

The equivalent *arrears* has also been in use from the 17th cent., as in English.

1631 *Va. House of Burg. Jrnl.* 125 The rents . . . should nowe be demaunded, with the arrerages. **1636** *Essex Inst. Coll.* IV. 113/1 Dischardging first theire arearages in the townes booke. **1671** *Plymouth Laws* 268 It shall be lawfull for the treasurer to distreyne for all arrearages of rates. **1691** *Boston Rec.* 206 [The] treasurer . . . to sue for all rents and arearages of rents acrewinge to the use of the towne. **1714** *Narrag. Hist. Reg.* III. 277 The committee chosen . . . to gather the arrearages of my sallary. **1721** *Mass. H. Repr. Journals* III. 179 Upon their paying in the arrearages of interest, . . . the commissioners do suspend the sale of the land for two years time. **1781** *Baltimore Town Rec.* 42 All arrearages for rent from the butchers must be paid to the clerk. **1807** *Ann. 10th Congress* 1 Sess. I. 672 In paying the arrearages of bounty to some of the men of my company. **1827** COOPER *Prairie* v, So I left him, without calling in the paymaster to settle my arrearages. **1861** *Army Regulations* 38 Debts . . . will be paid by the paymaster out of arrearages due to the soldier. **1881** *Salem Gazette* 10 June 1/1 No paper discontinued until all arrearages are paid.

+**b.** Matters that have been left untreated.

1843 *Yale Lit. Mag.* VIII. 355 We must now go back and bring up arrearages in the history of Jedediah Small.

* **3.** An amount that remains unpaid.

1710 J. BUCKINGHAM *Naval Exped.* 6 Nov., Paid to Mr. Campbell, post master, seven shillings, being the arrearage due for the year 1710. **1746** *N.Y. Ev. Post* 14 Sept., Those in arrear to this paper above one year, are desired to send in their arrearage. **1789** *Ann. 1st Congress* I. 368 This arrearage, together with the domestic debt, is of great magnitude. **1911** HARRISON *Queed* iii. 28 You have called to collect my arrearage for board?

+**Arriero.** *S.W.* [Sp.] A muleteer.

'The Mexicans, who are the most expert in this business, are invariably employed in Texas, and for all mule trains used in the commerce of the prairies' (B. '59).

1838 'TEXIAN' *Mexico* v. *Texas* 95 They were beginning to beat some of the arrieros and to pillage their loads; when he of the talismanic truncheon rushed in amongst them. **1844** KENDALL *Santa Fé Exped.* II. 169 It is singular . . . with what facility the arrieros, or muleteers, can confine almost any burden upon the backs of asses and mules. **1846** *Life & Corr. Quitman* 279 We found encamped here a good many arrieros, with their trains of mules, on their way to Monterey with corn. **1854** BARTLETT *Narr.* II. 64 The Mexican laborers are better arrieros, and understand all that appertains to the mule better than Americans.

* **Arroba.** *S. & S.W.* [Sp.] A weight of 25 pounds.

[**1772** ROMANS in Phillips *Notes* (1924) 125 A Spaniard . . . made up a cargo of two thousand arobas [*sic*] of red and black drum fish, dry'd and salted.] **1848** BRYANT *California* 283 The same amount of arrobas (twenty-five pounds) of tallow. *Ib.* 410 The pearl shells . . . are worth, at La Paz, one dollar and a half the arroba, or twenty-five pounds. **1881** RAYMOND *Mining Gloss.* s.v. **1909** 'O. HENRY' *Options* 112 They wash the gold . . . and then they pack it in buckskin sacks of one arroba each.

* **Arrow.**

* **1.** The slender pointed shaft, usu. barbed and feathered, used in shooting with a bow.

1605 J. ROSIER *True Relation* (1887) 118 When we went on shore to trade with them, in one of their canoas I saw their bowes and arrowes. **1622** 'MOURT' *Relation* 90 Two or three savages . . . whetted and rubbed their arrowes and strings, and made shew of defiance. **1630** [F. HIGGINSON] *New England* 19 For their weapons, they [=Indians] have bowes and arrowes, some of them headed with bone, and some with brasse. **1654** *N. Car. Col. Rec.* I. 18 Actual possession was solemnly given to them by the great commander, . . . in delivering them a turf of the earth with an arrow shot into it. **1677** *Maine Doc. Hist.* VI. 178 If the wolf kill any of your catell, you take away our gons for it & arrows. **1709** [see ARROW-WOOD *n.*]. **1723** *New-Eng. Courant* 2-9 Sept. 2/2 [The Indians] kill'd an ox with their bows and arrows, and boil'd him in the Common. **1785** MARSHALL *Amer. Grove* 160 *Viburnum dentatum.* . . . The young shoots . . . are generally used by the natives for arrows; whence it is known by the name of Arrow-wood. **1807** GASS *Journal* 63 The Indians . . . shoot them [=buffaloes] with bows and arrows. **1848** COOPER *Oak Openings* I. xiv. 215 More than half the savages of the west fought with arrows and spears. **1855** LONGFELLOW *Hiawatha* III. 165 Then Iagoo. . . . From an oak-bough made the arrows, Tipped with flint, and winged with feathers. **1869** BROWNE *Adv. Apache Country* 248 Their poison-dipped arrows are sufficiently destructive. These arrows are made of cane, tipped with feathers, and pointed with bone. **1886** ALCOTT *Jo's Boys* v, Ted and Josie . . . proceeded to astonish their friends by . . . skirmishes about the house and grounds with tomahawks and bows and arrows. **1907** C. C. ANDREWS *Recoll.* (1928) 134 The Indian boys were shooting arrows at a target.

b. A representation of this missile.

1705 BEVERLEY *Virginia* III. 23 The usual mark [on Va. Indians' shoulders] is one, two, or three arrows; one nation paints these arrows upwards, another downwards, a third sideways. **1835** SIMMS *Yemassee* I. 92 Throwing the loose hunting shirt open to the shoulder, he displayed . . . the curved arrow which is the badge of the Yemassees.

2. The flowering stem of the sugar-cane. {1779-}

1853 *Harper's Mag.* VII. 748/2 These upper and unripe portions, together with the last and elongated one, known as the 'arrow,' retain their green leaves. **1889** FARMER 22 Planters never cut their canes until the *arrow* is well out.

3. See BROAD ARROW.

+**Arrow-arum.** A plant or species of the genus *Peltandra*, marked by sagittate leaves; esp. the calla lily, *P. sagittifolia.* — **1857** GRAY *Botany* 427 *Peltandra*, Raf., Arrow Arum. **1890** *Cent.* s.v. *Peltandra*, [Of] the arrow-arum there are 3 species, natives of American swamps and river-borders from New York to Georgia. **1901** MOHR *Plant Life Ala.* 425 *Peltandra sagittifolia* (Michx.) . . . White Arrow-Arum. Wild Calla Lily. . . . [Found in] boggy borders of pine-barren streams.

* **Arrow-case.** A quiver. {-1578} — **1846** SAGE *Scenes Rocky Mts.* viii, The Medicine Soldier . . . slung his arrow-case over his naked shoulders. **1867** *Amer. Naturalist* Aug. 287 After being turned right-side out, it makes an elegant arrow-case.

+**Arrow-fishing.** The taking of fish by means of the bow and arrow. Also *arrow-fisher.* — **1846** THORPE *Myst. Backwoods* 30 When the water is at *b*, the lakes are formed, and arrow-fishing is pursued. *Ib.* 31 The lakes over which the arrow-fisher twangs his bow.

Arrow-grass.

1. A plant or species belonging to the genus *Triglochin* of marsh herbs with grass-like leaves. {*c*1800-}

1813 MUHLENBERG *Cat. Plants* 37 *Triglochin:* Arrow Grass, . . . triandrous. Can., Car. **1836** LINCOLN *Botany* App. 145 *Triglochin . . . palustre* (arrow-grass). . . . [Grows in] marshes. **1847** WOOD *Botany* 528 *Triglochin maritimum*, . . . Sea Arrow-grass, . . . has a sweetish taste, and cattle are fond of it. *Ib.*, *T. palustre.* Marsh Arrow-grass. **1857** *Mass. Bd. Agric. 4th Rep.* I. 109 The sea arrow grass is common in our salt marshes, having rush-like leaves of a sweetish taste, relished by cattle. **1901** MOHR *Plant Life Ala.* 329 Arrow-grass. Marsh plants of frigid and temperate regions. . . . North America [yields] 3 species.

+**2.** (See quotation.)

1889 VASEY *Agric. Grasses* 42 *Stipa spartea* is called porcupine grass, arrow grass, and devil's knitting-needles, from the long, stiff, twisted awns inclosing the seed.

* **Arrow-head, Arrowhead.**

* **1.** The head or pointed end of an arrow.

1658 GORGES *Briefe Narr.* 28 Disorderly persons . . . sell unto the savages, musquets, fowling-pieces, powder, shot, swords, arrow-heads, and other armes. **1817** S. BROWN *Western Gaz.* 170 One of these [mounds] having been opened, bones, stone-axes, arrow-heads, &c. were found in abundance. **1824** DODDRIDGE *Notes* 26 For a long time after the settlement of the country, the Indian arrow heads furnished the main supply of gun-flints. **1855** LONGFELLOW *Hiawatha* IV. 263 There the ancient Arrow-maker Made his arrow-heads of sandstone, Arrow-heads of chalcedony, Arrow-heads of flint and jasper. **1863** MITCHELL *My Farm* 121, I have turned up an arrow-head or two in the neighborhood, chipped from white quartz. **1897** *Outing* April 27/1 Thump, the arrow-head struck in the very middle of the fluff.

* **2.** A genus of aquatic plants (*Sagittaria*) having leaves shaped like the head of an arrow; a species or a plant of this genus, as *S. sagittifolia* or *S. variabilis.* {-1809}

1791 MUHLENBERG *Index Florae* 180 *Sagittaria*, Arrow-head. **1805** LEWIS & CLARK *Orig. Journals* (1904) III. II. 196 This root they call *Wap-pa-to*, the Bulb of which the Chinese cultivate in great quantities called the *Sa-git-ti-folia* [sic] or common arrowhead. **1832** WILLIAMSON *Maine* I. 130 Arrowhead, (*Sagittaria*,) is aquatic, . . . deriving its name from the leaves, which are formed like the head of an arrow. **1838** FLAGG *Far West* II. 30 The blood-red sumach . . . and the *sagittaria*, or arrow-head, with its three-leaved calyx . . . lend a finished richness of hue to the landscape. **1883** HOWELLS in *Harper's Mag.* Dec. 70/2 The cat-tails and arrow-heads in the 'ma'sh' at Ponkwasset.

b. Applied to other plants with leaves resembling arrow-heads.

1835 HOFFMAN *Winter in West* I. 171, I could fancy . . . the lilac-tinted adder's-tongue, and straw-colored arrow-head, shooting through the long grass between. **1904** STRATTON-PORTER *Freckles* 55 Grasses among which lifted the creamy spikes of the arrow-head.

+**Arrowing**, *vbl. n.* [f. ARROW 2.] The forming of the seed upon the sugar-cane. — **1856** OLMSTEAD *Slave States* 663 This function (called *arrowing*) it [=the sugar-cane] only performs in a very hot and steadily hot climate.

+**Arrow-leaf.**

1. =ARROWHEAD 2.

1880 *Harper's Mag.* June 70 The frog pond with lush growth of arrow leaves and pickerel weed. **1889** *Ib.* May 860/2 The yellow dock, white arrow-leaf, blue pickerel weed. **1894** *Amer. Folk-Lore* VII. 103 *Sagittaria variabilis*, . . . arrow-leaf, N.Y.

2. *attrib.* =ARROW-LEAVED *a.*

1869 FULLER *Flower Gatherers* 110 That is the Arrow-leaf-violet, *Viola Sagittata.* **1901** MOHR *Plant Life Ala.* 626 Arrow-leaf Violet. . . . Flowers blue. April; not frequent.

Arrow-leaved, *a.* Having arrow-shaped leaves; sagittate. — **1843** TORREY *Flora N.Y.* I. 71 *Viola sagittata*, Arrow-leaved Violet, . . . [grows] in fields and on dry hill-sides. *Ib.* II. 241 *Peltandra Virginica* . . . Arrow-leaved Arum. . . . Swamps and borders of ponds. **1847** DARLINGTON *Weeds & Plants* 282 Arrow-leaved Tear-thumb . . . [grows in] swampy meadows and thickets: New York to Florida. **1901** MOHR *Plant Life Ala.* 486 Arrow-leaved Tear-thumb . . . [grows in] low damp thickets.

Arrow-point.

1. The point or the head of an arrow.

1775 ADAIR *Indians* 425 One of those flint arrow-points is reckoned . . . a preservative against every kind of bewitching charm. **1824** DODDRIDGE *Notes* 26 The great number of those arrow points found all over the country. **1835** HOFFMAN *Winter in West* I. 279, I picked up on the side of the pass . . . several arrow-points. **1909** STRATTON-PORTER *Girl of Limberlost* iii. 51, I have a bushel of arrow points gathered, a stack of axes [etc.].

2. A point resembling that of an arrow.

1887 *Harper's Mag.* Nov. 944/2 When I met him at the arrow-point between Broadway and Fifth Avenue.

‖ **Arrow-quiver.** An arrow-case; a quiver. — **1867** *Amer. Naturalist* Aug. 287 A good many [lynxes] are killed by the Indians, who use their beautiful spotted skins for arrow-quivers.

Arrowroot.

1. A nutritious starch or medicinal food obtained from the fleshy roots of various species of *Maranta*, esp. *M. arundinacea.* {1811–}

1820 *Pharmacopœia of U.S.A.* 40 Arrow root. *Maranta arundinacea.* **1850** *Western Journal* IV. 264 Arrowroot, soon to become . . . an important article, among the products of [Florida]. *Ib.*, Bermuda arrowroot . . . is not better in appearance than the Florida article, and for culinary purposes is greatly inferior. **1876** M. F. HENDERSON *Cooking* 323 Add two heaping tea-spoonfuls of best arrowroot, rubbed smooth with a little cold water.

b. A plant, as *Maranta arundinacea*, having tubers from which this starch is obtained; also, its tubers. {1696–}

1850 *Western Journal* IV. 263 The culture of Arrowroot [in Florida] is likely to prove successful and profitable. *Ib.* 264 He who knows how to make a crop of corn, cannot fail to make a crop of arrowroot.

+**2.** The coontie, *Zamia integrifolia* (*Z. pumila*). Cf. 3 b.

1823 G. A. MCCALL *Lett. from Frontiers* (1868) 64 A half-worn sieve made of split cane, such as the Indian housewife used to bolt her flour, whether of corn or coonta-root, (a species of arrow-root). **1852** F. R. GOULDING *Young Marooners* xxvi. 173 Harold discovered a fine patch of Coontah or arrowroot from which a beautiful flour can be manufactured. **1871** DE VERE 411 The farina obtained from the so-called Arrow-Root.

+**b.** A starchy foodstuff obtained from its stems.

1826 G. A. MCCALL *Lett. from Frontiers* (1868) 157 The regions where the *coonta*, or arrow-root, the chief substitute for corn, or farinaceous food, is to be sought. **1860** CHAPMAN *Flora South. U.S.* 437 Coontie. . . . Low grounds, South Florida.—The stem abounds in starch, from which the Florida Arrowroot is obtained.

3. Attrib. with *jelly, preparation, water.*

1859 BARTLETT 98 An arrowroot preparation from the root of *Zamia integrifolia* by the Indians in Florida, where the plant is indigenous. *Ib.* 111 [Recipe for making] Arrow-root Water. **1876** M. F. HENDERSON *Cooking* 323 Arrowroot Jelly or Blanc-mange . . . may be flavored with lemon-juice if made with water.

+**b.** *Arrowroot palm, plant* (see quots. and sense 2).

1889 *Cent., Coontie, Coonty*, the *Zamia integrifolia*, or arrowroot-plant of Florida. **1901** MOHR *Plant Life Ala.* 137 The tropical so-called sago palm (*Cycas revoluta*) and arrowroot palm (*Zamia integrifolia*) of southern Florida add to the number of decorative evergreen plants.

+**Arrow-rush.** A rush with arrow-like stems. — **1846** EMORY *Military Reconn.* 11 The low grounds abound in . . . arrow rush.

‖ **Arrow-shield.** [ARROW 1.] **1832** CATLIN *Indians* I. 23 The Indian . . . mount[s] his snorting steed, with his bow and quiver slung, his arrow-shield upon his arm.

‖ **Arrow-stone.** A belemnite. — **1843** *Amer. Pioneer* II. 196 Several Indian flint arrow-stones . . . were discovered by . . . Mr. Gridley.

+**Arrow-tie.** 'A tie of hoop-iron used in baling cotton' (*Cent.*).

‖ **Arrow-tip.** An arrow-head. — **1880** *Scribner's Mo.* April 884 They [=flint-blocks] were doubtless split by the Indians from the oval nodules as materials for arrow-tips.

+**Arrow-weed. a.** The arrowhead, *Sagitta sagittifolia.* **b.** (See quotation 1876.)

1846 J. W. ABERT in Emory *Military Reconn.* 434 Some brackish pools . . . bordered with the cat-tail (*typha latifolia*) and arrow weed (*sagittaria sagittifolia*). **1869** BROWNE *Adv. Apache Country* 51 Thickets of arrow-weed lined the way, and forests of cotton-wood loomed up ahead. *Ib.* 55 An extensive alluvial valley, clothed with willow, cotton-wood, mesquit, and arrow-weed. **1876** *Field & Forest* II. 55 These Mexican jumping seeds . . . are derived from a plant called arrow weed, or *Yerba de flecha*, and *Colliguaja* by the Mexicans. **1886** S. W. MITCHELL *R. Blake* 263 Those pools close by with purpled arrow-weed.

+**Arrow-wood.**

1. One or other shrub or small tree bearing slender straight branches or shoots suitable for making arrows; esp. the viburnum (as *V. dentatum, pubescens*), also the flowering dogwood, etc.

1709 LAWSON *Carolina* 100 Arrow-wood, growing on the banks, is used, by the Indians, for arrows and gun-sticks. **1785** MARSHALL *Amer. Grove* 160 *Viburnum dentatum.* Toothed-leaved Viburnum, or Arrow Wood. This grows naturally in moist places. **1814** PURSH *Flora Amer.* I. 202 *Viburnum dentatum.* . . . Berries dark blue; known by the name of Arrow-wood. **1832** KENNEDY *Swallow Barn* I. xv. 226 Morasses . . . now over-grown with thickets of arrow-wood, nine-bark, and various other shrubs. **1850** *New Eng. Farmer* II. 60 The first [=dogwood] . . . is the Arrowwood; so called from the use once made of its straight shoots, by the Indians, for their arrows. **1850** AUDUBON *Western Journal* (1906) 218 On this ridge the grass is sparse, and 'arrow-wood' was plentiful. **1892** APGAR *Trees Northern U.S.* 114 Arrow-wood . . . [is] a shrub or small tree, 5 to 15 ft. high, with ash-colored bark.

2. (See quotations.)

1815 DRAKE *Cincinnati* ii. 77 [Plants growing in Miami country include] Indian arrow-wood. **1819** M'MURTRIE *Sk. Louisville* 217 *Euonymus carolinensis*, Indian Arrow Wood. **1884** SARGENT *Rep. Forests* 38 *Euonymus atropurpureus.* . . . Burning Bush. Wahoo. Spindle Tree. Arrow Wood.

+**Arroyo.** *S.W.* Also **arroya.** [Sp. Cf. ROYO.]

1. A rivulet, stream, or brook.

[**1806** *Ann. 10th Congress* 1 Sess. I. 571 The country east of the Sabine to the Arroyo Hondo.] **1846** SAGE *Scenes Rocky Mts.* xix, The banks of this *arroyo* are very steep and high, disclosing now and then, spreads of beautiful bottom lands with occasional groves of cottonwoods. **1849** MARCY *Rep.* (Ex. Doc. No. 64) 186 We crossed an 'arroyo' in which there were water and wood in abundance. **1854** BARTLETT *Narr.* I. 231 The *arroyo* . . . became so much swollen as to render it difficult to cross. **1878** BEADLE *Western Wilds* 68 The two days we followed the arroyo, grass was abundant. **1884** *Century Mag.* Sept. 657 A little valley, the *arroyo* of Santa Lucia, into which . . . comes through another *arroyo* of a few hundred yards in length the water from . . . the great spring.

2. The dry bed of a stream; a deep, dry channel; a gully. Freq. *dry arroyo.*

1843 FREMONT *Exped.* 252 We discovered . . . groves of oak trees on a dry arroyo. **1854** BARTLETT *Narr.* II. 130 In an arroyo, or place where there was a slight depression in the desert, marked by some mezquit bushes. **1859** MARCY *Prairie Traveler* 292 'New River,' though usually set down, is a dry arroya. **1869** BROWNE *Adv. Apache Country* 188 Roaring torrents have become dry arroyas. **1888** *Harper's Mag.* June 41/1 A mere sandy arroyo enters Kansas . . . and cuts its valley deeper as it descends the slope of the State. **1903** A. ADAMS *Log Cowboy* xx. 130 The point of the herd crossed the dry arroyo.

3. *Arroyo grape*, the riverside grape.

1885 HAVARD *Flora W. & S. Texas* 511 Arroyo Grape . . . [is a] thrifty climber, the small but excellent berries maturing in October. **1891** COULTER *Bot. W. Texas* I. 63 *Vitis riparia* . . . [grows on] stream banks or near water, common in most of the watered cañons of western Texas. Also known as 'arroyo grape.'

* **Arsenal.**

***1.** A building or establishment for the manufacture and storage, or for the storage only, of arms, equipment, and munitions of war.

1783 R. PUTNAM in *Memoirs* 201 Besides West Point there will undoubtedly be other arsinals . . . that will require small guards. **1787**

Constitution i. § 8 The erection of forts, magazines, arsenals, dockyards, and other needful buildings. **1790** *Ann. 1st Congress* I. 990 That the United States occupy a tract of land, on which are erected the fortifications and arsenal at West Point. **1816** *Ann. 14th Congress* 2 Sess. 271 There shall be erected . . . one or more arsenal or depot for arms, equipments, tents, and equipage, from which supplies shall be furnished. **1838** *Indiana H. Rep. J.* 116 To inquire whether the public good, and the security of the numerous public arms in this State do not require the establishment of a State Arsenal. **1852** *Harper's Mag.* V. 147/1 The new arsenal [at Springfield, Mass.], alone, is intended to contain three hundred thousand [muskets]. **1861** *Army Regulations* 152 Unserviceable arms will be sent to an arsenal for repair. **1881-5** McClellan *Own Story* 535, I signed a requisition for small arms and ammunition upon the commandant of the arsenal. **1895** M. A. Jackson *Memoirs* 615 They were citizen soldiery, . . . armed partly with what arms were found in the government arsenal.

b. Attrib. with *ground, port.*

1818 *Ann. 15th Congress* 1 Sess. I. 268 That two suitable stations may be selected for the establishment of arsenal ports. **1852** *Harper's Mag.* V. 159/2 The new arsenal . . . has already been alluded to in the description of the general view of the arsenal grounds.

‖**2.** The weapons carried by a person.

*a***1861** Winthrop *J. Brent* iv. 38 If he were but shaved and clipped, . . . disarmed of his dangerous looking arsenal, . . . seems to me I should know him.

Arsenic.** The grayish mineral so named. — **1842** *Niles' Nat. Reg.* 27 Aug. 416 Dr. Charles T. Jackson, [N.H.] State geologist, has lately examined a vein of Arsenic in Dunbarton. . . . Dr. Jackson says this may be easily mined. *c1857** Dana *Mineralogy* (1870) 225 Native arsenic, . . . in the United States, . . . has been observed at Haverhill, N.H., in mica slate, and also at Jackson in the same state. **1869** Browne *Adv. Apache Country* 208 The lode appears to be large, . . . and the ore . . . is composed of argentiferous galena, impregnated with arsenic.

***Arsesmart, Arsmart.** ?*Obs.* Also **asmart, ass smart.** One or other plant belonging to the genus *Polygonum;* esp. the common smartweed, *P. Hydropiper.*

1640 Parkinson *Theater of Plants* 857 Sharpe Arsmart of Virginia. *Ib.*, Shrub spotted Arsmart of Virginia with white flowers. **1784** Cutler in *Mem. Academy* I. 439 Arsmart . . . occasions severe smarting when rubbed on the flesh. . . . It dyes wool yellow. *Ib.* 440 Heartsease. Spotted Arsmart. . . . It will dye woollen cloth yellow, after the cloth has been dipped in a solution of alum. **1792** Imlay *Western Territory* 208 Of herbs, we have of the wild sort . . . dock, asmart, glass-wort, hellebore. **1804-6** Lewis & Clark *Orig. Journals* (1904) VI. i. 122 The ass smart is also found in the same neighborhood [=up to little Sioux River]. **1832** Williamson *Maine* I. 120 Arsmart, a well-known low herb, is said to dye a deep yellow.

+**Arse-up.** A species of woodpecker. — *a***1870** Chipman *Notes on Bartlett* 12 *Arse-up*, small slate-colored woodpecker; so named from its facility and habit of running upward upon a tree's trunk while its head is lower than its tail. Local in Connecticut.

Arson. The malicious burning of a dwelling, church, school, etc. {*a*1680-}

1785 *Mass. Perpetual Laws* (1788) 249 An act against arson, and other malicious burning. **1817** *Yankee Traveller* 88 A felon, charged with the high crime or misdemeanor of *arson* or man-slaughter. **1828** Webster s.v., In Connecticut, the burning not only of a dwelling house or contiguous building, but of a ship or other vessel, is declared to be arson, if human life is thereby destroyed or put to hazard. **1833** *Ill. Revised Laws* 181 Every person who shall wilfully and maliciously burn, or cause to be burned, any dwelling-house, kitchen, office [etc.] . . . shall be deemed guilty of arson. **1877** *Let.* in *N.Y. Herald* 25 July, P. M. Arthur . . . states that if Thomas A. Scott had gone himself to Pittsburgh, bloodshed and arson would have been averted. **1886** Logan *Great Conspiracy* 645 Riots and arson, were among the mildest methods proposed . . . to make the War for the Union a 'failure.'

+**Art editor.** The editor of a section dealing with art in a newspaper or periodical. — **1877** *Harper's Mag.* Dec. 53/2 The day editor [puts] . . . news relating to art in the hands of the art editor.

***Artemisia.**

1. A large genus of plants of the aster family, marked by a peculiar bitter or aromatic taste; a plant of this genus, esp. the sage-brush (*A. tridentata* or *A. cana*), common on the western plains. Also attrib. with *bush.* {1753-}

1817 J. Bradbury *Travels* 116 A species of Artemisia, common on the prairies, and known to the hunters by the name of Hyssop. **1828** Webster, *Absinthium* . . . a species of Artemisia. **1843** Fremont *Exped.* 71 The various artemisias . . . now in bloom, . . . give much gayety to the landscape of the plains. **1846** Emory *Military Reconn.* 15 The plains are covered with very short grass, . . . artemisia, in abundance. **1852** Marcy *Expl. Red River* (1854) 26 A continuous succession of barren sand-hills, producing no other herbage than the artemisia, and a dense growth of dwarf oak bushes. **1856** [G. H. Derby] *Phoenixiana* iii. 46 The sandy nature of the soil, sparsely dotted with bunches of cactus and artemisia.

attrib. **1843** Fremont *Exped.* 164 Uplands . . . covered with artemisia bushes. **1852** Stansbury *Gt. Salt Lake* 99 Wood was very scarce: we had but artemisia-bushes and a few charred sticks found amid the ashes of the extinguished fires left by the emigrants.

2. A species of chrysanthemum (see quotation).

1836 Lincoln *Botany* App. 87 *Chrysanthemum coronarium.* . . . Garden chrysanthemum, improperly called artemisia. Ex[otic].

+**Artemisie (-ishy).** [Var. of prec.] (See quotations.) — **1846** Sage *Scenes Rocky Mts.* xii, *Artemisie*, or rather *greasewood* of the mountaineers, became quite abundant, as did *absinthe.* or wild sage. **1889** R. T. Cooke *Steadfast* xxii. 236 A great bow-pot of early chrysanthemums, 'artemishys' Aunt Ruthy called them, filled the chimney.

+**Arter,** dialect variant of 'after.' — **1815** Humphreys *Yankey* 31 But arter all, now I think on't, I wish to know . . . what is your pertiklar calling. *Ib.* 103 Glossary, *Arter*, after. **1847** *Chunky's Fight* 137, I seen she [=a panther] were arter my throat! and with that I grabbed hern.

***Artery.**

+**1.** The chief river of a river-system.

1827 Cooper *Prairie* xxiv, The mighty arteries of the Missouri and Mississippi. *Ib.* xxxiv, Issuing from one stream into another, . . . they soon entered the grand artery of the Western waters. **1829** B. Hall *Travels in N. A.* III. 322 Not only of those great rivers, but of . . . hundreds of others, tributaries to this great artery [=the Mississippi], as it is well called by the American writers. **1850** G. Hines *Voyage* 329 This great artery of Oregon [=Columbia River] . . . receives the Cowilitz from the north.

+**2.** A main channel or passage in any branching system of communication, etc. {1885}

1850 Glisan *Jrnl. Army Life* 27 When many of those great arteries of commerce—the railroads—shall have centered in this well-located city. **1860** Maury *Phys. Geog. Sea* v. 100 These streams are the great arteries of inland commerce. **1887** George *40 Yrs. on Rail* 96 The little road . . . now boasts of being a main artery in the vast system of the Chicago and North-Western railway.

Artesian, *a.* {1830-}

1. *Artesian well*, a deep-bored well, in which the water is forced to the surface by natural internal pressure. {1860-}

1842 *Knickerb.* XIX. 160 In the attempts we have made at Artesian wells. **1843** *Niles' Nat. Reg.* 22 July 336 Artesian Wells. An experiment made at Norfolk, Va., has succeeded in bringing up excellent water. . . . The *Herald* urges the corporation to sink others. **1860** Abbott *South & North* 126 The Artesian well . . . pours forth an unintermitted stream of very clear, luke-warm water. **1869** Browne *Adv. Apache Country* 284 Artesian wells, . . . after all, must eventually be the salvation of Arizona. **1903** *Indian Laws & Tr.* III. 22 Labor [may be] employed for the construction of artesian wells, ditches, and other works for irrigation.

2. Pertaining to an artesian well. Also *fig.* {1830-}

1852 *Harper's Mag.* V. 337/2 My remark should be an Artesian bore to it. **1865** *Atlantic Mo.* XV. 393 A tubing of cast-iron artesian pipe.

***Artichoke.** Also †**hartichoke. a.** The Jerusalem artichoke (*Helianthus tuberosus*), native in Canada and the Mississippi valley. **b.** The artichoke proper (*Cynara scolymus*).

1649 *Descr. Virginia* 4 They have roots of severall kindes, . . . parsnips, onions, and hartichokes. **1698** G. Thomas *Acc. Penna. & N.J.* 21 Cucumbers, coshaws, artichokes, with many others, . . . besides what grows naturally wild in the country. **1724** H. Jones *Virginia* 60 The worst thing in their gardens, that I know, is the artichoke. **1737** Brickell *N. Carolina* 19 The artichoak I have observed but in two places in this Province. **1787** Washington *Diaries* III. 194 At Muddy hole the artichokes were planted. **1790** S. Deane *New-Eng. Farmer* 12 Artichoke, *helianthus tuberosus*, . . . a plant of the sun-flower kind, with an esculent root, that is perennial. It is said to be a native of America. **1832** Williamson *Maine* I. 129 The artichoke is somewhat tasteless; otherwise it resembles a small oblong potatoe. **1849** *Rep. Comm. Patents: Agric.* (1850) 451 Wild roots . . . that the Indians dig for food . . . [include] artichoke. **1850** L. Sawyer *Way Sketches* 93 The roots taste something like the artichoke found in the States. **1860** S. Mordecai *Virginia* xix. 211 Vegetables . . . such as . . . chickweed for bird fanciers and thistles —but not a good substitute for artichokes. **1886** P. G. Ebbutt *Kansas Emigrant Life* 72 On the prairies . . . artichokes, too, were abundant.

***Article,** *n.*

+**1.** An article *of* merchandise or property, in the person of a slave.

1837 H. Martineau *Society* II. 325 The creditors . . . answered that these young ladies [his 'quadroon' nieces] were 'a first-rate article,' too valuable to be relinquished. **1852** Stowe *Uncle Tom* i, There's an article now! You might make your fortune on that ar gal in Orleans, any day. *Ib.* xxx, [The trader] lifted up her curly hair, and pronounced her a first-rate article. **1856** — *Dred* I. 61 Milly's children, from their fine developments, were much coveted articles. **1869** Tourgee *Toinette* v. (1881) 64 The recognition of 'the nigger' as a human being, . . . instead of an article of merchandise.

+**2.** In conveyancing: (see quotation).

*a***1841** Buckingham *America* III. 103 The *article* was a device, of American origin, unknown in the English system of conveyancing; granting the possession, but not the fee of the land.

***Article,** *v. intr.* To stipulate in articles *for* something. *Obs.* {1656, 1770} — **1814** *Boston Spectator* 29 Jan. 20/1 Some of them in the lower classes . . . prostitute their bodies for money; whilst those of a higher degree article for it in their very marriage-contracts!

***Artificer.**

***1.** One who pursues an industrial handicraft; a craftsman or mechanic.

1633 *Mass. Bay Rec.* I. 109 And soe for other worke that shalbe done by the greate by any other artificer. **1639** *Md. Archives* I. 76 Provided that . . . no man (artificers excepted) be pressed to labour at the said building before November. **1660** *Springfield Rec.* I. 204 All carpenters, joyners, wheel wrights, or such like artificers. **1729** FRANKLIN *Busy-body* Wks. II. 129 There are among us great numbers of honest artificers. **1781** *Virginia State P.* I. 488 The artificers from Warwick are not yet arrived. **1794** WILLIAMS *Vermont* 176 The instruments and tools with which the artificers are furnished. **1809** KENDALL *Travels* I. 227 The inhabitants are principally artificers, as nailers, joiners and cartwrights. **1865** *Atlantic Mo.* XV. 603 Carpenters, upholsterers, and artificers await their will.

2. A military mechanic attached to the ordnance, artillery, or engineer service, for repairing or constructing materials of war. {1804–}

1758 *Lett. to Washington* II. 321 The 2d. Company of Artificers of the 2d. Regiment. **1775** *Journals Cont. Congress* III. 400 Artificers of different sorts have been employed in the army. **1802** *Ann. 7th Congress* App. 1306 Each company to consist of one captain, one first lieutenant, . . . four musicians, eight artificers. **1847** *Army Regulations* 24 No man, unless he be a carpenter, joiner, carriage-maker, blacksmith, saddler, or harness-maker, will be mustered as an 'artificer.' **1861** *Army Regulations* 520 Every volunteer non-commissioned officer, private, musician, and artificer, who enters the service.

Artificial, *n.* {1611–1743} +An artificial flower.

1842 *Amer. Pioneer* I. 274 After they have passed the lines of silks, laces and artificials. **1846–51** MRS. WHITCHER *Bedott P.* xxvi. 316 She had on a yaller bunnit, with a great pink artificial on it. **1857** B. YOUNG in *Jrnl. Discourses* V. 98 (Th.), [My wives will say] O dear, are there no ribbons coming? I want that artificial, quick. **1882** *Harper's Mag.* Feb. 436/2 She was going to the milliner's to buy some artificials. **1903** G. C. EGGLESTON *First of Hoosiers* 121 The preachers [a1853] used to denounce the sinful wearing of 'artificials' . . . in women's bonnets.

***Artificial,** *a.* Made or produced by art, in contrast to 'natural.'

In various applications, as *artificial fly* {1611–}, *flower* {1753–}, *teeth* {1684–}, etc.

(1) **1794** *Ann. 3rd Congress* 1472 Artificial flowers, feathers, and other ornaments for women's head-dresses. **1807** IRVING, etc. *Salmagundi* iii. 56 Mrs. Toole . . . sallies out under cover of a forest of artificial flowers. **1851** CIST *Cincinnati* 49 Artists, 25 [persons]; Artific. flowr. makers, 4. **1865** *Atlantic Mo.* XV. 321 The youngest . . . was a regular apprentice in an artificial-flower manufactory. **1880** *Harper's Mag.* June 30/2 The artificial-flower trade employs about four thousand women.

(2) **1837** *Harvardiana* III. 189 The tall pedagogue broke out a whole row of very white artificial teeth. **1857** [D. H. STROTHER] *Virginia* 18 A supply of artificial flies. **1883** *Century Mag.* July 383/2 On such a charming . . . river as this, the artificial fly alone should be used to lure the gamy bass.

(3) **1815** TICKNOR in *Life* I. 34 We reached the artificial lawn on which the house [of Mr. Jefferson] stands. **1818** *Niles' Reg.* XV. 23/1 A great number of artificial roads have been completed in the eastern and middle states. **1855** GLISAN *Jrnl. Army Life* 213 Its numerous artificial springs, or artesian wells, . . . are the finest in the Union.

(4) **1843** *Niles' Nat. Reg.* 29 July 348 In appearance the artificial ice closely resembles the natural; it is a semi-transparent body of crystal, composed of chemical salts.

Artillerist, *n.* {1778–} An artilleryman; a gunner.

1777 *Journals Cont. Congress* VIII. 692 Resolved, That General Washington be directed . . . to order . . . an experienced artillerist, to repair immediately to the city of Annapolis. **1794** *Ann. 3rd Congress* 86 An act providing for raising and organizing a Corps of Artillerists and Engineers. **1807** *Ann. 10th Congress* 1 Sess. I. 683 A second lieutenant in the regiment of artillerists. **1827** COOPER *Prairie* xxv, Would to Heaven that some of my trusty artillerists might fall upon this accursed encampment! **1862** NORTON *Army Lett.* 87 Our artillery and our artillerists are vastly superior to the rebels. **1881–5** MCCLELLAN *Own Story* 439 The artillerists had proved their heroism and devotion by standing to their guns.

***Artillery.** Also †**artilery, artillary.**

***1.** Large guns mounted on carriages; cannon; ordnance. (In early use with *great*.)

1652 *Boston Rec.* 113 Edward Hutchinson is . . . chosen Gentleman of the great Artillery of Boston. **1653** *Ib.* 114 What is contributed within this towne to repayr the great artilery and fortifiecasyon. **1689** *Maine Doc. Hist.* V. 47 This government [is] to have the first tender and refusal of the great artillery if drawn off the place. **1715** *Boston News-Letter* 6 June 2/1 Saturday last being His Majesty's Birth Day, . . . the artillery of the fort and of the man of war, were fired. **1755** WASHINGTON *Let.* Writings I. 166 Leaving the heavy artillery, baggage, &c. . . . to follow by slow and easy marches. **1776** *Journals Cont. Congress* VI. 876 That General Gates be informed, that Congress have it not in their power at present to supply him with the artillery he desires. **1797** *Ann. 5th Congress* I. 325 The bill for raising an additional force of artillery. **1807** *Ann. 10th Congress* 1 Sess. I. 482 He mentioned that with three pieces of artillery . . . he could defend any pass in the Allegany mountains. **1838** *Diplom. Corr. Texas* (1911) III. 1211 A severe and bloody battle fought in the open prairie without artillery and without cavalry on the part of Texas. **1865** BOUDRYE *Fifth N.Y. Cavalry* 59 The rebels . . . brought their artillery into position and commenced firing. **1881–5** MCCLELLAN *Own Story* 78 The artillery numbered 228 guns, but many of the batteries were still entirely unfit to take the field.

2. a. The Artillery Company of Boston. *Obs.*

1646 *Harvard Rec.* I. 26 Neither shall any without licence of the overseers of the colledge bee of the artillery or traine-band. **1653** [see ARMORY 1]. **1676** SEWALL *Diary* I. 13 Mr. Bendal [is chosen] ensign of the Artillery. **1709** *Ib.* II. 255, I dined with the artillery at Powells.

b. That branch of the military service which manages guns and other ordnance in war. {1786–}

1775 *Journals Cont. Congress* II. 220 That in the artillery the pay of captain be 26 . . . dollars per month. *Ib.* III. 399 That the regiment of artillery consist of one Colonel, two lieutenant Colonels, two Majors and twelve companies. **1800** *Ann. 6th Congress* 821 The second regiment of artillery and engineers shall consist but of three battalions. **1842** E. A. HITCHCOCK *Journal* (1930) 108 Major Peters passed the Point . . . with his company of artillery. **1868** *Mich. Agric. Rep.* VII. 336 The very brilliant review of artillery and infantry, held on the fair grounds.

3. Attrib., of things, activities, or persons connected with the use of artillery.

a. 1641 *Mass. Bay Rec.* I. 340 Mr. Flint . . . & Abraham Browne are appointed to accompany Mr. Oliver to see the artillery land layd out. **1686** SEWALL *Diary* I. 151 Artillery Training. Not one old captain there. **1703** *Ib.* II. 88 Artil. Training, I train'd in the forenoon. **1709** *Ib.* 254 Being Artillery day, and Mr. Higginson dead, I put on my mourning rapier. **1776** *Journals Cont. Congress* IV 112 If he [=General Schuyler] finds him capable, . . . to employ him in the artillery service. **1796** *Ann. 4th Congress* 2 Sess. 2571 The works consist of a fort, a citadel, a battery; . . . an artillery store, a guard house. **1861** WINTHROP *Open Air* 246 The two freight-cars we were using for artillery-wagons. **1861** *Army Regulations* 19 At the artillery school, Fort Monroe. **1863** NORTON *Army Lett.* 137 When Burnside got stuck in the mud, the artillery harness all broke. **1881–5** MCCLELLAN *Own Story* 414 A rapid artillery-fire . . . was maintained along the whole front.

b. 1649 *Mass. Bay Rec.* II. 270 The surveyer generall . . . lent one barrell & a halfe of the countryes store of powder to the artilery officers of Boston. **1778** *Journals Cont. Congress* X. 150 A commission of captain in Colonel Flower's regiment of artillery artificers. **1790** R. PUTNAM in *Memoirs* (1903) 241 An artillery core equel to a regiment of infentry in expence. **1855** SARGENT *Braddock's Exped.* 203 Four artillery-officers . . . were left with Dunbar. **1861** *Army Regulations* 19 The non-commissioned officers of bands for artillery regiments. **1865** *Atlantic Mo.* XV. 142 A certain artillery force that had come down the river. **1869** TOURGEE *Toinette* xxxv. (1881) 362 A gigantic artillery captain, bearded like the pard. **1881–5** MCCLELLAN *Own Story* 417 Robertson's and Tidball's horse-batteries from the artillery reserve.

c. *c*1876 in W. Allen *Chamberlain's Admin.* (1888) 383 The armed organizations which go under the names of 'Rifle Clubs,' 'Sabre Clubs,' and 'Artillery Clubs.'

Artillery company. A company of artillery. {1681–}

In earlier use only with reference to the Ancient and Honorable Artillery Company of Boston.

1650 *Mass. Bay Rec.* III. 186 The day of the meetinge of the Artilerie Company in Boston. **1660** J. HULL *Diary* 151, I was admitted into the Artillery Company. **1686** SEWALL *Diary* I. 151 The Artillery Company had like to have been broken up. **1717** *Mass. H. Repr. Journals* I. 219 A petition in behalf of the Artillery Company in Boston. **1763** *Boston Post-Boy* 13 June, Monday last, agreeable to ancient custom, the Artillery Company of the province appeared under arms, being the anniversary of the election of officers for the company. **1776** *Journals Cont. Congress* VI. 982 The brass pieces, with the artillery companies, . . . belonging to this state [Pennsylvania]. **1789** MORSE *Amer. Gazetteer* (1798) s.v. *Boston*, The Ancient and Honourable Artillery Company was incorporated in 1638. **1803** *Ann. 8th Congress* 2 Sess. 1509 Artillery company, with supernumeraries 120. **1848** MASON in E. Bryant *California* 462 A soldier of the artillery company returned here . . . from the mines. **1871** [L. H. BAGG] *At Yale* 507 The two guns of the artillery company . . . were stored in a barn.

+**Artillery election.** The election of officers of the Boston Artillery Company (see prec.).

In quotation 1673 *ellipt.*: cf. ARTILLERY SERMON.

1673 *Mass. H. S. Coll.* 4 Ser. I. 19 Mr. Seaborn Cotton preacht the Artillery Election at Boston. *c***1680** J. HULL *Diary* 202 So likewise did Mr. Higginson [preach a good sermon] upon the Artillery Election. **1686** C. MATHER *Diary* I. 132 Sermons at the artillery elections, in this countrey, have been things of considerable observation. **1772** A. G. WINSLOW *Diary* 66 Monday being Artillery Election I went to see the hall. **1816** *Harvard Laws* 11 The stated exercises . . . will not be required on . . . the days of . . . the general or artillery election. **1865** *Nation* I. 674 'Evacuation Day' . . . has long since ceased to have any historical value for the great body of the people, much like the holiday called 'artillery election' in Boston. **1883** BACON *King's Dict. Boston* 20/2 'Artillery Election Day' in June, and the 'Fall Field-Day' are the great occasions with the company during the year. **1901** O. A. ROBERTS *Ancient & Hon. Artillery Co.* IV. 487 Rev. Phillips Brooks, D.D., of Boston, . . . delivered the Artillery Election sermon in 1872.

Artillery horse. A horse for hauling a heavy gun, etc.

1792 *Ann. 2nd Congress* 1118 The artillery horses being very much reduced, and unable to undergo very much fatigue. **1815** *Boston Selectmen* 6 Oct. 153 There would be required . . . a quantity of forage for artillery horses. **1861** *Chicago Tribune* 19 July 1/7 Forty large artillery horses arrived here to-day. **1862** MCCLELLAN in *Own Story* 640 The importance of supplying cavalry and artillery horses to replace those broken down by hard service.

Artilleryman. A soldier belonging to the artillery; an artillerist. {1635–}

1642 *Conn. Public Rec.* I. 71 There shall be an artillary yard, where the Company shall haue liberty to exercise their arms . . . and chuse their officers according to the course of artillary men. **1654** JOHNSON *Wonder-w. Prov.* 192 A frequent instructer of the most martial troops of our artillery men. **1777** *Journals Cont. Congress* IX. 822 There are not a sufficient number to do the duty of artillery men in the army. **1865** GRANT in Logan *Great Conspiracy* 636 [To] allow the cavalry and artillery men to retain their horses. **1866** 'F. KIRKLAND' *Bk. Anecdotes* 395 Here artillery-men and marines were assembled; and on deck I left them to go below. **1892** M. A. JACKSON *Memoirs* xix. 379 A Confederate artilleryman . . . gives the following graphic picture of Jackson as he came on the field.

+**Artillery sermon.** *Obs.* A sermon preached on the day of the Artillery election. — **1644** *Mass. Bay Rec.* II. 71 The printer shall have leave to print the election sermon . . . & the artillery sermon. **1672** *Mass. H. S. Coll.* 4 Ser. I. 17 Mr. Oakes preached the artillery sermon at Boston. **1701** SEWALL *Diary* II. 35 Mr. Pemberton preaches the artillery sermon, from Luke 3. 14.

Artillery yard. A yard for the practice of artillerists. {1642} — **1642** [see ARTILLERYMAN]. **1776** *Journals Cont. Congress* VI. 987 A plan of an artillery yard being laid before Congress [it was resolved] that an artillery yard, with proper cover to exercise under in bad weather, be immediately erected.

* **Artist.** (In senses now obsolete.)

1. An expert in seamanship. {1723}

*a***1649** WINTHROP *Hist.* I. 164 They sent out a pinnace well manned . . . under the conduct of Mr. William Aspenwall, a good artist. **1721** *Amer. W. Mercury* 7 Feb. 2/2 Having no ballast, nor hatches, nor water in the sloop, nor any artist on board.

2. One skilled in surveying; a surveyor.

1658 *Lancaster Rec.* 59 Iff wee may choose an artist . . . to lay our townes bounds. **1662** *Boston Rec.* 8 Theare towne was reasolued to put it to the Generall Court, vnles theire artists could agree. **1665** *Dedham Rec.* IV. 102 It is this day agreed to tender to Lieft. Fisher as artist in that worke . . . tenn shillings . . . for euery daye he shall measure [etc.]. **1681** *Charlestown Land Rec.* 192 It will be necessary that the laying out of the proportions of land . . . be referred unto a committe . . . to be chosen together with the artist. **1714** *Essex Inst. Coll.* XXXVII. 106 Voated, that all the common lands in Salem . . . bee measured by an artist. **1716** *N. Car. Col. Rec.* II. 221 [An] impracticable wilderness . . . , where the best artists we have must have been at a loss to steer to the point designed. **1807** *Steele Papers* II. 523 While the artists were making these astronomical observations. **1813** *Ib.* 703 Enabling the commrs. and artists to be together at the termination of each day's work on the line.

3. A skilled workman or craftsman; an artisan. {1633–1815}

1687 *Conn. Col. Rec.* III. 407 Butchers, bakers, . . . barbers, millers and masons, with all other manual persons and artists. **1739** *Georgia Col. Rec.* IV. 677 The artists, who were excused from these works, wrought at their own trades. **1804** FESSENDEN *Terrible Tractoration* 33, I've shewn a mode . . . how the same again to botch, Just as an artist does a watch! **1815** *Niles' Reg.* VII. 340/1 Nothing seems wanting but artists, of all classes, especially smiths, carpenters and joiners, brick makers and layers, painters and glaziers.

Art-union. An association or society for the purpose of promoting art and encouraging artists, as by purchasing their works, usu. by lottery. {1837–}

'Such art-unions were at one time numerous in the United States, but they were generally declared by the courts to be of the nature of lotteries, and therefore illegal' (*Cent.*).

?*c***1842** WHITMAN *Prose Wks.* (1892) 372 Talk to an Art-Union. **1850** *Knickerb.* XXXV. 83 The rage for pictures, fostered by our rival art-unions. *Ib.*, The drawing and distribution of the American Art-Union have added still more to the excitement. **1852** *Harper's Mag.* V. 403/1 The Supreme Court . . . pronounced a judgment, by a majority, declaring the American Art-Union to be a lottery within the prohibition of the Constitution of the State. **1871** STOWE *Pink & White Tyranny* v. 59 The girls in his neighborhood with . . . their book-clubs and art-unions.

* **Arum.**

* **1.** A genus of plants belonging to the order *Araceæ*, distinguished by a large spathe; a plant or species of this genus.

1801 *Hodge & Boylan's N.C. Almanack* 37 The good woman infused . . . the root of arum, or poke in water. **1832** S. J. HALE *Flora* 22 Arum, *Dracontium*. Wake Robin. . . . Indigenous to . . . the warmer parts of Europe and America. **1835** BIRD *Hawks of Hawk-h.* I. vii. 91 A luxuriant array of arums, mandrakes, violets, and other plants that delight in cool and moist situations. **1860** HOLMES *E. Venner* iv, There were swamps . . . where the three-leaved arum and the skunk's cabbage grew broad and succulent. **1901** MOHR *Plant Life Ala.* 425 *Peltandra virginica*, . . . Green Arum, . . . [is found in] low muddy places.

+**2.** A plant belonging to any of several related genera: see quotations, and cf. ARROW-, DRAGON, WATER-ARUM.

1792 BELKNAP *Hist. N.H.* III. 127 The arum, or skunk cabbage, has been found very efficacious in asthmatic complaints. **1818** *Mass. H. S. Coll.* 2 Ser. VIII. 168 The latter part of May appear . . . the three-leaved arum or Indian turnip, the thimbleberry.

Ary, *a. dial.* Also **airy, ar'a.** [=*e'er a* 'ever a.' Cf. NARY, and vulgar E. (18th c.) *arrow.*] Any. {Also *s.* and *s.w. dial.*}

'A vulgarism used by the illiterate' (B. '48).

1818 FESSENDEN *Ladies Monitor* 171 Provincial words [include] *Ary*, for any or either. **1834** DAVIS *Lett. J. Downing* 37 He'd beat ary one on 'em. **1840** *S. Lit. Messenger* VI. 512/2 If I had ar' a weapon, you'd sing rather small. **1853** F. W. THOMAS *J. Randolph* 106, I know we'll catch that Toney stealing my rabbit if there's airy one in. **1864** TROWBRIDGE *Cudjo's Cave* xxxv. 361 'Can't see ary thing by this light,' replied Dan. **1865** 'MARK TWAIN' *Sk., Jumping Frog*, That feller'd . . . take ary side you please. **1899** *Cent.* s.v., I haven't seen ary one of them.

* **As,** *adv., conj.*, and *rel. pron.* In several uses now obs. or not recognized in standard speech or writing.

* **1.** *So . . . as*, in such a manner, to such an extent, . . . that. {–1777}

1631 WINTHROP *Letters* II. 60, I am so full of business here, as I can't think of mine owne affairs as I should. *a***1656** BRADFORD *Hist.* 169 Once she was so foundered in the sea as they all thought she would never rise againe. *Ib.* 488 Mr. Davison . . . found him so discreete and faithfull as he trusted him above all other. **1803** *Essex Inst. Coll.* XXXIX. 322 But he has been so vain & imprudent in his first setting out, as he will not easily get over.

* **b.** *So as, so 's*, so that. {–1797}

1636 *Winthrop Lett.* (1869) II. 154 The Indians killed up all their swine, so as Capt. Lovell had none. **1660** J. WINTHROP in *Winthrop P.* IV. 65 Furnishing out many vessells . . . so as those who come over may supply themselves at very reasonable rates. **1690** SEWALL *Diary* I. 319 It pleased God to clear the air, so as we saw our course. **1849** WILLIS *Rural Lett.* ii. 26 Why don't he cut down the trees so's he can see out? **1865** 'MARK TWAIN' *Sk., Jumping Frog*, Any way just so's he got a bet he was satisfied.

* **c.** *Like* (or *likes*) *as if*, as if.

*a***1846** *Quarter Race Kentucky*, etc. 190 He walked 'round catecorned-like—likes's if he was drivin for a plain plover.

* **2.** Introducing a noun clause, usually after *know* or *see* (with negative): That. {–1748; now *dial.*}

1782 *Essex Inst. Coll.* I. 13/2, I dont no [=know] as I shall [have a dollar] for six months to come. **1829** SANDS *Writings* II. 132, I don't know as I have any objections. **1845** JUDD *Margaret* I. xiv. 115, I don't know as I like the Meeting. **1861** STOWE *Pearl Orr's Isl.* I. iii. 15, I never knew as children was so engagin'! **1867–9** *Ill. Agric. Soc. Trans.* VII. 220, I don't know as I would be quite warranted in making that statement. **1888** *Harper's Mag.* Nov. 871/2, I don't know as I expected to take part in this debate. **1891** WILKINS *New Eng. Nun* 187, I don't see as he looked a mite different. **1904** W. H. SMITH *Promoters* ii. 57, I don't know as the profits of it ought to go into the Company.

b. *As how*, in the same sense. {1771–, *dial.*}

1781 WITHERSPOON *Druid P.* No. vi, He said as how it was his opinion. This absurd pleonasm is more common in Britain than in America. *c***1805** FESSENDEN *Orig. Poems* (1806) 81 Miss Sal, I's going to say as how We'll spark it here tonight. **1817** *Niles' Reg.* XII. 112/1 We are told . . . as how the bridegroom was bedecked with a nuptial favor. *Ib.*, We are told . . . as how the coachman, the horses, and the carriages were ornamented with ribbands. **1835** BIRD *Hawks of Hawk-h.* I. vi. 70 He said as how I must learn to be a gentleman, now I was in England, and never behave like a young savage no more. *Ib.* xix. 255 The rest is nothing, seeing as how they are in some of a panic already. **1839** *Lexington Observer* 10 April, I reckon as how I will. *a***1845** S. Smith *Theatr. Apprent.* 144, I think you told them there gentlemen of the jury as how I desarved being put in irons? **1866** C. H. SMITH *Bill Arp* 34 A spiritual medium in our camp says as how old Lucifer is preparing a factory. **1871** BRET HARTE *Roaring Camp* 50 The doctors came and said as how it was caused all along of his way of life.

3. So far as (I know, etc.).

1676 SEWALL *Diary* I. 16 He gave no answer, as I remember. **1686** *Ib.* 118 After much hot Dispute nothing at last done, as I know. **1702** *Essex Inst. Coll.* I. 14/1 He was not forbid the reading of it, . . . as I know. **1730** [see 4]. **1793** *Md. Hist. Mag.* VI. 356, I never agreed to bare any part of it as I no of. **1881** *Harper's Mag.* June 89/2 She handed back no words, as I could hear. **1901** RYAN *Montana* viii. 109, I saw her go into that room there quite a spell ago. . . . She hasn't passed out again, as I've seen.

*4. As a relative pronoun: That, which. {-1747; now *dial.*}

1630 WINTHROP *Lett.* (1869) II. 40, I found that love and respect from Capt. Milburne our master, as I may not forget. **1677** *Plymouth Rec.* 153 The uper old footpath as did formerly lead from the Towne of Plymouth. **1680** *Topsfield Rec.* 31 To sele wates and mesures by the toun standered as is now newli com from Ingland. **1730** J. COMER *Diary* (1923) 112 This evening . . . came on the most . . . amazing Northern light as ever was beheld in New England as I can learn. **1837** BIRD *Nick of Woods* I. 168, I am not one of them 'ere fellers as fears a big river. **1852** STOWE *Uncle Tom* i, I knew a real handsome gal once . . . , as was entirely ruined by this sort of handling. **1856** — *Dred* II. 23 That was a parson as *was* a parson. **1859** BARTLETT 13 Nobody as I ever heard on. This vulgarism is confined to the illiterate. **1865** *Atlantic Mo.* XV. 723, I mean the singers, Ma'am—them as sang at the concert to-night. **1872** EGGLESTON *Hoosier Schoolm.* x. 87 They was a man . . . as had a breakin'-out on his side.

*5. After comparatives: Than. {-1824; now *dial.*}

1895 *Dialect Notes* 376, I would rather see you as him. **1898** CANFIELD *Maid of Frontier* 15 Kin hol' more whiskey as a pork barrel. **1904** 'O. HENRY' *Heart of West* 291 Eleven years old and not bigger as a frankfurter.

***Asafetida, Asafoetida.** Also **assafoetida.** A drug having an offensive odor and an acrid taste, prepared from the milky juice of the roots of certain plants, and used esp. in allaying hysteria or in quieting the nerves, or occas. in a bag suspended from the neck to prevent disease.

1804 J. ROBERTS *Penna. Farmer* 66 A strong decoction of valerian and assafoetida may be given every three hours. **1836** J. HALL *Stat. West* ix. 115 The smell of burning assafoetida has a remarkable effect upon this animal [i.e. the black wolf]. **1867** HOLMES *Guardian Angel* 125 The old Withers stock,—good constitutions,—a little apt to be nervous, one or two of 'em. I've given 'em a good deal of valerian and assafoetida. *Ib.* 167 He had to lay in an extra stock of valerian and assafoetida whenever there was a young minister round. **1881** S. BONNER in *Harper's Mag.* April 736/1 From this mysterious bosom a strong odor of asafœtida exhaled as Sinai moved briskly about Dulcie's kitchen.

***Asbestos.** Also †**asbestus.**

1. A mineral used in making fireproof materials. {1667-}

1725 FRANKLIN *Let. to Sloane* 2 June, I have brought from thence [*sc.* N. America] a purse made of the stone asbestus. **1781-2** JEFFERSON *Notes Va.* (Bergh) II. 43 An asbestos of a ligneous texture, is sometimes to be met with. **1789** MORSE *Amer. Geog.* 183 At Newbury are beds of lime stone and asbestos. **1841** BUCKINGHAM *America* I. 249 Some quarries of asbestos are worked on Staten Island. **1885** *Harper's Mag.* March 551/2 But we have gold mines too— . . . and asbestos mines. There are ten acres of asbestos mines in Massachusetts.

2. *Radiated asbestos:* (see quotation).

1843 *Nat. Hist. N.Y., Geology* I. 582 The rock changes in character, . . . it becomes of a soft and fibrous texture, . . . [is] called by the inhabitants of the city [of New York] radiated asbestos.

Ascensionist. {1863} +One of a denomination of Christians (see quot.). — **1884** *Harper's Mag.* May 980/2 Some years ago, in Georgia, that band of Christians known as Ascensionists were having a . . . revival.

***Asclepias.** The milkweed.

1789 *Trans. Philos. Soc.* III. xxi, The Asclepias, called silkweed, has a fine white down in its pods, which in Massachusetts is carded and spun into very good wick-yarn. **1818** *Mass. H. S. Coll.* 2 Ser. VIII. 170 In July the lover of plants is gratified with . . . spear thistles, asclepias or milkweed. **1846** EMORY *Military Reconn.* 11 The low grounds abound in prickly rush, narrow leafed asclepias, &c. **1899** S. HALE *Letters* 346 The orange asclepias is still in bloom near Rochester.

+**Ascotch.** 'A name given by boys in New York to a small mass of wet gunpowder' (B. '77).

A-scouting: see A *prep.*[1] 4 and SCOUT *v.*, SCOUTING. — **1746** *N.H. Hist. Soc. Coll.* IX. 137, [I] went out into the woods a scouting. *Ib.* 212. **1758** in *Lett. to Washington* II. 348 In case any of his People should go a Scouting. **1885** 'CRADDOCK' *Prophet* i. 7 Ye war never so much ez seen a-scoutin' round the mourner's bench.

***Ash,** *n.*[1]

+1. A tree of the genus *Fraxinus*, various species of which are valued for timber and shade.

For various species, as *American, black, blue, prickly, white, yellow ash*, see under these headings.

1610 *Estate of Virginia* 54 The country yieldeth abundance of wood, as . . . ashe, sarsafrase, liue oake. **1622** 'MOURT' *Relation* 10 Excellent blacke earth all wooded with okes, pines, . . . vines, some ash. **1634** WOOD *New Eng. Prospect* I. v. 17 For that countrey ash, it is much different from the ash of England, being brittle and good for little. **1682** ASH *Carolina* 10 Trees for the service of building houses and shipping . . . [include] elm, ash, beech, and poplar. **1709** LAWSON *Carolina* 93 Of ash we have two sorts, agreeing nearly with the English in the grain. One of our sorts is tough, like the English, but differs . . . in the bark. **1738** CHALKLEY *Scotch-Irish Settlement Va.* II. 373 To a forked walnut by a black one, a hiccory, an ash by the riverside. **1750** WALKER *Journal* 26 April, On the lower side . . . is an ash mark'd T. W. **1765** R. ROGERS *Acc. N. Amer.* 42 Here may be found plenty of oak, ash and maple. **1778** CARVER *Travels* 497 The Ash. There are several sorts of this tree in these parts. *Ib.*, The yellow ash, which is only found near the head branches of the Mississippi. **1797** I. THOMAS *Newengland Farmer* 15 Ash, . . . a well known and useful tree natural to this climate; of which we reckon three sorts, the black, the white, and the yellow. **1802** ELLICOTT *Journal* 26 The timber growing on the river bottoms, is . . . ash (*fraxinus Americana*). **1865** *Atlantic Mo.* XV. 148 Scattered along the way are huge ashes, sycamores, elms. **1870** KEIM *Sheridan's Troopers* 159 Everywhere along the stream there was an abundance of . . . black walnut, ash and some locust. **1883** HALE *Woods & Timbers N.C.* 89 In this State they are all called simply *Ash*, without any discriminating adjuncts.

*2. The wood of the ash tree.

1744 FRANKLIN *Acc. Fire-Places* 20 Dry hickery, or ash, . . . are rather to be chosen. **1833** W. J. SNELLING *Expose of Gaming* 10 The prop table . . . was framed with rough ash or hickory, the bark on. **1838** J. HALL *Western States* x. 143 The ash is also an excellent wood both for fuel and for plank. **1846** THORPE *Myst. Backwoods* 39 An arrow of ash, three feet long, pointed with an iron spear of peculiar construction.

+b. *Baseball.* A bat made of ash wood.

1875 CHADWICK *Dime Base Ball Player* 45 Those handling the ash . . . have not been slow in discovering the open space between first and second bases.

3. *attrib.* a. Of ash. b. Made of ash wood.

1695 *Providence* (R.I.) *Rec.* XIV. 96 A great ash stake standing by the fence. *Ib.* 115 On the southwesterne corner . . . [is] an ash stock or small tree. **1709** *Derby* (Conn.) *Rec.* 428 An ash bush marked at the norwestward corner on three sides. **1825** NEAL *Bro. Jonathan* I. 275 Some tearing ash twigs, for basket work. **1835** BIRD *Hawks of Hawk-h.* I. ix. 120 Feel the lad's muscles; . . . you will find them as tough as ash-boughs. **1846** THORPE *Myst. Backwoods* 15 The *vacher*, armed with an ash stick, some seven feet in length, scours ahead of the flying cattle. **1848** Drake *Pioneer Life Ky.* v. 107 A Johnny-cake on a clean ash board. **1869** *Causes Reduct. Tonnage* (1870) 74 Ash oars. **1872** EGGLESTON *End of World* xvi. 109 When do you 'low to leave this terry-firmy and climb a ash-saplin'? **1881** TOURGEE *Zouri's Christmas* v, She's fearder o' fire nor a rattle-snake ob [=of] ash-bark.

***Ash,** *n.*[2]

+1. *pl.* Wood-ashes.

1828 WEBSTER s.v. *Wood-ashes*, In the U. States, where wood chiefly is burnt, the people usually say simply *ashes*. **1839** BUEL *Farmer's Companion* 203 Lime, gypsum, marl, and ashes are powerful auxiliaries, when applied to proper soils, or suitable crops. **1862** *Rep. Com. Patents: Agric.* 208 Ashes operate most beneficially upon worn-out, sandy soils. *Ib.*, Ashes are now but little used [as fertilizer], owing to the almost universal substitution of coal for fuel. **1865** *Atlantic Mo.* XV. 84 A less important . . . class of products entered New York during the same period, in the following amounts:— . . . Ashes, 1,401 Packages.

+2. The color of ashes.

1876 *Field & Forest* II. 41 Admitting that *tephrocotis* 'has the least ash on the head,' how can this fact be attributed to climatological influences?

Ash, *v.* {c1645, 1874} *tr.* To treat with ashes, especially in order to kill or drive off the cutworm or the budworm, or to fertilize the soil. — **1817** *Niles' Reg.* XII. 212/2 One hand may carefully ash three acres in a day, and . . . it will effectually destroy or drive away the cut worm. **1839** BUEL *Farmer's Comp.* 206 Marling, liming, or ashing increases the quantity. **1845** COOPER *Chainbearer* xxv, City-bred folks can't know nothin' of the toil and labor of the choppin', and loggin', and ashin', and gettin' in, and croppin' new lands.

A-shaped, *a.* Having the shape of the letter A. {Also E.} — **1869** *Ill. Agric. Soc. Trans.* VII. 109 A broad A-shaped scraper which . . . removed the loosened earth. **1876** INGRAM *Centennial Exp.* xii. 388 These side-frames are strong A-shaped castings.

+**Ash-barrel.** [ASH *n.*[2]] A barrel in which ashes are placed to be removed.

1870 F. FERN *Ginger-Snaps* 55 Garbage-heaps and ash-barrels before the door of poverty. **1876** 'MARK TWAIN' *Weather in Punch* (1878) ii. 16 You'll find that stranger down in the cellar with his head in the ash-barrel. **1891** *Scribner's Mag.* X. 117 A street where the ash-barrels lingered late on the sidewalk. **1900** C. C. MUNN *Uncle Terry* 33 A solitary window opening on an area devoted to ash barrels and garbage.

+**Ash-box.** [ASH *n.*[2]] A receptacle for ashes. — **1846** *Rep. Comm. Patents* (1847) 261 The chamber of combustion and its grate and ash-box. **1851** MELVILLE *Moby Dick* iii. (1926) 8 The first thing I did was to stumble over an ash-box in the porch. **1855** THOMPSON *Doesticks* 287, I was knocked bodily into an ash-box by the foreman of engine 73.

+**Ash breeze.** (See quotation.) — **1834** *Visit to Texas* xii. 105 We . . . took advantage of what is sometimes called the 'ash breeze': that is, our oars, and proceeded down the bay at a pretty good rate.

+**Ash-cake.** [ASH *n.*[2]] A cake of corn-bread baked in hot ashes.

1809 WEEMS *Marion* (1833) 50 A rasher of fat bacon from the coals, with a good stout lump of an ash cake, is nice enough for me. **1833** J. FINCH *Travels* 235 The ashes are swept off the hearth, and the cakes laid in rows upon it; they are then covered with the hot ashes, and are soon baked. They are called ash-cakes. **1840** *S. Lit. Messenger* VI. 385/2 This anniversary she is in the habit of celebrating by a dinner of fried middling and ash-cake. **1851** *Polly Peablossom* 70 All sorts of good things—bacon, an' possum fat, an' ash cake. **1853** RAMSEY *Tennessee* 719 Covered with hot ashes, the preparation is called the ash-cake. **1876** M. F. HENDERSON *Cooking* 326 Ash-cake . . . should be . . . wiped before eaten. There is no better food than this for dyspeptics. **1885** E. EGGLESTON in *Century Mag.* April 883/2 The baking of the 'ash-cake' under the ashes. **1904** GLASGOW *Deliverance* 21 You used to bake me ash-cakes when I was a little girl.

+**Ash-cart.** [ASH *n.*[2]] 'A cart that goes from door to door to collect ashes' (B. '59). {Also Sc.}

Ash-cat. *colloq.* [ASH *n.*[2]] A dirty or neglected child. {1808– *dial.* (Lancs. and Devon) in related sense} — **1869** 'MARK TWAIN' *Innocents Abroad* xxv. 262 They nurse one ash-cat [=child] at a time and the others scratch their backs against the door-post. **1876** — in *Atl. Mo.* June 642 Look here, you miserable ash-cat! **1881** — *Prince & Pauper* xvi. 195 The poor little ash-cat [=a pauper child] was already . . . wonted to his strange garret. **1899** GREENE *Va. Word-bk.* 45 *Ashcat*, a child that plays in the ashes, dirtying its hands, face, and clothes. **1910** C. HARRIS *Eve's Husband* 120 He came home late at night looking like an ash-cat-Sam.

Ash-colored, *a.* [ASH *n.*[2]] Of the color of ashes. {1611–} Freq. in specific names (see quots.).

1750 EDWARDS *Nat. Hist. Birds* III. 135 The ash-colour'd heron from North-America. **1812** WILSON *Ornithology* VI. 80 Ash-colored, or black-cap hawk, *Falco Atricapillus*. **1813** *Ib.* VII. 36 Ash-colored sandpiper, *Tringa Cinerea*, . . . inhabits both Europe and America. **1851** LAWRENCE in *Ann. Lyceum of Nat. Hist. N.Y.* V. 121 *Tyrannula cinerascens*, Ash-colored flycatcher, . . . frequents the borders of streams [in Western Texas]. **1892** APGAR *Trees Northern U.S.* 167 *Salix cinerea*, gray or ash-colored willow, . . . [is] occasionally cultivated; from Europe.

* **Ashen,** *a.* [ASH *n.*[1]]

1. Having a growth of ash trees. *Obs.*

1648 *Maine Doc. Hist.* VI. 4 From thence north westerlie hom to the ashen swamp.

2. Made of ash wood.

1731 J. SECCOMB *Father Abbey's Will* ii, An ashen pail, A threshing flail, An iron wedge and beetle. **1827** COOPER *Prairie* xviii, The long, delicate handle of an ashen lance. **1868** BEECHER *Norwood* 98 Pete . . . lifted a fish large enough to make the ashen spear-handle bend.

+**Ashery.** [ASH *n.*[2]] A manufacturing plant for pearl-ash or potash.

1828 A. SHERBURNE *Mem.* (1831) viii. 185, I much wished to set up an ashery, as there was none very near me. **1837** JENKINS *Ohio Gaz.* 421, 3 saw mills, 3 pot and pearl asheries. **1846** *Knickerb.* XXVIII. 279 The ashery . . . stands upon the brow of a steep hill. **1855** *Trans. Amer. Inst. N.Y.* 249 The burning of the primitive forest, and the gathering up of the ashes and the selling of them to the asheries for ten or twelve cents a bushel, is an evil that ought to be corrected. **1884** L. F. ALLEN *New Farm Bk.* 62 Spent lye of the asheries, is the liquid which remains after the combination of the lye and grease in manufacturing soap.

+**Ashes barrel.** =ASH-BARREL. — **1846** CORCORAN *Pickings* 61 O they were . . . knocking over the ashes barrels, shying stones at the lamps.

+**Ash furnace.** [ASH *n.*[2]] 'A furnace or oven used in glass-making' (W. '64). — **1814** BRACKENRIDGE *Views* 150 The three modes of smelting, to wit, the open furnace, the ash furnace, and the air furnace, (belonging to Mr. Austin,) have all been introduced since the Americans took possession of the country. **1819** SCHOOLCRAFT *Mo. Lead Mines* 73 On a visit to these mines, I observed the inside of the ash furnace beautifully tinged with a blue colour.

+**Ash-gum.** A receptacle for ashes made from a section of a hollow gum-tree. — **1851** HOOPER *Widow Rugby's Husb.* 42 A dozen fowls clustered on the top of the ash-gum.

+**Ash-hopper.** [ASH *n.*[2]] A receptacle for ashes, used in the making of soap. Also in phr. 'to work one's own ash-hopper,' to do one's own work, to be independent.

1804 in *Mineral. Journal* I. 105 Cubic salts, . . . thrown upon the ash-hoppers, . . . are supposed to assist in precipitating the lime. **1843** 'CARLTON' *New Purchase* I. ix. 63 Well! sort a allow not—most time, mam, you'll have to work your own ash-hopper. **1848** Drake *Pioneer Life Ky.* v. 96 The ash-hopper . . . was composed of clapboards, arranged in an inverted pyramid. **1866** C. H. SMITH *Bill Arp* 44, I'm told that there is about twelve hundred of you fellows skulking behind a parcel of ash hoppers. **1873** 'MARK TWAIN' & WARNER *Gilded Age* i. 18 There was an ash-hopper by the fence, and an iron pot for soap-boiling near it. **1880** *Harper's Mag.* June 23 A search was instituted—under the bed, in the bed . . . ; up the chimney and in the ash-hopper. **1891** *Ib.* June 70/1 The ash-hopper, the beehives all awry, the hay stack, were distinct.

+**Ash-house.** [ASH *n.*[2]] An outhouse in which ashes and refuse are placed. — **1807** IRVING, etc. *Salmagundi* iv. 73 He once shook down the ash-house, by an artificial earthquake. **1833** [see ASH-ROOM].

+**Ashlanders,** *n. pl.* A political club at Baltimore, Md., named 'from Ashland Square, near which they lived' (B. '77). — **1859** BARTLETT 13 *Ashlanders*, a club of Baltimore rowdies. **1888** LANE *Pol. Catch-Words* 13 Sept. 16 Ashlanders . . . took an active part in local politics; [their] . . . methods were like those of the Plug Uglies, etc.

Ash-leach. [ASH *n.*[2]] An ash-hopper. — **1805** *Pocumtuc Housewife* (1906) 47 In the spring, when the ash hole is cleared, have five or six bushels of ashes put in the ash leach, if you have one.

Ash-leaf. [ASH *n.*[1]] +*attrib.* =ASH-LEAVED. — **1855–6** *Ill. Agric. Soc. Trans.* VI. 390 The Box Elder of our river bottoms comes back to us under the name of . . . Ash Leaf maple.

Ash-leaved, *a.* [ASH *n.*[1]]

1. Having leaves resembling those of the ash.

1785 MARSHALL *Amer. Grove* 167 *Xanthoxylum fraxinifolium.* Ash-leaved tooth-ach tree. **1813** MUHLENBERG *Cat. Plants* 59 Ash-leaved trumpet-flower. *Ib.* 88. Ash-leaved walnut. **1846** BROWNE *Trees Amer.* 150 The ash-leaved xanthoxylum.

+**2.** *Ash-leaved maple*, or *negundo*, the box elder, *Rulac (Acer) negundo.*

1785 MARSHALL *Amer. Grove* 2 *Acer Negundo.* The ash-leaved maple. **1832** BROWNE *Sylva Amer.* 103 The ash-leaved maple attains the height of 40 or 50 feet. **1846** — *Trees Amer.* 106 The ash-leaved negundo . . . is seldom found growing wild in the northern parts of the union. **1857** GRAY *Botany* 85 Ash-leaved maple, box-elder, . . . [grows on] river-banks, Penn. to Wisconsin. **1892** APGAR *Trees Northern U.S.* 89 Ash-leaved maple, box-elder, . . . [is] a rather small, . . . rapidly growing tree, with light pea-green twigs.

+**Ash-man.** [ASH *n.*[2]] The collector of ashes.

1873 ALDRICH *Marj. Daw*, etc. 142 He has fought the ash-man's boy, the grocer's boy. **1879** B. F. TAYLOR *Summer-Savory* xxii. 178 No ash-man would pay as much for it. **1891** *Harper's Mag.* Dec. 47/2, I took him for the ashman, though the ashman always goes to the area door.

+**Ash maple.** [ASH *n.*[1]] The ash-leaved maple. — **1834** *S. Lit. Messenger* I. 98 On emerging from the wilderness, the customary variety of oak, ash maple, and hickory presents itself. **1861** *Ill. Agric. Soc. Trans.* IV. 449 The box elder or ash maple is decidedly and distinctly a maple, as its name—*Acer negundo*—indicates.

+**Ash oak.** An oak resembling the ash; the wood of this. — **1771** *N.H. Gazette* 30 Aug., Such persons as are desirous of contracting for white pine masts, yards and bowsprits, . . . lathwood, ash-oak rafters, etc.

A-shooting: see A *prep.*[1] 4 and SHOOT *v.* — **1738** STEPHENS *Proc. Georgia* 161 They went out in the woods a shooting. **1771** WASHINGTON *Diaries* II. 18 Went into the fields with Colo. Bassett a shooting. **1807** *Ann. 10th Congress* 1 Sess. I. 419 Some of the people went a shooting.

***Ashore,** *adv.* +*colloq.* At a standstill or complete stop; 'stranded.' **1856** GOODRICH *Recoll.* I. 96 A young New Englander found himself in the back parts of Pennsylvania, ashore as to the means of living. **1895** S. O. JEWETT *Life of Nancy* 314, I did feel all ashore when I found you'd promised.

Ash-pole. [ASH *n.*[1]] A rod or slender branch from the ash tree (used as a fishing-rod). — **1855** *Knickerb.* XLV. 579 The Sheriff and Archy pulled out their fish-lines, and an ash-pole from the brook-side, and tried their skill for trout.

+**Ash-pone.** [ASH *n.*[2]] A pone of corn-bread baked in the ashes.

1816 'A. SINGLETON' *Lett. from S. & W.* (1824) 78 What slaves I have seen, have fared coarsely upon their hoe-cakes and ash-pone. **1832** GOODRICH *Univ. Geog.* 260 Hoe-cake, . . . and ash-pone, a coarse cake baked under the ashes, are in common use, as bread. **1840** *S. Lit. Messenger* VI. 510/2 The center was filled with . . . various kinds of cornbread—such as hoecakes, ashpones, and johnnycakes.

+**Ash-rake.** [ASH *n.*[2]] An implement for raking ashes. — **1861** *Atlantic Mo.* April 438/2 There he stands . . . leaning on his ash-rake.

+**Ash-room.** A chamber for receiving ashes in a furnace. — **1833** SILLIMAN *Man. Sugar Cane* 50 It will be found advantageous, also, not to have the entrance for air united with the ash-room entrance. *Ib.*, The ash-room need not be large, as it will be found best to remove its contents at short intervals, into an ash-house built of brick.

+**Ash rust.** [ASH *n.*[1]] A fungous growth on certain ash-trees. — **1885** *Amer. Naturalist* XIX. 886 In Eastern Nebraska . . . [there] has been . . . great abundance of the ash rust (*Æcidium fraxini*) upon the leaves . . . of the green ash.

+**Ash swale.** [ASH *n.*[1]] A swale in which ash is the prevailing tree. — **1839** *Mich. Agric. Soc. Trans.* (1856) VII. 368 It follows mainly the course of two brooks, . . . and embraces the intervening ash swales.

+**Ash swamp.** [ASH *n.*[1]] A swamp in which ash is the predominant tree.

1668 *Oyster Bay Rec.* I. 4 That . . . the Surveors are to lay out the Ash Swamp & so much upland to it, as yt shall see[m] convenyent. **1699** *Waterbury Prop. Rec.* 47 Liberty to pitch on the hill at ashe swamp. **1708–9** *Lancaster Rec.* 305 Near the cartway that lyeth round Wataquatock hill in an ash swamp. **1724** *N.H. Probate Rec.* II. 229 Item I give to my son . . . twenty acres of land lying . . . in the ash swamp. **1789** MORSE *Amer. Geog.* 143 One species generally predominating in each soil, has originated the descriptive names of maple, ash, and cedar swamps.

+**Ash-throated,** *a.* [ASH *n.*[2]] The distinctive epithet of a tyrant flycatcher (*Myiarchus cinerascens*) of the Southwestern U.S. — **1858** BAIRD *Birds Pacific R.R.* 179 Ash-throated flycatcher. . . . The chin, throat, and fore part of the breast [are] ashy white. **1874** COUES *Birds N.W.* 239 [The] ash-throated flycatcher . . . is migratory, retiring to or beyond our boundary in the fall. **1881** *Amer. Naturalist* XV. 217, I also found a set of four eggs of another fly-catcher, the ash-throated fly-catcher.

***Ash tree.** [ASH *n.*[1]] =ASH *n.*[1] 1.

1667 *Providence Rec.* V. 317 Bounded on the south corner with an ash tree marked. **1699** *Derby* (Conn.) *Rec.* 202 The southered corner is an ash tree. **1785** MARSHALL *Amer. Grove* 50 *Fraxinus.* The ash-tree. . . . The flowers are hermaphrodite and female on different trees. **1796** *Ky. MS. Records* 5, I barked an ash tree . . . to salt meat on. **1803** *Ann. 9th Congress* 2 Sess. 988 Along the said boundary line . . . to an ash tree, at the distance of forty miles on the said line. **1805** PARKINSON *Tour* 374 There are ash-trees, but not in plenty. **1852** MITCHELL *Dream Life* 201 The ash tree grows crimson in color. **1893** E. L. WAKEMAN in *Columbus* (Ohio) *Dispatch* 20 April, One of the finest wide, high overarchings of ancient ash trees I have ever seen.

+Ash-water. [ASH *n.*[2]] Water or lye in which wood-ashes have been soaked. — **1852** MRS. ELLET *Pioneer Women* 331 They had nothing but corn, which they boiled in ash-water with a little salt.

Ash wood. [ASH *n.*[1]] Wood of the ash tree.

1689 SEWALL *Diary* I. 291 Ashwood, £5. 2. 0. **1741** *Georgia Col. Rec.* VI. 20 Leave to cut ash wood upon the said island to burn earthern ware with. **1823** COOPER *Pioneers* vii, In his hand he held a small basket of the ash-wood slips.

Ashy, *a. colloq.* [? ASH *n.*[2]] +Angry. — *a***1846** *Quarter Race Kentucky,* etc. 45 The feller . . . got rite ashy 'bout it, but I didn't mind him nor never paid no 'tention to him. **1903** *Dialect Notes* II. 305 He argued awhile and then he began to get ashy.

***Aside,** *adv.*

+1. *Aside from* (=Eng. 'apart from'). **a.** In addition to; without reckoning or including; besides.

1818 TICKNOR in *Life* I. 206 Indeed, aside from this, the mere show is more magnificent than can be seen at any other court in Europe. **1847** L. COLLINS *Kentucky* 507 The college . . . possesses revenues, aside from tuition, sufficient to maintain the faculty. **1852** *Mich. Agric. Soc. Trans.* III. 184 Humanity, aside from interest, would direct such a system of treatment. **1865–6** *Ill. Agric. Soc. Trans.* VI. 316 Aside from the lumber, it costs $15,000 to build it. **1869** *Amer. Naturalist* III. 4 Aside from the use of *Dentalium pretiosum* as money, I saw [etc.]. **1905** *Forum* April 598 The city, aside from being a great industrial . . . centre, enjoys . . . a high moral record. **1922** J. A. DUNN *Man Trap* iv. 44 Got the right kind of face; aside from good looks.

b. Except for.

1861 *Md. Hist. Mag.* V. 303 Aside from the upheavals made by our engineers, . . . I don't think I have ever seen a more dreary region. **1866** RICHARDSON *Secret Service* vii. 100 Aside from his negrophobia, the Southern gentleman is an agreeable companion. **1872** *Vermont Board Agric. Rep.* 674 Aside from those cuts the marble is very solid and sound. **1903** A. T. HADLEY *Freedom & Responsibility* 41 But aside from these exceptions, they recognized no limits to the principle of liberty and equality. **1906** *N.Y. Ev. Post* 21 Aug. 1 The Department [of State] is without information . . . aside from press dispatches.

+2. *Aside of,* by the side of, in comparison with.

1856 KANE *Arctic Expl.* II. i. 24 We . . . are mere carpet-knights aside of these indomitable savages.

***3.** Out of notice or consideration.

1860 MARSH *Eng. Lang.* 640 Leaving the question of competency aside. **1871** GRANT WHITE *Words & Uses* 21 But, pronouns . . . and 'auxiliary' verbs aside, it [Chaucer's English] is a mixture [etc.].

Asinico. [Sp.] An ass. {1606} — **1631** *Va. House Burg. Jrnl.* 125 Wee haue thought good to . . . furnish our selues with horses, Assinicoes, sheepe.

+Asking price. The price asked, as distinguished from the price that may be accepted.

1846 SAGE *Scenes Rocky Mts.* xx, The Americans, anxious to purchase a quantity of flour, offered to take it at the asking price. **1848** ARMSTRONG *Stocks* 19 Persons wishing to depress prices . . . agree to buy and sell to each other certain amounts at prices rather below the asking price. **1852** *Harper's Mag.* V. 534/1 The merchants . . . have two prices—an 'asking price' and a 'taking price.'

+A-sleighing: see A *prep.*[1] 4 and SLEIGHING. — **1764** J. ROWE *Diary* (1903) 71 Went with Mrs. Rowe a slaying. **1837** J. C. NEAL *Charcoal Sk.* (1838) 176 We ought to go a sleighing to encourage domestic manufactures. **1851** *Harper's Mag.* Sept. 571/1 'Eben' . . . obtained leave to use his master's sleigh and horses to take his sable inamorata a-sleighing to a neighboring road-side inn.

***Asp.** =ASPEN. (Also QUAKING ASP.)

1622 'MOURT' *Relation* 62 Hasell, holley, asp, sasifras, in abundance. **1634** WOOD *New Eng. Prospect* I. x. 42 There is . . . store of good oakes, wallnut, cædar, aspe, elme. **1671** *Providence Rec.* III. 215 Bounded round with the common and marked with two asps. **1699** *Ib.* IV. 183 A small bush, being an aspe or pople. **1889** *Cent. Dict.* 339/1 The white poplar, *P. alba,* is also sometimes called the 'white asp.'

***Asparagus.**

***1.** A plant of the genus *Asparagus* (garden variety, *officinalis*), cultivated for its tender shoots as food and producing graceful stems much used for decorations.

1709 LAWSON *Carolina* 77 Asparagus thrives to a miracle, without hot beds. **1724** *New-Eng. Courant* 10–17 Feb. 2/2 A good convenient garden in Boston, . . . which has in it . . . a very large bed of asparagus. **1788** J. MAY *Jour. & Lett.* 39 With it I had wild asparagus, which was very good. **1793** B. LINCOLN in *Mass. H.S. Coll.* 3 Ser. V. 110 We found a great plenty of asparagus and lettuce. **1845** *Knickerb.* XXV. 506 The asparagus which, with its delicate green, and its bright red berries, so often forms the ornament of New-England country-houses. **1853** B. F. TAYLOR *Jan. & June* 144 The asparagus is bundled out of the fire-place. **1862** *Rep. Comm. Patents: Agric.* 373 Few, perhaps, are aware of the labor, expense, and profit of cultivating the article asparagus for the New York market. **1879** B. F. TAYLOR *Summer-Savory* xxiii. 182 That ball-room on a Fourth of July night, . . . trimmed with asparagus, fresh flowers, and a national flag. **1891** FREEMAN *New Eng. Nun* 146 Great plumy bunches of asparagus waved over the tops of the looking glass. **1898** WESTCOTT *D. Harum,* David . . . lowered a stalk of the last asparagus of the year into his mouth.

2. Attrib. with *bough, bush, head, plant, plume, top,* etc.

1790 *Penna. Packet* 7 Dec. 3/3 Joseph Anthony, Junior, . . . has imported . . . snuffers, snuffer trays and inkstands, . . . asparagus and sugar tongs. **1832** KENNEDY *Swallow Barn* I. xix. 193 A tasteful screen of the tops of asparagus plants. **1855** *Trans. Amer. Inst. N.Y.* 524 Long Island yields excellent asparagus. . . . Till your soil ever so deep and the asparagus roots will go to the bottom. **1859** STOWE *Minister's Wooing* xxiv. 367, I opened my eyes, and saw the roses and asparagus-bushes on the manteltree-piece. **1863** 'M. HARLAND' *Husks* 44 In the fire place [was] a jar of asparagus boughs. **1865** MRS. WHITNEY *Gayworthys* vi. 58 Say had set her doll upon a moss throne, . . . and built a bower of asparagus plumes about her. **1878** *Amer. Home Cook Book* 12 A pint of asparagus-tops cut small. **1881** 'M. HARLAND' *Common Sense* 19 The remaining half of the asparagus heads. *Ib.* 19 Vegetable Soups . . . [Receipt for] Asparagus (White soup). **1904** A. DALE *Wanted, a Cook* 68 My wife whispered to the Zulu . . . : 'Asparagus soup for everybody.'

3. *Asparagus bean,* a bean (*Dolichos sesquipedalis*) indigenous to tropical America. *Asparagus bed,* a plot of ground in which asparagus is grown. {1761} *Asparagus beetle,* a leaf-beetle (*Crioceris asparagi* or *C. duodecimpunctata*) which feeds on the asparagus plant. {1815} +*Asparagus pea,* the asparagus bean.

1856 'COZZENS' *Sparrowgrass P.* vii. 85 The asparagus bean, a sort of long-winded esculent, inclined to be prolific in strings. — **1776** *N.J. Archives* 2 Ser. I. 88 The garden . . . has a very fine asparagus bed. **1779** *Ib.* IV. 39 A large garden, well stored with . . . asparagus beds. **1843** HAWTHORNE *Note-books* II. 128 In the garden are the old cabbages . . . and the withered stalks of the asparagus bed. **1847** L. COLLINS *Kentucky* 553 Woodford has been appropriately termed the 'asparagus bed' of Kentucky. **1904** GLASGOW *Deliverance* 25 Your asparagus bed is merely an item. — **1863** *Horticulturist* XVIII. 133 The Asparagus Beetle . . . [is] ready to begin . . . depredations on the first start of vegetation. *Ib.* 162 [If] the Asparagus Beetle . . . is left to itself, the destruction of Asparagus as a luxury for the table is quite certain. — **1859** A. VAN BUREN *Sojourn in South* 155 The Asparagus Pea, with a small round pod that grows from a foot to three in length, makes a choice dish at table.

***Aspen.** Also †**aspin(e, -an.** A tree of the poplar family (*Populus tremuloides*), notable for the tremulous motion of its leaves. (Cf. ASP.) Also attrib.

1709 LAWSON *Carolina* 100, I never saw any aspin, but in Rapahannock-River. **1785** WASHINGTON *Diaries* II. 345, [I] planted . . . some of the aspan, which had been brought here on Wednesday last. *a***1797** Imlay *Western Territory* (ed. 3) 144 The sugar maple-trees are generally found mixed with the beech, . . . aspen, butter nut, and wild cherry-trees. **1810**– [see AMERICAN ASPEN]. **1815** DRAKE *Cincinnati* ii. 83 The . . . leather wood and aspen seem to be confined to the more northern portions of this tract. **1846** WEBB *Altowan* I. vi. 164 In a small grove of aspen . . . two men . . . were sitting. **1846** SAGE *Scenes Rocky Mts.* xv, While winding among the ravines and aspen groves, we obtained an indistinct view of a . . . *'carcague.'* **1883** HALE *Woods & Timbers N.C.* 120 Those of them [poplars] called *Aspens* are remarkable for the easy vibration of the leaves when scarcely a breath of air is perceptible. **1904** GLASGOW *Deliverance* 48 Passing under the aspen where the turkeys stirred and fluttered in their sleep.

+Aspen poplar. The asp or aspen.

*a***1817** DWIGHT *Travels* I. 41 Varieties [of] poplar [are]: White, Aspen, Balsam or Black. **1848** E. BRYANT *California* x. 147 Groves of small aspen poplars . . . are a great relief to the eye. **1875** *Amer. Naturalist* IX. 203 The prevalent timber growth [in Utah] was made up of interrupted groves of Aspen poplar.

Aspen tree. =ASPEN.

1652 *Providence Rec.* II. 12, 3 acres . . . with an aspine tree at the south end. **1683** *Ib.* XIV. 39 The northermost corner bounded with an asppen tree. **1785** WASHINGTON *Diaries* II. 345 Brought down a number of young aspan trees from one Saml. Jenkin's. **1836** IRVING *Astoria* iii. 94 They found sufficient dry aspen trees to supply them with fire. **1850** L. SAWYER *Way Sketches* 61 There are some small aspen trees along the valley.

Asphalt. A composition (originally made from bituminous limestone, tar, and sand) used for paving streets and covering surfaces. {1847–} Also attrib.

Orig. (as in E.) in the Fr. form *asphalte.*

1838 *Niles' Nat. Reg.* 1 Dec. 224/1 Asphalte pavements. The composition of asphaltum and gravel has been laid in the portico of the Merchants' Exchange. **1878** *Harper's Mag.* Jan. 234 The benches and the asphalt walks [in Union Square, N.Y. City]. **1881** *Ib.* March 543/1 Children glide peacefully along the asphalt on roller-skates. **1906** 'O. HENRY' *Four Million* 92 Soapy . . . strolled out of the square across the level sea of asphalt, where Broadway and Fifth Avenue flow together.

Asphaltum. a. A bituminous mineral, in its native state usually a residue from evaporated petroleum. {1714–} **b.** =ASPHALT. Also attrib.

1838 [see ASPHALT]. **1847** *Knickerb.* XXIX. 384 Having heard . . . that a quantity of asphaltum could be procured upon the coast of the Republic [of Texas]. **1873** ABBOTT *C. Carson* 75 The roof was rendered impenetrable to rain, being covered with a thick coating of asphaltum, mingled with sand. **1876** INGRAM *Centennial Exp.* 569 The winged side of the structure . . . was . . . approached by a tier of asphaltum walks. **1886** POORE *Reminisc.* II. 262 Some ninety miles of the three hundred miles of half-made streets and avenues were graded and paved, some with wood and others with asphaltum. **1903** *Indian Laws & Tr.* III. 18 In the lands within the former Uncompahgre Indian reservation, in the State of Utah, containing gilsonite, asphaltum, elaterite [etc.].

+**Asp tree.** *Obs.* =ASPEN TREE. — **1662** *Providence Rec.* IV. 109 Marked with two asp and two white oake trees. **1675** *Ib.* XIV. 96 From the said walnut tree . . . to an aspe tree marked on two sides.

***Ass.** The jackass or donkey.

1639 *Maine Doc. Hist.* III. 156 Mr. Hingston tooke in 6 asses; . . . 2 of them died before they weare landed. **1743** CATESBY *Carolina* II. p. xxv, Beasts that were not in America, 'till they were introduced there from Europe: The Horse, Asse [etc.] **1805** LEWIS in *Ann. 9th Congress* 2 Sess. 1074 The Snake Indians . . . have, in addition [to buffaloes], immense quantities of horses, mules, and asses. **1868** *Colorado Gen. Laws* 584 Any ranchman . . . to whom any horses, mules, asses, cattle or sheep, shall be intrusted. **1883** ALLEN *Farm Book* 462 In this country, the ass is occasionally used in the cart, or as a beast of burden.

‖**Assassin collar.** ?A high stiff collar. — **a1860** *Songs of Yale* 14 The Junior . . . ; Now he spouts hog-latin: Wears assassin collars, Turns up Jack for trump, sir.

***Assault.** *Law.* An unlawful attack on the person of another. Often in the phr. 'assault and battery.'

1649 *Rhode I. Court Rec.* 5 John Stodder Pll: against Tho. Gorton in an action of assault and battery. **1655** *Ib.* 9 Richard Burden accused of asault . . . in the Court is . . . found guilty. **1784** *Mass. Laws* (1807) I. 159 It shall be . . . the duty of every Justice of the Peace . . . to punish . . . all assaults and batteries. **1827** *Ill. Revised Laws* (1833) 180 An assault, with an intent to commit murder, rape, mayhem, robbery, or larceny, shall subject the offender to confinement in the penitentiary. **1841** COOPER *Deerslayer* xi, His offences were confined to assaults and batteries, for several of which he had been imprisoned. **1853** *S. Lit. Messenger* XIX. 332/1 Indicted before Judge C., for an assault and battery committed on . . . one Phillip Cousins. **1872** HOLMES *Poet* i. 30 The school-books which have been so often the subjects of assault and battery.

***Assay,** *n.* The determination of the quantity of a certain metal or metals in coins, bullion, etc., or in crude ore. Freq. attrib.

1741 *N.J. Archives* 1 Ser. VI. 118 A table of the value of the several foreign coins, . . . and the assays made of them in our mint. **c1786** JEFFERSON *Writings* I. 250 The money Unit of these states shall be equal . . . to a Spanish milled dollar containing so much fine silver as the assay . . . shall show. **1795** *Ann. 3rd Congress* 1404 There are, besides, . . . the assay, melting, and refining furnaces. **1802** *Ann. 7th Congress* 2 Sess. 1242 Two sets assay scales, and sundry adjusting scales. **1869** BROWNE *Adv. Apache Country* 509 We don't go much on assays. Assays isn't worth shucks. *Ib.* 509, I know men in the assay line that keeps blank certificates, and fills 'em up accordin' to order. **1871** RAYMOND *3rd Rep. Mines* 264 The assay record at the mill, at least, indicates this. **1874** — *6th Rep. Mines* 415 Generally the assay-buttons from the slimes are worth much less per ounce than from the ore. **1883** *Harper's Mag.* March 497/1 The larger mines have extensive buildings . . . with handsome draughting and assay rooms. **1901** WHITE *Westerners* xxi. 194 An assay test in the School of Mines at Rapid.

***Assay,** *v.*

***1.** *tr.* To analyze (ore, etc.) in order to determine the proportion of certain metals in it.

1743 FRANKLIN *Proposal* Wks. 1905 II. 230 It is . . . proposed . . . that the subjects of the correspondence be: . . . brewing, and assaying of ores. **1792** *Ann. 2nd Congress* 69 The assayer . . . shall assay all such of them as may require it. **1875** RAYMOND *7th Rep. Mines* 74 Paid for assaying bars, $128.90.

+**2.** *intr.* To contain, as shown by analysis, a certain proportion of (usually precious) metal.

1882 *Rep. Precious Metals* 305, 2-foot vein of carbonates, that assay as high as $100 to the ton. **1885** *Harper's Mag.* April 698/2 They must assay thousands of dollars to the ton. **1901** WHITE *Claim Jumpers* ii. 23 None of the ore assayed very high.
fig. **1901** WHITE *Westerners* 112 He don't assay a cent a ton fo' sense!

***Assayer.** One whose duty is to make assays. {1618–}

1792 *Ann. 2nd Congress* 69 The assayer shall receive and give receipts for all metals which may lawfully be brought to the mint to be coined. **1793** JEFFERSON *Writings* III. 285 The treasurer . . . should receive the bullion; the assayer . . . is to ascertain its fineness. *Ib.*, It will be expedient . . . to lessen the pecuniary security required from the chief coiner and assayer. **1813** *Ann. 12th Congress* 2 Sess. 509 The report of the Assayer of the Mint. **1877** WM. WRIGHT *Big Bonanza* 33 In their cabin . . . they are said to have had . . . chemical apparatus and assayer's tools. **1893** M. HOWE *Honor* 272 He was the assayer of the San Diabolo mine during the term of years that Michael McFarren had served as its superintendent.

Assay-master. {1647–} +'An officer appointed . . . to test the quality of potash and pearlash intended for export, or the composition of the worms and still-heads used in distilling.' (*Cent.*) — **c1790** *Mem. Academy* II. I. 165 Having had frequent applications from the manufacturers of pot ash, to examine that article, when condemned by the assay masters. **1796** *Boston Directory* 298 Town Officers [include] . . . Assay-Masters: Joshua Witherle, John Welles.

+**Assay office.** [ASSAY *n.*] A government office at which ores and metals are assayed.

1852 *Harper's Mag.* Dec. 120 Instructions sent out from the Treasury Department to the collector [in San Fr.] not to receive the ingots stamped by the Assay Office, in payment of public dues. **1869** 'MARK TWAIN' *Innocents* xviii. 178 The cargoes of 'crude bullion' of the assay-offices of Nevada. **1882** *Rep. Precious Metals* 458 Deposited at the mints and assay offices as native gold from that State [=N.C.]. **1900** NELSON *A B C Wall St.* 10 Within this area . . . are . . . the United States Sub-Treasury, Assay Office and Custom House.

***Asseize,** *v. Obs. tr.* To seize upon as a legal process. {1590 only.} — **1666** *Boston Rec.* 30 John Crosse is hereby ordered to . . . asseize all forfeitures.

‖**Assemblage,** *v. intr.* To hold an assemblage. — **1812** ADAMS *Works* (1856) X. 23 The same northern and southern distinction will prevail; . . . the same lying and libelling, cursing and swearing, will still continue. The same caucusing, assemblaging, and conventioning.

***Assemble,** *v.* +*tr.* To put together, to make up, from separate parts into a complete form.

1852 *Harper's Mag.* V. 158/1 When the several parts are all finished, the operation of putting them together so as to make up the musket from them complete, is called 'assembling the musket.' **1888** *The Sun* 21 March (F.), The steel forgings have been made and turned over to our ordnance officers to assemble into guns. **1894** *Harper's Mag.* July 256/2 The partly assembled gun remains in the pit for forty-eight hours to cool off.

***ASSEMBLY.**

***1.** A gathering of persons elected as representatives for the conduct of public affairs.

1619– [see GENERAL ASSEMBLY]. **1638** *Md. Archives* I. 4 Certaine orders established by generall consent, to be observed during the Assembly. **a1647** F. GORGES *Descr. New-Eng.* iv. 47 No matter of moment can be determined . . . but by the advice and assent of the whole body of the Councell . . . called and summoned to the Assembly. **1665** *Md. Archives* II. 8 Wee doe . . . require yow that . . . yow repaire in person to the said Assembly. **1705** *Boston News-Letter* 1–8 Jan. 2/2 Our Governour was pleased to prorogue the Assembly of this Province unto Wednesday. **1766** in *S. Lit. Messenger* XXVII. 117/2 The gentleman who has filled that chair for several Assemblies, I hope is a good man. **1793** *Steele Papers* I. 100, I have heard a great deal that should have been said against you at the Assembly.

***2.** The body of persons thus assembled; a deliberative or legislative council.

In some states the 'General Assembly' is the whole legislature; in others the 'Assembly' is the lower house in the legislature. See also PRIMARY *a.*

1621– [see GENERAL ASSEMBLY]. **1636** *Dedham Rec.* 20 It is necessary that every man in our sayd assembly shold give Informacion. **1652** *Va. House of Burg. Jrnl.* 84 It is ordered by this Grand Assembly that Mr. Peter Ranson's pattent shall stand good. **1688** *Penna. Col. Rec.* I. 223 The Comittee presented to this board three bills which was brought to them from the Assembly. **1707** *Boston News-Letter* 3 Nov. 2/2 The Assembly of the Jerseys are now sitting. **1749** *Conn. Col. Rec.* IX. 453 It would . . . invest the Governor . . . with a power to negative all acts that should be passed in our Assembly. **1765** R. ROGERS *Acc. N. America* 134 At which three places their [=N.C.] general court or assembly for enacting laws sit alternately. **1776** *Journals Cont. Congress* V. 443 A committee of the assembly . . . have viewed the river Delaware. **1789** *Ann. 1st Congress* I. 60 Since his residence in Georgia, he has been repeatedly elected to the Assembly as a representative of the county of Chatham. **1823** J. THACHER *Military Jrnl.* 564 His funeral was attended by . . . the president and members of Congress, and of the Assembly of Pennsylvania. **1837** *Democratic Rev.* I. 18 Both in the Assembly, and among the people, Mr. Macon was distinguished for the high sternness of the remedies he proposed. **1876** *Colo. General Laws* (1877) 37 The manner prescribed by the laws of Colorado Territory regulating elections for members of the legislative assembly thereof.

***3.** A governing body in certain religious denominations.

1644 WINTHROP *Short Story* (title-p.), [How] the Antinomians . . . of

New England . . . were confuted by the Assembly of Ministers there. **1648** SHEPARD *Sunshine* 31 He [an Indian] was publikly brought forth before the Assembly [for beating his squaw]. **a1649** WINTHROP *Hist.* I. 232 The synod, called the assembly, began at Newtown [on Aug. 30, 1637]. **1783–4** *Md. Hist. Mag.* XXI. 34 Old Ladies . . . have drawn forth their broad back'd Robes, and crowded to the Assembly to gaze at the divinity. **1788** FRANKLIN *Autobiog.* 361 The laboured . . . endeavour . . . to prevail with our Quaker Assembly to pass a militia law. **1832** WILLIAMSON *Maine* II. 695 The highest court of appeals in the last resort, is the General Assembly;—and it consists of Commissioners from all the Presbyteries associated. It sits annually in Philadelphia. **1871** *Amer. Presbyterian Rev.* III. 478 Had the Assembly, when fresh and full, taken up this subject [ministerial relief]. **1895** *Minutes of Gen. Assembly Presb. Ch.* X. 421 The Assembly would utter a special warning against the danger.

4. a. A gathering of persons for worship; a church meeting. *Obs.* {1600–}

a1649 WINTHROP *Hist.* I. 392 Their church assemblies might ordinarily break up in such season, as people . . . might get home by daylight. **1654** JOHNSON *Wonder-w. Prov.* 42 The Church of Christ at Charles Town, having their Sabbath assemblies oftenest on the south side of the river. **1677** SEWALL *Diary* I. 43 One Torrey . . . gave a suddain . . . cry which disturbed the whole assembly.

‖**b.** A religious association; a church.

1823 *Baptist Mag.* IV. 198 Every separate church, or regularly organized assembly of Christians, is in itself a distinct body.

5. A gathering for social entertainment. {1718–}

1767 (*title*) An Address to Persons of Fashion, concerning frequenting of Plays, Balls, Assemblies, Card-Tables, &c. **1786** WASHINGTON *Diaries* III. 8 Shaw sent up to the dancing assembly at Alexandria. **1790** N. WEBSTER in Ford *Notes* I. 340 Assembly night, some altercation about wine, but a very brilliant [evening?]. **1807** IRVING, etc. *Salmagundi* i. 18 At the last assembly the company began to make some show about eight, but the most fashionable delayed their appearance until nine. **1817** BROWN *Western Gaz.* 93 Their assemblies and parties are conducted with . . . ease and grace. **1865** H. PHILLIPS *Hist. Paper Currency* II. 167 Gaiety pervaded the American camp . . . and an assembly was organized. **1891** S. M. WELCH *Recoll. 1830–40* 381 The leading young men in society during these later years of the decade of the thirties, inaugurated a series of 'Assèmblies' (dancing parties) of six, sometimes seven each winter, which continued far into the forties. **1898** PAGE *Red Rock* 146 The officers had given up hope of being invited to the assembly.

6. *Assembly call*, a summons, by drum or bugle, for soldiers to assemble. {=assembly, 1727–1803} *Assembly-club* (cf. sense 5), a club for dancing (*obs.*). *Assembly district*, an election district returning a member to the State legislature, as of New York.

1846 EMORY *Military Reconn.* 59 The assembly call was sounded, which seemed to settle all things. — **1864** T. L. NICHOLS *Amer. Life* I. 279 There are assembly-clubs of young men who unite for the sole purpose of dancing. — **1873** MCELROY & MCBRIDE *Life Sk.* 149 Mr. Blackie represents the thirteenth Assembly district of New York in the present Legislature. **1889** *Voice* (N.Y.) 8 Aug., The third and final day of the Republican re-enrollment in the 5th Assembly District.

Assemblyman. [ASSEMBLY 2.]

1. A member of an Assembly. {1647–}

1685 *Southampton* (N.Y.) *Rec.* II. 286 Major John Howell was chosen to be one of the Assemblymen for the county of Suffolk. **1696** SEWALL *Diary* I. 424 Town-meeting to chuse Assembly-men. **1708** *N. Car. Col. Rec.* I. 696 President Glover's writ for choosing Assembly men being read . . . the people went to electing. **1732** *Penna. Col. Rec.* III. 430 The Governor still apprehends some inconveniencies from the discharging the wages of Assembly men in the manner proposed by the bill. **1800** *Steele Papers* I. 197 Our Assembly men give a ball to-night. **1839** *Knickerb.* XIII. 498 The faction . . . had upon their ticket for assemblyman, the name of Mr. Silas Roe. **1861** *N.Y. Tribune* 18 Dec., A small party of the members of the Legislature, both Senators and Assemblymen, accompanied the Commissioners. **1880** *Harper's Mag.* Aug. 485 A shoe-maker had been elected Assemblyman. **1898** FORD *Hon. P. Stirling* 177 Three of the city's assemblymen and one of her senators had voted against the bills. **1905** D. G. PHILLIPS *Plum Tree* 28 'The old man's going to send you to the legislature, —lower house, of course.' I did not cheer up. An assemblyman got only a thousand a year.

+**2.** As a designation before a surname.

1899 *N.Y. Journal* 19 April 6/1 Assemblyman Adler . . . was quoted as saying: 'That's all right.'

Assembly room.

1. A room used for assemblies, either for legislative meetings or for social purposes. {1744–}

1740 W. SEWARD *Journal* 6 Having taken away the keys of the assembly-room, dancing-school, and musick-meeting. **1747** FRANKLIN *Letter* Wks. II. 356 The Assembly room in the State-house. **1775** BURNABY *Travels* 77 A good assembly-room belonging to the society of free-masons. **1789** WASHINGTON *Diaries* IV. 45, [I] dined with them and a large company [in Portsmouth, N.H.], at their assembly room, which is one of the best I have seen anywhere in the United States. **1791** *Salem Gazette* 18 Oct., Wax-Work . . . [held] at the Assembly Room, Salem. **1852** *Knickerb.* XXXIX. 152 The assembly-rooms [of a village hall]. **1863** S. C. MASSETT *Drifting About* 48 The Olympic Theatre . . . was located where the City Assembly Rooms now are. **1878** BEADLE *Western Wilds* 348 Bishop Warren was . . . thanking the Mormon 'Lord' in the ward assembly rooms.

+**b.** A large room or hall of a school, in which the pupils assemble.

1923 R. HERRICK *Lilla* 72 The assembly room where a hundred and fifty restive boys and girls were herded together for the purpose of study. *Ib.* 75 It was the custom to send all pupils detained . . . for failure in studies to the assembly room.

+**2.** A room in which the parts of a machine are fitted together.

1897 *Outing* June 279/2 We have reached one corner of the assembly-room, and here are the workmen lacing the spokes into the hubs.

***Assess,** *v.*

***1.** *tr.* To levy or impose (certain rates or taxes).

1634 *Boston Rec.* 2 The constable shall make and assess . . . a rate for the cowes keeping. **1692** BULKELEY *Will & Doom* 127 These rates are assessed in such a manner that . . . a penny in the pound in these assessments is much more than 12*d.* in the pound in England. **1707** *Boston News-Letter* 16 June 2/2 An Act for apportioning and assessing of three several taxes on polls and estates. **1719** *Mass. H. Repr. Journals* II. 122 To apportion, assess and levy the sum that shall be ordered by this court. **1789** FRANKLIN *Autobiog.* 438 They found the tax had been assess'd with perfect equity. **1856** *Ohio Statutes* (1860) II. 1545 To assess and collect a tax or charge on the . . . owners of any lots or lands. *Ib.*, The damages . . . may be assessed on all the lots or lands.

***2.** To rate (persons or property) according to means or value for the purpose of taxation or other levy.

1637 *Plymouth Col. Rec.* I. 61 To assesse men towardes the charges of the souldiers that are to be sent forth for the ayde of the Massachusetts Bay and Connectacutt. **1702** *Charlestown Land Rec.* 178 To pay all publick taxes to town, church and province said land shall be assessed. **1799** *Ann. 7th Congress* 2 Sess. 1415 Two acts of Congress; one for assessing houses, and the other for laying a direct tax. **1856** *Ohio Statutes* (1860) II. 1546 The value of such lots or lands as assessed for taxation. **1877** *Colo. General Laws* 744 Every assessor shall assess all personal property situate or being in his county on the first day of May in each year.

3. *absol.* To make assessments or levies.

1789 FRANKLIN *Autobiog.* 437 We reply'd that . . . the assessors were honest and discreet men under an oath to assess fairly and equitably. **1799** *Ann. 7th Congress* 2 Sess. 1434 We then proceeded to assess. **1882** *Nation* 31 Aug. 171/1 It is only when they [=rich men] represent . . . large corporations, and these . . . become liable to suffer from legislation, that the political striker sees his opening, and begins to 'assess.' . . . He began to levy his tolls in this State as soon as charters of incorporation began to be valuable.

***Assessment.**

***1.** The apportioning of the rate or amount of taxes; the amount so assessed.

1639 *Plymouth Laws* 68 They conceived they had not power to make assessments, rates and taxes. **1663** *Boston Rec.* 18 The neightbours . . . are to haue theare towne raite remitted for this next asseasment. **1692** BULKELEY *Will & Doom* 117 In executions of fines and assessments, and in civil actions. **1692** [see ASSESS *v.* 1]. **1710** *Boston News-Letter* 13 March 2/2 (*book-title*) A Guide to Constables in their . . . Collecting Rates & Assessments. **1788** FRANKLIN *Autobiog.* 381 In 1757 . . . [came] an alteration in the mode of assessment, which I thought not for the better. **1799** *Ann. 7th Congress* 2 Sess. 1430 We had taken between fifty and sixty assessments when we came to the house of Jacob Fries. **1809** KENDALL *Travels* II. 197 By assessments is meant those particular assessments which are made by the listers or by the general assembly. **1811** O. A. Rothert *Muhlenberg Co.* 167 The Court of Assessment of fines. **1856** *Ohio Statutes* (1860) II. 1547 If they determine to defray the expense of such work by an assessment. *Ib.*, The report and assessment shall be in writing. **1877** *Colo. General Laws* 751 Such instructions as shall be necessary to secure full and uniform assessments and returns.

+**2.** A levy made upon, a payment required from, members of an organization, business concern, etc.

1882 SALA *Amer. Revisited* (1883) I. 186 His salary . . . is subject to considerable reductions by the 'assessments' made on the policeman by the committees of the political organisation. **1883** *Harper's Mag.* Jan. 235/2 A . . . cashier had involved the bank in such complete ruin that, instead of dividends, an assessment was at once called for. **1890** *Nation* 10 April 291 The only thing . . . which Tammany leaders consider is . . . what 'assessments' the places or contracts can stand. **1905** D. G. PHILLIPS *Plum Tree* 131 My assessments upon the various members of my combine were sent, for several years, to me.

3. Attrib. with *bill, district* (see quots.).

1850 FOOTE *Sk. Virginia* 430 The bill to provide for the support of religion, commonly known as the General Assessment Bill, was engrossed for its third reading in 1784. **1864** *Statutes at Large* XIII. 224 Each assessor shall divide his district into a convenient number of assessment districts, which may be changed as often as may be deemed necessary.

+**b.** *Assessment work*, work done on a mining claim to maintain a possessory title.

1877 RAYMOND *Mines & Mining* 193 Most holders having contented themselves with doing the 'assessment-work.' **1882** *Rep. Precious Metals* 298 Promising locations of the district upon which assessment work only has been done. **1901** WHITE *Claim Jumpers* ii. 23 He did not see why they even did assessment work. **1923** B. M. BOWER *Parowan Bonanza* viii. 88 He would take care of the development work for her—at least the assessment work.

Assessor. One who assesses property for taxation. {1611–}

1646 *Mass. Bay Rec.* II. 174 *margin*, Who shalbe the assessors. **1687** *Huntington Rec.* I. 508 At a Cowrte of sessions . . . ordered that you send and impower an Assessor out of your town to meet with the Rest of the Assessors of the County. **1694** SEWALL *Diary* I. 391 Town-Meeting at Boston. Chose Assessors; Capt. Foster and I gave them their oaths. **1715** *Boston Rec.* 234 The Assessors may be left in a capacity of easing the poorer sort of persons. **1781** FRENEAU *Misc. Works* 391 *Quest.* What is your name? *Answ.* Titus Tax-grumbler. *Q.* Who gave you that name? *A.* The Assessor of our county. **1796** *Ann. 4th Congress* 2 Sess. 2697 The practice of combining the appointments of assessors and collectors in the same persons. **1834** *S. Lit. Messenger* I. 86 Its people in full town meeting elect a representative . . . in the legislature, . . . assessor and collector. **1849** WILLIS *Rural Lett.* ii. 25, I have just had a visit from the assessor. As if a man should be taxed for a house, who could be luxurious under a bridge! **1859** *Ohio Statutes* (1860) II. 1450 For the purpose of enabling the assessor to determine the value of buildings and other improvements. **1877** [see ASSESS *v.* 2]. **1904** *Newark Ev. News* 24 Aug. 6 A readjustment of local taxables recently completed by the city Board of Assessors.

***Assign,** *n.* Also †**assigne.** A person to whom property is legally transferred; an assignee.

1632 *Mass. Bay Rec.* I. 94 The heires and assigns of the said John Winthrop. **1633** *Ib.* 108 There is liberty graunted to Mr. John Winthrop, Junr., & to his assignes, to sett vp a trucking howss vpp Merrymak Ryver. **1637** *Essex Inst. Coll.* IX. 56 To allow his eyers, executors or assigns the value that the same shalbe worth. **1651** *Suffolk Deeds* I. 185 The sajd Richard Norton his heires and assignes . . . shall have all their wood . . . to be used in the sajd howse. **1720** *Mass. H. Repr. Journals* II. 251 The assigns of said White pretend to claim 700 acres. **1784** in *Rep. Comm. Patents* (1850) 531 Granting to your petitioner, his heirs and assigns, the sole right [etc.]. **1828** WEBSTER s.v., A deed to a man and his heirs and assigns. **1909** *Indian Laws & Tr.* III. 386 Said purchasers or their assigns shall be required to pay interest [etc.].

***Assign,** *v.* To affix one's signature; to sign; to subscribe. {–1633} — **1837** SHERWOOD *Gaz. Georgia* (ed. 3) 69 *Assign*, for sign; . . . to write the name. **1849** *S. Lit. Messenger* (De Vere), I will assign the paper, sir, as soon as you bring it to me, and then you can have it recorded in Court. **1871** DE VERE 580 To *assign*, is in the South used by illiterate persons and by an astounding number of men who ought to know better, instead of *sign*.

***Assignation.** =ASSIGNMENT 1. *Obs.* **1650** *Conn. Public Rec.* 512 Any debt . . . shall bee as good a debt and estate to the assignee as it was to the assigner, at the time of its assignation.

***Assignee.** One to whom property is legally transferred.

1640 *Suffolk Deeds* I. 50 The said John Turner his Executors, Administrators, or Assignees . . . shall enjoy the fourth part aboue demised. **1650** [see ASSIGNATION]. **1660** *Ib.* III. 375 To levy on the goods . . . to value of two hundred pounds and deliver the same to Richard Cooke assignee of Edward Lane. **1704** *N. Car. Col. Rec.* I. 605 John Falconer assignee of Coll. Robt. Quarry. **1790** *Ann. 1st Congress* II. 1231 An assignee was not always in as advantageous a situation as the assignor. **1822** *Ann. 17th Congress* 1 Sess. I. 157 Patents issued to said officers and soldiers, or their assignees. **1852** *Harper's Mag.* V. 694/2 A party of engineers was sent out by the American assignees, to complete the necessary surveys [of land grants]. **1884** *N.Y. Herald* 27 Oct. 2/1 Stock Farm: . . . assignee's sale November 1. **1900** C. C. MUNN *Uncle Terry* 60 Dad bought her for less than half that at an assignee's sale.

Assigner: see ASSIGNOR.

***Assignment.**

***1.** The transfer of one's interest in property to another, especially in arranging for the security of creditors.

1655 *Suffolk Deeds* II. 195 The first twenty pounds specified in the endorcement was for an assignment which Mr Riddan past vppon Mr Webb. **1694** *N. Car. Col. Rec.* I. 432 Capt. Thomas Relfe acknowledgeth his assignment of a patent to John Jenings. **1714** *Mass. Bay Currency Tracts* 73 The Trustees . . . shall have full power . . . [to] make what releases and assignments shall be thought necessary, for the use of this partnership. **1828** WEBSTER, *Convey*, . . . to pass a title to any thing from one person to another, as by deed, assignment, or otherwise. **1852** *Harper's Mag.* V. 694/2 After the assignment of the grant [of land] to American citizens. **1880** BARNET *Commercial Dict.* 26 Contracts frequently provide that there shall be no assignment without the consent of both parties.

+**2.** A duty assigned to one: **a.** In journalism, a task given to a reporter.

1897 *Scribner's Mag.* Aug. 232/2 The reporters . . . were waiting to be sent off on their first assignments before getting breakfast. **1911** HARRISON *Queed* iv. 44 Editorials he had written on assignment. **1917** SINCLAIR *King Coal* 207 You propose to have me shadowed while I'm working on this assignment?

b. An appointment to a particular position, as of a minister to a church or mission.

1904 *N.Y. Ev. Post* 11 May 9 He . . . went into the Presbyterian ministry, receiving assignments in various parts of the mining camp West.

Assignor. Also †**assigner.** A person who legally transfers property to another. {1668–}

1650 [see ASSIGNATION]. **1654** *Suffolk Deeds* II. 121 This assigner William Phillips did acknowledg this assignement to be his owne act. **1790** *Ann. 1st Congress* II. 1231 An assignee was not always in as advantageous a situation as the assignor. **1828** WEBSTER s.v., The assignor of a bill of exchange. **1858** *Rep. Comm. Patents* (1859) I. 654 Cyriel E. Brown, of Millbury, Massachusetts, assignor to himself, John Tenney and John Rhodes. **1880** BARNET *Commercial Dict.* 54 Where the assignee must sue in the name of the assignor, the assignor is liable for costs.

Assist, *n.* +In baseball (see quot. 1891). — **1877** *Constitution & By-laws Nat. League* 40 An assist should be given to each player who handles the ball in a run-out or other play of this kind. **1891** N. CRANE *Baseball* 79 *Assist*, the credit given by the scorer to a fielder who handles the ball in assisting to put out a player. **1896** KNOWLES & MORTON *Baseball* 101 The fielder who handles the ball in sufficient time to aid in retiring a base-runner is credited with an assist. **1917** MATHEWSON *Sec. Base Sloan* xiv. 187 Five strike-outs, three assists, and no errors was considered a fine record.

+**Assist,** *v.* +In baseball: (see quot. 1872). — **1872** CHADWICK *Dime Base-ball Player* 27 A fielder assists when he throws a ball to the baseman on which the runner is put out, or in any way assists a fielder to put a player out. **1877** *Const. & By-Laws of Nat. League* 40 The number of times a player assists shall be set down in the sixth column.

***Assistance.** *Writ of assistance*, a writ issued by a superior court during later colonial times, authorizing customs officers engaged in searching premises under certain laws to summon assistance. *Obs.*

1761 in J. Quincy *Mass. Rep.* (1865) 412 The Petitioners, Inhabitants of the Province of the Massachusetts Bay, humbly pray that they may be heard by themselves and Council upon the subject of Writs of Assistance. **1761** OTIS *Ib.* 413 Continuance of Writts and Proscesses proves no more nor so much as I grant a special Writ of ass. [*sic*] on special oath, for spec[ia]l Purpose. **1776** ADAMS *Works* (1854) IX. 418 The argument [in 1761] concerning writs of assistance in the superior court, which I have hitherto considered as the commencement of this controversy between Great Britain and America. **1818** — *Ib.* (1856) X. 276 Mr. Otis's oration against Writs of Assistance breathed into this nation the breath of life. [**1883** A. GILMAN *Hist. Amer. People* xi. 227 The customs' duties . . . became difficult to collect. This led, in 1761, to the 'Writs of Assistance,' under which search could be made for contraband goods . . . by the officer of the customs, or any one employed by him.]

***Assistant.**

***1.** One who assists another in some special capacity; a helper.

1639 *Springfield Rec.* I. 165 Henry Smith . . . shall have power to choose a Corporall for his asistant. **a1656** BRADFORD *Hist.* 122 William Bradford was chosen Governor . . . and . . . Isaak Allerton was chosen to be an Asistante unto him. **1704** *Boston Rec.* 29 Settleing a sallery upon an assistant to Mr. Chever in the government of the Lattin School. **1816** *Ann. 14th Congress* 1 Sess. 369 That Robert Tweedy [etc.], Assistants to the Sergeant-at-Arms, . . . be paid . . . two dollars a day. **1854** *Penna. Agric. Rep.* 230 Normal schools are founded for the express purpose of training teachers and assistants for the agricultural schools. **1890** RYAN *Told in Hills* 13, I was offered the position of assistant here to Doctor Grenier. **1902** *Harper's Mag.* Jan. 279/1 Mrs. Dud's pretty maids—she always had pretty ones, even to the cook's third assistant. **1905** *Indian Laws & Tr.* III. 130 For blacksmith and assistants, and tools, . . . five hundred dollars.

+**2.** An executive and judicial official in the colonies. *Obs.*

The first assistants of the Mass. Bay Colony were elected in England, as 'assisting' in the enterprise by representing the stockholders; on the transfer to New England they became managing heads of the government, along with the governor and deputy-governor.

*c*1618 STRACHEY *Virginia* 150 Sir W. Raleigh . . . also appointed unto him [John White] twelve assistents, unto whome he gave a charter, and incorporated them by the name of Governour and Assistents of the city Raleigh, in Virginia. **1629** *Mass. Charter* (1853) 10 There shalbe one Governor, one Deputy Governor, and eighteene Assistants of the same Company, to be from tyme to tyme constituted, elected, and chosen out of the freemen of the saide Company, for the tyme being. **1630** *Mass. Rec.* I. 75 Capt. Endicott beinge formerly chosen an Assistant did nowe take the oath of an Assistant in the presence of the Court. **a1647** F. GORGES *Descr. New-Eng.* iv. 46 Eight deputies [are] to be elected by the free-houlders of the severall counties, . . . to sit in any of the aforesaid Courts, and to be assistants. **1649** WINTHROP *Journal* I. 74 That no assistant could be chosen but by the freemen, who had power likewise to remove the assistants and put in others. **1654** JOHNSON *Wonder-W. Prov.* 39 The Governour Deputy and Assistants, held their second Court on the south-side of the river. **1672** *Portsmouth* (R.I.) *Town Rec.* 170 Mr. William Baulston the eldist Assistant in this towne is abscent. *c***1680** J. HULL *Diary* 163, I was also chosen by the country for an Assistant, and released my former service of Treasurer. **1722** *New-Eng. Courant* 7 May 2/2 The Freemen of the colony [R.I.] elected the following gentlemen for the ensuing year.... For Assistants, Jonathan Nichols Esq; [etc.]. **1741** *Georgia Col. Rec.* VI. 3 Proceedings of the President and Assistants for the town and county of Savannah in Georgia.

b. *Court of Assistants*, a judicial court held by these officials.

1630 *Mass. Col. Rec.* I. 74 That there should be a Court of Assistants helde att the Gouernors howse on the 7th day of September nexte. **1634** *Boston Rec.* 2 Chosen to serve as jurors at the next Court of Assistants. **1636** *Plymouth Laws* 41 That the Government, vizt. the generall courts and courts of Assistants be held at Plymouth. **1656** *Suffolk Deeds* II. 342 At which Court of Assistants held at Boston... the former judgment of the County Court was confirmed. **1669** *Boston Rec.* 45 The freemen of this towne... to meete togeather... for the choyce of jurymen for the next Court of Assistance [*sic*]. **1691** SEWALL *Diary* I. 354 The marriage of Hanna Owen with her husband's brother, is declar'd null by the Court of Assistants.

2. *Writ of assistants:* see ASSISTANCE. *Obs.*

1755 in J. Quincy *Mass. Reports* (1865) 402 Charles Paxton... prays he & his Deputys may be aided in the Execution of said office within his District by a Writ of Assistants under the Seal of this Superiour Court. **1761** *Ib.* 51 Paxton... applied to the Superiour Court for the Writ of Assistants, as by Act of Parliament to be granted to him. *Ib.* 56 This is properly a Writ of Assistants, not Assistance; not to give the Officers a greater Power, but as a check upon them.

3. Attrib. or adj. with names of offices, occupations, etc. {1710–}

1846 MACKENZIE *Life Van Buren* 223 In May and June, 1830, Jeromus Johnson,... and A. B. Mead, went into office as appraisers at New York, and Bernard J. Messerole, [etc.],... as assistant-appraisers. — **1828** SHERBURNE *Mem.* (1831) x. 221 In the year 1814, I was appointed one of the assistant assessors of the direct tax. — **1871** *Rep. Indian Affairs* (1872) 174 We have assistant associates with the agency. — **1808** *Ann. 10th Congress* 1 Sess. II. 1509 Resolved, that an Assistant Clerk be appointed by this House, who, during the necessary absence, or in case of the death of the Clerk of the House, shall perform the duties of the said Clerk. — **1789** *Ann. 1st Congress* I. 233 A petition... praying that the proper officer may be authorized to receive and examine their accounts as assistant-commissaries of issues. **1850** MILES *Journal* (1916) 16 Mr. Boyd, assistant commissary, came from town. — **1814** *Ann. 13th Congress* III. 123 Resolved, That the Senate... proceed to the choice of an assistant doorkeeper. — **1817** *N. Amer. Rev.* Nov. 147 The officers of the University are, at present, twenty professors, two tutors, librarian and assistant librarian. — **1828** SHERBURNE *Mem.* (1831) x. 216 In addition to the census, government had directed that the assistant marshal should also take an account of the several manufacturing establishments in their several divisions. **1845** HOOPER *Taking Census* i. 149 The assistant marshals... were employed to take the last census. — **1792** *Ann. 2nd Congress* 59 Be it further enacted, that... there shall be one Postmaster General, who shall have authority to appoint an assistant and deputy postmasters. **1825** *Statutes at Large* 18 Congress 2 Sess. lxiv. 113 No postmaster, assistant postmaster, or clerk... shall be... concerned in a contract for carrying the mail. **1853** *Executive Doc.* I. III. 701 The report of the second assistant Postmaster General. — **1850** HALE *M. Percival in Amer.* 140 At first sight, however, the prospect of securing for Miss Percival the position of 'assistant principal,' as, in the barbarous patois of the catalogue, it was called, did not seem very encouraging. — **1851** CIST *Cincinnati* 304 In September... he received the appointment of assistant professor of mathematics. **1879** *Scribner's Monthly* Dec. 202/2 Neither the title of 'assistant professor' nor that of 'tutor' exactly meets the case. **1891** *Univ. of Chicago Official Bull. No. I* 11 Lecturers and Teachers... shall be classified as follows:... (5) The Assistant Professor. — **1776** *Journals Cont. Congress* V. 419 Resolved, that the assistant quarter masters general be allowed captains pay. — **1784** FILSON *Kentucke* 38 A copy of the record must be... produced to the assistant register of the land-office in Kentucke. — **1792** *Statutes at Large* 2 Congress 1 Sess. vii. 238 Any public letter... may be franked by the Secretary of the Treasury, or the Assistant Secretary. **1812** *Ann. 12th Congress* II. 1330 It shall be the duty of the said Assistant Secretaries to aid and assist the Secretary of said department [of War]. — **1861** *Army Regulations* 287 The Secretary of War will designate the applicants to be examined for appointment of assistant surgeon. — **1845** *Knickerb.* XXV. 236 She remained at the school as an assistant-teacher. **1881** *Rep. Indian Affairs* xxxvi, To have suitable employment... for these youth at the various agencies as interpreters, apprentices, assistant-teachers, [etc.]. — **1821** *Boston Rec.* 205 The Selectmen... to make such compensation to the Assistant Town Clerk as they may think proper.

Assisted, *ppl. a.* +Of immigrants: Receiving financial or other assistance. — **1892** *Vermont Agric. Rep.* XII. 124 Neither do we want 'assisted Swedes' to attempt to clear our forests and starve in doing it.

***Assister.** ‖ An assistant (sense 2). *Obs.* — **1645** *Maine Doc. Hist.* IV. 9 The Jenerall Court shall eleckt there magistrats and assisters.

***Assize.**

***1.** (Usually in *pl.*) The sessions of a court of justice, corresponding to those still held in England. *Obs.* Also *Court of assize.*

1651 *East-Hampton Rec.* I. 17 The Assembly... choas... agents... to confer about and conclued such Matters to present to the Court of Assieses. **1669** *N.Y. State Col. Hist.* XII. 465 Still neither Mayor nor Aldermen [being] elected, the Grand Assizes like to be prorogued. **1687** *Mass. H. S. Coll.* 4 Ser. V. 159 There is but one place where the Grand Assize and Superior Court of Common Pleas is kept here. **1705** *Boston News-Letter* 12 Nov. 2/1 On Tuesday... there was held here the Superiour Court of Assize,... where the said Odell was arraigned for uttering counterfeit bills of credit on this province. **1724** *New-Eng. Courant* 1 June 2/1–2 Cecil County, Maryland.... At the Assizes held for this county on Friday... one Robert Dutch... was condemn'd to die for murdering one William Weden. **1743** FRANKLIN *Poor Richard 1744* 21 Courts of Assize in Maryland. **1754** *Maryland Archives* L. 507 Two of them [=offenders]... have recognized for their appearance at the next Assizes. **1784** *Va. House of Delegates J.* 10 Dec. (1828) 64 An act, for the establishment of Courts of Assize.

b. *Assize sermon*, a special sermon preached on the occasion of the Assizes.

1699 SEWALL *Letter-book* I. 216 Mr. Noyes... preached an excellent Assize Sermon.

***2.** The standard of quantity, measure, weight, etc., as of bread, casks, etc. *Obs.*

1687 *Conn. Public Rec.* III. 426 Such viewers shall have power to cast by all such staves as they judge not to be merchantable, either in respect of worm holes or want of assize. **1700** *Penna. Col. Rec.* I. 576 Complaint of the poor against the bakers of bread for sale not being of the law[fu]ll & due assize. **1705** *Boston News-Letter* 10 Dec. 4/1 An Act for regulating the assize of cask for tar, pitch, turpentine, and rozin, and for preventing frauds and deceit in said commodities. **1727** *Boston Rec.* 217 To viset the several bakers... and see that they conform to the law referring to the assize of bread.

***Associate,** *n.*

***1.** One associated with a magistrate or judge for the purpose of holding courts of justice. *Obs.*

1636 *Plymouth Laws* 54 Such a portion of land bounded so & so... was granted and in publick court confirmed by William Bradford and his Associats. **1641** *Mass. Liberties* 225 All Associates selected at any time to assist the Assistants in inferior Courts, shall be nominated by the townes belonging to that Court. **1650** *Mass. Rec.* III. 211 There shall also be a choyse of some meete persons for associates for each shire... which said associates... with one magistrate, shall... keepe all & every the sajd Shire Courts. **1659** *Maine H. S. Coll.* I. 389 There will be need of more associates for county courts than formerly. **1664** *N.H. Probate Rec.* I. 81 Afterwards this is refered to the Court of associats to order. **1686** *Plymouth Laws* 208 There shall be annually chosen by the Generall Court so many Associates as they shall see need of who shall sit in and act in the County Courts as the magistrates may.

***2.** One associated with others in an enterprise or business.

[**1670** DENTON *Descr. N.Y.* (1845) 17 The Governor... gives them a grant or patent for the said land, for themselves and associates.] **1792** *Ann. 2nd Congress* 486 The petition of the Directors of the Ohio Company of Associates. **1882** E. K. GODFREY *Nantucket* 164 The Mayhews... may not have been able to purchase the Indian or 'sachem rights,' but it is certain there were no 'associates' until 1659.

+**3.** As an academic title or degree.

The precise application varies in different academic institutions.

1879 *Scribner's Monthly* Dec. 202/2 A number of young men... have been gathered about the university under the title of associates. **1891** D. C. GILMAN *Johns Hopkins Univ.* 63 The number of associates, readers, and assistants has been very large. **1904** E. G. DEXTER *Hist. Educ. U.S.* 293 With the completion of the two years' course, a certificate is granted giving the title of associate in the University.

***Associate,** *a.*

***1.** Having a (freq. secondary or subordinate) position or function in association with another or others.

In early use with *justice* or *judge*.

1789 *Statutes at Large* 24 Sept. 73 The supreme court of the United States shall consist of a chief justice and five associate justices. **1789** *Ann. 1st Congress* I. 86, I nominate for the Supreme Court of the United States—For Associate Judges: John Rutledge,... James Wilson [etc.]. **1816** *Ann. 14th Congress* 2 Sess. 357 Chief Justice and Associate Justices of the Supreme Court of the United States shall cease to be Judges of the Circuit Courts of the United States. **1818** E. P. FORDHAM *Narr. Travels* 155 He is an associate Judge and sits on the bench with the circuit or law judge. **1837** PECK *New Guide* 248 The circuit courts [of Indiana] consist of a presiding judge in each judicial circuit... and two associate judges in each County. **1843** *Knickerb.* XXII. 494 We cannot permit the young associate-editor of that print... to misrepresent us. **1862** [NEWELL] *Orpheus C. Kerr* I. 25 Timothy Trot, licensed liquor dealer, and associate editor of the 'Lily of the Valley.' **1891** *Univ. of Chicago Official Bull. No. I* 11 Lecturers and Teachers... shall be classified as follows:... (4) The associate professor. **1904** *N.Y. Ev. Post* 23 July 4 He is associate editor of the *Evening Wisconsin.* **1906** *Ib.* 21 Aug. 3 Peter J. Dooling and William Dalton... agreed to drop their quarrel and become 'associate leaders' of the district. **1909** G. F. PARKER *G. Cleveland* 93 In like manner, L. Q. C. Lamar, then Secretary of the Interior, was appointed an associate Justice.

2. Associated; forming an association.

Applied spec. to a branch of the Presbyterian Church.

1798 [MASON] (*title*), Letters on frequent communion . . . to the Members of the Associate-Reformed Church. **1807** *Ann. 10th Congress* 1 Sess. I. 983 Mr. Findley presented a petition of the Associate Reformed or Presbyterian Congregation, in the city of Washington. **1811** MEASE *Philadelphia* 212 Sundry persons . . . made application to the associate synod in Edinburgh, for a supply of ministers. Two were accordingly sent, in 1754, and with ruling elders, constituted the 'Associate Presbytery of Pennsylvania.' **1824** R. H. BISHOP *Hist. Church Ky.* 172 He put himself under the care of the Kentucky Presbytery of the Associate Reformed Church. **1830** *Free Press* (Tarboro, N.C.) 19 Mar., A Camp Meeting . . . held by the Associate Reformed Methodists. **1837** PECK *Gaz. Illinois* (ed. 2) 74 There are also two or three societies of Associate Reformed Presbyterians, or Seceders. **1837** — *New Guide* 350 At Canonsburg [Pa.] is a seminary belonging to the Associate Church. **1857** C. VAUX *Villas* 104 The Associate Reformed Church proposed to be erected in Newburgh.

* **Associate,** *v. intr.* To become a member of an association, as of a religious body. {1653–}

1718 C. MATHER *Diary* II. 549 Animate my brother Samuel, to begin the work of associating, to serve the kingdome of God. **1751** M. Blake *Mendon Association* (1853) 41 Being thotful that it might tend to the advancement of the glory of Christ . . . in this vicinity, for them to associate . . . [they] voted themselves associated. **1832** WILLIAMSON *Hist. Maine* II. 695 From the church-session an appeal of right is allowable to the presbytery, . . . and from such others, if any, as have associated.

Associated, *a.* {1611–} Formed into, composing, an association.

1735 *Boston Rec.* 115 Jacob Wendell . . . laid before the town a letter to the committee, signed . . . in the name of the Associated Pastors. **1751** M. Blake *Mendon Association* (1853) 42 We, the subscribers, Associated Pastors of chhs. of Christ. **1796** (*title*), A Brief Account of the Associated Presbyteries. **1818–9** T. HULME *Journal* 61, I question whether the *associated* person of Mr. Rapp would not be in possession of as fine a domain . . . as the *incorporated* person of an Archbishop. **1859** BARTLETT 13 A number of newspaper establishments in New York and elsewhere, which have entered into a joint arrangement for procuring telegraphic and other news to be equally furnished to them all, have assumed the name of 'The Associated Press.' **1866** 'F. KIRKLAND' *Bk. Anecdotes* 30 An exact copy . . . was given to the agent of the associated press, and on the next morning it was read all over the North. **1882** 'M. HARLAND' *Eve's Daughters* 236 She is tempted to send the news to the Associated Press as 'An item of . . . interesting information.' **1888** W. LAWRENCE *A. A. Lawrence* 272 He became a Visitor of the Associated Charities in Roxbury.

* **Association.**

1. A union of persons or of groups for the purpose of advancing their common aims. {*a*1659–} **a.** A society of the clergymen of a neighborhood; occas., a meeting of such a society; also, in some denominations, an organized body of the churches of a region.

1693 C. MATHER *Wond. Invis. World* 10 Pastors . . . such as in their several neighborly Associations have had their meetings whereat ecclesiastical matters . . . are considered. **1737** E. PARKMAN *Diary* 14 Ensign Ward . . . here to obtain my evidence of what the Association . . . judged concerning Mr. Kent. **1747** *N.H. Hist. Soc. Coll.* IX. 4 We think it expedient . . . that they [the ministers of the Province] be formed into Associations to meet more frequently. **1798** A. HOLMES *E. Stiles* 19 Having received a license from the New-Haven Association of ministers, he preached his first sermon at West-Haven, in June. **1811** WEEMS *Lett.* III. 32 Learning that an immense Association of Divines was to sit in Columbia in Christmass, the idea struck me that [etc.]. **1824** *Amer. Baptist Mag.* IV. 242/2 Our present system of annual Associations, is capable . . . of being made to answer all the purposes which ought to be attempted by any system of ecclesiastical polity. **1832** WILLIAMSON *Hist. Maine* II. 699 Several [Universalist] churches sometimes, like those of congregationalists, form Associations. **1834** PECK *Gaz. Illinois* 89 The Baptist denomination includes nineteen associations, one hundred and ninety-five associated, and five unassociated churches. **1847** *Ind. Mag. Hist.* XXII. 419 In September 1843 me and my wife attended the Lost River association and heard old Nicholas Smith preach his celebrated sermon. **1869** STOWE *Oldtown Folks* 451 The first Association that Esther had to manage quite alone as sole mistress of the parsonage occurred while we were with her. **1874** B. F. TAYLOR *World on Wheels* I. xix. 141 But Elder Peck never could say 'Association.' You can shut your eyes and hear him: 'the brethren of the As-so-sa-shun will please to give their attention.'

b. An organization for a specific purpose. {1863–}

1747 FRANKLIN *Writings* II. 353 The writer . . . will, in a few days, lay before them [=his countrymen] a Form of an Association. **1775** *Journals Cont. Congress* II. 251 The convention of that Colony [=Ga.] agreed to enter into the general continental association. **1776** F. Moore *Diary of Revolution* (1860) I. 169 To sign, and so be safe; or to resolve . . . against 'associations,' And, by retreating, shun them. **1812** *Ann. 12th Congress* 1st Sess. I. 209 Mr. Dana . . . reported a bill respecting associations for maritime security. **1836** A. C. FLAGG in Mackenzie *Van Buren* 176 If the fetters are knocked off by the repeal of the Restraining Law, private banking associations may be formed. **1837** PECK *Gaz. Illinois* 73 Several lyceums and literary associations exist in this state. **1839** A. LAWRENCE *Diary & Corr.* 172, I will give to the Charitable Mechanic Association ten thousand dollars. **1848** *N.Y. Ev. Express* 22 Sept. 1/3 The 'American Association for the Advancement of Science,' met yesterday morning. **1866** 'F. KIRKLAND' *Bk. Anecdotes* 530 The Union Association of Colored Women. **1869** (*title*), American Philological Association. **1891** O'BEIRNE *Leaders Ind. Territory* 81/2 The Protective and Detective Association of Texas is under the management of Mr. Blossom in the Indian Territory. **1903** E. JOHNSON *Railway Transportation* 232 The organizations or 'associations' subsequently formed by competing railways in the West and other sections of the country.

***2.** A document by which the signers pledge themselves to combine for certain purposes. (Cf. 4.)

1696 SEWALL *Diary* I. 430 Mr. Blathwayts Letter recommending the subscribing the Association by all in public place and Trust. **1774** *Journals Cont. Congress* I. 75 The association being copied, was read and signed at the table. **1776** N. HALE in *Biogr. & Mem.* 142 In this city such as refuse to sign the Association have been required to deliver up their arms. **1788** FRANKLIN *Autobiog.* 361 A pamphlet . . . in which I . . . promis'd to propose in a few days an association, to be generally signed for that purpose. **1854** SIMMS *Southward Ho* 262, I will sign no association that shall make me lose my lands. *Ib.*, It's treason, I say, to sign any association.

3. 'In civil affairs, this word is much used at the present day, to denote the principle of uniting the producing classes in societies, for the purpose of obtaining for themselves a larger share of the fruits of their labor' (B. '48).

Bartlett's definition, and the quotations, refer to Fourierism.

1842 Commons, etc. *Doc. Hist.* (1910) VII. 185 The friends of Association in the City have founded a Society . . . to aid the propagation of the principles . . . of Association. . . . No responsibility is incurred by becoming a member of the Fourier Association. *a***1848** *N.Y. Tribune* (B.), Being firmly convinced that the Science taught by Fourier will ultimately lead us into true *Association*, if we follow it as a science.

4. Attrib. (in sense 1) with *meeting, paper* (=sense 2), *sermon, system.*

1776 *Docs. & Rec. rel. N.H.* 213 The Association Paper has been carried through this Town and these men refuse to sine. *Ib.* 235 The several persons abovenamed refuse signing the association paper. **1823** *Amer. Baptist Mag.* IV. 198/1 Having been called . . . to attend the meetings of some of the Baptist Associations in New-England, it has occurred to me, that a few remarks upon our general Association System, might be useful. **1824** *Ib.* 360/1(*title*), Association Sermon. **1878** STOWE *Poganuc People* xxi. 231 The Doctor . . . retreated to his study, where . . . he was preparing a paper to read at the next Association meeting.

+**Associational,** *a.* Pertaining to an association of clergymen or of churches.

1815 DWIGHT *Remarks Inchiquin's Lett.* 56 In order to obtain a license, and afterwards to be admitted to ordination, they [=students in divinity] must in each case pass through the Associational or Presbyterial examination, mentioned above. *a***1817** — *Travels* III. 520 The County of Fairfield . . . contains two Associational districts. The churches in the Western district [etc.]. **1853** M. BLAKE *Mendon Association* 44 The regular exercises at the Associational meetings have varied at different dates. **1896** *Peterson Mag.* VI. 312/1 Her tastes run largely to associational work, particularly in the field of charities. **1899** *Boston Transcript* 1 Dec. 9/2 The Year Book . . . gathers associational reports covering the year preceding.

+**Associationism.** [ASSOCIATION 1a.] The fact or practice of uniting societies of clergymen into a general association. — *a***1840** N. EMMONS in Park *Memoir* (1861) 163 Associationism leads to Consociationism; Consociationism leads to Presbyterianism.

Associationist. One who advocates the doctrine of association as taught by the Fourierites. Also *fig.*

1844 Commons, etc. *Doc. Hist.* VII. 198 Resolved . . . that the Name which . . . we adopt for ourselves . . . is, The Associationists of the United States of America. We do not call ourselves Fourierists. **1845** JUDD *Margaret* II. i. 186 She . . . stepped with a kind of caution among these groups of dumb, . . . industrious Associationists [=ants]. **1846** *Knickerb.* XXVIII. 16 This is contemplated, I believe, in all the Phalansteries of Unitative Associationists.

‖**Associatist.** =ASSOCIATIONIST. — **1848** *Howitt's Journal* III. 109 The *Harbinger*, the weekly organ of the American Associatists, a journal very ably conducted.

Associator. {1616–} One who associates with others in an enterprise. {1616–1683}

In Pennsylvania in the 18th cent. used (in pl.) for the militia, as the Quakers wished to avoid a military name.

1736 *Penna. Colonial Records* IV. 113 And, therefore, we think it proper that you call before you as many of the said Associators as possibly you can. **1756** Dinwiddie in *Lett. to Washington* I. 268 The Gentlemen Associators being Volunteers at their own Expence, I gave them no instructions. **1776** *Journals Cont. Congress* IV. 128 Resolved, That it be also recommended to the Committee of safety ... to send detachments of the four battalions of associators ... [from Phila.] to New York. *Ib.* V. 437 The commanding officer of the riffle batallion of associators in this city [=Lewistown]. **1788** Franklin *Autobiog.* 362 Colonel Lawrence ... and myself were sent [c1747] to New York by the associators, commission'd to borrow some cannon of Governor Clinton. **1847** Howe *Ohio* 169 'The Scioto Company' [consisted] ... at first of eight associators. **1865** Phillips *Hist. Paper Currency* II. 64 Even quondam associators refused to receive the money.

Assortment. An assorted or varied set of articles or goods. {1791–}

Replacing the older *sortment*, and perhaps actually earlier in American than English use.

1736 Murray *Letters* 33 As the most necessary things sell first, the remainder of my cargoe will want an assortment to help it of. **1742** *Boston News-Letter* 30 Dec. 2/1 To be sold by publick vendue ... this afternoon, ... a fine assortment of broad cloths, ... and almost all sorts of goods. **1751** *Boston Ev. Post* 23 Sept. 2/2 A large assortment of brass kettles. **1754** *S. C. Gazette* 1 Jan. 2/2 Samuel Peronneau hath just imported ... a large assortment of Irish linnens ... and long lawns. **1787** *Mass. Centinel* 3 Nov. 3/3 An assortment of ten plate and Franklin stoves. **1823** Cooper *Pioneers* viii, He had but little; ... but that little was enough to furnish, in the language of the country, an assortment for a store. **1858** *Theatrical Bijou* (Phila.) 13 Feb. 3/2 Their Autumn assortment of goods for boys, including cassimers, ... and fancy vestings. **1861** *Army Regulations* 123 The cargo of each [vessel] should be composed of an assortment of such stores as may be available for service.

***Assume,** *v.* +*tr.* To take over (the debts of another): cf. Assumption. — **1789** C. Gore in *Life R. King* (1894) I. 362 If the national government cou'd assume the different state debts, the consequence ... would be greatly beneficial to America. **1790** M. Cutler in *Life, Jrnls. & Corr.* (1888) I. 460 Congress are still on the question, whether the State debts shall be assumed.

Assumpsit. [L., 'he has taken on himself.'] **a.** A promise or contract, not under seal, which if broken may be a cause of a suit for damages. **b.** A suit for damages incurred through breach of such promise or contract. {1612–}

1649 *R.I. Court Rec.* 7 Either of them being bound in an assumpsit of 100 li. apiece to stand to the end these three made. **1828** Webster s.v., An assumpsit is express or implied. **1852** *S. Lit. Messenger* XVIII. 678/1 He had brought an action of assumpsit on a blacksmith's account. **1852** Dunlap *Bk. Forms* (1857) 298 Form of Declaration in Assumpsit, on Promissory Notes, approved by the Supreme Court of New Jersey.

***Assumption.** +The adoption of obligations by another. In the first years of the federal government, applied to the taking over of the state debts by the federal government.

1789 Gore in *Life R. King* (1894) I. 362 Till the intention of Congress is known relative to the assumption of funds, the State cannot, with propriety, make any arrangement for the payment of their debts. **1790** *Steele Papers* I. 64 Congress has been and still is extremely divided respecting the permanent residence of Government, the assumption of the State debts, the excise bill. *Ib.* 72 Were it possible to reject the assumption-project once more ... I would return to my fellow citizens perfectly satisfied. **1791** Washington *Diaries* IV. 159 The conduct of the Assembly respecting the assumption he thinks is condemned by them as intemperate and unwise. **1797** *Ann. 4th Congress* 2 Sess. 1808 The endearing arguments ... in favor of the assumption of the State debts. **1827** Sherwood *Gaz. Georgia* 74 All bonds, notes, promises and assumptions, made for medical services to persons ... shall be void.

+**Assumptionist,** *n.* One who advocates assumption (see prec.). — **1841** *Congress. Globe* Jan., App. 153/1 The distributionist, and the anti-distributionist—the assumptionist, and the anti-assumptionist, ... were united against the Democracy.

Aster. One or other plant of the genus *Aster*, having numerous species native to America. {1706–}

In Britain called *Michaelmas daisy*, the name *aster* being now restricted to the China aster.

1753 *Chambers' Cycl.* Suppl. s.v. *Star-wort*, The tall hairy New England aster with very large violet-purple flowers. **1784** Cutler in *Mem. Academy* I. 481 Bushy aster. Florets in ... the center yellow. By fences. September. *Ib.* 482 New England aster ... [grows in] borders of fields. **1818** *Mass. H. S. Coll.* 2 Ser. VIII. 170 In August the eye is gratified with ... numerous species of the aster. **1835** Bird *Hawks of Hawk-h.* I. vii. 91 Rock-daisies, and other plants, now in bloom, and, in the summer, their places would have been supplied by the aster and the golden-rod. **1852** Mitchell *Dream Life* 68 The last of the blue and purple asters shiver along the wall. **1869** Stowe *Oldtown Folks* 102 The golden-rod and the aster hung their plumage over the rough, rocky road. **1876** *Field & Forest* I. 65 By the last of August or first of September, the fields and woodsides of the Atlantic seaboard are whitened with low bushy Asters. **1884** Roe *Nature's Story* 282 Amy ... exulted in the extent and variety of their finely quilled and rose-like asters and dahlias. **1901** Mohr *Plant Life Ala.* 779 Aster. Starwort. From 200 to 250 species, recognized as valid; perennials; ... largely American.

+**Asthma weed.** Indian tobacco, used as a remedy for asthma. *Obs.* — **1819** *Western Rev.* I. 183 The *Lobelia inflata* or Asthma weed, a ... plant with alternate hairy leaves, blue flowers, and swelled seed vessels.

+**Astonisher.** *colloq.* Something that causes astonishment. {1871–} — **1860** J. D. Whitney in *Life* (1909) 178 The picture ... was an 'astonisher' to me, a sort of new revelation in landscape painting. **1889** 'Mark Twain' *Conn. Yankee* xxvii. 350 He was always ... breaking out with fresh astonishers.

+**Astorian.** [*Astoria*, Oregon, fur-trading station founded in 1811 by J. J. Astor.] A fur-trader attached to Astoria. — **1837** Irving *Bonneville* I. 24 The frightful hardships sustained by Wilson ... and other intrepid Astorians, in their ill-fated expeditions across the mountains. **1850** G. Hines *Voyage* 372 The arrival of the ship Beaver ... [with] supplies and reinforcements, encouraged the Astorians.

Astrachan. [The name of the Russian city and division *Astrakhan.*] +A variety of apple. Cf. Red Astrachan.

1852 *Horticulturist* VII. 437/2 Every householder who owns land ... ought to have one tree of the Astrachan apple, both on account of its earliness, and its excellence for cooking. **1856** *Rep. Comm. Patents: Agric.* 293 The best apples for this region are the 'Early Harvest,' ... 'Astrachan,' [etc.]. **1872** *Vermont Bd. Agric. Rep.* I. 99 The Astrachans are still early fall apples.

+**Astral. a.** Ellipt. for next.

1838 *Knickerb.* XII. 57 As she drew the flowers on the centre-table more under the light of the astral. **1854** B. F. Taylor *Jan. & June* 152 And what a lamp—no 'Astral,' but a true Lunar—is hung in the passage-way. **1854** Whittier *Maud Müller* xlvii, The weary wheel to a spinnet turned, The tallow candle an astral burned. **1865** *Atlantic Mo.* XV. 30 Mrs. Manlius ... reappeared with an astral, which turned the somewhat gloomy aspect of affairs into cheerful light.

b. *Astral lamp*, a lamp which has a ring-shaped reservoir for oil so placed that the descending light is not interrupted by it as in other lamps.

*c***1830** *Encycl. Amer.* (1835) VII. 398/1 In the astral and sinumbral lamps ... the oil is contained in a large horizontal ring, having a burner at the centre. **1840** Poe *Philos. Furniture* Wks. IX. 177 We mean, of course, the astral lamp proper, ... the lamp of Argand. **1841** R. Park *Pantology* 479 The astral lamps ... are covered with a spreading glass shade. **1850** Hawthorne *Note-books* II. 169 Through the white curtains may be seen the gleam of an astral-lamp, like a fixed star. **1856** M. J. Holmes *Gable-Roofed House* In Mr. Hubbell's parlor the astral lamp was lighted, and coals were heaped in the glowing grate.

+**Astral oil.** A grade of burning oil. — **1883** *N.Y. World* in *Glasgow Weekly Herald* 9 June 8/3 An ordinary tin can ... very like that in which astral oil is sold. **1889** *Scribner's Mag.* Aug. 192/2 A vessel of high-boiling petroleum-oil, like the well-known 'astral oil.'

Asylum. An institution for the care of orphans, the insane, the blind, or other afflicted persons. Also attrib. {1776–}

See also Insane, Lunatic, Orphan asylum.

'*Asylum* or *Home* is a word often used in America, when idea intended to be conveyed is that which an Englishman attaches to the word *alms-house*' (Clapin).

1811 *Freemasons Mag.* (Phila.) Nov. 97 The other proclaims its benevolent character in its name, 'The Orphan Asylum Society.' **1817** *Amer. Monthly Mag.* II. 34 The opening of the Connecticut Asylum, for the Education and Instruction of Deaf and Dumb persons. **1829** Channing *Works* (1884) 147 In Boston, there are two asylums for children. **1830** *Collegian* 119 Before dinner [I] went to the Asylum for the Deaf and Dumb. **1829** *Encycl. Amer.* I. 438/2 Asylum ... In England and the U. States, this name has been given to many charitable institutions for the relief of orphans, blind, or dumb and deaf persons, &c. **1847** L. Collins *Kentucky* 356 The Asylum for the Blind [in Jefferson County] is a noble institution, established by the State of Kentucky in 1842. **1870** M. E. Dodge in *Scribner's Mo.* I. 37 Of course there's a strong prejudice against the Asylum among the children of the poor. **1884** *Century Mag.* May 148 There is on foot just now in this State a benevolent movement for a State asylum for inebriates. **1905** *Bureau of Forestry Bull. No. 62*, 36 Of these latter grants there are four classes—public school lands, university lands, asylum lands, and county school lands.

***At,** *prep.*

I. +**1.** *Naut.* Of the wind: Blowing from (a specified point of the compass). ?*Obs.*

1635 R. Mather *Journal* 7 The wind continuing still at the west. *Ib.* 19 A fine gale of wind at north and by east. **1705** *Boston News-Letter* 16 April 2/2 It blows now very hard and cold at N. West. **1752** *Essex Inst. Coll.* XLII. 340 Meeting with a violent gale of wind at east, they were obliged to put back. **1752** Washington *Diaries* I. 31 The wind still at No. Wt. directly ahead. **1774** Fithian *Journal* I. 178 The day is vastly hot, the wind small at west. **1838** Cooper *Homeward B.* xxxii, Happy is the man who arrives on the coast of New York, with the wind at the southward, in ... November. **1849** Cooper *Sea Lions* ix, We do not know the reason why the wind at east should produce these phenomena.

+**b.** In (a part of the country designated by a point of the compass). Orig. in *at (the) eastward* (or *east*).

In very freq. use from *c*1700.

'The very common expressions 'at the North,' 'at the West,' instead of 'in the North,' 'in the West,' offend an English ear' (B. '59). 'This provincialism is not, however, promiscuously used, as, curiously enough, the better-known New-England States are generally spoken of as "in the East" ' (Clapin).

1636 *Mass. H. S. Coll.* 4 Ser. VI. 515 If Mr. Mayhew hath bought the provisions at the east. **1646** WINTHROP *Lett.* (1869) 357 Some hurt was done here, ... much fish and salt lost at eastward. **1697** *Essex Inst. Coll.* XI. 76 In going over a reaver [=river] at the southward. **1721** *Journals H. Repr. Mass.* III. 94 The forces at the eastward are without coverings, and scant of cloathing. **1782** *Essex Inst. Coll.* XXXVIII. 55 My companey being at the sotherd the money was drawn for them for 3 months. **1835** [INGRAHAM] *South-west* II. 213 The opinion, that their sons can be educated at the south by northern professors as well as at the north. **1839** COOPER *Home as Found* xxvii, He affected to believe I had given a false address at the West, when I was residing in the Middle States. **1841** S. SMITH *Theatr. Apprent.* (1845) 171 Certain 'brethren' at the East and North. **1851** HAWTHORNE *House Seven G.* xiii, A still unsettled claim to a very large extent of territory at the eastward. **1853** *Harper's Mag.* VII. 564/1 The following capital story is told of Mr. J. H. McVickar, an eccentric American humorist, well known at the West. **1878** B. F. TAYLOR *Between Gates* 97 Seventy miles in twenty-four hours at the East ... is a *Jehu* of a drive. **1885** EGGLESTON in *Century Mag.* April 880/2 The bright-blazing pitch-pine, called ... 'lightwood' at the South. **1887** *Nation* 14 April 307/3 If Southern laws of the land had been made at the North by Northerners. **1910** G. C. EGGLESTON *Confederate War* I. 20 Slavery existed and was defended at the South while it was antagonized at the North.

2. In (the stomach). {Also obs. E.} Cf. SICK *a.*

1731 *Essex Inst. Coll.* XLII. 224, I am something better to day than yesterday at my stomack. **1882** SWEET & KNOX *Texas Siftings* 80 When he is sick at his stomach ... he goes to Col. Andrews for advice.

+**3.** By (auction or sale; retail or wholesale).

1726– [see AUCTION 1]. **1825** NEAL *Bro. Jonathan* I. 12 The education, which they had been laying in, at wholesale, during the summer season. **1831** *Ill. Revised Laws* (1833) 438 No merchant ... shall hereafter be permitted to vend, sell, or retail, either at public auction or private sale, any goods ... without ... a license. **1886** WAYLAND & CHAPIN *Pol. Econ.* x. 121 It is ordinarily more economical to purchase supplies ... at retail, than at wholesale, though the prices are higher. **1900** DRANNAN *On Plains & Mts.* 476 As soon as we arrived at San Francisco we commenced selling our horses at private sale.

+**4.** With; attended by.

1903 LORIMER *Old Gorgon Graham* 146 When husband and wife both love the same person, and that person is the wife, it's usually a life sentence at hard labor for the husband.

5. Used redundantly after *where* ... {Also E. dial.}

'Often used ... in South and West' (B. '59).

1859 BARTLETT 14 Where is he at? **1898** A. NICHOLAS *Idyl of Wabash*, etc. 34 Where does he live at? **1903** *N.Y. Sun* 8 Nov. 6 The business world wants rest. It wants to know where it is at. **1916** BOWER *Phantom Herd* vi. 93 Where does Soul of Littlefoot Law come in at?

II. ***6.** *At after*, after. *Obs.* {Now *dial.*}

1659 *Lancaster Rec.* 70 If there was any medow left comon at after the 2 deuision was finished.

7. For miscellaneous uses as *at once* (=once), *at that*, etc., see the respective words.

+**At,** *v. colloq.*[2] [f. prec.] *tr.* To require or urge (a person) *to* do something. — **1873** M. HOLLEY *Betsy Bobbet* 206, I atted Josiah to sell the pork and get the money for that.

+**Atajo.** *S.W.* [Mex.-Sp., var. Sp. *hatajo* small herd (of cattle, etc.).] A train of mules or other pack-animals.— **1844** J. GREGG *Commerce of Prairies* II. 79 We engaged an *atajo* of mules at El Paso, upon which to convey our goods across. **1847** W. S. HENRY *Campaign Sk.* 303 A merchant with an atajo of mules laden with merchandise. **1847** RUXTON *Adv. Rocky M.* (1848) 60 The mozos rushed frantically here and there to collect the scattered atajo. **1859** BARTLETT 14.

+**Atamasco lily.** Also †**at(t)amusco lily.** [See quot. 1629.] The fairy lily, *Zephyranthes* (or *Atamosco*) *atamasco*, bearing a single lily-like flower, and found from Pennsylvania to Mexico.

[**1629** PARKINSON *Paradisus* 87 *Narcissus Virgineus.* The Virginia Daffodil. ... The Indians in Virginia do call it Attamusco.] **1743** CATESBY *Carolina* I. App. 112 The Attamusco Lilly is a native of Virginia and Carolina, where in particular places the pastures are ... thick sprinkled with them and martagons. **1775** BURNABY *Travels* 7 The woods [of Va.] ... are likewise adorned and beautified with ... atamusco-lillies, May-apples, and innumerable other sorts. **1813** MUHLENBERG *Cat. Plants* 34 Atamasco lily: Car. Georg. Pen.; fl. Jun. **1819** M'MURTRIE *Sk. Louisville* 211 Atamasco lily (hab. Indian territ.). **1857** GRAY *Botany* 513 Atamasco Lily ... Penn. (*Muhl.*) Virginia, and southward. June. **1901** MOHR *Plant Life Ala.* 123 On the shady borders of the hammock are found, flowering early in the spring, ... the Atamasco lily ... and hoary lupine.

Atanto, Ataunto, *adv.* 'Said of a vessel when she has all her light and tall masts and spars aloft' (1841 Dana *Manual* 129). {1836–; earlier *all a taunt*, 1622} — **1838** COOPER *Homeward B.* xxvii, With the exception of the sails, the ship was what is called a-tanto, forward. **1845** *Knickerb.* XXV. 424 The Boston ... lay in the stream, with every thing 'ataunto,' ready for sea. **1849** T. T. JOHNSON *Sights Gold Region* x. 100 Our gallant steamer plowed her way through the sea with yards ataunto. — *transf.* **1840** *Crockett Almanac* 10, I was rigged all-a-tanto.

+**A tent.** [f. A, *letter*, from the shape.] A tent the sides of which slope evenly from the center-pole or the ridge-pole to the ground.

1863 GRAY *War Letters* 187 Beside them was a lot of negro laborers (not even soldiers) in brand new A tents. **1865** KELLOGG *Rebel Prisons* 379 One Sibley tent and one 'A' tent were furnished to each squad of 100. **1888** J. D. BILLINGS *Hardtack* 48 The A or Wedge tents are yet quite common; ... it is *now* a canvas tent stretched over a horizontal bar. **1890** *Harper's Mag.* Oct. 658/2 Throwing the canvas of an 'A' tent over the frame, he looped the bottom of the tent to small pegs.

Ater, A'ter, reduced f. *after.* (Still dial.) — **1758** *Cal. Virginia State P.* I. 258 Soon ater we had come to a conclusion about it. **1804** FESSENDEN *Terrible Tractoration* 20 Oft inoculated ... with cow-pox matter, ... not one soul took small-pox a'ter! **1837** BIRD *Nick of Woods* II. 105, I'll take the back-track, and foller atter madam.

Athenaeum, -eum. [f. L. *Athenæum*, temple of Minerva.]

+**1.** 'An association of persons of literary or scientific tastes, for the purpose of mutual improvement' (W. '64).

1807 *Monthly Anthology* May 226 The Trustees with their associates are made a body corporate by the title of the Proprietors of the Boston Athenæum. **1810** *Mass. Commonwealth Laws* (1812) 148 An Act to incorporate certain persons, by the name of The Salem Athenæum. **1837** PECK *New Guide* 221 The Athenaeum [of Cincinnati] is an institution under the management of Roman Catholic priests. **1847** HOWE *Ohio* 390 The atheneum was commenced as a library company, by a few individuals, nearly twenty years ago, and soon becoming incorporated, put up a handsome two story brick building. **1882** E. K. GODFREY *Nantucket* 13 The Athenaeum and other literary societies have from time to time given courses of lectures.

+**2.** A building (or large room) in which books, magazines, and newspapers are kept for the use of members or of the public; a library; a reading-room.

1818 FLINT *Lett. from America* 112 The Atheneum, or reading-room [at Lexington, Ky.]. **1837** JENKINS *Ohio Gaz.* 112 There are also other public buildings, as follows: ... atheneum in Sycamore street, medical college in Sixth street. **1847** H. Howe *Ohio* 473 The other buildings of Western Reserve College are, ... divinity hall, president's house, athæneum. **1871** [L. H. BAGG] *At Yale* 15 In 1804 ... its present name, Athenæum, was then given to the old building. *Ib.* 21 The absolute necessity of providing some safe place ... for the society libraries in the Athenæum. **1883** 'MARK TWAIN' *Life on Miss.* lvii, A great mass meeting was to be held on a certain day in the new Athenæum [of Keokuk in 1861.]

Athens. [Capital of Greece.]

1. A city like or comparable to Athens, esp. for culture. Freq. applied to Boston, Mass. {Also occas. E.}

1817 PAULDING *Lett. from South* II. 112 Along the banks of the Ohio, the Mississippi, ... exists a race of men, ... with as much learning, genuine politeness, and various intelligence, as those who inhabit the Athens of America. **1818** DARBY *Emigrant's Guide* 206 Education made rapid advances in some places, particularly Lexington, insomuch as to obtain for that town the title of the Athens of the western states. **1826** FLINT *Recoll.* 48 If ... Lexington be, as she contends, the Athens of the west. *Ib.* 386 Boston, out of question, is the American Athens. **1838** C. NEWELL *Revol. Texas* 140 These, and other circumstances ... indicate this portion of the country [*i.e.*, Nacogdoches] as the future location of the 'Athens of Texas.' **1839** F. J. GRUND *Aristocracy in A.* II. 37 Why do you call Boston the Athens of the United States? **1840** THOMAS *Remin.* I. 263 New Haven [is] the Athens of the East, as Cincinnati is of the West. ... Here ... the arts have their abiding place. **1841** BUCKINGHAM *America* II. 399 However much in advance Boston may be of the three great cities named in its literary and scientific reputation, for which it is justly denominated 'The Athens of the West.' *c***1844** R. H. COLLYER *Amer. Life* 29 Boston has somehow obtained the name of the 'Literary Emporium' and the 'Athens of America.' **1853** *S. Lit. Messenger* XIX. 40/1 In Western Virginia, ... even about Lexington, the Cohee Athens—your Petitioner is well nigh discarded. **1859** L. WILMER *Press Gang* 18 Philadelphia, at that time [*c*1833], was called the 'Athens of America.' **1869** E. W. STEPHENS *Boone County History* 1915 As early as that period Columbia was denominated the 'Athens of Missouri.' **1872** *Atlantic Mo.* March 317 Marshall, called absurdly enough 'the Athens of Virginia.' **1877** BARTLETT 21 *Athens of America*, ... Boston, Massachusetts; also called *Modern Athens.* **1882** *Harper's Mag.* June 20/2, I have seen no women that equal the fair daughters of the Monumental City. They make Baltimore the so-called Athens of America.

+**2.** *Athens marble*, a variety of limestone quarried in Illinois.

1859 *New Amer. Cycl.* V. 67/1 The Athens marble, so called, is regarded as one of the finest building stones in the world. It is quarried only 20

m. from Chicago, directly on the banks of the canal. **1880** *Harper's Mag.* Oct. 717/1 Beautiful [Chicago] buildings of 'Athens marble'—nearly white—rose on all sides.

+**Atherton gag.** [C. G. *Atherton* (1804–53), U.S. Repr. and Senator (1836–49).] A resolution introduced into Congress by Atherton in 1838, and in force 1838–45, providing that all bills or petitions with reference to slavery should be tabled without debate. — **1865** SCOFIELD in *Congress. Globe* 6 Jan. 144/3 [Slavery] demanded silence in this House and in the Senate, and we adopted the 'Atherton gag.' **1867** SUMNER in *Congress. Globe* 5 July 493/2 The Senator from Maine [Mr. Fessenden] cannot have forgotten the Atherton gag. . . . If the Atherton gag was . . . odious . . . , then [etc.].

Athletic ground. A field or enclosed space where athletic contests, sports, etc., are held. — **1897** *N.Y. Journal* 5 Sept. 41/4 Captain Garrett Cochran will marshal a small army of gridiron warriors on the 'varsity athletic ground. **1899** QUINN *Pennsylv. Stories* 37 There stood on the old Athletic Grounds a rickety structure which bore without reproach the name of 'grand stand.'

+**Athleticize,** *v. tr.* To convert to the pursuit of athletics. — **1896** *Godey's Mag.* April 447/1 Are we to be so athleticized that we will disdain all fripperies. **1897** *Eclectic Mag.* Oct. 523 France, superficially, has become anglicized, athleticised.

Atlantic, *a.* {1601–}

1. Of or pertaining to, situated on, the Atlantic coast of the United States; hence, eastern.

1803 *Ann. 8th Congress* 2 Sess. 1503 The peltry procured in the Illinois is the best sent to the Atlantic market. **1823** M'KENNEY *Memoirs* (1846) I. App. 297 The goods received by him were generally charged . . . higher than they were worth in the Atlantic cities in 1822. **1841** LYELL *Trav. N. A.* (1845) I. 93 The region . . . sometimes called the 'Atlantic Slope.' **1841** *S. Lit. Messenger* VII. 551/1 It demands of our overgrown Atlantic towns, to throw open their advantages for the good of the distant country. **1851** CIST *Cincinnati* 73 The progress of improvement in Cincinnati is three times that of the great atlantic metropolis [=New York]. **1854** [W. BROMWELL] *Locomotive Sk.* 150 This zone . . . acquires a breadth of one hundred and one hundred and fifty miles in the southern States. . . . This is called the Atlantic plain. **1884** *Century Mag.* XXVII. 654/1 The low foreign element which forms the dregs of Atlantic cities. **1897** SUDWORTH *Arborescent Flora* 65 *Thuja occidentalis,* . . . (Atlantic) Arborvitæ. **1900** NELSON *A B C Wall St.* 126 *Atlantic ports,* Boston, New York, Philadelphia and Baltimore—the leading export points.

+**b.** *Atlantic States,* those bordering on the Atlantic Ocean.

Atlantic America: see AMERICA 1, quot. 1791.

1789 *Ann. 1st Congress* I. 153 The policy of taxing the navigation of the Atlantic States for the purpose of encouraging their agriculture. **1792** IMLAY *Western Territory* 141 The routes from the different Atlantic States to this country are various. **1803** *Ann. 7th Congress* 2 Sess. 114 The political subjugation of the Atlantic States. **1869** BROWNE *Adv. Apache Country* 336 The length of our stage-routes . . . would astonish the humdrum people of the Atlantic States. **1871** DE VERE 257 Another division, frequently found alluded to in books as well as in the daily press, . . . is that of Atlantic, Pacific, and Gulf States.

+**c.** Produced in the Atlantic States.

1852 REYNOLDS *Hist. Illinois* 92 This mill manufactured great quantities of flour . . . which would compare well with the Atlantic flour.

2. Crossing the Atlantic Ocean. {Also E.}

1839 *S. Lit. Messenger* V. 5/2 The packet owners have carried the Atlantic mail . . . for twenty years. **1852** *Harper's Mag.* V. 255/1 To grant a large increase of pay annually to the Collins line of Atlantic steamers. **1858** BUCHANAN in Prescott *Telegraph* 189 May the Atlantic Telegraph . . . prove to be a bond of perpetual peace and friendship. **1858** *Harper's Mag.* Oct. 700/2 We had learned articles proving that the Atlantic cable could never succeed under the existing conditions. **1891** *Scribner's Mag.* X. 3 The Atlantic greyhound of to-day is, in immersed form, substantially that of the viking's craft.

+**Atocha.** [Sp.] Esparto, *Stipa tenacissima.* Also attrib. with *grass, plant.* — **1868** *Rep. Commissioner Agric.* (1869) 262 There are two classes of this plant, the 'atocha,' properly so called, and the coarse or 'bastard' atocha. *Ib.,* The atocha grass, which is called esparto, is not cut like ordinary grass, but is pulled up from its socket. *Ib.* 264 It is at about this elevation [*sc.* 3,500 feet] where the snow usually commences, that the atocha plant ceases to grow.

+**Atole.** *S.W.* [Mex.-Sp., from Nahuatl *atolli.*] Ground or prepared corn-meal; gruel or porridge made of this.

1844 GREGG *Commerce of Prairies* I. 153 A sort of thin mush, called *atole,* made of Indian meal, is another article of diet. *Ib.* 154 The use . . . of atole is . . . [general] among the lower classes of Mexicans. **1847** RUXTON *Adv. Rocky M.* (1848) 197 The Indian family . . . prepared my supper of frijoles and atole, the last *the* dish of New Mexico. **1853** BREWERTON *With Kit Carson* (1930) 46 Atole is a kind of meal which when prepared forms a very nutritious dish not unlike 'mush,' both in taste and appearance. **1877** S. W. COZZENS *Young Trail Hunters* (1912) 38 (Bentley), Each man [was] provided with three days' rations, which consisted of about a quart of atole and a piece of jerked beef. **1881** *Amer. Naturalist* XV. 875 The scales [of sotol] . . . may be ground into atole.

Atop, *adv.* [A *prep.*[1] + TOP *n.*] On the top *of* something. {1672, 1708; now *dial.*} 'A vulgarism common in England and America' (B. '48).

1771 H. PELHAM in *Copley-Pelham Lett.* 162 There ought to be something taisty atop of the house. **1833** 'GREENE' *Dod. Duckworth* II. 151 Now it was one atop of two. **1837** *Crockett Almanac* 8 The infarnal critturs would get atop of our house. **1872** 'MARK TWAIN' *Roughing It* v. 48 We . . . climbed a-top of the flying coach. **1883** *Harper's Mag.* Feb. 349/1 Beyond this chasm is a round hole in the greensward atop of the cliff. **1912** MRS. WOODROW *Sally Salt* 124 The farmer laid his ten [dollars] atop of it.

Atop, *prep.* [Cf. prec.] On the top of. {1665–1713} — **1872** EGGLESTON *End of World* xxvi. 179 Parkins piled five twenty-dollar gold-pieces atop it. **1895** *Outing* XXVI. 333/2 There was a plaster stove with a bedframe atop it.

* **Attach,** *v.* Also †**atach.** * *tr.* To take or seize by legal authority; to arrest.

1635 *Plymouth Col. Rec.* I. 33 Twenty-seuen pounds of beuer . . . wer atached & deliuered vnto John Jeney. **1674** *Conn. Public Rec.* II. 232 This Court . . . impower Mr. Willys . . . to goe over to Block Island to attach Moweem who murdered a Pequit girle. **1675** SEWALL *Diary* I. 11 Father went to attach Ben Goodridge [etc.]. **1694** *N. Car. Col. Rec.* I. 405 Thomas Philips attached to answer Mr. Rich. Plater in a plea of debt. **1795** *Mass. Gen. Laws* (1823) I. 465 We command you to attach the goods and estate of A. B. **1798** *Laws N. Jersey* (1821) 356 The officer shall go to the house . . . and there declare . . . that he attaches the rights and credits, moneys and effects. **1852** STOWE *Uncle Tom* xxx, Susan and Emmeline were attached, and sent to the depot to await a general auction. **1860** *Ohio Statutes* II. 1005 The officer . . . shall make a true inventory and appraisement of all the property attached. **1880** BARNET *Commercial Dict.* 28 A writ . . . commanding the sheriff or other proper officer to attach the property, rights, credits or effects of the debtor to satisfy the creditor's demand.

Attaché. One who is attached to a staff as an aid or assistant. {1835–}

1835 [INGRAHAM] *South-West* I. 88 A statue of dazzling ebony, by name Antoine, . . . is on the whole, an extremely useful and efficient attaché. **1850** MITCHELL *Lorgnette* I. 3 The critical attachés to this amiable fraternity of town writers. **1880** CABLE *Grandissimes* xxxiv. 275 There came in . . . an attaché of his cousin Honoré's counting-room. **1891** *Century Mag.* April 849 Several attachés would immediately begin to search them [=letters].

* **Attachment.** Also †**-mente, atachment.**

* **1.** The taking of a person, goods, etc., into the control of a court to await judicial proceedings; apprehension, seizure.

1634 WOOD *New Eng. Prospect* II. vii. 72 A certaine man . . . layd himselfe open to the Kings lawes, fearing attachment, conviction, and consequently execution. **1662** *York Deeds* I. I. 137 Mr. Robert Jordan did by attachment take away . . . two oxen one bull & 3 cows. **1675** *Boston Rec.* 93 There was an action comenced . . . according to atachment. **1713** J. HEMPSTEAD *Diary* 21 Capt. Fish left an order of the assembly & a copy of father Edgcumbs attachment at my house. **1794** BLOOMFIELD *Rep.* 21 Court ordered an Attachment for contempt . . . for divers Expressions reflecting on the Authority of the Court. **1860** *Ohio Statutes* II. 1003 An order of attachment shall be made by the clerk of the court, in which the action is brought. **1880** BARNET *Commercial Dict.* 28 The creditor can acquire through his attachment no higher or better rights to the property or assets attached than his debtor had when the attachment took place, unless he can show some fraud or collusion by which his rights are impaired.

* **2.** The writ or precept authorizing such seizure.

1631 *Rec. Mass. Bay* I. 89 Euery Assistant shall haue power to graunt warrants, summons, & attatchments, as occacion shall require. **1642** *Newhaven Col. Rec.* 79 Itt is ordered that an attachmente be sent forth to detaine all the goods. **1655** *R.I. Court Rec.* 12 An action of debt uppon an attachment comenced by . . . Cranston against John Elton. **1686** SEWALL *Diary* I. 134 So an attachment ordered to go out for him against next Thursday. **1745** *Georgia Col. Rec.* VI. 128 An attachment was served . . . on Captain James Mackay . . . for the sum of twenty eight pounds. **1789** MACLAY *Deb. Senate* 100 The witness is subpoenaed, but does not attend. An attachment issues, but the party will . . . run to the woods . . . rather than attend. **1839** *Diplom. Corr. Texas* (1908) I. 433 They procured the attachment by giving as security the names of two individuals. **1871** *Ill. Revised Statutes* (1883) 151 In any court of record having competent jurisdiction, a creditor may have an attachment against the property of his debtor.

Attackt, *n. colloq.*[2] Also †**attact, atakt.** [Cf. next.] An attack. {1839–, *dial.*}

1706 *Virginia State P.* I. 107 It is most probable that the first attackt will be made upon the shipps in York River. **1776** R. LINCOLN *Papers* (1904) 3 Americans had about 7000 men on the island, when the atakt began. **1779** *Virginia State P.* I. 315 No attact to be made on the garrison at Kaskaskias until the spring. **1840** *Diplom. Corr. Texas* (1911) III. 1277, I . . . am now confined in my room by a very severe attact of rheumatism.

Attackt, *v. colloq.*[2] Also †**attact, atackt.** [f. *attack,* with excrescent *t.*] *tr.* To attack. {'Used by the vulgar in London' (Pick.).}

'This corruption . . . is, in our seaport towns, confined to the most illiterate people. . . . In the interior, it is sometimes heard among persons of somewhat higher class' (Pick.).

1689 *Maine Doc. Hist.* IV. 463 The enemy attacted Mr. Ffoxwells garison att Blwu pwinte. **1756** *Lett. to Washington* I. 220 There was . . . four hundred to attact me, and also four hundred to attact the upper fort Cocks. **1776** R. LINCOLN *Papers* (1904) 4 The British . . . were atackted and repulsed by a party of Americans. *c***1785** SARAH PEARS *Narrative* (MS.) 3 Seven bots . . . had agreed to keep togather for fear of being attacted by the Indians. **1832** KENNEDY *Swallow Barn* II. x. 140 Our militia was attackted, just as the day did break. **1839** *Knickerb.* XIII. 76 A company of circus-actors . . . were attackted by the town-officers, and sent packing. **1861** WINTHROP *Open Air* 241 If them Secessionists attackt us to-night, . . . they'll get in debt.

+**Attendance money.** A fee paid for attendance or service. — **1733** *Harvard Rec.* II. 607 Mr. Goffe [is] to have the travelling fees. 2*s.* for ten miles, & attendance money, viz. 2*s.* per day.

+**Attestant.** *Obs.* [ad. L. *attestant-*, *attestans* pr. pple.] One who makes attestation; an attester. {1880} — **1680** *New Castle Court Rec.* 388 The attestant thereupon left the land.

Attic. [Short for 'Attic story.']

1. The top or upper story of a building. {1817–}

1841 *Lowell Offering* I. 362 Well do I remember the old farm-house . . . and every room from the attic to the cellar. **1845** S. SMITH *J. Downing's Lett.* 38 One room in the basement, three in the third story, and one in the attic, if wanted. **1851** WARNER *Wide World* xxxv, The catnip's up in the store-room,—the furthest corner in the back attic. **1875** STOWE *We & Our Neighbors* 175 The child took him . . . up one or two rickety staircases, into an attic. **1907** C. C. ANDREWS *Recoll.* 211 The insurance regulations stipulated that a 'first class' house must have . . . an iron door for entrance to the attic.

2. Attrib. with *apartment*, *bedroom*, *room*, *suite*.

1853 FOWLER *Home for All* 104 A broad stair opening into the attic suite of rooms. **1854** M. CUMMINS *Lamplighter* xxvi. 235 Mrs. Jeremy . . . offered an attic-room for the storage of her furniture. **1857** C. VAUX *Villas* 87 Attic bedrooms . . . afford a valuable addition to the accommodation of a country house. **1865** STOWE *House & Home P.* 68 Poor little victims . . . consigned to some attic-apartment, called a play-room.

***Attorney**[1]. Also †**attorny, att-, aturney, atterney, attourny.**

***1.** One who is appointed or admitted in place of another to transact business for him. Chiefly and now only =ATTORNEY-AT-LAW.

'In the United States the term *barrister* is not used, the designation of a fully qualified lawyer being *attorney and counselor at law*' (Cent.).

1645 *York Deeds* I. ii. 11, I . . . ordayne Henry Boade gent. to be my lawfull atturney. **1648** *New Haven Col. Rec.* I. 371 Attornyes for the towne of Guilford . . . entreth an action . . . for certaine rates due vpon a lott. **1656** *R.I. Court Rec.* 19 The issue joyned by the aturnies not guilty of trespas. **1664** *Charlestown Land Rec.* 162 Granting unto my said atterney, full power and autheretie for me . . . to sue, arreste, implead, condemne and imprison everie of my debters. **1767** H. M. Brooks *Gleanings* 11 If those who are indebted to Mr. George Bray will pay what they owe him to me his attorney. **1793** HAMILTON in *State P.* (1819) I. 46 If she [the privateer] should do any thing beside this, it is immediately to be reported to the governour and the attorney of the district. **1801** *Spirit of Farmer's Museum* 197 Ask the attorney why he endeavours to clear a man from punishment, who evidently deserves it. **1832** WILLIAMSON *Maine* II. 690 The division into counsellors and attorneys, was established in 1806; . . . when they have practised two years as attorneys they may be admitted counsellors. **1846** COOPER *Redskins* vii, The principal speaker was a young man . . . of a sort of shabby-genteel air . . . whom I soon discovered to be the attorney of the neighborhood. **1860** *Ohio Statutes* II. 1047 Such court or judge shall appoint a competent attorney to examine the petition and prepare . . . cross interrogatories. **1898** CANFIELD *Maid of Frontier* 66 The nervous little attorney for the defense. **1906** *Indian Laws & Tr.* III. 750 There must be a judicial finding and judgment upon the question of attorney's fees. **1907** C. C. ANDREWS *Recoll.* 208, I had enough professional work as attorney to keep me busy.

2. =ATTORNEY-GENERAL *n.*

1704 *Boston News-Letter* 26 June 1/2 The Queen's attorney opened the case, and the court proceeded to the examination of the evidences for Her Majesty. **1705** SEWALL *Diary* II. 147 Mr Sheriff order'd the prisoners to be brought. Mr. Attorney spoke against them. **1790** *Kentucky Petitions* 163 A suit . . . against myself as Attorney for the Commonwealth. **1834** [R. BAIRD] *Valley Mississippi* xx. 256 There is an Attorney . . . for the United States.

***Attorney**[2]. Also †**atturney, attourney, atorney.** Legal authority granted to a person or persons to act or do business for another. Freq. in *letter* or *power of attorney.*

1640 T. Lechford *Note-Bk.* (1885) 377 Thomas Foster . . . makes a Letter of Attorney unto George Strange. **1654** *Suffolk Deeds* II. 122 This publique instrument of procuration or letter of atturney. **1694** *N. Car. Col. Rec.* I. 399 A letter of attorney proved in Court by the oath of Wm. Duckinfield. **1726** *Md. Hist. Mag.* XVIII. 218 You have . . . two letters . . . countermanding a power of attorney to him. **1726** *Manchester Rec.* I. 168 Reseved of Mr. Ezekel Goodale of Manchester forty-three pounds . . . in full atorney. **1747** FRANKLIN *Let.* Wks. 1887 II. 92 As he has your power of attorney, . . . I think to put your letter to Mr. Hughes into his hands. **1757** *Penna. Archives* I. 631 Power of attorney from Jersey Indians, to Tundy Tettamy & Capt. John, to sell their lands in Jersey. **1815** *Niles' Reg.* IX. 37/2 Where the power of attorney in question is executed before a notary public. **1835** *Ohio Statutes* (1860) II. 1276 The same force . . . as by law is given to . . . mortgages, powers of attorney, and other instruments of writing. **1860** *Ib.* II. 1053 No warrant of attorney executed by the person in custody . . . shall be of any force, unless [etc.].

Attorney-at-law. An attorney qualified to prosecute and to defend actions in a court of law. {1768–}

1771 *Md. Hist. Mag.* XVIII. 277 Mr. John Murray, attorney at law, . . . and his boy were all drowned. **1803** O. A. Rothert *Muhlenberg Co.* 52 [They] were on their motion admitted to practice as attorneys at law in this court. **1823** COOPER *Pioneers* xxxi, The little building that had a wooden sign over its door, with 'Chester Lippet, Attorney-at-law,' painted on it. **1846** MACKENZIE *Life Van Buren* 161 Mr. Hoyt . . . having taken out licenses, as an attorney-at-law, and as a solicitor-in-chancery. **1853** SIMMS *Sword & Distaff* 401 Stately and serious letters had been brought to Porgy, from dignitaries yclept attorneys-at-law. **1900** STOCKTON *Afield & Afloat* 282 A middle-aged man . . . introduced himself . . . as Romney C. Lloyd, attorney-at-law, of New York.

‖**Attorneydom.** The body of attorneys. {1881} — **1851** HALL *Manhattaner* 79 You . . . will see the happiest little judge in all Attorneydom.

***Attorney-general.**

***1.** The chief law-officer empowered to act for the government or the state in cases that affect it.

'In the United States he is a member of the cabinet appointed by the President, has the general management of the departments of justice throughout the country, advises the President and departments on questions of law, and appears for the government in the Supreme Court and Court of Claims. The individual States of the Union also have their attorneys-general' (*Cent.*)

(1) **1654** *Md. Council Proc.* 302 What his Lordship Should allow him for his pains as Attorney Generall for that year. **1686** *Papers rel. to Pemaquid* 130 The Attorney Generall hath perused this pattent. **1694** *N. Car. Col. Rec.* I. 424 Ordered that the attorney Generall forme an indictment on their Majesties behalf. **1721** *Mass. H. Repr. Journals* III. 111 The affairs of the Government requires the appointing an attorny general. **1726** FRANKLIN *Journal* Wks. II. 68 The attorney-general observed to the court, that [etc.]. **1792** IMLAY *Western Territory* 25 In 1782 the State of Virginia had given us a General Court, with judges and an attorney-general, to manage all legal affairs respecting the district. **1860** *Ohio Statutes* II. 1233 If payment thereof be not made in reasonable time, . . . the comptroller shall file such claim with the attorney general. **1865** *Atlantic Mo.* XV. 153 Roger Brooke Taney . . . had been attorney-general of Maryland.

(2) **1789** *Ann. 1st Congress* II. 2197 There shall also be appointed a meet person learned in the law to act as attorney-general for the United States. **1807** *Ann. 10th Congress* 1 Sess. I. 44 When the prosecutions against Aaron Burr . . . were instituted, I delivered to the attorney general all the evidence . . . which I had received. **1814** *Ann. 13th Congress* I. 766 An act to establish the permanent residence of the Attorney General of the United States at the seat of the general government. **1845** POLK *Diary* (1929) 36 The Cabinet held a regular meeting today; all the members present except the Attorney-General. **1866** 'F. KIRKLAND' *Bk. Anecdotes* 33 When the South Carolina 'ambassadors' came to Washington, Butler proposed to the Attorney-General to try them for treason.

+**2.** *Tennessee.* A State's attorney.

1903 *Nashville Banner* in *N.Y. Ev. Post* 14 Sept., It is a practice peculiar to Tennessee to dub all States' Attorneys Attorneys-General.

***Attractive,** *n.* An attractive feature; an attraction. {1598, 1765} — **1837** SHERWOOD *Gaz. Georgia* (ed. 3) 216 The Schools . . . were the attractives which drew the people here, to afford their children the advantages proferred.

+**Auburn system.** [*Auburn*, seat of a State prison, Cayuga County, N.Y.] A method of prison discipline based on the enforcement of silence among the prisoners.

1833 E. T. COKE *Subaltern's Furlough* xxv, The Concord [New Hampshire] prison . . . was conducted partly on the Auburn system. **1838** LIEBER in Buckingham *America* (1841) III. 140 The Auburn system acknowledges insulation as the fundamental principle of all sound prison discipline. **1842** BUCKINGHAM *E. & W. States* II. 306 The system of discipline pursued here, is that which is called the Auburn, or Silent System, in contradistinction to the Philadelphia, or Solitary System. **1851** J. F. W. JOHNSTON *Notes N. Amer.* II. 292 The Auburn system . . . is adopted here as in all the penitentiaries of New England, New York, Canada, and most of the north-western States. Solitary confinement at night and on Sundays, solitary meals every day, and constant but absolutely silent labour in company in large well-ventilated workshops, and under strict superintendence, form the essence of this system. **1869** HALL *Hist. Auburn* 352 The famous Auburn system then [1825] began to receive a careful trial.

***Auction,** *n.*

***1.** The procedure of publicly selling articles or property to the highest bidder.

The phrase *at auction* has now largely replaced *by auction* (the prevalent E. usage).

(*a*) **1709** *Leg. Council N.Y. Colony* (1861) I. 292 An Act to regulate the Sale of Goods by Publick outcry, Auction or Vendue in the city. **1721** *Boston News-Letter* 14 Aug. 4/2 To be sold by auction . . . a very curious . . . collection of books. **1731** *N.H. Probate Rec.* II. 340 The sale by auction of the estate by Capt. John Libby. **1737** [see AUCTIONEER *n.* 1] **1799** BROWN *A. Mervyn* xiv, The captured vessel . . . , as usual, would be sold by auction at a fifth or tenth of its real value. **1819** *Aurora General Advertiser* 16 Oct. 1/1 For sale by auction, . . . on Wednesday, . . . the elegant steam-boat Superior.

(*b*) **1726** *Boston News-Letter* 3 March, Valuable books, many more than a thousand, to be sold at auction. **1773** *Mass. Bay Acts & Resolves* V. 248 No person . . . shall sell, at public vendue, auction, or outcry, any goods [etc.]. **1781** *Essex Inst. Coll.* XXI. 283 Voated that the parish land should be desposed of at public occhun [*sic*]. **1822** *Ann. 17th Congress* 1 Sess. I. 318 The superintendent . . . is . . . to sell the furs . . . at public auction. **1825** in Commons, etc. *Doc. Hist.* I. 251 [A rice estate] will be sold at public auction, at the court house. **1852** STOWE *Uncle Tom* xxix, He and the lawyer think that the servants and furniture had better be put up at auction. **1862** *Rep. Comm. Patents: Agric.* 325 In December two of the swarms were sold at auction to settle up his estate. **1900** STOCKTON *Afield & Afloat* 360 The family . . . is dead and gone, and everything in it [=the family mansion] is to be sold at auction.

(*c*) **1774** *Assn. of Delegates of Colonies* 12 They shall be expected anew, Or sold auction-wise, for the good of the Loo. **1852** STOWE *Uncle Tom* xxviii, You may die or fail, and then Topsy be hustled off to auction. *Ib.* xxix, The trader . . . was going to make up a lot for auction.

* **b.** A public sale of this kind.

1775 *N.Y. Gazette* 23 Jan. 2/4 Public Auction, by Thomas William Moore, on Wednesday next. **1812** WEEMS *Letters* III. 76 With the sales of your books and auctions of ditto on a . . . large scale. **1852** [see ATTACH *v.*] **1871** DE VERE 299 A peculiar feature at genuine auctions is the so-called upset price. **1877** *Colorado General Laws* 96 Any person who may be licensed in this state to keep an auction, where horses, mules or cattle are sold.

2. Attrib. with *bell, day, hammer, shop,* etc.

1811 *Boston Selectmen* 11 Sept. 27 A number of applications for auction licenses were received. **1819** *Ib.* 6 Oct. 108 The application of John Cassell to remove his auction office . . . was granted. **1845** S. SMITH *Theatr. Apprent.* xii. 82 Promising me his custom and influence in the way of auction advertisements. **1855** THOMPSON *Doesticks* 135, [I] went on to the auction table, where [I] . . . succeeded in bidding in a China vase. **1855** *Knickerb.* XLV. 452 Heaps of old furniture scattered here and there, which reminded me that it was 'auction-day.' *Ib.* XLVI. 241 The loud and ceaseless din of the well-known auction-bell. **1861** [NEWELL] *Orpheus C. Kerr* I. 111, I'd like to know whether this is a public building . . . or a second-hand auction-shop. **1870** MEDBERY *Men of Wall St.* 276 The auction-hammer pattered; the brokers 'washed' the new issue up and up. **1884** *Century Mag.* June 277 You ought to hang that out for an auction flag.

Auction, *v. tr.* To sell by auction. Usu. with *off.* {1807–}

1862 LINCOLN in Logan *Great Conspiracy* 436, I am told that whenever the Rebels take any Black prisoners . . . they immediately auction them off! **1878** BEADLE *Western Wilds* 508 When he returned, the property at Cedar City had been auctioned off. **1895** G. KING *New Orleans* 189 The privateers . . . could so easily . . . sail up to the city, auction off their cargoes. *Ib.* 196 The cargoes . . . and slaves . . . were still auctioned at Grand Terre.

+**Auction-block.** A block or stand on which a slave stood on being sold by auction. — **1860** ABBOTT *South & North* 198 In case of disobedience, to send them to the whipping-post, or the auction-block. **1863** 'E. KIRKE' *Southern Friends* xxvi. 260 On the lawn . . . was the auction block—the carpenter's bench. **1873** 'MARK TWAIN' & WARNER *Gilded Age* vii. 78 The Hawkins hearts [had] been torn to see Uncle Dan'l and his wife pass from the auction-block into the hands of a negro trader.

+**Auction duty.** A duty or payment to public revenue levied on proceeds of sales by auction. — **1827** DRAKE & MANSF. *Cincinnati* iv. 30 The General Assembly . . . gave, for the permanent support of the establishment, half the auction duties of the city. **1851** CIST *Cincinnati* 149 Others are supported out of a portion of the auction duties, collected in Cincinnati.

Auctioneer.

1. One whose business is to expose or offer property or goods for sale by auction. {1708–}

1737 *Boston Selectmen* 27 June 54 Voted, That . . . Mr. Fleet be employed as the auctioneer in the sale of the three tracts of land, appointed to be sold by auction. **1773** *Ib.* 169 The Great and General Court . . . passed an act to . . . limit the number of auchtioners [*sic*]. **1787** *Baltimore Town Rec.* 61 Received from Thomas Yates auctioneer his accounts of town duties. **1822** *Ann. 17th Congress* 1 Sess. I. 253 That this government shall become their auctioneer for that purpose. **1848** *Knickerb.* XVIII. 379 These were the identical words that came rattling from the throat of . . . the auctioneer. **1863** NORTON *Army Lett.* 134 He rattled it [=his speech] off like an auctioneer. **1880** CABLE *Grandissimes* xl. 314 A sort of merchants' and auctioneers' coffee-house. **1904** *Century Mag.* Feb. 486/2 The auctioneer seemed to be in no hurry, and bidding was comparatively slow.

2. Attrib. or appositive with *gavel, peddler.*

1857 *Quinland* I. 118 A laughing crowd gathered about the wagon of an 'auctioneer-pedler.' **1870** MEDBERY *Men of Wall St.* 318 A bank whose shares . . . went plunging under the auctioneer-gavel to thirty-five.

Auctioneering, *vbl. n.* [AUCTIONEER.] A selling by auction. {*a*1733–}

1781 *Salem Gazette* 19 June, All voluntiers, who are pleased to encourage . . . polite literature, by the business of book auctioniering. *Ib.* Robert Bell, bookseller, . . . and professor of book-auctioniering. **1813** (*title*), The Ruinous Tendency of Auctioneering, and the Necessity of Restraining it. . . . New York, 1813. **1863** S. C. MASSETT *Drifting About* 127 The Captain having concluded to sell out his stock of merchandise, I was selected by his agent . . . to do the 'auctioneering' upon the occasion. *Ib.* 128, I am not going to laud my performances in the auctioneering line.

+**Auction-house.** A firm of auctioneers.

1848 *Knickerb.* XXXI. 185 Our friend Keese, of the auction-house of Cooley, Keese and Hill. **1851** *Ib.* XXXVIII. 20 The well-known New-York auction house, Leggett, Shotwell, Fox, and Company. **1861** *Chicago Tribune* 15 April 1 New auction and commission house, No. 107 Dearborn Street. **1891** *Harper's Weekly* 19 Sept. 710/2 Pawnbrokers, . . . like the auction houses, sell bad jewelry.

Auction-room. A room in which auctions are held. {1779–}

1775 J. ANDREWS *Letters* 81 The soldiers . . . took quarters with the royal Irish in Gould's auction room or store. **1788** FRENEAU *Misc. Works* 84 A book . . . set up at Bell's auction room to be disposed of to the highest bidder. **1795** *Boston Gazette* 28 Dec. 4/2 The vendue business will be continued at the auction room in Court Street. **1845** S. SMITH *Theatr. Apprent.* xi. 82 His auction-room . . . was crowded with people, for he had a night-sale. **1848** *Knickerb.* XVIII. 380 The wooden benches in Mr. Windmill's auction-room. **1877** HALE in *Harper's Mag.* Dec. 34/2 Ringgold . . . sold it [*sc.* flannel] in auction-rooms in twenty different cities as 'remnants.'

+**Auction-sale.** A sale by auction. {1898}

1820 *Ann. 16th Congress* 1 Sess. I. 367 The evils arising from auction sales. **1843** *Knickerb.* XXI. 445 Even at the auction-sale . . . he rarely loses his hilarity. **1866** 'F. KIRKLAND' *Bk. Anecdotes* 657 An auction sale . . . of a coffee, or tea set, and a quantity of silver plate, formerly used by Jefferson Davis. **1901** CHURCHILL *Crisis* 109 The incident of the auction sale.

+**Auction-stand.** A platform or the like from which an auction is conducted; an auction-block. — **1846** L. M. CHILD *Fact & Fiction* 74 The gentle girl . . . was ruthlessly seized by a sheriff, and placed on the public auction-stand in Savannah. **1848** LOWELL *Biglow P.* I. ix, How temptin' all on 'em would look upon an auction-stand!

+**Auction store.** A store in which commodities, etc., are sold by auction.

1785 *Penna. Packet* 24 Dec. 1/1 Northern-Liberty Auction Store, . . . at ten o'clock . . . will begin the sale of . . . merchandize . . . Alex. Boyd, auctioneer. **1790** *Ib.* 1 Jan. 3/4 At the city auction store, will be sold by public vendue . . . broadcloths, coatings, corduroys. **1839** BRIGGS *H. Franco* II. ii. 18 He . . . took me down to an auction store in Broad street, where there was a sale of lots. **1842** *Knickerb.* XX. 472 With all that is amusing about an auction-store, there is much that is sad too. **1878** COOKE *Happy Dodd* 150 Send 'em up to the auction store, and sell 'em.

Audience-chamber. A room in which audiences or formal receptions are held. {1753–} — **1789** *Ann. 1st Congress* I. 58 When the Senate and House of Representatives shall judge it proper to make a joint address to the President, it shall be presented to him in his audience chamber.

Audience-room. A room for the holding of audiences or meetings.

1790 MACLAY *Deb. Senate* 234, I got Henry, of Maryland, into the audience-room, and gave him a detail of what was going on. **1861** *Chicago Tribune* 15 April 1 The main audience room [of Bryan Hall, Chicago] is on the first floor. **1873** *Newton* (Kansas) *Kansan* 22 Aug. 1/4 Then the old serpent brings it about that the audience-room should be acoustically as bad as possible. **1883** 'MARK TWAIN' *Life on Miss.* ii. 39 The [Indian] chief's house contained an audience-room forty feet square. **1891** FREEMAN *New Eng. Nun* 20 When Alma went down into the audience-room, . . . the minister approached her.

***Audit.** Also †awditt. +A body of auditors of accounts. *Obs.* **1657** *R.I.Court Rec.* 32 This Court have constituted . . . Mr. Benedict Arnold presid[en]t, Mr. Samuell Gorton, Mr. John Easton and John Sanford to be an awditt to heare accompts. **1691** *Boston Rec.* 206 One of the audit apoynted to adjust and settle the accompts of the selectmen.

***Auditor.**

***1.** A person appointed or authorized to audit accounts.

1638 *Dorchester Rec.* 35 The cunstables shall give up their account to the foresayd auditors within one month. **1644** *Boston Rec.* 83 [They] are appointed auditors of Anthony Stodder late constable his accounts. **1720** SEWALL *Diary* III. 265, I . . . order'd notice to be given to the auditours, to pray their assistance. **1765** R. ROGERS *Concise. Acc.* 123 There are but three public officers [in Va.] . . . that are commissioned immediately from the King, viz. the Auditor of the Revenue, the Receiver General, and Secretary. **1789** *Ann. 1st Congress* I. 78, I nominate for the Department of the Treasury . . . Oliver Wolcott . . . Auditor. **1837** PECK *New Guide* 211 The annual report of the auditor of State [of Ohio]. **1846** M'KENNEY *Memoirs* I. 192, I sent my messenger to the office of the Second Auditor. **1849** CHAMBERLAIN *Indiana Gaz.* 305 D. Maguire, of the other [firm], is the Auditor of Public Accounts. **1863** *Huntington Rec.* III. 487 The object of the meeting being . . . to see what measure should be adopted by the Board of Auditors . . . for the relief of the indigent families. **1877** *Colorado General Laws* 89 The auditor of state shall draw his warrant upon the fund herein provided for.

+2. A money certificate. *Obs.*

1790 *Steele Papers* I. 57 They were giving for Auditors 5s. paper, interest not counted, . . . and for Auditors, after new coined, agreeable to our late Act, 3/8 for principal and ½ for Interest.

+3. [Sp.] An official in Louisiana under Spanish rule (see quot.). *Obs.*

1803 *Ann. 8th Congress* 2 Sess. 1521 The Auditor is the King's counsel, who is to furnish the Governor with legal advice in all cases of judicial proceedings, whether civil or military.

‖**Auditor,** *v. tr.* To approve, as an auditor. — **1799** *Kentucky Petitions* 180 An auditered [*sic*] certificate issued in favour of your petitioner.

***Auditor-general.** +The chief auditor of a state or other administrative unit.

1645 *Mass. Bay Rec.* II. 141 They have thought fit . . . to elect . . . Leift. Nathani[el] Duncan to be auditor generall for this country. **1652** *Ib.* IV. 113 The clarke for the Howse of Deputies shall account with the auditor generall for all such sommes. **1680** *N.H. Original Docs.* 115 Constituting him Surveyor & Auditor-General of all his Majesty['s] revenues in America. **1776** *Journals Cont. Congress* VI. 930 To John Gibson, Esqr., auditor general, for half a year's salary . . . , 533 30/90 dollars. **1868** *Mich. Agric. Rep.* VII. 473 The county treasurer . . . [shall] return all lands . . . delinquent for . . . tax, to the Auditor General. **1898** *Smull's Legislative Hand Book* 45 The duties of the Auditor General [of Penna.] are generally to examine and settle all accounts between the Commonwealth and any person, officer, department [etc.].

Auditorium. That part of a public building assigned to or occupied by the audience. {1881}

1854 IRVING in *Life & Lett.* (1864) IV. 181, I mingled in the crowd, and heard Bancroft's erudite address from the 'auditorium.' **1865** *Nation* I. 814 We do not quarrel with the word 'auditorium,' although it is not English; but we are seriously disposed to quarrel with a writer who tells us that 'the auditorium of the New York Circus has been enlarged.' People go to the horse-riding to *see* and not to *hear.* **1871** *Chicago Tribune* 11 Oct. 1 The Opera House auditorium had been completely renovated. **1883** *Harper's Mag.* Nov. 882/1 The auditorium [of the Metropolitan Opera-House] is quite the largest in the world. **1903** *Boston Herald* 20 Aug., The auditorium of the City Hall. **1903** *Boston Ev. Transcript* 22 August, The interior of the church is divided into an auditorium, Sunday school-room and pastor's study on the first floor.

+Audubon's warbler. [f. the name of the ornithologist J. J. Audubon (1780–1851).] A species of warbler, *Dendrœca auduboni*, native to the western states; the western yellowrump. — **1837** TOWNSEND in *Jrnl. Acad. Nat. Sci. Phila.* VII. 191 Audubon's Warbler . . . inhabits the forests of the Columbia river. **1839** AUDUBON *Ornith. Biog.* V. 52 Audubon's warbler . . . was discovered by Dr. Townsend, who has done me the honour of naming it after me. **1869** *Amer. Naturalist* III. 33 Audubon's Warbler (*Dendroica Audubonii*) . . . was very common [in Mont.] throughout the mountains.

+Audubon's woodpecker. [See prec.] The hairy woodpecker, *Picus villosus.* — **1849** AUDUBON *Ornith. Biog.* V. 194 Audubon's Woodpecker . . . was presented to me by its discoverer [Dr. James Trudeau].

***Auger.** Also †**augar, awger, augur, agur.**

***1.** A tool or instrument for boring holes larger than those bored by a gimlet.

1645 *Essex Inst. Coll.* L. 336, 2 augars, one gowge, 2 chissells. **1651** *Mayflower Descendants* X. 164 Axes, augers, tools and other housholdments. **1679** *Maine Wills* 78, I bequeath unto the aforesd. Peter Grant . . . my ads, & an inch & an halfe Auger. **1702** *Essex Inst. Coll.* XLII. 160 Inventory of ship . . . [includes] two augers. **1787** *Kentucky Gazette* 24 Nov. 2/3 Samuel Blair has for sale . . . augers and two foot rules, very cheap for cash. **1792** *Ann. 2nd Congress* 1043 In the centre of the lid a hole was bored . . . with an inch and half auger. **1846** *Knickerb.* XXVII. 268 Now stopping before a bale [of cotton] and boring down to the very heart of it with a long iron auger. **1862** *Rep. Comm. Patents: Agric.* 262 Maple trees . . . are usually tapped with a half inch auger, or bit. **1890** *Century Mag.* Dec. 171/2 To make the hole [in the cart-axle], an auger, gouge or chisel was sometimes used.

***2.** An instrument for boring through soil or rock.

1761 Eliot *Field-Husb.* App. 165 Bore into the Ground with an Auger that has a large Shank to it. **1829** CUMINGS *Western Pilot* 22 When the augar reaches the salt water, it immediately rises. **1838** J. HALL *Western States* i. 17 Its thick *strata* have never been pierced through, although the auger has penetrated into it . . . from four to six hundred feet. **1886** WINCHELL *Walks* 139 If the auger enters the upper part, gas escapes.

3. Attrib., etc. with *handle, maker, shank, stem.*

1704 *Boston News-Letter* 11 Sept. 2/2 Mr. Johnson took out of it an agur shank 4 foot long. **1818** FLINT *Lett. from Amer.* 61 The manufacturing people of Pittsburg [include] . . . 1 augur maker. **1883** *Century Mag.* July 329/2 The drilling tools consist of the 'bit,' . . . the 'auger stem,' an iron bar perhaps eight feet long screwed into the bit.

Auger-hole. A hole made by an auger. {1601–}

1815 *Niles' Reg.* VIII. 135/2 The first water that is struck in the auger hole is generally fresh. **1824** J. DODDRIDGE *Notes* 131 The table might be a large slab of timber, hewed out with a broad axe, supported by four sticks set in auger holes. **1835** [LONGSTREET] *Georgia Scenes* 227 An augur hole in the breech, served for a grease box. **1848** MASON in E. Bryant *California* 457 The sand and gold mixed together are then drawn off through auger holes into a pan below. **1865–6** *Ill. Agric. Soc. Trans.* VI. 646 Pieces of lumber that have augur holes near the ends should be measured for length between the holes.

Auk. A short-winged sea bird of the genus *Alca*, visiting the north and middle Atlantic states in winter; esp. the razor-billed species, *Alca torda.* {1678–}

1813 WILSON *Ornithology* IX. 94 Little Auk . . . is a very rare bird [with us], and when seen it is generally in the vicinity of the sea. **1828** WEBSTER s.v., The northern penguin or great auk, the little auk or black and white diver, the puffin. **1835** AUDUBON *Ornith. Biog.* III. 112 These Auks generally arrive on our Atlantic coast about the beginning of November. *Ib.* 115 The Razor-billed Auks. **1858** BAIRD *Birds Pacific R.R.* 918 The little auk . . . [is] one of the most abundant of the sea birds of northern America . . . , straying south in the winter occasionally to the coasts of the Middle States. **1882** E. K. GODFREY *Nantucket* 243 Later on [than Oct. 1] . . . the northerly storms bring . . . [the] old squaw, coot, ruddy duck, loon, greebes, auk.

+Aulone. *Calif.* (See quots. and cf. AVALONE, ABALONE.) — **1869** *Overland Monthly* III. 38 We went forth to 'pick up' whales, seals, aulones (*Haliotis*, a shell-fish in great repute among the Chinese). [**1883:** see ABALONE.]

***Aunt,** *n.*

1. Used in addressing elderly women not related to the speaker, as a term of courtesy or respect. Cf. AUNTIE 2.

1801 *Historical Review* (Cork) II. 189 People of Nantucket . . . always call each other cousin, uncle or aunt, which are become . . . common appellations. **1808** *Amer. Law Journal* I. 78 Thomas Hoag was at witness's house, was very intimate there, used to call her aunt. **1861** STOWE *Pearl of Orr's Island* I. 20 Aunt Roxy and Aunt Ruey . . . were not people of a dreamy kind. *Ib.* 21 These universally useful persons receive among us the title of 'aunt' by a sort of general consent.

+2. A term of address, or familiar designation, used or applied to elderly or mature colored women, esp. in former times in the South. Cf. AUNTIE 1.

1835 [LONGSTREET] *Georgia Scenes* 110, I want the keys, Miss 'V'lina, . . . said the cook. 'There they are, aunt* Clary,' said Evelina. *Ib.* note, 'Aunt' and 'mauma,' . . . are terms of respect, commonly used by children to aged negroes. The first generally prevails in the up country. **1837** *S. Lit. Messenger* III. 744 These two [blacks] were greeted always by the kind appelatives of . . . 'uncle and aunt.' **1852** STOWE *Uncle Tom* iv, Aunt Chloe . . . [had] come out . . . to 'get her ole man's supper.' **1874** 'MARK TWAIN' *True Story*, 'Aunt Rachel' was sitting . . . on the steps—for she was our servant, and colored. **1902** HARBEN *A. Daniel* 127 Mrs. Barclay sent up a tray of delicacies by Aunt Milly, the old colored woman.

+3. a. *Aunt Hannah*, a variety of winter apple.

1847 J. M. IVES *New Eng. Fruit* 47 Aunt Hannah. . . . We consider this to be one of the best eating winter apples of New England. **1849** *New Eng. Farmer* I. 32 Aunt Hannah is of excellent flavor, about equal to the famous Newtown Pippin. **1859** ELLIOTT *Western Fruit Book* 122 Aunt Hannah. From Massachusetts. . . . Flesh tender, crisp, sub-acid.

+b. *Aunt's apple*, a variety of apple (see quotations).

1817 W. COXE *Fruit Trees* 134 Aunts Apple. . . . is a beautiful and large apple. **1859** ELLIOTT *Western Fruit Book* 122 Aunt's Apple. Fruit, medium to large, . . . light yellow, streaked with red.

‖**Aunt,** *v.* [f. prec.] *tr.* To address (a negress) by the designation of 'aunt.' — **1835** [LONGSTREET] *Georgia Scenes* 111 'I'll starve for a week to save Clary's feelings,' said George, 'if you will only quit *aunting* her.'

Auntie, Aunty. {1792–}

+1. =AUNT *n.* 2. Also freq., a colored woman of the class addressed as 'auntie.'

1835 [INGRAHAM] *South-West* II. 241 Planters . . . always address them [*sc.* slaves] in a mild and pleasant manner—as 'Uncle,' or 'Aunty.' **1856** MURRAY *Lett. from U.S.* II. 159 This was an old nurse, an aunty, or mammy, as they are sometimes called (all ancient women of the darky kind here are addressed as aunties). **1857** M. J. HOLMES *Meadow-Brook* xxv, Jessie . . . flitted like a sunbeam from cabin to cabin, asking after this old Aunty, or that old Uncle. **1874** B. F. TAYLOR *World on Wheels* II. i. 176 The turbaned 'aunty,' who opened her mouth like a piano and laughed clear across the plantation. **1883** W. H. BISHOP in *Harper's Mag.* Oct. 728/2 The negro no longer submits with grace to be called 'uncle' and 'auntie' as of yore. **1905** N. DAVIS *Northerner* 202 Steaming apple-toddy and egg-nog, served by old-time 'aunties' in snowy white.

2. 'A familiar term often used in accosting an elderly woman' (B. '59). Cf. AUNT *n.* 1.

1868 BEECHER *Norwood* 19 Half the children in the village called her Auntie, and grew up with the impression that she was blood kin to them.

+**3.** With punning allusion to ANTI-.

1869 *Overland Monthly* Aug. 128/1 'Cousin Sal' . . . having been begotten by him [='Uncle Sam'] in the bonds of lawful wedlock with 'Aunty Extension.' **1899** *Review of Reviews* March p. xiv, In the States the Anti-Expansionists and Anti all other movements have been christened 'Aunties.'

Australian, *a.* {1814-}

1. Originating in, imported from, or associated with Australia.

1856 *Rep. Comm. Patents: Agric.* 194 In 1853, I obtained . . . 2 bushels each of 'Australian' and 'Gale's Early-flint' [*sc.* wheat]. **1863** *Ill. Agric. Soc. Trans.* V. 869 The chick-pea . . . has again been heralded as a valuable acquisition upon the prairies under the name of Illinois coffee, or 'Australian coffee.' **1889** VASEY *Agric. Grasses* 36 *Sorghum halepense* (Johnson Grass; Mean's Grass). . . . has been called . . . Australian Millet, and Morocco millet. **1894** COULTER *Bot. W. Texas* III. 548 *Bromus unioloides.* Rescue grass. Australian brome grass.

+**2.** *Australian ballot,* a system of voting by means of ballots intended to secure secrecy and prevent duplication of votes. Also attrib. with *bill, law, system.*

1888 POST (*title*), Election reform. Governor Hill's reasons for vetoing the Australian ballot bill. **1888** *Nation* 2 Aug. 91/2 By introducing the secret 'Australian ballot' in Congressional elections . . . the use of bribery in the choice of Congressmen might be discouraged to some extent. **1889** J. H. WIGMORE (*title*), The Australian Ballot System as embodied in the Legislation of various Countries. **1889** *Boston Alderm. pamphlet* Title-p., The so-called Australian ballot law. **1903** *Boston Ev. Transcript* 7 Oct. 3 The most important matter before the [Labor] convention to-day was the election of officers. The Australian ballot was used.

Austrian, *a.* Of or introduced from Austria (see quots.).

1832 S. J. HALE *Flora* 138 Austrian Rose, *Rosa bicolor.* . . . A genus of nearly 50 species. **1847** WOOD *Botany* 247 *Rosa eglanteria.* . . . Yellow Rose. Austrian Eglantine. . . . . From Germany. **1854** *Penna. Agric. Rep.* 163 The immediate progeny of foreign importations, comprising, in the tribe of barn-yard fowls, the . . . . Poland; the Austrian; the Hamburg. **1858** WARDER *Hedges & Evergreens* 247 *Pinus laricio Austriaca,* Black or Austrian Pine, is much admired for its sturdy habit and yellowish-green leaves. **1892** APGAR *Trees Northern U.S.* 175 *Pinus Austriaca,* Austrian or Black Pine. . . . A large cultivated tree, 60 to 80 ft. high.

* **Authority.**

1. A body of persons exercising civil power. {1652-} In New Eng. 'the magistracy or body of justices' (W. '06).

1666 *Boston Rec.* 31 You are to take such persons . . . befor Authority that they may be delt with according to the demerritt. **1672** *Mass. Colony Laws* 28 If any person shall willfully . . . deny any child . . . such children shall have liberty to complaine to Authority for redress. *Ib.* 84 If any person . . . shall . . . not legally prosecute the same [rude singers] before Authority. **1782** I. PUTNAM in Lossing *Encycl. U.S. Hist.* II. 1163/1 The authority of this town [Brookline] . . . have run into a great error in approbating an additional number of public houses. **1799** H. ADAMS *Hist. New-Eng.* 64 The authority required him to give bonds for his good behavior. **1806** WEBSTER s.v., [Used] in Con[necticut]. **1819** CLAY *Speeches* (1860) I. 122 If they were in the character imputed, they were alone amenable, and should have been turned over to the civil authority.

+**2.** (See quot. 1816.)

1804 *Laws of Middlebury College* 6 (Hall), Every Freshman shall be obliged to do any proper errand or message for the Authority of the College. **1816** PICKERING 40 *Authority* . . . is also used in some of the States, in speaking collectively of the professors &c. of our colleges, to whom the *government* of those institutions is entrusted.

+**Auto.** [Short for AUTOMOBILE *n.*]

1. An automobile or motor-car.

1899 *Boston Herald* 4 July 4/7 If we must Americanise and shorten the word, why not call them 'autos.' *Ib.* 9 July 6/3 The accident to Mr. W. K. Vanderbilt's 'auto' was due to . . . the driver. **1909** 'O. HENRY' *Options* 71 Watching the carriages and autos roll by in the street. **1910** WALCOTT *Open Door* xviii. 224 'My auto is waiting at the side door,' she said.

2. Attrib. with *robe, veil,* etc.

1912 W. IRWIN *Red Button* 197 A purple auto veil in my right hand. **1915** G. M. WHITE *Rose o' Paradise* 215 Theodore spread one of the auto robes on the ground.

+**Autobus.** An automobile omnibus or motor coach. — **1899** *Boston Herald* 12 July 6/5 We should have the new words . . . autobus, [etc.].

+**Autocar.** An automobile. Also attrib. — **1897** *Boston Transcript* 12 July 1/2 The works [in Paris] . . . caught fire today and sixty autocars were destroyed. **1907** *Pearson's Mag.* Jan. (Advt.) Auto Car Practice—'Homans, Self-Propelled Vehicles' . . . is the most complete book on the motor car.

+**Autocycle.** A cycle driven by motor power. {1905-} — **1900** *Outing* Nov. 122 A Recent Type of the Auto-Cycle. *Ib.* 208 Two New Types of Autocycles.

Autograph album. A blank book for recording autographs. — **1879** B. F. TAYLOR *Summer-Savory* xxvi. 209 The writer hopes the reader's name is not found in many autograph albums. **1891** FREEMAN *New Eng. Nun* 4 A square red autograph album.

Autograph-book. =prec. — **1858** HOLMES *Autocrat* i. 6 One of the lady-boarders . . . sent me her autograph-book. **1860** — *E. Venner* xxvi, This girl carried her autograph-book,—for she had one of those indispensable appendages of the boarding-school miss of every degree,—and asked Elsie to write her name in it. **1871** [L. H. BAGG] *At Yale* 475 Every Senior, too, used to procure him an 'autograph book,' and persuade his classmates to append their signatures to some 'happy sentiment' in prose or verse written therein by them.

+**Automobile,** *n.* [From next.]

1. A self-propelled vehicle for use on a street, roadway, etc.; a motor-car.

1897 *Boston Transcript* 17 May 12/6 The automobile is bound to be in general use before long. *Ib.,* The most successful automobiles made thus far are those in which electric motors are used. **1900** *Outing* Oct. 66 [Illustration of] Mr. H. H. Hunnewell in his Steam Automobile. *Ib.* 67 Mrs. Clement C. Moore in her Electric Automobile. *Ib.* 68 The automobile has already earned its right to be classed as another of our means of recreation. **1909** 'O. HENRY' *Options* 73, I never rode in an automobile in my life.

2. Attrib. with *club, show, veil,* etc.

1900 *Outing* Nov. 122 The influence of the Automobile Club of America. *Ib.* 368 [Article on] The Automobile Shows. **1915** D. R. CAMPBELL *Proving Virginia* 183 He was earning good wages . . . in an automobile factory. **1923** WYATT *Invis. Gods* IV. iii. 219 Dangling veils of the kind then [about 1903] known as 'automobile veils.'

+**Automobile,** *a.* [F.] Capable of moving itself by means of internal mechanical power; self-propelling. {Also in E. (1895), from F.}

1883 H. GREER *Dict. Electricity* 48 There are half a dozen systems of electric traction . . . in use. . . . 4. An auto-mobile car, with isolated rails. **1886** *Harper's Mag.* June 25/1 It is probable that the auto-mobile torpedo for our new navy will be an American invention. **1899** *Cent., Motorman,* . . . one whose business is to drive a motor-car, or automobile vehicle.

+**Automobile,** *v.* [f. the noun.] To drive, to ride or travel in, an automobile. — **1900** *N. Y. Journal* 11 Nov. 28/1 'Bubbling' . . . is the fashionable slang for automobling or locomobling or whatever you choose to call it. **1903** *N.Y. Times* 19 Dec. 9 Here is a hat for . . . the automobiling women. **1916** W. A. DU PUY *Uncle Sam* 122 The two men . . . automobiled about the city and dined at the resort of Fun Ken.

+**Automobilism** [f. AUTOMOBILE *n.* Cf. F. *automobilisme.*] The use of automobiles. {1899} — **1898** *Cosmopolitan* Sept. 483/2 As a sport, automobilism now occupies the foremost rank [in France]. **1900** *Outing* Oct. 66 The best that is in automobilism comes as the reward of experience.

Automobilist. One who uses or drives an automobile. {1897-} — **1898** *N.Y. Journal* 22 November 14/7 Laws for automobilists [in Paris]. **1899** *Ib.* 8 June 6/1 When a Winton carriage recently made its remarkable run between Cleveland and New York the French automobilists made light of the feat. **1904** *Newark Ev. News* 27 Aug. 6 The 'scorching' fever that afflicts so many automobilists.

+**Automobilize,** *v.* [f. as prec. +*-ize.*] *tr.* To habituate to the use of automobiles. — **1898** *Cosmopolitan* Sept. 480/1 It is scarcely an exaggeration to say that Paris is becoming 'automobilized.' **1902** *N.Y. Times* 26 March (C. D. Suppl.).

+**Auto-truck.** A motor truck. — **1899** *N.Y. Journal* 17 Jan. 5/2 The incorporation of the New York Auto-Truck Company. *Ib.* 8/3 The guardians of our language . . . will awake some morning to find the barbarous word 'auto-truck' . . . firmly fastened upon our suffering speech.

+**Auto-wagon.** A motor wagon. — **1900** *Engineering Mag.* XIX. 733 This objection . . . does not hold good with the auto-waggon, . . . which provides just that rapid and cheap form of independent direct transport for which so great a need exists at the present day.

* **Autumnal,** *a.* Occurring or appearing in autumn. *Autumnal fever*=FALL FEVER.

(1) **1772** J. HABERSHAM *Lett.* 163 The lands being flat and moist, . . . causes the white inhabitants in particular to be subject to severe Autumnal Fevers. **1831** PECK *Guide* 180 Miasma, which invariably produces yellow, bilious, intermittant, and other summer and autumnal fevers. **1851** CIST *Cincinnati* 29 In early times, autumnal fever, occurring every year, was seldom, except in some very limited spots.

(2) **1810** WEEMS *Lett.* III. 22, I w[oul]d gladly stay till the Autumnal Courts were all over.

(3) **1811** WILSON *Ornithology* III. 65 Autumnal Warbler, *Sylvia autumnalis:* This plain little species regularly visits Pennsylvania from the north in . . . October. **1814** MITCHILL *Fishes N.Y.* 451 Long-Island Herring. *Clupea mattowacca.* Called also the autumnal or fall herring. **1831** AUDUBON *Ornith. Biog.* I. 447 The Autumnal Warbler was so named . . . on account of its appearing in the neighbourhood of Philadelphia . . . during its migration from the northern States, where it breeds, to . . . Mexico, its winter residence. **1891** *Cent.* 6819/2 *Autumnal warbler,* the young of the bay-breasted warbler mistaken for a distinct species. *A. Wilson,* 1811.

(4) **1813** MUHLENBERG *Cat. Plants* 32 *Rhus autumnale.* Autumnal sumach.

Auxiliary. {1601} +A stage performer having no speaking part; a supernumerary. — **1845** S. SMITH *Theatr. Apprent.* i. 15 That useful, but much-despised class of individuals, indispensable in all theatres, called 'supers,' or more politely speaking 'auxiliaries.' **1854** E. Tompkins *Hist.*

Boston Theatre (1908) 15 Wanted—Several respectable young men for Auxiliaries.

*Avail, *v.*

+1. *tr.* To give or afford (a person) the knowledge, benefit, or advantage *of* something; to inform (one) of. *Obs.*

a1781 Witherspoon *Druid P.* No. 7, The members of a popular government should be continually availed of the situation and condition of every part. **1785** JEFFERSON *Writings* V. 114 It will rest, therefore, with you, to avail Mr. Barclay of that fund. **1806** *Ib.* XI. 106 If the present occasion be good, . . . your Majesty's character will not be wanting to avail the world of it. [**1840** MRS. TROLLOPE *Widow Married* xix, There is not a single one of them . . . but what shall be availed of your great obligingness.]

2. *intr.* To make use or take advantage (*of* something). Orig. in *p.p.* {1603, 1899–}

1848 BARTLETT 16 The newspapers sometimes say 'an offer . . . was made but not availed of.' **1860** EMERSON *Conduct, Fate*, Power . . . must be availed of, and not by any means let off and wasted. **1874** R. H. COLLINS *Kentucky* I. 114 Gen. Buell availed of the remarkably brilliant moonlight to bring up . . . the corps. **1902** C. H. PARKHURST *Sunny Side of Christianity* 58 One [quality] . . . which probably we can best avail of in illustrating the new point that now interests us. **1924** M. A. HOWE *B. Wendell* 28 The class availed of the departing professor's hospitality.

Availability. [1803–; f. next.] +'That qualification in a candidate which implies or supposes a strong probability of his success, apart from substantial merit—a probability resulting from mere personal or accidental popularity' (B. '48).

1844 *Congress. Globe* 4 June, App. 663/3 The *Eastern Argus* . . . describes the following as the traits of character which, in the estimation of the whigs, constitute the *ne plus ultra* of 'availability.' **1848** *N.Y. Herald* May (B.), Availability, not merit or qualifications, is the only requisite to secure a nomination. **1864** LOWELL in *N. Am. Rev.* Jan. 241 He was . . . nominated for his *availability*,—that is, because he had no history. **1884** G. T. CURTIS in *Century Mag.* Nov. 126 An accurate definition of this curious quality of political strength excludes the personal fitness of a man to be President of the United States, and includes his supposed 'availability.' **1904** *Phila. Public Ledger* 6 Aug. 8 Conceding that availability has too largely and too often dominated the choice of a Presidential candidate. **1905** *N.Y. Ev. Post* 13 Oct. 6 An illustration of the way in which what is called 'availability' is preferred to character and efficiency.

***Available,** *a.* +Having the requisite influence or strength, irrespective of merit, as a political candidate.

1837 *Baltimore Comm. Transcript* 20 June 2/2 (Th. S.), The New York papers are discussing whether the most talented, or the most available man, should be reëlected as candidate for the next presidency. **1844** *S.Lit. Messenger* X. 489/1 By consent . . . Jeptha Leathers, Esq. was regularly brought out as a candidate the next year. . . . So that he was the man for the times—an 'available candidate.' **1861** *Ill. Agric. Soc. Trans.* V. 381 We are compelled to vote for such politicians or 'available candidates' of a party as are selected for us, or throw our vote away! **1864** J. G. HOLLAND *Letters to Joneses* 278 Occasionally a patriot has been 'available' for carrying out the purposes of politicians. But often imbecility and rascality have been found 'available.' **1874** B. F. TAYLOR *World on Wheels* I. xvii. 123 By-the-by, is the 'available' aspirant for office always the cheapest? **1888** BRYCE *Amer. Commw.* III. lxx. II. 550 The man fittest to be adopted as candidate . . . is the man most likely to win, the man who, to use the technical term, is most 'available.'

Availableness. {1677} +=AVAILABILITY. — **1841** EMERSON *Ess., Conserv.* 470 Conservatism . . . goes for availableness in its candidate, not for worth; and for expediency in its measures, and not for right.

***Avails,** *n. pl.*

***1.** Profits or proceeds of any business, labor, investment, etc. {–*a*1733}

'*Avails*, . . . [used in] Con.' (W. '06). 'It is used in New England, for the proceeds of goods sold, or for rents, issues or profits' (W. '28). 'It is used in other parts of the country in like manner' (B. '48).

c1789 E. Baldwin *Yale College* 315 Avails of former donations . . . to purchase books, $114 98. **1798** HOLMES *Life E. Stiles* 398 In 1790 . . . Noah Webster, Esq. appropriated a certain proportion of the avails of his Grammatical Institute . . . as an annual premium. **1807** *Ann. 10th Congress* 1 Sess. I. 673 This corn . . . was sold . . . , and the avails placed in the quartermaster's hands. **1823** COOPER *Pioneers* ii, A mercantile house was established . . . with the avails of Mr. Effingham's personal property. **1841** CIST *Cincinnati* 124 The avails of manual labor are much affected by the state of business. **1863** 'E. KIRKE' *Southern Friends* 258 The avails will help me through with father's debts. **1876** *Vermont Bd. Agric. Rep.* III. 307 Most of us farmers need the avails of all our surplus produce. **1892** *Century Mag.* Jan. 326/2 Avails of [N.Y. Jews'] industry are pitiably meagre.

+**2.** Commodities; property.

1850 N. KINGSLEY *Diary* 99 If . . . she should not find profitable freight for Sacramento City, to take the avails of the company on board.

+**Avalanche.** *S.* (See quotations.)— **1859** BARTLETT 15 *Avalanche*, a Texan corruption of the French *Ambulance.* A spring waggon. **1872** DE VERE 580 *Avalanche*, a corruption of ambulance, was already before the late Civil War much used in Texas and the outlying territories. *Ib.*, Prince Polignac . . . showed very great excitement upon being informed by a [Southern] sergeant that the 'avalanche was just coming down the hill as fast as fury.'

+**Avalone** (**avelone, avallonia**), variants of ABALONE. — **1850** B. TAYLOR *Eldorado* xvii, The avelone, which is a univalve, found clinging to the sides of rocks, furnishes the finest mother-of-pearl. **1882** *Harper's Mag.* Oct. 728 They [Chinamen in S. California] prepare the avallonia meat and avallonia shells for their home market.

***Avens.** One or other species belonging to the genus *Geum* of perennial herbs, of which about twelve are native to the U.S. Freq. with distinguishing terms (see quotations).

1784 CUTLER in *Mem. Academy* I. 454 Common Avens. Herb-Bennet. Blossoms white or yellow. By fences and borders of fields. July. **1821** *Mass. H. S. Coll.* 2 Ser. IX. 150 Plants, which are indigenous in the township of Middlebury, [Vermont, include] . . . *Geum virginianum*, Avens; *strictum*, Upright avens; *rivale*, Purple avens. **1847** WOOD *Botany* 254 *G. rivale.* Water avens. Purple avens. . . . *G. strictum*, Ait. Yellow avens. . . . *G. Virginianum*, . . . White avens. . . . *G. macrophyllum*, Willd. Large-leaved yellow avens. **1868** GRAY *Field Botany* 122 *G. vernum*, spring avens. [Inhabits] thickets. . . . *G. strictum*, field avens. [Inhabits] moist grounds and fields.

Avenue, *n.*

1. An approach, as to a large country house or other residence, esp. when straight and having a row of trees on each side; a similar wide road in a park, etc. {1654–}

1769 WASHINGTON *Diaries* I. 308 At home all day, opening the avenue to the house. **1800** BROWN *A. Mervyn* xxix, In a short time I spied its painted roof and five chimneys through an avenue of *catalpas.* **1833** 'ELMWOOD' *Yankee among Nullifiers* 78 We reached the foot of the short avenue leading to the house. **1855** SIMMS *Forayers* 21 A great entrance, or carriage-way, . . . opening upon a noble avenue of oaks. **1861** HOLMES *E. Venner* x, A terraced garden, flanked at the left by an avenue of tall elms. **1884** CABLE *Dr. Sevier* lviii, Mary . . . was walking . . . down the central avenue of the old Girod cemetery. **1893** M. HOWE *Honor* 318 Seen from a carriage window as he drives . . . through the least-frequented avenues of the park.

attrib. **1801** *Steele Papers* I. 209 She has got . . . all the materials . . . for the avenue fence or pailing.

+**2.** A wide or a principal street, esp. one shaded with trees on each side; a broad thoroughfare. Also without reference to the character of the street, and freq. applied to thoroughfares running at right angles to others properly called 'streets.'

1780 J. MASON in *Boston Orations* (1785) 135 Till oppression stalked [in 1770] at noon-day through every avenue in your cities. **1793** *Ann. 6th Congress* 1335 Ground . . . on the northeast side of Massachusetts avenue [in Washington, D.C.]. *Ib.* 1336 Lots on the southwest of the said avenue. **1797** MORSE *Gazetteer* s.v. *Washington, D.C.*, The grand avenues . . . are from 130 to 160 feet wide, the other streets are from 90 to 110 feet wide. **1807** C. JANSON *Stranger in A.* 202 The entrance, or avenues, as they are pompously called, which lead to the American seat of government, are the worst roads I passed in the country. **1830** COOPER *Water Witch* ii, The wide avenue in which Olaff Van Staats dwelt was but a few hundred yards in length. . . . This avenue . . . was then, as it is still, called the Broadway. **1835** REED & MATHESON *Visit* I. 219 The main avenue, or street, is just a clearance from the woods. **1852** BRISTED *Upper Ten Th.* ii. 40 One of the broad avenues that intersect the upper part of the city longitudinally. **1890** *Harper's Mag.* June 140 They had bought up all the land in and around the village, had staked out avenues and town lots.

+**b.** A principal or fashionable street the name of which is shortened to 'the avenue.'

1852 *Knickerb.* XXXIX. 163 An old portrait which ornamented the back-parlor in Wooster-street, and which hangs in the basement upon the Avenue. **1863** 'M. HARLAND' *Husks* 8 Our block . . . is just the thing . . . and so convenient! So near the Avenue! **1884** *Century Mag.* Oct. 874/1 'Saw you on the Avenue this afternoon,' said Morris, passing a light. **1906** *Churchman* 3 Nov. 663 The Church would no longer be a class organization, with its rich congregation meeting on the avenue and its poor members gathering in some East Side chapel. **1909** 'O. HENRY' *Options* 80 The Avenue was as quiet as a street of Pompeii. Cabs now and then skimmed past . . . , and less frequent motor-cars.

+**c.** In the phr. 'the other end of the Avenue,' with reference to the position of the Capitol and the White House on Pennsylvania Ave., Washington, D.C.

1903 D. M. DEWITT *Impeachm. A. Johnson* 42 Thus far, it may be said, peace prevailed between the Capitol and 'the other end of the Avenue.' **1904** *N.Y. Ev. Post* 27 June 7 On the tariff question it seems almost certain that there will be a sharp difference of opinion between the White House group and the leaders at the other end of the avenue.

3. A way of access or approach. {–1678}

1783 *Boston Town Rec.* 304 The Inspector of the Markets . . . shall . . . pass through the several Market Places, the Avenues leading thereto, and the several publick Streets.

+**b.** A passageway.

1812 *Niles' Reg.* I. 329/1 He entered the semicircular avenue which leads to the door of the theatre. **1830** Cooper *Water Witch* III. viii. 232 The torrent of fire which was roaring among the avenues of the ship. **1850** *Western Journal* IV. 125 The avenues shall be ten feet wide, dividing the vineyard into squares of one hundred and twenty feet.

Avenue, *v. tr.* To form into an avenue. {1865} — **1859** A. Van Buren *Sojourn in South* 105 The walk to it from the gate was avenued by fine rows of arbor vitae trees.

+**Average,** *v.*

1. *intr.* 'To form a mean or medium sum or quantity' (W. '28); to be on an average. {1814–}

'The use of this as a *neuter* verb is not, as some persons have supposed, peculiar to us' (Pick., citing *London Star* of 1814).

1769 Washington *Diaries* I. 314 The above . . . appears to be no more than the worth of a fat wether—it being imagind, that woud average the above weight. **1800** Fessenden *Poems* (1806) 113 Each paper, take them as they rise, Will average at a hundred lies. **1867** *Iowa Agric. Soc. Rep.* (1868) 170 Barley . . . averages very well, but is not raised to any extent. **1872** *Vermont Bd. Agric. Rep.* I. 309 A deep cellar, divided into rooms, will average warmer than a shallow one not divided by partitions. **1873** Beadle *Undevel. West* 74 Society in Nebraska will average. . . . The standard of popular intelligence is high. *Ib.* 385 The recitations would average well in a white school. **1877** *Vermont Bd. Agric. Rep.* IV. 49 The cows average young, a very large proportion being still heifers. **1884** *Century Mag.* XXVII. 519/1 Neighbors called . . . to see how the flock 'evridged,' and to engage hands for their own shearing. **1898** Westcott *D. Harum* 231 But they [*sc.* 'the canalers'] averaged fer disposition 'bout like the ord'nary run o' folks; the' was mean ones an' clever ones.

2. *tr.* To distribute or select in proportional numbers or quantities.

1818 *Niles' Reg.* XIV. 174/1 The contributions for subsistence, if averaged on the families, would be 8 or 9 lbs of pork, and half a bushel of corn for a family of middling circumstances. **1828** Webster, To average a loss. **1865** Boudrye *Fifth N.Y. Cavalry* 52 We sent two hundred men on picket, averaging the number from the different companies.

3. To form a general opinion concerning; to 'size up.'

1869 'Mark Twain' *Innocents Abroad* xix. 189 Blucher said he guessed the old man could read the French of it and average the rest. **1881** — *Prince and Pauper* xxii. 276 The blacksmith averaged the stalwart soldier with a glance.

+**Average book.** At Harvard Univ., 'a book in which the marks received by each student . . . are entered; also the deductions from his rank resulting from misconduct' (Hall '56). *Obs.* — **1848** W. F. Allen in Hall *Coll. Words* (1856) 15 In vain the Prex's grave rebuke, Deductions from the average book.

Avocado. Also **avacado.** [See next.] The alligator or avocado pear.

(1) **1886** [H. G. Warner] *Florida Fruits* 239 The avacado . . . [is] often, but erroneously, called the alligator pear. *Ib.* 240 There are three varieties of the avacado, the red, purple, and green, the latter being most highly esteemed. **1899** E. J. Wickson *Calif. Fruits* (1900) 387 The avocado . . . is . . . one of the most promising of its class of fruits, as it is known to epicures.

(2) **1886** [H. G. Warner] *Florida Fruits* 240 As simply a shade tree the avacado is beautiful. **1910** *Yearbook Dept. Agric.* 431 The original tree of the Family avocado was found by Prof. P. H. Rolfs . . . on a place at Buena Vista near Miami, Fla.

Avocado pear. Also **avocardo, avagado, avigato pear.** [E. (1697), f. Sp. *abogado, aguacate,* ad. Nahuatl *ahuacatl.* Also later (*c*1838) taken directly from Mex.-Sp.]

1. The alligator pear.

[**1751** Washington *Diaries* I. 27 The Avagado pair is generally most admired [in Barbadoes].] **1838** 'Texian' *Mexico* v. *Texas* 10 In the orchards, the avigato pear, the citron and banana alternate with the apple, the plum and peach tree of Europe. **1838** M. Brooks *Idomen* (1843) 43 An avocado pear,—that fruit or vegetable marrow so cooling to the palate, when eaten with the light bread of Matanzas. **1859** Bartlett 7 Alligator Pear (*Laurus persea*). A West Indian fruit, . . . also called Avocado or Avigato Pear. **1896** in *Dept. Agric. 1904 Bull.* No. 61. 12 The alligator or avocado pear . . . is one of the most highly prized of all tropical fruits. **1902** *Fla. Hort. Soc. Proc.* XV. 64/2 The avocado pear . . . is to-day the most costly fruit on the American market.

2. The southern lauraceous tree *Persea persea* or *gratissima,* bearing the alligator pear.

1903 *Fla. Hort. Soc. Proc.* XVI. 63/1 The best plan for growing the avocado pear and the sapadillo. *Ib.* 64/2 The use of commercial fertilizers on avocado pears.

* **Avoirdupois.** +Personal weight.

Haber-de-pois is used in the same sense in Shaks. 2 *Hen. IV* II. iv. 276.

1861 Winthrop *Open Air* 69 We lightened the canoe by two men's avoirdupois, that it might dance. **1875** *Fur, Fin, & Feather* 105 The ladies' . . . avoirdupois will go steadily up while the wagon-springs settle steadily down. **1883** *Atlantic Mo.* May 681/2 Avoirdupois and strength are at a premium for rushing, blocking, and tackling. **1889** Farmer 26/2 She sat close by Mrs. Desbrough, a woman of solid avoirdupois. **1904** G. Stratton-Porter *Freckles* 228 A laugh is always good. . . . A little more avoirdupois won't hurt me.

fig. **1888** *Detroit Free Press* LXIII. No. 27. 1 In society . . . she was a leader by virtue of her wealth, family and a certain moral avoirdupois.

Avoset, Avocet. Also †**avosit.** [E. (1766), a. F. *avocette.*] +A wading-bird (*Recurvirostra americana*), allied to the snipes and stilts, and marked by the chestnut-brown color of the head.

1785– [see American avoset]. **1813** Wilson *Ornithology* VII. 48 Long-legged Avoset: *Recurvirostra himantopus;* . . . arrives on the sea coast of New Jersey about the twenty-fifth of April. **1839** Townsend *Narr.* iv. 184 We saw here great numbers of a beautiful brown and white avocet. **1874** Coues *Birds N.W.* 460 In the United States and northward the Avocet is chiefly a summer visitor. *Ib.*, Localities whence we have records of the 'White-necked Avocet' (*R. occidentalis*), which is . . . only the young of this species [*R. americana*]. **1883** P. Robinson in *Harper's Mag.* Oct. 714/1 The brackish marsh-lands are the haunt of curlews, avocets, plovers, and other wading birds.

+**Aw,** *interj. colloq.*[2] An exclamation of remonstrance, entreaty, or disgust. — **1852** Stowe *Uncle Tom* viii, 'Ugh! aw! like enough!' grunted his complaisant acquaintance. **1901** McCutcheon *Graustark* 41 'Aw, who are you?' demanded the conductor, belligerently. **1904** 'O. Henry' *Heart of West* 280 'Aw, come off,' said the boy, . . . 'I ain't no kid.'

* **Await,** *n.* or *adv. Obs.* +*Await of,* in wait or on the watch for. — **1775** *R.I. Hist. Soc.* VI. 19 We brought the remainder over, . . . tho' mighty difficult on account of the enemy lying await of us in the river.

* **Awakening,** *vbl. n.* +A spiritual revival.

1736 Edwards *Faithful Narr.* (1737) 5 In these two years there were near twenty . . . converted; but there was nothing of any General Awakening. *Ib.* 23 A Minister . . . told me of a very great awakening of many in a Place called the Mountains. **1741** — (*title*), Sinners in the hands of an angry God, a Sermon at Enfield, July 8, 1741, at a Time of Awakening. **1802** J. Cowles *Diary* 85 Timothy called here and told me of a late awakening in N.H. College. **1816** *N. Amer. Rev.* II. 365 A North-American Indian has a taste for intoxication, . . . and an inhabitant of Connecticut for *awakenings.* **1846** A. Wiley in *Indiana Mag. Hist.* XXIII. 428 He preached . . . until awakenings commenced, and the whole town . . . became religious.

Awares, *a. rare.* [Cf. E. *aware* a. and *unawares* adv.] **a.** Cognizant; aware. **b.** Watchful. — **1637** Morton *New Canaan* xvii. 295 [The Plymouth colonists] feared . . . hee would hinder the benefit of their Beaver trade . . . ere they were awares. **1737** E. Parkman *Diary* 9 That we may be awares & have our eyes open, our minds apprehensive, now.

* **Away,** *adv.* (See also 'Way *adv.*)

1. At a considerable distance in space; afar. +Freq. in colloq. phrases, as *away back, down, down east, south.*

1825 Neal *Bro. Jonathan* III. 145 A . . . he-yankee, from 'away down east.' **1825** [see Back settlement]. *c*1849 [Paige] *Dow's Sermons* I. 16 Away down in the south . . . is a great country called California. **1854** *Knickerb.* XLIII. 428, I am a miner, who wandered 'from away down-east.' **1871** Crofutt *Tourist's Guide* 154 An Eastern lumberman, from 'away down in Maine.' **1884** *Chicago Tribune* 15 May 7/3 A State-rights Bourbon Democrat from away back. **1905** Phillips *Social Secretary* 24 Even Tom don't seem natural any more, away off here in the East.

fig. **1904** H. Allaway in *N.Y. Tribune* 15 May 4 Manipulators desperately endeavoring to bring back recessions which will permit them to 'get even.' That they will make money is 'away back' in their calculations.

+**b.** *From away,* from a distance.

1888 *Boston Jrnl.* 6 Nov. 1/4 It is rumored that capitalists from away are making an effort to establish an industry in Rockland.

+**2.** *Away up,* far up; very high up.

1834 [Davis] *Lett. J. Downing* 189 It's a present to me . . . from Starks & Co., away up in York State. **1873** Beadle *Western Wilds* 450 Tourists by the Pacific Railway think themselves away up when at Sherman. **1902** O. Wister *Virginian* ix, All the ladies thought the world of her, and McLean had told him she was 'away up in G.' **1903** *N.Y. Sun* 26 Nov. 5 Turkeys are away up in price. **1904** *Minneapolis Times* 11 June 2 The rafters, away up high, were completely hidden under garlands of green.

+**3.** *Away back,* far back in time.

1882 Sweet & Knox *Texas Siftings* 45 Lawler . . . shot a deer, away back in 1840, on the spot where the capitol now stands. **1891** Ryan *Told in Hills* 234 A d—d good man, I may say, and a fighter from away back. **1903** W. F. Johnson *Century of Expansion* 81 He insisted upon this away back in the Revolution. **1904** *N.Y. Times* 12 May 3 Fessenden fixed his eyes upon the Senate away back in 1884.

+**4.** To a great extent; far.

1887 George *40 Years on Rail* vii. 130 Primitive railroading was away in advance of the stage-coaching that preceded it. **1906** *N.Y. Even. Post* 28 April, Manufacturers of all good cars are away behind in their deliveries.

* **Awful,** *a.* and *adv.* (In colloq. uses.)

+**1.** Very unpleasant or disagreeable; dreadfully ugly or objectionable. {1870–}

'This word . . . is never used except in conversation, and is far from being so common in the sea-ports now, as it was some years ago' (Pick.).

'Our common people use this word in the sense of frightful, ugly, detestable' (W. '28).

1809 FESSENDEN *Pills Poetical* 2, I fear our . . . nation Is in an awful situation. **1810** J. LAMBERT *Travels* (1813) II. 32 Awful weather, master, and sure enough your nose looks blue upon't. *Ib.* 505 Every thing that creates surprise is *awful* with them; 'what an *awful* wind! *awful* hole! *awful* hill! *awful* mouth! *awful* nose! &c.' **1816** PICKERING 42 In New England many people would call a disagreeable medicine, *awful. Ib.*, An ugly woman [is called] an awful looking woman. **1818** FEARON *Sketches* 124 She is not awful (ugly), I guess? [**1822** LAMB *Gentle Giantess* in *London Mag.* Dec. 529/1 She is indeed, as the Americans would express it, something awful.] **1828** WEBSTER s.v., Our common people use this word in the sense of frightful, ugly, detestable. **1881** 'MARK TWAIN' *Prince & Pauper* 29 He knew his father would . . . thrash him first, and that . . . the awful grandmother would do it all over again. **1886** ALCOTT *Jo's Boys* x. 195 She having a wholesome fear of her brother,—who could be rather awful when she went too far. **1889** 'MARK TWAIN' *Conn. Yankee* 574 It was awful—awfuler than you can ever imagine.

+**2.** Very great, intense, long, etc. {1845–}

1843 'CARLTON' *New Purchase* I. xix. 182 For potpie is the favourite [dish], and woodmen sharp set are *awful* eaters. **1847** FIELD *Drama in Pokerville*, etc. 103 We have never visited the town of Madison, Indiana, but we have an 'awful' curiosity to do so, from the 'awful' fact that we have never heard the place mentioned without the 'awful' accompaniment of this adjective! Madison is an 'awful place for revivals!' an 'awful place for Mesmerism!' an 'awful place for Mrs. Nichols' poems!' an 'awful place for politics!' and the following story will prove that it was, particularly, an 'awful place for Jackson!' **1856** *Yale Lit. Mag.* XXI. 147 (Th.), He's awful on possums; oh, I tell ye now, he's great. **1876** 'MARK TWAIN' & WARNER *Gilded Age* xxxiii. 307 It's an awful distance—ten or twelve hundred mile. **1886** *Outing* Nov. 101/1, I remember an awful fight between elk. **1891** WILKINS *New Eng. Nun* 201 You're an awful fool.

3. As *adv.* = AWFULLY. {*colloq.*}

'This sense of the word is peculiar to the West' (B. '48).

1818 J. PALMER *Travels in U.S.* 131 *note*, [It is] awful hot. **1837** *Democratic Rev.* I. 34 'Awful hot! Dreadful dusty!' answers the sympathetic toll-gatherer. **1846–51** WHITCHER *Bedott P.* ix. 89, I never thought *that* [*sc.* her face] was so awful handsome as some folks does. **1861** NORTON *Army Lett.* 15 He was awful mad. **1876** 'MARK TWAIN' *Tom Sawyer* ii. 13 She talks awful, but talk don't hurt. **1904** 'O. HENRY' *Heart of West* 61, I'd be awful edified to meet Miss Learight! **1921** PAINE *Comr. Rolling Ocean* iii. 39 A prairie town called Follansbee that looks awful good to me.

***Awfully,** *adv.* (In colloq. uses.)

+**1.** Very badly, terribly.

1816 PICKERING 42 A perverse, ill-natured child, that disobeys his parents, would be said to behave awfully. **1861** NORTON *Army Lett.* 32 His countenance was awfully disfigured.

+**2.** To a high or extreme degree; exceedingly; very; very much. {1830–}

1839 MARRYAT *Diary* II. 33 He dissipates awfully. **1867** S. HALE *Letters* 26 Cairo is delightful, awfully nicer than Alexandria. **1886–7** STOCKTON *Hundredth Man* xix, 'Oh, I like that!' said Gay, . . . 'and I am going to be awfully particular.' **1905** N. DAVIS *Northerner* 180 Are not these your trousseau clothes? It is aw-fully unlucky to wear them before the wedding!

A-whaling: see A *prep.*[1] 3 and WHALING *vbl. n.* — **1675** *East-Hampton Rec.* I. 380 Noe man . . . shall procure . . . any strange Indyan . . . to goe to sea a whaleing. **1687** *Doc. Hist. N.Y. State* (1849) I. 272 Those who were out the last yeare a whaling. **1718** J. HEMPSTEAD *Diary* 72 Comfort Davise hath hired my whale boat to go a whaling at fishers Island. **1770** *R.I. Commerce* I. 327 [If you do not] charter my Schooner, . . . I shall send her a whaling. **1851** MELVILLE *Moby Dick* xvi, Go a-whaling I must, and I would; and the Pequod was as good a ship as any.

+**Awheel,** *adv.* On a 'wheel' or bicycle.

1887 G. B. THAYER (*title*), Pedal and Path. Across the Continent Awheel and Afloat. **1896** *Ohio Chronicle* (Columbus) 23 May 2 Mr. S. . . . was talking of taking a trip awheel west. **1897** *Outing* XXX. 65 Awheel thro' the Tide-water of Virginia. *Ib.* 240 Across the Alleghanies awheel.

+**A-wheeling:** see A *prep.*[1] 4 and WHEELING. — **1896** *Voice* (N.Y.) 24 Sept. 7 Nowadays . . . [it is] eminently 'rational' to go a-wheeling in your shoes and stockings . . . unhampered by the one-time indispensable leg-covering.

Awkward squad. A military squad consisting of recruits or others undergoing training. {1796–} — **1836** HILDRETH *Campaigns Rocky Mts.* I. v. 41 The captain . . . ordered them in the awkward squad to have half an hour's extra drill. **1850** WATSON *Camp-fires Revol.* 260 It pictures the first marching of the 'awkward squad' enlisted for the continental service. **1861** *Chicago Tribune* 15 April 1 Awkward Squad drill, Monday, Wednesday and Friday evenings. **1888** BILLINGS *Hardtack* 208 Whenever they were out with a squad—usually the 'awkward squad'—for drill, they made business lively enough.

***Awl.** Also †aul(e, awle, all.

***1.** The slender boring-tool so named.

1647 *Essex Probate Rec.* I. 70, 3 aules, a gimblett. **1681** *New Castle Court Rec.* 462 Fower Kniues and fower alls. **1750** WALKER *Journal* 14 May, We had lost every Awl that we brought out. **1805** LEWIS in *Ann. 9th Congress* 2 Sess. 1064 They receive in return, . . . axes, kettles, awls, and other European manufactures. **1833** SILLIMAN *Man. Sugar Cane* 87 If there are lumps or loaves [of sugar], an awl is run up to relieve the liquor. **1850** GARRARD *Wah-To-Yah* iii. 49 The skins are . . . sewed together with an awl and sinew.

2. Attrib. with *blade, case, haft, hole.*

1633 *N.H. Doc. & Rec.* I. 79, 7 aule-blades. **1643** WILLIAMS *Key* 66 Stone formerly being to them [*sc.* Indians] in stead of Knives, Awle-blades, Hatchets and Howes. **1711** *Springfield Rec.* II. 41, 80 aul blades, 6 s. **1756** *Lett. to Washington* I. 364 Fine Indian Awl blades—@ 3/9 Gross not many left. **1761** *Essex Inst. Coll.* XLVIII. 96 To be sold . . . , awl blades, . . . awl hafts, . . . darning and knitting needles. **1762** H. M. Brooks *Gleanings* 128 The Door of the Box [of a Chaise] is pricked with Awl-Holes. **1849** *Rep. Comm. Patents* (1850) 213 What I claim . . . is a tool handle or awl haft. **1870** KEIM *Sheridan's Troopers* 198 The women wear belts . . . , suspended from which are an awl-case and paint-pouch.

Awlwort. The small stemless aquatic plant *Subularia aquatica*, with awl-shaped leaves. {1797} — **1847** WOOD *Botany* 163 *Subularia aquatica*, Awlwort. A small plant growing on the muddy shores of ponds in Maine, *Nutt.*, and near the White Mts., *Pickering.* **1857** GRAY *Botany* 39 *Subularia*, Awlwort. . . . June, July.

Awning.

1. A movable rooflike covering of canvas or like material serving as a protection from sun, rain, etc. {1608–}

1702 *Essex Inst. Coll.* XLII. 161 Inventory of ships . . . [includes] 14 irons for boats awning. **1740** STEPHENS *Proc. Georgia* 619 He saw a gentleman under the awning [of a boat]. **1806** LEWIS & CLARK *Orig. Journals* (1904) V. I. 39 The party formed themselves very comfortable tents with willow poles and grass in the form of the orning [*sic*] of a wagon. **1829** *American Traveller* 14 Sept., A Land Barge . . . with a Cabin, Births, etc. below . . . a promenade deck, awning, seats, etc. above. **1838** C. GILMAN *Recoll.* ii. 19 A richly-prepared table was laid under a decorated awning on a green in an enclosure. **1852** *Harper's Mag.* V. 188/1 A low balcony, now covered with a rough awning. **1870** *Scribner's Mo.* I. 124 A news-stand shaded by a red-fringed and white and blue striped awning. **1884** *Century Mag.* Oct. 879 The street [in Washington], with all its awnings out, was sultry, almost Oriental, in the hot mid-summer afternoons. **1906** F. LYNDE *Quickening* 27 The shops, with their false fronts and shabby lean-to awnings.

2. Attrib. with *cloth, maker,* and esp. *post.*

1702 *Essex Inst. Coll.* XLII. 161 A fine wrought awning cloth for the boat. — **1851** CIST *Cincinnati* 49 Occupations [include] . . . Awning makers, 9. — **1837** J. C. NEAL *Charcoal Sk.* (1838) 200, I'll have neither hand nor foot in hanging to an awning post. **1842** *Knickerb.* XX. 437 The awning-posts were dismantled of their drapery. **1884** 'MARK TWAIN' *Huck. Finn* xxi. 209 There was as many as one loafer leaning up against every awning-post.

***Ax, Axe,** *n.*

'In America *ax* is a very common spelling, though in England *axe* is still used almost exclusively' (W. '64).

***1.** The hewing-tool so named.

'The ax is of two kinds, the broad ax for hewing, and the narrow ax for rough hewing and cutting' (W. '28). See these and other distinguishing terms.

1639 *Maine Doc. Hist.* III. 201, I advized in my last for 6 axes. **1684** *Penna. Archives* I. 85 A party of men armed some with guns & others with axes. **1705** *Boston News-Letter* 19 Nov. 2/2 John Price . . . not being willing to proceed the Voyage, . . . with his Ax cut off his own Left hand. **1775** ROMANS *Florida* 147 The effects of the industrious ax and hoe in the hands of the Herculean sons of America. **1784** FRANKLIN *Autobiog.* 334 The man who, in buying an ax of a smith, my neighbor, desired to have the whole of its surface as bright as the edge. **1795** *Essex Inst. Coll.* LIV. 103 To the anchor works may be annexed . . . a suitable apparatus for making shovels, scythes, hoes, axes, etc. **1820** *Amer. Antiq. Soc. Coll.* 64 Then we delivered our presents, consisting of axes, knives [etc.]. **1841** E. A. HITCHCOCK *Journal* (1930) 52 They came and gave the Indian axes and the Indians wore them on their necks for ornaments. **1845** COOPER *Chainbearer* vi, The American ax! It has made more real and lasting conquests than the sword. . . . More than a million of square miles of territory have been opened up from the shades of the virgin forest. **1869** W. MURRAY *Adventures* 16 Wherever the axe sounds, the pride and beauty of the forest [=trees] disappear. **1904** G. STRATTON-PORTER *Freckles* 320 The clear, ringing echo of strongly swung axes.

+**b.** *An ax to grind*, a private purpose to serve; a selfish end to gain. {Hence in E.}

In allusion to the story in Franklin's *Autobiog.* 334.

1810 C. MINER *Who'll turn Grindstone* in *Life* (1916) 56 When I see a merchant, over polite to his customers . . . , thinks I, that man has an axe to grind. **1847** POLK *Diary* (1929) 203 He has always an ax to grind. **1854** *Congress. Globe* 15 Feb. 428 In passing the 'White House' . . . a few days ago, a friend, looking at its graceful columns and fine proportions, suddenly exclaimed, 'Axes Ground Here.' **1861** HOLLAND *Lessons in Life* i. 20 The Politicians and all that class of men who have axes to grind. **1871** *N.Y. Tribune* 23 March 4/5 The number of axes which are taken to the various State Capitols, to be ground at the public expense, is perfectly enormous. **1914** J. C. UNDERWOOD *Lit. & Insurgency* 82 Mr. James has been encouraged . . . by publisher's critics and readers who have axes to grind.

+**2.** A tomahawk or Indian ax.

1680 SEWALL in *N.E. Hist. Reg.* (1870) XXIV. 121 Major Pynchon . . . meeting with the Sachem the[y] came to an agreement and buried two Axes in the Ground; one for English another for themselves. *c***1689** S. G. Drake *Tragedies of Wilderness* (1841) 84 [The Indians] beat me again with the axe. **1826** COOPER *Mohicans* xii, The fifth and only Huron . . . sprang toward . . . Cora, sending his keen axe as the dreadful precursor of his approach. The tomahawk grazed her shoulder.

b. A native ax of stone or copper.

1705 BEVERLEY *Virginia* III. 60 Their Axes sharp Stones bound to the end of a Stick, and glued in with Turpentine. **1775** ADAIR *Indians* 405 The Indians formerly had stone axes, which in form resembled a smith's chisel. **1817** S. BROWN *Western Gaz.* 170 Bones, stone-axes, arrow-heads, &c., were found in abundance. **1834** PECK *Gaz. Illinois* 52 Stone axes and mallets, and other antiquities, are found in various parts of the state. **1872** *Amer. Naturalist* VI. 149 A majority of the axes found in New Jersey are water-worn pebbles. *Ib.*, In size, axes of this description vary very much. **1874** KNIGHT 195/2 Copper axes with single and double bits have been found in a *tumulus* near Chillicothe, Ohio. **1881** *Amer. Naturalist* XV. 686 The copper 'axes' so called (and very inappropriately, too) in no instances show any indications of having been put to any use as tools.

+**3.** (See quotation.)

1883 DE VERE in *Encycl. Brit., Amer. Suppl.* I. 200/1 The *axe*, or rather the *guillotine*, is made to represent the dismissal of Government officials upon the coming in of a new President or in case of some grave complication.

4. Attrib. with *blade, blaze, cloth, gang.*

1853 FOWLER *Home for All* 190 Father . . . took his linen ax-cloth for a strainer. **1894** FISKE *Holiday Stories* (1900) 86 As he reached out his foot . . . . an axe-blade crashed into his brain. **1901** WHITE *Westerners* xvi. 133 He must be pretty hot when his axe gang don't come any. **1903** — *Forest* xviii. 261 The fresh axe-blazes the Indian had made the day before.

Ax, Axe, *v.*[1] *tr.* To hew or cut with an ax. {1677–}

1838 *Yale Lit. Mag.* III. 86 You find him [Connecticut man] pioneering our population along the western prairies, and axing his way to the Pacific.

* **Ax,** *v.*[2] *dial.* or *colloq*[2] *tr.* and *intr.* To ask.

1789 WEBSTER *Diss. Eng. Language* 386 This word to *ax* is still frequent in New England. **1803** DAVIS *Travels U.S.* 318 But I [=a N.Y. landlady] never had the courage to ax him for the money. **1838** J. D. WHITNEY in Brewster *Life* 20 Praps you will ax what I have been doing this term.

‖**Axecraft, Axery.** Skill in the use of the ax. — **1843** 'CARLTON' *New Purchase* I. xx. 188 During the day, this winter, I took lessons in axecraft. *Ib.* 189 Tom had done in axery, what Horace pronounces in writing, the perfection of the art.

+**Axe-factory.** A factory for making axes. — **1833** *Niles' Reg.* XLIV. 359/1 Ax Factories at New Haven. **1847** HOWE *Hist. Coll. Ohio* 348 The village contains . . . 1 woollen and 1 axe factory. *Ib.* 420 Garrettsville . . . has . . . 1 axe factory.

+**Ax(e)-hammer.** A hammer-ax. — **1681** *New Castle Court Rec.* 476 Hee would beat him out with the ax hammer.

Ax(e)-handle. The handle or helve of an ax. {1865–}

1830 S. SMITH *Major Downing* 3 Ax handles dont fetch nothing. I could n't hardly give 'em away. **1843** 'CARLTON' *New Purchase* I. xiv. 109 The entire structure was . . . twenty feet square, as measured by an axe-handle. **1865** GRIGSBY *Smoked Yank* (1891) 191, [I] succeeded to-day in getting . . . Carr paroled to make axe handles for our squad. He made six good handles. **1904** GLASGOW *Deliverance* 161 The axe handle has broken again and I'll have to borrow Jim Weatherby's.

Ax(e)-head. The head of an ax. {1611–}

1865 MRS. WHITNEY *Gayworthys* vii. 74 In comes the old man . . . and calls for 'axe-heads. Six of 'em.' **1874** KNIGHT 196/1 The continuous blank, from which axe-heads may be cut. **1883** E. INGERSOLL in *Harper's Mag.* Jan. 201/1 Hurling their axe-heads deep into the gaping wound.

Ax(e)-helve. An ax-handle. Also attrib.

1730 J. HEMPSTEAD *Diary* 219, I made an ax helve for Gersk. **1788** J. MAY *Journal* 19 May 51 This day employed in making axe helves, hoe-handles, and sundry other . . . tools. **1823** COOPER *Pioneers* xxx, But I don't value the hollow piece of iron in your hand so much as a broken axe-helve. **1851** CARY *Clovernook* 129 His work. . . was the smoothing of an axe-helve with a broken piece of glass. **1874** B. F. TAYLOR *World on Wheels* I. ix. 72 A wine-cask . . . filled with oven-wood; to wit, wood split axe-helve size. **1888** EGGLESTON *Graysons* xix. 205 Hands calloused by axe-helve and plough-handle.

+**Axe-howe.** *Obs.* A form of hoe. — **1648** *Conn. Public Rec.* I. 492 An Inventory of the goods of Edward Chalkwell [includes] an axe howe, 6s.

+**Ax(e)man.** One who wields an ax in his work or employment; a woodman. {1878}

1671 *Essex Inst. Coll.* XX. 145 The time of meeting for ax men is to be by the Sun halfe an houre high. **1735** FRANKLIN *Penna. Gazette* 4 Feb., Firewards . . . direct the opening and stripping of Roofs by the Ax-Men. **1757** *Army Orders* 14 Twenty ax men of the Connecticutt troops to go over to the Island. **1760** *Boston Selectmen* 124 Nathl. Brown Master of Engine No. 2 applyd . . . to have a man added to the list of his men for an ax man. **1792** BELKNAP *New Hampshire* III. 76 Then follow the axe-men, who clear away the bushes and fell the trees. **1817** S. BROWN *Western Gaz.* 145 Axmen are sometimes obliged to erect scaffolds before they fall the tree. **1843** *Amer. Pioneer* II. 110 Colonel Brandt . . . finding him a superior axe-man and well acquainted with clearing new lands. **1861** *Md. Hist. Mag.* V. 303 The woods laid prostrate by our axeman. **1883** E. INGERSOLL in *Harper's Mag.* Jan. 200/2 'The first question . . . ,' said the . . . axe-man, . . . 'when we are going to fall a big tree, is where she'll lay.' **1906** F. LYNDE *Quickening* 37 Dabney had sent his ax-men to blaze the trees for his lordly boundaries.

+**Ax(e)-mark.** A mark cut by an ax; a blaze.

1832 *Louisville Directory* 107 Jacob Sodowsky . . . shewed a method of identifying the chops . . . made on the line and corner trees of old surveys, by cutting out the block containing the axe marks. **1837** BIRD *Nick of Woods* I. 98 The road . . . through this noble forest was . . . a mere path, designated, where the wood was open, by blazes or axe-marks on the trees. **1845** SIMMS *Wigwam & Cabin* 79 A race [of frontiers-men] too often confounded with the miserable runogates by whom the first explorations of the country are begun, but who seldom make the real axe-marks of the wilderness.

Axery: see AXE-CRAFT.

Ax(e)-sling. A sling for carrying an ax. — **1812** *Niles' Reg.* II. 131/1 Axes, axe slings, muskets . . . have been bought.

Ax(e)stone. [f. AX *n.*+STONE *n.*] A variety of hard stone from which the American Indians made stone axes. {1811–} — **1832** WILLIAMSON *Maine* I. 179 Axestone took its name from the circumstance of being used by the natives in lieu of iron, for edge-tools, such as axes, chisels and gouges.

* **Axletree.** Also †**axel-, axltree.** A cross-bar of a wagon, cart, etc., on the ends of which the wheels turn; †also, the axle of a grindstone.

1634 *N.H. Doc. & Rec.* I. 94 One grind-stone with iron handle and axltree. **1729** J. HEMPSTEAD *Diary* 215, I finisht the axletree foren[oon] & went to Court aftern[oon]. **1770** *Md. Hist. Mag.* XII. 353, I shall send them . . . with a carriage, that is upon an axel tree. **1784** CUTLER in *Mem. Academy* I. 471 The wood [of the locust tree is] . . . esteemed preferable for carriage axletrees. **1813** *Niles' Reg.* III. Add. 4/2 The wheels [were] fixed with wooden axletrees. **1849** PARKMAN *Oregon Trail* 43 Our English companions broke the axle-tree of their wagon, and down came the whole cumbrous machine. **1862** MCCLELLAN in *Own Story* 402 The guns sink up to their axle-trees. **1873** HOLLAND *A. Bonnicastle* iii, My little trunk was to be attached by straps to the axletree [of a chaise].

Axminster. [*Axminster*, Devon, E.] Designating a make of carpet 'with a flax or jute chain and a woolen or worsted filling which is formed into a pile' (Knight). {1818–} — **1852** MITCHELL *Dream Life* viii. 188 Libraries with . . . soft Axminster carpets. **1865** STOWE *House & Home P.* 99 No child is ever stimulated to draw or read by an Axminster carpet or a carved centre-table.

+**Ax-pin.** *Obs.* [f. E. (now dial.) *ax* 'axle.' Cf. EX-PIN.] An axle-pin. — **1659** *Essex Probate Rec.* I. 291 Quarter part of a harrow, linspins, axpins, washers.

* **Aye, Ay.** An affirmative response or vote. {1669–}

'The regular word used in voting "yes" in Congress. . . . The official terms, as in the Constitution, are *yea* and *nay;* but the more sonorous *aye* and *no* are preferred in making response' (*Cent.*).

1777 *Journals Cont. Congress* VIII. 676 If any member chooses to have the ayes and nayes taken upon any question, he shall move for the same [etc.]. **1778** *Ib.* X. 115 New Hampshire—Mr. Frost, ay; . . . Delaware,—Mr. M'Kean, ay. **1789** MACLAY *Deb. Senate* 122 Seven heads . . . were stated at the end of the paper, which the Senate were to give their advice and consent to. They were so framed that this could be done by aye or no. **1789** *Ann. 1st Congress* I. 336 The question was . . . passed in the affirmative: ayes 24, noes 22. **1804** *Essex Inst. Coll.* XXXIX. 327 The vote stood ays 73—nays 32. **1812** *Niles' Reg.* I. 376/2 The ayes and noes were called—yeas 96.—nays 25. **1863** WHITMAN *Diary* (1904) 49 At this moment the clerk is calling the ayes and noes. **1886** LOGAN *Great Conspiracy* 611 Governor English . . . responded with a clear-cut 'aye' on the passage of the Resolution. *Ib.*, When Ganson . . . and other Democrats, voted 'aye,' the applause was renewed.

Ayrshire. [*Ayrshire*, Scotland]. One of a breed of horned cattle that originated in the county of Ayr, valued for dairy farming. Orig. and occas. *Ayrshire cattle.* {Also E.}

1856 *Rep. Comm. Patents: Agric.* 24 Recently the Ayrshires have been introduced. *Ib.*, The Short-horns, Ayrshires, and Alderneys are considered the best for dairy purposes. **1865** *Atlantic Mo.* XV. 670/2 He had two beautiful Ayrshires, . . . clean heads, shining skins, and good milkers. **1868** *Conn. Bd. Agric. Rep.* 143 Is it then to be wondered at that the Ayrshires should be of unequaled excellence for dairy purposes? **1876** *Ill. Dep. Agric. Trans.* XIII. 322 A letter of Gov. Lincoln . . . in the *Union Agriculturist*, for 1841, shows that the former sent some crosses of Ayrshire and Short Horn cattle to a son in Alton that year, which was perhaps the first introduction of Ayrshire blood even in a diluted state.

+**Ayuntamiento.** *S.W.* [Sp.] The magistracy or administrative body of a town or city under Spanish jurisdiction; a town council.

1831 DEWEES *Letters fr. Texas* XV. 140 If, after two years from the date of the concession, the colonists should not have cultivated his land . . . the respective Ayuntamientos can grant it to another. **1836** EDWARD

Hist. Texas vii. 149 Those Ayuntamientos . . . shall consist of one alcalde, who shall be President, two Corregidors and one Procurator. **1838** C. NEWELL *Revol. Texas* 25 The next unconstitutional act of the military in Texas, was the annulling of one Ayuntamiento, legally established by authority of the Government. **1891** F. W. BLACKMAR *Sp. Institutions of S. W.* 189 Every town, of at least one thousand souls, had to establish an ayuntamiento.

Azalea. Also **azalia.** [mod. L. *azalea*, from Gr.] A shrub or plant of a large genus closely related to (and sometimes included with) the Rhododendrons. {1753-}

Native species include the clammy azalea or swamp honeysuckle (*A. viscosa*), the pinkster flower (*A. nudiflora*), the flame azalea (*A. lutea*), etc.

1785 MARSHALL *Amer. Grove* 15 *Azalea nudiflora.* Red-flowered Azalea. This grows most common upon a moist, clayey, gravelly soil. **1818** *Mass. H. S. Coll.* 2 Ser. VIII. 169 Among those, that flower in June, the most interesting are . . . the brilliant azalea or swamp pink, . . . and the mountain ash. **1846** *Spirit of Times* (N.Y.) 9 May 131/3 [He] has now for sale fine large plants of his new Hardy Azalias. **1868** BEECHER *Norwood* 92 A hardwood grove, full of wild azaleas and kalmias. **1869** ALCOTT *Little Women* II. xiv. 207 Amy looped her skirts with rosy clusters of azalea. **1878** STOWE *Poganuc People* xix. 209 The woods . . . were full of the pink and white azalea. **1880** *Harper's Mag.* June 80 The thicket of wild Azalea in the bog near by is crowned with a profusion of pink blossoms. **1901** MOHR *Plant Life Ala.* 71 A bushy low form of the common azalea or honeysuckle (*Azalea nudiflora*).

+**Azotea.** Orig. *S. W.* [Sp.] The flat roof of a house or other building, esp. as built in the Spanish-Mexican style.

1844 GREGG *Commerce on Prairies* II. 102, I perceived the *azotea* of the parochial church occupied by armed men. **1845** GREEN *Texian Exped.* xiii. 222 We ascended to the azotea . . . from which we had a splendid view of the city. **1850** GARRARD *Wah-To-Yah* xvii. 205 The spectators on the *azoteas* seemed scarcely to move. **1899** *Harper's Weekly* 27 May 523/1 Above all is an *azotea* of such admirable proportions and commanding such a superb view [of New York] that it is in imminent danger of being called a 'Roof Garden.' *Ib.*, Flowers and shrubs will be used to decorate the *azotea*.

***Azure,** *n.* and *a.* +**1.** A bluefish. *Obs.* **1720** *Broadside Verse* (1930) 161 Beside the Salmon, . . . Vast Shoals of Azures swim the Quinebauge. — +**2.** *Azure warbler*, the cerulean warbler, *Dendrœca cœrulea.* **1828** BONAPARTE *Ornithology* II. 28 The female Azure Warbler is four and three-quarter inches long. **1831** AUDUBON *Ornith. Biog.* I. 255 The Azure Warbler . . . arrives in the lower parts of the State of Louisiana, . . . breeds there, and sets out again about the beginning of October.

B

* **B.** The second letter of the alphabet.

1. As a brand or mark (see quotations).

1657 *Plymouth Col. Rec.* III. 112 Katheren Aines . . . for the blasphemos words that shee hath spoken, is centanced . . . to were a Roman B cutt out of ridd cloth and sowed to her vper garment on her right arme. **1671** *Plymouth Laws* 246 Such Offenders [=burglars] shall for the first offence be Branded on the right Hand with the letter B, and if he shall offend . . . the second time, he shall be branded on the other Hand and be severely whipped; and if either were committed on the Lord's day, his Brand to be set on his Forehead.

2. In the phrases (*not to*) *know a B from a buffalo's foot*, or *from a broomstick.*

Variants of Eng. *from a bull's foot* (1401), *from a battledore* (1609).

1832 PAULDING *Westward Ho* I. 101 You don't know a B from a buffalo's foot. **1846–51** WHITCHER *Bedott P.* xxv. 308 He didn't know B from a broomstick nor bran when the bag's open.

3. Used to denote grade or quality.

1886 *Harper's Mag.* June 93/1 'A' sugar is simply a term to designate the higher grades. . . . 'B' sugar is more brown.

‖**4.** (See quotation.)

1873 ALDRICH *Marj. Daw.*, etc. 122 Big Bethel and Bull Run and Ball's Bluff (the bloody B's, as we used to call them) hadn't taught us any better sense.

B.A. = Bachelor of Arts. See A.B. — **1761** Peirce *Hist. Harvard* 234 That Sir Sewall, B.A., be the Instructer in . . . learned languages for three years. **1885** *Cat. of Amherst* 9 The faculty [includes] . . . James H. Tufts, B.A. Walker Instructor in Mathematics. Ephraim L. Wood, B.A. Instructor in Latin.

* **Babe.** A baby.

In U.S. not so closely restricted to literary and poetic use as in later English. Additional examples are given by Thornton (also in Suppl.).

1799 *Gazette U.S.* 18 Oct. (Th.), Two bundles new babe clothes. **1816** *Mass. Spy* 24 Jan. (Th.), She was entombed with a babe in her arms. **1827** *Western Monthly Review* I. 74 She carried her babe, appended to her back, after the fashion of our Indians. **1861** NORTON *Army Lett.* 35 One was a babe and the eldest only nine. **1881** *Reinbeck* (Iowa) *Times* 6 Jan. 1/2 A few days ago the twin babes of Wm. and Fannie Johnson were frozen to death.

b. *pl.* 'The name of a set of Baltimore rowdies' (B. '59).

+**Baby act.** *To plead the baby act*, to set up a plea of legal infancy as a defence.

1873 *Congress. Globe* 26 Feb., App. 191/1 The gentleman from Ohio . . . did not plead ignorance or the baby act. **1888** *Congress. Rec.* 18 Aug., App. 440/1 [Mr. S. S. Cox] admits the authorship of that infamous work the 'Buckeye Abroad,' but pleads the baby act and says he was a boy when he wrote it. **1894** *Advance* (Chicago) 12 April, Had Gov. Tillman pleaded the baby act, . . . it would have been the directest way to encourage all kinds of lawlessness. **1901** *Forum* Jan. 592 One minute reading the riot act of manly independence, and the next pleading the baby act of thoughtless irresponsibility. **1904** SMITH *Promoters* xv. 229 That's business honor, and anything else is the baby act.

Baby-blue. A pale shade of blue. — **1889** CABLE in *Century Mag.* Mar. 748/2 The small, square manuscript sewed at the back with worsted of the pale tint known as 'baby-blue.'

+**Baby carriage.** A perambulator.

1882 HOWELLS *Modern Instance* xxiii, Bartley pushed Flavia about the sunny pavements in a baby carriage. **1882** SWEET & KNOX *Texas Siftings* 48 There is a great deal of buggy riding but comparatively little pushing about of baby carriages. **1909** 'O. HENRY' *Roads of Destiny* 146 A bottle of peptonized infant's food in the possession of an occupant of a baby carriage.

Baby-house. A doll's house. {1750–1801}

1772 A. G. WINSLOW *Diary* 63 My Papa has promised me, he will bring up my baby house with him. **1825** NEAL *Bro. Jonathan* I. 31 You were pretty sure to find Edith squatting in a corner, like a big doll in a baby-house. **1833** — *Down-Easters* I. p. vi, A short story or two by Flint—or myself—in our baby-house annuals. **1843** 'CARLTON' *New Purchase* I. ix. 60 As neat as a little girl's baby house. *Ib.* xvii. 123 True, I make-believe, like little girls, playing baby house. **1847** C. LANMAN *Summer in Wild.* xxv. 156 You happen to see a little girl arranging some rocky specimens in her baby-house. **1859** CARY *Country Life* iii. 66 He peeped curiously about, pleased as a child with a new baby-house. **1869** ALCOTT *Little Women* II. I. 14 Do you know I like this room best of all in my baby-house.

+**Babyhut.** *Obs.* (See quot.) — **1772** A. G. WINSLOW *Diary* 60 If she had wanted much to have seen me, she might have sent either one of her chaises, her chariot, or her babyhutt, one of which I see going by the door almost every day. [*Ib.*, *Note.* A baby hutt was a booby-hutch, a clumsy, ill-contrived covered carriage.]

+**Baby-jumper.** A device for supporting a baby and allowing him to exercise himself.

1847 *Rep. Comm. Patents* (1848) 47 Several patents have been granted for exercising machines, under the appellation of swings, baby-jumpers, &c. **1853** B. F. TAYLOR *Jan. & June* 214 Other babies tossed in a 'baby jumper.' **1854** [A. TRIPP] *Crests from Ocean-World* 365 Accosting them [Americans in London, 1848] I learned that they were true-blooded Connecticut Yankees, who were driving briskly their queer trade in the line of *Baby Jumpers*,—then a new invention. **1856** *Mich. Agric. Soc. Trans.* VII. 81 Wm. Phelps . . . [exhibited] baby jumper. **1870** A. B. EDWARDS *Debenham's Vow* II. 187 That sort of progress that is represented by steam-ploughs, baby-jumpers, and sewing machines.

+**Baby show.** (See quot. 1867.) — **1864** *New Mexican* 10 June 2/3 They awarded the highest prize at a recent baby show in Cincinnati, to a 'pickaninny'—a colored infant! **1867** W. H. DIXON *New America* II. 264 In a score of different places, people have founded an annual baby show at which they give prizes to the best specimen of baby-beauty.

+**Baby-tender.** A device for keeping a child in safety. — **1845** *Knickerb.* XXV. 406 Some stove, button, baby-tender, or other of the most ingenious mysteries of inventive man. **1849** *Rep. Comm. Patents* (1850) 210 Improvement in Locomotive Baby Tenders.

+**Baby-wagon.** A baby-carriage. — **1853** MCCONNEL *Western Char.* 282 A steam-engine would have been clogged by the weight of a baby-wagon. **1894** 'MARK TWAIN' *P. Wilson* ii, In front of Wilson's porch stood Roxy, with a . . . baby-wagon.

+**Baby-walker.** A device for supporting a child while learning to walk. — **1856** *Mich. Agric. Soc. Trans.* VII. 81 Wm. Phelps . . . [exhibited] 1 baby walker. **1874** KNIGHT *Dict. Mech.* 205/1.

Baccalaureate.

1. The University degree of bachelor. {1633–}

1702 C. MATHER *Magnalia* IV. Introd. (1852) 25 Among the laws, the reader will find the degrees of a baccalaureate and a doctorate, in divinity, provided for. **1849** *Cat. Wesleyan Univ.* 22 The Seniors will be examined for the Baccalaureate, four weeks before Commencement. **1907** *Elem. Sch. Teacher* 372 All of these four baccalaureates extend practically the same privileges to those who have obtained them.

+**b.** A sermon delivered at a baccalaureate exercise.

1892 E. A. TANNER *Baccalaureate & Other Sermons* 6 All of the baccalaureates of the ten years of his presidency at Illinois College are published.

c. Attrib. with *degree; address, discourse, sermon* (a discourse to a graduating class).

1851 *Harper's Mag.* III. 560/2 At Rutgers College the Baccalaureate Address was delivered to a graduating class of 18 members. — **1852** MITCHELL *Dream Life* 121 That proud entry upon our American life, which begins with the Baccalaureate degree. **1891** D. C. GILMAN *Johns Hopkins Univ.* 66 The manifold forms in which the baccalaureate degree is conferred. — **1871** [L. H. BAGG] *At Yale* 666 A third or more of every class were always absent from the 'baccalaureate discourse' and graduation exercises. — **1864** HOLMES *Soundings* 72 A baccalaureate sermon of President Hopkins. **1909** STRATTON-PORTER *Girl of Limberlost* x. 190 Every girl of the class would have three beautiful new frocks for Commencement: one for the baccalaureate sermon, another . . . for graduation exercises.

2. One who has the degree of bachelor.

1843 *Yale Lit. Mag.* VIII. 124 The talismanic words that transformed them from clowns to Baccalaureates.

+**Baccaro,** variant of BUCKAYRO. — **1850** COLTON *Three Years Calif.* xiv. 206 The lasso of our baccaros, thrown with unerring aim, brought him up all standing.

+**Bach,** *n.* Abbreviation of 'bachelor' (an unmarried man). Usually with *old.*

1855 *Knickerb.* XLV. 158 The President was an 'old bach.' of some sixty-five summers. **1856** STOWE *Dred* I. 11 As to the old bach—that smooth-dicky man—you see he can't be hurt. **1857** CHANDLESS *Visit Salt Lake* II. vi. 236 Mormons look upon a 'bach' with great suspicion . . . because they consider all men should marry. **1862** NORTON *Army Lett.* 127, I got in with J. H., a bilious, crotchety, quarrelsome old bach. **1874** J. C. MCCOY *Hist. Sketches* 14 Although young, Peryman is what the ladies term an 'Old Bach.' **1904** HARBEN *Georgians* 188, I . . . thought now was the time fer me, old bach' that I am, to . . . show them ladies I'd been about. **1911** LINCOLN *Cap'n Warren's Wards* xvii. 278, I'm an old bach, you say, and ain't had no experience.

b. *To keep bach*, to live as bachelors.

1879 I. L. BIRD *Rocky Mts.* 157 A cabin where two brothers and a 'hired man' were 'keeping bach.' **1883** EGGLESTON *Hoosier School-Boy* xvi. 106 Don't you know any house, or any place, where we could keep 'bach' together?

+Bach, *v.* [From the noun.] *intr.* To live as a bachelor; to keep house without the aid of a woman. Also *to bach it.*

1878 I. L. BIRD *Rocky Mts.* 156 The men don't like 'baching,' as it is called in the wilds—*i.e.* 'doing for themselves.' **1882** BAILLIE-GROHMAN *Camps in Rockies* 382 Burly pistol-girt miners, three or four 'baching' (bacheloring) in every hut. **1888** *Century Mag.* Jan. 412/2 He had always 'bached it' (lived as a bachelor). Next winter his nephew was coming to live with him. **1895** *Ib.* Sept. 674/2 That talk of Jack's . . . about his intentions to 'bach' it up there this winter, if he could coax his brother out . . . to bach with him. **1900** SMITHWICK *Evolution of a State* 93 The two men bached together. **1916** BOWER *Phantom Herd* ix. 143 Why don't you leave the hotel and come out here and bach with us, Luck?

+Bachelder, Batchelder, obsolete variants of 'bachelor.' — **1725** [see BACHELOR 1]. **1739** [see BACHELOR'S HALL]. **1795** B. DEARBORN *Columbian Grammar* 134 Improprieties, commonly called Vulgarisms, [include] . . . Batchelder for Batchelor.

***Bachelor.** Also †**ba(t)chelour.** (Cf. prec.)

***1.** One who has taken the lowest degree in arts, science, or other subject, at a college or university. Originally and usually = *Bachelor of Arts.*

(1) **1643** *New Eng. First Fruits* II. iv, Students . . . so were found worthy of the first degree, (commonly called Batchelour). **1650** Quincy *Hist. Harvard* (1840) I. 518 They, that expect to proceed Bachelors that year, to be examined of their sufficiency according to the laws of the College. **1674** SEWALL *Diary* I. 4 He should be suspended as to taking his degree of Bachelour. **1687** *Ib.* 181 Eleven Bachelors and seven Masters proceeded. **1725** Peirce *Hist. Harvard* 147 After which the President went up into the pulpit and called for the Salutatory Oration, and moderated one of the Batchelder's questions. **1734** *Harvard Rec.* I. 151 If Bachelours or Masters set an example of Idleness, extravagance, neglect of publick worship, or religious exercises. **1765** J. HABERSHAM *Lett.* 51 This I have also learnt from one Mr. Hutson, who took a Bachelors Degree at Nassau Hall the last Commencement. **1798** HOLMES *E. Stiles* 253 A congratulatory oration in Latin, by one of the Senior Bachelors. **1838** *S. Lit. Messenger* IV. 655/2 'Tis not a thing to be despised—A Bachelor's degree. **1892** *Univ. of Chicago Bulletin* IV. 5 A Bachelor's course, including an amount of Latin equivalent to that required for the Bachelor's degree in the University of Chicago.

(2) **1654** JOHNSON *Wonder-w. Prov.* 166 The present year 1651, on the twelfth of the sixth moneth, ten of them took the degree of Batchelors of Art. **1671** W. ADAMS *Mem.* 13. I was admitted to the degree of Batchelour of Arts in Harvard Colledge. **1720** D. NEAL *Hist. New Eng.* I. 185 The fourth [year at Harvard they bear the title] of Senior Sophisters, when they are admitted to the degree of Batchelor of Arts. **1766** CLAP *Ann. Yale* 27 The Rev. Mr. Woodbridge acted as Moderator; and he and Mr. Buckingham and other Ministers present, signed Certificates, that they judged them to be worthy of the Degree of Bachelor of Arts. **1798** HOLMES *E. Stiles* 13 The public examination of his class for the degree of Bachelor of Arts. **1818** *N. Amer. Rev.* March 429 A Degree of Bachelor of Laws is instituted in the University. **1825** TICKNOR in *Life* I. 356 It is . . . an unfortunate circumstance, that all our colleges have been so long considered merely places for obtaining a degree of Bachelor of Arts. **1855** *Harper's Mag.* X. 850/1 The graduating class at Old Yale . . . had a meeting the day before they were to be made into Bachelors of Arts. **1897** FLANDRAU *Harvard Episodes* 3 His absence [from Cambridge] rendered him frequently indifferent . . . to the outcome of examinations, to the degree of Bachelor of Arts.

+2. *Ohio valley.* The crappie, *Pomoxys annularis.*

1888 GOODE *Amer. Fishes* 71.

***Bachelor's button(s), Bachelor buttons.**

***1.** The name of several kinds of hardy annuals, such as the red campion, the yellow and the white ranunculus, the globe-amaranth, and the centaurea.

1832 HALE *Flora's Interpr.* 23 Bachelor's Button . . . Red or white field campion. **1836** LINCOLN *Botany* App. 100 *Gomphrena* . . . *globosa* (globe amaranth, bachelor's button). **1839** *S. Lit. Messenger* V. 751/2 Miss Bud with true feminine pride, had rendered bachelor hats and bachelor buttons contraband plants in her well organized flower knots. **1847** WOOD *Botany* 354 *Centaurea Cyanus.* Blue-bottle, Bachelor's-button. **1850** [S. F. COOPER] *Rural Hours* 127 You have . . . generally a cluster of pinks, bachelor's buttons, also, and a sweet pea, which is a great favorite. **1884** *Harper's Mag.* May 861/2 The Emperor . . . is a great friend of the cornflower (the bachelor's-button). **1896** E. HIGGINSON *Tales* 48 An' such flowers as she ust to have on both sides that walk! Lark-spurs, an' sweet-williams, an' bach'lor's-buttons, an' mournin'-widows.

2. *pl.* The seeds of the East Indian tree *Strychnos nux-vomica.*

1833 DUNGLISON *Med. Lexicon* (1839) 579/1 The seeds . . . have been long sold in the shops, under the names Nux vomica, Vomic nut, Poison nut, Bachelor's Buttons, &c. . . . For a long time, these seeds were used only for poisoning rats.

+Bachelor('s) hall. A bachelor's establishment. Chiefly in the phr. *to keep bachelor's hall.* (Cf. BACH *n.*)

[**1731** G. WEBB (*title*), Batchelors-Hall; a Poem. **1739** *Southampton Rec.* III. 13 The meadows on the beach lying between Coopers neck lane and Bachelders hall.] **1828** SHERBURNE *Mem.* (1831) vii. 136, I found him keeping bachelor's hall. **1835** [INGRAHAM] *South-West* II. 60 Here are congregated store-houses, boarding-houses, and bachelors' halls. **1843** *American Pioneer* II. 351 The same Indians . . . killed two men that were keeping batchelor's hall. **1852** REYNOLDS *Hist. Illinois* 174 His residence in Cahokia, was a medium between a 'bachelor hall,' and the staid mansion. **1857** CHANDLESS *Visit Salt Lake* II. vi. 235 Several of them kept 'bachelors' hall' together in a small house. **1881** *Harper's Mag.* May 879/1 Mr. Bob Beazley and his nephew Dick . . . had been keeping bachelors' hall together on the hill. **1887** *Lippincott's Mag.* Aug. 292 Let us pay a short visit to one of these 'bachelors' halls' [at Yale].

b. *transf.* of a beavers' abode.

1870 PINE *Beyond the West* 173 Several of them [beavers] called bachelors are sometimes found in one abode, which the trappers denominate bachelor's hall.

Bachelor('s) hat. A garden flower. — **1839** *S. Lit. Messenger* V. 751 Bachelors' hat with southernwood or old man, were conspicuous embellishments to almost every parterre. [See also BACHELOR'S BUTTON, quot. 1839.]

***Back,** *n.*

1. *On* (*upon*, or *to*) *the back of*, to the rear of, on the remote side of, behind or beyond. {1658, 1663}

1707 *Boston News-Letter* 10 Feb. 2/1 Our frontier towns . . . have been lately alarmed with apprehensions of danger from some of the Indians that are on the back of these towns. **1723** *Maine Doc. Hist.* XXIII. 148 We marched thro the woods on the Back of Wells; on the 10th we scouted on the back of York. **1734** *Penna. Col. Rec.* III. 564 So they acknowledged to several of the Inhabitants on the back of our Mountains. **1755** EVANS *Anal. Map Colonies* 15 The French . . . will turn their Forces, in Hopes of better Fortune, to the Back of Carolina. **1767** HUTCHINSON *Hist. Mass. Bay* iii. 281 Employed in marches upon the back of the frontiers. **1805** D. MCCLURE *Diary* (1899) 140 Walked up the hill, which lies on the back of the town.

2. *On* (*one's*) *back*, at the end of one's means or resources; in a helpless state.

1840 DANA *Two Years* xxviii. 312 He confessed the whole matter; acknowledged that he was on his back. **1862** MCCLELLAN in *Own Story* 457, I am still 'on my back' awaiting a decision from Washington. Burnside is still kept from me. **1904** *McClure's Mag.* Feb. 366/1 The employers of San Francisco are flat on their backs . . . ; when a labor leader makes a demand we give in without a word.

||**b.** *To turn on one's back*, to fall dead. *colloq.*

1848 RUXTON *Far West* i. 37 He turned on his back handsome, and Dick . . . blazes away, and drops another.

+3. In the colloq. phr. *to get one's back up*, to become, or to make one, angry.

Corresponding to E. *one's back is up* (1728–) and *to set* (1845–) or *to put* (1864–) *one's back up.*

1854 M. J. HOLMES *Tempest & Sunshine* xvi. 229 Her father saw she was in earnest [in her refusal], and replied, 'What's got your back up so high, Sunshine?' **1866** LOWELL *Biglow P.* II. xi. 242 Columby gut her back up so. **1869** STOWE *Oldtown Folks* xlii. 528 He's one o' yer dreadful ugly kind o' Christians, that, when they gits their backs up, will do worse things than sinners will. **1871** *Scribner's Mo.* II. 503 Those camels got their backs up at being employed in the slave-trade. **1875** STOWE *We & Neighbors* v. 65, I never opposed him openly—I never got his back up. You see, Eva, these men, if they *do* get their backs up, are terrible. **1889** FARMER 28/2 'Don't get your back up!' . . . a street catch phrase, at one time very popular.

4. *Mining.* (See first quotation.)

1843 *Nat. Hist. N.Y., Geology* I. 361 The 'back' in mining phraseology, means the mass of a vein that has not been removed, and lying above the galleries that have been opened. **1876** RAYMOND *8th Rep. Mines* 278 Between these [levels] a vast amount of stoping has been done, especially in the upper 'backs' near the surface.

5. The rear apartment of a 'floor.'

1885 *Century Mag.* Jan. 398 Miss Caledonia and Verona had the two second-story backs, and the third floor was given over to . . . Rose.

***BACK,** *a.* [BACK *n.* and *adv.*]

1. Situated behind some other thing or part, esp. **a.** Of outlying areas or their inhabitants.

See also BACK COUNTRY, -COUNTRYMAN, COUNTY, FARM, FARMER, INHABITANT, LAND, PARTS, SETTLEMENT, SETTLER, TOWN, WOODS, etc.

1634 in Neill *Virginia Carolorum* 119 He went not home as hee said, but to the back river. **1675 (1700)** *Md. Hist. Mag.* XIX. 368 At a point of a marsh at the mouth of Collett back Creek. **1700** *Virginia State P.* I. 70, I . . . have sent every way to search our ffrontears & back fforrist plantations. *Ib.* 71 Their ranging is . . . up to the uppermost inhabitants, soe down upon the back plantations. **1755** CROGHAN *Journal* 82 An Indian from Ohio . . . says that the French will . . . lay all the back frontiers in ruins this winter. **1770** *Md. Hist. Mag.* XIII. 67, I shall write to the back people by Mr. Roberts. **1775** *R.I. Hist. Soc.* VI. 17 This place . . .

is good land all to the back mountains. **1791** WASHINGTON *Diaries* IV. 165 The Convention ... made choice of a spot ... lower than the back members ... inclined to have it. **1817** PAULDING *Lett. from South* I. 82 Such [Atlantic States] as possess a back territory equal ... in fertility ... to the Western States. **1846** SAGE *Scenes Rocky Mts.* v, A dense band of buffalo cows made their appearance, from the back prairie. **1903** *N.Y. Ev. Post* 12 Sept., Rugs made by country women in the back districts.

b. Of parts of a house, farm, town, etc.

See also BACK-HOUSE, OFFICE, PARLOR, PORCH, ROAD, SHED, STREET, YARD.

1654 JOHNSON *Wonder-W. Providence* xxix. 65 The good man of the house ... was convay'd away by boate through a back lane. **1681** *Huntington Rec.* I. 318 My husband caryed it out a back dore and hide in the bushesh. **1704** *Boston News-Letter* 16 Oct. 2/2 A convenient back-dwelling house, with other accommodations ... to be lett. **1708** *Ib.* 13 Dec. 4/2 A convenient double dwelling house ... containing ... a back kitchin and wood-house. **1840** *Knickerb.* XVI. 255 There was the sound of a footstep on the back piazza. **1853** FOWLER *Home for All* 100 The square-house kitchen has an outside door, ... and a back-kitchen door. **1856** HALL *College Words* (ed. 2) 58 *Back Campus*, the privies [in College of New Jersey]. **1869** STOWE *Oldtown Folks* 160 There were spacious back buildings, which, joining the house, stretched far away in the shrubbery. **1871** — *Sam Lawson* 152 They'd seen her a walkin' out in the back garden. **1873** EGGLESTON *Myst. Metrop.* xxxvi. 307 When Mrs. Ferret came home from prayer-meeting she entered by the back gate. **1887** *Lippincott's Mag.* Sept. 421 We ... sot an' spit at each other, like two tom-cats on a back fence. **1894** 'MARK TWAIN' *P. Wilson* xviii, He said they were back-alley barbers disguised as nobilities. **1909** E. BANKS *F. Farrington* 142 Icicles hung from the back fence-boards.

2. Pertaining to past time; overdue, in arrears. {1525, 1841}

See also BACK-NUMBER, -PAY, -SALARY, -TAXES.

1779 *Mass. H. S. Coll.* 2 Ser. II. 460 [He] received 500 lashes, it being back allowance due to him. **1790** D. FANNING *Narrative* 48 All back plundering shall be void; as it is impossible to replace or restore all the plunder on either side. **1790** MACLAY *Deb. Senate* 231 The other back interest was to be funded. **1818** *Boston Selectmen* 1 Oct., That Mr. Tukesbury owed the town for back rent a sum sufficient to erect a story over the hall for bed rooms. **18—** *Harvard Reg.* 202 (Hall), A luxury ... which is sadly diminished by the anticipated necessity of making up back-lessons. **1845** COOPER *Chainbearer* xxiii, Unless he gives me ... a receipt in full ... for all back claims. **1850** N. KINGSLEY *Diary* 143 The back time of delinquent members ... will more than balance accounts. **1856** *Huntington Rec.* III. 431 To commence suit against Samuel P. Hartt for back lease rent. **1861** *Army Regulations* 246 When the supplies warrant it, back rations may be drawn. *a* **1909** 'O. HENRY' *Roads of Destiny* xvi, It's a long trail to follow trying to get back dues from the government. **1911** HARRISON *Queed* vi. 67, I gave you your supper at Mrs. Poynter's and afterwards collected twenty dollars from you for back board.

3. Leading or directed backwards; reversed, retraced; returning to the starting point.

See also BACK-ACTION, FURROW, LOADING, -SET, STRETCH, TRACK, TRAIL, -WATER.

1772 *Md. Hist. Mag.* XIV. 141 Let him ... specify the quantity that Hunters vessell may have a back freight.

+4. Pertaining to or connected with the back country.

1785 A. ELLICOTT in *Life & Lett.* 34 They expect in a short time to rival Hagers-town in the back trade.

***BACK**, *v.* [f. BACK *n.* or *adv.*]

***1.** *tr.* To mount or ride (a horse, etc.). {1592–1801}

1821 QUITMAN *Let.* in *Life & Corr.* 64 Nobody but myself has dared to back him. Perhaps I may get this nag for the journey. **1840** IRVING *Wolfert's Roost*, etc. (1855) 251 Seeing that it had something of a horse look, ... I determined to back it. **1889** *Century Mag.* April 899/2, I ... had not backed a horse for the year past.

+2. To carry on the back.

1840 DANA *Two Years* xx, We started off every morning ... and cut wood ... and after dinner ... carted and 'backed' it down until sunset. **1844** LEE & FROST *Oregon* xviii. 202 The Indians back heavy loads, confined by a strap over their foreheads. **1849** N. KINGSLEY *Diary* 46 We backed accross the space of a mile about 3/4 of a cord. **1861** G. W. WILDER *MS. Diary* 24 Feb., All turned out and backed rails. **1876** WARNER *Gold of Chickaree* 332 What do you think of a family of women and girls getting their own firing out of the woods, cutting it and backing it home? **1895** *Outing* Oct. 47/2 These hardy woodsmen, backing packs of from eighty to one hundred pounds each, tramped over the mountains.

3. To endorse (a document); to address (a letter). {1825– *Sc.*}

1829 SANDS *Writings* II. 136 By-the-way, you may as well back the paper and send what loose cash you have, besides. **1859** BARTLETT 17 To *back* a letter is Western for to 'direct' it. **1889** FARMER 28 The frequently-heard commercial phrase of *to back*, in the sense of 'to endorse.' **1902** CLAPIN.

+4. *To back and fill*, to go backwards and forwards, to recede and advance; *fig.* to vacillate or hesitate.

From the nautical terms *to back* (1707) and *fill* (1794) *the sails*. See also BACKING *vbl. n.* 1.

1848 DURIVAGE & BURNHAM *Stray Subjects* 174 The steam was well up upon both boats, which lay rolling, and backing, and filling, from the action of the paddles, at the dock. **1858** *Knickerb.* LI. 152 He wound up his wondrous performance [of dancing] by reeling gracefully up to the youthful countess ... and 'backing and filling' twice around her. **1875** 'MARK TWAIN' *Old Times on Miss.* iii. 55 Amidst the frenzy of the bells the engines began to back and fill in a furious way. **1890** *Harper's Mag.* Sept. 598/2 Nimble stewards back and fill from galley to pantry. **1903** *N.Y. Ev. Post* 24 Oct., The engine was backing and filling on a side track.

+5. *To back down*, to descend backwards; *fig.* to recede from a position one has taken up. Also *tr.* to make (one) recede or give way. {1880}

1849 LANMAN *Alleghany Mts.* xi. 90 When we got up about half way ... they all three of 'em backed down, and said I must not keep on. **1859** BARTLETT 17 *To back down*, to withdraw a charge, eat one's own words; as, 'I asked Jenkins, before witnesses, if he had called me a cheat; and he backed right down.' **1879** STOCKTON *Rudder Grange* x. 113 We're not going to back down. **1880** 'MARK TWAIN' *Tramp Abroad* xliv. 515, I said that as I had committed myself I would not back down. **1886** BRET HARTE *Snow-bound* 204 There's no backin' down here, Colonel Clinch, unless you and Hale kalkilate to back down the State of Californy! **1887** TOURGEE *Button's Inn* 188 Did anybody ever know J. Dewstowe to back down from a bargain? **1904** *N.Y. Times* 25 May 1, It is thought now that Mr. White wants to back down.

6. *To back out.* **a.** *intr.* To withdraw in face of difficulty or opposition; to refuse to fulfil a promise or engagement. {1818–}

1807 *Ann. 9th Congress* 2 Sess. 651 Our committee recommended to us to recede—to back out. **1815** HUMPHREYS *Yankey in Eng.* 33, I've bin up to the hub, and didn't flinch, ... nor won't back out now. **1829** WEEMS *B. Franklin* xxxii. 129 All at once [he] backed out of his promise to pay. **1834** PIKE *Prose Sk.* 25 Lewis had threatened to throw him into the fire, and would have done so had he not, as Lewis calls it, 'backed out.' **1845** HOOPER *Simon Sugg's Adv.* x. 129 Ante up! ante up, boys—friends I mean—don't back out! **1857** *Quinland* III. iv. II. 176 A man with the smallest amount of sensitiveness ... would have hastily retreated, ... but Hooker made it a principle never 'to back out.' **1862** NORTON *Army Lett.* 125, I'm not the one to back out because it's hard. **1883** EGGLESTON *Hoosier School-Boy* xv. 101 For a minute, Jack felt like backing out.

+b. *tr.* To force one to give up.

1835 LONGSTREET *Georgia Scenes* 27, I didn't care about trading; but you cut such high shines, that I thought I'd like to back you out. *Ib.* 28 Blossom swore he 'never would be backed out, for three dollars, after bantering a man'; and accordingly they closed the trade.

7. *To back up.* **a.** *tr.* To push or drive (a vehicle) backwards, esp. against a building, platform, etc.

1834 *Visit to Texas* xiii. 116 A small log building ... in the rear of which a cart was backed up on the Prairie. **1851** CIST *Cincinnati* 293 A four horse wagon was once backed up to our market, with two tons of strawberries, packed in cases of drawers. **1883** *Harper's Mag.* Aug. 400 The wagons were backed up against the walls.

+b. To stem or turn back.

1837 PECK *New Guide* 258 When the rivers [of Illinois] rise above their ordinary height, the waters of the smaller streams, which are backed up by the freshets of the former, break over their banks.

c. *intr.* To move or flow backward.

1864 'MARK TWAIN' *Sk., Killing Julius Caesar*, He then backed up against Pompey's statue, and squared himself to receive his assailants. **1887** GEORGE *40 Years on Rail* iv. 56 He had to back up till he could get momentum enough to carry him over the hill. **1903** *N.Y. Times* 17 Sept., The wind, swelling the tide, caused the water to back up into the cellars. **1906** 'O. HENRY' *Four Million* 5 'Twill be convenient in the way of greeting when he backs up to dump off the good luck.

8. *To back water*, 'to retreat, or withdraw; a Western metaphor, derived from steamboat language' (B. '59).

1867 'MARK TWAIN' *Letters* (1917) I. 124, I have taken the largest house in New York, and cannot back water.

***BACK**, *adv.*

+1. *Back of*, at the back of, in the rear of, back from, behind. (Cf. BACK *n.* 1.)

In common use from the middle of the 18th c. Copiously illustrated by Thornton (also in Suppl.) from 1774 onwards.

1694 *Va. State Papers* I. 44 We ranged on Ackoquane & so back of the inhabitants & the so[u]th. **1754** *Mass. H. S. Coll.* V. 120 The several tribes of Indians back of Pennsylvania ... will be entirely cut off. **1755** EVANS *Anal. Map Colonies* 29 If the Government has a Mind to preserve the Country back of Carolina, it should be looked to in Time. **1770** *Md. Hist. Mag.* XII. 354 Last Sunday & Monday exceeding hot & gusts back of us, but no rain here. **1775** *Biogr. N. Hale* 156 There is not one ... remaining in his lot back of his house. **1823** COOPER *Pioneers* xxvi, There's a place, a short two miles back of that very hill. **1850** G. HINES *Voyage* 362 The bay back of Cape Disappointment, they [=English explorers] called Baker's Bay. **1862** NORTON *Army Lett.* 71 Just back of me is a long bank of earth. **1868** *Putnam's Mag.* May 593/2 Back of the orange-groves ... are the rice-lands. **1879** TOURGEE *Fool's Errand* xxx.

191 Two children who were playing on the lawn back of the house. **1886** *Harper's Mag.* July 293/1 It was in a part of the city once truthfully, now conventionally, called 'back of town.' **1891** *Fur, Fin, & Feather* Mar. 195 As I am more familiar with the region back of Prospect, I will suppose he goes there. **1897** 'MARK TWAIN' *Following Equator* vii. 91 Back of it a graceful fringe of leaning palms.

b. In figurative uses.

1874 E. H. SEARS *Sermons & Songs* 40 The will . . . is the power that sits back of all his other powers. **1874** *Congress. Rec.* 16 June 5058/1 Is there anybody speculating back of this bill? **1884** W. M. PAYNE in *Chicago Dial* April 320/1 Back of the problems which it solves there are deeper ones left unsolved. *a***1904** WHITE *Blazed Trail Stories* ii. 23 His resolution to succeed has back of it this necessity of self-respect. **1907** M. H. NORRIS *The Veil* iv. 34 Back of his need of absolute rest, . . . Mr. Smith had another reason for having rented this property.

2. *Back and forth,* backwards and forwards; to and fro. {1839}

Illustrated in Thornton (also Suppl.) from 1846 to 1899.

1816 PICKERING 43 *Back and forth,* backwards and forwards. *Ex.* He was walking back and forth. This is a very common expression in New England; but it is used only in conversation. **1823** in *Trans. Ill. State Hist. Soc. 1910,* 173 Col. Kelly . . . walked back & forth for half an hour. **1836** DUNLAP *Water Drinker* (1837) I. 57, I am not one of your brook trout to be played back and forth with a hair line as her husband catches um. **1846** *Rep. Comm. Patents* (1847) 34 To employ a continuous sheet of it, laid back and forth . . . much above the thickness of the mattress when finished. **1865** MRS. WHITNEY *Gayworthys* 186 Didn't I lie . . . and hear you walking all the time over head,—back and forth, back and forth? **1893** *Congress. Rec.* Dec. 452/1 Through North River, at the place to which I am referring, the tide sweeps back and forth twice every day. **1907** UPTON SINCLAIR *Industrial Republic* xii, I would find myself comparing . . . the two eras, and transposing its leading figures back and forth.

||**b.** *Back and to,* in the same sense.

1856 M. J. HOLMES *L. Rivers* vi. 69 Causing grandma to wonder 'how the poor critters managed to carry victuals back and to when it was cold and slippery.'

3. a. Farther into the country. Cf. BACK *a.* 1.

1817 M. BIRKBECK *Journey in A.* 121 They begin already to talk of selling their 'improvements,' and getting farther 'back,' on finding that emigrants of another description are thickening about them. **1855** WILLIS *Convalescent* 63 With the freighting interests on the river, the lumber and butter interests 'up back,' . . . I think I have my share of political and county influence. **1907** W. LILLIBRIDGE *Trail* 160 But to take him clear back there . . . seems cruel.

b. Towards, or in, the area one has left.

1890 RYAN *Told in Hills* 28 'A Kentucky party, did you say, sir?' . . . 'Yes,' said Hardy turning toward him; 'relatives of mine from back East.' **1908** 'YESLAH' *Tenderfoot in S. California* ii. 22 Where one drop lights on you in a back east rain-storm, a bucketful strikes you in the same spot, out here. *Ib.* 24, I mean the real California sunshine, not a blinking, watery-eyed sun . . . (the back home kind).

4. *To go back on:* see GO *v.*

+**Back-action.** [BACK *a.* 3.]

1. Backward or reversed action, as in a machine. Usually attrib. and freq. *fig.*

1845 *Knickerb.* XXV. 406 The knowledge of some model, . . . some 'self-acting back-action saussage-stuffer.' **1861** [NEWELL] *Orpheus C. Kerr* I. 316 A double back-action machine standing in that chap's front entry. **1862** LOWELL *Biglow P.* II. v, The self-cockin', back-action style o' J. D. **1873** BEADLE *Undevel. West* 800 That sort of detraction has an awkward back-action about it. **1874** KNIGHT 205 Back-action Steam-engine. **1875** HOWELLS *Foregone Concl.* xiv. 240 A patent back-action apple-corer. **1889** *Harper's Mag.* Aug. 468/1 Don't you be tryin' no double-back-action tricks on me. **1909** 'O. HENRY' *Options* 58 The sheep had to be driven up to the ranch, and . . . Mexicans would snip the fur off of them with back-action scissors.

2. *Mining.* (See quotation.)

1877 WM. WRIGHT *Big Bonanza* 225 In that country [=Nevada] they have a way of hitching a second and smaller wagon behind the first, which second wagon is called a 'back-action.' Often as many as three and four wagons are thus coupled together in a train.

+**Back-basket.** [BACK *n.*] A basket for bearing on the back. — **1775** ADAIR *Indians* 90 The old [Indian] women pay their reputed prophet . . . a certain proportional quantity . . . of the new fruits, measured in the same large portable back-baskets, wherein they carried home the ripened fruits.

Back-board. [BACK *a.* 1]

1. 'A board placed across the after part of a boat' (W. '28). {1769-}

1854 *N.Y. Daily Tribune* 24 July 5/1 The scholastic mariners [of the 'Yale Navy'] repaired to the Pavilion Hotel, where the prizes were awarded. A beautifully carved back board to the Nautilus. **1865** *Atlantic Mo.* XV. 509 A . . . pleasure-boat . . . adorned by the builder with a . . . blue and gilt back-board of mahogany.

2. The tail-board of a wagon or cart. {1877}

1836 [J. K. PAULDING] *S. Nicholas* 84 The backboard of the wagon, ornamented with C. Y. in a true lover's knot. **1869** FULLER *Flower Gatherers* 147 He raised the back board, and fastened us in like a flock of sheep in a pen.

***Backbone.** [BACK *n.*]

1. The chief mountain range or watershed of a country or continent; the ridge of highest elevation in a locality; the summit of a mountain. {1684-}

1788 J. MAY *Jour. & Lett.* 29 These mountains I consider as the backbone of the continent. **1789** MORSE *Geog.* 51 The principal ridge is the Allegany, which has been descriptively called the back bone of the United States. **1816** U. BROWN *Journal* II. 359 Baker inform'd us, that Fairfaxes Stone . . . lay between what was called the back-bone & the Alleghany Mountain. **1817** PAULDING *Lett. from South* I. 150 The great chain which has been called with a happy aptitude, the backbone of America. **1822** J. FOWLER *Journal* 99 We came to the top or backbon of the mountain. **1838** *S. Lit. Messenger* IV. 292/2 It is not universally known that the most western waters of old Cohongaronta . . . rise on the *western* side of the great Backbone. **1849** LANMAN *Alleghany Mts.* Addenda 194 It appears that the valley of the French Broad is a trough, or depression, extending quite across the great back-bone of the United States. **1862** *Rep. Comm. Patents: Agric.* 154 The Rocky Mountain range—the great backbone of the North American continent. **1876** BOURKE *Journal* June 18 The numerous small bluffs and 'back bones,' separating the rivulets forming the Rosebud and Tongue from those paying tribute to the Little Big Horn. **1891** *Scribner's Mag.* X. 215 The road . . . re-crossed the main range, the highest ridge of the continental backbone. **1920** HUNTER *Trail Drivers of Texas* I. 150 When we arrived on the divide or the backbone.

attrib. **1873** MILLER *Amongst Modocs* xxix. 335 The Indian camp at the foot of the high backbone mountains of the McCloud.

+**2.** Strength of character; firmness; courage. {1865-}

Illustrated in Thornton (also Suppl.) from 1857 to 1912.

1857 *Republic* (B.) Backbone is the material which is designed to make an upright man. **1859** BARTLETT 17 *Backbone,* moral stamina. . . . A figurative expression recently much used in political writings. **1865** STOWE *House & Home P.* 19, I mentally resolved on opposing a great force of what our politicians call backbone to this pretty domestic conspiracy. **1871** S. HALE *Lett.* 70, I have *volumes* to write you, but no time and backbone since the fair. **1887** WILKINS *Humble Romance* 354 Nancy never had any backbone.

+**3.** *The Backbone Company,* 'the New Orleans, Baton Rouge, and Vicksburg R.R. Co.' (Th.).

1884 *Congress. Rec.* June 5639/2 Here was the grant to the Backbone company; the five years' limit had about expired. *Ib.* 5645/2 The Backbone people were unable . . . to construct their road. *Ib.* 5695 The vote by which the Backbone Railroad land-grant bill had failed to pass.

+**Back-cap,** *n. slang.* [BACK *a.*] *To give one a back-cap,* to disclose something to one's detriment; to run down, speak in depreciation of. — **1883** 'MARK TWAIN' *Life on Miss.* lii, Now I didn't fear no one giving me a back cap (exposing his past life) & running me off the job.

+**Back-cap,** *v. slang.* [f. prec.] *tr.* (See prec. and quot. 1889.) — **1889** *Cent., Backcap,* to depreciate or disparage. (U.S. slang.) **1891** *Boston Sunday Herald* 20 Sept. 4/5 Do you think you wouldn't say something that would backcap me? **1896** G. ADE *Artie* i. 7 Mrs. Morton got me a good seat and then backcapped the show a little before it opened up. *Ib.* xi. 99, I don't want to back-cap her.

+**Back country.** [BACK *a.* 1 a.]

1. The undeveloped or only partially developed districts lying to the rear of a peopled area.

1755 WASHINGTON *Let. to R. Orme* 2 April, I herewith send you a small map of the back country. **1771** J. HABERSHAM *Letters* 122 This Town has sometimes been almost impassible on foot and I suppose it must have been equally so in the back country. **1777** *Virginia State P.* I. 290 The people of Virginia had a right to the back country derived from their charter. **1784** J. SMYTH *Tour U.S.* II. 142, I agreed to accompany him on his return to the back country. **1790** D. FANNING *Narr.* 4 On the 1st of July, the Indians came down into the back country of South Carolina, and killed several families. **1813** *Niles' Reg.* IV. 401/1 The Creeks . . . surrounded by thick settlements of whites, without a back country to fly to, must be destroyed. **1820** *Ann. 16th Congress* 2 Sess., App. 1492 By clearing the rich and extensive forests of our back country, now lying useless. **1831** PECK *Guide* 292 It . . . has an abundance of excellent water, and a back country as range for stock. **1851** *S. Lit. Messenger* XVII. 687/2 The enterprise of man has extended the back country of New York from the sea to the lakes. **1876** *Congress. Rec.* 26 Jan. 668/2 West Point for all practical purposes is an isolated place. There is no back country to speak of. **1900** STOCKTON *Afield & Afloat* 35 They strolled on the beach, they took long walks in the back country.

b. In the plural. *Obs.*

1789 *Ann. 1st Congress* I. 169 How comes it, if the other articles are equally consumed in the back countries, that gentlemen did not urge the argument of expense on transportation? **1808** in *Niles' Reg.* XV. 57/1 The farmers of the back countries.

2. *attrib.* Constituting, belonging to, characteristic of, the 'back country.'

1787 in *Amer. Museum* (1789) II. *Chron.* 1/2 The back country people have killed three hundred Indians. **1800** *Raleigh* (N.C.) *Register* 8 July, Its policy is far from being apparent to a Back Country Farmer. **1806** *Ann. 9th Congress* 1 Sess. 1043 The first class . . . consists of back-country gentlemen, who live inland, all along from New Hampshire to Georgia. **1831** BUTTRICK *Travels* 79 Two wharves [were built] for the accommodation of the back country traders. **1847** HOWE *Ohio* 44 The internal improvement system of the state . . . has diverted the back country trade into other channels. **1863** MITCHELL *My Farm* 209 These back-country gentlemen have their families . . . educated. **1872** EGGLESTON *Hoosier Schoolm.* 5 It has been in my mind . . . to do something toward describing life in the back-country districts. **1887** *Harper's Mag.* Jan. 328/1 In a back-country town . . . there chanced to die one of the members of the community. **1895** *Century Mag.* July 323/1 To make this New Jersey holiday, assemble a thousand back-country vehicles, of all sorts.

+**Back-countryman.** [f. prec.] One living in, or coming from, the back country. — **1796** *Gazette U.S.* (Phil.) 19 Nov. (Th.), A new ballet dance, called the back countryman, or the new settlers. **1845** SIMMS *Wigwam & Cabin* I. 22 The boatman, who . . . knew by his dialect and dress that he was a back-countryman, came to his relief.

+**Back county.** [BACK *a.* 1 a.] A county lying to the rear of other counties or in the inland part of a state.

1755 FRANKLIN in *Autobiog.* 397 The people of these back counties have lately complained to the Assembly that a sufficient currency was wanting. **1782** DENNY *Journal* 47 Beef brought from the back counties of North Carolina. **1803** T. M. HARRIS *Tour* (1805) 59 In the back counties of Virginia, every planter depends upon his Negroes for the cultivation of his lands. **1812** *Niles' Reg.* III. 45/2 The back counties of Pennsylvania are making the most honorable exertion to redeem the character of our country. **1852** WATSON *Nights in Block-house* 165 The settlements along the Ohio, and some of the back counties, were preparing . . . to release him by force of arms. **1904** SMITH *Promoters* xx. 290 The little book agent . . . was working one of the brethren from some back county in great style.

attrib. **1775** *N.C. Gazette* (Newbern) 24 March, It has in one of the back county courts become a matter of legal enquiry. **1788** *Mass. Spy* 11 Nov. (Th.), A back county correspondent informs us that an expedition was set on foot against the Indians the beginning of last month.

+**Back-down.** [BACK *v.* 5.] An instance of backing down; tendency to back down. — **1862** GRAY *War Letters* 35 The President's message . . . seems to me clearly a case of back down. **1867** HALE *Ingham Papers* (1869) 138 Whatever else Frye is, he is a brave man, and he has very little back-down about him. **1884** 'MARK TWAIN' *H. Finn* xxviii. 265 She had the grit to pray for Judas, if she took the notion—there warn't no back-down to her, I judge. **1888** *Cleveland Leader* (F.), To-day's developments [in a strike] are looked upon as a square back down for the men. **1894** 'MARK TWAIN' *Pudd'nhead Wilson* xxi. 280 It's a clean back-down! he gives up without hitting a lick!

+**Back-draw.** [BACK *a.* 3.] A drawback, disadvantage. — **1883** *Century Mag.* Oct. 815/2 There are great back-draws to the bee business, the irregularities of the flowers being chief.

Back entry. [BACK *a.* 1 b.] A back entrance, or entranceway, to a house.

1854 CUMMINS *Lamplighter* xvi. 129 'Then where shall I keep the linen press?' 'Can't it stand in the back entry?' **1855** HOLMES *Poems* 191 The visions of morning [are] . . . Gone, like tenants that quit without warning, Down the back entry of time. **1904** *M. N.Y. Ev. Post* 8 Oct. 1 Every farmer who had a spare room or a cot in a back entry was able to dispose of them at any price.

attrib. **1853** FOWLER *Home for All* 127 From the center of the room toward the back-entry door to a door into the entry.

+**Back farm.** [BACK *a.* 1 a. Cf. next.] A farm in a back part of the country. — **1904** WALLER *Wood-carver* 4 The driver . . . summons the dwellers on the 'back farms' to the rough box nailed to the guide-post. *Ib.* 96 Strangers . . . who have come to me on this 'back farm' in New England.

+**Back farmer.** [BACK *a.* 1 a.] The occupant of a back farm. — **1770** *Md. Hist. Mag.* XII. 295 It is a generall complaint, not only here but among the back farmers.

+**Back fire.** [BACK *a.* 3.] A fire made to check an advancing prairie fire. (Cf. next.) Also fig. — **1839** KIRKLAND *New Home* xxv. 204 The winds, though light, favored the destroyer, and the more experienced of the neighbors . . . declared there was nothing now but to make a 'back-fire.' **1913** LA FOLLETTE *Autobiog.* 344 Thus starting a back fire on the Democratic legislators who were doubtful.

+**Back-firing.** [BACK *a.* 3.] The lighting of a fire to check an advancing prairie fire by depriving it of fuel. — **1891** EGGLESTON *Faith Doctor* iv. 49 As he rose to go, like a prairie traveller protecting himself by back-firing, he said [etc.]. **1892** *Boston Journal* 10 Oct. 9/3 By back-firing, the people of Hitchcok yesterday saved their town from being destroyed by the great prairie-fire then raging.

+**Back furrow.** [BACK *a.* 3.] A furrow ploughed in the reverse direction. — **1858** FLINT *Milch Cows* 191 When arrived at the end of the piece, a back furrow is turned up to the potatoes, and a good ploughman will cover nearly all without difficulty.

+**Back-furrow,** *v.* [Cf. prec.] *tr.* To plough (land) so that successive furrow-slices are laid against or towards each other. Also absol.

1861 *Ill. Agric. Soc. Trans.* IV. 113 Mr. K. K. Jones . . . had his land plowed deep, back furrowed it in beds twenty-four feet wide, [etc.]. *Ib.* 202 There were worked streets, back furrowed or turnpiked, . . . traversing the fields. **1867–9** *Ib.* VII. 169 In the spring, before setting, 'back-furrow,' slightly ridging the ground where the plants are to stand. **1872** *Vermont Bd. Agric.* I. 71 In the fall turn the furrows against the trees, and in the spring back-furrow and turn them away. **1877** BARTLETT 24 *Back-furrow*, to plough so that the second and fourth ridge of earth made is laid against or on the first and third ridges; to turn the soil every other time reversely.

+**Back-furrowing,** *vbl. n.* — **1855** *Ill. Agric. Soc. Trans.* I. 425 Plow first out from the row on both sides, then finish by *back-furrowing*, so as to leave the row a trifle higher than the surrounding surface. **1861** *Ib.* IV. 392 The sod should be broken with a prairie-plow, the furrows turned inward, overlapping in the centre of the road. This mode of plowing, (called 'back-furrowing,') is always to be observed when the track of the road is plowed.

Backgammon. The game so called. {*c*1645–}

1734 in *Harper's Mag.* March (1882) 485/2. I also frequent the coffee-house, to take a hitt at back-gammon. **1768** A. MACKRABIE in *Francis Letters* (1901) 97 They have a vile Practice here [=N.Y.], which is peculiar to this City: I mean that of playing at Back-Gammon . . . which is going forward in the public Coffee-House from Morning till Night. **1788** H. M. Brooks *Gleanings* 108 Reeds for hautboys, Men, Boxes and Dice for back-gammon. **1818** A. ROYALL *Lett. from Ala.* xix. (1830) 46 He is a merchant and generally drops in in the evening to take a game of back-gammon with Talbot. **1836** *S. Lit. Messenger* II. 188 Quoits and back-gammon are the only games indulged in. **1881** M. S[HERWOOD] *Home Amusements* 135 People who are fond of games stock their table drawers with cribbage boards and backgammon, cards of every variety.

b. Attrib. with *table* {1789}, *board* {1820}

1759 *Newport* (R.I.) *Mercury* 23 Jan. 3/2 To be dispos'd of, a back-gammon-table, with all the necessary furniture. **1766** E. Singleton *Social N.Y.* 265 James Rivington imported . . backgammon tables with men, boxes and dice. **1789** MORSE *Amer. Geog.* 390 At almost every tavern . . . there is . . . a backgammon table. **1868** MRS. WHITNEY *P. Strong* 153 Our old-fashioned backgammon table in the corner. **1790** *Penna. Packet* 10 May 4/3 John Sparhawk . . . has for sale . . . backgammon and chess boards. **1838** HAWTHORNE *Note-books* I. 103 In the smoking-room [are] two checker and backgammon boards. **1880** *Harper's Mag.* June 30/2 In New York . . . we find women employed in . . . finishing back-gammon boards.

Back-handed, *a.* and *adv.* [f. *back hand* BACK *a.* 3.] **a.** Not straightforward; not open(ly) or honest(ly). **b.** Acting like a back-hand stroke; coming back on one. {1865–} — **1800** *Ann. 6th Congress* 832 The fourth battalion had been raised in a back-handed way, and not in the fair regular manner that had been pretended. **1842** *Congress. Globe* 2 March, App. 189/1 This was called 'the franking privilege,' but to him it had become a back-handed privilege. . . . It was no slight labor to superscribe and frank several thousand documents. **1891** R. T. COOKE *Huckleberries* 97, I think he'd ought to have told her right out like a man, not to sneak off backhanded that way.

Back-house. [BACK *a.* 1 b.] A house, or part of one, lying behind the main building. {*a*1603–}

1683 *N.H. Probate Rec.* I. 263, I . . . give her . . . liberty to make use of the other back house as she shall have need. **1694** *Huntington Rec.* II. 132 A parcall of land . . . running north . . . to a fence by a littell back house. **1738** STEPHENS *Proc. Georgia* 121 They slipped out into the town from a back house where they lodged.

+**b.** A necessary; a privy (W. '47; B. '59).

Backing, *n.* (See quotation.) — **1867** *Congress. Globe* 21 Jan., App. 60/1 What run now [in distilling, after the doubling tub is removed] are called 'backings.' . . . These backings are too valuable to be lost, and are placed back into the still, run through again and come out doublings or proof whiskey.

Backing, *vbl. n.* [BACK *v.*]

+**1.** *Backing and filling:* see BACK *v.* 4. Also attrib.

1777 *Essex Inst. Coll.* XLII. 315 He was then ordered . . . to Stillwarter, then ordered from Stillwarter to Benington. . . . This, in the salers frase is backing & filling, [and] makes but poor way ahead. **1841** *Knickerb.* XVII. 49 Ha, ha! that was well done, and turned out well, notwithstanding the backing and filling of the lawyers and owners. **1854** *N.Y. Herald* 15 June (B.), There has been so much backing and filling not only upon the Cuba question, but upon every other, that [etc.]. *a*1859 *Maj. Downing* (B.), A backin' an fillin' and wrigglin' policy will never fetch any thing about. *a*1861 WINTHROP *J. Brent* i. 6 But enough backing and filling. Enter Richard Wade—myself—as Chorus. **1876** *Congress. Rec.* 3 Aug. 5125/1 Notwithstanding all of his 'backing and filling' . . . his testimony . . . was calculated to leave the impression [etc.]. **1897** *Congress. Globe* 22 Jan. 1056/2 The Government [will appear] as . . . backing and filling, to suit the circumstances of the politics in the country.

+**2.** *Backing down:* see BACK *v.* 5.

1883 *Harper's Mag.* Aug. 465/1 There's to be no backing down. **1886** [see BACK *v.* 5]. **1888** 'CRADDOCK' *Broomsedge Cove* xxiii. 425 Longwood deprecated a 'backing down' from this source.

3. *Backing out:* see BACK *v.* 6. Also attrib. and as adj.

1841 *Knickerb.* XVII. 374 Nor would her offended dignity be appeased by the self-imposed immolations of *backing-out.* **1845** S. SMITH *Theatr. Apprent.* 149, I don't come from a backing out country—I must have a showing for the money that's down. **1867** RICHARDSON *Beyond Missis-*

sippi i. 24, I won't back out—not one of the backing-out kind. **1880** TOURGEE *Invisible Empire* v. 413 In explanation of the backing-out process, he says it consisted simply in not going to any more meetings.

+**4.** *Backing baize,* baize used for backings. *Backing bell,* a bell giving the signal to back a vessel.

1833 *Niles' Reg.* XLIV. 381/1 Backing baizes—Charged at 7d. sterling per yard. **1883** 'MARK TWAIN' *Life on Miss.* xxiv, The pilot . . . putting his hand on a backing-bell rope.

+**Back inhabitant.** [BACK *a.* 1 a.] An inhabitant of the back country.

1745 *Baltimore Town Rec.* p. xvii, That the said towns are very conveniently situated in regard to the back inhabitants. **1753** WASHINGTON *Diaries* I. 46 The whole distance . . . is at least 135 or 140 miles from our back inhabitants. **1755** *Lett. to Washington* I. 159 The blood & burning of the back inhabitants has effectually rous'd the Pennsylvanians. **1789** *Ann. 1st Congress* I. 169 The back inhabitants consumed five times as much as those on the sea-coast.

+**Back land(s).** [BACK *a.* 1 a.] Land or lands lying behind the more settled or accessible areas.

1681 PENN *Acc. Penna.* Wks. 1782 IV. 301 The back-lands being . . . richer, than those that lie by navigable rivers. **1726** *N.J. Archives* 1 Ser. V. 113 Coll. Hunter . . . [said that] some of the Back Lands had Pine Trees & thick Bushes, but did not say that axes could not make a path throu them. **1775** *Maryland Hist. Mag.* X. 317 Allen Cameron . . . came to Virginia with an intention to purchase back lands and intended to go to Henderson for that purpose. **1780** J. JONES *Lett.* 9, I did not get the copy of the report passed the day before I came away respecting the cession of the back lands. **1789** *Ann. 1st Congress* I. 153 Our back lands are extremely well adapted to its cultivation [sc. of hemp]. **1800** *Raleigh* (N.C.) *Register* 4 Nov., Also about one thousand acres of back land, which commands a large outlet of good range for hogs and cattle. **1805** *Ann. 8th Congress* 2 Sess. 1444 In this Message the President states, that Georgia had passed an act for the disposal of some of their back lands. **1842** *Congress. Globe* 10 Jan., App. 78/1 When this Government acquired title to the back lands, as they were . . . called, . . . they became a permanent source of revenue.

+**Back lesson.** [BACK *a.* 2.] At Harvard: (see quot. 1851). — **1827** *Harvard Reg.* Sept. 202 They have indulged in the luxury of 'sleeping over,'—a luxury, however, which is sadly diminished by the anticipated necessity of making up 'back-lessons.' **1851** HALL *College Words* 14 *Back-lesson,* a lesson which has not been learned or recited; a lesson which has been omitted.

Back line. [BACK *a.* 1.] A line marking the rear boundary of a lot or piece of land. — **1709** *Cambridge Prop. Rec.* 263 Voted that the high ways laid out & described by back lines in the several platts . . . be recorded. **1769** WASHINGTON *Diaries* I. 320 Run the back line of Spencer and Washington's patent.

Back-load[1]. [BACK *n.*] An amount that can be carried, or a burden carried, on the back. {1725-}

1806 J. ORDWAY in *Journals of Lewis & Ordway* (1916) 359, I then returned with a back load of white roots to the Encampment. **1823** *Mass. Spy* 3 Dec. (Th.), A black fellow was taken up on suspicion, with a back load of live turkeys. **1840** DANA *Two Years* xix. 192 Having cut enough [wood] for a 'back-load,' the next thing was to make it well fast with the rope. . . . Two good back-loads apiece filled the hand-cart. **1847** Howe *Ohio* 47 They plied their labors there only a week at the time, or as long as a back load of provisions, that each carried, might happen to last. *a*1861 WINTHROP *Canoe & Saddle* xi. 242 Sweet youth, thou shalt have a back-load of trinkets to carry to thy Miranda when we part. **1870** COZZENS *Sayings* 11 Off goes the hidalgo, . . . and toils home under a back-load of the refuse [vanilla] beans from the trees. **1881** *Century Mag.* XXIII. 3 Many humble travelers on foot, trotting into Mexico with back-loads of market stuff. **1895** *Dialect Notes* I. 328 (Jerseyisms) *Back-load,* maximum quantity of game which a man can carry on his back; as, 'a back-load of ducks.' (Coast.)

fig. **1872** *Chicago Tribune* 6 Nov. 4/2 The October elections were too heavy a back-load to be borne by a party not organized and welded together.

Back load[2]. [BACK *a.* 3.] A return load. — **1800** TATHAM *Tobacco* 56 On their return, each one makes it his business to provide for his family, and for such neighbours as he can conveniently serve, by the conveyance of merchandize as part of their *back loads,* or returning freight.

+**Back loading.** [BACK *a.* 3.] A return cargo. — **1806** *Ann. 9th Congress* 1 Sess. 619 If they were not to be certain of the back loading in returning, they would not take the gift of the flour on condition of hauling it. **1842** *Amer. Pioneer* I. 70 Little did the first advocates of this system think, that . . . up river freight would be mere back loading.

+**Back log.** [BACK *a.* 1.] A log, usually of a large size, set at the back of a wood fire in a fire-place.

Further examples (1788–1878) are given by Thornton.

1684 I. MATHER *Providences* v. (1856) 115 The spit was carried up chimney, and came down with the point forward, and stuck in the backlog. **1744** FRANKLIN *Acc. Fire-places* 20 When you have laid a little backlog, . . . slide down your shutter as low as the dogs. **1777** *Essex Inst. Coll.* XLV. 208 The 17, our people got 2 the bigest backlogs on fire that I ever see on fire. **1793** *Mass. Spy* 7 March (Th.), He found his companion lying in a large body of live coals, her head on the back log and knees on the forestick. **1825** NEAL *Bro. Jonathan* I. 33 [She] was watching the current of sparks that rushed up the chimney whenever the 'back log' moved or the 'forestick' parted in the fire. **1838** DRAKE *Tales & Sk.* 177 No tree of the forest is equally valuable for 'backlogs,' which are the *sine qua non* of every good cabin fire. **1845** JUDD *Margaret* I. xvii. 158 In the cavernous fire-place burns a great fire, composed of a huge green back-log, a large green forestick, and a high cob-work of crooked and knotty refuse-wood. **1855** *Merry's Museum* XXX. 171 An old fashioned fireplace, in which a few huge 'back-logs' were burning. **1869** STOWE *Oldtown Folks* vi. 61 The fire was built according to architectural principles known to those days. First came an enormous back-log, rolled in with the strength of two men, on top of which was piled a smaller log. **1873** MILLER *Amongst Modocs* ix. 117 We had rolled a back log into the spacious fire-place. **1885** *Outing* Oct. 52/2 It is so brittle that . . . a half-dozen strokes of the ax will sever a respectable-sized backlog. **1904** WALLER *Wood-carver* 83 A back-log of hard maple, the girth of a man, and red as a live coal to the heart of it.

transf. **1883** *Wheelman* I. 294 The roads seemed to improve, and, the back-log of raw eggs and milk beginning to take effect, the pace was improved.

+**Back lot.** [BACK *a.* 1 b.] A lot lying behind others and away from a road or street.

1805 *Raleigh* (N.C.) *Register* 14 Jan., Back lots on the same square. **1861** STOWE *Pearl Orr's Isl.* I. xii. 100 She resembled more than anything one of those trotting chattering little brooks that enliven the 'back lot.' **1869** — *Oldtown Folks* 58 The apple-trees in our back lot.

+**Back-lotter.** [f. prec.] A dweller in a back lot. — **1850** JUDD *R. Edney* xi. 158 There are the Gum-chewers,—all backlotters, and vulgar.

+**Back number.** [BACK *a.* 2.]

1. An earlier number or copy of a periodical or newspaper.

1812 *Niles' Reg.* I. 392/2 To reprint certain back numbers of the register. **1837** *Knickerb.* X. 3 Back numbers have been re-printed to supply Volume Nine. **1842** *Yale Lit. Mag.* VIII. 96 On hand, two or three sets of back numbers. **1846** *Spirit of Times* (N.Y.) 4 July 218/2, I dare say some back-number of the 'Spirit' contains a history of a voyage of this kind. **1888** *Nation* 9 Aug. 115/3 He needs to be thrice armed who steps into the arena, as Mr. Lowell has done, laden with 'back numbers.' **1900** *Boston Direct.* Adv. 2329 Back numbers of all leading magazines.

2. *fig.* A person or thing that is antiquated or out of date.

1882 PECK *Peck's Sunshine* 153 There is always some old back number of a girl who has no fellow who wants to go. **1890** *Harper's Mag.* Feb. 439/2 If Galen should appear among us to-day, . . . he would be told he was a back number. **1893** *Advance* (Chicago) 21 Dec., If [Russia is] thought of as belonging to Europe, it is not to modern Europe. It is a back number by several centuries. **1896** KNOWLES & NORTON *Baseball* 89 Pitchers who were sarcastically referred to as 'back numbers.' **1903** *N.Y. Tribune* 6 Sept., He was told . . . that the talk about his being a back number was manufactured by Republicans. **1910** WALCOTT *Open Door* ix. 105 The Jellison divorce is a back number, and you could write it all out of your head by this time.

attrib. **1883** PECK *Bad Boy* 131 It was just like a old back number funeral. *Ib.* 136 Pa has been reading out of an old back number bible. **1911** QUICK *Yellowstone N.* xi. 286 When there's anything to be done . . . repugnant to some back number criminal law.

Back office. [BACK *a.* 1 b.] An office behind the main one, or toward the back of a building. Also attrib.

1846 *Knickerb.* XXVII. 58 Walk into my back office, Mister, and if I don't make your hair stand on eend I'm a demijohn. **1898** PAGE *Red Rock* 164 Leech . . . had the paper in his pocket, and had read it to Sherwood and Moses and Nicholas in his back office. **1910** C. HARRIS *Eve's Husband* 141 No one recalls the little back office attorney in this formidable judge.

+**Back-out.** [BACK *v.* 6.] An act or instance of backing out; withdrawing or retreating; inclination or tendency to give way.

1832 PAULDING *Westward Ho* II. 136 He could whip his weight in wild cats, there being no back out in him or any of his breed. **1836** CROCKETT *Exploits & Adv. Texas* 18 Now that idea . . . was a sort of cornering in which there was no back out. **1841** *Knickerb.* XVII. 27 There is no back out in the captain, no how. **1850** WATSON *Camp-fires Revol.* 63, I didn't like it much; but there was no back-out in me. **1855** BARNUM *Life* 115 The man knew that there was no back-out in the character of Hack Bailey. **1888** *Boston W. Globe* 28 March (F.), Mr. Barber's back-out has not much surprised me.

Back parlor. [BACK *a.* 1 b.] A parlor or sitting-room in the back part of a house. {1759-}

1839 BRIGGS *H. Franco* I. xiii. 95 They were made one by a Roman Catholic priest, in his back parlor, in Orange street. **1856** GOODRICH *Recoll.* II. 145 The scene opens in Miss Lucy's little back-parlor—a small, cozy, carpeted room, with two cushioned rocking-chairs, and a bright hickory fire. **1860** HOLMES *E. Venner* xviii, The young girl stepped into the back-parlor, where she found the great pewter flagon. **1865** MRS. WHITNEY *Gayworthys* xii. 110 With that he . . . walked off into the back parlor. **1875** *Scribner's Mo.* Dec. 345/1 Ridding their minds of the belief . . . that a front parlor must be just like a back one. **1887** N. PERRY *Flock of Girls* 109 Papa and Mamma both came into the back parlor and sat down before the fire.

*** Back part(s).** [BACK *a.* 1 a.] +The more remote portions *of* an area. Also without *of*=BACK COUNTRY.

(1) **1698** THOMAS *West N.J.* (1903) 79 Great Eggharbor River . . . runs by the back part of the Country into the Main Sea. **1742** *Virginia State P.* I. 235 We . . . hath ventred our lives & all that we have in settling the back parts of Virginia. **1755** EVANS *Anal. Map Colonies* 28 The Land from the Back-part of the Endless Mountains, Westward to Ohio. **1775** in *Amer. Hist. Review* I. 301 The inhabitants of Northampton and other back parts of Pennsylvania. **1789** *Ann. 1st Congress* I. 158 The back parts of the State are obliged to haul all they consume. **1807** *Ann. 10th Congress* 1 Sess. I. 469 My meeting with a William Davis, from the back part of the State of New York. **1825** NEAL *Bro. Jonathan* I. 72 A supper and a table . . . such as are still to be met with . . . throughout all the woods, and 'back parts' of America. **1856** GOODRICH *Recoll.* I. 96 Some years ago, a young New Englander found himself in the back parts of Pennsylvania, ashore as to the means of living.

(2) **1775** *Md. Hist. Mag.* X. 318 A regiment to be raised in the back parts and Canada. **1789** *Ann. 1st Congress* I. 167 The people on the sea-coast pursued merchandise; those in the back parts raised cattle. **c1812** PAULDING *Bucktails* v. ii. (1847) 81, I've liv'd in the back parts something. **1850** GERRARD *Wah-To-Yah* v. 83 But we were welcomed to the 'back part,' in true feeling of hospitality.

+Back pay. [BACK *a.* 2.]

1. Payment for past time or services; arrears of wages or salary. Also attrib.

1865 *Atlantic Mo.* XV. 237 The immense collection of back pay, bounties, pensions and prize-money . . . is Special Relief. **1873** ALDRICH *Marj. Daw*, etc. 103 The Good President commuted his sentence to imprisonment for life, with loss of prize-money and back pay. **1875** 'MARK TWAIN' *Sk., Pleasure Excursion*, Nearly all the back pay members contemplated making the round trip with us. **1881** *Harper's Mag.* Dec. 107/1 'Back pay!' chuckled Sam; 'that's what's accumulatin'—back pay! Let 'em hold off ten or a dozen years longer, and I'll be swimmin' in back pay.' **1899** T. HALL *Tales* 187 It seemed to him that he . . . might draw his back pay just as though he had been at work all the time. **1905** *N.Y. Ev. Post* 29 Nov. 10 Nearly two hundred claims for back pay have been left with the consulate.

2. *Back-pay grab:* (see quotation).

1890 *Cent.* s.v. *Grab, Back-pay grab, salary-grab*, in U.S. hist., a retroactive congressional act of 1873 for the increase of the salaries of congressmen: an opprobrious name.

Back porch. [BACK *a.* 1 b.] A porch at the back of a house.

1840 *S. Lit. Messenger* VI. 734/1 He was led by the hand into the back porch. **1872** EGGLESTON *End of World* xv. 103 Once on the back-porch she turned to the right and stood by Cynthy Ann's door. **1884** CABLE *Dr. Sevier* liii, They passed by a garden path up to the back porch and door of a small unpainted cottage.

Back road. [BACK *a.* 1 b.] A road, esp. an inferior one, leading or lying away from the main road.

1788 WASHINGTON *Diaries* III. 444 Began a survey of the road leading from my ferry to Cameron, and thence along the back road by Mr. Lund Washington's. **1827** J. HOWE *Journal* 15 Off we set on the back road. **1853** 'P. PAXTON' *Yankee in Texas* 196 On a back road, or 'street,' as they called it, stood two very comfortable dwelling-houses. **1865** BOUDRYE *Fifth N.Y. Cavalry* 169 This morning early we retreated on a back road. **1887** J. BURROUGHS in *Century Mag.* July 331 The road is what is called a 'back road,' and leads through woods most of the way.

Back room. [BACK *a.* 1 b.] A room at the rear of a house.

1788 FRENEAU *Misc. Works* 120 We . . . are shown into a back room, where the Bachelor sits by his fire-side in an arm-chair. **1852** *Harper's Mag.* IV. 577/2 There was no door leading from the room where Ellen was, directly into the back room. **1860** HOLMES *E. Venner* vii, The tables had been set in a back room. **1884** *N.Y. Herald* 27 Oct. 2/1 [To be let,] Store, Back Room and Basement; rent $37.

Back salary. [BACK *a.* 2.] Arrears of salary, or salary for past time. Also attrib. Cf. BACK PAY.

1873 *Newton* (Kansas) *Kansan* 26 June 2/1 If the people of the old Bay State don't lay this model back-salary grabber high and dry on the shelf, then we are mistaken. **1873** *Sat. Rev.* 27 Dec. 805/2 Congress . . . voted itself a few months ago an increase of pay, with retrospective effect—a proceeding known to American journalism as 'the back salary grab.' **1906** *N.Y. Ev. Post* 26 Dec. 8 It is a disgrace to the city that he should be compelled to sue for back salary.

Back seat. [BACK *a.* 1.]

1. A seat at the back of a vehicle or towards the back of a hall, etc.

1829 SANDS *Writings* II. 148 He had therefore ample room wherein to adjust himself and his properties on the back-seat. **1855** J. E. COOKE *Ellie* 421 His affectionate solicitude to see the children wrapped up, warmly and comfortably, in the back-seat, was touching to behold. **1860** HOLLAND *Miss Gilbert* xiii. 227 The double of Mrs. Gen. Cadwallader took the back seat to herself. **1878** STOWE *Poganuc People* xxxv. 337 The back seat of the creaking, tetering old stage on the way to Poganuc. **1898** CANFIELD *Maid of Frontier* 176 We took a back seat [in the meeting], me and my girl did.

+2. *fig.* A place of inferiority or insignificance. Usually in the phrase *to take a back seat.*

1859 *Harper's Mag.* June 54/2 This menagerie of . . . red skins, whom a score of indefatigable Coopers and Longfellows could never raise to merit a back seat in the heaven of romance. **a1863** *Southern Hist. Soc. P.* IX. 133, I tell you, those able-bodied men who are sleeping in feather beds to-night . . . must be content to take back seats when we get home. **1866** *Congress. Globe* 10 May 2536/3, I would disfranchise every voluntary rebel in the land, and place him . . . 'on the back seats.' **1882** HOWELLS *Modern Instance* xiv, Will you manage the bargaining from this on? . . . I'll take a back seat from this out. **1890** RYAN *Told in Hills* 171 But I couldn't sing Chinook, and the other fellow could, and for many consecutive days I had to take a back seat. **1904** *Pittsburg Gaz.* 8 Aug. 4 This fad for the Pomeranian . . . has given the broken-nosed pugs a back seat.

Back set, *n.* [BACK *adv.*]

1. A setting back; a check or reverse. {1721–, *Sc.*}

1816 CALHOUN *Works* II. 170 It would give a back set, and might . . . endanger their ultimate success. **1873** *Newton* (Kansas) *Kansan* 5 June 3/2 The recent rains have given this work a back-set. **1878** *Congress. Rec.* 7 Feb. 823/1 We cannot afford that there shall be another financial backset. **1885** *Rep. Indian Affairs* 142 But amid all the backsets I feel that we may be very hopeful of their future. **1891** EGGLESTON in *Century Mag.* Feb. 550 The backset to his ambition made him more sleepless than ever. **1904** HARBEN *Georgians* 37 Darley was a growing place. It was gradually recovering from the serious back-set given it by the war.

b. A relapse during convalescence. {*Sc.*}

1880 CABLE *Grandissimes* ii. 17 If you don't mind her you'll have a back-set, and the devil himself wouldn't engage to cure you.

+2. A counter-current in a stream or body of water.

1860 GREELEY *Overland Journey* 274 One of our fresh mules was sick, . . . and we contrived, by dexterous mismanagement, to get stuck in a bayou or back-set of the Humboldt Sink. **1882** *Harper's Mag.* 612/1 Of course much of this was slack water, or the backset caused by the overflow. **1903** WHITE *Forest* viii. 94 Jimmy . . . who was incontinently swept over a dam and into the boiling back-set of the eddy below.

+Back-set, *v.* [BACK *adv.*] *tr.* To restore (ridges of plowed prairie-land) to their original position by a later plowing. Also *Back-setting* vbl. n.

1880 *Harper's Mag.* Mar. 531/2 In Dakota . . . in the fall the decayed furrow is reversed, which is termed 'back-setting', and then the harrow is applied to break the turf to tatters. . . . The cost of breaking, backsetting, and harrowing is about four dollars per acre. **1883** *Lisbon* (Dakota) *Star* Sept., Contracts for large or small areas of backsetting or stubble plowing. **1884** *Ib.* 10 Oct., Farmers are now very busily engaged in plowing and backsetting and getting their land in readiness for crops next spring. **1894** *Congress. Globe* 31 July 8047/2 In some cases it will pay to 'break and back-set' the roadway to kill out the weeds.

+Back settlement. [BACK *a.* 1 a.] A settlement in the rear of the main settled area. Often in pl.

1759 Franklin *Works* (1847) III. 420 These were to be followed . . . by a large number of Indians and French . . . in order to fall on the back settlements of Pennsylvania and Virginia. **1763** C. SAUNDER *Cruelty of Indians* 7 It was agreed . . . to dispatch three of their number in quest of some, to the back Settlements adjoining the Forest. **1778** CARVER *Travels* 18 Those Parts of North America, . . . adjacent to the Back-Settlements, have been frequently described. **1792** IMLAY *Western Territory* 1 It will afford me an opportunity of contrasting the simple manners, and rational life of the Americans, in these back settlements, with the distorted and unnatural habits of the Europeans. **1803** *Lit. Mag.* (Phila.) Dec. 168 Philadelphia carries on a brisk trade with the interior country and her back settlements during the severest frosts. **1825** NEAL *Bro. Jonathan* II. 78 The family were in a bustle, with some news about a rising 'away up, in the back settlements.' **1832** KENNEDY *Swallow Barn* II. i. 1 His . . . family has moved off, with bag and baggage, to the back settlements.

attrib. **1896** 'MARK TWAIN' in *Harper's Mag.* Sept. 527/1 That was only a mud-turtle of a back-settlement lawyer.

+Back settler. [BACK *a.* 1 a.] One who has settled in the back country.

1755 WASHINGTON *Writings* (1931) I. 150, I tremble at the consequences that this defeat may have upon our back settlers. **1767** *Chron.* in *Ann. Reg.* 122/2 These miscreants are . . . a terror to the back-settlers. **1770** *Md. Hist. Mag.* XII. 370 You had immediately furnished a Body of the Militia with Arms, and ordered them . . . to protect the lives & Properties of the Back Settlers. **1792** *Affecting Hist. F. Manheim* 34 [They] commenced their horrid depredations and hostilities upon the back settlers. **1803** T. M. HARRIS *Tour* (1805) 59, I had often heard a degrading character of the Back settlers. **1811** R. SUTCLIFFE *Travels* (1815) iv. 92 Notwithstanding the homely fare of some of the back settlers, luxury is making rapid strides among them. **1845** *Knickerb.* XXV. 298 A party of the tribe just mentioned came in July, 1724, to work their usual butcheries upon the back settlers of New-Hampshire. **1853** RAMSEY *Tennessee* 148 Charles Robertson had emigrated from that Province, and it may have been, was known to some of the disaffected back-settlers there.

+**Back shad.** [BACK *a.* 3.] The common shad when descending a river after spawning. — **1868** B. LOSSING *Hudson* 145 They generally descend the river at the close of May, when they are called Back Shad.

Back shed. [BACK *a.* 1 b.] A shed at the back of a house.
1789 WASHINGTON *Diaries* IV. 30 The size [of the houses] generally is from 30 to 50 feet in length, and from 20 to 30 in width, exclusive of a back shed, which seems to be added as the family encreases. **1875** STOWE *We & Neighbors* liv. 480 He had leaped out of a window upon a back shed, and thence to the ground. **1894** *Outing* May 104/1, I'd given her a little one [*sc.* room] at the end of the second-story hall lookin' out on the back shed. **1904** WALLER *Wood-carver* 54 Aunt Lize has been busy making sausage-meat in the back shed.

***Backside.** [BACK *a.* 1.]

***1.** That side *of* a space or building which lies to the rear of it. {Now *dial.*}
1639 *Dedham Rec.* 70 Upland lying upon the backside of his furthest parcell of medowe. **1643** *York Deeds* I. 3 A creeke . . . is on the backside of his house. **1654** JOHNSON *Wonder-W. Prov.* 112 Chusing rather to dwell on the backside of this desert. **1672** *Conn. Public Rec.* II. 176 The begining of a plantation neare the backside of Norwalke. **1704** *Boston News-Letter* 4 Dec. 2/2 Yesterday arrived at the back-side of our Island, a French Prize. **1727** J. COMER *Diary* (1923) 32 On the back side of Cape Codd we were overtaken with an extreme storm of wind. **1746** *N.H. Hist. Soc. Coll.* IV. 210 From there ranged along the woods to the back-sides of Contoocook Mountains. **1825** NEAL *Bro. Jonathan* III. 79 By the North, or 'Backside' of the town, flows the Hudson. **1856** GOODRICH *Recoll.* I. 337, I sit, as you know, clear over the back-side of the meeting-house. **1869** TOURGEE *Toinette* vi. (1881) 69 There were two of these false windows also upon the back side of the building.

b. With *of* omitted.
1653 *Suffolk Deeds* I. 265 With all my land on the backside lyinge betwixt Mr. Webb and . . . Hugh Gunnisons. **1714** J. HEMPSTEAD *Diary* 37, I was mowing in the foren[oon] & cutting up bogs at the back side the lot and the boys in aftern[oon] raking & stacking.

***2.** The back premises, back yard, or space immediately behind a dwelling-house {Now *dial.*}
1634 *Cambridge Prop. Rec.* 1 The constable . . . shall make a surueyinge of the houses, backsids, . . . and other lands. **1642** *Boston Rec.* II. 69 It's granted to Capt. Gibones, John Davis, and John Smith to have the marish on their backsides to the water side. **1650** *Conn. Public Rec.* I. 514 Any other goods left out in orchyards, gardens, backsides, or other place in Howse or Feilds. **1684** *N.H. Hist. Soc. Coll.* VIII. 184 He is confined to his chamber, though not without leave to go down stairs, or into the back side. **1701** *Boston Rec.* 11 That no person whatsoever shall carry . . . any thing that may be an annoyance, out of thier houses, shops, yards, back-sides, or any of the dependancyes thereof. **1890** S. HALE *Lett.* 246 Only this stirs the back side to any activity.

3. As *adv.* At the back.
1805 *Pocumtuc Housewife* 20 A pot of beans can be baking back side, out of the way, with the rest.

Back-sight. [BACK *a.* 3.]

1. The rear sight of a rifle. {1860}
1851 GLISAN *Army Life* 59 A . . . very heavy and costly gun, with an elevating back sight for shooting at great distances. **1853** *Ib.* 118, I now . . . use a rifle, . . . having a plain open back-sight. **1874** KNIGHT 207/1 Other back-sights . . . have been made very different in form from those described.

2. In surveying: (see quot. 1867).
1867 MARSH in *N.Y. Nation* 9 May 373 A backsight is a sight or reading taken backwards; that is, in a direction opposite to that in which the levelling party is proceeding. **1882** FOOTE *Led-Horse Claim* vi. 101 The flag was placed here for what is called a 'back-sight,' to insure keeping the line ahead straight.

+**Backslope.** A font of type in which the letters slope backwards. — **1835** [H. C. TODD] *Notes* 14 A [printing] type called backslope is much used in the city [N.Y.]. **1869** *Bruce's Printing Types* 3 Job Fonts [of type include] . . . Backslope. **1907** *Types of the De Vinne Press* 337 Backslope can be used properly in a list of names of persons or of places in narrow columns [etc.]. *Ib.*, These Backslopes are not totally acceptable with the Roman types that have stems of upright lines.

+**Back stamping.** (See quotation.) — **1887** *Postal Laws & Reg.* 232 Back stamping.—Every postmaster, upon receipt of the mail, will immediately place the postmark of his office upon the back of every letter therein received, showing the date and hour of the day when the letter was received.

Backstay. [BACK *a.* 1.] A stay or rope 'running from a masthead to the vessel's side, slanting a little abaft' (Dana). {1626-}
To bring on backstays, to turn the sails so that they present no surface to the wind. (Obs. Eng. *abackstays, astays.*)
1650 *Mass. H. S. Coll.* 4 Ser. VI. 280 Mr. Throck: being a leage the formost, met vpon Point Judith with a gust from the souwest, which brought him on backstaues [*sic*], laid his vessell on one side. **1787** FRENEAU *Misc. Works* 419 For your back-stays and bob-stays I care not a pin. **1827** COOPER *Red Rover* III. iv. 102 What is this I see hereaway, atween the backstay and the vang? **1838** — *Homeward B.* xxviii, Here the mate returned, . . . leaped upon the rigging, and thence upon a back-stay. **1851** MELVILLE *Moby Dick* cxxxiv, The men, like shooting stars, slid to the deck, by the isolated backstays and halyards. **1890** *Century Mag.* Dec. 220 He did board her from our foreyard and slid down on one of her backstays. **1897** *Outing* July 358/2 As he begins to tend backstay, and occasionally to give a pull at the main or jib sheet, . . . his confidence increases.

+**Back-stick.** [BACK *a.* 1.] A large stick placed above a back-log on a hearth.
1852 *Harper's Mag.* VI. 132 What cared we for that, as we sat by the old-fashioned fire? Log, back-stick, fore-stick, top-stick, and superstructure, all in their places. **1859** COZZENS *Acadia* 167 Picton gave a great crunching blow with his boot-heel at the back-stick, and laid on a good supply of fuel. **1877** *Vermont Bd. Agric. Rep.* IV. 92 The boy would return to the wood-yard for the back stick and fore stick.

+**Back-stop.** [BACK *a.*] 'In base-ball, a fence placed a short distance behind the catcher to stop the ball if he fails to catch it' (*Cent.*) — **1889** REACH *Base Ball Guide* 142 Backstop must be ninety feet from home base. **1903** *Boston Ev. Transcript* 7 Oct. 17 Anybody who wishes to see the scores can find them painted up on the backstop of the baseball field at Agricultural College. — *transf.* **1890** H. PALMER *Stories of Base Ball Field* 46 Tom Daly was the greatest catcher . . . that the Chicago Club ever had, and a careful study of that back-stop's methods behind the bat to-day will help any young catcher.

Back strap, strapping. [BACK *a.*] A strap at the back of a boot. — **1805** in *Amer. Ind. Society* III. 368 Back Strap Boots, fair tops, 4 Dols. 00 Cts. Back Strappings the top of do, 0. Dols. 75 Cts. . . . Back Strap Bootees, 3 Dols. 50 Cts. **1806** in Commons, etc. *Doc. Hist.* III. 63 For making fancy boots, the sum of five dollars; for making back strap boots, the sum of four dollars.

Back-strap, *v.* [Cf. preceding.] **a.** *tr.* To beat (a person) with a back-strap. **b.** To remove a back strip from (pork). — **1807** IRVING, etc. *Salmagundi* x. 224 On his [=Crispin's] threatening to *backstrap* his adversary, the tailor was obliged to sheer off. **1865-6** *Ill. Agric. Soc. Trans.* VI. 639 Mess Pork shall be packed from sides of well fatted hogs, cut into strips not exceeding six and a half (6½) inches wide . . . and not back strapped.

Back street. [BACK *a.* 1 b.] A street lying in a back area or running behind the main buildings in a town.
1638 *Charlestown Land Rec.* 6 One acre and haulfe of earable land . . . butting south west upon the back streete. **1648** *Ib.* 99 The house and garden is bounded East by the back street which goes to the pitt where the Beasts drinke. **1708** *Boston News-Letter* 22-29 March 2/2 There is a convenient double dwelling house to be lett in the back-street be-north the mill-bridge. **1744** F. MOORE *Voy. Georgia* 114 Each family had a bower of palmetto leaves, finished upon the back street in their own lands. **1808** in *Niles' Reg.* (1818) XV. 51/2 A cheap aqueduct, of one arch, of 30 feet span, will carry the work across the creek into the back street. **1846** *Knickerb.* XXVIII. 111 The half-christianized youths of our back-streets. **1875** STOWE *We & Neighbors* ii. 27 We would also insist on . . . having a whole house to ourselves on a back street.

+**Back stretch.** [BACK *a.* 3.] In a racecourse, the portion farthest from the main body of spectators; contrasted with the 'home stretch.'
1868 H. WOODRUFF *Trotting Horse* xii. 122 On the back-stretch . . . Mr. Duffy asked me if I could ride it out without tiring. *Ib.* xiii. 134 The first sulky used broke down on the backstretch of the course. **1898** WESTCOTT *D. Harum* 282 What with . . . laggin' on the back stretch, an' ev'ry now an' then breakin' to a stan'still. **1903** A. ADAMS *Log Cowboy* xv. 100 He was speeding her on the back stretch.

+**Back swamp.** (See BACK *a.* 1 a.) — **1772** J. HABERSHAM *Letters* 213 You cannot suffer so much here or there, as planters in the back swamps. **1799** *Herald of Freedom* (Edenton, N.C.) 27 Mar., 2816 acres of land on the back swamp, beginning at a cypress on the west side of sandy or gravelly run, near the new road leading from muddy creek, to the rich lands of new river.

Backsword. *Obs.* [BACK *n.*] A sword with one cutting edge. {1611-1750} — **1650** *Conn. Public Rec.* I. 544 Each towne allso shall provide so many good firelocke muskitts and good backswords or cuttlasses, as the corseletts are they are charged with by this order. **1680** *Conn. Probate Rec.* I. 384, I give unto my son Job my musket and back sword.

+**Back talk.** [BACK *a.* 3.] Talk by way or reply or retort, esp. of a saucy or impudent kind.
1884 *Amer. Missionary* (N.Y.) April, There was saucy back-talk about 'preachers riding in their buggies Sunday.' **1888** *Harper's Mag.* Nov. 972/1 That'll do, my friend, I don't want no back talk. **1889** FARMER 30 'No back talk!'—A slang catch phrase indicating that the matter in question is closed to discussion; there's nothing more to be said. **1902** LORIMER *Lett. from Merchant* xiii. 177 That order for a carload of Spotless Snow Leaf from old Shorter is the kind of back talk I like. **1921** PAINE *Comr. Rolling Ocean* 33, I never stood any back-talk from foremast hands.

+**Back taxes.** [BACK *a.* 2.] Taxes for past time; arrears of taxes.
1788 G. R. MINOT *Insurrections in Mass.* 59 They completed an act providing for the payment of the back taxes in specifick articles. **1869** *Congress. Globe* 30 March 379/2, I do not like this changing of the laws to return back taxes which may be millions in value. **1898** PAGE *Red Rock* 218 The sum . . . was enough to pay all the back taxes and redemption fees on Mrs. Bellows's place. **1904** *N.Y. Tribune* 31 July, The Brooklyn

Rapid Transit was indebted to the municipality for back taxes amounting to several millions of dollars.

attrib. **1882** *Nation* 28 Dec. 544/3 The Grand Jury at Louisville, Kentucky, has found nine indictments against the Auditor, Back-Tax Collector, and Clerk of the Assessor's office of the city.

+**Back town.** [BACK *a.* 1 a.] A town in the back country.

1822 *Mass. Spy* 22 May (Th.), A gentleman from one of the back towns of this state. **1874** *Vermont Board Agric. Rep.* II. 444 The back towns are the only ones that export any appreciable quantity of timber. **1883** *Harper's Mag.* April 705/2 The prospect of an illness in that back town . . . was not alluring.

+**Back track.** [BACK *a.* 3.]

1. The track or path leading back towards the starting point or lying in the rear.

1724 *Lancaster Rec.* 230 We lay still and kept scouts upon our back tracks to see if there would any pursue. **1761** S. NILES *Indian Wars* II. 379 He that was appointed to watch their back track discovered the enemy. **1775** ADAIR *Indians* 346 One of our hunting white men . . . kept in their back-tracks, to trace them to their theatre of blood. **1802** *Balance* (Hudson, N.Y.) 6 April 106 (Th.), I must have been taking the course which hunters would call the Back Track. **1834** SIMMS *G. Rivers* I. 88 You know the back track to my house. **1840** HOFFMAN *Greyslaer* II. x. 28 They all united again, and trudged off as if to take up the back track once more afresh. **1850** GARRARD *Wah-To-Yah* xxiii. 275 Urging his horse in a full run on the back track, with three yelling Comanches at his heels. **1900** DRANNAN *Plains & Mts.* 504 After following the back-track two miles I found where the four mules had left it.

fig. **1867–9** *Ill. Agric. Soc. Trans.* VII. 422 The spring cattle trade had attained its climax, and was now on the 'back track.'

2. *To take the back track,* to return or retreat. Freq. *fig.*, to withdraw from an undertaking, position, etc.; to pursue a reverse line or policy.

(1) **1837** BIRD *Nick of Woods* II. 105, I'll take the back-track, and foller atter madam. **1842** *Amer. Pioneer* I. 430, I crawled off on my hands and feet until I got into the edge of the prairie . . . , when they raised the yell and took the back track. **1846** SAGE *Scenes Rocky Mts.* ii, Two of our party . . . wisely resolved to take the back track, and accordingly left for home. **1876** BURROUGHS *Winter Sunshine* IV. 97 Then the fox . . . , taking his back-track, fooled the dogs completely. **1903** WHITE *Forest* xviii, Two days we lingered, then took the back track.

(2) **1837** *Congress. Globe* 13 Oct., App. 322/2 Does he mean to follow them as my young friend from Tennessee [=Crockett] felicitously expresses it, 'by taking the back tracks?' **1857** *Knickerb.* L. 581 He has . . . a very praiseworthy aversion to taking the *back track*. **1869** *Congress. Globe* 26 Feb. 1606/1 We all have occasionally to take the back track. None of us are so proud as never to confess that we are wrong. **1871** *Harper's Mag.* Dec. 156/1 Now I don't think a man ought to go to the devil simply to prove that he isn't afraid to go to the devil. So I took the back track. **1892** *Congress. Rec.* 6 June, App. 444/2 You are arresting progress and taking the back track on civilization.

3. *To make back tracks* or *(a) back track,* to retrace one's steps. Also *fig.*

1840 HOFFMAN *Greyslaer* II. x. 28 After giving up the chase, I made back-tracks up the river. **1850** GERRARD *Wah-To-Yah* xix. 217 Things looked mity strange, an' I wanted to make back track. **1855** *Harper's Mag.* XI. 602/1 The bear couldn't climb up the steep bank, so he made a 'back track.' **1864** BROWNE *A. Ward, His Book* 196 So we shall hate to whip the naughty South, but we must do it if you don't make back tracks at onct. **1891** *Fur, Fin, & Feather* March 169 We reckoned upon giving the Englishmen their stomachs' full of bear before making back tracks to Custer.

+**Back trail.** [BACK *a.* 3.] =BACK TRACK. Also *fig.*

1847 Howe *Ohio* 202 They halted, and placed sentinels on their back trail, who remained there till late in the night, without seeing any signs of being pursued. The sentinels on the back trail returned to the camp. **1869** BRACE *New West* viii. 99 But we must be off. There's that darn'd mule on the back trail agin! **1891** RYAN *Told in Hills* III. ix. 254 You can strike the back trail as soon as you've a mind to. **1908** MULFORD *Orphan* xi. 132 One of his men . . . knelt behind a rock, his rifle covering the back trail. **1920** HUNTER *Trail Drivers of Texas* 128 The boss and I had a row and I decided I was ready for the back trail.

‖**Back-vine.** [BACK *a.* 1 b.] A vine, esp. a grapevine, growing at the back of a house or a lot. — **1851** *Knickerb.* Aug. 178 A large family of nameless flowers . . . between the 'house-vine' and the 'back-vine,' which creeps over its broad trellice, and suspends there, in long pendulous 'bunches,' its rich abundance of fruit.

* **Backwater, Back water.** [BACK *a.* 3.] The excess water of a stream or channel that is held or forced back by flooding or by a dam. {1629–} See also quot. 1872.

1654 *Southampton Rec.* I. 102 The said miller . . . ingageth to grind, notwithstanding the back water, soe long as the mill will goe. **1738** W. STEPHENS *Proc. Georgia* 162 They were mending the race for the back water to go off quick. **1783** W. FLEMING in *Travels Amer. Col.* 670 We could not cross Salt River lower on account of the back water from the Ohio. **1802** ELLICOTT *Journal* 15 The back water from the river also inundates the lick. **1816** U. BROWN *Journal* II. 49, [I] was obliged to pay . . . for ferry over on the back Water forced into said Gully by the River. **1834** BRACKENRIDGE *Recoll.* xix. 239 About half way we came to a stream, which, being filled by back water from the Mississippi, was not less than a hundred yards wide. **1850** N. KINGSLEY *Diary* 147 It . . . left a large space for the back water in the dam to suddenly go through. **1869** BROWNE *Adv. Apache Country* 251 The land is subject to overflow for many miles around, and is all cut up with sloughs and backwater. **1872** W. J. FLAGG *Good Investment* xxi. 95/1 Narrow lagoons, called 'backwater,' separate them [islands] from the mainland, and inlets from the sea into the backwater divide them from each other. **1873** BEADLE *Undevel. West* xxxvi. 767 Back-water from the Columbia often causes great rises, giving the surface of the stream a variation of thirty-two feet. **1883** *Century Mag.* XXVI. 420 Inundated either by a crevasse or by the rise of backwater on its northern side.

fig. **1902** HARBEN *A. Daniel* 136, I didn't honestly think there was a man in Georgia that could give me any tips about investments, but I had to take back water, and for a woman.

Backways, *adv.* Backwards. {*n. dial.* in related sense} — **1889** 'MARK TWAIN' *Conn. Yankee* ix. 106 A crab . . . couldn't travel any way but sideways or backways.

+**Backwood,** in attrib. use=BACKWOODS 2.

1792 BRACKENRIDGE *Adv. Capt. Farrago* xxv. 131 He thought it not amiss to make some inquiry, which by the by was rather an evidence of his backwood simplicity. **1820** FLINT *Lett. from Amer.* 189 The laying out of new counties . . . seems to be a gratifying duty to back-wood legislators. **1820** *Ib.* 207 His live-stock soon becomes much more numerous than that of his back-wood predecessor. **1836** T. POWER *Impressions* II. 165 These are commonly overlaid also . . . by a back-wood railway; that is, by trunks of trees packed closely side by side. **1836** *S. Lit. Messenger* II. 228/2 The oddities of a backwood reel are depicted with inimitable force. **1838** *Ib.* IV. 294 We were as well off as could be in these here backwood settlements. **1843** 'CARLTON' *New Purchase* I. xviii. 152 Perhaps a novice, . . . in backwood life, may be pardoned for feeling a momentary sickness when [etc.].

+**Back-wood-man.** =BACKWOODSMAN. — **1809** IRVING *Knickerb.* VI. ii, The back-wood-men of Kentucky are styled half man, half horse and half alligator, by the settlers on the Mississippi.

+**Backwoods, Back woods.** [BACK *a.* 1 a.]

1. The woods lying back from the more settled areas; the uncleared forest to the west of the earlier settlements.

'That part of Pennsylvania, west of the mountains, . . . was best known in New Jersey by the appellation *backwoods*' (1809 F. Cuming *Western Tour* 473). 'Thirty years ago the heart of Pennsylvania was considered as the "backwoods," ahd appeared as distant to the citizens of the Atlantic border, as the Mississippi does now' (1818 *Niles' Reg.* XV. 187/1).

1742 *Virginia State P.* I. 235 Severil of ous that were the first settlers of these back woods. **1768** *Boston Gazette* 25 Jan. (Th.), The chain of forts through the back woods. **1774** FITHIAN *Journal* I. 137 Breakfasted with us one Lee, a Gentleman of what they call here the back Woods—He seems indeed a little stiff in his manner. **1775** *Penna. Gazette* 16 Aug. 3/2 A formidable company of upwards of 130 men from the mountains and back woods, painted like Indians, armed with tomahawks and rifles, dressed in hunting shirts and mockasons. **1790** *Ann. 1st Congress* II. 1830 There could be no fear of individual settlers scattering and losing themselves in the back woods. **1819** *Niles' Reg.* XVI. 400/1 The 'backwoods' has almost become an obsolete term, though so familiar to all persons a little while ago. **1831** PECK *Guide* 219 Many persons on moving into the back woods . . . think it is little matter how they live, because no one sees them. **1834** [R. BAIRD] *Valley Mississippi* vii. 64 The idea is no longer entertained by Eastern people, that to go to the West, or the 'Back Woods,' as formerly it was called, is to move into a heathen land. **1845** S. SMITH *Theatr. Apprent.* 179 Here in America—and particularly here in the backwoods, we dislike any interference with our domestic affairs. **1854** BARTLETT *Narr.* II. 81 At the most miserable tavern in the back woods, I have found better accommodations than at this place. **1872** EGGLESTON *Hoosier Schoolm.* Pref. 6, I have not ventured to discuss the provincialisms of the Indiana backwoods. **1883** 'MARK TWAIN' *Life on Miss.* xxxvi. 387 He was a grazier or farmer from the back woods of some western State—doubtless Ohio. **1889** FARMER 30/2 The *backwoods* of the United States are rapidly disappearing, even if, practically, they have not already done so.

2. Attrib. with *farm, life,* etc. (Cf. BACKWOOD.)

1784 J. SMYTH *Tour U.S.* I. i. 12 The American soldiery, chiefly then back-woods riflemen. *Ib.*, The . . . savage depredation of a back-wood's mob of American soldiery. **1789** WEEMS *Letters* III. 418, I could not help observing the tyrannical manner of a backwoods husband. **1819** FLINT *Lett. from America* 135 A small degree of aversion to frivolous detail does not prevent me from describing a back-woods tavern. **1828** SHERBURNE *Mem.* (1831) ix. 201 There was a certain kind of backwoods modesty about us. **1831** PECK *Guide* 178 Eastern emigrants will sink as fast in the estimation of 'back-woods' people by such a course. **1842** MRS. KIRKLAND *Forest Life* II. 86 Our backwoods neighbors are less observant of their engagements. **1849** PARKMAN in *Knickerb.* XXXIII. 2 The backwoods lawyer was better fitted to conciliate the good will than to command the obedience of his men. **1855** THOMPSON *Doesticks* 218 A picture . . . which I mistook for a Kentucky backwoods girl. **1855** GLISAN *Jrnl. Army Life* 164, I must gradually come down to backwoods-life again. **1856** OLMSTED *Slave States* 393 It was a perfectly charming little backwoods farm-house. **1863** [P. RUYSDALE] *Pilgrimage over Prairies* II. 107 Whilst thus enjoying ourselves in the approved backwoods fashion, the form of some animal . . . was observed. **1865** *Nation* I. 651 The poor whites, whose local designation [in S.C.] is 'Backwoods People.' **1867** RICHARDSON *Beyond Mississippi* i. 24 A backwoods Missouri boy . . . throws the dice. **1873** 'MARK TWAIN' & WARNER *Gilded Age* xiii. 126 Harry at once found on landing that his backwoods costume would not be needed in St. Louis. **1875** 'MARK TWAIN' *Old Times Miss.* iv. 68 An agonized voice, with the backwoods 'whang' to it, would wail out. **1884** TROWBRIDGE in *Harper's Mag.* March 574/2 An old-fashioned backwoods house. **1888** BURROUGHS in *Century Mag.* Aug. 617/1 Backwoods cows and young cattle seem always to be famished for salt. **1902** WHITE *Blazed Trail* viii. 58 Too big for a little backwoods farm. *Ib.* xvii. 133 Regular old backwoods mossback.

+**Backwoodsman.** [BACKWOODS 2.] An inhabitant of the backwoods.

In early use also *backwood's man, back-woods-man.*

'*Backwoodsmen*, a name given by the people of the commercial towns in the United States, to those who inhabit the territory westward of the Allegany mountains. . . . This word is commonly used as a term of reproach (and that only, in the familiar style,) to designate those people, who, being at a distance from the sea and entirely agricultural, are considered as either hostile or indifferent to the interests of the commercial states' (Pick.).

1784 J. SMYTH *Tour U.S.* II. lvi. 108 Accompanied . . . by my faithful back-wood's man, whom at first I considered as little better than a savage. *Ib.*, These American back-wood's men can perform a little . . . almost in every handicraft, or necessary mechanical trade. *c***1790** FRENEAU *Poems* (1795) 431 Nor terror reign'd through each back-woodsman's hut, . . . Nor Indian's yells disturb'd our sad frontier. **1797** PRIEST *Travels* 55 They tell me the rifle-men of the western army were recruited from Kentucky . . . and are all experienced back-woods-men. **1801** F. AMES *Works* (1809) 144 The project of . . . converting sailors into back-woods-men, is not too monstrous for speculatists to conceive and desire. **1803** T. M. HARRIS *Tour* (1805) 59 Most of the 'Back-wood's men,' as they are called, are emigrants from foreign countries. **1809** F. CUMING *Western Tour* 118 The backwoodsmen, as the first emigrants from the eastward of the Allegheny mountains are called, are very similar in their habits and manners to the aborigines. **1834** *S. Lit. Messenger* I. 142 Theirs were not the fearless independence, and frank demeanor which marks the honest backwoodsman of our country. **1837** BIRD *Nick of Woods* I. 81 The original habitation of the back-woodsman seldom boasted more than two rooms in all. **1845** MRS. KIRKLAND *Western Clearings* 3 The backwoodsman made no mistakes, for to him a stump, or a stone, or a prostrate tree, has individuality. **1863** 'GAIL HAMILTON' *Gala-Days* 23 Do I look like a rough-hewn, unseasoned backwoodsman? **1872** EGGLESTON *End of World* xli. 261 He was a gentleman, though he had always been a backwoodsman. **1886** ROOSEVELT in *Outing* April 3/1 All of the five men were originally Easterners, backwoods men, stout, hardy fellows, but with only one cow-boy in the lot. **1902** 'MARK TWAIN' in *N.Amer. Rev.* April 434 No one can care less for a lord than the backwoodsman.

b. Hence *Backwoodsman-like* adj.

1848 PARKMAN in *Knickerb.* XXXI. 14 The impersonation of all that is wild and backwoodsman-like.

+**Backwoods woman.** [BACKWOODS 2.] A woman of the back woods. — **1840** *Knickerb.* XV. 292 All the endless drudgery belonging to the life of a backwoods-woman. **1884** HIGGINSON in *Harper's Mag.* July 281/1 Mrs. Jackson—a plain, estimable backwoodswoman, who sat smoking her corn-cob pipe.

+**Backwoodsy,** *a.* [BACKWOODS.] Pertaining to, characteristic of, the back woods. — **1862** B. TAYLOR *At Home & Abroad* 2 Ser. II. 72 Wild and backwoodsy as the place appeared, it was to us the welcome herald of breakfast. *a***1911** 'O. HENRY' *Rolling Stones* (1915) 201, I want a scrubby, ornery, low-down, snuff-dipping, back-woodsy, piebald gang. **1923** BOWER *Parowan Bonanza* xvi. 183 She would not sing the old songs Bill loved, because they were so absolutely backwoodsy.

‖ **Backwoody,** *a.* =prec. — **1832** WILLIAMSON *Maine* II. 645 He therefore spiked his guns, set fire to the Adams and the store-house, and retreated . . . through a back woody road, to Kennebeck.

Backy. *colloq.*[2] Abbrev. of TOBACCO. {baccy, 1833} — **1846** *Spirit of Times* (N.Y.) 4 July 228/2 Carrying my backy pipe with me to smoke. Well, you all know the old fellow is mighty fond of backy. . . . Says he 'D—d strong backy, Morgan!'

Back yard, Backyard. [BACK *a.* 1 b.] A yard at the back of a house or other building. {1679–}

1659 *Suffolk Deeds* III. 246 A back yard lying on the north side of the said dwelling house being tenn foote and a halfe wide. **1711** *Boston News-Letter* 8 Oct. 2/1 A fire broke out in an old tenement within a back yard in Cornhill [Boston]. **1768** in *Princeton Book* 14 The back yard of the College. **1812** *Niles' Reg.* II. 181/2 *Domestic* wines . . . can never be expected, from the few vines that can be raised in city gardens and back yards. **1837** *S. Lit. Messenger* III. 224, I found myself on a little piazza, in a back yard. **1853** THOMAS *J. Randolph*, etc. 256 He . . . led the way into the backyard of the jail, which is surrounded by a large wall. **1863** 'GAIL HAMILTON' *Gala-Days* 112 Now the water expands on all sides . . . as if the St. Lawrence had taken a turn into our back yard. **1882** 'M. HARLAND' *Eve's Daughters* 199 She . . . goes into the windy back-yard, perhaps covered with snow, to hang out the clothes. **1911** VANCE *Cynthia* 11 The dismal scenery of the backyard of Suzanne's, with its bare, unlovely fence, its network of clothesline, its parched patch of dejected grass.

* **BACON,** *n.*

* **1.** The cured flesh from the back and sides of a hog. Also occas. = ham.

1644 *Mass. H. S. Coll.* 4 Ser. VI. 376 As for porke or bacon, I haue none; I haue not yet killd any hoggs. **1685** T. BUDD *Penna. & N.J.* 34 Hams and bacon are also made much after the same manner as in West-Falia. **1730** J. SECCOMB *Abbey's Will* xi, A Leg of Pork, . . . And half a Flitch of Bacon. **1757** *Lett. to Washington* II. 157 He had not any fresh meat . . . but proposed to send Bacon; which the jailer said, most of the prisoners stomachs nauseate so much, that they cannot swallow it. **1766** J. BARNARD in *Mass. H. S. Coll.* 3 Ser. V. 204 She . . . wrote me a receipt, which, when I came home [from England], I scattered abroad; and from thence came all the right good bacon made in New England. **1775** ADAIR *Indians* 230 The Indian bacon . . . [is] more streaked, firm, and better tasted, than any we meet with in the English settlements. *c***1790** T. COXE *View U.S.* 62 The produce, manufactures, and exports of Pennsylvania are very many and various, viz. . . . herrings, tongues and sturgeon, hams and other bacon. **1806** *Austin Papers* (1924) I. 116 Bacon brought from Kentucky, in 97 sold at 20 to 25 Dollars pr Hundred. **1831** PECK *Guide* 172 Their method is to salt it [*sc.* pork] sufficiently to prepare it for smoking, and then to make bacon of hams, shoulders, and middlings or broadsides. **1839** *Diplom. Corr. Texas* (1908) I. 403 Messrs Campbell and Dean stored . . . twenty five thousand one hundred and ninety three pounds of bacon, and offered the same for sale. **1878** *Amer. Home Cook Book* 6 Bacon, like pork, should have a thin rind. **1882** THAYER *Log-Cabin to White House* xv. 164 They . . . carried . . . a quantity of ham, or 'bacon,' as the settlers called it.

b. *Bacon and eggs, b. and greens*, etc.

1778 MRS. DRINKER *Journal* 8 April, We dined on the usual fare, Bacon and Eggs. **1828** PAULDING *New Mirror* 27, I sighed for bacon and greens. **1835** HOFFMAN *Winter in West* II. 188 One who had . . . been . . . kept all his life on 'bacon and greens.' **1860** GREELEY *Overland Journey* 75 She gave us an excellent dinner of bacon and greens, . . . and pie. **1877** BARTLETT 132 In the South . . . 'bacon and collards' are a universal dish. **1902** LORIMER *Lett. Merchant* 272 He left home to get a few Indian scalps, and . . . came back for a little bacon and corn pone.

+**c.** Bear's meat similarly treated.

1737 BRICKELL *N. Carolina* 111 The Bacon made thereof is extraordinary good, but must be well saved, otherwise it will rust. **1818** SCHOOLCRAFT *Journal* 45 We have homony . . . and bear's bacon for dinner.

2. *To save one's bacon*, to keep oneself from harm, to escape without injury or loss. {1691–}

'A slang phrase very frequently heard in spite of its objectionable character' (De Vere 630).

1666 *Narr. Early Maryland* (1910) 341 To plead non compos mentis to save my bacon. **1707** *Mass. Prov. Laws* VIII. 725 A false story, to save your own bacon. **1755** *Lett. to Washington* I. 104, I saved my bacon by retreating to the fort. **1809** HORRY *Marion* (1833) 217 He forgot the cask, and turning tail, thought of nothing but to save his bacon! **1840** COOPER *Pathfinder* xi, 'You've saved your bacon, Quarter-master, as they say in the settlements of their creaturs,' cried Pathfinder. **1848** BARTLETT 20 'To save one's bacon,' a vulgar expression, meaning to save one's *flesh* from injury, to preserve one's *flesh* from harm or from punishment. **1867** EDWARDS *Shelby* xxiii. 410 Often, when just at the point of capture, a reckless and desperate resistance 'saved the bacon' of a chap who had no other escape.

+**3.** *Bacon and rice aristocracy*, a wealthy class who have made money by selling these commodities.

1853 POYES *Peep into Past* 37 Thomas Smith bought his brother's lot, and remained [in Charleston, S.C.] to build up the 'bacon and rice aristocracy.'

Bacon, *v.* [f. the n.] *tr.* To convert into bacon. — **1829** *Va. Lit. Museum* 16 Dec. 418 In Virginia, we hear of a man intending to '*bacon* his pork.' **1890** *Congress. Rec.* Aug. 8887/1 We consumed or sold our own pork, and we baconed it ourselves.

+**Bacon beetle.** A beetle of the genus *Dermestes*, the larvæ of which feed upon animal substances. — **1832** WILLIAMSON *Hist. Maine* I. 171 *Dermestes Lardarius*, Bacon Beetle. **1890** *Cent.* s.v. *Dermestes*, One species, *D. lardarius*, is known by the name of bacon beetle.

Bacon box. A box in which bacon is packed for transport. — **1888** SHERIDAN *Memoirs* I. 27 About all that reached the post was what came in the shape of bacon boxes, and the boards from these were reserved for coffins in which to bury our dead.

+**Bacon bug.** =BACON BEETLE. — **1837** WILLIAMS *Florida* 68 The Insects of Florida are numerous. . . . Those most common, are . . . Bacon Bug.—Dermestes. **1854** EMMONS *Agric. N.Y.* V. 60 The *Dermestes lardarius* commits its depredations in houses, usually in furs, meat, pork, bacon (whence it is sometimes called bacon bug).

‖**Bacon-color, -colored,** *a.* Having the color of bacon skin; brownish. — **1862** *N.Y. Tribune* 19 May (citing *Norfolk*, Va. *Daybook*), Maria is 18 years of age, very likely, has a very pleasant countenance, light bacon-colored skin. *Ib.*, Plato is about 19 years of age, and bacon color, squarely built.

Bacon-curer. One engaged in the curing of bacon — **1867–9** *Ill. Agric. Soc. Trans.* VII. 432, 4,118 hogs for bacon-curers and city consumption.

Bacon flitch, gammon. — **1768** FRENEAU *Poems* (1795) 10 Down he took his hams and bacon flitches, Resolv'd to fill the place with other riches. **1788** J. MAY *Journal & Lett.* 64 Amongst the solids were bacon gammon, venison tongues, roast and boiled lamb.

Bacon-ham. A cured ham. {1724 *Sc.*; 1796} — **1775** ROMANS *Nat. Hist. Florida* 331, I purchased some bear, bacon and venison hams of them. **1792** IMLAY *Topogr. Description of Western Territory* 153 Bacon, from 3½ d. to 4 d. Bacon hams, from 4 d. to 5½ d. **1805** SIBLEY in *Ann. 9th Congress* 2 Sess. 1097 We get from them some excellent bacon hams. **1823** JAMES *Exped.* I. 65 From him we obtained a plentiful supply of milk and some bacon hams. **1856** *Rep. Comm. Patents: Agric.* 413 Articles of merchandise . . . exported from Perth Amboy, New Jersey, in . . . 1855 [include] . . . Bacon hams, number, 1,500,000.

Bacon hog. A hog bred and raised for supplying bacon. {1709} — **1867–9** *Ill. Agric. Soc. Trans.* VII. 432 The weather became much warmer, thus lessening the demand for bacon hogs.

Baconish, *a.* [BACON *n.*] Bacon-colored. — **1848** *Ladies' Repository* VIII. 281 So constantly smoked, as they are, from morning to night, from their cradles to their graves, they nearly all look sallow, or baconish.

+**Baconist.** A follower of Nathaniel Bacon (*c*1642–1676) who opposed the arbitrary rule of representatives of the crown. — **1837** BANCROFT *Hist.* (1854) II. xiv. 241 The party of 'Baconists' had obtained great influence on the public mind.

Bacon side. The cured side of a hog. — **1853** STROTHER *Blackwater Chron.* ix. 124 Powell started the frying-pan . . . until at length the more delicate aroma of the hemlock was lost . . . in the ascendancy of the bacon-side. **1872** *Harper's Mag.* Aug. 349/1 Then for stock provisions we had a bacon side, cheese, biscuits, ground coffee, with the usual condiments.

Bacon skin. Skin from a side of bacon. — **1843** 'CARLTON' *New Purchase* I. xiv. 108 The door was hung not with iron, but with broad hinges of tough bacon skin. *Ib.* xxi. 196 To his . . . example was owing the loss of our original bacon-skin hinges.

***Bad,** *a.*

1. Of land: Unsuited for cultivation or occupation.

1651 *Southold Rec.* II. 16 His bad meadow lying at Corchaug containing four acres more or less. **1851** [see BAD LANDS]. **1870** KEIM *Sheridan's Troopers* 136 The tribes of the plains knew the country [in the Canadian River valley] as the 'bad ground.'

2. Sick; ill; suffering. {1748–}

1720 *Essex Inst. Coll.* LI. 287 Last night I was very bad but am better this morning. **1737** E. PARKMAN *Diary* 37, I was called away . . . to see old Capt. Byles, who was very bad with his throat. **1751** MACSPARRAN *Diary* 60, I am bad with a cold. **1840** DANA *Two Years* xxxii. 405 One of our watch was laid up for two or three days by a bad hand. **1859** ELWYN *Glossary* 18, 'I feel quite *bad*,' is a common expression in this country. **1872** EGGLESTON *Hoosier Schoolm.* ix. 83 'Why, how do you feel?' 'Kind o' bad and lonesome, and like as if I wanted to die.' **1886–7** STOCKTON *Hundredth Man* vii, 'She was very bad with the consumption, mum.'

3. Distressed, sorry, 'put out.' {*dial.*}

1839 MARRYAT *Diary* II. 33 *Bad* is used in an odd sense; it is employed for awkward, uncomfortable, sorry. **1887** WILKINS *Humble Romance* 138, I felt too bad to cry. **1889** *Harper's Mag.* Dec. 161/2 For one moment the valiant reporter felt 'pretty bad.'

+**4.** Of Indians: Unfriendly and dangerous.

1843 FREMONT *Exped.* 45 Our young men are bad, and, if they meet you, they . . . will fire upon you. **1900** DRANNAN *Plains & Mts.* 329 They told us the Utes were very bad farther West.

5. *To be in a bad box,* 'to be in a bad predicament' (B. '48).

1837 J. C. NEAL *Charcoal Sk.* (1838) 220 'Hey!—hello!—come out of that' said Lynx. . . . 'You are in a bad box, whoever you are.' *a***1848** *Maj. Downing* (B.), I began to be afraid now I'd got into rather a bad box. **1886** LOGAN *Great Conspiracy* 282 This done, the Enemy—if nothing worse ensues for him—will be in a 'bad box.' **1901** MCCUTCHEON *Graustark* 288 By my soul, you are in a bad box, sir.

***Bad,** *adv.* {1611–}

1. In a bad or faulty manner; poorly, wrongly.

1816 U. BROWN *Journal* I. 273 Land of not much account, farm'd bad. **1834** CROCKETT *Life* 58, I agreed with her, though, that the little varment had treated me so bad that I ought to forget her. **1840** *S. Lit. Messenger* VI. 386/1 She used to tap her with it on the hands, when she behaved bad, or did not say her lesson good. **1842** *Yale Lit. Mag.* VIII. 96 [The Editors] are privileged characters, and can write as bad as they know how—the more illegible the better. **1854** S. HALE *Lett.* (1919) 7 The children . . . during that time 'act as bad as they can.' **1890** RYAN *Told in Hills* 333, I was just mean enough to treat her pretty bad—flung her on the floor when she tried to stop me.

2. In an unfriendly or unfavorable manner.

1821 J. FOWLER *Journal* 18 These last Indeans appeer more unfriendly and talk sasy and bad to us. **1871** *Ill. Agric. Soc. Trans.* VIII 238 This speaks bad for our application of the art. **1883** C. F. WILDER *Sister Ridnour* 195, I'm afraid that you are getting to think bad of your fellow creturs.

3. Severely, seriously; strongly, much; to a great extent. {1681}

1845 HOOPER *Simon Sugg's Adv.* ii. 24 If . . . Bob kin do it, it's reasonable to s'pose that old Jed'diah Suggs won't be bothered *bad.* *Ib.* vii. 94 'Pshaw!' said Suggs, 'you aint bad hurt.' **1846** *Congress. Globe* 18 May 838/1 A man might *love* his country *so bad* as to be willing to cut the throats of one-half of the American citizens. **1880** CABLE *Grandissimes* lii. 397 'You've got it bad,' said Doctor Keene, mechanically. **1889** COOKE *Steadfast* xviii. 199 Ef he does she has the high-sterics proper bad, and then he flies round! **1890** RYAN *Told in Hills* 87 She has no injuries, I guess, only she's used up and needs rest bad. **1901** — *Montana* 3 There is one thing I want in this world, and want bad. **1904** STRATTON-PORTER *Freckles* 316, I'd be giving all me money in the bank for you! . . . or, at least, all but what I'm needing bad for something else.

4. *Bad off,* badly off, not in good circumstances or condition. {*dial.*} +*Bad off,* greatly desirous (to do something).

1815 HUMPHREYS *Yankey in Eng.* 77 Bad as I am off, I wouldn't swop conditions with that baddish woman for the world to boot. **1817** U. BROWN *Journal* II. 371 [Land] full of lime stone . . . bad off for timber & water. **1821** J. FOWLER *Journal* 15 Haveing left two behind, and three more unfitt for sarvice, makes us bad of for horses. **1845** HOOPER *Taking Census* i. 152 Yes, send for your marshal . . . if you're bad off to. **1863** 'E. KIRKE' *Southern Friends* i. 13 She's very bad off, very bad indeed. **1879** TOURGEE *Fool's Errand* xxix. 179 When I told him how bad off I was, owin' for some of the niggers . . . , he didn't wince. **1891** WILKINS *New Eng. Nun* 221 Eph couldn't be so dreadful bad off.

b. In a poor state of health; very ill.

1863 G. W. WILDER *MS. Diary* 30 Jan., H. has taken cold and is quite bad off.

Bad egg: see EGG *n.*

+**Baden corn.** [T. N. *Baden,* of Md.] (See quotations.) — **1837** *Cultivator* March 9/1 The Dutton and Baden corn . . . are valued for the economy with which they convert food into solid grain. **1838** ELLSWORTH *Valley N. Wabash* v. 46 Could we . . . by any process acclimate the 'Baden Corn,' your introduction of it will add more to the State than one-half her works of internal improvement. **1842** J. S. BUCKINGHAM *Slave States* II. 56 There had been lately introduced into this State [Georgia], a new description of grain, called Baden corn, from . . . a Mr. Baden, of Maryland, who had taken the pains to select the best ears or cobs of corn from his own fields, and plant them in the most favourable position.

+**Bad eye.** (See quot.) — **1875** MILLER *First Families* (1876) xv. 126 All of the following popular drinks, that is Old Tiger, Bad Eye, . . . , were all made from the same decoction of bad rum, worse tobacco, and first-class cayenne pepper.

***Badge.** +As a mark of an adulteress (see quotation and cf. A *letter* 1, AD *abbrev.*). — **1639** *Plymouth Col. Rec.* I. 132 Mary . . . Mendame, [having committed adultery] with Tinsin, an Indian, . . . the Bench doth therefore censure the said Mary to be whipt . . . and to weare a badge vpon her left sleeue.

+**Badge pin.** A fraternity pin. — **1871** [L. H. BAGG] *At Yale* 57 The badge pins worn by all the members constitute one of the most distinctive features of these societies. *Ib.* 172.

***Badger.**

***1.** The animal of that name.

1654 JOHNSON *Wonder-w. Prov.* xxi. 173 A receptacle for . . . Foxes, Rockoones, Bag[er]s, Bevers, Otters, and all kind of wild creatures. **1781–2** JEFFERSON *Notes on Va.* Writings II. 70 Kalm . . . tells us, that the lynx, badger, red fox, and flying squirrel, are the same in America as in Europe. **1807** GASS *Journal* 70 They say this animal which the French call a prarow, or brarow, is a species of the badger. **1819** E. DANA *Geog. Sketches* 51 The Badger, different species of Wolves, and a Hare, gray in summer and white in winter, are often seen in this country. **1845** DE SMET *Oregon Missions* (1847) 142 The badger, or the ground-hog, . . . digs the sandy soil. **1869** BROWNE *Adv. Apache Country* 421 Some Indians from Mono Lake came in . . . with a remarkably large badger, which they offered for sale to the miners. **1883** *Rep. Indian Affairs* 25 These peltries consist principally of muskrat, fox, polecat, and badger, and are obtained on the reservation. **1885** *Amer. Naturalist* Sept. 922 The Mexican badger, two specimens of which have been found in Central Kansas.

+**2.** A native or resident of the State of Wisconsin. *The Badger State,* Wisconsin.

Alleged to have been originally applied to lead-miners who made temporary dwellings by using or making holes in the hills.

1835 HOFFMAN *Winter in West* I. 176 There was . . . a keen-eyed, leather-belted 'badger' from the mines of Ouisconsin. **1844** *Knickerb.* XXIV. 286 Do you know that there is such a country as Wisconsin? . . . that the inhabitants are called 'badgers'? and that the forests they clear and the houses they rear fully attest their right to that title? **1856** EMERSON *Eng. Traits* iv. 54, I found abundant points of resemblance [in Tacitus] between the Germans of the Hercynian forest, and our *Hoosiers, Suckers,* and *Badgers* of the American woods. **1871** DE VERE 662 Wisconsin, abounding during early days in badgers, has ever since retained the name of 'Badger State.' *a***1881** *Madison* (Wis.) *Journal* (Th.), The characteristic term of 'badger' arose in the lead region. The miners were of two grades [etc.].

3. Attrib. and comb. with *-baiting, fight, -hunting.*

1835 HOFFMAN *Winter in West* I. 216 Fox-hunting on horseback . . . is the favourite sport; though wolf, bear, and badger-baiting have each their active followers. *Ib.* 314 They had struck the vein of ore which they were working, in badger-hunting. **1869** BROWNE *Adv. Apache Country* 421 At the town of Bodie I witnessed one of those impressive Sunday exhibitions which seem to be the popular mode of recreation in this country—a badger fight.

Badger hole. A burrow made by a badger; a hole in the ground resembling this. — **1823** W. KEATING *Narr.* 177 Many badger holes were observed. These we found to belong to the Menomone, or wild rice eaters. **1847** PARKMAN in *Knickerb.* XXIX. 395 His horse will step into badger-holes. **1904** 'O. HENRY' *Heart of West* 150 'Good-night,' said Ranse. 'Ride carefully over them badger holes.' **1913** W. C. BARNES *Western Grazing Grounds* 150 They should be free from prairie dog and badger holes, for many a tottering little lamb has fallen into such a hole and perished.

‖ **Bad Hearts.** (See quotation.) — **1852** MARCY *Explor. Red River* (1854) 3 We fell in with a party of Indians, of the nation of 'Kaskias,' or 'Bad Hearts.'

+**Bad Lands.** [tr. Fr. *mauvaises terres.*] Arid barren lands in certain parts of the west, characterized by erosion of the soft surface strata in varied and fantastic forms. Also attrib.

1851 OWEN *Geol. Survey of Wis.*, etc. (1852) 195 J. Evans . . . finally reached . . . the country of the 'Bad Lands' (Mauvaises Terres), lying high up on White River. **1868** RAYNOLDS *Explor. Yellowstone* 8 The much-dreaded and barren 'bad lands.' **1873** BEADLE *Undevel. West* xiv. 243 Northward and east of the Missouri are the 'Bad Lands' regions of desolation and death. **1888** ROOSEVELT in *Century Mag.* May 44/1 The extraordinary formation of the Bad Lands, with the ground cut up into gullies, serried walls, and battlemented hilltops, makes it the country of all others for hiding-places and ambuscades. **1888** *Harper's Mag.* March 567/1 We . . . found a land more broken, and interspersed with rocky land and bowlders—the only touch of 'bad lands' I recall on the route. **1895** KING *Fort Frayne* ii. 20 Two Indian scouts . . . had made their unerring way . . . through a labyrinth of Bad Lands. **1902** WISTER *Virginian* xv. 170 The night was established. The rolling bad-lands sank away in it. **1914** TARR *College Physiography* 102 Bad land tracts . . . are especially well developed and extensive in western Nebraska, North and South Dakota, and Wyoming.

* **Badly,** *adv.* [f. BAD *a.*] +*Badly off:* **a.** In poor condition or circumstances. Const. *for* (something deficient).

1852 STOWE *Uncle Tom* ix, They begin to flatter themselves that they are not so badly off after all. **1854** BARTLETT *Narr.* II. 490 We should have been badly off for fodder. **1855** KANE *Arctic Expl.* (1856) II. 50 We are so badly off for strong arms.

b. Ailing, ill.

1903 BURNHAM *Jewel* 125 'She's very badly off, very badly off, I'm afraid.' 'I hope not, sir. Children are always flighty if they have a little fever.'

Bad man. +*Western.* A lawless character, ready to fight or kill; a desperado.

1884 *Century Mag.* Dec. 194 The second was reputed to be decidedly a 'bad' man, an old-time Virginia City vigilante. **1888** ROOSEVELT *Ib.* Feb. 504/1 The 'bad men,' or professional fighters, and man-killers, are of a different stamp, quite a number of them being, according to their light, perfectly honest. **1891** *Harper's Mag.* July 211/1 Much of the vice attributed to the cowboy must be laid to the score of the 'bad man' of the Plains. **1898** CANFIELD *Maid of Frontier* 181, I've been what they call a bad man, . . . but I never did half of what was laid to me. **1901** WHITE *Westerners* ii. 12 They's a raft of bad men jest layin' fer a chance like that. *a***1909** 'O. HENRY' *Roads of Destiny* ix. 153 The 'bad man' of the Southwest does not run to extremes.

Bafta. An Oriental cotton fabric or muslin, of varying quality. {1612-} — **1768** FRENEAU *Poems* (1795) 11 Hum-hums are here—and muslins—what you please—Bandanas, baftas, pullcats, India teas. **1811** H. M. Brooks *Gleanings* 101 One bale . . . Chittabully Baftas. **1817** PAULDING *Lett. from South* I. 52 People . . . free from the intrusion of . . . sandahs, baftas, buglipoors, and all the jargon of East India commodities. **1823** M'KENNEY *Memoirs* (1846) I. App. 297 Do you know whether the samples you have exhibited to the committee, of calicoes and baftas, were, or were not from the fag ends of these goods?

* **Bag,** *n.* (In slang or special uses.)

* **1.** *To give* (one) *the bag*, to give (one) the slip, to run away from. {-1647}

1787 FRENEAU *Misc. Works* 414 As this was the case—he must give us the bag, Adhere to Old England, and sail with her flag. [*Footnote.*] A phrase common among seamen; importing to abscond or slip out of the way.

b. A rejection of advances or an offer of marriage; a refusal or dismissal of a suitor. Freq. *to give* (or *get*) *the bag.* {1825- *dial.*}

*a***1806** FESSENDEN *Poems* 39 'To give the bag' is an expression common with the lower classes in New England, and indicates that Miss Delia will not honour Mr. Damon with her company in a tete-a-tete conversation. *Ib.* 73 Jonathan . . . tumbled, sadly, all the way Lest he should get the bag, sir. **1825** NEAL *Bro. Jonathan* II. 277 Sent away, with a flea in your ear: some girl has given you the bag. *Ib.* 282, I would as lief slander all women, because one o' them had packed me off with a bag. **1828** *Yankee* Sept. 288/2, I never was courted but once in my life, and then I gave the bag. The poor fellow hadn't courage enough. **1839** J. S. JONES *People's Lawyer* I. i, Zack and I courted the same gal; . . . if she hadn't gin me the bag, John Ellsley might have been John Shingle.

2. *To give* (one) *the bag to hold* (or variants of this): **a.** To leave one to bear the brunt; to leave in the lurch or in an awkward situation.

1787 TYLER *Contrast* II. ii, General Shays has sneaked off and given us the bag to hold. **1793** JEFFERSON *Writings* X. 145 If the bankruptcies of England proceed to the length of an universal crush of their paper . . . she will leave Spain the bag to hold. **1851** HOOPER *Widow Rugby's Husband* 163 The rascals generally left him 'the bag to hold.' **1906** F. LYNDE *Quickening* 180 You have smashed Chiawassee Consolidated, and now you are going off to leave my father to hold the bag. **1922** TITUS *Timber* xvi. 152 'And Foraker's Folly is going to hold the bag?' 'Oh, I don't think he could work that, but maybe he'll make Helen trouble.'

b. = sense 1 b.

1813 PAULDING *Sc. Fiddle* IV. (1814) 82 But still she scorn'd his tender tale, . . . Flouted his suit with scorn so cold, And gave him oft the bag to hold. *Ib.* 193 If . . . she remains in the room with her parents, he is said, I know not for what special reason, 'to get the bag to hold.' *c***1840** MCCLINTOCK *Beedle's Marriage* (B.), Now and then one of the girls would promise, and then fly off at the handle; but most all contrived some reason for giving me the bag to hold.

3. *To carry the bag*, to have control.

1893 M. HOWE *Honor* 107 Did he not carry the bag? was he not the master of the situation?

+**4.** In base-ball, a bag of sand used to mark a base.

1874 CHADWICK *Base Ball Manual* 9 The other three bases are canvas bags, fastened to posts sunk in the ground [etc.]. **1912** MATHEWSON *Pitching* xii. 257 Half of base stealing is leaving the bag at the right time. **1917** — *Sec. Base Sloan* 255 Someone reported that the second base bag had broken away.

* **Bag,** *v.* +*tr.* To collect (bear-oil) in a skin bag. — **1842** HITCHCOCK *Journal* 164 Indians take skins from young does entire, and 'bag' the oil in them. *Ib.*, McClure says it is common to get fifteen or twenty gallons of oil from a bear—that thirty gallons have been 'bagged.'

Baga. [Short for *ruta-baga.*] The Swedish turnip, *Brassica campestris.* — **1853** *Michigan Agric. Soc. Trans.* (1854) 597 In the month of November half an acre was accurately set off by the chain, and the bagas taken up. **1862** *N.Y. Observer* 20 Feb., Roots (carrots, beets, or bagas).

Bagasse. [F. *bagasse*, Sp. *bagazo*, husks of olives, grapes, etc., after pressing.]

1. Sugar-cane that has been through all of the sugar-making operations; cane-trash. {1854-}

Now also applied to the waste pulp of sugar-beet.

1835 [INGRAHAM] *South-West* I. 239 The *baggasse* or cane-trash, (called in the West Indies *migass,*) is received into carts and conveyed to a distance . . . to be burnt. **1857-8** *Ill. Agric. Soc. Trans.* III. 522-3 A wide fire place, with corresponding doors, are desirable, as they permit the temporary smothering of the fire with green *begasse* [*sic*] at that juncture when the 'striking' is commenced. **1863** *Rep. Comm. Agric.* 134 Crushed cane or bagasse . . . is a very excellent stimulus to new growth. **1875** 'MARK TWAIN' *Old Times* 73 When they have finished grinding the cane, they form the refuse of the stalks (which they call *bagasse*) into great piles and set fire to them. **1884** *Rep. Comm. Agric.* 30 The bagasse, immediately after milling, was run through the cane-cutter.

2. Attrib. or comb. with *burner, cart, furnace.*

1833 SILLIMAN *Man. Sugar Cane* 15 Two boys at bagasse (ground cane) carts. **1858** *Rep. Comm. Patents* (1859) I. 709 Bagasse furnaces having the exit flue . . . located in the interior of the furnace. **1859** BARTLETT 19 *Bagasse Furnace*, a furnace arranged to burn the sugar-cane stalks. **1883** *Century Mag.* Jan. 391 The huge, square, red brick bagasse-burner, into which the residuum of crushed sugar cane passes continually. **1886** *Harper's Mag.* June 80/2 The now exhausted chips drop through a slide valve into begass carts below.

Bagatelle. [F. *bagatelle* trifle {*c* 1645}, It. *bagatella.*] A game played on a table with balls and cues. {1819} Also attrib. with *board, table.* — **1841** *Knickerb.* XVII. 402 How Captain Sherman's beautiful steamer would come along . . . to break up our game of 'bagatelle.' **1849** *Rep. Comm. Patents* (1850) 394, I claim . . . constructing a billiard or bagatelle table cushion. **1853** A. BUNN *Old Eng. & New Eng.* 45 Some thirty strong-minded women . . . asked him to discontinue the sale of liquor and the use of a 'bagatelle' board. **1862** *Trial C. M. Jefferds* 92 There are conveniences for playing cards, and a bagatelle table, and a bar.

Bagdad. [Name of the Oriental city.] Denoting a make of cigar. — **1834** CARRUTHERS *Kentuckians* I. 11 Bring me a gin sling, . . . and half-a-dozen Bagdad segars. **1854** 'O. OPTIC' *In Doors & Out* (1876) 197 She sent the Irish girl to the apothecary's shop for a bunch of 'Bagdad cigars.' *Ib.* 198 She took from the work basket, with an air as brave and solemn as a judge, one of the 'Bagdads.'

* **BAGGAGE.**

* **1.** The equipment of necessary or useful articles taken along by a party of explorers or Indians, or by a military force.

*c***1689** *Tragedies of Wilderness* (Drake, 1841) 83 Putting our baggage into them [=canoes, we] . . . went down to the fort. **1715** *Boston News-Letter* 26 Sept. 2/2 The English . . . went in several Pereagers in pursuit of them, . . . destroyed their Canoes and got a great deal of their Bagage. **1738** BYRD *Dividing Line* (1901) 27 The commissioners . . . left the men with . . . heavy baggage. **1750** WALKER *Journal* 6 March, Each man had a horse and we had two to carry the baggage. **1760** *Essex Inst. Coll.* XX. 294 This morning we struck our tents and put the bageg into the carts and marcht to Shambele. **1792** *Ann. 2nd Congress* 1141 The encampment was in a square with the baggage . . . in centre. **1805** Lewis in *Ann. 9th Congress* 2 Sess. 1038 Our baggage is all embarked on board six small canoes. **1811** *Ann. 12th Congress* 1 Sess. 2114, I had erected a block-house . . . as a depository for our heavy baggage and such of our provisions as we were unable to transport in wagons. **1826** Cooper *Mohicans* xvi, The garrison [were] to retain their arms, their colors, and their baggage. **1861** *Army Regulations* 163 The baggage to be transported is limited to camp and garrison equipage, and officers' baggage. **1865** Boudrye *Fifth N.Y. Cavalry* 61 Our tents were soon struck and sent to the rear with the baggage. **1895** M. A. Jackson *Memoirs* 548 [The] Pennsylvania Regiment . . . were trying to find their baggage and former place . . . in the log works.

*2. The collection of personal effects or similar articles, usually packed in bags, trunks, etc., taken by a person in travelling.

In Eng. use now generally replaced by 'luggage.'

'An American never uses the conversational term, *luggage*, but always speaks of his *impediments* as *baggage*' (1852 Bristed *Upper Ten Th.* iv. 81). 'Nor must luggage be asked for, or referred to under any other name than that of "baggage" ' (1870 W. F. Rae *Westward by Rail* 55).

1739 W. Stephens *Proc. Georgia* 410 The Captain . . . was carrying divers parcels of baggage to the water-side. **1750** *Georgia Col. Rec.* VI. 345 [He] had likewise given orders to the clerk of the store to provide a large boat, and use his utmost diligence to bring to this town the passengers and their baggage. **1765** Copley in *Copley-Pelham Lett.* 35, I have sent you the portrait of my brother by Mr. Haill, who has been so kind to take the care of it and put it among his own baggage. **1784** Washington *Diaries* II. 279 My equipage . . . consisting of 3 Servants and 6 horses, three of which carried my Baggage. **1806** *Ann. 10th Congress* 1 Sess. I. 425, I avail myself of . . . one of my attendants, who is going forward with my baggage, to offer compliments. **a1809** Freneau *Poems* I. 52 My baggage was stow'd in a cart very snug. **1835** *Essex Inst. Coll.* LIV. 199 No baggage can be taken except what belongs to passengers. **1860** M. J. Holmes *Maude* v. 53 The piles of baggage which the driver was depositing upon the stoop. **1871** *Scribner's Mo.* I. 594 All travelers carried baggage, so he thought he must do it, even if it necessitated the taking off of some of his clothing. **1875** 'Mark Twain' *Sk., Pleasure Excursion,* Baggage checked through to any point on the route. **1897** *Outing* May 197/2 The bicycle is carried free as personal baggage unless the regular weight limit is exceeded. **1907** *Springfield W. Repub.* 3 Oct. 2 Certainly the large amount of baggage which the American traveler is allowed to carry . . . puts a heavy burden upon the railroad, so long as passengers and baggage are transported in the same train.

||**3.** *slang.* Spoil, plunder.

1873 Beadle *Undevel. West* xxxi. 672 How even 'experts' were victimized, and how the swindlers 'got away with the baggage,' is it not all recorded . . .?

***4.** *colloq.* Foolish talk or opinions; 'trash'; 'bosh.' {1538–79}

1873 *Newton* (Kansas) *Kansan* 15 May 4/1 One of the representatives of the city stigmatized their report as 'bagage' [*sic*], or bosh.

+**Baggage agent.** [Baggage 2.] A railroad official or employee having charge of baggage or its transportation. — **1858** Smith *Railway Celebrations* Adv. 2 On almost all the trains will be found Baggage or Express Agents. **1871** De Vere 357 The stamped marks are entered into the baggage-agent's books. **1884** Cummings *Sk. Class 1862 Dartmouth Coll.* 45 From this position he was promoted to the responsible place of General Baggage Agent.

Baggage-animal. [Baggage 1, 2.] An animal used for the transportation of baggage. {1852} — **1846** Webb *Altowan* I. vii. 191 They had hoped to find the baggage-animals and the running-horses.

||**Baggage-blanket.** [Baggage 1.] A blanket in which baggage is carried. — **1761** Niles *Indian Wars* II. 563, 60 Indians . . . were lying in wait for them, and drying their baggage-blankets in the sun.

+**Baggage-car.** [Baggage 2.] A railway car used for transporting baggage and similar articles.

1835 [Ingraham] *South-West* I. 172 A long train of baggage or cargo-cars were in the rear of these. **1837** *S. Lit. Messenger* III. 658/2 In five minutes the baggage cars and the passengers were aboard a neat little steamer. **1846** *Mass. Stat.* 16 April 176 For passenger and baggage cars, per last report. **1857** M. J. Holmes *Meadow-Brook* xxxviii, The engine plunged down a steep embankment, throwing the train from the track and dragging after it the baggage car. **1877** *Harper's Mag.* Dec. 53/1 Sitting on one trunk in the baggage-car, with another trunk for a desk, he wrote . . . an article of the greatest importance. **1878** B. F. Taylor *Between Gates* 26 A Babel of trunks is surging toward the baggage-cars. **1888** E. B. Custer *Tenting on Plains* xx. 601 It was handed into the special coach, for there was no baggage-car. **1903** *N.Y. Times* 17 Aug., The baggage car was derailed and badly split.

Baggage cart. [Baggage 2.] A cart for the conveyance of baggage. {1749} — **1765** Otis *Considerations* 15 The driver of a baggage cart, on a crusade to the holy sepulchre. **1852** J. W. Bond *Minnesota* 257 To-day, our French-Canadians and half-breeds, who have charge of the provision and baggage-carts, have been . . . making new cart axles.

+**Baggage-check.** [Baggage 2.] A check of metal or card-board bearing a number which serves to identify a piece of baggage.

1854 *Instructions N.Y. & Erie R.R.* Rule 149, Baggage Checks must be kept at all times in a secure place. **1858** W. P. Smith *Bk. Railway Celebrations* Adv. 7 No other road issues Through baggage Checks, or can sell Through Tickets. **1886** Poore *Reminisc.* I. 41 Baggage checks and the checking of baggage were then unknown.

+**Baggage clerk.** =Baggage agent. — **1870** W. F. Rae *Westward by Rail* 77 Frantic efforts are made to attract the attention of the baggage clerk, and to induce him to attach the necessary check to the trunk or portmanteau, which has at length been discovered.

+**Baggage coach.** [Baggage 2.] A coach for the conveyance of baggage or the like. — **1878** Pinkerton *Strikers* 289 The inner track . . . was jammed full of engines, passenger and baggage coaches [etc.]

+**Baggage-crate.** [Baggage 2.] A crate or frame used to protect baggage in transportation. — **1839** *S. Lit. Messenger* V. 802/1 Our horses . . . were carried with the train in a large car partly filled with the baggage crates. **1845** P. Hone *Diary* II. 253, I found . . . that I had lost my trunk and dressing-case. I saw them put in the baggage-crate in New York. **1863** 'Gail Hamilton' *Gala-Days* 44, I suppose it [a trunk] would have kept on . . . had not Crene's dark eyes seen it tilting into a baggage-crate.

+**Baggage-express, -expressman.** (See quotations and Express *n.*) — **1859** *Harper's Mag.* Sept. 504/1 More and more parcels [are] addressed to the 'package-office of the Harlem Railroad,' . . . . This accounts for the influx to the cars of the gentlemanly-looking men you . . . have taken at first for the agents of a baggage-express. — **1872** T. W. Tucker *Waifs* 114 Countless hosts of travellers . . . 'rise up and bless' the baggage expressman, as he . . . relieves them of the . . . care of their numerous trunks, valises, and hat-boxes.

Baggage fish. *Obs.* [Earlier E. *baggage* (1553–).] Poor or worthless fish. {a1625} — **1702** C. Mather *Magnalia* (1853) I. i. 263 Eels, and other baggage fish, will stick in the mud.

Baggage-horse. [Baggage 1, 2.] A horse used for carrying baggage. {1640–}

1755 Franklin in *Autobiog.* 397 The waggons and baggage-horses . . . must march with the army, and no faster. **1780** W. Fleming in *Travels Amer. Col.* 636, I purchased a baggage horse from Thos. Carland. **1805** D. McClure *Diary* (1899) 58 We travelled leisurely, on account of the baggage horse. **1837** Bird *Nick of Woods* I. v. 86 His baggage-horses, under the charge of the younger of the two negroes, were sent on with the band. **1887** *Century Mag.* March 736/2 The guide went first, with four baggage horses and two riders.

+**Baggage-man.** [Baggage 2.] A man having charge of railroad baggage. .

1863 'Gail Hamilton' *Gala-Days* 45 'Well,' says the Baggage-man . . . 'you let me take your check.' **1877** *Harper's Mag.* Dec. 53/1 The baggage-men had been playing an uproarious game of euchre. **1887** George *40 Years on Rail* iv. 58, I . . . moved to Reading, Massachusetts, where I was baggageman on the Reading train. **1902** Wister *Virginian* i. 3 The baggage-man remarked that passengers often got astray from their trunks.

Baggage-master. [Baggage 1.] +An official having charge of the baggage at a railroad station or on board a train or steamboat.

Cf. Eng. *baggage-master* in military use. {1815}

1849 D. Nason *Journal* 112 Then the baggage master said he should charge for the tool-chest. **1858** *Texas Almanac 1859* 193 Railroad conductors, baggage masters, &c., are required to wear upon their hats some badge indicating their office. **1862–3** Hale *If, Yes, &c.* (1868) 25 Some pirate from the pier . . . had seized the waiting trunk . . . while the baggage-master's back was turned. **1883** *Wheelman* I. 253 As regards the exaction of a transportation tax, the baggage-master of the steamboat . . . demanded a half-dollar. **1891** Ellis *Check No. 2134* i. 5 On the first run made by Arthur Helmuth, in place of the regular express agent and baggage master. **1909** H. N. Casson *C. H. McCormick* 101 The train was about to start, when the baggage-master demanded pay for 200 pounds of surplus baggage.

+**Baggage-pony.** [Baggage 1.] A pony used to transport baggage. — **1840** Mrs. Kirkland in *Knickerb.* XVI. 212 As the cavalcade with its baggage-ponies . . . was getting into order for a march to the prairies. **1878** I. L. Bird *Rocky Mts.* 30 The bundled-up squaws riding astride on the baggage-ponies.

+**Baggage-rack.** [Baggage 2.] A rack in a railroad car or vehicle on which baggage is placed. — **1889** *Harper's Mag.* Feb. 430/2 The amazement of the driver . . . when he found a member of Congress standing on the baggage rack.

+**Baggage-room.** [Baggage 2.] A room for the storing of baggage, esp. on board a vessel or at a railroad station.

1838 Cooper *Homeward B.* xxiii, The trunks that contained their ordinary sea-attire, or those that were not stowed in the baggage-room. **1849** N. Kingsley *Diary* 25 Opened the baggage room to day—but found the things quite dry. **1855** *Knickerb.* XLV. 139 The rooms and halls [of the school] are full of girls; so you rush to the baggage-room, sit down on your trunk [etc.]. **1876** Ingram *Centennial Exp.* 701 It contained one very large room, ladies parlor, coat and baggage rooms [etc.]. **1902** Wister *Virginian* i. 3 He . . . left me planted in the baggage-room at Medicine Bow. **1908** *N.Y. Ev. Post* 4 Aug. 2 Piled high in the baggage room is a multitude of trunks.

+**Baggage-smasher.** *colloq.* [BAGGAGE 2.] One who handles baggage at a railway station, dock, etc.; a porter.

'So called from the reckless manner in which these persons handle the property of travellers' (B. '59).

1856 D. MACLEOD *F. Wood* 285 Baggage-smashers haunted the docks, tearing one's baggage about, stealing it sometimes. **1861** *N.Y. Tribune* 23 Nov., Emigrant-robbers, baggage-smashers, and all the worst classes of the city. **1869** HALE *Ingham Papers* 59 The Boston hackman of the best school . . . is a wholly different man from the baggage-smasher of Babel, or from the cabman of London. **1882** 'M. HARLAND' *Eve's Daughters* 350 Each . . . corded . . . with a power of muscle that would have insured a Saratoga trunk against the most energetic baggage-smasher. **1903** O. KILDARE *Mamie Rose* 242, I went to work at one of the boat piers as a baggageman—sometimes lovingly referred to as a baggage-smasher.

fig. **1874** B. F. TAYLOR *World on Wheels* II. vi. 229 The word 'sagacity' is completely ruined for all human uses. It belongs to the baggage-smashers of the brute creation.

+**Baggage-smashing,** *vbl. n.* (See first quot.) — **1883** *Ill. Revised Laws* 878 Baggage smashing. Any person employed by a railroad corporation in this state, who shall wilfully, carelessly or negligently break, injure, or destroy any baggage, shall be liable [etc.]. **1885** *Harper's Mag.* Aug. 418/2 His trunk . . . in a baggage-smashing melee . . . would, in the long run, come out victorious.

+**Baggage-tag.** [BAGGAGE 2.] A tag or card attached to a piece of baggage to identify it. — **1879** STOCKTON *Rudder Grange* vii. 75, I went up-stairs and got a baggage tag.

Baggage train. [BAGGAGE 1.] The line of baggage-laden animals, conveyances, etc., accompanying an army. {1863}

1841 PARK *Pantology* 506 The baggage train should be placed either in the column, or so near it that it may be speedily defended, in case of attack. **1847** *Army Regulations* 124 The wagons and pack-horses . . . together with . . . horses and carriages belonging to the corps . . . constitute the baggage train of an army. **1860** MORDECAI *Virginia* v. 66 The fleets of wagons that would assemble, in brisk times, near their stores, looked like the baggage train of a small army. **1888** ROOSEVELT in *Century Mag.* May 39/1 The trail made by Custer's baggage train is to this day one of the well-known landmarks.

+**Baggage-truck.** [BAGGAGE 1, 2.] A hand-truck for transporting baggage. — **1861** WINTHROP *Open Air* 228 The soldiers tramped forward and aft, danced on her decks, shot overboard a heavy baggage-truck.

Baggage wagon. [BAGGAGE 1, 2.]

1. A wagon used to transport army equipment and provisions. {1689-}

1776 *Journals Cont. Congress* IV. 46, 300 blankets, 64 pitching axes, and a baggage waggon. *Ib.* VI. 1010 For the hire of two baggage waggons. **1812** MARSHALL *Kentucky* 84 A most destructive fire unexpectedly opened from behind the baggage waggons. **1832** KENNEDY *Swallow Barn* II. i. 4 He became notorious for picking up stragglers, cutting off baggage-wagons. **1837** *S. Lit. Messenger* III. 238 For several days we saw a succession of troops, artillery, baggage-wagons, etc. passing through the village. **1847** FORD *Illinois* (1854) 130 Gen. Posey . . . marched back to Kellogg's Grove, to await the arrival of his baggage-wagons. **1862** NORTON *Army Lett.* 106 With their tents and all the baggage wagons . . . this field is pretty well filled up. **1889** *Century Mag.* Jan. 467/2 Up to this time I was still corporal of the guard, in charge of the baggage-wagon.

2. A wagon used for the transport of personal baggage.

1791 WASHINGTON *Diaries* IV. 149 My equipage and attendance consisted of a charriot . . . a light baggage waggon and two horses. **1805** *Columbian Centinel* 11 May 1/2 A baggage-wagon twice a week. **1845** S. SMITH *Theatr. Apprent.* 57 Next morning when about to pursue our journey, we were surprised to see quite a crowd collected about our baggage-wagon. **1853** *Harper's Mag.* VI. 434/1 The accommodating proprietor is at the pier, where baggage-wagon and omnibus are also in readiness to convey ourselves and baggage to the house. **1860** ABBOTT *South & North* 190 These men pray that the slaves may not be permitted to hire their own time, to own cabs, drays, and baggage-wagons, or to take contracts for work as mechanics. **1869** ALDRICH *Bad Boy* iv. (1877) 30 Our trunks were piled upon a baggage-wagon.

Bagging, *n.*

1. A coarse cloth used for making bags or for wrapping bales; sacking. {1732-}

'A coarse linen cloth, chiefly manufactured in Kentucky, for packing cotton in' (B. '48).

1792 *Ann. 2nd Congress* 1026 It would . . . be good policy to raise the duty . . . on the following articles: . . . canvas, brown rolls, bagging. **1812** *Niles' Reg.* II. 408/2 Twenty dollars for the best piece of twilled bagging, of hemp, flax, or cotton. **1839** H. CASWALL *America* 223 A staple article of produce is hemp, which is prepared and made into coarse 'bagging' by the slaves. This bagging is sold in the southern states, where it is employed in packing cotton for exportation. **1844** Cist *Cincinnati Misc.* 93 This establishment . . . produces annually, 800,000 yards Bagging and 100 tons of Bale Rope. **1857** Commons, etc. *Doc. Hist.* I. 279 The packing should be in square bales; . . . to be in two breadths of wide bagging, pressed until the side seams are well closed. **1862** *Ill. Agric. Soc. Trans.* V. 672 A very low grade of lint, unfit for anything but the very coarsest and lowest grades of bagging. **1884** ROE *Nature's Story* viii, The bagging round his wings and feet gave way.

2. Attrib. with *burlap, factory, loom, manufactory.*

1898 *Boston Transcript* 16 April 14/5 Mats made of rags or yarn drawn through bagging-burlap. — **1840** *Niles' Nat. Reg.* 5 Dec. 224/2 The bagging factory . . . at Lexington, Ky. took fire. **1844** Cist *Cincinnati Misc.* 94 In less than sixty days, a new Bagging Factory of equal capacity and extent with the present will be put in operation. **1862** *Rep. Comm. Patents: Agric.* 91 This kind of card is also used for carding hemp tow in Kentucky bagging factories. — **1847** *Rep. Comm. Patents* (1848) 162 The crop is certainly short of an adequate supply for the bagging looms and rope spinners now in operation. — **1817** BROWN *Western Gaz.* 98 There are several valuable rope walks, two bagging manufactories [etc.]. **1849** CHAMBERLAIN *Indiana Gaz.* 227 The principal manufactories are a bagging manufactory [etc.]. **1862** *Rep. Comm. Patents: Agric.* 101 A breaking machine . . . which was found very effective . . . at the bagging manufactory at Eaton, Ohio.

Bag holland. *Obs.* Holland cloth used for bags. — **1693** SEWALL *Letter Book* I. 137 One piece Shepard's Holland or course Bag-Holland. **1714** *Boston News-Letter* 24-31 May 2/2 Garlicks, Bagg Hollands, Ozinbrigs. **1741** *S.C. Gazette* 19-26 March, Just imported . . . and to be sold . . . bag hollands, brown hollands, table cloths.

‖**Baglegs,** *n. pl. Army slang.* (?) Baggy trousers. — **1861** NORTON *Army Lett.* 37 Bancroft, the great historian, came to see us. . . . We donned our 'baglegs' and went out with the rest of the brigade.

Bagonet. Chiefly *S.* Also **baggonet, bagnet.** Dialect forms of BAYONET *n.* {1692-; now *dial.*}

*a***1808** J. Lambert *Travels* (1813) II. 196 [A S. Carolinian asks] How can we charge bagonet without our guns? **1809** WEEMS *Marion* (1833) 121 They have got a tarnal nation sight of pistols! and bagonets. **1853** SIMMS *Sword & Distaff* 339 A pusson that can cut his way through an inimy's bloody bagnets, a whole regiment. **1871** EGGLESTON *Hoosier Schoolm.* xxix. 195 One of the blamed critters a punchin' his bagonet through it. **1878** C. COALE in *Ann. S.W. Va.* (1929) 1599 That bad man was riding behind him sticking a bagnet in him to make him keep up with their hosses.

+**b.** *Bagonet plant,* the Spanish bayonet or dagger. *Bagnet scraper,* a tool used in metal-work.

1823 W. FAUX *Memorable Days* 82 Hedges of bagonet plants and myrtles [on a S. C. island]. — **1886** *Scientific American* 6 March 145 The flat scraper should never be used for ornament—only the round nose and the 'bagnet' scrapers.

***Bag pudding.** A pudding boiled or steamed in a bag. {1598-1817; *dial.* 1877} — **1635** MATHER *Journal* 30 Sometimes wee used bacon & buttered pease, sometimes bag-pudding made with curraynes and raisins.

+**Bag-worm.** The larva of a lepidopterous insect, common in the northern states, which spins a bag for its protection. — **1862** *Congress. Globe* 8 Jan. 232/1 On the avenue and in the parks you will find the evergreen trees . . . being destroyed by the bag-worm. . . . We have no bird that can tear or penetrate the tough cocoon or covering in which it lives. **1871** STOWE *Sam Lawson* 68 Cut-worms, and bag-worms, and canker-worms, to say nothin' of rattlesnakes. **1876** *Vermont Bd. Agric. Rep.* III. 585 The Bagworm, *Thyridopterix ephemeræformis,* Haw., sometimes attacks the leaves of apple trees in other States. **1892** V. KELLOG *Kansas Insects* 104 The bag-worm has been known for several years as a shade-tree pest.

Bahama. Pertaining to, coming from, or associated with the Bahamas, a group of islands in the British West Indies. — **1789** MORSE *Amer. Geography* 59 American Birds [include] . . . Bahama Finch, American Gold-Finch. **1890** *Cent.* 2603/2 *Bahama grass,* . . . Bermuda grass. *Ib.* 5852/2 *Bahama sponge,* one of the three species or varieties of bath-sponges procured from the Bahamas. **1894** *Dept. Agric. Yearbook* 213 Among the birds [of s. Fla.] may be mentioned the white-crowned pigeon, . . . Bahama honey-creeper, and carcara eagle.

Baignoir. [F. *baignoire.*] A theater-box on the same level as the stalls. {1873-} Also attrib. — **1883** *Harper's Mag.* Nov. 884/1 There are three tiers and a half of boxes—122 altogether. The half-tier utilizes, in 'baignoir' boxes, the side walls of the parquet. *Ib.*, The baignoirs are expected to be especially attractive to clubs.

***Bail,** *n.*[1] Also †**bayle, baele, bale.**

***1.** Security given for an accused person to obtain his release from imprisonment pending his trial.

1638 *Mass. H.S. Coll.* 4 Ser. VI. 245 Holmes relates that William Baker, . . . for whome he gave bale &c. was hid againe . . . by Okace. *a***1656** BRADFORD *Hist.* 446 He was perswaded . . . they should be arested, and an action of such a summe layed upon them as they should not procure baele. **1671** *Plymouth Laws* 245 Whether they be in prison or under Bayle, his case shall be heard and determined at the next Court. **1678** *New Castle Court Rec.* 327 Itt is ordered to keepe him close prizoner without bayle or manprize. **1706** *Mass. H.S. Coll.* 2 Ser. VIII. 240 That William Rous . . . be committed to her Majesty's Gaol in Boston, there to remain in safe custody, without bail or mainprise. **1745** *Georgia Col. Rec.* VI. 145 A warrant was immediately granted to apprehend him, and he is now under bail. **1771** FRANKLIN *Autobiog.* 304 We gave bail, but saw that . . . the suit must soon come to a judgment and execution. **1787** *Md. Gazette* 1 June 3/2 Runaway from his Bail, a certain Morris Quill, about twenty-two years of age. **1789** *Ann. 1st Congress* I. 434 Excessive bail shall not be required, nor excessive fines imposed. **1827** DRAKE &

MANSF. *Cincinnati* vi. 49 Justices of the Peace. Of these there are three within the city. They are conservators of the peace, and can examine bail. **1840** *Diplom. Corr. Texas* (1908) I. 470, I have just heard that he is about to escape by giving bail. **1851** *Harper's Mag.* III. 127/2 The arrest of five persons, who were held to bail in the sum of $3000 each to appear for examination. **1898** PAGE *Red Rock* 495 Old Mr. Langstaff was released on his recognizance, Leech kindly offering the Commissioner to go his bail himself.

* **2.** The person or persons giving this security.

1705 BEVERLEY *Virginia* IV. 24 Upon the defendant's non-appearance, order goes against the bail. **1733** FRANKLIN *Poor Richard 1734* 23 Sold by the Printer . . . , counterbonds to save bail harmless. *a***1821** C. BIDDLE *Autobiog.* i. 1 He became bail for a Captain Turner. **1834** *Ohio Statutes* (1860) II. 1178 Any person . . . who shall and may be bail . . . for the appearance of any defendant. **1879** T. D. PRICE *MS. Diary* 8 Feb., Was appointed Guardian for Mrs. Rees, bond $2400. J. B. Jones & Jno. T. Evans Bails.

* **Bail,** *n.*[2] Also †**bayle, baile, bale.**

* **1.** The arched handle of a vessel extending from side to side over the mouth: often made of wire and attached so that it may fall to either side.

'A common word throughout New England' (B. '48).

1622 'MOURT' *Relation* 36 We found . . . an English Paile or Bucket; it wanted a bayle. **1646** *Early Conn. Probate Rec.* I. 16 [A] paile with an iron baile. **1819** *Niles' Reg.* XVI. Suppl. 187/2 It is supposed that the bail of the kettle was not in the bend of the hook, but only on the edge of it. **1840** *Knickerb.* XVI. 53 An iron pot, without a bale or cover. **1844** *Ib.* XXIII. 444 The clean white-pine buckets, without bails, into which the sap drips from the spiles, are made expressly for this use. **1873–4** *Vermont Bd. Agric. Rep.* II. 73 The pails . . . are smoothly made of the best of stock and supplied with bails, the ears for which are placed well down on the sides. **1879** B. F. TAYLOR *Summer Savory* xiii. 116, I hear footstoves tinkling down the aisle in winter, each swung in a black-gloved hand by its little bail. **1918** RIDEOUT *Key of Fields*, etc. 269 He snatched at the bail of a lantern that stood perched on a heap of mud.

* **2.** A ring or hoop.

1849 *Rep. Comm. Patents* (1850) 222 Said gudgeons being attached either to a railroad truck or the bail of crane.

* **Bail,** *v.* [BAIL *n.*[1]]

* **1.** *tr.* To admit to bail; to liberate on bail. {–1827} *arch.* or *Obs.*

1638 WILLIAMS *Letters* (1874) 86 Since which time (Seargeant Holmes baling him) he is again escaped. *a***1649** WINTHROP *Hist.* II. 192 Upon this two Englishmen . . . offered to be his sureties, whereupon he was bailed till he should be called for. *Ib.* 316 Mr. Smith and Mr. Dand . . . were bailed to the general court. **1705** SEWALL *Diary* II. 148 While we were deliberating in the Council-Chamber, P. Dudley writt a letter, that [he] would not bail them yet. **1773** TRUMBULL *Progress of Dulness* II. 37 Not all his compliments can bail, Or minuets dance him from the jail. **1781** *Virginia State P.* I. 565 He has in accordance with orders, arrested Overby and Wells, and bailed them in good security to appear for trial when called on. **1868** *Colo. General Laws* (1877) 320 Provided, that . . . the accused [be] . . . brought into court, . . . bailed or tried at the term.

* **2.** To get (one) *out* of prison by giving bail.

1709 *N.J. Archives* 1 Ser. III. 458 Which Writ was not delivered to him until . . . November last, long after Brown was bailed out of his custody. **1871** [L. H. BAGG] *At Yale* 258 There is always money enough in a crowd to 'bail out' any one who may be arrested. **1897** FLANDRAU *Harvard Episodes* 219 Procure all the money you can lay your hands on . . . and come bail me out. **1908** WHITE *Riverman* iii. 32, I'll just get along and bail the boys out of that village calaboose.

+**3.** To bind *over* by bail or security.

1889 *Cent.* s.v., To bail [one] over to keep the peace.

* **Bailable,** *a.* [BAIL *v.*]

* **1.** Entitled to be liberated on bail.

1647 *R.I. Col. Rec.* I. 194 He shall make his mittimus and send the offender to Gaile, vnless he be bailable, and then shall he baile him. **1666** *Md. Archives* II. 139 All criminalls accused of any offence . . . & not bayleable shall be . . . sent to the prison at St. Maries. **1686** SEWALL *Diary* I. 146 Council said he was not bailable. **1706** *Mass. H.S. Coll.* 2 Ser. VIII. 241 Notwithstanding the offence therein contained, they are bailable by law. **1787** *Northwest Ordinance* Art. 2, All persons shall be bailable unless for capital offences. **1836** EDWARD *Hist. Texas* 197 All persons shall be bailable by sufficient sureties.

2. Permitting of bail.

1827 *Ill. Revised Statutes* (1833) 210 It shall be the duty of the sheriff . . . to let him or them to bail, where the offence is bailable. **1868** *Colo. General Laws* (1877) 319 It shall be the duty of the district court . . . to make an order fixing the amount of bail, to each offense bailable by law.

b. (See quotations.)

1850 BURRILL *Law Dict.* (1859) I. 174/2 A bailable action is one in which a defendant may be obliged either to find bail on his arrest, or go to prison. *Ib.*, Bailable process is that upon which a defendant may be held to bail.

Bail-bond. [BAIL *n.*[1]] The bond entered into by one furnishing bail. {1709–1815}

1710 *Boston News-Letter* 13 March 2/2 How to make returns of all writts and warrants, form of bail bond, &c. **1733** FRANKLIN *Poor Richard 1734* 23 Sold by the Printer, . . . bail bonds. **1765** OTIS *Consideration of Colonists* 33 A rheam of bail bonds is now sold for about fifteen shillings sterling. **1834** *Ohio Statutes* (1860) II. 1178 To surrender . . . such defendant or defendants, in discharge of such recognizance bail bond. **1853** 'P. PAXTON' *Yankee in Texas* 359 The idea was universal that the bail-bond would be forfeited, and the criminal seek safety in flight. **1884** 'CRADDOCK' *Where Battle was Fought* 288 The law requires two sureties on a bail-bond.

+**Baile.** *S.W.* [Sp.] A dance; a dance hall.

1844 GREGG *Commerce of Prairies* I. 243 The musical instruments used at the *bailes* and *fandangos* are usually the fiddle and *bandolin*, or *guitarra*. **1846** MAGOFFIN *Santa Fe Trail* (1926) 165 The procession is broken up now, and all have gone off to the *bayle*, . . . *monte*, etc. **1867** J. MELINE *Santa Fé & Back* 105 On our arrival in the evening, a *baile* was immediately gotten up in our honor. They used to call these things fandangoes, but we are growing genteel, and now *baile* is the word. **1888** SHERIDAN *Memoirs* I. 30 On going to a house where a large *baille*, or dance, was going on we found among those present two of the Indians we had been chasing. **1895** REMINGTON *Pony Tracks* 73 One night the *patron* gave a *baile*. The *vaqueros* all came with their girls. **1907** WHITE *Arizona Nights* x. 166 We . . . built a *baile* and saloon and houses out of adobe.

* **Bailee.** *Law.* [f. *bail*, to deliver goods in trust.] One who is responsible for goods placed in his hands for a stated use.

1806 WEBSTER, *Bailee*, . . . one who receives goods in trust. **1845** *Ill. Revised Statutes* (1883) 399 If any bailee of any bank note, money or other property, shall convert the same to his own use. **1852**, etc. [see BAILOR]. **1865** *Atlantic Mo.* XV. 64, I must show him that I have not been a fraudulent bailee.

* **Bailie, Bailey, Baily.** *Obs.* **1.** An officer responsible for enforcing byelaws relating to fishing. (Cf. WATER-BAILEY.) **2.** An officer having charge of a bailiwick. — **(1) 1671** *Plymouth Laws* 284 It is further ordered, that the Master of any Vessel, that shall come here to fish, . . . shall . . . give under his hand to the Baily or his Deputy, for . . . due observance of the Orders of Court concerning their Fishing. **(2) 1672** *N.Y. State Col. Hist.* XII. 496 The said towne shall be erected into a Corporacon by the name of a Balywick, that is to say, it shall be governed by a Bailey & six assistants.

* **Bailiff.** Also †**baylif, -life, -liffe, balife.** An officer of justice under a sheriff, who carries out distraints or arrests, executes warrants, serves summonses, etc.

1634 *Dorchester Rec.* 8 Nicholas Upsall is chosen vnto the office of Baylife in this Plantation for the yeer ensuing, and is by vertue of this office to levie fines, amer[cements] & rates by way of destrayneing goods or impounding cattle for the [satis]fieing of them. **1638** *Md. Council Proc.* 73 Memorand. that this day Mr Sheriff hath appointed Robert Percy to be his bailiff or undersheriff until Xtmas next. **1656** *Dorchester Rec.* 85 It was voted by the towne . . . that it should bee the bailifes office to looke that Swine be yoaked and ringed accordinge to order. **1672** *Town Rec.* in Stiles *Windsor* (1891) I. 87 Ebenezer Dibble was by town vote chosen for town Baylif for this year ensuing, to go forth when required by the townsmen to fetch in town rates of those that refuse or neglect to pay their rates when demanded. **1725** *New-Eng. Courant* 1 Mar. 1/1 Perpetually haunted and dun'd by their creditors, and those frightful creatures call'd Bailiffs. **1741** *Georgia H. S. Coll.* II. 103 Sent James Shepherd to the guardhouse, for abusing this deponent and Mr. John Caldwell, third bailiff, in the execution of their office. **1773** TRUMBULL *Progress of Dulness* II. 37 Not all his oaths can duns dismay, Or deadly Bailiffs fright away. **1842** *Knickerb.* XX. 491 He then called up the bailiff, a tremendous-looking cracker . . . and proceeded to admonish him. **1885** *Rep. Indian Affairs* 204 The Captain of police acts as sheriff for the court, using as many of his police as necessary for bailiffs. **1910** J. HART *Vigilante Girl* 382 That man assaulted me, and this officer, who is the bailiff of my court, shot him.

Bailiffship. The office of bailiff. {1651–} — **1744** *Ga. Col. Rec.* VI. 97 As to the perpetual bayliffship which he pretends to, we could find no grounds for any such title.

* **Bailiwick.** [f. *bailie* bailiff, and *wick* place.] The district in which a sheriff (originally a bailie) has authority. Freq. used jocularly in a general sense: one's natural or proper place or sphere.

*a***1647** F. GORGES *Descr. New Eng.* iv. 47 The summons thereof to the severall Bailywicks, or Counties, is to be issued out in my name. **1672** *N.Y. State Col. Hist.* XII. 496 The said towne [of Newcastle] shall be erected into a corporacon by the name of a balywick. **1700** *N.J. Archives* 1 Ser. II. 335 To the sheriffe of the County: . . . you [shall] sumon twenty foure good & lawfull men of your bailewick . . . [to] appeare immediately before his majesties Justices. **1773** *Ann. S.W. Virginia* 205 That the Sheriff summon twenty four of the most capable freeholders in his bailiwick . . . to serve as a Grand Jury. **1816** *Niles' Reg.* IX. 370/2 We command you that you distrain the said president, directors, & Co. by all their lands and chattels within your bailiwick. **1840** [KENNEDY] *Quodlibet* vi. 86 To twenty writs placed . . . in the sheriff's hands, that functionary made his return . . . , 'Eloped under whip and spur out of the Bailiwick.' **1843** *Knickerb.* XXI. 589 A friend and correspondent inside the southern division of Mason and Dixon's 'bailiwick' gives us the following. **1851** *Ib.* XXXVIII. 554 In Belmont county, Ohio, immediately adjoining the bailiwick in which . . . Delaney exercised the functions of High Sheriff. **1867** 'T. LACKLAND' *Homespun* II. 213 In one place, the people are perhaps a little inclined to social gayety, or what would be esteemed such outside their own bailiwick. **1911** SAUNDERS *Col. Todhunter* ix. 119, I'm skeered to the marrow, . . . because I'm out o' my bailiwick.

***Bailment.**

***1.** The action or fact of admitting a person to bail.

1647 *R.I. Col. Rec.* I. 194 He shall certifie at the next Gaile delivery . . . such information, recognizance, and bailment.

2. 'A delivery of goods in trust' (W. 1806). {1602–}

1833 NEAL *Down-Easters* I. 26 A sort of law-lecture about general-average, common-carriers, bailment, etc. etc. **1859** BURRILL *Law Dict.* (ed. 2) I. 177/1 The restoration of the thing bailed to the bailor . . . does in fact constitute a part of the contract in nearly all the varieties of bailment. **1881** *Nation* 30 June 464/2 The modern doctrine of principal and agent appears; but this is to be construed with reference to the author's view of succession in status and of bailment.

Bailor. One who delivers goods to be used for a stated purpose. {1602–} — **1828** WEBSTER, *Bailor*, one who delivers goods to another in trust. **1852** BOUVIER in *Bacon's Abr.* I. 607 A mere naked bailee of goods is not liable to an action for them at the suit of the bailor, until after a demand and refusal. **1881** *Nation* 30 June 465/1 As he [=the thief] was responsible to the bailee from whom he took the property for breaking, he could not be proceeded against by the bailor. As the bailee had full protection . . . , so he was absolutely responsible to the bailor.

Bail-piece. a. A bail-bond {1768}, +or a court certificate attesting this. **+b.** A warrant authorizing a surety to arrest the person bailed by him.

*a*1821 C. BIDDLE *Autobiog.* i. 1 As he understood he was going off without settling the debt for which he was bound, my father took out a bail-piece. **1852** DUNLAP *Bk. Forms* (1857) 194 Aldermen and Justices of the Peace . . . cannot issue a bail piece to arrest the principal in any case. **1859** BURRILL *Law Dict.* 174/1 This undertaking of the bail is termed their *recognizance*, and is effected by executing and acknowledging what is called a bail-piece. **1904** *Baltimore American* 24 Aug. 2 He was later released on bail . . . but was again arrested last night . . . on a bail piece, issued by . . . [the] clerk of the Criminal Court.

Bail-writ. *Law.* A writ requiring one to find bail. — **1835** LONGSTREET *Georgia Scenes* 94 He's in for it; dead, sir; good bye to bail-writs and *sassiperaris!*' **1888** PERRIN *Ky. Pioneer Press* 35 He took out a bail writ against one Alfred Sebastian to secure a debt of $30.

Baire (=mosquito-net): see BEAR *n.*[3]

Bait-barrel, -bin, -box, -can. Receptacles for holding bait. — **1846** *Knickerb.* XXVII. 512 The mackerel and bait-barrels, and the 'doctor's' pots and kettles, begin to kick up a row. — **1881** *Amer. Naturalist* XV. 371 But most of the squid are sandwiched in layers of two or three deep between layers of finely broken ice in bait bins in the vessel's hold. — *a*1841 [W. HAWES] *Sporting Scenes* I. 41, I turned my bait box upside down. **1855** *Knickerb.* XLVI. 347 To become a disciple of the bait-box and grub. **1869** W. MURRAY *Adventures* Advt., Dealers in Fishing Tackle, . . . Snells, Bait-Boxes, Tackle-Books. **1871** LEWIS *Poultry Book* 172 If you have a chicken or fowl that has been killed by the mink . . . put that into the bait box and close the lid. — **1887** H. FREDERIC *Seth's Brother's Wife* 90 The poles were ready, the bait-can stood outside the shed door.

Baiter. [f. *bait* v.] One who baits fish-hooks. — **1888** GOODE *Amer. Fishes* 30 From these the anglers cast their squids and play their fish, attended by their 'baiters.'

Bait-fish, fish used as bait. **Bait-fisher,** one who fishes with bait. **Bait-fishing,** fishing with bait. **Bait-hook,** a hook furnished with bait. **Bait-hunting,** searching for fishing bait. — **1820** *Western Review* II. 235 (Ohio River fish), Fifty species of small fresh water fishes . . . [are] commonly called Minnies, Minnews, Bait-fish, Chubs, and Shiners. *Ib.* 241 *Rutilus compressus*, a small fish . . . called Fall-fish, Bait-fish, Minny, &c. **1871** *Penna. Game Laws* in *Fur, Fin & Feather* (1872) 110 It shall not be lawful for any person . . . to take any fish . . . by means of any seine . . . except bait fish to be used in angling. — **1883** *Century Mag.* July 378/1 Ignatius, who was a bait-fisher, jointed up an ash and lancewood rod of the same weight. — **1886** *Outing* May 160/1 To row a mile or so to the Narrows and then vary trolling with bait-fishing. — **1849** C. LANMAN *Alleghany Mts.* xviii. 149 In doing this, he handled the bait hook a little too roughly, and was consequently caught in the place of a bear. — **1881** *Amer. Naturalist* XV. 370 He spends twice as much time in sailing and bait-hunting as in the actual work of fishing.

***Baiting,** *vbl. n.*[1] A meal, or feed for an animal, on a journey or during an interval of work. {–1655}

1843 *Knickerb.* XXII. 430 The country tavern whose long shed and sanded hall give surety to the stranger and his beast of a comfortable noontide baiting. **1864** T. L. NICHOLS *Amer. Life* I. 33 The tavern-keeper could only charge for a baiting of hay and a lodging. **1868** BRACKETT *Farm Talk* 99 'Got your fodder all fed out?' 'Nearly. There's a hundred or two more of fodder corn, which I keep for baitings.' **1877** BARTLETT 26 *Baiting*, lunch in the field at hay-time.

Baiting, *vbl. n.*[2] +The laying in of a supply of bait. — **1881** *Amer. Naturalist* XV. 369 Our vessel, a small one, made three 'baitings,' fishing each time about two weeks. *Ib.* 371 Twenty-five or thirty thousand are thus cared for at a 'baiting' and will keep in fit condition for use from two to three weeks.

***Baiting-place.** [BAITING[1]] A stopping-place for rest and food. — **1825** NEAL *Bro. Jonathan* II. 95 When we come nigh the taverns; or baitin' places, or post offices. **1838** [INGRAHAM] *Burton* I. iv. 68 Indeed, the horses, with characteristic instinct, seemed to be equally aware, with Jaques, that they were approaching their journey's end, or, at least, a baiting-place.

Bait-knife. A knife for cutting bait. — **1857** *Harper's Mag.* Sept. 536/1 So we sat down upon two fish-barrels, I with . . . pencil in hand, he with a bait-knife. **1906** F. LYNDE *Quickening* 67 He got on his knees and picked out the exact spot in the dog's neck where he would drive the bait knife home.

+Bait-mill. A device used by fishermen for cutting fish, etc., into small pieces for bait. — **1846** *Knickerb.* XXVII. 513 Set the old bait-mill going. **1852** L. SABINE *Fisheries* (H. Doc. 23) 358 The bait-mill . . . was a box which was made to stand on end, and had a crank projecting through its side; while internally it had a wooden roller armed with small knives. **1874** KNIGHT 212/1.

+Bait-stealer. [BAIT *n.* 1.] The cunner or chogset, which nips the bait. — **1888** GOODE *Fishes* 297 At Salem they are called 'Nippers,' and occasionally here and elsewhere 'Bait-stealers.'

+Bait-stick. Part of a trap. — **1834** A. PIKE *Sketches* 33 Lewis placed his trap still deeper under the water, and covered it with moss, placing no bait-stick.

***Baize.** Also **†bayes, bays, baise, base.**

***1.** A coarse woolen cloth with a long nap, usually dyed green or red; used esp. as a lining and for house-furnishings.

1649 *Md. Archives* IV. 518 Thomas Pasmore . . . bought . . . soe much red cotton bayes or cloth as made his . . . wife . . . a wast coate. **1711** *Mass. H.S. Coll.* 6 Ser. V. 252, I haue wrapt the smale things in som of the black bays that covered the coach. **1755** *Essex Inst. Coll.* XLIII. 95 [He] had on a homespun brown striped cloth coat, lined with red bays, and breeches of the same, lined with red bays also. **1779** *R.I. Commerce* II. 71, [I] have . . . also receivd . . . one piece baize to outward appearance in good order. **1787** *Md. Gazette* 1 June 4/3 A drab-coloured cloth sleeve jacket, lined with green baize. **1803** *Ann. 7th Congress* 2 Sess. 349 Wool hats, . . . flannel, baize, half-thicks, and in truth all woolen cloths under 2*s* sterling per yard, pay an extra duty. **1849** *Rep. Comm. Patents: Agric.* (1850) 247 No. 5 [wool] . . . used for making coarse satinets, baises . . . 25 cents. **1910** HART *Vigilante Girl* iv. 54 His bed was laid on a faro layout set in green baize.

2. *attrib.* Made of baize. {1634–}

1642 *Md. Archives* IV. 154 Keeping from her one red base wastcoat lined with silk galon. **1732** *S.C. Gazette* 32/2 Run away . . . a Pawpaw negro woman, . . . having blue bays clothes. **1784** CUTLER in *Life & Corr.* I. 105, I put on a winter baize jacket. **1828** NEAL *R. Dyer* 70 A sailor-looking fellow, in a red baize shirt. **1843** 'CARLTON' *New Purchase* II. lx. 268 An uncommon abrasion of inexpressible-seats, and green baize leggins. **1866** 'F. KIRKLAND' *Bk. Anecdotes* 528 A motley assortment of baize jackets, ragged coats, and old trowsers. **1891** ELLIS *Check No. 2134* xxxvii. 259 He drew out a large green baize bag.

+Bake, *n.* [f. the vb.] **(1)** An act or the result of baking. **(2)** A social gathering at which a substantial meal is served. (Cf. CLAM-BAKE.) **1846** *Spirit of Times* (N.Y.) 6 June 174/3 In search of that five pound pickerel which he was bound to pull in every year, for the grand 'bake' at the village hotel. **1851** *Knickerb.* XXXVIII. 187 Saint Peter [in stained glass] is a little cracked . . . ; but I've got a first-rate bake on Paul. **1874** CODMAN *Mormon Country* 40 In the meantime one of Thompson's men 'started a bake.' Having the yeast already prepared from a powder, he mixed the flour in a frying-pan, and in less than fifteen minutes turned out a great cake of bread.

+Bake-beans, =*baked beans:* see below.—**1834** DAVIS *Lett. J. Downing* 26 Then we made the bake beans and salt pork fly.

***Baked,** *ppl. a.* Cooked by baking; spec. with *beans* (see also BOSTON) or *pork.*

(1) *a*1805 *Pocumtuc Housewife* (1906) 12 *Baked Beans.* Beans should be put in cold water and hung over the fire the night before they are baked. **1825** NEAL *Bro. Jonathan* II. 173 There were among the native preparations of the country, baked beans, . . . Indian pudding. **1832** L. M. CHILD *Frugal Housewife* 51 Baked beans are a very simple dish, yet few cook them well. **1846** *Yale Lit. Mag.* XI. 235 (Th.), Such affectionate mention of clam-chowder, roast-veal, and baked-beans. **1859** STOWE *Minister's Wooing* xvi, Burr . . . praised . . . the baked beans steaming from the oven. **1875** — *Deacon Pitkin* iv. 57 Indian bread, to accompany the pot of baked pork and beans. **1884** BARNES *Mem. Th. Weed* 79 Weed . . . enjoyed for dinner . . . codfish, supplemented by baked pork and beans. **1916** EASTMAN *From Deep Woods* 90/3 It may be some pies or Boston baked beans from your folks!

(2) **1828** E. LESLIE *Receipts* 23 Baked Apple Pudding. **1844** HAWTHORNE *Note-books* II. 148 We had some roast veal and baked rice-pudding on Sunday. **1860** M. J. HOLMES *Maude* v. 57 She ought to have a *relish*—preserves, jelly, baked-apple, or somethin'. **1882** MRS. OWENS *Cook Book* 28 [Recipe for] Baked Fish with Cream Sauce.

***Bake-house.** Also **†backe howse.** A building or part of one in which bread is baked; a bakery.

1649 *Suffolk Deeds* I. 122 A certaine parcell of land . . . together with the mansion house, millhouse & mill, bakehouse & all other the houses.

1660 *Portsmouth Rec.* 101 Tell he . . . showld sett up a brew howse or backe howse vpon the same. **1662** *Essex Probate Rec.* I. 378 A bake house, . . . an orchard. **1688** *Conn. Probate Rec.* I. 515, I give to my son John Warde . . . my part of my bake house. **1702** *Boston Rec.* 19 The bake-house belonging to the Revd. Mr. James Allen being on the back side of the town. **1735** FRANKLIN *Penna. Gaz.* Wks. II. 206 Where would be the damage, if . . . by regulating bakehouses . . . a clause were added to regulate all other houses. **1785** *Md. Hist. Mag.* XX. 46 He put on board her several scow loads of bread and flour which were taken from Elisha Hall's bake house on Jones's falls. **1819** M'MURTRIE *Sk. Louisville* 137 In Louisville . . . [are] six bake houses, ten blacksmiths' shops. **1861** *Army Regulations* 248 Ovens may be built or paid for by the Subsistence Department, but not bake-houses. **1885** *Rep. Indian Affairs* 198 One is a commodious bake-house with a large bake-oven in it.

+**Bake-kettle.** A vessel for baking bread, beans, potatoes, etc.

1846 SAGE *Scenes Rocky Mts.* xvii, On one occasion they carried off a bake-kettle to a distance of several hundred yards. **1847** Howe *Ohio* 152 She had but one fire-proof vessel in the house, an old broken bake kettle. **1852** STOWE *Uncle Tom* iv, Aunt Chloe whipped the cover off the bake-kettle. **1877** *Vermont Bd. Agric. Rep.* IV. 92 The warm biscuit and short cake . . . [were] baked in the bake kettle, with hot coals under the kettle and on the cover. **1889** COOKE *Steadfast* i. 13 On one side of the fire stood a bake-kettle and a four-legged pot.

+**Bake-oven.** [Perhaps after Du. *bakoven.*] An oven or pan used for baking. {1886 *dial.*}

'This term is often used in the West for the simple word *oven* in a bakery. It is also applied to the iron bake-pan' (B. '59).

1777 *N.J. Archives* 2 Ser. I. 335 A good two story brick-house, . . . [with] bake oven, a cedar log barn, and stables [etc.]. **1787** *Md. Gazette* 1 June 1/2 An excellent cellar, a large two-story brick kitchen and bake-oven. **1805** *Raleigh* (N.C.) *Register* 9 Sept., A dry cellar . . . in which is a bake oven, large enough to bake a barrel of flour at one heat. **1809** *Austin Papers* (1924) I. 164 Also of kitchen utensils, one table, two iron pots, one bake oven. **1812** *Mass. Spy* 2 Sept. (Th.), [He] threw it in the bake-oven, which had just before been heated to bake bread. **1848** E. BRYANT *California* 464 The furnaces are of the simplest construction exactly like a common bake-oven. **1885** *Rep. Indian Affairs* 50 The laundry and bakery . . . finished and furnished with stationary wash-tubs, bake-oven, troughs, and tables. **1891** RYAN *Told in Hills* 100 Without looking up from the eggs she was scrambling in the bake-oven of a few minutes before.

transf. **1845** *Knickerb.* XXV. 193 On the Illinois shore of the river, is a mass of rock, nearly sixty feet high, which from its peculiar shape, and from an aperture in the southern side, has obtained the appellation of 'The Devil's Bake-oven.'

***Bake-pan.** [BAKE *v.* Cf. Du. *bakpan.*] A pan or similar utensil in which bread, etc., can be baked. {1579 only.}

1790 *Penna. Packet* 1 March 3/3 William Robinson . . . hath for sale . . . iron castings, consisting of tea kettles, bake pans, spiders, skillets, dog irons, & flat irons. **1807** *Austin Papers* (1924) I. 132, 3 bake pans. **1840** DANA *Two Years* xxxv. 441 A cargo of fresh provisions, mules, tin bake-pans, and other notions. **1857** CHANDLESS *Visit Salt Lake* I. ii. 21 Our cooking utensils consisted of two or three camp-kettles, a frying-pan, skillet (or bake-pan), and a coffee-mill. **1879** BISHOP *4 Months in Sneak-box* 145 One of those flat-bottomed, three-legged, iron-covered vessels, which my reader will now recognize as the bake-pan, or Dutch oven.

***Baker.**

***1.** A person who bakes bread, cakes, pies, etc.

1645 *Suffolk Deeds* I. 61 Thomas Hawkins of Boston, Baker. **1654** JOHNSON *Wonder-W. Prov.* 209 Weavers, brewers, bakers, . . . are orderly turn'd to their trades. **1669** *Boston Rec.* 49 John Waite is prohibited to set vp the trade of a baker. **1675** *Penna. Mag.* VI. 89 Here you need not trouble the . . . bakers and brewers for beer and bread. **1723** *Weekly Mercury* 19–26 Feb. 4/1 The bakers there [=Boston] are under great apprehensions of being forbid baking any more bread, unless they will submit to the Secretary, as supervisor general and weigher of the dough. **1778** *Journals Cont. Congress* X. 206 Resolved, that a company of bakers be raised, to bake bread for the army. **1802** WEEMS *Letters* II. 225 Some of those [books] . . . look . . . like six penny loaves of baker's bread and feel to the full as light and spungy. **1810** M. DWIGHT *Journey* 35 We have nothing to eat & can get nothing but some slapjacks at a baker's some distance off. **1866** 'F. KIRKLAND' *Bk. Anecdotes* 602 She handed him . . . about a dozen bakers' cakes. **1880** *Harper's Mag.* Sept. 615 Bakers' buns being often upon the table. **1894** *Dept. Agric. Yearbook* 41 Very few accurate weighings and analyses of bakers' bread have been made in this country.

***b.** *Baker's dozen,* thirteen. {1599–} Also *baker's-dozenth,* thirteenth.

1865 *Atlantic Mo.* XV. 371 The political and religious prejudices of the people could not have called them a baker's dozen. **1871** BARNUM *Struggles* 713 What is thirteen but the traditional 'baker's dozen' indicating good measure? **1889** *Harper's Mag.* Feb. 492/1 With these thirteen, counting as twelve, we confidently challenge England to produce the Anglo-Saxon baker's-dozenth.

+**2.** A covered metal container used for baking.

'A small tin oven in which baking is performed' (W. '47).

1841 *Lowell Offering* I. 227 A peep into the baker told that the potatoes were cooked. **1852** *Harper's Mag.* March 446/2 There was a tin baker before this fire, with a pan of large apples in it. **1854** *Putnam's Mag.* Jan. 30, I . . . kicked off the hot cover of a baker . . . , and snatching the half-baked bread, . . . began to devour it. **1863** MRS. WHITNEY *F. Gartney* xxxii, She went straight to the tin-baker . . . , and lifted the cover, to see if her biscuits were ready for tea. **1879** *Scribner's Mo.* Nov. 23/2, I would advise . . . the taking of a stove, which with a baker . . . does not weigh over thirty-five pounds. **1887** TOURGEE *Button's Inn* 213 A tray of biscuit were showing circles of white flaky puff beneath the ardent reflections of a bright tin 'baker.' **1897** *Outing* Feb. 489/1 The cooking utensils, consisting of three dripping pans, one patented baker and one large coffee-pot.

+**Bakery.** [Perhaps after Du. *bakkerij.*] A place where baked products are made and sold; a bake-house or baker's shop. {1857–}

1827 DRAKE & MANSF. *Cincinnati* viii. 65 For the year 1826 . . . ten bakeries [employed] 28 hands. **1832** MRS. TROLLOPE *Domestic Manners* I. 85 There are no butchers, fishmongers, or indeed any shops for eatables except *bakeries,* as they are called, in the town. **1836** R. WESTON *Visit* 55 The signs above the different shop-doors, as I passed along, had a novel effect; 'Bakery,' denoting a baker's shop. **1846** *Knight's Penny Mag.* (N.S.) I. 101 The signs [in N.Y.] were no less striking to a stranger: . . . *Bakery* showed where one of life's great essentials could be bought. **1863** J. FISK *Exped. R. Mts.* 27 The city consists of one long and some short, irregular streets, . . . 'bakeries' and restaurants abounding for the floating population. **1865** *Atlantic Mo.* XV. 665/1 Everybody that ever travelled that road will remember Joseph German's bakery. **1881** *Harper's Mag.* Feb. 372/1 The occasion . . . was a fire in a brick building, . . . occupied as a bakery. **1923** K. D. WIGGIN *Garden of Memory* 112, I bought my luncheon at a different bakery every day.

+**Bake-shop.** [BAKE *v.*] A shop in which bread, pastry, etc. are sold.

1789 *Kentucky Gazette* 25 April 1/4 Nicholas Wood . . . keeps a Bake Shop in Lexington, . . . where may be had . . . several kinds of bread. **1862** *Norfolk* (Va.) *letter* in *N.Y. Tribune* 16 May, As a general thing, the stores are closed . . . The bake-shops, however, seem to be driving a brisk business. **1877** BARTLETT 27 *Bake-shop,* the place where articles made by bakers are sold. Southern. **1886** P. STAPLETON *Major's Christmas* 151 Jacob . . . stopped before a bake shop where two small youngsters stood . . . looking in at the window.

+**Bakhara,** var. BUCKAYRO. — **1827** DEWEES *Lett. from Texas* x. 66 These [rancheros] are surrounded by . . . peons and bakharas, or herdsmen.

***Baking,** *vbl. n.* **1.** *Whole baking,* a large number. (Cf. BILING *vbl. n.*) *colloq.* +**2.** The hardening of the pay-dirt at the bottom of the pan in gold-washing. — (1) **1843** [STEPHENS] *High Life N.Y.* II. xxii. 67 All to once, down cum a hull baking of posies, all around her, as thick as hops. (2) **1851** D. B. WOODS *At Gold Diggings* 51 It must be often stirred with the hands to prevent 'baking,' as the hardening of the mud at the bottom is called.

Baking-, the vbl. n. in attrib. use, as *baking-day, -dish, -iron, -kettle, -oven, -pan* {1601}, *-plate, -pot, -soda.*

1867 'T. LACKLAND' *Homespun* I. 34 If it so chances that it is baking-day, the scene can hardly be matched anywhere for its industry. **1900** DIX *Deacon Bradbury* 127 On Friday afternoons, Saturday being baking-day, the trade was busier. — **1859** ELWIN *Glossary* 35 A small baking-dish. **1879** MRS. WHITNEY *Just How* 175 Put the pieces of meat into a deep baking-dish. — **1633** *N.H. Doc. & Rec.* I. 79, 1 baking iron. — **1854** THOREAU *Walden* 69 'Mould it [=dough for kneaded bread], and bake it under a cover,' that is, in a baking-kettle. — **1852** STANBURY *Gt. Salt Lake* 63 Baking-ovens, cooking stoves without number, . . . were found [strewn by emigrants] along the road. — **1641** *Conn. Public Rec.* I. 443, 2 brass pans & a bakeing pan. **1650** *Mayflower Descendants* X. 173 One bakeing pan, 3 skillets. **1879** MRS. WHITNEY *Just How* 263 Put cherries or plums in layers, with the sugar strewed between, in deep earthen or stone baking-pans. — *Ib.* 29 When the cakes are done turn out each one and lay upon its reversed baking-plate. — **1875** KNIGHT 1583/1 A skillet or baking-pot used in cooking by wood coals on the hearth. — **1881** *Rep. Indian Affairs* 49 For weeks at a time, their storehouses were empty, with the exception of corn, baking soda, and soap.

Baking-powder. Any of various powders (differing as to ingredients) used to effect the raising of bread, biscuits, cake, etc. Also attrib.

1857 YOUMANS *Handbook of Household Science* 269 Preparations which are known as egg-powder, baking-powder, and custard-powders. **1864** *U.S. Patent* 13 Dec. 45,419 Baking powder. **1865** *Chicago Tribune* 10 April 1 [Using] Rogers' self rising flour, . . . you require no Baking Powder. **1873** *U.S. Patent* 143,580 Baking powder bread. **1880** *Scribner's Mo.* May 128/1 [In making] the bread, . . . baking-powder, not yeast, is used of course. **1884** *Harper's Mag.* June 81/2 A baking-powder box. **1900** *Sen. Doc. 56th Cong. 1 Sess. 303* 2 The effect of alum in baking powders is a matter at issue between the cream of tartar baking powder companies and the alum baking powder companies.

***Balance,** *n.* Also †**ballance.**

1. A political counterpoise or counteracting influence. {1677–}

Especially used in combination with *check:* see CHECK *n.*

1755 L. EVANS *Anal. Map Colonies* 31 Where there is no third State to hold the Ballance of Power. **1755** *Md. Hist. Mag.* III. 3 Pensylvania is truly in a hopeful condition, . . . and the Quakers are a blessed ballance. **1788** *Debates in Mass. Conv.* (1856) 204, I . . . had learnt something of the checks and balances of power, and I found them all here [in the U.S. Constitution]. **1789** R. H. LEE in J. Adams *Wks.* (1854) IX. 553, I think there is no doubt but that this legislature will be recommended to consist of the triple balance. **1802** *Ann. 7th Congress* 1 Sess. 532, I will agree that there are times when checks and balances are useful.

2. *In balance*, in debt. *Obs.*

1732 *Md. Hist. Mag.* XIX. 297, I am sorry to be so long in ballance to you wch I'm well asured you do not want, but hope to make you suitable returns for all favours.

+3. The remainder; what is left; the rest.

A transference from the commercial use (cf. 2). Copiously illustrated by Thornton from 1819 to 1882, and in Suppl. from 1807 to 1892. Comments on the use, by American and British writers, are frequent in the first half of the 19th c., e.g.: **1816** PICKERING 43 *Balance.* This mercantile word is much used by the people of the Southern States in conversation, as a general term signifying the *remainder* of *anything*. Ex. I spent a part of the evening at a friend's house, and the balance at home: A quarter part of the army were killed and the balance taken prisoners, &c. The word is also often used in the debates of Congress, as I am informed (but only by the Southern members) in the following manner: A member moves, that the first section of a bill should be amended, and the balance of the bill struck out. **1817** WEBSTER *Letter to Pickering* 12 *Balance.* The use of this word for *remainder* or *residue*, in a general sense, is forced, and not warranted by any good principle. **1842** BUCKINGHAM *Slave States* II. 132 The word balance is constantly used to signify the remainder of anything, as 'I shall spend the summer in the mountains, and the balance of the year on the sea-coast.' **1883** E. A. FREEMAN *Amer. Speech & Customs* I. 91, I doubt whether anyone in England would talk of 'the balance of the day,' a phrase which I have heard in America.

1788 *Penna. Mag. of Hist. & Biog.* (1894) XVIII. 62 Arose early and sent off the balance of our things at mother's. **1805–8** PIKE *Sources Miss.* 41, [I] sent four of my men with one canoe, loaded with the balance of nine deer, that had been killed. **1808** *Ib.* 184, I determined to . . . leave part of the baggage . . . and with the balance . . . cross the mountains on foot. **1813** *Conn. Courant* 5 Oct. 3/4 About 70 of our company will be able to go to Malden—the balance will be discharged. **1826** A. ROYALL *Sketches* 221 We walked through the balance of the hospital. **1829** — *Penna.* I. 12, I returned to the tavern and rested the balance of the day. **1839** *S. Lit. Messenger* V. 377/2 Come in and content yourself for the balance of the night. **1845** JUDD *Margaret* I. xiii. 96 Deacon Hadlock himself, hearing Obed's entreaties, consented to remit the balance of the penalty. **1849** Commons, etc. *Doc. Hist.* I. 254 The balance will average with any set of hands for good working and faithful subjects. **1857** J. H. GIHON *Geary & Kansas* 20 The balance of this reserve is now covered with squatters. **1862** *Ill. Agric. Soc. Trans.* V. 543 The balance of the bed you may sow with peppers and celery. **1878** SAWTELLE *Hist. Townsend, Mass.* 16 The balance of its territory is very rough and ledgy. **1884** NYE *Baled Hay* 73 The bird is constructed of an eagle's head, a canvas back duck's bust and feet, with the balance sage hen and baled hay. **1895** M. A. Jackson *Memoirs* 616 Lee, with D. H. Hill and the balance of his army, was to hold off McClellan. **1907** SINCLAIR *Industrial Republic* 47 We have been a century building them—you, and I, and the balance of the American people.

4. A movement in dancing. Cf. BALANCE *v.*

1900 STOCKTON *Afield & Afloat* 138 She and the ghost . . . opened the ball. Together they made the coupée, the high step, and the balance.

***Balance,** *v. intr.* Of partners in dancing: To advance and retire, or move in converse directions like the arms of a balance. {1775}

*c***1800** FESSENDEN *Poems* (1806) 24 Balance and foot it rigadoon and chassé, Brimful of rapture. *Ib.* 33 Balance Dick, then down the middle, . . . Balance Joe, to Lucy, to Lucy Wiggle. **1835** [LONGSTREET] *Georgia Scenes* 138 The strut prevailed most in balancing, the bobs, when balanced to; and the waddle, when going round. **1883** FOOTE *Led-Horse Claim* iv. 45 She was 'balancing' to one of the peripatetic partners in 'gentlemen to the left.' **1891** 'CRADDOCK' in *Harper's Magazine* Jan. 215/2 He might join the others on their round, dogging the steps of the youth he wished to forestall, both balancing to the lady of their choice. **1900** DRANNAN *Plains & Mts.* 190 The prompter called out, 'Balance all!' and I forgot to dance until all the others were most through balancing.

Balanced, *ppl. a. Naut.* Of a sail: Reduced by close reefing in order to steady the ship in bad weather. {1762–9} — **1750** *Essex Inst. Coll.* XLVI. 96 We were obliged to hand the jibb and lay too under ballanced mainsail. **1753** *Ib.* 120 Had a gale of wind at S.E. . . . ; lay too under balanc'd mainsail. **1802** ELLICOTT *Journal* 256 At break of day the wind shifted to the north, and continued with such violence that we had to heave too under a ballanced main-sail.

Balance-pole.

1. A pole used by a performer to assist in the preservation of balance. Also fig.

1832 KENNEDY *Swallow Barn* I. xii. 128 A man who addresses a woman must go at it like a French rope-dancer . . . and trust to the balance pole to preserve him through his flourishes. **1868** CHANNING *Recoll. Newport* 31 It was the custom of the time to use a balance-pole to steady the body when skating.

2. A well-sweep.

1832 KENNEDY *Swallow Barn* II. i. 40 The well grew to be choked up with weeds; the balance-pole waxed stiff, and creaked in its swivel.

Balance-reef, *n. Naut.* The closest reef of a fore-and-aft sail. — **1782** FRENEAU *Works* 387 He intends to provide my calash with what he calls single, double and balance-reef eyelet holes. **1840** COOPER *Pathfinder* xv, At two he was compelled to get a second reef aft; and by half-past two he had put a balance-reef in the sail.

Balance-reef, *v. Naut. tr.* To reduce (a sail) by the closest form of reefing. Also *balance-reefed* adj. =BALANCED. — **1814** *Log of 'Chasseur'* in *Md. Hist. Mag.* I. 169 Balance reefed the main sail, and took two reefs in the fore and aft fore sail. **1840** DANA *Two Years* v. 29 We . . . endeavored to beat to windward under close-reefed topsail, balance-reefed trysail.

Balance sail. *Naut.* A sail under a balance-reef. — **1761** *Essex Inst. Coll.* XLVII. 129 So we carried our ballance sails to keep clear of the land.

Balance-sheet. A tabulated statement of the debits and credits of a business, undertaking, etc. {1849–}

1838 *Democratic Rev.* I. 42 He becomes familiar with the various account books. . . . with trial balances, balance sheets [etc.]. **1854** 'O. OPTIC' *In Doors & Out* (1876) 49 Trial balance, balance sheet, every thing foots up without the variation of a penny. **1870** MEDBERY *Men of Wall St.* 325 Before winter the balance-sheets showed a clear gain, in a single season, of $1,300,000. **1877** *Harper's Mag.* Dec. 35/2 The balance-sheet for six months appeared in this form. **1898** WESTCOTT *D. Harum* 136 Would you kindly give me the last balance sheets of the two ledgers and the bill-book?

Balcony.

1. A platform jutting from a room or outside wall, supported by columns or consoles, and usually enclosed by a railing, balustrade, or parapet. {1618–, at first in the Ital. form *balcone.*} ‖(*b*) See quot. 1781.

1687 SEWALL *Diary* I. 169 This day several orders published at Boston, Governour and Council standing in Mr. Usher's balcony. **1719** *Ib.* III. 229 Govr. Phillips stood in Mr. Phillips's balcony hang'd with a carpet, and the officers saluted him as they passed by. **1736** *Boston Selectmen* 305 The balcony at the east end of the town house, fronting King Street. *Ib.* 316 The committee appointed for repair of the balcony of the town house. **1760** HUTCHINSON *Hist. Mass. Bay* iii. (1765) 387 A long declaration was read from the balcony or gallery of the town house. **1781** T. ANBUREY *Travels* (1923) II. 307 Most of the houses [in N.Y.] are built with brick . . . , several stories high; many of them have balconies on the roof, where company sit in the summer evenings. **1847** PARKMAN in *Knickerb.* XXX. 284 He walked up the steps, tramped along a rude balcony, and kicking open a door, displayed a large room. **1856** STOWE *Dred* I. 44 The outside of the house was built . . . with two tiers of balconies. **1860** HOLMES *Professor* ix. 282 On such a balcony or 'stoop,' one evening I walked with Iris. **1880** CABLE *Grandissimes* xv. 99 Rising over the levee willows . . . [the breeze] flutters among the balconies and in and out of dim Spanish arcades.

+b. A gallery (esp. the first gallery) in a theater.

1854 E. Tompkins *Boston Theatre* (1908) 15 Persons who purchase Tickets . . . for either the Parquette, Parquette Circle, Balcony [etc.]. **1883** *Harper's Mag.* Nov. 882/2 The three tiers of boxes and the balcony of which the [N.Y. Opera House] auditorium consists. **1906** *Springfield W. Republican* 13 June 14 The dress circle [in an English theatre], analogous to our balcony, has stall seats at ten and six.

+2. (See quotation.)

1830 J. F. WATSON *Philadelphia* 177 The 'cushion head dress' was of gauze stiffened out in cylindrical form with white spiral wire. The border of the cap was called the balcony.

+Bald, *n.* [BALD *a.* 1.] A bare or treeless mountain top, especially in the southern Appalachians. Sometimes as a proper name.

1838 *S. Lit. Messenger* IV. 231/2 At length, after considerable fatigue, we came to the top of the near Bald; from this we had an extensive and delightful prospect. *Ib.*, After a short pause, we went on to the far Bald, which we found a good deal higher than the near. **1849** C. LANMAN *Alleghany Mts.* Add. 184 The sides of the Roan, the Black, the Bald, and others . . . are covered with a deep rich vegetable mould. **1877** *Field & Forest* III. 39 We come out upon 'The Bald,' as it is called, a mountain meadow extending over the crest of the mountain. *Ib.* 40 These 'Balds' cover most of the summits of the mountains over 6000 feet in height . . . and are a marked feature of the Southern Appalachians. **1885** 'CRADDOCK' *Prophet* i. 2 She paused often, and looked idly about her, . . . sometimes still higher at the great 'bald' of the mountain. **1887** — *Keedon Bluffs* 169 For they were in truth near the summit, not ascending the great bald, but in a gap between two peaks. **1890–3** E. M. TABOR *Stowe Notes* 26 The Mountain is seen at its best in winter, with snow and ice along the rocky summit—the 'bald.'

***Bald,** *a.*

1. Destitute of vegetation or trees; bare. {1642–}

*c***1761** *N. C. Col. Rec.* VI. 608 At Bald head 2 miles north of the bar of

Cape Fear. **1780** R. PUTNAM in *Memoirs* 163, I shall be . . . at least as far as Peeks kill or the Bald Hill. **1784** BELKNAP in *Amer. Philos. Soc.* II. 43 On the northwest side seven summits are in plain view. . . . Of these four at least are bald. **1819** E. DANA *Geog. Sketches* 272 In this region, three-fourths of the banks of the Mississippi consist of open prairas, or rather bald hills. **1835** SIMMS *Yemassee* I. 102 Noble forests . . . hewn down by the axe to make way for the bald fields of the settlers. **1840** HOFFMAN *Greyslaer* I. x. 116 There's a ledge of bald rock to the left yonder. **1847** *S. Lit. Messenger* XIII. 97/1 The edge of the bald ground, about a mile from the top of the mountain. **1856** *Harper's Mag.* XIII. 294/1 The bald face of the mountain . . . is about one thousand one hundred feet above the level of the water. **1869** *Amer. Naturalist* II. 647 A few clumps of willows . . . are the only objects remaining . . . except the bald bluffs. **1872** EGGLESTON *End of World* xli. 257 A large bald hill overlooking the Ohio was to be the Mount of Ascension. **1901** MOHR *Plant Life Ala.* 104 The eminences of the lower swells of the plain with the strata of the limestone near the surface and destitute of arboreal growth are called bald prairies.

+**b.** *Bald place.* (See quotation.) *N.J.*

1813 WILSON *Ornithology* VII. 49 [Long-legged plovers] inhabit those particular parts of the salt marshes pretty high up towards the land, that are broken into numerous shallow pools. . . . In the vicinity of these 'bald places,' as they are called by the country people [of N.J.], . . . among the thick tufts of grass [etc.].

2. Of grain: Having no beard; awnless.

a1804 J. Roberts *Penna. Farmer* 114 What kind is the most productive, red, white, yellow, bearded or bald? **a1817** DWIGHT *Travels* I. 49 The best species . . . is that which has been commonly named the 'English bald-wheat.' **1856** *Mich. Agric. Soc.* VII. 805 He . . . raises . . . the little yellow kind of corn, . . . the old-fashioned bald or bearded wheat. **1863** *Rep. Comm. Agric.* 100 White Blue Stem is a variety of bald white wheat.

+**3.** Of birds: Having white feathers on the head.

See BALD COOT, BALD EAGLE, etc., below, and names of other birds, as FALL DUCK.

Bald brant. [BALD *a.* 3.] (See quotation.) — **1874** LONG *Wild-Fowl* 243 The younger [snow geese] . . . are further characteristically distinguished as bald brant or white-heads.

* **Bald coot.** Also †**ballcoot.** [BALD *a.* 3.] The American coot or mudhen, *Fulica americana.*

1709 LAWSON *Carolina* 149 Black Flusterers . . . Some call these the great bald Coot. **1782** JEFFERSON *Notes Va.* (1788) 118 Besides these [birds], we have the Royston crow, . . . black head, ballcoot [*sic*], sprigtail. **1789** MORSE *Amer. Geog.* 59 Upwards of one hundred and thirty American birds have been enumerated . . . [including] the bald coot. **1858** WILLIS *Convalescent* 387 He said there were thirty [kinds], naming, among others, the blue-wing, . . . the ball coot [etc.].

+**Bald cypress.** A coniferous tree, *Taxodium distichum,* common in the southern part of the United States, and in Mexico.

1709 LAWSON *Carolina* 96 Cypress is not an Ever-green with us, and is therefore call'd the Bald Cypress. **1810** MICHAUX *Arbres* I. 30 Cypress, denomination générale. Bald Cypress, nom moins usité. Black Cypress et White Cypress. **1832** BROWNE *Sylva Amer.* 143 It is called . . . in the ancient Southern States cypress, and sometimes bald cypress. **1875** *Amer. Naturalist* IX. 391 One more species completes the list of coniferae, the bald cypress, which grows along the Ohio and Mississippi. **1901** MOHR *Plant Life Ala.* 110 On the . . . banks of both of these rivers a fine timber growth of bald cypress frequently forms brakes of considerable extent, occasionally accompanied by the tupelo gum.

+**Bald eagle.** [BALD *a.* 3.] The white-headed eagle (*Haliaetus leucocephalus*), the bird emblematic of the United States.

1692 R. FRAME *Descr. Penna.* 27 The Turky-Buzard and Bald-Eagle high. **1705** BEVERLEY *Virginia* II. 34 In the Air you see a fishing-hawk flying away with a Fish, and a bald-eagle pursuing, to take it from him. **1709** LAWSON *Carolina* 137 The bald eagle [is] so call'd, because his head, to the middle of his neck, . . . is as white as snow. **1731** CATESBY *Carolina* I. 1 This bird is called the Bald Eagle, both in Virginia and Carolina, though his head is as much feather'd as the other parts of his body. **1783** *N.H. Hist. Soc. Coll.* VI. 285 Resolved, that the Bald Eagle, carrying the emblems on its breast, be established as the order of the Society. **1811** WILSON *Ornithology* IV. 89 White-headed, or bald eagle . . . is the most beautiful of his tribe in this part of the world, and the adopted emblem of our country. **1813** *Niles' Reg.* IV. 57 On the towering mast the bold Bald Eagle gloriously shall ride. **1826** FLINT *Recoll.* 6 The wolf, the bear, and the bald eagle, were the most frequent emblems on the tavern signs. **1846** SAGE *Scenes Rocky Mts.* xvii, Upon the opposite side of the river was a bald-eagle's nest, with two half-grown fledglings. **1850** [S. F. COOPER] *Rural Hours* 422 The Bald Eagle can scarcely be called a rare bird with us. **1867** *Amer. Naturalist* I. 41 The most beautiful . . . of our winter birds of prey, is the historical White-headed or Bald Eagle, . . . most inappropriately chosen for our national emblem. **1878** BEADLE *Western Wilds* xxx. 483 Small is the pleasure one can take . . . in the sweep of the bald eagle, where the next occupation of that eagle may be in picking the meat from his bones. **1884** ROE *Nature's Story* 50 We have only two species of the genuine eagle in this country, the bald, or American, and the golden, or ring-tailed.

Bald-face. {1690–}

+**1.** The whistling duck or American widgeon, *Mareca americana;* =BALD-PATE.

1709 LAWSON *Carolina* 151 The bald or white faces are a good fowl. They cannot dive. [Cf. *Ib.* 137 Water fowl are . . . sheldrakes, bald faces [etc.].] **1768** WASHINGTON *Diaries* I. 253 Went a ducking between breakfast and dinner and killd 2 mallards and 5 bald faces.

b. A horse having a white face or a conspicuous white mark on the face.

1785 WASHINGTON *Diaries* II. 436 Black bald face. **1894** *Outing* June 216/2, I jest had time to hitch old Bald Face into the cart and git here.

+**2.** A poor grade of whiskey; also called red-eye, pine-top, and lightning whiskey.

(*a*)**1845** HOOPER *Simon Sugg's Adv.* vii. 90 The Captain and 'Lewtenant Snipes' sat down, with a bottle of bald-face between them. **a1846** *Quarter Race Kentucky,* etc. 85 Who-oo-whoop! whar's the crock of bald-face, and that gourd of honey? **1851** *Polly Peablossom* 60 If you've got any more of that baldface, pour it out! **1856** *Harper's Mag.* XIII. 447/2 Skeeters and myself took a drink of bald-face together, which in these parts [Dismal Swamp of Virginia] is the sacred pledge of hospitality. **1892** *Amer. N. & Q.* VIII. 246, I have frequently heard *mean* whiskey called 'bald-face.'

(*b*)**1846** *S. Lit. Messenger* XII. 95/2 The loudest lungs were at a premium, and so was 'bald-face' whiskey. **1857** *Harper's Mag.* Nov. 859/1 He was addicted to . . . bald-face whisky, pug brandy, hard cider, etc.

+**3.** *Bald-face bear* (see quotation); *bald-face hornet,* the bald-faced hornet (see next).

1796 LATROBE *Journal* 104 The bald-face hornet. This dangerous fly is proverbially fierce. **1876** *Fur, Fin & Feather* Sept. 142 (citing *Idaho World*), A bear rarely seen in the mountains, which old hunters call the bald-face bear.

Bald-faced, *a.* {1677–} Of animals, etc.: Having a white face or white on the face.

1648 *Md. Archives* IV. 425 Making a priuate conueyance betweene themselues of a Bawld-facd heighfer. **1885** *Cent. Mag.* Nov. 60 He jogged along on his bald-faced bay in the bleak, untempered light. **1891** *Cent.* 6921 American widgeon, . . . also called locally bald-faced widgeon. **1913** BARNES *Western Grazing Grounds* 380 Bald-Faced . . . Horse with a white face.

+**b.** *Bald-faced hornet,* the white-faced hornet.

1861 *Ill. Agric. Soc. Trans.* IV. 341 The nest of our bald-faced hornet is occasionally suspended in a house to kill off the house-flies. **1902** L. O. HOWARD *Insect Book* 28 The bald-faced hornet (*Vespa maculata*) . . . builds the enormous paper nests commonly seen attached to the branches of the trees.

Bald-head. [BALD *a.*] +A bald-headed eagle. — **1850** GARRARD *Wah-To-Yah* xii. 157 The magnificent bald-head unfolded his wings slowly.

* **Bald-headed,** *a.* and *adv.*

+**1.** *Bald-headed eagle.* =BALD EAGLE.

1836 M. A. HOLLEY *Texas* v. 100 The bald-headed eagle and the Mexican eagle . . . are among the birds of prey, and are very common. **1847** ABERT in *H. R. Ex. Doc.* No. 41. 528 In the evening we saw a fine 'bald-headed eagle.' **1849** C. LANMAN *Alleghany Mts.* xx. 164 For an hour or more had I been watching the evolutions of a superb bald-headed eagle above the valley. **1873** *Newton* (Kansas) *Kansan* 19 June 3/2 Let patriots everywhere . . . prepare to do the clean thing by Uncle Sam and his bald headed eagle.

+**2.** =BALD *a.* 1.

1854 HAMMOND *Hills, Lakes,* etc. 79 One day we came to an old bald-headed mountain. **1862** F. Moore *Rebellion Rec.* V. II. 383, I received . . . an order to occupy the 'Bald-headed Hill' on my left.

+**3.** *adv.* Precipitately, impetuously, headlong. *slang.*

1848 LOWELL *Biglow P.* I. vi. 79, I scent wich pays the best, an' then Go into it baldheaded. **1867** *Ib.* II. Introduction p. lvii, 'To go it bald-headed'; in great haste, as where one rushes out without his hat. **1888** *Pall Mall Gaz.* 22 June (F.), The Chicago Republicans, to use an Americanism, have gone baldheaded for protection.

+**b.** *To snatch one bald-headed,* to manhandle one. *slang.*

1875 *Scribner's Mo.* Nov. 142/2 The throng then gave a specimen of calumny broke loose, And said I'd 'snatched him bald-headed.' **1889** FARMER 34 A somewhat different meaning is conveyed by *snatched bald-headed,* used of a person defeated in a street fight.

transf. **1909** 'MARK TWAIN' *Is Shakespeare Dead?* i. 6 Can't you keep away from that greasy water? Pull her down! snatch her! snatch her baldheaded!

* **Bald-pate.** [BALD *a.* 3.] +The widgeon; =BALD-FACE 1. — **1813** WILSON *Ornithology* VIII. 86 The canvass backs and widgeons, or as they are called round the [Chesapeake] bay, bald pates. *Ib.* IX. Index, Baldpate Duck. **1858** BAIRD *Birds Pacific R.R.* 783 Baldpate; . . . the top of the head from the bill is pale unspotted creamy white. **1883** *Century Mag.* Oct. 925/2 The little pools and creeks . . . furnish food for the blue and green winged teal, the black duck, mallard, baldpate and wood-duck.

+**Bald-rush.** (See quotation.) — **1857** GRAY *Botany* 503 Bald-rush, . . . *Psilocarpa scirpoides,* Torr., . . . [grows in] inundated places, Rhode Island and Plymouth, Massachusetts. July.

+**Baldwin.** A variety of eating apple originated *c*1800 by Loammi Baldwin of Woburn, Mass.; the Pecker or Woodpecker apple; also, the tree which bears this fruit.

1826 *Catal. Fruits in Garden Hort. Soc. London* 108, Apples, ... Baldwin's. **1837** COLMAN *Mass. Agric. Rep.* (1838) 61 The cold winter of 1833–4 was fatal to the Baldwin apple trees, throughout the county. **1848** LOWELL *Biglow P.* I. ix. end, Looking out through my study-window, I see Mr. Biglow at a distance busy in gathering his Baldwins. **1859** *Mich. Agric. Soc. Trans.* X. 254 Baldwin is a very popular market fruit in New England. **1861** *Ill. Agric. Soc. Trans.* IV. 468 Our farmers set in the early orchards of Wisconsin a large proportion of Roxbury Russets, Baldwins, ... and Spitzenbergs. **1880** *Harper's Mag.* Aug. 355/1 Outside were great orchards, ... the gnarled trees soon to redden with old fashioned Baldwins and Rambos. **1887** WILKINS *Humble Romance* 238 On the right of the garden were two old apple-trees, a Baldwin and a Porter.

+**Baldy.** [BALD *a.*] **1.** = BALD *n.* Also *attrib.* **2.** As the name of a horse. (Cf. BALD-FACE ib.) — **(1) 1875** J. J. STEVENSON in *U.S. Explorations & Surveys* III. 318 On the Rio Grande side ... is the group called Sierra Blanca, of which the most conspicuous is Old Baldy Mountain. **1884** L. B. PRINCE in *Encycl. Brit.* XVII. 399/2 The main range of the Rocky Mountains enters ... [N. Mexico] from the north, the highest peaks being the Costilla ... and Baldy. — **(2) 1894** *Outing* XXIV. 216/2 Well, I tried to wear it [= a whip] out on Baldy coming along. **1905** A. H. RICE *Sandy* 94, I d-drove dad's buggy ..., so he would come to the r-rescue, and he swung on to old B-Baldy's neck like he had been a race-horse.

* **Bale,** *n.* Also †**bail, bayl.** A large bundle or package of some article of merchandise done up compactly: **a.** In general use. **b.** Of cotton. **c.** Of hay.

a. 1704 *Boston News-Letter* 31 July 2/2, 124 bayls of dry goods and silks. **1705** *Ib.* 4 June 2/1 Some bails of paper. **1729** *Md. Hist. Mag.* XVIII. 336 Also half a bale of coffee if cheap. **1815** *Ib.* I. 233 Some shirts and two bales of purser's slops for the comfort ... of the wounded and others. **1838** COOPER *Homeward B.* xxix, The bales that had actually been got out of the ship having been put upon the bank with a view to lighten her. **1852** STOWE *Uncle Tom* xxix, The law regards him [= the Negro] ... as devoid of rights as a bale of merchandise. **1866** *Rep. Indian Affairs* 126 A bale of blankets and a sack of flour will accomplish more than its weight in gold. **1901** CHURCHILL *Crisis* 4 The floor was stacked high with bales of dry goods.

b. 1803 *Ann. 8th Congress* 2 Sess. 1523, 20,000 bales of cotton, of three cwt. each, at twenty cents per pound. **1810** WEEMS *Lett.* III. 15 Here in Augusta, they annually take forty thousand bales of cotton. **1825** *Austin Papers* (1924) II. 1078 In England they will fall more than 50,000 Bales short of the ordinary supply. **1832** CLAY *Amer. System* Sp. (1842) 175 The average produce of laborers engaged in the cultivation of cotton may be estimated at five bales, or fifteen hundred weight, to the hand. **1851** *Polly Peablossom* 143 Brother Crump, during the liveliest period of the cotton season, drove into Wetumpka and disposed of his 'crap' of ten bales. **1857** Commons, etc. *Doc. Hist.* I. 279 The packing should be in square bales; ... to be in two breadths of wide bagging, pressed until the side seams are well closed. **1867** EDWARDS *Shelby* xx. 365 And these commercial gentlemen usually kept count themselves of the number of bales sold. **1889** *Cent.* 428/2 The weight of a bale of American cotton is between 400 and 500 pounds, varying with the season of production. **1891** *Century Mag.* March 643 The cotton crop of Texas is over 1,000,000 bales.

c. 1834 *N.Y. City Ordinance* 15 April, All pressed hay, or hay in bales or bundles. **1865** *Atlantic Mo.* XV. 601 A brig, ... piled over with bales of hay, comes lazily down with the tide. **1874** KNIGHT 218/2 By these means the size of bale for a given weight of hay is materially reduced.

Bale, *v.* [BALE *n.*] *tr.* To make into bales. {1760–}

1806 WEBSTER, *Bale*, v., to put into bales. **1835** [INGRAHAM] *South-West* II. 290 To press and bale expeditiously requires at least four or five hands and one horse. **1862** *Rep. Comm. Patents: Agric.* 113 It will be found difficult to bale or ship flax in the sliver form. **1866** *Rep. Indian Affairs* 204 This year, however, the goods designed for them are properly baled and marked. **1874** KNIGHT 218/2 In baling forage rations, a feed of corn is placed in a feed of hay, and the whole condensed into the shape of a large brick. **1898** B. H. YOUNG *Jessamine Co., Ky.* 161 The bagging was used at that time in baling cotton.

+**Bale basket.** [See BAIL *n.*[2] 1.] — **1847** *Rep. Comm. Patents* 108 Take a half bushel of wheat in a bale basket, sink it gradually [in a half hogshead of salt water], stirring it with a paddle.

+**Bale cloth.** Cloth used for covering bales. — **1797** B. HAWKINS *Letters* 346, 8 yds. bale cloth to Harry Dergin, at 12½c., $1.00. **1818** DARBY *Emigrant's Guide* 205 The demand for cordage and bale cloth. **1862** *Ill. Agric. Soc. Trans.* V. 159 We have pressed the sirup from the sugar through fine bale-cloth.

+**Bale cotton.** Cotton packed in a bale or bales. — **1827** *Free Press* (Tarboro, N.C.) 22 Sept., Bale Cotton received and shipped to any merchant in Norfolk or elsewhere, for 12½ cents per bale.

Baled, *ppl. a.* [BALE *v.*] Made into bales, esp. of hay.

1828 *Free Press* (Tarboro, N.C.) 7 Nov., Cash given for Naval Stores, Cotton in the seed and baled Cotton, Beeswax, &c. **1872** EGGLESTON *End of World* xxx. 197 [The steamer] discharged her sugar and molasses, and took on a new cargo of baled hay and corn and flour. **1878** *Ill. Dept. Agric. Trans.* XIV. 29, I found upon investigation that to purchase bailed hay the cost ... would be burdensome. **1891** C. ROBERTS *Adrift America* 135, I was fortunate enough to be able to stow myself away in a car that was partly filled with baled hay. **1918** *Nation* 7 Feb. 168/1 Baled straw for the mattress ... being stored inside the barracks.

Bale-goods. [BALE *n.*] Merchandise made up in bales. ?*Obs.* {1694–1790}

1707 *Boston News-Letter* 19 May 2/1 The *Lowstaffe's* prize is said to be very valuable, being loaden with bale goods, beef and pork. **1720** *Weekly Mercury* 1 Sept. 1/1 The said pirates took out of the *Boston* ship bale goods to the value of near ten thousand pounds Sterling. **1745** *Essex Inst. Coll.* VI. 182/2 A large sloop laden with rum & molasses and bale goods. **1761** S. NILES *Indian Wars* II. 476 A large brig ... that had fur, deer-skins, with coarse bale-goods, on board. **1812** *Niles' Reg.* II. 168/2 A vessel ... has arrived at a port of the United States ... from Amsterdam, laden with ... a large quantity of cloths and bale goods. **1815** HUMPHREYS *Yankey in Eng.* 41 Of what articles was your lading composed? ... *Doo.* Staves and hoop-poles, with diverse bail goods.

+**Baler.** [BALE *n.* and *v.*]

‖**1.** One who produces (so many) bales of cotton.

1850 [H. C. LEWIS] *La. Swamp Doctor* 87 Every farmer in the South is a planter, from the 'thousand baler' to the rough, unshaved, unkempt squatter.

2. One of various kinds of machines used for baling paper, rags, hay, straw, etc.

1888 *Voice* (N.Y.) Why are not balers as common as threshers? I believe it is owing to ... manufacturers ... not pushing the balers. **1909** *Buckeye Informer* IX. 209 The Little Giant paper Baler is a daisy. It is just what we needed to take care of scrap paper.

3. One engaged in baling.

1889 *Cent.* s.v. **1899** *Boston Globe* 22 Oct. 36/4 A baler and shipper of hay.

+**Bale-rope.** [BALE *n.*] Rope used for binding bales, esp. of cotton.

1821 *Missouri Intell.* 25 Dec. 3/3 (Advt.) Bagging, Bale rope. **1824** *Ann. 18th Congress* 1 Sess. I. 1542 The price of cotton is higher than that of bagging and bale-rope; but, in selling cotton, the bagging and bale-rope are all weighed and sold as cotton. **1837** *Mass. Stat.* 12 April, A corporation, by the name of the Goulding Patent Bale Rope Manufacturing Company, for the purpose of manufacturing bale rope, in the towns of Roxbury and Brookline. **1862** *Rep. Comm. Patents: Agric.* 111 Flax-straw (which they generally ... converted into tow for bale-rope purposes). **1874** R. H. COLLINS *Kentucky* I. 48, 1,200 tons [of hemp] were manufactured into bagging or bale rope in Mason County.

Baling, *vbl. n.* [BALE *v.*] The process of putting up cotton, etc., in bales. {1879} Also attrib. with *cloth, linen, press, rope.*

1809 F. CUMING *Western Tour* 165 There is [in Lexington, Ky.] one manufacturer of baling cloth for cotton wool, who employs thirty-eight hands. **1809** *Ann. 11th Congress* 1 Sess. II. 2171 There is manufactured, in Kentucky, a quantity of baling linen sufficient for the consumption of the greater part of the cotton country. **1815** *Niles' Reg.* IX. 187/1 They are considered much superior to all other baling presses. **1836** J. S. Bassett *Plantation Overseer* 100 The am[oun]t of the Sale of all the Cotton ... is $3750 and the Bailing is to be taken out of that. **1851** *Ib.* 189, 1100 yards Coten bagginge; 1000 lbs baling rope. **1854** *Harper's Mag.* VIII. 456/1 The baling of the cotton ends the labor of its production on the plantation. **1874** KNIGHT 722/1 Double-acting baling-press ... has two boxes in which the material is compressed.

* **Balk.**[1] Also †**bawk.**

* **1.** A ridge between furrows; a strip of unplowed land serving as a boundary.

1636 *Boston Rec.* II. 13 Another layne to be left to goe from the water side up the balke or meare that goes up from the end of John Mylands house. **1654** *Suffolk Deeds* II. 5 With all and singuler houses, out houses, ... Leyes, balkes, lott grass, parting grass, meadowe [etc.]. **1788** WASHINGTON *Diaries* III. 355 All hands went to Hoeing up the Balks between, beginning on the No. side, next the Road. *a***1817** DWIGHT *Travels* II. 441 On the day, when the wheat was carried home, it was inconvenient to carry the chess; it was, therefore, thrown together upon a bawk, or head-land. **1857** *Lawrence* (Kansas) *Republican* 11 June 3 The plow [is] inclined to run out and leave those unsightly balks which disfigure some fields. **1884** *Vermont Agric. Rep.* VIII. 13 [He] prefers sod land for corn, and would insist that it be thoroughly done, with no balks.

* **2.** A wooden beam.

1862 *New Amer. Cycl.* III. 691/2 A pontoon train contains ... the balks and planks (chesses) to form the platform [etc.]. **1888** BILLINGS *Hardtack* 384 The floor timbers of the [pontoon] bridge, known as *Balks*, were twenty-five and one-half feet long. **1901** *Boston Globe* 2 Dec. 12/2 Timber dealers always talk of a large piece of mahogany or oak as a log, while a trunk of firwood is a firpole, and of other timber a balk.

+**Balk.**[2] [BALK *v.*] In base-ball: see quots. 1867–89. — **1845** in *Appleton's Ann. Cycl.* (1886) X. 77/2 A runner can not be put out ... when a balk is made by the pitcher. **1867** CHADWICK *Base Ball Player* 53 A balked Ball.—Should the pitcher move his foot in delivery—thereby making a 'balk'—and the Umpire call a 'balk' until the ball is returned to the pitcher, [etc.]. **1889** *Cent.*, *Balk*, [in] Base-ball, a motion made by the pitcher as if to pitch the ball, but without actually doing so. **1912** C. MATHEWSON *Pitching* x. 224 So one winter I spent some time every day out in the back yard getting that balk motion down.

Balked, *ppl. a.* +In base-ball: see BALK *n.*[2], quot. 1867.

+**Balker.** [BALK *v.*] A balky horse. — **1898** WESTCOTT *D. Harum* 5 'When you get a balker to dispose of,' said David gravely, 'you can't alwus pick an' choose.'

+**Balkiness.** [BALKY *a.*] The quality of being balky. — **1894** *Outing* July 349/1 The mules were the very embodiment of balkiness. **1909** LINCOLN *Keziah Coffin* x. 143, I, bein' a Hammond, with some of the Hammond balkiness in me, I set my foot down as hard as his.

+**Balking,** *vbl. n.* (See quotation and BALK *n.*[2]) — **1867** CHADWICK *Base Ball Player's Bk.* 91 *Balking.* The ball must be pitched, not jerked or thrown to the bat; . . . if he fails in either of these particulars then it shall be declared a balk.

+**Balky,** *a.* Also **baulky.** [f. E. *balk* (1843–), of a horse, to be restive.] Of a horse, mule, etc.: Given to stopping suddenly and refusing to go on.

1856 OLMSTED *Slave States* 197 Advice how to cure a balky horse. **1857** *Quinland* II. xvi. II. 117 The driver says one of his horses is baulky, and he can't go any farther. **1869** ALCOTT *Little Women* II. vi. 81 Of three [horses] left, one was lame, one blind, and the other so balky you had to put dirt in his mouth before he would start. **1873** BEADLE *Undevel. West* 743 The old conflict goes on, . . . first one side getting ahead and then the other, like a pair of balky oxen. **1897** PORTER in *Century Mag.* May 100 Like horses in a balky team, no two ever pulling together. **1902** MCFAUL *Ike Glidden* iv. 26 The horse was truly baulky, and evidently not worth a ten-cent piece.

***BALL,** *n.*[1]

***1.** A ball used in playing various games.

*c***1618** STRACHEY *Hist. Virginia* 78 They [=Indians] . . . forceably encounter with the foot to carry the ball the one from the other, and spurned yt to the goale. **1634** WOOD *New Eng. Prospect* II. xiv. 86 Their [*sc.* Indians'] Goales be a mile long . . . ; their ball is no bigger than a hand-ball, which sometimes they mount in the Aire with their naked feete. **1775** ADAIR *Indians* 400 The ball is made of a piece of scraped deer-skin, moistened, and stuffed hard with deer's hair. **1868** CHADWICK *Base Ball* 15 The pitcher is required by the rules to deliver the batsman a ball within the legitimate reach of his bat. **1891** *Triangle* December 127 Yale . . . carried the ball from the center of the field to Harvard's goal. **1897** *Outing* Aug. 481/1 [Unless] with the ability to race, . . . a pony will never get his rider 'on the ball' and run it up the full length of the field.

***b.** A game played with a ball; +now esp. baseball.

1737 BRICKELL *N. Car.* 336 Their [*sc.* Indians'] manner of playing Ball is after this manner. **1778** CARVER *Travels* 19 The Indians . . . drew near the Fort, and began a game at Ball, a pastime much used among them and not unlike tennis. **1802** ELLICOTT *Journal* 291 Athletic exercises were encouraged, particularly playing ball. **1807** IRVING *Salmagundi* xii. 266 Young seniors go down to the flag-staff . . . sometimes to play at ball. **1837** J. D. WHITNEY *Life* 20 It is about the time now for playing ball. **1859** ELWYN *Glossary* 18 Few of the games of ball in this country are the same as those in England. The one we used to call 'bat and ball,' may be an imperfect form of cricket. **1868** CHADWICK *Base Ball* 162 Our concluding remarks in this work on the National Game of ball of Americans. **1872** EGGLESTON *Hoosier Schoolm.* iv. 48 He could not catch well or bat well in ball. **1904** GLASGOW *Deliverance* 135 'Play ball with me; Will,' she said; 'I feel as if I were a child to-day.'

+**c.** In base-ball: A pitched ball, not struck at by the batter, which fails to pass over the home plate at a height between the knee and the shoulder.

1873 CHADWICK *De Witt's Base-ball Guide* 83 If the umpire calls three balls, and the ball on which the last call is made passes the catcher, the striker is at liberty . . . to run. *c***1886** — *Art of Pitching* 55 If a ball be bowled along the ground to the bat, the umpire is required to call a ball. **1891** N. CRANE *Baseball* 76 Every ball that is not hit by the batsman must be a 'strike' or a 'ball.'

d. In fig. phrases, as *to keep up the ball* {1781}, *to set*, or *keep*, *the ball rolling.*

1772–6 J. ANDREWS *Letters* 382 A discontented few, who make it their principal to keep up the Ball, . . . caus'd the whole day to be pass'd in altercation. **1840** *Log Cabin & Hard Cider Melodies* 58 Virginia will keep her ball rolling. **1850** W. COLTON *Deck & Port* xiv. 390 That courageous organization which set the ball of Anglo-Saxon supremacy rolling in California. **1871** STOWE *Pink & White Tyranny* xvi. 189 Bob Lennox . . . said he didn't 'care a hang who set a ball rolling, if only something was kept stirring.'

***2.** A cannon ball: a musket or rifle bullet.

1757 *Lett. to Washington* II. 75 The nine Waggon's loaded with as many iron Shot as can be sent (over and above the 50, three pound ball). **1758** *Ib.* 356, I beg you order me another barrel [of powder] as . . . in case of accident we have no remedy save two boxes of ball. **1795** *Ann. 3rd Congress* 1069 When Mr. Smith . . . ordered them to load, he found that fifty had put down the ball before the charge of powder. **1818** FLINT *Lett. from Amer.* 21 The vessel . . . is said to be furnished with apparatus for heating ball, . . . and to carry submarine guns. **1823** JAMES *Exped.* I. 69 Captain Calloway received in his body a ball that passed through his watch. **1825** NEAL *Bro. Jonathan* I. 177 [He took] down his gun, which always hung up, loaded with ball, over the doorway. **1843** N. BOONE *Journal* (1917) 209 His gun . . . having gone off, accidentally, and a ball, of about 12 to the pound, passed through his foot. **1851** GLISAN *Jrnl. Army Life* 92 The old Mississippi rifle, carrying a half-ounce ball, is a favorite with them. **1866** *Rep. Indian Affairs* 161 Willis is shot in the knee with a ball, and Cooley in the side with an arrow. **1891** *Century Mag.* Mar. 771 He bore the marks of balls and arrows.

3. Attrib. with *bat* (cf. BALL-STICK), *costume, match, tosser;* also (in sense 2) with *patch.*

1840 *Niles' Nat. Reg.* 4 April 74/1 [The] fatal shot . . . must have been near, as the ball-patch was sticking in her head. **1853** SCHOOLCRAFT *Indian Tribes* II. 78 The . . . Indians . . . all rush forward to catch it [the ball] in their ball-bats. *Ib.* 79 The ball-bat . . . [has] one end bent up in a circular form . . . in which is a net-work made of raw hide. **1871** [L. H. BAGG] *At Yale* 317 The vanquished party in a ball match always yields up its ball as a token of defeat. **1875** CHADWICK *Dime Base Ball Player* 32 The Prospect Park ten included several fine skaters, and one veteran ball-tosser. **1894** *Outing* June 213/2 The [Indian] athletes . . . got them into their ball costume, which consists of a breech clout.

Ball, *n.*[2]

1. A social gathering for the purpose of dancing. {1632–}

'The word is used in America, for a dance at the expense of the attendants' (W. '28).

1711 C. MATHER *Diary* II. 146 A number of people . . . had on the Christmas-night a frolick, a revelling feast, and ball, which discovers their corruption. **1771** FRANKLIN *Autobiog.* 237 But one does not dress for private company as for a publick ball. **1815** *Niles' Reg.* VIII. 56/1 The ward-room officers gave a splendid ball and supper. **1823** *Baptist Mag.* IV. 41 He restrained his children from balls and assemblies. **1856** GLISAN *Jrnl. Army Life* 282 Five of these attended a ball at the mouth of the river. **1859** STOWE *Minister's Wooing* viii, The fascinating Mrs. T., whose life is a whirl between ball and opera. **1867** EDWARDS *Shelby* xxix. 509 Balls, parties, picnics, and church going kept the gallants busily occupied until the bugles rang 'Boots and Saddles.' **1881** *Harper's Mag.* Jan. 204/1 Almost every engine company had an annual ball, but the ball of the season was the general ball for the fund [=Fire Department Fund].

fig: **1782** TRUMBULL *M'Fingal* III. 67 At Concord then, with manful popping, Discharg'd a round the ball to open. **1857** *Lawrence* (Kansas) *Republican* 9 July 3 Perrin wound up the ball by playing the political clown, and by insulting Foster.

2. Attrib. with *book, clothes, dress, gown,* etc.

1786 *Md. Hist. Mag.* XXI. 138 As my visit to Henny was entirely a nursing one, I took no Ball Cloaths with me. **1826** FLINT *Recoll.* 274 The French people [of Arkansas Post] generally came to the place of worship, arrayed in their ball-dresses, and went directly from worship to the ball. **1852** *Knickerb.* XXXIX. 151 For a month before the ball-season began, I made myself miserably happy. **1853** *Harper's Mag.* VI. 720/1 The dresses above described . . . are suited exclusively to full evening or ball costume. **1863** MRS. WHITNEY *F. Gartney* v, The graceful young figure of Edith Pemberton, in her floating ball-robes. **1869** ALCOTT *Little Women* II. 211 She showed him her ball-book with demure satisfaction when he strolled . . . up to claim her for the next. **1896** WILKINS *Madelon* 50 She looked also carefully at her pretty ball gown. **1904** WALLER *Woodcarver* 281 A girl of eighteen . . . in ball dress.

***Ball,** *v.*

1. *intr.* To get the soles, feet, or hoofs clogged with snow. Also with *up.* {*dial.*}

1760 *N. E. Hist. & Gen. Reg.* XXXVI. 31 A thaw, heavy travelling, the Snow shoes balling. **1788** WASHINGTON *Diaries* III. 297 Apprehension of the Horses balling with the Snow that had fallen, . . . induced me to relinquish the journey. **1828** [see above]. **1900** *Dialect Notes* II. 22 It probably comes from the 'balling up' of a horse in soft, new-fallen snow, when a snowball forms within each shoe.

+**b.** With *up:* (see quotation).

1856 HALL *College Words* (ed. 2) 19 *Ball up*, at Middlebury College, to fail at recitation or examination.

2. Of snow: To form into a ball below a horse's hoof. {1814–}

1828 WEBSTER s.v., We say the horse balls, or the snow balls. **1835** HOFFMAN *Winter in West* I. 179 The snow, being soft, would 'ball,' as it is called, beneath my horse's feet. **1855** WILLIS *Convalescent* 74 The snow happened to be of just that clayey consistency . . . which 'balls' in the horse's hoofs so as to set him on intermittent stilts. **1878** I. L. BIRD *Rocky Mts.* 168 The snow balled in Birdie's feet to such an extent that [etc.].

+**3.** *tr.* With *up:* To bring into a state of entanglement, confusion, or difficulty. *slang.*

1887 *Harper's Mag.* Sept. 605/2 'You seem balled up about something.' . . . 'Balled up! It's no word for it . . . I'm done for.' **1896** G. ADE *Artie* xi. 98 She had him balled up till he couldn't say a word. **1897** HOWELLS *Landlord at Lion's Head* 209 Are you consumed with the melancholy that seems to be balling up all the men? **1901** MERWIN & WEBSTER *Calumet K* ii. 20 Murphy's had the job and has balled himself up. **1911** H. QUICK *Yellowstone Nights* ix. 238 Every time old Hen stepped, he balled things up worse. **1922** A. BROWN *Old Crow* xlvi. 524 They got all balled up just as their intellectual betters do when they tackle theology.

Ball-alley. [BALL *n.*[1] 1.] An alley marked off for playing bowls. {1865} — **1802** ELLICOTT *Journal* 291 A convenient ball-alley was prepared. **1831** *Ohio Revised Statutes* I. 448 Any keeper of a public house ... [who] shall establish ... any ball or ninepin alley. **1876** *Scribner's Mo.* Jan. 310 The crowd ... escorted them in triumph to the ball-alley.

+**Ball and chain.** [BALL *n.*[1] 2.] An iron ball and the chain attaching it to a prisoner's legs, to prevent escape. Also fig. — **1835** INGRAHAM *South-West* II. 189 The threat of the Calaboose, or the 'ball and chain.' **1861** *Army Regulations* 126 The legal punishments for soldiers ... are—death; ... hard labor; ball and chain. **1866** RICHARDSON *Secret Service* xxxvi. 406 His being hand-cuffed and ballasted by a ball and chain, or confined in a filthy cell. **1873** BEADLE *Undevel. West* vii. 132 Those who had ... sent them to work with ball and chain, became apprehensive of legal vengeance. **1903** LEWIS *The Boss* iii. 26 W'at's the trouble with your heels? You aint got no ball an' chain on yet, you know. **1904** *Brooklyn Daily Eagle* 10 June 4 Tammany was ... whipped into line, and made work for him under ball and chain and in stripes, to the end.

+**Ballarag.** *colloq.* [Cf. E. *ballyrag* v. (1809), 'bullyrag.'] Abusive language. *Obs.* — **1744** *Conn. Col. Rec.* IX. 21 [If they are] members of the Assembly, ... I don't care. If I can't answer them by ballarag, I can by small sword.

* **Ballast,** *n.* Small broken stone, gravel, or other material, used to form the bed of a railroad. {1847–} Also attrib.

1847 GILLESPIE *Road-Making* (1858) 295 Upon this ballast are laid the supports of the rails.... Ships' ballast was first used for this purpose ... and from this circumstance the substitutes have retained the original name. **1872** HUNTINGTON *Road-Master's Assistant* 51 Ballast is frequently hauled a long distance, and wasted by dumping on a high, narrow embankment. *Ib.* 125 This class of accidents is mostly confined to new roads, ... where ballast trains, etc., are running.

* **Ballast,** *v. tr.* To fill in or form the bed of (a road, railroad, etc.) with gravel, broken stone, or similar materials. {Also E.}

1864 WEBSTER. **1872** HUNTINGTON *Road-Master's Assistant* 51 The importance of having tracks well ballasted is understood by all railroad men. **1881** *Chicago Times* 12 March, Nearly one hundred miles of road was newly ballasted.

+**Ballast-stone.** *Obs.* One of the stones used to ballast a vessel. — **1761** S. NILES *Indian Wars* II. 490 The boat ... with three Indians came under Captain Beale's stern; who, with small arms and ballast-stones, killed two of them. **1815** *Niles' Reg.* VIII. 140/1 Some of those which went to foreign ports were without cargoes; so that *ballast stones* were humorously 'quoted' in one of the papers ..., as being in great demand at $150 per ton.

Ball-cartridge. [BALL *n.*[1] 2.] A cartridge containing a ball or bullet. {1803–} — **1847** *Army Regulations* 30 No ball-cartridges are [to be] mixed with the blank cartridges issued to the men. **1861** NORTON *Army Lett.* 21 We have got out of ball-cartridges. **1884** *Century Mag.* Oct. 810/2 The Federal soldier ... frequently carried ... a twelve-pound musket, and eighty rounds of ball-cartridge.

+**Ball-club.** [BALL *n.*[1]]

1. A club or bat used in striking a ball.

1837 J. D. WHITNEY *Life & Lett.* 20, I can't see where the ball is coming soon enough to put the ball-club in its way. **1855** THOMPSON *Doesticks* 143 [As the] cripple ... was devoutly saying his prayers, a bad boy stole his crutch to make a ball club. **1878** B. F. TAYLOR *Between Gates* 256 The limbs [of the yucca] growing out ... from the trunk ..., sometimes live ball-clubs with the big ends farthest from the tree.

2. A club or team of baseball players.

1845–55 (*title*) Knickerbocker Ball [=baseball] Club. **1871** [L. H. BAGG] *At Yale* 318 An officer of the University ball club collected these emblems of victory. *Ib.* 384 The members of a victorious ball-club display, in connection with their own, the badges of the college they have vanquished. **1888** *Outing* July 356/1 The code of rules which now govern the play of every professional ball club in America.

Ball-coot, variant of BALD COOT.

Ball-court. [BALL *n.*[1]] A piece of ground marked off for the game of ball. {1677, 1721} — **1805–9** HENRY *Camp. Quebec* 170 We complete a ball court, which had been originally formed, as it were, by stealth.

Ballet.

1. An artistic dance, usually forming part of a theatrical or operatic performance. {1667–}

1827 *Md. Hist. Mag.* XVII. 241 At night went to Mr. Durrocher's ball, to see my niece Isabel Baron dance in the *ballet. Ib.*, There was an immense crowd, and great confusion, so that at one time it was feared there would not be room to dance the ballet. **1850** MITCHELL *Lorgnette* vii. 154 It was deemed advisable to drop the ballet which had uniformly belonged to the Opera in Europe. **1891** *Century Mag.* March 712 We never succeeded in putting on a first-class ballet.

2. Attrib. and comb. in *ballet dance, -dancer* {1836}, *-girl* {1848}.

1796 *Gazette U.S.* (Phila.) 19 Nov. (Th.), A new ballet dance, called the back countryman, or the new settlers. **1850** MITCHELL *Lorgnette* ii. 35 He may have the honor to do honor to a distinguished ballet-dancer. **1865** *Atlantic Mo.* XV. 621/1 Sometimes ... the gossamer dresses of these ballet-girls are caught in the blaze of the footlights.

Ball face. [BALD-FACE.] (A) white face. — **1658** *E. Hampton Rec.* I. 149 That coult ... was a reddish couler, ... and a ball face and wall eyes. **1819** *Missouri Intell.* 4 June 3/5 One bay horse ... a ball face. *a***1870** CHIPMAN *Notes on Bartlett* 20 *Ballface*, contemptuous epithet applied by negroes to white persons.—Salem, Mass., 1810–20.

Ball-faced, *a.* =BALD-FACED *a.* — **1658** *E. Hampton Rec.* I. 149 Are you a looking uppon that ball faced coult?

+**Ball-field.** [BALL *n.*[1] 1.] A field for playing baseball. — **1886** *Outing* June 365/2 The grand-stand ... is the finest ever seen on a ball-field. **1888** *Ib.* July 120/2 We have had exciting contests on the ball-field since then.

+**Ball game.** [BALL *n.*[1] 1.] A game of ball, now esp. baseball. (Cf. BALL-PLAY.)

1843 *Knickerb.* XVIII. 216 The boys suspend their ball game while he drives over the green. **1849** C. LANMAN *Alleghany Mts.* xiii. 100 Since my arrival here the Indians have had one of their ball games. **1894** *Outing* June 212–15 [Description of] An Indian Ball Game. **1898** SUSAN HALE *Letters* 335 These men were just like ... Harvard men, after the ball game has gone right for us. **1903** S. H. WARD *G. H. Hepworth* 19 Having to walk home from school the two friends did not join in ball games. **1912** C. MATHEWSON *Pitching* 209 Spectators at ball games who wonder at the marvellous fielding [etc.].

+**Ball ground.** [BALL *n.*[1] 1.]

1. A stretch of ground measured off for the Indian game of ball.

1772 D. TAITT in *Travels Amer. Col.* 546, [I] then went to a Ball ground ... where the Eutchie and Geehaw people were playing Ball. **1797** B. HAWKINS *Letters* 90 The heads of the town ordered the murderer to be put to death, and they appointed two men ... to execute him in the ball ground. **1845** HOOPER *Simon Sugg's Adv.* ix. 112 An Indian ball-play was announced to 'come off' within a few days, at the ball-ground near the river.

2. A space or field appropriated for playing ball games, esp. baseball.

1871 [L. H. BAGG] *4 Years at Yale* 316 The ball-ground, where all the matches and most of the practice games are played. **1879** *Harper's Mag.* August 402 We pass the Snuggery ball-ground animated with the shouts of victory. **1894** *Outing* June 213/1 The ball ground is laid out on a piece of level prairie and is marked by two goal posts about one thousand feet apart. **1917** MATHEWSON *Sec. Base Sloan* 218 A blue car buzzed past him bearing the legend 'Ball Grounds.'

+**Ball gun.** [BALL *n.*[1] 2.] A gun for firing ball cartridges. — **1897** *Outing* March 567, I had changed my single rifle for a double-barreled ball gun.

‖**Ballist.** *rare.* [BALL *n.*[1]] A 'baseballist.' — **1868** *New England Base Ballist* (Boston) 27 Aug., The title 'Ballist' is a verbal atrocity and bastard, and ought never to be uttered or printed.

Balloon, *n.*

1. A gas-bag with car for aerial ascents. {1783–}

1783 JAY *Corr.* III. 97, I have received the prints of the rise and fall of the balloon. **1784** *Independent Gazetteer* 17 July, The American Aerostatic balloon will rise from the New Work-house yard, with a person in it. **1789** MACLAY *Deb. Senate* 147 There was now a cry for adjournment, to see the balloon, and the Senate rose. **1790** WEBSTER in Ford *Notes* I. 335 Balloon ascends, takes fire & falls. *c***1837** CATLIN *Indians* II. 199 The 'travelled Indian' ... described ... the ascent of the balloon from Castle Garden. **1863** KETTELL *Hist. Rebellion* II. 491 During this battle the balloon was overlooking the strife, and was in telegraphic communication with General McClellan. **1881–5** MCCLELLAN *Own Story* 112 The various systems of communicating intelligence by signals, telegraph, balloons, etc. **1909** 'O. HENRY' *Options* 158 Old man Carr ... put all the money he had into dirigible balloons.

fig. **1791** HAMILTON *Works* (Lodge) VIII. 233 Raise it as high as possible by fictitious purchases, in order to take in the credulous.... Others are mounting the balloon as fast as possible.

b. An inflated bag or bladder used as a toy.

1860 HOLMES *Professor* v. 136 There was a very little boy who had one of those balloons you may have seen.

+**2.** (See quotation.) *Obs.*

1787 *Independent Gazetteer* 24 Feb. 3/1 Continental certificates (or what some term balloons) ... are those not adopted by any particular state.

+**3.** A 'balloon-frame.'

1855 *Trans. Amer. Inst. N.Y.* 405 While I start a balloon from the foundation and finish it to the roof.

Balloon, *v.* {1792} **1.** *intr.* To ascend in a balloon. In quotation *fig.* **2.** *tr.* **a.** (See quotation.) +**b.** To boom a candidate, as by fictitious favorable reports. (*Cent.* s.v. *Ballooning*). — (1) **1854** H. H. RILEY *Puddleford* 236 Mr. A. and B. are boating on the Mississippi, or 'ballooning' in some fancy speculation on the north shore of the Oregon. (2) **1870** MEDBERY *Men & Myst. Wall St.* 134 *Ballooning*, to work up a stock far beyond its intrinsic worth, by favorable stories, fictitious sales, or other cognate means.

‖**Balloonery.** [E. (*a*1846) ='management of balloons.'] (See quot.) — *c***1845** PORTER *Big Bear Arkansas* 140 The late editor ... occasionally indulges in a flight of fancy (which he appropriately terms 'balloonery.')

+**Balloon-frame.** [BALLOON *n.*]

1. A frame for a building, having light wood uprights secured by simple nailing; a house built in this way.

1853 J. W. BOND *Minnesota* 122 A little clump of shanties and balloon-frames in the neighborhood of the 'American house' [in St. Paul]. **1854** BOYNTON & MASON *Journey thro' Kansas* xi. 68 A comfortable log house . . . is a costly structure, and . . . the useless waste of timber, as compared with a light and suitable frame, 'balloon-frame,' is enormous. **1855** *Trans. Amer. Inst. N.Y.* 407 If it had not been for the knowledge of balloon frames, Chicago and San Francisco could never have arisen, as they did, from little villages to great cities in a single year. **1897** MOORE *How To Build* ii. 13 There are two methods of framing the beams, joists, and vertical timbers of wooden dwellings, viz., the 'braced' frame and the 'balloon' frame.

2. *Balloon-frame house*, a house so constructed.

1873 EGGLESTON *Myst. Metrop.* xxxv. 302 When at last he saw the familiar balloon-frame houses. **1883** *Rep. Indian Affairs* 150 Many of them live in good plank or 'balloon-frame' houses, such as most white farmers of this country inhabit.

+**Balloon framing.** =prec. 1. — **1855** *Trans. Amer. Inst. N.Y.* 394 The balloon framing used in the Western States and California.

+**Balloon hat.** *Obs.* [BALLOON *n.*] A former make of hat. — **1786** *Mass. Centinel* 15 July 3 The ladies are informed, that the present immensity of the balloon hat will be discarded totally.

+**Balloon house.** A house having a balloon-frame. — **1855** *Trans. Amer. Inst. N.Y.* 399, I have seen balloon houses put up, and was very much surprised at the facility, quickness, and strength of them.

Balloonist. [f. BALLOON *v.*] One who ascends in or observes from a balloon. {1828–} — **1860** *Amer. Almanac* (Boston) 391 Mr. Wise, the balloonist, with three companions, leaves St. Louis in the 'Airship Atlantic,' at 7.20 P.M. **1862** MCCLELLAN *Own Story* 395, I have been within six miles of the rebel capital, and our balloonists have been watching it all day. **1882** PECK *Sunshine* 212 The Advent preacher . . . when he saw the balloon of King, the balloonist, going through the air, thought it was the second coming of Christ.

+**Balloon sleeve.** [BALLOON *n.*] A bulging sleeve drawn in at or just above the wrist. {1860} — **1837** *S. Lit. Messenger* III. 3 Women came to the spring for water in great balloon sleeves and prunelle shoes.

+**Balloon vine.** The heartseed, *Cardiospermum halicacabum*, of the southern states. — **1836** LINCOLN *Botany* App. 84 Balloon vine, [native of] East Indies. . . . Flowers white and green. **1847** WOOD *Botany* 215 Heart-seed. Balloon-vine. . . . Native on the Missouri and its branches. **1901** MOHR *Plant Life Ala.* Balloon Vine . . . [grows in] Louisianian area, South Carolina, Florida, and Texas, [etc.].

***Ballot,** *n.*

***1.** A ticket, sheet of paper, or (orig.) small ball used in casting secret votes.

1776 *Journals Cont. Congress* VI. 880 The ballots being taken, George Measam was elected. **1803** *Ann. 8th Congress* 1 Sess. 168 As the Constitution stands each Elector is to write the names of two persons on a piece of paper called a ballot. **1837** *S. Lit. Messenger* III. 276 Mr. Randolph, who counted the ballots, . . . exclaimed 'It was impossible to win the game; . . . the cards were packed.' **1857** *Lawrence* (Kansas) *Republican* 18 June 3 The judges of the election shall provide suitable ballot-boxes wherein to deposit the ballots, cast at said election. **1864** in *Ev. Standard* 2 Nov., The voting was not very general, only 25,000 ballots being polled altogether. **1897** *Boston Ev. Record* 23 Dec. 1/7 These were ballots on which the only name crossed for alderman was that of Dixon.

***2.** The system or method of secret voting by the use of printed tickets, sheets of paper, or the like; the power of voting in this way.

1787 *Constitution* ii. §1 The Electors shall meet in their respective States, and vote by Ballot for two Persons, of whom one [etc.]. **1789** *Ann. 1st Congress* I. 21 All committees shall be appointed by ballot, and a plurality of votes shall make a choice. **1790** *Harv. Coll. Laws* 17 The President, Professors and Tutors, shall determine by ballot what Students have distinguished themselves. *a***1817** DWIGHT *Travels* I. 257 At that time and place, the Freemen, according to their warning, choose by ballot their Representatives to attend the Legislature. **1835** TICKNOR in *Life* I. 415 The subject of the ballot as practically managed in the United States. **1884** LOWELL *On Democracy* 12 Is it wise to give every man the ballot? **1898** PAGE *Red Rock* 199 One provision gave the ballot to the former slave, just as it was taken from the former master.

attrib. **1830** S. BRECK in *Recoll.* (1877) i. 29 Yet his friends, screened as they were by a ballot vote, did not wish bluntly to deny him.

b. A single instance of voting in this way.

1838 *Democratic Rev.* I. 238 The invalid had his bed removed to the capitol—where . . . he remained during the protracted struggle, depositing his vote in every ballot. **1852** *Harper's Mag.* V. 256/1 Unsuccessful ballotings were had for four days, and it was not until the forty-ninth ballot that General Franklin Pierce . . . received the nomination. **1904** H. L. WEST in *Forum* Oct. 169 The men who made Parker a possibility won for him the nomination on the first ballot. **1905** D. G. PHILLIPS *Plum Tree* 125 On the seventy-ninth ballot I got . . . two opposition votes.

3. The action or the result of balloting.

1787 M. CUTLER in *Life & Corr.* I. 331 As the former was more particularly known to the officers of the army, the ballot [for treasurer] closed in his favor. **1864** WEBSTER, *Ballot, n.* 1. Whole amount of votes cast. **1905** D. G. PHILLIPS *Plum Tree* 125 The ballot was: Dunkirk forty-one; Grassmere . . . thirty-six, [etc.].

***Ballot,** *v. intr.* To vote by ballot. {1695–}

1789 *Ann. 1st Congress* I. 18 The Senate proceeded to ballot for a Secretary. **1804** CLARK in *Lewis & C. Exped.* (1904) I. 12 The following individuals . . . being duly balloted for. **1884** G. T. CURTIS in *Century Mag.* Nov. 129 The Constitution . . . required them to meet and ballot in their respective States.

Ballot-box. [BALLOT *n.*]

1. A box into which each voter drops his ballot, or which is used in drawing lots. {*a*1680–}

1776 *Journals Cont. Congress* IV. 167 The Members having prepared Tickets . . . and put the same into the Ballot box. **1812** *Ann. 12th Congress* 2 Sess. 24 That the Secretary roll up, and put into the ballot box, two lots, No. 1 and No. 3. **1821** *Ann. 17th Congress* 1 Sess. I. 21 That the Secretary put into the ballot-box two papers of equal size, one of which shall be numbered two and the other shall be numbered three. **1838** A. BELL *Men & Things* (1862) 171 At election times, the ballot boxes as they are called (for balls are not used, but cards), are fixed at the different windows of this room. **1840** BUTLER in Mackenzie *Van Buren* 255 A system which was successful in enabling men to come here and deposit illegal votes in our ballot boxes. **1857** *Lawrence* (Kansas) *Republican* 11 June 2 He must bring back our ballot boxes from Missouri. **1860** HOLMES *Professor* ix. 262 When a man calls you names because you go to the ballot-box and vote for your candidate. **1865** *Nation* I. 72 Raids upon the ballot-box took the name of 'law and order.' **1890** H. O. WILLS *Twice Born* 111 He will steal the votes and stuff the ballot-box.

2. The system or practice of voting by ballot.

1834 *Congress. Deb.* 12 Mar. 888 There is no ballot-box in Virginia. **1856** GOODRICH *Recoll.* I. 245 On the whole, the ballot-box develops and represents a balance of good sense in the nation that outweighs even the multitudinous vices, follies, and foibles of individuals. **1857** *Lawrence* (Kansas) *Republican* 4 June 2 Hoping that the ballot-box—the priceless jewel of the American people—may yet be preserved . . . to every citizen of Kansas Territory. **1910** C. HARRIS *Eve's Husband* 139 You shall see women threaten the ballot box in the cause of temperance.

+**3.** *Ballot-box stuffer*, one who puts spurious ballots into a ballot-box (see next).

1856 *Harper's Mag.* XIII. 552/1 The members . . . bind themselves . . . to see to it that order is preserved, . . . and all criminals and ballot-box stuffers brought to punishment. **1858** *N.Y. Tribune* 30 Sept. (Th.), [They began] to rid the city of San Francisco of the pestilential presence of a band of shoulder-hitters and ballot-box stuffers. **1869** GREELEY *Let.* in *Congress. Rec.* 22 April (1879) 681/2 Between the rule of an emperor and the rule of a clique of ballot-box stuffers, every intelligent man must prefer the former. **1876** *Letter* in *N.Y. Tribune* Oct. (B.), Three or four men . . . who are in reality detectives sent on to look after the Democratic roughs and ballot-box stuffers. **1910** J. HART *Vigilante Girl* xix. 264 He is said to be a notorious ballot-box stuffer.

+**b.** *Ballot-box stuffing*, the insertion of spurious voting papers into a ballot-box by the party in charge.

'A new name for a new crime. This consists in the use of a box . . . so constructed with a false bottom and compartments as to permit the introduction of spurious ballots to any extent by the party having it in charge' (B. '59).

1856 GLISAN *Jrnl. Army Life* 353 Others known to have been engaged in ballot-box stuffing and false voting. **1873** EGGLESTON *Myst. Metrop.* xxvi. 218 Our readers will remember . . . wholesale bribery and corruption and nefarious ballot-box stuffing. **1886** LOGAN *Great Conspiracy* 664 Commensurate rewards for all the long years of . . . hard work in . . . 'nigger'-hangings, and ballot-box stuffings. **1888** *Fostoria Democrat* 8 March (F.), Ballot-box stuffing is an almost obsolete form of knavery in New York under its election system.

***Balloting,** *vbl. n.* Voting by ballot. Also attrib.

1789 MACLAY *Deb. Senate* 81 The balloting business . . . prevented my mentioning in order the more important debate on the tonnage act. **1792** *Steele Papers* I. 89 On your name being offered as a Senator, I freely said I believed no person was authorized to make the nomination. . . . However when the Balloting came on I had nothing to say. **1803** *Ib.* 416 A balloting has taken place for a Judge. **1838** *Democratic Rev.* I. 238 In the beginning of the contest they passed a resolution that the balloting should be continued without the adjournment of the House. **1872** HOLMES *Poet* ii. 58 Several close ballotings already; adjourned for a fortnight. **1884** G. T. CURTIS in *Century Mag.* Nov. 126 The ballotings in these nominating conventions often afford a curious study.

+**Ballot-stuffer.** A 'ballot-box stuffer.' — **1872** *Chicago Tribune* 11 Oct. 4/3 It is not Pennsylvania we have heard from, but merely an organized gang of ballot-stuffers. **1895** CHAMBLISS *Diary* 248, I could not afford to run the risk of being mistaken for a 'ballot stuffer.'

+**Ballot-stuffing.** 'Ballot-box stuffing' (BALLOT-BOX 3 b.). — **1876** NORDHOFF *Cotton States* 43/1 This small band of white men . . . have practiced all the basest arts of ballot-stuffing, false registration, and repeating, at election after election.

+**Ball park.** [BALL *n.*[1]] An enclosed ground, having accommodation for spectators, in which baseball games are played. — **1899** *Chicago News* 4 Aug. 6/1 Billy Phyle . . . went out to the ball park to see Burns this morning. **1906** *Washington Post* 28 May 3 The ball park was crowded with spectators when the game between Louisville and Toledo was called. **1912** C. MATHEWSON *Pitching* 197 When I reported at the ball park, the gates had been closed by order of the National Commission.

***Ball-play.**

+1. The game of Indian ball, original among N. A. Indians and the source of modern lacrosse.

1765 TIMBERLAKE *Mem.* 79, I was not a little pleased likewise with their ball-plays (in which they shew great dexterity) especially when the women played. **1772** D. TAITT in *Travels Amer. Col.* 552 In the afternoon I went to the Eutchies to see a ball play. **1775** ADAIR *Amer. Indians* 283 He heard a middle-aged Choktah warrior boast . . . at a public ball-play, of having artfully stolen several things from one and another trader. **1832** KENNEDY *Swallow Barn* I. xviii. 186 The Indians pretended they were going to have a ball play. **1841** HITCHCOCK *Journal* (1930) 56 An Osage Chief who had a son killed in a ball play got up for amusement of some officers . . . from Fort Gibson. **1850** GLISAN *Jrnl. Army Life* 38 We came across a party of Indians engaged in their national pastime, the ball-play. **1860** CLAIBORNE *Sam Dale* ii. 45, I had gone . . . to a great ball-play, on Hiwassee River, where more than a thousand Cherokees had assembled. **1899** CUSHMAN *Hist. Indians* 149 While en route, they unexpectedly came upon a large company of Choctaws at and assembled for a ball play.

+b. Attrib. and comb. in *ball-play dance, -goer, ground.*

c1836 CATLIN *Indians* II. 124, I rode out . . . to the ball-play-ground of the Choctaws. *Ib.*, Each party of players commenced the 'ball-play dance' . . . in their ball-play dress; rattling their ball-sticks together in the most violent manner. **1846** M'KENNEY *Memoirs* I. viii. 184 Fell in with flocks of wild turkeys, frightened from their retreats, doubtless, by the rush of the ball-play-goers, through all parts of the country.

2. =BALL-PLAYING 2.

1856 *Spirit of Times* (N.Y.) 22 Nov. 197/2 Thursday of this week was appointed . . . for the close of the season for ball-play.

Ball-player. {1619}

+1. One who plays at the Indian game of ball.

c1836 CATLIN *Indians* II. 125 The most distinguished ball-player of the Choctaw nation represented in his ball-play dress, with his ball-sticks in his hands. **1894** *Outing* June 212 The ball players . . . dashed forward at full speed, . . . brandishing their ball sticks.

2. One who plays ball, esp. baseball.

1837 J. D. WHITNEY *Life & Lett.* 20 For my part, I could never make a ball player. **1867** (*title*), The Ball Players' Chronicle. **1868** CHADWICK *Game of Base Ball* 126 That . . . impartial and resolute ball player, George Flanly, was chosen umpire. **1881** *Harper's Mag.* Jan. 314/1 Mr. Brooks's chronicle of *The Fairport Nine* . . . will be a favorite with incipient ball-players. **1887** *Lippincott's Mag.* Aug. 312 If ever he reappears as a professional ball-player it must be at the disposition of his former club.

Ball-playing, *vbl. n.* [BALL *n.*[1] Cf. prec.] The practice of the game of ball.

(1) **1827** McKENNEY *Tour to Lakes* 181 The little naked Indian boys . . . were meanwhile sporting over the green, playing ball,—*bag-gat-iway.* . . . This ball-playing is not unlike our game of bandy. **c1836** CATLIN *Indians* II. 123 Ball-playing . . . is the favorite one [*sc.* game] amongst all the tribes. **1846** SAGE *Scenes Rocky Mts.* xvi, Ball-playing [by squaws] was one of the games upon which heavy bets were made. **1849** C. LANMAN *Alleghany Mts.* xiii. 100 The manly game of ball-playing is still practiced after the ancient manner. **1899** H. B. CUSHMAN *Hist. Indians* 368 The training of their young men consisted of . . . War, hunting, and ball-playing.

(2) **1875** CHADWICK *Dime Base Ball Player* 43 The greatest evil . . . professional ball-playing ever encountered . . . is that arising from the pool-selling business. **1897** *Chicago News* 17 July 6/4 One Day of Good Ball Playing.

+Ball-post. [BALL *n.*[1]] A goal-post in the Indian game of ball. — **1899** CUSHMAN *Hist. Indians* 185 Pieces of timber were firmly planted together in the ground; these were called amlbi (Ball posts). *Ib.* 230 He could throw a spell or charm . . . over the ball-post.

+Ball-rolling beetle. The tumblebug. — **1850** [S. F. COOPER] *Rural Hours* 401 There is an insect very common in the lower parts of the State [of N.Y.] . . . : the ball-rolling beetle, so much resembling the sacred scarabæus of the Egyptians.

Ball-room. [BALL *n.*[2]] A large room for holding balls or dances. {1752-}

c1800 FESSENDEN *Poems* (1806) 32 Speak to landlord, and his lady, Bid them make the ball-room ready. **1818** — *Ladies Monitor* 57 Of frivolous ball-room flutterers beware. **1833** *Knickerb.* I. 157 One is now so crowded, squeezed, and pushed about in a ball-room. **1852** — XXXIX. 152 Beyond the dressing room was the ball-room itself, which might have measured fifty feet in length by thirty in breadth. **1896** WILKINS *Madelon* 31 Dorothy . . . stepped delicately . . . around the ball-room, with one little white hand on Burr Gordon's arm.

+Ball-screw. [BALL *n.*[1] 2.] A screw attachable to the end of a ramrod, for extracting bullets from the barrel of a gun. — **1846** SAGE *Scenes Rocky Mts.* ii. 18 Beneath the right arm hangs a powder-horn transversely from his shoulder, behind which, upon the strap attached to it, are affixed his bullet-mould, ball-screw, wiper, awl, etc. **1861** *Army Regulations* 467 Thirty-two ball-screws, thirty-two spring vices.

+Ball-signal. [BALL *n.*[1]] A type of signal at a railroad crossing. — **1864** *Mass. Statutes* lxv, The ball signal station, as it now stands.

+Ball-stick. [BALL *n.*[1] 1.] A racket used by Indians in their ball-play. Cf. CROSSE.

1775 ADAIR *Indians* 400 The ball-sticks are about two feet long, the lower end somewhat resembling the palm of a hand, and . . . worked with deer-skin thongs. Between these, they catch the ball, and throw it a great distance. **1800** B. HAWKINS *Sk. Creek Country* 82 [These] Indians . . . made ball sticks and played with them. **c1836** [see BALL-PLAY 2]. **1845** HOOPER *Simon Sugg's Adv.* ix. 113 They . . . knock down their antagonists with their ball-sticks. **1849** C. LANMAN *Alleghany Mts.* xiii. 102 Every individual [Cherokee] carried in his hand a pair of ball sticks, made with a braided bag at one end. **1894** *Outing* June 214/1 Around which [=goal posts] they circled, beating them with their ball sticks.

+Ball team. [BALL *n.*[1] 1.] A team of ball-players. — **1888** *Outing* July 356/1 The *personnel* of the average professional ball team . . . has improved very greatly from that of fifteen years ago. **1899** QUINN *Pennsylv. Stories* 37 Harvard had sent down its ball team, with an enthusiastic crowd of rooters. **1905** A. H. RICE *Sandy* 93 Is n't it grand he's going to be put on the ball team and the glee club!

+Ball-ticket. [BALL *n.*[2]] A ticket of invitation or admission to a ball. — **1835** [LONGSTREET] *Georgia Scenes* 130 For these assurances they look first to 'the face of the paper' (the ball-ticket), and if they do not find on it a goodly number of responsible names . . . they protest against it. **1860** *Harper's Mag.* Nov. 789/2 It was an ordination Ball Ticket, and read thus: 'Your company with lady is respectfully solicited at a ball [etc.].'

+Ball time. (See quotation.) — **1876** *Wide Awake* April 262/1 At the Naval Observatory in Washington [D.C., at noon] . . . a huge black ball, which is drawn up a few moments before, descends upon the dome of the Observatory; and hundreds all over the city stand, with watch in hand, to see it drop, to keep, as we say, 'ball time.'

+Ball willow. *local.* (See quotation.) — **1897** *Outing* XXIX. 538/1 A low swale filled with grass and a species of willow called locally [in north central states] 'ball' willow.

+Ballyhack. Used allusively for: An imaginary place far distant or out of the way. Usu. in *go to Ballyhack!*

'Go to Ballyhack; a common expression in New England. I know not its origin. It savors in sound, however, of the Emerald Isle' (B. '48).

c1845 THOMPSON *Chron. Pineville* 77 It was just the easiest thing . . . to blow . . . all . . . notions to Ballyhack. **1845** JUDD *Margaret* 55 'Obed is here too.' 'Let Obed go to Ballyhack. Come along out.' **1896** *Dialect Notes* 396 He knocked the plate all to ballyhack. . . . N. Y. C.

***Balm.**

***1.** The fragrant garden herb *Melissa.* (Cf. BEE-BALM 2.)

1637 MORTON *New Canaan* II. iii. 67 Hunnisuckles, balme, and divers other good herbes are there, that grow without the industry of man. **1709** LAWSON *Carolina* 77 Our Pot-herbs and others of use, which we already possess, are Angelica wild and tame, Balm, Buglos. **1813** MUHLENBERG *Cat. Plants* 56 *Melissa*: balm, . . . common. Pens. fl. Aug. Georg. **1840** DEWEY *Mass. Flowering Plants* 183 *Melissa officinalis*, L., The true Balm, from Italy. **1847** WOOD *Botany* 422 Balm. . . . A well known garden plant. . . . Flowers white or yellowish.

+2. The balsam poplar.

1873 MILLER *Amongst Modocs* xxxiii. 387 A stream . . . is foaming among the mossy rocks in a cañon below the house, with balm and madroño on its banks.

+Balm geranium. ?*Obs.* A scented geranium. — **1839** MRS. KIRKLAND *New Home* xx. (1840) 146 A lady to whom I offered a cutting of my noble balm geranium . . . declined the gift.

***Balm of Gilead.** [Jer. viii. 22. Cf. BALSAM OF GILEAD.]

+1. The balsam poplar (*Populus balsamifera*, or the variety *candicans*), which bears odorous buds covered with resin. (Occas. applied to other varieties.)

1784 CUTLER in *Mem. Acad.* I. 491 *Populus*, . . . the Black Poplar, commonly called, in the northern states, the Balm of Gilead. **a1817** DWIGHT *Travels* III. 315 A gum tree, of the kind which is here called the Balm of Gilead, or the black poplar, is now growing before the house of Mr. William Hunting, of this town. **1824** Z. THOMPSON *Vermont Gazetteer* 24 *Populus angulata.* Balm of Gilead. **1832** WILLIAMSON *Maine* I. 111 Sometimes it is called the Sycamore, or Balm of Gilead, and is found in the northern parts of the State. **1844** LEE & FROST *Oregon* x. 116 [The valley] is a kind of rolling prairie; . . . along its rivulets, [it is] fringed with the cottonwood or balm of Gilead. **1853** *Mich. Agric. Soc. Trans.* (1854) 130 The trees indigenous to the soil were . . . red elm and thorn on the dry land . . . and balm of gilead on the wet. **1861** *Ill. Agric. Soc. Trans.* IV. 448 The Balm of Gilead is hardy thousands of miles north of this. **1869** BROWNE *Adv. Apache Country* 456 The river is fringed with willow, sycamore, and a species of cotton-wood, resembling balm of Gilead. **1897** SUDWORTH *Arborescent Flora* 130 *Populus balsamifera.* . . . Common names [include] Balsam . . . , Balm of Gilead.

b. Attrib. with *buds.*

1832 L. M. CHILD *Frugal Housewife* 26 Balm-of-Gilead buds bottled up in N.E. rum, make the best cure in the world for fresh cuts and wounds. **1854** SHILLABER *Mrs. Partington* 27 The balm-of-gilead buds and rum, that occupied their position in the buffet, were not prepared for her. **1887** JEWETT in *Scribner's Mag.* Dec. 731/1 Just . . . pick me a handful o' balm o' Gilead buds. I want to put 'em in half a pint o' new rum.

+2. The balsam fir, *Abies balsamea*, or the resin obtained from this.

1832 BROWNE *Sylva Amer.* 96 This resin [of the silver fir] is sold in Europe and the United States under the name of Balm of Gilead. **1858**

WARDER *Hedges & Evergreens* 256 *Picea balsamea*, or Balm of Gilead, is the American Silver Fir. **1902** CLAPIN 35 *Balsam Fir*. . . . The tree itself is also known as *Balm of Gilead*, in imitation of the Eastern terebinth.

b. Attrib. with *fir* (*tree*).

1785 MARSHALL *Amer. Grove* 102 *Pinus-Abies Balsamea.* Balm of Gilead Fir-Tree. **1803** LAMBERT *Descr. Pinus* 48 Balm of Gilead Fir (*Pinus Balsamea.*) Habitat in Virginia, Canada. **1857** GRAY *Botany* 422 Balsam fir. . . . Also called Canada balsam or Balm-of-Gilead fir. **1894** *Amer. Folk-Lore* VII. 99 *Abies balsamea*, . . . blister pine, balm of Gilead fir. West Va.

‖**3.** A variety of balsam.

1836 EDWARD *Hist. Texas* ii. 42 Examples [of the herb varieties] are the balm of Gilead, the cinque-foil.

+**Balmony.** [?variant of E. *baldmoney*.] The turtlehead or snakehead, *Chelone glabra*. — **1842** MRS. KIRKLAND *Forest Life* I. 71 We stick to thoroughwort,—balmony,—soot tea,—'number six,'—and the like; and avoid, as if for the very life, all 'pothecary medicines.' **1857** GRAY *Botany* 285 Turtle-head, snake-head, . . . *Chelone glabra*. . . . Called also shell-flower, balmony, &c.

Balmoral, name of a royal residence in Scotland, used attrib. or ellipt. to designate various articles of apparel or wear. {1864–}

1866 MRS. WHITNEY *L. Goldthwaite* ii, On the bed lay her pretty balmoral suit, made purposely for mountain wear. *Ib.*, It's perfectly charming,—the loveliest balmoral I ever saw. *Ib.* v, It was nice . . . to have got her feet into rosetted slippers instead of heavy balmoral boots. **1867** BRET HARTE *Condensed Novels, &c.* 174 A pair of trousers, striped balmoral stockings. **1869** W. MURRAY *Adventures* 59 For a lady to wear in the wilderness . . . thick balmoral boots, with rubbers. **1874** KNIGHT 225/1 *Balmoral.* 1. . . . A striped woolen stuff. . . . 2. A sort of ladies' boot, lacing in front. **1877** *Rep. Indian Affairs* 340 Balmoral skirts, . . . 288. **1878** C. COALE in *Ann. S.W.Va.* (1929) 1589 The women wore . . . short gowns and petticoats instead of balmorals and hoop-skirts.

Balm-tea. A decoction of the common balm. {1752–}

1713 *Mass. H.S. Coll.* 6 Ser. V. 276 If the measeles coms amongst you, its best to giue sage and baum tea, with a little safron, and keep warm. **1770** J. ADAMS *Works* (1850) II. 240 Oated my horse, and drank balm tea at Treadwell's in Ipswich. **1775** C. MARSHALL *Diary* (1877) 43 Drank balm tea with my wife. Came home about dark. **1796** R. BAYLEY *Epidemic Fever in N.Y.* 117 The drinks which seemed the most grateful to the sick . . . were . . . molasses and water, balm-tea, &c. **1847** DARLINGTON *Weeds & Plants* 237 An infusion of the herb, or 'Balm Tea,' is a popular domestic medicine, and it is probably as efficacious as any other harmless warm drink in producing perspiration.

* **Balmy,** *a.* In colloq. or slang uses.

1. Soft or silly, as through the influence of drink; crazy. {1851–}

1850 JUDD *R. Edney* I. 453 The fellows there assembled had been drinking, and some of them were quite 'balmy.' **1857** *Quinland* I. x. I. 134 You are as *balmy* as a summer evening, as *shiny* as a new boot; you are *sprung* and *cut in the eye;* come, rouse yourself. **1895** S. O. JEWETT *Life of Nancy* 261 He got a little too much aboard . . . , and bragged to me an' another fellow when he was balmy. **1908** K. MCGAFFEY *Show Girl* 130 The poor dear is nearly balmy in the crumpet from worry.

+**2.** Uncomfortable; unpleasant.

1880 'MARK TWAIN' *Tramp Abroad* xxv. 252 Here was another balmy place to be in: I had forgotten the child's name; I hadn't imagined it would be needed again.

* **Balsam.** Also †**balsom, balsome.**

* **1.** An oily aromatic resin obtained from certain trees and shrubs (see 2), and used as a medicament or perfume.

1612 SMITH *Virginia* 12 Another tree . . . yeeldeth a very cleere and an odoriferous Gumme like Turpentine, which some called Balsom. **1647** *Maryland Archives* IV. 321 One glasse Balsome. **1730** *Virginia State P.* I. 383, I rec[eive]d the agreable balsam you sent by Major Harling, which all I have had this summer. **1789** MORSE *Amer. Geog.* 197 The clay lands produce fir . . . unfit for use, but it yields the balsam which is so much admired. This balsam is contained in small protuberances, like blisters, under the smooth bark of the tree. **1832** WILLIAMSON *Maine* I. 111 The Balsam, or black Poplar . . . is particularly celebrated for its balsam, which in the spring may be extracted from its buds, rich and fragrant as that of Peru. **1855** LONGFELLOW *Hiawatha* VII. 64 Give me . . . , O Fir-tree, Of your balsam and your resin. **1883** P. M. HALE *Woods & Timbers N.C.* 47 The turpentine or balsam is a clear thin liquid, obtained from small blisters on the bark of the trunk [of *Abies Fraseri*]. . . . It is of an acrid taste, and is much used by the inhabitants on cuts and sores.

* **b.** An aromatic medicinal preparation or ointment for healing wounds, etc.; a salve.

1708 TOMPSON *Poet. Works* 147 Were there a balsom, which all wounds could cure, Twas in this Asculapian hand be sure. **1759** *Newport* (R.I.) *Mercury* 26 June 4 Just imported . . . a large assortment of druggs, chymical and galenical medicines, Turlington's balsam. **1794** *Ann. 3rd Congress* 1472 There shall be levied . . . on all powders, pastes, . . . balsams, ointments, . . . 5 per cent. ad valorem. **1817** *Ann. 14th Congress* 2 Sess. 469 The good people of the United States suffer great impositions from the use of spurious and unwholesome balsams, from patent medicines, &c. **1840** DANA *Two Years* xv. 128 John . . . asked the steward to ask the captain to let him have some salve, or balsam, to put upon it. **1859** G. A. JACKSON *Diary* 521, [I] got balsam and put on Drum's wounds to-night.

c. *Balsam capivia* or *cop.*, copaiba balsam.

1806 CLARK in *Lewis & C. Exped.* (1904) IV. 365 A little girl with rhumatism whome I had . . . anointed . . . with balsom capivia. **1846** EMORY *Military Reconn.* 21 A plant which Dr. De Camp pointed out as being highly balsamic, . . . having collected quantities of it during his campaign to the Rocky mountains, and tested its efficacy as a substitute for balsam cop.

2. Any one of the various trees furnishing balsam or balsamic resin; esp. the balsam fir or the balsam poplar. {1651}

1785 MARSHALL *Amer. Grove* 107 *Populus balsamifera.* Balsam, or tacamahac-tree. This is a tree of but middling growth, covered with a light brown bark. **1805** CLARK in *Lewis & C. Exped.* (1904) III. 232 With a narrow bottom of alder & Small balsam between the Ponds and the Mountain. **1857** S. H. HAMMOND *Northern Scenes* 143 We . . . pitched our tent . . . among a cluster of spruce and balsam. **1860** OLMSTED *Back Country* 253 Above this, at a quarter of a mile from the top, begins a forest of balsam firs (popularly called 'balsams'). **1883** ZEIGLER & GROSSCUP *Alleghanies* 57 The balsam is one of the most beautiful of evergreens. **1890–3** TABOR *Stowe Notes* 32, I passed up on the edge of the old road through a small group of balsams. **1897** SUDWORTH *Arborescent Flora* 50 Fraser fir. . . . Common names: Balsam (N.C., S.C.). . . . She balsam (N.C.)

attrib. **1839** HOFFMAN *Wild Scenes* i. 113 We had Mackinaw-blankets, stretched upon balsam branches, to recline upon. **1869** W. MURRAY *Adventures* 23, I stretched myself upon my bed of balsam-boughs.

+**3.** The garden-balsam or lady's-slipper, *Impatiens balsamina.*

1840 DEWEY *Mass. Flowering Plants* 76 Garden Snapper, or Balsam; . . . 60 varieties . . . [are] sometimes found in one garden. **1857** GRAY *Botany* 74 The balsam or ladies' slipper of the garden. **1891** FREEMAN *New Eng. Nun* 125 Minty stopped and picked an enormous bouquet of zinnias and marigolds and balsams.

attrib. **1863** 'GAIL HAMILTON' *Gala-Days* 10 The marigold whispers his suspicion over to the balsam-buds. **1865** MRS. WHITNEY *Gayworthys* xxv. 243 They made fairy-slippers, . . . pulled from off the balsam-blossoms.

* **Balsam apple.**

* **1.** A small ornamental vine (*Momordica balsamina*) of the gourd family, originating in the East Indies.

1817–8 EATON *Botany* (1822) 356 *Momordica echinata*, balsam apple. **1836** LINCOLN *Botany* App. 117 Balsam apple; . . . pomaceous; berry angled, tubercled. **1840** DEWEY *Mass. Flowering Plants* 113 Balsam apple, wild cucumber, . . . blossoms in August. **1847** DARLINGTON *Weeds & Plants* 141 The balsam apple, . . . the red fruit of which, made into a tincture, was formerly used as an application to wounds.

+**2.** *Wild balsam-apple*, the white-flowered plant *Echinocystis lobata*, cultivated for ornament esp. in the eastern states.

1843 TORREY *Flora N.Y.* I. 250 Wild balsam-apple . . . [is] an ornamental plant when in full flower. **1857** GRAY *First Lessons* 115 A pollen-grain . . . of the wild balsam-apple.

+**Balsam fir.**

1. A cone-bearing tree (*Abies balsamea*) of the pine family, valued for its oily resin and its timber. Cf. BALM OF GILEAD 2.

1807 GASS *Journal* 138 The country is closely timbered with . . . what some call balsam-fir. **1839** HOFFMAN *Wild Scenes* 41 In a clump of birches and balsam firs . . . is our place to bivouac for the night. **1853** *Harper's Mag.* VI. 436/1 The balsam fir (*pinus balsamea*) . . . grows here, in its native air, with a vigor and beauty totally unknown below, where it is cultivated only as a shrub. **1863** B. TAYLOR *H. Thurston* iv. 55 Only the clumps of arbor-vitae and the solitary balsam-fir were allowed to display their hardy green. **1883** ZEIGLER & GROSSCUP *Alleghanies* 57 We now reached the edge of the great forests of the balsam firs. **1896** WILKINS *Madelon* 338 She said . . . that it was a pleasant day, and the smell of the balsam fir was good for him.

2. The Fraser fir or she-balsam, *Abies fraseri.*

1847 WOOD *Botany* 516 Fraser's or double balsam fir . . . [is] found on mountains, from N. Eng. to Car[olina]. **1858** WARDER *Hedges & Evergreens* 256 *Picea Fraseri*, the Double Balsam Fir, resembles the preceding [=American silver fir]. **1883** HALE *Woods & Timbers N.C.* 46 Balsam Fir (*Abies Fraseri*, Pursh) . . . is the handsomest of our Firs.

+**Balsam hickory.** The small pignut or hickory, *Hicoria odorata.* — **1785** MARSHALL *Amer. Grove* 68 *Juglans alba odorata.* Balsam hickery. . . . The timber . . . is used for axle-trees of carriages, etc., mill coggs and rounds. **1815** DRAKE *Cincinnati* ii. 80 Forest trees . . . of the Miami country . . . [include] Balsam hickory.

Balsamine. =BALSAM 3. {1794} — **1784** CUTLER in *Mem. Academy* I. 485 *Impatiens*. . . . Weathercock. Balsamine. Touch-me-not. Quick-in-the-hand. **1833** S. J. HALE *Flora* 25 Balsamine. *Impatiens* (Touch-me-not). . . . Stem tall and much branched. It is a native of the East Indies, China, Japan, and also of America. **1847** WOOD *Botany* 199 Garden balsamine . . . is one of the most beautiful of garden annuals.

+**Balsam of Gilead.** The balsam fir; =BALM OF GILEAD 2. — **1810** MICHAUX *Arbres* I. 18 Sylvir fir, . . . Fir balsam, . . . [ou] Balsam of Gilead tree (Baumier de gilead). Dénominations également en usage. **1814** PURSH *Flora Amer.* II. 639 *Pinus Balsamea.* . . . This elegant tree is known by the name of Balsam of Gilead Fir. . . . It grows to the height of about forty or fifty feet. **1832** BROWNE *Sylva Amer.* 95 This species of spruce . . . is called Silver Fir, Fir Balsam, and Balsam of Gilead.

Balsam of Peru. {1771} The leguminous tree *Myroxylon Pereiræ.* — **1775** BURNABY *Travels* 99 In the gardens is a very large collection of . . . balsams of Peru, aloes, pomegranates, and other tropical plants.

Balsam pear. A tropical plant (*Momordica charantia*) bearing a berry-like fruit. — **1890** *Cent.* 3827 Such are . . . the balsam apple, and . . . balsam pear, the best-known cultivated species. **1901** MOHR *Plant-Life Alabama* 747 Balsam Pear. [From] Tropical Asia, naturalized in warmer America. . . . Louisianian area. Georgia and Florida. Alabama.

+**Balsam pine.** The balsam fir. — **1805** CLARK in *Lewis & C. Exped.* (1904) III. 279 We continue to put up the streight butifull balsam pine on our houses. **1843** FREMONT *Exped.* 64 Ridges . . . covered with the dark green of the balsam pine. **1878** I. L. BIRD *Rocky Mts.* 15 Regal pines, straight as an arrow, with . . . firs and balsam pines filling up the spaces between them.

+**Balsam poplar.**

1. A native American tree (*Populus balsamifera*) bearing large buds covered with resin; the tacamahac.

[**1786** J. ABERCROMBIE *Arrangem.* in *Gard. Assist.* 32/1 Tacamahacca, or great balsam poplar. **1810** MICHAUX *Arbres* I. 40 Balsam poplar, . . . connu sous ce nom en Canada.] **1819** D. THOMAS *Travels* 93 The true balsam poplar differs greatly in the leaf [from *Populus angulata*]; but the buds of both . . . [are] resinous. **1847** WOOD *Botany* 506 The balsam-poplar, though nowhere abundant, is found in woods and fields, disseminated throughout N. England and Canada. **1850** [S. F. COOPER] *Rural Hours* 71 We have been looking and inquiring for the Tackamahac, the great northern or balsam poplar; it is found at Niagara and on Lake Champlain, but the farmers about here seem to know nothing of it. **1871** DE VERE 419 The Balsam Poplar [obtains its name] . . . from the resinous matter covering its buds. **1897** SUDWORTH *Arborescent Flora* 130 *Populus balsamifera* Linn. . . . Common names [include] . . . Balsam Poplar (N.H., Vt., Nebr., Minn.).

2. A variety of this, *P. candicans.*

1832 BROWNE *Sylva Amer.* 254 Heart-Leaved Balsam Poplar. *Populus candicans. Ib.*, This tree, which is a genuine balsam poplar, is commonly seen growing before the houses. **1848** *Knickerb.* XXXI. 31 We add . . . the northern cork-elm and the heart-leaved balsam-poplar.

+**Balsam-root.** *Calif.* A dwarf perennial herb or plant of the genus *Balsamorrhiza* of the thistle family. — **1889** *Cent., Balsam-root.* . . . They have deep thick roots which contain a terebinthinate balsam.

+**Balsam spruce.** The balsam fir. — **1847** WOOD *Botany* 516 *Abies balsamea.* . . , Fir balsam. Balsam spruce.

Balsam-tree. {1695–}

+**1.** The balsam poplar, *Populus balsamifera,* or a variety of this.

1766 STORK *Acc. E.-Florida* 46 Balsam-tree, of the same size and with leaves like the sycamore tree in England, yields the true balsam of Tolu. **1785** MARSHALL *Amer. Grove* 107 *Populus balsamifera.* Balsam, or Tacamahac Tree. *Ib.* 108 Lance-leaved balsam tree. **1813** MUHLENBERG *Cat. Plants* 95 *Clusia:* balsam tree . . . ; rose. Car.

+**2.** *N.W.* The white fir, *Abies concolor.*

1874 GLISAN *Jrnl. Army Life* 480 Thus the Coast Range [of Oregon] . . . is covered with evergreen forests . . . intermixed at places with Oregon alder, balsam tree, rhododendron, . . . Oregon ash. **1897** SUDWORTH *Arborescent Flora* 55.

+**Balsam-Weed.** (See quotations.) — **1817–8** EATON *Botany* (1822) 317 *Impatiens balsamina,* balsam weed. **1843** TORREY *Flora N.Y.* I. 25 *Impatiens fulva,* . . . Balsam-weed, Jewel-weed, . . . possess[es] active medicinal properties. **1889** *Cent., Balsam-weed,* a name of the common everlastings . . . , *Gnaphalium decurrens* and *G. polycephalum,* . . . also called 'sweet balsam.'

Baltimore. [The family title of the colonial proprietors of Maryland, and the name of the principal city of that state, founded in 1729.]

+**1.** *Baltimore bird, hangnest,* or (more usually) *oriole,* the hangbird or hangnest, *Icterus galbula.*

1706 KERSEY *Dict., Baltimore-Bird,* a beautiful Bird of Mary-land, with black and yellow Feathers, so call'd from the Colours of Or and Sable, in the coat of Arms, belonging to Lord Baltimore, Proprietour of that Province. **1709** LAWSON *Carolina* 145 The Baltimore-Bird. . . . They are the Bigness of a Linnet, with yellow Wings, and beautiful in other Colours. **c1728** CATESBY *Carolina* I. 48 The Baltimore Bird . . . breeds on the Branches of tall Trees, and usually on the Poplar or Tulip-tree. **1791** W. BARTRAM *Carolina* 302 Both species of the Baltimore bird . . . are spring birds of passage, and breed in Pennsylvania. **1808** WILSON *Ornithology* I. 23 Baltimore Oriole . . . is generally known [as] the Baltimore bird. *Ib.* VI. 89 The chief difference between the male and female Baltimore Oriole, is the superior brightness of the orange color of the former to that of the latter. **1844** J. P. GIRAUD *Birds L.I.* 142 Baltimore Hangnest, or Oriole, . . . is not very abundant on Long Island. **1868** *Amer. Naturalist* II. 381 Several times I have seen the Baltimore Oriole rapidly going over the bushes, giving each fresh flower a prick with the tip of his beak. **1874** Coues *Birds N.W.* 195 The highest style which the Baltimore Oriole has been able to accomplish the typical nest. **1886** *Century Mag.* June 274/2 32 The eggs of the Baltimore oriole, perhaps the most fantastically marked of all our birds' eggs. **1898** *Outing* April 71/2 A Baltimore oriole started to build his wonderful, pensile nest . . . in an apple-tree near her home.

+**b.** *ellipt.* =preceding sense.

1808 WILSON *Ornithology* I. 25 Orioles . . . with a few exceptions build pensile nests. Few of them, however, equal the Baltimore in the construction of these receptacles for their young. **1812** *Ib.* VI. 88 In the spring and summer of 1811, a Baltimore took up its abode in Mr. Bartram's garden. **1893** *Scribner's Mag.* June 765 The Baltimore . . . in plumage, song, and nest . . . is an especially remarkable bird.

+**2.** Attrib. in sense: Belonging to, produced in, or originating in Baltimore.

1744 *Md. Hist. Mag.* XXI. 248, I hope . . . that altho it be not of the Baltimore Iron yet I may have the same Price for it. **1849** A. MACKAY *Western World* I. 105 Baltimore . . . is said to be full of pretty women, a 'Baltimore beauty' being a sort of proverbial expression. **1859** *Harper's Mag.* April 688/1 Aaron V. Brown, Postmaster-General, . . . was chairman of the committee for constructing the 'Baltimore Platform.' **1862** *Rep. Comm. Patents: Agric.* 186 Baltimore Scarlet . . . and Burr's New Pine are good early strawberries. **1866** *Congress. Globe* 5 May 2406/3, I desire to present here the Baltimore platform upon which Andrew Johnson was elected.

+**3.** *Baltimore clipper,* a type of fast-sailing vessel constructed at Baltimore. Also *Baltimore buckeye, flyer.*

1814 *Niles' Reg.* VI. 175/2 With many vessels of war lying in the Chesapeake Bay, 19 out of 20 of our 'Baltimore flyers' have passed safely! **1815** *Ib.* VIII. 40/1 She appears to be a schooner of the 'Baltimore stamp.' **1832** F. A. BUTLER *Journal* II. 100 The Baltimore clippers are proverbial for their elegance and fleetness. **1841** BUCKINGHAM *America* I. 261 Its superiority in the fast-sailing qualities of its ships and schooners, known by the name of the 'Baltimore clippers,' gave it the advantage of effecting quicker voyages than the vessels of any other port could accomplish. **1851** E. S. WORTLEY *Travels in U.S.* xxiii. 138 Then there are the fairy, knowing-looking Baltimore clippers, their graceful masts clustered together [etc.]. **1882** *Century Mag.* July 352 The Baltimore clipper was the parent of several types of vessels. The famous oyster pungies of the Chesapeake are allied to it, but the latest phase of this form is the Baltimore buckeye.

+**4.** *Baltimore plan,* a plan proposed in 1894 by Baltimore financiers to procure a 'safe and elastic' currency by substituting a form of sinking fund in place of government bonds.

1895 *Congress. Rec.* App. 8 Jan. 169/1 Those who venture to argue that the Baltimore plan is good, because the present system of national banking has proved so under the stress of thirty years' experience are even further astray. **1896** *Congress. Rec.* App., 6 Feb. 489/1 What has become of the 'Baltimore plan' and the 'Carlisle plan' for banking currency?

+**5.** *Baltimore vine,* a species of vine or climbing plant.

1867 W. H. DIXON *New America* II. 85 Next come a host of gardens, in which the Baltimore vine runs joyously up poles and along espaliers.

+**Baltimorean.** [f. prec.] A native or resident of Baltimore.

1830 *Congress. Deb.* 25 Mar. 679/2 Last year the Legislature of Pennsylvania . . . refused to permit the patriotic Baltimoreans to make a railroad up into that State. **1846** *Spirit of Times* (N.Y.) 4 July 218/3 A rich joke . . . was played off by a Baltimorean on a Philadelphian. **1854** *S. Lit. Messenger* XX. 724/2 The Baltimorean . . . is a personage wholly unlike anybody else in the world. **1866** RICHARDSON *Secret Service* viii. 109 A number of Baltimoreans on board were returning home, after assisting at the capture of Sumter. **1898** ATHERTON *Californians* 316 Rose went East and triumphantly captured a Baltimorean of distinguished lineage and depleted exchequer.

* **Bamboo,** *n.*

1. +**a.** Any of various canes or cane-like plants, native in the south and south-east; esp. the greenbrier or bamboo brier. (Cf. sense 2.)

1709 LAWSON *Carolina* 101 Of canes and reeds we have many sorts. . . . The small bamboo is . . . a certain vine, . . . growing in low land. . . . Their root is a round Ball, which the Indians boil . . . , and eat them. **1784** SMYTH *Tour* I. 248 A deep miry swamp overgrown with briars, bambooes, and poisonous vines. **1833** SILLIMAN *Man. Sugar Cane* 7 The plant . . . was undoubtedly nothing more than a species of Bamboo, called the Wild Cane (*Miegia Macrospermia*). **1867** CRAWFORD *Mosby* 111 Lieutenant Smith . . . changed our camp . . . to a pine forest, with an undergrowth of briars, bamboo, and grape-vines so thick that a rabbit could scarcely pass through. **1883** HALE *Woods & Timbers N.C.* 186 Common bamboo or Green brier, (*Smilax rotundifolia,* Linn.). **1901** MOHR *Plant Life Ala.* 446 *Smilax laurifolia,* . . . Bay-leaf bamboo. . . . Flowers in May.

b. The common oriental bamboo; a fishing-rod made of this.

1869 W. MURRAY *Adventures* Advt., Calcutta bamboos, China lines, waterproofed braided silk lines, oiled silk lines. **1897** *Outing* June 221/2 Rods of split bamboo, bethabara, greenheart, steel, or lancewood, are all excellent.

+**2.** *Bamboo brier, briar,* the greenbrier, *Smilax bona-nox* or *S. rotundifolia,* a climbing plant with thick leaves and prickly stem.

1835 MARTIN *Descr. Virginia* 41 The eastern skirts of the Dismal Swamp are overgrown with reeds, ten to twelve feet high, interlaced everywhere with thorny bamboo briars. **1835** [LONGSTREET] *Georgia Scenes* 74 This came . . . over me, like a rake of bamboo briers. **1853** 'P. PAXTON' *Yankee in Texas* 57 Immense bamboo briers, like vegetable Pythons, twined and intertwined, crossed and recrossed, from tree to tree. **1871** DE VERE 410 Another name for it [i.e. bull-brier] is bamboo-briar, . . . because the very large briar attains, in the rich alluvial bottoms which it prefers, at times the size of the bamboo. **1901** MOHR *Plant Life Ala.* 68 Shrubby hawthorns, . . . persimmon, and black gum (*Nyssa multiflora*), entangled with the tough vines of bamboo briers.

3. Attrib. with *cane, fan, lounge, table, tribe, vine,* etc.

1759 *Newport* (R.I.) *Mercury* 10 April 4/2 To be sold . . . : Ivory-stick Fans, Bamboo ditto. **1799** F. Cuming *Western Tour* (1810) 327 We took our canoe and got a quantity of neat Bamboo canes, which we spent the day in trimming. **1852** STOWE *Uncle Tom* xxv, St. Clare was stretched on a bamboo lounge in the veranda, solacing himself with a cigar. *Ib.* xxvi, A light, fanciful bamboo table stood in the middle of the room. **1853** 'P. PAXTON' *Yankee in Texas* 22 His rude attempts at road-making whenever a mass of bull-brier or bamboo-vines, crossing and recrossing the cane, . . . called for action. **1855** THOMPSON *Doesticks* 19 An Oriental juggler, balancing a bamboo ladder on his nose. **1869** W. MURRAY *Adventures* Advt., Fine-spliced bamboo trout and salmon rods. **1901** MOHR *Plant Life Ala.* 45 The arborescent grasses of the bamboo tribe, the so-called cane.

+**Bamboo,** *v. tr.* 'To cheat; to bamboozle.—Conn.; but probably imported from the Southern States' (*a*1870 Chipman 20).

Bamboozle, *v.* {1703-} +**1.** To hustle in various directions. +**2.** In *p.p.* Inebriated; drunk. — **(1) 1833** S. SMITH *Major Downing* 130 The President [was] . . . bamboozled about from four o'clock in the morning till midnight, . . . and then . . . jammed into Funnel Hall two hours. **(2)** *a***1856** in Hall *Coll. Words* 461 The various words and phrases . . . in use, at one time or another, to signify some stage of inebriation [include]: . . . shot in the neck, bamboozled, weak-jointed.

+**Bamboula.** [Creole-Fr.] **1.** A small drum having a frame of bamboo, formerly used by slaves of Louisiana. **2.** A dance accompanied by such drum. — **1883** *Century Mag.* November 45/2 In New Orleans, . . . a minute's walk . . . will bring you to Congo square, the last green remnant of those famous Congo plains, where the negro slaves once held their bamboulas. *Ib.,* Every Sunday afternoon the bamboula dancers were summoned to a wood-yard on Dumaine street by a sort of drum-roll, made by rattling the ends of two great bones upon the head of an empty cask.

* **Banana.**

1. ***a.** The edible fruit of the tropical tree, *Musa sapientum.* **b.** The tree producing this. {1810-}

[**1776** FRENEAU *Poems* (1786) 141 The plantane and banana flourish here [i.e. Santa Cruz].] **1819** LATROBE *Journal* 163 Along the levee [were sold] . . . fish, bananas, piles of oranges, sugarcane. **1831** PECK *Guide* 47 The china-tree, catalpa, . . . banana, and orange, with their beauty and fragrance, charm the eye of the beholder [in La.]. *Ib.* 62 Crowds . . . of Negresses [in New Orleans] . . . carrying . . . oranges, and figs, and bananas or plantains. **1837** WILLIAMS *Florida* 114 The plantain and banana succeed to perfection in the southern district. **1851** *S. Lit. Messenger* XVII. 248 We had previously negotiated with a peripatetic fruit-woman for some bananas. **1855** GLISAN *Jrnl. Army Life* 191 Some thirty varieties of tropical plants are seen along the route; cocoanut, banana, orange, etc. **1868** *Rep. Comm. Agric.* 145 Of the banana and plantain, . . . several species [are grown in Florida]. *Ib.,* A plantation of bananas once established has never to be renewed. **1880** CABLE *Grandissimes* xxvi. 192 The lemon, . . . the banana, the fig . . . tossed their fragrant locks above the lilies and roses. **1904** GLASGOW *Deliverance* 118 She bought a couple of bananas for a few cents from a fruit-stand at the corner.

attrib. **1766** J. BARTRAM *E. Florida* (1769) 11 This was the fatal night that destroyed the lime, citron and banana-trees in Augustine. **1831** Peck *Guide* 60 You may see [in New Orleans] . . . the fig-tree, the olive, banana vegetable, the pomegranate, the orange, with much beautiful shrubbery. *a***1861** WINTHROP *Canoe & Saddle* 354 We had a most plentiful breakfast, in which a banana omelet figured nobly. **1877** PHELPS *Story of Avis* 408 The veiled crimson heart of the banana-blossom. **1881** *Harper's Mag.* 744/1 There were great banana-plants with long leaves. **1884** *Century Mag.* Sept. 657/2 Both banks of these two little valleys [at Monterey] grow trees, and canebrakes, and banana groves, and all manner of bushes.

+**c.** The name of a species of cotton.

1849 *Rep. Comm. Patents: Agric* (1850) 149 Cotton.—There have been some new varieties of seed introduced in this section, the banana and the sugar-loaf.

+**2.** *Mexican banana,* the Spanish bayonet, *Yucca baccata. S.W.*

1884 SARGENT *Rep. Forests* 219.

Banbury cake. [*Banbury,* Oxfordshire, England.] A small oval cake of rich pastry with a filling of mincemeat. {1615-} — **1706** SEWALL *Diary* II. 176, I gave him a Banberry cake, of which he eat pretty well. *Ib.* 177, I left the Banbury cake . . . with his wife.

+**Banco.** *Texas.* [Sp.] A bank of sand or silt in a river. — **1888** *Congress. Record* 25 Sept. 8937/1 Sometimes the stream will suddenly cut a new channel, . . . and . . . a tract or 'banco' of a hundred acres will be found to be on the other side of the river. *Ib.,* Some bancos increase by deposit; some wear away till they are entirely swept off.

* **BAND,** *n.*[1]

***1.** A small body of men in military training. See also TRAIN-BAND and TRAINED BAND.

1645 *Mass. H.S. Coll.* 4 Ser. VI. 150 There are some prest which are seruiceable men & they haue no armes. If the Clarke of the band were sent for & dealt with, . . . it were well. **1650** *Harvard Rec.* I. 27 Neither shal any schollar exercise himself in any Military band. **1654** JOHNSON *Wonder-W. Prov.* 191 Capt. Humphry Atherton, of the Band of Do[r]chester. **1665** *Conn. Public Rec.* II. 20 The person defectiue shal pay to the vse of the company to which he belongs 5s. . . . , vnles . . . he carry in pay to the clarke of the band to procure what he is wanting in. **1791** *Broadside Verse* (1930) 59/1 Sad to relate! our Federal Band, Were slain by Indians bold!

+**2.** A party of Indians.

1807 GASS *Journal* 44 At 10 o'clock we met the whole band. **1826** COOPER *Mohicans* ix, They stood surrounded by the whole band of the triumphant Hurons. **1837** IRVING *Bonneville* I. 152 It was expected he would meet the Shoshonie village or bands, on their yearly migrations. **1882** *Rep. Indian Affairs* 148 The Indians belonging to this agency are known as the Tabequache band of Utes. **1906** *Indian Laws & Tr.* III. 233 The proceeds therefrom shall be placed to the credit of the tribes or bands by whom such lands were ceded.

3. An organized company of musicians who play together on various instruments. Orig. (and occas. in later use) in *band of music.* {1660-}

1766 E. Singleton *Social N.Y.* 369 Ranelagh Gardens . . . are laid out at a great expence; . . . a complete band of music is engaged to perform. **1767** *Ib.* 298 The Royal American Band of Musick. **1807** GASS *Journal* 45 Their band of musick, or orchestra, was composed of about twelve persons beating on a buffaloe hide. **1847** *Army Regulations* 24 The musicians of the band will, for the time being, be dropped from company muster-rolls. **1866** 'F. KIRKLAND' *Bk. Anecdotes* 38/2 At the same moment the band struck up the 'Star Spangled Banner.' **1871** HOWELLS *Wedding Journey* vi. 155 In the old time . . . every table was full, and we dined to the music of a brass band. **1895** M. A. JACKSON *Memoirs* 630 Bands of music were interspersed and the whole pageant was . . . grand.

+**b.** *To beat the band,* to exceed or surpass everything. *colloq.*

1897 FLANDRAU *Harvard Episodes* 223, I was on the box-seat driving, you know,—lickety-split, to beat the band. **1900** G. BONNER *Hard Pan* iii. 81 Doesn't that beat the band? **1902** HARBEN *Abner Daniel* 44 He kept me waiting two days and hustled around to beat the band. **1904** W. H. SMITH *Promoters* xii. 185, I got help from outside, somehow, and it did the work to beat the band. **1911** SAUNDERS *Col. Todhunter* v. 64, I'm . . . primed for a campaign that'll . . . set 'em to whoopin' things up for you to beat the band.

+**4.** A division of a Methodist 'class.'

1832 WILLIAMSON *Maine* II. 697 A *Class* is a voluntary association of twelve or more, at whose head is a class-leader chosen by themselves, who is next below an exhorter; and the third part of a class is called a *Band.*

+**5.** A drove, flock, or troop of animals; a herd.

'In prairie parlance' (B. '59). 'Western U.S.' (*Cent.*). Possibly from or influenced by Fr. *bande.*

1823 W. H. KEATING *Narr.* 395 The term *band,* as applied to a herd of buffalo, has almost become technical, being the only one in use in the west. **1850** GARRARD *Wah-To-Yah* i. 13 Bransford and I . . . 'approached' a band of bulls. *a***1861** WINTHROP *J. Brent* ii. 13, I had come upon a band of horses feeding on the prairie. **1886** *Let.* in *N.Y. Ev. Post* Dec. (*Cent.*), In California every collection of animals of any sort is called a band. **1916** H. TITUS *I Conquered* vi. 79 The hunt for a band of mares with colts that should be branded.

* **Band,** *n.*[2] *A style of collar worn in the seventeenth and eighteenth centuries. *Obs.* {-1755}

1640 *Conn. Public Rec.* I. 453 The Inuentory of Tho. Johnson: . . . a shirt & band and hose yarne. **1648** *Ib.* 492 An Inventory of the goods of Edward Chalkwell: . . . a band and strings. *a***1649** WINTHROP *Hist.* II. 12 He came in his worst clothes, . . . without a band. **1685** *Conn. Probate Rec.* I. 377 A paire of Cotten Gloves that ware my huspan, and two of his bands. **1710** BUCKINGHAM *Naval Exped.* 79 An account of what I brought from Hartford: . . . a new pair of serge breeches, . . . 3 bands. **1768** COOPER in *Copley-Pelham Lett.* 71, I also send a gown, hood, and band, by which to finish the drapery. **1798** BENTLEY *Diary* II. 260 He [=a clergyman] . . . had a black cap & wide band, coat with small buttons on the cloaths. [**1869** STOWE *Oldtown Folks* 280, I called his attention to the picture of Mr. John Rogers in gown and bands.]

* **Band,** *n.*[3] +A number tied together; a bundle. — **1863** *Ill. Agric. Soc. Trans.* V. 668 The [tobacco] plants . . . are given to others, who strip off the remaining leaves, and tie them in bands of six or eight leaves.

1865–6 *Ib.* VI. 647 It is recommended that one-fourth (¼) M. bunches [of shingles] be packed in bands twenty (20) inches in length.

***Band,** *v.* +*tr.* To collect into a flock or herd. (Cf. BAND *n.*[1] 5.) — 1878 B. F. TAYLOR *Between Gates* 266, I leave him to 'band' his sheep and herd his bees as he pleases. **1902** CLAPIN 36 In prairie parlance, *to band* means to form, to assemble cattle, sheep, into vast flocks.

Bandanna, -ana. Also †**bandanno, -ano.**

1. A large (formerly silk) handkerchief, freq. of red, blue, or yellow with white spots or figures, originally imported from India. {1752–}

1741 *Penna. Gazette* 10 Sept. 4/2, Bandannoes. **1742** *Ib.* 12 Aug. 3/3. **1759** *Newport* (R.I.) *Mercury* 26 June 4/2 To be sold by Samuel Goldthwait, ... silk bandanoes, ... writing paper. **1788** H. M. Brooks *Gleanings* 59 A few pieces best India bandannoes. **1813** *Raleigh* (N.C.) *Minerva* 12 Nov., Cotton and silk bandanoes. **1835** *S. Lit. Messenger* IV. 89/2 One twists a yellow bandanna round his head for a night cap. **1853** 'P. PAXTON' *Yankee in Texas* 195 Each man armed with a huge bandanna, wiping off the fast gathering drops. **1864** NORTON *Army Lett.* 223 The men come in every day costume, but the women put on their brightest bandanas and calicoes. **1883** *Harper's Mag.* Oct. 728/2 The negro no longer ... wears the becoming bright-colored bandana and large golden ear-rings.

2. Attrib. with *cap, kerchief, pocket handkerchief.*

1839 BIRD *Robin Day* xxxvi, 'That dishclout turban' (meaning the bandanna cap). **1852** MITCHELL *Dream Life* 96 He ... clears his throat by a powerful ahem, followed by a powerful use of a bandanna pocket-handkerchief. **1865** *Nation* I. 72 The bandanna kerchief in which the negress envelopes her head, turban fashion.

b. *Bandanna handkerchief,* =1. {1824–}

1767 *Mass. Gazette* 23 April 3/2 Silk, bandanno, romall ... handkerchiefs, ... check line handkerchiefs. **1770** *Penna. Chron.* 10–17 Sept. 138/2 An English servant girl ... took away with her ... one white striped kenting handkerchief, one new bandano ditto. **1795** *Boston Gazette* 23 March 3/3 Sales at auction: ... bandanna & romal handkerchiefs. **1809** IRVING in *Knickerb.* (1927) Introd. p. xxv, He had in his hand a small bundle tied in a red bandana handkerchief. **1834** CARRUTHERS *Kentuckian* I. 19 He wore a large two-story hat, with a bandana handkerchief hanging out in front. **1856** STOWE *Dred* II. 322 [Frank proceeded] to tie around his throat a red bandanna silk handkerchief. **1880** *Harper's Mag.* Nov. 867 Wiping his white-fringed forehead with a red bandanna handkerchief. **1891** ROBERTS *Adrift America* 243 To urge them on I took a long bandanna handkerchief, and flicked the [ewe] nearest to me. **1907** WHITE *Arizona Nights* II. iii. 254 Jed Parker straightened his back, rolled up the bandana handkerchief.

+**c.** *Bandanna turban,* a head-dress fashioned from a bandanna, much worn in the south by Negro women.

1869 ALDRICH *Bad Boy* ii. (1877) 16 Aunt Chloe ... buried her face in the bright bandana turban. **1898** PAGE *Red Rock* 23 An old mammy in a white apron, with a tall bandanna turban around her head.

+**Bandan(n)aed,** *a.* Attired in a bandanna. — **1831** Peck *Guide* 62 Negresses [in New Orleans] ... carrying on their bandanaed heads ... a whole table ... covered with goodies.

Bandbox. [BAND *n.*[2]] {1631–}

1. a. A box in which bands were kept. *Obs.* **b.** The light kind of box in which hats, caps, etc., are commonly kept.

1636 *Essex Probate Rec.* I. 4 Inventory ... a band boxe, 2s. ... The child hath it. **1799** *N.Y. State Soc. Arts* I. 357 Those manufactures that depend upon it [*sc.* paper], as paper-hanging, marbled paper, band-boxes, book-binding, etc. **1809** [R. TYLER] *Yankey in London* 99 The band-boxes will come by the Galen. **1842** *Knickerb.* XIX. 522 She quitted the house with her band-box and her wages. **1849** *Rep. Comm. Patents* (1850) 332 Improvement in the manufacture of band boxes. **1883** C. F. WILDER *Sister Ridnour* 179 An old-fashioned band-box, made of thin wood, which was given my husband when a little boy by some aged relative. **1886** E. W. HOWE *Moonlight Boy* 289 The big red bandbox which stood on the bureau.

2. Used in the phr. *from* or *out of a* (or *the*) *bandbox* to designate anything noticeably neat or clean.

1825 WOODWORTH *Forest Rose* I. i, Why, he is a genteel, delightful looking fellow, neat as a starched tucker fresh from a banbox [*sic*]. **1833** *Knickerb.* I. 198 The old gentleman ... popped into the room, looking as if he had stepped out of a bandbox. **1851** *Polly Peablossom* 25 His blooming ruffles as neat and clean as if they had just come out of a band-box. **1869** 'MARK TWAIN' *Innocents* xxxviii. 410 They are all ... exceedingly neat and cleanly; they look as if they were just out of a bandbox. **1880** — *Tramp Abroad* i. 19 The street-car conductors and drivers wore pretty uniforms which seemed to be just out of the bandbox.

3. Attrib. with *hat, maker, officer* (cf. 2).

1838 *S. Lit. Messenger* IV. 638/2 To render fur caps and bandbox hats for winter ... articles of vital necessity. **1851** CIST *Cincinnati* 49 Occupations [include] ... bandbox makers, 2 [people]. **1866** GREGG *Life in Army* xiii. 106 The many starched-up, kid glove, and band-box officers of our army.

***Banded,** *ppl. a.* Of fishes, etc.: Marked by a band or bands (of color). {*a*1842–}

(1) **1814** MITCHILL *Fishes N.Y.* 427 Banded Mackerel. *Scomber zonatus.* ... Taken in the bay of New-York, occasionally, during the warm season. **1839** STORER *Mass. Fishes* 94 *Hydrargira nigro-fasciata.* Le Sueur. The banded minnow. **1842** *Nat. Hist. N.Y., Fauna* IV. 83 The Banded Drum, *Pogonias fasciatus,* ... [has] four dusky bands over the body. **1855** BAIRD in *Smithsonian Rep.* 324 Banded Sun-Fish. *Pomotis chætodon,* ... abundant in ... Cape May county, New Jersey. **1871** DE VERE 382 The banded garfish (*Belone truncata*) of the coast, also known as bill-fish. **1871** *Amer. Naturalist* IV. 720 In an aquarium the 'banded sunfish' (*Mesogonistius chætodon* Gill) is verily kaleidoscopic. The black bands actually sometimes wholly disappear! **1883** *Amer. Naturalist* XVII. 1254 As a fish for the aquarium the banded sunfishes are deservedly popular.

(2) **1823** James *Exped. Rocky Mts.* I. 267 *Crotalus horridus,* Banded rattlesnake. **1839** STORER *Mass. Reptiles* 247 *Salamandra fasciata.* Green. The banded Salamander. ... [I] think it must be a rare species with us. **1877** *Vermont Bd. Agric. Rep.* IV. 146 One of the leaf-rollers is not uncommon, that called the Banded Leaf-roller.

(3) **1844** *Nat. Hist. N.Y., Zoology* II. 191 The Banded Woodpecker, *Picus Hirsutus,* ... is a rare northern species. **1874** COUES *Birds N.W.* 284 *Picoides Americanus,* Brehm. Banded Three-toed Woodpecker, ... is very rare in the United States.

(4) **1871** RAYMOND *Mines* 41 So-called 'banded quartz' preponderates throughout the vein, and it is always found the richest in free gold and sulphurets.

+**Band-iron.** [BAND *n.*[2]] Iron in strips suitable for fashioning bands, collars, straps, or the like. — **1866** *Internal Revenue Guide* 104 On band, hoop and sheet iron, ... a tax of five dollars per ton. **1872** HUNTINGTON *Road-Master's Assistant* 28 It is a good plan to take hoop or band iron, 1 inch or 1½ inches wide.

***Banditti.** Also †**banditty.**

***1.** As *pl.* Robbers, desperadoes, or outlaws.

Freq. *c*1780–1820, applied to Indians outcast from their tribe or nation.

1755 *Lett. to Washington* I. 112, [I] am in hopes ... you will be able to drive those banditti from our frontiers. **1782** *Kentucky Petitions* 62 [They] continue to be invaded by the merciless banditty. **1790** *Ann. 1st Congress* II. 1729 Frequent incursions have been made on our frontier settlements by certain banditti of Indians. **1805** LEWIS in *Ann. 9th Congress* 2 Sess. 1043 At present they [=Kansas Indians] are a dissolute, lawless banditti. **1823** J. THACHER *Military Jrnl.* 285 They are continually exposed to the ravages and insults of infamous banditti, composed of royal refugees and tories. *c***1862** SHERIDAN in Bartlett *Americanisms* (1877) 321 The terms Jayhawker and Banditti were employed [by me] to distinguish them from the White League, a secret military organization.

2. A company of bandits or marauders. {1706–1826}

1758 *Lett. to Washington* II. 310 The horror and anxieties ... occasioned by these banditties of Cherokees who daily are traveling through our County. **1772** D. TAITT in *Travels Amer. Col.* 563 Greersons, who is captain of this banditto [*sic*], came ... to make an appologey. **1792** *Ann. 2nd Congress* 1048 A banditti, formed of Shawanese and outcast Cherokees, ... are solely the causes of the war. **1818** *Niles' Reg.* XIII. 362/2 Otis was basely assassinated ... by a well-dressed banditti, with a commissioner of the customs at their head. **1824** MARSHALL *Kentucky* I. 284 A banditti of these rude disturbers of domestic safety. **1832** WILLIAMSON *Maine* II. 256 The enemy, now partly Frenchmen, mostly natives, were considered a mere banditti. **1844** GREGG *Commerce of Prairies* II. 141 A band of that famous prairie banditti [=Pawnees].

+**Band-leader.** [BAND *n.*[1] 4.] A leader of a 'band' in the Methodist church. — **1774** ASBURY *Journal* I. 123 Though much afflicted, I met the band-leaders and body-bands; and we had a singular blessing.

+**Band-man.** [BAND *n.*[1] 3.] A player in a band. — **1886** HOWE *Moonlight Boy* 76 Preparing music, and training an occasional band man who found time to come to him.

+**Band-mill.** [BAND *n.*[2]] A mill driven by means of a band or rope instead of by a cogged wheel.

1823 JAMES *Exped.* I. 71 These [corn mills] are called band mills. **1837** PECK *New Guide* 127 A band-mill is the most simple [form of mill]. **1852** REYNOLDS *Hist. Illinois* 144 The band mill was so called; because a raw hide band twisted, was put on the large wheel, in the place of cogs. **1857** *Ill. Agric. Soc. Trans.* II. 314 Coeval with the band mill was the large wheel with cogs, drawn by horses.

***Bandoleer, -ier.** *Obs.* Also †**-aleer, -alier, -alere; -eleer, -elier; -ileer, -iler.** [F. *bandoulière.*] A shoulder-belt worn by an armed man to support a musket or carry cartridges.

In very frequent use from *c*1637 to *c*1680.

1633 *N.H. Doc. & Rec.* I. 77, 6 pr. of bandoleers. **1637** *Mass. H.S. Coll.* 4 Ser. VII. 323 One of the slane menn came driuinge by Saybrooke, ... his bandeleers about hime, & his sworde vnder his arme. **1639** *New Haven Col. Rec.* 25 Thatt every one that beares armes shall be compleatly furnished with ... a muskett, a sworde, bandaleers. **1653** *Boston Rec.* 6, I give ... five pounds ... to be layd out in pikes & bandaleers. **1689** *Mayflower Descendants* XI. 27, I leave ... to my well beloved son ... one gun, one sword and bandaleers. **1709** SEWALL *Diary* II. 258 Had that burnt it would have fired the ... bandaliers of powder.

Bandolero. *Obs.* Also **-elero, -eleero.** [It. *bandoliera,* Sp. *bandolera.*] =BANDOLEER. {17th c.} — **1632** *Plymouth Col. Rec.* I. 6 That every freeman ... provide for himselfe ... a sufficient musket, ... with bandeleroes, & other appurtenances. **1653** *Mayflower Descendants* XI. 155 One paier of bandeleeroes, a rest & a belt.

+**Bandowzer.** *Obs. slang.* A severe blow. — **1833** W. J. SNELLING *Exposé of Gaming* 26 We expected to see the man get a bounce on the nose, a dough bat, or a bandowzer.

+**Band-saw.** [BAND *n.*[2]] A narrow, endless steel band or belt, having saw teeth, which passes over and is driven by two large wheels. — **1864** WEBSTER s.v. *Saw.* **1874** KNIGHT 226/2 One advantage of the band-saw over the reciprocating saw. **1876** INGRAM *Centennial Expos.* 205 The band-saw is acknowledged to be best adapted for different work.

***Band-string.** *Obs.* [BAND *n.*[1]] A string for fastening a collar. — **1651** *Mayflower Descendants* XI. 6, 2 lased bands & one paire of band stringes. **1654** *Ib.* 205 Stuffe for bandstrings.

+**Band-tailed,** *a. W.* [BAND *n.*[2]] Denoting a wild pigeon (*Columba fasciata*) having a round tail marked by a blackish band or bar. — **1823** James *Exped.* II. 10 This species . . . may be distinguished by the name of band-tailed pigeon. **1828** BONAPARTE *Synopsis* 119 The band-tail [*sic*] pigeon . . . inhabits the Rocky Mountains. **1858** BAIRD *Birds Pacific R.R.* 597 Band-tailed Pigeon . . . [is found] from Rocky mountains to Pacific coast. **1874** COUES *Birds N.W.* 385 Band-tailed Pigeon, . . . a bird of the Rocky Mountains, . . . is common in many parts of the West.

+**Band-wagon.** [BAND *n.*[1] 3.]

1. A large wagon, usu. ornamented and high, with a deck to seat bandsmen, as in a circus parade.

1855 BARNUM *Life* viii. 205 At Vicksburg we sold all our land-conveyances, excepting four horses and the 'band wagon.' **1869** 'MARK TWAIN' *Innocents Abroad* xvii. 167 The tall van, plastered with fanciful bills and posters, that follows the band-wagon of a circus about a country village. **1905** *N.Y. Ev. Post* 21 Oct. 1 Jerome's band wagon began to move over the town to-day. It bears on its sides announcements of these mass meetings on Monday night.

2. In figurative (colloq. or slang) uses

1893 *Congress. Rec.* 25 Aug. 897/1 It is a lamentable fact that . . . our commercial enemy . . . should come along with a band wagon loaded with hobgoblins. **1903** *N.Y. Sun* 23 Nov. 12 Woolen makers are predicting brownish tints as the prime favorites in men's suits next winter. We're abreast the band wagon. **1906** in *N.Y. Ev. Post* 5 Sept. 4 Many of those Democrats . . . who rushed into the Bryan band-wagon . . . will now be seen crawling out over the tailboard. **1909** WHITE *Rules of Game* IV. ii, When you get to be as old as I am, you learn not to monkey with the band wagon.

attrib. **1908** *Nation* 16 April 343/1 Consequently, we shall now hear the 'band-wagon' argument for Taft more confidently than ever.

***Bandy,** *n.* The game of hockey. {1693–} Also attrib.

1827 McKENNEY *Tour to Lakes* 181 The little naked Indian boys . . . were meanwhile sporting over the green, playing ball. . . . This ball-playing is not unlike our game of bandy. **1832** C. S. STEWART *Sketches of Society* II. 102 Golf . . . is not dissimilar, however, to the game practised at the schools and colleges of America, called 'bandy.' **1839** *S. Lit. Messenger* V. 329/2, I stumpt it playing bandy. **1866** HALE *If, Yes, & Perhaps* (1868) 262, I supposed it was one of the boy's bandy holes.

+**Bandy porgy.** The moonfish (*Chætodipterus faber*) of the eastern coast. — **1883** GOODE *Fishery Industries* 70 A station for the artificial propagation of . . . the Spanish mackerel . . . and the bandy porgy.

Baneberry. A plant of the genus *Actæa,* which bears poisonous berries. {1755–} Also attrib.

1784 CUTLER in *Mem. Academy* I. 454 *Actæa.* . . . Christopher. Baneberries. . . . The root is useful in some nervous cases. **1821** *Jrnl. Science* III. 276 Plainfield, Mass. . . . June 6. The redberried actea or baneberry . . . [is] in flower. **1832** WILLIAMSON *Maine* I. 120 The Bane-berry . . . has green balls, as large as those of asparagus. **1840** DEWEY *Mass. Flowering Plants* 21 White Baneberry . . . grows in damp woods, and flowers in May. Astringent. **1847** WOOD *Botany* 146 *A. Rubra.* Bigelow . . . Red Bane-berry. **1887** *Harper's Mag.* July 303/2, I jumped out to secure some tall stalk of baneberry flowers. **1901** MOHR *Plant Life Ala.* 509 White Baneberry [has] . . . flowers white, April; berries white, ripe in July.

+**Bang,** *n.* [f. BANG *v.*[2]] The front hair cut short and worn down over the forehead; a fringe. {1880–} Usu. in *pl.*

1878 F. M. A. ROE *Army Lett.* 186 It had a heavy bang of fiery red hair. **1880** HOWELLS *Undisc. Country* viii. 113 When one lifted his hat . . . he showed his hair cut in front like a young lady's bang. **1883** *Harper's Mag.* Dec. 111/2 Miss Patty . . . [ran] her fingers over her 'bangs'—a very poor name for the lovely golden masses of wavy hair shading her brow and eyes. **1889** M. H. FOOTE in *Century Mag.* March 774/2 She swept up the bangs from her fair forehead. **1896** *Harper's Mag.* April 674/1 The Countess . . . had . . . a false and frizzled bang of light hair.

***Bang,** *v.*[1] In colloquial uses.

1. *tr.* To outdo or exceed in any quality or action; to 'beat.' {1779–}

1817 *Niles' Register* 18 January 337 We were not prepared for this —to use a sheer Yankee phrase, 'it bangs every thing.' **1829** A. ROYALL *Penna.* II. 96 But the boilers and cannon banged every thing. **1830** — *Southern Tour* I. 166 This bangs Walsh and Col. Stone all hollow. **1833** *Louisville Public Advt.* 2 Feb., This [mammoth hog] bangs the world!! **1848** BARTLETT 22 This bangs all things.—*Ohio.* **1862** *Knickerb.* LIX. 392 This bangs the Dutch of St. Louis. **1875** MILLER *First Families* (1876) xx. 180 Well, that bangs me all hollow! **1883** 'MARK TWAIN' *Life on Miss.* liii. 527 Don't it just bang anything you ever heard of?

+**b.** *To bang the bush,* to excel or surpass everything.

1836 HALIBURTON *Clockm.* 1 Ser. xxiv, My! said he, if that don't bang the bush. **1848** W. E. BURTON *Waggeries* 70 It happifies me to say that we bang the bush!

+**2.** *To bang away,* to discharge fire-arms.

1840 DANA *Two Years* xxxvi. 452 The watch on deck were banging away at the guns every few minutes. **1883** 'MARK TWAIN' *Life on Miss.* xxvi. 288 Firing back . . . and banging away with all their might. **1884** *Bismark* (Dakota) *Tribune* Aug., Preparing for the fray, he took aim and 'banged away.' **1902** LORIMER *Lett. Merchant* xiv. 200 He had banged away into . . . the flock, hoping to bring down those two birds.

3. *Banged up,* knocked about; in bad condition.

1886 *Harper's Mag.* June 107 Even the trig, irreproachable commercial drummer actually looks banged up and nothing of a man. **1886** E. L. DORSEY *Midshipman Bob* II. vii. 172 Then Young dragged himself on those banged up legs ever so far . . . to the Life-Saving Station.

+**Bang,** *v.*[2] *tr.* To cut (the hair) so as to form bangs or fringes. Chiefly in *p.p.*

1878 B. F. TAYLOR *Between Gates* 171 A Digger Indian's papoose, with . . . hair cat-black and 'banged.' **1881** *Harper's Mag.* June 110/1 The old woman with the big bags under her eyes . . . a-askin' you to bang her hair, sir! **1882** 'M. HARLAND' *Eve's Daughters* 110 Unsuspicious of this fact, she hides the unsightly clusters by 'banging' her hair. **1883** J. HAY *Bread-winners* ii. 30 His glance . . . would travel . . . to her hair, frizzed and banged down to her eyebrows. **1892** *Harper's Mag.* Feb. 442/1 See how they've tried to part her hair in the middle and bang it.

+**Bange,** *v. colloq. intr.* To spend time idly; to loaf, lounge. — **1886** S. JEWETT *White Heron* 9 Last winter she got the jay-birds to bangeing here. **1890** *Dialect Notes* I. 21 *Bange* . . . ; used in Central Maine: 'a pair of boots to bange round in.' **1897** HOWELLS *Landlord at Lion's Head* 187 It'll interest him to go out there; and we can make him believe it's just to bange around for the winter.

+**Banged,** *ppl. a.* [BANG *v.*[2]] (Having the hair) cut so as to form bangs. — [**1880** *Ev. Standard* 3 April 4 The present style of banged girl.] **1886** C. D. WARNER *Pilgrimage* v. (1887) 135 A very pretty black-eyed girl with banged hair.

Banger. {1814; f. BANG *v.*[1]} +*Yale slang.* 'A club like a cane or stick; a bludgeon' (Hall). — **1849** (*title*), The Yale Banger. **1853** *Yale Lit. Mag.* XIX. 2 (Th.), He is prone to sport a huge stick, suggestively called a 'Yale Banger.' **1855** *Ib.* XX. 75 A Sophomore gang . . . with faces masked and bangers stout, Had come resolved to smoke him [=a freshman] out. **1871** [L. H. BAGG] *At Yale* 258 When a solitary Fresh, carefully swinging his banger, is pounced upon by several Sophs. **1906** *Springfield W. Republican* 10 May 1 Secretary Taft . . . has rescued from some museum . . . his old 'banger' of student days.

attrib. **1871** [L. H. BAGG] *At Yale* 257 This challenge is accepted by the Sophomores and in the evening a 'banger rush' takes place.

+**Bangless,** *a.* [BANG *n.*] Having no bangs or fringes. — **1889** 'MARK TWAIN' *Conn. Yankee* xxvii. 344 The high classes wore their hair banged across the forehead; . . . the slaves were bangless.

+**Bango,** *interj.* 'A common exclamation among the negroes both North and South' (B. '59).

+**Bang-up,** *n.* {1835} A heavy overcoat.

1842 *Spirit of Times* (Phila.) 28 Jan. (Th.), That gentlemanly looking man in the snuff-colored bang-up, that's Mayor Scott. **1853** *Public Ledger* (Phila.) 11 June (De Vere), He was clothed in an old bang-up, black vest, grey pants, and straw hat. **1871** DE VERE 439 *Bang-up,* the old word for a heavy overcoat, . . . still survives in some parts of the Union.

Bang-up, *a. colloq.* {1812–43}

1. Of superior quality; first-class; excellent.

1830 Advt. in *Massachusetts Spy* 9 June (Th.), Forbes and Freeman: Bang-up cords. **1836** *Quarter Race Kentucky* (1846) 19 The watch is a bang-up lever. **1877** BARTLETT 28 This cloth is bang up. **1889** K. MUNROE *Golden Days* xvii. 181 It's going to be nifty, and high-toned, and run in a bang-up hotel style. **1902** WISTER *Virginian* xvi. 194 He . . . started in for a bang-up meal with champagne. **1921** PAINE *Comr. Rolling Ocean* vii. 118 The salaries are bang-up nowadays.

+**2.** *Prime bang up,* quite drunk or intoxicated. *Obs. slang.*

1825 PAULDING *J. Bull in Amer.* x. 116 The driver being at length 'prime bang up,' that is to say, as drunk as a lord.

+**3.** *colloq.* Of roads: (see quotation).

1835 ABDY *Journal* III. 65 The road was hilly and bad; great part of it being what is vulgarly called 'corduroy,' or 'bang-up,' or 'rail-road.'

+**4.** *slang.* Out of money; 'dead broke.'

1854 'O. OPTIC' *In Doors & Out* (1876) 98 The other person, who to use his own classic expression, was 'bang up,' and wanted to borrow fifty dollars. *Ib.* 105, I am 'bang up.' I have got a note of four hundred to pay [etc.].

***Banian, Banyan.** [Orig. attrib. use of *banian,* a Hindu trader or native broker.] A lounging gown, morning-robe, or the like, worn esp. during warm weather. {1725–1845}

1732 BYRD *Writings* (1901) 381, I found him in his night-cap and banian, which is his ordinary dress in that retired part of the country. **1733** *S.C. Gazette* 250/1 Just Imported . . . silk night Gowns or Banjans.

1744 *Mass. H.S. Coll.* VII. 191 [An Indian child], neatly dressed in a green banjan. 1774 Advt. in *Boston Gazette* 3 Oct. (Th.), Carried away with him a callico banyon, &c. 1833 J. F. WATSON *Hist. Tales Phila.* 117 In the summer season, men very often wore calico morning-gowns at all times of the day. . . . A damask banyan was much the same thing by another name. 1867 LOWELL *Fitz Adam's Story* 434 In summer-time a banyan loose he wore.

+**Banjo.** Also **banjou, bangy.** [Reduced form of BANJOR. Cf. West Indian *banshaw* (1764).]

1. A stringed musical instrument of the guitar kind, popular among Negroes of the South, played by plucking the strings with the fingers. {1846–}

1774 CRESSWELL *Journal* 30 A great number of young people met together [in Va.] with a fiddle and banjo played by two negroes. 1774 FITHIAN *Journal* I. 103 This evening . . . several negroes & Ben & Harry are playing on a banjo & dancing. 1808 T. ASHE *Travels* xi. 100 The music consisted of two bangies, played by negroes. 1833 *Sketches D. Crockett* 147 The banjo . . . , thrummed by some old trusty black. 1841 E. R. STEELE *Summer Journey* 210 The negro banjo . . . echoed from the lower deck. 1862 BROWNE *A. Ward his Book* 199, I saw a nigger sittin on a fence a-playin on a banjo. 1882 J. HAWTHORNE *Fortune's Fool* I. xi, He could play a goodly number of interesting tunes on his banjo. 1904 STRATTON-PORTER *Freckles* 193 The next time I am going to bring my banjo, and I'll play, and you'll sing . . . the songs I like best.

2. Attrib. with *picker, player.*

1859 BARTLETT 343 *Professor* . . . The application of the word to dancing-masters, conjurers, banjo-players, etc., has been called an Americanism. 1871 [L. H. BAGG] *At Yale* 300 Listening to . . . the music of an itinerant harpist, or banjo-player, or organ-grinder. 1890 *Harper's Mag.* Sept. 594/2 What a fallow field . . . for the banjo picker!

Banjoist. One who plays the banjo. {1880–} — 1888 BILLINGS *Hardtack* 69 There was probably not a regiment in the service that did not boast at least one violinist, one banjoist, and a bone player in its ranks.

+**Banjor.** *Obs.* Also **banger, banjer.** [Alteration of *bandore* {1591–1689}, from Sp. or Pg.] A banjo. {*c*1790, 1801}

1775 ADAIR *Indians* 175 One of their old sacred musical instruments . . . resembled the Negroe-Banger in shape. 1781–2 JEFFERSON *Notes Va.* (1788) 150 The instrument proper to them [*sc.* negroes] is the Banjor, which they brought hither from Africa. 1784 SMYTH *Tour* I. 46 Keeping time and cadence, most exactly, with the music of a banjor (a large hollow instrument with three strings). 1800 J. BOUCHER *Glossary* p. xlix, *Banjor*, a rude musical instrument, made of the shell of a large gourd, or pumpion, and strung somewhat in the manner of a violin: it is much used by negros. 1803 J. DAVIS *Travels* 379 My young master . . . made me learn to play the Banger.

***Bank,** *n.*[1]

1. (Usually *pl.*) The submarine plateau off the coast of Newfoundland, noted for its fishing grounds. {1702–}

1635 R. MATHER *Journal* 21 Conceiving thereby that wee were . . . on New-fondland banke, on the end of it neerer to New England. 1688 SEWALL *Diary* I. 239 Suppose ourselves very near the banks of New-found-Land. 1708 *Boston News-Letter* 24–31 May 2/2 Captain Michael Gill . . . bound for Newfoundland . . . designs to cruise upon the Banks there. 1729 FRANKLIN *Busy-body* No. 8, A sea-captain [said] . . . 'I esteem the Banks of Newfoundland to be a more valuable possession than the mountains of Potosi.' 1775 HUTCHINSON *Diary & Lett.* I. 411 The enquiry made into the great national advantages arising from the Newfoundland Fishery, has determined a great part of the Parl[iamen]t to exclude America from all the Banks. 1789 *Ann. 1st Congress* I. 139 The taking of fish on the banks is a very momentous concern. *Ib.* 209 Nine months are our fishermen employed on the Banks. 1840 DANA *Two Years* xxxiv. 429 What the whalemen on the Banks, . . . call 'a Cape Horn-er under a cloud of sail.' 1861 STOWE *Pearl of Orr's Island* I. 119 There'll be a splendid haul of fish at the Banks this year. 1880 [see BANKER[1] 1 b].

b. An oyster-bank or oyster-bed.

1799 WELD *Travels* 80 A bank of oysters in the [Potomac] river. 1881 E. INGERSOLL *Oyster Industry* 241 *Bed*, the *bank*, *reef*, or deposit of oysters in the water, either growing naturally or artificially, original or transplanted.

2. (See quot. 1881 and cf. COAL-BANK.)

1804 CLARK in *Lewis & Clark Exped.* (1904) I. i. 58 At 3 miles [we] passed a coal-mine, or bank of stone coal; . . . this bank appears to contain great quantity of fine coal. 1831 Peck *Guide* 193 Mr. Neilson's coal bank is immediately in the banks of the Big Muddy river, and is so convenient that the coal can be thrown from the bank into the boats. 1872 *Ill. Dept. Agric. Trans.* 151 Coal . . . sells at the 'banks' at six cents per bushel. 1881 RAYMOND *Mining Glossary*, *Bank*, an ore-deposit or coal-bed worked by surface excavations or drifts above water-level.

+**3.** A place where logs are piled to await transportation. (Cf. BANK *v.*[1] 3.)

1829 J. MACTAGGART *Three Years* I. 241 The Shantymen . . . cut down the pine trees, . . . and afterwards draw the logs to what is termed the *bank*, with oxen. 1902 WHITE *Blazed Trail* xiii. 91 An outline of the process after the logs have been piled on the banks.

4. A heap or long pile, usu. covered with earth.

1854 *Florida Plant. Rec.* 554/2, 2 banks of seed potatoes; 2 banks eating potatoes.

+**5.** *Out of bank:* (see quotation).

1859 BARTLETT 365 A stream is said to be 'out of ride' when it is past fording; 'out of bank,' is a still higher stage of water, i.e. over its banks.

+**6.** *To give* (one) *down the banks*, to scold or reprimand (a person). *colloq.*

1884 'MARK TWAIN' *H. Finn* xxvii. 280 He give me down the banks for not coming and telling him.

***BANK,** *n.*[2]

***1.** An establishment for the deposit and handling of money.

1688 *Penna. Col. Rec.* I. 236 The petition . . . was read, setting forth their designe in setting up a bank for money, &c. 1715 *Boston Rec.* 115 At a meeting . . . [it was] voted, that a town meeting be appointed to debate & declare whether they are for a publick or private bank. 1781 *Journals Cont. Congress* 26 May 546 The subscribers to the said bank shall be incorporated . . . under the name of The President, Directors and company of the bank of North-America. 1790 HAMILTON in *Ann. 1st Congress* II. 2045 There are at present three banks in the United States. *Ib.* 2049 The principles upon which a National Bank ought to be organized. *Ib.* 2050 The purposes of the Bank of the United States. 1794 *Mass. H.S. Coll.* III. 275 Massachusetts Bank. This was the first established in Boston, and incorporated by an act of the general court, February 7th, 1784. 1814 *Niles' Reg.* VI. 226/2 All the banks in New Orleans have made a stoppage of payment in specie. 1821 *Ann. 17th Congress* 1 Sess. I. 35 That Congress shall make no law to authorize any bank, or other moneyed institution, except in the District of Columbia. 1836 *Diplom. Corr. Texas* (1908) I. 73 A bank will give great facilities to the country in its monied affairs. 1857 GLISAN *Jrnl. Army Life* 391 Railroad stock was the first to suffer. . . . Next the banks and merchants in regular succession. 1865 *Atlantic Mo.* XV. 85/2 These banks are . . . the only ones in New York whose condition can be definitely ascertained. 1880 CABLE *Grandissimes* xl. 312 Claiborne will give us better money than that when he starts his bank.

***b.** *In bank*, in a bank; at the bank. {1563–1753}

1654 JOHNSON *Wonder-W. Prov.* 28 Onely this sum lies still in banke, and the other they have had the income againe. 1844 *Knickerb.* XXIII. 14 [She] claimed . . . among her chattels sundry shares in bank. 1856 D. MACLEOD *F. Wood* 177 For which [loan] we are still paying interest, notwithstanding the large amount now lying to the credit of the city in bank. 1886 S. W. MITCHELL *R. Blake* 240 My small reserve of money in bank has almost gone. 1902 WISTER *Virginian* xxiii. 273 Take my land away to-morrow, and I'd still have my savings in bank.

c. Occas. *bank of credit, deposit, issue,* etc.

1714 *Boston News-Letter* 1 Feb. 2/2 Whereas a project is on foot at Boston for erecting a Bank of Credit. *Ib.* 16–23 Aug. 2/2 A certain number of gentlemen and merchants are projecting a Bank of Credit, as they call it. 1841 PARK *Pantology* 125 Banks of deposite, receive money for safe keeping. *Ib.*, Banks of discount lend money, on security. 1841 F. WOOD in MacLeod *Biog.* 74 It had . . . proved unsafe as a public depository, unsound as a bank of emission. 1889 *Cent.*, *Bank of issue*, a bank or banking company duly authorized by law to issue bank-notes of its own.

2. a. The funds of the proprietor of a gaming-table, or of a gaming-house. {*c*1720–} **b.** A gambling establishment, or the proprietor(s) of it.

1835 [INGRAHAM] *South-West* I. 129 Each [gambling] house has a bank, as the amount of funds owned by it is termed. *a*1846 *Quarter Race Kentucky*, etc. 78 'Mr. Dealer,' I remarked, 'I have come to break up this bank.' 'The deuce you have!' replied the banker — 'let's see you do it.' 1849 AUDUBON *Western Journal* (1906) 197 The tables had changed hands in some instances, but the many are still sitting behind their 'banks.' 1854 *Harper's Mag.* VIII. 587/2 On either side of this apartment were ranged three tables for the convenience of the 'banks' and their customers. 1907 *Putnam's Mo.* July 482/2 Garish yellow lights showed where 'banks' were still running . . . [in] Manhattan.

fig. 1891 RYAN *Pagan* xiv. 176 That's why you cantered over to me; . . . but you've been playing on the wrong bank. I'm broke.

3. Attrib. and comb. (in sense 1): see BANK ACCOMMODATION, ACCOUNT, etc.

In the lack of an adjectival form, the attributive use of the noun is naturally very frequent, as in *bank cashier, deposit, discount, dividend, failure,* etc. The following, in addition to those entered below, are among the earlier or more significant of these.

1790 HAMILTON in *Ann. 1st Congress* II. 2057 There is an important fact, which exemplifies the fitness of the public debt for a bank fund. 1799 *Aurora* 15 March (Th.), Groups of pickpockets, bank-robbers, and hen-pecked dotards. 1802 *Ann. 7th Congress* 2 Sess. 1248 A sum, which, together with the bank dividends, shall be equal to the eight per cent annuity. 1811 *Ann. 11th Congress* 3 Sess. 612 Our State Legislatures are to be importuned to become bank jobbers and . . . copartners in the enterprise. 1813 WEEMS *Letters* III. 92 They may be worked off and in time to give you bank interest on your money. 1814 JEFFERSON *Letter* Wks. XIV. 77, I was derided as a maniac by the tribe of bank-mongers. 1817 PAULDING *Lett. from South* II. 174, I saw two or three bank notices, stuck up with an awl over his desk. 1833 *Deb. Congress* 24 Jan. 1337 The doctrines of the numerous veto messages . . . have been calculated to array one class of citizens against another, and none of these more so than the doctrines of the bank veto. *Ib.* 30 Dec. 2269 The bank statements do not show where the bills purchased by it are payable, but only the aggregate amounts. **1834** *Ib.* 20 March 1025 A certain description of paper . . . known by the appellation of 'bank drafts' . . . were made receivable in payment of the revenue. **1841** D. MacLeod *Biog. F. Wood* (1856) 89 The people have lost directly by bank failures, [$]108,885,721. *Ib.* 90 Men who . . . have been insnared into the temptation of a bank discount. **1844** *Indiana Senate J.* 280 To provide that . . . the bank be required to rely alone for the redemption of the bank scrip upon the sinking fund. **1847** *Knickerb.* XXX. 280 We are reminded . . . of a circumstance mentioned to us by an old bank-notary of this town. **1852** *Ib.* XXXIX. 54 Mr. Solomon Fudge is a bank-officer in Wall Street. **1853** *Harper's Mag.* Jan. 193 As if some invalid clergyman or bank-president, in white cravat, wished sedately to have his carriage called. **1863** *Century Mag.* Sept. (1885) 772 We went to H—'s office. . . . H— carried the bank box; I the case of matches. **1870** 'M. HARLAND' *For Better, for Worse* 254 Are you meditating sacrilege, or a bank robbery? **1880** BARNET *Commercial Dict.* 50 Authority to certify generally does not authorize a bank official to certify his own check. **1882** *Century Mag.* March 769/2 The bank-examiner . . . found very grave irregularities and delinquencies. **1883** C. F. WILDER *Sister Ridnour* 222 A book . . . that would do credit to a bank clerk. **1884** *Lisbon* (Dakota) *Star* 20 June, You . . . hadn't been a bank president and wanted to put an end to your existence? **1892** *Vermont Agric. Rep.* XII. 125 Something must be done for the farmer, . . . even though his mortgage, rather than his bank deposit, has grown.

Bank, *n.*[3] **1.** *In bank*, at a sitting of a court of justice. {1700–68} **2.** A shelf on which sheets are placed before or after printing.—(1) **1835** J. HALL *Sk. West* II. 198 All its functions, as a court, are performed in bank. It appoints its own clerk and reporter. (2) **1851** CIST *Cincinnati* 359 Place for Bank, from which the sheet is put on the tympan.

*** Bank,** *v.*[1]

+1. *tr.* To protect (a cellar, house, etc.), esp. against the cold of winter, by piling earth against it. Chiefly with *up.*

1720 *Canton* (Mass.) *Rec.* 6 Ten Pounds granted . . . to repaire the Roof of the meeting hovse and to bank the out side of the scils of said hovse. **1779** *Narrag. Hist. Reg.* I. 97 Banked up the cellar wall. **1845** KIRKLAND *Western Clearings* 103 He must . . . get up a 'bee' to bank up his beloved meeting-house. **1853** B. F. TAYLOR *Jan. & June* 143 They 'banked up' the house, yesterday; put the cabbages in the cellar, the day before. **1861** *Ill. Agric. Soc. Trans.* IV. 120 Mr. Smith . . . would use straw in the spring, but would bank up [the tree] with earth in the fall. **1863** 'GAIL HAMILTON' *Gala-Days* 156 He finds that he has to go and shovel a path, or bank up the cellar. *a*1869 A. D. RICHARDSON *Garnered Sheaves* (1871) 412 The landlord told me . . . he should be obliged to bank up the house to keep warm this winter.

2. To enclose with banks in order to protect, confine, or keep back. {1622–} Also with *out, up.*

1770 *Pennsylvania Chronicle* 10–17 September 138/3 A large quantity of swamp, or tide marsh, . . . now lies useless for want of banking, which, . . . if banked, would be of great value to the proprietors. **1771** J. HABERSHAM *Letters* 122, I think they are better situated to be banked to keep out the freshes than yours. **1802** ELLICOTT *Journal* 127 A number of adventurers . . . arrived, who began with spirit to bank out the river. **1865** 'GAIL HAMILTON' *New Atmosphere* ii. 19, I do not . . . wish to dam the river. But I would prevent it from being banked up here and banked up there, . . . till it bursts all bounds. **1884** *Harper's Mag.* July 196/2 The stream . . . has been banked.

+3. To stack or pile up (logs) on a river-bank or at a landing to await transportation.

1856 *Mich. Agric. Soc. Trans.* VII. 828 There will be logs enough cut and 'banked' for 100,000,000 feet of lumber. We are informed that the amount now banked daily, will amount to 2,500,000 feet. **1888** *Battle Creek Moon* 21 April, Wright & Davis . . . have purchased the logs banked at West Superior, Wis. *a*1904 WHITE *Blazed Trail Stories* ii. 25 Richard Darrell usually finished banking his season's cut a month earlier. *Ib.* iii. 40 The firm agreed to pay . . . for all saw-logs banked at a rollway. *transf.* **1895** KING *Fort Frayne* ii. 22 Double sacks of grain . . . were banked at the quartermaster's corral.

4. To store up (potatoes) in a bank or heap.

1851 *Florida Plant. Rec.* 418, 2 [slaves] banking potatoes and soforth.

Bank, *v.*[2] [f. BANK *n.*[2]]

1. *intr.* To engage in banking. {1727–}. +Also, to conduct the business of banking (or to gamble) *upon* capital.

1818 *Niles' Reg.* XIV. 14/2 The treasurer of the state has been loaning the funds deposited with him to private individuals on interest,—*i.e.* he has been *banking*, and is minus a considerable sum. **1831** *Deb. Congress* 2 Feb. 55 The name, the credit, and the revenues of the United States . . . constitute in themselves an immense capital to bank upon. **1834** *Ib.* 21 March 1065 Banking by one State compels all others to bank. **1838** *Democratic Rev.* I. 23 It being conceded that the banks must not hereafter, at any rate, bank upon the public money. **1853** *S. Lit. Messenger* XIX. 71/1 Simon found an opening on the thither side of a Faro table; and having disposed of the race mare for $300, banked on this capital.

+2. To count or rely *on* or *upon* (a person or thing) with confidence or assurance. Also with *that.*

1884 NYE *Baled Hay* 127 The man who ranks as a dignified snoozer and banks on winning wealth and a deathless name. **1892** *Congress. Rec.* April, App. 249/2, I am not banking heavily on [him] . . . as an honest man. **1898** *N.Y. Sun* 14 Sept. 1/3 The Democrats are banking upon this movement to help them out this fall. **1902** LORIMER *Lett. Merchant* xi. 151 An example of the fact that a fellow can't bank on getting a chance to go back. **1903** A. ADAMS *Log Cowboy* vi. 39, I was banking plenty strong . . . that next year . . . I'd take her home with me. **1906** *Md. Hist. Mag.* I. 110 As a public contractor he banked on the forbearance of the public. **1921** PAINE *Comr. Rolling Ocean* v. 81 You can bank on what I say, son. This vessel will either sink or swim.

+Bankable, *a.* [BANK *v.*[2]] Acceptable as cash or currency at a bank.

1828 WEBSTER, *Bankable*, receivable at a bank, as bills; or discountable, as notes. (Of recent origin.) **1832** *Deb. Congress* 7 March 2041 A currency . . . perhaps not bankable at all places. **1855** *Knickerb.* XLV. 469 Count 'em, Sir. Four hundred and ten dollars, good bankable money, Sir.

+Bank accommodation. [BANK *n.*[2]] Lending, or a loan, of money by a bank. — **1811** *Ann. 11th Congress* 3 Sess. 609 The revenue bonds outstanding . . . will not, cannot, be paid if bank accommodations are to stop. *Ib.* 612 By lessening or destroying bank accommodation, you transfer the credit from the city to the country. **1818** *Niles' Reg.* XIV. 1/2 A hundredth part of the bank-accommodation extended to one of these [men] . . . would 'put him on his feet.' **1851** CIST *Cincinnati* 322 A deficiency, at Cincinnati, of bank capital and bank accommodations, . . . has induced many steamboat owners to build elsewhere.

Bank account. [BANK *n.*[2]] An account with a bank; a sum of money deposited in a bank. {Also E.}

1799 BROWN *A. Mervyn* iv, Have I not seen his bank account? His deposits . . . amount to not less than half a million. **1865** *Atlantic Mo.* XV. 511 The servant who could manage his bank account. **1870** 'MARK TWAIN' *Sk., Widow's Protest*, She began to get miserly as her bank-account grew. **1904** STRATTON-PORTER *Freckles* 68 You needn't touch your bank account, Freckles.

Bank agent. [BANK *n.*[2] See AGENT *n.*] — **1819** Mackenzie *Van Buren* (1846) 159 It is true that the Bank has not extended to speculators and bank agents that prompt accommodation which [etc.].

+Bank-barn. [BANK *n.*[1]] A barn erected on sloping ground, so that three sides of the bottom story are enclosed by earth. — **1894** *Congress. Rec.* Jan. 1036/1 On my father's farm, when I was a boy, there stood a big bank-barn. **1903** *Forest & Stream* 21 Feb. p. iv/2 For Sale: Ideal game and fish preserve. Buildings . . . consisting of large house, bank barn, spring house and ice house.

Bank bill. [BANK *n.*[2]] A promissory note or certificate issued by a bank or banker; a bank note. {1696–1809}

'The term *bank-note* . . . at the present day [in England] is the only name given to what are called bank-*bills* in America' (Pick.).

1682 J. WOODBRIDGE in *Mass. Bay Currency Tracts* 7 And this . . . bank-bills, or payments therein, will effect, to all intents, as well as plenty of coin. **1714** P. DUDLEY *Ib.* 92 As to their bank-bills, I readily grant they are not money. *c*1720 *Ib.* 379 All paper bills whether province or bank bills are mutable in value, therefore delusive & injurious. **1790** MACLAY *Deb. Senate* 270 Bank bills are promissory notes, and of course not money. **1808** *Mass. Statutes* ch. xcix. Preamble, Jacob Perkins, of Newburyport, . . . hath invented . . . steel plates for the printing of bank-bills. **1819** D. THOMAS *Travels* 72 J. Swan had provided a quantity of small bank bills, which proved very convenient. **1839** BRIGGS *H. Franco* I. iv. 17 My father put a small roll of bank-bills into my hand. **1849** *Rep. Comm. Patents* (1850) 546 One of the most important of his inventions was the engraving of bank bills. **1882** THAYER *Log-Cabin to White House* viii. 88 Luck is like an old United States bank bill, of very uncertain value.

Bank-blasting. [BANK *n.*[1]] The application of an explosive to a bank to facilitate mining operations. — **1877** RAYMOND *Rep. Mines* 56 Bank-blasting is practiced. **1882** KING *Rep. Precious Metals* 627 The system of 'bank-blasting' generally in vogue.

Bank-book. [BANK *n.*[2]] A book for recording the deposits (or complete account) of a bank customer; a passbook. {1714–}

1793 HAMILTON in *Ann. 2nd Congress* 1203 A disagreement between a memorandum in the Treasurer's Bank Book and the statement reported by me. **1811** *Ann. 12th Congress* 1 Sess. 2062 As the Treasurer can keep no bank book, it is necessary that a weekly statement of his account be sent to him from the bank. **1857** M. J. HOLMES *Meadow-Brook* xiv, Did that in any way compensate him for the fifty dollars which stood on the Cr. side of his bank-book? **1865** *Atlantic Mo.* XV. 385 My blessing and my bank-book are your own. **1882** *Century Mag.* March 768/2 This board [of directors] seldom dip into the bank-books. **1904** WALLER *Woodcarver* 239, I drew out my bank-book . . . and showed her the balance of three hundred dollars.

+Bank capital. [BANK *n.*[2]] The capital of a banking establishment, or of a group of banks. — **1812** *Niles' Reg.* II. 77 The city of New-York already possesses a bank capital nearly double that of any other city in the Union. **1851** CIST *Cincinnati* 322 A deficiency . . . of bank capital . . . has induced many steamboat owners to build elsewhere. **1885** BROCKETT

Our Country's Progress 608 [The year] 1846, when the bank capital was at a low point.

Bank charter. [BANK *n.*[2]] A charter authorizing the founding of a bank. {1834–}

1812 *Niles' Reg.* II. 19/2 He said that no member would more cheerfully than himself grant to that association a bank charter. **1836** FLAGG in Mackenzie *Van Buren* 175 It has been pretty well settled, that a mould for running bank charters cannot be made constitutionally. **1837** *Diplom. Corr. Texas* (1908) I. 223 The length of the loan could be made for as long a time as the Bank Charter exists. **1871** [L. H. BAGG] *At Yale* 40 The last gift—of $7000, made in 1831—was of money received by the State as a bonus for a bank charter. **1882** *Nation* 20 July 41/1 An event of the week was the enactment of the Bank Charter Bill.

+**Bank check.** [BANK *n.*[2]] An order issued on a bank or banker to pay a designated sum of money.

1801 *Steele Papers* I. 225 Your letter enclosing a bank check of $100 . . . has been duly received. **1803** JEFFERSON in *Harper's Mag.* March (1885) 541/2, I enclose you a bank-check for twenty two and a half dollars. **1817** *Boston Comm. Gazette* 30 June (Advt.), Among them are . . . bills of lading, bank checks, check books. **1855** D. MacLeod *Biog. F. Wood* (1856) 289 And bank-checks they were, signed by one city official [etc.].

Bank clearings. [BANK *n.*[2]] (See quot. 1900.) — **1885** *Chicago Daily News* 5 Nov. 4/1 A fair amount was traded in on this basis. Associated bank clearings were $8,765,000. **1900** NELSON *A B C Wall St.* 127 *Bank clearings*, the total amount of the checks and drafts exchanged by banks (members of clearing-house association).

+**Bank cod.** [BANK *n.*[1]] The common cod, *Gadus morrhua*, from the Banks of Newfoundland (in contrast to *shore* or *native* cod). — **1814** MITCHILL *Fishes N.Y.* 367 Bank cod . . . is found at times in the New-York market, being caught in the sea near Nantucket, and beyond. **1842** *Nat. Hist. N.Y., Zoology* IV. 280 The Bank Cod. . . . Abdomen white. **1889** *Cent.* 1082 *Bank Cod*, a commercial term for cod caught on the banks of Newfoundland, of superior value.

+**Bank commissioner.** [BANK *n.*[2]] A commissioner for the supervision of banks.

1832 *Deb. Congress* 8 March 2070, I was an applicant for the situation of bank commissioner, under the New York Safety Fund. **1837** Buckingham *America* (1841) II. 282 The following statement is furnished by the bank commissioners for the purpose of showing the general condition of the banks. **1838** *Mass. Stat.* 23 Feb. 302 There shall be appointed by the Governor . . . three persons to be styled Bank Commissioners. **1862** *Amer. Ann. Cycl. 1861* 68/1 The bank commissioners notified the auditor of the failure of 17 banks. **1895** *Chicago Tribune* 6 April 1 The Bank Commissioner's report on the condition of the Nashua Savings Bank says that . . many investments . . . have increased largely in value.

+**Bank company.** [BANK *n.*[2]] A company formed to conduct banking business. — **1805** *Ann. 8th Congress* 2 Sess. 1088 The bank company was again heard by counsel in favor of their exclusive monopoly. **1835** [INGRAHAM] *South-West* I. xii. 129 Some of the houses . . . when likely to be hard run by heavy losses, can draw . . . upon the directors of the 'bank company.' **1837** PECK *New Guide* 205 The general revenue [of Ohio] is . . . collected . . . from insurance, bank and bridge companies, from lawyers, physicians, etc.

Bank credit. [BANK *n.*[2]] Credit given by a bank to one borrowing money from it. — **1811** *Ann. 11th Congress* 3 Sess. 612 In order to free the country from the mischiefs of an extended bank credit. **1858** *Mass. Acts* 178 Bank credits have contributed to the extension and the revulsion of trade. **1885** BROCKETT *Our Country's Progress* 605 [In] 1846 . . . bank credits had begun to multiply under the effects of the famine abroad.

Bank director. [BANK *n.*[2]] A director or executive of a bank. {1828–}

1817 PAULDING *Lett. from South* II. 95 Nearly as important a personage as . . . a Bank Director, or even a rich Money Broker. **1818** *Niles' Reg.* XIV. 2/1, I would rather be numbered among the slaves . . . than put my independence into the keeping of a board of bank directors. **1820** FLINT *Lett. from Amer.* 197 Twenty-four bank-directors still have it in their power to regulate the money value of all the property in the empire. **1833** Mackenzie *Van Buren* (1846) 242 You are surprised at the appointment of Mr. Alley as Bank Director. **1840** *Knickerb.* XVI. 207 A gentleman wearing the air of a bank-director. **1854** CUMMINS *Lamplighter* xvii. 131 Mr. Graham had gone to a meeting of bank-directors. **1881** W. O. STODDARD *E. Hardery* 24 A most satisfactory morning's work for a board of bank directors.

+**Bank district.** *local. Obs.* [BANK *n.*[2]] A district, usually consisting of two or more counties, served by a branch of a state bank. — **1838** *Indiana H. Rep. J.* 174 The expediency of providing by law, for the distribution of the fund in the several branch banks . . . in the several counties of the bank districts. **1844** *Indiana Senate J.* 322 A bill repealing certain acts relative to the establishment of bank districts.

Banker.[1] [BANK *n.*[1]]

1. A vessel engaged in cod-fishing on the Banks of Newfoundland. {1666–1769}

1704 *Boston News-Letter* 20 Nov. 2/2 The Advice man of war took a French Banker on the Banks of Newfoundland. **1725** *New-Eng. Courant* 24–31 July 2/2 Two ships . . . supply'd them with what . . . provisions they could spare, which you know could not be much from Bankers. **1802** *Mass. H.S. Coll.* VIII. 58 Sixteen bankers from the fishing banks, averaging 650 quintals each. **1815** J. Q. ADAMS *Duplicate Lett.* (1822) 219 The bankers . . . that go from the District of Maine, Connecticut and Rhode Island. *a***1848** Bartlett 22 There were employed in the fisheries 1,232 vessels; . . . the bankers may be put down at 36,540 tons. **1861** *Harper's Mag.* March 457/1 The fisheries on the banks of Newfoundland. . . . The crew of a 'banker' is generally composed of twelve men, including the 'skipper' or captain, who exercises no direct control over the others, but is recognized by them as the principal personage on board. **1880** *Ib.* Aug. 350/1 Still less could he [=the Maine islander] go the long voyages of the bankers to the bays of L'Escaut and Chaleurs.

+**b.** A person who fishes for cod on the Banks.

1861 *Harper's Mag.* March 461/2 On the banks of Newfoundland . . . some of the old bankers predicted a gale, which, by ten o'clock, began to blow. **1880** *Ib.* Aug. 338/1 The establishment of a 'banker' . . . whose occupation consisted in fishing in his schooner on the Grand Banks of Newfoundland.

+**2.** An inhabitant of the North Carolina sea-coast called the 'banks.'

1849 COOPER *Sea Lions* x, This term of 'Banker' applies to a scattering population of wreckers and fishermen, who dwell on the long, low, narrow beaches . . . from Cape Fear to near Cape Henry. **1871** DE VERE 334 The *bankers* of North Carolina . . . used to be wreckers of doubtful repute. They now combine the vocations of farming, fishing, and wrecking.

***Banker.**[2] [BANK *n.*[2]]

1. One who keeps or conducts a bank; a member of a banking establishment. {1671–}

In quots. 1714–6 applied to those who proposed to establish a bank.

1714 P. DUDLEY in *Mass. Bay Currency Tracts* 109, I understand the bankers have new modelled their projection. **1716** *Ib.* 170 This Bank seems projected more for the advantage of the bankers, than for the publick good. **1818** *Niles' Reg.* XIV. 3/1 A few of them are of the old class of bankers, . . . gentlemen who had money to spare when they entered into office. **1841** *Diplom. Corr. Texas* (1908) I. 501 The Agency of the Bankers is attempted to be placed in a doubtful position by questioning whether they have themselves assumed the Loan. **1875** STOWE *We & Neighbors* 446 With as much regularity and certainty as if checks had been drawn on a banker. **1881–5** MCCLELLAN *Own Story* 152 A committee of New York bankers were urging upon Secretary Chase the removal of Mr. Cameron.

2. One who deals or keeps the 'bank,' in certain games of chance. {1826–}

1806 LEWIS in *Lewis & C. Exped.* (1904) IV. 37 The individual who holds the peice [in an Indian gambling game] is a kind of banker and plays for a time being against all the others. *a***1846** [see BANK *n.*[2] 2]. **1849** AUDUBON *Western Journal* (1906) 197 We are all *bankers* here. **1854** *Harper's Mag.* VIII. 587/2 These tables were strongly built . . . with a parapet upon the three sides . . . partly, it may be, to put a stop to any undesirable scrutiny into the manipulations of the banker. **1887** KELLER *Draw Poker* 80 When the players have been allotted to their respective tables, it is the duty of the banker to furnish each with the same amount of chips.

+**Bank fisherman.** [BANK *n.*[1] 1.] A man or a vessel engaged in the bank fishery. — **1828** A. SHERBURNE *Mem.* (1831) ii. 35 She [=a vessel] had been a bank fisherman, but [was] . . . now finely painted, with a new and longer set of masts and spars. **1874** KNIGHT 212/1 Bait-mill [is] a machine used by the 'Bank' fishermen for cutting fish into bait.

Bank fishery. [BANK *n.*[1] 1.] The business or occupation of fishing for cod on the banks of Newfoundland. — **1792** *Ann. 2nd Congress* 66 An act for the encouragement of the bank and other cod fisheries. **1803** *Ann. 7th Congress* 2 Sess. 1335 Ships and vessels employed in the bank and cod fisheries. **1818** *Niles' Reg.* XIV. 15/2 A company was formed at Gloucester . . . for carrying on the bank fishery, with a capital of 50,000 dollars. **1861** *Amer. Cycl.* XII. 302/1 About . . . 80 [vessels are engaged] in the coast and bank fisheries.

***Bank-full,** *a.* Also **bankfull, -ful.** [BANK *n.*[1]] Full to the brink of the bank. {*c*1581, 1637, 1865}

App. in more extensive use in U.S. than in Eng.

1806–8 PIKE *Sources Miss.* 88 We could not cross the river, unless we rafted (it being bank full). **1816** U. BROWN *Journal* I. 224 Hughes River . . . this morning . . . was bankfull & no appearance of it falling. **1851** A. T. JACKSON *Forty-niner* (1920) 43 The creeks are running bank-full. **1883** 'MARK TWAIN' *Life on Miss.* xix. 228 Eagle Bend was two miles wide at this bank-full stage. **1903** *N.Y. Times* 28 Aug., Many of the small creeks have become bankfull, and are overflowing.

+**Bank halibut.** [BANK *n.*[1] 1.] The common halibut caught on the Banks of Newfoundland. — **1883** GOODE *Fish. Indust.* 51 These vessels salt down in their holds the Halibut which they obtain, and on their return it is smoked, producing smoked Halibut of the choicest kind—the so-called 'bank-halibut.'

Bank hours. [BANK *n.*[2]] The hours during which a bank is open to transact business. — **1845** M. M. NOAH *Gleanings* 51, I have seen a merchant . . . worn out with anxiety and fatigue, return to his house after bank hours, . . . finding no . . . cheerful voice to welcome him.

Banking, *vbl. n.*[1] [BANK *v.*[1]]

1. The construction of banks or embankments; the work of keeping *out* by making a bank. {1753–}

1802 ELLICOTT *Journal* 127 The banking out of the river had been carried on with great spirit. **1825** J. LORAIN *Pract. Husb.* 370 Banking and ditching are very injurious as well as very expensive. **1845** C. M. KIRKLAND *Western Clearings* 103 'Banking up' . . . consists in piling earth round the foundations so as to prevent the frosty winds from intruding below the floor. **1865** *Nation* I. 683 Then he . . . pulls up the earth on the listing. That's *banking*, and he has so much a task for banking.

2. A bulwark of earth; an embankment. {Also E.}

1853 KANE *Grinnell Exped.* 321, I observed one spot where the banking remained. **1872** *Vermont Bd. Agric. Rep.* I. 309 The exclusion of cold air should be possible without the annual banking that is put around most farm houses in the fall.

3. Attrib. with *shovel*.

1790 *Penna. Packet* 14 April 3/2 William Perkins, blacksmith, makes and sells . . . banking or ditching shovels, spades, [etc.].

Banking, *vbl. n.*[2] [BANK *v.*[2]]

1. The employment of a banker; the business of receiving, paying out, lending, and investing money. {1735–}

1818 *Niles' Reg.* XIV. 3/2 The despotism of banking will not allow the freedom of opinion, nor of the press. **1846** MACKENZIE *Life Van Buren* 174 Thad. Phelps on Free Banking. **1850** *Western Journal* IV. 212 The system of Free Banking originated in New York, and seems to be rapidly growing into favor in other States. **1865** *Atlantic Mo.* XV. 196/2 Morris might understand banking, but in taste he was absurdly deficient.

2. Business or transactions with or through a bank.

1898 WESTCOTT *D. Harum* 342 The new manufactories . . . did their banking with Mr. Harum.

3. Attrib.: **a.** In sense: Of or pertaining to a bank or banks.

1791 WASHINGTON *Diaries* IV. 196 Little was said of the Banking Act. **1808** *Steele Papers* II. 552, I . . . have not been able to learn whether you have embarked in the Banking-Business . . . or not. **1812** *Ann. 12th Congress* 1 Sess. 1423 He stated the amount of banking capital already in issue in the District at $4,500,000. **1814** *Niles' Reg.* VI. 47/2 The banking bill has at length passed the legislature of Pennsylvania. **1819** DANA *Geog. Sketches* 67 The company have been vested with banking powers. **1829** SANDS *Writings* II. 199 As he entered the banking room [etc.]. **1836** FLAGG in Mackenzie *Van Buren* 175 No private Banking System should be connected with this measure. **1839** *S. Lit. Messenger* V. 7/2 Philadelphia had the Bank of the United States; so that in banking capital New York was her inferior. **1840** *Niles' Reg.* 16 May 165/1 The general banking law of New York being based upon a system hitherto untried in this country. **1851** CIST *Cincinnati* 159 A spacious banking hall and offices. **1863** 'E. KIRKE' *Southern Friends* vii. 98 It was previous to banking hours. **1898** WESTCOTT *D. Harum* xiii. 113 The banking office consisted of two rooms.

b. In sense: Constituting a bank.

1806 WEBSTER, *Bank*, . . . a banking company, or their edifice. **1816** *Niles' Reg.* X. 18/1 The real amount of the banking concerns within the district of Columbia. **1818** *Ib.* XIV. 4/1 The multitude of banking institutions . . . made it desirable to have a currency which every man might know. **1836** FLAGG in Mackenzie *Van Buren* 176 If the fetters are knocked off by the repeal of the Restraining Law, private banking associations may be formed. **1841** D. MacLeod *Biog. F. Wood* (1856) 80 Brown, Brothers, & Co., another banking establishment, largely connected with capitalists across the Atlantic. **1851** CIST *Cincinnati* 89 The most important private Banking institutions of Cincinnati. **1860** HOLMES *E. Venner* xxxii, The great banking-firm, you know, Bilyuns Brothers and Forester. **1863** S. C. MASSETT *Drifting About* 157 The heaviest accounts in the city were kept at this pet banking-establishment. **1880** LAMPHERE *U.S. Govt.* 86/1 A National banking association may be formed by any number of persons not less than five.

‖**Banking game.** [Cf. BANK *n.*[2] 2.] A gambling game. — **1859** Wm. Wright *Big Bonanza* (1877) 71 No banking games, under any consideration, shall be allowed in this district.

+**Banking-ground.** [BANK *v.*[1] 3.] *Lumbering.* A place where logs are assembled for transportation. Also attrib. — **1880** *Lumberman's Gaz.* Jan. 728 The banking ground is about 125 feet above the bed of the river. **1893** *Scribner's Mag.* June 710/2 The logs are . . . placed by the banking-ground men in tiers. **1902** WHITE *Blazed Trail* xx. 148 Plenty [of lumber] . . . could be cut and travoyed directly to the banking ground. **1904** *Dialect Notes* II. 398 Logs . . . were piled in huge tiers on the banking grounds, as they were called on the Susquehanna.

Banking-house. [BANKING *vbl. n.*[2] 2.]

1. A house or building in which the operations of a bank are conducted. {1809–}

1812 *Niles' Reg.* II. 216/1 Stephen Girard . . . purchased the banking house of the late bank of the United States. **1817** BROWN *Western Gaz.* 147 The public buildings consist of three banking houses. **1847** L. COLLINS *Kentucky* 355 Louisville [contains] . . . one Jewish synagogue, five banking houses. **1863** S. C. MASSETT *Drifting About* 29, I had gone to collect an account at the Banking-house of Prime, Ward, and King, then the great guns in the banking line. **1881** J. W. BUEL *Border Outlaws* 118 Five determined men . . . hitched their horses in an alley near the banking-house of . . . Mitchell & Co.

2. A banking firm, company, or corporation. {1816–}

1818 *Niles' Reg.* XIV. 3/1 The secrets of the banking-house are imperfectly known. **1851** CIST *Cincinnati* 89 This Banking House has a large list of customers among the merchants. **1869** ALDRICH *Bad Boy* xx. (1877) 234 My father's banking-house went to pieces in the crash. **1893** M. HOWE *Honor* 52 The solid plain offices of the banking house of John Greyerstone.

+**Bankit.** *La.* [See BANQUETTE.] 'Sidewalk' (B. '77).

+**Bankite.** *Obs.* [BANK *n.*[2]] =BANK-MAN. Also attrib. — **1832** *Deb. Congress* 14 March 2156 The distinguished bankite leader in the House. **1838** 'UNCLE SAM' in *Bentley's Misc.* IV. 584 There were only two bankites besides myself in the regiment.

+**Bank land.** [BANK *n.*[1]] A stretch of land along a bank. — **1797** *Wilmington Gaz.* 8 June, Seven miles of bank land south of Cabbage-Inlet.

Bank lock. [BANK *n.*[2]] An intricate lock for bank offices, vaults, etc. — **1849** *Rep. Comm. Patents* I. 48 Improvements in bank locks. **1851** CIST *Cincinnati* 215 MacGregor & Lee . . . manufacture bank locks.

Bank-man. [BANK *n.*[2]]

+**1.** A supporter of a bank or banks, spec. of the second United States Bank (1816–36) in its contest with President Jackson. Cf. ANTI-BANK.

1837 F. B. CUTTING in W. L. Mackenzie *Life of Van Buren* (1846) 177 Take care how you write too freely to the Speaker. Time will show whether he goes with the bank-men or not. **1837** CALHOUN *Works* III. 79, I am neither a bank man, nor an anti-bank man. **1840** LYONS in Tyler *Lett. & Times* (1884) I. 609 The most distinguished supporters of Mr. Van Buren are avowed Bank men. **1856** *Harper's Mag.* XII. 413/2, I am a free-trader or a free-soiler, a tariff man or a bank man, upon my private convictions. **1864** T. L. NICHOLS *Amer. Life* II. 173 All the elements of opposition—the bank-men, the paper-money men, . . . united . . . to defeat Mr. Van Buren.

+**2.** *slang.* A burglar who robs banks.

1901 FLYNT *World of Graft* 78 Do you think Boston is as much of a bankman's hang-out as it used to be?

Bank martin. [BANK *n.*[1]] The bank swallow or the cliff swallow. {1774–} — **1806** CLARK in *Lewis & C. Exped.* (1904) V. 279 [We] saw several herds of buffalow, . . . also . . . bank martins.

Bank meadow. [BANK *n.*[1]] ?A meadow lying along a bank. — **1789** MORSE *Amer. Geog.* 295 The island . . . has four entrances over bridges and causeways, and a quantity of bank meadow adjoining.

Bank messenger. [BANK *n.*[2]] A messenger employed by a bank. — **1850** *Knickerb.* XXXV. 557 We knew a Wall-street bank-messenger . . . , whose feet looked like two parcels of shag-bark walnuts.

Bank note. [BANK *n.*[2]]

1. A promissory note or bill issued by a bank, commonly used as currency in place of coin. {1695–}

1714 *Mass. Bay Currency Tracts* 143 The Author . . . seems concerned about the Credit of the Bank Notes, and that for two Reasons. **1791** *Ann. 1st Congress* II. 2034 If there . . . are no bank notes which have a currency in both [places], the consequence is, that coin must be remitted. **1792** [see BANK POST-BILL]. **1812** *Ann. 12th Congress* 1 Sess. 1497 These Treasury notes . . . will be receivable for all debts due the United States. Bank notes are not so. **1817** *Niles' Reg.* XIII. 97/1 The people are inundated with paper, called bank notes, at almost every depreciated rate from ½ to 75 per cent. **1836** *Diplom. Corr. Texas* (1908) I. 68 Scrip of this kind, struck off like bank notes handsomely engraved, would . . . be a much sounder currency than some of the bank notes. **1876** *Scribner's Mo.* Feb. 600/1 The lady wrote . . . her own number, the price, the amount of the bank-note I handed her. **1884** ROE *Nature's Story* 287 Before he departed she slipped a bank-note into his hand with which to buy a dress for the baby. **1904** GLASGOW *Deliverance* 532 Will . . . unlocked the drawer of the old secretary and handed him a roll of banknotes.

attrib. **1819** *Plough Boy* I. 111 The experience they have had in bank note and other engraving. **1857** *Quinland* II. 127 The bill is an advertisement of our shoemaker . . . on bank note paper.

+**b.** *California bank note:* (see quotation).

1840 DANA *Two Years* xiii. 98 [Mexicans] at Monterey . . . have no circulating medium but silver and hides—which the sailors call 'California bank notes.'

+**2.** *Bank-note detector*, 'a periodical publication containing a description of worthless bank-notes, and intended to facilitate their detection' (W. '64). *Bank-note table*, a table giving the current value of the notes of various banks.

1834 *Deb. Congress* 23 Jan. 2523 Examine the bank note table which is almost daily furnished us in the public prints. **1854** *Penna. Agric. Rep.* 421 Variegated soaps and bank note detectors. **1894** *Congress. Rec.* 5 June 5790/2 One of the old bank-note detectors which have been so often referred to.

+**Bank oil.** [BANK *n.*[1]] 'Menhaden oil' (*Cent.*). — **1760** J. ROWE *Letters* 369, I desire it [=oil] may be of the pale sort or bank oyl.

Bank-paper, Bank paper. [BANK *n.*[2]]

1. Bank notes collectively; bills of exchange acceptable by a bank. {1790–}

1790 HAMILTON in *Ann. 1st Congress* II. 2033 Purchases and undertakings . . . can be carried on by any given sum of bank paper or credit, as effectually as by an equal sum of gold and silver. **1812** *Niles' Reg.* II. 19/2 Mr. Basset . . . deprecated the overwhelming torrent of bank paper, which flooded the country. **1816** BROWN *Journal* I. 356 This morning [he] . . . receives in bank paper of him $25.00 & his note . . . for seventy five dollars. **1838** *Indiana H. Rep. J.* 21 To see the State . . . flooded with depreciated or irredeemable Bank paper, the offspring of our own institutions. **1852** REYNOLDS *Hist. Illinois* 84 There was very little metallic currency in the country, and Bank paper was almost unknown. **1881** J. W. BUEL *Border Outlaws* 113 The evidence of bank-paper showed that the robbers had tarried a few moments to divide the spoils.

+**2.** Paper on which bank notes or bills are printed.

1851 CIST *Cincinnati* 216 A slip of bank paper suffices . . . to prevent that key from opening the lock to which it belongs.

+**Bank parlor.** [BANK *n.*[2]] The room in which a bank manager transacts business with his clients. — **1881** W. O. STODDARD *E. Hardery* 370 Ponsard and Uncle Madison were sitting by the table in the bank parlor. **1884** *Lisbon* (Dakota) *Clipper* 30 Oct. 2/3 The caution which has prevailed since last May in bank parlors. **1898** WESTCOTT *D. Harum* 118 The bank parlor was lighted by a window and a glazed door.

+**Bank party.** The political party which favored the continuance of the Second Bank of the United States (1816–36). — **1834** P. HONE *Diary* I. 97 He is a good candidate, and his success will be a triumph for the bank party.

+**Bank post-bill.** [BANK *n.*[2]] A bill issued by a bank for convenience in remitting money by post. — **1792** *Ann. 2nd Congress* 1 Sess. 62 If any person . . . destroy any letter, packet, bag, or mail of letters . . . containing any bank note, or bank post bill. **1794** *Ann. 3rd Congress* 1439.

+**Bank-rag.** Paper money issued by a bank. — **1845** *N.Y. Comm. Adv.* 13 Dec. (B.), The Senator was shinning around, to get gold for the rascally bank-rags which he was obliged to take.

Bank-runner. [BANK *n.*[2]] A bank messenger. — **1851** A. O. HALL *Manhattaner* 68 The jolly bank-runners carry their funds fearlessly under their arms, for the pickpockets are not to be found.

* **Bankrupt,** *n.* Any one, as a merchant or trader, unable to pay his debts in full, and thus liable to or under legal procedure for insolvency. {1707–}

1714 *Boston News-Letter* 1 March 2/2 An Act concerning Bankrupts, and for the Relief of the Creditors. **1732** J. HEMPSTEAD *Diary* 249, I was in town foren[oon] to administer the oath of a bankrupt to 2 prisoners. **1785** *Penna. Statutes* 16 Sept. 79 It shall be lawful for the commissioners . . . to break open the houses, . . . trunks or chests of the bankrupt. **1800** *Ann. 6th Congress* 1454 [If] there is reason to apprehend that the said bankrupt intends to abscond. **1829** *Encycl. Amer.* I. 551/1 From the day of his failure, the bankrupt is divested of all his interest and title in his property. **1849** A. LAWRENCE *Diary & Corr.* 47 He was in great anguish, considering himself a bankrupt for at least five thousand dollars. **1855** [PRAY] *Mem. J. G. Bennet* 68 Bankrupts were gazetted in abundance. **1893** M. HOWE *Honor* 58 Men who are courted as 'prominent financiers' on Monday and shunned as 'bankrupts' on Sunday.

* **Bankrupt,** *a.* Also †**bankerout.**

* **1.** Unable to meet the claims of creditors; insolvent.

1633 *Plymouth Laws* 33 In case a man die bankerout as afore considering the rawnes of the countrey. **1714** *Boston News-Letter* 1 Mar. 2/2 An Act . . . for the Relief of the Creditors, against such Persons as shall become Bankrupt. **1790** HAMILTON in *Ann. 1st Congress* II. 2035 The most serious of the charges [against banks] . . . are . . . that they give to bankrupt and fraudulent traders, a fictitious credit [etc.]. **1870** MEDBERY *Men of Wall St.* 71 If it sinks six per cent, they are bankrupt. **1901** CHURCHILL *Crisis* 91 If Colonel Carvel was doin' business in New England, . . . he'd been bankrupt long ago.

2. Of or pertaining to a bankrupt or to bankruptcy. {1809–}

1785 *Penna. Statutes* 16 Sept. 81 If the net proceeds of such bankrupt estate shall not amount to ten shillings in the pound. **1790** *Penna. Packet* 4 Jan. 4/2 The commissioners will attend on that day at the Bankrupt Office in the city of Philadelphia. **1790** MACLAY *Deb. Senate* 184 A memorial of one Tracy was read, praying a bankrupt law to be passed under the authority of the United States. **1798** *Ann. 5th Congress* III. 2546 A further postponement of the Bankrupt bill. **1818** *N. Amer. Rev.* VII. 38 Let Congress then pass a bankrupt law, . . . one which shall apply to merchants and traders. **1827** [G. MELLEN] *Chronicle of '26* 12 Next came the Bankrupt Bill . . . To keep poor debtors from the curse of pay. **1840** CALHOUN in *Congress. Globe* App., 2 June 692/3 What right has Congress to extend a bankrupt act over the incorporated institutions of the States? **1846** *S. Lit. Messenger* XII. 602/1 'Perhaps,' said Eliza Willis, looking askance at the old man, . . . 'perhaps he has taken the benefit of the bankrupt law!' **1877** PHELPS *Avis* 132 A gown she had bought at a bankrupt sale.

Bankruptcy. The state of being bankrupt; legal insolvency. {1700–}

1708 *N.C. Col. Rec.* I. 683 Her Majesty being pleased to recommend to the Generall Assembly an Act of Bankruptcy. **1785** *Penna. Statutes* 16 Sept., An act for the regulation of bankruptcy. **1787** *Constitution* i. § 8 The Congress shall have power . . . to establish . . . uniform laws on the subject of bankruptcies throughout the United States. **1790** *Ann. 1st Congress* I. 1143 A bill providing for a general system of Bankruptcy in the United States. **1818** *N. Amer. Rev.* VII. 38 Because a farmer, from a momentary inability to discharge a debt, should happen to commit an 'act of bankruptcy.' **1839** *Knickerb.* XIII. 1 The merchant [is] delayed in the collection of his valid claims, until whelmed in bankruptcy and ruin. **1856** D. MACLEOD *F. Wood* 35 A very large stock of goods, then in his store, depreciated . . . suddenly in value, and the result was bankruptcy. **1870** MEDBERY *Men of Wall St.* 71 This bankruptcy may not appear because the banks may not call in their loans. **1898** *U.S. Statutes* XXX. 559 The Attorney-General shall annually lay before Congress statistical tables showing . . . the number of cases during the year of voluntary and involuntary bankruptcy.

+**Bank share.** [BANK *n.*[2]] A share of stock in a bank.

1799 *Steele Papers* I. 173, I had made provision . . . by a sale of bank shares to be paid yesterday. **1803** *Ann. 7th Congress* 2 Sess. 666 The authority to make sale of the bank shares. **1845** M. M. NOAH *Gleanings* 22 [The father] had better buy that child a bank share, or invest it in some sure or profitable fund. **1875** *Rep. 43rd Congr., 2 Sess., H. of R.* No. 101. 7, The securities of the State have fallen in two years from 70 or 80 to 25; . . . while the fall in bank shares [and] railway shares, . . . have, in a degree, corresponded.

+**Bank snatcher, sneak.** [BANK *n.*[2]] A bank-robber. — **1890** R. WHEATLEY in *Harper's Mag.* Feb. 472/2 One of the most daring bank snatchers in the city effected two robberies in the course of a single day. — **1888** *Daily Inter-Ocean* 16 Feb. (F.), Buffalo officers to-day picked out . . . Jones, the notorious bank sneak and burglar known professionally in every city of the United States.

Bank stock. [BANK *n.*[2]] **a.** The capital of, or aggregate of shares in, a bank. **b.** A block or number of shares in a bank. {1705–}

1720 *Mass. Bay Currency Tracts* 385 By so doing in twenty-one years our bank-stock will be converted into bullion. **1790** HAMILTON in *Ann. 1st Congress* II. 2036 As the profits of bank stock exceed the legal rate of interest. **1800** WEEMS *Letters* II. 146 Did I not take out of bank all my little bank stock, for you? **1812** *Niles' Reg.* II. 78/2 The average price of bank-stock in the city of New-York is nineteen per cent above par. **1820** FLINT *Lett. from Amer.* 204 Among the objects of taxation quoted, that on bank stock is by the act limited to 'stock actually paid in.' **1842** *Knickerb.* XX. 339 There were large dividends declared on your bank-stock last week. **1862** *Rep. Comm. Patents: Agric.* 117 The five hundred millions invested in bank stocks. **1891** O'BEIRNE *Leaders Ind. Territory* 76/2 His property . . . being valued at thirty-five thousand, not including bank stock and investments.

Bank swallow. [BANK *n.*[1]] The sand martin, *Hirundo* or *Cotile riparia.* {1655–}

1812 WILSON *Ornithology* V. 46 The Bank Swallow . . . begins to build in April. . . . I met with this bird in considerable numbers on . . . the Kentucky river. **1839** PEABODY *Mass. Birds* 346 The Bank Swallow . . . is found wherever there is a sandy bank on the side of a pit or river. There it bores a hole with its bill. **1878** B. F. TAYLOR *Between Gates* 149 The rocks . . . are as full of holes as a bank-swallows' village.

+**Bank tax.** [BANK *n.*[2]] A tax levied on banks. — **1832** *Deb. Congress* 8 March 2073 The banks [of N.Y.] . . . consenting to come in [the safety fund association] on the condition of being relieved from the payment of the bank tax. **1842** DAVIS in *Mass. Acts & Resolves* 608 While the liabilities of the treasury were thus increased . . . its income, except from the bank tax, was diminished. **1844** *Indiana Senate J.* 154 Two resolutions, . . . one directing an enquiry in relation to the Bank tax fund.

Bank vault. [BANK *n.*[2]] The vault of a banking house. — **1842** *Knickerb.* XX. 340 No sooner has it [=money] . . . returned to the bank-vaults than it is again sent forth on another errand of iniquity. **1848** *S. Lit. Messenger* XIV. 643/2 The country was flooded with its paper, and the Bank vaults were innocent of specie. **1870** MEDBERY *Men of Wall St.* 2 A package of Boston and Maine R. R. stock stowed away in a bank-vault.

+**Bank Whig.** [BANK *n.*[2]] A Whig who supported the Bank of the United States. — **1835** *Louisville Public Adv.* 26 June, The cognomen of Bank Whigs is to be doffed.

* **Banner,** *n.*

* **1.** A flag or standard.

1687 *Conn. Public Rec.* III. 431 All captains . . . shall . . . provide for their companies and troops, . . . colours, trumpets, trumpeters and banners. **1814** KEY (*title*), The Star-spangled Banner. **1857** H. RILEY *Puddleford Papers* (1875) 253 A monument . . . covered with drums and fifes, and swords, and waving banners. **1864** EDWARDS *Shelby* 474 Missouri's stalwart sons will again rush to uphold the Confederate banner. **1881** THAYER *Log-Cabin to White House* xxiii. 269 The delegates of each state sat together, their banners bearing the name of their state. **1887** *Lippincott's Mag.* Aug. 298 Silk and satin banners, the trophies won by Yale's athletic organizations . . . , adorn the walls and balconies.

+**2.** A flag offered as a distinction for polling the largest majority for the Harrison ticket in the election of 1840. Hence fig., the foremost place or prize.

1840 *Log Cabin* (N.Y.) 5 Dec. 2/3 The Banner State. It is known that the Ladies of New Orleans early in the late contest offered a splendid Banner to the State which should give the largest relative majority for Harrison and Tyler in its popular vote for Presidential Electors. **1900** *Century Mag.* Feb. 636/1 Local authorities . . . united in the belief that . . . Ashtabula County might be accorded the banner.

+**3.** Attrib. in sense: Worthy of a banner as a distinction (cf. BANNER COUNTY, STATE); hence foremost, leading, preeminent in some respect: **a.** Of places.

1882 E. K. GODFREY *Nantucket* 208 Nantucket during the Rebellion sent into the army two hundred and thirteen men, . . . gaining for herself the proud distinction of 'banner town' of this Commonwealth. **1883** *Harper's Mag.* Jan. 282/1 It was the boast of the district that this constituency was solid for Bigler, and that this was the banner township of California. **1885** *Century Mag.* Nov. 28/1 The visitors . . . were mostly . . . miners on their way to the 'Banner district.' **1890** in *Congress. Globe* 26 June 6522/1 One of the arguments . . . is that Newcastle is the banner town of Crook County. **1892** *Vermont Agric. Rep.* XII. 128 Montgomery may be considered the banner town of the County for the manufacture of butter tubs. **1900** *Century Mag.* Feb. 636/1 [Article on] a Banner Divorce County. **1909** *St. Stephen's Leaflet* (Portland, Ore.) May (Th.), It is clear that the Good Shepherd is the banner parish in its offering on Easter Day.

b. In general use.

1843 *Knickerb.* XXII. 431 He who was for many years the banner-veteran of our worthies. **1850** *New Eng. Farmer* II. 360 A fine bunch of Kloss Blue Stem winter wheat, or Banner wheat, as generally called in Maine. **1886** *Harper's Mag.* July 237/2 She had the banner crop of tobacco in that county last year. **1901** WHITE *Westerners* xxiii. 212 The Great Snake . . . was admittedly the banner claim of the group. **1911** — *Bobby Orde* x. 128 On his banner day he brought down two fox-squirrels.

***Banner,** *v.* || *tr.* To send *away* by the waving of banners or the like. — **1859** A. VAN BUREN *Sojourn in South* 19 We were 'bannered' away by the waving of handkerchiefs of friends on the other steamers and the levee.

+**Banner county.** (See BANNER *n.* 2, 3.) — **1840** *Niles' Reg.* 5 Dec. 210/2 The Banner County.—Designation is claimed by Worcester, Massachusetts, which gave Harrison the largest aggregate majority, viz: 4,773. **1866** *Congress. Globe* 15 Jan. 241/3 [Mr. Price] came within a few votes of losing the banner county of his own State. **1875** *Clayton Courier* in *Congr. Rec.* App., 4 Feb. 19/1 Barbour County [Ala.] can be safely put down as the banner county.

+**Bannerite.** (See quotation.) — **1878** *Scribner's Mo.* XV. 636/2 My friend was a confirmed 'bannerite' as the printers term it—a careless, shiftless, strolling vagabond, here to-day and there to-morrow.

+**Banner state.** (See BANNER *n.* 2 and 3.) — **1840** *Niles' Reg.* 5 Dec. 210/1 The whigs . . . proposed to designate whichever state should give the Harrison ticket the largest majority, as The Banner State. There has been considerable rivalry for the honor. **1850** SEABROOK in *Life & Corr. Quitman* xiv. 37 Mississippi will be the banner state in the noble contest. **1851** J. F. W. JOHNSTON *Notes N. Amer.* II. 326 With more dignity, those of New Hampshire speak of their home as the Granite State; . . . of Kentucky as the Banner State. **1856** OLMSTEAD *Slave States* 535 The Banner State of the South [is Georgia]. **1887** GEORGE *40 Years on Rail* viii. 147 Obtaining the enormous land grant for Illinois, which makes her today the banner state of railroads. **1901** 'MARK TWAIN' *Speeches* (1910) 255, I was born in the 'Banner State,' and by 'Banner State' I mean Missouri.

+**Banner-stone.** [BANNER *n.* 1.] A prehistoric stone object supposed to have been used as a symbol of authority. — **1881** *Smithsonian Rep.* 657 Some banner-stones of striped slate have been found in Camillus, and one on Skaneateles Lake [N.Y.].

***Bannock.** (See quotations.) — (1) **1805** *Pocumtuc Housewife* (1906) 21 Indian Cake or Bannock is sweet and cheap food. **1848** BARTLETT 23 In New England, cakes of Indian meal, fried in lard, are called bannocks. **1907** *Dialect Notes* III. 240 *Bannock*, corn bread. Woodsmen's term. (Eastern Maine.) — (2) **1886** *Outing* Dec. 249/1 Pemmican, bannocks (simple flour, water, and salt), and hard biscuit are the staples, washed down with tea.

+**Banquet lamp.** An elaborate type of table lamp. — **1896** *New Eng. Mag.* Nov. (Advt.), Banquet lamps in Dresden, onyx, brass, silver, and wrought iron. **1903** K. D. WIGGIN *Rebecca* xiii. 139 The premiums . . . were three—a bookcase, a plush reclining chair, and a banquet lamp.

Banquette. Also **banquet.** [In sense 2, directly from Fr.]

1. *Mil.* A platform or raised way behind an earthwork or parapet, on which soldiers stand to fire at an enemy. {1629–}

1766 H. GORDON in *Travels Amer. Col.* 483 There is only a stockade round the place with a large banquet. **1842** *American Pioneer* I. 84 He stepped on to a narrow platform, or 'banquet,' running round the sides of the bulwark. **1847** PARKMAN in *Knickerb.* XXX. 284 The roofs of the apartments within, which are built close against them, serve the purpose of a banquette. **1867** EDWARDS *Shelby* 136 The banquettes of the earthwork . . . were blue with uniforms. **1884** 'CRADDOCK' *Where Battle was Fought* 84 Graffy stole cautiously out from . . . the powder-magazine, and lay at length on the banquette.

+**2.** *La.* A raised sidewalk or footpath.

1844 J. COWELL *Thirty Years* 95 Being knee-deep in mud in wading to the Banquette, then only curbed by the timbers of a broken-up flat-boat. **1875** 'MARK TWAIN' *Old Times* vi. 104 The young colored population of New Orleans were much given to flirting, at twilight, on the banquettes of the back streets. **1880** CABLE *Grandissimes* xiii. 81 When good luck has already been secured by smearing the front walk or the banquette with Venetian red. **1895** G. KING *New Orleans* 2 As we walk along the banquettes, our steps feel their footprints.

+**3.** An elevated platform of stonework.

1895–6 *17th Rep. Bureau Amer. Ethnol.* II. (1898) 541 Broad lateral banquettes are prominent features in the most complicated caves, and there are many recesses and small closets or cists.

Banter, *n.* {1690–}
'Southern and Western' (B. '59).

+**1.** A challenge, as to a fight, race, etc.; a dare.

1835 [LONGSTREET] *Georgia Scenes* 26 'Well!' said Blossom, 'make a pass at me.' 'No,' said Peter; 'you made the banter; now make your pass.' **1872** *Harper's Mag.* June 28/2 But, having a mind to try the mare a little stretch, I took up his banter. **1886** *Evening Post* 19 March, A youngster rushed in, and . . . said he 'had been down in the hollow making banters.' Upon inquiry, I learned he meant *challenges*.

+**2.** A match or contest.

1859 BARTLETT 21 'There will be a banter on the bare ground,' meaning a shooting-match.

Banter, *v.* {1676–}
'Southern and Western' (B. '59).

+**1.** *intr.* To argue or dispute as to terms; to haggle. Now *dial.*

1793 *Catskill Packet* in *Mass. Spy* 4 April 1/2 The husband, . . . after a few minutes bantering, accepted, in exchange for his wife, an old horse, with nine dollars in cash to boot. *c***1894** *Dialect Notes* I. 396 *Banter*, to haggle at a price.

+**2.** *tr.* To invite to a contest or the like; to challenge. {1881– *Ulster dial.*}

Further illustrated by Th. from 1836 to 1860.

1809 F. CUMING *Western Tour* 135 Two hunters sat down with us. . . . At last they bantered each other to go out and kill a deer. **1834** CARRUTHERS *Kentuckian* I. 183, I was thinking of walking out into the country and bantering somebody for a foot-race. **1872** EGGLESTON *End of World* xxvi. 177 The cards were put face down, and the company was bantered to bet the wine. **1891** *Boston Journal* July 2/3 At Augusta, Ga., a negro . . . was bantered to butt down the door of a saloon for a drink. **1901** HARBEN *Westerfelt* v. 69 He had bantered her to say what she thought about you. **1902** — *A. Daniel* 163 Colonel Barclay . . . bantered me for a trade time an' agin.

+**3.** *intr.* To make a challenge.

1836 *Quarter Race Kentucky* (1846) 14 A rough-hewn fellow . . . was bantering to run his mare against any horse that had ploughed as much that season.

+**4.** *tr.* To drive or clear *off* by banter.

1841 *Knickerb.* XVII. 27 They can't banter him off the track, no way they can fix it. **1843** STEPHENS *High Life N.Y.* I. xvi. 237 Miss Josephine Burgess understood the soft sodder principle like a book. She had a way of bantering off the bonnets and gim-cracks.

***Baptist.**

1. A member of a religious denomination whose most distinctive tenet is that baptism is valid only by immersion, following a personal profession of the Christian faith. {1654–} Cf. ANABAPTIST.

1679 *Mass. H.S. Coll.* 4 Ser. V. 30 Now he courts the Baptists; then he kicks off them, and flatters the Foxians. **1721** Quincy *Hist. Harvard* I. 435 It is what I wish the Baptists would do, though I have no great expectation. **1795** WINTERBOTHAM *Hist. View* II. 235 The Baptists are the most numerous of any denomination in the State [=R.I.]. **1831** Peck *Guide* 67 The Baptists have a good meeting-house [in N.O.]. **1847** L. COLLINS *Kentucky* 108 The Baptists were the pioneers of religion in Kentucky. **1883** *Schaff's Relig. Encycl.* I. 211/2 In America the earliest Baptists were found in the Massachusetts Colony, but were driven out.

2. Attrib. with *church, denomination, meeting-house,* etc.

1721 Quincy *Hist. Harvard* I. 435 The Baptist churches in Pennsylvania and the Jerseys. **1775** FITHIAN *Journal* II. 122 This settlement [=Fort Shirley] is broken with religious divisions—there is a Baptist Society, now under the direction of one Mr. Lane. **1802** JEFFERSON in *Harper's Mag.* March (1885) 542/2 A Baptist meeting house. **1823** *Baptist Mag.* IV. 28/2 The Baptist Education Society of the State of New York. **1837** PECK *Gaz. Illinois* 73 The Baptist denomination includes . . . 7,350 communicants. *a***1856** *N.Y. Times* in Olmsted *Slave States* 114 The Baptist Church generally gets the negroes. . . . Immersion strikes their fancy.

b. In appositive use with *minister, preacher,* etc. *Baptist seceder*, a Campbellite.

1787 in *Mag. Amer. Hist.* I. 435 Craig . . . is a Baptist preacher. **1797** *Mass. H. S. Coll.* V. 48 The plaintiff was a Baptist minister. **1815** Mills & Smith *Missionary Tour* 17 Baptist and Methodist preachers are considerably numerous. **1835** *S. Lit. Messenger* I. 259 The Baptist Seceders or followers of Alexander Campbell have 1 place of worship. **1837** PECK *Gaz. Illinois* 215 A charter has been obtained for a college, which is contemplated to be brought into operation by the Baptist Reformers. **1856** SIMMS *Charlemont* 435 Emma Loring married a baptist-preacher from Virginia. **1884** *Century Mag.* May 114/2 Seeing the notice of the Mormon elder's preaching, he resolved to invite the Baptist minister to go with him.

***BAR,** *n.*[1]

I. ***1.** A bar of wood or iron used for throwing as a trial of strength. *Obs.* {–1715}

a1656 BRADFORD *Hist.* 135 He found them in the streete at play, openly; some pitching the barr, & some at stoole-ball.

2. *pl.* A set of wooden rails which may be withdrawn to afford an opening through a fence or wall. {1711–} Cf. DRAW-BAR.

1639 *Conn. H. S. Coll.* VI. 5 All the fences & gates . . . to the bares shall be sufitiently mad up. **1660** *Providence* (R.I.) *Rec.* II. 139 Provided that they keepe a sufficient inlett of barres at each end of the highway for a cart to passe through. **1697** *Manchester Town Rec.* 78 Beniamin Woodberys most southerly bars that let out into the common land. **1703** *Providence* (R.I.) *Rec.* V. 109 [He] shall set up a gate or inlet of barrs in said fence. **1718** *Duxbury Rec.* 237 The said fence to be set up . . . , with privilege of a gate or bars convenient to open or draw. **1743** MACSPARRAN *Diary* 9 She sent Jack to open the gates and bars. **1785** WASHINGTON *Diaries* II. 338 The first drain beyond the bars in my lower pasture. **c1815** D. MCCLURE *Diary* (1899) 192 He walked with us to the road, took down the bars & took an affectionate leave. **1834** *Visit to Texas* xx. 191 We had . . . passed a fence or two, by letting down the bars. **1837** IRVING *Bonneville* III. 258 Giving the alarm, the whole party . . . hastened to the pens. The bars were down; but no enemy was to be seen or heard. **1853** 'P. PAXTON' *Yankee in Texas* 110 Riding up to the bars, I gave the usual 'hallo.' **1861** *Ill. Agric. Soc. Trans.* IV. 208 It is well fenced, . . . good gates or bars, good barns for hay. **1883** 'S. BONNER' *Dialect Tales* 51 As I reached the bars I turned an' looked back. **1887** WILKINS *Humble Romance* 315 The younger of the two old women let down the bars which separated the blooming field . . . from the road, and they passed through. **1904** GLASGOW *Deliverance* 332 He . . . returned slowly to the house. At the bars he met Sol Peterkin.

fig. **1878** R. T. COOKE *Happy Dodd* 389 Them kind of cattle don't like to find the bars up, now I tell ye. **1889** Farmer 41/2 Those foolish virgins, who . . . come up and piteously ask the Legislature to let down the bars.

b. Freq. *a pair of bars.*

A pair of drawbars occurs earlier (1671).

1722 *N.H. Probate Rec.* II. 143 Beginning att a pair of bars att the head of my old ffeild. **1741** *Ib.* III. 57 The plase where there was formerly a pare of bars. **1773** *Essex Inst. Coll.* XXI. 271 The Parish Committee shall . . . beuld a good pare of bars to go into the yard. **1821** COOPER *Spy* i, Riding through a pair of neglected bars, he knocked loudly at the outer door of a building. **1855** 'P. PAXTON' *Capt. Priest* 100 There was, to be sure, a slight ascent, and worse yet, a pair of bars must be surmounted. **1871** STOWE *Sam Lawson* 11 He got off the Boston road without knowin' it, and came out at a pair o' bars nigh upon Sherburn. **1880** *Scribner's Mo.* Feb. 511/1 The bar-way (in Yankee-land 'a pair of bars') seems to belong to the stone wall, rail and stump fences.

3. a. Elliptical for 'bar-iron.'

1771 *Md. Hist. Mag.* XIII. 256 He obtained 3 ton of bar from Hammond. **1772** *Ib.* XIV. 278 You have given away your barr. **1871** W. M. GROSVENOR *Protection* 295 In Cincinnati, rolled bar cost $55 a ton in 1842.

b. The handle of a printing-press.

1833 *Niles' Reg.* XLIV. 404/1 At that day, Harper was known as a '*driver*,' and well we remember the many long and hard *pulls* he gave us at the *bar*.

+c. In a bridle-bit, the mouthpiece which connects the two cheek-pieces.

1868 WOODRUFF *Trotting Horse* 391 A bar of moderate size, rather fine than thick, is what I have always preferred. **1898** P. L. FORD *Tattle-Tales* 35 He had had the reins buckled to the lower bar of the curb, so it must have been pretty bad for the grey.

d. The landside of a plough.

1876 *Ill. Dept. Agric. Trans.* XIII. 327 The French plow was destitute of iron, except a small piece . . . to cut the earth. . . . The bar, as it is called, was constructed of wood.

4. A transverse band of color. *The Bars*, the flag of the Confederacy (cf. STARS AND BARS).

1856 WHITTIER *Panorama*, Where'er our banner flaunts beneath the stars Its mimic splendors and its cloud-like bars. **1861** F. Moore *Rebellion Rec.* I. 120/1 Down your Black-a-moor Stripes and Stars! We'll up, instead, the Confederate Bars! **1863** WHITTIER *Barbara Frietchie* 14 Forty flags with their crimson bars. **a1864** F. Moore *Rebel Rhymes*, etc. 149 The Bars now in triumph shall wave O'er the land of the faithful and true. **1864** GRIGSBY *Smoked Yank* xxi. (1891) 185 On the bars there are thirteen stars.

II. *5. a. The rail in a court room at which prisoners are stationed for trial or sentence; the place assigned to a prisoner in court.

1669 *N.Y. State Col. Hist.* XII. 468 Let the Long Finne prisoner in the fort bee . . . brought to the barr. **1691** SEWALL *Diary* I. 350 Elisa. Emmerson was brought to the Bar to be sentenc'd. **1692** *Witchcraft Cases* 156 If she did but lean her breast against the seat, in the Meeting House, (being the Barr at which she stood,) they were afflicted. **1704** *Boston News-Letter* 26 June 1/2 The Court was cleared, and after advisement, the prisoner was again brought to the Bar. **1705** *Ib.* 23 July 2/1 After which the 7 Pirates of Quelch's crew remaining in goal were set to the Bar. **1799** *Ann. 7th Congress* 2 Sess. 1408 The prisoner at the bar was at the head of the infantry. **1823** COOPER *Pioneers* xxxiii, The Leather-stocking made his appearance, ushered into the criminal's bar under the custody of two constables. **1898** PAGE *Red Rock* 467 The Judge looked at Leech and waited. The latter put his hand on the bar.

b. *At the bar*, in the law-courts.

1767 CUTLER in *Life & Corr.* I. 18, [I] was employed in two cases at the Bar, at the Court of Common Pleas sitting here [=Edgarton]. **1786** FRENEAU *Poems* 83 Some at the bar a living gain, Perplexing what they should explain. **c1790** WITHERSPOON *Lect. M. Philos. & Eloquence* (1810) 172 The mere vulgarisms of discourse in the pulpit or at the bar. **1826** FLINT *Recoll.* 184 They have [in St. Charles], also, some acute lawyers at the bar. **1869** TOURGEE *Toinette* i. (1881) 17 You've got to promise to keep up the Hunter name at the bar of the circuit.

+c. The barrier marking off the area in front of the presiding officer in the houses of Congress.

1789 *Ann. 1st Congress* I. 24 When a bill shall be sent up by the House of Representatives to the Senate, it shall be carried by two members, who, at the bar of the Senate, shall make their obeisance to the President. *Ib.* 294 When a message shall come from the House of Representatives to the Senate, . . . the messenger or messengers, being a member or members of the House, shall be received within the bar. **1890** *Congress. Rec.* 1 Dec. 2/1 One of the secretaries of the President of the United States, appeared below the bar and said: Mr. President, I am directed . . . to deliver to the Senate a message.

***6.** The body of persons qualified or authorized to appear in court to plead cases; members of the legal profession sworn in some court of record.

1758 ADAMS *Works* (1850) II. 46, I will recommend you to the court; . . . I will speak to the bar; for the bar must be consulted. **1763** *Ib.* 142 If the bar was not agreed, the court could do nothing. **1789** MACLAY *Deb. Senate* 94 The gentlemen of the bar, in the House, seemed to have made a common cause of it, to push the power of Chancery as far as possible. **1797** *Penna. Mag.* VI. 112 If he means to be a great lawyer he should glory in opposing the whole Bar, and of all men his old Master. **1812** MARSHALL *Kentucky* 382 The leaders [of the party] . . . being members of the bench, or barr, of the Supreme Court. **1828** NEAL *R. Dyer* 102, I would have the bar, as you call it, above the trick and subterfuge of the law. **1835** HOFFMAN *Winter in West* I. 51, I passed an evening most agreeably at Wheeling with two or three prominent members of the Bar. **1851** *Polly Peablossom* 132 If he couldn't succeed while operating upon his own hook, the members of the bar would generally turn in and help him. **1898** PAGE *Red Rock* 455 It had been the practice in the County, when the Judge entered, for the Bar to rise and remain standing until he had mounted the bench. **1900** C. C. MUNN *Uncle Terry* 55, I tutored some, read law, and was admitted to the bar.

attrib. **1771** ADAMS *Works* (1850) II. 258 This evening at the bar meeting, I asked . . . the . . . consent of the bar to take Mr. Elisha Thayer . . . as a clerk. **1794** *Ann. 3rd Congress* 765 He hoped that the explanations of some gentlemen would be like what the lawyers call 'a bar dinner' at the end of the term. **1871** TOWNSEND *Mormon Trials* 9 At the bar table on one side sat Baskins and Maxwell.

***7.** The liquor-counter in a tavern, drinking-saloon, or the like. **+b.** The room containing this; a bar-room. {1835–}

1788 J. MAY *Journals & Lett.* 26 At length I roused the host, who, in coarse Dutch brogue, told me they were locked up in the bar. **1799** *Ann. 7th Congress* 2 Sess. 1412, [I] desired Mr. Levering (the tavern-keeper) to close the bar, thinking there was madness enough without stimulating it. **1817** S. BROWN *Western Gaz.* 72 There was a tavern, with cellars, bar, public and private rooms. **1829** B. HALL *Travels in N.A.* I. 125 The said album was placed in a sort of shed, . . . in what is denominated a bar, *anglicè*, a tap, or grog-shop. **1839** MATHEWS *Memoirs* IV. 331 The 'bar' of a hotel or steam-boat, or 'grocery,' is nothing more or less than a counter covered with spirituous liquors. **1856** OLMSTED *Slave States* 333 'What'll you drink, Baker?' said the lad, rising and going to the bar. **1865** *Atlantic Mo.* XV. 597/1 Phil . . . walks to the bar and calls for two tumblers of lemonade. **1880** CABLE *Grandissimes* xl. 312 Four men, leaning or standing at a small bar, were talking excitedly. **1898** WESTCOTT *D. Harum* 46 The contemplations of the lovers of art that frequent the bar of that hotel. **1925** TILGHMAN *Dugout* 38 Sulkily he eyed a resplendent Mexican . . . who leaned across the bar.

attrib. **1860** *Texas Almanac* 234 Choice whisky, tobacco, and bar stores generally.

III. *8. A bank of sand, gravel, or silt, esp. in a river or harbor, obstructing navigation or the flow of water.

In frequent use from *c*1800.

a1656 BRADFORD *Hist.* 262 They . . . toucht upon a barr of sand. **1707** *Boston News-Letter* 3 Nov. 2/1 The sea being very high and rough upon the bar, . . . the sloop was fill'd with water. **1751** GIST *Journals* 59 There is a bar of land at some distance from the shore. **1777** *Essex Inst. Coll.* XLV. 253 Dirty weather and much rain, with a bad bar, could not get out. **1781–2** JEFFERSON *Notes Va.* (1788) 3 A 40 gun ship goes to James town, and, lightening herself, may pass to Harrison's bar. **1789** MORSE *Amer. Geog.* 39 This lake is . . . navigable for large vessels, except a bar of sand towards the middle. **1802** *Mass. H.S. Coll.* 2 Ser. III. 1 On these bars the tide is from four to six feet deep at high water. **1815** DRAKE *Cincinnati* i. 35 The frequent formation of new bars, by the drifting of sand and gravel. **1821** NUTTALL *Travels* 60 These beds of sand, for the most part of the year under water, are what the boatmen term bars. **1857** CHANDLESS *Visit Salt Lake* I. i. 1 Boats, even if they do get aground now and then from the shifting of the bars, . . . can find their way up at last.

1875 'MARK TWAIN' *Old Times* iii. (1876) 59 Those tumbling 'boils' show a dissolving bar and a changing channel there. **1886** *Harper's Mag.* Sept. 625/1 The depth of water is deficient on bars in the Delaware between the island and the sea.

b. A similar obstruction due to a fall, a rocky ledge, or the like.

1671 *Springfield Rec.* II. 237 A piece of land ag[ains]t the great barr of the highest falls in the great river. **1823** JAMES *Exped.* I. 35 The navigation of the Ohio has a serious impediment . . . by a limestone bar extending across the river.

+**9.** A bank of sand or gravel in or beside a stream from which gold may be obtained by washing.

1850 J. L. TYSON *Diary in Calif.* 61 We came upon the 'Dry Diggings,' so called in contradistinction to the gold-washings on the bars of the rivers. **1859** G. A. JACKSON *Diary* 521 Marsh Cook is sluicing a little with two boxes on bar of Vasquez Fork. No good. **1871** RAYMOND *3rd Rep. Mines* 202 Rocky Bar . . . has suffered somewhat from the stampede to the bars of the Snake River. **1889** K. MUNROE *Golden Days* x. 109 In working the bars of a river, the upper layers of material must first be removed. **1907** WHITE *Arizona Nights* x. 164, I ran in a little bar and panned out some dust, so I camped a while.

+**Bar,** *n.*[2] Also **b'ar, baar, barr.** [Dialectal pron. of *bear.* This change of *êr* to *ār* is found in western E. dialects in such words as *bear* (v.), *tear* (v.), *swear* and *mare.*]

1. A bear.

'The common pronunciation in certain parts of the Southern and Western States' (B. '48).

1790 [see sense 3]. **1823** *Nat'l Intelligencer* 1 May 1/4 *Barr*, s., a . . . bear. **1837** BIRD *Nick of Woods* I. 89 Major Smalleye war as mad as a beaten b'ar. **1847** [ROBB] *Squatter Life* 75 He's safe as a skin'd bar. **1856** M. J. HOLMES *L. Rivers* ix. 108 'Crosser than a bar,' as the little darkies said, she flew back and forth. **1865** [C. H. SMITH] *Let.* in *Bill Arp* 133, I ain't no giant-killer. I ain't no Norwegian bar. **1917** H. T. COMSTOCK *The Man thou gavest* 9 She's responsible for more trouble than a b'ar with a sore head.

fig. **1846** CORCORAN *Pickings* 47 To skin the *bar* at once, can you give me . . . employment?

b. Without article, freq. in plural sense.

1843 'CARLTON' *New Purchase* I. xix. 154 They say you've no barr, no turkey . . . in Filledelfy? **1850** GARRARD *Wah-To-Yah* xx. 245 Ef you're for b'ar, grab your lightnin'-stock (my rifle) and make 'Pimo' tracks for yon butte. **1886** BRET HARTE *Snow-bound* 147 When b'ar or painters hang around nights and stampede the stock.

2. A bearish person.

1848 BARTLETT 392, I never knew a man from that State [=Arkansas] but he was a *bar*, and in fact the people are all *barish* to a degree.

3. Attrib. with *cub, fight, ham, hide, hunt* (also as vb.), *hunter, meat, skin,* etc. Also *bar's grease, oil.* (Cf. BEAR *n.*[1] and combs. there.)

(1) **1790** D. BOONE in *Amer. Speech* I. 314, I . . . depend on taking fur and baar skines for them this spring. **1844** FEATHERSTONHAUGH *Slave States* 81 He is 'to turn in' 15 gallons of *bar* (bear) oil. *c***1845** *Big Bear Arkansas* 21 Beside hog and hominy, you can have bar-ham, and bar-sausages, and a mattrass of bar-skins to sleep on. *Ib.* 24, I was . . . allowed to be decidedly the best bar hunter in my district. *a***1846** *Quarter Race Kentucky* 82 You may talk of your bar hunts . . . and your deer hunts. *Ib.* 88 Jim Smith . . . jist fell to huggin of hir bar fashion. *Ib.* 136, I remember when I couldn't bar hunt. **1847** [ROBB] *Squatter Life* 70 The 'bar' hunters of the southern section [of Missouri]. *Ib.* 106 Sich . . . drinkin' and eatin' *bar* steaks, and corn dodger. *Ib.* 134, I thort I'd send a present of my pet 'bar cub' over to Sally. **1850** [H. C. LEWIS] *La. Swamp Doctor* 170 Like bar-meat in summer without salt! *Ib.* 172 Thicker than har on a bar-hide. **1852** E. M. BENNET *Mike Fink* i. 10/1 Hang me up for bar-meat, ef I don't push off without 'em. **1860** *Harper's Mag.* March 442/1 Let's try our luck in the woods. Bar sign is plenty and fresh as paint. **1895** REMINGTON *Pony Tracks* 250 In the mornin' we'll strike his trail, and if we can git to him you'll shore see a bar-fight.

(2) *c***1845** *Big Bear Arkansas* 21 A skinfull of bar's grease. **1852** WATSON *Nights in Block-house* 32 H'yar, old Kentuck, gin us some o' that bar's-grease. *Ib.*, I had trapped and hunted for some weeks, gettin' plenty of beaver-tails and bar's-oil.

Bar, *n.*[3] [Variant of BEAR *n.*[3], perhaps by association with BAR *n.*[1]; but cf. BAR *n.*[2]] A mosquito-net.

1809 *Ann. 11th Congress* 2 Sess II. App. 2448, 95 musquito bars, at 4½ and 7 dollars each. **1819** LATROBE *Journal* 238 The bars are made either of coarse, open canvas, French lino . . . , open and figured gauze . . . , and most frequently of check muslin. **1835** [INGRAHAM] *South-West* II. 243 'Why are you at the . . . expense of having high-post bed-steads for your negroes?' . . . 'To suspend their "bars" from, that they may not be troubled with musquitoes.' **1851** A. O. HALL *Manhattaner* 62 There was no netting to the bedsteads! 'Why Jack . . . where is your "bar"; this is unpardonable neglect from the house.' **1866** GREGG *Life in Army* xv. 140 Nothing can exceed the luxury of lying down inside your 'bars' of a midsummer night, and feeling secure from their voracious bills. **1894** 'MARK TWAIN' *Those Twins* 415 Get their bed ready . . . and see that you drive all the mosquitoes out of their bar.

Bar, *n.*[4] *Texas.* [tr. Sp. *vara* rod, pole, bar.] =VARE. — **1836** HOLLEY *Texas* xi. 208 Should his only occupation be raising of stock, he shall only receive a superficies of grazing land, equal to twenty-four million square bars.

+**Bar,** *v.* [? f. BAR *n.*[1]] *tr.* (Usu. with *off.*) To clear (young cotton plants, etc.) from earth with a plough; to 'side.'

1835 [INGRAHAM] *South-West* II. 283 The process of scraping commences by running a light furrow close on each side of the row of young cotton, with the share of the plough next it, so as to throw the dirt from the cotton and trim off the scattering plants. . . . If there are many hoe-hands, there are several ploughs 'barring off,' as it is called. **1851** *Florida Plant. Rec.* 367 Commenced baring cotton this Evening. **1887** *Century Mag.* Nov. 111/1 In the stubble fields the first spring, work consists in 'barring off,' or moving the dirt away from the roots of the cane with plows and hoes.

+**Bar album.** *Obs.* [BAR *n.*[1] 7.] A register of guests at a hotel or the like. — **1835** C. COLTON *Four Years in Gt. Britain* (ed. 2) 94 In the United States, the moment a traveller arrives at an inn, before he can be assigned to his rooms, . . . the bar album is uniformly produced, and a pen put into his hand to record his name and residence!

+**Bar Association.** [BAR *n.*[1] 6.] An association of lawyers, judges, etc. — **1838** *S. Lit. Messenger* IV. 581/2 There exist, at divers places in the southern country, certain combinations among the gentlemen of the bar, commonly styled Bar Associations. **1878** BRISTOW, etc. in *Rep. Amer. Bar Assoc.* I. 4 The feasibility and expediency of establishing an American Bar Association.

+**Baratarian,** *a.* and *n.* (One) belonging to the pirates of Barataria Bay on the coast of Louisiana. — **1815** *Niles' Reg.* VII. 375/2 The privateering class, formerly yclept Baratarians, have produced a corps of skilful artillerists [at N.O.]. **1817** *Ib.* XIII. 289/1 The Barratarians, among whom the Lafittes may be classed foremost. *Ib.*, These steps of the officers of the port have irritated the Barratarian gentlemen.

***Barb.** +The kingfish, an eastern food-fish of the genus *Menticirrus*, bearing barbels on the chin. — **1888** GOODE *Amer. Fishes* 123 The king fish, . . . also known as . . . the 'Barb' about Barnegat.

***Barbacan.** *Obs.* An outer defence of a fortified place; a barbican. {–1633} — **1709** *N.H. Hist. Soc. Coll.* III. 47 Serg. Hugh Marsh [and others] . . . were slain . . . as they were going round an high rocky point above the barbacan. **1760** S. NILES *Indian Wars* I. 208 Mr. Patishal, as he lay in the barbacan with his vessel [at Pemmaquid fort in 1689], was taken and slain.

Barbadian. [See next.] A native or inhabitant of Barbados. — **1671** *S.C. Hist. Soc.* V. 299 Wee find that one of our servants wee brought out of England is worth 2 of the Barbadians.

Barbados, Barbadoes. [Name of the most easterly island of the West Indies, belonging to Great Britain.] Used attrib. to designate various products, etc., of the Barbados. †*Barbados distemper*, yellow fever.

1652 *Suffolk Deeds* I. 45 Forty parcells Barbadoes muscavadoes sugar. **1654** *Conn. Col. Rec.* (1850) I. 255 Berbados liquors, commonly called rum, kill deuill, or the like. **1671** *S. C. Hist. Soc.* V. 335 A rock like Barbadoes sandstone. **1699** in J. F. Watson *Philadelphia* (1830) 599 This is quite the Barbadoes distemper—they void and vomit blood. **1706** *Boston News-Letter* 25 Feb. 4/2 Good Barbadoes rhum by the hogshead or tearse, to be sold by Mr. Joseph Hiller. **1758** *Lett. to Washington* II. 400 For 1 hhd. & 1 barrell of punch consisting of 26 gals. best Barbadoes rum & 12½ lbs. s. ref[ine]d sugar. **1789** MORSE *Amer. Gazetteer* (1798) s.v. *Barbadoes,* The Barbadoes tar is a particular production of this island. **1795** J. SCOTT *U.S. Gazetteer* s.v. *Allegany County,* In this county is Oil creek: It flows from a spring much celebrated for a bitumen resembling Barbadoes tar. **1813** H. MUHLENBERG *Cat. Plants* 93 *Juniperus . . . Barbadensis, . . .* Juniper, . . . Barbadoes. Habitat, Florida. **1858** WARDER *Hedges & Evergreens* 270 The Barbadoes Juniper . . . is a large timber-tree.

***Barbarian,** *n.* +Applied, esp. by early writers, to the American Indian.

1643 WILLIAMS *Key* 39 The wild barbarians with no more Than nature, goe so farre. **1648** SHEPARD *Clear Sunshine* 31 It much affected all to see it [=penitent behavior] in a barbarian. *a***1656** BRADFORD *Hist.* 517 So that, unless they should . . . expose the colonies to contempte & danger from the barbarians, they cannot but exerciese force, when no other means will prevaile. **1675** WILLIAMS in *R.I. Hist. Soc. Publ.* VIII. 155 The barbarians have slain 14 persons. **1841** COOPER *Deerslayer* xix, Though daunted by these reproaches, the handsome barbarian could hardly be said to be penitent.

Barbecado, *v. Obs.* =BARBECUE *v.* — **1648** B. PLANTAGENET *New Albion* 25 The Indians in stead of salt doe barbecado or dry and smoak fish, to each house a reek or great pile.

BARBECUE, *n.* Also †**barbacue, -que, -kue, barbicue.** [Sp. *barbacoa,* of Carib origin; in various parts of Central and South America the name of a wooden grid on which meat is dried or roasted, or which is used as a couch or sleeping place; in the latter sense it is mentioned, in the forms *barbecu* and *borbecu,* by Dampier in 1697. The precise quarter from which the word was introduced into the Southern states is not clear.]

1. One or more hogs, oxen, or other animals, or fish, roasted in the open air, usually whole. {1764}

1709 LAWSON *Carolina* 36 The fire was surrounded with roast-meat, or barbakues. **1768** J. ROWE *Diary* 173, I . . . dind there on a barbicue with [23 others]. **1774** CRESSWELL *Journal* 30, I went with him [in Va.] and have been highly diverted. These barbecues are hogs, roasted whole. **1775** BURNABY *Travels* 37 Now and then [in Va.] a party of pleasure into the woods to partake of a barbacue. **1776** J. HARROWER *Diary* 107 At noon went to Snow Creek and the boys and dined at the spring on barbaque and fish. **1805** C. JANSON *Stranger in A.* (1807) 353 The citizens generally of all parties both in town and country, are respectfully invited to partake of a barbacue on Saturday next. **1833** *Niles' Reg.* XLIV. 190/1 A barbecue, in the old fashioned Virginia style, was prepared under an ample awning. **1850** E. P. BURKE *Reminisc. Georgia* 199 They are treated to a 'barbacue,' a term that means at the South, one or more swine roasted whole. **1871** 'MARK TWAIN' *Sk., Riley—Correspondent*, They ran up the Cannibal flag and had a grand human barbecue in honor of it. **1886** B. P. POORE *Reminisc.* I. 495 John S. Barbour, president of the road, invited a number of gentlemen to inspect it and partake of a barbecue. **1916** C. A. EASTMAN *From Deep Woods* 165 Two or three steers would be killed for a barbecue.

+**2.** A social gathering or entertainment at which the chief or distinctive fare consists of an animal or animals (as in sense 1) roasted or broiled in the open air.

1733 LYNDE *Diary* (1880) 138 Fair and hot; Browne, barbacue; hack overset. **1756** in *Boston Ev. Transcript* 16 Sept. (1908) 17/5 Coll. Scott with a number of regular officers had a barbecue upon an island. **1759** *Essex Inst. Coll.* XLIX. 9 A cloudy lowering day, another barbecue down at the Fort. **1769** WASHINGTON *Diaries* I. 326 Went up to Alexandria to a barbicue and stayed all night. **1773** *Ib.* II. 124 Went to a barbicue of my own giving at Accatinck. **1774** FITHIAN *Journal* I. 242, I was invited this morning by Captain Fibbs to a barbecue: this differs but little from the fish feasts; instead of fish the dinner is roasted pig, with the proper apendages, but the diversion & exercise are the same at both. **1799** WELD *Travels* 107 The people in this part of the country, bordering upon James River, are extremely fond of an entertainment which they call a barbacue. It consists in a large party meeting together, either under some trees, or in a house, to partake of a sturgeon or pig roasted in the open air, on a sort of hurdle, over a slow fire; this, however, is an entertainment chiefly confined to the lower ranks. **1809** IRVING *Knickerb.* IV. ix, They were engaged in a great 'barbecue,' a kind of festivity or carouse much practised in Merryland. **1833** J. HALL *Harpe's Head* 22 You surprise me, Mr. Fennimore; no taste for a barbecue! Well, that shows you were not raised in Virginia. . . . There's nothing in life equal to a barbecue, properly managed,—a good old Virginia barbecue. **1841** *S. Lit. Messenger* VII. 41/2 Among other entertainments in the country, barbecues frequently are given. **1851** HALL *Manhattaner* 170 [There are] dry jokes that are of great importance to the country subscribers who attend barbecues, and are expected to lead the 'toasts.' **1881** H. W. PIERSON *In the Brush* 3, I shall attempt to describe . . . their barbecues, basket-meetings, and weddings. **1884** SWEET & KNOX *Through Texas* xxxiii. 435 It was necessary that the reporter should attend a barbecue, held some ten miles from the city. **1902** WISTER *Virginian* ix. 104 The Swinton brothers were giving a barbecue at the Goose Egg outfit. **1910** C. HARRIS *Eve's Husband* 66 Chicken fighting ceased to be the side show and diversion at barbecues that year.

+**b.** A gathering of this nature serving as a political meeting.

1809 S. BRECK in *Recollections* (1877) App. 269 He had given a barbecue to two hundred people the day before as an election feast. **1834** BRACKENRIDGE *Recoll.* xv. 171, I witnessed, for the first time, what is called a *barbecue*, an assemblage of the people for the purpose of giving expression to political opinion. **1840** *Niles' Nat. Reg.* 1 Aug. 347 Eighteen tons of meats, venison, pies, hard cider, &c. were consumed by the great Harrison barbecue . . . at Zanesville. **1864** *Congress. Globe* 13 Jan. 182/3 This exhibition . . . would not elevate even the Senator [Mr. Davis] in a Kentucky barbecue. **1884** *Boston Jrnl.* 27 Oct. 2/3 At the Brooklyn barbecue, which Governor Cleveland recently attended, 5000 kegs of beer were dispensed.

3. Attrib. with *dance, dinner, feast, supper.*

1815 *Salem Gazette* 30 June 3/2 (Kentucky news), The subscriber . . . will prepare an elegant Barbacue Dinner on the Fourth of July. **1881** H. PIERSON *In the Brush* 90 On any occasion when the barbecue feast was to be the agreeable conclusion. *Ib.* 96 There have been uncounted barbecue-dances. *Ib.*, A large wedding, that was succeeded by a barbecue-supper.

Barbecue, *v.* Also †**barbacue, barbicue, barbikew.**

1. *tr.* To roast or broil (an animal) whole (cf. BARBECUE *n.* 1); to roast or broil (meat) slowly at an open fire. Also transf. {1661–}

1702 C. MATHER *Magnalia* VII. vi, When they came to see the bodies of so many of their countrymen terribly barbikew'd. **1705** BEVERLEY *Virginia* III. 13 Laying it upon sticks rais'd upon forks at some distance above the live coals, . . . heats more gently, and drys up the gravy; this they, and we also from them, call Barbacueing. **1713** *Boston Daily Courant* 11 Nov., A hog to be barbicue'd. **1724** B. LYNDE *Diary* (1880) 133 Hog barbacued at Col's farm, a great frolick. **1735** *New Voyage to Georgia* (1737) 22 We had the good fortune to kill one bear, some of which we barbecu'd for our suppers. **1737** W. STEPHENS *Proc. Georgia* 50 A young shote, barbacu'd over a fire in the wood, was set on the table. **1744** A. HAMILTON *Itin.* (1907) 107 They have a diversion here [in New York] very common, which is the barbecuing of a turtle. **1791** BARTRAM *Travels* 236 The ribs and the choice pieces of the three great fat bears already well barbecued or broiled, are brought to the banqueting house in the square. **1818** J. M. DUNCAN *Travels U.S.* I. 297 The meat to be *barbecued* is split open and pierced with two long slender rods, upon which it is suspended across the mouth of the pits, and turned from side to side till it is thoroughly broiled. **1825** NEAL *Bro. Jonathan* III. 137 Believing the evacuation itself, to be a genuine Yankee trick, which was to end 'right away,' in their being roasted alive, or barbecued. **1843** 'CARLTON' *New Purchase* II. lxiii. 288 It seemed as [if] all the edible creatures of the Purchase had taken an odd fit to come and be barbecued for the mere fun of it! **1872** HOLMES *Poet* i. 5, I've heard of political gatherings when they barbecued an ox. **1878** *Amer. Home Cook Book* 96 Underdone ham is nice barbecued. **1920** HUNTER *Trail Drivers of Texas* I. 82 A few days later we killed and barbecued a beef.

absol. **1883** *Harper's Mag.* Aug. 481/2 It would be a good thing if the politicians would clam-bake and barbecue, and make no speeches.

2. To dry or cure (flesh, etc.) by exposure to a slow fire. {1794}

1674 A. WOOD *Let.* in Alvord & Bidgood *Trans-Allegheny Region* 223 Here they killd many swine, sturgin and beavers and barbicued them, soe returned and were fifteen dayes running up a gainst the streame. **1709, 1737** [see BARBECUED *ppl. a.*]. **1775** ADAIR *Indians* 408 When the pompions are ripe they cut them into . . . slices, which they barbacue, or dry with a slow heat. **1886** Z. F. SMITH *Kentucky* 75 Halting a few days at Blue Licks to barbecue and jerk a supply of buffalo meat for their journey, they passed on.

Barbecued, *ppl. a.* Also †**barbacued, barbicued.** Cured by heat; roasted in the open air. {1732–}

1709 LAWSON *Carolina* 17 We found great store of . . . barbacu'd peaches, and peach-bread. **1737** WESLEY *Journal* 1 Jan., Having a little barbecued bear's flesh, (that is, dried in the sun), we boiled it. **1775** ADAIR *Indians* 395 All his war store of provisions consisted in three stands of *barbicued* venison. **1784** J. SMYTH *Tour U.S.* I. xiv. 105 Here I found a large table loaded with fat roasted turkies, . . . large hams, hung-beef, barbicued pig. **1791** BARTRAM *Travels* 134, I saved one or two barbecued trout. **1839** IRVING *Wolfert's Roost* (1855) 221 This was a family of Talahasochte, who had been out on a hunt, and were returning home loaded with barbacued meat, hides, and honey. **1855** *Knickerb.* XLV. 129 God of the barbacued, Scalloped, fried, broiled, and stewed! **1881** H. PIERSON *In the Brush* 67 Our bill of fare was cold, barbecued shoat. **1883** *Century Mag.* Aug. 545/1 Rounds of beef, barbacued pig, sirloin steaks, . . . were set forth. **1908** *Springfield W. Republican* 17 Sept. 10 A capable serving force handed out a barbecued beef sandwich in exchange for a ticket. **1920** HUNTER *Trail Drivers of Texas* I. 83 They made short work of our barbecued meat.

Barbed, *a.* {1611–}

+**1.** *Barbed mesquit:* (see quotation).

1877 BARTLETT 788 *Barbed Mesquit*, a species of grass, from two to three feet in height, found in Western Texas. It is a favorite winter grass, and is much sought for by stock of all kinds.

+**2.** *Barbed wire*, wire, or strands of wire twisted together, provided with barbs at intervals; much used in fencing. Also attrib., esp. in *barbed wire fence.* Cf. BARB-WIRE. {1883–}

1881 NYE *Baled Hay* 126 The students at this school will wear barbed-wire masks while practicing. **1884** *Nation* 24 Jan. 65/1 The 'barbed-wire fence war' which has broken out in Texas. **1886** STOCKTON *Mrs. Lecks* 73 They'd find it a good deal easier to take down a barbed-wire fence than a stone wall. **1893** B. TORREY *Foot-path Way* 41 After considerable wading and a clamber over a detestable barbed-wire fence. **1904** STRATTON-PORTER *Freckles* 10 We have . . . strung barbed wires securely about the extent of this lease. **1913** W. C. BARNES *Grazing Grounds* 116 The advent of the barbed wire fence probably did more to improve the condition of the open range stockman than any one thing that has come to him.

* **Barber.** One whose business is shaving and trimming beards and hair; a hair-dresser. Also attrib.

1642 *Md. Archives* IV. 177 John Elkin planter, John Robinson barber. **1654** *Essex Probate Rec.* I. 197 Barbers stuff, 5s.; 1 dieper bourd cloth, 16s. **1685** SEWALL *Diary* I. 111 Something of Bushnell, the barber's, relating to his estate was now also done. **1708** *Boston News-Letter* 5 April 2/2 [He] is by trade a barber and perriwig maker. **1723** *New-Eng. Courant* 2 Dec. 2/2 A journeyman barber lying drunk in the street. **1773** TRUMBULL *Progress of Dulness* II. 28 And who for beauty need repine, That's sold at every barber's sign? **1799** J. COWLES *Diary* 34 Mr. Gardiner, the barber, has just taken a horse to N.H. **1820** FLINT *Lett. from Amer.* 214 There are [in Cincinnati] . . . ten barbers and hair-dressers. **1838** HALIBURTON *Clockmaker* 2 Ser. iii, A member [of the legislature] . . . lookin' as wise as a barber's block with a new wig on it. **1852** STOWE *Uncle Tom* xlv, W—. Three-fourths black; barber and waiter; from Kentucky. **1893** POST *Harvard Stories* 68 He and Randolph . . . bought a barber's pole. They were careful to get a receipted bill from the barber. **1901** CHURCHILL *Crisis* 95 The wide arm of his mahogany barber chair. **1902** *Harper's Mag.* 989 A grand lady seated in a barber's chair.

Barber-chirurgeon. *Obs.* A barber-surgeon. {1627} — **1643** *Md. Archives* IV. 215 Rob[er]t Ellyson barber-chirurgeon demandeth . . . 1156 l. tob. due by acc[oun]t of chirurgery. **1654** JOHNSON *Wonder-W. Prov.* 138 Sending to Boston his servant maid for a barber-chirurgion, to draw his tooth. **1684** *Boston Rec.* 76 Cuthbert Garrett, barber churigion.

Barber-house. =BARBER-SHOP. — **1889** BRAYLEY *Boston Fire Dept.* 86 A fire at Gold's barber-house, in Southick's court, was put out by engine 6 during April.

Barberize, *v. dial. intr.* To ply the business of a barber. {*Sc.* 1640–98} — **1859** BARTLETT 22 To *Barberize*, a term among country hair-dressers. 'I can shoemake through the week, and barberize on public days'; that is, on days of public business, which call farmers to the country town.

Barber-pole. The striped pole serving as a barber's sign. Cf. BARBER'S POLE. Also transf. (quots. 1850).

1850 C. MATHEWS *Moneypenny* [35 He . . . wore . . . an olive coat, with long gaping pockets, . . . with a small pole constantly sticking out of one of them, which he kept poking into people's faces. *Ib.*] 61 Thrusting his hand and the barber-pole with fresh vigor to the bottom of his pocket. **1893** POST *Harvard Stories* 71 If your insulting remarks refer to this barber-pole . . . allow me to tell you that it belongs to us.

* **Barberry.** Also †**bareberri, barbery.** (See also BERBERRY.)

* **1.** The berry or fruit of the barberry-bush (see next).

1687 *Essex Inst. Coll.* I. 85 Fail not . . . in sending me . . . some aples and some barberyes. **1709** LAWSON *Carolina* 111 Barberry red, with stones, and without stones, grow here. **1774** FITHIAN *Journal* I. 259, I saw some barberry's, sloe's, & pomegranates, neither of which I had seen before. **1828** NEAL *R. Dyer* 55 Where the scarlet barberry glittered among the sharp green leaves. **1878** *Amer. Home Cook Book* 138 Take a quantity of barberries not over ripe.

* **2.** A prickly shrub of the genus *Berberis*, bearing small yellow flowers followed by oblong berries which turn red in the fall; esp. the common species *B. vulgaris.*

1714 SEWALL *Diary* II. 435 Let a Ditch . . . be made all on the outside of the Hedge, and set within Thorns or Barberries. **1784** CUTLER in *Mem. Academy* I. 435 *Berberis.* . . . Barberry. The berries are used for pickles. **1785** MARSHALL *Amer. Grove* 17 There is also a kind of barberry growing upon New-River in Virginia. **1832** WILLIAMSON *Maine* I. 114 Barberry is a briery bush . . . which bears . . . very acid berries. They are used for making pickles and for preserves. **1846** EMORY *Military Reconn.* 57 There were several new and beautiful varieties of cactus . . . and three-leaved barberry (*berberis trifoliolata*). **1858** WARDER *Hedges & Evergreens* 272 Holly-leaved Barberry is one of the most beautiful low evergreens. **1875** *Amer. Naturalist* IX. 199 The still more spiny-leaved Barberry (*Berberis Fremontii* Torr.). **1883** HALE *Woods & Timbers N.C.* 137 Barberry. (*Berberis Canadensis*, Pursh.) . . . It is not known to exist north of Virginia, and is the only native Barberry in the United States.

3. Attrib. with *bark, fungus, meadow*, etc.

1662 *Essex Probate Rec.* I. 400, 10 acres of meadow in the bareberri meadows. **1832** L. M. CHILD *Frugal Housewife* 28 Black cherry-tree bark, barberry bark, mustard seed . . . are excellent for the jaundice. **1869** *Amer. Naturalist* II. 637 The foreign barberry mildew, *Microsphoeria*, is here under several species. **1889** *Cent., Barberry fungus*, a fungus which attacks the leaves of the common barberry. . . . [It is] also called *barberry-rust* or *barberry cluster-cups.*

* **Barberry-bush.** =BARBERRY 2.

1661 *Providence Rec.* XV. 84 John Clawson was attacked with a broad ax by an Indian from behind barberry bushes near the Burying Place. **1737** [see BARBERRY-TREE]. **1789** MORSE *Amer. Geog.* 143 Lands of the third quality produce fir and pitch pine; the next, whortleberry and barberry bushes. **1799** G. Kittredge *Old Farmer* (1904) 328 Farmers . . . whose lands are overrun with barberry bushes. **1827** J. HOWE *Journal* 12 The last I saw of Smith was running through the barberry bushes to keep out of sight of the road. **1845** *Knickerb.* XXVI. 509 A stone-wall; against which the . . . tall barberry-bush with its scarlet fruit, delighted . . . to come and dwell. **1855** LONGFELLOW *Hiawatha* Introd. 103 The tangled barberry-bushes Hang their tufts of crimson berries Over stone walls. **1860** HOLMES *E. Venner* iv, Along the road-side were barberry-bushes, hung all over with bright red coral pendants in autumn and far into the winter. **1873** ALDRICH *Marj. Daw* 36 A winding road lined all the way with wild barberry-bushes.

+**Barberrying,** *vbl. n.* [BARBERRY.] The plucking or gathering of barberries. — **1859** THOREAU *Let. to H. Blake* 26 Sept., I am off—a-barberrying.

Barberry-tree. *Obs.* The barberry or barberry-bush. {1814–} — **1737** BRICKELL *N. Carolina* 106 The barberry-tree or bush, whereof we have two sorts which thrive well, *viz.* one with, and the other without stones. **1750** WALKER *Journal* 12 April, Some barberry trees on the east side of the river.

Barber shop. The shop of a barber.

Found in E. in 1579, but in Amer. use app. a new formation in place of the earlier BARBER'S SHOP.

1832 KENNEDY *Swallow Barn* I. Int. Ep. 8 A thorough-going violin . . . in an illuminated barber-shop, struggled in the contortions of a Virginia reel. **1855** THOMPSON *Doesticks* 50 There are waiters in the bar, in the washroom, in the barber-shop. **1865** *Nation* I. 137 As far as I have seen, in the hotels, at barber shops . . . the colored people appear good-natured. **1880** G. INGHAM *Digging Gold* xiv. 323 Even the barber shops were so full as to cause us considerable detention in getting our shave. **1893** 'MARK TWAIN' *P. Wilson* i, The candy-striped pole . . . indicated merely the humble barber shop. **1916** W. A. DU PUY *Uncle Sam* 55 His dark locks breathed forth odors of the lotions of cheap barber shops.

Barber's pole. {1684–} **1.** A barber-pole. **2.** ? A stick of candy having spiral stripes. — (1) **1846** *Spirit of Times* (N.Y.) 11 July 232/3 During my peregrinations through the camp, I neither saw a barber nor a barber's pole. **1855** THOMPSON *Doesticks* 165 The reptile's fiery tongue . . . resembles a barber's pole with the split end up. **1893** [see BARBER]. (2) **a1841** [W. HAWES] *Sporting Scenes* II. 68 Down went the lady-merchant, and down went her apples, peanuts and barbers'-poles. I felt sorry for the poor thing, but it was all her fault, for not getting out of the way.

Barber's shop. Now *rare.* A barber shop. {Still the current use.}

1648 *Suffolk Deeds* I. 100 Valentine Hill of Boston granted vnto David Sellecke . . . the barbers shopp & all thereto pertaineinge. **1712** *Boston Rec.* 173 Liberty . . . to set his windows for his barbers shop seventeen inches . . . into King Street. **1725** *New-Eng. Courant* 8–15 Feb. 1/1 He enters a barber's shop not as a customer. **1754** *Cambridge Prop. Rec.* 351 The north east end of John Morses barbars shop. **1856** OLMSTED *Slave States* 22 The adjoining hucksteries, barbers'-shops and bar-rooms, are evidently all the better patronized for this fine simplicity. **1861** WINTHROP *Open Air* 270 'The White House' . . . for the lodging and messing of the new artillery company,—its barbers' shops,—its offices.

+**Bar-bill.** [BAR *n.*[1] 7.] A bill for liquors or drinks at a bar. — **1836** *Public Ledger* (Phila.) 27 April (Th.), After boarding a day or two, and running up a bar-bill, he 'cut dirt.' **1847** FIELD *Drama in Pokerville* 122 These fellows owe four weeks board and their bar bills.

Bar-bit. (See BAR *n.*[1] 3 c.) — **1868** WOODRUFF *Trotting Horse* xlix. 391 With a big bar-bit in his mouth, he is more likely to hang on it.

Bar-boy. [BAR *n.*[1] 7.] A boy attendant at a bar. {1631} — **1851** HALL *Manhattaner* 10 These crowds appear . . . eating and drinking their way (lunchwise) into the early summer. Then the bar boys breathe less short.

+**Barb wire.** [Reduced f. *barbed wire.*] Barbed wire. Also attrib. with *fence, fencing.* {1883–}

1882 *Maine Bd. Agric. Rep.* XXVI. 249, I find only one closing consideration regarding barb wire fencing. . . . All attempts at barb wire that does not prick are sure to be . . . failures. **1902** LORIMER *Lett. Merchant* 7 A steer that's been . . . living on cactus and petrified wood till he's just a bunch of barb-wire and sole-leather. **1907** W. LILLIBRIDGE *Trail* 137 Landor . . . closed the gate of the barb wire fence surrounding the yard. **1920** HUNTER *Trail Drivers of Texas* I. 158 The innovation of the railways and barbwire fencing had greatly changed the conditions.

Barcalonga. *Obs.* Also †**barco longo, barque alongo.** [Sp.] A large Spanish fishing-boat. {1681–1790} — **1704** *Boston News-Letter* 22 May 2/1 The Spaniards going all ashore leaving him . . . on board, he stept & unloos'd the sails of the barque-alongo. **1711** *N.Car. Col. Rec.* I. 795 Having then a brigantine and barco longo mounted with canon and filled with armed men.

Barcelona. [A town in Spain.]

1. *Barcelona handkerchief, cravat,* or *neckcloth*, a handkerchief or neckerchief of soft twilled silk. {1816}

1761 E. Singleton *Social New York* (1902) 236 [Josiah Vavasor sold] black Barcelona handkercheifs. **1776** *New Jersey Archives* 2 Ser. I. 195 An assortment of dry goods, . . . among which are . . . Barcelona black cravats. **1780** E. PARKMAN *Diary* 219 Breck brot also a present of a Barcelona handkerchief to his mother from Samuel. **1802** H. M. Brooks *Gleanings* 99 Five Barcelona handkerchiefs. **1841** *S. Lit. Messenger* VII. 749/1 Around his neck was tied a black 'Barcelona' neckcloth, then much in vogue with tars.

2. In elliptical use. {1795, 1833}

1825 NEAL *Bro. Jonathan* III. 236 Loose, large trousers; a black barcelona—a checked shirt. **1841** *S. Lit. Messenger* VII. 768/1 Jim Guest himself, in the same spry dress, . . . tarpaulin hat, purser's pumps and Barcelona.

+**Bar diggings.** (See quotation and BAR *n.*[1] 9.) — **1881** RAYMOND *Mining Gloss., Bar-diggings*, Pac[ific], gold-washing claims located on the bars (shallows) of a stream, and worked when the water is low, or otherwise with the aid of coffer-dams. **1897** *U.S. Consular Report* October, 'Bar diggings' shall mean any part of a river over which the water extends when the water is in its flooded state and which is not covered at low water.

* **Bare,** *n.* [f. *bare* adj.] The bare skin. {–1611} — **1888** STOCKTON *Dusantes* 86 The idea . . . is worse than slidin' down a snow mountain, even if you had to do it on the bare of your back.

* **Bareback,** *adv.* and *a.*

* **1.** *adv.* On horseback without a saddle.

1768 *Essex Inst. Coll.* XIV. 262 Went to Boston in sley, thaw; came home bare back. **a1861** WINTHROP *Canoe & Saddle* xii. 249 Fudnun had thus far ridden the mission mare, while Gubbins pranced bare-back. **1880** 'MARK TWAIN' *Tramp Abroad* xxvi. 269 He could ride bareback and know and feel he was safe.

2. *adj.* Not furnished with, or assisted by, a saddle.

1880 CABLE *Grandissimes* lvi. 417 Errands were being carried by negro boys on bareback horses. **1923** J. H. COOK *On Old Frontier* 48 So bareback riding was the order of the day for some of the men.

‖**Bareback,** *v.* [f. prec.] *tr.* To ride (a horse) bareback. — *a***1861** WINTHROP *Canoe & Saddle* iii. 50 Because I could not ride the leagues . . . , barebacking the bonyness of prairie nags.

Bare-backed, *adv.* and *a.* {1628} =BAREBACK. — **1832** KENNEDY *Swallow Barn* II. iv. 61 A negro boy . . . mounted, bare-backed, upon a tall, full-blooded horse. **1834** CARRUTHERS *Kentuckian* II. 208, I would . . . rather ride a three-year-old filly bare-backed through a cane-brake. **1858** D. K. BENNETT *Chronol. N.Car.* 20 Wm. Mills . . . rode bare-backed horses.

* **Barefoot,** *a.* Also *dial.* **barfoot.**

+**1.** Of horses: Unshod.

1805 LEWIS in *L. & Clark Exped.* (1904) III. 15 Yet notwithstanding our horses traveled barefoot over them . . . fast . . . and did not detain us.

+**2.** Of a dance: Performed with bare feet.

1852 MRS. ELLET *Pioneer Women* 40 She would relate interesting anecdotes . . . of the 'barefoot and moccasin dance' and 'spice-wood tea-parties.'

+**3.** =BAREFOOTED *a.*

1866 LOWELL *Biglow P.* II. p. lxii, 'I take my tea barfoot,' said a backwoodsman when asked if he would have cream and sugar. **1888** *Chicago Herald* (F.), Never touch coffee unless you like it barefoot, that is, without sugar or milk. **1888** WHITMAN *November Boughs* 406 'Barefoot whiskey' is the Tennessee name for the undiluted stimulant.

* **Barefooted,** *a.* +Without addition or dilution; pure.

*c***1845** W. I. PAULDING *Madmen All* 194 Mostly [we drink] stone fence barefooted. . . . I thought even a Yankee knew that 'stone fence barefooted' is the polite English for whiskey uncontaminated—pure, sir! **1871** *Harper's Mag.* Dec. 160/1 'Will you take sugar and cream in your coffee?' . . . 'No, ma'am; I jest takes it barefooted and bald-headed.' **1878** BEADLE *Western Wilds* 183 It was sod corn [=whisky] barefooted. **1888** PERRIN *Ky. Pioneer Press* 32 It could be nothing else but an organ of the old Bourbon barefooted Democracy of the Jeffersonian type.

Barège. [*Barèges, Barège* (village in Fr. Pyrenees), where first made.] A light, silky or gauze-like dress-material. {1851–} Also attrib.

1839 'M. PENCIL' *White Sulphur P.* 83 Wanting some barège for veils this morning, C. and I went over to the store. **1858** VIELÉ *Following Drum* 81 Ladies . . . arrayed in the tasteful costume of black barege over white. **1870** MRS. STEPHENS *Married in Haste* lxi. 311 The traveling-veil . . . was of barege. **1891** FREEMAN *New Eng. Nun* 149 She wore a green barège bonnet, stiffened with rattans. **1892** M. DELAND in *Harper's Mag.* Jan. 272/1 She wore a hat with a blue barége veil tied around its . . . crown. **1898** — *Old Chester Tales* 235 Miss Jane . . . in her striped barege dress . . . began to protest.

***Bare-legged,** *a.* +=BAREFOOTED *a.* — **1704** S. KNIGHT *Journal* 47 But the pumpkin and Indian mixt bred had such an aspect, and the bare-legg'd punch so awkerd or rather awfull a sound, that we left both.

+**Bar-fish.** [BAR *n.*[1]] The calico-bass, *Pomoxys sparoides.* — **1888** GOODE *Amer. Fishes* 33 The yellow bass, . . . sometimes called bar-fish in the South.

+**Bargain-counter.** A counter in a store at which goods are displayed or sold at reduced prices. Also attrib. and fig.

1888 *Scribner's Mag.* Jan. 65/2 Ladies . . . in all the finery that the 'bargain counters' of Fourteenth Street could furnish. **1890** *Congress. Rec.* 28 Aug. 9258/1 You may go into any of the large mercantile establishments, . . . and you will find what they call a bargain-counter. **1900** *Ib.* App., 28 Feb. 77/2 Were the Spaniards right in their derisive epithets, calling us 'pigs' and 'a bargain-counter nation'? **1907** M. C. HARRIS *Tents of Wickedness* I. i. 16 France, chiefly memorable to most of them as a huge bargain-counter . . . across which they had passed much valuable money. **1914** G. ATHERTON *Perch of Devil* i. 22 Ida . . . divided her day between . . . the upholsterer, and the bargain counter.

+**Bargain day.** A particular day on which goods are offered at reduced prices. — **1898** C. A. BATES *Clothing Bk.* No. 1373, Instead of 'Dog Days' these twenty-four hours should be called 'bargain days.' *a***1906** 'O. HENRY' *Trimmed Lamp*, etc. 13 When I sell out it's not going to be on any bargain day. **1909** — *Options* 118 It's a bargain-day rush. I've got one more line of goods to offer before I shut up shop.

+**Bargain room.** (See quotation.) — **1880** Appel *Biogr. Wanamaker* (1930) 104 Bargain Room: . . . a place where remainders of lots are sold at smaller prices.

+**Bargain sale.** A sale of goods at reduced prices. — **1898** C. A. BATES *Clothing Bk.* No. 5211, Garments for which you pay the additional price at widely advertised 'bargain' sales. **1908** 'YESLAH' *Tenderfoot S. Calif.* iv. 42 It's a wonder to me that some of the fellars . . . don't buy an orange grove at some bargain sale price.

* **BARGE.** Also †**berge.**

* **1.** A flat-bottomed freight boat, suitable for river or canal traffic; esp. one of the kind formerly used on the Mississippi and its tributaries.

1690 SEWALL *Diary* I. 323 Go to Cambridge by water in the barge. **1737** *Weekly Journal* 8 March 2/2 To be sold, a very fine barge, with masts, sails, and six oars. **1775** *Essex Inst. Coll.* XLVIII. 51 We se the berges go up and down the river. **1787** HUTCHINS *Topogr. Descr. Va.* 9 This river is navigable with batteaux or barges to the foot of Laurel Hill. **1801** *Austin Papers* (1924) I. 71 This day I pass five barges and canoes bound up the river. **1823** JAMES *Exped.* I. 24 Arks and small barges descend, by the aid of skillful pilots, for great part of the year. **1828** FLINT *Western States* (1832) 151 The barge . . . had sails, masts and rigging not unlike a sea vessel, and carried from fifty to an hundred tons. **1835** J. HALL *Sk. of West* II. 71 Before the introduction of steamboats upon this river, its immense commerce was chiefly carried on by means of keel-boats, or of *barges*—large boats, calculated to descend as well as to ascend the stream. **1898** *Boston Herald* 11 Nov. 2/3 [The] master of one of the barges is reported to be in jail at Dawson, charged with broaching cargoes.

+**b.** (See quot. 1864.)

1864 WEBSTER, *Barge*, a double-decked passenger and freight vessel, without sails or power, and towed by a steamboat. **1903** *N.Y. Ev. Post* 24 Aug., The steamer was coming down the North River towing three barges crowded with excursionists. **1904** *Scribner's Mag.* May 561 During the heated days of August the towing of the big double-decked excursion barges became our chief occupation.

* **2.** The second boat of a man of war; a light boat used for communication between a vessel and the shore.

1761 S. NILES *Indian Wars* II. 432 The other three boats returned to the ships, leaving the 'Success's' barge in the enemy's possession. **1778** *Essex Inst. Coll.* LII. 6 This boat, which they & we took for a man of war's barge. **1823** COOPER *Pilot* II. xii. 197 Barnstable . . . ordered the long, low barge of Capt. Munson to be drawn upon the sand. **1838** INGRAHAM *Burton* II. iv. 56 The British fleet lay at anchor far down the Narrows, and the harbour was dotted with barges and light boats coursing in every direction. **1860** ABBOTT *South & North* 43 At eight o'clock we took one of these barges for the shore.

+**b.** 'A practice-boat used by crews in training for a race' (*Cent.* '89).

+**3.** *New Eng.* A large carriage; a picnic wagon.

1881 HOWELLS *Modern Instance* xxvii. 328 Marcia watched him drive off toward the station in the hotel barge. **1900** *Mass. Acts* 334 All stage coaches, tally-ho coaches, barges and other passenger vehicles. **1903** *Boston Herald* 19 Aug., The visitors were conveyed in barges to the crest of High Pole hill. **1907** *Springfield Weekly Republ.* 21 Feb. 16 [A sleigh-ride] which required every four-horse barge in the north half of the county.

4. Attrib. (in sense 1) with *boat, builder, canal,* etc.

1804 LEWIS in *L. & Clark Exped.* (1904) I. 128 These cooks as well as those previously appointed to the messes of the barge crew. **1809** F. CUMING *Western Tour* 223 Pittsburgh [has] . . . eight boat, barge, and ship builders. **1857** *Knickerb.* XLIX. 419 We saw chief-pilots . . . with Captain 'Dick,' and 'Bill Stall,' barge-officers. **1871** [L. H. BAGG] *At Yale* 353 In the barge race, Cymothoë won the first prize. **1874** R. H. COLLINS *Kentucky* I. 111 [Men] pour . . . over the pontoon bridge or bridge of barge-boats. **1903** E. JOHNSON *Railway Transportation* 16 Between 1830 and 1850 . . . the railroad had made its appearance and had begun to make the further construction of small barge canals inadvisable.

***Bargeman.** [BARGE 1.] 'A man who manages a barge' (W.) — **1827** MCKENNEY *Tour to Lakes* 238 On calling the voyageurs, I found they had gone across the isthmus to see the bargemen. **1852** *Knickerb.* XL. 196 It is but thirty-five years since New-Orleans was only known . . . through the semi-annual reports of returning bargemen.

‖**'Bargo.** *dial.* [Reduction of EMBARGO *n.*] *'Bargo times*, the period of an embargo. — **1820** *Hillsborough* (N.C.) *Recorder* 29 March, One [colored person] had a knife which he proposed to sell; but on mentioning the price, the other thought it rather extravagant, and said he could not give it, for 'it's 'bargo times.' . . . I could not help smiling at the expression.

Barilla. [Sp.] The saltwort (*Salsola Soda*) or the impure alkali obtained from this by burning. {1622–}

1765 in W. Stork *East-Florida* (1766) 79 The low lands are partly . . . salt-water marsh, full of the barilla, and the mangrove-tree. **1766** W. STORK *Ib.* 49 This herb resembles entirely our samphire in England, and is called barilla or kaly. **1791** BARTRAM *Travels* 68, I estimate nearly two thirds of it to consist of low salt plains, which produce barilla, sedge, rushes, &c. **1814** *N.Y. State Soc. Arts* III. 79 Barrilla . . . is made in the same manner as kelp, and employed for the same purposes. **1816** *Ann. 14th Congress* 1 Sess. 1874 The following articles shall be imported . . . free of duties: . . . barilla [etc.].

Bar iron. [BAR *n.*[1] 3a.] Iron wrought or rolled into the form of malleable bars. {1677–}

1653 *Suffolk Deeds* I. 306 Myne sow and barr iron, potts and other cast wares. **1657** *Mass. H.S. Coll.* 4 Ser. VII. 402, I am wiling to by youer iron in the sow, . . . if you haue no workmen to work it in to bar iron. **1671** J. WINTHROP *Letters* (1882) 141 Possibly by the like artifice . . . bar iron might be made out of cast iron. **1732** BYRD *Progress to Mines* (1901) 355, I askt my friend some questions about bar-iron. **1741** *N.J. Archives* VI. 141 Conveniences . . . for making the same [iron ore] into pigg mettal and barr iron. **1765** R. ROGERS *Acc. N. Amer.* 70 The commodities exported from hence [N.Y.] are . . . bar iron, and some copper. **1794** *Ann. 3rd Congress* 499 The committee appointed to consider . . . the propriety of remitting the duty on imported bar iron. **1812** *Ann. 12th Congress* 1 Sess. II. App. 2073 The Directors of the New Hampshire Iron Factory . . . erecting furnaces . . . for the purpose of manufacturing bar iron and various sorts of cast iron ware. **1837** W. JENKINS *Ohio Gazetteer* 52 Along this creek are . . . three furnaces . . . ; besides a forge for bar iron. **1849**

CHAMBERLAIN *Indiana Gazetteer* 337 About three tons of good bar iron a day are manufactured at a forge at Rochester. **1881** RAYMOND *Mining Gloss.* s.v. *Iron*, Wrought-iron, also called bar-iron and weld-iron, is the product of the forge or the puddling furnace.

* **BARK,** *n.*[1] Also †**barke, barque.**

1. The bark of various trees used for special purposes by the Indians or the settlers.

1637 MORTON *New Canaan* I. iv, The natives . . . put the great end of them [*sc.* poles] in the ground, placinge them in forme of a circle . . . ; they bind them together with the barke of walnut trees. **1643** WILLIAMS *Key* 42 They dry and eat this bark with the fat of beasts, and sometimes of men. **1648** SHEPARD *Clear Sunshine* 46 The wigwams . . . being built not with mats but barks of trees in good bignesse. **1669** *Plymouth Laws* 156 It is enacted . . . that noe barke nor board shalbe transported out of this Collonie. **1688** *Md. Hist. Mag.* XV. 124 It is supposed they will stay till the barque will peel that they can make canoes to goe over to the Northern Indians. **1694** *Huntington Rec.* II. 169 It is ordered that whome soever peeleth any standing trees for bark for their use of tanning . . . shall forfit five shillings for every tree found so peeled. **1738** BYRD *Dividing Line* (1901) 37 His habitation was a bower, cover'd with bark after the Indian fashion. *a***1772** WOOLMAN *Journal* 204 Forty [Indian] houses, . . . built mostly of split plank, one end . . . pinned to a plate on which rafters are laid, and then covered with bark. **1826** COOPER *Mohicans* v, The scout drew a canoe of bark from its place of concealment. **1840** — *Pathfinder* xix, These huts . . . had been roofed by bark brought from a distance. **1850** GARRARD *Wah-To-Yah* ii. 32 The pipe . . . was passed around, containing a mixture of tobacco and the bark of the red willow or swamp dogwood. **1864** 'PENNIMAN' *Tanner-Boy* 27 The bark of trees . . . is all dried, and then cut up in pieces, or ground into powder, and applied to the skins in places dug and boarded in the ground, called vats. **1885** *N.H. Forestry Comm. Rep.* June 10 To these should be added the large quantities of wood, fence-posts, and sleepers sold to railroads, telegraphy-poles, pulp-wood, bark, etc. **1919** *Maine my State* 48 There is nothing but huts here made of pickets and covered with the bark of trees or with skins.

fig. **1768** Morse *Amer. Geog.* (1789) 274 We [Indians] entered into a covenant chain of bark with you, and fastened your ship therewith.

b. Peruvian bark; quinine. {1704–}

1750 FRANKLIN in *Medical Side* (1911) 26 Don't imagine yourself thoroughly cured, and so omit the use of the bark too soon. **1786** WASHINGTON *Diaries* III. 110 Sent for Doctr. Craik, who . . . gave me a carthartick and directed the bark to be applied in the morning. **1800** WEEMS *Letters* II. 133 Your nerves are irritable—don't forget your bark. **1805** LEWIS & CLARK *Journals* (1904) II. 284 Capt. Clark is much better today. . . . I prevailed on him to take the barks which he has done. **1818** E. P. FORDHAM *Narr. Travels* 230 The fever soon became a regular intermittent, of which I was soon cured by bark and laudanum. **1901** *Harper's Mag.* Dec. 67 His incautious neglect to fortify himself against the swamp malaria by a glass of straight Bourbon with a pinch of bark in it.

2. In figurative phrases.

1822 *Ann. 17th Congress* 1 Sess. I. 75 A technical judge . . . may conceive it his duty to stick to the bark of the case. **1845** HOOPER *Simon Sugg's Adv.* i. 14 The old man's going to take the bark off both of us. *a***1846** *Quarter Race Kentucky*, etc. 140 The noise increased, until he said 'it sounded as if all h—l was pounding bark.' **1848** RUXTON *Far West* i. 35 They say he took the bark off the Shians when he cleared out of the village with old Beavertail's squaw. **1889** R. T. COOKE *Steadfast* vi. 76 The old sayin' is, 'don't ye never put in betwixt the bark and the tree.' {1562–1804} **1904** *N.Y. Ev. Post* 27 July 6 He sticks in the bark about the mortal peril of promising 'independence'; but he does promise 'self-government.'

b. *With the bark on*, in a rough, unpolished, or plain form. *colloq.*

1872 'MARK TWAIN' *Roughing it* xv. 124 That is the word with the bark on it. **1885** F. C. BAYLOR *On Both Sides* II. i, 'I don't like her, . . . and that is the truth, dear.' . . . 'With the bark on. No more do I.' **1903** *N.Y. Sun* 28 Nov. 7 Your Westerner with the bark on is fond of . . . picturesque figures of speech.

3. *ellipt.* +**a.** A section of the bark of a tree used as a drain.

1841 G. POWERS *Hist. Sk. Coos* 125 A bark had been laid down into the fountain, which conducted the water off.

+**b.** A basket made of bark.

1853 J. S. BARRY *Sketch of Hanover* (Mass.) 37 Children . . . may be seen daily . . . [going berrying] with baskets, or tin kettles, or barks on their arms.

4. Attrib. in the sense 'made of bark,' as *bark bowl, bridle, cabin, coffin, cord, cradle*, etc. See also BARK CANOE, HOUSE, HUT, etc.

1675 *Mass. H.S. Coll.* VI. 205 They have bark wigwams for shelter, and some mats. **1775** ADAIR *Indians* 406 The women however tether the horses with tough young bark-ropes, and confine the swine in convenient penns. **1819** SCHOOLCRAFT *Journal* 28 We encamped in an Indian bark tent. **1823** JAMES *Exped.* I. 113 Across these are laid long and slender sticks or twigs, attached parallel to each other by means of bark cord. **1827** MCKENNEY *Tour to Lakes* 344 Each [Indian] brought his bark bowl, and in this received his portion. **1834** *Knickerb.* IV. 372 As his mother swung Macoupin in his bark cradle. **1834** PECK *Gaz. Illinois* 339 They had secured provisions, but their only resource for water was by letting down vessels with bark ropes to the river. *c***1836** CATLIN *Indians* II. 138 The Chippeways struck their tents by taking them down and rolling up their bark coverings. **1841** COOPER *Deerslayer* viii, The building itself, the bark roof excepted, was not very combustible. **1843** 'CARLTON' *New Purchase* I. ii. 10 Enthusiasm for bark cabins and forest life. **1846** THORPE *Myst. Backwoods* 77 The open ends of the bark scroll are pressed together and fastened between clamps. **1847** HOWE *Ohio* 56 The dead were wrapped in white hickory bark, . . . and buried in their bark coffins. **1848** E. BRYANT *California* iv. 47 The bark-walls, on the inside, were ornamented with numerous charcoal-sketches. **1849** *Pres. Mess. Congress* II. 631, I built him a bark wigwam. **1859** *Harper's Mag.* July 282/1 A tall, gawky, long-legged [white], . . . riding a white mule, with a bark bridle and no saddle. **1877** JOHNSON *Anderson Co., Kansas* 18 In the neighborhood above they built some bark shanties. **1881** *Harper's Mag.* May 869/2 Facing the lake . . . stand the bark buildings. **1903** WHITE *Forest* xv. 215, I have seen a thoroughly . . . comfortable bark shelter made in about the time it would take one to pitch a tent.

* **Bark,** *n.*[2]

* **1.** A small sea-going sailing vessel, latterly one with three masts.

1622 'MOURT' *Relation* 63 At full sea, a barke of thirty tunne may goe vp. **1631** *Mass. Bay Rec.* I. 88 Noe person w[ha]tsoeuer shall buy corne . . . of any shipp or barke that comes into this bay, without leaue. *a***1649** WINTHROP *Hist.* I. 65 The governor built a bark at Mistick, which was launched this day, [July 4, 1631]. *a***1656** BRADFORD *Hist.* 425 Ther was a barke of this place, newly put in ther. **1687** SEWALL *Diary* I. 191 The master let his bark fall aground before he was aware. **1705** *Boston News-Letter* 12 March 2/2 There is a bark and briganteen seized at Suranam belonging to this place. **1708** *Ib.* 22 Nov. 4/2 They advise from Philadelphia, that Capt. Kearney in a bark was arrived there [=N.Y.]. **1820** *Coll. Amer. Antiq. Soc.* 66 Mr. de la Salle arrived from fort Frontinac with a great bark to supply us with provisions. **1838** HAWTHORNE *Note-books* I. 107 A wine-merchant . . . had arrived the day before in a bark from Copenhagen. **1869** *Causes Reduct. Tonnage* (1870) 15 Sixty barks, forty-three of them being foreign vessels.

* **2.** A boat or canoe.

1791 BARTRAM *Travels* 305 My trusty and fortunate bark I presented to the old interpreter, Job Wiggens, often my travelling companion. **1826** COOPER *Mohicans* x, They now bore the light bark from the upper end of the rock, and placed it in the water. **1840** — *Pathfinder* v, The light bark shot across the intervening space. . . . To secure the canoe, . . . occupied the friends but a moment. *a***1861** WINTHROP *Life in Open Air* viii. 63 Its current, unripplingly smooth, . . . bore on our bark.

* **Bark,** *n.*[3] +*pl.* The 'barking exercises' (BARKING *vbl. n.*[2]). — **1807** R. M'NEMAR *Ky. Revival* 63 The quickest method to find releasement from the jerks and barks, was to engage in the voluntary dance.

* **Bark,** *v.*[1] [BARK *n.*[1]]

* **1.** To strip (a tree) of bark; to take bark from (a tree).

'To make a circular incision through the bark so as to kill the tree. See *Girdle*' (B. '59).

1645 *New Haven Col. Rec.* 201 That none vnder the same penalties barke or cause to be barked any trees. **1669** *R.I. Col. Rec.* II. 272 Hee knew they were formerly his Indians, and had skill to bark cedar trees and to make bark houses. **1674** *Springfield Rec.* II. 120 There is graunted him the liberty of the Comons for getting bark . . . , the trees when barked to be free for any other. **1715** *Mass. Prov. Laws* II. 6 No person or persons may presume to . . . barke or box any pine tree or trees for the drawing of turpentine . . . without leave . . . from the owner. **1750** WALKER *Journal* 30 April, [There] is a large elm cut down and barked about 20 feet and another standing just by it. **1796** *Ky. MS. Rec.* 5, I barked an ash tree . . . to salt meat on. **1848** THOREAU *Maine Woods* 67 The trees were barked and splintered up to their tops. **1855** *Trans. Amer. Inst. N.Y.* 505 These [Mimosa] trees will grow any where, stand any cold and wind. Stock wont bark them. **1874** KNIGHT 622/2 The cork-tree at the age of twenty-five years is barked for the first time. **1902** WHITE *Blazed Trail* xiv. 99 'Don't you know, young man, that white pine logs on skids will spoil utterly in a summer? Worms get into 'em.' 'I do,' replied Thorpe. 'unless you bark them.'

fig. *c***1854** R. L. HALE *Log of Forty-Niner* 170 A little more head today and our ship would have barked an iceberg.

b. To strip (the shins, hand, etc.) of skin by striking with or against something rough or hard. {1850–}

1825 NEAL *Bro. Jonathan* II. 55 Oh, my shins!—oh—oh!—they're pootely barked, I wage. **1826** COOPER *Mohicans* v, A rifle bullet acts on a running animal, when it barks him, much the same as one of your spurs on a horse. **1850** B. TAYLOR *Eldorado* xvii. (1856) 171 After . . . barking my hand on the rough bark of a branchless pine . . . I started . . . to the top of a bald summit. **1857** *Lawrence* (Kansas) *Republican* 11 June 4 The light glared in his eyes and made him stumble, by which he barked his shins. **1866** 'F. KIRKLAND' *Bk. Anecdotes* 158 My son . . . had his nose badly barked and his hips broken . . . and now I am going to see if the rebels can bark the old man's nose. **1872** 'MARK TWAIN' *Roughing It* iv. 29 Every time it came it damaged somebody. One trip it 'barked' the Secretary's elbow. **1897** *Outing* May 173/2, I've barked my shins on every box and trunk you've got.

‖**c.** To divest (oneself) of clothing.

1859 *S. Lit. Messenger* XXVIII. 143/2 Bill sed he'd dive doun and rise the pole. So he barks hisself, and in he goes.

+**2.** To cover *over* with bark.

1832 *Louisville Directory* 107 This tree is well known to bark over its wounds very quickly, only darkening the external cover. **1847** Howe *Ohio* 151 The roof [of the hut] was barked over, strips being bent across from one eave over the ridge pole to the other and secured by poles on them.

+**3.** To bring down or kill (a squirrel) by striking the bark of the tree with a bullet.

'A common way of killing squirrels is . . . to strike with the ball the bark of the tree immediately beneath the squirrel; the concussion produced by which kills the animal instantly without mutilating it' (Audubon *Ornith. Biog.* I. 294).

1831 AUDUBON *Ornith. Biog.* I. 293 [Kentuckians] will *bark* off squirrels one after another, until satisfied with the number procured. **1840** 'UNCLE SAM' in *Bentley's Misc.* VII. 622 'What do you mean by barking a squirrel?' . . . 'I fires at the bark of the tree, jist by the squirl, so that the bark peels off, and so tarrifies the crittur, that down it comes in a kind of swoon.' **1845** *Yale Lit. Mag.* XI. 88 (Th.), [Daniel Boone] could 'bark off' squirrels with a rifle ball at any given distance. **1876** *Fur, Fin, & Feather* Sept. 167 The whole secret . . . of barking squirrels is to strike with the bullet immediately under that portion of the limb upon which the animal is stretched out. **1904** 'O. HENRY' *Heart of West* 309 Abel Wadkins used to kill squirrels that way—barkin' 'em, Abe called it.

* **Bark,** *v.*[2]

+**1.** *To bark up the wrong tree,* said of a dog which mistakes the tree in which the racoon, opossum, or other hunted animal is.

1833 *Sketches D. Crockett* 58, I told him . . . that he reminded me of the meanest thing on God's earth, an old coon dog, barking up the wrong tree. **1839** *Chemung* (N.Y.) *Democrat* 18 Sept. (Th.), The same reckless indifference which causes a puppy to bark up the wrong tree. **1855** SIMMS *Forayers* 447 Such a scout's no better than a mangy dog that barks up the wrong tree. **1866** [C. H. SMITH] *Bill Arp* 73 If my coon dog does sometimes bark up the wrong tree, he don't mean any harm by it.

+**b.** *fig.* To be mistaken in one's suspicions, ideas, or aims: to turn one's attention in a wrong direction.

1832 J. HALL *Legends of West* 46 You are barking up the wrong tree, Johnson. **1834** CROCKETT *Life* 61, I began to think I was barking up the wrong tree again. **1834** A. PIKE *Sketches* 34 [The Indians,] to use a western phrase, 'barked up the wrong tree,' when they got hold of Tom Smith. **1841** *Knickerb.* XVII. 27 He is barking up the wrong tree this time. **1853** SIMMS *Sword & Distaff* 249 You're barking up the wrong tree, Barton, if you thinks to scare me with your tongue. **1888** *Detroit Free Press* Oct. (F.), We ain't rich or pretty, but we are good, and the Professor is barking up the wrong tree. **1895** *Outing* Dec. 194/2 Whoever had even breathed the word 'wire' would soon have found he was barking up the wrong tree. **1900** H. LAWSON *Over Sliprails* 54 It gave me a lot of confidence in myself to see the law of the land barking up the wrong tree. **1904** *Baltimore American* 28 Oct. 6 The Democrats, with their usual sagacity, have barked up the wrong tree.

+**2.** Of squirrels: To utter a bark-like sound.

1857 *Rep. Comm. Patents: Agric.* 61 But, though active at this time [in cold, rainy weather] and apparently engaged in play, they [fox-squirrels] do not now 'bark,' as on warm and pleasant days. **1869** BRYANT *Among Trees* 76 And the brisk squirrel . . . barks with childish glee.

+**3.** To emit a sharp explosive sound.

1853 F. W. THOMAS *J. Randolph,* etc. 129 The Shelby [a boat] was 'barking' after us like a bloodhound from the slip. *Ib.* 132 These boats bark so you can hardly hear yourself talk. **1907** WHITE *Arizona Nights* III. xiii. 342 The Colt's forty-five barked once, and then again.

+**Bark-borer.** [BARK *n.*[1]] A species of black beetle that bores through the bark of trees. — **1857-8** *Ill. Agric. Soc. Trans.* III. 345 Another species is that sometimes called the bark borer, from its feeding exclusively upon the cambium immediately beneath the bark. **1867** *Amer. Naturalist* I. 110 Cylindrical bark borers, which are little round black weevil-like beetles, often causing 'fire-blight' in pears, etc.

+**Bark camp.** [BARK *n.*[1]] A bark hut. — **1842** *Amer. Pioneer* I. 79 Here we found an old hunter in a bark camp, 'solitary and alone.'

+**Bark canoe.** Also †**bark cannow, conoe.** [BARK *n.*[1] 3.] A canoe made of bark, esp. of the birch-tree.

1725 *Lancaster Rec.* 232 We traueld down the riuer and found a bark cannow. **1750** WALKER *Journal* 20 April, I thought it proper to cross the river and began a bark conoe. **1765** TIMBERLAKE *Mem.* 61 The bark canoes . . . are seldom used but by the northern Indians. **1765** R. ROGERS *Acc. N. America* 250 The bark-canoes, used by the Indians, seem for their curious workmanship to deserve particular notice. . . . Those made of elm are generally shorter than the others, and not so neatly constructed. **1817** S. BROWN *Western Gaz.* 253 This renders the communication impassable in summer, except with small bark canoes. **1846** M'KENNEY *Memoirs* I. iii. 62 The Indians . . . were out among the rapids, balancing their little bark canoes, with a foot upon each gunwale. **1857** HAMMOND *Northern Scenes* 172 It was tough work backin' my bark canoe over the carryin' places. **1858** WARDER *Hedges & Evergreens* 256 The Indians use it [=Canada balsam] for smearing their bark-canoes. **1869** W. MURRAY *Adventures* 205, I have boated much in bark canoe and cedar shell alike.

+**Bark chamber.** *Tanning.* (See quotation.) — **1849** *Rep. Comm. Patents* (1850) 231 The employment of the separate rising and falling bark chamber . . . for containing the bark, in combination with the main vat . . . containing the tan liquor.

+**Bark-cutter.** [BARK *n.*[1]] One occupied in cutting bark from trees. — **1847** Howe *Ohio* 28 The poor families of the bark cutters often exhibit the very picture of improvidence.

+**Bark-eater.** [BARK *n.*[1]] The yellow-bellied woodpecker, *Picus varius.* — **1862** *Ill. Agric. Soc. Trans.* V. 731 The head of . . . the true bark-eater and sap-sucker.

Barked, *ppl. a.* [BARK *v.*[1]] Stripped of bark; girdled. {1854} — **1829** COOPER *Wish-Ton-Wish* xvii, The half-reclaimed openings, with their blackened stubs and barked trees.

+**Barkeep, Bar-keep,** short for BARKEEPER.

1846 *Spirit of Times* (N.Y.) 4 July 218/2 We embarked . . . in company with . . . a *barkeep* to mix the l-q-rs. **1873** MILLER *Amongst Modocs* v. 62 A few sheaves of arrows in quivers were hung against the wall . . . at the back of the 'bar-keep.' **1883** 'MARK TWAIN' *Life on Miss.* xxii. 251 In my time they used to call the 'barkeep' Bill, or Joe, or Tom, and slap him on the shoulder. **1889** K. MUNROE *Golden Days* vii. 74 Drinks . . . were deftly compounded by the white-aproned 'bar-keeps.' **1903** C. T. BRADY *Bishop* xv. 286 We shuts down the saloons; . . . the barkeeps says they wants to go to church.

Barkeeper. Also **bar-keeper.** [BAR *n.*[1] 7.] One who serves liquors or refreshments at a bar; a bar-man. {1712, 1748}

1776 *Journals Cont. Congress* 20 Nov., To apprehend Bessonet, of Bristol, and his bar keeper. *Ib.* 27 Nov., To examine Mr. Bessonet and his bar keeper. **1803** J. DAVIS *Travels* 330 The bar-keeper brought me a note very carefully sealed. **1813** JEFFERSON *Writings* (1898) IX. 443 He is now bar-keeper to a tavern in Richmond. **1816** U. BROWN *Journal* II. 150 A good house of entertainment, the barkeeper not near as much of a gentleman as the hostler. **1839** HOFFMAN *Wild Scenes* 118 The principal hotel being in want of a bar-keeper, I was glad to fill a station. **1851** *Polly Peablossom* 182 She was assisted . . . by a lank, half-starved sucker, who officiated, in the absence of her lord, as major domo, barkeeper, and hostler. **1875** 'MARK TWAIN' *Old Times* iv. 14 The wholesale liquor-dealer's son became a barkeeper on a boat. **1898** PAGE *Red Rock* 444 The barkeeper heard him unmoved; but, when his customer left, he closed his door. **1904** *N.Y. Ev. Post* 14 Jan. 7 He went on to explain that his sister had married a barkeeper of that city.

+**Barken,** *ppl. a.* [BARK *n.*[1]] Made or consisting of bark. — **1755** T. FORBES in Gist *Journals* (1893) 148 Easter Tuesday we embarked to the number of six or 700 in about 300 Batteaus or Canoes (not barken). **1835** R. M. BIRD *Hawks of Hawk-h.* I. v. 61 Some tall and tawny hunter . . . may yet . . . urge his barken canoe over some cypress-fringed pool.

+**Barkentine.** Also †**barkenteen; barkantine, -quantine, -quentine.** [App. an alteration of older Eng. *bergantine* (16th c.), variant of *brigantine.* The history of the form between 1693 and 1852 is obscure.] A vessel somewhat resembling a bark.

1693 *Penna. Col. Rec.* I. 379 Having sailed from Barbadoes in the barkenteen Ann.

1867 SMYTH *Sailor's Word-bk.* 79 *Barkantine* or *Barquantine,* a name applied on the great lakes of North America to a vessel square-rigged on the foremast, and fore-and-aft rigged on the main and mizen masts. . . . They are long in proportion to their other dimensions. **1889** *Century Mag.* March 706/2 Office oil has been successfully used to still the waves by 82 steamers, . . . 6 barkentines, 11 brigs. **1900** *Scribner's Mag.* Sept. 286/1 She was a strange craft to our eyes; an auxiliary barkentine . . . of a little less than three hundred tons burden. **1903** *Boston Ev. Transcript* 6 Feb. 22/2 The first vessel ever built and rigged strictly a barkentine was the Leighton of 350 tons, built at Baltimore, Md. in 1852.

Barker.[1] [BARK *v.*[1]] One who removes the bark from trees or logs. {1611, 1829-}

1851 SPRINGER *Forest Life* 92 Then come the barker and loader, the men who hew off the bark from that part of the log which is to drag in the snow [etc.]. *Ib.* 94 The 'barkers' . . . are at once at work with their axes, hewing the bark [from the log]. **1860** *Harper's Mag.* March 444/2 The barker dexterously strips off the bark [from the trees]. **1874** KNIGHT 231/2 Besides the axe or hatchet, . . . the barker requires peeling-irons, which are thrust beneath the bark to loosen it.

* **Barker.**[2] [BARK *v.*[2]]

* **1.** An animal that barks. In quot. =a prairie dog.

1827 COOPER *Prairie* viii, Have you got a glimpse of any thing bigger than one of them burrowing barkers?

2. A pistol or revolver; a cannon. {1815}

1814 *Columbian Centinel* 5 Nov. 2 Travellers would do well to keep a pair of barkers in their retinue, and otherwise be prepared against highwaymen. **1842** COOPER *Wing-&-Wing* I. 75 Four more carronades, with two barkers for'ard. **1848** BURTON *Waggeries* 108 If ye've another barker convanient, we'll proceed. **1856** SIMMS *Charlemont* 364 Won't you fight? Pull out your barkers and blaze away, you small-souled scamps; I long to have a crack at you. **1859** BARTLETT 471 In flash language a pistol is 'a barker.' **1878** BEADLE *Western Wilds* 41 More'n once the robbers would tackle some gritty man that was handy with his 'barkers.' **1879**

BURDETTE *Hawkeyes* 121 Fearing he might ask to look at my revolver, I casually remarked that I never carried my barkers when I came East. **1886** DORSEY *Midshipman Bob* II. i. 101 The glittering brass 'barkers' ran swiftly after, impelled by dozens of sturdy arms.

3. One who makes announcements in a loud voice, esp. in order to advertise or to draw custom. {1822, 1855}

1897 HOWELLS *Landlord at Lion's Head* 247 The barker began to fill the night with hoarse cries of 'Miss Lynde's carriage; carriage for Miss Lynde!' **1902** LORIMER *Lett. Merchant* xii. 166 Munsterberg wasn't one of your common, coarse, county-fair barkers. **1910** WALCOTT *Open Door* xii. 151 Groups of men gathered about the doors before which loud-voiced 'barkers' set forth the attractions of cheap theaters.

+**Barkery.** [BARK *n.*[1]] =BARK-HOUSE a. — **1843** 'CARLTON' *New Purchase* I. xvi. 121 Such then was our barkery, our bark, and our bark grinder.

Barkey, Barky. [BARK *n.*[2]] A small barque. {1847, 1867} — **1838** COOPER *Homeward B.* v, Did you observe how the old barky jumped out of the way of those rovers in the cutter? **1839** BRIGGS *H. Franco* I. xvi. 155 She was a smaller ship, . . . but the old sailor . . . observed that she was a 'good wholesome lump of a barkey.' **1839** *Knickerb.* XIII. 39 The breeze is so fresh, and the sea so high, that the barky rolls and pitches *beautiful.*

***Bark house.** [BARK *n.*[1]] **a.** A building in which tan-bark is stored or prepared; a tan-house. +**b.** A house made of bark.

1660 *Boston Rec.* 155 Henry Bridgam . . . sett part of his barke house upon part of the townes land. **1669** *R.I. Col. Rec.* II. 272 Hee knew they were formerly his Indians, and had skill to bark cedar trees and to make bark houses. **1721** *Boston Selectmen* 83 Liberty [is] granted to Mr. Edward Procter to erect a bark house near Snow Hill. **1775** *Mass. H. Soc. Coll.* 2 Ser. II. 282 We found a good bark-house with one man in it. **1824** *Rouse's Point Harbinger* 17 Feb. 4/2 (Th. S.), A bark-house, and a good iron bark-mill. **1843** 'CARLTON' *New Purchase* I. xvi. 115 Our bark-house was of the Grecian architecture in its infancy. . . . Under this shelter was our store of bark. **1847** LANMAN *Summer in Wilderness* 89 The grove-city . . . consisted of seventy-six bark houses like those I have described.

+**Bark hut.** [BARK *n.*[1]] A hut built of the bark of trees.

[**1674** *S.C. Hist. Soc. Coll.* V. 457 The Indians being diligent in makeing two barke covered hutts, to shelter us from the injury of the weather.] **1744** F. MOORE *Voy. Georgia* 123 Here they met with some bark-huts, which our friendly Indians had some time since built for their lodging when they hunted there. **1807** IRVING, etc. *Salmagundi* xii. 266 This spot was inhabited by a race of aborigines, who dwelt in bark huts, . . . [and] danced buffalo dances. **1837** PECK *New Guide* 160 Some [Indians in Indian Territory] . . . live in bark huts, and are wretched. **1847** HOWE *Ohio* 492 They fell to work . . . erecting bark huts and log shanties. **1881** *Rep. Indian Affairs* 40 Their descendants live, not in bark huts, or skin 'tipi,' but in comfortable log houses.

***Barking,** *vbl. n.*[1] [BARK *v.*[1]]

***1.** The stripping of bark from trees. Also attrib. with *irons.*

Other attrib. uses, as *barking ax, bill, mallet, tools* are recorded by Knight and in the Cent. Dict.

1666 *Plymouth Rec.* 85 It was ordered . . . that . . . no . . . timber be spoyled by barkeing. **1790** *Penna. Packet* 1 May 1/1 The tanners of Philadelphia . . . request . . . the farmers to preserve such timber until the season for barking arrives. **1845** JUDD *Margaret* I. iii. 12 Here were a draw-shave, a crosscut saw, . . . barking irons, a scythe. **1889** FARMER 38 By *barking* (the phrase now mainly applies to the past) the settler facilitated the process of clearing the land of the primeval forest.

2. (See quotation and BARK *v.*[1] 3.)

1876 *Fur, Fin, & Feather* Sept. 167 Barking is an original method of killing squirrels pursued as a pastime . . . where these animals are numerous.

Barking, *vbl. n.*[2] [BARK *v.*[2]] +*Barking exercise(s)*: see quotations. — [**1807** R. M'NEMAR *Ky. Revival* 69 About the latter end of the year 1804, there were regular societies of these people in the state of Ohio, . . . praying, shouting, jerking, barking, or rolling.] **1834** *Biblical Repertory* VI. 350 A lady from Tennessee, who brought into a certain part of Virginia the barking exercise, immediately was imitated by certain of those affected with the jerks. *c***1843** B. W. STONE in Rogers *Biog.* (1847) 40 The barking exercise, (as opposers contemptuously called it,) was nothing but the jerks. **1847** COLLINS *Kentucky* 109 Those extraordinary and disgraceful scenes [of 1799] produced by the *jerks*, the *rolling* and the *barking exercises*, &c., which extensively obtained among some . . . persuasions of those days.

***Barking,** *ppl. a.* [BARK *v.*[2]] +*Barking iron*, a pistol {1847}. *Barking pup*, id. *Barking squirrel*, the prairie dog. *Barking wolf*, the coyote.

1825 [PAULDING] *John Bull in America* iv. 37 Seeing the barking iron, [he] shrunk back. — **1856** SIMMS *Charlemont* 443 He . . . amused himself by putting his two 'barking-pups' in order. — **1806** LEWIS in *L. & Clark Exped.* V. 177 The barking squirrel . . . [has] a false jaw or pocket between the skin and the mustle of the jaw. **1811–4** BRACKENRIDGE *Journal* 239 In the course of my ramble, I happened on a village of barking squirrels, or prairie dogs, as they have been called. — **1826** GODMAN *Nat. Hist.* I. 260 The Prairie or Barking Wolf, *Canis Latrans*, . . . frequents the prairies . . . of the west, where troops or packs . . . are frequently seen. **1867** *Amer. Naturalist* I. 289 The Prairie or Barking Wolf (*Canis latrans* Say) is by far the most abundant carnivorous animal . . . in almost every part of the West.

+**Bark lodge.** [BARK *n.*[1]] A lodge or hut constructed of the bark of trees. — **1846** M'KENNEY *Memoirs* I. iii. 67 To exchange the polish of courts of Europe for a bark lodge on Drummond's Island. **1873** HOWELLS *Chance Acquaintance* 130, I can only think of Eriecreek as an assemblage of huts and bark-lodges in contrast. *Ib.* 231 Mrs. Ellison . . . remained in the shadow of the bark-lodge.

Bark log. [BARK *n.*[1]] An undressed log. — **1674** *S. C. Hist. Soc. Coll.* V. 461 Wee our selfes carrying our trade upon barke logs swam over Ædistaw River.

+**Bark louse.** [BARK *n.*[1]] Any aphid that infests the bark of trees.

1841 HARRIS in Johnson *Farm Encycl.* (1868) 137/2 Early in the spring the bark lice are found apparently torpid, . . . sticking . . . closely to the bark. **1849** *Rep. Comm. Patents: Agric.* (1850) 438 The bark-louse is found on most Eastern trees. **1852** *Mich. Agric. Soc. Trans.* III. 199 [For] bark lice and caterpillar; wash them [=apple trees] with lye. **1862** *Rep. Comm. Patents: Agric.* 250 Bark lice attack the pear as well as the apple trees, . . . but the pear is also subject to another kind of bark louse. **1868** *Ill. Agric. Soc. Trans.* VII. 557 The apple tree bark louse has ceased to exist with us. **1884** *Rep. Comm. Agric.* 352 The ordinary food-plant of this species of bark-louse is the soft or silver maple.

+**Bark mill.** [BARK *n.*[1]] A mill for grinding bark, esp. for use by tanners and dyers.

1749 ELIOT *Field-Husb.* ii. 30 Take your Clover Hay to a Tanners Bark-mill, where they use a stone Wheel, grind it. **1819** *Plough Boy* I. 8 Constantly on hand, Potash Kettles . . . ; Bark Mills, of late improvement. **1832** KENNEDY *Swallow Barn* I. xxi. 209 He works hard when at his task; and goes at it with the reluctance of an old horse in a bark-mill. **1835** J. TODD *Student's Manual* 271 Walking is good, but not—if you must walk in a bark-mill. **1849** *Rep. Comm. Patents* (1850) 366 Having thus described the construction and operation of our bark mill, what we claim [etc.]. **1862** *Rep. Comm. Patents: Agric.* 308 The granulating mill is simple, like a bark-mill or corn-crusher. **1885** *Harper's Mag.* Jan. 276/1 Most tanners buy bark . . . and grind it in a bark mill, 'leaching' the bark to obtain the liquor.

+**Bark nutmeg.** [BARK *n.*[1]] An artificial 'wooden nutmeg.' — **1837** *S. Lit. Messenger* III. 414 We of the south are mistaken in the character of these people, when we think of them only as peddlers in horn flints and bark nutmegs.

Bark-peeler. [BARK *n.*[1]] One engaged in peeling bark for tanning. — **1862** *Rep. Comm. Patents: Agric.* 414 Tanneries sprang into existence along the streams, and the bark-peelers and teamsters engaged in this employment . . . made the whole region one of active and prosperous industry.

+**Bark-peeling.** [BARK *n.*[1]] A place where bark has been peeled from the trees. — **1876** BURROUGHS *Winter Sunshine* iii. 77 The red squirrel . . . is most abundant in old bark-peelings.

+**Bark shanty.** [BARK *n.*[1]] One constructed of bark. — **1840** *Knickerb.* XVI. 163 Bob Mosely's house was a tolerably large bark shanty, with a clap-board roof. **1840** HOFFMAN *Greyslaer* I. v. 61, I came, about night-fall, to a bark shanty, where some hunter had made a pretty good camp for the night, and left it standing.

+**Bark silk.** [BARK *n.*[1]] A fine fibre obtained from bark. — **1813** *Niles' Reg.* V. Suppl. 176/1 He showed me a fishing net made of bark silk.

+**Barkstone.** [BARK *n.*[1]] (See quotations.) — **1799** J. SMITH *Acc. Captivity* 38, I asked [him], what was the use of the beaver's stones, or glands, to them;—as the she beaver has two pair, which is commonly called the oil stones, and the bark stones? **1805** LEWIS in *L. & Clark Exped.* (1904) III. 319 The male beaver has six stones, two of which . . . are called the bark stones or castors. **1889** *Cent.*, *Barkstone*, the concrete musky secretion taken from the castor-glands of the beaver; castor; castoreum.

Bark tub. [BARK *n.*[1]] A tanner's vat. — **1662** *Essex Inst. Coll.* XLII. 133 It[em] in drest hempe. It[em] barke tubs.

Bark-wheel. [BARK *n.*[1]] A wheel for grinding bark. — **1843** 'CARLTON' *New Purchase* I. xviii. 149 A man who has already discovered two efficacious ways to make Christians—our bark-wheel, and now our boots!

Bar lead. [BAR *n.*[1]] Lead melted into the form of bars.

1714 *Boston News-Letter* 26 April 2/2 Four tunns of barr lead, five tunn of Sweeds iron. **1746** *Md. Hist. Mag.* XXI. 381, 2 hundred of barr lead; 2 hundred of sheet lead. **1761** *Essex Inst. Coll.* XLVIII. 95 The assortments are as follows, viz.:—gun powder; all sizes shot; bar lead [etc.]. **1768** J. ROWE *Diary* 154 Voted . . . that we will not for one year send for any European commodities excepting . . . bar lead [etc.]. **1819** SCHOOLCRAFT *Mo. Lead Mines* 43 The exports of Missouri Territory may be set down as follows: Pig and Bar Lead, . . . Flour, . . . Tow Cloth [etc.]. **1885** BROCKETT *Our Country's Progress* 466 Pig, bar, and sheet lead imported . . . [in] 1870, 58,310,464 lbs.

***BARLEY.** Also †**barly, -lie.**

***1.** The grain so named or the plant producing this.

1619 *Va. House of Burgesses* 17 Sending . . . greate store of all sortes of the best graine, as wheate, Barlie, Oates, and pease of all the best kindes. **1624** *Ib.* 28 They fell into extreame want, not havinge anything left to sustein them save a little ill conditioned Barley. *a***1649** WINTHROP

Hist. I. 90 This week [in Aug. 1632] they had in barley and oats, at Sagus, above twenty acres good corn, and sown with the plough. **1649** *Descr. Virginia* 14 We have many thousand of acres of cleer land, . . . and we sowe excellent Wheat, Barley, Rye. **1654** JOHNSON *Wonder-W. Prov.* 84 The want of English graine, Wheate, Barly and Rie proved a sore affliction to some stomacks. **1687** SEWALL *Letter-Book* I. 52 Much hurt has been done here this summer by a sort of worm. Much barly the ear eatt of. **1705** BEVERLEY *Virginia* IV. 57 Their richer sort generally brew their small-beer with malt, which they have from England, though they have as good barley of their own as any in the world. **1748** ELIOT *Field-Husb.* i. 14 Summer Wheat sowed with Barley is not apt to blast. **1781–2** JEFFERSON *Notes Va.* (1788) 40 Besides these plants, which are native, our farms produce wheat, rye, barley, . . . and Indian corn. **1831** PECK *Guide* 158 Barley is raised in St. Clair County for the St. Louis breweries. **1847** DARLINGTON *Weeds & Plants* (1860) 393, I understand that in Western New-York—the great Barley region of this country—it is usually called Six-rowed Barley. **1881** *Rep. Indian Affairs* 6 The Indians of this reservation have raised this season a good crop of wheat and barley.

2. Attrib. or comb. with **cake, candy, crusher,* **malt, mill, seeding* (=sowing), *stick* (=barley-candy), *straw* {*a*1721–}.

1850 *New Eng. Farmer* II. 374 In Pennsylvania, Western New York, and Ohio, . . . the farmers use only a limited quantity of their own wheat, and grow fat and hearty on rye and buckwheat and barley cakes. **1857** *Lawrence* (Kansas) *Republican* 6 Aug. 1 He'd rather have that one small barleycake you hold within your hand. — **1844** EMERSON *Lect., Young American,* One man buys . . . a land title . . . and makes his posterity princes; . . . and the other buys barley candy. **1883** HALE in *Harper's Mag.* Jan. 277/1 In it were . . . barley-candy statuettes, jumping-jacks, and other . . . toys. — **1885** *Rep. Indian Affairs* 145 The engine could be made useful if we had a good grist-mill and barley-crusher. — **1651** *Mass. H. S. Coll.* 4 Ser. VI. 362, I have putt aboard . . . sixe bushels of barly mault, sixe bushels of Indian mault, & one bushel of oatemeale. **1677** WINTHROP in *Phil. Trans.* XII. 1068 The Barly-Malt-Masters have used all their skill to make good Malt hereof the ordinary way; but cannot effect it. **1682** *Braintree Rec.* 22 To be payd . . . in current pay at . . . prises following, wheat 4s., rye 3s., barley mailte 3s. — **1881** *Harper's Mag.* Jan. 188/1 An old barley-mill . . . stood at the ford where Elizabeth Shipley crossed the stream. — **1786** WASHINGTON *Diaries* III. 40 The ground, in which the Barley seeding had commenced, has been plowed. — **1749** HEMPSTEAD *Diary* 538 At the cornfield . . . fencing Barley Stacks. — **1882** 'M. HARLAND' *Eve's Daughters* 112 We had lollypops and barley-sticks, and clear lemon-bars. — **1794** *N.Y. State Soc. Arts* I. 145 Barley-straw is hearty fodder for horned cattle in the winter. **1868** G. BRACKETT *Farm Talk* 129 Barley and wheat straw is only fit for bedding.

+**Barley-brand.** A species of blight affecting barley. — **1849** EMMONS *Agric. N.Y.* II. 131 Another diseased growth resembles the smut . . . and is called barley brand (*Uredo hordei*).

* **Barleycorn.**

***1.** A grain of barley. Also as a measure, one third of an inch.

1732 FRANKLIN *Poor Richard 1733* 4 All Measures of Longitude are deduced from Barley-corns. **1756** *Lett. to Washington* I. 364 Barley corn Beads black & white from 2/8 to 3/ per bunch. **1790** S. DEANE *New Eng. Farmer* 16/2 A few of the worst of the barley corns will be on the surface of the water. **1816** *News-clipping* in *Pettigrew P.* (N.C. Univ.), A small black mulatto man about 30 years old 5 feet 4 inches & a barley corn high. **1871** [L. H. BAGG] *At Yale* 267 'The shortest' [of the Freshmen] is then announced by name as president, and his 'hight' is mentioned in some absurd way as being so many 'barleycorns.'

+**2.** A particle; a whit.

1803 *Ann. 8th Congress* 1 Sess. 611 This is but the saving of a barleycorn, and ought not to be regarded. **1882** STOCKTON in *Century Mag.* III. 83/2 This man, who, every barleycorn a king, knew no tradition to which he owed . . . allegiance.

Barley earish. [Cf. E. *barley edish* (1669), *wheat ersh* (1597).] ? A field of barley stubble. — **1702** SEWALL *Diary* II. 62 Our dear sister . . . is the first buryed in this new burying place, a barley-earish, pure sand.

+**Barley grass.** The meadow barley, *Hordeum pratense* (*H. pusillum*). — **1795** WINTERBOTHAM *Hist. View* III. 401 Those which are found most common are the following: . . . Brome grass; . . . Lime grass; . . . Barley grass, *Hordeum pratense.* **1878** KILLEBREW *Tennessee Grasses* 196 Barley Grass, *Hordeum pusillum,* . . . looks very much like barley, and is much relished by cattle.

+**Barlow.** Short for 'Barlow knife.' — **1884** SWEET & KNOX *Through Texas* xxxiv. 463 By the sale of a damaged barlow . . . and a tailless kite, I became the possessor of twenty-five cents. **1890** *Congress. Rec.* 19 Aug. 8812/2 He did not want to carry a cheap and nasty knife, but the little fellow has to carry a 10 cent barlow. **1897** W. E. BARTON *Trouble at Roundstone* 83 [He] stood whittling the toprail with his Barlow when Eph rode up.

+**Barlow knife** (†**penknife**). [Name of the original maker.] A well-known make of pocket-knife in various sizes, having a single blade.

1779 *New Jersey Journal* 12 Oct., To be sold by Stephenson and Canfield, In Morris Town, . . . Barlow penknives, knives and forks. **1819** *Mass. Spy* 29 Dec. (Th.), A barlow knife, bloody, and another knife, rusty, lay along side of him. **1830** J. F. WATSON *Philadelphia* 201 The buck-handled Barlow penknives, . . . a source of great gratification to the boys. **1837** A. WETMORE *Gaz. Missouri* 311 Will you trade a little dried buffalo for a good Barlow knife? **1845** JUDD *Margaret* I. vi. 36 On the left were cuttoes, Barlow knives, iron candlesticks. *c***1865** G. W. BAGBY *Old Va. Gent.* etc. (1911) 49 Warts, which . . . he delights in trimming with a Barlow-knife, obtained by dint of hard swapping. **1876** 'MARK TWAIN' *Tom Sawyer* iv. 43 Mary gave him a brand-new 'Barlow' knife. **1896** HARRIS *Sister Jane* 229 On the side of the pew, were the letters W. W., which . . . I had carved with my barlow knife. **1906** *Washington Post* 28 May 1 In a duel . . . in which Sid Hoskins had a pitchfork and . . . Mc-Adams had a barlow knife.

+**Barlow pocket-knife.** =prec. — **1873** HOLLAND *A. Bonnicastle* iii, Before her, on the table, were a Barlow pocket-knife, a boy's playing-ball [etc.].

Bar-maid, Barmaid. [BAR *n.*[1] 7.] A female who serves food and drink at the bar of a tavern, hotel, etc. {1772–}

1784 A. ELLICOTT *Life & Lett.* 27 He has but three [beds], one occupied by himself and wife, one by the small children and the other by the bar-maid. **1825** NEAL *Bro. Jonathan* II. 290 It would be easier to destroy a woman of genius . . . than a bar-maid or a chamber-maid, so called. **1850** MITCHELL *Lorgnette* ii. 29 He boldly tips the wink to the bar-maid. **1858** VIELÉ *Following Drum* 94 Her pretty little granddaughter . . . who was receiving an education to fit her for the responsible situation of bar-maid to this 'Hotel Texan.' [**1895** *N.Y. Dramatic News* 19 Oct. 13/3 Billie Barlow introduced two new songs last week at the Pleasure Palace [N.Y.], 'Dorothy Dean' and 'The Barmaid.' The latter is hardly appreciated here, where the type is unknown.]

+**Bar-mining.** *W.* [BAR *n.*[1] 9.] 'The mining of river bars, usually between low and high waters, although the stream is sometimes deflected and the bar worked below water level' (Fay *Gloss. Mining Industry*). — **1871** RAYMOND *Mines* 199 It is not practical to carry on bar-mining in the Snake while the stream is high.

* **BARN.**

***1.** A covered building for the storage of grain or other farm produce, and often for stabling horses, cows, etc.

'The barns had a peculiar kind of construction: . . . in the middle was the threshing floor, and . . . in the loft or garret they put the corn . . . , the straw, or any thing else, according to the season: on one side were stables for the horses, and on the other for the cows' (1770 Forster tr. *Kalm's Travels* I. 223). 'In the northern states of America, the farmers generally use barns for stabling their horses and cattle; so that among them, a barn is both a cornhouse or grange, and a stable' (Webster, 1828). Cf. CATTLE-, COW-, HORSE-BARN.

In quot. 1668 applied to an underground place of storage.

1638 *Plymouth Laws* 59 If any shall be found or seene taking tobaccoe in the streets . . . or in any barne or outhouse. **1643** *Springfield Rec.* I. 173 It is ordered . . . that ther shall no Barnes . . . be set up or built in the high way. **1668** *East-Hampton Rec.* I. 302 The Indians that live att Montaukut shall fill up all their old barnes, and for the new ones they shall secure them from danger of cattill, or horses. **1710** *Boston Rec.* 68 He desires to build a Barn with wood, of twenty foot in front & forty foot backward . . . which will very much accomodate the s[ai]d Street. **1775** FITHIAN *Journal* II. 121 We held sermon in Mr. Fowley's barn. A rainy stormy day. **1828** A. ROYALL *Black Book* II. 71 Every farmer has his small wooden barn, under which name they include stables. **1835** HOFFMAN *Winter in West* I. 17 The barns into which their harvests are gathered are so spaciously and solidly built, that they want only architectural design to rival in appearance the most ambitious private mansions. **1877** *Rep. Indian Affairs* 60 There have been erected during the past summer a new barn, 22 by 400 feet, which the Indians are now filling with hay [etc.]. **1898** WESTCOTT *D. Harum* 295 If I was to go up to the barn all alone by myself an' look at the hoss. **1906** *Springfield W. Republican* 26 July 16 Thieves entered the barn . . . soon after midnight and stole a chestnut mare. **1907** C. C. ANDREWS *Recoll.* 144 At Maine Prairie I remember the meeting was in a barn.

phrases. **1854** 'O. OPTIC' *In Doors & Out* (1876) 317 Between you and I and the barn, as we say out west, I am no friend of such folks as these over here. **1901** M. D. BABCOCK *Thoughts* 17 Locking a barn seems no longer commonplace when the horse is stolen.

+**2.** A large shed or building for housing street cars.

1882 *Chicago Tribune,* In case the street car conductors get up another strike, you had better . . . head for the car barns. **1903** *N.Y. Tribune* 13 Sept., The signal to go ahead was given and the car shot into the barn.

3. Attrib.: **a.** With *bay, beam, dung, fodder, lantern,* etc.

1896 WILKINS *Madelon* 59 The mare, when she was saddled, danced an iron-bound dance in the barn bay. — **1824** *N.H. Hist. Soc. Coll.* 247 A piece of timber (apparently a part of a barn beam) . . . was carried . . . up the same hill. — **1879** B. F. TAYLOR *Summer-Savory* ii. 18 Like two little bundles of oats thrust in the elbows of a couple of barn-braces. — **1804** J. ROBERTS *Penna. Farmer* 204 Horses . . . when fed upon turnips are induced to eat the barn chaff, and other dry food. — **1802** *Mass. H. S. Coll.* 2 Ser. III. 3 The Indians use little barn dung; but about their hovels and stacks their land grows better. — **1821** *Ib.* IX. 145 Cows, in this way, may be supported through the winter at considerably less expense . . . than they can, when supplied wholly with barn fodder. — **1775** *Essex Inst. Coll.* XIII. 186, 1 Barn Lanthorn. — **1838** H. COLMAN *Mass. Agric. Rep.* (1839) 35 Drew on thirty loads short barn manure; principally the manure of sheep. — **1874** B. F. TAYLOR *World on Wheels*

II. viii. 252 The eaves, the chimneys and the peak of the barn-rafters should be full of the twitter of swallows. — **1859** A. CARY *Country Life* i. 8 Corncobs had been thrown at the daring roosters that ventured out from beneath the barn-sill.

b. In sense: That frequents or lives in a barn.

1855 *Knickerb.* XLVI. 224 The curlews (which species of snipe are larger than barn-pigeons). **1865** *Atlantic Mo.* XV. 527 A squirrel or bird or an unsuspecting barn-fowl. **1915** G. M. WHITE *Rose o' Paradise* 168 Jinnie spied a lean barn-cat, crossing the road.

+**Barnacle-back.** *slang.* [f. the *barnacle* which attaches itself to ships.] A sailor or marine. — **1846** *Spirit of Times* 6 June 177/1 The monotony of this place has been relieved . . . by the drilling of 'Uncle Samuel's' 'web feet,' or 'barnacle backs' that came here from the squadron. **1890** *Congress. Rec.* 21 April 3637/1 This old 'barnacle back' was as surly a growler as ever went aloft.

+**Barn-ball.** (See quot. 1879.)

1850 *Knickerb.* XXXV. 84 As we . . . never indulged in a game of chance . . . save the 'base-ball' . . . and 'barn-ball' of our boyhood. **1879** B. F. TAYLOR *Summer-Savory* xv. 122 The writer knew a boy who . . . never got farther than 'barn-ball,' which means throwing a ball at the gable and catching it when it returns. **1901** CHURCHILL *Crisis* 196 On a vacant lot near the station, a tall man . . . was playing barn-ball with some boys.

+**Barn-burner.** *colloq.* A member of the more progressive section of the Democratic party. Also attrib. Now *Hist.*

With allusion to the burning of well-stored barns that characterized the Dorr Rebellion, 1842. According to Thurlow Weed (letter to G. W. Curtis, 16 Dec. 1873) the title 'Barn-burners' was transferred by the 'Old Hunkers' to the progressive faction of the Democrats, and about 1843 accepted for the party by Col. Samuel Young: see *Autobiography of Weed*, p. 534. In popular belief, however, the name refers 'to the story of an old Dutchman who relieved himself of rats by burning down his barns which they infested' (*N.Y. Tribune* in B. '48).

1845 *Congress. Globe* 30 Dec. 117 The Whig party were no church-burners nor 'barn-burners' (a name which a certain portion of the Democratic party had delighted in taking to themselves). **1849** *Knickerb.* XXXIII. 302 My friend and I were thorough barn-burners, and specimens of this race being scarce in the heart of a slave-holding state, we were lionized. **1853** *Harper's Mag.* VIII. 125/1 To speak now of political corruption, or to denounce political corruption, is no evidence that a man is a Whig or a Democrat, a Hunker or a Barnburner, a Conservative or a Radical. **1863** B. TAYLOR *H. Thurston* iii. 42, I'm a Barnburner, . . . and since the split it seems like new parties, though we hold on to the old principles. **1876** *Congress. Rec.* 13 Jan. 404/1 The 'barn-burner democrats' in 1853 tried very hard to adhere to their anti-slavery principles in New York and still support the Pierce administration. **1886** B. P. POORE *Reminisc.* I. 347 The Massachusetts Abolitionists . . . with the Barnburner wing of the Democratic party in New York.

+**Barnburning,** *ppl. a.* [See prec.] Pertaining to or consisting of the radical reform Democrats. — **c1848** *N.Y. Tribune* (B.), They have gone into such depths of Barnburning Radicalism, that a large portion of the rank and file are determined not to follow. **1848** *Congress. Globe* App. 7 Aug. 1111/2 These Locofocos of the North have yielded everything, until now the Barnburning portion are in open revolt.

+**Barn-chamber.** =BARN-LOFT. — **1838** COLMAN *Mass. Agric. Rep.* 16 The best method of curing it [herds grass] . . . is to . . . tie it in bundles; and set it upright in a barn chamber. **1865** MRS. WHITNEY *Gayworthys* vi. 68 She had heard the whish of every truss of hay that he had thrust in . . . at the barn-chamber window. **1871** STOWE *Sam Lawson* 28 That afternoon beheld Sam arranged at full length on a pile of top-tow in the barn-chamber.

+**Barn-dance. a.** A dance of the nature of a schottische. **b.** A dance held in a barn. — **1895** L. Grove *Dancing* 424 'Barn dance' is an American designation; but as many other dances take place in barns out West, it is difficult to see why the title is specially applied to this Scotch lilt and schottische hops. **1900** C. C. MUNN *Uncle Terry* 19 The husking-bees, barn dances, or church sociables. *Ib.* 20 If it was a barn dance she was always there and never lacked partners.

***Barn-door.** The door of a barn. Also attrib., esp. with *fowl* {*c*1685-}.

1634 WOOD *New Eng. Prospect* II. xix. 95 Our hogges having found a way to unhindge their [*sc.* Indians'] barne doores, and robbe their garners. **1674** *Jamaica* (L.I.) *Rec.* I. 89 John Skidmore is . . . allsoe to make and hang a paire of barne doores to the barne. **1781** PETERS *Hist. Conn.* (1829) 193 All kinds of barn-door poultry. **1837** *S. Lit. Messenger* III. 588 A pot of boiling water in which she intended to scald a couple of barn-door fowls. **1847** LONGFELLOW *Evangeline* I. ii. 50 Heavily closed, with a jarring sound, the valves of the barn-doors. **1857-8** *Ill. Agric. Soc. Trans.* III. 540 Barn-door fowls are generally considered the best. **1882** PECK *Sunshine* 13 Mr. Crossman . . . saw the neighboring lady come out of the barn door head first.

b. *attrib.* as *adj.* Wide.

1865 MRS. WHITNEY *Gayworthys* xxvi. 256 Skirts were trodden on, and came out at the gathers; and there was more than one 'barn-door' rent. **1884** CABLE *Dr. Sevier* xxxix. (1885) 297 His high waisted, barn-door trowsers.

+**Barnegat.** *attrib.* Denoting a make of sneakboat orig. used in Barnegat Bay, N.J. — **1879** BISHOP *4 Months in Sneak-box* vi, One of the smallest and most comfortable of boats—a purely American model, developed by the bay-men of the New Jersey coast of the United States, and recently introduced to the gunning fraternity as the Barnegat Sneak-Box. **1889** *Scientific American* 6 April 219/1 The usual length of a Barnegat sneakboat is 12 feet. **1903** *Forest & Stream* 21 Feb. ix/4 For sale: . . . One bushwhack boat with curtains; one Barnegat sneakboat, 15 ft.

+**Bar netting.** [BAR *n.*[3]] Netting to keep off mosquitoes. — **1847** LANMAN *Summer in Wilderness* 143 As to musketoes, had I not taken with me a quantity of bar netting, . . . the creatures would have eaten me.

Barney, *n.* +(See quotations.) — (1) **1851** HALL *College Words* 15 *Barney.* At Harvard College, about the year 1810, this word was used to designate a bad recitation. (2) **1881** RAYMOND *Mining Gloss.*, *Barney*, a small car attached to a rope and used to push cars up a slope or inclined plane. **1889** *Cent.*, *Barney-pit*, in the anthracite mines of Pennsylvania, a pit at the bottom of a slope or plane into which the barney runs in order to allow the mine-car to run in over it to the foot of the plane.

+**Barney,** *v.* 'At Harvard College, about the year 1810, . . . to *barney* was to recite badly' (Hall *College Words*, 1851).

Barn-floor. The floor of a barn. {1611-} Also attrib.

1800 BROWN *A. Mervyn* xxv, Though a man, I . . . prefer knitting yarn to threshing . . . the barn-floor with a flail. **1840** THOMPSON *Green Mt. Boys* I. xi. 122 They unceremoniously tumbled him on a pile of hay on the barn floor. **1853** FOWLER *Home for All* 176 By arranging the floor on which the stock stand a foot or two below the barn floor, the cattle can feed off the barn floor. **1862** *Rep. Comm. Patents: Agric.* 134 There is scarcely a farm in New England that has not waste barn-floor room in which to winter forty or fifty sheep. **1872** *Vermont Bd. Agric. Rep.* I. 312 If an animal is ailing either from accident or ill treatment, the barn floor is the general hospital. **1887** TOURGEE *Button's Inn* 178 He . . . settled down to the work of husking corn upon the barn-floor.

+**Barn-grass.** The barn-yard grass (q.v.). — **1821** *Mass. H. S. Coll.* 2 Ser. IX. 153 Plants, which are indigenous in the township of Middlebury, [Vermont, include] . . . Dwarf groundnut. . . . Barn grass. **1832** WILLIAMSON *Maine* I. 132 Grasses.—Barn; Blue-eyed; Chess; [etc.]. **1836** LINCOLN *Botany* App. 122 *Panicum* . . . *crus-galli* (barn-grass, Au.); racemes alternate and in pairs. **1894** COULTER *Bot. W. Texas* III. 502 Barn-grass, Cock's foot, . . . [is] apparently native to the Southern States.

+**Barn-hill.** *attrib.* =Barn-door; barn-yard. — **1843** 'CARLTON' *New Purchase* I. xvi. 121 And this, after carrying barn-hill fowls a dozen at a time tied by the legs and dangling against his sides!

***Barnish,** *v. Obs.* [ME. (once); also in E. dialect {1839-}.] *intr.* To grow stout or plump. — **1649** *New Haven Col. Rec.* I. 478 Goodwife Charles wished ther was no more in the towne in Rebecka Turners case, for ther was a maide that satt neere her at meeting that did barnish apace; but she named nobody.

Barn-loft. The loft of a barn. {1837-} — **1743** MACSPARRAN *Diary* 12 The negro's put the wheat straw in the barn loft. **1873** BEADLE *Undevel. West* 75 The girl-matron 'reckoned . . . I could sleep in the barn-loft with brother Perry.'

+**Barn lot.** A lot of ground (for) containing a barn.

1724 *N.H. Probate Rec.* II. 250, I give to my Daughters . . . the other half part of my afores[aid] barn Lott in Salsbury. **1784** *Cambridge Prop. Rec.* 374 The line between Judge Trowbridge's house lot, & . . . Whittemore's Barn lot. **1867** CRAWFORD *Mosby* 78 His men . . . were feeding their horses in the barn-lot of a farm. **1879** TOURGEE *Fool's Errand* xxix. 179 You just . . . see that things is goin' right round the house and barn lot. **1906** F. LYNDE *Quickening* 19 The tree right back of Jim Stone's barn lot.

Barn-man. A laborer in a barn. {*c*1800-} — **1898** WESTCOTT *D. Harum* 9, I ast the barn man if he knowed who they was.

Barn-owl. {1674-} +The American species of owl (*Strix* or *Aluco pratincola*) related to the barn-owl of Europe.

Cf. AMERICAN BARN-OWL.

1812 WILSON *Ornithology* VI. 57 White, or Barn Owl, *Strix flammea*, . . . is said to make a blowing noise resembling the snoring of a man. **1858** BAIRD *Birds Pacific R.R.* 47 The Barn Owl, *Strix pratincola*, . . . [is found] throughout temperate North America. **1881** *Amer. Naturalist* XV. 210 The barn owl, while it remained in these thickets during the day, resorted more commonly to the bottom lands to breed. **1902** *Harper's Mag.* Feb. 489/1 The quail . . . must hide and keep very still when Strix, the barn-owl, comes about at night-time.

Barn-pass. A passage-way to a barn. — **1775** *Bristol* (Va.) *Vestry Bk.* 250 The shed to the stable & reperation of the barn pass.

Barn-plat, -plot. =BARN-LOT. — **1684** *Waterbury Prop. Rec.* 209 The land granted to Smith for a barn plat. **1676** *Hartford Land Distrib.* 543 All that land from the Corner of his Barn plott to the little riuer.

+**Barn-preacher.** [BARN *n.*] One who preaches in barns. — **1806** FESSENDEN *Democracy Unveiled* II. 173 We always possessed a violent antipathy to your bawling, itinerant, field and barn preachers.

+**Barn-raising.** The erection of the frame of a barn with the help of neighbors; a social gathering on this occasion. — **1856** T. D. PRICE *MS. Diary* 28 April, Went to D. D. Keller's barn raising. **1872** EGGLESTON *End of World* vi. 51, I never went to a corn-shucking, to a barn-raising, nor indeed to any of our rustic feasts.

Barn-roof. a. The roof of a barn. **b.** (See quot. 1889.) — **1889** *Century Mag.* Feb. 570 It is commonly known among factory people as a 'barn-roof,' consisting of an ordinary pitched roof made of rafters set eighteen inches or two feet apart on centers. **1896** WILKINS *Madelon* 22 He's hurt his arm. . . . He was clearing the snow off the barn roof and the ladder fell. **1909** 'O. HENRY' *Roads of Destiny* 308 Then I heard a sound like somebody ripping a clapboard off of a barn-roof.

Barn-room. Room or accommodation in a barn. — **1639** in T. Lechford *Note-Book* 66 Item, that the said William Coddington shall have barn roome for his corn there planted or sowen. **1741** *N.H. Probate Rec.* III. 43, I . . . bequeath unto my loving wife . . . the best Cow . . . & hay & barn room for keeping a Cow. **1853** FOWLER *Home for All* 177 Would not more barn-room pay many times over the interest on its cost?

***Barn-shovel.** A shovel for use in a barn. — **1848** *Knickerb.* XXXII. 90, I treed him [=a porcupine] under a haystack, and shot him with a barn-shovel.

Barnstable. Also **Barstable, Bastable.** [*Barnstable* (now 'Barnstaple'), Devon, England.] Made in or imported from Barnstaple, Eng. *Obs.*

1633 *N.H. Doc. & Rec.* I. 73, 6 barnstable blanketts. **1639** *Conn. Particular Ct. Rec.* 9, 6 cushions, 3 Barstable ruggs. **1634** WOOD *New Eng. Prospect* I. xii. 52 A great round shot called Bastable-shot, is the best; being made of a blacker Lead than ordinary shot. *a***1656** BRADFORD *Hist.* 320 In this ship [were] only 2 packs of Bastable ruggs, and 2 hoggsheads of meatheglin. **1675** JOSSELYN *Two Voyages* 210 When it is to be had . . . Barstable shot . . . is best for fowl.

+**Barnstorm,** *v.* [Cf. next.] *intr.* To make a rapid tour through rural districts, delivering campaign speeches and arousing political enthusiasm. — **1896** *Congress. Rec.* 7 April 3661/1 The last I heard of him [*sc.* a cabinet official, he] was barnstorming down in Georgia in favor of gold monometallism and what he saw fit to call 'honest money.'

+**Barnstormer.** An itinerant player who acts in a barn or a hall when a theater is lacking; hence, an inferior or second-rate actor. — **1884** 'DALY' *H. Irving in Eng. & Amer.* 159 A St. Louis writer . . . said that the advent of Mr. Irving had ended the career of the 'barn-stormers,' who, with their companies of 'sticks,' . . . were bidden to vanish for evermore. I should be . . . sorry to call Mr. Booth a 'barn-stormer.' **1890** JEFFERSON *Autobiog.* 58 A veteran barn-stormer of the olden time. **1902** LORIMER *Lett. Merchant* ix. 120 The nearest to a tragedy he had ever been was when he sat in the top gallery of a Chicago theatre and saw a lot of barnstormers play Othello.

+**Barn-storming,** *vbl. n.* (See quot. 1889.) Also attrib. — [**1884** *Pall Mall Gaz.* 6 June 5/1 If this be barn-storming, Betterton and Garrick were barn-stormers, and Mr. Daly's hero certainly is not.] **1889** *Cent.*, *Barn-storming*, the practice of acting in barns, as strolling players; hence, the practice of playing 'upon the road' or 'in the provinces.' **1914** M. S. GERRY *Masks of Love* 119 The next week gave Marjorie all the barnstorming experience she wanted.

Barn swallow. {1851} +The common swallow of the U.S., *Hirundo horreorum*, which usually affixes its nest to the beams or rafters of barns or old buildings.

1790 *Mem. Academy* II. I. 97 They were . . . chimney swallows. Their colour is much darker than that of the barn swallow. **1812** WILSON *Ornithology* V. 39 The Barn Swallow arrives in this part . . . [Phila.] from the south, on the last week in March, . . . and passes on to the North. **1839** PEABODY *Mass. Birds* 344 The Barn Swallow . . . is generally welcomed by the farmer, who knows that these birds are of incalculable service in protecting his cattle from the insects. *c***1849** [PAIGE] *Dow's Sermons* I. 165 Whatever comes must shortly go—disappear like barn-swallows at the latter end of summer. **1858** BAIRD *Birds Pacific R.R.* 308 Barn Swallow . . . inhabits North America from Atlantic to Pacific. **1874** COUES *Birds N.W.* 85 The Barn Swallow occurs throughout the Missouri region, especially during the migrations.

‖**Barnum.** *colloq.* [P. T. *Barnum* (1810–91), famous showman and 'Prince of Humbugs.'] A humbug. — **1856** BREWERTON *War in Kansas* 17 In short he believes the whole affair to be a 'Barnum'—alias humbug, of the most unmitigated kind.

+**Barnumism.** *colloq.* [See preceding.] Talk or advertising with bombast, like that of P. T. Barnum; showy or pompous advertisement. — **1893**– in Dictionaries. **1896** *Godey's Mag.* Feb. 118/2 The late P. T. Barnum, . . . whose picturesque methods have passed into proverb among more than one nation under the widely accepted word 'Barnumism.'

+**Barnumize,** *v.* [See BARNUM.] **1.** *tr.* To advertise in a showy, exaggerated, or bombastic manner. **2.** *intr.* (See quotation.) — (1) **1864** LOWELL *Prose Works* V. 99 They went to work deliberately to Barnumize their prospective candidate. **1892** *Nation* 4 Aug. 88 Paris has the best advertised literature in the world, and confers a renown like that of a writer for syndicates here, only glorified and Barnumized. (2) **1889** FARMER 40/1 To *barnumize* is to talk or assert oneself in the style popularly attributed to Barnum.

***Barn-yard.** Also **barnyard, barn yard.**

***1.** The yard surrounding or in front of a barn.

Common in older Scottish use (15–17th c.), and current in some English dialects, but not an ordinary E. term.

1663 *Huntington Rec.* I. 54 All my right and titell of house, house lott, barn yards, garden. **1683** *Conn. Probate Rec.* I. 344, I give my Barn yard equally to my sons. **1771** J. HABERSHAM *Letters* 122 The Governor has lost perhaps 200 barrels rice on his plantation . . . ; it was stacked in his Barnyards. **1789** *Mass. H. S. Coll.* IV. 145 As this will always be a grazing country, the manure from the barn yard will be a fruitful source. **1838** COLMAN *Mass. Agric. Rep.* 67 All the washings of the barn yard are received into the lower story or cellar. **1852** STOWE *Uncle Tom* vii, The whole party made a . . . descent into a barn-yard belonging to a large farming establishment. **1867** 'T. LACKLAND' *Homespun* III. 329 The city youth . . . supposes every farmer's barn-yard keeps at least one cow on purpose to give cream. **1889** *Century Mag.* April 839/1 In barnyard, kennels, stables, there is continual interest. **1907** C. C. ANDREWS *Recoll.* 19 A large sheltered watering trough in the barnyard was amply supplied with pure running water.

+**2.** *ellipt.* A barn-door or barn-yard fowl.

1868 *Putnam's Mag.* Feb. 241 An ale-house at Brooklyn, where the English mistress was superior in her choice of barnyards and their cooking.

+**3.** Attrib. with *bell, cleaning, goose,* etc.

1856 Commons, etc. *Doc. Hist.* I. 118 The barn-yard bell will be rung by the watchman . . . half an hour before sunrise. — **1855** *Knickerb.* XLVI. 305 A hen of the old barn-yard breed. — **1897** *Outing* April 60/1, I . . . thought of barn-yard cleaning in a wet-spring. — **1880** *Harper's Mag.* June 76 The swallows in the mud nests under the barn-yard eaves. — **1859** WILLIS *Convalescent* 451 Nothing could well be more ungraceful than the waddle of the barn-yard goose. — **1880** *Harper's Mag.* June 68/1 The laughing children riding on the big 'brush harrow' down through that barn-yard lane beyond. — **1888** *Vermont Agric. Rep.* X. 21 It is a bad practice to allow cows to be picking up barn-yard straw between meals. — **1886** *Outing* May 160/1 Then you drop overboard your minnow or 'barnyard tackle.'

+**b.** *Barn-yard fowl*, a domestic fowl, as the hen, duck, goose, or turkey; a barn-door fowl.

1843 *Knickerb.* XXI. 125 The chickens and tame barn-yard fowl were almost at his feet, scratching the soil. **1851** HAWTHORNE *Ho. Seven Gables* vi, These hens . . . would scorn to understand the vulgar language of a barn-yard fowl. **1858** VIELÉ *Following Drum* 126 A large garden . . . together with cattle and an enormous flock of barn-yard fowls, completed the scene. **1881** *Harper's Mag.* Jan. 305/1 Very much as a modest barnyard fowl might view a peacock. **1904** STRATTON-PORTER *Freckles* 32, I'll believe the birds . . . are tame as barnyard-fowl when I see it.

+**c.** *Barn-yard grass*, the cock-spur grass, *Panicum crus-galli;* also, the crab-grass or yard-grass, *Eleusine indica.*

1843 TORREY *Flora N.Y.* II. 424 Barnyard Grass . . . [grows in] wet places, and about barnyards: common; the rough-sheathed variety along ditches near the salt water. **1847** DARLINGTON *Weeds & Plants* 403 Cock's-foot Panicum. Barn-yard Grass. . . . [Grows in] moist grounds, meadows, drains of barn-yards, &c. **1889** VASEY *Agric. Grasses* 27 Barnyard Grass. . . . In the Southern States it is often employed, and is considered a valuable grass. **1901** MOHR *Plant Life Ala.* 357 Barnyard Grass, Cockspur Grass, . . . [grows in] low wet ground, cultivated places, border of marshes. *Ib.* 376 *Eleusine indica* (L.), . . . Barnyard Grass, . . . [grows in] Alabama: Over the State. Cultivated and waste places near dwellings.

+**d.** *Barn-yard manure*, a compost of dung, rotted straw, etc. Also *barn-yard compost.*

1819 *Amer. Farmer* I. 66 Plough in your barn yard or stable manure. **1849** *Rep. Comm. Patents: Agric.* (1850) 202 Barnyard manure, with lime, will produce the largest crops. **1872** *Vermont Bd. Agric. Rep.* 422 The meadow lands are generally dressed with common barn yard manure. **1883** SPOFFORD in *Harper's Mag.* Aug. 465/2 When you manure your hill of corn with barn-yard compost. **1884** ROE *Nature's Story* 103 No one wants anything better than barn-yard manure for most purposes.

***Baron.** +A commercial or financial magnate; one who dominates the trade in a specified commodity.

[**1776** J. ADAMS in *Familiar Lett.* 154 But the spirit of these Barons [=N.C. 'gentry'] is coming down, and it must submit.] **1818** *Niles' Reg.* XIV. 226/1 The name of a *Jew* and *'rag-baron'* is synonimous. **1885** *Century Mag.* Sept. 804 Who is responsible for [the depression]? . . . Is it the 'silver barons' or the 'gold bugs'? *c***1888** *Chicago Inter-Ocean* (F.), In all the 'steam rail baron's' reply to 'fair trade' . . . he calls upon the 'iron ore barons,' the 'coal and coke barons' and the 'labor barons' to aid him in meeting European competition. **1888** *N.Y. Life* 18 Feb. 27/2 One of the 'several times' a millionaire lumber 'Barons' of Michigan. **1898** CANFIELD *Maid of Frontier* 129 Having been used to the cattle baron or his immediate underling, they would have gone far and fared hard for him. **1906** *N.Y. Ev. Post* 29 June 7 The ice 'barons' of this city have again raised the price of ice to the dealers. **1904** 'O. HENRY' *Cabbages & Kings* 4 A rubber prince, a sarsaparilla, indigo, and mahogany baron.

***Barony.** *S.C.* and *Pa.* +A tract of land which formed part of the domain of a landgrave or cassique; a division of a county. Now *Hist.*

1669 J. LOCKE *Constitutions of Carolina*, Each county shall consist of eight signories, eight baronies and four precincts. *Ib.*, Each signory, barony, and colony shall consist of twelve thousand acres. **1669** *S. C. Hist. Soc. Coll.* V. 121 Each Square [of 12,000 acres] that shall be taken up by a Landgrave or Cassique is to be a Barrony. **1689** *Penna. Col. Rec.* I. 265 That the pretence thereof was they were a distinct Barony, which tho' they might be, yet that severall Baronys might be in one and the same County. **1707** ARCHDALE *New Descrip. Carolina* 13 These Landgraves are to have four Baronies annex'd to their Dignities, of 6000 Acres each Barony and the Cassocks two Baronies, of 3000 each. **1737** *S.C. Gazette* 16–23 July, I Landgrave Thomas Smith have laid out a Township on a Bluff of my Winyaw Barony. **1738** in *S.C. Hist. & Gen. Mag.* XIII. 10 What is still more remaining of my Barony Land I do empower my loving wife to sell. *c***1750** *Ib.* XI. 88 Under this Marble lieth the Body of Samuel

Wragg Esquire who . . . in 1717 purchased the Tract of Land called Ashley Barony. **1910** *S.C. Hist. & Gen. Mag.* XI. 75 [Article on] The Baronies of South Carolina, by Henry A. M. Smith.

Barouche, *n.* Also †**barouch, barrouche.** [G. dial. *barutsche.*] A four-wheeled carriage having a driver's seat in front and two seats facing each other behind, and furnished with a collapsible top. {1813–}

1824 *Missouri Intell.* 9 Oct. 1/5 The Mayor entered the carriage of the General which was a handsome Barrouche. **1831** A. ROYALL *Southern Tour* II. 122 He put his 'fiery colts,' as he calls them, to his barouch. **1835** HOFFMAN *Winter in West* II. 27 A tall rickety old barouche . . . stood waiting for us in a frozen swamp. **1846** *Knickerb.* XXVIII. 36 This jolly club, six in number, all went out to the races on the last day, in a barouche. **1863** WHITMAN *Specimen Days* (1883) 40 There were . . . a lot of children in barouches, and a squad of policemen. **1869** ALCOTT *Little Women* II. 116 He passes in his four-horse barouche. **1886** *Outing* April 66/1 The team of his barouche consisted of six horses. **1902** LORIMER *Lett. Merchant* xvi. 235 Then he bought a nice, open barouche.

+**Barouche,** *v. intr.* To ride in a barouche. — **1860** HOLMES *E. Venner* xxi, To think of seeing her barouching about Rockland behind a pair of long-tailed bays. **1881** HOWELLS *Modern Instance* xxvii. 334, I've been barouching round all over the moral vineyard with his friends.

‖**Bar-place.** [BAR *n.*[1] 2.] A place at which there are draw-bars. — **1863** MRS. WHITNEY *F. Gartney* xii, A little footpath that . . . stretched across the field, diagonally, to a bar-place and stile. *Ib.* xxviii, By and by, . . . she saw a chaise approaching. It was stopped at the corner, by the bar-place.

Bar-post. [BAR *n.*[1] 2.] One of the posts supporting a set of draw-bars. — **1847** WEBSTER. **1874** B. F. TAYLOR *World on Wheels* II. iv. 217 A little gray couple are busy building in the cleft of the bar-post. **1879** — *Summer-Savory* xvii. 138 Awkward H's like a pair of leaning bar-posts with one bar.

* **Barque.** [Fr. *barque.*]

* **1.** = BARK *n.*[2] 1.

1623 *Va. House of Burgesses* 22 The barques, and barges that then were built. **1637** *Plymouth Laws* 57 That there shall be thirty persons sent for land service, and as many others as shall be sufficient to manage the barque. **1654** *Suffolk Deeds* II. 54 To have & to hold the said barque Endeauer, & all her furniture. **1704** *Boston News-Letter* 4 Dec. 2/2 Captain Clavar in a barque . . . well mann'd, design[s] . . . to sayl on privateering. **1793** ASBURY *Journal* II. 184 The printed list of vessels in the harbor sets forth . . . seven snows, and two barques, besides pilot-boats and coasters. **1851** CIST *Cincinnati* 322 Within the last six years, the barque Muskingum, burthen 350 tons, was built at Marietta [etc.]. **1870** in *Scribner's Mo.* Feb. (1871) 414/2 The same storm [in the lake regions] . . . caused the total destruction of 2 propellers, 2 barques, 4 brigs.

+**2.** A raft. *Obs.*

1735 *New Voyage to Georgia* 46 We concluded to tie some trees together, and make a barque, as the Indians call it, to ford over to the main.

Barracan, -con. *Obs.* [Fr. *barracan*, med. *bouracan.*] BARRAGON. {1638, 1821} — **1705** *Boston News-Letter* 12 March 2/1 About 20 bails of divers sorts of wollen cloths, as Piecotoes, Perpetuanas, . . . Barracon and other woolens.

Barrack, *n.*[1] Also †**barrick, barrak, baruk.**

1. A building or set of buildings used for the accommodation of troops. In later use most commonly *barracks.* {1686–}

(1) **1758** *Lett. to Washington* II. 269 We have done all the joyners Work in the second Barrack. We are in great want of a Barrel of double tens for the last Barrack. **1778** *N.H. Comm. Safety Rec.* 164 Capt. Blunt . . . appointed to remove a barrack from fort Hancock to the light house in . . . New Castle. **1796** *Ann. 4th Congress* 2 Sess. 2572 Governor's Island has been fortified with a fort made of earth, . . . a large powder magazine, and barrack for the garrison. **1853** RAMSEY *Tennessee* 559 The barrack, and the Court house, and the grove, . . . were at first substituted for this purpose [*sc.* religious worship]. **1861** WINTHROP *Open Air* 34 We entered the barrack. Beneath its smoky roof-tree was a pervading aroma. **1902** *Harper's Mag.* Jan. 320/2 The brass railing that marked the entrance to the great barrack. **1916** EASTMAN *From Deep Woods* 76, I was shown to my quarters, which consisted of a bed-room, office, and dispensary, all in one continuous barrack.

(2) **1768** J. ROWE *Diary* 178 This day the troops went from Fanewill Hall into the Barracks. **1775** *N.J. Archives* 2 Ser. I. 5 The three companies now lying in said Barracks. **1788** FRENEAU *Misc. Works* 154 The boys of the barracks, those soldiers so bold. **1817** *Ann. 14th Congress* 2 Sess. 156 They are usefully employed in constructing military roads, barracks, fortifications, &c. **1850** L. SAWYER *Way Sketches* 30 The barracks at Fort Kearney are mere mud houses. **1884** *Harper's Mag.* Nov. 813/1 The college building had been seized for a barracks. **1891** *Century Mag.* Jan. 388 The soldiers erected barracks of tule, soon replaced by wood. **1907** C. C. ANDREWS *Recoll.* 214 Midsummer night was the only one, I was told, when soldiers were allowed to return to the barracks drunk.

2. Attrib. with *door, gate, hire,* etc.

1777 *N.H. Comm. Safety Rec.* 68 That . . . he leave the paying for Barrack room . . . to a special Committee. **1789** *Kentucky Petitions* 167 The claim of John Crow for maintenance of nine Indian prisoners & for Barracks hire. **1797** *Ann. 4th Congress* 2 Sess. 2324 The Army was in garrison, where there were barrack-houses convenient for the officers and men. **1852** *Harper's Mag.* May 849/1 Shortly after tattoo, sundry ladies . . . presented themselves at the barrack gate. **1860** LONGFELLOW *Paul Revere* 27 The muster of men at the barrack door. **1863** Hale *If, Yes, & Perhaps* (1868) 204 For next year, barrack-life was very tame to poor Nolan. **1886** *Harper's Mag.* Oct. 694/2 The men . . . have been removed to a new barrack building.

b. *Barrack-master*, an officer who superintends soldiers' barracks. {*a*1745–}

1774 J. ANDREWS *Letters* 72 The chimneys in the barracks are so ill-secur'd that the Barrack Master says that he shan't be surpris'd if fire breaks out in 'em very often. **1777** *Md. Hist. Mag.* V. 224 In case of a Storm it will be necessary to have the Barrack Masters House (without the Garrison) burnt. **1779** E. GERRY in *Warren-Adams Lett.* II. 124 The Departments of the Muster and Barrack Masters are abolished. **1816** *Ann. 14th Congress* 2 Sess. 27 It is impossible to settle the accounts of . . . the barrackmasters . . . employed with the same army. **1818** *Ann. 15th Congress* 1 Sess. II. 2541 So much of the act [of March 3, 1813] . . . as relates to . . . forage, wagon, and barrack masters, and their assistants, . . . is hereby repealed.

+**Barrack,** *n.*[2] [See HAY-BARRACK.] A structure for the shelter or storage of hay, straw, etc.; esp. one having a light, adjustable roof supported by four corner-posts. — **1854** *Harper's Mag.* IX. 849/2 We crept slyly around a 'barrack,' as it is called, of standing hay and by the pegs at a corner-post we climbed up to the top of the hay-mow. **1857** *Ohio Statutes* (1860) I. 425 If any person shall wilfully . . . burn . . . any barrack or stack of hay, wheat, rye, oats, . . . or grain of any kind. **1889** *Cent.* 457 *Barrack*, in Maryland, and perhaps elsewhere, . . . is used for a building of any kind intended for the storage of straw or hay.

Barrack, *v.* **1.** *tr.* To quarter (soldiers) in barracks. {1701, 1872} **2.** *intr.* Of troops: To lodge in barracks. {1834} — (1)**1777** *N.H. Comm. Safety Rec.* 79 Gave Col. Poor orders to barrack his reg[imen]t. **1781** *Ib.* 255 The Treasurer to let Mr. Noah Emery have sixty pounds new currency towards . . . paying Widow Hill for barracking soldiers. (2) **1777** in M. Cutler *Life & Corr.* I. 64 They barracked at Winter Hill.

+**Barraclade.** [Du. *baar, bare* bare, having no nap; *kleed* cloth.] 'A home-made woolen blanket without nap' (B. '48). 'This word is peculiar to New York City, and those parts of the State settled by the Dutch' (*Ib.*).

Barracuda. Also **barracouda, -coota, -cuta, baricoota.** Any of several voracious perch-like fishes constituting the genus *Sphyræna*, found in the seas of the southeastern and south-western coasts; esp. *S. barracuda* of Florida, etc., or *S. argentea* of the Pacific. {1678–}

1751 WASHINGTON *Diaries* I. 17 We . . . cou'd not intice with a baited hook two Baricootas which played under our Stern for some Hours. **1799** ELLICOTT *Life & Lett.* 186 [Off Florida] a great abundance and variety of fish may be taken: such as barracoota. **1842** *Nat. Hist. N.Y., Zoology* IV. 39 The Northern Barracuta . . . is a very active and voracious little fish. **1855** BAIRD in *Smithsonian Rep.* 326 Northern Barracuda, *Sphyræna borealis.* . . . They were taken from a small cove at Corson's inlet. **1887** GOODE *Fisheries & Fishery Industries* II. 600 The fish caught by trolling in summer [in S. Calif.] are chiefly barracuda, bonito, albicore, yellow-tail. **1895** *Outing* July 358/2 George proposes trolling for barracuda, the pike of Pacific waters.

+**Barrafou.** (See quotation.) — **1775** HARROWER *Diary* 93 [A Virginian] also made a Niger come and play on an Instrument call'd a Barrafou. The body of it is an oblong box with the mouth up and stands on four sticks put in bottom, and cross the top is laid 11 lose sticks upon which he beats.

Barragan. *Obs.* [Sp. *barragan* =obsolete Fr. *barracan*, BARRACAN.] A kind of camlet. {1787, 1840} Also attrib. — **1753** *N.J. Archives* XIX. 249 [He] had on when he went away, a good beaver hat, silk cap, baragon [*sic*] coat, and jacket, of a reddish brown colour. **1830** J. F. WATSON *Philadelphia* 179 From one advertisement of the year 1745, I take the following now unintelligible articles of dress: . . . prunelloe, barragons, druggets.

+**Barranca, -co.** *S.W.* [Sp.] A deep break or gully with steep sides made by running water, as from a heavy rainfall; a ravine or gorge.

[**1836** C. J. LATROBE *Rambler in Mexico* 90 One of the gentlemen . . . was precipitated in the darkness into a profound barranca. **1838** 'TEXIAN' *Mexico* v. *Texas* 64 A dreary looking *barranco*, thickly over-shadowed by acacia and ebony trees.] **1851** *Harper's Mag.* III. 461/1 During the night two of our best brigades had crept, unperceived, through the clay 'barrancas' close up to the rear of the enemy's camp. **1877** R. I. DODGE *Hunting Grounds* 166 The elk . . . will go easily in and out of the almost perpendicular 'barrancas' of the 'bad lands.' **1895** REMINGTON *Pony Tracks* 125 From the depths of a great *barranca* we begin the climb. **1907** WHITE *Arizona Nights* iv. 85 Larry had to lead his cavallo down the barranco to the main cañon.

* **Barrator, -er.** Also †**barettor.** One who vexatiously engages in, or incites to, lawsuits. *Obs.* or *arch.*

1641 *Mass. Body of Liberties* (1890) 41 If any man shall be proved and judged a commen Barrator vexing others with unjust frequent and endlesse suites, it shall be in the power of Courts . . . to punish him for his Barratry. **1647** *R.I. Col. Rec.* I. 178 They . . . are called Conspirators, Champerters, Embracers and common Barrettors. **1669** *R.I. Hist. Soc.*

X. 91 Wee much marvaile how hee escaped beinge indicted for a common barrator. **1852** DUNLAP *Bk. Forms* (1857) 258 A.B., of Beaver, . . . is a common barrator and daily disturber of the peace, vexing others with unjust and vexatious suits.

***Barratry.**

1. The offence of vexatiously raising or causing lawsuits. {1645-}

1641 [see BARRATOR]. **1711** *N.J. Archives* 1 Ser. IV. 88 May Bickley Gent. was indicted for barratrie. **1827** *Ill. Revised Laws* (1833) 195 If any person shall officiously intermeddle in any suit at common law . . . [he] shall be fined and punished as in cases of Common Barratry. **1827** *Western M. Rev.* I. 447 He was remarkably clever in working small matters up to a suit, or in other words, inclined to the easily besetting sin of lawyers, called barratry. **1876** *Colo. General Laws* (1877) 291 Every such person so offending shall be deemed to have committed the crime of common barratry.

2. Fraudulent or negligent dealing with a ship or cargo on the part of the master or mariners to the detriment of the owners. {1622-}

1647 *R.I. Col. Rec.* I. 159 Those Lawes that concern . . . Conveyances by Barratrie. **1792** Dallas *Reports* (1882) II. 138 In all cases respecting barratry, some circumstances of fraud . . . towards the owners were stated.

***Barred,** *ppl. a.* Marked with a bar or bars; striped. +In specific names (see quotations).

(1) **1811** WILSON *Ornithology* IV. 61 Barred Owl, *Strix nebulosa*, . . . is . . . frequently observed flying during day. **1856** [G. H. DERBY] *Phoenixiana* xxxiv. 210 A great barred owl, five feet from tip to tip, settled in the foliage [of the palmetto]. **1857** *Rep. Comm. Patents: Agric.* 120 The barred owl . . . on this continent extends its home at least as far southward as the limits of the United States. **1870** *Amer. Naturalist* III. 227 The Barred Owls station themselves in ambush on the coast.

(2) **1842** *Nat. Hist. N.Y., Zoology* IV. 218 The Barred Killifish, *Fundulus zebra* . . . is found in the salt water creeks about New York. *Ib.* 220 The Barred Minnow, *Hydrargira multifasciata*, . . . according to M. Lesueur, is also found in Saratoga lake. It may prove to be the young of the [transparent minnow]. **1871** DE VERE 67 The *Mummachog* is hardly known beyond the waters around Long Island; the small carp-like fish is more generally called the Barred Killy.

***BARREL,** *n.* Also **bar'l; †barrell, bar(r)iell, baril, beril.**

***1.** A cask. Freq. with *of* (the contents).

1619 *Va. House of Burgesses* 10 This . . . Assembly doth ordaine, that . . . all & every householder and householders have in store . . . one spare barrel of corne. **1622** 'MOURT' *Relation* 43 There being a little barrell of powder halfe full, scattered in and about the Cabbin. **1637** *Plymouth Laws* 27 The said parcell of herings, be it firkin, barrell, or hodgshead, or any other vessel. **1662** *Conn. Public Rec.* I. 391 He shall marke each Barrel that he packs, and for his paines he is to haue 8d. pr Barrell. **1684** I. MATHER *Providences* i. (1856) 15 A barrel of flour being cast on shore, they made cakes thereof. **1688** SEWALL *Diary* I. 225 Bespeak 3 Barrels of Apples of the Father and Andrew. **1713** *Boston Selectmen* 196 The Master of each Sloop . . . shall . . . send . . . of flower 1 barrell to each family. **1748** ELIOT *Field-Husb.* i. 14 A Barrel of Cyder of sweet Apples when made into Molasses, will be worth three Pounds. **1759** *Essex Inst. Coll.* XIX. 150 They also found about 200 barils of gunpowder but no Provision worth anything. **1806** *Austin Papers* (1924) I. 104, 1 barrel salted mackrell. **1842** HITCHCOCK *Journal* (1930) 104 Those who had taken him . . . sold him for a barrel of whiskey to some Spaniards. **1862** A. J. DICKSON *Across Plains* (1929) 41 The greater part of this she had packed in a barrel, putting flour around each can to lessen the jar. **1866** 'F. KIRKLAND' *Bk. Anecdotes* 573 There's no end to the . . . barrels of pork, and barrels of sugar and coffee, . . . he sends me. **1882** WORTHEN *Econ. Geol. Ill.* II. 41 Smith's cement mill . . . has capacity to grind two hundred barrels per day. **1892** M. A. JACKSON *Memoirs* 13 Cummins . . . proved [this] by lifting a barrel of cider and taking a drink from the bunghole. **1904** *Delineator* Aug. 296 Sometimes the regular travelling libraries have been sent, sometimes a barrel of books to form the nucleus of a local library.

2. A cask containing a specified or recognized quantity; +esp. five bushels of shelled, or one of unshelled, corn.

1641 *Md. Archives* 108 The Barrell to contein five of the said Bushell & no more or lesse. **1650** *Conn. Public Rec.* I. 515 Euery Casck commonly called Barrills or halfe hogsheads shall containe twenty eight gallons wine measure. **1775** J. HARROWER *Diary* 100 Of Corn there will be on this Plantation about 8 or 9 hundred Barrells at five Bushels to the Barrell. **1784** SMYTH *Tour* I. 292 Indian corn is the great staff of life in America, and is measured by what is called the barrel there, which contains just five bushels. **1828** WEBSTER s.v., In Connecticut, the barrel for liquors must contain 31½ gallons. . . . In New-York, a barrel of flour by statute must contain either 196 lb. or 228 lb. nett weight. The barrel of beef and pork in New-York and Connecticut, is 200 lbs. In general, the contents of barrels, as defined by statute, . . . must be from 28 to 31½ gallons. **1837** Commons, etc. *Doc. Hist.* I. 221 Begun picking corn of plantation hands, . . . their crop amounting to fifteen hundred barrels. **1848** J. S. ROBINSON *Santa Fe Exped.* 54 We found here large cribs of corn: some perhaps of a thousand barrels. **1857-8** *Ill. Agric. Soc. Trans.* III. 411 Often have I seen seventy-five bushels, or, as Kentuckians reckon, fifteen barrels, gathered from each acre. **1868** *Mich. Agric. Rep.* VII. 456 A barrel of fruit, roots, or vegetables, shall be two and one-half bushels. **1874** KNIGHT 238/1 *Barrel*, a measure of ear-corn in the Southern States, shelling 2½ bushels. **1900** NELSON *A B C Wall St.* 128 The standard or commercial barrel of pork is reckoned at 200 pounds. . . . A barrel of flour contains 196 pounds.

+3. A receptacle for waste paper.

1846 CORCORAN *Pickings from 'Picayune'* 38 No. 40 eagerly surveys the columns . . . for 'Lines to Eliza,' which he contributed, but . . . the editor had . . . consigned it to the 'barrel.'

+4. A cask of clothing, etc., (to be) sent to a missionary.

1877 PHELPS *Avis* 31 Some [people] take to zoology, and some take to religion. . . . John Rose says, in the Connecticut Valley, where he came from, it was missionary barrels.

+5. A large sum *of* money.

1877 *Congress. Rec.* App., 2 March 193/2 My colleague . . . might march upon Washington . . . to secure the inauguration of 'his man' who once had a 'bar'l of money.' **1904** *McClure's Mag.* Feb. 379 [A place] good enough for old Jayes to make barrels of money in.

+b. The sum of money provided by a candidate for election, to cover campaign expenses or bribe the voters.

'It is said to have originated in a dispatch to the St. Louis *Globe-Democrat* from Jefferson City about two weeks before the meeting of the Democratic Convention, in 1876, in St. Louis' (Lane *Pol. Catch-words* 16). 'In this sense often written and pronounced *bar'l*, in humorous imitation of vulgar speech' (*Cent.*).

1880 *Congress. Rec.* 3 April 2110/1 [They are] establishing 'peace on earth' among democrats . . . by a liberal use of the contents of Tilden's 'bar'l.' **1884** *Savannah News* Aug., It would be much better for General Butler if he would turn one of his barrels over to the Democratic campaign committee. **1888** *Florida Times* 11 Feb. (F.), It will be remembered that Mr. Flower was the nominal candidate of the anti-Cleveland men four years ago and with aid of his barrel they really did achieve some show of success. **1904** *Phila. Press* 14 June 5 If any delegates to the Republican county convention looked upon the anti-bribery movement as a joke, they realized their error to-night, when they reached here and found the 'barrels' they had hoped for missing. **1912** *N.Y. Ev. Post* 23 Sept. 1/1 Hinman is a relatively poor man, and could bring no money for the campaign. Clark has the requisite 'barrel,' and is credited with political ambitions.

***Barrel,** *v. tr.* To pack or store in a barrel or barrels, as for preservation, dispatch, etc.

1677 *Springfield Rec.* II. 131 In case they barrel up for market, they are to allow to the town twelve pence p[er] barrel for al that shal be transported. **1698** G. THOMAS *Penna.* 25 Their Merchandize chiefly consists in Horses, Pipe-Staves, Pork and Beef salted and barrelled up. **1743** CATESBY *Carolina* II. p. xxxiii, Drum Fish . . . are esteemed very good fish. . . . Many of them are yearly barrell'd up with salt, and sent to the West Indies. **1789** MORSE *Amer. Geog.* 352 These swine . . . are caught, killed, barrelled, and exported in great quantities. **1851** CIST *Cincinnati* 247 In these it stands to cool, after which it is barreled off for market. **1862** 'E. KIRKE' *Among Pines* 102 When barrelled, the turpentine is frequently sent to market in its crude state. **1864** *Examiner* 12 Jan., The offal of the hogs, which is fit for food, . . . is barreled and shipped to the soldiers. **1886** *Harper's Mag.* June 90/1 The sugar is now ready for barrelling.

Barrel beef. Beef packed in barrels. — **1715** *Boston News-Letter* 31 Oct. 2/2 Very good Barrel Beaff lately come from Ireland, to be sold at fifty shillings per barrel. **1721** *Mass. H. Rep. Journals* III. 64 The Inhabitants . . . shall have liberty . . . to pay the several Sums that shall be on them respectively assessed . . . in good Barrel Beef.

***Barrel-board.** A board suitable for making into barrel-staves. {1565} — **1628** *Va. House of Burgesses* 48 For pipestaves, barrell boords and Clapboords there hath formerly beene sent home of all sortes.

Barrel-bolt. A door-bolt fitting into a cylindrical socket. — **1853** FOWLER *Home for All* 113 The front door . . . secured with two barrel-bolts and a suitable sized front-door lock.

+Barrel bulk. A measure of capacity, as for freight, equivalent to five cubic feet. — **1853** *Harper's Mag.* VI. 581/2 Freights from Detroit to Lake Superior ports are usually $1 the barrel bulk—increased to $1 50 by the time of reaching the mines.

+Barrel cactus. [From the shape.] A species of cactus of the genus *Echinocactus*; esp. *E. Wislizeni* or *E. Emoryi*, yielding a refreshing drink. —**1881** *Amer. Naturalist* XV. 984 Another species of the family is one commonly called the 'nigger-head' or 'barrel' cactus, a Mammalaria. **1923** BOWER *Parowan Bonanza* ii. 19 Out there stood a barrel cactus, almost within reach of a gaunt yucca.

+Barrel campaign, candidate. (See quotations and BARREL *n.* 5 b.) — **1884** *Boston Jrnl.* 7 Nov. 7 The Fifth District Barrel Campaign. *Ib.*, We are accustomed to 'barrel' campaigns here. Nobody supposes this district to be Democratic, but the Democrats depend upon carrying it with money. . . . But another 'barrel' candidate was discovered. **1889** *Cent.* s.v., A *barrel* campaign is one in which money is lavishly employed to bribe voters.

+Barrel churn. A barrel-shaped churn.

1864 *Rep. Comm. Patents* I. 364 A barrel churn of that class which have a large opening in the side to admit of the ready removal of the dasher.

1873-4 *Vermont Bd. Agric. Rep.* II. 65 Inventors . . . making dairy men believe that they discovered something better than the barrel churn used by our fathers fifty years ago. **1888** *Ib.* X. 22 The butter was washed by rocking the barrel churn back and forth. **1891** CHASE & CLOW *Industry* II. 105 The barrel-churn was made with beaters inside which flew round and round as the handle outside was turned.

***Barreled, Barrelled,** *a.* Packed or stored in a barrel, esp. for commercial use.

1741 W. STEPHENS *Proc. Georgia* II. 144 Neither Corn, nor barrelled flesh, being any part of their Cargoes, what we chiefly got, was Biscuit and flour. **1798** [C. WILLIAMSON] *Descr. Genesee* iv, The proper articles for the Baltimore market are . . . fat cattle, barrelled beef and pork, flour. **1867-8** *Ill. Agric. Soc. Trans.* VII. 445 If converted into barreled pork, we get 998,753 barrels, of 200 lbs. each.

+**Barrel-fish.** (See first quotation.) The log-fish or rudder-fish, *Lirus perciformis*, found from Maine to Cape Hatteras. — **1885** Kingsley *Stand. Nat. Hist.* III. 191 They are most always found in the vicinity of floating barrels and spars, and sometimes inside of the barrels. Hence the fishermen call them barrel-fish, though the most usual name is rudder-fish. **1888** GOODE *Amer. Fishes* 223 The Black Rudder-fish . . . is also called by the fishermen 'Log-fish' and 'Barrel-fish.'

+**Barrel flour.** Flour put up in barrels and brought into a locality. — **1877** *Vermont Bd. Agric. Rep.* IV. 75 At nearly every family where I boarded after that, the woman of the house . . . let me understand that I should not fare as well with them as at the other place, for they had no barrel flour.

+**Barrel gin.** A form of cotton gin. — **1802** J. DRAYTON *S. Carolina* 133 Barrel gins are either worked by oxen or water; and may be said to be nothing more than foot gins, to which greater power is applied.

Barrel head. The round, flat head or end of a barrel.

1849 N. KINGSLEY *Diary* 76 Worked at getting out felloes for wheel-barrow wheels, . . . take old barrel heads for spokes. **1851** *Polly Peablossom* 124, I felt transfixed to the barrel-head. **1853** SIMMS *Sword & Distaff* 181 The hominy pot . . . now stood in the centre, resting upon a barrel-head. **1874** KNIGHT 239 Barrel-head cutter [is] a tool for rounding and chamfering barrel-heads.

Barrel-hoop. A hoop of a barrel. — **1856** STOWE *Dred* I. xxii. 296 Some barrel-hoops . . . [were] covered by coarse white cotton cloth. **1874** LONG *Wild-Fowl* 63 Pieces of flat barrel-hoops, or similar elastic material, are now bent over the top crosswise. **1884** 'MARK TWAIN' *H. Finn* xxxv. 360 If we make him a pen out of . . . a piece of an old iron barrel-hoop. **1897** BRODHEAD *Bound in Shallows* 27 A man was mending a fish-net . . . bulged to perfect rotundity with a barrel hoop.

+**Barrel-house.** A drinking place in which cheap liquor is sold. — **1883** PECK *Bad Boy* 120 After I had put a few things in his brandy he concluded it was cheaper to buy it, and he is now patronizing a barrel house. **1888** *Missouri Republican* 11 Feb. (F.), The West-Side police are still arresting barrel-house loafers. **1896** G. ADE *Artie* vi. 50, I see barrel-house boys goin' around for hand outs that was more on the level than you are.

+**Barreling-shed.** [BARREL *v.*] (See quotation.) — **1865** *Atlantic Mo.* XV. 398 The perfected oil is drawn to the tanks of the barreling-shed, and filled into casks ready for exportation.

‖**Barrel jacket.** [BARREL *n.* 1.] (See quotation.) — **1858** VIELÉ *Following Drum* 222 One delinquent was sentenced to wear a 'barrel jacket' every day. . . . It consisted of an old flour barrel with a hole cut for his head . . . and a pair of holes for his arms.

+**Barrel ore.** (See quotation and BARREL-WORK.) — **1849** *Pres. Mess. Congress* II. 460 The barrel ore [of copper] contains from 30 to 50 per cent of copper and the stamp work varies from 5 to 10 per cent. of a mixture of copper and silver.

Barrel organ. A hand organ in which the keys are acted on by pegs fixed in a revolving barrel, usually played by street musicians. {1772-}

1790 *Penna. Packet* 11 Dec. 3/2 Imported . . . by William Poyntell . . . , a chamber barrel organ which plays 40 tunes. **1842** DICKENS *Amer. Notes* vi, I remember [seeing in N.Y.] . . . one barrel-organ and a dancing-monkey. **1855** 'P. PAXTON' *Capt. Priest* 278 The hurdy-gurdy, barrel-organ, and jew's-harp, are grateful to our ears. **1878** *Harper's Mag.* Jan. 236 The one-armed soldier, whose barrel-organ has a hard time in making itself heard above the noise of the vehicles [on Broadway].

Barrel plate. a. An iron plate from which gun-barrels are made. **b.** In a machine-gun, a plate serving to hold the barrels in place. — **1852** *Harper's Mag.* V. 147/2 The barrels are made from plates of iron, of suitable form and size, called scalps or barrel plates. **1888** *Century Mag.* Oct. 886/1 The breech-ends are firmly screwed into a disk or rear barrel-plate, which is fastened to the shaft.

+**Barrel plow.** *Obs.* [BARREL *n.*] A form of drill-plow. — **1786** WASHINGTON *Diaries* III. 38, I tried my drill or Barrel plow; which requiring some alteration in the harrow, obliged me to bring it to the Smiths shop.

+**Barrel pork.** Pork packed or intended for packing in barrels. — **1851** CIST *Cincinnati* 228 The first floor . . . is used for cutting and packing barrel pork.

+**Barrel-seat.** A form of chair or seat cut out of a barrel. — **1868** BEECHER *Norwood* 148 He plumped Barton into his own barrel seat, with an emphasis.

‖**Barrel shirt.** [BARREL *n.* 1.] A 'barrel jacket.' — **1865** *Nation* I. 367 If he did n't, they'd put a barrel-shirt on him.

Barrel skirt. [BARREL *n.* 1.] A hoop skirt or petticoat. — **1867** W. H. DIXON *New America* II. 33 Our women . . . eat pearl-ash for bread, they drink ice-water for wine; they wear tight stays, thin shoes, and barrel skirts.

Barrel spring. A cylindrical spring. — **1773** *Boston Ev. Post.* 4 Oct., A genteel curricle with patent barrel springs.

Barrel stave. A stave shaped for, or used in, making a barrel.

1661 *Plymouth Laws* 132 That . . . six pence per hundred bee payed upon barrell staves and heading. **1709** LAWSON *Carolina* 92 We have red oak. . . . 'Tis not very durable; yet some use this . . . for pipe and barrel-staves. **1771** *N.H. Gazette* 30 Aug., Such persons as are desirous of contracting for . . . white oak pipe, hogshead and barrel staves, with heading. **1783** *Mass. Acts* xv, White oak hogshead and barrel staves. **1855** THOMPSON *Doesticks* 319 Several of the 'supes' . . . carried banners made of horse-blankets, nailed to barrel staves. **1884** *Rep. Comm. Agric.* 395 Churning with a barrel-stave was tried by some.

+**Barrel wheat.** [BARREL *n.*] — **1863** *Rep. Comm. Agric.* 90 The anecdote of the origin of the barrel wheat is well known. A farmer was in the habit of selecting his seed wheat by striking the sheaves across the head of an empty barrel; and as the largest, earliest matured, and the best grains shattered most easily, he thus selected them.

+**Barrel-work.** Pieces of copper ore sufficiently large to be sorted out by hand and freighted in barrels.

1849 *Pres. Mess. Congress* II. 468 The pieces which are raised to 30 per cent. of metal by beating off the rock are packed up in barrels, and this metal is called 'barrel-work.' **1853** *Harper's Mag.* VI. 448/2 In this way, the smaller pieces of mass copper, termed *barrel work*, the veinstone, and the poor stuff, are all raised. **1881** RAYMOND *Mining Gloss.*, *Barrel-work* . . . , native copper occurring in pieces of a size to be sorted out by hand in sufficient purity for smelting without mechanical concentration.

Barren, *n.* [f. the adj.]

+**1.** A tract of land having little or no natural vegetation except small trees or shrubs. Usually in *pl.*

The name is especially given to definite tracts in various parts of the country, sometimes with defining terms prefixed, as *pine-barrens*. The following are examples of the numerous definitions or descriptions given by earlier writers: **1797** F. BAILY *Tour* 355 Land . . . partaking more of the nature of what are more properly called *Barrens*, because the openness of the woods and the deficiency of timber arises more from a natural unfruitfulness than too great a luxuriance of soil. **1815** DRAKE *Cincinnati* i. 45 The northern parts abound in tracts . . . which, in contradistinction to the rich prairies, are called *barrens*. **1817** M. BIRKBECK *Journey in A.* 98 The road . . . is partly across 'barrens,' that is, land of middling quality, thinly set with timber. **1820** J. FLINT *Lett. from Amer.* 255 The name *barrens* must have arisen from the lands so denominated not producing such a large growth of vegetable matter as the forests, rather than from sterility. **1824** [W. N. BLANE] *Excursion U.S.* 142 Near this are some pretty extensive 'Barrens.' The Americans apply this term to those tracts of land, which, being covered with low shrubs and brushwood, much resemble what we call in England 'Copses.' **1836** J. HALL *Stat. West* vi. 92 The first settlers of Kentucky found large tracts of the country destitute of trees, and covered with bushes. Supposing that the want of timber was caused by the sterility of the soil, . . . they gave to these spots, the expressive name of 'the barrens,' and carefully avoided them in making their selections of land. **1844** Howe *Ohio* (1847) 163 A small tract, called 'the barrens,' so termed from the land being divested of undergrowth and tall timber; it is covered with a grass well adapted to pasturage. **1847** *Ib.* 469 These plains were covered with a thin growth of oak timber, and were denominated *barrens*, but, on cultivation, they produce fine crops of wheat.

(1) *pl.* **1697** *N. Eng. Hist. & Gen. Reg.* XXX. 65 As to the Soyle [of S.C.], . . . whether here and ther some rich Spot, and the Barrens are farr the greater in Quantitie, or how it may be [etc.]. **1705** LOGAN in *Penna. Hist. Soc. Mem.* X. 55 Those who have land to take up being now generally edged upon the barrens, are so clamorous that they will have it there or nowhere. **1724** H. JONES *Virginia* 35 Gentlemen and Planters love to build near the Water; though it be not altogether so healthy as the Uplands and Barrens, which serve for Ranges for Stock. **1784** FILSON *Kentucke* 20 Below a creek . . . on this river . . . a great territory begins, called Green River Barrens. **1796** Imlay *Western Territory* (ed. 3) 523 The Cumberland barrens, so called, where the land, though without timber, is frequently very good. **1811** *Niles' Reg.* I. 101/2 Our poorest barrens, plains and burnt lands will serve for sheep walks. **1833** *Ind. Q. Mag. Hist.* XV. 252 Travelling through barrens and small prairies, . . . I entered the heaviest growth of thick woods I have seen in the country. **1842** *Knickerb.* XX. 544 Emerging from the pine forests, over whose barrens I had ridden all the day. **1866** *Rep. Indian Affairs* 92 The balance of the land is sandy barrens, affording pasturage to a limited extent. **1879** *Scribner's Mo.* Nov. 20/1 The country, except on the barrens, furnishes a fine growth. **1902** MCFAUL *Ike Glidden* 100 The Barrens constitute the most remarkable feature of the Pine Tree State.

(2) *sing.* **1723** *Weekly Mercury* 4 July 4/1 An Orchard lying at the eastern end of the Loadstones Barren. **1784** JEFFERSON in Sparks *Corr. Rev.* IV. 63 Beyond these waters is a mountainous barren, which can never be inhabited. **1789** MORSE *Amer. Geog.* 286 As much as . . . one fourth of the whole state [=N.J.], is a sandy barren. **1801** ASBURY *Jour-*

nal III. 5 The land, though a barren, is of the most beautiful kind, and for range for cattle and for timber is very valuable. **1844** *Knickerb.* XXIII. 46 My arms were only sufficient to guide him a little in case he attempted the barren. **1876** HALE *P. Nolan's Friends* iv, The whole party were in the pines, through which, over a sandy barren, they were to ride for two days.

+**2.** Attrib. in names of trees, etc., growing on barrens, as *barren hickory, plum, white oak.* Cf. BARREN(S) OAK, etc.

1785 MARSHALL *Amer. Grove* 120 *Quercus alba minor,* Barren White Oak, . . . grows generally upon poor, barren, or waste land. **1792** IMLAY *Western Territory* 210 Barren, or red plumb. **1882** WORTHEN *Econ. Geol. Ill.* II. 105 The post-oak . . . prevails [in Clinton county] . . . together with black oak, some white oak, black jack, barren hickory.

* **Barren,** *a.*

***1.** Of land: Producing little or no vegetation; infertile; unproductive.

1638 *R.I. Col. Rec.* I. 33 It was upland from the water, and most of it barren and rockie. **1676** SEWALL *Diary* I. 26 An isthmus of about 3 miles and barren plain. **1755** EVANS *Anal. Map Colonies* 7 These plains . . . are a white sea-sand, . . . and perfectly barren, as no mixture of soil helps to enrich them. *a*1772 WOOLMAN *Journal* 193 As I rode over the barren hills. **1792** IMLAY *Western Territory* 52 The plain country . . . is considered as little better than barren land. **1826** Peck *Guide* (1831) 209 The Big Prairie in Missouri is . . . perhaps more properly barren land. **1868** RAYNOLDS *Explor. Yellowstone* 8 The much-dreaded and barren 'bad lands.' **1902** WHITE *Conjuror's House* xvii. 228 [Fort Rae] is a dreary spot, for the Barren Grounds are near.

+**b.** *Barren Lands,* in ironic use, =Canada.

1812 *Beauties of Brother Bull-us* 82 Jonathan . . . forthwith dispatched his chief bailiff, Benjamin Brave, into the Barren Lands of John Bull, with orders to annex them to Jonathan's farm.

+**2.** *Barren strawberry:* (see quotations).

1857 GRAY *Botany* 117 [The] Barren Strawberry . . . [grows on] wooded hill-sides, common northward, and southward along the Alleghanies. **1890** *Cent.* s.v. *Strawberry,* Barren strawberry, in England, [is] *Potentilla Fragariastrum* . . . ; in America, *Waldsteinia fragarioides.* . . . Neither has fleshy fruit. **1891** *Ib.* s.v. *Waldsteinia,* The barren strawberry . . . [is] widely diffused through northern and mountainous parts of the Eastern and Central States.

+**Barren(s) oak.** [BARREN *n.*]

1. The black-jack oak, *Quercus nigra.*

1797 PRIEST *Travels* 12 Water and barren oak are small and bushy, and only used for firing. **1810** MICHAUX *Arbres* I. 24 *Black jack oak,* seul nom en usage dans les Etats méridionaux. *Barrens Oak,* . . . à Philadelphie. **1814** PURSH *Flora Amer.* II. 629 The Barren Oak or Black Jack of the Virginians is of low growth, especially in the more northern states. **1832** BROWNE *Sylva* 269 In New Jersey and Pennsylvania it is called Barrens Oak. **1847** DARLINGTON *Weeds & Plants* 313 Barren Oak, . . . abundant in Maryland, and well known by the name of 'Black Jack,' is chiefly valuable for fuel. **1892** APGAR *Trees Northern U.S.* 158 Black Oak or Barren Oak. . . . A small tree, . . . with rough, very dark-colored bark.

b. The barrens scrub-oak.

1901 MOHR *Plant Life Ala.* 96 The turkey or barren oak and the blue jack . . . are frequent companions of the long-leaf pine.

2. *Dwarf barren oak:* (see quotation).

1785 MARSHALL *Amer. Grove* 123 *Quercus rubra nana.* Dwarf Barren Oak. This grows naturally upon dry barren ridges, and is found from five to ten feet high, generally growing very crooked.

+**Barren(s) scrub-oak.** [BARREN *n.*] The Turkey oak, *Quercus catesbæi.*

1810 MICHAUX *Arbres* I. 24 Barrens scrub oak. **1814** PURSH *Flora Amer.* II. 631 The Barren Scrub Oak is of shrubby growth, not above fifteen feet high. **1845** LINCOLN *Botany* App. 151 Barren scrub-oak. . . . Bark used by tanners. **1897** SUDWORTH *Arborescent Flora* 170 Turkey oak. . . . Common names [include] . . . Barren Scrub Oak (Tenn.).

+**Barrens white oak.** The post oak, *Quercus obtusiloba.* — **1847** DARLINGTON *Weeds & Plants* 308 Barrens White Oak. . . . Rough Oak. . . . This tree seems to be confined to barren hills, and exposed ridges.

Barreny, *a.* [BARREN *n.*] Of the nature of barrens. — **1882** WORTHEN *Econ. Geol. Ill.* II. 161 Rocks . . . may be found by digging to a small depth nearly all over the barreny hills.

* **Barricado,** *n.* Also †**baricado, barrocado.** A barricade. *Obs.*

1622 'MOURT' *Relation* 24 There we made our Randevous that night, making a great fire, and a Baricado to windward of vs. **1654** *Boston Rec.* 119 His grant of liberty to wharfe or make a barrocado before his land at Center haven. **1677** HUBBARD *Narrative* 18 The said Tropers . . . retired to the main Guard for that night, pitching in a Barricado about Mr. Miles his house. **1724** *New-Eng. Courant* 3-10 Aug. 2/1 They afterwards built a Barricado on Shore, from which they fought the English about 4 hours. **1731** *Boston Rec.* 25 The Wharf latly rebuilt by Mr. Brattle Oliver, upon the southerly end of the out Wharf or Barricado near the south Sconce or Battry.

Barricado, *v.* {1598} *tr.* To defend or fortify with a barricade; to obstruct or block up with a barrier. — **1684** I. MATHER *Providences* v. (1856) 102 People were sometimes barricado'd out of doors, when as yet there was nobody to do it. **1705** *Boston News-Letter* 27 Aug. 2/1 The French-men got on Shoar being 24, who baracado'd themselves, and defended the Sloop. **1776** *Journals Cont. Congress* IV. 203 The streets must be traversed and barricadoed, so as to prevent their coming on our flanks.

* **Barrier,** *n.* A boundary between colonies, etc.; a frontier. {1713-} Also attrib. with *settlement, town.*

1727 *Mass. H. S. Collections* 4 Ser. II. 176 The granting of two lines of barrier towns . . . will occasion long and tedious disputes. **1747** *Penna. Col. Rec.* V. 153 The colonies of New Jersey and Pennsylvania will have but a very thin barrier between them. **1775** ADAIR *Indians* 463 The present Quixote scheme . . . seems . . . to compel them [=the British Americans] to maintain a great body of imperious red coats to rule over them . . . without allowing them any militia, even on their barriers. *Ib.* 148 The barrier-settlements of Georgia. **1854** BENTON *30 Years' View* I. 15/1 The new boundaries . . . established a wilderness barrier between Missouri and New Mexico.

Barrier, *v. tr.* To barricade. {1869} — **1776** C. LEE in Sparks *Corr. Rev.* I. 153, I shall barrier the principal streets.

Barring-out. Shutting out a schoolmaster by barring or barricading the doors and windows of the school. {1728-} — **1834** BRACKENRIDGE *Recoll.* i. 14 The most prominent incident which fixed itself in my memory, was the barring out of the schoolmaster at Christmas, in order to bring him to terms on the subject of the holiday. **1851** *Knickerb.* XXXVII. 69/2 We have a great barring-out. We have held the building already for two days, and have enough poultry and cider laid in to hold out for at least a week. **1889** *Cent., Barring-out* . . . [is] a boyish sport . . . sometimes practised for mischief in parts of the United States.

* **Barrister.** A counselor at law; an attorney or lawyer. See note on ATTORNEY *n.*[1] 1.

1715 *Boston News-Letter* 17 Jan. 2/2 Robert Mompesson, Esq., Barrister at Law, . . . was esteemed the best Lawyer in North-America. **1768** in *Mass. H. S. Proc.* XIX. 149 It is agreed by the barristers and attorneys of this county that . . . the plaintiff have liberty . . . to amend the same. **1789** *Boston Directory* 206 Barristers at Law [include] Hon. Robert T. Paine, Attorney-General. **1838** *Democratic Rev.* I. 70 Richard Newcombe Gresly, Esq. Barrester at Law, Philadelphia. **1842** *Diplom. Corr. Texas* (1911) III. 1002 Dr. Adams is a leading barrister in the Admiralty courts. **1857** *Lawrence* (Kansas) *Republican* 4 June 1 James Christian, Barrister at Law and General Land Agent, Lawrence, K. T. **1891** H. W. SCOTT *Distinguished Lawyers* 173 Forty years ago Virginia was an old State and presented but few inducements to the young, ambitious barrister. **1893** 'MARK TWAIN' *P. Wilson* Introd., I was not willing to let the law chapters in this book go to press without first subjecting them to . . . correction by a trained barrister. **1900** STOCKTON *Afield & Afloat* 145 An unreasonable distrust for attorneys and barristers who might happen to be at the beginning of their careers.

+**Bar-room.** Also **barroom, bar room.** [BAR *n.*[1] 7.]

1. A room where liquors are kept ready to be drawn and sold at a counter. {E. *tap-room* or *bar*}

1807 ADAMS *Works* IX. 597, I sat down at a good fire in the bar-room to dry my great coat . . . till a fire could be made in my chamber. **1817** *Yankee Traveller* 76 Esquire Wrangle's bar-room, I found was not destitute of good company. **1832** KENNEDY *Swallow Barn* II. v. 80 Toll had imbibed some of the slang, and much of the boisterousness of the bar-room. *c*1840 NEAL *Beedle's Sleigh Ride* 3 As I was going past Mr. Josh Barter's tavern the other day, I heard a terrible noise in the bar-room. **1848** BURTON *Waggeries* 76 Rochester . . . lounged across the marble slabs of the bar-room. **1857** GUNN *N.Y. Boarding-Houses* 111 A showy bar-room, furnished with the usual amount of plate-glass. **1863** B. TAYLOR *H. Thurston* xviii. 232 The same placard was conspicuously displayed in the bar-room of the Ptolemy House. **1878** STOWE *Poganuc People* ix. 96 Loafers who . . . interspersed their observations . . . with visits to the bar-room of Glazier's tavern, which was doing a thriving business that morning. **1889** *Century Mag.* Jan. 451/1 At the rear of the store proper was a snugly fitted-up bar-room. **1907** C. C. ANDREWS *Recoll.* 82, I was greatly surprised to see the streets so desolate and to see so many bar-rooms open at different corners.

2. Attrib. **a.** With *counter, fight, stove,* etc. **b.** With *loafer, orator,* etc.

a. 1839 MRS. KIRKLAND *New Home* i. 11 When my husband . . . drew with a piece of chalk on the bar-room table at Danforth's the plan of the village. **1851** A. O. HALL *Manhattaner* 18 Down through various grades of . . . eating dens, to the more plebeian oyster-stand and bar-room counter. **1860** LOWELL *L'Envoi to the Muse* 77 Across the sand of bar-room floors 'Mid the stale reek of boosing boors. **1865** *Atlantic Mo.* XV. 510 The flaunting red curtains of a bar-room window. **1865** 'MARK TWAIN' *Sk., Jumping Frog,* I found Simon Wheeler dozing comfortably by the bar-room stove. **1877** *Harper's Mag.* Jan. 293/1 John Barnes retreated to hold council with the bar-room loungers. **1882** *Nation* 7 Dec. 485/2 The courtly duel will develop into a street or bar-room fight.

b. 1846 *Congress. Globe* 24 Dec. 86/2 He found the old threadbare charge . . . reechoed by . . . every brawling bar-room politician. **1852** *Knickerb.* XXXIX. 199 The bar-room orators of a little market-town. **1893** GUNTER *Miss Dividends* 109, I should think you would be ashamed . . . to admit associating with barroom loafers!

* **Barrow.**[1]

***1.** A castrated boar; a swine. {Now *dial.*}

'A male hog castrated; a word in common use' (W. '28).

1642 *Md. Archives* IV. 168 Of these piggs . . . none of them were barrowes. **1657** *Suffolk Deeds* I. 6 Three stray swine, on [*sic*] white sow, & two white barrowes. **1671** *Portsmouth* (R.I.) *Rec.* 423, I give a Sow and barrow to Mary and a Sow and barrow to Sarah. **1723** J. HEMPSTEAD *Diary* 134 Stephn drove my swine al into the woods, . . . 6 of them old white sows, 1 red barrow, & 3 white shoats. **1741** *Georgia H. S. Coll.* II. 106 Three sows . . . and three barrows were shot by one Pighly. **1763** WASHINGTON *Diaries* I. 184, 2 Sows 6 Barrows, 15 Pigs. **1854** *Penna. Agric. Rep.* 67 Two very large and fine fat barrows, . . . and two beautiful sow shoats. **1878** *Ill. Dept. Agric. Trans.* XIV. 211, I am confident if Windsor Castle had been altered to a barrow and fully fattened, he would have measured three feet and two inches high to top of rump. **1892** *Ky. Centenary Celebr. by Filson Club* 170 The fort's regular supply of pork habitually wandered around it . . . in the shape of huge white sows and barrows.

2. Appositive with *hog, shote, swine.*

1640 *Conn. Probate Rec.* I. 23 Twenty sixe barrowe hoggs, stores, & sowes. **1643** *Md. Archives* IV. 237 For non delivery of 5 breeding sowes & 5 barrow shotes. **1647** *N.H. Probate Rec.* I. 16 Also he sayeth he hath two barrow swine of a yeare ould and better. **1656** *Suffolk Deeds* II. 288 One barrow hogg & one sow & pigg.

* **Barrow.**[2] An aboriginal burial-mound.

1802 ELLICOTT *Journal* 13 There are several Indian mounds of earth, or barrows, within the vicinity of the village. **1808** ASHE *Travels* v. 42 Two barrows or burial places lie contiguous to the fort. **1879** *Harper's Mag.* July 162 Over by Silver Lake is a mound which the farmers declare must have been an Indian barrow.

* **Barrowist.** A follower of Henry Barrowe († 1593), one of the founders of Independency or Congregationalism. {1589–1645} — **1649** *Md. Archives* I. 245 Whatsoever person or persons shall . . . call or denominate any person . . . Calvenist, Anabaptist, Brownist, Antinomian, Barrowist, . . . Seperatist, or any other name in a reproachful manner relating to matter of religion.

+**Bar-share, Bar-shear.** [BAR *n.*[1]]

1. *Bar-share plow*, a plow having a share from the point of which a bar extends backwards.

1785 WASHINGTON *Diaries* II. 438 Tools and Implemts: . . . Bar Shear Plows, 9s. **1786** *Ib.* III. 80, I ordered . . . the Bar share plow to be used, till the common Corn was all crossed. *c*1797 LATROBE *Journal* 61 [Washington] gave the preference to the heavy Rotherham plow. . . . The Berkshire [*sic*] iron plow he held next in estimation. **1802** J. DRAYTON *S.Carolina* 140 The implements of husbandry, used in Carolina, . . . consist of various ploughs, such as bar-share, shovel, . . . cutter, and drill. **1857** *Ill. Agric. Soc. Trans.* II. 365 The shovel plow, that had been, in pioneer times, used considerably, was superseded by the barshear. **1867** *Iowa Agric. Soc. Rep.* (1868) 156 When the corn is up large enough it is cultivated according to the fancy of the farmers; some with shovel & some with barshear plows. **1876** *Ill. Dept. Agric. Trans.* XIII. 328 The barshare and shovel plow have been succeeded by the Cary, the Diamond . . . and a wonderful number of other earth turners.

ellipt. **1820** *Hillsborough* (N.C.) *Recorder* 12 July, When my corn is up, I run a barshear one round in each corn row.

2. A share fitted with a bar.

1850 *Cultivator* VII. 369 The 'Empire' ploughs with wrought steel mould boards, made with bar shares and wrought iron standards, . . . are superseding all other ploughs.

Bar-soap. [BAR *n.*[1]] Soap made up in bars. {1893–}

1824 *Catawba* (N.C.) *Journal* 26 October, 10 [dozen] Bar Soap. **1835** *Knickerb.* V. 297 He was an estimable individual, and did a good business in the line of bar-soap. **1872** 'MARK TWAIN' *Roughing It* iv. 41 Near it was a pail of water, and a piece of yellow bar-soap. **1881** *Harper's Mag.* Jan. 227/2 Her bar soap and scrubbing-brush were a horror to their eyes.

+**Bar-tender.** [BAR *n.*[1] 7.] One who serves liquors at a bar; a bar-keeper; a barman.

1855 J. E. COOKE *Ellie* 205 He had . . . accepted the office of bar-tender in a fashionable drinking saloon. *a*1861 WINTHROP *Canoe & Saddle* 17 He might have been taken for a decayed priest turned bar-tender. **1871** *Scribner's Mo.* I. 588 The English custom of female bar-tenders is to my mind horrible. **1887** F. FRANCIS *Saddle & Moccasin* 60 'At what time does the stage start for Magdalena?' I inquired of the bar-tender at the 'Metropolitan Hotel,' Tucson. **1903** *N.Y. Ev. Post* 2 Oct. 2 The assault upon a Park Row bar-tender, who refused to reveal the combination of the saloon safe. **1910** *Boston Transcript* 17 Nov. 1/6 The saloon has gone out of existence in Jersey City. . . . The bar tender has been done away with, now being known officially as a 'server.'

* **Barter,** *n.*

***1.** Traffic by exchange of commodities; trade by exchange; truck.

1682 [J. WOODBRIDGE] in *Mass. Bay Currency Tracts* 6 [Money] likewise . . . abrogateth the mystery of trucking, by sinking Barter, and reducing all bought, and sold, to the English Standard. **1823** E. JAMES *Exped.* I. 201 The man is the active agent in this barter, but he avails himself of the advice of his squaw. **1836** IRVING *Astoria* I. x. 165 Their packages of pounded salmon entered largely into the system of barter.

2. Attrib. with *trade* (=transaction).

1839 *Knickerb.* XIV. 71 Her whole crew . . . were on shore every day, . . . entering into various little barter-trades with the inhabitants.

* **Barter,** *v.*

***1.** *intr.* To engage in barter or traffic.

1654 JOHNSON *Wonder-W. Prov.* xxxvi. 83 As for flesh they looked not for any . . . unlesse they could barter with the Indians for venison or rockoons. **1714** *Boston News-Letter* 22 March 1, I have . . . to notify all Persons . . . that they do not . . . truk, barter, buy, sell, deal or trade with any Indian or Indians. **1835** SIMMS *Yemassee* I. 94 The English chief is a great chief, and does not barter for skins. **1840** DANA *Two Years* vii. 53 We . . . filled our jacket pockets with tobacco to barter with the people ashore. **1858** LONGFELLOW *Miles Standish* VII. 37 The traders Touching at times on the coast, to barter and chaffer for peltries. **1882** *Rep. Indian Affairs* 102 This year for the first time, they show a disposition to sell their ponies, instead of bartering.

***2.** *tr.* To give (a commodity) in exchange for another.

1721 *Mass. H. Repr. Journals* II. 368 A Bill to prevent the buying, selling, bartering or exchanging Silver Money or Bullion [etc.]. **1823** JAMES *Exped.* I. 166 They are on their way down the river to barter their beaver at Fort Osage. **1828** *Western Monthly Rev.* I. 724 Horses were so plenty that the Indians were willing to barter one for an axe. **1833** WYETH *Oregon* 84 The white trader barters a tawdry bauble of a few cents' value, for a skin worth fifty of it. **1885** *Rep. Indian Affairs* 162 Any store at which they can barter their fish, furs, hides, berries, etc., for groceries and other supplies that they may need.

+**Bartlett.** [See sense 1.]

1. *Bartlett pear*, a variety of luscious pear, native of England, and widely distributed here by Enoch Bartlett of Dorchester, Mass. Also ellipt.

1847 J. M. IVES *New Eng. Fruit* 56 The best four varieties, according to our estimation, are the Bloodgood, Bartlett, Bell Lucrative, and Winter Nelis. **1853** FOWLER *Home for All* 145 The Bartlet, a fine, noble, buttery, prolific fruit, among the best. **1867–8** *Ill. Agric. Soc. Trans.* VII. 506 Trees affected with this disease have been grafted with Bartlett and other pears. **1872** *Vermont Bd. Agric. Rep.* I. 114 The Bartlett, unlike the Flemish Beauty, is very tender. **1884** ROE *Nature's Story* 340 Sharing the honors . . . given to the peaches were the Bartlett and other early pears. **1901** CHURCHILL *Crisis* 135 Farmer Bell had the prize Bartlett pear tree . . . in that section.

b. A pear of this variety.

1862 *Rep. Comm. Patents: Agric.* 248 While his Bartletts were yielding him ten dollars a bushel in Boston. **1891** CHASE & CLOW *Industry* II. 131 Those yellow Bartletts which grew by your own door. **1901** CHURCHILL *Crisis* 135 He liked a luscious Bartlett.

2. The species of pear tree bearing this fruit.

1882 HOWELLS *Modern Instance* xxiii, I wonder the old Bartlett pear didn't burst into a palm-tree over your heads.

+**Bartram('s) oak.** [From its being found 'in a field belonging to a Mr. (William) Bartram, on the banks of the Schuylkill, 4 miles from Philadelphia.'] A species of oak-tree, *Quercus heterophylla* (Michaux).

1810 MICHAUX *Arbres* I. 24 Bartram's Oak . . . , sur la rivière Schuylkill. **1832** BROWNE *Sylva Amer.* 270 Certain species . . . are so little multiplied that they seem likely at no distant period to disappear from the earth. To this class belongs the Bartram oak. **1868** *Rep. U.S. Comm. Agric.* (1869) 202 Bartram oak. . . . This unique plant forms one of the most beautiful as well as the most interesting of all the oaks. **1901** MOHR *Plant Life Ala.* 473 Bartram Oak . . . [is] sparsely diffused and local from Staten Island to Delaware, North Carolina, northern Alabama, and northeastern Texas.

+**Bartram's sandpiper.** The upland plover or prairie pigeon, *Bartramia longicauda.* — **1813** WILSON *Ornithology* VII. 63 Bartram's Sandpiper . . . being as far as I can discover a new species . . . I have honored it with the name of my very worthy friend, near whose Botanic Gardens . . . I first found it. **1858** BAIRD *Birds* 737 Bartram's Sandpiper; Field Plover: . . . [inhabits] eastern North America. **1890** *Cent., Prairie-pigeon,* [or] Bartram's sandpiper, . . . abounds on the fertile alluvial prairies from Indiana and Illinois to the Dakotas.

+**Bartram's tattler.** =prec. — **1839** PEABODY *Mass. Birds* 370 Bartram's Tattler . . . is considered a great luxury. **1844** *Nat. Hist. N.Y., Zoology* II. 247 The Grey Plover. . . . In the books it is described under the names of Bartram's Tatler [*sic*] and Sandpiper. **1874** COUES *Birds N.W.* 503 Bartram's Tattler, or the 'Upland Plover,' as it is generally called by sportsmen, is a bird of wide and general dispersion in the Western Hemisphere.

+**Barvel.**[1] Also **barvil.** [Prob. a variant of *barbel.*] A New England lake-fish. — **1832** *N.H. Hist. Soc. Coll.* III. 85 The Barvil are taken in the spring of the year . . . with the spear. . . . Their average size is very nearly that of the pickerel. **1900** *Boston Transcript* 10 March 26/3, I think that the word barvel as applied to a fish, must be a localism rather peculiar to the region about Lake Winipiseogee. I remember that one day, more than fifty years ago, Horace Langley . . . brought into Concord a large number of barvels which had been taken from the lake at Alton, N.H.

Barvel.[2] *New Eng. loca* [Prob. repr. ME. *barmfell* 'lap-skin.'] A leather apron worn especially by fishermen. {1736–, *dial.*} — **1629** WINTHROP in *Mass. Col. Rec.* I. 404 We have now sent by these 3 shippes . . .

lynes, hookes, knives, bootes, & barvells, necessary for ffishinge. **1639** *Maine Doc. Hist.* III. 171 Our men lost many of their thinges in the bootes, barvells, ... bucketts, [etc.]. **1640** *Ib.* 297, 1 Calue skin for a barvell. [**1842** BUCKINGHAM *E. & W. States* I. 107 His [=Bay of Fundy fisherman's] knives are a *cut-throat* and *splitter*, his apron a *barrel* [sic].] **1896** *Dialect Notes* I. 412 *Barvel*, large leather apron worn by fishermen. ... Marblehead, Mass.

+**Bar-way.** [BAR *n.*[1] 2.] A passage closable by bars fitting into bar-posts; also, the bars thus used. — **1863** MITCHELL *My Farm* 207 Broken bar-ways have been replaced by new ones. **1880** [see BAR *n.*[1] 2b]. **1884** BURROUGHS in *Century Mag.* Dec. 218 Lines and boundaries are disregarded; gates and bar-ways are unclosed.

Basalt. A variety of trap-rock, frequent in columnar strata. {1789–} Also attrib.

1816 CLEAVELAND *Min. & Geol.* 283 Basalt ... is said to exist on the Stony Mountains. **1839** TOWNSEND *Narrative* v. 200 High walls and regular columns of basalt appear in many places. **1850** G. HINES *Voyage* 150 This astonishing pile of Basalt [=Mt. Hood]. **1856** GLISAN *Jrnl. Army Life* 365 At several places the river is confined by beautiful high, perpendicular columns of basalt. **1873** MILLER *Amongst Modocs* 351 My voice came back in strange echoes from the basalt bluffs.

Basaltes. Latin form of prec. {1601–} — **1837** IRVING *Bonneville* xxxvi, In this neighborhood, he saw ... several prismoids of basaltes, rising to the height of fifty or sixty feet.

Basaltic, *a.* Of the nature of basalt. {1772–}

1804 BROWN tr. *Volney's View of U.S.* 54 Accordingly we find basaltic masses in the vallies of the Allegheny [mountains]. **1815** *N. Amer. Rev.* I. 337 On the west side of Mount Holyoke ... is a series of basaltick columns. **1844** LEE & FROST *Oregon* xviii. 201 Basaltic and granitic rock abounds. **1849** AUDUBON *Western Journal* (1906), 108 We gazed then in silence at the superb cliffs, volcanic, basaltic, and sandstone. **1873** MILLER *Amongst Modocs* 349 The bluff of the river hung in basaltic columns a thousand feet above my head.

+**Bascule pan.** [E. and Fr. *bascule*.] A form of tilt-pan used in sugar-making. — **1833** SILLIMAN *Man. Sugar Cane* 38 Bascule pan of a circular form and moveable on its axis. *Ib.* 100 This is so elevated, that the syrup flows, readily, into the evaporating vessels—which are the (now well known,) bascule pans, called also, tilt or see-saw pans.

***Base,** *n.*[1]

+**1.** One of the stations in baseball.

1845 in *Appleton's Ann. Cycl.* (1886) X. 77/2 No ace or base can be made on a foul strike. *Ib.*, But one base [is] allowed [to be run] when the ball bounds out of the field when struck. **1856** *Spirit of Times* 6 Dec. 229/1 The bases shall be, from home to 2d base, 42 paces; from 1st to 3d base, 42 paces, equi-distant. **1867** CHADWICK *Base Ball Player* 10 The rule makes the base-bag the base, not the post to which it is fastened. **1887** *Outing* April 78/2 The pitcher ... cannot throw to a base and then throw to the bat with one simultaneous motion. **1917** MATHEWSON *Second Base Sloan* 146 It was Jim who praised Wayne's throws to first base.

fig. **1888** 'MARK TWAIN' in *Century Mag.* Jan. 463 It's about the gaudiest thing in the book, if you boom it right along and don't get left on a base.

+**2.** *To change one's base,* to retreat or decamp. *A change of base,* a retreat or departure. *colloq.*

A satirical allusion to the use of the phrase in military reports of operations during the Civil War, e.g.: **1862** MCCLELLAN in *Own Story* (1887) 485 Never did such a change of base, involving a retrograde movement, and under incessant attacks ... partake so little of disorder.

1869 BROWNE *Adv. Apache Country* 325 Sure 'nuff he got down at the next station and made tracks for Frisco. He changed his base—*he* did. *Ib.* 462 Chiv he looked black, but Pop had his turkey-buster well in hand; and Chiv changed his base and fell back on the town. **1888** *Notes & Queries* (London) 22 Sept. 250 This official style [by McClellan] of expressing a retreat furnished much laughter to the South. ... The polite euphuism for all fugacious displays came to be a 'change of base.' **1896** *N.Y. Dramatic News* 18 July 8/4 The change of base was brought about through a misunderstanding between Mr. Sheible and Mr. Cody. Mr. Sheible is at present in New York.

+**3.** *Off one's base,* absurdly wrong with respect to some idea. *slang.*

1882 PECK *Sunshine* 42 The Boston lady held up her hands in holy horror, and was going to explain ... how she was off her base. **1889** K. MUNROE *Golden Days* xxvi. 277 You must be clean off your base. **1907** M. C. HARRIS *Tents of Wickedness* III. iii. 251 Mrs. Butterbeans was so off her base about it, it was ludicrous.

+**Base,** *n.*[2] The game of ball or of prisoner's base. Also fig. — **1845** *Knickerb.* XXVI. 427 The motion very much resembles that of one who, in playing 'base,' screws his ball. **1848** BARTLETT 24 *Base,* a game of hand-ball [*sic*]. **1848** LOWELL *Fable for Critics* Wks. (1879) 131/2 He never was known ... to revel once in base, marbles, hockey. **1866** C. H. SMITH *Bill Arp* 129 Sherman was playin base around about Atlanta.

***Base,** *a.* Mixed or alloyed with inferior metal.

1683 *Penna. Col. Rec.* I. 88 This false, base and counterfitt Coyne. **1704** *Boston News-Letter* 31 July 2/2 Thomas Odell ... infamous for his making & uttering of base Money, absconds. **1876** RAYMOND *8th Rep. Mines* 267 Gold in base bullion. *Ib.*, Silver in base bullion.

***Base,** *v.* [f. E. *base* n.] *tr.* To lay or form a base for. {1587 ('bace'), 1878} — **1807** BARLOW *Columbiad* IV. 150 To base and build the commonwealth of man. *Ib.* 158 Long toils ... Must base the fabric of so vast a throne. **1816** PICKERING 46 To *Base,* to found, to build upon as a basis. A few of our writers have adopted this Gallicism; but it is not in common use.

+**Base-bag.** [BASE *n.*[1] 1.] A bag used to mark first, second, or third base. — **1867** CHADWICK *Base Ball Player* 10 The rule makes the base-bag the base, not the post to which it is fastened. **1886** *Appleton's Ann. Cycl.* X. 78/2 On each corner of ... [the] diamond field are placed the four bases, three of which are base-bags.

BASEBALL, *n.* [BASE *n.*[1] 1.]

1. The 'national game of the United States,' played with bat and ball by two sides of nine each.

The somewhat similar English game is named 'rounders,' although 'base-ball' was used by Jane Austen in *Northanger Abbey* (1803) i. 3. The history of the word in the U.S. before 1850 is obscure.

1850 *Knickerb.* XXXV. 84 As we ... never indulged in a game of chance ... save the 'bass-ball' ... and 'barn-ball' of our boyhood. **1864** T. L. NICHOLS *Amer. Life* I. 394 The American game of base-ball is played by hundreds of clubs. **1871** [L. H. BAGG] *At Yale* 316 The enthusiasm over base-ball was never as high at Yale as now, and the nine is confessedly superior to any other that has yet represented the college. **1881** *Harper's Mag.* Feb. 366/2 A pair of vases ... illustrate the national sport of base-ball. **1884** H. C. BUNNER in *Harper's Mag.* Jan. 298/2 On Murray Hill [N.Y.] ... base-ball and ten-pins are in no great favor. **1889** 'MARK TWAIN' *Speeches* (1923) 145 Baseball is the very symbol, the outward and visible expression of the drive and push and rush and struggle of the raging, tearing, booming nineteenth century. **1891** *Triangle* Feb. 1 The game of base ball has secured such a grasp on the American people that it bids fair to become a popular indoor winter game.

+**2.** The ball used in this game.

1863 'GAIL HAMILTON' *Gala-Days* 50 You may ... hurl the base-ball, follow the plough, ... and yet you may be a hero. **1883** *Harper's Mag.* Dec. 106/2 An oval ball ... a little larger than a base-ball.

+**3.** Attrib. with *bat, contest, game, ground,* etc.

1867 CHADWICK *Base Ball* 119 Base Ball Practice. **1868** CHANNING. *Newport* 38 We had base-ball contests, but without the systematic terminology of the present day. **1868** BEECHER *Norwood* 415 He was a leader on the base-ball ground—loud and merry in his outcry. **1871** [L. H. BAGG] *At Yale* 49 *University* ... [signifies] the picked base-ball nine. **1881** *Sun-beam* (Terre-Haute, Ind.) June 5/1 'Well,' observed the host, picking up a base-ball bat, 'How'll this suit you?' **1886** *Outing* July 490/1 Staten Island Athletic Club's base-ball nine. **1886** *Baltimore Amer.* in *Boston Journal* 21 July 2/3 Any respectable base ball game can attract from 2000 to 7000. **1887** *Lippincott's Mag.* Aug. 312 The four base-ball leagues then in existence. **1888** *Outing* XII. 117/1 The first regular professional baseball team ever established ... went into practical operation in 1868.

+**Baseball,** *v. intr.* To play at baseball. Also with *it.* — **1871** *Northern Vindicator* 22 March, The Blizzards are beginning to base-ball-it again this spring. **1896** *Ohio Chron.* (Columbus) 5 Dec., Even if he proposes to follow baseballing.

+**Baseball club.**

1. A club of baseball players and supporters.

1855 (*title*), Atlantic Base Ball Club, Jamaica, N.Y. **1871** DE VERE 438 The first Base-Ball Club was formed in the City of New York, and of course named the Knickerbocker Club. **1871** [L. H. BAGG] *At Yale* 313 The organization of a base-ball club is one of the first things accomplished by freshmen. **1873** BAILEY *Life in Danbury* 143 It afterward transpired that the grand cripple was the captain of a champion base-ball club. **1897** *Boston Journal* 8 June 4/5 Capt. Anson of the Chicago Base Ball Club.

2. The bat used in playing baseball.

1884 NYE *Baled Hay* 207 Should the immediate lime continue to remain deliberate, lay the water down on a stone and pound it with a base ball club. **1891** S. M. WELCH *Recoll. 1830–40* 173 They were hideous devices ... seeming to have been formed by dipping various sizes of bent base ball clubs in melted gum.

+**Baseballer.** One who plays or supports baseball. — **1888** *Battle Creek* (Mich.) *Journal* 12 Dec., Western Base Ballers. ... The managers of the Western Base Ball Association convened ... Saturday morning.

+**Baseballism.** **1.** The practice or pursuit of baseball. **2.** An expression used in baseball. — **(1) 1870** *Northern Vindicator* 14 May, We dis-serted briefly upon the present popular 'ism' of the day, viz.: base ballism, but deem it necessary to notice further [etc.]. **(2) 1898** *Boston Sunday Globe* 15 May 36/4 There are two kinds of salesmen, the 'pikers,' who grind away all the time, and the men who bunch their hits, to use a baseballism.

+**Baseballist.** A player or supporter of baseball. — **1868** (*title*), New England Base Ballist. A Weekly Journal. **1886** *Congress. Rec.* 2 April 3043/2 [He] is well known ... as a baseballist among constitutional lawyers and a constitutional lawyer among baseballists. **1896** *Ohio Chronicle* (Columbus) 5 Dec., The brilliant record our own Pickaway boy ... has made for himself as a crack base and footballist.

+**Baseball match.** A competitive game at baseball. — **1856** *Spirit of Times* (N.Y.) 1 Nov. 149/2 We continue to receive communications giving us notice of matches to come, and invitations to attend cricket and base ball matches. **1870** EMERSON *Society & Sol.* x. 209 Amiable boys, who had never encountered any rougher play than a base-ball match or a fishing excursion. **1886** STOCKTON *Hundredth Man* iv, If there were enough people here and in the neighborhood to get up a baseball match, . . . that would be something worth considering. **1894** 'MARK TWAIN' *Those Twins* v, Rogers bent himself . . . in the modern attitude of the catcher at a baseball match.

+**Baseball player.** One who plays baseball; *esp.* one proficient at baseball.

1859 (*title*), The Base Ball Player's Pocket Companion. **1867** CHADWICK *Base Ball Player* 71 The Model Base Ball Player. **1870** EMERSON *Plutarch* Wks. (Bohn) III. 347 They are like the baseball players, to whom the pitcher, the bat, the catcher, and the scout are equally important. **1872** HOLMES *Poet* i. 25 The ditch the baseball players of the present era jump over. **1887** *Lippincott's Mag.* Aug. 317 The relations which exist between base-ball players and the associations by which they are employed.

‖**Base bawler.** [With punning allusion to BASEBALLER.] (See quotation.) — **1868** CHADWICK *Base Ball* 107 Base bawlers—the men who, having lost some money in the late [baseball] match are asserting that they have been swindled.

+**Base-board.** The skirting-board next to the floor of a room; a similar board along the bottom of a fence, etc.

1853 FOWLER *Home for All* 159 After mop or base-boards are nailed on, and before lathing, fill in between these boards . . . with stone or mortar. **1857** C. VAUX *Villas* 60 One main thing that has to be attended to in wooden buildings is to make the corner-boards . . . and base-boards broad and heavy. **1884** CABLE *Dr. Sevier* lx. 466 A queer, clumsy patch in the plastering of one wall, near the base-board. **1887** TOURGEE *Button's Inn* 306 A narrow slat which served as a base-board in the room above. **1904** WALLER *Wood-carver* 104, I'm going to . . . fill the shelf around the three sides of the base-board with Aunt Lize's plants. **1925** BRYAN *Memoirs* 17 Our yard was enclosed in the old-fashioned paling fence with a baseboard about a foot high.

+**Base-burner.**

1. A stove in which the fuel is fed automatically from a hopper as the lower stratum is consumed.

1874 KNIGHT 242/1 The principle of the base-burner is also found in the furnace [etc.]. **1877** BARTLETT 32 *Base-burner*, a sheet-iron stove for burning anthracite coal. **1882** *Nation* 24 Aug. 147/2 The store 'base-burner' has been in every town and village . . . the nursery of political agitation and political harmony. **1893** 'O. THANET' *Stories Western Town* 34 We got to keep a fire in the base-burner good, all night, or the plants will freeze. **1922** TITUS *Timber* ii. 28 A gaunt man . . . was putting wood in the base burner as John and his companion entered.

2. Attrib. with *stove*.

1908 WHITE *Riverman* xxi. 188 When the very cold weather came and they had to light the base burner stove. **1911** — *Bobby Orde* i. (1916) 8 An iron 'base burner' stove occupied the middle of the room.

+**Base-burning,** *a.* In which the fuel burns at the base or bottom. — **1874** KNIGHT 242/1 *Base-burning Furnace*, a furnace or stove in which the fuel . . . is fed to the fire as the lower stratum burns. *Ib.* 242/2 Base-burning Stove. **1876** INGRAM *Centennial Expos.* 336 Mr. Ellis' base-burning boiler and self-acting draught regulator.

+**Base hit.** *Baseball.* A hit by which the batter makes first base. — **1875** *Chicago Tribune* 26 Oct. 2/7 The Philadelphians made twenty base hits to their opponents' six, and earned six runs. **1886** *Outing* July 489/1 The Harvard Freshmen . . . defeated the Yale Freshmen. . . . Base hits —Harvard, 3 for 4; Yale, 3 for 3. **1888** *Ib.* May 119/1 When Sweasy opened with a base hit things looked more promising.

Base line.

1. A measured line forming a base in surveying or land-measurement, spec. one running east and west (see quotations). {1785–}

1817 *Niles' Reg.* XII. 97/1 A standard line . . . is run due north and south, through the tract, . . . which line is crossed at right angles by another standard line, running due east and west, which is called the *base-line*. **1822** J. WOODS *English Prairie* 266 Next the ranges were ran [*sic*] into townships, six miles wide, beginning at the Indian boundary, called the base line. *Ib.*, The first line of townships from the base line is called town one. **1834** PECK *Gaz. Illinois* 93 In the surveys, 'meridian' lines . . . are intersected with 'base' lines. **1849** CHAMBERLAIN *Indiana Gazetteer* 22 The only base line running through the State crosses it from east to west. **1862** *Amer. Encycl.* XV. 204 The extensive territories of the United States are surveyed upon a peculiar system. . . . Each great survey is based upon a meridian line run due N. and S. . . . and upon a 'standard parallel' or base line, running E. and W. **1883** SMITH *Geol. Survey Ala.* 450 The narrow trough of Roup's Valley . . . is well defined as far south as the base line between the two surveys.

+**2.** *Baseball.* The line connecting one base with another.

1875 CHADWICK *Dime Base Ball Player* 29 The base lines are the lines running from base to base. **1912** MATHEWSON *Pitching* iv. 85 The ball rolled slowly down the third base line until Brown pounced on it.

+**Baseman.** *Baseball.* A player stationed at a base. — **1867** CHADWICK *Base Ball Player's Bk.* 84 Prepare your field for catches by placing your basemen out further, . . . and the second baseman play at right short. **1897** *Outing* May 204/1 Stagg has the problem of finding a catcher, a second baseman, short stop, third baseman, and a couple of . . . outfielders. **1899** QUINN *Penna. Stories* 45 Heidel, the third baseman of Penn, had just come to the bat. **1912** MATHEWSON *Pitching* 182 As he left the bag he spiked the first baseman. . . . The second baseman blocked the runner.

Basement.

1. A story below or partly below the level of the street, differing from a cellar in being lighter and better appointed. {1730–}

1833 *N.H. Hist. Soc. Coll.* V. 68 In the basement, or cellar, three rooms on the south side were filled with boxes. **1835** HOFFMAN *Winter in West* I. 94 There are a great many stores now building . . . with stone basements. **1837** *S. Lit. Messenger* III. 333 We must eat in the basement to keep the parlors in order for company. **1855** SIMMS *Forayers* 274 This building, a comfortable frame-work of two stories on a basement, . . . faced south and west. **1860** M. J. HOLMES *Rosamond* vi, Every apartment at — Hall, from basement to attic, was full, save two small rooms. **1884** *N.Y. Herald* 27 Oct. 2/2 Corner parlor floor and basement, very elegant, eight light rooms.

+**b.** *English basement:* see ENGLISH *a.*

2. Attrib. with *apartment, door, kitchen*, etc.

1840 *Knickerb.* XVI. 238 One [sign in Wall Street] which bore the name of Brothers Tuck, hanging against the basement office of a very high granite building. **1845** S. SMITH *J. Downing's Lett.* 59 So they went down to the basement door—that means a door that goes into a room about half-way between a cellar and a room above ground—most all the houses here in New York have 'em. **1852** *Knickerb.* XXXIX. 165 She does not allow match-girls . . . to be begging about the basement-windows. **1853** FOWLER *Home for All* 90 Our plan gives just the one [milk room] wanted, . . . near your basement kitchen. **1863** [C. C. HOPLEY] *Life in South* I. 4 Vast hotels rise bodily to admit a new foundation and a new suite of 'basement' apartments. **1863** 'E. KIRKE' *Southern Friends* i. 13 We reached the basement stairs, when everything became bare and dark and dirty. **1865** STOWE *House & Home P.* 269 Basement-kitchens are necessary evils, only to be tolerated in cities where land is too dear to afford any other. **1871** [L. H. BAGG] *At Yale* 293 Each man must . . . draw his own water at the college pump, or hydrant, or cistern or basement pump. **1880** *Harper's Mag.* May 868/2 In the spring of 1879 the building was finished, with the exception of the basement room. **1905** *Cleveland Plain Dealer* 13 Jan. 12, 'I will close any basement room that is opened by the board of education in the future,' said [the] Health Officer.

b. +*Basement house*, a house having a basement story. *Basement story:* (see sense 1).

1852 BRISTED *Upper Ten Th.* ii. 43 Even in a double house, or a house and a half, or a basement house, three different styles which would all admit of cloaking-rooms on the lower floor, no one ever thinks of having them there. **1853** *Harper's Mag.* VII. 129/2 What can be thought of that taste which would carve up such a town site . . . into rectangular squares, . . . and basement-houses tottering upon the meagre patches of grass? **1886** *Century Mag.* Feb. 549/1 We have since built basement-houses in not inconsiderable numbers, but they have never been really popular in New York. — **1826** G. POWERS *New York Prison at Auburn* 73 The basement story contains a kitchen, store-rooms, and pantries. **1833** *Niles' Reg.* XLIV. 178/1 The apartments [in Philadelphia] allotted to the office are in the basement story. **1853** SIMMS *Sword & Distaff* 363 He entered the house, . . . and going down to the basement story, seated himself beneath the piazza. **1872** HOLMES *Poet* x. 315, I am not writing for the basement story or the nursery.

+**Base-plate.** *Baseball.* 'One of the plates formerly often used to mark the bases; hence, by extension, one of the bases' (*Cent.*).

+**Base-player.** *Baseball.* A baseman. — **1867** CHADWICK *Base Ball Player's Bk.* 23 A base player taking a ball from a fielder. **1875** — *Dime Base Ball Player* 36 In appealing for judgment, base-players frequently make important errors.

+**Base-playing.** *Baseball.* Fielding at first, second, or third base. — **1868** CHADWICK *Game of Base Ball* 34 We now come to base playing, and we propose to show that each position has its peculiar points of play. **1891** *Triangle* Feb. 3 The special training should include . . . under base-playing: . . . avoiding the runner in playing base.

+**Base-runner.** *Baseball.* A player making the circuit of the bases. — **1867** CHADWICK *Base Ball Player* 129 The base-runner ceased to be forced to leave the base. **1887** *Outing* X. 78/2 He also commits a balk if he makes a feint to throw to a base occupied by a base-runner. **1912** MATHEWSON *Pitching* 255 A Club composed of good Base Runners.

+**Base-running.** *Baseball.* Running from one base to another. — **1886** CHADWICK (*title*), The Art of Batting and Base Running. **1888** *Outing* Aug. 407 It is only by . . . a lucky act of base-running . . . that a single run is obtained. **1891** *Triangle* Feb. 2 The special training should include . . . under base-running: start from the bat.

+**Base-stealing.** *Baseball.* Reaching a base without the aid of a hit or of an error. — **1891** *Triangle* Feb. 2 The special training should include . . . under base-running: . . . base-stealing. **1917** MATHEWSON *Sec. Base Sloan* xi. 145 He got to first and gave a very pretty exhibition of base-stealing a moment later.

+**Bashaba.** Also **bashabe, -ebe(s.** *Obs.* [Native word.] Titular name of a petty king of an Indian nation formerly inhabiting Maine. — **1605** ROSIER in *Mass. H. S. Coll.* 3 Ser. VIII. 142 [The Indians] often would . . . sign unto us, that their Bashebes (that is their king) had great plenty of furs. **1616** SMITH *Descr. New England* 8 They hold the Bashabes of Pennobscot, the chiefe and greatest amongst them. **1658** GORGES *Brie*

Narration II. vii, That part of the country we first seated in, seemed to be monarchical, by the name and title of a Bashaba. His extent was large. **a1704** HUBBARD *Hist. New England* vii. 30 In the places more eastward, they called the chief rulers . . . bashabeas. **1795** J. SULLIVAN *Hist. Maine* 88 Tribes . . . had above these [chiefs,] higher officers called Bashabas.

***Bashaw.** +A large catfish (*Leptops olivaris*) of the southern and western States. — **1888** GOODE *Amer. Fishes* 378 'The Mud Cat,' 'Yellow Cat,' 'Goujon' or 'Bashaw' is found in all the large rivers of the West and South.

***Basil.** +The mountain mint (*Pycnanthemum*), also called *American* and *wild basil*, or a species resembling this. Also attrib. with *weed.*

The European 'sweet basil' is mentioned by British and American writers from 1709 onwards.

1791 MUHLENBERG *Index Florae* 172 *Clinopodium vulgare*, Basil-weed. **1813** — *Cat. Plants* 56 Basilweed; wild basil; common. Pens.; fl. Aug. **1836** LINCOLN *Botany* App. 130 *Pycnanthemum . . . incanum* (wild basil, mountain mint . . .) leaves oblong-ovate . . . flowers in compound heads. **1847** WOOD *Botany* 419 Mountain Mint. Wild Basil. . . . Grows in rocky woods and hills, Can., N., Mid. and W. States. **1857** GRAY *Botany* 304 Mountain Mint. Basil. . . . Perennial upright herbs, with a pungent mint-like flavor. **1901** MOHR *Plant Life Ala.* 699 *Koellia pycnanthemoides* (Leavenw.) . . . Mountain Basil. . . . Carolinian and Louisianian areas [etc.]. *Ib.*, *Koellia albescens* (Torr. & Gr.) . . . Whitish Basil. [Grows in] Louisianian area. Florida to Texas and Arkansas.

***Basin.** Also **†bason, basan.**

***1.** A shallow circular vessel used esp. for holding water or other liquids. Cf. WASH-BASIN.

1640 *Conn. Public Rec.* I. 448, 7 small peuter dishes, 1 peuter bason. **1646** *Conn. Probate Rec.* I. 16 A trew and perfecte inventory [includes] . . . 2 salts, 3 porringers, 2 saucers & basan. **1693** SEWALL *Letter-Book* 140 A convenient number of basons and porengers. **1704** S. KNIGHT *Journal* 28 An earthen cupp, a small pewter Bason. **1759** H. M. Brooks *Gleanings* 34 A large Assortment of best London . . . pewter dishes, plates, basons, porringers, [etc.]. **1772** J. HABERSHAM *Letters* 200 The purchase of reels and copper basons to be distributed amongst those, who apply themselves to the culture of raw silk. **1851** A. CARY *Clovernook* 71 Taking a little tin basin . . . , the two went to the garden. The basin was by this time filled with currants. **1857** C. VAUX *Villas* 111 A bird-cage, or a basin of gold-fish, will also help to give an air of vitality to the whole room. **1863** MRS. WHITNEY *F. Gartney* xxviii, She turned a faucet that supplied a basin in the counting-room. **1890** BRET HARTE *Waif of Plains* 48 One of the wagons . . . [had] a china basin, and a cake of scented soap.

2. A large hollow or depression containing a body of water, freq. suitable as an anchoring or mooring place for vessels. {1725–}

1729 *Boston Rec.* 14 Voted that a Sum . . . be . . . paid . . . towards the raising the Pavement . . . so the wast[e] water may go over into the Bason. **1778** CARVER *Travels* 143 Small points of land, that . . . contribute, with the islands, to render this delightful bason (as it might be termed) calm and secure. **1785** *Md. Hist. Mag.* XX. 48 He is of opinion the Bason of Baltimore has filled up considerable since the time the aforesaid survey was executed. **1787** FRENEAU *Misc. Works* 429 The barque, . . . gaining the port [of New York] . . . Was safe in the bason, precisely at five. **1791** BARTRAM *Travels* 145 The creek . . . is wide and deep enough for a sloop to sail up into the bason. **1817** *Ann. 14th Congress* 2 Sess. 147 The bill authorizing vessels departing from . . . the basin of the Canal de Carondelet . . . to clear out at the custom-house, in the city of New Orleans. **1837** PECK *Gaz. Illinois* 56 A natural basin, of deep water, is at the mouth of Fox river. *Ib.*, A steamboat basin, or harbor, is to be constructed. **1849** T. T. JOHNSON *Sights Gold Region* xxvi. 248 Suddenly emerging into the bay . . . , we were in the midst of a fine circular basin . . . completely land-locked.

3. A geographical area having a depressed center. {1821–}

Great Basin, an elevated region, with an area of about 210,000 square miles, lying chiefly between the Wahsatch and the Sierra Nevada mountains, and having no drainage to the ocean.

1821 NUTTALL *Trav. Arkansa* 194 Beds of a slaty sandstone . . . inclined in opposite directions so as to form a basin, in which there are indications of coal. **1843** FREMONT *Exped.* 175 Great Basin—a term which I apply to the intermediate region between the Rocky Mountains and the next range, containing many lakes. **c1857** *Kit Carson's Own Story* (1926) 37 Trapped down Mary's River where [it] loses itself in the great basin. **1870** *Amer. Naturalist* IV. 27 The whole so-called basin is but a broad mountain top. **1879** *Scribner's Mo.* Dec. 243/1 The land descends into another swale or basin. **1888** *Nation* 5 Jan. 9/2 The central portion of the [National] Park is . . . accidented with broad depressed basins. **1902** WISTER *Virginian* xxxii. 407 We gained the rim of the basin. It lay below us, a great cup of country,—rock, woods, opens, and streams.

+b. *Basin State*, the State of Utah.

1852 STANSBURY *Gt. Salt Lake* 140 The sustenance of a population so numerous as . . . will ere long be congregated within the limits of the 'Basin State.'

4. The area drained by a river and its tributaries. {1830–}

1804 BROWN tr. *Volney's View* 67 This was subsequent to the formation of the rivers James, Susquehannah, and Delaware, because their basins, the vallies which supply them, are of a greater elevation. **1823** JAMES *Exped.* I. 37 That great formation of secondary rocks, which occupies the basin of the Mississippi and its tributaries. **1854** MARCY *Explor. Red River* 90 A map of the country embracing the basin of this river. **1857** *Lawrence* (Kansas) *Republican* 2 July 1 The great central city of the 'basin of the Mississippi,' which is to arise. **1883** SMITH *Geol. Survey Ala.* 214 The elevated rim, . . . called Sand Mountain, is the border of the Warrior Basin.

***BASKET.** Also **†baskett, -itt.**

***1.** A vessel or receptacle of varying capacity and design, made of interwoven or plaited pliant materials, as rushes, twigs, etc.

1612 W. S[IMMONDS] *Proceedings* vii. 50 They knew . . . how to convay them to trade with the Salvages, for furres, baskets [etc.]. **1622** 'MOURT' *Relation* 21 We found a little old Basket full of faire Indian Corne, and digged further & found a fine great new Basket; . . . the Basket . . . held about three or foure Bushels. **1634** WOOD *New Eng. Prospect* II. xix. 96 In Summer they [sc. Indian women] . . . make curious baskets with intermixed colours and portractures of antique Imagerie. **1667** *Watertown Rec.* I. 91 The Bridge att mill shall be built with Bassketts. **1683** *N.H. Hist. Soc. Coll.* VIII. 134 She turned and went toward the door, with a child and a little basket in her hand. **1716** *N.C. Col. Rec.* II. 259 No expenses [may] be allowed . . . him to buy baskets or any thing else among the Indians for his own use. **1739** *Boston Selectmen* 12 March, Selling coal in baskets commonly called two bushel baskets. **1788** FRANKLIN *Autobiog.* 353 A certain number of leather buckets, with strong bags and baskets (for packing and transporting of goods), which were to be brought to every fire. **1830** *Collegian* 94 Bring the wicker basket nigh, Piled with prose and verses high. **1857** C. VAUX *Villas* 111 A hanging-basket for flowers . . . will also help to give an air of vitality to the whole room. **1865** *Atlantic Mo.* XV. 95 We took a slice or two of bread and butter in a little basket. **1881** *Rep. Indian Affairs* 12 They manufacture from the roots of certain shrubs very strong and durable baskets.

b. A portable grate or cresset; a fire basket.

1875 KNIGHT 1012/1 A grated box or basket . . . in which fuel is burned. **1897** BRODHEAD *Bound in Shallows* 248 The sibilant cackling of the fire in the iron baskets along the bank.

2. A basket with its contents; the fill of a basket; a basketful (*of* something). {1725–}

1631 *Mass. Bay Rec.* I. 92 Plastowe shall (for stealeing 4 basketts of corne from the Indians) returne them 8 basketts againe. **1643** WILLIAMS *Key* 40 Every man carrying a little basket of this at his back. **1687** SEWALL *Diary* I. 181 Went to Hog-Iland; . . . brought home a Basket of Cherries. **1705** *Boston News-Letter* 20 Aug. 2/1 The loading . . . is said to consist of . . . 400 Baskets of Rezins, some Currants [etc.]. **1713** SEWALL *Letter-book* II. 22 A small Indian basket of summer fruit. **1815** *Austin Papers* (1924) I. 251 At Herculaneum I purchased 200 Baskets of Corn. **1867** RICHARDSON *Beyond Mississippi* xii. 147 The Judge . . . fined him twelve cans of oysters and two baskets of champagne. **1880** CABLE *Grandissimes* xviii. 132 A flat Indian basket of warm rice cakes. **1889** *Cent.*, *Basket*, a measure for fruit, equal in the United States to three fifths of a bushel.

+b. *A basket of chips*, in allusive use.

1800 *The Nightingale, or Rural Songster* 77 She smiled like a basket of chips. **1827** *Mass. Spy* 28 Nov. (Th.), The Yankee will say of a young lady, 'She is a real pretty girl, but she is as homely as a basket of chips.' **1840** *S. Lit. Messenger* VI. 513/1 'You look as smiling as a basket of chips,' said the wily brother. **1849** *Knickerb.* XXXIII. 171 His wife is as pleasant as a basket of chips. **1868** CHANNING *Recoll. Newport* 233 Her face was as smiling as a basket of chips on a frosty morning. **1880** *Harper's Mag.* Dec. 83/2 He pretends to be pious as a basket o' chips, but I hain't no vital faith in that kind o' pious. **1898** E. C. HALL *Aunt Jane* 45 There he was, as smilin' as a basket o' chips, if he did have to walk with a cane. **1902** HARBEN *A. Daniel* 18 She spoke to me as pleasin' as a basket o' chips.

3. *Basket-ball.* A goal consisting originally of a fruit basket, but now usually of a metal ring from which is suspended a cord netting open at the bottom.

1892 J. NAISMITH in *Triangle* Jan. 145 The baskets [are] hung up, one at each end on the railing. The goals are a couple of baskets or boxes about fifteen inches in diameter across the opening, and about fifteen inches deep. **1916** BANCROFT & PULVERMACHER *Handbook Athletic Games* 111 The baskets or goals are nets of cord fastened to metal rings 18 inches in diameter. These rings are attached to wooden backgrounds, or backstops. **1922** MATHER & MITCHELL *Basket Ball* 48 A team that carries the ball up the floor and then misses an easy basket has needlessly given the opponents a chance to control the ball.

4. Attrib. **a.** Having a frame of basketwork, as *basket barouche, carriage, cradle*, etc.

1837 *S. Lit. Messenger* III. 691 He, meanwhile, was lying in his basket cradle, his soft black eye following his sister. **1851** *Harper's Mag.* April 673/2 Why, I ask, is my unoffending infant so hedged into a basket-bedstead? **1869** ALCOTT *Little Women* II. 200 The equipages are as varied as the company, and attract as much attention, especially the low basket barouches. **1874** KNIGHT 244/1 Basket-carriage . . . [is] a small vehicle with a wicker bed, and adapted to be drawn by ponies.

+**b.** For which provisions are brought in a basket, as *basket dinner, lunch, picnic.*

1859 [see BASKET-MEETING]. **1868** *Congress. Globe* 6 Feb. 1008/3 In the southern part of Illinois . . . they have what they call basket parties, where every man carries his own refreshments. **1873** *Newton* (Kansas) *Kansan* 24 July 2/1 After a grand barbecue and basket picnic, addresses were made. **1904** *Boston Herald* 22 Aug. 6 A long political speech in the open air . . . at a basket picnic meeting in Ohio. **1904** *Charlotte Daily Observer* 21 Aug. 8 After the speech a basket dinner will be enjoyed by the picnickers. **1905** *Springfield W. Repub.* 11 Aug. 14 At noon a bountiful basket lunch was served under the trees in the park.

+**Basket-ball.** [Invented by James Naismith, 1891.]

1. A popular game, usu. played indoors, in which two opposing teams endeavor to score by tossing a ball through a 'basket' or ring elevated at either end of the court.

1892 NAISMITH in *Triangle* Jan. 144 Basket Ball [*article heading*]. We present to our readers a new game of ball. . . . It fills the same place in the gymnasium that foot ball does in the athletic field. Any number of men may play at it, and each one get plenty of exercise. **1893** *Physical Education* April 21 Basket Ball as an In-door Game for Winter Amusement and Exercise. *Ib.* 22 As Basket Ball originated at the Springfield Training School.

2. The inflated spherical ball used in this game.

1909 WEBSTER. **1916** BANCROFT & PULVERMACHER *Handbk. Ath. Games* 138 Basket balls range in price from $4.50 to $6.

Basket-chair. [BASKET 4a.] A chair made of basket-work. — **1783** E. PARKMAN *Diary* 298, 1 great chair 3s. Six lath basket chairs 24s. **1914** H. JAMES *Ivory Tower* I. i. 3 He now sat . . . in a low basket-chair which covered him in.

+**Basket clause.** A clause of a general or comprehensive character. — **1883** *Congress. Rec.* 13 Feb. 2580/1 This basket clause seems to be a sort of prophetic fine-comb with which to search all the possibilities of the future. **1897** *Ib.* 26 March 367/2 Mr. Bailey:—If we strike . . . [an item] from the dutiable list we transfer it to the 'basket clause' at 25 per cent. . . . Mr. Dingley:—There is no 'basket clause' to the free list.

||**Basket dance.** (?) — **1886** B. P. POORE *Reminiscences* I. 74 The '*minuet de la cour*' and stately 'quadrille' [at a Washington assembly] varied by the 'basket dance,' and, on exceptional occasions, the exhilarating 'cheat,' formed the staple for saltatorial performance, until the hour of eleven brought the concluding country dance.

+**Basket darning.** Darning with crossed interlacing threads. — **1884** *Harper's Mag.* Aug. 346/2 The darned threads are carried across either the woof or warp . . . and are not crossed by a returning thread, as in ordinary basket darning.

+**Basket-fish.** A species of sandstar found on the New England coast. — **1671** WINTHROP in *Phil. Trans.* VI. 2223 Until a fitter English name be found for it, why may it not be called . . . a Basket-Fish, or a Net Fish, or a Purs-net Fish? **1881** E. INGERSOLL *Oyster Industry* 241 Basket-Fish, *Astrophyton Agassizii*, a kind of many armed star-fish.

||**Basket horse.** (?) — **1847** FIELD *Drama in Pokerville* 188 A long, lumbering wagon, canvas-topped, &c., a 'basket-horse' snuffing the breeze out of the after end.

+**Basket-knife.** A knife having a basket or guard over the handle. — **1871** EGGLESTON *Hoosier Schoolm.* xvii. 133 The venerable . . . sentinel strode up and down . . . with his flintlock on his shoulder and his basket-knife in his belt.

Basket-maker. One who makes baskets. {1603-}

1829 COOPER *Wish-Ton-Wish* xx, The Mohicans are basket-makers for the Yengeese. **1851** CIST *Cincinnati* 49 Occupations [include] . . . Bandbox makers, 2 [persons]. Basket makers, 37. **1881** *Rep. Indian Affairs* 136 These Indians are skillful basket-makers. **1899** M. GOING *Flowers* 61 The basket-makers turn the willow's ability to produce adventitious buds to excellent account.

+**Basket-meeting.** [BASKET 4b.] A meeting, gathering, or picnic, for which the participants bring their provisions in a basket.

1859 BARTLETT 24 *Basket-meeting*, in the West, a sort of picnic, generally with some religious 'exercises.' **1868** BAKER *New Timothy* (1870) 74 Every body begins helping every body else to something; for it is 'a basket-meeting.' **1871** DE VERE 191 A corn-husking is announced . . . and the neighbors from far and near assemble, each bringing his provisions in a basket. From the latter feature these pic-nics derive their names of Basket-meetings. **1874** EGGLESTON *Circuit Rider* xxiii. 215 He had been to Jenkinsville t'other day to what the Methodis' called a 'basket meetin'.' **1881** H. PIERSON *In the Brush* 60 Religious meetings, popularly denominated 'basket-meetings,' were known and recognized as established institutions in the Brush. **1892** *Amer. Notes & Q.* VIII. 309 'Basket meetings' are not confined to the Southern negroes. On the contrary they are more common among the white people. Neither are they always religious. Quite frequently they are political, sometimes educational. When purely social they are called picnics.

+**Basket oak. a.** A species of oak tree (see quotation 1899). **b.** Strips of this for use in making basket-work or wickerwork. — **1856** *Florida Plantation Rec.* 506, 1 hand giting out basket oake today. **1892** APGAR *Trees Northern U.S.* 154 *Quercus Michauxii*, . . . Basket-oak, . . . [is] a large and valuable Oak with gray and flaky bark. **1894** COULTER *Bot. W. Texas* III. 414 Basket oak . . . [grows] along streams and swamps. **1899** SUDWORTH *Arborescent Flora* 158 *Quercus michauxii*, Cow Oak. . . . Common names [include] Basket Oak (Ala., Miss., La., Tex., Ark.). *Ib.* 159 *Quercus breviloba*, Durand Oak. . . . Common names [include] . . . Basket Oak (Ala., La., Tex.).

Basket phaeton. [BASKET 4a.] A phaeton having a body of basket-work. — **1878** B. F. TAYLOR *Between Gates* 77 Basket phaetons resembling runaway cradles are working in and out amid the great crashing wains. **1879** *Harper's Mag.* Aug. 386 Strange vehicles crowd the dépôt . . . from the veritable 'one-hoss shay' to the dainty basket-phaeton of fashion. **1887** N. PERRY *Flock of Girls* 64 The next moment the two girls were bowling along the avenue in the pretty basket phaeton.

+**Basket plant.** A species of orchid, *Stanhopea sigrina.* — **1862** *Ill. Agric. Soc. Trans.* V. 796 The *stanhopea sigrina* (or basket plant) is exceedingly rare and fragrant.

Basketry. Basket-making; basketwork. {1851-} — **1883** *Cat. Pedestal Fund Art Loan Exhib. N.Y.* 106 Zuni Basketry. **1893** K. SANBORN *S. Calif.* 104 The art of basketry is rapidly deteriorating, and will soon be lost unless Indian children in the reservation are taught something of the old skill by their grandmothers.

+**Basket-stuff.** Materials for making basket-work.

1824 *N. H. Hist. Soc. Coll.* I. 251 A few ash trees . . . were stripped of bark and limbs, and split literally into basket-stuff. **1846** L. M. CHILD *Fact & Fiction* 165 O-ge-hu-no-qua thought it no harm to gather basket-stuff in the same woods. **1877** *Vermont Bd. Agric. Rep.* IV. 91 The chairs were bottomed with elm bark, . . . or of split ash called basket stuff.

+**Basket timber.** Wood from which material for basket-making may be obtained. — **1845** *Cultivator* II. 303 What are they going to do when the supply of basket timber is exhausted?

Basket wagon. A wagon having a body of basket-work. — **1863** MRS. WHITNEY *F. Gartney* iv, One happy, little child . . . was riding over the lawn in her basket-wagon. **1876** WARNER *Gold of Chickaree* 58 The young lady detached herself at last, . . . and bowled away in her little basket-wagon.

Basket-ware. Ware constructed of or like basket-work. {1858} — **1839** HOFFMAN *Wild Scenes* iii, The patient pedestrian offered next some prettily woven basket-ware and carved wooden bowls, to tempt a purchase from the settler's wife. **1870** *Scribner's Mo.* I. 164 Where in the world did you pick up this old blue basket-ware china?

Basket-willow. The basket- or velvet osier, *Salix viminalis.*

1817-8 EATON *Botany* (1822) 440 *Salix viminalis*, basket willow. Cultivated. **1836** LINCOLN *Botany* App. 136 *Salix . . . viminalis* (osier, basket-willow) . . . Middle sized tree. Introduced [from Europe]. **1847** DARLINGTON *Weeds & Plants* 328 Basket Willow. A large shrub or small bushy tree, with long, straight and slender branches. **1853** J. W. BOND *Minnesota* 172 One kind of wood here . . . promises to be of much value; it is the basket-willow. **1869** FULLER *Flower Gatherers* 52 This branch of Willow (*Salix*) is the Osier, or Basket-Willow.

Basket-work. Anything made in the form or manner of a basket; wickerwork. {1769-}

1825 NEAL *Bro. Jonathan* I. 275 Some tearing ash twigs, for basket work. **1837** IRVING *Bonneville* xxix, The Shoshokoes . . . construct bowls and jugs out of a kind of basket-work formed from small strips of wood plaited. **1874** KNIGHT 243/1 Basket-work . . . is very commonly employed in the United States for the bodies of sleighs, and sometimes for pony phaetons. **1884** O. T. MASON in *U.S. Nat. Museum Rep.* 291-306 Basket-work of the North American Aborigines.

+**Basket-worm.** [BASKET 1.] (See quotations.) — **1862** T. HARRIS *Insects Injur. Veget.* 415 In Philadelphia and the vicinity . . . trees are often very much injured by the insects inhabiting them. These are there popularly called drop-worms and basket-worms. **1889** *Cent.* 420/3 The larva of a lepidopterous insect, *Thyridopteryx ephemeræformis* (Harris) . . . is called bag-worm because it spins a silken bag for its protection, and moves with it hanging downward; it has also received the names *basket-worm, drop-worm*, etc.

***BASS.**[1] Also †**basse, base.**

***1.** One or other of various fishes resembling the perch.

A number are distinguished by special names as *black, calico-, red, sea-, striped bass:* see under these words.

1616 SMITH *New England* 29 Herring, Mullet, Base [*sic*]. **1620** DERMER in Bradford *Hist.* 117 In the botume of the great bay is store of Codd & basse. **1630** [F. HIGGINSON] *New England* 11 There is a Fish called a Basse, a most sweet & wholesome Fish as euer I did eat. **1634** WOOD *New Eng. Prospect* I. ix. 34 The Basse is one of the best fishes in the countrey; . . . it is a delicate, fine, fat, fast fish. **1687** SEWALL *Letter-book* I. 72, [I] am in hopes you will sell that pickled Bass well. **1715** — *Diary* III. 55, I ordered a Bass to be dress'd; sent for Mr. Goodkin, with whom we dined very pleasantly. **1766** *Duxbury Rec.* 335 A petition to the General Court in order to prevent the distraction of the Bass in North river in the winter season. **1775** ROMANS *Nat. Hist. Florida* 187 The principal fish here, and of which the Spaniards make up the bulk of their cargoes, is the red drum, called in East Florida a bass, and in West Florida carp. **1788** J. MAY *Journal & Lett.* 34 Within ten rods of the house we catch any quantity of fish, . . . bass of two sorts, sturgeon of two sorts, and others. **1789** MORSE *Amer. Geog.* 276 Thirty waggon loads of bass have been caught in this bay at one draught. **1800** J. MAUDE *Niagara* 48 Well stocked with fish, as Bass (this is a favourite word with the Americans; they not only call trees by this name, but five or six distinct kinds of fish). **1807** *Mass. H.S. Coll.* 2 Ser. III. 56 The common bass is obtained through the whole year: it is found not only in the sea, but also in the lagunes, especially in the winter. **1834** PECK *Gaz. Illinois* 309 Peoria Lake ... abounds with various kinds of fish, such as sturgeon, buffalo, bass of several species. **1847** LANMAN *Summer in Wilderness* 74, I angled along its sandy shores a number of times, and could take nothing but bass. **1858** VIELÉ *Following Drum* 93 The present limited population [of Brazos Island] are principally ... fishermen who supply the Brownsville market with bass. **1868** CHANNING *Recoll. Newport* 66 Hereabouts were caught by Mr. Young, a celebrated Newport fisherman, the bass and tautog. **1871** *Amer. Naturalist* IV. 693 Bass, or Red-fish (*Corvina ocellata* Cuv.) ... is a very good fish on the table; rich, firm and delicate. **1883** *Century Mag.* July 376/2 There are but two well-defined species, the large-mouthed bass and the small-mouthed bass. **1897** *Outing* XXX. 219/2 The favorite haunts of the bass are about reefs, mats of weeds, submerged and floating logs.

2. Attrib. with *bar, fish, head, net, pole, rod, shoal, water.*

1634 WOOD *New Eng. Prospect* I. ix. 34 The English at the top of an high water do crosse the Creekes with long seanes or Bass Netts, which stop in the fish. **1688** SEWALL *Letter-book* I. 84 Received ... eight Barrels of Pickell'd Bass fish. **1764** HUTCHINSON *Hist. Mass* (1795) I. i. 90 All persons were restrained by a penalty from using cod or bass fish for manuring the ground. **1832** WILLIAMSON *Maine* I. 510 The broth of a boiled bass-head, thickened with homony, was called upaquontop. **1857** HAMMOND *Northern Scenes* 54 An English bass rod is the best, and with such ... the largest fish of these lakes may be secured. *Ib.* 338 He will supply himself with a strong bass-pole, a strong treble-action reel. *Ib.*, Near the upper end of Long Island are other prolific bass shoals, where the fisherman may enjoy himself. **1895** *Outing* XXVI. 371/2 We soon covered the distance and cast anchor on a famous bass-bar. **1897** *Ib.* XXX. 218/2 No attempt is made to give a complete list of the good bass-waters.

Bass.[2] [Alteration of *bast* {1691–}.]

+**1.** The lime-tree or linden, *Tilia americana.*

1778 CARVER *Travels* 499 The Bass or White Wood is a tree of a middling size, and the whitest and softest wood that grows. **1800** J. MAUDE *Niagara* 52 In the Winter, the Sugar-tree and the Bass are felled as fodder for cattle, which will greedily eat the greater part of the smaller branches. *a***1817** DWIGHT *Travels* IV. 83 The forests are beach, maple, bass, etc., but are shorter and less thrifty than in the preceding parts of our journey.

+**2.** Attrib. with *land, slat.*

*a***1817** DWIGHT *Travels* III. 178 The land between Utica and Laird's is what in New England is called beech and maple land, and here maple and bass land. **1874** *Vermont Bd. Agric. Rep.* II. 514 My corn crib ... is divided into two, and is made of three inch bass slats nailed fast.

+**Bassano.** A variety of beet. — **1857–8** *Ill. Agric. Soc. Trans.* III. 503 The early bassano ... comes the earliest. It is turnip shaped, light red, tender and sweet.

+**Bass bark.** [BASS.[2]] Bark of the basswood tree or lime-tree, *Tilia americana.* — **1794** W. BENTLEY *Diary* II. 111 Our country men from bass bark have manufactured wrapping paper. **1858** WARDER *Hedges & Evergreens* 64 The plants may be tied in bundles of one or two hundred with bass-bark or willow. **1863** *Horticulturist* March, Advt. 13 Bass Bark or Matting for budding and tying purposes ... for sale.

Bass boat. (?) A boat used in fishing for bass. — **1627** *Agreement* n Bradford *Hist.* 273 The above-said parties [Bradford, Standish, etc.] are to have and freely injoye the pinass latly builte, the boat at Manamett, and the shalop, called the Bass-boat.

Bass drum. A drum of low pitch. — **1804** BENTLEY *Diary* III. 68 The instrumental Music was provided in Town ... & consisted of the Bass Drum, Bassoon, Clarinet & flute. **1832** WILLIAMSON *Maine* II. 687 Formerly the fife and drum ... and the trumpet ... were the instruments of martial music. But in later years there have been introduced the bass-drum, bassoon, ... French horn and bugle. **1838** [INGRAHAM] *Burton* II. xi. 175 A bass-drum standing near the entrance, one or two bugles, and several swords ... lying about on the ground. **1884** CABLE *Dr. Sevier* liii, The soft boom of a bass-drum.

Bass-fisher, -fisherman. [BASS.[1]] One who fishes for bass.

1857 HAMMOND *Northern Scenes* 338 August is the best month in the year for the bass fishermen. **1884** ROE *Nature's Study* 128 A quick movement which an old bass-fisherman taught me. **1897** *Outing* XXX. 218/2 How well he [=the black bass] can do this the bass-fisher knows.

Bass-fishing. Fishing for bass.

*a***1656** BRADFORD *Hist.* 323 Bass fishing was never lookt at by them, but as soone as ever they heard on it, they looked at it as a vaine thing. *Ib.* 326 Mr. Allerton wente to the ship aboute his bass fishing. **1856** *Spirit of Times* (N.Y.) 11 Oct. 98/1 It is now the most interesting part of the bass-fishing season. **1895** *Outing* XXVI. 369/1 To lovers of bass fishing few fields offer more attractions than the lake region of Minnesota. **1897** *Ib.* XXX. 216 [Article on] Bass and Bass-Fishing.

Bass horn. {*a*1860} +*Humorously.* A piece of artillery. — **1862** NORTON *Army Lett.* 130 The rebs played on it with their 'brass bands' and 'bass horns.'

+**Bassing-ground.** 'Fishing-ground for bass; a place where bass may be caught' (*Cent.* s.v. *Ground*).

Bassoon. The musical instrument of that name. {1727–} — **1773** Singleton *Social N.Y.* 295 [Rivington had] bassoon, hautboy and bagpipe reeds, with and without cases. **1807** IRVING *Salmagundi* iv. 86 Like the sound of a French horn, bassoon, kettle-drum, and bass-viol, in our orchestra. **1832** [see BASS DRUM]. **1857** WILLIS *Convalescent* 241 A carnally common ... clarionet—bassoon and other nameless instruments in the background. **1885** F. M. A. ROE *Army Lett.* 339 We have two violins, oboe, and bassoon, the latter instrument giving the deep organ tones.

+**Bass rock.** *N.C.* ?The rockfish or striped bass. — **1784** J. SMYTH *Tour U.S.* I. xi. 89 Amazing numbers of those fishes, here called Bass-Rocks, coming up to the falls at the same time to spawn.

+**Bass tree.** [BASS.[2]] The basswood tree. — **1790** *N.H. Doc. & Rec.* VII. 716 Accordingly we marched till we found a large bass tree.

Bass viol. The musical instrument so named. — **1737** PARKMAN *Diary* 25 Mr. Hovey there with a Bass Viol. **1807** [see BASSOON]. **1840** J. D. WHITNEY *Life & Lett.* 44 [In] New Hampshire ... everybody scrapes the fiddle or bass-viol. **1871** STOWE *Sam Lawson* 56, I've walked ten miles ... jest to play the bass-viol in the same singers' seat with Huldy. **1885** HOLMES *Mortal Antipathy* Introd., A huge bass-viol which wallowed through the tune like a hippopotamus.

+**Basswood.** Also **bass-wood, bass wood.**

1. The wood of the American lime or linden, *Tilia americana.*

1670 [implied in BASSWOOD-TREE]. **1728** *Boston Rec.* 222 We are of opinion that no popler, chestnut, pine, henlock [*sic*], sassifax, black ash, basswood, or ceder shall be corded up. **1779** T. B. HAZARD in *Narrag. Hist. Reg.* I. 41 Made a hoe handle of bass wood. *a***1797** B. RUSH in Imlay *Western Territory* (ed. 3) 149 The sap ... is carried and poured into store troughs ... made of white ash, linden, bass wood, or white pine. **1847** *Knickerb.* XXIX. 377 The little fellows are gathering at evening now about the fire-side, to see their elders split and whittle the sweet-smelling pine and bass-wood. **1855** LONGFELLOW *Hiawatha* x. 153 Laughing Water ... gave them drink in bowls of bass-wood. **1879** B. F. TAYLOR *Summer-Savory* xi. 99 The E-flat bugle ... never sounded half so sweet to me as that bit of piping basswood. **1904** WALLER *Wood-Carver* 57 There are two planks of basswood under the eaves in the garret.

2. The tree yielding basswood.

1784 CUTLER in *Mem. Academy* I. 456 *Bixa.* ... Bass wood. White wood. Suggumug. **1814** PURSH *Flora Amer.* II. 362 *Tilia glabra.* ... This tree is known by the name of Lime- or Line-tree; Basswood; Spoonwood; and is both useful and ornamental. **1818** *Mass. H. S. Coll.* 2 Ser. VIII. 170 In July the lover of plants is gratified with ... the flowering raspberry, and among the trees the chesnut and basswood. **1841** COOPER *Deerslayer* ii, The trunk of a huge linden, or bass-wood, as it is termed in the language of the country. **1843** TORREY *Flora N.Y.* I. 116 *Tilia americana.* ... Whitewood. Basswood. ... The wood ... is used for chair seats and the pannels [*sic*] of coach bodies. **1851** J. S. SPRINGER *Forest Life* 31 The Balm of Gilead, ... the Ash and Bass-wood, ... all afford specimens of great magnitude. **1859** A. VAN BUREN *Sojourn in South* 43 The bay, or cucumber tree was pointed out to me. It looked like our bass-wood. **1890–3** TABOR *Stowe Notes* 19 After an hour's hard work, succeeded in bringing down the large basswood. **1897** *Outing* XXX. 224/2 Under the low-hanging basswood, where the three trees stand in the water.

3. Attrib., in sense 'made of basswood,' as *basswood ball, button, paddle, plank,* etc.

1824 *Microscope* (Albany, N.Y.) 27 March 4/1 (Th.), All the heroes of wooden nutmegs, horn gun-flint, and bass-wood button memory. **1833** 'ELMWOOD' *Yankee among Nullifiers* 40 They have been much in the habit of purchasing ... bass-wood pumpkin seeds. **1845** JUDD *Margaret* I. ii. 7 Chilion, her brother, who was at work with a piece of glass, smoothing a snow-white bass-wood paddle. **1849** *Knickerb.* XXXIII. 279 The bass-wood troughs or sweet-smelling cedar buckets. **1850** *Congress. Globe* 30 April 861/3 Wooden nutmegs, horn flints, and basswood hams. **1851** *Knickerb.* XXXVII. 377 The country-bred traveller ... smells the bass-wood 'spouts,' ... and inhales the odor of the red-cedar buckets. **1855** THOMPSON *Doesticks* 220 Magnificent forest scene— ... a mossy bank ... made of canvass, stretched over a basswood plank, and painted mud color. **1857** *Knickerb.* XLIX. 93 An old scow-built, bass-wood-bottomed canal-packet. *Ib.* 109 We have received, through a friend, four different kinds of basswood paper. **1879** B. F. TAYLOR *Summer-Savory* xi. 99 It looked like a basswood whistle, but it was bliss. **1895** *Outing* XXVI. 474/1 An hour in the saddle chasing the bounding basswood ball.

b. In depreciatory use.

*a***1859** B. YOUNG *Sermon* (B.), You Gentiles and hickory and basswood Mormons can write it down, if you please; but write it as I speak it. **1882** *Congress. Rec.* 2 Feb. 832/1 Every man who has ever practiced before a justice of the peace in a hog case in a bass-wood township would know [etc.].

+**Basswood log.** A log from a basswood tree.

1843 *Yale Lit. Mag.* VIII. 361 The half of a basswood log with the bark peeled off ... was placed under his head, in lieu of a pillow. **1846** *Knickerb.* XXVIII. 338 We proceeded ... to split bass-wood logs and hollow them. **1855** THOMPSON *Doesticks* 37 My arms fast asleep ... ; my other extremities with no more feeling in them than in a bass-wood log. **1892** *Vermont Agric. Rep.* XII. 155 The farmer of fifty years ago ... tapping his trees with an axe and catching the sap in troughs dug from bass wood logs.

+**Basswood tree.** =BASSWOOD 2.

1670 *Rowley Rec.* 210 The Northwest Angle is a basswood tree. **1740** *Lunenberg Proprietors' Rec.* 230 [The line] runs south some thirty degrees West on Common Land to a bass wood tree twenty two rod. **1778** CARVER *Travels* 26 They parcel it out into cakes, and inclosing them in leaves of the basswood tree, place them in hot embers. **1805** *Mass. Spy* 17 July 3/1 The main body [of birds] . . . appeared to be hovering round the top of an old bosswood [*sic*] tree. **1832** WILLIAMSON *Maine* I. 106 The Bass-wood tree is considered the same as the Linden or Lime-tree. **1837** IRVING *Bonneville* II. 146 The voyagers swept down . . . , arriving at the regions of . . . mulberry and basswood trees. **1885** *Harper's Mag.* July 194/2 The buffalo had at one time grazed in the shade of the basswood-trees.

+**Bassy,** *a.* [BASS.[1]] Frequented by bass. — **1897** *Outing* June 222/2 An opening in a mat of weeds, a shadowed nook . . . where a tree overhangs the water, into which insects may drop—these are very 'bassy' spots.

***Bastard,** *n.* +**1.** Bastard sugar. +**2.** A loggerhead turtle, *Thalassochelys (Colpochelys) kempi*, of the Gulf of Mexico. — (1) **1833** SILLIMAN *Man. Sugar Cane* 72 Two vacuum pans . . . will each refine . . . two and a half tons per day, . . . giving five days refining, and one day bastards. — (2) **1889** *Cent.* s.v.

***Bastard,** *a.* Applied specifically, as in general English use, to designate things, plants, trees, animals, etc., differing in some way from those properly entitled to the name or usually known by it.

*c***1728** CATESBY *Carolina* I. 49 *Icterus minor.* The Bastard Baltimore. Weighs thirteen pennyweight. **1808** WILSON *Ornithology* I. 23 Buffon, and Latham, have both described the male of the bastard Baltimore (*Oriolus spurius*), as the female Baltimore. — **1827** *Western Mo. Rev.* I. 209 It is a tall reedy . . . water-plant, not unlike the bastard cane of the southern countries. **1849** *Rep. Comm. Patents: Agric.* (1850) 169, I fear it will turn out to be, what we occasionally find in both varieties of the ribbon cane, a bastard cane, so called, always remaining of a light dun or dirty white color. — **1785** MARSHALL *Amer. Grove* 144 *Smilax Pseudo China.* Bastard China. — **1791** MUHLENBERG *Index Florae* 164 *Cynanchum tuberosum*, Bastard Dogs-bane. —**1823** *Missouri Intell.* 8 April 3 Drugs. Bastard emery. — **1774** HUTCHINSON *Diary & Lett.* I. 240 The grass appears unlike our salt grass: more like what some call bastard grass. — **1791** MUHLENBERG *Index Florae* 159 *Diathera americana.* Bastard Hedge-hysop. — **1888** CABLE *Bonaventure* 291 The maimed form and black and red markings of a 'bastard hornsnake.' — **1785** MARSHALL *Amer. Grove* 5 Shrubby Bastard Indigo. This grows naturally in Carolina, where it rises with many irregular stems, to the height of ten or twelve feet. **1806** *Ann. 9th Congress* 2 Sess. 1142 Wild carrot, wild onion, . . . wild cabbage, and bastard indigo. — **1847** DARLINGTON *Weeds & Plants* (1860) 256 Barbarian Lycium. Bastard Jasmine. **1894** *Amer. Folk-Lore* VII. 95 *Lycium vulgare*, . . . box-thorn, bastard jasmine. Iowa. — **1837** WILLIAMS *Florida* 39 Seven of them are covered with mangrove bushes and bastard lignumvitae. — **1882** WORTHEN *Econ. Geol. Ill.* II. 81, I observed . . . a layer of hard, firmly-cemented, calcareous sandstone. . . . It is generally called bastard limestone in this vicinity. — **1851** *S. Lit. Messenger* XVII. 374/2 The Mezquite . . . is not known to exist in our prairies; their frequenters have no name for it, except perhaps 'bastard locust.' — **1737** BRICKELL *N. Carolina* 20 In these Parts . . . [there are] Horehound, Melilot, Bastard-Lovage. — **1684** *Essex Inst. Coll.* XXII. 2 Also I give him . . . two acres of bastard and salt marsh or ruff meadow. — **1639** *Md. Archives* 77 One serviceable fixed gunne of bastard muskett boare. **1643** *Plymouth Laws* 74 Carbines and fouleing peeces . . . not above foure foote & a half long and not under bastard muskett or caliver bore. — **1901** MOHR *Plant Life Ala.* 470 *Quercus brevilobata*, Texan White Oak, Pin Oak, Bastard Oak, . . . [is] of some value for its timber. — **1784** CUTLER in *Mem. Acad.* I. 450 *Pyrus*, . . . Bastard Pear. Juniper. — *Ib.* 404 *Veronica*, Bastard-Peppergrass. — **1785** MARSHALL *Amer. Grove* 100 *Pinus echinata.* Three leaved prickly-coned Bastard Pine. This grows naturally in Virginia. **1884** SARGENT *Rep. Forests* 202 *Pinus Cubensis* . . . Bastard Pine. Meadow Pine. — **1724** *Wyllys Papers* 406 Our black girl Dinah . . . dyed (I think) of what they call a bastard plurisy. — **1791** BARTRAM *Travels* 274 The bastard rattle snake, by some called ground rattle snake, is a dangerous little creature. — **1737** BRICKELL *N. Carolina* 58 The Bastard Saffron is plenty in this Province. — **1882** WORTHEN *Econ. Geol. Ill.* II. 160 A hard calcareous sand rock, or, in the language of the people, a bastard sandstone. — **1832** *Louisville Public Advt.* 3 March, A general assortment of hardware . . . among which are mill, cross cut, bastard and hand saw. — **1888** GOODE *Amer. Fishes* 78 The Mangrove Snapper . . . of Charleston, called at Pensacola the 'Bastard Snapper.' *Ib.* 84 The Bream, or 'Bastard Snapper,' *Sparus aculeatus.* — **1709** LAWSON *Carolina* 92 Bastard-Spanish is an Oak betwixt the Spanish and Red-Oak. **1775** *Amer. Husbandry* I. 377 *Bastard Spanish oak*, used for rails and clapboards. — **1833** SILLIMAN *Man. Sugar Cane* 93 The language of the sugar refiners appears to be tolerably uniform, in applying the term bastard sugar to that which is formed from the first dripping of the lump. **1877** BURROUGHS *Taxation* 551 Bastard sugar is the residuum . . . of clayed sugars. — **1843** TORREY *Flora N.Y.* II. 160 *Comandra umbellata* . . . Bastard Toad-flax. . . . Dry rocky hill-sides, and in woods; frequent. **1846** WOOD *Botany* 479 Bastard, Toad-flax. . . . Plant about a foot high, in rocky woods.

Bastile, *n.* [From the *Bastille* in Paris.] A prison. {1790–1861} — **1884** SWEET & KNOX *Through Texas* 611 It took five policemen to show him the way to the bastile. **1884** *Ransom City* (Dakota) *Paper* 9 Feb., Fined $25, and ten days in the bastile, for selling liquor to the Indians.

Bastile, *v.* [Cf. prec.] *tr.* To imprison. {1742–98} — **1861** W. PHILLIPS *Speeches* (1863) 422 One thousand men . . . are 'bastiled' by an authority as despotic as that of Louis. **1889** FARMER 43 *To be bastilled* was the term which, during the Rebellion, was applied to the secret imprisonment inflicted by the military authorities upon those whose sympathies were assumed to lie with the Southern cause.

Basting ladle. A ladle for basting a roast of meat. — **1720** SEWALL *Letter-book* II. 106 One brass basting ladle; one larger brass ladle.

***Bastion.** A projecting part of a fortification having a pentagonal form.

1666 *Doc. Hist. N.Y. State* (1849) I. 74 At Albany . . . [there is] a small fort of foure bastions. **1678** ANDROS *Answer, Ib.* 89 Albany is a smale long stockadoed forte with foure bastions in it. **1708** *Boston News-Letter* 4 Oct. 4/2 They fired from the hill . . . , and wounded another man in the bastion. **1758** *Lett. to Washington* II. 268 The parapet on the last curtain is up, the last bastion is layd over with logs and two of the amburiers done. **1776** *Journals Cont. Congress* IV. 203 The north east and north west bastions, with the communicating curtain. **1789** MORSE *Amer. Geog.* 254 The fort . . . is a square with four bastions. **1819** E. DANA *Geogr. Sk.* 204 The town [St. Augustine] is fortified with bastions enclosed with a ditch, and defended by a castle. **1849** T. T. JOHNSON *Sights Gold Region* xv. 142 The purposes of defense against the simple warfare of the Indians being fully answered by bastions, the guns from which entirely commanded the walls. **1890** *Century Mag.* Dec. 170 Cannon . . . were pointed in every direction through embrasures in the walls and bastions.

***Bat,** *n.*[1]

***1.** The mouse-like quadruped of that name.

1709 LAWSON *Carolina* 125 The Bat or Rearmouse [is] the same as in England. *Ib.*, Roast a Bat on a Skewer, then pull the Skin off. **1792** BELKNAP *Hist. N.H.* III. 165 The only mamillary biped which we have, is the Bat. **1827** COOPER *Prairie* xxviii, He has never seen a buffalo change to a bat; he will never see a Pawnee become a Sioux. **1850** [S. F. COOPER] *Rural Hours* 342 There are said to be five different kinds of bats in this State. **1884** ROE *Nature's Story* 310 There are four species of bats to be mentioned, besides moles and shrews. **1885** *Amer. Naturalist* Sept. 922 The free-tailed bat, found in the north-eastern part of the State [of Kansas].

+**2.** The bull-bat or night-hawk, *Chordeiles virginianus.*

1709 LAWSON *Carolina* 144 East-Indian Bats or Musqueto Hawks, are the Bigness of a Cuckoo, and much of the same Colour. *c***1728** CATESBY *Carolina* I. 8 The Goat-Sucker of Carolina. . . . They are very numerous in Virginia and Carolina, and are called there East-India Bats. **1812** WILSON *Ornithology* V. 65 Night-Hawk. . . . This bird in Virginia and some of the southern districts, is called a bat. **1899** GREEN *Va. Word Book* 52 *Bat*, the night hawk.

***Bat,** *n.*[2]

***1.** The wooden implement used for striking the ball in various games, now esp. baseball.

1734–5 *Harvard Coll. Rec.* III. 383 Freshmen are to find the rest of the scholars with bats, balls, and footballs. **1786** *Independent Journal* (N.Y.) 19 April, To the Cricket Clubs: . . . batts and balls to sell. **1856** *Spirit of Times* (N.Y.) 6 Dec. 229/1 The bat or club [used in baseball] is of hickory or ash, about 3 feet long, tapering, . . . and round. **1865** *Atlantic Mo.* XV. 301 One of the bats which had done terrible execution on the tutor's windows. **1876** 'MARK TWAIN' *Tom Sawyer* xii. 107 He put his hoop away, and his bat: there was no joy in them any more. **1897** *Boston Journal* 8 June 4/5 Put McCormick behind the bat. Now . . . you'll win the pennant. **1905** VALENTINE *H. Sandwith* 393 Recess grounds . . . secured for Dunkirk youth with bat and ball.

fig. **1889** 'MARK TWAIN' *Conn. Yankee* xi. 516 Step to the bat, it's your innings. **1888** — in *Century Mag.* Jan. 459/1 [He] shall get a Meisterschaft answer—and hot from the bat! **1910** W. M. RAINE *B. O'Connor* 65 Turn loose your yarn at me hot off the bat.

+**b.** An Indian ball-stick.

1809 A. HENRY *Travels* 78 *Baggatiway* . . . is played with a bat and ball. . . . The bat is about four feet in length, curved, and terminating in a sort of racket. **1853** [cf. *ball-bat* s.v. *Ball n.*[1] 3].

2. *Bat and ball*, a juvenile game played by one or two batters and an opposing group of ball-servers and fielders. (Also allusively: quot. 1882.)

1791 BENTLEY *Diary* I. 254 Afterwards [i.e. after May] the Bat and Ball and the Game at Rickets. . . . The Bat & Ball as the weather begins to cool. **1832** WILLIAMSON *Maine* I. 507 The principal amusements among the natives are dancing, footracing, . . . and among the boys, bat and ball. **1882** G. C. EGGLESTON *Wreck of Red Bird* 129 The savage thought he would have a game of bat and ball with me . . . , so he took good aim and threw his club at me. *Ib.* 130, I suppose the savage don't know the rules of bat and ball.

3. *Baseball.* The turn of a player or team to bat. Usually in prep. phrases, esp. *at bat.* Also fig.

1875 *Chicago Tribune* 18 August 5/6 The fine play of the home nine for seven innings, . . . both in the field and at the bat. **1884** NYE *Baled Hay* 52 Common decency ought to govern conversation without its being necessary to hire an umpire to announce who is at bat and who is on deck. **1888** *Outing* May 118/2 Ferguson won the toss, sent the Cincinnatis to the bat, and at three P.M. . . . the contest began. *Ib.* 119/2 The Reds went to the bat, got in two runs [etc.]. **1903** A. H. LEWIS *The Boss* 186 You can tell by th' way they go to bat, whether th'

Blackberry has signed up to them to kill our franchise. **1904** *Chicago Ev. Post* 23 Aug. 2 Ordinarily, the first application filed is entitled to consideration.... The Democrats, of course, claim they were first at bat.

+**Bat,** *n.*[3] *slang.* Also **batt.** A spree or frolic.

1848 DURIVAGE & BURNHAM *Stray Subjects* 102 Zenas had been on 'a bat' during the night previous. **1869** WASHBURNE *Fair Harvard* 69 (Th.), I went to a 'bat' in S.'s room, and we smoked and drank till three. **1887** *New York Sun* June, Make the Hon. John P. St. John start upon a tearing 'batt.' **1891** *Harper's Mag.* Oct. 778/1 He had been on a bat, and all on earth that ailed him was that spree. **1893** HOWELLS *Coast of Bohemia* 261 He invited Charmian to take part in various *bats*, for the purpose of shocking the Pymantoning propriety of Cornelia. **1901** [P. L. FORD] *House Party* 188 We defied the Head and went off on the meekest and stupidest little bat you ever saw.

* **Bat,** *v.*[1] [BAT *n.*[2]]

1. *intr.* To use the bat in ball games. {1773–}

1872 EGGLESTON *Hoosier Schoolm.* iv. 48 He could not catch well or bat well in ball. **1887** *Courier-Journal* (Louisville) 27 May 2/4 The game was a terrific batting contest.... Werrick, Mack and Cross all batted in fine shape. **1917** MATHEWSON *Second Base Sloan* 241 Clover Jones?... He ain't so bad as some. He bats better'n Tim Leary.

* **2.** *tr.* To strike with a bat or otherwise.

1877 WM. WRIGHT *Big Bonanza* 62 When the book was not wanted..., those lounging about the saloon were in the habit of... 'batting' each other over the head with it. **1882** J. MCCABE *Nat. Encycl.* 572 All balls batted directly to the ground that bound or roll within the foul lines. **1887** *Scribner's Mag.* (F.), S'manthy just now was batting clothes on a block in front of the house. **1907** WHITE *Arizona Nights* xi. 168 Men got batted over the head often enough in those days.

+**3.** *Baseball.* To hit safely balls served by (a pitcher). Freq. in passive.

1887 *Courier-Journal* (Louisville) 27 May 2/4 Harkins started to pitch; ... after being batted for twenty-two hits the wearied pitcher surrendered up his post. *Ib.* 4 June 2/7 The Cleveland nine... batted Lynch freely and beat the Mets. **1896** *Cincinnati Enquirer* 5 July 2/5 Hart was batted freely, and that saved the game.

Bat, *v.*[2] *tr.* To close and open (the eyes) rapidly; to wink. {1847– *dial.*} Also simply, to close (the eyes).

1845 HOOPER *Simon Sugg's Adv.* xii. 143, I didn't say nuthin, but jist batted my eye at old Chamblin, and he laffed. **1848** LINCOLN in Carpenter *At White House* (1867) 271 General Cass... shakes his head, and bats his eyes, and blunders back. **1883** 'MARK TWAIN' *Life on Miss.* xliii. 438 Unhandkerchiefs one eye, bats it around tearfully over the stock. **1888** 'CRADDOCK' *Broomsedge Cove* xii. 208 If my patient can't sleep, not a soul in the house shall bat an eye all night. **1904** *N.Y. Sun* 7 Aug. 1 The Judge would say: 'That's interesting;... I hadn't heard of it.' But, as they say out West, 'he wouldn't bat an eye.' **1920** MULFORD *J. Nelson* xii. 126, I've seen you put away a dozen an' not bat an eye.

Batchelder, variant of BACHELDER.

+**Batea.** [Sp. (and Pg.) *batêa* tray, trough.] A shallow wooden trough used in California and Mexico for washing ore.

1844 GREGG *Commerce of Prairies* I. 169 A round wooden bowl called *batea*, about eighteen inches in diameter, is the washing vessel, which they [=Mexican Spanish] fill with earth [etc.]. **1864** MOWRY *Arizona & Sonora* 44 In the rubbish which was thrown out of the old mine, a comfortable subsistence is gained by washing in bateas. **1874** RAYMOND *6th Rep. Mines* 315 In these they wash the gravel and earth, by means of wooden bowls or *bateas*. **1898** *Engineering Mag.* XVI. 51 Wooden bateas about eighteen inches in diameter (probably used to carry the ore out of the mine).

+**Bateau.** Pl. **bateaux.** [Fr.] A light flat-bottomed boat for use on rivers. In early use more commonly BATTEAU.

1711 *N.J. Archives* 1 Ser. IV. 137 If you have not engaged Sloops for Albany they may go from hence in Bateaux. **1761** S. NILES *Indian Wars* II. 417 Colonel Bradstreet, coming from Oswego with 350 bateaux and 1,000 bateau-men, was attacked. **1775** Sparks *Corr. Revolution* I. 43 The sloop and schooner and ten bateaux with picked men, to lay in the river, ready to attack the enemy's schooner. **1817** FORDHAM *Narr. Travels* 108 It is navigable for keels nine and for bateaux and flats twelve months in the year. **1847** LANMAN *Summer in Wilderness* 171 At present they are navigable about half their length for small steamboats and bateaux. **1861** WINTHROP *Open Air* 25 We launched upon the Androscoggin, in a *bateau* of the old Canadian type. **1902** WHITE *Blazed Trail* xlvii. 334 On the surface of the river in the clear water floated two long graceful boats called bateaux.

b. Attrib., esp. with *man.*

1761 [see above]. **1791** *Mass. Spy* 6 Jan. (Th.), The bateaux men commonly hug the north shore. **1837** JENKINS *Ohio Gaz.* 397 A bateaux navigation upon this line of communication, has been... had with only four miles portage.

Bath bonnet. *Obs.* (See quot. 1830.) — **1751** Singleton *Social N.Y.* 213 Hats, Bath Bonnets, Hoods, and Pullareens for Ladies. **1830** WATSON *Philadelphia* 176, I have seen what was called a bath-bonnet, made of black satin, and so constructed to lay in folds that it could be set upon like a chapeau bras.

Bath-house. (Cf. BATHING-HOUSE.)

1. A house or building specially provided with arrangements for taking baths. {1705–}

1800 W. BENTLEY *Diary* II. 339, I bathed in the river this evening, & the Bath House was opened for the first time. **1816** U. BROWN *Journal* I. 267 Bath or Bathing Houses for each Sex are provided. **1839** 'M. PENCIL' *White Sulphur P.* 17 At our feet, on the other side, were the shining roofs of the cabins and bath-houses at the Warm Springs. **1851** CIST *Cincinnati* 167 Several of the hotels... have bathing rooms for the use of the public.... Besides these, there are several public bath houses. **1857** *Knickerb.* L. 456 A neighboring bath-house, kept by a live Yankee of the name of Martin. **1873** BEADLE *Undevel. West* 513 A commodious bath-house has been erected by the soldiers for general use. **1878** *Harper's Mag.* Jan. 200/2 When bath-houses were built,... it was necessary to have water of a higher temperature.

+**2.** A cabin, or a building containing a series of dressing rooms, for open-air bathers.

1884 SWEET & KNOX *Through Texas* 30 Although the beach was dotted with numerous bath-houses, few persons were disporting themselves in the brine. **1886** C. D. WARNER *Their Pilgrimage* xi, All down the shore were pavilions and bath-houses.

Bathing, *vbl. n.* Used attrib. with *beach, box, dress* {1859}, *establishment, machine* {1771}, *place* {1646}, *pool, suit,* etc.

1896 HOWELLS *Impressions & Exp.* 218 [The life-guard] was not... much in keeping with the inlander's ideal of bathing-beaches. — **1883** *Harper's Mag.* Feb. 336/2 Langland is... a lovely... spot, with... 'bathing-boxes' (as the sea-side cottages are called) perched about on the ... hill-sides. — **1864** T. L. NICHOLS *Amer. Life* I. 401 Ladies and gentlemen put on their bathing-dresses in these rooms. **1886** C. D. WARNER *Their Pilgrimage* xi, He would see women in their bathing dresses, wet and clinging, walking in the streets of the town. — **1821** *Jrnl. Science* III. 118 A smaller stream of water... separates the first bathing establishment from that which is now used. — **1840** DANA *Two Years* v. 33 The little brig... was no better than a bathing machine. **1856** MORDECAI *Virginia* (1860) i. 32 This bathing machine [=ducking-stool] fell into disuse many years ago. — **1880** *Scribner's Mo.* July 356/2 The Manhattan Beach bathing-pavilion is five hundred feet long. — **1869** BROWNE *Adv. Apache Country* 149 Deep pools in the river... were cleared out and made into bathing-places. — **1878** *Harper's Mag.* Jan. 200/1 A visitor to the springs... caused a building to be erected over one of the larger of the bathing pools. — **1886** C. D. WARNER *Their Pilgrimage* xi, He would also read placards along the beach explaining the reason why decency in bathing suits is desirable. **1911** VANCE *Cynthia* 308 A young ... woman, dressed in a bathing-suit that would have seemed not out of place on a Newport beach. — **1803** *Lit. Mag.* (Phila.) Oct. 12 Sun-rise and sun-set are the usual bathing-times [at Long Island].

Bathing-house.

1. =BATH-HOUSE 1.

1760 E. Singleton *Social N. Y.* 266 A cold Bathing-house... at the North River, is kept in order for the use of gentlemen or ladies. **1789** MORSE *Amer. Gazetteer* (1798), *Bath*, a village in the co. of Renssalaer, New-York.... A commodious bathing-house has been erected, at a considerable expence, containing hot, cold, and shower baths. **1816** U. BROWN *Journal* I. 267 Bath or Bathing Houses for each Sex are provided. **1833** *Niles' Reg.* XLIV. 314/2 We visited a bathing house, fitted up with much taste and elegance. **1863** CUMMING *Hospital Life* (1866) 82/2 Near the wash-house is a bathing-house [for convalescent soldiers, etc.].

2. =BATH-HOUSE 2.

1835 [INGRAHAM] *South-West* I. xvi. 174 The long white bathing-houses, which stretched along the south side of the pier. **1865** *Atlantic Mo.* XV. 547 'There be a fire up by the bathing houses, an' hot coffee,' said old Doctor Dennis. **1879** *Harper's Mag.* July 173 The stretch of water before the bathing-houses... offers a very cheering spectacle. **1891** *Scribner's Mag.* X. 195 The long sand-beach... lost itself in... a small dwelling, and a bathing-house or two.

+**Bathing-room.** =BATH-ROOM.

1791 BENTLEY *Diary* I. 250 The Cellars are in excellent order.... There is a bathing room under the apartments of the nursery, &c. **1839** *S. Lit. Messenger* V. 35/2 To M. and F.... was assigned the only carpetted apartment as compensation for their French couches,... dressing rooms, bathing-rooms, etc. at home. **1851** CIST *Cincinnati* 153 Still in the rear is a one story building,... used as a boys' bathing-room, and room for washing clothes. **1856** M. J. HOLMES *Homestead on Hillside* xii, Consulting with a carpenter about enlarging her bedroom and adding to it a bathing-room. **1865** STOWE *House & Home P.* 270 Mamma stands out for linen-closets and bathing-rooms and all that. **1873** BEADLE *Undevel. West* 288 The 'Cosmopolitan,' containing saloon, billiard hall, bathing rooms and barber shop.

* **Bathing-tub.** [Cf. BATHING *vbl. n.*] =BATH-TUB.

1832 CATLIN *Indians* I. 97 A crib or basket, much in the shape of a bathing-tub. **1846** *Rep. Comm. Patents* (1847) 363 What I do claim as new... is the special shape or configuration of my cast-iron bathing tub. **1854** *Penna. Agric. Rep.* 178 Also, one Bathing tub, which the committee recommend for its superior workmanship... and because they believe that its manufacture is among the first in this county. **1865** KELLOGG

Rebel Prisons 365 A row of tin wash-basins, and a wooden trough which served as a bathing-tub.

Bathman. A bath attendant. — **1878** *Harper's Mag.* Jan. 199 With the help of the negro bath-man he is soon in a hot bath. **1878** H. H. JACKSON *Travel At Home* 291 What an epitome of truth in the bathman's words!

Bath metal. *Obs.* [*Bath*, England.] An alloy containing 3 to 4 oz. of zinc to 1 lb. of copper. {1750-} — **1714** *Boston News-Letter* 7 June 2/2 A blew Coat ... with wrought Bath metal Butons gilt. **1714** *Essex Inst. Coll.* XLIII. 52, 1 Bathmettle Stone Necklace. **1725** *New-Eng. Courant* 17–24 May 2/2 New round toe'd Leather-heel'd Shoes, and Bath-mettal Buckles.

Bat-horse. ?*Obs.* [Fr. *bât* pack-saddle, *cheval de bât* pack-horse.] A horse used for carrying the baggage of military officers. {1863} Cf. BAT-MULE.

1757 WASHINGTON *Writings* I. 449, I should [be glad] to be informed ... if the officers ... provide bat-horses at their own expense. **1777** *Mass. H. S. Coll.* II. 25 The troops must take no tents, and what little baggage is carried by officers, must be on their own bat-horses. **1793** *Hapless Orphan* II. 95, I shall be obliged to leave all my baggage ... at this garrison, as we are not to have bat-horses. **1842** *S. Lit. Messenger* VIII. 657/1 Our bait-horses [*sic*] were immediately picketed in a body, and left under a guard.

Bath-room. A room containing a bath-tub and usually other toilet conveniences. {1780-}

1836 *Knickerb.* VIII. 706 In the rear, is quite a city of additions, in the shape of bed-rooms, bath-rooms, milk-rooms, buttery, pantry, etc. **1851** *Ib.* XXXVIII. 178 [We] must go and take a 'shower' in the adjoining bath-room. **1861** *Chicago Tribune* 19 July 1/8 A first-class residence ... with all the modern improvements: gas, water and bath rooms complete. **1885** *Harper's Mag.* Feb. 458/1 Quite a large number of houses contain seven rooms, and in these larger dwellings there is also a bath-room. **1902** *Harper's Mag.* May 887 Beyond [the bedroom] was the open door of a tiled bath-room.

+**Bath-tub.** A tub or other vessel, esp. one fitted in a bath-room, in which a bath can be taken. {=E. *bath*}

1870 'MARK TWAIN' *Sk., Ghost Story*, I ... was sorry that he was gone ... and sorrier still that he had carried off my red blanket and my bath-tub. **1884** *Century Mag.* Dec. 266/2 Most ... of the English earthenware bath-tubs imported into this country ... are furnished with an ingenious device for delivering the supply near the bottom of the tub. **1897** FLANDRAU *Harvard Episodes* 48 He hung clean towels over the edge of the bathtub. **1909** 'O. HENRY' *Roads of Destiny* 332 He removed his coat, ... and laid it upon the floor, ... as far as possible from the unused bathtub.

Batman. [Cf. BAT-HORSE.] A military servant of a cavalry officer. (Orig., a man having the charge of a bat-horse and its load.) {1809-} — **1755** *Lett. to Washington* I. 96 They have taken ... another man who was batman to Doct. Craik. **1757** WASHINGTON *Writings* I. 448, I should [be glad] to be informed ... how these bat-men are clothed, paid and victualled, and by whom?

Bat-money. *Obs.* (Cf. BAT-HORSE and prec.) An allowance for carrying baggage in the field. {1793-} — **1758** *Lett. to Washington* II. 351 As your Troops are allowed Bat money, I suppose that you may provide them with the necessary carrying Horses for their Tents.

Bat-mule. *Obs.* (Cf. BAT-HORSE.) A sumpter mule. {1879} — **1787** JEFFERSON *Let. to W. Short* 12 April, I am now in the act of putting my baggage into portable form for my bat-mule.

Batsman. [BAT *n.*[2]] One who wields the bat in certain games; the player at bat; +a batter in baseball. {1756-}

1856 *Spirit of the Times* (N.Y.) 6 December 229/1 He who strikes it [a fast ball pitched by Stevens] fairly must be a fine batsman. **1867** CHADWICK *Base Ball Player's Bk.* 12 If the batsman is in the habit of striking a very low or very high ball. *Ib.* 130 When the batsman makes his first base. **1887** *Outing* April 77/2 The penalty of giving a batsman a base is inflicted every time the pitcher hits the batsman with a pitched ball. **1917** MATHEWSON *Sec. Base Sloan* 180 When the first batsman was retired on an easy toss from Chase to Jim, she lost some of her ginger.

Bat-stick. [BAT *n.*[2]] A racket used as a bat; =BALL-STICK. — **1849** MARY EASTMAN *Dahcotah* 56 Each woman [of the Indian village playing the ball-game] has a long stick with a circular frame at the end of it; this they call a bat stick, and, simple as it looks, it requires great skill to manage it.

* **Battalion.**

1. A body of infantry, composed of several companies and forming a part of a regiment. {1708-}

1758 *Essex Inst. Coll.* XLVI. 211 [We] went over ... to Albany side, ... then marched with the whole bettaleon [*sic*] ... to Senacade. **1759** *Ib.* XIX. 151 This day a Centery of Coll. Rugles 2d Battelion [*sic*] shot a Highlander. **1776** *Journals Cont. Congress* VI. 861 A petition from Frederick Seegar desiring leave to resign ... as quarter master of the German batallion. **1790** *Ann. 1st Congress* II. 1815 Companies and battalions should be obliged to turn out only twice a year. **1847** *Army Regulations* 20 On the organization of a regiment or battalion, the companies will be designated by the letters of the alphabet. **1856** GLISAN *Jrnl. Army Life* 277 In southern Oregon the volunteer battalion have elected Bob Williams as their colonel. **1892** M. A. JACKSON *Memoirs* 223 Gen. Jackson started out with five battalions.

2. Attrib. with *commander, drill, man, muster.*

1793 *Ann. 2nd Congress* 779 They have formed into legionary corps, composed of horse, riflemen, light-infantry, and battalion-men. **1807** *Laws regulating Militia* 19 There shall be a battallion [*sic*] muster in every battallion ... in the month of May in each year. **1811** O. A. Rothert *Muhlenberg Co.* 167 You will have your Company parade ... in order to hold a Battalion Muster. **1865** *Atlantic Mo.* XV. 66 We have practised through all the main movements in battalion drill. *Ib.* 610 One of them a battalion-commander and the other a staff-officer. **1897** *Outing* Feb. 491 A bicyclist was detailed ... to ride forward ... and report the facts to the Battalion Commander.

+**Batteau.** Also †**battau.** Pl. **batteaux,** †**batteaus.** The usual spelling of BATEAU down to *c*1850. Cf. BATTOE.

1717 *N.J. Archives* IV. 318, I pressed all the carpenters in the place ... for the dispatch of these batteaux. **1726** PENHALLOW *Indian Wars* (1824) 73 Colonel Nicholson set out for New-York, and from thence for Albany, having ordered batteaux before. **1755** EVANS *Anal. Map Colonies* 18 This lake [Ontario] is best fitted for the Passage of Batteaux and Canoes, along the south side. **1765** CROGHAN *Journal* 14 In the least fresh, a batteau of any size may come and go. **1785** *Md. Hist. Mag.* XX. 53 He has passed down thro' said inside Channel in an empty Battau which drew about four Inches of water at a time. **1788** GORDON *History* (1789) I. 419 The stream was so rapid, that ... five or six batteaus filled and overset. **1807** *Ann. 10th Congress* 1 Sess. I. 463 He stated that there were two keels and four batteaux. **1816** U. BROWN *Journal* II. 222 Wm. Wells ... prevails with me to go with him down the River 1½ Miles to what he called a skift, I would said, a Batteau. **1819** *Missouri Intell.* 30 July 3/3 That the Independence is in point of size what a common batteaux [*sic*] would be to a keel boat of the larger size. **1837** IRVING *Bonneville* I. i. 25 In the old times ..., when the trade in furs was pursued chiefly about the lakes and rivers, the expeditions were carried on in batteaux and canoes. **1848** THOREAU *Maine Woods* 4 The making of batteaux is quite a business here for the supply of the Penobscot River. They are light and shapely vessels, calculated for rapid and rocky streams. **1857** [D. H. STROTHER] *Virginia* 232 The swarthy crew poled their batteau through the shallows. **1886** *Outing* April 58/1 Last and best is the 'batteau' of good length, little beam and flat bottom. **1905** G. E. COLE *Early Oregon* i. 12 As the batteau which was to bring our luggage would not be there for several hours, the Frenchman and myself started on foot.

attrib. **1776** C. CARROLL *Journal* (1845) 62 The water is shallow, but sufficiently deep for batteau navigation. **1848** THOREAU *Maine Woods* 4 At Oldtown we walked into a batteau-manufactory.

Batteau-man. ?*Obs.* Pl. **batteau(x)-men.** One occupied in navigating a bateau; a boatman.

1766 H. GORDON in *Travels Amer. Col.* 464 Having engaged the sufficient number of Batteau-men, we embarked on the Ohio. **1776** *Journals Cont. Congress* IV. 111 Resolved, That General Schuyler be desired to employ such batteau men as are in & near Albany. **1791** E. Watson *Western Canals* (1820) 62 The batteauxmen, who ply between Newtown and Middletown, in Pennsylvania, carry from six to eight hundred bushels. *a*1797 Imlay *Western Territory* (ed. 3) 73 During part of the summer and autumn, the batteaux-men drag their boats over the rock. **1817** PAULDING *Lett. from South* II. 89 The batteauxmen are for the most part composed of materials equally combustible. **1848** THOREAU *Maine Woods* 31 The most skilful boatman anywhere else would here be obliged to ... carry round a hundred times, ... where the practised batteau-man poles up with comparative ease.

Batten, *n.* Also †**batton.** [Variant of *baton.*]

1. A piece of squared timber; a bar or stout strip of wood. {1663-}

1684 I. MATHER *Providences* iii. (1856) 52 The battens next the chimney in the chamber were broken. **1742** *Bristol* (Va.) *Vestry Bk.* 111 Shetters ... fastened with wooden Boalts or Battons. **1891** *Scribner's Mag.* Sept. 318 The cracks between the boards are covered with battens.

+**2.** *spec.* 'A log less than 11 inches in diameter at the small end: Maine' (1905 *Forestry Bureau Bull. 61* s.v.).

Batten, *v.* Also †**batton.** [f. prec.] *tr.* To furnish or strengthen with battens. {1663-}

1674 *Md. Archives* II. 406 The doores all bottened [*sic*], with good substanciall hinges. **1675** *Plymouth Rec.* 147 He is to batten the walles and to make a small paire of staires. **1812** *Niles' Reg.* II. 5/1 The houses in general are built of wood, and many of them either shingled or battoned. **1857** *Ill. Agric. Soc. Trans.* II. 182 The house can be either shingled or battened with good sound boards. **1859** A. VAN BUREN *Sojourn in South* 41 The clefts between the logs are battened on the outside, with cypress shakes. **1876** *Vermont Bd. Agric. Rep.* III. 238 He either battens the crack or lines with coal tar sheathing.

Batten door. [BATTEN *n.* 1.] A door made of narrow boards secured by battens nailed across these. — **1835** [INGRAHAM] *South-West* II. 289 The lower sides of the press are composed of very strong batten doors. **1852** MRS. ELLET *Pioneer Women* 41 The bucket of cool water was ever on the shelf at the batten-door, which stood wide open, swung back upon its wooden hinges. **1880** CABLE *Grandissimes* xxiii. 170 Joseph Frowenfeld was making room on a narrow door-step for the outward opening of a pair of small batten doors.

Battened, *ppl. a.* [BATTEN *n.* or *v.*] Formed of, strengthened with, battens. {1663-} — **1859** A. VAN BUREN *Sojourn in South* 167 The floor . . . overhead is of cypress-shakes laid from joist to joist, like battened-work. **1891** 'THANET' *Otto the Knight*, etc. 317 Back of cotton-fields and garden, stands a comfortable battened house, the widow Brand's house.

Battening. [BATTEN *n.* or *v.*] A structure formed of battens. {1834} — **1845** JUDD *Margaret* I. iii. 11 The roof was a thatch composed of white-birch twigs, sweet-flag and straw wattled together, and overlaid with a slight battening of boards. **1880** HOWELLS *Undisc. Country* i. 29 'Mr. Hatch, will you put up the battening?' Hatch made haste to darken the windows completely with some light wooden sheathings prepared for the purpose.

+**Batten shutter.** [BATTEN *n.*] A shutter made of 'battens' or slats. Cf. next. — **1880** CABLE *Grandissimes* xvi. 117 The daughter presently threw open the batten shutters of its single street door. **1887** 'CRADDOCK' *Keedon Bluffs* 225 He . . . then opened the batten shutter of a little glassless window. **1891** — in *Harper's Mag.* Jan. 218/2 The batten shutters swayed gently in the wind.

+**Batten window.** [BATTEN *n.*] A window provided with batten shutters. — **1886** G. KING in *Harper's Mag.* July 293/2 They were too young to appreciate the fact that the batten windows were bowed only when they were there.

Batter. {1824-} = BATSMAN.

1856 *Spirit of Times* (N.Y.) 6 Dec. 229/1 De Bost . . . [is] a powerful batter, though often put out, from a tendency to raise the ball. **1887** CHADWICK in *Outing* April 78 The pitcher shall take his position facing the batter with both feet squarely upon the ground. **1890** H. PALMER *Stories of Base Ball Field* 50 Beckley . . . is also a strong batter and a good base-runner. **1912** MATHEWSON *Pitching* 157 The runner gets his start and the ball comes up so wide that the batter could not half reach it with a ten-foot club.

+**Batter-bread.** [Cf. next.] (See early quotations.) — **1899** GREEN *Va. Word Book* 52 *Batter-bread*, bread made of corn meal, eggs, and milk, and baked in a deep earthenware dish or tin pan. **1901** *Dialect Notes* II. 136 *Batter-bread*, a preparation like hominy, eaten with butter. **1904** GLASGOW *Deliverance* 30 The pert boy, beginning an assault upon an enormous dish of batterbread.

+**Batter-cake.** Chiefly *S.* [f. * *batter*, a culinary mixture.] A griddlecake.

1833 *Md. Hist. Mag.* XIII. 319 The servant will bring you hot muffins and corn batter cakes every 2 minutes. **1835** [LONGSTREET] *Georgia Scenes* 36 Waffles were handed to Ned, and he took one; batter-cakes were handed, and he took one. **1841** *S. Lit. Messenger* VII. 37/2 A little scrap of lard, if you please, mistress, for the batter-cakes. **1851** A. CARY *Clovernook* 112 Mrs. Tompkins stirred up a little jar of batter-cakes for breakfast, placing it on the hearth to rise. **1868** BAKER *New Timothy* (1870) 40 Now Miss Loo had eaten almost nothing since dinner, and there were rice batter-cakes for supper. **1880** *Harper's Mag.* Dec. 33/2 It was hard to make batter cakes over an open fire without the proper hanging griddle. **1897** 'MARK TWAIN' in *Autobiog.* (1924) I. 97 Biscuits, hot batter-cake, hot buckwheat cakes.

attrib. **1884** Z. F. SMITH *Kentucky* (1886) 122 There was corn bread in pone, in hoe cake, and in batter cake form.

+**Batter-pot.** [Cf. prec.] A pot in which batter is set to rise. — **1851** *Knickerb.* XXXVIII. 392 The civilizing encroachments of the batter-pot, that most persuasive of missionaries? *Ib.* 394 That old red earthen batter-pot! We see it now, as of yore it sat upon the kitchen hearth, capped with a pie-plate.

Batter-pudding. [Cf. prec.] A pudding made from batter. {1769-}

1828 E. LESLIE *Receipts* 28 [How to make] Indian pudding . . . Batter pudding. **1832** L. M. CHILD *Frugal Housewife* 61 Common flour pudding, or batter pudding, is easily made. **1838** C. GILMAN *Recoll.* xxvi. 175 They chatted together of batter-puddings, . . . Indian puddings, . . . rank butter [etc.]. **1876** M. F. HENDERSON *Practical Cooking* 274 [Recipe for making] Batter-puddings baked.

* **Battery.** Also †**batterie, battry, battree.**

* **1.** *Law.* The offence of beating or striking a person.

1631 *Mass. Bay Rec.* I. 86 A jury [was] impanneld to inquire concerneing an accion of battry. **1655** *R. I. Court Rec.* 9 Ralph Earll sen. accused of Batterie in the Court is by the Jurie found guiltie. **1675** *Plymouth Laws* 173 [Not] to try any action of defamation, battery, or that respects title of lands. **1784, 1841-1872** [see ASSAULT].

* **2.** A number of pieces of artillery grouped for combined action in firing.

1686 SEWALL *Diary* I. 140 The Frigot fires, then the Sconce and Ships, . . . Charlestown Battery, Frigot again [etc.]. **1718** *Boston Rec.* 133 Wheather they think it adviseable that a Battree be planted at the end of the long wharfe. **1777** *Md. Hist. Mag.* V. 213 They opened a small Battery & fired briskly. **1778** *Essex Inst. Coll.* LII. 15 While our batteries keep up a vigorous and almost incessant blaze ag[ain]st them. **1815** *Log of Chasseur* 231 We immediately opened our Battery of great guns, and began with the musketry. **1830** COOPER *Water Witch* III. 99 Then came gun after gun in view, until the whole broadside and the frowning battery of the Coquette were visible. **1861** *Army Regulations* 97 Batteries of artillery and their caissons move with the corps to which they are attached. **1871** W. L. GOSS *Soldier's Story* iii. 57 That evening a battery opened on Fort Gray. **1885** *Century Mag.* Feb. 632 A Federal battery of four or six guns unlimbered and horseless. **1895** REMINGTON *Pony Tracks* 207 Rawball's battery went into 'action front,' two sections to a street.

fig. **1880** *Harper's Mag.* May 935/1 The press opened its batteries upon him. **1888** *Nation* 19 Jan. 53/3 A permanent 'battery' of cameras such as was employed by Mr. Muybridge.

* **3.** The place, platform, or fortification on which a number of guns are mounted.

1654 JOHNSON *Wonder-W. Prov.* xx. 43 The one [hill] well fortified, . . . with store of great Artillery . . . , the other hath a very strong battery built of whole Timber. **1656** *Charlestown Land Rec.* 141, I . . . have sould . . . my former dwelling hous, with a garden and yeard anexed to it . . . forty feet from the corner post of the battery. **1689** *Mass. H. S. Coll.* 4 Ser. V. 194 The army divided, and part came up on the back side of the Fort, and part went underneath the hill to the lower battery. **1712** *Boston Rec.* 90 The Townes Wharfe, Dock and Flatts at the North Battree. **1771** FRANKLIN *Autobiog.* 362 A lottery to defray the expense of building a battery below the town, and furnishing it with cannon. **1776** *Journals Cont. Congress* IV. 203 A camp fortified by a chain of redoubts, . . . corresponding with the batteries on the New York side. **1826** COOPER *Mohicans* xiv, Batteries were already thrown up in their front. **1851** *Harper's Mag.* Sept. 465/2 A battery had been thrown up beside it. **1865** *Atlantic Mo.* XV 339 On three sides, the batteries are dashed against by the waves.

b. As the name of a particular locality, esp. in New York.

1787 TYLER *Contrast* I. i, But to . . . walk on the Battery [N.Y.], give me the luxurious, jaunty, flowing, bell-hoop. *Ib.*, I was dangling o'er the battery with Billy Dimple. **1807** IRVING, etc. *Salmagundi* v. (1860) 100 The Battery [N.Y.] . . . is so denominated . . . from having once been defended with formidable wooden bulwarks. **1828** *Englishman's Sketch-bk.* 9 The impression made on my mind as we approached the walk or point of the city [of N.Y.] called the Battery, was an agreeable one. **1833** E. T. COOKE *Subaltern's Furlough* I. 131 The former promenade is called the Battery, from having in the olden times of the Dutch settlers, or during the Revolutionary war, mounted a few guns. **1842** BUCKINGHAM *Slave States* I. 46 Charleston is seated on a projection of land, . . . there being, as at New York, a point at this junction, called 'The Battery,' forming an agreeable promenade. **1865** *Atlantic Mo.* XV. 76 Three small islands, extending from the Battery to the Narrows. **1880** *Harper's Mag.* July 287/2 The small but promising capitol which clustered about the Battery and overlooked the bay.

transf. **1842** COOPER *Wing-and-Wing* I. 11 Hundreds collected on the spot, which, in Manhattanese parlance, would probably have been called a battery. **1848** — *Oak Openings* I. xi. 160 Our language . . . has changed . . . public promenades on the water into 'batteries.'

+**4.** A boat, or special device attached to one, used in shooting wild ducks. (See quots. *a*1841, 1859 and 1897.)

*a*1841 [W. HAWES] *Sporting Scenes* I. 198 A machine, or battery, is a wooden box of the necessary dimensions to let a man lie down upon his back, just tightly fitting enough to let him rise again. **1851** LEWIS *Amer. Sportsman* 189 The Surface-boat, Coffin-boat, or Battery. . . . This artful contrivance for the destruction of ducks we claim as entirely American. **1859** BARTLETT 24 *Battery*, a sort of boat used . . . in the Chesapeake, in which the shooter lies below the surface of the water. **1866** *Va. Game Laws* in *Fur, Fin & Feather* (1872) 144 Any person shooting or using a skiff, box or battery while hunting wild fowl. **1875** *Fur, Fin & Feather* 120 Great slaughter has been done among them [raft ducks] by batteries. **1897** *Outing* Sept. 544/1 A stick . . . to which pieces of flat cedar are fixed . . . effectually hides his movements from any ducks in front of the boat. This in the local parlance is called a 'battery.'

+**5.** The smallest pan of the set used in sugar-boiling.

1833 SILLIMAN *Man. Sugar Cane* 33 The names appropriated to the different kettles are as follows: the largest is called the *grande*, . . . and the last the *battery*. **1862** *Rep. Comm. Patents: Agric.* 299 The juice is thrown forward through the successive pans, . . . until it reaches the smallest pan, called the 'strike' or 'battery.' **1888** CABLE *Bonaventure* 14 She was as sweet as the last dip of cane-juice from the boiling battery.

b. (See quotation.)

1886 *Harper's Mag.* June 80/2 These processes, in the old-fashioned plantation sugar-houses, are effected by what is known as a 'battery' of open pans or 'taches.'

+**6.** A set of stamps for pounding ore in a stamp-mill; the iron box in which the ore is pounded.

1853 *Harper's Mag.* VI. 578/2 There being openings in this opposite each cover or battery of stamps, the stone comes through, as fast as it is removed and shoveled into the covers. **1861** HITTELL *Mining in Pacific States* 160 In the Sierra Buttes mills two-thirds of the gold is caught in the batteries. **1869** BROWNE *Adv. Apache County* 396 The Real del Monte contains a battery of stamps; thirty-six Wheeler pans, and other machinery in proportion. **1872** 'MARK TWAIN' *Roughing It* xxxvi. 252 These [six rods] rose and fell, one after the other, . . . in an iron box called a 'battery.' . . . One of us stood by the battery all day long.

+**7.** The pitcher and catcher of a baseball team.

1868 CHADWICK *Base Ball* 90 He soon resumed his position, once more facing the battery of Lovett. **1886** — *Art of Pitching* 8 The 'battery' of a club's team. **1888** *Outing* May 117/1 The champion team . . . included Asa Brainard and Douglas Allison as the battery. **1891** *Triangle* Feb. 2 A 'cage,' . . . [where] the candidates would practice batting and throwing and the batteries would work together. **1912** MATHEW-

SON *Pitching* i. 14 Raymond and he could not get along together as a battery.

+8. Attrib. with *box*, *feeder*, *room* (sense 5), *gunner*, *shooting* (sense 3).

1871 RAYMOND *3rd Rep. Mines* 340 The battery box is . . . cast in one piece with the mortar-bed. **1874** LONG *Wild-Fowl* 71, I shall describe that in reference to battery-shooting. **1875** *Fur, Fin & Feather* 122 The battery gunner . . . has a great advantage over the fowler who shoots from the shore. **1877** RAYMOND *8th Rep. Mines* 330 Wages of two battery feeders. **1877** WM. WRIGHT *Big Bonanza* 341 In the battery-room are . . . six batteries of ten stamps each, or sixty stamps in all. **1885** *Forest & Stream* 1 Jan. 441 It would be far better, however, to decide upon some plan of action by which battery-shooting should be wholly done away with.

+**Bat-tick.** [BAT *n.*[1]] A small spider-like insect parasitic on bats. — **1852** T. HARRIS *Insects New Eng.* 501 A remarkable group of insects, which seems to connect the flies with the true ticks and spiders. Such are sheep-ticks and bat-ticks. **1868** *Amer. Naturalist* II. 198 The Bee-louse of Europe . . . [is] allied to . . . the wingless Bat-tick (*Nycteribia*).

+**Batting,** *n.* Cotton, wool, or other fibrous material, prepared in matted sheets, freq. used for making quilts or coverlets. Cf. COTTON BATTING.

1843 *Knickerb.* XXI. 408 Mine . . . cost me nothing but the batting and the quilting. **1846** *Rep. Comm. Patents* (1847) 212 This apparatus . . . has been employed for saturating . . . battings made of hempen and other coarse fibres. **1888** *Century Mag.* Sept. 767/2 Carding-combs of a rough pattern were constructed for the purpose of converting the raw cotton into batting.

Batting, *vbl. n.* The action of using a bat, esp. in a ball game. {1611–} Chiefly attrib. with *ball*, *list*, etc.; also *staff*, *stick* (cf. BATTLING *vbl. n.*).

1825 NEAL *Bro. Jonathan* II. 54 A keg that broke loose, began hopping about among their corns, like a 'battin' ball made of a sun-fish's nose.' **1867** CHADWICK *Base Ball Player's Bk.* 30 A regular scorer . . . should be competent to record the fielding as well as batting score of the game. *Ib.* 128 In taking his position for fielding, he will . . . be guided by the style of batting opposed to him. **1874** KNIGHT 251/1 *Batting-staff*, an implement used by laundresses for beating linen in washing. **1891** *Triangle* Feb. 2 The candidates would practice batting and throwing. **1902** HARBEN *A. Daniel* 192 A negro woman at the wash-place . . . was using a batting-stick on some clothing. **1917** MATHEWSON *Sec. Base Sloan* xiii. 173 Toonalta started the seventh with the head of her batting list up. *Ib.* 238 Wayne . . . bought a score-card which informed him of the batting order.

* **Battle axe.** A war hatchet; a tomahawk.

1813 *Ann. 12th Congress* 2 Sess. 47 They had only twenty pistols, and neither cutlasses, nor battle axes. **1827** COOPER *Prairie* xxx, Each [Indian chief] had his spear, his bow, his quiver, his little battle-axe, and his knife. **1870** KEIM *Sheridan's Troopers* 223 One had . . . two soldiers impaled on the end of his spear, and had hewn down several others with his battle-axe.

* **Battledore.**

* **1.** A small light racket used to drive a shuttlecock.

1658 *Southold Rec.* I. 449 An Inventorie of the personall estate whereof Elizabeth Payne widdow dyed possest: . . . a rollinge pinn, a battledore, a small paddle. **1790** *Penna. Packet* 11 Dec. 3/2 Imported . . . by William Poyntell, . . . drum battledores and shuttlecocks. **1838** *S. Lit. Messenger* IV. 654/1 Prints, chessmen, books, battledores and an antiquated harpsichord, complete the catalogue. **1877** HALE in *Harper's Mag.* March 580/2 In each house a hall . . . [with] a spinning-wheel, or a guitar, or a battledore.

2. A game in which two players drive a shuttlecock back and forth with such rackets. {1719–}

1838 *S. Lit. Messenger* IV. 654/2 Some play at battledore, or strum on an old harpsichord. **1879** *Harper's Mag.* July 166 The lawns . . . dotted with pretty figures . . . intent on croquet, lawn tennis, or battledoor [*sic*].

Battlefield. A field forming the site of a battle; a battle-ground. {1812–} +*Battlefield flower* (quot. 1893), the pansy.

1836 HAWTHORNE *Note-books* I. 24 Fortune . . . asking for them the sacrifice of health, of integrity, perhaps of life in the battle-field. **1857** H. W. HARRISON (*title*), The Battle-fields of the Republic; from Lexington to the City of Mexico. **1861** MCCLELLAN in *Own Story* 102 The rebels have chosen Virginia as their battle-field. **1870** KEIM *Sheridan's Troopers* 150 During the journey to the battle-field, a detachment found the bodies of a white woman and child. **1877** *Rep. Indian Affairs* 12 From this battle-field the Indians fled down the Bannack trail. **1892** M. A. JACKSON *Memoirs* 180 He took a view of the battle-field yesterday morning. **1893** *Amer. Folk-Lore* VI. 138 *Viola tricolor*, battlefield flower. Gordonsville, Va. [So named] because found so often on old battlefields, after the Civil War.

+**Battle-fish.** (See quotation.) — **1878** *Harper's Mag.* Jan. 203/1 In the creek [Hot Springs, Ark.] there are many species of fish, one of which, from its scales of red, white, and blue, is dubbed the 'battle-fish.'

Battle-flag. A flag carried in battle; esp. a regiment's standard. — **1862** MCCLELLAN in *Own Story* 614 My tent is filled quite to overflowing with trophies in the way of captured secesh battle-flags. **1865** BOUDRYE *Fifth N.Y. Cavalry* 170 Sixteen officers . . . fell into our hands, and also their battle flag. **1866** 'F. KIRKLAND' *Bk. Anecdotes* 103 The Ninth Texas regiment bore down . . . with their battle flag at the head of the column. *fig.* **1892** 'MARK TWAIN' *Amer. Claimant* xv. 161 Now, old fellow, take in your battle-flag out of the wet.

Battle-ground. A battle-field. {1865–}

1815 *Niles' Reg.* VII. Suppl. 84 Col. Lauderdale . . . having been buried on the battle ground [near New Orleans]. **1835** [LONGSTREET] *Georgia Scenes* 7 His plough . . . stood in the corner of the fence about fifty yards beyond the battle ground. **1870** KEIM *Sheridan's Troopers* 191 From the earliest times . . . the plains have been a common battle-ground. **1892** M. A. JACKSON *Memoirs* 196 Starting . . . on the Warrenton roads toward the battle-ground of Manassas.

fig. **1884** G. T. CURTIS in *Century Mag.* Nov. 125 That State which is supposed likely to be 'the battle-ground' or one of the battle-grounds of the election. **1885** *Ib.* Feb. 636 Ohio . . . has now become the battle-ground of the politicians.

+**Battle-hammed,** *a. Obs.* [Cf. E. *battle* (1575–1721), to grow fat.] Thick-hammed. — **1727** *New Eng. Weekly Journal* 11 Sept., Ran-away from his Master . . . a young Negro Man-Servant, about 20 Years of Age, a stout Fellow, speaks pretty good English, has thick Lips, battle-ham'd, and goes something waddling.

+**Battle-kneed,** *a. Obs.* [See BATTLE-HAMMED.] Thick-kneed. — **1743** *N.J. Archives* 1 Ser. XII. 181 They were stolen by one David Howell, . . . ruddy Complexion, light Hair, and battel-knee'd [*sic*].

Battle-lantern. A lantern at each gun of a warship, to light up the deck during a night engagement. — **1830** COOPER *Water Witch* III. vii, Lifting a lighted battle-lantern to his face, he saw that he slept. **1861** LOWELL *Washers of the Shroud* xxi, Let our Ship of State to harbor sweep, Her ports all up, her battle-lanterns lit. **1883** 'MARK TWAIN' *Life on Miss.* xlv. 465 He carried no battle-lanterns, but painted the decks of his ships white.

Battle-line. {1814–} The extended front of a body of troops ordered for battle. — **1866** 'F. KIRKLAND' *Bk. Anecdotes* 291 In another moment a rebel battle-line appears on the brow of the ridge above them. **1867** EDWARDS *Shelby* 120 Herron, in the low swampy ground where Shelby left him in the battle-line, took his own time to attack.

+**Battle pin.** A badge awarded for service in battle. — **1863** NORTON *Army Lett.* 188, I have another name to put on my battle pin (when I get it), that of 'Rappahannock Station, November 8th.'

Battleship. A war-vessel; esp. a ship of war built for fighting in the line of battle. — **1794** HUMPHREYS *Industry* 20 Give me the music, where the dock equips, With batt'ries black and strong, the battle-ships. **1898** *Boston Herald* 1 June 12/4 In her day she was a battleship, but she . . . would be little more than sport for a modern ironclad.

* **Battling,** *vbl. n.* The action of beating or striking with a batting-staff in the process of washing clothes. Attrib. with *bench*, *board*, *stick* (cf. BATTING *vbl. n.*)

1845 HOOPER *Taking Census* ii. 183 John Green's sister . . . goes to her battlin' bench. **1851** — *Widow Rugby's Husb.* 96 What a devil of a paddlin' the old woman giv him with the battlin'-stick. **1887** *Harper's Mag.* July 272/1 The splay-legged battling-boards fastened themselves firmer and firmer into the earth under the blows of the bats [of the washers of clothes]. *c*1895 *Dialect Notes* I. 370 (Tenn. words), *Battling-stick*, [one] with which clothes are beaten by the washwoman. **1924** J. W. RAINE *Land of Saddle-bags* 10 At the edge of the branch . . . is the big iron wash kettle and the 'battling' bench for the family laundry.

+**Battoe.** *Obs.* Frequent spelling variant of BATTEAU.

1711 *Boston News-Letter* 23–30 July 2/1 All our Battoes are finished, and several of them gone to Albany last week with several Indians. **1755** EVANS *Anal. Map Colonies* 27 Battoes, capable of carrying about three or four Tons, and drawing twelve Inches Water. **1760** CROGHAN *Journal* 106 We loaded our Boats, sent of the Battoes with the Provisions. **1774** FITHIAN *Journal* I. 209 It is a light neat Battoe elegantly painted & is rowed with four Oars. **1785** *Md. Hist. Mag.* XX. 52 He has passed both up and down . . . in a battaue [*sic*] . . . and that such battoe did not draw above ten or twelve inches when loaded. **1801** *Austin Papers* (1924) I. 72 [At] 12 O Clock this afternoon passed a Battoe in from New Orleans.

attrib. **1756** *Doc. Hist. N.Y. State* (1849) I. 478 A Party of 3 or 400 French & Indians . . . scalped five of the Battoe Guard.

+**Battoe,** *v. Obs.* [From prec.] **1.** *intr.* To proceed by bateau. **2.** *tr.* To convey by bateau. — **(1)** **1759** R. PUTNAM *Journal* (1886) 84 This day a detachment . . . marched up the Mohawk River in order to Battoe up that River. **(2)** **1764** F. B. HOUGH *Siege of Detroit* (1860) 280, I cannot discharge the Teamster & Waggoner . . . , being obliged to employ them at . . . Battoeing Provisions to Port Erie, making Hay, &c.

+**Battoe-man.** *Obs.* =BATTEAU-MAN. — **1756** *Doc. Hist. N.Y. State* (1849) I. 477 Upwards of 500 Battoe Men were sent different Ways into the Woods. **1759** *Essex Inst. Coll.* XIX. 188 We had a Rigmtl. Cort marshell upon a Battoman belonging to Coll. Bradstreet. **1760** *Ib.* XX. 199 This Day the Battoue men marchd off.

+**Battowing,** *vbl. n. Obs.* [BATTOE] The working of batteaux. — **1760** *Essex Inst. Coll.* XX. 199 To-day there was a draught out of our company for battowing from fort Miller to fort Edward.

+**Batture.** [Fr., the bottom of a sandy or rocky shallow.] On the Mississippi, a deposit of sediment adjacent to the river-bank, forming a bar or stretch of new ground.

[**1806** *Ann. 9th Congress* 2 Sess. 1115 In the afternoon of this day they passed three contiguous sand-bars, or beaches, called 'les trois battures.'] **1809** *Ann. 11th Congress* 1 Sess. I. 469 This piece of land under water, this piece of batture, has not yet arrived to that state of alluvion, which would authorize its being made a ground of claim as territory. **1814** *Western Gleaner* (Pittsburgh) I. 181 If the deposit be made, . . . it then becomes, what is called in the country, a *batture* or alluvion. These battures, low at first, gradually rise, by successive deposits. **1817** *Ann. 14th Congress* 2 Sess. 771 The expediency of granting . . . to the town of St. Louis . . . all the sand bar, or batture, formed by the recession of the Mississippi river between the said town and low water mark. **1829** B. HALL *Travels in N.A.* III. 343 At some little distance from the Levée, just where this new land, or batture, as it is called, was in the leisurely process of formation. **1849** KENNEDY *W. Wirt* I. 326 Certain works constructed by [E. Livingston at New Orleans, *c.* 1806] . . . upon the beach, or *batture*, as it was called. **1868** *Putnam's Mag.* I. 595 On the opposite side of the river is sure to be found a deposit of sediment, or a *batture.* **1887** *Harper's Mag.* March 607/1 When the river was high, and covered the batture in front of the levee, he took us to bathe.

attrib. **1854** *New Orleans Delta* 28 May, He says there are few . . . persons in Louisiana who are at all aware of the great capability of our batture lands for the production of rice.

Baufat, -att, variants of BOFFET. *Obs.*

+**Baum,** *v.* [Cf. E. *balm.*] (See quotation.) — **1851** HALL *College Words* 16 *Baum*, at Hamilton College, to fawn upon; to flatter; to court the favor of anyone.

+**Baumont-root.** =BOWMAN('S) ROOT. — **1789** *Amer. Philos. Soc.* III. p. xviii, *Spiræa trifoliata*, . . . Indian physic, Baumont-root, is an effectual and safe emetic.

Bawdacious, variant of BODACIOUS *a.*

*BAY, *n.*[1]

***1.** A recess in the coast of a sea or lake; a (usu.) wide-mouthed inlet.

1612 SMITH *Virginia* 4 A convenient harbour for fisher boats or smal boats at Kecoughtan . . . conveniently turneth it selfe into bayes and creeks. **1620** DERMER in Bradford *Hist.* 117 In the botume of that great bay is store of codd & basse, or mulett. **1637** MORTON *New Canaan* I. i, The Massachussetts . . . hath as yet the greatest number of inhabitants; and hath a very large bay to. **1654** JOHNSON *Wonder-w. Prov.* 43 Betwixt these two strong armes lies a large Cave [*sic*] or Bay, on which the chiefest part of this Town is built. **1684** *Mass. H. S. Coll.* 4 Ser. V. 123 It's commonly said by coasters, that there are in Virginia far greater bays than this of Narroganset, which are called rivers. **1701** *R.I. Col. Rec.* III. 437 No person . . . shall presume to go on board any ship . . . coming into . . . any bay or river within this Collony. **1747** *Penna. Col. Rec.* V. 103 Nor can we understand on what grounds you are pleased to alledge the length & difficulty of the Bay are less security than heretofore. **1771** FRANKLIN *Autobiog.* 250 In crossing the bay, we met with a squall. *a***1817** DWIGHT *Travels* I. 110 The coast also is finely indented with bays and harbours. **1817** *Ann. 14th Congress* 2 Sess. 127 With a seacoast . . . intersected by many deep bays and rivers, the country cannot be protected against depredations by any other . . . force. **1834** PECK *Gaz. Illinois* 103 [He] sailed through the lakes to Green Bay, there called the 'Bay of Puants.' **1840** COOPER *Pathfinder* viii, An unbroken outline of forest, with wide bays, and low headlands or points. **1881** McLEAN *Cape Cod Folks* i. 9 We could plainly hear the surf rolling in from the bay.

+**b.** *West.* San Francisco, as situated on the bay of that name.

1877 WM. WRIGHT *Big Bonanza* 398 Some one in the 'bear' interest has been telegraphing to the Bay [San Francisco] a pack of lies about the mines. **1900** DRANNAN *Plains & Mts.* 209 In those days persons speaking of going to San Francisco, always spoke of it as 'going to the bay.' **1910** J. HART *Vigilante Girl* xxi. 294 The miners up there look with much suspicion on the arrival of any lawyer from 'down at the Bay,' as they say.

+**c.** *Over the bay*, intoxicated. *slang.*

1833 GREENE *D. Duckworth* II. 176 He was seldom downright drunk; but was often—a little over the bay. **1896** *Dialect Notes* I. 398 'He was a little over the bay last night.' [Current in] Minn.; N.Y.

+**2.** The colony of Massachusetts Bay. *Obs.* except *Hist.*

So named with reference to the bay which is now Boston Harbor (**1859** J. G. Palfrey *New England* I. 185; **1890** J. WINSOR *Mem. Hist. Boston* I. 37). On 4 March 1629 the King incorporated 'the Governor and Company of the Mattachusetts Bay in Newe England.'

1636 *Maine Doc. Hist.* III. 79 No one place in the world comes neere itt; I meane in the Baye, where there is such a holly [=holy] walking. **1637** *Conn. Col. Rec.* I. 10 Mr. Haine & Mr. Ludlowe shall goe . . . to treate & conclude with our frendes of the Bay . . . and to parle with the bay aboute our settinge downe in the Pequoitt Countrey. **1638** UNDERHILL *Newes from America* 8 The governors of the Bay sent us to demand the heads of those persons that had slain Captain Norton. **1648** *New Haven Col. Rec.* I. 383 The governor was desired to wright to the governer in the Baye to know what they did ther aboute it. *a***1649** WINTHROP *Hist.* I. 58 Ever since this bay was planted by Englishmen. *a***1656** BRADFORD *Hist.* 434 The Gov[ernmen]t in the Bay were aquented with it but refferrd it hither. **1660** *New Haven Col. Rec.* II. 374 The maintaining children at the schooles or colledg in the Bay. **1680** *Conn. Prob. Rec.* 586, I give . . . what mony I have comeing to me in the bay.

+**3.** *S. C.* (See quotation.)

1910 *S. C. Hist. Mag.* XI. 44 From the description of the lots in this deed [dated 1744] it appears that one street, fronting on the river, was known as the 'Bay.' This word 'bay' . . . seems very generally to have been applied in Lower South Carolina at that period in towns on rivers or water courses, to the streets which fronted directly on the water.

+**4.** A part of a prairie or the like extending into and almost surrounded by a forest, wooded land, etc.

1850 W. COLTON *Three Years Calif.* 370 Still, in some of its [=San Joaquin valley's] bays, the evidences of fertility exist. **1852** *S. Lit. Messenger* XVIII. 314/1 We . . . turn into a sweet green *bay* (or bend) of fresh grass, and skirted with trees. **1853** 'P. PAXTON' *Yankee in Texas* 93 A strip of prairie extending into the woods is known as a 'Cove' or 'Bay.' **1874** B. F. TAYLOR *World on Wheels* 17 What there was of it [*i.e.* the village] in the old days lay in the bottom of a bay of land bounded . . . by wooded hills. **1907** *Dialect Notes* III. 209 *Bay*, a piece of land partly surrounded by woods (N.E. Ark.).

5. Attrib. (in early use in sense 2) with *city, coast, council, folk, government, salmon, soldier.*

1665 *Mass. Bay Rec.* IV. II. 249 [The king's commissioners] summoned the people . . . [and] possessed them of their innevitable ruine in case they continued vnder the Bay gouernment. **1675** *Conn. Public Rec.* II. 367 A covert to a letter from the Bay Councill to him. **1675** *Wyllys Papers* 223 The Indians . . . have slain & wounded nigh thirty men; most of them bay souldiers. **1680** *N.H. Hist. Soc. Coll.* VIII. 53 As for the Bay government, we have lived under the plague of the Bay government long enough. **1748** J. NORTON *Redeemed Captive* (1870) 44 Died John Jordan. . . . He belonged to the Bay government. **1781** *Virginia State Papers* I. 547 Consider our situation, surrounded on every side by enemies, the British on our Sea & Bay Coasts. **1835** *S. Lit. Messenger* I. 423 Wiser . . . than we, these 'Bay folk' have no courts . . . held by men who have not themselves studied the science they are to expound. **1857** *Harper's Mag.* Nov. 817/1 The bay salmon is larger than the cod in the bays of California. **1910** J. HART *Vigilante Girl* 199 When Yarrow held forth to Alden on the merits of the Bay City's [=San Francisco's] foreign restaurants he had not boasted unduly.

*Bay, *n.*[2]

***1.** A principal compartment or part of a building or other structure as marked off by beams, pillars, etc.

1665 Hutchinson *Coll. Orig. P.* (1769) 421 At Cambridg they have a wooden collidg and, in the yard, a brick pile of two bayes for the Indians. **1739** W. STEPHENS *Proc. Georgia* 403 The Work [=sawmill] was of sufficient Strength, . . . so was likewise the fore Bay, and the main Hatchway. **1857** C. VAUX *Villas* 297 This design . . . is to be executed . . . in brick and brown stone, with wooden trimmings to the roofs, bays, verandas, etc. **1879** *Scribner's Mo.* Dec. 170/1 The corridor . . . is lighted by seven large windows . . . which naturally divide it into bays of 20 feet square. Each bay is bounded by piers.

***2.** A division of a barn for the storage of hay, etc.

1693 *Groton Rec.* 107 Euery barn with one baye [shall be taxed] at one peney in the single. **1742** *N.H. Probate Rec.* III. 126 We have set off to Ann French . . . the westerly end of the Barn three bays through the barn. **1844** *Knickerb.* XXIII. 440 There goes Jim from the highest scaffold into the straw at the bottom of the 'deep bay.' **1865** MRS. WHITNEY *Gayworthys* 173 He spent nearly all his time in the bay of the old barn, lying there alone in the hay. **1867** 'T. LACKLAND' *Homespun* I. 85 Now he . . . sweeps ever so airily across the uppermost scaffold . . . , —and hangs . . . suspended over the yawning bay. **1896** *Vermont Agric. Rep.* XV. 116 Grass cut . . . and allowed to heat, and aired out a little can be put into a bay in large quantities.

+**3.** A sick bay.

1845 *Knickerb.* XXVI. 208 He was in the bay one day to see that all the sick was comfortably taken care of.

+**4.** (See quotation.)

1888 BILLINGS *Hardtack* 385 The distance between the centres of two boats [of a pontoon bridge] in position is called a *bay.*

*Bay, *n.*[3]

+**1.** Any of various trees and shrubs more or less resembling the laurel of southern Europe.

1634 WOOD *New Eng. Prospect* I. v. 13 In the woods, without eyther the art or the helpe of man, . . . [grow] mirtle, . . . bayes, &c. **1666** *S.C. Hist. Soc. Coll.* V. 63 The generallity of the timber being oake, maple, ash, wallnut, popler, bayes. **1682** ASH *Carolina* 6 There are many other fragrant smelling trees, the Myrtle, Bay and Lawrel. **1684** I. MATHER *Providences* vi. (1856) 118 Some . . . advised the poor woman to stick the house round with bayes, as an effectual preservative against the power of evil spirits. **1709** LAWSON *Carolina* 94 Bay and Laurel generally delight in a low, swampy ground. **1737** WESLEY *Journal* (1910) I. 402 The soil is a blackish sand, producing several kinds of oak . . . , bay, laurel, ash. **1801** ASBURY *Journal* III. 9 Pimeta swamps, with intermingled gums and cypress, variegated by evergreens of bay and laurel. **1838** W. B. DEWEES *Letters from Texas* xxii. 219 The timber is mostly live oak with an undergrowth of holly, wild-peach, and bay. **1853** SIMMS *Sword & Distaff* 151 A clump of bays, or dwarf-laurel. **1859** A. VAN BUREN *Sojourn in South* 43 The bay, or cucumber tree, . . . looked like our bass-wood. **1880** CABLE *Grandissimes* iv. 27 The queen sat down with them, clothed in her entire wardrobe . . . and odors of bay and sassafras.

+b. With specifying term: see quots. and *loblolly, red, swamp, sweet* (etc.) *bay*, and cf. BAY-TREE.

1629 PARKINSON *Paradisius* 599 The Virginia Bay, or Cherry Bay. *c***1728** CATESBY *Carolina* I. 39 The Sweet flowring Bay. *Ib.* 61 The Purple-berried Bay. **1781–2** JEFFERSON *Notes on Va.* (1788) 38 Portugal bay. *Laurus indica.* **1813** MUHLENBERG *Cat. Plants* 2 American olive (purple-berried bay).

+2. *S.E.* 'A piece of low, marshy ground producing large numbers of bay-trees' (B. '59); =BAY-GALL 1.

1795 ASBURY *Journal* II. 285 This Country [S. Carolina] abounds with bays, swamps, and drains. **1802** J. DRAYTON *S. Carolina* 7 They are called *bays*, from the quantities of bay trees which grow therein, and which are so tall and closely connected with each other, as to throw a continual shade over the lands below. Hence their soil is naturally sour and spungy. **1845** SIMMS *Wigwam & Cabin* I. 15 They found themselves on the edge of a very dense forest . . . , a portion of which was swallowed up in a deep bay—so called in the dialect of the country—a swamp bottom. **1855** — *Forayers* 354 The bay was the abiding place only of the reptile and the wild cat.

+b. *Florida.* (See quotation.)

1884 *Harper's Mag.* March 601/1 Swamp and 'bay' (the word applied in Florida to slough and water-grass meadows) amplify the area.

+3. Attrib. with *flower, thicket.*

1845 SIMMS *Wigwam & Cabin* I. 18 He proceeded to traverse the margin of the bay until he came to . . . the high-road. The youth . . . soon found himself on the opposite side of the bay thicket. **1851** *Polly Peablossom* 21 Polly was dressed in white, and wore a bay-flower with its green leaves in her hair.

***Bay,** *n.*[4] A bay horse or mare.

1780 W. FLEMING in *Travels Amer. Col.* 644 My horses missing. Advertized 30 dollars each. Heard of my two bays. **1832** J. F. WATSON *Hist. Tales N.Y.* 163 It was occasionally drawn by six horses, Virginia bays. **1835** [INGRAHAM] *South-West* I. 229 His own phaeton . . . was drawn by two beautiful long-tailed bays. **1881** W. O. STODDARD *E. Hardery* 364 A pair of handsome bays, with a light carriage behind them. **1904** STRATTON-PORTER *Freckles* 272 A stout, dark, red-faced man that drives a bay and a gray.

***Bay,** *a.* Of horses, mares, etc.: Reddish-brown, approaching chestnut.

1671 *Oyster Bay Records* I. 62 One three year old bay mare. **1707** *Boston News-Letter* 10 Feb. 2/2 The said Horse is a pretty large bright bay Gelding. **1746** *N.H. Probate Rec.* III. 416 My baye horse and furneture belonging to said horse. **1757** *N.J. Archives* XX. 160 Stray'd or stolen, . . . a natural pacing bay mare. **1788** V. B. Howard *Heroes* (1932) 41 Taken up, . . . an old bay mare about fourteen hands high. **1850** GARRARD *Wah-To-Yah* ii. 29 Roubideau wished to buy Paint, offering me a fine bay horse. **1892** M. A. JACKSON *Memoirs* xxi. 413 He rode over from headquarters upon his handsome bay horse. *a***1918** G. STUART *On Frontier* I. 176 Fred's bay filly . . . is lame.

***Bayberry.**

+1. The fruit or berry of the wax-myrtle (see 2).

Examples 1687, 1704, may belong to sense 2.

1687 *Manchester Town Rec.* 32 Near Vincsons baiberry medow . . . where the meeting house timber was cut. **1704** *Ib.* 106 The bounds of John Knowltons bay berry march which was formerly Nicolas Vinisons. **1709** LAWSON *Carolina* 89 The Bay-Berries yield a Wax, which besides its Use in Chirurgery, makes Candles that, in burning, give a fragrant Smell. **1746** *Brookhaven Rec.* 160 That the Inhabetents of Brookhaven do frequently destroy the Bay berys within the Township, by gathering them before they are groone to perfection. **1778** CARVER *Travels* 509 The Myrtle . . . bears small berries, which are generally called bay berries. **1802** *East-Hampton Rec.* IV. 316 Any person . . . detected in picking cranberries or ba[y]berries on Napeague beach or any of the common lands. **1894** 'MARK TWAIN' *Those Twins* vii, Take of . . . bay-berries . . . a dram and a half.

+2. The wax-myrtle or candleberry, *Myrica cerifera.*

1792 BELKNAP *Hist. N.H.* III. 123 The bayberry . . . the leaves of which yield an agreeable perfume, and the fruit a delicate green wax, which is made into candles. **1802** *Mass. H. S. Coll.* VIII. 197 The bushes are whortleberries, . . . bay-berries, and box-berries. **1832** WILLIAMSON *Maine* I. 114 The bayberry . . . bears clusters resembling berries. **1837** LINCOLN *Botany* App. 130/2 Bayberry . . . ; fruit globular, naked. On boiling, a pleasant-flavored wax is obtained. **1869** STOWE *Oldtown Folks* 577 The road was fringed . . . with great patches of the blue violet, and sweet-fern, and bayberry.

+b. (See quotation.)

1901 MOHR *Plant Life Ala.* 464 *Myrica caroliniensis*, . . . Bayberry, . . . Candleberry. . . . The bark of the root, as 'bayberry bark,' is used medicinally.

+3. *Bayberry bark* (see 2b and *b. root*); *b. bush*, =sense 2; *b. candle*, a candle made of bayberry wax; *b. day* (see quot.); *b. dip*, a dip formed of bayberry wax; *b. root* (see quot. and *b. bark*); *b. shrub*, =sense 2.

[**1770** FORSTER tr. *Kalm's Trav.* I. 192 Bayberry-bush, Candleberry Tree, . . . Tallow shrub.] **1830** J. F. WATSON *Philadelphia* 470 The ancient Swedes . . . made their candles generally from the bayberry bushes; the root they used to cure tooth ache. **1892** B. TORREY *Foot-path Way* 198, I began a stealthy approach . . . to a patch of bayberry bushes. — **1739** *Harvard Rec.* II. 689 To send to Mr. Mico, merchant in London, a box of thirty or fourty weight of Bay-berry Candles. **1773** *Advt.* in *Boston Gazette* 19 July (Th.), Mould, Dip, and Bayberry Candles. — **1911** *Boston Ev. Transcript* 27 May II. 3/7 In the annals of those [colonial] days, Sept. 15 was 'Bayberry Day,' when . . . old and young sallied forth with pail and basket, each eager to secure his share in this gift of nature. — **1903** *Boston Herald* 19 Aug., The bayberry dips are made by boiling bayberries down to a thick wax and dipping cords into the mixture. — **1792** *Mass. H. S. Coll.* III. 159 They took some bayberry root, and scraping off the bark, put it into a bottle. — **1855** *Knickerb.* XLVI. 221 An almost impenetrable under-growth of alders, briers, bay-berry shrubs, . . . grass and weeds.

+Bayberry tallow. Myrtle tallow; =next.

1720 *Mass. H. Repr. Journals* II. 333 The enhabitants of this province shall have liberty . . . to pay the several sums . . . in . . . oyl, whalebone, bayberry wax or tallow [etc.]. **1721** *Ib.* III. 45. **1828** WEBSTER, *Candleberry Tree*, . . . a shrub . . . from the berries of which a kind of wax or oil is procured, of which candles are made. . . . In popular language, this is called bay-berry tallow. **1847** WOOD *Botany* 500 Bayberry, wax myrtle. . . . The fruit . . . [has] a coating of whitish wax, which, being separated by boiling water, constitutes the bayberry tallow of commerce. **1859** BARTLETT 24 The berries [of *Myrica cerifera*], when boiled in water, yield a fragrant green wax, known as 'bayberry tallow,' used for making candles. **1891** *Amer. Notes & Q.* VI. 210, I have often heard old people tell about the former use of 'bayberry tallow,' or wax, for candle-making.

+Bayberry wax. Myrtle wax or myrtle tallow, used esp. for making candles. Also attrib.

1695 W. WINTHROP in *Winthrop P.* IV. 509, I shall send . . . a cake of the bayberry wax, about 23 lb, which is som I had by me since last year. **1712** *Mass. H. S. Coll.* 6 Ser. V. 257, I am now to beg . . . that you secure for me all the bayberry wax you can. **1720** [see prec.]. **1769** *Mass. Gazette* 21 Dec. (Th.), Bayberry-wax Candles [advertised]. **1785** FRANKLIN *Writings* IX. 326, I convey'd the Bayberry Wax to Abbé de Chalut, with your compliments. **1861** STOWE *Pearl Orr's Isl.* I. ix. 72 Look in a minute at Major Broad's and tell 'em to use bayberry wax for his blister. **1878** — *Poganuc People* xix. 217, I'm a comin' this year to make up her candles for her. . . . I've been tryin' out a lot o' bayberry wax to put in 'em. **1891** [see prec.]

+Bay-bird. [BAY *n.*[1] 5.] (See quotations.) — **1889** *Cent., Bay-birds*, a collective name of numerous small wading birds or shore-birds, chiefly of the snipe and plover families, which frequent the muddy shores of the bays and estuaries along the Atlantic coast of the United States. **1895** ELLIOT *N.A. Shore-Birds* 52 On the Atlantic seaboard, . . . this species [the Dowitcher] is one of the most common and well known of the 'Bay-birds.'

+Bay-breast. [See next.] The bay-breasted warbler. — **1892** TORREY *Foot-Path Way* 190 A hurried search showed . . . one yellow redpoll, and one clearly marked bay-breast.

+Bay-breasted, *a.* [BAY *a.*] *B. warbler* (see quotations). — **1810** WILSON *Ornithology* II. 97 Bay-Breasted Warbler. *Sylvia Castanea.* . . . This very rare species passes thro Pennsylvania about the beginning of May, and soon disappears. **1858** BAIRD *Birds Pacific R.R.* 276 *Dendroica castanea*, Baird. Bay Breasted Warbler. . . . [Inhabits] eastern United States to the Missouri. **1868** *Amer. Naturalist* June 173 Somewhat resembling the chestnut-sided warbler . . . is the Bay-breasted Warbler. **1892** B. TORREY *Foot-path Way* 6 We . . . soon were in the old forest, listening to bay-breasted warblers.

+Bay-bush. [BAY *n.*[3]] A bush of one or other species of bay; spec. the sweet gale. — **1688** *Huntington Rec.* I. 517 The east bounds is a hamake of bay bushes and a rocke. **1845** SIMMS *Cabin & Wigwam* I. 19 He heard something like a sudden breeze that rustled through the bay bushes at his feet.

+Bay colony. =BAY *n.*[1] 2. — **1777** *Hist. Pelham* (1898) 130 In the name of the People & Stats of the Bay Colony. **1899** E. S. BROOKS *Old Bay State* 101 Change does not always bring satisfaction. It did not to the Bay colony, which had become a royal province.

+Bay craft. [BAY *n.*[1]] A vessel built to navigate a bay.

1725 in *New Eng. Quarterly* (1929) II. 660 We met a Ship which they took and burnt then sending away what Prisoners they thought fit in a Bay Craft. **1784** J. SMYTH *Tour U.S.* II. 315 An illiterate rude skipper of a common bay craft, something resembling the coal lighters in the Thames. **1835** [INGRAHAM] *South-West* II. 150 The Gulf, 'accessible,' says Flint, 'by small vessels and bay-craft.'

+Bay-dam. *Obs.* [f. E. **bay* (now s. dial.) in the same sense.] A dam or bank to hold back water. — **1814** J. TAYLOR *Arator* 229 The place being made by bay-dams, was dug out to the precise level of low water, and the trunk accurately laid down upon it.

+Bayeau, Bayau, variants (after Fr.) of BAYOU. — **1804** CLARK in *Lewis & C. Exped.* (1904) I. 66 A Bayeau leading from a large Lake. **1806** T. ASHE *Travels* (1808) xl. 323 One of the most dangerous bayeaus on the Mississippi. **1810** F. CUMING *Western Tour* 271 The Mississippi . . . flows up a small canal or (in the language of the country) bayau.

+Bay-gall. *S.E. & S.* [BAY *n.*[3]]

1. A low-lying piece of boggy or spongy land overgrown with the sweet bay and other shrubs.

'Bay galls . . . are properly water courses, covered with a spungy earth, and mixed and bound with vegetable fibres. They tremble like a jelly for a considerable distance about the spot impressed' (1812 Stoddard *Sk. Louisiana* 124).

1775 Romans *Florida* 15, I shall treat of them by the names of pine land, hammock land, savannahs, swamps, marshes, and bay, or cypress galls. **1791** W. Bartram *Carolina* 197 Morasses . . . fed or occasioned by the great wet bay-gale [*sic*] or savanna Pine lands. **1800** B. Hawkins *Sk. Creek Country* 20 The eastern boundary of the Creek claims, is poor pine land, with cypress ponds and bay galls. **1817** S. Brown *Western Gaz.* 13 From thence down there are bay-galls, dwarf evergreens, and cypress ponds. **1837** Williams *Florida* 140 The sand hills and ridges rise to a considerable height, often chequered with ponds and bay galls. **1839** *S. Lit. Messenger* V. 375/2 On the left was a large bay-gall . . . thickly beset with cat-briers and undergrowth. **1863** *Rep. Comm. Agric.*, Low, flat, swampy regions, which are frequently studded with 'bay galls,' and are occasionally inundated. **1905** *Bureau of Forestry Bull. No. 64*, 14 Partially inundated depressions, locally known as 'bay galls,' . . . serve as the natural drainage channels of the flat longleaf pine land. *Ib.*, The bay galls, which receive their name from the sweet bay, . . . the characteristic tree of such situations, are of scarcely any economic importance at present.

2. The red bay (*Persea borbonia*) of the southern states.

1861 Wood *Botany* 620 Red Bay. Bay Galls. . . . *Persea Carolinensis* Mx. . . . Wood of a fine rose-color, once used in cabinet-work. **1897** Sudworth *Arborescent Flora* 201 Red bay [is called] . . . Bay Galls (Tenn.).

+**Bay ibis.** [Bay *n.*[1]] The glossy ibis, *Plegadis (Ibis) falcinellus.* — **1833** Bonaparte *Ornithology* IV. 36 The Bay or Glossy Ibis is twenty-six inches in length. **1874** Coues *Birds N.W.* 513 Two species of Ibis, the Wood and Bay, are known to occur . . . near the Missouri region.

+**Bay laurel.** A southern tree (see quotations). — **1836** Holley *Texas* 88 Among the underwood are found the bay laurel—the poet's own tree. **1859** Bartlett 24 *Bay Laurel*, . . . bay-tree. **1877** *Ib.* 33 Bay . . . [or] Bay laurel . . . is of the same family as the *Magnolia grandiflora*, which it resembles except in size.

***Bay-leaf. 1.** A bay tree. **2.** A leaf of this. {1636} — **(1)** **1832** S. J. Hale *Flora* 26 Bay Leaf, *Laurus* (Bay or Laurel tree). — **(2)** **1879** Webster s.v., [The] Bay-leaf . . . has . . . an aromatic taste, and is used in cookery and by confectioners. **1882** Mrs. Owens *Cook Book* 15 Add [to the broth] . . . a sprig of any kind of dried sweet herb, except sage, and one bay leaf. **1904** A. Dale *Wanted, a Cook* 242 Stew in a saucepan . . . one bay leaf, six whole peppers, . . . and, if handy, a hambone cut into pieces.

+**Bay line.** *Obs.* [Bay *n.*[1]] The boundary-line of Massachusetts. — **1725** *Providence* (R.I.) *Rec.* XIII. 24 The highway from Town to the Bay Line.

+**Bay lynx.** [Bay *a.*] The wildcat, *Lynx rufus.* — **1784** Pennant *Arctic Zoology* I. 51 Bay Lynx. . . . This species is found in the internal parts of the province of New York. **1823** James *Exped.* I. 261 *Felix rufa*, Bay lynx. **1838** *Mass. Zool. Survey Rep.* 28 Bay Lynx, . . . three times the size of the domestic cat, . . . stands high upon its legs. **1871** *Amer. Naturalist* V. 5 The Bay Lynx . . . [is] likewise rare on the prairies. **1890** *Cent.* s.v. *Lynx*, The common wildcat of North America is the bay lynx, . . . which runs into several varieties.

+**Bayman.**[1] [Bay *n.*[1]]

1. A man who resides on or close to a bay; esp. a native or resident of the colony of Massachusetts Bay.

1641 *Plymouth Col. Rec.* II. 23 That clause . . . which concerned the boundes from Narragansetts Bay to . . . Pockanockett, in regard the Bay men would haue had Sicquncke from us. **1643** Shirley in Bradford *Hist.* 486 Now it will fall out farr better for you . . . if you pay Mr. Andrews, or the Bay men, by his order, 544 li., which is his full demande. **1788** W. Gordon *History* I. 193 Scurrilous publications . . . were craftily calculated . . . , and suited the too levelling disposition of the Bay-men. *Ib.* 362 There is too great a nationality among the Bay-men: such a one might be unduly prejudiced in favor of his own colony. **a1841** [W. Hawes] *Sporting Scenes* I. 27 Inlets beloved by baymen, safe avenues of escape from the rough assaults of the puffy servants of Æolus. **a1889** *Shore Birds* 43 (*Cent.*), When the birds are traveling with the wind, or as baymen call it, a 'free wind.' **1904** *N.Y. Ev. Post* 11 June, Somers P'int, as the baymen call it, is one of several very attractive summer resorts that have grown up about the bay in recent years.

2. A mahogany-cutter of the Bay of Honduras. *Obs.*

1715 *Boston News-Letter* 10 Oct. 2/2 Huntington and . . . Holder . . . report that 250 of the Bay-Men . . . were designed to Campeche, to burn the Shipping there. **1723** *New-Eng. Courant* 13–20 May 2/1 The Privateer . . . returned to the Bay [of Honduras], . . . as Capt. Lyde was afterwards inform'd by some of the Bay-men. **1726** *Ib.* 23–30 Apr. 2/2 The Bay Men . . . immediately fitted out 2 boats. **a1821** C. Biddle *Autobiog.* i. 17 The baymen at this time would frequently sell their wood to two or three different captains.

+**Bayman.**[2] [Bay *n.*[2] 3] A sick-bay attendant or nurse. — [**1888** Churchward *Blackbirding* 25, I stole a beautiful knife from the sick bayman's locker.] **1889** *Cent.*, *Bayman*, . . . a sick-bay attendant; a nurse for sick or wounded men on a vessel of war. **1900** Webster *Suppl.* s.v., Bayman, in the United States navy, . . . [is] now officially designated as *hospital apprentice*.

Bayonet. {1611–}

1. A stabbing blade of steel, attachable to the muzzle of a rifle († or musket). {1672–} Cf. Bagonet.

1728 *Boston Rec.* 2 He did present to the Town two hundred and fifteen Firelocks with Bayonets fitted to them. **1758** *Essex Inst. Coll.* XLV. 157 These may inform those who may have the care of providing the bayonets for the Province, that Jacob Tyler . . . will provide the regiment. **1758** A. Fuller. *Ib.* XLVI. 214 The Regalors hove down their pak and fixed their bayarnits [*sic*]. **1775** *N.H. Prov. Papers* (1873) VII. 643 The bayonets to be 18 inches in the blade. **1826** Cooper *Mohicans* xxxii, 'In what manner would you set them [*sc.* soldiers] to work in this business?' 'The bayonet would make a road.' **1861** *Army Regulations* 64 A sentinel . . . will suffer no person to come nearer than within reach of his bayonet, until the person has given the countersign. **1867** Edwards *Shelby* 402 Spitting the lagging Confederates with bayonets as a French cook spits an ortolan. **1891** *Century Mag.* Jan. 425, I passed two sentinel fires and was pursued some distance at the point of the bayonet.

fig. **1807** *Ann. 9th Congress* 2 Sess. 551 If there shall be a collision between the press and the bayonet, it needs no prophetic spirit to say which will kick the beam.

b. A soldier armed with this weapon. {1780–}

1855 Simms *Forayers* 378 It needs but a thousand bayonets to expel him from the post of Orangeburg. **1884** *Century Mag.* XXVII. 499/2 His company numbered four thousand bayonets. **1892** M. A. Jackson *Memoirs* 356 Four pieces of artillery, supported by only a few hundred bayonets.

c. Attrib. with *belt, scabbard, sheath*, etc.

1775 *Essex Inst. Coll.* LIII. 83 May 23. Bo[ugh]t . . . a bayonett sheathe 5/. **1783** R. T. Durrett *Louisville* (1893) 147 [Military stores at Fort Nelson included] 385 Bayonet Belts. **1813** *Niles' Reg.* III. 295/2 Bayonet belts and scabbards, 42,127. **1825** Neal *Bro. Jonathan* II. 147 As the young soldier feels, when he sees a whole army moving forward . . . to the bayonet charge. **1861** *Army Regulations* 22 Cartridge-boxes and bayonet-scabbards will be polished with blacking. **1876** [Ingram] *Centennial Exp.* 143 The bayonet-grinder attracted hundreds about him.

2. See Spanish bayonet.

+**3.** *Bayonet fish, palmetto, rush:* (see quotations).

1829 B. Hall *Travels* III. 173 It is called on the spot [in S.C.], the bayonet palmetto, from each division of its broad leaf being in the form of that weapon. **1840** Dewey *Mass. Flowering Plants* 203 *Juncus militaris*, Bayonet rush, . . . flowers at the summit in a panicle. — **1888** Goode *Amer. Fishes* 390 The sword-fish and the bayonet-fish destroy many, rushing through the schools and striking right and left with their powerful swords.

+**Bayou.** *S.* Also †**bayoue, bayoe.** [Amer.-Fr. (1719), ad. Choctaw *bayuk* Bayouk. Cf. Bayeau, Bio.]

1. A stream or channel of water having little or no observable current, and freq. forming an inlet or outlet to a river or lake. Also in fig. context.

Comments on the word are:—**1818** T. Hulme *Journal* 1 July, This Bayou is a run out of the main river round a flat portion of land, which is sometimes overflowed. **1819** *McDonogh Papers* 36 The bayou itself being a handsome river of . . . two hundred feet in width. **1822** J. Woods *English Prairie* 234 A slue, or bayou (that is, where the water breaks out over a low place). **1826** T. Flint *Recoll.* 330 The term *Bayou* is understood here [in La.] to mean an alluvial stream with but little current, and sometimes running from the main river, and connected with it again, as a lateral canal. **1829** B. Hall *Travels in N.A.* III. 318 A sluggish creek, or what is called a Bayou—a sort of natural canal joining the lakes and rivers all over the Delta. **1833** T. Hamilton *Men & Manners* II. 235 These bayous are sluggish creeks which alternately supply nourishment to the Mississippi, and ease it of its load. **1835** Simms *Partisan* 317 The little lagune, or bayou, on the edge of which they . . . crouched. **1836** J. Hildreth *Campaigns Rocky Mts.* 84 A bayou or small intersecting stream. **1844** Mrs. Houstoun *Texas* (1845) 123 [Galveston] island is intersected with several inlets of the sea, or bayous, as they are called. **1850** [H. C. Lewis] *La. Swamp Doctor* 139 A lazy sluggish 'bayou'—as all the small water-courses in this country are Frenchifically termed. **1862** *Cornhill Mag.* VI. 476 Immense bayous, as they are termed—wide wastes of water and of marsh, covered with rushes.

1766 H. Gordon in *Travels Amer. Col.* 484 We left New Orleans . . . and lay that night at the Bayoue. **1792** J. Pope *Tour S. & W.* 42 In this *Bayoue* I counted seventy-three Alligators. **1803** *Ann. 8th Congress* 2 Sess. 1511 The Attakapas, . . . chiefly on the bayou or creek of Vermillion, about one hundred souls. **1805** Thoburn *Oklahoma* (1916) I. 29 A bayou of clear running water about fifty feet wide. **1819** E. Dana *Geog. Sk.* 18 The Arkansaw [river] . . . communicates with the White river by a bayou. **1822** *Missionary Herald* XVIII. 11 The hired men . . . wandered among the swamps and bayous of the Mississippi, till they and their horses had nearly perished. **1842** Longfellow *Quadroon Girl* ii, The Slaver . . . Watched the gray alligator slide Into the still bayou. **1848** *Indiana Gen. Ass. Doc.* II. 298 The building of the bridge across the bayou in Martin county. **1853** 'P. Paxton' *Yankee in Texas* 21 Joe and I . . . were upon the banks of a bayou, in a very dense thicket. **1865** G. Sabre *Prisoner of War* 11 The dead, slimy, green, vegetable, and animal decomposition of the bayous. **1885** *Outing* Oct. 64/1 In Tunica county, Mississippi, on the banks of a sluggish bayou . . . is my favorite hunting-ground. **1887** E. B. Custer *Tenting on Plains* ii. 86 There were seams and fissures in portions of the bayou, through which the moist mud oozed. **1901** White *Westerners* xiii. 93 In a word the broad sea of the wilderness has shrunken to bayous and bays.

b. In pl. *bayoux* (after Fr. usage).

1814 BRACKENRIDGE *Views La.* 39 Several settlements had been formed on the rivers and bayoux. **1817** J. BRADBURY *Travels* 238 Other *bayoux* that take water from this river above that city [=N.O.]. **1836** J. HALL *Stat. West* ii. 26 Below the Falls of Ohio . . . the river-bottoms . . . are intersected by *bayoux*, or deep inlets.

c. *Dry bayou:* (see quot. 1841).

1841 W. KENNEDY *Texas* I. 25 The word *bayou* . . . is rather loosely applied in the topography of Texas and the West. In strictness, I believe it means a deep inlet, which affords a channel for the water in time of flood, and remains dry, or nearly so, at other seasons. **1853** 'P. PAXTON' *Yankee in Texas* 29 Poke, so full of the chase that he had not noticed the dry bayou before him, pitched headlong down the precipitous bank.

2. (See quotations.)

1823 E. JAMES *Exped.* III. 93 The fertile but narrow eastern margin of the ravine, or as it would be called in the settlements of the Arkansa, *bayou*. *Ib.* 120 The Bayous, as they are named in this country, . . . are large and often very profound ravines or water courses.

3. An abandoned or isolated stretch of a river-course forming a lake or swamp.

1872 *Amer. Naturalist* VI. 725 This pond is a fine representative of a peculiar feature of the bottom-lands of the western and southern rivers, locally termed bayous, lagoons or ponds. **1904** CHAMBERLIN & SALISBURY *Geology* I. 181 [When] the abandoned channel-curve . . . contains standing water and has the proper form, it is called an ox-bow lake, . . . or sometimes a bayou. **1914** R. S. TARR *Physiography* 150 Some abandoned [river] courses along the lower Mississippi are called *bayous*.

4. Attrib. with *cabin*, *road*, etc.

1850 [H. C. LEWIS] *La. Swamp Doctor* 161, I saw the dust up the bayou road shaken up by a half-naked negro. **1886** *Harper's Mag.* Aug. 483/1 The following bayou version of one of the negro folk-lore stories is translated by a lady. **1883** *Century Mag.* July 376/2 The black bass . . . varies greatly, even in the same waters; . . . they have received names somewhat descriptive of their habitat, as . . . slough, bayou, moss, grass, and Oswego bass. **1888** CABLE *Bonaventure* 106 Sitting and pondering one evening in the little bayou cabin.

b. *Bayou blue*, alcoholic liquor. *slang.*

1870 NOWLAND *Indianapolis* 36 He thought (especially if he had taken a little 'bayou blue') he would weigh several ton.

+**Bayouk, Bayouc.** *Obs.* [Choctaw *bayuk*, *bayouque* (1699), river, creek, bayou.] =BAYOU *n.* — **1770** PITTMAN *Present State* 10 The entrance of the Bayouk of St. John is defended by a battery of six guns and a serjeant's guard. **1772** ROMANS in Phillips *Notes* (1924) 122 The Creek . . . is said to fall into the Alabama River, near to the Bayouc Cononga or Hesia. **1789** MORSE *Gazetteer* s.v. *John*, The entrance of the Bayouk of St. John is defended by a battery. . . . There are some plantations on the Bayouk.

+**Bayou State.** The state of Mississippi. — **1867** *Literary Record* (Trübner) 1 Aug. 1 Maine is popularly known as The Lumber or Pine-Tree State; . . . Mississippi as the Bayou State.

+**Bay Prairie.** [BAY *n.*[1] 4.] (See quotation.) — **1831** HOLLEY *Texas* (1833) vi. 58 This island constituted what is now called the Bay Prairie; a large, rich, and very beautiful prairie, lying between the timbered lands of Caney, and those of Colorado.

+**Bay rum.** [BAY *n.*[3]] An aromatic liquid obtained by distilling rum with the leaves of the Jamaica bayberry (*Pimenta acris*), or now also by blending certain oils; used esp. for cosmetic and medicinal purposes. Also attrib. with *bottle*.

1840 *Knickerb.* XVI. 34 Perfumed 'as to our locks' with the bay-rum or fragrant cologne. **1859** BARTLETT 24 Bay Rum . . . is chiefly used for the purposes of the toilet. **1871** 'MARK TWAIN' *Sk., About Barbers*, I read the greasy names on the private bay-rum bottles. **1883** *Harper's Mag.* Jan. 199 Erect pepper-woods, whose leaves . . . smell of bay-rum. **1902** HARBEN *A. Daniel* 99 When the barber finished he soaked my face in bay-rum.

+**Bay shilling.** *Obs.* [BAY *n.*[1] 2.] A silver coin formerly coined in Mass. — **1704** S. KNIGHT *Journal* 42 Mony is . . . Ryalls, or Boston or Bay shillings (as they call them,) or good hard money, as sometimes silver coin is termed by them.

+**Bay shiner.** [BAY *n.*[1]] (See quotation.) — **1842** *Nat. Hist. N.Y., Zoology* IV. 211 The Bay Shiner. *Leuciscus chrysopterus*. . . . This beautiful species is caught in the harbor of New York, and is popularly called Bay Shiner, or simply Shiner.

+**Bay shore.** [BAY *n.*[1] 1.] The coast of a bay. — **1823** DEWEES *Lett. from Texas* 33 We followed it [a trail] down on to the bay shore, till we came to a little grove. **1831** HOLLEY *Texas* (1833) vi. 70 All the lands . . . within ten leagues of the gulf or bay shore. **1850** FOOTE *Sk. Virginia* 357 The neighborhood must have been between the Blue Ridge and the Bay Shore.

Bay-side. [BAY *n.*[1]] The shore of a bay. {1883}

1677 *Md. Hist. Mag.* X. 285 The widdow of John Halfehead late of the bayside in St. Maries County. **1849** F. DOUGLASS *Life* 53 In August, 1832, my master attended a Methodist camp-meeting held in the Bay-side. **1899** GREEN *Va. Word-Book* 52 *Bay-side*, the Chesapeake Bay side of Accomack and Northampton counties.

+**Bay-snipe.** [BAY *n.*[1]] 'A bay-bird, or bay-birds collectively' (*Cent.* s.v. *Snipe*). — **1875** *Fur, Fin, & Feather* 121 It is also a capital place for bay-snipe shooting in summer.

+**Bay State.** [BAY *n.*[1] 2.] Massachusetts.

Also called *Old Bay State* (q.v.).

1801 *Spirit of Farmers' Museum* 198 The subscribers in Vermont, down here in the bay state and all about the country. **1828** COOPER *Notions* I. 113 We drove the English out of the Bay State in '76. **1838** Shields *S. S. Prentiss* (1883) 180 Come, what says the Bay State, time-honored Massachusetts? **1850** J. L. TYSON *Diary in Calif.* 11 Our captain . . . was a regular down-easter from the 'Bay State.' **1856** M. J. HOLMES *L. Rivers* Pref. 3 Reared among the rugged hills of the Bay State. **1891** HALE *Story of Mass.* 11 The Bay State [had its] . . . first permanent settlement . . . at Plymouth, by the colony of Independents.

b. Attrib. with *dialect*, *shawl*, etc.

*c*1848 LOWELL *'Look on who will'* ii, 'Tis but my Bay-State dialect,—our fathers spoke the same! **1858** HOLMES *Autocrat* i. 21 When I fling a Bay-State shawl over my shoulders. **1874** (*title*), Bay State Transportation League.

c. *ellipt.* A Bay-State shawl.

1877 BARTLETT 575 A tall man well bundled up in a Scotch plaid, or 'Bay State.'

+**Bay-Stater.** A native or resident of Massachusetts. — **1845** CIST *Cincinnati Misc.* I. 240 The inhabitants of Massachusetts are called Bay Staters. **1888** WHITMAN *November Boughs* 70 The soldiers . . . from . . . Massachusetts [were call'd] Bay Staters.

+**Bay swamp.** *S.* [BAY *n.*[3]] A tract of swampy ground overgrown with bay trees. — **1741** W. STEPHENS *Proc. Georgia* II. 237 The Land in these parts, setting aside the Pine-Barren, and some Bay-swamps, or the like, with proper cultivation, will yield a reasonable increase. **1791** BARTRAM *Travels* 18 A new . . . species of Annona . . . grows in abundance all over the moist savannas, but more especially near ponds and bay-swamps. **1832** BROWNE *Sylva* 164 In the pine-barrens, tracts 50 or 100 acres are met with at intervals, which, being lower than the adjacent ground, are kept constantly moist by the waters collected in them after the great rains. These spots are entirely covered with the loblolly bay, and are called Bay Swamps.

***Bay-tree.**

***1.** =BAY *n.*[3] 1.

1610 *Estate of Virginia* 54 The country yieldeth abundance of wood, as Oake, Wainscot, Walnut tres, Bay trees, Ashe. **1666** *S. C. H. S. Coll.* V. 77 Land . . . exceedingly timbred principally with live Oake and large Cedar and bay trees. **1709** LAWSON *Carolina* 26 There growing all over this Swamp, a tall, lofty Bay-tree, . . . these being in their Verdure all the Winter long. **1744** F. MOORE *Voy. Georgia* 94 The rest is woods in which there are many bay trees eighty foot high. **1785** MARSHALL *Amer. Grove* 72 *Laurus*. The Bay-Tree. . . . The Seed is a nut of a sharp pointed egg-shape. **1789** MORSE *Amer. Geog.* 415 The swamps abound with cypress and bay trees. The latter is an ever-green, and is food for cattle in winter. **1802** J. DRAYTON *S. Carolina* 6 Their soil is of very sandy nature; producing small pines and bay trees. **1869** FULLER *Flower Gatherers* 139 The Bay-tree of the Southern States is one of the finest American laurels, with large fragrant flowers. **1887** *Century Mag.* March 739/2 We set up our tabernacle in a group of bay-trees, and made our beds of the fragrant branches.

2. With specifying term: see quotations and *red*, *swamp*, *sweet*, *white* (etc.) *bay-tree*. (Cf. BAY *n.*[3] 1b.)

1785 MARSHALL *Amer. Grove* 73 *Laurus Borbonia*. Red-stalked Carolinian Bay-Tree. *Ib.* 114 Carolinian Evergreen Bay-Tree . . . is a beautiful evergreen shrub, but of small growth. **1890** *Cent.* s.v. *Laurel*, The California laurel or bay-tree, the mountain-laurel of the West, is *Umbellularia Californica*.

+**Bay tulip-tree.** *Obs.* ? The bull-bay or evergreen magnolia, *Magnolia fœtida*. — **1709** LAWSON *Carolina* 95 The Bay-Tulip-Tree is a fine ever-green which grows frequently here.

+**Bay vessel.** =BAY CRAFT. — **1789** *Advt.* in *Maryland Journal* 2 Jan. (Th.), I will exchange a small Bay vessel for a large one, and give the difference.

+**Bay wax.** [BAY *n.*[3]] Bayberry wax. — **1721** *New-Eng. Courant* 2–9 Oct. 2/2 We the Subscribers . . . [will] give our Attendance to assist any Person . . . that will come with . . . Eggs, Bees-Wax, Bay-Wax, or, in short, any Commodity that may be brought.

Bay willow. [BAY *n.*[3]] +(See quotation.) *local.* — **1892** APGAR *Trees Northern U. S.* 164 *Salix lucida*, Mühl. Shining or American Bay Willow. . . . New Jersey, north and westward.

***Bay window.** [BAY *n.*[2]]

***1.** A window filling or occupying a recess of a room, store, etc., and projecting outwards.

1828 WEBSTER, *Bay-window*, a window jutting out from the wall, as in shops. **1852** MITCHELL *Dream Life* viii. 187 Libraries with . . . fine views from bay windows. **1857** C. VAUX *Villas* 96 The bay-window is the peculiar feature next to the veranda that an American rural home loves to indulge in. **1860** HOLMES *E. Venner* xxii, Mr. Bernard and Miss Letty were having a snug *tête-à-tête* in the recess of a bay-window. **1873** HOLLAND *A. Bonnicastle* iii, There were thrifty plants and beautiful flowers in the bay-window. **1923** R. HERRICK *Lilla* 100 From the bay window of the front room, Lilla could see him . . . trot down the pavement.

2. *slang.* A large or protruding abdomen.

1889 FARMER 44 Bay Window . . . [is] applied to . . . men who, in English slang, have 'corporations.' **1902** LORIMER *Lett. Merchant* xi. 150 Josh . . . kept right on bulging out, building on an addition here and putting out a bay window there, all the time retiring new suits.

+**Bay-winged,** *a.* [BAY *a.*] Having wings of a bay color. Frequent in specific names.

1811 WILSON *Ornithology* IV. 51 Bay-winged Bunting, *Emberiza graminea,* . . . delights in frequenting grass and clover fields. **1839** PEABODY *Mass. Birds* 322 The Bay-winged Finch, *Fringilla graminea,* is . . . pleasant and unpretending in its song. **1844** *Nat. Hist. N.Y., Zoology* II. 151 The Bay-winged Sparrow, *Fringilla Graminea,* . . . [is] known in many parts of this State as the Grass-bird. **1858** BAIRD *Birds Pacific R.R.* 447 *Poocætes gramineus,* Baird. Grass Finch. Bay-winged Bunting. . . . [Inhabits] United States from Atlantic to the Pacific. **1889** *Cent.* s.v., Bay-winged longspur, . . . *Rhynchophanes maccowni,* a common fringilline bird of the western prairies. *Ib.,* Bay-winged summer-finch, *Peucæa carpalis* of Arizona.

* **Bazaar, Bazar.**

1. A store displaying an assortment of fancy goods. {1816-}

'*Bazar* is a word for which America is indebted to Mrs. Trollope, who established the first in Cincinnati—an enterprise which unfortunately did not succeed' (1871 De Vere 440).

1837 W. JENKINS *Ohio Gaz.* 112 Other public buildings [in Cincinnati include] . . . 4 market houses, bazar in Third street, theater. **1855** SIMMS *Forayers* 264 The Red-men, who were wont to assemble . . . at his dwelling—the bazar in question. *Ib.,* The Indian bazar of the old trader was usually thronged with his wild visiters. **1865** *Chicago Tribune* 15 April 1 Fans or the new style of Lumbard hair pins . . . [sold] at Noble's Notion & Toy Bazaar.

2. A fancy fair or sale of goods in aid of charities, or to raise funds for some special purpose. {1829-}

1865 *Atlantic Mo.* XV. 337/1 We had a 'money-box,'—not one of those pretty cedar inventions . . . that we now use at bazaars. **1875** STOWE *We & Our Neighbors* 474 The room . . . had been devoted to the reception of the wedding presents . . . and already it had assumed quite the appearance of a bazar. **1895** M. A. JACKSON *Memoirs* 637 Holding bazaars and entertainments that yielded large returns, which . . . they poured into the treasury of the association.

+**Bazoo.** *slang.* **1.** Allusively: A toy trumpet. Cf. *kazoo.* (Hence as a newspaper title.) **2.** Assertive or boastful talk. **3.** One's mouth. — **(1)** **1877** BARTLETT 49 *Blowin' his bazoo,* gasconade; braggadocio. Tennessee. **1884** NYE *Baled Hay* 237 People . . . listen to the silvery tinkle of his bazoo. **1888** WHITMAN *November Boughs* 407 Among the far-west newspapers, have been, or are, . . . *The Bazoo,* of Missouri. **1903** *Dialect Notes* II. 306 'He blows his own bazoo,' meaning that he is boastful and obtrusive. **(2)** **1902** HARBEN *A. Daniel* 81 You are jest my sort of a Christian—better'n me, a sight, fer you don't shoot off yore bazoo on one side or t'other. **1906** *Dialect Notes* III. 126 We've had enough of your bazoo. **(3)** **1906** *Dialect Notes* III. 126 Shut up your bazoo.

BB shot. A size of shot (intermediate between B and BBB), measuring .18 of an inch in diameter. — **1874** LONG *Wild-Fowl* 240 B or BB [shot] may with propriety be used in large or very close shooting guns. **1891** *Scribner's Mag.* X. 460 A Canada goose . . . had been struck with one 'BB' shot, which had penetrated the left ventricle.

* **Be,** *v.* In older or dialect use in the present tense =*am, is, are.*

1702 C. MATHER *Magnalia* (1853) I. 543, I been't afraid, I thank God, I been't afraid to die! **1789** WEBSTER *Diss. Eng. Lang.* 385 The verb *be* . . . is still [in New England] used after the ancient manner, I *be,* we *be,* you *be,* they *be.* **1815** HUMPHREYS *Yankey* 103 *Ban't, Ben't,* am, or is, or are not. **1816** PICKERING 46 This was formerly much used in New England instead of *am* and *are,* in phrases of this kind: *Be* you ready? *Be* you going? I *be,* &c. **1829** *Va. Literary Museum* 280 The top be smote from it and the branches be gone. **1833** S. SMITH *Major Downing* 155 Your Ant tells me she dont think Brother Joshua can be so strong of his age as I be. **1889** R. T. COOKE *Steadfast* vi. 75 Ain't you well off where you be? **1896** WILKINS *Madelon* 141 'Be you her brother?' questioned Mrs. Otis.

* **Beach.** Also †**beech.**

1. The gradually sloping bank of an inland stream or lake. {1771-}

1756 *Doc. Hist. N.Y. State* (1849) I. 478 Upwards of 1000 French and Indians appeared upon the Beech [of Lake Ontario]. [**1798** MORSE *Amer. Gazetteer* 37/1 Beach Fork, a branch of Salt R., . . . Kentucky.] **1823** JAMES *Exped.* I. 39 The beach or sloping part of the immediate bank of the Ohio . . . is of rather gradual ascent, and covered with timber a considerable distance below high water mark. **1823** COOPER *Pioneers* xxiv, 'No, no, Judge,' returned Natty, his tall figure stalking over the narrow beach. **1843** N. BOONE *Journal* (1917) 189 Captain Boone . . . commenced his march from the beach of Grand River opposite Fort Gibson at 11 o'clock. **1885** *Rep. Indian Affairs* 187 The lands are too mountainous . . . for cultivation, except a small area of sandy beach, the soil of which is very thin.

b. Attrib. (also in sense of 'sea-beach') with *fox, hotel, privilege.*

*a***1841** [W. HAWES] *Sporting Scenes* I. 84 Oliver and I had killed only some twenty coot, and a beach fox. **1882** *Nation* 10 Aug. 108/2 Their undertaking . . . [is] merely a 'business enterprise,' like a beach hotel. **1883** *Century Mag.* Sept. 654/1 There is a boundless field for disputes . . . in fishing and beach privileges.

+**2.** *New Jersey.* Any of the low sand islands which lie along or parallel to the coast; also, a portion of any of these.

1743 *N.J. Archives* VI. 155 A certain beach or island of sand lying next and adjoining to the main sea. **1855** *Knickerb.* XLVI. 221 The coast line of New-Jersey consists of a continuous chain of long narrow islands, known as 'beaches.' **1878** *Harper's Mag.* Feb. 330/1 The next island south is called Brigantine Beach. **1893** *Jerseyisms* in *Dialect Notes* I. 328 'Young' or 'little beach' is new-made beach containing younger timber; 'old beach,' parallel ridges crowned by old timber.

+**Beach apple.** A local Californian name for *Mesembryanthemum æquilaterale,* a fig-marigold. — **1893** *Amer. Folk-lore* VI. 142.

+**Beach-bird.** One or other of various sandpipers or other small birds that frequent the seashore.

1800 BENTLEY *Diary* II. 348 Dined . . . upon a Pie of beach birds. **1827** R. H. DANA *Poems* 97 The Little Beach-Bird. **1832** WILLIAMSON *Maine* I. 149 A Beach, or Sand-bird is about the size of a swallow, coloured white and gray; its flesh is eatable, though of a fishy flavour. **1837** HAWTHORNE *Note-Books* I. 77 Beach birds [were] flitting from place to place. **1844** *Nat. Hist. N.Y., Zoology* II. 210 The Piping Plover . . . or Beach-bird, as it is sometimes called on Long island. **1886** S. W. MITCHELL *R. Blake* xxii. 236 As to shooting, you can get a few beach-birds.

+**Beach-clam.** A local name for the surf-clam or sea-clam, *Mactra solidissima.* — **1791** *Huntington Rec.* III. 170 That no Beach Clams on the south side of the Islands . . . be catched by any Person whatsoever to sell to Boatmen. **1889** *Cent.* s.v.

Beach-comber. 1. A white man who lives as a loafer among the islands of the Pacific, and makes his living there often by disreputable means. {1847-}

'This is a term much in vogue among sailors in the Pacific. It is applied to certain roving characters, who, without attaching themselves permanently to any vessel, ship now and then for a short cruise in a whaler; but upon condition only of being honorably discharged the very next time the anchor takes hold of the bottom, no matter where they are' (Melville *Omoo* xxi. 109 *n.*).

1840 DANA *Two Years* xix. 177 In the twinkling of an eye, I was transformed from a sailor into a 'beach-comber' and a hide-curer. *Ib.* xxv. 266 We, being the most experienced 'beach-combers,' needed no help, and staid till the last. **1847** MELVILLE *Omoo* xxi. 109, I'm nothing more nor a bloody *beech-comber.* **1869** DANA *Two Years* (new ed.) 449 Poor Kanakas and sailors, the refuse of civilization, the outlaws and beach-combers of the Pacific! **1910** J. LONDON *House of Pride* (1912) 36 The Old Hypocrite! What difference between him and any beach-comber?

+**2.** *pl.* 'The long waves rolling in from the ocean' (B. '59).

+**Beach flea.** One of various small crustaceans found on the seacoast, esp. of the genus *Orchestiidæ;* a sand flea. — **1843** *Nat. Hist. N.Y., Zoology* VI. 35 Small crustaceans . . . known under the name of Sand-flea, or Beach-flea. *Ib.* 36 [The] Beach-flea . . . is frequently found concealed under stones and seaweed. **1890** *Cent.* 4140/3 *Orchestiidæ.* . . . The species are inhabitants of the littoral region, and some are known as 'beach-fleas.'

+**Beach grape.** (See quotation.) — **1819** SCHOOLCRAFT *Mo. Lead Mines* 29 Such are the poplar . . . and beach grape, which are only found to flourish on the rich alluvial lands composing the banks of rivers.

+**Beach grass.** A coarse grass (*Ammophila arenaria*) common on the sea-shore.

1681 *East-Hampton Rec.* II. 102 Thomas Bee doth . . . maintaine a sofisient three raile fence one the beach . . . down so low as any Beach grass groues. **1782** J. H. ST. JOHN *Lett.* 128 Those declining grounds which lead to the sea-shores [of Nantucket] abound with beach grass, a light fodder when cut and cured, but very good when fed green. **1791** *East-Hampton Rec.* IV. 269 If any person . . . shall . . . cut any beach grass on any of the beaches belonging to this town. **1802** *Mass. H. S. Coll.* VIII. 110 This ridge is well covered with beach grass; and appears to owe its existence to that vegetable. *Ib.,* Beach grass . . . grows about two feet and a half. **1833** *Mass. Statutes* 21 March, An Act to prevent the Destruction of Beach Grass, in the towns of Provincetown and Truro. **1839** *Ib.* 12 Feb., [They] are hereby made a corporation, by the name of the Massachusetts Beach Grass Paper Company, for the purpose of manufacturing paper from beach grass. **1863** *Ill. Agric. Soc. Trans.* V. 863 Beach-grass or mat grass is not valuable as an article of food for cattle. **1870** EMERSON *Soc. & Solitude* vii. 144 In Massachusetts, we fight the sea successfully with beach-grass and broom. **1892** B. TORREY *Footpath Way* 81 The rest of the vegetation was more or less familiar, I believe: . . . crisp-leaved tansy; beach grass [etc.].

+**Beach hill.** A small hill or dune on a beach. — **1815** *Mass. H. S. Coll.* 2 Ser. III. 173 Thus Shifting cove on the Manomet shore, where there are beach hills, is the outlet for Beaver-dam brook.

+**Beach ivy.** — **1802** *Mass. H. S. Coll.* VIII. 145 Beach grass, the beach pea, beach ivy, . . . grow here luxuriantly.

Beach land. Land lying on or adjacent to a beach. — **1658** *East-Hampton Rec.* I. 148 A certayne tract of beach land with all the rest of the grass that joynes to it not seperated from it by water. **1753** *Brook-*

haven Rec. 167 Several tracts or persels of . . . Swomp land, beach land, . . . situate within the township.

+**Beach lantern.** A lantern adapted for use on a sea-beach. — **1878** *Harper's Mag.* Feb. 331/2 Each patrolman will carry a beach lantern, also a red Coston hand-light.

+**Beach lot.** A lot on the water-front at San Francisco. — **1847** E. BRYANT *California* (1848) 438 All the ungranted tract of ground on the east front of the town of San Francisco, . . . known as the water and beach lots. *Ib.*, These beach lots were advertised immediately, and . . . sold at public auction. **1855** Soulé, etc. *Ann. San Fran.* 324 Those parts of the city called the Beach and Water Lots. **1910** J. HARTE *Vigilante Girl* 208 They say Burke has made a large fortune out of his beach and water lots.

+**Beach pea.** A species of wild pea (*Lathyrus maritimus*) growing on beaches.

1802 *Mass. H. S. Coll.* VIII. 145 Beach grass, the beach pea, beach ivy, . . . grow here luxuriantly. **1843** TORREY *Flora N.Y.* I. 157 *Lathyrus maritimus.* . . . Sea-side Vetchling. Beach Pea. . . . Sandy seacoast of Long Island. **1884** *Harper's Mag.* June 103/2 The beach pea is found along the North Shore [of Lake Superior], together with other plants and insects peculiar to the ocean. **1889** *Cent.* 3366/3 *L. maritimus*, of wide distribution on the sea-coast, is the beach-pea.

+**Beach plum.** The sand plum, *Prunus maritima.*

1784 CUTLER in *Mem. Academy* I. 448 *Prunus*, . . . Beach or Sea-Side Plum. The fruit of some of them, when fully ripe, is well-tasted. **1798** *Doc. Hist. N.Y. State* (1849) I. 674 The sand near the shore is blown into hills on which nothing grows but a grass called 'Beach Grass,' and a shrub bearing the Beach plum. **1810** *East-Hampton Rec.* IV. 365 No person . . . shall be permitted to pick or gather any cranberries, beach plums or bayberries on any of the common lands. **1817** *N. Amer. Rev.* V. 316 In the western end of the pond is a high islet . . . covered with a very rich soil, in which were growing the wild gooseberry, . . . beach plum, etc. **1828** BONAPARTE *Ornithology* III. 20 The white-crowned pigeon . . . on some of the Florida keys . . . feeds . . . on a kind of wild fruit, usually called beach plum. **1856** WHITTIER *Ranger* x, Where the purple of beach-plum mellows On the bluffs. **1862** THOREAU *Cape Cod* x. (1894) 326 Their companion a cow, their wealth a jag of drift-wood or a few beach-plums.

attrib. **1892** B. TORREY *Foot-path Way* 78 The beach-plum crop was a failure.

+**Beach sand.** Smooth-washed sand as found on the sea-shore or other beach.

1842 *Knickerb.* XX. 311 As to the mortar, it was as white and as hard as beach-sand could make it. **1853** FOWLER *Home for All* 148 My material was composed of one part Blake's black Ohio paint, to six parts fine beach sand. **1856** *Rep. Comm. Patents: Agric.* 181 The farms in the vicinity of the sea are partially manured with sea-weed, rock-weed, and beach sand. **1887** TOURGEE *Button's Inn* 2 An impetuous rivulet . . . gurgled . . . over rounded stones, with the shelving beach-sands crumbling into it.

+**Beach-wagon.** 'A light open wagon with two or more seats' (W. '79).

1869 ALCOTT *Little Women* II. 35, I shall hire a beach-wagon. **1871** *Scribner's Mo.* II. 634 He can drive you both down in the beach-wagon. **1884** HOWELLS *Silas Lapham* iv. 69 Lapham arrived on the ground in his four-seated beach-wagon.

* **Beacon.**

***1.** A signal-fire, or the material collected and placed for making one.

1635 *Mass. Col. Rec.* I. 137 There shalbe forthwith a beacon sett on the Sentry Hill att Boston, to giue notice to the country of any danger. **1644** *Plymouth Rec.* 18 When any of these places stand in neede of help . . . then a Beacon to be fyred. **1654** JOHNSON *Wonder-w. Prov.* 43 All three [hills] . . . keepe a constant watch to foresee the approach of forrein dangers, being furnished with a Beacon and lowd babling Guns. **1667** *R.I. Col. Rec.* II. 207 It shall be in the power of the Governor . . . to give forth an alarm to this Collony . . . by causing the beacon . . . to be fired, which shall be the directory to the rest of the beacons to be forthwith fired. **1707** *Boston News-Letter* 21 April 2/2 On the 6th Instant an Express came to our Governour from the Narraganset, acquainting his Honour that the beacon at Block-Island was on fire, and that they heard several guns go off. **1746** *N.J. Archives* VI. 373 Requesting . . . that for the more speedy intelligence and spreading the alarme of an invasion there might be erected a beacon on the Highlands of Neversinks. **1781** WAYNE in Sparks *Corr. Rev.* III. 192 The alarm-guns have been fired and the beacons kindled.

***2.** A mark erected on the sea-coast or along rivers to warn vessels of danger or to direct their course.

1667 *R.I. Col. Rec.* II. 207 To give order for the erecting of beacons in the most convenient places upon the coast . . . throughout the whole Collony, and pertickularly one upon the rocks at Sachuest. **1696** SEWALL *Diary* I. 429 Nantasket Beacon began. **1741** *Georgia Col. Rec.* VI. 14 We . . . appoint that the Sum of fifty Pounds be immediately issued for . . . the Expence of the Current Service, more particularly relating to the Beacon now erecting. **1789** *Ann. 1st Congress* I. 51 The Senate . . . had passed a bill for the establishment and support of light-houses, beacons, and buoys. **1805** *Ann. 8th Congress* 2 Sess. 1673 For erecting beacons in the harbor of New York . . . [an additional sum of] six thousand dollars. **1842** *Texas Diplom. Corr.* (1911) III. 1169 The necessity of a light house, or some other beacon, at Galveston, for the benefit of the navigators, entering that Port. **1869** DANA *Two Years* (new ed.) 433 On the whole coast of California there was not a light-house, a beacon, or a buoy.

3. Attrib. with *fire, light.*

1852 STANSBURY *Gt. Salt Lake* 209 A beacon-fire was lighted on a commanding eminence . . . , which was immediately responded to by a similar signal from Black Rock. — **1833** *Niles' Reg.* XLIV. 394 B[e]acon light at G. River, $364. **1841** *Congress. Globe* 20 Feb. 197/2 The bill authorising . . . the establishment of certain buoys and beacon lights. **1845** *Lowell Offering* V. 212 An island from which the beacon-lights twinkled dimly upon the white breakers. **1882** *Harper's Mag.* Jan. 166/1 A step recently taken by the General Government to lessen the dangers of the Ohio, Mississippi, and Missouri rivers. This consists in the establishment and maintenance of the 'beacon-light' system.

Beaconage. {1607, 1755} Toll paid for maintaining or providing a beacon. *Obs.* — **1661** *Virginia Statutes* II. 35 Every master of a shipp or vessel that shall anchor within Point Comfort having or not haveing a pilott to pay thirty shillings to the said pilott for beaconage.

* **Bead.**

1. A bead of glass, shell, or other material, as used in trading with Indians, or as made and worn by them.

A 'fathom of beads' was used as a standard of value.

1608 SMITH *Newes from Va.* Wks. (1884) I. 26 The King . . . described . . . how hee sent them ouer the Baye, for tribute Beades: and also what Countries paid him Beads, Copper, or Skins. **1619** *Va. House of Burgesses* 5 The Indians refusing to sell their Corne, those of the shallop . . . tooke it by force, . . . [giving] them satisfaction in Copper, Beades and other trucking Stuffe. **1622** 'MOURT' *Relation* 94 The King . . . [had] a great Chaine of white bone Beades about his necke. *Ib.* 104 They welcommed vs with such foode as they had, and we bestowed a small bracelet of Beades on them. **1637** *Mass. H. S. Coll.* 4 Ser. VI. 191 Sir, Miantunnomu desird me to giue you a hint that the 6 fathom of beades which he gaue for the slaying of Audsah be repaid him. *Ib.* 217 The 10 fathom of beades & one coate you may please at leasure to deliver to Mr. Throckmorton. **1640** *Ib.* VII. 339 No security being had, the officer seased vpon the beades and brought them away. **1682** *Indian Laws & Tr.* (1913) III. 696 Tênne bundles of Beads. **1709** LAWSON *Carolina* 71 The chief man amongst them made a long speech, [and] threw beads into our boat, which is a sign of great love and friendship. **1765** TIMBERLAKE *Mem.* 38 The headman . . . made a short discourse . . . and presented me with a string of beads. **1824** BRYANT *Indian at Burial-place* 40 Hither the silent Indian maid Brought wreaths of beads and flowers. *c*1836 CATLIN *Indians* II. 123 The Creeks . . . use a vast many beads, and other trinkets, to hang upon their necks, and ornament their moccasins and beautiful belts. **1855** LONGFELLOW *Hiawatha* XI. 27 Robes of fur and belts of wampum, . . . Beautiful with beads and tassels. **1877** *Rep. Indian Affairs* 50 The use of paint, beads, and blankets should be stopped, and strong, coarse clothing provided. **1878** *Ib.* 153 Among the Shoshones the trade in beads, paints, and trinkets has fallen off greatly during the last five years.

b. Attrib. with *basket, belt, gaiter, girdle,* etc.

1638 *Mass. H. S. Coll.* 4 Ser. VI. 250, 40 men were sent vp with their bead girdles to redeeme them. *c*1838 CATLIN *Indians* II. 219 His dress was chiefly of calicos, with a handsome bead sash or belt around his waist. **1842** HITCHCOCK *Journal* (1930) 144 Most of those I saw yesterday had on . . . a shirt of calico bound with a bead belt. *Ib.* 199 Moccasins or shoes, bead gaiters for the leggins. **1866** 'F. KIRKLAND' *Bk. Anecdotes* 605 A pretty Indian girl . . . exerting her persuasive powers . . . to induce a certain military gent . . . to buy of her a bead basket.

+**2.** The front sight of a gun, consisting of a small round knob on a thin stem.

1831 AUDUBON *Ornith. Biog.* I. 294 He raised his piece gradually, until the *bead* (that being the name given by the Kentuckians to the *sight*) of the barrel was brought to a line with the spot which he intended to hit. **1853** SIMMS *Sword & Distaff* 483 Each with the bead of his rifle prepared to tell upon an enemy's button.

+**b.** *To draw a bead on*, to take aim at. Also *to draw bead with, to have a bead on*, etc.

Illustrated by Thornton (s.v. *Draw*), with examples from 1841 to 1878.

1833 CATLIN *Indians* I. 77, I made several attempts to get near enough to 'draw a bead' upon one of them. **1835** [LONGSTREET] *Georgia Scenes* 219 Wait till you see him lift the old Soap-stick, and draw a bead upon the bull's-eye. **1846** *Spirit of Times* (N.Y.) 18 April 91/2 The percussion cap on their gun exploded without igniting the powder in the barrel, while they had a 'bead' on the game in question. **1869** MCCLURE *Rocky Mts.* 81 He did not fire, however, but told Steel to pass, which he did in safety, with a 'dead bead' drawn on him until he was out of range. **1878** BEADLE *Western Wilds* 415 'If Bob Rock draws a bead on him, he's gone,' was the general verdict. **1888** ROOSEVELT in *Century Mag.* May 40/1, I waited until the Indians were a hundred yards off, and then threw up my rifle and drew a bead on the foremost. **1889** *Harper's Mag.* Dec. 120/1 Billy Pitt drew a playful bead on Uncle Dicky with his stubby . . . rifle.

transf. **1853** *S. Lit. Messenger* XIX. 221/1 As Chuck levelled the pipe and drew a bead on them [=a crowd], and as it [the water] shot into the faces of the crowd—vip, vip, vip, they fell back.

3. A small bubble or bubbles on the surface of liquor. Also fig. *To raise a bead*, fig.: to bring to a head, to make succeed. {1753–}

'The figure is taken from brandy, rum, or other liquors, which will not "raise a bead," unless of the proper strength' (B. '48, p. 269).

1841 COOPER *Deerslayer* vi, That idee of your'n . . . carries a fine bead. **1846** [FIELD] *Drama in Pokerville* 56 Young Mr. Bagly had already broken three slim glasses, driving them through his hand in the attempt to raise 'a bead.' **1846** *N.Y. Tribune* (B.), If the convention had been then held, the party wouldn't have been able to raise a bead. **1866** *Congress. Globe* 4 June 2955/2 As we say out West, that kind of an argument will not *bear a bead;* it will not bear the touch-stone of truth; it has neither rhyme nor reason nor justice in it.

* **Beaded,** *a.* Consisting of or ornamented with beads.

1809 F. CUMING *Western Tour* 269 A pair of very handsome beaded mockesons. **1829** COOPER *Wish-Ton-Wish* xxvi, Belts of richly-beaded wampum. **1838** *S. Lit. Messenger* IV. 224/1 This warrior was a young man . . . with . . . a beautiful beaded shot-pouch over his shoulder. **1840** HOFFMAN *Greyslaer* I. i. 14 The terrible leg-knife, worn beneath the beaded garters of his companion. **1868** *Mich. Agric. Rep.* VII. 357 Mrs. W. H. Cleveland, Adrian, [exhibited a] beaded mat.

* **Beadle.** An assistant to an executive officer. *Obs.*

1630 *Mass. Bay Rec.* I. 74 His imployement [is] to be as a beadle to attend vpon the Governor, and alwaies to be ready to execute his commands in publique businesses. **1642** T. LECHFORD *Plain Dealing* 28 Jurors are returned by the Marshall, he was at first called the Bedle of the Societie. **1683** *N.H. Doc. & Rec.* I. 454 Fees of Court: . . . To the beadle, 6d.

+**Bead-line.** [BEAD 2.] The line of the front sight of a rifle. — **1866** 'F. KIRKLAND' *Bk. Anecdotes* 319 Our man was on the lookout for him; he had his rifle on the bead-line ready—pulled the trigger [etc.].

+**Bead ruby.** A small plant (*Maianthemum* or *Unifolium Canadense*) of the United States and Canada, having ruby-red berries. — **1850** [S. F. COOPER] *Rural Hours* 105 Violets . . . grow there, with . . . bead-ruby, squaw-vine, partridge-plant, pipsissiwa. **1894** *Amer. Folk-Lore* VII. 102.

+**Bead snake.** The coral snake, *Elaps fulvius.*

1736 CATESBY *Carolina* II. 49 The little brown Bead Snake . . . is an harmless Snake. *Ib.* 60 The Bead Snake. . . . They have nothing of a Viper, either in Form or Quality, but are very inoffensive. **1775** BURNABY *Travels* 18 Several snakes of this country [Virginia] are harmless and beautiful; such as the black snake, the wampum-snake, the bead-snake, the garter-snake, and some others. **1808** T. ASHE *Travels* xxviii. 243 The conversation as usual, turned on the serpent tribe, and we called the following at least to our recollection: . . . brown snake, little bead snake.

Bead tree. The China tree or false sycamore, *Melia Azedarach.* {1668–}

1737 BRICKELL *N. Carolina* 105 The Bead-Tree, so called from it's Fruit resembling Glass-Beads at a distance. . . . Their Fruit are as large as Peas, and hard when ripe, but easily drill'd, whereof are made Bracelets, and several other Toys. **1789** *Trans. Philos. Soc.* III. p. xxi, The *Melia azedarach* grows in the South, under the name of bead tree. **1847** DARLINGTON *Weeds & Plants* 69 Pride of India [or] Bead-tree . . . has been introduced into the Southern States as an ornamental shade tree, and is now perfectly naturalized there and west to Arkansas. **1901** MOHR *Plant Life Ala.* 588 Pride of China. Bead Tree. . . . Of some value for lumber. Ornamental shade tree.

Bead-work. Ornaments or designs made of beads. {1881–}

1840 DANA *Two Years* xxvi. 282 Buying Indian curiosities . . . such as bead-work, feathers of birds. **1853** *Harper's Mag.* VI. 585/2 All, men and women, are painted, and decorated with feathers in their hair and bead-work belts and leggings. **1866** *Rep. Indian Affairs* 234 The women were engaged in making various articles of beadwork. **1870** KEIM *Sheridan's Troopers* (1885) 170 While I was watching and admiring the bead-work of the squaws in the lodge.

* **Beagle.**

* **1.** A small hound formerly used in hunting hares. Also fig. and attrib.

1853 SIMMS *Sword & Distaff* 295 Dog of a somewhat mongrel aspect, a sort of cross of wolf, cur, and beagle. **1856** [H. W. HERBERT] *Manual for Sportsmen* 211 When large, he [the harrier] is often called a foxhound, when small a beagle—the latter animal, in a perfectly pure state, being very rare and indeed almost unknown in America. **1897** *Outing* April 95/2 The following experts attended to the judging: . . . Geo B. Post, Jr., beagles; H. W. Lacy, poodles. **1902** WHITE *Blazed Trail* xxxi. 221 When he departed he left behind him four little long-eared, short-legged beagle hounds.

+**2.** A nickname for an inhabitant of Virginia.

1845 Cist *Cincinnati Misc.* 240.

* **Beaked,** *a.* Of plants, fishes, etc.: Provided with a beak. {1841–}

1817–8 EATON *Botany* (1822) 253 Beaked hazel. *Ib.* 514 Beaked violet. **1840** DEWEY *Mass. Flowering Plants* 79 *Viola rostrata*, Beaked Violet . . . ; hills and woods; May. **1842** *Nat. Hist. N.Y., Zoology* IV. 312 The Beaked Eel, *Anguilla rostrata*, . . . 'is esteemed for the table.' **1843** TORREY *Flora N.Y.* II. 187 *Corylus rostrata*, . . . Beaked Hazel-nut. . . . Mountain woods and banks of rivers. *Ib.* 347 *Eleocharis rostellata*, . . . Beaked Spike-rush. **1858** THOREAU *Maine Woods* 119, I saw the aster puniceus and the beaked hazel, as we paddled along. **1901** MOHR *Plant Life Ala.* 406 *Rhynchospora* [includes] . . . Humble Beaked Rush, . . . Divergent Beaked Rush, . . . Chapman's Beaked Rush.

* **Beaker.** Also †**beker.** A drinking vessel, a goblet. Also *b. glass.*

Apparently the word survived in vernacular in America longer than in England.

1646 *Early Conn. Probate Rec.* I. 16, 1 pewter quart, 1 halfe pinte, 1 beker. **1674** *Harvard Rec.* I. 62 Butterie Utensils [include] . . . 2 Beakers, one marked IB; the other W. W. **1801** *Spirit of Farmers' Museum* 235 Set the cups, and beaker glass, The pumpkin, and the apple sauce. **1816** PICKERING 47 *Beaker*, a tumbler. Not many years ago this word was in common use in New England, and, I believe, in some other parts of the United States; but it is now seldom heard except among old people.

Beak-horn, variant of BICKERN. *Obs.* {1781 bickhorn, 1547 bycorne} — **1636** WINTHROP *Life & Lett.* II. 156 Here was an anvil, with a beak horn at the end of it, which I think was carried to Con[necticu]t. **1646** *Essex Probate Rec.* I. 49 One smale beakhorne, 2 hamers.

Beak rush. {1830} A species of the genus *Rhynchospora* of sedge-like plants; the beaked rush. — **1843** TORREY *Flora N.Y.* II. 363 Small Capillary Beak-rush. . . . White Beak-rush. *Ib.* 364 Brown Beak-rush. . . . Round-headed Beak-rush. *Ib.* 365 Tall Slender Beak-rush. **1857** GRAY *Botany* 504 *Rhynchospora*, Beak-rush. [Ten species detailed.] **1899** M. GOING *Flowers* 193 The 'beak-rush,' which we may find growing near the 'wool-grass.'

* **Beam.**

1. A shaped block upon which hides are fixed to be scraped or shaved in preparation for tanning. {1875}

1671 *Plymouth Laws* 277 Such [leather] as though tanned enough, is in some other respect defective, either by over-liming, or for want of being well wrought upon the Beam. **1868** *Amer. Naturalist* II. 474 The skin is dried and . . . spread out on anything answering to the currier's beam. **1885** [see BEAMING]. **1891** CHASE & CLOW *Industry* II. 68 Sloping and curved blocks . . . form 'beams' over which the soft hides are stretched by the fleshers and hairers.

+**2.** (See quotation.)

1844 *Lowell Offering* IV. 169 These rooms are kept very warm, and are disagreeably scented with the 'sizing,' or starch, which stiffens the 'beams,' or unwoven webs.

3. *Beam-house, -room*, a house or a room containing the beam or beams used in scraping or shaving hides.

1885 *Harper's Mag.* Jan. 274/2 After the hair-loosening the besmeared tip-cart again makes its appearance, . . . ready to take a load [of hides] to the beam-house. **1891** CHASE & CLOW *Industry* II. 68 Here they are in the beam-house among the 'hairers' and 'fleshers.' — **1885** *Harper's Mag.* Jan. 274/2 But for unsavory odors a beam-room might pass for a laundry.

* **Beaming,** *vbl. n.* The process of removing the hair from skins. Also attrib. with *knife.* — **1841** PARK *Pantology* 476 Leather, is made by the process of tanning: the skin being first cleansed of hair and flesh, by the action of lime and the beaming knife. **1885** *Harper's Mag.* Jan. 274/2 'Beaming,' or unhairing, derives its name from an inclined convex wooden form called a 'beam,' on which the hide is spread during the operation.

+**Beamster.** [BEAM 1.] A man who prepares hides at a beam. — **1885** *Harper's Mag.* Jan. 274/2 The beamsters, bending to their task, look as if they had taken in a large week's washing.

* **Bean.**

* **1.** The seed of the leguminous plant *Faba vulgaris* and allied plants, in common use as an article of food.

1616 SMITH *New England* 16 The hearbes and fruits are of many sorts and kindes: as . . . gourds, strawberries, beans, pease, and mayze. **1643** WILLIAMS *Key* 24 From the South-west came their Corne, and Beanes out of their Great God Cautantowwits field. **1654** JOHNSON *Wonder-w. Prov.* 173 Indian Beans at 16 s. per bushel. **1677** HUBBARD *Narr.* 57 The Troop . . . brought in daily much of the enemies Corn and Beans which they had hid in Barns under the ground. **1764** HUTCHINSON *Hist. Mass.* (1795) I. vi. 413 In summer they had fish from the sea, . . . berries of all sorts, green corn, beans and squashes. **1778** CARVER *Travels* 263 Unripe corn . . . and beans in the same state, boiled together with bears flesh. . . . They call this food Succatosh. **1805** *Pocumtuc Housewife* 20 A pot of Beans can be baking back side, out of the way, with the rest. **1834** A. PIKE *Sketches* 56 We bought some meat and mesquito meal, made by grinding the beans between two stones. **1855** BARNUM *Life* 89 He always carried a 'bean' in his box which, he insisted, imparted a much improved flavor to the snuff. **1860** HOLMES *Professor* iii. 78 The tutor breakfasts on coffee made of beans. **1865** KELLOGG *Rebel Prisons* 187, I . . . invested my little fortune in beans and salt, and for that day I had something good to eat. **1886** STOCKTON *Mrs. Lecks* 27 Cold baked beans and lukewarm water ain't exactly company vittles.

* **b.** Used in voting. {1580–1660}

1832 WILLIAMSON *Maine* I. 373 The freemen [*c*1650] voted by way of *corns* and *beans;* the former being counted for him and the latter against him.

2. In various phrases: +**a.** *Not to know beans*, to be very ignorant. *To know beans*, to know what is what, to be wide awake.

1833 GREENE *D. Duckworth* II. 66 He don't know beans. **1844** *Knickerb.* XXIII. 71 If, agriculturally speaking, you do n't 'know beans,' he will annihilate you with his rural wisdom. **1855** *Yale Lit. Mag.* XX. 192 (Th.), Whatever he knows of Euclid and Greek, In Latin he don't know beans. **1856** *Knickerb.* XLVIII. 315 We never saw, and our metropolitan friends, (country-born, and 'knowing beans,' tomatoes, etc.,) say they never saw, such a sight. **1888** *Portland Transcript* 7 March (F.), A dainty Boston girl who, of course, knows beans. **1888** *Chicago Herald* (F.), One has to know beans to be successful in the latest Washington novelty for entertainment at luncheons. **1909** STRATTON-PORTER *Girl of Limberlost* xxv. 454 This [violin] . . . don't know 'beans,' as mother would say, about the Limberlost.

+**b.** *To care a bean* or *beans, to be worth* or *to amount to beans*, indicating a small or the least amount.

Also with *hill of beans:* see HILL *n.*

1857 *Knickerb.* XLIX. 138, I don't care beans for the rail-road. **1876** BRET HARTE *G. Conroy* VI. ii, Thet paper don't 'mount ter beans, no how! **1902** LORIMER *Lett. Merchant* 239 Because a fellow cuts ice on the Arctic Circle, it doesn't follow that he's going to be worth beans on the Back Bay. **1909** WASON *Happy Hawkins* 200 They didn't care a blue bean what the prevailin' style in opinions happened to be.

c. In miscellaneous uses.

1842 'UNCLE SAM' *Peculiarities* I. 98, I . . . was at the battle of New Orleans, when we gave the British beans. **1860** HOLLAND *Miss Gilbert* xxvi. 454, I felt meaner than beans about it. **1868** W. BAKER *New Timothy* (1870) 122 He'll never say 'beans' again! **1878** R. T. COOKE *Happy Dodd* 73 They don't think no small beans o' themselves.

+**Bean-blow.** The flower of the bean plant. — **a1854** [PAIGE] *Dow's Sermons* IV. 73 (Th.), As gently as a breeze ever scupped a bean-blow.

***Bean bread.** A coarse kind of bread made with bean meal.

1796 B. HAWKINS *Letters* 38 They sent me a present of bean bread and dumplins. **c1849** [PAIGE] *Dow's Sermons* I. 74 Any hungry saint would much rather dine with a sinner upon a good haunch of venison, than with an angel, and get nothing but bean soup and bean bread.

+**Bean club.** *slang.* [Cf. *beans* (slang), money.] A club or group of boodlers or politicians. — **1875** *Chicago Tribune* 1 Sept. 4/3 These persons can well afford to . . . join hands in the bean-club in the common cause of plunder.

+**Beanite.** *slang.* A member of the 'Bean club' (q.v.); a boodler. — **1875** *Chicago Tribune* 1 Sept. 3/4 Boss Tweed held about the same relationship to the Americus which the Head-Centre of the beanites holds to the Union.

+**Bean-patch, plot.** A piece of ground on which beans are grown. — **1850** *Knickerb.* XXXV. 23, I know that rank corn is now grown on the bean-patch below. — **1775** ADAIR *Indians* 232 Their young married people . . . had . . . broke down and polluted many of the honest neighbours bean-plots.

+**Bean-poker.** [See POKER.] A card-game (see quotation). — **1877** WM. WRIGHT *Big Bonanza* 104 The stoves of the saloons and lodging-houses were well patronized. Bean-poker and old sledge were the principal amusements.

+**Bean pole.**

1. A pole upon which bean-vines climb.

1821 *Mass. H. S. Coll.* 2 Ser. IX. 143 This [sprout] when it rises sufficiently high, should be tied to a strong stake or pole, similar to a bean pole. **1849** LANMAN *Alleghany Mts.* ii. 22 She immediately seized a bean pole, and by a single blow deprived the doe of life. **1855** WILLIS *Convalescent* 48 The bright green thickets might turn out something, as we ride along, besides estimates of bean-poles and fire-wood. **1865** TROWBRIDGE *Three Scouts* xi. 114 Enos came rushing to the spot, flourishing a bean-pole. **1874** *Vt. Bd. Agric. Rep.* II. 547 Year after year the farmer gets bean poles, hop poles, fence rails, building timber and fire wood from such a swamp. **1890-3** E. M. TABOR *Stowe Notes* 7 One [bird] lit on a bean-pole, with a cry harsh and peculiar. **1900** E. BRUNCKEN *N. Amer. Forests* 61 Hop poles, bean poles, Christmas trees find ready sales in many places.

phrases. **1834** C. A. DAVIS *Lett. J. Downing* 324 If the Senate had ben like tother house . . . 'The Government' would a ben as strait as a bean-pole. **1860** *Harper's Mag.* April 581/2 A tall, gaunt specimen of humanity. . . . His costume was as singular as his figure, and hung upon him 'like a shirt upon a bean-pole.'

2. *fig.* A tall, thin person.

1837 HALIBURTON *Clockmaker* 1 Ser. xxix, Mr. Jehiel, a bean pole of a lawyer, was at the bottom of it. **1838** *Knickerb.* XII. 228 'Green peas, gen'lemen—green peas!' squeaked a bean-pole waiter. **1881** STODDARD *E. Hardery* 62 Not till she's married, and goodness knows when that'll be, the great, stuck-up beanpole.

+**Bean-porridge.** Porridge made from bean-meal.

1828 *Yankee* March 83/3 A sandy complexioned boy . . . eating bean-porridge with a pewter spoon. **c1849** [PAIGE] *Dow's Sermons* I. 195 You have souls susceptible of the beauty of bean-porridge hot. **1877** *Vt. Bd. Agric. Rep.* IV. 92 Here the dinner pot was boiled, . . . and the bean porridge made. **1878** B. F. TAYLOR *Between Gates* 286 Two days more would . . . ripen bean-porridge to the fine perfection of 'nine days old.'

+**Bean-pot.** A pot in which beans are cooked. — **1829** *Frugal Housewife* (Boston) 42. **a1846** *Quarter Race Kentucky*, etc. 85 Jim Smith, hand over that spoon, an quit a lickin it like 'sank in a bean-pot.' **1883** HOWELLS *Woman's Reason* ix, Perhaps you'll find that they've begun to give bean-pots an aesthetic shape. **1904** 'O. HENRY' *Heart of West* 88 He's got pots of money—bean-pots full of it.

+**Bean-shell.** A bean-pod: *fig.* a small or flimsy vessel. — **1777** *Md. Journal* 25 Feb. (Th.), The Continental bean-shells, mann'd with Yankies, and armed with innocent pop-guns.

+**Bean-shooter.** (See first quotation.) — **1889** *Cent.* 488/3 *Bean-shooter*, a toy for shooting beans, shot, or other small missiles; a pea-shooter. **1890** *Congress. Rec.* 4 March 1920/1, I have not excused this rudeness or shooting with a bean-shooter. *Ib.* 5 Sept. 9744/2 Judge Benjamin . . . was . . . shot in the forehead with a leaden bullet from a weapon known as a 'bean-shooter.'

+**Bean soup.** Soup of which the principal ingredient is beans.

1837 J. C. NEAL *Charcoal Sk.* (1838) 98 Hollering oysters and bean soup has guv' me a splendid voice. **1852** STANSBURY *Gt. Salt Lake* 26 Wild-onion . . . we found . . . quite palatable in flavouring our bean-soup. **1865** KELLOGG *Rebel Prisons* 363, I have seen men . . . draw their bean-soup in their shoes, for the want of a cup . . . to put it in. **1888** GRIGSBY *Smoked Yank* xiii. (1891) 104 'Right this way, gentlemen, for your hot chicken soup! Bean Soup!'

Bean-tree. {1616} +A variety of catalpa (*C. bignonioides* or *catalpa*) having bean-like pods.

1847 DARLINGTON *Weeds & Plants* 222 Bignonia-like Catalpa. Catawba. Bean-tree. . . . Cultivated as a shade tree, but indigenous in the South-west. **1865-6** *Ill. Agric. Soc. Trans.* VI. 390 Do you want a Bean Tree, send for the Catalpa to the neighboring nursery. **1897** SUDWORTH *Arborescent Flora* 335 Common Catalpa. . . . Common names [include] . . . Beantree (N.J., Del., Pa., Va., La., Nebr.).

+**Bean-vine.** The vine of the bean plant.

1828 WEBSTER s.v. *Vine*, Thus we speak of the hop vine [and] the bean vine. **1838** HAWTHORNE *Note-books* I. 127 These factories have . . . boarding-houses near them, . . . often with bean-vines running up round the doors. **1845** JUDD *Margaret* I. iv. 19 Wait till the flowers is gone, they wouldn't be worth more'n your toad-flax and bean vines. **1849** *Knickerb.* XXXIII. 131 Even the very roses and bean-vines know better than to twine themselves about those grand-looking pillars. **1868** *Amer. Naturalist* II. 469 Deer . . . sometimes trespass on cornfields, where they crop the bean-vines. **1912** MRS. WOODROW *Sally Salt* 181 The bean vines, twining in luxuriant wreaths and festoons over their tall poles.

+**Bean-weevil.** A species of beetle, as *Bruchus fabæ* or *B. obsoletus*, harmful to beans. — **1870** PACKARD in *Mass. Agric. Rep.* I. 370, I sent specimens of the bean weevil . . . to Dr. G. A. Horn, of Philadelphia, who pronounces it to be . . . a native species (*B. varicornis* of Leconte). **1873** — in *Amer. Naturalist* VII. 536 The Bean-weevil. . . . How extremely injurious this weevil . . . still threatens to be, appears from both Mr. Riley's and my reports. **1892** V. KELLOG *Kansas Insects* 4 This stage is passed . . . in some place of shelter beneath stones, or boards, or even buried in seeds (as with the Pea- and Bean-weevils).

***BEAR,** *n.*[1] (See also BAR *n.*[2])

***1.** The well-known quadruped of the genus *Ursus*.

For *American, black, brown, cinnamon, grizzly* (etc.) *bear*, see these headings.

?**1607** PERCY in *Smith's Works* (1884) I. p. lxix, There are Beares, Foxes, Otters, . . . and wild beasts vnknowne. **1634** WOOD *New Eng. Prospect* I. vi. 19 For Beares they be common, being a great blacke kind of Beare, which be most feirce in Strawberry time, at which time they have young ones. **1637** MORTON *New Canaan* II. v, The beare is a tyrant at a lobster, and at low water will downe to the rocks and groape after them with great diligence. **1676** GLOVER *Acc. Va.* in *Phil. Trans.* XI. 631 There are also several sorts of ravenous Beasts, as Wolves, . . . and in the Northern most parts of the Countrey some Bears. **1701** C. W[OLLEY] *Journal N.Y.* (1902) 37 The Skins of . . . Bears, Bevers, Rackoons, [etc.] . . . they bring upon their backs to New-York. **1750** WALKER *Journal* 7 April, In the Evening our dogs caught a large He Bear, which before we could come up to shoot him had wounded a dog of mine. **1772** WASHINGTON *Diaries* II. 49 Found both a Bear and Fox but got neither. **1818** SCHOOLCRAFT *Journal* 18 We discovered, in a ravine below, four bears upon trees. **1832** WILLIAMSON *Maine* I. 133 Of the Bear kind, are three species: 1. the Bear itself. . . . Its flesh is good, and its skin and its grease is valuable. **1866** *Rep. Indian Affairs* 299 Bears are very plentiful this fall. **1891** *Scribner's Mag.* Oct. 450/1 Bear seek their winter quarters in Bad Lands and in the mountains.

b. *Bear's bacon, claw, flesh, foot, lard, steak.* See also BEAR'S FAT, BEAR'S GREASE, BEAR'S MEAT, BEAR'S OIL.

1709 LAWSON *Carolina* 95 Bears-Flesh is a very well-tasted food. **1733** BYRD *Journey to Eden* (1901) 308 But Bears' flesh needs something of the farinaceous, to make it pass easily off the Stomach. **1816** U. BROWN *Journal* I. 282 The persons that do it ought to be . . . fed on the beef of Rattle snakes & bears foot soop. **1818** SCHOOLCRAFT *Journal* 45 We have homony . . . and bear's bacon for dinner. **1823** COOPER *Pioneer* xvi, Bear's hams makes the best of food. **1835** IRVING *Tour of Prairies* xxxiii. 306 Fritters of flour fried in bear's lard. **1839** *S. Lit. Messenger* V. 450/1 The old Negro placed a hot bear's-steak . . . on the table. **1890** RYAN *Told in Hills* 55 The necklace of bear's claws that adorned the bronze throat of the gentleman.

c. Phr. *as cross* or *as hungry as a bear* (or *bear cub*).

1845 C. M. KIRKLAND *Western Clearings* 78 They've had the agur, . . . and they're as cross as bear-cubs. **1854** CUMMINS *Lamplighter* xix. 155

Well! folks do say that first-rate cooks and nurses are allers as cross as bears! **1859** G. A. JACKSON *Diary* 522 Phil has been as cross as a bear all day. **1902** HARBEN *Abner Daniel* 255, I'm as hungry as a bear.

d. Attrib. with *chase, cub, fight, rib.*

1845 [see prec.] **1852** BOND *Minn.* 257 We found it a very hard march, with the bear-chase, the bad roads. *Ib.* 307 The regular dinner consisted of broiled bear-ribs, eggs, coffee, etc. **1855** SIMMS *Forayers* 373 It'll be a bear fight first, I tell you—tooth and nail! **1888** *Cincinnati Enquirer* (F.), A bear cub had accidently got into one of my traps.

2. *ellipt.* Bear's meat.

1733 BYRD *Journey to Eden* (1901) 310 For those Stomachs . . . there was plenty of fat Bear, we having kill'd two in this day's March. **1737** BRICKELL *N. Carolina* 111 The next day we were invited to another planter's house, who told us he had the finest piece of bear that could be, just roasted and ready for the table. **1750** WALKER *Journal* 23 April, Then Ambrose Powell . . . and I departed, leaving the others to provide and salt some Bear.

3. On the stock exchange, one who sells for future delivery with the expectation that prices will fall in the meantime. Also attrib. with *raid, panic,* etc. {1744-}

Originally {1709-31} applied to the stock sold, also called *bear-skin* {1719-26}.

1805 *Ann. 8th Congress* 2 Sess. 1103 As well may your buyers and sellers of stock, your bulls and your bears of the alley, require indemnification for their losses at the hands of the nation. **1828** [PAULDING] *New Mirror* 136 Your banking capital can . . . put the *bulls* and *bears* on tiptoe. **1870** MEDBERY *Men of Wall St.* 92 Half the Assembly entered on a bear raid against Harlem. **1875** *Scribner's Mo.* July 271/2 California street is the speculator's paradise, or perdition. Here the bulls bellow and the bears growl their loudest. **1902** LORIMER *Lett. Merchant* 178 Four or five years ago little Jim Jackson had the bears in the provision pit hibernating.

* **Bear,** *n.*[2] {Chiefly *Sc.* and *northern*} Barley of the four- or six-rowed varieties.

1765 ROGERS *Acc. N.Amer.* 85 The chief articles exported from this province [=Penna.], are wheat, flour, bear, pig and bar iron, hogshead and pipe staves. **1787** WASHINGTON *Diaries* III. 192 The westermost [was sowed] ½ with a Barley . . . sent me by Genl. Spotswood under the denomination of Bear, and which in appearance was very much like the Rhode Island . . . barley. **1788** *Ib.* 348 A large rough grain, called by some of the People about me Bear, and esteemed a Winter grain. **1849** *Rep. Comm. Patents: Agric.* (1850) 153 Have tried some half dozen sorts [of barley], as also *bear* or *big,* imported from Scotland, not worth the trouble and expense.

+**Bear,** *n.*[3] Also **bère, baire.** [Creole-Fr. *baire* (1727), *berre* (1719), *ber:* W. A. Read *Louisiana-French* 3. Cf. BAR *n.*[3] and BIER.] A gauze net used or suitable for keeping out mosquitoes.

1775 ROMANS *Florida* 189 Where musketoes are plenty, have a close covering, called in this country a *Bère,* and made in form of a musketo net, to put up over your bed. *Ib.* 228 *note, Baires* are a kind of tent made of light coarse cloth, like canvas gauze, called by the French *villemontiers.* **1797** F. BAILY *Tour* 309 The bedrooms [of New Orleans] . . . are furnished with nothing but a hard-stuffed bed, . . . covered with a clean, white sheet; and over the whole there is a large gauze net (called a *bear*), which is intended as a defence against the mosquitos. **1798** ELLICOTT in *Life & Lett.* 158 Our beds are all surrounded with a kind of thin curtains called bears to keep them off when we go to rest. **1806** CLARK in *Lewis & C. Exped.* (1904) V. 181 The Musquetors has been so troublesome . . . that we . . . cant write except under our bears. [**1895** G. KING *New Orleans* 65 The oarsmen [*c.* 1726] made their mosquito *baires* for them, by bending long canes, fixing the ends in the ground over their mattresses, and covering the frame with a linen which they securely tucked in all around.]

+**Bear,** *n.*[4] =BAR *n.*[1] 8.— **1803** LEWIS in *Journals of L. & Ordway* 32 [We passed] another bear or ripple.

* **Bear,** *v.*[1]

1. *intr.* Of ice (or snow): To support the weight of a person, etc. {*Sc.*}

1768 WASHINGTON *Diaries* I. 246 Attempted to go into the Neck on the Ice but it w[oul]d not bear. **1775** *Essex Inst. Coll.* LIII. 88 Our men attempted to go to Bunker's hill, but did not get there, as the ice would [not] bear. **1878** H. H. JACKSON *Travel at Home* 38 'Oh!' said I, 'you have been off on the snow.' . . . 'And it "bears" everywhere. I jumped on the "crust" with all my weight.'

+**2.** *tr.* With *off:* (see quotation).

1869 *Overland Mo.* III. 126 Another rides in, selects a stray brand, and 'cuts it out,' by chasing it out with his horse. At other times they 'bear off' a single animal, by riding between it and the herd, when in motion.

Bear, *v.*[2] [BEAR *n.*[1] 3.] *tr.* To produce a fall of prices in (the market, stocks). {1884; *intr.*, *a*1842}

1848 W. ARMSTRONG *Stocks* 19 This is perhaps the grand theatre for bulling and bearing stocks. **1861** *N.Y. Tribune* 29 Nov. (B.), His Lordship is wholly guiltless of the charge which the 'Herald,' in its anxiety to bear the market, has brought against him. **1867-9** *Ill. Agric. Soc. Trans.* VII. 431 The strong influences which were used to 'bear' the hog market. **1870** MEDBERY *Men of Wall St.* 163 He habitually 'bulled' stocks and 'beared' gold. **1881** *Chicago Times* 4 June, If we succeed in bulling silver we shall also succeed in bearing gold to the same extent.

+**Bear bacon.** [BEAR *n.*[1] 1.] Meat from the back and sides of a bear.

1772 ROMANS in Phillips *Notes* (1924) 124 The Hickory Nut they make a kind of Milk of; which they esteem next to their Bear Bacon above all things in the World. **1775** ADAIR *Indians* 415 In the spring of the year, bear-bacon is a favorite dish with the traders. **1837** *Knickerb.* X. 414 The woodsman had exerted himself violently in the chase, to secure his supply of bear bacon, while the Indian Summer lasted. **1859** G. A. JACKSON *Diary* (MS.) 10 Swapped bear bacon for scissors. **1886** Z. F. SMITH *Kentucky* 690 That which was not so paid was probably commuted for bear bacon, buffalo steak, or jerked venison.

* **Bear baiting.** [BEAR *n.*[1] 1.] The sport of setting dogs on a captive bear.

[**1634** WOOD *New Eng. Prospect* I. vi. 19 Beares . . . at this time likewise . . . will . . . swimme to the Islands; which if the Indians see, there will be more sportfull Beare bayting than Paris Garden can affoard.] **1835** HOFFMAN *Winter in West* I. 216 Fox-hunting on horseback, with full packs of hounds, is the favourite sport; though wolf, bear, and badger-baiting have each their active followers. **1835** *Ohio Revised Statutes* (1860) I. 449 Any person or persons who shall hereafter confine . . . any bull, steer, or other domestic or domesticated animal . . . for the purpose of bull baiting, bear baiting, or other purpose of torture. **1879** *Scribner's Mo.* Oct. 823/1 One Sunday there was [in Leadville, Colo.] a bear-baiting and another a boxing-match.

Bear-berry. [BEAR *n.*[1] 1.]

1. The trailing shrub *Arctostaphylos uva-ursi;* sometimes also, an allied or similar plant, as the arbutus. {1625-}

1672 JOSSELYN *New Eng. Rarities* 65 Cran Berry, or Bear Berry, because Bears use much to feed upon them, is a small trayling plant that grows in Salt Marshes. **1785** MARSHALL *Amer. Grove* 12 The Bear-berry. This grows naturally in the Jerseys. **1832** WILLIAMSON *Maine* I. 120 The Bearberry, or Bear's grape, trails on the ground, putting forth roots from its prominent stems. *a***1862** THOREAU *Maine Woods* 181 The plants which chiefly attracted our attention were the . . . beautiful harebells, . . . bear-berry [etc.]. **1878** H. H. JACKSON *Travel at Home* 289 The ground was gay with yellow lupines, daisies, and great mats of killikinnick vines (the bear-berry). **1892** B. TORREY *Foot-path Way* 72 Broad patches of bearberry showing at a little distance like beds of mountain cranberry.

attrib. **1892** TORREY *Foot-Path Way* 78 One needed only to look at the bearberry patches to perceive that Cape Cod sand was not wanting in fertility after a manner of its own.

+**2.** A species of rhamnus (*R. Purshiana*) native to the Pacific States; bearwood.

1884 SARGENT *Rep. Forests* 41 *Rhamnus Purshiana.* . . . Bearberry. Bear Wood. Shittim Wood. **1893** *Amer. Folk-Lore* VI. 139 *Rhamnus Californica,* wild coffee; bearberry. S. Barbara Co., Cal.

+**3.** (See quotation.)

1883 HALE *Woods & Timbers N. C.* 140 Bear Huckleberry, Bearberry (*Gaylussacia ursina,* Gray); . . . the berry is purplish or dark red, insipid and dry, ripening in July and August.

+**Bear-blanket.** [BEAR *n.*[1] 1.] A bearskin used as a blanket. — **1850** [H. C. LEWIS] *La. Swamp Doctor* 168 The quantity of bear-blankets in the neighbouring cabins.

+**Bear-chowder.** [BEAR *n.*[1] 1.] A soup made with bear-meat. — **1847** LANMAN *Summer in Wilderness* xiv. 88 When the bear chowder was done, it was equally distributed among the assembled crowd.

Bear-claw. A bear's claw (cf. BEAR *n.*[1] 1 b.) — **1890** RYAN *Told in Hills* 94 To the rafters were fastened some beaver-paws and bear-claws. **1901** *Harper's Mag.* April 741/1 Medicine Bear . . . put his feather in his head and the bear-claw on his neck.

+**Bear dance.** [BEAR *n.*[1] 1.] A kind of dance practiced by the Indians. — *a***1820** in *Western Rev.* II. 161 There are a number of other [Indian] dances, such as the bear dance, the Turkey dance. **1823** W. H. KEATING *Narr.* 283 He witnessed part of a very interesting ceremony known by the name of the bear dance. **1833** CATLIN *Indians* I. 245 And they all like the fine pleasure of a bear hunt, and also a participation in the bear dance, which is given several days in succession, previous to their starting out.

* **Bearded,** *a.* Of plants: Provided with bristles or hairy tufts; awned.

1709 LAWSON *Carolina* 75 There are several sorts of Rice, some bearded, others not, besides the red and white. **1768** *Amer. Philos. Soc.* I. 287 . . . Those gentlemen who tell us that bearded wheat has been destroyed by the fly-weevil. **1802** J. DRAYTON *S. Carolina* 125 They are called Guinea rice, bearded rice, a short grained rice. **1805** LEWIS in *L. & Clark Exped.* (1904) II. 272 The uplands are covered with prickly pears and twisted or bearded grass. **1856** *Mich. Agric. Soc.* VII. 805 He . . . raises . . . the little yellow kind of corn, . . . the old-fashioned bald or bearded wheat.

+**Beard-grass.** One of various grasses belonging to the genera *Polypogon* {1841-}, *Andropogon,* and *Atheropogon.*

1791 MUHLENBERG *Index Florae* 181 *Andropogon,* Beard-grass. **1839** in *Mich. Agric. Soc.* VII. (1856) 400 *Andropogon nutans.* Beard-grass. *Atheropogon apludoides.* Beard-grass. **1843** TORREY *Flora N.Y.* II. 478 *Andropogon Virginicus,* . . . Virginian Beard-grass, . . . [grows in] sterile soils and exsiccated swamps. **1847** WOOD *Botany* 622 *Andropogon nutans,*

Beard Grass, ... [grows in] sandy fields, U.S. and Canada. **1863** *Ill. Agric. Soc.* V. 867 *Andropogon scoparius*, Broom, Beard-grass. **1889** VASEY *Agric. Grasses* 121 *Andropogon argenteus*, Silver Beard Grass. **1889** *Cent.*, *Beard-grass*, ... some species of *Polypogon*, especially *P. Monspeliensis* and *P. littoralis*, from the densely bearded appearance of the close panicles. **1901** MOHR *Plant Life Ala.* 369 *Polypogon monspeliensis*, French Beard-grass.... *Ib.*, *Polypogon littoralis*, Seaside Beard-grass.

Beardless, *a.* In specific names of fishes or birds (see quotations). — **1814** MITCHILL *Fishes N.Y.* 411 Beardless Drum. *Sciaena imberbis*.... It affords excellent eating. *Ib.*, [The] Beardless Drum ... has a row of teeth in each lip, and patches of teeth in the throat, and the general features of the drum. **1889** *Cent.* s.v., The beardless flycatcher, *Ornithium imberbe.*

Bear-dog. [BEAR *n.*[1] 1.] A dog used in hunting bears. {1673}

1837 *Knickerb.* X. 410 About the hour of midnight, the 'whole team of bear-dogs' opened a boisterous greeting as the roistering captain approached his cabin. **1852** MARCY *Explor. Red River* (1854) 53 We were so unfortunate yesterday as to lose an excellent bear-dog. **1872** *Harper's Mag.* June 29/2 My bear-dog, old Howler, happened to be layin' there asleep. **1885** *Outing* Oct. 65/2 A bear dog belongs to no particular breed; he is an accident. **1895** *Ib.* XXVIII. 74/2 A good bear dog ... must be a mongrel; a cross of the hound with the mastiff or bull-dog is the best.

+**Beard tongue.** A perennial herb of the genus *Pentstemon.* — **1821** *Mass. H. S. Coll.* 2 Ser. IX. 153 *Pentstemon pubescens*, Beard tongue. **1840** DEWEY *Mass. Flowering Plants* 160 Beard-tongue ... ; hills and banks and valleys; June; a beautiful plant for borders. **1847** WOOD *Botany* 400 Beard-tongue ... [grows on] river banks, bluffs, hills, and barrens, Western N.Y. to Ohio, Iowa and Illinois. **1901** MOHR *Plant Life Ala.* 718 *Pentstemon hirsutus*, ... Pubescent Beard-tongue, ... [grows on] dry sandy or gravelly soil.

***Beareager.** *Obs.* [f. *bear* BEER.] Vinegar made from beer. {-1593} — **1639** *Md. Archives* IV. 78 It[em] 1. rondlett beareager cont. 16. gns.

***Bearer.**

1. One who helps to carry the corpse at a funeral. {1633-}

1676 SEWALL *Diary* I. 17 Bearers, Henry Philips [etc.]. **1700** *Ib.* II. 9 She is buried between 5 and 6 p.m. Bearers ... Mr. Russel [etc.]. **1708** *Essex Inst. Coll.* X. 81, I was bearer to Mrs. Roff. **1726** *N.H. Probate Rec.* II. 285 Besides the scarfs and gloves that shall be given to my bearers. **1737** E. PARKMAN *Diary* 28 This Joseph Amsden was one of the Bearers of ... the young woman that dyed at Deacon James Wood's. **1780** *Ib.* 199 The Mourners, Bearers, &c. came to my House, to hear the Will. **1821** COOPER *Spy* xiv, Captain Lawton sat in his saddle ..., until the bearers came opposite to his position. **1843** *Knickerb.* XXI. 73 Softly, gentlemen bearers! set me down softly. **1868** G. G. CHANNING *Recoll. Newport* 21, I call to mind the gloves laid upon the coffin, a customary gratuity to the 'bearers.' **1879** B. F. TAYLOR *Summer-Savory* ix. 80 There was no plumed hearse, ... but only 'bearers.' **1897** BRODHEAD *Bound in Shallows* 224 Just now the throng appeared to be drawing towards the open grave. The lodgemen surrounded it, forming a hollow line as the bearers advanced.

2. An attendant on a child. {1811-, with ref. to India}

1835 [INGRAHAM] *South-West* II. 92 The Africans ... whom they have had for their nurses, play-fellows, and 'bearers.'

+**Bear-fat.** Fat from a bear. (Cf. BEAR *n.*[1] 1 b.)

1780 W. FLEMING in *Travels Amer. Col.* 640 Bear fat is preserved sweet and pure by putting in a bunch of the Slippery Elem bark into it when rendering. *a***1846** *Quarter Race Kentucky*, etc. 144 He took a long wooden skewer, and having thrust its point through a small piece of bear fat, he then followed it by a small piece of the liver. **1852** WATSON *Nights in Block-house* 135 Then bear-meat, looking very much like pork; bear-fat in separate dishes; a few squirrels; ... filled up the rest of the table.

+**Bear flag.** [BEAR *n.*[1] 1.] A flag bearing the emblem of a bear, adopted as a standard by California insurgents. *Obs.* — **1848** *Calif. Claims* (Senate Rep. 23 Feb.) [27 A settler ... had hoisted a flag—a grizzly bear upon a white field—as the insignia of the new State. *Ib.*] 50 The most valuable portion of the beautiful valley ... and the wealthy missions of the country would have been ceded and granted away, but for the opportune hoisting of the bear flag.

+**Bear-grass.** [BEAR *n.*[1] 1.] **a.** A plant of the genus *Yucca*, esp. *Y. filamentosa* (also called SILK-GRASS), or of the allied *Dasylirion* of Texas. **b.** The camas or quamash.

1750 WALKER *Journal* 12 April, On the Banks is some Bear-Grass. **1802** DRAYTON *S. Carolina* 67 Silk grass, or bear grass. (*Yucca filamentosa.*) ... Its root is used instead of soap, for washing woollens; and its leaves after being a little roasted, are sometimes twisted into horse traces. **1807** GASS *Journal* xvi. 167 One of them had a hat made of the bark of white cedar and bear-grass, very handsomely wrought and water proof. **1832** R. COX *Adv. Columbia River* 155 The head is covered by a species of helmet made of cedar bark, bear grass, and leather. **1836** IRVING *Astoria* x. (1850) 62 Hither also, the tribes from the Rocky Mountains brought down bear-grass, quamash, and other commodities of the interior. *Ib.* xl. 221 Some [Indians] wore a corslet, formed of pieces of hard wood, laced together with bear grass. **1847** *Rep. Comm. Patents* (1848) 162 Some interesting statements have been made respecting the bear grass or Florida hemp. **1881** *Amer. Naturalist* XV. 874 The first experience of the traveller with the bear-grass, whose hooks scratch and tear everything they touch, is a disagreeable one. **1885** HAVARD *Flora W. & S. Texas* 517 *Dasylirion Texanum.* Bear Grass; the Sotol of the Mexicans.... Abundant west of the Pecos ... ; the most striking botanical feature of the country.

+**Bear grease.** =BEAR'S GREASE. — **1763** *Boston Post-Boy* 12 Dec., Black sattin Baggs for the Hair, ... & Bear Grees.

+**Bear-greased,** *ppl. a.* Lubricated with bear's grease. — **1833** CATLIN *Indians* I. 203 His irresistible importunities have brought me, night after night, to the only alternative of using his bedaubed and bear-greased body for a pillow.

+**Bear-ground.** [BEAR *n.*[1] 1.] A place frequented by bears. — **1797** B. HAWKINS *Lett.* 70 This was our beloved bear ground, and reserved as such as long as it was of value for bear. **1800** — *Sk. Creek Country* 33 It ... was preserved by the Indians for bears, and called the beloved bear-ground. **1923** J. H. COOK *On Old Frontier* 137 When we reached the place where I knew there was good bear ground, I instructed the men to move in line with me.

+**Bear-ham.** A bear's ham. — **1766** W. STORK *Acc. East-Florida* 50 It is reckoned very good food, especially the bear hams, &c. **1850** [H. C. LEWIS] *La. Swamp Doctor* 165 From the joists depended bear-hams and tongues innumerable.

+**Bear-hunt.** [BEAR *n.*[1] 1.] A hunt after a bear or bears.

1803 *Lit. Mag.* (Phila.) Oct. 64 A grand bear hunt is proposed on the third Wednesday in October [at Portsmouth, N.H.]. **1818** SCHOOLCRAFT *Journal* 32 We found our host and his sons early busied in equipping themselves for a bear-hunt up the Great North Fork. **1834** *S. Lit. Messenger* I. 97 We were not without hope of being treated to the novelty of a bear hunt. **1845** MRS. KIRKLAND *Western Clearings* 125 They were going to have a bear-hunt out there. **1878** C. COALE in *Ann. S.W. Va.* (1929) 1542 A friend who took his first and last bear-hunt with Wilburn Waters. **1900** DRANNAN *Plains & Mts.* 89 Many times during the winter I was reminded of the bear hunt, in which the bear hunted me.

+**Bear-hunter.** [BEAR *n.*[1] 1.] One who hunts bears.

1765 ROGERS *Acc. N. America* 259 An alliance with a noted bear-hunter, who has killed several in one day, is ... eagerly sought after. **1837** PECK *New Guide* 42 Col. Crockett was a famous bear-hunter in western Tennessee. **1847** HOWE *Hist. Coll. Ohio* 367 Volney ... was under the guidance of two Virginia bear hunters through the wilderness. **1851** *Polly Peablossom* 146 Besides being a great bear-hunter ... Mike professed to be 'considerable' of a fighter. **1864** TROWBRIDGE *Cudjo's Cave* 297 Pomp ... arrived, bringing the bag of meal ... which the bear-hunters had forsaken. **1901** MCCUTCHEON *Graustark* 9 A group of Indian bear hunters created considerable interest.

+**Bear-hunting.** [BEAR *n.*[1] 1.] The hunting of bears. (Also in participial use.)

1705 BEVERLEY *Virginia* IV. 65 Some few years agoe, I was a Bear-Hunting in the Woods above the Inhabitants. **1709** LAWSON *Carolina* 117 Bear-hunting is a great Sport in America, both with the English and Indians. **1857** *Harper's Mag.* Nov. 819/2 Bear hunting is sport only for those who set little value upon life. **1891** *Scribner's Mag.* Oct. 448/2 Bear hunting, as a general rule, I do not think would appeal to most sportsmen. **1900** DRANNAN *Plains & Mts.* 216, I spent the next three days bear hunting, and saw any amount of sign, but only saw one bear.

Bearing blanket, cloth {1601-11}. A blanket or (baptismal) cloth for carrying a child. — **1644** *Essex Probate Rec.* I. 38, 1 red bearing blanket with 2 gr. Laces. **1647** *Ib.* 78 A bearinge Cloth, ... three Peticots, fowre wescots, a whood & an apren.

+**Bearing tree.** A tree by which bearings are taken. — **1817** *Niles' Reg.* XII. 98/2 At each corner the courses are taken to two trees, in opposite directions as nearly as may be, and their distance from the post measured. These trees are called 'bearing trees,' and are blazed on the side next the post. **1878** *Harper's Mag.* Jan. 210/2 A 'bearing' tree has been blocked to get at a 'blaze' made in the spring of '38.

Bearish, *a.* [BEAR *n.*[1] 3.] Inclined or tending to 'bear' the market. {1884} — **1848** W. ARMSTRONG *Stocks* 21 A small portion of the experience of an individual of bearish propensities. **1881** *Chicago Times* 30 April, The movement was bearish, and prices all averaged a trifle lower. **1882** *Century Mag.* Aug. 539 He's bullish to-day; he'll be bearish tomorrow.

+**Bear-meat.** [BEAR *n.*[1] 1.] The flesh of a bear. Cf. BEAR'S MEAT.

1787 Ramsey *Tennessee* (1853) 504 Good bear meat, without bones, eight dollars per hundred wt. **1809** F. CUMING *Western Tour* 155 It is only fourteen or fifteen years since no other except buffalo or bear meat was used by the inhabitants of this country. **1849** LANMAN *Alleghany Mts.* xi. 90 We remained a sufficient length of time to enjoy one supper and one breakfast; the first was composed of corn bread and bear meat. **1868** *Amer. Naturalist* II. 529 Some bear-meat, obtained at 'Hell gate,' was of this species. **1884** ROE *Nature's Story* 134 Adjacent buildings are for the storage of furs, bear-meat, and the accommodation of Indian hunters. **1890** RYAN *Told in Hills* 96 Jimmy brought out ... some bits of salt meat—evidently bear-meat.

+**Bear mouse.** [BEAR *n.*[1]] The field mouse. — **1857** *Rep. Comm. Patents: Agric.* 84 Where several species [of meadow-mice] are found in one locality, they are commonly considered by farmers as one animal, known under various names, as 'short-tailed field rats or mice,' 'bear mice,' 'bull-headed mice,' 'ground mice,' 'bog mice,' &c.

+**Bear oak.** [BEAR *n.*[1] 1.] The black scrub-oak, *Quercus ilicifolia.*

1810 MICHAUX *Arbres* I. 24 Bear' oak (Chêne d'ours), connu sous ce nom dans les Etats de New-Jersey et de New-York. **1814** PURSH *Flora Amer.* II. 631 *Quercus Banisteri.* . . . This shrub . . . is known by the name of bear oak, black scrub oak, and dwarf red oak. **1832** BROWNE *Sylva* 263 The ordinary height of the bear oak is 3 or 4 feet. **1847** DARLINGTON *Weeds & Plants* 315 The dwarf species, known as Scrub Oak, or Bear Oak, is *Q. ilicifolia,* Wang. . . . It is a worthless little species, . . . abounding on poor soils. **1892** TORREY *Foot-path Way* 81 The rest of the vegetation was more or less familiar, I believe: . . . bear oak; chinquapin.

+**Bear root.** [BEAR *n.*[1] 1.] Swamp hellebore. — **1751** ELIOT *Field-Husb.* iii. 66 Take the Roots of Swamp Hellebore, sometimes called Skunk Cabbage, Tickle Weed, Bear Root.

+**Bear-rough.** [BEAR *n.*[1] 1.] A thicket such as shelters bears. — **1837** *Knickerb.* X. 413 Here security was made doubly sure by the bear-rough that sheltered them.

+**Bear's bush.** — **1787** CUTLER in *Life,* etc. I. 201 [We] brought home Bear's-bush and two species of Sumach.

Bear's-claw. [BEAR *n.*[1] 1 b. Cf. E. *bear-claw* (1589), brank-ursine.] (?) A species of delphinium. — **1806** LEWIS in *L. & Clark Exped.* (1904) IV. 234 A speceis of the bearsclaw of which I preserved a specemine . . . is in blume.

+**Bear's fat.** [BEAR *n.*[1] 1 b.] Bear fat; bear's grease.

1709 LAWSON *Carolina* 207 A roasted or barbakued Turkey, eaten with Bears Fat, is held a good dish. **1743** CATESBY *Carolina* App. p. ix, At their going on enterprizes of war, . . . [Indians daub] their hair with bear's fat. **1754** *Records of Moravians* II. (N.C. Hist. Comm.) 533 We must do with melted butter, which is not to be compared with bears fat. **1791** Jillson *Dark & Bl. Ground* 109 The windows are of heavy paper greased with bear's fat. **1806** *Ann. 9th Congress* 2 Sess. 1116 The hunters count much on their profits from the oil drawn from the bear's fat.

***Bear's foot.** [BEAR *n.*[1] 1 b.] An herb of the genus *Helleborus.* — **1787** CUTLER in *Life,* etc. I. 201 Brought home savin and bear's-foot, and planted them in garden. **1824** *New Eng. Farmer* II. 199 A child was lately poisoned in Pennsylvania by its mother's administering the herb called Bear's Foot, as an antidote for worms.

+**Bear's grape.** =BEAR-BERRY. — **1842** BUCKINGHAM *E. & W. States* I. 161 The bear's grape, which trails on the ground, is effective in dysentery.

***Bear's grease.** [BEAR *n.*[1] 1 b.] The fat of the bear, esp. as used for medical and cosmetic purposes; sometimes (as in quot. 1855) made synthetically.

1674 JOSSELYN *Two Voyages* (1675) 92 Purchace . . . cured himself of the Sciatica with Bears-greese, keeping some of it continually in his groine. **1709** LAWSON *Carolina* 207 The Bears Greese is the sweetest and least offensive to the stomach . . . of any Fat of animals I ever tasted. **1724** *New-Eng. Courant* 9–16 Nov. 2/2 If any Persons have any Bears Grease to sell, the said Boylston will give them 8 s. per Gallon. **1768** J. LEES *Journal* 43 On the voyage down they are allowed nothing but Indian Corn and Bears Grease, which they boil up together. **1791** J. LONG *Voyages* 45 A feast is prepared of dog's flesh boiled in bear's grease, with huckle berries. **1839** BRIGGS *H. Franco* II. 142 The first thing I did was to purchase a bottle of Cologne water, and a box of bear's grease. **1855** BARNUM *Life* 208 Proler . . . was a manufacturer of paste-blacking, . . . Cologne water, and bear's grease. **1878** *Decorum* 316 In the way of a pomatum bear's grease is as pleasant as anything. **1902** LORIMER *Lett. Merchant* 166 [He] had nice, curly black hair and didn't spare the bear's grease.

+**Bear's handkerchief.** [BEAR *n.*[1] 1.] The caul of a bear. — *a***1846** *Quarter Race Kentucky,* etc. 144 He opened the 'bear's handkerchief,' or caul, and wrapped it round the whole [skewer of fat and liver], and thus roasted it before the fire.

Bear-shooting. The shooting of bears. — **1887** *Century Mag.* March 738/2 He rode in silence for some time and then he gave a short, scornful laugh. 'I don't call that any kind of bear-shooting.'

+**Bear-sign.** [BEAR *n.*[1] 1.]

1. A track, or other indication of its presence, made by a bear. Also collectively.

1839 *S. Lit. Messenger* V. 377/1 To be sure I did see a powerful sight of bear signs. **1853** 'P. PAXTON' *Yankee in Texas* 21 We have fallen upon the hereinbefore-mentioned 'bear-sign.' There could be no more timber-hunting that day. Fresh bear-sign . . . proved too much for Joe's newly born spirit of industry. **1855** *Harper's Mag.* XI. 596/2 The old he-bears have a habit . . . of biting the bark of certain forest-trees at the highest point they can reach when standing on their hind legs. These 'bear signs' are perfectly indicative to the experienced hunter of the size of the bear. **1887** *Scribner's Mag.* Sept. 305/1 They reported any amount of bear-sign on the slopes leading to the river. **1895** REMINGTON *Pony Tracks* 256 The advance consists of six or eight big blood-hounds, . . . with Dan and Mr. Cooper to blow the horn, look out for 'bear sign' [etc.].

2. *transf.* A doughnut.

1903 A. ADAMS *Log Cowboy* xviii. 279 She asked me to make the bear sign—doughnuts, she called them—and I did. *Ib.* 283 He rolled his dough, cut his dough, and turned out the fine brown bear sign to the satisfaction of all.

Bearskin. [BEAR *n.*[1] 1.]

1. The skin of a bear; freq. one prepared for use as a rug or covering. {1823–}

1647 *Boston Rec.* 405 Shipped . . . 1 puncheon bever. 3 C seventy foure moose skins. 1 pack beare skins. **1667** *Southampton Rec.* I. 157 The said beare skin was carryed to Shenecock Indians by Southold Indians whoe tooke the beare. **1742** in *Travels Amer. Col.* 220 They brought us to Logs which they had placed for that purpose covered with Bear Skins and desired us to sit down. **1765** TIMBERLAKE *Mem.* 15, I lay . . . with an Indian on a large bear-skin. **1796** B. HAWKINS *Lett.* 15 There I added to my traveling stock a bear skin. **1806** PIKE *Sources Miss.* 84 They also demanded ten dollars for a bear skin (the most beautiful I ever saw, which I wanted to mount a saddle). **1812** MARSHALL *Kentucky* 150 Much use was made of the deer-skins in dress—while the bear-skin was consigned to the floor, for a bed. **1826** FLINT *Recoll.* 142 Some tribes covered their tents with bear-skins. **1844** LEE & FROST *Oregon* xvii. 191 Sitting on the ground, sometimes with a mat or a bear-skin spread beneath them. **1884** BRET HARTE *Carquinez Woods* 16 In one corner lay a bearskin and blanket. **1896** WILKINS *Madelon* 141 I've got a bearskin here to wrap her up in.

2. A rough woollen cloth used for overcoats.

1762 H. M. Brooks *Gleanings* 37 Broad cloths, German serges, bear-skins, beaver coating, half-thick, red shagg, bayes. **1771** *Penna. Gazette* 26 Sept. 3/1 The sale of a large assortment of coarse and fine broad-cloths, bearskins, coatings, naps. **1779** E. PARKMAN *Diary* 108 Mrs. P. . . . purchases — yds. of bear skin to make him [Elias] a straight bodyd coat. **1805** PARKINSON *Tour* 381 A top-coat for a boy twelve years old, of the cloth called bear-skin, eight dollars.

3. Attrib. =Made of, covered or trimmed with, bear-skin (usually in sense 1).

1752 *N.C. Gazette* (Newbern) 13 March, Three Coats, one a Broad-cloth or Sarge, one a Bear-skin Cape-coat. **1757** *Ib.* 15 April, Had on when he went away, a new Bear-skin Vest and Breeches. **1775** ADAIR *Indians* 390 The victors . . . put on their feet a pair of bear-skin maccaseenes. **1789** FRENEAU *Poems* (1795) 321 A bear-skin coat was round his carcase roll'd. **1821** *Hillsborough* (N.C.) *Recorder* 10 Jan., A dark brown bearskin great coat, lined with red flannel. **1825** NEAL *Bro. Jonathan* I. 104 The stranger . . . [took] off a large bear skin cap. **1834** *Knickerb.* IV. 372 His mother . . . strapped him by bear-skin thongs in a box made from a hollow limb, to her back. **1840** EMMONS *Mass. Quadrupeds* 24 A Bear-skin robe which is made out of the best parts of good skins, sells from thirty to fifty dollars. **1851** *Harper's Mag.* Aug. 390/1 At night they lay on the ground, covered with their thick bear-skin cloaks. **1851** MELVILLE *Moby Dick* xvii, I took my bearskin jacket and threw it over him. **1857** *Quinland* I. 28 Shaking the snow right and left, from his bearskin over-coat. **1890** E. B. CUSTER *Following Guidon* 55 One of the officers said that he thought you would . . . think it was the man . . . who gave the President the bear-skin chair.

+**Bear's meat.** [BEAR *n.*[1] 1 b.] =BEAR-MEAT.

1772 D. TAITT in *Travels Amer. Col.* 513 One of the head men intertained us at his house with some bears meat for breakfast. **1819** SCHOOLCRAFT *Mo. Lead Mines* 250 Bears' meat was sold at $10 per cwt. **1829** T. FLINT *G. Mason* 13 Tender pieces of venison and bear's-meat smoked on the table. **1840** *Knickerb.* XVI. 162 By the opening of Spring we would generally have quantities of bear's meat and venison salted, dried, and smoked, and numerous packs of skins. **1855** WILLIS *Convalescent* 48 We still have venison in plenty, bear's-meat occasionally. **1864** TROWBRIDGE *Cudjo's Cave* xxv. 229, I have some salted bear's meat that you'll be welcome to. **1880** CABLE *Grandissimes* iv. 26 They sat down to bear's meat, sagamite and beans.

+**Bear's oil.** [BEAR *n.*[1] 1 b.] Liquid fat from the bear, used as food, as medicine, and as ointment for the hair.

1674 Alvord & Bidgood *Trans-Allegheny Region* 213 Aboundance of corne [was brought] . . . with fish, flesh and beares oyle for the horse to feed upon. **1705** BEVERLEY *Virginia* III. 18 Their sauce to this dry Meat . . . is only a little Bears Oyl, or Oyl of Acorns. **1724** JONES *Virginia* 11 Their Hair is very black, coarse and long; and they are all over daubed frequently with Bear's Oil. **1750** WALKER *Journal* 20 June, My riding Horse was bit by a Snake this day, and having no Bear's Oil I rub'd the place with a piece of fat meat, which had the desired effect. **1765** TIMBERLAKE *Mem.* 14 We supped with the Indians on dried venison dipped in bears oil, which served for sauce. **1780** W. FLEMING in *Travels Amer. Col.* 640 Hunters that preserve a great quantity of bears oil and take every method to get the largest quantity and sweet let the fat lye till it is quite tender. **1800** HAWKINS *Sk. Creek Country* 42 Which [root] the women mix with bears' oil, to redden their hair. **1821** J. FOWLER *Journal* 44 We dryed out the bares oil and caryed it with us. **1842** *Amer. Pioneer* I. 428 A kettle of bear's oil and some craclins were set before us, and we began eating, they first chewing the meat, then dipping it into the bear's oil. **1888** EGGLESTON in *Century Mag.* July 341/2 His hair was well kept in place by bear's oil.

+**Bear State.** [BEAR *n.*[1] 1.] A nickname of the state of Arkansas (also of California). — **1848** BARTLETT 392, I once asked a Western man if Arkansas abounded in bears, that it should be designated as the 'Bear State.' **1872** DE VERE 658 Arkansas is called the *Bear State,* though within its limits and throughout the West the name is pronounced *Bar* State. . . . California enjoys the same title.

+**Bear-steak.** [BEAR *n.*[1] 1.] A piece of bear-meat.

1788 J. MAY *Journal & Lett.* 59 Had an elegant dinner. Amongst the variety was . . . boiled fish, bear-steak, roast venison, etc. **1844** *Knickerb.* XXIII. 89 A dinner, which consisted partly of clams, bear-steak, etc.

1883 ZEIGLER & GROSSCUP *Alleghanies* 48 By the following night . . . the drivers and standers [may be] toasting bear steaks in their cabins.

+**Bear story.** A tale (alarming or improbable) concerning a bear or bears. Also transf. — **1856** *S. Lit. Messenger* XXII. 349/1 There is a bear story connected with a hollow sycamore. **1857** *Lawrence* (Kansas) *Republican* 13 Aug. 3 Somebody has evidently frightened you by telling 'bear-stories' about him, just as mothers sometimes do their little ones. **1871** *Atlantic Mo.* Nov. 564/2 A company of hunters . . . went on in their old eternal way of making bear-stories out of whole cloth.

+**Bear-track.** [BEAR *n.*[1] 1.] A track made by a bear; bear-sign. — **1850** GARRARD *Wah-To-Yah* xx. 246 Searching for fresh 'sign' among the huge beartracks. **1885** *Century Mag.* June 224/2 The spot where the bear-tracks were so plenty.

+**Bear-trap.** [BEAR *n.*[1] 1.]

1. A trap for catching bears. Also fig.

1825 NEAL *Bro. Jonathan* I. 108 What are ye arter there, squattin' so; jess like a cub in a bear trap? **1835** BIRD *Hawks of Hawk-h.* I. 269 Look you, boy, you are in a bear-trap, and the log will soon be on your back. **1849** LANMAN *Alleghany Mts.* xviii. 149 Having come to one of his bear-traps . . . he thoughtlessly . . . went under the trap to arrange his bait. **1860** HOLMES *E. Venner* iii, A sudden flash of his foot that clashed the yellow dog's white teeth together like the springing of a bear-trap.

2. (See quot. 1841 and BEAR *n.*[1] 3.)

1841 *Week in Wall St.* 81 Bear-traps . . . signifies . . . [brokers who] have sold stock which they have not got, and trust to circumstances to be able to supply it. **1848** W. ARMSTRONG *Stocks* 22 As soon as the debtor had gone out, he thrust his hands into his pockets, . . . and . . . muttered to himself, 'I'm in a bear trap—this won't do.'

+**Bear tree.** [BEAR *n.*[1] 1.] (See quot. 1832.) — **1808** F. CUMING *Western Tour* 423 About five miles from our hut I found a bear tree. **1832** J. A. MCCLUNG *Sk. Western Adventure* 24 Their only resource then, was to hunt bear trees; that is, for large hollow trees in which bears lay concealed during the winter. **1834** CROCKETT *Life* 182, I found a small tree which I thought I could fall so as to lodge against my bear tree. **1860** *Harper's Mag.* March 447/2 Sunday also comes to relieve the daily routine of camp life. . . . Visits are made to neighboring camps, bear-trees routed of their tenants, and traps inspected.

+**Bear venison.** [BEAR *n.*[1] 1.] =BEAR'S MEAT. — **1709** LAWSON *Carolina* 38 They brought in great store of loblolly, . . . stewed peaches, bear venison, &c.

+**Bear-wallow.** [BEAR *n.*[1] 1.] A shallow depression attributed to the wallowing of bears.

1843 'CARLTON' *New Purchase* I. xxvii. 247 Mail . . . had indeed come, but with only one letter, and that maybe for the Big-Bear-wallow settlement! **1872** W. J. FLAGG *Good Investment* i. 46/2 Sometimes he will meet with one of those almost mysterious shallow basins of water called 'bear-wallows.' **1880** *Scribner's Mo.* April 883/1 The guide exhibited to . . . us some remarkable depressions . . . each being a yard wide by a foot deep. These, as he said, were the bear-wallows. **1891** RYAN *Pagan* v. 62 He rode . . . on through the columns of white-oaks, whose feet are caressed by feathers of fern in the long, desolate 'bear-wallows.'

+**Bear-weed.** [BEAR *n.*[1] 1.] The yerba santa (*Eriodictyon californicum*), native to California. — **1887** BURROUGHS in *Century Mag.* July 325 The stem [is] two feet high, very leafy, and coarser than bear-weed.

+**Bearwood.** [BEAR *n.*[1] 1.] =BEAR-BERRY 2. — **1869** *Amer. Naturalist* III. 407 Oregon Bearwood (*Frangula Purshiana*). This species of Buckthorn occurs on both slopes of the Coeur d'Alene Mountains. **1884** SARGENT *Rep. Forests* 41 *Rhamnus Purshiana.* . . . Bearberry. Bear Wood. Shittim Wood.

Beasling, variant of BEASTLING.

* **Beast.**

* **1.** An animal of the ox kind.

1633 *Plymouth Col. Rec.* I. 9 Hatherly . . . hath sold unto John Barnes . . . one heyfer, . . . the said John standing to the adventure of the beast. **1638** *R. I. Col. Rec.* I. 54 Every one . . . shall have for his present use one acre of Medow for a Beast, one acre for a sheep, and one acre and a half for a Horse. **1648** *Conn. Public Rec.* I. 476 An Inuentory . . . [includes] foure cowes, foure oxen, four young beasts, one mare, nine swyne.

* **2.** A horse.

'A common name for a horse in the Southern States' (B. '48).

1684 I. Mather *Providences* ii. (1856) 29 They had a horse near by, . . . but . . . the beast was slow and dull. **1820** *Amer. Farmer* I. 369 The frequent custom of husband and wife going a junketing on the same horse or 'beast,' as in those days it was more commonly called. **1826** COOPER *Mohicans* ii, The ungainly man . . . came into view, with as much rapidity as he could excite his meagre beast to endure. **1835** [LONGSTREET] *Georgia Scenes* 22 Do you want to swap hosses? . . . I believe I've got a beast I'd trade with you. **1887** N. PERRY *Flock of Girls* 99 Your ma . . . was out with . . . the two horses, and something scared the beasts.

* **Beastings,** *n. pl.* Beestings. (See quotation.) — **1838** H. COLMAN *Mass. Agric. Rep.* (1839) 72, I found . . . among the farmers . . . that by a class of customers . . . the *beastings*, that is the first drawings of the milk from the udder after parturition, were always bargained for beforehand.

Beastlings, *n. pl.* Also **beas-, beesling(s).** =BEASTINGS. {1641–; now *dial.*} Also attrib. in sing., =imbibed from birth.

1723 *New-Eng. Courant* 18–25 Nov. 2/1 She does not know . . . how to boil a Skillet of Beaslings without letting it turn. **1809** WEEMS *Marion* (1833) 130 Unless they are well worked and scoured of their mother milk, or beastling partiality to the English, they are lost. **1899** GREEN *Va. Word-Book* 32 To make a young cow gentle and a good milch-cow, pour the beeslings on her rump.

Beat, *n.* {1615–}

1. A regular route or round traversed or frequented by a person. {1825–} Also transf.

Usually, as in E., the round of a policeman or sentry.

1721 *New-Eng. Courant* 2–9 Oct. 2/2 The several Clerks of the Train-Bands made a strict Enquiry at all the Houses within their respective Beats. *c***1845** W. T. THOMPSON *Chron. Pineville* 45 On muster-days he was in great requisition in his beat, and . . . few could beat him on that soul-stirring, ear-piercing instrument. *a***1846** *Quarter Race Ky.*, etc. 178 Long Ben, an old negro, who had fiddled for that 'beat' for the last quarter of a century. **1850** [H. C. LEWIS] *La. Swamp Doctor* 148 [The country doctor] became the repository of all the . . . secrets of the neighbourhood, which he was expected to retail out as required for the moral edification of the females of his 'beat.' **1870** *Amer. Naturalist* IV. 71 The white hunter builds his two log cabins, one near the southern limits of his *beat* and the other at its northern terminus. **1872** 'MARK TWAIN' *Roughing It* vi. 54 His beat or jurisdiction of two hundred and fifty miles was called a 'division' [*i.e.* of a stagecoach route]. **1900** SMITHWICK *Evolution of a State* 159 The Indians were not depredating in our beat.

fig. **1869** BROWNE *Adv. Apache Country* 27 We have thus far followed up our intended beat from the time of the early Spaniards to the passage of the act . . . establishing the Territorial government.

+**b.** In Alabama and Mississippi, a division of a county; a voting-precinct. (Cf. next.)

1860 CLAIBORNE *Sam. Dale* x. 166 Governor Holmes appointed me colonel of the militia, . . . and commissioner to take the census and organize beats or precincts. **1896** *Congress. Rec.* 13 March 2788/1 Testimony was taken to show that fraud was committed in certain beats,—the River beat, Union, and one or two others.

attrib. **1865** Fleming *Hist. Reconstruction* I. 288 All contracts . . . shall be . . . in duplicate attested and read . . . by a beat, city or county officer.

+**c.** *Captain's beat:* (see quotation).

1859 BARTLETT 68 *Captain's Beat,* the limits within which the members of a military company reside. Within the same limits the votes are received on election days. Southern.

+**2.** A path or track made by animals.

[**1736** *Smithtown Rec.* 299 May the 15 day 1736, then layd out to Job Smith a certain tract of land . . . by the place called the Horse beat.] **1838** *Knickerb.* XII. 293 The deer subsist upon the leaves of this evergreen plant [=ground-hemlock], . . . treading the snow from around its branches, as often as it falls during the season. This spot is called the deer or moose *beat*, by the hunters. **1857** *Harper's Mag.* Nov. 819/1 The bear goes to and from his den or cover . . . by certain paths, called 'beats.' A bear will use the same beat for years, going by night on one beat, and in the day taking another, more circuitous.

+**3.** *The beat of,* anything to surpass or excel (the thing or person in question). Freq. with *to see* or *hear.* *colloq.*

1833 S. SMITH *Major Downing* 129, I never see the beat of it. **1847** *Knickerb.* XXIX. 62, I suppose this Teeples ha'n't got his beat in old Potter. **1847** *Billy Warrick's Courtship* 100 (Th.), You don't tell me so! Did I ever hear the beat o' that! *c***1848** MRS. WHITCHER *Bedott P.* xi. 112 Here's that silk; did ye ever see the beat on't? *a***1859** *Yankee Hill's Stories* (B.), Sam Slick was a queer chap. I never see the beat of him. **1876** 'MARK TWAIN' *Tom Sawyer* i. 2, I never did see the beat of that boy. **1887** *Century Mag.* July 407/1 There wasn't his beat for fun on this side the mountains. **1894** 'MARK TWAIN' *Those Twins* vii, Why, I never heard the beat of it. **1902** L. RICHARDS *Mrs. Tree* 70 'There! you hear her!' murmured Direxia. 'Oh, she is the beat of all!'

+**4.** In journalism, the securing and publishing of a piece of news before one's competitors; the exclusive item itself.

1875 STOWE *We & Our Neighbors* 292 Here are four or five big dailies . . . , and if any one of them gets a bit of news before another, it's a victory—a beat. **1877** *Harper's Mag.* Dec. 48 A beat in a third [paper]—i.e. some news which his own paper does not contain. **1881** *Ib.* March 550/2 Not one of them [=newspaper correspondents] goes to bed . . . without fearing he has suffered a 'beat.' **1887** *Detroit Tribune* 27 June 3/2 They finally succeeded, and cheered lustily as the Ocean King steamed for New York with a big 'beat' for the Times. The office was safely reached, & the 'beat' appeared that morning. **1895** *St. Louis Star* 6 May 4 This was the largest price paid for a newspaper 'beat' up to that time. **1899** HOWELLS in *Literature* 1 July 691 Within the limits of fiction or of fact the highest achievement of a reporter is to make his story a *beat.* **1910** WALCOTT *Open Door* x. 121 If she won't see the other reporters, so much the better for me. It'll be a beat.

b. *To get a beat on* (one), to get the advantage of. *slang.*

1889 FARMER 46 As used by thieves and their associates, *to get a beat on one* . . . also implies that the point has been scored by underhand, secret, or unlawful means.

+**5.** *colloq.* A lazy, shiftless or broken-down fellow; a loafer. (Cf. DEAD-BEAT *n.*)

1870 O. Logan *Before Footlights* 371 The landlord's good nature and kindness are tested. First, he must sift the 'beats' from their more worthy brethren. [**1871** [Bagg] *At Yale* 138 In sophomore year, Beta Xi men are called 'Dead Beats,' or simply 'Beats,' by those of Theta Psi.] **1872** *Chicago Tribune* 22 Oct. 3/4 The latter endeavored to show him up as a drunkard and a beat. **1880** A. Hayes in *Harper's Mag.* Feb. 389 But he said that these beats, when they were at home, had old squirrel rifles . . . with flint-locks. **1886** *Century Mag.* Feb. 514/2 He was all the more likely on that account to be a beat; the expression was probably such as a beat would put on in approaching his intended prey. **1888** Billings *Hardtack* 95 The original idea of beat was that of a lazy man or a shirk, who would by hook or by crook get rid of all military or fatigue duty that he could; but the term grew to have a broader significance. **1888** Whitman *November Boughs* 407 Among the crowd were . . . three Virginia beats. **1897** *Outing* Sept. 630/2 Colonel Barfleigh is an old beat, but somehow I enjoy listening to the old fellow talk.

+**6.** *colloq.* One who fails to pay his bills.

1887 *Courier-Journal* 15 Feb. 3. Police on the lookout for professional hotel beats. **1901** J. Riis *Making of an American* 139 When the grocer on my corner complained that he was being ruined by 'beats' who did not pay their bills . . . I started in at once to make those beats pay up.

* **Beat,** *v.*

* **1.** *tr.* To pound (corn) into meal. Also with *bread* as object.

1619 *Va. House Burgesses* 10 In case they [=Indians] will of themselves come . . . to doe service, in killing of Deere, Fishing, beatting Corne, & other workes. **1633** *Plymouth Col. Rec.* I. 8 Stephen Deane, desiring to set up a water worke, to beate corne uppon the brooke. **1642** *Md. Archives* IV. 166 Richard Browne did covenant . . . to serve him . . . and to doe all labours except beating bread. **1643** Williams *Key* 65 Their women constantly beat all their corne with their hand. **1661** *Md. Council Proc.* 441 Ordered that the said Euerett be . . . comitted into the Sherriffs hands . . . and in the meane tyme the said Euerett to be kept in Chaynes and beate his owne Bread. **1709** *N.C. Col. Rec.* I. 714 Their bread [is] of Indian corn which they are forced for want of mills to beat. **1838** *S. Lit. Messenger* IV. 465/1 He was employed in beating corn into a kind of coarse meal.

+**b.** To thresh (rice). Also with *out.*

1796 J. Pettigrew *MS. Let.* 12 April (N. C. Univ.), I am in hopes you have been over, got your rice beat out, and returned before now. **1805** C. Pettigrew *MS. Let. to E. P.* 21 March (N. C. Univ.), We . . . have this morning ascertained the quantity of the rice . . . I wish now to have it beat the first bad weather for it is high time.

2. To rouse *up* and collect (recruits, companions, etc.). {1885–}

Earlier E. use is to beat up *for* volunteers {1696}, recruits {1711}, etc.

1809 Irving *Knickerb.* III. v. (1849) 171 He tarried . . . to beat up recruits for his colony. **1843** [F. L. Hawks] *D. Boone* 53 It is not wonderful that the Boones found difficulty in beating up companions. **1857** Hammond *Northern Scenes* 24 'Suppose,' said the doctor, 'we beat up Smith and Spalding, and take them along.'

3. *colloq.* **a.** To surpass or excel, in phr. *to beat all, anything, everything, the Jews, the world.* Also with complement as *blind, to death,* etc. {c1800–}

To beat the band, the Dutch: see Band *n.*[1] 3 b, Dutch *n.*

(*a*) **1843** [Stephens] *High Life N.Y.* II. 28 Now if this don't beat all, ain't I the beatermost feller for losing things? **1845** Mrs. Kirkland *Western Clearings* 49 'Why! that beats all!' exclaimed Mr. George. . . . 'Why didn't she come?' **1871** Barnum *Struggles & Triumphs* 414 'Well, I declare,' said he, 'that beats all; you are the luckiest man I ever heard of.' **1875** 'Mark Twain' *Old Times Miss.* ii. (1876) 28 Well, this beats any thing. **1883** *Harper's Mag.* Nov. 970/1 Well, ef that don't beat the Jews! **1891** Freeman *New Eng. Nun* 5 'You do beat everything,' said Dagget, trying to laugh again. **1910** McCutcheon *Rose in Ring* 259 'Well, you *do* beat the world,' he exclaimed. 'In the name of heaven, where did you come from?' **1912** Mulford & Clay *Buck Peters* i. 24 Don't it beat all how different luck will run for different people?

(*b*) **a1846** *Quarter Race Kentucky,* etc. 82 If a regular bilt frolick in the Nobs of 'Old Knox' don't beat 'em all blind for fun, then I'm no judge of fun, that's all! **1847** Field *Drama in Pokerville,* etc. 14 Each one declared that it just beat any thing 'this side of Orleens,' to death! *Ib.* 93 Its court-house . . . beats its big hotel all to smash.

+**b.** *It beats my time,* it surpasses my comprehension; it amazes, astonishes, or surprises me.

1869 'Mark Twain' *Innocents Abroad* lvii. 616 Well, you take it along—but I swear it beats my time, though. **1872** Eggleston *Hoosier Schoolm.* iv. 50 'Licked him all to smash!' said Bud . . . 'That beats my time all holler.' **1898** Page *Red Rock* 224 It clean beats my time. I don't know what's got into her.

+**c.** To get the better of (a person) by trickery; to cheat or defraud.

1873 *Newton* (Kansas) *Kansan* 1 May 2/2 Johnson . . . left with his wife . . . for the east, after having beat several creditors. **1886** *Century Mag.* Feb. 513 How do I know you ain't trying to beat me? **1888** *Chicago Inter-Ocean* 23 March (F.), Two boys . . . were each fined twenty-five dollars. . . . They have been beating boarding-houses all over the West Side. **1891** C. Roberts *Adrift America* 53 To beat one's way, or to beat the conductor or the railroad, are equivalent phrases for travelling in the cars without paying any fare. **1904** *Columbus Ev. Dispatch* 29 June 4 The . . . people who try to beat the street car conductors out of their fare.

d. To get ahead of, to arrive or act before (another).

+In recent use (1904–) common in *to beat* (one) *to it.*

1898 Canfield *Maid of Frontier* i. 21 He's watching the rangers . . . and will probably try to beat them here. **1904** *McClure's Mag.* March 556/2 'They simply beat us to it,' complained Barrett, as we rode south.

+**e.** *To beat out,* to get the better of; to defeat, surpass, excel; also, to get the start of.

1893 *Outing* May 155/2 The act of starting consisted in beating out the pistol. It was a footless sprinter then who could not steal a fifth of a second on the start. **1898** *Boston Transcript* 27 Sept. 4/5 One of the papers this morning . . . says that one of the candidates for office was last evening 'beat out.' **1902** McFaul *Ike Glidden* xxii. 190 Since I have driven him I've become satisfied that he can beat out any horse in the State. **1905** N. Davis *Northerner* 227 Jiminy! . . . This beats out all creation!

+**4.** *To beat* (one's) *way,* to travel without paying for one's transportation. *colloq.* or *slang.*

1887 M. Roberts *Western Avernus* 235, I could walk or 'beat my way' on the train. **1891** C. Roberts *Adrift America* 195 There was nothing for it but to start out and beat my way there. *Ib.* 247 He was one of those who do not use the railroad and 'beat their way.' **1895** Chambliss *Diary* 48, I did not come out on one of those railroad passes especially designed for the accommodation of senators. . . . I did not beat my way out, either. **1899** Tarkington *Gentleman from Ind.* xii. 202 Slattery . . . gave in that they beat their way on that freight [=train]. **1906** *N. Y. Ev. Post* 7 Sept. 2 He had come from the West, and had beaten his way from Syracuse to this city by 'trains and turnpike.'

* **Beat,** *ppl. a.*

+**1.** Overcome by astonishment; taken aback. *colloq.*[2]

1835 [Longstreet] *Georgia Scenes* 212 Well, the law me, I'm clear beat! **1848** Bartlett 28, 'I was quite beat,' i.e. utterly astonished. **1881** A. Hayes *New Colorado* ii. 25 When the feller . . . got the light on the [railroad] pass, . . . he was the wust beat feller you ever see.

+**2.** With *out:* Exhausted; worn out by fatigue.

1758 *Essex Inst. Coll.* XVIII. 92 This day arrived at Flatt Bush Colo. Bagley's Regiment, generally in health and high spirits, tho' some was very much beat out by their march from Northampton. **1780** Clinton in Sparks *Corr. Rev.* III. 132 The militia . . . were so beat out with fatigue, having marched at least fifty miles in less than twenty-four hours. **1833** S. Smith *Major Downing* 127 At last he got so beat out he couldn't only wrinkle his forehead and wink. **1865** Mrs. Whitney *Gayworthys* x. 93 She's clear beat out . . . and she must go to bed, herself, this minute. **1878** Beadle *Western Wilds* 39 We got to the Mormon City all beat out. **1891** Ryan *Pagan* ix. 123 'I'm beat out,' he acknowledged; 'and I ain't a going to keep up this sort of canter the whole trip.'

+**3.** *Beat biscuit,* =beaten biscuit.

1888 Hargis *Graded Cook Book* 226 Now, Miss Bene, you are always axing me how I makes beat biscuits. **1898** Page *Red Rock* 99 Mrs. Dockett's fried chicken and beat-biscuit . . . before his eyes. **1923** Watts *Luther Nichols* 306 A delicacy known all over the South as beat biscuit.

+**Beatemest, -omest,** *a. colloq.*[2] [Prob. from *beat 'em* (= them), Beat *v.* 3 a; cf. Eng. dial. *beatem* n., 'victor' {1828–}. See also Beatenest, Beatermost.] Best, finest, greatest.

1833 Neal *Down-Easters* I. 62 Famous wrastler he was too, . . . beatemest feller ever you see for some things. **1833** S. Smith *Major Downing* 123 He's got the beat'em-est tongue that I ever see. **1838** Drake *Tales & Sk.* 30 Why your the beatomest shakes, I ever seed. **1843** [Stephens] *High Life N.Y.* I. 113 Wal, . . . if this York ain't the beautumest [*sic*] place that ever I did see. **1845** *Lowell Offering* V. 82 Uncle Peter would reel off 'the beatemist yarns' (to use an expression of his own) you ever heard. **1851** Judd *Margaret* (ed. 2) III. v. 245 Take it by and large fifty head a season, and she is the beatomest [*ed.* 1845: the beater of all].

* **Beaten,** *ppl. a.* [Beat *v.* 1.]

1. Pounded.

1654 Johnson *Wonder-W. Prov.* xi. *109 They . . . were entertain'd royally, . . . boyling Puddings made of beaten corne. **1678** *New Castle Court Rec.* 362 A lb. of beaten ginger.

2. Worn hard by frequent passage. {1748–}

1685 *Duxbury Rec.* 59 We marked a red oak on the westwardly side of the road, so laying out the beaten road, or old cart way. **1878** I. L. Bird *Rocky Mts.* 158 My sailing orders were 'steer south, and keep to the best beaten track.'

+**3.** *Beaten biscuit,* a hard biscuit made of dough consisting of flour, shortening, and water, lightened by thorough beating and frequent folding. *S.*

1876 M. F. Henderson *Practical Cooking* 69 Little machines . . . for the purpose of making beaten biscuit. **1887** *Century Mag.* Nov. 16/2 A procession of little darkies [at Mount Vernon, Va.] . . . supporting plates of . . . love-puffs, beaten biscuit, laplands. **1898** E. C. Hall *Aunt Jane* 175 Sam's soda biscuits was as good as mine; and when it come to beaten biscuits, why nobody could equal Sam. **1902** G. C. Eggleston *D. South* 312 Slipping a surreptitious beaten biscuit into his pocket, [he] retreated.

+**Beatenest, Beatin'est,** later forms of BEATEMEST *a.*
1860 *Harper's Mag.* 135 A countryman . . . attracted by the white slab . . . exclaimed, 'Well, if this ain't the beatenest town I ever saw!' **1869** STOWE *Oldtown Folks* 99 Wh–a–t? . . . If there ain't the beatin'est name ever I heard. **1874** EGGLESTON *Circuit-Rider* 119, I reckon I am the beatin'est man to ax questions in this neck of timber. **1884** 'MARK TWAIN' *Huck. Finn* xiii, It's the beatenest thing I ever struck. **1898** E. C. HALL *Aunt Jane* 33 Of all the preachers that ever I heard, he certainly is the beatenest. **1908** K. D. WIGGIN *Rebecca* xix. 209 Ain't she the beatin'est creetur that ever was born int' the world!'

* **Beater.** [BEAT *v.*]

+**1.** A slave driver. *Obs.*
1644 *Md. Archives* IV. 275 P[ai]d the beater for the gang, for wages.

+**2.** A thresher.
1796 J. PETTIGREW *MS. Let.* 12 April (N. C. Univ.), It has been so warm that the rice I suppose broke very much, & it was also very laborious for the beaters.

+**3.** One who excels others. Also with plural.
1845 JUDD *Margaret* II. v. 283 Take it by and large, fifty head a season, and she is the beater of all. **1859** STOWE *Minister's Wooing* xv, Well, if you a'n't the beaters! up just as early as ever, and everything cleared away! **1869** — *Oldtown Folks* 359 She never see the beater of him for allus goin' off in his best clothes. **1882** *Century Mag.* March 766/2 All the relations from far and near was there. . . . Well, it beat the beater! **1886** *Harper's Mag.* Nov. 835/1 Well, for getting sunthin outer northing, she's a beater!

+**4.** One of the vats used in the making of indigo. Cf. *beating-vat* s.v. BEATING *vbl. n.* (quot. 1797).
1784 J. SMYTH *Tour U.S.* II. 60 They judge that the fermentation has attained its due pitch . . . ; this directs the managers to open a cock, and let off the water into another vat which is called the *beater*. **1835** [INGRAHAM] *South-West* I. 273 The liquor is at length drawn off into another vat, called the beater.

+**5.** *Beater press,* 'a press for beating bales into smaller bulk' (Knight).
1865 *Chicago Tribune* 10 April 1, A No. 1 Beater Hay Press. **1865** *Rep. Comm. Patents* I. 506 A beater press of toggle levers. **1867** *Ib.* II. 1504/1 The combination of a compressing and beater press.

+**Beateree.** *colloq.*[2] That which surpasses. — **1861** R. COOKE in *Atl. Mo.* Aug. 159/2 That was the beateree of all the weddin'-towers I ever heerd tell on. **1878** — *Happy Dodd* x. 99 Mis' Potter sent that, and it is the beateree for bread, but 'tain't rye.

+**Beatermost,** *a. colloq.*[2] =BEATEMEST. — **1843** [STEPHENS] *High Life N.Y.* II. xix. 28 Now if this don't beat all, aint I the beatermost feller for losing things? **1845** MRS. KIRKLAND *Western Clearings* 98 The Maineman . . . will declare [his cow] to be the 'beatermost critter under the canopy.'

* **Beating,** *vbl. n.* [BEAT *v.*] Used attrib. in names of implements or machines.
1790 S. DEANE *New-Eng. Farmer* 30/2 The turfs of swarded land are cut up with a kind of hoe called a beating axe. **1797** IMLAY *Western Territory* (ed. 3) 250 In this second or beating vat, as soon as the liquor [indigo] is in, it must be beat or stirred by a process similar to churning. **1846** *Rep. Comm. Patents* (1847) 251, I do not claim the use of beating-wings with roughened surfaces for cleaning wheat of smut, garlic, &c. **1874** KNIGHT 260 *Beating-engine,* an engine for cutting rags to pieces. *Ib., Beating-machine,* a machine for . . . cleaning cotton from dust or other rubbish. **1885** *Harper's Mag.* Jan. 284/1 The fine outline of a shoe depends largely on the iron lasts and corresponding forms of a 'beating-out machine.'

Beau, *n.* {1687–}

1. An attendant on a lady; a suitor or sweetheart. {?1720–*a*1845}
'This word, nearly obsolete in England, is in common use with us' (B. '59).
1732 *S. C. Gazette* 45/1 If I marry the Man of Worth . . . I shall oblige my Parents and improve my Fortune; but with my dear Beau I promise myself Happiness. **1828** WEBSTER, *Beau,* . . . in familiar language, a man who attends a lady. **1846** COOPER *Redskins* vi, Oh! lose my way? . . . It looks so, to see a young lady walking in the streets without a beau! **1854** M. J. HOLMES *Tempest & Sunshine* xviii. 251 She must look to her father for a beau that evening. **1857** — *Meadow-Brook* ix, As her brother Charlie said, . . . 'gals always run off and spit on their hair, when they saw their beaux coming.' **1884** *Harper's Mag.* Feb. 411/2 She must have been surprised to have a beau. **1891** FREEMAN *New Eng. Nun* 212 Anyhow, she didn't write quite so often, and then I heard she'd got a beau. **1904** E. D. DELAND in *Delineator* Oct. 546 Land's sakes, . . . Emmeline's got a beau!

2. Attrib. with *catcher, killer* (see quotations), *knot.*
1845 MRS. KIRKLAND *Western Clearings* 119 Our damsels might have saved themselves the trouble of curling their beau-killers, and slipping off their aprons as he approached. **1857** M. J. HOLMES *Meadow-Brook* ii, When she herself stood before the glass a whole half hour, arranging just in front of her ears two spit curls, sometimes called 'beau catchers.' **1872** EGGLESTON *End of World* vi. 52 A man can not dress well unless he has a talent for it. And I never had a genius of beau-knots.

Beau, *v.* [f. the noun.] *tr.* To act as an escort or sweetheart to (a lady). {1843–}
1856 M. J. HOLMES *L. Rivers* xii. 167 John Jr. was . . . whispering to Nellie, that 'he had no idea of beauing a medicine chest.' This he said, referring to Mabel's ill-health. **1860** HOLLAND *Miss Gilbert* xix. 350, I'm beauing her around and sort of bringing her up. **1898** WESTCOTT *D. Harum* 322 It come about that I got to beauin' her 'round quite a consid'able. **1914** ATHERTON *Perch of Devil* xvii. 106 Mark . . . beaued my sister who died, for a year or two.

Beaufet. {*a*1720–1863} A buffet.
The origin of the spelling, usual in Eng. in the 18th cent., is not clear.
1715 *Boston News-Letter* 2 May 2/2 Cabbinetts, Escrutoires, Chests-of-Drawers, Tables, Beaufetts, Writing Desks. **1832** J. F. WATSON *Hist. Tales N.Y.* 160 Another corner was occupied by a beaufet, which was a corner closet with a glass door, in which all the china of the family and the plate were intended to be displayed for ornament as well as use. **1845** *Lowell Offering* V. 147 In one corner of the room was the beaufet, which contained the most antique specimens of ware that I have ever seen. **1869** STOWE *Oldtown Folks* iv. 34 He knew . . . how many silver table-spoons and teaspoons graced the beaufet in the corner.

+**Beaut.** *colloq.*[2] [Abbrev. of *beauty* {1753–}.] Some thing or some one fine or splendid. (Often ironical.)
1866 'F. KIRKLAND' *Bk. Anecdotes* 178 Hopeful is not a beauty, and he knows it; and though some of the rustic wits call him 'Beaut,' he is well aware that they intend it for irony. **1896** G. ADE *Artie* i. 5 They was beauts too. **1903** C. L. BURNHAM *Jewel* 18 'Ain't she a beaut!' exclaimed Zeke as he led out the mare. **1911** HARRISON *Queed* vii. 87 That eye you got. She'll be a beaut to-morrow—skin's broke too.

* **Beautiful,** *a.* and *adv. colloq.* **a.** Fine, excellent; delightful.
1816 U. BROWN *Journal* I. 276 The beautifulest stone coal I ever saw is here from 8 to 12 cents pr bushel. ***a*1846** *Quarter Race Ky.,* etc. 88 It makes my mouth water now to think what a beautiful row we had.

b. Beautifully, finely, etc.
1839 *Knickerb.* XIII. 39 Though the breeze is so fresh . . . that the barky rolls and pitches *beautiful,* and so mars my penmanship. **1875** 'MARK TWAIN' *Old Times Miss.* vii. (1876) 39 Oh, it was done beautiful—beautiful.

* **BEAVER.** Also †**bever, beavor, beavour.**

* **1.** The well-known amphibious rodent, *Castor fiber.*
***c*1608** WINGFIELD in *Smith's Works* (1884) I. p. lxxvi, The President likewise bought . . . dear of the Indyans, beavers, and other flesh. **1622** 'MOURT' *Relation* 87 He promised . . . to bring . . . such beuers skins as they had to trucke with vs. ***a*1649** WINTHROP *Hist.* I. 73 The beavers had shorn down divers great trees there, and made divers dams across the brook. **1676** GLOVER *Acc. Va.* in *Phil. Trans.* XI. 626 There likewise keep in the rivers Bevers and Otters. **1709** LAWSON *Carolina* 120 Bevers are very numerous in Carolina, there being abundance of their Dams in all Parts of the Country. **1765** R. ROGERS *Acc. N. America* 164 This invites hither the greatest plenty of deer, elks, buffaloes, wild cows, bears, beavers, &c. **1789** MORSE *Amer. Geog.* 58 The largest beavers are nearly four feet in length, about fourteen or fifteen inches in breadth over the haunches, and weigh fifty or sixty pounds. **1818** SCHOOLCRAFT *Journal* 26 Two large and beautiful beavers . . . were sporting in the water. **1831** PATTIE *Personal Narr.* 24 Here we caught a beaver, the first I had ever seen. **1837** IRVING *Bonneville* I. xxi. 202 From the middle of June to the middle of September, all trapping is suspended; for the beavers are then shedding their furs, and their skins are of little value. **1883** *Amer. Naturalist* Nov. 1197 At early twilight five beavers came out from holes in the bank.

b. As a generic term, or in collective sense.
1612 SMITH *Virginia* 14 The Beaver is as bigge as an ordinary water dogge, but his legges exceeding short. ***a*1649** WINTHROP *Hist.* I. 61 A sagamore . . . offered to give them yearly eighty skins of beaver. **1672** JOSSELYN *New Eng. Rarities* 18 The Beaver, whose old ones are as big as an Otter. **1770** WASHINGTON *Diaries* I. 441 Then Bever catch it in there way up, which frequently brings them into the Month of May. **1807** GASS *Journal* 23 The hunters killed five deer and caught two beaver. **1825** NEAL *Bro. Jonathan* III. 409 The buffaloe take to the plain—and the beaver dive into the water—for they know me. **1840** HOFFMAN *Greyslaer* I. v. 60, I had gone clean up to Racket Lake, . . . hoping to get a few beaver . . . on my own account. ***c*1856** *Kit Carson's Life* 15 We trapped down the San Joaquin . . . and found but little beaver. **1878** BEADLE *Western Wilds* xii. 188 Then Clear Creek, Colorado, was lively with beaver. **1885** *Rep. Indian Affairs* 68 They also trap a few beaver.

+**2.** A beaver skin.
[**1616** SMITH *New England* 12 Of Beuers, Otters, Martins, Blacke Foxes, and Furres of price, may yearely be had 6 or 7000.] **1634** WINTHROP *Letters* (1869) II. 126 The Pekods . . . offered us a great present . . . of beavers. **1677** *New Castle Court Rec.* 53 The Plt. demands of the def[endan]t . . . the sume or quantity of fifty five Bevers or thirteen hundered and twenty Gilders. **1687** *Doc. Hist. N.Y. State* (1849) I. 164 The custom . . . upon every beaver skin commonly called a whole Beaver, nine pence. **1692** *Md. Hist. Mag.* XIII. 211 They presented him with a beaver in expectation of having some corn. **1721** *Mass. Ho. Repr. Jrnls.* III. 111 Thou didst . . . promise to remit those four men, by giving thee two hundred Beavers.

*b. Beaver skins collectively; beaver fur.

Common in the 17th century, and to some extent later, as an article of trade or standard of value.

1630 *Mass. Bay Rec.* I. 76 It was ordered that those . . . whoe bought certayne cattell . . . shall pay . . . 9l. of beauer, for the keepeing of the said cattell. **1631** T. DUDLEY in *N.H. Hist. Soc. Coll.* IV. 234 Beauer beeinge valued at 6 shilling a pound, wee made laws . . . to leaue the price of beauer at libertie. **1637** *Conn. Public Rec.* I. 12 The payment to be made either in monney, in Wampum at fower a penny, or in good and marchantable beaver. **1645** *Newhaven Col. Rec.* 170 Richard Beech acknowledged the debt & his promise to pay beaver, but professed he could not gett beaver. **1674** Alvord & Bidgood *Trans-Allegheny Region* 213 The Tomahittans sent twenty men laden with beavor to the white people. **1686** SEWALL *Letter-Book* 32 A small trus of Bever in a box weighing sixteen pounds or better. **1716** CHURCH *Philip's War* 73 Having enquired where all their best Bever was? They said, it was carried away to make a present to the Bay of Fondy Indians. **1744** A. DOBBS *Hudson's Bay* 39 He had four Packs of Beaver of 40 each. **1789** *Ann. 1st Congress* I. 167 It was agreed to lay an impost of seven and a half per cent . . . upon . . . all hats of beaver. **1819** *Niles' Reg.* XVI. 407/1 If an Indian has a good pack of beaver, the trader will not fail to get it from him upon the best terms he can. **1834** A. PIKE *Sketches* 10 Here and there an individual, by buying beaver, . . . returns home a gainer. *c*1856 *Kit Carson's Life* 19 We went to the mines, found Robert McKnight and there left our beaver with him. **1891** *Century Mag.* Nov. 60 Exchanging brass rods . . . and pain-killer for beaver.

+c. An amount equivalent in value to a beaver pelt.

1902 WHITE *Conjuror's House* iii. 26 He too reported of the trade—so many 'beaver' of tobacco, of powder, of lead, of pork.

*3. A hat made of beaver fur or of an imitation of it.

'The modern silk hat was commonly called a *beaver* until recently' (*Cent.*).

1651 *Suffolk Deeds* I. 190 Seventy pounds to be pajd in felts & castors . . . and thirty pounds to be pajd in bevors within the sajd terme. **1723** *New-Eng. Courant* 2 Dec. 1/1 That a Captain should stand in the Hold of a Vessel, . . . without Shoes on his Feet or Beaver on his Head. **1739** FRANKLIN *Poor Richard 1740* 18 William Reynolds, at the 'Hat and Feather,' . . . makes and sells all sorts of Hats, Beavers, Castors, and Felts. **1809** *Boston Gazette* 2 March (Advt.), American beavers. **1832** KENNEDY *Swallow Barn* II. i. 4 Mike brandished his blade above his beaver, and made it glitter in the sun. **1846** *Spirit of Times* (N.Y.) 6 June 170/2 My hat—my new, five dollar beaver—purchased that night, and worn for the first time, was missing! **1869** ALCOTT *Little Women* II. x. 144 Two of the young men were settling their beavers before the hall mirror. **1884** CABLE *Dr. Sevier* xxxix. 294 A small, alert fellow, in a rakish beaver and very smart coat. **1898** PAGE *Red Rock* 549 They were both dressed in long black broad-cloth coats, and the negro wore a shiny new beaver.

+4. In phrases: a. *To work like a beaver*, to work hard and steadily.

Further examples, from 1835 to 1888, are given by Thornton, p. 955.

1741 Brooks *Days of Spinning-Wheel* (1886) 31 To be sold . . . , the very best negro woman in this town, who . . . will work like a beaver. **1771** COPLEY in *Copley-Pelham Lett.* 161, I must work like a Beaver. **1838** *Knickerb.* XII. 228 A dozen of those around us had at once commenced on the solids; which of course made the rest work like beavers to finish their soup. **1866** 'F. KIRKLAND' *Bk. Anecdotes* 274 Davis saw Grant's army . . . across the valley, working like beavers on their fortifications. **1877** RAYMOND *8th Rep. Mines* 225 The new superintendent has worked like a beaver since he assumed the management. **1888** ROOSEVELT in *Century Mag.* April 861/2 The calf-wrestlers, grimy with blood, dust, and sweat, work like beavers.

b. *Busy*, or *industrious, as a beaver.*

1817 PAULDING *Lett. from South* I. 68 His competitor . . . was heavy and cunning, but as industrious as a beaver. **1879** in *Congressional Rec.* 28 April (1881) 419/1 Another member of my society was as busy as a beaver circulating statements that I had . . . lied to him.

c. *Mad as a beaver*, etc.

1809 *Mass. Spy* 5 July (Th.), He is naturally as mad as a beaver, and will scold like a termagant. **1877** BARTLETT 809 As lonely as a catamount, and as dull as a bachelor beaver.

5. In miscellaneous uses (see quotations).

1837 IRVING *Bonneville* II. i. 16 The trapper now gives up the contest of ingenuity, and shouldering his traps, marches off, admitting that he is not yet 'up to beaver.' **1848** RUXTON *Far West* ii. 86 From that moment he was 'gone beaver'; 'he felt queer,' he said, 'all over, like a buffalo shot in the lights.' *Ib.* iii. 99 'Ho, boys! hyar's a deck, and hyar's the beaver' (rattling the coin). **1850** GARRARD *Wah-To-Yah* viii. 107 'Wagh! Indians, by beaver!' hurriedly said he, changing his tone. *Ib.* ix. 116 With the skins under my arm, I bowed myself out, and 'made beaver' for Mr. Bent's lodge. *Ib.* xix. 216 Why, the old beaver [=fellow] says as how he was in hell once. **1857** *Harper's Mag.* Oct. 645/2 We are 'gone beaver,' sure—the whole of us! The Indians are inside the fort!

6. Attrib. (esp. in sense 2 b) with *cloak, cloth, flesh, fustian, overcoat, strip*, etc.

1634 WOOD *New Eng. Prospect* II. xix. 96 If a husband [sc. an Indian] have a minde to sell his wives Beaver petticote, as sometimes he doth. **1790** *Penna. Packet* 24 April 1/4 William and John Sitgreaves . . . have just received for Sale . . . Manchester Goods, consisting of . . . pillow and beaver fustians. **1809** A. HENRY *Travels* 56 Two families . . . occasionally brought bever-flesh for sale. **1850** GARRARD *Wah-To-Yah* vi. 88 The pipe was lavishly decorated with beaver strips, beads, and porcupine quills. **1856** *Spirit of Times* (N.Y.) 25 Oct. 135/1 Just received from Paris a large assortment of Beaver Silk Hats. **1856** *Spirit of Times* (N.Y.) 29 Nov. 207/1 The 'Coronation Cloak' . . .is made of black beaver cloth. **1875** *Chicago Tribune* 7 Dec. 5/7 A full line of Fur Beaver and Chinchilla Cloaks, very cheap. **1886** BRET HARTE *Snowbound* 153 Falkner had exchanged his . . . picturesque *serape* for a beaver overcoat.

+**Beaver blanket.** A blanket or rug of beaver skins. — **1752** W. TRENT *Journal* 96 The Twightwees made the following speech, with a beaver blanket, with a green painted spot in the middle. **1778** CARVER *Travels* 24 He prayed '. . . that I might lie down, by night, on a beaver blanket.'

+**Beaver canal.** A canal resulting from the constructions of beavers. — **1868** *Amer. Naturalist* May 157 Is there not some evidence of a progress in knowledge to be found in the beaver-canal and the beaver-slide? **1889** *Harper's Mag.* Jan. 234/2 It is not so easy to determine what is and what is not a beaver canal.

+**Beaver coat.** A coat made from beaver skins.

1634 WOOD *New Eng. Prospect* II. ii. 60 Some of our English . . . to uncloathe them [*sc.* Indians] of their beaver coates, clad them with the infection of swearing and drinking, which was never in fashion with them before. **1637** MORTON *New Canaan* III. xix, This man . . . espied a Salvage come in with a good Beaver coate. *Ib.*, Hee made a shifte to get that Beaver coate, which their mouthes watered at. **1748** WEISER *Journal* 36 The Delawares made a Speech to me & presented a Beaver Coat & a String of Wampum.

+**Beaver coating.** A material imitative of beaver fur. — **1759** *Newport Mercury* 5 June 4/1 To be Sold, . . . Bearskins, Beaver Coating, knap'd Ditto. **1762** H. M. Brooks *Gleanings* 37 German Serges, Bearskins, Beaver Coating. **1784** *Mass. Centinel* (Extra.) 12 May 2/3 To the Hatters of Town and Country. An opportunity now offers of their supplying themselves with Beaver Coating, by applying immediately to Samuel Wallace.

+**Beaver country.** Country rich in, or suitable for trapping, beaver. — **1761** NILES *Indian Wars* II. 541 [The fort] stands in the midst of the extensive territories of the Six Nations, and commands their beaver country entirely. **1837** IRVING *Bonneville* I. viii. 96 The upper part of the Salmon River was represented as far more eligible, beside being in an excellent beaver country.

+**Beaver cutting.** The gnawing of small trees by beavers; *pl.* the trees, branches, etc., so cut. — **1845** FREMONT *Exped.* 220 There were no beaver cuttings on the river. **1846** SAGE *Scenes Rocky Mts.* iv, Near our night-camp I noticed fresh beaver 'cuttings,' some of which consisted of trees, six inches in diameter, levelled by these sagacious animals. **1889** *Harper's Mag.* Jan. 234/2 Not unless severed roots and other marks of beaver-cutting are found is this conclusive.

+**Beaver-dam.** A dam made by beavers.

1660 *Essex Probate Rec.* I. 314 A farme at Bever Damme neere Readinge. **1664** *Plymouth Rec.* 75 A small brooke . . . called the beaver dam brooke. **1675** *Providence Rec.* IV. 33 On the north side of the Ridge of ground or banke called the beauer Damm. **1703** *Virginia State P.* I. 83 West . . . to three white oakes, by the East side of the Tuckahoe Bever Dam. **1746** *N. H. Probate Rec.* II. 615 Bounding on a swampy meadow to a pich pine tree . . . standing near a beaver dam. **1778** CARVER *Travels* 105 Having stopped up several old beaver dams which had been broken down by the hunters, I was enabled to proceed for some miles. **1797** B. HAWKINS *Letters* 87 We . . . take a small path to the left to facilitate the crossing of the beaver dam. **1805** LEWIS in *L. & Clark Exped.* (1904) II. 245 He saw a number of beaver dams succeeding each other in close order and extending . . . far up those streams. **1839** LEONARD *Adventures* (1904) 70 They had meandered the creek till they came to beaver dams. **1868** *Amer. Naturalist* II. 534 Near the source of the Little Blackfoot river were many ponds formed by beaver-dams. **1878** BEADLE *Western Wilds* 188 It was the good old time . . . when beaver dams adorned every stream in the mountains. **1903** WHITE *Forest* xvi. 231 He knows the beaver-dams, how many animals each harbors.

+**Beaver den.** A den or resort of beavers. — **1804** CLARK in *Lewis & C. Exped.* (1904) I. 104 [We] camped on the L. S. above a Beaver Den.

+**Beaver-eater.** *Obs.* The wolverine, *Gulo luscus.*

1771 PENNANT *Synopsis* 197 Wolverene . . . in America is called the Beaver-Eater; watching those animals as they come out of their houses, . . . [it] devours them. **1791** LONG *Voyages* 41 The country every where abounds with wild animals, particularly bears, . . . beaver, beaver eaters, lynx, [etc.]. **1796** MORSE *Univ. Geog.* I. 196 The Wolverene, called . . . by hunters the Beaver eater. **1804–5** CLARK in *Lewis & C. Exped.* (1904) VI. i. 107 Carkajous, wolverine or beaver eaters . . . or links.

+**Beaveret.** *Obs.* Also **-ett, -it. a.** A material like beaver fur, used for making hats. Usu. attrib. with *hat.* **b.** A hat made of this.

1718 *Md. Hist. Mag.* XVIII. 202 One new Beaveret, cost prime 1 £ Ster[ling]. **1722** *N.J. Archives* XI. 67 Run away, . . . a Negro Man. . . . He wears . . . Sheep-russet Stocking, new Shoes and an old Beveret Hat. **1731** *New Eng. W. Journal* 18 Oct. 2/2 Several sorts of English goods, as, Beverits, Castor Hats. **1761** *Essex Inst. Coll.* XLVIII. 95 The assortments are as follows, viz.: . . . mens and boys fine castor & beaverit hats. **1770** *Mass. Gazette* 15 Jan. 4/2 Castor & Beverett Hatts. **1820** *Boston Daily Advertiser* 19 May 2/6 (Advt.), Beaveretts.

+**Beaver field-mouse.** (See quotation.) — **1842** *Nat. Hist. N.Y., Zoology* I. 86–88 The Beaver Field-mouse, *Arvicola hirsutus*. . . . The popular name of Beaver rat or Beaver mouse, is derived from the abundance and fineness of its fur.

+**Beaver fur.** =BEAVER SKIN. {1855} — **1747** NEAL *Hist. New-Eng.* (ed. 2) I. 104 The Natives treated them with great Humanity, and traded with them for a considerable Quantity of Bever-Furs. **1805** *Austin Papers* (1924) I. 140, 33 lb. Beaver furs, $33. **1822** J. FOWLER *Journal* 166 Last night's rain wett all our bagage as well as the bever furr.

* **Beaver hat.** A hat made of beaver; =BEAVER 3.

1639 *Md. Archives* IV. 78 An old beaver hatt & stuff coate. **1678** *New Castle Court Rec.* 267 One gray bever hatt. **1688** *N.H. Probate Rec.* I. 325, I give . . . to Robert Fulton . . . my best Bever hat. **1715** *Boston News-Letter* 9 May 2/2 [He] had on . . . an old beaver hat, and a course linen shirt. **1740** in *Mass. H. S. Proc.* V. 111 They are chiefly employed in making up beaver-hats, which are sold cheaper here than in England. **1769** J. ROWE *Diary* 185, I laid a Wager of a Beaver Hat with Sam Swift. **1775** BURNABY *Travels* 137 [In Boston] they fabricate beaver-hats, which they sell for a moidore a piece. **1806** FESSENDEN *Democracy Unveiled* I. 163 'I'll bet a beaver hat' he's right. **1824** MARSHALL *Kentucky* I. 124 The price of a beaver hat was five hundred dollars. **1835** [H. C. TODD] *Notes* 59 The best beaver hats, and in large quantities, are made at Reading, Massachusetts. **1857** *Quinland* I. 103 Last of all appeared the white beaver-hat, with a very narrow brim, with a very high bell crown, and surmounted with a white feather, tipped with red. **1858** VIELÉ *Following Drum* 55 A beaver hat, with a broad gold band and cockade, complete their stylish outfit. **1868** G. G. CHANNING *Recoll. Newport* 151 The beaver-hats in my day were very costly. **1891** 'THANET' *Otto the Knight*, etc. 90 He had pushed his shining black beaver hat obliquely backward over his ears.

+**Beaver house.** =BEAVER LODGE. — **1765** R. ROGERS *Acc. N. America* 258 Sometimes the Indians open the ice near the beaver-houses. **1809** A. HENRY *Travels* 29 In passing one of them, we saw many beaver-houses and dams.

+**Beaver hunt.** A hunting expedition after beaver. — **1848** PARKMAN in *Knickerb.* XXXI. 194 He and three or four of his companions were out on a beaver hunt.

+**Beaver hunter.**

1. One who hunts for beaver.

1687 *N.Y. State Doc. Hist.* (1849) I. 258 The French King . . . has built a Fort . . . where all our Traders & Beaver Hunters must pass. **1805** LEWIS in *Ann. 9th Congress*, 2 Sess. 1071 Algonquins . . . are not esteemed good beaver hunters. **1837** IRVING *Bonneville* I. vi. 77 Wyeth . . . and his New-England band of beaver hunters and salmon fishers. **1841** COOPER *Deerslayer* v, Why may not a beaver-hunter be as respectable as a governor? **1847** RUXTON *Adv. Rocky Mts.* (1848) 234 The beaver-hunter has set his traps in every creek and stream.

2. *pl.* The name of an Indian tribe.

1845 DE SMET *Oregon Missions* (1847) 164 Within the limits . . . are found the Black-Feet, Crees, . . . Beaver Hunters, Flat-side Dogs, Slaves, and Deer-Skins.

+**Beaver hunting.** The hunting of beavers. Also attrib. — **1722** D. COXE *Carolina* 46 On this River and the Branches thereof, is one of the greatest Beavour Huntings in America. **1726** *Doc. Hist. N.Y. State* (1849) I. 773 The Sachems of the Five Nations did . . . render up all their Land where the Beaver hunting is. **1774** *Ib.* 742 The Five Nations . . . Beaver hunting country being bounded to the West by that Lake [=Lake Huron].

+**Beavering,** *vbl. n.* The hunting of beavers. — **1841** COOPER *Deerslayer* ii, The old man and I out-knowledge the beaver. . . . I do a little beavering myself, as occasion offers.

+**Beaver lands.** (See quotation.) — **1873** BEADLE *Undevel. West* 764 In the lower portions of the valley the road traverses what are called 'Beaver Lands,' said to be the choicest of all the lands in Oregon.

+**Beaver lodge.** A habitation of beavers.

1805 ORDWAY in *Journals* 257 [We] saw abundance of beaver lodges. **1809** A. HENRY *Travels* 256 Beaver lodges were numerous. **1826** COOPER *Mohicans* xxxii, A bullet came whizzing from among some beaver lodges . . . situated in the clearing. **1837** IRVING *Bonneville* I. xvii. 174 The Indian hunters of his party were in the habit of exploring all the streams along which they passed, in search of 'beaver lodges.' **1846** SAGE *Scenes Rocky Mts.* xxviii, Beaver lodges are commonly constructed in holes carefully excavated in the banks of streams, in such a manner that the entrances are entirely covered by water.

+**Beaver maker.** [BEAVER *n.* .] A maker of beaver hats. — **1652** *Suffolk Deeds* I. 235 Theodore Atkinson of Boston, . . . beauer maker. [Elsewhere called 'hatter' and 'feltmaker.']

+**Beaver meadow.** (See quot. 1809.)

1644 *New Haven Col. Rec.* I. 126 A proposition . . . thatt they may have the Bever meadowes granted to them. **1656** *New Haven Rec.* 279 A peece of land lying betwixt the great pond and the beauour meddow. **1690** *Waterbury Prop. Rec.* 221 That lot lying in beaver meadow. **1809** KENDALL *Travels* III. 176 The dams being in the end abandoned by the beaver, and broken through by the water, large tracts of meadow-land are formed, which, from their origin, are described as beaver-meadows. **1853** *Harper's Mag.* VI. 442 Smooth patches of beaver meadow, lying snugly among the forests. **1876** *Fur, Fin, & Feather* Sept. 141 While walking through an old beaver meadow . . . he saw . . . that some large body was approaching him.

+**Beaver medicine.** Bait used in the trapping of beaver. — **1877** J. S. CAMPION *On Frontier* 157 The 'beaver medicine,' for so the bait is called, requires extraordinary care in its preparation.

+**Beaver mouse.** The beaver field-mouse (q.v.).

+**Beaver path.** [BEAVER I.] A path made and used by beaver. — **1889** *Harper's Mag.* Jan. 238/2 The jaws of the trap are so placed that their length coincides with the direction of the beaver path.

+**Beaver pay.** *Obs.* [BEAVER *n.* 2 b.] Payment in beaver or at the value of it. (Cf. BEAVER PRICE.) — **1662** *Jamaica* (L.I.) *Rec.* I. 14 [They] are to pay twentie three pounds in bever pay that is to say wheat at sixe shillings & indian corn at three shillings sixe pence the bushell. **1685** *N.J. Archives* I Ser. I. 504 The disbursemen off four pounds a peice in bever pay.

+**Beaver-plew.** [See PLEW.] =BEAVER SKIN. — **1850** GARRARD *Wah-To-Yah* xix. 220 The rocks on the sides was pecked as smooth as a beaverplew rubbed with the grain.

+**Beaver-poison.** The water-hemlock, *Cicuta maculata*. — **1857** GRAY *Botany* 157 Spotted cowbane. Musquash-root. Beaver-poison. . . . The root is a deadly poison.

+**Beaver pond.** Also †**pound.** The pond made by a beaver dam.

1640 *New Haven Col. Rec.* I. 27 The cow pasture shall begin on the hither side of the Beever ponds. **1656** *Jamaica* (L.I.) *Rec.* I. 170 The new Plantation neare unto the Bever pond. **1659** *New Haven Rec.* 381 A peice of land betwixt the hill & the Beavour pound. **1700** *Waterbury Prop. Rec.* 211 Teen acers of land joyning to his eyght acer lot at the bever ponds. **1748** ELIOT *Field-Husb.* i. 8, I think there is reason to believe that the shaking Meadows have been formerly Bever Ponds. **1765** CROGHAN *Journal* 18 Our course was through a thick woody country, crossing a great many swamps, morasses, and beaver ponds. **1800** HAWKINS *Sk. Creek Country* 21 In the old beaver ponds, in thick boggy places, they have the bog potatoe. **1851** CIST *Cincinnati* 29 The encampment of twenty-six men, by the side of a beaver pond, has grown into a city. **1899** CUSHMAN *Hist. Indians* 192 The beaver-pond was left in undisputed possession of the Choctaws.

+**Beaver price.** (See quotation and cf. BEAVER PAY.) — **1662** *Hempstead Town Rec.* I. 127, I William Smith do prise the halfe of the mill at ffourty pounds sterling, to be paid in beaver or cattell at beaver prise.

+**Beaver rat.** The beaver field-mouse (q.v.).

+**Beaver robe. a.** A robe of beaver skin. **b.** (See quot. 1918.)

1791 J. LONG *Voyages* 136 The father covers them with a beaver robe. **1806–8** PIKE *Sources Miss.* 98 The *Aile Rouge* had a beaver robe and pipe prepared to present. **1818** EASTBURN *Yamoyden* (1834) I. 189 On the beaver robe outspread Our remnant rest beneath its shade. **1918** Connelley *Hist. Kansas* I. 290 Of [buffalo] hides, one of the rarest was the 'Beaver-robe', a soft fur resembling the animal it was named for.

+**Beaver-root.** The yellow pond-lily, *Nuphar advena*. — **1832** WILLIAMSON *Maine* I. 126 Of the Lily tribe, we have several species . . . such as the yellow water-lily, or dog-lily, or beaver-root.

+**Beaver-shot.** Shot used for killing beaver. — **1725** *New-Eng. Courant* 17–24 May 1/2 He . . . slightly wounded Capt. Lovewell and one of his Men with Beaver Shot.

+**Beaver sign.** Tracks, gnawed trees, etc., indicating the presence of beavers.

1822 J. FOWLER *Journal* 126 The ice begins to thaw and all [are] makeing for the bever sign. **a1848** RUXTON *Far West* (1849) 28 Thar plans is plain to this child as beaver sign. **1890** D'OYLE *Notches* 66, I . . . had taken good stock of the beaver 'sign' and such things. **1900** DRANNAN *Plains & Mts.* 49 From Arkansas river . . . carefully examining every stream we came to for beaver sign.

+**Beaver skin.** A (or the) skin of a beaver.

(1) [1605 J. ROSIER *True Relation* (1887) 110 Their clothing is Beavers skins, or Deares skins, cast over them like a mantle.] **1616** SMITH *New England* (1865) 20 Wee got for trifles neer 1100 Beuer skinnes. **1620** — *New Eng. Trials* Wks. 1884 I. 243 From Cannada and New England hath come neare twenty thousand Beuer Skinnes, within these fiue yeares. **a1649** WINTHROP *Hist.* I. 60 John Sagamore . . . came to the governour to desire his letter for recovery of twenty beaver skins. **1666** *Md. Archives* II. 18 An act prohibiting the exportation of all sorts of hydes & skins . . . except Beaver skins and Otter skins. **1692** *Md. Hist. Mag.* XIII. 208 The Indians had hired a guide for one good beaver skin. **1726** PENHALLOW *Indian Wars* (1824) 89 [They] returned him a belt of wampum, with some beaver skins. **1766** ROGERS *Ponteach* I. i, What is your Price for Beaver Skins per Pound? **1837** IRVING *Bonneville* I. xix. 198 His men were continually stealing away thither, with whatever beaver skins they could secrete or lay their hands on. **1847** RUXTON *Adv. Rocky Mts.* (1848) 216 The depreciation in the value of beaver-skins has thrown the great body of trappers out of employment. **1861** WINTHROP *Open Air* 25, I had three years before floated down the magnificent Columbia to Vancouver, bedded on bales of beaver-skins.

(2) **1785** Ramsey *Tennessee* (1853) 297 It shall . . . be lawful for the aforesaid land tax . . . to be paid in the following manner: . . . good, clean beaver skin, six shillings. **1836** IRVING *Astoria* II. xxxviii. 264 They could meet with no game, and subsisted for a time on strips of beaver skin.

+**Beaver slide.** A sloping passage constructed by beaver. — **1868** [see BEAVER CANAL].

+**Beaver stream.** A stream frequented by beaver.

1837 Irving *Bonneville* I. xxi. 210 [The exploration] would be attended with great profit, from the numerous beaver streams with which the [Great Salt] lake must be fringed. **1850** Garrard *Wah-To-Yah* x. 130 The hardy frequenters of the Rocky Mountain hunting grounds and beaver streams. **1916** Thoburn *Hist. Oklahoma* II. 27 They ascended the courses of the rivers and of the tributary beaver streams.

+**Beaver tail.** Also **beaver's tail.** The tail of a beaver, sometimes used as an article of diet.

1805–9 Henry *Camp. Quebec* 23 They returned two fresh beaver tails, which when boiled, renewed ideas, imbibed with the May butter of our own country. **1817** Paulding *Lett. from South* I. 196, I neither like terrapins, tripe, beavers' tails, . . . nor any other o {the great dishes. **1827** Cooper *Prairie* vii, Beavers' tails and minks' flesh may do to talk about before a maple fire and a quiet hearth. **1850** Garrard *Wah-To-Yah* xiii. 167 When his arm wasn't no bigger 'an a beaver tail.

+**Beaver trade.** *Obs.* **a.** Beaver as an article of trade. **b.** Trade in beaver skins.

1632 *Mass. H. S. Coll.* 2 Ser. VIII. 231 Received for beaver trade at 12*d* per lb of Mr. Turner of Sagus . . . £1. 6. 6. **1645** Winslow in *Winthrop P.* 178 The determinacon of our Court concerning the beaver trade. **1671** Alvord & Bidgood *Trans-Allegheny Region* 195 The French . . . will in a short time be absolutely Masters of the Beaver trade, the greatest number of Beavers being caught there. **1687** *Doc. Hist. N.Y. State* (1849) I. 173 Finding such contest between the Government of Canada & this about the Beaver trade.

+**Beaver-trading,** *vbl. n.* Trading for beaver skins. — **1687** *Doc. Hist. N.Y. State* (1849) I. 259 Major McGregory . . . went with 60 of the young men of Albany, and some of the Albany Indians a Beaver trading.

+**Beaver trap.** A trap used in catching beavers.

1709 Lawson *Carolina* 48 The old King . . . went to look after his Bever-Traps, there being abundance of those amphibious Animals in this River. **1790** Washington *Diaries* IV. 141 At another place some Bever traps and skins were taken at an Indian camp. **1821** J. Fowler *Journal* 9 We this morning berryed or cashed [*sic*], as the French call it, 32 bever traps. **1848** Parkman in *Knickerb.* XXXI. 328 A buffalo-robe was rolled up behind them, and a bundle of beaver traps slung at the pommel. **1859** G. A. Jackson *Diary* 523 His mouth is as tight as a No. 4 beaver trap. **1871** *Rep. Indian Affairs* (1872) 418 The amount expended for beaver-traps, if used for the purchase of sheet-iron kettles, would be of much more service to the Indians.

+**Beaver-trapper.** One engaged in trapping beaver. — **1819** Schoolcraft *Journal* 63 It is by a skilful preparation of [sweet-scented herbs and spicy barks] . . . that beaver-trappers are enabled to take such quantities of them. **1856** J. B. Jones *Western Scenes* 70 An old beaver trapper and deer hunter took it into his head that [etc.].

+**Beaver-trapping.** The trapping of beavers. — **1823** E. James *Exped.* I. 162 He remained . . . a considerable time after his nation had departed down the river to their beaver trapping. **1850** Garrard *Wah-To-Yah* xx. 247 Kit Carson, . . . whose prowess in scalptaking and beaver-trapping is the theme of many campfires.

+**Beaver tree.** The bay tree, *Magnolia glauca.*

1753 Kalm *N. Amerika* II. 324 *Magnolia*, . . . Beaver-Tree. **1801** *Hist. Review & Directory* I. 238 The Beaver Tree grows in the Swamps, and Flora's court is scarce decorated with a fairer or sweeter flower. **1850** *New Eng. Farmer* II. 109 The doctor informed his friend that he had seen it at the south, and it was there called the Beaver-Tree. **1897** Sudworth *Arborescent Flora* 195 Sweet Magnolia. . . . Common names [include] . . . Beaver Tree (Del., S.C., Miss.). **1901** Mohr *Plant Life Ala.* 505 White Bay. Sweet Bay. Beaver Tree. . . . The bark is used medicinally.

+**Beaver wood.**

1. The beaver tree; the wood of this tree.

1810 Michaux *Arbres* I. 33 Small magnolia . . . ou Beaver wood, nom tombé en désuétude, autrefois dans le New Jersey. **1832** Browne *Sylva Amer.* 209 In Philadelphia and New York and in their vicinity, this tree is called Magnolia, which denomination has entirely superseded those of Swamp sassafras and Beaver wood. **1859** Bartlett 27 Beaver-tree . . . [is] called also Beaver-wood, and sometimes Castor-wood, probably from the preference shown by the beavers for the bark as food, or for the wood as useful in their structures.

2. The hackberry.

1813 Muhlenberg *Cat. Plants* 95 Beaver wood [or] hoop ash. **1843** Torrey *Flora N.Y.* II. 167 Sugar-berry. Beaver-wood. . . . Woods, particularly in rocky situations on the banks of rivers. **1894** *Amer. Folk-Lore* VII. 98 *Celtis occidentalis*, . . . hoop-ash, beaver-wood, N.Y.

+**Beaver works.** (See quotation.) — **1889** *Harper's Mag.* Jan. 230/1 These burrows, of which there are several in every 'beaver-works,' as the trappers call the range of land and water occupied by a colony of beavers, open into the water.

+**Beccasse.** [F. *bécasse* woodcock; *bécassine* snipe.] (See quotation.) — **1841** *S. Lit. Messenger* VII. 77/1, Innumerable species of the snipe are . . . met with, from the little Bobtail of the sandbar, up to the Beccasse of the plain.

+**Beckhorn, Beckorne.** =Beak-horn, Bickern. — **1661** *Jamaica* (L.I.) *Rec.* I. 102 The Smiths goods prized by these men . . . [include] a beck horn, o 05 00. **1669** *York Deeds* II. 69 The Smyths shopp with bellows, anvell, beckorne, vice, sledg hammer & some ould irons.

***Bed,** *n.*

1. In earlier use sometimes written *beed* or *bead*, indicating a long vowel as occas. in older Scottish. *Obs.*

1657 *East-Hampton Rec.* I. 116 One beed & boulster. **1661** *Southampton Rec.* II. 24 An envoice . . . [including] hangings for bead, cubbard, beadsteads. **1667** *N.H. Probate Rec.* I. 705 A roufe that belongeth to the same beed. **1685** *Conn. Probate Rec.* I. 377, I will and bequeath to my Cousen Samuel Hubart the beed and furnitur to it. **1744** *N.H. Probate Rec.* III. 203, I give to my beloved Wife . . . one Bead, viz.: that on which we generally lodg, & the Bead Cloths & furniture belonging to it. **1821** J. Fowler 7 A crick . . . , with an extensive beed of stone coal in its bottom. **1822** *Ib.* 75, I . . . drew one of the men from his beed by the top of his head.

+**2.** The body or box of a wagon, or the lower part of one.

1835 Carruthers *Cavaliers of Va.* I. 79 They found several ox-carts standing in the street, in the beds of which were stretched the dead bodies of eight Indians. **1856** P. Cartwright *Autobiog.* xxiv. 358 The great mass . . . wanted a preacher that could . . . stand in the bed of a wagon. **1870** Nowland *Indianapolis* 12 The only possible way of getting over was to unload the wagon and take it to pieces . . . ; then the large body or bed was floated over. **1888** C. D. Ferguson *Exp. Forty-niner* iii. 40 We camped there on the north bank that night, sending over our wagons with boxes and beds all made water-tight. **1904** W. H. Smith *Promoters* xviii. 270 Some of these beds will hold more than a hundred bushels.

+**3.** A kind of knot.

1913 Barnes *Western Grazing Grounds* 368 There are an endless number of hitches used by western men, as the squaw, the stirrup, the bed and the basco; all are good and for their purposes quite as satisfactory in every way as the diamond.

***Bed,** *v.* [f. Bed *n.*]

+**1.** *Forestry.* To furnish (a tree) with a 'bed' to fall on when felled.

1792 Belknap *Hist. N.H.* III. 103 When a mast tree is to be felled, . . . the workmen have a contrivance which they call *bedding* the tree; . . . they cut down a number of smaller trees . . . and place them so that the falling tree may lodge on their branches. **1905** *Forestry Bureau Bull. 61* B s.v., To bed a tree.

+**2.** To plow (ground, esp. for cotton) in beds or broad ridges. Also with *up.*

1830 W. Edwards *MS. Diary* 13 April (N.C.H.C.), Bedding low grounds. **1847** Commons, etc. *Doc. Hist.* I. 195 March: 1, 2, 3, bedding cotton ground. **1847** *Florida Plantation Rec.* 231, 18 plows beding cotton land. **1852** *Ib.* 62 The little peace of new ground . . . which I will plant in cotton as soon as I get it broke and bedded up. **1856** *Ib.* 448, 6 hand beding up for corn. **1858** *Texas Almanac 1859* 81 The ploughs . . . should be started to bed up the ground. **1884** 'Craddock' *Where Battle was Fought* 8 A ploughman going out to bed up land for cotton.

+**3.** (With *down.*) To make a bed for (a horse, cattle, etc.); to furnish with a bed or bedding. Also absol.

1865 Trowbridge in *Atl. Mo.* Sept. 267/2 Accordingly, after bedding down the horse and fastening the barn, he returned to the kitchen. **1898** Canfield *Maid of Frontier* 97 When I . . . rode up the lane, I always found her . . . waitin' to give me a kiss afore I bedded down for the night.

+**4.** (Usually with *down.*) In cattle-raising on the plains, to collect (cattle) and guard them until they lie down to sleep.

1888 Roosevelt in *Century Mag.* April 862/2 The first guards have to bed the cattle down; . . . it simply consists in hemming them into as small a space as possible, and then riding round them until they lie down and fall asleep. *Ib.* 864/1 We got them bedded down without difficulty. **1903** A. Adams *Log of Cowboy* ii. 18 Flood and all the herd men turned out to bed down the cattle for our first night. **1920** Hunter *Trail Drivers of Texas* I. 62, I picked the wrong place to bed the herd.

+**b.** *intr.* Of cattle: To lie *down* for the night.

1903 A. Adams *Log of Cowboy* viii. 110 Not a hoof would bed down. **1920** Mulford *J. Nelson* xxiii. 256 The beef cut . . . was headed for a rise, where in due time it bedded down and prepared to spend a quiet peaceful night.

+**5.** (See quotations.) Also with *down.*

1881 E. Ingersoll *Oyster Industry* 241 *Bedding*, transplanting oysters of any size to beds prepared for them, from which they are to be removed before the frosts of the ensuing winter. *Ib.*, Bedding-down [oysters].

Bed-blanket. A blanket for use on a bed. {1701}

1770 *Carroll P.* in *Md. Hist. Mag.* XIII. 68, 6 pair of the best Bed Blankets. **1850** Judd *R. Edney* ii. 28 She went half a mile, with a bed-blanket, before tea. **1857** *Quinland* I. 28 The women . . . 'bundled' themselves up in shawls and bed-blankets.

Bed-board. *Obs.* The front board of a bedstead. — **1684** Mather *Providences* v. (1856) 104 When the man was a bed, he was . . . pinched and scratched, and his bed-board was taken away from him. *Ib.* 106 He was attended with the same iterated loss of his clothes, shaking off his bed-board [etc.].

***Bed bolster.** The bolster of a bed. — **1733** *N.H. Probate Rec.* II. 496 One Bed Boulster, two Pillows. **1758** in *Mayflower Descendants* X. 87 My next best bed bolster & one Coverlid.

Bed-bug.

1. An insect (*Cimex lectularius*) that infests houses and beds. {1813–}

Chiefly U.S., since in English *bug* is now restricted to this sense.

1808 R. B. THOMAS *Farmer's Almanac 1809* July, Ladies, for mercy's sake, see about the bed bugs. **1812** ASBURY *Journal* III. 393, I could have wished to sleep without annoyance from fleas or bed-bugs. **1837** *Knickerb.* X. 30, I felt as one who, in the midst of a delightful dream, is assailed by a bed-bug. **1867** *Amer. Naturalist* Aug. 284 They are accused of harboring about their bodies quantities of those nocturnal pests, the bed-bugs. **1877** BARTLETT 803 The interviewer ... will hunt you sharper, and worry you worse, than a canal-boat bed-bug. **a1918** G. STUART *On Frontier* I. 50 The confounded bed bugs ran us out of the beds in the house, and we all slept out in the yard.

attrib. **1863** BOUDRYE *Fifth N.Y. Cavalry* 348 With wise discrimination he can trace The difference 'twixt the louse and bedbug race. **1884** NYE *Baled Hay* 58 It seems the house ... has a lot of bedbug tonic.

+2. In phrases, as *crazy as a bed-bug*, etc.

1832 S. SMITH *Major Downing* 104 Nabby run about from house to house like a crazy bed-bug. **1833** *Ib.* 139 Van Buren has cleared out and gone back ... to New York ... with a bed bug in his ear. **1859** BARTLETT 524 As crazy as a bedbug. **1904** *Buffalo Commercial* 2 Aug. 6 On the subject of the relations of organized capital and organized labor it [the N.Y. *Sun*] is as crazy as a bed-bug.

+Bed bunt. *Obs.* [LG. *bunt*, Du. *bont*, printed material (now usually of cotton). The comb. *beddebont* occurs in Frisian.] A colored linen or cotton stuff used for bed-covers. — **1761** *Newport* (R.I.) *Mercury* 3 Nov. 4/2 To be sold by Naphtael Hart, jun., ... Flanders Bedtick, Bed Bunt, ... superfine and middling Camblets. **1770** *Md. Hist. Mag.* III. 146 We will not hereafter ... import ... Cotton and Linen Stuff, Bed-Bunts, and Bed-Tickin of all sorts. **1787** *Maryland Gazette* 1 June 3/3 Callicoes and Printed Linens; Bed-ticking and Bed Bunts; ... Bar-Iron and Steel; Iron Castings.

+Bed cap. ?A night-cap. — **1820** *Missouri Intell.* 18 April 4/1 A general Assortment of Merchandise, ... Bed Caps, ... Buttons, coat, pantaloon & Vest.

***Bed-case.** A bed-tick.

1640 *Conn. Public Rec.* I. 449, An Inventory of the goods ... of James Olmestead ... [includes] 6 blanketts, ... a course bedcase. **1661** *Southampton Rec.* II. 9, I give my wife Alce at her request a bed case made of hemp with boulster. **1664** *Essex Probate Rec.* I. 453, 1 Cotten Rugge & a Canvas bedcase. **1806** WEBSTER, *Ticking*, a strong cloth for bed cases.

***Bed-chamber.** A bedroom or sleeping room. {*arch.* in 19th c.}

1683 *N.H. Hist. Soc. Coll.* VIII. 160 [They] went into another room: viz., the bed chamber, to see if they could agree. **1696** SEWALL *Diary* I. 442 This day I remove poor little Sarah into my Bed-Chamber. **1709** *Ib.* II. 258, I slipt on my Cloaths ... and run ... below Stairs, and still found all well but my own Bed-chamber. **1747** *N.J. Archives* 1 Ser. VII. 59 From my bed chamber I have a prospect for 10 miles up and down the river. **1809** F. CUMING *Western Tour* 110 The other four rooms ... are intended ... for bed chambers. **1841** H. PLAYFAIR *Papers* I. 9 And then last of all, and very late, to the bed-chamber, as the courtly Yankees term a bed-room. **1841** A. BACHE *Fire-Screen* 67 The parlour in which I was placed, with a handsome bed-chamber adjoining, were more expensively fitted up than the rest of the house. **1864** T. L. NICHOLS *Amer. Life* I. 245, I was shown to a large and thoroughly-furnished state room, as comfortable as any bed-chamber need be.

+Bed-clothing. Bedclothes. — **1852** STOWE *Uncle Tom* xxxii, A tattered blanket ... formed his only bed-clothing. **1863** 'E. KIRKE' *Southern Friends* i. 19 Turning down the bed-clothing, she showed him sleeping quietly by her side. **1876** HABBERTON *Jericho Road* 16 The Parson ... awoke, and accused Slim of appropriating his bed-clothing.

Bed-cord. A stout cord or rope passing from side to side of a bed-frame to support the mattress. {a1625–1720}

1645 *Essex Inst. Coll.* L. 327 Delivered to Deborah ... 1 bed cord, 1s. 8d. **1656** *Essex Probate Rec.* I. 242, 2 bedsteeds with bedcords. **1726** *Boston News-Letter* 8–15 Dec. 2/2 Bedcords, ... lately imported from London, to be sold. **1783** FRENEAU *Poems* (1786) 325 Rebels ... have hung up his subjects with bed-cords & halters. **1807** IRVING, etc. *Salmagundi* iv. 75 Hints to travellers about packing their trunks; straps, buckles, and bed-cords. **1832** WILLIAMSON *Maine* I. 107 [The elm's] inner bark is strong and fibrous, and is wrought into bed-cords and chair-bottoms. **1857** *Lawrence* (Kansas) *Republican* 6 Aug. 4 Northrup & Chick ... have in store ... 300 doz. bed cords. **1874** LONG *Wild-Fowl* 107 All you need to carry besides your ordinary bed-clothes is a common bed-cord. **1886** *Harper's Mag.* June 58/2 Traces are made of hickory or papaw, as also are bed-cords.

Bed-cover. =next. {1837–}

1828 WEBSTER, *Rug*, ... in America, I believe, ... is applied only to a bed cover for ordinary beds, and to a covering before a fire-place. **1879** *Scribner's Mo.* Nov. 136/2 A few dried apples Sarah had brought in the box with the dishes and bed-covers. **1896** J. C. HARRIS *Sister Jane* 51 William, ... turn down the bed-cover in the next room.

+Bed-covering. A covering for a bed; *pl.* bedclothes.

a1656 BRADFORD *Hist.* 157 Many sould away their cloathes and bed coverings. **1863** 'M. HARLAND' *Husks* 80 The bed-coverings were clean and fresh. **1865** KELLOGG *Rebel Prisons* 382 The room ... was hung round with filthy rags, tattered quilts and blankets, ... which the wretched inmates used as clothes and bed-covering. **1882** 'M. HARLAND' *Eve's Daughters* 359 Immediately upon rising, the bed-coverings should be removed, shaken, and spread out over foot-board or chairs.

Bed-curtain. A curtain that encloses a bed.

1790 *Columbian Centinel* 29 Sept. 19 [For Sale,] Mahogany Chairs, ... card Tables, one suit of purple and white copper-plate Bed Curtains. **1838** *S. Lit. Messenger* IV. 60/1 The bed-curtains were closely drawn. **1843** *Knickerb.* XXII. 145 The married noses ... pealed a lullaby through the bed-curtains. **1865** *Atlantic Mo.* XV. 608 Suddenly drawing the bed-curtains and flapping an old love-letter in her eyes. **1896** WILKINS *Madelon* 168 Margaret Bean peered around the bed-curtain.

Bedding. In earlier use sometimes written *beeding* or *beading* (cf. BED *n.* 1). — **1660** *N.H. Probate Rec.* I. 44, I give ... unto my daughter my best feather bead boulster & beading belonging unto it. **1666** P. SANFORD *Letter Book* 16, I desiere yo to send me a good Sadle and Furniture ... and Sixe or Eight pownds worth of good Beeding as Ruggs and blankets.

Bedding cloth(e)s. *Obs.* Bedclothes. — **1659** *Essex Probate Rec.* I. 295 One Bed and Beding Cloths. **1746** *N.H. Probate Rec.* III. 339 All the beding cloaths that we have made sience we were marriade.

Bedding goods. *Obs.* The furnishings of a bed. — **1671** *Oyster Bay Rec.* I. 62 All the rest of Bedding goods and household Stuff ... are to remain in my hands.

+Bedding-ground. =BED-GROUND. — **1884** W. SHEPHERD *Prairie Exper.* 199 In the afternoon the same programme for the sheep; and for the bedding-ground a bare open spot. **1920** HUNTER *Trail Drivers of Texas* 215 It looked like a 'round up' when turning them off of the bedding ground.

+Bed-ground. [Cf. BED *v.* 3.] In cattle-raising, a place where cattle sleep for the night. Also fig. — **1880** *Scribner's Mo.* March 770/2 There the cattle are huddled together or 'rounded up' in as small a compass as possible, called 'the bed-ground,' and the herders stand guard over them ... until morning comes. **1903** A. ADAMS *Log of Cowboy* ii. 18 He could use the poorest judgement in selecting a bed ground for our blankets. **1920** HUNTER *Trail Drivers of Texas* I. 62, I had everything in the saddle to move the herd off the bed ground.

+Bed-ice. A layer of ice on the surface of water. — **1874** LONG *Wild-Fowl* 52 If the ice is thin ... shallow grooves should be cut in the bed-ice, and the ends of the cakes [of ice] placed therein.

Bed lace, lacing. *Obs.* ?A slender kind of bed-cord. — **1790** *Penna. Packet* 8 March 4/2 The Subscriber ... continues to make White Rope of all kinds, Bed-Cords, Bed-Laces, Plow Lines and Plow-Traces. — **1777** *N.J. Archives* 2 Ser. I. 516 Halters, plough-lines, bed-lacings, ... sold by Edward Pole, ... Burlington.

Bed-line. *Obs.* =BED-CORD. — **1647** *Essex Probate Rec.* I. 89, 2 bedsteeds & 2 bed lines. **1651** *Ib.* 128 A bedsted & a trundle bed & bedlyne.

+Bed log. A log forming the foundation of a structure. — **1883** *Amer. Naturalist* Nov. 1197 Five beavers came out from holes in the bank.... The[ir] first effort was to get back to its place the bed log.

Bed-maker. A college servant whose work includes bed-making. {1691–} — **1731** J. SECCOMB *Father Abbey*, Mr. Matthew Abbey ... had for a great Number of Years served the College [=Harvard] in Quality of Bed-maker and Sweeper.

Bed-ore. Ore forming, or taken from, a bottom stratum. — **1794** *Mass. H. S. Coll.* IV. 48 Having procured a quantity of earth, or loam ... —(it resembled bed-ore, though not impregnated with particles of iron)—he laid it on a flat rock.

***Bed-pan.**

***1.** A warming pan. *Obs.* {–1699}

1635 *Essex Probate Rec.* I. 5 A bedd pan, 5s. **1648** in *Mayflower Descendants* X. 199 Item one bedpan, [5s.]. **1679** *New Castle Court Rec.* 297, 1 smoothing yron & bed pan. **1684** *Essex Inst. Coll.* XXV. 154 In the New house in the hall. Imprimis: ... a bason, six Pewter platters, a bed pan.

2. A sanitary vessel for use in bed. {1883}

1678 *New Castle Court Rec.* 361 Twoo Earthen bed Pans. **1711** *Essex Inst. Coll.* IV. 187/1 A bed pan & stool pan. **1756** *Lett. to Washington* I. 168 Half a dozen Bed-panns for the Hospital. **1759** H. M. Brooks *Gleanings* 34 Tea-pots and spoons, bed and close stool pans, measures, &c. **1816** *Austin Papers* (1924) I. 263, 2 Bed Pans at 25c.

Bed-piece.

1. A foundation plate or structure in a machine, etc.; a sole-plate.

1846 *Rep. Comm. Patents* (1847) 91 One of these is for an improvement in jointing staves by bending them over a bed-piece. **1849** *Ib.* (1850) 203, I do not claim the bed piece, the tumbler, the folding slide or the lever. **1851** J. H. ROSS *In New York* 203 The largest castings made by this company are 'bed-pieces' for steam-ships. Upon these bed-pieces the engine, boilers, and all the machinery rest.

+2. (See quotation and BED *v.* 1.)

1851 J. S. SPRINGER *Forest Life* 94 Before felling the Pine, small trees are cut for bed-pieces, the Pine-tree falling across them transversely.

Bed-plate. =BED-PIECE. — **1849** *Rep. Comm. Patents* (1850) 211 This is combined with the bed plate for guiding and keeping the edge of the tire true. **1850** N. KINGSLEY *Diary* 107, I gave up and went to putting in timbers to set the bed-plates to the enjines. **1876** INGRAM *Centennial Exp.* vi. 165 The shaped envelopes were placed on packages on a bed-plate.

Bedquilt. A quilt for use on a bed. {*a*1847–}
1765 E. Singleton *Social N.Y.* 334 [Mrs. Thomas Carroll taught . . . French quilting, knoting for Bed Quilts or Toilets [etc.]. **1788** *Mass. Centinel* 30 April, All his Goods . . . among which are some elegant Mersailles Bed-quilts. **1803** MRS. E. S. BOWNE *Life* 164 One poor bed quilt is all I have towards housekeeping. **1825** NEAL *Bro. Jonathan* I. 54 The women gather about her; and . . . 'turn out' a handsome bed-quilt for her, sometimes in a single afternoon. **1837** A. WETMORE *Gaz. Missouri* 295 An advertisement 'of the size of a bed-quilt' . . . gave promise of a show unparalleled in village annals. **1867** 'T. LACKLAND' *Homespun* II. 202 Wonders of industrious ingenuity in the bed-quilt line hang . . . about the different rooms. **1876** INGRAHAM *Centennial Exp.* 367 A lady from Alabama exhibited a rich crocheted bed-quilt. **1898** E. C. HALL *Aunt Jane* 72 There was a old woman down here in Kentucky usin' his patterns to make a bedquilt.

+**Bed-quilting.** A social gathering for the purpose of making quilts. — **1819** *Mass. Spy* 12 May (Th.), They were to assist at a bed-quilting he intended to have at his raising.

+**Bedrock.**

1. *Mining.* The solid rock underlying loose detrital beds or strata. {1879–}
1850 N. KINGSLEY *Diary* 154 We go down but we are in for seeing the bed rock all along the bottom. **1859** G. A. JACKSON *Diary* 521 Clear day. [I] removed fire embers and dug into rim on bed rock. **1870** 'MARK TWAIN' *Sk., Petrified Man,* This stuff had run under him and cemented him fast to the 'bed-rock.' **1873** MILLER *Amongst Modocs* xiii. 161 It is a great task in the placer mines, . . . particularly in the streams, to get on the bed-rock to open a claim and strike a lead. **1891** *Century Mag.* Feb. 533 It is only where there is a steep grade that the rich stratum on the bed-rock can be conveniently prospected and washed.

attrib. **1871** RAYMOND *Mines* 69 The running of a bed-rock tunnel to drain . . . these diggings. **1873** MILLER *Amongst Modocs* xxxii. 368 The waters of the Sacramento, that boiled and foamed in a bed-rock flume.

2. *fig.* The fundamental or essential part; the bottom or basis.
1873 MILLER *Amongst Modocs* vi. 71 But I have thought it all out, clean down to the bed-rock. **1877** BRET HARTE *Story of a Mine,* etc. 421 He's clean gold on the bed rock after all! **1884** SWEET & KNOX *Through Texas* xx. 268 They do not reach the hard-pan of wickedness, the bed-rock of depravity, at once. **1887** *Century Mag.* April 861/1 The new discussion . . . touched the very bed-rock of primary human rights. *a***1909** 'O. HENRY' *Roads of Destiny* iii. 52 From general topics the conversation concentrated to the bed-rock of grim personalities.

attrib. **1896** *Congress. Rec.* 5 Feb. 1329/1 Taxation and representation must go together, according to the very bedrock definition of republican government.

b. In the phr. *to come* (or *get*) *down to* (*the*) *bedrock.*
1871 BRET HARTE *Roaring Camp,* etc. 63 To come down to bed-rock, it's just this. **1875** *Scribner's Mo.* July 277/1 [In San Francisco] getting at the real character of a man is 'coming down to the bed rock.' **1889** 'MARK TWAIN' *Conn. Yankee* xix. 234 When you come right down to the bed-rock, knight-errantry is worse than pork. **1902** S. G. FISHER *True Hist. Amer. Rev.* 126 Both sides got down to bed-rock, and in this period we find the best and strongest pamphlets.

c. Something solid or excellent.
1902 WISTER *Virginian* xxvii. 346 That play is bed-rock, ma'am! Have you got something like that?

3. *transf.* The lowest limit or extremity.
1869 S. BOWLES *Our New West* v. 99 We came down to 'bed-rock,' as the miners say, i.e. an extra flannel shirt and a pocket-comb. **1873** MILLER *Amongst Modocs* iv. 43 'Are you really dead-broke?' 'Skinned clean down to the bed-rock.' **1883** HAY *Bread-Winners* iv. 54 The family is about down to bedrock. **1884** NYE *Baled Hay* 65 Whenever the dead-beat poet strikes bedrock. **1911** HARRISON *Queed* xxv. 319 The people . . . are howling economy and saying that all expenses must go to bed-rock.

attrib. **1881** *Chicago Times* 11 June, The transactions . . . having been based on bed-rock prices.

Bed-rope. *Obs.* A bed-cord. — **1642** *Md. Archives* IV. 97, 6 bed ropes and 3 fishing lines.

Bed-rug. A rug for covering a bed.
1647 *Essex Probate Rec.* I. 78 An old Straw bed and Creadle Rugg with an old Bed Rugg. **1687** *Conn. Public Rec.* I. 299, I give unto my daughter . . . my bed rug. **1850** *Knickerb.* XXXVI. 73 Open the door and the gentle breeze from without will waft aside the blue woollen 'bed-rug.' **1899** GREEN *Va. Word-Book* 54

+**Bed-sack.** A sack made to hold (army) bedclothes for convenience of carrying them.
1661 *Essex Probate Rec.* I. 323 A bead sacke, . . . a cheste. **1811** *Niles' Reg.* I. 45/2 In this valuable class of cotton goods are included . . . bed sacks. **1814** *Ib.* VI. 320/2 A paper . . . was found in the clothing store at New London, printed [? pinned] to one of the bed sacks furnished for the soldiers. **1861** *Army Regulations* 169 Bed-sacks are provided for troops in garrison. **1888** [see BEEF-STOCK].

Bed-sick, *a.* {1611} Confined to bed by illness. — **1814** ASBURY *Journal* III. 436, I would have preached today at Fountain Head, but I was bed sick.

+**Bed-spread.** [Perhaps after Du. *beddesprei,* L.G. *bedsprêd.*] A coverlet or counterpane. {1887–}
*c***1845** *Big Bear Ark.,* etc. 30, I made a bed-spread of his skin, and the way it used to cover my bar mattress . . . would have delighted you. **1848** BARTLETT 28 *Bed-spread,* in the interior parts of the country, the common name for a bed-quilt, or coverlet. **1856** *Mich. Agric. Soc. Trans.* VII. 701 One bed-spread of beautiful crochet work, made by a little girl ten years of age. **1877** *Rep. Indian Affairs* 344 Bed-spreads, 1,500. **1904** *N.Y. Times* 9 May 3 (Advt.), 500 honeycomb and crocheted bed-spreads, hemmed, double bed size.

Bedstick. A bedstaff. {1887, *dial.*} — **1899** GREEN *Va. Word-Book* 54 Bedstick . . . [was] a long stick used for smoothing the bedclothes when bedsteads were too high and broad to be reached with the hand.

***Bedstraw.** A plant of the genus *Galium.*
1817–8 EATON *Botany* (1822) 285 Bedstraw. *Ib.* 286 Rough bedstraw. **1821** *Mass. H. S. Coll.* 2 Ser. IX. 150 Plants, which are indigenous in the township of Middlebury [Vt., include] Bed straw, . . . Rough bed straw. **1840** DEWEY *Mass. Flowering Plants* 144 *Galium verum,* Yellow Bedstraw . . . ; probably not indigenous here as in Europe. **1843** TORREY *Flora N.Y.* I. 310 *Galium trifidum,* . . . Small bedstraw. . . . Swamps and moist shady woods. **1846** Emory *Military Reconn.* 391 Here we collected some beautiful flowers, amongst which were . . . the delicate bed straw (*galium tinctorum*). **1883** *Century Mag.* Sept. 720/2 The bed-straw . . . [has a] jointed stem . . . ringed with circles of lance-shaped leaves. **1901** MOHR *Plant Life Ala.* 741 *Galium trifidium,* Small Bedstraw. . . . Open marshes. *Ib.* 742 *Galium triflorum,* Sweet-scented Bedstraw.

Bed-tester. Also †**teaster.** The fittings at the head of a bed or the canopy over a bed. {1704–}
The form *teaster* or *teester* is still locally current, as in Eng. dialect.
1649 *Essex Probate Rec.* I. 111 One bed teaster & vallance. **1650** in *Mayflower Descendants* X. 172, I give and bequeath unto my Daughter Judith . . . my bed teaster. **1758** J. WILLIAMS *Hist. Captivity* 3, I reach'd up my Hands to the Bed-tester, for my Pistol. **1842** *American Pioneer* I. 125 He snatched a pistol from his bed-tester, . . . and snapped it.

***Bee**[1].

***1.** An insect of the order *Hymenoptera,* esp. the well-known honey-bee, *Apis mellifica* or *mellifera.*
1644 *Conn. Public Rec.* I. 460 An Inuentory of the Goods of Ephraim Huit . . . [includes] 3 stocks of bees. **1685** T. BUDD *Penna. & N.J.* 35 Bees are found by the experience of several that keep them, to thrive very well. **1705** BEVERLEY *Virginia* IV. 81 Bees thrive there abundantly, and will very easily yield to the careful Huswife, two crops of Honey in a Year. **1747** *N.H. Probate Rec.* III. 471, I also give her the best swarm of Bees. **1789** ANBUREY *Travels* II. 282 The bee is not natural to America, for the first planters never observed a single one in the immense tract of wood they cleared; . . . the Indians . . . have no word for a bee, and they therefore call them by the name of the *Englishman's Fly.* **1844** GREGG *Commerce of Prairies* II. 233 The *bee,* among Western pioneers, is the proverbial precursor of the Anglo-American population. **1846** THORPE *Myst. Backwoods* 151 The hunter . . . prepares a candle, which he makes out of the wax taken from the comb of wild bees. **1848** COOPER *Oak Openings* I. iii. 52 The air above and around him was absolutely darkened by the cloud of bees that was collected to defend their treasures. **1878** B. TAYLOR *Between the Gates* 267 The bee is the most overworked animal in California, and is miserably imposed upon by the only creature that can match him in geometry. **1881** BURROUGHS *Pepacton* (1895) 66 When you touch the 'business end' of a bee, it will sting even though its head be off.

+**b.** Phr. *brisk* (or *busy*) *as a bee.*
1844 P. HONE *Diary* II. 211 James Gerard, brisk as a bee and loquacious as a whip-poor-will. **1859** L. WILMER *Press Gang* 199 He established a Democratic paper, and . . . made himself 'as busy as a bee in a tar-barrel.' **1868** MRS. WHITNEY *P. Strong* 41 The dear little mother, brisk as a bee, . . . has gone downstairs with Emery Ann. **1899** GREEN *Va. Word-Book* 21 Virginia Folk-sayings [include] . . . Brisk as a bee.

+**2.** =BEE-LINE.
1850 [H. C. LEWIS] *La. Swamp Doctor* 93, I'd take a 'bee' for home, an' come to this slew, an' then have to head it.

3. Attrib. with *acre, business.*
1841 *Niles' Nat. Reg.* 31 July 352/1 The Bee Business. Mr. Rice . . . has an extensive establishment for keeping bees. **1882** *Century Mag.* June 226/2 Around the lofty redwood walls of these little bee-acres there is usually a fringe of chestnut-oak. **1883** *Ib.* Oct. 816/2 Nobody need think the bee business is all play.

+**Bee.**[2] [Of obscure origin. There is no evidence for the suggestion, which is of late date, that it is an allusion to the social and industrious habits of the bee.]

1. A meeting of neighbors or friends for the purpose of accomplishing some task in common, esp. by way of assisting one of the number; a social gathering for this or other purposes.
Also with defining terms as *apple-, husking-, logging-, paring-, quilting-, raising-, spelling-bee:* see these words.
1769 *Boston Gazette* 16 Oct. (Th.), Last Thursday about twenty young Ladies met at the House of Mr. L., on purpose for a Spinning Match;

(or what is called in the Country a Bee). **1816** Kittredge *Old Farmer* (1904) 169 Husking is now a business for us all. If you make what some call a *Bee*, it will be necessary to keep an eye on the boys, or you may have to husk over again the whole heap. **1837** H. MARTINEAU *Society* II. 99 Every one has heard of the 'frolic' or 'bee,' by means of which the clearing of lots, the raising of houses, the harvesting of crops is achieved. **1841** G. POWERS *Hist. Sk. Coös Co.* 111 They . . . made what is defined, in the Yankee vocabulary, 'a bee,' for picking pigeons; and two or three times a week the people of Haverhill were invited down to Mr. Tyler's to pick pigeons. **1846** *Knickerb.* XXVIII. 338 They came cheerfully to the 'bee,' and after the usual amount of eating, drinking, swearing, and joking, the house . . . was raised and covered in. **1856** GOODRICH *Recoll.* I. 76 The cellar of our new house was dug by a *bee* in a single day, and that was Christmas. **1856** A. A. LAWRENCE in *Life* (1888) 109 In many towns the ladies are having 'Bees' to sew for Kansas. **1866** MRS. WHITNEY *L. Goldthwaite* xiii, Two hours later she came meekly to Miss Craydocke's room, where the 'bee' was gathered,—for mere companionship to-day, with chess and fancy-work. **1890** E. B. CUSTER *Following Guidon* 257 If one of us was plunged into difficulties . . . the rest came in for a 'bee,' and made light work about the sewing-machine.

transf. **1906** *N.Y. Ev. Post* 25 Jan. 1 'We can never head off the probing of the Railroad Commission . . . and such an investigation bee spells ruin,' was the grim comment of another senator.

2. A combined presentation of gifts to a minister by members of the congregation.

'*Bee*, . . . joint, voluntary, and gratuitous aid afforded by neighbors to their minister' (W. '47).

1823 I. HOLMES *Account* 358 For the clergy, in country places, once or twice a year, they have what they denominate a 'bee,' or 'hive.' . . . The members of his congregation . . . repair to the minister's dwelling, each person taking something, either an article of clothing or victuals. **1846** WHITCHER *Widow Bedott P.* ii. 26, I remember once when Parson Porter had a bee, I sent him an amazin' great cheese. **1852** MRS. DUNCAN *America* 160 With such people it is much easier to give gifts to their pastor, than to insure him a regular money income. From this circumstance has arisen the plan of having what has got the name of 'A Bee,' once a year.

Bee-bait. [BEE[1].] Honey used to attract wild bees. — **1900** SMITHWICK *Evolution of a State* 292, I had occasion to speak of 'bee bait.' . . . When we went out in search of a 'bee tree' we took along a vessel containing honey; this we placed . . . to attract the attention of any bee.

+**Bee-balm.** An aromatic plant of the genus *Monarda* or *Melissa*.

(1) **1847** DARLINGTON *Weeds & Plants* 232 *Monarda didyma*, . . . Oswego Tea, Bee Balm. . . . New England West and South. July–August. A very showy plant, . . . very common in gardens. **1887** BURROUGHS in *Century Mag.* July 328, I have never found it [=cardinal-flower] with its only rival in color, the monarda or bee-balm, a species of mint. **1904** WALLER *Wood-carver* 264 Some stalks of the bee-balm stand in my pitcher on the bench.

(2) **1868** *Rep. Comm. Agric.* (1869) 281 Plants from which bees gather honey and pollen . . . [include] bee-balm (*Melissa officinalis*). **1889** *Cent.* 433/2 The garden or lemon-balm, bee-balm, or balm-mint, is *Melissa officinalis*.

Bee-bird. The spotted fly-catcher or other allied bird. {1789–} — **1862** *Ill. Agric. Soc. Trans.* V. (1865) 734 The Bee bird will eat bees, and working bees even, when he cannot get drones. **1881** *Amer. Naturalist* XV. 215 The Arkansas fly-catcher (*Tyrannus verticalis*)—the Western bee-bird—is everywhere common. **1883** *Century Mag.* Oct. 816/2 The bee . . . is an irresistible treat to the bee-bird.

***Beech.** Also †**beach.**

***1.** A forest-tree of the genus *Fagus*, esp. the American variety *F. ferruginea* or *americana*.

Used collectively, or applied to a single tree.

For *American, blue, red* (etc.) *beech*, see these headings.

(*a*) **1622** 'MOURT' *Relation* 60 This Harbour is . . . compassed with a goodly Land . . . wherein are nothing but . . . Beech, Sasifras, Vines, and other trees which wee know not. **1637** MORTON *New Canaan* II. ii, Beech there is of two sorts, redd and white. **1709** LAWSON *Carolina* 94 Beech is here frequent, and very large. The Grain seems exactly the same as that in Europe. We make little Use thereof, save for Fire-wood. **1763** R. T. Durrett *Louisville* (1893) 132 Thence South . . . to a beech and buckeye. **1796** B. HAWKINS *Letters* 25, I crossed this branch . . . thro' some low rich bottom land, among some of the tallest and largest beech I ever saw. **1832** WILLIAMSON *Maine* I. 106 The Beech is of three varieties;—the red and the white, both larger than the ash, and excellent fuel; the black, which is tough and small. **1836** J. HALL *Statist. West* x. 140 The foliation of the beech is probably one of the best standards of comparison between different places. **1852** MITCHELL *Dream Life* 201 The beeches . . . guard their foliage, until each leaf whistles white, in the November gales. **1862** NORTON *Army Lett.* 115 We . . . [were] lying on the ground with no covering, heads pillowed on the roots of oaks and beeches. **1883** HALE *Woods & Timbers N.C.* 79 [Of] the Beech (*Fagus ferruginea*), . . . the wood is . . . well adapted for plane-stocks, shoe-lasts, and the handles of mechanical implements.

(*b*) **1781–2** JEFFERSON *Notes Va.* (1788) 39 Beach, *Fagus sylvatica.* **1817** *Ann. 14th Congress* 2 Sess. 1012 There may now be had from it . . . beach, poplar [etc.]. **1826** COOPER *Mohicans* vii, Seat yourselves in the shade, which the moon throws from yonder beach—'tis thicker than that of the pines. **1837** JENKINS *Ohio Gaz.* 167 The timber is sugar, beach, black walnut, blue and white ash.

b. The wood of this tree. {1607–}

1816 *Ann. 14th Congress* 2 Sess. 1196 There may be small variations, according as . . . beech . . . or any other wood is employed.

2. Attrib. with *bark, bud, forest, leaf, log*, etc.

1718 *N.H. Probate Rec.* II. 58 One of the said lotts begins at a Beach Stump spotted and numbered two. **1790** E. DENNY *Journal* 144 Difficult march this day over beech roots and brush. **1790** *Penna. Packet* 1 May 1/1 Wanted by the tanners of Philadelphia, a large quantity of . . . Birch and Beach Bark. **1798** I. ALLEN *Vermont* 27 Their punishment sometimes consisted in whipping severely with beech twigs. *c***1805** R. PUTNAM *Memoirs* 19 We had northing to eat sence morning, but beech buds and a few high cranberries. **1813** *Niles' Reg.* V. 131/1 The road passes through a beach forest without any clearing. **1847** *Knickerb.* XXIX. 377 Would that we were there 'sponking' glowing maple-coals on the green beech-logs. **1872** EGGLESTON *End of World* xxxvii. 233 Even as a tyrannical backwoods schoolmaster straightens his long beech-rod relishfully before applying it. **1880** *Harper's Mag.* June 72 How well I recall the 'tat-tat' upon the dry carpet of beech leaves.

+**Beech bottom.** A bottom abounding in beech trees.

1770 WASHINGTON *Diaries* I. 442 Beach Bottoms are excepted against, on acct. of the difficulty of clearing them. **1779** W. FLEMING in *Travels Amer. Col.* 619 Went through beach bottoms, on the river on each side. **1809** F. CUMING *Western Tour* 188 The next two miles was through a beech bottom. **1841** *American Pioneer* I. 39 The tree is sixty-five feet high; it stands on a flat beech bottom, with many other trees of the same kind near it.

+**Beech-drops.**

1. A plant (*Epiphegus Virginiana*) parasitic on the roots of the beech.

1815 DRAKE *Cincinnati* ii. 86 Plants useful in medicine [include] . . . Beech-drops, the root. **1836** LINCOLN *Botany* App. 96 Beech-drops, cancer root. . . . The whole plant is yellowish-white. **1843** TORREY *Flora N.Y.* II. 24 *Epiphegus Americana*. . . . Beechdrops. Cancer-root. . . . Shady beech woods. **1901** MOHR *Plant Life Ala.* 731 Beech-drops . . . [grow] clustered on roots of beech.

2. See ALBANY, CAROLINA BEECH-DROPS.

3. *False beech-drops*, the pinesap, *Hypopitys lanuginosus*.

1857 GRAY *Botany* 262 *Monotropa Hypopitys*. Pine-sap. False Beechdrops. . . . Oak and pine woods; common. **1892** COULTER *Bot. W. Texas* II. 254 False beech-drops [are] somewhat pubescent or downy, tawny, whitish, or reddish, commonly fragrant plants.

+**Beecher.** *S.E.* [BEECH 1.] One of a class of 'poor whites' in North Carolina. — **1868** *Putnam's Mag.* June 709/2 Its low-down class is by no means so degraded as . . . the 'beechers,' and other wild paupers of North Carolina.

+**Beecher's Bible.** *Obs.* A Sharp's rifle.

App. with sarcastic or humorous allusion to Henry Ward Beecher's belief that 'the Sharp rifle was a truly moral agency, . . . [containing] more moral power . . . , so far as the slaveholders of Kansas were concerned, than a hundred Bibles' (*N.Y. Ev. Post*, Feb. 1856, quoted in Wilder *Ann. Kansas* (1886), p. 109).

1857 CHANDLESS *Visit Salt Lake* I. i. 7 A Bible—not a 'Beecher's Bible' (*i. e.* Sharp's rifle), as the collocation might suggest. **1872** R. J. HINTON *Flanking S. Carolina* in *Kansas Mag.* Feb. 103 Stowell opened our rifle-boxes, and each man received a 'Beecher-Bible' for the first time. **1879** *Congress. Rec.* 5 April 262/1 You marched an armed body of men into my town before ever a 'Beecher's bible' was sent to Kan. . . . Then, thank God, Beecher did send his 'bibles.' **1910** O. G. VILLARD *John Brown* 306 Successes at the polls were more effective than 'Beecher's Bibles.'

+**Beech flat.** A flat on which the beech is the prevailing tree.

1847 *Ind. H. S. Publ.* III. 440 The knobs and beech flats of some poorer sections of the State. **1849** CHAMBERLAIN *Ind. Gazetteer* 274 The country is . . . moderately fertile, except in the beech flats, at the head of the streams, where it is only fit for grass.

+**Beech ground.** =BEECH LAND. — *a***1817** DWIGHT *Travels* IV. 60 The beech and maple grounds were too wet to be burned.

+**Beech knob.** [BEECH 1.] A knob or hummock of beech trees. — **1779** W. FLEMING in *Travels Amer. Col.* 623 [We] fell on a Creek that emptied into Chaplains Fork of Salt River over bad beach knobs.

+**Beech land.** Land on which the beech tree predominates.

1789 MORSE *Amer. Geog.* 143 One species generally predominating in each soil, has originated the descriptive names of birch, beach, and chesnut lands. **1790** E. DENNY *Journal* 143 Beech and white oak land generally, and no running water. *Ib.* 144 March through beech and swamp oak land. **1808** F. CUMING *Western Tour* 416 Some plats of beech land, that appears to be second rate, as it frequently produces spice-wood.

***Beech mast.** Beechnuts.

1819 E. DANA *Geographical Sks.* 190 These swamps afford the finest stock range imaginable, particularly for hogs, . . . besides the immense quantity of oak and beech mast [etc.]. **1849** CHAMBERLAIN *Ind. Gazetteer* 17 Oaks and beech mast is found in such quantities as to contribute largely both to feeding and fattening hogs. **1874** LONG *Wild-Fowl* 198

Beech-mast . . . is often very abundant, but the trees are as often on the hills far from water as near by.

Beechnut. The nut of the beech; †the beech tree. Also attrib. {c1865–}

1778 CARVER *Travels* 501 The Beech nut. Though this tree grows exactly like that of the same name in Europe, yet it produces nuts equally as good as chesnuts. **1798** I. ALLEN *Vermont* 276 A good beech nut year may be called a good swine year. *Ib.*, As soon as the acorns, beech-nuts, &c. begin to fall, they are driven to the woods . . . to feed on them. **1820** FLINT *Lett. from Amer.* 208 Hogs . . . become fat by feeding on the acorns and beech nuts which strow the ground in autumn. **1851** J. S. SPRINGER *Forest Life* 29 Burned and cracked, the Beech-nut makes a very good substitute for coffee. **1857** HAMMOND *Northern Scenes* 333 A black squirrel came hopping along with his mouth full of beech nuts. **1880** *Scribner's Mo.* April 921/1 You're as full of envy 'n back-bitin' as a beech-nut's full of meat.

+**Beech ridge.** A ridge on which beech trees grow. — **1789** MORSE *Amer. Geog.* 197 The interior parts are interspersed with beech ridges. **1805** PARKINSON *Tour* 113 There are likewise a great many swamps in the beech-ridge, which occasioned me very often to lie wet.

+**Beech-seal,** *n. Vermont.* A beech rod. *Obs.* — **1840** D. P. THOMPSON *Green Mt. Boys* I. iii. 34 A prisoner in the hands of the Green Mountain Boys, a fair candidate for the honor of the Beech-seal. *Ib.* 41 The usual number of stripes, . . . faithfully applied to the back of the offender with a green beech rod, termed, as before mentioned, the Beech-seal. **1856** *Congress. Globe* App. 30 April 552 The Vermonters . . . caught one of the [N.Y.] officers and tied him to a tree, and laid upon him what they called a 'beech seal,' which grows in the woods in the shape of what boys call switches. **1893** J. AULD *Picturesque Burlington* 17 The 'land grabbers' . . . were often admonished and sometimes punished by whippings—'the beech seal.'

+**Beech-seal,** *v. tr.* To whip with a beech rod. Hence **beech-sealer.** — **1840** THOMPSON *Green Mt. Boys* I. v. 54 Why, he was the one that so handsomely beech-sealed one of the York authorities down Bennington way, last year. *Ib.* xiii. 145 Boys, you may as well be getting a brace of genteel beech-sealers; for I feel very confident of a decision in my favor.

+**Beech swamp.** A swamp in which beech trees predominate. — **1805** ASBURY *Journal* III. 201 [In Ohio] we had a beach-swamp [*sic*], mud up to the hubs, stumps as high as the wagon-body, logs, trees. **1819** E. DANA *Geog. Sk.* 190 The principal of these are the Catoma . . . and Big Swamp creek, all of which afford extensive bottoms of rich cane brake, and beech swamp. **1823** KEATING *Narr.* 158 The beech swamp . . . offered us such difficulties during the last four hours of our ride. **1843** 'CARLTON' *New Purchase* II. xliv. 95 The cream-coloured mud in beech swamps, the black mud and water in bayous.

***Beech tree.** A single tree of the beech kind.

1648 *Portsmouth Rec.* 39 Leaveinge that [land] . . . from the marked beech tree . . . out of the sayed parcell. **1699** *Conn. Col. Rec.* IV. 304 The southwest corner a beech tree marked A. P. **1718** *N.H. Probate Rec.* II. 58 One of the said lotts . . . runs south-easterly . . . to a Beach tree spotted and numbered three. **1750** WALKER *Journal* 1 April, I marked my Name, the day of the Month, and date of the year on several Beech Trees. **1835** BIRD *Hawks of Hawk-h.* I. xix. 254 You turn off from the road at a place where a fresh blazed beech tree grows by a rock. **1851** CIST *Cincinnati* 29 In sixty years, the encampment . . . beneath a dense forest of beech trees, has grown into a city.

attrib. **1783** W. FLEMING in *Travels Amer. Col.* 667 The inhabitants tan leather with beach tree bark.

Beech wood.

1. A forest of beech trees. (Usually *pl.*).

1805 *Ann. 8th Congress* 2 Sess. 1087 But after they had paid the swindlers, and cleared the heavy beach-woods, to make a living, they were ejected. **1819** C. B. JOHNSON *Lett. from Penna.* 48 You then pass into what are called 'the beech woods,' which are composed of various kinds of timber, but take their name from that which predominates. **1843** 'CARLTON' *New Purchase* I. x. 66 Beyond the water was a low, marshy and, at present, a truly terrific beech-wood, . . . known to be necessarily uninhabited. **1843** [see BEECH DROPS 1].

2. a. The beech tree. **b.** The wood of this. {1712–}

1849 EMMONS *Agric. N.Y.* II. 313 Beech wood, *Fagus sylvestris.* **1856** *Rep. Comm. Patents: Agric.* 282, I had a rude mill put up with two beech-wood rollers. **1868** BEECHER *Norwood* 533 The white-wood dishes, the beechwood ladles and scoops.

Bee comb. [BEE[1].] A honeycomb. — **1823** *Missouri Intell.* 10 June 1/3, I found about a peck of bee combs hanging on a limb.

+**Bee culture.** The keeping of bees; apiculture.

1856 *Rep. Comm. Patents: Agric.* 121 My profits from bee culture seldom fail from the loss of colonies in winter. **1861** J. S. HARBISON (*title*), The Bee-keeper's Directory; or, the Theory and Practice of Bee-culture. **1868** [see BEE-MOTH]. **1880** *Harper's Mag.* Oct. 777/2 He pried off the top of the old box hive, . . . and the whole science of bee culture was exemplified. **1884** ROE *Nature's Story* 219 Your swarm of bees . . . will take care of themselves, and help take care of you. That's the beauty of bee-culture.

Bee-eater. {1768–} =BEE-BIRD. — **1811** R. SUTCLIFF *Travels* (1815) xiv. 272 His bee-hives [in Penna.] having been considerably annoyed by a bird, called the bee-eater, he . . . shot one of them.

***Beef,** *n.*

***1.** A steer, bull, or other animal of the ox kind. Pl. *beeves* (†*beaves, beves*) or *beefs* (†*beeffs*).

In England this sense is archaic or technical, and the singular has been obsolescent since the 18th cent.

a. *sing.* **1758** C. REA *Journal* 15 Six men . . . put under Guard on suspicion of killing a young Beef and 2 Calves. **1760** WASHINGTON *Diaries* I. 138 Wm. Lodwick and the boy . . . went up for the lame Beef they left upon the Road coming down. **1769** *Md. Hist. Mag.* XII. 281 Molly desires a beef may be sent down the 21 of next month. **1790** *Ann. 1st Congress* II. 1330 The inhabitants were not left a spare blanket, a bushel of corn, or a single beef. **1831** PECK *Guide* 168 It is common at camp and other large meetings, to kill a beef and three or four hogs for the subsistence of friends from a distance. **1849** N. KINGSLEY *Diary* 39 Had half of a beef sent aboard which . . . was quite a treat. **1862** *Congress. Globe* 12 July 3305/1 Every slaughtered beef he [=the farmer] may sell, 'hide, hoof, and horns,' is subject to a tax. **1885** *Outing* Oct. 22/1 With no noise other than a single bellow, . . . the beef would fall forward upon its knees, dead. *a*1909 'O. HENRY' *Roads of Destiny* xiii. 212 He dug his trench on the plaza, and got half a beef on the coals for an all-night roast.

b. *pl.* (1) **1704** *Boston News-Letter* 3 July 2/2 There's arriv'd . . . another prize; . . . her loading consists of . . . 32 beaves hides [etc.]. **1736** *Virginia State P.* I. 228 Corn being very scarce with me, I did not put up my beeves to fatten. **1787** JEFFERSON *Writings* (1855) II. 142 In some parts they kill beeves for the skin only. **1798** I. ALLEN *Vermont* 103 He must . . . find horses to mount his cavalry and beeves for his army. **1816** E. PETTIGREW *Let. to Ann Pettigrew* Jan. (Pettigrew P.), I send you all the things you sent for also 2 small Beves Tongues. **1821** *Murphey Papers* I. 226 Two beeves were killed and orders given for the men to cook and eat as quick as possible. **1853** 'P. PAXTON' *Yankee in Texas* 117 [The Texan] *hunts* bees, cattle, a missing pair of oxen (he calls them *beeves*), or a doctor. **1857** D. BRAMAN *Texas* iv. 68 Steers, at three and four years old, are considered beeves. **1899** CUSHMAN *Hist. Indians* 466 Also 250 horses and 50 beeves sent from Natchitoches, were lost en route.

(2) **1713** *N.C. Col. Rec.* II. 3 Benjamin Tull . . . hath impress'd and kill'd severall Beefs of which he hath rendred noe account. **1740** *S.C. H. S. Coll.* IV. 163 Altho' Beefs were very plenty, it was with great difficulty the Volunteers could obtain any fresh Provisions. **1755** *Lett. to Washington* I. 109 After devouring 2 beeffs & a sufficient quantity of potatoes. **1822** J. WOODS *English Prairie* 346 *Judge.* Well, what trucks have you got to trade away to make money? *Esq.* I have got a few beefs, and a tolerable chance of corn.

2. Without article, in generic or collective sense.

1840 Buel *Farmer's Companion* 318/2 Index, The fattening of beef. **1853** 'P. PAXTON' *Stray Yankee in Texas* 42 For a man who shoots 'beef' instead of 'deer' is for ever after a laughing-stock to the settlement. **1902** A. MACGOWAN *Last Word* 9 It was shipping time, and . . . a dozen ranches were . . . getting the long trains of 'beef' off to Kansas City and Chicago. **1907** WHITE *Arizona Nights* ii. 30 We was just gettin' back from drivin' some beef up to the troops.

3. Attrib. with *barrel, fat, grease, herd, house.*

1833 J. S. JONES *Green Mt. Boy* I. iii, Hog's lard, beef fat, and taller. **1838** FLAGG *Far West* II. 211 The remains . . . occupying their stone coffin much as the subject of scientific dissection occupies a beef-barrel. **1850** GARRARD *Wah-To-Yah* xii. 159 The beef grease and sand certainly excluded the browning effects of the sun. **1885** ROOSEVELT *Hunting Trips* (1910) 91 We had driven in a beef herd (which we wished to ship to the cattle yards). **1888** *Outing* May 101 The porcupines that alternately gnawed and squeaked at an ancient beef-barrel not far from our tent. **1902** LORIMER *Lett. Merchant* 224 Tell our people at the Beef House to look into this export cattle business.

Beef, *v.* [f. the noun.] +**1.** *tr.* To put more muscle into; to drive harder. *College slang.* (Cf. *beef* = muscle, strength, in recent slang: 1900–.) +**2.** To slaughter (cattle) for meat. — (1) **1860** *Yale Lit. Mag.* XXVI. 83 (Th.), The first boat in is the winner of the race, so round they turn, and 'beef her' for the home stretch. (2) **1889** FARMER 48/1 *To beef,* to kill oxen, and convert their flesh into beef. **1916** BOWER *Phantom Herd* xvi. 268, I calc'late I'd better beef another critter.

+**Beef animal.** A cow, bull, or ox, etc. — **1837** COLMAN *Mass. Agric. Rep.* 73 They agree to pay 32 cents for the offal of every beef animal there slaughtered. **1920** M. J. S. DELANEY *Survivor's Recollections* 14 Joe Stansfield went out that morning to drive in a beef animal from the range to be killed.

+**Beef-biscuit.** A biscuit made with beef; a meat-biscuit. — **1856** [GOODRICH] *G. Go-Ahead* 191 A sort of meat-bread, like the beef-biscuit made in Texas.

+**Beef cattle.** Cattle intended to be slaughtered for beef, or of a breed suitable for this. {1880}

1776 *N.C. Hist. Comm.* XVII. 1356, I have been talking to Mr. Bloom about some Beef Cattle; he thinks they can be had. **1789** WASHINGTON *Diaries* IV. 21 We met four droves of Beef Cattle for the New York Market (about 38 in a drove). **1820** *Missouri Intell.* 23 April 3/3 Proposals will be received at this office for the delivery of 200 head of beef cattle. **1854** BARTLETT *Narr.* II. 289 Three mules with their packs, two donkeys, and our three remaining beef-cattle, were missing. **1873–4** *Vermont Bd. Agric. Rep.* II. 205 The beef cattle need a little extra keeping to bring the price we anticipated in the spring. **1899** *Scribner's Mag.* XXV. 116/2 We passed a herd of fine beef cattle on their way to Santiago. **1909** WA-

SON *Happy Hawkins* 21 Well, you'll see me trail in this bunch o' beef cattle.

attrib. **1811** *Niles' Reg.* I. 101/2 We can . . . discontinue . . . some of our cotton and beef cattle farming. **1861** *N.Y. Tribune* 5 Dec., The beef-cattle market for the week closed yesterday.

+**Beef-chuck.** (See CHUCK *n.*) — **1886** HOWELLS in *Century Mag.* April 861/1 'Refrigerator in the next room,' the mate lectured on. 'Best beef-chucks in the market; fish for Fridays.'

+**Beef contract.** A contract to supply beef. Also attrib. — *c***1867** 'MARK TWAIN' *Sk., Great Beef Contract,* He had nothing to do with beef contracts for General Sherman. *Ib.,* You are the beef contract man. **1902** WISTER *Virginian* xxiv. 278 The friends of the editors get the hay and beef contracts. **1903** A. ADAMS *Log Cowboy* ii. 12 The contract called for a thousand she cattle . . . and two thousand . . . beeves, estimated as sufficient to fill a million-pound beef contract.

+**Beef contractor.** One who contracts to supply beef. — **1881** *Rep. Indian Affairs* 80 The beef contractor failed to deliver the cattle on the regular day of issue.

+**Beef cow.** A cow raised for meat. — **1785** in Summers *Ann. S.W. Virginia* 788 Proof being made . . . that David Crouch is entitled to three pounds ten shillings for one beef cow. **1894** *Vermont Agric. Rep.* XIV. 64 Cows may be divided into two classes, beef cows and milk cows. **1902** McFAUL *Ike Glidden* ix. 71 To inquire . . . if he cared to buy a beef cow that he was fatting.

+**Beef-creature.** An animal serving for beef. — **1782** *N.H. Comm. Safety Rec.* 299 Authorized Colo. Badger to dispose of one beef Creature towards his own Expenses. **1816** PICKERING 73 A correspondent also observes, 'He has killed a beef-creatur (or creature) today, is a New England expression.' **1833** *Trial E. K. Avery* 23 When killing a beef creature we sometimes use such a hitch to hang up the quarters. **1858** *Harper's Mag.* May 854/2 Here [central Mass.] in the country, when one of the neighbors kills a 'beef creature,' he is expected to send a piece to each one of the families near by.

+**Beef-curer.** One who cures meat. — **1851** CIST *Cincinnati* 228 There are as many as thirty-three pork and beef packers and ham and beef curers on a large scale.

+**Beef-dodger.** =BEEF-BISCUIT. — **1853** BENTON *Sp.* 7 May (B.), It is a small party, but . . . goes unincumbered with superfluities: . . . pinole, pemmican, and beef-dodgers for their principal support.

+**Beef-head.** Nickname for a native of Texas. — **1872** *Harper's Mag.* Jan. 318/1.

+**Beef-headed,** *a.* Thick-headed, stupid. — **1828** MRS. ROYALL *Black Book* II. 114 Such a great beef-headed fellow as you editor of a paper.

+**Beef-issue.** The issue of cattle to the Indians for food. — **1895** R. H. DAVIS in *Congress. Rec.* 15 Jan. 1005/2 A beef issue is not a pretty thing to watch. **1911** QUICK *Yellowstone N.* xii. 299 The 'O. M.' Mr. Elkins . . . casually landed a juicy contract with Uncle Sam f'r supplyin' beef-issue cattle over on the Rosebud.

Bee-flower. {1626–} +The New England aster, *Aster novae angliae.* — **1840** DEWEY *Mass. Flowering Plants* 135 The most beautiful of our species [of asters], . . . called by the people, bee-flower, because it is in September so sought for by the honey-bee.

+**Bee-fly.** [BEE[1].] An insect of the family *Bombyliidae.* — **1868** *Rep. Comm. Agric.* (1869) 317 The bee-flies, *Bombyliidæ,* are to be met with in April and May, in sunny paths in woods. **1881** *Amer. Naturalist* XV. 143 The 'parasitism' of these bee-flies upon locust-eggs.

+**Beef ox.** An ox intended for beef. — **1834** S. SMITH *Major Downing* 124 Quick as ever you see a beef ox knocked down with an ax.

+**Beef-packer.** One who packs meat for preservation and sale. — **1796** *Boston Directory* 271 Nutt, Isaac, beef packer. **1851** CIST *Cincinnati* 229 S. Davis, Jr. & Co., beef and pork packers, commission merchants, and curers of extra family hams. **1904** *N.Y. Tribune* 17 July 8 Now even many rural districts are as dependent on the beef packer, the vegetable canner, . . . as the veriest cockney.

+**Beef packing.** The packing of meat for preservation and sale. — **1851** CIST *Cincinnati* 229 Their avowed business is pork and beef packing on commission, for the home and foreign markets.

+**Beef-raising.** The raising of cattle to supply beef. — **1892** *Vermont Agric. Rep.* XII. 144 When beef raising was remunerative, here the Shorthorn cattle grew to perfection.

+**Beef stall.** A stall for the sale of beef. — **1812** *Boston Selectmen* 29 July 69 The Clerk of the Market is directed to lease the vacant beef stalls in Ann street. **1813** *Ib.* 10 Nov. 103 Remonstrance . . . relative to beef stalls . . . in Union Street.

+**Beefsteak house.** An eating-house supplying beefsteaks. — **1764** E. Singleton *Social N.Y.* 366 Wm. Adams opens, at the Sign of General Monckton, . . . a Beef-Steak House. **1834** H. J. NOTT *Novellettes* I. 94 He can escape from the empty pageant to the substantial and homely comforts of a beefsteak or oyster house. **1860** MORDECAI *Virginia* iv. 58 The Globe Tavern . . . closed its career, a few years ago, as an 'oyster and beef-steak house, with other refreshments.'

Beef-steer. A steer raised for beef. {1880} — **1885** *Century Mag.* June 222/2 Bears caused him severe loss, killing with ease even full-grown beef-steers. **1888** ROOSEVELT *Ib.* March 666/2 The cattle are fattest and in best condition during the fall, and it is then that the bulk of the beef steers are gathered and shipped. **1904** 'O. HENRY' *Heart of West* 5, I can't sell even a beef-steer to a party of campers.

+**Beef stock.** **1.** Extract or essence of beef. **2.** Beef cattle. — (1) **1888** BILLINGS *Hardtack* 304 Each ambulance was required to carry . . . the following articles:— . . . six 2-pound cans beef-stock [etc.]. — (2) **1891** O'BEIRNE *Leaders Ind. Territory* 29/2 He also owns five thousand head of cattle, three thousand of which are beef stock. **1916** THOBURN *Hist. Oklahoma* II. 368 The beef stock from Texas was driven from the overstocked ranges into Oklahoma during the grazing season.

+**Beef store.** A store for the sale of beef. — **1796** *Boston Directory* 295 Windship, Jonathan, beef store, Nathan Spear's wharf.

+**Beef tax.** *Obs.* A tax payable in beef. — **1781** *Virginia State P.* I. 530 Convinced of the impossibility of collecting the Beef Tax, in this County, I have agreed to accept of the People, the same quantity of Pork. **1782** *Mass. Acts & Resolves* 7 May (1890) 983 Where execution hath been levied . . . on any town Treasurer . . . for either of the two first beef-taxes. **1782** *N.H. Comm. Safety Rec.* 278 Ordered . . . to discount . . . four thousand . . . pounds weight of beef out of their beef tax for 1781.

+**Beef ticket.** A ticket issued to Indians authorizing the drawing of beef from a government contractor. — **1842** E. A. HITCHCOCK *Journal* (1930) 79 Thompson came to an understanding with the contractor's agent, that they should be paid three cents per pound for all the beef tickets they could purchase.

+**Beef worm.** (See quotation.) — **1872** MORRELL *Flowers & Fruits* 381 A fly, . . . about double the size of a house-fly, infests certain localities among the brush, and deposits a worm on the human flesh every opportunity; that is known as the 'beef worm,' and it immediately bores into the flesh.

+**Bee-gum.** [BEE[1].]

1. A gum-tree which houses a swarm of bees, or from which beehives are made.

1817 WEEMS *Letters* III. 215 To be run . . . round & round the circumference of a Bee-Gum like a Dog in chase of his tail, is enough to try the patience of ten Jobs. **1851** *Polly Peablossom* 103 Maybe you know whar a bee-gum is? **1859** BARTLETT 27 *Bee-gum,* in the South and West, . . . a species of the gum-tree from which beehives were made. **1888** C. D. WARNER *On Horseback* 92 Big Tom was always on the alert to discover and mark a bee-gum.

2. A beehive; originally, one made from a section of the hollow trunk of a gum-tree.

1848 [THOMPSON] *Major Jones's Sk. Travel* 143 (Th.), A fisherman's house . . . lookin' 'bout as big as a beegum agin the everlastin stone wall. **1850** *Wilmington* (N.C.) *Commercial* 28 March 2/5 (Th. S.), M. A. received twenty lashes on Saturday, for stealing a bee-gum and its contents. **1859** BARTLETT 27 *Bee-gum,* in the South and West, a term . . . now [applied] to beehives made of any kind of boards. **1866** C. H. SMITH *Bill Arp* 75 Let him . . . observe the horse cavalry as they wind about the corn-patches and potato-patches, the bee-gums and chicken-coops. **1884** EGGLESTON in *Century Mag.* Jan. 442/2 The bees were for the most part rudely hived in cross-sections of the gum-tree, hollowed by natural decay; whence, in the South and West, a bee-hive of any kind is often called a bee-gum. **1888** 'CRADDOCK' *Despot* i. 14 The little cabin . . . with . . . its few bee-gums awry along the rickety rail fence. **1913** M. W. MORLEY *Carolina Mts.* 180 Neither are there 'hives' in the mountains, only 'bee-gums,' which the bees fill with 'right smart of honey.'

b. *transf.* A tall hat.

1900 SMITHWICK *Evolution of a State* 110 A tall *beegum* rode familiarly beside a coonskin cap.

+**Bee-harvest.** [BEE[1].] The common ox-eye daisy. — *a***1847** H. Howe *Hist. Coll. Ohio* 358 The white-weed or bee-harvest, as it is called, so profusely spread over our bottom and wood lands, was not then seen among us.

***Beehive.** [BEE[1].]

***1.** A receptacle for housing honey-bees; =HIVE *n.*

Formerly made of straw (cf. BEE-SKEP) and dome-shaped, or =BEE-GUM. Now usually a wooden box of special make with inside fittings.

1791 BARTRAM *Travels* 60 Each side of the avenue was lined with bee-hives. **1796** B. HAWKINS *Letters* 40, I saw at Mr. Bailey's 20 bee hives; he says . . . there are wild bees in the country in every direction. **1802** ELLICOTT *Journal* 285 Some [cypress knees] . . . are eight or ten feet high, and being hollow are used for bee-hives. **1850** *New Eng. Farmer* II. 303, I have been engaged in selling the patent bee-hive, known as 'Colton's,' for a few years. **1863** MITCHELL *My Farm* 49 A shelf, on which rested five bee-hives with their buzzing swarms, stood beside a clump of lilacs. **1898** HARPER *S. B. Anthony* I. 7 On all the farms were fine orchards . . . among which stood long rows of beehives with their wealth of honey.

attrib. **1879** *Harper's Mag.* Dec. 63/2 Here too is the portrait of her daughter, a coquettish woman in a 'bee-hive' head-dress.

2. *transf.* A place swarming with busy people.

1725 *New-Eng. Courant* 8 March 1 If we could be so happy as to make that Building [the Town-house] a Bee-Hive of Business but one Hour in a Day. **1838** H. COLMAN *Mass. Agric. Rep.* (1839) 81 The little manufacturing bee-hive of South Lee [Mass.]. **1867** W. H. DIXON *New America* I. 249 [Brigham] Young's house is called the Beehive; in it no drone ever finds a place; for the Prophet's wives are bound to support themselves [etc.]. **1920** *Nat. Geographic Mag.* 203–245 [Article on] Massachusetts—Beehive of Business.

3. A kind of fireworks. *Obs.*

1766 *R.I. Col. Rec.* VI. 494 In the evening, one hundred and eight sky-rockets, with a bee-hive, containing one hundred and six serpents, was [*sic*] played off before the court house.

Bee-hiving. [f. prec.] The keeping of bees in hives. — **1868** *Rep. Comm. Agric.* (1869) 275 To make bee-hiving successful, it is necessary to have strong swarms early in spring.

Bee-house. [BEE[1].] A house in which beehives are kept. {1675–}

1782 J. H. ST. JOHN *Letters* 33 My common place of rest is under my locust-trees, close by my bee-house. **1790** S. DEANE *New-Eng. Farmer* 24 A bee-house should be situated at a good distance from places where cattle are kept. **1849** *New Eng. Farmer* I. 42 A bee-house eight feet square and eight feet high, surmounted by a roof running up into a spire. **1883** *Encycl. Brit., Amer. Suppl.* I. 481/2 Bees are often kept through the winter in cellars . . . or in . . . warm bee-houses.

+**Bee-hunt.** [BEE[1].] A search for wild bees for the sake of their honey.

1837 IRVING *Bonneville* I. ii. 37 In the autumn, when the harvest is over, these frontier settlers . . . prepare for a bee hunt. **1845** MRS. KIRKLAND *Western Clearings* 68 One of the greatest temptations to our friend Silas, and to most of his class, is a bee-hunt. **1846** THORPE *Myst. Backwoods* 190 We have also seen Tom Owen triumphantly engaged in a bee-hunt. **1884** ROE *Nature's Story* 347 Nutting expeditions will soon be in order, and we have a bee-hunt on the programme.

Bee-hunter. [BEE[1].] One who hunts wild bees for their honey. {1776–}

1824 J. DODDRIDGE *Notes* 71 We formerly had some professed bee hunters; but the amount of honey obtained from the woods was never considerable owing to the want of a sufficient quantity of flowers to furnish it. **1827** COOPER *Prairie* iii, 'A bee-hunter!' observed the latter, with a readiness that proved he understood the nature of the occupation. **1837** A. WETMORE *Gaz. Missouri* 58 The bee-hunters . . . have made sad havoc with the timber of Missouri. **1846** THORPE *Myst. Backwoods* 185 As a country becomes cleared up and settled bee-hunters disappear. **1880** BURNETT *Old Pioneer* 17 My uncle was a veteran bee-hunter.

Bee-hunting. [BEE[1].] A search for bee-trees and wild honey.

1824 [W. N. BLANE] *Excursion U.S.* 239 It is a favourite amusement, at a particular season of the year, to go bee-hunting; and great quantities of honey are then collected. **1826** Commons, etc. *Doc. Hist.* II. 277 They were generally bound for the head waters of . . . the Des Moines rivers, a bee hunting. **1836** J. HALL *Statist. West.* ix. 122 On the verge of civilization, bee-hunting furnishes employment to many individuals during several months of the year. **1853** *Knickerb.* XLII. 368 In October, Venison, myself, his honey-box, and axes, set out 'a bee-hunting,' as he called it. **1860** OLMSTED *Back Country* 211 Sometimes he 'took up bee-huntin' for a spell.' **1887** *Century Mag.* Jan. 438/1 He had most special fondness for . . . bee-hunting. In this sport he was as successful as fond.

Beek-iron. *Obs.* =BEAK-HORN, BICKERN. {beak-iron, 1667} — **1714** *Boston News-Letter* 11–18 Oct. 2/2 To be sold by Mr. Jonathan Belcher . . . Anvils, Beek Irons, Frying Pans.

Bee-larkspur. [BEE[1].] A kind of larkspur, *Delphinium elatum.* {1846} — **1836** LINCOLN *Botany* App. 93 Bee larkspur . . . [is originally] a native of Siberia. **1840** DEWEY *Mass. Flowering Plants* 28 The Bee Larkspur bears a flower which has at a little distance, a striking resemblance to a *bee.* **1850** [S. F. COOPER] *Rural Hours* 117 They are partial to the bee larkspur also, with the wild bergamot or Oswego tea.

+**Bee-line.** [BEE[1].]

1. The direct course taken by a bee in returning to its hive.

*c***1845** *Big Bear Ark.*, etc. 118 He watches for the honey-bee, takes his 'bee line,' and follows for half a mile. **1846** *Spirit of Times* (N.Y.) 4 July 223/2 The wife of a regular backwoodsman . . . could shoot a catamount, fell a tree, or 'follow a Bee-line,' with unerring precision. **1848** DRAKE *Life in Kentucky* (1870) 135 When the bee has sucked its fill, it rises, makes two or three circuits, and then moves off in a straight, a 'bee-line,' to the swarm of which it is a member. **1900** SMITHWICK *Evolution of a State* 292 A laden bee flies in a 'bee line.'

2. A direct or straight line.

Usually in the phrases *in* or *on a bee-line; to make, take,* or *strike a bee-line.*

1830 *Mass. Spy* 24 Nov. (Th.), The squirrel took a bee line, and reached the ground six feet ahead. **1837** *Yale Lit. Mag.* II. 141 (Th.), [They will be] engaged in investigating the nature of what is vulgarly called a 'bee line,' drawn in the directions of their several domicils. **1841** *Georgian* (Savannah) 25 Jan. (Th.), Guide, draw a bee-line for home, and see that you take us there by the shortest route. **1847** LANMAN *Summer in Wilderness* 193 We . . . make a bee-line for the log cabin of our intended host. ?**1851** J. J. HOOPER *Simon Sugg's Adv.* (1928) xii. 103, I maid a brake [=made a break] on a bee line for Urwinton. **1856** COZZENS *Sparrowgrass P.* v. 63 The finny prey disappeared through the rent, and made a bee-line for the Hudson. *a***1861** WINTHROP *Canoe & Saddle* xi. 216 Le Play House is on the Atinam, twenty miles in a bee-line from camp. **1873** ALDRICH *Marj. Daw*, etc. 110, I do not believe there was a moment, day or night, when he could not have made a bee-line for Faneuil Hall. **1883** *Harper's Mag.* May 889/2 Are you going round the world in a bee-line? **1889** K. MUNROE *Golden Days* xxxii. 346 Thurston . . . had started on a bee-line . . . for the opposite side of the room.

fig. **1853** THOMAS *J. Randolph*, etc. 122 You'll have a bee line drawed upon you some of these days, in consequence of that tongue of yours. **1854** SHILLABER *Mrs. Partington* 157 The portrait of the deceased corporal . . . looked straight forward, as if indicating a bee-line of duty. **1863** MRS. WHITNEY *F. Gartney* xxviii. 292 Does not God work out our human fate by the bee-lines of his providence?

attrib. **1862** LOWELL *Biglow P.* II. ii. 52 Concord Bridge, thet Davis . . . Found was the bee-line track to heaven an' fame.

+**Bee-martin.** [BEE[1].] The kingbird, *Tyrannus carolinensis.*

1805 LEWIS in *L. & C. Exped.* (1904) II. 141 The bee martin or king-bird is common to this country; tho' there are no bees . . . , nor have we met with a honey bee since we passed the entrance of the Osage River. **1820** *Western Carolinian* (Salisbury) 11 July, A son of Mr. Thomas Sparks, of Franklin county, took down his gun to shoot a bee martin. **1834** MINOR *Diary* in *Atl. Mo.* XXVI. 339 Bee-martins, and red-headed woodpeckers—gave me a vivid reminiscence of my poor, good old commonwealth. **1856** *Rep. Comm. Patents: Agric.* 67 Mocking-birds and bee-martins catch and destroy the boll-worm moth. **1893** *Scribner's Mag.* June 765/1 Every farmer knows the king-bird, or bee-martin.

b. *Bee-martin pole*, a pole supporting a nesting place of the bee-martin.

1851 *Polly Peablossom* 121 Had she a d—d tall thing like a bee-martin pole stuck up forard?

+**Bee-moth.** [BEE[1].] A moth (*Galleria cereana* or *mellonella*) that infests beehives.

1829 *W. Carolinian* in *Mass. Spy* 27 May (Th.), Instinct teaches the bee-moth to secrete herself, during the day, in the corners of the hive. **1837** COLMAN *Mass. Agric. Rep.* 71 The bee moth is to be guarded against by making the crevices of the hive tight with putty or glue. **1850** *New Eng. Farmer* II. 218 He calls the attention of the public to a new mode of preventing the depredations of the bee-moth. **1868** *Rep. Comm. Agric.* (1869) 275 Patent bee-palaces, moth-traps, and self-dividers have done as much as the bee-moth . . . to hinder the progress of bee-culture in this country. **1889** *Cent.* s.v. *Galeria*, The bee-moth [is] a great pest in apiculture, the destructive larvæ of which feed on the wax.

Been, ellipt. in dial. use for *have* or *has been.* (Cf. BEN and BIN.) — **1802** *Steele Papers* I. 250, I have had but one bushel & half of sault sence I been under your dirrection for the stock. **1904** 'O. HENRY' *Heart of West* 4 We been runnin' on the same range, and ridin' the same trails since we was boys.

* **Beer.** Also †**beere, bear(e.**

***1.** An alcoholic beverage brewed esp. from malt and usually flavored with hops.

1622 'MOURT' *Relation* 67 Munday the 25. being Christmas day, we began to drinke water aboord, but at night the Master caused vs to haue some Beere. **1633** *Plymouth Laws* 35 That no beer be sold in any such place to exceed two pence the Winchester quart. **1643** WILLIAMS *Key* 120 Of the Chips of the Walnut-Tree . . . some English in the Countrey make excellent Beere. **1654** JOHNSON *Wonder-w. Prov.* ix. 20 Most began to repent when their strong Beere and full cups ran as small as water in a arge Land. **1677** WINTHROP in *Phil. Trans.* XII. 1068 The English have also found out a way to make very good Beer of Grain: that is, either of Bread made hereof, or else by Malting it. **1702** SEWALL *Diary* II. 63 Call'd at Mr Woodbridges and drank a glass of very good beer. **1737** BRICKELL *N. Carolina* 38 The following are made in Country, viz. Cyder, Persimon-Beer, made of the Fruit of that Tree, Ceder-Beer, made of Ceder-Berries; they also make Beer of the green Stalks of Indian-Corn which they bruise and boyle. **1789** *Ann. 1st Congress* I. 224 Shall it be said that the General Government descends to small beer for its revenue, while strong beer remains duty free? **1809** F. CUMING *Western Tour* 211 So I walked to a small house, where I had observed on a sign 'Beer and Cakes.' **1815** *View N.Y. State Prison* 37 The Agent has given premiums of one pint of wholesome beer to each man for over-work to a certain extent. **1850** GARRARD *Wah-To-Yah* xviii. 210 The beer, manufactured from wheat, was tolerably good. **1880** CABLE *Grandissimes* xxii. 167 She would have liked . . . to pour upon the door-sill an oblation of beer sweetened with black molasses to Papa Lébat.

‖**2.** A liquor obtained in making molasses from wheat.

1819 *Niles' Reg.* XVII. 64/1 As soon as the mash arrives at the highest state of saccharine fermentation, it is strained, and the beer (as it is called) boiled down to molasses.

3. Attrib., esp. with names of vessels for containing beer, as *barrel* {1602–}, *bowl, cask, cup,* etc.

1636 *Essex Probate Rec.* I. 5 Towe beare vessells. **1640** *Conn. Public Rec.* I. 448, An Inventory . . . of James Olmestead [includes] . . . 2 beare hogs-heads, two beare barrells. **1647** *Essex Probate Rec.* I. 66, 6 beare cups, 4 wine cups. **1651** in *Mayflower Descendants* X. 163, I bequeath to Edward Buckley a silver beerbowle. **1656** *Harvard Rec.* I. 207 [Given] by Mr. Thomas Langham . . . one silver Beer Bowl. **1662** *Essex Inst. Coll.* XLII. 133 Two keelirs, . . . 2 beere vessels & pails. **1716** *Mass. Bay Currency Tracts* 174 Glass-works . . . in its several parts, as Window-Glass, Beer-Glasses and Bottles. *c***1728** *MS. Inv. Toxhall's Estate, Bertie Co.* (N.C.H. C.), One Bear cask. **1775** *Essex Inst. Coll.* XIII. 187 A few Casks & a Beer barrel. **1865** *Atlantic Mo.* XV. 536 There was one woman in the store, sitting on a beer-cask. **1871** HOWELLS *Wedding Journey* v. 111 On a table before them stood a pair of beer-glasses. **1872** *Chicago Tribune* 17 Oct. 3/3 Defendant, before he could drink the beer, struck him . . . with a beer-mallet. **1882** SWEET & KNOX *Texas Siftings* 205, I've heard it from . . . the bunghole of a beer-keg. **1883** *Harper's Mag.* July 261 The inventions for rolling beer kegs upstairs in a jiffy. **1883** *Century Mag.* Oct. 957/1 The beer-sellers have been openly retailing their wares without license under the sign of 'Bottling Works.'

+**b.** *Beer and cake store*, a tavern. *Obs.*

1825 J. Pickering *Inquiries Emigrant* (1831) 31 Almost all the roads leading to a town in America are full of houses on their sides, called 'taverns,' or 'liquor,' 'beer and cake,' or 'grocery,' stores.

+**Bee-ranch.** A ranch devoted to beekeeping or bee-culture. — **1883** *Encycl. Brit., Amer. Suppl.* I. 477/2 The four southernmost counties of California in 1880 produced more than 4,000,000 pounds of honey. There are probably more than 500 bee-ranches in those counties. **1887** *Century Mag.* March 737/2 The wagon-track, in fact, was made for the convenience of a few bee-ranches set up here.

+**Bee-range.** [BEE[1].] A row of beehives. — **1845** JUDD *Margaret* III. i. 402 In the garden is a large bee-range.

Beer-cellar. [Cf. G. *bierkeller*, Du. *bierkelder.*] A beer-shop located in a cellar or basement. {1865}

1732 *S. C. Gazette* 28/2 At the Beer Cellar, over against Mr. Elliot's Bridge on the Bay. **1776** *N.J. Archives* 2 Ser. I. 74 A good beer-cellar, the floor of which is paved with brick. **1817** PAULDING *Lett. from South* II. 57 Diving into stews and beer-cellars, to acquire views of vice.

+**Beer fountain.** A device for drawing up beer from the cask; a beer-pump. — **1849** *Rep. Comm. Patents* (1850) 243 Improvement in portable beer fountains.

+**Beer-garden.** [After G. *biergarten.*] An open-air spot furnished with tables and chairs where beer is retailed.

1870 *Scribner's Mo.* I. 115/2 When the war broke out . . . photographs of Bismarck were speedily for sale in all the great German beer-gardens on the Bowery. **1877** PHELPS *Avis* 377 She saw him . . . drumming with his finger to the music in a beer-garden. **1881** *Harper's Mag.* March 545 The grounds are used for a negro beer garden. *Ib.* April 715/1 The beer gardens there [*sc.* at Milwaukee] did then—and yet do—a very thriving business. **1884** *Ib.* Jan. 299/1 The bowling-alley is, as a rule, an adjunct of what is known [in New York] as a beer garden.

+**Beer-hall.** [G. *bierhalle*, Du. *bierhal.*] A beer-house. — **1896** *N.Y. Dramatic News* 11 July 4/1 Bicyclists who are making the concert gardens and beer halls in the suburbs flourish.

* **Beer-house.** A house at which beer is sold. {1494, 1864}

1779 *N.J. Archives* III. 713 Instead of taking command of the militia, . . . he ought immediately to abscond into some other state, and skulk about there in beer-houses. **1781** *Essex Inst. Coll.* XIII. 231 The Beer houses demand hard [money] for a pot of drink. **1809** IRVING *Knickerb.* IV. vi, The great business of politics went bravely on—the parties assembling in separate beer-houses. **1816** WEEMS *Letters* III. 150 You are a plain man and wont have your proposals stuck up in beer houses & grog pips. **1867** L. BAKER *U.S. Secret Service* 49 My escort . . . fell asleep on the stoop of the beer-house, leaving me to go unmolested on my way. **1883** R. G. WHITE in *Century Mag.* Oct. 855/2 Rose street, [N.Y., is] . . . filled now with beer-houses and tenement-houses.

+**Beer-jerker.** *slang.* **a.** One who draws beer. ‖**b.** 'A tippler' (F.). — **1873** *Newton* (Kansas) *Kansan* 15 May 2/1 You will have the beer jerker at a disadvantage. **1887** *Courier-Journal* 11 Jan. 3/4 The Beer Jerker Skips.

Beer measure. A measure of capacity, the gallon containing 282 cubic inches. — **1673** *Plymouth Laws* 170 It is enacted by the Court that 15 Gallons beer measure shalbe a settled Gage for Tarr barrells. **1858** FLINT *Milch Cows* 19 One of the four cows . . . gave in one year 3864 quarts, beer measure.

Beer quart. A quart by beer measure. — **1708** *Boston News-Letter* 8–15 Mar. 2/2 [The stolen tankard] held about a Beer quart, and weighed about 25 Ounces. **1858** FLINT *Milch Cows* 19 An average of over ten and a half beer quarts a day for the whole year.

+**Beer saloon.** A saloon in which beer is sold. — **1861** NORTON *Army Lett.* 15 Night before last a row broke out in a beer saloon near the depot. **1881** *Harper's Mag.* May 814/1 Its stores and cellars were turned into beer saloons, cheap restaurants, clothing stores, etc. **1891** *Century Mag.* April 932 Beer saloons, cheap grocery stores, . . . marked the increasing poverty . . . of the population [in New York].

Beer-shop. A retail store for beer. {1848–} — **1843** *Knickerb.* XXII. 3 A more miserable collection . . . of filthy beer shops than are clustered together . . . it would be difficult to find. **1865** *Atlantic Mo.* XV. 678 Beer-shops, stripped of their male bar-tenders, have adopted female substitutes. **1867** L. BAKER *U.S. Secret Service* 49 A beer shop by the roadside tempted the guard, and we all entered it.

+**Beer-slinger.** *slang.* One who serves beer. — **1875** *Scribner's Mo.* July 277/1 In the slang vernacular, . . . a 'pretty waiter girl' is a 'beer-slinger.' **1875** *Chicago Tribune* 18 Sept. 10/1 Leaning over the bar, with all the dignity of a Teutonic beer-slinger.

+**Beer spruce.** [Cf. SPRUCE BEER.] A variety of spruce-fir. — **1787** SARGENT in *Mem. Academy* II. I. 158 Spruce Pine grows on cliffs near heads of waters [in the n.w. Ohio valley], and is of the same qualities with the northern Beer spruce; it is from one to three feet diameter.

Beer stall. *Obs.* A stand for a beer cask. {1630} — **1646** *Essex Probate Rec.* I. 64, 2 beere vessells & beerestall. **1655** *Ib.* 224 Beere stalls & some lumber.

+**Beer wagon.** A wagon for conveying barrels of beer. — **1861** [NEWELL] *Orpheus C. Kerr* I. 290 The brigade is formed in the shape of a clamshell, with the right resting on a beer wagon. **1883** *Harper's Mag.* Oct. 718/2 The ambitious cockney setting out for a brush on Harlem Lane, beaten by an ash cart or beer wagon.

Bee-skep. A straw bee-hive. {*c*1640–} — **1658** *Southold Rec.* I. 446 An Inventorie [includes] . . . 2 pare of cards; 4 bee skeps.

Beeslings, variant of BEASTLINGS.

Bee stand. [BEE[1].] A group of bee-hives. — **1882** *Harper's Mag.* Nov. 970/1 He ran right over a bee stand just the other side of the cypress bush.

* **Beet.** Also †**beat.**

* **1.** A vegetable of the genus *Beta*, cultivated for its root and for its tops as greens; a single root of this.

The plural *beets*, still common in American use, has in English been discontinued in favor of *beetroot*. 'In the United States *beets* are served at table as a vegetable, while in Great Britain *beet root* is served' (**1892** B. Matthews *Americanisms* 24).

(1) *sing.* **1709** LAWSON *Carolina* 77 The Garden-Roots that thrive well in Carolina, are . . . Radishes, Horse-Radish, Beet, both sorts. **1790** S. DEANE *New-Eng. Farmer* 27/2 *Beet*, a well known esculent root. **1835** *Harvardiana* I. 189 The spot on his nose assuming the color of a full-grown beet. **1855** *Trans. Amer. Inst. N.Y.* 197 Those materials which the cabbage rejects are good pabulum for the beet. **1897** R. M. STUART *Simpkinsville* 228 The deacon's . . . pale face resembled nothing so much as a fibrous and gnarled beet. **1917** *Dept. Agric. Yearbook* 406 The amount of sugar that a given beet will store.

(2) *pl.* **1737** BRICKELL *N.Carolina* 18 The Garden Roots that thrive here are . . . wild Onions, Beets, and most other Roots that are to be met with in Europe. **1788** MARY DEWEES *Journal* (MS.) 8 Those who chose had a dish of cold ham and pickled beats. **1833** *Md. Hist. Mag.* XIII. 320 You may choose for yourself, ham, beef, turkey, . . . for vegetables, potatoes, beets, hominy. **1834** PECK *Gaz. Illinois* 29 Beets often exceed twelve inches in circumference. **1850** *Western Journal* IV. 14 This newly discovered method of extracting sugar . . . from beets. **1883** *Rep. Indian Affairs* 17 They will raise about 100 bushels of beets, 50 bushels of turnips [etc.]. **1904** *N.Y. Ev. Post* 26 March, Cold chopped beets with lettuce make a good supper salad. **1917** *Dept. Agric. Yearbook* 405 The development of desirable strains of beets.

2. Attrib. with *bank, bed, grower, vinegar*, etc.

1836 *Niles' Reg.* 1 October 80/3 If they [=beets] are to be raised by the aid of a *beet bank*, we fear more attention will be paid to it than to the beet-beds. **1871** *Rep. Comm. Agric.* 98 The Department has received several letters from various beet cultivators. **1884** OWENS *Cook Book* 356 [Recipe for making] Beet vinegar. **1917** *Dept. Agric. Yearbook* 402 In this country two problems are confronting the beet growers and sugar producers.

+**Beetle bug.** A weevil of the genus *Curculio.* — **1824** DODDRIDGE *Notes* 85 The beetle bug, or curculio, an insect unknown to the country, at its first settlement, . . . perforates the green fruit, for the deposition of its egg.

* **Beetle-head.** +*local.* The Swiss plover, *Squatarola helvetica.* — **1829** TICKNOR in *Life* I. 386 Mr. Webster has been out shooting all day, and brought home a fine quantity of beetle-heads, curlews, and other things. **1844** *Nat. Hist. N.Y., Zoology* II. 218 The large Whistling Plover, or Bull and Beetle-head Plover as it is called in its autumnal dress. **1874** COUES *Birds N.W.* 449 Beetle-head, Bull-head Plover, . . . will be immediately recognized by the presence of a small hind toe.

* **Beetle-headed,** *a.* +*local.* (See prec.) — **1839** PEABODY *Mass. Birds* 361 The beetle-headed plovers . . . toward the last of September . . . collect in great flocks, preparatory to their migration.

Beetle-ring. A ring placed round the end of a beetle or mallet to prevent splitting. Usu. in *pl.*

1641 *Conn. Public Rec.* I. 444, 2 wedges, 2 betel rings, 2 sawes. **1645** *Early Conn. Probate Rec.* I. 31 My long cross cut saw, and my betell rings, and three wedges. **1677** *Essex Inst. Coll.* XLII. 145 A pair of beetle rings, one shilling six pance. **1684** *Hempstead Town Rec.* I. 433 Four iron wedgess and two betle rings, 8s. **1823** COOPER *Pioneers* xxx, I don't care the valie of a beetlering for you and your parjury too. **1881** *Rep. Indian Affairs* 93 By the blacksmith: Twenty-three beetle-rings, forty-eight wedges.

+**Bee-tree.** [BEE[1].] A tree in which wild bees have a nest.

1782 J. H. ST. JOHN *Letters* 37 If we find any where in the woods (no matter on whose land) what is called a bee-tree, we must mark it. **1796** B. HAWKINS *Letters* 47 The last season a bee tree was taken in this neighborhood and all who eat of the honey sickened instantaneously. **1819** SCHOOLCRAFT *Journal* 59 A bee-tree, which Mr. Pettibone and myself chopped down, . . . contained several gallons of honey. **1830** DEWEES *Lett. from Texas* xiii. 122 They found a bee tree where the bees went in about three feet from the ground. **1845** MRS. KIRKLAND *Western Clearings* 68 The slightest hint of a bee-tree will entice Silas Ashburn and his sons from the most profitable job of the season. **1884** ROE *Nature's Story* 226 If a hive is to be emptied . . . or a bee tree to be cut down, the act is described as 'taking up' the hive or tree. **1900** SMITHWICK *Evolution of a State* 16 The men had the excitement of . . . cutting bee trees.

* **Beetroot, Beet root.**

* **1.** The beet or its root. Also attrib. with *sugar* =beet-sugar.

1839 *Diplom. Corr. Texas* (1911) III. 1267 Belgium consumes thirty millions pounds of sugar, five of which only is beet root. **1840** *Niles' Reg.* Index p. iv, Beet root sugar. **1853** *Harper's Mag.* July 266/2 The culture of beet-root and the extraction of sugar have been commenced [in Utah] with favorable prospects. **1878** *Amer. Home Cook Book* 125 If convenient add a beetroot sliced. **1917** *Dept. Agric. Yearbook* 410 After seed harvest the beet roots and stalks remain in the ground . . . for live-stock feed.

2. Attrib. with *factory, juice, vinegar.*

1863 *Rep. Comm. Agric.* 636 Beet-root juice . . . contains . . . cane sugar. **1886** *Harper's Mag.* June 92/2 The census of 1880 reported four beet-root factories, . . . employing 350 hands. **1889** *Cent.* 504/3 *Beet-root vinegar,* vinegar prepared from the juice of the sugar-beet.

Beet-sugar. Sugar extracted from the root of the sugar beet. {1833-}

1832 *Debates in Congress* 15 June 3595/1 An honorable member from Alabama has been pleased to read . . . a passage from some obscure pamphleteer in France, on . . . the manufacture of beet sugar. The author treats as an absurdity the making of beet sugar. **1837** COLMAN *Mass. Agric. Rep.* (1838) 71 A few pounds of beet Sugar, the first probably made in New England, were made this year in Salem by Pickering Dodge. **1880** *Vermont Agric. Rep.* VI. 117 The manufacture of beet sugar may become profitable in some portions of the country. **1886** *Harper's Mag.* June 92/2 The production of beet sugar, where bounties are not paid, will probably be limited by the fact that [etc.]. **1911** *Dept. Agric. Yearbook* 18 The refined beet sugar made this year nearly equals 600,000 short tons, the largest amount ever made.

attrib. **1838** ELLSWORTH *Valley of Wabash* iv. 43 Beet sugar manufacture offers another advantageous mode for the investment of capital. *Ib.* viii. 97 Small beet sugar manufactories could be established on farms. **1871** *Rep. Comm. Agric.* 210 [Article on] The Beet-sugar Industry. **1877** *Ib.* 157 Beet-sugar production is scarcely yet past the experimental stage. **1880** *Vermont Agric. Rep.* VI. 220 The total expenditure in the state upon beet sugar factories will probably reach a million of dollars. **1886** *Harper's Mag.* June 92/1 The beet-sugar industry has scarcely made a start in this country yet. **1899** *Chicago Record* 31 Jan. 10/1 The beet sugar bounty is another important matter to which the [Michigan] legislature will give attention. **1917** *Dept. Agric. Yearbook* 400 The first permanent beet-sugar mill was established in America in 1879.

Beeves, pl. of BEEF *n.*

‖**Beeve tallow.** [f. *beeves,* pl. of BEEF *n.*] Tallow from animals of the ox kind. — **1836** EDWARD *Hist. Texas* 73 The wax thus obtained is . . . valuable to the farmer by hardening his beeve tallow candles.

Beggar lice. {1851-, *local*} + BEGGAR'S LICE 1, 2.

1859 BARTLETT 27 A species of *Desmodium* whose pods break at the joints . . . is sometimes called Beggar-Lice. **1868** *Florida Plant. Rec.* 177 Write to Horger I wish the cotton crop worked late, so as to keep down the beggar lice. **1871** *Ib.* 187 [The mules] are still fed on 'Beggar lice,' together with what they get in pasture between meals. **1889** [see BEGGAR-WEED].

+**Beggar's dance.** (See quot. 1788.) — **1788** W. BIGGS *Captivity* 31 They took me with them to dance what is called the 'Beggar's Dance.' It is a practice for the Indians every spring, when they come in from their hunting ground, to go to the trading towns and dance for presents. **1833** CATLIN *Indians* I. 245 The Indian has surpassed us in honesty by christening it in his own country, the 'beggar's dance.' **1847** Emory *Military Reconn.* 537 Some of the subordinates came to dance the 'beggar's dance' before the chief's lodge.

Beggar's lice.

+**1.** A weed (*Cynoglossum morrisoni*) which gives off prickles that stick to clothing.

1847 DARLINGTON *Weeds & Plants* 245 Beggar's Lice . . . [grows in] fence-rows and borders of thickets: Northern and Middle States. **1857** GRAY *Botany* 325 Beggar's Lice . . . [is] a vile weed. **1872** *Vermont Bd. Agric. Rep.* I. 285 *Cynoglossum officinale,* Hound's Tongue, and *C. Morisoni,* Beggar's Lice, are common in open woods. **1901** MOHR *Plant Life Ala.* 690 Beggar's Lice [grows in the] Alleghenian to Louisianian area.

+**2.** A weed of the genus *Desmodium.*

1893 *Amer. Folk-Lore* VI. 140 *Desmodium Canadense,* beggar's lice. Concord, Mass.

Beggars' presses. *colloq.* Wrinkles or creases in garments. { =beggars' plaits, *dial.*} — **1870** EGGLESTON *Queer Stories* iv. 28 She had put it [a dress] away carelessly and it was all in 'beggars' presses.'

+**Beggar's tick.** One of the prickly awns of *Bidens frondosa* or similar plants. Also *pl.,* the plant itself.

1869 FULLER *Flower Gatherers* 273 The lower flowers had gone to seed, and first attracted our attention by their prickly capsules, which clung to us like beggar's ticks. **1881** *Harper's Mag.* Oct. 645/2 Ask them if they have ever seen a *beggar's tick.* **1886** *Ib.* Dec. 101/2 Who, in spite of himself, has not brought home the 'beggars-ticks' (*Desmodium accuminatus*) [*sic*]? **1893** *Amer. Folk-Lore* VI. 141 *Agrimonia Eupatoria,* stick seed; beggar's ticks. West Va. **1894** TORREY *Fla. Sketch-Book* 27, I came upon some white beggar's-ticks—like daisies.

Beggar's velvet. *Obs.* Some cheap material resembling velvet. {1711} — **1721** *Weekly Mercury* 3-10 Aug. 2/2 He had a Pair of spare Britches of Beggars Velvet.

+**Beggar-tick(s.**

1. A coarse weed of the genus *Bidens,* having awns that cling to clothing. Cf. BEGGAR'S TICK.

1836 LINCOLN *Botany* App. 76 *Bidens cernua,* . . . water beggar-ticks. . . . Ponds and ditches. **1847** DARLINGTON *Weeds & Plants* 183 *Bidens chrysanthemoides.* . . . Chrysanthemum-like Bidens. Beggar-ticks. **1854** THOREAU *Walden* xiv. 282 A garden . . . over-run with Roman wormwood and beggar-ticks, which last stuck to my clothes. **1863** RANDALL *Pract. Shepherd* 142 The common Burdock . . . and the wild Bur-marigold, Beggar-ticks, or Cuckold, (*Bidens frondosa,*) are peculiarly injurious to wool. **1872** *Vermont Bd. Agric. Rep.* I. 280 *Bidens frondosa,* Beggar-ticks, common in rich waste places and cultivated fields. **1901** MOHR *Plant Life Ala.* 807 *Bidens frondosa,* . . . Stick-tight, Common Beggar Tick, . . . [grows in] low rich soil, borders of fields.

2. =BEGGAR'S LICE 2.

1859 BARTLETT 27 *Beggar-ticks* . . . is also applied to a species of *Desmodium* whose pods break at the joints. **1889** [see next].

Beggar-weed. {In E. ='door-weed,' etc.} + BEGGAR-TICK(S 2. — **1889** VASEY *Agric. Grasses* 94 *Desmodium* . . . There are about forty species native in the United States. . . . These are often called beggar-tick, beggar-lice, beggar weed, or tick-weed.

+**Begging dance.** =BEGGAR'S DANCE. — **1820** *Western Rev.* II. 161 The begging dance is performed by young men and boys, who dress like warriors and go about through the village singing war songs and dancing. *c***1838** CATLIN *Indians* II. 214 The Begging Dance, is a frequent amusement, and one that has been practiced with some considerable success at this time. **1844** S. M. FULLER *Summer on Lakes* 121 Part of the same band I had seen in Milwaukee, on a begging dance. **1847** LANMAN *Summer in Wilderness* 72 The only Indian ceremony I have witnessed at this place, is called the Begging Dance.

+**Begging party.** (See quotation and cf. preceding.) — **1831** *Illinois M. Mag.* 459 In the spring of '14 a calumet party of about twenty Grand Pawnees paid them [=Ponca Indians] a visit in their village. . . . These are generally called by whites *begging parties,* but . . . I would ascribe to them less degrading motives: for though custom decrees that presents be made on such occasions, all alike give and receive. The visitors were . . . feasted on fat dogs, and then they danced.

* **Begin,** *v.*

+**1.** *intr.* With preceding negative and infinitive following: To make any, or the least, approach (*to* be or do something), to have the slightest pretension to.

1833 *Niles' Reg.* XLIV. 348/1 The one in Bleecker street . . . cost ten thousand dollars, and that does not begin to be as expensive as this. **1849** *Wilmington* (N.C.) *Commercial* 5 April 2 (Th.S.), We can't begin to come up to the prospectus. **1857** *Knickerb.* XLIX. 273 He can shut Thompson up on personal abuse, a thing that nothing short of a dozen Tombs lawyers could ever begin to do. **1863** NORTON *Army Lett.* 148 The regulars . . . don't begin to come up to the volunteers in soldierly bearing and appearance. **1868** *Putnam's Mag.* June 672/2 These girls . . . didn't begin to be as strong as Marthy. **1887** *Harper's Mag.* May 869/2 The whole of Switzerland . . . would not begin to compare with the glories of the National Park. **1895** KING *Fort Frayne* iii. 46 We did not begin to know he had so many warriors close at hand. **1907** HOWELLS *Through Eye of Needle* 43 Often there's a . . . dinner that you couldn't begin to get for the same price anywhere else.

+**2.** *ellipt.* To compare at all (*with* something).

1862 NORTON *Army Lett.* 47 There is no other man whom I would be so much pleased to have taken as . . . Floyd. Jeff Davis wouldn't begin. **1897** 'MARK TWAIN' *Following Equator* xxxviii. 347 Indeed, our working-women cannot begin with her as a road-decoration.

+**Beginning tree.** *Obs.* A tree from which descriptions of land are reckoned. — **1769** *Md. Hist. Mag.* XII. 284 The former [plot] . . . calls for the beginning tree of Concord at the end of the second course. *Ib.* 285 If the beginning tree of Concord should be fixed at C.

+**Behaving party.** (See quotation.) — **1829** T. FLINT *G. Mason* 148 They had been present at what are there [New Orleans] very significantly termed 'behaving parties.' In these, as the name imports, the persons present are supposed to be on their good behaviour.

+**Beheader.** One who cuts off the heads of fish. — **1765** R. ROGERS *Acc. N. America* 21 One of them [fishermen], who is called the Beheader, opens the fish with a two-edged knife, and cuts off his head.

+**Behindments,** *n. pl.* Payments in arrear. — **1758** *Essex Inst. Coll.* XXI. 159 Henry William, Mr. Frances Pool, . . . [to] be a Committe to make up with the treasurer consarning the be-hindments of the Parish taxes for years past. **1877** BARTLETT 37 *Behindments,* arrearages.

* **Beholden,** *a.* Under obligation. {-1741; now *dial.*}

1835 KENNEDY *Horse Shoe Robinson* II. 222, I am much beholden to your lordship's generosity. **1855** J. E. COOKE *Ellie* 202 Well, I'm much beholden to her on your account, daughter. **1873** F. HALL *Mod. English* 101 We are beholden to the happy daring of translators, for the amplitude and variety of our diction. **1878** R. T. COOKE *Happy Dodd* 203, I'm a livin' woman this day, beholden to nobody.

* **Behoove,** *v.* {Former variant of *behove,* which is now the exclusive form in England.} To be incumbent on (one).

1712 SEWALL *Diary* II. 358 It behooves us that we do not disgrace our Alma Mater. **1828** WEBSTER s.v., Let him behave as it behooveth. **1845** COOPER *Chainbearer* xxviii, Forgive it all, my man; forgive it all, as behooves a good Christian. **1858** H. REED *Lect. Eng. Lit.* i. 28 What books does it behoove me to know? **1863** *Maine Bd. Agric. Rep.* 135 For this there must be adequate reasons, and it behooves us to ascertain . . . what they are. **1865** NORTON *Army Lett.* 249 It behooved me to be careful in my issue [of clothing]. **1888** E. B. CUSTER *Tenting on Plains* vii. 212 In a land of venomous serpents, it behooved a man to carry his own abatis everywhere.

+**Beignet.** [Fr.] (See quotation.) — **1835** IRVING *Tour Prairies* xxxiii. 306 We . . . supped heartily upon stewed buffalo meat, roasted venison, beignets, or fritters of flour fried in bear's lard.

* **Being,** *pres. pple.* used as *conj.*

* **1.** *colloq.*[2] or *dial.* Seeing that, since, inasmuch *as.* {-1815; now *dial.*}

1658 *R.I. Rec.* 396 The collonies . . . seeme to be ofended with us, beinge the sayd people [=Quakers] have theire liberty amongst us. *Ib.* 398 And beinge a barrill of furrs was returned in that shippe . . . the collony hath taken order for the recruitinge of that loss. **1707** ARCHDALE *Carolina* 7 It is Pity they should be farther thin'd with civil Quarrels, being their Service is in all Respects so necessary. **1830** S. SMITH *Major Downing* (1834) 9 You may take 'em at 9d, being it's you. ?**1834** *Maj. Downing* (B. '48), The mug cost 15d. . . . , but bein it had a crack in it, I told her she neednt pay but a shilling for it. **1845** JUDD *Margaret* I. iv. 20 Bein' ye'll help Obed, I'll give ye the honey. **1879** TOURGEE *Fool's Errand* x. 44, I thought it would be no more than neighborly, being as you were strangers as I may say. **1889** FARMER 50 Being as you are going to town I need not trouble myself.

‖**2.** If.

1845 JUDD *Margaret* I. xvi. 141, I got two of um, and should have got the rest bein Dr. Spoor hadn't a come in.

+**Belduque.** *S.W.* [ad. Sp. *verdugo* (*Dialect Notes* I. 188).] A sheath knife. — **1838** 'TEXIAN' *Mexico v. Texas* 218 Away went the quarteroon, armed with a large knife, or *belduque*, to dig up the roots. *c***1892** *Dialect Notes* I. 188 *Belduque.* . . . This word is in very common use in Western Texas. **1894** *Scribner's Mag.* May 606/2 The smuggler . . . quickly drew his terrible 'belduque,' and slashing right and left he made his escape.

Belefelde. [f. *Bielefeld* in Westphalia.] A kind of linen. — **1833** *Niles' Reg.* XLIV. 269/1 Linens to be admitted at an ad valorem duty of 15 per cent. . . . [include] Britagnes: belefeldes: bodenwerders.

* **Belfry.** Also †**belvery, bellfary, belfrey.** A tower or cupola for a bell.

1692 *Manchester Rec.* 45 The s[ai]d house to be in the same form . . . of Wenham meeting hous with a . . . belvery on the top of s[ai]d house suteable for a good bell. **1704** *Boston News-Letter* 6 Nov. 2/2 There happened a Fire in Harvard Colledge . . . and the soot being blown into the Belfrey, fired some old Boards. **1713** *Narrag. Hist. Reg.* III. 276 The Terret or Bellfary on the Meeting House. **1809** F. CUMING *Western Tour* 95 The court-house of stone with a small belfry, has nothing in beauty to boast of. **1846** COOPER *Redskins* xiv, On top of this tower stood a long-legged belfry, which had got very dangerous. **1891** *Century Mag.* Jan. 402, I ascended one of the towers to the belfry.

Belgian, *a.* +Denoting a block of granite, trap, or other hard stone used for paving, or a pavement made of such blocks. Also absol. — **1864** A. DALY in *Life* (1917) 62 As full of rocks . . . as Broadway when Russ or Belgian is being laid. **1875** KNIGHT 1641 The pavements now in common use [include] . . . *Belgian,* similar to ashlar, but of smaller blocks. **1899** *Cent.* 512/3 Belgian blocks . . . for pavements. **1904** *Brooklyn Daily Eagle* 5 June, It ought also to be possible to leave well-defined routes of belgian blocks over which heavy loads may be drawn to every part of the city.

* **Believe,** *v.* In the phrase *you'd better believe:* see BETTER *adv.*

* **Beliked,** *a.* Well thought of; liked. {Now *dial.*} — **1818** ANN PETTIGREW *Let. to E. Pettigrew* 17 March (MS.), Mr. Mason, the new parson, has arrived and is very much beliked. **1843** 'CARLTON' *New Purchase* I. xix. 173, I do believe me and Nancy was beliked by them [Indians]. *a***1859** *Baltimore Cor.* in *N.Y. Herald* (B.), This gentleman is generally beliked by his fellow-citizens.

+**Belittle,** *v.*

1. *tr.* To make small, to reduce in size.

1781-2 JEFFERSON *Notes on Va.* (1788) 69 So far the Count de Buffon has carried this new theory of the tendency of nature to belittle her productions on this side the Atlantic. **1816** PICKERING 48 To *Belittle* . . . is sometimes heard here in conversation; but in writing, it is, I believe, peculiar to that gentleman [=Jefferson]. **1856** GOODRICH *Recoll.* I. 309 Every thing looked belittled, degenerated in dimensions. The house [=church] seemed small, the galleries low, the pulpit mean. *a***1859** *Brook Eastford* 124 (B.), We fear men's minds grow really belittled, where they ought to be enlarged. **1866** *N.Y. Herald* Jan., His occupation is not absolutely gone; but the end of the war has belittled it sadly.

2. To cause to appear small.

1850 S. COOPER *Rural Hours* I. 127 The hills . . . [do not] belittle the sheet of water. **1875** HOWELLS *Foregone Conclusion* 256 The simple tale of sickness and death inexpressibly belittled his passionate woes. **1883** H. GEORGE *Social Problems* (1884) 20 We have already corporations whose revenues and pay-rolls belittle those of the greatest States.

3. To speak slightingly of; to disparage. {1862-}

1797 *Independent Chron.* 30 March, [He] is . . . an honorable man, . . . let the writers . . . endeavour to belittle him as much as they please. **1834** *Knickerb.* IV. 57, I have said that, to be a contemporary, is to be belittled. **1857** *N.Y. Times* 10 Jan. (B.), The usual efforts were made to belittle the press, and treat its censures with contempt. **1870** R. G. WHITE *Words* 219 A certain time is spent by each party in belittling and reviling the candidates of its opponents. **1884** *Harper's Mag.* May 864/1 Persistent efforts to belittle it, or regard it as exaggerated, have failed.

+**Belittling,** *a.* **a.** Reducing in size. **b.** Disparaging; discrediting.

1796 MORSE *Amer. Univ. Geog.* I. 230 The Abbe Raynal, in a former edition of his works, supposed this belittling tendency or influence had its effect on the race of whites transplanted from Europe. **1843** *Knickerb.* XXI. 411 A condition even more inevitably belittling (if we may be allowed the use of a kitchen word in a utilitarian discussion) than any mechanical employment. **1856** S. WARNER *Hills Shatemuc* 175, I never heard such a belittling character of the profession.

* **Bell.**

* **1.** A bell to be rung, or to ring, for various purposes, esp. to give general notice of a meeting.

1632 *Cambridge Rec.* 24 Dec. 4 Every person . . . shall be . . . within the meeting-house in the afternoon within half an ouer [=hour] after the ringing of the bell. **1654** JOHNSON *Wonder-w. Prov.* 103 They had as yet no Bell to call Men to meeting. **1680** *Dedham Rec.* V. 104 The Town did disire that a meete person should . . . ringe the Bell constantly att nine of the clock euery night. **1702** *Boston Rec.* 25 It being proposed . . . dureing the present sickness . . . that there be only a first and second bell tol'd at each Funerall. **1734** *Harvard Rec.* I. 137 No undergraduates shall go to the meeting House on the Lords day, before the ringing of the second bell. *a***1772** WOOLMAN *Journal* 120 In the woods we were under some disadvantage, having no fire-works nor bells for our horses. **1777** *Journals Cont. Congress* VIII. 741 An order to remove all public bells, in Philadelphia, to a place of security, upon a near approach of the enemy. **1813** *N.Y. State Soc. Arts* III. 22 A foundery for casting bells was erected more than forty years since in Massachusetts, and the business has been continued in that state ever since. **1828** WEBSTER s.v., In private houses, bells are used to call servants, either hung and moved by a wire, or as hand-bells. **1860** A. Redford *Hist. Methodism Ky.* (1870) II. 436 The stills were worked up into bells and stew-kettles. **1866** 'F. KIRKLAND' *Bk. Anecdotes* 260 He . . . eluded the Confederate pickets, by wearing a big sheep's bell on his head, and bleating away over the mountains. **1884** ROE *Nature's Story* 87 The horses' bells now chiming musically in the still air.

+**b.** As an ornament worn by Indians.

1809 F. CUMING *Western Tour* 246 We walked to the Indian burying ground . . . and picked up some of the small copper bells, used by the natives for ornament.

+**c.** *transf.* (See quotation.)

1895 *Outing* Dec. 218/2 [The caribou's] coat was a beautiful mouse color, . . . and he had a fine bell—*i.e.,* long, hanging white hair under the throat.

+**2.** *pl.* The rings forming the rattle of a rattlesnake. *Obs.*

1781 S. PETERS *Hist. Conn.* 261 Before they bite, they [rattlesnakes] rattle their bells three or four times.

Belladine. *Obs.* {1721 'Bellandine, or white Turkey Silk'} A silk fabric. Usu. *Belladine silk.* — **1733** *S.C. Gazette* 282/1 Just Imported, . . . white and black alamode, . . . beladine silk. **1759** *Newport* (R.I.) *Mercury* 26 June 4/3 To be sold by Jacob Richardson, . . . best Belladine sewing Silks. **1762** *Ib.* 7 Sept. 3/2 To be sold . . . , broglio's, light and cloth colour'd belladine.

+**Bell-boy.**

1. A boy who rings a bell.

1851 MELVILLE *Moby Dick* xxxix, Eight bells there! d'ye hear, bell-boy?

2. A boy who answers the bell in a hotel.

1879 B. F. TAYLOR *Summer-Savory* x. 90 [The bustler] degrades me in the sight of the bell-boys . . . and the office lounger. **1886** *Harper's Mag.* Dec. 147/2 Neither of them had observed the bell-boy's face as Beryl ordered her ice-water. **1889** *Century Mag.* March 664/1, I dance in the hall, swear at the bell-boy, and finally fall asleep in my clothes. **1897** BRODHEAD *Bound in Shallows* 57 Issuing loud orders to the small negro boy who filled the offices of bell-boy, waiter, and porter in the hotel. **1904** W. H. SMITH *Promoters* iii. 63 A hotel . . . where porters or bell-boys would do any service for a commensurate tip. **1913** LA FOLLETTE *Autobiog.* 154 Sunday evening I was surprised to receive a note from Harshaw brought to me by a bellboy from the Park Hotel, Madison.

Bell-buoy. A buoy with a bell attached to it, sounding by the motion of the waves.

1838 FLAGG *Far West* I. 22 The hated clang of the bell-boy [*sic*] was soon after heard resounding far and wide in querulous and deafening clamour throughout the cabins [of an Ohio river boat]. **1882** *Harper's Mag.* Sept. 593/1 Away far off in the distance she thought she heard the measured clang of the bell buoy. **1897** *Outing* May 162/2 The tolling of the bell-buoy marking the inner bar floated tremulously, mournfully across the darkened waters. **1910** J. HART *Vigilante Girl* 12 The sound of bells also came over the water . . . as the waves tumbled a bell-buoy half over, and then tumbled it back again.

+**Bell-button.**

1. A small bell worn as a button by Indians. *Obs.*

1775 ADAIR *Indians* 7 The beaus . . . choose bell-buttons, to give a greater sound. *Ib.* 171 The young warriors now frequently fasten bell-buttons, or pieces of tinkling brass to their maccaseenes, and to the outside of their boots.

2. An ornamental button having the shape of a globular bell.

1839 *S. Lit. Messenger* V. 329/1, I had on, for the first time, a pair of new blue breeches . . . adorned with bell-buttons. *Ib.*, I just began to move in, glittering (that is the bell-buttons) like the morning star. **1851** MELVILLE *Moby Dick* vi. 36 In bespeaking his sea-outfit, he orders bell-buttons to his waistcoats. **1852** MITCHELL *Dream Life* vi. 89 Among the boys . . . a blue jacket that you wear, with bell buttons of white metal, is their especial wonderment. **1871** D. E. Wood *West Point Scrap-Book* 65 So sets of 'bell buttons' for dresses Are exchanged [by cadets] for a lock of your hair. **1904** *Cent. Mil. Acad. at West Point* I. 519 [In 1863] acting assistant instructors (Cadets) wore rows of buttons containing double the regulation number of bell buttons on their dress coats. **1917** R. C. RICHARDSON *West Point* 97 The present list includes . . . a single-breasted coat of blue gray cloth, with three rows of gilt bell buttons in front.

+**Bell-buttoned,** *a.* (See preceding, sense 2.) — **1871** O. E. Wood *West Point Scrap Book* 111 The bell-buttoned brevity of the cadet's coat-tail.

+**Bell cart.** *Obs.* A cart announced by the ringing of a bell. — **1766** J. T. Buckingham *Newspaper Lit.* I. 35 The Bell Cart will go through Boston before the end of next month, to collect Rags for the Paper-Mill at Milton.

+**Bell-collar.** A collar, usu. of leather, for suspending a bell from the neck of a horse, cow, etc. — **1839** FOOTE *Sk. Virginia* (1850) 514, I took hold of the horse by the bell collar, and then he [=an Indian] came running up and scared the horse away.

+**Bell cord.** A cord to be pulled in order to ring a bell; spec. one running through a passenger car. Also fig.

1843 *Knickerb.* XXI. 332 The man . . . look'd for a bell-rope to summon the host [of the inn] for writing materials; but he found no bell-cord to pull. **1875** *Chicago Tribune* 2 July 8/1 When a half-drunken man has hold of the bell-cord instead of the strap to steady himself by. **1887** GEORGE 40 *Years on Rail* ii. 32 In the old cars the bell-cord ran over the top and was wound on a reel. **1891** E. S. ELLIS *Check No. 2134* xiii. 88 A brakeman . . . with the bell cord grasped, ready to give the signal.

+**Bell-cow.** A cow with a bell suspended from her neck. Also transf.

1878 H. H. JACKSON *Travel at Home* 313 It is the faint and distant tinkle of the bell-cow's bell. **1896** G. ADE *Artie* xi. 103 If you can't travel with the bell-cows, why stick to the gang? **1904** T. WATSON *Bethany* 20, I hear the 'toll, tolang, toll, tolang,' of the bell-cow down in the meadow by the creek.

+**Bell-crown.** A bell-shaped crown on a hat; a hat with this kind of crown. Also attrib.

1843 [STEPHENS] *High Life N.Y.* II. xxviii. 170 There I sot, with the old bell-crown atween my knees. **1843** *Knickerb.* XXI. 585, I love it, I love it, and who shall frown, Because I still sport that old bell-crown? **1857** *Quinland* I. 103 Last of all appeared the white beaver-hat, with a very narrow brim, with a very high bell crown. *c***1870** BAGBY *Old Va. Gentleman* 27 The typical Yankee, in bell-crown hat, swallow-tail coat. **1879** B. F. TAYLOR *Summer-Savory* vi. 51 The roomy bell-crowns, that flared like an old-time wooden churn bottom side up.

+**Bell-crowned,** *a.* Of a hat: Having a crown shaped like an inverted bell.

1821 DODDRIDGE *Backwoodsman & Dandy*, Betsy . . . said it was a thing called a Dandy, . . . with your bell crowned hat. **1840** *S. Lit. Messenger* VI. 733/1 His bell-crowned hat was tilted over his left eyebrow when he walked. **1843** *Knickerb.* XXI. 333 Lusty young farmers . . . in blue frocks and white bell-crowned hats. **1855** *S. Lit. Messenger* XXI. 221 His hat might have been originally a bell-crowned black beaver. **1865** 'MARK TWAIN' in *Sk. Sixties* (1926) xiv. 203 Pictures . . . of men with swallow-tailed coats and bell-crowned hats.

Belled, *a.* [BELL 2.] +*Belled snake*, a rattlesnake. *Obs.* — **1781** S. PETERS *Hist. Conn.* 260 The belled or rattle snakes are large.

+**Belle-fleur.** [F.] A variety of apple. Cf. BELL-FLOWER². — **1856** *Rep. Comm. Patents: Agric.* 292 Winter apples [include] . . . Ortley, or White Belle-fleur. **1864** *Ohio Agric. Rep.* XVIII. App. 49 The Bellefleur apple grafted upon the Sweet Bough was less acid than usual.

+**Bell factory.** A bell foundry. — **1841** *Niles' Nat. Reg.* 24 July 336/2 The destruction by fire, of the bell factory in Madison county, Ala.

* **Bell-flower¹.** A flower of one or other species of the genus *Campanula.*

1741 MILLER *Gardener's Dict.* (ed. 2) I. s.v., *Campanula minor Americana*, . . . Dwarf American Bell-flower, with rigid Leaves, and blue Flowers. *Ib.*, Dwarf American Bell-flower, with rigid Leaves, and white Flowers. **1821** *Mass. H. S. Coll.* 2 Ser. IX. 147–8 Plants, which are indigenous in the township of Middlebury, [Vermont, include] . . . *Campanula erinoides*, Prickly bell-flower. . . . *Campanula perfoliata*, Clasping bell-flower. **1839** in *Mich. Agric. Soc. Trans.* VII. (1856) 402 *Campanula erinoides*, Prickly bell-flower. *C. rotundifolia*, Flax bell-flower. **1840** DEWEY *Mass. Flowering Plants* 109 *Campanula medium*, common Bell Flower, . . . is a very beautiful flower of different colors. **1867** *Amer. Naturalist* I. 406, I examined some half a dozen or more species of Bellflower, or Campanula. **1896** WILKINS *Madelon* 31 Her blue brocade petticoat tilting airily . . . like an inverted bell-flower.

+**Bell-flower².** Also **belleflower.**

1. =BELLE-FLEUR. Also attrib. with *apple, pippin.*

1817 W. COXE *Fruit Trees* 120 *Bell-Flower*, a remarkably large, beautiful and excellent apple, both for the dessert and for cooking. **1847** IVES *New Eng. Fruit* 41 Bellflower . . . is a large and beautiful apple. The form is very oblong, tapering to the eye. **1857** WARDER *Pomology* 712 Bellflower Pippin . . . [is cultivated in] Ind. **1864** LOWELL *Fireside Travels* 34 There's the bell-flower apple, and folks that like a sweet apple generally like that. **1868** *Mich. Agric. Rep.* VII. 430 Tested fruits recommended by the Western Michigan Lake-Shore Association [include] Apples: . . . Yellow Bellflower, Canada Red. **1875** STOWE *Deacon Pitkin* vii. 81, I was up to the store with some o' Squire Jones's bell flowers.

2. The tree bearing this variety of apple.

1876 BURROUGHS *Winter Sunshine* vii. 163 The thick . . . top of the belleflower, with its equally rich, sprightly, uncloying fruit. **1884** ROE *Nature's Story* 400 Those [trees] that are rather long and slender branching are yellow bell-flowers.

* **Bell-founder.** One who casts bells. — **1851** CIST *Cincinnati* 297 He engaged in business with T. B. & H. B. Coffin as bell and brassfounders.

Bell foundry (†**foundery**). A foundry in which bells are cast. — **1796** *Boston Directory* 277 Revere, Paul, bell and cannon foundry. **1827** DRAKE & MANSF. *Cincinnati* viii. 65 One brass and bell foundery. **1851** CIST *Cincinnati* 172 This is the only bell-foundery in the United States, in which bells are constructed upon purely scientific principles.

+**Bell-frog.** *S.* and *S.E.* A species of frog (see quots. 1791, 1827). — **1791** BARTRAM *Travels through Carolina*, etc. 277 The bell frog, so called because their voice is fancied to be exactly like the sound of a loud cow bell. **1827** WILLIAMS *West Florida* 29 The Bell or Virginia frog, is only found in the eastern district; and there they are not numerous. **1853** *Harper's Mag.* Nov. 771/1 The tinkling of the bell-frog, and the chirp of the savanna-cricket—all fell upon my ear [in s. La.].

Bell-hanger. One whose business is to hang bells.

1789 *Boston Rec.* 202 Whall, William, smith and bell-hanger. **1791** JEFFERSON in *Harper's Mag.* March (1885) 534/2 Paid a bell hanger on a/c., 5s. **1841** BUCKINGHAM *America* I. xii. 223 Locksmiths and bell-hangers are a class of workmen that also go their rounds. **1851** W. IRVING in *Life* IV. 71 Plumbers and bellhangers [are] to attack the vitals of the house. **1906** *Boston Directory* 2151 Locksmiths' and Bell Hangers' Supplies.

+**Bell-horse.** A horse furnished with a bell, serving as leader to a pack-train. Cf. BELL-MARE.

1775 ADAIR *Indians* 337 But they [*sc.* the Choctaw Indians] used an artful stratagem, . . . for they stole one of the bell horses, and led it away. **1857** MRS. BATES *On Pacific Coast* 237 These trains are led by a horse, with a bell attached to his neck. He is designated the bell-horse, and these mules have such an affection for him, that they will follow anywhere he goes. **1884** F. M. A. ROE *Army Lett.* 320 The bell horse leads, and wherever it goes the mules will follow. **1891** *Harper's Mag.* Nov. 890/1 The pack trains consisted of a 'bell-horse' and boy, and six horses following.

+**Belling,** *vbl. n.* [BELL.] A charivari. — **1862** G. W. WILDER *MS. Diary* 18 July, E. thought we would probably get a belling.

* **Bell-maker.** A bell-founder. — **1809** F. CUMING *Western Tour* 222 Pittsburgh [has] . . . one bell maker; three tallow-chandlers.

* **Bellman.** A man who goes about a town ringing a bell as a means of giving public notice; a night-watchman (*obs.*); a town-crier.

1653 *Boston Rec.* 115 The Seleckt men are to provid a bellman for to goe about the towne in the night from tenn unto five a Clocke in the morning at such times in Winter as thear is noe wach kept in the towne. **1663** *Ib.* 18 Edward Dauis and Joseph Gridly . . . to be the Bellmen of the Towne. **1698** SEWALL *Diary* I. 486 Davis, the Bell-man, told me of it when he [came] . . . to call me to Court. **1701** *Ib.* II. 27 [The] Bell-man said these [New Year] verses a little before break-a-day. **1705** in *Hist. Charlestown* (1845–9) 244 David Ray to be bellman, to go about the town with his bell every night from eleven o'clock until five in the morning, to keep watch for alarums and fires, and give timely notice thereof. **1730** *Boston Rec.* 17 The Scavengers have power to order a bellman or some propper Person to warn the People to rake up their Dirt. *a***1821** BIDDLE *Autobiog.* iv. 237, I called on him for the money; upon which he sent a bell-man round the town, sold a hogshead of rum [etc.]. **1846** *Knickerb.* XXVII. 174 The first thing he did was to despatch a bell-man through the streets [of Cincinnati], giving notice that the exhibition would take place that evening. **1863** MASSETT *Drifting About* 156 The bellman, to whom I had paid five dollars for ringing in the people, . . . had just informed me that the house was full. **1881** *Harper's Mag.* Jan. 181/2 Only a few years since the old town bellman was a dignitary of considerable importance . . . as he walked along the stony streets ringing his bell.

+**Bell-mare.** A mare provided with a bell, serving as leader to a pack-train. Cf. BELL-HORSE.

1853 BREWERTON *With Kit Carson* (1930) 41 The wily Californians . . . are in the habit of employing a steady old white mare . . . to act as a kind of mother and guide to each drove of unruly mules. This animal is sometimes called the 'bell-mare' from a large bell they attach to her neck. **1859** MARCY *Prairie Traveler* iv. 102 In crossing rivers the bell-mare should pass first, after which the mules are easily induced to take to the water. **1876** BOURKE *Journal* Feb. 27 In organizing the trains, 'bell-mares' . . . are provided: these are most preferably white mares having bells hung around their necks. The mules speedily learn the sound of their proper bell and rarely fail to heed its warning. **1880** *Scribner's Mo.*

May 126/2 He mounted the bell-mare and started off, the train of pack animals filed along behind.

*Bell metal.** An alloy of copper and tin used for making bells, and for other purposes. Freq. attrib. =made of this metal.

1646 *Conn. Public Rec.* I. 482 One bell mettell morter. **1647** *Essex Probate Rec.* I. 70, 3 brasse potts, one bell metle skillett, on[e] litle bell skillet. **1684** *Essex Inst. Coll.* XXV. 154 In the kitchen [are] three brasse ketles, a bel metle pot. **1701** *N.H. Probate Rec.* I. 474 My great Bell-mettal-mortar and Pistill. **1711** *Springfield Rec.* II. 41 Three Dozen of Belmettle Buttons at 7d the dozen. **1720** SEWALL *Letter-book* II. 106 One bell-metal skillet of two quarts. **1790** *Gazette U.S.* 16 Jan. 1/3 It seems to me that his throat is lined with bell metal. **1825** NEAL *Bro. Jonathan* I. 82 The clock sounded—a cumbrous old affair, with a bell-metal face. **1868** G. G. CHANNING *Recoll. Newport* 160 The sirup . . . being ready in a bell-metal skillet, each piece of the prepared quince was dropped gently into it.

+**Bell-mule.** Cf. BELL-HORSE, -MARE. — **1876** MILLER *First Families* iii. 23 She had ridden the bell mule of the pack-train.

Bellows fish. {1684-} *New Eng.* and *N.Y.* +The American angler, *Lophius piscatorius.*

1807 *Mass. H. S. Coll.* 2 Ser. III. 55 The puff fish, or swell fish, or bellows fish, is a cartilaginous fish. It is seven inches long; and . . . its proportions are those of a sculpion nearly. **1814** MITCHILL *Fishes N.Y.* 466 [The] common Angler . . . is called by some the bellows-fish, . . . from a power to . . . swell himself immediately after being taken out of water. **1842** *Nat. Hist. N.Y., Zoology* IV. 163 The American Angler. . . . Its monstrous form has given rise to many popular names, such as Sea Devil, Fishing Frog, Bellows-fish. **1871** *Harper's Mag.* June 30 The lophius, or bellows-fish, which seems to be mostly mouth, is properly named angler. **1889** *Cent.* 516/3 *Bellows fish,* . . . a local name in Rhode Island of the angler, *Lophius piscatorius.*

+**Bellows top. 1.** A collapsible top of a chaise. **2.** Egg-flip. — **(1)** **1815** *Columbian Centinel* 28 June 3/3 (Advt.), 4 new bellows top chaises. **1890** *Harper's Mag.* Oct. 718/1 Willis . . . drove a square-topped gig, being that two-wheeled vehicle known as a Boston 'chaise,' but with a square instead of a bellows top. **(2)** **1873** JOEL PARKER *Centenn. Address* (B.), When egg was beaten in it, it was called bellows-top; partly, perhaps, from its superior quality and partly from the greater quantity of white froth that swelled to the top of it.

Bellows trousers. (See quotation.) — **1861** *Vanity Fair* 26 Jan. 45/1 The original pair [of trousers were] . . . plaited prominently over the hips and gathered in with a drawing-string round the ankles. They were called bellows trowsers in those days, from their form.

+**Bell pear.** A variety of pear; the tree bearing this.

1786 WASHINGTON *Diaries* III. 24 In the No. Et. square of this garden, . . . 7 Row, 3 Bell Pears East. [**1849** *New Eng. Farmer* I. 79 It has been done, with good success, in this town, on a pear-tree of the Bell variety.] **1856** COZZENS *Sparrowgrass P.* xi. 146 He takes kindly to his feed, and has already eaten himself into the shape of a bell-pear.

Bell-pull. A handle or cord by which a bell is rung. {1832-} — **1842** *Knickerb.* XX. 437 Not a brass knob, knocker or bell-pull but brightly reflected its neighbor on the opposite side of the way. **1881** STODDARD *E. Hardery* 286 Black crape on the bell-pull to-day. **1908** WHITE *Riverman* viii. 71 He returned . . . and pulled at the old-fashioned wire bell-pull.

+**Bell-puller.** A bell-pull. — **1843** *Amer. Pioneer* II. 91 He rapped with his knuckles, for knockers and bell-pullers were unknown.

+**Bell-punch.** An instrument that punches and rings a bell, such as a conductor on a street car uses in collecting fares. — **1877** BARTLETT 253 *Gong-Punch,* an instrument used by conductors [etc.] . . . ; a bell-punch. **1880** *Harper's Mag.* Feb. 438/1 Happily for them, the Cosmopolitan had not then introduced the bell-punch. **1883** *Ib.* Sept. 643/2 'I don't believe they would trust *me* to take up a collection.' . . . 'They would—if you had a bell-punch.'

*Bell-ringer.** One whose duty is to ring a bell, usually at stated intervals for a special purpose.

1656 *Essex Inst. Coll.* IX. 190 The belringere is to digge the graues to interr the dead. **1667** *Harvard Rec.* I. 48 The Bel-Ringers office is, to ring the bell (except for meales), to keep the clock, & to call the president to prayers. **1695** SEWALL *Diary* I. 411 Robt. Williams the Bell-Ringer, Publisher, and Grave-digger died this morn. **1717** *Boston Selectmen* 22 Ordered, that the T. clerk do supply the several sextons or bell ringers . . . with the penall order . . . relating to regulating of Buryalls. **1855** *Harvard Mag.* I. 56 The College bell-ringer . . . discovered that the flame of love had heated his tender sensibilities. **1871** [L. H. BAGG] *At Yale* 17 The room of the bell ringer, upon the second floor, is the only one used as a dormitory. **1894** 'MARK TWAIN' *P. Wilson* v, Tom . . . found the old deformed negro bell-ringer straddling along in his wake.

Bell-ringing. The ringing of a bell; the time at which a bell is rung (for church). — **1833** *Niles' Reg.* XLIV. 14/2 They left Mr. Bradlee's house on Sunday morning, at bell-ringing, proposing to go to Trinity Church.

Bell-rope. A rope by means of which a bell is rung; a bell-cord or bell-pull. {1638-}

1647 *Watertown Rec.* 17 Due to ould Knop . . . for a bellroope [*sic*], and for mending the Meeting house dore, . . . 6s. 6d. **1721** J. HEMPSTEAD *Diary* 110 I p[ai]d him 3s . . . for a Bell-rope. **1837** *Harvardiana* IV. 4 She pulled the bell rope. **1843** [see BELL-CORD]. **1856** M. J. HOLMES *Homestead on Hillside* i, Mrs. Hamilton's hand involuntarily sought the bell-rope, to summon some one else to her room. **1887** GEORGE *40 Yrs. on Rail* 227, I pulled the bell-rope [on the train] and forced him off.

+**Bell's finch, greenlet.** [Named by Audubon for J. G. *Bell.*] (See quotations.) — **1844** AUDUBON *Birds of Am.* VII. 333 Bell's Vireo or Greenlet, *Vireo Bellii,* . . . is usually found in the bottom lands along the shores of the Upper Missouri river. **1858** BAIRD *Birds Pacific R.R.* 470 Bell's Finch. . . . *Hab.*—Southern California and valley of Gila and Colorado to Fort Thorn. **1869** *Amer. Naturalist* III. 184 A new bird . . . running on the ground with much the appearance of Snow-birds. This was Bell's Finch (*Poospiza Bellii*), one of the more southern group. — **1873** *Ib.* VII. 199 Bell's greenlet (*Vireo Bellii*); a species of the plains.

+**Bell-squash.** A species of squash shaped like a bell. — **1843** [STEPHENS] *High Life N.Y.* II. xxi. 52 A great smashing bunch of posies as big as a bell-squash choked in at the neck.

Bell strap. A strap by which a bell is rung on a street-car, etc. — **1888** WHITMAN *November Boughs* 406 [The conductor's] characteristic duty is to constantly pull or snatch the bell-strap, to stop or go on.

+**Bell's vireo.** =Bell's greenlet (q.v.). — **1844** [see above]. **1858** BAIRD *Birds Pacific R. R.* 337 *Vireo Belli,* Aud. Bell's Vireo. . . . *Hab.*—Missouri river and eastern Texas. **1874** COUES *Birds N.W.* 101 Bell's Vireo . . . [is] abundant in Kansas.

Bell tent. A tent shaped like a bell. {1785-} — **1778** *Journals Cont. Congress* X. 20 The Deputy Quarter Master General [is] . . . to provide one thousand good bell Tents and send them to the Army. **1888** BILLINGS *Hardtack* 47 On account of its [the Sibley tent's] resemblance to a huge bell, it has sometimes been called a Bell Tent.

+**Bell time.** The time, announced by a bell, for resuming or ceasing work, etc. — **1845** *Lowell Offering* V. 98 Just look at the clock and you will find that it is but five minutes to 'bell time.'

*Bell wheel.** The wheel attached to the yoke of a church bell in order to ring it. — **1665** *Rowley Rec.* 162 William Boynton for . . . tending about . . . and sucoring windowes and the bell wheel. **1725** *Md. Hist. Mag.* VII. 277 To . . . makeing a Door to the Belfrey & mending the Bell wheel.

Bellwort. {*c*1840 (Lindley)}

+**1.** A plant of the genus *Uvularia,* native to the eastern and central states.

1784 CUTLER in *Mem. Academy* I. 434 *Uvularia,* . . . Bellwort, Sweet-smelling Solomon's Seal, Jacob's Ladder. **1818** *Mass. H. S. Coll.* 2 Ser. VIII. 168 At the same time appear the blossoms of the alder, hazel, and poplar; soon after those of the uvularia or bellwort. **1843** TORREY *Flora N.Y.* II. 319 *Uvularia perfoliata,* . . . Perfoliate Bellwort. **1850** JUDD *R. Edney* xxvi. 277 He . . . adorned their hats with bellworts and laurels. *a*1862 THOREAU *Maine Woods* 320 *Uvularia grandiflora,* large-flowered bellwort. **1901** MOHR *Plant Life Ala.* 438 *Uvularia* . . . [includes] Large-flowered bellwort, . . . Perfoliate bellwort, . . . Mountain bellwort, . . . Oakes's bellwort.

2. A plant of the family *Campanulaceae.* {1884}

1869 FULLER *Flower Gatherers* 219 The *Campanulaceae,* or Bell-worts, a family remarkable for beauty rather than for any very valuable qualities.

+**Bellyache root.** A species of angelica (see quotations). — **1775** ADAIR *Indians* 412 None of the Indians however eat any kind of raw sallads; . . . few of them have gardens, and it is but of late they have any angelica, or bellyach-root; this is one of their physical greens, which they call *Looksooshe.* **1789** *Amer. Philos. Soc.* III. p. xviii, Cholick is removed, by the oil of the Spicewood-berries: the flatulent and hysteric kind, eminently so by Angelica *lucida* . . . , called therefore *belly-ach-root.*

+**Belly bacon.** Pork from the belly of a hog. — *a*1775 J. BOUCHER *Glossary* 50 At dinner, let me that best buck-skin dish, Broth, . . . cat-fish, . . . and belly bacon see.

+**Belly-bender.** 'Floating pieces of ice, or weak ice, which bend under one, as he passes from one cake to another. Boys take great pleasure in this precarious amusement' (B. '77).

+**Belly-bumbo, -bump(s), -bunt, -flumps.** *colloq.*[2] A way of coasting down hill while lying face downwards. Also *belly-bump* v.

Other variants, as *belly-bunk, -buster, -flop, -flounder, -gutter, -plumper, -whack, -whopper,* are given by Bartlett (1877) and in *Dial. Notes* I. 60, 235, 377, 412.

1855 WILLIS *Convalescent* 75 The only attitude he patronizes on his sled ('belly-flumps') is slightly apoplectic. **1877** BARTLETT 39 Belly-bumbo. **1888** *Chicago Inter-Ocean* (F.), Barney had his sled out yesterday, belly-bumping on a little patch of ice and snow. **1890** *Dialect Notes* I. 60 In Maine and Massachusetts are used 'to go belly-bump' and 'to go belly-bunt.' **1904** WALLER *Wood-carver* 63 There is a fine coast for good two thirds of the way down the Pent Road; . . . she tells me she always slides 'bellybump.'

+**Belly-bumper.** *colloq.*[2] **1.** (See quot. 1890.) **2.** =BELLY-BUMBO. — **(1)** **1868** G. G. CHANNING *Recoll. Newport* 33 The boy who happened to make the 'belly-bumper' movement, as it was termed, was ejected from the circle. **1890** *Dialect Notes* I. 60 *Belly-bumper,* an awkward dive, when the boy, instead of cleaving the water with his hands and head, falls flat on his stomach with a splash. Common in Philadelphia. **(2)** *c*1892 *Ib.* 211 *Setters, steerers, belly-bumpers,* three ways of coasting. Salem.

+**Belly-guts.** *colloq.*[2] **1.** *Penna.* Molasses candy. **2.** =BELLY-BUMBO. — **(1)** **1849** WM. DUANE *Let. to Bartlett* (MS.) 22 Jan., *Belly Guts,* a Pennsylvania word, now becoming obsolete, being supplanted by the more elegant, though perhaps not quite correct, name of molasses candy. **1870** *Nation* 4 Aug. 73/1 'Hippen' does not belong to us. 'Belly-guts' still survives. (Your *belles-gouttes* is very ingenious.) — (2) **1859** BARTLETT 29 *Belly-guts*, . . . a term applied by boys to the manner of sliding down hill on their sleds, when lying on their bellies. **1892** *Jrnl. Amer. Folk-Lore* V. 145 *Bellygut, Bellyhump*, terms used [in Mass.] in 'coasting.' To lie on a sled with the face down.

* **Belong,** *v.* +*intr.* To have natural connection or association *with* something; to be in its (or one's) proper place or sphere.

1821 COOPER *Spy* xxvi, I have never known whether he belonged above or below. **1845** — *Chainbearer* vi, Most of the craft on the Hudson belonged up the river. **1861** HOLMES *E. Venner* xxvii, You belong with the last [set], and got accidentally shuffled in with the others. **1866** A. WILSON *St. Elmo* x, To replace it in the glass box where it belongs. **1889** WHITMAN in *Century Mag.* Jan. (1911) 256/2 He was not a closet man, belonged out-of-doors. **1903** K. D. WIGGIN *Rebecca* xxvi. 290, I'll put dumplings round the aidge; they're turrible fillin', though they don't belong with boiled chicken.

* **Beloved,** *a.* Loved, dear. +Used freq. in the literal translation of Indian phrases, as 'beloved bear-ground,' 'beloved ground,' 'beloved man.'

1733 *Georgia Col. Rec.* III. 381 Their Chief and his beloved Man . . . desire to be instructed in the Christian Religion. **1749** *Ib.* VI. 266 They then were told, that to morrow [Sunday] was our great Beloved Day, on which we did no Business. *Ib.* 267 The Great King had sent these Goods to the Beloved Men here. **1772** TAITT in *Travels Amer. Col.* 527, I was not a beloved man but some runaway. **1797** [see BEAR-GROUND]. **1800** B. HAWKINS *Sk. Creek Country* 70 The cabin of the beloved men . . . fronts the north. **1813** *Niles' Reg.* V. 284/1 There were assembled at Autosse, warriors from eight towns for its defence, it being their beloved ground.

* **Below,** *adv.*

+**1.** At or to a lower point on a river.

1645 *Springfield Rec.* I. 164 The brooke in the longe meddow . . . and the brooke a little below on the other side. **1665–70** *Lancaster Rec.* 297 His enteruail lott . . . lyeth below upon the River. **1755** *Lett. to Washington* I. 152, I could not engage the wintering of them below through the scarcity of Fodder. **1777** in *S. Lit. Messenger* XXVII. 253/1 The whole militia here, lately called below, were of volunteers without a single draft. **1816** BRACKENRIDGE *Journal Voy. Missouri* 197 There must . . . be a hiatus between the settlements which may hereafter be made above, and those below. **1819** *Niles' Reg.* XVII. 112/1 A late Nashville paper notices the arrival there of . . . 'Line boat, No. 11,' with full cargoes of dry goods, sugars, &c. from below. **1827** COOPER *Prairie* ii, They told us, below, we should find settlers something thinnish here-away. *Ib.* xxxiii, I had hoped and believed that you would have accompanied us below. **1845** SIMMS *Wigwam & Cabin* 14 His course seemed like their own to lie below. **1846** LYELL *Second Visit* (1849) II. 111 'A fine opportunity of going below,' . . . he explained, . . . merely signifies 'going down the river.'

+**2.** Off a port or shore. *Obs.*

1711 *Boston News-Letter* 25 June 2/1 New-York, June 18. . . . A Pink is below from Maderas. **1714** *Ib.* 6 September 2/1 Capt. James Goold is arrived below from Boston. **1716** SEWALL *Diary* III. 104 Capt. Belchar told me, there was a Ship below, suppos'd twas the Gov[erno]r. **1857** *Harper's Mag.* Feb. 348/1 When the packet-ship *Bunkum* was announced as 'below,' there was a great stir at the Astor House.

Below, *prep.* Lower down (on a river) than. {1691–}

1672 *Topsfield Rec.* 14 Doune to the bridg that goeth ouer the riuer below old Goodman Townes. **1684** *Manchester Rec.* 15 The Landing Place at the water side blow [*sic*] the town bridge. **1759** *Essex Inst. Coll.* XIX. 67 We travelled from Half moon to the place called the 3 mile house bellow Stillwater. **1777** *Virginia State P.* I. 283 The Deponent . . . proposed purchasing the lands below the Kentuckey. **1807** *Ann. 10th Congress* 1 Sess. I. 445 Tyler's boats lay below our own about seven or eight rods. **1809** F. CUMING *Western Tour* 244 Highland creek . . . is three miles below Slim island. **1821** COOPER *Spy* iv, Were you ignorant, Captain Wharton, that our pickets have been below you for several days? **1898** CANFIELD *Maid of Frontier* 168 On the banks of the Jim Ned [creek], five miles below town.

+**Belshnickle, Belsh Nichel.** [G. (Palatinate and Saar) dial. *Pelznickel*, f. *pelz* fur, *Nickel* Nicholas.] Santa Claus. — **1823** James *Long's Exped.* I. 188 Our Belshnickles, who make their appearance on Christmas-eve. **1830** J. F. WATSON *Philadelphia* 242 The 'Belsh Nichel' and St. Nicholas has been a time of Christmas amusement from time immemorial among us. *Ib.*, Every father in his turn remembers the excitements of his youth in Belsh-nichel and Christkinkle nights.

Belt, *n.*

* **1.** A strip of leather or other flexible material worn round the waist and holding weapons, etc.; in later quotations esp. with reference to frontier or western use.

1637 *Conn. Public Rec.* 12 Gones, swordes, belts, Bandilers, . . . are to be delivered into the handes of the saide Constables. **1688** *Conn. Probate Rec.* 442, I do give to my son . . . two swords & two belts; also my great Bible. **1777** *Rec. N.H. Comm. Safety* 92 One Hundred Pounds to buy Belts for the Soldiers. **1837** BIRD *Nick of Woods* I. iv. 63 Bloody Nathan . . . had a long rifle on his shoulder, and a knife in his belt. **1852** *Knickerb.* XXXIX. 224 Buckling on my pistol-belt, with its trusty revolver, I mounted a fine-limbed, powerful gray. **1869** 'MARK TWAIN' *Sk., Journalism in Tenn.*, He snatched a navy revolver from his belt and fired. **1880** HAYES *New Colorado* ix. (1881) 120 Among the passengers was a . . . fierce-looking man, girded with a belt full of revolvers and cartridges, and clearly a road agent.

+**b.** An Indian belt composed of wampum, used esp. as a token of friendship. See quot. 1778 and cf. WAMPUM-BELT.

Usually in such phrases as 'belt of wampum,' 'belt of peake' (i.e. wampumpeag), 'belt of peace.'

1663 *Md. Archives* 472 A vast Expence of 70 Belts of Peake. **1664** *Md. Council Proc.* 499 Hee . . . had brought a present for the Christians of forty Beavers & bealts of peake. **1685** T. BUDD *Penna. & N.J.* 65 The Indian Kings . . . had prepared four Belts of Wampum (so their current Money is called, being black and white Beads made of a Fish shell). **1723** *New-Eng. Courant* 2–9 Sept. 2/1 They [the Mohawks] have left a Belt of Wampumpeeg to be presented to his Majesty by the first Opportunity. **1747** *Penna. Col. Rec.* V. 147 We therefore present this Belt to desire that we may be furnished with better Weapons. **1753** GIST *Journals* 82 Our Indians . . . ordered them to deliver up to the French the belt, with the marks of the four towns. **1778** CARVER *Travels* 362 These belts are made of shells found on the coasts of New England and Virginia, which are sawed out into beads of an oblong form, about a quarter of an inch long, and round like other beads. Being strung on leather strings, and several of them sewed neatly together with fine sinewy threads, they then compose what is termed a Belt of Wampum. **1798** B. HAWKINS *Letters* 310 A broad belt of peace arrived from all of them and was very favourably received. **1813** *Niles' Reg.* IV. 75/2 The black belt of wampum, stained with American blood, is now before your eyes. **1855** LONGFELLOW *Hiawatha* II. 8 He had stolen the Belt of Wampum From the neck of Mishe-Mokwa. **1891** S. M. WELCH *Recoll. 1830–40* 121 A young Indian, a brave or chief, would improve upon this dress by wearing belts of wampum.

c. (See quotation.) *Obs.*

1797 *State P.* (1819) III. 403, I have it from indubitable authority, that a large belt (by which he meant a speech) from the Spaniards is now travelling through the different nations.

2. An extended stretch of country; a zone. Often with a defining term, as BLACK BELT, CORN BELT, COTTON BELT, etc. {1810, 1834}

1827 COOPER *Prairie* i, The measure had made us the masters of a belt of fertile country. **1830** *Deb. Congress* 5 May 895/1 A belt of country extending from 37 degrees north to 37 degrees south latitude. **1834** [R. BAIRD] *Valley Mississippi* xii. 132 The mountainous belt, in Virginia, is about 120 miles in width. **1869** BROWNE *Adv. Apache Country* 50 About fifteen miles beyond Cook's Wells, after coursing along the belt of the great sand-desert on the left, we struck into the Colorado bottom. **1882** WORTHEN *Econ. Geol. Ill.* II. 59 A broad belt of alluvial bottom lands, from three to four miles in width, skirt . . . the Illinois river. **1892** *Vermont Agric. Rep.* XII. 121 Then there is a splendid belt of farming land along the bank of the Connecticut.

fig. **1900** G. BONNER *Hard Pan* ii. 41, I've run into bad-luck belts before, but never as wide a one as this.

b. Common in phr. 'belt of timber.'

1834 A. PIKE *Sketches* 13 These Cross Timbers are a belt of timber, extending from the Canadian, or a little further north, to an unknown distance south of Red River. **1843** N. BOONE *Journal* 236 Country passed over prairie, with the exception of belts of timber along the various creeks intersecting our road. **1870** KEIM *Sheridan's Troopers* 115 A fine belt of timber grew immediately upon its borders. **1873** CUSTER in E. B. Custer *Boots & Saddles* 285 Bivouacking in a belt of timber on the river bank, we waited.

3. The prize or winning place in a contest. {1850}

Originally the 'champion's belt' in a boxing-match.

1890 *Harper's Mag.* March 613/1 A sufficient number of miles . . . to have assured him the belt at any of our walking matches. **1902** LORIMER *Lett. Merchant* 97 He would have held the belt in his Sunday-school for long-distance verse-reciting if [etc.]. *Ib.* 216 It wasn't any walk-over to hold the belt in those days.

* **Belt,** *v.*

+**1.** *tr.* To make a circular incision around (a tree) through the outer bark and the cortex in order to kill it; to girdle.

1812 MARSHALL *Kentucky* 14 These improvements . . . consisted principally in cutting the under brush, and belting the larger trees. **1837** IRVING *Bonneville* II. i. 12 The beaver . . . was evidently engaged in 'belting' the tree, and his first incision had been on the side nearest to the water. *Ib.* 13 The beaver . . . makes incisions round them, or, in technical phrase, belts them with his teeth. **1853** STROTHER *Blackwater Chron.* xiv. 216 One man, therefore, in a hundred days, would belt or deaden one hundred acres. **1880** BURNETT *Old Pioneer* 14 The large trees were belted around with the axe.

2. *slang.* To put under one's belt; to swallow.

*a***1846** *Quarter Race Kentucky*, etc. 82 He can belt six shillins worth of corn-juice at still-house rates and travel.

3. *colloq.* To hasten; to rush forward without taking care or thought. {*dial.*}

1894 *Outing* April 57/2, I belted along as fast as the waders and treacherous footing would allow.

+**Belt axe.** An axe carried at the belt. — **1859** G. A. JACKSON *Diary* 521, [I] marked the big fir tree with belt axe and knife. *Ib.*, I had broken his back with belt axe.

* **Belted,** *a.* Having a belt-like mark round the body; esp. +*belted kingfisher.*

(1) **1811** WILSON *Ornithology* III. 59 Belted Kingsfisher, *Alcedo Alcyon*, ... is the only species of its tribe found within the United States. **1839** PEABODY *Mass. Birds* 342 The Belted Kingfisher ... is found in the neighborhood of fresh waters over all the United States. **1878** *Proc. U.S. Nat'l Museum* I. 432 Belted Kingfisher ... is a common resident at Stockton. **1885** M. THOMPSON *By Ways & Bird Notes* 82 A belted kingfisher, that most beautiful of all our birds of the streams, suddenly appeared. *Ib.* 94 The belted halcyon turned aside in his flight.

(2) **1878** *Ill. Dept. Agric. Trans.* XIV. 296 Mr. Mitchell asked the difference between the Holstein and Belted cattle. **1879** *Webster's Suppl.* 1545/1 *Belted cattle*, cattle, originally from Dutch stock, having a broad band of white round the middle, while the rest of the body is black.

Belting, *vbl. n.* +The girdling of a tree. — **1829** *Va. Lit. Museum* 16 Dec. 418 *Belting* in Virginia—the same as *girdling.* **1839** *S. Lit. Messenger* V. 314/1 Fine spreading trees ... they extirpate ... sometimes by the slow torture of belting. **1855** *Ib.* XXI. 662/2 Killing the larger forest trees without removal, by the process of belting, or girdling.

+**Belt knife.** A knife carried at the belt. — **1859** *Harper's Mag.* Aug. 425/1 The Judge ... whipped out his belt-knife and made at the aggressor. **1859** G. A. JACKSON *Diary* 521 Dug and panned today until my belt knife was worn out.

+**Belt pistol.** A pistol carried at the belt. — **1775** ADAIR *Indians* 326 In the middle of the river, I was forced to throw away one of my belt-pistols. **1837** A. WETMORE *Gaz. Missouri* 85 The belt-pistol he mistook for a butcher-knife. **1848** F. BRYANT *California* 466 A revolving belt pistol may be found useful.

+**Belt plate.** A plate or buckle affixed to a waist-belt. — **1866** 'F. KIRKLAND' *Bk. Anecdotes* 212 His cap box had slipped from his belt plate. **1884** *Century Mag.* Oct. 809/1 Some men ... were ... constantly polishing buttons and belt-plates.

+**Belt-saw.** A band-saw. — **1819** *Niles' Reg.* XVI. 93/2 The editor ... was invited a few days since, to see the newly invented Belt or Strap saw, in operation. **1874** KNIGHT 273/2.

‖**Ben,** *v. Obs. tr.* To refit or repair (a mill) in some manner. — **1660** *Huntington* (L.I.) *Rec.* I. 31 The defendant ... did git a work-man in the spring to ben the mill. *Ib.*, He did ... send to Henery Lininton ... to come to ben the mill. *Ib.*, The defendant is bound to git Goodman Webb to ben the mill if posable.

* **Ben, b'en,** dialect variant of BEEN *p.p.* {-17th c. (*north dial.*)}

1778 *Mass. H. S. Coll.* 2 Ser. II. 447 Mr. Aaron Thompson liked to ben killed breaking a colt. **1779** *Ib.* 456 The late Prisoner has ben 8 days without any food. **1845** COOPER *Chainbearer* ix, Yes, sir, religion ... has b'en too long neglected among us. **1859** ELWYN *Glossary* 21 *Ben*, for 'been,' ... may be heard very commonly here. **1898** WESTCOTT *D. Harum* 340 But I ben losin' him over an' agin all these years. What he'd 'a' ben when he was *so* old [etc.]. **1901** *Harper's Mag.* Dec. 45 There's b'en a bee tree discovered.

* **Bench,** *n.*

***1.** The seat in court occupied by a judge, justice, or magistrate, or a body of these.

*a*1649 WINTHROP *Hist.* II. 44 The secretary ... being unwilling to command him [=the governor] publicly to go off the bench, and yet not thinking it fit he should sit as a judge. **1686** SEWALL *Diary* I. 119 When Mr. Jenner came in, the Magistrates went all off the Bench to hear his News in the Lobby. **1702** *Ib.* II. 68 Mr Sheriff Dyar officiats with his white wand. Sits on the Bench for want of a seat. **1787** *Amer. Museum* I. 244/1, I had hopes he would have appeared this day on the bench ... to moderate the court in my favour. **1821** COOPER *Spy* ii, Laying aside the sword, to assume the ermine on the benches of the highest judicial authority. **1839** *Knickerb.* XIII. 7 The judge sits quietly on his 'bench,' possibly looks on. **1891** O'BEIRNE *Leaders Ind. Territory* 142/1 He was elected county judge, occupying the bench until his election to the House of Representatives. **1898** PAGE *Red Rock* 455 The counsel ... were ranged along the bar, fronting the bench and the jury-box.

***b.** The occupant(s) of a judicial bench; the body of judges, etc., sitting on the bench.

1636 *Plymouth Laws* 47 That such be ... accordingly punished or fined or both by the discrecon of the bench. **1639** *Plymouth Col. Rec.* I. 132 The Bench doth therefore censure the said Mary to be whipt. **1670** *Huntington Rec.* I. 164 May it please the worshipfull Bench wee ... cannot see cause [etc.]. **1675** *N.Y. State Col. Hist.* XII. 539 There may be more Magistrates named in this Towne for the completing the Bench. **1708** *Boston News-Letter* 1 March 2/2 His Excellency in Council has been pleased to appoint ... the Honorouble Jonathan Corwin Esqr. one of the Justices of the said Court, to fill up the Vacancies in that Bench. **1787** *Amer. Museum* I. 243/1 May it please the honourable bench to indulge me in a few words. I ... have no money to fee lawyers to plead for me. **1822** *Ann. 17th Congress* 1 Sess. I. 73, I do not design in any way to impugn the learned members of the bench, when I admit the possibility of the same propensity remaining with them. **1851** *Polly Peablossom* 133 Some younger barristers, fond of a 'practical,' and not much afraid of the bench, transferred all the silver spoons of Sterritt to the Judge's coat pocket. **1865** *Atlantic Mo.* XV. 557 Our judiciary consisted of a bench of three judges. **1905** S. E. BALDWIN *Amer. Judiciary* 328 The lawyers, as a body, are always anxious for their own sake to have an able and independent bench.

+**2.** A level stretch of land between a stream and higher ground or in a mountainous area; a natural terrace.

1811 *Ann. 12th Congress* 1 Sess. 2116 Towards the left flank this bench of high land widened considerably. **1828** A. SHERBURNE *Mem.* xi. (1831) 243 He was a powerful animal, and reached the shore and drew me up a very steep bank on to a bench of the river. **1837** JENKINS *Ohio Gaz.* 148 [Coshocton] is ... laid out on four flats or benches running parallel with the river from north to south. *a*1842 O. RUSSEL *Journal* v. (1921) 29 The bench where we were encamped contained about 500 acres nearly level. **1853** J. W. BOND *Minnesota* 111 From the lower landing of St. Paul, we rise upon a bench some seventy-five feet above the river. **1870** BEADLE *Utah* 164 From this place he passed out into the main valley, and from the 'bench' northwest of Ogden ... caught his first view of Great Salt Lake. **1873** MILLER *Amongst Modocs* xiv. 174 He would ... cut to right and left ... until we had reached the rim of a bench in the mountain. **1897** *McClure's Mag.* Sept. 963 Claims ... are limited practically only by the width of the ground between the two 'benches' or sides of the hills, that close in the stream. **1905** VALENTINE *H. Sandwith* 321 Snow Shoe was on a bench of the Alleghanies.

+**3.** A stope of a mine.

1882 C. KING *Rep. Precious Metals* 627 Where the banks are worked in 'benches,' or stopes, vertical shafts ... are sunk from the surface of the deposit.

4. (See quotations and cf. BENCH SHOW.)

1876 INGRAM *Centennial Exp.* 675 The dogs were in stalls on an elevated floor or 'bench,' as it is technically styled. **1879** *Webster's Suppl.* 1545/1 *Bench*, a collection or group of dogs exhibited to the public; so named because the animals are usually placed on benches or raised platforms.

***Bench,** *v.* [BENCH *n.* 1.] +*tr.* To raise to the bench; to appoint as a judge. — **1846** M'KENNEY *Memoirs* I. ii. 54 To the question asked of a member of the Hickory club in Washington—What are you going to do with Mr. M'Lean? the answer was, 'D—n him, we'll bench him.'

+**Bench-bottom.** [BENCH *n.* 2.] Ground forming a bench beside a river. — **1867** *Iowa Agric. Soc. Rep.* (1868) 160 On the second or bench-bottoms on the Missouri ... are our best wheat lands.

***Benching.** +Furniture in the form of benches. — **1881** HOWELLS *Modern Instance* xii. 150 They sank on the benching that ran round the wall. **1886** *Century Mag.* April 860/1 A large, square room, with benching against the wall for them to sit on.

+**Bench-judging.** [BENCH *n.* 4.] Judging at a bench-show. — **1897** *Outing* May 125/1 Feet and legs are therefore the prime points in bench-judging and score the highest.

+**Bench-land.** [BENCH *n.* 2.] Land that forms, or is situated on, a bench.

1857 CHANDLESS *Visit Salt Lake* II. x. 326 The coast is walled by steep mountain ridges; ... sometimes with bench-land fifty or hundred feet above the water-level intervening. **1868** [W. E. WATERS] *Life among Mormons* 71 The entire valley, with all the bench-lands, and the mountains surrounding these. **1892** *Harper's Mag.* June 96/2 The bench lands [in Montana] form the bulk of what remains. **1905** *Springfield W. Republican* 1 Dec. 3 He turned his herd loose among the [Montana] bottoms and foothills and benchlands.

+**Bench-legged,** *a.* Of a dog, mule, or other animal: Having the legs wide apart. — **1866** C. H. SMITH *Bill Arp* 159 Dodds says before he'd pull a trigger for Thad Stevens he'd have his soul transmigrated to a bench-leg'd fice. **1881** TOURGEE *'Zouri's Christmas* iii, A bench-legged fice, with one upward-pointing and one drooping ear. **1889** *Harper's Mag.* Aug. 485/2 Selling his little bench-legged mule to a travelling showman. **1903** A. ADAMS *Log Cowboy* xii. 184 The Indians' little bench-legged ponies were no match for them. *Ib.* xv. 238 A long, bench-legged black dog with a Dutch name.

+**Bench show.** [BENCH *n.* 4.] A dog show. — **1879** *Webster Suppl.* 1545/1 *Bench-show*, an exhibition of dogs or other animals. **1887** *Harper's Mag.* May 934/1 The American bench shows furnish an opportunity to most readers to see the best mastiffs in the country. **1897** *Outing* Feb. 481/1 Field-trials and bench-shows have been powerful factors in the improvement of the dogs. **1906** *N.Y. Ev. Post* 12 Feb. 1 The opening of the thirteenth annual bench show of the Westminster Kennel Club in Madison Square Garden.

Bench-vise, -vice. A vise adapted for use on a work-table, as of a carpenter or other mechanic.

1742 *Md. Hist. Mag.* XX. 260 A Bench Vice for a smith; A Hand Vice. **1762** *Essex Inst. Coll.* XLIX. 276 To be sold, ... Smith's Anvils and Bench Vices. **1790** *Penna. Packet* 7 May 3/3 Imported and to be sold by John Wood, Clock and Watch Maker, ... bench vizes, turn benches. **1874** KNIGHT 274/2, *d c* are the screws of a bench-vise, by which work is held.

Bench warrant, *n.* [BENCH *n.* 1.] A warrant issued by a judge. {1696} — **1784** Ramsey *Tennessee* (1853) 278 Ordered, that a Bench Warrant issue to Captain John Newman, to take suspected persons. **1859** *Harper's Mag.* June 119/1 The Court ... has had occasion to issue bench warrants to arrest persons connected with the Parrish murders. **1878**

BEADLE *Western Wilds* xxxii. 514 Another called for the immediate arrest of Brigham on a bench warrant, before he could fly the country. **1910** J. HART *Vigilante Girl* 315, I shall at once issue a bench warrant for his arrest.

+**Bench-warrant,** *v.* [f. prec.] *tr.* To issue a bench-warrant for (a person). — **1862** *Trial C. M. Jefferds* 145 The District Attorney has not bench-warranted me yet.

***Bend,** *n.*

1. A turn in the course of a river. (Cf. BENT *n.*[2] 1.)

*c*1665 *Lancaster Rec.* 297 His enteruail Lott . . . foloweth the Riuer to an elbo or bend in the Riuer. **1682** *Oyster Bay Rec.* I. 186 He is to run or range upon a strayght line south . . . to the first bend of the river. **1803** *Ann. 8th Congress* 2 Sess. 1500 The city [of New Orleans] . . . is situated on the east bank, on a bend, of the river. **1809** F. CUMING *Western Tour* 263 The second bluffs . . . form the interior of a great bend of the river. **1821** NUTTALL *Trav. Arkansa* xvi. 288 To-day we passed seven bends, making about 28 miles. *Ib.*, We again arrived at the lower end of the Eagle's-nest bend. **1846** THORPE *Myst. Backwoods* 127 The boat was securely fastened in some little bend or bay in the shore [of the river]. **1865** MRS. WHITNEY *Gayworthys* vi. 67 They wouldn't get across before she should come. They meant to have a row up the bend, first. **1906** F. LYNDE *Quickening* 71 There was a foot log just around the next bend above, . . . and thither he led the way.

attrib. **1838** [E. FLAGG] *Far West* I. 82 The stream generally infringes on the bend-side, and throws up a sandbar on the shore opposite.

***b.** A tract of land within a turn of a river.

1789 *Steele Papers* I. 41 They both also claim the great Bend of Tennessee but that is nothing to you as it is not within the limits of North Carolina. **1797** B. HAWKINS *Lett.* 134 They are about to settle the bend of Tennessee. **1828** *Western M. Rev.* I. 512 Accidental circumstances shift the impetus of its current, and propel it upon the point of an island, bend or sandbar. **1900** DRANNAN *On Plains & Mts.* 299 That night we drove all our horses into the bend [of the Arkansas].

2. One of the outer timbers of a vessel; the part between the water-line and the bulwarks. {1626-}

1800 *Essex Inst. Coll.* XIII. 72 Healed the ship and payed the Mainwheels, bends, and black streaks. **1812** *Niles' Reg.* II. 350/2 She is a fine new vessel, coppered to the bend.

+**3.** *Above (one's) bend,* beyond one's abilities.

1835 CROCKETT *Tour Down East* 44, I shall not attempt to describe the curiosities here [at Peale's Museum]; it is above my bend. **1848** BARTLETT 1 *Above one's bend,* out of one's power; beyond reach. A common expression in the Western States. **1848** COOPER *Oak Openings* (De Vere), It would be above my bend to attempt telling you all we saw among the Redskins. **1871** DE VERE 577 *Above one's bend* means, above one's power of bending all his strength to a certain purpose.

4. A bow (of the body).

1847 [ROBB] *Squatter Life* 98, I gin her the best bend I had in me, and raised my bran new hat as peert and perlite as a minister.

+**5.** *slang.* A spree. (Cf. BENDER 1.)

1887 F. FRANCIS, JR. *Saddle & Moccasin* 84 They do say as he was 'customed to go on a scoop—on a bend, occasionally, as it were.

***Bend,** *v.* +**1.** *tr.* To curve over (corn injured by birds, squirrels, etc.) to protect the ears from rain. **2.** To infringe slightly. — (1) **1833** Commons, etc. *Doc. Hist.* I. 218 Bending corn on the 23d. **1852** *Ib.* 227 Weeding peas and bending corn with gang of women. (2) **1864** NORTON *Army Lett.* 242 Perhaps you think it bending the Sabbath to build while I should be at church.

***Bender.** (In slang uses.)

+**1.** A drinking frolic; a spree.

1846 CORCORAN *Pickings* 62, I was on an almighty big bender last night . . . and the way we *did* walk into the highly concentrated hard cider. **1848** BARTLETT 30 To go on a bender, is, to go on a spree. **1855** THOMPSON *Doesticks* xx. 169 Said boat being fast aground on a sand-bar, . . . crew all on a 'bender' in the engine room, firemen all drunk on the boiler deck. **1861** LOWELL *Biglow P.* II. i. 31 To go off on benders . . . an' waste their time in foolin'. **1868** [A. B. CONDICT] *P. Eckert* 116 Now's our time, Phil, . . . for a *regular bender.* We'll have a high old time . . . and won't go home till morning, eh? **1873** MILLER *Amongst Modocs* v. 61 'You look as pale as a ghost. . . . Been on a bender last night; no?' cried an old sailor, glass in hand. *Ib.* xiii. 162 He never 'got on any glorious benders,' with the western men. **1886** J. HATTON *Old Ho. Sandwich* I. 82 The boss of Drummond's Gulch may be said to have begun his 'bender,' as a bout of drunken dissipation was called in these regions. **1902** MCFAUL *Ike Glidden* xv. 177 Jim took the money, and started for the city on an old fashioned bender.

fig. **1857** *Knickerb.* XLIX. 43 It was one of the times such as we read of —a regular Thanksgiving made perfect—a bender of friendship preserved in the syrup of pleasant recollections. **1870** W. W. FOWLER *Ten Years in Wall Street* 438 The bears were on a bender that day.

||**2.** A leg.

1849 LONGFELLOW *Kavanagh* xii, Young ladies are not allowed to cross their benders in school.

+**Bene.** [L. *bene,* well.] — 'A word sometimes attached to a written college exercise, by the instructor, as a mark of approbation' (Hall). — **1837** *Harvardiana* III. 402 When I look back upon my college life, And think that I one starveling *bene* got. **1840** DANA *Two Years* xi. 89, I . . . heard the 'well done' of the mate . . . with as much satisfaction as I ever felt at Cambridge on seeing a '*bene*' at the foot of a Latin exercise.

+**Beneficial society.** A society whose members are entitled to certain benefits in return for their payments to its funds. {=benefit society, 1845-} — **1811** MEASE *Philadelphia* 278 The following Benefit Societies also exist in Philadelphia. American Beneficial Society, 105 members, . . . Union Beneficial Society, [etc.]. **1842** *Niles' Reg.* 21 May 181/2 About two hundred more [passengers], among whom were the Calvert beneficial society. **1865** *Atlantic Mo.* XV. 317 Varick had in better days become a member of a beneficial society which allowed forty dollars to a widow for the funeral expenses of her husband.

Beneficiary. {1662-} +(See quotations.)

1798 *Harvard Laws* 34 No one, who is a College Beneficiary, shall remain such any longer than he shall continue exemplary for sobriety, diligence, and good order. **1814** *Ib.* 37 The Beneficiaries appointed by the immediate government, or by the President and Tutors. **1834** PECK *Gaz. Illinois* 85 Of this number [of students], ten are beneficiaries, who are aided by education societies, with a view to the gospel ministry. **1851** HALL *College Words* 18 In American colleges, students who are supported on established foundations are called beneficiaries. **1852** C. A. BRISTED *Five Years in Univ.* II. 159 A particular class of students, the 'beneficiaries,' as they are commonly called, men who adopt the intention of becoming clergymen at a comparatively late period of life, and are assisted in their collegiate course by charitable contributions. **1856** OLMSTED *Slave States* 606 Another young man, who looked like a beneficiary of the Education Society. **1871** [L. H. BAGG] *At Yale* 34 [Certain students] also receive . . . an additional $100 a year in case they are the beneficiaries of the American Educational Society.

+**Beneficiate,** *v.* [Sp. *beneficiar.*] *tr.* To reduce (ores). — **1871** RAYMOND, etc. *Trans. Amer. Mining Eng.* I. 91 This paper will treat of such works only as beneficiate ores directly in the mining districts. **1876** — *8th Rep. Mines* 317 Mr. Keck has completed his beneficiating works. *Ib.*, This ore is now . . . subjected to the rest of the beneficiating process. **1883** W. BISHOP *Old Mexico* 238 His ancient beneficiating hacienda of Regla.

+**Beneficiation.** [Cf. prec.] The reduction of ores. — **1881** RAYMOND *Mining Gloss.* s.v.

***Benefit.**

1. A theatrical performance for the profit of some person (as a special actor), group, or fund. {18th c.-}

1751 *Weekly Postboy* (N.Y.) 28 Jan., For the Benefit of Mrs. Taylor . . . will be presented a comedy called Love for Love. *Ib.*, Those Gentlemen and Ladies who please to favor this Benefit. **1828** *Yankee* July 215/1 The 'Benefits' . . . are all tricks of the trade. Generally the 'Benefits' are shared with the company or the managers. **1833** IRVING in *Life & Lett.* (1866) III. 58 We had a benefit here, lately, for Cooper and his family, which netted nearly four thousand dollars. **1850** NORTHALL *Yankee Hill* 78 A complimentary benefit tendered to his old friend . . . Samuel Woodworth, Esq. **1886** P. STAPLETON *Major's Christmas* 14 The printed notice that Miss Eva May . . . would take a benefit in 'Romeo and Juliet.'

attrib. **1828** *Yankee* July 239/2 One, who in a society where they are playing for each other, has nothing but a pair of pretty legs to contribute to the common stock . . . on a benefit-night. **1903** T. A. BROWN *N.Y. Stage* I. 96, July 16 [1853] a benefit performance took place for the relief of the unfortunate Chinese Dramatic Company, and July 21 a second benefit entertainment in their aid was given.

b. A collection of gifts for one in financial difficulties.

1846 *Spirit of Times* (N.Y.) 18 April 91/2 A disposition prevails to give him a sort of 'benefit' as an offset to the late loss he sustained by fire.

+**2.** *To take the benefit,* to take advantage of the bankruptcy laws.

1823 I. HOLMES *Account* 215 To shew the extreme facility of obtaining the benefit of the Insolvent Act, an attorney . . . informed me, that a person applied to him to assist him 'in taking the benefit,' as it is termed, of the act. **1844** 'UNCLE SAM' *Peculiarities* I. 82 When citizens who are insolvents release themselves by law from their debts, they are said to 'take the benefit'—a very simple matter, as they have only to give a short notice, and swear they are not worth anything beyond clothing, necessary furniture, and the instruments of their trade. **1846** COOPER *Redskins* xii, I took 'the benefit,' as it is called, myself.

3. *Benefit Society,* a society for mutual insurance against financial distress in sickness or old age. {1845-}

1811 MEASE *Philadelphia* 276 Other Mutual Benefit Societies . . . are numerous and annually increasing. *Ib.* 278 The following Benefit Societies also exist in Philadelphia. **1909** *23rd Rep. Comm. Labor* 665 The industrial benefit societies differ from the labor union . . . in that the membership . . . is not as a rule dependent upon membership in any particular union.

+**Benevolence circle.** =next. — **1872** *Harper's Mag.* March 637/1 The wife . . . after a time joined a ladies' 'benevolence circle,' of which she was elected secretary.

***Benevolent,** *a.* +*Benevolent society* or *association,* a society organized for benevolent or charitable purposes.

1811 MEASE *Philadelphia* 277 Columbian Benevolent Society [was] instituted 1804. All well known, healthy citizens of Pennsylvania are eligible. *Ib.* 287 St. Patrick's Benevolent Society [was] incorporated 1804. **1835** MARTIN *Descr. Virginia* 159 There is a benevolent society, which holds its meetings at this place. c**1850** A. A. LAWRENCE in *Life* (1888) 54 The Young Men's Benevolent Society chose me president again. **1865** *Atlantic Mo.* XV. 86 Thirty benevolent societies, (and we are in that respect far behind London). **1872** BRACE *Dangerous Classes N.Y.* 371 Some benevolent associations have obtained this by . . . an 'annuity insurance' of the life of their agents. **1882** E. K. GODFREY *Nantucket* 299 The Union Benevolent Society . . . was formed for the sole purpose of assisting children. **1895** *N.Y. Dramatic News* 23 Nov. 14/3 Two boxes in the Pleasure Palace have been donated the fairs given by the Ladies' Benevolent Sewing society.

Bengal grass. Italian millet (*Setaria Italica*), originally native to Asia. — **1847** WOOD *Botany* 607 Bengal Grass . . . [grows] in fields, not often cultivated. **1857** GRAY *Botany* 581 *Setaria Italica* . . . [is] sometimes cultivated under the name of . . . Bengal Grass. **1890** *Cent.* s.v. *Grass*, Bengal grass . . . [is] now very extensively cultivated as a forage-plant.

Benjamin[1]. **a.** An overcoat worn by men. **b.** A shoulder-cape. {1817–41; in later use *slang*}

1843 *Knickerb.* XXI. 214 A jolly heart, beneath a shaggy benjamin, bade defiance . . . to cold. **1883** J. HAWTHORNE *Dust* I. 9 The glimpses of his attire that showed beneath the layers of benjamins in which his . . . person was enveloped. **1897** *Outing* May 110/2 A typical old road coachman's . . . 'upper benjamin' (shoulder cape) never flies up into his face, as do the Inverness capes of his passengers.

+**Benjamin**[2]. *New Eng.* A plant of the genus *Trillium*, esp. the strong-scented wake-robin, *T. erectum.* Usu. *pl.* — **1887** *Harper's Mag.* July 303/1 In the woods [of N.H.] the painted trilliums—the 'Benjamins' of the country folk—were unfolding their delicate pink and white flowers. **1891** *Amer. Folk-Lore* IV. 149 My father used to gather the early plants [*T. erectum*, in Gilsum, N.H.] for greens, and called them Benjamins. **1892** *Ib.* V. 104 *Trillium erectum*, . . . Benjamins. So. Vt.

+**Benjamin bush.** [Corruption of *benjoin*, earlier form of *benzoin*.] The spicewood, spicebush, or feverbush, *Benzoin benzoin.* — **1857** GRAY *Botany* 379 Benjamin-bush . . . [grows in] damp woods; rather common. **1890** *Cent.* 3462 Benjamin-bush has a pleasant aromatic scent and taste, especially its bark and berries. **1892** APGAR *Trees Northern U.S.* 131 Benjamin-bush: Leaves . . . very spicy in odor and taste. . . . Flowers in early spring, before the leaves expand.

+**Benjamin tree.** =preceding. — **1640** PARKINSON *Theatr. Bot.* 1572 The fruite of this Benjamin-tree, or of the browne American Balsame before set down. **1693** *Phil. Trans.* XVII. 619 There are no less than six sorts of *Anona* . . . [including] the Benjamin-Tree . . . from the Continent of Virginia. **1741** MILLER *Gardener's Dict.* (ed. 2) I., *Benzoin*, the Benjamin-tree. . . . This Tree was brought from Virginia into England, some Years since. **1785** MARSHALL *Amer. Grove* 73 The Benjamin-Tree, or Spice-Wood, . . . grows naturally in moist places, and rises often to the height of eight or ten feet. **1789** *Amer. Philos. Soc.* III. p. xvii, The best recommended remedies against intermittent fevers are . . . Spicewood, Benjamin-tree, Benzoin.

+**Benne.** Also **bene, benni, benny.** [Mende (Sierra Leone) *bene.*] The sesame (*Sesamum Indicum*), from whose seeds oil is extracted. Also attrib. with *seed.* {1874–} Cf. BHENÉ.

1769 in *Amer. Philos. Soc.* I. 309, I send you a small keg of Bene or Bene Seed, which you will please to present to your Society for their inspection. **1775** ROMANS *Florida* 130 The negroes use it as food either raw, toasted, or boiled in their soups and are very fond of it; they call it *Benni.* **1827** *Western M. Rev.* I. 81 Benne, an African plant, which yields an oil, it is affirmed, not inferior to that of olives, has been tried and succeeds well. **1828** WEBSTER s.v. *Sesamum*, One species of it is cultivated in Carolina, and the blacks use the seeds for food. It is called there bene. **1856** *Rep. Comm. Patents: Agric.* 276 The pea-nut, or pindar, the palma-christi, the bene, or other leguminous plants, adapted to the climate. *Ib.* 287 Last spring, I planted [in La.] my bene seeds (*Sesamum orientale*) about a month later than I should have done, on the 1st of May. **1889** *Cent.* 526/2 *Benne, Bene.* . . . Large quantities of both oil and seeds are imported into . . . the United States, and are used chiefly in the manufacture of soap and for the adulteration of olive-oil.

***Bent,** *n.*[1] **1.** =BENT GRASS 1. +**2.** A rush or reed. — (1) **1749** FRANKLIN *Letter* Wks. 1905 II. 386, I threw in . . . a peck of Burden-grass or blue bent, and two Pints of Red Clover. **1796** MORSE *Amer. Geog.* I. 186 Cultivated grasses in the Eastern and Middle States [include] . . . many species of Bent (*Agrostis*) particularly the Rhode Island Bent (*Agrostis interrupta?*). **1861** WOOD *Botany* 774 *Agrostis alba*, White Bent. . . . A common and valuable grass in old fields. *Ib.*, *A. canina*, Brown Bent, Dog's Bent. **1890** *Cent.* 5024 Redtop, at least in the United States, is a highly valued pasture-grass, and is also sown for hay. It . . . is . . . also called fine bent, fine-top-grass, and herd's-grass. (U.S.) **1899** *Dept. Agric. Yearbook* 494 Creeping bent (*Agrostis stolonifera*) and Rhode Island bent (*A. canina*) are much prized for lawns. (2) **1896** P. A. BRUCE *Econ. Hist. Va.* I. 146 The ordinary dwelling, however, was protected by mats woven from bents gathered in the woods.

***Bent,** *n.*[2]

+**1.** A curve or bend in a river. *Obs.*

1669 *Dedham Rec.* IV. 177 We mett vpon the Line at the bent of Charles Riuer. **1708** *Providence Rec.* VII. 3 That Piece of land . . . which lieth at the bent of the River below the Bridge. **1755** EVANS *Map Colonies* 5 Near the great Bent of Potomack. **1770** WASHINGTON *Diaries* I. 404 Went round what is calld the Great Bent.

+**2.** One of the transverse parts of a framed building or structure.

'One section of the frame of a building, which is put together on the ground or foundation and then raised by holding the feet of the posts, and elevating the upper portion. A bent consists of posts united by the beams which pass transversely across the building' (Knight).

1815 *Niles' Reg.* IX. 200/2 The floats were placed at proper distances, with their ends to the shore, and on each of them were raised two bents or frames. *Ib.*, This made sixteen bents, on which the grand and enormous structure was raised. **1842** MRS. KIRKLAND *Forest Life* I. xvii. 136 An immense bent was about to be raised, . . . and as many men as could find hands-breadths on its edge were applying their united energies to the task. **1845** COOPER *Chainbearer* x, The 'people' had just taken their stands at the first bent, ready for a lift, while trusty men stood at the feet of the posts. **1848** — *Oak Openings* I. xiv. 211 Pinning together his palisades, making them into manageable bents, and then setting them up on their legs. **1901** MERWIN & WEBSTER *Calumet K* viii. 148 Then she came into view through an opening between two 'bents' of timber.

***Bent,** *a.* +Tipsy. *colloq.*[2] (Cf. BEND *n.* 5.) — **1833** GREENE *Dod. Duckworth* II. 176 He was seldom downright drunk; but was often . . . confoundedly bent.

Bent grass. [BENT *n.*[1]]

1. A pasture grass of the genus *Agrostis*, esp. *A. vulgaris* and *A. canina.* {1778–}

1791 MUHLENBERG *Index* 160 *Agrostis*, Bentgrass. **1802** J. DRAYTON *S. Car.* 61 Plants . . . flourishing within the boundaries of this state [include] . . . Bent grass (*Agrostis*). **1843** TORREY *Flora N.Y.* II. 442 *Agrostis stricta*, . . . Upright-flowered Bent-grass. . . . Sandy field near the outlet of Oneida Lake. **1847** WOOD *Botany* 597 Bent grass [is] . . . a common and very valuable grass, spread over hills, vales, and meadows, forming a soft, dense turf. **1889** VASEY *Agric. Grasses* 46 Herds grass [of Pennsylvania], Bent Grass, . . . is extensively cultivated. **1901** MOHR *Plant Life Ala.* 370 *Agrostis alba*, Fiorin, White Bent Grass, . . . [grows on] low damp banks. *Ib. Agrostis intermedia*, Upland Bent Grass. *Ib.* 371 *Agrostis altissima*, Tall Bent Grass.

2. a. A grass with a stiff or wiry stem. **b.** The reed, *Arundo phragmites.*

1797 TRUMBULL *Hist. Conn.* (1898) I. iii. 19 Where lands were thus burned there grew bent grass, or as some called it, thatch, two, three and four feet high. **1871** *Rep. Comm. Agric.* 423 Bent grass. . . . This species of reed, which grows abundantly around St. Thomas, in Southern Utah, during the summer months, produces a kind of white, sweet gum.

Berberry, variant (after L. *Berberis*) of BARBERRY. Also attrib. with *bush.* {1725, 1830}

1843 TORREY *Flora N.Y.* I. 33 *Berberis vulgaris*, . . . Common Berberry, . . . [grows in] hedges, fields, and road sides. **1846** BROWNE *Trees Amer.* 34 The common Berberry, in its wild state, is seldom found higher than six to ten feet. *Ib.* 35 The wood of the berberry is hard and brittle. **1847** WOOD *Botany* 152 *Berberis vulgaris.* Berberry Bush. . . . A well known bushy, ornamental shrub, in hard, gravelly soils, Northern States. **1863** *Rep. Comm. Agric.* 157 The May apple . . . belongs to this class, as does the red berried plant well known as Berberry.

+**Bergall.** *local.* The cunner, chogset, or bluefish, *Ctenolabrus adspersus*, or related species.

1814 MITCHILL *Fishes N.Y.* 402 Bergall of New-York, *Labrus chogset.* Chogset of the Mohigans. Bluefish. *Ib.* 403 Yellow bergall. *Labrus chogset fulva.* **1842** *Nat. Hist. N.Y., Zoology* IV. 172 The bergall is very common on our coast. The larger fish are held in some repute. *a***1888** DOREN in Goode *Amer. Fishes* 131 Like the bergall the Spot bites at the hook with a sly tentative nibble.

Bergaloo, alteration of VERGALOO (pear).

Bergamot.[1] Also †**-mont, burgamot.** A variety of pear. Also attrib. {1616–} — **1786** WASHINGTON *Diaries* III. 24, 5th Row, 2 Cooks pears . . . and 2 . . . green Burgamot. **1818** *Jrnl. Science* I. 362 September 6. Bergamont pears fully ripe. **1872** *Vermont Bd. Agric. Rep.* I. 107 Man . . . has transformed it and produced the rich sugary, melting, delicious Bergamots and Seckels.

Bergamot.[2] {1696–} Also **burgamot.** +An odorous herb of the genus *Monarda.*

1822 J. WOODS *English Prairie* 218 The prairie-roses, balm, here called bergamot, and sassafras-wood, are exceptions, and have all powerful scents. **1838** FLAGG *Far West* II. 29 The orchis, the balmy thyme, the burgamot, and the asters of every tint, . . . then prevail. **1843** TORREY *Flora N.Y.* II. 59 *Monarda Fistulosa.* . . . Horse-mint. Wild Bergamot. . . . Hill-sides, and rocky banks of rivers. **1857** GRAY *Botany* 310 Wild Bergamot [grows in] . . . woods and rocky banks, W. Vermont to Wisconsin. **1892** COULTER *Bot. W. Texas* II. 339 *Monarda fistulosa* . . . [grows in] dry soil. . . . 'Wild bergamot.'

Bergamy, burgamy, obs. variants of BERGAMOT[1]. {1677} — **1676** GLOVER *Acc. Va.* in *Phil. Trans.* XI. 628 There are some sorts of Pears, but at very few Plantations; I have seen the Bergamy, Warden, and two or three other sorts. **1760** WASHINGTON *Diaries* I. 147 Grafted 10 of the Bergamy Pears from Collo. Mason's. **1786** *Ib.* III. 13 On the same side are burgamy pears, grafted the first April last yr.

Bergère. Also †**burgair.** [Fr. *bergère.*] A large easy chair. {1813–41} — **1773** E. Singleton *Social N.Y.* 83 [Joseph Cox from London] makes all sorts of . . . settees, couches, burgairs [etc.]. **1842** Buckingham *E. & W.*

States III. xx. 434 A bulky alderman . . . placing his corporation within the generous dimensions of a bergere. **1876** WARNER *Gold of Chickaree* 179 Sit down, please, in this bergère, and let me sit here.

* **Berkshire.** The name of the English county, used attrib. or absol. to designate a variety of bean and a breed of swine.

(1) **1788** WASHINGTON *Diaries* III. 311 The next land to this a bushel of Berkshire Beans from Mr. Peachy was sown.

(2) **1843** *Knickerb.* XXI. 116 The Berkshire is in the garden. *Ib.* 120 Having driven the Berkshire pig out of the garden. **1850** *New Eng. Farmer* II. 56 He bought this kind at Brighton, and he says that his neighbors call them the Berkshire breed. **1871** EGGLESTON *Hoosier Schoolm.* xxvi. 180 You can't make . . . a China hog into a Berkshire. **1879** *Diseases of Swine* 33, I succeeded finally . . . in buying . . . three Berkshire sowpigs. **1882** SWEET & KNOX *Texas Siftings* 17 The slow and stately step of the patrician Berkshire. **1913** G. STRATTON-PORTER *Laddie* iv, The pigs . . . chanked up every peach that fell there. Those peaches were too good to feed even father's finest Berkshires.

Berlin.

1. The name of the capital of Prussia, used attrib. to designate various articles. †Also absol. =Berlin coach, a four-wheeled covered carriage. {1731–46}

1724 JONES *Virginia* 32 Most Families of any Note having a Coach, Chariot, Berlin, or Chaise. **1772** *Mass. Gazette* 20 Feb., A genteel Berlin coach, commodious, for six persons. **1829** R. C. SANDS *Writings* II. 163 Her girdle was fastened in front with a massive shining clasp of Berlin ware. **1847** BRIGGS *Tom Pepper* I. 151 Some worked, or made-believe work, with Berlin wool and beads. **1852** *Knickerb.* XXXIX. 166 On ordinary days he wears a white apron, but on great occasions he is ornamented with a blue coat and Berlin gloves. *c***1870** BAGBY *Old Va. Gentleman* 257 [A] beard . . . like Berlin wire, tough and hard. **1876** *Wide Awake* 215/2 This was the first meeting of the 'Busy Bees,' and they were in full buzz over Berlin wools, crotcheted mats, embroidered slippers.

2. *Berlin work*, 'worsted embroidery' (W. '79).

1880 *Harper's Mag.* Oct. 656/1 It used to be a 'pattern' she worked, in the days of Berlin-work, and she needed only to buy a certain number of shades of wool.

Berme. [F.] A narrow path between the bottom of a rampart and the ditch, or between a stream and its bank. {berm, 1729–} — **1775** R. MONTGOMERY in Sparks *Corr. Rev.* (1853) I. 470 By the time we arrived there, the fraise around the berme would be destroyed. **1884** 'CRADDOCK' *Where Battle was Fought* 124 They paused on the berme to rest, and stood there motionless for an instant. **1890** MERRITT in *Harper's Mag.* April 725/1 In most wild mountain regions the narrow berme on the edge of streams . . . is the only passable route.

+**Berm(e)-bank.** Also **birm-.** [Cf. prec.] The bank of a canal opposite the towing path. — **1854** in *N. & Q.* 1 Ser. IX. 12/2 The bank of a canal opposite to the towing-path is called the birm-bank. **1877** *Engineer* 3 Aug. 89/1 To lay a rail upon the berme bank (the bank opposite the towing path). **1883** *Williamsport* (Pa.) *Gaz.* 30 March (Th.), The horse plunged over the berm bank into the bed of the canal.

Bermuda (also **Bermudas**), the name of the islands in the Atlantic, used attrib. or absol. to designate varieties of currants, potatoes, etc.

1737 BRICKELL *N. Carolina* 89 Bermudas—Currans, so call'd from their growing plentifully in that Island, are very common in the Woods of Carolina. **1797** IMLAY *Western Territory* (ed. 3) 261, 4. Purple potatoe, having that colour throughout; . . . 5. Bermudas, or round white potatoe. **1854** *Penna. Agric. Rep.* 206 Robert Wallace, for a lot of Bermuda potatoes. **1883** HALE *Woods & Timbers N.C.* 143 Bermuda or French Mulberry (*Callicarpa Americana*) [is] quite common in light soils and dry, open woods.

+**b.** *Bermuda grass*, a coarse perennial grass (*Cynodon Dactylon*) that grows in sandy places.

1835 [INGRAHAM] *South-West* II. 88 A thick bluish green grass, termed Bermuda grass. **1847** *Knickerb.* XXIX. 453 Underneath the Bermuda-grass grows vigorously. **1856** *Rep. Comm. Patents: Agric.* 252 The Bermuda grass, . . . in this State, far excels the celebrated Kentucky blue-grass, either for summer or winter pasture. **1861** WOOD *Botany* 804 Bermuda grass [is] . . . a vigorous creeper, in sands and hard soils, Penn. to the Gulf. **1883** ALLEN *Farm Book* 116 Bermuda Grass . . . is the most nutritive grass known, and to the river planter it is invaluable. **1901** MOHR *Plant Life Ala.* 105 The old fields exhausted by the continuous practice of the one-crop system are . . . being converted into wide pastures of Bermuda grass. **1906** F. LYNDE *Quickening* 11 The dooryard with its thick turf of uncut Bermuda grass.

Bermudian, *n.* and *a.*

1. A trading vessel belonging to the Bermuda Islands.

1777 J. ADAMS in *Warren-Adams Lett.* I. 313 Many French Vessells have arrived there [=S.C.], some Bermudians, and some of their own.

2. *Bermudian mulberry*, French mulberry (*Callicarpa americana*). *Bermudian Vine* (see quot. 1859).

1802 ELLICOTT *Journal* 287 Bermudian mulberry (*callicarpa americana*). **1818** NUTTALL *N. Amer. Plants* 101 Bermudian Mulberry. . . . Tomentose shrubs with opposite leaves. **1859** BARTLETT 77 The sterile vine [of the river-grape, *Vitis riparia*] is cultivated for its sweet-scented blossoms, and is then called Bermudian Vine.

* **Berry.**

* **1.** A wild berry, esp. a cranberry, blueberry, or huckleberry.

See BERRY-FIELD, BERRYING, etc., below.

b. Attrib. with *cake, pail, roll.*

1876 MRS. HENDERSON *Practical Cooking* 274 [Recipe for] Baked Berry Rolls. **1873** E. S. PHELPS *Trotty's Wedding* xiii, There's berry-cake for supper. **1892** WILKINS *Jane Field* 261 Three barefooted boys loping along in the dust, with berry-pails.

2. A grain or kernel (esp. of wheat). {1691–}

1855 *Trans. Amer. Inst. N.Y.* 590 Another fall variety [of wheat], . . . having larger berries. **1867** *Iowa Agric. Soc. Rep.* (1868) 145 The wheat crop was light: . . . a full berry; good weight but light yield. **1873–4** *Vermont Bd. Agric. Rep.* II. 226 Dr. Hoskins . . . highly approved of salt as a fertilizer for wheat. It brightens and strengthens the straw, and gives a nice berry.

+**Berry-field.** A field in which berries grow or are cultivated. — **1861** *Harper's Mag.* Aug. 363/2 Granny Woodban . . . living in the berry fields all summer, and wandering off no one knew where in winter. **1869** FULLER *Flower Gatherers* 260 Wild Indigo, or *Baptisia*, . . . we had been accustomed to see in dry pastures and berry-fields. **1879** *Harper's Mag.* June 68/2 They are a merry, jolly, happy-go-lucky tribe, . . . finding food in the berry [*i.e.* strawberry] fields.

+**Berry-house.** (See quotation.) — **1879** *Harper's Mag.* June 69/2 In the berry-house where the packing of boxes is done, a huge pile of empty crates reaches nearly to the roof.

+**Berrying,** *vbl. n.*

1. The gathering of wild berries.

1847 EMERSON (*title*), [Poem on] Berrying. **1880** 'MARK TWAIN' in *Atl. Mo.* XLVI. 226 Swimming, skating, picnicking, berrying, circusing, and all sorts of things which boys delight in.

2. Attrib. with *crowd, excursion, frolic, party, time*, etc.

1845 COOPER *Chainbearer* xxi, It's berryin' time now. I'll run and get a basket. **1848** *Knickerb.* XVIII. 217 The berrying parties in the dull days of July . . . furnish sources of enjoyment. **1880** *Harper's Mag.* Dec. 89/2 The younger people had their berrying frolics, . . . nuttings, and the like. **1884** *Lisbon* (Dakota) *Star* 25 July, Several . . . drove out to Fort Ransom . . . on a berrying and picnic excursion. **1890** RYAN *Told in Hills* 58 After their stop at the Indian camp, which Genesee explained was a berrying crowd from the Kootenai tribe. **1891** *Fur, Fin, & Feather* March 169 They are regular berrying parties, and they reckons to clean out the ripest fruit and berries as they works their way gradually down stream.

+**Berrying,** *pres. pple.* =A-BERRYING. — *c***1853** MISS SEDGWICK in *Life & Lett.* (1871) 44, I went with herds of school-girls nutting, and berrying, and bathing by moonlight. **1868** *Amer. Naturalist* May 133 A man who had been out berrying stated that he suddenly came across a Rattlesnake with her young. **1880** *Harper's Mag.* March 546/1 With no companions but another woman, who had 'gone berrying.' **1880** *Ib.* Aug. 339/1 Little children going 'berrying' along the single, central road.

+**Berry lot.** [BERRY[1]. Cf. BERRY PATCH.] — **1845** COOPER *Chainbearer* xxiii, I went a berryin' this forenoon, and up ag'in the berry lot . . . I saw a young woman.

‖**Berry-money.** Money earned by picking berries. — **1886** P. STAPLETON *Major's Christmas* 168 The things she bought us one Christmas with the berry-money she arnt herself.

+**Berry-moth.** The moth of the cranberry fruit-worm (*Acrobasis vaccinii*). — **1884** *Rep. Comm. Agric.* 395 Where the water was taken off [the bogs] early, the berry-moth was found in some numbers.

+**Berry party.** [BERRY 1.] A berrying party. — **1860** *Harper's Mag.* Nov. 789/1 My brothers came one morning for me to . . . make one of a whortleberry party to the mountain. . . . Aunt Tabby . . . inquired what she could give me to make me . . . not mind the berry party.

+**Berry pasture, patch.** [BERRY 1.] — **1880** HOWELLS *Undiscovered Country* 204 The women went, five or six in a wagon, . . . to the berry pasture a mile or two away. **1893** B. TORREY *Foot-path Way* 176 The thrasher is silent in the berry pasture. — **1896** WILKINS *Madelon* 344 She resolved that she would go away . . . to another berry patch that she knew of. **1902** MCFAUL *Ike Glidden* xiv. 110, I'd rather tramp the berry patch than study double rule.

Berry-picker. One who picks berries as an occupation.

1867 'T. LACKLAND' *Homespun* I. 73 It is right here in the open air . . . that the berry-pickers chat as they work. **1879** *Harper's Mag.* June 68/2 The berry-pickers, mostly negroes, are a peculiar class of people. **1895** *Outing* August 479/2 The poor berry-picker who gathers his brood under one small tent. **1902** MCFAUL *Ike Glidden* xiv. 102 The scene was dotted by the white tents and the covered wagons of the berry pickers.

Berry-picking, *vbl. n.* The picking of berries. Also attrib. — **1885** *Rep. Indian Affairs* 113 They obtain a livelihood by farming in a small way, . . . berry-picking, and . . . trapping. **1902** MCFAUL *Ike Glidden* xiv. 100 The people of the district had gone on their annual berry-picking expedition.

+**Berry-pie.** A pie made with berries — **1876** MRS. HENDERSON *Practical Cooking* 237 Fruit and Berry Pies, or Tarts. **1881** MRS. OWENS *Cook Book* 146 [Recipe for] Berry pie. **1900** DIX *Deacon Bradbury* 13 She reentered with half a berry-pie, hot from the oven. **1902** MCFAUL *Ike Glidden* xiv. 111 Fish is jes' as good to eat As any berry pie.

+**Berry season.** The time of year in which berries are picked. — **1875** *Amer. Naturalist* IX. 1 It was the berry season, and persons from the pines were on board. **1878** *Rep. Indian Affairs* 74 During the berry season the women and children make considerable additions to their income by picking berries for the market. **1902** McFaul *Ike Glidden* xiv. 101 During the berry season two thousand people, including men, women and children, are usually scattered over this vast area.

Berry-spoon. A spoon used for serving berries. — **1875** Stowe *We & Our Neighbors* 474 Of course the reader knows that there were the usual amount of berry-spoons, and pie-knives, and crumb-scrapers.

Berth. Also †**birth.**

1. A situation or post on board a ship. {1720–}

1722 *New-Eng. Courant* 8–15 Jan. 1/1 The Letter was detained by the Post-Master several Weeks, ... so the poor Man lost his Birth [as 'master of a vessel']. **1800** J. Boucher *Glossary* p. xlix, A *Berth*, a station, or employment; a term much used among seamen.

b. A situation, post, appointment. {1778–}

1745 *Md. Hist. Mag.* VI. 220 When the old parson dies, w[hi]ch he will in a very little time, I hope he'll get the Birth. **1775** in *Biogr. N. Hale* 157 Was I qualified for a birth and of influence sufficient to procure one, I would accept it with all my heart. **1788** Jefferson *Writings* VII. 236 Both will prefer their present berths. **1852** Stowe *Uncle Tom* iv, I'll do the very best I can in gettin' Tom a good berth.

2. A place for sleeping in a ship. {1809–}

(*a*) **1791** Washington *Diaries* IV. 151 Having lain all night ... in a birth not long enough for me by the head. **1799** in F. Cuming *Western Tour* (1810) 337 Captain Mason politely gave up his birth in the cabin to me. **1811** *Niles' Reg.* I. 151/1 It happened that he was lying in a birth to the windward. **1825** Paulding *J. Bull in America* iv. 46 When we came to draw lots for our births, ... I drew a birth in a remote part of the vessel. **1828** A. Sherburne *Mem.* iii. (1831) 72 The carpenter and boatswain have each a birth, viz. a kind of small room by themselves, forward of the fore hatchway. **1838** *S. Lit. Messenger* IV. 26/1 They slept in the same birth spanking, quarrelling and kicking half the night, to the diversion of the passengers.

(*b*) **1771** Franklin *Autobiog.* 274 Ralph and I were forced to take up with a berth in the steerage, ... none on board knowing us. **1803** *Ann. 7th Congress* 2 Sess. 1340 Their provisions spoiling during the West India voyages ... render the berths and quarters of the men unhealthy. **1830** S. H. Collins *Emigrant's Guide* 79 The bed places in the steerage are called *berths.* **1835** A. Parker *Trip to Texas* 85 Forward is the place for deck passengers, having berths but no bedding. **1847** [Robb] *Squatter Life* 88 The captain suggested a locker berth, as the most comfortable. **1865** Mrs. Whitney *Gayworthys* xx. 193 He came down into the forecastle and ... stopped beside my berth.

b. A sleeping place in a building or on a railroad car. {1885–}

(1) **1805–9** Henry *Camp. Quebec* 144 There were four rooms below, all capacious and well supplied with births or bulks, in the common method of barracks. **1806–8** Pike *Sources Miss.* 81 We returned to the Chief's lodge, and found a birth provided for each of us. **1865** *Atlantic Mo.* XV. 237 There is a large room containing ninety-six berths, where any soldier ... can obtain decent lodging free of expense. *c***1900** R. L. Hale *Log of Forty-Niner* 77 We occupied the same room, in which there were two bunks or berths.

(2) **1849** A. Mackay *Western World* II. 55 When this line was first put in operation, some of the carriages were so constructed that at night they could be fitted up with small berths at the sides, after the fashion of a canal boat, on which passengers by the night trains might repose. **1866** *Pathfinder* (Boston) Dec. 30 Double or single berths or sections in sleeping cars. **1876** Crofutt *Trans-Continental Tourist* 87 At Ogden passengers are allowed one hour to eat, change cars, ... and secure seats or berths in the ... sleeping-coaches of the Central Pacific. **1901** Churchill *Crisis* 324 In Shreve's time the cabins were curtained off, just like these new-fangled sleeping-car berths.

3. (See quotation.)

*a***1862** Thoreau *Maine Woods* 234 The chopper ... speaks of a 'berth' of timber, a good place for him to get into, just as a worm might.

+**4.** *Berth deck*, a deck upon which the berths in a vessel are situated; the crew occupying this deck.

1814 *Niles' Reg.* VI. 36/1 Captain Lambert and Mr. Waldo were the only wounded persons not removed to the *birth deck*, on this occasion. **1815** *Ib.* IX. 108/1 The impropriety of obliging the crew of a ship of war ... to sleep on the *birth-deck.* **1830** Cooper *Water Witch* III. i. 21 What is the opinion of the berth-deck concerning this strange brigantine? **1856** Olmsted *Slave States* 550 Not unfrequently, a bale ... would be thrown up, ... scattering the passengers on the berth deck. **1885** *Century Mag.* Aug. 642/2 The second [shell] ranged ... through the ward-room and steerage and out upon the berth-deck.

Beryl.** A precious stone of pale green color. — *a1817** Dwight *Travels* I. 35 Beryls, some of them very fine specimens, have been picked up at Brookfield [Conn.]. **1829** *Encycl. Amer.* II. 84 Some of the most remarkable localities of beryl are found ... in Massachusetts, Maine and New Hampshire in the U. States. **1868** Dana *Min.* 246 Beryls of gigantic dimensions have been found in the United States; ... one beryl from Grafton weighs 2,900 lbs. **1880** *Harper's Mag.* Nov. 880/2 Then there are beautiful specimens of beryl [at Chesterfield, Mass.].

+**Beshow.** [Indian *bishowk*, in the Makah dialect of the Wakashan stock.] The candle-fish, *Anoplopoma fimbria*, found along the west coast of North America. — [**1884** Goode *Fisheries U.S.* I. 268 Black Candle-fish ... in the Straits of Fuca ... is called by the Indians 'Beshow.'] **1888** — *Amer. Fishes* 271 The Beshow ... is generally known in Puget Sound by the name of 'Horse-mackerel.'

Bespeak. A request (for a particular play). {1839–} — **1846** S. Smith *Theatr. Apprent.* 97, I consented to accompany him to the governor's house to 'request a bespeak.' *Ib.*, I had been told a 'bespeak' from 'his excellency' would fill the theatre.

+**Best chamber.** The best bedchamber. — **1815** J. Hutton *Fashionable Follies* II. ii, Run, Robert, and put his bed in the best chamber. **1856** M. J. Holmes *L. Rivers* xxvii. 291 Did she think she was spiting her by showing what muss she could keep the 'best chamber' in if she chose?

+**Best parlor (parlour).** =next. — **1771** Copley in *Copley-Pelham Lett.* 137, I should like to have one window in the best Parlour. **1839** *S. Lit. Messenger* V. 794/2 When within the front door, you had on your left hand the best parlor. **1841** *Knickerb.* XVII. 389 The main part of the house, containing the 'best parlor,' and other rooms which were not in constant use, was shut up.

+**Best room.** The best finished and furnished room in a house, freq. reserved for Sundays and special occasions; a parlor. Also attrib.

1719 Sewall *Diary* III. 233 Moodey and I ... were married ... in the best room below stairs. ... Had a very good Dinner ... in the best room. **1764** *N.H. Hist. Soc. Coll.* IX. 170 Jno. Kimball came to help me lay my best room floor. **1771** Copley in *Copley-Pelham Lett.* 142 The door from the best room cannot be opposite to those steps. **1833** *Knickerb.* I. 305 The room in which they were incarcerated was the parlor, or 'best room,' of his paternal home. **1845** *Ib.* XXV. 506 His handsome hostess conducted him to his sleeping-room. It was a large chamber, the best room' of the log cabin. **1861** Stowe *Pearl Orr's Island* I. ii. 10 Here is the front room of the house, set apart as its place of especial social hilarity and sanctity—'the best room.' **1867** 'T. Lackland' *Homespun* III. 315 The 'best room' of the farmer's house is open then, though both sunshine and fire-light be kept out through the rest of the week. **1872** *Harper's Mag.* Oct. 684/1 There is a paneled door in the middle of the house, and on each side of the entry a parlor, or 'best room.' **1896** Wilkins *Madelon* 37 She passed Parson Fair's house, and the best-room windows were lighted.

***Bet,** *v.*

1. *tr.* To wager (one's life, money, pile, etc.) on something.

See also Boot, Bottom dollar.

1852 *Columbian* (Olympia, W. T.) 2 Oct. (Th.), They will all be faithfully preserved, and frequently referred to—and 'bet your life' on that. **1868** Bret Harte *Poems, Tale of a Pony* 78 Smart! You bet your life 'twas that! **1870** W. Boyd in *Boston Daily Times* 10 Aug., Every Mayflower native ... may safely 'bet his pile' ... that England won't stand still. **1890** Ryan *Told in Hills* 12 You can bet your money on that!

+**2.** *You bet (you)*, certainly, most assuredly. Also *you can bet.*

(1) **1868** *N. & Q.* 4 Ser. I. 293/2 The expression 'You bet!' is a Californian contraction of the sentence, 'You may bet on the truth of what I say.' **1869** *Overland Mo.* III. 185, I've been in this country since '41, and am posted, you bet! **1869** Browne *Adv. Apache Country* 296 You bet I'll seize a few of those glittering [silver] bricks. **1872** 'Mark Twain' *Roughing it* ii. 27 'The mosquitoes are pretty bad, about here, madam.' 'You bet!' 'What did I understand you to say, madam?' 'You Bet!' **1876** *Scribner's Mo.* Nov. 142/1 Instead of simply yea or nay, he gruffly said, 'You bet!' **1886–7** Stockton *Hundredth Man* xxxv, 'You bet he did!' said Enoch, 'but that's neither here nor there.' **1895** Remington *Pony Tracks* 210 'Did you hit him?' 'Well, you kin bet!'

(2) **1872** 'Mark Twain' *Roughing it* xx. 152 'I'll get you there on time' and you bet you he did, too. **1909** White *Rules of Game* v. xxxiv, 'He's a quick thinker, then,' said Bob. 'You bet you!'

Bethel. {*a*1617–} +A place where religious services are held for seamen. Also attrib. with *flag, union*, etc.

1823 *Amer. Baptist Mag.* IV. 178/2 New-Orleans Bethel Union, in the establishment of which the friends of seamen have great cause of rejoicing. *Ib.* 179 Having received from the New York Bethel Union ... a Bethel Flag. **1840** Dana *Two Years* xxxvii. 479 The establishment of Bethels in most of our own seaports, and in many foreign ports frequented by our vessels. **1856** Olmstead *Slave States* 143 Though there are two 'Bethels' [in Norfolk, Va., there is] no 'home' for its seamen. **1875** Emerson *Lett. & Social Aims* iii. 93 You may find him in some lowly Bethel, by the seaside.

+**Bethlemite.** One of a community of the Moravian Brethren settled at Bethlehem, Pennsylvania. — **1816** 'Scene painter' *Emigrant's Guide* 37 A sect denominated Bethlemites, from the name of a parish or township called Bethlem, which they exclusively inhabit, a few miles from Philadelphia, follow the example of the primitive Christians, by throwing their property into one common stock.

***Betony.** Also †**bittany.** One or other American plant resembling the European betony. Also attrib. with *tea.*

1778 Carver *Travels* 515 Herbs ... [include] Betony, Scabious, Mullen. **1794** Asbury *Journal* II. 216, I made use of flax-seed, and afterward of betony-tea, both of which were of use to me. **1832** Williamson *Maine* I. 120 Betony, the stalk of which is much shorter, has ... a purple blowth,—a tea of it will relieve the headach.

+**Betrustment.** A trust, something entrusted; the act of entrusting. — **1702** C. MATHER *Magnalia* v. II. (1852) 255 To make over church-betrustments 'unto faithful men.' **1711** — *Diary* II. 59 The grand Provision . . . for my Orphans, is in the following Deed of Betrustment. **1731** *Suffield Doc. Hist.* 246 In pursuance of which betrustment reposed in us, we have indeavoured to confirm. **1802** [L. LINCOLN] *Farmer's Lett. to People* 8 Be impressed with a sense of this interesting betrustment.

* **Better,** *a.* More. In the phrases *and better, better than.* In later use *colloq.* or *dial.* {Now *dial.*}

(1) **1670** *Conn. Public Rec.* II. 129 She hath not heard from her late husband Thomas Huitt for the space of eight yeares and better. **1699** *Virginia State P.* I. 64 Its aboutt a mile long or sumething better. **1774** FITHIAN *Journal* I. 139 At twelve I rode out, with Ben, an hour & better. **1890** *Harper's Mag.* Feb. 348/2, I tackled Greek once, twenty years ago now and better. **1895** *Century Mag.* Sept. 676/1 Jack Waring hain't fetched his bones this way for two months and better.

(2) **1751** GIST *Journals* 58 The tooth . . . was a Jaw Tooth of better than four Pounds Weight. **1770** WASHINGTON *Diaries* I. 363, [I] found a Fox at Muddy hole and killd her . . . after a chace of better than two hours. **1775** *Essex Inst. Coll.* XIII. 195 He . . . has sold . . . better than two tons Oil. **1859** ELWYN *Glossary* 21 *Better,* for 'more than' is common in New England, as, 'better than ten bushels.' **1879** TOURGEE *Fool's Errand* xxxviii. 280, I was at Mr. Hoyt's school—had been there better than a year.

* **Better,** *adv.* In colloq. uses.

+**1.** In the idiom, *I, you, he,* etc., *had better,* the *had* is often omitted.

1831 S. SMITH *Major Downing* 65 My clothes had got so shabby, I thought I better hire out a few days and get slicked up a little. **1845** HOOPER *Taking Census* i. 154 You better mind the holes in them ere rocks. **1853** *S. Lit. Messenger* XIX. 89/1 When I tell you a thing, Blass, you better believe it, you had. **1888** *Vermont Agric. Rep.* X. 14 If a man has a cheese factory he better keep it. **1911** R. D. SAUNDERS *Col. Todhunter* iv. 54 You better mind your own business. **1916** BOWER *Phantom Herd* i. 7 What you better do is this.

+**2.** Phr. *You'd better believe,* you may be sure; most assuredly; without doubt.

1856 *Yale Lit. Mag.* XXI. 171 (Th.), If I catch your daughter from home, You'd better believe, I'll live in the clover. **1857** *Knickerb.* XLIX. 69, I settled his hash, now you'd better believe, quick! **1862** *Major Jack Downing* 26 May (1867) 70 You'd better believe we've been in an awful excitement here. **1872** HOLMES *Poet* x. 331 My old gentleman means to be Mayor . . . before he goes off the handle, you'd better b'lieve.

3. *To go better* (in poker): see GO *v.*

Bettering house. {1735–}

+**1.** An institution which cares for necessitous people and assists them to develop habits of industry.

Originally and usually applied to that at Philadelphia.

1774 S. DEANE *Corr.* 177 What is called the Bettering House, in other words a poor-house. **1776** CRESSWELL *Journal* 155 Here is a good building they call a Bettering House, where all strolling and disorderly people are confined to labour till they can give a sufficient account of themselves. **1795** WINTERBOTHAM *Hist. View* II. 419 The following interesting account of the Quaker's Hospital, or Bettering House, as it is properly called. **1799** WELD *Travels* 7 The Bettering House, which is under the care of the overseers of the poor, stands in the same neighbourhood. **1806** Commons, etc. *Doc. Hist.* III. 75 My family must perish, or go to the bettering house. **1830** Watson *Annals Phila.* (1870) I. 103 The square fronting northward of the late Bettering-house was a great apple orchard in his time.

2. A reformatory. {1735–}

1826 *Missouri Intell.* 26 May 3/4 A correspondent is glad to perceive that a 'Penitentiary' or Bettering House is about to be established at Washington, by the authority . . . of Congress.

* **Betterment.**

+**1.** An improvement on real property. (Usually pl.)

'This term was first used, as I have understood, in the State of Vermont; but it has for a long time been common in the State of New Hampshire: And it has been getting into use in some parts of Massachusetts, since the passing of the late law, similar to the Betterment Acts (as they are called) of the states abovementioned' (Pickering).

1785 *Vermont State P.* (1823) 499 An Act to secure Daniel Marsh, in the possession of a certain farm, until he shall have opportunity of recovering his betterments. *Ib.* 501 The value of the improvements and betterments made on such lands by such possessor or possessors. **1809** KENDALL *Travels* III. 160 These men . . . demand either to be left owners of the soil or paid for their betterments, that is, for what they have done towards clearing the ground. **1823** COOPER *Pioneers* Introd., The shiftless, bargaining, discontented seller of his 'betterments.' **1839** *Vt. Revised Statutes* (1840) 218 The court shall appoint a committee . . . who shall, on oath, ascertain what would then be the value of such land, if no betterments had been made thereon. **1845** COOPER *Chainbearer* vii, Some folks call us squatters . . . but I do not. We have bought the betterments of a man who hadn't much of a title. ?**1882** S. L. PHILLIPS *Mechanics' Liens* (1893) 305 The term 'improvements,' as here used, does not mean an addition or betterment of a building, but some independent erection on the land. **1900** DIX *Deacon Bradbury* 162 The small amount . . . melted away under his hands in absolutely required replenishments and betterments.

2. Improvement; amelioration. {–1669}

1865 CARY *Ballads & Lyrics* 304 Each man should live for all men's betterment. **1877** Pinkerton *Molly Maguires* ii. 26 Mr. Pinkerton is after sending me to England, as he kindly says, for the betterment of my health. **1892** *Columbus* (Ohio) *Dispatch* 18 Aug., Authorities differ not only widely but vituperously as to the origin of practical effort for their betterment. **1910** *N.Y. Ev. Post* 27 Jan. (Th.), A man prominently identified with the betterment of the city.

+**3.** Attrib. (in sense 1) with *act, law, tax.*

1816 PICKERING (see sense 1). **1854** KENT *Commentaries* (ed. 8) 393 The statute law in Massachusetts, New Hampshire and Vermont is called the 'Betterment Law.' **1885** *U.S. Reports* CXV. 399 The Betterment Act of this Territory [Dakota] contained these provisions in §641 of the Code of Civil Procedure. **1890** J. RAE in *Contemporary Rev.* May 644 The betterment tax . . . has been known in America for two hundred years.

Bettermost, *a.* Best; greatest. *colloq.* or *dial.* {1762–; chiefly *dial.*}

1838 HALIBURTON *Clockmaker* II. xviii, I put on my bettermost clothes. *a***1848** MRS. KIRKLAND (B.), The bettermost cow, an expression we do not find in Shakspeare or Milton. **1855** SIMMS *Forayers* 113 The bettermost part b'longed to Miss Carrie here. **1859** BARTLETT 31 Sometimes is heard the expression *bettermost best,* as, 'These girls are dressed in their bettermost best.' *a***1871** STOWE (De Vere), I stopped the bettermost part of the time with my cousin, the deacon.

Bettor. One who bets or takes part in betting. {1640–} — **1894** *Outing* June 214/2 One of the features of the day is the 'bettor' or go-between. He is mounted on a pony, . . . and carries anything and everything that is betted. *a***1906** 'O. HENRY' *Trimmed Lamp* 171 'What'll be done to you'll be a plenty,' said a bettor, with anticipatory glee.

Betty. 1. A Florence flask. (Cf. BLACK BETTY.) {1725} **2.** A womanish man. — (1) **1848** BARTLETT 31 *Betty,* . . . a pear-shaped bottle wound around with straw, in which olive oil is brought from Italy. Called by chemists a Florence flask. (2) **1873** HOWELLS *Chance Acquaintance* ii. (1874) 49, I'll thank you, Colonel Ellison, not to be a Betty. . . . I don't think it's manly to be always noticing ladies' clothes.

* **Between,** *prep. Between you and me* (or *I*) *and the* (*bed-*) *post,* in confidence. {1832}

1801 *Sp. Farmers' Museum* 289, I heard Ben Burgler whisper, . . . 'That was a cursed treaty—Between you and I, and the post.' **1830** A. ROYALL *Lett. from Alabama* 136 Between you and I and the bed post, I begin to think it all a plot of the priests. **1833** NEAL *Down Easters* I. 23 Between you an' me an' the post I've taken a sort of a likin' to you. **1843** [STEPHENS] *High Life N.Y.* II. 112 And between you and I and the post, . . . my ginuine opinion is [etc.].

‖**Between-days.** The days between certain specified times. — **1894** 'MARK TWAIN' *P. Wilson* x, Every now and then she paid him a visit there on between-days, also.

+**Between-lands.** Lands lying between those on a lower and higher level. — *c***1900** R. L. HALE *Log of Forty-Niner* 86 These higher, or between lands [near Portland, Oregon], as they are called, are unhealthy.

* **Betwixt,** *prep.* Between. *archaic, dial.* (as in Eng.), or *colloq.* — **1830** S. SMITH *Major Downing* (1834) 9 Facin the Sargent is my own likeness, with the likeness of Deacon Willoby betwixt us. **1833** *Ib.* 194 The steamboat President runnin betwixt New York and Providence. **1881** *Harper's Mag.* May 879/1 There's a mighty power o' defference betwixt a man and a boy. **1884** 'MARK TWAIN' *Huck. Finn* ii. 9 So he set down on the ground betwixt me and Tom.

* **Bever,** *n.* At Harvard, a light repast, esp. between breakfast and dinner; a lunch. *Obs.* — **1646** *Harvard Rec.* I. 27 No Scholars shall . . . bee absent from his studyes or appointed exercises above an houre at Morning-Bever, halfe an houre at afternoone-Bever; an houre and an halfe at Dinner. **1650** Quincy *Hist. Harvard* (1840) I. 548 [The butler] is not bound to stay above half an hour at bevers in the buttery after the tolling of the bell. **1851** HALL *College Words* 19 At the appointed hour for bevers, there was a general rush for the buttery.

Bever, *v.* {1607, 1632} *intr.* 'To take a small repast between meals' (Hall *College Words,* citing Wallis). *Obs.*

* **Beverage.** +(See quotations.) — **1800** J. BOUCHER *Glossary* p. xlix, *Beveridge,* or *Beverage* . . . , a drink made of spring-water, white sugar, and the juice of lemons, limes, or oranges. **1885** E. EGGLESTON in *Century Mag.* April 884/1 In many places in 1656 the distressed traveler could find nothing stronger than water, or milk and water, or 'beverige,' which last appears to have been a drink made of molasses and water.

+**Bewick's wren.** [Named for Thomas *Bewick,* English wood-engraver (1753–1828).] A species of wren (*Thryothorus bewickii*) abundant in the south and the middle west. — **1831** AUDUBON *Ornith. Biog.* I. 96 Bewick's Wren, *Troglodytes Bewickii.* . . . In shape, colour and movements, it nearly resembles the Great Carolina Wren. **1858** BAIRD *Birds Pacific R. R.* 363 Bewick's Wren . . . is very strongly marked among all the North American wrens by the very long black tail, varied only on the exterior with whitish. **1898** TORREY in *Atlantic Mo.* April 457/1 The singer was at home for the season: . . . a Bewick's wren, as I had guessed.

+**Bhené,** obs. variant of BENNE. — **1818** DARBY *Emigrant's Guide* 185 That species of sesamum, called oriental bhené. *Ib.,* The bhené is certainly one of the most productive vegetables that ever was cultivated by man. It is known in Louisiana, but much neglected.

+**B'hoy.** *colloq.*[2] [Irish pronunc. of *boy.*] A tough character or rowdy.

'*B'hoys*, . . . a name applied to a class of noisy young men of the lower ranks of society in the city of New York' (B. '48).

Extensively illustrated by Thornton from 1846 to 1866.

a1846 *Quarter Race Kentucky*, etc. 117 As the colt was known to be a sharp one, and his owner 'one of the b'hoys' for a quarter race, . . . he had the call in the betting at six to four. *Ib.* 120 Hold your hosses, b'hoys! **1846** *Knickerb.* XXVIII. 557 A friend of ours . . . was much struck, and not a little amused, by 'The B'hoys,' returning from their Sunday drives. **1852** Bristed *Upper Ten Th.* i. 29 Its occupants are of the not-to-be-mistaken Bowery cut—veritable b'hoys. **1861** Winthrop *Open Air* 145 To the front stepped Mr. William Tarbox . . . no longer a bhoy, but an . . . erect, fine-looking fellow. *Ib.* 221 At the corner of Grand Street . . . a 'bhoy' in red flannel shirt . . . called me. **1895** Howells in Crane *Maggie*, etc. (1931) 136 Her brother, . . . who . . . is what the b'hoy of former times has become in our more strenuously policed days.

***Bib.**

***1.** A cloth placed under a child's chin; a cloth worn over the breast by adults.

1772 Winslow *Diary* 13, I was dress'd in my yellow coat, my black bib and apron. **1863** 'M. Harland' *Husks* 24 It was not a sumptuous repast to which Sarah sat down after she had placed Jeannie in her high chair and tied the great gingham bib around her neck.

2. Phr. *best* (or *company*) *bib and tucker* (or *band*), one's best clothes. {1854–, *dial.*}

1795 *Art of Courting* (Newburyport, Mass.) 175 The old gentleman put on his best bib and band. **1809** Weems *Marion* (1833) 42 We all put on our 'best bibs and tuckers.' **1822** *National Gazette* in *Massachusetts Spy* 27 Feb. (Th.), It is not in the evenings only that they are to be encountered in 'the best bib and tucker.' **1833** *Sketches of Crockett* 38 Both girls and boys had on their best bib and tucker. **1843** in Commons, etc. *Doc. Hist.* VIII. 219 The fair operatives in the factories at Chicopee . . . formed in solemn column, arrayed in their best bibs and tuckers. **1875** Stowe *We & Our Neighbors* 160 Even the moderate 'tea-fight' . . . necessitated . . . a mustering and review of best 'bibs and tuckers,' through the neighborhood. **1886** Stockton *Mrs. Lecks* 127 Mrs. Lecks and Mrs. Aleshine put on their best bibs and tuckers. **1902** A. MacGowan *Last Word* 63 Beside her at the dinner-table, magnificent in company bib and tucker, . . . sat the sovereign Teddy.

Bib-apron. An apron with a top piece that serves as a bib. {1750–} — **1866** Mrs. Whitney *L. Goldthwaite* x, They got her into a bright violet print and a white bib-apron. **1904** Waller *Wood-carver* 242 She came in, demure in her great bib-apron.

+**Bible agent.** A seller of Bibles. — **1847** Briggs *Tom Pepper* I. 16, I turned a bible agent out of the schooner the day before we left.

Bible-back. [Cf. next.] A hump-backed or round-shouldered person. {1896, *dial.*} — **1890** *Buckskin Mose* x. 145 We in a few days started, pitching our camp . . . at La Due Very's, generally known as 'Old Bible-back.' **1903** *Dialect Notes* II. 349 *Bible-back*, a round-shouldered, hump-backed person, [is current in] N.Y., . . . N.J.

Bible-backed, *a.* [Cf. Sc. dial. *beugle-backed* (1709).] Hump-backed. {1873, *dial.*} — **1857** *Olympia* (Wash.) *Pioneer & Democrat* 11 Dec. (Th.), We might, in consequence [of lack of funds], become somewhat round-shouldered and 'bible-backed.'

+**Bible Christian.** One of 'a sect closely resembling the Methodists, from whom they differ merely in having a more popular form of Church government' (Schaff). — **c1819** in Metcalfe *Out of Clouds* (1872) 27 The preaching of a man who professed to be a 'Bible-Christian.' **1828** in *Hist. Phila. Bible-Christian Church* (1922) 140 A Sick Club . . . formed of members of the Bible-Christian Church alone. **1848** Bartlett 31 Bible Christians . . . 'abstain from all animal food and spirituous liquors.' **1883** *Schaff's Relig. Encycl.* I. 257 Bible Christians. . . . In the United States there is only one congregation, which is in Philadelphia.

+**Bible-class.** A class for the study of the Bible, either as part of a Sunday school or as a separate organization.

1824 *Baptist Mag.* IV. 371, I intimated my intention to establish . . . Bible classes for the study of the sacred oracles. **1865** *Atlantic Mo.* XV. 684 Some evening appointment at Bible class or other such gathering. **1870** Eggleston *Blake's Walking-Stick* v. 38 The young men's and the young women's Bible classes undertook to supply Sitles with a broom-machine. **1873** 'Mark Twain' & Warner *Gilded Age* liii. 478 The Senator wrought in Bible classes, and nothing could keep him away from the Sunday-schools. **1893** J. Auld *Picturesque Burlington* 126 The president [of the Y.M.C.A.] also conducts a voluntary Bible Class every Sunday afternoon.

+**Bible Communist.** One of a sect founded by the social reformer John H. Noyes (1811–86), whose followers held property in common; a Perfectionist. — **1867** Dixon *New America* II. 262 The Family at Oneida Creek consists of about three hundred members, a number which these Bible Communists say is [etc.]. **1869** J. H. Noyes *Hist. Amer. Socialisms* 631 Bible Communists are not held responsible for the proceedings of those who meddle with the sexual question, before [etc.].

Bible oath. An oath taken on a Bible. {1698–}

1836 C. Gilman *Recoll.* xvi. 109, I can take my Bible oath that I saw your ring on the gentleman's little finger, ma'am. **1840** Simms *Border Beagles* 394, I'll take Bible-oath to it, ma'am. I'll kiss the book to it. **1847** [Robb] *Squatter Life* 137, I jest swar a bible oath, I'd spile his pictur' so he couldn't enjoy campmeetin' much. **1872** Holmes *Poet* ix. 293, I would hold my right hand up and take my Bible-oath, if it was not busy with the pen at this moment.

Bible-reader. One who visits the poor or sick in order to read the Bible to them. — **1868** [A. B. Condict] *P. Eckert* 76 'The Lord is ever faithful,' responded the Bible-reader—for their visitor was one of those good Christian women sometimes found in our great cities, who . . . continually go about doing good.

Bible society. An organization for the distribution of Bibles, or sometimes for the study of the Bible. {1780–} Also attrib.

1811 Mease *Philadelphia* 287 Bible Society. In December, 1808, a society was formed for the distribution of the Bible among the poor. **1815** Dwight in *Q. Review* 175 In this country there are . . . at least sixty-five Bible Societies. **1816** *Amer. Bible Soc. Ann. Rep.* (1838) I. 10 The American Bible Society, of which the sole object shall be, to encourage a wider circulation of the Holy Scriptures without note or comment. **1834** *Knickerb.* III. 113 The Rev. Dr. Miller preached a Bible Society sermon. **1840** *Niles' Reg.* 21 March 48/1 Union of the American Bible society and Philadelphia Bible society. **1862** Jackson in M. A. Jackson *Life* 360, I also hope that . . . large contributions were made to our Bible Society. **1882** Bitting *Bible Societies & Baptists* 114 The Society . . . buying the cheaper editions published by the American Bible Society.

***Bickern.** *Obs.* An anvil with tapering ends. Cf. Beak-iron, Beckorne. — **1678** *New Castle Court Rec.* 267 Smiths Tooles: one pr. of bellowes, one anvill, . . . one bickeren, 2 hamners [*sic*].

Bicknell apple. (See quotation.) — **1816** *Mass. H. S. Coll.* 2 Ser. VII. 116 The 'Bicknell apple,' so termed, is here cultivated. It yields a great proportion of juice, but as to quality is rather watery.

Bicycle, *n.*

1. A machine of two wheels, one behind the other, propelled by means of pedals; a cycle. {1868–}

[**1868** *Scientific American* 16 Dec. 389 The connecting apparatus differs from that of the French bycycle.] **1877** *Scientific Amer. Suppl.* 21 July 1283/3 The silence of the bicycle . . . constitutes its chief danger to pedestrians. **1883** *Wheelman* I. 401 The revival of velocipeding, the advent of the modern bicycle, in this country, was in the latter half of 1877. **1886** *N.Y. Herald* in *Cyclist* 3 Nov. 82/1 Crocker was paced by Woodside, Rowe, and Hendee on bicycles. **1896** *Godey's Mag.* April 430/2 He has passed into the second and higher stage of riding a bicycle.

2. Attrib. with *cap*, *club*, *corps*, etc.

1876 *Scientific Amer. Suppl.* 19 Feb. 128/2 Bicycle-riding . . . is a sport confined to a select few in this country; but in England it is extensively practised. **1877** *Ib.* 21 July 1283/3 In a country with good roads . . ., the bicycle-rider . . . might be very useful in war as a scout. **1882** *Wheelman* I. 26 At agricultural fairs, . . . bicycle-races are becoming a regular part of the entertainment. **1883** *Ib.* 412 Our club . . . reorganized as a bicycle club. **1884** *Springfield Wheelmen's Gaz.* Nov. 105/2 Minneapolis is to have . . . a first class bicycle track. **1890** *Harper's Mag.* Oct. 656/2 We each wore . . . ribbed bicycle stockings that came to our knees. **1895** *N.Y. Dramatic News* 6 July 5/3 Friday evening was 'bicycle night,' and Maggie sang some of her famous bicycle songs. *Ib.* 7/2 Weston and his wife . . . have caught the bicycle fever. **1897** *Boston Journal* 22 Jan. 3/4 Several of the bicycle stores are being newly painted. **1906** 'O. Henry' *Four Million* 234 He touched the brim of the old plaid bicycle cap perched on the back of his head. **1909** — *Options* 292, I suppose . . . your idea of rural sport is to have a little whirl between bicycle cops in Central Park.

Bicycle, *v.* [f. prec.] *intr.* To ride a bicycle. Hence *Bicycling* vbl. n.

1879 *Lippincott's Mag.* Nov. 626/1 At present Boston is the centre of bicycling. **1880** *Scribner's Mo.* Feb. 496/2 The bicycling song, written by our Highland Laddie, was rendered to the air of 'Dearest Mac.' **1881** *Harper's Mag.* July 286/2 The influence of an increasing interest in the practice of bicycling will be . . . powerful in effecting the improvement of the roads all over the country. **1883** *Wheelman* April 6/1 We donned our knickerbockers, . . . and bicycled to the wharf. **1897** *Outing* Aug. 447/2 But nobody asks her to bicycle or anything else.

+**Bicycler.** One who rides a bicycle.

1879 *Lippincott's Mag.* Nov. 626/1 Two bicyclers rode one hundred miles in the suburbs of Boston in twelve hours. **1881** *Harper's Mag.* July 284/2 'Taking a header' . . . is an experience which any bicycler knows may occur to him at any time. **1882** *Advance* (Chicago) 1 June (editorial), The grand convention of 'bicyclers,' held in this city this week. **1884** *Springfield Wheelmen's Gaz.* Nov. 104/3 Philadelphia bicyclers cannot ride more than two abreast through their park.

Bicyclist. [f. Bicycle *n.*] =Bicycler. {1876–} — **1879** *Webster's Suppl.* **1881** *Harper's Mag.* July 283/2 The bicyclist should feel for his machine a tender sense of gratitude for the service it has done him. **1881** *Nation* 23 June 442 An axiom for bicyclists which holds equally good for pedestrians—viz., the object of journeying is . . . to enjoy one's self. **1897** *Chicago Tribune* 14 July 6 The bicyclists of the city have been making a strenuous fight against the proposition to levy a tax of $1 a year.

Bicycular, *a.* **a.** Two-wheeled. **b.** Pertaining to bicycles or bicycling. — **1869** *Scientific American* 20 Feb. 117 Astonishing the citizens of Davenport, Iowa, by her skillful management of the bicycular Velocipede.

1884 *Springfield Wheelmen's Gazette* Nov. 105/2 Minneapolis . . . expects to eclipse Chicago in matters bicycular.

Bid, *n.*

1. The offer of a price, esp. at an auction, or of something for a certain sum; the amount offered. {1837–}

1788 Jefferson *Writings* VII. 95 He . . . thought to obtain a high bid by saying he was called for in America. **1805** *Ann. 9th Congress* 2 Sess. 1025 The highest sum resulting from the bids was seven cents, for a square foot. **1852** Stowe *Uncle Tom* v, 'The fellow made me a high bid on Eliza, if that would suit you any better,' said Mr. Shelby. 'The wretch!' said Mrs. Shelby. **1861** *Army Regulations* 155 When sealed bids are required, the time of opening them shall be specified. **1882** *Nation* 19 Oct. 331/1 The time for receiving bids for $100,000 loan . . . expired to-day. But no bids were offered. **1906** *Indian Laws & Tr.* III. 622 The bids for the lands offered will be opened at the Vernal, Utah, land office.

+**2.** An application or request for employment.

1855 J. E. Cooke *Ellie* 67 Mrs. Brown had more 'bids' for her work, at the moment, than she could supply.

+**3.** An invitation.

1887 *Lippincott's Mag.* July 100 Our new man has a 'bid,' and . . . must be initiated into the mysteries of a 'dyke.' *Ib.* Nov. 739 The student . . . may even secure 'bids' to some small and half-formal gatherings during the winter. **1893** *Kansas University Q.* Jan. 136 A bid to the wedding.

* **Bid,** *v.*

+**1.** *Bid to,* in p.p., denoting the receipt of an invitation. *Obs.*

1729 J. Comer *Diary* (1923) 81 A child's funeral bid to. *Ib.* 98 This morning Gideon Wanton's child's funeral bid to.

+**2.** *Bid off:* **a.** To dispose of at auction.

1780 *N.H. Comm. Safety* 235 Provided the heirs of Joseph Simmes . . . should bid off at Vendue any of said Estate laying in the town of Middletown. **1819** *Niles' Reg.* XVI. 320/2, 101 lots were bid off for an aggregate of upwards of 96,000 dollars. **1833** *Ib.* XLIV. 347/1 The school master is often 'bid off' or 'put up at auction,' as are our paupers—and the *lowest* bidder in the district takes him. **1857** *Lawrence* (Kansas) *Republican* 28 May 3 The other day . . . they were sold, being bid off mainly for wrapping paper.

+**b.** To obtain by bidding at auction.

1855 *Harper's Mag.* X. 853/1 At an auction in the country a fiddle was put up for sale. It was 'bid off' by a green-looking Yankee. **1872** Flagg *Good Investment* xii. 548/1 They were a portion of the library of the late Peyton Simms, Esq., which Mr. Damarin had chanced to bid off at an auction sale in Cincinnati. **1892** Howells *Mercy* 209 Those things of their own that the sisters had meant to sacrifice, were bidden off, and restored to them. **1907** C. C. Andrews *Recoll.* 276 It was bid-off by the lumber-men themselves, who formed a combination to prevent it from falling into the hands of other purchasers.

+**3.** *Bid in,* to buy at an auction.

1855 Thompson *Doesticks* 135 [I] succeeded in bidding in a China vase. **1857** *Quinland* I. 139 If any can pay, well and good. Farms are to be bid in at not more than half of their estimated value, and as much under as possible. **1875** *Chicago Tribune* 1 Oct. 2/3 The stallion Glaymore . . . was knocked down for $2,500, understood to have been bid in for Gen. Grant. **1917** J. F. Daly *Life A. Daly* 345 The costly books which were bid in at the sale of 1878.

Biddy[1]. *colloq.* or *jocular.* A hen or chicken. (Cf. He-biddy.) {1601–; now *dial.*}

1844 *Spirit of Times* (Philad.) 9 Sept. (Th.), The way that factory at the Masonic Hall turns out the chickens [by steam heat] is a caution to 'biddies.' **1853** B. F. Taylor *Jan. & June* 94 Sacred to the memory of . . . a little Biddy, drowned to death, July 10th. **1867** Holmes *Guardian Angel* 4 A hen at Four Corners had just laid an egg measuring 7 by 8 inches. Fetch on your biddies! **1884** Roe *Nature's Story* ii, You don't catch her wasting a sitting of eggs under a fickle biddy. **1894** *Vermont Agric. Rep.* XIV. 175 Hang up a head of cabbage and let the hens pick it, or throw in a few apples to supply biddy with green food.

Biddy[2]. [Familiar form of *Bridget.*] An Irish servant-girl. Also transf. {1711 (Swift)} — **1858** Holmes *Autocrat* xii. 363 Poor Bridget, or Biddy, our red-armed maid-of-all-work! **1861** Winthrop *Open Air* 261 Our thousand [soldiers] did the Capitol little harm that a corporal's guard of Biddies with mops and tubs could not repair in a forenoon's campaign. **1865–6** *Ill. Agric. Soc. Trans.* VI 294 Two dollars a week would not tempt even the greenest Biddy to leave her church. **1902** Bret Harte in *Harper's Mag.* April 733 He's . . . puttin' up a high-toned house on the hill . . . with a Chinese cook, and a Biddy, and a Mexican *vaquero* to look after his horse.

Biennial, *a.* and *n.*

1. *adj.* Occurring, held, or appearing every two years. {1750}

1715 *N.C. Laws* (1791) 9 A General Biennial Assembly, held . . . at Little-River. **1735** *N.C. Col. Rec.* IV. 88 An Act relating to Biennial and other Assemblyes. **1788** *Mass. Debates & Proc.* (1856) 101 Mr. Parsons . . . said the subject in debate was the expediency of biennial elections. **1814** *Portsmouth Oracle* 24 Sept. 3/3 The Biennial Convention of the Protestant Episcopal Church. **1840** *Niles' Reg.* 4 April 78/1 They contracted with the department of state to print and bind the last Biennial Register (or Blue Book). **1854** *Presentation Day Songs* (Yale) 14 June, Olmsted served an apprenticeship setting up types, For the schemes of Bien. Examination. **1873** *Harper's Mag.* XLVI. 573 There has been a change from *annual* to *biennial* sessions in thirteen of the States. **1906** *Indian Laws & Tr.* III. 258 There shall be a biennial election of officers for the Osage Tribe.

b. Involving a period of two years.

1737 *N.C. Col. Rec.* IV. 270 Read the Repeal of the Biennial Act; ordered that a Proclamation issue to give notice thereof. **1792** Jefferson in *Writings of Washington* (1892) XII. 100 *n.*, The biennial bill furnishing money for the support of the foreign establishment.

c. *Bot.* Continuing for two years.

1843 Torrey *Flora N.Y.* I. 236 *Gaura biennis*, . . . Biennial Gaura. . . . Dry soil, banks of the Mohawk.

+**2.** *n.* A biennial examination at Yale.

1853 *Songs of Yale* 4 The 'Biennial' is an Examination occurring twice during the course,—at the close of the Sophomore and of the Senior years,—in all the studies pursued during the two years previous. It was established in 1850. **1853** *Cent. Anniv. Linonian Soc.* (Yale) 70 (Hall) The system of examinations has been made more rigid, especially by the introduction of biennials. **1871** [Bagg] *At Yale* 277 As the 'Biennial' was superseded by the 'Annual' examinations, so the 'Biennial caps' gave way to 'Annual caps.' *Ib.*, In the time when Biennials . . . were in vogue. **1876** W. S. Tyler *Amherst Coll.* 237 Amherst had already led the way in dispensing with biennials and senior examinations in the whole curriculum.

+**Biennialist.** One who favors biennial rather than annual sessions of a legislative body. — **1894** *Columbus* (Ohio) *Dispatch* 7 March, The Lieutenant Governor, an intensely partisan biennialist, told him he need not answer any questions.

+**Bier.**[1] A gauze or netting to keep out mosquitoes. Cf. Bear *n.*[3] and Bar *n.*[2] — **1805** *Lewis & Clark Exped.* (1893) II. 417 *note*, I had left my bier, of course suffered considerably. **1821** Nuttall *Trav. Arkansa* 191 Two very handsome young men of the Osages . . . endeavoured, though ineffectually, to hook off a musquetoe bier.

Bier.[2] *Obs.* [Cf. E. *bere, beare* (–*c* 1600), framework for carrying.] +A portable cradle of basket-work. — **1805** Lewis in *L. & Clark Exped.* (1904) II. 197 The bier in which the [Indian] woman carrys her child and all it's cloathes wer swept away.

Bier way. The right of way for a funeral. *Obs.* — **1664** *Dedham Rec.* IV. 98 It is by voate granted that a way from the meeting house to the Buriall place one Rode broade shall be layed out . . . for free vse for a Beere way [*margin* Burial place way].

+**Biff,** *interj.* and *n.*

1. *interj.* imitative of the sound of a blow.

1847 [Robb] *Squatter Life* 137, I didn't wait till he finished afore I hit him, *biff*, alongside his smeller.

2. A blow. Also fig.

1890 *Dialect Notes* I. 72 *Bif*, . . . oftenest used in such phrases as 'to give one a biff in the ear.' *c***1893** *Ib.* 234 Hit 'im a biff. **1904** W. H. Smith *Promoters* x. 165 What an idiot a man can be when he gets a biff that takes his wind. **1904** F. Lynde *Grafters* xxviii. 368 But Hawk's next biff was more to the purpose. . . . The plan was [etc.].

+**Biff,** *v.* [f. the noun.] *tr.* To strike, deal a blow to. — *c***1892** *Dialect Notes* I. 214 He biffed him on the ear. **1902** Clapin 50 *Bif, Biff, Bift,* current in several parts of the States in sense of to strike, and especially to give a quick blow. **1910** McCutcheon *Rose in Ring* 337 Jimmie Parsons . . . tried to stop him after he biffed me. Jimmie's got two wonderful black eyes as a result.

* **Big,** *a.*

'This adjective is generally used by the people of the Southern States, in cases where a New Englander would use *great* or *large.* Ex. A big man, &c. We should say in New England, a *large* man' (Pickering).

* **1.** Used to designate a large thing of its kind as distinguished from a smaller one.

1821 J. Fowler *Journal* 16 The Indeans advise us to cross the Arkensaw at the big timber. **1836** *Knickerb.* VIII. 45 We were compelled to pick up our meals at the houses of the scattering planters . . . where corn-cake and 'big hominy' is the universal provender. **1841** *Ib.* XVII. 33 He proposes to meet those who are desirous of instruction in music, at the Big-room of the Tavern. **1848** J. Mitchell *Nantucketisms* 40 *Big General*, the largest bill of a fishing vessel. **1850** Garrard *Wah-To-Yah* xxiii. 286 St. Vrain told me you was in Taos, on guard, when the old *palous* were hung, and that you cut a 'big swath' generally. **1859** Greeley *Overland Journey* (1860) 359 The chances for 'big strikes' in the mines are few, and greenhorns cannot share them. **1859** Bartlett 31 The 'big horn,' for the last trumpet, is almost profane. *c***1866** Bagby *Old Va. Gentleman* 51 The traveller enters this domain [of grassland] through a rickety 'big-gate.' **1880** G. Ingham *Digging Gold* i. 41 The great richness of the gold-fields . . . enabled some lucky miners to make rich strikes and proportionately 'big pay.' **1889** *Harper's Mag.* May 878/1 Thus we see on all sides . . . our 'big game' diminishing with terrible rapidity. **1923** J. H. Cook *On Old Frontier* 55 This first year that I was on the trail, every river from the Red River to the Arkansas was 'big swimming,' as the boys termed it.

b. In specific names of animals, plants, etc.

1814 Mitchill *Fishes N.Y.* 404 Big Porgee of New-York, *Labrus versicolor.* **1832** Browne *Sylva* 226 Large Buckeye . . . is here [in the Southern states] called Big Buckeye, to distinguish it from the *Pavia rubra.*

1842 *Nat. Hist. N.Y., Zoology* IV. 80 The Big Drum, *Pogonias chromis*, . . . is a large and deep fish. **1844** *Ib.* II. 285 The Great Diver, or Big Loon, may be regarded as a perpetual resident in this State. **1855** BAIRD in *Smithsonian Rep.* 333 The Big Porgee, *Pagrus argyrops.* The flesh of the porgee is excellent when fresh. **1874** COUES *Birds N.W.* 573 *Fuligula Marila*, . . . Greater Scaup Duck; Big Black-head. **1884** SARGENT *Rep. Forests* 133 *Carya sulcata*, . . . Big Shellbark. *Ib.* 175 *Populus monilifera*, . . . Big Cottonwood. **1901** MOHR *Plant Life Ala.* 465 *Populus deltoides*, Carolina Poplar, Big Cottonwood, . . . [is] a timber tree.

+**c.** In Indian talk.

See also BIG KNIFE, BIG TALK, and MEDICINE.

1813 *Niles' Reg.* V. 78/2 The Indians . . . being determined to see which of the *big canoes* had the command of the lake. **1837** IRVING *Bonneville* II. vii. 81 The old chief . . . did all that he could to glorify the Big Hearts of the East. **1899** CUSHMAN *Hist. Indians* 66 Their forefathers came from a country beyond the 'Big Waters' far to the north-west.

d. In colloquial uses.

1845 HOOPER *Taking Census* ii. 167 Throw a meal-bag . . . over your head, twell my little 'squire gits sorter usen to the big ugly! **1877** BARTLETT 42 D. D. F. — is the biggest toad in the puddle. **1883** J. HAY *Bread-winners* ii. 20 You'd a big sight better let me alone. **1891** *Fur, Fin, & Feather* March 170 They thought we were giving them a big stiff. **1900** ROOSEVELT in Pringle *Roosevelt* (1931) 214 I have always been fond of the West African proverb: 'Speak softly and carry a big stick; you will go far.' **1902** HARBEN *Abner Daniel* 72 He's a big Ike in some church in Atlanta. **1904** W. IRWIN *Random Rhymes* (1906) 181 Theodore did say, 'Now tell me quick by the Big Stick Why dost thou refuse to pay?' **1912** C. MATHEWSON *Pitching* i. 1 During his first two years in the big show . . . [he] looked like a cripple at the plate.

+**2.** Excellent in quality; fine, 'great.' *colloq.*

1848 RUXTON *Far West* (1849) 128 The valley [contains] . . . many thermal . . . springs, . . . considered, moreover, to be the 'biggest kind' of 'medicine' to be found in the mountains. **1863** NORTON *Army Lett.* 183 The brigade was flying round, getting into line, drums beating and a big time generally. *Ib.* 190 We had big times that night for fires. **1888** *Washington* (Pa.) *Review* (F.), The *Pittsburg Times* . . . is the biggest little paper we are acquainted with. **1889** FARMER 53 What in England would be called fine old whiskey and brandy would, in America, be designated 'big whiskey.'

3. Great, important. *colloq.*

1881 BUEL *Border Outlaws* 155 When Thursday, which is always the 'big day' of the Exposition, arrived, every incoming train poured hundreds of new arrivals into the city. **1914** H. JAMES *Ivory Tower* II. i. 77 What was before him at the least was a 'big' experience.

Big Belly. [tr. Fr. *Gros Ventres*, 'great bellies.'] +One of a tribe of Indians of Algonquian stock now settled in Montana; also, one of the Hidatsa or Minitari of Dakota; a Grosventre Indian. — **1805** CLARK in *Lewis & C. Exped.* (1904) I. 248 The grand Chief of the Big bellies . . . spoke slightly of the Americans, saying if we would give our great flag to him he would come to see us. **1807** GASS *Journal* 76 This forenoon we passed two villages of the Grossventers, or Big-belly's nation of Indians.

Big bore. [BIG *a.* I.] A rifle of large calibre. — **1843** 'CARLTON' *New Purchase* II. xxxvi. 31, I had a powerful big bore to fix for a feller going out West.

+**Big bug.** *colloq.* [BIG *a.* 3.] A person of importance.

In common use from 1830. Fully illustrated by Thornton from 1830 to 1861.

1827 *Harvard Reg.* Oct. 247 He who desires to be a big-Bug, rattling in a natty gig, No-top, or chaise, or tandem. **1832** CATLIN *Indians* I. 40 You must see the magic dress of this Indian 'big bug' [=medicine man]. **1835** D. P. THOMPSON *Adv. I. Peacock* 40, I was rather fearful when you went from here that you would not be able to do much with the big-bugs there in the village. **1841** GREELEY in *Corr. R. W. Griswold* (1898) 53 He has been round boring every big-bug in the State to bone for him. **1852** BRISTED *Upper Ten Th.* ix. 207 For the biggest bugs of the Papist set Were not convinced by their primate yet. **1853** *Harper's Mag.* Aug. 425/1 The subject, we take it, is the 'merchant' of a country-store; quite a different variety from the big bugs of the trade in the Great Metropolis. **1868** [A. B. CONDICT] *P. Eckert* 151 'Oh, ho! you've got in with the grandees and big bugs, have you?' sneered Dan. **1876** MILLER *First Families* xxi. 189 The great Washington, Cæsar, Horace Greeley, all sich big-bugs, it might take one, two, three years. **1884** HOWELLS *Silas Lapham* ii. 44 There's all kinds of people on Beacon Street; you mustn't think they're all big-bugs. **1896** J. C. HARRIS *Sister Jane* 24 He don't belong to the big-bugs. **1907** C. C. ANDREWS *Recoll.* 51 After the governor had entered and most of the big bugs including invited guests, the undergraduates thought it time for them to go in. **1923** BOWER *Parowan Bonanza* xi. 132 Then he was just married to-day—this morning, upstairs in the parlor—with all the big bugs in town present.

attrib. **1848** E. JUDSON *Mysteries N.Y.* I. 13, I haven't lifted nuthin' . . . but I mauled some o' the bigbug swells a bit ago.

‖**Bigbuggery.** [f. prec.] The condition of being a big bug; conceit, arrogance. — **1843** 'CARLTON' *New Purchase* I. xxv. 235 No one would have become so popular in the New Purchase, but for mistaken opinions in the neighbours about 'Mr. Carlton's bigbuggery and stuckupness.'

+**Big Devils.** A tribe of the Sioux Indians. — **1814** Biddle *Lewis & Clark Exped.* I. 61 Yanktons of the (North or) Plains, or Big Devils, who rove on the heads of the Sioux, Jacques, and Red rivers; the most numerous of all the tribes, numbering about 500 men.

Big ditch. [BIG *a.* I.] +**1.** The Erie canal. +**2.** The Atlantic Ocean. — **(1) 1835** [H. TODD] *Notes* 64 The Erie canal—here called *canol*—was at first attempted to be laughed down, under the cognomen of 'The Big, and Clinton's Ditch.' **1845** *Knickerb.* XXVI. 268 The population appears to have doubled within the last twenty years; this is, since the 'big ditch' was completed. **1872** *Harper's Mag.* May 841/1 Tammany used the 'big ditch' scheme as one of the most effective weapons against him [=Clinton]. **(2) 1909** WASON *Happy Hawkins* 11, I'm the biggest fool this side o' the big ditch.

Big dog. *slang.* [BIG *a.* I.] +*fig.* A person of great, or the greatest, importance. Also with additions, as *of the tanyard.*

1845 HOOPER *Simon Sugg's Adv.* x. 126 Pointing to the reverend gentleman who had so successfully carried the unbeliever through the Old and New Testament, and who Simon was convinced was the 'big dog of the tanyard.' **1847** FIELD *Drama in Pokerville*, etc. 35 At any rate, he belonged to 'one of the first families in Virginia,' . . . and [was], altogether, the 'big dog' at Pokerville. **1851** *Knickerb.* XXXVIII. 555 He cut his market associations, bought lots up town, now lives in the Fifth Avenue, and is a 'big dog.' **1859** BARTLETT 31 In some parts of the country the principal man of a place or in an undertaking is called the 'big dog with a brass collar,' as opposed to the little curs not thought worthy of a collar.

Big drink. *colloq.* [BIG *a.* I.] +The Mississippi River. — **1846** *Oregon Spectator* 2 May (Th.), There never would have been any Atlantic Ocean if it hadn't been for the Mississippi, nor ever will be after we've turned the waters of that big drink in the Mammoth Cavern. **1853** 'P. PAXTON' *Yankee in Texas* 121, [I] went through Massassippi, crossed the 'Big Drink,' came to now and then, when the chill come it too strong. **1859** BARTLETT 131 'The Big Drink' is a common term applied by South-Western people to the Mississippi River.

+**Big dust.** *slang.* [BIG *a.* I.] A 'fine specimen.' — **1844** M. C. FIELD in Sol. Smith *Theatr. Apprent.* 207 'Well, you're a big dust of a doorkeeper!' said the rowdy as he went in.

Big end. [BIG *a.* I.] +(See HORN *n.*) — **1852** *Journal of Discourses* I. 16 (Th.), We have commenced at the little end of the horn, and by and bye we shall come out at the big end. **1856** COZZENS *Sparrowgrass P.* iv. 51 That is the first time that I see an original idea come out at the big end.

Bigeye. [BIG *a.* I b.] +(See quotations.) Also attrib. — **1818** *Jrnl. Science* I. 79 The big-eye herring (*Clupea megalops*) begin to be seen at the fish-market. **1889** *Cent.* 4718 *Priacanthus macrophthalmus*, the bigeye of the West Indies, occasional on the coast of the United States.

Big figure. [BIG *a.* 3.] +*The big figure*, a grand scale or style. Usu. with *to go* or *on.*

1836 CROCKETT *Exploits* 52 When a man sets about going the big figure, halfway measures won't answer no how. *Ib.* 119 He had met him a few weeks before down at Baton Rouge, where the fellow was going the big figure. **1837** NEAL *Charcoal Sk.* (1838) 33 What's right on the big figger must be right on the small scale. **1843** [W. J. THOMPSON] *Maj. Jones's Courtship* (B.), Well, I glory in her spunk, but it's monstrous expensive and unpleasant to do things on the big figure that she's on now. **1848** BURTON *Waggeries* 71 Why, our senators go the big figger on fried oysters and whisky punch.

Big fish. *slang.* [BIG *a.* I.] +A 'big bug.' — **1836** HOWARD *Stewart* 139 He is a big fish—anything he says will be believed.

Big four. [BIG *a.* 3.]

+**1.** A combination of four important things, persons, or companies.

1886 *Outing* Nov. 156/1 The trial races . . . proved beyond a doubt that the *Mayflower* was the queen of the 'big four.' **1890** *Congress. Rec.* 10 May 4540/1 The monopolist who usurps and controls the markets as the 'big four' have controlled the beef market of the country. **1890** *Nation* 20 March 235/2 It is less than a year since *Harper's Weekly* . . . astonished its readers by publishing portraits of Tammany's Big Four. **1894** P. L. FORD *Hon. P. Stirling* 232 Because you are willing to do that, you are one of the 'big four.' **1904** *N.Y. Times* 14 June 16 The 'big four,' Senators Platt and Depew, Gov. Odell and ex-Gov. Black, will go to Chicago on the Southwestern Limited.

+**2.** *spec.* The name of a railroad connecting Cleveland, Cincinnati, Chicago, and St. Louis, now part of the New York Central Railroad system.

Fully illustrated in Thornton's Supplement from 1890 to 1913.

1890 WHEELER & CARDWILL *W. A. W.* p. vi, Big 4 Route. . . . Best Modern Day Coaches on all Trains. **1892** *Columbus* (O.) *Dispatch* 30 Jan., Reference is elsewhere made to the doubtful rumor of the acquisition of the Columbus, Hocking Valley & Toledo Railroad by the Big Four. **1898** A. NICHOLAS *Idyl of Wabash* 208 Joe Little, brake-man on the Big Four railroad. **1905** *Chicago Tribune* in *N.Y. Ev. Post* 4 April 13 The Big Four will parallel the tracks of the Chicago and Eastern Illinois. **1915** RIPLEY *Railroads* 476 The Lake Shore road . . . held only approximately 40 per cent. of the common stock of the Big Four road.

+**Biggity.** *colloq.* [Cf. E. *bigoted*, also *big* = 'pompous'] Self-important; conceited; proud. ('A negro term': Farmer.) — **1880** HARRIS *Uncle Remus* xviii, Like po'in' [=pouring] spring water on one er deze yer biggity fices. **1883** 'MARK TWAIN' *Life on Miss.* lviii. 570 The captains were very independent and airy—pretty 'biggity,' as Uncle Remus would say. **1899** CHESNUTT *Conjure Woman* 206 He'd swell roun' 'er in a biggity way.

+**Big Greasy,** designating a special cut in card-playing. — *a*1846 *Quarter Race Kentucky*, etc. 92 He gin 'em [=the cards] the Sunflower 'shuffle,' and I the Big Greasy 'cut,' and pushed 'em back.

Big gun. [BIG *a.* 1, 3.]

1. A firearm of large size.

1861 *Ohio Acts* LVIII. 125 It shall also be unlawful for any person . . . by the aid or use of any swivel, punt gun, big gun (so-called), . . . to catch, kill, wound or destroy . . . any wild goose [etc.].

+2. A man of importance.

1834 *Knickerb.* III. 439 The big guns of the nation are there [=Washington]. **1857** GLISAN *Jrnl. Army Life* 379 At Salem I attended a dancing party, . . . and had the pleasure of seeing all the elite of the town, and the 'big guns' of the Oregon Legislature. **1865** S. HALE *Letters* 16, I have been two trips around the big guns of the parish. **1888** *Texas Siftings* 13 Oct. (F.), You don't consider that insignificant ink-slinger . . . a big gun, do you? *a***1918** G. STUART *On Frontier* II. 221 They had all the fun of stealing the horses and were then safely escorted through the danger zone to their reservation and turned loose, there to be a 'big gun' in the tribe.

Big head. [BIG *a.*]

+1. A bone disease in horses and cattle, causing a swelling in the head.

1805 *Lancaster* (Pa.) *Intelligencer* 3 Dec. (Advt.) [A brown steer had] what they call the Big Head. **1824** *New Eng. Farmer* II. 388 An inquiry . . . as to the cause of, and remedy for the disease 'called Big Head in horses.' **1867, 1879** [see BIG JAW]. **1887** *Courier-Journal* 16 Jan. 16/6 A veterinary authority tells us that 'the "big-head" of the Mississippi valley is the manifestation of a general fault in nutrition.'

+2. A fish having a large head.

1820 RAFINESQUE *Ichth. Ohiensis* 49 Bighead Chubby [of the Ohio River], *Semotilus cephalus*. . . . Vulgar names, Chub, Big-mouth, and Big-head. It has really the largest head and mouth of this tribe. **1842** *Nat. Hist. N.Y., Zoology* IV. 214 Chub, Big-head, *Leuciscus cephalus*. **1889** *Cent.* 549/3 *Bighead*, a local name of a Californian species of sculpin, *Scorpænichthys marmoratus*, a fish of the family *Cottidæ*. Also called *cabezon*.

+3. *fig.* Conceit; egotism. *colloq.*

1850 [H. C. LEWIS] *La. Swamp Doctor* 157 Pride, that busy devil that . . . lets human nature die of the big-head before common sense can bleed freely. **1853** B. YOUNG in *Jrnl. Discourses* I. 338 (Th.), Were I to use a Western term, I would say they were troubled with a big head. **1881** H. PIERSON *In the Brush* 173 They were sent there if they were thought to be lacking in humility, or, in the language of the Brush, if they had the *big-head*. **1884** BRET HARTE *On Frontier* 201 But Spencer had got the 'big head.' **1896** *Congress. Rec.* 20 March 3030/2 There are men holding subordinate places in the government of the U.S. today . . . [who] have got the 'big head,' and got it bad. **1902** LORIMER *Lett. Merchant* 226 A boss with a case of big-head will fill an office full of sore heads.

‖**Bigheadism.** A manner of action or conduct characterized by conceit. — **1856** P. CARTWRIGHT *Autobiog.* xxviii. 431 It was surely begotten in the regions, or sprang from the soil of 'Bigheadism.'

+Big-horn. [BIG *a.*] The Rocky Mountain sheep, *Ovis montana.*

1805 CLARK in *Lewis & C. Exped.* (1904) I. 282, 4 horns of the mountain ram or big horn. **1807** GASS *Journal* xxi. 222 They saw a number of deer, and of the ibex or big-horn. **1823** JAMES *Exped.* II. 31 Numerous tracks were seen resembling those of the common deer, but they most probably have been those of the big-horn. **1853** *Harper's Mag.* VII. 326/1 From the party who here visited us, we managed to obtain a portion of a Rocky-Mountain sheep, or 'big-horn,' as it is often called. **1857** *Rep. Explor. R.R. Route to Pacific* VI. IV. 72 The big-horn, as this sheep is there [i.e. in Calif.] called. **1868** *Amer. Naturalist* Dec. 538 The Bighorn is common in the rugged bare hills along the Missouri from Fort Union west. **1888** ROOSEVELT *Ranch Life* 155 The big-horn . . . is the sole American representative of the different kinds of mountain sheep that are found in the Old World.

b. Attrib. with *sheep.* (Cf. next.)

1859 SUCKLEY & COOPER *Nat. Hist. Wash. Territory* 137 *Ovis Montana*, . . . Mountain Sheep, . . . the Bighorn Sheep.

Big-horned, *a.* +Having big horns. (Cf. prec.) — **1805** LEWIS in *L. & Clark Exped.* (1904) II. 92 We have met with great abundance of the argalia or bighorned animals. **1805** — in *Ann. 9th Congress* 2 Sess. 1061 A few grizzly bear, skins of the white bear, and big-horned antelopes. **1822** J. FOWLER *Journal* 114 We find nothing to kill exsept two of the Big Horned Sheep, one of which Robert Fowler shot but cold not git it.

Big house. [BIG *a.* 1.] A house notable for its size; +*spec.* on a plantation, the house of the master as opposed to those of the servants or slaves.

1823 COOPER *Pioneers* xli, Yes! the big house has rung with merriment this month past! **1887** *Century Mag.* Nov. 116/2 Their whitewashed cabins . . . are as dear to them as is the 'big house.' **1888** *Ib.* June 277/1 The plantation was usually not too large for the owner . . . to visit the 'quarters,' which were not very far from the 'big house.' **1898** PAGE *Red Rock* 484 The prisoners were first marched to Leech's big house.

***Bight.** Also †**bite.** An inward bend in a coast-line; a recess in a coast or bay.

1640 *Md. Hist. Mag.* VI. 68 A line drawn from the head of Prior's Creak east into a bite called Adam's bite. ?**1786** *Ib.* XIX. 265 At the bounded Tree at the bite which was a considerable distance from the shore. **1827** COOPER *Red Rover* ii, This is a pretty bight of a basin. **1840** DANA *Two Years* vii. 57 Two small bights of land on each side of the main bay (sometimes dignified by the name of bays). **1849** T. T. JOHNSON *Sights Gold Region* x. 99 The succeeding night we entered the bay, or rather bight of Monterey. **1899** GREEN *Va. Word-Book* 58 We put the boat in the bight, out of the way of the ice.

Big jaw. [BIG *a.* 1.] +BIG HEAD 1. — **1867** *Iowa Agric. Soc. Rep.* (1868) 130, I have not lost but two of the bovine species . . . ; one in 1861 had big head or jaw. **1879** *Diseases of Swine* 199 Yazoo.—A great many horses die annually in this county from a disease called big-head or big-jaw—an enlargement and softening of the bones. It is caused by feeding corn exclusively.

Big knife. [BIG *a.* 1.]

+1. An Indian name for: (*a*) a Virginian; (*b*) an American (in contrast to an English) white man. Cf. GREAT KNIFE, LONG KNIFE. *Obs.* except *Hist.*

For a discussion of the terms *Big knife, Great knife, Long knife*, see Albert Matthews' contribution to *The Nation* 14 March 1901, pp. 213–4.

1750 GIST *Journals* 36 Upon his understanding I came from Virginia, he [a Frenchman married to an Indian woman] called me the Big Knife. **1774** A. ST. CLAIR in *St. Clair Papers* (1882) I. 297 They lay all to the charge of the Big Knife, as they call the Virginians. **1779** G. R. CLARK *Campaign* (1869) 38 If they thought of giving their hands to the Big Knives, [they were] to give their hearts also, and . . . I did not doubt but after being acquainted, that they would find that the Big Knives [were] of better principals than what the bad Birds, the English, had taught them to believe. **1786** *Mass. Gazette* 17 Oct., General Clarke, of Virginia, whom the Indians dread, and stile the *Big-Knife*. **1791** J. LONG *Voyages* 169 At the commencement of the war, the Big Knives (meaning the Americans), had advised him to turn his heart from the English. **1817** BRADBURY *Trav.* 75 The Americans are called 'the Big Knives' by the Indians of the Missouri. **1818** *Niles' Reg.* XIV. 389/1 Since my remembrance my heart . . . has been that of an Englishman; . . . but the Big Knives (the Americans) returned again, masters of my land. **1827** COOPER *Prairie* xviii, It is farther to the towns of the Big-knives.

+2. An Indian attached to the American side.

1779 *Virginia State P.* I. 316 The Grand Kite and his Nation living at Port St. Vincent told Mr. Hamilton that he and his people was Big Knives and would not give their hands any more to the English.

Big laurel.

+1. A species of large magnolia, *M. grandiflora.*

1810 MICHAUX *Arbres* I. 32 The large magnolia, . . . [or] Big laurel. **1813** MUHLENBERG *Cat. Plants* 53 Big laurel, evergreen tulip-tree [grows in] Georgia [and] Mississippi. **1832** BROWNE *Sylva* 210 Of all the trees of North America, east of the Mississippi, the Big Laurel is the most remarkable for the majesty of its form. **1861** WOOD *Botany* 214 Big laurel . . . [is] a stately and beautiful tree, attaining the hight of 70–90 f. **1883** HALE *Woods & Timbers N.C.* 110 *Magnolia grandiflora*. . . . Farther south it is often called Big Laurel.

+2. The rose-bay, *Rhododendron maximum.*

1853 STROTHER *Blackwater Chron.* vii. 89 This dale is girt round . . . by a broad belt of the *Rhododendron*—commonly called the big laurel out here.

Big meeting. +'Common in the West for "protracted meeting"' (B. '59). — **1857** *Magazine of Travel* April 230 A peculiar feature of the [Iowa] country is the Methodist camp meetings, usually called 'big meetins,' to which the whole country flock indiscriminately.

+Big money. [BIG *a.*] A large amount of money; large profits, high wages or salary. — **1882** E. INGERSOLL in *Harper's Mag.* April 691/1 In those days [=the winter of 1880–1881] the ranchman had as good a mine as any on the sources of his river, and made 'big money.' **1889** FARMER 54 A speaker advocating the claims of the Y.M.C.A. said that to accomplish certain objects 'big money must be subscribed.' **1904** HARBEN *Georgians* 26, I always thought . . . that Eric was allowed to handle money too early in life—big money, I mean. **1921** PAINE *Comr. Rolling Ocean* viii. 130 Two hundred dollars was coming to me as my bit, Jud, and it looked like big money.

Big-mouth. +(See quotations.) — **1820** [see BIG HEAD 2]. **1888** GOODE *Amer. Fishes* 67 *Chænobryttus anistius*, a species also called 'Warmouth,' 'Big-mouth,' . . . abounds in the tributaries of the Upper Mississippi.

+Big Muddy. [Descriptive; also based upon an erroneous interpretation of the Indian name.] The Missouri River.

1825 in [S. F. Cooper] *Rural Hours* (1850) 481 Ye plains where sweet Big-Muddy rolls along, And Teapot, one day to be found in song. **1857–8** *Ill. Agric. Soc. Trans.* III. 352 In the winter of '55–6, when one wide sweep of destruction laid dead most of the orchard trees north of the Big Muddy. **1861–2** *Ib.* V. 167 This part . . . , lying between the Big Muddy river on the south and the line of chalk-like soil . . . extending [etc.]. **1868** *Congress. Globe* 1 June 2755/3 The train that brings the rich ore to Indiana carries back to Missouri coal superior even to that of the Big Muddy. **1870** RAE *Westward by Rail* 67 The Missouri . . . has been called mighty, which it doubtless is, . . . yet the appellation of 'Big Muddy,' which is current here, is the one which more truthfully characterizes it. **1897** *Outing* March 568/2 The people of this little town on the banks of the 'Big Muddy' were in attendance.

Bignonia. {1835–}

1. One or other plant belonging to the genus *Bignonia* of climbing shrubs bearing showy, trumpet-shaped flowers.

1785 MARSHALL *Amer. Grove* 22 *Bignonia sempervirens*, Ever-green Bignonia, or Yellow Jasmine. **1802** M. CUTLER in *Life & Corr.* II. 104 [We] went to Mr. Holt's garden and collected a number of trees, magnolias, bignonias, Liriodendrons, etc. **1826** T. FLINT *F. Berrian* (1834) I. 217 Beautiful stone cottages, clustered with the bignonia in full flower. **1865** PARKMAN *Huguenots* iv. (1875) 52 From out the shadowy thickets hung the scarlet trumpets of the bignonia.

+**2.** The trumpet creeper, *Tecoma radicans.*

1847 DARLINGTON *Weeds & Plants* 221 Rooting Bignonia, Trumpet creeper.... This beautiful climber ... is cultivated extensively, and readily bears the climate of New England.

Big Pasture. [BIG *a.* 1.] +That part of the prairie region lying immediately to the east of the Rocky Mountains. (See quotation.) — **1873** BEADLE *Undevel. West* xxii. 436 Our route this afternoon and to-night is through the 'Big Pasture' of America. It extends from latitude 52°, in British America, to Texas, and has an average width of 250 miles.

Big pond. [BIG *a.* 1.] +Humorously, the Atlantic Ocean. (Cf. MILL-POND.)

1840 HALIBURTON *Clockmaker* III. xviii, He is ... the best live one that ever cut dirt this side of the big pond. **a1862** THOREAU *Cape Cod* x. 251 It is but a step from the glassy surface of the Herring Ponds to the big Atlantic Pond. **1902** *Outing* June 345/1 Irish and Gordon setters of late years have hardly sustained their reputation on either side of the big pond.

Big road. Chiefly *S.* [BIG *a.* 1.] +A main road; a highway.

1818 W. T. Harris *Remarks* (1821) 104 Oh, I guess you can't miss it, stranger; only keep the Big Road. **1871** EGGLESTON *Hoosier Schoolm.* iv. 41 The 'big road' (Hoosier for *highway*) ran along the north-west side. **1885** 'CRADDOCK' *Prophet* xii. 232 Jacob's tyranny in insisting that his unshod steed should keep straight up the rocky 'big road.' **1904** T. WATSON *Bethany* 11 Old people, even now, speak of the enormous numbers of hills of potatoes that stood in triple rows between his cow-lot and the Big Road. **1906** L. BELL *C. Lee* 299 The Barnwells' carryall went slowly out ... into the 'big road' which led to Sunnymede.

+**Big stiff, strike:** see STIFF *n.*, STRIKE *n.*

+**Big talk.** [BIG *a.* 1.]

1. A conference or discussion with, or among, Indians.

1837 IRVING *Bonneville* I. xxii. 216 The military were stationed at some little distance from the scene of the 'big talk'; ... the general and the chiefs were smoking pipes and making speeches. **1844** GREGG *Commerce of Prairies* I. 77 After our 'big talk' was concluded, and dinner dispatched, we again set out southward. **1872** EGGLESTON *End of World* xv. 104 When an Indian has announced his intention of having a 'big talk' he immediately lights his pipe and relapses into silence until the big talk shall break out accidentally and naturally. **1899** CUSHMAN *Hist. Indians* 141 The council was convened, the 'big talk' had, and the whiskey banished from Choctaw Nation.

2. Prolonged or 'tall' talk.

1860 HOLLAND *Miss Gilbert* x. 173 He sort o' stands round, and spreads, and lets off all the big talk he hears. **a1861** WINTHROP *Canoe & Saddle* vii. 154 Hamitchou recounted his legend, ... motioning, in expressive pantomime, at the close, that he was dry with big talk, and would gladly wet his whistle.

+**Big thing.** *colloq.* [BIG *a.* 1.] (See quots. 1875 and 1877.) — **1875** BURNHAM *Three Years* iv, *Big Thing*, a very good prospect; a promising scheme. **1877** BARTLETT 776 *Big thing*, a grand speculation or profitable acquisition; an affair of special advantage. **1877** WM. WRIGHT *Big Bonanza* 81 Comstock ... was always ready to join every expedition that was fitted out to explore new regions, as the 'big thing' seemed to him to be ever just ahead. **1884** NYE *Baled Hay* 65 If it could be so arranged ... it would be a big thing for humanity.

+**Big top.** *colloq.* The main tent of a circus. — **1896** *N.Y. Dramatic News* 29 Aug. 6/1 If times were not so hard the large 'big top' would not have held the people. **1920** C. R. COOPER (*title*), Under the Big Top.

Big tree. [BIG *a.* 1.] +The sequoia tree of the Sierra Nevada. Also attrib.

1860 HUTCHINGS *Scenes Calif.* (1870) 37 'All aboard for ... the Calaveras Big-Tree Grove,' cries the coachman. *Ib.* 85 The road to the Mariposa Grove of Big Trees. **1865** 'MARK TWAIN' *Sketches* (1926) 163 Calaveras possesses some of the grandest natural features ... such as the Big Trees. **1875** *Field & Forest* I. 44 One [redwood] recently described ... as equalling the largest known specimen of the 'big tree' proper. **1897** *Outing* Sept. 539/2 Huge cedars suggest the famed 'big trees' of California. **1904** *N.Y. Ev. Post* 15 July 7 In fine contrast to the old way of treating the 'big trees' of California.

+**Bike,** *n. colloq.* A bicycle. Also **bike,** *v.i.*, to ride on a bicycle; **biker,** a bicycler; **biking,** bicycling. — **1882** *Wheelman* I. 189 Much I should like To know why you ... take such a header From off your 'bike.' **1895** *N.Y. Dramatic News* 9 Nov. 15/1 Mrs. Tony Pastor ... can be seen on her favorite 'bike' daily. — **1895** *Ib.* 6 July 7/2 Frank Weston and his wife, Effie Essler, ... are to be seen 'biking' it nearly every evening on the Boulevard. — **1883** *Wheelman* I. 336 It seemed as if Nature had rallied all her forces for one grand attack on us three poor, miserable 'bikers.' *Ib.* 339 There must be by this time at least eighteen inches of snow in the mountains, and all 'bikers' know what that means. — *Ib.* 340 We very modestly declined, informing them that 'biking' and drinking are inconsistent.

* **Bilberry.**

* **1.** The fruit of several species of *Vaccinium*, esp. *V. myrtilloides*, *V. cæspitosum*, and *V. uliginosum;* the bush bearing this fruit.

1634 WOOD *New Eng. Prospect* I. v. 14 In other seasons there bee Gooseberries, Bilberries, Resberies. **1682** ASH *Carolina* 14 Strawberries, Rasberries, Billberries, and Blackberries grow frequently up and down the Woods. **1709** LAWSON *Carolina* 208 The wild Fruits ... are now brought into the Field; as are likewise ... Bilberries dry'd, of which they stew and make ... Cakes. **1784** CUTLER in *Mem. Academy* I. 439 *Vaccinium*, ... the Bilberry or Blueberry. These shrubs are low when they grow on high land, but tall in swamps. **1789** MORSE *Amer. Geog.* 54 Apples are the most common fruit in the United States.... Besides apples are ... billberries, whortleberries [etc.]. **1832** WILLIAMSON *Maine* I. 115 Bilberries, as well as blueberries, are blue, being the largest and sweetest of these three species. **1847** WOOD *Botany* 368 *V. corymbosum.*... Blue Bilberry. High Whortleberry.... Berries large, black, often with a tinge of purple, subacid. **1857** GRAY *Botany* 249 *V. cæspitosum*, Dwarf Bilberry.... Alpine region of the White Mountains, New Hampshire; and high northward. **1901** MOHR *Plant Life Ala.* 107 The rocky ground is sparingly covered by the following shrubs, all of them bushes ... : deerberry, ... dwarf huckleberry, ... bilberry [etc.].

attrib. **1787** CUTLER in *Life & Corr.* I. 278, On the sides of the hill, are many blueberry, whortleberry, and bilberry bushes.

2. (See quotations.)

1850 *New Eng. Farmer* II. 346 Will you be so good as to give us the correct name of the shrub known here, with some by the name of bilberry, with others by that of Indian plum? **1889** *Cent.*, *Bilberry*, a name sometimes given in the United States to the fruit of the shad-bush, *Amelanchier Canadensis.*

Bilboa. [Former name for *Bilbao* in Spain.] A variety of potato. — **1830** J. F. WATSON *Philadelphia* 718 Probably about 65 years ago, they then first introduced a larger kind, more like the present in use, which were called, in New England, the bilboa.... In Pennsylvania the same kind of potatoes were called Spanish potatoes.

Bilbo-bolt. *Obs.* (Cf. next.) {1772–84} — **1702** *Essex Inst. Coll.* XLII. 161 Inventory of ship ... [includes] a Bilbo bolt.

* **Bilbo(e)s, Bil(l)bow(e)s,** *n. pl. Obs.* An iron bar furnished with sliding shackles used to secure prisoners. — **1630** *Mass. Bay Rec.* I. 75 It is ordered by this present Court, that Thomas Morton ... shall presently be sett into the bilbowes. **1631** T. DUDLEY in *N.H. Hist. Soc. Coll.* IV. 235 For the satisfacon of the Indians wherein ... wee caused his hands to be bound ... and set his feet in the bill bowes. **1642** *Md. Archives* 159 He shall be imprisoned or sett in the stocks or bilbos. **1673** *Southampton Rec.* II. 202 The Smith is to make manacls for theire hands, and Bilboes for theire feet. **1683** *N.H. Hist. Soc. Coll.* VIII. 135, I am abused ... by being in irons, ... which irons are called bilboes, exceeding large.

* **Bile,** *n. dial.* A boil. {–1748; now *dial.*}

1778 *Md. Jrnl.* 13 Oct. Advt. (Th.), Has a scar on one of his cheeks, occasioned by a bile or something like it. **1805** CLARK in *Lewis & C. Exped.* III. ii. 277 Jo. Fields with biles on his legs. **1817** S. BROWN *Western Gaz.* 200 One of his men ... was afflicted with biles. **c1849** [PAIGE] *Dow's Sermons* I. 161 Ancient Job was smitten with sore biles. **1872** BRET HARTE in *Atlantic Mo.* March 352 I've got a fevier. And childblains.... And biles!

* **Bile,** *v.* Colloq. variant of *boil* v. {Now *dial.*}

1759 *Essex Inst. Coll.* XIX. 67 Roberson and I biled ris for the Lewten[ant]. **1779** *Mass. H. S. Coll.* 2 Ser. II. 452 Lie[utenan]t Carter began to bile sugar. **1835** HOFFMAN *Winter in West* II. 119 You might bile down cr'ation and not get such another state out of it. **1886** STOCKTON *Mrs. Lecks* 59 By the time we've got a little dried off, the kettle will bile. **1895** *Century Mag.* Sept. 674/2, I'll bet she don't bile his shirts or cook his dinners, not much.

Biled, *a. colloq.*[2] or *dial.* =BOILED *a.*

(1) **1836** *Quarter Race Ky.* (1846) 14 Colonel, let us have some of your byled corn [=whiskey]—pour me out a buck load.

(2) **1851** A. T. JACKSON *Forty-niner* (1920) 113 He had shaved his beard off, except his mustache, and was dressed up in a 'biled shirt.' **1862** BROWNE *A. Ward His Book* 130, I ... put on a clean biled rag to attend Miss Picklehomony's grate musical sorry at the Melodeon. *Ib.* 224 Accordinly I put on a clean biled shirt and started for Washinton. **1872** 'MARK TWAIN' *Roughing it* lvii. 416 The miners [of Calif.] ... had a particular and malignant animosity toward what they called a 'biled shirt.' **1890** E. B. CUSTER *Following Guidon* 172 The frontiersmen ... discussed the 'biled shirts,' and viewed the whole party with lofty scorn. **1899** T. HALL *Tales* 263 There had been a constant call at the single store in Lander for 'biled shirts,' linen collars, [etc.].

(3) **1862** BROWNE *A. Ward His Book* 114 Mike gits as drunk as a biled owl.

(4) **1878** *Harper's Mag.* LVII. 575 Slabs of fat ... adding savour and strength to a b'iled dinner. **1889** R. T. COOKE *Steadfast* vi. 74 A 'b'iled dinner' was her glory. **1895** A. BROWN *Meadow-Grass* 269 Do you remember how you used to come over an' eat cold b'iled dish for supper?

(5) **1895** *Dialect Notes* I. 387 Doughnut . . . was biled-cakes if in twisted form . . . on Cape Cod, and generally in Eastern Mass.

+**Biler.** *colloq. To burst* (or *bust*) *one's biler* (see BOILER 1 b). — **1834** CARRUTHERS *Kentuckian* I. 218 That'll make them think somebody's busted their biler. **1840** MARRYAT *Second Diary* 108, I reckon he'd burst the biler. **1847** [ROBB] *Squatter Life* 142 A fellar that's . . . mity likely to git his fires dampened, or bust his biler.

Biling, *vbl. n. colloq.*[2] Also **bilin', bylin'.** [dial. var. of BOILING.] *The whole biling*, the entire group; all. {*dial.* 1839}

1833 NEAL *Down Easters* I. 61 Gage was the biggest gentleman ever you see, and so's the whole bylin' of 'em. **1840** HOFFMAN *Greyslaer* II. x. 31 You may . . . go away the hull biling on ye. **1848** BURTON *Waggeries* 70 We grow the hull biling of those fixings. **1873** 'MARK TWAIN' & WARNER *Gilded Age* xvii. 164, I thought maybe you'd fetch the whole bilin' along with you. **1884** 'MARK TWAIN' *Huck. Finn* xxix. 304 The whole bilin' of 'm 's frauds!

Bilious fever. A disease characterized by feverishness and general debility, formerly supposed to be due to a disorder of the liver. {1732}

Frequently mentioned between 1800 and 1845.

1779 E. PARKMAN *Diary* 145 He is ill of bilious Fever and Camp-Distemper. **1789** MORSE *Amer. Geog.* 310 It has been observed that [in] Pennsylvania . . . bilious and remitting fevers, which a few years ago, appeared chiefly in the neighborhood of rivers, creeks and mill ponds, now appear in parts remote. **1802** DRAYTON *S. Carolina* 27 The *typhus icterodes*, or putrid bilious or yellow fever, is however particularly local to Charleston. **1823** *Baptist Mag.* IV. 150 His disease . . . was the malignant bilious fever. **1836** *Niles' Reg.* 22 Oct. 128/3 The bilious fever and measles have been almost as destructive as the cholera [near Charleston]. **1849** [CHAMBERLAIN] *Indiana Gazetteer* 119 The prevailing diseases were bilious and intermitting fevers, the former in many cases differing very little from the yellow fever of New Orleans.

Bilk. *slang.* One who cheats by evading payment; a swindler. {1790-} — **1869** McCLURE *Through Rocky Mts.* 211 A bilk is a man who never misses a meal and never pays a cent. **1873** BEADLE *Undevel. West* 78 Nineteen hotels and restaurants were in operation, and at every one of them 'bilks' abounded. **1883** PECK *Bad Boy* 191 You are a high-toned, gentlemanly sort of a bilk. **1902** 'MARK TWAIN' in *Harper's Mag.* Feb. 441 Just about eligible to travel with this bilk here— . . . this loud-mouthed sneak.

***Bill,** *n.*

***1.** The draft of a measure presented to a legislative body.

1638 *Md. Archives* I. 4 No man shall . . . speake above once to one bill or matter at one reading. **1688** *Penna. Col. Rec.* I. 223 The Bill for continuance of the Laws. **1689** SEWALL *Diary* I. 266 Such a thing as this might make them more desperately eger to hinder the Bill. **1739** *Boston Rec.* 251 Voted, that it be recommended . . . to bring forward, and procure a Bill to be pass'd for the more just admeasurement of Grain. **1747** *Penna. Col. Rec.* V. 64 We have had divers Bills under our consideration, which when passed into Laws will, we judge, be for the general good of the Province. **1787** *Constitution* i. §7 Every bill which shall have passed the House of Representatives and the Senate, shall, before it become a law, be presented to the President of the United States. *a*1817 DWIGHT *Travels* III. 277 All Bills, which have passed the Senate and Assembly, are presented to them for examination. **1846** POLK *Diary* (1929) 87 If the bill which had passed the house today should also pass the Senate. **1855** GLISAN *Jrnl. Army Life* 172 Very few bills pass Congress on their merits alone. **1881** *Rep. Indian Affairs* p. lxix, This bill, as well as others of a kindred nature, died a natural death at the close of the last Congress.

***2.** A bill of exchange; a promissory note.

1631 *Mass. Bay Rec.* I. 90 The party that giveth such bills shall renewe them vpon demaund & deliuery in of the olde bill. **1649** ELIOT *Glorious Progress* 88 This 10. l. bill Captain Harding paid here, and was to take it at London. **1651** *Suffolk Deeds* I. 293 A list of seuerall bills & notes assigned vnto Mr. Laurence Hanaton per mee Peter Mudd. **1663** *Plymouth Laws* 143 The same time that they . . . give a bill under theire hand for the payment therof in some short time after. **1705** *N.C. Col. Rec.* I. 621 John Privett proves a Bill of four pounds payable from Thomas Houghton. **1745** *Penna. Col. Rec.* V. 6 Admiral Warren . . . thinks himself authorized . . . to draw Bills for defraying the Expence. **1798** B. HAWKINS *Letters* 297, I cannot sell a bill on you where I am, and have sent the bills to him to obtain the money for them. **1865** *Atlantic Mo.* XV. 583 No sooner had Congress begun to receive money from Europe than it began to draw bills upon its agents there.

+**3.** A government note or a bank-note. Cf. PAPER BILL.

1682 in *Mass. Bay Currency Tracts* 7 Secondly, that Credit pass'd in Fund, by Book, & Bills, (as afore) will fully supply the defect of Money. **1714** P. DUDLEY *Ib.* 105 We have had twelve Years Experience already of Publick Bills, with great Honour, Safety, and Success. **1716** *Mass. H. Repr. Journals* I. 114 That the Bills be of the same tenour with those that are already emitted. **1729** *N.H. Provincial P.* (1870) IV. 553 The vote of the House sent up yesterday for re-emitting some bills at loan [was] non-concurred. **1755** *Lett. to Washington* I. 141 Some part in small bills will be necessary as change is hard to be got. **1790** *Ann. 1st Congress* II. 2055 The bills and notes of the bank, originally made payable, or which shall have become payable on demand in gold and silver coin, shall be receivable in all payments to the United States. **1817** S. BROWN *Western Gaz.* 112 The notes of this bank are in excellent credit, but bills from the neighboring states . . . have a free and extensive circulation. **1851** *Polly Peablossom* 32 The little man took from his pocket a hundred-dollar bill. **1852** STOWE *Uncle Tom* xxxix, Cassy . . . unlocked the desk, took from it a roll of bills, which she counted over rapidly. **1865** *Atlantic Mo.* XV. 3 The New York coarsely printed bills which he took in payment. **1900** DIX *Deacon Bradbury* 66 The bills seemed alive. . . . The few new, stiff ones among them gave out the most delicious crackle. **1920** MULFORD *J. Nelson* xxvi. 263 'Cash it is,' said Ridley. 'Gold or bills?' 'Make it bills,' answered Big Tom. *Ib.* 271 He's got bills, wads an' wads of bills. Quite some over six thousand, I reckon, in bills.

b. A paper medium of exchange.

1856 GOODRICH *Recoll.* I. 493 [During the war of 1812] barbers put out bills, payable in shaving, and various institutions adopted a similar course.

***4.** A public announcement; a poster, a hand-bill; *spec.* a play-bill.

1828 *Yankee* July 239/2 They were not in the bills of the day—they were not expected to appear. **1845** S. SMITH *Theatr. Apprent.* vii. 55 The time fixed upon for the curtain to rise was 'Eight o'clock precisely,' as the bills have it. **1855** BARNUM *Life* 144 The moment you see a bill up, indicating that the house is 'To Let,' ring the bell. **1865** *Atlantic Mo.* XV. 719 As I handed the [concert-] bill back to Max, he whispered to my maid. **1883** SHIELDS *S. S. Prentiss* 34, I have seen an ordinary steamboat 'poster' (bill), with the usual wood-cut picture of the boat, carefully hung up to adorn the walls.

+**b.** *Theatrical.* The acts or numbers collectively announced on a program; the performance as a whole; also, a single play.

1875 *Chicago Tribune* 13 Sept. 7/3 Hooley's Theatre: . . . California Minstrels, in a Bill of Rare Ethiopian Sketches. **1880** *Ib.* 10 May 5/7 Carrie Swain, of 'The Tourists,' captivated the people; but she was only an item in the bill. **1889** *Ib.* 8 Sept. 27/1 The bill for the week will be . . . [the] familiar Irish drama, 'The Paymaster.' **1896** *N.Y. Dramatic News* 4 April 14/2 Vernona Jarbeau fairly led Keith's bill.

+**5.** *To fill the bill:* see FILL *v.*

+**6.** An order to a saw-mill for wood cut to specified sizes; the wood so cut. Also attrib. with *stuff.*

1881 *Chicago Times* 16 April, Last fall our mills shut down with contracts for bill stuff still on their order books. **1897** BRODHEAD *Bound in Shallows* 217, I'll put this log into planks, and get up some fresh wood for the bill. **1901** MERWIN & WEBSTER *Calumet K* i. 5 We're expecting a big bill of cribbing. *Ib.* vi. 113, I shouldn't be surprised to see the rest of the bill coming in by rail any time now.

+**7.** A decree of divorce. Freq. *to get a bill* (*of divorce*). *colloq.* (Cf. BILL *v.* 4.)

Cf. the biblical reference to 'a bill of divorce' (Jer. iii. 8).

1891 'THANET' *Otto the Knight*, etc. 19 She went off and she got a bill of divorce—for desertion and non-support. **1894** *Dial. Notes* I. 341 *To get a bill*, to get a divorce. . . . Western Connecticutt. *c*1908 *Ib.* III. 241 (E. Maine), *Bill*, bill of divorce. As soon as he got his bill, her engagement was announced.

***Bill,** *v.* [f. BILL *n.*]

1. *To bill out*, to allocate or assign in or by a bill.

1735 *N.H. Hist. Soc. Coll.* II. 76 [A committee was] appointed to bill out this money according to the proprietors' directions.

+**2.** To enter (freight) on a way-bill; to consign by rail to a destination.

1867 *Vermont Rep.* XL. 326 The Station agent . . . billed the plaintiff's goods through to Charlestown, Mass. *Ib.* 329 That the plaintiff's freight on this occasion was . . . entered on the books and billed as prepaid through. **1881** *Chicago Times* 17 June, All live stock will be billed subject to the usual minimum weights. **1902** LORIMER *Lett. Merchant* x. 134 The chances are that the car weighed out more than it was billed. **1922** TITUS *Timber* xviii. 165 Thursday afternoon John was in Pancake, billing out another shipment of his lumber.

+**3.** To cover (a town) by distributing or fixing up bills or posters.

1863 MASSETT *Drifting About* 127 We had 'billed' the city pretty well. **1884** *Harper's Mag.* Sept. 509/2 The . . . agent thought this town . . . would be a good place for his man, and so he 'billed' it, which I learn is the proper expression for posting announcements . . . of any exhibition.

+**4.** *colloq.* To divorce (a wife). Cf. BILL *n.* 7.

1885 H. H. JACKSON *Zeph* ii. 42 He's a blamed fool he don't bill her [i.e. a runaway wife].

+**Bill-board.** [BILL *n.* 4.] A board to which notices or posters are affixed.

1851 W. K. NORTHALL *Curtain* 15 With excusable vanity, the bill-boards of the Park . . . still continued to style the Park 'The Theatre.' *a*1877 *Rome* (N.Y.) *Sentinel* (B.), People who fail . . . to edit a bill-board are firmly convinced that they could edit a newspaper. **1886** P. STAPLETON *Major's Christmas* 173 Big, staring letters on a bill-board across the street. **1898** M. DELAND *Old Chester Tales* 245 Well, I was advertised all round; you ought to have seen the bill-boards. **1902** McFAUL *Ike Glidden* xvi. 122 When they were passing a gorgeously hued circus poster on a bill board along the roadside, the colt shied off sideways.

1906 *Springfield W. Republican* 6 Dec. 1 That a bill be introduced in Congress eliminating pictures from the billboards of that city.

attrib. **1902** HARBEN *Abner Daniel* 58 Jack Ass in bill-board letters would come nearer to it than anything that occurs to me now. **1911** *Amer. Year Book* 1910 237/2 Billboard Advertising.—Missouri's Supreme Court has sustained the St. Louis billboard ordinance.

Bill-book. {1774–} A book in which bills are entered; also, a pocket-book. — **1847** WEBSTER (citing Bouvier). **1887** *Postal Laws* 410 The entries on pouch bills will be made by writing with a hard lead-pencil, after placing carbon paper between the bill and the record sheet of the bill book. **1898** WESTCOTT *D. Harum* 116 It's all ben left to me: . . . gen'ral ledger, bill-book, discount register, . . . drawin' off statemunts f'm the ledgers an' bill-book. **1905** *N.Y. Times* 3 Feb. 3 In a billbook in an inside pocket were many checks for various sums on Plainfield banks.

+**Bill-broker.** {1833} A broker who discounts bills. — **1861** *Harper's Mag.* Oct. 642/1 Roger Lovatt was a bill-broker, irreverently termed by the vulgar a note-shaver.

+**Bill-bug. 1.** (See quotation.) **2.** One or other species of snout-beetle belonging to the genus *Sphenophorus;* esp. *S. sculptilis* and *robustus,* which feed upon corn. — **(1) 1861** *Harper's Mag.* Aug. 319/1 The next . . . belongs to the family of *Rhyncophorus,* or 'Weevils.' . . . It is familiarly called at the South and West, 'Bill-bug,' 'Corn-borer,' and 'Cane-piercer.' **(2) 1882** *Rep. Comm. Agric.* 138 For many years several species . . . have damaged the corn crop in various parts of the United States, more particularly at the South, where they are all known as 'Bill-bugs.' **1884** *Ib.* 413 Corn Bill-Bugs . . . are . . . often found about fallen green pine timber [in N.C.]. **1909** *Cent. Suppl.* 133/3 The genus *Sphenophorus* [includes] . . . Blue-grass bill-bug, . . . Calloused bill-bug, . . . Clay-colored bill-bug, . . . Sculptured corn bill-bug, . . . Tenacious bill-bug.

* **Billet,** *v. tr.* To quarter (soldiers) on householders. Also with *out.*

*a***1649** WINTHROP *Hist.* II. 33 The Dutch would not be thus pacified, but prepared to send soldiers to be billeted at their house. **1690** *Plymouth Laws* 224, 18 bushells of wheat . . . paid to Capt. John Jacob . . . in Consideration of his qua[r]tering or Billeting Souldiers. **1709** *Boston Rec.* 90 Pursuant to an order of his Excel[len]cy . . . for billeting out of ninety of the Soldiers, . . . the Select men do assigne them to be billeted at . . . severll Houses. **1761** NILES *Indian Wars* II. 367 He was returning from Boston with a considerable sum of money for billeting soldiers. **1775** *Journals Cont. Congress* III. 288 A Committee of three . . . appointed to report the best method of billeting the soldiers for the continental army. **1778** *Deane Papers* 125 The Navy-Gentlemen . . . are billeted over the Town which makes it difficult to quarter the men.

Billeting, *vbl. n.* [f. prec.] The assignment of soldiers to lodgings. {1640–}

1721 *Mass. H. Repr. Journals* III. 112 Thomas Witherel's [accompt] for billiting. **1724** *Talcott Papers* 13 The billeting of the garison soldiers to be considered as a debt due from the government. **1756** WASHINGTON *Let. to Dinwiddie* 23 Sept., The billeting, quartering, and dieting of soldiers upon the inhabitants, . . . in many cases, cannot be avoided. **1776** TRUMBULL in Sparks *Corr. Rev.* (1853) I. 120 That they should be entitled to the same pay, wages, and billeting allowed the troops before Boston. **1916** *Manual for Quartermaster Corps* I. 146 Subsisting troops by billeting can generally be resorted to only in case of small commands, or where troops are scattered.

b. Attrib. with *money.*

1746 *N.H. Hist. Soc. Coll.* IV. 212 We paid off the men their billetting money. **1759** *Essex Inst. Coll.* III. 101 Part of the fleet sailed, . . . and we received our billeting money. **1776** *Journals Cont. Congress* IV. 39 The contract . . . to allow one twelfth part of a dollar per day, for billeting money to every one of the men.

+**Bill-fish.** One or other fish having a bill-like snout, esp. one or other species of gar-fish.

[**1782** P. H. BRUCE *emoirs* xii. 424 The sea hereabouts [Bahamas, etc.] abounds with fish unknown to us in Europe, . . . bill-fish, hound-fish, etc.] **1793** *Mass. H. S. Coll.* III. 119 We also have the bill-fish in great plenty in the month of October. **1807** *Ib.* 2 Ser. III. 57 There are the bill fish and the gar; the latter opening a small mouth; the former opening its mouth like a snipe; being in other respects like each other. **1832** WILLIAMSON *Maine* I. 157 The Bill-fish is a small, rare salt water fish, weighing only about half a pound; . . . its flesh is dark coloured, and in flavour rather rank to the taste. **1847** LANMAN *Summer in Wilderness* 112 With the sturgeon [in the upper Mississippi] . . . I am disposed to class the sun-fish, bill-fish, bull-head, and chub. **1870** *Amer. Naturalist* IV. 520 The Bill-fish (*Scomberesox Storerii*) . . . has gradually decreased [in numbers]. **1871** *Ib.* V. 439 A fine specimen of *Belone truncata,* 'Green bone,' 'Billfish,' or 'Salt water Gar,' . . . was taken . . . in the Connecticut River. **1884** GOODE *Amer. Fishes* I. 458 'Bill-fish' . . . is also applied by our fishermen to the slender species [of silver garfishes] of the sword-fish family. *Ib.* 663 The Long-nosed Gar-pike, *Lepidosteus osseus,* . . . is known as 'Gar-pike,' 'Bill-fish,' 'Sword-fish,' etc.

Bill-head. A paper on which the name, address, etc., of a person or firm are printed, with space below for writing in an account or other matter. {1879–}

1845 J. W. NORRIS *Chicago Directory* 136 Job Printing. Cards of all sizes, Circulars, Bill Heads, Hand Bills [etc.]. **1845** *Knickerb.* XXVI. 82 Some wag had obtained possession of one of its blank bill-heads, and . . . had substituted the following for the regular 'carte' of the day. **1857** *Lawrence* (Kansas) *Republican* 13 Aug. 3 Bill Heads ruled to any pattern, at J. Dodsworth's Book Bindery.

+**Bill-holder.** One who holds a bill or acceptance; the possessor of bills issued by a bank. — **1846** W. L. MACKENZIE *Life Van Buren* 157 Butler rebukes the avaricious bill-holders—'We pay in specie.' **1850** *Western Journal* IV. 214 In case of the insolvency of any bank . . . , the bill-holders thereof shall be entitled to preference in payment over all other creditors. **1855** *Mass. Acts & Resolves* 996 It is the duty of a depositor to ascertain the solvency of any bank he intrusts with his property; but the bill-holder . . . trusts solely to the law for protection.

Billiard-ball. The small hard ball with which the game of billiards is played. {*a*1637–} — **1781** *Salem Gazette* 3 July, Isaac Greenwood . . . makes . . . backgammon boxes men and dies, chess men, billiard-balls [etc.]. **1849** AUDUBON *Western Journal* (1906) 52 We reached Brownsville where the rolling of bowling-alleys and the cannoning of billiard balls was all that seemed to enliven the village at that hour.

+**Billiard hall.** A hall in which billiards are played. — **1873** *Winfield* (Kansas) *Courier* 18 Jan. 3/2 The lower room [of the gallery building] will soon be occupied . . . as a saloon and billiard hall. **1881** *Sunbeam* (Terre Haute, Ind.) June 8/1 Frisbie's Billiard Hall and Sample Room. **1882** *Wheelman* I. 103 The smoky and spirituous atmosphere of the card-room or billiard-hall.

+**Billiardist.** One who plays billiards. — **1879** *N.Y. Ev. Express Almanac* 371 October 1 [1878], J. B. Cyrille Dion, billiardist, died. **1888** *St. Louis Globe Democrat* 24 Jan. (Farmer), Each competitor has put up fifty dollars entrance money in Billiardist Daly's hands. **1898** *N.Y. Journal* 29 Aug. 8/3 Two wonderful little billiardists.

Billiard-marker. One who keeps the score at billiards. {1775–} — **1877** *Harper's Mag.* Dec. 109/2 Better than being a billiard marker, and I've been that for an hour. **1898** P. L. FORD *Tattle-Tales* 125, I suppose some devoted friend of mine has told you I'm only a billiard-marker?

Billiard-playing. The playing of billiards. — **1807** J. R. SHAW *Life* (1930) 76 Men of diabolical principles and practices from almost all quarters, employed in . . . horse-racing, billiard-playing [etc.].

Billiard-room. A room in which billiards are played. {1848–}

1816 U. BROWN *Journal* I. 265 Dined & fed at Jesse Brown's Hotel, an Inn kept in high Stile with Billiard Room. **1847** FIELD *Drama in Pokerville,* etc. 14 The three taverns, and thirty-three bar-rooms, of Pokerville, exclusive of a billiard-room and ten-pin-alley, were alive at an early hour. **1878** H. H. JACKSON *Travel at Home* 138 The 'Cosmopolitan Saloon' . . . consists of nine rooms, a billiard-room, where are two fine billiard-tables [etc.]. **1902** 'MARK TWAIN' in *Harper's Mag.* Jan. 267 The scene is in the tavern billiard-room.

* **Billiards.** A game in which ivory balls are driven about on a cloth-covered table by means of cues in accordance with certain rules.

1722 *New-Eng. Courant* 16–23 April 2/2 Any Gentlemen or others that have a Mind to recreate themselves with a Game of Billiards, if they will repair to the House where David Melvill did formerly live, . . . shall meet with civil Entertainment. **1780** FRANKLIN *Writings* VIII. 155 You ought to walk or ride, or, if the weather prevents that, play at billiards. **1825** NEAL *Bro. Jonathan* II. 385 They had been wasting their money, or that of their employers, . . . playing billiards. **1865** *Nation* I. 13 There is a great deal of whist and billiards played in the clubs of New York. **1902** 'MARK TWAIN' in *Harper's Mag.* Jan. 265 [They play] billiards, for there is a table, crossed all over with torn places repaired with court-plaster.

+**b.** *Presbyterian billiards,* croquet.

1873 *Winfield* (Kansas) *Courier* 31 July 1/7 That transcendently interesting amusement commonly called croquet, but vulgarly signified 'Presbyterian billiards.'

+**Billiard saloon.** An establishment in which billiards are played.

1847 *Santa Fe Republican* 10 Sept. 3/1 Missouri House and Billiard saloon. . . . In connection with the Hotel are two superior Billiard Tables. **1867** J. MELINE *Santa Fé & Back* 36 Julesburg has six houses, including a store, adobe-yard, blacksmith shop and—billiard saloon! **1870** [R. TOMES] *Decorum* 121 The frequenters of the bar-rooms, billiard saloon, and gambling-tables. **1875** 'MARK TWAIN' *Old Times on Miss.* xvii. (1876) 144 Bogart's billiard-saloon was a great resort for pilots in those days.

Billiard-table. An oblong table having a top covered by a green cloth and surrounded by a ledge, on which the game of billiards is played. {1677–}

1748 FRANKLIN *Writings* II. 371 If he sees you at a billiard-table, . . . he sends for his money the next day. **1789** MORSE *Amer. Geog.* 390 At almost every tavern . . . on the public road [in Va.], there is a billiard-table. **1793** BENTLEY *Diary* II. 21 Within a year past Billiard Tables have been indulged in the public houses, & the consequences have been serious to several families, & young persons. **1850** GARRARD *Wah-To-Yah* ii. 41 There was a billiard table in a small house on top of the fort. **1865** *Atlantic Mo.* XV. 64 There are magnificent saloons, containing five, ten, and sometimes twenty billiard-tables. **1889** BRAYLEY *Boston Fire Dept.* 317 In many of these rooms the members, at their own expense, placed billiard tables.

attrib. **1851** CIST *Cincinnati* 49 Occupations [include] . . . Billiard-table keepers, 2 [people]. Billiard-table marker, 1 [person].

Billion. +[After French usage] A thousand millions. {1690–, in sense 'a million millions'}

1834 DAVIES *School Arithmetic* 13, 6,245,289,421 [reads] 6 Billions, 245 millions, 289 thousand, 421. **1840** *Congress. Globe* 6 Jan., App. 89/1 We may begin with the hundred and twelve millions, and then proceed . . . until we have bought and divided that billion of acres. **1860** WORCESTER, *Billion*, according to the French method of numeration in use on the continent of Europe and in the U.S. a thousand millions, or 1,000,000,000. **1889** 'MARK TWAIN' *Conn. Yankee* ix. 112, I sat under the telling of it hundreds and thousands and millions and billions of times. **1893** *Congress. Rec.* App. 103/1 Such headlines as these, 'The Billion Congress,' . . . 'The Indelible Billion.' **1897** *Ib.* 19 March 89/1 The first 'billion-dollar Congress. **1904** *Providence Journal* 2 Aug. 6 The announcement that the trust funds in the American Treasury have now reached the unexampled sum of over a billion dollars.

+**Billionaire.** One whose wealth amounts to a billion dollars or more. — **1860** HOLMES *E. Venner* vii, One would like to give a party now and then, if one could be a billionnaire. **1887** — in *Atlantic Mo.* LX. 219 The man before whom millionaires tremble as they calculate, and billionaires pause and consider.

+**Bill-poster.** One who puts up advertisements or other notices. {1864–}

1809 *Longworth's N.Y. Directory* 370 Samuel Walker, bill-poster, 80 Wall. *c***1845** W. T. THOMPSON *Chron. Pineville* 17 He soon relieved the fit of curiosity . . . by relating . . . his close intimacy with the bill-poster of the company who had just arrived in town. **1895** *N.Y. Dramatic News* 12 Oct. 12/2 The billposters' war has been settled in Chicago. **1920** C. R. COOPER *Under Big Top* 4 A 'brigade' of billposters being dropped at one town to look after the billposting.

+**Bill-posting,** *vbl. n.* The occupation of posting up bills. — **1869** BROWNE *Adv. Apache Country* 352 Bill-posting is one of the fine arts. . . . To one who witnesses this bill-mania for the first time the effect is rather peculiar. **1896** *N.Y. Dramatic News* 29 Aug. 12/2 Carroll has closed a contract to do the billposting the coming season. **1920** [see BILL-POSTER].

+**Bill puffing.** [BILL *n.* 4.] 'Puffing' by advertising in playbills. — **1855** W. B. WOOD *Recoll. Stage* 451 Newspaper and bill puffing and lying, and every other possible sort of vaunting, swaggering, and imposition.

+**Billstead.** (See quotation and cf. BILSTED.) — **1832** J. F. WATSON *Hist. Tales N.Y.* 164 The general furniture [about 1780] was made of 'billstead,' another name for maple.

Bill-sticker. A bill-poster. {1774–} — **1840** C. MATHEWS *Politicians* II. ii, Would a bill-sticker . . . change his mind to please this upstart? **1855** THOMPSON *Doesticks* xx. 171 Sandie . . . had fallen asleep in Nassau street, and the bill-stickers had nearly overlaid him with show-bills. **1869** BROWNE *Adv. Apache Country* 346 Bill-stickers are sticking up bills of auctions, theatres, and new saloons.

Bill-sticking, *vbl. n.* and *ppl. a.* Bill-posting. {1864–} — **1869** BROWNE *Adv. Apache Country* 354 My friend the Professor was an artist in the line of bill-sticking, and carefully studied effects. **1873** W. MATHEWS *Getting on in World* xiii. 180 This puffing, advertising, bill-sticking part of creation.

Billy. *slang.* {1795–}

+**1.** A policeman's club.

*a***1859** *N.Y. Herald* (B.), A day or two since a poor German was taken to prison, and, on examining him, it was discovered that he was a victim to the billy. **1871** [BAGG] *At Yale* 294 The walls are adorned with . . . policemen's caps and 'billies.' **1877** 'E. MARTIN' *Hist. Great Riots* 143 The officers drew their billies and cowed the mob. **1903** *N.Y. Times* 11 Sept., Eight men set upon a policeman this morning and after taking his revolver and billy away from him kicked and beat him.

+**2.** (See quotation.)

1848 [E. JUDSON] *Mysteries N.Y.* IV. 49 The foremost villain . . . broke down her guard with a short iron crowbar, or 'billy' as the burglars term it.

+**Bilsted.** Also †**boilsted.** [Of obscure origin. Cf. BILLSTEAD.] The sweet gum.

1765 R. ROGERS *Acc. N. America* 138 This soil [in N. & S.C.] is a blackish sand, producing . . . ash, laurel, boilsted, &c. **1843** TORREY *Flora N.Y.* II. 217 Common Sweet-gum. Bilsted. . . . Moist woods and borders of swamps. **1857** GRAY *Botany* 148 Bilsted . . . [grows in] moist woods, Connecticut to Virginia, and southward. **1884** SARGENT *Rep. Forests* 86 Sweet Gum. . . . Liquidamber. Red Gum. Bilsted. **1901** MOHR *Plant Life Ala.* 538 Bilsted . . . [is a] valuable timber tree.

+**Bimbo.** [Later variant of BUMBO.] A kind of punch.

1837 *Baltimore Commerc. Transcript* 5 Sept. 2/3 The *U.S. Gazette* asks what is *bimbo?* Not toddy, we hope. . . . *Bimbo* is a rascally compound of brandy and sugar, flavored with lemon peal [*sic*]. An invention of the devil to make drunkards. **1846** *Spirit of Times* (N.Y.) 4 July 217/3 At the request of a 'temperance member' of that 'Sodality,' the 'Committee on Bimbo' have determined upon the introduction of a small portion of 'aqua fortis' into the admixture. **1853** [G. H. DERBY] *Phoenixiana* (1856) xxviii. 173 After imbibing my morning glass of bimbo (a temperance drink, composed of 'three parts of root beer and two of water-gruel, thickened with a little soft squash, and strained through a cane-bottomed chair').

+**Bime-by, Bimeby,** variant of BYME-BY *adv.*

1722 *Broadside Verse* (1930) 115/2 Indian bimeby take Captain Westbrook's fort; Some kill, some captive take. **1824** *Nantucket Inquirer* 5 Jan. (Th.), Well, bimeby he took notion to hab my darter. . . . Well, bimeby I found em out. **1841** *Knickerb.* XVII. 38, I was going to give you some exercises in beating time; Old Hundred bime-by. *Ib.* 455 First I wanted to go out, but bime-by I got used to it. **1845** S. SMITH *J. Downing's Lett.* 49 For if they brought in much more we should all get mixed up . . . bime by. **1856** M. J. HOLMES *L. Rivers* xxxvii. 401 Bimeby he cum to, and says he, 'Where did you get that?' **1878** BEADLE *Western Wilds* 28 Bimeby one chap says: 'Oh, yes, I know Mr. Darnell.' **1900** C. C. MUNN *Uncle Terry* 173 Mr. Page is comin' back here bimeby.

Bimetallic, *a.* [F. *bimétallique* (1869).] Pertaining to, using, etc., two metallic bases of currency. {1876–}

1877 S. HORTON *Silver & Gold* (ed. 2) 149 The relative amounts of the stock of Bi-metallic countries and of Mono-metallic countries. *Ib.* 156 The Bi-metallic Standard . . . answers the highest requirements of Money. **1878** *N.Amer. Rev.* CXXVI. 161 The superior advantages of a bi-metallic, double or alternative standard of value. **1882** *Nation* 6 July 7/3 Some of its promoters maintain . . . that the bi-metallic cause never looked more hopeful than at this very moment. **1899** *Chicago Daily News Almanac* 154/1 Bimetallic League of the Ohio Valley . . . advocated the nomination of Mr. Bryan for the presidency in 1900.

Bimetallism. The use of a bimetallic standard of currency. {1876–}

1877 S. HORTON *Silver & Gold* (ed. 2) 155 Bi-metallism and the Standard of Desiderata. **1882** *Nation* 6 July 7/3 The negotiations for the establishment of universal bi-metallism have ended in a somewhat mysterious manner. **1897** W. E. CHANDLER *Remarks* (title-page), The use of silver as well as gold as standard money, free coinage of both, under a system of bimetallism. **1914** MCLAUGHLIN & HART *Cycl. Amer. Govt.* I. 132 Bimetallism necessarily establishes what has been called a limping standard.

Bi-metallist. One who advocates a double metal standard of currency. Also as *adj.* {1879–}

1877 *Nation* 22 Nov. 313/2 Our Western bi-metallists . . . propose . . . to defy the experience of mankind as to the limits of legislative power. **1878** *N. Amer. Rev.* CXXVI. 163 The bi-metalists denounce it . . . for postponing the restoration of both. **1882** *Nation* 6 July 7/3 If this could now be witnessed somewhere, it would do more for the bi-metallists than any number of pamphlets. **1894** E. B. ANDREWS *Honest Dollar* 32 Upon many points, wide dissidence of view still separates bimetallists from the theorists who oppose them. **1914** MCLAUGHLIN & HART *Cycl. Amer. Govt.* I. 131 The weakness in the arguments of the bimetallists is their assumption [etc.].

Bi-monthly, *a.* Occurring or produced every two months. {1878–} — **1851** CIST *Cincinnati* 118 Here are regularly received fifteen Quarterly, one Bi-Monthly . . . and two Weekly magazines.

***Bin,** *p.p.* =BEEN, BEN. {16–18th c.; now *rare* exc. *dial.*}

Still the standard pronunciation, though usu. written *been.*

1622 'Mourt' *Relation* 11 Having bin forced to cut her downe in bestowing her betwixt the decks. **1637** MORTON *New Canaan* II. vii, The Mackarels . . . have bin chased into the shallow waters . . . [and] whole hoggesheads have bin taken up on the Sands. **1656** *N.H. Probate Rec.* I. 33 The portion that should have bin theirs is to be divided. **1676** *Conn. Public Rec.* II. 470, I have not bin a great while fitt to travaile. **1704** S. KNIGHT *Journal* 25 Who was as sparing of his words as his daughters had bin. **1798** W. MANNING *Key of Liberty* 3, I have bin a constant Reader of publick Newspapers. **1815** HUMPHREYS *Yankey* 33, I've bin up to the hub, and didn't flinch. **1886** P. STAPLETON *Major's Christmas* 18, I've bin janitor here fifty year. **1900** C. C. MUNN *Uncle Terry* 203 My pertector and my staff have bin taken from me.

***Bind,** *v.*[1]

***1.** *tr.* To make liable for a payment or the discharge of an obligation.

1642 *Springfield Rec.* I. 154 The said Thomas Cooper doth binde himselfe and executors to pay £10 in Corne. **1654** *Suffolk* (Mass.) *Probate Reg.* N.S. 1/74 [I, Benjamin Scott] binde myself, heires, [etc.] . . . by these presents. *a***1656** BRADFORD *Hist.* 266 To disingage them of those great sumes which they stood charged with, and bound for. **1771** FRANKLIN *Autobiog.* 275 He had half ruin'd Miss Read's father by persuading him to be bound for him. **1790** *Ann. 1st Congress* 10 Feb. 1, 160, I mentioned also the case of a bond, and supposed that we were bound to the punctual payment of Government notes, . . . as a person would be bound to the payment of a bond, when it is exhibited in court. **1852** DUNLAP *Bk. Forms* (1857) 207 To which payment, well and truly to be made and done, I do bind myself . . . firmly by these presents. **1861** *Army Regulations* 147 The sureties to the bond shall be bound jointly and severally for the whole amount of the bond. **1900** DIX *Deacon Bradbury* 20 Know all men . . . that I . . . am held and firmly bound unto John Lee . . . in the sum of . . . two thousand dollars.

***2.** To put under bond to keep the peace or answer to a charge.

1667 *Conn. Public Rec.* II. 60 Noe particular minister of justice shal inflict any punishment other than imprisonment or stocking or binding them to the peace or good behavior. **1670** *Witchcraft Cases* 51 Katherine Harryson bound over to appeare . . . upon suspicion of Witch-craft. **1705** SEWALL *Diary* II. 148, I could hardly be brought to their being bound to their good behaviour. **1712** *Ib.* 337, [I] bound him over to the Sessions in £50. to answer for . . . pronouncing a Mock-Sermon. **1774** J. DAVID *Justice of Peace* 53 Any two Justices, at their Discretion, may bind any person over to the County Court. *Ib.* 59 A Justice of Peace . . . may bind to the good Behaviour any Person [etc.]. **1845** *Ill. Rev. Statutes* (1883) 421 The defendant . . . shall not be bound over to the next court unless he is also charged with some other offense. **1896** *Cincinnati Enquirer* 15 Aug. 6/2 Charged with housebreaking and larceny, [he] was bound over to the Criminal Court in the sum of $500.

*3. To indenture (some one) to a master; to apprentice. Often with *out*.

1631 *Mass. Bay Rec.* I. 90 Lucy Smith is bound as an apprentice with Mr. Roger Ludlowe for 7 yeares. **1674** SEWALL *Diary* I. 7 My Brother Stephen was bound Apprentice to Mr. Edmund Batter, Merch[ant]. **1706** *Boston News-Letter* 18 March 2/2 Any Person that wants to bind out a Lad or Lads to learn the Trade of a Man or Womans Tailour. **1742** *N.H. Probate Rec.* III. 89 Likewise for her to keep the stock together until my three sons come of age (if she can keep them with her) but if she binds them out then to divide it among them. **1771** FRANKLIN *Autobiog.* 239 To prevent the apprehended effect of such an inclination, my father was impatient to have me bound to my brother. **1811** MEASE *Philadelphia* 268 The children of members deceased . . . are . . . bound out to such trades as may suit their situation. **1818** FLINT *Lett. from Amer.* 98 Some of the children of the more necessitous families are bound out to labour for other people. **1852** DUNLAP *Bk. Forms* (1857) 164 Thomas Jones . . . by these presents doth bind and put himself apprentice to William Burns, of Reading. **1871** STOWE *Sam Lawson* 83 My mother she wanted to bind me out to a blacksmith. **1884** 'MARK TWAIN' *Huck. Finn* xi. 93 Then I told her my father and mother was dead, and the law had bound me out to a mean old farmer in the country. **1890** FIELD *Bright Skies* 123 The black man was no longer a slave, but an 'apprentice,' who could be 'bound out' to hard labor under conditions.

4. To sew (boots or shoes).

1815 Commons, etc. *Doc. Hist.* IV. 48, I employ a woman for binding boots. **1865** *Atlantic Mo.* XV. 616 Thousands among us are engaged in binding shoes.

+**Bind,** *v.*[2] [Substituted for BOUND *v.*, by confusion between this and the p.p. *bound.*] *intr.* To have the boundary, to border, *on* a place.

1677 *N.Y. State Col. Hist.* XII. 574 From thence southwest binding vpon a little Creeke one hundred & eighty five pertches to a marked white oake. **1746** *N.H. Probate Rec.* III. 454 His single share . . . runs North . . . then binding on said way by the water side. **1750** GIST *Journals* 31 Take the Courses of the River and Mountains on which it binds in Order to judge the Quantity. **1782** *Baltimore Town Rec.* 45 To lay out the foundation of a House . . . which house was intended to be built binding on the said Street. **1803** *Steele Papers* I. 396 One Tract of about 600 Acres . . . binds on the river. **1808** *Ann. 10th Congress* 1 Sess. II. 2119 The State of New York . . . binds on Lake Erie to Niagara, on the whole extent of Lake Ontario. *Ib.*, Vermont binds on lakes which communicate with Canada. **1832** *Louisville Public Advt.* 7 March, To lease, . . . Lots binding on the Ohio River. **1899** GREEN *Va. Word-Book* 59 Land binding on the north side of the inlet.

* **Binder.**

1. Some article of male attire. *Obs.*

In Eng. use (1695, 1787) as a form of head-dress, or part of a cap.

1688 SEWALL *Diary* I. 240 Shifted my Linen this day, Shirt, Drawers, N. Wastcoat, Binder. **1689** *Ib.* 287 Plimouth, deliver'd to be wash'd 2 Shirts, 2 Handkerchiefs, 5 Crevats, 1 Cap, 1 Binder.

2. *a. A bookbinder.

1788 FRENEAU *Misc. Works* 140 Now from the binder's, hurried home In neat array, my leaves are come. **1818** JEFFERSON *Anas* (1903) 23 These scraps . . . I had bound with the others by a binder. **1865** KELLOGG *Rebel Prisons* 399 Paper has advanced 120 per cent., binders' cloth 400 per cent., binders' board 190 per cent. **1888** PERRIN *Ky. Pioneer Press* 51 He held the office of Public Printer and Binder for a number of years by successive elections.

b. One who binds up sheaves of grain. {1611–}

1798 I. ALLEN *Hist. Vermont* 274 There is one part of the world where the reaper and the binder are held in proper degree of estimation.

c. An appliance or machine for binding sheaves.

1857 *Ill. Agric. Soc. Trans.* II. 120 A self raker, and even a binder, may be just as simple in its structure as some *hand raker*, considering what it does. **1884** KNIGHT *Suppl.* 795/1 To show to what immense proportions the manufacture of binders, reapers, and mowers has grown in the United States. **1894** C. MERIWETHER in *Nation* 16 Aug. 116/3 One man on the binder, another to drive, and three to shock, will harvest as many acres as thirty hands did when they reaped with the cradle.

3. A means of binding or fastening; a band or cover, etc. {1642–}

1837 *U.S. Patent* 26 Dec., Binder for newspapers. **1840** THOMPSON *Green Mt. Boys* II. xii. 321 Cut the fastenings of the outside binders of the roof. **1845** MRS. KIRKLAND *Western Clearings* 96 One of the more active youths climbs the tall stack to toss down the sheaves; the next hand cuts the 'binder,' and passes the sheaf to the 'feeder.'

+**Bindery.** [Cf. Du. *binderij.*] An establishment where books are bound; a book-bindery. {1882–}

1810 I. THOMAS *Printing* I. 402 At Worcester [Mass.], he . . . set up a bindery. **1815** *Mass. H. S. Coll.* 2 Ser. III. 177 One bookstore and bindery in the place has a circulating library. **1826** *Boston News Letter* 28 Oct., Smith, Reed & Gaylor will receive at their Bindery . . . orders . . . to bind any quantity of books, in any style, at reasonable prices. **1851** CIST *Cincinnati* 175 Fifteen binderies, with 136 hands. **1865** *Atlantic Mo.* XV. 166/1 Working with other girls in factories, or binderies, or other places where girls are largely employed. **1871** *Scribner's Mo.* I. 367 Before long the Mercantile Library Association will have a bindery of its own. **1885** L. W. CHAMPNEY in *Harper's Mag.* Feb. 370/1 Flavilla . . . took her death sloppin' to and from the bindery.

* **Binding,** *vbl. n.*

*1. A protective edging for a fabric; a braid.

1658 *Southold Rec.* I. 440 An inventory [includes] . . . 2 paire of stockings, many other bindings. **1711** *Springfield Rec.* II. 41, 18 yards of woosted Binding. **1714** *Boston News-Letter* 22–29 March 2/2 Blue binding for Bedding. **1746** E. Singleton *Social N.Y.* 187 A blue Broadcloth coat, . . . the binding on the right side is much wore. **1764** *Md. Hist. Mag.* X. 41 Eight yards of India crimson Tafferty . . . and six yards of silk crimson Binding. **1796** B. HAWKINS *Letters* 18 They sell the fowls grown, 2 for 2½ yards of binding worth 2 cents. **1809** F. CUMING *Western Tour* 322 The Indians . . . are paid in . . . handkerchiefs, and worsted binding of various colours. **1881** *Art Interchange* (N.Y.) 27 Oct. 90/1 Pale blue cretonne, finished off with a binding of the same colored velvet.

2. Attrib. with *wire.* +*Binding twine*, a coarse or heavy kind of twine, esp. that used in harvesting machines.

1767 H. M. Brooks *Gleanings* 31 Binding Wire; Brass and Iron ditto. **1890** *Congress. Rec.* Aug. 9260/1 The observations of the Senator from Minnesota in respect to binding-twine are also very important to the people of Louisiana.

* **Bindweed.**

*1. A slender, twining herb belonging to the genus *Convolvulus*, esp. the common species *C. sepium* and *C. arvensis.*

*c*1729 CATESBY *Carolina* I. 35 The Purple Bindweed of Carolina. The Flower of this *Convulvulus* [sic] is of a reddish purple, and of the size and shape of common white Bindweed. They blow in June. **1784** CUTLER in *Mem. Academy* I. 416 Bindweed. . . . Small Convolvulus. Blossoms white or striped. **1789** *Amer. Philos. Soc.* III. p. xix, Purple bindweed is very powerful, if the Indians can handle rattle snakes after anointing the hands with its juice. **1843** TORREY *Flora N.Y.* II. 96 Common Bindweed . . . is often a troublesome weed; the roots being very deep and spreading. *Ib.* 97 *Calystegia Sepium*, . . . Great Bindweed, . . . [grows] sometimes as a weed in cultivated grounds. **1847** DARLINGTON *Weeds & Plants* 247 Field Convolvulus. Bind-weed. . . . This foreigner has been introduced into some portions of our country,—and may give the farmers some trouble, if they do not guard against it. **1856** *Rep. Comm. Patents: Agric.* 92 Another span-worm . . . feeds upon the bind-weed flower, (*convolvulus*,) and does not disturb cotton. **1880** CABLE *Grandissimes* xxix. 244 A frenzied mob of weeds and thorns: . . . smart-weed, sneeze-weed, bind-weed [etc.]. **1901** MOHR *Plant Life Ala.* 682 Common Field Bindweed . . . [is] spreading slowly to waste places and likely to become a troublesome weed.

2. A species of the genus *Smilax* of liliaceous plants, as the greenbrier. {1601–}

1737 BRICKELL *N. Carolina* 96 Prickley Bind-weed, or Sarsaparilla, is a kind of Prickley Vine, not unlike the former [Small Bamboo]. **1785** MARSHALL *Amer. Grove* 142 *Smilax Sarsaparilla.* Ivy leaved rough Bindweed, or Sarsaparilla. This grows naturally in Virginia and to the southward. **1847** DARLINGTON *Weeds & Plants* 350 *Smilax rotundifolia.* . . . Green-brier. Rough Bind-weed. . . . This rugged shrubby vine is often abundant in moist low grounds.

+**Bin(n)acle, Binocle.** *local.* Also **binnekill.** [Du. *binne(n)-* inner, *kil* channel.] A side channel of a river; an inlet from a river into flat land.

1860 *Delaware County Deeds* LIII. 358 Commencing on the bank of the Delaware River . . . to a point at the mouth of the binacle, thence up along the western side of said binacle at low water mark. **1881** J. BURROUGHS *Pepacton* i. (1895) 19 There was a whirlpool, a rock eddy, and a binocle within a mile. *Ib.* 20 The boys . . . came down to . . . see me go through the whirlpool and pass the binocle. **1899** *Walton* (N.Y.) *Reporter* 14 Oct., A car load of brown trout . . . were placed in the river above and below Walton village, and in the binnacles opening into the river. **1901** *Utilitarian* (Margetville, N.Y.) 25 April, They [boys] ventured to enter the binnacle and the current at once began to take them down the stream. **1901** *Dialect Notes* II. 134 There was a binnekill in the meadow near by.

+**Bio,** variant spelling of BAYOU. — **1792** *Amer. Philos. Soc.* III. 217 A place called the Bio-Piere. **1843** 'CARLTON' *New Purchase* I. xii. 91 Keep . . . along the bottim till you come to the bio. *Ib.* xxviii. 268 The blasted fool . . . wades clean in all through the bio!

* **Birch,** *n.* Also †**burch, burtch.**

*1. A hardy northern tree of the genus *Betula;* a single tree of this kind, or the wood obtained from it.

Also with distinctive names as *black, dwarf, red, white, yellow birch,* q.v.

1616 SMITH *New England* 16 Oke, is the chiefe wood; . . . walnut, chesnut, birch . . . and many other sorts. **1637** MORTON *New Canaan* II. ii, Birch: of this there is plenty in divers parts of the Country. Of the barck of these the Salvages of the Northerne parts make their delicate Canowes. **1700** *Md. Hist. Mag.* XIX. 356, 400 acr. sur[veyed] . . . beginning at a bounded burch at the mouth of Deer Creek. **1703** *Cambridge Prop. Rec.* 220 A Burtch on the uper Side. **1709** LAWSON *Carolina* 99 The Birch grows all on the Banks of our Rivers, very high up. I never saw a Tree on the Salts. **1788** J. MAY *Journal & Lett.* 69 Have not seen any chestnuts, nor any birch or alders, in this part of our settlement. **1816** *Ann. 14th Congress* 2 Sess. 1196 There may be small variations, according as . . . birch . . . or any other wood is employed. **1839** HOFFMAN *Wild Scenes* 45 The flames . . . lighting up the stems of the pale birches. **1859** A. L. HILLHOUSE tr. *Michaux's Sylva* II. 67 Of the seven species of Birch which have been discovered in North America, five may be ranked among tall trees. **1865** MRS. WHITNEY *Gayworthys* xxvii. 264 She had 'swung birches' before, many a time in sport; she was tossed down, fifteen feet, and dropped. **1883** *Wheelman* I. 285 Dale Creek is perfectly obscured in a labyrinth of willows, birch, and cherry trees.

2. A switch of birch wood. {1648-}

1819 [A. PEIRCE] *Rebelliad* 58 With 'birches' we will baste their hides, And 'tar and feather' them besides. **1845** MRS. KIRKLAND *Western Clearings* 5 The Schoolmaster laid down his birch.

+**3.** A canoe made of birch bark.

1861 WINTHROP *Open Air* 50 Now, in a birch we would slide down the Penobscot, . . . camp at Katahdin, . . . and speed down the river to tidewater. **1864** LOWELL *Fireside Trav.* 129 Never use the word *canoe* if you wish to retain your self-respect. *Birch* is the term among us backwoodsmen. **1875** HOLLAND *Sevenoaks* iv. 54, I jest shoved over in a birch, an' ye must be perlite enough to return the call. **1895** *Outing* Oct. 47/1 The precious birch was secured to its sled, and anxiously watched by all hands.

4. Attrib. and comb. with *bucket, builder* (sense 3), *measure, rind, rod,* etc.

1654 JOHNSON *Wonder-w. Prov.* 15 Light cannowes, (which are a kinde of Boates made of Birch Rindes, and sowed together with the rootes of white Cedar-Trees). **1695** *Duxbury Rec.* 68 We ran south . . . until we came to a birch sapling, . . . which we marked on four sides. **1707** *Mass. H. S. Coll.* 5 Ser. VI. 60* Her Squa Mistress . . . allow'd her a little Birch-Rind. **1793** BENTLEY *Diary* II. 50 Some [Indians] do appear at the Colleges of whom Capt. Pratt purchased a Birch milkpan. The bottom is square. **1832** WILLIAMSON *Maine* I. 523 The savages taking a cart, . . . filled the body [of it] with the birch-rinds, straw and fire-matches. **1858** THOREAU *Maine Woods* 101 While Joe was preparing his birch-horn . . . we collected fuel. **1861** WINTHROP *Open Air* 49 These aborigines are the birch-builders. **1865** *Atlantic Mo.* XV. 687 He had reached down for the birch rod . . . and had called in Reuben for extraordinary discipline. **1866** *Rep. Indian Affairs* 293 The mococks (birch buckets) hold from sixty to eighty pounds of sugar. **1867** 'T. LACKLAND' *Homespun* I. 71 The good home-folk take along baskets and birch-measures on their arms. **1881** *Harper's Mag.* April 642/1 The littleness . . . is soon dismissed in the glow and crackle of a birch-wood fire.

Birch, *v.* +With *it.* To journey in a birch-bark canoe. — **1861** WINTHROP *Open Air* 50 Iglesias . . . had birched it down to Lake Chestuncook in bygone summers, to see Katahdin [mountain] distant.

Birch bark.

+**1.** The bark of the birch tree used for various purposes.

1643 WILLIAMS *Key* 67 Others make slighter doores of Burch or Chestnut barke, which they make fast with a cord in the night time. **1674** GOOKIN *Indians* iii, Their pails to fetch their water in, are made of birch barks. **1675** JOSSELYN *Two Voyages* 27 We had the sight of an Indian-Pinnace sailing by us made of Birch-bark. **1705** BEVERLEY *Virginia* III. 19 They make Canoas of Birch Bark, by slipping it whole off the Tree. **1753** WASHINGTON *Diaries* I. 59 They . . . told 50 [canoes] of Birch Bark, and 170 of Pine. **1773** H. FINLAY *Journal* 6 Our chief guide drew a sketch of the next day's route on a sheet of smooth birch bark with charcoal. **1837** *S. Lit. Messenger* III. 733 Along the shore were Indian lodges, of a conical form, and covered with birch bark. **1857** HAMMOND *Northern Scenes* 256 The meat was . . . served up on clean birch bark, just peeled from the trees, in the place of platters. **1866** MRS. WHITNEY *L. Goldthwaite* vi, A flag basket at her feet holds strips and rolls of delicate birch-bark. **1880** *Harper's Mag.* July 180/1 The party camped . . . , making huts of birch bark.

b. Attrib., esp. with *canoe.*

*a***1800** *Spirit Farmers' Museum* (1801) 244 With panniers . . . Laden with birch bark boxes, berries tart. **1805-9** HENRY *Camp. Quebec* 193 The birch-bark canoe . . . is not only a curious, but a most ingenious machine. **1837** *S. Lit. Messenger* III. 733 They came, some of them from a great distance in their birch bark canoes. **1846** L. M. CHILD *Fact & Fiction* 168 Her mother used to sing to her, when she swung from the boughs in her queer little birch-bark cradle. **1867** HOLMES *Guardian Angel* 361 It's easier to get a birch-bark canoe off the shallows than a big ship off the rocks. **1880** *Harper's Mag.* July 181/2 She and Sarah were soon sound asleep in their birch-bark hut. **1903** WHITE *Forest* iii. 26 In a loft a birch-bark mokok . . . dispenses a faint perfume. *Ib.* x. 128 This birch-bark package contains maple sugar. **1907** C. C. ANDREWS *Recoll.* 121 A caravan of Red Lake Indians, who . . . were encamped round in tents or birch bark lodges.

+**2.** A birch-bark canoe.

1902 WHITE *Conjuror's House* ii. 16 As the swift rush of the birch-barks brought them almost to their journey's end, they burst . . . into whoops of delight.

+**Birch beer.** A beverage prepared with an extract from the birch tree. — **1883** *Wheelman* I. 392 We [bicyclers] reached Bushkill at 12:30 P.M., stopping—for birch beer—at odd places.

+**Birch broom.** A broom made of birch twigs.

1809 IRVING *Knickerb.* III. v, The long alley of poplars . . . like so many birch brooms standing on end diffused a melancholy and lugubrious shade. **1846** *Knickerb.* XXVII. 458 Ply the birch-broom and the shovel. **1852** *Harper's Mag.* Feb. 292/1 He found . . . a poor woman sweeping the pavement with a birch broom.

+**Birch canoe.** A canoe made of birch bark. Also attrib.

*a***1649** WINTHROP *Hist.* II. 85 Mr. Gorge and Mr. Vines . . . went up Saco river in birch canoes. **1675** JOSSELYN *Two Voyages* 102 Thither the Indian goes in his Birch-Canow when the Moon shines clear. **1698** SEWALL *Diary* I. 475 Went to Hog Island with Mr. John White in his Birch canoe. **1715** *Boston News-Letter* 11 July 2/1 The French of Canada are come into our Onandago Country with 50 Birch Cannoo's. **1752** P. STEVENS in *Travels Amer. Col.* 310 We are told that 200 large birch canoes and batteaux are gone up the river this spring. **1775** *Mass. H. S. Coll.* 2 Ser. II. 281 Here I found a fine Birch Canoe carefully laid up. **1815** *Niles' Reg.* IX. 114/1 The birch canoe party proceeded to the end of the point. **1838** J. HALL *Western States* xii. 218 The birch canoe is peculiar to the northern regions, where the tree that supplies the bark is found. **1849** PARKMAN *Oregon Trail* 19 A birch canoe was as familiar to us as a steam-boat. **1875** HOLLAND *Sevenoaks* vii. 83 The birch canoe in which he had expected to ascend the river. **1916** C. A. EASTMAN *From Deep Woods* 178, I set out with an Ojibway guide in his birch canoe.

* **Birchen,** *a.* Also †**bur(t)chen, burching.**

1. +**a.** Having a growth of birch trees. *Obs.*

1657 *Warwick* (R.I.) *Rec.* 297 A 6 acre Lott, on the south side bounded with his owin Birchin ffeeld. **1673** *Springfield Rec.* II. 245 Jeremy Horton hath graunted unto him twenty acres of land in the birchen playn above Skeepmuck.

b. That is a birch; consisting of birches.

1663 *Plymouth Rec.* 57 The bounds of the land . . . is as followeth on the southwest corner with a burchen tree marked. **1852** *Harper's Mag.* V. 5/1 Just before reaching the hotel, we see through the fine birchen groves.

2. Made from birch bark or birch wood. +*Birchen canoe* =BIRCH CANOE.

1634 WOOD *New Eng. Prospect* II. xvi. 90 In the night time they [=Indians] betake them to their Burtchen Cannows . . . [to catch] the Sturgeon. **1675** JOSSELYN *Two Voyages* 70 Many of these trees are stript of their bark by the Indians, who make of it their canows, kettles, and birchen-dishes. *Ib.* 140 The Lobsters they take in large bayes, . . . going out in their birchen-canows. **1684** I. MATHER *Providences* i. (1856) 15 Thus did they patch up a boat, in fashion like a birchen canoe. **1709** *N.H. Hist. Soc. Coll.* III. 46 Going off with a small birchen canoe into Pemaquid Sound [they] were . . . both drowned. **1818** EASTBURN *Yamoyden* II. vii, He skims the blue tide in his birchen canoe. **1855** *Knickerb.* XLV. 173 Her captor, who intended soon to claim her for his wife, had built a light birchen-canoe. **1865** PARKMAN *Pioneers of France* 300 Indefatigable canoe-men, in their birchen vessels, light as egg-shells.

3. Obtained from the birch.

1643 WILLIAMS *Key* 61 Burching barke, and Chesnut barke which they dresse finely, and make a Summer-covering for their houses. **1705** *Boston News-Letter* 12 Nov. 2/2 We will humbly move, that . . . it may be laid on after the Dutch-fashion; that is with good Burchen Rods. **1826** COOPER *Mohicans* xx, You showed knowledge in the shaping of birchen bark, Uncas, when you chose this from among the Huron canoes. **1843** *Knickerb.* XXI. 344 The birchen rod . . . is not now a terror to juvenile offender. **1870** LOWELL *Study Windows* 304 How would birchen bark, as an educational tonic, have fallen in repute!

+**Bircher.** One who operates a (birch-bark) canoe. — **1861** WINTHROP *Open Air* 51 Cancut, though for this summer boatman or bircher, had other strings to his bow.

+**Birch land.** Land on which the birch tree predominates. — **1789** MORSE *Amer. Geog.* 143 One species generally predominating in each soil, has originated the descriptive names of . . . birch, beach and chesnut lands.

+**Birch stump.** The stump of a birch tree (used as a boundary mark). — **1684** *Manchester Rec.* 15 From s[ai]d tree cros the Neck . . . to a burtch stump. And from s[ai]d burtch stump to a pine stump. **1690** *Duxbury Rec.* 66 Land . . . butted on the northerly side with a birch stump near the mill. **1760** *N.H. Probate Rec.* III. 375 Thence northeasterly about seventy Rods to a Birch Stump with Stones.

+**Birch swamp.** A swamp in which the birch tree predominates.

1660 *Warwick* (R.I.) *Rec.* 326 Bounded . . . on the southeast towards the burch Swamp. **1666** *Portsmouth Rec.* 133 On achre of land nere adioyninge to the Birch Swamp. **1740** *N.H. Probate Rec.* II. 240 Fifteen acres of land laying above the Birch Swamp so called.

* **Birch tree.** A tree of one or other species of birch.

1654 *Providence Rec.* II. 78 On the south Corner a small Birch tree. **1661** *Portsmouth* (R.I.) *Rec.* 105 A winde falen birch tree which is the upermost Corner. **1677** *Providence Rec.* XIV. 8 A Burch tree marked standing on the Eastern side of the runn. **1704** *Ib.* IV. 156 The southeast Corner . . . is a Burch Tree marked & stones laid about it. **1764** HUTCHINSON *Hist. Mass.* (1765) I. 467 The other sort [of canoes] were made of the bark or rind of the birch tree, with knees or ribs. **1837** *Crockett Almanac* 20 It occurred to him . . . to run around a small birch tree . . . as tight as he could spring. **1890** RYAN *Told in Hills* 41 The girl walked away to where their traps and sachels were stacked under a birch tree. **1893** M. HOWE *Honor* 162 Avis is straight and flexible as a young birch tree.

***Bird.**

+1. a. *Bird of freedom, of America, of our country,* the bald-headed eagle. *Bird of Washington* (quots. 1831, 1874), the bald eagle in its immature stage.

Bird of freedom is implied in the name of 'Birdofredom Sawin' in Lowell's *Biglow Papers* (1846–7).

1831 AUDUBON *Ornith. Biog.* I. 58 This new species of Eagle, 'The Bird of Washington,' . . . is indisputably the noblest bird of its genus that has yet been discovered in the United States. *Ib.* 60–61. **1846** LOWELL *Biglow P.* I. ii, Our country's bird alookin' on an' singin' out hosanner. **1847** *Ib.* iv, Ef the bird of our country could ketch him, she'd skin him. **1848** PARKMAN in *Knickerb.* XXXII. 514 Tête Rouge declaring that he would kill the bird of America, borrowed Delorier's gun and set out on his unpatriotic mission. **1853** B. F. TAYLOR *Jan. & June* 120 The Bird of Freedom inclined his body forward, his wings spread out like a sail. **1874** COUES *Birds N.W.* 370 From the circumstance that several years . . . are required for the gaining of the perfect plumage, when the head and tail are entirely white, . . . 'Gray Eagles' and 'Birds of Washington' are much the more frequently met with [than 'Bald Eagles']. **1906** H. M. ALDEN in *Harper's Mag.* March 638 We are . . . proud of . . . the 'Bird of Freedom.'

+b. A gold coin with an eagle stamped on it. Cf. EAGLE.

1853 SIMMS *Sword & Distaff* 496, I won't trust you . . . ontel the money's put down here, the yellow birds, all a-flying about me. **1857** *Quinland* II. 73 'Excellent; and here is a bird for you,' Morley said, carelessly dropping a golden eagle into his red horny hand.

+2. *slang.* **a.** A person of particular quality or excellence; a first-rate thing. (Freq. ironical.)

1842 *Spirit of Times* 12 Feb. (Th.), Chippendale slept in the watch-house. . . . Chippendale is certainly a bird. **1852** *Knickerb.* XL. 320 Talking of fast men, that Williams is a bird. **1855** 'P. PAXTON' *Captain Priest* 319 The Perfect Bird has no wings, yet he is considered 'fly' upon all sporting matters. **1856** *Knickerb.* XLVII. 429 A sleigh, drawn by a 'perfect bird' of a three-mile bay mare. **1889** 'MARK TWAIN' *Conn. Yankee* vii. 85 Raphael was a bird. We had several of his chromos. **1903** A. H. LEWIS *The Boss* 124 Say! . . . that young Morton beats four kings an' an ace. He's a bird! **1911** QUICK *Yellowstone N.* ix. 230 He's got a disguise that's a bird.

+b. A person.

1852 BRISTED *Upper Ten Th.* vi. 128 The same reason . . . kept Mr. Simpson, and other 'birds' of his set, out of the exclusive society. **1854** SHILLABER *Mrs. Partington* 309 Miss Pidgin—A bird too tough for sentiment. **1860** HOLLAND *Miss Gilbert* xix. 349 She's no such kind of a bird as you've been talking about. **1921** PAINE *Comr. Rolling Ocean* iii. 41 You and I will get on great. How about these other birds? **1922** R. PARRISH *Case & the Girl* 223 He's the bird all right. I never lamped him but once before myself.

+c. (See quotation.)

1887 A. JENKS in *Lippincott's Mag.* Aug. 291 There are men in every college, of whom Yale has its full number, denominated in student slang as 'birds.' The 'birds' are firm believers in the old Epicurean theory that everything in life is subservient to pleasure.

+Bird bank. (See quotation.) — **1835** AUDUBON *Ornith. Biog.* III. 242 They flew directly towards their place of rest [in Cole's Island, S.C.], called the 'Bird Banks.'

+Bird-bell. A plant of the genus *Nabalus* or *Prenanthes.* — **1850** [S. F. COOPER] *Rural Hours* 283 Another flower, common in our woods just now, is the Bird-bell, the Nabalus of botanists. *Ib.*, These plants are sometimes called lion's-foot, rattlesnake-root, &c., but the name of Bird-bell is the most pleasing. **1894** *Amer. Folk-Lore* VII. 92 *Prenanthes altissima,* . . . bird-bell. N.Y.

Bird cherry(-tree). One or other variety of wild cherry. {1597, birds cherry tree}

1785 MARSHALL *Amer. Grove* 112 *Prunus Cerasus Virginiana,* Virginian Bird-Cherry-Tree. . . . The timber is . . . used by joiners, cabinet-makers, etc. for many purposes. *Ib.* 113 *Prunus-cerasus montana.* Mountain Bird-Cherry-Tree. . . . The fruit is . . . of a red colour, and an extremely acid taste. **1843** TORREY *Flora N.Y.* I. 196 *Cerasus Pennsylvanica,* . . . Bird Cherry. . . . Fruit the size of a large pea, red, austere, scarcely eatable. **1850** *New Eng. Farmer* II. 221 Of the various kinds of cherry, the laurel or bird cherry is the most dangerous. **1892** APGAR *Trees Northern U.S.* 99 *Prunus avium* (Bird-cherry or English Cherry) . . . [has] fruit of various colors, somewhat heart-shaped. **1893** *Amer. Folk-Lore* VI. 140 *Prunus Pennsylvanicus,* bird cherry. Penobscot Co., Me. **1897** SUDWORTH *Arborescent Flora* 240 Wild Red Cherry . . . [is also called] Bird Cherry (Me., N.H., N.Y., Pa., Minn., Iowa).

+Bird-dog. A dog, as a setter or pointer, used in hunting game-birds. — **1889** *Cent.* **1897** *Outing* May 126/1 It is comparatively an easy matter to judge a bird-dog which is always within sight or call.

Bird-egging. The searching for wild birds' eggs. — **1860** *Harper's Mag.* Nov. 753/1 We had choice of a cruise on the Sound for scup fishing, or a bird-egging frolic to Muskegeet.

Bird-eyed, *a.* Cf. BIRD'S-EYE. — **1744** *Md. Hist. Mag.* XXI. 245 One peice of Bird Ey'd India Handkerchief. **1746** *Ib.* 379, 2 p[s] Bird Eyed India Handkerchief.

+Bird-foot violet. The bird's-foot violet (q.v.). — **1817–8** EATON *Botany* (1822) 512 *Viola pedata,* birdfoot violet. **1840** DEWEY *Mass. Flowering Plants* 78 Bird-foot Violet . . . blossoms in May, grows in woods and dry soils; flowers large and blue. **1857** GRAY *Botany* 43 Bird-foot Violet . . . [grows in] sandy or gravelly soil, New England to Illinois and southward. May. **1889** *Cent.* 561 The leaves of the bird-foot violet.

+Bird grass. A variety of grass (see later quotations).

1785 WASHINGTON *Diaries* II. 361 Sowed 5 rows and a small piece of the bird grass seed. *Ib.* 362, I planted the everlasting pea . . . by the side of the bird grass. **1790** S. DEANE *New-Eng. Farmer* 28/2 Bird-grass, usually known in the country by the name Fowl-meadow Grass. **1797** I. THOMAS *Newengland Farmer* 33 Bird Grass, *Poa avaria, spicalis subbifloris.* Usually known in this country by the name Fowl Meadow Grass. It acquired this name by being supposed to be brought to a piece of meadow in Dedham, by ducks, and other wild water fowl. **1890** *Cent.* 4575/3 *Poa trivialis* [is cultivated] as 'bird-grass.'

+Bird-gun. A light gun used for bird-shooting. — **1853** SIMMS *Sword & Distaff* 115 This Frenchman . . . owned . . . a miserable little single-barrel bird-gun, small in bore, but something taller than its owner. **1886** DORSEY *Midshipman Bob* II. ii. 117 A small, light bird-gun, and a short oar, until his muscles come up, sir. **1904** GLASGOW *Deliverance* 193 Christopher . . . had waited with his bird-gun in the bushes to shoot Fletcher when he came in sight.

+Bird-hawk. A bird of the genus *Cuculus.* — **1832** WILLIAMSON *Maine* I. 141 The Whetsaw . . . frequents logging camps; and is thought to be the same as the Bird-hawk, though as to this naturalists differ.

Bird-house. A small house or box for birds to nest in. — **1870** 'F. FERN' *Ginger-Snaps* 54, I look at that elaborate little bird-house for sparrows. **1916** EATON *Bird House Man* (1917) 14 Alec . . . pushing his half-finished bird house to the back of the bench.

***Birding,** *vbl. n.*

1. Attrib. (with *piece, shot*), =Used for shooting birds.

1642 *Essex Inst. Coll.* L. 236, 2 muskitts, 1 birding pese. **1651** *Mayflower Descendants* X. 161 One byrding peece, one sword, one halbert. **1684** *N.H. Probate Rec.* I. 278 A chest . . . together with a Birding Peice. **1742** *Md. Hist. Mag.* XX. 173 There is somewhat less than four ton thereof, chiefly Birding Shott. **1770** *Carroll P., Ib.* XIII. 68, 4 lbs of the smallest Birding shot. **1809** WEEMS *Marion* (1833) 82 The Carolinians, with no other than birding pieces, . . . were comparatively feeble.

+2. *Birding grass,* =BIRD GRASS.

1787 WASHINGTON *Diaries* III. 198, I sowed . . . 19 rows of the Birding-grass sent me by Mr. Sprigg of Annapolis.

***Bird-lime.** A viscous substance spread upon twigs or rods in order to catch birds.

1631 WINTHROP in *Hist.* (1853) I. 458 If you could bring . . . some birdlime. **1737** BRICKELL *N.Carolina* 23 Misseltoe of the Oak, in great Plenty all over this Province, whereof good Birdlime is made. **1785** MARSHALL *Amer. Grove* 63 Of the bark of common Holly is made Birdlime, which is better than that made of Misletoe. **1837** J. L. WILLIAMS *Florida* 98 Gum Elemi, called by the inhabitants Gumbo-limbo, is a large spreading tree, with a smooth brown bark. . . . The juice, which is a white milk, is converted into birdlime by boiling it to the consistency of a soft gum.

Bird of Paradise. +(See quotation.) — **1858** BAIRD *Birds Pacific R.R.* 169 *Milvulus forficatus,* Scissor-tail, Swallow-tailed Flycatcher, . . . [is the] 'Bird of Paradise' of the Texans.

Bird pepper. One or other kind of capsicum. {1786}

1785 WASHINGTON *Diaries* II. 383 Next to this are two rows of the Bird pepper. **1845** LINCOLN *Botany* App. 85/1 *Capsicum baccatum,* bird pepper, . . . [grows in] Florida. **1890** *Harper's Mag.* July 230/2 The tiny bird-peppers, brilliant in hue, small as a pea, hot as fire. **1892** COULTER *Bot. W. Texas* II. 299 Bird pepper . . . [is] sparsely found in southern and southwestern Texas.

+Bird's-egging. *fig.* One's business, affairs, story, etc. — **1854** S. SMITH *Down East* 32 So now go on with your birds'-egging, and make your Christmas as fast as you please. **1896** *Dialect Notes* I. 412 'That's none of my bird's-egging,' that's none of my affair. 'Go on with your bird's-egging,' go on with your story.

***Bird's eye.**

1. A marking fancied to resemble the eye of a bird. Usually attrib. {1665–}

1635 *Boston Rec.* 238 One piece of birdseye fustian cont[aining] 20 yds. **1843** *Lowell Offering* III. 90 She also had towels and table linen . . . done in patterns manifold. There was . . . diamond, bird's eye, lock and compass [etc.]. **1879** B. F. TAYLOR *Summer-Savory* viii. 77, I have a looking-glass, . . . and the frame of it . . . was as full of birds' eyes as a pigeon-roost in full feather.

+2. *Bird's-eye limestone* (or *marble*), 'a formation in the New York system of geology' (B. '59). Also ellipt.

1843 *Nat. Hist. N.Y., Geology* III. 38 At Fort-Plain . . . the change from Birdseye to Trenton limestone is perfectly abrupt. *Ib.*, The surface of the upper layers of birdseye, at its point of connection with the superior rock. *Ib.* IV. 28 Black-river Limestone Group . . . consisting of the Birdseye and Chozy limestone. **1857** DANA *Mineralogy* (1872) 365 The bird's-eye marble of Western New York is a compact limestone, with crystalline points scattered through it.

+Bird's-eyed, *a.* (See next.) — **1855** *Trans. Mich. Agric. Soc.* VI. 528 Much of this [maple] timber is curled, and some bird's-eyed.

+**Bird's-eye maple.** Wood of the maple when filled with little eye-like spots.

1820 *Niles' Reg.* XVIII. 152/1 The case . . . is of that kind of wood called bird's eye maple. **1823** *New Eng. Farmer* II. 67 Birds Eye Maple. . . . This beautiful wood is becoming a very valuable article of Cabinet furniture. **1841** *S. Lit. Messenger* VII. 16/1 Packet-ships . . . are built, fitted and found in the most elegant manner, with bulk-heads of bird's-eye maple. **1848** D. P. THOMPSON *L. Amsden* 20 A small, neatly-made, oblong box, holding, perhaps, about a pint, which he had chiseled and cut out from a solid billet of the beautiful bird's-eye maple. **1876** INGRAM *Centennial Exp.* 362 Pacific Slope Exhibits. . . . There was one beautiful specimen of bird's-eye maple, which was so hard and fine that it resembled marble. **1904** STRATTON-PORTER *Freckles* 74 They tak', . . . for instance, a burl maple—bird's-eye they call it in the factory.

Bird's-eye primrose. (See quotations.) — **1817-8** EATON *Botany* (1822) 409 *Primula farinosa*, bird's eye primrose; . . . leaves rugose, . . . mealy beneath. **1857** GRAY *Botany* 271 Bird's-eye Primrose . . . : corolla pale lilac with a yellow eye. **1890** *Cent.* 4728/1 Bird's-eye primrose . . . [is] a pretty plant . . . , the flower-stalks . . . bearing compact umbels of lilac-purple yellow-eyed flowers.

+**Bird's-foot violet.** {1882-} The large-flowered stemless violet, *Viola pedata.* (Cf. BIRD-FOOT VIOLET.) — **1882** *Century Mag.* May 153/2 Mr. Robinson recommends a score or more of American plants as suitable for English woods, . . . [including] pond-lily, bird's-foot violet, Canada violet. **1901** MOHR *Plant Life Ala.* 626 Bird's-foot Violet . . . [grows in] Carolinian and Louisianian area; Southern New England, New Jersey, and southern Missouri [etc.].

Bird-shot. Shot suitable for shooting small birds.

1630 WINTHROP in *Hist.* (1853) I. 452 We have powder and pieces enough, but want flints and birdshot. **1761** *Essex Inst. Coll.* XLVIII. 96 To be sold byGeorge Deblois . . . best gunpowder and flints, bird, pigeon, duck, and goose shot. **1874** R. H. COLLINS *Kentucky* I. 217/2, 7 Radical negroes, at 2 A.M., called out of his house one who voted the Democratic ticket, and kukluxed him by shooting him with bird-shot.

***Bird's nest.**

+**1.** Indian pipe (*Monotropa uniflora* or *hypopitys*), parasitic on roots and vegetable mold.

1784 CUTLER in *Mem. Academy* I. 442 Birdsnest. Blossoms yellow. About Great Ossapy pond, in . . . New-Hampshire. **1837** LINCOLN *Botany* 129 *Monotropa uniflora*, bird's nest, Indian-pipe; . . . whole plant ivory white at first. **1847** WOOD *Botany* 380 Bird's-nest . . . [is] a small, succulent plant, . . . common in woods, near the base of trees, on whose roots it is said to be parasitic. **1889** *Cent.* 561/3 Bird's-nest . . . [is] a parasitic ericaceous plant . . . the leafless stalks of which resemble a nest of sticks.

***2.** The wild carrot, *Daucus carota.*

1802 J. DRAYTON *S. Carolina* 65 Wild carrot, or bird's nest (*Daucus*). **1894** *Amer. Folk-Lore* VII. 89 *Daucus Carota* . . . bird's nest; N.J.

3. Attrib. or ellipt., denoting articles of food made like, or fancied to resemble, birds' nests.

1832 L. M. CHILD *Frugal Housewife* 63 If you wish to make what is called 'bird's nest puddings,' prepare your custard [etc.]. **1882** MRS. OWENS *Cook Book* 235 [Recipe for] Bird's Nest Pudding. *Ib.* 236 [Recipe for] Bird's Nest. **1896** *Dialect Notes* I. 412 *Bird's-nest*, a fruit pudding, in which any kind of pudding fruit may be used.

+**Bird-thrashing,** *pr. pple.* Beating bushes to drive out birds. — **1886** *Century Mag.* Feb. 586/1 The boys were off in the thickets bird-thrashing.

Birmingham. [Name of the industrial city in England.] +Pittsburgh, manufacturing city in Pennsylvania.

1814 *Niles' Reg.* VI. 208/1 Pittsburg, sometimes emphatically called the 'Birmingham of America,' will probably become the greatest manufacturing town in the world. **1818** FEARON *Sketches* 199 Though it [Pittsburgh] is not at present a 'Birmingham,' as the natives bombastically call it. **1829** B. HALL *Travels in N.A.* III. 390 We reached Pittsburg, appropriately called the Birmingham of America. **1837** PECK *New Guide* 174 Pittsburgh, . . . from its manufacturing enterprise, especially in iron wares, has been denominated the 'Birmingham of the West.' **1853** A. BUNN *Old Eng. & New Eng.* 100 We told you, some time ago, that New York was one of the dirtiest places we ever happened to have been in, but the Iron City (as Pittsburg is called), this 'Birmingham of America,' throws it completely into shade.

Birth, obs. variant of BERTH *n.* **Birth deck,** variant of BERTH DECK.

Birth-night. A night kept as the anniversary of some person's birth. Also attrib. with *ball.* {1628-1818}

In early use spec. the evening of a royal birthday. {1712-30}

1724 JONES *Virginia* 31 A good cupola or Lanthorn, illuminated with most of the Town, upon Birth-Nights, and other Nights of occasional Rejoicings. **1763** JEFFERSON *Letter* Writings IV. 7, I have some thoughts of going to Petersburg. . . . If I do, . . . I may keep on to Williamsburg, as the birth night will be near. **1769** WASHINGTON *Diaries* I. 325 Went to the Queen's Birth Night at the Palace. **1797** *Ib.* IV. 252 Went in the evening to an elegant entertainment given on my birth night. **1798** JEFFERSON in *Harper's Mag.* (1885) March 536/2 Subscription for General Washington's birth night 5 D[ollars]. **1807** IRVING, etc. *Salmagundi* xv. 348 He had not passed so pleasant an evening since the birthnight ball of the beauteous empress of Hayti. **1847** POLK *Diary* (1929) 199 It has been customary for the President to attend the birth-night ball, and thus pay his respects to the memory of the father of his country.

Birthplace. {1607-} +*The Birthplace of Liberty*, Philadelphia. — **1876** INGRAM *Centennial Exp.* 746 By holding an International Exhibition in the 'Birth-place of Liberty.'

+**Birthroot.** Indian balm, *Trillium erectum.*

1822 *Jrnl. Science* IV. 62 Plants collected by Professor B. Douglass . . . around the great Lakes . . . [include] Birth root: Black Rock, May 3d. **1855** *Mich. Agric. Soc. Trans.* VI. 149 In the lower grounds are skunk cabbage, birth root, wild turnip. **1857** GRAY *Botany* 464 Purple Trillium, Birthroot, . . . [is] common northward, especially westward, and along the Alleghanies. **1894** *Amer. Folk-Lore* VII. 102 *Trillium erectum*, . . . birth-root, nosebleed; N.Y.

***Birthwort.** A shrub of the genus *Aristolochia.*

1785 MARSHALL *Amer. Grove* 12 *Aristolochia frutescens.* Pennsylvanian Shrubby Birthwort. This grows naturally near Pittsburg. **1847** WOOD *Botany* 465 Birthworts . . . are successfully employed in medicine. **1847** DARLINGTON *Weeds & Plants* 68 Birthwort Family [are] herbs or shrubby plants. **1882** *Century Mag.* May 153/2 Mr. Robinson recommends a score or more of American plants as suitable for English woods, . . . [including] birthwort, Virginia creeper, dwarf cornel. **1901** MOHR *Plant Life Ala.* 480 Birthwort Family . . . [includes] Virginia Snakeroot, . . . Large-leaved Pipe Vine [etc.].

Biscake. *Obs.* [Alteration of *biscuit* or *biscuit-cake.*] Biscuit. {1657-81} — **1684** I. MATHER *Providences* 50 He gave me a bit of Biscake, as big as a Walnut. **1716** CHURCH *Philip's War* (1865) I. 58 Plymouth Forces had not so much as one Biscake left. **1724** in Sheldon *Hist. Deerfield* I. 419 We have some stores provided in each Town: especially of Indian Shoes and Biscake. **1823** *Nat'l Intelligencer* 1 May 1/4 *Biscake*, [Western dialect for] Biscuit.

***Biscuit.** Also †**bis-, bysket(t), biskit, bisquit.**

***1.** A crisp dry bread baked hard in thin cakes; hard-tack.

Originally bread baked twice [=rusks], and so perhaps in some of the earlier examples.

1622 'MOURT' *Relation* 17 Our victuals was onely Bisket and Holland cheese. **1644** *Conn. Public Rec.* I. 119 It is ordered by this Court, that noe grayne or byskett shalbe laden by any aboard any vessell in this Riuer. **1675** *Ib.* II. 354 The Councill . . . desire that there may be biskit prepared at New Hauen and Milford, a thowsand in each place. **1714** *Boston News-Letter* 1-8 Nov. 2/1 The Troops in Arms were entertained with Wine and Bisket, and an Ox roasted whole. **1721** *Boston Selectmen* 83 The clarks of the markit are directed to make alowance for the Biskit wel baked, three quarters of an Ounce on each Biskit. **1751** *Boston Ev. Post* 23 Sept., Then Biscuit next, which must be soak'd some Time. **1788** MARY DEWEES *Journal* (MS.) 3, I . . . can take my bit of ham and Biscuit with any of them. **1799** ASBURY *Journal* II. 407 To travel thirty miles in such a cold day without fire, and no food, except a bit of biscuit, is serious. **1805** PIKE *Sources Miss.* 7, [I] gave them one quart of made whiskey, a few biscuit and some salt. **1849** J. B. JONES *Wild West Scenes* iii. 33 The furniture consisted of a few trunks, . . . two camp beds, four barrels of hard biscuit. **1889** BRAYLEY *Boston Fire Dept.* 45 It broke out in the bakehouse of Mr. Brattle Oliver. . . . A large amount of flour, biscuit, and household goods were destroyed.

b. A single cake of this; a cracker.

*a***1649** WINTHROP *Hist.* I. 42 A servant . . . had bargained with a child to sell him a box worth 3*d.* for three biscuits a day all the voyage. **1677** HUBBARD *Narr.* 87 The rest of the Forces had but one Bisket a man to bring them to this place. **1685** SEWALL *Diary* I. 77 Friday May 22d . . . : distributed some Biskets, and Beer, Cider, Wine. **1759** *Essex Inst. Coll.* XX. 156 They said they could have throughn a Bisket into the mouth of the Canon. **1781-2** JEFFERSON *Notes on Va.* Writings 1905 II. 28 A hill . . . so steep that you may pitch a biscuit from its summit into the river which washes its base. **1805** D. MCCLURE *Diary* (1899) 6, I . . . asked for a pint of milk . . . , & with a biscuit . . . I made a comfortable breakfast. **1840** COOPER *Pathfinder* ii, He is as good a fellow as ever broke a biscuit, in his way. **1890** RYAN *Told in Hills* 284 Can you give me a bottle of brandy and some biscuits?

+**2.** A small soft cake of quick bread, made of dough raised by baking powder, soda, or similar leavening agent.

'The name, in England, is given to a composition of flour, eggs, and sugar. With us the name is given to a composition of flour and butter, made and baked in private families. But the compositions under this denomination are very various' (W. '28).

1818 E. P. FORDHAM *Narr. Travels* 226 Perhaps he must carry his horse-load of wheat 30 miles to the mill,—and his wife . . . must make biscuits of it on his return. **1835** [LONGSTREET] *Georgia Scenes* 111 The first supper . . . consisted of smoked tea, half-baked biscuit, butter, and sliced venison. **1843** 'CARLTON' *New Purchase* I. v. 27 Hot rolls came, a novelty then, but much like biscuits in parts of the Far West, viz. a composition of oak bark on the outside, and hot putty within. **1850** SIMMS *Charlemont* 342 Biscuits hot, of best Ohio flour, are smoking on his plate. **1860** OLMSTED *Back Country* 161 Besides this, either at breakfast or supper, a fried fowl, 'biscuit' of wheat flour, with butter were added—the biscuit invariably made heavy, doughy and indigestible with shortening. **1875** STOWE *We & Our Neighbors* 313, I tried my hand in making those little biscuit Mary gets up. . . . Mary makes them with sour milk and soda. **1886** STOCKTON *Mrs. Lecks* 62 Mrs. Aleshine was just taking a pan of newly baked biscuits from a small iron oven. **1903** *N.Y. Sun* 1 Dec. 8

Did he never spread cream ham gravy on his hot biscuits whose taste and delicious odor united to delight his palate?

3. *Biscuit-baker*, a baker of biscuits. {1707-} *Biscuit barrel*, a barrel for holding biscuit or hard tack. *Biscuit bench, block*, a bench or block on which biscuits are prepared for baking. *Biscuit cake*, a biscuit or cracker (*Obs.*).

1652 *Suffolk Deeds* I. 208 Wee . . . graunt, confirme, and make ouer vnto James Oliuer of Boston biskett baker, one white mare. **1660** *Ib.* III. 420 Thomas Haukins of Boston . . . Biscet baker. — **1787** JEFFERSON *Corr.* Writings VI. 302 He has contrived a varnish, also, for lining biscuit barrels, which preserves the biscuit good, and keeps it free from insects. **1840** HAWTHORNE in *Harper's Mag.* XLV. 690/2 Sometimes I . . . warmed myself by a red-hot stove, among biscuit-barrels, pots and kettles. — **1887** *Century Mag.* Oct. 858/1 When he stood by the biscuit bench while she . . . made him marvelous geese of dough. — **1895** 'CRADDOCK' *Myst. Witch-Face Mts.*, etc. 219 Mrs. Blakely . . . had observed him at the gate, while she stood at the biscuit-block in the shed-room. — **1654** JOHNSON *Wonder-w. Prov.* 171 They were brought so neer the shore for convenient landing, that they might have heaved a Bisket cake on land. **a1656** BRADFORD *Hist.* 128 So they were all landed; but ther was not so much as bisket-cake or any other victialls for them.

+**Biscuit potato.** (See quotation.) — **1838** COLMAN *Mass. Agric. Rep.* 33 The Biscuit potato, a round potato with brown rough skin, mealy and productive.

+**Biscuit root.** An edible root found in the Pacific northwest, as camass (*Camassia esculenta*) or cowish (*Peucedanum*). — **1837** IRVING *Bonneville* II. ix. 90 [Indians] use . . . the cowish, also, or biscuit root, about the size of a walnut, which they reduce to a very palatable flour. *Ib.* xviii. 189 The old housewife . . . produced a pot of parched flour and a string of biscuit roots. **1845** DE SMET *Oregon Missions* (1847) 116 The bitter root . . . grows in light, dry, sandy soil, as also the caious or biscuit root. **1846** WEBB *Altowan* I. iv. 141 Their contents consisted of . . . the biscuit root, tasting exactly like a New York cracker newly baked.

+**Biscuit-shooter.** *slang.* **1.** A waitress in a restaurant, eating-house, or the like. **2.** (See quotation.) — **(1) 1898** WISTER *Lin McLean* 53 A biscuit-shooter! . . . I'm told that's what the yard-hands of the railroad call them poor waiter-girls. **1904** STEEDMAN *Bucking the Sagebrush* 49 The 'hash-slinger' (if a gentleman) or 'biscuit-shooter' (if a lady) repeated a list of the grub as piled. **(2) 1920** HUNTER *Trail Drivers of Texas* I. 299 *Biscuit shooter*, name for cook in cow camp.

+**Biscuit stuff.** Flour for baking biscuits. — **1773** WASHINGTON *Writings* (1931) III. 109 The stoage of the sloop is unknown; perhaps there may be about 200 barrels of super fine burr; . . . and 50 of bisquet stuff.

* **Bishop.**

1. * **a.** In certain churches (as the Anglican and Roman Catholic), an ecclesiastical dignitary having administrative power in a diocese. +**b.** In some non-episcopal sects, following New Testament usage, a pastor with or without special administrative duties.

1769 FRANKLIN *Let.* 23 Feb. (MS.), I do not conceive that Bishops residing in America would either be of such Advantage to Episcopalians, or such Disadvantage to Anti-episcopalians, as either seems to imagine. **1776** TRUMBULL *M'Fingal* II. 35 Has not Gage . . . made the Amer'can bishop's see grow, By many a new-converted Negro? **1785** in *S. Lit. Messenger* XXVIII. 38/1 One would not have expected that the first American Bishop had come to New England. **1797** MORSE *Amer. Gazetteer* s.v. *Philadelphia*, The African church . . . is supplied with a negro clergyman, who has been lately ordained by the bishop. **1807** JANSON *Stranger in Amer.* 25 Titles of honour are given to legislators; and that of bishop to the dignified clergy, in America. **1832** WILLIAMSON *Maine* II. 697 Their clerical order consists of Bishops, who are at the head of the Methodist connection;—Elders . . . and Deacons. **1835** REED & MATHESON *Visit* II. 76 The terms, church, clergy, and bishop, . . . are used promiscuously in the churches of America. The Presbyterian church gives officially the style of bishops to her pastors. **1837** PECK *New Guide* 364 From general information I estimate the number of their [the Newlights'] 'bishops' and 'proclaimers' at three hundred. **1844** RUPP *Relig. Denominations* 486 The Rev Christian Herr, of Pequea, Lancaster county, [is] a Bishop of the Mennonite Church. **1877** [MCCABE] *Hist. Great Riots* 111 One of the most earnest workers . . . to put a stop to the disorder was the Roman Catholic Bishop of Pittsburgh. **1905** VALENTINE *H. Sandwith* 336, I am glad . . . you persuaded the bishop to allow Ned to be confirmed.

+**2.** A lady's bustle. *Obs.*

Illustrated by Thornton from 1790 to 1848.

1787 *Newport Herald* 11 Oct. 1/4 Tear off that load of horse-hair foolishly called a *bishop*, from thy back. **1788** *Columbian Mag.* Jan. 35 A young lady of diminutive size, has quitted a ball-room in the extremest mortification, because her *bishop* was not as large as Mrs. M'Rump's. **1790** *Mass. Spy* 16 Sept. (Th.), I know not how to describe the ideas that were excited in my mind by the sight of a Bishop. Agreeably to your directions I fixed it upon my hips: but my sister and two brothers ran out of the room to avoid me. **1807** *Balance* 8 Sept. 281 (Th.), Some years ago, I am informed that the ladies wore what they called bishops; but am not informed as to their real shape, size, and use. **1828** PAULDING *New Mirror* (1868) 68 They say . . . bishops and pads are coming into fashion. **1830** J. F. WATSON *Philadelphia* 175 When the ladies first began to lay off their cumbrous hoops, they supplied their place with successive succedaneums. . . . First came bishops—a thing stuffed or padded with horse hair [etc.]. **a1845** *Big Bear Ark.*, etc. 105 What is the fashuns in Tennysee; the biggist sort of Biships is the go here. **1846** SAXE *Progress* (1847) 22 If by her 'bishop,' or her 'grace' alone, 'A genuine lady, or a church, is known.'

+**Bishoped,** *p.p.* [BISHOP 2.] Furnished with a bustle. — **1807** IRVING, etc. *Salmagundi* ii. 40 When our ladies in stays, and in bodice well laced, When bishop'd, and cushion'd, and hoop'd to the chin.

+**Bishop's cap.** The miterwort, *Mitella diphylla* or *nuda.*

1839 LONGFELLOW *Voices of Night* Prelude viii, When . . . Bishops-caps have golden rings. **1843** TORREY *Flora N.Y.* I. 257 *Mitella nuda*, . . . Stoloniferous Bishop's-cap, . . . [grows in] moist shady woods, and in sphagnous swamps. **1847** WOOD *Botany* 280 Bishop's Cap . . . [is] very common in the woods of N. Eng. to Can. and Ky. **1869** FULLER *Flower Gatherers* 45 The flowers of the 'Bishop's Cap' are small and white, and grow usually upon wet rocks.

+**Bishop sleeve.** A wide sleeve resembling that of a bishop's robe. — **1846** CORCORAN *Pickings from 'Picayune'* 56 Instead of making the sleeves tight they are the old fashioned *bishop* sleeves; and instead of putting in the Elssler buttons, she has substituted hooks and eyes.

Bishop's weed. {1614-} +(See quotations.) — **1889** *Cent.* 564/3 Bishop's weed . . . [is] a name given . . . in the United States to a somewhat similar umbelliferous plant, *Discopleura capillacea.* **1901** MOHR *Plant Life Ala.* 648 *Ptilimnium capillaceum*, . . . Mock Bishop's Weed. . . . Flowers white; May, June. *Ib.* 649 *Ammi visnaga*, . . . Toothpick Bishop's Weed, . . . [is] adventive on ballast. *Ib.*, *Ammi majus*, . . . Greater Bishop's Weed, . . . [is] a showy annual.

+**Bishop-weed.** [Cf. prec.] The mock bishop's weed, *Ptilimnium capillaceum.* — **1833** EATON *Botany* (ed. 6) 127 *Discopleura capillacea*, bishop weed. **1840** DEWEY *Mass. Flowering Plants* 19 *Discopleura capillacea*, . . . Bishop Weed, . . . grows in wet places or bogs, near New Bedford. **1847** WOOD *Botany* 286 Bishopweed . . . [grows] in swamps near the coast, Mass. to Ga. **1857** GRAY *Botany* 156 Mock Bishopweed, . . . *D. capillacea.* . . . Brackish swamps, Massachusetts to Virginia, and southward.

+**Bisnaga (biznaga).** *S.W.* [Sp. *viznaga.*] A species of cactus, *Echinocactus viznaga* or *ingens.* — **1845** FREMONT *Exped.* 266 We ate occasionally the *bisnada* [sic], and moistened our mouths with the acid of the sour dock (*rumex venosus*). **1883** *Harper's Mag.* March 502/2 The bisnaga is a thorny cactus like an immense water-melon set on end. **c1893** *Dialect Notes* I. 253 (citing *Guide* of Eagle Pass, Texas), Viznaga or biznaga . . . are armed with formidable spines.

* **Bison.**

1. A wild ox (*Bison americanus*), formerly abundant over most of North America. Popularly called BUFFALO. {1774-}

'Few now remain, and it has been ascertained that of the millions which once roamed the prairies of the West scarcely a hundred survive' (F.).

[**1774** GOLDSMITH *Hist. Earth* (1822) II. 241 In America . . . the bison is well known. The American bison, however, is found to be rather less than that of the ancient continent.]

1796 MORSE *Univ. Geog.* I. 195 Bison, or Wild Ox. This animal has generally been called the Buffalo, but very improperly. . . . [It] is found in the middle States. **a1805** *Steele Papers* II. 864 The exhibition of a most extraordinary and curious animal called the Bison, never seen in this part of the country before. **1806** *Ann. 9th Congress* 2 Sess. 1136 The great western prairies . . . [have] herds of wild cattle, (bison, commonly called buffalo). **1823** BRYANT *Indian Girl* 26 With wampum-belts I crossed thy breast, And wrapped thee in the bison's hide. **1828** J. GODMAN *Nat. Hist.* III. 4 Of all the parts of the bison that are eaten, the hump is the most famed for its peculiar richness and delicacy. **1832** CATLIN *Indians* I. iv. 24 The buffalo (or more correctly speaking bison) is a noble animal, that roams over the vast prairies. **1846** WEBB *Altowan* I. vi. 178 A man who carries his bed on his saddle, and expects his horse to course down the hart and the bison. **1870** KEIM *Sheridan's Troopers* xxv. (1885) 176 These Indians live in tents of the skin of bison, tanned, and live by the chase. **1887** E. B. CUSTER *Tenting on Plains* xii. 361 The hurricanes . . . have scattered the bleached bones of the bison.

+**b.** The 'mountain buffalo' or 'mountain bison,' formerly regarded (by error) a distinct species.

1877 R. I. DODGE *Plains of Gt. West* 144 In various portions of the Rocky Mountains . . . is found an animal which old mountaineers call the 'bison.' This animal bears about the same relation to a plains buffalo as a sturdy mountain pony does to an American horse. **1878** I. L. BIRD *Rocky Mts.* 200 The last great haunt of the magnificent mountain bison. **1900** DRANNAN *Plains & Mts.* 50 Bison . . . is the distinctive name in that region for mountain buffalo, all buffalo belonging to the bison family. *Ib.* 107 Had I only known the nature of bison, which I learned afterward were not so vicious as buffalo, [etc].

+**2.** Attrib. with *bull, path, robe, trace.*

1821 NUTTALL *Trav. Arkansa* 162 We . . . kept up along the banks of the Kiamesha, by a bison path. *Ib.* 212 We proceeded along a blind bison trace. **1823** JAMES *Exped.* I. 114 Large wooden bowls, which were placed on bison robes or mats. **1827** COOPER *Prairie* xix, A few enormous bison-bulls were first observed. **1846** WEBB *Altowan* I. vi. 178 A large robe of a young bison bull.

+**Bison skin.** The skin of a buffalo. — **1823** JAMES *Exped.* I. 113 Bison-skins supply them with a comfortable bedding. **1835** COOPER *Monikins* x. 114 There were a couple of good large bison-skins among my effects. **1858** HOLMES *Autocrat* xi. 296 Thoroughbrace bison-skin, thick and wide.

* **Bistort.** The herbaceous plant *Polygonum bistortoides* (snakeweed) or the alpine variety, *P. viviparum.*

1784 CUTLER in *Mem. Academy* I. 439 *Polygonum.* . . . Bistort. Snakeweed. . . . The root is said to be one of the strongest vegetable astringents. **1795** WINTERBOTHAM *Hist. View* III. 398 The native and uncultivated plants of New-England . . . employed for medical purposes . . . [include] Bistort. **1847** WOOD *Botany* 475 *P. viviparum,* viviparous bistort, . . . [is found in] White Mts. N. to Arc. Am. **1857** GRAY *Botany* 371 *P. viviparum,* Alpine Bistort. . . . Alpine summits of the White Mountains, New Hampshire, shore of Lake Superior, and northward.

* **Bit,** *n.*

I. ‖**1.** Pasture for sheep or cattle. In the phrase *bit of mouth* (=E. 'bite of grass'). *Obs.*

1689 *Oyster Bay Rec.* I. 550 All the lott of land . . . with all my right of cominage, woods, underwoods, bit of mouth and turburd [=turbary].

II. +**2.** *Bit of eight,* a piece of eight; a Spanish dollar. *Obs.*

1676 TOMPSON *Poet. Works* 50 Twas ere a Barge had made so rich a fraight As chocholatte, dust-gold, and bitts of eight.

+**3.** A small Spanish silver coin (the real) or a substitute for this, and latterly (esp. in the West) a nominal coin or amount, having the value of 12½ cents. (Cf. *Spanish bit.*)

Originally *bit* was apparently (as in sense 2) a rendering of the Spanish *pieza,* but its general use was probably assisted by the fact that the 'bit' was sometimes the result of dividing a coin of greater value. For the value in relation to former coins see quotations 1773–1835, and cf. *fip(p)enny bit.*

1683 *Md. Hist. Mag.* I. 101 [In this one the grantee was put in possession by the delivery of a silver coin] called in Spanish a Bitt fixed on the Seal of these presents. **1699** *East-Hampton Rec.* II. 460 Cost of two pieces of writting 5 bitts. **1704** *Brookhaven Rec.* 5 Fine for 1 hour [lateness at town meeting] 1 bitt; for all day, 2 bitts. **1705** *Boston News-Letter* 30 April 2/1 A Proclamation, prohibiting the Importation of any clipt Money of Bitts or double Bitts into this Colony. **1723** *Smithtown Rec.* 80 Shuball Marchant, Pounder, . . . doth oblige himself to have but half a bit for turning of the key. **1731** J. COMER *Diary* (1923) 117 [The outing] cost me two bitts. **1773** FITHIAN *Journal* I. 72, I gave to Dennis the boy who waits at Table half a Bit. . . . A Bit is a pisterene bisected; or an English sixpence, & passes here for seven pence Halfpenny. *Ib.* 92. **1790** *R.I. Commerce* II. 430, [I] have sold . . . Cheese at one bitt and ¼ to 1¼ bit per lb. **1824** 'SINGLETON' *Lett. South & West* 127 A bit is the Pennsylvanian *eleven-pence,* the New York *shilling,* and the New England *nine-pence.* **1835** P. SHIRREFF *Tour* p. iii, The dollar of Illinois is divided as in the State of New York, but the shilling is often called a 'bit' and the sixpence a 'piccayune.' **1846** EMORY *Military Reconn.* 35 At all hours of the day may be seen jackasses passing laden with wood, which is sold at two bits (twenty-five cents) the load. **1855** M. THOMPSON *Doesticks* xxiii. 202 A stranger must disburse an avalanche of 'bits,' 'pics,' and 'levys,' before he can get even a plate of cold victuals. **1860** MORDECAI *Virginia* xxvii. 277 'Bits' were in semi-circular form; 'half bits' in quadrants. **1875** *Scribner's Mo.* July 277/1 The bit is a mythical quantity. It is neither twelve and a-half cents, nor half of twenty-five; it is neither fifteen cents nor ten cents. **1883** BEADLE *Western Wilds* xxxvi. 590 We doubt if it would go around but for the innumerable saloons which furnish beer and whisky at a bit (12½ cents) a drink, the two bit (25 cents) place being the exception. **1902** LORIMER *Lett. Merchant* 267 An old yellow woman, who would go into a trance for four bits. **1907** *Notes & Queries* 27 July 64/1 In the Gulf States the quarter dollar is universally two bits, and also in the West.

+**b.** *Short bit,* ten cents; *long bit,* fifteen cents.

*c*1854 [PAIGE] *Dow's Sermons* IV. 219 (Th.), The will, that cuts off an expectant heir with a 'short bit.' **1859** MRS. DUNIWAY *Capt. Gray's Coy.* 158 Let 'em fight it out, daddy. I'd give a long bit myself to see 'em pull hair. **1877** WM. WRIGHT *Big Bonanza* 89 The stakes . . . were two short bits (twenty cents). **1906** *N.Y. Ev. Post.* 20 July 4 The dime, or 'short bit,' has made its way to the Pacific Coast, become the minimum coin of general circulation in the nineties, and has since been cut under by five and one-cent pieces in fair abundance.

+**Bit,** *v.* To bore a hole in (a tree, etc.) with a bit or auger. — **1857** *Lawrence* (Kansas) *Republican* 11 June 4 Of course, he hadn't any auger to bit or tap the trees.

* **Bite,** *n.*[1] A deception, an imposition; also, a cheater. *Obs.* {1711–1790; now *n. dial.*}

1723 *New-Eng. Courant* 15–22 April 2/1 After the Proclamation was readd at the Corner of School-Street, a Negro, who stood to hear it, cry'd out, 'A Bite, a Bite': Upon which he was immediately seiz'd. **1755** *Essex Inst. Coll.* LII. 81, I'm told horse dealers here are great *Bites.* **1792** BRACKENRIDGE *Capt. Farrago* i. 3 The jockeys suspected from this speech, that the horse was what they call a bite, and that under the appearance of leanness and stiffness, there was concealed some hidden quality of swiftness uncommon. **1853** *Knickerb.* XLII. 434 The plaintiff's attorney, on perusing the plea, saw that it was meant for a 'bite,' . . . and demurred to it!

+**Bite,** *n.*[2] [Prob. for *bight* bend, loop of a rope, etc.] (See quotations.) — **1851** SPRINGER *Forest Life* 104 In other instances loads are eased down hill sides by the use of 'tackle and fall,' or by a strong 'warp,' taking a 'bite' round a tree, and hitching to one yoke of the oxen. **1858** *Rep. Comm. Patents* (1859) I. 358 The ears of corn are allowed to descend by their own gravity down the 'bite' or angle formed by the contact of the wheel and rollers.

* **Bite,** *v.* (In colloq. uses.)

+**1.** With *off.* To conclude speaking.

1843 [STEPHENS] *High Life N.Y.* II. xxi. 48, I had to bite off short, for a chap come aboard the sloop with Captin Doolittle. **1845** MRS. KIRKLAND *Western Clearings* 16 In vain the lecturer told his audience that he was 'just going to bite off.' **1911** VANCE *Cynthia* 172 'Ah, bite that off!' Rhode interrupted impatiently.

2. *To bite off more than one can chew,* to undertake a task beyond one's powers.

1877 BEADLE *Western Wilds* ii. 42 Men, you've bit off more'n you can chaw. **1878** STOWE *Poganuc People* iii. 33 They've bit off more'n they can chaw, that's all. **1898** HAMBLEN *Gen. Manager's Story* 115, I'll tell you one thing. . . . You've bit off more'n you can chew this time. **1905** *Hartford Courant* 10 Feb. 8 Young Lawyer Comerford . .. bit off more than he could chew. . . . He could not make good when called on for proof. **1908** WHITE *Riverman* iii. 29 You're biting off more than you can chew. Skedaddle!

+**3.** With *in.* To moderate or modify one's words or talk.

1843 [STEPHENS] *High Life N.Y.* I. i. 11 'You seem to be a stranger in the city,' sez he, a trying to bite in, for I s'pose he see that my dander was a getting up.

+**Bit house.** [BIT *n.* 3.] (See quotation.) — **1877** WM. WRIGHT *Big Bonanza* 354 In Virginia City, . . . the majority of these saloons are what are called 'bit houses'; that is, drinks of all kinds and cigars are one bit—twelve and one-half cents. The dime, however, passes as a 'bit' in all of these houses.

Bittell-ring, variant of BEETLE-RING. — **1654** *Essex Probate Rec.* I. 190 Bittell Ringes and Saw.

Bitter, *n.* =BITTERS. — **1784** CUTLER in *Mem. Academy* I. 455 An infusion of the [puccoon] root in rum or brandy makes a good bitter. **1898** WESTCOTT *D. Harum* 25 He was hungry, having had no luncheon but a couple of biscuits and a glass of 'bitter.'

Bitter, *a.* Used in combination with names of plants, etc., as *almond, cottonwood, cress, dock, elm, hickory, oak, pecan,* to denote species or varieties of these.

1807 *Mass. H. S. Coll.* 2 Ser. III. 50 More than one half of these two townships is covered with shrub oak and bitter oak. **1813** MUHLENBERG *Cat. Plants* 88 *Juglans sulcata, amara:* bitter hickory, white, [grows in] Pens. **1843** N. BOONE *Journal* (1917) 222 The grove near our camp has mulberry, bitter elm, & dogwood. **1843** TORREY *Flora N.Y.* I. 57 *Cardamine pratensis,* Common Bitter Cress; Cuckoo-flower. **1844** GREGG *Commerce of Prairies* I. 159–60 Another [cottonwood] . . . found on the mountain streams of New Mexico . . . has been called willow-leaf or bitter cottonwood, and has been reckoned by some a species of cinchona. **1847** DARLINGTON *Weeds & Plants* 284 Bitter Dock. Broad-leaved Dock. [Grows in] grass lots; gardens, meadows, &c. **1851** BARRY *Fruit Garden* 351 The Bitter Almond . . . is hardy and productive; nut . . . bitter, and only useful in confectionery or medicine. **1861** WOOD *Botany* 230 Bitter Cress [is] common in streams and springy places throughout the country. **1884** SARGENT *Rep. Forests* 136 *Carya aquatica.* . . . Water Hickory. Swamp Hickory. Bitter Pecan. **1901** MOHR *Plant Life Ala.* 96 In sheltered situations, the sweet and bitter orange and loquat . . . are cultivated. *Ib.* 832 *Citrus bigaradia,* Bitter Orange.

+**Bittered sling.** A cocktail. — **1806** *Balance* (Hudson, N.Y.) 13 May 146 (Th.), Cocktail is a stimulating liquor, composed of spirits of any kind, sugar, water, and bitters—it is vulgarly called bittered sling, and is supposed to be an excellent electioneering potion.

Bitter end. [App. f. *bitter* 'the turne of a cable about the bits, . . . and the bitters end is that part of the cable doth stay within boord' (1627 Capt. J. Smith); but now associated with *bitter* adj.] *To the bitter end,* to the last extremity. — **1849** *Congress. Globe* 12 Dec. 23/2, I am unfortunately among those who voted for the gentleman from Indiana—even 'to the bitter end.' **1857** *Lawrence* (Kansas) *Republican* 2 July 2 Even his own police, who seemed at the beginning so eager to support him to the bitter end, received clear light.

+**Bitter-ender.** One who holds out to the very last in some cause. — **1850** *Congress. Globe* App. 12 March 303/3 The disunionist looks to a southern Confederacy; the bitter-ender to the triumph of his party, and the downfall of as honest . . . an Executive, as this country has known since the days of Washington.

+**Bitter-head.** The strawberry bass, *Pomoxys sparoides.* — **1888** GOODE *Amer. Fishes* 69 The names 'Bitter Head' and 'Lamplighter' are also ascribed to it.

+**Bitter land.** Sour land or soil. — **1837** WILLIAMS *Florida* 89 The third kind of swamps are those spongy tracts, where the waters continually ooze through the soil, and finally collect in streams and pass off. These are properly termed galls, sometimes sour, sometimes bitter lands.

* **Bittern**[1]. Also †**bitter.** A wading-bird of the heron kind (sub-family *Botaurinæ*).

1610 *Estate of Virginia* 13 The riuers . . . are couered with flocks of Wild-foule: as . . . teal, wigeons, hearens, bitters. **1709** LAWSON *Carolina* 148 We have three sorts of Bitterns in Carolina. *c*1730 CATESBY *Carolina* I. 78 The brown Bittern. . . . These Birds frequent fresh Rivers and Ponds in the upper parts of the Country, remote from the Sea. *Ib.* 79 The crested Bittern. . . . These Birds are seen in Carolina in the rainy seasons. **1753** ELIOT *Field-Husb.* iv. 94 The baleful Thickets of Brambles, and the dreary Shades of larger Growth [in a swamp]; the Dwelling-Place of the Owl and the Bittern. **1813** WILSON *Ornith.* VII. 97 The Green Bittern makes its first appearance in Pennsylvania early in April. *Ib.* VIII. 37 [The] Least Bittern, *Ardea exilis*, . . . is commonly found in fresh water meadows. **1813-** [see AMERICAN BITTERN]. *c***1849** [PAIGE] *Dow's Sermons* I. 57 You . . . manage to keep upon such scripture-forbidden creatures as . . . sea-gulls, shitepokes, cranes, bitterns, and owls. **1870** *Amer. Naturalist* III. 231 Of the Herons, five at least are summer residents near our sea-coast. . . . These are the Green, the Night, and the great Blue Herons, the Least and the Common Bittern. **1892** TORREY *Foot-path Way* 71 Up from the reeds a bittern will now and then start.

Bittern².

1. The lye remaining after the making of common salt from sea-water or brine. {1682-}

1798 *N.Y. State Soc. Arts* I. 281 Nothing now remains in the pot but a small quantity of bittern, which is thrown away. **1804** J. ROBERTS *Penna. Farmer* 80 The bittern, as it is called, tends to foul, make rancid, corrode and corrupt meat. **1809** KENDALL *Travels* II. 133 The entire period of the process is usually about three weeks. In the spring, the same water, or, as, after leaving the pickle-rooms, it is called, the *bittern*, will yield two or three rakings. **1830** *Va. Lit. Museum* 736 Specimens of salt, salt-water, and bittern were sent to the laboratory of this institution by Judge Summers. *Ib.*, From the bittern it [bromine] has been separated in considerable quantity.

+2. A liquid manufactured by the Indians from horse chestnuts and various roots to be put in water in order to stupefy fish. *Obs.*

1775 ADAIR *Indians* 403 They scatter this mixture over the surface of a middle-sized pond, and stir it about with poles, till the water is sufficiently impregnated with the intoxicating bittern.

+Bitternut. The swamp hickory, *Carya amara* (*Hicoria minima*). Also **bitternut hickory.**

1810 MICHAUX *Arbres* I. 19 Bitter nut hickory . . . , seul nom en usage dans N.Y. **1814** PURSH *Flora Amer.* II. 638 *Juglans amara.* . . . This is known by the name of Bitter Nut, White or Swamp Hickory. **1819** E. DANA *Geog. Sketches* 171 The timber growth on the bottoms consists principally of . . . hackberry, bitter nut, hickory. **1832** BROWNE *Sylva* 170 The inhabitants of New Jersey give it the name of Bitternut, which, as it indicates one of the peculiar properties of the fruit, we have chosen to retain. *Ib.*, This species is generally known in New Jersey by the name of Bitternut Hickory. **1847** DARLINGTON *Weeds & Plants* 306 The Bitternut . . . is another species resembling the Pig-nut, having the small thin-shelled nuts, the kernels of which are intensely bitter. **1892** APGAR *Trees Northern U.S.* 143 Bitternut . . . [is a] large tree with orange-yellow winter buds. **1901** MOHR *Plant Life Ala.* 463 Bitternut . . . [is] of little value except for fuel. *Ib.* 100 Bottoms . . . heavily timbered with . . . mockernut (*Hickoria alba*) and bitternut hickory (*Hickoria minima*), all draped with Spanish moss.

+Bitter-root. [tr. Fr. *racine amère.*] Tobacco-root (*Lewisia rediviva*), found in Oregon, Idaho, and adjacent regions.

1845 DE SMET *Oregon Missions* (1847) 116 The bitter root, whose appellation sufficiently denotes its peculiar quality, is, however, very healthy. **1878** *Rep. Indian Affairs* 88 A large prairie . . . furnishes them with camas and bitter-root, which they dig and dry in the spring for winter use. **1885** *Century Mag.* Jan. 447 It was too late [in June] to find the exquisite camellia-like flower of the bitter-root, which in May stars the ground. **1895** *Montana Codes & Statutes* I. 425 The flower known as *lewisia rediviva* (bitter root) shall be the floral emblem of the state of Montana. *a***1918** G. STUART *On Frontier* I. 178 The wild flax and bitter-root are in full bloom.

+Bitter rot. A kind of rot that attacks apples, grapes, etc. — **1861** *Ill. Agric. Soc. Trans.* IV. 115 The bitter rot makes its appearance as a brown spot on the side of the apple. *Ib.* 117. **1890** *Cent.* 5235/3 The bitter rot [of the grape is caused] by *Greeneria fuliginea.*

Bitters.

1. A medicine or tonic, consisting of spirits and a vegetable infusion. {1713-}

Sometimes used euphemistically for whiskey or other alcoholic beverages.

1739 D. WADSWORTH *Diary* 40 Mr. Eliot . . . here advises me to take . . . bitters, as gentian, camamile, &c. in powder or steeped in wine. **1776** FITHIAN *Journal* II. 195, I take claret in bitters which sensibly helps me. *Ib.*, I find myself much recovered & strengthened by the bitters. **1785** MARSHALL *Amer. Grove* 78 Virginian Tulip-Tree. . . . The bark of the roots is used . . . in bitters. **1809** F. CUMING *Western Tour* 44 They returned, drank whiskey under the name of bitters, and resumed their beds on the floor. **1818** FLINT *Lett. from Amer.* 54 Some Americans [were] drinking their morning's bitters, (spirits with rue, wormwood, or other vegetable infusion). **1827** J. PICKERING *Inquiries Emigrant* (1831) 93 Let him give out drams of whisky, . . . 'bitters' (any kind of liquor taken in a morning ostensibly for procuring an appetite). **1835** LATROBE *Rambler* II. 61 It was agreed by the majority of the good people of Tallahassee, to go on drinking and stimulating with mint-julep, mint-sling, bitters. **1842** MRS. KIRKLAND *Forest Life* II. xxxii. 7 The counter at the post-office . . . served as well for the dispensation of 'bitters' and tobacco as of letters. **1855** BARNUM *Life* 81 Noah purchased a quart of Santa Cruz rum, at the same time enjoining 'Squire Hoyt to be sure and bring over some fresh tanzy . . . for bitters. **1873** 'MARK TWAIN' & WARNER *Gilded Age* xvi. 154 A habit of taking every morning before breakfast a dose of bitters, composed of whisky and asafoetida, out of the acclimation jug. **1896** *McClure's Mag.* VI. 486/2 Mrs. Stillman grew paler and weaker, until even her husband noticed it, and brought her a bottle of bitters. **1904** GLASGOW *Deliverance* 60, I believe he means the brown bitters mother used to make for chills and fever. **1910** C. HARRIS *Eve's Husband* 109 Mother and I . . . invariably knew . . . when father had been drinking too much of his own 'bitters.'

+2. A beverage of bitter taste (see quotation). Also called *prairie bitters.*

1846 SAGE *Scenes Rocky Mts.* xvi. 132 A kind of beverage very common among mountaineers, . . . 'bitters.' . . . It is prepared by the following simple process, viz.: with one pint of water mix one-fourth gill of buffalo-gall, and you will then have before you a wholesome and exhilarating drink.

+3. *To get one's bitters,* to meet one's deserts or fate.

1812 *Md. Hist. Reg.* IX. 70 You might get your bitters in Baltimore Town. *c***1812** PAULDING *Bucktails* v. ii. (1847) 79 Take that, honey, for your pains—(*knocks himself down.*)—Fait—I think you've got your bitters now, Mister Whack. **1813** — *J. Bull & Br. Jon.* iii. (ed. 2) 16 At last this old fellow got his bitters. *a***1846** *Quarter Race Ky.* etc. 194 The seal soon got his bitters, and the captin cut a big hunk off the tail eend.

***Bittersweet.**

***1.** The woody nightshade, *Solanum dulcamara.*

1766 BARTRAM *Journal* 41 Bitter sweets . . . are next in goodness to the china. **1766** *Ib.* 44 On a bluff . . . we gathered good bitter-sweets. **1784** CUTLER in *Mem. Academy* I. 420 Bittersweet [is] common about fences in moist land. **1818** EASTBURN *Yamoyden* III. xxxii, The many-coated columbine, And bittersweet luxuriant sprung, Robust and statelier vines among. **1832** WILLIAMSON *Maine* I. 120 Bitter-sweet, a hardy climbing plant of five feet high and shrubby, is good for rheumatism, asthma, and jaundice, and in diet-drink. **1852** MITCHELL *Dream Life* 201 The bitter-sweet hangs its bare and leaf-less tendrils from rock to tree, and sways with the weight of its brazen berries. **1875** STOWE *We & Our Neighbors* 339 Bright bunches of vermilion bittersweet, and the crimson-studded branches of the black alder, added color to the picture. **1904** STRATTON-PORTER *Freckles* 83 About the case he planted wild clematis, bitter-sweet, and wild grapevines.

+2. The climbing shrub, *Celastrus scandens.*

1813 MUHLENBERG *Cat. Plants* 25 Climbing Stafftree or bittersweet. **1815** DRAKE *Cincinnati* 77 Forest of the Miami Country . . . [contains] Staff tree or bittersweet. **1843** TORREY *Flora N.Y.* I. 140 Bittersweet, Wax-work; . . . sometimes employed as a domestic medicine in the Western States. **1857** GRAY *Botany* 81 Climbing Bitter-sweet. The opening orange-colored pods, displaying the scarlet covering of the seeds, are very ornamental in autumn. **1870** *Amer. Naturalist* June 215 Bittersweet (*Celastrus scandens*), also called Roxbury Waxwork, . . . is a hardy climber. **1901** MOHR *Plant Life Ala.* 605 Wax-work. False Bitter-sweet. . . . The bark is used as a domestic medicine.

+Bitter-water. =BITTERN² 1. — **1802** ELLICOTT *Journal* 15 But the greatest difficulty they found, was with the bitter water, which I supposed was what the manufacturers of salt in England, call bittern, and drains from the salt after it is granulated.

Bitter-weed.

+1. Ragweed or hogweed, *Ambrosia artemisiæfolia.*

1821 NUTTALL *Travels* 204 We struck across the desiccated corner of the pond; here the *Ambrosias* or bitter weeds were higher than my head on horseback. **1836** EDWARD *Hist. Texas* 19 The connection . . . enables them to form . . . a low, sandy, bitter-weed island. **1857** GRAY *Botany* 212 Bitter-weed . . . [is found in] waste places everywhere. **1892** COULTER *Bot. W. Texas* II. 210 Hog-weed, Bitter-weed, . . . a common weed of waste grounds. Extremely variable. **1901** MOHR *Plant Life Ala.* 757 Hog-weed, Bitterweed, . . . [is] the commonest of weeds.

+2. The sneezeweed, *Helenium tenuifolium.*

1901 MOHR *Plant Life Ala.* 54 The bitterweed, . . . , originally from the sunny plains . . . south of the Arkansas valley, was first observed in Mobile in 1866. *Ib.* 810 Bitterweed . . . [is] one of the most obnoxious of weeds.

***Bitumen.** Mineral pitch, or other hydrocarbon, such as petroleum and allied substances.

1789 MORSE *Amer. Gazetteer* 407 Three springs or ponds of bitumen near Green river, [Ky.,] . . . empty themselves into a common reservoir. **1792** IMLAY *Western Territory* 53 There is in it [=s. Ky.] a most valuable lead mine, and several salt springs, and two of bitumen, which, when analyzed, is found to be amber. **1795** J. SCOTT *Gazetteer* s.v. *Allegany County*, In this county is Oil creek: It flows from a spring much celebrated for a bitumen resembling Barbadoes tar, and is known by the name of Seneca Oil. **1806** *Ann. 9th Congress* 2 Sess. 1120 This stratum of coal . . . does not appear sufficiently impregnated with bitumen, but may be considered as vegetable matter in the process of transmutation to coal. **1848** E. BRYANT *California* 393 We passed several warm springs which throw up large quantities of bitumen or mineral tar. **1857** DANA *Mineralogy* (1872) 85 Bituminous coal varies much and indefinitely in the amount of bitumen it contains. **1870** KEIM *Sheridan's Troopers* xxxiv. (1885) 248 The bitumen, however, was less easily to be found.

Bituminous, *a.* {1620–} Of the nature of, or containing, bitumen. Applied spec. to coal and oil.

(1) **1827** DRAKE & MANSF. *Cincinnati* i. 11 Bituminous coal of a good quality, and in large quantities, abounds in those parts of the state. **1838** J. HALL *Western States* iv. 59 The neighboring hills furnish an inexhaustible supply of bituminous coal. **1852** MARCY *Explor. Red River* (1854) 123 After leaving this ridge the road crosses the Brazos near very extensive fields of bituminous coal. **1880** DANA *Mineralogy* 754 Bituminous Coals ... have the common characteristic of burning in the fire with a yellow, smoky flame.

ellipt. **1854** B. F. TAYLOR *Jan. & June* 197 We shall be fossils by and by. ... And when we get to that, shall we give light like the poor Anthracite, or Bituminous, or Lignite, or whatever it is?

(2) **1837** IRVING *Bonneville* I. xxiii. 223 The bituminous oil, called petrolium [*sic*] or naphtha, which forms a principal ingredient in the potent medicine called British Oil. ... In the State of New York, it is called Seneca Oil, from being found near the Seneca lake.

(3) **1844** GREGG *Commerce of Prairies* II. 184 In some of the regions bordering the Neosho river ... there are also said to be a few singular bituminous or 'tar springs,' as they are sometimes called by the hunters.

+**Biue,** obs. variant spelling of BAYOU. (Cf. BIO.) — *c***1805** R. PUTNAM *Memoirs* 43 Sunday April 25th [1773] we ... passed another small Biue; which in high water communicates with the Lake of Homocheto.

Bivalve, *n.* {1683–} *spec.* An oyster or clam. — **1841** *Big Bear Arkansas* (1845) 81 He indulged in a long stare at the man opening the bivalves. **1857** HAMMOND *Northern Scenes* 142 Some of these [clams] we opened, and found the living bivalves in appearance precisely like their kindred of the salt water. **1874** PINKERTON *Expressman & Detective* 125 Franklin gave his orders, and the delicious bivalves were soon smoking before them.

Bivouac, *n.* A military or other encampment for the night in the open air. {1811– *Mil.;* 1853–}

1826 COOPER *Mohicans* xiii, The luminary which was shedding its mild light through the opening in the trees, directly on their bivouac. **1837** IRVING *Bonneville* II. 20 They ... then trimmed and replenished their fire, as if for a bivouac. **1843** FREMONT *Exped.* 14 We made our bivouac in the midst of some well-timbered ravines. **1861** *Army Regulations* 72 Heavy cavalry ... is covered, when necessary, in marches, camps, or bivouacs, by light troops. **1881–5** MCCLELLAN *Own Story* 582 The 12th corps and Sedgwick's division bivouacked around Bolivar. **1885** *Century Mag.* XXX. 447/1 The confederate divisions remained in bivouac all the next day.

attrib. **1862** MCCLELLAN *Own Story* 394 This evening, when the bivouac-fires were lighted, the scene was grand beyond description. **1865** *Atlantic Mo.* XV. 751 It was much better for the *morale* of the army than to sit by bivouac-fires waiting for sunny skies.

Bivouac, *v.*

1. *intr.* To encamp, or camp out, for the night, esp. in the open air. {1809– *Mil.;* 1814–}

1835 IRVING *Tour Prairies* xxxi. 293 The young Count ... had wandered about until dark, when he thought of bivouacking. **1837** — *Bonneville* I. i. 26 Accustomed to live in tents, or to bivouac in the open air, he [the mountaineer] despises the comforts ... of the log-house. **1846** M'KENNEY *Memoirs* I. ii. 45 They halted,—began to bivouac, sling their kettles, &c., &c. **1856** WHIPPLE *Explor. Ry. Route* II. 37 Near station 5 there are springs, in the vicinity of which the reconnoitring party bivouacked. **1867** CRAWFORD *Mosby* 23 The notorious Jim Lane of Kansas, with one hundred of his desperadoes, bivouacked in the East Room of the White House, as a body guard for his Excellency the President. **1892** M. A. JACKSON *Gen. Jackson* 223 The soldiers bivouacked under the cold winter sky without tents or blankets.

2. *tr.* To post or dispose (troops, etc.) in a bivouac.

1878 C. COALE in *Ann. S. W. Va.* (1929) 1611 He bivouacked his little command of five hundred men a short distance from the village, and entered the town.

Bi-weekly, *a.* **1.** Occurring, running, etc., twice in a week. **2.** Occurring, appearing, etc., every two weeks. — **(1) 1832** W. T. BARRY in *Amer. State P.* XV. (1834) 348 The line of stages ... has been increased from a bi-weekly to a tri-weekly line to Eastville. *Ib.*, A bi-weekly line of four-horse post coaches. **(2) 1889** *Cent.* s.v., A bi-weekly magazine.

+**Biz.** Colloq. abbreviation of *business.*

1862 BROWNE *A. Ward His Book* 222, I must forth to my Biz. **1873** LELAND *Egyptian Sketch-book* 35 No. IV. made it his 'biz' to fall upon the old hands. **1877** BEADLE *Western Wilds* iii. 46 He had what he called a 'big biz' at each successive terminus town. **1881** STODDARD *E. Hardery* 308 He kin beat any chap I know of mindin' his own biz, and not tellin' about it arterwards. **1890** *Harper's Mag.* April 813/1, I'll go down to the sale, if I can leave my biz. **1898** P. L. FORD *Tattle-Tales* 87, I knew he meant biz. **1910** RAINE *B. O'Connor* 39 The bunch borrowed a mighty good .45 of mine I need in my biz.

+**Blab school.** *S.E.* [E. *blab n. or v.] A school in which the pupils learn the lessons by repeating them aloud; a 'vocal school.' — **1890** F. E. JENKINS in *Congress. Rec.* 10 Feb. 1165/1 You are riding along a mountain road ... and you ... distinguish human voices mingling together in loud discord. ... [It is] a school at study and all studying at the top of their voices. Such a din! This is a 'blab' school. *Ib.*, Of these mountain children in our mission schools ... I never talked with one who had not been accustomed to the blab school, except the younger ones.

***Black,** *n.* [f. the adj.]

1. A Negro. {1625–} Chiefly in *pl.*

(1) *pl.* **1671** in *Virginia Car.* (1886) 335 What number of people have yearly died, within your plantation, ... both whites and blacks? **1674** Alvord & Bidgood *Trans-Allegheny Region* 214 They have many blacks among them. **1715** *Boston News-Letter* 15 Aug. 2/2 [In] South Carolina ... they are still daily battling with the Indian Enemy, wherein they have lost a great many Whites & Blacks. **1760** Commons, etc. *Doc. Hist.* I. 309 The poor blacks have died very fast even by inoculation but the people in Chrs [=Charles] Town were inoculation mad. **1775** HABERSHAM *Letters* 241 This will be a great Comfort to me, as the souls of my poor benighted Blacks have long lain heavy on my Heart. **1782** J. H. ST. JOHN *Letters* 224 We do not want you to teach us what we are to do with our blacks. **1795** *Mass. H. S. Coll.* IV. 199 It became necessary to put the blacks with the Indians, into the fourth column. **1803** *Ann. 8th Congress* 2 Sess. 1503 In proportion to the distance from the capital [of Louisiana] the number of blacks diminishes below that of the whites. **1812** BRACKENRIDGE *Louisiana* (1814) 175 The disproportion of the whites to the blacks [is] of course increasing. **1815** DRAKE *Cincinnati* i. 32 In Ohio the blacks were only nineteen hundred, being to the whites as eighty-three to one thousand. **1827** MCKENNEY *Tour to Lakes* 72 The old gentleman then asked me ... 'what did I think of a colony for the blacks, somewhere, far off in the West?' **1850** [S. F. COOPER] *Rural Hours* 111 The blacks were allowed full liberty to frolic, for several days in Whitsunweek. **1861** S. COX *In Congress* (1865) 27 Nor will I discuss whether the blacks have been bettered by their precipitate freedom. **1865** *Nation* I. 33 At Savannah, Gen. Woodford provides the blacks with the same facilities for education as the whites. **1869** W. H. BREWER *Rocky Mt. Lett.* 7 A better farming region with many humble cabins, not a few inhabited by blacks, perhaps escaped slaves of former days. **1898** PAGE *Red Rock* 190 The marauders ... were quickly almost as obnoxious to the blacks as to the whites.

(2) *sing.* **1758** *Lett. to Washington* II. 329 The Black [a French negro] is arrived. **1780** R. PUTNAM in *Memoirs* 169 A Black who calls him self Robert sais he belongs to Colo. Moyland. **1818** FEARON *Sketches* 58 The barber enquired if he wanted the proprietor ..., who was also a black. **1821** COOPER *Spy* vii, He noticed the approach of the black ... with a smile of contempt. **1843** MISS SIDDONS *Female Warrior* 7, I told Mary (the black) that I should first go to Mobile. **1856** OLMSTED *Slave States* 129 The free black does not, in general, feel himself superior to the slave.

2. A black part.

1753 WASHINGTON *Diaries* I. 49 You say this land belongs to you, but there is not the Black of my nail yours.

3. A black horse.

1845 HOOPER *Taking Census* i. 153 Forthwith mounting our old black, we determined to give the old soul a parting fire. *a***1861** WINTHROP *J. Brent* iii. 31 The black was within the corral, pawing the ground, neighing, and whinnying. **1873–4** *Vermont Bd. Agric. Rep.* II. 211 They are able to ride in grand carriages with their three minute blacks hitched thereto.

4. *In black:* +**a.** Having a black skin. +**b.** Having the skin blackened, as for Negro minstrelsy. +**c.** Allusively, with reference to slave-owning.

a. 1881 in *Bibliog. of Negro Amer.* (1905) 26 Our brother in black.
b. *c***1874** C. H. DAY (*title*), Fun in Black; or, Sketches of Minstrel Life.
c. 1899 CHESNUTT *Wife of His Youth* 201 The wholesale nature of the transaction carried consternation to the hearts of those [slave-owners] whose ledgers were chiefly bound in black.

***Black,** *a.*

***1.** Black-skinned; belonging to the Negro race. See also BLACK MAN, PEOPLE.

1671 BERKELEY in *Virginia Car.* (1886) 335 We suppose ... that there is in Virginia ... two thousand black slaves. *c***1705** *Mass. Bay Acts* (1869) I. 580 *note*, That the importation of white Servants be encouraged, & that the Importation of black servants be discouraged. **1748** *Georgia Col. Rec.* VI. 207 Those (they call Servants) are black Slaves. **1797** *Wilmington* (N.C.) *Gazette* 23 March, Two good black carpenters. **1812** *Niles' Reg.* III. 107/1 It is now ascertained that black troops ... have arrived from Cuba. **1823** E. JAMES *Exped.* I. 179 A negro belonging to the Fur Company coming in on an errand, they spoke of him as the 'black white man.' *c***1824** G. W. Rauck *Boonesborough* (1901) 165 One of our men ... was discovered ..., by a black woman belonging to Colonel Callaway, while gathering some wood. **1838** [INGRAHAM] *Burton* II. vi. 89 A heavily-built coach, drawn by a pair of large bay horses and driven by a black coachman. **1849** F. DOUGLASS *Life* 35 The girls seldom passed her without her saying, 'Move faster, you black gip!' **1859** BARTLETT 144 *Black Fellow*, a black man. Southern. **1875** *Chicago Tribune* 6 Nov. 3 District Attorneys ... denounce negroes, ... against whom no offense is proven by the laws of the State [of Texas], as 'black hellions.' **1880** CABLE *Grandissimes* 16 The blue-turbaned black nurse was tucking the covering about his feet. **1881** *Harper's Mag.* 659 A young colonel of the Union army ... stood on the wheel-house of a transport with his black regiment ... on the deck below. **1893** HOWELLS *Coast of Bohemia* 63 The black porter of the sleeping-car caught up her bag and carried it out for her. **1907** C. C. ANDREWS *Recoll.* 205 It did not degrade white soldiers because black soldiers had equal military rights, nor will it degrade white citizens if blacks have equal rights.

absol. **1865** GRANT in Fleming *Hist. Reconstruction* I. 52 The white and the black mutually require the protection of the general government. **1881** *Harper's Mag.* Sept. 439/1 Great was the joy with white and black when Mrs. Peacock . . . arrived at the gate.

+**b.** *Black flesh, stock,* Negro slaves.

1827 COOPER *Prairie* viii, The newspapers of Kentuck have called you a dealer in black flesh a hundred times, but little did they reckon that you drove the trade into white families. **1861** VICTOR *Southern Rebellion* I. 234 The oldest families in the State—the true F. F. V.'s—derived their chief revenue from their annual sales of 'black stock.'

c. Pertaining to, connected with, the Negro.

1816 W. BENTLEY *Diary* IV. 383 Mrs. Mins keeps the African School in this quarter. It is properly our black town. **1844** *McDonogh Papers* 72 We keep an agent employed whose business it is to visit every black settlement . . . for the purpose of instructing them more perfectly in agriculture . . . and religion. **1861** H. GREELEY in *Independent* 14 Nov., They . . . predict that the downfall of Black bondage is not far distant. **1864** S. COX *In Congress* (1865) 357 No charitable black scheme can wash out the color of the negro, change his inferior nature. **1871** *Rep. Indian Affairs* (1872) 245 That said Peter did not claim to be of white or black admixture, but of pure Chippewa blood. **1888** *Congress. Rec.* 26 Sept 8947/1 Justices of the peace in the black counties . . . converted their offices into engines of oppression to both races.

2. In the distinctive names of many varieties of trees or plants, birds or other animals.

For the more important of these, as *black alder, ash, bass, bear,* etc., see the separate entries below. Also combined with other names of color, as *black and white creeper, black and yellow warbler:* for these see the nouns.

(1) **1622** 'MOURT' *Relation* 136 Plums of three sorts, with [? white] blacke and red, being almost as good as a Damsen. **1683** *Mass. H. S. Coll.* 4 Ser. V. 113 For the mouth, we take strawberry-leaves, . . . blackbrier leaves, sorrel,—of each, a like quantity boiled in spring water. **1698** G. THOMAS *Penna. & N.J.* 16 The several sorts of Wild Fruits, as excellent Grapes, Red, Black, White, Muscadel, and Fox. **1699** *Boston Rec.* VII. 237 A black elm [as a corner-tree]. **1705** BEVERLEY *Virginia* II. 14 The Black and the Murrey Plum . . . are small, and have much the same Relish with the Damasine. **1736** P. COLLINSON in Darlington *Memorials* (1849) 73 All the sorts of Ash, Sugar tree, Wild Roses, Black Beech, or Hornbeam. **1769** *Amer. Philos. Soc.* I. 190 The vines proper for these countries [of New England] are . . . the black Orleans, . . . the black Hamburgh, [etc.]. **1785** MARSHALL *Amer. Grove* 153 American black Lime, or Linden-Tree. **1786** WASHINGTON *Diaries* III. 132 That 3 pecks of the black spelt had been sowed yesterday in the drilled Corn. **1791** J. BREVARD *MS. Diary* 26 July (N.C. Univ.), The black clover is to be seen growing all over this country. **1814** *Lewis & Clark Exped.* I. 316 Abundant . . . too are red and black gooseberries. **1820** *Let. to Ebenezer Pettigrew* 10 April, You can have hundred Bushels of the black peas . . . at fifty cents. **1831** AUDUBON *Ornith. Biog.* I. 151 The male and female moving through the twigs of the Common Briar, usually called the Black Briar. **1840** DEWEY *Mass. Flowering Plants* 141 Black Knapweed [is] a coarse and troublesome weed . . . naturalized in a few places. . . . July and August. **1847** DARLINGTON *Weeds & Plants* 115 Black Apricot . . . is reputed to be a more certain fruit-bearer; but I have not found it so. *Ib.* 288 Black Purslane . . . has been suspected of being the cause of salivation, or slabbering, with which horses are often affected, in the latter part of summer. **1863** GRAY *Botany* p. xliv, Egyptian or Black Bean, cultivated for ornament, rarely for its beans, is a smooth twiner. **1876** BURROUGHS *Winter Sunshine* VII. 155 The ranker, hardier kinds [of apples], like the northern spy, the greening, or the black apple. **1892** APGAR *Trees Northern U.S.* 106 *Cratægus tomentosa,* Black or Pear Hawthorn; . . . wild in western New York, west and south. **1897** SUDWORTH *Arborescent Flora* 336 *Crescentia ovata,* . . . Black Calabash Tree (Fla.). **1901** MOHR *Plant Life Ala.* 799 *Brauneria purpurea,* Black Sampson, Purple Cone-flower. . . . Open woods and prairies.

(2) **1778** CARVER *Travels* 479 The Rattle Snake. There appears to be two species of this reptile; one of which is commonly termed the Black, and the other the Yellow. **1789** MORSE *Amer. Geog.* 287 Black turtle, crabs and oysters. **1791** J. LONG *Voyages* 160 The black water snake is used by the Indians when they go to war. **1806** LEWIS in *L. & Clark Exped.* (1905) V. i. 87 The black beatle usually called the tumble bug. **1832** WILLIAMSON *Maine* I. 172 Spiders: several species, such as black, gray, . . . jumping, rose Spiders. **1837** WILLIAMS *Florida* 105 [Of] the Rock Crab . . . the meat is stronger and less delicate than the Black Crab. **1842** *Nat. Hist. N.Y., Zoology* I. 116 The Moose . . . is known with us under the various names of *Flat-Horned Elk, Black Elk* [etc.]. *Ib.* IV. 203 *Catostomus elongatus.* The Missouri Sucker, Black Horse and Black Buffalo. *Ib.* 185 The Black Catfish, *Pimelodus atrarius,* . . . occurs commonly in Wappingers creek. **1868** *Amer. Naturalist* II. 115 The Spotted-cricket . . . appears [in New England] simultaneously with the Black-cricket (*Gryllus niger*). **1878** *Proc. U.S. Nat. Museum* I. 182 The Black Grouper (*Epinephelius nigritus*) of the Southern Coast. **1884** GOODE *Fisheries U.S.* I. 268 Black Candle-fish (*Anoplopoma fimbria*)—This species is known in Puget Sound by the name of 'Horse-mackerel.' At San Francisco it is usually called 'Candle-fish.'

(3) **1743** CATESBY *Carolina* App. p. xxxvii, The Coast of Virginia and Carolina in Winter [is visited by] . . . Black Duck, Black Flutterers, Whistlers. **1805** CLARK in *Lewis & C. Exped.* (1905) III. 139 A great number of Pelicons . . . and black Comerants. **1822** J. WOODS *English Prairie* 196 The birds are . . . paroquets, . . . wood-peckers, black-martins, and a few other small birds. **1839** PEABODY *Mass. Birds* 285 The Black Oriole, *Quiscalus baritus,* . . . probably rests here . . . on its annual migrations. **1844** *Nat. Hist. N.Y., Zoology* II. 300 The Black Tern, *Sterna nigra,* . . . appears to prefer the marshes of the interior. **1850** BROWNE *Poultry Yard* 70 The Black Bantam . . . is most pugnacious of its whole tribe. **1869** *Amer. Naturalist* III. 183 About the gardens [in California] are the House Finch . . . , the Black Pewee (*Sayornis nigricans*) [etc.]. *Ib.* VII. 634 The Black Snowbird breeds on the Graylock Range. **1878** *Proc. U.S. Nat. Museum* I. 398 *Phainopepla nitens,* Black Ptilogony, . . . [is a] common resident of the chaparral belt. **1889** *Cent.* 296 *Archibuteo sancti-johannis* is the black buzzard of America.

3. In adjectival compounds, as *black-backed, -bellied, -billed,* etc., used to form specific names.

Also less frequently in attributive compounds, as *black-breast* (plover), *black-cap* (warbler). For the more important examples of both types, see the separate entries below.

1813 MUHLENBERG *Cat. Plants* 49 Black-fruited Pear. **1839** AUDUBON *Ornith. Biography* V. 327 Black-footed albatross, *Diomedea nigripes.* **1840** DEWEY *Mass. Flowering Plants* 205 *Luzula melanocarpa,* Black-fruited Rush, has a black capsule. **1842** *Nat. Hist. N.Y., Zoology* IV. 205 The Black-nosed Dace. *Leuciscus atronasus.* **1843** TORREY *Flora N.Y.* II. 520 *Eleocharis melanocarpa,* . . . Black-fruited Eleocharis. **1844** *Nat. Hist. N.Y., Zoology* II. 227 The Black-crowned Night-Heron, or Quawk. **1858** BAIRD *Birds Pacific R. R.* 37 The Black-shouldered Hawk . . . [has] lesser wing coverts glossy black, which forms a large oblong patch from the shoulder. *Ib.* 133 *Trochilus Alexandri,* Black-chinned Humming Bird. *Ib.* 396 *Psaltriparus Melanotis,* Black-cheeked Tit. **1885** *Amer. Naturalist* Sept. 922 The long lost black-footed ferret, or prairie dog-hunter, of Western Kansas, whose rediscovery was recorded a few years since.

+**Black alder.** [BLACK *a.* 2.]

1. A deciduous berry-bearing shrub, *Ilex verticillata* (or *Prinos verticillatus*), the Virginia winterberry.

1805 LEWIS in *L. & Clark Exped.* (1905) III. 261 The large black alder. **1810** WILSON *Ornithology* II. 133 [The] Pine Finch . . . seeks the seeds of the black alder, on the borders of swamps, creeks and rivulets. **1814** BIDDLE *Lewis & Clark Exped.* II. 159 The stem of the black alder arrives to a great size. **1822** J. FOWLER *Journal* 143 In the bottoms along the cricks, cotten wood, black alder and willows. **1832** WILLIAMSON *Maine* I. 113 The black Alder is found in swamps; . . . the bark is bitter and a decoction of it is reputed to be a tonic. **1832** BROWNE *Sylva* 114 The Black Alder which is unknown in the Southern, and rare in the Middle States, is not uncommon in Massachusetts, New Hampshire, and Vermont. **1847** LOWELL *Indian-Summer Reverie* 84 Hard by, with coral beads, the prim black-alders shine. **1850** *New Eng. Farmer* II. 60 The Black Alder, and the Single Berry Black Alder, are handsome shrubs. **1891** *Cent.* 6943 The winterberry especially so named is *I. verticillata,* otherwise called *black alder.*

b. Attrib. with *bark* (see quotation).

1901 MOHR *Plant Life Ala.* 604 The bark [of *Ilex verticillata*] was officially recognized in earlier editions of the United States Pharmacopœia under the name of black alder bark.

2. (See quotation.)

1889 *Cent.* 134/1 In the eastern United States the common species are the smooth alder, *Alnus serrulata,* and the speckled alder, *A. incana.* Both are also known as black alder.

Black and tan. +**1.** *attrib.* Attended or frequented by blacks and whites. +**2.** (See quots.) — (1) **1890** *Why the Solid South?* 328 [Such] men . . . were shining exceptions to the rule of ignorance and depravity which pervaded what became memorable as the Black and Tan Convention. **1902** J. W. GARNER *Reconstruction in Miss.* 186 The reconstruction convention, locally known as the 'Black and Tan' convention. **1925** W. C. RECKLESS *Nat. Hist. Vice Areas in Chicago* 273 The so-called Black and Tan cabarets. **1928** H. ASBURY *Gangs of N.Y.* 18 The Black and Tan [a New York dive *c* 1875] . . . was largely frequented by Negroes, but the women were all white. (2) **1884** *Gringo & Greaser* 15 Feb. 1/2 The old black-and-tan bugaboo of miscegenation. **1914** MCLAUGHLIN & HART *Cycl. Govt.* I. 133/1 *Black and Tan Republicans.* Since about 1890 the Southern Republicans have been divided into the two factions of Lily Whites and Black and Tan. *Ib.,* The Black and Tans predominate in the counties with a large black population.

+**Black ash.** [BLACK *a.* 2.]

1. A species of ash (*Fraxinus nigra*), also called *basket-ash* and *hoop-ash.*

1673 *Essex Inst. Coll.* VI. 178/2 A forked Black ash which is also Osmund Trask his bound. **1688** *Maine Doc. Hist.* VI. 323 Another parcell of land . . . two rodd to a black Ash. **1728** *Boston Rec.* 222 We are of opinion That no Popler, Chestnut, Pine, Henlock [*sic*], Sassifax, Black ash, Basswood, or Ceder shall be corded up. **1765** J. BARTRAM *Journal* (1769) 6 Here and near the river's bank grows the . . . elm and black-ash, with most of the South-Carolina plants. **1785** MARSHALL *Amer. Grove* 51 *Fraxinus Nigra,* Black Ash. This kind grows in moist places. **1802** ELLICOTT *Journal* 284 Black-ash . . . not in great abundance, and becomes more scarce as you descend the river. **1821** NUTTALL *Trav. Arkansa* 229 Many bends indeed presented nothing but cypress and black ash. **1832** BROWNE *Sylva* 157 The black ash requires a moister soil than the white ash. **1848** *New Eng. Farmer* I. 5 Your hackmatack . . . combines strength with durability. . . . The alder, black ash, and cedar are its neighbors. *a*1862 THOREAU *Maine Woods* 308 The elm and black ash were very common along the lower and stiller parts of the streams. **1900** E. BRUNCKEN *N. Amer. Forests* 16 A few, like the black ash or bald cypress, will grow lustily on swamps wet the year through.

2. Attrib. with *ladder-pole, swamp, tree, tub.*

1737 J. HEMPSTEAD *Diary* 316, I cut a black ash ladder pole. **1779** *N.J. Archives* III. 272 Five hundred acres of land . . . ; a great part has been a black-ash swamp. **1872** *Vermont Bd. Agric. Rep.* I. 154 An experiment had been tried by a Cornwall farmer, packing butter in spruce, oak and black ash tubs. **1904** WALLER *Wood-carver* 114 The two black ash trees that grow by the fence.

Black back. +A species of alewife. — **1815** *Mass. H. S. Coll.* 2 Ser. IV. 294 The second [kind of alewife], less in size, and usually called 'black backs,' equally true to instinct, as invariably seek the Agawaam.

Black-backed, *a.* (See BLACK *a.* 3.)

1828 BONAPARTE *Synopsis* 362 The Black-backed Gull, *Larus marinus*, . . . inhabits both continents: not uncommon during winter in the middle states. **1839** PEABODY *Mass. Birds* 381 The Black-backed Gull, *Larus marinus*, . . . devours voraciously all sorts of food except vegetables. **1858** BAIRD *Birds Pacific R. R.* 98 *Picoides Arcticus.* Black Backed Three-toed Woodpecker. **1870** *Amer. Naturalist* III. 572 Black-backed three-toed woodpecker. . . . Mr. Scott took two specimens . . . of this northern species at Westfield in 1867. **1872** COUES *Birds* 312 Great Black-backed Gull. Saddle-back. Coffin-carrier. **1874** — *Birds N.W.* 368 Black-backed Eagle.

Black ball. +The disease of smut in wheat. — **1856** *Rep. Comm. Patents: Agric.* 186 The spores of parasitical fungi . . . may still be present in sufficient quantities to produce 'black-ball,' or 'smut,' in the succeeding crop.

+**Black balsam.** [BLACK *a.* 2.] ?The balsam fir, *Abies balsamea.* — **1883** ZEIGLER & GROSSCUP *Alleghanies* 57 Every grove is composed of both black and white balsams, and no single tree is widely separated from its opposite sex. **1888** C. D. WARNER *On Horseback* 50 The black balsam [of Car. or Va.] is neither a cheerful nor a picturesque tree.

+**Black bass.** [BLACK *a.* 2.]

1. A fish of either species of the genus *Micropterus*, valued as food.

1815 *Trans. Lit. & Phil. Soc. N.Y.* I. 146 Basse, is a Dutch word, signifying perch. Black, or Oswego, basse, a fine fish, like our black fish. **1817** S. BROWN *Western Gazetteer* 347 There are [in Lake Superior] . . . pike, red and white carp, black bass, herrings, &c. &c. **1819** EVANS *Pedestrious Tour* 181 In Lake Ontario are principally white fish and black bass. **1842** *Nat. Hist. N.Y., Zoology* IV. 28 The Black Fresh-Water Bass, *Centrarchus fasciatus*, . . . is common in the great lakes: . . . in this State . . . it is generally known under the name of Black Bass. **1847** LANMAN *Summer in Wilderness* 115 We happened to be in the vicinity of a deep hole, out of which we brought fine black-bass. **1857** HAMMOND *Northern Scenes* 337 The black bass of the St. Lawrence and Ontario, are the 'gamest' fish that swim. **1881** *Harper's Mag.* Sept. 511/2 The short dark form of the much-prized black bass. **1888** *Boston Journal* 17 People who like fish in Atlanta are eating . . . channel-cat and black bass. **1889** *Cent.* 571 Two species are known, the large-mouthed black-bass, *Micropterus salmoides*, . . . and the small-mouthed black-bass, *Micropterus dolomieu.* **1897** *Outing* Aug. 438/1 [To] the boys . . . large and small-mouth black bass were known as 'green' bass.

2. (See quotations.)

1855 BAIRD in *Smithsonian Rep.* 323 Black Bass, Sea-Bass, *Centropristes nigricans.* . . . The black fish, as an article of food, may be reckoned among the best of the fishes of the coast. **1889** *Cent.* 571 *Black-bass*, a local name, along portions of the Pacific coast of the United States, of a scorpænoid fish, *Sebastichthys melanops*, or black rock-fish. **1897** *Outing* Aug. 438/1 The boys called the rock-bass the 'black bass.'

+**Black bear.** [BLACK *a.* 2.] The common American bear (*Ursus americanus*), usually having a black coat and a tawny snout.

1805 LEWIS in *Ann. 9th Congress* 2 Sess. 1041 Skins of the small deer, black bear, some beaver. **1846** THORPE *Myst. Backwoods* 152 So tenacious of life is the common black bear, that it is frequently wounded in its most vital parts, and will still escape. **1854** MARCY *Expl. Red River* vi. 57 Several anecdotes . . . , concerning the habits of the black bear, would seem to entitle him to a higher position in the scale of animal instinct and sagacity than that of almost any other quadruped. **1870** KEIM *Sheridan's Troopers* 246 Game was evidently abundant, including black bear and panther. **1885** *Century Mag.* April 837 The black bear is not dangerous unless it be a she-bear with cubs.

Black-bellied, *a.* (See BLACK *a.* 3.)

1813 WILSON *Ornithology* VII. 41 Black-bellied Plover, *Charadrius apricarius*; . . . called by many gunners along the coast the Black-bellied Kildeer. *Ib.* IX. 79 Black-bellied Darter, or Snake-bird: *Plotus melanogaster.* **1814** MITCHILL *Fishes N.Y.* 390 Black-bellied Flounder. *Pleuronectes melanogaster.* **1869** *Amer. Naturalist* III. 231 The Golden, the Black-bellied, and the Ring Plover, are only spring and autumn visitants to our [New England] coast. **1874** COUES *Birds N.W.* 122 *Plectrophanes Ornatus*, Chestnut-collared Bunting; Black-bellied Longspur. *Ib.* 489 *Tringa Alpina* var. *Americana*, . . . Black-bellied or Red-breasted Sandpiper.

Black belt. [BLACK *a.* 1; BELT *n.* 2.]

+**1.** That portion of the southern states (see quot. 1905) in which the colored population is most numerous; the part of this included in one state or other area.

Thornton (*Suppl.*) also gives examples of the attrib. use with *county, country, Democrat* (1890).

1875 *Congress. Rec.* 8 Jan. 342/1 During this last campaign . . . I made a number of speeches in Georgia. I spoke in what is known as the 'Black Belt.' **1878** *Ib.* 17 Dec. 241/2 There is one region of country to which no man emigrates, and that is what is called the 'black belt,' that is where the negro population is very dense. **1890** FIELD *Bright Skies* 107 As I came up from the Gulf States, I had crossed the Black Belt—the portion of the South most densely populated by the black race. **1905** *N.Y. Ev. Post* 21 Nov. 3 The Black Belt has a curiously irregular shape. Extending from Virginia across North and South Carolina, Georgia, Alabama, to Mississippi and Southern Louisiana, it stretches a narrow arm across the river and up into Southern and central Arkansas. **1910** *Ib.* 14 Dec. 7 Snow Hill Institute, which has accomplished much for negro education, is located in Wilcox County, Ala., in what is known as the 'black belt' of the State.

2. A belt of fertile black soil in certain states, as Alabama and Mississippi.

1883 SMITH *Geol. Survey Ala.* 268 The Black Belt or Canebrake Region. This division of the prairie region is underlaid by the Rotten Limestone before described, and in its topography and soils shows considerable uniformity. *Ib.*, The canebrake or black belt. **1887** *Harper's Mag.* July 243 Alabama turns her poorest side to the railways. . . . But we will soon skirt the 'Black Belt,' which is full of rich plantations under scientific cultivation. **1888** GRIGSBY *Smoked Yank* x. (1891) 80, I had always supposed that the 'black belt' of Alabama was a region where black negroes were thicker than elsewhere. It is the region of black soil. **1901** B. T. WASHINGTON *Up from Slavery* 108 The term 'Black Belt,' so far as I can learn, . . . was first used to designate a part of the country which was distinguished by the colour of the soil.

Blackberried elder. +A shrub (*Sambucus Canadensis*) with black-purple berries. {In Eng. applied to *S. nigra*} — **1785** MARSHALL *Amer. Grove* 141 *Sambucus nigra*, American Black-berried Elder. This rises generally to the height of six or eight feet. **1813** MUHLENBERG *Cat. Plants* 33. **1821** *Jrnl. Science* III. 278 Floral . . . Calendar for Plainfield, Mass. . . . July 3. Blackberried elder . . . in blossom. **1874** GLISAN *Jrnl. Army Life* 480 We find . . . black berried alder [*sic*] and red elm along the tributary streams.

***Blackberry.**

+**1.** A single fruit of one or other of the American species of blackberry vine or bush (*Rubus*).

High, Low (etc.) *blackberry:* see these words. In the first quotation perhaps = black currant, as in Scotland and the north of England.

1654 JOHNSON *Wonder-W. Prov.* vi. 109* They . . . were entertain'd royally, with respect to the Indian manner, . . . boyling Puddings made of beaten corne, putting therein great store of black-berryes, somewhat like Currants. **1682** ASH *Carolina* 15 Strawberries, Rasberries, Billberries and Blackberries grow frequently up and down the Woods. **1709** LAWSON *Carolina* 105 The Black-Berries are bitterish, and not so palatable, as in England. **1743** CATESBY *Carolina* App. p. xxi, There are three or four kinds of blackberries in the woods, of better flavour than those in England. **1788** J. MAY *Journal & Lett.* 97 Blackberries of a very good quality are very plenty in the woods. **1824** J. DODDRIDGE *Notes* 85 Blackberries grew in abundance in those places where shortly before the settlement of the county the timber had been blown down. **1836** IRVING *Astoria* II. xxxiv. 207 A small beaver supplied them with a scanty meal, which they eked out with frozen blackberries, haws, and chokecherries. **1846** *Spirit of Times* (N.Y.) 11 July 229/1 Lived eight days on one poor hawk and three blackberries. **1868** MRS. WHITNEY *P. Strong* 36 In the August ripening there are blackberries and thimbleberries under the walls everywhere. **1874** GLISAN *Jrnl. Army Life* 490 Blackberries, both wild and cultivated, are abundant, large and delicious. **1891** FREEMAN *New Eng. Nun* 127 They could pick plenty of blackberries to eat with them along the road. **1907** C. C. ANDREWS *Recoll.* 163 It was in the mountains, where toward evening we had been allowed to go a short distance to pick blackberries.

***b.** In the phr. *as plenty* (or *thick*) *as blackberries.*

1834 DAVIS *Lett. J. Downing* 102 Where money is as plenty as blackberries. **1837** J. C. NEAL *Charcoal Sk.* 192 For constables are as thick as blackberries. **c1845** *Big Bear Ark.*, etc. 18 He represented them to be 'about as plenty as blackberries.' **1866** 'F. KIRKLAND' *Bk. Anecdotes* 302/1 The Yankee sharpshooters, armed with rifles of a long range, . . . were 'thick as blackberries' in the woods to the front. **1886** *N.Y. Critic* 16 Oct. 183 In the more favored Canadian region they are as plenty as blackberries.

2. As a generic name, or denoting the plant bearing the berry. Usually with *the.*

Also with specific terms, as *creeping, garden, running*, etc.: see these words.

1784 CUTLER in *Mem. Academy* I. 453 Blackberry. The fruit is well tasted. **1831** PECK *Guide* 139 The gooseberry, strawberry and blackberry grow wild and in great profusion. **1841** COOPER *Deerslayer* xxvii, As well might you expect to see . . . the blackberry growing on the pine. **1865** MRS. WHITNEY *Gayworthys* xxiii. 214 These dainties [include] . . . wine of elderberry, blackberry, and currant. **1883** ZEIGLER & GROSSCUP *Alleghanies* 63 A rail fence where every corner had been . . . left for nature to plant with the hazel and blackberry. **1901** MOHR *Plant Life Ala.* 540 The common blackberry of the market [is] used fresh and for preserves and for making cordial and wine.

b. A blackberry bush or blackberry vine.

1799 in F. Cuming *Western Tour* (1810) 325, I took a walk on the shore, and found it covered with . . . blackberries. **1850** C. MATHEWS *Money-penny* 178 The two blackberries were not visible. **1889** CABLE in *Century Mag.* Jan. 362/1 Presently Suzanne uttered a cry and recoiled with affright from a thicket of blackberries.

3. Attrib. with *brandy, cane, cordial,* etc.

1791 *Trans. Philos. Soc.* III. 75 Whether he had found . . . relief from the pain of the stone, from the Blackberry Jam, of which he took large quantities. **1828** NEAL *R. Dyer* 188 They . . . spend half their play-time in the blackberry-swamp. **1839** *S. Lit. Messenger* V. 753/2 She continued to attest . . . her housekeeping abilities, by blackberry cordial. **1840** C. MATHEWS *Politicians* III. v, Overpowering a man's understanding with detachments of roast-beef and blackberry-pudding. **1846** THORPE *Myst. Backwoods* 134 Mike himself was a good deal cut up with the Indian's knife; but he called his wounds blackberry scratches. **1861** JACKSON in M. A. Jackson *Life* 194, I received . . . a bottle of blackberry vinegar from the Misses B—. **1866** 'F. KIRKLAND' *Bk. Anecdotes* 463/1 Pastry—pea-meal pudding, blackberry sauce. . . . Dessert—white oak acorns; beech nuts; blackberry leaf tea. **1873** 'GAIL HAMILTON' *Twelve Miles* viii. 128 What do you care for blackberry-patches? **1876** HABBERTON *Jericho Road* xvi. 151 A blackberry cane that attached itself to his coat. **1898** ATHERTON *Californians* 131, I know so many remedies for a cold,—blackberry brandy, or currant wine. **1898** E. C. HALL *Aunt Jane* 6, I took the premium on my salt-risin' bread and sponge cake. . . . I ricollect 'twas in blackberry time. **1899** CHESNUTT *Wife of His Youth* 136 It occurred to her that her granddaddy would like a blackberry pudding for dinner.

Blackberry brier. The blackberry bush, or one of the prickly stems of this. — **1784** CUTLER in *Mem. Academy* I. 452 *Rubus*. . . . Small Bramble. Blackberry Brier. Dewberry. **1865** BOUDRYE *Fifth N.Y. Cavalry* 153 We sought the shelter of tall, thick-grown blackberry briars.

* **Blackberry bush.** A (or the) bush on which blackberries grow; a bramble-bush.

1785 MARSHALL *Amer. Grove* 137 *Rubus fruticosus.* Common Blackberry Bush. This rises generally (with several stalks from the same root) to the height of four or five feet. **1825** NEAL *Bro. Jonathan* I. 127 A loose irregular hedge of blackberry-bushes, and briar, which had come up of themselves. **1848** *Knickerb.* Sept. 226 Bruff scratched his shins with the blackberry bushes and brambles. **1855** 'P. PAXTON' *Capt. Priest* 164 He . . . was nearly lost amid a maze of underbrush and blackberry bushes. **1856** M. J. HOLMES *Rice Corner* i, The road . . . was skirted on either side with . . . flowering dogwood, blackberry bushes, and frost grapevines. **1870** R. H. DAVIS in *Scribner's Mo.* I. 168 On the top of the hill she found her mother engaged in active conflict with a blackberry-bush that had caught her . . . trimming.

Blackberrying, *vbl. n.* (and *pres. pple.*) Gathering blackberries. Also attrib. {1861–}

1828 *Yankee* July 227/1 It is new for city girls to go a black-berrying. **c1845** *Big Bear Ark.*, etc. 103 Who went blackberryin and huckleberryin with me? **1853** B. F. TAYLOR *Jan. & June* 231 Those 'black-berryings' in summer and snowy battles in winter. **1867** RICHARDSON *Beyond Mississippi* xi. 137 One delicate lady . . . who on blackberrying expeditions in the woods, frequently killed huge rattlesnakes. **1895** 'CRADDOCK' *Myst. Witch-Face Mt.* iii. 51, I war a-blackberrying, thar bein' only a few lef' yet.

Blackberry pie. A pie made with blackberries.

1749 HEMPSTEAD *Diary* 525 A blackberry pie after meat for Diner. **1863** [C. C. HOPLEY] *Life in South* II. 119 He told us that a countryman had come into camp with a quantity of 'blackberry pies.' Blackberries in America are a much finer fruit than those ripened by our faint English sun. **1864** NICHOLS *Amer. Life* II. 217 In the way of refreshments there was gingerbread, blackberry pies, and whisky. **1881** 'M. HARLAND' *Common Sense in Household* 355 Blackberry, Raspberry, and Plum Pies are made in the same manner [as the cherry pie].

+**Blackberry vine.** One of the prickly stems of a blackberry bush; a blackberry brier.

1839 HAWTHORNE *Note-books* I. 206 A ground-sparrow's nest in the slope of a bank . . . hidden by a blackberry-vine trailing over it. **1847** EMERSON *Poems* 64 Caught among the blackberry vines, Feeding on the Ethiops sweet, Pleasant fancies overtook me. **1868** BEECHER *Norwood* 15 At the upturned roots was a tangle of blackberry vines. **1880** *Harper's Mag.* Aug. 333/1 The undergrowth of blackberry vines and wild-rose bushes. **1893** POST *Harvard Stories* 221 Dick showed me a blackberry vine, or some sort of a bramble that ran across the face of the rock. **1905** *Bureau of Forestry Bul. No. 63,* 11 Grass, pigeon moss, . . . and trailing blackberry vines commonly make up the ground cover.

Blackberry wine. Wine made from blackberries. — **1805** *Pocumtuc Housewife* (1906) 30 [Recipe for] Blackberry Wine. **1854** *Penna. Agric. Rep.* 93 His blackberry, elderberry and currant wines, are excellent. **1888** HARGIS *Graded Cook Book* 475 Blackberry wine: To every gallon of berries, . . . [add] one quart of boiling water.

+**Black Betts.** [Cf. next.] Alcoholic liquor. — **1845** L. CRAWFORD *Hist. White Mts.* 45 There I was loaded . . . with a plenty of what some call 'Black Betts,' or 'O be joyful,' as it was the fashion in those days, to make use of this kind of stuff.

+**Black Betty.** *Obs. slang.* A spirit bottle. — **1821** DODDRIDGE *Backwoodsman & Dandy,* He that got first to the bride's house, got black betty. *Ib.*, The company stopt and every boy and girl, old and young, . . . must kiss black betty; that is to take a good slug of dram. **1824** — *Notes* 123 If any wanted to help himself to a dram, . . . he would call out 'Where is black Betty?' **1827** [see BETTY].

Black-billed, *a.* (See BLACK *a.* 3.) — **1811** WILSON *Ornithology* IV. 16 Black-billed cuckoo: *Cuculus erythrophthalma;* . . . fond of . . . creeks, feeding on small shell fish. **1839** PEABODY *Mass. Birds* 333 The Black-billed Cuckoo . . . is often found near the edge of water. **1869** *Amer. Naturalist* April 80 Black-billed Magpie (*Pica Hudsonica*) . . . continued common throughout the route westward [from the Bad Lands].

Black bindweed. {1794–} +The ivy-bindweed, *Polygonum convolvulus.* — **1843** TORREY *Flora N.Y.* II. 146 Black Bindweed . . . [grows in] cultivated grounds and sandy fields; very common. **1857** GRAY *Botany* 375 Black Bindweed . . . [grows on] cultivated and waste grounds; common. July, Aug. Nat. from Europe. **1901** MOHR *Plant Life Ala.* 486 Black Bind Weed . . . [grows] in waste places. . . . June to August; frequent. Annual.

Black birch. [BLACK *a.* 2.]

+**1.** The cherry birch (*Betula lenta*), or tree of an allied species.

1675 JOSSELYN *Two Voyages* 69 The Birch-tree is of two kinds, ordinary Birch, and black Birch. **1685** *Manchester Rec.* 20 From thence easterly to a black burch near the river. **1711** *Boston Rec.* 86 A blackburch on the Side of a Swamp. **1748** in Chalkley *Scotch-Irish Settlement Va.* III. 267 Corner to Wm. Worwick's land; black birch; black oak and thorn. **1785** MARSHALL *Amer. Grove* 18 *Betula nigra.* Black, or Sweet-Birch. . . . The natives often make their canoes of the bark of this tree. **1789** *Mass. H. S. Coll.* IV. 146 These lands abound with timber, and other necessary articles for ship building, of which it was thought deficient, until, by repeated experiments, *black birch* is found to answer the purpose. **1832** WILLIAMSON *Maine* I. 106 The black Birch is a very superiour wood for articles of household furniture; its heart is of a dark brown. **1850** [S. F. COOPER] *Rural Hours* 72 The black birch is faintly tinged with russet at first, the others are quite green. **1861** *Ill. Agric. Soc. Trans.* IV. 453 Mr. Phœnix recommended . . . the American Black and Yellow Birches. **1889** *Cent.* 560 Other prominent species [of birch include] . . . the black birch, *B. occidentalis,* of the Rocky Mountains and westward. **1897** SUDWORTH *Arborescent Flora* 141 *Betula nigra,* River Birch. . . . Common names [include] . . . Black Birch (Fla., Tenn., Tex., Iowa). **1904** WALLER *Wood-carver* 85, I've often wondered what became of it. It was a black birch, wasn't it?

2. Attrib. with *bough, bush, tree,* etc.

1721 *Braintree Rec.* 152 From thence we run to a black burch Tree by the side of a swamp. **1736** *Providence Rec.* IX. 72 West thirty two degrees south eighty six pole to a Black birch bush marked. **1828** SHERBURNE *Mem.* (1831) vii. 148, I discovered a very large black birch tree. **1867** 'T. LACKLAND' *Homespun* I. 32 The drops of rain fringe the black birch . . . boughs like lines of bells. **1906** F. LYNDE *Quickening* 279 The orchardist, . . . chewing a black birch twig as he makes the leisurely round of his line fence.

* **Blackbird.** +One or other of various birds belonging to the family *Icteridæ*, esp. the crow-blackbird or grackle (*Quiscalus purpureus*), or the marsh-blackbird.

Also with distinguishing terms as *Brewer's, crow, marsh, red-shouldered, red-wing(ed), rusty(-winged), swamp, yellow-headed black-bird* (q.v.).

1602 BRERETON *Discovery of N. Virginia* 12 We saw in the country . . . Doves, Sea-pies, Blacke-birds with carnation wings. **1612** SMITH *Map of Virginia* 15 There are [in Virginia] woosels or blackbirds with red shoulders, thrushes, and diuerse sorts of small birds, some red, some blew. **1643** WILLIAMS *Key* xv. 89 Blackbirds. Of this sort there be millions, which are great devourers of the Indian corne as soon as it appears out of the ground. **1659** *Dedham Rec.* IV. 7 The Constable . . . desbursed . . . the remaynder for killing black birds according to Towne order. **1668** *Watertown Rec.* 93 Whosoever kill any black-birds in our towne shall be pay[ed] by the towne. **1673** *Plymouth Rec.* I. 131 The Towne ordered that every man . . . shall procure twelve black birds heads, six of them by the first of June next and six of them by the first of October. **1697** *Portsmouth Rec.* 309 Every housholder in this Town of Portsmouth . . . shall kill twelve blackbirds between this and the tenth of May next. **1709** LAWSON *Carolina* 139 Black-Birds. Of these we have two sorts, which are the worst Vermine in America. They fly sometimes in such Flocks, that they destroy every thing before them. **1732** *N.H. Hist. Soc. Coll.* I. 163 [A penny per head voted] for the encouragement of killing of blackbirds within the township. **1778** CARVER *Travels* 473 The Blackbird. There are three sorts of birds in North America that bear this name. . . . The crow blackbird . . . is quite black, and of the same size and shape of those in Europe [etc]. **1786** FRENEAU *Poems* 86 Where the Blackbird roosts at night, In groves of half distinguish'd light. **1807** GASS *Journal* 103 There is in the bottoms a great quantity of spear-mint and currant bushes. Also multitudes of blackbirds. **1824** DODDRIDGE *Notes* 71 Crows and black birds have of late become very plenty. They were not natives of the wilderness. **1836** *S. Lit. Messenger* II. 358 They possess two qualities . . . in common with certain birds, such as rooks, crows, and blackbirds, that is, they are gregarious and marvellously noisy. **1852** MITCHELL *Dream Life* 201 The lazy black-birds skip after the loitering cow, watchful of the crickets, that her slow steps start to danger. **1858** VIELÉ *Following Drum* 135 Rows of blackbirds would perch on his sharp backbone, unmolested by the feeble switches of his scanty tail! **1880** *Harper's Mag.* June 69/1 The noisy blackbirds hold high carnival in the top of the old pine-tree. **1902** WISTER *Virginian* xxv. 295 He stepped to the door carefully, and saw the crowding blackbirds begin their walk. **1912** MRS. WOODROW *Sally Salt* 268 All about her . . . were great pumpkins, and a flock of blackbirds, glistening metallically, walked mincingly among them.

Black boy.

+1. Among the Indians of Maryland: (see quotation). *Obs.*

1635 *Relat. Maryland* v. 34 The Children live with their Parents; the Boyes untill they come to the full growth of men; then they are put into the number of Bow-men, and are called Black-boyes.

+2. One of those frontiersmen who, under the leadership of James Smith, acted to prevent trading with the Indians of Pennsylvania from 1763 to 1769.

The name was derived from the practice of blacking the face, in imitation of the Indians.

1769 *Penna. Gazette* 2 Nov., An extract of a letter from Bedford . . . relative to James Smith, as being apprehended on suspicion of being a black boy. *Ib.*, James Smith . . . is stiled the principal ring leader of the black boys. **1799** JAMES SMITH *Captivity* (1870) 119, I collected eighteen of my old black-boys, that I had seen tried in the Indian war. *Ib.* 122, etc. **1812** *Niles' Reg.* III. 57/2 Col. James Smith, . . . who was one of the Black boys, of the Sideling Hill expedition in Pennsylvania, . . . has gone to join our army.

3. A Negro.

1856 OLMSTED *Slave States* 141 The 'old Ab' was manned by one black boy, sixty years old.

+**Black brant.** [BLACK *a.* 2.] 1. The brant-goose, or a variety of this. 2. (See quotation.) — (1) **1858** BAIRD *Birds Pacific R.R.* 767 *Bernicla Nigricans*, Black Brant. . . . [Inhabits] Pacific coast of North America. Very rare on the Atlantic coast. **1869** Coues *Birds N.W.* 557 The Black Brant is said to come in immense flocks, and to afford more profitable sport [etc.]. (2) **1872** *Amer. Naturalist* July 401 Two other interesting birds found here are the double-crested cormorant and the white pelican, the former bearing the singular local name of 'black brant!'

+**Black-breast.** (See BLACK *a.* 3.) — **1844** *Nat. Hist. N.Y., Zoology* II. 240 This species [of sandpiper, *Tringa cinclus*] is common on the coast of New-York, which it reaches in April, and is then called Black-breast. **1856** *Spirit of Times* (N.Y.) 6 Sept. 9/2 Great sport is also to be had at curlew, black-breasts, red-breasted snipe. **1882** GODFREY *Nantucket* 157 In May, spring black-breast plover are at times numerous.

Black-breasted, *a.* (See BLACK *a.* 3.) — **1844** *Nat. Hist. N.Y., Zoology* II. 240 The Black-Breasted Sandpiper, *Tringa Cinclus*, . . . returns to us in the autumn, . . . and is then called Winter Snipe. **1874** COUES *Birds N.W.* 491 *Tringa Ptilocnemis*, Black-breasted Sandpiper. *Ib.* 288 *Sphyrapicus Thyroideus*, Black-breasted or Williamson's Woodpecker.

+**Black brush.** Some species of prickly shrub or bush. *N.J.* — **1856** *Spirit of Times* (N.Y.) 8 Nov. 161/1 The next day we worked . . . until our poor pointers were . . . cut up by the bog-grass and sharp *black brush.*

+**Black bug.** [BLACK *a.* 2.] A small black insect. (In quots. applied to species attacking turpentine trees and wheat.) — **1859** G. W. PERRY *Turpentine Farming* 103 Black Bug.—This insect is found as small as a hair up to its full-grown state, which is about the size of a common straw, and a quarter of an inch long. It will cut through the thickest kind of bark to the skin at any size, and commences to do so at the appearance of warm weather. **1861** *Ill. Agric. Soc. Trans.* IV. 316 When the black bug is plenty, you may expect the grub in three years.

+**Blackburnian,** *a.* and *n.* [f. the name of Mrs. *Blackburn*, 'an English lady.'] *Bl. warbler*, a North American warbler (*Dendroica blackburniæ*). Also absol. as *n.*

1783 LATHAM *Gen. Syn. Birds* II. II. 461. **1811** WILSON *Ornithology* III. 64 Blackburnian Warbler. *Sylvia Blackburniae.* . . . This is another scarce species in Pennsylvania, making its appearance here about the beginning of May; and again in September on its return. . . . Inhabits also the state of New York, from whence it was first sent to Europe. **1844** *Nat. Hist. N.Y., Zoology* II. 93 The Blackburnian Warbler . . . was first discovered by an English collector named Ashton Blackburn. **1868** *Amer. Naturalist* June 179 The Blackburnian Warbler (*Dendroica Blackburniae*) is one of the most beautiful of all the warblers, for none can show more pleasing colors than the orange of its throat and breast. **1892** TORREY *Foot-path Way* 6 We . . . soon were in the old forest, listening to bay-breasted warblers, Blackburnians, black-polls, and so on. *Ib.* 16 A Blackburnian warbler perched, as usual, at the very top of a tall spruce, his orange throat flashing fire as he faced the sun.

Black-cap. [BLACK *a.* 3.]

1. *attrib.* Of various birds: Having black feathers on the top or the crown of the head.

*c***1730** CATESBY *Carolina* I. 53 *Muscicapa nigrescens.* The Black-cap Flycatcher. . . . They feed on Flies and other Insects. They breed in Carolina. **1812** WILSON *Ornithology* VI. 80 Ash-Colored, or Black-Cap Hawk. *Falco Atricapillus.* . . . The Black-cap Hawk is twenty-one inches in length; . . . crown black. **1839** PEABODY *Mass. Birds* 288 The Black-cap Titmouse . . . is better known by the name of Chicadee. *Ib.* 297 The Green Black-Cap Flycatcher, *Muscicapa Wilsonii*, . . . is . . . common enough in Maine. **1844** *Nat. Hist. N.Y., Zoology* II. 60 The Black-Cap Tit . . . builds its nest usually in the hole of a squirrel or woodpecker. **1869** *Amer. Naturalist* III. 384 Black-cap Tit (*Parus atricapillus*), the commonest of our [Utica, N.Y.] winter birds. *Ib.* 480 May 20th I first saw [in Calif.] the . . . Black-cap Warbler (*Myiodioctes pusillus*). **1892** TORREY *Foot-path Way* 186 Wilson's black-cap warbler is one of the less common of our regular Massachusetts migrants.

b. The black-capped titmouse, *Parus atricapillus.*

1845 JUDD *Margaret* I. i. 3 A black-cap is seen to fly over it.

+2. The black raspberry. Also attrib.

1847 DARLINGTON *Weeds & Plants* 127 *Rubus occidentalis.* . . . Wild or Black Raspberry. Thimble-berry. Black Caps. **1862** *Rep. Comm. Patents: Agric.* 169 The common wild black raspberry, . . . the Black-cap, as it is familiarly called, is very largely grown for market. **1867** *Iowa Agric. Soc. Rep.* (1868) 194 A row of Black Cap raspberries . . . will well pay for the trouble of setting . . . them. **1871** *Ill. Agric. Soc. Trans.* VIII. 173 The principal varieties that are cultivated in the West are the Black-caps. **1901** MOHR *Plant Life Ala.* 541 *Rubus occidentalis*, Black Raspberry, . . . [grows in] Alabama; mountain region; rocky places. . . . This is the blackcap raspberry.

Black-capped, *a.* [BLACK *a.* 3.] = BLACK-CAP I.

1808 WILSON *Ornithology* I. 134 [The] Black-Capt Titmouse, *Parus Atricapillus*, . . . is one of our resident birds, active, noisy and restless. **1811** *Ib.* III. 103 [The] Green Black-Capt Flycatcher, *Muscicapa Pusilla*, . . . is an inhabitant of the swamps of the southern states. **1828** BONAPARTE *Synopsis* 29 The Ash-coloured Hawk. Black-capped Hawk. *Falco atricapillus. Ib.* 96 The White-breasted black-capped Nuthatch, *Sitta carolinensis*, . . . inhabits throughout North America. **1870** *Amer. Naturalist* IV. 543 In the depths of winter they and . . . the Black-capped Titmouse (*Parus atricapillus*), enliven the woods. **1874** COUES *Birds N.W.* 20 *Parus Atricapillus*, . . . Black-capped Chickadee. *Ib.* 232 *Myiodioctes Pusillus*, Green Black-capped Flycatcher. **1878** *Proc. U.S. Nat'l Museum* I. 407 *Myiodioctes pusillus*, (var.) *pileolata.*—Californian Black-capped Green Warbler. **1884** ROE *Nature's Story* iv, We all know the lively black-capped chickadees.

Black cat. [BLACK *a.* 2.]

+1. A large blackish marten (*Mustela pennanti*) of the northerly parts of N. America. Also called *black fox*, *fisher*, and *pekan.*

1791 *Mass. Laws* (1801) I. 509 No person . . . shall hereafter, in either of the months of June, July, August or September, . . . kill any Otter, Beaver, Minks, Sable or Martin, Fisher or Black-Cat [etc.]. **1832** WILLIAMSON *Maine* I. 135 The Black-Cat is much larger in size than the wild-cat, very ravenous and fierce, . . . called by the natives *Wooleneag.* **1842** *Nat. Hist. N.Y., Zoology* I. 31 The Fisher or Black Cat . . . is a large and powerful animal, standing nearly a foot from the ground. **1850** [S. F. COOPER] *Rural Hours* 234 Some of those animals whose furs are most valued, as the ermine and sable, are nocturnal; so is the black-cat, and the rare wolverine also. **1882** *Century Mag.* March 719/2 The black cat is the most successful cub slayer.

2. A black domestic cat. +In the phr. (*as*) *dark as a stack of black cats.*

1847 [ROBB] *Squatter Life* 65 All was dark as a stack of black cats.

Black cattle. a. Beef cattle, as distinguished from dairy cattle. {1725–} b. Cattle having a black hide.

1741 *Georgia H. S. Coll.* II. 110 Daniel Cannon . . . having lost fifty [hogs] and upwards, . . . besides black cattle. **1747** *Georgia Col. Rec.* VI. 190 [He] hath at this Time a considerable Stock of Horses and black Cattle. **1765** R. ROGERS *Acc. N. Amer.* 50 The produce of the soil [of N.H.] is chiefly Indian corn, rye . . . ; they also . . . breed black cattle. **1784** J. SMYTH *Tour U.S.* I. xxxviii. 291 Some few black cattle are also brought from this part of the frontiers, but in no considerable numbers. **1798** I. ALLEN *Hist. Vermont* 270 The breed of black cattle is daily improving. **1836** HOLLEY *Texas* iii. 53 It is considered to be fully equal to the level region for raising black cattle and hogs. **1856** *Spirit of Times* (N.Y.) 4 Oct. 81/1 There is a kind of black cattle with long glossy hair, the hides of which . . . are now occasionally seen in use as robes. **1918** *Journal of Agric. Research* 7 Oct. 22 The general experiences of those who have bred black cattle and fawn or red colored animals together.

Black cherry. [BLACK *a.* 2.]

+1. A species of cherry tree, *Prunus serotina.*

*c***1729** CATESBY *Carolina* I. 28 The Cluster'd Black Cherry . . . [grows] in the thick woods of Carolina; where these trees most abound. **1784** CUTLER in *Mem. Academy* I. 449 *Prunus.* . . . The Small Black Cherry. The tree is small and shrubby. **1802** J. DRAYTON *S. Carolina* 71 Common black cherry (*Prunus Virginica*) grows in the upper country, in dry strong soils. **1805** SIBLEY in *Ann. 9th Congress* 2 Sess. 1096 The top, a gravel loam, of considerable extent, on which grow large oaks, hickory, black cherry, and grape vines. **1827** *Western Monthly Rev.* I. 322 The leaves somewhat resemble those of the wild black cherry. **1850** *New Eng. Farmer* II. 187 Wadsworth . . . had three cows and two setters poisoned by eating the twigs of the black cherry. **1905** *Bureau of Forestry Bul. No.* 60, 20 About fifteen years ago some fine black cherry was lumbered on . . . Grandfather Mountain.

+2. The fruit of this. Also attrib. with *brandy.*

1720 SEWALL *Diary* III. 272 She gave me a Dram of Black-Cherry Brandy, and gave me a lump of the Sugar that was in it. *c***1730** CATESBY *Carolina* I. 75 The Bullet-Bush. . . . The berries . . . are globular, somewhat larger than a Black Cherry. **1784** CUTLER in *Mem. Academy* I. 449 The fruit [of the small black cherry] is not so well flavoured as the large black cherry. **1821** *Jrnl. Science* III. 281 Floral . . . Calendar for Plainfield, Mass. . . . September 6, . . . Black cherries ripe.

+**Black cherry tree.** =BLACK CHERRY 1. Also attrib.
1719 HEMPSTEAD *Diary* 86, I dug up a white grape vine . . . & set it . . . by a black Cherry tree. **1737** *Ib.* 316, I went out to my Island & fell 2 black Cherry Trees. **1821** *Jrnl. Science* III. 283 June 5, . . . Black cherry tree and white flowered oxalis in blossom. **1832** L. M. CHILD *Frugal Housewife* 28 Black cherry-tree bark, barberry bark, mustard-seed, . . . are excellent for the jaundice. **1844** *Knickerb.* XXIII. 442 The canal . . . leads to the old mills down to the right yonder, where you see that grove of black-cherry trees.

Black-coat. A depreciative term for a clergyman. {1627–}
1654 JOHNSON *Wonder-w. Prov.* 96, I'le bring you to a Woman that Preaches better Gospell then any of your black-coates that have been at the Ninneversity. **1701** *N.J. Archives* 1 Ser. II. 383 If they vote not ag[ain]st us, . . . we shall bring the Black Coats or Preists (as they [= Quakers] call them) & a militia. **1811** 'RED JACKET' in *Freemasons Mag.* (Phila.) March (1812) 462 We listened to the talk you delivered to us from the Council of Black Coats in New York. . . . [*Note.*] The appellation given to clergymen by the Indians. **1828** A. ROYALL *Black Book* II. 60 She is the only woman of accomplishments, I have met with, who favor those black coats [=clergymen]. *c***1836** CATLIN *Indians* II. 106 Red Jacket . . . alleging, that the 'black coats' (as he calls the clergymen) did more mischief than good [among the Indians]. **1870** EMERSON *Society & Sol.* ix. 197 The black-coats are good company only for black-coats.

+**Black cockade.** (See quotations.) — **1840** KENNEDY *Quodlibet* 48 What was generally, at that time, denominated and known by the appellation of the Old Federal Party, and what, in common parlance, has been sometimes scoffingly termed, The Black Cockade. *Ib.* 52 And so, Mr. Flam avers, is every one of his black cockade friends who have got an office. **1850** J. T. BUCKINGHAM *Newspaper Lit.* II. 73 The year 1798 has been signalized by the opponents of Adams's administration as the 'Era of the Black Cockade';—perhaps not inappropriately, as that badge was generally worn by the Federalists of Massachusetts.

+**Black code.** [tr. Fr. *code noir* (1685). Cf. BLACK *a.* 1 b.] A legal code applying to the colored population, esp. to that of a southern state before emancipation.
1840 *Picayune* 30 July 2/1 A black man . . . has been arrested and . . . [will] be tried before Judge Preval, under the Black Code.' **1852** *S. Lit. Messenger* XVIII. 634/2 In the Code Noir (Black Code) of Louisiana, under the head of Crimes . . . , it is laid down that [etc.]. **1866** GREGG *Life in Army* 238 To show the friends of freedom, how the South has degenerated . . . , I will present a synoptical view of the pertinently named Black Code of Louisiana. **1871** DE VERE 152 A word as hideous in sound as of import, connected with the negro, is the famous Black Code, a collection of laws first made by Bienville in Louisiana. . . . This system of laws . . . is still the authority in the parts of America settled by Spaniards. **1876** *Congress. Rec.* 9 Aug. 5347/2 The act which is known all over this country and all over the world as the 'black code' of South Carolina, a code that should disgrace every one of its authors. **1879** TOURGEE *Fool's Errand* xxi. 119 It was done in the very face of the 'Black Codes.' **1889** *Century Mag.* April 875/1 Connecticut repealed the 'black code.' From a few hundred in 1835, the antislavery societies rose to two thousand in 1837.

+**Black cohosh.** [BLACK *a.* 2.] =BLACK SNAKE-ROOT. — **1851** CIST *Cincinnati* 211 Jacob S. Merrel, Steam Drug mills, prepares . . . concentrated extracts of vegetable medical articles . . . such as . . . macrotin or black cohosh, leptandrin or black-root extracts. **1859** BARTLETT 91 Black Cohosh or Black Snake-root (*Cimicifuga racemosa*) [is] a well-known medicinal plant. **1884** *Rep. Commissioner Agric.* 135 Tall Snake-Root; Black Snake-root; Black Cohosh; . . . a tall herbaceous perennial, growing in rich woods in nearly all the wooded and mountainous districts.

Black-crested, *a.* (See BLACK *a.* 3.) — **1858** BAIRD *Birds Pacific R.R.* 385 *Lophophanes Atricristatus*, Black-crested Tit. **1881** *Amer. Naturalist* XV. 214 At Indio I likewise first noticed a bird which became more common and familiar in Arizona, viz., the black-crested fly-catcher.

Black currant. [BLACK *a.* 2.]
+**1.** The fruit of a wild American species of *Ribes*, or the shrub bearing it.
1675 JOSSELYN *Two Voyages* 20 Falling upon a piece of ground overgrown with bushes, called there black currence. . . . I set my piece against a stately Oake, with a resolution to fill my belly. **1705** BEVERLEY *Virginia* II. 15 There grow naturally Two Sorts of Currants, one red, and the other black, far more pleasant than those of the same Colour in England. **1778** CARVER *Travels* 30 There also grow around the Lake gooseberries, black currants, and an abundance of juniper. **1785** MARSHALL *Amer. Grove* 132 Pennsylvanian Black Currants. . . . The flowers grow in loose bunches, and are succeeded by oblong, black fruit when ripe. **1822** J. FOWLER *Journal* 143 In the bottoms . . . [grow] the chock cherry, black curren, [etc.]. **1836** LINCOLN *Bot.* 133 *Ribes floridum*, wild black-currant. **1843** TORREY *Flora N.Y.* I. 248 Wild Black Currant. . . . Borders of woods, fences, etc., sometimes in low grounds. **1857** GRAY *Botany* 137 Wild Black Currant . . . [grows in] woods. . . . Much like the Black Currant of the gardens, which the berries resemble in smell and flavor.

2. The cultivated European species, *Ribes nigrum.* {1768–}
1836 EATON *Botany* (ed. 7) 487 *Ribes nigrum*, black currant. . . . Berries black. **1847** DARLINGTON *Weeds & Plants* 137 Black Ribes, Black Currant, . . . affords a jelly which is a popular and useful remedy for sore throat, colds, &c. **1863** GRAY *Botany* p. lii, *R[ibes] nigrum*, Garden Black Currant, has black berries, like those of our *R. floridum.* **1900** WICKSON *Calif. Fruits* (ed. 3) 396 Black currants are but little grown, the market demand for them being very light.

+**Black cypress.** [BLACK *a.* 2.] A species of bald cypress, *Taxodium distichum.*
1810 MICHAUX *Arbres* I. 30 Cypress, . . . Bald Cypress, . . . [*ou*] Black *et* White Cypress. **1832** BROWNE *Sylva* 145 The others, of which the bark is browner and the wood heavier, more resinous, and of a duskier hue, are called Black Cypresses. **1853** [POYAS] *Peep into Past* 56 The 1st (St. Philip's) [church] . . . built in 1682 of black Cypress upon a brick foundation. **1884** SARGENT *Rep. Forests* 184 *Taxodium distichum.* . . . Bald Cypress. Black Cypress. **1901** MOHR *Plant Life Ala.* 325 *Taxodium distichum* . . . Black Cypress. . . . Most valuable timber tree, the largest of Atlantic North America.

+**Black dance.** (See quotation.) — **1778** CARVER *Travels* 270 The nations to the westward of the Mississippi, and on the borders of Lake Superior, still continue to make use of the Pawwaw or Black Dance. The people of the colonies tell a thousand ridiculous stories of the devil being raised in this dance by the Indians.

Black diamonds. {1849} 'Lumps, small or large, of anthracite coal' (B. '77). — **1842** *Niles' Nat. Reg.* 16 April 112 A fleet of boats laden with the black diamonds of the Alleghany. **1860** EMERSON *Conduct of Life, Power*, We may well call it [=coal] black diamonds. Every basket is power and civilization.

Black dolphin. {1784–} =BLACK FLY b. — **1849** *Rep. Comm. Patents: Agric.* (1850) 339 The latter seldom escape the attacks of another species, which, from their sooty color, are called the black-flies, black dolphins, or colliers.

Black drink. +A decoction of the leaves of the yaupon (*Ilex cassine*), formerly used by the Indians of the southern states as a ceremonial drink and as a medicine. Also attrib. with *ceremony, cup.*
1772 D. TAITT in *Travels Amer. Col.* 503, I went this morning to the Hot house and stayed there about two hours smoking and drinking black drink. *Ib.* 553 You had throwed him away in not sending him the rifle and Black drink Cups you had promised him. **1775** ROMANS *Florida* 95 When they drink it at their assemblies in the square, they call it black drink. **1797** B. HAWKINS *Letters* 55 They sent to inform me they would expect to see me in the morning at the ceremony of the black drink. **1826** FLINT *Recoll.* 142 Their religious ceremonial of roasting a dog, and, in some places, drinking what is called the 'black drink,' before they commence any important enterprize. **1842** E. A. HITCHCOCK *Journal* (1930) 114 One of the sheds is appropriated, or two parts of the three in which it is divided, to the preservation of articles used in the preparation and drinking of the 'black drink.' **1857** GRAY *Botany* 263 Cassena. Yaupon. . . . Leaves used for tea, as they were to make the celebrated black drink of the North Carolina Indians. **1906** Hodge *Handbook Indians* I. 150/2 Personal names referring to the black-drink ceremony were very common.

Black drum. [BLACK *a.* 2.] +The common drumfish, *Sciœna atra*, found along the Atlantic coast.
1709 LAWSON *Carolina* 156 Black Drums are . . . shap'd like a fat pig; they are . . . not so common with us as to the Northward. **1743** CATESBY *Carolina* App. p. xxxii, Common Names of . . . Sea Fish [of Carolina include] . . . Drum, black, Drum, red, Angel-fish. **1772** ROMANS in Phillips *Notes* (1924) 123 Black and Red Drum, this Last miscalled in this Country the Carp. **1814** MITCHILL *Fishes N.Y.* 409 The black drum . . . swims in numerous shoals in the shallow bays on the south side of Long-Island, where fishermen . . . can find them almost like a flock of sheep. **1842** *Nat. Hist. N.Y., Zoology* IV. 81 The Big Drum, *Pogonias chromis.* There are two strongly marked varieties: one dark brown, the Black Drum of the fishermen; . . . the other the Red Drum. **1884** GOODE *Aquat. Animals* 367 The adult is known as the 'Black Drum,' the young as the 'Striped Drum.'

Black duck. [BLACK *a.* 2.]
+**1.** The dusky duck, *Anas obscura.*
1637 MORTON *New Canaan* II. iv, Ducks there are of three kindes, pide Ducks, gray Ducks, and black Ducks in great abundance. **1743** CATESBY *Carolina* App. p. xxxvii, The Black Duck . . . is esteemed . . . for the goodness of its flesh, which never tastes fishy. **1792** *N.Y. State Soc. Arts* I. 34 Teal, and black-ducks, might probably be easily tamed, if attempts were judiciously made. **1794** *Mass. H. S. Coll.* III. 199 Sea fowl are plenty on the shores and in the bay; particularly the gannet, curlew, brant, black duck, sea duck, [etc.]. **1813** WILSON *Ornithology* VIII. 141 [The] Dusky Duck, *Anas Obscura*, . . . is generally known along the sea coast of New Jersey and the neighboring country by the name of the Black Duck, being the most common . . . of all those of its tribe that frequent the salt marshes. **1839** TOWNSEND *Narr.* v. 201 In the small streams near the bases of the hills, the common canvass-back duck, shoveller, and black duck, (*Anas obscura,*) were feeding their young. **1843** *Knickerb.* XXII. 33 Tertulian insisted upon my going with him to shoot black duck. **1844** *Nat. Hist. N.Y., Zoology* II. 344 The Black Duck, as it is universally called except in the books, is very abundant in this State. **1882** E. K. GODFREY *Nantucket* 158 Although the black duck breed here in considerable numbers, yet, when the first of September arrives, the birds are missing. **1893** POST *Harvard Stories* 43 Then I want half a black duck. Tell the cook it is for me.

+2. The surf duck or sea coot.

1785 PENNANT *Arctic Zoology* II. 556 Black Duck . . . extends to New York, and even to South Carolina. **1813** WILSON *Ornithology* VIII. 49 Black, or Surf Duck, *Anas perspicillata*, . . . is peculiar to America, and altogether confined to the shores and bays of the sea, particularly where the waves roll over the sandy beach. **1828** BONAPARTE *Synopsis* 389 The Black Duck . . . inhabits the Arctic regions of America, whence it migrates periodically in great numbers, all along the coasts of the union.

+3. *transf.* (See quotation.)

1767 HUTCHINSON *Hist. Mass.* (1795) II. iii. 267 From this or a like action, probably took rise a common expression among English soldiers and sometimes English hunters, who, when they have killed an Indian, make their boast of having killed a black duck.

+**Black eagle.** [BLACK *a.* 2.] The golden eagle. — **1693** CLAYTON *Acc. Va.* in *Phil. Trans.* XVII. 989 The Third is the Black Eagle, resembling most the *English* Eagle; they build their Nests . . . generally at the top of some tall old Tree . . . and the People fall the Tree generally when they take the young. **1874** COUES *Birds N.W.* 368 *Aquila chrysaetus*, Golden Eagle, . . . Black Eagle.

Black-eared, *a.* (See BLACK *a.* 3.) — **1818** MITCHILL in *Amer. Monthly Mag.* II. 247 Black eared Pond-Fish, *Labrus appendix.* **1842** *Nat. Hist. N.Y., Zoology* IV. 32 The Black-Eared Pondfish. *Pomotis appendix.* . . . Its broad appendix distinguishes it. **1877** *Field & Forest* II. 189 The common red and black-eared Sunfish.

Black-ears. +(See quotation.) — **1820** RAFINESQUE in *Western Rev.* II. 49 Big-ear Sunfish, *Icthelis megalotis*, . . . a fine species, called Red-belly, Black-ears, Black-tail Sunfish, &c. It lives in the Kentucky, Licking, and Sandy rivers, &c.

+**Blackee,** variant of BLACKIE. — **1824** *Nantucket Inquirer* 8 March (Th.), The blackee, turning round suddenly, gave him a severe blow. **1835** HOFFMAN *Winter in West* II. 252 A gang of dandy-looking blackees, each with an enormous cudgel. **1835** [INGRAHAM] *South-West* I. 102 The shining face of a blackee may be seen glistening from among his vegetables.

+**Black elder.** [BLACK *a.* 2.] A species of elder, *Sambucus canadensis.*

1807 GASS *Journal* 136 There are black elder, and bore-tree, pitch and spruce pine, all growing together on these mountains. **1818** *Jrnl. Science* I. 365 July 4. Black elder (*Sambucus canadensis*) in full flower. **1821** *Mass. H. S. Coll.* 2 Ser. IX. 155 Plants which are indigenous in the township of Middlebury [include] . . . *Sambucus canadensis*, Black Elder. **1832** WILLIAMSON *Maine* I. 107 The Elder is of two species, the black and red. *a***1862** THOREAU *Maine Woods* 310 The prevailing shrubs and small trees along the shore were: . . . *Sambucus Canadensis* (black elder), rose, . . . etc.

Blackey, variant of BLACKIE *n.*

Black eye.

+1. (?)The cow-pea, *Vigna sinensis.* (Cf. BLACK-EYED *a.* 1.)

1788 WASHINGTON *Diaries* III. 357 Finished planting of Pease here yesterday; . . . two . . . were of the large and early blackeye.

2. *fig.* **a.** A rebuff or set-back. **b.** A bad reputation or character.

1795 *Mass. Spy* 18 Feb. 4/2 Massachusetts beaten; and a black eye for Connecticut. **1876** *Congress. Rec.* 3 Feb. 854/1 Somebody was threatening to give a black eye to these 3.65 bonds. **1888** *Battle Creek Journal* 29 Feb., It is a subject for . . . congratulation that one gigantic monopoly was given a black eye, Thursday. **1892** *Congress. Rec.* App. 18 April 231/2 You, Mr. Chairman, gave that precedent a very black eye. **1904** W. H. SMITH *Promoters* xxii. 312 None of us must be cut up if his pet plan gets a black eye. **1907** M. C. HARRIS *Tents of Wickedness* 83 That's what I call making a fool of herself and getting a black eye that she'll never get rid of.

+3. *Black-eye sunfish:* (see quotation).

1819 *Western Rev.* I. 376 Blackeye Sunfish, *Icthelis melanops.* Vulgar names, blue-fish, black-eyes, sun-fish, blue-bass, &c.

Black-eyed, *a.* [BLACK *a.* 3.] {*a*1667–}

+1. Of a variety of pea: Having a black spot.

1743 *Md. Hist. Mag.* XX. 367 One Hundred Ninety One & half Bushels Black Eyed Pease in the sconer Annapolis. **1786** WASHINGTON *Diaries* III. 56 They proceed to sow the small black eyed pea and finished with them. **1797** IMLAY *Western Territory* (ed. 3) 240 Some kinds, such as the small white sort, . . . the white black-eyed pea, . . . and many others, are undoubtedly at least as good [as the European]. **1813** *Niles' Reg.* V. Add. A 7/2 The said cups or buckets were of a size large enough to carry about three grains of Indian corn, or five of black-eyed peas. **1841** *S. Lit. Messenger* VII. 775/1 The most substantial vegetables, . . . such as potatoes, cabbages, tomatoes, black-eyed peas, and the like. **1898** PAGE *Red Rock* 61 Her mênu, in which, corn-bread, dried fruit, black-eyed pease, and welcome figured as the principal dishes.

+2. *Black-eyed Susan.* **a.** One or other of several plants having flowers with a black or dark center.

1891 *Cent.* s.v. *Thunbergia*, The hardy annual *T. alata*, known locally by the name *black-eyed Susan* from its buff, orange, or white flowers with a purplish-black center. **1892** *Amer. Folk-Lore* V. 93 *Hibiscus trionum*, black-eyed Susan. N.H.; N.B. *Ib.* 98 *Rudbeckia hirta*, . . . black-eyed Susans. N. Vt.; Cape Cod. **1906** PITTMAN *Belle of Blue Grass C.* xvi. 241, I found all of the waste places now covered with black-eyed susans, and thus converted into veritable fields of the cloth of gold. **1918** *Maryland Laws* 949 The *Rudbeckia hirta* or Black-Eyed Susan . . . is hereby designated and adopted as the flower emblem of the State of Maryland. **1923** WYATT *Invis. Gods* 16 A clump or two of golden-rod, of black-eyed Susan and purple-panicled timothy.

b. 'Texan for a revolver' (F.).

Black-eyes. +The black-eye sunfish: see BLACK-EYE 3.

Black-face. [BLACK *a.* 1.] {1844–, of sheep}

+1. A Negro.

1704 S. KNIGHT *Journal* 40 Order the master to pay 40s to black face. **1899** CUSHMAN *Hist. Indians* 312 Do they not even now kick and strike us as they do their black-faces?

+2. An exaggerated make-up used by white (and sometimes black) performers of comic Negro parts. Usu. attrib.

1869 DUMONT *Benedict's Congress Songster* 9 Lew made his first bow before the public at the Metropolitan Theatre in a black face. **1895** *N.Y. Dramatic News* 16 Nov. 7/4 An old-time black-face actor died in Bellevue hospital. *Ib.* 14 Dec. 5/3 A decidedly . . . amusing black face musical sketch. **1897** *Chicago Tribune* 18 July 33/2 Black face comedians. **1917** J. F. DALY *Life A. Daly* 352 Emmet . . . organized the first black-face minstrel band.

+**Blackfeet,** *n. pl.* (Cf. BLACKFOOT.) [Transl. of Indian name *siksika*, from *siksinam* 'black,' and *ka*, root of *oqkatsh* 'foot'.] A tribe, or group of tribes, of Algonquian Indians, whose home was the northern plains east of the Rocky Mountains.

1813 *Niles' Reg.* IV. 265/2 Avoiding even the probability of seeing their enemies the Black Feet. **1835** *S. Lit. Messenger* I. 393 Sometime during the autumn of 1832, a young blood Indian (of the race of the Black-feet) arrived at the fort all alone. **1837** IRVING *Bonneville* II. iii. 40 The Blackfeet, in this affair, do not appear to have acted up to the character which has rendered them objects of such terror. **1845** DE SMET *Oregon Missions* (1847) 93 He indicated the day, the place, and the number of *Blackfeet* who would attack their camp. **1872** *Amer. Naturalist* VI. 180 The Indians . . . considered them [i.e., white people] . . . immortal, until they saw one of them killed by the Blackfeet. **1894** J. MOONEY *Siouan Tribes* 12 The Blackfeet, Cheyenne, and Arapaho have moved out from the Saskatchewan and Red river and occupied the plains. **1910** HODGE *Handbook* II. 570/2 The Blackfeet have been roving buffalo hunters, . . . shifting periodically from place to place.

attrib. **1835** HOFFMAN *Winter in West* II. 70 One of their number . . . had been . . . badly wounded in one encounter with the Blackfeet Indians. **1837** IRVING *Bonneville* II. xxiv. 234 The Blackfeet marauders discovered his cantonment. **1844** LEE & FROST *Oregon* xii. 127 Their perpetual wars with the Blackfeet Indians had prevented their increase. **1847** D. COYNER *Lost Trappers* 86 The Black-feet Indian is an embodiment of every quality that is offensive to the feelings of civilized man.

+**Black fin.** (See quotation.) — **1875** *Amer. Naturalist* IX. 135 This Indiana Argyrosomus appears to be quite distinct from the species found in Lake Michigan; i.e., the shallow-water 'herring' . . . and 'black fin' (*A. nigripennis*).

* **Black-fish.** [BLACK *a.* 2.]

+1. A small species of whale.

1688 SEWALL *Diary* I. 239 [We saw] Birds, and a number of Fishes called Bottle-noses. Some say they are Cow-fish, or Black-fish. **1793** *Mass. H. S. Coll.* III. 121 It would be curious indeed to a countryman, who lives at a distance from the sea, to be acquainted with the method of killing black-fish. Their size is from four to five tons weight, when full grown. **1809** KENDALL *Travels* II. 149 As we approached the mouth of the inlet, the vertebres of a small species of whale, here called *black-fish*, became frequent on the beach. **1832** WILLIAMSON *Maine* I. 164 The Black-fish . . . is shaped like a whale, and has a large fin upon the back. One of common size will yield half a dozen barrels of oil. **1869** 'MARK TWAIN' *Innocents Abroad* v. 48 We saw the usual sharks, blackfish, porpoises, &c., of course, and . . . large schools of Portuguese men-of-war. **1880** *Harper's Mag.* Sept. 504/1 [In Maine] the sinister shark is on thy track; the porpoise lunges from the right; dogfish, blue-fish, black-fish, from the left.

+2. The tautog.

1765 R. ROGERS *Acc. N. America* 68 In the sea adjacent to this island [L.I.] are sea-bass and black-fish in great plenty. **1775** BURNABY *Travels* 121 Fish [at R.I.] are in the greatest plenty and perfection, particularly the tataag or black-fish. **1789** MORSE *Amer. Geog.* 205 In the rivers and bays are plenty of sheeps-head, black-fish, herring [etc.]. **1807** *Mass. H. S. Coll.* 2 Ser. III. 57 The black fish, called the crow fish at Nantucket, is caught in the Sound and harbours in May and June. **1842** *Nat. Hist. N.Y., Zoology* IV. 176 The Common Black-fish, or Tautog, . . . is a well known and savory fish, affording equal pleasure to the angler and the epicure. *a***1846** *Quarter Race Ky.*, etc. 26, I once crossed over to Faulkner's island to fish for tautaugs, as the north-side people call black fish. **1854** SIMMS *Southward Ho* 471 One hurries home, bearing a string of blackfish. He has pleasant anticipations of a fry that night. **1878** *Harper's Mag.* Feb. 335/1 The tautog or black-fish . . . is taken with bait in large numbers both in summer and winter. **1897** *Outing* May 160/2 These fishermen, who think that God made blackfish for them exclusively, cut it [=a buoy] loose.

+3. The sea-bass.

1855 [see BLACK BASS 2]. **1867** *Common Sense Cook Book* 12 Rock-fish, or Striped Bass, Black fish, Halibut, Cod, . . . may be cooked like shad. **1886** *Nat. Museum Proc.* VIII. 202 *Perca atraria*, . . . Black Fish, . . . is the southern form of the sea bass. **1888** GOODE *Amer. Fishes* 39 The Sea Bass is also known south of Cape Hatteras as the 'Blackfish.'

+**Black flower.** *Obs.* The bunch-flower, *Melanthium Virginicum.* — **1817** S. BROWN *Western Gaz.* 322 Mr. Granger enumerates the following species [found in New Connecticut], viz.: . . . Seneca snake root, black flower, white hellebore, [etc.]. **1836** LINCOLN *Botany* App. 115 Black flower; . . . leaves long; . . . flowers become black.

Black fly. [BLACK *a.* 2.]

+**1.** An insect, *Simulium molestum*, found in northern wooded regions, annoying because of its painful bite.

1789 *Mass. H. S. Coll.* IV. 148 Objections have been made to these counties, on account of the black flies, and other insects. **1807** GASS *Journal* 230 A small black fly in this country . . . so torments our horses, that they can get no rest. **1845** JUDD *Margaret* II. vii. 309, I recollect when we was in the Provinces down to Arcady, where the Black Flies come out as thick as birds arter a thunder-storm. **1851** SPRINGER *Forest Life* 56 The black fly and the musquito can only reach the exposed parts of the body. **1854** HAMMOND *Hills, Lakes,* etc. 23 A smudge protected us from the musquitoes and black flies, and our slumbers were unbroken. **1869** W. MURRAY *Adventures* 56 Gnats . . . are much worse than the black fly or mosquito. **1870** *Amer. Naturalist* III. 399 The black-flies of the Lake Superior swamps . . . we had met on their own ground. **1876** *Fur, Fin, & Feather* Sept. 139 At Calais, Maine, last fall ruffed grouse were as thick as black-flies in August.

+**2.** The collier or dolphin fly, *Aphis fabæ.*

1849 [see BLACK DOLPHIN].

Blackfoot. Also †**Black-foot, black foot.**

+**1.** A diseased condition of a horse's hoof. *Obs.*

1820 *Plough Boy* I. 320 A correspondent has sent us the following receipt for curing a disease now prevalent among horses, called the black foot.

+**2.** An Indian of the Blackfeet tribe. (Cf. BLACKFEET.)

1837 IRVING *Bonneville* I. xii. 133 But the heart of a Blackfoot is a lie, and his tongue is a trap. If he says peace, it is to deceive. **1842** *S. Lit. Messenger* VIII. 584/1 Those pioneers, who . . . seek their pleasure in the hunt of a Blackfoot of the Rocky Mountains. **1845** DE SMET *Oregon Missions* (1847) 180 In speaking of the departed, a Black-Foot never says, such a one is dead. **1890** RYAN *Told in Hills* 187 Genesee bought her of a beast of a Blackfoot.

b. *attrib.* Belonging to the Blackfeet.

1805 LEWIS in *L. & C. Exped.* (1904) II. 98 The Minetares or black foot Indians who inhabit the country watered by the Suskashawan. **1814** BIDDLE *Lewis & Clark Exped.* II. 344 The Blackfoot Indians . . . are vicious and profligate rovers. **1836** IRVING *Astoria* I. xv. 246 Colter . . . [had] some knowledge of the Blackfoot language. **1837**—*Bonneville* I. xviii. 182 A band of braves enlisted . . . to penetrate into the Blackfoot country. **1845** DE SMET *Oregon Missions* (1847) 180 The Black-Foot heaven is a country composed of sandy hills. **a1918** G. STUART *On Frontier* I. 134 Here we built a corral, strong enough to bid defiance to the Blackfoot Indians.

+**Black fox.** [BLACK *a.* 2.]

1. A color variety of the red fox, *Vulpes fulvus.* Also attrib. with *skin.*

1602 BRERETON *Virginia* 13 Such commodities as we saw in the country . . . [include] Beares, . . . Luzernes, Blacke Foxes. **1616** SMITH *New England* 20 Of Beuers, Otters, Martins, Blacke Foxes, and Furres of price, may yearely be had 6 or 7000. **1633** *N.H. Doc. & Rec.* I. 73 Capt. Neale had . . . 17 martins, one black-fox skin. **a1656** BRADFORD *Hist.* 409 They sente . . . 200 otter skins, besids sundrie small furrs, as . . . black foxe skins, &c. **1675** JOSSELYN *Two Voyages* 82 The black Fox is of much esteem. **1752** GIST *Journals* 76 We killed a black Fox & two Bears. **1805** PARKINSON *Tour* 305 There are many kinds of . . . foxes (the flying fox, black, red, great grey, and little grey fox). **1826** GODMAN *Nat. Hist.* I. 276 The black fox is found throughout the northern parts of America, . . . where it is considered among the richest and most valuable of furs. **1851** GLISAN *Jrnl. Army Life* 89 Animals not usually eatable are . . . black fox [etc.]. **1892** HERRICK *Mammals Minn.* 81 Complete melanism gives us the Black or Silver-Gray Fox (*Vulpes argentatus*). In high latitudes often quite black save the tip of the tail. **1922** BARNES *Mammals of Utah* 120 Black Fox, Silver Fox, *Vulpes fulva argentata*, . . . [is] uniform lustrous black with a distinct white tip to the tail.

2. =BLACK CAT I. (*Cent.* '89.)

Black frost. a. A frost not accompanied by rime (in contrast to a *white* or *hoar frost*). **b.** A frost so severe that it blackens vegetation.

1709 LAWSON *Carolina* 156 The Blue-Fish . . . come (in the fall of the year) generally after there has been one black frost. **1787** WASHINGTON *Diaries* III. 198 This Morning there was a small white frost and a black one which was so severe as to stop brick laying. **1791** Imlay *Western Territory* (1797) 467 The severe weather generally sets in about the beginning of December, with sharp cold, black frosts, and falls of snow. **1829** SANDS *Writings* II. 124 A favorite myrtle which was menaced by . . . an unexpected black frost. **1833** SILLIMAN *Sugar Cane* 13 As soon as the black frosts are over, . . . the covering of the Cane . . . is reduced to one or two inches. **1842** *S. Lit. Messenger* VIII. 467/1 The weather was very cold, and we had generally black frosts. **1875** STOWE *We & our Neighbors* v. 52 Like the entrance of a black frost into a flower garden. **a1918** G. STUART *On Frontier* I. 175 Another deadly black frost last night.

Black gown. {1710} +A Jesuit missionary among the Indians of the West. — **1845** DE SMET *Oregon Missions* (1847) 106 Within the last four years, considerable numbers of these Indians were visited by the 'black-gowns.' **1847** *Ib.* Introd. 18 The savages assembled . . . to behold the 'black gowns' of whom so much had been said. **1872** *Amer. Naturalist* VI. 94 Everywhere among the western Indians the Jesuits were known by the name of Blackgowns. **1880** CABLE *Grandissimes* iv. 25 When the year 1682 saw a humble 'black gown' dragging and splashing his way with La Salle and Tonti, through the swamps of Louisiana, holding forth the crucifix and backed by French carbines.

+**Black grama.** [BLACK *a.* 2.] One of the two chief species of grama-grass. (See also quotation 1913.) — **1885** HAVARD *Flora W. & S. Texas* 528 Black Grama (*Bouteloua hirsuta*): hardly distinguishable from the last [=Blue Grama] in appearance and equally good. **1894** *Amer. Folk-Lore* VII. 104 *Bouteloua hirsuta*, . . . black grama grass. Neb. **1913** W. C. BARNES *Western Grazing Grounds* 49 Take black grama, for instance. Most stockmen apply this name to the ordinary grama which is most prevalent.

+**Black grass.** [BLACK *a.* 2.] A species of rush (*Juncus Gerardi* or *bulbosus*) growing in salt marshes.

1807 *Mass. H. S. Coll.* 2 Ser. III. 51 This black grass is frequently overflowed by the water of the ponds. **1837** COLMAN *Mass. Agric. Rep.* (1838) 18 Black-grass (deemed the best product) grows on the higher parts of the marsh, where it is only occasionally flooded by the tide. **1843** TORREY *Flora N.Y.* II. 330 Black Grass . . . [grows on] borders of creeks and ditches in salt marshes. **1857** GRAY *Botany* 483 *Juncus bulbosus*, Black Grass, . . . [grows on] salt marshes; common along the coast from New Jersey northward. **1871** DE VERE 408 Salt-Hay, a very important product of salt-marshes, is of two principal sorts, called *salt-grass* and *black-grass.*

+**Black growth.** (See quotations.) — **1814** *Mass. H. S. Coll.* 2 Ser. III. 121 The wood is chiefly black growth, viz. hemlock and spruce; but there is some rock maple and beach. **1851** JUDD *Margaret* (ed. 2) I. xvii. 136 Yet there are, what by a kind of provincial misnomer is called the black growth, pines and firs. **a1862** THOREAU *Maine Woods* 307 The fir has the darkest foliage, and, together with the spruce, makes a very dense 'black growth.'

+**Black grunts.** *local.* The black perch, *Lobotes surinamensis.* — **1814** MITCHILL *Fishes N.Y.* 419 Some of the fishermen call him black grunts.

Black guillemot. [BLACK *a.* 2.] The sea-pigeon (*Uria grylle*) of the North Atlantic. {1766–}

1828 BONAPARTE *Synopsis* 423 The Black Guillemot . . . [is] not uncommon during winter along the coasts of the United States. **1839** PEABODY *Mass. Birds* 399 The Black Guillemot, *Uria grylle*, . . . are sea-birds, . . . hardly ever going inland, except to breed. **1844** *Nat. Hist. N.Y., Zoology* II. 278 The Black Guillemot, as it appears occasionally on our coast during severe winters, is subject to great variations in the quantity of white or black in its plumage. **1868** *Amer. Naturalist* II. 162 The albinotic condition of the Black Guillemot must not be confounded with its normal winter plumage, which is nearly white.

+**Black gum, Blackgum.** (Also with hyphen.) [BLACK *a.* 2.]

1. A tree, *Nyssa multiflora*, etc., of the dogwood family, known for its tough wood and dark blue berries.

1709 LAWSON *Carolina* 95 Of the Black Gum there grows, with us, two sorts. . . . The one bears a black well-tasted Berry. . . . The Bears crop these trees for the Berries, which they mightily covet. *Ib.* 213 He added, that no wood or Tree could withstand it [*i.e.*, lightning], except the black Gum. **1784** J. SMYTH *Tour U.S.* I. xii. 93 On the inferior high land . . . , lofty pines . . . mixed with scrubby oaks and black-gum. **1817** *Ann. 14th Congress* 2 Sess. 1012 There may now be had from it . . . poplar, black and sweet gum, [etc.]. **1832** BROWNE *Sylva* 223 It is designated by the name of Black Gum, Yellow Gum and Sour Gum. *Ib.* 224 The black gum is much superior in size to the tupelo. **1835** [INGRAHAM] *South-West* II. 79 A fine though dusty road . . . bordered with noble forests of oak, black gum, etc. **1861** *Ill. Agric. Soc. Trans.* IV. 453 Mr. Freeman moved to recommend the Black and Sweet Gum for ornamental trees in South Illinois. **1885** 'CRADDOCK' *Prophet* xv. 281 The hickory trees . . . were a lustrous contrast to the sombre pine, . . . or the vivid crimson of the black-gum. **1901** MOHR *Plant Life Ala.* 32 Chestnut . . . and black gum (*Nyssa sylvatica*) are common. *Ib.* 117 The deciduous black gum (*Nyssa biflora*).

b. The berries of this tree.

1868 *Amer. Naturalist* II. 122 Only severe hunger will force him to eat the meat of a bear that has lapped black-gum.

2. A single tree of this genus.

1785 WASHINGTON *Diaries* II. 346 Planted all the . . . Blackgums in my Serpentine Walks. **1799** *Herald of Freedom* (Edenton, N.C.) 27 March, 640 acres in Dover pocosin, beginning at a black gum in gum swamp. **1835** *Survey of Property* Nov., in *Pettigrew P.* (N.C. Univ.), To an old Pine stump and a little black Gum on the east side of the old road. **1883** ZEIGLER & GROSSCUP *Alleghanies* 312 The stream flows through its center, overhung with oaks, . . . black gums, and a dozen other varieties of trees. **1906** F. LYNDE *Quickening* 161 Groves of oaks and hickories, tulip trees and sweet- and black-gums.

3. Attrib. with *berry, switch, tree.*

1737 BRICKELL *N. Carolina* 70 The Black Gum Tree, whereof there are two sorts. **1785** WASHINGTON *Diaries* II. 392 The black Gum Trees, . . . which put out leaf and looked well at first, are all dead. **1868** *Amer. Naturalist* II. 122 When mast is not plenty, they [*sc.* bears] lap black-gum berries (*Nyssa multiflora?*) **1872** Tourgee *Invisible Empire* (1880) viii. 444 One of them took a bundle of black-gum switches.

+**Black Harry.** (See quotations.) — **1814** MITCHILL *Fishes N.Y.* 416 Black harry, hannahills, and blue-fish, are some of the names by which he [=sea bass] is known. **1842** *Nat. Hist. N.Y., Zoology* IV. 25 The Black Sea Bass, *Centropristes nigricans*, . . . [is] sometimes called Blue-fish, Black Harry. **1888** GOODE *Amer. Fishes* 39 In the Middle States the Sea Bass is called . . . 'Black Harry.'

+**Black haw.** [BLACK *a.* 2.]

1. The fruit of a species of viburnum (*V. prunifolium*).

1709 LAWSON *Carolina* 107 A slender Tree . . . bears the black Haw, which People eat, and the Birds covet also. **1775** ADAIR *Indians* 361 Black haws grow here [*ante* 'Mississippi lands'] in clusters, free from prickles. **1824** DODDRIDGE *Notes* 86 Black haws grew on large bushes along the moist bottoms of small water courses. **1841** DRAKE *Tecumseh* 58 A part of his captors rambled around the place of their encampment in search of blackhaws. **1849** PRITTS *Border Life* 396 The squaws and boys were scattered out in the bottoms, hunting red haws, black haws, and hickory nuts. **1891** *Fur, Fin, & Feather* March 169 A bear likes wild plums and black haws.

2. The tree bearing this; or the southern species, *V. rufomentosum;* also, the sweet viburnum, *V. lentago.*

1785 MARSHALL *Amer. Grove* 160 *Viburnum prunifolium*, Black Haw. This I take to be our common, small black Haw. **1787** SARGENT in *Mem. Academy* II. I. 159 Black Haw, four inches diameter, and producing good fruit. **1818** SCHOOLCRAFT *Journal* 21 Our approach to a warmer climate is indicated by several green plants . . . and particularly by the black haw, which we have this day found in great perfection. **1848** E. BRYANT *California* v. 66 The growth of timber on the western bank of the river is . . . cotton-wood, the black-haw, (in bloom,) dog-wood. **1857** *Ill. Agric. Soc. Trans.* II. 631 Squirrels . . . are also very fond of the berries of the black-haw (*Viburnum lentago*). **1883** HALE *Woods & Timbers N.C.* 146 Black Haw [is] common in rather dry rich soils from the coast to the lower part of the Upper District. **1901** MOHR *Plant Life Ala.* 88 An undergrowth of dogwood, black haw, sourwood, and sumach.

attrib. **1872** EGGLESTON *End of World* xxi. 145 The black-haw bushes hung over the roadside. **1901** MOHR *Plant Life Ala.* 743 The bark . . . is used in medicine [as] 'black-haw bark.'

b. A single tree of this kind.

1785 WASHINGTON *Diaries* II. 346 Planted . . . all the black haws, all the large berried thorns. **1786** *Ib.* III. 34 Replaced the following trees in my Shrubberies: . . . 5 black haws. **1817** S. BROWN *Western Gaz.* 26 Spice wood, sassafras, black and white haws, . . . are common to the best soils.

+**Black hawk.** [BLACK *a.* 2.] A species of buzzard, *Archibuteo sancti-johannis*, in its melanistic phase.

1812 WILSON *Ornithology* VI. 82 [The] Black Hawk, *Falco niger*, . . . is . . . found most frequently along the marshy shores of our large rivers. *Ib.*, The Black Hawk . . . is a native of North America alone. **1844** *Nat. Hist. N.Y., Zoology* II. 8 The Rough-legged Buzzard, or Black Hawk, is a Northern species, rarely found beyond Carolina. **1857** *Rep. Comm. Patents: Agric.* 87 Dr. Hoy . . . observed . . . a flock of black-hawks, (*Archibuteo sancti-joannis,*) . . . to frequent a high knoll to which numerous meadow-mice had been driven by the inundation. **1869** *Amer. Naturalist* III. 228 The Black-hawk, by some supposed to be only a darker race of this species [=Rough-legged Buzzard], and once occasionally to be met with, is now unknown [in New England]. **1874** COUES *Birds N.W.* 362 The Black Hawk being simply the melanotic condition of the Rough-legged.

Black-head. {1658-}

+**1. a.** The greater or lesser scaup duck. **b.** The shoveler.

1781-2 JEFFERSON *Notes on Va.* (1788) 77 Black head. **1844** *Nat. Hist. N.Y., Zoology* II. 323 The Broadbill, *Fuligula Marila.* On the Chesapeake . . . it is called Black-head. . . . It is highly prized by epicures on this coast. **1848** *Knickerb.* XXXII. 331 Good enough duck, for the matter of that, seeing it be but a black-head; but, my city youngster, let's look at the shot you use. **1852** BAIRD in Stansbury *Gt. Salt Lake* 324 Little Black-head; Shuffler. Found across the continent; very common throughout the interior. **1874** COUES *Birds N.W.* 573, I frequently saw Black heads in Dakota and Montana, especially during the migrations. **1874** LONG *Wild-Fowl* 251 The black-heads tole the most readily, then the red-heads, next the canvas-backs, and the bald-pates rarely.

2. The black-headed gull.

1813 WILSON *Ornithology* IX. 90 The Black-heads may be seen . . . coursing along the river shores, gleaning up the refuse of the fishermen.

3. *attrib.* =BLACK-HEADED *a.*

1827 WILLIAMS *West Florida* 30 Black-head fly catcher. **1835** MARTIN *Descr. Virginia* 483 A great variety of ducks, as the canvass back, the red head shoveler, the black head shoveler. **1852** BAIRD in Stansbury *Gt. Salt Lake* 316 *Parus septentrionalis*, Black-head Titmouse, . . . is the largest of the American species of true Black-cap Titmice.

Black-headed, *a.* (BLACK *a.* 3.) {1774-}

1808 WILSON *Ornithology* I. 136 Having shot him . . . I found it to be the black-headed titmouse. **1813** *Ib.* IX. 90 The Black-headed Gull is the most beautiful and most sociable of its genus. **1823** E. JAMES *Exped.* I. 61 We were somewhat surprised to see here a flock of blackheaded terns. **1842** *Nat. Hist. N.Y., Zoology* IV. 210 The Black-headed Dace, *Leuciscus atromaculatus*, . . . varies much in size. **1855** *Knickerb.* XLVI. 222 In the marshes the . . . black-headed gull, and clapper-rail or mud-hen rear their young. **1856** CASSIN *N. Amer. Birds* pl. 24 The Black-headed Vireo, *Vireo atricapillus.* **1858** BAIRD *Birds Pacific R.R.* 337 *Vireo Atricapillus*, . . . Black-headed Flycatcher. *Ib.* 498 *Guiraca Melanocephala*, . . . Black-headed Grosbeak. **1869** *Amer. Naturalist* III. 75 The habits of the Black-headed grosbeak are quite different. *Ib.* 234 The Black-headed Gull, a southern and somewhat rare species. **1881** *Ib.* XV. 214 Another minute little bird . . . is the black-headed gnat-catcher (*Polioptila melanura*).

Black-heart. [BLACK *a.* 3 b.] Used attrib. and absol. to denote a dark variety of cultivated cherry.

(1) **1786** WASHINGTON *Diaries* III. 13 A black heart May cherry, grafted at the same time. **1836** HOLLEY *Texas* v. 88 The fruit [of the wild peach] resembles a large black-heart cherry. **1860** HOLMES *Professor* iii. 64 Joe, with his cheeks like lady apples and his eyes like black-heart cherries. **1868** CHANNING *Recoll. Newport* 160 The black-heart or mazard cherry, grown on the island, was as good as the best. *c***1870** BAGBY *Old Va. Gentleman* 258 He leaves my face as bloody as a black-heart cherry, just skinned.

(2) **1833** *Md. Hist. Mag.* XIII. 377 Here were . . . numerous trees of ripe cherries, black hearts and red hearts. **1852** *Knickerb.* XL. 190 When from aloft ox-hearts and black-hearts nodded . . . a kindly invitation. **1865** *Atlantic Mo.* XV. 437 Drinking the black-heart's wine.

Black-hearted, *a.* (See quot. 1872.) — **1872** *Vermont Bd. Agric. Rep.* I. 94 The lower branches are suffered to grow until of such size that a dry, dead knot is left when they are cut off, which sometimes kills the center of the tree, making it 'black-hearted.' **1874** *Ib.* II. 290 He expressed the opinion that all the trees that split from frost are black hearted, and that a tree not black hearted will not split from frost.

Black hellebore. [BLACK *a.* 2.] The Christmas rose, *Helleborus niger*, the rootstock of which is used in medicine. — **1778** CARVER *Travels* 511 Garlick, Wild Parsnips, Mandrakes, Hellebore White and Black. **1820** *Pharmacopoeia of U.S.* 231 Tincture of Black Hellebore. Take of Black hellebore sliced, four ounces [etc.]. **1836** EDWARD *Hist. Texas* ii. 43 The hellebore white and black, and Solomon's seal. **1890** *Cent.* 2779 Black hellebore, . . . common in gardens, . . . is a native of Europe.

+**Black hickory.** [BLACK *a.* 2.] One or other species of hickory, esp. the mockernut or pignut.

1787 W. SARGENT in *Mem. Acad.* II. I. 157 Black Hickory [of the Ohio valley], with a small thin shell nut. **1818** DARBY *Emigrant's Guide* 34 The most common timber trees found in the basin of the Mobile [include] . . . Black hickory, . . . Black walnut, . . . Black sugar maple. **1819** E. DANA *Geog. Sketches* 228 On a little stream called Petite Anse . . . are . . . more than 40 different species of trees, including the live oak, walnut, white and black hickory, and sweet gum. **1884** SARGENT *Rep. Forests* 134 *Carya tomentosa.* . . . Mocker Nut. Black Hickory. *Ib.*, *Carya porcina.* . . . Black Hickory. Switch-bud Hickory. **1897** SUDWORTH *Arborescent Flora* 114 *Hicoria alba*, Mockernut (Hickory), . . . [is also called] Black Hickory (Tex., Miss., La., Mo.). *Ib.* 115 *Hickoria glabra*, Pignut (Hickory) . . . [is also called] Black Hickory (Miss., La., Ark., Mo., Ind., Iowa).

***Black horehound.** The stinking horehound, *Ballota nigra*, characterized by dull purple flowers. — **1837** LINCOLN *Bot.* App. 81 Black horehound. **1840** DEWEY *Mass. Flowering Plants* 179 Black Horehound . . . [has an] offensive odor. **1857** GRAY *Botany* 318 Black Horehound . . . [grows in] waste places: . . . scarce. Adventitious from Europe. **1901** MOHR *Plant Life Ala.* 706 Black Hoarhound . . . [is] naturalized in New England, New York, and Pennsylvania.

Black horse (cavalry). +**1.** *S.E.* (See quotations.) *Obs.* **2.** A clique or coterie of members of a state legislature who exact money from the supporters of any measure by threatening its defeat. — **(1) 1862** in S. Cox *In Congress* (1865) 221 A cry was raised that the Black Horse, a formidable body of the rebel cavalry, . . . were charging upon us. **1867** L. BAKER *U.S. Secret Service* 52 The famous, and by the Union army much dreaded, black-horse cavalry. — **1866** *39th Congress 2 Sess.* 6 Sen. Ex. Doc. 55 Bands of men styling themselves 'Regulators,' 'Jayhawkers,' and 'Black-horse cavalry,' have infested different parts of the State [Ga.], committing the most fiendish and diabolical outrages on the freedmen. **(2) 1893** *Congress. Rec.* Dec. 453 Speaking for New Jersey, I know something of the black-horse cavalry force and the way they do their work at Trenton sometimes. I know . . . the way the black horse does business around about Legislatures. **1907** BROWN & STRAUSS *Dict. Politics* 45 Black Horse Cavalry . . . [are] more or less numerous in every legislative body. . . . Their number is frequently great enough to be of considerable influence.

+**Black huckleberry.** [BLACK *a.* 2.] The high-bush huckleberry, *Gaylussacia resinosa*, or its fruit.

1847 DARLINGTON *Weeds & Plants* 209 The plant which furnishes the larger share of the 'black huckleberries' of the northern markets. **1847** [see BLACK WHORTLEBERRY]. **1855** R. GLISAN *Jrnl. Army Life* (1874) 249 Berries afford them a good substitute for bread; such as the black-berry, . . . and red and black huckleberries. **1858** HOLMES *Autocrat* xii. 357 On lifting this, each boarder found a small heap of solemn black huckleberries. **1889** *Cent.* 2909/1 The common high-bush huckleberry or black huckleberry of the markets.

Blackie, Black(e)y. [f. BLACK *a.* 1. Cf. BLACKEE.] A Negro. {1815-}

(*a*) **1817** PAULDING *Lett. from South* I. 122, I worked hard for it, and sold many a poor d—l of a blacky to Carolina and Georgia to scrape it together. **1836** GILMAN *Recollections* xvi. 107, I was to visit some infirm negroes; as I advanced towards their houses, a little regiment of blackies . . . came marching toward me. **1840** R. BIRD *Robin Day* xxiii. 40 One of the blackies remained on watch over me, armed with a poker. **1852** BRISTED *Upper Ten Th.* ix. 226 No sign of a groom or a servant of any kind, but a number of boys, mostly blackies, about one to every ten horses. **1862** *Beaufort* (N.C.) *let.* in *N.Y. Tribune* 13 June, Helpless misses and masters, who have needed Blackie to pull on their stockings and brush their hair.

(*b*) **1825** WOODWORTH *Forest Rose* I. Finale, That's you my little blackey. Come—tune up. **1833** NEAL *Down-Easters* I. 95 What'll you have now sir, said another blackey, in passing our part of the table. **1842** HITCHCOCK *Journal* (1930) 201 It was plain that it did the blackey good, in her tattered dress and dirty as she was, to see a white man. **1846** M'KENNEY *Memories* I. 186 By the aid of this little old blackey, . . . I reached Tuscaloosa.

Black jack, blackjack. (Also with hyphen.)

*1. A leather jug for holding liquor. *Obs.* {Now *Hist.*}

1759 *Newport* (R.I.) *Mercury* 26 June 4/3 Imported . . . and to be sold by Jacob Richardson, . . . Tea-chests, Table-chests, Japan'd Waiters and Black Jacks. **1775** *Essex Inst. Coll.* L. 107 Last even[in]g we left a pint black jack ab[ou]t half full of water.

+2. =BLACK JACK OAK.

1786 WASHINGTON *Diaries* III. 131 The Wood part . . . is tolerably full of rail timber and wood (chiefly spanish Oak and black Jack). **1789** MORSE *Amer. Geog.* 415 A species of oak grows in the moist, gravelly soil, called Black Jack. It seldom grows larger than 8 or 9 inches diameter. **1796** B. HAWKINS *Letters* 51 The growth pine, not large, with blackjack and willow leaved hickory. **1814** PURSH *Flora Amer.* II. 629 *Quercus nigra.* . . . The Barren Oak or Black Jack of the Virginians is of low growth, especially in the more northern states. **1823** E. JAMES *Exped.* I. 54 The borders of this plain begin to be overrun with a humble growth of black jack and witch hazel. **1834** PECK *Gaz. Illinois* 24 Of oaks there are several species, as . . . the black jack, a dwarfish, knarled looking tree, excellent for fuel, but good for nothing else. **1843** N. BOONE *Journal* 226 On the ridge we passed a thicket of low blackjack. **1863** *Rep. Comm. Agric.* 62 High rolling sandy districts, which are sparsely covered with a stunted growth of 'black jack' and pine. **1882** WORTHEN *Econ. Geol. Illinois* II. 2 Stretches of upland, which are very sparsely timbered with post oak . . . and interspersed with black-jack. **1923** J. H. COOK *On Old Frontier* 6 This timber was a sort of scrub oak or blackjack.

attrib. **1775** ROMANS *Florida* 156 *Silk Grass* grows on the most barren sand hills of Florida (called black Jack ridges). **1818** DARBY *Emigrant's Guide* 86 Pine again occurs in great abundance interspersed with black-jack ridges [in s. Louisiana]. **1837** WILLIAMS *Florida* 126 The peninsula . . . is covered with pine and black jack timber. **1838** *S. Lit. Messenger* IV. 161 As hard as eight horses can eat the bark off a black jack tree. **1883** HALE *Woods N.C.* 215 The most abundant kinds being the red and black-jack varieties. **1903** A. ADAMS *Log of Cowboy* 193 The piney woods and black-jack sections . . . making classification [of cattle] easy. **1906** 'O. HENRY' *Four Million* 131, I must have that girl, dad, or this town is a blackjack swamp for evermore. *a***1909** — *Roads of Destiny* x. 165 A little town five miles off the railroad down in the black-jack country of Arkansas.

+b. A single tree of this species.

1775 ROMANS *Florida* 306 This morning we came past some good low grounds, and saw the first oaks of the kind called black jacks. **1791** WASHINGTON *Diaries* IV. 199 [The lands] appear to be of a thinner quality and more inclined to black Jacks. **1799** *Herald of Freedom* (Edenton, N.C.) 27 March, 460 acres joining the Onslow county line, beginning at a black jack. **1828** COOPER *Notions* II. 192 Charging at the battle of Eutaw into a thicket of black-jacks, (a sort of thorny bush,) where the English infantry had thrown themselves. **1834** H. J. NOTT *Novellettes* I. 180 A shot that would hardly knock a squirrel out of a black jack. **1862** *N.Y. Observer* 5 June, If the rebel troops become guerillas, they will have to be hung. The black-jacks will be far more fatal to them than yellow-jack to our troops. **1887** *Scribner's Mag.* May 571/2 A wood of black-oaks, or 'black-jacks.' **1896** J. C. HARRIS *Sister Jane* 221 It was a stunted black-jack.

fig. **1835** KENNEDY *Horse Shoe Robinson* II. xvii. 142 Stop your bawling, you stunted black-jack!

+c. The wood of this tree. Also attrib.

1802 B. HAWKINS *Letters* 426 One peck of blackjack ashes to a hide. **1879** TOURGEE *Fool's Errand* xv. 75 The wide fireplace, in which the dry hickory and black-jack was blazing brightly. **1880** *Harper's Mag.* Jan. 179/1 In the wide hearth a 'black-jack' fire was reflected in the brass andirons.

+3. *Fork-leaf, forked-leaf* or *-leaved black jack*, the turkey-oak, *Q. catesbæi.*

1883 SMITH *Geol. Survey Ala.* 293 Fork-leaf black-jack, turkey oak. **1884** SARGENT *Rep. Forests* 151 Turkey Oak. Scrub Oak. Forked-leaf Black Jack. **1894** *Amer. Folk-Lore* VII. 99 *Quercus Catesbæi*, . . . forked-leaved black jack, S.C. **1901** MOHR *Plant Life Ala.* 471 Forked-leaf Black Jack. . . . Small tree. Abundant in sandy pine barrens.

4. Sulphide of zinc; zinc-blende. {1747-}

1819 SCHOOLCRAFT *Mo. Lead Mines* 197 Accompanying the lead ores of several mines in Washington county . . . is found a sulphuret of zinc, which is the 'black jack' or 'mock lead' of miners. **1837** FEATHERSTONHAUGH *Canoe Voyage* II. 120 Galena . . . mixed up with what they call 'dry bones,' and 'black Jack.' *a***1877** Black Hills Corr. in *Phila. Times* (B.), We found . . . a large underlayer of black-jack of too poor a quality to work. **1878** BEADLE *Western Wilds* 485 'Black-jack,' or zinc blende, is a very troublesome combination.

+5. =BLACK STRAP.

1863 'E. KIRKE' *Southern Friends* ix. 112 'Then he does pray better for a little whiskey?' 'Yes; a mug of "black jack" helps him amazingly.' **1877** BARTLETT 45 *Black-Jack*, . . . rum sweetened with molasses. New England. **1880** *Scribner's Mo.* June 293/1 A father whose sole object in life was to vie with his neighbors in the consumption of 'black jack' and corn whisky.

+6. A species of dark-colored fish (cf. JACK *n.*)

1883 *Harper's Mag.* July 319/2 Mr. Jefferson . . . [displayed] an intimate knowledge of 'black-jack.' *Ib.*, Jefferson happened to ask him if he liked 'black jack' fishing.

+7. A short pliable shaft with a weighted head used as a bludgeon.

Hence in later use (1905-) as a verb: to strike with a blackjack.

1895 *Denver Times* 5 March 8/5 During the scuffle, Miss Alderfer . . . saw the 'black jack' up his sleeve, . . . and as a result, swore out the concealed weapons charge. **1897** *Boston Post* 17 Oct. 24 Kelly [was] in the act of striking cashier Stickney with a blackjack. **1903** A. H. LEWIS *The Boss* iii. 27 'What did he assault you with?' 'With a blackjack, your honor.'

+**Black jack oak.** Also **black-jack** or **blackjack oak.** A species of oak, *Quercus nigra* or *marylandica;* =prec. 2.

1782 JEFFERSON *Virginia* (1788) 62 Black jack oak. *Quercus aquatica.* **1792** IMLAY *Western Territory* 216 The more broken and hilly country . . . [produces] black jack oak, fir, &c. **1810** MICHAUX *Arbres* I. 24 Black jack oak, seul nom en usage dans les Etats meridionaux. **1819** E. DANA *Geog. Sketches* 222 Black jack oak, mixed with pine, grow along the Nezpique. **1832** BROWNE *Sylva* 269 The black jack oak is sometimes 30 feet high and 8 or 10 inches in diameter. **1843** TORREY *Flora N.Y.* II. 188 Black Jack Oak, . . . when of sufficient size, . . . is much esteemed for fuel. **1856** OLMSTED *Slave States* 383 The shrubby black-jack oak, with broad leaves, brown and dead, yet glossy, and reflecting the sun-beams. **1883** SMITH *Geol. Survey Ala.* 358 The prevailing timber is the longleaf pine, with its associates, black-jack and post oaks.

attrib. **1843** N. BOONE *Journal* 222 Came this afternoon to some black jack oak groves, some of the trees two feet in diameter.

+**Black Joke.** *Obs.* The name of some popular song. — **1799** JAMES SMITH *Acc. Captivity* 62 The following song was composed by Mr. George Campbell (an Irish gentleman . . .) and was frequently sung to the tune of the Black Joke. *c***1800** J. PLUMMER *Life & Adv.* 75, I had no hope . . . that I should get any favor from him by praying, any sooner than I should by spending the same time in singing the black joke, or whistling the tune of Wilkes's wriggle. **1855** SIMMS *Forayers* 391 There he was last night, lively as ever, sitting upon the end of a whiskey-barrel, and going 'the Black Joke' at race-horse speed.

+**Black knot.**

1. A fungoid disease of plum and cherry trees, producing black excrescences on the branches.

1851 BARRY *Fruit Garden* 364 The Plum Wart or Black Knot . . . originates . . . from an imperfect circulation of the sap, induced by violent changes of temperature. **1856** *Mich. Agric. Soc. Trans.* VII. 714 In the eastern States the black knot not only disfigures the trees, but is sapping their vitality. **1865-6** *Ill. Agric. Soc. Trans.* VI. 408, I am not prepared to suggest a remedy for the 'Black Knot,' or protecting fruit buds from the frost. **1868** G. BRACKETT *Farm Talk* 88 The common cherry and plum tree is affected with a parasitic disease, popularly known as the black-knot. **1890** *Cent.* 5821/3 *Sphæria morbosa*, the destructive black-knot of plum- and cherry-trees.

2. One of these excrescences.

1864 *Maine Ann. Agric. Rep.* 25 [He] had never seen a black knot on any of his trees, where he used salt.

+**Black land.** Land having a black soil. — **1803** *Mass. H. S. Coll.* IX. 140 On the low, or, what is commonly called, black land, the timber is chiefly white and Norway pine, spruce, and hemlock. **1873** BEADLE *Undevel. West* 794 The country . . . [is] about one-fifth in timber, alternating 'black lands' and sandy loam. **1883** SMITH *Geol. Survey Ala.* 269 The yield of seed-cotton of the fresh black land.

+**Black larch.** The tamarack or hackmatack.

1785 MARSHALL *Amer. Grove* 104 Black American Larch-Tree. This is also a variety differing in having dark coloured cones. **1803** LAMBERT *Descr. Genus Pinus* 56 Black Larch, *P[inus] pendula*, . . . shews itself only in the cold mountainous parts of North America. **1828** BECK in *Trans. Albany Inst.* I. 18 As we reach Pennsylvania, New-Jersey, and New-York, . . . the *Pinus rigida*, [etc.] . . . rise to their native height on the lowlands. The same may be said of the . . . *P. pendula* (red and black larch). **1837** COLMAN *Mass. Agric. Rep.* (1838) 116 The Larch referred to in the text . . . resembles our Hackmetack or Black Larch, (*Larix Pendula,*) in the value of its timber and bark. **1847** DARLINGTON *Weeds & Plants* 339 American or Black Larch. . . . A slender tree, 20–50 feet high. . . . Canada to Virginia. **1884** SARGENT *Rep. Forests* 215 *Larix Americana*. . . . Larch. Black Larch. Tamarack. Hackmatack. **1897** SUDWORTH *Arborescent Flora* 32 *Larix laricina*, Tamarack. . . . Common names [include] . . . Black Larch (Minn.).

+**Black law(s).** [BLACK *a.* 1 b.] A law or laws regulating or forbidding the admission of colored persons to a state or other area.

1852 T. HUGHES in J. Ludlow *Hist. U.S.* 342 The Topeka constitution . . . contained one article . . . which must not be passed over. I mean that commonly known as the 'black law,' by which coloured people were excluded from the territory. **1854** Hambleton *H. A. Wise* 403 So far as the repeal of the black laws is concerned, . . . by which bonds were required for the good behavior of every colored person coming into the state [=Ohio]. **1856** *S. Lit. Messenger* XXII. 8/1 Witness the Black laws of Indiana, Illinois, Ohio, and Delaware. **1867** Fleming *Hist. Reconstruction* II. 18 In the Western States . . . what are called the 'Black Laws' exist, which forbid colored people to live there. **1887** *Courier-Journal* 17 Feb. 5 The [Ohio] Legislature today passed a bill repealing the black laws. **1888** M. LANE in *America* 20 Sept. 16 *Black Laws* . . . were state laws, such as were in Illinois, by which persons could bring slaves within the territory and hold them as indentured servants.

attrib. **1877** *Kansas Hist. Coll.* VI. 295 None but democrats, whigs of the old school, black-law men, could be fellowshipped.

***Black lead, Blacklead.** (Also with hyphen.) Plumbago, graphite.

1634 WOOD *New Eng. Prospect* I. v. 14 The Indians informe us that they can leade us to the mountaines of blacke Lead. **1637** MORTON *New Canaan* II. vi, Black Leade I have likewise found very good, which the Salvages use to paint their faces with. **1643** *New Eng. First Fruits* 22 Black-lead . . . for the improving of which, we are now about to carry over Servants and instruments with us. **1674** J. HULL in *Amer. Antiq. Soc. Trans.* (1857) III. 127 Unless you and any of the partners will join me in sending home the black lead, either to England or Holland. **1789** MORSE *Amer. Geog.* 370 Considerable quantities of black lead are taken occasionally for use. **1806** *Murphy Papers* (N.C.H.S.) I. 6, I spoke again to Guthrie about the black-lead; he promised to send it up by the first Waggon passing up this way. **1875** KNIGHT 1010/1 Graphite . . . is well known in the mechanic arts as plumbago and black-lead. **1883** *Amer. Cycl.* XIII. 246 Lead pencils, so called because made of graphite or black lead.

b. Attrib. with *crucible, mine, pot.*

1658 *Mass. H. S. Coll.* 4 Ser. VII. 405 When Matthew Grissel comes vnto the Blacke Lead mine, if hee bee willinge still to digge it vpon thirdes, & to let us haue his parte of Leade, wee will allow him. **1715** *Mass. H. Repr. Journals* I. 21 To lay out Four Miles Square of land which shall include the Black Lead Mines. **1744** FRANKLIN *Acc. Fire-Places* 36 Get some Powder of Black-Lead, (broken Bits of Black-Lead Crucibles from the Silversmiths, pounded fine, will do). **1761** H. M. Brooks *Gleanings* 26 Crucibles and Black Led Potts. **1785** *Deane Papers* 214 The Affair of the Black Lead Mine. **1883** *Amer. Cycl.* VIII. 165/1 Mansell's black-lead mine near the same locality [=Attleboro, Pa.].

Blackleg, black leg, *n.* (Also with hyphen.)

1. A swindler or sharper; a professional gambler. {1771–1857}

In common use 1835–1870.

1786 ASBURY *Journal* I. 506 We lodged where there were a set of gamblers. . . . We left these blacklegs early next morning. **1817** PAULDING *Lett. from South* I. 39 As it is not customary to dress fine at the Springs or elsewhere: those who do, are apt to be taken for Black Legs, or Horse Jockeys. **1833** *Niles' Reg.* XLIV. 370/1 Allied gangs of 'black legs,' and other sharpers, including counterfeiters of bank notes, were well known to exist. **1845** S. Smith *Theatr. Apprent.* 147 A slight suspicion had crossed my mind that some of our card party might possibly be blacklegs—in other words, gamblers. **1852** *Harper's Mag.* V. 535/2 Mr. Randolph . . . hated the very sight of a gambler, or, as he always phrased them, 'black-legs.' **1866** RICHARDSON *Secret Service* iv. 67 There were some professional slave dealers, and many nondescript who would represent the various shades between loafers and blacklegs in any free community. **1872** EGGLESTON *End of World* xvi. 113, I admonish you not to believe a blackleg. **1884** SWEET & KNOX *Through Texas* xxv. 339 He takes steps toward future distinction as a blackleg by gambling with marbles.

2. +**a.** Scurvy.

1847 RUXTON *Adv. Rocky Mts.* (1848) 279 The wagons now returning were filled with sick men suffering from attacks of scurvy, . . . called 'Black Leg' in Missouri.

b. A disease in cattle affecting the legs. {*a*1722–}

1858 FLINT *Milch Cows*, etc. 281 Typhoid fever . . . is sometimes followed by diseases known as black tongue, black leg, or quarter evil. **1868** *Rep. Comm. Agric.* (1869) 36 Black tongue, black leg, hollow horn, . . . are reported, but not to the usual extent. **1913** BARNES *Western Grazing Grounds* 286 There are but three diseases among western range cattle which can be considered general: Big jaw (actinomycosis), bloating (tympanites) and black-leg.

Blackleg, *v. intr.* To act as a blackleg {1865–} or a 'scab' during a strike. — **1888** in Farmer *Americanisms* (1889) 58 Knights of Labor who had determined to blackleg it, regardless of the jeers and threats of their companions.

Black-legged, *a.* (Cf. BLACKLEG *n.* 1.) — **1834** H. J. NOTT *Novellettes* I. 42, I was able to inform him that his new acquaintance was Lee, the famous Virginian sportsman, as they politely term such black-legged cattle. *a***1854** TATNALL in Benton *30 Years' View* I. 73/1, I applied to the administration the epithet, 'puritanic-diplomatic-black-legged administration.'

+**Black-liner.** [BLACK *n.* 2.] One who in drawing the color line gives an advantage or preference to the Negro. — **1875** *44th Congress 2 Sess.* 45 Sen. Misc. Doc. 583 Warren County . . . [in an election] made a clean sweep of the county officers for the black-liners, and to-day scores of their ignorant dupes lie buried in the ditches.

Black list, black-list, *n.* {1692–} +An employers' list of undesirable workmen, esp. on account of their being trade-unionists or agitators. — **1888** *Atlantic Mo.* Nov. 611/2 Worn out with the long struggle with poverty, he had got his name taken off from the black-list. **1888** ALEX. JOHNSTON in *Encycl. Brit.* XXIII. 786/2 The half-understood, but heartily dreaded, weapon known as the 'black list,' by which combinations of employers, especially of corporations, drove employees inclined to 'agitation' out of employment. **1895** *Chicago Strike of 1894* 49 The Illinois Central and Rock Island . . . have a blacklist; . . . they do exchange these and blacklist people as between each other. **1921** *Public Opinion & Steel Strike* 7 Some 600 under-cover reports were on file, together with copies of contracts with the agencies, blacklists, etc.

Black-list, *v.* [f. prec.] +*tr.* To place on a black list (of workmen). Also *black-listed* ppl. a., *black-listing* vbl. n. — **1884** *Milnor* (Dakota) *Teller* 30 July, All the clerks making application [for work at other stores] were spotted and blacklisted and many have been dismissed. **1888** *Atlantic Mo.* Nov. 608/1 The manufacturers . . . had retaliated for some 'labor troubles' . . . by 'black-listing' about thirty men. *Ib.*, Mr. H. informed us that he was a 'black-listed' man. *Ib.* 608/2 The increase of evil in the world thus resulting from the black-listing scheme. **1889** Salmons *Burlington Strike* 454 The company will not follow up, black list, or . . . proscribe those who were concerned in the strike. **1895** [see BLACK LIST *n.*]. **1921** *Public Opinion & Steel Strike* 8 Undercover men's reports may blacklist a man or land him in jail.

+**Black locust.** [BLACK *a.* 2.]

1. The common locust or false acacia, *Robinia pseudacacia*, valued for its wood and as an ornamental shade tree.

1787 W. SARGENT in *Mem. Acad.* II. I. 157 The Black Locust . . . grows from six inches to two feet and a half diameter. **1789** MORSE *Amer. Geog.* 404 The soil is deep and black, and the natural growth . . . black locust, poplar. **1827** DRAKE & MANSF. *Cincinnati* x. 73 The black locust, which is here so abundant and excellent, is not found in the neighborhood of Pittsburgh. **1831** PECK *Guide* 128 The black locust, a native growth of Ohio and Kentucky, may be raised [in Ill.] from the seed. **1838** FLAGG *Far West* II. 184 An enormous black-locust on the right of the pathway. **1849** [CHAMBERLAIN] *Indiana Gazetteer* 16 The black locust is abundant near the Ohio River, but not found in the interior until it is cultivated, but then grows well in dry, rich soil. **1887** *Scribner's Mag.* May 572/1 Some species [of forest trees]—as . . . the black-locust—are extensively subjected to insect enemies. **1901** MOHR *Plant Life Ala.* 77 On its flanks [Lookout Mt.] the black locust (*Robinia pseudacacia*) is found, one of the few localities in Alabama where it can be considered to be indigenous.

attrib. **1848** J. S. ROBINSON *Santa Fé Exped.* 18 Black locust and cottonwood timber abounds.

b. The wood of this tree.

1787 W. SARGENT in *Mem. Acad.* II. I. 157 The Black Locust is a very durable wood, and in use for pins and gate posts. **1820** FLINT *Lett. from Amer.* 229 The black locust is strong, heavy, not much subject to warping, and resists the effects of the weather for a long period of time. **1846** THORPE *Myst. Backwoods* 38–9 The implements of the arrow-fisherman are a strong bow, five or six feet long, made of black locust or of cedar, (the latter being preferred).

2. The honey-locust, *Gleditsia triacanthos.*

1884 SARGENT *Rep. Forests* 59 Honey Locust. Black Locust. Three-thorned Acacia.

+**Black mammy.** [BLACK *a.* 1.] A colored nurse. — **1886** B. P. POORE *Reminisc.* I. 538 He loved his 'old black mammy,' and she loved him. **1901** R. D. EVANS *Sailor's Log* i. 3 Like most Southern children, I was brought up and cared for by a black 'mammy.' **1904** F. LYNDE *Grafters* vi. 81 Old Chloe . . . was my black mammy.

***Black man, †Blackman.** [BLACK *a.* 1.]

1. The devil. *Obs.*

1692 *Witchcraft Cases* 159 The afflicted persons said, the Black Man whispered to her in the Assembly. **1702** C. MATHER *Magnalia* (1853) I. 206 The spectres under the command of that *blackman*, as they called him, would apply themselves to torture them. [**1865** *Atlantic Mo.* XV. 2 The Indian medicine-men . . . were supposed to draw their knowledge from no gracious source, the Black Man himself being the principal professor in their medical school.]

2. A Negro.

(*a*) **1775** J. HABERSHAM *Letters* 241, I hope that your Blackman David may be blessed, as he seems to be very anxious to be instrumental of good to your Ladyships Negroes. **1802** *Charlestown Land Rec.* 250 From

William Smiths (black-man) over to Capt. David Goodwin's . . . is 40 feet. **1807** GASS *Journal* 130 Capt. Clarke's blackman's feet became so sore that he had to ride on horseback.

(*b*) **1778** in Logan *Great Conspiracy* 511 A well-chosen body of 5,000 black men, properly officer'd, to act as light troops. **1807** *Boston Selectmen* 15 April 332 An application from several free black men was made to the Board. **1818** *Niles' Reg.* XV. 139/2 The fire is said to have originated from the carelessness of a black man. **1857** E. STONE *Howland* vi. 107 A Southern state had a right to imprison and sell into slavery a free colored or black man from the North. **1893** *Congress. Rec.* Feb. 2301/1 The black man . . . is being educated, and can see where his political affiliation can best be allied. **1907** C. C. ANDREWS *Recoll.* 203 On another trip we saw a middle-aged black man shaving shingles on a 'shaving horse.'

+**Black maple.** [BLACK *a.* 2.] The black sugar-maple (q.v.).

a1817 DWIGHT *Travels* I. 40 The Hard Maple, sometimes called the Black, is extensively called the Sugar Maple, in this country. **1832** WILLIAMSON *Maine* I. 108 The black, or rock Maple is the most valuable of either; . . . the saccharine quality of its sap has . . . surnamed it the sugar Maple. **1845** LINCOLN *Botany* App. 69/1 Sweet tree, black maple. . . . Large tree, affording almost as much sugar as the sugar maple. **1897** SUDWORTH *Arborescent Flora* 284 Sugar maple. Common names [include] . . . Black maple (Fla., Ky., N.C.). **1898** N. E. JONES *Squirrel Hunters of Ohio* 21 Sugar manufactured in those days was made from the black maple or sugar tree.

Black Maria. *colloq.* A prison van. {1874–}

1847 *Boston Ev. Traveller* 25 Sept. 2/3 A new Black Maria, . . . a new wagon for the conveyance of prisoners to and from the courts of justice. **1877** BARTLETT 45 *Black Maria*, a close, box-carriage, generally painted black, used for carrying convicts to a prison or penitentiary. **1890** E. B. CUSTER *Following Guidon* 160 Our escort . . . hurried us out of what seemed like a 'Black Maria,' it was so dismal in the carriage. **1902** A. MACGOWAN *Last Word* 332 The bench where the sentenced ones wait for the black Maria.

Black medick. [BLACK *a.* 2.] {1816–} The nonesuch, *Medicago lupulina.* — **1843** TORREY *Flora N.Y.* I. 172 Black Medick. . . . Cultivated grounds. **1857** GRAY *Botany* 93 Black Medick . . . [grows in] waste places; sparingly. Adventitious from Europe. **1882** *Rep. Comm. Agric.* 254 In the black medick the pods are kidney-shaped, and when mature become of a blackish color. **1901** MOHR *Plant Life Ala.* 560 Black medick . . . [grows on] dry open banks, roadsides, waste places.

Black-mixed, *a.* and *n.* A very dark grey (cloth), known in England as *Oxford mixture* {1837–}. — **1822** *Law Harvard Coll.* (1824) 18 The surtout or great coat of black mixed, with not more than two capes. **1856** HALL *College Words* (ed. 2) 171 The black-mixed, otherwise called *Oxford Mixed* cloth, is explained under the latter title.

+**Black money.** *Obs.* Paper money printed in black. — **1782** *Maryland Journal* 31 Dec. (Th.), The House is against taking either black or red Money in Payment for taxes. **1787** *Ib.* 28 Sept., Advt. (Th.), Cash given for black and Continental State Money.

+**Black moose.** A color-variety of the moose, *Alces americanus.*

1724 Kidder *Exped. Lovewell* (1865) 16 [We] killed a Black Moose that day. **1743** CATESBY *Carolina* App. p. xxviii, The Moose or Elk . . . [they] in New England . . . call the black Moose. **1842** *Nat. Hist. N.Y., Zoology* I. 116 The Moose . . . is known with us under the various names of Flat-Horned Elk, Black Elk, Moose, and Black Moose. **1858** THOREAU *Maine Woods* 141 He had the horns of what he called 'the black moose that goes in low lands.' . . . The 'red moose' was another kind.

+**Black moose-bush.** (See quotation and cf. MOOSE-BUSH.) — **a1817** DWIGHT *Travels* II. 418 Here, also, I first observed the black-moose bush; a pretty shrub with a rich pulpy leaf, and a tuft of brilliant white flowers at the end of every branch.

+**Black moss.** The Spanish moss of the southern states.

1774–6 [JANET SCHAW] *Journal of Lady of Quality* (1923) 152 The trees that keep clear from this black moss (as it is called) are crowned with the Mistletoe. **1849** D. NASON *Journal* 23 We saw black moss to any amount. **1857** GRAY *Botany* 458 Common Long Moss or Black Moss . . . [is] a characteristic plant of the Southern States. **1894** COULTER *Bot. W. Texas* III. 426 Common Long-moss. Black moss. . . . Hanging on trees, forming long tufts; southern Texas.

+**Blackmouth dance.** (See quotation.) — **1899** CUSHMAN *Hist. Indians* 499 The Chickasaws had two dances sacred to women alone and in which they only participated—one was called . . . Blackwood Dance; the other, . . . Blackmouth Dance.

+**Black muck.** (See quot. 1855.) — **1849** CHAMBERLAIN *Indiana Gazetteer* 283 The soil being a mixture of clay, marl, and black muck. **1855** *Trans. Amer. Inst. N.Y.* 343 The Newark meadows . . . are formed of black, carbonaceous soil, usually known as black muck.

* **Black mulberry.** A species of mulberry (as *Morus nigra*) yielding a dark-colored fruit.

1705 BEVERLEY *Virginia* II. 15 Our Mulberries are of three sorts, two Black and one White; the long Black sort are the best. **1741** *Georgia H. S. Coll.* II. 250 The white mulberry, which serves to feed the silk worms; the black is about the size of a black cherry. **1765** R. ROGERS *Acc. N. America* 138 On these lands are found the black mulberry, the American cherry, fox and cluster grapes. **1808** T. ASHE *Travels* xxviii. 240 Besides these, I met with the honey locust, black mulberry, and wild cherry. **1831** PECK *Guide* 139 The black mulberry grows in most parts [of Illinois], and is used for the feeding of silk worms with success. **1846** BROWNE *Trees Amer.* 438 The leaves of the black mulberry are sufficiently succulent for the purpose [of nourishing the silk worm]. **1890** *Cent.* 3890 The black mulberry, *Morus nigra*, native somewhere in western Asia, . . . has been to some extent introduced into the United States. **1901** MOHR *Plant Life Ala.* 831 *Morus nigra*, Black Mulberry, Russian Mulberry, [is] most frequent in the pine belt.

b. Attrib. with *tree.*

1775 ADAIR *Indians* 360 The black mulberry-tree . . . is high, and, if it had proper air and sun-shine, the boughs would be very spreading.

Black mustard. [BLACK *a.* 2.] A species of mustard, *Brassica nigra.*

1784 CUTLER in *Mem. Academy* I. 468 Black mustard. The imported mustard, so common at tables, and which is generally preferred to our own, is the pulverized seed of this species. **1843** TORREY *Flora N.Y.* I. 61 Black Mustard . . . [grows in] fields and waste places. . . . The seeds afford mustard, so well known as a stimulating condiment. **1847** DARLINGTON *Weeds & Plants* 47 These two species, known as Black and White Mustard, from the color of the seeds, are naturalized in many places, having escaped from gardens. **1857** GRAY *Botany* 36 Black Mustard. . . . The acrid seeds furnish the mustard of our tables, etc. **1901** MOHR *Plant Life Ala.* 523 Black Mustard . . . [is] extensively naturalized in fields and waste places in the Northern States.

Black-necked, *a.* [BLACK *a.* 3.] — **1839** PEABODY *Mass. Birds* 358 The Black Necked Stilt, *Himantopus nigricollis.* **1858** BAIRD *Birds Pacific R. R.* 704 Black Necked Stilt. **1870** *Amer. Naturalist* III. 638 Black-necked Stilt, . . . one of the rarest of all our visitors, . . . [is] properly a southern and south-western species.

Black nightshade. [BLACK *a.* 2.] The common nightshade, *Solanum nigrum.* — **1818** *Mass. H. S. Coll.* 2 Ser. VIII. 170 In July the lover of plants is gratified with . . . the common iris, the woody and black nightshades. **1840** DEWEY *Mass. Flowering Plants* 165 Black Night-shade [grows] in waste places, about fields, . . . [and] has the characters of a poisonous plant. **1847** WOOD *Botany* 448 Black Nightshade. . . . A weed-like plant without beauty and of suspicious aspect, about rubbish, in old fields, N. and W. States. **1849** *New Eng. Farmer* I. 191 Bittersweet, or woody nightshade, . . . belongs to the same genus as black nightshade, . . . a poisonous plant. **1890** *Cent.* 5751/3 The cosmopolitan weed *S. nigrum*, the common or black nightshade, [is] the original type of the genus.

+**Black nurse.** [BLACK *a.* 2.] A shark of inactive habits (family *Scymnidæ*). — **1883** C. F. HOLDER in *Harper's Mag.* Jan. 186/2 One of the most interesting luminous fishes is a shark . . . that resembles the black nurse, or scymnus, that I have often caught on the Florida coast.

+**Black oak.** [BLACK *a.* 2.]

1. One or other species of oak tree, as the dyer's oak (*Quercus tinctoria* or *velutina*), black jack (*Q. nigra*), and red oak (*Q. rubra*), valued for their timber.

1634 WOOD *New Eng. Prospect* I. v. 16 Of Oakes there be three kindes, the red Oake, white, and black. **1682** ASH *Carolina* 10 They have . . . Oak of three sorts, the White, Black and Live Oak. **1709** LAWSON *Carolina* 92 The next is Black Oak, which is esteem'd a durable Wood, under Water; but sometimes it is used in House-work. **1775** ROMANS *Florida* 18 Black oak, with leaves serrated, and their tops almost triangular. **1785** MARSHALL *Amer. Grove* 120 *Quercus nigra.* . . . Our common Black Oak is used much (where cedar is scarce) for making shingles, and also for rails, etc. **1790** S. DEANE *New-Eng. Farmer* 191/1 The black oak has a very dark-coloured hard and rough outer bark. **1821** NUTTALL *Trav. Arkansa* 71, I entered upon an oak swamp . . . with some red and scarlet, as well as black and post oak on the knolls. **1832** BROWNE *Sylva* 289 This species is found throughout the United States on both sides of the Alleghanies and is everywhere called Black Oak. **1839** J. PLUMBE *Sk. Iowa* 32 The timber [of Iowa] . . . is principally white, burr, red and black oak, hickory and black walnut; some maple, ash, elm, birch and basswood. **1849** CHAMBERLAIN *Indiana Gazetteer* 160 The more hilly part of the country has a clay soil, and the timber there is white and black oak. **1882** Worthen *Econ. Geol. Ill.* II. 105 Some regular post-oak flats . . . covered with post-oak and black-jack, and a few black-oak. **1897** SUDWORTH *Arborescent Flora* 174 Black Jack . . . [is also called] Black Oak. (Ark., Wis.) **1901** MOHR *Plant Life Ala.* 84 Oaks form the predominating forest growth of these highlands—white oak, mountain oak, and fine black oak.

b. Applied to other species of oaks (see quotations).

1884 SARGENT *Rep. Forests* 146 *Quercus Emoryi*, . . . Black Oak. **1897** SUDWORTH *Arborescent Flora* 168 *Quercus coccinea*, Scarlet Oak, . . . [is also called] Black Oak (Mo., Ill., Iowa, Wis.). *Ib.* 169 *Quercus californica*, . . . [called] Black oak (Cal., Oreg.), Mountain Black Oak (Cal.), . . . California Black Oak (Cal.).

c. Attrib. with *bush, pole, spire, tree,* etc.

(1) **1666** *Warwick Rec.* (1926) 323 Land . . . bounded one the southwest side by a blacke oake tree. **1694** *Hartford Land Distrib.* 296 On the South west corner upon the Top of the Hill we marked a black oake Tree. **1703** *Conn. Col. Rec.* IV. 422 A black oak tree by a ledge of rocks on the side of a hill. **1730** *Providence Rec.* XVI. 423 Beginning att a black oake tree then running east . . . to a heape of stones. **1853** RAMSEY *Tennessee* 593 The rest of the family, six in number, were buried in one grave under a black-oak tree, still standing.

(2) **1693** *Derby* (Conn.) *Rec.* 162 A black oak bush standing upon the high way. **1704** *Ib.* 228 It runs to another black oake spire with stones at the root. **1705** *Duxbury Rec.* 201 Bigining at the foot next the Bay, the first is a small black oak stump. **1723** *Providence Rec.* IX. 69 Thence south fifteene degrees East ten Rods to a black oake pole. **1725** *Ib.* XVI. 400 Southward to a small black oake bush marked on two sides. **1755** Chalkley *Scotch-Irish Settlement Va.* III. 338 Between a white oak and a black oak saplin. **1800** B. Hawkins *Sk. Creek Country* 20 Between these rivers, there is some good post and black oak land. **1809** F. Cuming *Western Tour* 198 The road runs through . . . miry black oak woods. **1811** Mease *Philadelphia* 66 No ground black oak bark may be shipped, except such, as in the opinion of the inspector, shall have been shaved, clean from the ross, or outside bark. **1862** *Rep. Comm. Patents: Agric.* 599 Fig. 32 is the larva, . . . usually found . . . more particularly in black oak wood or in old stumps. **1868** *Rep. Comm. Agric.* (1869) 100 The larva of our native *Centronopus calcaratus* (Lec.) inhabits black-oak stumps.

2. A single tree belonging to any of these species.

1659 *Portsmouth Rec.* 377 Fortie fower acres of land . . . bounded . . . north ward towards the mill with a littel black oake. **1664** *Plymouth Rec.* 74 A great blacke oake standing in the meddow. **1695** *Conn. Col. Rec.* IV. 153 Thence runing to Preston five mile corner tree, which is a black oake marked on two sides standing between two rocks. **1734** J. Hempstead *Diary* 275 The Line . . . ought to run . . . to the great Black oak on the Hill. **1782** *Steele Papers* II. 750 Beginning at a small red Oak . . . and runing thence South . . . to a small black Oak. **1792** Imlay *Western Territory* 36 The country is broken and steril, producing scarce any other timber than the fir tree, or pine and knotty black oaks, which are generally deemed symptoms of a bad soil. **1821** Nuttall *Trav. Arkansa* 152 We now continued south-east, about 20 miles, over hilly woods covered with dwarfish post and black oaks. **1887** *Scribner's Mag.* May 571/2 A wood of black-oaks, or 'black-jacks.'

3. The wood of this tree. Also attrib.

1711 Sewall *Diary* II. 302, I was supply'd with . . . a Load of black oak by Nath. Sparhawk. **1829** Cooper *Wish-Ton-Wish* iii. 39 Walls that were wainscoted in the black oak of the country. **1902** *Harper's Mag.* May 885 The Governor sat at the head of the big black-oak table in his big stately library.

+**Black oat-grass.** [Black *a.* 2.] An oat-grass, *Stipa avenacea*, common in the eastern and southern states.

1843 Torrey *Flora N.Y.* II. 433 Black Oat-grass . . . [is found in] dry sandy or rocky woods, not uncommon in the valley of the Hudson. **1857** Gray *Botany* 549 Black Oat-Grass . . . [grows in] dry or sandy woods, S. New England to Wisconsin, and (chiefly) southward. **1890** *Cent.* 5951 The only common species of the eastern United States is *Stipa avenacea*, the black oat-grass. **1901** Mohr *Plant Life Ala.* 366 Black Oat Grass. . . . Carolinian and Louisianian areas.

+**Black ore.** A variety of iron ore. — **1804** *Mass. H. S. Coll.* IX. 255 Black ore [is] found in deep water on a muddy bottom in cakes of a dirty black colour, and of an earthy appearance.

Black people. [Black *a.* 1.] **a.** Negroes. +**b.** Spaniards. (See quot. 1778.) — **1775** J. Habersham *Letters* 241 Mr. Knox . . . has sent over two Moravian Brethern . . . to instruct his Black People. **1778** Carver *Travels* 35 Whilst they were crossing a plain, they discovered a body of men on horseback, who belonged to the Black People; for so they [*sc.* the Indians] call the Spaniards.

***Black pepper.** +Attrib. with *tea*, denoting a decoction used as a drink. — **1851** Springer *Forest Life* 66 The night was cold, but by our exertions to keep up a brilliant fire, and copious draughts of black pepper tea, . . . we kept quite comfortable.

+**Black perch.** [Black *a.* 1.] A name applied to various dark-skinned fishes of or resembling the perch kind, esp. the black sea bass, *Centropristis striatus*, the small-mouthed black bass, *Micropterus dolomieu*, or the flasher, *Lobotes surinamensis.*

1780 W. Fleming in *Travels Amer. Col.* 646 The Inhabitants of this place [in Ky.] catched numbers of fish yesterday and today, all cat fish except a black perch such as in Roanoke. **1814** Mitchill *Fishes N.Y.* 421 Red Perch. *Bodianus rufus.* . . . When the fish is not in the breeding season, the colours are browner and darker; leading the people to call him the 'black perch.' **1817** S. Brown *Western Gaz.* 121 The fish consist principally of the cat, pike, . . . and white and black perch. **1839** Storer *Mass. Fishes* 9 *Centropristis nigricans.* The Black Perch. The only specimen . . . [was] sent me from Holmes Hole, where it is called black fish and black basse. **1842** *Nat. Hist. N.Y., Zoology* iv. 13 The Small Black Bass, *Labrax nigricans*, . . . is commonly known under the name of Black Perch. **1846** Thorpe *Myst. Backwoods* 158 Struggling upon our line is a black perch. **1849** Lanman *Alleghany Mts.* ix. 65 Their black perch is but another name for the black or Oswego bass. **1883** *Century Mag.* July 376/2, I have heard them [=black bass] called black perch, yellow perch, and jumping perch up the Rockcastle and Cumberland rivers, and white and black trout in Tennessee.

+**Black persimmon.** (See quots.) — **1884** Sargent *Rep. Forests* 105 *Diospyros Texana*, . . . Black Persimmon. **1892** Coulter *Bot. W. Texas* ii. 257 [Growing in] woods along streams, . . . the 'chapote' of the Mexicans [is] also known as 'black persimmon.' **1897** Sudworth *Arborescent Flora* 321 *Diospyros texana*, Mexican Persimmon. . . . Common names [include] . . . Black Persimmon (Tex.), Chapote (Tex.).

+**Black pine.** [Black *a.* 2.] One of several varieties of pine, as the jack pine, pitch pine, lodgepole pine, etc.

1681 *N.H. Probate Rec.* I. 47 From that 48 Pole S.W. to a black Pine Stump on the West. **1781–2** Jefferson *Notes on Va.* (1788) 39 Black, or pitch-pine, *Pinus taeda.* **1809** Kendall *Travels* III. 146 The black pine or pitch pine (*pinus tæda*) grows in sands, has a very long leaf, and a bark in very large scales. **1832** Browne *Sylva* 237 This species is known in all the United States by the name of Pitch Pine, and sometimes in Virginia by that of Black Pine. **1854** Glisan *Jrnl. Army Life* 152 In Arkansas—the birch, honey-locust, cyprus, black and white pine. **1892** Apgar *Trees Northern U.S.* 175 *Pinus Austriaca*, . . . Austrian or Black Pine. . . . A large cultivated tree, 60 to 80 ft. high, hardy throughout. [Brought from] Europe.

Black-poll. [Black *a.* 3.]

1. *Black-poll warbler*, a North American warbler, the male of which has a black head when in full plumage.

[**1785** Pennant *Arctic Zoology* II. 401 Black-poll Warbler. . . . Inhabits during summer, Newfoundland and New York.] **1811** Wilson *Ornithology* IV. 40 Black-poll Warbler, *Sylvia striata*, . . . has considerable affinity to the Flycatchers in its habits. **1844** *Nat. Hist. N.Y., Zoology* ii. 95 The Black-poll or Black-headed Warbler . . . is highly useful in destroying cankerworms and other noxious insects. **1867** *Amer. Naturalist* I. 121 All around Eastport [Maine], and especially on the islands, the Black-Poll Warbler is one of the most common birds. **1892** Torrey *Foot-path Way* 99 Two birds dashed by me—a blackpoll warbler in hot pursuit of an olive-backed thrush.

+**2.** *absol.* =sense 1.

1868 *Amer. Naturalist* II. 180 It is very quick, scarcely less so than the black-poll. **1892** Torrey *Foot-path Way* 16 The feeble, sharp song of the black-poll is a singular affair. **1895** *Outing* April 69/2, I made out the blue yellow-back, . . . the blackpoll and the black-throated green.

Black-polled, *a.* [Black *a.* 3.] =prec. 1. — **1868** *Amer. Naturalist* II. 179 The Black-polled Warbler (*Dendroica striata*), is the last of the tribe to arrive in spring, seldom appearing before the twentieth of May.

Black pony. +In obscure allusions (see quotations). — **1833** *Niles' Reg.* XLIV. 345/2 Another black poney [*sic*].—The new brig John Gilpin, built at Baltimore, left that port in June, 1832. **1834** [C. A. Davis] *Lett. J. Downing* 137, I wish you'd git a 'black pony' goin this season, like the folks did last year, who print a paper down-cellar under yourn.

***Black poplar.** [Black *a.* 2.] A species of poplar, *Populus nigra.*

*c***1730** Catesby *Carolina* I. 34 The Black Poplar of Carolina. This Tree grows only near Rivers, above the inhabited parts of Carolina. **1781–2** Jefferson *Notes on Va.* (1788) 39 Black poplar. **1785** Marshall *Amer. Grove* 107 Black Poplar . . . is not of very large growth, but covered with a darkish rough bark. **1792** J. Pope *Tour S. & W.* 94 Black Poplar. . . . Large Potions of a Decoction from the Bark of this Tree, especially the Root, is a sovereign Antidote to the Bite of the Rattle-Snake. **1810–** [see American black poplar]. **1817** S. Brown *Western Gaz.* 321 The timber of these tracts [in Ohio], consists of . . . honey locust, aspin, black poplar, birch. **1892** Apgar *Trees Northern U.S.* 170 Black Poplar. . . . A very variable, large (50 to 80 ft. high), rapidly growing tree with spreading branches. Occasionally planted. From Europe.

Black pox. *Obs.* =Black smallpox. — **1672** Josselyn *New Eng. Rarities* 63 The Black Pox, the Spotted Feaver, the Griping of the Guts, the Dropsie, and the Sciatica, are the killing Deseases in New-England.

Black pup. (See quotation.) — **1869** *Overland Monthly* III. 391 The young [seals] of nearly a year old, called 'gray' or 'silvered pups'; and before their coats are changed to this shade, called 'black-pups.'

+**Black racer.** [Black *a.* 2.] A fleet sub-species (*Coluber constrictor*) of the black snake. — **1849** J. B. Jones *Wild West Scenes* xvii. 246 Dod, they ain't pisen! . . . They're nearly all black racers, and they don't bite. **1849** Lanman *Alleghany Mts.* ii. 22, I saw one [snake fight], Monday was a week, between a black-racer and a rattle snake. **1908** [see Black runner].

+**Black raspberry.** [Black *a.* 2.] The blackcap or thimbleberry, *Rubus occidentalis.* — **1781–2** Jefferson *Notes Va.* (1788) 37 Native plants [of Va. include] Black raspberries, . . . Blackberries, . . . Dewberries. **1836** Lincoln *Botany* App. 134 Black raspberry [has] branches and petioles glaucous and prickly. **1847** Darlington *Weeds & Plants* 127 Wild or Black Raspberry. . . . The fruit of this is . . . sweet and agreeable. The plant, however, is generally treated as a weed, on all neat farms. **1901** Mohr *Plant Life Ala.* 541 Black Raspberry . . . [was] frequently transplanted by the settlers to their gardens.

Black rat. [Black *a.* 2.] The black European or American species of the common rat, *Mus rattus* {1774–} or *Mus americanus.*

1774 Goldsmith *Hist. Earth* (1822) III. 180 The Black Rat [has] . . . propagated in America in great numbers, being originally introduced from Europe. **1826** J. Godman *Nat. Hist.* II. 83 The Black Rat, *Mus Rattus*, . . . found only in situations to which the brown rat has not extended its emigrations. **1842** *Nat. Hist. N.Y., Zoology* i. 80 The Black Rat, . . . originally . . . derived from Europe, . . . is now exceedingly rare. *Ib.* 81 The American Black Rat, *Mus americanus* . . . ; the species . . . [is] confounded with the imported Black Rat of Europe. It is very rare. **1857** *Rep. Comm. Patents: Agric.* 110 The black-rat was once abundant in parts of the United States, but is now unknown in many localities where it formerly bred. **1898** *Yearbook Dept. Agric.* 92 The black, or house, rat . . . by the middle of the present century was known as far north as Halifax and Montreal, Canada, and on the Pacific coast at San Diego and Humboldt Bay, California.

+**Black Republican,** *n.* and *a.*

1. *n.* A contemptuous name (current esp. 1856–66) for a member of the Republican party. Freq. in *pl.*

'The later name of "Black Republican" was given to the present Republican Party as one of reproach, just before the Rebellion, by Major Heiss of the Washington *Union,* and the well-known George N. Sanders. . . . "If the Republicans of France are red," said Sanders, "ours must be black"' (**1873** F. HUDSON *Journalism U.S.* 275). '*Black Republican,* a contemptuous Southern nickname for Republicans, owing to their friendliness toward the cause of negro emancipation' (**1890** NORTON *Polit. Americanisms* 13).

1856 *Congress. Globe* 3 Jan. 141/2 Now, these gentlemen denounce us as 'Black Republicans.' **1858** QUITMAN in *Life & Corr.* (1860) II. xix. 252 The Black Republicans, or the Anti-Slavery party under some other name, will sweep every free state at the next contest. **1860** ABBOTT *South & North* 115 Rather than let this Union be dissolved, they will drive into Canada every Black Republican, every abolitionist. **1864** T. L. NICHOLS *Amer. Life* I. 259, I listened to a foolish and furious speech from Lovejoy, one of the most ultra of the Black Republicans. **1867** L. BAKER *U.S. Secret Service* 583 Appealing to all his previous prejudice against Black Republicans and Abolitionists. **1905** *N.Y. Ev. Post* 27 Oct. 6 [President Roosevelt] is one of the blackest of black Republicans. For example, he had closed a Mississippi post-office because some whites had made trouble for the colored postmistress.

2. *adj.* Designating, or belonging to, the Republican party.

1856 *Congress. Globe* 27 Aug. 52/2 With what face, or show of justice or truth, can one of this Free-Soil or Black Republican party rise and condemn that fugitive law? **1861** A. ELY *Journal* (1862) 43 An article in the Dispatch . . . states that I represent one of the ultra Black Republican districts in New York State. **1866** RICHARDSON *Secret Service* iii. 55 As for a Black Republican flag—why that is . . . not to be endured.

+**Black Republicanism.** [f. prec.] The principles of the Republican party. — **1858** LINCOLN in Logan *Great Conspiracy* 62 All the hard names that Judge Douglas has called them [=Republicans] by, . . . all his declarations of Black Republicanism. **1860** in Logan *Ib.* 128 We will meet . . . all the myrmidons of Abolitionism and Black Republicanism everywhere upon our own soil. **1860** *Richmond Enquirer* 6 Nov. 1/5 (Th.), Will you follow Little Sandy Rives into Black Republicanism?

+**Black-ride.** *Obs.* A performance of 'black riding' (q.v.). — **1857** *Letter* in E. L. Green *Hist. Univ. S.C.* 243 Friday night we had a beautiful sight—a black-ride in the Campus. There were four or five riders half masked with their faces blacked. . . . It was a splendid sight to see them galloping up and down the Campus, waving their flambeaux. *Ib.,* This morning some four or five were called up before the faculty . . . to answer as to the part they took in the blackride.

‖**Black rider.** One of a band of mounted banditti represented as operating during the Revolutionary war. — **1841** SIMMS *Kinsmen* v. (1882) 51 The Black Riders of Congaree . . . were dressed in complete black—each carried . . . all the usual equipments of the well-mounted dragoon. *Ib.* 65 The chief of the Black Riders.

+**Black riding.** (See quotation.) *Obs.* — **1851** HALL *Coll. Words* 20 At the College of South Carolina, it has until within a few years been customary for the students, disguised and painted black, to ride across the college-yard at midnight, on horseback, with vociferations and the sound of horns. *Black riding* is recognized by the laws of the College as a very high offence.

+**Black root.**

1. A perennial herb, *Pterocaulon pycnostachyum* (or *undulatum*), common in the southern states.

1833 EATON *Botany* (ed. 6) 288 *Pterocaulon pycnostachya,* black root. **1837** WILLIAMS *Florida* 93 Black Root, *Pterocaulon pychnostachyum.*—The famous Indian remedy for pulmonary disorders. **1861** WOOD *Botany* 439 Black-root . . . [grows on] sandy soils, S.Car. to Fla. A curious plant, 2 to 3 f. high. **1901** MOHR *Plant Life Ala.* 790 Black Root . . . [grows on] dry open grassy pine barrens.

2. (See quotation and cf. KOOYAH.)

1843 T. TALBOT *Journals* 45 We traded some Kooyah or Black root, . . . a black, sticky, suspicious looking compound, of very disagreeable odor. . . . It is a very palatable and soon a favorite mess.

3. The root of *Veronica (Leptandra) virginica;* also, a bitter glucoside obtained from this.

1851 [see BLACK COHOSH]. **1891** *Cent.* s.v. *Veronica,* A few [species] are of medicinal repute, especially *V. Virginica,* known as black-root and Culver's-root or Culver's-physic, . . . occurring in Canada, the eastern and central United States [etc.]. **1901** MOHR *Plant Life Ala.* 724 *Leptandra virginica,* . . . Culver's-Root. . . . The root is the 'blackroot' or 'Leptandra' of the United States Pharmacopœia.

4. The white star grass or colic root.

1864 WEBSTER, *Blackroot,* a plant of an intense bitter taste, the *Aletris farinosa.*

+**Black rot.** **1.** A form of rot in various fruits and plants. **2.** A disease affecting poultry (see quotation). — **(1) 1849** *Rep. Comm. Patents: Agric.* (1850) 438 In the southern part of the State winter apples are very liable to the black-rot, spots, [etc.]. **1889** *Cent.* s.v. *Grape-rot,* The black-rot fungus is *Phoma uvicola,* which causes the grapes to shrivel and turn blackish. . . . In America this is the most destructive rot. **1893** *Rep. Secretary Agric.* 249 Experiments in the Treatment of Black Rot of the Grape. **(2) 1871** LEWIS *Poultry Book* 97 Black Rot.—The symptoms of this disease are blackening of the comb, resembling mortification [etc.].

+**Black runner.** [BLACK *a.* 2.] =BLACK RACER. — **1835** LATROBE *Rambler in N.A.* II. 46 He would tell us . . . of the powers of the black-runner in destroying the rattle-snake, by the inconceivable swiftness of its motions. **1908** *Dialect Notes* III. 291 *Black-runner,* a black snake noted for fleetness. Also called *black racer,* or simply *racer.*

+**Black rush.** One or other species of *Juncus* (see quots. and cf. BLACK GRASS). — **1840** DEWEY *Mass. Flowering Plants* 204 *Juncus bulbosus,* Black Rush, . . . [grows] about salt marshes, and 'makes good hay.' **1861** WOOD *Botany* 724 *Juncus maritimus,* Black Rush. . . . In brackish marshes, Va. to Fla. . . . Flowers dark brown. **1901** MOHR *Plant Life Ala.* 50 Paludial plants confined to the salt marshes of the seashore . . . [include] black rush (*Juncus roemerianus*).

+**Black rust.** A fungoid blight attacking wheat and other cereals, etc. — **1790** S. DEANE *New-Eng. Farmer* 20/1 The pods are liable to be hurt by a black rust, if they are exposed much to the sun. **1817–8** EATON *Botany* (1822) 415 *Puccinia graminis,* blight, black rust. . . . In the culm of wheat and various other grasses. **1847** *Rep. Comm. Patents* (1848) 108 If followed by wet weather the black rust or smut is produced, or if by dry weather the red rust. **1890** *Cent.* 5280 Black rust . . . [is] the final or teleutospore stage of *Puccinia graminis,* or grain-blight.

+**Black sage.** [BLACK *a.* 2.] A woolly-leaved, labiate plant (*Trichostema lanatum*) of the mint family, growing in the western states. — **1876** J. G. BOURKE *Journal* 12 March, We now found ourselves well across the Southern boundary of Montana, in a region well grassed with gramma and the 'black sage,' a plant almost as nutritious as oats. **1891** *Cent.,* *Trichostema lanatum,* with a striking purple-woolly spike, is known in California as 'black sage.'

+**Black salmon.** [BLACK *a.* 2.] (See quotations.) — **1832** WILLIAMSON *Maine* I. 160 There are three varieties; the black Salmon, which is smallest; the hawkbill . . . ; and the smoothnosed. **1856** *Spirit of Times* (N.Y.) 20 Dec. 253/1 We have two kinds of this fish [the pike-perch, in the Ohio River]; one is called the white, the other the black salmon. **1890** *Cent.* 5315/1 Black salmon, a local name of the great lake-trout, *Salvelinus (Cristivomer) namaycush.*

+**Black-salter.** [f. next.] A maker of black salts. — **1880** 'E. KIRKE' *Garfield* 6 The boy overcame her scruples, and thus our future President became prime-minister to a black-salter. **1882** [see next].

+**Black salts.** The black residuum obtained from wood ashes after lixiviation and evaporation; crude potash. — **1864** T. L. NICHOLS *Amer. Life* II. 213 The process . . . of boiling the lye into black salts, was commonplace. **1882** THAYER *From Log Cabin* x. 150 Large kettles for boiling the lye, reducing it to potash, which, in its crude state, was called 'black-salts.' The manufacturer of the article was called a 'black-salter.'

***Black saltwort.** The sea-milkwort, *Glaux maritima.* — **1836** LINCOLN *Botany* App. 100 Black salt-wort. . . . Marshes on the sea-coast. **1847** WOOD *Botany* 386 *G[laux] maritima,* Black Saltwort, [is] a small, smooth, fleshy plant, found occasionally in the salt marshes on our sea-coast, Can. to N.J. . . . Leaves . . . smooth, fleshy and darkly glaucous.

+**Black sampson.** The purple cone-flower, *Brauneria (Echinacea) purpurea.* — **1857** GRAY *Botany* 214 Purple cone-flower. . . . Root thick, black, very pungent to the taste, used in popular medicine under the name of Black Sampson. **1901** MOHR *Plant Life Ala.* 799 Black Sampson, . . . Open woods and prairies.

Black sand. +A black-colored sand; esp. an oxide of iron containing gold.

1849 *Rep. Comm. Patents* (1850) 405 Much of the black sand now in use is colored, and is common silicious sand, but the best article is a ferruginous sand. **1852** [H. V. HUNTLEY] *California* (1856) II. 155 With regard to the amount of gold found in the 'iron oxyde, called blacksand,' I differ from the writer. **1854** MARCY *Explor. Red River* 20 Specimens of quartz and black sand were collected in the mountains. **1875** BOURKE *Journal* June 14 Another 'sign' of importance has been that all the streams now have quartz gravel beds altho' no 'black sand' is visible. **1877** WM. WRIGHT *Big Bonanza* 541 At last all was panned out, even to the last grain of 'black sand,' and nought remained.

+**Black scrub-oak.** [BLACK *a.* 2.] A dwarf species of oak, *Quercus ilicifolia.*

1810 MICHAUX *Arbres* I. 24 Bear Oak, . . . Black Scrub Oak. **1832** BROWNE *Sylva* 263 This diminutive species is known in the Northern and Middle States by the name of Bear Oak, Black Scrub Oak and Dwarf Oak. **1892** APGAR *Trees Northern U.S.* 157 Bear or Black Scrub-oak. . . . Sandy barrens and rocky hills. New England to Ohio, and south.

+**Black sea bass.** [BLACK *a.* 2.] (See quotation.) — **1842** *Nat. Hist. N.Y., Zoology* IV. 24 The Black Sea Bass, *Centropristis nigricans,* . . . is one of the most savory and delicate of the fishes which appear in our markets from May to July.

Black seed, Black-seed. [BLACK *a.* 3.]

+**1.** *Black seed grass, millet grass* (see quotations).

1775 ROMANS *Florida* 129 A grass not ill resembling silver hair grass, which is called from the colour of its seed, black seed grass, makes an excellent pasture on the meanest sand we find in the country. — **1833**

EATON *Botany* (ed. 6) 266 *Piptatherum racemosum*, clustered millet-grass, black-seed millet-grass.

+**2.** *Black seed (cotton)*, the native sea-island or long-stapled cotton.

1796 B. HAWKINS *Letters* 30, I advised him, . . . as from his information the black seed cotton will not do here, to plant only the green seed. **1800** — *Sk. Creek Country* 44 He plants the green-seed cotton, it being too cold for the blackseed. **1802** *Steele Papers* I. 341 Black Seed or Long Staple Cotton is in demand. **1827** SHERWOOD *Gaz. Georgia* 10 The sea-island or black-seed cotton, which is generally worth double as much as the green-seed, grows kindly in all the lower parts of this section. **1847** EMORY *Military Reconn.* 129 There are but two distinct species: the black seed, which is the native American, and found as such no where else, and the green seed, which adheres to the staple, of Asiatic origin. **1858** *Texas Almanac 1859* 84 We have omitted to mention the numerous experiments now being made to grow the Sea-Island or black-seed cotton on our coast lands. **1882** *Century Mag.* Feb. 573/1 The long staple or black-seed cotton of the Sea Island variety.

‖**3.** Dark-skinned people.

1809 IRVING *Knickerb.* I. v, These miscreants [=aboriginal Americans] . . . were a perverse, illiterate, dumb, beardless, black-seed.

+**Black skimmer.** [BLACK *a.* 2.] The shearwater. — **1813** WILSON *Ornithology* VII. 85 Black Skimmer, or Sheerwater: *Rhynchops nigra;* . . . is a truly singular fowl. **1858** BAIRD *Birds Pacific R.R.* 866 The Black Skimmer. *Hab.*—From Texas to New Jersey. **1874** COUES *Birds N.W.* 715 Black Skimmer; Cut-water. . . . In North America, Gulf and Atlantic coasts regularly to New Jersey; casually, if at all, to New England. **1883** *Century Mag.* Sept. 652/2 On Cape Cod . . . are many rare ones for the North, such as the black skimmer, or shear-water.

+**Black slash.** (See quotation and SLASH *n.*) —**1849** *New Eng. Farmer* I. 235 A large portion of the land in Indiana, as well as some other of the Western States, is technically called 'flat woods,' 'wet lands,' 'black slashes,' &c.

Black smallpox. [Cf. BLACK POX.] Hemorrhagic smallpox; variola. — **1881** *Harper's Mag.* Jan. 196 Presently one of the assistants cried out that the sleepers had 'the black small-pox.'

* **Blacksmith.**

* **1.** A smith who works in 'black metal' or iron.

1634 WOOD *New Eng. Prospect* I. xii. 52 Though all these be made in the Countrey (there being divers Blacke-smiths) yet . . . it is cheaper to carry such commodities out of England. **1638** *R.I. Col. Rec.* I. 66 Richard Maxon, Blacksmith, . . . was accordingly detected for his oppression in the way of his trade. **1675** *Penna. Mag.* VI. 88 For Tradesmen there be none but live happily there, as Carpenters, Blacksmiths, Masons, . . . and so any other Trade. **1708** *Boston News-Letter* 17–24 May 2/2 A Clothier's Iron Skrew for a hot Press to be Seen and Sold by Nathaniel Ayres Black-smith at his Shop near the Salutation in North Boston. **1715** *Ib.* 12 Sept. 2/2 Six Negro Men aged about 20 Years, one of them a Black-smith by Trade, to be Sold. **1782** J. H. ST. JOHN *Letters* 14 It is not in the noisy shop of a blacksmith or of a carpenter, that these studious moments can be enjoyed. *c*1792 T. COXE *View U.S.* 314 Five or six blacksmiths—one employed in plating saddle trees. **1798** H. M. Brooks *Gleanings* 72 Wanted, a Blacksmith, to contract for doing all the Iron Work at the Salem Frigate. **1831** PECK *Guide* 294 Bituminous coal of a good quality and in common use by the blacksmiths, exists in abundance. **1854** BARTLETT *Narr.* I. 289, I applied to a blacksmith . . . to repair our broken wheel. **1883** *Wheelman* I. 433, I helped a blacksmith pull into shape a very badly bent crank.

b. Attrib. (also *blacksmith's*) with *coal, tools, work.*

1749 *N.H. Probate Rec.* III. 684 My Barn and shop with all my black smiths tools and implements. **1797** *Ann. 4th Congress* 2 Sess. 2047 Bar iron, &c. for blacksmith, mill-wright, and machinery work. **1822** *Ann. 17th Congress* 1 Sess. I. 186 Praying for the payment of one hundred and twenty dollars for blacksmith's work. **1882** Worthen *Econ. Geol. Illinois* II. 173 Shelton's coal-digging . . . supplies the country for miles around with its blacksmith coal. *a*1918 G. STUART *On Frontier* I. 217 He left his blacksmith tools and other things with me.

+**2.** (See quotation.)

1888 GOODE *Amer. Fishes* 300 Another somewhat noteworthy species [of fish] is known in California, on account of its dusky colors, as the 'Blacksmith,' *Chromis punctipinnis.*

+**Blacksmithery.** [f. prec.] **1.** Blacksmith's work. **2.** A blacksmith's shop. — (1) **1869** *Overland Monthly* III. 10 In North Carolina, as in the North, blacksmithery, wagon-making, coopery, and other sorts of hard-handed industry, were in noisy blast. **1889** *Advance* (Chicago) 21 March 229 Carpentry, blacksmithery, and carriage making are also chief industries for the Indian on the plain. (2) **1871** *Rep. Indian Affairs* (1872) 327 The fixed property of this reservation consists of agents quarters, 3 dwellings, 2 blacksmitheries.

Blacksmithing. [f. BLACKSMITH.] The work of a blacksmith, or the doing of this. {1830–}

1764 in Bittinger *Hist. Haverhill* [N.H.] (1888) 177 One right of land [was voted to Wm. Wheeler on condition that he would] follow the business of blacksmithing for ten years, or some one else for him. **1841** CIST *Cincinnati* 131 Among the manufactures . . . [was] blacksmithing. **1849** F. DOUGLASS *Life* 12 The blacksmithing, cart-wrighting, coopering, and grain-grinding, were all performed by slaves. **1853** *Knickerb.* XLII. 450 He is an Aristocrat, worth twenty-five thousand dollars made at the blacksmithing. **1864** *Narr. Privations of Prisoners of War* 51 Under the temptation to secure double rations, many worked at their trades of blacksmithing and shoemaking for the rebel army. **1882** Worthen *Econ. Geol. Illinois* II. 30 At some localities it contains considerable sulphuret of iron, and cannot be used for blacksmithing. **1917** SINCLAIR *King Coal* 49 He was charged a certain sum for 'black-smithing'—the keeping of his tools in order.

attrib. **1866** 'F. KIRKLAND' *Bk. Anecdotes* 164/1 The blacksmithing business might go to the d—l, but the farm must be looked after.

+**Blacksmith('s) shop.** The workshop of a blacksmith; a smithy.

(*a*) **1752** *N.H. Probate Rec.* III. 454 One Peice of Land . . . with the Blacksmiths Shop which stand[s] on the home lot. **1781** *Md. Hist. Mag.* V. 130 They came on board, took out the prisoners and carrying them up to a blacksmith's shop, there had them put in irons. **1813** PAULDING *J. Bull & Br. Jonathan* (ed. 2) xxiii. 123 At the taverns, blacksmiths' shops, and . . . at the church-doors. **1836** *S. Lit. Messenger* II. 303/2 Mr. Buckskin, you, sir, dodging behind the blacksmith's shop, I summon you on the jury. **1853** FOWLER *Home for All* 20 He erected a blacksmith's shop, and finally a block of stores and dwellings. **1861** WINTHROP *Open Air* 13 The cinders before the blacksmith's shop opposite had yielded their black dye to the dismal puddles. **1880** CABLE *Grandissimes* xx. 152 Opposite a blacksmith's shop . . . Aurore Nancanou . . . had halted. **1881** M. J. HOLMES *Madeline* iv. 61 Near by was a blacksmith's shop, and thither Guy ordered his driver to take the broken-down wagon.

(*b*) **1791** FRENEAU *Poems* (1795) 421 Unless the [stage-]driver . . . Has made some business for the black-smith-shop. **1809** WEEMS *Letters* II. 413 Each store sh[oul]d have 2 to 300 to stick up at × roads, Blacksmith shops, Mills, taverns, &c. **1836** *S. Lit. Messenger* II. 303/1 A store, a tavern, and a blacksmith shop, the common ingredients of a county town. **1850** GARRARD *Wah-To-Yah* i. 8 On the west skirt of the belt of timber . . . was a diminutive blacksmith shop. **1866** *Rep. Indian Affairs* 83 The blacksmith shop is old and useless, affording no protection from the rains and cold weather. **1876** HABBERTON *Jericho Road* xvi. 145 He walked so fast that the boys at the blacksmith shop stopped work to stare. **1889** *Harper's Mag.* Aug. 390/1 Perhaps he had better ride over to the blacksmith shop. **1902** MCFAUL *Ike Glidden* iii. 22 The stranger wandered carelessly among the stalls and blacksmith shops that lined the square.

+**Black snake, Black-snake,** *n.* [BLACK *a.* 2.]

1. One or other of several snakes having a black skin, esp. the large non-venomous species *Coluber (Bascanion) constrictor*, the black racer, *C. constrictor*, and the pilot-snake, *Coluber obsoletus (Elaphe obsoleta).*

1634 WOOD *New Eng. Prospect* I. xi. 46 A great long blacke snake, two yards in length, which will glide through the woods very swiftly. **1676** GLOVER *Acc. Va.* in *Phil. Trans.* XI. 631 There are also long black Snakes, short and thick black Snakes; this latter sort often times sucks the Cows, and causes them to give bloody milk. **1685** T. BUDD *Penna. & N.J.* 74 As to the other Snake, the most plentiful is a black Snake; its bite, 'tis said, does no more harm than the prick of a Pin. **1705** BEVERLEY *Virginia* IV. 64 Several other Snakes . . . have little or no hurt in them, viz. such as they call Black-Snakes, Water-Snakes, and Corn-Snakes. **1736** CATESBY *Carolina* II. 48 The Black Snake. . . . They are all over of a shining black. . . . They are the most numerous of all the Snakes. **1775** A. BURNABY *Trav. N. Amer.* 30, I observed a large black-snake, about six feet long, lying cross the stump of a tree by the road side. **1794** *Amer. Philos. Soc.* IV. 111 The black-snake is a serpent of much more activity than the rattle-snake. **1822** J. WOODS *English Prairie* 290 The black snakes are often six feet long. I have heard of their twining themselves round a man's leg so hard that he could scarcely move. **1832** KENNEDY *Swallow Barn* I. xxiii. 239 As to the black snake . . . you may amuse yourself with taking them in your hand. **1847** LANMAN *Summer in Wilderness* 114 On opening one of my prizes, an immense black snake was found in his bowels. **1866** GREGG *Life in Army* i. 18 The Black Snake was found often from ten to twelve feet in length, with a white ring round the neck: this species were called racers on account of their great speed. **1884** ROE *Nature's Story* 254 While those large black-snakes are not poisonous, they are ugly customers sometimes. **1891** *Boston Journal* Nov., The snakes had chosen the hollow tree for their winter home. There were fifty-eight large rattlers and eight black snakes.

attrib. **1857** *Atlantic Mo.* I. 97/1 Somewhere in the copse there is a black-snake hole.

2. An Abolitionist. *Obs.*

Introduced as a retort to 'Copperhead,' the adj. being suggested by 'Black Republican.'

1863 *Crisis* 18 March 63 (article-heading), 'Copperhead' Victory in Sullivan! 'Black Snakes' cleaned out. *Ib.* 1 April 77 The Abolition Black-snakes are now using every effort to obtain subscribers to a new *ism. Ib.*, The Black-snake editors appear to be urging their followers up to 'blood letting' among us. *Ib.* 6 May 119 The Black Republicans . . . are now very industriously applying the term 'Copperheads' to the Democrats. . . . Now, the representative of the Republicans, opposite to the Copperhead, is the Blacksnake.

3. A strong pliant whip made of black leather strips braided together, and tapering from the butt to the snapper.

1863 J. FISK *Exped. R. Mts.* 5 A 'black snake' . . . brought him on his legs. **1869** BROWNE *Adv. Apache Country* 45 His black-snake whizzes through the air and down on the back of the lagging wheeler. **1873** BEADLE *Undevel. West* 98 The writer seated on his 'nigh-wheeler,' and wielding a 'big-bellied blacksnake' over the backs of six mules. **1883** *Harper's Mag.* March 495/1 The Mexican-looking drivers trudged beside them . . . , cracking huge 'blacksnakes' at the animals. **1894** *Outing* June 216/2 'You see this blacksnake?' (a long whip made of braided leather thongs). **1904** STRATTON-PORTER *Freckles* 266 She only gripped the hames, . . . and slashed away with the blacksnake.

attrib. **1901** WHITE *Westerners* xxxiv. 310 He snapped the lash of his black-snake whip. **1906** PITTMAN *Belle of Blue Grass C.* iv. 84 In his hand he carried a long 'black-snake whip,' which he was whirling around his head, cracking it in the most scientific manner.

+**Blacksnake,** *v.* [f. prec. 3.] *tr.* To lash with a black-snake whip. — **1870** 'MARK TWAIN' *Sk., History repeats Itself,* I lay I'll blacksnake you within an inch of your life! **1901** *Kansas H. S. Coll.* VII. 49 One wagon boss blacksnaked him [a thieving Indian].

+**Black snake-root.** [BLACK *a.* 2.] Either of two plants, the sanicle, *Sanicula Marilandica,* and the black cohosh, *Cimicifuga racemosa,* which possess medicinal properties.

1698 G. THOMAS *Penna. & N.J.* 19 There grows also in great plenty the Black Snake-Root, (fam'd for its sometimes preserving, but often curing the Plague, being infused only in Wine, Brandy or Rumm). **1781-2** JEFFERSON *Notes on Va.* (1788) 36 Black snake-root, *Actaea racemosa.* **1798** ASBURY *Journal* II. 365 A handful of black snakeroot, one handful of fennel seed, and one handful of wormwood. **1840** DEWEY *Mass. Flowering Plants* 21 Cohosh. Black Snakeroot. . . . Strong medicinal purposes. **1843** T. TALBOT *Journals* 29 The Indians in addition use many roots. . . . I will here mention a few of them to be taken internally. The Actaea Racemosa or Black Snake root [etc.]. **1859,** etc. [see BLACK COHOSH]. **1863** *Rep. Comm. Agric.* 157 The Black Snake root (*cimicifuga*) is also a very pretty plant of this family [*Ranunculus*].

+**Black snapper.** [BLACK *a.* 2.] A valuable fish found along the coast of Florida, *Lutjanus caxis.* — **1799** A. ELLICOTT in *Life & Lett.* 186 Along the Florida Reef, and among the Keys, a great abundance and variety of fish may be taken: such as . . . black, red, and gray snappers. **1888** GOODE *Amer. Fishes* 79 The Gray Snapper, *Lutjanus caxis,* . . . is called the 'Gray Snapper' in South Florida, and the 'Black Snapper' at Pensacola.

+**Black snipe.** [BLACK *a.* 2.] (See quot.) — **1872** *Amer. Naturalist* VI. 400 The glossy ibis (called 'black snipe!') is now a common summer bird.

Black Spanish. [BLACK *a.* 2.] A breed of domestic fowls. — **1849** *New Eng. Farmer* I. 385 Italian, or Black Spanish, were exhibited by Daniel Buxton. **1856** *Rep. Comm. Patents: Agric.* 63 Of all the fancy fowls, I prefer either the 'Black Spanish,' or the 'Polands.' **1871** W. M. LEWIS *Poultry Book* 58 The Black Spanish . . . is one of our best black breeds of fowls, laying as they do a large sized and meaty egg. **1890** *Cent.* 5794 Spanish fowl . . . [is] more exactly called 'white-faced black Spanish.'

+**Black spot. 1.** The area over which slavery was prevalent. **2.** A member of a former lawless organization in the coal-mining sections of Pennsylvania, suppressed in 1877. — (1) **1851** A. LAWRENCE *Diary & Corr.* 307 We have allowed the 'black spot' to be too far spread over our land; it should have been restrained more than thirty years ago. (2) **1888** M. LANE in *America* 18 Oct. 15 They were known in one locality as 'Blackspots,' and in another as 'Buckshots,' and committed all sorts of murders, and outrages.

+**Black spruce.** [BLACK *a.* 2.] A species of spruce (*Picea mariana* or *nigra*), found in the northern states and Canada. Also attrib. with *fir.*

1765 R. ROGERS *Acc. N. America* 48 You will find beach, hemlock, and some white pines; higher up [in N.H.] the growth is chiefly black spruce. **1792** BELKNAP *New Hampshire* III. 110 The black spruce is used only for beer. . . . Of this spruce, is made the essence, which is as well known in Europe as in America. **1803** LAMBERT *Descr. Genus Pinus* 41 Black Spruce Fir, *P. nigra,* grows wild only in New England, Canada, Nova Scotia. **a1817** DWIGHT *Travels* I. 37 The black spruce . . . is extensively used as an ingredient of Beer. **1832** BROWNE *Sylva* 99 The distinguishing properties of the wood of black spruce are strength, lightness, and elasticity. **1834** *S. Lit. Messenger* I. 97 Black spruce and hemlock pines, of dark funereal aspect, tower above the soil [in Va.] like an army of Titans. **1857** *Rep. Comm. Patents: Agric.* 68 It loves to take up its residence among evergreens, the cones of which form its favorite food, those of the black-spruce particularly. **1861** *Ill. Agric. Soc. Trans.* IV. 460 The Black Spruce of Maine . . . is one of, if not the most beautiful of the Spruce tribe. **1869** *Amer. Naturalist* III. 410 Black Spruce (*Abies Menziesii*). This Black Spruce is as abundant on the higher parts of the Cœur d'Aleñe as on the coast. **1892** APGAR *Trees Northern U.S.* 179 Black or Double Spruce . . . : wild in the North and along the Alleghanies; often cultivated.

+**Black squirrel.** [BLACK *a.* 2.] A color variety of the fox-squirrel, *Sciurus niger,* or the grey squirrel, *S. carolinensis.*

[**1602** BRERETON *Virginia* 16 Squirrels, which to the Northward are blacke, and accounted very rich furres.] **1682** ASH *Carolina* 22 There are . . . the flying Squirrel, . . . the Red, the Grey, the Fox and Black Squirrels. **1738** CATESBY *Carolina* II. 73 The Black-Squirrel. . . . These, with the grey Fox-Squirrel, are very numerous and destructive to corn in the fields. **1788** J. MAY *Journal & Lett.* 72 Our luck has been heretofore to have good provisions— . . . fine venison, and turkeys—when we pleased; also, gray and black squirrels at any time. **1820** *Amer. Antiq. Soc. Coll.* 64 [The Iroquois wear] a sort of robe made of beavers' and wolves' skins, or black squirrels. **1842** *S. Lit. Messenger* VIII. 405/1 Numberless black squirrels . . . sharing the rich fruits of those many corn-crowned hills. **1850** [S. F. COOPER] *Rural Hours* 288 The black squirrel is small, only a foot long; its fur is of a glossy jet black. **1851** GLISAN *Jrnl. Army Life* 89 Animals . . . that are good for food . . . [include] black and fox squirrel. **1857** *Rep. Comm. Patents: Agric.* 66 The black-squirrel has been observed through the Middle States, in Michigan and Wisconsin.

Black staff. *Obs.* A staff or stave to be carried by a constable; the officer carrying one of these. — **1646** *Essex Inst. Coll.* IX. 147 Its agreed that two blackstaues of sixe foot long or therabout be prouided for the Constables [of Salem]. **1666** *Groton Rec.* 19 [A payment] toe black staffe. **1670** *R.I. Col. Rec.* II. 344 There came doune . . . George Bull and Tho. Mumford, with his black stafe, and . . . would have paniled the jury.

+**Black state.** [BLACK *a.* 1 b.] One of the Southern States, in reference to the Negro population. — **1814** *Niles' Reg.* VI. 189/1 The exports of the 'black' state of South Carolina. **1830** *Deb. Congress* 24 Feb. 194/2 The sectional tirade against the South as 'black States.'

Black strake, streak. *Naut.* In *pl.,* 'a range of planks immediately above the wales in a ship's side' (Falconer). — **1796** *Ann. 4th Congress* 2 Sess. 2785 The whole of the frame is raised; the wales, black strakes, flush, quarter, and fore drifs, on and dressed off. **1800** *Essex Inst. Coll.* XIII. 72 Healed the ship and payed the main-wheels, bends and black streaks.

Black-strap. +A mixture of rum and molasses used as a liquor.

In quot. 1725 perhaps in the older English sense of port or common red wine {1785-}.

1725 *New-Eng. Courant* 1-8 Feb. 1/2 The common Tipler had rather his Back should half freeze than want a little Black-Strap to warm his Belly. **1827** *Harvard Reg.* Oct. 235 Let black-strap's sable god deplore Those engine-heroes so renowned of yore! **1828** *Yankee* 16 July 227/1 This is the baby-drink, call'd black-strap and molasses, for the boys. **1830** [N. AMES] *Mariner's Sketches* 151 The mate was compounding a large tin pot of hot 'blackstrap,' when a [seal] . . . bolted in among us. *Ib.* 156 A solemn and somewhat 'lengthy' application to the mate's tin pot of hot blackstrap . . . restored the dormant circulation. **1833** W. J. SNELLING *Exposé of Gaming* 10 He was taking mighty pulls at a huge tankard of blackstrap which stood beside him. **a1849** HILL *Yankee Stories* (B.), I guess you never drink'd no blackstrap, did you? Why, bless you, it's the sweetest drink that ever streaked down a gullet. **1856** HALL *College Words* (ed. 2) 178 The favorite beverage at fires was rum and molasses, commonly called 'black-strap.' **1887** TOURGEE *Button's Inn* 137 The self-confident tradesman . . . mixed a glass of 'black-strap.' *Ib.* 146 Not a few jorums of black-strap had been mixed.

+**Black sucker.** [BLACK *a.* 2.] A cyprinoid fish, *Catostomus nigricans.* — **1839** STORER *Mass. Fishes* 86 *Cyprinus nigricans.* . . . The Black Sucker. . . . Color of the back, black; sides reddish yellow. **1842** *Nat. Hist. N.Y., Zoology* IV. 202 The Black Sucker . . . is common in Lake Erie, where it is frequently called by the whimsical name of Shoemaker. **1870** *Amer. Naturalist* IV. 386 Mud-loving species . . . common to the Delaware and its tributaries . . . [include] Black Sucker.

+**Black sugar-maple.** [BLACK *a.* 2.] A variety of sugar-maple, *Acer saccharinum* var. *nigrum.* Cf. next and BLACK MAPLE.

1818 [see BLACK HICKORY]. **1832** BROWNE *Sylva* 104 Black Sugar Maple . . . [is so called,] probably, on account of the dark color of its leaves in comparison with those of the sugar maple. **1846** — *Trees Amer.* 84 From the dark hue of its leaves, it was very appropriately designated by Mr. Loudon, under the name of . . . Black Sugar Maple. **1850** [S. F. COOPER] *Rural Hours* 65 The sugar, and the black sugar maples, are all included among our trees. **1892** APGAR *Trees Northern U.S.* 86 Black Sugar-maple. . . . Found with the other Sugar-maple, and quite variable.

+**Black sugar-tree.** [BLACK *a.* 2.] =prec. — **1780** W. FLEMING in *Travels Amer. Col.* 631 There is two sort of sugar trees cald black and white, from the Colours of the bark, and it is thought the black yields the strongest water. **1810** MICHAUX *Arbres* I. 29 Black sugar tree, . . . nom secondaire mais qui doit être préféré. **1832** BROWNE *Sylva* 104 In the Western States, and the parts of Pennsylvania, between the mountains and the Ohio, this species is called . . . Black Sugar Tree.

Black-tail. [BLACK *a.* 2.] {1661-}

+**1.** *attrib.* =BLACK-TAILED *a.*

1819 *Western Rev.* I. 235 The black-tail fox is of mixed grizzled color on the back. **1826** J. GODMAN *Nat. Hist.* II. 304 The Black-tail Deer, *Cervus Macrotis.* **1871** DE VERE 371 The variety found on the Pacific Coast (*Cervus columbianus*) is more commonly designated as the Black-tail Deer, from the black tip to its tail. **1886** ROOSEVELT in *Outing* May 131/1 The black-tail deer were more plentiful in my immediate neighborhood. **1895** *Ib.* Oct. 45/2 Next morning we . . . had two large black-tail bucks and a doe lying before our little tent.

+**b.** *Black-tail chub, fall-fish, sunfish* (see quotations).

1820 RAFINESQUE in *Western Rev.* II. 49 Big-ear Sunfish, *Icthelis megalotis.* . . . A fine species, called Red-belly, Black-ears, Black-tail Sunfish, &c. It lives in the Kentucky, Licking, and Sandy rivers, &c. *Ib.* 241 Blacktail Fallfish, *Rutilus melanurus.* . . . Vulgar name Blacktail Chub. In the Ohio and Muskingum, &c.

2. A (or the) black-tailed deer.

1850 GARRARD *Wah-To-Yah* x. 133 A band of black-tail, . . . clattering adown, with graceful motions, sped across the plain. **1878** I. L. BIRD *Rocky Mts.* 120 Graceful 'black-tails,' swift of foot. **1883** *Wheelman* I. 339 The prettiest sight of all, perhaps, was a band of deer . . . of the species familiarly known as Blacktails. **1886** *Outing* Nov. 102/2 Ye must track and kill a 'black-tail,' Captain.

Black-tailed, *a.* [BLACK *a.* 3.]

+1. *Black-tailed deer*, the Columbian deer (*Cervus columbianus*) or the mule-deer (*C. macrotis*). Cf. BLACK-TAIL.

1806 LEWIS in *L. & Clark Exped.* (1905) IV. 87 The black tailed fallow deer. **1807** GASS *Journal* iii. 40 The black-tailed, or mule deer have much larger ears than the common deer and tails almost without hair, except at the end, where there is a bunch of black hair. **1834** A. PIKE *Sketches* 24 Black-tailed deer . . . are larger than the deer which are found in the United States, and in fact their skin sometimes is so large that it might be mistaken for an elk-skin. **1837** IRVING *Bonneville* I. iii. 44 In these rugged and elevated regions they began to see the black-tailed deer, a species larger than the ordinary kind, and chiefly found in rocky and mountainous countries. **1848** PARKMAN in *Knickerb.* XXXI. 333 Two black-tailed deer bounded away among the rocks. **1870** *Amer. Naturalist* III. 164 The black-tailed deer is found in this vicinity [i.e., plains of Kansas]. **1879** B. F. TAYLOR *Summer-Savory* iii. 31 At Cheyenne . . . we got our first steak of the black-tailed deer—rich, juicy, dark, a luxury.

+b. *Black-tailed roebuck*, =prec.

1845 DE SMET *Oregon Missions* (1847) 134 The black-tailed roe-buck, as well as its red-tailed relative.

+2. Applied to other animals or birds.

1828 BONAPARTE *Synopsis* 327 The Black-tailed Godwit, *Limosa aegocephala.* **1846** EMORY *Military Reconn.* 15 The only animals seen were one black-tailed rabbit and an antelope. **1859** BARTLETT 218 Jackass Rabbit (*Lepus callotis*) . . . is known also by the names of Mule Rabbit, Texan Hare, and Black-tailed Hare. **1874** COUES *Birds N.W.* 494 *Limosa Hudsonica*, Hudsonian or Black-tailed Godwit.

+**Black tan.** [BLACK *a.* 2.] A black-and-tan dog. — **1856** *Spirit of Times* (N.Y.) 1 Nov. 140/2 Dan brought home two of the finest *black tans* you ever laid your eyes on.

+**Black tariff.** The tariff of 1842. 'This was a high tariff, odious to the Democrats, in which the duties averaged 33 per cent.' (Th.). — **1846** *Congress. Globe* App. Jan. 92 Let this state of things once come, and . . . we shall hear no more about the 'black tariff.' *Ib.* App. 1 July 1043/1, I might compromise a little rather than see the country longer consigned to the tender mercies of the black tariff of 1842!

Black tea. The leaves of the tea plant prepared by withering and fermenting; a beverage made from this. {1785-} — **1789** *Ann. 1st Congress* I. 168 On bohea tea, per pound, [a duty of] six cents; on all souchong and other black teas, ten cents. **1816** *Ann. 14th Congress* 1 Sess. 1873 On tea, from China, . . . souchong and other black, [a duty of] twenty-five cents per pound. **1848** *Encycl. Amer.* XII. 161 The black teas, usually imported by Europeans and Americans, are . . . bohea, congo, campo, souchong, pouchong, pekoe. **1881** *Rep. Indian Affairs* 118 An Indian is just as intemperate in the use of black tea as he would be in the use of whiskey.

* **Black thorn, Blackthorn.** [BLACK *a.* 2.]

+1. An American species of hawthorn.

The application in quot. 1737 is doubtful.

1737 BRICKELL *N. Carolina* 79 The Black Thorn, or Sloe Tree grows plentifully in several parts of this Province, . . . but is quite different from our Sloe Tree in Ireland. **1798** *N.Y. State Soc. Arts* I. 228 The black thorn has been destroyed by a worm that preys upon its twigs. **1807** C. SCHULTZ *Travels* II. 24, I noticed on the banks of the Ohio . . . black thorn, Jerusalem oak, . . . and of willows an endless variety. **1843** TORREY *Flora N.Y.* I. 222 *Crataegus tomentosa*, . . . Black Thorn. . . . Wet thickets; western part of the State. **1857** GRAY *Botany* 124 Black or Pear Thorn. [Grows in] thickets; common. May, June. **1884** SARGENT *Rep. Forests* 79 Black Thorn. Pear Haw. **1885** HAVARD *Flora W. & S. Texas* 512 *Cratægus subvillosa*, . . . Texas Black Thorn, [is a] small tree. **1901** MOHR *Plant Life Ala.* 99 *Crataegus molle* (black thorn) . . . [is] rarely found north of the Central Pine belt.

+2. The sweet acacia or sponge-tree.

1833 EATON *Botany* 1 *A. farnesiana*, black thorn. . . . New Orleans. **1845** LINCOLN *Botany* App. 69/1 *Acacia farnesiana*, (black thorn). . . . Flowers fragrant; legumes fusiform. *S.*

*3. The European sloe, *Prunus spinosa.*

1847 WOOD *Botany* 241 Black Thorn. Sloe. . . . Hedgerows and cultivated grounds, Penn. **1892** APGAR *Trees Northern U.S.* 98 Sloe, Blackthorn, . . . is becoming naturalized along roadsides and waste places; from Europe.

Black-throated, *a.* [BLACK *a.* 3.] Of various birds (esp. buntings or warblers): Having a black throat.

[**1785** PENNANT *Arctic Zoology* II. 363 Black-throated bunting. . . . Inhabits New York.] **1808** WILSON *Ornithology* I. 54 Black-throated Bunting, *Emberiza Americana*, . . . arrive[s] in Pennsylvania from the south about the middle of May. **1810** *Ib.* II. 115 Black-Throated Blue Warbler, *Sylvia Canadensis. Ib.* 137 Black-Throated Green Warbler, *Sylvia Virens.* **1839** PEABODY *Mass. Birds* 398 The Black-throated Diver, *Colymbus septentrionalis*, . . . [is] at all times shy and watchful. **1844** *Nat. Hist. N.Y., Zoology* II. 43 The Black-Throated Waxwing, *Bombycilla Garrula.* **1858** BAIRD *Birds Pacific R.R.* 130 *Lampornis Mango*, . . . Black-throated Humming Bird. *Ib.* 470 *Poospiza Bilineata*, . . . Black-throated Sparrow. **1868** *Amer. Naturalist* II. 172 The Black-throated Blue Warbler . . . arrives about the first week in May. **1869** *Ib.* III. 189 The only other bird of interest seen east of this was the pretty Black-throated Finch. **1878** *Proc. U.S. Nat. Museum* I. 406 *Dendrœca nigrescens*, Black-throated Gray Warbler. **1892** TORREY *Foot-path Way* 16 During all that time [I] saw and heard . . . black-throated blues, black-throated greens [*sc.* warblers].

Black tin. +(See quotation.) — **1844** FEATHERSTONHAUGH *Slave States* 80 Mr. M'Faddin showed me pieces of galena that he had ploughed up in his lands; zinc also and manganese are found, which last the settlers call *black tin.*

Black tongue. An affection of the tongue, in human beings or cattle, symptomatic of various diseases. — **1853** in *Mich. Agric. Soc. Trans.* VII. 297 Occasionally, on the lake shore, black tongue, with other forms of erysipelas, appears in winter and spring. **1858** [see BLACK LEG 2 b]. **1879** *Diseases of Swine* 208 Cattle are affected with murrain and blacktongue and nearly all die. **1888** BILLINGS *Hardtack* 294 Glanders took off a great many [mules], and black tongue, a disease peculiar to them, caused the death of many more.

Black tooth. (See quotation.) — **1877** *Vermont Dairym. Assoc. Rep.* VIII. 107 Black tooth is a popular disease of swine.

+**Black tree.** The black mangrove. — **1884** SARGENT *Rep. Forests* 117 *Avicennia nitida.* . . . Black Mangrove. Black Tree. Black Wood. **1897** SUDWORTH *Arborescent Flora* 334 Blackwood. . . . Common names [include] Blackwood (Fla.), Blacktree (Fla.).

Black trout. [BLACK *a.* 2.] +One or other species of trout having a very dark skin. — **1849** LANMAN *Alleghany Mts.* ix. 65 On inquiring of a homespun angler what fish the river did produce, he replied: 'Salmon, black-trout, red horse, hog-fish, suckers and cat-fish.' **1878** *Proc. U.S. Nat. Museum* I. 72 *Salmo Tsuppitch.* Tsuppitch Salmon. Black Trout of Lake Tahoe. **1883** *Century Mag.* July 376/2, I have heard them [=black bass] called . . . white and black trout in Tennessee. **1891** *Cent.* 6503 *Black trout*, the Lake Tahoe trout; specified as *Salmo henshawi.*

Black vomit. One of the symptoms in serious cases of yellow fever; also, the disease itself. {1749-}

1799 BROWN *A. Mervyn* xviii, The sheets were tinged . . . with that substance which is said to be characteristic of this disease, the gangrenous or black vomit. **1832** J. F. WATSON *Hist. Tales N.Y.* 118 In 1743 a yellow fever, as it was called, visited New York. . . . They had black vomit and spots. **1836** E. L. JOHNSTON *Recoll. Georgia Loyalist* vi. 97 Andrew had been taken with the black vomit, fatal symptom! in the night. **1854** SIMMS *Southward Ho* i. 3 Can you really prefer black vomit to an easy and agreeable death from charcoal? **1878** *Harper's Mag.* Dec. 130/1 The dreaded symptom of black-vomit is almost surely a fatal one: after this occurs, not more than two or three out of a hundred recover.

Black vulture. [BLACK *a.* 2.] The urubu or carrion crow, *Catharista atrata*, of the southern states.

1791 BARTRAM *Travels* (1928) 237 These breed and continue the year round in Pennsylvania: . . . *Vultur atratus*, black vulture, or carrion crow; [etc.]. **1813** WILSON *Ornithology* IX. 105 It is said that the Black Vultures sometimes attack young pigs, and eat off their ears and tails. **1858** BAIRD *Birds Pacific R.R.* 5 *Cathartes atratus*, the Black Vulture, the Carrion Crow, . . . [is] abundant in the Southern States. **1869** *Amer. Naturalist* III. 498, I had sent me . . . a good specimen of the Black Vulture . . . , the first one I ever knew so far east.

+**Black walnut.** [BLACK *a.* 2.]

1. A species of walnut, *Juglans nigra*, having a brown wood turning blackish with age.

1624 *Va. House of Burgesses* 28 [We] weare . . . wholly imployed in cuttinge downe of masts, cedar, black wallnutt, clapboarde. **1634** A. WHITE *Brief Rel. Maryland* (1910) 40 The ground is heare, as in very many places, covered . . . with ackhornes, black walnut, cedar, . . . and such like. **1682** ASH *Carolina* 7 Wallnut Trees there are of two or three sorts; but the Black Wallnut for its Grain, is most esteem'd. *c*1730 CATESBY *Carolina* I. 67 The Black Walnut. . . . The wood . . . approaches nearer to black than any other wood that affords so large timber. **1787** SARGENT in *Mem. Academy* II. I. 157 Black Walnut [grows in the n.w. Ohio valley] from two to six feet diameter. **1807** GASS *Journal* 18 On the north the land is level and well timbered, with ash, sugar tree, black walnut . . . and some other timber. **1820** FLINT *Lett. from Amer.* 229 Black walnut grows to a great size, and is considered a mark of the excellence of the soil on which it grows. **1823** JAMES *Exped.* I. 71 The black walnut attains, in the Missouri bottoms, its greatest magnitude. **1843** N. BOONE *Journal* 225 On this we found . . . a sort of black walnut with many appearances to indicate its being a new variety. **1857-8** *Ill. Agric. Soc. Trans.* III. 479 The black walnut and white walnut or butternut flourish finely upon our prairies, and the value of their timber renders them very desirable in cultivation. **1870** KEIM *Sheridan's Troopers* 159 Everywhere along the stream there was an abundance of wood, . . . black walnut, ash and some locust. **1885** *Amer. Naturalist* XIX. 136 The mite gall found on the black walnut. **1887** [see BLACK ASH]. **1892** APGAR *Trees Northern U.S.* 141 Black Walnut [is] . . . more common west than east of the Alleghanies; often planted.

b. Attrib. with *grove, timber.*

1779 *Coll. N.H. Hist. Soc.* VI. 320 The finest black walnut timber grows on the intervale that I ever saw. **1905** VALENTINE *H. Sandwith* 59 The stone mansion [seen] through trunks of a stately black-walnut grove.

2. A single tree of this species.

1700 *Md. Hist. Mag.* XIX. 350 Halls ridge neck . . . [beginning] at a bounded black wallnut standing on a ridge. **1738** Chalkley *Scotch-Irish Settlement Va.* II. 373 To a forked Walnut by a black one, a Hiccory, an Ash by the riverside. **1785** V. B. Howard *Heroes* (1932) 143 Then west . . . to a large black walnut. **1876** WHITMAN *Specimen Days* (1892) 93 The rich dark green of the tulip-trees, . . . the dull hues of the sycamores and black-walnuts!

b. One of the nuts from this tree.

1737 BRICKELL *N. Carolina* 69 The Indians gather great Quantities of these Nuts, and the Black Wall-nuts (being ripe in Autumn). **1792** IMLAY *Western Territory* 90 Several kinds of nuts grow in the forests, such as chesnuts, hickory, and black walnuts. **1824** DODDRIDGE *Notes* 27 Of black walnuts [we had] many varieties as to size, and amount of kernal. **1851** *Knickerb.* XXXVII. 183 A deep box, containing 'black' and 'shag-bark' walnuts, chesnuts, . . . and hazel-nuts.

3. The wood of this tree.

1832 BROWNE *Sylva* 180 The black walnut is also employed for the stocks of military muskets. **1834** PECK *Gaz. Illinois* 24 The black walnut is much used for building materials and cabinet work, and sustains a fine polish. **1850** [S. F. COOPER] *Rural Hours* 65 A few years back, maple ranked next to mahogany for these purposes, but lately black walnut has been more in favor. **1858** WILLIS *Convalescent* 416 He explained that the present demand of black-walnut . . . affected his class of chopping very considerably. **1871** [L. H. BAGG] *At Yale* 166 The same design, enlarged, carved in black-walnut . . . , was displayed in the rooms of members.

b. Attrib. with names of articles of furniture, etc.

1704 SEWALL *Diary* II. 113 Mrs. Zachary . . . is brought in a black walnut coffin to the south-end of the town. **1720** — *Letter-book* II. 106 A true looking glass of black walnut frame of the newest fashion (if the fashion be good), as good as can be bought for five or six pounds. **1835** HOFFMAN *Winter in West* I. 140 The black walnut stand, upon which I am writing, occupies the centre of the room. **1855** *S. Lit. Messenger* XXI. 374/2 An old black-walnut cupboard, which may have been used as a wardrobe. **1870** MEDBERY *Men of Wall St.* 117 Customers may enter behind the black-walnut or other screens which shut out the profane public. **1880** BURNETT *Old Pioneer* 9 After the sugar was molded into cakes or grained, it was carefully deposited in the black walnut 'sugar-chest.' *Ib.* 15 Taking the . . . trusty old rifle, with its black-walnut stock and flint-lock, we started into the hills. **1907** C. C. ANDREWS *Recoll.* 89 Indian houses were built of black-walnut logs.

+Black-walnut tree. =prec. 1, 2.

1624 SMITH *Generall Historie* 25 There is [in Va.] also some Elme, some blacke Walnut tree, and some Ash. **1775** ADAIR *Indians* 360 Lands of a loose black soil, . . . well shaded with large and high . . . black walnut-trees. **1790** S. DEANE *New-England Farmer* 190/1 The black walnut tree is said to grow naturally in Virginia. **1847** HOWE *Hist. Coll. Ohio* 295 A black walnut tree . . . was . . . carried across the creek [by a storm]. **1888** *Detroit Free Press* 30 March (F.), The black walnut-tree will cut a figure on our farms in the future. It can be made as profitable as the apple-tree in localities where it will thrive at all.

+Black warrior. [BLACK *a.* 2.] A large black hawk, *Buteo borealis harlani*, of the southern states. — **1831** AUDUBON *Ornith. Biog.* I. 441 The Black Warrior has been seen to pounce on a fowl, kill it almost instantly, and . . . conceal it. *Ib.* 442. **1839** PEABODY *Mass. Birds* 269 The Black Warrior . . . subsists on poultry, partridges, and other birds. **1858** BAIRD *Birds Pacific R.R.* 24 Black Warrior. The specimens . . . were obtained . . . in New Mexico. **1874** COUES *Birds N.W.* 352 Harlan's Buzzard; Black Warrior. . . . I regard the claims of this species to validity as not yet established.

Black wart. +A black excrescence on certain fruit-trees. — **1861** *Ill. Agric. Soc. Trans.* IV. 454 The Black Cherry . . . is sometimes affected by the black wart. **1862** *Rep. Comm. Patents: Agric.* 255 Plums and cherries are infested with the curculio and the black wart. **1867** *Amer. Naturalist* April 112 The members then discussed the origin of the Black Wart on the Plum Tree.

+Blackwash, *v.* [Suggested by *whitewash.*] *tr.* To blacken in character. — **1839** *Congress. Globe* App., 17 Jan. 103/3, I am confident . . . every effort will be used . . . to whitewash the black frauds . . . of Swartwout, and blackwash the Administration. [Also in recent use (1927).]

+Black wasp. [BLACK *a.* 2.] — **1789** MORSE *Amer. Geog.* 62 Insects found in America . . . [include the] Black wasp. [**1850** [S. F. COOPER] *Rural Hours* 252 We have but few wasps here; our most common kind is this black variety.]

+Black weevil. [BLACK *a.* 2.] (See quotation.) — **1849** *Rep. Comm. Patents: Agric.* (1850) 153 These are the *Calandra oryzae*, the true rice weevil; distinguished from his European cousin by the two reddish spots on each wing-cover, and known among us as the 'black weevil.'

+Black whortleberry. The black huckleberry (q.v.). — **1784** CUTLER in *Mem. Academy* I. 438 The Black Whortleberry. **1818** *Jrnl. Science* I. 362 July 16, Black whortleberries (*Vaccinium resinosum*) ripening. **1847** WOOD *Botany* 368 *Vaccinium resinosum*, Black Whortleberry or Huckleberry. . . . Berries black, globose, sweet and eatable, ripe in August.

+Black willow. [BLACK *a.* 2.]

1. A species of willow, *Salix nigra*, with dark bark.

1802 ELLICOTT *Journal* 284 Black-willow . . . [is] not in great abundance, and becomes more scarce as you descend the river. **1828** BECK in *Trans. Albany Inst.* I. 18 Elliott remarks, that the *Salix nigra* (black willow,) is the only species which is found in the low country of Carolina, except [etc.]. **1846** EMORY *Mil. Reconn.* 77 It is principally of deep dust and sand, overgrown with cotton wood, . . . willow, and the black willow. **1861** *Ill. Agric. Soc. Trans.* IV. 447 A Black Willow, introduced from Pennsylvania, is said to be a rapid grower here. **1892** APGAR *Trees Northern U.S.* 163 Black Willow. . . . Common along streams, southward, but rare in the northern range of States. **1901** MOHR *Plant Life Ala.* 125 Black willow and cottonwood cover the recent alluvium.

attrib. **1901** MOHR *Plant Life Ala.* 465 *Salix nigra*, Black Willow. . . . The bark, as 'black willow bark,' is used medicinally.

2. (See quotations.)

1884 SARGENT *Rep. Forests* 170 *Salix flavescens*, . . . Black Willow. **1892** APGAR *Trees Northern U.S.* 163 *Salix amygdaloides*, . . . Western Black Willow, . . . is the common Black Willow of the streams of Ohio to Missouri. **1894** *Amer. Folk-Lore* VII. 91 *Baccharis viminea*, . . . black willow; Santa Barbara Co., Cal. **1897** SUDWORTH *Arborescent Flora* 120 *Salix lasiandra*, Western Black Willow.

Black-winged, *a.* (See BLACK *a.* 3.) — **1828** BONAPARTE *Synopsis* 31 The Black-winged Hawk, *Falco melanopterus*, . . . inhabits the southern states. **1844** *Nat. Hist. N.Y., Zoology* II. 176 The Black-winged Redbird, or Fire-bird and Tanager, as it is often called.

+Black wolf. [BLACK *a.* 2.] A variety of the gray wolf, *Canis lupus*, having a black coat.

[**1634** WOOD *New Eng. Prospect* I. vi. 24 The Woolfe being a blacke one, he was loath to spoyle his furre with a second shot, his skinne being worth five or sixe pound Sterling.] **1637** MORTON *New Canaan* II. v, By the Salvages . . . the skinne of the black wolfe . . . is esteemed a present for a prince. **1684** *Conn. Public Rec.* III. 149 Those on the west side of the sayd river fell to the Mohegans, and for about forty five yeares have payd tributt, acknowledgments, and white deer skinns and bear skinns and black wolfe skinns. **1823** James *Exped. Rocky Mts.* I. 261 *Canis lycaon*, Black wolf. **1831** PECK *Guide* 162 In Illinois . . . the black wolf . . . is scarce. Occasionally they are killed by our hunters. **1836** J. HALL *Statist. West* ix. 114 The common, or black wolf . . . is a large fierce animal, and very destructive to sheep, pigs, calves, poultry, and even young colts. **1845** *Knickerb.* XXV. 236 A black wolf, of the largest size, the skin of which he brought off as a trophy. **1846** SAGE *Scenes Rocky Mts.* vi, The black wolf . . . is fully as large as the common cur-dog.

+Blackwood, Black wood. [BLACK *a.* 2.]

1. The black mangrove, *Avicennia nitida*, of Florida.

1775 ROMANS *Florida* 268 Here we begin to see a few of the tropical plants, such as *carica, borassus, capsicum*, mangles and blackwood. **1884, 1897** [see BLACK TREE].

b. Attrib. with *bush.*

1775 ROMANS *Florida* App. 27 There are some mangrove and blackwood bushes on them. *Ib.* 80 The chief growth on the keys are mangrove and blackwood bushes.

2. (See quotations and cf. BLACK GROWTH.) Also attrib.

1812 F. A. MICHAUX *Arbres de l'Amérique* II. 220 On désigne ces terreins sous le nom de *Black wood lands*, terreins à essence noire. **1848** BARTLETT 33 *Black wood*, hemlock, pine, spruce, and fir. Maine. **1859** HILLHOUSE tr. *Michaux's Sylva* I. 154 The first class comprises the resinous trees, such as Pines and Spruces, and covers the low grounds and bottoms of the valleys; these forests are called Black-wood lands.

3. *Blackwood dance* (see BLACKMOUTH DANCE).

+Black woodcock. [BLACK *a.* 2.] The pileated woodpecker, *Hylotomus pileatus.* — **1811** WILSON *Ornithology* IV. 27 In Pennsylvania and the northern states he is called the Black Woodcock; in the southern states, the Log-cock. **1858** BAIRD *Birds Pacific R.R.* 107 Black Wood Cock; Log Cock. *Hab.*—North America from Atlantic to Pacific.

+Black worm. [BLACK *a.* 2.] One or other of several black grubs attacking plants or trees.

1790 S. DEANE *New-Eng. Farmer* 148/1 The black worm, an insect so called, is an ash coloured worm, with a stripe almost black upon its back. . . . The greatest mischief that they commonly do, is to young cabbages. **1791** N. WEBSTER in Ford *Notes* I. 346, [I] find great multitudes of black worms devouring fields of grass & corn. **1817** in Fitch *Rep. Insects N.Y.* (1865) 116 Worchester, May 22d. We learn that the black worm is making great ravages on some farms in this town. **1859** G. W. PERRY *Turpentine Farming* 106 Black Worm . . . is to be found on green pines in the latter part of spring, from which time, during the remainder of the season, they may be seen wherever scars reach the wood. **1861** *Ill. Agric. Soc. Trans.* V. 476 The army worm . . . has probably existed there [=New England] for a century, . . . being known by the popular name of 'black-worm.'

***Bladder.** A prepared animal bladder used as a container for liquor, etc. — **1833** NEAL *Down-Easters* I. 20 'What d'ye give a bladder [of snuff]?' 'A bladder! Oh—ah—I understand now; I don't buy it by the bladder.' . . . 'How then?' 'By the box.' **1839** BRIGGS *H. Franco* I. xxiii. 253 The little skiff . . . landed . . . some dozens of bladders well filled with Aquadente.

Bladder campion. {1762–} A species of campion (*Silene inflata*), with a globular inflated calyx. — **1817** EATON *Botany* (1822) 256 *Cucubalus behen*, bladder campion. **1840** DEWEY *Mass. Flowering Plants* 87 Bladder Campion . . . [grows] about fences and roads; . . . introduced; substitute for asparagus and green peas. **1857** GRAY *Botany* 55 Bladder Campion. . . . Fields and road-sides; E. New England. July. . . . Nat. from Eu[rope].

Bladder fern. {1828} A fern of the genus *Cystopteris* (esp. *C. bulbifera*), having an inflated indusium. — **1843** TORREY *Flora N.Y.* II. 501 *Cystopteris bulbifera*, . . . Bulb-bearing Bladder-fern. . . . Shady rocky places: frequent. *Ib.*, *Cystopteris fragilis*, . . . Brittle Bladder-fern. . . . Crevices of moist rocks: not common. **1868** *Amer. Naturalist* II. 527 The Bladder Ferns (*Cystopteris*) appear in . . . two [species]; . . . one, the fragile Bladder Fern, creeping out of limestone and granite crevices alike, and from the interstices of old walls; and a bulb-bearing one. **1889** *Cent.* 574 [Of the] bladder-fern . . . Great Britain and North America have three [species] each, and of these two are common to both countries.

Bladder ketmia. {1829} A species of *Hibiscus* with an inflated fruiting calyx. — **1817–8** EATON *Botany* (1822) 306 Bladder ketmia, flower of an hour. **1843** TORREY *Flora N.Y.* I. 115 *Hibiscus trionum* . . . Bladder Ketmia. Venetian Mallow. . . . In gardens and cultivated grounds: Partially naturalized. A native of the south of Europe and Africa. **1847** DARLINGTON *Weeds & Plants* 67 Three-lobed Hibiscus. Bladder Ketmia. Flower-of-an-hour. . . . Formerly cultivated in gardens, and not rare as a weed in cultivated grounds. **1857** GRAY *Botany* 69 Bladder Ketmia. . . . Escaped from gardens into cultivated grounds.

*** Bladder-nut.**

1. A shrub (*Staphylea trifolia*) bearing its seeds in large inflated pods.

1791 MUHLENBERG *Index Florae* 166 Bladder-nut. **1821** *Mass. H. S. Coll.* 2 Ser. IX. 156 Plants . . . indigenous in the township of Middlebury [Vermont, include the] . . . Bladder-nut. **1850** *New Eng. Farmer* II. 60 The Bladder Nut is a shrub of easy cultivation. **1883** HALE *Woods & Timbers N.C.* 173 Bladder Nut . . . is probably to be found along streams through the Middle District. **1896** *Godey's Mag.* April 400/2 There is a bush, common in some parts along streams and marshes, that botanists call *Staphylea trifolia*, or 'bladder-nut.' **1901** MOHR *Plant Life Ala.* 605 American Bladder Nut . . . [grows in] moist shady borders of woods and copses. . . . Shrub 8 to 10 feet high.

2. Attrib. with *tree.*

1785 MARSHALL *Amer. Grove* 147 *Staphylaea.* Bladder-Nut-Tree. *Ib.* 148 *Staphylaea trifoliata.* Three-leaved Bladder-nut-Tree. **1815** DRAKE *Cincinnati* 77 Forest of the Miami country [contains] . . . Bladdernut tree, . . . Poison Vine [etc.].

+Bladder plum. A disease in plums, etc., by which the stone is aborted, leaving a hollow cavity; plum pocket. — **1889** BASTIN *College Botany* 315 *Exoascus*, one species of which produces the disease called 'bladder-plum,' in the fruits of various species of Prunus.

Bladder-pod. {1866} A low-growing herb (*Vesicaria Shortii*) bearing a small globose pod. — **1857** GRAY *Botany* 37. **1861** WOOD *Botany* 237. **1891** *Cent.* 6738 *Vesicaria.* . . . The flowers are large and golden-yellow in the American species. . . . They are known as bladder-pod, especially *V. Shortii*, in America.

+Bladder-tree. = BLADDER-NUT. — **1824** BIGELOW *Florula Bostoniensis* (ed. 2) 121 *Staphylea trifolia*, Bladder tree, . . . a handsome shrub from six to ten feet high, remarkable for its large inflated capsules.

Bladder-weed. A species of sea-weed, with air-bladders in the fronds. — **1858** HOLMES *Autocrat* 190 As I don't want my wreck to be washed up on one of the beaches, in company with devil's-aprons, bladder-weeds . . . and bleached crab-shells, I turn about.

Bladder-wort. {1776–} A genus of water-plants (*Utricularia*), having small air-bladders on the leaves.

1784 CUTLER in *Mem. Academy* I. 405 *Utricularia.* . . . Purple Bladderwort. Lesser hooded Milfoil. . . . In muddy ponds. **1821** *Mass. H. S. Coll.* 2 Ser. IX. 157 Plants . . . indigenous in the township of Middlebury [Vermont, include] . . . Bladderwort. **1824** BIGELOW *Florula Bostoniensis* (ed. 2) 7 *Utricularia vulgaris*, Bladder-wort. . . . An aquatic plant, appearing above water only with its stalk and flowers. **1843** TORREY *Flora N.Y.* II. 20 *Utricularia vulgaris.* . . . Common Bladderwort. . . . Ponds and slowly flowing streams; rather common. *Ib.* 21 *Utricularia striata.* . . . Striated Bladderwort. . . . Swamps and shallow waters. **1869** *Amer. Naturalist* III. 375 The three kinds of plants which are the best suited for the aquarium, of all our natives, are . . . Bladderwort [etc.]. **1894** TORREY *Fla. Sketch-Book* 29 Here and there a pool was yellow with bladder-wort.

*** Blade, *n.***

+1. *pl.* The leaves of Indian corn, much used as fodder.

'In this sense much used in the Southern States' (W. '28).

1724 H. JONES *Virginia* 40 Indian Corn is the best Food for Cattle . . . and the Blades and Tops are excellent Fodder, when well cured. **1805** PARKINSON *Tour* 39 It was natural for me now to inquire, what they [= inhabitants of Norfolk, Va.] kept their cows and horses on during the winter. They told me—their horses on blades, and their cows on slops. **1818** PALMER *Travels U.S.* 119 Where we breakfasted [in Tenn. or W.Va.], the landlord . . . gave our horses some *blades*, i.e. large dried leaves of Indian corn. **1831** PECK *Guide* 155 About the middle of September, the cornfields [of the Central West] are again entered to gather the 'blades'; —the leaves—which are . . . saved for fodder. This is the common, rough food, in addition to corn, given to horses, calves, &c. **1885** 'CRADDOCK' *Prophet* i. 14 The dew had dried from the long, keen blades of the Indian corn. **1894** *Vt. Agric. Rep.* XIV. 42 [Corn] stalks . . . are divided into . . . the leaves or blades (stripped from the stalks, below the ears), the tops, . . . the husks or shucks, and the butts.

+b. Attrib. (in singular) with *fodder, house.*

1823 Commons, etc. *Doc. Hist.* I. 256 For example, the tops are not cut from the corn. The blade fodder only is pulled, and that not always. **1865** *Nation* I. 333 Later in the day they could be seen coming up out of the fields, carrying on their heads great stacks of the dried fodder, which is at once stowed away in blade-houses. These are small buildings with walls of logs, between which are left wide apertures for the admission of air, as the fodder is apt to grow musty. **1897** W. E. BARTON *Hero in Homespun* 184 [They] gave them [the horses] some 'roughness,' as John called the bundles of blade fodder.

+2. (See quotation.)

1805–9 HENRY *Camp. Quebec* 192 About midway of the horn [of the moose] from the crown of the head, there is a broad flat part of the horn, called the blade.

Blade, *v.* [f. the noun.] {1841–, *local*} *+tr.* To strip (corn-stalks) of the leaves. — **1791** Imlay *Western Territory* (1797) 477 August . . . he sows his turnips, tops his indian corn, and blades it for the cattle.

*** Blame, *v. slang* or *colloq.*[2]** [Probably a substitute for *blast.*]

1. Used as a mild imprecation in the optative or imperative mood. {1865–, *dial.*}

1829 SANDS *Writings* II. 149 Goy blame it all, I guess they'm chiefly done dinner to humm. **1835** [LONGSTREET] *Georgia Scenes* 26 'Blame my buttons,' said Blossom, 'if I like them eyes.' **1857** HAMMOND *Northern Scenes* 59 Blame me, if he [i.e. a fish] hadn't taken a double hitch of the line around his eye tooth. **1865** 'MARK TWAIN' *Sk., Jumping Frog*, Why, blame my cats if he don't weigh five pound. **1866** [C. H. SMITH] *Bill Arp* 47 Blame my skin if I wasn't joking. **1876** 'MARK TWAIN' *Tom Sawyer* vii. 67 Blame it, I ain't going to stir him much. **1884** — *Huck. Finn* ii. 14 Why, blame it all, we've *got* to do it. **1891** 'THANET' *Otto the Knight*, etc. 266 That's so, blame his skin!

b. In passive, in phr. (*I'm*) *blamed if* (etc.). {1867–}

1843 STEPHENS *High Life N.Y.* I. iii. 31, I'll be blamed if you've the least bit of Yankee in you. **1848** BARTLETT 34, I'll be blamed, if . . . **1876** 'MAX ADELER' *Elbow Room* xv, Blamed if I haven't forgotten that word. **1894** 'MARK TWAIN' *P. Wilson* xiii, But I'm blamed if I can see my way through it. **1904** H. R. MARTIN *Tillie* 322, I'm blamed if I dare adwise you.

+2. Used as *adv.* = BLAMED 2. Also as an intensive with *please.*

*a***1861** WINTHROP *J. Brent* viii. 85 It's a free country and I shall say what I blame please. **1876** 'MARK TWAIN' *Tom Sawyer* vii. 67 He's my tick and I'll do what I blame please with him, or die! **1881** *Harper's Mag.* May 881/1 Mrs. Brinkly and her cousin are two blame fine women. **1909** WASON *Happy Hawkins* 135 They must 'a' been blame poor shots.

+3. Used as *adj.* = BLAMED 1.

1876 'MARK TWAIN' *Tom Sawyer* vi. 65 Talk about trying to cure warts with spunk-water such a blame-fool way as that! **1886** J. C. HARRIS in *Century Mag.* Jan. 427/1, I got a dockyment here that'll fetch you a blame sight quicker 'n your dockyment'll fetch me. *a***1909** 'O. HENRY' *Roads of Destiny* xxi. 351 You're a blame Yankee, ain't you? **1912** WASON *Friar Tuck* viii. 68 You blame little squab, you!

Blamed, *ppl. a.* and *adv. slang* or *colloq.*[2] [Cf. prec.]

1. *ppl. a.* Confounded. {1883–, *dial.*}

1862–3 HALE *If, Yes & Perhaps* (1868) 20 This adjective 'blamed' is the virtuous oath by which simple people, who are improving their habits, cure themselves of a stronger epithet. **1880** 'MARK TWAIN' *Tramp Abroad* xxvi. 270, I'd a blamed sight ruther carry the claim myself. **1887** H. FREDERIC *Seth's Brother's Wife* 339 He's the blamedest fool in th' caounty. **1904** LORIMER *Gorgon Graham* 200 They've an ache or a pain in every blamed joint. **1922** A. BROWN *Old Crow* iii. 31 There isn't a blamed thing I can do. . . . I hate the whole blamed show.

2. *adv.* Confoundedly; excessively. {1884–, *dial.*}

1833 *Knickerb.* I. 303, I thought I mought reach it with greater safety by dressing myself up in disguise, which I now look upon as a blamed foolish notion. **1835** [LONGSTREET] *Georgia Scenes* 223 Yes, a blamed good shot! *c***1845** W. I. PAULDING *Noble Exile* 139, I advised you not to answer that invitation, . . . but you're so blamed fierce, you would do it. **1845** MRS. KIRKLAND *Western Clearings* 70, I wasn't a goin' to let Dean know; because he'd ha' thought himself so blam'd cunning. **1876** 'MAX ADELER' *Elbow Room* xv, The pistol looked so blamed dangerous when I cocked it that I changed my mind. **1904** STRATTON-PORTER *Freckles* 51, I am . . . so blamed ignorant I don't know which ones go in pairs. **1911** R. D. SAUNDERS *Col. Todhunter* iii. 52 Always ready to wrastle our blamedest for whatever's worth havin'.

+Blamenation, *n.* and *adv.* [f. BLAME *v.*, after *damnation.*] Used as an expletive or mild oath. — **1837** J. C. NEAL *Charcoal Sk.* (1838) 106 Don't stand . . . all day a blockin' up the gangvay, or I'll drive right over you—blamenation if I don't! **1837** *Knickerb.* X. 167, I think she's blamenation elegint! **1863** 'E. KIRKE' *Southern Friends* iv. 63, I'll lamn ye like blamenation. *Ib.*, But, blamenation, ye ar!

+Bland dollar. [From the name of R. P. *Bland*, joint author of the silver bill of 1878.] A silver dollar containing 412½ grains Troy of standard silver. — **1879** *Congress. Rec.* 15 May 1369/2 Notwithstanding this sad fate of the Bland silver dollar, it is now seriously proposed to repeat that folly on a much larger scale. **1882** *Ib.* App., May 303/2 The Bland dollar . . . is worth in the market some 20 cents more than the trade dollar. **1896** *Ib.* May 4935/2, I simply call the attention of the Senate to the fact that the so-called Bland dollar was never a full legal tender.

***Blank,** *n.*

***1.** A written or printed document or form with spaces left blank to be filled in as required; a blank form or sheet. {–1711}

Frequently with defining terms, as *question, receipt, telegraph blank,* q.v. **a1649** WINTHROP *Hist.* I. 292 They procured many hands in Weymouth to a blank, intending to have Mr. Lenthall's advice to the frame of their call. **1733–4** *Penna. Gazette* 4/2 Blanks in the most authentic forms, and correctly printed. **1771** FRANKLIN *Autobiog.* 307, I had in it blanks of all sorts, the correctest that ever appear'd among us. **1775** J. BELCHER in *Biog. N. Hale* 165, [I] should be glad if our Company is not near compleated, you would send me over some more Blanks, as I expect next Monday, to make my Number, 30, at least. **1796** B. HAWKINS *Letters* 14 If you approve of this, you can send him some blanks, and request of him to postpone this session. **1841** CIST *Cincinnati* Advt., Cards, Blanks, Pamphlets, . . . and every variety of book and job printing. **1845** HOOPER *Taking Census* i. 150 Arming us with the proper quantity of blanks, [he] sent us forth to count the noses of all the men, [etc.]. *Ib.* 151 Drawing our blanks from their case, we proceeded [etc.]. **1873** RAYMOND *Silver & Gold* 13 A set of blanks, . . . embracing under appropriate headings the class of information desired, were sent . . . to persons engaged in mining in various parts of the State. **1880** [see BLANK AGENCY]. **1904** P. H. HANUS *Modern School* 128 By means of question blanks sent to the parents, much information . . . is secured by the teachers.

2. A zero score in a game.

1875 *Chicago Tribune* 15 July 5/5 The Chicagos, having been neatly retired for a blank. **1888** *Outing* May 119/2 The tenth innings had seen both sides retire for blanks.

***Blank,** *v.* +*tr.* To retire (a team) without a score. — **1887** *Courier-Journal* 26 May 2/6 In the eighth and ninth innings both [baseball] teams were blanked.

+Blank agency. [BLANK *n.* 1.] (See quot. 1880.) — **1868** *Statutes at Large* 27 July XV. 196 The Postmaster-General . . . is hereby authorized . . . to establish a blank agency for the Post-Office Department . . . ; and all other blank agencies are hereby abolished. **1880** LAMPHERE *U.S. Govt.* 240/1 The Blank Agency, to which is assigned the duty of supplying the post-offices entitled thereto with blanks.

+Blank agent. [See prec.] A postal official having charge of the issue of blank forms. — **1854** *Statutes at Large* 22 April X. 276 That the stamp and blank agent for the Post Office Department receive the same salary as clerks of the second class.

+Blank book, blank-book. [Cf. BLANK *n.* 1.]

1. A book of clean writing paper in which to make entries, keep accounts, etc.

1712 C. MATHER *Diary* II. 199, I would scarce lett a day pass me, without obliging my son, Increase, to transcribe . . . into a blank book, some instructive passage. **1768** *Md. Hist. Mag.* X. 132 To a Seven Quire Blank Book for a Register, £1. 5. 0. **1775** *N.H. Comm. Safety* 16 One of the Blank books of Records for Deeds. **1789** *Ann. 1st Congress* I. 167 It was agreed to lay an impost of seven and a half per cent. ad valorem on blank books. **1811** *Steele Papers* II. 657 These are blank books of a single quire each. **1837** *Knickerb.* IX. 293 It was a blank-book, and the two first pages were devoted to memoranda of disposed-of millinett. **1850** GARRARD *Wah-To-Yah* ii. 39 To . . . scrawl a few words in a blank book of the events of the day. **1867** S. HALE *Letters* 26 Charley gave me a lovely fat blank book with drawing-paper leaves, for a kind of journal of this trip. **1876** [G. H. TRIPP] *Student-Life* 11 A paper with printed questions and a blank-book were soon placed before each candidate. **1886** S. W. MITCHELL *R. Blake* ii. 14 He spent a few minutes more over the details of daily duty set out in a little blank-book.

2. Attrib. and comb. with *binder, bindery, manufacturer,* etc.

1831 *Boston Directory* Advt. p. 18 Blank book manufacturers. **1848** *Philadelphia Almanac,* Blank book binder. **1851** CIST *Cincinnati* 175 J. F. Desilver, blank-book bindery. *Ib.,* Booksellers and stationers in the blank-book, pamphlet and job line. **1886** *Standard Guide of Washington* 225 Paper Rulers and Blank Book Manufacturers.

***Blanket,** *n.*

***1.** One of the ordinary (usually woolen) coverings of a bed.

Also applied to a similar covering made of another material (as *gum* or *rubber blanket*) or used for another purpose (as *ironing, saddle blanket*).

1640 *Conn. Public Rec.* I. 449, 6 blanketts, one p[ai]re of curtens & curten rods, & a course bedcase. **1642** *Md. Archives* IV. 99 A very old quilt & pillow, 2 overworne blanketts & a coverlett. **1674** *Essex Inst. Coll.* XXXVII. 98 A truckle bedsteed, a fether bed with the pillowes, blanketts & coverled. **1733** *N.H. Probate Rec.* II. 496, I give unto Sarah Beck . . . a blanket and two Rugs. **1766** Chalkley *Scotch-Irish Settlement Va.* I. 127 Four wooden noggins, also . . . one Dutch blanket. **1780** W. FLEMING in *Travels Amer. Col.* 641 Left a double blanket with Mrs. Logan when there. **1803** *Ann. 7th Congress* 2 Sess. 349 Blankets—a bale of ten pieces will cost about £40 sterling. **1836** *Diplom. Corr. Texas* (1908) I. 144 Without a place to sleep, except on the naked deck—without any thing but two little blankets to answer for both bed and covering. **1847** RUXTON *Adv. Rocky Mts.* (1848) 213 All night long the wind roared through the cañon, and at times swept the blankets from our chilled bodies. **1860** CLAIBORNE *Sam. Dale* ix. 149, I set out the same night, taking with me only a blanket, my flint and steel [etc.] **1875** HIGGINSON *Hist. U.S.* xxi. 205 Officers on parade sometimes wore old blankets or faded bedquilts to cover them. **1893** *Outing* May 133/1 Each man sleeps between two blankets, with shoes and clothes all on. **1902** WISTER *Virginian* xxvi. 300 He . . . continued his preparations for departure, washing the dishes, rolling the blankets [etc.].

b. Attrib. and comb. with *bed, cap, case, cloth, covering, money, suit,* etc.

1648 *Conn. Public Rec.* I. 490, 4 yards ½ of blankitt cloth. **1776** *N.H. Comm. Safety* 52 Ordered, . . . To pay his recruits Blanket money. **1812** *Niles' Reg.* II. 9/1 This will contribute to render our blanket wool cheaper. **1840** HOFFMAN *Greyslaer* III. i. 99 He was a strong-featured, bull-necked fellow, whose . . . blanket-cloth overcoat indicated the occupation of a teamster or drover. **1842** *American Pioneer* I. 427 My friend . . . took out a sort of blanket cap, and put it on my head. **1843** S. M. FULLER *Summer on Lakes* 170 The children creeping out from beneath the blanket-door of the lodge. **1861** *Army Regulations* 307 [Supplies of] Blankets, woolen, [and] Blanket-cases. **1850** GARRARD *Wah-To-Yah* xiii. 173 For months I had enveloped myself with blankets in the open air, pulling off no clothing but the blue blanket topcoat, which, with my saddle, served as a pillow. **1850** G. HINES *Voyage* 150 We committed ourselves to sleep on our blanket beds upon the ground. **1884** *Century Mag.* Oct. 803/1 It is not easy for him to forget the fatigue, . . . the blanket-bed by the roadside. **1887** *Lippincott's Mag.* Oct. 577 Out of doors [at Williams College], workmen have been busy constructing the toboggan slide, which is soon occupied by a gay crowd in the regulation blanket suits and *toques.*

+2. A blanket belonging to an Indian, and usually worn as a garment.

1704 *Boston News-Letter* 14 Aug. 2/2 The Company . . . kill'd 2 Indians, . . . & took 5 or 6 Guns, & 9 or 10 blankets from the Enemy. **1721** SEWALL *Diary* III. 288 If the Indian must go . . . you are directed to take up a Blanket and Shirt for him, of Col. Fitch. **1726** PENHALLOW *Indian Wars* (1824) 50 They . . . put the enemy in such a terror that they not only quitted their plunder and blankets, but the other captive also. **1756** *Doc. Hist. N.Y. State* (1849) I. 484 The whole party [of Indians] soon took to their Heels, . . . some leaving behind their Arms, others their Blankets. **1807** IRVING, etc. *Salmagundi* iii. 58 The shawl scarlet, . . . thrown over one shoulder, like an Indian blanket, with one end dragging on the ground. **1835** IRVING *Tour Prairies* v. 32 [As] the Osage . . . rode, with his blanket wrapped round his loins, his naked bust would have furnished a model for a statuary. **1841** COOPER *Deerslayer* xxx, This blanket that I wear is not the blanket of a common squaw. **1859** BARTLETT 34 To say of one's father or mother that they 'wore the blanket,' implies that they were but half civilized Indians. Western. **1870** KEIM *Sheridan's Troopers* 169 Her squaws wore new and bright red blankets. **1871** *Rep. Indian Affairs* (1872) 170 Some of these Indians dress like white people, but a large portion still wear the blanket from want of funds to provide themselves with other garments. **1885** *Ib.* 79 Nearly all wear blankets, but many have on some single garment of civilization. **1896** WILKINS *Madelon* 245 Madelon . . . would have held an old ragged blanket of one of her Indian grandmothers like the bridal gown of a queen.

+b. Attrib. with *brave, tribe,* etc. Also BLANKET INDIAN.

1866 *Rep. Indian Affairs* 173 There is . . . great ignorance concerning the location of the prairie or blanket tribes. **1891** RYAN *Told in Hills* 166 You should hear her talking Chinook to a blanket brave. **1891** *Scribner's Mag.* Dec. 769 The sheep . . . made of a race of nomad savages [in New Mexico] the foremost of blanket weavers. **1905** A. ADAMS *Outlet* 81 On our left was the reservation of three blanket tribes of Indians.

+3. A coarse blanket used to catch the gold dust in gold-washing apparatus. Freq. attrib. (see quotations).

1873 RAYMOND *Silver & Gold* 283 Blankets are used, and the blanket-washings are treated in two arrastras. **1874** *Vt. Bd. Agric. Rep.* II. 757 What gold escapes in passing through the blanket boxes, deposits itself with the heavy black sand near the upper end of the concentrator boxes. **1876** RAYMOND *8th Rep. Mines* 333 Blanket-tailings run through Bartolo pans. **1881** — *Mining Gloss., Blanket-sluices,* sluices in which coarse blankets are laid, to catch the fine but heavy particles of gold, amalgam, etc., in the slime passing over them. **1882** C. KING *Rep. Precious Metals* 606 The blanket washings can be passed through a simple machine.

+4. Attrib. in the sense: Covering, inclusive.

1886 *Sec. Treasury Rep.* I. p. xli, Suitable annual appropriations . . . require no blanket clause to justify or cover them. **1889** *Cent., Blanket-mortgage,* a mortgage intended to cover an aggregation of property, or secure or provide for indebtedness previously existing in various forms. **1896** *Congress. Rec.* 4 May 4783/2 Messrs Morgan & Co. had given a blanket bid to cover the whole amount. . . . Under the terms of the blanket bid, which covered all bids where there was a failure to take the bonds [etc.]. **1900** NELSON *A B C Wall St.* 24 The issue of a general or 'blanket' mortgage is usually resorted to with the . . . aim of obtaining new capital. **1903** E. JOHNSON *Railway Transportation* 79 The creditor may hold equipment bonds, terminal bonds, or a general or 'blanket' bond. **1903** A. B. HART *Actual Government* 308 The U.S. courts have repeatedly issued blanket injunctions, forbidding all persons from interference with particular federal functions. **1904** W. H. SMITH *Promoters* i. 25 When the people who have granted a blanket charter that has more in it than dreamed of wake up to the real facts. **1907** WHITE *Arizona Nights* vii. 136 'What?' says I. 'Elucidate, my bucko. I don't take no such blanket order.' **1914**

McLaughlin & Hart *Cycl. Amer. Govt.* I. 101 Nine out of ten of the states have provided for an official 'blanket ballot.'

Blanket, *v.* [f. the noun.]

1. *tr.* To cover with a blanket or similar covering. {1605–}

1854 Simms *Southward Ho* 331 Get thee behind us, Texas—blanket thyself and be silent. **1874** *Vt. Bd. Agric. Rep.* II. 513 The great advantage of this barn is the comfort of my horses, which I never have to blanket at all. **1886** *Leslie's Mo.* Jan. 66/1 The driver . . . and . . . passengers were well blanketed. **1894** *Vt. Agric. Rep.* XIV. 104 It is a better way to keep them [*sc.* colts] than shod and blanketed all winter. **1907** W. Lillibridge *Trail* 32 The wiry little mustang he rode [was] all but blanketed under the big army saddle.

+**2.** To include under one head or category; to take inclusively.

1892 *N.Y. Law Journal* in *Law Times* XCIII. 413/1 A bona fide immigrant . . . blanketed the aforesaid quarter-section with his own claim, and the court held that the blanketer . . . was *potior in jure.* **1913** La Follette *Autobiog.* 365 The employees then holding office were not blanketed into the service.

+**Blanket-bag.** A bag made from blanket material, or used for carrying blankets; a sleeping-bag.

1724 *New-Eng. Courant* 5 Oct. 2/2 My Wife . . . made Preparation (by making sundry Blanket Baggs) to transport away what Goods she could. **1856** Kane *Arctic Explor.* I. 193 Other skins and blanket-bags were thrown above them. **1880** 'Mark Twain' *Tramp Abroad* xxxvi. 413 There must be some porters, to carry . . . blanket bags for the party to sleep in. **1885** *Outing* Oct. 77/2, I crept into my blanket-bag, and slept . . . soundly.

+**Blanket capeau, capot.** *Obs.* =next. — **1807** Pike *Exped.* III. App. 62 Presented to the commandant-general in a blanket cappot. **1821** Nuttall *Travels Arkansa* 79 The dresses of the men consist of blanket capeaus, buckskin pantaloons, and mockasins. **1835** Hoffman *Winter in West* I. 127 The French settlers, with their elf-locks and blanket capotes, might at a distance be well taken for aborigines.

+**Blanket-coat.**

1. A coat made of blanket material.

'A coat made from a blanket, common in the West, and often seen with the black stripe of the border of the original blanket crossing various parts of the garment' (B. '59).

1805–9 Henry *Camp. Quebec* 109 Having on a fine white blanket coat . . . made me, as it were, invisible in the snow. **1821** Nuttall *Travels Arkansa* 238 The men, as usual, are commonly dressed in blanket coats, and the women wear handkerchiefs around their heads instead of bonnets. **1835** Hoffman *Winter in West* II. 86 The majority were dressed in rough blanket-coats of every possible colour. **1851** *Polly Peablossom* 119 Clad in the bright-green blanket-coat, and broad-brimmed hat, which form the principal features in the costume of the elegants of their section, . . . they started. **1855** J. Reynolds *Own Times* (1879) 39 The white blanket-coat, known as the capot, was the universal and eternal coat. **1871** De Vere 194 Mackinaw blankets, . . . being very thick and well made, . . . served not only for beds but also for overcoats, which were called Blanket-Coats. **1888** Roosevelt in *Century Mag.* Oct. 834/2 A powerfully-built trapper, . . . who wore a gayly coloured capote, or blanket-coat.

attrib. **1831** Royall *Southern Tour* II. 125, I could not but admire the gallantry of . . . one of those blanket-coat stage-drivers.

2. *transf.* One wearing a blanket-coat.

1837 Bird *Nick of Woods* I. 58, I'm for any man that insults me! log-leg or leather-breeches, green-shirt, or blanket-coat.

+**Blanket deposit.** *Mining.* [Blanket *n.*] 'The name given . . . in Colorado and Utah to deposits of ore occurring in a form having some of the characters of those elsewhere designated as flat sheets, bedded veins, beds, or flat masses' (*Cent.*).

Blanketed, *ppl. a.* **1.** Covered with a blanket; furnished with blankets. +**2.** Of cattle: Having a broad belt of white round the middle. — **(1) 1835** [Ingraham] *South-West* II. 176 His blanketed saddle is his cabriolet. **1874** *Vt. Bd. Agric. Rep.* II. 757 The heavy black sand . . . in passing through the blanketed sluice boxes deposits another portion of fine gold. **1890** Ryan *Told in Hills* 245 The party . . . galloped past in all ignorance of moody eyes watching them from the side of a blanketed horse. **(2) 1887** *O.E.D.*

Blanketeer. One who carries a blanket for sleeping in the open air. {1822–33} — **a1861** Winthrop *Canoe & Saddle* 113 'Many blanketeers, by a fire, I behold,' he whispered. *Ib.* 210 Ferdinand was . . . making good his claim as a blanketeer.

+**Blanketer.** (See Blanket *v.* 2, quot. 1892.)

+**Blanket grass.** (See quotation.) — **1889** Vasey *Agric. Grasses* 23 *Papsalum platycaule* . . . forms such a thick turf that it is called here [n. Fla.] 'blanket grass.'

+**Blanket Indian.** [Blanket *n.* 2.] An Indian who still uses the blanket as a garment instead of the ordinary dress of the whites, and remains in a primitive state of civilization.

Illustrated in Thornton *Suppl.* from 1875 to 1898.

1859 Bartlett 35 *Blanket-Indian*, a wild Indian, whose principal article of dress is the blanket. **1873** Roe *Army Lett.* 95 The everyday dress of the genuine blanket Indians. **1875** *Congress. Rec.* 2 Feb. 912/2 [Mr. McCreery's] argument applies to reservations made for what we call in the West 'blanket Indians.' **1885** *Rep. Indian Affairs* 75 These are nearly all 'Blanket Indians.' **1886** *Congress. Rec.* March 2273/1 The boys and girls [on leaving school] go back to barbarism, back to the tepee, back to the blanket Indians. What have you done to enable him [*sic*] to go back to anything but a blanket Indian? **1906** *Atlantic Mo.* March 328/2 Only 26,000 blanket Indians are left in the United States. **1919** *Dialect Notes* V. 31 'Blanket Indians' are no longer found among the Cherokees.

Blanketing, *n.* [Blanket *n.* 1.] Material for blankets. {1677–}

1666 P. Sanford *Letter Book* 15 Three peces of good stript blancketting of the beest sort, two peces of good blew duffalls. **1673** *Essex Inst. Coll.* XXXV. 213 To bring . . . som Rugs and blainckiting of trucking cloth. **1730** *Md. Hist. Mag.* XIX. 185 To Mr. Phil Smith Merc[han]t . . . 50 yards Blanketing. **1775** *S.C. Hist. Soc. Coll.* II. 49 Mr. Drayton had purchased . . . a considerable quantity of blanketing and plains which were likewise under orders to proceed to Charles-Town. **1812** *Niles' Reg.* II. 9/2 The flushings or lion skins for great coats . . . are nothing more than good tweeled blanketing.

Blanketing, *vbl. n. Obs. slang.* (See quotation.) — **1835** Abdy *Journal* I. 38 The new-comers [in the prison on Blackwell's Island, N.Y.] are regaled with what is called a *blanketing*.—When left alone with the other prisoners, . . . they are suddenly surrounded by the most abandoned and daring, covered with a blanket, and robbed of every thing they may have about them of value.

+**Blanket overcoat.** =Blanket coat. — **1822** Quitman in *Life & Corr.* 72 Straw hats and no neck-cloths in summer, and in winter coarse shoes and blanket overcoats. **1850** Garrard *Wah-To-Yah* v. 71 A stiff wind . . . caused me to pull up the collar of my blue blanket overcoat. **1889** Cable in *Century Mag.* Jan. 364/1 While the younger was muffling himself in an old blanket-overcoat such as we give to plantation negroes.

Blanket-roll. [Blanket *n.* 1.] A blanket made up into a roll. — **1891** *Harper's Mag.* June 8/1 His bridle hand is raised by the blanket roll or carbine. **1899** *Scribner's Mag.* Jan. 27/1 These men about him were taking it all quite seriously, and making ready to disembark, carrying their blanket-rolls and rifles with them.

+**Blanket shawl.** [Blanket *n.* 1.] A shawl made of blanket or thick woolen cloth.

1837 *S. Lit. Messenger* III. 660 The blanket shawls with their varied coloring looked pretty and comfortable. **1843** S. M. Fuller *Summer on Lakes* 41 England sat up all night wrapped in her blanket shawl. **1858** Holmes *Autocrat* i. 21 A *blanket*-shawl we call it, and not a plaid; and we wear it like the aborigines, and not like the Highlanders. **1863** 'E. Kirke' *Southern Friends* i. 10 He hid his little face in the big blanket-shawl which he wore. **1881** Pierson *In the Brush* 33 With a large blanket-shawl rolled compactly together, and strapped with my umbrella behind my saddle. **1898** Westcott *D. Harum* 165 Hullo, John! what you got there? . . . Slips, blanket-shawl, petticut, stockin's.

+**Blanket sheet.** 'A large newspaper in folio form.' Also attrib. with *newspaper.* — **1870** Maverick *Raymond & N.Y. Press* 36 The heavy, old-fashioned, 'blanket sheet' newspaper. **1873** F. Hudson *Journalism* 344 The blanket sheets made their appearance in the city of New York in 1827. **1901** Churchill *Crisis* 342 Black headlines, and grim lists three columns long,—three columns of a blanket sheet!

+**Blanket-tent.** [Blanket *n.* 1.] A tent made from blankets. — **1852** *Knickerb.* XL. 390 We discovered the blanket-tents of the Indians. **1865** Kellogg *Rebel Prisons* 143 A man who was quietly sleeping in his little blanket tent. *Ib.* 302 The sick men had to strike their blanket tents, and put them up again as best they could.

+**Blanket-waisted,** *a.* =Blanketed *ppl. a.* 2. — **1877** Bartlett 776 *Blanket-waisted.* Cattle distinguished by a broad band of white hair completely encircling the body.

Blanket-washer. [Blanket *n.*] **1.** An apparatus for washing blankets. +**2.** One who washes for gold by means of a coarse blanket. — **(1) 1876** Ingram *Centennial Exp.* 345 A blanket-washer, a mangle, a frame for stretching and dyeing lace curtains, etc. **(2) 1876** Raymond *8th Rep. Mines* 330 For 24 hours . . . Wages of two blanket-washers [were] $4.

+**Blank work.** [Blank 1.] The printing of blank forms. — **1873** *Winfield* (Kansas) *Courier* 11 Jan. 1/7 The Courier Job Office . . . [is] prepared to do all kinds of job work, Blank work, Circulars, Posters, etc., at reduced rates.

Blare, *v. intr.* To flare. {1721; now *dial.*} — **1744** Franklin *Fire-places* 76 The Flame burns quite upright, and does not blare and run the Tallow down.

* **Blast,** *n.*

1. a. A single operation of smelting iron ore.

1657 *Mass. H. S. Coll.* 4 Ser. VII. 403 Pray forward that work at Nue Hauene, that thay may try a blast in the spring of the yere. *Ib.*, [I] am lick to haue on[e] halfe of the hol works at Lin and at Brantre, and soe intend to mack a blast here. **1806** Webster, *Blast*, . . . one smelting of ore. **1828** — *Blast*, . . . the whole blowing of a forge necessary to melt one supply of ore; a common use of the word among workmen in forges in America.

b. *In blast*, of a smelting furnace: In operation, working. *Out of blast*, not working.

1780 *Virginia State P.* I. 370 If Mr. Ross can get in Blast time enough to make it worth his while to work for these United States . . . he shall be paid for Shot Twenty five pounds pr: ton Pensylvania Currency. **1796** Morse *Amer. Geog.* I. 652 At present there are four or five furnaces in the state [of N.C.] that are in blast. **1815** *Austin Papers* (1924) I. 248 When the Furnace is out of Blast, you will see that the Lead is removed. **1881** RAYMOND *Mining Gloss., Blast,* the period during which a blast furnace is *in blast,* that is, in operation.

c. *transf.* (Usually *in full blast.*)

1839 MARRYAT *Diary in Am.* II. 36 In *full blast*—something in the extreme. 'When she came to meeting, with her yellow hat and feathers, was'n't she in *full blast?*' **1845** HOOPER *Simon Sugg's Adv.* x. 119 Suggs ... was on his way to a camp-meeting, then in full blast on Sandy creek. **1850** *Congress. Globe* App., 5 July 1096/2 The chance ... that slavery may be extended ... will be sufficient to keep all the elements of agitation in full blast at the North. **1865** *Chicago Tribune* 10 April 1 Manager Ogden has re-opened his theater, and Buckley & Budd's minstrel house is in blast. **1890** *Congress. Rec.* 18 July 7436/2 Cities like Topeka, in Kansas, where the school-boys never saw saloons and where the jails are empty, now have these original-package saloons in full blast.

***2.** A blight or similar withering infection of growing plants. {–1815}

1702 C. MATHER *Magnalia* v. iv. (1852) 316 Some of the principal grains, especially our wheat and our pease, fell under an unaccountable blast. **1749** DOUGLAS *British Settlements N.A.* (1753) 206 New England wheat is subject to blast. **1789** MORSE *Amer. Geog.* 144 Wheat ... on the sea coast ... has never been cultivated with success, being subject to blasts. **1810** J. LAMBERT *Travels thro' U.S.* III. 55 In dry seasons, the rice is liable to attacks from a small bug, equally injurious to it as the Hessian fly is said to be to wheat, or the blast to sugar canes. **1829** *Va. Lit. Museum* 179 When the weather has been very wet, late in the season, a disease called *blast,* (and occasioned by the insects of the genus *Aphis*) proves very fatal.

+**3.** Blasting powder; a quantity of this placed to cause an explosion.

1851 *Polly Peablossom* 117 Fur we had five kegs ov blast along. **1871** RAYMOND *3rd Rep. Mines* 121 A blast put into the limestone threw off a thin cap. **1882** C. KING *Rep. Precious Metals* 110 Tunnels have traversed this rock 100 or 200 feet without exploding a blast.

* **Blast,** *v.*

***1.** *intr.* To undergo blasting or blighting. {–*c*1630}

1748 ELIOT *Field-Husb.* i. 14, I have been told that Summer Wheat sowed with Barley is not apt to blast, and do well together. **1774** HUTCHINSON *Diary & Lett.* I. 171 K[ing]—What is the reason you raise no wheat in your Province? H[utchinson].—In most places, especially near the sea, it blasts. *Ib.*, When the grain is so forward as to be out of milk the beginning of July, it seldom blasts. **1838** FLAGG *Far West* II. 217 Maize seems the appropriate production for the soil; all of the smaller grains, on account of the rank luxuriance of the growth, being liable to blast before the harvesting.

***2.** *tr.* To affect (vegetation) with blight; to blight, wither.

1757 HEMPSTEAD *Diary* 688 In the morning they ... raked the blasted sumer wheat: **1828** WEBSTER s.v. *Smut,* Sometimes the whole ear [of corn] is blasted and converted into smut. **1905** [E. W. PRINGLE] *Rice Planter* 246 The vines are being cut for hay.... It has not been cold enough yet to blast them.

3. *intr.* To be engaged in blowing up rock.

1884 BRET HARTE *On Frontier* 272 And what if I happen to know that the Excelsior boys ain't blastin' today?

+**Blasted,** *adv.* {1682– as adj.} Confoundedly, damnably. — **1854** M. J. HOLMES *Tempest & Sunshine* xv. 204 Lord's sake be spry, for I'm blasted hungry. **1856** *Spirit of Times* (N.Y.) 4 Oct. 69/2 Our boys had been working on 'fatigue' all night, and were blasted tired. **1886** *Leslie's Mo.* Jan. 67/2 He's too blasted smart for an Indian.

Blast-engine. [Cf. BLAST *n.* 1 a.] A machine for blowing up the fire in a furnace. — **1873** RAYMOND *Silver & Gold* 385 The only blast-engines in use in Nevada and Utah are the different sizes of Sturtevant's fan and Root's pressure-blower.

Blast-furnace. [Cf. BLAST *n.* 1 a.] A smelting furnace into which a blast of air is artificially driven. {1706–}

1802 *Ann. 7th Congress* 2 Sess. 1239 There are also seven blast furnaces now carried on. **1849** CHAMBERLAIN *Ind. Gazetteer* 319 Mishawaka ... contains two large blast furnaces, two cupola furnaces, one forge. **1871** RAYMOND *Mines* 438 The blast furnace is the best adapted for the smelting of the rich argentiferous lead ores, or of mixtures of lead ores. **1880** *Harper's Mag.* Dec. 56 This coal ... is ... a fuel that finds its way to the blast-furnaces of Lake Champlain. **1906** F. LYNDE *Quickening* 378 Farther on, the recurring flare from the tall vent of the blast-furnace lighted the haze depths weirdly.

* **Blasting,** *vbl. n.*

***1.** Injury to growth by blight, etc. {–1669; now *arch.*}

1670 *Conn. Public Rec.* II. 125 The Lord's holy hand is still lifted up against us, as may evidently appeare by the continuations of blasting and cattmillows. **1675** *Ib.* 259 It hath pleased the Most High to continue ... blastings and mildues upon the fruits of the feild. **1700** SEWALL *Letter-book* I. 240 We are ... something afflicted ... by reason of the blasting of Wheat and Rye. **1702** LOGAN in *Penna. H. S. Mem.* IX. 81 All or most of the parterres are dead by blasting. **1725** *New-Eng. Courant* 14–21 Aug. 2/1 The Scarcity of other mediums of Exchange, by reason of Blastings, Droughts, Luxury, &c. **1828** WEBSTER s.v. *Blast,* The blasting of plants.

2. The blowing up of rocks by an explosive material. Also attrib. with *cotton, powder, stick.* {1824–}

1815 *N. Amer. Rev.* I. 336 The rock is so hard that it can be worked only by drilling and blasting. **1846** *Rep. Comm. Patents* (1847) 23 Four qualities of gun-cotton were used: ... No. 4, blasting cotton. **1869** 'MARK TWAIN' *Innocents Abroad* xxvii. 284 We bought a two-horse wagon and put eighteen hundred pounds of bacon, flour, beans, blasting-powder, picks, and shovels in it. **1881** RAYMOND *Mining Gloss., Blasting-stick,* a simple form of fuse. **1902** 'MARK TWAIN' in *Harper's Mag.* Jan. 266 A tin can of blasting-powder, which they placed upon the candle-box.

+**Blast-wall.** (See quotations.) — **1852** *Harper's Mag.* April 643/1 A great black slanting structure ... [forms] a 'blast-wall.' *Ib.* 644/2 A structure of black timber ... set up in the shape of an acute angle. This is a 'blast-wall,' intended to offer some resistance to a rush of air in case of an explosion [at the powder-mill].

+**Blat,** *v.* Also **blatt, blaat, blät.** [Imitative.]

1. *intr.* To bleat, or make similar sounds.

1846 in Northall *Yankee Hill* 102 Your fellow-countrymen ... are not allowed to emigrate north of the Columbia River, on account of a raging he-calf who is bla-ting on the other side. **1867** 'T. LACKLAND' *Homespun* II. 198 You begin at the head of the row with some fine calves, bläting in your face and eyes. **1888** *San Fran. News Letter* 4 Feb. (F.), One of these insects of an hour rears up and blatts. **1907** WHITE *Arizona Nights* viii. 149 Perhaps the calf blatted a little as the heat scorched. **1911** QUICK *Yellowstone Nights* 126 The first little blizzard, they'll hump up an' blat for home and mother. **1916** BOWER *Phantom Herd* ii. 24 The stock-yards where a bunch of sheep blatted now in the thirst of mid-afternoon.

2. *tr.* To blurt *out.*

1879 HOWELLS *Lady of Aroostook* I. v. 50 Now, if I have anything on my mind, I have to blat it right out, as you may say.

Blatherskite. Also **-skyte.** [Eng. dial. *blatherskite,* Sc. *bletherskate, bladderskate* (*a*1680), f. *blather, blether,* to talk nonsense; also Irish dial. *bletherumskite* nonsense (1825).]

'The Scotch song *Maggie Lauder,* in which this word occurs, was a favourite ditty in the American Camp during the War of Independence (J. Grant Wilson *Poets and Poetry of Scotland* I. 82); from this ... *blatherskite* became a familiar colloquialism in U.S.' (O.E.D.).

1. 'A blustering, noisy, talkative fellow' (B. '48). Also attrib. as adj.

(1) **1791** J. BREVARD *MS. Diary* 28 July (N. C. Univ.), On the same seat with a Blatherskite Irishman (who kept constantly jawing to & teasing the girl all the way). **1888** *N.Y. Herald* 29 July (F.), Every Blatherskite Republican is filled to the brim and spouting high protection.

(2) **1841** *Knickerb.* XVII. 340 That intense *blatherskite,* 'Mr. George Jones, of Stratford-on-Avon and the Virginia Theatres.' **1879** *Louisville Home & Farm* 15 April, Max revealed ... a large bluish knob 'on the back of his head.' ... He resumed ... when that blatherskite Dan gave me this 'bump of destruction.' **1886** *Boston Journal* 16 Aug. 2/1 Irish Americans ... should be wary of listening to the appeals of blatherskites whose counsel, if accepted, would work the greatest injury to Ireland. **1889** 'MARK TWAIN' *Conn. Yankee* xii. 147 She was a perfect blatherskite; I mean for jaw, jaw, jaw, talk, talk. **1906** *N.Y. Ev. Post* 30 March 1 The cheap, noisy, disagreeable, and unreasonable labor blatherskite. **1911** HARRISON *Queed* xviii. 229 A glance ... showed that the blatherskites had pounded him harder than ever.

2. Nonsensical talk; 'bunkum.'

1861 *N.Y. Tribune* 28 Dec., To wit, our proving, not by verbal blatherskyte, but by facts, that the C. S. A. is dependent on us.

Blatter, *v.* [Imitative.] *intr.* To talk volubly or idly. *colloq.* {Now *rare*} Also **Blatterer** {1627}, **Blattering** *ppl. a.* — **1836** *S. Lit. Messenger* II. 362/1 The Blatterers;—although this word is now nearly obsolete, ... I venture to use it here. *Ib.*, But let me return to the description of the Blattering order. **1867** *Nation* 3 Jan. 2/2 The most impudent of all the famous blatterers and swindlers who have ever crossed the water to ply their vocation on American soil. **1884** 'MARK TWAIN' *Huck. Finn* xxv. 248 So the king he blattered [*some eds.* blatted] along, and managed to inquire about pretty much everybody and dog in town.

Blaze, *n.*[1] Also **blaeze, blaize, blease.** [Related to ON. *blesi,* MDu. *blesse,* Du. *bles,* G. *blässe, blesse.*]

1. A white spot or mark on the face of a horse. {1639–}

1677 *East-Hampton Rec.* I. 403 A bay Mare ... [having] a white blase downe her face. *Ib.*, The upper part of the white blase. **1707** *Boston News-Letter* 10 Feb. 2/2 The said Horse is a prety large Bright Bay Gelding ... with a white Blaze in his Face. **1748** *Braintree Rec.* 147 A stray mayr ... of a brownish or mouse couler, with a small streak or blaze in the face. **1785** WASHINGTON *Diaries* II. 441 Bay [horse]—long blaze. *Ib.*, Brown Boy—crooked blaze, 13 hands high. *c***1845** *Big Bear Ark.* etc. 36 He knew the colonel's old sorrel riding-horse ... by the blaze on his face. **1868** WOODRUFF *Trotting Horse* xiv. 140 Oneida Chief was a handsome chestnut, with three white legs and a blaze. **1898** PAGE *Red Rock* 85 Blood-bay, with three white feet and a blaze on his nose.

b. A similar mark elsewhere on the body.

1855 SIMMS *Forayers* 257 'A most glorious black, black without a spot.' 'Yes, a blaze on his right shoulder.'

+**2.** A white mark made on a tree by slicing off a piece of bark, to distinguish it as a boundary-mark or to indicate a path in a forest.

1662 *Groton Rec.* 7 The meetinge house shall be set . . . by a small whit oak marked **at** the souwest side with two notches and a blaze. **1737** J. WESLEY *Journal* 3 Dec., We came into a large swamp, without path or blaze, where we wandered up and down near three hours. **1750** WALKER *Journal* 26 April, Besides several Trees blazed several ways with 3 chops over each blaze. **1781** L. Summers *Ann. S.W. Virginia* (1929) 1084 Ordered that . . . [he] mark the said road with Bleases. **1817** *Niles' Reg.* XII. 98/2 A blaze, large enough for the purpose, is made on the tree, and on the blaze the letter R. is made, with the number of the range annexed. **1833** FLINT *D. Boone* 79 The brothers left such traces—or blazes as they are technically called—of their course as they thought would enable them to find it again. **1843** 'CARLTON' *New Purchase* I. xii. 87 The blaze is a longitudinal cut on trees at convenient intervals made by cutting off the bark with an axe or hatchet: three blazes in a perpendicular line on the same tree indicating a legislative road, the single blaze, a settlement or neighborhood road. **1865** *Atlantic Mo.* XV. 508 When I was in Florida a peculiar set of marks, like the technical 'blaze,' were found on certain trees. **1880** G. INGHAM *Digging Gold* xvi. 368 Here the trail appeared to branch, two sets of blazes appearing, one path bearing to the right, and another to the left. **1891** *Fur, Fin, & Feather* March 197 The trail is a series of plain blazes on the trees which any one could follow. **1903** WHITE *Forest* xii. 155 Our blazes alone continue the initial short cut of the Fur Trail.

+**b.** A blazed trail or road.

1853 'P. PAXTON' *Yankee in Texas* 100 He will see them pouring in . . . by every possible road, . . . wagon roads, main roads, 'cow trails,' and 'blazes.' *Ib.* 126 Two horses that come up the road and turned into the 'blaze,' went up a little piece to a big water-hole.

‖**3.** A metal shield on a (fireman's) cap.

1764 *Boston Selectmen* 121 Such person . . . shall . . . at every Fire wear a black leather jocky cap with a pewter blaze in the front of it.

***Blaze,** *n.*[2] Also **blais.** [f. BLAZE *v.*[2]] +A continuous or sustained firing. — **1777** *Md. Hist. Mag.* VI. 141 Thay maid two or three attempts to rush on us, but we kept up such a blais on them, that thay wair repulsed every time. **1777** *Md. Journal* 2 Sept. (Th.), [They] kept up such a blaze upon the enemy, that they were forced to retreat.

+**Blaze,** *n.*[3] (See quotation.) — **1887** KELLER *Draw Poker* 9 *Blaze,* a hand consisting of five court cards.

+**Blaze,** *v.*[1] [f. BLAZE *n.*[1]]

1. *tr.* To mark (a tree) by slicing off a piece of bark.

1750 WALKER *Journal* 13 April, On the top of the Ridge are Laurel Trees marked with crosses, others Blazed and several Figures on them. *Ib.* 23 May, I blazed several Trees in the Fork and marked T. W. on a Sycomore Tree. **1777** ANBUREY *Trav. Amer.* (1791) I. 263 For the more easy discovery of their way back again, their tomahawks are continually blazing the trees, which is cutting off a small piece of the bark. **1793** *Hapless Orphan* II. 77 We were impeded in our march, by reason of the surveyors not having blazed the trees, or opened the road. **1805-9** HENRY *Camp. Quebec* 24 We . . . found a path tolerably distinct, which we made more so by blazing the trees. **1823** JAMES *Exped.* I. 178 They observed stakes stuck in the ground at certain distances, and trees blazed as far as they went up the trail. **1867** RICHARDSON *Beyond Mississippi* i. 20 It is one vast wilderness with a tree blazed here and there. **1880** *Lumberman's Gazette* Jan. 28 The limits are marked by trees blazed on four sides. **1895** *Outing* Oct. 44/2 Jake had blazed the trees for three or four miles through this wonderful mass of timber, and by his marks we wended our way in single file.

2. To mark or indicate (a path, etc.) by making blazes on trees. Also transf.

1750 WALKER *Journal* 30 April, I blazed a way from our House to the River. **1756** *Lett. to Washington* I. 272 The Indians have blazed a path from the Crossing. **1805-9** HENRY *Camp. Quebec* 24 We ascended the river rapidly, blazing every carrying-place. **1819** *N. Amer. Rev.* VIII. 14 After the surveyor has staked or blazed out the line, the work is commenced. **1853** STROTHER *Blackwater Chron.* vi. 73 A man could walk about for a week . . . and never . . . be five miles from where he started, unless he blazed his way. **1861** WINTHROP *Open Air* 99 Still we plodded on, following a path blazed by the Bostonians. **1879** BRET HARTE *Drift from Two Shores* 57 The first settler . . . declared that the Saints were afore his time, and occupied a cabin in the brush when he 'blazed' his way to the North Fork. **1887** *Harper's Mag.* April 664/1 By the route he had blazed, a force of five hundred and fifty men soon followed.

b. *fig.* To mark out (a way, etc.) for others to follow.

1850 J. C. NOTT *Chronology* 36 (B.), Champollion died in 1832, having done little more than blaze out the road to be travelled by others. **1886** Z. F. SMITH *Kentucky* 28 Pioneers who formed the vanguard, and who blazed the way to future conquest. **1902** W. L. MEAD *How Words Grow* p. vi, Professor Bréal has blazed the way for future explorers in the wilderness of philology. **1909** H. N. CASSON *Life C. H. McCormick* 42 These inventors . . . failed, but . . . doubtless blazed the way by their failures to the final success of McCormick. **1920** HUNTER *Trail Drivers of Texas* I. 15 Mr. Goodnight's allusion to my 'blazing' the trail for the Joe McCoy herd.

3. To mark *out* (a claim) by blazes on trees.

1871 DE VERE 169 The new-comer, having selected his future home, would, in the language of the day, 'at once *blaze out* on the tree-trunks his pre-emption claim.'

4. *absol.* To cut blazes on trees.

1796 F. BAILY *Tour* 156 A person well used to it will blaze as he rides along.

***Blaze,** *v.*[2] *colloq.* [Cf. BLAZE *n.*[2]] *intr.* With *away:* To fire rapidly or continuously. Freq. fig., to proceed or continue to do something with great vigor. {1826-}

1776 *Battle of Brooklyn* II. i, We . . . saw something move; we bid them stand and blazed away like brave boys. **1812** DUNLAP *Yankee Chronology* 8 [The British ship] blazed away like a barn a fire—we stuck to her like true Yankee tars—every shot told. **1834** C. A. DAVIS *Lett. J. Downing* 147 He blaz'd away like all wrath, for an hour; and . . . stop'd to take breath. **1834** CARRUTHERS *Kentuckian* I. 25 The tune would take a quick turn, like one I knowed afore, so I used to blaze away at it. **1835** BIRD *Hawks of Hawk-H.* I. vi. 70 Just as he stooped down to scratch it, we blazed away again, me and Hy. **1845** S. SMITH *Theatr. Apprent.* ii. 31, I had promised to blaze away at him in the next 'Sun.' **1853** 'P. PAXTON' *Yankee in Texas* 23, I raised my hatchet, took deliberate aim, and blazed away. My shot was perfectly innocuous, for, ducking their heads, the hatchet passed over them. **1865** *Atlantic Mo.* XV. 287 The guard nails you with a bullet; and as they like that sort of thing, they blaze away whenever they get a chance. **1883** 'MARK TWAIN' *Life on Miss.* liv. 531 The elements . . . rattled and banged and blazed away in the most blind and frantic manner.

Blazed, *ppl. a.* [f. BLAZE *v.*[1]]

1. Having a blaze on the face. {1685-1727} Cf. BLAZE FACE.

1780 *Va. House of Delegates Jrnl.* 16 Nov. 19 A bay horse, with a blazed face. **1787** WASHINGTON *Diaries* III. 155 A sorrel mare, blazed face, off hind foot white. **1869** *Overland Mo.* III. 126, I had seen . . . an old gray mare, considerably flea-bitten, with a blazed face and a docked tail.

+**2.** Of a tree, etc.: Marked with a blaze.

1737 W. STEPHENS *Proc. Georgia* 50 This Land . . . bounded on the North by the River, on the South by several blazed Trees. **1748** WASHINGTON *Diaries* I. 10 Phillip Moors house bears No. 86 Wt. No. 23 Wt. 48 po. to a Blazed Tree. **1792** J. POPE *Tour S. & W.* 49 The Goals . . . consist of two blazed Saplings fixed in the Ground. **1833** *Knickerb.* I. 88 Here and there a *blased* tree formed my sole means of direction. **1835** BIRD *Hawks of Hawk-H.* I. xix. 260 He made his way to the roadside, almost at the very spot where a blazed beech tree flung its silver limbs over a rock. **1850** E. P. BURKE *Reminisc. Georgia* 215 At the South . . . one often hears the remark made, 'that it takes only a few blazed trees to make a city.' **1884** BRET HARTE *Carquinez Woods* 172 They proceeded cautiously, at right angles with the 'blazed' tree, for ten minutes more. **1901** WHITE *Claim Jumpers* iii. 33 By the time you have walked six thousand feet . . . your little blazed stake in a pile of stones is likely to be almost anywhere.

+**3.** Of a path, line, etc.: Indicated by blazes on the trees.

1819 J. FLINT *Lett. from Amer.* 154 Not neglecting to carry with him a pocket-compass, to enable him to follow the blazed lines marked out by the surveyor. **1832** J. F. WATSON *Hist. Tales N.Y.* 41 From Utica to Canandaigua they travelled . . . by 'blazed paths.' **1853** 'P. PAXTON' *Yankee in Texas* 122, I went up country a bit, struck 'Trammel's Trace'—nothing but a blazed road then. **1880** G. INGHAM *Digging Gold* xvi. 369 The summit of the mountain . . . where we discovered a blazed trail. **1884** SWEET & KNOX *Through Texas* ix. 119 There are notched roads and blazed roads. **1887** *Scribner's Mag.* Sept. 305/1 A blazed trail leads up to it from the park. **1905** *Bureau of Forestry Bul. No. 60* 24 Cut no timber outside the blazed line.

Blaze face. [f. BLAZE *n.*[1] 1.] A face with a white spot or mark on it. — **1787** WASHINGTON *Diaries* III. 155 A sorrell Stallion, a blaze face, 2 hind feet and off fore foot white. **1856** *Spirit of Times* (N.Y.) 25 Oct. 131/1 The three came down the quarter-stretch at a great flight of speed, . . . each having a blaze-face, or a stripe and snip. **1884** *N.Y. Puck* Aug., The bay gelding with a blaze face.

Blaze-faced, *a.* [f. prec.] Having a blaze on the face. — **1870** EGGLESTON *Queer Stories* viii. 65 If she were rich, she would buy an omnibus with four 'blaze-faced,' sorrel horses.

+**Blazer**[1]. [f. BLAZE *v.*[1]] One who blazes trees. — **1775** ROMANS *Florida* 195 These same two men serve as chain-bearers, and two as blazers.

Blazer[2]. [f. BLAZE *v.*[2]]

+**1.** Something which blazes up (in fig. sense), is glaringly prominent, etc. *colloq.*

1845 MRS. KIRKLAND *Western Clearings* 127 T'other gal is likely enough, but the mother's a blazer! **1903** A. ADAMS *Log Cowboy* vi. 81 'Are you sure you wasn't running a blazer yourself?' . . . inquired Durham. **1906** *Springfield W. Republican* 19 April 1 The Kaiser's telegram to Count Goluchowski recalls some of his blazers [=errors] in the past. **1907** WHITE *Arizona Nights* 11 It was just a cold, raw blazer [=lie].

2. A bright-colored sports jacket. {1880-}

1888 HOWELLS *A. Kilburn* x, A rather raw-boned, wooden-faced young man in a flannel blazer.

+**3.** A dish used for cooking over a flame.

1889 *Cent., Blazer,* . . . a dish under which there is a receptacle for coals to keep it hot. **1895** *Harper's Mag.* May 885/1 Delicacies which Tom prided himself on being able to prepare on a blazer.

+**Blaze road.** (See BLAZED *a.* 3.) — **1817** E. P. FORDHAM *Narr.* 100 [Indiana] is one vast forest, intersected by a few Blaze roads and two or three open roads. Blaze roads are merely lines, marked through the forests by slices of bark, like a blaze, being chopped off the trees.

Blazes, plural of BLAZE *n.*[2], used chiefly in exclamations, as *blazes, by blazes, in (blue) blazes,* or in comparisons, *as blazes, like blazes.* Also *blue blazes.* {1838–} *colloq.*

(1) **1837** J. C. NEAL *Charcoal Sk.* (1838) 134 Here I've been serving my country . . . these ten years, like a patriot— . . . hurraing my daylights out, and getting as blue as blazes. *c***1845** W. T. THOMPSON *Chron. Pineville* 49 All the hair [was] off his head and his face [was] as black as the very old blazes. **1849** N. KINGSLEY *Diary* 19 Hot as blazes—glad to get under awnings. **1849** JONES *Wild West Scenes* iii. 47, I was hunting after muskrats in the ponds out here, when the fire came like blazes. **1853** SIMMS *Sword & Distaff* 345 He kin shoot like blazes, rifle or Ingin bow. **1855** — *Forayers* 138, I'm as cool as blazes. **1896** *N.Y. Dramatic News* 4 July 7/1 This afternoon was as hot as blazes. **1922** A. BROWN *Old Crow* xliv. 504 You went by 'fore light, drivin' like blazes.

(2) **1853** SIMMS *Sword & Distaff* 421, I'll hev' my rights, by blazes, whenever I gits a chaince! **1875** 'MARK TWAIN' *Old Times Miss.* iii. (1876) 53 Look sharp, I tell you! Oh blazes, there you go! **1883** — *Life on Miss.* xxviii. 302 Where in blazes are you going with that barrel now? **1885** *Harper's Mag.* Aug. 397/2 Hannah-Maria-Jemimy! goldarn an' blue blazes! **1911** SAUNDERS *Col. Todhunter* ix. 123 What in blue blazes and Sam Hill is that man a-doin' there?

(3) **1835** [LONGSTREET] *Georgia Scenes* 58 Dod eternally durn my soul, . . . if I didn't drive blue blazes through him in less than no time.

+**Blazing,** *vbl. n.* [f. BLAZE *v.*[1]] The operation of marking trees with blazes; the set of marks thus made.

1772 ROMANS in Phillips *Notes* (1924) 121 To make a Road from C to B all that seems to be wanting is the Blazing of the Trees. **1799** *Aurora* (Phila.) 22 May (Th.), Gashing, notching, and blazing, are fallacious, futile, hurtful. **1818** J. PALMER *Travels U.S.* 139 Blazing is a common practice in America; it consists of taking about a foot of bark off every third or fourth tree on each side of a path. **1836** *Knickerb.* VIII. 276 These 'blazings' are the guide-boards and milestones of the wild woods.

Blazing, *ppl. a.* [BLAZE *v.*[2]] *slang.* Used adverbially as an intensive with *drunk.* — **1857** in *Lawrence* (Kansas) *Republican* 28 May 4 The brave official had become what is sometimes termed 'blazing drunk.'

+**Blazing iron.** *Obs.* [BLAZE *v.*[2]] A firearm. — **1778** ANBUREY *Travels* II. 218 To meet a New Englander riding in the woods with his blazing iron (the term they give to a musket or gun) you might mistake him for the knight of the Woeful Countenance.

* **Blazing star.** [In Eng. use in the sense of 'comet' (1502–1762), or applied *fig.* to a person or thing.]

+**1.** One or other of the plants *Aletris farinosa* (or its root), *Chamælirium luteum,* or *Liatris squarrosa.*

(1) **1789** *Amer. Philos. Soc.* III. p. xx, The root of *Aletris farinosa* is taken in powder, or bruised and steeped in liquor: this root is called star-root, blazing star, devil's bit; and greatly esteemed . . . for many qualities. **1859** BARTLETT 36 Blazing Star (*Aletris farinosa*) . . . is also called Devil's Bit. Both names are also applied to other and very different plants.

(2) **1817–8** EATON *Botany* (1822) 303 Blazing star, false unicorn root. **1832** WILLIAMSON *Maine* I. 124 The leaves of the last [star-grass] spread near the ground and look not unlike a 'blazing' star. **1840** DEWEY *Mass. Flowering Plants* 205 *Helonias dioica,* Blazing Star, Devil's Bit, Unicorn's Horn; . . . wet situations on hills. **1857** GRAY *Botany* 478 *Chamælirium luteum.* Blazing-Star. . . . Low grounds, W. New England to Illinois, and Southward. **1869** FULLER *Flower Gatherers* 170 The country people usually know it as 'The Blazing Star,' or 'Unicorn Plant.'

(3) **1836** LINCOLN *Botany* App. 110 *Liatris scariosa,* blue blazing star. **1847** WOOD *Botany* 317 Blazing Star. . . . A splendid plant, . . . with brilliant purple flowers. **1901** MOHR *Plant Life Ala.* 115 The forests . . . brilliant with the purple spikes of the blazing stars (*Lacinaria*). *Ib.* 767 *Lacinaria graminifolia,* . . . Narrow-leaf Blazing Star. . . . Flowers pale rose; September. **1904** STRATTON-PORTER *Freckles* 328 These [vases] she filled with fringed gentians, blazing-star, asters, goldenrod, and ferns.

+**2.** *West.* A stampede of pack-mules or other animals from a center.

1889 *Cent.* **1901** *Munsey's Mag.* XXV. 403/2 The herd . . . burst like a bombshell into that most disastrous of all plains mishaps—a 'blazing star.' The solid herd streamed suddenly in all directions, scattered in knots and bunches, and twos and threes, and vanished into the storm and darkness.

+**Bleach,** *n.* [f. the verb.] A quantity of linen, etc., laid out to bleach or hung up to dry. — **1849** WILLIS *Rural Lett.* xii. 112 The breachy ox has run over the 'bleach and lavender' of a seven days' wear and washing. **1902** CLAPIN.

***Bleach,** *v.* **1.** *To bleach high:* (meaning obscure). +**2.** (See quot. 1851.) — (1) **1805** in *Ann. 10th Congress* 1 Sess. I. 646 When I proceeded farther, to 'bleach high,' I blushed to the fingers' ends. (2) **1836** *Harvardiana* III. 123 'Tis sweet Commencement parts to reach, But, oh! 'tis doubly sweet to *Bleach.* **1851** HALL *College Words* 20 At Harvard College, he was formerly said to *bleach* who preferred to be *spiritually* rather than *bodily* present at morning prayers.

* **Bleacher.**

+**1.** A container used in bleaching.

1883 *Century Mag.* Oct. 812/2 The nuts are then poured into bleachers —boxes with perforated bottoms.

+**2.** One of a roofless set of benches for spectators on an athletic field, esp. at baseball and football games, bleached by exposure to sun and rain. Usually in plural.

Hence in later use (1909–) *bleacherite,* an occupant of the bleachers; *bleachery,* the bleachers.

1889 *Chicago Tribune* 1 Sept. 14 'You lie!' yelled a fat man on the bleachers. **1892** *Alumni Weekly* (New Haven) 1 March, These Yale patrons . . . buy seats for the game . . . on bleachers and grand stand close to the enemy's goal. **1897** FLANDRAU *Harvard Episodes* 52 Spavins . . . was all the time behind the bleachers absorbed in putting the shot. **1904** *N.Y. American* 5 May 13 The bleachers of the club grounds have been so enlarged this season as to accommodate about 12000 persons. **1911** *N.Y. Ev. Post* 14 Sept. (Th. S.), The democracy of the game is at its best on the bleachers and in the grandstand.

attrib. **1917** MATHEWSON *Sec. Base Sloan* xviii. 238 More than half of the bleacher seats were empty.

b. *transf.* In *pl.,* the occupants of these seats.

1889 *Chicago Tribune* 1 Sept. 14/7 Instead of cheering him for his gallant attempt, the bleachers sent up a groan. **1890** H. PALMER *Stories of Base Ball Field* 11 The discovery by the 'bleachers' of a silk hat in the grand stand was the signal for a whole afternoon of sport at the wearer's expense.

+**Bleaching board.** =BLEACHER 2. Usually in plural. — **1888** *Cosmopolitan* Oct. 445 [Illustration of] B. B. Audience—The Bleaching Boards. **1889** *Chicago Tribune* 1 Sept. 14/6 Cudworth dodged the ball, and it rolled clear to the bleaching boards.

Bleary. {1825, *Sc.*} (See quots.) — **1809** HENRY *Camp. Quebec* 65 Our kettle, boiling a bleary, which was no other than flour and water, . . . without salt. *Ib.,* This morning . . . breakfasting on our bleary, we took up the line of march.

***Bleat,** *n.* +A 'call' for imitating the bleating of a deer. — **1852** MARCY *Explor. Red River* (1854) 54, I took out my bleat and commenced exercising my powers in imitating the cry of the fawn.

***Bleat,** *v.* +*To bleat up,* to decoy by imitative bleating. — **1806** LEWIS in *L. & Clark Exped.* (1905) V. 156 The does now having their fawns the hunters can bleat them up and in that manner kill them with more facility and ease.

Bled, *ppl. a.* [BLEED *v.*] Drained of resin or turpentine. — **1894** *Pop. Science Mo.* June 284 A series of tests and examinations of bled and unbled timber has been carried on.

* **Bleed,** *v.*

1. *intr.* Of trees: To emit or lose sap when pruned or wounded. {1674–1796}

1828 WEBSTER s.v., A tree or a vine bleeds. **1874** *Vt. Bd. Agric. Rep.* II. 289 The best results [with apple orchards] are obtained by pruning in March and April. If pruned later the trees will often 'bleed,' though it is stated that a perfectly healthy tree will not bleed if pruned at any season. *Ib.,* Mr. Start said he had pruned in May without injury to trees from bleeding.

2. *tr.* To draw sap, gum, etc., from (a tree) by wounding it.

1856 *Spirit of Times* (N.Y.) 22 Nov. 198/2 Bleeding Trees to make them bear, consists in cutting the bark up and down the tree, from the limbs to the ground, about the 1st of May. **1895** *Yearbook Dept. Agric. 1894* 45 The pineries of the Southern States which are being 'bled' for turpentine.

3. To cheat or drain of money. {1680–1849}

1875 BURNHAM *Three Years* p. iv, *Bleed,* to cheat, over-reach, victimise, or extort money from. **1880** CABLE *Grandissimes* xlviii, The policy they then adopted . . . bled them to penury. **1901** MERWIN & WEBSTER *Calumet K* xii. 224 Men will take every opportunity to bleed a corporation.

Bleeder. [BLEED *v.* 3.] One who extorts money from another. — **1894** *Columbus* (Ohio) *Dispatch* 5 Oct., It seems that the police of New York were not the only bleeders. The agents of the Gerry Society for the Suppression of Vice were also at it.

* **Bleeding,** *ppl. a.* [BLEED *v.*] +Applied to Kansas during the period (1854–60) when the question of allowing slavery within the territory was being debated. Now *Hist.*

The title of 'Bleeding Kansas' was used by the Free-State party to excite sympathy, and by the other side in derision. It was first used by the New York *Tribune* (LANE in *America* 20 Sept. 1888, p. 15).

1857 GOV. WALKER in *Lawrence* (Kansas) *Republican* 4 June 4 Does she want to be 'bleeding Kansas' for the benefit of political agitators within or out of her limits? *Ib.* 25 June 3 Democracy that . . . never alluded to our Territory except to tauntingly and contemptuously stigmatize it as 'bleeding Kansas.' **1860** Connelley *Hist. Kansas* (1918) I. 173 Landing in Bleeding Kansas—she still bleeds—we fell at once into 'Emigration Road.' **1873** BEADLE *Undevel. West* xix. 366 It appeared as if 'Bleeding Kansas' was about to bleed again in the cause of municipal reform. **1882** BAILLIE-GROHMAN *Camps in Rockies* 16 He was 'riz' in West Kansas in its earliest days, when the eastern portion of that State was the 'bleeding Kansas' of which twenty years ago we heard so much. **1896** *Congress. Rec.* 16 Jan. 748/1 Kansas, 'bleeding Kansas,' pays $277,633.81 internal revenue, and she gets back in the form of pensions $6,084,592.16.

Bleeding heart. {1825–}

1. A variety of cultivated cherry.

1847 DARLINGTON *Weeds & Plants* 118 Birds' Prunus, English Cherry, Bleeding-heart, &c. **1859** ELLIOTT *Western Fruit Book* 228 Bleeding heart. . . . Fruit, medium, long, pointed heart shape, dark red mottled.

2. One or other species of the genus *Dicentra* of delicate perennial herbs, esp. *D. spectabilis.* {1884}

1887 J. BURROUGHS in *Century Mag.* July 325, I have an eye out for the white-hearts (related to the bleeding-hearts of the gardens, and absurdly called 'Dutchman's breeches') the last week in April. **1897** *Outing* Dec. 318/2 She held out a rose to Ferguson, but to Jonathan she gave a bleeding-heart. **1923** E. F. WYATT *Invis. Gods* 16 An aster bed in the center of its lawn surrounded by the rosy foam of peonies, the sprays of bleeding heart.

+**3.** The burning bush or wahoo.

1897 SUDWORTH *Arborescent Flora* 281 *Evonymus atropurpureus,* . . . Bleeding Heart (N.C.).

Blenny. {1769} A spiny-finned sea-fish of the genus *Blennius.*

1814 MITCHILL *Fishes N.Y.* 375 Large-lipped Blenny, *Blennius labrosus,* . . . was taken at sea among the cod fishes. **1839** STORER *Mass. Fishes* 67 *Zoarcus anguillaris.* The eel-shaped Blenny. . . . When young, its flesh is very sweet and palatable. **1842** *Nat. Hist. N.Y., Zoology* IV. 149 The Sea Weed Blenny. *Blennius fucorum. Ib.* 156 The Fringed Blenny, *B. ciliatus,* . . . is invariably smaller than the other species.

+**Blickey, -ie.** *N.Y.* and *N.J.* [Du. *blikje,* f. *blik* tin.] (See quotations.) — **1859** BARTLETT 36 *Blickey,* . . . in New York, a tin pail. **1877** *Ib.* 707 Tin blickey. **1889** *Cent., Blickie,* . . . a small pail or bucket. (New Jersey.) **1896** *Jerseyisms* in *Dialect Notes* I. 328 *Blicky* (*blickie, blickey*) . . . [is] said to be Dutch in its origin, but [it is] used extensively in S. J., where there are no Dutch. *Ib.* 382, The variety is distinguished by an adjective, as 'wooden' or 'tin' blickey.

Blifustier, error for *flibustier* FILIBUSTER. — **1835** SIMMS *Yemassee* I. 138 Your face did wear a most Blifustier expression. *Ib.* note, *Blifustier* was one of the names conferred by the Dutch, by which the early bucaniers of America were known. *Ib.* 150 A good wind, sir, would carry this Blifustier beyond the fort.

Blight, *n.*

1. A diseased condition in plants, usually caused by fungoid parasites. Also in *pl.* {1611–}

1804 J. ROBERTS *Penn. Farmer* 38, I have found the following [steeps] to be the most fertilizing, and effectual to prevent blights and smuts. **1837** COLMAN *Mass. Agric. Rep.* (1838) 28 The blights or shrivelling of the kernel . . . are in some cases occasioned by the want of lime in the soil. **1854** Commons, etc. *Doc. Hist.* I. 272 Among the diseases to which Long Cotton is subject blight, rust and blue may arise from some defect in the soil. **1863** MITCHELL *My Farm* 142 Every apple is patched with a mouldy blight. **1878** *Rep. Indian Affairs* 121 Early varieties are already ripe and late ones more than half grown, with, as yet, no indication of blight. **1891** 'THANET' *Otto the Knight,* etc. 119 The blight, the mildew, the rust, . . . what misery they wrought!

+**b.** See AMERICAN BLIGHT.

+**2.** *pl.* A rash.

1828 WEBSTER s.v., In America, I have often heard a cutaneous eruption of the human skin called by the name of *blights.*

Blight, *v.* [f. the noun.] *intr.* To suffer from blight. {*tr.* 1695–} — **1857–8** *Ill. Agric. Soc. Trans.* III. 337 The next year it was free from blight, but the fourth year it blighted down to where it had been budded.

* **Blind,** *n.*

1. A screen serving as a protection from the fire of an enemy; a blindage. {1644–1802}

1756 *Lett. to Washington* I. 311 A Blind like a Ravelin necessary to conceal the Sally Port. **1760** *Essex Inst. Coll.* III. 197 The Gen'l . . . began to lay waste the garrison of Louisbourg beginning at the blind opposite the South gate. **1777** *Md. Hist. Mag.* V. 215, [I] threw up a Blind on the Platform which . . . will in some Measure make the Men . . . secure.

2. a. A wooden screen for a window. {1786–}

Usually applied to each of two slatted and hinged frames, the pair being called 'the blinds.'

1771 COPLEY in *Copley-Pelham Lett.* 142 Those Windows having new fassioned Blinds such as you see in Mr. Clarke's Keeping room. **1823** COOPER *Pioneers* iii, Some three or four of the better sort of buildings, in addition to the uniformity of their colour, were fitted with green blinds. **1840** *Knickerb.* XVI. 245 To add to his gloomy feelings, it was a dark, dull day, and the wind moaned sadly through the blinds of his windows. **1857** *Lawrence* (Kansas) *Republican* 4 June 1 Burnett & Bailey, Dealers in Windows, Doors and Blinds. **1865** *Atlantic Mo.* XV. 492/2 That room . . . whose blinds are closed the whole year round. **1875** STOWE *We & Our Neighbors* i. 9 Jack . . . must learn not to get up and bark through those blinds. **1883** E. W. HOWE *Country Town* (1926) 50 There were thick wooden blinds at all the windows. **1892** *Vt. Agric. Rep.* XII. 114 Vergennes . . . is largely engaged in the manufacture of horse nails, curtain rollers, doors, sash, blinds, and furniture. **1898** PAGE *Red Rock* 123 There he flung open the blinds and rummaged in the drawers. **1901** CHURCHILL *Crisis* 282 Then the blinds were flung aside, and a young lady . . . stood in the window, smiling.

attrib. **1858** *Rep. Comm. Patents* (1859) I. 575 Improvement in Staples for Blind-Slats. **1863** in *Century Mag.* Sept. (1885) 770 They . . . tried every door, peeped in the windows, . . . while I watched them through the blind-slats.

b. A length of material mounted on a roller and capable of being pulled up or down; a shade.

1845 C. M. KIRKLAND *Western Clearings* 142 Ashdod Cockles had not thought it prudent to suspend more than a single candle within the chintz curtains and the gauze blind. **1875** STOWE *We & Our Neighbors* 49, I . . . sometimes wish I could go right into some . . . dark church, and pull down all the blinds, and shut all the doors. **1880** *Harper's Mag.* July 262/2 The gas was lighted in your parlor before the blinds were down, and the policeman saw him . . . standing on the hearth rug. **1902** 'MARK TWAIN' *Ib.* Feb. 429 Mr. Holmes's blinds were down; but by-and-by he raised them.

3. A hiding-place or covert used or made by a hunter or fowler to conceal himself from the game; also, a place of ambush. {1697}

1818 *Niles' Reg.* XV. 64/2 Col. Boon rode to a deer lick, seated himself within a blind raised to conceal him from the game. **1824** DODDRIDGE *Notes* 22 When watching a deer lick from his blind at night, the formidable panther was often his rival. **1847** H. Howe *Hist. Coll. Ohio* 455 McArthur went to a deer lick, . . . made a blind, behind which he concealed himself, and waited for game. **1853** A. BUNN *Old Eng. & New Eng.* 106 The legitimate mode of shooting these birds is from the interior of a sort of pen, called a blind. **1869** *Penna. Laws* 21 April 85 No person shall . . . build blinds for the purpose of killing or to trap or snare any wild turkey. **1874** LONG *Wild-Fowl* 45 Ingenuity in the providing of proper ambush, or blind, as all such hiding places are generally termed by wild-fowlers. **1887** *Harper's Mag.* June 55/2 The Indians made a 'blind,' or hiding-place of bushes, behind which they lay in wait for the whites. **1897** *Outing* Feb. 516/2 By that time the chill has left the air, and a body can sit comfortably in his blind, smoking the pipe of peace.

4. A blinker for a horse. {1796–, *dial.*} Cf. BLIND BRIDLE.

1828 WEBSTER s.v., A blind . . . for a horse. **1848** *Congress. Globe* App., 30 June 820/1 [Mr. Polk] was worked into the Presidency with Oregon and Texas on either side, as a horse is worked with blinds. **1881** J. W. BUEL *Border Outlaws* 61 It had originally been a blind-bridle, but now one of the blinds had fallen off. **1901** *Munsey's Mag.* XXV. 739/1 A halter has a soft leather-covered bit, and is without blinds.

+**5.** In poker, the stake put up by the elder hand (the 'age') before the deal, and thus without seeing the cards.

1857 *Hoyle's Games* (Amer. ed.) 289 Should a party see fit to call the blind, [he] must put twice the number in the pool, with the privilege of running over the blind. **1859** *Harper's Mag.* Sept. 572/2 Mike . . . concluded he could bluff; and, says he, I'll make my blind good and see your *Simon,* and go you ten better. **1872** 'MARK TWAIN' *Roughing It* xlvii. 333 Now you talk! You see my blind and straddle it like a man. **1884** 'CRADDOCK' *Where Battle was Fought* 35 Estwick . . . raised the blind one hundred dollars. **1889** FARMER 62 To make a blind good costs double the amount of the ante, and to make a straddle good costs four times the amount of the blind. **1894** *Congress. Rec.* 4 May 4408/2 When the fourth [school] boy . . . handed in his composition, it read, 'Put up your blind. It is my deal.'

+**6.** A blind baggage-car (BLIND *a.* 2 b).

*c***1894** *Dialect Notes* I. 390 *Jump the blind,* to steal a ride on platform of baggage-car. West.

* **Blind,** *a.*

* **1.** Not visible or obvious; hidden; obscure.

*a***1656** BRADFORD *Hist.* 262 It pleased God . . . they came right before a small blind harbore, that lyes aboute the midle of Manamoyake Bay. **1702** C. MATHER *Magnalia* (1853) I. iii. 308 He was taken with . . . an odd fit, which caused him to stop at a blind house of entertainment on the road. **1714** *Boston News-Letter* 5 April 2/1 On Friday last the Ferry Boat of Seaconet . . . struck on a blind Rock at some distance from Land. **1826** COOPER *Mohicans* xiii, The hunter . . . seemed to select among the blind signs of their wild route with a species of instinct. **1852** *Mich. Agric. Soc. Trans.* III. 188, I have drained with open and blind ditches. **1872** 'MARK TWAIN' *Roughing It* xl. 280 A 'blind lead' is a lead or ledge that does not 'crop out' above the surface. **1883** BEADLE *Western Wilds* xxxiv. 561 Sometimes a blind lode is traced by a faint outcrop in a neighboring gulch. **1884** BRET HARTE *On Frontier* 232 He was out . . . all night, prospecting in the moonlight for blind leads.

* **b.** Not easy to trace, follow, or find one's way in.

1736 *Duxbury Rec.* 160 About 39 rods, to a stake and stones, by an old blind path. **1784** WASHINGTON *Diaries* II. 304 The path it is said is very blind and exceedingly grown with briers. **1797** B. HAWKINS *Letters* 112 Continue on a blind tract thro' hilly . . . land and down a stream. **1829** COOPER *Wish-Ton-Wish* ii. 34 The blind road . . . led to one of the distant settlements. **1835** SIMMS *Yemassee* II. 143 He was on the blind path in the woods—I heard him cry . . . for the scouts. **1875** 'MARK TWAIN' *Old Times Miss.* ix. (1876) 60 How is a body ever going to get through this blind place at night? **1877** BRET HARTE *Story of a Mine,* etc. 313 You know yourself, dad, it's a blind trail. **1890** H. M. FIELD *Bright Skies* 288 It was pitch dark; but I picked my way over the blind roads, till about midnight I reached the place.

c. Uncertain, indefinite.

1846 POLK *Diary* (1929) 177 He answered that he would pay a blind sum and would not stand on a few million dollars.

2. Closed at one end. {1668–}

The figurative use of *blind alley* has been known in Eng. from at least 1854.

1770 WASHINGTON *Diaries* I. 365, [I] found a fox at the head of the blind Pocoson. **1837** *S. Lit. Messenger* III. 224, I found myself . . . in a back yard, opening by a gate . . . into a blind alley. **1842** *Knickerb.* XX. 309 He had had some experience in 'blind' bayous. **1853** [COZZENS] *Prismatics* 37 We came to a blind alley or entry. **1883** *Century Mag.* Sept. 651/2 Sometimes you are tempted to pursue such a way until it turns out a 'blind road.'

+b. Of a baggage-car on a train: (see first quotation.)

1901 *Scribner's Mag.* April 429/1 The train's got a blind baggage-car on. . . . That's a car that ain't got no door in the end that's next the engine. **1910** H. A. FRANCK *Vagabond Journey* 361 He was not long in convincing both Rice and me that he knew the secrets of the 'blind baggage' and the ways of railroad 'bulls.' **1912** MATHEWSON *Pitching* xi. 249 He had come all the way either by side-door special or blind baggage.

Blind, *adv.* +Blindly; heedlessly; recklessly. *Go it blind:* see GO *v.* — **1853** *S. Lit. Messenger* XIX. 334/1, I had a vague idea that a woman was mixed up in the matter, . . . so I led out blind to find out. **1859** *Harper's Mag.* Sept. 572/2 He riffled the kurds, and Mike went blind.

Blind, *v.* **+1.** *tr.* (See quotation.) **2.** To remove (buds) from a plant. — **(1) 1859** BARTLETT 36 *To Blind a trail,* to conceal a person's foot-prints, or to give them the appearance of going in a different direction; figuratively, to deceive a person by putting him on the wrong track. **(2) 1862** *Rep. Comm. Patents: Agric.* 513 The eyes on these canes (except the two on the top) should be rubbed off, or, as it is technically called, 'blinded,' so as to concentrate the strength into the two.

+Blind bridle. A bridle fitted with blinds or blinkers. {Cf. *blind halters,* 1711; *blinder bridal,* 1839– n. dial.}

1833 J. HALL *Harpe's Head* 30 Some rode with blind-bridles. **1847** Emory *Military Reconn.* 540 This mule had a blind bridle on its head. **1861** *Ill. Agric. Soc. Trans.* IV. 376 A blind bridle may be tolerated on a blind horse. **1866** 'F. KIRKLAND' *Bk. Anecdotes* 277 He came upon a very fine horse in the bottom, tied by a blind-bridle. **1881** BUEL *Border Outlaws* 61 It had originally been a blind-bridle, but now one of the blinds had fallen off. **1894** *Congress. Rec.* 20 Jan. 1148/2 An old blind bridle being the first hangman's rope he could find, he tied one end of it around his neck.

+Blind chisel. ? A 'blind-slat chisel' (Knight), a hollow chisel for cutting the mortises to receive the slat-ends. — **1851** CIST *Cincinnati* 258 Brand, stamp, and blind chisel makers.

+Blind door. [BLIND *n.*] An outside door made of slats. — **1881** *Century Mag.* Nov. 131/1 One of those deceptive New England cottages . . . with its front hall, now cooled by the light sea-breeze drifting through the blind-door.

Blind eel. +(See quotations.) — **1865** *Atlantic Mo.* Jan. 96 A new hook had been put on mine [*sc.* fishing line], as on the last excursion the old one had caught in what the boys call a 'blind eel,' that is, a sunken log. **1877** BARTLETT 47 When a fisherman brings up a piece of sea-weed on his hook, he is said to have caught a blind eel.

Blinder.

+1. A window shutter or blind.

1790 BENTLEY *Diary* I. 187 Whether blinders upon the outside of windows are not more troublesome than within?

2. A covering for the eyes, esp. a blind or blinker for a horse. {1788–, *dial.*}

1809 BARLOW *Columbiad* x. 414 Now the race at last Shake off their manacles, their blinders cast. **1812** *Boston Gazette* 9 July 3/4 (Advt.), [The cow,] when she went away, had on a board blinder. **1854** BARTLETT *Narr.* I. 359 A blinder is slipped over the eyes of the mule, which renders him perfectly docile. **1856** EMERSON *Eng. Traits* v. 92 In common, the horse works best with blinders. **1869** ALDRICH *Bad Boy* (1877) 114 The Captain interrupted Miss Abigail . . . , directing her to make a shade out of card-board and black silk, to tie over my eye. . . . She turned out no less than six of these blinders. **1884** 'MARK TWAIN' *Huck. Finn* xi. 96, I took off the sun-bonnet, for I didn't want no blinders on then. **1895** *Outing* Aug. 478/1 Spurs, like blinders, should be banished from the polo field.

+Blind fast. [BLIND *n.*] ?A fastener for a blind. — **1846** *Knickerb.* Sept. 279 A. Fuller . . . has fitted up a [machine] shop at his house . . . where he will attend to the manufacture of Blind Fasts.

+Blind fish. A fish (*Amblyopsis spelæus*) with only rudimentary sightless eyes, found in the Mammoth Cave of Ky. — **1843** *Journal of Sci.* 94 Description of a 'Blind Fish,' from a cave in Kentucky. **1847** L. COLLINS *Kentucky* 157 In this river or pool are found 'blind fish,' without the slightest appearance of eyes. **1897** HOVEY & CALL *Mammoth Cave* 100 Soon after the rivers were discovered, . . . the earliest specimens of crayfish and blind-fish were also found.

+Blind hand. The player who bets before examining his hand in blind poker. — **1882** *Poker* 88 For some reasons players never give the blind hand credit for a good or even an average hand.

+Blind mess. *Obs.* (See quotation.) — **1828** A. SHERBURNE *Mem.* (1831) iv. 86 The messes in rotation, send one of their number into the cook room every day. The mess which sends the man, is called the blind mess [because the lots of meat were indicated by a blindfolded man].

Blind pig. *colloq.* [From the professed object of exhibition.] +A place used for the illicit sale of liquor. Cf. BLIND TIGER. — **1887** *Minn. Gen. Statutes Suppl.* (1888) 248 Whoever shall attempt to evade or violate any of the laws of this state . . . by means of the artifice or contrivance known as the 'Blind Pig' or 'Hole in the Wall' . . . shall . . . be punished. **1897** *Chicago Tribune* 11 Aug. 2/6 Meyers, alleged proprietor of a 'blind pig' in 'No Man's Land,' . . . gave a constable . . . the slip yesterday. **1901** *Dialect Notes* II. 136 *Blind pig,* a speak-easy; . . . [a] saloon without a license. **1904** *Minneapolis Times* 7 June 2 The petition charges incompetency, arguing that he has for years permitted 'blind pigs' to flourish in that prohibited district.

+Blind-pigger. *colloq.* [See prec.] One who keeps a 'blind pig.' — **1894** *Voice* (N.Y.) 6 Dec. 1/5 By a mob . . . headed by one of the blind-piggers who was under arrest, Rev. McNamara was severely beaten. **1917** D. PICKETT *Cycl. of Temperance* 55 The blind pigger in wet territory can procure his liquor shipments without exciting suspicion.

+Blind poker. (See quotation.) — **1871** DE VERE 328 Poker, when played by betting before looking at one's hand, is called *Blind Poker;* and this has given rise to the very common phrase, to *go it blind,* used whenever an enterprise is undertaken without previous inquiry.

+Blind pool. *colloq.* A pool the purpose of which is known only to the organizers, to whom the other members leave its management. — **1882** *Nation* 31 Aug. 168/1 He denies the charge that he managed the 'blind pool' dishonorably, and declares that although made up on paper, it never went into effect. **1883** *Harper's Mag.* Nov. 940/1 How Henry Villard and the Oregon company obtained control of the Northern Pacific, . . . the story of the 'blind pool,' has often been told.

Blind robin. +(See quotation.) *colloq.* — **1889** RILEY *Pipes o'Pan* 32 A reputed banquet whose menu's range confined itself to herrings, or 'blind robins,' dried beef, and cheese.

Blind snipe. +(See quotations.) — **(1)** *a***1841** [W. HAWES] *Sporting Scenes* I. 179 Sportsmen, generally, among themselves, talk of killing a 'cock'; but if they meet an old woman in the woods, . . . they ask her if she has seen any 'blind snipes.' **1844** *Nat. Hist. N.Y., Zoology* II. 258 The American Woodcock, *Rusticola minor,* . . . in some parts of the State . . . is known under the name of Blind Snipe; but for what reason I have not been able to discover. **(2) 1890** *Cent.* 5731/3 *Blind snipe,* the stilt-sandpiper, *Micropalama himantopus.*

+Blind staggers. {*staggers,* 1577–} One or other ailment in domestic animals causing a staggering gait and apparent blindness; in sheep caused by hydatids in the brain.

1815 HUMPHREYS *Yankey* 30 *New.* Megrims. . . . Vapours. . . . *Doo.* Blind staggers! **1835** [LONGSTREET] *Georgia Scenes* 214 They'd . . . tilt right over backwards . . . and die right away, . . . with a sort o' somethin' like the blind staggers. **1838** COLMAN *Mass. Agric. Rep.* (1839) 75 [The swine] having no exercise, it tends to produce the blind staggers. **1860** CLAIBORNE *Sam. Dale* ii. 32 We built our cabin and made a clearing, but the blind staggers got among our horses and killed all but one. **1868** *Rep. Comm. Agric.* 41 Blind staggers has been somewhat fatal in the south and west. **1874** *Vt. Bd. Agric. Rep.* II. 431 The disease [in sheep] is frequently called 'blind staggers.' **1905** VALENTINE *H. Sandwith* 33 Archy McSwords called me down to the stables to see one of the mules bled for the blind staggers. **1912** MRS. WOODROW *Sally Salt* 322 My Pegasus can't stay up long; he gets blind staggers in the air and tumbles down very soon.

+Blind teeth. *S.* (See quotations.) — **1843** *Cultivator* Dec. 198/1 One [horse] had gone entirely blind before I was apprised of the cause, and the other two I relieved by immediately extracting the *blind teeth. Ib.,* Hundreds of instances could be adduced of the existence of blind teeth, and the destruction of sight when not extracted.

Blind tiger. *colloq.* +BLIND PIG. — **1883** *Arkansas Digest Laws* (1884) 493 Any person . . . who shall sell . . . any alcohol . . . by such device as is known as 'the blind tiger,' . . . shall be deemed guilty of a misdemeanor. **1892** *Evening Echo* 30 June 1/7 The proprietor of a 'blind tiger' . . . in Lancaster . . . has been fined in 577 cases. **1902** LORIMER *Lett. Merchant* 217 [He] ran . . . a blind tiger in the back room with moonshine whiskey. **1909** *N.Y. Ev. Post* 28 Jan. (Th.), A 'blind tiger' is a private residence, a shed, a tent, or an office room in a building, occupied temporarily and stocked with beer and whiskey for sale to friends of the proprietor.

+Blink. *local.* A mackerel when about a year old. — **1856** Goode *Fisheries* (1884) 298 The mackerel . . . are not sold by weight, but are culled, and are denominated as follows: Large ones, second size, tinkers, and blinks. **1888** ATWOOD in Goode *Fishes* 174 Fish of this size are sometimes called 'Spikes.' . . . The next year I think they are the 'Blinks,' being one year old.

***Blister.**

+1. An irritating or annoying person or animal; a nuisance. *colloq.*

1854 *Yale Lit. Mag.* XX. 29 (Th.), Here's Mrs. Grind now,—rooms to let,—good rooms, but the dowager's a blister. **1877** J. M. BEARD *K. K. K. Sketches* 182 Having been damned for a 'blister,' and a 'cooter,' and a 'scorpion,' [K. K. Kain] wandered forth. **1884** 'MARK TWAIN' *Huck. Finn* xxix. 303 Well, I never see anything like that old blister for clean out-and-out cheek. **1889** — *Conn. Yankee* xx. 247 We got the hogs home just at dark—most of them. The princess . . . was missing, and two of her ladies in waiting: . . . a couple of the tryingest blisters to drive that I ever saw.

+2. A small oyster.

1881 E. INGERSOLL *Oyster Industry* 241 *Blister*, a young oyster, not larger than a quarter dollar. . . . (Barnegat to Cape May.)

+3. *Blister and curl:* (see quotation).

1864 *Ohio Agric. Rep.* XVIII. 460 For some years, in this country, the disease which produces the 'Blister and Curl' in the peach leaf, and decay in the peach fruit, has . . . produced extensive ravages.

Blister-beetle. {1816–} One or other of various beetles yielding a poison which is used in medicine to raise blisters on the skin; in the imago state they are frequently destructive to field and garden crops.

1868 *Amer. Entomologist* I. 24 The blister-beetles . . . are . . . poisonous when taken internally in large doses. *Ib.*, The Ash-gray Blister-beetle (*Lytta cinerea*) . . . attacks not only potato vines, but also honey-locusts. **1869** *Amer. Naturalist* III. 99 The Blister Beetles frequently feed on potato bugs. **1876** *Vt. Bd. Agric. Rep.* III. 569 Perhaps the most common of these beetles in the United States is the striped blister beetle (*Lytta vittata*). **1881** *Amer. Naturalist* XV. 143 Others, as the true blister-beetles, (*Lyttini*), feed on locust eggs.

Blistered, *ppl. a.* [f. *blister* n. or v.] Of steel: Having the surface covered with small blisters. {1837–} — **1744** *Md. Hist. Mag.* XXI. 243 Ironware: 6 good . . . gardin spades; 3 ffaggotts Blistered Steel. **1770** *Carroll P.* Ib. XIII. 65 My Smiths say the Bristol or Blister'd steel sent to us is very bad. **1787** *Steele Papers* I. 15 Respecting the Steel it is right, you must certainly mean Blistered Steel which comes, at or near the price you mention. German Steel never was bought so low.

+**Blisterer.** One who reprimands severely. — **1883** EGGLESTON *Hoosier School-Boy* xxiii. 157 Bob Halliday said 'the young master was a blisterer.'

Blister-fly. {1862–} A fly of the genus *Cantharis;* the Spanish fly or related species. — **1836** EDWARD *Texas* 88 Next comes the Spanish or blister fly, to be found in greater numbers, quite innoxious to the beholder, but dangerous to be handled. **1856** *Rep. Comm. Patents: Agric.* 88 Several blister-flies, or cantharides, found in Columbia, South Carolina, were seen to devour the petals of the cotton-flower. **1868** *Rep. Comm. Agric.* (1869) 103 The black Cantharis, or Blister-fly, . . . devours the foliage of the potato and various flowers.

***Blistering,** *ppl. a.* [f. *blister* v.] Raising blisters. *Blistering beetle* =BLISTER BEETLE. *Blistering fly* =BLISTER-FLY.

1820 *U.S. Pharmacopoeia* 269 Index, Blistering Cerate, . . . cerate of Cantharides. **1847** *Florida Plantation Rec.* 573 Medison wanting on Eldistina: . . . Blistering ointment. **1851** *Ib.* 439 One small roll of blistering salve. **1854** EMMONS *Agric. N.Y.* V. 96 The *cantharides*, or blistering flies used in medicine. **1869** *Amer. Naturalist* III. 96 Of the Blistering Beetles (*Cantharidæ*), I have observed this year the Striped Cantharis . . . unusually abundant. **1876** *Vt. Bd. Agric. Rep.* III. 569 There is quite a large group of beetles known as blistering beetles. These are mostly long, narrow insects running or flying with speed.

+**Blister pine.** *W.Va.* The balsam fir, *Picea balsamea.* — **1894** *Amer. Folk-Lore* VII. 99 *Abies balsamea*, . . . blister pine, balm of Gilead fir, West Va.

Blister steel. (See BLISTERED.) {1821–} — **1742** *Md. Hist. Mag.* XX. 173, I request . . . you will send me . . . 3 Dozen Smiths Warding Files, . . . 2 [ditto] Blister Steel. **1874** KNIGHT 501 Cast-steel [is] blister steel which has been . . . cast into ingots, and rolled.

+**Blizz.** [Of obscure origin. Cf. next.] A violent shower. — **1770** L. CARTER *Diary* 31 May (*William & Mary Coll. Hist. Mag.* XIII. 51), At last a mighty blizz of rain.

+**Blizzard,** *n.* [Cf. BLIZZ and E. dial. *blizzer, blizzom*, a blaze, a flash.]

Articles on this word, by Allen Walker Read, appeared in *American Speech* III. 191–217, V. 232–5.

1. A sharp blow; a shot or volley of shot.

1829 *Va. Lit. Museum* 16 Dec. 418 *Blizzard*, a violent blow. . . . *Kentucky.* **1834** CROCKETT *Life* 152, I saw two more bucks, very large fellows, too. I took a blizzard at one of them, and up he tumbled. **1846** *Spirit of Times* 6 June 177/3 We turned one of our 18 pounders to bear on the mass and gave them a 'blizzard' to help them along. **1863** J. B. JONES *Western Scenes* 76 (Th.), I'd gin him a blizzard, if I died for it the next minit. **1863** *Boston Sunday Herald* 8 Feb. 4/4 Give them a blizzard right at their shins at short range, and then let them have the bayonet. **1866** J. J. CRAVEN *Prison Life of Jeff. Davis* 13 He had ridden right in on top of the 6th Conn. regiment, and our boys had given him what we called 'a blizzard.' **1881** *Nation* 14 April 260 In 1836 I first heard the word 'blizzard' among the young men at Illinois College, Jacksonville. If one struck a ball a severe blow in playing town-ball it would be said 'That's a blizzard.' **1887** *N.Y. Ev. Post* 24 March (*Cent.*), Along the Atlantic coast, among the gunners who often hunt in parties stationed near together behind blinds, waiting for flocks of migratory birds, the word *blizzard* means a general discharge of all guns, nearly but not quite together—a rattling volley, differing from a broadside in not being quite simultaneous.

attrib. **1897** *Outing* Feb. 516/2 In my younger days I participated in several of these blizzard shoots, one of which I will relate.

b. In *pl.* as the name of a baseball club.

1871 *Northern Vindicator* (Estherville, Iowa) 22 March, The Blizzards are beginning to base-ball-it again this spring.

2. *fig.* a. A squelching speech, retort, or remark.

1835 CROCKETT *Tour down East* 16 During dinner the parson . . . called on me for a toast. Not knowing whether he intended to . . . have some fun at my expense, I concluded to go ahead, and give him and his likes a blizzard. **1851** *Polly Peablossom* 175, I resolved to give him a parting 'blizzard.' I shouted, 'Hello, old cock; you have good victuals and a fine family, your galls in particular.'

b. A drink of intoxicating liquor.

1881 *Nation* 31 March 220 There has been an extensive use of the word in Pennsylvania for many years, as witness the following: (1) A drink of any intoxicant, generally applied to whiskey. . . . 'Let's take a blizzard.'

3. A violent storm of fine driving snow accompanied by intense cold.

'Common in winter on the great plains of the States and Territories of the northwestern United States east of the Rocky Mountains, especially Dakota' (*Cent.*).

1870 *Northern Vindicator* (Estherville, Iowa) 23 April, Campbell has had too much experience with northwestern 'blizards' [*sic*] to be caught in such a trap. *Ib.* 30 April, The unfortunate victim of the March 'blizzard' . . . is rapidly improving. **1873** F. M. A. ROE *Army Letters* 88 Our rooms were facing just right to catch the full force of the blizzard. **1874** *Dubuque* (Iowa) *Telegraph* 9 March, When a gentleman predicted that they would be visited by a 'blizzard,' the remark only created fun. **1876** *Wright Co. Monitor* (Clarion, Iowa) 13 Dec., A genuine blizzard sat on its hind legs and howled for twelve or fourteen hours while the mercury lurked at from ten to fourteen degrees below zero. **1881** *Rep. Indian Affairs* 125 Wheat . . . was destroyed by the unprecedented cold weather of the past winter, supplemented by numerous blizzards. **1884** *Harper's Weekly* 15 March 175/1 The last blizzard which struck us started from the plains of Texas, and made a bee-line for the Jersey coast. **1886** BRET HARTE *Snow-bound* 102 This is no blizzard, but a regular two days' snifter! *c*1900 R. L. HALE *Log of Forty-Niner* 74 There we stood, looking . . . like two snow images made by boys at play in a New England blizzard. **1916** C. A. EASTMAN *From Deep Woods* 110 There was a blizzard, in the midst of which I was ordered out with several Indian police. **1922** QUICK *Vandemark's Folly* 268 He was staying all night with me to help me get my stock through a bad storm; it was a blizzard.

b. *The Blizzard State*, South Dakota.

1907 *Boston Transcript* 9 Nov.

4. *Western blizzard:* (see quotation).

1888 H. CLEWS *28 Years in Wall St.* 5 My advent in Wall Street was on the heels of the panic of 1857. That panic was known as the 'Western Blizzard.'

+**Blizzard,** *v.* 1. *intr.* To whizz through the air; to go off smartly. 2. In *p.p.* 'Blowed'; 'confounded.' *colloq.* — (1) **1881** *Nation* March 208 An impatient boy will say 'Let her blizzard' to his comrade who hesitates in throwing him a ball. . . . 'When I got near enough I let her blizzard and shot it dead.' . . . It is with us largely a boy's phrase, and is well known. (2) **1893** GUNTER *Miss Dividends* 67 Then he suddenly ejaculates, 'Well, I'm blizzarded!'

+**Blizzardly,** *a.* Having the characteristics of a blizzard. — **1883** *Letter* in *Advance* (Chicago) 1 March, The rain changed to driving snow, with very blizzardly tendencies, the mercury dropped forty-three degrees. **1885** *Milnor* (Dakota) *Teller* 2 Jan. 3/2 A trifle blizzardly this week.

+**Blizzardous,** *a.* Marked by blizzards. — **1883** *Dansville* (Ohio) *Advertiser*, I'm hazardous and blizzardous. . . . I'm bad and my name is March.

+**Blizzardy,** *a.* Blizzardly. — **1888** *San Fran. News Letter* (F.), I should like to have seen the Colonel's face when he got that very cold, blizzardy letter.

+**Bloat.** [f. *bloat* v.] A bloated person; a drunkard.

*a*1861 WINTHROP *Open Air* 147 When I think . . . what a mean bloat I was, going to the stub-tail dogs with my hat over my eyes. **1862** NORTON *Army Lett.* 89, I have an idea that the fellow, who is the veriest bloat and bully in the company, will conclude to let me alone. **1871** *Congress. Globe* App., 15 Feb. 129/1 Wife-whippers, penitentiary birds, street vagabonds, beastly bloats, and convicted felons thronged Chambers street [N.Y.]. **1872** 'MARK TWAIN' *Roughing It* lxxi. 513 The red sun looked . . . through the tall, clean stems of the cocoanut trees, like a blooming whisky bloat through the bars of a city prison. **1889** FARMER 64 *Bloat* (Cant), a drowned body; also a drunkard.

Bloated, *ppl. a.* +*Bloated eels*, 'eels skinned and eviscerated. Connecticut' (B. '77).

Bloater. {1832–} +Applied to a mackerel. — **1857** *Harper's Mag.* Sept. 539/2 They are hauling in mackerel, genuine bloaters, as fast as they can. *Ib.* 540/1 The captain shouted, 'Here they are, boys!' and with the word landed a real bloater.

Bloating, *vbl. n.* {1753} Distention of the abdomen in cattle. — **1896** *Diseases of Cattle* (U.S. Dept. of Agric.) 30 When the bloating is not too great, gentle walking exercise will facilitate the removal of the gas. **1913** BARNES *Western Grazing Grounds* 286 There are but three diseases among western range cattle which can be considered general: Big jaw (actinomycosis), bloating (tympanites) and black-leg.

***Blob.** +A miller's thumb or similar small fish. — **1881** *Amer. Naturalist* Nov. 879 These [s. Tenn. fishes] were the common blob, *Potamocottus meridionalis*, and sucker, *Catostomus teres.* **1888** GOODE *Amer. Fishes* 302 *Uranidea* and allied genera, known in some localities by the

English name of 'Miller's Thumb,' also called 'Bull-heads,' 'Goblins,' 'Blobs,' and 'Muffle-jaws.'

* **Block,** *n.*

+**1.** A connected or compact mass of houses or other buildings, in later use esp. one mainly or wholly occupying the space bounded by four streets. Freq. *block of buildings* or *houses.*

1796 *Aurora* (Phila.) 13 Dec. (Th.), The whole block of buildings included between that slip, Front Street, and the Fly Market. **1801** CUTLER in *Life* II. 50 The buildings [in Washington] are brick, and erected in what are called large blocks, that is, from two to five or six houses joined together, and appear like one long building. **1833** J. E. ALEXANDER *Transatlantic Sk.* II. 121, I was tempted to stay in Louisville by an offer of an introduction to certain young ladies with blocks of houses, (a block is half a dozen or a dozen contiguous dwellings built on the same plan). **1833** *Niles' Reg.* XLIV. 406/1 The post office at Oswego, together with one whole block of stores, were burnt last night. **1844** Cist *Cincinnati Misc.* 78 The absolute want of room elsewhere . . . gave an impulse to warehouse building in the eastern and southern parts of the Ward, which is filling them up with many and extensive improvements, in blocks as well as single houses. **1857** HAMMOND *Northern Scenes* 115 The landlord of the premises was the owner of a block of twelve houses—six on Pearl Street, and six on Broadway, the lots meeting midway between the two streets. **1865** MRS. WHITNEY *Gayworthys* xli. 378 She entered by the brick alley that tunnelled the block half a dozen doors below in the side street. **1871** HOWELLS *Their Wedding Journey* 47 At last they were . . . seeking the nearest car by endless blocks of brownstone fronts. **1881** *Harper's Mag.* April 712/2 In the case of Milwaukee . . . solid blocks of houses flush with the sidewalk are very few. **1911** LINCOLN *Cap'n Warren* xi. 171 The block had evidently been, in its time, the homes of well-to-do people.

+**b.** One of the rectangular areas in which towns are commonly laid out. In early use occas. *block of lots.*

1815 DRAKE *Cincinnati* vi. 202 The principal wall or embankment, encloses an entire block of lots and some fractions. **1817** S. BROWN *Western Gaz.* 101 Each block of lots has the advantage of two 16 feet alleys. **1823** COOPER *Pioneers* viii, The village had been formally laid out into the streets and *blocks* that resembled a city. **1844** *Indiana Senate J.* 303 The committee are informed that the block in the town of Indianapolis, donated for the institution of a lunatic asylum, contains four acres. **1852** BRISTED *Upper Ten Th.* ii. 42 The desire to make one's house a little superior to the ordinary standard has caused many of the lots in the newer and more fashionable streets to be arranged, wherever the size of the 'blocks' will permit it, with fronts of twenty-six or twenty-seven feet. **1857** CHANDLESS *Visit Salt Lake* 151 The whole space occupied is about four square miles laid out in 'blocks' (squares) of ten acres. **1873** EGGLESTON *Myst. Metrop.* v. 49 He thought he would like to buy half of block 26. **1896** J. C. HARRIS *Sister Jane* 8 Colonel Cephas Bullard . . ., although he lived at the far end of the block, was our nearest neighbor. **1899** *Metropolitan Mag.* Feb. 139 Seven years ago these one hundred and fifty blocks were planted with shacks and, at best, a tumble-down cottage or two. **1901** *Munsey's Mag.* XXIV. 530/1 A map of New York . . . looks like a big chessboard. Most of it is divided off into rectangular 'blocks,' as they are called.

+**c.** Used as a measure of distance in a town.

1843 C. MATHEWS *Writings* 276 'I was standing in my shop-door—if the court please— . . . when about two blocks off I saw'—'Two blocks?' interrupted the district attorney. 'Yes, sir, two blocks,' retorted the crockery-dealer. **1848** *Knickerb.* XVIII. 190 The postman . . . sometimes holds up a letter half a block off. **1855** 'P. PAXTON' *Capt. Priest* 237 The traveller . . . would . . . be run over some three times in one block. *c***1867** 'MARK TWAIN' *Sk., Fine Old Man,* He walked five blocks in a rain-storm. **1886** *Century Mag.* April 868/2 He stopped half a block short of his own door. **1888** *Outing* May 119/1 The shouts from the now excited crowd . . . might have been heard blocks off. **1893** 'MARK TWAIN' *P. Wilson* i, The main street, one block back from the river, . . . was the sole business street. **1917** MATHEWSON *Sec. Base Sloan* xvi. 215 Congress House was far uptown and many blocks away.

+**d.** A continuous portion of land.

[**1829** J. MACTAGGART *Three Years* II. 283 In some of the new townships in the western part of [Upper Canada], . . . that seventh part of the land . . . was laid out in blocks, . . . containing from 2000 to 10,000 acres.] **1902** MCFAUL *Ike Glidden* vii. 45 Ansel explained that he owned the east half of the two-thousand-acre block, and the deacon owned the west half. **1925** BRYAN *Memoirs* 34 Our farm contained five hundred twenty acres in one block.

+**e.** *La.* A section of a sugar plantation.

1887 *Century Mag.* Nov. 115/1 A sugar plantation is divided by main ditches and roads into sections known in some parishes . . . as 'blocks.'

+**2.** A blockhouse.

1829 COOPER *Wish-Ton-Wish* vii. 108 He . . . will take but little [rest] . . . until his head be safely housed within some such building as yon block. **1840** — *Pathfinder* xxiv, He next examined the door of the block, to ascertain its security. **1845** SIMMS *Wigwam & Cabin* I. 59 When I thought of our wives and children in the block . . . I got wolfish. **1852** WATSON *Nights in Block-house* 27 D'ye see, arter Vansan and I left the block, we paddled up the stream.

3. a. In ship-building, one of the solid pieces of timber placed under the keel. {*c* 1850–}

1795 *Ann. 4th Congress* 2 Sess. 2575 The keel is completed and laid on the blocks. **1827** COOPER *Red Rover* viii, I know the whole history of the ship, from the day they laid the blocks for her keel to the minute when she let her anchor go where you now see her. **1849** LONGFELLOW *Building of Ship* 95 Thus . . . will we build this ship! Lay square the blocks upon the slip [etc.].

+**b.** The stand on which a slave stood when being sold by auction.

1853 *Chambers's Jrnl.* Oct. 39 Boy mounts the block; . . . the auctioneer kindly lends him a hand. **1857** *Lawrence* (Kansas) *Republican* 30 July 1 Well, the slaves were taken to New Orleans, were put upon the block and dispersed to the four winds. **1860–** [see AUCTION-BLOCK]. **1863** 'E. KIRKE' *Southern Friends* xxiv. 251 The negroes were to be put on the block at nine o'clock the next morning. **1866** BRYANT *Death of Slavery* 79 There shall the grim block remain At which the slave was sold.

fig. **1875** *Chicago Tribune* 22 July 2/5 The gold is not cried orally from 'the block' by our auction-treasurer.

c. A large upright piece of wood used for various domestic purposes.

1845 JUDD *Margaret* I. iii. 11 The kitchen or commons . . . also contained the table-board, block, and rag-cotton chairs.

d. A clog to impede an animal's movements. Also fig.

*c***1845** *Big Bear Ark.* etc. 60 The dog had a big block and chain to him. **1885** 'CRADDOCK' *Prophet* 115 The dragging block and chain of his jeopardized prospects.

||**4.** A section cut from the side of a tree. Cf. BLOCK *v.* 1 b.

1832 *Louisville Directory* 107 By cutting out the block containing the axe marks, and counting the circles, or annulations. *Ib.*, Sodowsky . . . cut out a block above and below the chops of the axe on the corner tree. *Ib.*, He produced his block in open court.

5. *Block and tackle,* a pulley and ropes used in hoisting. Also fig.

1838 *Knickerb.* XII. 373 The diver began to don his submarine habiliments, which were swung inward from the vessel's side . . . by means of a block-and-tackle. **1864** NORTON *Army Lett.* 221 General Birney seems to consider the Eighth as . . . block and tackle by which to hoist his favorites into place and power.

6. A quantity or number taken as a unit or group, or dealt with at one time; esp. a large number of shares of stock bought or sold in a lump.

For further illustration of *blocks of five* (sc. voters bribed to vote as desired), see Thornton *Suppl.* s.v.

1870 MEDBERY *Men Wall St.* 14 Three years before a block of a million dollars in United States funds had been purchased, and the transaction was still town talk. **1875** HOLLAND *Seven Oaks* xxiv. 331 The combination began by selling large blocks of the stock for future delivery. **1885** *Harper's Mag.* Nov. 841/1 A broker or operator . . . buying heavily, perhaps in 'blocks' composed of any number of shares—say 5000 or 10,000—bought in a lump. **1888** *Congress. Rec.* Jan. (1890) 450/2 Divide the floaters into blocks of five and put a trusted man with necessary funds in charge of these five. **1889** *Century Mag.* Feb. 624/1 The 'ten thousand floaters' of Indiana, who . . . were corralled and conducted to the polls in 'blocks of five.' **1901** MERWIN & WEBSTER *Calumet K* iii. 40 For a long time they were at me to take a big block of treasury stock. **1904** W. H. SMITH *Promoters* vii. 135 All he cares for is to make sure that the block of stuff he stands behind will sell.

+**7.** *Baseball.* (See quotation.)

1893 W. CAMP *College Sports* 296 A block is a batted or thrown ball that is stopped or handled by any person not engaged in the game.

Block, *v.*

1. *To block out,* to make or design in a rough or preliminary manner; also, to lay out, plan. {1837–; in earlier Sc. without the adv.}

1753 WASHINGTON *Diaries* I. 59 They . . . told 50 [canoes] . . . besides many others which were blocked-out, in Readiness to make. **1829** *Mass. Spy* 16 Dec. (Th.), There are portions [of the Message] which bear the marks of having been 'blocked out' by General Jackson. **1868** *Congress. Globe* 22 July 4344/2, I blocked out the present Territory, gave it the name of Wyoming, and attached it to the Territory of Dakota. **1873** 'MARK TWAIN' & WARNER *Gilded Age* lxi. 558 Into the law the subscriber is going. . . . Practice first in Hawkeye, . . . and wind up on the Supreme bench. . . . That's the way I block it out, sir. **1879** STOCKTON *Rudder Grange* xvi. 194, I've blocked out the whole of the rest of it [=bridal trip]. **1887** *Harper's Mag.* Dec. 125/1 She'll never be married. . . . No man ain't blocked out fit for Her. **1911** HARRISON *Queed* iv. 49, I wish you would block out a series of articles . . . designed to prepare the public mind for a thorough-going reform.

b. To cut out a section from the side of (a tree); also, to cut *out* a piece containing (axe marks). Cf. BLOCK *n.* 4.

1832 *Louisville Directory* 107 The practice of blocking out the chops on the corner and line trees of surveys, has been universally adopted. **1878** *Harper's Mag.* Jan. 210/2 A 'bearing' tree has been blocked to get at a 'blaze' made in the spring of '38.

c. To shape (material) *into* some form.

1859 HAWTHORNE *Marble Faun* xiii. (1883) 144 As if the marble had never been blocked into the guise of human heads.

+**2.** *To block one's game,* to thwart one's plans.

[**1844** KENDALL *Santa Fé Exped.* II. 260 Soon after [he] ordered his own men to leave the gambling cot of the leper, and by this means 'blocked the game.'] **1862** LOWELL *Biglow P.* II. iii. 107 It ain't your twenty millions thet'll ever block Jeff's game. **1869** *Congress. Globe* 19 March 166/2, I invoke Congress to 'block this game' [of appropriations]. **1884** *Boston Journal* 20 Dec. 2/2 Their little game was blocked.

+**3.** *To block off,* to head off, stop.

1893 POST *Harvard Stories* 86 The two opposing crowds . . . swept across the diamond, 'blocking off' the owners of the two dogs. **1899** QUINN *Penna. Stories* 190, I tried to fix up two or three things with Miss Fitzgerald and she blocked me off each time, very nicely, it is true, but still she blocked me off.

Blockade, *n.* {1693–}

1. The blocking of a harbor or the watching of a line of coast by enemy ships as a war measure; also, a beleaguerment.

1775 in Sparks *Corr. Amer. Rev.* I. 485 Were a blockade alone to be the measure adopted. **1803** *Ann. 7th Congress* 2 Sess. 220 The ocean was put in a state of blockade to us. **1814** *Ann. 13th Congress* II. 1479 It was their *paper* blockades, against which this Government contended. **1836** *Diplom. Corr. Texas* (1908) I. 118, I transmit to you a decree of Blockade of the Port of Matamoros. **1861** LINCOLN *Proclamation* 27 April, For the reasons assigned . . . , a blockade of the ports of the states of South Carolina, Georgia, Florida, Alabama, Louisiana, Mississippi, and Texas, was ordered to be established. *Ib.*, An efficient blockade of the ports of these states [=Va. and N.C.]. **1861** in Logan *Great Conspiracy* 136 You suppose we shall sit quietly down and submit to a blockade. **1862** KETTELL *Hist. Rebellion* I. 294 It had been long manifest that the blockade of the South could not be complete until the transit of supplies by this route [=Louisville and Nashville railroad] was cut off. **1892** M. A. JACKSON *Memoirs* 212 In those war times of blockade and scarcity, such things [=clothing] were doubly prized.

+**b.** *To run the blockade,* to enter or leave a blockaded port or area by eluding the blockading force.

1861 *Harper's Mag.* Sept. 547/1 The 'Sumter' . . . succeeded in running the blockade of the mouth of the Mississippi. **1862** *Ann. Cycl.* I. 72/2 Whether a citizen of the Confederate States . . . had a right to come into a prize court . . . , and establish that the vessel was not attempting to run the blockade. **1865** *Atlantic Mo.* XV. 430 A Rebel steamer . . . lying somewhere up the river, and awaiting her chance to run the blockade. **1883** *Century Mag.* Nov. 142/1 Colonel Thorburn . . . afterward became engaged in running the blockade, bringing supplies into the Confederate States.

c. Attrib. in sense: Held up by a blockade.

1865 *Chicago Tribune* 10 April 1 It may fairly be inferred . . . that the patriotic citizens making these donations . . . had the choice of . . . taking blockade cotton at government prices.

+**2.** *ellipt.* Blockade whisky.

1867 CRAWFORD *Mosby* 217 The guard got drunk on 'blockade.' *Ib.* 220 One fellow . . . seeing the excellent 'blockade' poured into the streets, thought it a wanton destruction. **1913** M. W. MORLEY *Carolina Mts.* 66 For corn . . . supplies as well that important beverage, variously known as . . . 'blockade,' 'brush whiskey,' and in the outer world, 'corn-whiskey.'

+**3.** A block or stoppage of transport or traffic, esp. on a railroad by snow or some accident.

1867–9 *Ill. Agric. Soc. Trans.* VII. 419 An effectual snow blockade around the city, and on nearly all our Western railroads. **1873** BEADLE *Undevel. West* 350 With the snow sheds since constructed, and other precautions, we may reasonably expect no more blockades. **1882** PECK *Sunshine* 194 Seventy-five traveling men were snowed in at Green Bay during a late blockade. **1910** *N.Y. Ev. Post* 13 Dec. 3 When a drawbar on the middle car of a Third Avenue elevated train broke . . . a long blockade began.

attrib. **1882** PECK *Sunshine* 197 As long as the memory of that blockade Sunday [at Green Bay, Wis.] remains green with the good people there. **1893** GUNTER *Miss Dividends* 271 The two . . . wade through the snow to . . . a palace car . . . crowded with the *élite* of the blockaded passengers, all in their blockade best. **1904** *N.Y. Times* 5 May 3 After it had become known that the system was paralyzed, 'blockade signs' were hung out at all the stations.

+**4.** A barrier on a river.

1871 *N.C. Game Laws* in *Fur, Fin, & Feather* (1872) 153 It shall not be lawful for any person to draw a seine . . . between the blockade near Hill's Point . . . and the falls at Wm. S. Battle's factory.

Blockade, *v.* {1680–}

1. *tr.* To subject to a naval or a military blockade.

1777 *R.I. Col. Rec.* VIII. 295 This State is . . . blockaded by a considerable naval and land force. **1803** *Ann. 7th Congress* 2 Sess. 181 You must have a war. . . . Seaports will be blockaded, and the Mississippi shut. **1861** in Logan *Great Conspiracy* 136 You are going to blockade our ports, you say. **1861** *Harper's Mag.* July 259/1 This Act [prohibiting export of cotton except through seaports] . . . is to continue in force so long as any ports of the Confederate States are blockaded by the United States.

+**2.** To block by ice or snow. (Cf. BLOCKADE *n.* 3.)

1816 *Niles' Reg.* X. 216/2 In consequence of the vast body of ice with which it [the harbor] is yet *blockaded,* they were unable to get in. **1872** *Vt. Bd. Agric. Rep.* I. 24 An exceedingly severe snow storm having completely blockaded many of the roads, many were prevented from attending the meetings. **1874** GLISAN *Jrnl. Army Life* 497 Many weary miners . . . would occasionally get blockaded by deep snows.

Blockader. [f. BLOCKADE *v.* and *n.*]

1. One that blockades; a blockading vessel. {1849}

1863 *Ann. Cycl.* II. 630/1 The steamer, from her excellent machinery and light draught, proved a valuable acquisition to the blockaders. **1864** *Continental Mo.* July 46–55 (heading), Life on a Blockader. **1886** COFFIN in *Outing* April 46/1, I've passed within twenty feet of a blockader off Wilmington.

+**2.** *S.* (*local*). An illicit distiller (cf. *blockade whisky*) or dealer in tobacco.

1883 ZEIGLER & GROSSCUP *Alleghanies* 141 In the wilderness, we would be taken for revenue officers and, as such, shot on sight by blockaders. **1886** *Boston Beacon* 2 Jan., 'The dealers in illicit tobacco, who flourished principally in North Carolina, were called *blockaders*,' and the illicit tobacco *blockade tobacco.* **1924** J. W. RAINE *Land of Saddle-bags* 132 There are always men in the neighborhood that might give information to the sheriff . . . to satisfy some grievance or grudge against the 'blockader.'

+**Blockade-run,** *a.* [Cf. next.] Brought in through a blockade. — **1865** *Atlantic Mo.* XV. 508/2, I should like to see the negroes whom I knew most thoroughly intrusted with blockade-run rifles, just by way of experiment.

+**Blockade-runner.** [BLOCKADE *n.* 1 b.] A vessel engaged in running a blockade; the captain or one of the crew of such a vessel.

1863 *Rep. Secy. of Navy* p. v, Not a single blockade-runner has succeeded in reaching the city [of Charleston] for months. **1864** PORTER in *Ann. Cycl.* IV. 566/2 A blockade-runner going in right ahead of him, the forts making the blockade-runner signals. **1865** *Atlantic Mo.* XV. 512 Blockade-runners had better apply immediately. **1877** (*title*), The Narrative of a Blockade-Runner. By J. Wilkinson, Captain in the Late Confederate States Navy. **1877** Raymond *8th Rep. Mines* 363 Our cruisers . . . were able to spy and pursue the blockade-runners, whose thick clouds of escaping bituminous smoke betrayed them. **1889** *Century Mag.* Feb. 601/1 She was built for a blockade-runner, I suppose you know.

+**Blockade-running,** *vbl. n.* [BLOCKADE *n.* 1 b.] The action of getting, or attempting to get, through a blockade.

1864 *Rep. Secy. of Navy* p. xvii, It is scarcely possible to wholly prevent this species of illicit traffic and blockade running. **1865** *Ann. Cycl.* IV. 562/2 An official statement of the results of blockade-running at Wilmington. **1867** CRAWFORD *Mosby* 229 The Secretary of War . . . had written . . . for an officer to go on the Northern Neck to break up the blockade-running carried on in that quarter. **1881–5** MCCLELLAN *Own Story* 203 Which would give us the . . . advantage of preventing blockade-running at those points. **1886** *Outing* April 46/2, I've rambled off into the blockade runnin' business.

+**Blockade-running,** *ppl. a.* [BLOCKADE *n.* 1 b.] Engaged in running a blockade. — **1864** *Nautical Almanac* 505/1 The Anglo-Confederate blockade-running steamer Chatham is captured by the United States gunboat Huron.

+**Blockade tobacco** (*S., local*): see BLOCKADER 2.

+**Blockade whisky.** [BLOCKADE *n.* 1, 2.] Illicit whisky. Also attrib. with *still.* — **1883** ZEIGLER & GROSSCUP *Alleghanies* 52 Like blockade whisky, a ball outer thet black bore allus goes to the spot. *Ib.* 325 You will follow the Chatooga river, . . . along a picturesque course, where the unbroken solitude breeds blockade whisky stills. **1896** *Congress. Rec.* 31 March 3408/2, I ask . . . if it is not infinitely better that we should have a little blockade whisky occasionally.

Blockading, *vbl. n.* [BLOCKADE *v.* and *n.* 2.] **a.** The action or fact of maintaining a blockade. Also attrib. +**b.** The production of illicit liquor.

a. 1810 *Steele Papers* II. 645 Not a word is said relative to the Blockading system of April 1806. **1861** *Rep. Secy. of Navy 1862* (1863) 164 The vessels . . . will be released and employed on blockading duty as soon as Otter and Tybee islands are held by the army. **1886** *Harper's Mag.* June 3/1 A large fleet of cruising ships for blockading purposes was extemporized during our civil war.

b. 1883 ZEIGLER & GROSSCUP *Alleghanies* 141 Blockading, or 'moonshining' as it is sometimes called, . . . is not as prevalent in these mountains as is generally supposed. *Ib.* 357 While Redmond, the famous moonshiner, lived in the neighborhood, and a little blockading was still going on in the Balsams. **1887** *Courier-Journal* 24 Jan. 1/7 Suspicion rests against certain parties, . . . engaged in 'blockading,' as the guilty ones.

Blockading, *ppl. a.* [BLOCKADE *v.*] Maintaining a blockade. {1708–}

1812 *Norfolk Democr. Herald* in *Raleigh* (N.C.) *Minerva* 31 July, We may momently expect a blockading squadron on our coast. **1813** CUTLER in *Life* II. 319 A vessel taken by the Chesapeake Blockading Fleet. **1838**

Diplom. Corr. Texas (1911) III. 1217 The absence of the Blockading squadron from the Texian coast. **1846** *Commercial Rev.* I. 501 Subjecting the offending party to rightful capture by any of the forces of the blockading power on . . . the high seas. **1861** *Chicago Tribune* 19 July 1/2 Position of the blockading vessels. *Ib.*, The Atlantic blockading squadron . . . consists of twenty-two vessels. **1862** *Ann. Cycl.* II. 637/1 Flag-Officer, Western Gulf Blockading Squadron. **1865** *Ib.* V. 601 There were in the several blockading squadrons in January last, . . . four hundred and seventy-one vessels.

+**Block coal.** [BLOCK *n.*] A variety of coal readily mined in large blocks and specially suitable for iron-smelting. Also attrib.

1871 *Amer. Naturalist* V. 177 On this excursion [to Terre Haute] a visit will be made to the celebrated Block-coal field (iron smelting coal) and Blast furnaces, of Clay County. *Ib.* 554 Block coal has a laminated structure and is composed of alternate thin layers of vitreous, dull black coal, and fibrous, mineral charcoal. **1873** *Amer. Cycl.* IV. 726/2 The splint or block coal of N.W. Pennsylvania, Ohio, and Indiana. **1874** R. H. COLLINS *Kentucky* I. 210 The Peach Orchard coal, the cannel coal, and the block coal (now best known at Ashland and used in the raw state for smelting iron ore), are among the finest in the world, and could be brought out in immense quantities—if [etc.].

+**Block committee.** (See quotation and BLOCK *n.* 1.) — **1839** T. BROTHERS *United States* 134 The politicians, or office-hunters, form their 'block committees,' the duty of each of which committees is to organise and drill all the whigs, or democrats, as the case may be, that live in a certain number of houses adjoining each other, which they are pleased to call 'blocks.'

+**Block fort.** *Obs.* A blockhouse. — **1798** I. ALLEN *Hist. Vermont* 41 He, with a number of men, repaired to New Haven falls, and built a block fort.

* **Blockhouse.**

* **1.** A building, usually constructed of logs with loopholes or embrasures, serving as a place of safety and defence against an attacking enemy. Now chiefly *Hist.*

*c*1622 PORY *Plymouth & New Eng.* (1918) 42 The quality of the people . . . and their industrie . . . appeareth by their building . . . a blockhouse . . . erected in the highest place of the towne. [**1670** *N.Y. State Col. Hist.* XII. 474 It was thought the market place . . . was the most convenient place in New-Castle to erect block-houses for defensive purposes.] **1675** ANDROS in Easton *Indian War* 98 All Towns and Villages [are] . . . to fortify and make compleat . . . a block or palizadoed House, or Place for a Retreat to Women and Children, etc. and keeping good Watch and Ward. **1694** *Mass. H. S. Coll.* 4 Ser. I. 105 There are five block-houses, 2 north, by two of the forementioned gates, and 3 south. **1708** *Boston News-Letter* 4 Oct. 4/2, 3 Cannoa's of Indians put off from 2 small adjacent Islands in open view within large Musket-shot of our Block-house. **1721** J. BAXTER in *New Eng. Hist. Reg.* (1867) XXI. 57 All Hands went briskly to work, to finish the log-work in the Lower Block-house. **1734** *Mass. Ho. Repr. Journals* 8 Could the Line of Block-Houses so often proposed, be effected, it would be a fine Cover to a great number of our Infant Plantations. **1756** *Lett. to Washington* I. 303 The Council are of opinion a Block-house may be found necessary to secure the passage of the River. . . . The Council are of opinion that it will be found necessary to maintain a Blockhouse at Pearsalls. **1765** ROGERS *Acc. N. America* 176 At the east-end of this lake stands a royal blockhouse, which is garrisoned to keep up a communication with the lakes. **1785** E. DENNY *Journal* 59 All hands set to work chopping, clearing &c., and preparing timber for block-houses and pickets. **1797** *Ann. 4th Congress* 2 Sess. 2325 A blockhouse was as good a fortification against the Indians as any other. **1812** *Letter* in *Raleigh* (N.C.) *Minerva* 31 July, A regiment goes ahead by turns to open the road and erect a block house at every twenty miles. **1823** JAMES *Exped.* I. 75 The women and children fled in consternation to the block-houses. **1847** PARKMAN in *Knickerb.* XXX. 284 The little fort is built of bricks dried in the sun, and externally is of an oblong form, with bastions of clay in the form of ordinary block-houses. **1861** MCCLELLAN in *Own Story* 240 The railway . . . to be at once repaired and put in running order, all the bridges to be protected by block-houses. **1871** *Rep. Indian Affairs* (1872) 279 A block-house should be built at the Agency. **1902** WHITE *Conjuror's House* iv. 39 The fort itself, a medley of heavy-timbered stockades and square block-houses.

attrib. **1812** MARSHALL *Kentucky* 160 Bryant's Station . . . had a bastion at either end, composed of strong logs, built in the block house form, with necessary loop holes. **1852** WATSON *Nights in Block-house* 361 Ezra, give these raw men some notion of block-house sieges, can't you? **1904** WHITE *Silent Places* i. 4 There scarcely needed . . . the block-house stockade . . . to inform the initiated that this . . . was a post of the Honourable the Hudson's Bay Company.

+**2.** A house built of squared logs. (See also quot. 1826.)

1821 Z. HAWLEY *Jrnl. of Tour* (1822) 52 A block-house [in Ohio] differs from a log one in this particular: in the former the logs are hewn square, so that they are smooth within and without, and the latter are hewn only within, having the bark on the outside. **1826** J. BRADFORD *Ky. Notes* 74 *Blockhouse*, a strong log house the second story of which overjuts or protrudes beyond the first 18 inches or more all round. **1857** *Mich. Agric. Soc. Trans.* VIII. 398 The house that Mr. Campau built is yet standing; it is what is called a block-house, *i.e.*, a house built of logs that have been hewed square before being laid up.

Blocking. [BLOCK *n.* 3 a.] The set of blocks used in shipbuilding. — **1706** SEWALL *Diary* II. 156 A great ship, . . . building at Salem, runs off her blocking in the night. **1883** *Harper's Mag.* May 937/2 The blocking is knocked away.

+**Blocking-man.** (See quotation.) — **1835** in Hoffman *Winter in West* II. 117 The hogs are . . . then passed to the 'blocking-men,' who place them on the several blocks . . . when they are received by the 'cutters.'

Block-maker. [BLOCK *n.* 5.] A maker of blocks or pulleys. {*a*1687–}

1682 *Suffolk Deeds* XII. 289 Jonathan Adams of Boston in the County of Suffolke in New England Blockmaker. **1683** *Boston Rec.* 59 Albert Lawsen . . . lodgeth at Wm. Whatine, Block maker. **1714** *Boston News-Letter* 13–20 Sept. 2/2 The Hull of the Ship Hanover . . . with Smiths work, Blockmakers, Joyners, Carvers work, and a Long Boat suitable for the Ship. **1742** *Md. Hist. Mag.* XX. 176 Send me . . . the Blockmakers Account that thereby I may know how to sell some. **1794** *Mass. H. S. Coll.* III. 273 Tradesmen, such as ropemakers, coopers, carpenters, blockmakers, riggers . . . &c. should not occupy wooden shops or sheds within the vicinity of dwelling houses. **1817** *Ann. 14th Congress* 2 Sess. 780 After having been launched . . . the riggers fit and put over head the rigging; and the blockmakers, sailmakers, and blacksmiths, furnish their several parts. **1850** HAWTHORNE *Scarlet Letter* Introd., All three give glimpses of the shops of grocers, block-makers, slop-sellers, and ship-chandlers. **1884** *Harper's Mag.* Jan. 220/2 The agent owning, say, an eighth of [an Atlantic packet], . . . the block-maker and sail-maker each a sixteenth, perhaps.

Block-ship. [f. *block* v.] A ship intended to block the entrance to a port. {1801} — **1816** *Ann. 14th Congress* 1 Sess. 1887 The President is further authorized to cause to be completed . . . the block ship now on the stocks, near New Orleans. **1876** INGRAM *Centennial Exp.* 138 Fulton's system included . . . 'blockship' torpedoes, to be carried on spars projecting from a peculiar kind of vessel, and exploded by contact with the enemy.

Block stool. [BLOCK *n.* 3.] A stool made from a block of wood. — **1872** FLAGG *Good Investment* xxiv. 232/1 On a block stool by the fire-place, and back of Hagan and Robert, . . . Betsey sat apart smoking her pipe.

‖**Block truck.** A solid wooden wheel. — **1860** *Harper's Mag.* Jan. 282/2 In Kentucky . . . there is a region so rocky and rough that the people do most of their hauling on . . . a frame mounted on wide block trucks sawed from a log.

* **Blood.**

1. A trail of blood.

1746 *N.H. Hist. Soc. Coll.* IV. 208 On the 12th day, early in the morning, went up and took the blood of [the] Indian and followed along by the drag and blood of the Indian about a mile.

* **2.** A fast or showy young man, esp. one inclined to be disorderly.

1797 *Farmer's W. Museum* 21 Aug., A kind of cudgel worn, or rather borne, by the bloods of a certain college in New England. **1804** *Monthly Anthology* (Boston) I. 154 On the evening of the Exhibition I resorted to a tavern, and with some rakes from Boston and a few College *bloods*, I got very drunk. **1834** CARRUTHERS *Kentuckian* I. 17 The 'bloods' looked fierce, and exchanged pugnacious looks, but all chance of a collision was prevented by the return of the hostess. **1851** *Harper's Mag.* Jan. 187/2 It is the boast of the bloods of the town of Rackinsack, in Arkansas, that they are born with skins like alligators. **1876** BOURKE *Journal* 28 July–8 Sept., The view entertained generally is that a young 'blood' emphasizes his claims by imitating the snobbery of dress and drawl of the English swell.

+**b.** *slang.* (See quotation.)

1851 HALL *College Words* 178 At Washington College, Penn., students of a religious character are called *lap-ears* or *donkeys*. The opposite class are known by the common name of *bloods*.

+**3.** *slang.* (See quotation.)

1851 HALL *College Words* 20 *Blood*. At some of the Western colleges, this word signifies excellent; as a *blood* recitation. A student who recites well is said to *make a blood*.

4. A thoroughbred horse or other blooded animal. {*c*1865–}

1860 CLAIBORNE *Life & Corr. Quitman* 171 Great power is required to carry these ponderous masses, and great speed; and only bloods, and half-bloods well crossed, are accepted. **1873** BEADLE *Undevel. West* xxi. 405 Hated the loss of his sheep wuss'n anything else—fine bloods—couldn't get others like 'em.

+**5.** A Blood Indian. (Cf. 8 b.)

1863 *Amer. Philos. Soc. Trans.* n.s. XII. 249 The Blackfeet inhabit a portion of country farther north than the Bloods. **1892** *Amer. Anthropologist* April 153 Originally there was but one tribe of these people, the Blackfeet; . . . the Bloods and Piegans are offshoots of this main tribe. *Ib.* 159 This old Blood used to say that he had often heard his father speak of the trouble. **1910** HODGE *Handbook* II. 570 An important Algonquian confederacy . . . consisting of . . . the Siksika proper or Blackfeet, the Kainah or Bloods, and the Piegan, the whole body being popularly known as Blackfeet.

+6. *Blood and thunder*, used attrib. to designate low-class fiction or drama characterized by bloodshed and violence.

'The term [is] generally applied to works dealing with the exploits of desperadoes, cut-throats, and other criminals' (F.).

1857 *Quinland* II. 76 Mrs. Bill, left to herself, resumed reading a blood and thunder romance. **1861** [NEWELL] *Orpheus C. Kerr* I. 38 There seems to be enough danger laying around loose on Arlington Heights to make a very good blood-and-thunder fiction in numerous pages. **1870** 'FERN' *Ginger-Snaps* 206 May they remonstrate if . . . a person . . . reads aloud to a companion some blood-and-thunder novel? **1873** *Newton* (Kansas) *Kansan* 15 May 1/5 Murat Halsted . . . wrote blood-and-thunder stories. **1880** *Harper's Mag.* July 193/1 The modern kind would flee from a policeman's club, and would not make a hero for a juvenile 'blood-and-thunder' weekly. **1900** *Congress. Rec.* 21 March 3144/2 This bill . . . fosters the blood-and-thunder stories which inflame the minds and allure the hearts of the youth of the land.

b. Applied to persons whose action or conduct is marked by violence or noisy menace.

1857 *Quinland* II. 130 There comes Jupiter Bellows, the blood-and-thunder actor of the Great Republican Union Theatre. **1870** *Nation* 13 Jan. 17/2 They put the most ferocious blood-and-thunder Unionist in the whole South in the Governor's chair. **1917** H. T. COMSTOCK *The Man* 96 Of course this would never do. White, or one of the blood-and-thunder raiders, might appear.

+7. *Blood-and-wounds*, a species of bull-frog. *S.*

1872 FLAGG *Good Investment* xx. 901/1 [On the Great Pedee] monstrous frogs, named 'blood-an-'ounds,' from the sounds they utter, called in loud, deep bass for 'blood and wounds.' **1909** *Cent. Suppl.* 145/2 *Bloodnoun*, a local name of the bullfrog, *Rana catesbiana.* (Southern U.S.)

8. Attrib. **a.** Of horses: =BLOODED *a.* 1. (Cf. BLOOD HORSE.) {1800–}

1792 *Steele Papers* II. 763 The noted running horse Statesburg—a fine blood bay about five feet high, 10 years old. **1817** FORDHAM *Narr. Travels* 97 Some of the Miamies . . . ride blood ponies. **1825** *Missouri Intell.* 7 May 3/4 We appraised one blood bay mare. **1851** *Knickerb.* XXXVIII. 179 [An excursion] to Mount Fordham, in Westchester, on the recent occasion of the Annual Sale of Blood-Stock. **1868** WOODRUFF *Trotting Horse* xxix. 244 Trustee's dam was one of the most famous blood-mares. **1898** PAGE *Red Rock* 85 This horse . . . [is a] blood bay, with three white feet.

+**b.** Denoting a tribe of the Blackfeet Indians. (Cf. 5.)

1791 *Mass. H. S. Coll.* 1 Ser. III. 24 The tribes of Indians which he passed through [between Montreal and the Lake of the Woods], were called . . . Blood Indians, the Blackfeet tribe, . . . and several others. **1832** CATLIN *Indians* I. 52 The Blackfeet proper are divided into four bands or families, as follow:—. . . the 'Blood' band, of 450 lodges; and the 'Small Robes.' **1846** [STEWART] *Altowan* I. 173 The blood Indians are to have a thousand lodges on the Horse Plains. **1863** *Amer. Philos. Soc. Trans.* n.s. XII. 249 The Blood Indians range through the district along Maria, Teton, and Belly Rivers. **1892** *Amer. Anthropologist* April 156 The Blackfoot name for the Blood tribe is Kainah. The term Blood was probably given them by the Hudson Bay people on account of their custom of painting their faces with a red streak extending from ear to ear.

+**c.** *Blood atoner*, a Mormon who holds that certain sins can be atoned for only by shedding of the sinner's blood.

1900 *Congress Rec.* 24 Jan. 1131/1 The 'Blood Atoners' silenced in death the voice of apostacy. *Ib.*, Mr. Eldredge was a Danite. Mr. Eldredge was a Blood Atoner.

+**Blood beet.** The ordinary red beet.

1829 *Free Press* (Tarboro, N.C.) 20 Feb., Blood Beets. **1831** PECK *Guide* 141 It is instantly perceived that the onion is more mild [in Illinois than in the more northern states], and the blood beet less deeply colored. **1837** COLMAN *Mass. Agric. Rep.* (1838) 39 Other milk men speak of trials with the common blood-beet for the feed of milch cows with great advantage. **1854** *Penna. Agric. Rep.* 88 For the best twelve half-long blood Beets. **1868** *Mich. Agric. Rep.* VII. 349 John Ford, Detroit, [exhibited] 12 blood beets.

***Blood bulk.** *Obs.* {1563–75} The softer part of the human body; the lower part of the trunk. — **1637** *Md. Archives* IV. 10 John Bryant by the fall of a tree had his bloud bulke broken.

Blooded, *a.*

+**1.** Of horses (or other animals): Of good blood; of a pure or superior breed or stock.

1778 *Maryland Journal* 20 Jan., Advt. (Th.), Several blooded mares and fillies will also be sold. **1784** *Ib.* 2 Nov., Advt. (Th.), A natural trotter but not free spirited, though part blooded. **1796** B. HAWKINS *Letters* 42 Mr. Weatherford showed me this morning some fine horses raised by him, on his plantation; they were blooded nearly full. **1816** *Niles' Reg.* X. 8/2 The wool of native sheep is estimated at 50 cents per lb.; of half-blooded, at 62½; of three-fourths blooded at 75. **1832** KENNEDY *Swallow Barn* II. xvi. 208 My blooded colts . . . are of the finest breed in Virginia. **1836** *S. Lit. Messenger* II. 161, I will get one of the blooded plough-horses, and he will make out as well as any. **1849** AUDUBON *Western Journal* (1906) 100 A second man was in grand Spanish costume, on a small but blooded grey horse. **1858** [see BLOOD-HORSE]. **1872** FLAGG *Good Investment* xxii. 99/1 One of those sales of 'blooded stock' which are often held at county seats in the blue-grass region of Kentucky. **1879** B. F. TAYLOR *Summer-Savory* x. 92 Blooded dogs—lean, liver-colored, and as full of points as a hedge-hog—lie gaping about the floor. **1898** PAGE *Red Rock* 43 Jacquelin, on a blooded colt, was trying to keep . . . in line with him.

+**2.** Applied to persons. (Cf. BLOOD *n.* 2.)

1804 *Massachusetts Spy* 11 Jan. (Th.), When one of our blooded young fellows separates from the crowd, he only, &c. **1899** CHESNUTT *Wife of His Youth* 292 'Pears ter me Ben gettin' mighty blooded, . . . drivin' a hoss an' buggy.

+**Bloodee.** *Obs.* (See quotations.) — **1797** *Farmer's W. Museum* (Walpole, N.H.) 21 Aug. (Hall), Seniors about to take degrees Not by their wits, but by *bloodees*. *Ib.* (footnote), A kind of cudgel . . . borne . . . by the bloods of a certain college in New England, 2 feet 5 inches in length, . . . with a huge piece of lead at one end.

+**Bloodgood.** [See quot. 1847.] A variety of pear. — **1847** IVES *New Eng. Fruit* 58 *Bloodgood*. This pear was first brought into notice by the late James Bloodgood, of Flushing, Long Island. **1852** *Horticulturist* VII. 122 Bloodgood [is] a capital pear, of the first quality. **1867–8** *Ill. Agric. Soc. Trans.* VII. 523, I got four dollars per box for Bloodgoods last year.

Blood horse. [BLOOD *n.* 8.] A blooded horse. {1800–} — **1833** *Niles' Reg.* XLIV. 357/1 John Randolph, at the time of his death, was in possession of . . . 180 horses, of which 120 were blood horses. **1841** FOOTE *Texas & Texans* II. 383 They [wild horses] . . . are . . . inferior to the American blood-horse in volume of muscle. **1858** HOLMES *Autocrat* ii. 40 Let me beg you . . . not to speak of a 'thorough-bred' as a 'blooded' horse. . . . I consent to your saying 'blood horse,' if you like. **1860** — *Professor* iii. 65 Admiral Sir Isaac Coffin sent out two fine blood-horses . . . to Massachusetts. **1868** WOODRUFF *Trotting Horse* v. 72 Those strains which are related more or less closely to the blood-horse may be trained at an earlier period.

* **Bloodhound.** A dog of a large keen-scented breed used in tracking men or beasts.

1619 *Va. House of Burgesses* 13 That no man do sell or give . . . to the Indians, . . . any English dog of quality, as a Mastive, Greyhound, Blood hounde, lande or water Spaniel. **1812** *Niles' Reg.* II. 119/2 Four blood hounds, being unconfined, lately attacked and dreadfully mangled a lad. **1840** *Deb. Congress* 28 Feb. 226/1 Mr. W[ebster] also presented a remonstrance against the use of bloodhounds in the Florida war. **1840** *Niles' Nat. Reg.* 28 Nov. 201 Three white men . . . had been scented out by the bloodhounds, and were brought in—the first proof of the utility of the dogs. **1853** SIMMS *Sword & Distaff* 141, I would give the last hundred guineas for a couple of good Scotch blood-hounds. **1865** *Atlantic Mo.* XV. 6242 A man . . . having come . . . out of slavery to our lines, with rifle-bullets whizzing round him, and bloodhounds on the trail behind. **1880** *Harper's Mag.* June 23/1 There was a superannuated blood-hound . . that they kept tied up all day under a delusion that he was fierce. **1904** STRATTON-PORTER *Freckles* 278 Then McLean sent for a pack of bloodhounds and put them on the trail of Black Jack.

Blood orange. A variety of sweet orange having a deep-red pulp. — **1877** *Harper's Mag.* Jan. 287/2, I'll put some blood oranges there. . . . The sun sucks its sweetness into these oranges.

* **Bloodroot.**

+**1.** The red puccoon, *Sanguinaria canadensis;* also, its rootstock.

1722 DUDLEY in *Phil. Trans.* XXXII. 295 Remedies for the Sting of a Rattlesnake; among others, is a Root they call Blood-root. **1778** CARVER *Travels* 515 Blood Root, a sort of plantain that springs out of the ground in six or seven long rough leaves, the veins of which are red. **1789** MORSE *Amer. Geog.* 53 Besides these are several other roots and plants of a medicinal kind, such as . . . horse-radish and blood-root. **1824** J. DODDRIDGE *Notes* 148 Indian physick . . . was frequently used for a vomit and sometimes the pocoon or blood root. **1834** *Indian Captivity of O. M. Spencer* (1917) 36 In April, the ground was covered with May apple, bloodroot, ginseng, violets, and a great variety of herbs and flowers. **1837** BIRD *Nick of Woods* I. 25 Dyed as red as blood-root could make them. **1855** *Harvard Mag.* I. 232 The Bloodroot . . . perhaps may be considered our earliest spring flower. **1865** PARKMAN *Pioneers of France* 307 The white stars of the bloodroot gleamed among dank, fallen leaves. **1880** *Harper's Mag.* June 72 Who does not know the bloodroot—that shy recluse hiding away among the mountain nooks? **1884** *Rep. Comm. Agric.* 133 Blood-root [is] a low perennial herb, with a thick fleshy prostrate root-stock, filled with a reddish orange-colored juice. **1898** TORREY in *Atlantic Mo.* April 460/2 Day by day the sun's heat did its work, melting the snow of the shadbushes and the bloodroot.

attrib. **1868** BEECHER *Norwood* 15 Down on the south side . . . were blood-root blossoms, white as snow.

+**2.** A preparation of this root, used in medicine as a stimulant, expectorant, and emetic.

1832 WILLIAMSON *Maine* I. 120 The *Blood-root* is an acrid narcotic; and a large dose of it occasions nausea, heart-burn, and faintness. **1851** Cist *Cincinnati* 211 Merrell . . . prepares concentrated extracts of vegetable medical articles, such as . . . sanguinarin or blood-root, macrotin or black cohosh. **1871** DE VERE 61 Bloodroot . . . continues to be a favorite remedy with all who deal in simples.

Bloodshot. ?*Obs.* An effusion of blood in the eye. {1607–71} — **1801** Cist *Cincinnati* (1841) 187 They [head-lice] will not occasion more pain than an eye-stone, but will so gorge themselves with the film, or bloodshots, that, in the morning, they will be discharged dead from the eye.

*Bloodstone. +Hematite, red iron ore. — **1709** LAWSON *Carolina* 31 Here is likewise the true Blood-Stone, and considerable Quantities of Fullers-Earth. **1800** D. R. D'ERES *Memoirs* 17 [There] are discovered large rocks of a reddish cast, which our Indians called blood-stone. **1822** *Jrnl. Science* IV. 47 The hæmatite of Lake George may very possibly answer for blood stones, so much used in polishing gilded buttons, etc.

+Blood-tubs. *Obs.* A gang of roughs formerly active in Baltimore. — **1861** F. Moore *Rebellion Rec.* I. III. 73/1 'Blood-tubs' and 'Plug-Uglies,' and others galore, Are sick for a thrashing in sweet Baltimore. **1866** 'F. KIRKLAND' *Bk. Anecdotes* 529 Thus equipped, they were enabled to go out in search of their companions, without danger of attack from the Plug Uglies and Blood Tubs. **a1877** *New York Paper* (B.), The disguise of Plug-uglies and Blood-tubs in the garments of reform. [**1888** M. LANE in *America* 20 Sept. 15 Blood-tubs . . . got the name by dipping the head of an obnoxious German in a tub of blood and then chasing him along the streets. At one time these gangs of roughs, like the Ashlanders and Plug Uglies, practically controlled the ward politics of Baltimore.]

+Blood turnip. A globular variety of blood beet. — **1857-8** *Ill. Agric. Soc. Trans.* III. 503 The early blood turnip is a standard sort [of beet], turnip shaped, blood red, very tender and good for early use and late keeping.

***Bloodwort.**

+1. The bloodroot or red puccoon.

1705 BEVERLEY *Virginia* IV. 56 Others degenerate, and will not continue above a year or two at the most; such are July-Flowers, . . . Clary, and Bloodwort. **1778** CARVER *Travels* 515 Herbs . . . [include] Wild Dock, Rock Liverwort, Noble Liverwort, Bloodwort. **1814** PURSH *Flora Amer.* II. 366 *Sanguinaria stenopetala* . . . is known by the name of Blood-wort. **1836** EDWARD *Hist. Texas* ii. 42 Examples of [herbs include] . . . the bloodwort, the plantain.

2. *pl.* or *attrib.* (See quotations.)

1857 GRAY *Botany* 457 *Hæmodoraceæ* (Bloodwort Family) . . . [includes] . . . Red-root, . . . Lophiola, . . . Colic-root. **1861** WOOD *Botany* 696 Bloodworts . . . [include] Red-root, . . . Crest-flower, . . . Star-grass. **1901** MOHR *Plant Life Ala.* 446 Bloodwort Family . . . [includes] Red Root. . . . Flowers yellowish, rhizoma bloody red.

+3. The rattlesnake weed, *Hieracium venosum.*

1833 EATON *Botany* (ed. 6) 174 Vein-leaf hawkweed, bloodwort. . . . *S.* **1839** in *Mich. Agric. Soc. Trans.* VII. 409 *Hieracium venosum*, Bloodwort. **1889** *Cent.* 594 Bloodwort, the leaves of which are veined with red.

***Bloody,** *a.*

***1.** *Bloody flux*, dysentery. *Obs.*

1624 *Va. House of Burgesses* 34 With them was brought a most pestilent disease (called the Bloody flux) which infected all most all the whole Collonye. **1690** SEWALL *Diary* I. 337 A Souldier from Canada died of the bloody flux. **1715** *Boston News-Letter* 18 July 2/2 The Camp up the Country is said to be very sickly with the Bloody Flux, &c. **1756** *Lett. to Washington* I. 326 The Bloody Flux spreads amongst our Men. Ten of them are now ill with it. **1775** FITHIAN *Journal* II. 32 The bloody-flux is already very bad in Maryland. **1797** R. THOMAS in *Ga. H. S. Coll.* IX. 457 Yesterday I received an express from T. B. informing me of his laying very ill with the Bloody Flux. **1847** DE SMET *Oregon Missions* 82 We arrived in the Oregon Territory during the prevalence of a disease (bloody flux).

+2. Stained with blood as the result of fighting. Attributed esp. to Indian speech with reference to paths or ground, spec. in *the Bloody Ground*=Kentucky. (See also DARK *a.*)

1751 C. GIST *Journals* 51 Their Father . . . said the Road [in Ohio] was clear, but he understood it was made foul and bloody, and by them. **1777** *Virginia State P.* I. 283 The Dragging Canoe told them it was the bloody Ground, and would be dark, and difficult to settle it. *Ib.* 286 [The Indians] also observing it was a bloody Country, and if he went to it they would not hold him by the hand any longer. **1784** J. FILSON *Kentucke* 10 This region was formerly claimed by various tribes of Indians. . . . Hence this fertile spot became an object of contention, a theatre of war, from which it was properly denominated the Bloody-Grounds. **1802** J. DRAYTON *S. Carolina* 14 The path over this mountain, has been crooked and straight, bloody and clean; (according to the Indian talks). **1836** IRVING *Astoria* I. xviii. 301 Edward Robinson . . . had been one of the first settlers of Kentucky, and engaged in many of the conflicts of the Indians on 'The Bloody Ground.' **1840** *Knickerb.* XVI. 161 He . . . had signalized himself in the hard conflicts with the Indians, which gained Kentucky the appellation of 'the Bloody Ground.' **1855** *Herald of Freedom* 18 Aug. 2/4 The bloody land [=Kansas. Cf. BLEEDING].

***3.** Involving, connected or associated with bloodshed: **a.** Of harsh laws; spec. *the bloody bill* (see quots. 1833).

1781 PETERS *Hist. Conn.* 69 Of such sort were the laws made by the people of Newhaven. . . . They . . . were very properly termed *Blue Laws,* i.e. *bloody Laws;* for they were all sanctified with . . . whippings, cutting off the ears, burning the tongue, and death. **1833** *Niles' Reg.* XLIV. 36/1 The law 'further to provide for the collection of duties on imports,' is called 'the bloody bill,' by all the nullifiers, and some yet talk about letting blood, because of its passage! *Ib.* 384/1 May those who voted for the bloody bill to coerce South Carolina, a free and sovereign state, into shameful submission, never go down to their graves in peace. **1855** *S. Lit. Messenger* XXI. 2 At the time in question no Southern State was as much noted for subserviency to the Bloody Code as Mississippi.

+b. *The bloody chasm*, the estrangement between North and South caused by the Civil War.

Fully illustrated by Thornton *Suppl.*, 1876-88.

1876 *Congress. Rec.* 14 June 3791/1 This measure is one of conciliation. It reunites; it fills up the 'bloody chasm.' **1888** *Ib.* Dec. 161/1, I hope I will be excused to-day from again shaking hands across the 'bloody chasm.'

+c. *The bloody shirt*, the symbol of continued hostility, or of the desire to provoke it, between opposing parties, spec. between the North and South after the Civil War.

With reference to the actual exhibition of the blood-stained shirt of one who has been killed, in order to arouse or keep alive the desire for revenge. (*a*1586-) The Amer. use is fully illustrated by Thornton *Suppl.*, 1876-90.

1875 J. S. Reynolds *Reconstruction S.C.* (1905) 304 A diligent attempt is now being made to hide with the 'bloody shirt' the appalling wrongs committed by the Republican party. **1876** *Congress. Rec.* 17 April 2523/2 The 'bloody shirt' is freely used at one end of the Capitol, and here, at this end, is the bugaboo of State rights. **1879** TOURGEE *Fool's Errand* xxxviii. 285 He who chanced to refer to so old and exploded a joke was greeted with the laughter-provoking cry of the 'bloody shirt.' **1880** *Harper's Mag.* Sept. 538/1 You'll see no waving of 'the bloody shirt' among that class. **1882** HOWELLS *Modern Instance* xxxi, He had cared nothing about the canvass from the beginning, having an equal contempt for the bloody shirt of the Republicans and the reform pretensions of the Democrats. **1887** *Nation* Dec. 514/1 The speech . . . was devoted to the waving of the bloody shirt. **1890** *Congress. Rec.* June 5598-9 If you complain about stuffing ballot-boxes, that is 'waving the bloody shirt.' **1904** *Indianapolis News* 23 June 6 To those that remember campaigns a few years ago, this is very much like the 'bloody shirt,' which did duty for so many years.

attrib. **1877** J. M. BEARD *K.K.K. Sketches* 156 These men . . . lay their knives at the throats of a sufficient number of innocents to afford a text for bloody-shirt invectives. **1887** *Courier-Journal* 16 Feb. 1/2 Senator Hoar's bloody-shirt investigation about imagined outrages in Washington county, Texas.

4. *slang.* (See quotation.) *Obs.*

1819 [A. PEIRCE] *Rebelliad* 44 Arriving at Lord Bibo's study, They thought they'd be a little bloody. . . . [*Footnote*] Formerly a College term for daring, rowdy, impudent. *Ib.* 76.

5. In names of plants, fishes, etc.: (see quotations).

(*a*) **1774** *Boston Ev. Post* 4 April (Th.), [Susannah Benken sells garden seeds including] early frame, white goss, early green goss, large green goss, bloody goss, Aleppo goss. **1784** CUTLER in *Mem. Academy* I. 490 *Amaranthus*, . . . Bloody Amaranthus. Love-lies-a-bleeding. Princes Feather. **1817-8** EATON *Botany* (1822) 181 *Aronia sanguinea*, bloody choak-berry. *Ib.* 289 *Geranium sanguineum*, bloody geranium. **1852** MITCHELL *Dream Life* 199 The golden rod, the orchis, the dahlia, and the bloody cardinal of the swamp-lands.

(*b*) **1839** STORER *Mass. Fishes* 31 *Gasterosteus apeltes*, the bloody stickleback; . . . found . . . in large numbers in creeks, to which the sea had access.

(*c*) **1881** E. INGERSOLL *Oyster Industry* 242 *Bloody clam*, the Blood Quahaug; the young and small specimens of various species of *Arcidæ*, supposed to be choicest food of the starfishes. (Narragansett bay.)

+Bloody-back. *Obs.* An abusive term for a British soldier. — **1770** *Mass. Gazette Extraordinary* 21 June 2/2 The Mob still increased, and were outrageous . . . calling out 'Come, you Rascals, you bloody Backs, you Lobster Scoundrels; fire if you dare.' **1781** PETERS *Hist. Conn.* (1829) 292 That the lead of it [=George III.'s statue] should be run into bullets, for the destruction of the English bloody-backs.

+Bloomer. [From the name of Mrs. Amelia *Bloomer* (1818-94) of Seneca Falls, N.Y.]

1. Attrib. with *costume, dress,* etc., denoting a style of female costume comprising a short skirt and loose trousers gathered closely round the ankles.

Mrs. Bloomer 'did not invent it, was not the first to wear it, and protested against its being called by her name. . . . For some years she edited and published, at Seneca Falls, N.Y., a magazine called *The Lily*, in which (Feb. 1851) the new costume appears to have been first mentioned in print' (Th.).

1851 *Boston Transcript* 26 May 2/3 The daughter of Dr. Hanson, of this city, appeared in the Bloomer suit at a convention in South Reading last week. *Ib.* 31 May 2/4 Quite a large number of young ladies in that city [=Lowell] have made arrangements to attend church tomorrow in the Bloomer costume. **1852** *Harper's Mag.* June 10/2 This feat of passing under the rock is always a very damp one, though during the season, troops of damsels may be seen bravely accomplishing it, . . . and doing it too without the confident freedom of the *Bloomer dress!* **1852** J. B. JONES *Col. Vanderbomb* 69, I thought if the Bloomer trousers were fit for anything in the world, it was to go into such holes as that. **1857** *Harper's Mag.* Jan. 283/2 The lady-speakers who adopted the Bloomer costume would not come under this clerical interdict. **1863** B. TAYLOR *H. Thurston* v. 65 She is quite pretty, and wears the new Bloomer dress. **1882** *Harper's Mag.* March 557/2 All the women were compelled to wear the short skirts and ample pantalets of the Bloomer costume.

2. The Bloomer costume or trousers. Freq. *pl.* Now *Hist.*

(*a*) **1851** *Harper's Mag.* Sept. 576/2 The ladies seem determined to reduce the volume of their dresses. This is manifested . . . at home by the general favor in which the 'Bloomers' are held. **1851** Mrs. L. Clappe *Lett. from Calif.* 25 Nov. 143 How can they so far forget the sweet, shy coquetries of shrinking womanhood as to don those horrid bloomers? **1855** *Chicago Times* 29 March 3/2 Perhaps Lawrence [Kansas] is the only city in America, where a majority of the ladies wear Bloomers. **1864** Hale *If, Yes, and Perhaps* (1868) 246 We laughed more, till the oldest woman tumbled in her bear-skin bloomers, and came with a smash right on the little cast-iron frame. **1873** *Winfield* (Kansas) *Courier* 26 June 2/2 The dress is bloomers or American costume. *c***1900** M. J. Holmes *Aikenside* i. 13 Like his Aunt Margaret, who sometimes wore bloomers, and advocated women's rights.

(*b*) **1851** *Worcester Spy* in *Boston Transcript* 29 May 2/4 The first 'Bloomer' made its appearance in our city yesterday. **1852** *Knickerb.* Sept. 241 None but the most graceful females can hope to assume the Bloomer. **1853** B. F. Taylor *Jan. & June* 85 [I] shouldn't be surprised to see a Bantam out in Bloomer any morning.

b. *pl.* Short baggy breeches of lightweight material gathered about the knees, freq. worn by women in sports, cycling, etc.

1889 *Cent.* 595/2 *Bloomer*, . . . 3. *pl.*, specifically, the light trousers, now commonly buttoned below the knee. **1895** Chambliss *Diary* 102 Let our would-be mannish ladies, who wear bloomers and ride bicycles, take warning. **1910** *Sears, Roebuck & Co. Catalog No. 121* 239 Black sateen bloomers.

attrib. **1895** *N.Y. Dramatic News* 26 Oct. 12/4 The company has been well advertised, . . . the 'bloomer girl' having attracted much attention.

3. A wearer of bloomers.

1852 *Knickerb.* September 241 The Bloomers once triumphant, no prophetic ken will be required to read their future tactics. **1854** *Congress. Globe* 20 May, App. 717 Bloomers wearing the apparel of men, and men wrapped in the apparel of women. **1860** Holmes *Professor* vii. 195, I don't like the Bloomers any too well,—in fact, I never saw but one, and she . . . had a mob of boys after her.

4. Attrib., applied to a form of fence, and to a divided stern of a yacht.

1862 *Ill. Agric. Soc. Trans.* (1865) V. 692 Many men . . . are compelled to make . . . 'Shanghai' or 'Bloomer' fences (two-boarded fences) which every one knows is but little better than no fence. **1897** *Outing* April 9/1 Tartar was generally recognized to have won her races without benefit from the 'bloomer stern,' which had excited so much adverse criticism earlier in the year.

+**Bloomered,** *a.* [f. prec.] Characterized by wearing bloomers. — **1895** S. T. Kidder in *Advance* (Chicago) 6 June 1287 The 'new woman,' . . . though not necessarily of the bloomered type, is marching . . . to victory in Wisconsin.

+**Bloomerism.** [f. Bloomer.] The practice or advocacy of wearing the Bloomer costume. — **1851** (*title*), 'Bloomerism,' or The New Female Costume of 1851. **1852** *Knickerb.* XL. 240 We consider Bloomerism as the most dangerous of modern 'isms.' **1852** *Corr. R. W. Griswold* (1898) 281 Bloomerism gains many converts *in opinion* here. **1855** Hambleton *H. A. Wise* 452 A rush of fanatics from Boston and New York would be let loose to propagate Abolitionism, Bloomerism, Fourierism and every pestilent device. **1864** T. L. Nichols *Amer. Life* I. 69 Lectures on Women's Rights, Bloomerism, Free-love, and Heaven knows what.

* **Bloomery, -ary.** [f. *bloom* a mass of iron after the first smelting or hammering.]

1. A forge in which iron is converted into blooms.

*c***1644** *Mass. H. S. Proc.* 2 Ser. VIII. 15 Provided that they doe within 10 yeares set up an iron furnace & forge . . . & not a bloomery only. **1749** W. Douglass *Brit. Settlements in N. A.* (1755) I. 540 Iron is a considerable article in our manufactures; it consists of these general branches: . . . 3. Bloomeries, which from bog or swamp ore . . . reduce it into a bloom or semiliquidated lump. **1757** *Doc. Hist. N.Y. State* (1849) I. 731 There were two Furnaces in the Mannor of Cortland & several Bloomeries. **1760** Washington *Diaries* I. 160 Called at the Bloomery and got Mr. Wm. Crawford to shew me the place . . . for erecting an Iron Work upon. **1812** *Niles' Reg.* I. 343/1 Upon the best authority we state the furnaces, forges, and bloomeries in the United States to be 530. **1871** W. M. Grosvenor *Protection* 171 In 1731 there were . . . in New England, nineteen forges or bloomeries. **1883** Zeigler & Grosscup *Alleghanies* 206 During the war it was wrought in bloomeries and manufactured into spikes, cannon, and shafts for the iron-clads.

2. Attrib. with *bar iron, forge, iron, tool.*

1740 *Mass. Bay Acts & Resolves* (1874) II. 1015 The inhabitants of this province shall have liberty . . . to pay the several sums . . . assessed, in . . . good bloomery bar iron, at three pounds per hundred. **1778** *Coll. N.H. Hist. Soc.* IX. 290 Bloomery Iron at the place of manufacture. **1779** *N.J. Archives* III. 535 One lot . . . includes . . . the remains of a bloomary forge and saw-mill. **1881** Raymond *Mining Gloss., Bosh,* a trough in which bloomary tools . . . are cooled.

Blooming, *vbl. n.* [f. *bloom* v.; cf. prec.] The reduction of iron to the form of blooms. {1812–} Also attrib. with *mill.* — **1871** *Trans. Inst. Mining Eng.* I. 203 This first reduction or blooming is usually done in this country in a 30-inch 3-high rolling mill. **1880** *Harper's Mag.* Dec. 62 A brisk little locomotive . . . speeds away with the ingots to the 'blooming' and 'rail' mill.

Bloom-iron. [Cf. prec.] Iron in the form of blooms. — **1835** Hoffman *Winter in West* I. 77 Bloom-iron . . . is brought hither [=to Pittsburgh] for manufacture from the forges on the Juniata. **1863** *Mich. Gen. Statutes* (1882) I. 1025. Pig, bloom, or other iron manufactured in this state, shall be free from specific tax.

+**Blossom.** **1.** Radiated quartz. **2.** (See quot. 1881 and cf. Blossom rock.) — **(1) 1819** Schoolcraft *Mo. Lead Mines* 71 This variety of quartz . . . has acquired the popular name of blossom of lead, or mineral blossom. *Ib.* 91 In searching for ore, the soil, the slope of the hills, spar, blossom, trees, etc. are taken as guides. *Ib.* 184 Radiated Quartz . . . is particularly abundant in Washington County, where it is known under the popular name of mineral blossom. **(2) 1881** R. Raymond *Mining Glossary, Blossom,* the oxidized or decomposed outcrop of a vein or coal-bed, more frequently the latter. **1883** Beadle *Western Wilds* xxxiv. 560 We are certainly near the outcrop from which the 'blossom' was broken.

Blossom hemp. Male hemp, carl hemp. — **1766** Washington *Diaries* I. 228 Began to pull Hemp at the Mill and at Muddy hole—too late for the blossom Hemp by three Weeks or a Month. **1862** *Rep. Comm. Patents: Agric.* 114 The male [hemp] is called the blossom-hemp, and the female the seed-hemp. When the blossom-hemp has shed its pollen, it dies.

+**Blossom rock.** =Blossom *n.* 2. — **1872** *Harper's Mag.* XLVI. 23 A vein . . . exhibiting 'blossom rock,' a yellow, spongy mass, charged with iron rust formed by the oxidation of the pyrites. **1876** *Atl. Mo.* Dec. 678 Found blossom rock up there yesterday, . . . true blossom rock. The assayer, he was up, an' he says it's the real mineral, no mistake. **1878** Beadle *Western Wilds* 479 Men were let down from above to 'prospect,' a crevice was found with 'blossom' rock. **1880** A. A. Hayes in *Harper's Mag.* Feb. 380/1 If he had only had a keen eye for 'blossom rock' and other indications . . . how differently history might have read. **1883** Beadle *Western Wilds* xxxiv. 560 As we hunt up the mountain side we encounter some 'blossom rock,' which is merely float of such size, richness, and generally ragged contour as to show that it has not rolled far.

Blotted, *ppl. a.* [f. *blot* v.] Partially obliterated; defaced. — **1720** *Weekly Mercury* 21 July 3/2 They have felloniously taken with them . . . one black Coloured Gelding with a Star in his forehead, has a sore back and a blotted brand on one of his buttocks.

* **Blotter.**

1. A daybook or letter book; a book of record or entry. Also attrib. with *entry.* {1847–}

1678 *Connecticut Public Rec.* III. 498 The number on each article therein, directing to Journal page, wherein every particular of the parcels thereof is, also the number of each debenture, order, account, or blotter entry. **1769** *Md. Hist. Mag.* XII. 284 In looking over the blotter I found your agree[men]t with Rumsey to sell Deerhill for £50. **1770** *Ib.* 294 To prevent mistakes make a M^n of this in y[ou]r Blotter. **1806** Weems *Letters* II. 335 They had never been enter[e]d in his blotter, or never posted. **1811** *Steele Papers* II. 657, 2 blank blotters 35 cts. each, $.70. These are blank books of a single quire each with pasteboard covers and altho' I have called them *blotters,* they are more properly day books. **1882** *Century Mag.* July 369/1 [Thoreau's] journal . . . does not consist of mere scraps, . . . like the blotter most literary men keep, but of finished work. **1900** Nelson *A B C Wall St.* 35 The blotter contains the amounts of all stocks received and delivered, the names of the firms, and, for identification, the certificate and bond numbers of all securities delivered. **1906** *Atlantic Mo.* Feb. 264 It was necessary . . . to examine the daybook or blotter in the chief clerk's office [at the Patent Office].

+**b.** The record book of a police station, spec. the list of arrests and charges.

1887 *Harper's Mag.* March 500/2 Every item of police duty, and of civil or criminal occurrence, is inscribed on the 'blotter.' **1901** J. Riis *Making of an American* 232 For hours I lingered about the record clerk's room where they kept the old station-house blotters, unable to tear myself away. **1901** *Munsey's Mag.* XXIV. 540/2 It is a month of uncommon virtue when the blotter shows as few as a hundred arrests. *a***1906** 'O. Henry' *Trimmed Lamp* 112 His objections came to be spread finally upon some police station blotter or a hospital register.

2. A sheet of blotting paper; a blotting pad. {1859–}

1872 [Bagg] *At Yale* 557 An ink-bottle, . . . a blotter, and a dozen or twenty half-sheets of quarto-post, lie upon every table. **1879** B. F. Taylor *Summer-Savory* xvii. 138 A big blotter spread open upon the lid, goose-quill pens, a sand-box and a pewter inkstand within reach. **1884** *Boston Lit. World* 19 April 132/2 Reade's . . . pen spluttered, . . . and he used no blotter. **1901** Merwin & Webster *Calumet K* xiii. 247 Bannon was sitting in the office chair with his feet on the draughting-table, figuring on the back of a blotter.

* **Blotting paper.** The absorbent paper used for drying writing. Also fig.

1770 J. Habersham *Letters* 94 Small Memorandum Books . . . bound with thin red Leather, and a blotting Paper, between each leaf. *c***1790** T. Coxe *View U.S.* 62 Wrapping, blotting, sheathing and hanging paper. **1843** *Knickerb.* XXI. 119 'Them buttons, Sir, them buttons?' replied the tailor, looking at one through the blotting-paper. **1871** Stowe *Pink & White Tyranny* xii. 129 You may . . . become a mere sheet of blotting-paper all your life.

Blouse. [Fr.] A loose upper garment, usu. of a light material, resembling a shirt or smock frock. {1875–}

In earlier English use (1840–) only with reference to France.

1848 Bartlett 36 *Blouse,* a loose garment made of brown linen, fastened round the waist with a belt; worn by men and boys in France, and lately introduced partially into this country. **1861** *Chicago Tribune* 26 May 1/3 Cassinet pants are supplied the volunteers.... They cost the State $5, and blouses made of shoddy, with pants, $10. **1862** NORTON *Army Lett.* 105 All there is on the shoulders of my blouse is a threadbare spot where the musket rubs. **1884** 'CRADDOCK' *Where Battle was Fought* 310 Edgar... stood upon the front steps in... brown linen knickerbockers and blouse. **1894** *Outing* Sept. 471 The uniform of the enlisted men [of Ill. Naval Reserve] is composed of white duck pantaloons and blouse. **1905** VALENTINE *H. Sandwith* 251 Walking the furrows was a solitary young figure in blue blouse and straw hat. **1919** *Sears, Roebuck & Co. Catalog No. 138*, 395 A handsome durable boys' blouse that will look good on most every boy.

Blow, *n.*[1]

1. A strong blowing of wind; a gale. {1660-}

'This also is a legitimate word, in general use in the U. States' (W. '28). 'Originally a seaman's word, but now come into general use' (B. '48).

1806 WEBSTER, *Blow*, ... gale of wind. **1818** E. PETTIGREW *Let. to Ann Pettigrew* 12 Feb., The Lake is at this time higher by two inches than I ever saw it and ... we had a most tremendious blow on shore. **1840** DANA *Two Years* iv. 31 This was the first blow, that I had seen, which could really be called a gale. **1854** S. SMITH *Down East* 192 And when it [the wind] comes on a blow, what a stirring time there is! **1874** LONG *Wild-Fowl* 61 It will ... be well to give a few directions as to the management of the boat when taking up decoys in a heavy 'blow.' **1888** P. H. SHERIDAN *Memoirs* I. 18 Generally the *blow* lasts for three days, and the cold becomes intense and piercing. **1900** STOCKTON *Afield & Afloat* 299 You two are caught in a heavy blow and I've offered you a port of refuge.

||**b.** *What's the blow?* What is the matter? *colloq.*

1852 STOWE *Uncle Tom* viii, A body may be pretty sure of that, when *you* 're glad to see 'em.... What's the blow now?

+**2.** *College slang.* 'A merry frolic with drinking; a spree' (Hall). *Obs.*

1827 *Harvard Reg.* Aug. 172 My fellow-students had been engaged at a 'blow' till the stage horn had summoned them to depart. *Ib.* Oct. 235 And, if no coming *blow* his thoughts engage, [the idling student] Lights candle and cigar. **1848** *R.I. Words* (Bartlett MS.), *Free Blow*, eating or drinking free of Expense.

+**b.** 'The person who engages in a blow.' *Obs.*

1830 *Collegian* 231 Wishing that I could see, in the long vista of the past, .. the many honest *digs* who had in this room consumed the midnight oil,—the many hardened *blows* who had rioted here around the festive board.

+**3.** A breathing space.

1855 *Knickerb.* Aug. 146, I seized her bridle, and brought the whole party to a stand. I determined that the horses should now have a good 'blow,' ... and resolutely held on.

4. The blowing of a steamer or a whale.

1847 FIELD *Drama in Pokerville*, etc. 175 Now her 'blow' is heard, like a suppressed curse of struggle and defiance. **1853** KANE *Grinnell Exp.* 359 It had more of voice mingled with its sibilant 'blow' than I had ever heard.

+**5.** The sending of a blast of air through crude molten cast iron so as to burn out the excess of carbon.

1874 KNIGHT 277/2 The completion of the blow and the exhaustion of the impurities is denoted almost instantaneously by a change in the whiteness of the flame.

Blow, *n.*[2] {1710-}

1. A blossom; a flower. {1797}

'This word is in general use in the U. States, and legitimate' (W. '28). Also with defining word, as *bean-blow*, etc.

1824 *Old Colony Memorial* 6 March (Th.), As thick as seven bumble bees on a punkin-blow. **1832** WILLIAMSON *Maine* I. 126 May-weed, a low plant with white blows. **1849** N. KINGSLEY *Diary* 15 The fruit grows on the extreme top with a blow or flower resembling our Skunks Cabbage. **1856** *Knickerb.* Sept. 226 Phil suggested to her that 'the large blow' was inconvenient to be carried. **1869** STOWE *Oldtown Folks* viii. 102 Miss Asphyxia had one word for all flowers. She called them all 'blows.' **1878** R. T. COOKE *Happy Dodd* xii. 122 Feelin's ain't worth a red cent without they come to facts, no more'n flowers that ain't fruit-blows. **1891** — *Huckleberries* 291, I should be gettin' flower seeds and things; I'm kinder fond of blows in the time of 'em.

2. Bloom, blossom. *In (the) blow*, in bloom. {1759-}

1804 LEWIS in *L. & Clark Exped.* (1905) VI. 173 The violet, the doves foot, & cowslip are in bloe [*sic*]. **1852** *Mich. Agric. Soc. Trans.* III. 198, I generally cut my grass when in the blow. **1917** WILKINS & KINGSLEY *Alabaster Box* x. 139 My! you can smell it a mile off when it's in blow.

* **Blow,** *v.*

The use of *blowed* as p.t. and p.p., illustrated by the following examples, was current in E. down to the close of the 18th century, and is still common in dialect, or in illiterate speech:—**1775** *R.I. Hist. Soc.* VI. 3 The weather, accompanied by a fog and heavy rain, blowed very fresh. **1806** LEWIS in *L. & Clark Exped.* (1905) IV. 352 It rained... and blowed with great violence. **1829** WEEMS *B. Franklin* viii. 24 Collins blowed upon the idea. He said it was all *stuff*. **1836** EDWARD *Hist. Texas* vi. 103 They consequently blowed his brains out. *a***1862** THOREAU *Maine Woods* 244 One thunder-storm ... blowed hard against the northern shore. **1878** [see sense 10]. **1902** O. WISTER *Virginian* p. ix, The wages ... were squandered hard,—half a year's pay sometimes gone in a night,—'blown in,' as he expressed it, or 'blowed in,' to be perfectly accurate. **1911** QUICK *Yellowstone N.* ix. 241 A witness ... from outside the jurisdiction had blowed in.

I. *intr.* **1. a.** *Blow high, blow low*, whatever may happen.

1774 FITHIAN *Journal* I. 235 Ben is in a wonderful Fluster lest he shall have no company tomorrow at the Dance—But blow high, blow low, he need not be afraid; Virginians are of genuine blood—They will dance or die! **1851** *Knickerb.* XXXVII. 488 The Captain had determined to reach Ithaca that night, and held on his course, as the popular phrase is, 'blow high, or blow low.' *a***1861** WINTHROP *J. Brent* vi. 63, I've booked Brother John fur Paradise; Brother Joseph's got a white robe fur him, blow high, blow low! **1921** PAINE *Comr. Rolling Ocean* x. 171 Here were three musketeers ... who were blithely resolved to stand by each other through thick and thin, blow high, blow low.

b. *colloq.* To move as if carried or impelled by the wind. +*To blow in*, to appear or turn up unexpectedly; to drop in.

1844 *Knickerb.* XXIII. 51, I was half awake... when Bob came in, blew about the room for awhile, and cried out. **1868** S. HALE *Lett.* 42 She is a picturesque looking creature.... Why she blows up and down the Nile year in and year out, ... I dunno. **1895** REMINGTON *Pony Tracks* 104 We were all very busy when William 'blew in' with a great sputtering. **1904** LORIMER *Gorgon Graham* 47 Yesterday our old college friend, Clarence, blew in from Monte Carlo. **1911** VANCE *Cynthia* 340 'That's just the way she's been goin' on ever sinst I blew in here!' he declared.

2. a. Of persons: To take breath. {1523-1786 of horses}

1774 FITHIAN *Journal* I. 211 In the mean Time tho' (as Workman say) I must blow a little, for to be sure I am fatigued. **1860** HOLLAND *Miss Gilbert* ii. 29, I'll sit here and blow, till he comes round.

+**b.** Of deer: (see quotation).

1868 *Amer. Naturalist* Oct. 467 Another sound is a kind of snort,—a forcible emission of air from the nostrils. The hunter says he 'blows'; it may be a note of anger or defiance. At the season when the doe is rearing her young, ... she will stand and 'blow.' ... The bucks also blow, but less frequently.

3. *fig.* To talk boastfully; to boast or brag.

Examples of this sense occur in ME., and it is current in modern Northern dialects, but English writers of the later 19th cent. regarded it as colonial. Cf. BLOWER and BLOWING.

1859 BARTLETT 36 *To blow*, to boast, brag; to 'talk big.' You blow behind my back, but dare not say any thing to my face. **1862** BROWNE *A. Ward His Book* (1865) 108 'People!' sed the stranger, 'I'm the Juke d' Moses!' 'Old hoss!' sed a passenger, 'methinks thou art blowin!' **1872** 'MARK TWAIN' *Roughing It* xxxi. 224 What's your idea for ... blowin' about your father? **1884** HOWELLS *Silas Lapham* i. 13 Well, I ain't a-going to brag up my paint; I don't suppose you came here to hear me blow.

4. a. To go off, to burst or gush out, explosively or with force. Freq. with *off* or *out*.

1835 [LONGSTREET] *Georgia Scenes* 224 I don't say that I'll win beef; but if my piece don't blow, I'll eat the paper; or be mighty apt to do it. **1873** BEADLE *Undevel. West* 333 The fluid turned aside to existing crevices, or 'blew out' through hollow chambers. **1886** WINCHELL *Walks & Talks* 143 Personal information from Mr. Neff ... assured me that these wells continued to 'blow.'

b. *fig.* With *off* or *out*. To speak out angrily.

1847 [ROBB] *Squatter Life* 143, I fired up and generated an inch or two more steam, and then blew off at him. **1875** STOWE *We & Our Neighbors* 99 You must n't let St. John and me run too much together, or I shall blow out.

c. To get *up* steam.

1898 HAMBLEN *Gen'l Manager's Story* 301 There wasn't an engine of the whole three that could go over the sixty mile division without stopping half a dozen times to 'blow up.'

5. With *off*. To cease or stop a fight.

1845 HOOPER *Simon Sugg's Adv.* iv, 48 When we blowd off, I judge he had the wust of it.

6. *fig.* With *out*. To become spent or exhausted.

1845 SIMMS *Wigwam & Cabin* I. 58, I reckon I was clean gone, if it hadn't been that she [=a stabbed bear] blowed out before me. **1857** *Ill. Agric. Soc. Trans.* II. 364 In 1826 a great excitement was started ... at the discovery of copper.... It has all blown out. **1883** FULTON *Sam Hobart* 50 Though at times he ... profaned God's name in the most terrible way, so that those next him turned from him and left him to *blow out* (as they say of a locomotive).

II. *tr.* **7. a.** To break *up* by a rush of water. *Obs.*

1739 W. STEPHENS *Proc. Georgia* 402 A great and uncommon Flood came down upon them, and had blown up the Mill. **1788** WASHINGTON *Diaries* III. 329 The heavy rain of last Night had blown up my lower tumbling dam, or waste.

b. To break up by explosion; to blast. *Obs.* {1799}

1770 *Md. Hist. Mag.* XII. 353 Pray send me a 2" of the Course Gunpowder to Blow the lime stone. **1785** WASHINGTON *Diaries* II. 415 [We] passed down the Seneca falls to the place where the workmen were blowing rocks. **1798** BENTLEY *Diary* II. 288 They are blowing the rocks on the neck in the road to Winter Island.

+**8.** To send (a ball), make (a hole), *through* a person.

1790 FANNING *Narrative* 7 They threatened blowing a ball through me every instant, if I did not surrender. **1860** CLAIBORNE *Sam. Dale* iv. 73 Fall back, or I will blow you through. **1871** BRET HARTE *East & West Poems* 18 Walker of Murphy's blew a hole through Peters For telling him he lied. **1891** ROBERTS *Adrift in Amer.* 153 If you talk to me like that, I'll blow a hole through you that a rat could crawl through.

9. *slang.* To peach; to turn informer. {1859}

1848 E. JUDSON *Mysteries N.Y.* II. 48 To 'blow' would be to tell of some of my stealing; and to get me 'sent up,' means to get sent to the states prison.

+**10.** To praise boastfully; to extol.

1878 BEADLE *Western Wilds* 126 This [State], the most loudly blowed and persistently advertised of the whole sisterhood. *Ib.* 194 In Kansas or Nebraska we should see . . . one or two live journals blowing the place as the 'future metropolis of the boundless west.'

+**11.** *slang. To blow in*, to spend (money) freely or completely; to squander. Also absol.

In later use (1902–) freq. without *in*, to spend. {1874–}

1887 F. FRANCIS *Saddle & Moccasin* 144 'Sam went off on a bend.' 'To blow in?' Jake laughed assent. **1889** *Century Mag.* March 784/1 His story was that the brother sold out his share and 'blew it all in' in about a week. **1892** *Congress. Rec.* 2 Feb. 784/1 They amassed a surplus of more than $100,000,000, and quietly turned it over to our Republican friends to blow it in the next year. **1902** WHITE *Blazed Trail* xxvi. 184 Awaiting the time soon to come when, his stake 'blown-in,' . . . the shanty boy would again start for the woods. **1905** D. G. PHILLIPS *Plum Tree* 88 Something in the expression of the mouth suggested thoughts of how he was going to enjoy himself as he 'blew in' his winnings.

+**12.** To treat (oneself or another). Also with *to* (something). *slang.*

1896 *Dialect Notes* I. 412 'To *blow* oneself,' to spend money freely. **1903** C. L. BURNHAM *Jewel* 97 'Father took me to the horse show.' 'He did, eh?' 'Yes, he told mother he was going to blow me to it.'

Blowback. [BLOW *v.*] A backward draught or current of air. — **1883** FULTON *Sam Hobart* 224 The flames originated from the '*blow back*' on the engine, forcing the flames out of the furnace when the door was opened.

+**Blow-bladder.** An inflatable bladder. — **1877** BARTLETT 776 'A blow-bladder figure for it,' a price inflated beyond all reason.

+**Blowdown.** [BLOW *v.*] A place encumbered with trees that have been blown down. — **1895** *Outing* Aug. 448/2 After that, a line of blazes wanders erratically back and forth up the side of the mountain, dodging '*blow-downs*' and ledges. **1900** *Scribner's Mag.* Sept. 264/1 The horses picking their way carefully over blow-downs and through the wet snow.

***Blower.** [BLOW *v.*] +**1.** *local.* (See quotations.) **2.** A boaster or braggart. Also attrib. — **(1)** **1842** *Nat. Hist. N.Y., Zoology* IV. 327 The Common Puffer. *Tetradon turgidus.* . . . This curious fish receives its popular names of Puffer and Blower from its being enabled to inflate itself when taken from the water. **1869** *Amer. Naturalist* III. 555 A female snake, *Heterodon platyrhinus*, commonly known in this locality [Lancaster, Penna.] as the 'Blower,' or 'Blowing Viper,' was killed in Martic Township. **(2)** **1856** *Spirit of Times* (N.Y.) 4 Oct. 66/3 When some . . . vain fellow, or successful 'blower,' has a few friends who want to elevate him. *c*1863 WHITMAN *Specimen Days* (1882) 45, I am continually lost at the absence of blowing and blowers among these old-young American militaires. **1863** 'MANHATTAN' in *Ev. Standard* 10 Dec., General Grant . . . is not one of the 'blower' generals.

Blowfly. A flesh fly. {1858}

The first quotation is from an English traveler.

1821 NUTTALL *Travels Arkansa* 201 The green blow-flies, attracted by the meat brought to our camp, exceeded every thing that can be conceived. **1846** ABERT in Emory *Military Reconn.* 397 The blowfly had peopled our blankets with living masses of corruption. **1859** *Amer. Cycl.* VII. 579/2 The blue-bottle or blow fly . . . is found in summer about slaughter houses. **1879** BISHOP 4 *Months in Sneak-box* 225 Another insect scavenger, found along the low shores of the Gulf, is the blow-fly, and one very useful to man.

Blowgun. [BLOW *v.*] A tube from which arrows are propelled by blowing with the breath. {1864}

1846 M'KENNEY *Memoirs* I. vii. 163, I had never before seen what those Indians call a blow-gun. . . . It is a reed of from eight to ten feet long. Here, among the [Chickasaw] little boys, it was in common use. **1877** *Harper's Mag.* Dec. 79/2, I made a sketch of an Indian who came in with his blow-gun and some skins. **1899** CUSHMAN *Hist. Indians* 216 The boys strolled through the woods with their blow-guns and bow and arrows.

+**Blowhard,** *a.* and *n. colloq.*[2] [BLOW *v.*[3]]

1. *adj.* Blustering, boastful.

1855 *Oregon Weekly* 21 July (Th.), The *Oregonian* of last week has a blowhard article on the subject. **1921** PAINE *Comr. Rolling Ocean* vi. 105 He don't get by with his blow-hard stuff, but I'll have to say he is entertaining.

2. *n.* A blustering person; a braggart.

1884 SWEET & KNOX *Through Texas* i. 19 Parker . . . instructing the druggist to 'tell that blowhard that he has been fooling with Phil Parker of —,' . . . returned to finish his game. **1893** 'O. THANET' *Stories Western Town* 50, I told him Richards was a blowhard. **1894** *Congress. Rec.* 23 Jan. 1238/2 Anyone who will read the whole testimony will see that . . . [this man] was a mere braggart, a pretender, a blow-hard. **1919** T. K. HOLMES *Man from Tall Timber* xiii. 154 Of all the old blow-hards that ever come into this neck o' woods. **1922** MULFORD *Tex* 32 He fairly burned to turn his poker craft against this blowhard's invitation, to wipe from that self-complacent face its look of omniscience.

Blowing, *vbl. n.* [BLOW *v.*]

1. Being carried off by a flood. (Cf. BLOW *v.* 7 a.) *Obs.*

1760 WASHINGTON *Diaries* I. 150 A messenger came to inform me that my Mill was in great danger of blowing.

2. Breaking up by explosion; blasting. *Obs.* {1799}

1788 WASHINGTON *Diaries* III. 361 From hence we proceeded . . . to the Seneca falls, where much digging and blowing had been performed for the purpose of conducting the Navigation through one of the Marshes. **1805** SIBLEY in *Ann. 9th Congress* 2 Sess. 1103 We often heard a noise like the explosion of a cannon, . . . which, I afterwards was informed, was the blowing of the mines, as it is called. **1808** in *Niles' Reg.* XV. 50/1 The least expensive and most obvious means of removing the former, are the blowing of the most prominent rocks.

3. Emission or eruption (of natural gas).

1806 *Ann. 9th Congress* 2 Sess. 1139 Not rarely a curious phenomenon is seen, which is termed the blowing of the mountains; it is confined elastic gas forcing a passage through the side or top of a hill.

4. Boasting, bragging. {1873}. Also attrib.

1840 *Congress. Globe* App., 9 Jan. 50/1 [I advise them] to treat with contempt and scorn, all the blasting, blowing, blustering, and bullying displays they may see here or elsewhere. **1867** HARTE *Condensed Novels* 301 All this with that ingenious candor which is perfectly justifiable in a barbarian, but which a Greek might feel inclined to look upon as 'blowing.' **1878** BEADLE *Western Wilds* 134 Its bright and saucy editorials excelled all specimens extant of Kansas blowing.

+**5.** *Blowing-out*, =BLOW *n.*[1] 5.

1905 VALENTINE *H. Sandwith* 9 Passing the Works Mr. Hallett had been attracted by the spectacle of the blowing-out. *Ib.* 13 The illumined sky . . . on this night [was] a signal for them to join in the celebration of the blowing-out.

Blowing, *ppl. a.* [BLOW *v.*] {1604–}

+**1.** *Blowing adder, snake, viper*, a snake of the genus *Heterodon*, esp. *H. platyrhinus* of the eastern states.

1688 J. CLAYTON *Acc. Va.* in *Phil. Trans.* XVIII. 134 The Blowing-Snake [is] an absolute species of a Viper, but larger than any I have seen in Europe. **1806** CLARK in *Lewis & C. Exped.* (1905) VI. 224, 7th . . . [we] saw a blowing snake. **1869** [see BLOWER 1]. **1882** *Amer. Naturalist* XVI. 566 Of all strange habits in snakes, none equals that observed in the blowing adder (*Heterodon simus*). **1884** *Public Opinion* 5 Sept. 305/1 The blowing adder was formerly common in . . . Orange County, New York.

+**b.** *Blowing fly*, the blow-fly or flesh fly.

1805 LEWIS in *L. & Clark Exped.* (1904) II. 51 This stream we named Blowing Fly Creek, from the immence quantities of these insects found in this neighbourhood. **1823** JAMES *Exped.* I. 108 The blowing flies swarmed in inconceivable numbers, attacking . . . the provision of the party.

+**2.** *Blowing cave* or *cavern*, one from (or into) which a strong current of air issues (or enters).

1781–2 JEFFERSON *Notes on Va.* (1788) 22 There is another blowing cave in the Cumberland mountain. **1805** CLARK in *Lewis & C. Exped.* (1904) II. 176 A nois . . . [as] might be caused by running water in some of the caverns . . . , on the principal of the blowing caverns. **1835** MARTIN *Descr. Va.* 25 The blowing cave at the Panther's gap in Rockbridge, admits perpetually a strong current of air. **1843** *Nat. Hist. N.Y., Geology* I. 107 If the outlet of the cave be left open, it will form a blowing cave.

+**3.** *Blowing sands*, sand or sand-hills which are shifted by the wind.

1839 BUEL *Farmer's Comp.* 89 We have used the blue clay upon blowing sands. **1861** in *Maine Bd. Agric. Rep.* X. (1865) 149 The most striking geological characteristic on the road from Winthrop to the Androscoggin River, are the sand hills, or 'blowing sands' of Wayne and South Livermore.

4. Boasting, bragging.

1882 WHITMAN *Specimen Days*, etc. 259 The members who composed it were . . . the meanest kind of bawling and blowing office-holders, office-seekers, . . . kept editors [etc.].

+**Blowing horn.** [BLOWING *vbl. n.*] A horn sounded by blowing. — **1836** C. GILMAN *Recollections* xxx. 209 The usual dress of a hunter is composed of a cap, a frock coat, . . . boots, spurs, and blowing-horn. **1854** *Harper's Mag.* VIII. 422/1, I took the 'blowing-horn,' which stuck in the crack of the wall, close by the door, and gave it a 'toot' or two, which reverberated far around the cane and swamp.

Blowing up. [BLOW *v.*] *colloq.* A severe rating or scolding. {1874–}

1822 J. WOODS *English Prairie* 95 He then gave them, as he called it, a good *blowing up*, and came on board in a very bad humour. **1846** CORCORAN *Pickings* 121, I thought I could stand a blowing up pretty well—I have had some experience in that way, as the old woman's tongue can testify. **1893** POST *Harvard Stories* 28 Then the governor would pay my bills at Christmas and give me a blowing up.

Blowout. [BLOW *v.*]

1. *slang.* An outbreak of disagreement, disorder, or loud noise; a row. {1826}

1825 PAULDING *John Bull in Amer.* 137 We had a *blow out* here last Sunday, and half a dozen troublesome fellows, they call justices, were done for by the brave *rowdies.* **1837** J. C. NEAL *Charcoal Sk.* (1838) 165 He has a prompt alacrity at a 'blow-out' and has been skyed in a 'blow-up.' **1840** SIMMS *Border Beagles* 133 This evening there was a strange blow-out that has made the chap furious as a wild beast. **1842** *Spirit of Times* 15 Feb. (Th.), I've had five breezes, seven blow-outs, nine shindies, and a dozen ructions on this $1 Relief note. **1885** *Harper's Mag.* June 137 Thar was another lung tearin', ear bustin' blowouts [in an opera]. Men, women, and children rushed in singin' at the top of their voices.

b. An outcry.

1857 *Knickerb.* XLIX. 35 They [eventuations] came a few weeks after . . . followed by a grand blow-out in all the papers on the impropriety of stealing in general.

2. *slang.* An occasion of unusual or lavish indulgence in food or drink; a jollification, spree, or convivial party. {1856-}

1834 H. J. NOTT *Novellettes* I. 47 Tommy and myself had had a blow-out on the fourth. **1836** *Knickerb.* VIII. 203 He took a regular blow out, and was not sober for a month. **1837** *Ib.* IX. 127 The first attempt of a freshman, who would imitate the higher classes, in what, in college, is called a 'blow-out.' **1846** CORCORAN *Pickings* 104 Mr. Bouligny, the sheriff, gave them on Christmas-day what is termed in flash phrase 'a blow out.' **1852** STOWE *Uncle Tom* viii, Get us hot water, and sugar, and cigars, and plenty of the real stuff, and we'll have a blow-out. **1863** MASSETT *Drifting About* 132, I determined to give a 'blow-out' to one or two old New York friends. **1876** 'MARK TWAIN' *Tom Sawyer* xxxiv. 264 'What's all this blow-out about anyway?' 'It's one of the widow's parties that she's always having.' **1909** 'O. HENRY' *Roads of Destiny* 133 With three hundred dollars he had gone to Laredo for his regular 'blowout.' **1913** MULFORD *Coming of Cassidy* vii. 112, I'll clean you out an' have a real, genuine blow-out on your money.

b. *transf.* A longer indulgence than usual.

1840 DANA *Two Years* xx. 203 We . . . had, besides, what the sailors call 'a blow-out on sleep'; not turning out in the morning until breakfast was ready.

+3. *Mining.* A portion of a lode where the mineral appears to have been dislodged by some eruptive force.

1873 BEADLE *Undevel. West* 333 All the strange terms in mining parlance: 'true lodes, . . . blow-outs.' **a1904** WHITE *Blazed Trail Stories* xii. 233 The doubtful spot on the *Jim Crow* was not a blow-out, but a 'horse.'

+4. A hollow made by the wind in an area of shifting sand or in the top of a butte. Also attrib. with *grass*, etc.

1892 SMITH & POUND *Bot. Survey Nebraska* II. 8 If a spot on a dry hill becomes bare, the loose sand is blown away, a small hollow is made, the surrounding grass dies from drought. . . . Such blow outs were seen 100 meters in diameter and 15 . . . meters deep. **1895** RYDBERG in *Nat. Herb.* III. 135 It sometimes happens that settlers [in the sand-hill region] a few years after breaking their land find a field transformed into a big blow-out. **1897** POUND & CLEMENTS *Phytogeography of Nebraska* (1898) 248 A small number of grasses are especially adapted to these localities and are uniformly to be found in such blow outs. . . . These grasses mark a second formation, which may be called the blow out formation. *Ib.*, The blow out grasses . . . bind the sand together with their roots.

+Blow snake. The blowing adder, snake, or viper. Cf. BLOWING *ppl. a.* 1. — **1899** *Animal & Plant Lore* 86 The breath of a 'blow snake' . . . is 'sure death' to the one who breathes it. Illinois.

Blowth. [Cf. BLOW *n.*[2]] Bloom, blossom. Usu. collective. {1602- (blooth), 1614- (blowth); now *dial.*}

1828 WEBSTER, s.v., Thus we say, trees are now in their blowth, or they have a full blowth. **1832** WILLIAMSON *Maine* I. 106 Alder . . . is a species of the birch kind, having in its blowth the same number of stamens. *Ib.* 120 Betony . . . has . . . a purple blowth. **1862** LOWELL *Biglow P.* II. p. xxviii, With us a single blossom is a *blow,* while *blowth* means the blossoming in general. A farmer would say that there was a good blowth on his fruit trees. The word retreats farther inland and away from the railways, year by year. **1878** R. T. COOKE *Happy Dodd* 144 It's sprouts a heavy blow breaks down, not tough old boughs like me, that's had their growth an' their blowth and got used to winds. **1889** *Harper's Mag.* Oct. 693/1 Mine don't show a speck o' blowth yet.

Blowup. [BLOW *v.*]

+1. A failure in business; a bankruptcy.

1821 *Niles' Reg.* 15 Sept. 38/1 Bank of Missouri. We have the particulars of the blow up of this institution. **1895** *N.Y. Dramatic News* 7 Dec. 18/1 The People's theatre and everybody connected with it are still head-over-ears in trouble and the grand blow-up may be expected at any time.

2. An explosion; usu. *fig.*, a rupture, disturbance, or quarrel. Cf. BLOWOUT 1. {1809-}

1837 [see BLOW-OUT 1]. **1838** *Yale Lit. Mag.* III. 268 Of all stations commend me to that of a *Magazine* editor, provided he can get along smoothly—without any blow-ups. **1843** *American Pioneer* II. 282 All the offices filled by the Spanish authorities were to be filled by western citizens. . . . Before the great blow up of 1806, I heard many named who were tendered appointments. **1846** *Knickerb.* XXVII. 174 All the time rage is gnawing at his heart, and every circumstance portends that there will shortly be a grand blow-up. **1854** 'O. OPTIC' *In Doors & Out* (1876) 35 He was not in a condition to appreciate a regular matrimonial 'blow up.' **1916** WILSON *Red Gap* 127 Only a year ago, . . . there was a lovely blow-up and Ellabelle says to me in her hysteria: 'Once a Scotchman, always a Scotchman!'

+b. =BLOWING UP.

1835 BIRD *Hawks of Hawk-h.* II. i. 6, I am as ready for a blow-up now as another time; only that we must blow fast, so as to run up to Hal, to be scolded before bed-time. **1840** DANA *Two Years* iv. 28 The Captain . . . gave him a grand blow-up, in true nautical style.

+3. A pan used in dissolving raw sugar for refining, having perforated pipes through the holes of which steam is blown into the sugar.

1833 SILLIMAN *Man. Sugar Cane* 77 The vats, or blow-ups, as they are called, containing the sugar, . . . are heated by steam tubes passing through them. **1857-8** *Ill. Agric. Soc. Trans.* III. 524 The syrup is now emptied into a tub or tank, called a 'blow up,' in the bottom of which is a wrought metal pipe [etc.]. **1886** *Harper's Mag.* June 82/2 These 'mixers' or 'blow-ups' are really great stew-pans set in the ground.

***Blue,** *n.*

I. 1. One wearing a blue uniform or colors, or maintaining loyal adherence to a party. {1755-}

1758-[see JERSEY BLUE]. **1765** TIMBERLAKE *Memoirs* 2, I made my first campaign in the year 1756, with a company of gentlemen called the Patriot Blues, who served the country at their own expence. **1775** *Md. Hist. Mag.* V. 153 Capt. Thomas Ennalls of the Cambridge Blues produced to the Council a Paper. **1806** *Ann. 9th Congress* 1 Sess. 702 At that time, too, we heard a great deal about the spirit of the nation, and saw a something of the spirit then talked of, in a corps called the — Blues. **1815** *Niles' Reg.* VIII. 39/2 Among those who devoted themselves to their country, the 'Brownsville Blues' are entitled to at least as much distinction and regard as any. **1840** *Niles' Nat. Reg.* 9 May 154/3 The regiment of 'Delaware Blues' was so called from their *blue* uniforms.

2. A bluestocking. {1788-} *Obs.*

1829 *Maysville Eagle* 24 Nov., The lady is a *blue*—she cannot talk of these commonplace matters. **1833** *Knickerb.* II. 58 Being herself a little bit of 'a blue,' she was endeavouring to set off the sparkles of her wit. **1846** MRS. BANCROFT *Letters* (1904) 28 [English] women . . . are much more cultivated than our women as a body, not our blues. **1856** STOWE *Dred* I. xi. 148, I have no opinion of making *blues* of young ladies; but still, I think . . . that a little useful information adds greatly to their charms.

+3. *slang.* A student (at Dartmouth or Yale) of a strict or serious character. *Obs.*

1842 *Dartmouth* IV. 117 The students here are divided into two parties, . . . the *Rowes* and the *Blues.* The Rowes are very liberal in their notions; the *Blues* more strict. *Ib.* 118 Lucian called him a *Blue,* and fell back in his chair in a pouting fit. **1848** *Yale Gallinipper* Nov., Each jolly soul of them, save the blues, Were doffing their coats, vests, pants, and shoes. **1850** *Yale Lit. Mag.* XV. 81, I would n't carry a novel into chapel to read, . . . because some of the blues might see you. **1856** [see BLUE-SKIN 4].

+4. A blue coat (with long tails). *Obs.*

1836 HOLMES *Centennial Song* vi. 46 They did not rattle round in gigs Or dash in long-tail blues. **1845** *Lowell Offering* V. 148 In their eagerness to make a man of him at once they had hurried him into a 'long-tailed-blue,' though he was but about three years of age. **1860** CLAIBORNE *Sam. Dale* i. 27 The negro wore a 'long-tail blue,' the skirts flying out as he fled. [**1867** *Atlantic Mo.* Nov. 610/2 A companion piece, followed speedily by 'Lucy Long,' . . . 'Long-Tail Blue,' and so on.]

+5. The blue uniform worn by U.S. soldiers in distinction from the gray uniform of the Confederates (or the West Point cadets). Freq. in *the boys in blue.* (Cf. ARMY BLUE.)

(1) **1848** *West Point Graduating Class Song,* But with right stout hearts we'll play our parts, When we change the Grey for the Blue. **1865** KELLOGG *Rebel Prisons* 352 We were marched in a row to the counter, where each man was given a new suit of Uncle Sam's blue. **1867** F. M. FINCH in *Atlantic Mo.* Sept. 369 (*title*), The Blue and the Grey. **1879** TOURGEE *Fool's Errand* xxv. 153 In the course of another decade, one will almost be ashamed to confess that he wore the blue. **1880** *Harper's Mag.* Feb. 478/1 The humor of the war continues to crop out here and there, and is relished equally by the gray-coats, and by those who wore the blue. **1888** *Chicago Inter-Ocean* (F.), If designing Democratic politicians had kept their hands off, and let the men of the blue and gray settle things, there would not be to-day one-half the bad blood that exists.

(2) **1866** *Congress. Globe* 27 Jan. 460/1 The brave 'boys in blue' fought manfully, and through their efforts . . . the Union has been preserved. **1866** 'F. KIRKLAND' *Bk. Anecdotes* 159 After a solemn promise that her 'brave boy in blue' would ever . . . regard her as his affianced. **1880** HAYES in *Harper's Mag.* Jan. 199/2 Uncle Sam gave the soldiers in the Civil War the right to 160 acres each. . . . Some of the boys in blue only took up portions. **1893** *Congress. Rec.* 30 Sept. 1971/1, I do not wonder that there is great dissatisfaction among the boys in blue, the men who fought to sustain the Union.

II. +**6. a.** A blueberry.

1709 LAWSON *Carolina* 104 The Hurts, Huckle-Berries, or Blues of this Country, are four sorts, which we are well acquainted withal.

b. A blue-skinned variety of potato.

1838 COLEMAN *Mass. Agric. Rep.* 34 The Chenango [potato], sometimes called Mercer, or Pennsylvania Blue.

c. A blue warbler.

1892 TORREY *Foot-path Way* 16, I . . . saw and heard only . . . Canada warblers (near the base), black-throated blues, black-throated greens [etc.].

d. A blue-fish.

1897 *Outing* Sept. 546/1 The blues are here! . . . an' they're bitin' like savages.

7. *The blues*, depressed spirits, despondency, melancholy. {Cf. *blue devils*, 1787–}

1807 IRVING *Salmagundi* xv, [He] concluded his harangue with a sigh, and I saw he was still under the influence of a whole legion of the blues. **1820** *Western Carolinian* 18 July, The fact is, he was but recently convalescent from a severe spell of the *blues.* **1837** *S. Lit. Messenger* III. 387, I shall have a fit of the blues if I stay here. **1850** N. KINGSLEY *Diary* 143 Some are beginning to get the blues on most horribly. **1866** GREGG *Life in Army* v. 39 It was well for me that day that I was enabled to look on the brightest side of the case, and avoid a severe attack of the blues. **1871** *Scribner's Mo.* I. 589 The silence alone is enough to give a well man the blues. **1883** *Harper's Mag.* Dec. 55 Come to me when you have the blues.

***8.** A blue or bluish color. +In special senses (see quotations).

1854 Commons, etc. *Doc. Hist.* I. 272 Among the diseases to which Long Cotton is subject blight, rust and blue may arise from some defect in the soil. **1868** *Amer. Naturalist* Oct. 468 The fawn is similar in color, with two rows of white spots, and scattering ones on each side, which it retains often long after the winter-coat is assumed. This is called the blue. It is rather ashy-gray, or near a slate-color. **1877** CATON *Antelope & Deer of Am.* (1881) 149 There is a bluish shade observed on the Common Deer, which is so prevalent as to have given the winter coat the general appellation . . . of the *blue*, among frontiersmen and hunters, who say the deer is in the *red* or the *blue*, as it may be in the summer or the winter coat.

***Blue,** *a.*

I. Used as a distinctive epithet. **1. a.** In the names of trees, plants, or flowers, as BLUE ASH, BEECH, -BERRY, FLAG, etc. Also *blue aster, dogwood, squash,* etc.

1769 *Amer. Philos. Soc.* I. 190 The vines proper for these countries [=northern New England] are, . . . 2. The black Orleans, 3. The blue Cluster. **1784** CUTLER in *Mem. Academy* I. 476 *Crepis*, . . . Blue Succory. Blossoms blue. . . . It is said to be a good stomachic. **1814** BENTLEY *Diary* IV. 280 This squash is commonly known by the name of the Blue Squash, . . . and is also called the African Squash. **1832** HALE *Flora* 75 Blue Hyacinth . . . [is] cultivated in our gardens. *Ib.* 123 Blue Periwinkle. . . . Flowers deep blue, white in the centre—scentless. **1836** LINCOLN *Botany* App. 110 *Liatris scariosa*, blue blazing star. **1840** DEWEY *Mass. Flowering Plants* 246 *Poa compressa*, is the Blue Grass, or Blue Spear Grass; . . . bluish-green color. **1859** *Harper's Mag.* Aug. 319 A magnificent cluster of the blue aster. **1890** *Cent.* 3422 *Blue lettuce*, a plant of the section *Mulgedium* of the genus *Lactuca*, with blue flowers. (U.S.) **1897** SUDWORTH *Arborescent Flora* 198 Tulip Tree; . . . Blue Poplar. *Ib.* 262 *Robinia . . . glaucescens*, Blue Locust. *Ib.* 309 *Cornus alternifolia*, Blue Dogwood. **1901** MOHR *Plant Life Ala.* 15 There he [W. Bartram] also found the blue sage, *Salvia azurea*, 'with its spikes of flowers of celestial blue.'

b. In the names of birds, fishes, or other animals, as BLUEBIRD, BLUE BREAM, CAT, CRANE, -FISH, etc. Also *blue crow, goose, hawk, kite; blue herring, pike,* etc.

1794 *Amer. Philos. Soc.* IV. 102 The blue motacilla (blue-bird), the torchepot and others, build in the hollows of trees. **1805** LEWIS in *L. & Clark Exped.* (1904) II. 140, I saw a small bird . . . about the size of the blue thrush or catbird. **1814** MITCHILL *Fishes N.Y.* 457 Blue Herring (*Clupea cærulea*). . . . The skin is free from spots and stripes; and is a bluish colour. *Ib.* 480 [This] Blue Lump-fish (*Cyclopterus cæruleus*) . . . was taken in the bay of New-York, with the shad. *Ib.* 487 [The] Small blue Shark . . . is often taken in our waters. **1821** NUTTALL *Travels Arkansa* 71 The birds were singing from every bush, more particularly . . . the blue sparrow (*Motacilla sialis*). **1828** BONAPARTE *Ornithology* II. 30 Blue Hawk, or Hen Harrier, *Falco Cyaneus*. . . . In the Southern parts of the Union, and especially in Florida, they are rather common in all their varieties of plumage. **1832** WILLIAMSON *Maine* I. 171 Mill beetle.—*Staphylinus*, several species, black, blue, or striped beetle, &c. **1842** *Nat. Hist. N.Y., Zoology* IV. 19 The Yellow Pike-Perch. *Lucioperca americana.* . . . Fishermen enumerate . . . three species or kinds. The Blue Pike . . . [I] consider as an aged individual of the present species. **1873** *Amer. Naturalist* VII. 202 Soaring gracefully above them with a similar flight were smaller numbers of the 'blue kite' (*Ictinia Mississippiensis*). **1874** COUES *Birds N.W.* 209 *Gymnokitta Cyanocephala*, . . . Blue Crow; Cassin's Jay; Maximilian's Jay. *Ib.* 553 *Anser Cærulescens*, Blue Goose. **1892** TORREY *Foot-path Way* 83, I saw at different times an adult male blue yellow-backed warbler. *Ib.* 178 The blue golden-winged warblers that sang daily on the edge of the wood.

2. With the name of some part (esp. of the body) or accessory, forming an attributive or absolute compound, as BLUE BACK, -BELLY, -BILL, CLAW, etc.

3. As the first element in adjectival compounds of the type BLUE-BACKED, -BELLIED, -BERRIED, -COATED, etc., freq. in use as distinctive names. Also *blue-flowered, -spotted, -striped,* etc.

1805 LEWIS in *L. & Clark Exped.* II. 7 From it's [the Missouri's] mouth to this place I have neither seen the blue crested fisher nor a fishing hawk. **1813** MUHLENBERG *Cat. Plants* 59 Blue-flowered trumpet flower. **1839** STORER *Mass. Reptiles* 252 *Salamandra glutinosa.* The blue spotted Salamander. **1840** DEWEY *Mass. Flowering Plants* 80 Passion Flower. Two species are often cultivated in gardens. *Passiflora Cærulea*, Blue-flowered, from Brazil. **1843** TORREY *Flora N.Y.* I. 188 *Baptisia australis.* . . . Blue-flowered False Indigo. **1844** *Nat. Hist. N.Y., Zoology* II. 162 The Blue-Striped Bunting. *Emberiza Lincolni.* . . . This bunting is very rare. **1901** MOHR *Plant Life Ala.* 663 *Anagallis arvensis cærulea*, Blue-flowered Pimpernel. *Ib.* 749 *Lobelia syphilitica*, Large Blue-flowered Lobelia.

II. In *slang* or *colloq.* uses. **4.** *Till all is blue,* to the last extreme. {1838–}

Perhaps originally with reference to the effects of drinking, as in quot. 1859.

1806 *Balance* (Hudson, N.Y.) 22 July 232 (Th.), The land we till is all our own; . . . Therefore we'll fight till all is blue, Should any dare invade it. **1859** BARTLETT 37 To drink 'till all's blue' is to get exceedingly tipsy. **1862** LOWELL *Biglow P.* II. iii. 94 You Thet waller in your low idees, an' will till all is blue. **1888** HOWELLS *Annie Kilburn* iv, They kept the supply a-goin' till all was blue, before they could settle on anybody.

+**5.** Intoxicated, drunk.

1838 *Knickerb.* XII. 549 The bar-room, where the landlord stood, And sued me, when I got So blue upon my birth-day. **1844** J. C. NEAL *Peter Ploddy* 147 You must be snapt now—any man that acts so queer, must be blue. **1847** [ROBB] *Squatter Life* 154 Then he would . . . take another pull at the whiskey, until . . . he not only got *blue*, but everything he looked at was multiplying. **1848** W. E. BURTON *Waggeries* 24 Another yeller feller . . . was . . . dreadful blue. **1851** *Polly Peablossom* 105 The blue tickets he sold out to some upper-country flatboatmen who were pretty *blue.*

+**6.** (See quotations.)

1851 HALL *College Words* 21 'Our real delvers, midnight students,' says a correspondent from Williams College, 'are called *blue.*' *Ib.* 130 At Princeton College, the word *blue* is used with *fizzle*, to render it intensive; as, he made a *blue fizzle*, he *fizzled blue.*

7. Of the wind or its direction: Cold, chilling.

1854 SHILLABER *Mrs. Partington* 63 One day, with the wind blue east, the window was open all day. **1898** CANFIELD *Maid of Frontier* 105 The blue wind that comes down on a man and runs around him like a knife with a saw-edge on it. **1910** 'O. HENRY' *Strictly Business* 93 Yes, it's a comfortable town. It's different from the plains in a blue norther.

8. Unpromising, discouraging. Esp. in *to look blue.* {1833–}

Cf. the sense of 'depressed, low-spirited' common from at least 1831, and in E. use from 1682.

1873 BEADLE *Undevel. West* 528 The Agency employés had not been paid for a year, and as they have to buy their own provisions, things looked blue for them. **1877** *Harper's Mag.* Dec. 42/1 In that horrible second year, when every thing was so blue, things were very different. **1878** BEADLE *Western Wilds* 175 Night came on suddenly . . . and the situation looked blue. **1910** J. HART *Vigilante Girl* vii. 106 Things look pretty blue, but never mind. . . . Cheer up.

+**Blue ash.** [BLUE *a.* 1.]

1. A species of ash, *Fraxinus quadrangulata;* a tree of this species. Also attrib.

1783 W. FLEMING in *Travels Amer. Col.* 667 Blue Ash a spieces of the White Ash and called so from the bark tinging water of that colour, grows to be a large tree. **1819** D. THOMAS *Travels* 93 Ten miles west of New-Lancaster, we first observed the blue ash. It is a fine stately tree of two or three feet diameter, generally of a straight grain, and may be easily split into rails. **1832** BROWNE *Sylva* 156 The Blue Ash is unknown to the Atlantic parts of the United States. **1847** in Drake *Pioneer Life Ky.* ii. 34 We charged upon the beautiful blue-ash and buckeye groves. **1849** CHAMBERLAIN *Ind. Gazetteer* 160 Where the tall and thinly scattered walnut, blue ash, and sugar trees no more interrupted travellers on horseback or in carriages. **1868** A. REDFORD *Hist. Methodism Ky.* I. 398 The first house was built of blue-ash logs. **1887** *Scribner's Mag.* May 571/1 Where blue-ash, black-walnut, or coffee trees abounded, they [=early settlers] knew that they had the most fertile soils.

2. *local.* The green ash, *Fraxinus lanceolata.*

1897 SUDWORTH *Arborescent Flora* 330.

***Blueback.** [BLUE *a.* 2.]

+**1. a.** A herring, trout, or salmon having a bluish back. Also attrib. **b.** A variety of lobster. **c.** A blue-backed warbler.

1812 BENTLEY *Diary* IV. 125 Mr. Osgood . . . had taken great numbers of the Herrings called Bluebacks at the mills this season. **1843** *Nat. Hist. N.Y., Zoology* v. 24 There is a variety of the Lobster, termed Bluebacks, on account of their dark bluish color. They are derived from the coast about Cape Cod, have comparatively thin shells, and are highly prized by epicures. **1871** *Fur, Fin & Feather* (1872) 158 This section shall not apply to the taking of blue back trout in Franklin and Oxford counties. **1881** *Amer. Naturalist* XV. 178 The blue-back and the dog salmon probably seek deeper water. *Ib.* 180 Little blue-backs of every size down to six inches are also found in the Upper Columbia in the fall. **1883** *Century Mag.* Sept. 684/1 The blue-back's nest was scarcely a foot from the ground. **1888** *Amer. Naturalist* XXII. 308 The blue-back or red fish, *O. nerka*, extends northward at least to the Yukon and southward to the Columbia. **1890** *Cent.* 2550/1 The blue-back, *Clupea æstivalis*, . . . [is] closely related to the alewife.

+**2.** A paper note of the Confederate States.

1871 De Vere 47 During the Civil War, . . . the original Blue Backs of the Confederacy (so-called in opposition to *Green Backs* of the Union) soon became known as Shucks.

Blue-backed, *a.* [Blue *a.* 3.]

1858 *Harper's Mag.* May 724/1 The scholars sat on rough-hewn benches conning their well-thumbed primers, or blue-backed spelling-books. **1865** *Atlantic Mo.* XV. 521, I miss in the woods . . . the Blue-Backed Warbler, the Green-Backed Warbler, . . . and many others. **1890** *Cent., Oquassa*, . . . the blue-backed trout, *Salmo oquassa.* (Rangeley Lake, Maine.)

+**Blue beech.** [Blue *a.* 1.] The hornbeam or iron-wood, *Carpinus americana* or *caroliniana.*

1821 *Mass. H. S. Coll.* 2 Ser. IX. 148 Plants, which are indigenous in the township of Middlebury, [Vermont, include] *Carpinus americana*, Blue beech. **1855** *Mich. Agric. Soc. Trans.* VI. 149 The shrubs are crab-apple, thorn apple, blue beech. **1857** Gray *Botany* 409 American Hornbeam, Blue or Water Beech, . . . [grows] along streams; common. . . . [Has] very hard whitish wood. **1884** Sargent *Rep. Forests* 159 *Carpinus Caroliniana.* . . . Hornbeam. Blue Beech. Water Beech. Iron Wood. **1892** Apgar *Trees Northern U.S.* 151 American hornbeam, Blue or Water Beech. . . . The wood is very hard and whitish. Common along streams; sometimes cultivated.

* **Bluebell.** One or other plant having bell-shaped flowers of a blue color (see quotations).

1784 Cutler in *Mem. Academy* I. 411 *Cissus.* . . . Meadow Bluebells. . . . In moist land. Not common. September. **1806** Lewis in *L. & Clark Exped.* (1905) VI. 138 In the fore part of the day I observed the Collumbine, the blue bells [*Campanula rotundifolia*], and the yelow flowering pea in blume. **1837** Lincoln *Botany* App. 181 Blue-bell, *Campanula.* **1877** *Harper's Mag.* Jan. 287/1 Their old spicy garden, with its . . . bluebells and hollyhocks. **1892** *Amer. Folk-Lore* V. 101 *Polemonium reptans*, bluebell. Mansfield, O. **1894** *Ib.* VII. 96 *Veronica Americana*, . . . bluebells. Fort Fairfield, Me.

Blue-bellied, *a.* [Blue *a.* 3.] +*Blue-bellied Yankee*, etc. = next. — **1852** *S. Lit. Messenger* XVIII. 681/1, I'd disgrace the party—and am no better than a dratted, blue-bellied, federal whig! **1857** T. Gladstone *Englishman in Kansas* 47 To fight for . . . our glorious constitution, and rid the place of those cowardly blue-bellied Yankees. **1866** Richardson *Secret Service* viii. 111 Throw three or four shells among those blue-bellied Yankees and they will scatter like a flock of sheep. **1866** C. H. Smith *Bill Arp* 4 Did you suppose it was going to take a year to whip a parcel of blue-bellied Yankees? **1923** J. H. Cook *On Old Frontier* 14 A 'blue-bellied Yankee,' even if he were but a boy, was about the most unpopular thing in Texas at that period.

+**Blue-belly.** [Blue *a.* 2.]

1. An American or Yankee.

1827 J. Pickering *Inquiries Emigrant* (1831) 92 The inhabitants are chiefly Americans, . . . some 'I guess,' from the 'States' prison,' and some that have 'broke the limits.' . . . In short 'blue bellies' of all sorts and condition, equal to any of the frontier towns on both sides of the 'lines.' **1857** T. Gladstone *Englishman in Kansas* 43 No highfalutin' airs here, you know. Keep that for them Blue-bellies down East. *Ib.*, This here tool of mine [=a pistol], it isn't the first time it has seen a Blue-belly.

2. A soldier in blue army uniform.

In earlier use a Southern nickname for a Northern or Federal soldier during the Civil War.

1866 Richardson *Secret Service* xxv. 303 The Rebels held Fredericksburg, on the south bank. The men conversed freely across the stream. One day I heard a dialogue like this: 'Halloo, butternut!' 'Halloo, bluebelly!' **1866** 'F. Kirkland' *Bk. Anecdotes* 234/1 The door was opened, and the graybacks were not a little astonished at the sight of the 'blue bellies,' as they were pleased to call the Yankees in their sportive moods. **1871** De Vere 280 The Northerners were Yanks, or Bluebellies (from their blue uniform), or Boys in Blue. **1905** Rex Beach *Pardners* ii. 54 Well! them bodies has got to be hid, or we'll have the tribe [of Indians] and the blue-bellies from the fort a scouring these hills.

Blue-berried, *a.* [Blue *a.* 3.] Bearing blue berries. — **1785** Marshall *Amer. Grove* 39 *Cupressus Thyoides.* Maryland Blue-berried Cypress. **1813** Muhlenberg *Cat. Plants* 17 *C. sericea*, Blue-berried Swamp Dogwood. **1859** Hillhouse tr. *Michaux's Sylva* I. 178 An analysis of the bark . . . of the Blue-berried Dogwood.

+**Blueberry.** [Blue *a.* Cf. G. *blaubeere*, Du. *blauwbes.*]

1. a. The fruit of several species of *Vaccinium*, esp. *V. corymbosum;* the bilberry. **b.** One or other of the plants producing this berry. {*c*1784}

1709 Lawson *Carolina* 104 The first sort is the same Blue or Bilberry, that grows plentifully in the North of England, and in other Places. **1784** Cutler in *Mem. Academy* I. 439 *Vaccinium*, . . . the Bilberry or Blueberry. These shrubs are low when they grow on high land, but tall in swamps. **1832** Williamson *Maine* I. 93 The party . . . found as they ascended, a variety of wild fruits, such as raspberries, blue, and wortleberries. **1836** Lincoln *Bot.* App. 148 *Vaccinium pennsylvanica*, low blueberry; . . . berries large, blue, somewhat glaucous. Dry hills. N.Y. to Geo. **1842** *Lowell Offering* II. 131 We want to spread currants and blueberries on the table to be dried. **1844** S. M. Fuller *Summer on Lakes* 29 Highly-finished little blossoms, as pretty as those of the blueberry. **1847** Wood *Botany* 369 *V. uliginosum.* Mountain Blueberry. *Ib.* 370 *V. Canadense.* Canadian Blueberry. **1848** Thoreau *Maine Woods* 59 Blueberries were distributed along our whole route; . . . the bushes were drooping with the weight of the fruit. **1851** Springer *Forest Life* 203 A bed of blueberries also presented itself, and we stopped to dine upon them. **1871** *Rep. Comm. Agric.* 415 Blueberry (*Vaccinium Pennsylvanicum*) grows abundantly along the northwest coast. **1884** *Harper's Mag.* July 202/1 The bear wanders about in his search for blueberries. **1902** McFaul *Ike Glidden* xiv. 101 Blueberries grow in abundance [in Maine], and the yield of this vast vineyard is one of the most prolific in America.

2. Attrib. with *bush, flat, land, patch, plain, swamp.*

1787 Cutler in *Life*, etc. I. 278 Under the trees and on the sides of the hill, are many blueberry, whortleberry, and bilberry bushes. **1828** *Western M. Rev.* II. 206 Unenclosed and naked pastures, looking for all the world like New-England blueberry swamps. **1841** Hawthorne *Note-books* II. 33 These red spots are the blueberry and whortleberry bushes. **1866** Mrs. Whitney *L. Goldthwaite* vi, An enormous valley, . . . over whose tall pines and cedars one looked, as if they were but juniper and blueberry bushes. **1873** 'Gail Hamilton' *Twelve Miles* viii. 126 You are cutting through the . . . blueberry-swamps. **1887** *Harper's Mag.* May 938/2 We mustn't forget the blueberry patch. **1895** *Outing* Dec. 217/1 We put in the next day hunting over the blue-berry flats after bear. **1902** McFaul *Ike Glidden* vii. 45 This blueberry land seems to me to be characterized as wild land. *Ib.* 100 The blueberry plains. *Ib.* 101 This peculiar tract of land . . . is entirely covered with wild blueberry bushes.

+**Blueberrying,** *vbl. n.* [f. prec.] The gathering of blueberries. — **1861** *Harper's Mag.* Jan. 188/1 Several acres . . . had long been put to no other use than that of a general 'blue-berrying' region. **1887** *Ib.* April 791/2 Are you used to blueberrying?

+**Bluebill.** [Blue *a.* 2.] The blackhead or scaup duck.

1813 Wilson *Ornithology* VIII. 84 Scaup Duck. . . . This Duck is better known among us by the name of the Blue Bill. It is an excellent diver. **1844** *Nat. Hist. N.Y., Zoology* II. 323 It is only known on this coast under the name of Broad-bill, and more rarely Blue-bill. It is highly prized by epicures on this coast. **1861** *Ohio Acts* LVIII. 125 It shall be unlawful for any person . . . to catch . . . any wild goose, . . . blue-bill, or other wild duck. **1874** Long *Wild-Fowl* 274 Blue-bills are also very partial to over-flowed prairies and corn-fields. **1895** *Outing* Dec. 211/2 Then through the willows came a flock of blue-bill.

attrib. **1874** Long *Wild-Fowl* 273 Blue-bill shooting . . . is one of the prettiest of sports; they come in to the decoys so readily [etc.]. **1894** *Outing* April 73/1 An oft-tried sporting friend . . . had asked us to join him in a day's bluebill shooting.

+**Bluebird, Blue-bird.** [Blue *a.* 1.]

1. A songbird (*Sialia sialis*) of predominantly blue color.

1688 Clayton *Va.* in *Phil. Trans.* XVII. 996 They have a Bird they call a Blew-bird, of a curious azure colour about the bigness of a Chafinch. **1709** Lawson *Car.* 144 A Blue-Bird is the exact Bigness of a Robin-red-breast. **1774** Fithian *Journal* 121 The finest morning we have yet had; the Robbins, & blue Birds singing all around us. **1778** Anburey *Travels* II. 198 The most remarkable are the Fire-bird, Hanging-bird, Blue-bird and Humming-bird. **1808** Wilson *Ornithology* I. 56 Blue-bird . . . [is] one of the first messengers of spring. *Ib.* 62 The Blue-bird is . . . regularly seen in winter, after . . . a few days of mild and open weather. **1823** Cooper *Pioneers* xxiii, The gay and fluttering blue-bird, the social robin, and the industrious little wren, were all to be seen. *c***1825** Longfellow *Autumn* 27 Aloud From cottage roofs the warbling blue-bird sings. **1852** Mitchell *Dream Life* 34 The old year . . . lingers upon the lap of spring; and is only fairly gone, . . . when the blue-birds have chanted his requiem. **1868** *Amer. Naturalist* II. 667 The Blue-bird . . . made its appearance in Massachusetts once as early as the 15th of February. **1892** Torrey *Foot-Path Way* 179 Bluebirds are several times as abundant [in August] as in June. **1896** J. C. Harris *Sister Jane* 68 One of the first intimations [of spring] was the fluttering of a pair of bluebirds around a hollow post in the garden. **1904** Glasgow *Deliverance* 298 Ah! there's the bluebird . . . whistling in the meadow. **1904** C. W. Beebe in *N.Y. Tribune* 13 March 31 The bluebird's note will always be spring's dearest herald.

attrib. **1883** *Harper's Mag.* Oct. 710/2 A notch . . . for a bunch of bluebird feathers.

fig. **1903** Aldrich *Ponkapog Papers* 111 A shy New England bluebird [=a poetess], shifting its light load of song, has for the moment been mistaken for a stray nightingale.

b. *Rocky Mountain* or *Western bluebird:* (see quotations 1858).

1839 AUDUBON *Ornith. Biog.* V. 41 Western Blue Bird, *Sylvia Occidentalis.* The Western Blue Bird possesses many of the habits of our common kind. . . . In the small rocky prairies of the Columbia . . . I saw them in considerable numbers. **1858** BAIRD *Birds Pacific R.R.* 223 *Sialia Mexicana,* Western Blue Bird. . . . In perfectly mature males the blue of the throat is as bright as that of the crown. *Ib.* 224 *Sialia arctica,* Rocky Mountain Blue Bird. . . . Rocky mountains range and south to Mexico. **1874** COUES *Birds N.W.* 14 The Western Bluebird apparently inhabits only a limited area in the southwestern part of the Missouri region. *Ib.*, Rocky Mountain Bluebird . . . [inhabits] eastern foot-hills of the Rocky Mountains to the Pacific.

2. One serving in the Northern army during the Civil War. (Cf. BLUE *n.* 5.)

1861 [NEWELL] *Orpheus C. Kerr* I. 199, I reached the side of the Commander of the Accomac. . . . 'How are you, my blue-bird; and what do you think of this brilliant assemblage?' **1867** CRAWFORD *Mosby* 129 John Munson and Walter Whaley brought in two bluebirds, one walking and the other riding. The one riding was a guard and bearer of despatches to General Gregg's headquarters.

Blue book, Blue-book. {1715-}

+**1.** The 'Biennial Register' of information about the U.S. government.

1836 BENTON in *Deb. Congress* June 1719 An array of names more numerous . . . than was to be found in the 'Blue Book,' with the Army and Navy Register inclusive. **1840** *Niles' Nat. Reg.* 4 April 78/1 A memorial . . . setting forth that they contracted with the department of state to print and bind the last Biennial Register (or Blue Book). **1848** BARTLETT 37 *Blue-Book,* a printed book containing the names of all the persons holding office under the Government of the United States, with the amount of their pay. It answers to the Red-Book of England. [ed. 1859 adds: The distinction in color was made at the suggestion of Peter Force, Esq., of Washington.] **1880** LAMPHERE *U.S. Govt.* 192/2 The Secretary is charged with the compilation and printing, in each year in which a new congress assembles, of the Biennial Register or Blue Book of the United States. **1904** *Brooklyn Eagle* 7 Sept. 5 The bulky Blue Book of the present day . . . is in two volumes, each of more than 1,000 pages. **1912** F. J. HASKIN *Amer. Govt.* 323 A graphic illustration of the growth of the civil service of the United States is afforded by a contrast of the Government Blue Books published in 1816 and 1905. The one published in 1816 is not much larger than a child's 'reader,' and had but 176 pages. The one for 1905 had 4,219 pages.

+**2.** A register of a similar character published by various states.

1879 (*title*), The Blue Book of the State of Wisconsin for 1879. **1891** *Calif. Statutes* 31 March 454 The Secretary of State is hereby authorized to compile, publish, and distribute one thousand copies of a State Blue Book or Roster. **1915** (*title*), The Nebraska Blue Book and Historical Register.

+**3.** A directory of persons of social prominence.

1882 HOWELLS *Modern Instance* xxi, I suppose you won't refuse to come because I don't ask the whole Blue Book to meet them. **1890** (*title*), The Chicago Blue Book of Selected Names. **1893** POST *Harvard Stories* 51 Reader, dost thou know aught of the ancient town of Boston? If not, look some time into a Boston Blue Book, open anywhere, and see what Holworthy saw.

+**4.** A directory of a business or a professional class.

1895 (*title*), Blue Book: Official Directory of the Practicing Dental Profession of Chicago, Ill. **1896** *Blue Bk. Amer. Shipping* 2 Patrons of the Blue Book are privileged to ask . . . for any information that we may have in hand. **1909** (*title*), Manufacturers' Record's Annual Blue Book of Southern Progress.

+**5.** A blank book having a blue cover, freq. used in examinations.

1893 POST *Harvard Stories* 240 Jack . . . walked up to the desk at the end of the [examination] room, and put his blue book on the pile of others. **1897** FLANDRAU *Harvard Episodes* 106 Sears . . . consumed them all [=history facts] like an ogre at his dinner . . . until he could disgorge . . . the facts of five hundred years on his blue book.

***Bluebottle.**

***1.** The blue cornflower, *Centaurea cyanus.*

1817-18 EATON *Botany* (1822) 230 *Centaurea cyanus,* blue bottle. **1828** WEBSTER, *Blue-bottle,* a plant, a species of Centaurea, called Cyanus, which grows among corn. **1840** DEWEY *Mass. Flowering Plants* 141 Blue Bottle [is] a common ornamental flower in gardens, . . . partially naturalized. **1847** DARLINGTON *Weeds & Plants* 194 Blue Centaurea, Blue-bottle, . . . is often seen in gardens, and in some places is gradually straggling into the cultivated fields. **1857** GRAY *Botany* 232 Bluebottle . . . [grows on] road-sides, escaped from gardens. July.

2. The blue flesh fly or meat fly, *Musca vomitoria.* {c1720-} Freq. *bluebottle fly.*

[**1824** IRVING *Bracebridge Hall* II. 199 The buzzing of a stout blue-bottle fly.] **1837** BIRD *Nick of Woods* I. 218 The squabbling of seed-ticks and blue-bottle flies. **1859** [see BLOW-FLY]. **1872** *Newton* (Kansas) *Kansan* 19 Sept. 4/3 The unerring instinct of a blue bottle-fly in pursuit of tainted meat. **1885** CRADDOCK *Prophet* x. 179 The drone of a blue-bottle, fluttering in and out of the window. **1888** *Outing* May 105 Myriads of blue-bottles . . . ready to pounce on fish or flesh and deposit their eggs.

+**Blue bream.** [BLUE *a.* 1.] (See quotation.) — **1888** GOODE *Amer. Fishes* 67 The Blue Sun-fish, *Lepomis pallidus,* is also known as the 'Blue Bream.'

+**Blue cat, Blue-cat.** [BLUE *a.* 1 b.] A kind of catfish. — **1835** MARTIN *Descr. Va.* 347 This river is also remarkable for its fine fish, particularly the mud and blue cat, which are very much celebrated among travellers for their fine flavor and astonishing size. **1855** SIMMS *Forayers* 275 In this sat a youth, . . . fishing for blue-cat and perch. . . . The blue-cat of the Edisto is one of the nicest fish that swims. **1889** *Cent.* 852/3 *Blue cat,* . . . a local name in the United States of the channel catfish. *Ictalurus punctatus.*

+**Blue catfish.** [BLUE *a.* 1 b.] (See quotations and cf. prec.) — **1836** KIRTLAND in *Ohio Geol. Survey* 169 *Pimelobus cerulescens,* Rafinesque; Blue Cat-fish. *Ib.* 194 The blue catfish is common to the Ohio and the lake waters, and is universally known. **1836** HOLLEY *Texas* v. 101 Yellow, white and blue catfish are furnished commonly by the rivers and streams in this country.

+**Blue chickens:** see BLUE HEN 1, quot. 1840.

+**Blue claw.** *local.* [BLUE *a.* 2.] A species of crab. — **1807** *Mass. H. S. Coll.* 2 Ser. III. 58 There is the large crab, called here [Dukes Co., Mass.] the blue claw.

Blue clay. A common variety of clay, of a bluish color. Also attrib.

1778 CARVER *Travels* 101 This country likewise abounds with a milk white clay, . . . and also with a blue clay that serves the Indians for paint. **1799** DE WITT in *Mem. Academy* II. II. 79 A curious annular stone . . . in the centre of a bed of blue clay. **1806** *Ann. 9th Congress* 2 Sess. 1121 On digging through about four feet of blue clay, the salt water oozed from a quicksand. **1836** HOLLEY *Texas* ii. 33 The substratum beneath the sand of the bar is blue clay, as is also that between the bar and the beach. **1840** *S. Lit. Messenger* VI. 192/2 The fossil bones of the blue clay stratum, are manifestly antediluvian. **1843** N. BOONE *Journal* 204 The only out crop of rock passed over was a sort of blue clay slate dipping to the S.W. **1879** *Scribner's Mo.* Dec. 242/2 Then I excavated great deep holes, but came to a blue clay that held water like rubber.

***Bluecoat.** [BLUE *a.* 2.]

1. One wearing a blue coat as part of a military uniform. {1699}

+In later use either one serving in the army of the United States, or, during the Civil War, one of the Northern troops.

(1) **1676** TOMPSON *Poet. Works* 57 Thither retir'd The stragling blew-coats when their guns were fir'd. **1686** SEWALL *Diary* I. 165 Suppose this to be the first Funeral Govr. Andros has been at, Blew-Coats going before him. **1687** *Ib.* 193 His Excellency with Sundry of the Council, Justices and other Gentlemen, four Blew-coats, two Trumpeters . . . set forth for Woodcocks. **1723** *New-Eng. Courant* 7 Jan. 1/1 All Persons are hereby caution'd to be very circumspect, with respect to their Discourse, when in Company with a certain Blue Coat Feather-Cap.

(2) **1833** CATLIN *Indians* I. 240 The United States and British governments . . . paid them [*sc.* Indians] . . . for every 'scalp' of a 'red' or a 'blue coat' they could bring in! **1851** GLISAN *Jrnl. Army Life* 87 The latter threaten to . . . drive the blue-coats out of the country. **1868** *Putnam's Mag.* June 705/1 A soldier's marriage . . . is frequently but a temporary contract. . . . Occasionally a female of decent connections espouses a blue-coat. **1880** *Harper's Mag.* Dec. 31 Successive companies of soldiers had vainly fought the climate in an agricultural way, red-coats of England and blue-coats of the United States.

(3) **1865** G. W. NICHOLS *Story Gt. March* 154 So we jogged on for awhile and then . . . we descried a blue coat and a white-eared mule approaching. **1866** 'F. KIRKLAND' *Bk. Anecdotes* 137 'It's very well to tell me that, with all those blue-coats coming up the hill; but were you not all Secesh yesterday?' 'No, Sir! we were always Union.' **1879** TOURGEE *Fool's Errand* xxi. 122 But only wait until . . . the 'Blue Coats' are out of the way. **1887** GEORGE *40 Yrs. on Rail* 103 In a few days the country was filled with volunteers. My train began to carry the 'blue coats.'

+**b.** *colloq.* A policeman.

1875 *Chicago Tribune* 29 Aug. 5/4 Occasionally one of the blue coats would attempt to put back the crowd, but they would not be put back. **1878** PINKERTON *Strikers,* etc. (1884) 400 The rioters . . . clambered to the tops of houses and hurled stones upon the blue-coats. **1890** *Buckskin Mose* xiii. 203 As the boys were dismounting for active business, a blue-coat suddenly appeared upon the scene. **1903** A. H. LEWIS *The Boss* 15 With that, the bluecoat seized Sheeny Joe, and there we were, one in each of his hands.

+**2.** A bluish color of the coat in deer at a certain time of the year. Cf. BLUE *n.* 8.

1870 *Amer. Naturalist* May 190 The spike-horn was shot just as deer were attaining the 'blue coat.'

Blue-coated, *a.* [BLUE *a.* 3.] Wearing a blue coat (+as part of the Federal uniform). {1691-}

1869 TOURGEE *Toinette* xl. (1881) 408 Was his intense Southern pride to be thus baffled and humbled . . . by the blue-coated surgeon? **1882** *Uncle Rufus & Ma* 55 On its very verge was a white tent, before which paced a blue-coated soldier. *a***1892** M. A. Jackson *Gen. Jackson* 382 In front . . . you see the blue-coated Federal lines extended, well-armed, well-equipped.

+**Blue cohosh.** [BLUE *a.* 1.]

1. A perennial herb (*Caulophyllum thalictroides*), reputed to have medicinal properties.

1821 *Mass. H. S. Coll.* 2 Ser. IX. 148 Plants, which are indigenous in the township of Middlebury, [Vermont, include] . . . *Caulophyllum thalictroides*, Blue cohosh. **1843** TORREY *Flora N.Y.* I. 33 Blue Cohosh. Pappoose root. . . . *Leontice thalictroides*. . . . The root . . . is in some repute as a diuretic and bitter. **1857** GRAY *Botany* 20 Blue Cohosh. . . . Also called Pappoose-root. . . . [Grows in] deep rich woods. **1859** BARTLETT 91 Black Cohosh . . . [is] a well-known medicinal plant. There are also White and Blue Cohosh, other allied plants. **1889** *Cent.* s.v. *Caulophyllum*, The American species, . . . known as blue cohosh, is reputed to have medicinal properties.

2. (See quotation.)

1901 MOHR *Plant Life Ala.* 517 *Caulophyllum thalictroides*. . . . The rhizoma and roots are the blue cohosh of medicine.

+**Blue crab.** [BLUE *a.* 1.] An edible crab of a blue color belonging to the genus *Callinectes*, esp. *C. sapidus* or *C. hastatus*, found on the Atlantic coast. — **1883** RATHBUN in *U.S. Museum Bulletin 27* 109 The most valuable of these are the Blue Crab (*Callinectes hastatus*), Lady Crab [etc.]. *Ib.*, The Blue Crab is the common edible crab of the Atlantic Coast, and ranges from Massachusetts Bay to the Gulf of Mexico. **1883** GOODE *Fisheries U.S.* 20 With the exception of the oyster, the clams, the lobster and the blue-crab, the value of these is at present not fully realised.

+**Blue crane.** [BLUE *a.* 1.] The blue heron.

1781–2 JEFFERSON *Notes Va.* (1788) 74 *Ardea caerulea*, . . . Blue heron [or] Crane. **1806** CLARK in *Lewis & C. Exped.* (1905) IV. 139 The large Blue . . . Herons or crains as they are usialy [*sic*] called in the U. States. **1813** WILSON *Ornithology* VII. 117 Blue Crane, or Heron, . . . [often seen] on the muddy shores of the Mississippi, from Baton Rouge downwards to New Orleans. **1835** AUDUBON *Ornith. Biog.* III. 87 Great Blue Heron. . . . The 'Blue Crane' (by which name this species is generally known in the United States) is met with in every part of the Union. **1869** *Amer. Naturalist* III. 401 The great Blue Crane . . . [is] found in this part of the state [Florida] around the shores of the bay and gulf.

+**Blue curls.** [BLUE *a.* 2.]

1. The bastard pennyroyal, *Trichostema dichotomum*.

1817 EATON *Botany* (1822) 490 *Trichostema dichotoma*, blue curls. **1840** DEWEY *Mass. Flowering Plants* 180 Blue Curls . . . [grow in] pastures and hills of light soil; June. **1859** BARTLETT 37 *Blue curls*. . . . From the shape and color of its flowers. A common plant resembling pennyroyal, and hence called bastard pennyroyal. **1863** *Rep. Comm. Agric.* 160 The 'Blue Curls' . . . abounds in most grain fields, blooming in August. **1901** MOHR *Plant Life Ala.* 707 Common Blue Curls . . . [grow in] sandy fields and pastures.

b. (See quotation.)

1901 MOHR *Plant Life Ala.* 707 *Trichostema lineare*, . . . Linear-leaved Blue Curls; . . . [frequent in] sandy pastures, borders of fields, dry copses.

2. The self-heal or heal-all, *Brunella vulgaris*.

1847 WOOD *Botany* 424 Self-heal. Blue curls. A very common plant, in meadows and low grounds. **1894** *Amer. Folk-Lore* VII. 96 *Brunella vulgaris*, . . . blue curls; somewhat general.

+**Blue dangle(s).** =Blue tangle(s). — **1861** WOOD *Botany* 481 *Gaylussacia frondosa*. . . . Blue Dangles. . . . Grows in open woods, N. Eng. to Fla. and La. . . . May, Jn.

Blue devil, *n.* {1616}

+**1.** As a plant-name (see quotations).

1847 DARLINGTON *Weeds & Plants* 242 Blue-weed. Viper's Bugloss. Blue Devils. . . . Fields and road-sides: introduced. Native of Europe. **1894** *Amer. Folk-Lore* VII. 95 *Echium vulgare*, . . . blue devils, blue weed; Iowa. *Ib.* 91 *Aster cordifolius*. . . . Blue Devil, stick-weed, bee-weed, Fall Aster; West Va.

+**2.** One of those who took part in the cutting of fences in Texas in 1883.

1884 *Nation* 24 Jan. 65/1 The fence-cutters, or 'blue devils,' as they are called, represent the primitive Texas of the ante-bellum period. *Ib.* 65/2 It is evident that the blue devils . . . are endeavoring to give the fence war the air of a struggle between poverty and banded wealth.

+**Blue devil,** *v. tr.* To make despondent. *colloq.* — **1836** in *Journal of Southern History* (1935) I. 364 To be hemmed up in a strange place without . . . anything to interest you, expecting every minute to get off and every minute disappointed, is enough to Blue Devil one.

+**Blue dog. 1.** *Jersey Blue Dog* =JERSEY BLUE. **2.** (See quotation 1875.) — **(1) 1798** *Aurora* (Philad.) 13 Dec. (Th.), They said I was a Jarzy Blue Dog, and they would cut my head off. **(2) 1875** *Chicago Tribune* 24 Aug. 6/1 'Blue Dog' was a State issue for canal extension. **1893** *Congress. Rec.* 25 Aug. 936/2 Then we had the Michigan wild-cat money; then we had throughout Indiana, Illinois, and Ohio what is known as blue-dog and yellow-pup.

Blue dyer. One who dyes fabrics blue. — **1788** *Kentucky Gazette* 15 March 1/3 The subscriber . . . has set up the blue diers business . . . and will take in Hemp, Flax and Cotton thread to dye. **1809** F. CUMING *Western Tour* 164 There is one excellent umbrella manufactory. . . . Three blue-dyers. Five hatters [etc.]. *Ib.* 223 Pittsburgh [has] . . . thirteen weavers; ten blue-dyers.

Blue-eyed, *a.* [BLUE *a.* 3.]

+**1.** Denoting a species of warbler.

1810 WILSON *Ornithology* II. 111 Blue-Eyed Yellow Warbler, *Sylvia Citrinella*. . . . This is a very common summer species. . . . It arrives in Pennsylvania about the beginning of May. **1828** BONAPARTE *Synopsis* 83 The Blue-eyed Yellow Warbler . . . inhabits North America as high as the Arctic circle during summer: very common.

+**2. a.** *Blue-eyed grass*, one or other species of iridaceous grass-like plants of the genus *Sisyrinchium* with small, delicate blue flowers.

1784 CUTLER in *Mem. Academy* I. 487 *Sisyrinchium*. . . . Blue-Eyed Grass. Blossoms blue. In grass lands. . . . It makes very pretty edging for borders in gardens. **1818** *Mass. H. S. Coll.* 2 Ser. VIII. 169 Among those that flower in June, the most interesting are . . . two species of crowfoot, the blue-eyed grass. **1840** DEWEY *Mass. Flowering Plants* 195 Blue-eyed Grass . . . growing over pastures and upland meadows, with a few fine blue flowers. . . . July. **1843** TORREY *Flora N.Y.* II. 291 *Sisyrinchium Bermudiana*, . . . Common Blue-eyed Grass. . . . In moist meadows, among grass, and in woods. **1869** FULLER *Flower Gatherers* 127 'That will separate them,' said Uncle John, 'and put the little . . . blue-eyed grass into the family of *Irida*.' **1894** TORREY *Fla. Sketch-Book* 30 Beside the railway track were blue-eyed grass and pipewort. **1901** MOHR *Plant Life Ala.* 450 *Sisyrinchium graminoides*, Stout Blue-eyed Grass, . . . [grows] in grassy pine woods. **1923** CATHER *Lost Lady* ii. 17 The blue-eyed grass was in purple flower.

+**b.** (See quotations.)

1892 *Amer. Folk-Lore* V. 97 *Houstonia cœrulea*, blue-eyed babies. Springfield, Mass. **1894** *Ib.* VII. 96 *Collinsia verna*, . . . blue-eyed Marys. Anderson, Ind.

+**3.** *slang.* Inebriated.

*a***1856** *Burlington Sentinel* in Hall *Coll. Words* (ed. 2) 461 Words and phrases which have been in use . . . to signify some stage of inebriation [include] . . . fogmatic, blue-eyed, a passenger in the Cape-Ann stage.

+**Blue-fin.** 'A local name in the United States of the lake-herring or whitefish of Lake Michigan, *Coregonus nigripinnis*' (*Cent.*). — **1884** GOODE *Fisheries U.S.* I. 541 The 'Blue-fin' or 'Black-fin' . . . has . . . been taken only in the deeper waters of Lake Michigan.

Bluefish, Blue-fish. [BLUE *a.* 1.]

+**1.** A common salt-water fish (*Pomatomus saltatrix*) with a bluish back.

*c***1622** PORY *Plymouth & New Eng.* (1918) 39 As concerning the blew fish, in delicacie it excelleth all kinde of fish that ever I tasted. [**1639** *Plymouth Col. Rec.* XI. 34 To erect wares to take fish at Mortons hole, Blewfish Riuer.] **1672** JOSSELYN *New Eng. Rarities* 96 Blew fish, or Horse. I did never see any of them in England; they are as big usually as the Salmon, and better Meat by far: It is common in New-England and esteemed the best sort of Fish next to Rock Cod. **1675** — *Two Voy. New-Eng.* 141 The Bass and Blew-fish they take in harbours. **1709** LAWSON *Carolina* 155 The Blue-Fish . . . come (in the fall of the year). . . . They are called Blue-Fish, because they are of that Colour, and have a forked Tail, and are shaped like a Dolphin. **1714** J. HEMPSTEAD *Diary* 38 Wm. Pendal . . . fell out of a small Boat in the horserace catching bluefish. **1792** *Mass. H.S. Coll.* III. 159 A large fat fish, called the blue fish, thirty of which would fill a barrel, was caught in great plenty all round the island. **1837** *Knickerb.* IX. 345 A group of blue fish had gathered just before him. **1844** *Ib.* XXIV. 482 Better still I love, . . . With hempen string and bait of fat manhaden To throw for bass or blue-fish. **1858** VIELÉ *Following the Drum* 92 We caught a number of blue-fish, and of course cat-fish. **1870** *Amer. Naturalist* IV. 519 The Bluefish . . . which inhabits our waters from the last of June till September, has had very marked periodic variations in numbers. **1880** *Harper's Mag.* July 210/2 We went out into the channel, . . . and came back with thirty odd blue-fish. **1886** *Leslie's Mo.* Feb. 206 There was a dinner of savory chowder, baked blue-fish, hot corncake and coffee. **1891** *Scribner's Mag.* X. 211 His instinct of the whereabouts of the blue-fish was unerring. **1897** *Outing* Sept. 546/1 The captain and I have trolled and chummed for bluefish.

+**2.** Applied to various other fishes, as the weakfish and sea bass.

1814 MITCHILL *Fishes N.Y.* 424 Horse Mackerel. (*Scomber plumbeus.*) With . . . colour of the head and body such that they often call him blue-fish. **1819** *Western Rev.* I. 376 *Ichthelis cyanella*, . . . a small species hardly three inches, called Blue-fish or Sunfish. I found it on the Ohio at the falls. Appearing entirely blue at a distance. **1855** BAIRD in *Smithsonian Rep.* 329 Squeteague, Blue Fish, . . . as a table fish, . . . is very much inferior to almost any other captured on the coast. **1859** BARTLETT 37 On the Jersey coast, the name *Blue-fish* is applied to the Weak-fish, or Squeteague. **1871** *Amer. Naturalist* V. 398 At Great Egg Harbor [N.J.] . . . Weak-fish (*Cynoscion regalis*) [is] called 'Blue-fish.' **1888** GOODE *Amer. Fishes* 39 In the Middle States the Sea Bass is called 'Black Will,' . . . about Newport and New Bedford, 'Bluefish.'

+**3.** *Blue-fish shark*, ?the blue shark.

1856 *Spirit of Times* (N.Y.) 29 Nov. 205/1 It was a shoal of blue sharks, or blue-fish sharks, and the tail of the one caught by us was shaped precisely like that of a horse-mackerel.

+**Bluefisher.** [f. prec.] (See quotation.) — **1898** *Boston Transcript* 9 April 9/6 Bluefisher, (as the boats engaged in catching this class of fish are officially known).

+**Bluefishing.** [f. as prec.] Fishing for bluefish.
1860 *Harper's Mag.* July 194/2 Us . . . who spent three or four weeks at Muskeogue every summer for the sake of the bluefishing. **1880** *Ib.* Sept. 590 Three [children] had been lost in a boat out blue-fishing. **1882** GODFREY *Nantucket* 146 Come here to Nantucket, . . . and go out for a day's sport,—either bluefishing, sharking, or scupping, or all combined. **1886** *Outing* Oct. 73/2 From him we learned . . . that the best bluefishing was to be had right there. **1897** *Ib.* Sept. 546 [Article on] Bluefishing off Fire Island.

+**Blue flag.** [BLUE *a.* 1.]

1. One or other of two species of wild iris, *Iris versicolor* and *Virginica.*
1784 CUTLER in *Mem. Academy* I. 406 *Iris*, . . . Blue Flag. . . . A decoction of the fresh roots is a powerful cathartic. **1821** *Jrnl. Science* III. 277 Calendar for Plainfield, Mass. . . . June 9. . . . Common iris or blue flag in flower. **1832** WILLIAMSON *Maine* I. 123 The blue Flag (or flower-de-luce) . . . sends up a stem 3 feet high. . . . Its root . . . is an active cathartic and an Indian diuretic. **1840** DEWEY *Mass. Flowering Plants* 194 Blue or Poison Flag. Common on wet grounds, and about sluggish water. **1855** SIMMS *Forayers* 485 The yellow and purple saracenia, and the blue flag, you will gather along the swamp. **a1862** THOREAU *Maine Woods* 212 In the water on the meadows grew . . . the common blue-flag abundantly, its flower just showing itself above the high water, as if it were a blue water-lily. **1880** *Harper's Mag.* June 70 We see the frog pond with lush growth of arrow leaves and . . . flat blades of blue-flag. **1904** WALLER *Wood-carver* 114 The great blue-flag is found there three and four feet high.
attrib. **1869** FULLER *Flower Gatherers* 91 Shall we not have time to examine this blue-flag blossom today? **1881** *Harper's Mag.* Sept. 585/2 A few weeks ago we were dressing the skiff with wild roses and blue-flag flowers. **1901** MOHR *Plant Life Ala.* 449 *Iris versicolor*, Blue Flag. . . . The rhizoma, under the name of 'blue flag root,' is used medicinally.

2. (See quot. 1889.)
1861 H. MACARTHY *Song, The Bonnie Blue Flag* i, Hurrah for the Bonnie Blue Flag that bears a Single Star! **1870** LOGAN *Before Footlights* 229, I would have sung the Bonny Blue Flag with joy, . . . if I had been acquainted with . . . the words. **1889** FARMER 75 *Bonny Blue Flag*, the Blue Flag, the standard of the Confederates, was thus affectionately named. Round it gathered the whole sentiment and earnestness of the Southern cause.

Blue fly. [BLUE *a.* 1.] A bluebottle fly. {1759}
1836 *Knickerb.* VIII. 395 You might hear the blue-flies, with their droning hum, all day in the air. **1848** J. S. ROBINSON *Santa Fé Exped.* 70 Deliver me from that Mexican plague the blue fly. **1856** STOWE *Dred* I. xii. 163 He just puts me in mind of one of these blue-flies, whirring and whisking about. **1905** VALENTINE *H. Sandwith* 147 Above the general noises could be heard the brassy buzz of blue flies.

Blue fox. [BLUE *a.* 1.] A variety of the Arctic fox; the fur of this. {1863} — **1865** *Atlantic Mo.* XV. 211 'Here's a'—hawk, I thought he said, and caught up my gun. But what? Fox? Yes,—'blue fox.'

+**Blue gentian.** [BLUE *a.* 1.] **1.** False pennyroyal. **2.** One or other species of the genus *Gentiana* having blue flowers; the fringed gentian or the soapwort gentian. — **1817-8** EATON *Botany* (1822) 320 *Isanthus cœruleus*, blue gentian, false pennyroyal. Along the Hudson. . . . Odour resembles the spikenard. **1824** BRYANT *November* 7 The blue gentian-flower, that, on the breeze, Nods lonely. **1869** FULLER *Flower Gatherers* 289 We . . . sat down to examine a common Blue Gentian, while they explored the marsh. **1880** *Harper's Mag.* Sept. 557 See how eyes shine out from fair young faces In gentians blue, that catch the thistle's feather.

+**Blue grama (grass).** [BLUE *a.* 1.] Mesquite grass (*Bouteloua oligostachya*) and other low grasses of the Southwest. — **1872** BOURKE *Journal* December 15 Hills today well grassed with blue and white gramma. **1885** HAVARD *Flora W. & S. Texas* 528 Common or Blue Grama . . . grows everywhere throughout Texas, wherever grass can fairly grow. . . . It forms a large proportion of the hay . . . and is considered the best obtainable. **1894** *Amer. Folk-Lore* VII. 104 *Bouteloua oligostachya*, . . . blue grama grass; Neb.

+**Blue grass, Blue-grass.** [BLUE *a.* 1.]

1. A field grass (*Poa pratensis*), characteristic especially of Kentucky and Virginia; June grass. Also the wire grass, *Poa compressa.*
1751 GIST *Journals* 47 All the Way from the Shannoah Town to this Place . . . is well watered, . . . full of beautiful natural Meadows, covered with wild Rye, blue Grass and Clover. **1751** ELIOT *Field-Husb.* iii. 61 The Land that you would improve this way, must be intirely free from Blue Grass, called by some Dutch Grass, or Wire Grass. **1784** *Md. Jrnl.* 17 Aug., Advt. (Th.), This land lies open to the barrens, where there are many hundred acres without timber, and thick set with blue grass. **1792** IMLAY *Western Territory* 207 The latter kinds [of grass] . . . form excellent pastures; and are also capable of being made into hay, particularly the spear and blue grass. **1805-9** HENRY *Camp. Quebec* 168 The production of a basket-full of the ordinary blue-grass of our country. **1835** HOFFMAN *Winter in West* II. 130 This was the grazing portion of the farm, and the hardy blue grass, even thus early, afforded a rich sward beneath the boughs. **1847** L. COLLINS *Kentucky* 494 Lands . . . well adapted for grasses of all kinds, and particularly the blue grass, the favorite of stock raisers. **1868** *Mich. Agric. Rep.* VII. 99 The field had been used as meadow; the herbage consisting of a mixture of clover, timothy and blue grass. **1873** BEADLE *Undevel. West* 656, I found good blue grass, which is very rare everywhere in the Rocky mountains. **1889** *Harper's Mag.* Jan. 259/1 The blue-grass . . . blooms toward the middle of June in a bluish, almost a peacock blue, blossom, which gives to the fields an exquisite hue. **1898** *Congress. Rec.* March 2417/2 The blue grass of Kentucky, which when more grazed is always better.

b. With distinguishing term: (see quotations).
1864 *Ohio Agric. Rep.* XVIII. 461 Under and near the peach trees were noticed the leaves of the Ohio Blue Grass (*Poa pratense*). **1882** *Rep. Comm. Agric.* 231 The *Poa arachnifera*, locally called Texas blue grass, has been known for many years as one of the native grasses of Texas. **1885** HAVARD *Flora W. & S. Texas* 530 Other grasses highly prized for pasture or hay . . . [include] Texas Blue Grass, . . . , native on the prairies of the Brazos. **1889** *Cent.* s.v., The red-topped blue-grass of Montana and westward is *Poa tenuifolia*. **1901** MOHR *Plant Life Ala.* 384 *Poa compressa*, English Blue Grass. . . . Valuable pasture grass. *Ib.* 826 *Poa compressa*, Canada Blue Grass. Prairie region and northward, [grown] for pasture.

2. The region of the blue grass; *spec.* the state of Kentucky.
1871 DE VERE 407 Both the region where it grows naturally, and the settlers there, are known as *Blue-Grass* simply, and hence the State of Kentucky is often thus designated. **1886** Z. F. SMITH *Kentucky* 199 By a kind of natural selection, the first Kentuckians took and held the 'Blue-grass.' **1894** *Outing* June 275/1 'In old Fayette,' the heart of the Blue-grass, in the grand old commonwealth of Kentucky. **1897** BRODHEAD *Bound in Shallows* 17 Even her I don't see much of; she's mostly visiting her kin in the blue grass.

3. Attrib. with *country, county, land, pasture, region,* etc.
(1) **1823** DEWEES *Lett. from Texas* 35 The musquit grass grows very thick and about three feet high, and looks very much like a blue grass pasture. **1842** *Cultivator* IX. 82 In the latter part of November I turned this stock on a blue grass pasture of about two hundred acres. **1872** EGGLESTON *Hoosier Schoolm.* v. 60 They took the usual short-cut through the 'blue-grass pasture.' **1879** *Congress. Rec.* 12 April 402/1 The most valuable herds of cattle . . . are to be found in the 'blue grass' pastures of that State [=Ky.]. **1901** MOHR *Plant Life Ala.* 824 North of the Tennessee river the establishment of the blue grass pasture becomes possible.
(2) **1867** 'E. KIRKE' *On Border* xvii. 238 He was in an 'opening' of the bluegrass region. **1884** *Meteorological Journal* I. 8 An especially severe tornado passed over the Kentucky bluegrass region. **1888** P. H. SHERIDAN *Memoirs* I. 192 Orders were issued for an advance upon the enemy with . . . the hope of destroying him within the limits of the 'blue grass' region, and, failing in that, to drive him from Kentucky.
(3) **1883** *Harper's Mag.* Oct. 715/1 The blue-grass country is reached by traversing central Virginia and Kentucky. **1897** *Outing* Sept. 627/2 There are magnificent pictures of the Kentucky mountains; the rare beauty of the blue grass country.
(4) **1884** *Rep. Comm. Agric.* 201 The other cattle . . . which were examined were pastured on 160 acres of blue-grass land. **1895** *Century Mag.* Aug. 621/2 One of the many knobs from which Daniel Boone is said to have looked first over the Blue Grass land.
(5) **1880** *Harper's Mag.* Sept. 645/1 The following amusing examination recently occurred in a court-room in one of the Blue Grass counties of Kentucky. **1886** *Ib.* Sept. 541/2 They were highly approved, and bred to the native cows of the 'blue-grass' counties.
(6) **1856-7** D. OWEN *Geol. Survey Ky.* (B.), We even hear the inhabitants of this part of Kentucky frequently styled 'Blue-grass men' in contra-distinction to the 'Mountain men,' residents of the adjacent hill and mountain country. **1883** *Harper's Mag.* Oct. 721 The theory of breeding [horses] upon which the leading blue-grass residents are mainly agreed in their practice. **1894** *Outing* June 279/1 The Bluegrass gentleman, like his English forefather, must own an estate. *Ib.*, As a people, the Blue-grass Kentuckians are distinctively cultivated.

b. Attrib. with *farm, hay, meadow, seed, sod,* etc.
1772 *Penna. Gazette* 16 April 4/3 Timothy and blue grass hay to be sold. **1788** WASHINGTON *Diaries* III. 322, I sowed 3½ bushels of Blue grass Seeds. **1861-2** *Ill. Agric. Soc. Trans.* V. 212 A stiff blue grass sod is not as conducive to the growth of an orchard tree as might be. *Ib.* 213 They swept the timothy and blue grass meadows and pastures clean. **1887** E. B. CUSTER *Tenting on Plains* 340 A Blue-grass farm with blooded horses, etc., . . . was my husband's ideal home.

c. *The Blue Grass State*, Kentucky.
1889 FARMER 68 Kentucky . . . thus derives its name of the Blue Grass State. **1907** *Springfield W. Repub.* 3 Oct. 3 Missouri, which adjoins the Blue Grass state along a stretch of the Mississippi river.

4. *ellipt.* as *adj.* Belonging to or in the blue grass country; having the characteristics of this.
1889 *Harper's Mag.* Aug. 459/2 Bud rode into the yard on Mollie. . . . 'Blue-grass all over. I wonder how he came by her.' **1913** STRATTON-PORTER *Laddie* x. 274 There's a strain of Arab in the father, . . . and the mother is bluegrass.

‖**Bluegrassdom.** The blue grass region; =BLUE GRASS 2. — **1887** *Courier-Journal* 19 Feb. 6/7 The first time people in Bluegrassdom were ever assessed for anything like what they are worth.

+**Bluegravel.** *Mining.* (See quotation.) — **1874** RAYMOND *6th Rep. Mines* 15 The term 'blue-gravel' has come into general use among hydraulic miners, to distinguish . . . the lower and richer portions [of a deposit] which have often, but not always, a peculiar bluish color.

Blue-gray, -grey, *a.* +Used to denote certain species of birds.

1810 WILSON *Ornithology* II. 164 [The] Small Blue Grey Flycatcher, *Muscicapa Caerulea*, . . . is a very dexterous Flycatcher. **1831** AUDUBON *Ornith. Biog.* I. 431 The Blue-grey Fly-catcher arrives in the neighbourhood of New Orleans about the middle of March. **1844** *Nat. Hist. N.Y., Zoology* II. 92 The Blue-Grey Warbler, *Sylvicola cærulea*, . . . reaches Louisiana from Mexico in the spring. **1874** COUES *Birds N.W.* 17 *Polioptila Cærulea*, . . . Blue-gray Gnat-catcher.

+**Blue grosbeak.** [BLUE *a.* 1.] A scarce variety of grosbeak, *Guiraca cærulea.*

*c***1729** CATESBY *Carolina* I. 39 The blue Gross-beak. . . . I have not seen any of these Birds in any parts of America but Carolina. **1781–2** JEFFERSON *Notes Va.* (1788) 75 *Coccothraustes cærulea*, . . . Blue grass [*sic*] beak. **1811** WILSON *Ornithology* III. 78 Blue Grosbeak. *Loxia Cærulea*. . . . In the United States . . . it is a scarce species. **1839** AUDUBON *Ornith. Biog.* V. 508 The Blue Grosbeak extends to the Rocky Mountains. . . . I found it abundant and breeding in the Texas. **1857** *Rep. Comm. Patents: Agric.* 125 The blue-grosbeak is a somewhat rare bird. It arrives in the lower parts of Louisiana about the middle of March. **1874** COUES *Birds N.W.* 169 *Goniaphea Cærulea*, . . . Blue Grosbeak. *Hab.*—United States, southerly, from Atlantic to Pacific. **1882** *Century Mag.* Jan. 359/2 Of these birds, all except the . . . blue grosbeak are familiar summer songsters throughout the Middle and Eastern States.

+**Blue grouse.** [BLUE *a.* 1.] A variety of grouse, *Tetrao obscurus.* — **1860** in Coues *Birds N.W.* 395 This bird, called generally in Oregon the Blue Grouse, and also known as the Pine Grouse, Dusky Grouse, &c. **1874** GLISAN *Jrnl. Army Life* 493 There is an abundance of game along the coast, such as . . . white-fronted goose, blue grouse, quail. **1888** ROOSEVELT in *Century Mag.* June 210/1 There were many grouse in the woods, of three kinds,—blue, spruce, and ruffed.

+**Bluehead.** *slang.* Intoxicating liquor. — **1856** *Spirit of Times* (N.Y.) 6 Sept. 7/1, I thought I would ask you if you wouldn't swallow a 'slug' of Carthage blue-head.

Blue-headed, *a.* [BLUE *a.* 3.] +Used to designate certain species or varieties of birds.

1858 BAIRD *Birds Pacific R.R.* 340 *Vireo solitarius*, Blue-headed Flycatcher. *Ib.* 608 *Starnoenas cyanocephala*, Blue-headed Pigeon. **1872** COUES *Key* 120 Blue-headed or Solitary Vireo. **1874** — *Birds N.W.* 199 *Scolecophagus Cyanocephalus*, . . . Blue-headed Grackle. **1889** *Cent.* 1419/3 The blue crow of North America, . . . *Gymnocitta cyanocephala*, . . . [is] also called blue-headed jay or piñon jay. **1892** TORREY *Foot-path Way* 244 Solitary (or blue-headed) Vireo.

+**Bluehearts.** A perennial plant (*Buchnera americana*) with purple flowers, or a related species.

1817 EATON *Botany* (1822) 213 *B. americana*, blue hearts. **1843** TORREY *Flora N.Y.* II. 39 Blue Hearts. . . . [grows in] moist meadows. **1861** WOOD *Botany* 528 Blue-hearts. . . . N.Y. to Ga. and La. . . . Blackens in drying. **1901** MOHR *Plant Life Ala.* 728 *Buchnera americana*. . . . Blue-hearts. [Grows in] dry open woods. . . . Flowers violet, May to July. *Ib.*, *Buchnera elongata*. . . . Southern Blue-hearts. . . . [Grows in] dry pine woods. . . . Flowers violet to deep blue.

+**Blue Hen.** [BLUE *a.* 1.]

Alleged to have originated from the insistence of a Delaware Revolutionary officer named Caldwell, a breeder of gamecocks, that 'no cock could be truly game unless its mother was a blue hen' (*Delaware State Journal*, July, 1860, in B. '77).

1. *Blue hen's chickens*, soldiers or natives of the state of Delaware; cf. also quot. 1844.

1840 *Niles' Nat. Reg.* 154 In the revolutionary war, . . . Captain Caldwell had a company recruited from Kent and Sussex, called by the rest 'Caldwell's game cocks,' and the regiment after a time in Carolina was nicknamed from this 'the blue hen's chickens' and the 'blue chickens.' . . . But after they had been distinguished in the south the name of the *Blue Hen* was applied to the state. **1844** *Ib.* May 183 The Blue Hen's Chickens, was the name of a club from Kent county, having with them a significant banner, representing a chicken coop. **1856** *Congress. Globe* App., 12 July 1056/2 The blue hen's chickens—the descendants of the cocks which crowed and fought so bravely in the times which tried men's souls; and game ones at that. **1861** *Delaware Inquirer* 5 May (B.), Delaware's honor is in your hands. . . . Blue-Hen's Chickens to the front! Forward! March! **1864** *Congress. Globe* June 2968/2, I remember the early history of the 'Blue Hen's Chickens.' . . . The record is as proud as that of the early 'Jersey Blues.'

b. In transf. use: A fiery, quick-tempered person.

1830 A. ROYALL *Lett. from Ala.* 69 [Andrew Jackson said] he was 'one of the blue hen's chickens.'

2. *Blue Hen* (*State*), the state of Delaware.

1840 [see sense 1]. **1840** *Niles' Reg.* 9 May 154/3 The whigs of the revolution never ceased to boast of the Blue Hen and her chickens. **1867** *Literary Record* (Trübner) 1 Aug., [Delaware] is popularly known . . . as The Blue Hen or Diamond State. **1897** *Congress. Rec.* App. 23 March 68, I am thankful to the gentleman from the 'Blue Hen State' for his suggestion. **1904** *N.Y. Ev. Post.* 10 Nov. 1 The most reliable information . . . from the Blue Hen State indicates [etc.].

+**Blue heron.** [BLUE *a.* 1.] One or the other of two species of heron (*Ardea cærulea* and *herodias*) with bluish plumage.

*c***1730** CATESBY *Carolina* I. 76 *Ardea cærulea.* The blue Heron. . . . These Birds are not numerous in Carolina, and are rarely seen but in the Spring of the Year. **1781–1835** [see BLUE CRANE]. **1839** PEABODY *Mass. Birds* 362 The Great Blue Heron, *Ardea herodias*, . . . is a shy and suspicious bird. **1844** *Nat. Hist. N.Y., Zoology* II. 222 The Blue Heron, *Ardea Cerulea*, . . . is a rare visitor to our coast. **1869** *Amer. Naturalist* II. 401 Stalking along the muddy margin of the stream may frequently be seen the Blue Heron. **1874** COUES *Birds N.W.* 518 The breeding places of the Great Blue Heron on the Colorado River. **1892** TORREY *Foot-path Way* 198 The great blue heron is . . . a big bird, standing almost as high as an ordinary man.

+**Blue huckleberry.** (See quotations.) — **1883** HALE *Woods & Timbers N.C.* 139 Blue Huckleberry (*Gaylussacia frondosa*). . . . The berries are dark blue, large and sweet. **1897** WILLIS *Flowering Plants* II. 384 The *Vaccinium pennsylvanicum* . . . is called the blue huckleberry.

Bluejack. [BLUE *a.* 1.]

||**1.** A sea fish having a blue skin.

1871 *Harper's Mag.* June 32 The little *blue-jacks* manoeuvre within, among the tentacles [of the physalia].

+**2.** A species of small oak (*Quercus cinerea* or *brevifolia*) growing in the southern states.

1884 SARGENT *Rep. Forests* 153 *Quercus cinerea*. . . . Upland Willow Oak. Blue Jack. Sand Jack. **1897** SUDWORTH *Arborescent Flora* 175 *Quercus brevifolia*. . . . Common names [include] . . . Blue Jack (N.C., Fla., Tex., Ga.). **1901** MOHR *Plant Life Ala.* 91 The upland willow oak or blue jack, common in the lower Coast Pine belt, in this isolated pine forest reaches its most northern station.

+**Blue jay, Blue-jay.** [BLUE *a.* 1.] A North American jay, *Cyanurus cristatus* (*Cyanocitta cristata*).

1709 *Bristol Rec.* in *Narrag. Hist. Reg.* III. 211 The same order shall extend to the killing of blew Jawes [*sic*]. *c***1728** CATESBY *Carolina* I. 15 The Blew Jay is full as big, or bigger than a Starling. **1778** CARVER *Travels* 472 The Blue Jay. This bird is shaped nearly like the European jay, only that its tail is longer. **1808** WILSON *Ornithology* I. 12 The Blue Jay is an . . . inhabitant of the woods . . . where his squalling voice often alarms the deer. **1836** HOLLEY *Texas* v. 101 Crows . . . —starlings—blue jay . . . — swallows and wrens abound. **1846** THORPE *Myst. Backwoods* 71 Out starts, alarmed by the noise, a blue jay, who squalls as he passes in waving lines before you. **1856** WILLIS *Convalescent* 102 My two aristocrats, particularly—the king-fisher with his crown and the blue jay with his brilliant plumage—were supremely handsome. **1865** *Atlantic Mo.* XV. 515, I have seen a Blue Jay alone, saluting and admiring himself in the mirror of a little pool. **1871** LOWELL *Study Windows* 40 A blue-jay shrills *cah cah* in his corvine trebles. **1879** B. F. TAYLOR *Summer-Savory* x. 92 One of those fellows that possess all a blue-jay's impudence and none of its beauty. **1884** ROE *Nature's Story* 115 That handsome bird, the blue jay, so wild at the East, is as tame and domestic as the robin in many parts of the West. **1897** BRODHEAD *Bound in Shallows* 1 The murmur of the leaves mixed confusedly with the cries of a blue-jay. **1905** N. DAVIS *Northerner* 45 Silence reigned for five minutes; unbroken save for the blue jays, who screamed their joyous maledictions across the sunny air.

Blue John. {1672–} +*local.* (See quot.) — **1869** *Overland Mo.* III. 129 North Carolinians call skim milk 'blue John.' **1891** *Amer. Notes & Q.* VIII. 62 Blue-john is a thin blue milk that has been skimmed, that is, 'sour sweet-milk.'

+**Bluejoint.** [BLUE *a.* 2.] *Bluejoint* (*grass*), a tall bluish-stemmed grass (*Calamagrostis canadensis*); a similar grass of the western states (*Agropyrum glaucum*).

1832 *N.H. Hist. Soc. Coll.* III. 205 Hay of good quality is cut upon the upland; . . . in the intervals and meadows . . . bluejoint and several other kinds of grasses. **1849** *Pres. Mess. Congress* II. 844 Many of the drained beaver-ponds have become meadows, from which several tons of blue-joint or marsh grass may be annually cut. **1855** *Mich. Agric. Soc. Trans.* VI. 149 The plants on the uplands are columbo . . . and two kinds of bluejoint grass. **1868** *Rep. Comm. Agric.* (1869) 177 The blue-joint grass (*Calamagrostis Canadensis*) also reaches the latitude of Kotzebue Sound, and grows on the coast of Norton Sound with a truly surprising luxuriance. **1880** *Hist. Dane Co., Wis.* 858 The entire town was covered with a sweet and nutritious grass called blue-joint. **1889** VASEY *Agric. Grasses* 48 *Agropyrum glaucum* (Blue Stem, Bluejoint) . . . occurs nearly everywhere, but sparsely, on the plains, and extending quite up into the mountains. *a***1918** G. STUART *On Frontier* II. 127 Blue joint grass in the bottom but not usually thick enough for hay.

+**Blue law(s).**

1. The severe puritanical regulations alleged to have been in force at New Haven, Conn., and its neighborhood, in the seventeenth and eighteenth centuries. Also occas. extended to similar regulations elsewhere at later dates.

A number of the laws are given by Peters, who is the earliest authority for them and for the name. Further information is given in *True and False Blue Laws*, and *Rev. Samuel Peters*, by J. Hammond Trumbull (Hartford 1876–7), *An Examination of Peters's Blue Laws*, by W. F. Prince (Wash., 1899), and *Ye Olden Blue Laws*, by G. Myers (N.Y., 1921).

1781 PETERS *Hist. Conn.* 43 Even the rigid fanatics of Boston, and the mad zealots of Hertford, . . . christened them the *Blue Laws.* **1787** *Amer. Museum* III. 524/1 *note,* The above laws [of the New Haven colony] were originally printed on blue paper, on which account they were called 'blue laws.' **1788** *Kentucky Gazette* 28 June 1/3 A correspondent has favoured us with a memorandum of what are termed 'the blue laws' of New Haven. **1804** W. AUSTIN *Lett. from London* 65 You know the Connecticut Blue Laws made it death for a priest, meaning a clergyman of the Church of England, to be found within that state! [*Footnote*] So called from their being stitched in blue paper. **1809** KENDALL *Travels* I. 275 Some celebrity attaches itself to Newhaven, in consequence of the code of laws to which she had the honour of giving birth while an independent colony, and which are opprobriously denominated *blue-laws.* **1814** JEFFERSON *Let.* Writings XIV. 75 Connecticut, in her blue laws, laying it down as a principle that the laws of God should be the laws of their land. **1815** *Niles' Reg.* VIII. 363/1 This is a notable instance of the efficacy of *blue laws.* **1818** FESSENDEN *Ladies Monitor* 85 His blue laws, never sanction'd by rewards, Seem form'd by Athens' sanguinary sage. **1822** (*title*), The Code of 1650, &c., To which is added, some Extracts from the Laws . . . commonly called Blue Laws. **1826** FLINT *Recoll.* 269 They were re-enacting in that distant and turbulent region, what they would call 'the blue laws' of old Virginia, relating to gambling, breach of the Sabbath, and the like. **1835** [INGRAHAM] *South-West* II. 54 In 'Natchez under the hill,' the Sabbath . . . is not observed according to the strictest letter of the old 'blue laws.' **1845** *Lowell Offering* V. 87 Uncle Peter . . . was conversant with the 'blue laws,' and could relate many a ludicrous incident concerning them. **1847** *Knickerb.* XXIX. 2 We are coming back to the spirit of Connecticut Blue Laws. **1855** BARNUM *Life* 65, I don't think it any sin to dodge your Yankee blue-laws. **1869** STOWE *Oldtown Folks* 58 We may rail at Blue Laws and Puritan strictness as much as we please, but [etc.]. **1871** BARNUM *Struggles & Triumphs* 53 The following scene makes a chapter in the history of Connecticut, as the State was when 'blue-laws' were something more than a dead letter. **1886** *Harper's Mag.* Sept. 637/2 Even the wind in summer fears to be a Sabbath-breaker. It is an enchanted realm. Have the blue-laws such vitality? **1902** *N.Y. Tribune, Weekly Rev.* 26 April 1/2 The bad attack of the blue laws under which Boston suffered last Sunday. **1904** *N.Y. Ev. Post* 7 June 1 Mr. York claimed that conditions were not the same as when the 'blue laws' were passed, and characterized Sunday ball playing as a harmless recreation, encouraged in Chicago and Cincinnati with beneficial results.

+**b.** In *singular.* A strict or severe law.

1895 *N.Y. Dramatic News* 7 Dec. 2/2 The arrest was made under an old blue law, which provides for the punishment of those who commit adultery.

2. *The Blue Law State,* Connecticut.

1839 BRIGGS *H. Franco* II. xviii. 180 'But, you were not a member of the Hartford convention?' exclaimed Mr. Bloodbutton. . . . 'Never was in the Bluelaw State in my life, sir.' **1854** *Congress. Globe* 6 July 1618/1, I know that Connecticut, in the olden time, was libeled by a Tory renegade, . . . as the Blue Law State.

+**Blue lead.** *Mining.* (See quot. 1874.) — **1871** RAYMOND *3rd Rep. Mines* 88 The latter claim has 5,000 feet of what appears to be a blue lead channel. **1874** — *6th Rep. Mines* 16 The term 'great blue-lead' is employed by the miners to distinguish those portions of the alluvium which are found to rest in a well-defined channel, on the 'bed-rock.' **1880** G. INGHAM *Digging Gold* ii. 46 The class of deposits known as the ancient river channels or the 'blue lead' of California . . . are gold-bearing gravels found deep beneath the surface.

Blue light(s). {1805-}

+**1.** The lights reported to have been shown at New London, Conn., as a signal to the British fleet during the war of 1812-5. Hence later in allusive use to suggest disloyalty or treason, or to designate New England federalists.

1813 DECATUR *Let.* in *Niles' Reg.* (1814) V. 302 In the course of the evening [of 12 Dec.] two blue lights were burnt on both the points at the harbor's mouth as signals to the enemy, and there is not a doubt, but that they have, by signals and otherwise, instantaneous information of our movements. **1813** *Norwich* (Conn.) *Courier* in *Columbian Centinel* 25 Dec. 2/2 The reports . . . of the exhibition of blue lights on the heights near New-London, as signals to the enemy's squadron, are wholly incorrect. **1814** *Ann. 13th Congress* 1 Sess. I. 1123 The *blue lights,* so called, which are said to have been displayed at or near the harbor of New London. **1814** *Niles' Reg.* V. 311/2 It is astonishing to observe the efforts made to invalidate the truth of the report respecting the 'blue lights' exhibited on the shores of New-London.

1814 *Niles' Reg.* VI. 2/1 Such is the universal sentiment of our invincible and invaluable seamen. They hate 'blue-lights' and traitors. **1815** *Ib.* VIII. 140/2 Many of our best and most patriotic citizens are emigrants from New England; and even a very 'blue light' loses that factious, grumbling and suspicious spirit that distinguished him at home. **1832** *Congress. Deb.* 12 March 2116 Mr J[enifer] said he should not expect hereafter to hear anything more in relation to the 'federalists,' 'the Hartford convention,' or 'blue lights,' from that quarter. **1833** NEAL *Down-Easters* I. 47 Forthwith a political set-to began, . . . calling one another blue-lights, jacobins, tories, democrats and enemies to the country. **1834** *Louisville Public Advt.* 27 Feb., In the North, the old Blue Lights are charmed with the prospect of Mr. Webster's success. **1838** DRAKE *Tales from Queen City* 91 An adventurer from the land of 'blue-lights' and Hartford Conventions. **1847** *Congress. Globe* 20 Jan., App. 252/1 Where, tell me where, have you buried the sins of these 'old blue lights' of New Hampshire? With what magic wand have you changed their Federalism into modern Democracy? **1856** GOODRICH *Recoll.* I. 484 *Blue Lights,* meaning treason on the part of Connecticut federalism during the war [of 1812], is a standard word in the flash dictionary of low democracy.

+**b.** Attrib., esp. in *Blue light men.*

1817 Fearon *Sketches* (1818) 145 It is an unholy league between apostates and political traitors on one part, and on the other the anglo-federalists, . . . the Hartford conventionalists, the blue-light men [etc.]. **1818** FEARON *Ib.* 139 Federalists, called also 'Tories,' 'Hertford Conventionalists,' and 'Blue Light Men.' **1835** [H. C. TODD] *Notes* 8 The party phrase *Blue-light* men, employed by democrats against federalists, originated in Connecticut. **1844** *Congress. Globe* App., 6 March 399/2 J. C. Wright [was] . . . as rank a blue-light federal whig as ever justified the Hartford convention. **1848** *Ib.* 2 March 418/2 The late war with Great Britain was unpopular with the blue-light Federalists. *Ib.* 22 June 866/1 There were birds of every feather there [in the Philadelphia Convention] —blue-light Federalists, no-territory men, abolitionists, &c. *a***1859** *N.Y. Herald* (B.), Horace Greeley, and a train of real blue light Clayites from your State, have arrived this morning.

+**2.** *College slang.* (See quotations.)

1856 HALL (ed. 2) 30 At the University of Vermont this term is used, writes a correspondent, to designate 'a boy who sneaks about college, and reports to the Faculty the short-comings of his fellow students.' **1900** *Dialect Notes* II. 23 *Blue-light,* a student who seeks to ingratiate himself with the faculty by informing.

Blue limestone. A variety of limestone of a bluish-grey color. Also attrib.

*a***1817** DWIGHT *Travels* II. 480 The rock over which the Hudson descends at this place, is a vast mass of blue limestone, horizontally stratified. **1843** *Nat. Hist. N.Y., Geology* IV. 503 Numerous localities are presented . . . , where the blue limestone exists in great force. **1850** *Cultivator* VII. 369 An undulating beech clay soil, resting upon blue limestone. **1883** *Harper's Mag.* Oct. 719/1 The Kentucky blue-limestone too is a quarry for the turnpike-roads. *Ib.* 719/2 The blue-grass . . . is not blue at all. . . . It is 'blue limestone grass' properly.

+**Blue linnet.** [BLUE *a.* 1.] **a.** The indigo bird, *Cyanospiza cyanea.* **b.** The lazuli finch, *C. amœna.*

*c***1730** CATESBY *Carolina* I. 45 The blue Linnet . . . is rather less than a Gold-finch. . . . The whole Bird appears, at a little Distance, of an intire blue Colour. **1781-2** JEFFERSON *Notes Va.* (1788) 75 *Linaria cœrulea.* . . . Blue linnet. **1808** WILSON *Ornithology* I. 100 Indigo Bird. *Fringilla Cyanea.* . . . Blue Linnet. **1868** WOOD *Homes without Hands* xxix. 550 The Indigo Bird or Blue Linnet of America (*Spiza cyanea*). **1869** *Amer. Naturalist* III. 77 Blue Linnet (*Cyanospiza amœna*). I saw this bird on the eastern slope of the Rocky Mountains.

+**Blue lodge(s).** A secret society formed in Missouri in 1854 to carry Kansas for slavery. — **1855** *Herald of Freedom* 1 April 4 In the slave States, . . . what is called the 'Blue Lodge' . . . is now lending every energy, to make Kansas a slave State. **1857** *Lawrence* (Kansas) *Repub.* 25 June 2 Every step in the 'blue lodge' scheme to foist a slave Constitution upon Kansas has proved the wisdom of that policy. *Ib.* 13 Aug. 2 The blue lodges are again in full blast upon the Missouri border, planning another invasion. **1867** DIXON *New America* I. 24 Ten years since a gang of Blue Lodges started from the opposite bank, landed on this levée, took possession of the town [etc.]. **1887** *Century Mag.* April 871/2 The conspirators had already [in Oct. 1854] spent some months in organizing their 'Blue Lodges.'

+**Blue lupine.** [BLUE *a.* 1 a.] A species of lupine, esp. *Lupinus perennis,* having blue flowers. — **1852** STANSBURY *Gt. Salt Lake* 27 A blue lupine and a white mallow were also gathered. **1878** I. L. BIRD *Rocky Mts.* 15 A dusty blue lupin here and there reminded me of earth's fairer children.

Blue marl. +(See quotations.) — **1883** SMITH *Geol. Survey Ala.* 269 The unchanged rock [=rotten limestone] . . . is frequently spoken of as the blue-marl rock. *Ib.* 488 These subsoils frequently have limy concretions and are underlaid with a blue marl (Rotten Limestone) at ten to twelve feet depth.

+**Blue-mass pill.** =BLUE PILL. — *c***1865** 'MARK TWAIN' *Sk., Answers to Correspondents* A female baby . . . commenced by eating one dozen large blue-mass pills, box and all. **1881** *Phila. Record* No. 3470, 3 This incident was a plunge into a bath after taking a blue-mass pill, which caused the death of Mr. Byrnes in less than half an hour.

+**Blue Monday.** *colloq.* A Monday regarded as depressing or trying, esp. by reason of reaction from undue indulgence or taxing work on the previous day.

1869 BRACE *New West* xvii. 218 They never have, like the whites, a Sunday spree and a 'blue Monday.' **1870** 'F. FERN' *Ginger-Snaps* 66-74 [Essay on] Blue Monday. *Ib.* 67 'Blue Monday!' By this name clergymen designate the day; . . . the worn-out clergyman takes Monday for a day of rest, for truly the Sabbath is none. *Ib.,* But Blue Monday does not belong exclusively to clergymen. **1879** B. F. TAYLOR *Summer-Savory* xv. 130 Hearing something under the left side of your jacket *thud, thud,* like the old-fashioned 'pounder' on blue Mondays. **1893** *Advance* (Chicago) 16 Nov., The Blue Monday Musings of 'Deacon Pugh' sometimes seem to be the output of a mental, perhaps physical, dyspepsia. **1898** M. DELAND *Old Chester Tales* 136 Dr. Lavendar never had 'blue Mondays'— perhaps because he preached old sermons.

+**Bluemouths.** (See quotation.) *Obs.* — **1740** *Ga. Col. Rec.* IV. 663 The Eastern and Southern Parts of it [*sc.* Georgia, are] inhabited by the Creek Indians; . . . the Western by the Chactaws, the Blewmouths, and other Indian Nations, to South-Sea.

Blue mud. (See quotations.) — **1882** WORTHEN *Econ. Geol. Illinois* I. 521 Below these beds of clay and gravel, a deposit is often met with in this county [=Jackson], . . . consisting of a dark blue or black mud, containing branches of trees. *Ib.* II. 4 Below these beds we find at some localities the same 'blue mud.'

+**Blue myrtle.** (See quot. 1889.) — **1884** SARGENT *Rep. Forests* 41 *Ceanothus thyrsiflorus*, . . . Blue Myrtle. **1889** *Cent.* 874/2 The blue myrtle of California, *Ceanothus thyrsiflorus*, becomes a small tree.

Blue norther: see NORTHER.

+**Blue-nose, Bluenose.** [BLUE *a.* 2.]

1. *slang.* A native of Nova Scotia or New Brunswick. Also (quot. 1830), a native of New England. Cf. BLUE-NOSED *a.*, quots. 1809, 1866.

1830 *Northern Watchman* (Troy, N.Y.) 30 Nov. (Th.), A real 'blue-nose,' fresh from the land of steady habits. **1837** HAWTHORNE *Note-books* I. 48 Personages at the tavern: the Governor; . . . two young Blue-Noses from Canada or the Provinces. **1842** *Life in West* 82 We have two pilots on board, our own old fellow and the long blue-nose. **1848** *Knickerb.* XXXI. 450 One . . . stated the accident to have happened in consequence of the officer having mistaken the 'Blue-nose' for a *bear!* **1873** BEADLE *Undevel. West* 711 The Yankee shudders as he thinks of the hard fate of the 'Canucks' and 'Blue-noses' of British America. **1883** E. INGERSOLL in *Harper's Mag.* Jan. 206/2 The Americans employed are very often graduates of the Maine woods, or 'Bluenoses' from Lower Canada. **1904** W. Z. RIPLEY in *Atlantic Mo.* March 302 The 'Bluenoses' who come down from Nova Scotia to work in competition with American carpenters.

attrib. **1840** HALIBURTON *Clockmaker* III. xi, I broke my leg a-ridin' a cussed Blue-nose hoss. **1905** *Nation* 9 Feb. 105/1 The Blue-nose fishermen would doubtless be glad to sell the herring direct.

b. 'A Nova Scotian vessel' (*Cent.* '89).

2. A variety of blue-skinned potato.

*c***1840** HALIBURTON *Sam Slick* (B.), 'Blue Noses' . . . is the name of a potatoe . . . which they [=Nova Scotians] produce in great perfection. **1843** STEPHENS *High Life N.Y.* I. v. 52 So he filled up the hold with potaters, real blue noses. **1844** *Knickerb.* XXIII. 32 Are they kidneys, blue-noses, or fox?—and will they bu'st open white and mealy? **1848** LOWELL *Biglow P.* I. ii. 21, I'd give a year's pay fer a smell o' one good blue-nose tater. **1863** *Maine Agric. Rep.* 9 In raising White Blue Nose potatoes . . . I never . . . could perceive that small seed was not equally as good as large. **1872** *Vt. Bd. Agric. Rep.* I. 232 He . . . sighs for a potato that will yield as much and cook as well as the old Blue Noses used to do forty years ago.

3. A variety of clam.

1883 *Leisure Hour* XXXII. 252/1 The coarsest is the mud clam, or blue nose.

Blue-nosed, *a.* [BLUE *a.* 3.] **a.** Having a blue nose. +Applied esp. as a term of contempt. +**b.** *Blue-nosed potato*, =BLUE-NOSE 2.

1809 IRVING *Knickerb.* III. ii, As a mouse eats his way into a comfortable lodgment in a goodly, blue-nosed, skim'd milk, New England cheese. **1833** J. S. JONES *Green Mt. Boy* I. ii, We can raise more . . . blue-nosed potatoes than we can harvest, a darned sight. **1841** *Knickerb.* XVII. 49 A face whose combined features strikingly resembled a half-peck of blue-nosed potatoes. **1866** C. H. SMITH *Bill Arp* 87 General Johnston was retreating and the blue-nosed Yankees were to pollute our sacred soil the next morning. **1890** *Amer. Notes & Q.* V. 6 Can you tell me why Presbyterians are sometimes called 'blue-nosed?'

+**Blue oak.** [BLUE *a.* 1.] **a.** The bur oak. **b.** The Californian rock-oak, *Quercus Douglasii.* — **1817** S. BROWN *Western Gaz.* 25 Sugar maple, blue and white oak, black locust. **1884** SARGENT *Rep. Forests* 143 *Quercus Douglasii.* . . . Mountain White Oak. Blue Oak.

+**Blue palmetto.** *S.E.* **1.** The fan palm, *Rhapidophyllum hystrix.* **2.** The dwarf palmetto, *Sabal adansoni.* — (1) **1861** WOOD *Botany* 667 *Chamærops.* Blue Palmetto. **1890** *Cent.* s.v. *Palmetto*, Blue palmetto . . . [is] a species with an erect or creeping stem, 2 or 3 feet long, and leaves circular in outline. (2) **1901** MOHR *Plant Life Ala.* 96 The appearance of the dwarf or blue palmetto (*Sabal adansonii*) . . . indicates that the subtropical region of the State has been entered. *Ib.* 125 [In] these swamps . . . the blue palmetto reaches its perfection.

+**Blue pearmain.** [BLUE *a.* 1.] A variety of autumn apple. — **1847** J. M. IVES *New Eng. Fruit* 40 Blue Pearmain.—This fruit is large, the form round. **1876** BURROUGHS *Winter Sunshine* 165 Late in November he found a blue-pearmain tree growing within the edge of a swamp.

+**Blue perch.** [BLUE *a.* 1 b.] The cunner, *Ctenolabrus adspersus.* — **1839** STORER *Mass. Fishes* 78 *Crenilabrus burgall.* . . . The Conner. Blue Perch. Chogset. It . . . is an excellent fish for the table. **1842** *Nat. Hist. N.Y., Zoology* IV. 173 The Common Bergall . . . at Boston . . . is often called Blue Perch. **1859** BARTLETT 58 *Burgall*, a small fish, very common in New York. . . . In New England . . . [it is called] Blue Perch and Conner.

+**Blue-Peter.** (See quot.) — **1709** LAWSON *Carolina* 151 Blue-Peters. the same as you call Water-Hens in England, are here very numerous, and not regarded for eating. [Hence in Jefferson, Morse, etc.]

Blue pigeon. *Naut.* The deep-sea lead. {1897} — **1856** *Harper's Mag.* XIII. 589/1 The speed [of the ship] was slackened, and the 'blue pigeon' kept constantly moving.

Blue pill.

1. An anti-bilious mercurial pill. (Cf. BLUE-MASS PILL.) {*a*1824–}

1820 *U.S. Pharmacopoeia* 181 [Recipe for] Mercurial pills (blue pills). **1833** NEAL *Down-Easters* I. 15 A large box, with a lead-colored pigment, blue pill or opodeldoc perhaps. **1845** *Knickerb.* XXV. 107 One blue pill every night for a week; seidlitz-powder in the morning. **1898** I. H. HARPER *S. B. Anthony* I. 40 It recommends plenty of blue pills and boneset for the ague.

‖**b.** *pl.* Used in addressing a druggist.

1861 [NEWELL] *Orpheus C. Kerr* I. 316 'See here, old blue-pills,' says one of the firemen pleasantly, 'if you don't let us in, your own crib will go to blazes in ten minutes.'

+**2.** *slang.* A bullet.

1834 'J. DOWNING' *Andrew Jackson* 111 They saw no hopes from fitin, they wern't fond of blue pills, and . . . were preparin tu take care of *number one.* **1861** *Missouri let.* in *N.Y. Tribune* 19 Nov., Between blue pills, halters and the penitentiary, we shall soon work of[f] this element of rascaldom.

+**Blue-Point, Bluepoint.** [The headland of that name near Great South Bay, Long Island.] A small oyster, of a superior flavor, obtained from the beds off Blue Point or from the south shore of Long Island. Orig. attrib. with *oyster.*

1805 PARKINSON *Tour* 315 One sort, which they call Blue-Point oysters, is very good, and esteemed by some Englishmen superior to any they ever tasted. **1823** I. HOLMES *Account* 256 Their oysters are both excellent and numerous. The Blue Point oyster of New York excels any other in the world. **1832** J. F. WATSON *Hist. Tales N.Y.* 165 The largest 'Blue-Point' oysters could be bought, opened to your hand, for 2s. a hundred. **1880** 'MARK TWAIN' *Tramp Abroad* xlix. 574, I have selected a few dishes, . . . as follows: . . . Blue points, on the half shell. Cherry-stone clam. *a***1909** 'O. HENRY' *Roads of Destiny* 343 He got along fine with the olives and celery and the bluepoints.

+**Blue-pointer.** =BLUE-POINT. — **1844** *Knickerb.* XXIII. 500 Here we are with our Prince's Boys, . . . our Shrewsburys, and Blue pointers, a shilling's worth of either worth all the shell-fish that ever grew on the French coast. **1853** *Harper's Mag.* VII. 275/2, I am told that, . . . when a demijohn of brandy had been burst, a large blue pointer was found lying in a little pool of liquor, just drunk enough to be careless of consequences.

+**Blue pup.** (See quotations.) — **1848** BARTLETT 272 In Michigan, they apply the term 'blue pup money' to bank notes having a blue stamp on their backs. **1875** *Chicago Tribune* 24 Aug. 6/1 'Blue Pup' was a shinplaster currency issued by canal contractors, and redeemable in 'Blue Dog.' *Ib.* 26 Aug. 4/1 The grand mass-meeting in Detroit in favor of cheap imitation money of the 'blue-pup' and 'yellow-dog' variety.

+**Blue quail.** [BLUE *a.* 1.] The scaled quail (*Callipepla squamata*), found in the Southwest. — **1846** EMORY *Military Reconn.* 62 We saw here also, in great numbers, the blue quail. **1874** COUES *Birds N.W.* 441 Blue Quail . . . is also called the Scaled Quail, from the peculiar appearance of the plumage of the under parts. **1898** CANFIELD *Maid of Frontier* 190 He ran almost as fast as the blue quail flies.

+**Blue racer.** *W.* [BLUE *a.* 1.] A variety of the common black-snake. — **1886** EBBUTT *Emigrant Life in Kansas* 66 The 'blue-racer' snake . . . is a quick traveller; in fact, it is no sooner seen than gone, like a flash of greased lightning with the brake off. **1886** *Leslie's Mo.* Feb. 149/2, I mind the time when thare was blue racers thare. **1904** STRATTON-PORTER *Freckles* 146 Daily Freckles was compelled to drive big black snakes and blue racers from the nests of his chickens.

+**Blue robin.** [BLUE *a.* 1.] The bluebird. — **1844** *Nat. Hist. N.Y., Zoology* II. 65 The Bluebird, or Blue Robin as it is called in the western counties, . . . is hailed with us as the first harbinger of spring. **1884** ROE *Nature's Story* 95 He resembles your English redbreast closely both in appearance and habits, and our New England forefathers called him the 'blue robin.'

Blue ruin. *slang.* {1819–} Intoxicating liquor, esp. of an inferior quality.

1827 [see BETTY]. **1837** A. WETMORE *Gaz. Missouri* 290 The disturber known in the west by the name of 'long green' and 'blue ruin.' **1863** 'E. KIRKE' *Southern Friends* iii. 49 Thirsty natives, imbibing certain fluids known at the South as blue ruin, bust-head, . . . and devil's dye. **1875** G. P. BURNHAM *Three Years* vi, Jersey Lightning, a peculiar New Jersey drink; 'blue ruin.' **1875** *Chicago Tribune* 25 Aug. 5/2 Blue Ruin at the Golden Gate, [involving] extensive swindling on the part of distillers and revenue agents.

+**Blue-skin, Blueskin.** *colloq.* or *slang.*

1. One who ardently supported the Revolution. *Obs.*

1782 *Loyal Verses* (1860) 100 Tho' the Colour's unlike both Christian and Jew Skin, Yet it greatly resembles a true Rebel Blue-Skin. **1783** FRENEAU *Poems* (1786) 349 James Rivington, printer, of late, to the king, But now a republican—under your wing—Let him stand where he is . . . And he'll turn a true Blue-Skin.

2. A person of strict morals; a Presbyterian. *Obs.*

1787 TYLER *Contrast* II. ii, It is no shame, my dear Blueskin, for a man to amuse himself with a little gallantry. **1830** A. ROYALL *Lett. from Ala.* 203 Every blue skin of them is still in office. **1830** — *Southern Tour* I. 7 We laughed at my race from Betsy Chase and the Blueskins. **1846–51** WHITCHER *Bedott P.* ix. 93 They call 'em 'Harrington blue-skins.' **1848** BARTLETT 39 *Blue-skins*, a nickname applied to the Presbyterians, from their alleged grave deportment. **1855** BARNUM *Life* 50 There the congregation would sit and shiver, and their faces would look so blue, that it is no wonder 'the world's people' sometimes called them 'blue skins.'

3. A Negro. *Obs.*

1821 COOPER *Spy* vii, You seem very careful of that beautiful person of yours, Mr. Blueskin. **1835** *Knickerb.* VI. 22, 'I say, blue-skin,' squeaked little Martin, as the negro was about to raise his gun. **1847** [ROBB] *Squatter Life* 111 'What, Missus dar, *too!*' shouted the nigger, . . . and off the cussed blueskin started fur the house.

4. =BLUE *n.* 3. *Obs.*

1823 *Crayon* (Yale) 22, I . . . issued from my cell, To see if we could over-hear, Or make some blue-skin tell. **1856** HALL (ed. 2) 31 *Blue-skin* . . . was formerly in use at some American colleges, with the meaning now given to the word *Blue.*

b. A toady. *Obs.*

1871 [G. R. CUTTING] *Student Life at Amherst College* 132 During the years from 1821 to 1826. . . . It was the practice to hang in effigy those students who, by special attention to the Faculty, had gained the obnoxious name of 'Blue-skins.'

5. A Federal soldier, esp. one from New England. *Obs.*

1863 J. L. FISK *Exped. Rocky Mts.* 31, I went to the tabernacle and heard Bishop Woolley incite his flock to sneer at the 'blue skins' (meaning our soldiers stationed there). **1866** 'F. KIRKLAND' *Bk. Anecdotes* 302 Darn the blueskins, any how; who's scared of the blue-bellies? (That is, Eastern men.)

+**Blue spike.** [BLUE *a.* 2.] An aquatic plant bearing a dense spike of blue flowers. — **1784** CUTLER in *Mem. Academy* I. 433 *Pontederia.* . . . Pickerelweed. Blue Spike. Blossoms blue. Common on the borders of ponds and rivers. July.

+**Blue spruce.** (See quotations.) — **1884** SARGENT *Rep. Forests* 205 *Picea pungens.* . . . White Spruce. Blue Spruce. **1886** *Century Mag.* May 245 Up on the terrace, near the gleaming blue spruce. **1897** SUDWORTH *Arborescent Flora* 34 *Picea mariana*, Black Spruce. . . . Common names [include] . . . Blue Spruce (Wis.).

+**Blue stem, blue-stem, bluestem.** [BLUE *a.* 2.]

1. A variety of wheat. Orig. attrib.

1853 *Mich. Agric. Soc. Trans.* (1854) 72, 2 bushels blue stem wheat. **1856** *Rep. Comm. Patents: Agric.* 194 In 1853, I obtained from Baltimore 2 bushels of 'White Blue-stem' wheat. **1861–2** *Ill. Agric. Soc. Trans.* V. 209 Mr. C. sows the Blue Stem and the May or Alabama, in about equal quantities.

2. One or other of several grasses, esp. *Andropogon furcatus* and *Agropyrum glaucum* of the western states.

1864 A. J. DICKSON *Across Plains* (1929) 191, I was not a little proud of my skill as the lush bluestem and red top, waist high, fell in neat windrows at the swing of my scythe. **1879** H. KING in *Scribner's Mo.* Nov. 138/2 A fire . . . grasps a belt of the tall, thick blue-stem, and the flame leaps suddenly . . . out above the smoke. **1888** *Harper's Mag.* Feb. 348/2 The beautiful carpet of natural grasses, buffalo, gramma, and blue stem. **1889** VASEY *Agric. Grasses* 35 *Agropyrum glaucum* (Blue Stem; Bluejoint) . . . is commonly cut for winter use. **1894** *Amer. Folk-Lore* VII. 103 *Andropogon scoparius*, . . . big blue stem, big blue joint; Central Neb. **1916** THOBURN *Oklahoma* II. 15 The most common wild grass in the central and eastern sections is the ordinary bunch grass, though bluestem, goldentop and other species are by no means uncommon.

3. *Blue-stem golden-rod* (see quotations and cf. next).

1817–8 EATON *Botany* (1822) 467 *Solidago caesia*, blue-stem golden-rod. **1845** LINCOLN *Botany* App. 170/2 Blue-stem golden-rod; . . . stem smooth; tinged with purple; sub-glaucous. **1901** MOHR *Plant Life Ala.* 772 Blue-stem Golden-rod . . . [grows in] open damp woods; . . . flowers July, August. *Ib.*, *Solidago cæsia paniculata*, Southern Blue-stem Golden-rod.

Blue-stemmed, *a.* (See prec. 3 and cf. BLUE *a.* 3.) — **1846** WOOD *Botany* 329 *Solidago cæsia*, Blue-stemmed Goldenrod. . . . Flowers of a deep, rich yellow.

Bluestocking.

1. A woman with literary tastes or pretensions. {1790–} Also attrib. {1804–}

1809 IRVING *Knickerb.* v. i, A blue-stocking lady would have been regarded with as much wonder as a horned frog. **1832** BRYANT *Letter to Wife* 31 May (MS.), The daughter [of T. Flint] is . . . the 'great blue stocking of the west.' . . . She is very intelligent . . . and talks remarkably well. **1835** *Knickerb.* V. 120 A blue-stocking, on being asked if she had read any of Charles Brockden Brown's novels, absolutely laughed in the inquirer's face. **1838** DRAKE *Tales & Sk.* 57 After a copious flow of small talk, the 'blue-stockings' retired to their respective cottages to pore over the new novel and the last review. **1865** *Atlantic Mo.* XV. 459 The Miss Hapgoods, who were the blue-stockings of the place, were charmed to have such an addition. **1871** *Scribner's Mo.* II. 630 We've got a first-rate chance to see how a blue-stocking keeps house.

+**2.** A professing Christian. Also attrib. *Obs.*

1829 A. ROYALL *Pennsylvania* I. 152 The sole and all-weighing cause of my partiality for the Germans, is their aversion to the gray coats, or, as they are called in Pennsylvania, *blue stockings.* **1830** — *Lett. from Ala.* 189 Honorable Joseph Laurence of the blue-stocking county, Washington, Pennsylvania, is a tall good figure.

+**3.** *local.* The avocet.

1844 *Nat. Hist. N.Y., Zoology* II. 267 The American Avoset, or Blue-stocking as it is called in New Jersey, is a scarce bird on the shores of this State. **1848** BARTLETT 39 *Blue stocking*, the American avoset. **1872** COUES *Key* 247.

Bluestone.

+**1.** A bluish argillaceous sandstone, used as a building material and for flagstones.

1709 LAWSON *Carolina* 50 This [river] is call'd Heighwaree, and affords as good blue Stone for Mill-Stones, as that from Cologn. **1733** BYRD *Journey to Eden* 287 A new Entry I had made upon Blue Stone Creek. **1851** A. CARY *Clovernook* 106 A little puddle of water had thawed from his boots and soiled the bluestone hearth. **1864** C. VAUX *Villas* (ed. 2) 117 At Newburgh, on the Hudson, a church . . . has been built. . . . The body of the work is constructed of a grayish bluestone. **1883** *Harper's Mag.* May 816/1 The Bank of California [in San Fran.] . . . is two stories in height, of 'blue stone,' of a pleasant color.

2. Sulphate of copper. {1883}

1839 DUNGLISON *Med. Lex.* (ed. 2) 177/1 *Cupri Sulphas*, . . . Blue Stone, Blue Vitriol, . . . as a tonic, . . . has been used in epilepsy, intermittents, &c. **1873** *Rep. Comm. Agric.* (1874) 159 The best remedy against these insects, however, is . . . by dropping a mixture of 'blue stone' of the druggists . . . into the flower of the Jamestown weed.

+**Blue streak.** *colloq.* or *slang.*

1. A streak of light caused by rapid movement.

1830 *Kentuckian* 14 May, A gentleman . . . has only to get into a Sunday Mail Coach . . . to pass Mr. Rowan with such rapidity as not even to leave a 'blue streak' behind him.

2. A rapid rush, a swift course.

1842 *Knickerb.* XX. 306, I . . . decided . . . to go up the river 'with a rush,' over the mountains 'with a whirl,' and make a 'blue streak' for home.

3. A continuous stream or incessant flow (of words). Freq. as an adverbial complement with *talk*, etc.

1847 *Knickerb.* XXX. 178 Interspersing his vehement comments with a 'blue streak' of oaths. **1883** J. HAY *Bread-Winners* 276, I admire your pluck, and I'll swear a bluestreak for you when the time comes. **1886** DORSEY *Midshipman Bob* I. 88 He turned on him in a towering rage . . . and told him *he'd* teach him to treat his superior officers with disrespect (and then he swore a blue streak). **1895** *Century Mag.* Sept. 676/1 He calmly lied to me a blue streak, and he knew that I knew he was lying. **1895** S. HALE *Letters* 289, I . . . drove in her sort of . . . carryall, . . . talking a blue streak two miles to her house. **1914** ATHERTON *Perch of Devil* i. 24 You must be considerable in earnest to talk a blue streak!

+**Blue stripe.** (See quotation and cf. BLUEBELLY.) — **1878** BEADLE *Western Wilds* 443 There will, perhaps, be the Yankee type: the people north and east of Pennsylvania, . . . with that traditional 'blue stripe on the belly.'

+**Blue stuff.** *Mining.* Sulphuret of silver. — **1877** WM. WRIGHT *Big Bonanza* 52 They, however, did not know that the 'blue stuff,' . . . which they had dug into, was of any value. **1876** RAYMOND *8th Rep. Mines* 19 The celebrated 'blue stuff' . . . vexed and bewildered Comstock and his companions, when working below the great Washoe lode.

Bluet. {1727–, the corn bluebottle}

The plural form has frequently been taken as a singular.

+**1.** A small plant (*Houstonia cærulea*) with 'delicate little flowers, light blue, pale lilac, or nearly white with a yellowish eye' (Gray).

1821 BARTON *Flora* I. 119 Fairy-flax. Bluett. Innocence. Venus' Pride. **1857** GRAY *Botany* 174 Bluets. . . . A delicate little herb, producing in spring a profusion of light-blue flowers. **1863** *Rep. Comm. Agric.* 159 The 'Bluets,' 'Innocence,' 'Dwarf Pink,' with, perhaps, some other common name, is one of the prettiest ornaments of our spring meadows. **1869** FULLER *Flower Gatherers* 83 One day, when we were going home from school, Jimmy Carroll came running back with a cluster of Bluets in his hand. **1887** BURROUGHS in *Century Mag.* July 333 We have one flower which grows in vast multitudes, yet which is exquisitely delicate and beautiful in and of itself, I mean the houstonia, or bluets. **1901** MOHR *Plant Life Ala.* 738 *Houstonia minor*, Southern Bluets. . . . Flowers cerulean blue. *Ib.*, *Houstonia minima*, Smallest Bluets. . . . Flowers sky blue.

2. A similar plant of the genus *Oldenlandia* (al. *Hedyotis*).

1843 TORREY *Flora N.Y.* I. 315 *Hedyotis caerulea.* . . . Common Bluets. Dwarf Risk. *Ib.* 316 *Hedyotis longifolia.* . . . Long-leaved Bluets [etc.]. **1857** GRAY *Botany* 172 Bluets, . . . *O. glomerata*, . . . [grows in] wet places, S. New York to Virginia near the coast, and southward.

+**3.** The farkleberry.

From Amer.-Fr. *bluet*, with reference to the blue ripe fruit.

1897 SUDWORTH *Arborescent Flora* 312 *Vaccinium arboreum*, . . . Tree Huckleberry, . . . Bluet (La.).

+**Bluetail.** The blue-tailed lizard (see next.) — **1738** CATESBY *Carolina* II. 67 *Lacertus cauda cærulea.* The Blue-Tail Lizard. . . . They are seen often on the ground, and frequent hollow trees. . . . They are found in Virginia and Carolina. **1890** *Cent.*, *Eumeces*, . . . a genus of skinks, of the family *Scincidæ*. It contains small harmless lizards known as blue-tails and scorpions.

Blue-tailed, *a.* [BLUE *a.* 3.] +*B. lizard* or *skink*, a variety of skink, *Eumeces* (*Scincus*) *fasciatus*.

1789 MORSE *Amer. Geog.* 63 The Blue-tailed Lizard, and the Lion Lizard are found in the southern states. **1827** WILLIAMS *West Florida* 28 The northern blue tailed lizard is sometimes, but rarely, seen. **1842** *Nat. Hist. N.Y., Zoology* III. 29 Blue-tailed Skink. . . . This harmless little animal, miscalled the Blue-tailed Lizard and Striped Lizard, is not uncommon in the southern counties of the State. **1890** *Cent.* s.v. *Skink*, Common skinks in the United States are the blue-tailed, *Eumeces fasciatus*, and the ground-skink, *Oligosoma laterale*.

+**Blue tangle(s).** [BLUE *a.* 2.] The dangleberry or blue huckleberry. — **1814** PURSH *Flora Amer.* I. 286 *Vaccinium lanceolatum*. . . . About three feet high; . . . berries large, blue, globular, eatable; called by the country people Blue-tangles. **1847** DARLINGTON *Weeds & Plants* 208 *Gaylussacia frondosa*. . . . Dangle-berry, Blue Tangles. **1857** GRAY *Botany* 247 Blue Tangle, Dangleberry, . . . [grows in] low copses, coast of New England to Kentucky, and southward.

Blue vervain. [BLUE *a.* 1.] The common vervain, *Verbena hastata*. — **1843** TORREY *Flora N.Y.* II. 51 *Verbena hastata*, . . . Tall Blue Vervain, Simpler's Joy. **1857** GRAY *Botany* 298 Blue Vervain . . . [grows in] low and waste grounds, common. July–Sept. *a***1862** THOREAU *Maine Woods* 311 Plants commonly regarded as introduced from Europe . . . [include] blue vervain. **1891** *Cent.* 6737/3 The blue vervain, a tallish slender plant with small blue flowers.

Blue violet. [BLUE *a.* 1.] A species of violet having blue flowers; esp. the wood-violet, *Viola palmata*.

1818 *Jrnl. Science* I. 360 March 21. Blue violet (*Viola cucullata*) in full flower. **1832** HALE *Flora* 183 Blue Violet, *Viola odorata*. . . . The genus Viola within its proper limits is almost equally divided between Europe and the temperate parts of North America. **1839** in *Mich. Agric. Soc. Trans.* VII. 422 *Viola cucullata*. Blue violet. **1869** STOWE *Oldtown Folks* 577 The road was fringed . . . with great patches of the blue violet, and sweet-fern, and bayberry. **1891** COULTER *Bot. W. Texas* I. 25 Common blue violet . . . [grows] in low ground, common almost everywhere.

+**Blue warbler.** [BLUE *a.* 1.] A species of warbler with blue plumage.

1810 [see BLACK-THROATED]. **1831** AUDUBON *Ornith. Biog.* I. 78 As soon as the foliage of the forests begins to expand, the Blue Yellow-backed Warbler flies to the tops of the trees, and there remains during the season. **1858** BAIRD *Birds Pacific R.R.* 280 *Dendroica Cærulea*, Blue Warbler. *Hab.*—Eastern United States to the Missouri river. **1868** *Amer. Naturalist* II. 176 The Blue Warbler; . . . its natural home . . . [is] the south and the south-west, where it is extremely abundant. **1874** COUES *Birds N.W.* 233 Blue Warbler . . . is tolerably common in Central Ohio. **1892** TORREY *Foot-Path Way* 191, I came upon . . . three goodly throngs, including . . . black-throated blue warblers, pine warblers [etc.].

Blueweed. [BLUE *a.* 1.]

1. Viper's bugloss (*Echium vulgare*), a plant of European origin.

1843 TORREY *Flora N.Y.* II. 84 Blue-weed, Viper's Bugloss, [or] Blue Thistle . . . ; rare: introduced from Europe. A very ornamental plant when in full flower, but sometimes a troublesome weed. **1847** DARLINGTON *Weeds & Plants* 242 Blue weed, Viper's Bugloss, [or] Blue Devils . . . of late years . . . has become abundant in New York. **1850** [S. F. COOPER] *Rural Hours* 106 It will be easy to name a number of these: . . . bugloss, blue-weed, and the pigeon-weed of the grain-fields. **1857** GRAY *Botany* 320 Blue-weed [is] . . . rather rare northward; a troublesome weed in Virginia.

2. (See quotation.)

1877 BARTLETT 53 *Blue Weed* (Chicorium). Wild endive, bearing a large dark-blue flower. New England.

+**Blue whistler.** *slang.* A bullet. — **1850** [H. C. LEWIS] *La. Swamp Doctor* 44, I determined to go this time for the 'antlered monarch,' by loading one barrel with fifteen 'blue whistlers,' reserving the other [shot] for small game.

+**Blue whortleberry.** The dwarf huckleberry, *Gaylussacia dumosa*. — **1818** *Jrnl. Science* I. 371 July 4. . . . Blue whortleberries . . . beginning to ripen. **1821** *Mass. H. S. Coll.* 2 Ser. IX. 157 *Vaccinium frondosum*, Blue whortleberry.

+**Bluewing.** [BLUE *a.* 1, 2.]

1. A North American variety of teal.

1709 LAWSON *Carolina* 148 The Blue-Wings are less than a Duck, but fine Meat. These are the first Fowls that appear to us in the Fall of the Leaf. **1724** JONES *Virginia* 42 These exceed in wild Geese and Ducks, Cohoncks, Blew-Wings, Teal, Swans, and Mallards. **1768** WASHINGTON *Diaries* I. 294 Went into the Neck and up the Creek after Blew Wings. **1775** BURNABY *Travels* 16 The American shell-drake and blue-wing exceed all of the duck kind whatsoever. **1851** *S. Lit. Messenger* XVII. 659/2 Mallards, blue-wing, and some other tolerably good ducks. **1874** LONG *Wild-Fowl* xv. 192 They are a trifle smaller than the blue-wings.

2. *attrib.* =BLUE-WINGED *a.*

*c***1731** CATESBY *Carolina* I. 96 *Anas Americanus luto rostro*, the Blue-wing Shoveler. . . . The upper part of the wing is covered with pale blue feathers. *Ib.* 99 *Querquedula Americana fusca*, the Blue-wing Teal, . . . in August . . . come in great plenty to Carolina. **1781–2** JEFFERSON *Notes Va.* (1788) 73 Blue wing teal. **1895** *Outing* Oct. 43/1 A bunch of blue-wing teal rose from the ice-pond.

Blue-winged, *a.* [BLUE *a.* 3.] (See quotations and BLUEWING 2.)

1637 MORTON *New Canaan* II. iv, Teales there are of two sorts, green winged, and blew winged; but a dainty bird. **1789** MORSE *Amer. Geog.* 59 The Blue winged teal. *Ib.*, The Blue winged shoveller. **1810** WILSON *Ornithology* II. 109 Blue-Winged Yellow Warbler. *Sylvia Solitaria*. . . . This bird has been mistaken for the *Pine Creeper* of Catesby. **1813** *Ib.* VIII. 66 The Blue winged Shoveller is twenty inches long, and two feet six inches in extent. **1844** *Nat. Hist. N.Y., Zoology* II. 83 The Blue-Winged Warbler. *Vermivora solitaria*. *Ib.* 350 The Snow Goose, or White Brant and Blue-winged Goose, as it is occasionally called. **1865** *Atlantic Mo.* May 521, I have met here many of the rarer species, such as the . . . Blue-Winged Swamp-Warbler, the Worm-Eating Warbler, the Fox-Sparrow, etc. **1868** *Amer. Naturalist* II. 175 The blue-winged yellow warbler is one of those that spend the summer with us. **1874** LONG *Wild-Fowl* 185 The flesh of the blue-winged teal is considered by epicures to be superior in delicacy of flavor to that of most water-fowl. **1877** *Harper's Mag.* Jan. 214/2 Blue-winged flies darting in and out of the oozy floats.

+**Bluewood.** [BLUE *a.* 1.] A small tree or shrub (*Condalia obovata*) of Texas and other southwestern states. — **1884** SARGENT *Rep. Forests* 4 *Condalia obovata*, . . . Blue Wood, Log Wood, Purple Haw. **1885** HAVARD *Flora W. & S. Texas* 457 Mixed with it [=mezquit] are the hardly less common Lote-bush and Brasil or Blue Wood.

+**Bluff,** *n.*[1] [f. the adj.]

1. A steep bank or shore; the steep bank of a river or a sharp rise in the level of land; the top of such a rise.

Rare before 1700 but in common use after that date, also in place-names as *Bear, Dachee, Edisto, Utaw, Walnut Bluff*. All the earlier instances are from South Carolina and Georgia, and many of them relate to Savannah.

1687 in *S.C. Hist. & Gen. Mag.* (July, 1929) 131 April 26. . . . We landed on a Bluffe where some shads were. . . . At night with the Ebb we came to a Bluffe [etc.]. *Ib.* 132, 30. This morning . . . we came . . . to ane old Indian plantation on a Bluffe. **1699** *S.C. Warrants for Lands* (1915) 155 That Point of Land, lying on Port-Royall River below the Bluff. **1707** *Ib.* 206 One hundred acres of land on the uppermost bluff on the south side of Blake River. **1733** *Ga. Col. Rec.* III. 380 The River here [at Savannah] forms an Half-moon, along the South side of which the Banks are about Forty Feet high, and on the Top a Flat, which they call a Bluff. **1735** F. MOORE in *Ga. H. S. Coll.* I. 94, I took a view of the town of Savannah. . . . It stands upon the flat of a hill, the bank of the river (which they in barbarous English call a bluff) is steep and about forty-five foot perpendicular. **1737** WESLEY *Journal* 2 Dec. (1775) 54 Savannah stands on a flat *Bluff* (so they term any high-land hanging over a creek or river) which rises 45 feet perpendicular from the river. **1765** J. BARTRAM *Journal* 19 Dec. (1766) 2 These grew on a high bluff 8 or 10 foot above the surface of the river. **1776** M'ROBERT *Tour* 34 From this we travelled along the shore, which rises into headlands, or bluffs, as they are called here [in New England]. **1779** in *Loyal Verses* (1860) 53 Incessant thunders rend the frighted sky, And bluffs and hillocks to the sound reply. **1797** F. BAILY *Tour* (1856) 261 'Bluff' is a name given in this country [on the Mississippi] to any promontory of land that terminates almost perpendicularly. **1807** GASS *Journal* i. 22 On the south side we passed high handsome banks or bluffs of red and blue strata. *Ib.* (footnote), By Bluffs in the Western Country is understood high steep banks, which come close to and are washed at their base by the rivers. **1817** A. ROYALL *Lett. from Ala.* (1830) viii. 19 Nashville is built on a high bluff. . . . The citizens have cut a passage through this bluff. **1829** J. MACAULEY *Hist. N.Y.* I. 20 The Alleghanian or Appalachian mountains . . . end in bluffs and rocky steeps. **1839** Z. LEONARD *Adventures* (1904) 71 We attempted to follow the river through the mountain, but we soon found this to be impossible, as the bluffs of huge rocks projecting several hundred feet high, closed it to the very current. **1853** *N.H. Hist. Soc. Coll.* VII. 433 The river made a sudden curve, . . . throwing the water with great force against a high bluff of clay and gravel. **1867** RICHARDSON *Beyond Mississippi* i. 18 Wherever the sharp bluffs of Missouri slope to the southward, they are specially adapted to vine-growing. **1881** *Rep. Indian Affairs* 37 The bottom lands here are about one and one-fourth of a mile wide, the land rising with a gentle slope from the river to the bluffs in the rear. **1890** E. B. CUSTER *Following Guidon* 44 The Indians were assembling . . . on the bluffs overlooking the command. **1897** *Outing* Sept. 587/2 Long Island shore . . . rises in majestic bluff and promontory to overlook the azure at Montauk Point. **1905** G. E. COLE *Early Oregon* iv. 54 [The creek] was walled in by perpendicular bluffs on both sides.

2. Attrib. with *country, crest, deposit, formation, point.*

1861–4 *Ill. Agric. Soc. Trans.* V. 628 The term loess is applied to a deposit which . . . has been sometimes called the 'bluff' deposit. **1869** *Amer. Naturalist* Feb. 646 Leaving Sioux city and going northward . . . , we soon pass the northern limit of the bluff formation. **1884** *Century Mag.* April 822/2 Large landed estates, with slaves, were features of the high bluff country. **1886** *Outing* May 131/1 One of my foremen shot a mountain ram on a ragged bluff-crest but half a mile away.

b. Attrib. in sense: Situated on a bluff.

1859 *Harper's Mag.* March 571/2 The Shelby Agricultural Society's fair grounds, a mile and a half from this, the 'Bluff City' [=Memphis]. **1871** DE VERE 663 Hannibal, in Missouri, is known as the *Bluff City*, being built on high bluffs overhanging the river.

+Bluff, *n.*[2] [f. BLUFF *v.*[2]]

1. The game of poker.

1845 Sol. Smith *Theatr. Apprent.* 148 The reader who does not understand the game of 'bluff' or 'poker,' as it is most generally called, may as well leave off here. **1856** Olmsted *Slave States* 52 In some of the parties he saw grown men and small boys playing bluff. **1857** *Quinland* II. 79 In the farther room several persons were sitting round a table, playing at cards. The game was 'bluff,' and they were playing high. **1864** T. L. NICHOLS *Amer. Life* I. 170 Those who need the excitement of betting play at games of bluff and poker. **1885** *Century Mag.* Aug. 639/1 Sutler's pasteboard checks were very useful in playing the game of 'bluff.'

fig. **1859** *Harper's Mag.* Oct. 713/2 Hazlit [High-constable] felt abashed at the formidable appearance of the culprit, but determined to *play bluff.* **1866** *Harvard Mem. Biographies* I. 400 It is a very magnificent game of Bluff that we are playing.

2. An instance of, or the practice of, bluffing in poker.

To call a bluff: see CALL *v.*

1879 BRET HARTE *Drift from Shores* 204, I used to slap 'em down on the boys for a bluff in a game of draw poker. **1885** *N.Y. Wkly. Sun* 13 May 2 The terrible thing about this . . . game for the unsophisticated foreigner is the 'bluff.' **1895** *Boston Herald* in *Westminster Gazette* 31 July 8/1 The difficulty we all experienced in playing 'poker' with Grant . . . [was] that he watched his adversaries narrowly, and could detect a 'bluff' with unerring certainty.

b. *fig.* An attempt to impress or intimidate another, without the actual power or intention of carrying out the action suggested.

1873 MILLER *Amongst Modocs* 200 You . . . called us on a dead hand, . . . but this was no bluff of mine. **1876** BRET HARTE *G. Conroy* xl, 'No more I did,' responded the gambler; . . . 'this is only a little bluff!' **1887** F. FRANCIS, JR. *Saddle & Moccasin* 130 'You got the stock, though?' 'Oh—yes! I run a bluff on 'em.' **1889** 'MARK TWAIN' *Conn. Yankee* xxxix. 506 It was a 'bluff,' you know. At such a time it is sound judgment to put on a bold face. **1897** FLANDRAU *Harvard Episodes* 232 Billy's face . . . told him that he was perfectly safe in making a 'bluff' at changing the subject. **1901** McCUTCHEON *Graustark* 434 'And you—you did all that "on a bluff"?' gasped the other. **1903** C. T. BRADY *Bishop* 19 It was bravado—a bluff pure and simple—but well done. **1911** VANCE *Cynthia* 71 Why didn't you try it, anyhow—throw the bluff, at least?

c. A bluffer, pretender.

*a*1904 WHITE *Blazed Trail Stories* ii. 27 'You're a bluff!' he said insultingly.

3. A stake in a card game; a bid.

1870 NOWLAND *Indianapolis* 163 While playing he kept his money in his mouth, it held just twenty dollars in silver; his usual 'bluff' was a mouthful, which he emptied from his mouth on to the table.

Bluff, *a.* Also **blufe, bluft, bloffe.** {1627–, of ships.}

1. Of a shore or riverbank: Rising steeply. {1658–} Usually attrib. with *bank, head, point.*

(1) **1664** W. HILTON *Rel. Discovery* (1907) 10 The said head-land is bluft, and seems steep, as though the trees hung over the water. **1666** *S.C. Hist. Soc. Coll.* V. 70 The Coast hence . . . appeares even and bluffe with trees when you are in the offing. **1805** SIBLEY in *Ann. 9th Congress* 2 Sess. 1099 When the oak and pine woods come bluff to the river for about five miles. **1808** F. CUMING *Western Tour* 378 The sides of the hill are more bluff as you come nearer the river. **1879** *Harper's Mag.* June 70/1 The shores are generally bluff, with narrow strips of sand beach.

(2) **1664** W. HILTON *Rel. Discovery* (1907) 11 If you . . . stand in N. N. W. with the bluft head aforesaid. **1703** *S.C. Warrants for Lands* (1915) 182 A warrant for 500 acres of land . . . lying in . . . the bluff part of the swamp and part of the level ground over the swamp. **1738** BYRD *Dividing Line* (1901) 32 The high land terminated in a bluff point. **1792** *Let.* in Imlay *Western Territory* (ed. 2) II. 121 The bottoms of the Wabash on the opposite side are confined by a bluff bank nearly two hundred feet. **1809** BARLOW *Columbiad* I. 267 Round each bluff base the sloping ravine bends. **1809** F. CUMING *Western Tour* 255 The Chalk bank, which is a whitish brown bluff cliff, rising from the water's edge. **1819** SCHOOLCRAFT *Mo. Lead Mines* 155 It is . . . a high bluff rock. **1828** *Western M. Rev.* II. 323 These ponds generally terminate in a bluff bank, where the ripple, or shoal, commences. **1840** *Knickerb.* XVI. 270 Between the lofty and picturesque bluff-points . . . Lake Superior pours out the St. Marys. **1853** 'P. PAXTON' *Yankee in Texas* 69 The banks of the river . . . did not rise at once or precipitously, bearing no resemblance to the bold bluff shores that confine nearly all southern rivers. **1872** *Ill. Dept. Agric. Trans.* 135 The bluff lands and the intermediate lands between bluff and bottom are peculiarly adapted to the culture of winter wheat. **1873** BEADLE *Undevel. West* 739 Mr. Mann's train was camped on the bluff bank.

2. Of the face: Broad and flat. *Obs.* {1664–87}

1729 *N.J. Archives* XI. 162 Run away . . . John Harris, . . . much Pockfretten, a bluff Face, short Hair.

+Bluff, *v.*[1] [f. BLUFF *n.*[1]] *tr.* To raise in the form of a bluff. — **1809** BARLOW *Columbiad* I. 643 Where dread Niagara bluffs high his brow.

Bluff, *v.*[2] [Perh. from Eng. dial. *bluff* 'to blindfold or hoodwink' (1674–).]

1. *tr.* To scare *off,* alarm, or discourage (an opponent in poker) by misleading him as to the value of the hand one holds.

(1) **1845** S. Smith *Theatr. Apprent.* 149 Therefore, inasmuch as I believe you are only trying to bluff me off, I go two hundred. **1871** DE VERE 328 The first tries to *bluff* him off by a still higher bet, and thus the stake rises rapidly to often enormous sums.

(2) *a*1859 *N.Y. Spirit of Times* (B.), 'I goes you five dollars this time,' says Jim. . . . 'I . . . goes you ten better,' said Bill; 'you ain't agoin' to bluff dis child.' **1885** *N.Y. Weekly Sun* 13 May 2/7 One evening . . . he went his whole heart, soul, and pocket on three aces and was bluffed by his opponent with a pair of trays.

fig. **1890** RYAN *Told in Hills* 224, I think it's playing it pretty low down on Providence to bluff him on an empty hand.

b. To impress or impose upon (one) by pretence or a mere show of strength. Also with *off.*

(1) **1846** [FIELD] *Drama in Pokerville* 87 'Go it!' cried a dozen voices; . . . 'Can't bluff you, old hoss.' 'No back out,' &c. &c. **1852** *Knickerb.* XXXIX. 474 In a recent murder-trial in this city, . . . where the usual course of intimidating or 'bluffing' the adverse witnesses was frequently resorted to. **1866** C. H. SMITH *Bill Arp* 39 The General bluffed 'em, and ever since that game was played the little town close by has been called Cedar Bluff. **1888** J. KIRKLAND *McVeys* 244 Does he think he can bluff me? He'd better try it! **1908** W. A. WHITE in *Kansas City Star* 31 May, He defied them. He would not be bluffed into offending Wall Street.

(2) **1839** *Observer & Repub.* (Louisville, Ky.) 18 May, I've stood three pluck one too often to be bluffed off even if there was forty against me. **1848** E. JUDSON *Mysteries N.Y.* II. 73 No! I've been fairly bluffed off by that little stuck up thing, the sewing girl. **1850** GARRARD *Wah-To-Yah* xxiii. 287 That's a great old way to bluff a fellow off, when he's half froze to see his girl. **1887** *Century Mag.* March 974 He would propose such a sort of fight as would bluff off Shields.

2. *intr.* To act so as to bluff another.

1854 *Congress. Globe* 3 May 1070 We both know how that game [of brag] is played. I thought I would bluff back on him. **1885** BRET HARTE *Ship of '49* v, Far from bluffing, Sleight, I am throwing my cards on the table. **1886** *Knowledge* 1 March 161/1 *Bluff,* verb, to bet on a worthless hand. This is regarded as a creditable achievement at the noble game of poker. **1889** 'MARK TWAIN' *Conn. Yankee* xl. 512, I was not bluffing this time. I meant what I said; I could do what I promised. **1893** POST *Harvard Stories* 237 Write only on those questions that you can answer. . . . Don't try to bluff on the questions that you don't know.

+Bluffer. [f. BLUFF *v.*[2]] One who bluffs (at poker or otherwise).

1850 GARRARD *Wah-To-Yah* ix. 122 Others . . . gasconaded and looked fierce enough to stare a mad 'bluffer' out of countenance. **1887** KELLER *Draw Poker* 11 *Playing Pat,* playing an original hand without drawing cards. A favorite device of bluffers. **1888** *Detroit Free Press* 5 May (F.), The American man-of-war . . . could be blown out of the water in five minutes by the guns of the Moors. Is Uncle Sam a bluffer? **1895** KING *Fort Frayne* ii. 24 The Eleventh . . . had surrounded and disarmed Tall Bull's little band of ugly 'bluffers.' *a*1906 'O. HENRY' *Trimmed Lamp* 34 They knew every verse of the old bluffer by heart.

+Bluff game. [BLUFF *n.*[2] and *v.*[2]] A game in which bluffing is practiced. Usu. fig. — **1845** HOOPER *Simon Sugg's Adv.* x. 129 'No!' said Simon. . . . 'The bluff game ain't played here!' **1857** *Knickerb.* XLIX. 41 The hard bluff game he had been playing against life single-handed. **1888** *St. Louis Globe Democrat* 29 April (F.), They . . . thought he could outnumber them. It was a bluff game and he won. **1889** K. MUNROE *Golden Days* 123 We was playing a bluff game.

+Bluffing, *vbl. n.* [BLUFF *v.*[2]] The action of using bluff. Also attrib. with *game, method, system.*

1850 *Congress. Globe* App., 14 May 606/1, I cannot look upon the effort of Texas in any other light than a bluffing, brow-beating game. *c*1850 *Southern Sketches* 137 (Bartlett 1859), Jim . . . tried the bluffing system; but Joe said he . . . would put up with no more insults from his bullying neighbor. **1882** *Nation* 12 Oct. 301/1 The other method, which might be called the bluffing method, . . . has been frequently applied to civil-service reform. **1887** KELLER *Draw Poker* 6 It must be remembered that in poker 'bluffing' or betting on nothing, is not only permissible, but is one of the most seductive features of the game.

+Bluff land. [BLUFF *a.* 1 and *n.*[1] 2.] Land that rises steeply; *pl.* lands rising sharply from bottom land. — **1666** *S.C. Hist. Soc. Coll.* V. 62 The North East side is a bluffe land, rounding from the River. **1685** *Let.* in *S.C. Hist. & Gen. Mag.* XXIX. 73 We settled ourselves altogether in a verie convenient place for a town [=Stuartstown, S.C.] . . . , a high bloffe land excellently weell [*sic*] watered. **1884** *Encycl. Brit.* XVII. 309/2 These so-called 'bluff-lands' [in Nebraska], composed of loess materials.

Bluffy, *a.* {1844} +Resembling bluffs; steep. — **1851** *Knickerb.* XXXVII. 182 The shores have a bluffy appearance, and the river has scooped out hollows all along the banks. **1882** *Century Mag.* Sept. 707 The Penobscot winds around the bluffy headlands.

Bluing, Blueing, (*vbl.*) *n.* {1862–} The use of blue matter in laundrywork; the blue matter itself. Also attrib. with *bag, powder, water.*

1842 MRS. KIRKLAND in *Knickerb.* XX. 419 The harvest-moon . . . is like 'the yelk of an egg that's been froze, and then dropt into a great tub o' bluin'-water.' **1868** *Mich. Agric. Rep.* VII. 351 James Pyle, New York

City, [exhibited] blueing powder. **1870** 'FERN' *Ginger-Snaps* 263 A professional laundress, . . . up to the mysteries of bluing, rinsing, clear-starching and ironing. *Ib.*, That shirt-bosom, with its streaks of bluing, its little globules of starch. **1881** *Harper's Mag.* Dec. 73/2 In color the meloe is of a deep indigo blue, rotund in form—indeed, facetiously suggesting a small bluing-bag. **1913** STRATTON-PORTER *Laddie* i, The bluing settled in the rinse water and stained her white clothes.

Blunderbuss. {1654–}

1. A short gun (or pistol) with a large bore, firing a number of balls or slugs. Now *hist.*

1702 *Essex Inst. Coll.* XLII. 160 Inventory of ship: . . . three brass Blunderbusses, one iron ditto. **1774** *Mass. Gazette* 3/3 A few . . . coach guns or blunderbusses. **1780** *Virginia State P.* I. 407 List of Ordnance Stores sent to Richmond from the Magazine in Wms burg: . . . Guns, Bayonets, Pistols, Buck Shott, . . . Blunderbusses. **1787** *Boston Gazette* 5 March 3/3 Lost. A small Pocket Blunderbuss, or Pocket Pistol, ab. 8 or 9 inches in length fr. the butt of the stock to the muzzle. **1805** LEWIS in *L. & Clark Exped.* (1904) II. 91 The buffaloe in passing had . . . shattered the stock of one of the blunderbushes [*sic*]. **1807** *Ann. 10th Congress* 1 Sess. I. 434 Mr. Blannerhasset took away with him two blunderbusses, one pair of horse pistols, a pair of pocket pistols, and a dirk. **1834** *S. Lit. Messenger* I. 157 Their arms were of divers descriptions; double barrelled guns, deer guns, ducking guns, and a blunderbuss. **1850** GARRARD *Wah-To-Yah* xxiv. 301 A set of green men . . . poorly and scantily armed with government blunderbusses. **1854** BARTLETT *Narr.* II. 444 In their midst a huge blunderbuss mounted on a swivel.

2. A talkative or blundering person. {1685–1768; now *dial.* or *colloq.*}

1775 TRUMBULL *M'Fingal* II. (1785) 45 How loud a blunderbuss is Graves! **1873** *Newton* (Kansas) *Kansan* 17 July 3/4 The people may not be bored every other day by some traveling newspaper blunderbuss. **1894** P. L. FORD *P. Stirling* 18, I want the dear old blunderbuss to see how nice a really nice girl can be.

‖**3.** *Blunderbuss boots*, ? wide-topped boots.

1873 *Newton* (Kansas) *Kansan* 31 July 3/3 Geo[rge] Hagerty [was] in hunting trim with his cow hide blunderbuss boots on.

Blunt, *a.* Of cartridges: Blank. — **1799** *Aurora* (Philad.) 9 July 2/5 The Militia Legion will form on its parade . . . , provided as heretofore with blunt cartridge. **1800** *Ib.* 30 April.

* **Board,** *n.*

* **1.** A thin flat piece of lumber having greater length than breadth.

1622 'MOURT' *Relation* 33 A graue . . . was also covered with boords. **1640** *Plymouth Laws* 44 That no man . . . sell out of the Colony's any kind of boards planks or timber. **1643** WILLIAMS *Key* 67 Many of them get English boards and nailes and make artificiall dorres and bolts themselves. **1661** *Plymouth Laws* 133 That a sufficient man in every town, bee appointed to take up what excise shalbee due to the Countrey whether Iron Tarr boards oysters &c. **1714** SEWALL *Diary* III. 6 This Court the Deputies . . . complain of a Duty laid on Boards . . . by . . . New-Hampshire. **1747** *N.H. Probate Rec.* III. 508, I give unto John Odlin . . . all the boards in & about the house. **1784** FILSON *Kentucke* 23 The wild cherry-tree . . . supplies the inhabitants with boards for all their buildings. **1831** PECK *Guide* 126 A farm is about to be enclosed within a few miles from my residence, with plank, or as a New Englander would say, boards, sawed at the mill. **1865** *Atlantic Mo.* XV. 75 Some recall how they crossed other parts of the swamp on boards. **1882** *Century Mag.* Sept. 764/1 An awning of canvas covered the few bottles that stood on the rough boards constituting this 'bar.'

collect. **1627** *Plymouth Col. Rec.* XII. 8 From henceforward no dwelling-house was to be couered with any kind of thatche as straw, reed, &c. but with either bord, or pale. **1649** ELIOT *Glorious Progress* 16 These poor Indians . . . saw very good board and planke. **1698** *East-Hampton Rec.* II. 393 To Cornelios Stretton for 100 borde to the Meeting hous.

+**b.** (See quotations.)

1853 'P. PAXTON' *Yankee in Texas* 65 This . . . camp was . . . formed by setting up a few crotches to sustain a rude roof of undressed shingles, . . . there known as 'boards.' **1859** BARTLETT 40 In the South-west, boards are strips of wood from two to four feet in length riven from blocks, and differing only in size from shingles. All sawed stuff, which at the North is called *boards*, is here called *plank*. **1889** *Cent.* 604 To riven pieces of this kind, not more than 3 feet long, used for roofing, the name *board* is exclusively applied in the southern United States.

c. *pl.* The stage of a theater. {*a*1779–}

1798 *Commercial Advertiser* (N.Y.) 11 Dec., Mrs. Barrett made likewise her first appearance on our boards, and . . . she was as well received as the Play [*The Stranger*]. **1842** *Knickerb.* XX. 492 Mr. Vandenhoff . . . [had] the most wretched support upon the stage that any actor of pretension ever encountered upon the Park boards. **1845** S. SMITH *Theatr. Apprent.* ii. 33, I longed for an opportunity to tread the boards again. **1875** *Chicago Tribune* 21 Sept. 8/2 At the New Chicago Theatre, 'Pauline' keeps the boards. **1889** *Century Mag.* March 752/2 Under the fostering care of the amateur stage the American society drama has obtained a foothold on the professional boards.

+**d.** The board upon which the market quotations in a stock exchange are posted.

1865 *Atlantic Mo.* XV. 575 The artist is like the stock which is to be quoted at the board and thrown upon the market. **1870** MEDBERY *Men Wall St.* 14 The par value of annual sales, made at the boards and 'over the counter,' are computed as . . . exceeding $22,000,000,000.

+**e.** A board room.

1882 *Century Mag.* Aug. 538 'Twill not be long now ere Mr. Briggs returns. He's in the 'board,' sir.

+**f.** *Printing.* (See quotation.)

1893 M. Philips *Making of a Newspaper* 103 The 'copy-cutter' cut the despatch into two parts . . . , and then laid them upon 'the board,' a sort of counter where the compositors came to be supplied with copy.

2. A company of persons meeting at a council table; a body of persons officially constituted for a specific purpose. {1613–}

1683 *Penna. Col. Rec.* I. 84 That it was convenient Warrant should be sent from this board. **1715** *Mass. Ho. Repr. Jrnls.* I. 63 If there be . . . [no business] to come down from the Board, the House desire to be dismist. **1792** *Ann. 2nd Congress* 1033 To constitute a fund for the operations of a Board to be established, for promoting arts, agriculture, manufactures and commerce. **1819** Mackenzie *Life Van Buren* (1846) 152 After a long discussion . . . the board very gravely decided that I was not yet *naturalized*. **1823** *Baptist Mag.* IV. 21 We have now but three foreign missionaries in the employment of the Board. **1848** W. ARMSTRONG *Stocks* 8 The Old Board, as its name indicates, was first established and has been in existence since 17—. **1861** *Army Regulations* 18 Captains . . . [are] subject to the temporary details of service, as for courts-martial, military boards, &c. **1902** G. M. MARTIN *Emmy Lou* 189 Her papa furnished pokers and shovels for the schools, and her papa would call on the Board.

b. Const. *of* the sphere of action or business (as *of agriculture*, *of health*, etc.) or the members constituting the board (as *of advisers*, *of aldermen*, etc.)

(**a**) **1776** *Journals Cont. Congress* VI. 860 Resolved, that the Board of War be directed to send to the commissary of Stores, . . . 10 Tons . . . powder. **1787** CUTLER in *Life & Corr.* I. 240 Mr. Osgood, President of the Board of Treasury. **1797** *Ann. 4th Congress* 2 Sess. 1835 A Board, to consist of not more than thirty persons, which shall be called 'A Board of Agriculture.' **1809** KENDALL *Travels* II. 257 A board of health is annually formed, by the election of one member from each of the twelve wards into which the town [=Boston] is divided. **1812** *Ann. 12th Congress* 1 Sess. 2284 The corporation of the City of Washington shall be composed of a mayor, a board of aldermen, and a board of common council. **1819** *N. Amer. Rev.* VIII. 3 The Board of Public Works in the State of Virginia was established by an act of the General Assembly, passed February 1816. **1840** *Niles' Nat. Reg.* 19 Sept. 48/1 The receipts of the American board of missions, during the past year, have amounted to $241,991. **1872** BRACE *Dangerous Classes N.Y.* 53 The excellent Reports of the Metropolitan Board of Health. *Ib.* 360 Four different classes of officers, . . . , namely, School-Visitors, the Board of Education, State Attorneys, and Grand Jurors. **1884** BISBEE & SIMONDS *Board of Trade* 97 The corporation known as the Chicago Board of Trade was organized more than a quarter of a century ago. . . . The business done upon the floor of this board of trade has become a great . . . factor in fixing the prices or value of grain, meats, and other commodities . . . throughout the United States. **1886** J. L. NICHOLS *Business Guide* (1891) 129 Boards of Trade and Stock Exchanges . . . instead of blessing and benefiting mankind . . . have become gigantic engines of robbery and oppression. **1911** *Okla. Session Laws* 3 Legisl. 121 The Board of Control for the School for the Deaf at Sulphur . . . shall have all the powers, rights and privileges heretofore legally exercised by said board.

(**b**) **1789** MORSE *Amer. Gazetteer* (1798) 31/1 The affairs of the town [=Baltimore] are managed by a board of town commissioners, a board of special commissioners, and a board of wardens. **1807** *Ann. 10th Congress* 1 Sess. I. 1206 Mr. Newton, . . . to whom was referred, on the twentieth ultimo, the petition of the Board of Trustees of the University of Vincennes, . . . made a report thereon. **1812** [see (*a*)]. **1835** *Biogr. Isaac Hill* 64 The same board of selectmen who had accused him of misrepresentation would be again supported. **1846** *Knickerb.* XXVIII. 121 Gentlemen . . . have adopted this plan [=the use of blackball] for preserving their union clubs, boards of directors, and other select and *distingué* associations, from any admixture. **1851** HALL *College Words* 304 In many American colleges the general government is vested in a board of trustees, appointed differently in different colleges. **1851** CIST *Cincinnati* 341 It was not the intention of the Board of Directors to proceed with the building, until [etc.]. **1852** D. G. MITCHELL *Dream Life* 84 No important measure can pass the board of select-men without the Squire's approval. **1863** MASSETT *Drifting About* 143, I was waited upon by the Mayor of the city, assisted by Alderman Queen, and one of the Board of Supervisors. **1877** JOHNSON *Anderson Co., Kansas* 88 The county board of commissioners was changed [in 1858] to a board of supervisors. **1885** *Rep. Indian Affairs* 60 As with the police and 'Indian court' so will it be in regard to the present opposition to the 'board of advisors.' *c*1887 Board of Brokers [see BOARD-BOOK]. **1892** M. A. JACKSON *Jackson* 55 [He] found him much perplexed in consequence of a difference between himself and the Board of Visitors. **1911** *Okla. Session Laws* 3 Legisl. 121 The Board of Regents of the State University . . . shall have the following additional power and duties [etc.].

* **3.** The ordinary meals furnished to a person in a house or

other establishment on the basis of some understanding or agreement, usually at a stipulated rate.

1698 *East-Hampton Rec.* II. 397 Payed by John Parsons for Sarah Whitehaires Borde at Flat bush in 1699. **1723** *Md. Hist. Mag.* XVIII. 204 To your Negro womans Board, and chyrurgicall Aplycations, £6. o. o. **1759** *Boston Gazette* 13 Aug., The said Todd and Purcell having spare Room in said House, can accommodate young Ladies with Board and Lodging at a reasonable Rate. **1818** *N. Amer. Rev.* March 426 The college charges [at Harvard] are . . . Board in commons 38 weeks of term time at about $3 per week, $114. **1870** O. LOGAN *Before Footlights* 286 The slavery of waiting to be married merely to have one's board and lodging paid.

+**b.** Applied to the keeping of horses.

1856 SIMMS *Charlemont* 113 John Cross . . . had made terms with Squire Hinkley for the board and lodging of Brother Stevens and his horse. **1899** *Chicago Record* 4 Jan. 11/3, I will pay $18 per month for the board of my family and road horse 'Judson' until my return from abroad. . . . As I do not care to pay board for two horses, I will sell my . . . mare.

4. In card games.

1852 *Harper's Mag.* V. 535/2 Mr. Randolph . . . asked whether he had money enough to make good the 'board' if he lost. **1857** *Hoyle's Games* (Amer. ed.) 288 *Treble Head.*—When the cards have been twice dealt, and no bets for the pool &c., the pool always belonging to the *board* until a bet is made. **1873** MILLER *Amongst Modocs* 44 It seemed like robbing, to take their money on four aces, and I told them to not set it too deep, but they . . . came to the centre and called me to the board. **1893** K. SANDBORN *S. Calif.* 103 The owner was implored to sit down and gamble himself, hoping in this way to win more money and get back the board.

+**5.** *On board* =ABOARD *adv.*

1860 MRS. S. COWELL *Diary* 168 At Island Point . . . the custom house officer . . . came 'on board' as the Yankees say. **1863** [C. C. HOPLEY] *Life in South* I. 200 Conductor, have you a lady 'on board' who is going to get out here? **1869** 'MARK TWAIN' *Innocents* xii. 108 Once on board, the train will not start till your ticket has been examined. **1883** *Harper's Mag.* Jan. 170/2 The . . . scream of the . . . train warned us to the station and we were soon on board again. **1884** SWEET & KNOX *Through Texas* i. 21, I at once decided . . . to take a trip through the comparatively unknown wilds of Texas on board of a Mexican mustang. **1904** *N.Y. Times* 11 May 3 Half a dozen . . . guards and three private detectives were on board the train when it left Boston.

6. Attrib. in the sense: Made of boards (or from a board), as *board bookcase, door, house, partition,* etc. Also BOARD FENCE, FLOOR, etc.

The corresponding English term is usually *wooden.*

1698 CHAMBERLAIN *Lithobolia* (1914) 64 Another Battery . . . issuing with so prodigious a Noise against the thin Board-wall of my chamber. **1704** S. KNIGHT *Journal* 22 My Apartment . . . was a little Room parted from the Kitchen by a single bord partition. **1812** *Boston Gazette* 9 July 3/4 (*advt.*), The other [cow], when she went away, had on a board blinder. **1825** J. NEAL *Bro. Jonathan* I. 8 The snow was . . . driving through every nook and crevice of the board-work. **1852** STOWE *Uncle Tom* xvii, George and Jim [were] placed on a rough board seat in front. **1859** A. VAN BUREN *Sojourn in South* 93 Sitting on a board-shelf, resting on pegs driven into the logs, . . . you . . . find a water-pail. **1863** 'E. KIRKE' *Southern Friends* i. 12 An old, weather-worn building . . . hermetically sealed by green board shutters. **1869** J. R. BROWNE *Adv. Apache Country* 402 Push open the rough board or slab door, and you have before you the . . . domestic life of the honest miner. **1881** E. INGERSOLL *Oyster Industry* 242 *Board Bank,* a platform set in the bank, or otherwise arranged so as to be alternately covered by tide and flooded with fresh water for freshening oysters before selling. (Cape May.) **1883** *Century Mag.* Aug. 547/1 The absence of glass, the board shutters being painted in imitation of windows, tells of a primitive period. **1883** *Rep. Indian Affairs* 19 The Indians are all living in board houses, with fire-places and chimneys. **1888** GRIGSBY *Smoked Yank* iii. (1891) 25 The barracks were large board shanties. **1898** PAGE *Red Rock* 282 A plain, white board bookcase filled with old books stood on one side. **1912** MRS. WOODROW *Sally Salt* 148 Hidden deep in the woods was a board shack roughly put together.

b. Dealing in boards.

1790 *Penna. Packet* 24 Aug. 3/4 The Partnership of M'Culloh and Peterson, board merchants, is this day disolved by mutual consent.

* **Board,** *v.*

***1.** *tr.* To cover or enclose with boards. Also absol. with *in.*

1646 *Springfield Rec.* I. 185 A shop for a Smith, which is . . . to be boarded both roofe and sides. *Ib.* 200 Mr. John Pynchon will make a chamber over the meeting howse and board it. **1705** *Mass. Prov. Laws* 468 Built with hewed logs up to the eves, the roof boarded and shingled. **1716** *Narragansett Hist. Reg.* III. 278 Mr. Nathaniel Jacobs did sometime past pull down a pane of glass in the Meeting house, and board up the place. **1761** in E. Hyde *Hist. Winchendon* (1849) 96 Voted, That the Committee be empowered to see that the said meeting house be hewed, framed and raised, the outside boarded, shingled, and clapboarded. **1876** MRS. WHITNEY *Sights & Insights* I. 340 Out West . . . we get up a frame, and board in; then we finish off as fast as we can, specially inside.

***2.** To supply (a person) with meals, or meals and lodging; also, to arrange for the board of (someone).

1661 *Jamaica* (L.I.) *Rec.* I. 104 The Town are to board him by turns ffor the sayd time according to the Number of Cattell ye have. **1771** FRANKLIN *Autobiog.* 243 My brother . . . did not keep house, but boarded himself and his apprentices in another family. **1777** *N.H. Comm. Safety Rec.* 73 Ordered . . . to pay . . . £6. 15, for boarding five officers. **1820** IRVING *Sk.-Bk., Sleepy Hollow,* To help out his maintenance, he [the schoolmaster] was, according to country custom in those parts, boarded and lodged at the houses of the farmers. **1845** MRS. KIRKLAND *Western Clearings* 58 [The cow] is doomed to the knife at this season of 'boarding hands.' **1854** M. J. HOLMES *Tempest & Sunshine* ii. 28, I find I can get boarded for a dollar and a half a week. **1856** P. CARTWRIGHT *Autobiog.* ii. 28 My father sent me to school, boarding me at Dr. Beverly Allen's. **1898** PAGE *Red Rock* 546 She did not board any Yankees now—except Captain Thurston, of course.

***3.** *intr.* To obtain one's meals, or meals and lodging, in the house of another, usually at a fixed rate.

1655 *Harvard Coll. Rec.* III. 331 Noe Student shall board or lye out of the Colledge without just Cause allowed by the President. **1714** SEWALL *Diary* III. 15, I . . . had boarded at Mr. Oakes's. **1734** *Harvard Rec.* I. 140 No Undergraduate shall lodge or board out of the College. **1771** FRANKLIN *Autobiog.* 265 He continu'd lodging and boarding at the same house with me, and at my expense. **1787** TYLER *Contrast* IV. i, A gentleman, who, it seems, boards in the same house with him, saw him coming out of our door. **1840** DANA *Two Years* xxxvi. 450 I'm going to knock off grog, and go and board at the Home. **1865** *Atlantic Mo.* XV. 511 Boarding at the same hotel with the General, I sat also at the same table. **1879** STOCKTON *Rudder Grange* i. 3 For some months after our marriage, Euphemia and I boarded. **1907** C. C. ANDREWS *Recoll.* 153 He boarded in a private family, where were a few other boarders.

+**4.** *To board out:* **a.** To secure meals away from one's room or home, or outside of a college dormitory.

1774 MRS. A. ADAMS *Letters* (1848) 22, I suppose they would not choose to be at the expense of boarding out. **1818** J. M. DUNCAN *Travels U.S.* I. 146 'Boarding out' . . . is now much less necessary, in consequence of the erection of two new buildings, with . . . sleeping apartments. **1854** 'O. OPTIC' *In Doors & Out* (1876) 107 This fine furniture was all sold, and he was obliged to board out. **1871** EGGLESTON *Hoosier Schoolm.* ix. 81 Ralph would not find it very pleasant 'boarding out' all the time he was entitled to spend at Pete Jones's.

+**b.** *tr.* To recover (a debt) by boarding with the debtor.

1864 TROWBRIDGE *Cudjo's Cave* ix. 83 It would be equally impossible for him ever to board it out.

+**5.** *To board round* or *around:* **a.** *tr.* To furnish (a schoolmaster) with meals and lodging in different homes in turn.

1833 *Niles' Reg.* XLIV. 347/1 Our schoolmasters are . . . 'boarded round,' so as to save the drawing the pay of the schoolmaster's board from the school fund. **1876** 'JOSH BILLINGS' *Wks.* 325 (F.), The school-committee . . . board him around the neighborhood.

b. *intr.* Of a schoolmaster, etc.: To have meals and lodging in different families in succession.

1839 MRS. KIRKLAND *New Home* xlv. (1840) 319 A dignitary who had 'boarded round' till there was very little of him left. **1845** *S. Lit. Messenger* XI. 754/2 The trustees . . . insisted that . . . I should 'board round' among the employers. **1848** *Knickerb.* XVIII. 68 He . . . taught Stokeville school, and received therefor the sum of nine dollars per month, and 'boarded round!' **1857** *Quinland* I. 274, I am to 'board round,' which is the most disagreeable part of a schoolmaster's life. **1864** T. L. NICHOLS *Amer. Life* I. 60 This amount was often saved . . . by the master or mistress boarding round—taking turns of a week or two at the houses of his or her pupils. **1871** EGGLESTON *Hoosier Schoolm.* 15 It was as well for Ralph that he began to 'board round' by stopping at Mrs. Means's. **1882** THAYER *From Log-Cabin* iv. 59 Teachers always 'boarded round,' dividing the time equally among the families. **1898** I. H. HARPER *S. B. Anthony* I. 24 The next summer she taught a district school at the neighboring village . . . for $1.50 a week and 'boarded round.'

+**6.** *tr.* To keep and feed (horses).

1875 *Cincinnati Daily Times* 1 July 2/8 Metropolitan Livery, Boarding and Sale Stables. . . . Special attention given monthly and day boarding horses. **1880** HOWELLS *Undiscovered Country* 261 The mare . . . was consequently boarded out of town a good deal. **1905** *N.Y. Ev. Post* 24 Feb. 1 The owner of a large stable . . . said that . . . he had recently had some seventy horses to board.

+**7.** To go on or into a vehicle, train, etc.

1879 in *Good Words* (London) Jan. 50 The tramps had boarded a train 50 miles away. **1882** *Nation* 17 Aug. 124/3 A bar-tender, named Reddington, . . . tried to board the train at Bleecker Street [N.Y.]. **1901** MCCUTCHEON *Graustark* i, Mr. Grenfall Lorry boarded the east-bound express at Denver with all the air of a martyr. **1909** *Public Ledger* (Phila.) 24 June 7/1 The two men boarded a car on 20th street.

+**Board bill.** [BOARD *n.* 3.] The charge made, or amount due, for board.

1833 E. T. COKE *Subaltern's Furlough* ii, He has gone away without paying his tailor's bill, or his board bill. **1866** 'F. KIRKLAND' *Bk. Anecdotes* 644 An order for stopping the pay of a Treasury clerk, who owes her a board bill of about seventy dollars! **1871** [L. H. BAGG] *At Yale* 244 The board bills are payable partly in advance, that is at the middle instead of the end of each term. **1890** *Harper's Mag.* May 908/1 All these brothers were earning their own board bills.

+**Board-book.** [BOARD *n.* 2.] A book in which a member of the Board of Brokers recorded daily sales at the Exchange. — **1872** TALMAGE *Abom. Mod. Society* 112 The inevitable board-book that the operator carries in his hand may be as pure as the clothing merchant's ledger. [*c***1887** E. V. SMITH *Plain Truths* 13 The Board of Brokers, as it was called before it claimed to be entitled the New York Stock Exchange, commenced business with eighteen members. . . . The Board met at 11 a.m. and adjourned at 12. Each broker carried a small book in which the prices current and transactions of the day were recorded.]

***Boarded,** *ppl. a.* [BOARD *n.* or *v.*] Made of or covered with boards. Also *boarded-up.*

1636 *Essex Probate Rec.* I. 5, 2 borded Canow. *a***1656** BRADFORD *Hist.* 402 A mighty storme . . . tooke of the borded roofe of a house. *c***1728** CATESBY *Carolina* I. 20 The Red-headed Wood-pecker[s] . . . taking a peculiar delight in ratling with their bill on the boarded houses. **1830** *Collegian* 226 Having crossed the bridge and the boarded walks that succeed. **1890** JEWETT in *Harper's Mag.* Dec. 102 The dismal little boarded-up spidery coquina house was as clean as a whistle.

***Boarder.** [BOARD *v.* 3.]

***1.** One who has meals, or meals and lodging, in the home of another or in a hotel.

*a***1649** WINTHROP *Hist.* I. 312 Being also questioned about the ill and scant diet of his boarders . . . he put it off to his wife. **1677** *New Castle Court Rec.* 123 One John Cooper dying . . . at his house where the said John Cooper was a border. **1722** FRANKLIN *Dogood P.* Wks. II. 9 Discoursing the other Day at Dinner with my Reverend Boarder, . . . I ask'd his Advice about my young Son William. **1762** Peirce *Hist. Harvard* 266 There are above ninety of the Under-Graduates who cannot be accommodated with chambers, but are obliged to live as boarders in private families. **1796** F. BAILY *Tour* (1856) 100 Persons who put up at any of the taverns in America, when they stop two or three days, pay the same per day, whether they eat anything in the house or not; hence the general term 'boarders.' **1848** W. E. BURTON *Waggeries* 79 The clanging of the gong summoned the boarders to the dinner-table. *c***1852** *Corr. R. W. Griswold* (1898) 287, I was merely a boarder [at Brook Farm], having made an arrangement of half work, half pay. **1871** DE VERE 516 Permanent boarders, as persons are called who live for any length of time in a boarding-house or hotel. **1883** HOWELLS *Woman's Reason* xv, I earned money enough to come to Boston and study Art . . . by helpin' mother take boarders. **1909** 'O. HENRY' *Options* 308 Jacks and I were regular boarders at the restaurant, of course.

***2.** A pupil who receives meals and lodging in the school he attends.

*c***1819** D. McCLURE *Diary* (1899) 185 In the summer attended to the instruction of a few pupils, . . . 2 or 3 boarders. **1834** PECK *Gaz. Illinois* 184 Belleville has two select schools; one for boarders half a mile distant. **1849** [CHAMBERLAIN] *Indiana Gazetteer* 54 The terms of tuition in the common branches for boarders are $100 per annum; for half boarders $40. **1851** CIST *Cincinnati* 67 Of these scholars, one hundred and four are boarders, principally from distant places. **1866** *Rep. Indian Affairs* 313 At the beginning of last winter my pupils (who are all boarders) numbered forty-eight.

+**3.** A horse that is cared for at a livery-stable.

1903 *N.Y. Tribune* 20 Sept., Advt., Boarders wanted at Rochville Boarding Stable.

+**Board fence.** [BOARD *n.* 6.] A fence made of boards.

1718 *Boston Selectmen* 48 They . . . shall . . . maintain a substanciall board fence . . . from the Barn to three rods distant southerly from the dwelling house. **1725** *Manchester Rec.* 165 On the esterly side by the highway as the stone wall & board fence now stand. **1775** *Mass. H. S. Coll.* I. 260 A board fence hid him from the Indians. **1790** S. DEANE *New-Eng. Farmer* 90/1 Board fences are of two kinds: They are built either with posts and spikes or with slender stakes and withes. **1823** *New Eng. Farmer* II. 20 The usual method of making board-fence, is to put the posts firmly into the ground, and then attach the boards to them in a direct line. **1843** *Knickerb.* XXI. 481 A plain board-fence . . . is one of the commonest objects in nature. **1866** MOORE *Women of War* 507 They quickly scaled the high board fence, one standing on the other's shoulders. **1891** S. M. WELCH *Recoll. 1830–40* 68, I distinctly remember a long, weather-beaten, tight board fence, on the lower half of this block [in Buffalo]. **1916** W. A. DU PUY *Uncle Sam* 107 When the officer gained those steps he but looked into a blank board fence.

+**Board fencing.** [Cf. prec.] Fencing made of boards. — **1871** *Ill. Agric. Soc. Trans.* VIII. 232 By means of hedging and movable board fencing, keep up a great deal of pasturage.

+**Board floor.** [BOARD *n.* 6.] A floor made of boards.

1836 *Knickerb.* VIII. 150 The trail from St. Augustine to this great bend, about thirty miles, is almost as level as a board floor. **1840** DANA *Two Years* xiii. 100 Some of the more wealthy inhabitants have glass to their windows and board floors. **1866** MOORE *Women of War* 299 Our colonel had had his quarters arranged in the best camp style; . . . good board floor. **1882** *Century Mag.* March 793/2 In preparing cellars or basements, it is often desirable to have board-floors.

+**Board foot.** [BOARD *n.* 1.] The volume of wood in a piece of timber 12″×12″×1″. (A unit employed in measuring lumber.) — **1896** *Vt. Agric. Rep.* XV. 83 About 24 cubic feet per acre is added . . . annually—this means about 150 board feet. *a***1904** WHITE *Blazed Trail Stories* iii. 46 His business was . . . to ascertain . . . the number of board feet put in by the contractor.

***Boarding,** *vbl. n.* [BOARD *v.* 2.]

***1.** The providing of board, or living as a boarder.

1715 *Boston News-Letter* 17 Oct. 2/2 Very good Lodging Chambers fit for any Gentleman, and Boarding likewise. **1790** *Penna. Packet* 31 May 3/4 Genteel Boarding & Lodging for single Gentlemen or a small Family. Enquire of the widow Lesher in Germantown. **1805** PARKINSON *Tour* 566 It is customary when you . . . lodge in a tavern to pay a regular price, dine or not, for every meal, which is called boarding in the house. **1824** [W. N. BLANE] *Excursion U.S.* 26 This custom of 'boarding,' as it is termed, I disliked very much, as it deprived me of many a meal when I was desirous of going to see sights. **1831** PECK *Guide* 246 The cost of boarding and tuition is seventy-five dollars per annum. **1845** S. SMITH *Theatrical Apprent.* i. 21 My landlord hinted that I was in his debt for two weeks boarding and lodging. **1861** [J. B. JONES] *Rebel War Clerk's Diary* I. 55 The boarding of my family, alone, comes to more than my salary.

2. Attrib. with *bill, car, cottage, shanty, table, woman.*

1844 *Lowell Offering* IV. 146 The boarding women are always 'dreadful good' to the new boarder. **1848** MASON in E. Bryant *California* 457 A store was erected, and several boarding shanties in operation. **1857** *Quinland* II. 159, I have finished with Dr. Spooney, my boarding bill is paid, a few dollars are left in my pocket. **1873** BEADLE *Undevel. West* 367 We ate in the 'Pioneer boarding car,' and slept in another car attached. **1878** *Harper's Mag.* Feb. 336/1 The hotels, saloons, restaurants, and boarding cottages [of Atlantic City] . . . are innumerable. **1886** JAMES *Bostonians* 28 She had gone out to her supper; she got her supper at a boarding-table about two blocks off. **1900** *Engineering Mag.* XIX 794/1 Double deck boarding cars built by and in use on the St. Paul & Duluth R.R.

+**b.** *Boarding-stable:* (see quotations and BOARDING-HOUSE 2).

1903 *N.Y. Tribune* 20 Sept., Advt., Boarders wanted at Rochville Boarding Stable. **1905** *N.Y. Ev. Post* 27 Sept. 5 Many horses were suffocated . . . when fire destroyed the two-story boarding stable.

+**Boarding-hall.** A residence for students in which meals are served. — **1868** *Mich. Agric. Rep.* VII. 17 Bill of boarding hall, $79.49. **1871** *Rep. Indian Affairs* (1872) 444, I opened a boarding-hall for them, remodeling some of our old mission buildings for the purpose. **1882** *Dakota Mission Conf. of M. E. Ch.* 3 Sess. 19 Two college boarding halls—one for ladies and one for gentlemen—are carried on [at Cornell College, Iowa]; . . . most excellent board is secured for $2 per week.

Boardinghouse. [BOARDING *vbl. n.* 2.]

1. A house in which people board, or board and lodge. {1823–}

1787 CUTLER in *Life*, etc. I. 325 The best boarding-house in Newport. **1789** MACLAY *Deb. Senate* 127 Izard . . . said that the members of the Senate went to boarding-houses, lodged in holes and corners. **1799** *Ann. 5th Congress* III. 2924 The gentleman from South Carolina, he presumed, had no information on this subject, except what he got from boarding-houses. **1810** BENTLEY *Diary* III. 488 During her widowhood she for many years kept a genteel boarding house. **1835** [LONGSTREET] *Georgia Scenes* 146 The horns of the several boarding-houses began to sound. **1848** JUDSON *Mysteries N.Y.* 1. 105 [She] was reduced, as she was ever saying, to the unfortunate necessity of keeping a boarding-house. **1873** 'MARK TWAIN' & WARNER *Gilded Age* xxiv. 222 There are more boarding-houses to the square acre in Washington than there are in any other city in the land. **1873** *Newton Kansan* 17 July 3/2 A poetical genius [who] takes his hash at a cheap boarding house. **1901** WHITE *Claim Jumpers* i. 1 In a fifth-story sitting room of a New York boarding house four youths were holding a discussion.

+**2.** A stable where horses are put up and fed.

1853 A. BUNN *Old Eng. & New Eng.* 64 Instead of the familiar sign of 'horses taken in to bait and stand at livery,' you may read stuck up, 'boarding-house for horses,' as if they were a set of human beings.

3. Attrib. and comb. with *cook, keeper, runner; fare, table, tavern,* etc.

1811 MEASE *Philadelphia* 136 Boarding house keepers must report persons who are taken sick in their houses. **1838** HAWTHORNE *Note-books* I. 71 At — a nice, comfortable, boarding-house tavern, without a bar or any sort of wines or spirits. **1840** DANA *Two Years* xxxvi. 459 The decks were filled with people; custom-house officers; . . . and boarding-house runners. **1863** HALE *If, Yes & Perhaps* (1868) 29 You forget that I cannot borrow of you any more than of a boarding-house-keeper. **1881** *Harper's Mag.* May 867/2 He . . . had stood the strain of newspaper work and boarding-house fare. **1882** SWEET & KNOX *Texas Siftings* 18 The hair [of a razor-back hog] has been scalded off by the enraged boarding-house cook. **1901** CHURCHILL *Crisis* 13 He was . . . too shrewd to be dragged into political discussions at the boarding-house table.

+**Boarding place.** A home, hotel, etc., where people board.

1854 M. CUMMINS *Lamplighter* xx. 170 [I] represented to her that I wanted a boarding-place for the winter. **1857** M. J. HOLMES *Meadow-Brook* v, When school was out, I started for my boarding-place quite contented with teachers generally. **1877** *Harper's Mag.* March 604/1 My aunt didn't like my boarding place, and wasn't pleased with my boarding mistress. **1911** H. S. HARRISON *Queed* iii. 28 She runs this boarding-place, and people of various kinds come to her.

+**Boarding round.** [BOARD *v.* 5.] Of a schoolmaster: The practice of having meals and room in successive families. — **1845** *S. Lit. Messenger* XI. 755/1, I was formally appointed 'schoolmaster' of the 'Octagon Schoolhouse,' upon the half a dollar per month and 'boarding round' basis.

Boarding school. [BOARDING *vbl. n.*]

1. A school in which pupils are boarded and taught. {1677-}

1714 *Boston News-Letter* 12–19 April 2/2 At the House of Mr. James Ivers . . . is now set up a Boarding School, where will be carefully taught, Flourishing, Embroidery [etc.]. **1723** *New-Eng. Courant* 18–25 Nov. 1/1, I . . . spent several Summers in my younger Years at the Boarding Schools in Boston. **1780** *N.J. Archives* 2 Ser. IV. 332 A Boarding School will be opened on Monday the 24th inst. **1833** in *Century Mag.* Sept. (1885) 780/1, I am, sir, . . . permitted to be the Principal of the Canterbury (Conn.) Female Boarding School. **1848** COOPER *Oak Openings* II. xxx. 217 The girls had been to an 'eastern' boarding-school, that particular feature of civilization not yet flourishing in the north-western states. **1863** 'M. HARLAND' *Husks* 52, I am sick to death of the dollish 'sweet creatures' every boarding-school turns out by the score. **1873** E. S. PHELPS *Trotty's Wedding* vii, Jem [was] . . . stranded for a year in this awful Massachusetts boarding-school. **1892** M. A. JACKSON *Memoirs* vii. 90 The girls were old enough to be sent to boarding-school and the boys to college. **1900** C. C. MUNN *Uncle Terry* 18 Alice . . . had been sent to a boarding-school for two years, where she devoted most of her time to music.

2. Attrib. with *girl, madam, miss,* etc.

1757 *Duxbury Rec.* 321 Briggs Alden, Boarding School Master. **1807** IRVING, etc. *Salmagundi* xix. 510 This dissertation shall be . . . distributed gratis among boarding-school madams. **1835** HOFFMAN *Winter in West* I. 13, I was . . . a little . . . confused at being thus exposed to the full broadside gaze of a hundred 'boarding-school misses.' **1848** *Knickerb.* XXXI. 225 Who has not seen the eyes of the boarding-school boy almost suffused with tears as he gazed upon the codfish dinner, alias 'Nantucket owls'? **1861** WINTHROP *Open Air* 85 The rocks in the current were only as thick as the plums in a boarding-school pudding. **1882** *Wheelman* I. 93 The only fresh-air exercise left for the boarding-school girl is the proverbial walk.

+**Board log.** [BOARD *n.* 1.] A log from which boards may be obtained. — **1647** *Springfield Rec.* I. 190 No man shall hence forth transport out of the town to other places, any buildinge tymber, board loggs, or sawn boardes or planks. **1832** WILLIAMSON *Maine* II. 25 The General Court [in 1693] thought it expedient to encourage him, by permitting him to take board-logs from the public lands.

Board measure. [BOARD *n.* 1.] +The standard of measurement applied to boards; measurement of timber in board-feet (see BOARD-FOOT). Abbreviated as B. M.

1809 F. CUMING *Western Tour* 10 Eight hundred thousand feet of timber, board measure, were employed in and about it. **1813** *Ann. 13th Congress* 1 Sess. I. 379 If you judge of its merits by its superficial contents, . . . length and breadth, by the foot, board measure, the speech has rarely been matched. **1859** *Mass. Resolves* 1 April 52 Stumpage . . . at the rate of . . . four dollars per thousand feet, board measure, for logs. **1898** *Engineering Mag.* XVI. 95 The completed raft contains 450,000 lineal feet of timber, or in the neighborhood of 3,000,000 feet, board-measure.

***Board nail.** [BOARD *n.* 1.]

***1.** A nail of a size suitable for nailing boards. {-1540}

1770 *Mass. Gazette* 29 Jan. (Th.), A Moses Boat, with the larboard Gunwale broke, and mended with Board Nails amidships. **1850** *New Eng. Farmer* II. 319 A wheel . . . was filled with board nails, (cut nails,) with their points projecting outwards. **1867** LOWELL *Fitz Adam's Story* 417 He had been known to cut a fig in two, And change a board-nail for a shingle-nail.

+**2.** *colloq.* In the phrases 'cross (angry, gritty, etc.) enough to bite a board nail off.'

1833 S. SMITH *Major Downing* 193 Two of the Senators . . . looked cross enough for a week to bite a board nail off. **1845** — *J. Downing's Lett.* 48 At that he looked as if he'd bite a board nail off. **1854** — *Way Down East* 62 Then father would look gritty enough to bite a board-nail off.

+**Board pine.** *Obs.* [BOARD *n.* 1.] A pine tree suitable for cutting into boards; ?the white pine. — **1672** JOSSELYN *New Eng. Rarities* 61 Board Pine, is a very large Tree two or three Fadom about. . . . It yields a very soveraign Turpentine for the curing of desperate Wounds. **1675** — *Two Voyages* 64 The Pine-Tree challengeth the next place, and that sort which is called Board-pine is the principal. *Ib.* 65 Take the bark of a Board-pine-Tree [etc.].

+**Board room.** [BOARD *n.* 1d.] The main room or hall of a stock exchange building. — **1883** *Harper's Mag.* May 816/1 The board-room within is amphitheatre-shaped, and a bronze railing protects the circle of seats. **1885** *Ib.* November 844/2 This same juvenile section is addicted to horse-play with unconscious intruders into the Board Room. **1900** S. A. NELSON *A B C Wall St.* 13 Most of the building, however, is an immense board room or hall.

+**Board rule.** 'A figured scale for finding the number of square feet in a board without calculation' (W. '47 citing Haldiman).

+**Board sidewalk.** [BOARD *n.* 6.] A sidewalk made of boards. — **1883** 'MARK TWAIN' *Life on Miss.* xxx. 295 The board sidewalks on the ground level were loose and ruinous. *a***1904** WHITE *Blazed Trail Stories* i. 3 The . . . high board sidewalks of the lumber town were filled . . . with people.

+**Board timber.** [BOARD *n.* 1.] Timber from which boards may be obtained. — **1856** *Florida Plant. Rec.* 458, 2 [men] sawing bord timber.

+**Boardwalk.** [BOARD *n.* 6.] A footway or sidewalk made of boards.

1872 F. M. A. ROE *Army Letters* 53 We reached a narrow board walk that was supposed to run along by her side fence. **1888** *American Humorist* 1 September (F.), Perhaps the greatest attraction of Asbury Park is the board-walk. It runs along the beach for over two miles. **1895** C. KING *Fort Frayne* vii. 98 The back gate stood open, . . . and the board walk leading from it to the rear door was visible. **1898** M. DELAND *Old Chester Tales* 332, I tripped on the board walk on the common; it had a hole in it. **1899** HALL & BLOODGOOD *Atlantic City* 69 No other promenade in the country is so unique and enjoyable as Atlantic City's Boardwalk. It was first built in 1870. **1923** C. J. DUTTON *Shadow on Glass* 59, I went down the long boardwalk past the bathing houses.

+**Board-yard.** *Obs.* [BOARD *n.* 1.] A place where boards and other lumber are stored and sold; a lumberyard. Also attrib. — **1790** *Penna. Packet* 24 Aug. 3/4 The board-yard business is now carried on by John M'Culloh, at Mr. Thomas Morris's wharf. **1811** MEASE *Philadelphia* p. xii, An open space near the Delaware, in the southern part of the city, . . . has been rented for a board yard!! **1830** J. F. WATSON *Philadelphia* 208 It is only within the last 25 years that board yards and wood yards have been opened in the western part of the city. **1850** H. C. WATSON *Camp-Fires Revol.* 86 Jack White and I were peeping from behind a pile of logs in the old board-yard.

+**Boasting dance.** A dance by Indians. — **1833** CATLIN *Indians* I. 126 Dancing . . . may be seen in a variety of forms: such as the buffalo dance, the boasting dance, the begging dance, etc.

Boaston, variant of BOSTON.

***Boat,** *n.*

***1.** A small vessel, propelled usually by oars or sails.

1622 'MOURT' *Relation* 115 The Sauages here came very thicke amongst vs, and were earnest with vs to bring in our Boate. **1630** *Mass. Bay Rec.* I. 74 Noe person shall vse or take away any boate or cannoe without leaue from the owner thereof. **1636** *Springfield Rec.* I. 157 In case the said house and boats [=*supra* greate shallops] be not soe satisfyed for, then soe much meddowe [is] to be sett out. **1654** JOHNSON *Wonder-w. Prov.* 15 Their light cannowes . . . are a kinde of Boates made of Birch Rindes, and sowed together with the roots of white Cedar-Trees. **1708** *Boston News-Letter* 4 Oct. 4/2 On Thursday last there came a small Boat with 2 Salem men & 3 others, to Bristol. **1781–2** JEFFERSON *Notes Va.* (1788) 13 Cheat river . . . is navigable for boats, except in dry seasons. **1840** COOPER *Pathfinder* iii, As soon as the boat was in the stream, Pathfinder sank on his knees, continuing to use the paddle. **1883** [see BONNET 2].

2. A large (sailing or steam) vessel for river or sea traffic.

1836 *Diplom. Corr. Texas* (1908) I. 93, I waited [in Nashville] for the arrival of a Boat which was expected. **1856** GLISAN *Jrnl. Army Life* 366 There are but two boats plying between this and the latter place [Portland] at present. **1857** *Lawrence* (Kansas) *Republican* 4 June 2 From St. Louis to Jefferson City . . . is a pleasant afternoon ride, arriving in time for the evening boat to Kansas. **1884** 'MARK TWAIN' *H. Finn* xxiv. 241 She's a big Orleans boat, and I was afeard she mightn't stop there. **1900** C. C. MUNN *Uncle Terry* 60, I am surprised at the size of your boat; . . . she is large enough for an ocean voyage.

3. Attrib. with various nouns denoting things or persons connected with boats. See also BOAT-BATTERY, BOOK, -BUILDER, etc.

(1) **1636** *Plymouth Laws* 55 The cutt at Greenes Harbor for a boat passage shall be eighteen foote wide. **1638** *Md. Archives* IV. 86, 5 boat hooks, 2 p[air] rudder irons. **1649** *Southampton Rec.* I. 40 The towne reconed with Joshua Barnes for his boat hier. **1787** *Md. Gazette* 1 June 1/2 Nails, Sprigs, and Brads, . . . Boat and Sheathing Nails, of all kinds. **1788** in *Rep. Comm. Patents* (1850) 537 He does not pretend to have begun his boat engine until Mr. Buckly had sent notice. **1789** Cist *Cincinnati* (1841) 204 We raised what in this country is called a camp, by . . . leaning boat-boards . . . against the ridge-pole. **1816** *Niles' Reg.* IX. Suppl. 164/1 To confine the water in such manner as to form a good boat navigation down the [Conn.] River. **1832** *Louisville Public Advt.* 17 March, Wrought Boat Spikes 12 Casks, well ass'd, for sale. **1842** *Knickerb.* XX. 309 We shall take a boat-compass along. **1847** H. Howe *Ohio* 212 The floor [of the Presbyterian church] was of boat plank, resting on wooden blocks. **1848** W. E. BURTON *Waggeries* 85 His nerves were somewhat shocked when he heard the helmsman chattering with the driver of the [canal-]boat horses. **1857** *Harper's Mag.* Nov. 817/2, I rolled myself in my boat-cloak, and lay down on the slope of the mountain. **1865** MRS. WHITNEY *Gayworthys* xlii. 392 The fishermen came; holding themselves off . . . with their stout boat-poles planted againt the ledge. **1871** *Harper's Mag.* July 186 The winning boat's crew in the senior race are presented with the champion boat-flag. **1874** LONG *Wild-Fowl* 21 In boat-shooting, . . . he uses *two* muzzle-loaders. **1884** *Century Mag.* Dec. 281 [On] the first boat-bridge thrown out in active service of the army . . . the army of General Banks crossed to the Virginia shore in 1862.

(2) **1778** *Essex Inst. Coll.* LII. 7 The boatcrew invited . . . [our people]

on shore. **1840** DANA *Two Years* xxv. 263 The mates, of course, and the boat-steerers . . . had been to sea before. **1844** J. COWELL *Thirty Years* 93 A lieutenant in the navy, on his way to Pensacola to join his ship, was one of our boat-mates. **1872** in *Fur, Fin & Feather: Game Laws* 184 The boat-tender, or other persons found on board the vessel, boat, float, canoe, or craft. **1882** J. NIVEN in Godfrey *Nantucket* 354 The boat keepers, contrary to orders, cast off their painters. **1884** *Harper's Mag.* March 524/2 The boat-masters . . . come into the smoky little parlor.

Boat, *v.*

1. *tr.* To put on board a boat; to convey by boat. {1613–}

1656 *Portsmouth Rec.* 73 The suruayers ar to se the cattell boated. **1745** MACSPARRAN *Diary* 26, I may have better Fortune in boating this wood than the last. **1800** *Raleigh* (N.C.) *Register* 22 April, The Lumber can be boated from the Mills to Georgetown. **1815** DRAKE *Cincinnati* iii. 140 The principal part [of the wood] is rafted and boated down the Ohio and Licking rivers. **1842** *Amer. Pioneer* I. 346 The Indians . . . rendered it hazardous boating provisions from the older settlements on the Monongahela. **1865** *Atlantic Mo.* XV. 394/1 The oil drawn into barrels . . . is boated to the railway. **1866** *Congress. Globe* 24 July 4098/1 Stone . . . had become captain of a company which he had raised and boated down to Pittsburg. **1884** *Century Mag.* Jan. 435/2 The navigable rivers . . . of the Chesapeake and Albemarle regions enabled the planters to ship their bulky hogsheads direct from their own barns, or to boat them to the inspector's warehouse.

2. *intr.* To go by means of a boat; to row. {1673–}

1827 COOPER *Prairie* ii, I once met a man that had boated on the river he names. **1851** A. O. HALL *Manhattaner* 154 Two thousand of the enemy, with General Keane, had boated through Canal Bienvenue. **1869** W. MURRAY *Adventures* 10, I have boated up and down that wilderness, going ashore only to 'carry' around a fall.

+**3.** To engage in the business of conveying by boat.

1885 *Graceville* (Minn.) *Transcript* 3 June 2/1 Scores of men who have grown up on the canal are disposing of their boats at a sacrifice, and will boat no longer [on N.Y. canals].

+**Boatable,** *a.* Navigable by boat.

1683 PENN *Descr. Penna.* Wks. (1782) IV. 315 The Schuylkill being an hundred miles boatable above the falls. **1683** — *Frame of Govt.* §22 Libertie to draw . . . their fish to shoare on any man's Lands, . . . except such lands as doe lye upon inland Rivulets, that are not boatable. **1789** MORSE *Amer. Geog.* I. 306 The Seneca Indians . . . can walk four times in a day, from the boatable waters of the Ohio, to those of the Tyoga. *a***1800** T. TWINING *Visit* 390 The Susquehannah . . . is navigable, or, as the Americans say, *boatable*, down the stream, nearly from its rise. **1826** FLINT *Recoll.* 299 Some of them [=bayous of the Miss. R.] are boatable, and, like the parent stream, have high and cultivated banks. **1849** THOREAU *Week on Concord* Wed. 271 We had poled ourselves through the canal . . . to the boatable part of the river. **1888** *Harper's Mag.* Sept. 510/1 Occasionally a caribou is killed . . . while seeking the grass growing in some boatable stream.

+**Boat-battery.** A vessel heavily armed and armored designed for bombarding purposes. — **1864** 'PENNIMAN' *Tanner-Boy* 178 The commanding officer . . . was authorized to turn him over to the captain of some boat-battery or transport.

+**Boat book.** *Obs.* A book for keeping accounts and other records on board a river-boat. — **1831** *Louisville Public Advt.* 1 July, Boat Books.—Ledgers, journals, freight, passage books.

Boatbuilder. One who builds boats. {1679–}

1708 SEWALL *Diary* II. 236, I . . . fear'd that our Warehouse was a-fire: but it proves a smith's shop . . . and a Boat-builder's Shed. **1740** *N.H. Probate Rec.* III. 783 John Stickney of Newbury, Mass., boat-builder. **1780** *Virginia State P.* I. 390 He has consulted experienced Boat-builders. **1822** *Ann. 17th Congress* 1 Sess. I. 279 The amount paid for labor, . . . mast makers, boat builders, . . . and other laborers. **1878** *Harper's Mag.* Feb. 324/2 The inhabitants [of West Creek, N.J.] are fishermen, farmers, and boat-builders properly.

Boatbuilding. The building of boats. {1863–}

1780 *Virginia State P.* I. 391 It is absolutely necessary that the 'Boat-building business' be pushed, to perfect the 'designed Expedition.' **1834** PECK *Gaz. Illinois* 48 Boat building will soon become a branch of business in this state. **1841** CIST *Cincinnati* 252 The science of boat-building has . . . improved. **1879** BISHOP *4 Months in Sneak-Box* 9 The favorite material for boat-building in the United States is white cedar.

+**Boat canal.** An artificial navigable waterway for boats. — **1813** *Ann. 13th Congress* 1 Sess. I. 49 The supply of water drawn from Elk river, by a feeder six miles in length, (already completed, which is itself a boat canal). **1841** PARK *Pantology* 450 Ship Canals are usually 20 feet deep; sloop canals, 8 or 10 feet; and boat canals, from 3 to 6 feet deep.

Boat club. A club composed of those who enjoy rowing, sailing, etc.

1833 *Knickerb.* I. 147 Jack came fuming into the office every morning . . . puffing and blowing, like one of the young gentlemen of the boat club after a hard row. **1865** *Atlantic Mo.* XV. 483 So I . . . accepted my naval establishment, as if it were a new form of boat-club. **1886** *Standard Guide of Washington* 167 The Boat Clubs are in a most flourishing condition, . . . several of them owning Club Houses.

+**Boat corn.** Corn brought south by boat. — **1849** *Rep. Comm. Patents: Agric.* (1850) 164 Every planter [of Miss.] . . . may secure a supply, at least six weeks before his main crop will ripen, by planting a few acres of *boat corn*, that is, corn . . . of a more northern climate, most commonly of Ohio or Kentucky.

+**Boat hand.** A laborer employed aboard a boat. — **1821** *Ann. 17th Congress* 1 Sess. I. 46 This admiralty jurisdiction had done much to ruin those who were engaged in . . . [steamboat] navigation, by making the boat-hands unfaithful. **1875** 'MARK TWAIN' *Old Times Miss.* iv. 73 The passengers had an hour's recreation . . . while the boat-hands chopped the bridge away. **1880** *Harper's Mag.* Dec. 53 This simile is borne out by the action of the double stream of . . . colored boat-hands.

Boatheader. A sailor in command of a whaleboat. — **1851** MELVILLE *Moby Dick* 83 Rising from a little cabin-boy . . . to a harpooner; . . . from that becoming boat-header, chief-mate, and captain. **1869** *Overland Mo.* III. 41 The light lance darted from the boat-header's hands. **1906** *Harper's Mag.* April 678/1 The mate [of a whaleboat] 'heads'—that is, commands—the boat, and so is called the 'boat-header.'

+**Boat horn.**

1. A horn used by river boatmen for signaling. *Obs.*

1835 CROCKETT *Tour* 87 One fellow tried to sing, that was not half up to a Mississippi boat-horn. **1836** C. GILMAN *Recoll.* 69 The call of a night-bird to its mate, a boat-horn waking the echoes, . . . were the only sounds abroad. **1888** *Harper's Mag.* Dec. 48/1 The outline of his long boat-horn caught his eye, and picking it up he sounded its winding largo voice.

2. (See quotation.)

1838 [C. MATHEWS] *Motley Bk.* (1840) 149 A boat-horn . . . consists of the horn of an ox attached to the extremity of a wooden handle, and is used in our sloops and other river craft to wet the sails.

Boathouse. A house or shed beside or near the water where or in which boats are kept. {1824–}

1840 *S. Lit. Messenger* VI. 223/2 At the extremity of the lake stood a boat-house where picnic parties sometimes take their luncheon. **1851** *Knickerb.* XXXVIII. 25 The unpainted wooden boat-house at the place where the little glen is terminated by the beach. **1887** J. HAWTHORNE in *Century Mag.* June 178/2 The boat-house was a long shed, built on piles over the water and destitute of a floor. **1900** C. C. MUNN *Uncle Terry* 305 Telly, . . . unlocking a small annex to Uncle Terry's boathouse, showed him a dainty cedar craft.

Boating, *vbl. n.* {1788–}

1. Journeying or going by boat; in later use, using a boat for pleasure.

1637 [see 3]. **1789** *Kentucky Gazette* 25 April 1/4 Nicholas Wood . . . keeps a Bake Shop in Lexington, . . . where may be had . . . hard bread for Boating. **1802** ELLICOTT *Journal* 18 The river [is] in much better order for boating. **1856** KANE *Arctic Explor.* I. 92 We came to the end of our boating. **1873** HOLLAND *A. Bonnicastle* xxv, Bathing, boating, ball-playing and eating . . . constituted the round of waking delights. **1886** *Harper's Mag.* Oct. 795 The boating and balling . . . left him no time for study.

+**2.** Transporting by boat.

1660 *Virginia Statutes* II. 10 Ordered, That . . . the people . . . bring the corne to such convenient places for boating as they [the commissioners] shall appoint. **1735** *R.I. Col. Rec.* IV. 510 Voted . . . [that] said committee dispose of all the said timber, . . . the charge of boating, &c., to be paid out of the general treasury. **1758** *N.J. Archives* 1 Ser. XX. 178 There is on the said Plantation, a . . . good new Dock, very convenient for boating. **1806** WEBSTER, *Boating*, conveying, or the practice of transporting in boats. **1808** *Niles' Reg.* XV. (1818) 57/1 By the canal, it would cost in boating fifteen cents, for 300 miles. **1829** *Va. Lit. Museum* 16 Dec. 418 *Boating*, 'Conveying by boats,'—not in use in England, but as good a word as *carting* or *ploughing*. **1840** DANA *Two Years* xiv. 110 There is always more or less of boating, in small boats; and if heavy goods are to be taken ashore [etc.].

3. Attrib. (chiefly in recent use).

1637 *Dedham Rec.* 29 To bring the Milstones from Watertowne Mill by land unto the boateing place. **1685** in *Hist. Northampton* (1898) I. 198 [The] boating place below the falls. **1755** *N.J. Archives* 1 Ser. XIX. 488 To be sold, . . . a House . . . very convenient for Shop-Keeping and Boating Business, lies near the Water side. **1827** COOPER *Prairie* xiv, Paul . . . [stood] whistling . . . the air of a boating song. **1846** CORCORAN *Pickings from 'Picayune'* 188 They talked of nothing but pic-nics at Hoboken, drives to Harlem, boating parties to Staten Island, etc. **1870** MEDBERY *Men of Wall St.* 290 The start was what boating-men call a 'spurt.' **1876** [G. H. Tripp] *Student-Life* 378 There are the 'boating set,' and the 'ball men.' **1887** J. HAWTHORNE in *Century Mag.* June 179/1 After we had assumed the proper boating-costume . . . we lowered the boat into the water.

+**Boat landing.** A landing place used by boats; esp. the place on the bank of a river where boats stop to discharge or take on freight, passengers, etc.

1826 FLINT *Recoll.* 13 The first thing that strikes a stranger . . . , arrived at the boat-landing [in Pittsburg], is the . . . spectacle of the varieties of water-craft. **1848** E. BRYANT *California* 44 The wagons were hauled as near the boat-landing as they could be by the teams. **1881** *Harper's Mag.* Oct. 687/1 Below, and nearer the boat-landing, were the Guides' shanty, the kitchen, and the pantry. **1910** J. HART *Vigilante Girl* 283 They found a boat-landing, and Bascom brought forth a boatman.

Boatload. The load of a boat; as much as a boat can contain or carry.

1680 *New Castle Court Rec.* 442 Wee have sent away a boat load [of corn] with Hancock the other day. **1728** *Braintree Rec.* 123 Another of said committee agreed with Samuel Savel Jun[io]r for a parcel of Stones, . . . being near three Boat loads, at thirty shillings. **1745** MacSparran *Diary* 27 In the last boat load . . . I lost my dear servant. **1775** *Essex Inst. Coll.* L. 118 The particulars he could not learn but they saw nineteen boat load of wounded Regulars bro[ugh]t back to Boston. **1847** C. Lanman *Summer in Wilderness* 159 You may accuse me of telling a large story when I speak of boat-loads of trout. **1857** *Quinland* II. 23 One of those great mills, in which sixteen 'run of stones' turn out a whole boat-load of flour every twenty-four hours. **1887** Bret Harte *Crusade of Excelsior* 71 Get the last boat-load ready, and report to me.

* **Boatman.** A man employed aboard a boat.

*a*1649 Winthrop *Hist.* II. 138 Two of the boatmen going up to the houses were shot and killed. **1679** *Portsmouth Rec.* 200 Noe boat man shall view any cattle, sheep, or swine which is caryed of in his boat except a nother viewer help to vew them which is not a boat man. **1723** *New-Eng. Courant* 2 Dec. 1/1 Every Boatman, who commands his Dog and his Boy on board a Wood-Sloop, . . . arrogantly assumes . . . the Title of Captain. **1773** *Broadside Verse* (1930) 53 At Salem, near Boston, . . . William Ward, Boatman, [was drowned]. **1829** *Western M. Review* III. 16 He served as a boatman on the Ohio and Mississippi rivers. **1835** Hoffman *Winter in West* II. 69 Here . . . more than one 'last of the boatmen' still lingers. **1844** *Indiana Senate J.* 232 The existence . . . of a boatmen's infirmary at Lafayette. **1877** 'E. Martin' *Hist. Great Riots* 73 Early in June the boatmen on the Chesapeake & Ohio Canal . . . refused to transport coal for less than $1 per ton. **1910** [see Boat-landing].

Boat race. A race between river steamers (*obs.*) or boats. {1861–}

1854 M. J. Holmes *Tempest & Sunshine* xix. 270 Our readers . . . will not refuse, again, to run the risk of its [the Mississippi's] floating snags, sandbars, and boat-races. **1858** A. A. Lawrence in *Life* (1888) 149 This afternoon we drove down upon the Western Avenue to see the regatta. . . . 'The Harvard' beat in the large boat race. **1880** *Harper's Mag.* July 216/1 The game sports of the club . . . include . . . boat-races on the pond [etc.]. **1887** *Lippincott's Mag.* Aug. 296 Yale has perhaps defeated Harvard or Princeton in base-ball or has won the boat-race at New London.

+**Boat ride.** A sail or row in a boat. — **1842** *Lowell Offering* III. 59 The released captive [a turtle] was gratified with a boat-ride. **1874** Pinkerton *Expressman & Detective* 40 He was told by a slave that 'Massa Simon' and the 'Missus' had shortly before gone down the river for a boat ride. **1883** C. E. Wilder *Sister Ridnour* 144 A series of invitations were given to go to picnics, clam chowders, boat rides, fishing excursions.

+**Boat-stores,** *n. pl.* Equipment, supplies, etc., needed aboard ship. — **1835** A. Parker *Trip to Texas* 12 They are all ornamented with grog-shops, containing, among other miscellaneous matter, an abundant supply of 'boat-stores.' **1841** Cist *Cincinnati* 42 Dealers in boat-stores, iron, [etc.].

* **Boatswain.**

* **1.** An under officer on a ship who has charge of the deck force.

1646 *New Haven Col. Rec.* 258, Goodman Walker testified that he went into the cellar with the boatswayne to shew him the meate. **1684** I. Mather *Providences* i. 27 The master, the mate, the boat-swain, the cook, two fore-mast-men and a boy. **1723** *Weekly Mercury* 6 June 2/2 Evans and his Boatswain quarreling the Crew divided, one part for the Captain and the other for the Boatswain. **1774** J. Andrews *Letters* 60 The Boatswain's whistle call'd all hands upon deck. **1836** Irving *Astoria* I. 105 The Eleanor . . . then sailed; concluding, no doubt, that the boatswain had deserted.

2. a. *Boatswain's mate,* a petty officer ranking next below a boatswain; a boatswain's assistant. {1652–}

1794 *Ann. 3rd Congress* 1426 The following petty officers . . . shall be appointed by the captains of the ships: . . . one captain's clerk, two boatswain's mates, one cockswain. **1796** *Ann. 4th Congress* 2 Sess. 2786, 4 Boatswain's Mates, $13. **1823** Cooper *Pilot* I. iii. 31 The shrill whistle of the boatswain's mate. **1840** Dana *Two Years* i. 4 A naval officer . . . hardly speaks to a sailor except through a boatswain's mate.

b. *Boatswain's chair,* a plank slung by ropes on which a sailor sits when at work aloft.

1878 *Harper's Mag.* Feb. 334/1 The 'boatswain's chair' and the 'breeches buoy' are similar, though older and less efficacious, devices.

+**Boattail.** [See next.] The boat-tailed grackle. Also attrib. — **1857** *Rep. Comm. Patents: Agric.* 129 They [the red-winged starlings] move more gracefully and quickly than either the purple-grackle or the 'boat-tail' of the Southern States. **1887** *Harper's Mag.* Feb. 351/1 Most conspicuous of all [was] the handsome boat-tail grackle.

+**Boat-tailed,** *a.* Having a keel-shaped tail when spread: the distinctive feature of certain grackles. — **1839** Audubon *Ornith. Biog.* V. 48 Boat-Tailed Grakle. *Quiscalus Major. Ib.,* The name of Boat-tailed Grakle has been of late given to our Common Crow Blackbird, *Quiscalus versicolor.* **1857** *Rep. Comm. Patents: Agric.* 131 The crow-blackbird, or 'Boat-tailed Grackle,' is an inhabitant of the Southern States, to the maritime portions of which it is more particularly attached. **1870** *Amer. Naturalist* III. 636 Boat-tailed Grackle. . . . I now seriously question the occurrence of this southern species in Massachusetts. **1894** Torrey *Fla. Sketch-Book* 107 In the leafy top of a pine sat a boat-tailed grackle, splendidly iridescent, engaged in a musical performance.

+**Boat-water.** Water navigable by boats. — **1804** *Mass. H. S. Coll.* 2 Ser. VIII. 112 We left our canoes at the head of boat-waters, in a small clear stream of spring water.

* **Boatwright.** *Obs.* A boat-builder. {–1606} — **1647** *Md. Hist. Mag.* VI. 367 Robert Kedger of the Prouince of Mary-Land Bote-wright. **1681** *Southold Rec.* I. 278 Abraham Whittier, boat wright, did sell unto Thomas Moore a certain percell of land. **1781** *Virginia State P.* I. 495 Boat wrights of the best kind, 3s 6d [of pay].

+**Boatyard.** A yard in which boatbuilding is done.

1805 R. H. Collins *Kentucky* (1874) I. 408 There are also . . . a coal yard and boat yard; and, it is said, several saltpetre caves. **1831** Peck *Guide* 295 Land is reserved [at lower Alton] for a large boat yard. **1842** *S. Lit. Messenger* VIII. 95/2 Other measures no less important . . . are the establishment of a National Boat-Yard on the Mississippi, [etc.]. **1847** L. Collins *Kentucky* 335 [At] West Point . . . there has been an extensive boat yard established, which is doing a flourishing business. **1897** *Outing* XXX. 5/2 Before there was a sign of activity about any of the boatyards, a rumor was afloat . . . that six contracts had been let for first-class sloops.

Bob, *n.*[1]

1. a. A bunch or cluster of hair, thread, worms, etc., used on a line in fishing. {1660–9; dial. *bab,* 1882–3}

1791 Bartram *Travels* 108 These [hooks] are . . . covered with the white hair of a deer's tail, shreds of a red garter, and some parti-coloured feathers, all which form a tuft or tassel, nearly as large as one's fist . . . : this is called a bob. **1828** Webster, *Bob:* . . . our common people apply the word to a knot of worms, on a string, used in fishing for eels. **1859** Bartlett 41 *Bob,* a knot of worms or chicken-guts on a string, used in fishing for eels, and in the South for trout. **1883** *Century Mag.* July 383 The man using the bob is seated in the bow of a boat. *Ib.,* The bob . . . is formed by tying three hooks together, back to back, and covering their shanks with a portion of deer's tail.

b. A small float attached to a fishing line.

1843 in Shields *S. S. Prentiss* (1883) 324 They are mere bobs upon the surface, showing where the big fish were nibbling at the bait below.

+**2.** An attachment to the tail of a kite, serving to ballast it.

1844 *Knickerb.* XXIV. 260 Once in a while a bob gets reinforced, just as the kite has nearly reached the ground. **1848** Lowell *Biglow P.* Notices of Press 1 To delay attaching the *bobs* until the second attempt at flying the kite would indicate but a slender experience in that useful art. **1865** Mrs. Whitney *Gayworthys* viii. 85 They had their own kite to fly, now; and there was nothing to remind them that they had ever helped to tie a bob to the tail of anybody's else. **1867** Holmes *Guardian Angel* 198 Cut off the bobs of your kite . . . and see if it doesn't pitch, and stagger, and come down head-foremost.

+**Bob,** *n.*[2]

1. A short, stout sleigh runner.

1857 *Knickerb.* XLIX. 67 The 'stage' consisted of a rickety pair of bobs —an open box, of course—two miserably gaunt horses, and a Dutchman. *c*1873 De Vere *MS. Notes* 186 *Bobs,* short, stout sleds, 2 of which are gen[erally] placed under 1 sleighbox or wagon box and called a pair of bobs. **1885** E. B. Custer *Boots & Saddles* 112 The rudest bobs were ironed by the company blacksmith. **1889** Farmer 71/1 A sleigh used in the West for conveying large timber, its special characteristic being two pairs of *bobs* or short runners. **1906** *N.Y. Ev. Post* 19 May 9 The same spruce and hemlock logs drawn on bobs.

2. A bobsled or bobsleigh.

1887 *Harper's Mag.* Dec. 113/2 The Captain's sleigh went townward toward evening, and the butcher's 'bob' tore an ugly groove along the lower edge [of the plain]. **1888** *Ib.* May 973/1 Telling the little ones how they might have been mangled by one of the swift 'bobs.'

attrib. **1888** *Troy Daily Times* 31 Jan. (F.), All the village bobbing clubs will participate in the carnival at Albany to-morrow and Thursday nights, when the ice-yacht contest will be held. The bob race will be held in the evening.

b. In plural form in singular sense.

1911 White *Bobby Orde* xvii. (1916) 194 Bobby saw bearing down on him a magnificent bobs. . . . Its board was twelve feet long. *Ib.* 195 If the bobs upset, or the horse went too fast, he could detach the bobs.

Bob, *n.*[3] A light, bounding motion. +In the phrase *on the bob.* — **1834** [Carruthers] *Kentuckian* I. 21 You see he always took 'em on the bob, jist as you would shoot a diving bird. **1864** O. W. Norton *Army Letters* 240 The status of the poor quartermaster may be graphically described as 'on the bob' from morning till night.

+**Bob,** *n.*[4] Short for Bobwhite. — **1883** *Century Mag.* Aug. 483/2 The European partridge . . . weighs twice as much as Bob White, but he has not Bob's sturdy, rapid . . . flight. **1902** E. Sandys & Van Dyke *Upland Game Birds* 9 Then brave, brown Bob . . . enters Love's fateful lists.

+**Bob,** *interj.* An intensive enclitic. — **1857** *Baltimore Sun* 30 March (B.), 'Sir, are you drunk?' The juror straightening himself up, . . . replied, 'No sir-ree, bob!' *Ib.,* Well, . . . I fine you five dollars for the 'ree' and ten for the 'bob.'

Bob, *v.*[1] *intr.* To fish with a bob. {1614–}

The humorous phrase 'to bob for whale' echoes English usage {1766}.

1788 *Mass. Centinel* 13 Dec. 104/1 His rod he drew, . . . and sat upon a rock, and bob'd for a whale. **1834** *Knickerb.* IV. 118 We understand they sometimes 'bob for whales' in the vicinity of Nantucket. *c***1849** J. G. SAXE *Cold Water-Man* Poems (1853) 96 He ne'er had learned the art to 'bob' For anything but eels. **1857** HAMMOND *Northern Scenes* 88, I believe there are no whale; but you can bob for trout.

Bob *v.*[2] *tr.* To cut short, dock (a horse's tail, etc.). Also with *off*. {1675–96}

1822 J. FOWLER *Journal* 112 We this day seen six wild Horses, tho two of them must have been in Hands, as their tails ware bobed short. **1889** *Cent.* 606/2 *Bob*, . . . to cut short; dock: often with off: as, to *bob* or *bob off* a horse's tail. **1894** *Congress. Globe* App. 11 Jan. 43/1 The [Republican] party . . . have adopted every English 'fad,' from a gold standard down to 'bobbing' their horses' tails.

***Bob,** *v.*[3] +In the phrase *to bob around*, to go from place to place; to knock about. — **1857** *Harper's Mag.* March 443/2 You may take me if you can catch me while I'm bobbin' around, but I can't stop for you. **1869** BROWNE *Adv. Apache Country* 182 She had prospected awhile in Australia, and bobbed around Frisco for the last few years. **1871** DE VERE 585 'Bobbing around' is . . . a favorite expression in the United States.

+**Bob,** *v.*[4] [BOB *n.*[2]] *intr.* To ride or coast on a bobsled. — **1880** *Wisconsin Rep.* 254 For injuries suffered . . . by collision with persons 'bobbing' or 'coasting' on such street, the city is not liable.

Bobbed, *a.* Cut off short; docked. {1675–96}

Bobbed-tail (quot. 1908): see BOBTAIL 4, 5d.

1768 WASHINGTON *Diaries* I. 256 Hunting again, and catchd a fox with a bobd tail and cut ears. **1894** *Outing* XXIV. 193/1 There is nothing more hideous than a bobbed jib. **1897** *Ib.* XXIX. 464/2 Small boys strutting about in tall beavers with bobbed-off coats, looking . . . like tailless sparrows. **1908** 'YESLAH' *Tenderfoot S. Calif.* 67 Then began a foot race for another dinky car, a bobbed tail electric this time.

Bobber. [BOB *n.*[1]] A float used in angling. {1837–}

1873 W. C. PRIME *I Go A-Fishing* 248 A strong fellow [=a trout] struck the bobber and carried away the leader. **1881** *Harper's Mag.* Oct. 654/1 You can see the bobber dance upon the ripples. **1884** ROE *Nature's Story* 195 In smooth water it's like fishing with one of your little cork bobbers there on your lines. **1913** G. STRATTON-PORTER *Laddie* viii. 145 He bought me . . . a real fishing line, several hooks, and a red bobber.

Bobbinet. A cotton lace, having a six-sided mesh. Also attrib. with *lace*. {1836–} — **1827** *Hallowell* (Maine) *Gaz.* 20 June 4/5 Goods; among which are . . . elegant wide blk. and white Bobinett Laces: Threa[d] and Bobinett Laces, edgings and insertings. **1868** MRS. WHITNEY *P. Strong* 172 Patience, won't you just see whether Emery Ann has done pressing out that piece of bobbinet?

Bobbing, *vbl. n.*[1] [BOB *v.*[1]] Fishing with a bob. {1653–}

1814 MITCHILL *Fishes N.Y.* 360 The eel . . . is also taken . . . by a bunch of tough-bait, after a manner called *bobbing*. **1832** J. F. WATSON *Hist. Tales N.Y.* 54 They had the art of catching fish by torch-light . . . in the way we call *bobbing*. **1883** *Century Mag.* July 383/1 The Floridians . . . use a long rod or pole for still-fishing, skittering, and bobbing.

+**Bobbing,** *vbl. n.*[2] [BOB *n.*[2]] The pastime of riding on a bobsleigh or sled. Attrib. with *club*, *party*, etc. — **1888** *Troy Daily Times* 31 Jan. (F.), All the village bobbing clubs will participate in the carnival at Albany to-morrow. . . . There are seventy-eight entries for the bobbing parade. **1888** *Harper's Mag.* May 973/1 Ruby and Ned displeased their mother by joining a 'bobbing' party on a neighbouring 'hill' street.

Bobbin lace, †lacing. Lace made by means of bobbins; bone lace. — **1678** *New Castle Court Rec.* 362, 11 doz. thred Laces & 11 peces of bobing Laceing. **1725** SEWALL *Diary* III. 369 Madame Franklyn . . . comes to me, shews me her Bobbin-Lace: What she has made up.

+**Bobcat.** [f. *bob* a short or docked tail {1711–}; cf. BOB *v.*[2]] The bay lynx (*Lynx rufus*), having a short tail. Also transf. — **1888** ROOSEVELT in *Century Mag.* March 656 We also keep hens, which, in spite of the damaging inroads of hawks, bob-cats, and foxes, supply us with eggs. **1901** O. WISTER *Members of Family* vii. (1911) 250, I came for a box of matches, y'u bawlin' bobcat. **1907** WHITE *Arizona Nights* xvi. 232 By now the coyotes and bob-cats had nailed the straight-breds. **1918** MULFORD *Man from Bar 20* 23, I was just as happy as a bobcat in a trap—an' about as peaceful.

+**Bob-coat.** A bob-tailed coat. — **1835** LONGFELLOW *Outre-Mer* I. 64 The procession was led by a long orang-outang of a man, in a straw hat and white dimity bob-coat.

‖**Bob-crackery.** *colloq.* ?*Obs.* A trifling article. — **1837** *Harvardiana* III. 238, I was dispatched . . . for a load of pumpkins and such other bob-crackeries.

+**Bobolink.** Also **boblinco(l)n, -o-lincoln, -o-link-horn, -a-linkum; boblink, bob-a-link, -o-link, -o'-linck.** [An imitation of the 'metallic clinking' note of the bird.]

1. The reed-bird or rice-bird (*Dolichonyx oryzivorus*), well-known for its song.

(*a*) **1774** J. ADAMS *Works* II. 401 Young Ned Rutledge is a perfect Bob-o-Lincoln,—a swallow, a sparrow, a peacock. *a***1801** FESSENDEN *Orig. Poems* (1806) 146 In strains as sad as you can think on, In unison with bob-o-link horn. **1821** *Jrnl. Science* III. 275 Floral . . . Calendar for Plainfield, Mass. . . . May 24 . . . the bob of lincoln [*sic*] and kingbird, seen for the first time. **1840** HOFFMAN *Greyslaer* II. 104 There he goes . . . singing for all the world like a Bob-a-linkum on the wing. **1843** L. M. CHILD *Lett. New York* 272 He will love . . . the merry bob-o' lincoln better than stuffed birds from Araby the blest. **1850** MITCHELL *Reveries* 151 The black-and-white coated Bob-o-Lincoln, is wheeling his musical flight, while his quieter mate sits swaying on the topmost twigs.

(*b*) **1792** J. BELKNAP *New Hampshire* III. 173 Boblincoln, *Emberiza oryzivora*. **1809** IRVING *Knickerb.* II. v, In the merry month of June . . . when . . . the luxurious little Boblincon revels among the clover blossoms of the meadows. **1830** PAULDING *Chron. Gotham* 103 They went away as gay as boblincons in a clover meadow. **1839** IRVING *Wolfert's R.* (1855) 33 The happiest bird in our spring, however, and one that rivals the European lark in my estimation, is the Boblincon, or Boblink, as he is commonly called.

(*c*) **1844** *Nat. Hist. N.Y., Zoology* II. 144 The Boblink, or Bob-o' link as it is called in this State, is known in others by the various names of Reed-bird, May-bird, Meadow-bird, [etc.]. **1846** FARNHAM *Prairie Land* 217 These will give the bobo'-link, brown thrasher, robin, whip-poor-will, &c., ample encouragement to visit you. **1848** BARTLETT 40 *Bobolink*, the popular name of the rice-bunting (*icterus*), a bird which frequents the wild rice and marshes. . . . It is called [also] the skunk-blackbird. **1874** COUES *Birds* 179 The Bobolink makes a rude and flimsy nest of dried grass on the ground. *Ib.*, They are now songless—who ever heard Bobolink music in the fall? **1877** BURROUGHS *Birds & Poets* 102 The bobolink . . . has . . . on the high grass lands of the interior of the state [=N.Y.], quite a different strain—clearer, . . . and running off with more sparkle and liltingness. **1885** *Milnor* (Dak.) *Free Press* 25 April 3/1 It is said that the bobolinks, which are such dandylike, rollicking birds in the summer, go south in the autumn, take off their gaudy uniform, put on suits of rusty black, change their name, and become either reed or rice birds.

(*d*) **1810** WILSON *Ornithology* II. 48 Rice Bunting, *Emberiza Oryzivora*. This is the *Boblink* of the eastern and northern states, and the *Rice* and *Reed*-bird of Pennsylvania and the southern states. **1841** *Knickerb.* XVII. 157 The boblink, who sinks up and down on a 'long flaunting weed' in the opposite clover field, cannot endure the parody on his sweet notes. **1844** [see *c*].

(*e*) **1826** FLINT *Recoll.* 243, I saw early in the spring a flock of those merry and chattering birds, that we call bob-a-link, or French black-bird.

2. The call note of this bird.

1855 BRYANT *Robert of Lincoln* i, Robert of Lincoln is telling his name: Bob-o'-link, bob-o'-link, Spink, spank, spink.

+**Bobolition.** *Obs.* An alleged Negro variant of ABOLITION. — **1818** (*title*), Bobolition of Slavery!!! Grand selebrashum by de Africum Shocietee!!! Boston. **1819** W. FAUX *Memorable Days* 9 A recent anniversary in Boston of Free Blacks, met to celebrate the abolition, or as they term it the *Boblition* of the slave-trade. **1821** (*title*), Grand bobalition, or great annibersary fussible! . . . Boston. **1839** F. J. GRUND *Aristocracy* II. 137 For G—d's sake! cried the old gentleman; let us not have *bobolition*. **1861** F. Moore *Rebellion Record* I. III. 126/2 Wake up, I tell yer! Git up, Jefferson! Bobolishion's comin'—Bob-o-lish-i-on.

+**Bob sawyer.** *local.* [BOB *v.*[3]] =SAWYER. — **1879** BISHOP *4 Months in Sneak-box* 65 This trap for careless sailors is a tree, with its roots held in the river's bottom, and its broken top bobbing up and down with the undulations of the current. Boatmen give it the euphonious title of 'bob sawyer' because of the bobbing and sawing motions imparted to it by the pulsations of the water.

+**Bobsled,** *n.* [BOB *n.*[2]]

1. A sled, having two pairs of short runners, used in transporting timber, etc.

1848 BARTLETT 40 *Bob-sled*, a sled prepared for the transportation of large timber from the forest to a river or public road. *Maine*. **1849** WILLIS *Rural Letters* i. 20 Then there would be wear and tear of bob-sled, teamster's wages, and your dead-pull springs, the horses' knees. **1851** SPRINGER *Forest Life* 94 The teams [draw] after them a short sled, called a 'bob-sled': probably so named for the bobbing motion it has while drawn over the rough ground. **1851** *Harper's Mag.* Sept. 518/1 The yokes and chains are carried up by the workmen, and also the bob-sled in pieces. **1860** *Ib.* March 444/1 The unearthly shrieks of the bob-sleds as they groan beneath their ponderous burdens [logs]. **1879** F. M. A. ROE *Army Lett.* 230, I was at the saw-mill four days, and then we all came in together and on bob sleds.

2. A sled for coasting made of two pairs of runners connected by a long board.

1890 *Dialect Notes* I. 72 *Bob-sled*, a 'double-runner' (only of a boy's sled). **1891** *Amer. Folk-Lore* IV. 160 The 'double-runner' of New England becomes, however, on Long Island, a 'bob-sled,' or even a 'bob.' **1904** *N.Y. Ev. Post* 21 Jan. 11 Three boys are in the Englewood Hospital as the result of a collision between two bob sleds.

+**Bobsled,** *v. intr.* To ride or coast on a bobsled; =BOB *v.*[4] — **1883** PECK *Bad Boy* 154 You have got to be darn careful when you have the mumps, and not go out bob-sledding.

+**Bobsleigh.** (See first quotation.) — **1889** *Cent.* 607/2 *Bob-sleigh*, a sleigh constructed upon the same principle as a bob-sled. **1890** H. FREDERIC *Lawton Girl* 14 The expressman who halted his bob-sleigh at the cutting in front of her . . . seemed a long time making up his mind to speak.

+**Bob-squirt.** *colloq.* [See SQUIRT *n.*] A worthless young man; a whipper-snapper. — **1891** WILKINS *New Eng. Nun*, etc. 26 S'pose they should turn you out in your old age an' call in some young bob squirt, how'd you feel? **1905** — *Debtor* 469 But you look as if you could do more and better work in an hour than that young bob-squirt.

* **Bobtail.**

+**1.** A bobtail coat. (See 5 b.)

1824 *Free Press* (Halifax, N.C.) 17 Sept., Bobtails and hunting shirts! you are a set of d—d ignorant fellows. **1850** C. MATHEWS *Moneypenny* 61 The checker-board hat was changed to a fall beaver; . . . but the bob-tail and barber-pole were on duty in strong force.

+**b.** *pl.* A nickname of the early Virginian rangers.

1880 *Harper's Mag.* Feb. 358/1 Braddock's . . . troops nicknamed the Virginia rangers, in derision at the scanty coats which Dinwiddie had given them, 'Bobtails.'

+**2.** A variety of snipe.

1841 *S. Lit. Messenger* VII. 77/1 Innumerable species of the snipe are every where to be met with, from the little Bobtail of the sandbar, up to the Beccasse of the plain.

3. =BOB *n.*[1] 2.

1844 *Knickerb.* XXIV. 251 'Brother Jonathan' made a long 'bobtail' [for the kite].

+**4.** A bobtail car (see 5 d).

1875 *Chicago Tribune* 16 Oct. 11/3 Witness . . . [had] been conductor on a two-horse car since last May; . . . [and not] conductor on a 'bobtail.'

5. *attrib.* **a.** Of a horse or other animal: Having a bobbed tail.

1845 HOOPER *Simon Sugg's Adv.* vii. 83 There goes old man Simmons . . . in a cart drawn by a bob-tail, gray pony. **1866** C. H. SMITH *Bill Arp* 81 Just pitch in freely . . . , bet it on some bob-tail nag if you want to. **1872** *Newton Kansan* 31 Oct. 2/3 [He] flew around the room like a bob tail bull in fly time. **1882** PECK *Sunshine* 67 The docking of that badger's tail, and setting it up like a bob-tail horse. **1910** C. HARRIS *Eve's Husband* 306 He'll come back like Bo-peep's other lost bobtail sheep if you can wait and behave properly.

+**b.** Of a coat: Having short square skirts. (Cf. sense 1.)

1832 KENNEDY *Swallow Barn* II. 5 A shad-bellied blue bobtail coat . . . was well adapted to show the breadth of his brawny chest. **1846** LOWELL *Biglow P.* I. i. 6, I dunno' but wut it's pooty Trainin' round in bobtail coats. **1880** 'MARK TWAIN' *Tramp Abroad* xxxv. 400 They gave my bobtail coat to somebody else, and sent me an ulster suitable for a giraffe.

‖**c.** Of persons: Short in stature.

1856 *Spirit of Times* (N.Y.) 25 Oct. 130/2 He was a leetle yaller bobtail cuss, but he could run.

+**d.** Of a car (or train): Shorter or smaller than the usual type. (Cf. 4.)

'The popular name for a small tram-car horsed by a single animal, and on which the only official is a driver' (F.).

1873 *Newton Kansan* 5 June 3/3 The 'bob-tail' train to Hutchinson. **1875** *Chicago Tribune* 8 Sept. 8/2 The bobtail cars ought to be taken off the streets right away, or conductors put on them. **1883** *Phila. Ev. Star* 13 Feb. 3/4 We have been sincerely interested in the old familiar bob-tail cars that furnish transportation for the hurrying multitudes of [New Orleans]. **1887** *Harper's Mag.* Sept. 646/1 In a New York bobtail car. **1888** *Christian at Work* (F.), Congress . . . might try the experiment of abolishing bobtail cars. **1901** CHURCHILL *Crisis* 263 Little 'bob-tail' yellow cars were drawn by plodding mules to an inclosure in a timbered valley, . . . known as Lindell Grove.

+**e.** (See quotations.)

1880 *Congress. Record* 6 May 3078/2 The Territories have only a part of what is called here 'bobtail' representation, a power to speak but not to vote. **1886** *Outing* Dec. 227/2 Upon the expiration of his first enlistment, he was given what is called a *bobtail* discharge, a discharge without character.

f. In poker: Consisting of four cards of one suit and one of another. (Cf. BOBTAILED *a.*, quot. 1873.)

1887 *Courier-Journal* 20 Jan. 4/1 The Confederates would . . . bet away the Washington monument on a 'bob-tail flush.' **1894** CHOPIN *Bayou Folk* 2 Mr. Wallace Offdean hurried to the bank in order to replenish his portemonnaie which had been materially lightened at the club through the medium of unpropitious jack-pots and bobtail flushes.

Bobtailed, *a.* {1640–1702} =BOBTAIL 5.

1796 WEEMS *Letters* II. 47 Your allowance to me . . . is rather of this lean and bobtailed kind. **1841** *S. Lit. Messenger* VII. 219/1 A little rough-coated, bob-tailed chunk of a Canadian poney. **1843** [STEPHENS] *High Life N.Y.* II. 203, I got on my figgered vest and my little bob-tailed coat. **1856** 'SNODGRASS' ['Mark Twain'] in *Keokuk Sat. Post* 1 Nov. 9 Then some soldiers with bob-tailed tin coats on (high water coats we used to call 'em in Keokuk) come in. **1873** *Winfield* (Kansas) *Courier* 15 Feb. 1/5 For a little man Senator Allen could play a pretty large game. The clerical part of the House was also well up in all the mysteries of a 'pair' or a 'bob-tailed flush.' **1875** *Chicago Tribune* 16 Oct. 11/3 The witness professed ignorance in regard to public feeling being against 'bobtailed' cars. **1894** ROBLEY *Bourbon Co., Kansas* 63 The stage, an old bob-tailed ,jerky,' . . . made the trip once a week. **1901** WHITE *Westerners* i. 4 He owned . . . a light, two-wheeled wagon of the bob-tailed type.

+**Bob veal.** Veal so immature as to be unfit for food. — **1888** *San Francisco W. Exam.* 22 March (F.), It is time this traffic in shrimp and bob-veal was stopped. **1911** *N.Y. Ev. Post* 13 Oct. 1 A former butcher was sentenced . . . for . . . shipping . . . the carcasses of five bob veal calves to this city.

+**Bobwhite.** [Imitative of the bird's note.]

1. The call or note of the quail or partridge.

1812 WILSON *Ornithol.* VI. 25 The quail . . . will sometimes sit, repeating, at short intervals, 'Bob White,' for half an hour at a time. **1846** FARNHAM *Prairie Land* 72 He looks about a moment, and repeats in a higher and more intense key, 'Bob White!' **1874** COUES *Birds N. W.* 437 These notes [of the plumed quail] . . . are analogous to the 'bob-white' of the Eastern Quail.

2. A popular name of the quail or partridge, *Ortyx virginianus.*

1856 *Spirit of Times* (N.Y.) 22 Nov. 193/1 But never does he, like dear, beautiful Bob White, visit our barns. *Ib.* 27 Dec. 269/2. **1858** BAIRD *Birds Pacific R. R.* 641 It would be much better . . . to select names for the American birds which have not been used for other species; such, perhaps, as Bob white for the *Ortyx.* **1876** *Fur, Fin, & Feather* Sept. 144 The cultivated fields [near Forest City, Ark.] are tenanted with Bob Whites. **1883** *Century Mag.* Aug. 483 Bob White, The Game Bird of America. *Ib.*, In the North and East, he is called Quail; in the South and West, he is Partridge; while everywhere, he is known as Bob White. **1904** *Phila. Press* 30 May 7 Ornithologists have been making an investigation of the economic value of the bob white.

+**Bock (beer).** [G. *bockbier.*] A variety of dark lager beer of more than the usual alcoholic content which is sold in spring. — **1883** DE VERE in *Enc. Br. Suppl.* I. 198/1 The same is true of their [=Germans'] favorite drink, and no American can plead ignorance of what lager and bock beer mean. **1887** H. FREDERIC *Seth's Brother's Wife* 111 The beverage was bitter. . . . They discussed the merits of this new 'bock.' **1897** F. NORRIS *Stories & Sk.* (1931) 65 An open car had appeared on the crosstown cable line and Bock beer was on draught at the 'Wein Stube,' and Polk Street knew that Spring was at hand.

+**Bockey.** [Du. *bakje*, dim. of *bak*, trough, tray.] (See quotation.) — **1848** BARTLETT 41 *Bockey*, a bowl or vessel made from a gourd. A term probably derived from the Dutch, as it is peculiar to the city of New York and its vicinity.

Bocking. ?*Obs.* [Named from the village *Bocking* in Essex, England.] A kind of coarse woolen cloth, used to protect floors and carpets. {1759–}

1820 *Columbian Centinel* 5 Jan. 4 Foster . . . has for sale . . . Bockings. **1832** in *Niles' Reg.* LXIV. 379/2 This country consumes largely of an article called 'bockings,' well known to the New England people. **1844** *Congress. Globe* 11 March 360/2 On flannels, . . . and on bockings and baizes, there shall be levied a duty of thirty per centum ad valorem. **1848** BARTLETT 41 *Bocking*, a kind of baize, or woollen cloth, . . . used to cover floors or to protect carpets. **1864** MRS. STOWE in *Atlantic Mo.* Jan. 43/2 The large cloth which covered the middle of the floor, and which the women call a bocking, had been . . . nailed down there. **1873** E. S. PHELPS *Trotty's Wedding* xviii, We . . . put down a strip of bocking where Bib had worn the front stair-carpet through.

+**Bodacious,** *adv.* and *a.* Also **bowd-, bawdacious.** [Cf. next.] **1.** *adv.* In a high degree; very. **2.** *adj.* Complete; thorough. — (1) *c*1845 W. T. THOMPSON *Chron. Pineville* 178 She's so bowdacious unreasonable when she's raised. (2) **1887** 'CRADDOCK' *Keedon Bluffs* 153 Air ye turned a bodacious idjit, Skimp? **1896** POOL *In Buncombe County* 239, I'm er bawdacious fool.

+**Bodaciously,** *adv. dial.* [Perhaps a fanciful expansion of *bodily;* cf. BODYACIOUSLY.] Completely, thoroughly, wholly.

1837 SHERWOOD *Gaz. Georgia* (ed. 3) 69 *Bodaciously*, wholly. **1840** *Congress. Globe* 20 July 545/2 Have we not heard it proclaimed . . . that the Administration is bodaciously used up. **1843** 'CARLTON' *New Purchase* I. xix. 175 It was now snowing so bodaciously fast as to kiver [my tracks] as fast as I made them. **1845** J. J. HOOPER *Simon Sugg's Adv.* xii. 147 Ef you don't want to be eet up boddaciously, . . . you'd better git a-top of . . . [your horse] and slope! **1878** BEADLE *Western Wilds* 118, I saw a man . . . , who had been 'bodaciously chawed up' to use his own language, by a grizzly bear. **1883** *Ib.* 615 Not a smidgeon [of corn] left—just bodaciously chawed up and spit out. **1884** 'CRADDOCK' *Tenn. Mts.* I. 28 An' now ye hev gone an' bodaciously slaughtered pore Jubal Tynes! **1891** *Harper's Mag.* June 67/2 The whole posse, prisoner an' all, would bodaciously roll over the rocks into some o' them gorges. **1904** W. N. HARBEN *Georgians* 69 You was ruinin' yoreselves bodaciously.

+**Bodewash.** *local.* =BOIS DE VACHE. — **1871** DE VERE 110 *Bodewash* . . . [is] the *Buffalo Chips* of the Western hunter and trader. **1877** BARTLETT 56 *Bodewash.* (Fr. *bois de vache.*) Dried cow-dung, used for fuel on the treeless plains of the Far West.

Bodice maker. *Obs.* One who makes bodices. {1672–1758.} — **1680** *Boston Rec.* Misc. P. X. 58 James Ferry, Bodice Maker. **1686** SEWALL *Diary* I. 146 Wm. Harrison the Bodies-maker is buried.

+**Bodock, Bodok.** =BOIS D'ARC, BOWDARK.

1847 DARLINGTON *Weeds & Plants* (1860) 297 Orange-like Maclura. Osage-orange. Bow-wood. Bodock. **1871** DE VERE 110 Its wood being specially well adapted for the bows used by the Indians, it [the Osage Orange] was called *bois d'arc* by French settlers; the unfamiliar name became in the hands of English hunters *Bowdark*, . . . and finally it settled down into the still shorter *Bodok* which is now the common designation in many parts of the Union. **1889** FARMER 72 *Bodok, Bowdark*, . . . the osage orange. A beautiful shrub, which flourishes in Missouri and Arkansas, . . . and is . . . much used for hedge-rows. **1897** SUDWORTH *Arborescent Flora* 190 *Toxylon pomiferum*. . . . Common names. . . . Bois D'Arc (La., Tex., Mo.). Bodock (Kans.).

* **Body.**

* **1.** The trunk of a tree, etc. {-1697}

1656 *Jamaica* (L.I.) *Rec.* I. 169 Whosoever shall fell any trees in the high wayse shall take both top and body out of the highway. **1671** W. ADAMS *Memoir* 14 A violent hurricane . . . tearing up by the roots, or breaking the bodyes of almost all trees within its compasse. **1708** *Topsfield Rec.* I. 162 Persons belonging to the Town shall have liberty to . . . fall wood . . . provided they carry away the Tops of what they fall as well as the Bodies. **1847** *Rep. Comm. Patents* (1848) 198 The body of the vine [of the mustang grape] oftentimes attains to six inches in diameter. **1898** PAGE *Red Rock* 315 She let the bough go and edged in toward the body of the tree.

+**2.** An area or region *of* land or timber.

1700 *Providence Rec.* IV. 199 A heape of stones neere a small rock . . . is the norwesterne Cornner of the said Body of land. **1750** C. GIST *Journals* 32 After finding a large Body of good level Land, you are not to stop. **1772** *Town & Country Mag.* 161 A large body of land, extending thirty miles up the Coosaw river. **1834** PECK *Gaz. Illinois* 164 Vermilion county . . . contains large bodies of excellent land. **1837** W. JENKINS *Ohio Gaz.* 134 Columbia, a new town, . . . is surrounded by an extensive body of excellent land. **1857** *Lawrence* (Kansas) *Republican* 4 June 3 It is beautifully situated . . . near a heavy body of timber.

+**3.** *Body and breeches*, wholly, entirely. *colloq.*

1878 *Congress. Rec.* 12 April 2492/1 The Yankee notions produced by Newark every year will buy out, body and breeches, any thoroughly Democratic State in the Union. **1901** W. A. WHITE in *McClure's Mag.* Dec. 151/2 Platt . . . got nearly to the door; then turned back, and surrendered, body and breeches.

+**Bodyaciously, -aceously,** *adv.* =BODACIOUSLY *adv.* — **1833** J. HALL *Leg. West* 38 It's a mercy, Miss, that the cowardly varments hadn't used you up body-aciously. *Ib.* 82 The misery in my tooth . . . seems like it would jist use me up *bodyaciously*. **1866** *Congress. Globe* 17 March 1473/3 When she [S.C.] went out of the Union she did not pick herself up bodyaceously, walk off, and locate in some . . . other hemisphere.

+**Body-meeting.** *Hist.* (See quotation.) — **1823** TUDOR *Otis* 418 [At Boston in 1773] a body-meeting was an assembly after public notification, at which any citizens might attend, and at which many of the principal inhabitants of the neighbouring towns attended. . . . These body meetings were in fact, only an orderly, well regulated mob.

+**Body pew.** (See quot. 1877.)

1823 *Baptist Mag.* IV. 145 Elder A— requested those who were willing to own themselves concerned for their souls, to seat themselves in the body pews. **1843** *Knickerb.* XXI. 72 The young lady . . . looked down at the coffin . . . , and at the same time . . . cast stolen glances at a young physician in one of the body-pews. **1877** BARTLETT 608 *Slip*, . . . in New England, a long seat or narrow pew in a church with or without doors, in contradistinction to the old-fashioned 'square' or 'body pew.' **1891** WILKINS *New Eng. Nun* 108 In one of the foremost body-pews sat John Arnold.

Body servant. A favorite Negro acting as the personal servant of his master. {1760-}

1856 OLMSTED *Slave-States* 58 He was seriously contemplating to sell out, retaining only his foster-mother and a body-servant. **1861** *Chicago Tribune* 19 July 1/5, 12 of McNell's force were wounded, including his colored body servant. **1869** TOURGEE *Toinette* iii (1881) 39 He directed his body-servant, Bob, to have everything in readiness to return to Lovett Lodge the next morning. **1883** *Harper's Mag.* Aug. 484/1 His body-servant . . . was constantly straying over to a neighboring plantation and, it was reported, had taken a new wife over there. **1890** *Century Mag.* Nov. 62 He is assisted by his negro servant Chad, . . . who is chambermaid, cook, butler, body-servant, and boots. **1898** PAGE *Red Rock* 41 His old body-servant, Tarquin, silent and dark, brought a light and set it conveniently for him.

+**Boffet.** *Obs.* Also **bofat, baufat, -att.** {a1720 (beaufette), 1745-1863 (beaufet)} =BEAUFET. — **1725** *New-Eng. Courant* 1 Mar. 1/2 We have very little [gold or silver] left in the Country besides the Plate that adorn our Boffets. **1785** *Lower Norfolk* (Va.) *Antiquary* I. 135, 1 small pine baufatt, 3s. **1828** WEBSTER, *Buffet*, a cupboard; . . . the name has become, in a great measure, obsolete, except among the common people, by whom it is pronounced *bofat*. **1848** G. E. ELLIS *Letter* (Bartlett MS.), Our old ladies in the country have a sort of corner cupboard, or *dresser* wh[ich] they call a *baufat* [sic], probably derived from the French *buffet*. **1880** *Harper's Mag.* Nov. 879/2 Being asked . . . how the settlers in that region were prospering, he replied that they were 'as poor as the devil's bofat.' . . . A bofat . . . is a little corner closet where the family rum was generally kept.

* **Bog,** *n.*

* **1.** An expanse of wet, spongy ground; a morass.

1623 *Va. House Burgesses* 23 The Creeks are rather useful, than noisome; and no Bogs have been seen here by any. **1676** B. TOMPSON *New-Englands Crisis* 17 A . . . dismal swamp . . . Nurst up with springs, quick boggs & miery plashes. **1738** BYRD *Dividing Line* (1901) 29 Those Netherlands were full of bogs, of marshes and swamps. **1790** S. DEANE *New-Eng. Farmer* 29/2 Some bogs when they have a sward of grass-roots, will shake and tremble under the foot. **1807** *Mass. H. S. Coll.* 2 Ser. III. 94 They annually sell a hundred or two hundred bushels of craneberries, which grow in great plenty in their craneberry bogs. **1860** [see BOG-GRASS]. **1880** *Harper's Mag.* June 80 A thicket of wild azalea in the bog near by is crowned with a profusion of pink blossoms. **1916** THOBURN *Oklahoma* III. 783 The roadbed had been built mostly through bog and swamp.

+**2.** A small hummock in a marsh or meadow.

'This is a common use of the word in New England' (W. '28).

1714 J. HEMPSTEAD *Diary* 37, I was mowing in the foren[oon] & cutting up Bogs at the back side the lot. **1748** ELIOT *Field-Husb.* i. 4 The Bog Meadow [will be] the next in Charge, because the Bogs must be cut up with a Bog Plough or with the Hoe. **1828** WEBSTER, *Bog*, 2. A little elevated spot or clump of earth, in marshes and swamps, filled with roots and grass. **1842** *Knickerb.* XX. 361 He strode and jumped from one bog to another. **1846** *Ib.* XXVII. 56 They carry the dead man to the misty grave-yard, dig a hole in the moist earth, [and] throw a few bogs over him. **1874** *Vt. Bd. Agric. Rep.* II. 550 The hard, grassy tussocks, tufts or bogs, were then cut off evenly and carted away to the upland. . . . Over six hundred loads of these bogs were cut from the meadow.

3. Attrib. with *meadow, mud, pasture, pond, soil.*

1653 *Essex Probate Rec.* I. 159 A peece of meadow at bog pond. **1837** COLMAN *Mass. Agric. Rep.* (1838) 54 A trap door is in the barn floor, so that the bog-mud, litter, or other refuse may be easily thrown in. **1860** *Harper's Mag.* April 583/2 They . . . found themselves in an open space of bog meadow. **1869** FULLER *Flower Gatherers* 58 This . . . False Honeysuckle . . . I suppose you found in some swamp or bog-pasture. **1883** *Century Mag.* Sept. 650/2 Six inches of clear sand are carted on, to cover the heavy bog soil.

b. With names of plants, as *bog asphodel, bilberry, cranberry,* etc.

1817-8 EATON *Botany* (1822) 480 *Stellaria uliginosa*, bog starwort. **1832** WILLIAMSON *Maine* I. 93 The party . . . found as they ascended, a variety of wild fruits, such as . . . black currants, box berries, and bog cranberries. **1833** EATON *Botany* (ed. 6) 231 *Myrica gale*, sweet gale, bog myrtle. **1857** GRAY *Botany* 249 *Vaccinium uliginosum*, Bog Bilberry. . . . Alpine tops of the high mountains of New England and New York, and northward. *Ib.* 479 *Narthecium*, Bog-asphodel.

Bog, *v.* [f. the noun.]

1. *intr.* (or in *pass.*) To be sunk or mired in a bog. {1603-} +Also with *down, in.*

1655 *Plymouth Rec.* 29 The cow John Dunhame had was also boged and dyed. **1836** DEWEES *Lett. from Texas* 204 Here might be seen delicate ladies wading through mud and dirt, striving to hasten their footsteps and free themselves from the marshes; but at every step they would bog in deeper and deeper. **1845** T. GREEN *Texian Exped.* vi. 67 His whole command came near starving, many . . . having their horses broken down and bogged. **1903** A. ADAMS *Log Cowboy* xii. 179 Bob Blades attempted to ride out of the river below the crossing, when his horse bogged down.

2. *tr.* To level or drain (a meadow).

1680 *Springfield Rec.* I. 430 Denton is to . . . occupy & improve the whole said medow, provided he do bog & clean the said medow.

+**3.** *intr.* To remove hummocks in a meadow (cf. BOG *n.* 2.).

1854 THOREAU *Walden* 221 My host . . . worked 'bogging' for a neighboring farmer, turning up a meadow with a spade or bog hoe.

+**Bog birch.** *local.* [BOG *n.* 1.] The Indian cherry or yellow wood, *Rhamnus caroliniana.* — **1897** SUDWORTH *Arborescent Flora* 298 *Rhamnus Caroliniana*. . . . Common names [are] . . . Stinkwood (La.), Bog Birch (Minn.).

+**Bog evergreen.** [BOG *n.* 1.] A variety of Andromeda found in marshes and bogs. — **1784** CUTLER in *Mem. Academy* I. 443 *Andromeda*, . . . Gardrobe, Bog Ever-green, [is] . . . common in fens and quagmires. **1795** WINTERBOTHAM *Hist. View* III. 391 Flowering Trees, Shrubs, &c. . . . : Red-bud andromeda, . . . Bog evergreen.

+**Bog gale.** [BOG *n.* 1.] The sweet gale, *Myrica gale.* — **1785** MARSHALL *Amer. Grove* 95 *Myrica Gale*, American Bog Gale, . . . grows naturally in bogs and swamps.

Bog grass. [BOG *n.* 1.] One or other species of coarse grass or sedge growing in bogs or swamps.

1821 *Mass. H. S. Coll.* 2 Ser. IX. 149 Plants, which are indigenous in the township of Middlebury, [Vermont, include] . . . *Cyperus poaeformis*, (Pursh,) . . . Bog grass, [etc.]. **1857** E. STONE *Life of Howland* 247 They had no grass for winter fodder, but bog or salt meadow or thatch. **1860** *Harper's Mag.* April 583/2 The bogs were breast-high, and were covered with a dense growth of bog grass equally high.

* **Boggy,** *a.* Also †**bog(g)ie, bog(e)y, baugey.** Marshy, swampy. In early use esp. with *meadow.*

(1) **1637** WINTHROP *Lett.* (1869) II. 198 The swamp was so thick with shrubs, & boggy withal, that some stuck fast, & received many shot. **1654** JOHNSON *Wonder-W. Prov.* II. vi. 115* They slew many more of their enemies, the residue flying into a very thick swamp, being unaccessible, by reason of the boggy holes of water. **1758** *Essex Inst. Coll.* XVIII. 193 There was a party detach'd & sent to mowe a boggy Swamp. **1772** D. TAITT in *Travels Amer. Col.* 497 [We] continued our course, . . . crosing severall small creeks and bogey runs, which fall into Scambia

River. **1865** *Maine Agric. Rep.* X. 135 In the northeast corner is an extensive marsh, in the middle of which is a boggy pond. **1880** *Harper's Mag.* June 70 We see the frog pond, with . . . flat blades of blue-flag just starting from the boggy earth.

(2) **1640** *Hartford Land Distrib.* 25 The fore sayd parsells . . . abutting on the bogey medow on the west. **1682** *Conn. Probate Rec.* I. 281 All the woodlands & boggy meadow shall be settled upon both of them. **1700** *Waterbury Prop. Rec.* 51 A peice of land . . . betwein his peic of bogey meadow and the path. **1717** *Providence* (R.I.) *Rec.* XVI. 135 Bounded . . . partly on a baugey meadow . . . and partly on the seder pond.

+**Bog hoe.** [Bog *n.* 2.] A hoe used in cutting up and removing hummocks in bogs. — **1854** [see Bog *v.* 3]. **1874** *Vt. Bd. Agric. Rep.* II. 551 Then with axes, potato hooks, and bog hoes, the turf was all peeled off.

Boghole. [Bog *n.* 1.] A sink, hole, or depression, having a bottom of soft, spongy consistency. — **1839** Mrs. Kirkland *New Home* i. 17, I was getting cross and tired . . . when down came our good horse to the very chin in a bog-hole. **1855** Baird in *Smithsonian Rep.* 342 Ditches in the prairies of Wisconsin, or mere bog-holes apparently affording lodgment to nothing beyond tadpoles, may thus be found filled with melanuras. **1913** W. C. Barnes *Western Grazing Grounds* 26 What the winter storms did not kill, the 'bog holes' caught in the spring.

Bog iron. [Bog *n.* 1.]

1. = Bog iron ore (see sense 2).

1795 Winterbotham *Hist. View* (1796) II. 215 Mountain and bog iron are found in several parts of this district [in Maine]. **1843** *Nat. Hist. N.Y., Geology* IV. 419 About one mile east of Lockville, bog iron occurs, covering about an acre; it is in large solid masses near the surface, and is frequently turned up by the plough. **1890** *Cent.* 3460/2 Limonite . . . [is] an important iron ore which . . . forms the bog-iron of existing marshes.

2. *Bog iron ore*, a variety of iron ore found in bogs or swampy places. {1789-} Cf. Bog-ore.

1813 *N.Y. State Soc. Arts* III. 15 The ores of iron which are found in this country, are . . . magnetic iron stone, brown haematite, and bog iron ore. **1817** *N.Amer. Rev.* V. 313 Assawampset pond is very shallow and its bottom consists of bog iron ore, which has been an article of commerce ever since its discovery in 1747. **1843** *Nat. Hist. N.Y., Geology* IV. 437 Several deposits of bog iron ore occur in solid masses one mile west of Albion. **1863** *Rep. Comm. Agric.* 40 Bog-iron ore is so common as to be put down as occurring in almost every County in the State [Me.].

+**Bog lime.** [Bog *n.* 1.] A mixture of clay and lime obtained from bogs. — **1840** in *Mich. Agric. Soc. Trans.* V. (1853) 298 This condition is that which is very commonly designated as '*bog-lime.*' **1856** *Ib.* VII. 367 It is . . . scarcely known to our farmers that marl, or bog lime, may be used with . . . profit.

+**Bog meadow.** [Bog *n.* 1.] Meadow that contains bogs; boggy meadow.

1749 Eliot *Field-Husb.* ii. 35 The way to get out of this Difficulty . . . is by clearing and dreining Swamps, Cran-berry and Bog Meadows. **1761** in Eliot *Field-Husb.* App. 161 To endeavour to propagate Wheat on a wet Bog Meadow and fresh Meadow Grass on a high Sand Hill are equal Absurdities. **1783** Tenney in *Mem. Academy* II. I. 44 The [mineral] springs are situated . . . at Saratoga, in a kind of bog meadow. **1843** *Nat. Hist. N.Y., Geology* I. 371 The argillite portion of the county of Orange embraces an unusual number . . . of swamps, or, as they are called, bog meadows. **1850** *New Eng. Farmer* II. 137 We have many bog meadows that require it [*sc.* draining], which may be made to produce merchantable hay. **1860** *Harper's Mag.* April 583/2 They turned short to the left in the direction of the road, and in a few moments found themselves in an open space of bog meadow.

*__Bog mine.__ *Obs.* [Bog *n.* 1.] Bog iron ore. {-1762} — [*c*1644 *Mass. H. S. Proc.* 2 Ser. VIII. 14 This sort of ore at Braintre is of the same sorte which they call in Ireland the Bogge mine.] **1681** *Topsfield Rec.* 33 The Towne has ordered that there shall bee noe boge mine doge in the Towne but by some townes man. *Ib.*, To dig twente tun of bogmine.

Bog moss. [Bog *n.* 1.] A moss belonging to the genus *Sphagnum* found in peat bogs and marshes. — **1791** Muhlenberg *Index Florae* 183 *Sphagnum palustre*, Bog-moss. **1856** *Rep. Comm. Patents: Agric.* 247 In order to keep . . . [the seeds] moist, I spread over the surface of the pot a regular layer of sphagnum, or bog-moss. **1901** Mohr *Plant Life Ala.* 294 Bog or Peat Mosses.

+**Bog mouse.** *local.* [Bog *n.* 1.] One or other of various species of meadow mice. — **1857** *Rep. Comm. Patents: Agric.* 84 Where several species [of meadow-mice] are found in one locality, they are commonly considered by farmers as one animal, known under various names, as . . . 'Ground Mice,' 'Bog Mice,' &c.

+**Bog onion.** *local.* [Bog *n.* 1.] **a.** The root of a variety of fern (*Pteris aquilina*). **b.** The royal fern (*Osmunda regalis*). **c.** The Indian turnip (*Arisæma triphyllum*).

1832 Williamson *Maine* I. 120 The Brake, of which there are several varieties, the root of which is sometimes called the 'bog-onion,' . . . is good for sprains. **1890** *Cent.* 4167/3 Six species are known, of which three are found in North America, *Osmunda regalis* being the royal fern or osmund royal, also called *bog-onion*, *buckhorn-brake*, *ditch-fern*, and *king-fern*. **1892** *Amer. Folk-Lore* V. 104 *Arisæma triphyllum*, bog onion. Worcester Co.

Bog ore. [Bog *n.* 1.] = Bog iron ore. {1772}

1734 *Doc. Hist. N.Y. State* (1849) I. 734 We have a great many Iron mines both of the bogg, and of the Mountain Oar. **1748** Eliot *Field-Husb.* i. 2 After a while Bog Oar of a better sort and of a more kindly nature and temper was found. **1791** Bartram *Travels* 223 The higher ridges of hills afford great quantities of a species of iron ore, of that kind found in New Jersey and Pennsylvania, and there called bog ore. **1804** *Mass. H. S. Coll.* IX. 255 Bog ore abounds in swamps and other low places, subject to an overflow of water issuing from springs. **1827** Drake & Mansf. *Cincinnati* i. 11 All the iron of the state is obtained from argillaceous or bog ores. **1849** *Rep. Comm. Patents: Agric.* (1850) 197 Our marshes constitute a singular feature of our region of country [Ind.]. In many places they abound with bog-ore.

+**Bog plow.** [Bog *n.* 2.] A kind of plow used in removing bogs from land. — **1748** Eliot *Field-Husb.* i. 4 The Bog Meadow [will be] the next in Charge, because the Bogs must be cut up with a Bog Plough or with the Hoe.

+**Bog potato.** *Obs.* [Bog *n.* 1.] A species of wild potato growing in swampy places. — **1800** B. Hawkins *Sk. Creek Country* 21 In the old beaver ponds, in thick boggy places, they have the bog potatoe.

Bog rush. [Bog *n.* 1.]

1. The soft rush, *Juncus effusus*, or closely related species.

1817-8 Eaton *Botany* (1822) 450 *Schœnus setaceus*, bog-rush. **1843** Torrey *Flora N.Y.* II. 325 *Juncus effusus*. . . . Bog-rush. Soft-rush. . . . Low moist grounds: very common. **1845** Frémont *Exped.* 252 We found abundant water in small ponds . . . bordered with bog rushes (*juncus effusus*). **1857** Gray *Botany* 480 *Juncus*, Rush, Bog Rush . . . [includes] common or soft rush, . . . black grass.

2. *False bog rush:* (see quotation).

1817-8 Eaton *Botany* (1822) 428 *Rhynchospora sparsa*, false bog-rush.

Bog sedge. [Bog *n.* 1.] One or other variety of sedge growing in boggy ground. — **1840** Dewey *Mass. Flowering Plants* 264 *Carex acuta*, Bog Sedge. Grows in dense bogs. **1843** Torrey *Flora N.Y.* II. 387 *Carex angustata*. . . . Large Bog Sedge. . . . Wet meadows; very common. *Ib.* 388 *Carex caespitosa*. . . . Smaller Bog Sedge. . . . Banks of streams, and in swamps; northern and western counties.

+**Bogue,** *n. S.* [Choctaw *bok*, *bouk*, stream.]

1. A stream; a river, creek, etc.

1826 Flint *Recoll.* 317 The rivers that run through these level and swampy pine forests, are called, in the Indian language, 'Bogue,' with some attribute denoting the character of the stream. *Ib.*, There are a number of Bogues that are navigable by schooners for some distance into the country.

2. *transf.* A nickname for an inhabitant of western Florida.

1826 Flint *Recoll.* 319 They are a wild race, with but little order or morals among them; they are generally denominated 'Bogues,' and call themselves 'rosin heels.'

+**Bogue,** *v. colloq.* or *dial.* [Of obscure origin.] *intr.* To go around, to walk about, to take part *in*.

1775 G. W. Rauck *Boonesborough* 179 [We] were four days boguing in the woods seeking the way. **1867** Lowell *Biglow P.* II. p. lvii, I don't git much done 'thout I *bogue* right in along 'th my men. **1889** *Harper's Mag.* Dec. 120/1 He does bogue roun' thar mighty studdy a-s'archin' for them turkles [turtle-shaped stones]. **1889** *Cent.* 611/2 *To bogue in*, to 'sail in'; take a hand; engage in a work. (Local, New England.)

+**Bogus,** *n.*[1] and *a.* [Of obscure origin.]

The suggestions that it is connected with *bogy* or the dialect *tantra bogus* (the devil), or is derived from the personal names *Bogus* or *Borghese*, are not supported by any direct evidence.

I. 1. *n.* An apparatus used in making counterfeit coins. *Obs.*

1827 *Painesville* (Ohio) *Telegraph* 6 July, He never procured the casting of a Bogus at one of our furnaces. *Ib.* 2 Nov., The eight or ten boguses which have been for some time in operation.

b. *Bogus press*, *machine* = prec.

1844 *Spirit of Times* 12 Oct. (Th.), A bogus press for making counterfeit money was dug up near Lyme, Huron County, Pa., on Monday last. **1850** *Frontier Guardian* 23 Jan. (Th.), We employed that same Bill Hickman to ferret out a bogus press and a gang of counterfeiters. . . . A part of the bogus machine has been found here in Mulholland's possession.

2. Money made on a bogus; counterfeit coin or notes. Also fig.

1839 Mrs. Kirkland *New Home* xxxii. (1840) 227 The boxes of the 'real stuff' . . . contained a heavy charge of broken glass and tenpenny nails, covered above and below with half-dollars, principally 'bogus.' **1842** *Life in West* 297 They had attempted to pass bogus (base coin). **1848** W. E. Burton *Waggeries* 90 No luggage, nor no nothing, but a roll of bogus. **1853** B. Young in *Journal Discourses* I. 270 (Th.), [The Magicians of Egypt] produced a very good bogus, but it was not quite the true coin. **1867** [see 3]. **1875** G. P. Burnham *Three Years* p. iv, *Bogus*, counterfeit bank notes, or false coins of any kind.

b. Attrib. and comb. with *business*, *maker*, *molder*.

1841 *S. Lit. Messenger* VII. 54/1, I am a minter, A bogus moulder, from about Sandusky. **1844** *Nauvoo Neighbor* 12 June (Th.), To bolster up the interests of blacklegs and bogus-makers. **1850** *Frontier Guardian* 23 Jan. (Th.), James M. Mulholland was one of the principal actors in the bogus business.

c. A counterfeit article.

1857 *Knickerb.* XLIX. 278 Don't run your bogus [*sc.* cigars] on me this time.

II. 3. *adj.* Of coin, currency, or gold-dust: Spurious, counterfeit.

1842 J. A. CLARK *Gleanings by Way* 340 Cowdery, Whitmer, and others, were guilty of perjury, cheating, selling bogus money, (base coin), and even stones and sand for bogus! **1848** BARTLETT 41 *Bogus money*, counterfeit silver coin. A few years since, a large quantity of this coin was in circulation at the West, where it received this name. **1857** *Herald of Freedom* (Lawrence, Kansas) 22 Aug. (Th.), I must have paid you for my supper with a bogus half-dollar. **1867** McClure *Rocky Mts.* 378 More Bogus. Joe Logan was arrested a week ago by 'X', for manufacturing bogus gold dust.

b. In general use: Counterfeit, not genuine, fraudulent, deceptive.

In early use (group 1) frequent with *legislature* or other political terms.

(1) **1857** *Lawrence* (Kansas) *Republican* 28 May 1 A code of laws was enacted by the bogus legislature. *Ib.* 18 June 3 It claims to be a Free-State paper, though it advocates voting at the bogus election. **1859** J. B. JONES *Southern Scenes* 370 The bogus Cabinet at Washington. **1860** *Richmond Enquirer* 2 Nov. 1/8 (Th.), Remember that Stephen A. Douglas is a bolter from the party, is a bogus Democrat. **1866** *Cosmopolitan* 28 April 472/2 The official presence of representatives from the *bogus* State of Western Virginia illegalises its functions. **1867** A. D. RICHARDSON *Beyond Miss.* v. 74 Lawrence people, without any authority from the bogus laws, had formed a municipal organization. **1870** BEADLE *Utah* 166 The Mormon civil authorities could find pretences for bogus legal actions. **1873** *Winfield* (Kansas) *Courier* 2 Oct. 2/4 The bogus Wisconsin grangers and reformers have set up an independent state ticket. **1877** JOHNSON *Anderson Co., Kansas* 24 It was immediately adjourned to the Shawnee Manuel [sic] Labor School Mission, . . . and there passed the first code of laws for the Territory commonly known as the 'bogus laws.' **1894** ROBLEY *Bourbon Co., Kansas* 39 By the 1st of September they had finished their labors which resulted in the preparation of an immense code of 'laws,' which have always been called and known as the 'Bogus Statute of 1855.'

(2) *c***1849** [PAIGE] *Dow's Sermons* IV. 216 (Th.), Crocodile tears are bogus. **1856** *Spirit of Times* (N.Y.) 20 Dec. 261/3 A firm, called Henry W. Manchester & Co., . . . have flooded the Southern and South Western States with bogus [lottery] tickets. **1859** L. WILMER *Press Gang* 150 'Bogus' Life Insurance Companies . . . do a flourishing business in some of our principal cities. **1860** GREELEY *Overland Journey* 36 The manufacture of paper-cities and bogus corner-lots. **1860** MRS. S. COWELL *Diary* 96 The articles sold consist of 'Bogus' jewellery. **1861** WINTHROP *C. Dreeme* 45 Dora and . . . Hall . . . inspected me critically. Was I bogus? *a***1862** THOREAU *Maine Woods* 188 The last name . . . had a bogus sound, too much like sectarian to me. **1871** 'MARK TWAIN' *Sk., About Barbers* 259 He had figured . . . the night before, in red cambric and bogus ermine, as some kind of a king. **1872** *Newton Kansan* 22 Aug. 4/3 A bogus dispatch announcing a Democratic victory in North Carolina. **1874** GLISAN *Jrnl. Army Life* 448 They devised a cunning scheme to gain a bogus reputation for themselves. **1877** WM. WRIGHT *Big Bonanza* 48 They thought that, after all, what they had found might be some sort of 'bogus stuff'—base metal of some new and strange kind. **1891** *Scribner's Mag.* X. 215 There had sprung up a sort of bogus metropolis of the mountains. **1895** CHAMBLISS *Diary* 31 Apropos of bogus Chinese 'certificates of previous residence,' I have seen with my own eyes numbers of them.

+**Bogus,** *n.*[2] (See quotations.) — **1848** BARTLETT 41 *Bogus*, a liquor made of rum and molasses. **1871** DE VERE 444 *Bogus*, the name of a beverage . . . , is occasionally heard in the Eastern States, especially among fishermen.

+**Bogusly,** *adv.* [BOGUS *a.*] In a fraudulent manner. — **1862** *N.Y. Herald* 2 May, When this [post] office came under the rebel government, and the oath was sent to us, we filed it bogously [*sic*], and sent it to Richmond without swearing to it.

+**Bogus maker, molder, press:** see BOGUS *n.*[1]

+**Bog willow.** (See quotations.) — **1833** EATON *Botany* (ed. 6) 319 *S. discolor*, bog willow, red-root willow. **1845** LINCOLN *Botany* App. 161/1 *Salix discolor*, bog willow, Ap[ril]; leaves oblong, rather obtuse. **1892** APGAR *Trees Northern U.S.* 166 Glaucous or Bog Willow . . . [is] a very variable species, common in low meadows and on river banks; usually a shrub, but occasionally 15 ft. high.

Bohea. [Fuhkien Chinese *Bu-i*, variant of *Wu-i:* see def.]

1. A black tea, originally of the finest kind from the Wu-i hills in the north of Fuhkien, but latterly the lowest quality among the black teas. **a.** Attrib. with *tea.* {1704–73}

1720 *Weekly Mercury* 19 Jan. 2/2 Price currant at Philadelphia. Very good Bohea Tea—24s. per pound. **1759** *Boston Post-Boy* 15 Nov., The Ships . . . from London, brought over no less than 206 Chests of Green and Bohea Teas. **1767** *Boston Gazette* 2 Nov. 2/2 There is a certain Herb, lately found in this Province, which begins already to take Place in the Room of Green and Bohea Tea. . . . It is called Labrador. **1775** TRUMBULL *M'Fingal* I. 21 Addresses signed, then chose Committees, To stop all drinking of Bohea-teas. **1779** JAMES WARREN in *Warren-Adams Lett.* II. 105 Bohea Tea 40 dollars per lb. **1802** CUTLER in *Life & Corr.* II. 60 A motion to inquire whether it be expedient to reduce duties on Bohea Tea, Brown Sugar, and Coffee. **1842** *Lowell Offering* II. 144 Abigail's package contained a Chinese silk hat, the crown of which was full of Bohea tea. **1891** S. M. WELCH *Recoll. 1830–40* 183 The use of snuff . . . was a common habit; indeed the elderly ladies used it, sometimes to excess as they did Bohea or Hyson teas.

b. Ellipt. {1701–} Also as prepared for drinking. {1706–}

1767 *Newport* (R.I.) *Mercury* 28 Dec. 3/3 Where Scandal and Detraction now prevail, And noxious Bohea sheds a pois'nous Stream. **1787** FRENEAU *Misc. Works* 425 But then—he could never put up with Bohea, La, Madam, is this the best tea that you keep? **1807** IRVING, etc. *Salmagundi* xix. 444 The wives of our cits of inferior degree, Will soak up repute in a little bohea. **1832** J. F. WATSON *Hist. Tales N.Y.* 125 The kettle was invariably set on the fire for tea, of Bohea, which was . . . punctually furnished at three o'clock. **1841** A. BACHE *Fire-Screen* 79 We will have brown bread and bohea for breakfast. **1854** S. SMITH *Down East* 336 It's tea! as true as I'm alive, it's the real bohea.

+**2.** The carrion flower.

1833 EATON *Botany* (ed. 6) 343 *Smilax herbacea*, bohea tea. **1839** in *Mich. Agric. Soc. Trans.* VII. 419.

Bohemian chatterer, waxwing. A northern bird of passage, *Ampelis garrulus.* {1841–} — **1858** BAIRD *Birds Pacific R.R.* 317 Wax-wing [or] Bohemian Chatterer . . . [is] seen in the United States only in severe winters, except along the great lakes. **1866** — *Review of Birds* I. 406 For many years authentic eggs of the Bohemian Chatterer were greatly sought after. — **1828** BONAPARTE *Ornithology* III. 10 Whence does the Bohemian Wax-wing come at the long and irregular periods of its migrations? **1869** *Amer. Naturalist* III. 473, I was . . . pleased to obtain a beautiful specimen of the Bohemian Waxwing. **1874** COUES *Birds N.W.* 91 Bohemian Waxwing . . . [is] a species of circumpolar distribution, wandering irregularly southward in flocks, in winter, to about 35° north in America.

Bohn. *Obs. slang.* (See quotation 1856.) — **1855** *Songs of Yale* (1860) 40 'Twas plenty of skin with a good deal of Bohn. **1856** HALL *College Words* (ed. 2) 32 *Bohn*, a translation; a pony. The volumes of Bohn's Classical Library are in such general use among undergraduates in American colleges, that *Bohn* has come to be a common name for a translation.

+**Bo-hoy,** variant of BHOY. — **1846** *Spirit of Times* (N.Y.) 4 July 219/1 The bo-hoys . . . flourish in the region of the rail road depot. **1846** *Knickerb.* XXVII. 467 He answered, with a smile on his lip peculiar to 'one of the bo-hoys.'

***Boil,** *n.* +A turbulent swirl or eddy in the Mississippi River.

1805 CLARK in *Lewis & C. Exped.* (1905) III. 151 In those narrows the water was agitated in a most shocking manner, boils, swells, & whorlpools [*sic*]. **1826** T. FLINT *Recoll.* 87 The Mississippi . . . is full of singular boils, where the water rises with a strong circular motion. **1829** — *George Mason* 124 He studied the currents, the *boils* and eddies, the marks of shallow and deep water. **1850** JUDD *R. Edney* xvi. 205 At its foot was the rabid 'boil' and terrific undertow. **1853** *Putnam's Mo.* Aug. 188/2 These 'boils,' as the boatmen call them, are immense upheavings of the moving waters [of the Mississippi]. **1875** 'MARK TWAIN' *Old Times* iii. (1876) 59 Those tumbling 'boils' show a dissolving bar and a changing channel there.

***Boiled,** *ppl. a.* [f. *boil* v. Cf. BILED.] Prepared by, subjected to, boiling. In some special applications.

+**1.** *Boiled cider*, cider that has been boiled to increase its alcoholic content. (Cf. CIDER ROYAL.)

1705 *Lancaster Rec.* 153 They drank a barell of boyled Cyder & a barell of Strong bear. **1832** *Louisville Public Advt.* 13 March, 25 bbls. boiled cider, for sale.

+**2.** *Boiled dinner*, a dinner of which the chief course consists in meat and vegetables boiled together. Also attrib.

1805 *Pocumtuc Housewife* (1906) 9 Directions for a Boiled Dinner may seem unnecessary. **1882** HOWELLS *Modern Instance* ix, I'm goin' to give 'em potatoes and cabbage to-day—kind of a boiled-dinner day. **1886** B. P. POORE *Reminisc.* I. 384 She could make a regal Cape Cod chowder, . . . or prepare the old-fashioned New Hampshire 'boiled dinner.' **1897** HOWELLS *Landlord Lion's Head* iii, The woman brought in a good boiled dinner of corned beef, potatoes, turnips, and carrots. **1906** CHURCHILL *Coniston* 120 He attacked the boiled dinner with a ferocity which should have been exercised against Jethro.

+**3.** *Boiled shirt*, a white or a dress shirt.

1861 *Harper's Mag.* Jan. 155/1 Here and there . . . a San Francisco dandy of the 'boiled shirt' and 'stove-pipe' pattern loomed up. **1869** A. K. MCCLURE *Rocky Mts.* 412 In order to attend the Governor's reception, I borrowed a boiled shirt. **1873** MILLER *Amongst Modocs* 130 The Judge . . . wore a 'stove pipe' hat and a 'boiled shirt.' **1876** *Fur, Fin, & Feather* Sept. 129 If a member puts on a 'boiled shirt' it signifies he is not going fishing again. **1886** P. G. EBBUTT *Emigrant Life* 114 Miss Black made me quite a fancy 'boiled' shirt for Sundays. **1893** POST *Harvard Stories* 55 He grabbed his evening clothes and shoes, a 'boiled' shirt and tie. **1903** *N.Y. Ev. Post* 22 Sept., The fact is that Tammany Hall has merely progressed from shirtsleeves to the 'boiled shirt.'

+**b.** *Boiled rag*, in the same sense.

1886 *Outing* May 167/1 For the first time since leaving port I wore 'boiled rags' as the mate calls them.

+**4.** *Boiled crow, owl:* see CROW *n.*, OWL *n.*

***Boiler.**

1. The container used to generate steam for an engine. {1757–}

1813 *Niles' Reg.* IV. 111/1, I construct the boilers of my steam engines of strong metalic plates. **1827** [G. MELLEN] *Chronicle of '26* 22, I think these steam-boats are unruly things, Having a boiler. **1831** Mackenzie *Van Buren* (1846) 228 We shall have our locomotive at work by the end of the week. The boiler went back to the road to-day. **1851** E. S. WORTLEY *Travels in U.S.* 112 In the papers you will often see a whole column headed 'snagged.' . . . Then follows sometimes a list of 'boilers burst.' **1866** MOORE *Women of War* 275 Three transports were to be sent, with large river steamers, their boilers well protected with cotton bales. **1871** HOWELLS *Wedding Journey* iii. 59 The steamboat berth into which he gets with his pantaloons on, and out of which he may be blown by an exploding boiler at any moment. **1891** *Harper's Weekly* 19 Sept. 714/2 The iron covering of the boiler was turned inside out. . . . A wrecking train soon removed the débris.

+b. *To burst one's boiler*, etc., to break down seriously; to come, or bring, to grief. Cf. BILER.

1824 *Cheraw Intelligencer* in *Franklin* (Greenfield, Mass.) *Herald* 2 March (giving 'a short essay, repeating this phrase at the end o levery paragraph': Thornton.) *c***1845** W. I. PAULDING *Madmen All* 189 May my boiler be eternally busted, if there isn't that are young lady.

2. One who makes salt; a salt boiler.

1847 in H. Howe *Hist. Coll. Ohio* 263 A person, who had come on horseback . . . to the salt-works to purchase salt, had his pack-saddle stolen by the boilers.

3. Attrib. with *maker* (also fig.), *roof, wiper*.

1867 W. H. DIXON *New America* II. 85 The [Shaker] church . . . with a boiler roof. **1877** 'E. MARTIN' *Hist. Great Riots* 143 Robert Jamieson, a boiler-maker, . . . [was] placed under arrest. **1887** *Courier-Journal* 6 Jan. 2/3 Thomas Feeney, a boiler wiper. **1902** LORIMER *Lett. Merchant* 131 Knowing how many rounds the Old 'Un can last against the Boiler-Maker.

+Boiler deck. [BOILER 1.] The deck of a steamboat immediately above the boiler or boilers.

1830 *Steamboat Disasters* (1846) 127 The boiler-deck—being that part of the upper deck situated immediately over the boilers. **1840** *Knickerb.* XV. 295 She had struck on a snag, and . . . it had forced its way through every obstacle, until it pierced the boiler deck. **1844** J. COWELL *Thirty Years* II. 91 [The] piazza . . . forms a promenade all round the boat, and joins the boiler-deck, where you can lounge with your cigar. **1851** A. O. HALL *Manhattaner* 174, [I] stood upon the boiler-deck. **1868** *Ill. Agric. Soc. Trans.* VII. 143 Six hundred head [of cattle] were crowded upon the boiler deck, kept extremely hot by the boiler and engines. **1870** 'O. OPTIC' *Field & Forest* 124, I saw two ladies and three gentlemen . . . coming down the steps from the boiler deck. **1875** 'MARK TWAIN' *Old Times* ii. (1876) 32 The boiler deck (*i.e.*, the second story of the boat, so to speak) was as spacious as a church.

+Boilerhouse. [BOILER 1.] A building containing a boiler or boilers. — **1880** LAMPHERE *U.S. Govt.* 227/1 The buildings connected with the hospital, not occupied by patients, are a boiler-house, a laundry. **1901** *Scribner's Mag.* April 409/2 He . . . saw the flicker of a lantern down in the boiler-house.

Boiler iron. Iron suitable for making boilers. Also attrib.

1851 C. CIST *Cincinnati* 213 The yearly products are . . . five hundred tons boiler-iron, heads, etc. **1873** RAYMOND *Silver & Gold* 34 The rim of the [Cox] pan is made of boiler-iron, and it has a perforated cast-iron bottom. **1876** 'MARK TWAIN' *Tom Sawyer* xxxii. 251, I had its big door sheathed with boiler iron two weeks ago. **1883** *Harper's Mag.* Aug. 332/2 The Cambria Iron Company . . . produced in 1881 . . . steel springs in quantity, boiler iron, [etc.]. **1902** 'MARK TWAIN' in *Harper's Mag.* Jan. 267/2 The boiler-iron stove . . . is distributing a grateful warmth.

Boiler plate. {1855–} +*slang.* Stereotyped matter issued to the newspaper press. Also attrib. and fig.

1893 *Congress. Rec.* 18 Aug. 465/1 The country weeklies have been sent tons of 'boiler plates,' accompanied by . . . wily letters asking the editors to use the matter as news. **1897** *Ib.* 6 Jan. 518/1 Your 'boiler-plate' literary bureau seems to have syndicated the 'protest' business. **1905** D. G. PHILLIPS *Plum Tree* 190 He attended to the subsidizing of news agencies that supplied thousands of country papers with boiler-plate matter to fill their inside pages. **1909** 'O. HENRY' *Options* 250 The ancients are discredited; Plato is boiler-plate.

Boilery. {1628–} A place where brine is boiled — **1714** SEWALL *Diary* III. 18 Went to the Meeting of the owners of the Salt-works. . . . Agreed to pay £10. apiece towards a Boylery.

Boiler yard. A place where boilers for steam engines are made. — **1851** C. CIST *Cincinnati* 174 There are ten boiler yards, employing ninety-seven hands.

***Boiling,** *vbl. n.*

1. The process of boiling maple sap or the juice of the sugar cane, for the production of sugar or syrup.

1823 COOPER *Pioneers* xx, The underwood had been entirely removed from this grove, or bush, as, in conjunction with the simple arrangements for boiling, it was called. **1845** *Cultivator* n.s. III. 17 Over 100 lbs. per day was made at four successive boilings. **1874** *Vt. Bd. Agric. Rep.* II. 730 Have the most careful and trusty hand take charge of the boiling [of the maple sap].

b. Attrib. with *pan, room, stick.*

1791 in Imlay *Western Territory* (ed. 3, 1797) 473 The mature state of the boiling is known by taking a little of the syrup from the boiling-stick, and trying if it ropes or draws into a thread between the finger and thumb. **1833** B. SILLIMAN *Sugar Cane* 32 The cane juice is run off by a spout into . . . vats, situated in the mill room, near the partition which divides it from the boiling room. **1849** *Rep. Comm. Patents* (1850) 244 Pipes or tubes [pass] through the whole length of the series of boiling pans.

2. The entire company or group. {*dial.*} Cf. BILING.

1786 *New Haven Gazette* 13 April 75/3 (Th.), The d—l ran a hunting with the boiling of them.

+Boiling arch. [BOILING *vbl. n.* 1.] A type of furnace arch upon which the kettles used in making maple sugar rest. — **1874** *Vt. Bd. Agric. Rep.* II. 728 Boiling arches should be of good depth, not filled up at back end.

‖**Boiling frolic.** A bee or frolic for making apple-butter. — **1857** [D. H. STROTHER] *Virginia* 202 Whether you saw her carrying eggs to market . . . or helping to stir apple-butter at a boiling frolic.

Boiling-house. [BOILING *vbl. n.* 1.] A house in which sugar is made by boiling cane juice or maple sap. {1647–1712, for soap}

[**1687** R. BLOME *Isles & Terr. in Amer.* 33 The Sugar-Canes are planted all the year round, the making of which is . . . subject to casualties . . . in the Boyling-House.] **1779** *N.J. Archives* 2 Ser. IV. 8 The buildings are . . . in good order, consisting of a dwelling-house, boiling-house, drying-house, two store-houses. **1791** *Amer. Phil. Soc. Trans.* III. 70 It has been a subject of inquiry whether the maple sugar might not be improved in its quality and increased in its quantity by the establishment of boiling houses in the sugar maple country. **1837** WILLIAMS *Terr. of Florida* 249 A huge column of flame arose from the boiling-house. **1862** *Rep. Comm. Patents: Agric.* 310 There is a large room into which the cooling or granulating vats are conveyed from the boiling-house on a tramway.

+Boiling place. [BOILING *vbl. n.* 1.] The place where maple sap is boiled in making sugar. — **1844** *Knickerb.* XXIII. 444 And now we are at the 'boiling place.' . . . The cauldron . . . is filled with the fresh sap two or three times a day. **1848** D. P. THOMPSON *L. Amsden* 11 The boiling place . . . [was] indicated by the cloud of mingled smoke and steam which rose from the seething kettles. **1876** BURROUGHS *Winter Sunshine* v. 123 The 'boiling-place,' with its delightful camp-features, is just beyond the first line [of maple trees].

+Boiling pot. A place in a river where the water is violently agitated; =BOIL *n.*

1790 WASHINGTON *Diaries* IV. 78 A place called the Suck, or boiling pot, where the [Holstein] river runs through the Cumberland Mountains. *a***1817** DWIGHT *Travels* III. 206 [The] Great boiling pot . . . is a vast cavity in a mass of lime-stone, forming the bed of the mill-stream. **1837** BIRD *Nick of Woods* I. 225 Thar's a boiling-pot above and a boiling-pot below.

Boiling spring. A spring which gives out water at a high temperature. {1839–}

1823 JAMES *Exped.* I. 25 While we were waiting at the rapids, several of our party made an excursion to visit the boiling spring. **1846** SAGE *Scenes Rocky Mts.* xxv, Numerous boiling springs are also found . . . whose waters are frequently so hot that meat may be cooked in a very few minutes by submersion in them. **1848** E. BRYANT *California* xv. 204 What produced the remarkable verdure was the water flowing from a number of boiling springs. [**1895** A. BROWN *Meadow-Grass* 113 She had reached the spot . . . where lay 'Peggy's b'ilin' spring.']

Boilsted, early variant of BILSTED.

+Bois brulé. [F., ='burnt wood.'] A Canadian half-breed Indian, esp. one of French and Indian extraction. Also attrib.

1805 LEWIS in *Ann. 9th Congress* 2 Sess. 1047 The Tetons Bois brûlè killed and took about 60 of them last summer. **1840** HOFFMAN *Greyslaer* II. 260 Of Guisbert . . . , as the '*Bois-brulé*,' or half-blood child was generally called, we have . . . been enabled to gather but few traditions. **1852** J. W. BOND *Minnesota* 283 Prepared for a start down the river . . . in a bark canoe, with two *Bois Brulés* as voyageurs. **1860** *Harper's Mag.* Oct. 585/1 Fired by contagious enthusiasm, a black-eyed beauty in blue calico, and a strapping *bois brulé*, would jump up from the floor and outdo their predecessors in vigor and velocity. **1871** EGGLESTON *Duffels* (1893) iv. 99 The *bois brûlés* began to be too much softened with whiskey. **1878** BEADLE *Western Wilds* 379 In July, 1859, I . . . watched the long trains of Bois Brules from Pembina, slowly descending that stream [=Rum R.] to St. Paul. *Ib.* 380 Most of the drivers were of the pure Bois Brules stock. **1881** *Amer. Naturalist* XV. 123 Buffalo make good tractable work cattle when caught young, and the *Bois Brules* frequently use them as such.

+Bois d'arc. [F., 'bow-wood'.] The osage orange, the wood of which was used by the Indians for making bows. Cf. BODOCK and BOWDARK.

1805 in *Ann. 9th Congress.* 2 Sess. 1138 At this place Mr. Dunbar obtained one or two slips of the '*bois d'arc*,' (bow wood, or yellow wood,) from the Missouri. **1829** *Western M. Rev.* III. 57 An area of three acres, shaded with laurier almond, and Bois d'arcs, the most beautiful trees of the American forest. *c*1835 CATLIN *Indians* II. 91 The most luxuriant and picturesque foliage, consisting of the lofty bois d'arcs and elms. 1856 WHIPPLE *Explor. Ry. Route* I. 22 Two Indians . . . were painted with vermilion, and carried bows of bois d'arc three feet long. 1870 KEIM *Sheridan's Troopers* xxxi. 229 Bows are made of various materials, but principally of bois d'arc or Osage orange. 1880 CABLE *Grandissimes* xxvi. 193 Lofty hedges of Cherokee rose or bois-d'arc. 1885 M. THOMPSON *By-Ways* 152, A lonely purple finch twittering in a hedge of *bois d'arc*.

attrib. 1842 E. A. HITCHCOCK *Journal* (1930) 74 His party . . . used bows and arrows for killing buffalo—bow made of the bois d'arc wood. 1844 GREGG *Commerce of Prairies* II. 283 Bows . . . of buffalo ribs . . . are not equal to bows of the bois-d'arc tree. 1885 M. THOMPSON *By-Ways* 158 The cat-bird . . . is . . . the musical deity of our blackberry jungles and *bois d'arc* hedges.

Bois de vache. [F., 'cow-wood.'] =BUFFALO CHIPS. (Cf. BODEWASH.) Also attrib. with *fire*.

1843 FRÉMONT *Exped.* 22 Our fires were partially made of the *bois de vache*, . . . a very good substitute for wood, burning like turf. 1846 SAGE *Scenes Rocky Mts.* v, The lack of wood . . . was readily met by the great abundance of *bois de vache*. 1850 GARRARD *Wah-To-Yah* i. 11 [We used] *bois de vache* (buffalo chips) for want of better fuel. *Ib.* i. 19 We made a small bois de vache fire. 1852 STANSBURY *Gt. Salt Lake* 37 Four old lodge-poles, . . . eked out by bois de vache for fuel, served to give us a capital roast of buffalo-meat.

Bokhara clover. [*Bokhara*, western Asia.] The sweet clover, *Melilotus alba.* — 1884 *Rep. Comm. Agric.* 125 Bokhara clover . . . has recently been considerably cultivated [in some parts of the South] and apparently with satisfactory results. 1894 *Ib.* 440 Melilotus (*Melilotus alba*) is also known as Bokhara clover, sweet clover, and large white clover.

* **Bold,** *a.* +Of water: Having a strong current. *Obs.* — 1805 CLARK in *Lewis & C. Exped.* (1904) I. 298 The little Missouri . . . is 134 yards wide at it's Mouth and sets in with a bould current. *Ib.* 362 A beautiful bold runing stream. 1821 J. FOWLER *Journal* 28 A streem of bold running watter one hundred and fifty feet wid[e]. *Ib.* 146 At twelve miles we crosed a bold streem of watter.

+**Bold hives.** *colloq.* [See HIVES.] The croup. — 1824 J. DODDRIDGE *Notes* 148 The croup, or what was then [*c*1775] called the 'Bold hives' was a common disease among the children, many of whom died of it.

Bolingbroke. +(See quot.) — 1823 *New Eng. Farmer* II. 85 Our city has been much amused with a low tripod-kind of a hat, made of fine beaver, and worn by our Bang-ups. Some call them the *Touch*, others the *Gape and Stare*, the real name is the Bolingbroke.

+**Bolivar.** *Obs.* [Simon *Bolivar*, Venezuelan patriot (1783–1830).] **1.** *Bolivar hat*, a kind of broad-brimmed leghorn hat. Also ellipt. **2.** A style of gentleman's coat. — (1) 1827 *Hallowell* (Maine) *Gaz.* 20 June 3/5 Advt., 1 case more of those elegant Bolivar Hats for Ladies. 1829 A. ROYALL *Pennsylvania* I. 85 Here a Bolivar with a forest or flower garden on the top, there a little scooped out thing called a bonnet, then the high-crowned dandy hat. 1848 BARTLETT 393 *Bolivar Hat*, a Leghorn bonnet, with a broad brim, worn a few years since. (2) 1886 B. P. POORE *Reminisc.* I. 75 Those gentlemen [at Washington, D.C., *c*1827] who dressed fashionably wore 'Bolivar' frock-coats of some gay-colored cloth.

* **Boll.** Also †**bowl, bole.** +The seed vessel of the cotton plant. {1865–}

1796 B. HAWKINS *Letters* 30 The staple of the cotton good, tho' not so much so as it would have been, had it been thined and toped. The bowls or pods would then have been larger. 1818 SCHOOLCRAFT *Journal* 27 The bowls were handsomely filled with cotton of fine quality. 1834 in J. S. Bassett *Plantation Overseer* 73, I have seean grown boles in it yesterday nearly waste high. 1835 J. H. INGRAHAM *South-West* II. 284 The pericarp or boll of cotton . . . is generally matured in eight or ten weeks. 1856 in Commons, etc. *Doc. Hist.* I. 127 When picking out cotton, do not allow the hands to pull the Boles off the Stalk. 1862 in *Ill. Agric. Soc. Trans.* V. (1865) 509 The late planted [cotton] will only produce a small return of bolls. 1869 J. R. BROWNE *Adv. Apache Country* 241 We saw fine bolls of cotton growing wild in this uninhabited region. 1911 *Dept. of Agric. Yearbook* 57 Some of the new types produce larger bolls and longer lint than any of the varieties now generally cultivated in Texas.

* **Bolled,** *ppl. a.* {–1639} +Of cotton: Furnished with bolls. — 1854 *Florida Plant. Rec.* 90 All so the cotton crop is good and it seames to be groing finly at present and is bold well.

+**Boll rot.** 'A disease to which the boll of the cotton-plant is liable, manifesting itself . . . by a slight discoloration . . . and the discharge of a putrid mass' (*Cent.*).

+**Boll weevil.**

1. The cotton-boll weevil, *Anthonomus grandis*, a well-known insect destructive to the cotton plant.

[1895 *Insect Life* March 295 Report on the Mexican Cotton-Boll Weevil in Texas, . . . by C. H. Tyler Townsend, . . . [dated] December 20, 1894.] 1903 W. D. HUNTER *U.S. Farmers' Bulletin* 163 Methods of Controlling the Boll Weevil: Advice based on the work of 1902. 1903 (*title*), Proceedings of the Boll Weevil Convention . . . in New Orleans, Louisiana, Nov. 30th and Dec. 1st, 1903. 1904 W. D. HUNTER *Mexican Cotton Boll Weevil* 10 Up to the present time (January, 1904) the boll weevil has been found outside of the State of Texas in only three instances. 1911 *Dept. Agric. Yearbook* 81 When the boll weevil came, bankers and business men lost confidence and extensive local panics resulted.

2. *Boll weevil Democrat:* (see quotation).

1906 *Springfield W. Republican* 19 July 16 The 'boll-weevil democrats' is the term of opprobrium which a southern paper applies to democrats who favor Hearst.

+**Bollworm.** The larva of the moth *Heliothis armigera*, which feeds upon cotton bolls; also called corn-ear worm, corn worm.

1847 *Rep. Comm. Patents: Agriculture* (1848) 171 In view then of . . . the destruction caused by the boll worm . . . the receipts will show another short crop. 1849 *Ib.* (1850) 9 Such insects as . . . army and boll worms, annually destroy crops to the amount of twenty millions of dollars. 1852 *Florida Plant. Rec.* 77, I notice that the bowl worm is making the cotton throw off a great many small boles. 1856 *Rep. Comm. Patents: Agric.* 64 Insects injurious to the cotton-plant consist of . . . the boll-worm, cotton caterpillar, and some others. 1883 SMITH *Geol. Survey Ala.* 547 The boll-worm is not often very damaging. 1899 *Dept. Agric. Yearbook* 256 Late fall plowing is of value in ridding infested fields of the boll worm.

attrib. 1856 *Rep. Comm. Patents: Agric.* 67 Mocking-birds and bee-martins catch and destroy the boll-worm moth. 1899 *Dept. Agric. Yearbook* 256 The habit of the boll worm larva of feeding in concealment renders it practically impossible to kill it with poisons.

Bologna. {Bolognian sausage, 1596–; Bologna s., 1842}

1. *Bologna sausage*, a large sausage of mixed meat, spiced and enclosed in a skin.

1758 in R. Rogers *Jrnls.* 95 All our provisions from the beginning was only a small Bologna sausage, and a little ginger. 1839 C. F. BRIGGS *Harry Franco* II. 203 An abundance of what is called refreshments, viz.: claret and whiskey, Bologna sausages, and segars. 1857 HAMMOND *Northern Scenes* 117 Each [cat] . . . had a tail bigger than a Bologna sausage. 1897 *Outing* XXIX. 489/1 The provisions . . . [included] three cans deviled ham, ten lbs. bologna sausage. 1902 LORIMER *Lett. Merchant* 71 A man can't have his head . . . stuffed full of odds and ends like a bologna sausage, and do his work right.

2. *ellipt.* =prec.

Now colloquially called *bolony*.

1850 *Knickerb.* XXXV. 23 Relishing 'Bolognas,' will he plead that a jelly-eyed roaster is disgusting? 1867 J. N. EDWARDS *Shelby*, etc. 87 Five thousand as pretty Dutch as ever bolted a bologna. 1874 PINKERTON *Expressman & Detective* 64 Before embarking on the Walsh he laid in a stock of 'bolognas.' 1916 SANDBURG *Chicago Poems* 24 The dago shovelman finishes the dry bread and bologna.

+**Bolongaro.** 'A kind of snuff made of various grades of leaves and stalks of tobacco' (*Cent.*). — 1833 *Knickerb.* II. 57 A villainous snuff-box rolled from my pocket, and scattered . . . a thousand pinches of Bolongaro, full in the face of Miss Tabby.

+**Bolson.** *S.W.* [Sp. *bolsón*, augmentative of *bolsa* purse.] A low area or basin completely surrounded by higher ground or mountains. Also attrib. with *plain.* — 1899 *Boston Transcr.* 8 Aug. 24 Between the ranges [cut by the Rio Grande] are dry plains called 'bolsons'—a Spanish word signifying purses or enclosed basins. 1904 *Amer. Geologist* Sept. 164 The bolson plains may be considered as sections of an upraised peneplain surface in its earliest infancy.

* **Bolt,** *n.*[1]

1. A piece of wood suitable for splitting up into boards, shingles, clapboards, etc. {1688–}

1639 *Portsmouth Rec.* 10 A shipp lood of . . . pipe stauffes & clabboard boults. 1663 *Charlestown Land Rec.* 84 Granted vnto Josias Wood to cutt, and per tickett carrie ten trees for bolts from of our wood interest. 1670 *Plymouth Rec.* I. 114 Noe bolts, boards or single shalbe transported out of the Townshipp. 1682 *Ib.* 172 Noe Indians shall hencforth be sett to worke . . . making of shingles or bolts. 1832 WILLIAMSON *Maine* I. 524 Wincoln and his men, overpowered by numbers, retired and took shelter behind a pile of shingle bolts. 1853 *Mich. Agric. Soc. Trans.* IV. 156 This machine cuts, dresses & joints a stave in a perfect manner, . . . feeding itself from a bolt of wood. 1875 TEMPLE & SHELDON *Northfield, Mass.* 65 These clap-boards, or cleft-boards, were split from oak bolts, or cuts.

2. A form of earmark for animals. *Obs.*

1732 *Edgecombe Co. Marks & Brands* 15 Aug. (N.C.H.C.), A Bolt in the left & the right ear cut off.

* **Bolt,** *n.*[2] [See BOLT *v.*]

+**1.** An act or instance of 'bolting' in politics; a desertion of, or revolt against, a candidate or party.

1858 *N.Y. Tribune* 8 Jan. 2/3 (Th.), It is known that there would have been some such a bolt from the nominations, had the nominations been made. *Ib.* 1 April 3/3 (Th.), The Lecomptonists and the 'anti-Lecompton' Democracy of Lecompton went off on this bolt, doing it secretly. 1872 *Chicago Tribune* 10 Oct. 4/6 Stanard . . . is a strong party man, and only got into the bolt of 1870 through a misapprehension. 1884 *Lisbon* (Dakota) *Star* 22 Aug. The Irish bolt continues. The Telegraph, a paper whose proprietors are Irish and Catholic, . . . entered the canvass for Cleveland. 1887 *Scribner's Mag.* May 625/1 If journalists and journals were in the market, . . . there would be no such widespread bolt against your machine ticket to-day. 1903 A. H. LEWIS *Boss* 116 You can say that we . . . are goin' to make a bolt for better government.

+**2.** *slang.* (See quotation.)

1851 HALL *College Words* 22 *Bolt*, an omission of a recitation or lecture.

Bolt, *n.*[3] A machine for sifting flour. {1847}

1777 *N.J. Archives* 2 Ser. I. 451 To be sold, the Cranberry Mills, ... [having] four new bolting cloths, and all the bolts work by water. **1803** *Mass. H. S. Coll.* IX. 114 After having descended into a long trough, it [the wheat] is conducted up into the bolts, and thence to a large cooling room. **1813** *Niles' Reg.* V. Add. A. 10/1 At that time there was no machine in her to feed the bolts. **1849** *Rep. Comm. Patents* (1850) 303, I claim as my invention ... the process of re-grinding the offal of wheat, immediately after it has passed from the 'bolts.'

* **Bolt,** *v.*

+**1.** *tr.* To avoid (an issue) by not voting.

1813 *Portsmouth* (N.H.) *Oracle* 20 Nov. 2/3 (Th.), Others, ashamed to make further opposition, but without sufficient courage to do their duty, bolted the question.

b. *intr.* To draw back *from* an agreement.

1849 T. T. JOHNSON *Sights Gold Region* ii. 16 Surprised at our facile compliance with their original demand, they determined at once to bolt from their contract.

+**2.** *intr.* To break away from a political party or its representative; to desert or go over to the opposition party.

1833 *Louisville Herald* 17 Oct., Does the Doctor apprehend that the editor is about to 'bolt'? **1845** BENNETT in Mackenzie *Van Buren* (1846) 236 Before the summer was over, however, Mr. Webb bolted from the democratic party on the United States bank question. **1848** *Knickerb.* XVIII. 515 Didn't Best swear that he'd 'bolt,' because he wasn't nominated for constable last spring? **1862** [BROWNE] *A. Ward his Book* 219 The Old Flag ... had allers bin on the ticket he'd voted, and he was too old to Bolt now. **1875** *Scribner's Mo.* Nov. 124/2 Voters, even though they have little to do with forming platforms and nominating men, can bolt. **1890** *Spectator* 27 Sept. 398/1 Both Democrats and Republicans have ... been thrown into a fever of alarm lest the agricultural interest should 'bolt,' as it is termed.

+**3.** *tr.* To break away from, desert, turn against (a party, program, or candidate).

1847 *Congress. Globe* 4 Feb. 322/2, I had never bolted a regular nomination of the Democratic party, from President to constable. **1857** *Lawrence* (Kansas) *Republican* 25 June 2 The judge bolts popular sovereignty—when applied to Utah. **1867** *Congress. Globe* 16 April 847/1, I did not follow ... [Mr. Fessenden] in his leadership on that occasion. I have no recollection of ever having bolted my leader until that time, but then I did. **1872** *Newton Kansan* 17 Oct. 2/1 The Democrats bolted the Greeley ticket in large numbers. **1885** HOWELLS *Indian Summer* i. 3 No one had much fault to find when the *Democrat-Republican* bolted the nomination of a certain politician of its party for Congress. **1901** W. A. WHITE in *McClure's Mag.* Dec. 149 If he bolts the caucus, a new man often appears from his district the next session. **1913** LA FOLLETTE *Autobiog.* 322 The opposition was laying the foundation either for stealing the state convention or else bolting it and placing a third ticket in the field.

Bolter. [BOLT *v.*] +One who 'bolts' in politics.

The exact sense in the following quotation is not clear: **1812** *Salem Gaz.* 10 July 4/1 (Th.), D. Tompkins would ... send home the bolters by new prorogation. (Cf. BOLT *v.* 1.)

1858 *N.Y. Tribune* 12 Jan. 2/3 (Th.), An attempt ... to make the people go into the election and harmonize the bolters. **1860** *Richmond Engineer* 2 Nov. 1/8 (Th.), Remember that Stephen A. Douglas is a bolter from the party. **1875** NORDHOFF *Cotton States* 22/2 The restive negro's name is sent ... through the country or district, with 'Bolter' affixed to it; and this fixes upon him the stigma of treason. **1884** *Century Mag.* Nov. 126 The few who will neither surrender their principles nor bury them in silence are stigmatized by a term borrowed from the turf ... as 'bolters.' **1886** LOGAN *Great Conspiracy* 91 On the 11th of June [1860] ... the Democratic Bolters' Convention met at Richmond.

* **Bolting,** *vbl. n.*[1] [f. *bolt* to sift. Cf. BOLT *n.*[3]] The process of sifting meal or flour. Used attrib. in various collocations having a more general or later currency than in England, esp. *bolting mill.*

(1) **1711** *Harvard Rec.* I. 397 Voted, ... that what Charge the Steward has bin at in purchasing a Bolting-Mill for the Use of the College be allow'd him. **1725** *New-Eng. Courant* 19 June 2/2 A Bolting Mill and Cloths to be sold. **1775** BURNABY *Travels* 47 There is [near Colchester, Va.] an iron furnace, a forge, two saw-mills, and a bolting-mill. **1798** *Smithtown Rec.* 351 The grist mill house to be ... so constructed as to carry three run of stones with three Bolting mills. **1885** E. EGGLESTON in *Century Mag.* April 881/2 The New England town community in some cases provided bolting-mills where each man might bolt his own flour.

(2) **1722** *New-Eng. Courant* 21 May 2/1 A Fire broke out at Bristol, which burnt down ... a Bolting-House and two other Houses. **1786** in *Rep. Comm. Patents* (1850) 573 He can erect ... a machine to attend the bolting hopper with regularity. **1790** *Penna. Packet* 2 Feb. 3/3 The mill-house ... [contains] three boulting chests, hoisting gears, a rolling screen, and a fan. **1813** *Niles' Reg.* V. Add. A. 10/1 A machine to feed the bolting chests in the mill. **1846** *Rep. Comm. Patents* (1847) 100 Patents have been granted this year for improvements in bolting machines. **1875** KNIGHT 1143/2 *Hutch,* ... the case of a flour bolt; a bolting-hutch. **1900** SMITHWICK *Evol. of State* 237 George Glasscock ... put up the first bolting works in that part of the country [=Texas].

Bolting, *vbl. n.*[2] [BOLT *v.*] +Desertion of party. Also attrib. with *ticket.* — **1845** BENNETT in Mackenzie *Van Buren* (1846) 236, I stuck to the movement, and left the *Courier and Enquirer* on account of this bolting. **1858** *N.Y. Tribune* 12 Jan. 2/3 (Th.), The Delegate Convention determined not to vote. A few disaffected got up a bolting ticket. **1875** *Scribner's Mo.* Nov. 124/2 We have arrived at the golden age of bolting, and voters ... can bolt. **1884** *N.Y. Times* 24 June 1/2 Why, Sir, bolting is the very safety of the Union. This caucus system of ours is a despotism, tempered only by bolting. **1895** A. O. MYERS *Bosses & Boodle* 55 Cash is paid for the vote as promised. This is an evasion of a very strict law.... Bolting is the only remedy.

Bolting, *ppl. a.* [BOLT *v.*] +Making a political 'bolt.' — **1867** *Congress. Globe* 16 Feb. 1445/2 This bolting convention of Radicals at Cleveland was condemned ... by the great mass of the Union Party. **1886** LOGAN *Great Conspiracy* 90 After the withdrawal of the bolting delegates at Baltimore, the Convention proceeded to ballot for President.

* **Bolting cloth.** [BOLTING *vbl. n.*[1]] A silk, linen, or hair cloth used by millers for sifting meal, flour, etc.

1730 *Md. Hist. Mag.* XIX. 185 A fine bolting cloth for merchants work. **1770** *Ib.* III. 146 We will not hereafter ... import ... Muslin, Kenting, Gauze of all Kinds, except Boulting-Clothes. **1813** *Niles' Reg.* V. Add. A. 14/1 The mill stones and bolting cloths being the only agents in separating from each other the constituent parts of the wheat. **1832** *Louisville Directory* 98 [Ground wheat] was sifted through a gauze handkerchief ... as the best bolting cloth to be had. **1849** *Rep. Comm. Patents: Agric.* (1850) 67 The wheat was ground ... and twice passed through a bolting-cloth sieve. **1881** *Rep. Indian Affairs* 176 A new bolting-cloth for the grist-mill.

attrib. **1858** *S. Lit. Messenger* XXVII. 354/1, I packed my sole-leather trunk, with the bolting-cloth cover, and made my *congé.*

Bolt iron. Round bar iron suitable for being made into bolts. {1793} — **1810** *Columbian Centinel* 17 Jan. 3 William Little ... has for sale ... Tub Steel, ... Bolt Iron. **1818** *Niles' Reg.* XV. 106/1, 665,503 lbs. of bolt iron to follow augurs from 5-8 to 3 1-2 inches. **1833** *Ib.* XLIV. 365/2 Bolt or chain iron [is] of various diameters cut up in ends of different lengths.

* **Bombardier.**

* **1.** A gunner in the artillery.

1777 *N.J. Archives* 2 Ser. I. 290 Williams is about 5 feet, 8 or 9 inches high, says he has been a bombadeer [*sic*]. **1796** A. BARTON *Disappointment* I. i, I'm acquainted with an old artillery-man, who told me his father was a bombardier. **1855** SARGENT *Braddock's Exped.* 136 A matross is an artillery soldier of a rank inferior to the bombardier or gunner.

2. (See quotations.) Also attrib. with *beetle.*

1854 EMMONS *Agric. N.Y.* V. 41 *Brachinides;* ... when pursued, they suddenly discharge from behind a highly volatile and elastic fluid, possessing considerable pungency.... From this singular mode of defence, these insects have received the name of bombardiers. **1868** *Amer. Naturalist* April 111 The curious Bombardier beetle. **1889** *Cent.* 617/1 *Bombardier-beetle,* the common name of many coleopterous insects, family *Carabidæ* and genera *Brachinus* and *Aptinus,* found under stones.

Bombazette, -et(t). *Obs.* [Cf. next.]

1. A kind of thin woolen cloth.

1811 *Niles' Reg.* I. 46/1 Bombazetts, bombazines, ... caps and mittens and other useful goods can only be made of wool long enough to be combed. **1812** *Ib.* II. 9/1 Wool ... wrought into ... bombazettes. **1824** *Harvard Univ. Laws* 18 Pantaloons of black mixed or of black bombazet. **1827** *Hallowell* (Maine) *Gaz.* 20 June 4/4 Advt., Received ... twilled Bombazett; some very superior Haskin Gloves.

2. *attrib.* Made of this material.

1829 in *Advance* (Chicago) 16 May 1895, St. Clair Female Seminary: ... Dress of young ladies ... two black bombazette frocks, and one white one. **1839** *S. Lit. Messenger* V. 36/1 The room was illuminated by eight windows with ... nothing but the dark scarlet bombazet demi-curtain. **1848** *Knickerb.* XXXII. 81 There was a dun-colored calico gown belonging to the face, with a black bombazet apron in front.

* **Bombazine.** Also †**bombazin, -bazeen.**

* **1.** A fine cloth made of silk and wool or wool and cotton.

1754 *S.C. Gazette* 1 Jan. 4/2 The goods on hand consist in check mantuas and Irish stuffs, everlastings, bombazine. **1759** in H. M. Brooks *Gleanings* 33 Lastings of all colours, bombazine, ... English oznabrigs. **1762** *Ib.* 37 Bombazeen, Allopeen, colour'd Russells. **1787** FRENEAU *Misc. Works* 423 Where ... ge'mmen go dress'd in your black bombazeen. **1811** *Niles' Reg.* 21 Sept. I. 46/1 Bombazines, worsted hosiery, caps and mittens ... can only be made of wool long enough to be combed. **1829** A. ROYALL *Pennsylvania* I. 118 Some of the citizen-ladies were dressed ... in calico, some in bombazeen, and some in silk. **1858** *Amer. Cycl.* III. 454/2 Bombazine ... is now usually composed wholly of woollen. **1901** CHURCHILL *Crisis* 10 Miss Crane, tall, with all the severity of side curls and bombazine, stood ... at the gate.

b. *attrib.* Made of bombazine.

1837 *S. Lit. Messenger* III. 513, I loosened her bombazin dress to the waist. **1840** *Knickerb.* XVI. 241 The appearance ... was accompanied by a middle-aged gentleman, in a black bombazine suit. **1856** A. CARY *Married* 107 The bombazine mourning gown worn for her deceased husband.

2. A dress made of this material.

1845 C. M. KIRKLAND *Western Clearings* 48 Millbank, the tailor's lady, ... wore an elegant black bombazine, with pink satin bows on the shoulders. **1863** B. TAYLOR *H. Thurston* ii. 33 Mrs. Fortitude Babb had made her appearance, clad in the black bombazine which she had purchased for Jason's funeral. **1887** *Century Mag.* XXXIV. 335/1 Twenty ladies shook to the breeze the camphored folds of twenty bombazines, alpacas, and venerable silks. **1904** E. GLASGOW *Deliverance* 4 A lean and high-featured matron, encased in the rigidity of her Sunday bombazine.

Bomb battery. A battery discharging bombs. — **1740** *S.C. Hist. Soc.* IV. 56 He said it [the utmost point] was two miles Distance from the Castle, and therefore not fit for a Bomb Battery. **1777** *Md. Hist. Mag.* V. 217 They have since continued a fire from their two Bomb Batteries & Red Hot Balls.

Bomb-cracker. A cracker that explodes like a bomb. — **1889** *Harper's Mag.* May 977/2 He would roll down hill to enjoy himself, but crown his delight by tossing up bomb-crackers as he rolled.

Bombo, variant of BUMBO.

Bombproof, *n.* [From the adj.]

1. A bombproof structure; a place affording protection from enemy bombs or gunfire. {1811-}

1780 *Heath P.* 8 The magazine ... is in that end of the bomb proof. **1781** E. DENNY *Journal* 43 Shot and shell raked the town in every direction. Bomb-proofs the only place of safety. **1809** BARLOW *Columbiad* VII. 618 A strong high citadel still thundering stood, ... And housed in bomb-proof all the host she bore. **a1817** DWIGHT *Travels* II. 444 The bomb-proof, which was extensive, ... [is] partly fallen in. **1842** *Amer. Pioneer* I. 26 An arsenal built of large logs and covered with earth, stood ... near the guard-house, and answered as a 'bomb-proof' or magazine for the protection of their powder. **1865** *Atlantic Mo.* XV. 425 These iron bars formed an invulnerable roof for magazines and bomb-proofs of the fort. **1888** J. D. BILLINGS *Hardtack* 57 These bomb-proofs ... were made of logs heavily banked with earth and having a door ... on the side away from the enemy.

+b. A place of safety; a situation or occupation not exposing one to danger. (Cf. 2.)

1891 *Scribner's Mag.* X. 367 Mrs. Wagoner's husband had been in a bomb-proof during the war.

+2. In the Southern States, one who occupied a place or position of safety during the Civil War.

1869 *Overland Mo.* III. 128 In the cis-Mississippi States [such Southerners] ... were generally dubbed 'bomb-proofs.' **1871** *Congress. Globe* 21 Jan. 656/3 [In Va., when] those who have been engaged in behalf of the 'lost cause' ... cannot be found, 'bomb-proofs' are patronized in their stead, in preference to Union men. **1871** DE VERE *Americanisms* 281 Officials, who were not expected to expose themselves to the fire of the enemy, like quartermasters, commissaries, etc., were nicknamed *bomb-proofs*. **1876** *Southern Hist. Soc. P.* II. 229 While the war lasted, it was the delight of some of the stoutly built fellows to go home for a few days, and kick and cuff and tongue-lash the able-bodied bomb-proofs.

Bombproof, *a.*

1. Strong enough to resist the effect of bombs or shells. {1755-}

1741 *S.C. Hist. Soc.* IV. 11 The Rampart ... casemated underneath for Lodgings, arched over, and of late said to be made Bomb-proof. **1777** in Sparks *Corresp. Amer. Rev.* II. 43 A bomb-proof magazine is nearly finished; no other security in the post against shells. **1818** FLINT *Lett. from Amer.* 21 The vessel is bomb-proof, impelled by a powerful steam-engine.

+b. Safe from the risks of fighting.

1868 *Putnam's Mag.* I. 715/1 During the late war the Simminses did their share of the fighting, for ... none of them had influence to get 'bomb-proof' places, and keep in the rear. **1889** *Century Mag.* Feb. 587/1 Much ill-feeling existed towards men who remained in the capital in what were called bomb-proof offices. **1895** *Congress. Rec.* 11 Jan. 887/2 He asked to be relieved from a bombproof situation under the Government in order to join his regiment.

2. Of persons: (see BOMBPROOF *n.* 2).

1869 *Congress. Globe* 6 Feb. 950/2 These sleek, bomb-proof patriots, who fight the battles of their country by strutting about the avenue here.

Bonaclapper, dialect variant of BONNY-CLABBER. — **1883** *Harper's Mag.* Oct. 806/2 We [Kentuckians] used to call it bonaclapper.

+Bonanza. [Sp., 'fair or calm weather,' 'good fortune.']

1. *In bonanza*, of a mine: Producing very profitable ore. [Sp. *en bonanza*.]

1844 GREGG *Commerce of Prairies* I. 170 When the Placer was in its greatest *bonanza*—yielding very large profits to those engaged in the business. **1876** RAYMOND *8th Rep. Mines* 193 The great Aurora vein or channel has been in *bonanza* this summer, ... yielding monthly some $100,000. **1888** J. J. WEBB *Adventures* 101 The products of gold mines ... did not amount to more than $200,000 dollars a year when in 'bonanza,' and very seldom to anything near that amount.

2. Good luck in goldmining; the accidental discovery of a rich vein or pocket.

1847 RUXTON *Adv. Rocky Mts.* (1848) 148 Their gains depend entirely upon the bonanza, or the chance of striking a rich vein, which ... is a rare event. **1881** RAYMOND *Mining Glossary, Bonanza*, in miners' phrase, good luck.

3. A valuable find of ore; a rich vein or lode, or portion of one.

1875 *Scribner's Mo.* July 272/1 A great 'bonanza' stretching across both mines was discovered. **1876** RAYMOND *8th Rep. Mines* 274, I judge that the lot referred to must have been rather an accidental bonanza in the vein. **1878** BEADLE *Western Wilds* 46 He ... was sinking on the vein with tireless energy, in the daily hope of striking a bonanza. **1880** *Harper's Mag.* Feb. 381/2 He will seek a 'claim,' and fondly see a bonanza in the smallest and shallowest of his 'prospect holes.' **1887** F. FRANCIS *Saddle & Moccasin* 56 As soon as he 'struck a Bonanza,' he meant to sit around and reflect on week-days too.

4. *fig.* A 'mine' of something; a valuable thing; a source of wealth or profit.

1875 *Chicago Tribune* 1 Sept. 4/1 Justices of the Peace who manifest a determination to cut off the big bonanzas which the Collector, Assessor and Supervisor have enjoyed. **1880** 'MARK TWAIN' *Tramp Abroad* xxii. 212 Digging, three days agone, I struck a manure mine!—a Golconda, a limitless Bonanza, of solid manure. **1884** SWEET & KNOX *Through Texas* 154 As a mine of knowledge in the matter of cattle, he was a bonanza. **1896** *Chicago Record* 4 July 7/3 The engagement [of *The Gay Parisians*] is proving a bonanza for Manager Charles Frohman. **1904** *Boston Herald* 18 Oct. 6 We blundered into this Philippine business ... partly because it was thought ... a commercial bonanza was to be obtained by the annexation of this archipelago.

5. *attrib.* Applied to persons who have made fortunes through mining operations.

1876 *Boston Post* 5 May (B.), The Bonanza king was bitterly indignant at the means employed to depreciate his mines. **1883** *Harper's Mag.* May 816/1 The Nevada Bank, the lever of the Bonanza kings, ... is found to be a four-story and Mansard-roof iron façade. **1884** NYE *Baled Hay* 39 Colorado, ... dwelling place of the bonanza Senator. **1884** *Cent. Mag.* Sept. 796 The railroad king, ... the bonanza mine owner, the Texas rancher, and the Pennsylvania iron prince. **1898** ATHERTON *Californians* 61 A 'Bonanza' family, whose huge fortune, made out of the Nevada mines, had recently lifted it from obscurity to social fame.

b. In sense: Yielding much profit or large interest.

1876 *Boston Post* 5 May (B.) The recent decline in Bonanza stocks in the San Francisco market. **1877** WM. WRIGHT *Big Bonanza* 18 The history of the famous Comstock silver lode ... and of the bonanza mines, situated on that lode. **1883** MRS. FOOTE *Led-Horse Claim* i. 9 The ark of the mining interests ... had drifted about unsteadily after the break in bonanza stocks in the summer of 1877.

c. *Bonanza farm*, a farm on a large scale, worked with modern appliances. Hence *bonanza farmer*.

1882 *Century Mag.* Aug. 505/1 Except on the big 'bonanza farms,' owned and operated by capitalists, it is rare to find any sheds for implements. **1882** *Uncle Rufus & Ma* 46 The large 'bonanza' farmers in Cass County have been successful. **1883** *Fisheries Exhibition Cat.* 79 The bonanza farms of America, where every kind of agricultural process is accomplished by steam. **1904** *Minneapolis Times* 8 July 4 The 'bonanza' farm, not many years ago a subject of much boasting in the west, is a thing of the past, and from now on intensified instead of expansive farming will prevail.

Bonaparte. [The name of the naturalist Bonaparte (1803-1857).] Used in the possessive (or attrib.) in bird-names, as *Bonaparte's flycatcher, gull, sandpiper.*

1839 PEABODY *Mass. Birds* 379 Bonaparte's Gull, *Larus Bonapartii*, is seen occasionally, early in autumn, on the coast of this State. **1844** *Nat. Hist. N.Y., Zoology* II. 311 Bonaparte's Gull ... is a northern species, breeding from Maine to the arctic circle.... It is one of the most common species on our coast. **1858** BAIRD *Birds Pacific R.R.* 295 *Myiodioctes Bonapartii*.... Bonaparte's Flycatcher. **1874** COUES *Birds N.W.* 655 *Larus ... Philadelphia*.... Bonaparte's Gull. *Ib.* 487 *Tringa Fuscicollis*. ... Bonaparte's Sandpiper. **1917** *Dial. Notes* IV. 423 Bonaparte gull (*Larus philadelphia*).

Bonavist. *Obs.* Also **-vis, bonnivis.** A kind of bean native to the tropical parts of America. {1700-}

1682 ASH *Carolina* 14 Pulse they have of great Variety, ... viz. Beans, Pease, Callavance, Figdlaes, and Bonavist, &c. **1709** LAWSON *Carolina* 76 The Bonavis, Calavancies, Nanticokes, and abundance of other Pulse, too tedious here to name, ... we found the Indians possess'd of, when first we settled in America. **1737** BRICKELL *Nat. Hist. N. Carolina* (1911) 17 The Bonavis is another kind of Pulse and yields a great Increase. **1743** CATESBY *Carolina* App. p. xvi, After the [Indian] corn is come up some small height, there are drop'd into every hill two or three beans called *Bonavis*, which as they shoot up are supported by the stalks of the corn. **1800** J. BOUCHER *Glossary* xlix, *Bonniviss*, (pronounced *bonny-bess*); a kind of kidney-beans; first brought, as may be supposed, from the Island Bonavista.

***Bond,** *n.*

***1.** A formal document by which a person undertakes to perform a certain act, or to act in a certain way, under a specified monetary penalty in case of breach or failure.

1653 *Boston Rec.* 11 The Townesmen ... may refuse to give bond though it be for a publique good. **1660** *Mass. H. S. Coll.* 4 Ser. VII. 247 Mr. Alen and Mr. Migat is bound in 50*li.* bond. **1689** *Ib.* 224 He was bound in £500 bond to answer it, and to his behavior for the future. **1714** SEWALL *Diary* III. 22 Treasurers must give Bond, for the faithful discharge of their Trust. **1792** CHIPMAN *Amer. Law Rep.* (1871) 27 The bond was taken for the prisoner's good behavior. **1834** in *Army Regulations* (1861) 517 If such person is a trader, his license shall be revoked and his bond put in suit. **1901** CHURCHILL *Crisis* 65 'Then he set her free,' said Miss Carvel, contemptuously. 'Judge Whipple went on her bond to-day.'

*2. A document by which a person agrees to pay a specified sum of money at an appointed time.

1630 WINTHROP *Let.* in *Hist.* I. 449 She hath a bond of £400. Yet you know there is not so much due to her. **1682** *New Plymouth Laws* 196 Tradsmen have noe opportunity to take bonds, bills, or witnes of the delivery of theire goods. **1704** SEWALL *Diary* II. 94 Reckon'd with the tenants of the saw-mill at Braintry, and took their bonds for the arrears. **1790** *Ann. 1st Congress* I. 1260 When one man owes another an account, and gives his bond for the balance, the account is no longer of force. **1873** HOLLAND *A. Bonnicastle* vii, One ponderous bundle of papers I found to be composed entirely of bonds and mortgages. **1898** PAGE *Red Rock* 202 Still's reply to the contempt that was visited on him was to bring suit on the bonds he held.

b. A document of this nature issued by a government, corporation, company, etc., for the purpose of borrowing money. {1651–}

1691 C. MATHER in *Mass. Bay Currency Tracts* 13 'Twas an honest and good method you took, to pay by Bonds what you could not by Ready Cash. *Ib.* 14 All the Inhabitants of the Land, taken as one Body are the Principals, who reap the Benefits, . . . and are the Security in their Publick Bonds. **1790** *Ann. 1st Congress* I. 1160, I mentioned also the case of a bond, and supposed that we were bound to the punctual payment of government notes. **1857** *Mass. Acts & Resolves* 727 Let preference, then, be given to our own State scrip, . . . selecting next our county, city and town bonds. **1861** *U.S. Statutes* 8 Feb. 129 The Secretary of the Treasury is hereby authorized . . . to exchange at par bonds of the United States. **1892** M. A. JACKSON *Memoirs* 206 You had better not sell your coupons from the bonds.

attrib. **1898** ALTGELD *Live Questions* (1899) 795 (*heading*), Forcing bond issues. *Ib.*, The bond speculators are said to have made between thirty and forty millions of dollars, clear profit, out of these bond transactions. **1905** N. DAVIS *Northerner* 106 Adairville returned a solid vote in favor of the bond issue.

Bond, *v.* [f. the noun.]

1. *intr.* To issue bonds.

1812 *Ann. 12th Congress* 2 Sess. 1273 We have only bonded for three thousand seven hundred and fifty dollars.

2. *tr.* To issue bonds upon (property); to finance by means of bonds.

1883 *Harper's Mag.* Nov. 939/1 Conservative investors . . . said the [Northern Pacific] road . . . was too heavily bonded.

b. To accept another's bond or bonds for.

1880 G. INGHAM *Digging Gold* xvii. 386 Gold parties . . . who bought [the Dakota lode] . . . , when approached in regard to selling it, would not offer to bond it for less than one hundred thousand dollars.

3. To bind (one) by a legal bond; to put under a bond.

1896 *N. Amer. Rev.* CLXIII. 711 The [Western] settlers who were so willing to bond themselves. **1916** W. A. DU PUY *Uncle Sam* 217 As book-keeper, Tollman . . . was . . . not considered as being in a position of trust. He was not even bonded.

Bonded, *ppl. a.* [BOND *n.* and *v.*]

1. *Bonded debt*, the debt represented by the bonds which have been issued by a corporation, etc. Also *bonded indebtedness*.

1873 *Newton Kansan* 13 March 3/2 Harvey County has less bonded indebtedness than any organized county in Southern Kansas. **1875** *Chicago Tribune* 7 Sept. 2/2 It is deemed important to build a city-hall, . . . and an addition of say $2,000,000 is made to the bonded debt. **1886** *Harper's Mag.* July 197/2 This income will, of course, increase as the bonded debt decreases.

2. *Bonded warehouse*, a warehouse in which various goods subject to duty are held until the duty is paid. {1868–}

1865 *Internal Revenue Guide* (1866) 159 Lucifer or friction matches . . . may be transferred . . . directly from the place of manufacture to a bonded warehouse. **1865** *Atlantic Mo.* XV. 80 Something like a quarter of all New York imports go in the first instance to the bonded warehouse. **1884** *Harper's Mag.* June 58/2 Of bonded warehouses . . . in New York, Brooklyn, Jersey City, and Hoboken, the number is fifty-nine.

Bondholder. [BOND *n.* 2.] One who owns a bond issued by a government, corporation, company, or individual. {1865–}

1838 *Diplom. Corr. Texas* (1911) III. 830 The proposition would be accepted by a part of the Bondholders. **1844** *N. Amer. Rev.* Jan. 139 This law amounted to a contract made by the State and the Banks with every bond-holder. **1855** [PRAY] *Mem. J. G. Bennet* 334 Honest debts to foreign bond-holders should be first liquidated. **1878** *N. Amer. Rev.* CXXVI. 498 The South had bonds and bondholders as well as the North.

***Bondman.** +A Negro slave. *Obs.* — **1862** GREELEY in Logan *Great Conspiracy* 433 Let them impress this as a truth in the great mass of their ignorant and credulous Bondmen, and the Union will never be restored. **1866** BRYANT *Death of Slavery* 17 Fields where the bondman's toil No more shall trench the soil. **1867** A. D. RICHARDSON *Beyond Mississippi* 43 In the entire Territory, there were not a hundred bondmen.

Bondslavery. [Cf. *bondslave* {1561–}.] The holding of bondmen or slaves. — **1641** *Mass. Liberties* 231 There shall never be any bond slaverie, villinage or Captivitie amongst us.

Bondsman. [BOND *n.* 1.] One who becomes surety for another. {1754–}

1713 HEMPSTEAD *Diary* 28 The latter p[ar]t of the day [I was] with Jno Pendall at the Court of Probates to be his bondsman w[i]th Capt Hough. **1753** *Duxbury Rec.* 314 To see that said persons procure some good able bondsmen for the money aforesaid, with the interest thereof. **1808** *Ann. 10th Congress* 2 Sess. 251 The trade would in many instances be abandoned from inability of the owners of vessels to procure such bondsmen as would be acceptable to the collector. **1875** *Chicago Tribune* 2 July 4/1 The 'corner' transactions were nothing more than gambling contracts . . . and therefore the law will not enforce the claim against the bondsmen. **1906** 'O. HENRY' *Four Million* 174, I noticed at one side a gathering of professional bondsmen in solemn black and collars that buttoned behind.

***Bondwoman.** +A Negro female slave. *Obs.* — **1850** *Harper's Mag.* Nov. 725/1 One who, though a dark Child of Africa and a bondwoman, received the most polite attention from the Commander-in-Chief. **1869** TOURGEE *Toinette* xiv. (1881) 159 The wonderful beauty of his young bond-woman.

***Bone,** *n.*

+**1.** *To feel it* (etc.) *in one's bones*, to feel certain about, to have an intuition of, something. Also of the thing, *to be in one's bones*.

1844 Barnes *Mem. Thurlow Weed* (1884) 123 It was in my bones all summer. **1857** *Quinland* II. 169, I feel it in my bones that the next election will be the making of me. **1875** HOLLAND *Sevenoaks* 315, I know the thing is coming. I can feel the thing in my bones. **1878** BEADLE *Western Wilds* 42, I felt in my bones no good could come of it. **1902** H. L. WILSON *Spenders* 466 It is a happy man who has divined the leisure of eternity, so he feels it, like what you say, 'in his bones.' **1912** MULFORD & CLAY *Buck Peters* 57 Son, there's a big time due in these parts; I feel it in my bones.

***2.** *pl.* Pieces of bone, etc., rattled together to form an accompaniment to a banjo, guitar, etc.

a1859 *Negro Melody* (B.), The fiddle there, and den de bones, And de merry tambourine. **1869** *Atlantic Mo.* July 72/2 The musical instruments . . . consisted, if I well recollect, of the banjo . . . , three sets of bones, a tambourine, a triangle, and an accordion. **1880** E. JAMES *Negro Minstrel's Guide* 4 The following schedule of prices . . . will be of considerable interest and value to young amateurs: . . . rosewood bones, 50 & 75 cts. per set; ebony bones, $1; tamborines, from $2 each.

+**b.** A performer who uses bones; *spec.*, the right-hand endman in a Negro minstrel company.

1880 E. JAMES *Negro Minstrel's Guide* 2 An amateur Negro minstrel band may consist of from seven to thirteen . . . performers, arranged on the stage as follows: . . . Bone-player on the extreme right; Triangle-player next to Bones' end. **1891** S. M. WELCH *Recoll. 1830–40* 371 Mr. Rice . . . was the man who first instituted negro minstrelsy as an occupation or profession. He was the leader of a band of five, as his son George was the bones of it. **1915** B. MATTHEWS in *Scribner's Mag.* June 756/1 Bones captured the chair at one end and Tambo pre-empted that on the other; and they began their wordy skirmish with the middle-man.

+**c.** Attrib. with *convention, performer, player*, etc.; also *bone end* (cf. 2 b).

1846 *Spirit of Times* 25 April 100/1 He is brother to the *bone* performer belonging to the troupe of Ethiopian Serenaders. **1867** *N.Y. World* 14 Dec. 2/1 The Virginia Bones and Banjo Convention is in its first stage [at Richmond, Va.]. **1880** E. JAMES *Negro Minstrel's Guide* 6 Much . . . depends on the drolleries and antics of the Tambo and Bone ends to insure a good time for the spectators. **1888** BILLINGS *Hardtack* 69 There was probably not a regiment in the service that did not boast at least one violinist, one banjoist, and a bone player in its ranks.

***Bone,** *v.*

‖**1.** *tr.* To drive in to the bone.

1839 *Knickerb.* XIII. 387, I was straitening for a second lunge my lance, which I had 'boned' in the first.

+**2.** *intr.* To work hard; to apply oneself closely or strenuously. Freq. with *in, into,* or *down. colloq.*

1841 GREELEY in *Corr. R. W. Griswold* (1898) 53 Webb wants to be Postmaster; . . . he has been round boring every big-bug in the State to bone for him. **a1861** WINTHROP *Open Air* 148 We was about sick of putty-heads and sneaks that . . . didn't dare to make us stand round and bone in. **a1870** CHIPMAN *Notes on Bartlett* 42 *Bone*, to apply one's self closely. 'To bone into it.' **1883** *Century Mag.* June 273 'I suppose you'll keep up your reading along with your law?' 'No, . . . I'm going to bone right down to it.'

+**b.** To study hard; to get *up* a subject by close study.

1886 E. L. Dorsey *Midshipman Bob* 72 Mr. Dugald . . . said a few weeks' more 'boning' would brace me up to the mark. (That's what they call studying here.) **1887** E. B. Custer *Tenting on Plains* ix. 286, I have known the General to 'bone-up,' as his West Point phrase expressed it, on the smallest details of some question at issue.

3. *tr.* To annoy or pester (a person). *colloq.* {1863–, *dial.*}

1858 *Harper's Mag.* March 566/1 You had better go to the head-waiter, and he will give you some [raisins]. . . . And if he don't give you some, *bone* him! **1884** 'Craddock' *Where Battle was Fought* 292 Estwicke . . . was a trifle confused to be boned on a point like this.

Bone dust. Bones ground for use as a fertilizer. {1834–}

1839 Buel *Farmer's Comp.* 71 Bone-dust is comparatively a new manure. **1856** *Rep. Comm. Patents: Agric.* 276 The lower-priced guanos and bone-dust are best adapted to supply the phosphates. **1884** *Rep. Comm. Agric.* 408 The materials used being old rotted sod made into compost, with the usual proportion of bone-dust.

Bone felon. [**felon* in same sense.] An extremely painful abscess or boil on the finger. {*dial.*} — **1854** *Florida Plant. Rec.* 117 Biner is sick from cold, and old Betty with a bone fellon on one of her fingers. **1897** R. M. Stuart *Simpkinsville* 19 My wife she had a finger wrapped up, an' he . . . give her a recipe for bone-felon.

+**Bonefish.** [Bone *n.*] **a.** One or other of various sea fishes (see quotations). **b.** A whale yielding whalebone; a 'right' whale.

1734 *Phil. Trans.* XXXVIII. 317 *Mormyrus, ex cinereo nigricans,* the Bone-Fish. **1802** Ellicott *Journal* 255 Along the Florida Reef, and among the Keys, a great . . . variety of fish may be taken: such as . . . black, red, and gray snappers, mullets, bone-fish, etc. **1809** E. A. Kendall *Travels* II. 204 The species of whale taken was . . . that which is technically called the *bone-fish,* or fish valued for the article called in commerce *whale-bone.* **1884** Goode *Aquatic Animals* 279 The 'Bone-fish' of Key West, according to Stearns, belongs to this [sturgeon] family and genus. *Ib.* 674 In Southern New England this fish [=the dogfish] is called the 'Bone-fish.' **1897** *Outing* XXIX. 331/1 The bone-fish somewhat resembles a whiting in shape, with the mouth of a sucker and no teeth.

+**Bone gathering.** *Obs.* Among Indians: (see quotation). — **1775** Adair *Indians* 180 Those who lose their people at war . . . are so observant of this kindred duty, as to appropriate some time to collect the bones of their relations; which they call *bone gathering.*

+**Bone-headed,** *a. colloq.* [Bone *n.* Cf. recent *bonehead,* 'blockhead.'] Thickheaded, obstinate, stupid. — [**1864** A. J. Dickson *Across Plains* (1929) 143 If some boneheaded mule displayed characteristic traits, the muleskinner was very expert with his long lash.] **1903** *Smart Set* IX. 96 You talk like a bone-headed fool!

Bone house. {1799–} +A place where some tribes of American Indians preserved the bones of their dead. — **1775** Adair *Indians* 183 Those bone-houses are scaffolds raised on durable pitch-pine forked posts, in the form of a house covered a-top, but open at both ends. **1899** H. B. Cushman *Hist. Indians* 225 As soon as the bone-houses of the neighboring villages were filled, a general burial of bones took place.

***Bone lace.** [Bone *n.*] Lace made with bobbins, originally of bone. Also attrib.

1636 *Mass. Bay Rec.* I. 183 No person . . . shall make or sell any bone lace, or other lace, to bee worne vpon any garment. **1676** *Conn. Rec.* II. 283 What person soever shall wear gold or siluer lace . . . or any bone lace . . . the list makers of the respectiue townes are hereby required to assesse such persons . . . at one hundred and fifty pownd estate. **1758** *Essex Inst. Coll.* XLV. 344 Sundry Pieces of fine wide black Bone Lace. **1762** in H. M. Brooks *Gleanings* 37 Black and white Bone Lace, . . . Silk and Cotton Laces. **1796** H. Wansey *Excursion U.S.* 48 There is also in this town [Ipswich, Mass.] . . . a large bone-lace manufactory.

+**Bone meal.** [Bone *n.*] Bones ground for fertilizing purposes. — **1850** *New Eng. Farmer* II. 44 On Mr. Preston's farm, . . . they began to use bone-meal. **1868** *Rep. Comm. Agric.* (1869) 401 Bone-meal prepared by high-pressure steam contains not much less nitrogen than ordinary bone dust.

Bone-mill. [Bone *n.*] A place where bone products are manufactured. — **1884** Sweet & Knox *Through Texas* 634 The animal must be a superannuated plug, . . . fit only for the bone-mill.

+**Bone picker.** [Bone *n.*] Among some of the American Indians, one who stripped the flesh from the bones of corpses.

1809 F. Cuming *Western Tour* 261 Some priest or privileged person, who was called the bone picker, was always sent for to the nation to come and cleanse the bones from the flesh [of a corpse] . . . that the bones might be carried home and interred in the general cemetery. **1818** Schoolcraft *Mo. Lead Mines* (1819) 288 There existed an order of men [among the Indian tribes] . . . called bone-pickers, with long nails like claws, whose business and profession it was to clean the unconsumed flesh from the bones, previous to burial. **1821** Nuttall *Travels Arkansa* 294 The Choctaws, till very late years, had a practice . . . of exposing their dead upon scaffolds till such time as the flesh decayed, which was then separated from the bones by a set of old men, who . . . were called 'bone-pickers.' **1899** H. B. Cushman *Hist. Indians* 225 The Bone-Picker never trimmed the nails of his thumbs, index and middle fingers, which accordingly grew an astonishing length.

Bone-pit. [Bone *n.*] (See quotation.) — **1889** Farmer 74 *Bone-pits,* Indian places of interment. These bone-pits are found scattered throughout the United States and Canada.

+**Bones.** A student organization at Yale University. Also attrib. with *men.* — **1871** [L. H. Bagg] *At Yale* 145 Popularly the society is known as 'Bones,' and its members as 'Bones men.' *Ib.* 148 A half-dozen extra men are chosen in Bones, in addition to the regular fifteen. **1902** J. Corbin *American at Oxford* 26 The would-be host circulates the room tapping the elect on the shoulder and speaking a quiet word as they select Bones men at Yale.

Boneset. {1670–, comfrey.}

+**1.** The North American thoroughwort, valued for its medicinal properties.

1817–8 Eaton *Botany* (1822) 278 Boneset, thoroughwort. **1839** Briggs *H. Franco* II. 135 My malady was not one that could be affected by a warming pan, nor by that best of all herbs, boneset. **1857** Gray *Botany* 187 *E. sessilifolium,* Upland Boneset; . . copses and banks, Massachusetts to Ohio, and southward along the mountains. **1880** Gibson in *Harper's Mag.* June 80 Out in the swamp meadow the tall clumps of boneset show their dull white crests. **1888** *Century Mag.* XXXVI. 764/1 Directions for the use of boneset as a substitute for quinine. **1901** Mohr *Plant Life Ala.* 761 *Eupatorium purpureum,* Trumpet-weed, Purple Boneset, . . . [grows in] low thickets and shaded banks. *Ib.* 764 *Eupatorium perfoliatum* . . . is the boneset or Eupatorium of the United States Pharmacopœia.

+**b.** *Boneset tea,* a decoction of the leaves of this plant.

1839 Briggs *H. Franco* II. 153 'Dear soul,' said the good woman, 'let me warm your bed, and give you some boneset tea.' **1865** Stowe in *Atlantic Mo.* XV. 496 Well, Jane, you've probably got a cold; go into the kitchen and make yourself some good boneset tea. **1877** *Vt. Dairymen's Assoc.* VIII. 53 Boneset tea is a good vehicle in which to give salts. **1886** Howells *Minister's Charge* 214, I guess if you don't want any boneset tea, a little of the other kind won't hurt any of us.

+**2.** *ellipt.* Boneset leaves or tea.

*c*1850 Whitcher *Bedott P.* xiii. 136, I send you herewith a paper o' boneset. **1876** M. F. Henderson *Cooking* 327 Pour one and one-half pints of boiling water on a ten-cent package of boneset. **1890** *Harper's Mag.* April 713/2 Dosin' with ginger tea, an' boneset an' sage an' saffron.

***Bonesetter.** [Bone *n.*] One who sets broken and dislocated bones. — **1688** *Conn. Probate Rec.* I. 498 Daniel Porter, Bonesetter, of Farmington. **1722** *Essex Inst. Coll.* XXXVII. 217 [Edward Mould,] marriner & Bonesetter. **1868** Channing *Recoll. Newport* 131 A famous bone-setter, by the name of Sweet.

+**Bone shark.** The basking shark, *Cetorhinus maximus.* — **1802** *Mass. H. S. Coll.* VIII. 199 There is a large shark in the harbour, named the bone-shark, and similar in shape to the man-eating shark, but harmless. **1814** Mitchill *Fishes N.Y.* 486 [The] Basking Shark . . . is remarkable for having something within his mouth resembling the horny substance called whale-bone, which has led some persons to call him the bone-shark. **1889** *Cent.* 621/3 *Bone-shark,* a common name along the New England coast of . . . the basking shark.

+**Bone yard.** [Bone *n.*]

1. A yard or place in which the bones of dead animals (esp. horses or cattle) are collected for subsequent use.

1862 *Rep. Comm. Patents: Agric.* 127 After that, to commence a liberal supply of grain, will doubtless hasten many of them to the bone-yard. **1903** *N.Y. Ev. Post* 7 Oct. 7 A dilapidated horse saved from the bone-yard.

b. A place in the forest where the bones of animals are abundant.

1903 W. J. Long *Beasts of Field* 70, I have met men . . . who speak of 'bone yards' which they have discovered—places where they can go at any time and be sure of finding a good set of caribou antlers. And they say that the caribou go there to die.

c. *jocular.* 'In the game of dominoes, the pieces reserved to draw from' (*Cent.*).

2. A burial place, cemetery. *slang.*

1872 'Mark Twain' *Roughing It* xlvii. 334 When some roughs jumped the Catholic bone-yard and started in to stake out town-lots in it he went for 'em! **1874** Eggleston *Circuit Rider* v. 59 You or me'll have to go to the bone-yard. **1898** Westcott *D. Harum* 370, 'I ain't quite to the bone-yard yet myself,' he added with a grin. **1903** A. H. Lewis *Boss* 205 Along comes a scientist an' tells him it's all off an' nothin' for it but the boneyard!

***Bonito, Bonita.** [Sp.]

1. One or other species of tunny, esp. *Sarda mediterranea* of the Atlantic Ocean and *Sarda chilensis* of the Pacific Ocean.

1635 R. Mather *Journal* (1850) 20 Wee saw this morning a great many of Bonnyetoes leaping and playing about the ship: Bonyetoe [*sic*] is a fish somewhat bigger than a cod but lesse than a porpuise [*sic*]. **1709** Lawson *Carolina* 155 Boneto's are a very palatable Fish, and near a yard long. They . . . are killed with the Harpoon, and Fishgig. **1842** D. Webster *Private Corr.* II. (1856) 133 In the Washington market this morning at five o'clock, I saw for the first time the bonita. He is a long, slender, round fish. **1871** *Germantown Telegraph* 2 Aug., The people of Rhode

Island are happy in consequence of the appearance in their waters of that excellent fish, the Bonita. **1882** E. K. GODFREY *Nantucket* 145 At rare intervals the bonita, Spanish mackerel, flying fish, and other varieties belonging farther south, have been captured. *a***1884** JORDAN in Goode *Fisheries U.S.* I. 319 This fish [*Sarda chilensis*] is everywhere known as the Bonito. The names 'Spanish Mackerel,' 'Skipjack,' and 'Tuna' are also sometimes applied to it. . . . It ranges from San Francisco southward to Chile, being abundant in Monterey Bay.

+**2.** *local.* The cobia or sergeant fish, *Elacate atlantica.*

1884 GOODE *Fisheries U.S.* I. 444 The cobia or crab-eater—*Elacate canada.* This fish, known in the Chesapeake Bay as the 'Bonito' and 'Coal-fish,' and as the 'Sergeant-fish' in Southern and Eastern Florida, . . . is considered one of the most important food-fishes of Maryland and Virginia.

***Bonnet.** Also *dial.* **bunnet.**

***1.** A woman's outdoor head-covering, without a brim and usually having strings.

1723 *Weekly Mercury* 7 Nov. 4/2 Run away, . . . a Negro Woman . . . having on a Stuff Gown and a new Bonnett Lined with red Silk. **1792** *Columbian Centinel* 30 June 3/4 This Day opened, and for Sale, . . . an extensive and elegant variety of fashionable Ladies' Hats, and Bonnets. **1812** *Emporium Arts & Sci.* (Phila.) May 73 In Massachusetts . . . the forming of bonnets from that material [straw] seems to have first begun. *c***1850** MRS. WHITCHER *Bedott P.* xxvi. 316 She had on a yaller bunnit, with a great pink artificial on it. **1880** CABLE *Grandissimes* xiii. 87 The flaring bonnet and loose ribbons gave her a more girlish look than ever.

b. Attrib. with *curtain, paper, pasteboard.*

1780 *N.J. Archives* 2 Ser. IV. 316 Parchment and Bonnet Pasteboard, to be sold at the Printing-Office. **1790** *Penna. Packet* 21 April 4/4 Robert Campbell, Bookseller and Stationer, . . . has just received . . . Bonnet Papers, Quills, Wax & Wafers. **1843** [STEPHENS] *High Life N.Y.* II. xxxi. 235 'The tickets,' sez he, a pintin tu the papers. 'What! these leetle queer chunks of bunnet paper?' **1845** MRS. KIRKLAND *Western Clearings* 19, I was 'a-goin' to want that 'ere flowery white bunnet-curting [curtain]' of mine.

+**2.** *Florida.* A variety of yellow water lily.

1822 [see BONNET LEAF]. **1836** *Knickerb.* VIII. 283 The banks of the river [near Rolls Town] are . . . lined with 'bonnets,' as they are called there. **1883** *Century Mag.* July 383/1 The boatman rows the boat . . . along the edges of the saw-grass, water-lettuce, bonnets, or other aquatic plants which border the . . . lakes of Florida.

+**Bonnet grass.** A variety of bent grass, *Agrostis alba.* — **1836** EATON *Botany* (ed. 7) 147 *Agrostis alba,* white top, bonnet grass. **1889** *Cent.* 623/1.

+**Bonnethead.** Also **bonnet-headed shark.** The shovelhead shark. — **1878** *Proc. U.S. Nat'l Museum* I. 387 *Reniceps Tiburo,*—Shovel-headed Shark, Bonnet-head. Abundant [near Beaufort Harbor, N.C.]. **1890** *Cent.* 5552/2 Bonnet-headed shark [is] a hammer-headed shark of the genus *Reniceps.*

+**Bonnet leaf.** =BONNET *n.* 2. — **1822** [W. H. SIMMONS] *Notices of E. Fla.* 29 (Th.S.), The bonnet leaf, a species of lotus, abounds in the dead water formed by the meeting currents.

+**Bonnet-worm.** [BONNET *n.* 2.] An insect larva occurring on the yellow water lily. — **1888** GOODE *Amer. Fishes* 58 In Florida . . . [black bass] feed on a grub called the 'bonnet-worm.'

Bonnyclabber. Also **bonyclabber, bonny clapper.** [1631–, *Anglo-Irish* =Ir. Gael. *bainne clabair,* f. *bainne* milk, *clabar* sour thick milk.] Milk that has thickened on becoming sour.

1731 *Essex Inst. Coll.* XLII. 233 Today we din'd . . . upon roast Mutton, & for Sauce a Sallet, mixed with Bonyclabber sweetned with Molasses. **1769** *Md. Hist. Mag.* XII. 280 His stomach was neither overcharged with Bonny Clabber nor Scotch Cale, but rather with some of Mr. Dick's Claret. **1800** J. BOUCHER *Glossary* p. l, For breakfast . . . bonny clabber with molasses sweet. **1807** C. JANSON *Stranger in A.* 181 The morning's milk turns to curd in the evening. This they call 'bonny clabber,' and eat it with honey, sugar, or molasses. **1834** *Visit to Texas* xiii. 118 'Bonny clapper' . . . I had ere this become fond of. **1849** *Knickerb.* Feb. 172 Some of those who did train, looked as sour as bonny-clabber. **1859** A. VAN BUREN *Sojourn in South* 154 But they have a much pleasanter name for what we call loppered milk—bonny clabber. **1872** *Harper's Mag.* Nov. 814/1, [In the Appalachian Mts.] I found the table garnished with some ill-looking hunks of boiled meat, a corn pone, and a crock of bonny-clabber. **1883** *Ib.* March 603/2, I had so much bonny-clabber, or curdled milk [in New Jersey], that I did not know what to do with it. **1904** M. D. CONWAY *Autobiog.* 18 We had our supper in summer under the apple-trees—griddle-cake and molasses, bonnyclabber, preserves.

Bonus. {1773–} +A bounty. — **1847** [ROBB] *Squatter Life* 80 [Every man shall be] made pay a license to the state before he can git a bonus for wolf-scalps.

+**Bony,** *n.* A mixture of sand-rock and shale. (Cf. next.) — **1874** RAYMOND *6th Rep. Mines* 39 The coal . . . is interstratified with sand-rock and shale. In some of the mines the roof consists of a mixture of the two, called by the men 'bony.' *Ib.* 41 The Black Diamond vein has for roof and floor shale, slate, and 'bony.'

***Bony,** *a.* [Cf. prec.] Of coal: Shaly. — **1857** *Harper's Mag.* Sept. 463/1 Much of the slate and 'bony coal' that occurs in the vein is separated . . . and thrown around the slope [in Penna.].

+**Bony fish.** The menhaden or mossbunker.

1814 MITCHILL *Fishes N.Y.* 453 Bony-fish, Hard-heads, or Marsbankers . . . [are] about fourteen inches long. **1842** *Nat. Hist. N.Y., Zoology* IV. 259 *Alosa menhaden.* Bony-fish or Mossbonker. **1871** *N.Y. Laws* II. 1674 Bony fish, or moss bunkers . . . are exempted from the operation of this section. **1884** L. F. ALLEN *New Farm Bk.* 80 The moss-bonker, or bony-fish, . . . are caught in seines, and sold to the farmers by the wagon load.

+**Bony fishing.** 'The menhaden-fishery' (*Cent.*).

+**Bony gar.** (See quotation and cf. next.) — **1821** NUTTALL *Travels Arkansa* 177 The boney gar (*Esox osseus*), and the large grey cat-fish, are also sufficiently common.

+**Bony pike.** A species of garfish common in the rivers and lakes of North America, also called the garpike, bill-fish, etc. — **1842** *Nat. Hist. N.Y., Zoology* IV. 272 The Buffalo Bony Pike, *Lepisosteus bison,* . . . was obtained at Buffalo, Lake Erie, where it is called the Bony Pike, Alligator and Alligator Gar. **1889** *Cent.* 2459 *Garpike,* any fish of the family *Lepidosteidæ;* a gar. Also called *bony pike.*

***Booby.**

1. One or other species of gannet (see quotations). {1634–}

1731 CATESBY *Carolina* I. 86 *Anseri bassano congener Avis fluvatilis.* The Great Booby. . . . They frequent the Rivers and Sea Coast of Florida. **1828** BONAPARTE *Synopsis* 408 The Booby, *Sula fusca,* . . . [is] common in summer on the coasts of the southern states. **1889** *Cent.* 623/3 The common booby of the United States is *Sula leucogastra,* a well-known species of the South Atlantic coast.

+**2.** *New England.* (See first quotation and cf. BOOBY HUT.)

1889 *Cent.* 623/3 *Booby,* . . . a hack on runners; a sleigh kept for hire. **1892** HOWELLS *Quality of Mercy* 39, I thought you'd ride better in the booby; it's a little mite chilly for the cutter.

+**Booby-hack.** =BOOBY 2. — **1888** *Boston Globe* (F.), A party . . . coming down the steep grade . . . on a double ripper, . . . collided with Crowley's booby hack.

+**Booby hut.** *Obs.* [Alteration of next.] A covered or enclosed sleigh, formerly used in New England, esp. in Boston.

1795 *Columbian Centinel* 24 Jan. 3/4 Two second hand Booby-Huts. **1812** *Boston Gazette* 28 Dec. (Th.), He has on hand, for sale, a number of Booby Huts and Carriages. **1826** *Missouri Intell.* 8 March 1/4 The others in carriages, the bodies of which are exactly like Boston Booby Huts (a kind of large close sleigh used there). **1835** in C. Mathews *Memoirs* (1839) IV. 325, I induced him on Wednesday to accompany Mrs. Eliot and myself in a 'Booby Hut' (for so a covered sleigh is called.) **1846** G. WARBURTON *Hochelaga* II. vi. 146 Some of the ladies of the wealthy classes [in Boston] are seen in the very cold weather driving about in a covered conveyance, enclosed partly with glass; . . . it is called a 'Booby-hut.' **1859** BARTLETT 43 Booby-hut, a carriage body put upon sleigh runners. New England.

Booby hutch. *Obs.* [In former E. use a small or clumsy carriage.] =BOOBY HUT. — **1766** *Boston Gazette* 29 Dec. (Th.), A very neat Booby-hutch to be sold cheap for Cash. **1767** *Mass. Gazette* 12 Feb. 4/2 A close Sleigh, or Booby-Hutch, to go with either one or two horses, . . . to be sold.

+**Boodle.** Also †**boedel.** [Du. *boedel,* in sense 1.]

1. Property, goods, effects. *Obs.*

1699 Mansell *Ann. Albany* (1852) III. 53 Elisabeth . . . hath the Boedel of Jan Verbeek, deceased, in hands.

2. *The whole boodle,* the whole lot, number, or amount. *slang.* (See also KIT.)

1833 J. NEAL *Down-Easters* I. 61, I know a feller 'twould whip the whool boodle of 'em an' give 'em six. **1833** S. SMITH *Major Downing* 108 He pulled off his coat and threw it down, and declared he'd fight the whole boodle of 'em. **1847** D. P. THOMPSON *Locke Amsden* 76 [He] stumped all the rest to come on, one at a time, and there wasn't a soul of the whole boodle that dared do it. **1858** HOLMES *Autocrat* v. 139 He would like to have the whole boodle of them (I remonstrated against this word, but the Professor said it was a diabolish good word, and he would have no other) . . . shipwrecked on a remote island. **1884** HALE *Xmas in Narragansett* 272 At eleven o'clock the 'whole boodle of them,' as Uncle Nahum called the caravan, . . . had to boot and spur for church.

3. *slang.* Counterfeit money; money obtained by underhand or dishonest means; money in general.

1858 *Harper's Weekly* 3 April 222/1 'Boodle' is a flash term used by counterfeiters. *Ib.* 222/2 The leaders [of the band] were the manufacturers and bankers of the 'boodle.' **1884** *Mag. Amer. Hist.* XII. 566/2 *Boodle,* a slang word adapted to political usage from the *argot* of counterfeiters. Originally it meant the main portion of the counterfeit money, and by an easy translation has come to mean a large roll of bills such as political managers are supposed to divide among their retainers. **1888** J. J. WEBB *Adv.* 229 The custom-house officers were notorious for their rascality and cunning in drawing strangers into their foils for the purpose of collecting boodle. *Ib.* 230 This would have . . . enabled them to demand a large sum by way of boodle or 'consideracion' for our release. **1888** *St. Louis Globe Democrat* (F.), She presented a draft for 2000 dols. drawn upon a Detroit bank, and received the cash. Immediately after that she left for the East with the boodle. **1891** S. FISKE *Holiday Stories* (1900) 158 A few diamonds, and a lot of jewelry; in fact . . . the whole boodle that we have been searching for so long. **1902** HARBEN *Abner Daniel* 58 Poverty on one side, boodle on the other. **1909** 'O. HENRY' *Roads of Destiny* viii. 138 My skill as a tattooer is worth half the boodle [=money stolen].

4. *slang.* Money used as a means of carrying on political bribery and corruption, or obtained as political spoils.

1884 [see 3 above]. **1886** *N. Amer. Rev.* July 94 The 'aqueduct job' . . . will furnish the financial sinews (or what they briefly term 'the party boodle') to make Mr. Hill the next President of the United States. **1887** *Congress. Rec.* 25 Jan. 1025/1 [In Rhode Island] the man who is bribed you could not punish, while the man who furnished the 'boodle' was liable to indictment. **1894** *Ib.* 10 Jan. 667/2 Republican conventions have always 'pointed with pride' to any channel that floated boodle their way. **1904** 'O. HENRY' *Cabbages & Kings* (1916) 94 Homer P. Mellinger takes up the bundle of boodle and slams it in the governor man's face.

attrib. **1887** *Nation* 14 April 307/3 New York is better known all over the . . . world for boodle Aldermen and municipal rings than for anything else. **1895** *Denver Times* 5 March 5/3 The Ogden gas ordinance . . . has aroused warm opposition . . . on the ground that it is a 'boodle' measure. **1904** STEFFENS in *McClure's Mag.* April 591/1 'Driftwood' was boodle bills for business men, and some of it was blackmail, but it was all irregular.

b. The use of 'boodle'; bribery.

Also in recent use (1904–) as verb: to bribe, to use bribery.

1904 W. H. SMITH *Promoters* iii. 72 The game of boodle isn't near as easy to play as it used to be. **1904** STEFFENS in *McClure's Mag.* April 587/1 No wonder Minneapolis, having cleaned out its police ring of vice grafters, now discovers boodle in the council!

+**Boodleism.** [f. prec. 4.] The practice of political bribery and corruption. — **1894** *Congress. Rec.* App. 13 Aug. 1229/1 What we call the Government of the people . . . has become a government . . . for the benefit of boodleism. **1898** ALTGELD *Live Questions* (1899) 824 Boodleism is a crime. *Ib.*, He helped to break up boodleism in Illinois. **1904** *Minneapolis Times* 6 July 6 He has been making war on boodleism for political effect.

+**Boodleistic,** *a.* [f. BOODLE 4.] Characterized by boodleism. — **1898** *Congress. Rec.* 28 April 4385/1 The barking of this mangy Wall street boodleistic cur . . . reminds me of a lonely coyote baying the moon.

+**Boodleize,** *v.* [f. BOODLE 4.] *tr.* To corrupt, bribe, or influence illegally or improperly. — **1886** *Congress. Rec.* 21 July 7730/1 [The *Cincinnati Commercial* says in effect that] we seven men have been boodleized, and there are no seven men in the State of Ohio, unless they were boodleized, who would agree to any such proposition. **1895** A. O. MYERS *Bosses & Boodle* 290 Mr. Brice took Mr. Payne's thoroughly boodleized seat in 1891.

+**Boodler.** *slang.* [f. BOODLE 3, 4.]

1. One who tries to obtain money by improper means.

1888 J. J. WEBB *Adv.* 230 We were fortunate enough not to be drawn into any compromise . . . and left the next morning in high spirits, and the boodlers mortified.

2. One who practices political bribery and corruption.

1887 *Courier-Journal* (Louisville) 6 May 4/8 Chicago Boodler Trials. **1887** *Nation* 17 Nov. 386/3 It is suspected that 'boodlers' are at work undermining the enterprise so far as public officials control it. **1888** *Omaha World* (F.), We have elections and campaigns, and political parties, and bosses, and ringsters, and boodlers. **1896** G. ADE *Artie* xii. 108 He turned out to be a boodler, eh? **1898** ALTGELD *Live Questions* (1899) 824 Governor, you would better not say so much against these boodlers. **1904** STEFFENS in *McClure's Mag.* April 588/2 If he had confined his chase to that unprotected bird, the petty boodler, all might have been well.

+**Boodlerism, Boodlery.** [f. prec.] The practice of bribery and corruption in politics. — **1887** *Advance* (Chicago) 30 June 408 'Boodlerism' in the management of our city and county and State affairs. *Ib.*, Let her not plead great conscience . . . but grant open licence to boodlery.

+**Boodling.** *slang.* [f. BOODLE 4.] The use of fraud and corruption in politics. — **1890** *School Board* Feb., Something akin to 'boodling' has been unearthed in the public educational system of New York city. **1903** *N.Y. Ev. Post* 31 Aug., We fancy that the people of Missouri will conclude to diminish boodling rather by taking from than adding to the powers of the dominant machine.

+**Booger, -ar.** *dial.* [Cf. Eng. dial. *buggard, -art.*] A bogy, bogle. — **1866** C. H. SMITH *Bill Arp* 78 Imagining that . . . their bones are . . . to rot in some thicket, far, far away, where ghosts and boogers go dodging around. **1891** *Harper's Mag.* Oct. 825/1 The *boogah* hole, . . . the hiding place of cats and of children fleeing from justice, and of 'boogars' or 'boogahs,' whatever these mysterious beings may have been. **1904** T. E. WATSON *Bethany* 15 Old Isom himself had . . . to make certain that no 'boogers' darted in and caught me.

***Book.**

1. The book used in claiming 'benefit of clergy.' *Obs.* {1601–1710}

1639 *Md. Archives* 35 Then was read the Bill . . . for allowing Book to certain Felonies. **1703** *N.C. Col. Rec.* I. 595 Thomas Dewham haveing yesterday been convicted of Manslaughter, & sav'd by his Book, and Sentens suspended.

***2.** An account book as a record of money owing.

1655 *Suffolk Deeds* II. 172, I . . . acquit Michall Rayner . . . of all debts dues and demands what so euer due . . . vpon booke, bond or bill. **1748** *N.H. Probate Rec.* III. 557, I also give to my said wife all money due to me by Book, Bonds, or other ways due to me. **1762** in H. M. Brooks *Gleanings* 36 Persons who have far exceeded their Contracts either on Book or Notes of Hand.

3. *Like a book.* **a.** Elegantly.

1829 *Mass. Spy* 28 Jan. (Th.), You talk like a book, Mr. Bond. **1833** NEAL *Down-Easters* 26 An educated and travelled Yankee . . . talking like a book, even to his washerwoman. **1841** *S. Lit. Messenger* VII. 768/2 You dance like a book. **1847** *Knickerb.* XXX. 279 Small novelists . . . who not only 'talk like a book,' but what is a good deal more to be dreaded, like one of their own books.

b. Thoroughly, perfectly.

1839 BRIGGS *H. Franco* I. 73 Know him like a book, replied Mr. Lummucks. **1857** *Knickerb.* XLIX. 42 Why, I know her and her husband like a book. *a*1859 *Spirit of Times* (B.), He knew the woods like a book.

+**4.** A pack of folded hides.

1840 DANA *Two Years* xxix. 329 A large 'book' was made of from twenty-five to fifty hides, doubled at the backs, and put into one another, like the leaves of a book.

+**5.** A pack of cards.

1853 SIMMS *Sword & Distaff* 241 'Hev' you any *books?*' Books meant cards in the vernacular of the forest.

+**6.** *ellipt.* Book muslin.

1875 *Chicago Tribune* 26 July 1/1 We are offering splendid Bargains in . . Lawns, Swisses, Books, Nainsooks, [etc.].

Book account, †accompt. [BOOK *n.* 2.] A statement of accounts recorded in a book.

1672 *Mass. Col. Laws* (1887) 39 On complaint . . . of sundry Inconveniences . . . through want of seasonable examination and balancing of Book accompts. **1741** *N.H. Probate Rec.* III. 86, I order my book accompt standing against James Ried of this town to be paid to the Rev[eren]d Mr. David Magregor. **1819** *Missouri Intell.* 24 Sept. 3/4 All persons indebted to us by note or book account will please call and settle the same immediately. Those who may not have it in their power to discharge their book accounts at this time, will call & give their notes. **1883** C. F. WILDER *Sister Ridnour* 232 The treasurer . . . keeps a correct book-account of all moneys taken and expended.

+**Book agent.** A person who sells books, usually by going from house to house.

a. 1848 *Phila. Almanac* Advt. 2 Book canvassers and agents wanted. **1880** *Harper's Mag.* Dec. 159/2 The visits of itinerant pedlar and book-agents . . . were to her welcome incidents in the daily monotony. **1882** PECK *Sunshine* 46 We shall . . . throw the first book agent down stairs head first that tries to shove off on us one of these new-fangled, go as you please Bibles. **1887** M. ROBERTS *Western Avernus* 302, I went to a great bookseller's in town and undertook the work of a 'book agent.' I had to wander round the city with a large sample atlas under my arm. **1892** S. HALE *Letters* 272 'No, she is not,' said a young person, . . . treating me exactly as if I were a book agent. **1910** MULFORD *Hopalong Cassidy* vii. 50 Was you ever an auctioneer . . . or a book agent?

b. 1856 P. CARTWRIGHT *Autobiog.* 460 He received the appointment of book agent in Cincinnati. **1876** WHITMAN *Prose Wks.* (1882) 316 All through this illness, my book-agents for three years in New York successively, badly cheated me.

Book auction. A sale of books by auction. {1809–} Also attrib. — **1790** *Penna. Packet* 31 Dec. 3/4 N.B. Book-auction will continue during the season. The stated evenings for sale will be Tuesday and Friday evenings. *a*1841 [W. HAWES] *Sporting Scenes* II. 44 Dictionaries are so common that boys buy them at book-auctions, and study the definitions as they carry home your marketing. **1889** *Boston Journal* 29 Oct. 2/3 Happening into a book auction sale in Boston.

Book auctioneer. One who sells books by auction. {1880–} — **1781** *Salem Gazette* 19 June, The Book-Auctionier intends also to exhibit a Collection of Books by Auction. **1840** *Knickerb.* XVI. 228 But with the theory, the similarity between the sentiments of the Ancient and Modern Book-Auctioneer vanishes.

***Bookbinder.** One who binds books.

1637 *Boston Rec.* 19 Leave is granted to Richard Fairbank to sell his shopp to — Saunders, a booke-bynder. **1671** *Ib.* 64 Wm. Nowell & Thomas Rand, Booke binders, are to be returned as above. **1685** *Ib.* 78 George Pordage, merchant, became surety . . . for Bartholomew Sprint, a Booke Binder. **1720** *Weekly Mercury* 21 April 2/2 The first is a Bookbinder, the other a Printer by Trade and were late Servants to Mr. Bradford of Philadelphia. **1750** FRANKLIN *Writings* II. 440 We . . . fix'd them tight in a bookbinder's small press. **1798** WEEMS *Letters* II. 100, I am in arrears to Mr. Conrad the book binder. **1812** *Niles' Reg.* I. 390/1 The public are respectfully informed, that the subscriber has . . . for sale, plane irons, . . . also book-binder's knives. **1849** CHAMBERLAIN *Indiana Gazetteer* 401 There are in [Tippecanoe County] . . . 13 printers and book binders. **1889** BRAYLEY *Boston Fire Dept.* 285 The building at 3 Cornhill, occupied by Rand & Avery, printers and book-binders.

+**Bookbindery.** [Cf. Dutch *boek-binderij* and BINDERY.] A place where books are bound.

1815 *Niles' Reg.* VIII. 141/2 There are [in Pittsburg] . . . 5 printing offices; 4 book binderies. **1817** S. BROWN *Western Gaz.* 311 Zanesville . . . has a . . . post-office, book-bindery, [and] two printing-offices. **1845** [see BOOKBINDING]. **1846** LYELL *Second Visit* (1849) II. 250 [Harpers] manufacture their own types and paper, and have a 'bookbindery' under the same roof. **1865** *Atlantic Mo.* XV. 616 The book-binderies reckon three thousand in their various establishments, who fold and sew the sheets. **1885** *Harper's Mag.* Feb. 370/1 Flavilla . . . served an apprenticeship at the book-bindery.

||**b.** The binding of books; the product of the bookbinder's art.

1887 *Courier-Journal* 2 May 5/2 It is a sad thing that some of the most beautiful book-bindery and some of the finest rhetoric have been brought to make sin attractive.

Bookbinding. The process of binding books. {1787–}

1771 FRANKLIN *Autobiog.* 290 Meredith was to work at press, Potts at book-binding. **1808** *Ann. 10th Congress* 2 Sess. 90 Works in pelts and skins, such as leather, . . . and book-binding, are carried on to wide extent. **1845** J. W. NORRIS *Chicago Directory* 93 Chicago Book Bindery . . . is now prepared to execute Book Binding, in all its varieties, in the best manner. **1880** *Harper's Mag.* June 32/1 The second class [of industries] may be said to include such trades as . . . book-binding, printing, dress-making.

Book business. The buying and selling of books; the book-trade. — **1865** Kellogg *Rebel Prisons* 399 We have lost $6,000 in the book business the past four or five years. **1866** [A. M. KEILEY] *In Vinculis* (ed. 2) 136 Lieutenant Haverty . . . [was] a whole-souled Fenian, formerly in the book-business in New York.

Book club. A club formed for the purpose of facilitating the reading or discussion of books by its members. {1792–} — **1817** E. P. FORDHAM *Narr.* 129 In the state of Indiana, in which there is but one town that is of six years standing, there are several Book-clubs. **1835** P. HONE *Diary* I. 134, I went to the Book Club . . . at nine o'clock. This is a club which meets every other Thursday evening at Washington Hotel, where they sup, drink champagne and whiskey punch, [and] talk as well as they know how. **1883** *Century Mag.* May 156/1 Two book clubs, and several musical associations and reading societies, keep . . . this one village from . . . intellectual stagnation.

+**Book concern.** An establishment engaged in publishing or selling books.

1844 Rupp *Relig. Denominations* 449 The General Conference . . . shall not appropriate the produce of the Book Concern . . . to any purpose other than for the benefit of the travelling supernumerary. **1851** *Congress. Globe* 4 Jan. 170 This House has become the greatest 'book concern' in the Union. **1852** *Harper's Mag.* V. 835/1 A decision was obtained . . . , establishing the right of the Methodist Episcopal Church South to an equitable portion of the Book Concern. **1872** *Congress. Rec.* 27 May 3909/3 Every book published by the Methodist Book Concern . . . is published on sized paper. **1900** *Ib.* 20 March 3096/2 The little fellow who is attempting to establish a book concern at another place might be crushed.

+**Book factor.** =BOOK AGENT (a). — **1797** WEEMS *Letters* II. 86, I . . . think you have borne much harder upon me than upon the rest of your Book Factors.

+**Book farmer.** A farmer who studies agriculture from books and farms in accordance with what he learns from these.

1849 *Rep. Comm. Patents: Agric.* (1850) 17 Washington was eminently a 'book-farmer,' and was anxious to gain knowledge from the educated agriculturists of Europe. **1856** *Mich. Agric. Soc. Trans.* VII. 806 A notorious book farmer succeeded in making one of the best farms in the State of New York. **1865** 'GAIL HAMILTON' *Skirmishes* ix. 133 We want them to be practical farmers, book-farmers and gentlemen-farmers in one.

+**Book farming.** Farming in accordance with information obtained from books.

1854 *Penna. Agric. Rep.* 113 Such men are the most given to sneer at what they call, in derision, 'Book-farming.' **1859** *Mich. Agric. Soc. Trans.* X. 537 Another man . . . summarily pronounces all book farming a humbug. **1867** *Iowa Agric. Soc. Rep.* 125 The reason that so many take no particular pains to improve their stock is . . . they don't believe in book-farming.

Book-folder. One employed in folding the sheets of books for binding. — **1872** BRACE *Dangerous Classes N.Y.* 166 She went to be a book-folder downtown. **1880** *Harper's Mag.* June 28/2 Book-folders have not been able to earn more than three dollars a week.

***Bookkeeper.**

***1.** A person who keeps the accounts of a business, firm, or other establishment.

1666 *Md. Archives* II. 50 His bookes being avouched by his booke Keepers oath. **1697** *N.C. Col. Rec.* I. 486 Ordered that James Fuget bookkeper give credit for the said sum. **1728** *New-Eng. Courant* 10–17 May 2/2 A young Man, . . . employ'd as a Bookkeeper to a Merchant in this Place, hang'd himself. **1773** J. ROWE *Diary* 243 My old Bookeeper, James Perkins, was buried this afternoon. **1870** 'F. FERN' *Ginger-Snaps* 147 If she has no money, . . . she is a book-keeper, or she sets types. **1884** CABLE *Dr. Sevier* xxxii. (1885) 251 'Book-keeper to a baker.' . . . It somehow vexed him to see Richling so happy in so low a station. **1900** STOCKTON *Afield & Afloat* 343 One morning I was sitting in my countinghouse alone, for my bookkeeper had a holiday. **1916** W. A. DUPUY *Uncle Sam* 217 The disappearance of the bookkeeper . . . fixed attention on him.

+**2.** At Harvard College, a student appointed to record the names of those students who did not return to their rooms by a specified hour in the evening. *Obs.*

1830 *Collegian* 225, I strode over the bridge, with a rapidity which grew with . . . my anxiety to reach my goal ere . . . the book-keeper's light should disappear from his window.

Book-kenting. *Obs.* A fine linen cloth, folded like book-muslin. — **1746** *Md. Hist. Mag.* XXI. 379 Invoice of goods: . . . 2 p[iece]s book Kenting; 1 p[iece] Cambrick.

Book muslin. A kind of fine muslin, so called from the booklike manner in which it is folded. {1836–} Also attrib.

1759 *Newport Mercury* 10 April 4/2 To be sold by Simon Pease, jun., . . . Book Muslin, Cambricks, Silk Ferrets. **1790** *Phila. Packet* 2 Jan. 4/4 Just imported . . . olive coloured and black velverets, Book muslin. **1842** *Knickerb.* XX. 119, I do hate of all things a washed book-muslin. **1852** BRISTED *Upper Ten Th.* iv. 87 Though new to society, she had none of the book-muslin timidity about her. **1864** B. TAYLOR *H. Thurston* iv. 56 The spotless book-muslin handkerchief, many-folded, covered her neck and breast. **1871** *Harper's Mag.* Dec. 116/1 White book-muslin curtains tied up with blue ribbons.

+**Book peddler, pedlar.** One who travels about selling books. — **1844** *Lowell Offering* IV. 146 Some book-pedlers, shoe-pedlers, essence-pedlers, and candy boys came in. **1845** *Knickerb.* XXV. 198 There was the travelling book pedlar, better acquainted with the world. **1889** *Century Mag.* April 847/1 First seen in the neighborhood of Alexandria [Va.] as a book-peddler for a Philadelphia firm.

+**Bookrack.** A device for holding books. — **1880** TOURGEE *Bricks* 233 That lamp-stand and little book-rack . . . were Hesden's notions. **1885** *Harper's Mag.* March 543/1, I had made up my mind to nothing but a book-rack, or a paltry little toilet set. **1904** M. E. WALLER *Wood-carver* 149 Do you think you could find time for the carving of . . . book-racks, magazine-cutters, or photograph frames?

***Bookseller.** One who sells books.

1685 *Boston Rec.* 79 Francis Burrowes . . . became surety . . . for John Dunton, Booke seller. **1705** SEWALL *Letter-book* I. 322, I have now reprinted the Sentiments of the Athenian Society, which I had not seen nor heard of, till I saw it in a Book-Sellers Shop last Fall. **1728** *Boston Selectmen* 179 The Brick Shop or Tenement . . . now in the Possession of Benja[min] Gray Book seller. **1814** *Harvard Laws* App. 9 The university bookseller furnishes one copy of the books used in the several classes to those students, who apply. **1834** H. J. NOTT *Novellettes* I. 174, I made an arrangement with a New-York bookseller. **1877** *Harper's Mag.* April 722/2 In 1652 Hezekiah Usher, the first book-seller, began his business in Boston. **1907** C. C. ANDREWS *Recoll.* 172 The bookseller in a courteous manner gave me the freedom of his store.

Bookstall. A stall on which books are displayed for sale. {1800–} — **1843** *Knickerb.* XXII. 81 A dilapidated book-stall volume before us, . . . thus illustrates the position of our valued correspondent. **1850** JUDD *R. Edney* xxxv. 369 In a book-stall . . . he took up a volume entitled 'Poems.' **1891** CHASE & CLOW *Industry* II. 176 Railway stations, at home and abroad, are furnished with book-stalls.

+**Bookstore.** A store or shop where books are sold; a bookshop.

1763 *Boston Ev. Post* 3/3. **1765** in A. Ellicott *Life & Lett.* (1908) 51 Examined several Book stores. **1793** T. COXE *View U.S.* 160 The advertisement of a single book-store in Philadelphia . . . contains seventy editions of different books printed in the United States. **1818** W. DARBY *Tour to Detroit* (1819) 22 Bookstores afford . . . the best data, from which can be calculated the state of public literary improvement. **1847** L. COLLINS *Kentucky* 449 Harrodsburg . . . contains . . . two book and drug stores, one printing office. **1871** [L. H. BAGG] *Four Years at Yale* 210 An enclosure for the College Bookstore was built in the middle. **1907** C. C. ANDREWS *Recoll.* 165 The very first day I was in prison, I obtained permission to send to the village bookstore for a copy of Shakespeare.

attrib. **1895** WILLIAMS *Princeton Stories* 149 They were all nice new copies, with the book-store smell about them.

+**Booky,** *a.* Fond of books; bookish; derived from books. — **1832** PAULDING *Westward Ho* I. 194 You're one of the booky fellers that think of one thing while they are talking about another. **1898** ATHERTON *Californians* 28 It became known that she was 'booky,'—a social crime in San Francisco.

Boom, *n.*[1] {c1645–}

+**1.** A barrier formed by connected logs placed across a stream or round an area of water to retain floating logs.

1676 SEWALL *Diary* I. 23 Squaw and Sonne taken at Salmon Falls Mill, being seen as they went over the Boom. **1702** C. Mather *Magnalia* VII. App. (1852) II. 592 She stole along by the river side, until she came to a boom, where she passed over. **1765** R. ROGERS *Journals* (1883) 138, I . . . intended to . . . saw off their boom, for which end I had taken saws with me, the boom being made with logs of timber. **1789** *Mass. Acts* (1894) V. 94 The laying a boom across the River Androscoggin . . . for the purpose of stopping and securing logs and other lumber. **1832** WILLIAMSON *Maine* I. 46 To secure floating logs, and stop flood-wood, piers are sunk . . . , and large timbers in joints so fastened to them with irons as to form an impassable boom. **1851** SPRINGER *Forest Life* 159 When hauled on to the lakes, they [logs] are laid together as compactly as possible, and inclosed in a 'boom.' **1869** W. MURRAY *Adventures* 16 The rivers are blockaded with 'booms' and lodged timber, stamped all over the ends with the owner's 'mark.' **1889** *Wis. Annot. Statutes* I. 966/2 In no case can a riparian proprietor . . . extend booms completely across a navigable stream. **1903** WHITE *Riverman* vi. 54 The drive of which Orde had charge was to be delivered at the booms of Morrison and Daly.

2. A barrier placed in a river, or at the entrance to a harbor, to obstruct the passage of boats or ships in time of war. {*c*1645–}

1775 *N.H. Comm. Safety Rec.* 19 It is tho't expedient to lay a Boom across the River from Peirce's to Seevey's Island, strong enough to hinder the passage of Vessels. **1775** *Journals Cont. Congress* III. 486 Deane doubts the practicability of obstructing it [=Hudson R.] with booms. **1823** THACHER *Military Jrnl.* 96 A boom composed of large pieces of Timber well secured together by riveted bolts, is placed on the north side of the bridge [at Mt. Independence in June, 1777].

+**Boom,** *n.*[2] [BOOM *v.*[2] 2.]

1. In gold mining, a rush of water collected in a reservoir. (Cf. BOOMING *vbl. n.*[2] 1.) Also attrib. with *flume.*

1874 RAYMOND *6th Rep. Mines* 302 The use of a boom permits the working of ground that could by no other means be made to pay. **1876** — *8th Rep. Mines* 318 A force of thirty-five men was set at work . . . building boom-flumes and reservoirs.

2. A sudden increase in business activity; a rapid rise in prices; a sudden, and occas. artificial, inflation of real-estate values.

1879 *Lumberman's Gaz.* 19 Dec., There has not been the 'boom' upon lumber experienced in many other articles of merchandise. **1881** *Harper's Mag.* April 756/2 During war times and in the after 'boom,' there were many abortive attempts on the part of adventurers to embark in this [=life-insurance] business. **1883** 'MARK TWAIN' *Life on Miss.* xli. 298 The 'boom' was something wonderful. Everybody bought, everybody sold. **1886** *Kansas H. S. Trans.* III. 398 When we wish to express in a superlative degree, any great movement in trade, in manufacture, in real estate, in the rapid growth of cities, or what not, we call it a 'boom.' **1887** *Courier-Jrnl.* 5 Jan. 4 A speculator finds a 'site' for a 'boom.' **1894** ROBLEY *Bourbon Co., Kansas* 9 Rogers thought he was in the midst of a 'boom,' and he asked them $1,000 an acre. **1901** DUNCAN & SCOTT *Allen & Woodson Co., Kansas* 15 As a result of this large immigration Allen county during this summer [1857] experienced its first 'boom.' Times were flush. Money was abundant.

b. Attrib. and comb. with *city, magic, maker, time.* Also BOOM TOWN.

1886 *Leslie's Mo.* March 306/1 Cities . . . whose inhabitants had yet to be gathered in from the four corners of the earth by boom magic. **1891** *Anthony's Photogr. Ann.* IV. 23 The old town of San Juan Capistrano I found had been divided in the 'boom' times. **1895** *Century Mag.* Aug. 638/2 The troop of boom makers has actively given its perennial leisure to extravagant schemes of town-platting. **1896** *N. Amer. Rev.* CLXIII. 711 The West is harvesting the fruitage of the seed sown in the boom time of seven . . . years ago. **1904** *Public Ledger* (Phila.) 14 June 8 No 'boom city' of the West can boast such a record of amazing and substantial growth.

3. A rush by claim seekers to occupy unsettled lands in Oklahoma. Cf. BOOMER[1] 2. *Obs.* exc. hist.

1885 *Century Mag.* Aug. 603/2 An organized movement, known as 'the Oklahoma boom,' has been made to seize and colonize a large body of the territorial lands.

4. Enthusiastic support of, or admiration for, a particular person; esp. great or rapidly increasing sentiment in favor of a political candidate.

1879 *Daily Telegraph* (Lond.) 26 Dec., The Grant 'Boom' may be succeeded by the Sherman 'Boom.' **1884** *Reading* (Penna.) *Herald* 15 April, Blaine's book was issued yesterday, just at the critical moment in his boom for the Presidency. **1888** *Battle Creek Journal* 7 March, Working Up a Little Boom for Cullom. . . . It is said that a decided Cullom boom was developed at the recent caucus of the Republican members of congress. **1901** W. A. WHITE in *McClure's Mag.* Dec. 147 The two herders picketed their legislators to a temporary boom for Platt for senator.

attrib. **1880** *Nation* XXXI. 285/1 Forward the boom brigade; 'Vote for Grant,' Conkling said.

Boom, *v.*[1] [BOOM *n.*[1] 1.]

+**1.** *tr.* To impound (logs) in a boom.

1850 JUDD *R. Edney* xxviii. 312 It was arranged that the elder Edney should furnish the logs, Chuk boom them, and Richard saw them. **1858** *Mich. Gen. Statutes* (1882) I. 995 Persons whose logs, timber or lumber have been run, driven, boomed, rafted, cleared from the banks. **1865** *Ib.* 999 The business of driving, booming, rafting, and running logs, timber, lumber or other floatables.

+**2.** To equip (a river, lake, etc.) with a boom for stopping floating timber.

1879 *Lumberman's Gaz.* 1 Oct., Numerous lakes communicating with the main Slough have been boomed.

***Boom,** *v.*[2]

1. *intr.* To go under full sail or at full speed. {1617–1706}

1823 COOPER *Pilot* II. iii. 44, I'll make him . . . open both [eyes] wider than if . . . the Flying Dutchman was booming down on him. **1838** POE *Narr. A. G. Pym* 13 Under the jib only, I now boomed along before the wind. **1875** 'MARK TWAIN' *Old Times Miss.* ii. 36 We went booming along, taking a good many chances, for we were anxious to 'get out of the river.' **1884** — *H. Finn* xiii, We boomed along down the river, watching for lights and watching for our raft.

+**b.** Of a river: To rush strongly. Also of logs carried down by a river. (Cf. BOOMING *ppl. a.* 1.)

1852 *Knickerb.* XL. 154 The Licking added her tribute very modestly to the total, which, not now estopped . . . by the 'gorge' on the bar, went booming by. **1879** *Lumberman's Gaz.* 19 Dec., The three drives . . . are all this side of Big Rapids, and with plenty of water come booming along at a most lively rate. **1884** SWEET & KNOX *Through Texas* xl. 562 The Rio Grande is booming, sixty feet deep, and five miles wide. **1902** WHITE *Blazed Trail* liii. 371 Just as soon as they find out thát the river is booming, . . . they'll let loose those twelve million on us.

+**c.** To move with speed or vigor. Also fig.

1873 'MARK TWAIN' & WARNER *Gilded Age* xvii. 60 Mr. Jeff Thompson was the most popular engineer who could be found for his work. . . . In his own language he 'just went booming.' **1904** W. H. SMITH *Promoters* xi. 175 His spirits boomed to the top notch.

+**2.** To display sudden activity or briskness; to rise rapidly into notice or prosperity.

1873 'MARK TWAIN' & WARNER *Gilded Age* xxvii. 244 There's $200,000 coming, and that will set things booming again. **1875** *Scribner's Mo.* X. 277 When stocks are active, they are said to be 'booming.' **1878** J. B. McCULLAGH in *St. Louis Globe Democrat* 18 July (*Cent.*), The Republicans of every other State are of the same way of thinking. The fact is, the Grant movement [for a third term of the presidency] is booming. **1879** *Lumberman's Gaz.* 12 Nov., New life and energy has been infused into all channels of business—things are booming. **1880** G. INGHAM *Digging Gold* xi. 276 The town gradually increased in size, and about the middle of October, 1878, began to 'boom.' **1885** BRET HARTE *Maruja* 154 He'd got things boomin' with that railroad and his manufactory company. **1891** EGGLESTON *Faith Dr.* v, Hilbrough's face was of that . . . sort which always seems to indicate that things are booming, to borrow a phrase from our modern argot. **1911** H. S. HARRISON *Queed* 215 The boarding-house business is booming these days.

+**3.** To show enthusiasm *for* a candidate, etc.

1879 *Indianapolis Journal* 23 April, The rest [of the stalwarts] are in varying degrees positive, if not all 'booming' for U. S. Grant. **1889** FARMER 78/1 The whole State is booming for Smith. *Ib.*, The boys have whooped up the State to boom for Smith.

+**4.** *tr.* To bring prominently into public notice; to support or promote in this way; to cause a 'boom' in.

1882 E. V. SMALLEY in *Century Mag.* Aug. 506/1 To 'boom' a town in Dakota is an art requiring a little money, a good deal of printer's ink, and no end of push and cheek. *Ib.*, Fargo is said to be the best-boomed town in Dakota. **1884** *Boston Journal* 22 Nov. 2/4 The World is booming Mr. Conkling for United States Senator. **1886** *Kansas H. S. Trans.* III. 405 So much modesty and so much progress never met before to boom a State. **1887** *Courier-Journal* 12 Jan. 5/3 The *World's* effort to boom 'Lord' Roscoe for the United States Senate [etc.]. **1893** HOWELLS *Coast of Bohemia* 146 What an imprudence, . . . when I'd just been booming you! **1906** *N.Y. Ev. Post* 9 Jan. 2 Spencer Eddy . . . is being boomed to succeed John A. G. Leishmann as minister to Turkey. **1909** H. N. CASSON *Life McCormick* 190 Then the sudden scarcity of laborers created a panic among the farmers, and boomed the sale of all manner of farm machinery.

+**Boomage.** [BOOM *n.*[1] 1.] Toll for the use of a boom in which logs are stored. — **1818** *Mass. Laws* (1822) VIII. 51 A toll or boomage . . . is hereby granted . . . for the benefit of the said proprietors . . . according to the rates following. **1862** *Penna. Statutes* 396 To prevent collecting boomage upon non-marked lumber. **1864** C. L. FLINT *Eighty Years* 74 The boom is owned by an individual, who derives a large profit from the boomage, which is 35 cents per thousand on all logs coming into it.

+**Boomer**[1]**.** [BOOM *v.*[2] 4.]

1. One who 'booms' a town, enterprise, cause, individual, etc.; an enthusiastic supporter or advocate.

1882 *Century Mag.* Aug. 508 Bismarck [N.D.] has a 'boomer.' He is hired . . . to ride upon the trains east of Fargo and talk to emigrants about the advantages of settling near the Banner City. **1889** *Anthony's Photogr. Bull.* 191 The secretary should be an enthusiast, a 'boomer.' **1893** *Harper's Mag.* April 712/3 Professional 'boomers' . . . invaded the State [=Kansas], bought and platted additions, which they sold at exorbitant prices. **1903** *N.Y. Tribune* 6 Sept., The boomers of W. R. Hearst for President did not inject the Presidential proposition into the proceedings. **1917** WILKINS & KINGSLEY *Alabaster Box* v. 56 Guess we'll have to set the Deacon down for a right smart real-estate boomer.

2. A claim seeker participating in a rush for unsettled lands in Oklahoma. (Cf. BOOM *n.*[2] 3.) *Obs.* exc. hist.

1885 *Century Mag.* Aug. 604/2 The Oklahoma 'boomers,' on their way to the Kansas border, passed over desirable thousands of acres. **1885** *Boston Journal* 19 Aug. 2/4 The intention of the Oklahoma boomers to abandon attempts to invade Oklahoma or violate the President's proclamation. **1890** J. K. BANGS in *Harper's Mag.* Dec. 160/1 Donkey parties in the temporary canvas residences of the fashionable boomers had been held. **1891** *Scribner's Mag.* Sept. 313/1 Seeking . . . their lawful heritage under the home-stead laws of Oklahoma, boomers faced the heat of the August sun. **1892** *San Francisco Chron.* 18 April, Thousands of Boomers on the Border [of Okla.]. Not enough Claims to go around.

3. An unusual or phenomenal success.

1887 *Courier-Journal* 30 Jan. 8/4 This sale will be a boomer for the very finest soft or stiff hat goes for $1.98.

Boomer[2]**.** Also **booma.**

+1. *S.E.* The red squirrel or chickaree, *Sciurus hudsonius.*

1858 D. K. Bennett *Chronology N.C.* 94 The only inhabitants we saw on these high points were pheasants, cross bills, . . . and mountain boomers, a sort of squirrel. **1878** C. Coale in *Ann. S.W. Va.* (1929) 1544 The formidable animal proved to be a boomer, a species of mountain squirrel. **1883** Zeigler & Grosscup *Alleghanies* 64 The most curious noise of these forests is that of the boomer, . . . native to the Alleghanies. **1889** Farmer 78 *Booma* . . . is a North Carolina term for the little red squirrel. . . . *Booma* is the Indian name.

+2. The Rocky Mountain beaver or sewellel.

1889 *Cent.* 626/3 *Boomer,* . . . a name of the showt'l or mountain beaver, *Haplodon rufus* or *Aplodontia leporina.*

+Boom-gatherer. [Boom *n.*[1] 1.] One who assembles logs in booms. — **1850** Judd *R. Edney* xviii. 220 This flood was both spring-time and harvest for log-drivers, boom-gatherers, and lumber-men generally.

Boom-head. +(See quotation.) — **1848** Thoreau *Maine Woods* 42 The logs . . . are thus towed altogether . . . across the lake . . . by a windlass or boom-head such as we sometimes saw standing on an island or head-land.

+Boom-house. [Boom *n.*[1] 1.] The abode of those engaged in work upon a boom. — **1897** E. W. Brodhead *Bound in Shallows* 118 The man who had succeeded Bohun in the management of the boom-house paddled by in a dugout.

Booming, *vbl. n.*[1] [Boom *n.*[1] 1.]

1. The formation of a boom, or the material used for one.

1798 *Boston Rec.* 45 That . . . the said Corporation be allowed the Privilege of securing by booming their logs on such parts of the beach at the foot of the Common . . . as the Selectmen . . . may appoint.

+2. The impounding of logs in a boom. Also attrib.

1850 Judd *R. Edney* xxviii. 312 Bill Stonners' Point was the best booming privilege on the River. **1864** *Mich. Gen. Statutes* (1882) I. 1000 The amount of such charges . . . for driving, booming, rafting and running of said logs, timber or lumber. **1879** *Ib.* 550 Each log running or booming company doing business on any waters on which the logs or timber are floated or run.

+Booming, *vbl. n.*[2] [Boom *v.*[2]]

1. A method of using impounded water in placer mining. (See first quotation.)

1874 Raymond *6th Rep. Mines* 299 The practice of booming has permitted the successful working of poorer ground than has been before worked in the county. [*Note,*] A rude form of hydraulic mining, in which a torrent of water, obtained by the accumulation of smaller supplies, is suffered to escape from the reservoir at intervals. *Ib.* 302 Booming may be considered as the best labor-saving invention introduced into the country of late years.

2. The fact of flourishing by a boom; the creation of a boom or the attempt to make one. Also attrib.

1873 *Newton Kansan* 3 July 1/6 'Booming' is the name of an operation with which probably our readers are not generally familiar. **1880** *Harper's Mag.* Feb. 383 This little town [Rosita, Colo.] was founded in 1872, and led a quiet existence, with occasional episodes of what is here called 'booming.' **1881** *Chicago Times* 1 June, The Texas market is also advised as active, and in some cases excited, but most of the trade here seem to think this 'booming' tendency is at least a little premature. **1888** *St. Paul Globe* 22 Jan., If every man in St. Paul would only do a little booming for the coming ice palace the amount of good it would do is almost incalculable. **1888** *Chicago Herald* (F.), Ben Butterworth, of Ohio, one of the mainstays of John Sherman's booming squad.

Booming, *ppl. a.* [Boom *v.*[2]]

+1. Of a river: Rushing strongly.

1831 Audubon *Ornith. Biog.* I. 155 To give you some idea of a *Booming Flood* of these gigantic streams, it is necessary to state the causes which give rise to it. **1850** *Congress. Globe* App. 4 April 531 Shall the army which finds itself on the wrong side of a booming river, rush headlong in? **1868** *Putnam's Mag.* I. 596/1 The chutes, the landslides, the booming torrents [of the Miss. R.] . . . —all these supply . . . themes of conversation.

+2. Splendid, grand. Also as intensive *adv.*

1884 'Mark Twain' *H. Finn* xvii. 151 We can just have booming times —they don't have no school now. *Ib.* xxiv. 242 They was booming mad, and gave us a cussing.

+3. Flourishing by a boom.

1891 *Harper's Mag.* Aug. 485/2 The office of the Spread Eagle Hotel in the booming border town of Centropolis.

+Boomlet. [Boom *n.*[2] 2, 4.] An attempted 'boom'; one that does not attain the proportions expected. — **1887** *Saginaw Ev. Jrnl.* 7 Dec., The boomlet of W. R. Burt for governor grows about an inch a day. **1904** *Brooklyn Eagle* 9 June 4 A brief survey of the New York situation did for the McClellan boomlet. **1907** *Collier's Weekly* IX. 28 He [Gov. Hughes] was introduced by Chanler who has a Presidential boomlet of his own, and was hailed as our next President.

+Boom-master. [Boom *n.*[1] 1.] The man in charge of collecting logs in a boom. — **1851** Springer *Forest Life* 175 It is the duty of the boom-master . . . to raft the logs of each individual in parcels by themselves.

‖**Boomopolis.** [Boom *n.*[2] 2 b.] A boom city or boom town. — **1890** J. K. Bangs in *Harper's Mag.* Dec. 160 A Boomopolis Wedding. *Ib.*, The undisputed belle of Boomopolis . . . that Eden of sand and corner lots.

+Boomster. [Boom *n.*[2] 2.] One who works up a boom. — **1879** *Nation* 9 Oct. 236 The trickery and usurpation . . . of the leading boomster. **1880** *Ib.* 12 Feb. 105/2 Moreover, he . . . dismissed him 'when under fire'— . . . an act which every boomster must regard with loathing. **1887** *Courier-Journal* 8 Jan. 4/4 Henry Watterson goes for the Southern boom in his usual style. . . . A few of his favorite epithets . . . for the progressive men of the South are: . . . 'Boomsters,' 'Ringsters,' [etc.].

+Boomstick. [Boom *n.*[1] 1.] A piece of heavy timber used in making a boom for impounding logs. — **1850** Judd *R. Edney* xvi. 207 They found Chuk in trouble; his guys had parted, and his boom-sticks were broken. **1860** *Harper's Mag.* March 454/1 The boom . . . is so constructed—by means of long boom-sticks run from pier to pier—as to intercept all logs floating down the river. **1879** *Mich. Public Acts* 28 May 214 It shall be unlawful for any person other than the owner thereof . . . to take possession of . . . any log, spar, boomstick, etc., . . . in any . . . waters in this State. **1897** E. W. Brodhead *Bound in Shallows* 10 She could walk the boom-sticks like a cat, and ride on the log cars in a most amazing fashion.

+Boom town. *W.* [Boom *n.*[2] 2 b.] A town originating in, or flourishing as the result of, a boom in land or mining. — **1900** Smithwick *Evol. of State* 19 Colonel De Witt was as enthusiastic as the real estate dealer in a boom town nowadays. **1906** *N.Y. Ev. Post* 4 Aug. 4 Quite as melancholy as the moss-grown ruins of older civilizations are the frame-built 'boom' towns of the West.

+Boonder. ?*Obs.* [Du. *boender.*] A brush used in scrubbing. — **1791** Freneau *Poems* (1795) 423 Fate early had pronounc'd this building's doom, Ne'er to be vex'd with boonder, brush, or broom. **1859** Bartlett 43 *Boonder* or *Bounder*, a scrubbing-brush. New York. **1889** Farmer 78 *Boonder,* . . . a brush. Still commonly used in New York and New Jersey.

Boor. *Obs.* [Du. *boer.*] +A Dutch colonist of the farming class. — *a***1649** Winthrop *Hist.* II. 161 We were then informed also of a Dutch ship lately arrived at Hudson's river sent to the free boors at Fort Orange. **1701** C. Wolley *Journal N.Y.* (1902) 66, I cannot say I observed any swearing or quarrelling . . . except once betwixt two Dutch Boors.

+Boost, *n. colloq.* [f. the verb.] A push or shove that assists one to rise; assistance towards success or reputation.

1825 Neal *Bro. Jonathan* II. 101 What say you, mayor?—shall I give him a boost?—or no? **1831** S. Smith *Major Downing* 63, I got a pretty good boost in Boston, by the editors giving me recommendations. *c***1849** [Paige] *Dow's Sermons* I. 105 It is remarkable what a boost the sudden possession of a few dollars can give to a chap. **1867** Lowell *Familiar Epistle* iv, Bacchus (that now is scarce induced To give Eld's lagging blood a boost). **1884** *Boston Journal* 20 Sept., I believe that . . . Grov' Cleveland was fully justified in giving the Standard Oil Co. a boost. *c***1888** *Santa Fé Times* (undated clipping), Finally he [a bucking bronco] gave us one grand, farewell boost and we clove the firmament. **1904** *N.Y. Sun* 9 Aug. 3 To-night Mr. Woodruff's boom for the Governorship is to get a strong boost at the meeting of the county committee. **1908** 'Yeslah' *Tenderfoot S. Calif.* 134 These baskets of flowers on the street corners in the middle of winter, are the biggest boost to the Angel City it could possibly have.

b. A ride along one's way; a lift.

1891 Garland *Main-travelled Roads* (1922) 73 'Want a boost?' 'Well, yes. Are you down with a team?' 'Yep. 'Bout goin' home. Climb right in.'

+Boost, *v. colloq.* [Of obscure origin.]

1. *tr.* To raise or lift; to hoist, push, or shove *up.*

Abundant evidence for the recent currency of both noun and verb (and derivatives) is collected in *American Speech* I. 661–72.

1815 Humphreys *Yankey* 103 *Boost,* raise up, lift up, exalt. **1847** Field *Drama in Pokerville,* etc. 117 [He clambered] back into the box, . . . the sanctimonious manager assisting to 'boost him' with the most friendly solicitude. **1860** J. C. Adams *Adventures* 306 (Th.), Proceeding much the same as persons who load saw-logs, we managed to boost the cage up. **1872** 'Mark Twain' *Roughing It* vii, You ought to have seen the bull . . . tearing up the earth, and boosting up the sand like a whirlwind! **1882** *Harper's Mag.* Sept. 594/1 A hack was chartered, and we boosted him in, and I guess he is all right now. **1890** *Ib.* April 714/1, I used to bring her her doses an' drinks, an' boost up her head to take 'em. **1903** K. D. Wiggin *Rebecca* i. 8 He helped her out, 'boosted' her up to the front seat [of a stagecoach], and resumed his own place.

b. In figurative contexts.

1835 Cooper *Monikins* vi, He did not boost his philosophy on the leaping-staff of impulse. **1843** *Yale Lit. Mag.* VIII. 356 An unexpected piece of good fortune . . . has been often known to boost men of genius up the ladder of wealth and distinction. **1857** *Knickerb.* XLIX. 42 It was thus with cheerful counsel that Hiram began to boost Sam up the tree of virtue. **1868** Mrs. Whitney *P. Strong* 131, I took her deliberately away to West Street, . . . [and] 'boosted' up her conscience to buy.

2. *fig.* To raise *into* a higher position; to assist to get on or to rise in the world.

a1859 *N.Y. Herald* (B.), Lord Palmerston was boosted into power by the agricultural interest of England. **a1861** WINTHROP *J. Brent* 299 We still hold together, with a common purpose to boost civilization, so far as our shoulders will do it. **1873** W. MATHEWS *Getting on in World* 204 But do not, while thus 'boosted' into, boast of your success. **1894** P. L. FORD *P. Stirling* 258, I began by loaning the fund to people . . . who could be boosted a little by help. **1902** LORIMER *Lett. Merchant* 8 While the lack of a college education can't keep No. 1 down, having it boosts No. 2 up.

b. To praise *up;* to laud or extol. Also absol.

1887 F. FRANCIS *Saddle & Moccasin* 121 You think that I'm trying to boost the place up because it belongs to us. **1903** G. ADE *People You Know* 93 He could Knock better than he could Boost.

c. To cheer *up;* to encourage.

1887 N. PERRY *Flock of Girls* 239 She did talk about herself when she cried herself down, and we were always boosting her up to make her feel better.

d. To raise in amount.

1907 *Phila. Inquirer* 28 Nov. (Th.), Little disposition to boost the cost of this or that musty, dog-eared volume was apparent. **1910** *Springfield W. Republican* 15 Dec. 16 The proposition then was to boost the salary figures to $5,000.

3. To push or shove *along.*

1833 S. SMITH *Major Downing* 139 You . . . give me a lift into public life, and you've been a boosting me along ever since. **1856** *Knickerb.* Sept. 286 Hiram Twine, who had 'boosted' me along before him by the shoulders.

+**Booster.** [BOOST *v.*] **1.** *Electr.* (See quotation.) **2.** One who supports or promotes the interests of a person, cause, etc. — (1) **1896** S. P. THOMPSON *Dynamo-Electric Mach.* (ed. 5) 726 Motor-dynamos are employed . . . to compensate the drop in voltage on long mains by inserting into the main at a distant point a series motor. . . . American electricians term it a 'booster.' (2) **1908** 'YESLAH' *Tenderfoot S. Calif.* 147 He must have been a native—a truthful man, and likewise a 'Booster.' **1917** *Nation* 25 Jan., President Lowell of Harvard continues to be one of the best boosters of unpopular causes. **1922** S. LEWIS *Babbitt* i. 19 He stuck in his lapel the Boosters' Club button.

* **Boot**[1].

* **1.** A leather covering for the foot and lower part of the leg.

In more recent usage generally designating foot-wear which extends at least to the middle of the calf of the leg.

1640 *Conn. Public Rec.* 453, 1 paire of shues and boots. **1715** *Boston News-Letter* 17 Oct. 2/2 Samuel Stebbins has set up a Translators Shop . . . . where all Persons may have Boots, Shoes, Pattoons, or any thing belonging to that Trade mended. **1784** *Mass. Centinel* 28 Aug. 3/3 Will be sold at the American Coffee-House . . . this Day . . . 1 pair silver buckles for boots. **1853** 'P. PAXTON' *Yankee in Texas* 25 He had, for the occasion, divested his feet of a heavy pair of 'pot metal' boots. **1881** *Harper's Mag.* Jan. 192/1 Putting liquor in one's boots turns out to be an old recipe for keeping the feet from freezing. **1892** J. E. COOKE *B. Hallam* 231 He seldom wore boots, then rapidly becoming the fashion among all classes.

b. *colloq.* In various figurative phrases.

To get the boot on the wrong leg, to make a mistake in attribution. *The boot is on the other foot,* the situation is reversed. *To move* or *start one's boots,* to set off; to depart. *To go it boots,* to act quickly or vigorously. *To die in one's boots* or *with one's boots on,* to die by violence. *Big in one's boots,* proud, conceited. *To beat out of one's boots,* to beat decisively. *To go down in one's boots,* to be scared.

(1) **1834** CARRUTHERS *Kentuckian* I. 97 He's got the boot on the wrong leg. — **1866** MOORE *Women of War* 173 'Ah,' replied the jolly rebel, 'the boot is on the other foot now.' — **1851** *Alta Californian* 29 July, It needed not this display to assure the spectators that they were bent on 'moving their boots.' **1886** *Leslie's Mo.* May 614/2 Now start your boots, and go home. — **1851** *Polly Peablossom* 72, I tell you what, ef he didn't go it *boots* that time I don't know! — **1873** BEADLE *Undevel. West* 435 It will be said in Western dialect, 'They died in their Boots.' **1873** MILLER *Amongst Modocs* vi. 75 If you keep on slinging your six-shooter around loose . . . , you will . . . die with your boots on. **1886** BRET HARTE *Snow-bound* 93, I'm not going to shoot you now, . . . so you will have a chance to die with your boots on, if you are superstitious. — **1879** TOURGEE *Fool's Errand* 84 They are gittin so big in ther boots they cant rest. — **1890** *Adrian* (Mich.) *Times* 6 March, 'Gov. Luce,' he said, '. . . can beat Barnes out of his boots.' — **1901** WHITE *Claim Jumpers* viii. 113 'You hits hard, sonny,' said he, 'and you don't go down in your boots a little bit.'

(2) **1856** *Spirit of Times* (N.Y.) 6 Sept. 3/3 You may bet your old boots on that. **1860** *Harper's Mag.* Sept. 565/1 Toodles . . . played some intensely funny trick on Lemons. . . . Lemons at length made use of the Captain as a lever to raise Toodles out of his boots. **1875** *Chicago Tribune* 2 Nov. 8/2 Little children (bless their souls and bother their boots) patter an accompaniment with their tiny feet. **1883** *Harper's Mag.* Sept. 592/2 Russell . . . now felt his courage oozing out at the seams of his boots.

+**2.** (See quotations.)

'This . . . application is local and improper' (W. '28).

1828 WEBSTER, *Boot,* . . . an apron or leathern cover for a gig or chair, to defend persons from rain and mud. **1911** LINCOLN *Cap'n Warren* 9 The 'boot' was a rubber curtain buttoned across the front of the buggy, extending from the dashboard to just below the level of the driver's eyes.

+**3.** *In the boot,* of wheat: In the stage of putting out leaves.

1858 *Texas Almanac 1859* 70 A severe frost fell in Northern Texas on the 5th of April, 1857, when the wheat was in the boot.

* **Boot**[2].

* **1.** *To boot,* in addition, besides.

1667 *Southold Rec.* I. 450 John Swezy exchanged with Capt John Tooker a gray hors . . . for a baye hors. . . . John Swazy is to give Cpt. Tooker two peeces of roope to boote. **1713** *Essex Inst. Coll.* X. 101, I am to give him 3£. 10 shil. to boot. **1741** HEMPSTEAD *Diary* 384, I . . . exchanged a 2 y[ea]r old Steer with Stephen Bennet for one of his . . . & give him 40s to Boot. **1883** BRET HARTE *Poet. Works* 145 And all of Smith's pigs were skyugled to boot. **1898** WESTCOTT *D. Harum* 229, I got another equine wonder an' fifteen dollars to boot fer my old plug.

* **2.** Something additional given in a trade (esp. in horses) to make the exchange equal. {–1726; now *dial.*} Also attrib. with *note.*

1811 A. GRAYDON *Memoirs* (1846) 30 He picked up six or eight of my marbles, . . . throwing me down three or four times the number of his own, the amount of boot being apparently wholly unworthy of calculation. **1835** [LONGSTREET] *Georgia Scenes* 27 Blossom swore absolutely, roundly and profanely, that he never would give boot. **1848** DRAKE in *Pioneer Life Ky.* 82 My father's necessities for an abler horse led him . . . to swop her off, and by giving some boot, to get an abler horse. **1859** *Harper's Mag.* June 137/1 Jones Adare was a great swapper of horses. . . . Jones kept on trading and having his boot-notes shaved. **1888** C. D. FERGUSON *Exp. Forty-niner* 63 He made much money out of them [=Mormons] by trading in horses, taking their worn out ones and getting the full value of his in money as 'boot.' **1899** CHESTNUTT *Conjure Woman* 42 But de spekilator had gin 'im big boot.

b. A difference in value.

c1840 NEAL *Beedle's Sleigh Ride* 13 For my part, I think there is not much boot between them.

Boot-and-shoe. [BOOT[1] 1.] *attrib.* Connected with the making or sale of boots and shoes.

1789 *Boston Directory* 174 Baxter John and Com. boot and shoe-store, No. 14, State-street. **1809** F. CUMING *Western Tour* 223 Pittsburgh [has] . . . twenty-one boot and shoe-makers. **1827** DRAKE & MANSF. *Cincinnati* 57 [In Cincinnati in 1826 there were] twenty-nine Boot and Shoe Shops, . . . [and] two Boot and Shoe Tree Factories. **1891** WILKINS *New Eng. Nun* 109 There was a new boot-and-shoe manufactory there. **1898** B. H. YOUNG *Jessamine Co., Ky.* 194 [He] was engaged in the boot and shoe business in Nicholasville in 1826.

+**Bootblack.** [BOOT[1] 1.] One who blacks and polishes shoes; a shoeblack.

1817 *Essex Inst. Coll.* VIII. 246 At the house where we stopped they had a boot-black and barber. **c1849** [PAIGE] *Dow's Sermons* I. 110 Even a boot-black is bound to shine in his profession. **1869** S. BOWLES *Our New West* 279 The boot-blacks and baths and barbers are of European standards. **1883** *Harper's Mag.* July 817/1 The San Francisco boot-blacks seem quite a model to their class. **1887** *Courier-Journal* 13 Jan. 2/6 One member . . . sent out at once for a bootblack to put an extra polish on his shoes.

+**Bootblacking.** [BOOT[1] 1.] Polishing boots and shoes with blacking. Also attrib. — **1866** GREGG *Life in Army* 139 Here are . . . candy shops, peanut stands, cake wagons, and boot-blacking establishments. **1870** O. LOGAN *Before Footlights* 173 Men have the whole field of labor before them, from Wall street speculation down—or up—to boot-blacking.

+**Bootbrush.** [BOOT[1] 1.] A shoebrush. — **1865** NORTON *Army Lett.* 268 Mr. Brown . . . (handles the boot brush) under the auspices of my friend Burrows.

+**Boot cleaner.** [BOOT[1] 1.] One who cleans boots. — **1837** *S. Lit. Messenger* III. 656 They . . . are willing to remain the boot-cleaners and the bottle-washers of the whites. **1845** M. M. NOAH *Gleanings* 85, I shortly after perceived Cuff, my boot cleaner, with a row of polished boots arranged on his pole.

+**Boot crimp.** A device used in boot-making for bending or molding leather into proper shapes (patented 7 June 1839). — **1847** WEBSTER. **1849** *Rep. Comm. Patents* (1850) 212 Improvement in Boot Crimps. **1868** *Mich. Agric. Rep.* VII. 363 A. M. R. Fitzsimmons, Reading, [exhibited a] boot crimp. **1874** KNIGHT 335/2 *Boot-crimp,* a tool or a machine for giving the shape to the pieces of leather designed for boot uppers.

+**Boot crimper.** A person or a device that crimps boot leather. — **1830** *U.S. Patents* 19 Feb. **1841** *Boston Almanac* 53 Boot Crimpers. Ross, Jacob, Wilson lane [etc.].

+**Bootee.** [f. BOOT[1] 1. Cf. *coatee,* etc.] A half boot or high shoe, covering the ankle but not the leg.

1799 *Aurora* (Phila.) 15 Nov. (Th.), For sale, 180 pairs of bootees. **1844** *Congress. Globe* 11 March 361/3 On men's boots or bootees of leather, . . . women's boots or bootees, . . . children's boots, bootees, and shoes, . . . there shall be levied a duty. **1861** *Army Regulations* 238 Mounted men may receive one pair of 'boots' and two pair of 'bootees,' instead of four pair of bootees. **1889** *Cent.* 628/2 *Bootee*, a trade-name for a half or short boot for women.

Boother, dialect variant of *booder*, BOWLDER. {*c*1680–} — **1826** *Penna. H. S. Mem.* I. 293 Different kinds of stone, by continual rolling and wearing, have become smooth and round, and are called boothers.

+**Boot hook.** [BOOT[1] 1.] (See quot. 1874.) — **1851** *Polly Peablossom* 188 The first article that presented itself was a pair of boot-hooks. **1855** M. THOMPSON *Doesticks* 297, I could forgive . . . thy pantaloons so tight thou hadst to pull them on with boot-hooks. **1874** KNIGHT 336/1 *Boot-hook*, a device for drawing on boots and shoes, consisting essentially of a stout wire bent into a hooked form and provided with a handle.

***Boothose.** *Obs.* [BOOT[1] 1.] An overstocking covering the leg like a boot. Also allusively. Occas. attrib. with *top.* {1815} — **1638** *Md. Archives* IV. 46, 3. p[air] bootehose. **1650** *Southampton Rec.* I. 68 Touells and 1 paire of boote hose tops. **1788** FRENEAU *Misc. Works* 86 The lee strap of my larboard boot hose.

Bootjack.

1. A contrivance for pulling off a boot. {*a*1841–}

1845 *Knickerb.* XXV. 444 The great clothes-horse stood behind the door, and my grandfather's boot-jack in its old corner kept it company. **1855** M. THOMPSON *Doesticks* 52 My frantic eye caught sight of my cast-iron boot-jack. **1867** COZZENS *Sayings* 75 Here [is] Mr. Timmins, with one boot in his hand and the other in the boot-jack.

+**2.** *slang.* A dolt; a blockhead.

1842 *Dartmouth* IV. 116 A stupid fellow, a dolt, a boot-jack, an ignoramus, is called here a *gonus.*

+**3.** In railroading, the place where two rails cross or come very near each other. Also attrib.

1890 T. M. Cooley, etc. *Railways Amer.* 222 At all places where two rails cross or approach each other . . . dangerous boot-jacks are formed by the rail-heads. **1898** *Engineering Mag.* XVI. 161/2 The 'Bootjack' Signals of the Lake Shore and Michigan Southern Ry.

+**Bootleg.** [BOOT[1] 1.]

1. The leg of a tall boot, or the leather cut out for one.

1843 *Knickerb.* XXI. 523 His legs [were] encased in a pair of massive boots, which were surmounted by a pair of linsey-woolsey breeches plunged into his boot-legs. **1855** M. THOMPSON *Doesticks* 181 The man who would . . . hopefully essay the concoction of a satisfactory stew from jack-knife-handles and bootlegs. **1882** *Century Mag.* Sept. 765/1 If I don't . . . see Maine and Maria again, and with a boot-leg full o' gold-dust, too, I'm a Dutchman. **1887** *Harper's Mag.* Dec. 78/2 Timothy . . . drew his 'shootin-iron' from his boot-leg, and cocked it with a metallic click. **1888** 'CRADDOCK' *Broomsedge Cove* 65 He . . . paused only to slip into his long boot-leg a 'shootin' iron.' **1889** F. REMINGTON in *Century Mag.* April 905/2 Pipes were filled, smoked, and returned to that cavalryman's grip-sack, the boot-leg.

2. *attrib.* **a.** Of liquor or its sale: Illicit.

With reference to carrying a flask in the leg of a boot. Cf. BOOTLEGGER. Freq. in recent use.

*a***1889** *Omaha Herald* (B. & L.), There is as much whisky consumed in Iowa now . . . on the boot-leg plan. **1922** SANDBURG *Slabs of Sunburnt West* 25 Burnt like a shot of bootleg booze.

b. Inferior, bad.

1895 CHAMBLISS *Diary* 324 The menu at the meal stations along through Texas and Arizona consists of whit-leather steak, overdue eggs, bad-smelling butter, corn dodgers, and 'boot-leg' coffee.

+**Bootlegger.** *slang.* [Cf. prec. 2 a.] One who carries liquor in his bootleg; an illicit dealer in liquor.

Also in recent use *bootlegging* vbl. n. and ppl. a.

1889 SANGER *Rep.* in Thoburn *Hist. Oklahoma* I. 223 Gamblers, liquor dealers (or as they are called here 'boot-leggers'), lot-jumpers. **1890** *Voice* (N.Y.) 17 July, The 'bootlegger' is a grim spectre to the anti-Prohibitionist. **1891** *Cycl. of Temperance* 508/2 'Bootlegger' is a Kansas name for the sneaking itinerant peddler of illicit whiskey. It is the practice of these contemptible wretches to carry flasks concealed about the person, frequently in the bootleg—hence the name. **1904** *Topeka Capital* 29 May 4 A United States marshall arrested a bootlegger at Osborne for selling whisky without a government licence. . . . Bootlegging is a bad business.

+**Bootlick,** *n. slang.* [BOOT[1] 1.] **1.** One who curries favor with another; a toady. (Orig. college slang.) **2.** (See quotation.) — (1) **1849** *Yale Banger* 6 Nov. 6 The rites of Wooden Spoon we next recite, When Boot-lick hypocrites upraised their might. **1850** *Yale Battery* 14 Feb., Then he arose, and offered himself as a '*boot lick,*' to the Faculty. **1851** [see BOOTLICKING *vbl. n.*]. **1859** BARTLETT 44 *Boot-lick*, . . . a lickspittle, a toady. **1899** GREEN *Va. Word-Book* 64 *Bootlick*, a person who tries to gain favour by mean behavior. (2) **1851** HALL *College Words* 24 At Yale, and other colleges, a tutor or any other officer who informs against the students, or acts as a spy upon their conduct, is also called a *bootlick.*

+**Bootlick,** *v. slang.* [BOOT[1] 1.] **a.** *tr.* To curry favor with, toady to (a person). **b.** *intr.* To be a toady. — **1845** HOOPER *Simon Suggs' Adv.* v. 58 A young man . . . was inclined to boot-lick anybody suspected of having money. **1851** HALL *College Words* 24 *Bootlick*, to fawn upon; to court favor. **1885** *Milnor* (Dakota) *Teller* 1 May 2/3 They must drink, truckle, and bootlick to keep their greatness uppermost. **1915** *N.Y. Tribune* 24 March 5/3 It . . . accused 'The Spectator's' staff of grafting and bootlicking their advertisers.

+**Bootlicker.** *slang.* [BOOT[1] 1.] =BOOTLICK *n.* — **1848** *Yale Banger* 23 Oct., Three or four boot-lickers rise. *c***1850** MRS. WHITCHER *Widow Bedott P.* xxvii. 331 Sweezer's very intimit with the squire's folks—a kind o' bootlicker tew 'em. **1924** B. J. HENDRICK *W. H. Page* I. 19 The recipient is either a humbug or a bootlicker.

+**Bootlicking,** *vbl. n. slang.* [BOOT[1] 1.] Toadying. — **1851** HALL *College Words* 24 Some [students are] . . . very apt to linger after recitation to get a clearer knowledge of some passage. They are *Bootlicks*, and that is known as *Bootlicking.* **1894** *Current Hist.* IV. 472 Working his way by scheming and bootlicking into the good graces of . . . a young idiot of a lord.

+**Bootlicking,** *ppl. a. slang.* [BOOT[1] 1.] Given to toadying. — **1849** *Gallinipper* Dec., The 'Wooden Spoon' exhibition passed off without any such hub-bub, except where the pieces were of such a character as to offend the delicacy and modesty of some of those crouching, fawning, boot-licking hypocrites.

Bootmaker. [BOOT[1] 1.] One whose occupation is making boots. {1630–}

1789 *Boston Directory* 173 Archer, Moses, boot and shoe-maker, Adams-street. **1845** *Knickerb.* XXVI. 377 A journeyman boot-maker is the presiding officer. **1866** 'F. KIRKLAND' *Bk. Anecdotes* 282/2 The reputation of Young . . . was not of the best, and the bootmaker would do nothing for him. **1882** *Century Mag.* July 480/2 My slippers . . . cost me just a round five dollars more than a new pair had cost at my boot-maker's shop.

Boot money. [BOOT[2].] A sum given as boot. {1878–, *n. dial.*} — **1853** 'P. PAXTON' *Yankee in Texas* 47 He would usually put off the winner with . . . a dubious note that he had received as 'lanyappe' (*Anglice*, boot money).

Boot-room. [BOOT[1] 1.] A room in which boots are kept or polished. — **1818** FEARON *Sketches* 250 The public rooms [of hotels] are—a news-room, a boot-room, in which the bar is situated, and a dining-room. **1907** M. C. HARRIS *Tents of Wickedness* 301 Having things when he wanted them, . . . was the key-note of the boot-room of Oscar Hungerford, Esq.

Boot-scraper. An iron fixture for scraping mud, etc., from the soles of shoes. — **1882** THAYER *From Log-Cabin* 345 How many boot-scrapers are there at the door?

Booty race. [From the phrase *to play booty*, to lose a race, etc., intentionally.] A race not run fairly to win. — **1812** *Mass. Spy* 30 Sept. (Th.), He by pure feats of running (not at a booty race) found shelter in a tavern. **1838** J. McDONALD *Biographical Sk.* 40 Edgington did not run a booty race. For about a mile the Indians stepped in his tracks almost before the bending grass could rise.

Booze. *colloq.* {1732–}

+**1.** Alcoholic spirits.

1890 WEBSTER. **1896** *Voice* (N.Y.) 16 July 1/6 The Duckworth club . . . consumed large quantities of booze. **1904** *N.Y. Sun* 7 Aug. 18 The quality of the booze is excellent. **1907** S. E. WHITE *Arizona Nights* 322 But he's quit his gun fighting As well as his Booze. *a***1909** 'O HENRY' *Roads of Destiny* 374 They'll drink you up like a bottle of booze.

+**2.** Attrib. with *fight, fighter, joint, traffic.*

1895 *Voice* (N.Y.) 9 May 5/4 Drunkards . . . paving the floors of Hades with lost souls—lost through the booze traffic. **1896** G. ADE *Artie* xii. 110 He's . . . dug up the long green and he's puttin it out at the booze joints. **1916** SANDBURG *Chicago Poems* 170 Cooped in the same cell with me was . . . a booze-fighter. **1922** H. L. FOSTER *Adv. Trop. Tramp* ix. 127 Riotous booze-fights . . . were less in evidence.

***Borage.** Also **burrage.** One or other plant of the genus *Borago;* esp. the species *B. officinalis*, sometimes cultivated for its bright blue flowers.

1731 J. SECOMB *Father Abbey's Will* x, An old Black Muff, some Garden Stuff, A Quantity of Burrage [*rime* Porridge]. **1791** MUHLENBERG *Index Florae* 163 *Borago officinalis*, Borage. **1812** *Niles' Reg.* II. 393/2 Having found, from some former experiments, that the herb vulgarly called *burrage*, contained a considerably [*sic*] quantity of this gas, . . . I concluded to make a trial of it. **1846** WOOD *Botany* 431 Common Borage . . . [is] with us a common inhabitant of the garden. *Ib.*, *Borago orientalis*, Oriental Borage, . . . an ornamental garden plant. . . . Flowers blue, appearing in the spring months. **1889** *Cent.* 629/3 Borage . . . is sometimes used as a salad, occasionally in medicine in acute fevers, etc., and also in making claret-cup.

***Borax.** Biborate of soda or sodium tetraborate, a crystalline salt, colorless or white when pure, used as a flux, antiseptic, etc. — **1867** *Ann. Cycl. 1866* 85/1 Borax was discovered in California in 1856. **1883** *Encycl. Brit., Amer. Suppl.* I. 693/2 While borax, the biborate of soda, is found at several places in California, only in . . . the Slate Range Marsh, San Bernardino co., does it occur in such quantity . . . as to render it of much commercial value. **1889** *Cent.* 630/1 The United States is now almost wholly supplied with borax from California.

***Border.**

***1.** The boundary or frontier of a district or of the country at a particular place. Also in *pl.* +In later use freq. of the western frontier.

1648 *Conn. Col. Rec.* I. 163 Ther are certen farms to be sett forth uppon the borders or within the limitts of Fayerfield. **1671** ELIOT *Progress of Gospel* 31 Magunkukquok is another of our Praying-Towns at the remotest westerly borders of Natick. **1805** *Ann. 8th Congress* 2 Sess. 1097 The Spaniards were on its border [i.e. of Indian land in Ga.], and a part of it was actually occupied by settlers under Spanish and British grants.

1819 A. LAWRENCE *Diary & Corr.* 71, I shall go across the Alleghanies, or journey through the interior to the northern border of this country. **1836** *Diplom. Corr. Texas* (1908) I. 163 All the advantages . . . would be forever lost to the United States and important advantages given to a Power on her Southern border which already confines her on the North. **1839** HOFFMAN *Wild Scenes* 52 Snow-shoes [are] . . . only manufactured in perfection by the Indians, who drive quite a trade in them along the Canada border. **1857** W. CHANDLESS *Visit Salt Lake* I. 122 The valley was very picturesque, with the russet colouring and round yet rocky hills characteristic of the 'borders.' **1862** M. A. Jackson *Memoirs* 371 But, I assure you, this thing of being on the border, and subject at any time to be taken captives again, is indeed dreadful. **1874** GLISAN *Jrnl. Army Life* 446 At the time of my sojourn on the western border.

2. *attrib.* (Chiefly of the western frontier, but occas. of the Southern States bordering on the Northern.) **a.** Of persons: Living on or belonging to the borders. See also BORDERMAN, RUFFIAN.

1827 COOPER *Prairie* ii, The indirect manner so much in use by the border inhabitants. *Ib.* x, The yellow fringes and ornaments that were sometimes seen among the border-troops of the confederacy. **1837** IRVING *Bonneville* II. 106 He had . . . betaken himself to the society of the border Indians. **1841** *Knickerb.* Jan. 30 [The coat] around the 'border' chief its shelter cast, In proud defiance of the northern blast. **1843** *Amer. Pioneer* II. 131 To the chagrin and disappointment of the border woman, she pulled out the lost article, rolled up in her dingy bedding. **1849** PARKMAN *Oregon Trail* 19, I was . . . already familiar with many of the border tribes. **1856** SIMMS *Charlemont* 425 His garb was picturesque, that of a bold border-hunter. **1870** R. PUMPELLY *Across Amer. & Asia* i. 1 A border bully, armed with revolver, knife, and rifle. **1870** *Congress. Globe* App. 26 March 225/2 The marbles of our western border have heretofore served as 'chimney rock' for the cabin of the luxurious border farmer, and for fencing for his field. **1874** GLISAN *Jrnl. Army Life* 432 Then comes the counter feeling of vengeance on the part of the border settlers. **1881** J. W. BUEL *Border Outlaws* 143 Armed bands of vindictive border residents were almost constantly prowling about the Younger residence. **1916** EASTMAN *From Deep Woods* 127 The border ranchmen called me in now and then.

b. Of places: Situated on the borders.

1826 COOPER *Mohicans* x. 97 Sometimes he fancied the wary savage . . . was holding his way towards a well known border settlement. **1839** *Diplom. Corr. Texas* (1908) I. 400 This government would not . . . insist on an equal right with the United States to the navigation of that border stream. **1846** SAGE *Scenes Rocky Mts.* i, I shall never forget the pleasing sensations produced by my first visit to the border-prairies. **1847** [ROBB] *Squatter Life* 71 Hoss Allen counted strong on the border counties, while his [political] antagonist built his hopes on the centre. **1857** *Lawrence* (Kansas) *Republican* 11 June 2 Already the pro-slavery papers of Border Missouri raise a shout of expected triumph. **1867** J. M CRAWFORD *Mosby* 13 Having spent the last two years in guerilla warfare, in the border counties of Virginia. **1869** BROWNE *Adv. Apache Countyr* 268, I scarcely think they would waste time in stealing ore of little value, and transporting it across the border line through an Apache country. **1873** *Newton Kansan* 17 July 2/2 Mr. Gross describes the life and fortunes of the homesteaders in the border counties of Kansas. **1879** TAYLOR *Summer-Savory* 92 Were you ever a guest at a border tavern? The landlord is a tall Kentucky hunter. **1885** *Century Mag.* XXX. 725/1 Two young men were riding along the wood road of the border land in Virginia. **1891** Border town [see BOOMING *ppl. a.* 3]. **1907** WHITE *Arizona Nights* 256, I'm looking for a man with sand enough . . . to lead a posse after cattle-rustlers into the border country. **1924** R. CUMMINS *Sky-High Corral* 17 He's from the border country, where men who pack guns know how to use 'em.

c. Of actions, incidents, etc.: Happening or taking place on, connected with, the borders.

1835 HOFFMAN *Winter in West* I. 270, I had previously . . . seen stockades erected in the open prairie . . . with other similar marks of the late border-strife. **1838** DRAKE *Tales & Sk.* 118, I must return from this long digression among the border forays of the West. **1842** *Amer. Pioneer* I. 210 You may expect to hear from him, on border incidents. **1852** WATSON *Nights in Block-House* 300 The man who says that story is not nateral to border fightin', don't know any thing about the matter. **1874** B. F. TAYLOR *World on Wheels* I. vi. 46 You hear border talk and see border manners, in cars finished to the last touch of pier-glass polish. **1907** WHITE *Arizona Nights* II. 251 He was . . . rather neatly dressed in the border costume.

* **Borderer.** An inhabitant of a border or frontier region; +esp., a frontiersman, a backwoodsman.

1738 BYRD *Dividing Line* (1901) 30 We had the fortune to meet with a borderer upon North Carolina, who made a rough sketch of that part of the country. **1827** COOPER *Prairie* vi, The resemblance between the American borderer and his European prototype is singular, though not always uniform. **1835** HOFFMAN *Winter in West* I. 244 A hard-featured borderer . . . sat smoking a pipe on the other side of the fireplace. **1847** HOWE *Hist. Coll. Ohio* 56 Belmont has been the scene of at least two of the daring adventures of this far-famed borderer [=Lewis Wetzel]. **1852** MRS. ELLET *Pioneer Women* 202 An old tavern . . . well known to the early pack-horsemen and borderers of that region. **1857** *Lawrence* (Kansas) *Republican* 6 Aug. 2 Fearful . . . that the Free-State sentiment of Douglas County . . . might prove too much for Johnson County, even though overrun by borderers from Missouri. **1888** ROOSEVELT in *Century Mag.* Feb. 500/1 The restless, aimless craving for change . . . [is] deeply grafted in the breast of the American borderer.

+**Border life.** [BORDER 2 c.] Life on the borders, esp. on the western frontier of the United States.

1827 COOPER *Prairie* x, Unlike most of those who live a border life, he united the better instead of the worst qualities of the two people. **1841** — *Deerslayer* i, Though his manner necessarily partook of the rudeness of a border-life. **1856** SIMMS *Charlemont* 426 Seeking his fortune in such adventures as make border-life in our country something like the more civilized life of the middle ages. **1872** *Ill. Dept. Agric. Trans.* 155 Many of the farmers are men who prefer something akin to border life. **1887** TOURGEE *Button's Inn* 236 Our American border-life was peculiarly fecund in such religious movements.

Borderman. [BORDER 2 a.] An inhabitant of the frontier or border. {1620}

1827 COOPER *Prairie* ii, Whatever may be the other qualities of a border man, he is seldom deficient in the virtue of hospitality. **1836** *Knickerb.* VIII. 281, I was asked one day, by a borderman, what I would do were I to be attacked by him. **1845** COOPER *Chainbearer* xxiii, Those experienced bordermen well knew it was not possible for me to cross the open ground and to reach the woods in the short interval of time. **1867** EDWARDS *Shelby* 33 Major Ben Elliot . . . had recruited a battalion of notorious scouts and bordermen.

+**Border ruffian.** [BORDER 2 a.]

1. A member of the pro-slavery party in Missouri who in 1854–58 often crossed the border into Kansas to vote illegally and to intimidate the opponents of slavery. Now hist.

1856 *Congress. Globe* 5 March 585/3 The Missouri 'border ruffians,' as they have been termed. **1857** *Lawrence* (Kansas) *Republican* 28 May 1 The leading border ruffians . . . issued a proclamation to the Missourians . . . and marched again towards Lawrence. **1860** ABBOTT *South & North* 251 In a small town near the borders of Missouri, where the 'border ruffians' of that State could guide their [=legislators'] movements. **1862** KETTELL *Hist. Rebellion* I. 33 The Southern emigrants, aided by organized bands, known as 'border ruffians,' . . . soon came in collision with the Northern settlers. **1870** *Congress. Globe* 4 April 2391/1 While Senators were denying the existence of border-ruffianism in Kansas border ruffians were laying waste and murdering people. **1888** GRIGSBY *Smoked Yank* ii. (1891) 18, I used to urge my father to take me with him out to Kansas so that we might help to put down the 'border ruffians' from Missouri. **1901** CHURCHILL *Crisis* 31 There was a gentleman on the steamboat who said that it took more courage to enter the Judge's private office than to fight a Border Ruffian.

2. Attrib. (or as adj.) with *decision, state,* etc.

1856 *Spirit of Times* (N.Y.) 27 Dec. 269/3, I wonder if there is any chance for an outsider of the 'Border Ruffian' State to come in? **1858** *N.Y. Tribune* 12 July 6/5 (*headlines*), Jack Henderson discharged. A Border-Ruffian Decision. **1860** GREELEY *Overland Journey* 18 [Atchison, Kansas] was long a Border-Ruffian nest. **1867** A. D. RICHARDSON *Beyond Miss.* 27 Now, his paper was emphatically 'border ruffian.' *Ib.* 28, I asked if there was any doubt about the border ruffian incursions.

+**Border-ruffianism.** [BORDER 2 c. Cf. prec.] The acts of violence that characterized the border strife in Kansas and Missouri over slavery. Now hist.

1861 in *Diary of Mrs. S. Cowell* 377 With the power thus given him he would have had the state of Missouri, by this time under all the terrors of Kansas border ruffianism. **1863** Amer. Corr. in *Times* (London) 10 April, In the days when the Border-ruffianism of Kansas was the staple subject of the denunciations of the Republican party. **1866** A. D. RICHARDSON *Secret Service* 17 Many former shining lights of Border Ruffianism were now . . . lurid torches in the early bonfires of Secession. **1871** EGGLESTON *Hoosier Schoolm.* vi. 71 It is out of these materials [=desperadoes and thieves] that border ruffianism has grown. **1905** VALENTINE *H. Sandwith* 162 The *Tribune* was eagerly scanned by pious Republicans for latest exaggerations of Border ruffianism.

+**Border state.** [BORDER 2 b.]

1. A southern state that borders on the northern states, or a state bordering on Canada. Usu. in *pl.*

1849 *Niles' Reg.* 14 Feb. 97/3 The border States of the South. **1860** *Congress. Globe* 19 Dec. 139/3 It is an intimidation to the border States, alluding especially . . . to Virginia, Maryland, Kentucky, and Missouri. They constitute the first tier of the border slave States. **1861** F. Moore *Rebellion Rec.* I. III. 122 In all the range of Border States, . . . The staunch, unflinching Delaware's The only one that's trusty. **1862** 'E. KIRKE' *Among Pines* 36 The other Cotton States are with us, and the leaders in the Border States are pledged to Secession. **1866** F. CARPENTER *At White House* 77 Action in reference to enlisting blacks in the Border States. **1884** BLAINE *20 Years of Congress* I. 25 The emancipation of negroes . . . received . . . the patronage of leading men among the slave-holders of the Border States.

2. Attrib. with *accent, convention, Democrat, manners,* etc.

1861 *Chicago Tribune* 26 May 1/6 The Border State Convention meets at Frankfort on Monday. **1862** KETTELL *Hist. Rebellion* I. 73 Neither the Crittendon resolutions, nor the border state propositions were, however, destined to pass Congress. **1875** *Chicago Tribune* 8 Dec. 1/5 'Here we are again!' . . . Deacon Pogram, with his band of Border-State Democrats. **1884** BLAINE *20 Years of Congress* I. 467 If the border-state policy of Mr. Lincoln . . . had not required [etc.]. **1886** LOGAN *Great Conspiracy* 555 In both Houses of Congress . . . they had been striving . . . to poison the loyal Northern and Border-State mind. **1888** A. C. GUNTER *Mr. Potter* viii, Miss Potter still keeps her Border-State accent and her Border-State manners.

fig. **1863** 'G. HAMILTON' *Gala-Days* 92 For these Border State men . . . I have a profound contempt.

+**Border tier.** [BORDER 2 b.] (See quotation.) — **1873** BEADLE *Undevel. West* 203 [The] Gulf Railroad runs . . . in a few places within five miles of the Missouri line, and is popularly known here as the 'border tier road.'

Border war. [BORDER 2 c.] A war carried on upon the frontier, esp. against Indian tribes.

1809 IRVING *Knickerb.* v. ii, All the other catalogue of heart-rending cruelties that disgraced these border wars. **1835** HOFFMAN *Winter in West* I. 113 Detroit, . . . a frontier post . . . which has witnessed so many scenes of border war. **1839** *Diplom. Corr. Texas* (1908) I. 362 He placed their arms in the hands of the U.S. Agent until the border war was over. **1845** *Cincinnati Misc.* 236 The border war between the whites and Indians, had for many years prior to 1782 been waged by small parties. **1859** J. B. JONES (*title*), Wild Southern Scenes: a Tale of Disunion! and Border War!

Border warfare. [Cf. prec.] Warfare conducted on the frontier. — **1835** *S. Lit. Messenger* I. 439 They frequently accompanied each other in hunting excursions . . . always taking along the eldest sons . . . to teach them some of the rudiments . . . of border warfare. **1858** *82nd Anniv. Independence* (Boston) 53 Save us from border warfare and from foreign war. **1879** *Harper's Mag.* Aug. 324 The possession of these forts [on Lake George] was the cause of much border warfare.

+**Bore,** *n. Obs. slang.* [f. BORE *v.*] A hoax, trick, deception. — **1800** *Aurora* (Phila.) 3 July (Th.), A Federal bore [concerning the reported death of Jefferson]. **1811** *Mass. Spy* 1 May (Th.), Tis thus that Hymen cracks his joke, A hoax, a quiz, a bore.

***Bore,** *v. tr.* To hoax or deceive; to make sport of, to tease. {1602–1622} — **1800** *Aurora* (Phila.) 12 Sept. (Th.), The institution of the Lazy Society was a mere sportive hoax, to bore some of the laziness of the District. **1801** *Sp. Farmers' Museum* 63 We should advise adventurers to be cautious how they purchase, as . . . we think there is a probability of their being bored. **1836** *Knickerb.* VIII. 558 If he returned without firing a shot, after all his preparations, . . . he would be bored for life. **1844** *Cincinnati Misc.* 21 'You are not boring me, Mr. Sutton, I hope.' . . . 'Rest assured that I . . . am perfectly serious.'

Bored, *ppl. a.* +Of a well: Formed by drilling or boring. (Cf. BORE-WELL.) — **1883** SMITH *Geol. Survey Ala.* 444 Drinking water in this region is obtained from bored or artesian wells. **1922** T. A. MCNEAL *When Kansas was Young* 205 A fair-haired child who was so unfortunate as to fall into a bored well out in western Kansas.

***Borer.** [f. *bore* v.]

1. A name given to various insects that bore into wood, plants, etc. {1789–}

1838 *Mass. Zool. Survey Rep.* 89 The larvae [of capricorn beetles], in common language called borers, are eminently wood-eaters, and exceedingly injurious to vegetation. **1850** [S. F. COOPER] *Rural Hours* 126 In many parts of the country these beautiful trees have been very much injured of late years by a worm called the borer. **1868** G. BRACKETT *Farm Talk* 58 The borer is a grub, which lives in the bark and wood of the apple tree, near the roots. **1878** *Congress. Rec.* 5 Feb. 773 If you allow the logs to lie on the ground one year . . . the borers have taken out one-third of the value of your logs. **1892** V. KELLOG *Kansas Insects* 70 Flat-headed apple-tree borer (*Chrysobothris femorata*) . . . deposits its eggs during the middle of the day, and only during warm, sunny days. **1898** DELAND *Old Chester Tales* 287 He had the stoop which comes from bending over cold frames and poking about roots for borers. **1908** WHITE *Riverman* ii. 15 There's borers, for one thing, to spoil a good many of the logs.

+**2.** *slang.* **a.** A traveling salesman; a drummer. *Obs.*

1836 *Public Ledger* (Phila.) 23 Aug. (Th.), [In Philadelphia drummers] are called borers, probably from some resemblance in qualities to a worm that infests fruit trees. **1856** *Knickerb.* Oct. 407 Felicien B. blessed the drummers and borers of New York.

+**b.** A lobbyist. *Obs.* (Cf. BORING *vbl. n.*)

1854 *Congress. Globe* App. 20 May 893/2, I should like to say a few words about these 'legislative borers.'

Boretree. [Eng. dial., variant of *bourtree.*] The elder. {1691–} — **1807** GASS *Journal* 136 There are black elder and bore-tree, pitch and spruce pine all growing together on these mountains. **1849** PRITTS *Border Life* 466 Get a rod of bortree, well seasoned.

+**Bore-well.** [Cf. BORED *ppl. a.*] A bored well. — **1873** *Winfield* (Kansas) *Courier* 18 Jan. 2/2 At Bunker Hill . . . they have a bore-well two hundred and seventy feet deep.

+**Bore-worm.** =BORER 1. — **1856** *Rep. Comm. Patents: Agric.* 86 This [dropping off of young cotton-buds] has been attributed to the agency of the young larvæ of the 'bore-worm.'

Boring, *vbl. n.* [Cf. BORER 2b.] +The practice of trying to influence members of a legislature. — **1841** in G. Combe *Notes U.S.* I. 322 Great impediments are thrown in the way of the fulfilment of imperative duties by the monstrous increase of boring and lobbying on behalf of the interests of corporate associations.

***Borough.**

+**1.** In Connecticut, Pennsylvania, and a few other states, an incorporated town or municipality having less population than a city and being differently governed.

1718 *Penna. Col. Rec.* III. 58 The said town [Bristol] might be erected into a Borough by a Charter of Incorporacon. **1789** *Ann. 1st Congress* I. 73 Mr. Maclay presented a draft of ten miles square, including the borough of Lancaster. **1796** *Ann. 4th Congress* 2 Sess. 2694 These . . . lands, lots, and buildings, lying within any city, village, or borough, are assessed in detail. **1828** WEBSTER s.v., In Connecticut, this word, *borough*, is used for a town or a part of a town, or a village, incorporated with certain privileges, distinct from those of other towns and of cities; as the *Borough* of Bridgeport. **1840** *Niles' Nat. Reg.* 12 Sept. 32/2 The population of the borough of Norfolk, according to the census just taken, is . . . 10,573. **1879** *Harper's Mag.* Sept. 520 Not far above the borough—now town—of Chester, there stood a quaint old-fashioned . . . house. **1919** MENCKEN *Amer. Lang.* 296 This is now [spelled] . . . Allegheny for the Pittsburg borough and the Pennsylvania county.

+**2.** Any one of the five major administrative subdivisions of New York City.

1897 N. M. BUTLER in *Independent* 11 March 306/1 The Charter provides . . . that the Borough of Brooklyn may have a professionally conducted school system. **1898** VAN PELT *Leslie's Hist. N.Y.* II. 360 On January 1, 1898, Brooklyn ceased to be a city, becoming one of the five boroughs of the greater City of New York. **1901** *Outlook* 5 Oct. 275/2 The great problem which has confronted the people of New York is the bringing of this great city, with all its boroughs, together. **1914** McLaughlin & Hart *Cycl. Amer. Govt.* I. 144/1 In each borough [of N.Y.] there is elected by popular vote a borough president who holds office for four years.

3. Attrib. with *law, system* (sense 2), etc.

1819 *Missouri Intell.* 17 Dec. 2/4 It was expected that they in turn would have shewn some hesitation in the making of their borough laws. **1897** N. M. BUTLER in *Independent* 11 March 306/3 The immediate care and supervision of the Borough School Boards. **1900** *Nation* 6 Dec. 439/2 The borough system has been for the most part a failure thus far.

+**Bos.** *slang.* (See quotation.) — **1851** HALL *College Words* 25 At the University of Virginia, the desserts which the students . . . are allowed twice per week, are respectively called the senior and junior *bos.*

+**Bosaal.** *S.W.* [Sp. *bozal* muzzle.] 'A peculiar kind of halter, used in breaking and riding unruly horses' (B. '59). — **1853** 'P. PAXTON' *Yankee in Texas* 117 A fish spear is to him [the Texan] a *groin;* . . . a halter, a *bosaal;* a whip, a *quirt;* a house, no house, but a *log-pen.* **1909** 'O. HENRY' *Roads of Destiny* 149 It required but a few moments to contrive the rope into an ingenious nose-bridle, after the style of the Mexican *borsal* [sic].

+**Bosman,** †**Bosseman.** [Fr. *bosseman*, from G. *bootsmann* boatswain.] =BOWSMAN. — **1876** HALE *P. Nolan's Friends* i, A man in the bow called the bosman, who generally wielded a sort of boathook, watched the course. **1904** in *Kansas H. S. Trans.* IX. 272 The captain of the boat [early 19th c.], called the 'patron,' did the steering, and his assistant, called the 'bosseman,' stood on the bow, pole in hand, and gave directions to the men at the cordelle.

***Bosom.** +The front of a shirt. (Also *shirt bosom.*) Also attrib.

1863 *Horticulturist* Dec. 4 Shirt and Bosom makers. **1865** *Atlantic Mo.* XV. 466 More than thirty other girls were employed in making bosoms, wristbands and collars for shirts. **1872** *N.Y. Times* 24 April 8 (Hoppe), Shirts made to order, with beautifully embroidered Bosoms. **1896** WILKINS *Madelon* 351 None of the others have bosoms and wristbands stitched like these. **1903** *N.Y. Tribune* 27 Sept., The waiters did not wear . . . shirts with soiled bosoms. **1905** *N.Y. Ev. Post* 26 May 12 Men's Unlaundered Shirts. . . . Three-ply linen bosoms reinforced back and front.

+**Bosom board.** A board upon which the bosoms of shirts, waists, etc., may be ironed. — **1869** E. PUTNAM *Receipt Bk.* 319 For the washroom, have . . . an ironing blanket and sheet; a dress-board and bosom-board well covered. *a***1918** G. STUART *On Frontier* I. 256, I have been called upon to make a 'bosom board,' . . . and she has starched front, neck, and wristbands of our shirts.

‖**Bosom bottle.** ?A small bottle for carrying in the bosom. — **1714** *Essex Inst. Coll.* XLIII. 52, 2 diamond cut Bottles 24/, 7 Bosome ditto 7/.

+**Bosom-piece.** =BOSOM. — **1850** JUDD *R. Edney* xi. 154 Richard fairly struck his high colors to the persuasions of his sister, and ran up instead a white collar and bosom-piece.

+**Bosom-pin.** A breastpin. — **1855** BARNUM *Life* 123 What a fool I was to give you that finger-ring and bosom-pin. **1868** G. G. CHANNING *Recoll. Newport* 242 Bosom-pins, of various patterns, were common. **1889** CUSTER *Tenting on Plains* 213 This cambric finery, ornamented with three old-fashioned bosom-pins.

+**Bosque.** [Sp. *bosque.*] A wood or forest; a clump or grove of trees. — **1863** *Rio Abajo Press* 3 March 2 Jose Maria Chaves . . . has a commodious and comfortable house, corral, bosque, and farming land. **1888** J. J. WEBB *Adv.* 286 A second feed of corn was given them, and they were turned into the *bosque* to pick up what they could find in the way of grass, sprouts, etc.

+**Boss,** *n.*[1] Also **bos.** [Du. *baas* master, foreman.]

1. An employer or foreman; one in charge of men or work.

Early comments on the use of the word are given in the first group of quotations.

(1) **1818** FLINT *Lett. from Amer.* 9 *Master* is not a word in the vocabulary of hired people. *Bos*, a Dutch one of similar import, is substituted. **1823** I. HOLMES *Account* 342 No one, in this republican country, will use the term master or mistress; 'employers,' and the Dutch word 'boss,' are used instead. **1824** A. ROYALL *Lett. from Ala.* (1830) 173 Boss, in the Atlantic States, is a word applied to an overseer or manager. **1833** HAMILTON *Men & Manners* I. 234 Such words as *slick, kedge,* and *boss* . . . are rarely used by the better orders. **1838** COOPER *Amer. Democrat* 122 So far has this prejudice gone, that in lieu of the latter [term, viz. master], they have resorted to the use of the word *boss*, which has precisely the same meaning in Dutch!

(2) **1806** IRVING *Life & Lett.* (1862) I. 96, I had completely forgotten the errand, . . . so I had to return, make an awkward apology to *boss*, and look like a nincompoop. **1818** FEARON *Sketches of America* 58 The barber enquired if he wanted the proprietor or his *boss*, as he termed him, who was also a black. **1839** HOFFMAN *Wild Scenes* 109, I was sent packing by my bos before I was fifteen. **1845** *Knickerb.* Nov. 415 You peer through the gloom, and discover the 'boss' and two or three 'jours,' each seated on a low form. **1854** S. SMITH *Down East* 289 The clerk laughed, and told him he must ask the boss about that. **1873** BEADLE *Undevel. West* 718 Every 'boss' has his own particular mark cut in the bark. **1884** 'MARK TWAIN' *H. Finn* vi, He said he would show who was Huck Finn's boss. **1891** 'THANET' *Otto the Knight*, etc. 18 By and by come the big strike over the boss taking on some non-union men. **1920** HUNTER *Trail Drivers of Texas* I. 298 In a cattle outfit the owner is called the 'big boss.'

transf. **1850** *N.Y. Herald* 24 May (B.), Rothschild is the real Pope and boss of all Europe.

2. As a term of address.

Often used in addressing a superior. In quots. freq. applied to a stranger. 'The blacks often employ it in addressing white men in the Northern States' (B. '77).

1839 C. F. BRIGGS *H. Franco* I. 31 'Why don't you get in, boss?' said one of the men on the dock. **1862** [BROWNE] *A. Ward his Book* 199 'Yes, boss,' he replied, 'an' I wish 'em honorable graves!' **1875** *Chicago Tribune* 3 Dec. 3/4 Boss, does you want some one to husk corn? **1880** 'MARK TWAIN' *Tramp Abroad* xxiii. 225 Why, boss, he's ben the pizenest kind of a Free-will Baptis' for forty year. **1888** *Amer. Humorist* (F.), 'Didn't I rent you the land for a third of the crop?' 'Yes, boss,' said the man. **1891** 'THANET' *Otto the Knight*, etc. 328 That's my chile! Take him 'way, boss!

3. The manager or dictator of a political organization.

1875 HOLLAND *Sevenoaks* 103 The custom which makes . . . 'bosses' of men who control election gangs. **1875** *Chicago Tribune* 9 Nov. 4/6 The overthrow of the 'Bosses' in the late elections in New York, Brooklyn, and Chicago. **1878** *N. Amer. Rev.* Aug. 12 An oligarchy might set up itself; but it would be one made up of the 'boss,' the 'railroad king,' and the bonanza Croesus. **1881** *Harper's Mag.* May 819/2 Athens saw the rise of 'bosses' and 'henchmen' in her degenerate days. **1888** LOWELL *Political Essays* 304 Could we only have a travelling exhibition of our Bosses, and say to the American people, 'Behold the shapers of your national destiny!' **1895** CHAMBLISS *Diary* 235 Owing to the disreputable character of the 'bosses' who put them up for election, they stand no show of ever being re-elected. **1906** *Springfield W. Republican* 22 Feb. 5 The democratic Ohio Senate intends to 'Lexow' Cincinnati, so long under the control of the republican boss. **1911** H. S. HARRISON *Queed* 320 Of the boss's sincerity he never entertained a doubt.

4. *attrib.* **a.** Of persons: Chief or master; holding a high place or rank in any line of work or action.

1836 in Commons, etc. *Doc. Hist.* IV. 287, I am a boss shoemaker. **1837** J. C. NEAL *Charcoal Sk.* (1838) 137 It isn't saying much for your boss politicianer that he chose you. **1840** J. P. KENNEDY *Quodlibet* 221 Charley Moggs, long known as the boss loafer of Bickerbray. **1843** [STEPHENS] *High Life N.Y.* II. 1 All the boss milliners in York got into a tantrum and kicked up . . . a darned rumpus. **1853** *Knickerb.* XLII. 632 The orchestra consisted of three fiddlers; an old gentleman, boss-fiddler, and two younger fiddlers. **1859** BARTLETT 44 Hence we hear of a *boss*-carpenter, a *boss*-bricklayer, a *boss*-shoemaker, etc., instead of master-carpenter, etc. **1861** F. Moore *Rebellion Rec.* I. III. 21 The first application was made to the 'boss laborer' who informed them that his department was full at present. **1880** 'MARK TWAIN' *Tramp Abroad* xxvi. 263 Old boss sign-painters, who flourished before the decadence of art. **1902** [G. H. LORIMER] *Lett. from Merchant* 263 So I called over the boss painter and between us we cooked up a nice little ad.

b. Of things: Of the best kind; first-class; supreme.

1867 *Iowa Agric. Soc. Rep.* (1868) 129 If all are fed together, the 'boss' cattle fill themselves. **1880** *Harper's Mag.* March 552/2 He returned, and said that he 'had a boss time.' **1883** J. HAY *Bread-Winners* 270, I've been at the variety show, and it was the boss-fraud of the season. **1884** SWEET & KNOX *Through Texas* 102 It was a boss sight to see how mad that old mud-cat was. **1886** *Outing* Dec. 198/1 He war makin' boss time, too, when he seen a slim figger away ahead uv him. **1897** WISTER *Lin McLean* 127 We'll show you the boss place [=restaurant] in Market Street. *Ib.* 128 [The place] was not boss, precisely.

Boss, *n.*[2] [Cf. E. dial. (s.w.) *boss, buss* calf. Cf. BOSSY *n.*] **1.** (See quot. 1848.) **2.** A word used in calling or soothing a cow. — (1) **1846** SAGE *Scenes Rocky Mts.* iii, 'Come, boss!—Poor boss!—bossy, bossy!' addressing the buffalo, which commenced advancing. **1848** BARTLETT 44 *Boss* (Lat. *bos*), among the hunters of the prairies, a name for the buffalo. (2) **1874** *Vt. Bd. Agric. Rep.* II. 706 So-o-o boss! There, you've kicked it over—All that milk, now, I declare! **1901** HEMPL in *Nation* 18 April 314/2 The call 'Co' boss' is familiar to most of the inhabitants of our Northern States and Canada.

***Boss,** *n.*[3] +The hump of a buffalo. — **1846** SAGE *Scenes Rocky Mts.* v, The operator then commenced his labors by gathering the long hair of the '*boss*,' and severing a piece obliquely at the junction of the neck and shoulders. **1848** RUXTON *Far West* iii. 111 Gathering the long hair of the boss in one hand, the skin was separated from the shoulder.

+**Boss,** *v.* [Boss *n.*[1]] *tr.* To manage, control, direct. Also with *it:* To be in command, to exercise authority.

1856 [M. THOMPSON] *Plu-ri-bus-tah* 222 He 'bossed' a splendid 'ked'n'-try.' **1856** *Nat. Intelligencer* 3 Nov. (B.), The little fellow that sits up in the pulpit and kinder bosses it over the crowd gin us a talk. **1867** LOWELL *Fitz Adam's Story* xx, 'Sence I have bossed the business here,' says he, 'No fairer load was ever seen by me.' **1873** 'MARK TWAIN' & WARNER *Gilded Age* viii, [To] buy up all the growing crops and just boss the market when they mature. **1877** *Harper's Mag.* Dec. 60/1 She always wants to boss us too much. **1883** 'MARK TWAIN' *Life on Miss.* xxviii, They conceive that they can fetter and handcuff that river and boss him. **1897** FLANDRAU *Harvard Episodes* 124 It amused Wolcott every now and then to have Haydock 'boss' him. **1903** A. ADAMS *Log Cowboy* 11 Robert himself was to boss a herd up the trail. **1907** M. C. HARRIS *Tents of Wickedness* I. 74 There she has her fill of bossing it over the workmen's families.

+**Bossdom.** [Boss *n.*[1] 3.] The position or influence of a political boss; the control of politics by bosses. — **1888** BRYCE *Amer. Commonwealth* II. lxiii. 462 The extinction of the Boss himself and of bossdom. **1894** *Citizen* (Albion, Mich.) 293 It is not healthy for a party, if the few are allowed to do all and say all. That way Rings and Bossdom lie.

+**Bossism.** [Boss *n.*[1] 3.] The system of political control by bosses.

1881 *Scribner's Mo.* Aug. 626/1 The event shows, also, that the days of 'bossism' are closing. **1882** *Nation* 16 Nov. 414/2 He regarded the result of the elections as a complete and final overthrow of 'bossism.' **1890** *Harper's Mag.* Nov. 925/1 Political 'bossism' would be a deadly calling here [=Switzerland]. **1893** *Congress. Rec.* 3 Feb. 1144/2 No party leader could have been freer [than Senator Barbour] from just imputation of attempting bossism.

+**Boss(e)loper.** *Obs.* [?Du. *boschlooper.* Cf. BUSHLOPER.] ?A settler in the woods. — **1687** *Doc. Hist. N.Y. State* (1849) I. 254 The Governour of Canida sent for all the Bosslopers that were at Ottawawa. **1690** *N.Y Hist. Soc. Coll.* II. 175 Four hundred men were gone from Quebek under command of Mons. Pirneusse, and Monsieur Courtimanche, being all Bosse-lopers Inhabitants and Indians. **1691** *Mass. Bay Currency Tracts* 26 Had they not gone with the Fleet to Canada, a thousand Boss-Lopers had been upon our Country Towns and laid them waste.

+**Boss rule.** [Boss *n.*[1] 3.] Political rule by party bosses. — **1882** *Nation* 6 July 4/2 The platform contains a protest against the spoils system of politics and the boss-rule of party. **1886** ROOSEVELT in *Century Mag.* Nov. 75/1 In New York, as well as in most of our other great cities, the conditions favor the growth of ring or boss rule. **1888** M. LANE in *America* 20 Sept. 15 *Boss-Rule*, signifies a political authority that rules the party. It is said to have been first applied by Wayne McVeigh and used in political speeches in Chicago.

+**Boss-ship.** [Boss *n.*[1] 3.] The position or domination of a boss, especially in politics. — **1882** *Nation* 2 Nov. 371/3 The gross and wholesale prostitution of the service . . . to enable Mahone to build up a new and repudiating boss-ship in Virginia. **1889** 'MARK TWAIN' *Conn. Yankee* xiii. 160 The thing that would have best suited . . . my nature would have been to resign the Boss-ship and get up an insurrection. **1894** *Voice* (N.Y.) 6 Sept., It was thought to be an auspicious time to shake off the 'boss-ship' exercised by Mr. Platt for many years. **1904** *N.Y. Ev. Post.* 16 Dec. 6 [To] make the time ripe for a party to revolt against a hideous boss-ship.

Bossy, *n.* [Eng. dial. (s.-w.), dim. of *boss*. Cf. Boss *n.*[2]]

1. A calf or cow; the call used to one of these. Also attrib. with *calf.*

1843 [STEPHENS] *High Life N.Y.* II. 181 She only bust out in a new spot; and, like a great bossy calf, I had to jine in agin. **1848** BARTLETT 44 *Bossy*, a familiar name applied to a calf. **1863** 'G. HAMILTON' *Gala-Days* 95 Bossy starts from the post, tail up, in a hand gallop. **1907** *N.Y. Ev. Post* 25 Feb. 3 He . . . will go out to interview a bossy who has eaten her last wisp of hay. **1911** H. QUICK *Yellowstone N.* xii. 314 Nothin' but actual experience can impart any remote approach to a notion o' what it means to incorporate the fruit of the nest [=eggs] with the bossy.

2. (See Boss *n.*[2] 1, quot. 1846.)

+**Bossy,** *a.* [Boss *n.*[1]] Inclined to boss, to manage, or to dictate.

1882 *Harper's Mag.* Dec. 108/1 There was a lady manager who was dreadfully bossy. **1900** E. A. DIX *Deacon Bradbury* 44 Wasn't she horrid and bossy this morning, trying to make us all just pack that box her own way? **1911** J. C. LINCOLN *Cap'n Warren's Wards* 124 If I'd known you war callin' Caroline, I shouldn't have been quite so bossy.

Bost, *v.* [Eng. *boast* (1823–), of uncertain origin.] *tr.* To hew roughly. — **1808** *Ann. 10th Congress* 1 Sess. II. 2750 Of the 24 Corinthian columns . . . fourteen are only rough-hewn or bosted.

Boston.

+**1.** The name of the capital of Massachusetts, used attrib. to designate things belonging to, characteristic of, or associated with, that city. Cf. BOSTONIAN *a.*

For terms with specific meanings, or in distinctive use, see BOSTON BEANS, BROWN BREAD, etc.

1697 *Conn. Probate Rec.* I. 551 To my daughter Hannah my warming pan and my Boston Kettle. **1788** FRANKLIN *Let. to Lathrop* 31 May, The Boston manner, turn of phrase, and even tone of voice, and accent in pronunciation, all please, and seem to refresh and revive me. **1850** G. HINES *Voyage* 167 Their dresses were an imitation of the Boston fashions. **1862** 'E. KIRKE' *Among Pines* 166 The vehicle . . . was mounted on wheels that had probably served their time on a Boston dray. **1868** MRS. WHITNEY *P. Strong* 124 People who go [to Boston] every day or two keep 'Boston bonnets' of a meaner sort. **1886** *Harper's Mag.* Nov. 946/1 What is the Boston philosophy? Why, it is not to care about anything you do care about. **1901** CHURCHILL *Crisis* 151 Graven on his face was what is called the 'Boston scorn.'

2. A card game, somewhat resembling whist.

'A game of cards was invented in Versailles, and called in honour of the town, *Boston*' (1821 W. Tudor *Lett. E. States* 364 *n.*). 'Said to be so called from Boston, Mass., and to have been invented by officers of the French army in America during the time of the Revolutionary war' (W. '79).

1821 W. TUDOR *Lett. E. States* 364 *Boston* . . . was composed partly of whist, and partly of quadrille, though partaking most of the former. As it is almost unknown in this country [etc.]. **1873** *Winfield* (Kansas) *Courier* 15 Feb. 1/4 Dozens of over-worked city officials would spend the whole summer . . . skinning each other at poker. Some times the inferior game of 'Boston' was resorted to. [**1879** *Mag. Amer. Hist.* III. 762 The Boston Club of New Orleans was named after this game, and is one of the oldest social clubs in that city.]

+**3.** A former designation among the natives of Oregon and Alaska of a white inhabitant of the U.S. Freq. pl. Also attrib. (Cf. BOSTONIAN *n.* 2.)

'Perhaps the term originated at the time when Massachusetts sent her enterprising sons—mostly from Boston—on trading voyages to the Northwest coast' (De Vere).

1844 LEE & FROST *Oregon* 148 He boasted that the 'Bostons,' as he termed us, 'should never make him good.' **1870** *Overland Mo.* March 204 (De Vere), We marched out into the Indian country, trusting that although the savages were at war with the Bostons [etc.]. **1885** *Century Mag.* April 834 'Boston man' was the Chinook term for all Americans,—Englishmen and Canadians being called 'King George men.' **1887** *North Star* (Sitka) Dec. 3/3 The people of the United States are known among the natives of Alaska as 'Boston people.'

+**4.** Bostonese; learned talk.

1861 *Harper's Mag.* May 726/1 In short — to use the phrase of an envious and gibing New Yorker — 'we talked Bosting' enough in an hour to have lasted reasonable people a month.

+**5.** A kind of waltz.

1885 [see BOSTON DIP]. **1887** *Courier-Journal* (Louisville) 8 May 12/8 The young English baron . . . [was] dancing the Boston with Miss Bazaine. **1911** HARRISON *Queed* 108 She could make even 'the Boston' look graceful. **1913** E. SCOTT *All about the Boston* 24 The term 'Boston' is applied to the kind of movement that in its best and most graceful form would be far more consistently described as Rectilineal or Diagonal waltzing.

+**Boston (baked) beans.** Navy beans cooked with pork and molasses.

1876 M. F. HENDERSON *Cooking* 162 [Recipe for] Boston Baked Beans. **1882** MRS. OWENS *Cook Book* 108–9. **1902** E. L. BANKS *Newspaper Girl* 166 Your Boston beans done in an earthen pot with the middle-piece-pork just rightly browned. **1903** *N.Y. Ev. Sun* 7 Nov. 4 Has the shipping to England of 500 pots of Boston baked beans anything to do with the recent visit of the Honourables of London? **1904** *Omaha Bee* 16 Aug. 4 The maker of Boston baked bean pots is dead, but the fame of the Boston baked bean is perpetual.

+**Boston brown bread.** Bread made by long steaming from corn meal, rye, wheat, etc., molasses and other ingredients. — **1856** *Rep. Comm. Patents: Agric.* 163 The 'Boston Brown Bread' contains two parts of corn to one of rye-meal, by measurement. **1877** BARTLETT 70 *Brown-bread,* bread made of rye meal and Indian meal (maize) baked very slowly in an iron vessel. Much used in New England, hence, in other States, it is generally called Boston Brown Bread. **1879** F. M. ROE *Army Lett.* 231 A few days before Faye went to the mill I made some Boston brown bread. **1894** RICHARDS & TALBOT *Food in Student Life* 17/1, 12 loaves Boston brown bread, 77 [cents].

+**Boston chaise, cloak, coat, coffee.** (See quotations.) — **1890** *Harper's Mag.* Oct. 718/1 That two-wheeled vehicle known as a Boston 'chaise.' — **1836** T. POWER *Impressions* I. 190 Each [was] carrying a small valise, a carpet-bag, [and] a long Boston coat or cloak. — **1830** N. A[MES] *Mariner's Sk.* 132 She [=a boat] was supplied with . . . a keg of molasses, another of 'Boston particular,' 'lacking six days of being a week old' and a quantity of Boston coffee, videlicet rye.

+**Boston chip.** A kind of shingle. — **1813** *Ann. 12th Congress* 2 Sess. 1118 On shingles, called *Boston chips,* not more than 12 inches in length, per thousand, £ 0 3 4.

+**Boston cracker.** A kind of hard biscuit made in Boston.

1818 FEARON *Sketches of A.* 44 In the evening . . . the table is filled with cheese, biscuits (called Boston crackers,) molasses, and slices of raw dried beef. **1845** *Knickerb.* XXVI. 182 He bought three lobsters and as many Boston 'crackers,' with which he returned to the sloop. **1860** S. N. CARVALHO *Travels & Adv.* 32, I . . . could not get anything to eat except some Boston crackers. **1868** W. BAKER *New Timothy* (1870) 14 Long tables lined with students . . . eating Boston crackers. **1886** *Delineator* Nov. 389 Add three soda biscuits or three Boston crackers rolled very fine and sifted.

+**Boston dip.** In dancing (see quotation). — **1885** DODWORTH *Dancing* 73 *Boston.* . . . When stepping with the right foot, the left knee is slightly bent, producing the dip, from which the name Boston Dip was derived.

+**Bostoner.** ?*Obs.* An inhabitant of Boston. — **1758** *Micmakis & Maricheets* 65 On condition of the Bostoners returning to Petitpas. **1765** OTIS *Vindication of British Colonies* iv, The Sentiments even of the most seditious Part of the Bostoners themselves.

+**Bostonese. 1.** Inhabitants of Boston. **2.** The mode of speech regarded as characteristic of the people of Boston. — **(1) 1888** *N.Y. Herald* 29 July 7/6 There were a number of people present at a lawn party, principally Bostonese. **(2) 1889** FARMER 79/2 Bostonese . . . is a method of speech or manners supposed to be specially affected by the residents of that city. **1892** HOWELLS in *Harper's Mag.* Jan. 250/2 I speak Bostonese, at present.

Bostonian, *n.* [*Boston,* Mass.]

+**1.** An inhabitant or native of Boston.

1682 J. W. *Lett. from New-Eng.* 7 In short, Sir, these Bostonians enrich themselves by the ruine of Strangers. **1702** C. MATHER *Magnalia* (1852) I. 102 Yet it may be said of the Bostonians, as it was of the Macedonians [etc.]. **1775** J. ADAMS *Fam. Lett. to Wife* (1875) 59 Poor Bostonians! My heart bleeds for them day and night. God preserve and bless them! **1778** S. CURWEN *Journal & Lett.* 205 The Bostonians are said to be out of humor with their new friends and allies [the French], and no wonder. **1794** J. DRAYTON *Letters* 92 With such heavy taxes as the Bostonians labour under, much more might be done for their convenience. **1815** *N. Amer. Rev.* II. 77 The Bostonians will regret that he should have said nothing of their beautiful environs. **1817** *Ib.* V. 316 It is too brackish even for the palate of a Bostonian. **1856** P. CARTWRIGHT *Autobiog.* 478, I found the Bostonians to be a liberal people. **1865** *Nation* I. 12 The erudition of the members does not bristle out like that of Bostonians. **1897** FLANDRAU *Harvard Episodes* 18 You are not a Bostonian. . . . When I say 'a Bostonian,' . . . I mean of course a Bostonian that one knows.

+**2.** A term formerly applied by the French and Indians to all Americans, and particularly to those of New England.

1787 E. DENNY *Journal* 106 Five of the Indian chiefs each made a reply . . . , expressing their gladness at being taken by the hand by their fathers the Bostonians. **1799** *Mass. H. S. Coll.* VI. 150 In the years 1775 and 1776, the French . . . called all the inhabitants belonging to the then thirteen revolted colonies, by the general name of *Bostonians.* **1820** W. TUDOR *Lett. E. States* 307 Americans were then, in France, often called *Bostonians,* the term by which they are designated in Canada to this day.

Bostonian, *a.* +Pertaining to Boston, Massachusetts.

1698 C. MATHER (*title*), The Bostonian Ebenezer. Some Historical Remarks on the state of Boston. **1781** PETERS *Hist. Conn.* (1829) 202 This [regulation] gives the New-York and Bostonian merchants an opportunity of taking out the best part of the Connecticut pork. **1794** HUMPHREYS *Industry* 15 Where Bostonian maids, with songs, prepare The canvass wings to wanton wide in air. **1881** *Harper's Mag.* April 648/2 She uttered 'culture' with the sibilant Bostonian twang.

+**Bostonianism.** [f. prec.] Features or traits characteristic of Boston. — **1845** W. I. PAULDING *Noble Exile* 107 When we get abroad in Europe, we are ready enough to copy: not but that we do mingle a little Bostonianism in every style we assume. **1881** *Harper's Mag.* April 712/2 A third [house or shop-front in Milwaukee] adopts a peculiar bit of Bostonianism.

+**Bostonism.** =prec. — **1881** *Harper's Mag.* Feb. 381/2 There is such a thing as New York Bostonism.

+**Bostonite.** An inhabitant or native of Boston. — **1848** *Knickerb.* XXXI. 175 Part of his cargo was living pork for the Bostonites. **1884** *Boston Journal* 12 Sept., Wuston is the Iroquis name for Boston, and Wustonaka or Bostonites represents to these Indians the whole American people, since Boston was in the early days the rallying place of Americans.

+**Bostonized,** *ppl. a.* Rendered like Boston, Massachusetts, or its inhabitants.

1679 *N.C. Col. Rec.* I. 245 The rest of His Majesty's people so trading must become Bostoniz'd or relinquish dealing. **1825** *Boston Mo. Mag.* I. 145 In plain language, my outward man was not quite *Bostonized.* **1882** *Boston Ev. Transcript* 18 Jan. 2 To show how the villages of the Massachusetts sea coast were being 'Bostonized.'

+**Boston money.** *Obs.* Money of the standard current at Boston.

1679 *East-Hampton Rec.* II. 87 In consideration of the sume of five pounds in boston monney to mee in hand paid. **1683** *Penna. Col. Rec.* I. 85 The Gov[erno]r telleth Ch. Pickering & Sam[ue]ll Buckley of their abuse to the Governm[en]t in quining of Spanish Bitts and Boston money. **1833** *Niles' Reg.* XLIV. 316/2 A piece of British cotton shirting, bought

. . . in the autumn of 1813, at eighty-five cents per yard, cash, (Boston money or specie).

+**Boston news.** Out-of-date or stale news. — **1846** *Spirit of Times* 16 May 138/2 Preserving the freshness, novelty, and interest of the subject, which by age . . . may be deprived of its interest, and rank among 'Boston news' to you.

+**Boston notions.** (See NOTION and cf. *Yankee notions.*) — **1889** FARMER 80/1 *Boston Notions* . . . is a well-known expression and dates back many years. It was used during the last century, and even at that time had become proverbial.

+**Boston particular.** *Obs.* [Cf. PARTICULAR *n.*] A blend of alcoholic liquor. — **1830** N. A[MES] *Mariner's Sk.* 132 The boat was supplied with a keg of molasses, another of 'Boston particular,' lacking six days of being a week old.

+**Boston pine.** A variety of cultivated strawberry. — **1852** *Horticulturist* 352 Boston Pine has done nobly this season. **1853** FOWLER *Home for All* 140 The Boston Pine is another excellent kind—large, rich, and prolific. **1862** *Rep. Comm. Patents: Agric.* 186 For medium season: Brighton Pine, Boston Pine [etc.].

+**Boston shilling.** *Obs.* The Bay shilling (q.v.). — **1704** S. KNIGHT *Journal* 42 Mony is pieces of Eight, Ryalls, or Boston or Bay shillings (as they [=people of Conn.] call them).

+**Boston truck.** *Obs.* (See quotation.) — **1860** E. EVERETT *Mt. Vernon Papers* iii. 24 The Boston truck is constructed of two parallel shafts, hewn from the best of oak.

+**Boston white.** A variety of potato. — **1856** *Rep. Comm. Patents: Agric.* 221 The 'Boston Whites' are . . . early, good flavored, and yield well.

Botanic, *a.* {1656–}

1. =BOTANICAL *a.* 1. {1789 (E. Darwin)}

1814 *Niles' Reg.* VI. 152/2 To Columbia College, [is granted] a tract of land in the city of New York, known by the name of the Botanick Garden. **1815** *Trans. Lit. & Phil. Soc. N.Y.* I. 81 The first institution in the United States established as a repository of the native vegetable productions of this country . . . was the Elgin Botanic Garden, founded in 1801. **1829** S. CUMINGS *Western Pilot* 45 They had even the luxury of a botanic garden, and a green house. **1855** *Harvard Mag.* I. 232 Specimens may be seen in flower at the Botanic Garden.

2. =BOTANICAL *a.* 3. *Obs.*

1835 *Stimpson's Boston Directory* 17 (*advt.*), Mass. Botanic Infirmary, or Thomsonian Hospital—for the reception of the sick and the lame. **1877** BARTLETT 702 *Thomsonian System,* a peculiar treatment of diseases, so named from its inventor, Samuel Thomson, a native of . . . New Hampshire. . . . His followers have discarded much that he adopted, and are now known as Eclectic or Botanic physicians.

Botanical, *a.* {1658–}

1. *Botanical garden,* a garden in which plants are grown for use in the study of botany. {1797–}

1785 WASHINGTON *Diaries* II. 407, I began to make good the missing spaces of what was sowed in my small or Botanical Garden. **1872** *Atlantic Mo.* Jan. 18 William Bartram . . . [founded] on the banks of the Schuylkill the first botanical garden of America. **1884** *Century Mag.* XXVII. 654/1 The dark past of the ante-bellum period, when slaves were herded in pens on the grounds now used as a botanical garden at the foot of the Capitol.

2. Prepared from medicinal plants.

1796 R. THOMAS in *Ga. H. S. Coll.* IX. 448 Dr. Brodum's botanical syrup & nervous cordial, at £1.2.

3. Using plants or herbs in medicine.

1836 M. A. HOLLEY *Texas* v. 89 Where every man, in time of sickness, becomes a 'botanical quack and steam doctor.' **1849** [CHAMBERLAIN] *Indiana Gazetteer* 374 There are . . . five botanical and 12 other physicians.

Botanist. {1682–} An herb doctor. — **1860** MRS. S. COWELL *Diary* 4 Frame houses, with odd signs,—such as 'Groceries, flour, and feed,' 'Botanist and horse doctor.'

Botfly. One or other of the insects whose eggs produce bots or maggots in living animals. {1819–} — **1869** *Amer. Naturalist* II. 595 The Bot-fly of the horse . . . is pale yellowish, spotted with red. **1913** W. C. BARNES *Western Grazing Grounds* 323 Heel flies . . . do an immense amount of damage to cattle, both domestic and range, every year. They are also locally known as 'bot' flies and 'warble flies.'

***Bots, Botts,** *n. pl.* [Plural of *bot* maggot. Cf. BOT-FLY.] An ailment in horses, cattle, and sheep, caused by the maggots of botflies. Also transf.

(*a*) **1788** CUTLER in *Life & Corr.* I. 433, I rather thought the symptoms were those of bots. **1856** *Spirit of Times* (N.Y.) 6 Dec. 230/2 An inquiry is made of Dr. Holmes the editor of the 'Maine Farmer,' about destroying bots in horses. **1884** NYE *Baled Hay* 198 A scientific work upon 'The Rise and Fall of Botts in America.'

(*b*) **1829** Mackenzie *Life Van Buren* (1846) 210, I've got the bots, . . . halt and founders; and I assure you if I can only keep my own leggs, I shall do well. **1838** *Lexington Observer & Rep.* 2 June, An old woman died of the bots or sum such disease. **1866** [C. H. SMITH] *Bill Arp* 68 He wants a lot of tallow-faced gentlemen who've got the gout, or the blind-piles . . . or the botts.

Bottle-brush grass. A species of grass, *Hystrix* (*Elymus,* or *Gymnostichum*) *hystrix,* so called from the shape of its flowering spikes. — **1843** TORREY *Flora N.Y.* II. 478 Bottle-brush Grass. . . . Moist, rocky woods, and along shady ravines: not rare. *Fl.* July. **1857** GRAY *Botany* 571 Bottle-Brush Grass . . . [grows in] moist woodlands; rather common. July. **1878** KILLIBREW *Tennessee Grasses* 223 Bottle-brush grass . . . [makes] good forage. **1901** MOHR *Plant Life Ala.* 389 Bottle Brush Grass, . . . grows from New England to Nebraska, south to Florida and Texas.

+**Bottle fly.** A bluebottle, bluefly. — **1849** HOLMES *Stethoscope Song* iii, The first was a bottle fly, big and blue. **1852** J. BOND *Minnesota* 262 The sun was very hot, huge bottle-flies and gnats very bad, and our horses most used up. **1872** MORRELL *Flowers & Fruits* 382 The bottle fly very much resembles the buffalo gnat of Texas and other southern States.

+**Bottle gourd.** The common gourd, *Lagenaria vulgaris.* — **1847** DARLINGTON *Weeds & Plants* 138 Common Lagenaria. Calabash. Bottle Gourd. . . . Whole plant somewhat viscid, and emitting a fetid musky odor. **1863** GRAY *Botany* p. liii, Bottle Gourd is well marked by its large white flowers on long peduncles, and its hard-rinded fruit of diverse shapes, used for bottles, dippers, &c. **1901** MOHR *Plant Life Ala.* 831 Bottle gourd . . . [grows in] Louisianian area.

+**Bottle grass.** A variety of foxtail grass (see quotations).

1840 DEWEY *Mass. Flowering Plants* 244 *Setaria.* Bottle Grass. . . . Four species of the grass, *viridis, glauca, Italica, verticillata* . . . are pretty common. . . . *S. viridis,* is found in the vicinity of Boston. **1847** WOOD *Botany* 607 *S*[*etaria*] *Glauca,* Bottle Grass. . . . Fields and roadsides, N. Eng. to Ohio. **1863** *Ill. Agric. Soc. Trans.* V. (1865) 867 *Setaria viridis,* Green Fox-tail or Bottle-grass, is from the South of Europe.

Bottlehead. {1654–} +The black-bellied plover, *Squatarola helvetica.* — **1877** BARTLETT 777 Bottle-Head . . . [is] also called 'beetlehead' and 'green head.'

Bottlenose. {1668–} +A river fish having a bottle-shaped nose. — **1805** LEWIS in *L. & Clark Exped.* (1904) II. 304 A species of scale fish of a white colour and a remarkable small long mouth which one of our men inform us are the same with the species called in the Eastern states *bottlenose.* **1805** CLARK *Ib.* 306 Some fish, trout & bottle nose.

+**Bottle stopper.** (See quotation.) — **1875** *Amer. Naturalist* IX. 143 The singular fistulous-stemmed species *Eriogonum inflatum* . . . from the peculiar bulging appearance of its main stalk and upper branches . . . has received the fanciful popular name of 'bottle stoppers.'

Bottling works. A place where beverages are bottled. — **1883** *Century Mag.* Oct. 957/1 The beer-sellers have been openly retailing their wares without license under the sign of 'Bottling Works.'

***Bottom,** *n.*

***1.** A stretch of low-lying land, usually along a river or other stream. (Cf. RIVER-BOTTOM.) {–1732; now *dial.*}

'The intervals or what the people of this country call bottoms, are from one half to three quarters of a mile wide' (**1788** Imlay *Western Territory* (1797) 595). 'The term "bottom" is used throughout the west to denote the alluvial soil on the margin of rivers' (**1834** Peck *Gaz. Illinois* 4).

1634 *Boston Rec.* IV. 9 The hedgey ground that lies in the bottom betwixt his house and the water. **1666** *Springfield Rec.* I. 341 Forty acres of Land granted him in a low Peice of ground or Bottom havinge a brooke run thorow it. **1700** *Providence* (R.I.) *Rec.* IV. 141 The other 3 acres . . . is a Bottom betweene two hills of Rocks. **1750** GIST *Journals* 34 The Land from Shannopin's Town is good along the River, but the Bottoms [are] not broad. **1807** GASS *Journal* 31 Our camp is in a wide bottom, in which are large elm and oak trees. **1845** *Indiana Mag. Hist.* XXIII. 11 The rich, fresh bottoms yielded such amounts of corn as the natives of older and poorer parts of the Union would have been astonished to see. **1877** JOHNSON *Anderson Co., Kansas* 131 On the first of June the rain had been so heavy that the North Pottowatomie overflowed its banks and bottoms. **1885** M. THOMPSON *Byways & Bird Notes* 162 Along the Wabash river, in the broad, wooded 'bottoms,' I have heard it [=Wilson thrush] singing long after sunset. **1891** *Century Mag.* March 650 Terrorized ranchmen . . . endeavored to till a few acres of barley or corn in the bottoms . . . with cocked revolvers on hip. **1907** MULFORD *Bar-20* 200 They crawled to the last line of brush and looked out over an extensive bottom.

+**b.** *First, second, third bottom:* (see quotations).

1788 *Let.* in Imlay *Western Territory* (1797) 595 Next to these are what is called second bottoms, which are elevated plains, and gentle risings of the richest uplands, and as free from stone as the low or first bottom. **1792** *Cincinnati Misc.* 51, I hear that the people of Cincinnati are voting on this question—whether the jail shall be built on the first bottom or the second bank? **1803** LEWIS in *Journals of L. & Ordway* 34 What is called the third bottom is more properly the high benches of the large range of hills. **1804** CLARK in *Lewis & C. Exped.* (1904) I. 54 The . . . Lands on each Side of the river . . . may be classed as follows, viz.: the low or overflown points or bottom land, . . . the 2nd or high bottom of rich furtile Soile, . . . the third or high Lands. **1808** F. CUMING *Western Tour* 377 When wide they [=benches] constitute what are called bottoms, as first, second and third bottom counting from the river upwards.

c. =BOTTOM LAND 1.

1835 HOFFMAN *Winter in West* II. 105 The increased windings of the stream, with its picturesque alternations of 'bluff' and 'bottom.' **1838** FLAGG *Far West* I. 83 Her 'man' was proprietor of some thousands of acres of 'bottom' in the vicinity. **1875** *Chicago Tribune* 11 Sept. 2/5 The grant [of land to the Santa Fe line] comprised about 3,000,000 acres, more than one-third of which is river valley land, or what is generally designated as 'bottom.' **1879** TOURGEE *Fool's Errand* 47 The rest . . .

is very well fitted to cut up into little farms . . . for colored men, giving them . . . a piece of good bottom to cultivate.

d. Attrib. with *brook, country, farmer*, etc. Also BOTTOM GROUND, LAND, etc.

1784 CUTLER in *Mem. Academy* I. 436 Water Dock [grows] in muddy bottom brooks. **1804** CLARK in *Lewis & C. Exped.* (1904) I. 49 Next to the river is an ellegent bottom Plain which extends several miles in length. **1818** MELISH *Trav. U.S.* 485 To the south along the creek are handsome rich bottom lots. **1844** *Cincinnati Misc.* 5 This statement . . . would not give an adequate idea how far the brow of the hill overhung the bottom region. **1855** *Knickerb.* Feb. 190 The clearing was a large bottom-tract. **1862** 'E. KIRKE' *Among Pines* 211 We had passed through a dense forest of pines, but were emerging into a 'bottom country.' **1872** W. J. FLAGG *Good Investment* iv. 221/2 The bottom farmers is got a'most all their land into hay since the war begun. **1883** SMITH *Geol. Survey Ala.* 249 The bottom soils of this region vary with the surrounding uplands. **1885** *Century Mag.* April 845 He . . . got tired . . . of sputin about water-gaps, and stock a-breakin' in bottom fields. **1897** BRODHEAD *Bound in Shallows* 17, I never mix with the bottom people. . . . And the hill folks—oh!

***2.** A ship or vessel, usually with designation of nationality.

1658 *Suffolk Deeds* III. 133 The ship Oaketree . . . arriving in the Port of Boston . . . [is] a flemish bottom. **1696** *Cal. Virginia State P.* I. 51 In the Collony of Virginia, by virtue of the said Act, . . . he hath power to enter into any Ship, Bottome, Boat or other Vessell. **1787** JEFFERSON *Writings* VI. 409 Nor is the idea unpleasing . . . of naturalizing American bottoms, and American citizens in France. **1792** *Ann. 2nd Congress* 694 It may be proper to impose a small additional duty of tonnage on every American bottom, perhaps one cent per ton. **1842** *Diplom. Corr. Texas* (1908) I. 620 Commerce and merchandise is carried in American bottoms from American ports. **1883** *American* VII. 162 We have abolished all the discriminating duties against goods imported in foreign bottoms.

3. The seat of a chair. {1885} Also attrib.

1790 *Penna. Packet* 1 Jan. 1/2 John Mason, Upholsterer, . . . has for sale and makes Sacking Bottoms of the best kind. **1838** HALIBURTON *Clockmaker* 2 Ser. 265 'A foundationalist, . . . what is that?' . . . 'It's a bottom maker. He only made bottoms, he didn't make arm and legs.'

+**4.** The foundation on which a state of things, financial scheme, etc., rests. In phrases denoting the failure or destruction of this.

1867 *Iowa Agric. Soc. Rep.* 64 The bottom has at length dropped out of this humbug. **1872** 'MARK TWAIN' *Roughing It* lviii. 420 What a gambling carnival it was! . . . And then—all of a sudden, out went the bottom and everything and everybody went to ruin and destruction! **1879** TOURGEE *Fool's Errand* 279 The bottom has fallen out at last! **1883** *Harper's Mag.* May 816/2 The 'bottom had dropped out' of the famous 'Comstocks.' **1884** *Boston Journal* 1 Nov. 12/3 'What, betting on election?' said a well-known bookmaker to-day. . . . 'Why, the bottom has fallen out of it.' **1888** *Cleveland Leader* (F.), The declination of Mr. Blaine has knocked the bottom out of Mugwumpery. **1902** LORIMER *Lett. Merchant* 178 A cigarette and a pint of champagne knock the bottom out of a million-dollar pork corner.

+**5.** The lowest point or figure. Also attrib. with *figure, price*, etc.

1868–9 *Ill. Agric. Soc. Trans.* VII. 433 Hogs touched bottom, or the lowest point during the summer of 1868. **1875** *Chicago Tribune* 19 Nov. 5/7 Advt., Underwear at Bottom Prices. *Ib.* 1 Dec. 1/2 We shall and must succeed if Bottom Notch Prices Will Do It. **1895** *N.Y. Dramatic News* 14 Dec. 5/3, I don't know whether the limit has been reached in 'bottom prices' yet. **1898** WESTCOTT *D. Harum* 353 There came a day when it [*i.e.* the price of pork] . . . 'looked like going lower' than ever (as such things usually do when the 'bottom' is pretty nearly reached). **1902** WISTER *Virginian* xxv. 291 'No, sir,' mumbled Shorty. . . . 'A hundred dollars is bottom figures.'

6. In technical uses: **a.** A sieve-bottom.

1688 SEWALL *Letter-Book* I. 96 Am importuned to send for fourty Duz. of Course four foot Hair Bottoms.

+**b.** A vat used in salt-making.

1833 *Niles' Reg.* XLIV. 395/1 The vat, or bottom, as it is generally called, was constructed 100 feet in length and 10 in width and all on the same level.

+**c.** *pl.* 'The impure metallic copper . . . which separates from the matt, and is found below it' (Raymond).

1876 RAYMOND *8th Rep. Mines* 393 Four tons of white metal, from the Ziervogel treatment, give 600 pounds of bottoms.

***Bottom,** *v.* [BOTTOM *n.*]

1. *tr.* To supply (a chair) with a bottom.

1732 J. HEMPSTEAD *Diary* 251, I went . . . to the Indian Town to get a Squaw to botom Chairs [for] Brother Talmage. **1766** J. BARTRAM *Journal* (1769) 31 We soon came to Forbes's bluff, where grows a good sort of rush to bottom chairs with, or make mats. **1884** CABLE *Dr. Sevier* liv. (1885) 409 She produced a chair bottomed with raw-hide.

2. To be at the bottom of; to underlie.

1876 RAYMOND *8th Rep. Mines* 56 The company is extending and straightening the bed-rock tunnel, so that it . . . will 'bottom' all the land on this end of the claim.

+**Bottom dollar.** [BOTTOM *n.* 5.] The last dollar which one possesses. Freq. in the phrase *to bet one's bottom dollar.*

1866 [C. H. SMITH] *Bill Arp* 119 This is a big thing certain, and I will invest my bottom dollar in this kind of money. **1866** *Congress. Globe* March 1474/1 His opinion is that a State can go out of the Union, and he is willing to bet his bottom dollar on his judgment. **1877** BARTLETT 61 When a man's money is gone, he will say, 'I've seen my bottom dollar.' **1886** *Leslie's Mo.* Dec. 684/2, I came suddenly on a grizzly not ten rods away. You can just bet your bottom dollar, . . . I was just skeered. **1902** BRET HARTE in *Harper's Mag.* April 737, I'll bet my bottom dollar he has been advertised for afore this.

+**Bottom facts,** *n. pl.* Fundamental or basic facts. — **1877** *N.Y. Tribune* 17 March 4/4 Curiosity has been on tip-toe these many weeks to know the 'bottom facts' in [the case of Sen. Grover of Oregon]. **1883** 'MARK TWAIN' *Life on Miss.* xlii. 393 Though there ain't only one or two ways when you come down to the bottom facts of it. **1896** *Congress. Rec.* 26 Feb. 2182/2, I am only giving what I believe to be the bottom facts.

***Bottom grass.** [BOTTOM *n.* 1 d.] Grass growing in low ground or in a bottom. — **1850** GARRARD *Wah-To-Yah* 279 Eleven hundred horses capering, rolling, and cropping the sweet bottom grass. **1877** J. S. CAMPION *On Frontier* 20 It was . . . covered with a carpet of coarse 'bottom grass,' nearly waist-high in many places. **1904** 'O. HENRY' *Heart of West* 180 The bottom grass and the chaparral and the lonesome timber crowded all around it.

+**Bottom ground.** [BOTTOM *n.* 1 d.] Low-lying ground; bottom land. — **1637** MORTON *New Canaan* II. ii, If any man be desirous to finde out in what part of the Country the best Cedars are, he must get into the bottom grounds. **1823** JAMES *Exped.* I. 80 Above this both shores [of the Mo. R.] are low bottom grounds. **1843** *Amer. Pioneer* II. 253 They concluded to leave the bottom grounds.

+**Bottom land, Bottom-land.** [BOTTOM *n.* 1 d.]

1. Low-lying land, usually along a river.

1728 *Boston News-Letter* 23–30 May 2/2 To be sold, fifty Acres of extraordinary good Meadows and Meadow Bottom Land. **1792** IMLAY *Western Territory* 45 Few places on it [the Kentucky] have any bottom land, as the rock rises mostly contiguous to the bed of the river. **1815** DRAKE *Cincinnati* 43 Dayton, the chief town, is laid off on a fine tract of bottom land. **1834** *Visit to Texas* iii. 30 The soil was here, as below, very rich bottom land, black, and 20 feet deep. **1867** *Iowa Agric. Soc. Rep.* (1868) 141 On rich prairie or bottom-land forty bushels per acre would be an average. **1870** *Amer. Naturalist* III. 7 There we shall doubtless find . . . a tract of what is called in western parlance 'bottom land.' **1890** BRET HARTE *Waif of Plains* 98 Before them opened a vast expanse of bottom land, slightly sloping on the right to a distant half-filled lagoon.

attrib. **1903** WHITE *Forest* xviii. 261 Our way led . . . through a quarter mile of bottom-land thicket. **1903** *N.Y. Ev. Post* 19 Sept., To complete the maturity of the bottomland crops.

2. A stretch of low-lying ground; a bottom. Usually in pl.

1785 A. ELLICOTT in *Life & Lett.* 40 The Bottom-Lands on this Stream are very good but they are narrow. **1796** *Ib.* 142 The flat, or bottom lands on the Ohio, are not surpassed by any in the United States for fertility. **1818–9** T. HULME *Journal* 70 These, like all the *bottom* lands, having a coat of sediment from their river in addition to the original soil, are by far the richest. **1846** FARNHAM *Prairie Land* 257 The fevers took their most malignant and fatal character in the 'bottom lands.' **1866** *Rep. Indian Affairs* 243 The soil of the bottom lands of the Missouri and Niobrara rivers . . . are peculiarly adapted to produce corn. **1891** 'THANET' *Otto the Knight*, etc. 250 She knew it was in the bottom-lands, and she sent the boots, begging the warden to let her boy have them. **1903** *N.Y. Ev. Post* 12 Sept., The tract consists of a bottom land along the Ohio River, and a plateau elevated 300 feet above the bottom land.

+**Bottom prairie.** [BOTTOM *n.* 1 d.] A low-lying prairie; one not much elevated above neighboring watercourses. — **1807** GASS *Journal* 36 We . . . passed a handsome bottom prairie. **1838** H. W. ELLSWORTH *Valley of Wabash* i. 5 Much of the prairie land . . . varies in depth from three to thirteen feet, according to its position, as upland or bottom prairie. **1882** WORTHEN *Econ. Geol. Ill.* II. 73 The latter are the so-called 'ridge prairies,' while the former are sometimes designated as 'bottom prairies.'

+**Bottom rail.** In the South after the Civil War the phrase *bottom rail on top* denoted the changed relations between former slaves and those who had owned them. — **1879** TOURGEE *Fool's Errand* xi. 50 It is . . . reported that he has been sent down here . . . to assist in overturning our institutions, and putting the bottom rail on top. **1884** *Century Mag.* April 861/2 It was the period of negro supremacy. . . . 'The bottom rail was on top.' **1898** PAGE *Red Rock* 321 Yes, the, bottom rail is on top, and we mean to keep it so till the fence rots down.

+**Bottom rock.** [Cf. BEDROCK and ROCK BOTTOM.] The lowest stratum of rock. Also fig. — **1864** DANA *Geology* (1874) 45 The whole thickness above the unfossiliferous bottom-rocks. **1887** C. B. GEORGE *40 Years on Rail* 93 About the time I had reached bottom rock in my financial troubles, . . . I met A. B. Pullman.

+**Bottom timber.** [BOTTOM *n.* 1 d.] Timber growing in a bottom. — **1837** PECK *Gaz. Illinois* 125 The bottom timber consists of oaks. **1867** *Iowa Agric. Soc. Rep.* (1868) 129 When they [=cattle] run out in the bottom timber they often eat the buckeye balls, and are badly poisoned. **1874** LONG *Wild-Fowl* 150 How much better walking it is in this bottom-timber than in the woods of New England.

Botts, variant of BOTS *n. pl.*

+**Bot-worm.** A grub or larva of the botfly (q.v.). — **1799** *N.Y. State Soc. Arts* I. 391, I think it out of doubt . . . that the egg on the horses hair produces the bot-worm. **1877** *Vt. Dairym. Assoc. Rep.* VIII. 105 Grub-in-the-head is a bot-worm, . . . cousin to the bots in horses.

+**Boudin.** [F. *boudin* sausage, blood pudding.] Buffalo intestines prepared as a sausage. Usu. in pl. *Obs.* — **1843** Frémont *Exped.* 22 The hunters came in with a fat cow; and . . . we enjoyed well a supper of roasted ribs and *boudins*, the *chef d'oeuvre* of a prairie cook. **1846** Sage *Scenes Rocky Mts.* v, Marrow-bones, *boudins*, and *intestinum medulæ* . . . [are] choice selections with mountaineers. **1848** Ruxton *Far West* iii. 108 The theme of conversation being the well-remembered merits of good buffalo-meat, . . . of delicious 'boudins,' and marrow-bones. **1852** Stansbury *Gt. Salt Lake* 35 Today the hunters killed their first buffalo . . . and a busy scene ensued of roasting, boiling, and making boudin, which is a sort of sausage boiled and eaten hot.

+**Boudoir car.** A railroad coach having elegantly furnished sections. — **1887** C. B. George *40 Yrs. on Rail* 248 Smoking, buffet, drawing-room, boudoir, dining and sleeping cars have all been added to meet the needs and tastes of this enterprising age. **1893** M. Philips *Making of a Newspaper* 179 The train . . . had one of the Mann boudoir cars; I engaged a section [and] adjusted the table.

+**Boudoir theater.** A small, elegantly furnished theater. — **1856** *Spirit of Times* (N.Y.) 22 Nov. 200/1 This beautiful boudoir theatre has been placed by him under my guardianship.

+**Bough,** *v. tr.* With *down:* To lay or cover with boughs. — **1861** Winthrop *Open Air* 89 Iglesias and I stripped off armfuls of boughs and twigs from the spruces to 'bough down' our camp. 'Boughing down' is shingling the floor elaborately with evergreen foliage.

+**Bough house.** A temporary structure made of boughs, serving as a blind in wild-fowl shooting or as a camp.

1811 Wilson *Ornithology* III. 111 Their destroyers construct for themselves lurking holes made of pine branches, called *bough-houses*. . . . Hither they repair with their fowling-pieces . . . and wait the appearance of the birds. *c***1835** S. Fobes *Arnold's Exped.* 38 At night we struck up a fire, built us a bough-house, . . . and half-boiled one piece of meat. **1844** *Knickerb.* XXIII. 444 Now for a quiet smoke on the plank settle in the bough-house. **1859** G. A. Jackson *Diary* 520 In camp all day. Built bough house, and ate fat sheep. **1894** *Outing* July 281/1 Down in the bough house the campers reclined in attitudes comfortable if not always picturesque.

Boughten, *a. dial.* [For *bought:* current in Eng. dial., and occas. used in verse (1793–).] Bought or purchased at a store or from a dealer; not homemade.

1801 *Spirit Farmers' Mus.* 235 Jotham, get your boughten shirt. **1825** Neal *Bro. Jonathan* I. 131 Their large, flashy buckles; ribbons, leather shoes; and white 'boughten' stockings. **1839** *S. Lit. Messenger* V. 431/2 For calico, tea . . . and other 'boughten' articles of use . . . he goes . . . to Sebec. **1859** A. Cary *Country Life* 55 The eldest son [was] proud of his darkening beard, and 'boughten' coat. **1865** *Atlantic Mo.* XV. 346 My father having . . . promised me a boughten writing book as it was called, instead of a sheet of paper folded at home. **1880** R. T. Cooke *Steadfast* 165, I'd ruther live in my own boughten hogshead than in another person's four-story mansion. **1906** Pittman *Belle of Blue Grass C.* 146 His wife [is] . . . calkerlatin to come in next week and get some boughten stuff for herself.

Boulder: see Bowlder.

Boulevard. {1772– (with reference to Paris).} A broad, well-made street, avenue, or main road.

'Now sometimes extended to . . . a street which is of especial width, is given a park-like appearance by reserving spaces at the sides or center for shade-trees, flowers, seats, and the like, and is not used for heavy teaming' (*Cent.*).

1875 *Scribner's Mo.* Sept. 541/2 The boulevard which started from Lincoln Park, connects the Central and Douglas Parks. **1879** *Harper's Mag.* Dec. 39/2 To view the town [=Atlanta] itself, let me commend a ride along the new 'boulevard' on the eastern edge. **1880** [W. B. Vickers, etc.] *Hist. Denver, Col.* 199/1 A famous drive is the North Denver and Highland *boulevard*, a wide avenue, nearly five miles long, in a straight line. **1903** A. B. Hart *Actual Govt.* 328 Hence have grown up systems of boulevards, broad, winding, and well-surfaced, reaching from park to park and often from city to city.

Bounce, *n.*[1] {1798– (cherry bounce)} A kind of cordial, usu. flavored with the juice of certain fruits. (Cf. Cherry bounce.) — **1800** *Mass. H. S. Coll.* VII. 247 The usual drink of the fishermen [of Shoals Islands], at that period [*c.* 1730–], was a liquor which they called *bounce*, composed of two thirds spruce beer and one third wine. **1835** Bird *Hawks of Hawk-H.* II. 171 Here I've mixed you a brandy cock-tail, and you've spilled the bounce into it. **1888** Hargis *Graded Cook Book* 474 [In making] blackberry bounce, . . . to two quarts of juice put about three-fourths of a pound of sugar.

Bounce, *n.*[2] [f. Bounce *v.*] +*slang.* Abrupt or decided dismissal from employment or some other position or relationship. Frequently *grand bounce.* — **1877** Bartlett *Dict. Amer.* 777 To get the *grand bounce* is to be dismissed from service; particularly from an office under government. **1883** J. Hay *Bread-Winners* 256 They can only take me for a tramp and give me the grand bounce. **1889** Howells *Hazard of Fortunes* II. 308 Well, I guess she's given him the grand bounce at last. **1894** 'Mark Twain' *Twins* Introd., There was no possible way of crowding her in. . . . I saw I must simply give her the grand bounce. **1910** 'O. Henry' *Rolling Stones* 122 'Had you ever thought,' I asks, . . . 'of giving her the bounce yourself?'

Bounce, *v.* +(In colloq. or slang uses.)

1. *intr.* **a.** To start or spring *at* a person, etc.; to be startled, give a start.

1834 Simms *Guy Rivers* II. xl. 278 She was mighty sprigh And she bounced at many a feller Who came a fighting-shy. **1835** Kennedy *Horse Shoe Robinson* I. 78 Now, never bounce at that, man! *a***1846** *Quarter Race Ky.* etc. 94 Darn him, I hadden't no time to think afore I bounced at him!

b. To set *out* smartly.

1859 G. A. Jackson *Diary* 523 [They] want us to move down [to a newly-forming town]. No town for us. We will bounce out for the head of Vasquez in the early spring.

2. *tr.* To cause to start from cover.

1840 *Crockett Almanac* 11 The rest of the time he spent in . . . bouncing deer. **1858** *Harper's Mag.* Oct. 615/2 It is a common thing for still-hunters, when a deer is suddenly 'bounced up,' . . . to bleat, imitating the noise of the fawn.

3. To eject forcibly; to throw out; to evict.

'A word now extensively used for the forcible excluding of a troublesome or noisy person, from a house or bar-room, a car, &c.' (B. '77).

1877 Bartlett 62, I daresn't go in there; the bar-tender's drunk, and I might get bounced. **1887** M. Roberts *Western Avernus* 238 If you'll give me a dollar and a quarter . . . I'll let you ride. If you get bounced by M— before then, it will be my loss. **1891** *Harper's Mag.* Jan. 324/2 He was grabbed roughly by the shoulders and 'bounced' from the shop. **1899** Stockton *Associate Hermits* 110 As soon as I agreed to Corona's coming I determined to bounce that man. *a***1906** 'O. Henry' *Trimmed Lamp* 48 A certain man named Adam, whom the cherubim bounced from the orchard. **1911** H. S. Harrison *Queed* 20 What is the name of this young man—the one I may be compelled to bounce?

b. To discharge or dismiss summarily from an employment or post.

1876 *Congress. Rec.* 10 Aug. 5403/1 Where are the soldiers of the Union army . . . ? Nearly all gone, a clean sweep; to use a phrase that I never heard before, although I am told it is common in some sections of the country, they are 'bounced.' **1881** *Daily Oregonian* 30 March (Th. S.), It now seems probable that the Senate will never be organized till Gorham is 'bounced.' **1886** Poore *Reminisc.* I. 112 Van Buren, when he came into power, promptly 'bounced' him. **1889** Howells *Hazard of Fortunes* II. 156 He says that if he consents to *my* bouncing the old fellow it's the same as if *he* bounced him.

c. To eject from membership (in a church).

1882 Peck *Sunshine* 29 (*caption*), Bounced from church for dancing.

d. To cast off, throw over (a suitor).

1893 'Thanet' *Stories Western Town* 213 You don't suppose it would be any use to offer Esther a cool hundred thousand to promise to bounce this young fellow? **1906** Wilkins *Doc. Gordon* i. 11 Sometimes they say things to me that their fine young lady friends would bounce 'em for.

4. To 'jump' (a claim).

1889 K. Munroe *Golden Days* 69 We've got to . . . stake out the others [=lots] so the Injuns can't bounce 'em.

5. With *it.* To blurt out.

1879 Tourgee *Fool's Errand* 43 At length he 'bounced it squarely,' as the country-people hereabout say, with the statement [etc.].

+**Bouncer.** *slang.* [f. Bounce *v.* 3.] A man employed in a hotel, theater, saloon, etc., to eject undesirables, or otherwise maintain order. — **1888** Gunter *Mr. Potter* xx, Several of the fighting brigade of the establishment, that in American slang would be termed 'bouncers.' **1890** E. B. Custer *Following Guidon* 31 One of the frontiersmen . . . describes a person called the 'bouncer,' who seems to be a well-recognized functionary in such [boarding] establishments. . . . His duties consist in bringing to time people who neglect to pay their bill, and for this service he is boarded without charge. **1898** Westcott *D. Harum* 45 The very mild-mannered and gentlemanlike 'bouncer' at the Altman House [is] an ex-prize-fighter. **1902** White *Blazed Trail* iii. 18 He was seized by the collar and trousers in the grip known to 'bouncers' everywhere.

Bouncing Bet. A popular name for the soapwort. — **1817–8** Eaton *Botany* (1822) 447 *Saponaria officinalis*, soapwort, bouncing bet. **1881** *Harper's Mag.* Oct. 648 See this long bouquet of Bouncing-Bet, stramonium, and pansy. **1884** *Ib.* Oct. 740/2 The bouncing-bets and sweet-williams on either side of the front door. **1899** M. Going *Flowers* 221 The pretty roadside saponaria, familiarly known as 'bouncing-Bet,' expands about sundown.

***Bound,** *n.* Also †**bownd, boun.**

***1.** *pl.* The line(s) or limits of a definite area or piece of ground; a boundary.

In early records very common of the limits of townships: see also Town-bounds.

1632 *Mass. Bay Rec.* I. 94 The bounds of Charles Towne shall end att a tree marked by the said pale. **1653** *Conn. Col. Rec.* I. 246 Without the bounds of the libbertyes of the plantatyons. **1659** *R. I. Col. Rec.* I. 417 That fower men be apoynted to marke out the westward bownds of our collony as our charter bowndeth it. **1685** *Providence* (R.I.) *Rec.* V. 47 One halfe of forty five acres of upland, the boundes thereof knowne by heapes of stones. **1707** *Ib.* IV. 79 A little hill . . . being also the Norweste boundes thereof. **1738** BYRD *Dividing Line* (1901) 23 No lands at all should be granted within the disputed bounds. **1740** *Bristol Vestry Bk.* (Va.) 102 [They] did agree that the old Lines in dispute . . . shall be Lines & bounds of their Lands forever. **1807** *Smithtown Rec.* 228 Whereas there are Deversity & Contrariety of opinion . . . respecting the true Bounds. **1911** *Okla. Session Laws* 3 Legisl. 75 The Governor shall cause to be placed upon the ballots . . . the metes and bounds of the proposed new territory.

b. The area included within the defined limits.

1643 *Providence* (R.I.) *Rec.* II. 7 All the land that he hath lying in the Bounds of Providence excepting his house share and housing. **1665** *Conn. Col. Rec.* II. 511 To prohibitt the Connecticut Indians from huntinge vpon Vncus his bounds. **1703** *Ib.* IV. 448 Five roods of meadow lying in the bounds of Stanford. **1833** *Ohio Revised Statutes* (1860) 1211 The limits of the prison bounds of the several counties in this state. **1853** in Winthrop *Hist.* (1853) I. 2 *n.*, He maintained a small plantation for fishing at Mistick, in the present bounds of Malden.

*2. One of the limits or boundary lines of a piece of ground, township, etc. *Obs.*

1659 *Portsmouth* (R.I.) *Rec.* 379 One Acre of land . . . bounded . . . the one Side with the bound of Tho. Lawton. **1661** *Providence* (R.I.) *Rec.* I. 95 Unto the Rest of the bound which was formerly ffixed. **1702** *Ib.* XI. 71 To set the westerne bound of our plantations & to run the line. **1746** *Waterbury Prop. Rec.* 164 To remove their bound East or West to bring them into the line of said high wayes.

*3. A boundary mark, usually a tree, stake, or stone. (See also CORNER-BOUND.) *Obs.*

1637 *R.I. Col. Rec.* I. 28 We have . . . agreed . . . to run vppon a streight line . . . to an oake tree . . . having four marks with an axe, till some other land marke be set for a certaine bound. **1663** *Plymouth Rec.* 57 The western bound . . . is a walnut tree, . . . the northermost bound a white oake. **1684** *Providence* (R.I.) *Rec.* XIV. 90 Bounding on the north easterne Corner with an old Stumpe, which was a former bound. **1705** *Derby* (Conn.) *Rec.* 232 We . . . set up bounds where the high way should go into the long lott.

4. In *pl.* with *a* or *that:* A boundary mark or boundary. *Obs.*

1640 *Providence* (R.I.) *Rec.* XV. 2 The oake Tree having ffowre markes with an Axe: tell some other land marke bee sett for a certaine boundes. **1662** WINTHROP *Letters* 76 He consents to take it [a charter] at that bounds sett downe . . . in their paper. **1671** *Ib.* I. 25 The north easterne Corner Bound . . . shall be a devideing Boundes betweene me & the aforesayd Joseph Williames. **1702** *Topsfield Rec.* 126 Making a bounds at every forty rods end.

* **Bound,** *v.* [BOUND *n.*]

*1. *tr.* To mark or lay out the bounds of (land); to delimit. *Obs.*

1636 *Plymouth Laws* 54 To have and to hold the said portion of land so granted, bounded and recorded as aforesaid. **1665** *Topsfield Rec.* 8 Wee have so don and bounded it as followeth. **1703** *N.H. Probate Rec.* I. 503, I give to my beloved son . . . about eleven Acres of Land as it is alredy bounded and in his possession.

+**b.** To name the boundaries of.

1877 *Harper's Mag.* March 558 Lessons literally went in at one ear and out of the other; if she bounded Pennsylvania correctly to-day . . . she was as likely to put Texas on the east and Georgia on the north of it tomorrow.

2. *intr.* To have the boundary at a certain place; to adjoin or abut.

1647 *Charlestown Land Rec.* 109, I . . . have sould . . . one hay lott, lying and scituate in the high marshes, which lotts bounds up to Mr Winthrops orchard. **1792** JEFFERSON *Writings* VIII. 327 They [=Spanish territories] bound on us between two and three thousand miles.

Bound, *ppl. a.* [BIND *v.* 3.] Of a boy or girl: Articled to service.

1843 *Amer. Pioneer* II. 140 Our family consisted of my father, mother, and three children, . . . and a bound boy of fourteen. **1846** *Congress. Globe* 6 Feb. 322/3 He has to stand by, as we say in the West, 'like a bound boy at a husking.' **1871** EGGLESTON *Hoosier Schoolm.* iv. 51 Ralph recognized Hannah, the bound girl at old Jack Means's. **1878** BEADLE *Western Wilds* 329 Willie . . . concluded that she must be a 'bound girl' as he had been a 'bound boy,' and that some harsh master was taking her away from home. **1886** WILKINS *Adv. of Ann* 10 They had been revolving this scheme of taking 'a bound girl' for some time in their minds. **1896** S. O. JEWETT *Country of Pointed Firs* 157 A scatter-witted little bound girl came running to the meetin'-house door.

Bound, *p.p.* +Determined; resolved. — **1856** STOWE *Dred* I. iv. 49, I'm on the way to be as sombre and solemn as you are, but I'm bound to have a good time first. *c***1873** DE VERE *MS. Notes* 445 'He is *bound* to do it.' . . . In the West =he is resolved to do it. **1889** *Cent.* 642/1 He is bound to do it.

Boundary. Also †**boundery, bowndary.** {1626–, *fig.*}

1. The line which marks the limits of a town, settlement, state, etc.

1643 *R.I. Col. Rec.* I. 130 The South bounds ffrom the sea shoare of each boundary uppon a straight lyne westward twentie miles. **1671** *Ib.* II. 402 The western boundary whereof is Pawcatuck alias Narragansett river. **1693** *Conn. Col. Rec.* IV. 108 A great difference groweing . . . about land and bowndaries of land. **1741** *N.H. Prov. Papers* V. 927 Those Boundarys which his Majesty in Council has settled in so solemn a manner after nine years troublesome Legitation [*sic*]. **1754** *Waterbury Rec.* 185 Capt. Judd and Lieut. Jno. Scovill were appointed to make Search and Enquiry about that antient boundary. **1794** *Ann. 3rd Congress* 108 An act for determining the Northern boundary of the Territory ceded to the United States by the State of North Carolina. **1836** *Diplom. Corr. Texas* (1908) I. 132 As regards the boundaries of Texas, perhaps this question cannot be definitely settled at present. **1870** EMERSON *Soc. & Solitude* vi. 134 The selectmen have once in every five years perambulated the boundaries. **1902** *Indian Laws & Tr.* III. 671 Thence in a Northerly direction along the Western boundary 13 miles to a point.

+**2.** A boundary mark; =BOUND *n.* 3.

1670 *Conn. Prob. Rec.* 66 From a tree marked N.F. being a boundary between Wethersfield and Hartford. **1680** *Providence* (R.I.) *Rec.* XIV. 54 A Black oak Tree marked on foure sides, being alsoe a Boundery of the sayd Benedict Arnold his Land. **1702** *Derby* (Conn.) *Rec.* 218 A great stone layd close by a rock is the boundary of my upper division. **1707** *Providence* (R.I.) *Rec.* IV. 79 The said (called) Elbo Tree shall and must be the boundary there. **1772** *Carroll P.* in *Md. Hist. Mag.* XIV. 365 Davis . . . went with me to the Post placed in the roome of a white Oake & Hickory, Boundaries of Kendalls Delight.

3. *attrib.* **a.** Serving as a boundary or boundary mark.

1825 NEAL *Bro. Jonathan* I. 157 We'll have your name put up on all the boundary trees for having broken the laws of our association. **1858** WARDER *Hedges & Evergreens* 156 Boundary-fences, in Louisiana, are made at the expense of the adjacent estates, if they be inclosed. **1883** *Ill. Revised Statutes* 1191 Jurisdiction over boundary waters . . . of cities, villages, and towns. **1883** *Century Mag.* Sept. 687/1 The glimpses of a boundary river show like partial seams in an almost seamless whole.

b. Connected, or dealing, with boundaries.

1852 *Harper's Mag.* V. 119/1 The gentlemen attached to the Boundary Commission had left San Francisco for San Diego. **1877** *Ib.* Dec. 88/1 The American physician (attached to the Boundary Commission) was for iced drinks. *Ib.*, Mr. Grey, one of the Boundary Commissioners.

Boundary line. An established line that marks the limits of a town, state, etc. {1842–}

1705 *R.I. Col. Rec.* III. 528 The boundary lines between this her Majesty's Collony . . . and her Majesty's Province of the Massachusetts Bay. **1763** J. HABERSHAM *Letters* 14 A kind of temporary or rather Boundary Line, beyond which the white People agreed not to settle. **1781** in Ramsey *Tennessee* (1853) 267 To give him time to meet them with a flag-guard, on Holston River, at the boundary line. **1805** *Steele Papers* I. 456 One of the Commissioners appointed by this State to extend the boundary line of this State and the State of South Carolina. **1818** *Ann. 15th Congress* 1 Sess. I. 882 Under the Treaty of Ghent, certain Commissioners had been appointed to ascertain the boundary lines between the United States and the British northern provinces. **1856** GLISAN *Jrnl. Army Life* 362 It was then concluded . . . that the forty-ninth degree of north latitude should be the boundary line. **1894** ROBLEY *Bourbon Co., Kansas* 17 The boundary line of the Nation (in 1843) was almost exactly 150 miles west of Fort Scott. **1906** *Indian Laws & Tr.* III. 231 The boundary line between the Creek Nation, Indian Territory, and the Territory of Oklahoma.

+**Bound-corner.** *Obs.* [BOUND *n.* 2.] The meeting point of two boundary lines. — **1670** *Rowley Rec.* 207 The bound corners at that end is a great red oake. **1677** *Topsfield Rec.* I. 21 His bound Corner of his farm should be now this on and twente Rod from the small oke to the bound stake. *Ib.* 20 That popeler is his bound Cornar tree.

Bounded, *ppl. a.* [BOUND *n.* or *v.*] +Of trees: Selected or distinguished as a boundary mark. *local.* — **1674** *Md. Hist. Mag.* I. 9 Beginning at the northernmost bounded tree of the land . . . and running north . . . to a bounded oak by a small branch. **1700** *Ib.* XIX. 353 Goodmans Adventure, . . . beginging at a bounded white oak and runing south west. **1742** *Ib.* XX. 262 The Bounded Locusts stood . . . near a small mash. **1786** *Ib.* XIX. 262 If he had cut it down he could have been hung, as it was a bounded tree.

***Bounder**[1]. *Obs.* [Cf. BOUND *n.*] A limit; a boundary. {–1635; now *dial.*} — **1654** *R.I. Col. Rec.* I. 132 Which bay is the East bounder. **1658** *Providence* (R.I.) *Rec.* I. 79 A little runnett . . . is the Bounder betwixt the sayd land, and a percell of meaddow. **1667** *Warwick* (R.I.) *Rec.* 408 Which sandy point is the second bounder. **1733** *Providence* (R.I.) *Rec.* IX. 68 On the North Easterly Side of the aboue mentioned bounders.

***Bounder**[2]. *Obs.* [f. BOUND *v.* 1.] One selected to establish bounds or boundaries. — **1692** *Derby Rec.* 159 Further tha hav chosen John Pringle bounder.

+**Bounder**[3]. **a.** A device causing objects to rebound. **b.** In baseball: A batted ball which bounds over the ground. — **(a) 1858** *Rep. Comm. Patents* (1859) I. 364, I claim the inclined plane and bounder . . . for bounding cranberries, to separate the good from the bad. **(b) 1868** CHADWICK *Base Ball* 37 The short-stop, too, has to field more ground balls and short bounders that any other fielder. *Ib.* 74 Hatfield . . . , hitting a 'bounder' to Pike, near third base, dropped his bat and ran for first base. **1875** *Chicago Tribune* 15 July 5/5 George Wright [made] . . . one of his unapproachable stops and throws off a bounder.

+**Bound-house.** *Obs.* [BOUND *n.*] A house erected to mark the bounds of a corporation. — **1665** *N.H. Doc. & Rec.* I. 249 The fixing, nameing, and owning a Bound-house 3 large miles north from Merrimack River . . . must necessarily determine the limitts of the said [Massachusetts] Corporation. **1676** *Ib.* 325 They thought fit at length to declare themselves mistaken in what they had done in the year 1631, when they erected bound-houses.

+**Bound line.** *Obs.* [BOUND *n.*] A boundary line. — **1664** *Dedham Rec.* IV. 84 Whereas the grante made and layed out seuerall years since to Ensi: Francis Chickering . . . haue bene . . . altered in its bounde Lines. **1667** *Ib.* 131 Deputed, to new runne . . . the bounde lynes, . . . the men vnder written. **1680** *Waterbury Prop. Rec.* 15 To . . . determin a Bounde Lyne twixt you.

Bound mark. Also **bounds mark.** [BOUND *n.*] Something that marks a boundary. {1623, 1826}

1640 *Conn. H. S. Coll.* VI. 33 To se that a sufficientt bund marke be sett bettwene man & man, att ech end of theare medow a greate ston sett in a houle. **1661** *Providence* (R.I.) *Rec.* I. 11 Haueing these Bound markes; one the Easte a small wallnut Tree [etc.]. **1679** *Plymouth Rec.* 162 A younge white oake tree . . . which is the said Abrahams bounds marke. **1695** *Providence* (R.I.) *Rec.* IV. 166 Said heape of stones & the tree marked is the south-easterne cornner & a bound marke or land marke. **1703** SEWALL *Diary* II. 76 Helping to carry the Chain and lay Stones for Bound-Marks. **1735** *Boston Selectmen* 273 They . . . are impowered to run the Line, and renew the Bound-marks between the Town of Boston and the Town of Lynn. **1858** THOREAU *Maine Woods* 156 Old bound-marks may be found every forty rods, if you will search.

+**Bound-marked,** *a.* [BOUND *n.*] Marked to serve as a bound. — **1666** *Conn. Col. Rec.* II. 512 Upon the west side of the riuer up northward unto a bound marked tree.

Bound-out, *ppl. a.* =BOUND *ppl. a.* — **1898** DELAND *Old Chester Tales* 169 A child don't eat much, and I guess they've made her work; a bound-out child works her passage every time.

Bound servant. [BOUND *ppl. a.*] A servant under compulsion or contract. — [**1720** *Weekly Mercury* 24 Nov. 2/1 The Dying Speech of Edward Hunt formerly taken in the Rebellion at Prellon and transported a bound Servant to the Island of Antigua.] **1815** *Niles' Reg.* VIII. 65/2 If the southern states . . . placed them [=slaves] on the footing of bound-servants, they would be entitled to representation. **1817** E. P. FORDHAM *Narr. Travels* 125 They [=families from Ky.] generally spoil the tempers of their bound servants, whom they do not have so much under command.

+**Bound stake.** *Obs.* [BOUND *n.*] A stake serving as a boundary mark. — **1655** *Suffolk Deeds* II. 205 With fower or six foote of the garden place . . . south to the bound stake standing therein. **1668** *East-Hampton Rec.* I. 274 Thay marked a pine tree for the bound stake betwene the plantations. **1677** *Topsfield Rec.* 21 From the small oke to the bound stake and from this bound stak . . . strat on . . . westward. **1782** *Southampton Rec.* III. 290 The Trustees finally determined that the line shall run from the bound stake at Setuck . . . to Peaconneck Great River.

+**Bound tree.** *Obs.* [BOUND *n.*] A tree serving as a boundary mark. — **1663** *Watertown Rec.* VI. 79 Seirgt Bright was apoynted to warne Goodman Egeles . . . to answer for fellinge a bound tree between Cambridge and Watertowne. **1671** *Providence* (R.I.) *Rec.* I. 25 Sayd bound Tree is by joynte Agrement betwixt us marked with these letters [etc.]. **1687** SEWALL *Diary* I. 191 Set an H on a sear Pine, which said Morse shewed me that it was certainly our Bound-Tree. **1707** *Providence* (R.I.) *Rec.* V. 6 A white oake tree . . . is also a bound tree of the land of Sammell Comstock. **1723** *Braintree Rec.* 154 Then proceeded on said line till it meets with the old Road, at a noted black oak Bound Tree.

* **Bounty,** *n.*

1. A sum of money paid by a government to merchants or manufacturers to encourage the export or production of certain articles of trade. {1718-}

The payment of a bounty to the 'Northern Colonies,' to encourage their export of 'naval stores' to Britain, was suggested in 1718 by William Wood in his *Survey of Trade* 150.

1723 *Doc. Hist. N.Y. State* (1849) I. 721 The Commissioners of the Navy [ought] to appoint a Factor at New York . . . who shall yearly publish the prices he will give for any of these commoditys & the Government to save themselves the Benefit of the Bounty. **1741** *Ga. Col. Rec.* VI. 16 Mr. Causton . . . requested that the Sum of thirty six Pounds and eleven Shillings remaining unpaid to him of the Bounty on Corn . . . might be paid. **1789** *Ann. 1st Congress* I. 147 He conceived it [steel] more deserving a bounty to increase the quantity, than an impost which would lessen the consumption and make it dearer also. **1817** *Ann. 15th Congress* 1 Sess. I. 509 To inquire into the expediency of granting bounties to manufacturers who manufacture a given number of yards of woollen and cotton cloths of a certain width. **1860** in Logan *Great Conspiracy* 221 The first [of these evils] was the Fishing Bounties, paid mostly to the sailors of New England. **1884** *Century Mag.* Jan. 433/1 A filature was built in Savannah, and bounties were paid, by which means the price of silk was doubled.

b. A grant of land to encourage settlers.

1803 LEWIS in *Journals of L. & Ordway* 60 They [=settlers from Ky. & Tenn.] are allowed a bounty in lands proportioned to the number of their respective familys which are called head rights.

2. A gratuity given to one entering upon military or naval service, or a reward given for such service. {1702-}

1747 *N.J. Archives* 1 Ser. VI. 438 We . . . gave a bounty of six pounds a man to each man so to be inlisted to incourage their inlistment. **1775** *Journals Cont. Congress* III. 387 If an inferior officer, marine, or sailor, lose a limb or be . . . disabled, . . . they shall receive a bounty of 200 dollars. **1777** *N.J. Archives* 2 Ser. I. 442 To induce the Light Horse Men to inlist, it was reported they should receive twenty dollars bounty, a coat, jerkin, pair of buckskin breeches [etc.]. **1798** *Ann. 5th Congress* I. 542 Progress has been made by the Surveyor General in surveying the lands allotted for the satisfaction of military bounties. **1818** *Ann. 15th Congress* 2 Sess. I. 411 A bill, allowing to each non-commissioned officer, musician, and private, . . . a bounty in land, as in other cases. **1836** *Diplom. Corr. Texas* (1908) I. 70 On my arrival here I enquired of Maj. Miller for the law under which he was offering 800 acres of land and twenty four dollars bounty. **1865** *Atlantic Mo.* Feb. 239/2 This includes the collection of bounties for discharged soldiers, of pensions for wounded soldiers, of bounty, back pay, and pensions for families of deceased soldiers. **1881-5** MCCLELLAN *Own Story* 259 Out of these wholesale drafts grew the system of substitutes and bounties, which cost so many unnecessary millions to the country.

+**3.** A premium or reward given to encourage the slaying of wild animals or Indians.

1726 PENHALLOW *Indian Wars* 106 Capt. Lovewell [and 30 men] . . . came on . . . two Indians, one of which they killed and . . . for which they received the promised bounty of one hundred pounds a scalp. **1767** HUTCHINSON *Hist. Mass. Bay* II. 142 To encourage small parties of the English to go out and hunt the Indians, the general court promised a bounty or reward, no less than forty pounds, for every Indian scalp. **1790** S. DEANE *New Eng. Farmer* 327/1 Notwithstanding the bounties that have been given by government for destroying them [=wolves], the settlements bordering on the wilderness are still subject to their mischievous incursions. **1841** COOPER *Deerslayer* vi, I've such a big and bushy head that it's quite likely they'll indivor to get two scalps off it, for the bounty is a tempting thing. **1846** *Knickerb.* XXVII. 276, I took off his [the panther's] hide and carried it to Monroe county, For which I got twenty-five dollars bounty. **1873** *Newton Kansan* 20 Feb. 4/1 The bounty of 15 cents on gopher scalps is said to have cost Nebraska $25,000 in two years. **1901** DUNCAN & SCOTT *Allen & Woodson Co., Kansas* 15 They [the county board] . . . offered a bounty of twenty-five cents for wolf scalps.

4. Attrib. with *act, grant, reward, tract.* See also BOUNTY-LAND, etc.

1726 PENHALLOW *Indian Wars* 99 The frontiers being thus alarmed, two companies of volunteers went from New-Hampshire on the bounty act, one hundred pounds a scalp. **1761** S. NILES *Indian Wars* II. 354 A fresh company . . . soon found the Indian Ashley had shot, and scalped him; for which he received an hundred-pound bounty reward, according to the order of the Assembly. **1831** PECK *Guide* 319 The Military Bounty Tract . . . was set aside by Congress and patented for soldiers who served in the last war. **1837** BIRD *Nick of Woods* I. 47 The bounty-grants earned by himself in virtue of military service rendered in the army of his native State. **1863** F. Moore *Rebellion Rec.* V. I. 48 A large amount of money was subscribed to the bounty fund.

+**Bounty,** *v.* [f. the noun.] *tr.* To assist, encourage, or reward with a bounty. — **1788** JEFFERSON *Writings* VII. 210 The eighty-five ships, . . . bountied, as the English are, will require a sacrifice of twelve hundred and eighty-five thousand two hundred livres a year. **1863** NORTON *Army Lett.* 180 The government may get considerable money to bounty volunteers, but they will be too late.

+**Bounty-broker.** *Obs.* [BOUNTY *n.* 2.] One who traded in the enlistment of soldiers at the time of the Civil War. — **1864** SALA in *Daily Telegraph* (Lond.) 9 Aug., A bounty-broker is simply a crimp, or what the recruiting sergeants in Charles-street, Westminster, call a 'bringer.' **1865** in L. Baker *U.S. Secret Service* (1867) 398 In detecting and bringing to punishment men who are violating the laws as bounty brokers and bounty jumpers. **1865** *Congress. Globe* 7 Feb. 633/2 There has been a great deal of rascality perpetrated by bounty brokers. **1866** 'F. KIRKLAND' *Bk. Anecdotes* 172 It now appeared there were sharper ones to look after than the bounty-brokers.

+**Bounty jumper.** [BOUNTY *n.* 2.] One who enlists as a soldier, obtains the bounty paid to recruits, and then deserts.

1864 WHITMAN *November Boughs* (1888) 80 There are many hundreds of 'bounty jumpers,' and . . . eighty thousand deserters! **1865** *Congress. Globe* 24 Feb. 1083/2 [We have been] putting bounty jumpers into the army as substitutes, to desert from time to time. **1866** A. D. RICHARDSON *Secret Service* 393 Several days of our confinement . . . were spent in a little cell with burglars, thieves, 'bounty-jumpers,' and confidence men. **1878** BEADLE *Western Wilds* 532 All the really valuable survivors of the volunteer army had returned to civil life; only the malingerers, the bounty-jumpers, . . . remained. **1890** *Harper's Mag.* Dec. 162/2 The colonel ordered six of us to accompany him to a neighboring town to catch some bounty-jumpers. **1891** *Century Mag.* April 845 We spend several weary days . . . being forced to associate with a miserable lot of union deserters, bounty-jumpers and criminals. **1911** *N.Y. Ev. Post* 11 Jan. 6 The bummers and deserters and bounty-jumpers . . . are cheek by jowl with the real fighters.

fig. **1917** B. MATTHEWS *These Many Years* 83 Like other substitutes, they were often only bounty-jumpers.

+**Bounty jumping,** *vbl. n.* [Cf. prec.] The practice of enlisting to obtain the bounty and then deserting. — **1865** 'P. V. NASBY' *Struggles* 169 Vallandigum and Voorhees hev gone into the law; I shel embark into bounty-jumpin. **1881** *Congress. Rec.* Feb. 1292/2 We had in some of our large cities men who were pursuing the very profitable industry of 'bounty jumping.' **1888** GRIGSBY *Smoked Yank* xiv. 114 A small band of roughs from New York City who had been engaged previous to their capture in what was called bounty jumping.

attrib. **1881** 'MARK TWAIN' in *Century Mag.* Nov. 38/1 Four days full of bounty-jumping excitements and irritations.

+**Bounty-jumping,** *a.* (See prec. and BOUNTY-JUMPER.) — **1867** Goss *Soldier's Story* 157 Thus ended the lesson of retribution that . . . broke up a gang of bounty-jumping desperadoes.

+**Bounty land.** [BOUNTY *n.* 2.]

1. Land given as bounty for military service.

1779 *Ky. Petitions* 49 This would entitle every man to draw a free lott in Town, and also entitle him to his Bounty Land. **1791** *Ann. 1st Congress* II. 1746 A petition of sundry officers . . . on the subject of bounty lands allotted to them. **1816** *Ann. 14th Congress* 2 Sess. 268 Resolved, that a committee be appointed to inquire into the expediency of authorizing a commutation for money of the bounty land to soldiers. **1836** *Diplom. Corr. Texas* (1908) I. 96 Your volunteers will, therefore, be entitled to bounty lands in proportion to their services. **1850** *U.S. Statutes* IX. 520 An Act granting Bounty Land to certain Officers and Soldiers who have been engaged in the Military Service of the United States. **1885** *Harper's Mag.* Sept. 552/2 He . . . sought . . . to induce Congress to grant the petition of the officers for the bestowal of their bounty lands.

2. Attrib. with *act, bill, bureau, claim.*

1836 *Niles' Nat. Reg.* 24 Sept. 62/1 [Appropriation] for messenger in the bounty land bureau, [$]400. **1842** *Ib.* 25 June 269/2 The expenditures made in satisfaction of the bounty land claims allowed by the state of Virginia. **1873** *Newton Kansan* 27 Feb. 2/1 The soldier's bounty land bill has been adversely reported. **1889** *Cent.* 642/3 *Bounty Land Act*, a United States statute of 1850 (9 Stat., 520), granting lands to those engaged in the military service, or to their widows or minor children.

+**Bounty lot.** [BOUNTY *n.* 2.] A lot consisting of bounty land. — **1820** *Missouri Intell.* 27 May 2/3 The Lands in the Military Tract . . . could not be distributed to soldiers, being . . . too small or too large for bounty lots. **1832** WILLIAMSON *Maine* II. 543, 80 settlers, who were entitled to the bounty-lots of government.

Bounty money. Money given as a bounty, esp. as a gratuity in return for military service. {1692-}

1688 SEWALL *Letter-Book* I. 91 Am sorry [he] is like to have no lift from the Bounty money. **1698** *Ib.* 206, I pray you to use suitable applications, that if there be any Bounty Money, ours may share in it. **1720** *Mass. Bay Currency Tracts* 387 Middling Hemp will raise above 1000 Weight on one Acre, besides the Bounty Money given 2 d. per Pound. **1755** WASHINGTON *Order to Troops* 18 Oct., George West's claim to a man said to be his servant, now in the guard; which if he makes good, they are to deliver him up, and he to return the bounty-money. **1757** in *Lett. to Washington* II. 151 The number of Drafts . . . that were paid the Bounty Money & had their Regimentals before they deserted. **1780** *Heath Papers* III. 38 There is at present some impediments to the recruiting service which is principally . . . some difficulty in obtaining bounty money and clothing for the recruits. **1845** MRS. KIRKLAND *Western Clearings* 210 You bought that 'ere fine broadcloth coat out of bounty money, didn't ye? **1863** F. Moore *Rebellion Rec.* V. I. 62 The Board . . . assembled at Troy, appropriated seventy-five thousand dollars as bounty money, to be paid to volunteers enlisting into the army. **1881** 'MARK TWAIN' in *Century Mag.* Nov. 35/1 A recruit could pay a sentinel three or four hundred dollars to let him escape, and still have enough of his bounty-money left to constitute a fortune for a poor man.

Bourbon. Also **Burbon.**

+**1.** A kind of whisky, originally made in Bourbon County, Kentucky. (Cf. BOURBON WHISKY.)

1850 [H. C. LEWIS] *La. Swamp Doctor* 45 We . . . kept secret, having put it [=a cave] in requisition as the depository of a jug of 'old Bourbon.' **1860** HOLMES *Professor* vii. 208 The young man John . . . asked me to come up one day and try some 'old Burbon' which he said was A 1. **1866** A. D. RICHARDSON *Secret Service* 50 Three of the officers . . . invited us into their quarters to discuss political affairs over their Bourbon and cigars. **1871** *Harper's Mag.* June 39 'What baskets are those?' 'Grub.' 'And the bottles?' 'Ale and Bourbon.' **1881** H. W. PIERSON *In the Brush* 266 These Baptists were of the anti-mission class . . . but favored good Bourbon. **1881** *Harper's Mag.* May 958/2 At the appointed word their leader, well charged with Bourbon, started. **1891** C. ROBERTS *Adrift Amer.* 150 Taking an occasional overdose of Bourbon was his one particular failing. **1909** 'O. HENRY' *Roads of Destiny* 46 There was two quarts of the finest old silk-velvet Bourbon in that satchel. **1923** WATTS *L. Nichols* 304, I take it the Turkey trot is a place for other refreshment besides chicken-gumbo and Bourbon.

+**b.** Attrib. with *cocktail, liquor.*

1862 *Congress. Globe* May 2288/3 One barrel of genuine Bourbon liquor. **1867** W. H. DIXON *New America* II. 96 These people say they want no Cherokee medicines, no plantation bitters, no Bourbon cocktails.

+**2.** A conservative in politics, esp. a Democrat of old-fashioned or extremely conservative principles.

In allusion to the Bourbon royal family of France.

1871 DE VERE 111 We find the name of the royal *Bourbons* applied, now politically to any old-fashioned party which acts unmindful of past experience. **1873** PIKE *Prostrate State* 13 It must be said of the Southern Bourbon of the Legislature that he comports himself with a dignity, a reserve, and a decorum, that command admiration. **1875** *Congress. Rec.* 10 Feb. 37/2 If any American . . . longs for something like the republic of the fathers, he is hooted at as a 'Bourbon.' **1882** *Congress. Rec.* App. 2 June 334/1 One [Negro] comes to join the Bourbons with a lien on his crop, or assailed by the grasshopper and boll-worm. **1884** NYE *Baled Hay* 140 Colonel Thomas . . . Dayton entered the democratic headquarters, . . . the stamping ground of the bourbons. **1911** HARRISON *Queed* 222 These old Bourbons whom we call leaders are mill-stones around our necks.

attrib. **1859** *Olympia* (W. T.) *Pioneer & Democrat* 15 April (Th.), The 'Bourbon' family have attempted to rule this territory from the earliest hour of its creation. **1875** *Congress. Rec.* 2 March 2111/1 Baxter's success depended upon the influence of his Bourbon allies. **1881** *Congress. Rec.* 7 Feb. 1305/2, I am not sufficiently acquainted with history to know why a man should dislike to be called a 'Bourbon' democrat. **1883** *Century Mag.* July 398/1 A man's opinions on . . . the Bourbon régime in the South, were no test of his fitness to collect taxes. **1884** *Boston Journal* 20 Sept., That chief of Bourbon organs, the Charleston (S.C.) News. *Ib.* 23 Sept., Major J. W. McDaniel of Virginia, the Bourbon candidate for Governor three years ago. **1892** *Ib.* 7 Aug. 4/3 The Bourbon Democrats are out for wild-cat currency.

3. *attrib.* Denoting varieties of sugar cane and cotton, possibly introduced from the Isle of Bourbon.

1814 *Niles' Reg.* VI. 200/1 Thirteen years ago some Bourbon canes were given to Mr. Couper, of St. Simons, by a gentleman who had emigrated from one of the Bahama Islands. **1853** *Harper's Mag.* VII. 749/1 The Bourbon cane is of a dark purplish color. — **1818** J. PALMER *Travels U.S.* 443 Cotton, Bourbon and other foreign [varieties]. **1856** *Rep. Comm. Patents: Agric.* 227 In the earlier experiments, the Bourbon cotton was mainly relied upon.

+**Bourbonism.** [BOURBON 2.] Obstinate conservatism in politics. Also, in recent use (1906), *bourbonish* adj., *bourbonize* v. — **1884** *Boston Journal* 18 Sept., The brevet Democrats catch the spirit of pro-slavery Bourbonism naturally. **1904** *Buffalo Commercial* 22 Nov. 8 If the young and liberal men in the South are encouraged to throw off the yoke of Bourbonism.

+**Bourbon whisky.** =BOURBON 1. — **1850** [H. C. LEWIS] *La. Swamp Doctor* 37, I would have sworn it was good old Bourbon whiskey. **1851** *Knickerb.* XXXVII. 280 A somewhat free-drinker in Kentucky . . . purchased a hogshead of the 'Bourbon whiskey' of that region. **1880** *Congress. Rec.* May 2938/2 It requires nearly three years to produce a Bourbon whisky which is ready for consumption. **1901** CHURCHILL *Crisis* 74 He always had three fingers of the best Bourbon whiskey . . . every evening.

Bourgeois. +Formerly, the chief trader in charge of a fur company's trading post in the Northwest Territory. — **1839** TOWNSEND *Narrative* 183 On its smooth, perpendicular sides, we see carved the names of most of the mountain bourgeois. **1847** PARKMAN in *Knickerb.* XXX. 129 Papin was the *bourgeois* of Fort Laramie. He had come down the river with the buffalo-robes and the beaver, the produce of the last winter's trading. **1850** GARRARD *Wah-To-Yah* ii. 42 There was a billiard table in a small house on top of the fort, where the bourgeois and visitors amused themselves.

Bouse, variant of BOWSE *v.*

***Bout.** A course or round in knitting a stocking. {mod. dial.} — **1861** STOWE *Pearl Orr's Isl.* I. 57 Sally [is] . . . evidently more intent on what her father is producing than on the evening task of 'ten bouts.'

***Boute.** *Obs.* [Variant of *bought* = Du. *bocht*, G. *bucht.*] A bend of a coast-line or river. — **1675** *Penna. Archives* I. 34 Two Necks or points of land, lying and being in this River of Delaware and on the east-side thereof over ag[ains]t the Boute above Verdrick-teige-hooke.

+**Bouting row.** A row made by the going and returning of the plow; a bout. {*bouting*, 1834} — **1767** WASHINGTON *Diaries* I. 240 Sowed the bouling [*sic*] Rows at Do[eg Run] with 1½ Bushels. *Ib.* III. 440 Both plows and Hoes were employed in breaking up the bouting Roes along the fence.

Bovey coal. [Named from the parish of *Bovey*, in Devonshire, England.] Lignite. {1760-} — **1816** CLEAVELAND *Mineral. & Geol.* 414-5 Brown lignite. . . . Bovey Coal, or compact carbonated wood. Kirwan. . . . Small quantities have been observed in the alluvial earths of the U. States. **1821** NUTTALL *Travels Arkansa* 54 A sand-bar, . . . scattered in every direction with lignite or bovey coal, washed probably from the basis of the Bluffs. *Ib.* 222 Species of oyster . . . contained specks of bovey coal. **1828** WEBSTER s.v. Coal, Under . . . [brown coal or lignite] are included many varieties, such as cannel coal, bovey coal, jet, &c.

***Bow.**

***1.** The ordinary weapon for shooting arrows, used esp. by Indians. Freq. coupled with *arrow.*

(1) 1634 WOOD *New Eng. Prospect* II. v. 66 A Sagamore with . . . his bow in his hand, his quiver at his back. **1647** *R.I. Col. Rec.* I. 186 To the end that we may come to outshoot these natives in their owne bow; be it enacted . . . that that statute touching Archerie, shall be revived. **1654** JOHNSON *Wonder-W. Prov.* 114 Facing the English Fort built on the mouth of the River in their large Cannowes, with their Bowes and long Shafts. **1676** B. TOMPSON *Poet. Writ.* 54 Let neighbouring Sachems know, And every one that hath club, gun or bow. **1765** TIMBERLAKE *Memoirs* 60 Their bows [*i.e.*, of Cherokee Indians] are of several sorts of wood, dipped in bears oil, and seasoned before the fire. **1827** COOPER *Prairie* viii, The Indian . . . leaned lightly with one hand on a short hickory bow.

1834 [R. BAIRD] *Valley Mississippi* 278 Those streets . . . are somewhat in the shape of an Indian's bow, except that the extremes form large angles, instead of curves. 1883 BANCROFT *Native Races* Wks. I. 164 Bows are made [by the Haidahs] of cedar, with sinew glued along one side.

(2) 1605 J. ROSIER *True Relation* (1887) 118 When we went on shore to trade with them, in one of their canoas I saw their bowes and arrowes. 1630, etc. [see ARROW 1]. 1676 GLOVER *Acc. Va.* in *Phil. Trans.* XI. 633 The Indians . . . having nothing . . . but Bows and Arrows, wherewith they killed their Deer and other wild Beasts. 1783 R. PUTNAM in *Memoirs* 218 The [Indian] natives . . . will be very sorry to be reduced to the disagreeable necessity of useing the bow and arrow as the only means for killing their gaim. 1849 WILLIS *Rural Lett.* 312 They [=half-breeds] make baskets, fans, bows-and-arrows, etc., for sale.

attrib. 1856 *Harper's Mag.* XIII. 589/1 The men [of the Chetkoe tribe] sported the bow and arrow armor with a coyote or fox-skin for a quiver. *a*1862 THOREAU *Maine Woods* 173 There was . . . much of the Indian accent resounding through his English, . . . much of the 'bow-arrow tang' as my neighbor calls it.

+**2.** *pl.* The rims or framing of a pair of spectacles.

1711 *Essex Inst. Coll.* IV. 187/1 To Madam Rebekah Brown, I give my spectacles with gold bows. 1847 LONGFELLOW *Evangeline* I. iii. 4 Glasses with horn bows Sat astride on his nose. 1861 STOWE *Pearl Orr's Isl.* I. 65 Mrs. Kittredge glared through the horn bows of her glasses. 1890 *Harper's Mag.* Oct. 720/1 A pair of ancient silver-rimmed spectacles from which the bows were lost.

***3.** A U-shaped contrivance, made of wood, which partially encircles the neck of an ox and connects it with the yoke above.

1676 *Hempstead Rec.* I. 305 Jeames Beat is to provide what bous and youcks is nedfull for the oxen. 1746 *N.H. Probate Rec.* III. 420, I also give to my said Wife all my Tools . . . excepting one Yoke, Bows, & Tackling belonging unto it. 1775 J. STEVENS *Jrnl.* in *Essex Inst. Coll.* XLVIII. 63 This Day I fixed som bos for the oxen. 1857 *Lawrence* (Kansas) *Republican* 11 June 3 See that he [=an ox] does not have . . . a bow so wide or deep that it will gall his shoulders.

+**4.** A bent strip of wood serving as an arch to support the canvas or tilt of a covered wagon.

1856 WHIPPLE *Explor. Ry. Route* I. 10 As our wagons were packed to the bows, . . . we offered to purchase his wagon and horses. 1859–60 MRS. WITHER *MS. Letters* 2 We put a rag carpet over the bows of the wagon. 1864 A. J. DICKSON *Across Plains* (1929) 138 The whole was surmounted by a canvas cover supported by bows which widened outward if the box was flaring. 1877 F. M. A. ROE *Army Lett.* 161 The high top will be of canvas drawn over 'bows,' in true emigrant fashion.

5. A bend or curve.

1727 *Braintree Rec.* 120 Eighty rods straight thorow said Penniman's Land, there being a considerable bow in her fence. 1819 E. DANA *Geogr. Sk.* 207 The city stands on the east bank of the Mississippi, at one end of a southern bow in the river.

***Bow case.** [BOW 1.] A case or covering for a bow. — 1622 'MOURT' *Relation* 88 [The Indians] brought with them in a thing like a Bow-case . . . a little of their Corne. 1870 KEIM *Sheridan's Troopers* 169 The chief with great pride took down his other quiver and bow case.

Bowdacious, variant of BODACIOUS.

+**Bowdark,** variant of BOIS D'ARC. — 1844 GREGG *Commerce of Prairies* II. 199 In many of the rich bottoms from the Canadian to Red River, . . . is found the celebrated *bois-d'arc* . . . , usually corrupted in pronunciation to *bowdark*. 1848 BARTLETT 46 Bow-dark tree. 1871 DE VERE 110 The Osage Orange . . . was called *bois d'arc* by French settlers; the unfamiliar name became in the hands of English hunters *Bowdark*.

Bowed, *a.* [BOW 2.] +Of spectacles: Having 'bows' or rims of a specified kind. — 1840 *Knickerb.* XVI. 296 In addition to this, he had a pair of large bowed spectacles, resting upon the tip of his ruby nose. 1852 *Ib.* XXXIX. 54 His gold-bowed spectacles will be raised upon the upper part of his forehead. 1860 HOLLAND *Miss Gilbert's Career* 4 Then came the Rev. Jonas Sliter . . . looking very severe behind his . . . gold-bowed spectacles.

***Bowel.** *Obs. slang.* +(See quotation.) — 1856 HALL *College Words* (ed. 2) 37 At Harvard College, a student in common parlance will express his destitution or poverty by saying, 'I have not a bowel.' The use of the word with this signification has arisen, probably, from a jocular reference to a quaint Scriptural expression.

+**Bower.** [G. *bauer*, peasant, knave in cards.] One of the highest cards in euchre. The *right bower* is the knave of trumps, and the *left bower* is the knave of the suit having the same color as the trump suit.

1844 J. COWELL *Thirty Years* 101 When diamonds are trumps at a game at uker [*sic*], I always think of Charley, if I happen to have the left bower guarded. 1847 [ROBB] *Squatter Life* 129 The stranger . . . dealt and turned up the right bower—his antagonist passed, and the stranger raising the bower, bid him play. 1858 *Congress. Globe* 28 May 2460/2 He uses terms which I do not understand: talking about the 'right bower,' and 'ace,' and all that sort of thing. 1868 BRET HARTE *Luck of Roaring Camp* Sandy Tipton . . . for a moment rose superior to the fact that he had an ace and two bowers in his sleeve. 1871 — *Poems* 81 Till at last he put down a right bower, which the same Nye had dealt unto me. 1873 MILLER *Amongst Modocs* 138 The prisoner was named 'Spades.' . . . I should say he was indebted to his likeness to that right or left bower for his name. 1898 WESTCOTT *D. Harum* 36 We have played . . . fifteen hundred games, in which he had held both bowers and the ace of trumps . . . fourteen hundred times.

b. *fig.* In various applications.

1850 [H. C. LEWIS] *La. Swamp Doctor* 125 'What is calomel?' 'A drug, sir, that may be called the right bower of quackery.' 1869 BRET HARTE *Tennessee's Partner* Wks. (1872) 43 'What have you got there?—I call,' said Tennessee quietly. 'Two bowers and an ace,' said the stranger, . . . showing two revolvers and a bowie-knife. 1870 R. H. DAVIS in *Scribner's Mo.* I. 66 She is his right bower. He means to play her some day and win. 1884 *Milnor* (Dakota) *Teller* 8 Aug., Little Maud S. . . . once again reigns as the queen of the turf and holds a right bower over the King. 1902 HARBEN *A. Daniel* 75 A feller that used to be my right bower in my still business left me when I swore off.

+**Bowery.** Also **bowry, bowerie.** [Du. *bouwerij* husbandry, farm.]

1. A farm in the early Dutch settlements in the state of New York.

1654 R. WILLIAMS *Letters* (1874) 272 But before we weighed anchor, their boweries were in flames; Dutch and English were slain. 1668 *N.Y. State Col. Hist.* XIII. 418 For the Preachers Bowry which is at the New Dorpe. 1675 *Ib.* 490 The boweryes or farmes of Schanechtade are to pay . . . four Bushells of winter wheate per Annum as a quitt Rent. [1832 J. F. WATSON *Hist. Tales N.Y.* 135 The old Dutch records sufficiently show, that in primitive days all the rear of the town was cast into farms, say six in number, called 'Bouwerys.'] 1841 BANCROFT *Hist. U.S.* II. 294 Stuyvesant thought it no wrong to his employers to purchase of them at a small price an extensive bowery just beyond the coppices. 1876 *Scribner's Mo.* Feb. 461/1 The descendant built in 1763 this snug 'bowerie' of the Beekmans at a point distant enough from the busy little city to lose its clamor.

b. The farm or countryseat of Governor Stuyvesant of New York, afterwards a resort of pleasure parties from the city.

1704 S. KNIGHT *Journal* 55 Their Diversions in the Winter is riding Sleys about three or four Miles out of Town, where they have Houses of entertainment at a place called the Bowery. 1890 *Century Mag.* Nov. 46 Their adoration took the form of steady pilgrimages to Mynheer Van Witt's mansion, 'Bovenkirk,' just beyond Governor Stuyvesant's 'Bowery.'

c. The street or region in the city of New York occupying the site of the Governor's farm.

1787 CUTLER in *Life & Corr.* I. 305, I . . . left the city by way of the Bowery. 1803 J. DAVIS *Travels in the U.S.A.* 28 The fatal event [= murder and suicide] took place at a house in the Bowery. 1839 *N.Y. City Ordinance* 2 May, The Police Office in the city of New York shall be held and kept at . . . the building corner of Third Street and the Bowery. 1850 C. MATHEWS *Moneypenny* 15 When he came to Union square he dismounted . . . [and] proceeded on foot for the Bowery. 1875 G. P. BURNHAM *Three Years* 125 The residents and passers-by in the Bowery, on Hestor Street, and along the byways adjacent thereto, will not have forgotten a limping, oldish man. 1899 C. H. ROBBINS *The Gam* 81 They would simply make the nations 'rush the growler' for them, as they say in the Bowery.

attrib. 1852 BRISTED *Upper Ten Th.* 29 Its occupants are of not-to-be-mistaken Bowery cut—veritable 'b'hoys.' 1856 [M. THOMPSON] *Plu-ri-bus-tah* 40 On the sea-shore stood . . . America, . . . Swearing, in good Bowery English, Fearful oaths of direst vengeance. 1859 *Harper's Mag.* April 616/2 As they drove by, one of them, with a most remarkable 'Bowery twang,' sang out [etc.]. 1891 *Ib.* Dec. 41/1 The shining bodies of men, bare naked, and frescoed like a Bowery bar-room, were not lacking.

2. A large shelter or building erected for the purpose of accommodating those attending a gathering or meeting.

1788 J. MAY *Jour. & Lett.* 78 Our long bowery is built on the east bank of the Miskingum; a table laid sixty feet long, in plain sight of the garrison. 1809 F. CUMING *Western Tour* 227 What adds to the beauty . . . is a handsome grove . . . through the middle of which runs a long frame bowery. . . . Here a portion of citizens meet each 4th of July. 1852 STANSBURY *Gt. Salt Lake* 130 An immense shed had been erected upon posts, which was capable of containing three thousand persons. It was called 'The Bowery,' and served as a temporary place of worship. 1867 W. H. DIXON *New America* I. 188 The [Mormon] Temple block is covered with temporary buildings and erections—the old tabernacle, the great bowery, the new tabernacle, [etc.]. 1878 BEADLE *Western Wilds* 341 At once the brethren were called together in the bowery—an open shed where they usually worshiped.

+**Bowery boy.** [BOWERY 1 c.] A young rough or rowdy of the type at one time characteristic of the Bowery in New York.

1840 *Picayune* (New Orleans) 28 Aug. 2/1 The Bowery boys of New York have, in our opinion, eclipsed the nice young men of Baltimore. 1848 BARTLETT 279 *Round Rimmers*, . . . in New York, a name applied to a large class of dissipated young men, by others called Bowery boys and Soap-locks. 1855 M. THOMPSON *Doesticks* xxi. 186 In this particular vehicle, a fashionably dressed Miss, had, from necessity, taken her seat in the lap of a Bowery boy. **1862** NORTON *Army Lett.* 48 The Twenty-fifth New York is composed of New York roughs, Bowery boys, 'Dead Rabbits,' etc. **1891** S. M. WELCH *Recoll. 1830–40* 30 Long hair and ear-locks . . . were . . . deemed vulgar, except for the dudes and 'Bowery boys' of those days.

+**Bowery-boy-ish,** *a.* Of or pertaining to a Bowery boy. — **1852** *Knickerb.* Aug. 187 There was something very 'Bowery-boy'-ish in a question asked by one 'soap-lock' of another.

+**Boweryish,** *a.* [BOWERY 1 c.] Suggestive of the Bowery in New York. — **1846** POE *Literati, L. G. Clark,* Its best friends are forced to admit [this 'Editor's Table'] is a little Boweryish.

Bow fast. A rope or line used to fasten a boat at the bow to a dock, etc. — **1822** *Western M. Review* III. 354 His bow-fast (a grape vine) parted, and his frail bark put to sea without a pilot. **1835** HOFFMAN *Winter in West* II. 103 The bow of the steamer approached near enough to the abrupt margin for one of the crew to leap to land with a bow-fast in his hand.

+**Bowfin.** A freshwater fish, *Amia calva.* — **1889** *Cent.* 176/2 [The] *Amiidæ* . . . is an archaic type represented now by a single living species, . . . the bowfin or mudfish, inhabiting the fresh waters of North America. **1897** *Outing* Aug. 437 This fish, the bowfin . . . , was always termed 'dog-fish,' and he was an ugly-looking fellow. His greenish-yellow, snaky-looking body was not pleasant to contemplate, and there was an ugly expression about his big mouth.

+**Bowie.** =BOWIE-KNIFE.

*a***1846** *Quarter Race Ky.,* etc. 115 Uncle Billy drew a bowie and intimated a desire to see the chap willing to undertake the job. **1853** BALDWIN *Flush Times Ala.* 190 Most men would have seized their gun, or bowie, on such terrible aggravation. **1856** [M. THOMPSON] *Plu-ri-bus-tah* 97 Hear them argue with their rifles, And debate with three-foot bowies. **1867** A. D. RICHARDSON *Beyond Miss.* 24 You have won that splendid enamel-cased ivory-handled bowie. **1886** *Outing* IX. 109/1 With bare arms I drove the 'bowie' deep into the grizzly's carcass and the blood came pouring forth. **1901** *Munsey's Mag.* XXIV. 450/2 The term 'bowie' came to mean almost any kind of a knife carried in a sheath. The real bowie is from nine to ten inches long, with one edge.

+**Bowie knife.** (bō'i, bū'i) [Named after Col. James *Bowie,* killed at the Alamo on March 6, 1836.] A heavy sheath-knife with a slightly curved point, usually from ten to fifteen inches in length; also loosely, any large sheath knife.

The name is further illustrated by Thornton from 1836 to 1899. Cf. also *American Speech* XII (1937), 77 ff.

1836 *Niles' Register* 4 June 234 [A duel] with two large Bowie-knives (an instrument about twelve inches in length, and an inch and a half wide, with two edges tapering to a sharp point). **1837** [see ARKANSAS 6]. **1838** REZIN P. BOWIE *Letter* in *Niles' Register* 29 Sept. 70 The first Bowie knife was made by myself. **1839** C. F. BRIGGS *H. Franco* II. 168 An ivory-handled bowie-knife was found by my side by the watchman who picked me up. **1845** SIMMS *Wigwam & Cabin* 204, I had been well provided with pistols and bowie knife before leaving home. **1856** [M. THOMPSON] *Plu-ri-bus-tah* xxii, Editors, and Congress members With their bowie-knives and horsewhips. **1857** *Lawrence* (Kansas) *Republican* 28 May 1 This was on the 31st of March . . . when the invading hordes . . . with bowieknives and revolvers bore down upon the polls. **1865** in W. R. Jillson *Lincoln* (1932) 99 He advanced toward Mr. Lincoln with a six barrelled revolver in his right-hand, and a bowie knife in his left. **1889** K. MUNROE *Golden Days* 151 With bowie-knife in hand [he] ran in to complete his work. **1910** J. HART *Vigilante Girl* 322 Tower . . . had drawn his bowie knife, and was just about to use it on Hawke.

attrib. **1837** in Commons, etc. *Doc. Hist.* II. 299 The introduction of their lawless customs among us, in the shape of gamblers and bowie knife assassins.

+**Bow-key.** [Bow 3.] =BOWPIN. — **1857** J. YOUNG in *Journal Discourses* VI. 230 You that have on such a yoke had better pull out the bow-keys. **1921** H. QUICK *Vandemark's Folly* 304, I would be gosh-blasted if I wouldn't, by Golding's bow-key! *Footn.,* 'By Golding's bow-key' was a very solemn objurgation. . . . It harks back to the time when every man who had oxen named them Buck and Golding, and the bow-key held the yoke on.

***Bowknot.** {–1768} Applied fig. to an awkward position of the human body. — **1839** *Knickerb.* XIII. 75 Ay, ay, you're right there, and he can tie himself into a bow knot. **1861** STOWE *Pearl Orr's Isl.* I. 30 When he had once seated himself in a double bow-knot at a neighbour's evening fireside. **1896** *Godey's Mag.* April 446/2 A woman with her back doubled into a bow-knot.

***Bowl.**+A game played by American Indians. — **1778** CARVER *Travels* 365 The game of the Bowl or Platter . . . is played between two persons only. Each person has six or eight little bones . . . two of the sides of which are coloured black, and the others white. These they throw up into the air, from whence they fall into a bowl or platter placed underneath. **1851** SCHOOLCRAFT *Indians* 188 Pugasaing, or, the game of the bowl . . . is the principal game of hazard among the northern tribes. **1855** LONGFELLOW *Hiawatha* XVI. vii, Then from out his pouch of wolf-skin Forth he drew . . . All the game of Bowl and Counters.

Bowlder, Boulder. {Orig. *boulder-stone* (*a*1300–). The spelling *bowlder,* formerly usual, is now rare or obsolete.}

1. A large detached stone or mass of rock, usually abraded or weather-worn. {1813–}

(*a*) **1828** WEBSTER s.v., Bowlders of Granite, often of great size, are very common on the surface of the most recent formations. **1837** PECK *New Guide* 236 Delaware [Co., Ind.]: . . . some limestone, and granite bowlders scattered over the surface. **1878** H. H. JACKSON *Travel at Home* 148 Enormous bowlders lie here and there. **1884** *Century Mag.* Dec. 196/1 To dive from a great protruding bowlder into the limpid depth of the lake. **1890** RYAN *Told in Hills* 36 She amused herself by hopping bird-like from one round, insecure bowlder to another, and sending several bounding . . . into the gully. **1897** *Outing* May 129/1 The huntsmen across the valley have clambered atop of their bowlder to get a more commanding view of the approaching race.

(*b*) **1831** PECK *Guide* 137 These stones are denominated boulders in mineralogy. **1852** in MARCY *Explor. Red River* (1854) 174 [We] saw today a number of boulders, mostly composed of hard granite. **1870** KEIM *Sheridan's Troopers* 258 We began the ascent on horseback, winding among rocks, scaling boulders, moving along dizzy ledges.

attrib. **1849** LANMAN *Alleghany Mts.* 51 He climbed upon an immense boulder-rock (weighing perhaps fifty tons), which stood on the very brow of a hill side. **1902** WHITE *Conjuror's House* i. 1 A chaos of bowlder-splits. **1903** — *Forest* xv. 217 The result is a series of roaring, dashing boulder rapids and waterfalls.

2. A rounded waterworn stone of the sort used for paving or building; a cobblestone. {1617–} Chiefly attrib.

1840 *S. Lit. Messenger* VI. 192/2 These evidences are below the alluvial, and above the boulder strata. **1851** CIST *Cincinnati* 338 Of late years . . . the introduction of bowlder pavement . . . is gradually changing the whole surface of the city. *a***1861** WINTHROP *Canoe & Saddle* 191 On pebble boulders we must make our couch. **1874** KNIGHT 347/1 Boulder-paving [is] paving with round water-worn boulders, set on a graded bottom of gravel.

Bowldered, Bouldered, *a.* [BOWLDER 2.] Paved with cobblestones. — **1873** BEADLE *Undevel. West* 682 There is not a foot of regular turnpike, a rod of bowldered street, or a mile of navigable canal in the entire Territory.

***Bowling alley.** {–1703} An area or inclosure equipped for bowling.

[**1671** *S.C. Hist. Soc. Coll.* V. 308 The Country soe plaine & leuyll that it may be compared to a Bowling ally.] **1825** J. PICKERING *Inquiries Emigrant* (1831) 15 Almost every tavern keeps a bowling-alley. **1849** AUDUBON *Western Journal* (1906) 52 We reached Brownsville where the rolling of bowling-alleys and the cannoning of billiard balls was all that seemed to enliven the village. **1857** WILLIS *Convalescent* 255 We saw one other peculiarity of 'Sconset—a *whittling room;* or the Nantucket substitute for billiards or bowling-alley. **1868** H. WOODRUFF *Trotting Horse* 61 You will find them [=race tracks] so ordered as to be as smooth as a bowling-alley. **1884** H. C. BUNNER in *Harper's Mag.* Jan. 298/2 The establishment of a good bowling-alley is the signal for the appearance of . . . new bowling clubs. **1904** *McClure's Mag.* Feb. 375/1 [The] company shipped a load of finely dressed wood from its factory in the East for a bowling alley.

Bowling green. An area of grass with a smooth, level surface suitable for playing bowls. {1646–}

[**1654** JOHNSON *Wonder-w. Prov.* 164 The scituation of this Colledg is very pleasant, at the end of a spacious plain, more like a bowling green, then a Wilderness.] **1714** SEWALL *Diary* II. 417 Meeting . . . was now held at Mr. Stevens's beyond the Bowling Green. **1724** JONES *Virginia* 31 A Market Place; near which is a . . . good Bowling Green. **1785** WASHINGTON *Diaries* II. 418 Began again to smooth the Face of the Lawn, or Bolling Green, on the west front of my House. **1815** in Kittredge *Old Farmer* (1904) 276 Bowling-greens have become of late mightily in fashion. **1841** BUCKINGHAM *America* I. 42 The Bowling Green [in New York] is a confined space of 200 feet long by 150 broad.

+**Bowling saloon.** A building equipped with bowling alleys where patrons may engage in bowling. — **1846** *Knickerb.* XXVII. 274 'Speaking of horns' reminds us of 'Horn's Bowling Saloon,' at No. 333 Broadway. **1852** *Ib.* XXXIX. 106 Let them who licensed the bowling-saloon answer with the conflagration still staring them into the face! **1855** J. HOLBROOK *Among Mail Bags* 58 In the basement of the hotel was a bowling saloon. **1889** BRAYLEY *Boston Fire Dept.* 211 The same day fire originated in a wooden building used for bowling-alleys, and known as the 'Neptune Bowling Saloon.'

+**Bowlist.** A member of a former New England religious sect. — **1781** PETERS *Hist. Conn.* 280 The Bowlists, Separatists and Davisonians, are peculiar to the Colony. The first allow neither singing nor prayer.

***Bowman**[1]. [Bow 1.] +An Indian warrior, armed with a bow.

1623–4 *Va. House Burgesses* 33 They had formerly agreed . . . to paye us yearlye tribute, viz. a bushell of corne for every Boweman. **1654** JOHNSON *Wonder-w. Prov.* vi. *114 Boldly they rushed on, and found the passages guarded at each place with an Indian Bow-man. **1699** *Va. State P.* I. 62 A just and full account of . . . what number of Cabbins & Indians there are, especially Bowmen. **1833** CATLIN *Indians* I. 142 The great object of practice is to enable the bowman to draw the bow with suddenness and instant effect.

||**Bowman**[2]. *Obs.* [Prob. for *bâtman* BATMAN, with *bât* pronounced as in French.] (See quotation.) — *a***1859** *Sk. Virginia* (B.), Each captain and lieutenant [in Va.] was entitled, and I believe is so now, to select from the rank of his company a soldier to wait on him, to carry messages, to

cater for him, and to cook for him; and the soldier thus selected was called *bowman.*

+**Bowman root.** [Cf. the earlier BAUMONT ROOT.] =next. — **1824** DODDRIDGE *Notes* 148 Indian physick, or bowman root, a species of epicacuanha [*sic*] was frequently used for a vomit.

+**Bowman's root.** A name given to various common plants, esp. a species of *Gillenia.*

1815 DRAKE *Cincinnati* ii. 87 [In the] forest of the Miami country [grows] *Euphorbia colorata,* Bowman's root. **1843** TORREY *Flora N.Y.* I. 200 *Gillenia trifoliata*. . . . Indian Physic. Bowman's-root. . . . The root . . . acts as an emetic or a cathartic, according to the dose. **1847** WOOD *Botany* 257 *G. stipulacea,* Bowman's Root. . . . Western N.Y. to Ala. . . . Flowers fewer, rose-colored. **1901** MOHR *Plant Life Ala.* 539 *Porteranthus trifoliatus*. . . . Bowman's Root. *Spiraea trifoliata*. . . . *Gillenia trifoliata*. . . . Alleghenian and Carolinian areas; . . . rare west of the Alleghanies.

Bow oar. The oarsman nearest the bow. — **1886** *Century Mag.* Nov. 35/1 Nobody knew what to do with the disaster except 'the bow-oar,' who is described as a gigantic youth.

+**Bowpin.** [Bow 3.] A small flat piece of some hard, tough wood used for attaching an oxbow to its yoke. Also fig. — **1856** *Mich. Agric. Soc. Trans.* VII. 55 D. O. & W. S. Penfield . . . [exhibited] sample bow pins. **1857** F. D. RICHARDS in *Journal Discourses* V. 47 You will not be so likely . . . to lose your bow-pins, chains, or axe. **1857** H. C. KIMBALL in *ib.* V. 217 (Th.), The bow-pin has dropped out of old Bright's bow, . . . and the yoke is now on old Buckanan's neck.

Bowse, *v.* Also **bouse, bouze.** [Sc. and northern Eng. dial.] *intr.* To rush, come or go with a rush. {1807-} — **1774** FITHIAN *Journal* I. 264 He saw a Light in my Chamber—up he bouzes, with a Bottle of Rum in his hand. **c1850** WHITCHER *Bedott P.* xxvi. 316 The very Miss Hawkins they'd ben talkin' about come bowsin' into the room. **1859** A. VAN BUREN *Sojourn in South* 174 Hotly besieged he first 'boused' among the shrubs and bushes, then rolled on the ground.

+**Bowsman.** [Alteration of Fr. *bosseman* BOSMAN, mistaken for *bow's-man* bowman, oarsman near the bow.] The mate of a boat. — **1804** LEWIS in *L. & Clark Exped.* (1904) I. 34 The one not engaged at the oar [of the 'batteaux'] will attend as the Bows-man. **1819** *Missouri Intell.* 24 Sept. 1/4 As soon as he got out of the water and mud, [he] began cursing the patroon, bowsman, boat, and owner, . . . and demanded his wages, saying he would leave the boat. **1840** *Knickerb.* XVI. 270 The delicious white-fish are so numerous, that the bow's-man takes his scoop-net and literally dips them into the boat. **1846** M'KENNEY *Memoirs* I. 97, I ordered the bowsman to stick a pole down in the river. **1902** WHITE *Conjuror's House* ii. 16 New leggings, of holiday pattern, were intermittently visible on the bowsmen and steersmen.

Bowstick. [Bow 1.] A bowstaff. — **1729** *Essex Inst. Coll.* XLII. 132 The storm . . . obliged them to clear & heave what was in her over board as Apples, Bow Sticks, &c.

Bow-timber. [Bow 1.] Wood for making bows. — **1846** SAGE *Scenes Rocky Mts.* iii, We . . . encamped at Big Vermilion for the purpose of procuring a quantity of hickory for gun-sticks and bow-timber.

Bow-whip. (See quotation.) — **1890** *Harper's Mag.* Oct. 718/1 His whip was the fashionable 'bow-whip' of the period, common enough now, to be sure, with a long lash, tapering down to a fine silk 'snapper' on the end.

+**Bowwood.** [Bow 1.] The Osage orange, bois d'arc, or yellowwood, *Maclura aurantiaca.*

1806 *Ann 9th Congress* 2 Sess. 1138 One or two slips of the bois d'arc, bow wood, or yellow wood, from the Missouri. **1821** NUTTALL *Travels Arkansa* 168 In a small prairie . . . a single tree of the bow-wood (or *Maclura*) existed, having a trunk of about 18 inches diameter. **1827** *Western M. Rev.* I. 253 Bow-wood is a striking and beautiful tree, found on the upper courses of the Washita [and] the middle regions of Arkansas. **1857** GRAY *Botany* 398 The Osage Orange, or Bow-wood of Arkansas, is sparingly cultivated for hedges. **1892** APGAR *Trees Northern U.S.* 137 Osage Orange. Bow-wood. . . . [Has] fruit as large as an orange, golden-yellow when ripe.

***Box,** *n.*[1] A small evergreen tree or shrub of the genus *Buxus,* esp. *B. sempervirens.*

1791 MUHLENBERG *Index Florae* 179. **1821** NUTTALL *Travels Arkansa* 76 We entered the alluvial forest, containing oak, hickory, box, [etc.]. **1832** HALE *Flora* 27 The arborescent Box grows to the height of 12 or 16 feet. *Ib.,* The Dwarf Box . . . is used to divide beds from the walks of flower-gardens. **1898** WESTCOTT *D. Harum* 385 The April sun, deliciously warm, drew a smoky odor from the hedge of box with which the parapet walk was bordered.

b. Attrib. and comb. with *bordered, lined; bush.*

1839 *S. Lit. Messenger* V. 794/2 The garden [was] a pleasant sight to see, with its rectangular box-lined gravel walks. **1884** *Harper's Mag.* Oct. 661/2 A rose bloom in a box-bordered plat. **1885** *Century Mag.* Sept. 730/1 Small panes of glass, shadowed without by a massive clump of box-bushes.

***Box,** *n.*[2]

+**1.** A cavity made in the trunk of a tree, usually a maple tree or pine, for collecting sap or turpentine.

1720 P. DUDLEY in *Phil. Trans.* XXXI. 27 You box the tree, as we call it. . . . The Box you make may hold about a Pint. **1775** ROMANS *Nat. Hist. Florida* 150 A hole is cut in the tree on the side most exposed to the solar rays. . . . This hole is called a box, and the turpentine is dipped out of it. **1832** BROWNE *Sylva* 232 The remainder of the year is occupied . . . in making the *boxes* . . . in the base of each [pine] tree. **1857** *Harper's Mag.* May 745/1 The liquid turpentine runs into the notches, or boxes, as they are technically called, each holding from a quart to half a gallon. **1859** G. W. PERRY *Turpentine Farming* 77 When chipping is commenced on the faces, it is called 'hacking boxes.' **1865** *Nation* I. 651 He . . . had a turpentine orchard containing a hundred thousand boxes. **1872** *Vt. Bd. Agric. Rep.* I. 215 He would cut some four or five boxes or gashes, one above the other. **1896** *Pop. Science Mo.* Feb. 478 The French turpentine workman does not cut a big, deep, broad box into the tree [as our southern workman does].

+**2.** A sort of raft formerly used on the Connecticut river. *Obs.*

1809 E. A. KENDALL *Travels* III. 218 Rafts, composed of boards and other lumber, are called *boxes.*

+**3.** A receptacle or pigeonhole in a post office in which a subscriber's mail is placed.

1833 *Trial E. K. Avery* 43 E. K. Avery had a private box at my office. **1862** *Congress. Globe* 9 Jan. 258/1 The class of men who have boxes in post offices, who go there regularly [etc.]. **1871** [L. H. BAGG] *At Yale* 213 A branch post-office was connected with the Bookstore, the 'boxes' whereof were rented for a dollar each, or one half the price of those in the general office. **1897** BRODHEAD *Bound in Shallows* 242 The following evening Dillon found in his post-office box a letter of one line.

attrib. **1884** CABLE *Dr. Sevier* (1885) 341 The small hand-holes of the box-delivery were in the wide tessellated passage. **1887** *Postal Laws* 214 Each postmaster must keep in his office . . . a list of box holders.

+**4.** A kind of boat used in duck-shooting; a sink box.

1859 BARTLETT 47 *Box,* a boat for duck-shooting. **1874** LONG *Wild-Fowl* 52 Perhaps the very best blind . . . is the sunken box, . . . a deep box of pine. *Ib.* 253 The box in which the shooter lies should be of pine.

+**5.** The body of a wagon.

1869 J. R. BROWNE *Adv. Apache Country* 193 One of the escort picked up a few sticks of wood . . . and threw them in the box of the forage-wagon. **1888** C. D. FERGUSON *Exp. Forty-niner* 38 And we would have to unload and carry everything to a sand bar, then take the wheels off and float the box down. **1899** *Mo. So. Dakotan* I. 175 The box is in the slough and the hind axle hangs on the demolished harvester.

+**6.** In baseball, the station occupied by the pitcher.

1886 *Outing* May 239/1 In the absence of Hovey . . . Boyer occupied the box and did some effective work. **1894** *Chicago Record* 15 May 3/1 The Clevelands knocked Breitenstein out of the box in the fifth inning. **1897** *Outing* May 203/1 The team is fairly strong all round except in the box. **1897** *Boston Journal* 8 June 4/5 He ought to be given a show in the box. . . . Change Ryan to shortstop and put McCormick behind the bat. **1903** *N.Y. Ev. Post* 17 Sept. 5 It was a pitcher's battle, with Ewing in the box for Cincinnati.

7. *In* (or *into*) *a box,* in (or into) a difficult situation or 'fix.' *colloq.* {1887-}

Cf. *in a bad box* (1837-) s.v. BAD *a.* 5, and Eng. *in a* (or *the*) *wrong box* (1554-).

1864 WEBSTER 156/3 *In a box,* in a perplexity or embarrassing position; in difficulty. **1891** WILKINS *New Eng. Nun,* etc. 124 It's a mean kind of box I've got you into. **1896** *N.Y. Dramatic News* 4 July 8/2 Owing to the mixed up state of affairs, [they] are both somewhat in a 'box.' **1907** WILKINS *By Light of Soul* 227 But say, M'ria, you be in an awful box.

***Box,** *v.*

+**1.** *tr.* To make an incision in (the trunk of a tree) preparatory to collecting the sap or turpentine. Also *intr.*: To cut *into.*

1700 *Springfield Rec.* II. 357 No Stranger . . . shal box any trees or improve the sam for Turpentine. **1720** P. DUDLEY in *Phil. Trans.* XXXI. 27 You box the Tree, as we call it, i.e. make a hole with an Axe, or chizzel, into the side of the Tree. **1737** BRICKELL *N. Carolina* 265 Negroes cut large Cavities on each side of the Pitch-Pine Tree (which they term Boxing of the Tree) wherein the Turpentine runs. **1862** 'E. KIRKE' *Among Pines* 102 The trees are 'boxed' and 'tapped' early in the year, while the frost is still in the ground. **1892** *Harper's Mag.* Aug. 398/2 The pines . . . bear a large amount of wounding. To extract the turpentine, the axeman boxes them. **1896** *Vt. Agric. Rep.* XV. 35 The person wanted to know . . . 'If the maple trees were boxed into to make a receptacle for holding sap.' **1906** L. BELL *C. Lee* 282 Carolina rode forward fearlessly, glancing sharply at the trees for signs of their having been boxed by thieving negroes [for turpentine].

+**2.** To provide with planking to prevent caving.

1816 *Boston Selectmen* 18 April 179 The ground having been boxed last fall and the well sunk to the depth of about 30 feet. **1821** *Ib.* 7 Sept. 216 After consideration . . . of the probable cost of digging and boxing a cellar under the building [etc.].

+**Box alder.** =BOX ELDER. — **1805** CLARK in *Lewis & C. Exped.* (1904) I. 299 There is some timber in it's bottom lands, which consists of . . . small Ash and box alder. **1847** J. PALMER *Rocky Mts.* 65 The streams are lined with cotton wood, willow and boxalder. **1867** *Iowa Agric. Soc. Rep.* (1868) 437 The smaller groves . . . consist principally of soft maple, . . . box-alder and willow. **1884** *Fargo* (Dakota) *Argus* 27 May, I have . . . five hundred eight-foot cottonwood and box-alders for shade-trees.

+**Boxberry.** The wintergreen or checkerberry. Also attrib. with *bread, cake, swamp*, etc.

1706 *Plymouth Rec.* 26 Thirty six acres of land . . . bounded from a stake in the range of said Cooks land in boxberry swamp. **1802** *Mass. H. S. Coll.* VIII. 197 The bushes are whortleberries, . . . bay-berries, and box-berries. **1804** *Ib.* 2 Ser. VIII. 114 A variety of fruits, such as raspberries, . . . boxberries, and bog cranberries. **1832** CHILD *Frugal Housewife* 86 Boxberry, fever-bush, sweet fern, and horse-radish make a good and healthy diet-drink. **1847** WOOD *Botany* 373 Box-berry . . . [is] common in woods and pastures. Can. to Penn. and Ky. **1852** MRS. ELLET *Pioneer Women* 206 The 'box-berries' still showed their bright scarlet faces, peeping out beneath the snow and ice. **1881** MCLEAN *Cape Cod Folks* 243 We had boxberry bread, boxberry stews and pies, and one day, I caught a glimpse of Grandma . . . frying boxberry griddle-cakes.

+**Boxboard.** A board suitable for making boxes. — **1853** FOWLER *Home for All* 34 [When] you . . . are ready for your walls, procure common pine box boards, . . . and cut them off to the length required for your wall. *Ib.* 35 Driving a nail down through these cross pieces, into each box board. **1905** *Bureau of Forestry Bul.* No. 63, 15 The lumber is usually of a low grade, but it is always in demand at good prices for match blocks, pail staves, and box boards.

+**Box cañon.** A cañon having a comparatively flat bottom and vertical sides. — **1873** BOURKE *Journal* 21 March, We descended into a box cañon and made camp. **1887** *Outing* April 11/1 It turned out to be an ugly hole at the end of a box cañon, with but one way in and out. **1889** *Century Mag.* April 904/2 We then continued our journey down the mountains through a box-cañon. **1907** WHITE *Arizona Nights* 3 We . . . followed it [=a watercourse] into box canons between rim-rock carved fantastically. **1916** BOWER *Phantom Herd* 243 You're holding 'em in a box cañon . . . waiting for a chance to drive them outa the country.

+**Boxcar.** A railroad car for carrying freight, resembling a huge box.

1856 *Mich. Agric. Soc. Trans.* VII. 334 There are on the road . . . 11 four-wheeled box cars. **1863** CUMMING *Hospital Life* (1866) 89/2 We are in a box-car. **1865** R. H. KELLOGG *Rebel Prisons* 283 They were merely common box-cars, such as are used at the North for transporting freight. **1874** B. F. TAYLOR *World on Wheels* I. 51 Box-cars, with sliding doors on the sides. **1878** PINKERTON *Strikers*, etc. 309 A meeting of fully four thousand strikers . . . was held, . . . the leaders speaking from the top of box-cars. **1884** *Century Mag.* April 861/1 His dwelling is an old freight box-car, lifted from its wheels and shoved aside from the busy railroad track. **1888** GRIGSBY *Smoked Yank* (1891) 90 We were put . . . in box cars, and started . . . to Savannah to be exchanged. **1889** C. L. MARSH *Opening Oyster* 34 In stealing rides on freight-trains, box-car or gondola, it was all one to us. **1901** MERWIN & WEBSTER *Calumet K* 293 Long strings of box cars filled the belt line sidings.

attrib. **1898** *Engineering Mag.* XVI. 69 The Illinois Central equipment was of the standard box-car type. **1904** T. WATSON *Bethany* (1920) 171 Box-car travel had not proven a luxury. **1921** *Rural Organization* 133 Eight million . . . children attend one- and two-teacher rural schools, scattered over the continent in 210,000 box-car buildings.

+**Box cart.** A two-wheeled vehicle having a box-shaped body. — **1890** *Harper's Mag.* March 569/2 Jim . . . returned with the box-cart and horse.

Box coat. *Obs.* A heavy overcoat, or one with a cape, formerly worn by coachmen on the box, or by those riding outside a coach. {1825}

[**1822** IRVING *Bracebridge Hall* I. 101 The travellers'-room is garnished . . . with box coats, whips of all kinds, . . . and oil-cloth covered hats.] **1840** SIMMS *Border Beagles* I. 14 The sharp militia colonel in his new box-coat . . . [was] seeking to find favour in the regiment. **1849** WILLIS *Rural Lett.* 43 We can leave our box-coats at home. **1860** EMERSON *Conduct of Life* 130 There are advantages in the old hat and box-coat. . . . Dress makes a little restraint. . . . But the box-coat . . . unlocks the tongue. **1877** BARTLETT 64 *Box-Coat*, a heavy overcoat, originally worn by coachmen; when not in use, usually carried by teamsters and drivers under their box or seat.

+**Box coot.** (See quotation.) — **1844** *Nat. Hist. N.Y., Zoology* II. 335 The Box Coot, Spectacle Duck, . . . is very common on the coast of New-York during the winter.

+**Box crab.** One or other species of crab of the genus *Calappa* resembling a box when at rest. — **1889** *Cent.* 759/1 *C. depressa* and *C. granulata* are among the species known as *box-crabs*.

+**Box elder.**

1. The ash-leaved maple, *Acer negundo*.

1787 SARGENT in *Mem. Academy* II. I. 158 Box Elder, from six inches to two feet, and a very crooked tree. **1810** MICHAUX *Arbres* I. 29 *Box elder*, seule dénomination dans les Etats de l'Ouest. **1818** DARBY *Emigrant's Guide* 34 The most common timber trees found in the basin of the Mobile [include] . . . *Acer negundo*, Box elder, [etc.]. **1848** E. BRYANT *California* 119 The timber which fringes the margin of the stream is chiefly box-elder and large willows. **1860** *Ill. Agric. Soc. Trans.* IV. 450 The Ash Leaf Maple or Box Elder . . . is easily grown from cuttings, hardy, fine form, grows large, and is desirable. **1875** *Chicago Tribune* 14 Oct. 7/2 Its valley [*i.e.*, of the Belle Fourche, is] . . . divided here and there by dry creeks filled with box-elders and plum-bushes. **1885** HAVARD *Flora W. & S. Texas* 458 Of the Maple family, the Box-Elder, a small tree near the water, is the only representative.

2. A tree of this species.

1871 EGGLESTON *Hoosier Schoolm.* 69 That box-elder . . . stood just in sight. **1878** BEADLE *Western Wilds* 351 Three figures appeared in the shadow between the ward meeting-house and the line of box-elders beside it. **1884** *Century Mag.* March 649/2 There are large numbers of elms, lindens, box elders, and buttonwoods, besides other varieties. **1888** *Scribner's Mag.* (F.), Bob McCord had stopped in the darkness under the shade of a box elder.

+**Box-elder bug.** (See quotation.) — **1892** V. KELLOG *Kansas Insects* 99 Box-elder bug (*Leptocoris trivittatus*). . . . In winter the bugs frequent houses, and many appear in sunny places on warm days.

+**Box freight car.** =BOX CAR. — **1858** W. P. SMITH *Railway Celebrations* 92 Equipment of the Marietta and Cincinnati Railway: . . . Cars, . . . Box Freight (or 'House'), 221. **1866** W. REID *After the War* 365 We had been traveling . . . in third-class passenger cars. Now we came down to box freight cars. **1903** E. JOHNSON *Ry. Transportation* 141 In the military and fourth classes the coaches are but little better than box freight-cars.

+**Box house.** A house of a simple pattern and structure, somewhat resembling a huge box. — **1881** *Rep. Indian Affairs* 83 The school was . . . conducted in . . . the house formerly used by the agent, and some box-houses constructed for the purpose. **1904** 'O. HENRY' *Heart of West* 306 Not far away was the little railroad station, its building a strong box house. **1909** — *Options* 303 There was a four-room, unpainted . . . box house in which the family lived.

Boxing, *vbl. n.* [BOX *v.*]

+**1.** The practice or method of making boxes in the trunks of trees to collect turpentine or sap.

1708 *Springfield Rec.* II. 376 It was voted to restraine the boxing of Turpentine Trees within the inmost Comons. **1880** *Vt. Agric. Rep.* VI. 112 An aged maple tree may be found with the scars made by an axe in tapping by the method then known as 'boxing.'

2. A protective casing or conduit of wood, stone, etc.

1816 *Boston Selectmen* 18 April 179 The water contained in the ground outside of the boxing . . . flowed in as fast as they attempted to take it out. **1865–6** *Ill. Agric. Soc. Trans.* VI. 319 A water pipe or boxing eighteen inches in the clear is laid under ground to the centre of the yard. **1884** *Century Mag.* March 649/2 This [planting of trees] was systematically done, the trees being carefully selected by experts, . . . planted with great care, and protected by boxing. **1893** 'MARK TWAIN' *P. Wilson* i, All along the streets . . . stood locust trees with trunks protected by wooden boxing. **1907** M. H. NORRIS *Veil* 44 He felt he knew its depth [*i.e.* of a well]; knew its slimy, moss-covered stone boxing.

+**3.** The enclosing of printed lists, tables, etc., within rules.

1888 *2nd Ann. Rep. Interstate Com. Commission* 271 (*Cent.* s.v. *Table*), The use of miscellaneous in the boxing of this table requires a word of explanation.

Box iron. A smoothing iron having a boxlike receptacle for the heating iron. {1746–}

1666 *Essex Inst. Coll.* XXV. 147 Inventory of Gou[erno]r Endecott household. . . . It[em] boxe Iron & heaters. **1687** *Conn. Probate Rec.* I. 353, I give to my daughter . . . a fire slice, box Iron & heaters. **1720** SEWALL *Letter-Book* II. 107 Item a good box-iron to iron with. **1874** KNIGHT 351 *Box-iron*, a hollow smoothing-iron, heated by a hot iron within.

+**Box letter.** [BOX *n.*[2] 3.] A letter intended to be placed in a private box at the post office. — **1832** *U.S. Postal Regul.* 43 Box-letters. **1843** *P.O. Laws & Reg.* II. 17 All letters placed in a post office, to be delivered from it to the persons addressed [are] called 'Box letters.' *Ib.* 28 Drop and box letters are not to be advertised.

+**Box martin.** The common American martin, *Progne subis*. — **a1857** *R.I. Rev. Stat.* lxxxiii. §2 Any person who shall take, kill or destroy any swallow or box martin, between the first day of May and the first day of October, shall forfeit for every such bird two dollars.

+**Box oak.** Post oak. — **1785** WASHINGTON *Diaries* II. 360 These [acorns] grew on a tree resembling the box Oak. **1810** MICHAUX *Arbres* I. 22 Post oak, . . . Iron Oak, . . . Box oak (chêne buis), [ou] Box White Oak . . . dans l'Etat de Maryland.

+**Box oyster.** *local.* (See quotation.) — **1881** E. INGERSOLL *Oyster Industry* 242 *Box Oyster*, an oyster from seven to ten years old, of round, handsome shape, not less than three inches wide and five inches long. (Connecticut and New York) . . . The name is due to the fact that many years ago it was customary to ship oysters of this grade to New York in boxes instead of the ordinary barrel.

+**Box-rent.** [BOX *n.*[2] 3.] Rent paid for a post-office box. — **1841** *Congress. Globe* App. 20 Feb. 343/2 This House was constrained . . . to adopt my proposition to cure the abuse growing out of box-rents. **1880** LAMPHERE *U.S. Govt.* 231/1 Officers of the fourth class receive no fixed salary, but are allowed their box-rents and commissions on cancelled stamps. **1887** *Postal Laws* 18 The Division of Salaries and Allowances . . . prepares orders for regulation of box-rents rates.

+**Box settle.** A covered box serving as a settle and bed. — **1860** HOLMES *E. Venner* v, A man slept in a box-settle at night, to wake up early passengers. **1877** BARTLETT 64 *Box-Settle*, a settle whose seat is the cover of a box (*i.e.* a bunk).

+**Box sledge, sleigh.** A sledge or sleigh with a boxlike body. — **1855** *Knickerb.* Feb. 168 The widow and he were often seen riding side by side, on fine moon-light evenings, in Mr. Lean's large box-sleigh. **1884**

ROE *Nature's Story* 11 After seeing that her trunks were safely bestowed in a large box-sledge, . . . he drove rapidly homewards.

+**Box stall.** A large stall for horses or cattle, in which they can be left untied; a 'loose box.' — **1885** *Harper's Mag.* May 949/2 His choicest colt . . . had been fed from his birth in a box stall. **1889** W. WARFIELD *Cattle-Breeding* 309 It consists of a double row of box-stalls, ten by twelve feet, each . . . fitted with two stanchions. **1890** *Harper's Mag.* Sept. 559/1 Those great box-stalls, with quilts hung before them. **1897** *Outing* XXX. 84/2 Let the horse have his day as at Forest Park Farm he well may, and take a turn round the box-stalls.

+**Box stove.** A stove somewhat resembling a box in shape. — **1820** *Columbian Centinel* 1 Jan. 3/3 Oblong and oval Box Stoves. **1842** *Knickerb.* XIX. 306 This room is warmed by a box-stove. **1867** 'T. LACKLAND' *Homespun* I. 137 The dry, baking heat of the iron box-stove. **1873** MILLER *Amongst Modocs* 61 There was an enormous box-stove there in the middle of the room, with a drum like a steam boiler above. **1885** E. B. CUSTER *Boots & Saddles* 175 Each room had an old-fashioned box-stove.

+**Box suit.** A man's suit, the coat having box pleats in the back. — **1887** *Courier-Journal* 8 May 1/1 All box suits at half price.

Boxthorn. [BOX *n.*[1]] A common name for the *Lycium barbarum*, and related species. {1678–}

1814 O. O. RICH *Amer. Plants* 14. **1818** NUTTALL *N. A. Plants* 101 Box-Thorn (*Lycium Carolinianum*), shrub (without thorns). **1847** DARLINGTON *Weeds & Plants* 256 Barbary Box-thorn . . . [is] rather difficult to get rid of when once established, [and] is often something of a nuisance. **1857** GRAY *Botany* 341 *Lycium Barbarum*, L. (Barbary Box-thorn, or Matrimony-vine), a slightly thorny trailing shrubby vine, well known in cultivated gardens, is yet hardly spontaneous. **1894** *Amer. Folk-Lore* VII. 95 *Lycium vulgare*, . . . box-thorn, bastard jasmine, Iowa.

Box tortoise. A species of land tortoise (*Cistudo*) capable of closing itself up in its shell. {1843–} — **1839** STORER *Mass. Reptiles* 214 From the circumstance of the sternum being divided into two portions, . . . enabling the animal when disturbed, to encase itself entirely within its shell, the species is generally known under the name of 'box tortoise.' **1842** *Nat. Hist. N.Y., Zoology* III. 24 The Box Tortoise is common everywhere on dry land, although it is also occasionally met with in swamps and moist places. **1885** *Amer. Naturalist* XIX. 37 The common box tortoise, called also 'land tortoise' and 'terrapin,' according to locality, hibernates regularly in Southern Indiana.

+**Box trap.** A trap that employs a box for catching birds and small animals. — **1840** [W. HAWES] *Sporting Scenes* I. 112 The poor quail has to contend with . . . 'figure-y 4' box-traps of vagabond hen-roost pilferers. **1857** GLISAN *Jrnl. Army Life* 394, I have returned the compliment by preparing for them, every night, a nice little piece of meat in a box trap. **1871** LEWIS *Poultry Book* 173 Fasten it to the treadle of a steel trap, or to a common box trap. **1876** BURROUGHS *Winter Sunshine* I. 22, I come upon their snares, dead-falls, and rude box-traps. **1884** ROE *Nature's Story* 41 Webb helped him make two box-traps, and the boy concealed them in the copse where the rabbit-tracks were thickest.

Box trunk. *Obs.* A trunk of a box-like form. — **1783** in *Mass. H. S. Collections* I. 178 What will be the charge of land transportation of a box trunk?

Box-tubing. (Cf. BOXING *vbl. n.* 2.) — **1874** *Vt. Bd. Agric. Rep.* II. 520 Mr. Andrews used a box-tubing, twelve inches square, to the roof to ventilate his barns.

+**Box turtle.** =BOX TORTOISE. Also fig. — **1833** *Niles' Reg.* XLIV. 374/2 The turtle is of the species commonly called the box turtle, having the upper shell very crowning, and the lower shell flat. **1856** EMERSON *Eng. Traits* 125 The same men . . . shut down their valve, as soon as the conversation approaches the English church. After that, you talk with a box-turtle. **1869** *Amer. Naturalist* III. 279 A large Box Turtle (*Cistuda Virginica*) was unearthed while digging in the barn-yard.

+**Box wagon.** A wagon having a box-like body. — **1846** BUSHNELL *Work & Play* (1864) 246 If you will make up your mind to . . . live on the coarsest fare, to ride in a box wagon or cart [etc.]. **1871** *Lippincott's Mag.* Nov. 479/2 'Bragg,' he called, 'get out the double harness and the box wagon.' **1874** *Congress. Rec.* 25 April 3377/2 [It] was a small . . . covered carriage, sufficient to enable a Bureau officer to come to the Capitol . . . and not be soaked in a 'box-wagon.'

+**Box white oak.** Post oak, BOX OAK. — **1810** [see BOX OAK]. **1832** BROWNE *Sylva* 275 In Maryland and a great part of Virginia where it abounds, . . . it is called Box White Oak, and sometimes Iron Oak and Post Oak. **1892** APGAR *Trees Northern U.S.* 153 *Quercus stellata*, . . . Post-Oak, Rough or Box White Oak, . . . [is] a medium-sized tree, 40 to 50 ft. high, with very hard, durable wood.

Boxwood. {1652–}

1. The box or box tree; also, the wood of this.

1846 BROWNE *Trees of Amer.* 433 A great portion of the box-wood of commerce, sold in the European and American markets as 'Turkey box,' is grown in Circassia and Georgia. **1892** APGAR *Trees Northern U.S.* 133 *Buxus sempervirens* (Boxwood). . . . This plant is a native of Europe, and in its tree form furnishes the white wood used for wood-engraving.

+**2.** The flowering dogwood.

1832 BROWNE *Sylva* 141 In the United States at large, it is known by the name of Dogwood, and in Connecticut it is also called Box Wood. **1832** WILLIAMSON *Maine* I. 114 Among the shrubs of the largest size is the *Boxwood*, or 'shad-blossom' (sometimes erroneously taken for 'common Dogwood'). **1883** HALE *Woods & Timbers N.C.* 101 Dogwood. . . . Common throughout the United States, and mostly known by this name, but sometimes called *Boxwood*. **1884** SARGENT *Rep. Forests* 91 *Cornus florida*, . . . Flowering Dogwood, Box Wood.

+**3.** The yellowwood of Florida.

1884 SARGENT *Rep. Forests* 39 *Schaefferia frutescens*, . . . Yellow wood, Box wood. **1890** *Cent.* 5386/3 *S. frutescens*, a small tree of southern Florida and the neighboring islands, produces a valuable wood which from its color and hardness is known by the names of *yellow-wood* and *boxwood*.

***Boy.**

+**1.** A male slave; a Negro.

1764 JEFFERSON *Writings* IV. 15 You mentioned one letter which you wrote last Friday, and sent by the Secretary's boy. **1835** [INGRAHAM] *South-West* II. 242 They always address . . . as 'boy' and 'girl' . . . all [slaves] under forty years of age. **1845** in Lyell *Second Visit* I. 221 A liberal reward will be given for the arrest of a boy named Dick. . . . He is about thirty years of age. **1855** *Knickerb.* XLV. 190 Reared from childhood in the arms of my 'boy,' I was attached to him by no common feelings. **1862** 'E. KIRKE' *Among Pines* 34 The newcomer . . . had, at the solicitation of his 'boys,' . . . who were afraid to proceed, called to ask shelter for the night. **1879** TOURGEE *Fool's Errand* 35 Enough corn, meat, and forage to subsist himself and the two 'boys' (slaves) whom he kept to help him. **1888** *Harper's Mag.* April 705/2, I will defend this boy. I know nothing whatever of the case, but I happen to know something of the negro.

2. *The boys*, used to designate youths or men as members of a company, crew, or class. {1730–}

Also used in the vocative, *boys*, in addressing a company or number of men.

1819 W. COBBETT *Year's Residence U.S.* 321 The farmer here generally is at the head of his 'boys,' as they, in the kind language of the country, are called. **1841** DANA *Seaman's Man.* 139 The men are divided as equally as possible with reference to their qualities as able seamen, ordinary seamen, or boys (as all green hands are called, whatever their age may be). **1843** *Knickerb.* XXII. 160 The man who makes money [by farming] . . . must rise in the morning with the 'boys.' **1846** [W. STEWART] *Altowan* I. vi. 174 He was camp-keeper to some of the boys who were out on some of the sources of the Missouri. **1850** N. KINGSLEY *Diary* 111 The boys are haveing good success at killing ducks now-a-days. **1867** W. H. DIXON *New America* I. 2 These Western boys (every man living beyond the Missouri is a Boy, just as every woman is a Lady). **1887** C. B. GEORGE *40 Yrs. on Rail* 167 All 'the boys' on the road will swear by their superintendents. **1889** *Harper's Mag.* Dec. 119/2 The boys, long, lank, and middle aged for the most part, . . . sat in an irregular semicircle about the hearth. **1901** M. E. RYAN *Montana* 97 These ladies and their husbands, together with the better class of the 'boys,' were the people whom Mr. Lyster expected to meet.

+**b.** Men in the army; soldiers. Freq. in *the boys in blue* (cf. BLUE *n.*)

1861 O. W. NORTON *Army Lett.* 19 It was then announced that the whole thing was a canard, started just to keep the boys quiet. **1861** *Chicago Tribune* 19 July 1/4 The firing was at Bull's Run, . . . [and was] commenced by a skirmish-party of Michigan boys. **1865** TROWBRIDGE *Three Scouts* i. 8 'Pile on the sticks, boys! Rebel fences make good Union fires!' . . . All were 'boys' in the regiment. **1866** *Congress. Globe* 27 Jan. 460/1 The brave 'boys in blue' fought manfully, and through their efforts, thank God, the Union has been preserved. **1876** J. E. TODD *John Todd* 428 'My Secesh gun' . . . fired its last shot at the 'boys in blue,' and was picked up on the fields of Newbern. **1888** *Missouri Republ.* 3 March (F.), One of our most popular preachers tells a rich one of some of the boys who wore the gray. **1893** *Congress. Rec.* 30 Sept. 1971/1, I do not wonder that there is great dissatisfaction among the boys in blue, the men who fought to sustain the Union. **1901** CHURCHILL *Crisis* 478 On our march to the sea, if the orders were ever given to turn northward, 'the boys' would get very much depressed.

+**c.** Loungers about taverns; town loafers. (Cf. B'HOY and BOWERY BOY.)

1834 *Knickerb.* III. 34 The landlord after telling me several times not to mind the *boys*, went about his business. **1845** J. J. HOOPER *Simon Sugg's Adv.* xii. 142, I wouldn't care a dried-apple d—m for 'the boys' to know it. **1846** *Spirit of Times* 25 April 101/1 James was what is commonly called 'one of the boys'—that is, he was a gentleman of the town, with no visible means of support. *Ib.* 9 May 121/1 The 'boys' have carried sufficient 'stones in their hats' . . . to make a strong fortification on the Battery. **1851** *Polly Peablossom* 98 The old man . . . was apt, when he got among 'the boys' in town, to take more than he could conveniently carry. **1853** J. G. BALDWIN *Flush Times Ala.* 7 He was the man for the 'boys,'—then a numerous and influential class.

+**d.** Political followers; hangers-on.

1885 *Mag. Amer. Hist.* Jan. 98/1 *Boys* . . . is often used nowadays to designate the political hangers-on of a candidate or party. **1888** BRYCE *Amer. Commonwealth* II. 451 He has entered the large and active class called technically, 'workers,' or more affectionately, 'the Boys.' **1888** M. LANE in *America* 20 Sept. 15 It is often considered highly expedient for a candidate to make it all right with 'the boys.' **1897** *Chicago Tribune* 9 July 6/3 (caption), Powers as the agent of the 'boys'. . . . The ordinance could not possibly pass unless 'the boys' were liberally rewarded. **1906** *N.Y. Ev. Post* 1 March 8 Machine politicians . . . always want some one who will be kind to 'the boys.'

Boy's-love. A popular name for southernwood. {1863-} — **1883** *Century Mag.* Oct. 959/1 Whosoe'er I first do meet With the Boy's-Love in my shoe, He's the one I'm sure to wed. **1887** WILKINS *Humble Romance* 25 Boys'-love, sweet-williams, and pinks were the fashionable and prevailing flowers. **1889** *Cent.* 650/1 *Boy's-love,* . . . the southernwood; . . . an ointment made with its ashes [is] used by young men to promote the growth of a beard. **1892** *Amer. Folk-Lore* V. 22 In Maine and in Woburn, Mass., this herb is called boy's love. . . . In other parts of Massachusetts it is said that if a girl puts a piece of southernwood down her back she will marry the first boy whom she meets.

***Brace,** *n.*[1] [F. *brasse.*] A measure of length, 5,318 feet. {-1710} — **1805** CLARK in *Lewis & C. Exped.* (1904) I. 269 He . . . had received . . . from M. Chaboillez . . . the following articles 3 Brace of Cloth 1 Brace of Scarlet a par Corduroy overalls.

+**Brace,** *n.*[2] *colloq.* [f. BRACE *v.* 1.] **1.** *To take a brace,* to pull oneself together, make a fresh start, mend one's ways. **2.** =BRACER. — **(1) 1884** *Century Mag.* Nov. 154 Vane 'takes a brace.' He goes to America in the steerage, . . . sternly lives in down-town lodgings [etc.]. **1907** WHITE *Arizona Nights* III. 282 'It's time we took a brace here,' he growled. **1910** RAINE *B. O'Connor* 49 You want to take a brace and act like a man. **(2) 1890** RYAN *Told in Hills* 183 They needed that swallow of brandy as a brace against the cold wind of the hills. **1897** 'THANET' *Missionary Sheriff* 123 He passed the tumbler to Harned, who shook his head. 'Don't need a brace?'

* **Brace,** *v.*

+**1.** *intr.* With *up:* **a.** To take liquor or a tonic to brace the nerves or system. Also fig.

1809 *Ann. 10th Congress* 2 Sess. 1148 We have been home, and bracing up; we have had plenty of good wine. **1817** S. R. Brown *Western Gaz.* 354 If the stomach be foul . . . take an emetic and then brace up with bark. **1856** E. G. PARKER *4 July Orat.* (Boston) 7 By drinking of the true herotonic—the sentiments of the Revolution—we may brace up for one day. **1888** *Texas Siftings* 18 Aug. (F.), Let's go over to the saloon and brace up with a snifter.

b. To pull oneself together; to prepare for an effort; to pluck up courage.

1816 U. BROWN *Journal* II. 44 He minutely examines the same & began to brace up in the following Manner; said it was the opinion of divers [etc.]. **1830** COOPER *Water Witch* III. 122 'Brace up,' said Ludlow, in the calm tones that denote a forced tranquillity. **1887** *Harper's Mag.* May 938/2 When I have a strong pressure to bear I can brace up and do almost anything. **1893** 'MARK TWAIN' *£1,000,000 Bank-Note* 30 He gripped my hand hard, and braced up, and was all right and lively after that for the dinner. **1901** *Emporia* (Kansas) *Gazette* 19 July, So brace up, gentle reader, Leave off groaning over the mulligrubs.

+**2.** *tr.* To press or plant firmly; to render firm by pressure. Also *intr.* for *refl.*

a1846 *Quarter Race Ky.* etc. 97 Braced back in my phaeton, . . . I touches her [=the mare] up On an elegant 'raw.' **1849** THOREAU *Week on Concord* Thurs. 315 With their fore feet braced, they sustained the rushing torrent in their rear. **1857** M. J. HOLMES *Meadow-Brook* xxviii, Bolt upright upon the box, with his brawny feet firmly braced against the dash-board so as to give him more power, sat Bill. **1885** 'MARK TWAIN' in *Century Mag.* Dec. 196/2 It would sit down and brace back, and no one could budge it.

+**Brace game.** A card game in which at least one player is cheated. Also fig. — **1875** *Chicago Tribune* 25 Aug. 8/1 The brace game flourishes for no other purpose than to cheat the gambling fraternity. **1882** PECK *Sunshine* 38 How does he know but the same deacon is playing a brace game on him on the hereafter? **1908** WHITE *Riverman* vi. 58 I tell you, you can't win! . . . It's a brace game pure and simple.

Bracer. [Cf. BRACE *v.* 1.] A drink of something that braces one up. {1740-, of medicine}

1829 *Savannah* (Ga.) *Mercury* 1 July (Th.), If I take a settler after my coffee, a cooler at nine, [and] a bracer at ten, . . . who has a right to complain? **1834** *Western Mo. Mag.* 573 The soldier . . . set to with keen relish, having whetted the appetite with divers bracers. **1877** HABBERTON *Jericho Road* 12 Take Slim up to the bar and treat him to whisky; he needs a bracer—bad. **1894** 'O. HENRY' *Cabbages & Kings* 202 Take a bracer, anyway, before you go. **1907** MULFORD *Bar-20* 232 The members of the outfit . . . gave their uproarious sanction, all needing bracers to sustain them.

***Brack.** *dial.* A flaw or fault in a piece of cloth or other fabric. {Now *dial.*} — **1816** PICKERING 51 This old English word is still used colloquially in many parts of New England, where it is commonly applied to a breach or flaw in a piece of cloth. **a1859** *New Eng. Tales* (B.), The calico was beautiful, while not a brack could be found in it. **1871** STOWE *Sam Lawson* 59 There warn't a brack in his silk stockin's. **1883** JEWETT *Mate of the Daylight,* etc. (1885) 46 There aint a spot on 'em [=blankets], nor a brack in 'em.

Brackel, variant of BROCKLE *a. Obs.* — **1665** *Hempstead Rec.* I. 164 Date the same sold by Moosses Moodg to Ellias Douty wone cow coolered black with a brackel face with a slip coot out onder the ofe aer branded with :SS:.

‖**Bracket shoe.** *Obs.* App., a snowshoe or racket. — **1648** *Good News from New Eng.* in *Mass. H. S. Coll.* 4 Ser. I. 203 The tripping Deer . . . burst through frozen snow, Hunters pursue with bracket shoes.

Bradish, *v. local.* [Cf. Eng. dial. *braddishing,* variant of *brattishing, bratticing.*] *tr.* To enclose or close up with planking or canvas. — **1888** *Missouri Republican* 31 March (F.), After the settling the west entrance was not safe to work in, but timbers were put in and it was bradished, or hermetically sealed.

* **Brag,** *n.*

1. A braggart, boaster. {1671, and mod. dial.}

1817 A. ROYALL *Lett. from Ala.* 42 The Kentuckyans are great brags. **1873-4** *Vt. Bd. Agric. Rep.* II. 213 [He was] very communicative in regard to himself, being what we should call something of a brag. **1910** 'O. HENRY' *Rolling Stones* (1912) 117 George is the vainest man I ever see, and the biggest brag.

2. A game at cards, resembling poker. {1734-}

1845 *Congress. Globe* 30 Dec. 112/2 This looked like playing the game of brag, while the negotiation was pending. **1852** JACKSON *Forty-niner* (1920) 159 They play poker and 'Brag' for big stakes. **1871** BARNUM *Struggles & Triumphs* 312 Soon after I went to bed five or six men came into the room with cards and a candle and asked permission . . . to sit down and play a quiet game of 'brag.' **1887** *Courier-Journal* 23 Jan. 15/7 Poker . . . is an American improvement on the game of brag.

b. A challenge made in this game.

a1846 *Quarter Race Ky.* etc. 201 Making a large brag on no pair, he observed Brown lean back in his chair.

3. *fig.* Esp. *to play brag,* to boast; to try to get the better of another by a boastful attitude. {1883-}

1814 J. Q. ADAMS *Diary* (1929) 148 He was for playing brag with the British Plenipotentiaries. **1866** C. H. SMITH *Bill Arp* 7 Both sections were playing 'brag' as well as 'battle.'

+**Brag,** *a.* [f. BRAG *n.* or *v.*] Fine, excellent, first-rate.

(1) 1838 *Jeffersonian* 5 May 96 The Moselle was a new *brag* boat and had recently made several exceedingly quick trips. **1847** FIELD *Drama in Pokerville,* etc. 174 The water at a 'good stage,' and out for a 'brag trip,' with a rival boat behind. **1892** 'MARK TWAIN' *£1,000,000 Bank-Note,* etc. (1893) 199, I remember the brag run of a steamer which I travelled in once on the Pacific.

(2) 1845 SIMMS *Wigwam & Cabin* II. 142, I'm no brag dog—nor I don't want to be a biting dog. **a1846** *Quarter Race Ky.* etc. 200 Brown had bantered the hardy mountaineer, who was said to be a brag player, for a game of poker. **1857** *Knickerb.* L. 292 Isaac had once been the 'brag hand' of the plantation. **1872** *Harper's Mag.* Sept. 508/1 She's our brag gal over here, she is, and strangers like to hear about her. **1893** *Outing* May 92/1 His sire [*i.e.* of a puppy] . . . was the brag runner of the country. **1904** HARBEN *Georgians* 291 Our brag murderer, who recently laid low one of our most popular citizens.

(3) 1848 D. P. THOMPSON *L. Amsden* 14, I took the syrup from the kettle . . . and filled up anew [with sap], thinking I would boil down a few pounds as nice as I could for brag-sugar. **1848** *Knickerb.* XXXII. 329 Over my head was a pair of huge antlers, from which were suspended . . . some stalks of 'brag wheat.' **1872** *Vt. Bd. Agric. Rep.* I. 570 The 'brag crops' of the West are small, even with manure applied liberally. **1874** *Ib.* II. 732 Encourage them to make some 'brag sugar,' and see the enthusiasm it will kindle in them.

* **Brag,** *v.*

1. *intr.* With *on.* **a.** To boast of or about. *colloq.* {1786; now *dial.*}

1850 H. C. WATSON *Camp-Fires Revol.* 49 It would have been somethin' to brag on, I know. **1853** BALDWIN *Flush Times Ala.* 24 He bragged largely on Virginia. **1860** GREELEY *Overland Journey* 20 Kansas brags on its thunder and lightening; and the boast is well founded. **1898** WESTCOTT *D. Harum* 191 'You have been very generous all through, Mr. Harum.' 'Nothin' to brag on,' he replied, 'nothin' to brag on.'

+**b.** To flatter, praise up.

1876 *Dodge City Times* in *Sat. Ev. Post* 8 March (1930) 146 Mr. Morphy, for the defendant, . . . bragged on the court, winked at the witnesses and thought he had a good case. **1895** *Century Mag.* Aug. 573/2 The other [side] loudly voices its belief and admiration, the latter act being described in the vernacular as 'bragging on him up.'

+**2.** *tr.* To stake in the game of brag.

1845 SOL. SMITH *Theatr. Apprent.* 148, I commenced the game by bragging a dollar.

+**Bragger.** [Cf. BRAG *n.* 2, *v.* 2.] In the game of brag, a nine or knave. — **1807** IRVING, etc. *Salmagundi* 501 Presently one of them . . . exclaimed triumphantly, 'Two bullets and a bragger!' and swept all the money into his pocket. **1844** Shields *S. S. Prentiss* (1883) 334 You can't expect me to take a hand in this game when he . . . holds two bullets and a bragger. **1883** SHIELDS *Ib.* 23 [The timid player] failing to do so [i.e. meet the bluff], the bragger wins, and takes the pile upon the table.

Brahma. Also **Bramah.** A variety of chickens said to have been brought in 1846 from Lakhimpur on the Brahmaputra River in India. The full form *Brahmaputra* sometimes occurs. {1851-} Also attrib. — **1854** *Penna. Agric. Rep.* 205 D. Miller for best pair Brahmah Pootra chickens. **1869** *Comm. Agric. Rep.* 485 The Bristol Central Committee recommend the Brahmas and Dorkings for the table. **1879** B. F. TAYLOR *Summer-Savory* 190 Now we met another [steamer] with a brood of barges about her like a hen with a small family of exaggerated Bramahs. **1894** *Vt. Agric. Rep.* XIV. 173 If for roasters, then select the Brahma, Cochin, Langshan, or Plymouth Rocks.

* **Brahmin,** *a.* and *n.*

+**1.** *adj.* Of New Englanders: Exclusive in respect of culture and society.

1861 HOLMES *E. Venner* i, The other young man . . . comes of the Brahmin Caste of New England. This is the harmless, inoffensive, untitled aristocracy to which I have referred. *Ib.* ii, The New England Brahmin caste often gets blended with connections of political influence or commercial distinction. **1903** TRENT *Hist. Amer. Lit.* 112 The fact . . . bears testimony to the growing tolerance of New England, but it does not prove that the Brahmin clergy had by any means been driven from the field. **1905** GREENSLET *Lowell* 46 Lowell's democratic sympathies, as well as the character of his new friends, were separating him . . . from the 'Brahmin' caste to which by inheritance he belonged.

+**2.** *n.* A New Englander belonging to the aristocratic, conservative class.

1881 R. H. STODDARD *Homes* 155 To be a missionary of Boston culture, rather than the apostle of political or theological revolution, must have pleased the anxious thought of this medical Brahmin. **1900** HOWELLS *Literary Friends* 278 This light and joyous creature could not but be a Pariah among our Brahmins, and I . . . never met him in any of the great Cambridge houses. **1920** MENCKEN *Prejudices* 2 Ser. 21 The criticism that supports this decaying caste of literary Brahmins is grounded almost entirely upon ethical criteria.

3. A species of cattle, orig. imported from India.

1893 G. W. CURTIS *Horses*, etc. 210 Dr. James Bolton Davis, of Charleston, S.C., . . . imported [in 1849] the first pair of Brahmins ever brought to the United States. *Ib.*, The name 'Brahmin,' however, is . . . firmly fixed among those who have bred or known them in the Southern States.

Brahminical, *a.* {1809-} +BRAHMIN *a.* — **1900** HOWELLS *Literary Friends* 272 He was ancestrally of the Swiss 'Brahminical caste,' as so many of his friends in Cambridge were of the Brahminical caste of New England.

***Braid,** *n.* +A string of corn, onions, etc., tied together. — **1857** HAMMOND *Northern Scenes* 149 The stories contained in that work hang together so like a string of onions, or a braid of seed corn. **1871** *Ill. Agric. Soc. Trans.* VIII. 177 Onions, in our climate, . . . are best kept thinly spread, or in braids, in a dry place.

Braid, *v. tr.* To beat, stir, mix. {East Angl. dial., 1830-} — **1869** E. PUTNAM *Receipt Bk.* 27 Add a quarter of a pound of butter and two spoonfuls of flour, braided together. **1902** CLAPIN 72 Instead of beating the eggs, the women in New England often say *braiding* the eggs or *cutting* them.

Braided rug. A homemade rug composed of long strips of cloth braided and sewed together. — **1884** WILKINS in *Harper's Mag.* July 307/2 She wants some braided rugs. **1895** A. BROWN *Meadow-Grass* 173 Mrs. Blair . . . marched back and forth through the room, . . . pulling the braided rug to one side or the other.

+**Brail.** [F. *brelle.*] A number of logs forming part of a raft. — **1879** *Lumberman's Gaz.* 1 Oct., This part of the Slough is wide and deep, and is used for coupling up the strings into brails and rafts. **1881** T. B. WALKER *Letter* 4 June, A brail of logs is a crib of loose logs surrounded by a boom of longer ones whose ends are fastened together. . . . Three or four brails are put side by side and fastened together to form a raft and towed by steam tugs. **1905** *Forestry Bureau Bul.* 61 *Brail,* a section of a log raft, six of which make an average tow.

* **Brain,** *n.*

1. *To have* or *take . . . on the brain,* to be obsessed by.

1865-6 *Ill. Agric. Soc. Trans.* VI. 279 Everybody don't at once take 'tree planting on the brain' the natural way. **1869** *Congress. Rec.* 5 Jan. 182/2 The [Cincinnati] Gazette seems to have the franking privilege 'on the brain.' **1870** *Ib.* 2 March 1643/3 [This] is a volunteer statement from one of the somewhat notorious 'peace commission,' who seem to have 'Indian on the brain.' **1872** BRACE *Dangerous Classes N.Y.* 287 The writer of this had had the Reading-room 'on the brain' for many years.

+**2.** *To take brains,* to absorb the boiled brains of the deer (or other animal) used in dressing the skin.

1868 *Amer. Naturalist* Oct. 474 The [deer-] skin . . . should be stretched and broken still more, while drying, that it may 'take brains' more readily.

***Brain,** *v.* +*tr.* To treat (skins) with brains in the process of tanning. — **1868** *Amer. Naturalist* Oct. 474 There are three principal operations: graining, braining, and smoking. *Ib.*, It is known when the skin is brained in this manner.

+**Brain-dressed,** *a.* [Cf. prec. and BRAIN *n.* 2.] Of skins: Dressed with a liquor obtained by boiling deer brains. — **1887** *Harper's Mag.* June 61/2 These [deerskin leggings] were prepared of brain-dressed skins that perfectly turned the rain and dew.

+**Brainfag.** Mental exhaustion. — **1851** DUNGLISON *Med. Lex.* 596 A hypochondriacal condition . . . termed by some *cerebropathy;* by others, *brain-fag.* **1876** *Congress. Rec.* 3 Aug. 5124/1 Whether he has been actually prostrated by a protracted attack of 'brain fag' . . . I do not know. **1884** W. JAMES in *Mind* IX. 17 In states of extreme brain-fag the horizon is narrowed almost to the passing word.

+**Brain-tanned,** *a.* =BRAIN-DRESSED. — **1880** *Harper's Mag.* Dec. 159 The picturesque hunting shirt, with the brain-tanned moccasin and belt, . . . were as sure to put in their appearance . . . as the hunter himself.

+**Brainy,** *a.* Well equipped with brains; possessing intellectual ability; showing great intelligence.

1874 J. W. HOWE *Sex & Education* 25 Men here are for the most part wiry, sinewy, nervous, and brainy. **1877** *Albany Jrnl.* in *N.Y. Tribune* 16 March, A fresh, clean, brainy, courageous, forceful man. **1885** HOWELLS *Silas Lapham* i. 14 He's about as brainy as any of us, I guess. **1888** *St. Louis Globe Dem.* 29 April (F.), The brainy paragraphs thrown off by one society reporter. **1891** *Anthony's Photog. Bull. Ann.* IV. 179 Soon after the war there was, I thought, a marked development of the nervous, 'brainy' children. **1906** *Atlantic Mo.* Nov. 588 No profession is to-day so singled out . . . by ambitious, brainy young men, as that of the law.

* **Brake,** *n.*[1] Also **break.**

***1.** An instrument for breaking flax or hemp.

1634 WINTHROP *Letters* II. 126 Divers things, which we . . . have need of, [include] . . . a brake for hemp. **1838** H. W. ELLSWORTH *Valley of Wabash* 90 In the new method of reducing flax . . . less care in gathering will be required; especially if the 'brakes' are improved by the addition of transverse rollers. **1863** *Rep. Comm. Agric.* 116 The process consists in fermentation, by soaking in water till the gluten is dissolved . . . so that the brake or hatchel can detach it in fragments.

***2.** An apparatus or contrivance used in kneading dough, working butter, etc. {-1617; now *dial.*}

1650 *Essex Inst. Coll.* XLIII. 71 The Inventory of the goods of Edmund Lewis [includes] . . . too tubes, a brake & a crackell. **1652** *Suffolk Deeds* I. 137 In the brew house . . . one kneading trough, one dresser, one brake. **1837** S. GRAHAM *Bread* 93 The machine which the bakers call the break, used in making crackers and sea-bread. **1876** *Vt. Bd. Agric. Rep.* III. 97 The working [of the butter] can be done equally as well with the hands or on the well constructed brake, by one who has experience. **1909** *Cent. Suppl.* 160/1 *Brake,* in cracker-baking, a machine for rolling dough [etc.].

* **Brake,** *n.*[2] Fern or bracken.

1748 ELIOT *Field-Husb.* i. 3 The lower part next the Salt Marsh is Rushes, the next are Reeds, then large Brakes and Bushes. **1790** S. DEANE *New-Eng. Farmer* 93/2 Fern, or Brakes, a well known sort of weeds. **1838** HAWTHORNE *Note-books* I. 60 In the interstices grow brake and broad-leaved forest-grass. **1845** LYELL *Second Visit* I. 60 The sweet fern . . . was replaced by the true fern, called here [in the White Mts.] 'brake.' **1853** 'P. PAXTON' *Yankee in Texas* 59 The brake is always upon low ground, or rather in a swale, which, during the rainy season, is filled with water. **a1862** THOREAU *Maine Woods* 310 The characteristic flowers in swamps were: . . . *Pteris aquilina* (Common brake), [etc.]. **1887** WILKINS *Humble Romance* 110 Jest look at all them brakes under the winders; they allers grow whar it's damp. **1903** WHITE *Forest* xiii. 172 Our way had led through unbroken forest oppressed by low brush and an underfooting of brakes.

* **Brake,** *n.*[3]

***1.** A thicket or copse; an area covered with bushes, briers, reeds, etc.

1757 J. CARVER *Massacre of English* 36, I threw myself into a brake, and lay for some minutes apparently at the last gasp. **1827** COOPER *Prairie* v, Not the smallest sound of life arose out of the calm and darkness which enveloped the brake. **1876** BOURKE *Journal* 31 May, Country . . . destitute of timber, except in the 'brakes,' where a few scrub juniper trees can be found secreted. **1886** *Harper's Mag.* June 64/2 Here is the only opening through Pine Mountain from 'the brakes' of Sandy to the Tennessee line.

+**2.** A canebrake.

1852 REYNOLDS *Hist. Illinois* 195 The cane grew so thick and strong that man, or beast, could scarcely penetrate it. These were called brakes.

Brake, *n.*[4] Also **break.** A device for lessening the speed of a vehicle by retarding the revolution of the wheels. {1772-}. *To put down* or *on* =apply (the brake). Also *down* or *on brakes* as a signal or direction to apply these.

1850 *Knickerb.* XXXVI. 577 We had run over an obstruction in the road, . . . which had broken the 'break' to the baggage-car entirely off. **1870** KEIM *Sheridan's Troopers* 20 The locomotive whistled down breaks. **1878** PINKERTON *Strikers* 208 Scarcely had the strikers' engineer a second in which to sound 'down brakes,' before the thundering crash came. *Ib.* 318 These trains were intercepted . . . by men jumping upon them, putting on the brakes [etc.]. **1894** P. L. FORD *P. Stirling* 285 He whistled 'on brakes' to his train, so that it should be held on the grade safely.

fig. **1871** BRET HARTE *Luck of Roaring Camp* 101 But it's loving her, and seeing her, day arter day, goin' on at this rate, and no one to put down the brake; that's what gits me! **1886** LOGAN *Great Conspiracy* 180 It seems strange that Mr. Lincoln's Inaugural address did not . . . sufficiently strengthen the Union-loving people . . . to put the 'brakes' down on Rebellion. **1887** *Harper's Mag.* July 238/2 Mrs. Ely . . . usually was only a dumb, smiling adjunct to her enthusiastic husband. But there were times when she felt it necessary to put down the brakes.

Brake, *v.* [BRAKE *n.*[4]] {1868-}

+**1.** *intr.* Of a train: To slow *up* under the application of the brakes.

1891 E. S. ELLIS *Check No. 2134* 86 The conductor discovered the strange blunder the moment the cars began braking up.

+2. To perform the duties of a brakeman on a train.
1889 SALMONS *Burlington Strike* 379 He had been braking on the Wabash when I first knew him. **1892** GUNTER *Miss Dividends* 263, I'm braking on the Burlington again, and we're bound for Chicago.

Brake beam. (See first quot.) — **1874** KNIGHT 357 *Brake-beam*, . . . the transverse beam connecting the shoes of opposite wheels. A brake bar. **1895** REMINGTON *Pony Tracks* 149 While riding in an army ambulance . . . the brake-beam broke on the descent of a hill. **1898** HAMBLEN *Gen'l Manager's Story* 29 Oh, came in on a break beam, did you?

+**Brakeman.** Also **breakman.** [BRAKE *n.*[4]] A railroad employee whose chief duty is to set or apply the brakes on the cars. Cf. BRAKESMAN.
1843 *Western R.R. Corp. Proc.* 48 Amount paid Brakemen on all the trains, . . . [$]11,276.04. **1856** M. J. HOLMES *L. Rivers* 416 Jerry Langley has changed his occupation of driver for that of a brakeman on the railroad between Canandaigua and Niagara Falls. **1865** TROWBRIDGE *Three Scouts* 188 The train slackened speed; the brakemen screwed up the breaks. **1874** B. F. TAYLOR *World on Wheels* I. 58 [He] goes away from home by the cars, and afflicts the conductor and the brakeman and his traveling companions. **1883** *Harper's Mag.* Jan. 212/2 The brakeman bawled out, 'Tannery Town!' **1893** GUNTER *Miss Dividends* 225 He doesn't wake even after the train has arrived at Ogden, till he is roused by the brakeman. **1904** *Boston Globe* 28 Feb. 40/6 There is a chair there [in the monitor of a caboose] placed on a swivel and the rear brakeman, or the conductor, may sit in it and see what is going on.

+**Brake shoe.** [BRAKE *n.*[4]] The lining of a brake; that part which bears the friction involved in braking. — **1874** KNIGHT 357 *Brake-shoe*, that part of a brake which is brought in contact with the object whose motion is to be restrained. **1881** HAYES *New Colorado* 95 He had . . . insisted on having an extra brake-shoe at Fairplay. **1888** *Century Mag.* XXXVI. 247/1 His tail got nipped between the brake-shoe and the carwheel. **1910** J. HART *Vigilante Girl* 147 As the brake-shoes left the wheel-tires, the heavy coach lurched forward.

Brakesman. Also **breaksman.** {1851-} =BRAKEMAN.
1848 W. TEMPLETON *Locomot. Eng.* (ed. 2) 81 The amount of wages for breaksmen. **1857** [D. H. STROTHER] *Virginia* 276 Horace Woodward, engineer; John Weaver, fireman, and G. G. Frithey, brakesman. **1880** TOURGEE *Invisible Empire* 416 They did not intend to allow any negro route agents . . . or negro brakesmen. **1891** ROBERTS *Adrift Amer.* 93 No business I ever saw is, to my way of thinking, so hazardous as that of a brakesman. **1897** BRODHEAD *Bound in Shallows* 56 Some of them revealed themselves as brakesmen by the slight swaying of their gait.

+**Brake wheel.** [BRAKE *n.*[4]] A hand wheel, on the platform or roof of a railroad car, by means of which the brake is controlled. — **1872** HUNTINGTON *Road-Master's Asst.* 114 Brakemen, instead of taking the most comfortable vacant seat they can find, sit astride the brake-wheel. **1891** C. ROBERTS *Adrift Amer.* 78 The very devil of mischief . . . put it into Mr. Hiram's head to pick up the oil can and pour a stream of oil on the brake-wheel.

+**Brakey.** *colloq.* Also **brakie, breaky.** A brakeman on a train. — **1887** M. ROBERTS *Western Avernus* 238 The brakie came down a step and made a kick at him. **1891** C. ROBERTS *Adrift Amer.* 92 Jumping an east bound freight, . . . I managed to . . . keep on it till I got to . . . Alaméda, where I was spotted by an avaricious 'breaky.' **1898** HAMBLEN *Gen'l Manager's Story* 16 You don't see but mighty few brakeys as old as we be. **1911** H. QUICK *Yellowstone N.* 315 An' me ostrichized by the very brakey in the caboose.

* **Bramble.**

1. 'Any rough prickly shrub' (W. '28).
*a***1649** WINTHROP *Hist.* I. 237 He had a scratch on the left side of his nose, . . . he said it was with a bramble. **1753** ELIOT *Field-Husb.* iv. 94 The baleful Thickets of Brambles, and the dreary Shades of larger Growth [in a swamp]. **1841** COOPER *Deerslayer* xxvi, The wanderings of a warrior ar'n't altogether among brambles. **1865** *Atlantic Mo.* XV. 257 They had wandered into spots where the brambles were thick. **1880** *Harper's Mag.* June 78 The brambles, and the fragrant creeping-clover show their alluring colors.

2. A shrubby or trailing plant, furnished with prickles, of the genus *Rubus;* a blackberry bush or vine.
1784 CUTLER in Mem. *Academy* I. 452 *Rubus* . . . Bramble. Upright Briar. **1828** WEBSTER, *Bramble*, the raspberry bush or blackberry bush. **1847** DARLINGTON *Weeds & Plants* 125 *Rubus*, Bramble [includes raspberries, blackberries, and the dewberry]. **1857** GRAY *Botany* 120 *Rubus*, Bramble [includes various species of raspberry, blackberry, cloudberry].

* **Brambleberry.** *Obs.* {-1727; now *dial.*} The blackberry or black raspberry, or its fruit. — **1723** *Weekly Mercury* 16 May 4 He will truck for . . . all sorts of ripe Grapes, Peaches, . . . Mullberry's, and Brambleberry's. **1832** WILLIAMSON *Maine* I. 114 Of the Bramble kind we have seven species: . . . 5 the Brambleberry.

* **Branch.**

I. 1. A tributary of a creek or river, related to it as the branch of a tree to a trunk; one or other of the streams which flow into, or unite to form, a river.
1642 *Md. Hist. Mag.* V. 171 A Line drawn . . . unto a branch of St. George's Creek called Weston's branch. **1654** JOHNSON *Wonder-w. Prov.* 46 Seaventh Church . . . was at Water-Towne, scituate upon one of the Branches of Charles River. **1745** *Baltimore Town Rec.* p. xvii, The said Towns are very conveniently situated on the Head of the North-West Branch of Patapsco River, and only parted by the Head of the said Branch. **1852** WATSON *Nights in Block-House* 233 On proceeding farther, they discovered that it was a fork or branch of the river, probably the Kiskeminetas.

+**2.** A small stream; a brook.
1663 *N.C. Col. Rec.* I. 20 That Parcell of land lying and being on the same Neck, Beginning at a small creek or Branch. **1674** *Md. Hist. Mag.* I. 10 Running north and by east fifty perches to a bounded oak by a small branch. **1699** *Virginia St. P.* I. 64 We came to a broad Branch of a bout fifty or sixty yards wide. **1724** JONES *Virginia* 34 These Creeks are supplied with the Tide . . . and also with fresh Water-runs, replenished with Branches issuing from the Springs. **1770** *Md. Hist. Mag.* III. 279 Upon a small branch descending into the said Run the said John Howard killed a rattlesnake. **1833** HALL *Leg. of West* 27 He proceeded cautiously towards a rivulet, or in the vernacular of the country, a *branch*, that meandered along the foot of the hill. **1859** R. B. MARCY *Prairie Traveler* 301 It is a small running branch, but always affords good water. **1881** *Rep. Indian Affairs* 87 The numerous small streams and little branches are most generally marked by lines, or belts, or groves of timber. **1892** HARRIS *On the Plantation* 174 They found a little stream of water running at the bottom. It was what you call a branch. **1913** M. W. MORLEY *Carolina Mts.* 177 'Branch' means any stream of water smaller than a river.

attrib. **1880** *New Virginians* I. 82 The land being what is called branch-bottom, i.e. alluvial in character.

3. A side railroad (or stage route) connecting with a main one.
1827 *Badger & Porter's Stage Register* xiv. 2/1 Canandaigua (a branch thence to Rochester) to Buffalo. **1885** *Harper's Mag.* April 689/1 A short train dashes . . . off on the branch.

b. Attrib. with *line, railroad, train,* etc.
1857 *Harper's Mag.* Aug. 419/1 The lady . . . wished our friend to see her trunk transferred to the car of the branch train. **1879** *Ib.* July 165 Mills brought about a branch railroad from Kingston. **1883** *Ib.* Nov. 944/2 After the completion of the Pacific railroads there will be only a few branch lines left to be built in the far West.

II. +**4.** A chapter of a Greek letter fraternity. (In common use until *c* 1880.) Also attrib. with *chapter.*
1779 in *Cat. of Harvard Chap. of ΦBK* (1912) 90 Petition of Mr. Parmelie for a Charter Party to institute a Branch of this Society at Cambridge in Massachusetts, granted. **1835** *Cat. of Conn. Alpha of ΦBK* 3 The branches of the Society at the present time, are six in number. **1856** *Cat. of ΦBK Alpha of Mass.* 58 No person who is a Graduate or Undergraduate of any other University or College where there is a branch of this Society, shall be elected a member of this branch. **1871** [L. H. BAGG] *At Yale* 55 Sigma Eps at Yale, calling itself the 'Kappa' chapter, established a branch 'Alpha' chapter at Amherst.

5. The upper or lower house of a legislative body. {1768-}
1747 *N.J. Archives* 1 Ser. VII. 89 Any number of persons coming to present petitions or lay complaints before any branch of the Legislature [etc.]. **1815** *Niles' Reg.* IX. 260/1 The popular branch of the legislature of this state, is said to consist of 62 republicans and 55 federalists. **1824** B. F. BUTLER in Mackenzie *Life Van Buren* (1846) 168 We have in the two branches of the Legisl. about 105 members who are thorough-going Caucus men. **1836** *Diplom. Corr. Texas* (1908) I. 123 Wm. H. Wharton is thought to be elected to the Senate—his brother and Dr. Archer to the other branch. **1870** *Nation* 20. Jan. 33/1 When the condition of the various irons he has in the fire in the lower branch will permit it, he transfers himself swiftly to the Senate Chamber.

6. A local place of business, store, bank, etc., established by a larger concern and remaining subordinate to it. {1817-}
1811 CLAY *Speeches* (1842) 31 Not one cent . . . was in the vaults of the Bank of the United States, or in any of its branches. **1832** *Deb. Congress* 8 March 2073 Their great rival competitor, a branch of the Bank of the United States. **1853** *Harper's Mag.* VII. 562/2 The proprietor . . . sometimes . . . would visit his country-store, or 'branch.'

b. Attrib. with *depot, house, library, mint, office,* etc. See also BRANCH BANK, etc.
1842 *Niles' Nat. Reg.* 9 April 94/1 A bill to abolish the branch mints. **1865** *Atlantic Mo.* XV. 242 The branch depots . . . established in each army corps. **1877** *Boston Globe* 26 May 2/2 To establish [telephonic] communication between the several branch libraries and the Central Library. **1884** *Century Mag.* Feb. 585/2 In short, nearly half the convicts are scattered about in 'branch prisons.' **1890** *Buckskin Mose* 217 Wells, Fargo and Company one of whose branch-offices was in this place.

7. A certificate given by the proper authority to a pilot who has successfully passed an examination given to test his competency; hence, a grade or division of the pilot service. {1865-} Cf. BRANCH PILOT.
1783 *Mass. Statutes* 11 July 528 The Governor . . . is empowered . . . to give to each of the said Pilots branches or warrants for the due execution of the duties of their respective offices. **1811** MEASE *Philadelphia* 72 Previously to granting any license, the pilot must conduct a square rigged

Vessel, twice up and down the river, under the inspection of a pilot of the first branch.

+**8.** (See quotation.)

1822 MORSE *Rep. Indian Affairs* I. 55 A half point blanket is sold for four skins. . . . Five branches, or two hundred and fifty grains of wampum, one skin. . . . Forty branches of white beads, one skin.

Branch bank. [BRANCH 6 b.] A bank established as a branch of another, originally of the Bank of the United States.

1796 *Boston Directory* 302 Branch Bank, State street. **1801** *Steele Papers* I. 215 Will you . . . send me soon a form of a power of Attorney, which will enable me to receive my Salary at the Branch Bank of New York? **1812** *Niles' Reg.* II. 77/2 The late branch bank of the United States at New-York . . . controled the commercial enterprise of that great city. **1832** *Congress. Deb.* 8 March 2073 This branch bank was the great burden of their complaint [*i.e.* of the N.Y. banks]. **1844** *Indiana Senate J.* 59 What measures have been taken to prohibit the collecting officers and legal advisers of the several branch banks from acting as directors thereof. **1911** WICKERSHAM in *Opinions Attorneys General* XXIX. 94 The same capital is required to run the branch bank as to operate the parent bank. **1923** *U.S. Reports* CCLXIII. 649 If a national bank should attempt to establish and operate a branch bank [etc.].

attrib. **1832** *Deb. Congress* 20 Jan. 128, I have . . . brought this branch bank currency to the test of several provisions in the charter. *Ib.* 7 March 2041 The branch bank orders . . . had been considered . . . an abuse of the charter of the [U.S.] bank.

+**Branch church.** In the Christian Science Ch., a local congregation; a branch of the Mother Church. — **1895** EDDY *Church Manual* 27 Branch churches shall not take the title of *The* First Church of Christ, Scientist. **1909** *Ib.* (ed. 81) 73 Each branch church shall be distinctly democratic in its government. **1914** *New Eng. Mag.* LI. 59 Many instances might be given where the organization of a branch church can be traced directly to a single case of healing.

+**Branch grass.** *local.* A kind of grass so called from its many branches. — **1837** COLMAN *Rep. Agric. Mass.* (1838) 18 *Branch Grass*, a short reedy grass, resembling much the fox grass.

Branch pilot. [BRANCH 7.] A pilot holding a certificate of competency. {1864–}

1783 *Mass. Statutes* 11 July 528 Each of the said branch Pilots shall enter into bonds. **1793** *State P.* (1819) I. 116 Benedict Wheatley . . . qualified as a branch pilot for the Chesapeake bay and Potowmac river. **1805** *Mariner's Dict., Branch Pilot*, a grade in the station of pilots, which implies superior experience and skill; one who is duly authorized to pilot ships up particular channels and rivers. **1811** MEASE *Philadelphia* 72 If carried to sea, first branch pilots receive captain's wages until their death, or return. **1859** *Harper's Mag.* Sept. 571/2 The Captain asked him if he was the *branch* pilot for the place, when he exclaimed, 'No, Sir-ee! I'se de real *root*, an' no mistake.'

+**Branch road.** [BRANCH 3.] A road or railroad which is a minor division of a larger system. — **1831** *Congress. Deb.* 1 March 830 The right of Congress to pass laws hereafter for the opening of branch roads [etc.]. **1851** SPRINGER *Forest Life* 83 Next in order comes the business of looking out and cutting the 'main,' and some of the principal 'branch roads.' **1865** KELLOGG *Rebel Prisons* 47 [Tarboro, N.C.] is in railroad connection with the South by a short branch road. **1878** R. T. COOKE *Happy Dodd* 386 Happy took the train of a branch road leading to Siloam. **1902** HARBEN *A. Daniel* 137 Wanting to know if there were not many branch roads that did not own their rolling stock.

+**Branch store.** [BRANCH 6 b.] A store that is a part or branch of a larger institution. — **1842** E. A. HITCHCOCK *Journal* 109, I find Chapman is here in charge of Hill's branch store. **1853** *Harper's Mag.* VII. 562/2 He opened a branch-store in a town in the north part of the State. **1873** *Newton Kansan* 3 April 3/2 Hall and Willey . . . have started a branch store at Halstead. *a***1918** G. STUART *On Frontier* I. 216 Warden and Higgins concluded to start a branch store in our village and leave a portion of their goods here.

+**Branch swamp.** [BRANCH 2.] A swamp on a small stream or branch. — **1832** BROWNE *Sylva* 195 Red Bay . . . is profusely multiplied in the branch swamps. *Ib.* 248 Farther south, it [=the buttonwood tree] . . . is not seen in the branch swamps. **1883** HALE *Woods N.C.* 132 Loblolly Bay [is] . . . confined, I think, to the branch-swamps and bays within 100 miles of the coast.

+**Branch water.** [BRANCH 2.] The water of a small stream or branch. — **1866** C. H. SMITH *Bill Arp* 29 They will eat roots and drink branch-water. **1887** EGGLESTON *Graysons* xiii, I hain't had nuthin' to drink to-day 'ceppin' jes branch water. **1902** CLAPIN 73 *Branch-water*, a Southern expression for stream-water, as distinguished from well water. **1903** A. ADAMS *Log Cowboy* 86, I had scarcely drunk anything in three months but branch water.

* **Brand,** *n.*

* **1.** A distinguishing mark impressed on an animal or thing by the application of a heated iron, esp. a mark of ownership made in this way on a horse, steer, cow, etc.

(1) **1667** *Conn. Public Rec.* II. 58 This Court orders that . . . for their brand of horses they shal have the letter V on the near buttock. **1707** *Boston News-Letter* 10 Feb. 2/2 The said Horse is a pretty large bright bay Gelding, having a Brand on his near Buttock of this form d. **1743** *Ga. Col. Rec.* VI. 80 Barker has branded a Colt of one of those Mares with (GL) being one of the Brands he has for his own private use. **1788** V. B. HOWARD *Heroes* (1932) 41 Taken up, . . . an old bay mare . . . no brands perceivable. **1806** LEWIS in *L. & Clark Exped.* (1905) IV. 74 Among the Sosones . . . we saw several horses with spanish brands on them which we supposed had been stolen from the inhabitants of Mexeco. **1834** *Visit to Texas* vi. 59 As the brands on horses afford the only evidence of their identity, . . . the rules observed in respect to them are very strict. **1869** C. L. BRACE *New West* 288 The brands, both of cattle and horses, . . . are controlled by law in California. **1878** BEADLE *Western Wilds* 538 They came, in a few hours, upon two dead horses with the cavalry brand. **1905** *Boston Ev. Traveler* 27 Jan. 11/2 'Rustler,' . . . means a man who steals other people's cattle and puts his own brand on them.

(2) **1728** *Braintree Rec.* 126 It was also voted that the Brands of the Town for Shingles & Clapboards be a small [B]. **1811** MEASE *Philadelphia* 58 These brands [for flour-casks] are to be registered with the clerk of the Quarter Sessions of the County. **1905** *Forestry Bureau Bul. 61, Brand*, . . . a letter or sign indicating ownership, which is stamped on the ends of logs.

+**b.** A herd of cattle having a particular brand.

1885 *Rep. Indian Affairs* 166 They have many small brands of cattle. **1898** CANFIELD *Maid of Frontier* 142 He had a hundred brands of cattle and horses. **1903** A. ADAMS *Log Cowboy* 90, I must have inspection papers before I can move a brand out of the county in which it is bred.

* **2.** A sign or mark impressed on an offender with a hot iron.

1680 *N.H. Hist. Soc. Coll.* VIII. 13 If either [offence] were committed on the Lord's day his brand shall be sett on his forehead. **1705** *Boston News-Letter* 12 Nov. 2/1 A remarkable Person truly! One marked with a Brand in the Cheek.

3. The instrument used for branding; a branding iron. {1824–}

1692 *Conn. Probate Rec.* 456, I . . . give unto my beloved son Samuel Halle my Muskit and my two Horse Brands. **1718** *Boston Selectmen* 35 One brand, 3 Stamps, 2 large hand hammers [etc.]. **1913** W. C. BARNES *Western Grazing Grounds* 380 *Cooney*, a raw hide . . . in which the cook carries his iron dutch-ovens and other heavy utensils. Often the brands are carried in it also.

* **Brand,** *v.*

* **1.** To burn or stamp (a person on the face, hand, etc.) as a punishment.

1632 *Mass. Bay Rec.* I. 99 Richard Hopkins shalbe seuerely whipt, & branded with a hott iron on one of his cheekes, for selling peeces & powder & shott to the Indians. **1650** *Conn. Public Rec.* I. 513 If any person shall committ Burglary . . . such a person . . . [shall] bee branded on the forehead with the Letter (B). **1694** *N.C. Col. Rec.* I. 401 Ordered that they be branded in the hand with the letter T. **1711** *Boston News-Letter* 11 June 2/2 Ran-away from William Gardner of Kingstown in the Colony of Rhode-Island . . . a Molatto Man of middle stature branded on the Cheek with the Letter G. **1743** HEMPSTEAD *Diary* 411 Nath[anie]ll Richard of Norwich . . . was whiped 25 stripes & branded on the forehead with A on a hot Iron. **1796** MORSE *Amer. Geog.* I. 469 For the second offence [*i.e.* of a Quaker engaging in business in Conn. without a license], the person was to be branded in the hand with the letter H. **1852** MRS. STOWE *Uncle Tom* xi. 91 A very light mulatto, . . . deeply scarred on his back and shoulders; has been branded in his right hand with the letter H.

2. To stamp (articles) with a hot iron as a mark of ownership, identification, or indication of quality.

1653 *Boston Rec.* 114 The seleckt men shall forthwith provide six good and long ladders . . . in Case of fier, thes ladders to be branded with the town marke. **1771** J. HABERSHAM *Letters* 152, I think the casks branded on the head with a Gun barrel O or OO is something better than the other casks blindly branded JOH.

b. To impress (a mark or lettering) in this way.

1811 MEASE *Philadelphia* 58 Corn, intended to be ground into meal, must be first kiln dried, and when ground, the words 'kiln dried,' must be branded on the cask.

3. To place a mark of ownership upon (horses, cattle, etc.), usually by means of a hot iron or brand.

1644–5 *Conn. Rec.* I. 118 The owners of any Catle within thes Plantations shall earemarke or brand all their Cattle and swyne that are above halfe a yeare old (except horsses). **1660** *Mass. H. S. Coll.* 4 Ser. VII. 244 Bring in all your horses & mares, & brand them with this mark. **1743** *Ga. Col. Rec.* VI. 80 Barker has branded a Colt of one of those Mares with (GL). **1765** WASHINGTON *Diaries* I. 216 In all 24 head [of cattle] branded on the Buttock GW. **1800** B. HAWKINS *Sk. Creek Country* 45 Thence they are collected together by their owners, to mark and brand the young ones. **1839** Z. LEONARD *Adventures* (1904) 225 [The wild horses] are divided to each man, who brands and hobbles them, and then turns them loose upon the prairie. **1867–9** *Ill. Agric. Soc. Trans.* VII. 221 The laws of Texas require cattle to be branded when a year old. **1878** BEADLE *Western Wilds* 508 Fifty head of the emigrants' stock were branded with the church brand. **1902** WISTER *Virginian* 54 We emerged from a narrow cañon suddenly upon . . . some cow-boys branding calves by a fire in a corral.

+**Bran-dance.** A dance performed on ground covered to the depth of several inches with moistened bran. — **1833** *Sketches of Crockett* 148 This is the famous bran-dance of the west, and derives its name from the fact that the ground is generally sprinkled with the husk of Indian meal. **1841** *S. Lit. Messenger* VII. 567/2 A phrase which, we fear, a large part of our readers have never yet heard, to wit: a bran-dance. **1851** *Arkansas Doctor* 52 (Th.), There I stood, looking kin to a fool at a bran-dance. **1883** 'S. BONNER' *Dialect Tales* 152 We were ready to cut pigeon wings in a bran dance until the bran flew about our ears as dry as the dust of a powdered mummy.

+**Brand book.** [BRAND *n.* 1.] A book recording the brands used and registered by the owners of horses or cattle. — **1665** *Conn. Public Rec.* II. 28 They shal enter such saile within 10 daies in the said brand booke, with the artificial and natural marks, coulor and age of such horses. **1674** *Ib.* 245 The markes of the creatures . . . shall be entered with the keeper of the brand booke. **1889** FARMER 85 *Brand-book,* a register of the multitudinous marks used in branding. **1913** W. C. BARNES *Western Grazing Grounds* 186 Following are pages taken from the Brand Books of different live stock associations.

Branded, *ppl. a.* [BRAND *v.*] +Of certain fishes: Having spots suggestive of brand marks. — **1814** MITCHELL *Fishes N.Y.* 411 Beardless Drum. *Sciaena imberbis* . . . upon the upper part of the tail, on each side, is a black spot, . . . resembling the brand of a hot iron upon wood; whence he has been called the *branded* drum. **1842** *Nat. Hist. N.Y., Zoology* IV. 75 The Branded Corvina. *Corvina ocellata.* . . . This beautiful fish, which appears but occasionally on our coast, is more common at the south. **1890** *Cent.* 1782/1 The branded drum or beardless drum, *Sciæna ocellata,* [is] the redfish of south Atlantic and Gulf States.

+**Brander.** [BRAND *v.* 3.] One who brands horses and cattle. {1860}

1681 *Conn. Rec.* III. 79 It shall be done by the publique officer appoynted to brand horses, . . . and the sayd brander shall record all such horss kind as he markes or brands. **1692** *Ib.* IV. 85 Whereas information is given to this Court the branders hath taken, branded, and sold horses [etc.]. **1902** A. MACGOWAN *Last Word* 231, I heard . . . the voices of the herder, . . . the brander, [etc.]. **1920** HUNTER *Trail Drivers of Texas* I. 297 The flanker and assistants . . . call out 'hot iron' or 'sharp knife,' the brander responding, 'Right here with the goods.'

* **Branding,** *vbl. n.* [BRAND *v.*]

1. The action of placing brands upon horses, cattle, etc.

1740 W. STEPHENS *Proc. Georgia* 513 They were not of his branding. **1797** I. THOMAS *Newengland Farmer* 200, I have known no other marking used for horses than branding with a hot iron, on the shoulder or thigh. **1841** *S. Lit. Messenger* VII. 77/2 Our stranger friend was on his way to the branding. **1869** C. L. BRACE *New West* 287 Driving them together every spring . . . on a certain ranch, and having a branding. **1898** CANFIELD *Maid of Frontier* 153 The spring branding was over. . . . The hearts of the honest cattle-folk were happy. **1910** J. HART *Vigilante Girl* 195 Branding is not so unpleasant as slaughtering.

+**2.** Attrib. with *camp, crew, day,* etc.

1849 *Rep. Comm. Patents* (1850) 416 Branding tools are usually heated in the fire preparatory to use. **1878** I. L. BIRD *Rocky Mts.* 147 The calf is bullied into the branding pen, and the hot iron burns into his shrinking flesh. **1904** 'O. HENRY' *Heart of West* 16 A portable furnace, such as are seen in branding-camps. **1907** WHITE *Arizona Nights* 146 Three branding crews were told to brand the calves we had collected. **1910** J. HART *Vigilante Girl* 195 It's not even a branding day.

+**Branding chute.** A narrow enclosure into which cattle are driven to be branded. — **1893** *Stand.* 326/2 *Branding-chute,* a corral narrowing inward, into which cattle are driven to be branded. **1900** *Congress. Rec.* App. 10 Jan 22/1 [Judge Greene] was just as much at home standing on a branding shute backed up against a sod corral out on the range [etc.]. **1905** A. ADAMS *Outlet* 36 This branding-chute was long enough to chamber eight beeves. . . . A high platform ran along either side of the branding-chute, on which the men stood while handling the irons. **1920** HUNTER *Trail Drivers of Texas* I. 297 A branding chute where an arrangement for holding the cattle while they are being branded is called a 'squeezer.'

* **Branding iron.** An iron used in branding, esp. in marking cattle.

(1) **1686** *Narrag. Hist. Reg.* III. 105, 2 draft chains & branding irons. **1797** I. THOMAS *Newengland Farmer* 201 The marking of neat cattle on the horn, with the branding iron, is so easily done. **1834** *Visit to Texas* xiii. 119 Advantage is taken . . . to apply the branding iron to their flanks and mark them for life. **1888** T. ROOSEVELT in *Century Mag.* Feb. 495/2 Cowboys and branding-irons take the place of fences. **1904** 'O. HENRY' *Heart of West* 17 She ran swiftly to her furnace at the gate and brought the branding-iron, queerly-shaped and white hot.

(2) **1840** *Knickerb.* XVI. 359 It is an abuse, especially in a republic, which calls for the whip and the branding-iron. **1863** W. PHILLIPS *Speeches* 259 He showed me his broad bosom scarred all over with the branding-iron. **1865** *Atlantic Mo.* XV. 505 The former [=welts] were made by the whip and branding-irons of a Virginia planter.

‖**Branding new,** *a.* Brand-new, bran-new. — **1809** WEEMS *Marion* (1833) 109 A branding new scow and boat. **1814** — *Letters* III. 108, I can get the[m] branding new & of better sorts at 45. **1829** — *B. Franklin* 54 Ben . . . went to see him at his printing-office [wearing] . . . a complete suit of broad cloath, branding new.

***Brandlet.** *Obs.* [Variant of *brandreth.*] A gridiron. — **1650** in *Mayflower Desc.* X. 173 One brandlet, one Rostiron. **1651** in *ib.* X. 161, 2 shakes, one brandlet.

Brandling. A small red worm with rings of bright coloring. {1651–} — **1832** WILLIAMSON *Maine* I. 168 We have among us, in summer, a variety of native Worms. . . . These are the Grub; the Earthworm; the Brandling; the Angleworm [etc.].

Brand-mark, *n.* [BRAND *n.* 1.] A mark made with a branding iron. {1655–} — **1658** *New Plymouth Laws* 117 Every Towne in this Government shall have some publicke brand marke for theire horse to distinguish them from other townes. **1662** *East-Hampton Rec.* I. 192 The colt beinge a horse colt hath the same eare marke and brandmarke. **1667** *Lancaster Rec.* 80 On the motion . . . that the letter Lc be allowed . . . brand marke for the sajd towne of Lancaster, the court orders the same so to be. **1680** *N.H. Hist. Soc. Coll.* VIII. 21 It is ordered . . . that the brand markes mentioned in the Law, title horses, to brand horses, . . . shall be as followeth.

Brand-mark, *v.* [Cf. prec.] *tr.* To brand (an animal, cask, etc.) with a special mark. {1678} — **1663** *East-Hampton Rec.* I. 209 Brand marked with the letter T on the neare thigh. **1673** *Mass. Col. Rec.* IV. II. 553 Every . . . licensed person shall brand marke all caske wherein it [=sturgeon] is packed with the letters of his name.

+**Brand-reader.** [BRAND *n.* 1.] One skilled in distinguishing the brand on cattle. — **1888** ROOSEVELT in *Century Mag.* April 860 A man must have natural gifts, as well as great experience, before he becomes a good brand-reader and is able to really 'clean up a herd.'

Brand's-end. *Obs.* The end of a burnt or burning piece of wood. {*a*1674} — **1723** *New-Eng. Courant* 22–29 April 2/1 A brand's-end of Fire, cover'd with dry Flags, was laid at the side of a Bake-House near the Mill-Pond. **1735** FRANKLIN *Writings* II. 205, I would advise 'em to take care how they suffer living Brands ends . . . to be carried out of one Room into another. **1736** *Md. Hist. Mag.* III. 45 This Deponant looking on the Shead Ruff of Capt. Cressap's house he see a large brand's End of fire.

Brandt, (Brand,) variant of BRANT. — **1698** G. THOMAS *Acc. Pensilvania* 13 There are an infinite Number of Sea and Land Fowl, of most sorts, *viz.* . . . Geese, Divers, Brands. **1834** *Visit to Texas* ii. 19 The shore of a pond . . . offered a convenient retreat to thousands of wild ducks, geese, brandt and other fowl. **1836** IRVING *Astoria* I. 163 These islands . . . at certain seasons abound with swan, geese, brandts, . . . and other wild fowl. **1854** BARTLETT *Narr.* I. 85 We had seen great quantities of wild ducks, . . . also two large brandt. **1877** R. J. DODGE *Hunting Grounds Gt. West* 241 Of these [migratory birds] the 'Brandt goose' is the largest.

+**Bran duster.** A machine for separating flour and bran. Also attrib. — **1849** *Rep. Comm. Patents* 374 No. 6952.—Improvement in Bran Dusters. . . . Robt. M. Dempsey. **1853** *Mich. Agric. Soc. Trans.* IV. 35 E. R. Benton, Cleveland, O., bran duster. **1884** *Rep. Comm. Agric.* 99 The bran-duster flour is a dirty, lumpy by-product.

Brandy, *n.* {1657–; earlier *brandy wine, brandewine,* Du. *brandewijn*} The spirit originally distilled from wine or grapes, later also from peaches, apples, or other fruits.

See also APPLE-, CHERRY-, PEACH-BRANDY.

1666 *Md. Archives* II. 124 For wine per gallon. . . . For Brandy per gallon. **1675** *Boston Rec.* 95 Capt. William Hudson and Lt. John Smith [are licensed] to sell beere wine and brandy. **1689** *New Plymouth Laws* 222 Whosoever shall . . . sell & deliver a less quantity . . . than 5 Gallons of Wine, Brandy, Rum or strong liquors &c. . . . is by law . . . accounted a retailer. **1761** J. ROWE *Letters* 400 As to Brandy it will fetch here a Dollar per Gallon. **1799** WELD *Travels* 105 From the peaches they make brandy. . . . They give it a very delicious flavour in this part of the country by infusing dried pears in it. **1840** *Niles' Nat. Reg.* 7 Nov. 160/1 Brandy from Potato Starch. . . . Potato flour or starch is capable . . . of yielding a very pure and well tasted spirit. **1850** GARRARD *Wah-To-Yah* i. 6 But for brandy and other liquors, fever and ague would have predominated. **1887** *Courier-Journal* 15 Feb. 6/3 The brandies of California did not strike me very favorably.

Brandy, *v.* **a.** *tr.* To refresh or supply with brandy. {1837–} **b.** *intr.* To partake of brandy. — **1829** B. HALL *Travels in U. S.* II. 92 At dusk . . . we stopped to water the horses and brandy the gentlemen. **1840** C. MATHEWS *Politicians* I. i, Brandy with those in Scammel street, and take your supper of cutlets and pale ale at Work's. **1862** B. TAYLOR *Home & Abroad* 2 Ser. ii. 120 At the Six-Mile House, our horses were watered, and the passengers brandied.

Brandy-cherry. The rum cherry. {*a*1687} — **1853** *Harper's Mag.* VII. 275/2 A swine drunk on brandy-cherry stones is disgusting.

Brandy grapes. Grapes from which brandy is made. — **1867** *Iowa Agric. Soc. Rep.* (1868) 207 The price paid for wine grapes . . . is five cents a pound; while brandy grapes, . . . which include all the refuse, are only three cents a pound.

Brandy house. A place where brandy is sold. — **1841** *S. Lit. Messenger* VII. 767/2 The groggeries and brandy houses were lighted up.

Brandy peach. A peach preserved in brandy. {1781–} — **1841** *S. Lit. Messenger* VII. 219/2 Third course: . . . sweet meats, brandy-peaches and cheese. **1857** HOLMES *Prologue* i, The lorn damsel, with a frantic screech And cheeks as hueless as a brandy-peach, [etc.]. **1876** M. F. HENDERSON *Pract. Cooking* 253 [Recipe for] Brandy Peaches.

Brandy punch. Punch the alcoholic ingredient of which is brandy. {1818–} — **[1689** SEWALL *Diary* I. 306 In the Lord's Hall Guy's Pot was filled with Brandy Punch.] **1701** WOLLEY *Journal N.Y.* (1860) 35 Their quaffing liquors are Rum-punch and Brandy-punch. **1726** *New-Eng. Courant* 19–26 Feb. 1/2 The quantitys of Wine and Brandy-Punch drank (or rather destroy'd) by these Clubs, is incredible. [**1849** HOLMES *Nux Postcoenatica* xvii, The warm champagny, old-particular brandy-punchy feeling.]

+**Brandy sling.** A drink composed of brandy, water, sugar and sometimes lemon. — **1810** M. V. H. DWIGHT *Journey* 49 He . . . invited us into the house & call'd for some brandy sling—we did not drink, which he appeared not to like. **1832** FERRALL *Ramble thro' U.S.* 33, I drank my 'brandy sling,' and retreated. **1847** *Knickerb.* XXIX. 382 The old toper . . . [was] licking out the sugar from the spoon that contained the last of his brandy sling. **1851** W. K. NORTHALL *Curtain* 219 With trembling lips [he] called for a brandy sling.

+**Brandy smash.** (See quot. 1909.) — **1850** THAXTER *Poem before Iadma* 7 Or didst thou at the Pemberton absorb a brandy-smash? **1865** *Nation* I. 371 The versatile whiskey is transforming itself into brandy-smashes. **1872** *Newton Kansan* 22 Aug. 5/3 The way he'll sling the flowing bowl, deal out brandy smashes and cock(ed) tails won't be slow. **1873** MILLER *Amongst Modocs* 141 All ranged themselves . . . before the bar, calling out 'Cocktail,' . . . 'Brandy-smash,' . . . and so on. **1909** *Century Suppl.* 161/1 *Brandy-smash*, a drink made by mixing brandy with crushed ice and putting a few sprigs of mint in the glass.

+**Brandy smasher.**=BRANDY SMASH. — **1846** *Knickerb.* XXVII. 59 Another banner shall be stationed opposite the hotels and coffee-houses. . . . 'Beware of Cock-Tails and Brandy Smashers!' **1847** C. F. BRIGGS *Tom Pepper* I. 212, I should be working for him now, if it hadn't been for brandy smashers.

+**Brandy sour.** A drink composed of brandy, lime or lemon juice, bitters and carbonated water. — **1861** [NEWELL] *Orpheus C. Kerr* I. 212 [The South Carolina gentleman] . . . clears a mighty track of everything that bears the shape of whiskey-skin, gin-and-sugar, brandy-sour, [etc.].

Brandy toddy. Brandy mixed with hot water and sweetened. — **1840** *Picayune* 23 Aug. 2 He was suffering . . . for a stiff brandy toddy. **1846** CORCORAN *Pickings* 95 Ned Brown was . . . as *blue* as brandy toddies could make him. **1856** BAGSBY *Old Va. Gentleman* 221 A bed . . . whose counterpane secretes its primitive tints under a sweet and greasy scum of spermaceti and spilled brandy-toddies.

Bran-fire-new, *a.* Brand-new. {dial. *brand-fire-new*} — **1825** NEAL *Bro. Jonathan* I. 151 We have alluded once to the calico waistcoat in which he appeared before the preacher. 'My stars!' cried Miriam. . . . 'Bran-fire noo, as I'm alive!' **1834** CROCKETT *Life* x. 76, I therefore gave up all I had, and took a bran-fire new start. *Ib.* xii. 88 This is . . . a bran-fire new way of doing business. **1843** [STEPHENS] *High Life N.Y.* I. 236 Eenamost every Sabberday she would go to meeting in a bran-fire new bonnet.

* **Brant.**

* **1.** The smallest northern wild goose (*Bernicla brenta*), or one of the American varieties of this.

Used in the sing. as a generic or collective name.

1672 JOSSELYN *New Eng. Rarities* 9 There are three kinds; the Gray Goose, the White Goose, and the Brant. **1781–2** JEFFERSON *Notes Va.* (1788) 6 [The Mississippi R.] also abounds in herons, cranes, ducks, brant, geese, and swans. **1813** WILSON *Ornithology* VIII. 131 The Brant is expected at Egg Harbour on the coast of New Jersey about the first of October. **1877** *Field & Forest* II. 193 Brant are found in market, but it does not follow that they were got here. **1897** *Outing* XXX. 94/2 According to the story, the Coosa River for many miles is frequented by hosts of brant, geese, and duck. **1901** WHITE *Westerners* v. 33 Their hysterical cackle rose like the crying of an indignant band of brant.

2. A goose of this species.

1612 SMITH *Virginia* 15 In winter there are great plenty of Swans, Craynes gray and white with blacke wings, Herons, Geese, Brants, [etc.]. **1676** GLOVER *Acc. Va.* in *Phil. Trans.* XI. 626 On the Bay and Rivers feed . . . Swans and Geese, Cormorants, Brants, . . . with many others. **1778** CARVER *Travels* 55 Great numbers of fowl frequent also this Lake and rivers adjacent, such as storks, swans, geese, brants, and ducks. **1807** GASS *Journal* 161 The men went out and killed nine brants. . . . Three of the brants were quite white except the points of their wings, which were black. **1833** WYETH *Oregon* 75 They will pick a goose, or a brant, and run a stick through its body and so roast it, without taking out its entrails. **1884** ROE *Nature's Story* 169, I do not know what a brant is, nor much about its habits.

3. Attrib. and comb. with *shot, shooting.*

1762 *Essex Inst. Coll.* XLIX 276 To be sold . . . Goose and Brant Shott. **1874** LONG *Wild-Fowl* 245 No. 3 shot . . . is sufficiently large for brant shooting. **1875** *Fur, Fin & Feather* 122 There are several good points on the coast for brant shooting.

+**Brant bird.** *local.* The turnstone. — **1844** *Nat. Hist. N.Y., Zoology* II. 216 The Turnstone . . . is known among our gunners . . . under the names of Brant-bird, Heart-bird, Horsefoot Snipe, and Beach-bird. **1891** *Cent.* 6543/1.

* **Brant goose.** =BRANT.

1637 MORTON *New Canaan* 46 There are Geese of three sorts, vize brant Geese, which are pide, and white Geese which are bigger, and gray Geese. **1839** PEABODY *Mass. Birds* 386 The Brant Goose, *Anser bernicla*, a bird well known on our markets. **1871** LEWIS *Poultry Book* 96 The Brant Goose and the Barnacle goose are the smallest of their tribe yet introduced to our aquatic aviaries.

Braro, -ow. [F. *blaireau* badger.] The American badger, *Taxidea americanus.* — **1804** WHITEHOUSE in *Lewis & Clark Exped.* (1905) VII. 67 Capt. Clark killed a Deer and a brarow. **1805** LEWIS *Ib.* IV. 110 The *Braro* so called by the French engages is an . . . inhabitant of the open plains of the Columbia as they are those of the Missouri.

* **Brash,** *a.*[1]

1. Of wood, vegetables, etc.: Brittle, fragile, easily broken.

1816 PICKERING 52 This term is used in some parts of New England, in speaking of wood, or timber, that is brittle. **1829** *Va. Lit. Museum* 16 Dec. 418 *Brash*, 'brittle.' In this sense the word is American. **1848** BARTLETT 46 *Brash*, brittle. . . . In New York it is often heard in the markets, applied to vegetables. Ex. 'These radishes are brash.' **1871** STOWE *Sam Lawson* 178 Taking off his old torn hat, and rubbing the loose shock of brash and grizzled hair.

2. Indisposed; sickly. *dial.*

1889 FARMER. **1895** *Dial. Notes* 384.

Brash, *a.*[2] *dial.*

1. Hasty, rash, impetuous. {1824–, *dial.*}

1837 BIRD *Nick of Woods* I. 120 Strannger [*sic*] thar's as brash as a new hound in a b'ar fight. **1872** *Harper's Mag.* June 28/2 Now Pogue's colt, bein' young and brash, got about two jumps ahead in the start. **1888** 'CRADDOCK' *Broomsedge Cove* 27 Ye notice how terrible brash Josiah Preen be, can't wait for pa'son to summons him.

2. Harsh or hard in action; rough; rude.

1880 TOURGEE *Bricks* 116 He was pretty brash wid me, an 'llowed ter hit me wid a stick. **1896** G. ADE *Artie* iii. 23, I swore I'd get next, no matter what kind of a brash play I had to make. **1897** *Congress. Rec.* March 190/2 [Such duties] are too low and mild on the things of the South, and too high and brash on the things of the North. **1901** *Munsey's Mag.* XXIV. 481/1 Ordinarily, he had an impudent swagger, and was inclined to be 'brash' towards his fellow men. **1904** W. H. SMITH *Promoters* 51 We won't rob 'em entirely; there isn't any use in being altogether too brash.

+**3.** Active, nimble, quick. Also as *adv.*

1884 'MARK TWAIN' *H. Finn* 62 When I got to camp I warn't feeling very brash, there warn't much sand in my craw. **1887** 'CRADDOCK' *Keedon Bluffs* 63 Whar's that buckeye tree ye war a-goin' ter cut down fur me so brash? **1891** RYAN *Pagan Alleghanies* 118, I ain't so brash in the timber as I'd like to be.

+**Brashly,** *adv.* [BRASH *a.*[2] I.] Hastily, rashly. — **1865** 'MARK TWAIN' *Sketches* (1926) 179, I mixed into this business a little too brashly —so to speak—and without due reflection.

Brashness[1]. [BRASH *a.*[1] I.] Brittleness. — **1864** *Maine Agric. Soc. Ret.* 54 They [=sheep] become very fat in the summer, which increases the brashness of the wool.

Brashness[2]. [BRASH *a.*[2] I.] Impetuosity, rashness. — **1890** *Congress. Rec.* April 3638/1 Lieutenant Davis went into the war with great brashness. **1894** FORD *P. Stirling* 258 'That is a bargain,' he said, with a brashness simply disgraceful in a good business man.

+**Brash oak.** *local.* The post oak, *Quercus minor.* — **1897** SUDWORTH *Arborescent Flora* 154 *Quercus minor*. . . . Common names [include] . . . Box Oak (Md.)., Brash Oak (Md.).

Brasier, obs. variant of BRAZIER.

+**Brasil.** *Texas.* [Sp.] (See quotation.) — **1891** COULTER *Bot. W. Texas* I. 58 *Condalia obovata*, . . . known as 'brasil' and 'logwood' . . . [is] one of the common 'chaparral' plants of western Texas.

Brasilet, -alette. *Obs.* {1686} =BRAZILETTO. — **1687** *Doc. Hist. N.Y. State* (1849) I. 163 Upon all merchandizes imported . . . the summ of forty shillings . . . for every hundred pounds valued at prime cost except . . . brasalette [etc.]. **1705** *Boston News-Letter* 10 Dec. 4/2 To be sold in Boston . . . Indigo, Brasilet, Cocoa, Chocolat, with all sorts of Spice.

Brass band. A band of musicians who perform on wind instruments of brass. Also allusively (quot. 1909). {1861–}

1837 HAWTHORNE in *Democratic Rev.* Oct. 35 A company of summer soldiers, marching from village to village . . . , attended by the 'brass band.' **1856** OLMSTED *Slave States* 552 The military parades are usually accompanied by a negro brass band. **1874** GLISAN *Jrnl. Army Life* 452 At some distant frontier post where they can only hear the fife and drum, or, at most, a brass band. **1897** E. W. BRODHEAD *Bound in Shallows* 208 A continual outpour of music came from the brass-band beside the race-track. **1909** G. F. PARKER *G. Cleveland* 158 A campaign which had been carried on for nearly three years without any of the methods of the brass band.

Brass bass: see BRASSY BASS.

+**Brasseye.** *local.* The whistling coot or goldeneye, *Bucephala clangula.* — **1844** *Nat. Hist. N.Y., Zoology* II. 330 *Fuligula clangula*, the Brass-eye, Whistler or Great-head, . . . is another northern species.

+**Brass-eyed,** *a.* (See quotation and preceding.) — **1839** PEABODY *Mass. Birds* 393 The Golden Eye . . . [has also] the name of Brass-eyed Whistler.

Brass founder. One who casts articles in brass. {1601–}

1720 *Weekly Mercury* 5 May 4/1 Very good Lamp-black to be sold by John Hyatt Brass Founder in the High Street near the Prison. **1792** *Ann. 2nd Congress* 1021 Brass founders . . . are numerous in the United States. **1808** *Ann. 10th Congress* 2 Sess. 90 The brass-founder, the copper-smith, the jeweller, and the wire-worker, have made distinguished progress in their respective arts. **1851** CIST *Cincinnati* 297 He engaged in business with T. B. & H. B. Coffin as bell and brassfounders.

Brass foundry. A manufacturing plant equipped for making brass castings. {1716–} — **1809** F. CUMING *Western Tour* 222 Pittsburgh [has] . . . seven coppersmiths, . . . one brass foundery. **1827** DRAKE & MANSF.

Cincinnati 65 One Cotton Spinning and Brass Foundry. **1838** COLTON *Ind. Delineated* 21 Here are several large iron and brass foundries.

+**Brass knuckles.** A contrivance made of brass, used to protect the knuckles in striking a severe blow. — **1855** *Chicago Times* 13 March 3/1 That new implement in modern *Mohawkism*—brass knuckles. **1861** *All Year Round* 13 July 372 What the crew most feared, was the free use of the 'brass knuckles' or 'knuckle dusters.' . . .These are brass finger-guards; . . . they constitute a regular portion of the equipment of an officer of the American mercantile marine. **1872** *Chicago Tribune* 15 Oct. 2/2 He thinks . . . that the way to hold the South is with an iron hand and brass knuckles. **1890** *Buckskin Mose* 30, I . . . dealt him a heavy blow with my brass-knuckles under the jaw.

+**Brass wood.** =BOW-WOOD. — **1844** *Congress. Globe* App. 31 May 500/1 On the Arkansas and Red rivers, an extremely valuable wood, . . . called the bois d'arc, or brass wood, grows in great quantities.

+**Brass(y)-bass.** (See quotations.) — **1884** GOODE *Fisheries U.S.* I. 424 The Brassy Bass of the Lower Mississippi Valley, *Roccus interruptus.* **1889** *Cent.* 664/1 *Brass-bass*, a percoideous fish, *Morone interrupta:* so called from its bright brassy color, tinged with blue on the back. . . . It attains the size of the common white perch, and inhabits fresh waters of the Mississippi valley.

* **Brave.**

+**1.** An Indian warrior.

1819 SCHOOLCRAFT *Mo. Lead Mines* 176 Their warriors are called braves, to which honour no one can arrive, without having previously plundered or stolen from the enemy. **1821** J. FOWLER *Journal* 67 The Ietan cheef has not viseted us since he moved up the river, . . . but the braves appeer friendly. **1844** GREGG *Commerce of Prairies* II. 292 The 'braves' are those who commonly deck themselves with the most gaudy trappings, and would usually be taken by a stranger for the chiefs of the band. **1853** RAMSEY *Tennessee* 455 The braves were decorated with eagle feathers on their heads, and other insignia of their rank. **1860** GREELEY *Overland Journey* 153 The 'brave,' whether civilized or savage, is not a worker, a producer. **1870** KEIM *Sheridan's Troopers* 212 The boys who are to become braves, are never punished, whatever may be their offense. **1901** WHITE *Westerners* ix. 63 Let them equally enjoy the chase, the other branch of a brave's education.

2. A brave soldier or fighting man.

1847 D. COYNER *Lost Trappers* 54 The Mandan chief . . . expected that the burial of a white brave would have been accompanied with more pride and ceremony. **1866** 'F. KIRKLAND' *Bk. Anecdotes* 67 Almost instantly after the concealed forces rushed out and surrounded the astounded Captain and his braves. **1898** CANFIELD *Maid of Frontier* 33 There were braves among them, and he loved courage in any form.

+**3.** A member of the Tammany Society.

1871 *N.Y. Times* 5 July 5/1 The Tammany Society. Celebration by the Braves'—Reading of the Declaration of Independence. **1895** *N.Y. Tribune* 26 Jan. 2 The braves and warriors who assembled in the big audience chamber of the . . . Tammany temple . . . had plenty of room. **1907** BROWN & STRAUSS *Dict. Amer. Politics* 390 Its organization [*i.e.* of Tammany Society] was supposed in a general way to imitate Indian customs, . . . the members being called braves, its meeting place the wigwam, etc.

+**Brazen bullhead.** A species of small sculpin, *Acantho* (or *Cottus*) *aeneus.* — **1814** MITCHILL *Fishes N.Y.* 380 Brazen Bullhead, *Cottus aeneus.* With brass-coloured complexion, thorny head, and rusty blotches over the sides. **1839** STORER *Mass. Fishes* 20 The brazen Bullhead . . . is very voracious, catching at almost any kind of bait offered to it, and distending itself immensely with food.

* **Brazier.** Also †**brassier, brasier.** A maker of articles of brass.

1646 *Essex Probate Rec.* I. 51 Hee is the brassiers bro. at Boston. *a***1649** WINTHROP *Hist.* II. 272 The Narragansetts . . . sold their kettles to a brazier in Boston. **1705** SEWALL *Diary* II. 120 Tedman, the Brazier, opens his Shop and dies. **1771** FRANKLIN *Autobiog.* 237 He . . . sometimes took me to walk with him, and see joiners, bricklayers, turners, braziers, etc., at their work. **1833** *Niles' Reg.* XLIV. 366/1 The straight links he considered brazier's rods, but in commerce they would not be known as such.

Braziery. Brazier's work. {1795–} — **1767** *Boston Gazette* 13 July, Just imported, . . . a fine Assortment of Braziery, Ironmongery, and Cutlery Ware.

Braziletto. {1656–} An inferior kind of brazilwood yielding a dyestuff. — **1790** *Penna. Packet* 1 Jan. 4/2 For Sale by John Leamy, . . . Braziletto Dye wood, . . . Spanish Hydes [etc.]. *Ib.* 6 May 1/4 R. Henderson has for sale, Brazilletto by the ton.

Brazilian, *a.* In specific names (see quotations). — **1871** LEWIS *Poultry Book* 85 The Musk or Brazilian Duck . . . is of a very dark, rich, blue-black prismatic [color]. **1901** MOHR *Plant Life Ala.* 614 *Malva brasiliensis,* . . . Brazilian Mallow. Fugitive on ballast from the tropics. Mobile, first collected June, 1893.

+**Breachy,** *a.* Of horses, cattle, or sheep: Apt to break out of enclosures or through fences.

1780 E. PARKMAN *Diary* 275 To my sorrow, my Oxen have been breachy at Mr. Isaac Parker's and let in Cattle with them, into his Cornfield. **1816** PICKERING 52 This is a common word among the farmers of New England, in speaking of oxen, &c. that are unruly, and apt to *break* through their enclosures. **1846** *Knickerb.* XXVIII. 343 [He] had sold me a yoke of 'breachy' oxen, notorious for their deeds throughout the settlement. **1863** H. S. RANDALL *Pract. Shepherd* 193 One 'breachy' sheep will rapidly teach its habits to the whole flock. **1874** *Vt. Bd. Agric. Rep.* II. 378 The cows are unusually gentle and very fond of being petted. Never knew one to be breachy. **1899** A. BROWN *Tiverton Tales* 133 That fence was all done up in the spring, but that cussed breachy cow o' Tolman's hooked it down.

fig. **1846** LOWELL *Biglow P.* I. vii. 61 Pledges air awfle breachy cattle. **1879** *Congress. Rec.* 10 June 1895/2 There are one or two breachy men who will insist upon leading your party into the very jaws of death and destruction.

* **Bread,** *n.*

1. a. Biscuit, esp. sea biscuit. *Obs.* except in *hard bread* q.v. {1651–1793}

*a***1656** BRADFORD *Hist.* 151 It arose but to a quarter of a pound of bread a day to each person. **1684** I. MATHER *Providences* 19 The seven in the boat . . . having neither sails nor oars, neither bread nor water. **1718** HEMPSTEAD *Diary* 72, I opened a bb white bread & took out 10 dozn & 4. **1851** SPRINGER *Forest Life* 60 The bread-barrel, although scuttled, was but half full of bread.

b. A variety of bread, including cakes, rolls, etc. See also INDIAN BREAD.

1789 *Kentucky Gazette* 25 April 1/4 The several kinds of bread, viz. loaf bread, Butter Biscuit, Cakes of different kinds, hard bread for Boating, crackers and Biscuit suitable for Travellers. **1835** [LONGSTREET] *Georgia Scenes* 36 He ate his meat and *breads* in the usual way, but he drank his liquids in all ways. **1863** [C. C. HOPLEY] *Life in South* II. 237 'Breads,' as all the variety of corn cakes, waffles, hot rolls, and hominy are called.

c. Bread made with special ingredients.

1643 WILLIAMS *Key* (1866) 121 The Indians bruise them [=strawberries] in a morter, and mixe them with meale and make Strawberry bread. **1705** BEVERLEY *Virginia* III. 14 They make their Bread of the Indian Corn, Wild Oats, or the Seed of the Sunflower.

2. *In good bread,* in a good living or position. *In bad bread,* in a bad state, in difficulties. ?*Obs.* {1825–, *dial.*}

1763 *Essex Inst. Coll.* XLIX. 139 Mr. Barnard . . . is now in good bread, and seems loth to affront his people by telling them plainly of these public sins. **1778** *Ib.* XLIII. 11 Old England I beleve is got into bad Bread for Mr. Frenchman at last is put a Trick on them in declaring our independant. *Ib.* 16 Hope it is the French Fleet, if not we shall be in bad Bread.

+**3.** *Bread-and-butter,* used attrib. with *brigade* or *men* as a contemptuous designation for office seekers.

1866 *Congress. Globe* 19 Dec. 206/3 There are gentlemen here, who in the last political contest went over the country saying that a certain party was a 'bread and butter brigade.' **1867** *Ib.* 12 April 834/2 [What Senator Howe] said nearly a year ago, when he invented . . . a phrase, when he spoke of the 'bread and butter brigade.' *Ib.* 835/3 [They] were removed by Andrew Johnson to make place for unreliable, irresponsible Copperheads in most cases, or bread-and-butter men, who are worse.

+**4.** *Bread-and-cheese apple* (see quotation).

1817 W. COXE *Fruit Trees* 116 [The] Rambo, or Romanite . . . is much cultivated in Delaware. . . . It is in some parts of the country, called the Bread and Cheese apple.

+**Bread,** *v. tr.* To supply with bread.

1797 *Steele Papers* I. 152, I cannot return you corn again this fall, as what I have . . . will scarcely bread the Negroes and feed the Work Horses. **1842** BUCKINGHAM *Slave States* II. 167 He always grows enough to *bread* his own people for a year at least, and sells the balance. **1879** TOURGEE *Fool's Errand* 91 They had enough to bread themselves. **1885** *Rep. Indian Affairs* 148 These Indians raised sufficient amount of wheat last year to bread them until the present crop is gathered.

Bread bag. A bag in which bread or biscuit is kept by sailors or travellers. {1864–} — **1828** A. SHERBURNE *Memoirs* 69 Three times a day Capt. Marsh would set down with the bread bag between his legs. **1840** DANA *Two Years* xxiii. 225 All hands were called again; the kids, pots, bread-bags, etc., stowed away. *a***1861** WINTHROP *Canoe & Saddle* 68, I was standing . . . in the centre of a group of tin pots, . . . blankets, bread-bags, bridles, spurs, and toggery. **1866** 'MARK TWAIN' in *Harper's Mag.* Dec. 109/2 This A.M. the bread-bag was found open and some bread missing.

+**Breadboard.** A board on which dough is kneaded. — **1869** E. PUTNAM *Receipt Bk.* 4 Mix . . . the dough; roll it, on a bread-board, about an inch thick. **1883** PECK *Bad Boy* 109, I told my chum that we couldn't hold the bread-board over the clothes basket much longer.

+**Bread-bowl.** A bowl in which the ingredients for making bread are mixed; a mixing bowl. — **1819** PEIRCE *Rebelliad* 15 The bread-bowls fly at woful rate. **1863** MRS. WHITNEY *F. Gartney* xi, Glory's hands were busy in the bread bowl, and her brain kneading its secret thoughts. **1879** — *Just How* 41 Two heaping cups of 'Arlington meal,' or graham flour, unsifted, in bread-bowl. **1896** WILKINS *Madelon* 14 She passed him with the bread-bowl on her hip and her soft arm curved around it.

+**Bread-cake.** A cake made with bread dough. — **1876** M. F. HENDERSON *Cooking* 298 [Recipe for making] Bread-cake. **1877** PHELPS *Story of Avis* 134 Avis held the skimmer suspended at a rash angle over a plate of bread-cake.

+**Bread cask.** A cask for holding bread. — **1778** *Journals Cont. Congress* X. 249 Bread casks with lining hoops, each, 3/90ths of a dollar.

‖**Bread colony.** *Obs.* A colony furnishing breadstuffs. — **1769** *Amer. Philos. Soc.* I. 190 All the foregoing sorts [of vines] will do very well for the three bread colonies, viz. New-York, New-Jersey, Pennsylvania.

∗ **Bread corn.** Grain, esp. maize, used in, or suitable for, making bread.

1668 *East-Hampton Rec.* I. 288 Whosoever shall grind Malte at the mill shall after[wards] . . . clear the mill with at least halfe apeck of bread corne. **1711** *Boston Rec.* 143 There is but little bread corn now in the Town. **1775** ADAIR *Indians* 407 The third [kind of corn grown by the Indians] is the largest, of a very white and soft grain, termed 'bread-corn.' **1823** KEATING *Narr.* 193 Our bread-corn had been consumed. **1853** RAMSEY *Tennessee* 144 Their bread-corn was brought from the neighborhood where Abingdon now stands.

+**Bread grain.** Wheat, maize, rye, etc., used for making bread. — **1793** JEFFERSON *Writings* III. 263 Bread-stuff, that is to say bread-grains, meals, and bread. **1814** J. TAYLOR *Arator* 175 Their food [*i.e.* of horned cattle] for half the year consists of the coarse offal of bread grain.

+**Bread line.** A line of poor people waiting to receive bread, coffee, etc. (Common in later use.) — **1900** *Lippincott's Mag.* LXV. 3 [Story by A. B. Paine entitled] The Bread Line. *Ib.* 12 That's the bread line. They get a cup of coffee and a loaf of bread every night at twelve o'clock. **1904** *Charleston News & Courier* 5 Sept. 4 The 'bread line' . . . nightly forms in front of Fleischmann's bakery in New York. *a***1906** 'O. HENRY' *Trimmed Lamp* etc. 188 The Bread Line moved forward slowly, its leathern feet sliding on the stones.

Bread riot. A riot caused by want of bread. — **1859** L. WILMER *Press Gang* 122 Do you think that we should ever have had a 'bread riot' in the United States, if we had never had an incorporated bank. **1883** J. D. FULTON *Sam Hobart* 124 Everybody saw in 1877 that if the capabilities of the railroads were destroyed, in a short time bread riots, starvation, . . . and suffering would become terrible facts.

+**Breadroot.** A leguminous plant (*Psoralea esculenta*) of the western plains, having a tuberous edible root; the prairie turnip or Cree potato. — **1829** EATON *Botany* (ed. 5) 349 *Psoralea esculenta*, bread root. . . . The root affords a staple article of diet to the western Indians. **1841** *Penny Cycl.* XIX. 94/2 The bread-root of North America is cultivated along the banks of the Missouri. **1843** FRÉMONT *Exped.* 50 During the day, I had occasionally remarked among the hills the . . . bread-root of the Indians. **1846** SAGE *Scenes Rocky Mts.* vi, A specimen of the bread-root . . . was procured from the creek-bank. . . . This . . . attains a size from twenty to thirty inches in circumference.

+**Breadstuff.**

1. Cereals, flour, meal, etc., out of which bread is made; also, bread of all kinds.

1793 JEFFERSON *Writings* IX. 20 France receives favorably our bread stuff, rice, wood, [etc.]. **1807** MARSHALL *Life Washington* V. 519 One great objection to the conduct of Britain was, her prohibitory duty on the importation of bread-stuff. **1815** *Mass. H. S. Coll.* 2 Ser. III. 205 Probably one third the bread-stuff consumed, is imported; flour from Boston; corn, from the neighboring towns. **1856** P. CARTWRIGHT *Autobiog.* 254 Some of the people had to go sixty miles for their grinding and bread-stuff. **1866** *Rep. Indian Affairs* 97 Their principal want is bread-stuff, and I have furnished them with wheat raised at this place. **1900** SMITHWICK *Evol. of State* 15 When the colonists used up the breadstuff they brought with them they had to do without until they raised it.

b. Attrib. with *country, farm, farmer, market.*

1814 J. TAYLOR *Arator* 92 The three resources . . . common to every bread stuff farm. *Ib.* 102 The most abundant source of artificial manure within the reach of a bread-stuff farmer. *Ib.* 170 The bread stuff country of the United States. **1887** *Courier-Journal* 11 Jan. 4/1 The breadstuff markets were without decided tendencies.

2. *pl.* The various kinds of grain used for this purpose. Also rarely in *sing.* of one of these.

1831 P. HONE *Diary* I. 31 The farmer . . . availing himself of the increased price of bread-stuffs, occasioned by the brisk foreign demand. **1847** *Rep. Comm. Patents* (1848) 125 Its [=buckwheat's] use as a bread-stuff is confined principally to the cakes which are made of it. **1854** THOREAU *Walden* 69 Every New Englander might easily raise all his own breadstuffs in this land of rye and Indian corn. **1863** *Rep. Comm. Agric.* 9 Nor could the people . . . with no foreign demand for breadstuffs, be expected to make much progress in tilling the soil. **1904** *N.Y. Times* 13 May 11 For April the decrease in our exports of bread-stuffs was $11,319,993. The foreigners can get wheat cheaper elsewhere.

∗ **Breadth.** A tract of cultivated land regarded in terms of its breadth alone. {1813–} — **1785** WASHINGTON *Diaries* II. 361, I sowed half a bushel of orchard grass seed . . . in a breadth through the Field. **1861** *Ill. Agric. Soc. Trans.* IV. 254 Our Corn crop for 1860 was an immense one, an unusually large breadth having been planted. **1867** *Iowa Agric. Soc. Rep.* (1868) 373 A greater breadth of wheat was sown than in any previous year.

Bread ticket. A ticket entitling the possessor to bread. — **1855** *Chicago Times* 21 March 3/1 To await trial for entering a bakeshop and stealing therefrom bread tickets to the value of $16.

Bread tray. +A large shallow wooden receptacle in which dough is kneaded. — **1879** B. F. TAYLOR *Summer-Savory* 157 On the narrow ledge, guiltless of trimming as a wooden bread-tray, lies the Bible. **1898** PAGE *Red Rock* 182 Her sleeves were rolled up, showing her round, white arms. She was busy with a bread-tray.

+**Bread trough.** ?*Obs.* A bread tray; a kneading trough. — **1638** *Md. Council Proc.* 76, I have seised . . . a bread troughe [and] . . . a reaping hooke. **1775** *Essex Inst. Coll.* XIII. 187 A Cloath's Horse, a Bread Trough, [etc.]. **1783** E. PARKMAN *Diary* 299 A Meal Sieve /6. Bread Trough /8.

+**Bread weigher.** An official charged with supervision of the weight of bread offered for sale. — **1725** *New-Eng. Courant* 7 Aug. 1/1 Bread very often wants near a quarter Part of its due Weight, notwithstanding the extraordinary Diligence of the Bread-weighers, who daily seize great Quantities of it.

Bread wheat. Wheat used for making bread. — **1814** J. TAYLOR *Arator* 153 The best bread and seed wheat, is invariably that gotten out and cleaned within a day or two after it is cut.

∗ **Break,** *n.*[1] [f. BREAK *v.*]

I. 1. A sudden gap, interruption, or drop in a chain of hills, mountain slope, the bed of a stream, etc. {1688–}

1760 in *N. E. Hist. & Gen. Register* XXXVI. 32 On arriving on the Lake, I took the bearing of a Notch or Break in the Mountains. **1781** WASHINGTON *Diaries* II. 251 These hills have very few interstices or Breaks in them. **1828** A. SHERBURNE *Memoirs* 65 A mountain . . . so steep and abounding with breaks and precipices, that it was very difficult for a man to ascend it in any place. **1897** BRODHEAD *Bound in Shallows* 238 Logs blackened the stream, showing the terrific speed of the current as they dashed over the break.

+**b.** *pl.* In the West: A series or succession of sharp interruptions of the terrain; broken country.

In recent use (1902–) also in the singular.

1854 MARCY *Expl. Red River* 5 Manuel . . . pointed out to him breaks or bluffs upon a stream to the south of the Canadian. **1869** BROWNE *Adv. Apache Country* 226 Not far beyond the mesa we entered upon a rugged region, abounding in breaks and arroyas very rocky and difficult for our horses. **1888** J. J. WEBB *Adventures* 296 We saw a man on horseback ascend a butte some distance on our right, near the breaks of the Arkansas. **1895** C. KING *Fort Frayne* 221 He was allowed for his winter range only the south bank of the Platte from Frayne to the breaks of the Medicine Bow.

+**2.** An agitated or disturbed area on the surface of water, as that made by the rising of a fish, or by a snag.

1852 *Mich. Agric. Soc. Trans.* III. 231 They will make a break in the water near the shore with their tail. **1875** 'MARK TWAIN' *Old Times* ix. 71 That silver streak in the shadow of the forest is the 'break' from a new snag. **1890** *Harper's Mag.* April 715/1, I run off once with my tackle, an' I'd jest throwed in my line an' seed a break, when mother calls out. **1894** 'MARK TWAIN' *P. Wilson* xvi, She passed many a snag whose 'break' could have told her a thing to break her heart. **1900** F. NORRIS *Blix* 144 The two watching from the boat . . . saw that most inspiriting of sights —the 'break' of a salmon-trout.

+**3.** (See first quotation.)

1859 BARTLETT 48 *Break*, a regular sale of tobacco at the 'breaking' or opening of the hogsheads. Local in Virginia. **1886** *Amer. Philological Assoc.* XVII. 45 Common Southern expressions [include] . . . *Break*, a sale of tobacco [etc.].

+**4.** One of the supporting stalks around which sorghum, corn, etc., is shocked.

1862 *Ill. Agric. Soc. Trans.* (1865) V. 160, I selected the gallows stalks, or breaks of my shocks [of sorghum].

II. +**5.** A rush or dash away from a place; an attempt to escape.

1833 *Sketches of Crockett* 82 Just before I got there, the old bear made a break and got loose. **1853** 'P. PAXTON' *Yankee in Texas* 98 Ef thar's a bright moon he'll keep shady tell nigh sun up, and then he'll make a break. **1878** E. B. TUTTLE *Border Tales* 46 Finally, the leader [*i.e.* of elk] will make a break in one direction or another. . . . Having made one break . . . their wits are exhausted. **1888** ROOSEVELT in *Century Mag.* May 49 Our three men . . . understood perfectly that the slightest attempt at a break would result in their being shot down. **1920** MULFORD *J. Nelson* 47 Oh, if you'll only make a break, or give me half an excuse to throw lead!

+**b.** A rush or dash *for* a place or person; an attack made in a rush.

1845 J. J. HOOPER *Simon Sugg's Adv.* xii. 143, I maid a brake on a bee line for Urwinton. **1883** 'MARK TWAIN' *Life on Miss.* iii, He said he could lam any thief in the lot. They was all about to make a break for him. **1889** FARMER 86 [Bears] can smell a man a long way off, and as soon as they can do this they make a break for him. **1899** A. H. QUINN *Penn. Stories* 50 Field, in the meantime, had made a break for third and reached it safely.

+**c.** An attempt or try *at* something.

1886 P. STAPLETON *Major's Christmas* 27 Maybe now a cornerser [=connoisseur] . . . would give you more, but I'll make a break at it as best I know how.

III. +**6.** A breakdown; a failure. ?*Obs.*

1827 J. RANDOLPH in *Life* (1851) II. 289, I am of opinion that (as we say in Virginia) we have made 'a great break.' In fact the administration have succeeded in no one measure.

+**7.** A sudden change in gait or speed on the part of a horse, esp. of a race horse.

1868 H. WOODRUFF *Trotting Horse* 41 The penalty of a break was such that the rider . . . would be afraid to push his horse up to the top of his speed. **1876** *Vt. Bd. Agric. Rep.* II. 143 His superior trotting motion and instinct, that is not disturbed by any attending circumstances into a break. **1884** BRET HARTE *On the Frontier* 117 He presently struck into the long swinging pace of his kind, and kept it throughout without 'break' or acceleration. **1902** MCFAUL *Ike Glidden* 200 When rounding into the home stretch his horse broke, and suddenly went to a wild swerving break that carried him to the complete outside of the track.

+**8.** A sudden decline in the price of stocks on the stock exchange.

1870 MEDBERRY *Men of Wall St.* 203 It is partly for want of courage to endure an occasional 'break' in stocks, . . . that . . . the outsiders . . . meet with misfortune. **1882** [see BONANZA 5b]. **1900** S. A. NELSON *A B C Wall St.* 130 The attack of a bear crowd or the actual inability of the holders will produce a decline, which is called 'a break.'

+**9.** A mistake, an error. Usually *a bad break.*

1884 NYE *Baled Hay* 200 Possibly science may be wrong. We have known science to make bad little breaks. **1898** HAMBLEN *Genl. Manager's Story* 136 He kept this kind of thing [*i.e.* an examination] up for a good hour. . . . On the whole, I didn't make any very bad breaks. **1901** RYAN *Montana* 263 No one here seems to know about the bad break he made over there; but, Lord! **1902** LORIMER *Lett. Merchant* 311 When a clerk makes a fool break, I don't want to beg his pardon for calling his attention to it. **1903** G. ADE *In Babel* 174 They could retail the grammatical errors and the social 'breaks' of the family that lately had come in from the country town. **1911** HARRISON *Queed* 255 He would be almost certain to make some serious error, some fatal break, which would impair his usefulness.

+**10.** A critical or decisive point or moment.

1888 BRYCE *Amer. Commonwealth* II. 568 One balloting follows another till what is called 'the break' comes. . . . The break, when it comes, comes with fierce intensity. **1912** C. MATHEWSON *Pitching* 54 In most Big League ball games, there comes an inning on which hangs victory or defeat. Certain intellectual fans call it the crisis. . . . Big League managers mention it as the 'break,' and pitchers speak of the 'pinch.'

+**Break,** *n.*[2] [prob. from *brake* v., to dress hemp.] The hemp produced in one year. — **1796** *Mass. Mercury* 29 April (*Cent.*), Best St. Petersburg clean Hemp of the break of the year 1796. **1907** *Daily Chronicle* 7 March 6/6 A 'break' of hemp, which in America means the quantity sold in a year.

*BREAK, *v.*

The former (now dial.) p. p. *broke,* and the irregular *breaked,* are illustrated in the following quotations: **1697** *Virginia State P.* I. 53 It [an impostume] is lately break'd. **1723** *New-Eng. Courant* 5-12 Aug. 2/2 Several houses [are] blown down and broke. **1751** FRANKLIN *Electrical Experiments* 64 It was broke in several places. **1758** *Essex Inst. Coll.* XVIII. 92 A man . . . had his legg brok. **1777** *N.H. Comm. Safety Rec.* 79 There was 42 Squares of Glass broke, 2 Stairs broke, . . . & plastering broke down in several rooms. **1823** COOPER *Pioneers* xxviii, You've broke the law. **1847** [see sense 1]. **1855** M. THOMPSON *Doesticks* 44, [I] was necessitated to get a bill broke.

I. 1. *tr.* To beat and crush flax. {17th c.}

By confusion with **brake* in the same sense.

1719 *Mass. Bay Currency Tracts* 201 As to Flax there is Labour in . . . breaking, hatchelling, spining, weaving, &c. before we use it for Cloathing. **1775** in Commons, etc. *Doc. Hist.* I. 189 This morning 3 men went to work to break, swingle and heckle flax. **1788** WASHINGTON *Diaries* III. 295 The ground being too hard to ditch the Dutchman came home and broke flax. **1845** JUDD *Margaret* I. iii. 13 Mr. Hart . . . helped Hash on the farm, broke flax, made shoes, . . . and drank excessively. **1847** in DRAKE *Pioneer Life Ky.* 69 The flax was dried . . . , sunk below the surface of the ground, and 'broke.' **1862** *Ill. Agric. Soc. Trans.* (1865) V. 675 The last and crowning operation—the breaking and dressing the fibre or lint for the market. 1911 *Dept. Agric. Yearbook* (1912) 199 The straw . . . passes through a series of automatic machines which . . . break, scutch, and partly hackle the fiber.

2. In figurative or allusive phrases: **a.** *Break(ing) the Pope's neck* (see quotations).

1773 P. V. FITHIAN *Journal* I. 65 Mr. Lee, by the voice of the Company, was chosen Pope, . . . and the rest of the company were appointed Friars, in the Play call'd 'break the Pope's neck.' **1833** GREENE *Dod Duckworth* II. 167 To the orthodox amusement of breaking the Pope's neck, succeeded various others; such as . . . blindman's buff. **1890** *Amer. Notes & Q.* VI. 53 There used to be a game played by young persons of either sex in New England called 'Break the Pope's Neck.' . . . It was an in-door game, played of a winter's evening in country places, and I think a pewter plate was twirled in a certain way at one stage of the game.

+**b.** *To break another's nose,* to administer a check or set-back to a person.

1864 NORTON *Army Letters* 217 The new major 'has broken the doctor's nose' and given him to understand that his duties are to attend to the sick.

+**c.** *To break the slate,* to refuse to support a list of candidates approved by one's political party (cf. 15b).

1888 BRYCE *Amer. Commonwealth* II. 458 The list so settled is now a slate, unless some discontented magnate objects and threatens to withdraw. To do so is called 'breaking the slate.'

transf. **1888** A. C. GUNTER *Mr. Potter* xxii, It's a desperate dodge, but I think it'll 'break the slate!' *Ib.* xxiii, Mr. Potter is arranging to 'break the slate.'

+**d.** *Stock exchange.* To cause a sharp fall in (a price or prices).

1885 *Harper's Mag.* Nov. 841/2 He . . . 'spills stock' when he throws great quantities upon the market, either from necessity or to 'break,' i.e., lower, the price. **1902** NORRIS *Pit* ix, How are we going to unload our big line of wheat without breaking the price on us?

3. *To break joint(s),* to lay stones, bricks, etc., so that one set overlaps another.

*a***1817** DWIGHT *Travels* III. 93 After one row [of beach-grass] was set, others were placed behind it in such a manner, as to shut up the interstices; or, as a carpenter would say, 'so as to break the joints.' **1842** *Amer. Pioneer* I. 163 It is constructed of hewed yellow poplar logs. . . . They are placed so as to break joints, like stone work or masonry. **1856** OLMSTED *Slave States* 668 Planting is done by laying the cuttings . . . three always together, with the eyes of each a little removed from those of the others, that is, all 'breaking joints.' **1874** *Vt. Bd. Agric. Rep.* II. 511 After placing sills on the foundation, begin to lay on slats as above mentioned breaking joints each time.

+**4.** *To break corn,* to remove the ears from the stalks.

1837 in Commons, etc. *Doc. Hist.* I. 221 Through breaking corn on the 18th, . . . and begun picking corn of plantation hands. **1847** *Florida Plant. Rec.* 294, 4 [hands] brake corn, 8 halling in corn. **1854** *Ib.* 103, I had to stop and brak corn so the gin could ketch up.

***5.** To render obedient, to tame or train (horses, etc., also formerly slaves). Cf. 18b, 19a.

(1) **1831** PECK *Guide* 164 The poor French, who monopolize the business of catching and breaking these horses, make them an article of traffic. **1850** W. MILES *Journal* (1916) 13 Day after day passed in catching [mules] and hitching to wagons to break them. **1868** H. WOODRUFF *Trotting Horse* 53 When the colt is broken to the saddle, his work in harness is to be commenced. **1883** E. W. HOWE *Country Town* (1926) 24 Sometimes he came by the school on a winter evening, with a rude sled, to which he had young horses attached to break them. **1903** [E. W. PRINGLE] *Rice Planter* 57, I have always broken my colts myself.

(2) **1845** F. DOUGLASS *Life* 57 Mr. Covey had acquired a very high reputation for breaking young slaves.

+**6.** To soften hard water.

1848 in DRAKE *Pioneer Life Ky.* 94 Much [of the water] had to be brought from the spring and broke with ashes. **1853** *Harper's Mag.* VI. 582/2 The water of Lake Superior . . . being . . . entirely unfit for the laundry without a previous 'breaking,' by soda or other means.

+**7.** Of a horse: To alter (its gait). Cf. 15 and BREAK *n.*[1] 7.

1868 H. WOODRUFF *Trotting Horse* 54 At this time, you will often see him break his gait.

II. 8. To free (a road, path, etc.) from snow or other obstructions; to open up, make. {1698–} Cf. 20c.

1779 *Mass. H.S. Coll.* 2 Ser. II. 478 The roads [were] very bad this day, and not broke. **1780** E. PARKMAN *Diary* 195 Neighbors with Cattle and Shovels to break the Roads. **1853** B. YOUNG in *Jrnl. Discourses* I. 83 Who broke the roads to these valleys? . . . We broke the roads to this country. **1855** *Chicago Times* 24 Jan. 3/1 To many of us who have lived in the snowy down east, 'breaking roads' has been a familiar sight. *c***1856** M. J. HOLMES *Homestead on H.*, Old Red House ii, Several more days passed before the process of 'breaking roads' was gone through with sufficiently to admit of a passage from one house to another. **1896** *Vt. Agric. Rep.* XV. 35 The sugar maker should . . . not spend the first week of the sugar season breaking roads. **1911** ROLT-WHEELER *Boy with Census* 264 When you try to break trail and have to keep ahead of a dog-team . . . , it's just about the hardest kind of work there is.

+**9.** To prepare (land) for cultivation. Also absol.

In earlier use with *up:* see sense 21a.

1846 FARNHAM *Prairie Land* 214 You would see the heavy team of three and four yokes of oxen traveling slowly over a tract, dragging after them a plough, which if you have never seen 'breaking' done, is an entire stranger to you. **1849** [CHAMBERLAIN] *Indiana Gazetteer* 15 In clearing land, breaking prairies and hauling freight in muddy roads, oxen have been preferred to horses. **1857** *Lawrence* (Kansas) *Republican* 11 June 3 Those who are breaking prairie this year in Kansas. *Ib.* 18 June 4 Prairie should be broke at least four inches deep. **1880** *Harper's Mag.* March 531/2 An acre and a half could be 'broken' in a day. **1880** *Scribner's Mo.* June 213/2 In one instance, in Graham county, a man 'broke' five acres of raw prairie with a common spade.

+**10.** To break up (a camp, etc.) in order to move elsewhere.

1864 A. J. DICKSON *Across Plains* (1929) 108 Everyone was now growing impatient of further delay, and it was decided to break corral. **1872** BOURKE *Journal* 22 Nov., Broke camp at sun-up. **1920** HUNTER *Trail Drivers of Texas* I. 273 He did not hear us breaking camp.

+b. *To break yard*, of moose: (see quot. and MOOSE-YARD).
1887 *Harper's Mag.* Feb. 459/1 They 'break yard,' as it is called, and falling in one behind the other, start down the mountain in close column.

+11. To open (tobacco hogsheads).
1871 DE VERE 447 *Break*, to, is in Virginia, and other tobacco-raising States, applied to the opening of the hogsheads, as they are sent from the plantations, previous to a public sale.

+12. To open (a breech-loading gun or pistol).
1889 *Cent.* 669/1 *To break a gun*, to open it by the action.

III. *intr.* **+13. a.** Of a hunting dog: To break away after game.
1809 F. CUMING *Western Tour* 135 A fine dog, led by a string to prevent his breaking (or hunting the game beyond the reach of their rifles).

+b. To make a rush or dash; to run.
1834 CROCKETT *Life* xiv. 96 When my lead dog found him [*sc.* a bear] and raised his yell, all the rest [of the dogs] broke to him. **1836** *Quarter Race Ky.* (1846) 20 He broke down the track to his mare, slacked her girths, and led her back. **1846** W. STEWART *Altowan* I. vi. 174 He . . . looked out, and saw a robe!—broke, leaped into the river. **1890** *Buckskin Mose* ix. 136 We accordingly 'broke' in its direction. **1907** WHITE *Arizona Nights* v. 98 The cattle would attempt to 'break' past the end and up the valley.

+c. To make a dash *for* a place.
To break for high or *tall timber:* see TIMBER.
1835 [LONGSTREET] *Georgia Scenes* 125 The way she [a horse] now broke, for Springfield 'is nothing to nobody.' **1851** *Polly Peablossom* 179 He . . . 'broke' for the well. *c***1856** *Kit Carson's Life* 34 We broke for our arms, they for theirs. **1857** 'MARK TWAIN' *Adv. of Snodgrass* (1928) 44 So I gathered up the traps and broke for home like a quarter-hoss. **1902** LORIMER *Lett. Merchant* xvi. 237 Just as the crowd yelled and broke for the house, two patrol wagons full of policemen got there.

+d. To break up, disperse.
1881 H. W. PIERSON *In the Brush* 177 The benediction was then pronounced, and, in their vernacular, the 'meeting broke.'

+e. *Lumbering.* Of logs: To move readily or freely.
1893 *Scribner's Mag.* June 710/2 This is active work and requires . . . care in so placing the logs that they will 'break' or roll in easily when the ice goes out.

+14. Of fish: To come to the surface of the water.
1885 *Outing* Oct. 75/2 Just then a trout broke under the alders. **1885** *Harper's Mag.* Jan. 216/1 Once I tried to fool them with sham colored feathers; but no, sir, they [the fish] never broke.

+15. Of a horse, esp. in racing: To change gait; to lose a level stride. (Cf. 7.)
1852 BRISTED *Upper Ten Th.* 26 Suddenly the pacer stops short and capers. He is used up and has 'broken.' **1856** *Spirit of Times* (N.Y.) 25 Oct. 131/1 Rocket unfortunately broke, caught again splendidly, but could not recover his previous advantage. **1868** H. WOODRUFF *Trotting Horse* 42 If the horse . . . when he breaks . . . is to be immediately pulled to a trot, or pulled up, I think it will be better to teach him not to break. **1876** BRET HARTE *G. Conroy* II. VI. v, The springs creaked, the wheels rattled, the mare broke, plunged, and recovered herself. **1908** *Springfield W. Republican* 8 Oct. 2 A trotter in a race breaks, that is, loses his level stride and reverts to an impossible kind of gallop which is not permitted by the rules of harness racing.
fig. **1902** LORIMER *Lett. Merchant* 60 Never start off at a gait that you can't improve on, but move along strong and well in hand to the quarter. . . . Take it calm enough up to the half not to break.

+b. *fig.* To break away from a party and vote differently from what is expected. (Cf. 2c.)
1904 *N.Y. Ev. Post* 17 May 1 Kane County deserted Yates. . . . Will County broke also, and gave twenty-six votes for Lowden. **1908** *Springfield W. Republican* 8 Oct. 2 The word 'break' applied to political campaigners has the same meaning [as in horse-racing].

+16. Of prices of commodities, stocks, etc.: To fall suddenly or sharply.
1892 *Courier-Journal* 1 Oct. 11/5 When wheat broke under 76c the corn bulls quickly sold out again. **1902** LORIMER *Lett. Merchant* 23 He is the chap that's buying wheat at ninety-seven cents the day before the market breaks.

IV. With adverbs.

17. *Break away.* +Of the weather: To clear up, become fair. ?*Obs.*
1758 *Essex Inst. Coll.* XVIII. 98 Cloudy cool Morning wind west northerly breaks away about Noon. **1768** WASHINGTON *Diaries* I. 249 Very like to snow but broke away abt. Sun Set. **1775** W. A. Pusey *Road to Ky.* (1921) 43 Wednesday the 5th breaks away fair & we go down the valey. **1816** U. BROWN *Journal* II. 221 This morning rains very much, about ten o'Clock breaks away.

18. *Break down.* **+a.** To dance, or perform (a dance), in a violent, stamping manner.
1838 *Lexington Observer & Rep.* 8 Aug., He got to 'breaking down' so hard toward the end of his dance, that the head [of the barrel] went in. **1873** 'MARK TWAIN' & WARNER *Gilded Age* xvi, The twang of a banjo became audible as they drew nearer, and they saw a couple of negroes, from some neighboring plantation, 'breaking down' a juba.

+b. To break in (a horse). *Obs.*
*c***1835** CATLIN *Indians* II. 59 This 'breaking down' or taming, however, is not without the most desperate trial on the part of the horse.

c. Of a hill, mountain, etc.: To drop to a lower level.
1853 D. H. STROTHER *Blackwater Chron.* 24 Passing through the North mountain, . . . where it breaks down almost on a level with the valley . . . , we entered the mountain region.

19. *Break in.* **a.** =sense 5. {1785–} Also transf.
1852 MRS. STOWE *Uncle Tom* xix. 198, I broke a fellow in, once . . . that all the overseers and masters had tried their hands on in vain. **1858** VIELÉ *Following the Drum* 122 The Indian lassos his horse, jumps on the wild restive creature's back, and remains there till he is in a measure broken in. **1898** WESTCOTT *D. Harum* 100, I would rather break him in myself, and if he's willing and sound and no vice, I can get him into shape.

+b. To wear (boots or shoes) until they are comfortably adjusted to the feet.
1846 *Spirit of Times* (N.Y.) 25 April 99/2 A pair of his new boots require no 'breaking in.' **1884** NYE *Baled Hay* 119, I had . . . been breaking in a pair of new boots that day.

20. *Break out.* **a.** To get out (articles) from a place of storage; to open up and clear out (a receptacle).
1840 DANA *Two Years* xiv, Then there is always a good deal to be done in the hold: goods to be broken out. **1849** N. KINGSLEY *Diary* 22 Broke out our chests to day, found all our things in good order. *Ib.* 73 They broke out the baggage room to day to get iron for various purposes.

b. To form or make by breaking through a wall.
1727 *Md. Hist. Mag.* VII. 399 It is ordered . . . that they be at the Expence of breaking out a window near the pulpit.

c. To free (a path, road, etc.) from snow; to open up after a heavy snow. (Cf. 8.)
1852 *Harper's Mag.* April 582/2 Hugh had broken out a road to the place by means of the oxen. **1867** 'T. LACKLAND' *Homespun* I. 135 Their grandparents . . . would be out on the bleak country roads, helping the men 'break out' with ox teams. **1867** S. HALE *Letters* 19 She reported that Walnut Street had been broken out, . . . by snow ploughs. **1888** HOWELLS *A. Kilburn* iii, The sidewalks . . . were promptly broken out in winter by the public snow-plough.

+d. *Lumbering.* To clear of jammed logs.
1901 *Munsey's Mag.* XXV. 393/2 Bold men with peevies 'break out' the rollways; the logs rattle down.

+e. *intr.* (See quotations.)
*a***1870** CHIPMAN *Notes on Bartlett* 49 *To break out in a new spot*, to do some new thing; to do something else.—C[onnecticu]t. **1878** I. L. BIRD *Rocky Mts.* 215 Even their [*sc.* Indians'] 'reservations' do not escape seizure practically; for if gold 'breaks out' on them they are 'rushed.'

21. *Break up.* ***a.** To begin to cultivate (ground) by digging or plowing; esp. to open up for the first time with a heavy plough. (Cf. 9.)
'To plough up land that has lain long as a meadow, is the sense as understood in the United States' (B. '48).
1636 *Cambridge Prop. Rec.* 40 Nyne Acc[r]es of land not yett brocken vpp. **1638** *New Haven Col. Rec.* 2 Neither setting up any wigwam, nor breaking up any ground to plant corne, [etc.]. **1640** *Southampton Rec.* I. 14 The Indians above named shall have libertie to break up ground for theire use. **1716** *Mass. Bay Currency Tracts* 174 The improving the sowing of Hemp and Flax . . . is much obstructed by the inability of many to break up Land suitable. **1750** T. WALKER *Journal* (1898) 55 The People I left had . . . clear'd and broke up some ground, & planted Corn. **1802** *Steele Papers* I. 250, I have broken up . . . the feeld this Side of your house. **1842** MRS. KIRKLAND *Forest Life* II. 72 The wheat land which I bought at a large additional cost in consideration of their being broken up and planted. **1872** EGGLESTON *End of World* 13 Had she noticed that August Wehle, who was 'breaking up' her father's north field, was just ploughing down the west side of his land?
absol. **1719** HEMPSTEAD *Diary* 87, I was about home fitting my plow & Looking my Steer & getting oxen to break up. **1764** *N.H. Hist. Soc. Coll.* IX. 167, [I] began breaking up.

b. To make (a person) nervous, dejected, or unstrung.
1860 HOLMES *Professor* i. 12 This episode broke me up, as the jockeys say. **1886** *Boston Journal* 10 July, The ladies suffered greatly from nervous excitement, and all were pretty badly broken up. **1891** S. M. WELCH *Recoll. 1830–40* 323 They both seemed all broke up by my awkwardness.

+Breakback. A roof (usually on the rear side of a house) having the lower portion of a different slope from the upper. — **1856** GOODRICH *Recoll.* I. 78 The house itself was a low edifice . . . ; the rear being what was called a *breakback*, that is, sloping down to a height of ten feet; this low part furnishing a shelter for garden tools, and various household instruments. **1859** BARTLETT 48 *Break-back*, a term applied to a peculiar roof, common in the country, where the rear portion is extended beyond the line of the opposite side, and at a different angle.

+Breakbone fever. An infectious fever found in warm climates; the dengue. — **1862** *Cincinnati let.* in *N.Y. Tribune* 16 May, The warm weather is adding . . . another fever, to which the natives [of the south-western states] give the name (said to be very graphic) of Breakbone, in which every bone in the body feels as if it were broken. **1866** A. FLINT *Princ. Med.* (1880) 1073 During this stage, . . . acute, often excruciating, pains in the head, eyes, muscles of the neck, loins, and extremities are prominent traits of the affection; hence the name *breakbone fever.* **1895** *Outing* XXVI. 402/1 My hand shook as if I had had the breakbone fever for years.

Breakdown. {1832–} +A noisy rollicking dance of rustic origin.

Also, 'a dance in the peculiar style of the negroes' (B. '59).

1819 QUITMAN in *Life & Corr.* I. 42 Lay at Point Pleasant, where Whiting and I visited a Virginia 'break-down.' **1840** in Buckingham *E. & W. States* (1842) II. 28 The match . . . will consist of a variety of Break-downs, Jigs, Reels, &c. **1847** FIELD *Drama in Pokerville*, etc. 180 There were river yarns, and boatmen songs, and 'nigger break-downs.' **1875** *Chicago Tribune* 30 Sept. 5/1 Lotta, the charming little actress who plays the banjo and dances break-downs. **1889** E. B. CUSTER *Tenting on Plains* 234 The fattest darkey of all waddled down next and did a break-down. **1899** BRET HARTE *Hamlin's Mediation* 102 The dancing of the girl suggested a negro 'break-down' rather than any known sylvan measures. **1920** C. R. COOPER *Under Big Top* 5 Lidge Dawsey was holding a supper and breakdown.

attrib. **1864** T. L. NICHOLS *Amer. Life* I. 227 She . . . heard a long impromptu song composed in her honour, with a banjo and breakdown accompaniment.

***Breaker.** [f. BREAK *v.*]

+**1.** One engaged in breaking hemp. *Obs.*

1720 *Mass. Bay Currency Tracts* 389 Two breakers for 1 day 6 s.

2. A reef or bank on which the waves break. ?*Obs.* {1681}

1722 *New-Eng. Courant* 7–14 May 4/2 Soon after (it happening to be Tide of Ebb) they were left bare upon a Breaker; but the Waves dashing over them much bruised their Bodies. **1834** *Visit to Texas* xii. 112 On the western breaker the soundings are six feet.

+**3.** A kind of plow used in breaking land.

1857 *Lawrence* (Kansas) *Republican* 28 May 3 A large assortment of Breakers of all sizes, especially of my extra Two-Horse Moldboard Breakers. **1873** *Newton Kansan* 13 Feb. 3/3 All sizes of breakers and old ground plows, at S. Lehman & Co's.

+**4.** A horse that breaks from a level stride.

1868 H. WOODRUFF *Trotting Horse* 201 Although a trotter of remarkably fine speed and power, he was such a bad breaker, . . . that at first he was beaten by horses much inferior to himself. *Ib.* 398 Whether you should make a puller of him . . . or whether you shall suffer him to become a bad, losing breaker.

+**Breakfast cap.** ?*Obs.* A small fancy cap worn by women at breakfast time. — **1863** 'G. HAMILTON' *Gala-Days* 28 What had I to do with breakfast-caps? . . . If I had wanted breakfast-caps, shouldn't I have asked for breakfast-caps? **1873** C. D. WARNER *Backlog Studies* 71 The Mistress, in a pretty little breakfast-cap, is moving about the room with a feather-duster.

+**Breakfast horn.** [See HORN *n.*] A horn sounded as a summons to breakfast. — **1845** M. M. NOAH *Gleanings* 78 We returned to the house, warned by the shrill echo of the breakfast horn. **1884** 'MARK TWAIN' *H. Finn* 361 He broke off there, because we heard the breakfast-horn blowing.

Breakfasting, *vbl. n.* {1732–*a*1771} Attrib. with *hall, house* {1732}, *room.* — **1830** *Collegian* 120 At seven we stopped at the breakfasting-house. **1834** CARRUTHERS *Kentuckian* I. 14 The gentlemen of the stage-coach found their way into the long breakfasting-hall of the establishment. **1835** *S. Lit. Messenger* I. 724 The members of the Kitchen Cabinet and the black Alguazils of the breakfasting-room.

Breakfast room. The room in a house in which breakfast is served. {1837} — **1836** SIMMS *Mellichampe* xvi, Descending to the breakfast-room, the first person who encountered his glance was the fair Janet. **1863** MRS. WHITNEY *F. Gartney* xii, A bright little breakfast-room. **1915** D. R. CAMPBELL *Proving Virginia* 16 The little round table in the cozy breakfast-room.

+**Breakfast station.** A place on a stage route where breakfast is obtained. — **1872** 'MARK TWAIN' *Roughing It* xii, 97 Just beyond the breakfast-station we overtook a Mormon emigrant train of thirty-three wagons. **1891** *Scribner's Mag.* X. 216 Gerard talked with him until they reached the breakfast station.

Breakfast table. A table at which breakfast is served. {1838–}

1775 *Essex Inst. Coll.* XIII. 186 A Breakfast Table. **1790** *Penna. Packet* 29 March 1/1 Mahogany dining tables, card and breakfast tables. **1809** KENDALL *Travels* I. xv. 170 The breakfast-table is spread at eight-o'clock. **1821** COOPER *Spy* v, The officers were invited to take their morning's repast at the family breakfast table. **1884** ROE *Nature's Story* 93 A happy group gathered at the breakfast-table that morning.

+**Breakfast-tea.** A kind of tea used for breakfast. *English breakfast-tea,* souchong. — **1865** STOWE *House & Home P.* 262 Breakfast-tea must be boiled! **1877** PHELPS *Story of Avis* 169 Barbara [was] . . . capable of bringing the English breakfast-tea in a lotus-leaf.

Breaking, (*vbl.*) *n.* [BREAK *v.*]

+**1.** Land newly broken up by the plough.

1860 GREELEY *Overland Journey* 10 Despite the hard times, Illinois is growing. There are new blocks in her cities, . . . new breakings on this or that edge of almost every prairie. **1861** *Ill. Agric. Soc. Trans.* IV. 318 If it is new breaking, it should be plowed in the fall. **1867** *Putnam's Mag.* May (De Vere), Wide spaces of breaking showed the tender green of young wheat. **1880** *Harper's Mag.* May 817/2 Here and there a great square of black earth was exposed in a new 'breaking.'

+**2.** *attrib.* (See quotation and cf. BREAK *v.* 13 d, BREAKING-UP 3.)

1881 H. W. PIERSON *In the Brush* 253 These 'breaking' or parting exercises have afforded me the opportunity of hearing the grandest . . . African melodies to which I have ever listened.

+**Breaking plow.** [BREAK *v.* 9.] A heavy plow used in breaking up land. — **1853** *Knickerb.* XLII. 593 The great 'breaking-plough,' with its dozen yoke of cattle, in the first place, goes tearing and groaning through the roots and grubs that lie twisted under it. **1867** *Iowa Agric. Soc. Rep.* (1868) 431 Mr. Cole is running a breaking-plow in its season with five yoke of Herefords. **1881** *Rep. Indian Affairs* 88, I have retained the control of the work-oxen and breaking-plows. **1891** C. ROBERTS *Adrift Amer.* 43 There had been an old breaking plough left just outside the house.

+**Breaking team.** [BREAK *v.* 9.] A team drawing a breaking plow or the like. — **1839** J. PLUMBE *Sk. Iowa* 40 This route would also answer well for persons . . . wishing to purchase their breaking-team, plow, &c. at the West. **1860** GREELEY *Overland Journey* 65 The squatter can give you a hundred good excuses for his miserable condition: he has no breaking-team; [etc.]. **1896** *Congress. Rec.* 5 May 4843/2, I do not brag of my voice. I came honestly by it driving breaking teams.

Breaking up, *vbl. n.* (Cf. BREAK *v.* 21 a.)

1. The process of plowing or opening land.

1716 *Mass. Bay Currency Tracts* 181 One Branch of which, (*viz.*) that of breaking up of Land, . . . would Yearly save the Country [etc.]. **1847** in DRAKE *Pioneer Life Ky.* 45 After a first 'breaking up' with the coultered plow, the shovel plow was in general use.

+**b.** Attrib. with *hoe, plough, team.*

1764 *N.H. Hist. Soc. Coll.* IX. 168, [I] mustered my breaking up team. **1790** S. DEANE *New-Eng. Farmer* 127/1 It [=a narrow hoe] has also the name of a breaking-up hoe. **1854** B. J. TAYLOR *Jan. & June* 41 For a few days past, they have kept a thing . . . going in the Clover Field, that they call a 'breaking-up plough.' **1861** *Harper's Mag.* Nov. 854/1 Old Deacon Cole had a 'breaking-up team,' consisting of six yoke of oxen.

2. The giving way, or moderating in severity, of the cold of winter.

1708 *Boston News-Letter* 19–26 Jan. 2/2 The Season setting in cold, and freezing hard, has hindered the Mast Fleet, who design upon the breaking up of the Weather . . . to imbrace the first opportunity of Sailing for Great Britain. **1755** L. EVANS *Anal. Map Colonies* 26 The late or early Breaking up of the Winter. **1874** LONG *Wild-Fowl,* Upon the breaking up of winter, however, they begin to arrive.

3. Dissolution, disruption, dispersal (of a party, meeting, etc.). (Cf. BREAKING *vbl. n.* 2.) Also attrib.

1872 *Harper's Mag.* March 496/1 Mr. Buchanan's administration was embarrassed by a monetary revulsion only less severe than that of 1837. Its close was amidst the stirring 'breaking up' which preceded Mr. Lincoln's inauguration. **1904** M. E. WALLER *Wood-Carver* 41, I remember that week in which she took me to the camp-meeting. . . . I was just fifteen, and on Sunday before 'breaking-up Monday,' I got religion.

Breakup. {1795–} +The Civil War. *Obs. colloq.* — **1869** J. R. BROWNE *Adv. Apache Country* 133 It [=Tucson] became during the few years preceding the 'break-up' quite a place of resort for traders, speculators, [etc.]. **1884** SWEET & KNOX *Through Texas* 74 Before the civil war, or, as a Texan would say, "fore the break-up,' [etc.].

***Bream.**

+**1.** One or other of various fishes resembling the common European bream, esp. the common fresh-water sunfish.

[**1622** 'MOURT' *Relation* 108 Massasoyt brought two fishes that he had shot, they were like Breame but three times so bigge.] **1634** WOOD *New Eng. Prospect* II. xvi. 90 In frostie weather they [=Indians] cut round holes in the yce, about which they wil sit . . . catching of Pikes, Pearches, Breames, and other sorts of fresh water fish. **1643** WILLIAMS *Key* (1866) 138 Breame. Of this fish there is an abundance which the Natives drie in the Sunne and smoake. **1772** ROMANS in Phillips *Notes* (1924) 123 Those [river fish] peculiar to America are three Species of the Bream, one of which is here called Perch, the Striped Rock, and a kind of Fish . . . on which there is not a Name yet fixed. **1792** *Mass. H. S. Coll.* I. 113 It [the lake] is supplied with pickerel, large perch, eels, shiners, breams, pouts. **1832** WILLIAMSON *Maine* I. 158 The Bream is a scaled fresh water horn-back fish, . . . [and] is as good to the taste as the perch and less bony. **1854** THOREAU *Walden* 199 There have been caught in Walden . . . shiners, chivins or roach (*Leuciscus pulchellus*), a very few breams, and a couple of eels, one weighing four pounds. **1860** *Harper's Mag.* March 488/2 Our cousins in Massachusetts call this fish [the sun-fish] 'bream,' but it is totally distinct from the European fish which bears that name. **1885** M. THOMPSON *Byways & Bird Notes* 126 Speaking of bream, as the Southerners call the blue-perch, . . . you find it in the eddies and swirls of those Georgian brooks and rivers.

+**2.** With various distinctive names.

1791 BARTRAM *Travels* 176 The golden bream or sun-fish, the red bellied bream . . . also abound here. **1842** *Nat. Hist. N.Y., Zoology* IV. 93 The Rhomboidal Porgee. *Sargus rhomboides.* Salt-water Bream. *Ib.* 191 The

Variegated Bream, *Abramis versicolor*, ... appears occasionally in the New-York market, from the Connecticut and Hudson river and the streams of Long Island. **1888** GOODE *Amer. Fishes* 67 The Blue Sunfish, *Lepomis pallidus*, is also known as the 'Blue Bream' and 'Copper-nosed Bream.'

* **Breast,** *n.*

1. The face or most exposed portion of a dam, drift, etc.

1815–6 *Niles' Reg.* IX. Suppl. 164/2 The other ends [are bolted] upon the breast of the dam. **1857** *Harper's Mag.* Sept. 462/1 Two miners and a laborer generally work in a 'breast,' or 'slope,' which is usually forty feet in width. **1873** RAYMOND *Silver & Gold* 63 The gravel is brought from the 'head' or 'breasts' of the drifts by a car drawn by a mule to the foot of the incline. **1880** G. INGHAM *Digging Gold* 258 The new owners [of the Desmet Mine] pushed their development from this breast, already exposed. **1903** WHITE *Forest* viii. 94 The men were working at the breast of it [*i.e.* of a jam], some underneath, some on top.

+**2.** A spikelet of wheat.

1868 S. E. TODD *Amer. Wheat Culturist* 24 In some sections of the country, a spikelet is better understood if it is spoken of as a *breast of wheat.*

* **Breast,** *v.*

1. *tr.* To face or oppose manfully or courageously.

1842 *Amer. Pioneer* I. 80 We had set out with a determination to breast with fortitude the hardships we might have to encounter. **1847** PRESCOTT *Peru* II. 29 Prepared to breast the difficulties of the sierra. **1888** *Congress. Rec.* 31 July 7104/1 Gentlemen ... may lash themselves into a fury ... and talk about breasting the Senate. Why, you can not breast anybody on that.

2. To push or force *aside*, *off*, or *up*. Also *intr.*

1840 DANA *Two Years* xxiv, Slipping down sometimes with hand and feet round the rope, and sometimes breasting off with one hand and foot against the precipice, [etc.]. **1840** COOPER *Pathfinder* xxv, The cutter, catching the current under her lee bow, was breasted up to her course. **1853** KANE *Grinnell Exp.* xliv. (1856) 406 We gradually force ahead, breasting aside the floes.

‖**3.** *Mining.* To take *out* from the breast of a drift.

1882 C. KING *Rep. Prec. Metals* 641 The gravel is broken or breasted out from that side of a block farthest from the main drift.

+**Breast complaint.** Consumption; tuberculosis. — **1837** SHERWOOD *Gaz. Georgia* (ed. 3) 82 Dyspepsy carries off some; consumption, or breast complaint, as it is termed, affects some persons.

+**Breasting,** *vbl. n.* A method of hunting deer in which the hunters ride abreast and shoot from horseback. — *a***1889** G. B. GRINNELL *Gun & Rod* 152 (*Cent.*), Breasting is employed where the deer make their home in very high grass, such as is to be found on some of the prairies in the South-west.

Breastpin. {1825–} +A brooch. — **1873** BAILEY *Life in Danbury* 257 A lady living on Spring Street lost a valuable breast pin. **1909** *Sears, Roebuck & Co. Catalogue No. 118* 83 Ladies' warranted rolled gold plate, gold front and gold filled fancy brooches or breast pins.

***Breastplate.** +A plate worn as an ornament on the breast. — **1765** TIMBERLAKE *Memoirs* 50 They [=Cherokees] that can afford it wear a collar of wampum, ... a silver breast-plate, and bracelets on their arms and wrists of the same metal. **1807** *Ann. 10th Congress* 1 Sess. I. 458 He made me a present of a silver breastplate. *Ib.* 639 Mr. Owens ... presented me with a very handsome breastplate.

+**Breastweed.** Lizard's tail, *Saururus cernuus.* — **1829** EATON *Botany* (ed. 5) 509 Lizard's tail, breast weed.... Rare in New York east of Cayuga Lake—abundant west of it. **1889** *Cent.* 672 Breastweed [is] a name given to the lizard's-tail of the United States ... from its use as a remedy in mammary inflammation.

Breastwork.

1. A field work or fortification of a few feet in height, made or thrown up as a protection against an enemy. {1642–}

1653 *New Plymouth Laws* 97 The townesmen ... shall make and fully finnish a place or places for defence ... videlecet, a brest worke with flankers. **1687** *Doc. Hist. N.Y. State* (1849) I. 149 At New York there is a fortification ... with sods as a breast-work well & pleasantly situated for the defence of our Harbor. **1715** *Mass. H. Repr. Journals* I. 8 That a Breast-work for Six Guns be erected in some convenient place. **1740–1** *Boston Rec.* 271 The Platform and Breast-Work which they propose to be of wood, the Breast Work of Square Pine Timber, and the Platform of Oak Plank. **1765** TIMBERLAKE *Memoirs* 87 The northern Indians ... were then actually building a breastwork within quarter of a mile of Fort Robinson. **1777** *Md. Hist. Mag.* V. 215 The Enemy threw up a long Breast work on the high Ground at Province Island. **1806–8** PIKE *Sources Miss.* 194 We continued to go on with the works of our stockade or breast work. **1853** RAMSEY *Tennessee* 218 A rude and hasty breast-work of brush and old logs was immediately constructed. **1881–5** MCCLELLAN *Own Story* 592 In the fields between was a long line of stone fences, continued by breastworks of rails, which covered the enemy's infantry from our musketry.

‖**2.** A breast-high partition.

1747 *Md. Hist. Reg.* IX. 52 [The Vestrymen] ordered that a Breast-Work be erected in the Chapel of this Parish.

+**3.** The breast of a fireplace.

1806 *Mass. Spy* 23 July (Th.), On the breastwork over the fire-place was the distinct impression of a bloody hand. **1824** *N.H. Hist. Soc. Coll.* I. 249 At the same instant the breast work and chimney gave way.

***Breath,** *n.* +In the phrase, *to take one's breath*, to overcome with sudden emotion. — **1898** 'MARK TWAIN' *Myst. Stranger* (1916) 14 He said it placidly, but it took our breath for a moment and made our hearts beat. **1905** T. DIXON *Clansman* 351 The daring campaign these men were waging took his breath.

+**Breath-taking,** *a.* [BREATH *n.*] Tending to produce sudden emotion. {1897–} — **1880** 'MARK TWAIN' *Tramp Abroad* xxxiii. 359 It was a sort of breath-taking surprise.

Breech-band. Also †**britch-band.** A strong leather band that passes around the breech of a harness animal; breeching. — **1812** WEEMS *Letters* III. 65 What shou'd it be but the rubbing of the britchband against his tail!! **1869** STOWE *Oldtown Folks* 355, I just wanted to borrow your breech-band, 'cause ours is broke.

+**Breechcloth.** A breechclout or loincloth.

1793 B. LINCOLN in *Mass. H.S. Coll.* 3 Ser. V. 152 They all have Indian stockings, made of woollen cloth; the males a breech cloth and the females a woollen petticoat. **1812** MARSHALL *Kentucky* 158 All the Indians ... had a right ... of bringing away the skins with which to buy legings, breach-cloths, and blankets. **1823** JAMES *Exped.* I. 118 The ordinary dress of the men is a breech cloth of blue or red cloth, secured in its place by a girdle, [etc.]. **1878** *Rep. Indian Affairs* 31 No painted Indian with long hair, feathers, or breech-cloth can be found in the settlement. **1890** *Harper's Mag.* April 730/2 Stripped to their breech-cloths, ... the Indian scouts ... surrounded and guarded the sullen renegade guide.

+**Breechclout.** A cloth worn round the breech as an article of clothing, esp. by Indians. (Cf. BREECHCLOTH.)

(1) **1757** PUTNAM *Memoirs* (1903) 12 Nothing to cover us from the Natts & Musketoes but a Shirt and Breech-Clout. **1758** in *Lett. to Washington* II. 358, I wish you would order by the first Opportunity Breech-Clouts for the men [of the 1st Va. Regiment]. (2) **1797** F. BAILY *Tour* 272 Printed calico shirts ... (together with what they call a breech-clout) formed the whole of their dress. **1804** CLARK in *Lewis & C. Exped.* (1904) I. 112 Those People are all naked, covered only with Breech Clouts Blankets or Buffalow Roabes. **1836** IRVING *Astoria* II. 221 That worthy sachem landed in princely state, arrayed in a bright blue blanket and red breech clout. **1873** F. M. A. ROE *Army Lett.* 116 He was in full war dress—that is, no dress at all except the breech clout and moccasins. **1889** *Century Mag.* April 908/2 Lieutenant Jim only needed breech-clout and long hair in order to draw rations at the agency.

+**Breechesflower.** Dutchman's-breeches. — **1814** PURSH *Flora Amer.* II. 462 *Corydalis Cucullaria.* ... This singularly constructed flower is known among the inhabitants by the name of Breeches-flower or Yellow-breeches. **1843** TORREY *Flora N.Y.* I. 45 Dutchman's Breeches, Breeches-flower, ... [grows in] shady woods, in rich soils, particularly among rocks; common in most parts of the state. **1893** *Amer. Folk-Lore* VI. 137 *Dicentra cucullaria*, little boy's breeches. Central Iowa. Breeches flower. N.Y.

Breeches maker. One who makes breeches. {1831–} — **1727** *Boston Selectmen* 162 John Allwood Briches maker from Castle William is admitted by the Select men. **1774** in Chalkley *Scotch-Irish Settlement Va.* I. 180 Charles Beard to be bound ... to learn trade of breeches makers and skin dressers. **1781** JOSEPH JONES *Letters* 73, I bespoke a pair of leather breeches of a breeches maker whose name I have forgot. **1809** F. CUMING *Western Tour* 223 Pittsburgh [has] ... thirteen tailors; one breeches maker and skin-dresser.

Breeching. =BREECHCLOTH, -CLOUT. — **1842** *Amer. Pioneer* I. 47 On going to bed the men [Indians] pull off all but their breeching, and the women all but their shrouds.

+**Breech piece.** =BREECHCLOTH, -CLOUT. — **1846** COOPER *Redskins* xx, Habitually he wore his Indian vestments; the leggings, moccasins, breech-piece, blanket or calico shirt, according to the season.

+**Breed.** +A person of mixed racial descent, esp. one of Indian and white blood. — **1892** *Harper's Mag.* Feb. 387/2 One-quarter of the number of 'breeds' could read and write. **1903** WHITE *Forest* viii. 93 We had supper at a table with three Forest Rangers, two lumber-jacks, and a cat-like handsome 'breed.'

* **Breeder.**

1. An animal kept for breeding purposes. {1641}

1787 WASHINGTON *Diaries* III. 285 Ordered ... 1 sow which appeared to be with pig to be turned out for a breeder. **1831** PECK *Guide* 171 Thousands of hogs are raised without any expense, except a few breeders to start with. **1857** *Ill. Agric. Soc. Trans.* II. 373 Never permit a male animal to come on the farm, as a breeder, unless he equals ... the females. **1894** *Vt. Agric. Rep.* XIV. 100 As soon as a mare proves not to be a valuable breeder ... it is wise to stop breeding her.

***2.** One who engages in the breeding of cattle, hogs, etc.

1856 *Rep. Comm. Patents: Agric.* 40 At weaning time, breeders generally sell their mule colts to men who buy up lots every fall for raising. **1885** *Harper's Mag.* May 900/2 Several remarkable cases of enormous butter capacity shown by Jersey cows ... [have] opened the eyes of breeders. **1894** *Vt. Agric. Rep.* XIV. 100 The real horse is cultivated by the mind of the breeder.

***Breeding,** *ppl. a.* Producing offspring. (Cf. BREEDER 1.) — **1743** *Ga. Col. Rec.* VI. 80 Barker claims four breeding mares. **1831** PECK *Guide* 165 Breeding mares are profitable stocks. **1856** OLMSTED *Slave States* 55 A breeding woman is worth from one-sixth to one-fourth more than one that does not breed. **1894** *Vt. Agric. Rep.* XIV. 103 Breeders paid no attention to the soundness of breeding animals.

***Breeze,** *n.* +**a.** In the phrase *a breeze of luck,* a period of success, prosperity, good fortune. **b.** *To get up a breeze,* to stir up agitation; to exert pressure. — **(a) 1834** CROCKETT *Narr. Life* 61, I now began to think we had struck a breeze of luck. **1850** [H. C. LEWIS] *La. Swamp Doctor* 83, I'se struck a breeze of luck, sure, to get it [a tooth] 'stracted without hurtin'. **(b) 1875** *Chicago Tribune* 3 Sept. 2/5 To get up a breeze near the commission that shall have its proper influence.

* **Breeze,** *v.* In the phrase *to breeze up* (of the wind), to freshen, become stronger. {1859–}

1752 WASHINGTON *Diaries* I. 31 At noon the Wind breezed up at So. and clouded. **1761** S. NILES *Indian Wars* II. 316 The wind breezing up, they soon get out of their reach. **1831** T. BUTTRICK *Travels* 22 The wind soon began to breeze up ahead, all hands were called to put the vessel under close sail. **1879** S. O. JEWETT *Old Friends* (1885) 258 It's breezing up and it'll be cooler than it is in the house.

+**Brelaw.** [F. *blaireau.* Cf. BRARO.] The American badger. — **1805** PIKE *Sources Miss.* 30 Killed three geese and one racoon, also a brelaw, an animal I had never before seen.

Brent (goose), variant of BRANT (GOOSE). — **1856** *Spirit of Times* (N.Y.) 13 Dec. 242/1 The Canada goose, generally known in America as the wild goose, . . . and the Brent goose, better known as the Brant. **1873** *Kansas Mag.* Feb. 103 The sullen gray bars of the river were vocal with sonorous flocks of brent.

+**Brer.** Also **bre'er.** Negro pronunciation of *brother.* — **1880** HARRIS *Uncle Remus* i. (1881) 2 Arter Brer Fox bin doin' all dat he could fer ter ketch Brer Rabbit. **1880** TOURGEE *Bricks* 186 'Bre'er Nimbus' was still the heart and life of the community. **1889** 'MARK TWAIN' *Conn. Yankee* vii. 86 It turned Brer Merlin green with envy. **1890** — in *Harper's Mag.* Feb. 440/1 If you read what this author says about Brer Albucasis.

Brethren. +A German-American religious sect, also known as German Baptists and Dunkers.

1822 *Ann. 17th Congress* 1 Sess. I. 230 The Brethren (for by that name they began to be known) established themselves in [Shekomeko, 50 miles west of Hartford, Conn.]. **1844** Rupp *Relig. Denominations* 92 The German Baptists, or Brethren, . . . are commonly called Dunkers; but they have assumed for themselves the name of 'Brethren.' *Ib.* 94 The German Baptists, or Brethren, have now dispersed themselves almost through every State in the Union, more or less; but they are most numerous in Pennsylvania, Maryland, Virginia, Ohio, and Indiana. **1867** W. H. DIXON *New America* II. 184 Among themselves, they are known as Brethren; the spirit of their association being that of fraternal love. **1884** *Schaff's Relig. Encycl.* III. 2401/2 The name originally adopted by themselves [i.e. the Dunkers], and . . . now generally used, is simply 'The Brethren'; but they frequently use the term 'German Baptists,' even in their official documents.

attrib. **1844** Rupp *Relig. Denominations* 697 The Brethren Church is . . . comparatively small, owing to the fact, that until within twenty years, its religious exercises have all been conducted in the German language.

Brett. 'A four-wheeled carriage having a calash top and seats for four besides the driver's seat' (Knight). — **1865** MRS. WHITNEY *Gayworthys* xxx. 301 Mrs. Topliff drove an open English brett; one fine September day she offered Say a seat in it.

* **Brevet,** *n.*

1. A document conferring a nominal rank on a military officer without a right to additional pay. {1811–}

'Such commissions were given to the officers of the American Army at the close of the war, giving them a grade of rank above that which they had held during service' (W. '28.).

1776 *Journals Cont. Congress* V. 800 Officers having brevets, or commissions of a prior date to those of the regiment in which they now serve. **1777** *Ib.* VII. 196 Resolved, that Monsieur Faneuil have the rank of a colonel by brevet in the continental army, without pay or rations. **1847** *Army Regulations* 4 Officers having rank . . . by brevet . . . will not assume the command unless specially put on duty. **1850** *Harper's Mag.* Aug. 299/2 [Capt. Z. Taylor's defense of Fort Harrison] procured from President Madison a preferment to the rank of brevet major, the first brevet, it is said, ever conferred in the American army. **1856** [see BREVET *v.* 2.] **1861** *Army Regulations* 10 Officers having brevets . . . may take place in courts-martial and on detachments, . . . according to the ranks given them in their brevets. **a1892** M. A. Jackson *Gen. Jackson* 44 This storming of Chapultepec . . . won him the brevet of major.

2. *attrib.* **a.** With *commission, officer, pay, rank.*

1781 HAMILTON in Sparks *Corr. Rev.* III. 303 Congress seem, however, to have made a distinction; they only give a kind of warrant to those whom they designate as Brevet Officers. **1784** *Mass. Centinel* 5 June 1/3 All commissioned and brevet officers of the army and navy. **1818** *U.S. Statutes* III. 427 The officers of the army, who have brevet commissions, shall . . . receive the pay and emoluments of their brevet rank when on duty. **1847** POLK *Diary* (1929) 187 Each claiming the office . . . by virtue . . . of his brevet rank. **1861** *Army Regulations* 342 Officers charging brevet pay.

b. With rank of officers appointed by brevet.

1819 *Niles' Reg.* XVI. 40/2 Brevet general James Miller, at present a colonel in the army, is appointed to be governor of the new territory of Arkansaw. **1850** GLISAN *Jrnl. Army Life* 5 Fort McHenry . . . was then garrisoned by two companies of light artillery—Brevet-majors Hays and Sedgwick's. **1862** STANTON in McClellan *Own Story* 475 Brevet major-general of the regular service and . . . brevet brigadiers in the regular service. **1881–5** MCCLELLAN *op. cit.* 290 Such reconnoissances as I did at Vera Cruz (when a brevet second lieutenant of engineers). **1886** *Outing* Oct. 54/2 Brevet General Forsyth, of the Fourth Cavalry . . . arrived in camp this afternoon on a tour of inspection.

c. (See quotations.)

1871 DE VERE 284 The 'boys,' with a witty turn of the military significance of the word, were in the habit of terming a battle a brevet-hell. **1884** *Boston Jrnl.* 18 Sept., The brevet Democrats catch the spirit of pro-slavery Bourbonism naturally.

Brevet, *v.* [f. prec.]

1. *tr.* To raise to a specified military rank by brevet. {1839–} Also fig.

1854 BARTLETT *Narr.* II. 146 He [Lt. Col. Craig] soon attained the rank of captain, and was breveted Lieutenant Colonel for gallant service. **1874** B. TAYLOR *World on Wheels* 46 The men that get aboard [a Western train] . . . talk deer, horse, bear, turkey. They brevet you, and you become captain or colonel by the breath of their mouths, which is tobacco. **1879** TOURGEE *Fool's Errand* 18 He is colonel now; has been breveted a brigadier-general. **a1892** M. A. Jackson *Gen. Jackson* 44 Lieutenant Jackson had been brevetted a captain.

‖**2.** *intr.* To confer a brevet.

1856 *Spirit of Times* (N.Y.) 1 Nov. 149/3 He may not win a brevet for fighting Indians, (for the Government do not brevet for that, though it is the most dangerous service).

* **Brewer.** One whose occupation is brewing.

1653 JOHNSON *Wonder-w. Prov.* 209 Weavers, Brewers, Bakers, . . . are orderly turn'd to their trades. **1714** *Boston News-Letter* 1–8 Feb. 2/2 A House and Barn having an Acre of Land adjoyning it, fit for a Brewer or any other Trade. **1789** *Ann. 1st Congress* I. 144 Upon the whole, he concluded so high a duty as nine cents would give the brewers here a monopoly. **1813** *Niles' Reg.* IV. 295/1 What will lord Sheffield think of a brewer in Cincinnati advertising and wishing to contract for 20,000 bushels of barley? **1881** *Harper's Mag.* April 716/2 For . . . 1879 the records of the collector of internal revenue show a total of 548,770 barrels of beer sold by the brewers of Milwaukee. **1897** *Outing* XXX. 370/1 It seemed like a quiet country lane to me, after my experience of Broadway cable-cars and brewers' wagons.

+**Brewer's blackbird.** [Named after T. M. *Brewer,* 1814–80.] The blue-headed grackle, *Scolecophagus cyanocephalus.* — **1858** BAIRD *Birds Pacific R.R.* 552. **1874** COUES *Birds N.W.* 199. **1895** *Dept. Agric. Yearbook 1894* 234 The redwing . . . , Brewer's blackbird . . . , and rusty blackbird . . . often associate with them [=the crow blackbird].

+**Brewer's sparrow.** [See prec.] Brewer's bunting, found in the Rocky Mountain region. — **1858** BAIRD *Birds Pacific R.R.* 475 *Spizella Breweri,* . . . Brewer's Sparrow. **1869** *Amer. Naturalist* III. 77 Brewer's Sparrow. . . . I found flocks, apparently of this species, on the eastern slope of the mountains only, migrating South in August. **1874** COUES *Birds N.W.* 115 Brewer's Sparrow . . . [inhabits] southern Rocky Mountain region, especially New Mexico and Arizona.

Brewery. An establishment where brewing is carried on as a business. {1658–}

1780 *N.J. Archives* 2 Ser. IV. 508 She . . . is to be met with at the Brewery. **1789** *Ann. 1st Congress* I. 211 There are no breweries in our country [*sc.* New England]. *Ib.* 211 We have done something on this occasion to favor the breweries in the Middle States. **1794** *N.Y. State Soc. Arts* I. 152 In the city of New-York there are at present a number of very large and respectable breweries established. **1818** DARBY *Emigrant's Guide* 258 [Pittsburgh has] three breweries, in which are made an immense quantity of beer, porter, and ale. **1886** *Boston Herald* 17 July, The men employed in the Cincinnati breweries are discontented because . . . they are denied the . . . right to drink more than 10 glasses of beer in one day.

* **Brewhouse.** A house in which brewing is done.

1638 *Charlestown Rec.* 2 One roode of grounde . . . with a dwelling-house, Brew House and other apurtinances. **1654** *Boston Rec.* 12 His dwelling house with a little brewhouse standing neere the brooke. **1677** SEWALL *Diary* I. 40 Met with the Watch at Mr. Rocks Brew house. **1734** *Harvard Rec.* I. 148 He shall Allow to the College for the Kitchen, Brewhouse, [etc.] . . . so much per Annum as the Corporation shall direct. **1776** *N.J. Archives* 2 Ser. I. 74 The dwelling-house contains . . . an entry and good kitchen, . . . the brew-house is 70 feet by 50, with a malting cellar 70 feet in length and 16 feet wide.

***Brewis.** +In New England, a porridge made of bread, milk, and molasses. — **1805** *Pocumtuc Housewife* (1906) 7 Get some rice Porridge or brewis and cold meat. **1859** ELWYN *Glossary* 25 *Brewis.* . . . In New England, in our school days, it meant flinty crusts of rye and Indian bread softened with milk and eaten with molasses. **1874** MRS. WHITNEY *We Girls* 130 One [frying-pan] was set on with the milk for the brewis, into which, when it boiled up white and drifting, went the sweet fresh butter and the salt . . . and then the bread-crumbs. . . . The end of it . . . [was] a light savoury bread-porridge.

Brewster. +A make of a hat. — **1840** KENNEDY *Quodlibet* 110 William was smoothing the nap of his glossy black Brewster, with a brush as soft as silk.

Brewsterite. +A follower of James C. Brewster, a dissenting Mormon, who with others formed a new church in 1849. — **1870** BEADLE

Utah 124 Most of the other aspirants took off various sects, known in the Brighamite church as . . . 'Brewsterites,' 'Cutlerites,' 'Gatherers,' etc.

Briar, frequent variant of BRIER.

*** Brick.**

***1.** A molded block of clay, burned in a kiln or dried in the sun, for use as a building material.

1630 [F. HIGGINSON] *New-England* 7 At this instant we are setting a Bricke-Kill on worke to make Brickes and Tyles for the building of our Houses. **1645** *New Haven Col. Rec.* 226 It was propownded that Edw. Chipperfield might have libertie to make bricks in the playnes vnder the West Rocke. **1704** S. KNIGHT *Journal* 52 The bricks in some of the Houses are of divers Coullers and laid in Checkers, being glazed look very agreeable. **1794** T. COXE *View U. S.* 25 Bricks, tiles, . . . are tending to greater perfection, and will soon be sold so cheap as to throw foreign goods of the same kind entirely out of the market. **1857** *Lawrence* (Kansas) *Republican* 2 July 1 The large and economical adobe brick, hardened in the sun and without fire, supersedes other material for walls and fences in this dry atmosphere. **1865** *Atlantic Mo.* March 314/2, I found the people [of Circleville, O.] using the clay from the wall of the square inclosure for making brick and streets.

***2.** Building material in this form.

1639 *Va. Mag. of Hist.* (1895) III. 30 Since which order there are twelve houses and stores built in the Towne, one of brick by the Secretarye. **1704** S. KNIGHT *Journal* 52 The Buildings [of New York are] Brick generaly, very stately and high. **1883** *Rep. Indian Affairs* 72 A large force is now being used making brick for the Wichita school-house.

+b. *transf.* (See quotation.)

1888 *Harper's Mag.* July 235/1 A house built of squares of sod taken from the prairie—Nebraska or Kansas brick, as they are facetiously termed.

3. In colloq. or slang expressions: **+a.** *Like a thousand of brick* or *bricks*, violently; with extreme vigor.

1842 MRS. KIRKLAND *Forest Life* I. 135 If folks is sassy, we walk right into 'em like a thousand o' brick. **1847** [ROBB] *Squatter Life* 37 To use a classical expression he lit upon the upper town and its member [of the legislature] 'like a thousand of brick!' **1863** NORTON *Army Lett.* 173, I, like every loyal soldier, am down on every opposer of the war 'like a thousand of brick.' **1867** *Congress. Globe* 18 Feb. 1513/3, I had no expectation . . . of bringing down upon myself, 'like a thousand of brick,' the torrent of his indignant eloquence. **1896** H. FREDERIC *Damnation of T. Ware* 158 You've got to be mighty particular in such matters, you know, or you'll have the trustees down on you like a 'thousand of bricks.'

b. *Like bricks*, vigorously, with good will. {1836–}

1846 *Spirit of Times* 18 April 88/1 He accordingly took him under his arm, and walked him off like 'bricks.'

+c. *To have* (etc.) *a brick in one's hat*, *(to be) tight as a brick*, to be intoxicated or tipsy.

1847 *Knickerb.* XXIX. 569 A youth who came home one night, prepared 'to build,' having 'a brick in his hat.' **1849** LONGFELLOW *Kavanagh* xxix. 148 Her husband had taken to the tavern, and often came home very late, 'with a brick in his hat,' as Sally expressed it. **1857** *Quinland* I. 134 Shame on you, Tom. . . . You have got a brick in your hat. **1869** BROWNE *Adv. Apache Country* 448 The Doctor had taken a new kink, and was off about town in search of an additional brick to put in his hat. **1894** 'MARK TWAIN' *Those Twins* Introd., Her half had never drunk a drop in his life, and, although tight as a brick three days in the week, was wholly innocent of blame.

‖**d.** *To feel like bricks*, to feel wretched or miserable. *?Obs.*

1846 *Spirit of Times* (N.Y.) 11 July 232/1, I have been hard at work all day—I feel like bricks—had no supper.

+4. A brick house.

1845 *Cincinnati Misc.* 114 The tearing down of Frames to make way for Bricks, and the great excess of new bricks over new frame buildings, will increase the disparity between the two. **1869** 'MARK TWAIN' *Innocents* xlviii. 504 When I read that they let a bedridden man down through the roof of a house . . . I generally had a three-story brick in mind. **1881** *Harper's Mag.* April 713/1 The big Grecian house, . . . the square topped fort-like brick, . . . are all absent. **1883** *Cent. Mag.* XXVII. 43/2 It creates the impression that its builder commenced it with the intention of erecting a three-story brick.

+5. A rectangular block (of gold or silver). Also fig.

1869 BROWNE *Adv. Apache Country* 295 'Struck it rich!' 'Silver bricks!' and 'Pay rock!' hummed and drummed through the air. **1876** RAYMOND *8th Rep. Mines* 354 Individuals are constantly carrying out bags of gold and gold bricks and some silver bricks. **1878** F. M. A. ROE *Army Lett.* 206 We went to the assay building the other day to see a brick of gold taken from the furnace. **1902** LORIMER *Lett. Merchant* 18 They would swap the talent for a gold brick and lose the napkin.

***6.** Attrib. in the sense: Made of brick.

1623–4 *Va. House of Burgesses* 32 Bricke Church [was] intended to be built. **1642** *Plymouth Rec.* 11 To repaire the watchouse and make a brick chimney to it. **1649** *Suffolk Deeds* I. 117 The highway . . . along to Edw. Bendalls brick house. **1721** SEWALL *Diary* III. 286 His wife and he now dwell together again; he being return'd to her from his brick Buildings. **1738** *Boston Rec.* 215 The petition . . . for Liberty . . . to raise a good Brick Fence in the Front of the old Burying Place. **1745** *Itinerant Observ.* 43 The Parson of the Parish . . . has the only Brick-House in Town. **1763** *Boston Post-Boy* 7 May, A large and comodious Brick Dwelling-House, pleasently scituated in Corn-Hill. **1787** *Md. Gazette* 1 June 1/2 The House is adjoining the French Consul's [and] has . . . a large two-story Brick Kitchen. **1803** *Ann. 8th Congress* 2 Sess. 1507 Two very extensive brick stores, from one hundred and sixty to one hundred and eighty feet in length. **1810** WEEMS *Letters* III. 14 Doctor Murrays grand Brick building. **1862** MCCLELLAN in *Own Story* 468, Of the old settlement of Jamestown there is nothing left . . . but the brick tower of the church. **1879** *Harper's Mag.* June 67/1 Its antiquity [is] attested by the old brick houses, . . . beside the banks of one of the numerous creeks. **1884** *Century Mag.* April 830/1 The houses were all examined, and old St. Thomas's brick buildings . . . were ransacked. **1892** M. A. JACKSON *Memoirs* 11 Jonathan Jackson began housekeeping with his young wife in a neat brick cottage of three rooms.

Brick bread. *?Obs.* Bread in the form of a brick. (Cf. BRICK LOAF.) — **1762** *Boston Selectmen* 29 Nov. 236 A 4d. loaf of Brick Bread is 3 oz. less than a 4d. White Loaf.

***Brick burner.** A brickmaker. {–1703} — **1841** SIMMS *Scout* vi, It leads by the clay diggings of the old Dutchman—the brick-burner.

Brick clay. Clay suitable for making bricks. {1837–} — *c*1790 T. COXE *View U.S.* 75 From our new country we have . . . potters clay, brick clay, &c. **1815** DRAKE *Cincinnati* 44 Good brick clay is scarce, and hence the buildings are principally of wood. **1868** LOSSING *Hudson* 206 Its banks yield some of the finest brick-clay in the country.

Brick earth. =BRICK-CLAY. {1667–} — **1640** *Dedham Rec.* III. 74 Twoe of them are deputed to search for Bricke earth & provide a place necessary to burne bricke vpon.

***Brickkiln.** Also †**brick kill, brickill, bricke kell.** A furnace in which bricks are burned.

1630 [see BRICK 1]. **1643** *Dedham Rec.* III. 98 All that are enclosed by the s[ai]d fence in the Island nere the Brick Kill. **1663** *Boston Rec.* 17 A parcell of Land . . . ouer against the Bricke-kells. **1671** *Springfield Rec.* II. 231 A convenient high way to the old clay pitts or place where the old brick kilne was. **1676** *Huntington Rec.* I. 223 A lot near the brickill in the west neck. **1701** *Boston Rec.* 12 No person shall . . . erect and burn any brick Kiln, but in such place . . . as the select men . . . shall approve. **1757** *General Orders* 21 The Covering Party at the Brickill to take Post within the Stockaids at the Retreet Beating. **1830** *Collegian* 59 An unpicturesque brick-kiln occupied the site of the famous hanging bridge. **1868** BRACKETT *Farm Talk* 73 There's . . . a clay bank over in the corner. There was a 'brick kill' down there a good many years ago. **1901** CHURCHILL *Crisis* 128 That tavern . . . was long and low . . . , and hot that night as the inside of a brick-kiln.

***Bricklayer.** One who builds with brick.

1630 *Mass. Bay Rec.* I. 74 Carpenters, joyners, brickelayers, sawers, and thatchers shall not take above 2s aday. **1676** *Boston Rec.* 105 The severall persons above . . . [may] call any bricklayer or bricklayers . . . to veiue and judge of any chimneys that are suspected to be defective. **1720** *Weekly Mercury* 12 May 4/2 He pretends to be a Bricklayer by Trade. **1783** *S.C. Gazette* 3 June 1/1 For private Sale . . . a Negro Fellow who is a good Bricklayer. **1857** *Lawrence* (Kansas) *Republican* 25 June 3 Several good brick-layers can find steady and profitable employment in this city. **1872** *Harper's Mag.* XLVI. 151/2 The strike of the bricklayers in Chicago. **1887** *Courier-Journal* 3 May 3/5 Wanted—a large number of Stone Masons and Red Bricklayers.

+Brick loaf. Bread made into loaves resembling a brick in shape. — **1761** *Boston Selectmen* 15 April 145 Four penny brick loaf. 1 l. 14 oz. 8 dr. **1873** MRS. WHITNEY *Other Girls* iii, I never would make a brick loaf; that always seemed to me a man's perversion of the idea of bread. **1879** — *Just How* 24, I like the 'brick-loaf' pans.

Brickly, -ley, *a. dial.* Brittle. {1825–, *dial.*} — **1837** SHERWOOD *Gaz. Georgia* Glossary, *Brickly*, brittle. **1871** DEVERE 586 The 'brickly ware,' which is met with in Southern writers. **1884** SARGENT *Rep. Forests* 218 *Thrinax argentea*. . . . Silver-top Palmetto. Brickley Thatch. Brittle Thatch.

***Brickmaker.** One who makes brick.

1634 WOOD *New Eng. Prospect* xii. 53 Men . . . most fit for these plantations [include] . . . a good Brickmaker, a Tyler [etc.]. **1640** *Dedham Rec.* III. 74 Twoe of them are deputed to search for Bricke earth [etc.] . . . in the greate Iland wher conveniently they maye be had to the satisfaction of the Brickemaker Thomas Eames. **1661** *Boston Rec.* 1 The motion of Rich. Gridley & the rest of the brick makers in the Towne for to rent some part of the Townes land in the Common to make brickes. **1693** *Ib.* 213 Inspectors of Brickemacors,—John Gooding, Rich. Scates. **1834** WEBSTER in Benton *30 Years' View* I. 419/1 This meeting consisted of three thousand persons, and was composed of carpenters, masons, brickmakers, . . . and others, whose occupations are connected with the building of houses. **1877** *Rep. Indian Affairs* 60 A skilled brickmaker was engaged to examine all the clays in the vicinity of the agency.

Brickmason. One who builds with brick; a bricklayer. {1605–}

1638 *Md. Archives* I. 3 John Halfe-head, of St. Maries hundred, brickmason. **1837** PECK *New Guide* 319 A carpenter or brick mason wants no other capital to do first-rate business . . . than a set of tools, and habits of industry. **1883** 'MARK TWAIN' *Life on Miss.* xxv. 280 Sunday-schools have done a good work in Cairo, as well as brick-masons.

+Brick pond. A pond in connection with a brickyard. — [1731: see BRICKYARD.] **1811** *Mass. Spy* 9 Jan. 3/3 Two boys . . . were drowned in a brick pond in the vicinity of the city [=Philadelphia]. **1841** A. BACHE

Fire-Screen 43 It would be so pleasant on the brick-pond. **1850** *Wilmington* (N.C.) *Commercial* 5 Sept. 2/3 (Th.S.), Water brought from the neighbouring brick-ponds [at Philadelphia] in buckets.

Brick-striker. A workman or machine that molds bricks. — **1638** *Dedham Rec.* III. 48 Joseph Moyse, Joyner,—Weeden brickstrieker. **1874** *Index of Patents* I. 148 [A] brick-striker [was patented by] P. Sweet, Ashtabula, Ohio, Feb. 20, 1835.

+**Brick-wood.** Firewood used in a brickkiln. — **1788** WASHINGTON *Diaries* III. 295 The Negro Men were employed in cutting Rail stuff and Brick Wood.

Brickyard. A place where bricks are made; a brickfield. {1864–}

1731 *Essex Inst. Coll.* XLII. 229 The water here . . . is as thick of mudd & Clay as in the Pond of a Brick yard. **1788** WASHINGTON *Diaries* III. 330 Rode to all the Plantations, to the Mill, Brick yard, and fishing landing. **1809** F. CUMING *Western Tour* 165 There are seven brick yards which employ sixty hands, and make annually two million five hundred thousand bricks. **1848** J. S. ROBINSON *Santa Fé Exped.* 21 The city at a little distance more resembles a parcel of brick yards than any thing else. **1871** *Rep. Indian Affairs* (1872) 531, I have had a brick-yard made, and a kiln of one hundred thousand is ready to burn.

+**Bridal rose.** A variety of *Rubus* grown for its white flowers. — **1832** HALE *Flora* 139. **1845** *Lowell Offering* V. 257 Her rose geranium in a great blue waterpail, and her bridal rose in a cracked beanpot. **1861** WOOD *Botany* 240 *Bridal Rose*. . . . A delicate house plant, with snow white double flowers. Native of Mauritius. **1899** *Animal & Plant Lore* 107 When the 'bridal rose' blossoms, there will follow a death in the family. Massachusetts.

+**Bridal tour.** A journey taken for pleasure by a newly married couple. — **1856** M. J. HOLMES *Homestead on H.*, Gilberts v, The next morning Mr. and Mrs. Sherwood departed on their bridal tour. **1865** *Atlantic Mo.* XV. 491 And so Emmy was wheeled away from us on the bridal tour. **1880** 'MARK TWAIN' *Tramp Abroad* xxxv. 388 She was newly married, and was on her bridal tour.

Bridal wreath. A shrub (*Spiraea hypericifolia*) which has many panicles of small white flowers. — **1889** *Cent.* **1892** WILKINS *Jane Field* 143 Bushes of bridal-wreath sent out white spikes. **1898** ATHERTON *Californians* 262 Over a high bush on the lawn . . . the long 'bridal wreaths' tumbled.

+**Bride-perch.** *local.* (See quotations.) — **1819** *Western Rev.* I. 375 Dotted Painted Tail. *Calliurus punctulatuse*. . . . Vulgar names, painted-tail or bride-perch. **1820** *Ib.* II. 54 Ohio Red-eye, *Aplocentrus calliops*, . . . lives in the lower parts of the Ohio, in Green river, &c. Vulgar names Red-eyes, Bride perch, Batchelor's pearch, Green bass, &c.

***Bridewell.** A prison, workhouse, or house of correction.

'The name is now generally given to a prison in connection with a police-station, for the temporary detention of those who have been arrested by the police' (*Cent.*).

1653 *Boston Rec.* 26 My thoughts . . . have beene about . . . the setting up of a Bridewell or Workehouse for Prisonrs Malefactors & some sort of poore people. **1712** *Ib.* 93 'Tis now made a Bridewell & House of Correction, which obstructs many honest poor peoples going there. **1775** BURNABY *Travels* 134 The chief public buildings [in Boston] are, . . . a bridewell; a public granary; and a very fine wharf. **1803** in *Century Mag.* (1884) April 867/1 That the said building be erected on the vacant ground between the jail and bridewell. **1873** ALDRICH *Marj. Daw*, etc. 78 The police-station (bridewell is the local [N.E.] term). **1891** *Cycl. Temperance* 17/2 Visit our station-houses, bridewells, jails, [etc.], . . . and you will witness the effects of this horror of horrors.

***Bridge,** *n.*[1] Also †**bridg, brig; bredg, breadg(e).**

***1.** A structure of stone, wood, or metal, serving as a means of crossing a stream, river, ravine, or similar obstruction to the passage of persons or vehicles.

The forms *bredg*, *breadg(e)*, from southeastern English dialect, occur in the records of Hartford, Conn., from 1643 to 1651. (*Conn. H. S. Coll.* VI. 66, 94; XIV. 80, 419).

1622 'MOURT' *Relation* 104 When wee came to any small Brooke where no Bridge was, two of them desired to carry vs through. **1654** JOHNSON *Wonder-w. Prov.* 197 The constant penetrating farther into this Wilderness, hath caused . . . the large rivers to be over-laid with Bridges passeable, both for horse and foot. **1664** *Conn. Col. Rec.* I. 417 To make two Bridges, . . . in each Bridge to lay three trees, so hewed that they may be sufficient for horses to passe safe ouer. **1677** *Conn. H. S. Coll.* VI. 177 To consult with som able workmen about the building of a Stone bridge. **1704** S. KNIGHT *Journal* 58 Here wee ridd over a Bridge made of one entire stone of such a Breadth that a cart might pass with safety and to spare. **1808** PIKE *Sources of Miss.* III. 21 On the top of the pillars were laid pine logs lengthways squared on two sides, and being joined pretty close, made a tolerable bridge for horses. **1885** *Rep. Indian Affairs* 168, I have sent into the Salmon River Country the first lumber that ever went there, except some fence, bridge, or house washed down the river.

‖**b.** *colloq.* (See quotation.)

1863 NORTON *Army Lett.* 148 Yesterday Abraham paid us a visit, or rather he didn't. He reviewed all the other regiments in the brigade, but by some blunder of Colonel Stockton's he made a bridge of our nose.

+**2.** A causeway or corduroy road.

1839 MRS. KIRKLAND *New Home* (1840) ii. 19 The 'beautiful bridge,' a newly-laid causeway of large round logs. *Ib.* vii. 40 A marsh which we were crossing by the usual bridge of poles, or *corduroy* as it is here termed. **1885** M. THOMPSON *Byways & Bird Notes* 72 The mud looked deep and treacherous. . . . I fell to work, carrying pieces of logs, rails, fallen boughs, etc., until I had made a quite respectable corduroy bridge.

Bridge, *n.*[2] [Of obscure origin.] Bridge whist, a card game derived from whist. In later use ellipt. for *auction* and *contract bridge*. {1894–}

1898 DICK *Amer. Hoyle* 521 Bridge is played by four persons, two of them being partners opposed to the other two as partners. **1903** *Outlook* LXXIV. 885/1, I play bridge for money because almost every one else does. **1916** KITTREDGE *Gawain & Green Knight* p. iii, The author does not play bridge, — and it is impossible to swim or to sail a boat in a New England winter.

ellipt. **1911** FERBER *Dawn O'Hara* 50, I'm spoiled for sewing bees and church sociables and afternoon bridges.

attrib. **1903** *Evanston* (Ill.) *Press* 11 April, Bridge score tablets—each 35c. **1903** *Outlook* LXXIV. 885/1, I put my bridge winnings into the marketing, and once this spring I ran the house on them for two weeks. **1909** *American Mag.* LXVIII. 221 All you need in a bridge game is good guessing. *Ib.*, The bridge players were not so easy to identify. *Ib.*, The member of the Racquet Club had referred a point of play to Mr. Buskirk after being cut out of the bridge table. **1918** *Lit. Digest* 14 Sept. 43 The combined facts that I have lived most of the time in the country, that I have been ill a good deal, . . . have kept me from becoming a 'bridge-fiend.'

***Bridge,** *v.* +To form a passageway over (a marsh or bog). — **1809** KENDAL *Travels* I. 235 Here, a sufficient, though not very agreeable road, is formed by causeys of logs; or, in the language of the country, it is *bridged*.

+**Bridge company.** A company formed to build bridges. — **1817** *Niles' Reg.* XII. 142/1 Among the laws passed were 24 for incorporating turnpike and bridge companies. **1837** PECK *New Guide* 205 The general revenue is obtained from moderate taxes . . . collected from insurance, bank and bridge companies [etc.].

Bridge-jumper. One who indulges in sensational leaps, usually from bridges. — **1887** *Courier-Journal* 19 Feb. 4/5 Lawrence Donovan, the Brooklyn bridge-jumper, leaped into the Schuylkill river.

+**Bridge perch.** *local.* (See quotation.) — **1888** GOODE *Amer. Fishes* 71 *Pomoxys annularis* . . . has other names of local application as 'Tin Mouth,' 'Bridge Perch.'

+**Bridge pewee.** The phoebe, *Sayornis fuscus*, so called from its habit of building nests under bridges. — **1867** *Amer. Naturalist* I. 54 Ornithological Calendar for March—Meadow Larks, Bridge Pewees or Phoebes, [arrive].

+**Bridge spectacles.** Eyeglasses or spectacles having no side frames but held on the nose by a spring. — **1830** J. F. WATSON *Philadelphia* 180 In her early years [*c*1750] the only spectacles she ever saw were called 'bridge spectacles,' without any side supporters, and held on the nose solely by nipping the bridge of the nose. **1845** JUDD *Margaret* I. xiv. 103 She provided him with a pair of broad horn-bowed bridge spectacles.

+**Bridge-tender.** One who has charge of a drawbridge. — **1853** A. BUNN *Old Eng. & New Eng.* 149 The draw was opened by the bridge-tender for the passage of the steam-boat. **1856** *Knickerb.* XLVII. 633 (Th.), The bridge-tender vociferates, 'Hurry up! vessels coming! bridge must open!' **1872** HUNTINGTON *Road-Master's Assistant* 131 Some of the most lamentable [accidents] that ever happened in this country have taken place at drawbridges, owing to the neglect of the bridge-tender. **1875** *Chicago Tribune* 15 Aug. 16/4 The bridge-tenders . . . were paid off at the Exposition Building yesterday. **1887** *Century Mag.* Aug. 495/1 The bridge-tender, called in for consultation, thought the *Cowles* 'a little mite' longer than that laker.

Bridge whist. =BRIDGE *n.*[2] — **1899** CHAMPLIN & BOSTWICK *Young Folks' Cycl. Games* (ed. 2) 770/1 *Bridge Whist*, a game that is played, after the lead of the first card, like Dummy Whist. **1903** *Outlook* LXXIV. 885/1 The Spectator had heard of bridge whist and the women gamblers it produced. **1918** *Lit. Digest* 14 Sept. 42 That part of the body politic, or impolitic, which finds one of its most strenuous recreations in bridge whist is beginning to search its conscience.

+**Bridled tern.** A species of tern found in the warmer parts of N. America, *Sterna anaethetus melanoptera*. — **1869** *Amer. Naturalist* III. 340 When Dr. Gambel found out that it was different from both these species, he bestowed upon it the title of the Bridled Tern (*S. frenata*). **1874** COUES *Birds N.W.* 701. **1891** *Cent.* 5937/2 Some middle-sized terns with dark upper parts, widely distributed in tropical and warm temperate regions, are the subgenus *Haliplana*, as the common sooty and bridled terns.

Bridle-leather. Leather suitable for making bridles. — **1760** in Chalkley *Scotch-Irish Settlement Va.* III. 63, 19 hides tanned leather, 16 sides soal leather, 11 sides bridle leather. **1853** *Mich. Agric. Soc.* (1854) 55 Ladue & Eldred, Detroit, [exhibited] . . . 6 sides bridle leather. **1874** LONG *Wild-Fowl* 163 A narrow strip of bridle-leather about two feet in length.

Bridle path. A path that can be traveled on horseback, but not with a vehicle. {1811–}

1833 J. HALL *Harpe's Head* 77 The best roads were mere bridle-paths, beaten by the feet of pack-horses. **1843** FRÉMONT *Exped.* 60, I had determined to cross the dividing ridge by a bridle-path. **1886** B. P. POORE *Reminisc.* I. 217 Many of his mail-routes were but little more than bridle-paths. **1891** M. E. RYAN *Pagan of Alleghanies* 19 Get out into the bridle-paths if you want to find originality.

+**Bridle-post.** A hitching post. — **1866** WHITTIER *Snowbound* line 60 The bridle-post an old man sat With loose-flung coat and high cocked hat.

+**Bridle-rack.** A hitching-bar. — **1832** KENNEDY *Swallow Barn* I. 21 A bridle-rack stands on the outer side of the gate.

Bridle road. =BRIDLE PATH. {1833-} — **1775** FITHIAN *Journal* II. 37 Thence I rode onward thro' a dark blind path, they call it here a 'Bridle Road.' **1817** S. BROWN *Western Gaz.* 155 On the north bank . . . there is a bridle road to Detroit. **1852** *Harper's Mag.* June 11/2 The coming season, however, will supply tourists with two bridle-roads, from the Lafayette House and the Flume House. **1880** *Ib.* Sept. 532/2 They concluded to call it a bridle-road.

+**Bridle track.** =BRIDLE PATH. — **1837** W. JENKINS *Ohio Gaz.* 321 The country was yet a wilderness, with no other ingress than by Indian trails, and bridle tracks, opened by themselves. **1885** *Century Mag.* Oct. 917 Wheelways ample, smooth, clean, a springy bridle-track adjoining the road [etc.] . . . —these are the essential physical features of a grand promenade.

Bridle way. =BRIDLE PATH. {1760} — **1703** *Providence Rec.* V. 108 A free passage through the . . . said land . . . for a bridle way. **1775** *Ann. S. W. Virginia* 249 A bridle way from Camp Union . . . is established. **1867** 'E. KIRKE' *On Border* 192 We had to come by a bridle-way over the mountain. **1876** BANCROFT *Hist. U.S.* I. xx. 542 The paths were bridleways rather than roads.

+**Bridle-wisdom.** [f. next.] The quality of being bridle-wise. — **1895** *Outing* XXVI. 477/1 Not that in the heat of play one relies upon this bridle-wisdom [of a polo-pony].

+**Bridle-wise,** *a.* Of a horse: Readily guided by, or responding to, a touch of the bridle.

'Applied to a horse which is guided by pressure of the bridle against his neck instead of by pulling on the bit' (*Cent.*).

1840 *Picayune* 6 Oct. 2 Phrases in use among the 'natives' [of Ill.]: . . . The horse was not fit for a lady to ride; he was not *bridle wise.* **1843** 'CARLTON' *New Purchase* I. vi. 39 A noble-looking young man, mounted on a spirited horse, scarcely broken, and certainly not 'bridle-wise.' **1879** TOURGEE *Fool's Errand* 42 Comfort had gone into town early with my little bridle-wise mare Jack. **1884** SWEET & KNOX *Through Texas* 62 They had been trained to the extent of being what is called 'bridle-wise.' **1895** *Century Mag.* Aug. 626/1 His bridle has one rein, his horse is bridle-wise.

fig. **1898** H. S. CANFIELD *Maid of Frontier* 100 Just like a woman. You can't never make 'em bridle-wise.

* **Brief,** *n.*

+**1.** 'A summary of arguments and cases filed by counsel in an appellate court; called in Pennsylvania a "paper-book"' (Th.).

1821 *American* (N.Y.) 22 Aug. 2/3 (Th.), I do not think much of the legal acquirements of that man, who, after being furnished with the briefs of counsel, and picking the brains of the bar, is able . . . to tack together as much law as will make a good opinion. **1877** W. M. EVARTS *Electoral Commission Proc.* 108/1 (Th.), The Ore. brief . . . comes up again to prove that, when an ineligible person is elected, there is no election. **1892** *Congress. Rec.* 16 March 2130/1, I had the honor to be one of the attorneys in the case, and filed a brief against the bonds.

2. 'A letter patent, from proper authority, authorizing a public collection or charitable contribution of money for any public or private purpose. *New-England*' (W. '28).

* **Brief,** *a.*

1. Of epidemic diseases: Common, prevalent, rife. {1706-, *dial.*}

1722 *New Eng. Courant* 9-16 April 2/2 Sundry evil minded Persons have of late industriously reported in the Country Towns, that the Small Pox is again very brief in this Town [=Boston]. **1774** FITHIAN *Journal* I. 235, I hear nothing of the Ague abroad, it seems to go by turns, sometimes brief, then exceedingly scarce. **1816** PICKERING 53 *Brief* . . . is much used in New England by the illiterate, in speaking of a rumour or report, as well as of epidemical diseases. . . . A correspondent informs me, that *brief* is used by the illiterate in Virginia as well.

2. Of the wind or air: Strong, keen.

1829 *Va. Lit. Museum* 16 Dec. 419 *Brief,* is a *North of Englandism*—as 'the wind is brief'—that is, is prevalent or strong. **1888** 'CRADDOCK' *Broomsedge Cove* 159 This air a powerful rough kentry, an' the air is brief.

+**Brieflet.** A brief news item. — **1882** *Boston Transcript* 18 Jan. 1/3 [Heading], Brieflets. **1888** *Voice* 5 Jan., [Heading], Business Brieflets. **1890** *Register* (Whitewater, Wis.) 12 June, [Heading], Wisconsin Brieflets. Interesting Items Gathered from various Sources.

* **Brier, Briar.** Also †**bryer.**

***1.** A prickly or thorny bush or shrub, esp. a blackberry or wild rose bush; a bramble.

(*a*) **1704** S. KNIGHT *Journal* 22 There grew a Brier there, of a prodigious Highth and bigness, the like hardly ever known, called by the Indians Narragansett. **1713** HEMPSTEAD *Diary* 28, I was with the boys att Holmes's Lot mowing Bryers. **1796** MORSE *Amer. Geog.* I. 651 A species of the sensitive plant is also found here [in N.C.]; it is a sort of brier. **1853** RAMSEY *Tennessee* 462 He crawled into a bunch of briers. **1871** *Scribner's Mo.* II. 181 The path, too, is tangled with briers.

(*b*) **1752** W. TRENT *Journal* 79 [The Indians] had come through briars, thickets, and great waters to see me. **1806** in *Ann. 9th Congress* 2 Sess. 1117 The banks of the [Washita] river are covered with cane, or thick underbrush, frequently so interwoven with thorns and briars as to be impenetrable. **1856** *Florida Plant. Rec.* 447, 1 [slave] gon to Col. Gadsden with wagon for Briars. [*Note.* Thorny plants, intended for setting a hedge.]

b. Attrib. and comb. with *blackberry, copse,* etc.

1795 WINTERBOTHAM *Hist. View* III. 395 Flowering Trees, and Shrubs, &c. [include the] . . . Briar blackberry. **1829** T. FLINT *George Mason* 29 The red-bird, springing away from the briar copse, which he began to disturb with his grubbing-hoe. **1839** HOFFMAN *Wild Scenes* 173 The cat-bird from the brier-thicket replied in mocking notes. **1889** *Century Mag.* April 932/1 Our route wound here and there past fodder-stacked corn-fields, brier-grown old pastures [etc.].

2. A thorn of a brier. In phr. *keen* or *sharp as a brier.*

1900 C. C. MUNN *Uncle Terry* 76 Children are in some ways as keen as briers. **1902** HARBEN *A. Daniel* 257 She's pretty, an' stylish, an' as sharp as a brier.

* **Brier-, Briar-bush.** Also †**bryer-,** †**bryar-.** A brier growing as a bush.

1700 *Manchester Town Rec.* 96 The highway that goes to the fresh meddow and so . . . westerly to a heap of stons by a bryer bush. **1704** *Cambridge Prop. Rec.* 265 About 7 foot Westward of a Bryar bush. **1767** *Ib.* 325 An other Stake & heap of Stones near a Bryer Bush. **1856** *Mich. Agric. Soc. Trans.* VII. 807 The corners of the fences decorate themselves with elders, briar-bushes, popples, and other ill-shaped shrubbery. **1870** 'F. FERN' *Ginger-Snaps* 280 She had encountered a fierce briar-bush; she had got her hands scratched in the conflict.

+**Brier-, Briar-hook.** [BRIER 1 b.] A kind of reaping hook for cutting briers. Also fig., a razor. — **1819** *Plough Boy* I. 130 The common red pea . . . should be cut with a small briar-hook. **1843** 'CARLTON' *New Purchase* II. xxxvii. 42 With a genuine far-east barber's flourish, [I] touched the vile old briar-hook to my cheek.

+**Brier-, Briar-patch.** [BRIER 1 b.] A piece of ground overgrown with briers.

*c***1845** *Big Bear Ark.*, etc. 20 Pitch me naked into a briar patch if the steam didn't come out of the bullet-hole. **1846** T. B. THORPE *Myst. Backwoods* 159 The infinite bones that spread under his gay exterior as confusedly as the stems of a brier-patch. **1853** C. W. WEBBER *Tales* 173 (Th.), Hurrah for our captain! He's some in a brier-patch. **1881** *Harper's Mag.* April 729/2 Kill me if you will . . . but don't frow me inter de brier patch. *a***1909** 'O. HENRY' *Roads of Destiny* xxi. 354 We struck a brier-patch and had to sit down.

Brier rose. [BRIER 1 b.] A common variety of wild rose, the dog-rose. {1810-} — **1737** BRICKELL *N. Carolina* 90 The Brier-Rose, or Hip-Tree, is to be met with in some places, especially on dry Lands, but is generally of a Dwarfish kind. **1825** BRYANT *Death of Flowers* The brier-rose and the orchis died amid the summer glow. **1867** WHITTIER *Palatine* line 21 The hills are sweet with the brier-rose.

+**Brier-, Briar-scythe.** [BRIER 1 b.] A scythe for cutting down briers. — **1813** *Niles' Reg.* III. 296/1 [List of military supplies], 50 briar scythes. **1858** WARDER *Hedges & Evergreens* 181 The best method of cutting the tops off is to use a mowing-machine or briar-scythe. **1876** *Ill. Dept. Agric. Trans.* XIII. 301 The weeds were kept down with the hoe or briar scythe.

Brig[1]. [Abbreviation of BRIGANTINE.] A vessel with two square-rigged masts, carrying also a fore-and-aft sail on the mainmast. {1720-}

1712 HEMPSTEAD *Diary* 10 News came of a french Brigg, 150 men, [at] Tarpolian Coave. **1722** *New-Eng. Courant* 4-11 June 2/2 [The pirates] promise him his Brig again when they have taken a better Vessel. **1741** W. STEPHENS *Proc. Georgia* II. 97 A large Brig laden with Provisions being lately wrecked on that Coast near Savannah River. **1775** *Journals Cont. Congress* III. 278 Certain intelligence of the sailing of two north country built Brigs. **1794** *Ann. 3rd Congress* 1445 Eleven hogsheads of coffee were imported in the brig Jason. **1819** E. DANA *Geogr. Sk.* 99 Several large brigs have been built here, and sent to New-Orleans. **1835** HOFFMAN *Winter in West* I. 276 A line of four steam-boats, . . . and regular lines of brigs and schooners, are now established between that port [Chicago] and the principal ports of the lower lakes. **1877** *Harper's Mag.* Jan. 284/1 We chose to stay there . . . and make a home for father when he should . . . be ready to put another master in the brig.

+**Brig**[2], **Brigg.** [Of obscure origin.] A place for the confinement of prisoners (orig. on board a vessel); a nautical or military prison. — **1852** *Knickerb.* XXXIX. 404 In less than a minute I was in the 'brig,' in double irons. *Ib.*, They call the place where prisoners are confined, 'the brig.' **1921** R. D. PAINE *Comr. Rolling Ocean* 62 The master-at-arms stowed them for safe-keeping in a small building with barred windows which he called the brig. *Ib.* 109 Better break away before that loud friend of yours lands you in the ship's brig. **1923** WATTS *Luther Nichols* 136 His routine [of army work] was broken into once or twice by a sojourn in the brigg.

Brigade, *n.*

1. A subdivision of an army. {1637-}

'Two regiments of infantry, or cavalry, shall constitute a brigade, and shall be commanded by a major-general' (1799 in *Military Laws* (1858)

95). 'A brigade shall be composed of four regiments of infantry, one regiment of riflemen, one battallion of artillery,' [etc.] (1816 *Ann. 14th Congress* 2 Sess. 271). 'A brigade is formed of two or more regiments' (1861 *Army Regulations* 71). 'The body of troops commanded by a brigadier-general, comprising two or more regiments' (1890 *Columbian Cycl.* s.v.).

1776 G. CLINTON in Sparks *Corr. Rev.* (1855) I. 261, I issued orders to all the regiments in my brigade to stand ready to march on a moment's warning. **1811** *Ann. 12th Congress* 1 Sess. 2119 The whole of the infantry formed a small brigade under the immediate orders of Colonel Boyd. **1836** *Diplom. Corr. Texas* (1908) I. 97 Before this occurred we had a call from Gen[era]l Gains for a brigade to defend the western borders. **1863** S. COX *In Congress* (1865) 325 The people are not yet so degraded as to desire to save their Government by the aid of black brigades. **1876** INGRAM *Centennial Expos.* 612 At four o'clock in the evening the entire brigade, under the command of Brigadier-general William Randall Smith, entered the grounds.

+**2.** A group or band of trappers or hunters.

1836 IRVING *Astoria* II. 198 After the departure of the different detachments, or *brigades*, as they are called by the fur traders, the Beaver prepared for her voyage. **1837** — *Bonneville* I. i. 22 They detach bands, or 'brigades' as they are termed, of trappers in various directions, assigning to each a portion of country as a hunting, or trapping ground. **1860** *Harper's Mag.* Oct. 587/2 The hunter ... never goes alone. He and his friends and neighbors make up a brigade—large or small, it is called a brigade. **1902** WHITE *Conjuror's House* i. 4 From the wilderness came the brigades bearing their pelts, the hardy traders of the winter posts.

+**3.** A train of wagons or railroad cars.

1780 *Md. Hist. Reg.* IX. 242 This is to inform your Excellency that we have sent of two Brigades of waggons loaded with flour. **1887** GEORGE *40 Years on Rail* 31 Freight cars in the early days were called 'burthen cars' and trains were known as 'brigades.'

4. Attrib. (in sense 1): **a.** With *band, camp, color, headquarters, parade*, etc.

1848 [N. AMES] *Childe Harvard* 17 The 'Brigade Band' pours forth a melodious blast Above the pulpit. **1861** *Army Regulations* 59 Grand guards, and other brigade guards, are organized and mounted on the brigade parade by the staff officer of the parade. **1862** NORTON *Army Lett.* 80 At sunrise buglers at brigade headquarters sound the 'brigade call' and the 'reveille.' **1863** *Ib.* 133 To furnish me a horse that I could carry the brigade colors on. **1863** CUMMING *Hospital Life* (1866) 98/2 They informed me that from what they had heard of many of the other brigade hospitals, the men were in a much worse plight than theirs. **1886** LOGAN *Great Conspiracy* 351 Baker, of Oregon, ... having reached the Capitol, direct from his Brigade-camp, entered the Senate Chamber, in his uniform.

b. With *color-bearer, commander, inspector, major, paymaster, postmaster, quartermaster*, etc.

1775 *Journals Cont. Congress* II. 186 A deputy adjutant general or a Brigade Major, for the army in the New York Department. **1778** *Ib.* XI. 749 Motion was made, that the pay of the Rev. Mr. Hunter commence from the date of the resolution for appointing brigade chaplains. **1794** *Ann. 4th Congress* 2 Sess. 2829 To every judge, justice, sheriff, brigade inspector—in short, to every public officer residing in the western counties, a letter was addressed. **1797** *Ib.* 2330 There shall be one Brigade Quartermaster, one Brigade Paymaster, and one Judge Advocate. **1816** *Ann. 14th Congress* 2 Sess. 273 It shall be the duty of the brigade major of such brigade to inspect and muster the same, and sign the muster rolls. *Ib.*, Brigade quartermasters [shall be entitled] to the pay ... of an assistant deputy quartermaster general. **1861** MCCLELLAN *Own Story* 70 Brigade commanders will be held responsible for the strict execution of this order. **1863** NORTON *Army Lett.* 133, I am now the brigade color-bearer and bugler. *Ib.* 140 He had been a bugler, an orderly, and the brigade postmaster since he came out, and has never drilled at all. **1913** *Army Regulations* (1917) 52 A brigade commander ... will command his brigade and will be responsible for its ... preparedness for war service.

Brigade, *v.* +**1.** *tr.* To group (wagons) in a train. +**2.** To command in a brigade. — **(1) 1781** *Cal. Virginia St. P.* I. 594 You will therefore lose no time in sending them [=public wagons] to the Army, properly brigaded, with good Conductors and drivers. **(2) 1864** NICHOLS *Amer. Life* II. 156, I'll be d—d if I will be brigaded by a man who kept a — in Washington, and killed his best customer.

Brigadier.

1. An officer who commands a brigade; a brigadier general. {1678-}

1780 in Ramsey *Tennessee* (1853) 212 To raise one hundred men, agreeable to command of the Hon. Brigadier Rutherford, to send to the aid of South-Carolina. **1797** *Ann. 4th Congress* 2 Sess. 2330 All such parts of the said act which relate to the light dragoons, ... as may be construed to affect the Brigadier. **1812** *Ann. 12th Congress* 1 Sess. 1324 The oldest Brigadier (General Wilkinson) received much less pay than those on the two additional establishments. **1867** A. D. RICHARDSON *Beyond Miss.* 88 A military board, consisting of ... eight brigadiers. **1874** G. C. EGGLESTON *Rebel's Recoll.* 166 General Ripley stood less upon rule ... than any other brigadier I ever met. **1884** BLAINE *20 Years of Congress* I. 104 General Pierce ... was one of President Polk's political brigadiers.

+**b.** *Rebel brigadier:* see REBEL *a.*

2. *Brigadier general:* =sense 1. {1690-}

1776 *Journals Cont. Congress* IV. 181 The Congress then proceeded to the election of Brigadier Generals. **1778** *Ib.* X. 366 The pay of the brigadier general of cavalry ... 156¼ dollars per month. **1798** A. HOLMES *E. Stiles* 15 Wooster ... was ... made a brigadier-general in the continental service. **1802** *Ann. 7th Congress* App. 1306 There shall be one brigadier general with one aid-de-camp who shall be taken from the captains or subalterns of the line. **1812** *Niles' Reg.* II. 383/1 Brigadier-general Armstrong has arrived in this city. **1861** *Army Regulations* 40 A Brigadier-General is to be received—by cavalry, with sabres presented. **1861** LEE in M. A. Jackson *Gen. Jackson* 166, I have the pleasure of sending you a commission of brigadier-general in the Provisional Army. **1862** KETTELL *Hist. Rebellion* 125 In the Confederate army there was but one grade of general—that of brigadier-general. **1884** *Century Mag.* Nov. 110 Brigadier-generals were more numerous there than I ever knew them to be at the front.

Brigadiership. The office or rank of brigadier. {1826-} — **1776** in *Amer. Hist. Review* I. 307 The two vacant Brigadierships were now filled up.

***Brigantine.** Also †**brig(g)anteen, brigenteen(e); brigateen, briggatine.** A two-masted vessel, having the foremast and aftermast of different types and latterly with different rigs.

(*a*) **1685** SEWALL *Diary* I. 86 [They were] to go with Mr. Patteshol's Brigenteen to fetch in two privateers. **1688** — *Letter-Book* I. 3 Invoice of Goods shiped on Board the Brigenteene Freindship, ... bound for Barbadoes. **1705** *Boston News-Letter* 25 June 1/2 They tell us a new Briganteen from New-York was carried in to Martinico ... which we fear is Capt. Perkins in a fine Briganteen the 1st Voyage, & bound for Barbadoes. **1726** *Ib.* 27 Oct. 2/2 A briganteen about 80 tons.

(*b*) **1687** *Doc. Hist. N.Y. State* (1849) I. 254 The day following they saw a Brigantine att anker, and all the army went ashore and lay there that night. **1704** *Boston News Letter* 24 April 2/2 His Honour ... immediately caused the Drum to beat for Voluntiers, ... and in 3 or four hours time, fitted and man'd a Brigantine with 70 brisk young men. **1762** in H. M. Brooks *Gleanings* 10 The Brigantine *Tartar*, a prime Sailer, mounting fourteen Six Pounders, [and] twenty Cohorns. **1790** *Columbian Centinel* 2 Oct. 23/3 For sale, an excellent double-decked Brigantine, of about 120 tons burthen, almost new. **1830** COOPER *Water Witch* I. viii, The ... mysterious craft was a brigantine of that mixed construction ... which is no where seen to display the same beauty of form and symmetry of equipment as on the coasts of this Union. **1853** SIMMS *Sword & Distaff* xxxix, That arm of the sea which afforded harborage to the brigantines, or transport vessels, to which, he and others ... were about to furnish stolen cargo. **1904** M. E. WALLER *Wood-carver* 163, I ... shipped as cabin-boy on a brigantine bound for Australia.

(*c*) **1704** *Boston News-Letter* 1 May 2/2 Richard Smith, Brigateen Drag ... for Antigua. **1771** J. ROWE *Diary* 217 Capt. Brown sail'd for Oporto in my new Briggatine this morning.

+**Brigaty, -etty, -ity,** *a. dial.* [Cf. BIGGITY *a.*] Spirited; audacious. — **1884** 'CRADDOCK' *Tenn. Mountains* 189 Did you tell Tom to put up your 'beastis'? He is so 'brigaty' that he might not stand. **1888** — *Broomsedge Cove* 333 Waal, sir, they [=lynchers] be powerful brigetty an' bold. **1898** DUNBAR *Folks from Dixie* 63 My 'Lias done got right brigity an' talk about bein' somep'n'.

+**Brighamite.** A follower or adherent of the Mormon leader Brigham Young. Also attrib. — **1854** SIMMS *Southward Ho* 181 He was driving ... with one of his wives—and, to do him justice, we must assure the reader that, unlike our modern Brighamites, he had but one at a time. **1878** BEADLE *Western Wilds* 342 The cannon and long-range rifles of the Brighamite militia completely raked the interior of the camp. **1890** *Congress. Rec.* 2 April 2933/1 The Mormons are divided into two classes, known as Josephites and Brighamites. ... It is the ... Brighamites alone who believe in bigamy and in polygamy.

***Bright,** *a.*

1. Quick-witted, intelligent, smart. {1741-}

'Bright, ingenious; possessing an active mind.—*Webster.* This is a common use of the word in the United States' (B. '48). 'In standard English used chiefly in speaking of children or one's inferiors' (O.E.D.).

1805 D. MCCLURE *Diary* (1899) 123 The doctor is a man of bright parts. **1815** HUMPHREYS *Yankey in Eng.* 32 You are tarnation bright. **1824** IRVING *Tales of Traveller* I. 203, I began life unluckily by being the wag and bright fellow at school. **1872** F. M. A. ROE *Army Lett.* 37 It was very bright in her to think of this unusual *divertissement* for our guests. **1880** *Congress. Rec.* 22 Jan. 483/1, I recognize the gentleman from Virginia as one of the brightest gentlemen on the floor. **1887** STOCKTON *Hundredth Man* x, She was so bright and quick at seeing what ought to be done.

b. Used ironically.

1878 BEADLE *Western Wilds* 425 Among other bright laws, was one that no planter in Texas should sow more than one bushel of tobacco seed. **1921** R. D. PAINE *Comr. Rolling Ocean* 40 What's the bright idea?

2. In the phrase *bright lookout:* Sharp, alert, watchful.

1781 *Md. Hist. Mag.* V. 129 He was much frightened and kept a bright look-out to avoid the catastrophe. **1840** DANA *Two Years* xix. 195 The Kanakas ... getting long sticks ... went into the bush, and keeping a bright look-out, stood within a few feet of him. **1903** C. T. BRADY *Bishop* iv. 74 Cautioning Corporal White and the men left behind ... to keep close in the fort ... and keep a bright lookout for Indians.

3.+**a.** Applied to tobacco of a certain degree of excellence as indicated by its color.

1822 *Missouri Intell.* 17 Dec. 1/3 None but the brightest tobacco is now worth marketing. **1849** *Rep. Comm. Patents: Agric.* (1850) 322 There ought, if the quality of the crop will permit, to be four sorts of tobacco, 'Yellow,' 'Bright,' 'Dull,' and 'Second.' **1911** *Dept. Agric. Yearbook* 231 The Norfolk fine sandy loam . . . is used for the production of corn, winter oats, cowpeas, peanuts, and the bright cigarette tobacco.

+**b.** Used with reference to the complexion of mulattoes.

1831 *Georgian* (Savannah) 5 April 3/3 For sale, a bright Mulatto Man. **1888** C. D. WARNER *On Horseback* 116 Mary, the 'bright' woman (this is the universal designation of the light mulatto), was a pleasing but bold yellow girl. **1899** CHESTNUTT *Wife of His Youth* 144 He's mos' lackly one er dem bright mulatters. **1911** HARRISON *Queed* 211 Now a young bright-skin negro wishes to marry Laura.

* **Bright,** *adv.* +*Bright and early*, very early in the morning.

1837 IRVING *Bonneville* II. ii. 17 Captain Bonneville and his three companions set out, bright and early, to rejoin the main party. **1845** *Knickerb.* XXV. 449, I was up bright and early. **1855** *Ib.* XLV. 638 Bright and early the gong of the Massassoit House called all hands to breakfast. **1869** STOWE *Oldtown Folks* 175, I'll be up bright and early with my old horse and wagon. **1891** *Fur, Fin, & Feather* March 168 So I hitched up bright and early and started back. **1917** MCCUTCHEON *Green Fancy* 50 All three promised to be up bright and early in the morning to speed him on his way.

Brighten, *v.* +*To brighten the chain*, to renew old acquaintances or friendships. — **1846** *Spirit of Times* 18 April 96/2 At Petersburg, he had brightened the chain with his old friend Dr. Minge, one of nature's noblemen.

+**Brightwork.** Metal objects aboard ship that are kept bright by polishing. — **1841** *S. Lit. Messenger* VII. 769/2 It was a part of my duty, when I had to watch, to superintend the cleaning of the 'bright work.' **1911** VANCE *Cynthia* 123 [The dining-saloon] was also dingy . . . , the lustre of its brightwork dulled, its white paint tarnished.

+**Brilliantine. a.** A superior quality of dress fabric, resembling alpaca. **b.** An oily preparation used to smooth and give gloss to the hair. — **(a) 1873** MRS. WHITNEY *Other Girls* iii. 15 Nobody really looked down to see that the underskirt was the identical black brilliantine that had done service all the spring. **1908** *Sears, Roebuck & Co. Catalogue No. 118* 898 White mohair brilliantine, natural finished fabric. **(b) 1884** *Harper's Mag.* Oct 706/1 The same devotion to starch and brilliantine. **1905** *Sears, Roebuck & Co. Catalogue No. 115* 391 Brilliantine, an imported French hair oil for making the hair soft and glossy.

+**Brim.** The long-eared sunfish, *Lepomis auritus.* — **1887** *Harper's Mag.* July 270/1 If they could slip away . . . there would be a diminished number of 'brim' and 'goggle-eye,' in the ditch. **1894** *Outing* XXIII. 403/2 Besides these, there was the brim, a small, red fish, which is excellent fried.

* **Brimstone,** *n.*

***1.** Sulphur. Also attrib. with *kiln, mine.*

1637 MORTON *New Canaan* II. vi, Brimstone mines there are likewise. **1677** HUBBARD *Narr.* 22 They had for two days assaulted that poor handful of helpless people . . . thrusting poles with Fire brands and rags dipped in brimstone tied to the ends of them to fire the house. **1730** HEMPSTEAD *Diary* 226, I . . . have been daubing with Brimstone for the Itch. **1775** *Journals Cont. Congress* II. 85 That it be recommended to the committees of the several towns . . . to collect all the salt petre and brimstone in their several towns. **1775** FITHIAN *Journal* II. 99 The brimstone . . . found [in Penn.] . . . is very pure, & of the brightest yellow, the Piece which I saw was in the Stone, & burned very clear & entire. **1807** IRVING, etc. *Salmagundi* XV. 347 The story of his once having smoked out a country singing-school with brimstone and assafœtida. **1919** *Tariff Comm. Information conc. Pyrites* 19 The crude brimstone produced in this country . . . is guaranteed to contain 95.5 per cent pure sulphur and often grades as high as 99.9 per cent.

2. In allusive uses: (see quotations).

1843 'UNCLE SAM' *Peculiarities* I. 161, I'm all brimstone, and drive the roughest rocking-horse in any three of these United States. **a1846** *Quarter Race Ky.*, etc. 85 [At a Tenn. frolic], 'Go it while you'r young!' 'Hurraw for the brimstone kiln—every man praise his country!' **1856** P. CARTWRIGHT *Autobiog.* 202, [I] shook my brimstone wallet over him [=I threatened him with hell] till he was sick and tired of it.

+**Brimstone,** *v. tr.* To smoke with brimstone. — **1868** *Rep. Comm. Agric.* (1869) 275 The yield is principally derived from hives that are 'brimstoned' in the fall, or from old combs that are unfit for use. **1880** *Harper's Mag.* Oct. 777/1 This fearless being, however, knew only one way to 'take up the honey,' viz., to brimstone the bees, killing every one.

+**Brindle-tail.** Used attrib. with *party*, etc., to denote a former faction of the Republican party in Arkansas. — **1871** *Congress Globe* 7 Jan. 350/1 The 'Brindle-tail party,' as it is called, . . . opposed Governor Clayton's usurpations of power. *Ib.*, The Lieutenant-Governor . . . still remains in the Republican party, but belongs to the 'Brindle-tail' wing of that party. **1872** *Ib.* 9 Feb. 935/2 In the township of Ashley, more than in any other . . . did the 'Brindle-tail' mob hold high carnival.

Brine spring. A spring the waters of which are impregnated with salt. {1817–} — **1823** JAMES *Exped.* I. 14 As far northward as the brine springs of Onondago. **1839** in *Mich. Agric. Soc. Trans.* (1856) VII. 371 We would refer to the whole subject of brine springs as presented in that report. **1843** *Nat. Hist. N.Y., Geology* IV. 34 This rock gives origin to brine springs throughout its whole range.

* **Bring,** *v.*

1. *tr.* * **a.** Of land: To produce or yield. {1535 only}

1738 BYRD *Dividing Line* (1901) [The ridge] is so wretchedly poor that it will not bring potatoes. **1831** PECK *Guide* 47 The bottoms . . . will bring three or four crops of corn without manure.

+**b.** To produce (curd) from milk.

1855 *Mich. Agric. Soc. Trans.* VI. 183 The milk for cheese is made into curd . . . by adding sufficient rennet to 'bring' it in about fifteen minutes.

***2.** To give birth to; to bear. {1523–1795}

1843 *Amer. Pioneer* II. 172 The moose is an animal similar to the deer or elk, except vastly larger. . . . They usually bring two young at a time.

3. *Bring down the house*, etc., to cause vigorous applause, laughter, etc.

1865 *Atlantic Mo.* XV. 575 Those tresses that brought down the house when your talents might have failed to do so, are now frosted with the snow of years. **1870** LOWELL *Study Windows* 384 Every sentence brought down the house, as I never saw one brought down before. **1880** *Harper's Mag.* Feb. 480/1 He once 'brought down the house' at Convention by saying [etc.]. **1887** *Ib.* March 653/2 The old man's criticism 'brought down' that part of the congregation in convulsions of laughter.

+**4.** *Bring on*, to bring forward, produce, show.

1886 *Chicago Tribune* 13 Sept. 4/3 Bring On Your Bears. What with offensive Ministers and erratic Consuls, . . . burden after burden of trouble has been laid upon Secretary Bayard's shoulders. *Ib.*, He can request England or Canada . . . to bring on their bears.

+**5.** *Bring round*, to occupy; to while away.

1847 FIELD *Drama in Pokerville*, etc. 73 Juleps, milk punches, and tenpins . . . brought round the evening.

+**6.** *Bring to*, to get (land) into suitable condition for cultivation.

1837 COLMAN *Mass. Agric. Rep.* (1838) 77 One of these gentlemen . . . has found this sort of land, after it was thus 'brought to,' extremely favorable to the growth of rye.

+**Bringer.** (brindger) *S.* **1.** A name for a dog, especially one of a vicious or courageous disposition. **2.** *Like Bringer*, furiously. — **1851** *Polly Peablossom* 52 He 'gin pickin' up rocks an' slingin' um at the dogs like bringer! **1880** HARRIS *Uncle Remus* (1883) 190 Nuthin' neber 'sturbs his mine, Twel he hear ole Bringer bark.

Brister, colloq. variant of *Bristow*, the older form of Bristol (in England). (Cf. BRISTOWMAN.) — **1805** LEWIS in *L. & Clark Exped.* (1904) II. 216 White Circular spots, about the size of a brister blue shot. **1845** GREEN *Texian Exped.* 322 We saw the blood oozing from an orifice the size of a brister shot. — **1823** COOPER *Pioneers* vi, Why, considering, . . . I must say that it was ship-shape, and Brister-fashion. [**1840** DANA *Two Years* xiv. 122 Ship-shape and Bristol fashion. *Ib.* xx. 205.]

Bristly, *a.* Used in the specific names of plants, etc., bearing bristles.

1814 MITCHILL *Fishes N.Y.* 384 Bristly Dory, *Zeus setapinnis*, . . . [is] taken in the bay of New-York. **1833** EATON *Botany* (ed. 6) 310 *Rubus setosus*, bristly raspberry. **1840** DEWEY *Mass. Flowering Plants* 27 *Ranunculus Pennsylvanicus*, Bristly Crowfoot, flowers in August in woods and meadows. **a1862** THOREAU *Maine Woods* 315 *Aralia hispida* (bristly sarsaparilla). **1878** Killebrew *Tennessee Grasses* 218 *Setaria Verticillata*, Bristly Foxtails, . . . is one of the foxtail grasses, some of which are very good grazing when young. **1883** HALE *Woods & Timbers N.C.* 139 Bristly currant (*R. resinosum*). . . . It is covered in every part, not excepting the fruit, with resinous glandular hairs, by which it may be recognized. **1892** APGAR *Trees Northern U.S.* 94 *Robinia hispida* (Bristly Locust, Rose-Acacia), with bristly leafstalks and branchlets.

Bristowman. *Obs.* [Cf. BRISTER.] A vessel from Bristol. — **1685** SEWALL *Diary* I. 88 A Bristow-man comes in this day and fires five Guns at the Castle. **1691** — *Letter-Book* 124 Sent a Letter to Cousin Hull and Madam Usher per the Bristowman.

Britannia. Also **Brittania, Brittany.**

1. A kind of linen; Britannia linen. {1676 only}

1754 *S. C. Gazette* 1 Jan. 2/3 Christopher Jolliff has just imported . . . a variety of checked and striped Linnens, Silesias, Britannias. **1817** *Niles' Reg.* XIII. 289/2 The prizes made by the privateers under the Mexican flag, are to a very large amount of merchandize, such as jewelry, laces, silks, linen, britanias, [etc.].

2. *pl.* ? Trousers of Britannia linen. *Obs.*

1798 B. HAWKINS *Letters* 352 One pair of Britannias . . . $3.50.

3. Attrib. (esp. with *ware*): Made of Britannia metal, an alloy of tin and regulus of antimony, resembling silver in appearance.

(1) 1814 BENTLEY *Diary* IV. 237 Capt. Bowditch . . . informed me this day that he had begun the work of the Britania Ware. **1819** SCHOOLCRAFT *Mo. Lead Mines* 141 The recent invention and introduction into general use, of Britannia and other wares, has now almost superseded the use of pot-metal. **1841** C. CIST *Cincinnati* Advt., All kinds of Brittania Ware repaired at short notice. *Ib.*, Brittania ware factory. **1848** *Boston Directory* App. 8 Table Cutlery, Britannia Ware, . . . and Furnishing Goods generally. **1858** *Texas Almanac* Advt., Glassware, Britannia-ware. **(2) 1840** *Picayune* 28 July 1 Salt Spoons; Britannia Table and Tea Spoons. **1851** A. CARY *Clovernook* 235 [Shall we use] the plain china or the gilt, the tin or the britannia coffee-pot? **1853** B. F. TAYLOR *Jan. & June* (1871) 52 The ignoble purpose of polishing brass andirons and Britannia tea-urns. **1887** WILKINS *Humble Romance* 107 Pouring the tea from the shiny britannia teapot into the best pink china cups. **1891** — *New Eng. Nun* 91, 'I had a Brittany teapot,' returned Mrs. Handy.

4. Table articles made of Britannia metal; Britannia ware.

1851 A. CARY *Clovernook* 91 The cupboard with its open doors, where the china and britannia were wisely set for show.

+**Briticism.** A word or expression characteristic of, or peculiar to, Great Britain. — **1868** R. G. WHITE in *Galaxy* March 335 This use of the word is a widespread Briticism. **1883** *Boston Journal* 17 Sept., The smaller of the two [books] is a well arranged handbook of Briticisms, Americanisms, Colloquial Phrases, &c.

British, *a.* +With reference to American Indians: Acting as allies of Great Britain. — **1835** HOFFMAN *Winter in West* I. 277 Behind these the British Indians lay concealed. **1852** J. REYNOLDS *Hist. Illinois* 9 It was a band of these natives, called the 'British,' or 'Black Hawk Band,' that caused so much trouble and expense to the United States.

British America.

1. The part of North America originally occupied by British settlers or claimed by Britain. *Obs.*

1764 OTIS *Rights* (1766) 77 The ministry [of Gt. Britain] . . . may rely on it, that British America will never prove undutiful, till driven to it. **1766** J. ADAMS *Diary* 28 March, The genius and guardian angel of Britain and British America. **1782** J. H. ST. JOHN *Letters* 53 British America is divided into many provinces. **1784** SMYTH *Tour* II. 34 The houses here [in Florida] have a very singular appearance within, being floored with a kind of reddish stucco, . . . no where else to be met with in British America.

2. The part of North America still included in the British dominions; Canada.

1869 BOWLES *Our New West* 23 From British America on the north to Mexico on the south is from one thousand to twelve hundred miles.

British American, *a.* and *n.*

1. *adj.* Forming part of, belonging to, British America.

1765 J. HABERSHAM *Letters* 45 We are speaking of the indefeasible Birth Right of a Brittish American Subject. **1789** MORSE *Amer. Geog.* 473 (*caption*), British American dominions.

2. *n.* A person of British extraction born or resident in America.

1764 O. THACHER (*title*), The Sentiments of a British American. **1764** OTIS *Rights* (1766) 86 The names of his present Majesty, and his royal Grandfather, will be ever dear to every loyal British American, for the protection they afforded us. **1775** ADAIR *Indians* 261 The conduct of the Christian French has fixed many of the Muskohge in a strong native hatred to the British Americans. **1784** SMYTH *Tour* I. 346 The Indians indeed do not appear to entertain any dislike to the British or French . . . ; nor have the real British or French any particular aversion to them, as the British Americans have.

+**Britisher.** A native of Great Britain; a person of British origin.

The American origin or currency of this form has sometimes been questioned by American writers.

1829 MARRYAT *F. Mildmay* xx, [American mate speaking,] 'Are we going to be bullied by these . . . Britishers?' **1838** *Knickerb.* XII. 173 As we passed the village of Niagara, even the juvenile 'Britishers' on the wharves indulged in terms that were scarcely civil toward the 'd—d yankees.' **1843** *Yale Lit. Mag.* IX. 79 (Th.), Is that the way the Britishers larnt ye to treat a gal, blast your infernal pictur? **1847** *Knickerb.* XXIX. 578 We are doing our best to make the 'Britishers' a little more alike than they are. **1871** EGGLESTON *Hoosier Schoolm.* xi. 96 Your father was a miserable Britisher. **1884** *Boston Journal* 26 Nov. 2/2 A Britisher has discovered that North America was at one time colonized by the Romans. **1903** *Boston Herald* 20 Aug., The Britishers say the challenger is a remarkable boat to windward. **1922** H. ROBINSON *Development Brit. Empire* 1 In this way there was added another distinct stock to form the composite Britisher.

+**Britishism,** variant of BRITICISM. — **1894** *Harper's Mag.* Jan. 315 Doubtless he could use 'Britishisms' if he chose. *Ib.*, Nor should we advise an American statesman to attempt a 'Britishism.'

British merchant. +(See quotation.) — **1860** S. MORDECAI *Virginia* II. 33 The term 'British merchants' is here used *not* in its general acceptation, but as it was formerly applied in Virginia to those who had establishments here and who in fact had the monopoly of trade in the Southern States.

+**British oil.** A patent medicine the chief ingredient of which was petroleum. — **1787** *Kentucky Gazette* 15 Dec. 2/3 Robert Barr . . . has lately received a general assortment of Grocery and Dye Stuffs with the following medicines, viz. Glauber salts, . . . British oil, [etc.]. **1809** F. CUMING *Western Tour* 444 Natural curiosities are a sulphur spring; a spring, from which is collected a bituminous substance resembling in properties and appearance, British oil. **1837** IRVING *Bonneville* I. xxiii. 223 The bituminous oil, called petrolium or naphtha, which forms a principal ingredient in the potent medicine called British Oil.

Brittle salix, willow. The crack willow, *Salix fragilis.* — **1847** DARLINGTON *Weeds & Plants* 329 Brittle Salix, Bedford Willow, . . . is one of the species cultivated for basket work. — **1857** GRAY *Botany* 416 Brittle Willow . . . [is] a tall and handsome tree, with smooth polished branches. **1891** *Cent.* 6929/1 Brittle willow . . . [is] so called because the twigs break easily from the branches.

+**Brittlewood.** A local name for the Indian cherry. — **1897** SUDWORTH *Arborescent Flora* 298 *Rhamnus caroliniana,* . . . Indian Cherry. . . . Common names [include] . . . Brittlewood.

+**'Broad, Broad,** *n. dial.* [From an erroneous division of *abroad.*] A going abroad or away; a journey, a trip. — **1823** COOPER *Pioneers* xv, I heer'n say that the Judge was gone a great 'broad, and that he meant to bring his darter hum. **1841** *S. Lit. Messenger* VII. 40/1 You must give up your *broad* to-day, Coral]y, for I want to have rails right away to fix the fences. **1921** C. GREER-PETRIE *Angeline at Seelbach* 25, I was sorry the Jedge was in sich a swivvit to git back to Louisville, bekase I didn't half git my broad out.

***Broad,** *adv.* Broadcast. — **1737** WASHINGTON *Diaries* III. 205 The New river grass which was sown broad with Oats . . . was also coming up.

+**Broad aisle.** The main aisle or passageway in a church. Also attrib.

1807 *Mass. Spy* 25 March 4/1 [For sale] Another Pew at the right hand of the broad aisle, esteemed the pleasantest in said house. **1825** NEAL *Bro. Jonathan* II. 19 Right under the middle of our new meetin' house; in the very centre of the broad aisle. **1847** *Knickerb.* XXX. 14, I got a stand in the broad-aisle near the pulpit. **1850** JUDD *R. Edney* ix. 141 Then there was Mrs. Tunny, . . . who owned a broad-aisle pew in Dr. Broadwell's Church. **1868** G. G. CHANNING *Recoll. Newport* 77 The outsiders would enter, and make their way through the broad and side aisles. **1889** *Harper's Mag.* Dec. 147/1 When I see her parade up the broad aisle, I want to stick out my tongue at her.

transf. **1866** LOWELL *Biglow P.* II. xi. 244 No white man sets in airth's broad aisle Thet I ain't willin' t' own ez brother.

+**Broad alley.** =BROAD AISLE. *Obs.*

1731 *Suffield Doc. Hist.* 250 It being put to the Town whether the Broad alley in the meeting House should be fil'd up, it pass'd in the Negative. **1763** *Essex Inst. Coll.* XLIX. 139 With what face can you require a young woman to stand in the broad alley and there confess fornication? **1776** TRUMBULL *M'Fingal* (1785) I. 26 More groans than haunted church-yard vallies, And more confessions than broad-alleys. **1806** *Intelligencer* (Lancaster, Pa.) 21 Oct. (Th.), Mr. Deming was sitting in the Pew east of the broad Alley.

Broad arrow. 1. The symbol of an arrowhead used to denote the property of the King. *Obs.* {1687–} +**2.** The symbol or badge of an Indian tribe. — **(1) 1642** *Md. Archives* I. 196 The Sheriff or his deputy . . . shall mark it [=tobacco] with a broad arrow, to signifie the seisure of it. **1671** *N. J. Archives* 1 Ser. I. 69 The defendant alleageth that his said vessell . . . is not lawfully arested . . . for there is nor was not any broad arrow sett upo' her main mast. **1678** *New Castle Court Rec.* 253 The widdow . . . daring to medle therewith the broad Ar[row] being put on the house [attached by the sheriff]. **1691** *Virginia State P.* I. 27 The Broad Arrow being their Ma[jesty]s perticuler marke. **(2) 1835** SIMMS *Yemassee* I. 97 Does Sanutee speak for the Yemassee—and where are the other chiefs of the broad-arrow?

***Broadax.** An ax having a broad blade (*i.e.*, with a long cutting edge), used for hewing timber.

1638 *Md. Archives* IV. 74 An old broad axe. **1641** *Conn. Public Rec.* I. 444 A broad axe, two narrow axes. **1702** MATHER *Magnalia* (1852) I. 221 Were it not that I am to do service for the publick, I should be much easier in returning to my broad-ax again. **1775** *Essex Inst. Coll.* L. 123 On his right was a highland piper . . . making a most horrid noise with his bagpipes, & on his left Costen with his broad ax on his shoulder. **1845** SIMMS *Wigwam & Cabin* 1 Ser. 99, I threw down the broad-axe, for I had been hewing out some door-facings. **1878** B. F. TAYLOR *Between Gates* 126 A puncheon floor hewn out with broadaxes.

Broadbill. {1634–}

1. a. The scaup duck or related species; called also black-head, bluebill, raft duck, etc. **b.** The spoonbill. **c.** The shoveler duck.

1831 P. HONE *Diary* I. 30 A man had . . . six hundred broad-bills. **1844** *Nat. Hist. N.Y., Zoology* II. 323 *Fuligula Marila* . . . is only known on this coast under the name of Broad-bill, and more rarely Blue-bill. **1848** BARTLETT 49 Broadbill (*Anas marila*), the common name of a wild duck, which appears on our coast in large numbers in October. **1886** ROOSEVELT in *Outing* Aug. 522/2 The mallard duck, shoveler duck, and broad bill are also common [along the Little Missouri R.], and afford excellent sport.

2. *attrib.* =BROAD-BILLED *a.*

1854 *Calif. General Laws* (1865) I. 480 Spoon-bill duck, and all other broad-bill ducks.

Broad-billed, *a.* Of birds: Having a broad bill. (Cf. prec.) — **1839** PEABODY *Mass. Birds* 367 The Broad billed Sandpiper, *Tringa platyrhinca,* is very rare in the United States. **1844** *Nat. Hist. N.Y., Zoology* II. 336 *Fuligula Americana* . . . is known on this coast under the name of Broad-billed Coot.

Broad bottom. +A member of the Anti-federalist party. — **1816** *Mass. Spy* 10 Jan. (Th.), The Broad Bottoms are increasing in strength. The Federalists rest on their oars.

Broad-bottomed, *a.* +Anti-federalist. — **1819** *Mass. Spy* 13 Jan. (Th.), Many broad-bottomed measures have been enacted.

Broadbrim.

1. One who wears a broad-brimmed hat; esp. a clergyman or Quaker. {1797–}

1774 ADAMS *Works* (1850) II. 400 Two or three broad-brims over against me at table. **1776** *Battle of Brooklyn* I. iv, Down goes Episcopacy and Quakerism, at least. I hope you won't leave one broad-brim on the continent. **1835** BIRD *Hawks of Hawk-H.* II. i. 7 Falconer, clapping him on the back, swore, with the favorite oath of his friend Caliver, he 'had never seen a jollier old broad-brim.' **1848** *S. Lit. Messenger* XIV. 91/2, I left Broad-brim salting his cattle in the hills, and came down to have a word or two with you.

2. A broad-brimmed hat. {1855}

1834 *Knickerb.* III. 83, I shouldn't wonder to see you . . . rig out in a methodist's broad brim and straight togs. **1847** BRIGGS *Tom Pepper* I. 127 Finding Wilson's broad-brim hanging in the hall, [I] clapped it on my head. **1876** *Scribner's Mo.* Nov. 142/2 When he slapped my broad-brim off, . . . it roused the Adam in me. **1880** HOWELLS *Undiscovered Country* 118 'Did you notice them, Mr. Hatch?' . . . 'Parties in broad-brims? Yes, I saw them.' **1895** C. KING *Fort Frayne* 46 The tall stalwart captain . . . took off his broad brim.

3. *attrib.* =BROAD-BRIMMED *a.*

1842 *Knickerb.* Nov. 491 A tremendous-looking cracker, wearing a broad-brim white hat.

Broad-brimmed, *a.* Of a hat: Having a broad brim. (Cf. prec.) {1716–} — **1809** IRVING *Knickerb.* III. iv, A low-crowned, broad-brimmed hat overshadowed his burly visage. **1848** THOREAU *Maine Woods* 78 They might have been taken for Quakers, with their broad-brimmed hats, and overcoats with broad capes. **1866** A. D. RICHARDSON *Secret Service* 268 The guests . . . regarded with much curiosity the . . . rural-looking man in cotton coat and broad-brimmed hat. **1880** HOWELLS *Undiscovered Country* 112 Two men . . . wore low-crowned, broad-brimmed hats of beaver.

Broad-brimmer. =BROADBRIM 2. {1860} — **1847** [ROBB] *Squatter Life* 68 An 'old hat' is, in fact, dangerous—so is a new one of a peculiar shape—so was Sol.'s broad brimmer.

Broadcast, *a.* Of machines: Adapted for sowing grain broadcast. — **1856** *Mich. Agric. Soc. Trans.* VII. 56 C. B. Seymour, Scio, [exhibited a] broadcast sower. **1867** *Iowa Agric. Soc. Rep.* (1868) 149 Broad-cast sowers are favorites. **1868** *Mich. Agric. Rep.* VII. 346 Peter Low, Adrian, [exhibited a] broad-cast seeder cultivator and roller. **1905** [E. W. PRINGLE] *Rice Planter* 162, I bought a Cahoon broad-cast seeder, and have tried to make Willing . . . understand the directions.

* **Broadcloth.**

* **1.** A finely woven woolen cloth, usually 54 inches or more in width.

1634 in Winthrop *Hist.* (1853) I. 475, I took and bestowed [the powder] first in a tent, which I made of mine own broadcloth. **1659** *Oyster Bay Rec.* I. 162 Jo: Dickinson hath payde unto ye sayd John Hincksman in broadcloth at 18s per yard. **1691** SEWALL *Letter-Book* I. 122, I entreat you to send me an end of colourd Broad-Cloth . . . rather inclining to sad than light colour. **1762** in BROOKS *Gleanings* 128 The Chaise has standing Posts with a canvass Top, the Lining is cloth coloured Broad-Cloth. **1815** *Niles' Reg.* IX. 36/1 An extensive woolen manufactory, designed and calculated to yield 60 yards of broad cloth per day, will be in operation the ensuing winter. **1835** [H. C. TODD] *Notes* 9 Superfine broad cloth is made in the village of Fishkill. *a***1862** THOREAU *Maine Woods* 274 Polis picked up a gun-case of blue broadcloth. **1901** CHURCHILL *Crisis* 113 Mr. Eliphalet Hopper, in Sunday broadcloth, was seated on the landing.

2. a. A piece or variety of broadcloth.

1651 *Suffolk Deeds* II. 167 Those twelue broade Cloathes. that I haue sold vnto him. **1714** *Boston News-Letter* 11–18 Jan. 2/2 To be sold by Mr. Thomas Cushing at his Shop . . . : Broad Cloths, Druggets, Shalloons and Triming. **1790** *Columbian Centinel* 29 Sept. 20/4 [For sale,] Low-priced, and middling Broadcloths. **1817** S. BROWN *Western Gaz.* 94 The woolen manufactury [in Lexington, Ky.] . . . manufactures broadcloths, cassimeres, [etc.]. **1863** RANDALL *Pract. Shepherd* 73 There has been a steadily increasing tendency . . . to substitute for the broadcloths and fine black cassimeres . . . comparatively coarse cassimeres of various, and . . . 'fancy' colors.

b. A broadcloth coat or suit.

1856 [M. THOMPSON] *Plu-ri-bus-tah* 115 Keeping bright his Christian armor, In the closet with his broadcloth, With his Sunday boots and broadcloth. **1877** *Harper's Mag.* March 560/2 This temporary pastor . . . whose broadcloth, eyeglass, manners, and customs were the theme of every Basset tea table. **1904** E. GLASGOW *Deliverance* 112, I met him in the turnpike last Sunday in a brand new broadcloth.

3. Attrib., esp. in the sense: Made of broadcloth.

(1) 1639 *R.I. Col. Rec.* I. 48 Tenn fathom of wampumpeage and one broadcloth coate. **1704** *Boston News-Letter* 13 Nov. 2/2 [He] has on a black broad Cloath Jacket, under that a frize Jacket and Breeches. **1787** *Md. Gazette* 1 June 4/1 A good claret coloured broadcloth coat, lined with white. **1835** HOFFMAN *Winter in West* I. 215 A smartly dressed young man . . . whose handsome broadcloth suit, worn as a travelling dress, bespoke the favoured beau of some country village. **1856** STOWE *Dred* II. 89 Do they think broadcloth coats and gold watches can comfort a man for all this? **1893** 'THANET' *Stories* 36 The long black, broadcloth cloak in which she had taken pride for the last five years.

(2) 1811 *Niles' Reg.* I. 118/2 A large stage drawn by oxen, carrying on it a large broad cloth loom. **1863** H. S. RANDALL *Pract. Shepherd* 73 Our broad-cloth manufactories sunk under the horizontal tariff of 1846.

(3) 1870 MEDBERY *Men of Wall St.* 139 Benevolent institutions . . . send their broadcloth beggars into the down-town offices by swarms.

(4) 1870 MEDBERY *Men of Wall St.* 41 Supple youths . . . making a loan, . . . then . . . like lightning disappearing in the broadcloth darkness. **1873** MILLER *Amongst Modocs* x. 153 This Alcade . . . was only a broadcloth sort of a man. A new arrival from the States.

Broad gauge. {1846 (Royal Comm. Rep.); 1864–}

1. A width between the rails greater than the usual standard (4′ $8\frac{1}{2}$″) of railroads. Also in fig. context.

1847 GILLESPIE *Road-Making* 284 Objections to the broad gauge, More ground is required [etc.]. **1858** BRANNAN in *Tall Tales of S.W.* (1930) 255 [The 'hard-shell' religion is] not like the Methodists, what specks to get to heaven by hollerin' hell-fire, nor like the Univarsalists, that get on the broad gage and goes the hull hog-ah! **1865** *Atlantic Mo.* Jan. 78/1 This uniform broad-guage of twelve hundred miles . . . apparently decides the main channel by which the West is to discharge her riches into New York.

2. *attrib.* **a.** With *locomotive, mail train, road.*

1847 GILLESPIE *Road-Making* 284 The larger engines of the broad gauge roads. **1860** HOLMES *Professor* v. 145 The President of the United States is only the engine-driver of our broad-gauge mail train. **1870** MEDBERY *Men of Wall St.* 84 He is told that a broad-gauge road is always a good purchase. **1887** *Courier-Journal* 5 May 3/3 Its construction has overthrown the old idea that a broad-gauge road could not be built through the Rockies. **1894** *Poor's Man. of Railroads* 41 (*advt.*), Compound locomotives. Broad and narrow gauge locomotives.

b. *fig.* On a large or liberal scale; large-minded, etc. Also as adj.

*c***1873** [see BROAD GAUGER]. **1879** B. F. TAYLOR *Summer-Savory* 41 The Denver and Rio Grande railroad, a cunning narrow-gauge, while its officers are broad-gauge. **1887** GEORGE *40 Years on Rail* 234 Out West everthing is done on the broad-gauge plan. **1889** *Harper's Mag.* May 989/1 Those who have . . . known English men and women of the broad-gauge variety.

Broad-gauged, *a.* =BROAD GAUGE 2b. — **1870** *Congress. Globe* 18 June 4578/2 In our broad-gauged and reckless way of counting cost and reckoning money, three cents is a sum hardly counted as anything. **1881** *Chicago Times* 4 June, Everything broad-gauged and in liberal proportions. **1902** LORIMER *Lett. Merchant* 40, I hadn't been broad-gauged enough to see that it was a better way.

+**Broad-gauger.** (See quotation and cf. BROAD GAUGE 1, quot. 1858.) — *c***1873** DE VERE *MS. Notes* 242 *Broad Gauge* church in [the] West = Universalist or no church. A Broad Gauger may be an infidel, atheist, etc.

Broad hoe. +A hoe having a blade about a foot wide, used in the cultivation of corn, cotton, tobacco, etc.

1672 *Oyster Bay Rec.* I. 69 A broade hooe. **1754** *S.C. Gazette* 1 Jan. 2/2 Just imported . . . a large assortment of . . . broad hoes. **1772** *Carroll P.* in *Md. Hist. Mag.* XIV. 147 Order 35 fathom of Prize Rope & two Dozen of Broad Hoes. **1800** W. TATHAM *Tobacco* 13 The third kind of hoe is the *broad* or *weeding* hoe. **1899** GREEN *Va. Word-Book* 70 *Broad-hoe,* a hoe with a blade a foot wide, and long handle for weeding corn.

Broadhorn.

+**1.** A kind of flatboat formerly used on American rivers, especially the Mississippi and the Ohio.

1819 DEWEES *Lett. from Texas* 11 The vessels upon this river consist in part of barges and keel boats; but mostly of upper country flat boats, (generally called broad-horns). **1820** J. HALL *Lett. West* (1828) 324 The flat-bottom boat is a mere raft. . . . An immense oar is placed on the roof on each side, near the bow (which has given these boats the nickname of 'broad horns'). **1834** [R. BAIRD] *Valley Mississippi* 127 Hundreds of flat bottomed boats (called in the Western boatman's dialect, 'broad horns,') annually float down from a thousand places on the Ohio. **1847** FIELD *Drama in Pokerville,* etc. 178 In the year 1822, steamboats having left the 'keels' and 'broad-horns' entirely 'out of sight' [etc.]. **1884** *Harper's Mag.* June 124/2 There was the Kentucky 'broad-horn,' compared by the emigrants of that day to a New England pig-sty set afloat, and sometimes built one hundred feet long, and carrying seventy tons.

+**2.** A kind of river boat, somewhat similar to the earlier boat of the same name, but designed for carrying coal.

1851 *Knickerb.* XXXVII. 182 The river is dark as night; but we see, every now and then, 'broad-horns' and coal-flats, with a twinkling light. **1880** *U.S. Census* VIII. 183 For coal boats, or broad-horns, the standard size is 170 feet in length. **1883** *Encycl. Amer.* I. 440/2 When the coal mines in the vicinity of Pittsburg began to ship coal to Southern markets, the 'broad-horn,' or 'coal-boat,' was invented.

+**3.** The bighorn or Rocky Mountain sheep.

1847 *Knickerb.* XXX. 141 He had wandered some distance up the mountain in search of wild sheep, or 'broad-horns.'

+**4.** A longhorn; Texas longhorn.

1900 GARLAND *Eagle's Heart* 164 Reynolds and Mose rode out toward the slowly 'milling' herd, a hungry, hot, and restless mob of broadhorns, which required careful treatment.

Broadleaf. 1. Used attrib. with names of plants (see quotations). **2.** A kind of tobacco. — **(1) 1804** LEWIS in *L. & Clark Exped.* (1905) VI.

154 Broadleaf Willow found on the Missouri not so common as the Narrow leaf willow but grows much larger. **1817–8** EATON *Botany* (1822) 469 *Solidago latifolia*, broad-leaf golden-rod. **1883** SMITH *Geol. Survey Ala.* 293 *Q[uercus] nigra* (broadleaf black-jack, or simply black-jack). **(2) 1864** *Ohio Agric. Rep.* XVIII. 148 The Maryland Broadleaf, as far as it has been tried, gives promise of being a valuable kind.

Broad-leafed, *a.* =BROAD-LEAVED *a.* 1. — **1814** *Lewis & Clark Exped.* I. 289 An almost impenetrable thicket of the broad-leafed willow. **1840** COOPER *Pathfinder* i, The broad-leafed linden known in the parlance of the country as the basswood. **1852** STANSBURY *Gt. Salt Lake* 221 The broad-leafed dock of the eastern prairies abounds here. **1890** *Cent.* 3622/2 Broad-leafed maple [is] a fine species . . . of California and Oregon, the wood of which is largely used locally for furniture, etc. **1891** *Ib.* 6362/3 *Broad-leafed tobacco*, the Maryland tobacco.

***Broad-leaved,** *a.*

***1.** Having broad leaves; extensively used in the specific names of plants, trees, etc.

*c***1728** CATESBY *Carolina* I. 13 The broad-leaved Candle-berry Myrtle . . . grows usually not above three foot high, . . . having a broader leaf than the tall Candle-berry Myrtle. **1785** MARSHALL *Amer. Grove* 44 *Euonymus latifolius.* Broad-leaved Spindle Tree. *Ib.* 72 *Kalmia latifolia.* Broad leaved Kalmia. **1818** *Jrnl. Science* I. 366 Broad-leaved panic grass (*Panicum latifolium*). **1823** JAMES *Exped.* I. 10 The deep umbrageous hue of hemlock spruce . . . is exchanged for the livelier verdure of the broad-leaved laurel. **1833** EATON *Botany* (ed. 6) 299 *Ranunculus palmatus*, broad leaved crowfoot. **1837** HAWTHORNE in *Atlantic Mo.* March (1866) 259/2 In the interstices grow brake and broad-leaved forest grass. **1843** TORREY *Flora N.Y.* II. 14 *Plantago Major.* . . . Broad-leaved or Common Plantain. *Ib.* 155 *Rumex obtusifolius*, . . . Broad-leaved Dock. *Ib.* 209 *Salix lucida.* . . . Glossy Broad-leaved Willow. **1884** SARGENT *Rep. Forests* 47 *Acer macrophyllum.* . . . Broad-leaved Maple. **1894** COULTER *Bot. W. Texas* III. 545 *Uniola latifolia.* (Broad-leaved spike-grass.)

‖**2.** Broad-brimmed.

1840 HOFFMAN *Greyslaer* I. 128 Shoes without buckles, and a broad-leaved chip hat . . . marked him.

Broad road. +Main road or highway. *colloq.* — **1871** STOWE *Pink & White Tyranny* 292 The bustle and animation . . . on the turnpike, spoken of familiarly as the 'broad road,' will be somewhat increased.

+**Broad seal war.** 'A contest in the House of Representatives, in December, 1839, as to the admission or exclusion of five Whig members from New Jersey, who had certificates of election under the broad seal of the State' (*Cent.*). — **1877** RAUM *New Jersey* II. 399 The Whigs refused to vote; but the question was decided by the rest of the House in favor of the Democratic claimants. . . . This was called Governor Pennington's 'broad seal war.'

***Broadside.** +The part of an animal, esp. a hog, that lies between the ham and the shoulder; a side of bacon. — **1831** PECK *Guide* 172 Their method is to salt it [=pork] sufficiently to prepare it for smoking, and then to make bacon of hams, shoulders, and midlings or broadsides. **1846** MELVILLE *Typee* I. viii. 69 A rapidity and loudness of utterance that almost led me to suspect he had been slyly devouring the broadside of an ox in some of the adjoining thickets. **1853** *Harper's Mag.* VII. 276/2 The old Doctor quietly obeyed directions and layer after layer of fat 'broadside' was hoisted out to him.

Broad-tailed, *a.* Having a broad tail; spec. with *humming-bird, sheep.* {1802} — **1858** BAIRD *Birds Pacific R.R.* 135 *Selasphorus Platycercus*, . . . Broad-tailed Humming Bird. **1881** *Harper's Mag.* June 27/1 Doctor Coues describes a similar antic practiced by the broad-tailed humming bird . . . of the Rocky Mountains. — **1863** RANDALL *Pract. Shepherd* 53 A variety of the Broad-Tailed sheep . . . was bred for a considerable period in the United States.

+**Broad-tread.** Attrib. of cars, etc.: Having wheels with a wide bearing surface. — **1866** W. REID *After the War* 471 Great 'broad-tread' carts, with a stout mule hitched in the shafts and a pair of lighter ones in front, are used to haul the cane to the mill. **1875** *Chicago Tribune* 11 Sept. 3/6 The cars . . . are new and of 'broad tread.'

+**Broadway.** [A well-known street in New York City.]

1. In transf. sense: A street resembling this in some way, esp. in having theaters and other places of amusement.

1839 *Knickerb.* XIV. 436 The principal street in the village is called Broadway. **1884** *Century Mag.* March 678/2 No sooner is the 'Interocean City' of some farthest Western frontier of civilization out of the log-cabin period, than it has at once a Broadway, a Fifth Avenue, and an Academy of Music.

2. Attrib. in sense: Located on, similar to, or characteristic of Broadway; latterly esp. of the actors and theaters of Broadway.

1849 A. MACKAY *Western World* I. 67 It is impossible to meet with a more finished coxcomb than a Broadway exquisite, or a 'Broadway swell,' which is the designation attached to him on the spot. **1881** *Harper's Mag.* April 712/2 Another suggests some Broadway idea. **1891** LOVETT *U.S. Pictures* 34 The 'Broadway Squad'—that is, the stalwart policemen whose duty it is to pilot pedestrians across. **1904** *N.Y. Ev. Post* 9 May 7 Mr. Townsend of Chemulpo, an American who has lived out here twenty years without any Broadway nostalgia. **1913** *Nation* XCVI. 352/3 No one who has spent an hour at a Broadway cabaret can doubt that we are splendidly casting off the shackles of academicism.

Broad-winged, *a.* {1816} +Denoting a small hen hawk or buzzard, *Buteo platypterus.* — **1812** WILSON *Ornithology* VI. 92 [This] Broad-Winged Hawk, *Falco Pennsylvanicus*, . . . was perched on the dead limb of a high tree. **1844** *Nat. Hist. N.Y., Zoology* II. 11 The Broad-winged Buzzard, *Buteo Pennsylvanicus*, . . . is a rare species in our State. . . . In Virginia and Maryland, it is more common. **1874** COUES *Birds N.W.* 360 Broad-winged Buzzard. *Ib.*, The Broad-winged Hawk is apparently more numerous along the Atlantic coast than elsewhere, especially in New England. **1895** *Dept. Agric. Yearbook 1894* 222 The broad-winged hawk . . . feeds largely on insects, small mammals, snakes, toads, and frogs.

Brocade. The rich textile fabric of that name. {1695–}

1726 *New-Eng. Courant* 5–12 March 2/2 Edward Carter, Silk-Dyer and Scowerer, . . . dyes and scowers all sorts of Brocades, Velvets [etc.]. **1739** W. STEPHENS *Proc. Georgia* 477 They shared four hundred Dollars apiece . . . and many rich Brocades, etc. **1803** *Ann. 7th Congress* 2 Sess. 221 A lady may like a fine transparent muslin, or a shawl, or brocade. **1841** COOPER *Deerslayer* xii, A beautiful dress of brocade, a little the worse from negligent treatment, followed. **1896** WILKINS *Madelon* 11 Not a girl . . . could wear a gown of brocade with the grace . . . with which Madelon Hautville wore indigo cotton.

attrib. **1714** *Essex Inst. Coll.* XLIII. 52, 20 yards Brocade Ribon. **1841** COOPER *Deerslayer* xxxi, She looked like a queen in that brocade dress in which we met her. **1869** STOWE *Oldtown Folks* 167 Harry brought in a quantity of fruit . . . and, like two squirrels, they stored it under the old brocade sofa.

+**Brocadilla.** [Sp. *brocadillo.*] =BROCATELLE 2. Also attrib. — **1872** *Vt. Board Agric. Rep.* 658 No other marble quarried in Rutland county resembling it except the brocatelle, known to the trade as 'brocadilla.' *Ib.* 660 The 6th layer is of brocadilla marble, green and white varied.

Brocatelle. [F.] **1.** An imitation of brocade. Also attrib. {1669–} +**2.** A kind of ornamental marble found to some extent in Vermont. — **(1) 1852** STOWE *Uncle Tom* xiii, A real comfortable . . . old chair, and worth . . . a dozen of your plush or brocatelle drawing-room gentry. **1865** — *House & Home P.* 106 John, happily, had no money to buy brocatelle curtains. **1881** M. J. HOLMES *Madeline* 58 It was his first introduction to rosewood, velvet, and brocatelle. **(2) 1872** [see BROCADILLA].

Broccoli. A form of cabbage very much like cauliflower. {1699–} — **1792** IMLAY *Western Territory* 88 Of culinary plants and vegetables, there are [on the upper Ohio] . . . cabbages, brocali [*sic*], celery and sallads. **1839** E. J. HOOPER *Practical Farmer* 32 *Brocoli*, There are three sorts in this country, viz. early white, early purple, and large cape. **1855** BROWNE in *Trans. Amer. Inst. N.Y.* 610 There have been imported from England three varieties of Broccoli. **1918** *Dept. of Agric. Bulletin No. 667* 12 Total car-lot shipments of fruits and vegetables [in 1916] by States . . . : Broccoli, California 2; Oregon 48.

***Broche.** *local.* [Variant of *broach, brooch.*] A removable covering, usually of corn husk, placed upon the spindle of a spinning wheel to receive the thread as it is spun; the covering and its thread. {Now *dial.*} Also comb. — **1885** 'CRADDOCK' *Prophet* xiii. 237 She had a broche in her hand, just taken from the spindle. *Ib.*, For the lack of the more modern broche-holder she thrust a stick through the tunnel of the shuck on which the yarn was wound.

Brockeled, *pp. a.* =next. — **1899** *Mo. So. Dakotan* I. 176 [He] walked slowly 'round and lovingly rubbed the brockeled face of the off ox.

Brockle, -ell, *a.* [Cf. Sc. dial. *brockit, brocked.*] Of mixed black and white. — **1665** *Hempstead Rec.* I. 166 One cow coolered black with a brockell face. **1749** HEMPSTEAD *Diary* 539 [I] set out with my cattle . . . 1 black brockle faced.

+**Brogan.** Also **broghan.** [Sc. and Ir. Gael. *brógan*, dim. of *bróg* shoe.]

1. A stout coarse shoe.

1835 HOFFMAN *Winter in West* I. 200 In another [corner of the room], a pair of Cinderella-like slippers would *chassez* cross with a brace of thick-soled broghans. **1835** INGRAHAM *South-West* II. 99 Slippers, brogans, a pillow . . . filled up the picture. **1841** *S. Lit. Messenger* VII. 775/2 Our slaves in the South-West are annually supplied with . . . two pair of brogans. **1845** SOL. SMITH *Theatr. Apprent.* 101 Not having sandals prepared, he permitted them to wear their own coarse brogans. **1853** 'P. PAXTON' *Yankee in Texas* 25 He had . . . divested his feet of a heavy pair of 'pot metal' boots, and invested them in two old, worn-out, slip-shod brogans. *c***1869** 'MARK TWAIN' *Sk., Niagara* 67 He wore a slouch hat and brogans, and had a short black pipe in his mouth. **1881** *Harper's Mag.* March 638/1 A rural statesman entered the hall with his No. 12. brogans covered with the soil of his native hills. **1891** *Century Mag.* Feb. 489 A fashionable bonnet . . . is donned with her best cotton robe and brogans. **1921** C. GREER-PETRIE *Angeline at Seelbach* 17, I waked up jest in time to ketch that ar darky in the act of a-makin' way with them brogans.

attrib. **1855** *S. Lit. Messenger* XXI. 222 A shapeless and dilapidated waistcoat, and brogan shoes, completed his attire.

2. *local.* (See quotation.)

1881 E. INGERSOLL *Oyster Industry* 242 *Brogan*, a kind of large boat used by the oystermen of the Chesapeake.

+**Broglio.** A kind of cloth. — **1759** in H. M. Brooks *Gleanings* 33 Cross-bar'd stuffs, rich brunets, broglios, stript & plain camblets & cambleteens. **1762** *Newport Mercury* 7 Sept. 3/2 To be sold by Gideon, . . . figur'd . . . broglio's, light and cloth colour'd belladine.

+**Brogue,** *v. dial. intr.* To crawl. — **1883** ZEIGLER & GROSSCUP *Alleghanies* 51 'I've brogued it through every briar patch an' laurel thicket.' . . . 'What do you mean by "brogued it"?' . . . 'Crawled, thet's what hit means.'

Broiler. {1671–}

+**1.** A utensil for broiling meat, etc.

[**1828** WEBSTER, *Broiler*, that which dresses by broiling.] **1846** WORCESTER, *Broiler*, . . . a gridiron. **1902** *Harper's Mag.* May 966 Phil . . . shot away from her and into the kitchen to turn the wire broiler. *a***1906** 'O. HENRY' *Trimmed Lamp*, etc. 64 Two minutes longer on the broiler would have made this steak fit to be eaten by a gentleman.

+**2.** A chicken suitable for broiling.

1876 *Vt. Bd. Agric. Rep.* III. 244 The cockerels should be sold for broilers when large enough. **1882** 'M. HARLAND' *Eve's Daughters* 72 Jack raises chickens and sells the eggs and 'broilers' to Mamma. **1894** *Vt. Agric. Rep.* XIV. 167 To-day there is more money in eggs than in poultry, unless your home markets are open for broilers.

***Broke,** *ppl. a.* [ME. and dial. variant of *broken*. See the introductory note to BREAK *v.*]

1. Ruined financially; bankrupt; completely out of money. Also *flat broke* (cf. DEAD BROKE). {1851–}

1821 *Murphey P.* in *N.C. Hist. Comm.* I. 220, I have been broke now twelve Months, as every one thought: yet I move on in the old way. **1846** *Spirit of Times* 25 April 101/2, I unfortunately am short of funds, flat broke, busted, collapsed. **1860** MRS. S. COWELL *Diary* 210 When he did see him, said frankly that he was 'broke' and had not time to send to New York for money. **1865** 'MARK TWAIN' *Sk., Answers to Correspondents*, So he was cleaned out, as you may say, and he struck the home-trail, cheerful but flat broke. **1884** SWEET & KNOX *Through Texas* 16 Unlike most professional gamblers, he was seldom 'broke.' **1898** *New York Journal* 16 Sept. 14/1 Mike Dwyer . . . is about 'broke.' . . . He still hopes to win out, but the prospect is dubious. **1902** LORIMER *Lett. Merchant* 194 A man's got to lose more than money to be broke. **1907** WHITE *Arizona Nights* vii. 133 It took me six weeks and two days to go broke.

+**2.** Of animals: Broken to harness.

1833 M. A. HOLLEY *Texas* v. 97 This brutal process is repeated until the animal is thoroughly broke and rendered docile. **1834** CROCKETT *Life* 68 They were both broke to the halter. **1850** W. MILES *Journal* (1916) 12, 500 broke mules were to be in readiness. **1856** *Mich. Agric. Soc. Trans.* VII. 275 Oxen exhibited as working cattle, for their being the best broke, must be hitched to either a wagon or cart. **1893** ROOSEVELT *Wilderness Hunter* 426 The light-hearted belief . . . that any animal which by main force has been saddled and ridden, or harnessed and driven a couple of times, is a 'broke horse.'

+**b.** Trained as a hunting dog.

1856 *Spirit of Times* (N.Y.) 11 Oct. 97/1 It is, therefore, requisite that they [cocker spaniels] . . . should be extremely well broke.

***Broken,** *ppl. a.*

1. Interrupted by periods of time; given at intervals.

1677 R. WILLIAMS *Unpub. Lett.* (1881) 55, I have had £28. in broken parcels in 5 years. **1806** LEWIS in *L. & Clark Exped.* (1905) IV. 73 We gave him broken dozes of diluted nitre. *Ib.* VI. 94 Charbons an[d] La-Page returned, having made a broken voyage.

+**2.** *Broken days*, among the American Indians, the time appointed for the fulfilment of an arrangement made by two parties.

1775 ADAIR *Indians* 318 Seventeen were the broken days, according to the Indian phrase, when the Choktah engaged to return with the French scalps. *Ib.* 329, I . . . arrived in the Choktah country before the expiration of the broken days, or time we had appointed. **1798** B. HAWKINS *Letters* 318 The chiefs request the agent . . . that when he sends a written notice to them, he will send the broken days to the head man. *Ib.*, When the broken days are out they are to commence their journey of banishment. **1842** E. A. HITCHCOCK *Journal* 132 On the fourth meeting they give out the 'broken days' for the Busk.

3. *Broken breast*, inflammation of the mammary glands.

1877 *Vt. Dairymen's Assoc. Rep.* VIII. 105 In the human subject this is known as 'broken breast.'

4. *Broken land*, land prepared for cultivation.

1898 *Mo. So. Dakotan* I. 52 Each succeeding year had seen a larger field in crop and a new strip of broken land.

‖**Broken bone fever.** Dengue or breakbone fever. — **1872** *Newton Kansan* 22 Aug. 4/2 Dengue fever—what is known in South Carolina and Georgia as 'Broken Bone' fever—is still on the increase in Calcutta and the neighborhood.

***Broker.** One who acts as a middleman or intermediary in the transaction of business between individuals or parties.

1787 TYLER *Contrast* (1790) I. ii, Sir, Mr. Transfer, the broker, is below. **1788** CUTLER in *Life & Corr.* I. 381, Individual adventurers should not apply to the *Brokers*, but deposit their hard money in the hands of one man only. **1796** *Ann. 4th Congress* 2 Sess. 2697 On every hundred dollars value of foreign wares, . . . sold, bargained, or trafficked for, by factors and brokers, eighteen and three-quarter cents. **1836** *Congress. Deb.* 8 June 1719 Then came the profits to the brokers, first cousins to the bankers, for changing notes for money. **1843** W. ARMSTRONG *Stocks* 7 We have given a sketch of the different Boards of Brokers, their rules and regulations. **1855** *Chicago Times* 29 March 1/4 The orders for Stocks from abroad . . . were sensibly felt at the Broker's Board, and prices went up 1 per cent. **1869** BROWNE *Adv. Apache Country* 530 Brokers and horse-jockeys generally make their profits from the credulity of their fellow-men. **1886** A. DALY *Nancy & Company* 11 My daughter . . . shall live in the shadow of marble pillars—under frescoed ceilings and gilded cornices with her placid broker. **1902** LORIMER *Lett. Merchant* 179 Some one saw him drinking a small bottle just before he went on 'Change, and told it round among the brokers on the floor.

Broma. [From *theobroma*, the name of the cacao plant.] A preparation of chocolate. — **1888** J. D. BILLINGS *Hardtack* 218 As to the contents [of a box from home], I find on the back of an old envelope a partial list . . . condensed milk, sugar, broma, butter [etc.].

Brome grass. One or other species of oatlike grasses belonging to the genus *Bromus*. {1759–} — **1791** MUHLENBERG *Index Florae* 161 *Bromus*, Brome-grass. **1795** WINTERBOTHAM *Hist. View* III. 401 [In list of native grasses of New England.] **1802** J. DRAYTON *S. Carolina* 61 [In list of indigenous grasses.] **1832** WILLIAMSON *Maine* I. 124 To these may be added Brome, Bent, . . . Quaking, Panic, and Soft Grasses. **1843** TORREY *Flora N.Y.* II. 467 *Bromus ciliatus*, . . . Fringed Brome-grass, . . . [grows in] woods and rocky hills: frequent. *Ib.* 468 *Bromus sterilis*, . . . Barren Brome-grass, . . . [is found in] Penn-Yan, Yates county. *Ib.* 468 *Bromus purgans*, . . . Hairy-flowered Brome-grass, . . . [grows in] woods and river-banks, northern and western counties. **1868** GRAY *Field Botany* 355 *Bromus*, Brome grass. . . . Coarse grasses: two or three wild species are common, and . . . [four] are weeds of cultivation, from Europe.

+**Bronc(h).** *colloq.* Also **bronk.** =BRONCO.

1893 ROOSEVELT *Wilderness Hunter* 418, I saddled up the bronc' and lit out for home. **1903** 'O. HENRY' in *McClure's Mag.* Dec. 142, I gets on my bronc and pushes the wind. **1911** QUICK *Yellowstone N.* 301 She was agitatin' herself about the bronks' feelin's. **1921** MULFORD *Bar-20 Three* 242 Got to go easy with it for awhile, bronch. . . . Water can't be so terrible far ahead.

b. Attrib. with *train, twister*. Also as adj.

1910 MULFORD *Hopalong Cassidy* 138 That ain't a bad cayuse you got there. . . . Is it very bronc? **1913** — *Coming of Cassidy* 153 That's shore a long time to ride this bronc train. **1916** H. TITUS *I Conquered* 92 You'd have made a fine bronc twister.

+**Bronco, Broncho.** [Sp. *bronco* rough, rude.]

1. *W.* A small wild or half-wild horse or pony of the western states; an unbroken or imperfectly broken horse of this kind. (Cf. BRONC.)

(*a*) ?**1850** *Life in Rocky Mts.* 41 (Bentley), A buggy drawn by light broncos. **1875** BOURKE *Journal* 13 May, American horses . . . should be superseded by the California Broncos, which can well endure every hardship this country has to present. **1893** CHITTENDEN *Ranch Verses* (1905) 29 He is fond of his horse—'tis a bronco, of course. **1899** *Boston Journal* 6 Aug. 6/1 The term 'bronco,' which is generally used as representing the cayuse or low-bred Mexican or Spanish horse, is simply the Spanish for wild horse. **1904** STEEDMAN *Bucking the Sagebrush* 109 One of the peculiarities of a bronco is that he doesn't like a loose rope.

(*b*) **1869** S. BOWLES *Our New West* 101 A well-broken Indian pony or a 'broncho' (a California half-breed horse) can be got. **1871** *Scribner's Mo.* II. 2 Our provisions . . . were securely lashed to the backs of twelve bronchos. **1886** ROOSEVELT in *Century Mag.* July 340/1 In sitting a bucking broncho . . . the cowboy is absolutely unequaled. **1887** *Outing* May 2/1 Charlie B— was your typical country Englishman and the only thing American about him was the broncho he rode.

+**2.** Attrib. with *breaker, mare, mule, pony*, etc.

1869 S. BOWLES *Our New West* 101 The mule and the Indian and 'broncho' ponies will live on the rich grasses of the country. **1878** I. L. BIRD *Rocky Mts.* 54 Their live stock consists of two wretched horses, a fairly good *broncho* mare, a mule, four badly-bred cows. **1879** *Harper's Mag.* Nov. 886/2 Swift and sure-footed horses . . . of the *broncho* type—a mixture of the American horse and the mustang. **1885** F. M. A. ROE *Army Lett.* 337 He had been ridden only three or four times when we bought him, and probably by a 'bronco breaker.' **1891** *Century Mag.* Feb. 539 Its wearisomeness [was] occasionally relieved by a runaway among the half-trained bronco teams. **1895** *Outing* XXVII. 244/2 The indefatigable Apache scouts . . . left camp with their pack train . . . composed of hardy little 'broncho' mules.

b. As *adj.* Unruly, wild; untrained, raw.

1886 *Outing* Dec. 230/2 This morning I witnessed for the first time the milking of a *bronco* or undomesticated cow. **1887** F. FRANCIS *Saddle & Moccasin* 46 Sam's too broncho: he gets all-fired mean sometimes when he's full. **1902** A. MACGOWAN *Last Word* 37, I was fresh and green from my Texas pastures; too broncho to feel any awe of him.

+**Broncobuster.** *colloq.* One who breaks broncos to the saddle. — **1888** ROOSEVELT in *Century Mag.* Feb. 507 The flash riders, or horse-breakers, always called 'bronco busters,' can perform really marvelous feats. **1891** *Harper's Mag.* July 208/1 The bronco buster may be a 'professional' . . . or he may be a cow-puncher in slack times. **1907** WHITE *Arizona Nights* 303 A broncho buster . . . was engaged in roping and throwing some wild mustangs.

+**Bronco busting.** *colloq.* The process of breaking broncos to the saddle. — **1891** *Harper's Mag.* July 208/1 Bronco busting is a distinct art. **1902** A. MAC GOWAN *Last Word* 48, I shouldn't have allowed myself to be drawn into any talk on broncho busting. **1911** H. Quick *Yellowstone N.* 301, I had been asked to give a exhibition of broncho bustin'.

+**Bronze backer.** The smallmouth black bass. — **1888** Goode *Amer. Fishes* 56 'Bronze-backer' is one of its pet names among the anglers.

+**Bronzed grackle.** A widely distributed subspecies of the grackle. — **1895** *Dept. Agric. Yearbook 1894* 233 The common purple grackle ... and its two subspecies, the bronzed grackle (*Quiscalus q. æneus*) and the Florida grackle.

+**Bronze John.** *slang.* The yellow fever. — **1869** *Overland Mo.* Aug. 130/1 'Bronze John' is pretty well known [in the South] for yellow fever.

Brooder. +A heated boxlike contrivance used in raising chicks hatched in an incubator. — **1880** H. Tomlinson *Artificial Incubation* 32 [Chickens] may ... be transferred to an artificial mother, or *brooder* as the Yankees call it. **1894** *Vt. Agric. Rep.* XIV. 173 If you want to raise but a few, the old hen is the best, but if a large number is required, she must give way to the incubator and brooder.

+**Brood frame.** One of the frames in a patent bee hive. — **1861** *Ill. Agric. Soc. Trans.* IV. 82 Cut E is the brood frame. Little *g* represents the upper one full of comb.

Brood mare. A mare used for breeding. {1878}

1821 *Missouri Intell.* 18 Dec. 1/1 (*Advt.*), Brood mares, cows, swine. **1831** Peck *Guide* 166 Some farmers keep a stallion and eight or ten brood mares. **1848** E. Bryant *California* 377 We crossed in the course of the day a wide flat plain, upon which were grazing large herds of brood-mares (*manadas*) and cattle. **1857** D. Braman *Inf. Texas* 44 Land here can be purchased at from $1 to $2 per acre, ... and brood-mares for $25 each. **1876** Ingram *Centennial Exp.* 673 There were quite a number of the imported percheron stallions and brood mares. **1907** White *Arizona Nights* viii. 317 Senor Johnson owned ... perhaps half a thousand quite unbroken [horses]—brood mares, stallions [etc.].

* **Brook.** A small stream; a branch.

1828 Webster s.v., In some parts of America, *run* is used in a like sense; but *run* is also applied to larger streams than *brook.* **1871** De Vere 80 The *kill* of New York is a *brook* in New England, a *run* in Virginia, and, alas! a *crick*, or creek, almost everywhere else.

1622 'Mourt' *Relation* 59 We ... found divers corne fields, and little running brookes. **1668** *Derby* (Conn.) *Rec.* 10 A little Brook or spring that runs into the beaver River. **1682** *Providence Rec.* XIV. 64 A small Run of water called Ventor Brook. **1734** *Boston Rec.* 71 All Fish caught in Rivers, Ponds, and Brooks, shall be ... sold in the Market. **1796** Morse *Amer. Geog.* I. 450 These rivers are fed by numberless brooks. *a***1817** Dwight *Travels* II. 149 It is impossible for a brook of this size to be modelled into more diversified, or more delightful, forms. **1880** *Harper's Mag.* July 212/2 Its brooks and forests [*i.e.* of Long Island, were] popular with the hunting denizens of Manhattan. **1908** G. H. Palmer *Alice F. Palmer* 277 West of New York everything that runs is a 'creek.' Brook, as a spoken word, is gone.

+**Brook-drive.** (See quotation.) — **1851** Springer *Forest Life* 164 Brook-drives are ... usually distinct parcels of logs belonging to an individual or company.

+**Brook-driving.** Floating logs down a brook in time of high water. — **1851** Springer *Forest Life* 156 In brook-driving it is necessary to begin early, in order to get the logs in to the ... current of the main river while the freshet is yet up.

+**Brook-fish.** A fish frequenting brooks; also *spec.* (See quotation 1889.) — **1846** *Knickerb.* XXVIII. 177 In that stream ... lurk scores of the aristocracy of brook-fish, which are to dangle upon our lines tomorrow. **1889** *Cent.* 695/1 *Brook-fish*, a fish of the family *Cyprinodontidæ* and genus *Fundulus:* same as *killifish* and *mummychog.* (Local U.S.)

+**Brook-fishing.** Fishing in a brook. — **1857** [D. H. Strother] *Virginia* 17, I have a rod here, ... the very thing for brook-fishing, for whipping the smaller streams. **1857** S. H. Hammond *Northern Scenes* 112 Let him rig for brook-fishing and take to that stream.

* **Brooklime.** +A species of speedwell, *Veronica americana.*

1622 'Mourt' *Relation* 62 We found heere ... Caruell, Brook-lime, Liver-wort. **1784** Cutler in *Mem. Academy* I. 403 Brooklime. Water Speedwell. Blossoms whitish or purplish. In swamps. **1817–8** Eaton *Botany* (1822) 508 Brooklime. ... Flowers large. Wet [grounds]. **1843** Torrey *Flora N.Y.* II. 41 Brooklime ... [grows in] muddy borders of small streams, and about springs; frequent. **1891** *Cent.* 6732 Brooklime, a petiolate aquatic with purple-striped pale-blue flowers, [is] distributed from Virginia and New Mexico to Alaska.

+**Brooklynite.** An inhabitant of Brooklyn, N.Y. — **1835** W. L. Garrison in *Life* II. 67 Mr. and Mrs. May sat at my right hand, propounding many questions about the Brooklynites. **1881** *Harper's Mag.* May 817/1 With the exception of a few Brooklynites ... the place [= Coney Island] had been abandoned to cardsharpers and the roughest class from New York.

+**Brook pimpernel.** The water speedwell, *Veronica anagallis.* — **1817–8** Eaton *Botany* (1822) 508. **1836** Lincoln *Botany* App. 148. **1839** in *Mich. Agric. Soc. Trans.* VII. 422.

+**Brook trout.** The speckled trout (*Salvelinus fontinalis*), or related species of the genus *Salmo.*

1836 Dunlap *Mem. Water Drinker* I. 57, I am not one of your brook trout to be played back and forth with a hair line. **1839** Hoffman *Wild Scenes* 31 Storing our canoe with a good supply of brook and lake trout. **1856** *Spirit of Times* (N.Y.) 8 Nov. 161/1 The yellow perch ... are extinct already; as, surely and speedily, soon will be the beautiful red-spotted brook-trout. **1857** S. H. Hammond *Northern Scenes* 99 The sweetest fish that swims is the brook trout, weighing from a quarter of a pound down. *c***1908** F. M. Canton *Frontier Trails* 170 The golden trout of Alaska ... are about the size of the brook trout in Colorado and Wyoming.

+**Brook-trouting,** *vbl. n.* [f. prec.] Fishing for brook trout. — **1855** *Knickerb.* XLVI. 308 In brook-trouting it is always better to pass on, and not seek to get all the fish out of any one hole.

Brookweed. Water pimpernel, *Samolus valerandi.* — **1791** Muhlenberg *Index Florae* 164. **1817–8** Eaton *Botany* (1822) 446 Brookweed. ... Damp [grounds]. **1845** Lincoln *Botany* App. 162/1 Water pimpernell, brook-weed, ... racemes many-flowered. **1857** Gray *Botany* 274 Water Pimpernel. Brook-weed ... *S. Valerandi* ... Var. *Americanus.* ... Wet places; common. June–Sept.

+**Broom,** *v.* [Cf. Broomed *ppl. a.*] *tr.* To fray or splinter. — **1823** Cooper *Pilot* I. xvii. 228, I would rather drop my anchor on a bottom that won't broom a keel.

+**Broom birch.** The red birch (*Betula rubra*) or related species. — **1810** Michaux *Arbres* I. 26 *Red birch*, ... dans New York et Penn. *Broom birch*, nom secondaire. **1813** H. Muhlenberg *Cat. Plants* 88 Broom birch [or] poplar-leaved birch (*Betula populifolia*).

+**Broom brush. 1.** A shrubby American species of St. John's Wort. **2.** (See quotation.) — **(1) 1888** *New York World* (F.), The Shakers ... were the first to make brooms of broom brush, and, in fact, originated the entire broom business. **1893** *Amer. Folk-Lore* VI. 138 *Hypericum proliferum*, broom brush, West Va. **(2) 1889** *Cent.* 695/1 *Broom-brush* a whisk-broom or clothes-brush made from broom-corn.

+**Broom clover.** Wild indigo or yellow broom, *Baptisia tinctoria.* — **1790** S. Deane *New-Eng. Farmer* 25/2 Broom clover and mustard are said to afford bees an excellent pasture.

+**Broomcorn.** A variety of millet (*Sorghum vulgare*), the panicles of which are used as brooms, brushes, etc.

1781–2 Jefferson *Notes Va.* (1788) 40 Our farms produce wheat, rye, barley, oats, buck wheat, broom corn, and Indian corn. **1822** J. Woods *English Prairie* 302 Broom-corn ... resembles Indian corn, but is slighter. I have seen it upwards of ten feet high, the corn comes on the top of it. **1830** J. F. Watson *Philadelphia* 718 Charles Thomson ... well remembered the circumstance of the first introduction of broom corn into our country. Dr. B. Franklin chanced to see an imported corn whisk ... [and] espied a grain of it still attached to the stalk. This he took and planted, and so we at length have got it in abundance. **1850** [S. F. Cooper] *Rural Hours* 511 Every head of a family among the blacks had a little patch of land allotted to him expressly for the purpose of raising broom-corn. **1863** *Rep. Comm. Agric.* 134 Care, therefore, must be observed, not to allow scattering stalks of broom corn to be grown near the sugar-cane. **1879** B. F. Taylor *Summer-Savory* 177 A million or two of wild brooms, the clean and yellow plumage of the broom corn, ... that shall by and by be girded into besoms for kitchen floors and whisks for garments. **1891** *Century Mag.* Jan. 416 As they passed a field of broom-corn several men suddenly disappeared.

attrib. **1836** *Niles' Nat. Reg.* 3 Sept. 16/3 *Broom corn* speculations have been made in this region.

+**Broom crowberry.** A shrub (*Corema Conradii*) much resembling the common crowberry. — **1857** Gray *Botany* 393 *Corema*, Broom-Crowberry. ... Much-branched little shrubs. **1892** B. Torrey *Foot-Path Way* 80 Equally new to me ... were the broom crowberry and the greener kind of poverty grass.

+**Broomed,** *ppl. a.* [Cf. Broom *v.*] Frayed or splintered at the end so as to suggest a broom. — **1796** J. Dabney *Address* 25 Stir the liquor with a broomed stick, until it shall be found to ferment. **1850** Judd *R. Edney* xviii. 221 The logs, with the bark bruised off and the ends 'broomed' up. **1872** Huntington *Road-Master's Assistant* 95 When a rail gets badly broomed at the ends, it is taken to a shop and repaired by welding on a piece of bar-iron.

+**Broom grass.** One or other species of the genus *Andropogon* of perennial grasses; esp. broom sedge, *A. scoparius* or *A. macrourus.*

1793 *N.Y. State Soc. Arts* I. 181 Broomgrass, two species (*bromi*). **1829** Eaton *Botany* (ed. 5) 106 *Andropogon scoparius*, broom-grass ... *S.* **1853** Simms *Sword & Distaff* 215 Much of the roofing had decayed, and the openings were thatched with broom-grass and pine straw. **1854** — *Southward Ho* 276 A natural meadow ... was covered with a rank forest of broom-grass, parched and dried by the sun. **1889** Vasey *Agric. Grasses* 35 *Andropogon macrourus*, or heavy-topped broom grass, is frequent near the coast. **1901** Mohr *Plant Life Ala.* 336 Broom-Grass. ... Over the State, on poor sandy soil. Common everywhere.

+**Broom hickory.** A species of hickory (*Hicoria glabra*), formerly used for making brooms. — **1813** H. Muhlenberg *Cat. Plants* 88 Heart hickory, or Broom hickory. **1832** Browne *Sylva* 182 This tree is generally known in the United States by the name of Pignut and Hognut Hickory, sometimes of that of Broom Hickory. **1847** Darlington *Weeds & Plants* 306 Pig-nut Hickory. Broom Hickory. ... The young saplings of this species were much used, formerly, for making splint brooms. **1897** Sudworth *Arborescent Flora* 115 *Hicoria glabra*, Pignut (Hickory). ... Common names [include] ... Broom Hickory (Mo.).

+**Broom pine.** The long-leaved or Georgia pine, *Pinus palustris.* — **1791** Bartram *Travels* 58 The trees were tall, and generally of the species called Broompine. **1802** Ellicott *Journal* 279 The upland is generally of an inferior quality, producing little besides wire-grass, pitch-pine (*pinus*) and broom pine (*pinus palustris*). **1810** MICHAUX *Arbres* I. 16 Broom pine (*Pin à balais*). **1829** EATON *Botany* (ed. 5) 331 Long leaved, yellow pitch or broom pine. **1832** BROWNE *Sylva* 229 This invaluable tree ... is called Long-leaved Pine ... and Broom Pine.

* **Broomrape.** A species or plant of the genus *Orobanche*, parasitic on the roots of broom, clover, etc.

*c***1729** CATESBY *Carolina* I. 36 Broom-rape ... rises to the height of eight to ten inches; and is of a flesh-colour. **1833** EATON *Botany* (ed. 6) 242 *Orobanche uniflora*, squaw-root, broom rape, cancer-root. ... About 3 inches high, of a yellowish white color. S[outh]. **1840** DEWEY *Mass. Flowering Plants* 156 Broomrape. ... Being parasites they often destroy the plants they feed on. **1868** GRAY *Botany* 680 *Orobanche Minor*, Lesser Broom-rape, is parasitic on clover in the vicinity of Washington, ... and has been met with in New Jersey. **1890** *Cent.* 4159 *O. caryophyllacea* is the clove-scented broom-rape, growing on species of *Galium*.

+**Broom sedge.** Also *erron.* **-sage.**

1. A species of coarse grass of the genus *Andropogon* or *Aristida;* broom grass.

1819 'AGRICOLA' *Ess. Agriculture* 26 Worn-out fields, which have ... grown up in broom sedge, may be highly improved by ... ploughing them deep. **1834** MINOR *Diary* in *Atl. Mo.* XXVI. 339/2 Gullies, red hillsides, bare of soil—broom-sedge—persimmon, sassafras, ... —gave me a vivid reminiscence of my poor, good old commonwealth. **1849** *Rep. Comm. Patents: Agric.* (1850) 462 Corn brooms are driving broom-sedge, as an article for sweeping floors, out of every humble dwelling in the Union. **1860** ABBOTT *South & North* 181 Fields once fertile, now unfenced, abandoned, and covered with those evil harbingers—fox-tail and broom-sedge. **1875** *Field & Forest* I. 54 An economic use of *Andropogon Virginiacus*, called wrongly Broom Sedge, and used for making brooms in Virginia. **1889** VASEY *Agric. Grasses* 35 Broom Sedge ... is common on the Western prairies, growing in dense tufts.

2. Attrib. with *grass.*

1859 G. W. PERRY *Turpentine Farming* 9 Every kind of turf should be turned over, such as ... wire grass, savanna grass and broom-sage grass. **1897** *Outing* XXX. 68/1 The country was flat and sandy, alternating between pine forests and fields of broom-sedge grass.

+**Broomstraw.**

1. =BROOM GRASS. Also attrib. in fig. use.

1785 WASHINGTON *Diaries* II. 365 Had the Roots, shrubs (which had been grubbed) and tussics of broom Straw ... raked of[f] and burnt. **1837** *S. Lit. Messenger* III. 217 In the centre of a large field of broom-straw ... stood the house. **1839** BUEL *Farmer's Companion* 18 They still produce what we call hengrass, broom-straw, and ... a starveling pine or cedar bush. **1855** *S. Lit. Messenger* XXI. 222 A sham society, with 'broom-straw' aristocracy, whose wealth, refinement, and education the schoolmaster estimated as a mathematically minus quantity. **1869** TOURGEE *Toinette* xxviii. (1881) 291 A great arm-chair, made of broom-straw by some ingenious plantation hand. **1902** W. S. GORDON *Recoll. Lynchburg* 9 Gentle hills covered with young pines, sassafras bushes, and broom-straw.

2. A single stalk of this.

1845 J. J. HOOPER *Simon Sugg's Adv.* iii. 38 In two hours more he wont be able to step over the butt cut of a broomstraw. **1869** STOWE *Oldtown Folks* 391 Sam was beguiled to amuse himself by tickling his nose with a broom-straw. **1881** TOURGEE *'Zouri's Christmas* iv, From the interstices in which the broom-straws had been stuck now rose a fragrant steam.

* **Brother.**

1. Placed before a person's name as a designation, usually denoting membership in a religious body.

1640 *New Haven Col. Rec.* 33 Liberty granted to Mr. Gregson, bro: Andrewes and Goodman Warde. **1856** SIMMS *Charlemont* 62 Call me not Mr., I pray thee. ... If thou wilt call me Brother Cross, my heart shall acknowledge the bonds between us. **1872** EGGLESTON *End of World* 246, I don't believe in all of Brother Goshorn's nonsense about wearing veils and artificials.

+**2.** Applied by Indians to white men or to each other.

1684 I. MATHER *Providences* (1856) ii. 39 When the Indian was set free, he came to me, ... and said I was his brother. **1826** COOPER *Mohicans* xxviii, Let her be sent to my squaws, if she gives trouble to my brother. **1848** — *Oak Openings* I. 121 'Has my brother lost a warrior?' was the calm reply.

+**3.** A member of a college fraternity.

1779 in Shepardson *Phi Beta Kappa* (1915) 12 Brother: It is an uncommon pleasure which I feel in being able to address you by this tender appellation. *Ib.*, You are to become the brother of unalienable Brothers. **1899** A. H. QUINN *Penna. Stories* 74 He was a member of Kappa Phi, and ... he had a right to anything his brothers could give him.

Brother-chip. (See quot. 1848.) — **1848** BARTLETT 49 *Brother-chip*, a fellow-carpenter; in a more general sense, a person of the same trade. **1858** *Harper's Mag.* April 709 His friend, the lawyer, gave him a letter of introduction to a brother chip practicing at D—.

***Brotherhood. a.** A group or community of Christians of like belief; a benevolent society. **b.** A trade-union, esp. one of several unions of railroad employees. — **(a) 1723** *New-Eng. Courant* 9 Sept. 2 Some of our Clergy have asserted ... that they have Power to admit Members ..., without the Knowledge or Consent of the Brotherhood. **1750** WALKER *Journal* 16 March, A mill ... lately built by the Sect of People, who call themselves of the Brotherhood of Euphrates, and are commonly called the Duncards. **1891** *Atlantic Mo.* June 814/1 The colored people have developed a laudable disposition to take care of their own poor. ... Brotherhoods, Good Samaritan societies, and mutual benefit organizations are established. **(b) 1895** ROBINSON *Men Born Equal* 60 It used to be the case that any ... reasonably intelligent young fellow who went into railroading at the bottom and attended to his business was sure of promotion. ... But the brotherhoods have changed all that. *Ib.*, A young fellow ... has not been in the service long before the brotherhood is after him.

+**Brother Jonathan.** [See JONATHAN.]

The statement that the ordinary use of the phrase (see below) originated in Washington's reference to Jonathan Trumbull as 'Brother Jonathan' is of late appearance (1846) and not supported by any of the actual instances. (Cf. A. Matthews in *Publ. Mass. Hist. Soc.* VII. 94–125.) The following is a natural example of the collocation: **1771** COPLEY in *Copley-Pelham Lett.* 141, I have wrote to Brother Jona'n [*sc.* Jonathan Clarke] and it is now late.

1. The typical representative of the New Englanders or Yankees, or of the American people as a whole.

1802 [J.] T. CALLENDER *Lett. to Hamilton* ii. 20, I am not ... very much alarmed at the ... furious thunderbolts of brother Jonathan. **1812** PAULDING (*title*), The Diverting History of John Bull and Brother Jonathan. **1815** *Mass. Spy* 17 May (Th.), [In verse is told an incident] highly characteristic of John Bull and Brother Jonathan. **1815** HUMPHREYS *Yankee in England* 19 You were a nation wiser than brother Jonathan. **1817** PAULDING *Lett. from South* I. 83 When they [the aborigines] have exhausted one hunting-ground, [they] pull up stakes, and incontinently march off to another ... where game is plenty. So with honest brother Jonathan. **1824** *Ann. 18th Congress* 1 Sess. 2024 Suppose the West procures the passage [of the protective tariff], do you suppose Brother Jonathan will not reap the advantages of it? The people of New England have the necessary capital. **1828** A. LAWRENCE *Diary & Corr.* 83, I wish to see you, as long as you live, a well-bred, upright Yankee. Brother Jonathan should never forget his self-respect. **1830** S. BRECK in *Recollections* (1877) 24 Every vulgar story told by John Bull ... was implicitly believed by Brother Jonathan. **1833** *Niles' Reg.* XLIV. 321/2 'Brother Jonathan,' we think, will soon grapple one of them [*i.e.* sea-serpents]—for he fears nothing that swims. **1854** *Harper's Mag.* IX. 674/2 The colonists, who ... have petitioned their government to forbid the further encroachments of enterprising Brother Jonathan on these vast preserves. **1865** *U.S. Service Mag.* IV. 27 Brother Jonathan is dead. Born in another age, and of the day of small things, he has passed away. **1871** *Overland Mo.* March 273/1 Since that day, a great many people have found 'Brother Jonathan' a very helpful relative in time of need.

2. An individual Yankee or American.

1780 *Royal Gazette* (N.Y.) 5 July 3/1 Many of the republican families in East Jersey have lost their daddies and brother Jonathans. **1788** *Amer. Museum* Aug. 184/2 A person whispered his companion, ... [who replied,] 'By nowns, brother Jonathan, there would not be a single point of the compass that would suit him.' **1819** *Plough Boy* I. 191 The balloon landed again the same evening in the garden of colonel Johnson, at Bozrah, Connecticut. Brother Jonathan was not a little surprised at the ærial visitant. **1825** NEAL *Bro. Jonathan* II. 46 His look was that of a lubberly country boy—a 'jinooine' Brother Jonathan—going forth from his home, to 'undertake' a school for the winter.

‖**Brother Jonathanism.** [f. prec.] Exaggerated nationalism. — **1886** RICHARDSON *Amer. Lit.* (1891) II. 295 American literature, between 1775 and 1825, veered swiftly to and fro between humble subservience to European ... leadership, and a self-conscious indignant 'Brother-Jonathanism.'

Brotherly, *a.*

1. *The City of Brotherly Love,* Philadelphia.

A translation of the name after its sense in Greek.

1799 *Aurora* (Phila.) 28 Sept. (Th.), A great wonder appeared in the city which is called Brotherly Love. **1820** *Amer. Farmer* I. 395 Young 'Virginia Doctors,' ... are made the scape goats in the city of Brotherly love, for all sorts of devilment. **1837** *S. Lit. Messenger* III. 260/1 An affair which has just been exciting a good deal of commotion in our excellent city of brotherly love. **1855** *Knickerb.* XLV. 216 A recent gossippy letter from a genial friend in the 'city of brotherly-love.' **1866** GREGG *Life in Army* 114 The staid and regular character of the city of Brotherly Love. **1887** *Harper's Mag.* Oct. 658/1 There arrived a dog ... from the City of Brotherly Love.

2. *Brotherly-love vireo* or *greenlet,* an eastern species of vireo, *V. Philadelphicus.*

1874 COUES *Birds N.W.* 97, 233. **1882** *Century Mag.* Jan. 361/2 New England song-birds [include] ... Brotherly love vireo, solitary vireo. **1891** *Cent.* 6763/3 *Philadelphia vireo*, the brotherly-love greenlet, discovered [*c.* 1851] by John Cassin near the city of that name.

Brougham. [Named after Lord *Brougham*, 1778–1868.] A light, closed, one-horse carriage. {1851–} Also, an automobile of a type resembling this. — **1865** *Atlantic Mo.* XV. 61 Nor barouche, nor mail-phaeton, nay, nor soft-cushioned brougham delighted me. **1886** *Outing* VIII. 62/1 Before the glories of dress coaches ... had been spoiled by such economical expedients as landaus and broughams. **1897** *Ib.* XXX. 640/1 Their new premises, Broadway, New York ... are in evidence, with greatly increased ... stock of broughams, cabriolets, victorias [etc.].

1903 *Encycl. Americana* II. s.v. *Automobiles*, Its success has been demonstrated in the form of runabouts, broughams, and similar urban automobiles.

***Brown,** *n.* **1.** A piece or kind of brown holland cloth. **2.** A brown-skinned person; a mulatto. — (1) **1817** *Cape-Fear Recorder* 5 April, A handsome assortment of Linens, . . . Ticklenburgs, Osnaburgs, Browns, and Burlaps. (2) **1862** *Independent* 10 April, The jealousy between the blacks and browns, which has done so much mischief in the West Indies, is not fostered by American people of color.

***Brown,** *a.* (and *adv.*).

1. In the distinctive names of many species of birds, fishes, etc., and trees or plants.

For the more important of these, as BROWN ASH, BAT, BEAR, BERRY, CAT (FISH), etc., see the separate entries following.

(1) **1709** LAWSON *Carolina* 159 The brown Pearch, which some call Welch-men, are the largest sort of Pearches that we have, and very firm, white and sweet fish. **1736** CATESBY *Carolina* II. 45 *Vipera fusca.* The Brown Viper. . . . They are found in Virginia and Carolina, in the last of which Places they are called the Trunchion Snake. They prey on Lizards, Efts, and other Animals. **1778** CARVER *Travels* 471 There are three sorts of partridges here, the brown, the red, and the black, the first of which are most esteemed. **1814** MITCHILL *Fishes N.Y.* 369 *Gadus tomcodus fuscus*, or brown tom cod; with the back and upper parts of the sides a mottled brown or olive. **1839** AUDUBON *Ornith. Biog.* V. 22 Brown Song Sparrow, *Fringilla Cinerea*, . . . inhabits the woody districts of the Columbia . . . and continues as far south as Upper California. **1846** SAGE *Scenes Rocky Mts.* vi, The black wolf . . . nearly equals the white and brown in size. **1850** [S. F. COOPER] *Rural Hours* 252 The large, brown wasps, so abundant elsewhere, are scarce about the village. **1881** *Amer. Naturalist* XV. 212 A very common bird from the mountains to the coast, in California, is the brown towhee (*Pipilo fuscus*). **1882** GODFREY *Nantucket* 157 Large numbers of the upland gray-back, otherwise known as the brown-bird, made their appearance here on the marshes. *Ib.* 339 Fish which live near the shore . . . are called 'shoal-water cod,' 'Shore cod,' 'Inshore cod,' 'Worm-cod,' 'Clam-cod,' 'Brown cod.'

(2) **1817-8** EATON *Botany* (1822) 182 *Arum atrorubens*, brown dragon. **1842** BUCKINGHAM *Slave States* I. 177 The Georgia pitch-pine is abundant, and it is . . . called by a great variety of names, such as the southern, the red, the brown, the yellow, and the long-leaved pine. **1857** GRAY *Botany* 544 *Agrostis canina*, Brown Bent-Grass, . . . grows in meadows, &c., E. New England: scarce. Nat. from Europe. **1897** SUDWORTH *Arborescent Flora* 30 *Pinus palustris*, Longleaf Pine. . . . Common names [include] . . . Brown Pine (Tenn.); Hard Pine (Ala., Miss., La.). *Ib.* 115 Pignut Hickory; . . . [also called] Brown Hickory.

b. In adjectival compounds, as *brown-headed*, *-masked*, *-spotted*, used to form specific names.

1810 WILSON *Ornithology* II. 105 Brown-Headed Nuthatch, *Sitta Pusilla*, . . . is chiefly an inhabitant of Virginia and the southern states. **1828** BONAPARTE *Synopsis* 358 The Brown-masked Gull, *Larus capistratus*, . . . not very rare during autumn on the Delaware, and especially the Chesapeake. **1839** STORER *Mass. Reptiles* 252 *Salamandra maculata*, the brown spotted Salamander, . . . feed[s] upon insects. **1858** BAIRD *Birds Pacific R.R.* 106 *Sphyrapicus Thyroideus*, Brown-headed woodpecker, . . . [inhabits] Cascade and Coast ranges of California and Oregon.

***2.** Brown-skinned; mulatto. (Cf. BROWN *n.* 2.)

1838 C. GILMAN *Recoll.* 270 (*note*), I have known *brown people*, as they are termed, feel too great a contempt for a black leader to become a class-leader. **1898** DUNBAR *Folks from Dixie* 4 Her brown skin was as smooth and soft as silk. *Ib.*, Do not gather from this that it was Sam alone who paid his *devoirs* to this brown beauty.

3. *To do (up) brown.* **a.** To 'roast' thoroughly; to deal severely with. {1837-40}

1846 *Knickerb.* XXVII. 173 His enemies are getting the dripping-pan and basting-spoon ready for his roasting, and he is at that moment being regularly 'done brown.' **1851** *Arkansas Doctor* 162 (Th.), From the way the negro acted and looked at me, I thought he was doin' up the rascal very brown. **1854** *Weekly Oregonian* 17 June (Th.), All I have got to say is, you did me up brown,—a good deal browner than I expected. **1857** *Ill. Agric. Soc. Trans.* II. 232, I'm afeard so—mine are 'done brown' now—pretty much used up, I tell you. **1902** HARBEN *Abner Daniel* 55 Well, you will before I'm through with you, and I'll do you up brown.

+**b.** To do thoroughly or properly; to do to perfection.

1840 *Picayune* 15 Aug. 2 [It was] the most magnificent . . . Flounder that we ever saw. . . . We sent it to Hewlitt's, where it was 'done up brown.' *c***1849** [PAIGE] *Dow's Sermons* I. 188 Nature seemed to take particular pains to have everything as it should be—'done up brown,' as they say in the Bowery. **1850** N. KINGSLEY *Diary* 160 Worked down on the bar at clearing off to be ready for washing on Monday, they are doing it up brown and no mistake. **1851** A. O. HALL *Manhattaner* 82 *Manhattaner.* Is litigation attended here with much formality? *Red-faced Clerk.* We do it up here as brown as they do it anywhere. *a***1859** *Southern Sketches* 57 (B.), Well, I think Ellen's a doin' it up brown! There'll be another weddin' soon, I guess. **1873** *Newton Kansan* 30 Jan. 3/2 The play . . . will be done up brown.

‖**4.** (Meaning obscure.)

1848 [N. AMES] *Childe Harvard* 94 But then, they reap the harvest,—glory, too!—and the Historian will write it 'brown.'

+**Brown ash.** The elder-leaved American ash, *Fraxinus sambucifolia.* — **1832** BROWNE *Sylva* 157 In . . . the provinces of New Brunswick and Nova Scotia the White Ash and the Black Ash, which is sometimes called Water Ash and Brown Ash, are the most abundant in the forests. **1874** *Vt. Bd. Agric. Rep.* II. 549 In Whiting part of this swamp produces brown ash, birch, soft maple and elm.

Brownback. +**1.** The red-breasted snipe or dowitcher in summer plumage. +**2.** The largest known species of godwit. — (1) **1844** *Nat. Hist. N.Y., Zoology* II. 255 The Dowitchee, Red-breasted Snipe, Quail Snipe, or Brown-back, arrives on the coast of New-York towards the latter part of April. **1872** COUES *N. Amer. Birds* 252 *Macrorhamphus*, . . . Gray Snipe, Brown-back. (2) **1889** *Cent.* 697/3 *Brownback*, . . . a name of the great marbled godwit, *Limosa fedoa.*

Brown bat. (See quotations.) — **1842** *Nat. Hist. N.Y., Zoology* I. 8 The Little Brown Bat, *Vespertilio subulatus. Ib.* 9 The Little Brown Bat appears to be subject to great variations in size and color. **1867** *Amer. Naturalist* I. 284 The well-known little Brown Bat (*V. subulatus* Say) is generally and abundantly distributed throughout the territory [of Arizona].

Brown bear. +A variety of the common black bear (*Ursus americanus*) having a brownish coat.

1805 LEWIS in *Ann. 9th Congress* 2 Sess. 1066 Some brown, white, and grizly bear, deer and lynx. **1807** GASS *Journal* 84 Here we killed a very large brown bear, which measured three feet five inches round the head. **1817** S. BROWN *Western Gaz.* 199 The great brown bear of the Upper Missouri, is a terrible animal. **1837** PECK *New Guide* 42 The brown bear is still hunted in some parts of the Western States. **1874** GLISAN *Jrnl. Army Life* 493 There is an abundance of game along the Coast, such as . . . brown and cinnamon bear.

+**Brown berry.** (See quotations.) — **1785** WASHINGTON *Diaries* II. 342 Planted eight young Pair Trees . . . in the following places . . . 3 Brown Berries in the west square in the Second plat. **1806** CLARK in *Lewis & C. Exped.* (1905) IV. 13 The Vineing or low brown berry, a light brown berry rather larger and much the Shape of a black haw.

+**Brown Bet.** [Cf. BETTY, and BLACK BETTY.] A brown jug. — **1807** J. R. SHAW *Life* (1930) By tipping me a little out of brown Bet, which contained some double fortified stimulous [etc].

+**Brown Betty.** A pudding of apples and bread crumbs. — **1864** *Yale Lit. Mag.* XXIX. 187 [In training] tea, coffee, pies and 'brown Betty' must next be sacrificed. **1884** F. E. OWENS *Cook Book* 192 [Recipe for] Brown Betty. **1911** WHITE *Bobby Orde* x. 126 It was the season of apple-sauce with cinnamon, and baked apples . . . , and apple-tapioca and Brown Betty.

Brown bread. Bread of a brownish color; +*spec.* a bread composed of wheat (usu. graham) flour and rye or corn meal, molasses, soda and water or milk, not baked but steamed for several hours.

'The component parts of the American comestible of this name are two-thirds maize meal and one-third rye meal; formerly confined to New England, and now, in consequence, known in other parts of the Union as Boston-bread' (F.). Cf. BOSTON BROWN BREAD.

1719 *Weekly Mercury* 29 Dec. 2/2 Price Currant at Philadelphia. Middleing Bread, 14*s.* per Hundred. Brown —, 12*s.* per Hundred. **1746** *Boston Selectmen* 7 Jan. 150 A six penny loaf (old tenor) of Major Thwing's brown bread [etc.]. **1763** *Ib.* 3 Jan. 242 Loaf of brown bread [must be] 3/4 wheat the other 1/4 rye. **1832** L. M. CHILD *Frugal Housewife* 76 Six quarts of meal will make two good sized loaves of Brown Bread. **1869** STOWE *Oldtown Folks* 78 He had a vast internal capacity for the stowing away of beans and brown bread. *c***1891** 'THANET' *Otto the Knight*, etc. 162 'The brown bread, ma'am,' sobbed Mizzie. . . . 'I put it in the steamer, like—you all—tole me; but—it dropped through an' spread out.' **1904** M. E. WALLER *Wood-Carver* 43 Hot roast potatoes, fresh brown-bread, and a slice of Uncle Shim's well-cured bacon.

+**Brown cat, catfish.** (See quotations.) — **1820** RAFINESQUE in *Western Rev.* II. 359 *Silurus nebulosus* . . . is a large fish, from two to four feet long, and commonly called Yellow Cat, Mud Cat, and Brown Cat; but these names are common to other species. — **1842** *Nat. Hist. N.Y., Zoology* IV. 184 The Brown Catfish, *Pimelodus pullus*, . . . is very common in Lake Pleasant, Lake Janet, and many other lakes in the northern districts of the State.

+**Brown corn.** An early maturing variety of Indian corn. — **1849** *Rep. Comm. Patents: Agric.* (1850) 87 The common eight-rowed, mixed with a kind called the 'Brown corn,' does the best. **1856** *Ib.* p. xi, The Improved King Philip or Brown Corn . . . was extensively disseminated in all the States north of New Jersey, and throughout the mountainous districts of Pennsylvania, Maryland, and Virginia.

+**Brown crane.** The sand-hill crane (see quot. 1890). — **1805** LEWIS in *L. & Clark Exped.* (1904) II. 255 Saw several of the large brown or sandhill Crain today with their young. **1813** WILSON *Ornithology* VIII. 22 It is . . . probable that the . . . Brown Crane (*Ardea Canadensis*), is nothing more than the young of the Whooping Crane. **1852** BAIRD in Stansbury *Gt. Salt Lake* 319 *Grus canadensis*, Brown Crane, occurs in large flocks throughout the whole interior of North America. **1874** GLISAN *Jrnl. Army Life* 493 There is an abundance of game along the coast, such as . . . brown crane. **1890** *Cent.* 5330/3 *Grus canadensis* . . . properly applies only to the northern brown or sand-hill crane, somewhat smaller and otherwise different from the southern brown or sand-hill crane, *Grus mexicanus* or *G. pratensis.*

+**Brown creeper.** A variety of the common tree creeper, *Certhia familiaris.*

1808 WILSON *Ornithology* I. 122 The Brown Creeper is an extremely active and restless little bird. **1828** BONAPARTE *Synopsis* 95 The Brown Creeper, . . . inhabits the north of both continents; more common in . . . the western and northern states, than in Pennsylvania. **1837** J. L. WILLIAMS *Florida* 74 There are many birds in Florida, . . . Nuthatch, . . . Brown Creeper [etc.]. **1869** *Amer. Naturalist* III. 511 The Brown Creeper, and the Hairy and Downy Woodpecker, etc., in Massachusetts, are represented . . . by different sets of individuals. **1885** *Harper's Mag.* Dec. 78/2 With the insectivorous birds, such as the nut-hatch, the brown creeper, . . . the food supply is not so materially affected by the deep snows. **1892** TORREY *Foot-Path Way* 49 Throughout the winter, brown creepers . . . were surprisingly abundant.

+**Brown curlew.** (See quotations.) — **1731** CATESBY *Carolina* I. 83 *Numenius fuscus.* The Brown Curlew. . . . They . . . come annually about the middle of September, and frequent the watery Savannas in numerous flights, continuing about six weeks, and then retire. **1805** LEWIS in *L. & Clark Exped.* (1904) II. 119 Brown curloos, a small species of curloo or plover of a brown colour about the size of a common snipe and not unlike it.

+**Brown eagle. a.** The osprey, *Pandion haliaëtus.* **b.** The bald eagle, *Haliaëtus leucocephalus.* — **(a) 1815** *Mass. H.S. Coll.* 2 Ser. IV. 274 It is probably the brown, or 'fisher eagle,' we have noticed in the winter season. **(b) 1844** *Nat. Hist. N.Y., Zoology* II. 5 The Brown or Bald Eagle . . . found in every part of the United States, feeding upon fish, wild fowl and small quadrupeds.

+**Brown flycatcher.** (See quot. 1730.) — *c***1730** CATESBY *Carolina* I. 54 *Muscicapa fusca.* The little brown Fly-catcher. . . . All the upper part of the body [is] of a dark ash-colour. . . . These breed in Carolina, and retire Southward in Winter. **1832** WILLIAMSON *Maine* I. 143 The brown Fly-catcher . . . caught them [=flies] and cleared them all out of the chamber in one day.

+**Brown hawk. a.** The sharp-shinned or pigeon hawk, *Accipiter (Falco) fuscus.* **b.** (See quotations.) — **(a) 1828** BONAPARTE *Synopsis* 434 The American Brown Hawk, *Falco fuscus.* **1839** PEABODY *Mass. Birds* 266 The American Brown, or Slate Colored Hawk, *Falco fuscus* . . . is said to abound in the thinly settled parts of the southern states, where it often makes great havoc among the domestic poultry. **(b)** [**1874** COUES *Birds N.W.* 357, I took no specimens [of Swainson's buzzard] in the melanistic state of plumage in which the bird has been described as another supposed species (*B[uteo] insignatus*).] **1881** *Amer. Naturalist* XV. 209 The brown hawk (*Buteo insignatus*) is not . . . [seen often] owing to its frequenting quiet secluded places.

Brownism. [From the name of Robert *Brown*, 1550–1633.] The ecclesiastical system based upon the beliefs and principles advocated by Robert Brown. {*a*1617–} — **1670** R. MATHER *Journal* 82 He was for the true Congregational-way, in opposition to both the Extremes of Brownism on the one hand, and Presbyterianism on the other hand. **1702** C. MATHER *Magnalia* (1853) I. iii. 63 The leaven of that rigid thing they call Brownism has prevailed sometimes. **1764** HUTCHINSON *Hist. Mass.* (1795) I. iv. 370 This was called the middle way between brownism and presbyterianism.

***Brownist.** [Cf. prec.] A believer in the ecclesiastical principles of Robert Brown.

1637 MORTON *New Canaan* I. iii, This mortality was not ended when the Brownists of new Plimouth were setled at Patuxet in New England. **1642** T. LECHFORD *Plain Dealing* 22 Another of them for saying one of the Ministers of the Bay was a Brownist, or had a Brownisticall head, . . . was whipt. **1702** C. MATHER *Magnalia* (1853) I. iii. 64, I must also advise you to abandon, avoid and shake off the name of Brownist. **1787** BENTLEY *Diary* I. 64 In this Town is an Assembly of Brownists so called from the head of the sect.

Brownistic(al), *a.* Pertaining to Brownism. {1636–} — **1642** [see prec.]. **1702** C. MATHER *Magnalia* (1853) I. ii. 115 About the time of Governour Bradford's death, religion it self had like to have died in that colony, through a libertine and Brownistick spirit then prevailing among the people.

+**Brown lark.** The pipit or titlark, *Anthus ludovicianus.* — **1812** WILSON *Ornithology* V. 89 Brown Lark: *Alauda rufa* . . . flies in loose scattered flocks; is strongly attached to flat, newly-ploughed fields. **1839** PEABODY *Mass. Birds* 317 The Brown Lark, *Anthus spinoletta*, is one of those birds which arrive from the north. **1874** COUES *Birds N.W.* 231 Brown Lark, [is] abundant; migratory; breeds in great numbers above timber-line.

Brown loam. Brown soil comprised of clay and sand. Used attrib. — **1883** SMITH *Geol. Survey Ala.* 206 *Sandy Brown-loam Soil* (Trenton) from three miles west of Birmingham, Jefferson county. . . . Color, brown at top, passing into yellow at three inches depth. *Ib.* 406 The brown-loam lands of Yellow creek bottom make a tenth of the region reported upon.

+**Brown meal.** (See quotation.) — **1839** MARRYAT *Diary* II. 35 In the West, when you stop at an inn, they say—'What will you have? Brown Meal and common doings, or white wheat and chicken fixings';—that is, 'Will you have pork and brown bread, or white bread and fried chicken?'

+**Brown pelican.** A species of pelican, *Pelecanus fuscus.* — **1823** James *Exped. Rocky Mts.* I. 266 Brown pelican. **1828** BONAPARTE *Synopsis* 401 The Brown Pelican . . . [is] common in southern states, where it breeds. **1835** AUDUBON *Ornith. Biog.* III. 376 The Brown Pelican, which is one of the most interesting of our American birds, is a constant resident in the Floridas. **1870** *Amer. Naturalist* IV. 58 The Brown Pelican I have not known to occur previously so far north [*i.e.* Mass.].

Brown rat. The Norway, or wharf, rat, *Rattus norvegicus* (*Mus decumanus*). — **1826** J. GODMAN *Nat. Hist.* II. 78 The common, brown, or Norway rat, . . . [is] extensively diffused over this country. **1842** *Nat. Hist. N.Y., Zoology* I. 79 The Brown Rat . . . is frequently known as the Dock Rat. **1857** *Rep. Comm. Patents: Agric.* 109 Farmers are occasionally surprised by the sudden and entire disappearance of the brown-rats from their houses, where they were abundant a short time before. **1898** *Dept. Agric. Yearbook* 91 The brown rat . . . reached the eastern coast of the United States about 1775.

Brown roll. (Cf. BROWN *n.* 1.) — **1792** *Ann. 2nd Congress* 1026 It would . . . be good policy to raise the duty . . . [on] brown rolls, bagging, and upon all other linens.

+**Brown snake.** A snake of a brown color, usually the *Haldea striatula.* — **1832** WILLIAMSON *Maine* I. 170 Eight species of Serpents have been seen among us: viz. . . . 5. the little brown Snake. **1839** STORER *Mass. Reptiles* 223 *Coluber ordinatus.* Lin. The little brown Snake. **1842** *Nat. Hist. N.Y., Zoology* III. 46 The Small Brown Snake, *Tropidonotus dekayi*, . . . has been noticed in Massachusetts, Michigan and Louisiana. **1868** *Amer. Naturalist* II. 136 On opening a large Black-snake . . . a full-sized Brown-snake (*Tropidonotus occipitomaculatus*) was found in its stomach. **1890** *Cent.* 5724/3 Brown snake, *Haldea striatula* of the southern United States.

+**Brown snapper.** A brownish-colored fish (*Epinephelus morio*), found in the south Atlantic and Gulf coast waters. — **1884** GOODE *Nat. Hist. Aquat. Anim.* 410 The Red Grouper . . . north of Florida . . . is called the 'Brown Snapper,' or 'Red-bellied Snapper.' **1885** C. F. HOLDER *Marvels of Animal Life* 176 Snappers, red and brown.

+**Brownstone, Brown-stone, Brown stone.**

1. Various kinds of brown sandstone extensively used as a building material; also, a piece of this.

1836 *Knickerb.* VIII. 390 His poor remains may be found in one corner of a doctor's garden—a brown stone at his head and foot. **1851** J. H. ROSS *In New York* 207 The stone on which the man was at work was a brown, or what is frequently called red stone. **1857** C. VAUX *Villas* 69 Houses that are built of squared brown stone have a melancholy, dingy, monotonous, and uninteresting look. **1871** *N.Y. Tribune* 19 Jan. (De Vere), The brown stone, now so fashionable, is perhaps the most perishable of all materials used in New York house-building. **1886** *Century Mag.* Feb. 550/1 We once admired our brown-stone very heartily; it became, indeed, an almost proverbial synonym for all that is desirable and elegant. **1894** 'O. HENRY' *Cabbages & Kings* 244 The Casa Morena . . . was a building of brown stone, luxurious as a palace in its interior.

2. Attrib., usually in the sense: Made or built of brownstone.

1860 HOLLAND *Miss Gilbert's Career* 375 If we look in upon a New York household, situated in the most opulent and fashionable quarter of the city, we shall find in the brown-stone dwelling of Mrs. Kilgore [etc.]. **1868** *Rep. Comm. Agric.* 191 The material is pressed brick, with brownstone base, belts, trimmings, and cornices. **1876** INGRAM *Centennial Exp.* 69 The Public Ledger Building . . . is an imposing brown-stone structure. **1883** *Harper's Mag.* Sept. 561/1 People talk as if . . . the brown-stone high-stoop house with its bloated detail . . . had been done by educated architects. **1884** *Century Mag.* March 678/2 Its ambitious citizens begin to erect shapeless, roofless houses, . . . which . . . they paint as nearly as possible brown-stone color. **1891** *Scribner's Mag.* X. 118 The distant brown-stone spire seemed melting in the fluid yellow of the west. *a***1906** 'O. HENRY' *Trimmed Lamp*, etc. 55 He lived in rented rooms in one of the decayed old family brownstone mansions in one of the quiet streets east of the park.

b. *Brownstone front*, a house front of this material, or a house with such a front. Also attrib. in sense: Having a front of brown stone.

(a) 1866 J. E. COOKE *Surry* 361 What would you give to be looked at in that manner by a Virginia girl, good friend? I think it would be better than to have a 'brown-stone front' on Fifth or any other avenue. **1872** HOWELLS *Wedding Journey* 47 At last they were aware . . . of seeking the nearest car by endless blocks of brownstone fronts, . . . with their eternal brown-stone flights of steps. **1880** *Scribner's Mo.* Oct. 855/1 A few pioneer brown-stone fronts, with their great Doric high-stoops . . . stare, tenantless, out of blank, astonished windows. **1883** *Century Mag.* Oct. 859/2 That series of architectural horrors known as 'brown-stone fronts.' **1887** *Harper's Mag.* Nov. 947/1 The dream that life is wholly an affair of smooth-swept flags and imbecile brown-stone fronts. **1906** 'O. HENRY' *Four Million* 177 Dulcie went up to her room—the third floor back in a West Side brownstone-front.

(b) 1870 'F. FERN' *Ginger-Snaps* 308 Everybody's baby in the United States, without distinction of brown-stone-front houses. **1884** *Century Mag.* March 678/2 The place which the brown-stone-front house fills in the history of our domestic architecture. **1909** 'O. HENRY' *Options* 22 The (so-called) Vallambrosa Apartment House . . . is composed of two old-fashioned, brownstone-front residences welded into one.

3. *attrib.* Belonging or pertaining to the well-to-do class.

1865 'G. HAMILTON' *New Atmosphere* 32 The brown-stone friends are shocked and scandalized, which is probably the best thing that could happen to them. **1873** *Winfield* (Kansas) *Courier* 15 Feb. 1/4 There has been some poker in the Manhattan Club, but the brownstone members of that institution have pretty generally attempted to keep it a secret. **1888** BRYCE *Amer. Commonwealth* II. III. lxii. 443 *n.*, The so-called 'brownstone districts' in New York City have, I believe, good [political] Machines. **1909** *N.Y. Sun* 3 Nov. 6 The 'brownstone vote,' as it is called, is cast as completely as is the vote of the most crowded tenement house districts.

Brown stout. A variety of porter made from brown malt. {1803}— **1800** *Columbian Centinel* 25 Jan. 3/3 For Sale, a few Casks of excellent Brown Stout. **1861** *Vanity Fair* 23 March 134/2 That person ... produced all that was necessary to satisfy hunger or thirst, in the shape of sandwiches, brown-stout, [etc.].

Brown sugar. Cane sugar in an unrefined or partly refined state. {1704-}

1725 *New-Eng. Courant* 5-12 April 2/2 To be sold ... Powder Sugar, all sorts of Brown Sugar, fine and course Sirrup. **1795** *Ann. 3rd Congress* 1085 People who now buy loaf sugar, would then buy brown sugar. **1820** *Hillsborough* (N.C.) *Recorder* 10 May, They have on consignment and for sale ... 3 hogsheads of Brown Sugar. **1860** S. MORDECAI *Virginia* 323 Brown sugar sold at twenty-five cents or more per pound. *a***1862** THOREAU *Maine Woods* 246 They were unwilling to spare more than four pounds of brown sugar. **1917** *Jrnl. Home Econ.* IX. 375 The English account suggests using brown sugar, but this was not found advisable in the experiments. It gives a darker color to the jam.

+**Brown thrasher.** [See THRASHER.] The common thrasher or sandy mockingbird, *Harporhynchus rufus.*

1810 WILSON *Ornithology* II. 83 [The] Ferruginous Thrush, *Turdus Rufus*, ... is the Brown Thrush, or Thrasher of the middle and eastern states. **1824** BRYANT *Rivulet* 13 List the brown thrasher's vernal hymn. **1839** PEABODY *Mass. Birds* 300 The Brown Thrush or Thrasher, ... must be regarded as the finest of our singing birds. **1854** THOREAU *Walden* 171 Near at hand, upon the topmost spray of a birch, sings the brown-thrasher—or red mavis, as some love to call him—all the morning. **1883** *Century Mag.* Sept. 684/1 Years pass without my finding a brown-thrasher's nest.

transf. **1850** C. MATHEWS *Moneypenny* 9 Yes, my little brown-thrasher, said the other.

+**Brown thrush.** =BROWN THRASHER.

1805 LEWIS in *L. & Clark Exped.* (1905) VI. 190, 18th [April] ... the brown thrush or mocking bird has appeared. **1810, 1839** [see prec.]. **1857** S. H. HAMMOND *Northern Scenes* 28 You will hear the voice of the catbird, the brown thrush, the chewink. **1868** *Amer. Naturalist* I. 143 We also welcome the Red Mavis, or Brown Thrush, to the hedges. **1885** M. THOMPSON *Byways & Bird Notes* 156 The brown-thrush, next to the mocking-bird, [is] the most famous singer of our woods.

+**Brown titlark.** A brown titling or pipit. — **1831** AUDUBON *Ornith. Biog.* I. 49 The Brown Titlark, *Anthus Spinoletta*, ... is met with in every portion of the United States which I have visited. **1844** *Nat. Hist. N.Y., Zoology* II. 76 The Little Brown Titlark winters in Louisiana, and as far south as Brazil.

***Browse,** *n.* The small shoots, twigs, etc., of trees and shrubs upon which horses and cattle may feed. {-1837}

1721 DUDLEY in *Phil. Trans.* XXXI. 168 In the Winter they [*sc.* moose] live upon Browse, or the tops of Bushes and young Trees. **1789** *Mass. H.S. Coll.* IV. 145 In it there is not only the browse, common to all wood lands, but a full supply of common plants. **1827** COOPER *Prairie* i, All old journeyers, like myself, know the virtue of sweet water, and a good browse for the cattle. **1847** *Knickerb.* XXIX. 201 During the most of the year they [=cattle] range at large, and live on browse and wild grass. **1857** *Lawrence* (Kansas) *Republican* 11 June 4 Part [of the stock] lived upon 'browse.' **1866** *Rep. Indian Affairs* 299 Their ponies are small-sized, but very hardy, capable of living in winter in thick timber on browse. **1876** *Vt. Bd. Agric. Rep.* III. 74 As browse grew scarce, they were under the necessity, when there was a scarcity of hay, to resort to the feeding of grain of some sort. **1884** EGGLESTON in *Century Mag.* Jan. 443 In all the colonies the wild grass and the browse of the woods was the main dependence. *a***1904** WHITE *Blazed Trail Stories* ix. 162 His two ponies cropped browse and pawed for grass.

***Browse,** *v. tr.* To provide cattle with twigs, branches, etc. {-1669} — **1819** C. B. JOHNSON *Letters fr. Penna.* 75 It frequently occurs ... that his cattle are fed principally with the branches of trees, which he cuts down for that purpose, and which they appear to relish tolerably well: this is called browsing. **1876** *Vt. Bd. Agric. Rep.* III. 74 It was customary, in years past, when farmers were short of hay, to browse their cattle, as it was called; they took them to the woods, where they had been getting wood, and ... felled trees on purpose for the brush, to use as feed for their stock.

+**Bruised,** *ppl. a. slang.* Intoxicated. — *a***1856** *Burlington Sentinel* in Hall *Coll. Words* (ed. 2) 461 We give a list of a few of the various words and phrases which have been in use ... to signify some stage of inebriation: ... Boosy, bruised, screwed [etc.].

***Bruiser.**

+**1.** A rowdy; a tough.

'A generic name in large cities for a rowdy or bully. Sometimes, however, the term has been limited in its application to a particular band of ruffians. This was the case once in Baltimore' (F.).

In England {1744-} a professional boxer or prize fighter.

1836 J. HILDRETH *Campaigns Rocky Mts.* I. 237 From this I imagined that he was a regular bruiser, and no one cared to oppose him. **1860** EMERSON *Cond. of Life* 55 The 'bruisers,' who have run the gauntlet of caucus and tavern through the county or the state. **1875** *Scribner's Mo.* X. 267 'Bruisers' from New York and 'plug uglies' from Philadelphia ... swooped down, a hideous brood, upon the infant city. **1887** *Courier-Journal* 20 Jan. 1/7 The hall of the House was well supplied with local Republican thugs and toughs this morning. These bruisers were well distributed throughout the hall. **1903** A. H. LEWIS *Boss* 49 There began to collect about me a coterie of halfway bruisers.

+**2.** (See quotation.)

1879 P. L. ISAAC *Notes on Shipping* 65 The old-fashioned bluff-bowed craft, sometimes called 'bruisers.'

+**3.** (See quotations.)

1881 E. INGERSOLL *Oyster Industry* 242 *Bruiser*, a short paddle used for beating sponges in process of cleaning. (Florida.) **1883** RATHBUN in *U.S. Museum Bul. 27* 125 Saturdays are spent in ... squeezing the sponges and beating them with a short heavy stick, called a 'bruiser.'

+**Brulé.** Also **Brulie.** [F.] A subtribe of the Teton division of the Dakota or Sioux Indians. Also attrib. with *Sioux.* — **1847** PARKMAN in *Knickerb.* XXX. 290 The *Brulé*, and other western bands of the *Dahcotahs*, are thorough savages. **1854** *33d Cong. 2d Sess.* H. R. Ex. Doc. 36, 3 The Brulies have 200 lodges, and the Wah-sah-zhe, a branch of the Brulies, ... have 75 lodges. **1855** SCHOOLCRAFT *Indian Tribes* V. 494 Broulè Sioux [live near] Platte River and Valley.

+**Brummer.** *Pa.* [Cf. G. *brummen* to hum, buzz, etc.] A blast furnace. — **1898** *Lebanon* (Pa.) *News* 20 Jan. in *Congress. Rec.* Feb. 1506/1 Our people can again hear the sweet familiar sounds of the 'brummer,' which to many is more agreeable music than any of the Wagner compositions.

Brunonian, *n.* and *a.* {1799-} +**1.** *n.* A student or alumnus of Brown University, Providence, R.I. +**2.** *adj.* Pertaining to Brown University. — **(1)** **1829** (*title*), The Brunonian. Edited by the Students of Brown University. **1889** *Cent.* 699/2. **1900** *Brown Alumni Mo.* I. 6/1 (*caption*), Brunonians far and near. **(2)** **1909** *Memories of Brown* 8 The editors ... have desired to ... create in the contemporary mind a fuller consciousness of the continuity of Brunonian tradition and aspiration. **1917** *Brown Alumni Mo.* XVII. 259/1 To the consternation of the Brunonian rooters, Umpire Lanigan called it a ball.

+**Brunswick stew.** A stew composed of mixed vegetables and meat. — *c***1870** BAGBY *Old Va. Gentleman* 10 The crack of the gun was heard continually—the boys were shooting squirrels for Brunswick stew. **1909** F. B. CALHOUN *Miss Minerva* 23 Me an' Wilkes Booth Lincoln been eatin' chitlins ... an' Brunswick stew ever sence we's born.

***Brush,** *n.*[1]

***1.** Branches of trees cut off; small trees, shrubs, etc., cut down for firewood, fencing, etc. {-1830; now *dial.*}

1624 J. SMITH *Virginia* IV. 160 With a few withered leaves, reeds, and brush, make a small fire. **1689** *Huntington Rec.* II. 23 It was voated ... that all from 14 years old and upwards shall the 2d munday an tusday in June next cutt brush. **1701** *Providence Rec.* XI. 62 Concerning the high way ... obstructed by William Harris his daming the River by throwing in of Brush. **1774** *Newport Mercury* 30 May 1/2 Heretofore the north orchard was hired to be pruned, and they that did the labour had the brush for their pains. **1792** BELKNAP *New Hampshire* III. 259 The same defence [against mosquitoes] is used for the cattle; smokes of leaves and brush are made in the pastures where they feed by day. **1826** COOPER *Mohicans* xxiii, Large piles of brush lay scattered about the clearing, and a ... squaw was occupied in firing as many as might serve to light the coming exhibition. **1861** NORTON *Army Lett.* 37, I was out in the woods after brush and came across the field. **1879** *Scribner's Mo.* Dec. 241/1 Trees have been felled and brush burned.

***2.** Small growing trees, bushes, shrubs, etc. {-1820}

1622 'MOURT' *Relation* 17 We came into a deepe Valley, full of brush. **1672** *Hempstead Rec.* I. 288 Upon a training day theaire was given to John Jonson a home lot in the brush by his fathers Champins lot. **1725** in Kidder *Exped. Lovewell* (1865) 32 There were few Trees and scarce any Brush. **1751** ELIOT *Field-Husb.* iii. 61 If a Swamp be full of small Brush, and but few great Trees, the cheapest and best Way is to flow it, and kill it with the Water. **1818** SCHOOLCRAFT *Journal* 17 Feeling somewhat fatigued from ... tearing our way through the brush and green briar. **1835** HOFFMAN *Winter in West* I. 207 Their lessening figures were hid from our view by the low brush which in some places skirted its banks. **1846** THORPE *Myst. Backwoods* 70 You can observe some green brush that looks as if it grew out of the very decayed wood; in this 'brush' is hidden away the deadly rifle. *c***1856** *Kit Carson's Life* 46 We secured ourselves and animals in the brush, then commenced the fight. **1873** BOURKE *Journal* 6 Jan., Country passed through today was an open plain covered with brush. **1886** BRET HARTE *Snow-bound* 9 No rustle in the wayside 'brush,' nor echo from the rocky cañon below, betrayed a sound of their flight. **1891** M. E. RYAN *Pagan of Alleghanies* 290 He's got a friend hiding in the brush there; he'll see to him. **1900** *Bureau of Statistics* (Dept. of Commerce) *Mo. Summary* 1116 The swampers ... clear away the brush and other obstructions from around the tree, so that the logs can be gotten to the nearest skid road.

+**b.** *S.W.* Backwoods; a sparsely settled wooded region or district.

1881 H. W. PIERSON *In the Brush* 9, I was once present at an ecclesiastical meeting in the Brush. *Ib.*, My experiences in the Brush.

3. *attrib.* and *comb.* **a.** In sense 1, esp.: Made or covered with brush.

1805 LEWIS in *L. & Clark Exped.* (1905) III. 6 At the distance of five miles he arrived at some brush lodges of the Shoshones. **1811** *Niles' Reg.* I. 101/1 The brush scythe or brush cutter would be better always in our sheep keepers hands. **1825** NEAL *Bro. Jonathan* III. 407 After many weeks of incredible hardship, he slept in a brush cabin, where he found part of a mocassin. **1835** *S. Lit. Messenger* I. 581 The pony . . . moves homeward . . . leaping every obstacle in his way to his brush stable. **1850** L. SAWYER *Way Sketches* 94 These enterprising traders had just arrived and set up a brush shade for a house. **1854** MARCY *Expl. Red River* 34 It occurred to me that the plan of erecting our brush dams must have been originally suggested from witnessing those of the beavers. **1857** HAMMOND *Northern Scenes* 111 Our boatman built for our accommodation, a brush shanty in the place of our tents. **1873** BEADLE *Undevel. West* 654 John D. Lee has pre-empted the pool, and has his wife Rachel living there in a sort of brush tent. **1877** W. WRIGHT *Big Bonanza* 65 Some . . . did their cooking in the open air under a brush-shed. **1895** *Outing* XXVII. 231/2 Daybreak . . . found us ensconced in a brush blind on the spot where the flock had been scattered. **1903** A. ADAMS *Log Cowboy* 16 When we reached the brush chute, all hands started them on a run for the water.

b. In sense 2.

1856 B. YOUNG in *Jrnl. Discourses* III. 324 (Th.), You know that, when they get a little brush-whipped, they are apt to become angry. **1859** A. CARY *Country Life* 7 [The half-holiday] was less welcome than as if it had brought a log-rolling, brush-burning, or stone quarrying with it. **1867** J. N. EDWARDS *Shelby* 206 Furloughed militia darted out from every haystack and brush patch to have one good shout for Lincoln. **1868** *Amer. Naturalist* II. 176 The Green Black-capped Warbler . . . is fond of haunting thickets and open brush-fields. **1868** *Rep. Comm. Agric.* 257 Much of the trimming from the under side, to let the brush sapling into its place, is saved. **1878** BEADLE *Western Wilds* 36 Didn't you come sneakin' along the brush-road from Nauvoo t'other day, then? **1881** H. W. PIERSON *In the Brush* 6 Father A— . . . is an old Brush-Breaker. . . . He has broken a right smart chance of brush. *Ib.* 29 The women were dressed as I have seen thousands of Brush-women dressed. **1907** WHITE *Arizona Nights* 10 And me squatting behind that ore dump about as formidable as a brush rabbit.

* **Brush,** *n.*[2] [Cf. BRUSH *v.*[2]]

1. A slight attack of illness. {1733}

1831 PECK *Guide* 7 'But are not your family now sick?' 'No, they only have a little brush of the ague.'

2. A short and rapid run or race.

*a***1846** *Quarter Race Ky.*, etc. 50 He had me at the first brush, for I told you the brown horse was a mighty fast one for a little ways. **1852** BRISTED *Upper Ten Th.* 26 His nag has less foot for a brush than the pacer. **1853** *Knickerb.* XLIII. 53 There were a good many nags about that could beat him on a brush, but for long drives he had few equals. **1868** H. WOODRUFF *Trotting Horse* 105 He may have a couple of brushes of a quarter of a mile each. **1903** *N.Y. Times* 7 Sept., Mr Dodge . . . got into a brush with a passing horseman. . . . His horse continued the brush for about ten yards. **1906** *N.Y. Ev. Post* 16 June, Apart from the annual regatta, there are endless minor 'brushes' for 'fresh-water sailormen.'

+**Brush,** *v.*[1] [f. BRUSH *n.*[1]] **1.** *tr.* To mend, repair, or cover with brush. **2.** To drag brushwood over land in order to level it, break clods, etc. **3.** To provide with brush to climb on. **4.** In *p.p.*: Lost as in brush.

(1) **1730** HEMPSTEAD *Diary* 219 Jno. Larkins workt cutting of fenceing Stuff & brushing fence. **1905** *Forestry Bureau Bul. 61* s.v., *To brush a road*, to cover with brush the mud-holes and swampy places in a logging road, to make it solid. (N[orthern] F[orest]). (2) **1857–8** *Ill. Agric. Soc. Trans.* III. 490 The ground [in the nursery] should be fresh plowed, harrowed and rolled, or brushed, as the planting proceeds. (3) **1889** *Cent.* 700/1 To brush peas. (4) **1881** H. W. PIERSON *In the Brush* 7 Didn't you think the Bishop got badly *brushed* in the first part of his sermon? . . . It's a comfort to a beginner to know that an old preacher sometimes gets brushed.

* **Brush,** *v.*[2] [Cf. BRUSH *n.*[2] 2.]

+**1.** *tr.* To force on; to drive hard or briskly.

1755 *Conn. Gazette* 29 Nov. (De Vere), As tending to beget ill will, and brushing a disunion in the several governments in America. **1827** COOPER *Prairie* x, I have at this moment a dog brushing a deer, not far from this. **1868** WOODRUFF *Trotting Horse* 70 Eight or ten days prior to the race . . . brush him half a mile. **1904** *N.Y. Times* 28 Nov. 5 The drivers . . . spent a couple of hours before dusk brushing their fast steppers on the upper stretch.

2. *intr.* To ride, run or move quickly. {*dial.* 1809–}

1838 *N.Y. Advertiser & Express* 31 March 2/2 Forty-two race horses were brushing on the Eclipse course yesterday morning. *a***1846** *Quarter Race Ky.*, etc. 124 You'd have laughed . . . to have seen me in that race—to see the fire leave me at times and then to see me brushin' up on her agin. **1856** SIMMS *Charlemont* 344, I'm pretty certain that Stevens will be riding out to-day. . . . I'll take my chance for it, therefore, and brush out ahead of him.

b. *To brush round*, to bestir oneself. *colloq.* {1805}

1833 S. SMITH *Major Downing* 167 The gineral is *brushin round* now, and says the message must be finished and printed offhand. **1875** HOLLAND *Sevenoaks* 127 If the feller that only had one talent had brushed round, he could 'a' made a spec on it. *Ib.* 156 You an' me has got to be brushin' round.

* **Brush,** *v.*[3]

+**1.** *To brush over*, to cultivate rapidly and superficially.

1788 WASHINGTON *Diaries* III. 416 The other hands [were] brushing over the Potatoes in the Corn.

+**2.** *tr.* To explore, reconnoiter, search (woods).

1829 COOPER *Wish-Ton-Wish* xxviii, There was a party sent to brush the woods on the trail of Indians. **1855** SIMMS *Forayers* 207 Whether knocked up or not, we must brush that wood before dark.

+**3.** *intr.* With *up*. To make oneself more tidy; to keep abreast of the times; to refresh one's memory.

1840 *Knickerb.* XVI. 162, I thought I must brush up for the occasion. **1855** GLISAN *Jrnl. Army Life* 164 Knowing such an opportunity to brush up in my profession might not occur again for years. **1856** *Mich. Agric. Soc. Trans.* VII. 619 All began to feel a stronger desire to brush up and to keep stirring with the progressing times. **1858** THOREAU *Maine Woods* 86 We brushed up and watched the first signs of dawn through an open port. **1878** BEADLE *Western Wilds* 265 We here overhauled our kit, brushed up a little, and put on our best gear for a visit. **1898** DELAND *Old Chester Tales* 122 Of course I shall have to brush up a little. **1903** *Dial* 1 Sept. (Advt.), If you wish to brush up on your English you will find nothing better. **1906** *N.Y. Ev. Post* 12 Dec. 8 Now that your busy season is about to open, Senator, I presume you are beginning to brush up on your oratory.

+**4.** *tr.* To beat, flog. Also with *up*.

1865 KELLOGG *Rebel Prisons* 196 The Surgeon, himself, said that he 'brushed his [slaves] up a little when they needed it.' **1908** *Dialect Notes* III. 294 *Brush*, to beat with a switch or brush.

***Brush bill.** [BRUSH *n.*[1]] An implement for cutting brushwood. {1588} — **1647** *Essex Probate Rec.* I. 85 One Spitt & one brush bill. **1845** JUDD *Margaret* I. iii. 12 Here were . . . a scythe, rakes, a brush-bill, fox-traps, [etc.].

+**Brush camp.** [BRUSH *n.*[1]] A temporary shelter or camp made of brush. — **1776** *Essex Inst. Coll.* LIII. 89 Marched to Lake Champlain, 10 miles. . . . Staid in a brush camp. **1873** BEADLE *Undevel. West* 657 By it [was] the brush camp of his tribe, a horribly filthy and repulsive gang of some forty savages. **1897** *Outing* XXX. 190/2 The outfit from Maine, log-cabin, brush-camps, guides and all, was busy at the old stand.

+**Brush drag.** [BRUSH *n.*[1]] A device made of brush used for catching fish. — **1801** *Mass. Spy* 21 Oct. (Th.), They had met at Franklin with a view of fishing the Miami with what is called a brush drag.

+**Brushed,** *a.* [BRUSH *n.*[1]] Overgrown with brush. — **1666** *Duxbury Rec.* 16 A certain parcel of land . . . marked with divers trees, until you come to a low brushed swamp. **1888** *Century Mag.* Jan. 453/1 A cañon, liberally wooded or 'brushed' with wild plums.

+**Brush ends.** [BRUSH *n.*[1]] The tips or points of brushwood. — **1868** *Rep. Comm. Agric.* 256 In single-line hedge the saplings are so wound between as to press against the stakes, the tips or brush ends being all turned to the beveled or slanting side. **1889** *Harper's Mag.* Jan. 230/2 The brush ends inclined towards the bottom of the stream.

+**Brush fence.** [BRUSH *n.*[1]] A fence made of brush.

1729 HEMPSTEAD *Diary* 212, I made 42 Rod Brush fence from the Hill of Rocks at the old orch[ar]d towards the new. **1802** *Mass. H. S. Coll.* VIII. 114 In the midst of the hollow the sand has been raised by a brush fence. **1828** NEAL *R. Dyer* 162, I am sorely afraid of that narrow green lane there, with a brush-fence on the upper side of it. *c***1845** *Big Bear Ark.*, etc. 38, I look like having ran into a brush fence of a dark night. **1880** *Scribner's Mo.* Feb. 504/1 A lawful brush fence must be a rod wide, with no specification as to its height.

+**Brush fire.** [BRUSH *n.*[1]] A fire in brush, or fed by brush. — **1850** GARRARD *Wah-To-Yah* xviii. 213 The spiral smoke, turning gray in the twilight, rose from the brushfire through Louey's exertions. **1869** BROWNE *Adv. Apache Country* 123 A brush-fire was made over the grave to destroy the traces. **1881** *Rep. Indian Affairs* 96 In the center of a circle a brush fire was burning while the Indians danced around it.

+**Brush harrow.** [BRUSH *n.*[1]] A harrow made of brush. — **1761** WASHINGTON *Diaries* I. 178 The seed was harrowed in with a Brush Harrow. **1880** *Harper's Mag.* June 68/1 Rather would we listen to the musical ring of the laughing children riding on the big 'brush harrow.'

+**Brush heap.** [BRUSH *n.*[1]] A heap or pile of brush.

1812 *Ann. 12th Congress* 2 Sess. 147 Every swamp—nay, every brush-heap surrounded with weeds furnishes a hiding place. **1845** MRS. KIRKLAND *Western Clearings* 67 His own sallow helpmate goes barefoot and bonnetless to the brush-heap to fill her ragged apron with miserable fuel. **1858** D. K. BENNETT *Chronology of N.C.* 13 A mischievous fox that had taken refuge in a brush-heap near his poultry-yard. **1883** 'S. BONNER' *Dialect Tales* 125 A queer sort of fence made of . . . broad planks and narrow planks, old fence-rails, sticks of wood and brush-heaps.

+**Brush house.** [BRUSH *n.*[1]] A house made of brush. — **1862** NORTON *Army Lett.* 64 When we came back we burned all the log barracks and brush houses at the forts. **1871** *Rep. Indian Affairs* 342 Ossuna is a very old man, living in a brush-house and cultivating a small piece of land. **1880** G. INGHAM *Digging Gold* 381 The . . . mountaineers . . . had erected a brush house; that is, an enclosure covered on top and at the sides with pine boughs which . . . made a very comfortable shelter. **1883** *Rep. In-*

dian Affairs 21 While these Indians live entirely in tents, tepes, and brush houses, . . . they are fast adopting the customs of whites in manner of dress.

+**Brush hut.** [BRUSH *n.*[1]] An Indian dwelling made of brush. — **1889** *Century Mag.* April 908/2 We were never out of sight of the brush huts of the Indians. **1893** K. SANBORN *S. California* 140 They had substantial brush huts, supported by pillars.

+**Brushing,** *vbl. n.* [BRUSH *v.*[3] 4.] A thrashing; a whipping. — **1842** *Amer. Pioneer* I. 183 During the Christmas holydays, Washington thought the Hessians would be drinking, and it would be a good time to give them a brushing. **1879** TOURGEE *Fool's Errand* xv. 80, I heard afterwards that they did break up the meeting, and give the preachers a little brushing.

Brushing, *ppl. a.* [BRUSH *v.*[2] 2.] Brisk; lively. {1792–1824} — **1845** SIMMS *Wigwam & Cabin* I. 85 'Twas a pleasure to cross him and streak it away, at a brushing canter, . . . for a good five miles at a stretch. **1868** H. WOODRUFF *Trotting Horse* 124 Paul Pry was at no time a horse of brushing speed.

+**Brushland.** [BRUSH *n.*[1]] Land covered with brush. — **1853** *Mich. Agric. Soc. Trans.* 631 The fields . . . look more like what is commonly called brush land than they do like a white man's improvements. **1867** *Iowa Agric. Soc. Rep.* 154 Fall [wheat] does the best on our timber and brush lands. **1877** JOHNSON *Anderson Co., Kansas* 58 Dewey, Baer and Williams cleared off three or four acres of brush land and planted it in corn.

Brushmaker. One who makes brushes. {1709}

1729 *Boston Selectmen* 182 William Clark . . . was admitted an inhabitant of this Town & to . . . exercise his calling of a Brushmaker. **1743** FRANKLIN *Poor Rich. Alm. 1744* 23 John Wilkinson, Brush-Maker. **1820** FLINT *Lett. from Amer.* 213 There are [in Cincinnati] . . . five painters and glaziers; two brush-makers. **1837** W. JENKINS *Ohio Gaz.* 95 Burlington contains . . . one brush maker.

Brushmaking, *vbl. n.* The manufacture of brushes. — **1815** *View N.Y. State Prison* 33 The business of brush-making has also increased greatly within the last four years [in the prison].

Brush manufacturer. One who makes or manufactures brushes. — **1796** *Boston Directory* 283 Spear, Richard, brush manufacturer, No. 63, Marlborough street.

+**Brush meeting.** [BRUSH *n.*[1]] A meeting held in the woods. — **1890** *Congress. Rec.* 9 May 4376/2, I remember in 1887 attending a great prohibition meeting that was held over in Virginia, called a brush meeting.

+**Brush net.** =BRUSH DRAG. — **1807** GASS *Journal* 29 What [fish] we caught were taken with trails or brush nets.

+**Brush pile.** [BRUSH *n.*[1]] A pile of brush; a brush heap. — **1865** WHITTIER *Snow-Bound* line 59 A smooth white mound the brush-pile showed. **1865** MRS. WHITNEY *Gayworthys* xxxviii. 361 The very chickens run under the fences and the brushpile, and only the ducks are abroad and gay. **1874** LONG *Wild-Fowl* 135 He [a dog] found them [=ducks] hiding in some old brush-pile.

+**Brush plain.** [BRUSH *n.*[1]] A plain the natural growth on which is brush. — **1684** *Manchester Town Rec.* 19 Sixteen acurs on the brushe plaine. **1842** *Nat. Hist. N.Y., Zoology* III. 38 This beautiful snake . . . is also found, but rarely, in what are called the Brush plains of Long Island. **1856** *Spirit of Times* (N.Y.) 18 Oct. 113/1 Rabbit . . . can only now be found . . . where there are extensive brush-plains.

***Brush scythe.** [BRUSH *n.*[1]] A scythe used in removing brush, brambles, undergrowth, etc. {1573} — **1634** in Winthrop *Hist.* (1853) I. 464 Sithes for grass, and two brush sithes. **1811** *Niles' Reg.* I. 101/1 The brush scythe will cut up the brambles. **1858** WARDER *Hedges & Evergreens* 63 They must be cut off near the ground either with a brush-scythe or with the mowing-machine.

+**Brush whisky.** [BRUSH *n.*[1]] Whisky made in the brush; moonshine whisky. — **1885** 'CRADDOCK' *Prophet* 22 The brush whiskey [was] warming his heart. **1895** — *Myst. Witch-Face Mt.* 24 His liability to the Federal law for making brush whiskey. **1913** M. W. MORLEY *Carolina Mts.* 66 That important beverage, variously known as . . . 'blockade,' 'brush whiskey,' and in the outer world, 'corn-whiskey,' which is extracted from the grain and surreptitiously distributed.

Brushwood. [BRUSH *n.*[1]]

1. Branches of trees or bushes cut or broken off; small wood. {*a*1613–} Also attrib.

1637 MORTON *New Canaan* II. v, They [beavers] build up a howse, . . . placed in some pond to which they make a damme of brush wood, like a hedge. **1744** FRANKLIN *Acc. of Fire-Places* 20 A dry Faggot of Brushwood . . . is very advantageous. **1823** JAMES *Exped.* I. 96 During the severe wintry weather, he affirmed that bears make for themselves a shelter of brushwood. **1850** GARRARD *Wah-To-Yah* xx. 250 Their ox teams did most worthy service in hauling logs and brushwood to the dam. **1869** BROWNE *Adv. Apache Country* 463 Their wives and children are dwelling . . . under a bunch of willows or a brush-wood wigwam.

2. Small growing saplings, bushes, trees, etc. {1732–}

1772 D. TAITT in *Travels Amer. Col.* 500 We . . . went NNE thirteen miles and a quarter to a riseing ground clear of trees or brush wood. **1824** MARSHALL *Kentucky* I. 139 It was covered by a forest of oak trees of middling size, and the ravines with small saplings or brushwood. **1858** D. K. BENNETT *Chronology of N.C.* 22 Once his house was beset by Indians in the night; . . . and his family escaped and fled to a hill or brushwood near by. **1867** J. N. EDWARDS *Shelby*, etc. 85 Everywhere amid the heavy brushwood a silent scene of killing was enacted.

Brushy, *a.* [BRUSH *n.*[1]]

+**1.** Overgrown or covered with brush or brushwood.

1658 *Essex Inst. Coll.* IX. 221 A swampy brushy meadow in the great swampe near Wenham. **1661** *Manchester Town Rec.* 15 The way that gose to and through the brushee plain. **1693** *Mass. Prov. Acts* VII. 397 Though the way [was] now most hideous, sometimes swampy, then stony & horibly brushy scarce passable for Horses. **1706** *Derby* (Conn.) *Rec.* 390 Bounded . . . east by a brushye hill side. **1723** *Braintree Rec.* 154 It being brushy or bushy land we opened it by cutting away the bushes where the way is to go. **1785** A. ELLICOTT in *Life & Lett.* 47 The Hills extreme brushy, and no inhabitants within many miles. **1806** CLARK in *Lewis & C. Exped.* (1905) III. 250 All around this great bend is high land thickly timbered brushey & almost impossible to penetrate. **1839** *Knickerb.* XIII. 246, I slowly wound my way up a brushy slope, some three hundred yards in length. **1874** Coues *Birds N.W.* 145 The White-winged Snowbird . . . frequents brushy hill-tops and mountain-sides.

||**2.** Forming small twigs. (Cf. BRUSH ENDS.)

1879 *Scribner's Mo.* Nov. 52/1 In placing the willows the brushy tops are laid so as to project three or four feet outside the frame [of the mattress].

Brussels. [The capital of Belgium.]

1. *Brussels (lace)*, a fine variety of pillow lace. {1748–}

1756 E. Singleton *Social N.Y.* 245 Turn your lawns into gauze, let your Brussels be blond. **1789** *Md. Hist. Mag.* XXI. 240 She was not pretty this Afternoon, tho' adorn'd with pink Sattin Tambour muslin and Brussell's Lace. **1871** *Harper's Mag.* XLIII. 25/1 This old robe . . . [was] made thick and comfortable by innumerable layers of the finest Brussels lace. **1893** *Chicago Tribune* 23 April 44/4 Some odd pairs of Irish Point, Nottingham, and Brussels at one-half price. **1902** L. RICHARDS *Mrs. Tree* 14 This tiny old woman, . . . with the acanthus-leaf in finest Brussels nodding over her brows.

2. *Brussels (carpet)*, a kind of carpet having an upper surface of wool on a backing of strong linen thread. {1831–} Also *B. carpeting*.

(1) **1824** *Ann. 18th Congress* 1 Sess. 961 There shall be levied . . . the following duties . . . on Brussels, Venetian, Turkey, and Wilton carpets and carpeting, fifty cents per square yard. **1854** 'O. OPTIC' *In Doors & Out* (1876) 101 With a nice new Brussels carpet and the new furniture, Mrs. Weston's little parlor looked exceedingly pleasant. **1860** M. J. HOLMES *Maude* xv. 168, I also told Mr. Jenks to buy me one hundred yards of Brussels carpeting, in New York. **1865** STOWE *House & Home P.* I A roll of Brussels carpet which was spread out in flowery lengths on the floor of Messrs. Ketcham & Co. **1891** WILKINS *New Eng. Nun* 90 There I had a whole house, with Brussels carpets on all the rooms except the kitchen.

(2) **1827** *Harvard Reg.* Dec. 307 The embroidered Brussels of a drawing-room. **1847** *Knickerb.* XXX. 209 The floor was carpeted with rich Brussels, deep as clover and soft as velvet. **1856** M. J. HOLMES *Homestead on H.*, House at Snowdon v, The glowing grate, whose bright blaze rendered still more brilliant the flowers of the costly Brussels. **1866** RICHARDSON *Secret Service* 39 Lo, the pictures and statues, the Brussels and rosewoods which his money has bought! **1883** HOWELLS *Woman's Reason* viii, The reception-room of these ladies was respectable in threadbare brussels and green reps.

3. *Brussels sprouts*, the small cabbagelike heads which grow on the stem of the plant *Brassica oleracea* var. *gemmiflora;* the plant itself. {1796–}

1839 E. J. HOOPER *Practical Farmer* 34 Brussels Sprouts [are] used as winter greens. **1855** BROWNE in *Trans. Amer. Inst. N.Y.* 611 Brussels Sprouts . . . from France . . . is a variety of cabbage . . . little cultivated in this country. **1871** *Rep. Comm. Agric.* 531 Cauliflowers, Brussels sprouts, and kale, in the selection of the soil and manure, and in cultivation, require generally the same treatment as cabbages. **1887** *Amer. Naturalist* XXI. 441 Brussels sprouts. . . . This vegetable [is] in this country only grown in the gardens of amateurs.

***Brute.** +A farm animal, as an ox or a cow. — **1867–8** *Ill. Agric. Soc. Trans.* VII. 223, I have been dealing with cattle . . . since 1861, and . . . did not lose a brute until the past summer.

+**Bub.** *colloq.* [See BUBBY; cf. BUD *n.*[1] and German *bube*, a boy.]

1. A playful form of address used to boys and young men.

A pun in 1837 *Knickerbocker* X. 521, rendering *syllabub* by *idiot-brother*, evidently associates *bub* with BUD *n.*[1] Cf. Bartlett's '*Bub* and *Bubby*, contractions for brother' ('59, p. 51).

1846–51 MRS. WHITCHER *Bedott P.* 287 Come here and see me, bub. **1847** C. F. BRIGGS *Tom Pepper* I. 98 'Where are you going, Bub?' said one of them. **1869** STOWE *Oldtown Folks* 138 'Hulloah, bub!' shouted they, 'where ye goin'?' **1872** HOLMES *Poet* i. 9 Many eminently genteel persons . . . are in the habit of addressing all unknown children by one of the two terms, 'bub' and 'sis,' which they consider endears them greatly to the young people. **1875** HOLLAND *Sevenoaks* 37 'Well, bub,' said he tenderly, 'how fare ye?' **1889** *Century Mag.* Jan. 411/2 'Lookee here, bub,' said one o' the men, 'that won't do.' **1896** *McClure's Mag.* VI. 485/2, 'I wouldn't if I were you, bub,' said Margaret. . . . She always called him 'bub' when she wanted to vex him. *a***1904** WHITE *Blazed Trail Stories* 4 Say, bub, you look as interested as a man killing snakes.

2. A baby, child, or young person. Also transf.

1845 *St. Louis Reveille* 4 Aug. (Th.), Letters from a Baby, [signed] Bub. **c1871** 'MARK TWAIN' *Sketches* Wks. XIX. 72 You may see stately pictures of papa and mamma, Johnny and Bub. **1876** *Congress. Rec.* Jan. 725/2 You [=Eugene Hale of Maine] have been known in the last three or four Congresses as 'Blaine's little bub.'

Bubble and squeak. {1785–} *New Eng.* +'Hash or minced meat' (*Cent.*).

Bubbler. +(See quotations.) — **1819** *Western Rev.* I. 372 Grunting Bubbler, *Amblodon grunniens*.... The vulgar names of this fish are white perch, ... bubbler, and muscle-eater. **1832** FLINT *Miss. Valley* I. 79 Bubbler *amblodon*, Buffalo perch. Found in all the waters of the Ohio. ... It is a fine fish for the table. **1871** DE VERE 383 The Bubbler, ... when drawn from the waters of the Ohio, ... makes an extraordinary bubbling noise, as if protesting against such treatment.

+Bubby. *colloq.* =BUB.

1841 *Knickerb.* XVII. 39 'Bubby,' added he, looking at a white-headed little boy with ... affectionate good humor. **1863** MRS. WHITNEY *F. Gartney* iv, 'Bubby,' otherwise Master Herbert Clarence Grubbling. **1888** 'CRADDOCK' *Broomsedge C.* 232 Ye ain't agoin hongry this winter air ye, bubby? **1888** *San Fran. Weekly Exam.* (F.), When she was ready to go home, she did so without carriage or baby. Shortly after Bubby kicked up high jinks.

transf. **1895** 'CRADDOCK' *Myst. Witch-Face Mt.* 28 In the distance, a tree-toad called ... for rain. 'Ye'll git it, bubby,' Con addressed the creature.

+Bubby flower. [f. *bubby* woman's breast {1686–}.] (See quotation. Cf. N.C. dialect *bubbybush*, species of *Calycanthus* and *Evonymus*.) — **1791** ANBURY *Travels* II. 352 A shrub peculiar to this province [Va.] ... bears a small flower, which the inhabitants term the bubby flower; ... the name ... arises from a custom that the women have of putting this flower down their bosoms, ... till it has lost all its grateful perfume.

Buccan, *v.* Also †**bucan.** [F. *boucaner.*] *tr.* To cook meat on a boucan or low hurdle; to barbecue. {1761–} — **1791** BARTRAM *Travels* 349 Breakfasting on excellent coffee, relished with bucanned venison [etc.]. **1887** *Harper's Mag.* Aug. 357/2 There they established themselves, spending the time alternately in hunting the wild cattle and buccanning the meat.

Buccaneer. Also **bucaneer, buc(c)anier.** [F. *boucanier*, originally applied to the hunters of San Domingo and West India islands.]

1. A pirate frequenting the West Indies or coasts of Spanish America. {1690–} Now hist.

1764 HUTCHINSON *Hist. Mass.* (1795) I. i. 164 The trade of the province increasing, especially with the West-Indies, where the bucaneers or pirates at this time were numerous. **1796** MORSE *Amer. Geog.* I. 773 The Isle of Providence [in the Bahama Islands] became an harbour for the buccaneers, or pirates. **1824** IRVING *Tales Traveller* I. IV. 240 Among these [adventurers in New Netherlands], the foremost were the buccaneers. **1841** COOPER *Deerslayer* xxiv, Have you never heard any fearful stories about Thomas Hutter's having once been concerned with the people they call buccaneers? **1851** *Ann. 5th Congress* 277 When they were considering the best mode of defending our merchants against pirates and bucaniers, no nation had a right to take offence at them. **1884** SWEET & KNOX *Through Texas* 23 On this lonely shore the gentle buccaneer ... buried his treasures, and despatched his prisoners.

+2. A long-barreled musket. *Obs.*

1806 *Mass. H. S. Coll.* 1 Ser. X. 139 One Woodcock discharged his long musquet, called in those days [c1675] a buccaneer.

3. Attrib. with *crew, piece, race.*

1828 A. SHERBURNE *Memoirs* (1831) ii. 48 They soon began to fire upon us, with long buccanier pieces, into which they put eight or ten musket balls for a charge. **1858** VIELÉ *Following the Drum* 48 They seem to be the last traces left, in North America, of the bucaneer or sea-robber race. *Ib.* 227 When fairly out at sea, he discovered that he formed part of a bucanier crew.

Buccaneering, *vbl. n.* [f. prec.] The occupation of a buccaneer; the practice of piracy. {1758–} Also attrib. — **1767** HUTCHINSON *Hist. Mass.* II. 116 There succeeded a general abhorrence of bucaneering. **1800** WEEMS *Washington* (1867) 8 The history of his capturing Cornwallis and Tarleton, with their buccaneering legions. **1824** IRVING *Tales Traveller* II. 259 A mighty rich man ... who made a vulgar display of wealth, which it was whispered he had acquired by buccaneering. **1850** E. P. WHIPPLE *Ess. & Reviews* II. 195 It was essentially a buccaneering expedition, whose object was plunder and murder.

‖**Buccarebou.** *Obs.* =CARIBOU. — **1796** MORSE *Amer. Geog.* I. 388 An animal called by the natives, buccarebou, of a size between the moose and the deer, was formerly found in this country [Maine].

***Buck,** *n.*[1]

***1.** A male deer.

1622 'MOURT' *Relation* 25 We saw three Bucks, but we had rather haue had one of them. **1677** *Conn. Public Rec.* II. 308 It is fownd to be very prejudiciall to the pub[lic] weale to transport out of this Colony the skinns of bucks. **1681** *Penna. Mag.* VI. 175, I have seen four Bucks bought for less than 5s., the Indians killing them only for their skins. **1733** BYRD *Journey to Eden* (1901) 295 Our Hunters knockt down a Brace of Bucks, wherewith we made ourselves amends for our scanty Supper the afore-going Night. **1758** *Essex Inst. Coll.* XVIII. 180 We were alarm'd ... by a number of Rangers fireing at a Buck. **1809** WEEMS *Marion* (1833) 145 He would make nothing, at a hundred yards, to stop you a buck at full tilt through the woods. **1846** T. B. THORPE *Myst. Backwoods* 155 The swelled-neck buck, bearing his proud antlers aloft. **1885** *Outing* Oct. 68/1 He carefully examined the sign where a big buck had scraped the earth with his sharp hoofs.

+b. A buckskin, as a standard of value among the Indians.

1748 C. WEISER *Journal* 41 He has been robbed of the value of 300 Bucks, & you [Indians] all know by whom. *Ib.*, Every cask of Whiskey shall be sold to you [Indians] for 5 Bucks in your town. **1789** in Cist *Cincinnati* 215 Another Indian ... was forced to pay two bucks more. **1834** *Mass. H. S. Coll.* 3 Ser. VI. 147 If they [the Indians] took him away so that he should lose him, he would make them pay him a thousand bucks.

+c. *Hearty as a buck*, strong, vigorous.

1835 CROCKETT *Tour* 8 So, so middlin'. I'm hearty as a buck, but can't jump jest so high. **1871** DE VERE 208 The 'buck' suggests to the hunter the idea of being 'hearty as a buck.'

+2. A male sheep; a ram. [So G. *bock* and *schafbock*.]

1812 *Niles' Reg.* II. 240/1 The product [of wool] was as follows: a Buck (*Judas*) 12 lbs. 4 oz. **1817** *Ib.* XII. 287/1 A merino buck ... was sheared on the 23d ult. of a fleece weighing fourteen pounds. **1851** *Mich. Agric. Soc. Trans.* III. 95 Sheep.... Best buck over 2 years old. **1866** *Rep. Indian Affairs* 150 That the ewes be purchased in New Mexico, and the bucks in the States, in order to improve the stock. **1881** HAYES *New Colorado* 60 His 'bucks' (say about three to each hundred ewes) will generally be Merinos.

***b.** A male goat, he-goat. {–1551} [So G. *bock*, Du. *bok*.]

1869 BRACE *New West* 237 In the fall of 1861, W. Landrum obtained two bucks from a grower in the State of Georgia.

3. A gay or dashing fellow; a dandy. {1725–} Also in general sense, a fellow.

1774 FITHIAN *Journal* I. 89 Balantine, either to shew himself a true full-blooded Buck, or out of mere wantonness & pastime turned the Bones ... into many improper and indecent postures. **1789** S. LOW *Politician Outwitted* IV. ii, I am Dick Worthnought, esquire; a gentleman, a buck of the blood. **1803** WEEMS *Letters* II. 263, I shall, God willing, be dashing away among the Winchester Bucks. **1870** NOWLAND *Indianapolis* 148 Mr. Walpole having several daughters in the heyday of life, caused a considerable sensation with the young bucks of the settlement. **1888** 'CRADDOCK' *Broomsedge Cove* 55 Suddenly addressing the two men on the log, 'I seen ye two bucks thar ... at the baptizin'.' **1902** C. MORRIS *Stage Confidences* 164 Beaux, bucks, lady-killers, Johnnies,—all these terms have been applied at different periods to the self-proclaimed fascinator of women.

+b. Used as a familiar form of address.

1840 *S. Lit. Messenger* VI. 508/1 'Pay your own slug, buck,' said Hopper, snapping down a six-and-a-quarter cent piece on the table. **1852** WATSON *Nights in Block-House* 169 'No; go on with the story, my buck,' said Hurlbut. **1855** SIMMS *Forayers* 136 How are you, old buck, this warm weather? **1904** STRATTON-PORTER *Freckles* 243 'Remember that you're covered every move you make, my buck,' he cautioned.

+4. a. A male Indian.

1850 A. T. JACKSON *Forty-Niner* (1920) 10 The Indians burn their dead and I went over to the ridge ... to a buck's funeral Friday night. *Ib.*, They ... wrapped the buck in a blanket. **1869** S. BOWLES *Our New West* 115 Our beautiful Indian princess ... was only a plain young 'buck,'—not even a maiden. **1875** *Chicago Tribune* 19 Oct. 7/3 An old and wrinkled 'buck' ... monotonously repeated that he was a 'heap good Injun.' **1880** *Harper's Mag.* March 500/1 The bucks lie listlessly about, while the squaws scratch their heads. **1885** *Rep. Indian Affairs* 79 The squaws take charge of the carcass, dry the meat, and the 'buck' takes the hide to the traders. **1897** *Congress. Rec.* April 715/2 All of these Indians,—the bucks, the squaws, and the papooses,—were blanket Indians. **1903** WHITE *Forest* xv. 204 In the stern sit two or three bucks wearing shirts, jean trousers, and broad black hats.

b. A male Negro.

[**1842** *Spirit of Times* (Phila.) 18 April (Th.), A 'long nine' with a fierce looking buck of a colored fellow hanging to the end of it.] **1880** *Congress. Rec.* June 4147/1, I told the boys that we wanted 20,000 'bucks,' buck niggers, in Indiana this year. **1904** HARBEN *Georgians* 116 A big black buck was a-leanin' over the side fence with a cigar in his mouth. **1909** *Dialect Notes* III. 393 *Buck*, ... now applied almost exclusively to male negroes as the opposite of *wench*.

+5. *ellipt.* for BUCKSKIN, BUCKSHOT.

(1) **1845** J. W. NORRIS *Chicago Directory* 119 Retail dealers in ... buffalo robes, buffalo overshoes, buck mitts.

(2) **1845** SIMMS *Wigwam & Cabin* II. 107 On using big buck, he numbered two sevens for a load; the small buck, three. **1855** — *Forayers* 195 Emptied one barrel of buck upon a fellow who was sneaking off among the box in the garden. **1876** *Fur, Fin, & Feather* Sept. 135 The doctor soon drew a bird charge from his gun and loaded it with buck, and fired. **1889** *Cent.* 704/3 *Buck-and-ball*, a cartridge for smooth-bore firearms containing a spherical bullet and three buckshot: now little used. **1895** *Outing* Dec. 214/2, I vainly searched for a charge of buck.

6. Attrib. or appositive with *antelope, fawn, track* (sense 1); *lamb* (sense 2); *lad, nun, parson, party* (sense 3); *brethren, warrior* (sense 4a); *load* (sense 5(2)).

1890 CUSTER *Following Guidon* 216 Day before yesterday I saw a fine buck antelope. — *c***1850** *Dow's Sermons* (F.), You see my buck brethren, that the women are bound to get the better of us. — **1786** WASHINGTON *Diaries* III. 11 The largest of my Buck fauns . . . [had] its left knee broke. — **1872** *Chicago Tribune* 10 Oct. 5/3 The young and nearly illiterate buck-lads interpret the grumble into a moral and parental encouragement. — **1852** *Mich. Agric. Soc. Trans.* III. 25 Best pen of 5 buck lambs. — **1836** *Quarter Race Ky.* (1846) 14 Colonel, let us have some of your *byled* corn—pour me out a buck load—there—never mind about the water. — **1907** WHITE *Arizona Nights* III. iii. 286, I might as well go be a buck nun and be done with it. — **1836** *S. Lit. Messenger* II. 463 Such as this diocese was . . . when wine-bibbing and buck-parsons were sent out to preach 'a dry clatter of morality.' **1837** J. C. NEAL *Charcoal Sk.* (1838) 26 It's a buck party, if I may use the expression,—a buck party entirely. — **1897** *Outing* XXIX. 438/2 The largest and freshest buck-track he could find. — **1876** *Congress. Rec.* June 3505/1 As soon as these buck warriors smell the warpath [etc.].

+Buck, *n.*[2] [Du. *zaag-bok*, G. *sägebock* or *bock*.] A sawhorse; a sawbuck. — **1839** C. F. BRIGGS *H. Franco* II. i. 2 There were also wood sawyers sitting listlessly on their bucks. **1848** BARTLETT 393 *Buck*, a frame or stand of peculiar construction on which wood is sawn for fuel. In New England it is called a *saw-horse*.

+Buck, *n.*[3] [Cf. BUCKBOARD.] A long board adapted for use on snow by having runners attached to it. — **1881** *Harper's Mag.* April 786/2 The 'buck' is a more modern word to describe the long plank attached to runners—a device . . . developed from the old custom of holding the small single sleds together in a train.

+Buck *n.*[4] [f. BUCK *v.*[4]] The act of bucking, or power to buck.

1884 SWEET & KNOX *Through Texas* 69 If there had been any buck in them, it would have developed itself at an early stage in the journey. **1890** L. C. D'OYLE *Notches* 34 In two months from now the worst 'buckers' amongst them will not have a 'buck' left in them. **1891** *Harper's Mag.* July 206/2 After a series of bucks, more or less severe, during which his spurs go time and again into the pony's flanks [etc.].

+Buck, *n.*[5] [Of obscure origin.] *To pass the buck:* **a.** (See quot. 1887.) **b.** *fig.* To shift responsibility *to* someone else.

(a) 1872 'MARK TWAIN' *Roughing It* xlvii. 332, I reckon I can't call that hand. Ante and pass the buck. **1876** MILLER *First Families* 94 The head man of the company . . . jumped a first-class poker game, where he was playing at twenty dollars ante and pass the buck, to come in. **1887** KELLER *Draw Poker* 38 They resort to the bold and ludicrous experiment of 'passing the buck.' The 'buck' is any inanimate object, usually knife or pencil, which is thrown into a jack pot and temporarily taken by the winner of the pot. Whenever the deal reaches the holder of the 'buck,' a new jack pot must be made. **(b) 1912** W. IRWIN *Red Button* 341 The Big Commissioner will get roasted by the papers and hand it to the Deputy Comish, and the Deputy will pass the buck down to me, and I'll have to report how it happened. **1920** MULFORD *J. Nelson* 60 Bein' a stranger down here, I reckoned they'd pass the buck to you.

+Buck, *n.*[6] *slang.* [Of obscure origin.] A dollar. — **1896** G. ADE *Artie* 106 Jimmy can afford to buy wine at four bucks a throw when he's only gettin' three a week out o' the job. **1903** *McClure's Mag.* Feb. 428 A man . . . passed around some gold watches. . . . Twenty bucks they cost you over the counter. **1911** J. F. WILSON *Land Claimers* 2 'There's my eight hundred bucks,' he said.

Buck, *a.* [Cf. BUCK *n.*[1] 6.] (See quotation.) — **1851** HALL *College Words* 39 At Princeton College, anything which is in an intensive degree good, excellent, pleasant, or agreeable, is called *buck*.

Buck, *v.*[1] *colloq.*

1. *Buck up*, to take courage, recover one's spirits; to exert oneself. {1815– *dial.* and *colloq.;* now common}

1844 J. C. NEAL in *Graham's Mag.* Jan. 38 'Well, now, for my part, I don't see the trouble,' said Mrs. Fitzgig, 'why can't a man buck up?' **1902** LORIMER *Lett. Merchant* 153, I want to see you grow . . . so strong and big that you will force us to see that you are out of place among the little fellows. Buck up! **1921** PAINE *Comr. Rolling Ocean* 152 Now buck up and go tell the yarn to the crowd. **1922** A. BROWN *Old Crow* 385 Buck up, old man. Here's another chance for you.

+2. *Buck up to*, to stand up to; to make up to (a person), spec. in courting. {1865–, *dial.*}

*a***1846** *Quarter Race Ky.*, etc. 45, I didn't mind him . . . , till he bucked up too me an give me a feller rite under the ear. **1848** *R. I. Words* (Bartlett MS.), *Buck up*, to make oneself agreeable to—to pay close attention—first step in courting. **1868** PAULDING *Book of Vagaries* 265 Single gentlemen . . . should beware how they 'buck up' to widows.

+Buck, *v.*[2] (Cf. BUCK *n.*[5])

1. *tr.* To throw away or lose (money) by gambling. Orig. with *off*.

1851 *Alta Californian* 8 July, The money Percy took to the El Dorado [San Francisco saloon], where he duly bucked it off against a faro bank. **1851** J. J. HOOPER *Widow Rugby's Husb.* 20 No matter how I make an honest rise, I'm sure to 'buck it off' at farrer. **1851** MRS. CLAPPE *Lett. from Calif.* 121 Little John was then at the Humboldt betting, or, to speak technically, 'bucking' away large sums at monte.

2. *intr.* To play or gamble *at* monte, faro, etc.

1863 *Rio Abajo Press* 12 May 1 Do you expect me to believe a Saint would buck at monte? **1871** DE VERE 327 The fact that players at Three-Card Monte . . . are said to *buck* at monte, causes the familiar phrase of *bucking* at anything.

b. With *against*. Also =next.

1871 BRET HARTE *Luck of Roaring Camp*, etc. 95 Why don't you say you want to buck agin' Faro? **1873** BEADLE *Undevel. West* 92, I am never weary of watching the game, and the various fortunes of those who 'buck against the tiger.'

fig. **1898** CANFIELD *Maid of Frontier* 109 The man who bucks against that kind of game is a fool.

3. *To buck the tiger*, to play against the bank at monte or faro; hence, to play cards; to gamble.

1863 *Rocky Mt. News* 29 Jan. (Th.), At night [in Denver] you have a choice of two theatres, perhaps a dance, . . . most anything, even to bucking the tiger. **1888** C. D. FERGUSON *Exper. of Forty-Niner* 136, I ought perhaps to balance the foregoing instance by relating another a little more cheering, on account of the tender age of one who boldly *bucked the tiger*. **1902** LORIMER *Lett. Merchant* 188 He had already collected everything that was due this week and had lost it bucking the tiger. **1910** *N.Y. Ev. Post* 19 May (Th.), Could not resist numerous inducements to 'buck the tiger' in New York.

Buck, *v.*[3] [Possibly, as suggested by Bartlett, the same as *buck*, to butt, recorded in Eng. use from 1750.]

+1. *intr.* To display disinclination or resistance; to be recalcitrant; to make a fuss about something.

In later use partly *fig.* from BUCK *v.*[4]

1851 A. T. JACKSON *Forty-Niner* 89 Anderson has been asked to deliver the oration and although he bucked at first he finally accepted. **1869** BRACE *New West* 204 There was a woman and child inside the coach who commenced bucking so, and there ain't none of them passengers as ever have pistols. **1898** *Boston Journal* 10 July 10/1 Even when uniformed men of this generation mutiny, or buck, in a body, they very rarely make their point stick. **1902** LORIMER *Lett. Merchant* 195, I know you'll think the old man is bucking and kicking up a lot of dust over a harmless little flyer. **1904** 'O. HENRY' *Heart of West* 244 There was a bank examiner . . . nosing around our place to-day, and he bucked a sight about that note of yours.

+b. *To buck up*, to back out, draw back.

1902 MCFAUL *Ike Glidden* 169 All I know is, they say he bucked up on that race they started him in.

+2. To exert oneself *against* or *at* something; to push or drive hard *against*.

1859 BARTLETT 51 *To Buck* [is] used instead of *butt*, [and is] applied to animals pushing with their head and horns, and metaphorically of players at football and such games, pugilists, etc. **1870** in De Vere 327 You'll have to buck at it like a whole team, gentlemen, or you won't hear the whistle near your diggings for many a year. **1873** BEADLE *Undevel. West* 772 A salmon is never found with head down stream—'always bucking agin the current,' says the natives. **1908** MULFORD *Orphan* 33 It would be far more pleasant to skirt the thorns than to buck against them. **1921** PAINE *Comr. Rolling Ocean* 106 A good many of the boys seem to look up to you as a sort of leader since we bucked through that big gale of wind.

+b. *fig.* To strive *against* a person, power, etc.

1882 'MARK TWAIN' *Stolen White Elephant* 192 It ain't no use. We can't buck agin him. **1899** A. H. QUINN *Penna. Stories* 201 In the few cases in which you dare to buck up against us you call us a lot of drunkards. **1900** G. BONNER *Hard Pan* 41 There's no good bucking against bad luck. **1909** 'O. HENRY' *Roads of Destiny* x. 163 We had that protest from Springfield to buck against, and the governor nearly balked.

+c. To spring *over* (an obstacle); to run *into* (a person).

1886 ROOSEVELT in *Century Mag.* July 338/1 The horse generally has to be brought to a canter . . . , and then bucks over the obstacle by sheer strength. **1904** G. STRATTON-PORTER *Freckles* 100 If you was to buck into Mr. McLean in your prisint state, without me there to explain matters, the chance is he'd cut the liver out of you.

+3. *tr.* To drive or rush into, force one's way or try one's strength against (something). Also fig.

1861 *Harper's Mag.* July 276/1 Mr. Fusilbury . . . was in a dream of philosophy, bucking a lamp-post, and gazing intently at that block of houses. **1885** E. B. CUSTER *Boots & Saddles* 254 They began what they called 'bucking the drifts.' **1887** *Courier-Journal* 28 Jan. 3/2 The Northern Pacific railroad special train with three engines and one snow-plow bucked snow for six days to get to Cinnabar to relieve the expedition which got into Livingston yesterday. **1891** ROBERTS *Adrift Amer.* 114 There was a snow plough with two engines to it 'bucking the snow' (as the expression goes here) in front of us. **1902** LORIMER *Lett. Merchant* 32 Jim's father had a lot of money till he started out to buck the universe and corner wheat. **1904** 'O. HENRY' *Cabbages & Kings* (1916) 95, 'I'm going to buck centre,' says Henry, in his football idioms. **1907** MULFORD *Bar-20* 107, I won't buck the cavalry, but I'll keep it busy huntin' for me. **1911** LINCOLN *Cap'n Warren's Wards* 105 If this big, simple minded country man had come to New York to buck the stock market, it was time to sound a warning. **1913** LA FOLLETTE *Autobiog.* 75 If he thinks he can buck a railroad company with 5,000 miles of line, he'll find out his mistake.

+**4.** To thrust or force (one) *in.*

1897 FLANDRAU *Harvard Episodes* 158 He wanted Sears Wolcott on the Signet [club]. . . . His best motives for wishing to 'buck' Sears in were hardly formulated in his own mind.

Buck, *v.*[4]

1. *intr.* Of a horse or mule: To make a sudden leap upwards and come down with the hind legs in the air, the fore legs stiff, and the head held low, in an effort to cast off the rider or load. {1859 in Australian use}

1864 DICKSON *Across Plains* (1929) 118 While the animals reared back, twisted, bucked and bowled simultaneously. **1869** C. L. BRACE *New West* 97 They . . . flogged him with a cartwhip, but it wasn't of no use, he jist bucked whenever you got on him. **1869** *Overland Mo.* III. 127 A mustang is generally any thing in the world but 'religious,' for he will both 'sull,' (have the sulks) and 'buck.' **1884** SWEET & KNOX *Through Texas* 68 The majority of Texas ponies buck, or pitch as it is sometimes termed. **1885** *Century Mag.* Nov. 32/2, I've wished Joe Enselman would bring me an injun pony—a good one that won't buck. **1893** ROOSEVELT *Wilderness Hunter* 352 He bucked so under the saddle that nobody on the ranch could ride him.

transf. **1871** BRET HARTE *Poems* 59 Why, ef he'd a straddled that fence-rail the derned thing'ed get up and buck. **1901** MERWIN & WEBSTER *Calumet 'K'* 6 Every muscle in his body from the ankles up had helped to deal the blow, and the big stick bucked.

2. *tr.* To toss about, to throw *off*, by bucking.

1871 *Atlantic Mo.* Nov. 570 [The colt] had 'nearly bucked her to pieces.' **1885** BRET HARTE *Maruja* 101, 'I'll bet he don't buck his saddle off with me on it,' said the Doctor, grimly. **1889** *Century Mag.* Jan. 338/2 A person who had just been 'bucked' violently from the back of a descendant of the Barbs. **1902** WISTER *Virginian* xxvi. 301 Some'll buck you off, and some'll roll with you, and some'll fight you with their forefeet. **1909** *N.Y. Ev. Post* 18 Feb., Provided the sure-footed little cayuse . . . refrains from 'bucking' you off.

+**Buck,** *v.*[5]

1. *tr.* To punish by tying the wrists together, passing the arms over the bent knees, and inserting a stick over the arms and beneath the knees.

1853 M. REID *Rifle Rangers* lx, Wud yez jist ordher me to be gagged and 'bucked?' **1863** CUMMING *Hospital Life* (1866) 69/2 His method of punishing the men [is] by bucking and gagging. **1865** *Morning Star* Oct., He also saw men bucked by order of Wirtz for attempting to escape [from Andersonville]. **1867** W. L. GOSS *Soldier's Story* 47 To punish him for his attempt at escape, he was 'bucked.' **1888** J. D. BILLINGS *Hardtack* 146 Some [military judges] would *buck and gag* their victims.

2. To hold or tie (a person) securely across a log, preparatory to flogging.

1879 TOURGEE *Fool's Errand* 80 Is the rest of the incident true,—that about dragging the ministers from the pulpit, bucking them across a log, and beating them? *Ib.*, They might have bucked 'em across a log; . . . it's a powerful handy way to larrup a man.

+**Buck,** *v.*[6] [BUCK *n.*[1] 2.] *tr.* To put (ewes) to the ram. Also absol. and with *up.* — **1867** T. D. PRICE *MS. Diary* 5 Oct., Commenced bucking in afternoon. **1913** W. C. BARNES *Western Grazing Grounds* 380 *Bucking up,* placing the bucks with the ewes. A band of sheep is sold 'bucked up' to lamb on certain dates.

+**Buck,** *v.*[7] [BUCK *n.*[2]] *tr.* To saw wood, originally with the aid of a buck. — **1870** *Phila. Press* 8 Jan., [The] Pennsylvanian does not saw wood; he 'bucks' it. **1905** *Forestry Bureau Bul. 61* s.v., *Buck,* to saw felled trees into logs (Pacific Coast Forest).

+**Buck,** *v.*[8] *S. tr.* To bend or crook. — **1883** *American* VI. 237 (*Cent.*), To *buck,* meaning to bend, is a common word in the South.

+**Buck ague.** [BUCK *n.*[1] 1. Cf. BUCK FEVER.] Nervous excitement felt by an inexperienced hunter at the sight of game, orig. deer.

1844 GREGG *Commerce of Prairies* II. 24, I have often heard backwoodsmen speak of the 'buck ague,' but commend me to the 'buffalo fever' of the Prairies for novelty and amusement. **1851** *S. Lit. Messenger* XVII. 46/1 It is not everyone who can stand and look upon large game, in momentary expectation of shooting;—the heart thumps harder, the throat parches, . . . there is an undoubted case of *Buck-ague.* **1855** *Knickerb.* XLV. 316 If you have a prescription for the 'buck-ague,' prepare it to-night. **1872** MORRELL *Flowers & Fruits* 275 By this time I had what old Texans called 'the buck ague.' **1883** *Wheelman* I. 339 Our friend Charlie was seized with a severe attack of 'buck-ague,' as it is termed, they being the first deer he had ever seen. **1894** *Outing* XXIV. 344/1 My confusion . . . was the direct result of the buck-ague and an insane desire to possess myself of that elk.

+**Buck and wing.** A kind of tap dance (app. of Negro origin) performed with wooden or fiber-soled shoes. Orig. and usu. attrib. with *dance, dancer, dancing,* etc.

1895 *N.Y. Dramatic News* 23 Nov. 13/4 Burt Jordon, an exceedingly agile buck and wing dancer, was a hit at Keith's last week. **1897** *Chicago Tribune* 9 Aug. 10/4 Cake walking, 'buck' and 'wing' dancing . . . are the main features presented. **1907** MULFORD *Bar-20* 110 In the centre of the room was a large man dancing a fair buck-and-wing. *Ib.* 112 Up by the door Bigfoot Baker, elated at winning the buck-and-wing contest, was endeavouring to learn a new step. **1910** 'O. HENRY' *Strictly Business* 10 A mixed-up act comprising a monologue, three lightning changes with songs . . . and a buck-and-wing dance. **1918** SANDBURG *Cornhuskers* 35 Why do I always think of niggers and buck-and-wing dancing whenever I see watermelon?

+**Buckayro, Buckaroo.** Also **buckhara, bukkarer, buccahro, buccaroo, buckeroo.** [Corruption of VAQUERO.] A cowboy. Also attrib. (See BACCARO, BAKHARA.)

(*a*) *a***1861** WINTHROP *J. Brent* 21 The bukkarer, as Gerrian's Spanish entitled Hozay, comprehended enough of the order to know that he was to drive up the horses. **1889** *Cent.* 704/3 Buckayro. **1890** FARMER *Slang,* Buckhara. **1890** *Buckskin Mose* xii. 172 A large stock of cattle . . . had been in the charge of five good trusty *Buccahros* or herdsmen. **1904** *N.Y. Tribune* 17 July, He was herding a big bunch of cattle there with the help of half a dozen buckayros. **1910** J. HART *Vigilante Girl* 60, I can talk what they call 'buckayro' Spanish.

(*b*) **1900** WISTER *Jimmyjohn Boss* 18 Buccaroos? . . . Yep. Cow-punchers. Vaqueros. Buccaroos in Oregon. Bastard Spanish word, you see, drifted up from Mexico. **1907** WHITE *Arizona Nights* 51 If you were going to be a buckeroo, you couldn't go into harder training. **1913** W. C. BARNES *Western Grazing Ground* 200 Buckaroo. **1916** H. L. WILSON *Somewhere in Red Gap* 129 Nothing ever did worry that buckaroo as long as his fingers wasn't too cold to roll a cigarette.

+**Buck bass.** [BUCK *n.*[1]] A species of black bass. — **1883** *Century Mag.* July 376/2 Other names have been conferred on account of their pugnacity or voracity, as, tiger, bull, sow, and buck bass.

Buck bean.** The bog bean or marsh trefoil, *Menyanthes trifoliata.* — **1817–8** EATON *Botany* (1822) 352 Buck-bean . . . [grows in] stagnant waters. **1832** WILLIAMSON *Maine* I. 121 The Buckbean, or Marsh Trefoil prefers always wet spongy soils. . . . The plant holds a high place as a bitter or tonic. *a1848** Thoreau *Maine Woods* 26 We pushed our boat through an acre or more of buck-beans, which had taken root at the bottom, and bloomed above the surface. **1869** FULLER *Flower Gatherers* 133 This is the 'Buck-bean,' or *Menyanthes trifoliata,* the only American plant of the genus.

+**Buck beech.** A species of beech. — **1709** LAWSON *Carolina* 94 Beech. . . . Another sort call'd Buck-Beech is here found. **1835** *Survey of Property* Nov., *Pettigrew P.* (N.C. Univ.), To a maple & 2 buck beaches corner Trees.

+**Buck beer.** =BOCK BEER. — **1859** BARTLETT 51 *Buck beer,* (German, *bock bier,*) the strongest kind of German beer. . . . It is, of course, intoxicating.

+**Buckberry.** (See quot. 1824.) — **1824** J. DODDRIDGE *Notes* 86 An indifferent kind of fruit, called buckberries used to grow on small shrubs. . . . This fruit has nearly vanished from the settled parts of the country. **1920** STEPHENS *Life at Laurel Town* 14 Such substitutes as nature . . . is able to plant in Kansas—sumach and buckberry [etc.].

+**Buckboard.** [Cf. BUCK *n.*[3]]

1. (See quotation.)

1839 HOFFMAN *Wild Scenes* i. 10 Did he ever see a teamster riding upon a buckboard? a stout, springy plank, laid upon the bare bolsters of a wagon?

2. A very light four-wheeled buggy.

1869 TOURGEE *Toinette* iv. (1881) 45 The kind-hearted old slave woman folded her sooty arms about the shivering, splattered figure on the 'buck-board.' **1880** *Congress. Rec.* 26 Feb. 1165/2 The mail [in the Southwest] is carried in buckboards drawn by one or two ponies or mules. To stock the entire route with buckboards, mules and other outfit does not cost . . . $30,000. **1883** M. F. SWEETSER *Summer Days* 126 The buckboard which . . . some one else calls 'a cross between a see-saw and a hammock,' is the favorite vehicle for driving parties. **1892** ALLEN *Blue-Grass Region* 284, I made my way towards this mountain town, now riding on a buck-board, now on a horse. **1899** HOWELLS *Ragged Lady* 99 They sent her in a buckboard, with one of the stablemen to drive her. The landlord put her neat bundle under the seat of the buckboard with his own hand. **1903** A. ADAMS *Log Cowboy* 187, I'll make inquiry for you daily from men coming in, or from the buck board which carries the mail to Supply. **1923** R. HERRICK *Lilla* 23 She sat glumly with Dan on the front seat of the old buckboard.

3. Attrib. with *buggy, ride, wagon.*

1871 *Republican Daily Journal* (Kansas) 25 Aug., Dr. Wilder was indulging yesterday in a new buckboard buggy. **1885** *Outing* Oct. 74/2 At 2.20 exchanged my seat in a . . . railway carriage, for a place beside Frank Johnson, in a long buck-board wagon. **1890** C. KING *Sunset Pass* 9 Officers . . . had to . . . take a four or five days' 'buckboard' ride across the dusty deserts of Colorado. **1891** *Harper's Mag.* Dec. 29/2 Then we hired a buck-board wagon, and made ready for the journey.

+**Buckbrush.** [BUCK *n.*[1] 1.] Brush upon which deer feed. Applied specifically to several different plants or shrubs.

1874 LONG *Wild-Fowl* 179 He may find good shooting, . . . when the buck-brush is so close that the boat cannot be easily pushed through it. **1894** *Amer. Folk-Lore* VII. 90 *Symphoricarpus occidentalis,* . . . wolfberry, buck-brush, W. Neb. **1913** W. C. BARNES *Western Grazing Grounds* 61 The buck brush (*Cowania mexicana*), also called quinine bush, service berry (*Amelanchier*), . . . all furnish a large amount of excellent forage.

1916 BOWER *Phantom Herd* 185 The cat jumped out from behind a buck brush.

+**Buck dancer, dancing:** see BUCK AND WING. — **1896** *N.Y. Dramatic News* 29 Aug. 8/3 Conwell and O'Day, buck dancers, made a gigantic hit at Ferris Wheel park. **1897** G. ADE *Pink Marsh* 73, I use' to know cullud boy in Tuhkish bath place 'at got job on' e stage doin' buck-dancin'. **1925** J. BLACK *You Can't Win* iv. (1926) 39 The young negroes began singing and buck dancing.

+**Buck elk.** [BUCK *n.*[1]] A male elk.

1750 T. WALKER *Journal* 26 May 64 Our Dogs roused a large Buck Elk. **1751** C. GIST *Journals* 60 We killed a Buck Elk here and took out his Tongue to carry with us. **1804** CLARK in *Lewis & C. Exped.* (1904) I. 148, I Killed a Buck Elk & Deer. **1821** NUTTALL *Travels Arkansa* 210 A fat buck elk, which my companion had contrived to kill. **1839** L. LEONARD *Adventures* (1904) 62, I have killed two big Buck Elk!

+**Bucker**[1]. [BUCK *v.*[4]] A horse that bucks.

1884 *Harper's Mag.* July 301/1 If we should chance to select 'a bucker,' the probabilities are that we will come to grief. **1888** ROOSEVELT in *Century Mag.* April 851 The third [horse] turned out to be one of the worst buckers on the ranch. **1891** *Harper's Mag.* July 208/1 It is a common feat for him . . . to ride a vigorous bucker. **1907** WHITE *Arizona Nights* v. 95 He was a very hard bucker, and made some spectacular jumps.

+**Bucker**[2]. [BUCK *v.*[3] or *v.*[4]] **a.** One who refuses to follow his party leaders; a bolter. **b.** One who is insubordinate or has a grievance. — **1887** *Scribner's Mag.* Oct. 508 So I heard, last year, a politician speak of a bolter of the Republican ticket as a 'bucker.' **1898** *Boston Journal* 10 July 10/1 Yet the army is never without its buckers.

+**Bucker**[3]. [BUCK *v.*[2]] One who plays at games of chance like monte, faro, etc. — **1898** BRET HARTE *Stories in Light* 91 The unfortunate 'bucker' was cleared out not only of his gains, but of his original investment. **1900** SMITHWICK *Evolution of State* 75 One of the buckers was in my shop one day and . . . was struck with an idea.

* **Bucket.**

* **1.** A vessel for holding liquids; a pail.

'The term is applied, in the South and West, to all kinds of pails and cans holding over a gallon' (B. '59).

1622 'MOURT' *Relation* 36 We found . . . also an English Paile or Bucket. **1699** *Brookhaven Rec.* 63 Moses Owen shall have privilidge of drawing water att the aforesaide well, provided that hee . . . doe beare an equall proportion of the charge of . . . mainetaining buckitts & well ropes. **1781–2** JEFFERSON *Notes Va.* (1788) 35 It is used with a bucket and windlass as an ordinary well. **1832** KENNEDY *Swallow Barn* I. 296 The tall post . . . still supported the long piece of timber that balanced the bucket. **1853** RAMSEY *Tennessee* 513 His being a small tin bucket, I dipped it in first . . . and, never looking at the Indians, dipped up my bucket full. **1904** *McClure's Mag.* Feb. 382 Lunch-baskets and demijohns were piled in a neat heap, together with . . . two galvanized iron buckets.

attrib. **1903** G. ADE *In Babel* 317 Heinmiller depended somewhat upon the bucket trade.

2. *spec.* **a.** One for carrying water to extinguish fires. Also attrib. with *carriage, company, man.*

1782 TRUMBULL *M'Fingal* (1785) 88 Whence to and fro the waiters run, Like bucket-men at fires in town. **1870** O. LOGAN *Before Footlights* 274 There was rather a promiscuous display; 'hose companies,' 'hook-and-ladder companies,' and, I suppose, 'bucket companies.' **1881** *Harper's Mag.* Jan. 198/2 The law then, and until 1835, required each householder to keep in the hall . . . two leather buckets and to throw them into the street when an alarm of fire was heard. **1889** BRAYLEY *Boston Fire Dept.* 200 There were three bucket-carriages in the service.

+**b.** The vessel in which the sap from the sugar maple is collected.

1853 *Harper's Mag.* VI. 562/1 Now [=March] is the smell of red cedar 'spouts' through which the nectar is to distill into the 'bucket,' the stone-trough, and the potash kettle. **1880** *Ib.* LXI. 66 The lumbering ox-team and sled wind through the woods from tree to tree to relieve the over-flowing buckets.

3. One of the compartments of a water wheel. {1759–} +Also attrib. with *plank, wheel.*

1814 in *Scribner's Mag.* (1887) May 518/1 Water-wheel, 16 feet diameter, length of bucket 14 feet. **1826** FLINT *Recoll.* 105 It is now common to see flat-boats worked by a bucket wheel, and a horse power, after the fashion of steamboat movement. **1901** CHURCHILL *Crisis* 322 The bells clanged and the bucket-planks churned, and the great New Orleans packet crept slowly to the *Barbara's* side.

+**Bucket letter.** (See quotation.) — **1865** A. H. STEPHENS *Diary* (1910) 380 Dave Holt [*c*1830] was author of the letters signed 'Ned Bucket,' and published all over the country. . . . Anonymous letters came to be called 'Bucket letters.'

Bucketmaker. One who makes buckets.

1789 *Boston Directory* 184 Fenno, John, Cordwainer, leather bucket-maker. **1843** *Niles' Nat. Reg.* 80/1 The Mackerel Fishery has failed this year. Hingham, the head quarters of mackerel fishers and bucket makers, suffers.

+**b.** A nickname for an inhabitant of Hingham, Mass.

1840 DANA *Two Years* xxiii. 229 He was born in Hingham, and of course was called 'Bucketmaker.' *Ib.* xxxvi. 453 One of our boys was the son of a bucket-maker.

+**Bucket shop.** [BUCKET *n.*[1] 1.]

1. In New York City, a place where liquor was obtained in buckets, bottles, etc., brought by the patrons.

1875 STOWE *We & Our Neighbors* 380 The lowest, the most dreadful of all, was what they called the bucket shops. There the vilest of liquors are mixed in buckets and sold to wretched, crazed people. **1879** *Congress. Rec.* 14 May 1320/2 All the carriers of slung-shots, dirks, and bludgeons, all the fraternity of bucket-shops. **1881** *N.Y. Ev. Post* Oct. (Th.), A 'bucket-shop' in New York is a low 'gin-mill,' or 'distillery,' where small quantities of spirits are dispensed in pitchers and pails (buckets). When the shops for dealing in one-share or five-share lots of stocks were opened, these dispensaries of smaller lots than could be got from regular dealers were at once named 'bucket-shops.'

2. A brokerage establishment which does not execute a customer's orders but holds his money with the intent of pocketing it when the market goes against him.

1881 [see sense 1]. **1884** *Congress. Rec.* App., June 406/2 As between a bucket-shop and a put-and-call establishment, as between a margin-dealer and a roulette player, there is little or no moral difference. If there be any, it is in favor of the bucket-shop and the roulette-wheel. **1886** *Boston Journal* 11 Nov. 2/2 A new plan to suppress bucket-shops and restore speculative trading to former channels is being agitated by a number of members of the Board of Trade. **1887** *Courier-Journal* 7 Jan. 7/7 [As to] the character of business done by a 'bucket shop,' . . . the proprietor is . . . engaged instead in 'a species of gambling.' **1894** *Congress. Rec.* App. June 934/2 The bucket-shops . . . have demoralized more youth than all the gambling dens of the universe. **1902** LORIMER *Lett. Merchant* 115 When he chooses a father-in-law who plays the bucket shops, [etc.]. **1910** *N.Y. Ev. Post* 4 April 4 What . . . our people call a bucket-shop, is not only a gambling establishment pure and simple but is in most cases a gambling establishment which pretends to be something else.

+**Buckey.** *local.* The alewife. — **1877** BARTLETT 71 *Buckey*, an alewife. Western Connecticut. **1889** S. HALE *Letters* 227, I walked down to the beach for fish and came back bringing a stick of buckeys.

+**Buckeye, Buck-eye.** [BUCK *n.*[1] 1.]

1. One or other species of horse chestnut native to the United States, esp. the sweet buckeye (*Æsculus flava*) and the Ohio buckeye (*Æ. glabra*).

'The tree was so called on account of the resemblance which its dark-brown nut bears to a buck's eye, when the shell first cracks and exposes it to sight' (Clapin).

1784 J. FILSON *Kentucke* 23 Here also is the buck-eye, an exceeding soft wood, bearing a remarkable black fruit. **1792** IMLAY *Western Territory* 128 By the middle of the month [March], the buck-eye or horse chesnut is clad in its summer's livery. **1802** ELLICOTT *Journal* 286 Buck eye, (*aesculus pavia,*) this [*i.e.* of the Mississippi] is sometimes confounded with the buck eye, (*aesculus flava,*) of the Ohio; they are not the same. **1832** BROWNE *Sylva* 226 Large Buckeye . . . is here [in the southern states] called Big Buckeye, to distinguish it from the *Pavia rubra.* **1873** BEADLE *Undevel. West* 751 In times of scarcity they eat . . . the balls of the mountain buckeye. **1895** A. O. MYERS *Bosses & Boodle* 65 *Pavia Ohioensis*, the Ohio buckeye, or American horse-chestnut, is a native of the Ohio Valley. **1901** MOHR *Plant Life Ala.* 92 The delicate white-flowered spikes of the small-flowered buckeye (*Æsculus parviflora*).

b. Attrib. with *ball, bush, grove, leaf, log, nut, poison, tree.*

1785 WASHINGTON *Diaries* II. 360 Sowed . . . the following things: . . . Six buck eye nuts. **1804** *Md. Hist. Mag.* IV. 15 Sugar trees of enormous size . . . blue ash, oak, buckeye trees . . . all very large. **1838** E. S. Thomas *Reminiscences* I. 100 The Doctor had resolved on both giving and getting a stump speech, and had therefore supplied himself with the stump of the Buck Eye tree. **1847** in Drake *Pion. Life Ky.* 34 We charged upon the beautiful blue-ash and buckeye groves. **1850** N. KINGSLEY *Diary* 104 A short Buckeye stick which is celebrated for its handsome curl in its grain. **1867** *Iowa Agric. Soc. Rep.* 129 Cattle have few diseases in this locality except the 'buck eye' poison. *Ib.* 129 When they run out in the bottom timber they often eat the buck eye balls and are badly poisoned. **1882** *Amer. Naturalist* XVI. 913 The Buckeye Leaf Stem Borer. . . . We gave a short abstract of Mr. E. W. Claypole's paper on the above insect. **1897** BRODHEAD *Bound in Shallows* 142 'Bout like a buckeye log that'll rot at one end while it sprouts at the other.

2. A single tree of this kind.

1763 in R. T. Durrett *Louisville* (1893) 132 Beginning at a hoopashe and buckeye, the lower corner of Major Edward Ward's land [etc.]. **1780** W. FLEMING in *Travels Amer. Col.* 651 Warrant for 1000 acres . . . beginning at a Sugar tree, Ash, Elm and Buck Eye on the side of a hill corner. **1807** C. SCHULTZ *Travels* II. 24 The following are the natural fruit and forest trees, which I noticed on the banks of the Ohio: . . . black and white haws, buck-eyes, papaws. **1839** HOFFMAN *Wild Scenes* iii, The Buck-eyes make better bowls than you can carve from your Yankee poplars. **1878** B. F. TAYLOR *Between Gates* 214 Beneath avenues of live-oaks, among the junipers, the buckeyes and the buckthorns. **1886** BRET HARTE *Snowbound* 185 The trail . . . was passable the day before yesterday . . . for I discovered it, and went as far as the buck-eyes.

3. The nut or fruit of the buckeye. Also attrib.

1817 U. BROWN *Journal* II. 375, I have left in thy Counting Room . . . five Buck Eyes, alias Horse Chestnuts that also grew on the 472 Acres in

Harrison, Va. **1884** 'CRADDOCK' *Tenn. Mts.* 60 Buck-eyes were falling, and the ashy 'Indian pipes' silvered the roots of the trees. **1892** *Amer. Folk-Lore* V. 20 In Talladega, Alabama, the negroes believe that if one carries buckeyes in the pocket he will have no chills through the year. **1910** 'O. HENRY' *Strictly Business* 36, I'd be . . . better satisfied if the citizens . . . run more to velveteen vests and buckeye watch charms.

4. A native or inhabitant of Ohio. (Cf. BUCKEYE STATE.) In early use sometimes in wider application: see quots. 1828, 1857.

1823 JAMES *Exped.* I. 20 In allusion to this circumstance, the indigenous backwoodsman is sometimes called buck-eye, in distinction from the numerous emigrants who are introducing themselves from the eastern states. **1828** T. FLINT *Arthur Clenning* 171 [She] put into his arms a third boy, a fine Illinois buckeye too. **1835** HOFFMAN *Winter in West* I. 177 Nothing was wanting but a 'buckeye' from Ohio. **1846** FARNHAM *Prairie Land* 155 The Yankee Colony . . . bore off the prize for which the open-mouthed Kentuckians, Tennesseeans and Buckeyes were disputing. **1852** S. S. COX *Buckeye Abroad* 84 About twenty French men and women, all jolly, sat around us Buckeyes. **1857** *S. Lit. Messenger* XXIV. 317 A handsome young Buckeye Who lived in the West, in the State of Kentucky. **1871** BARNUM *Struggles & Triumphs* 347 You may fool the New Orleans folks, but you can't come it over the Buckeyes. **1882** *Congress. Rec.* 8 July 5811/1 The regenerated statesmanship of the modern Buckeye could be aroused by nothing less than the Presidency of the U.S. **1895** A. O. MYERS *Bosses & Boodle* 64 It has been claimed that this device [a buckeye tree] on this seal [*i.e.*, of Gov. St. Clair] gave the appellation of 'Buckeyes' to Ohio and her people.

b. *attrib.* Belonging to, characteristic of, Ohio.

1834 *Western Mo. Mag.* 145 Our own Buckeye population. **1838** DRAKE *Tales & Sk.* 59 A young Buckeye flower of the Miami valley, whose . . . beaming black eye . . . had won many hearts. **1841** *Arcturus* II. 53 (Th.), Far in the stern you see flitting about three or four gentle hoosiers or buckeye fair ones. **1842** *Amer. Pioneer* I. 436 His son of that name was my school-mate at a buckeye log cabin school-house. **1842** *Knickerb.* XIX. 223 The liquor was called for—a pint of buck-eye whiskey. **1852** S. S. COX *Buckeye Abroad* 11 We had not gone far before a singular phenomena—singular at least to our Buckeye eye—appeared. **1877** R. B. HAYES *Speech* 28 June (B.), Here and now I give you a hearty Buckeye shake [of the hands]. **1893** *Columbus* (O.) *Dispatch* 6 Sept., The Buckeye place-seekers can now and then be seen peering down upon the occupant of the Vice President's chair.

5. A variety of potato.

1868 *Rep. Comm. Agric.* 240.

6. A type of schooner: (see quotation 1889, and cf. BUGEYE.)

1885 C. P. KUNHARDT *Small Yachts* 234 (*Cent.*), The buckeyes . . . are an exaggeration of the dugout canoe. **1889** *Cent.* 705/2 *Buckeye*, . . . a flat-bottomed centerboard schooner of small size . . . decked over, and with a cabin aft, used in oyster-fishing in Chesapeake Bay.

7. A cheap, commercial oil painting. Also attrib.

1881 *N. Y. Ev. Post* 7 June (Th.). **1906** *Atlantic Mo.* Nov. 640 The serious painters whose work is found in exhibitions, and the despised 'buckeye' painter who paints for department stores and cheap picture shops.

‖**Buckeyed,** *a.* [BUCKEYE 1 b.] Poisoned from eating buckeyes. — **1867** *Iowa Agric. Soc. Rep.* 129 From half a pound to one pound of lard put down the animal's throat when 'buckeyed' is a pretty safe antidote for the poison.

+**Buckeye State.** [Cf. BUCKEYE 4.] The state of Ohio.

1840 HARRISON *Melodies* 59. **1843** *Amer. Pioneer* II. 64 For aught we know, it was the first furnace in the 'Buckeye state.' **1851** *Polly Peablossom* 180 Thus terminated the last meeting on the 'field of honour' that ever came off in the 'Bonnie Buckeye State.' **1875** *Chicago Tribune* 15 Nov. 5/2 Gov. Hayes . . . stated . . . that the educational question had given the Republicans a victory in the Buckeye State. **1894** *Congress. Rec.* App. 26 Jan. 79/1 The very author of the tariff plank in the Chicago platform was last fall buried beneath more than 80,000 votes in that grand old 'Buckeye' State. **1907** *Chicago Tribune* 8 May 8 When the secretary of war [=W. H. Taft] was in the Buckeye state a week ago he . . . got in touch with the people.

+**Buck fever.** [BUCK *n.*[1] 1.] =BUCK AGUE.

1841 *S. Lit. Messenger* VII. 224/2 'If you see a deer, Ellit,' said the scout, laughing, 'you'll be sure to git the buck fever.' **1857** HAMMOND *Northern Scenes* 127 Smith blazed away at him . . . ; but the deer dashed forward. . . . Smith acknowledged to a severe attack of the Buck fever. **1890** CUSTER *Following Guidon* 218 The elks were so much larger than other game that the officers often lost their first shots from buck-fever. **1902** WHITE *Blazed Trail* xix. 140 What few running shots offered, he missed, mainly because of buck fever.

+**Buck fly.** [BUCK *n.*[1] 1.] (See quotation.) — **1859** BARTLETT 52 *Buck fly*, an insect which torments the deer at certain seasons.

+**Buck-handled,** *a.* [BUCK *n.*[1] 1.] Having a handle made of buckhorn. — **1840** *S. Lit. Messenger* VI. 507/1 Joe Curry . . . was a tall strapping fellow, with a mouth always standing half-open, like an old case of buck-handled knives. **1845** *Knickerb.* XXVI. 513 To these were afterwards added . . . an excellent buck-handled carving-knife and fork. **1865** STOWE *House & Home P.* 42 We have all the cracked plates, . . . cracked teacups and old buck-handled knives that can be raised out of chaos.

***Buckhorn.** [BUCK *n.*[1] 1.] Cf. BUCK'S-HORN.

1. The material of a male deer's horn. Chiefly attrib. or comb. {1613, 1820–}

1756 in *Lett. to Washington* I. 364 Buck horn handled Cutlasses @ 2/6—but few left. **1827** COOPER *Prairie* i, The buck-horn haft of his knife was profusely decorated with plates of silver. **1846** *Spirit of Times* (N.Y.) 4 July 223/2 She took from its Buck-horn rack a six foot rifle. **1866** GREGG *Life in Army* 265 Like the little boy's old knife which needed new blades, new spring, and a bran new buck-horn handle! **1880** *Scribner's Mo.* April 884/1 Quantities of flint-chips, such as the old arrow-head makers used to spring off from the block by adroitly handling creased tips of buckhorn.

***2.** The horn of a male deer.

1824 DODDRIDGE *Notes* 124 The rifle, which was always suspended to a joist by a couple of buck horns, or little forks. **1853** *Knickerb.* XLII. 326 He sent us the abundant ears of the lofty prairie-corn, which embellished the buck-horns in our town-sanctum during the fall and winter months!

+**3.** A type of rifle sight having a branching projection on each side of the sight notch. Also attrib.

1877 R. I. DODGE *Hunting Grounds Gt. West* vii. 105 The very best sight, and the one almost universally in use by sportsmen and professional hunters on the plains, is the plain 'buckhorn.' *Ib.*, Sportsmen who use the 'buckhorn' must learn to sight 'on the barrel.' **1901** WHITE *Westerners* xi. 78 Innumerable times he had viewed the doctor, Prue, and the scout through the buck-horn sights of his long rifle.

+**4.** As a plant name, or used attrib. to designate varieties of plants: (see quotations).

1712 PETIVER in *Phil. Trans.* XXVII. 424 Virginia Sumach. . . . The first-branches are very soft and velvety, like the horns of a young deer, for which reason it is called Buckhorn by the country people. **1847** DARLINGTON *Weeds & Plants* 220 *Plantago lanceolata*, . . . Ribgrass, English Plantain, Buckhorn Plantain. **1889** *Cent.* 658/2 Buckhorn brake [is] a name sometimes applied to the flowering fern, *Osmunda regalis*. *Ib.* 705/2 *Buckhorn*, a name for the club-moss, *Lycopodium clavatum*. **1892** *Amer. Folk-Lore* V. 105 *Osmunda regalis*, buck-horn. Worcester Co., Mass.

+**Buck Indian.** [BUCK *n.*[1] 4 a.] A male Indian.

1840 HOFFMAN *Greyslaer* II. 54 There they lay on the grass, six big buck Injuns, likely fellows all. **1857** CHANDLESS *Visit Salt Lake* I. 98 You could not mistake a squaw for a buck Indian. **1869** *Congress. Globe* 27 Feb. 1707/3 Chasing the fourteen year old buck Indians across the plains for the purpose of catching them and putting blue breeches on them. **1882** *Congress. Rec.* 26 July 6540/1 The commissioners provided a pound of striped candy for each buck Indian in order to be certain of his assent. **1899** T. HALL *Tales* 276 Judge Leander Quinn was lured away from a monte game with a couple of buck Indians. **1902** 'MARK TWAIN' in *Harper's Mag.* Jan. 264 The camp has about . . . five squaws, and a dozen vagrant buck Indians in rabbit-skin robes.

+**Bucking,** *vbl. n.*[1] [BUCK *v.*[4]] The action, on the part of a horse or mule, of trying to throw the rider over its head. Also attrib.

1869 MCCLURE *Rocky Mts.* 302 The native horses become singularly skilled in 'bucking,' and there are few riders who can keep the saddle or make them yield to the lines. **1870** KEIM *Sheridan's Troopers* 232 The animal made several violent dashes in advance, at the same time indulging in that resolute manoeuvre known as 'bucking.' **1873** BEADLE *Undevel. West* 284 A saddle, not carefully girted, slipped back and the mule straightway went to 'bucking.' **1902** WISTER *Virginian* 291 Stooping to investigate the bucking-strap on his saddle—a superfluous performance, for Pedro never bucked.

transf. **1907** WHITE *Arizona Nights* viii. 151 Naturally Mr. Calf entered his objections, which took the form of . . . the most comical bucking.

+**Bucking,** *vbl. n.*[2] [BUCK *v.*[5]]

1. (See quot. 1864 and BUCK *v.*[5] 1.)

1864 PITTENGER *Daring & Suffering* 228 The guards came up, and seizing Pierce, . . . and tying his hands before his knees, with a stick inserted across under his knees and over his arms, in the way that soldiers call 'bucking,' they left him there all night. **1865** KELLOGG *Rebel Prisons* 113 One of the camp thieves or 'raiders' would be . . . carried to the brook, to endure the process of 'gagging' and 'bucking.' **1921** R. M. JONES *Later Period of Quakerism* II. 744 The bucking-down was resorted to for two hours.

2. *Bucking paddle* (cf. BUCK *v.*[5] 2).

1861 [H. JACOBS] *Life Slave Girl* 98 Others were tied hand and feet, and tortured with a bucking paddle.

+**Bucking,** *vbl. n.*[3] [BUCK *v.*[3] 2.] The action of forcing one's way against obstacles. — **1882** *Harper's Mag.* Dec. 3/2 Presently the swiftest water is reached, the race of the rapid. Now commences what Western steamboat men call 'bucking.'

+**Bucking,** *vbl. n.*[4] (See quotation.) — **1888** *Troy Daily Times* 8 Feb. (F.), The queerest thing about the poor white is, that not one was ever known to make any kind of religious profession. There is, as far as I know, but one thing in which they believe, and that is what is termed further South voudouism, or, as they term it here, bucking.

+**Bucking,** *a.* [BUCK *v.*[4]] Inclined or accustomed to buck; pertaining to bucking.

1877 W. WRIGHT *Big Bonanza* 87 He was killed . . . by being thrown from a 'bucking' mustang. **1884** SWEET & KNOX *Through Texas* 68 For it dispelled fears and misgivings we had, that our lately acquired purchases might have been 'bucking ponies.' **1895** REMINGTON *Pony Tracks* 12 When you put a man . . . on the 'bucking' horse, . . . he must have a (tight) seat on his mount. **1901** WHITE *Claim Jumpers* v. 74 The curley-haired young man who had lent him the bucking horse.

+**Buckjump,** *n.* [BUCK *v.*[4]] A leap, spring, or plunge made by a bucking animal. — **1861** *Harper's Mag.* June 8/1 The Captain . . . generally rides downhill at full gallop, and when that is impracticable, compels his animal to slide or make 'buck jumps' over the worst places.

+**Buckjump,** *v.* =BUCK *v.*[4] Also transf. — **1890** JEFFERSON *Autob.* 468 As a rider of buck-jumping ponies he was a wonder either with or without a saddle. **1897** *Outing* XXX. 217 Lordly salmon, gamy trout and buck-jumping ouananiche are fit for any man to play. **1903** *McClure's Mag.* Nov. 97/2 They tried me with a pencil and paper, but I balked, laid my ears back, and buck-jumped. **1907** WHITE *Arizona Nights* v. 96 Sometimes we skipped and hopped and buck-jumped through and over little gullies.

Buckjumper. [BUCK *v.*[4]] A horse that bucks. — **1878** I. L. BIRD *Rocky Mts.* 147 Two stockmen from the Plains, one of whom rode a violent buck-jumper. **1882** *Detroit W. Free Press* 2 Dec. 1/6 That pony is a mustang and buck-jumper.

Buckle, *n.* +*To make buckle and tongue meet,* to make both ends meet. — **1888** *Harper's Mag.* Apr. 703/1 Beginning without money, he had as much as he could do to make 'buckle and tongue meet,' as the phrase goes.

* **Buckle,** *v.*

1. *intr.* +**a.** *To buckle to,* to lay hold of; to grasp firmly; to apply oneself to.

1825 NEAL *Bro. Jonathan* I. 266 Don't buckle to the great brute, whatever he may do. **1838** *S. Lit. Messenger* IV. 407 Each man must buckle to his man, and not a soul of them will be able to save himself. **1884** 'MARK TWAIN' *H. Finn* 138 Come, buckle to your paddle, and let's get along.

+**b.** To settle *down to,* or set to work seriously or steadily at, something.

1865 *Atlantic Mo.* XV. 301 If he would only buckle down to serious study. **1871** BRET HARTE *Poems* 55 Chiquita Buckled right down to her work. **1886** DORSEY *Midshipman Bob* II. viii. 188 In a few days the boys buckled down to hard work, which was not remitted until the June examinations were over. **1889** CUSTER *Tenting on Plains* 145, I was constantly mystified . . . how our officers . . . could, as they expressed it, 'buckle-down' to the dull, exhausting days of a monotonous march.

+**2.** *To buckle in.* **a.** 'To close in; to embrace or seize the body, as in a scuffle. A popular use in America' (W. '28).

+**b.** To set to work.

More usually *to buckle to,* in use from 1845. {1712–}

1880 'MARK TWAIN' *Tramp Abroad* xx, I buckled in and read all of those books, because he wanted me to.

Buck leather. [BUCK *n.*[1] 1.] =BUCKSKIN. — **1647** *Essex Probate Rec.* I. 92, I giue to my Brother James Baly . . . one paire of buck lether Breches.

+**Buck mouse.** [BUCK *n.*[1] 1.] The jumping mouse, *Zapus hudsonius.* — **1857** *Rep. Comm. Patents: Agric.* 90 The white-footed wood-mouse is known under the names of 'Deer Mouse,' 'Buck Mouse,' 'White-footed Field Mouse.'

Buck neck. [BUCK *n.*[1] 1.] The skin from the neck of a buck. — **1670** *Southampton Rec.* II. 56 For every season they will give vnto vs . . . one pair of shoes or a buck neck to make them.

+**Buck Negro, nigger.** [BUCK *n.*[1] 4 b.] A male Negro.

1853 *S. Lit. Messenger* XIX. 221/2 A big buck negro struck with all his might, with the back of the axe, to knock it [the door] off its hinges. **1860** *Richmond Enquirer* 30 Nov. 2/4 (Th.), He let drop from the canvas an unmistakable small, nappy-headed buck negro. **1863** 'KIRKE' *Southern Friends* 66 Scented, bedevilled-up buck niggers. **1884** J. C. HARRIS in *Century Mag.* Nov. 123 A mighty purty pass it's come tọ, when great big buck niggers can lie a-snorin' in the woods all day. **1904** *N.Y. Ev. Post* 5 Sept. 4 If a buck nigger should offer to escort a young white woman to church, her father, if he were a true Southern white man, would kill the brute as he would a mad dog.

+**Bucko.** *slang.*

1. *Naut.* A ship's officer (esp. a mate) who treats his men brutally.

1899 M. ROBERTSON *Where Angels Fear,* etc. (1921) 107 Stand by here, mates. These buckoes'll kill some one yet. Look out for their brass knuckles and guns. **1905** — in *Cosmopolitan* May 49/1 Mr. Rollins, when sober, was a capable first officer, but, drunk or sober, a brute — a 'bucko,' as sailors call his kind.

b. Attrib. with *mate.*

1911 VANCE *Cynthia* 242 You're said to be a fighter, a bully, a bucko mate: prove it. **1921** PAINE *Comr. Rolling Ocean* 47 After this episode he addressed the autocratic Judson as 'the bucko mate.'

2. =BUCK *n.*[1] 3 (but with disparaging connotation).

1902 NORRIS *Pit* (1922) iii, This time I want to . . . get a twist on those Porteous buckoes, and raise 'em right out of their boots. **1907** WHITE *Arizona Nights* vii. 136 'What?' says I. "Elucidate my bucko. I don't take no such blanket order.' **1910** MCCUTCHEON *Rose in Ring* 384 ['Jail is] just where you'll land, my handsome bucko,' said the malevolent Colonel.

Buckra, Buckrah. Also †**boccarorra.** [Of African origin.] {1736 Antigua use in *S.C. Gazette* 23 April 1737; 1794– in O.E.D.}

1. Among southern Negroes: A white man.

1795 WINTERBOTHAM *Hist. View* III. 298 [Americans] are pleased with the observation of a negro, and frequently mention it, that 'Boccarorra (meaning the white man) . . . make ebery ting workee, only de hog.' **1800** BROWN *A. Mervyn* xli, Bob said, in a whining, beseeching tone, 'Why, missee, massa buckra wanna go for doo, dan he winna go fo' wee.' **1836** SIMMS *Mellichampe* xlvii, 'Tis only poor buckrah dat does trouble nigger. **1836** GILMAN *Recoll.* (1838) 104 'Ole Maus Osborne dead, . . . and one buckra been come to mak de bounds of de land.' **1855** SIMMS *Forayers* 182 Like the servants of most of the lordly planters of that day, Benny Bowlegs had but small esteem for the class whom he described as 'poor *buckrah.*' **1865** *Atlantic Mo.* Jan. 69/1 Am he a buckra? **1899** CHESNUTT *Conjure Woman* 14 Dey wuz a settlement er free niggers en po' buckrahs down by de Wim'l'ton Road.

b. Master. Also transf.

1886 *Amer. Philol. Assoc.* XVII. 45 *Buck-ra* (for boss or master in South Carolina). **1892** HARRIS *On the Plantation* 75 Miss Chicken Hawk she coyspon' wid Mr. Eagle, which he was de big buckra er all de birds.

2. Attrib. with *man, people, woman,* etc.

1835 [LONGSTREET] *Georgia Scenes* 48 Fedder fly all ober de buckeraman meat. **1836** GILMAN *Recoll.* (1838) 127 Miss Neely, one buckra woman want for track up all de clean floor. **1845** *Knickerb.* XXVI. 332 So thought Mr. Thomas Rice, a 'buckra gemman' of great imitative powers. **1846** CHILD *Fact & Fiction* 197 Myself found the body of my likeliest boy under the tree where buckra rifles reached him. **1872** W. J. FLAGG *Good Investment* 549/2 No mo' . . . dan . . . de buckra people 'bout yere kin be like Miss Bella.

b. *transf.* Attrib. with names of objects.

1871 DE VERE 151 Negroes thus speak of buckra yam, with the understanding, however, that it is not only white, but peculiarly good also.

Buck rabbit. [BUCK *n.*[1]] A male jack rabbit.

1838 *Knickerb.* XI. 447 Your land is so poor, that a single buck-rabbit would make a famine in your whole county. **1841** *S. Lit. Messenger* VII. 39/2 What the plague then makes her run and stomp about the house like a buck-rabbit? **1874** B. F. TAYLOR *World on Wheels* vi. 46 Three or four exaggerated creatures lie in a heap in a corner. . . . They are ears with bodies to them. It is your first sight of a buck-rabbit.

attrib. **1878** PINKERTON *Strikers* 318 The train [is] called through that locality the 'buck-rabbit' train, from the fact that it stops at every little station.

* **Buckram.** Also †**bucrum, buckrum.**

* **1.** A coarse linen fabric stiffened with paste.

1644 *Conn. Public Rec.* I. 459 In bucrum, 10 s. **1710** BUCKINGHAM *Naval Exped.* 81 To Buckram, tape, silk, mowhair and making the coat. **1724** *New-Eng. Courant* 5–12 Oct. 2/2 All Persons that have Occasion to have Cloth made into Buckrum, or have Occasion for any Buckrum ready made [etc.]. **1807** IRVING, etc. *Salmagundi* v. 117 Being braced up in the fashionable style, with whalebone, stay-tape, and buckram, [she] looked like an apple-pudding tied in the middle.

comb. **1726** *New Eng. Courant* 5–12 March 2/2 Samuel Hall, buckram-stiffner and glass-maker. **1880** *Harper's Mag.* Dec. 36/2 The old buckram-backed rhymed versions of the psalms.

+**b.** *In buckram:* (see quotation).

*c***1830** GODMAN in *Waldie's Select Library* II. 87/3 Twelve hours later the shell is sufficiently stiffened to require some slight force to bend it, and the crab is said to be in *buckram.*

+**2.** One who was inclined to favor metallic rather than paper currency. *Obs.*

1855 Hambleton *H. A. Wise* 448 Some Softs who are 'Buckrams,' tending to Hards.

+**Bucksaw.** [BUCK *n.*[2]] A saw fitted in a frame and operated with both hands.

1857 UNDERHILL & THOMPSON *Elephant Club* 62 The boys . . . carry their anatomical investigations to the extent of cutting off a leg or two, . . . with a buck-saw. **1884** SWEET & KNOX *Through Texas* 487 The cross-eyed negro with . . . a bucksaw in his hand, begins sawing wood in the backyard of the saloon. **1891** *Century Mag.* March 711 Rations of wood were brought in daily and to each mess was delivered an ax and a bucksaw. **1891** ROBERTS *Adrift Amer.* 198 He would put me to saw wood with a bucksaw.

‖**Buck-scrape.** [BUCK *n.*[1] 1.] A place where the ground has been scraped by deer. — **1885** *Outing* Oct. 68/1 We had walked about a quarter of a mile when we found a fresh buck-scrape.

+**Buck's-eye.** =BUCKEYE 1. — **1781–2** JEFFERSON *Notes Va.* (1788) 38, I will sketch out those [plants] which would principally attract notice . . . : Red flowering maple, *Acer rubrum;* Horse-chesnut, or Buck's-eye, *Æsculus pavia.* **1814** PURSH *Flora Amer.* I. 255 *Æsculus macrostachya.* . . . The whole of this genus is known in their native countries by the name of Buck's-eye-tree. **1836** LATROBE *Rambler* II. 8 The buck's eye, a shrub with bright green leaves and red flower-buds, and the red-berry, covered with peach-coloured blossoms, were seen every where.

*Buck's-horn. [BUCK n.[1] 1.]

*1. =BUCKHORN 1, 2. Also attrib.

1637 MORTON *New Canaan* III. xiv, A goodly pine tree of 80 foote longe was reared up [as a Maypole] with a peare of buckshorns nayled one somewhat neare unto the top of it. 1824 DODDRIDGE *Notes* 114 This awl with its buckshorn handle was an appendage of every shot pouch strap.

+2. In plant names: (see quotations).

1629 PARKINSON *Paradisus* 611 *Rhus Virginiana.* The Virginia Sumach, or Buckes horne tree of Virginia. 1821 *Mass. H. S. Coll.* 2 Ser. IX. 153 *Onoclea struthiopteris.* Buck's horn brake. 1890 *Cent.* 3552/2 *Lycopodium clavatum* . . . has also been called stag's horn, buck's horn, fox's claws, foxtail, etc.

+Buck-shot, Buckshot, *n.* [BUCK n.[1] 1.]

1. Shot of large size used in shooting deer.

1775 *Gaine's Mercury* 14 Aug. (B.), The reason that so many more of the King's troops were wounded than killed . . . is that the Americans use a small shot, called buck-shot, which is much smaller than the soldiers' bullets. 1776 *Journals Cont. Congress* VI. 860 Resolved, that the Board of War be directed to send to the Commissary of Stores, . . . 20 Tons Buck shot. 1810 WEEMS *Washington* (ed. 10) 75 With fowling pieces loaded with ball and buckshot. *c*1836 CATLIN *Indians* II. 141 One of them . . . levelled it [=his gun] at us, and gave us a charge of buck-shot about our ears. 1869 BROWNE *Adv. Apache Country* 99 They had but one gun with them, which . . . was charged with buck-shot. 1873 MILLER *Amongst Modocs* 170 The Prince procured a great double-barrelled shot gun, throwing buck-shot by the handfull, for himself. 1887 *Courier-Journal* 3 May 1/1 Lincoln threatened to kill the first man who came near, but a load of buckshot placed him beyond carrying out his threat. 1910 HART *Vigilante Girl* 171 His injuries . . . were flesh-wounds, as Alden had been partly shielded from the buckshot by a rug across his knees.

2. A single bullet of this kind.

The plural is usually without *-s.*

1777 *Essex Inst. Coll.* XLV. 210 One Buck Shot went through his Hat. 1797 B. HAWKINS *Letters* 275 There were two balls thro' the dead man, and the wounded men, one with a ball, and the other a buck shot. 1811 *Ann. 12th Congress* 1 Sess. 2122 Our infantry used, principally, cartridges containing twelve buck shot. 1846 M'KENNEY *Memoirs* I. 74 The ball being only the size of a buck-shot, he could see no place of entrance. 1866 RICHARDSON *Secret Service* 54 We purchased a few buckshots and fragments of shells from the ancient Ethiop. 1871 NAPHEYS *Prevention of Disease* III. 740 A piece about the size of a buckshot is the ordinary dose.

3. *Buckshot war*, an election disturbance in Harrisburgh, Pa., in 1838, in which troops called out to quell the riot were ordered to use cartridges containing buckshot.

1842 *Congress. Globe* June 609/1 Mr. B. [=Benton] believed that was the phrase used in Pennsylvania, in time of the buckshot war. 1868 *Ib.* Dec. 141/1 Mr. [Thaddeus] Stevens made the capital mistake of his life, in determining to treat the election as if it had not occurred. This brought on the 'buckshot war.' 1875 *Congress. Rec.* March 38/1 This buckshot war was a ridiculous affair from beginning to end.

4. *Buckshot soil, cotton land:* (see quotations).

1871 R. SOMERS *Southern States since War* 144 The soil is a dry deep red loam—what is called, in the language of the country, 'a buckshot soil.' 1884 'CRADDOCK' *Where Battle Was Fought* 13 Comparing Tennessee soil to the alluvial richness of the buckshot cotton lands of Mississippi.

5. =BLACK SPOT 2.

1888 M. LANE in *America* 18 Oct. 15 They were known in one locality as 'Blackspots,' and in another as 'Buckshots,' and committed all sorts of murders, and outrages.

‖Buckshot, *v. colloq.* [BUCKSHOT n.] *tr.* To shoot with buckshot. — 1887 *Courier-Journal* 8 May 4/7 He was buck-shotted to death on Friday afternoon at his home near Kerrville.

*Buckskin. [BUCK n.[1] 1.]

*1. The skin of a male deer.

1646 *Mass. H. S. Coll.* 4 Ser. VI. 334 Wequash Cooks brother tooke from him . . . 1 greatt buckskynn and two doe skynns. 1678 *New Castle Court Rec.* 349, 80 drest buckskines at 2s 6d. 1709 LAWSON *Carolina* 224 Those that buy Rum of them have so many Mouthfuls for a Buck-Skin. 1750 *Cal. Virginia St. P.* I. 243 There came a number of Indiens to the sd: house and did . . . take out of it . . . two Buck Skins in Parchment. 1772 D. TAITT in *Travels Amer. Col.* 508 A Blanket which is commonly sold for six pound of drest skins they would sell for a buck skin in the Hair. 1837 *Knickerb.* X. 413 The fabrication of jeans by one party, and the dressing of buck-skins by the other, furnished profitable amusement.

2. Leather made from the skin of a buck. {1804-}

1705 BEVERLEY *Virginia* III. 3 Their Shoes, when they wear any, are made of an entire piece of Buck-Skin. 1747 FRANKLIN *Electrical Exper.* (1751) 17 We rub our tubes with buckskin. 1813 *Austin Papers* (1924) I. 223 Indian dressed Buckskin for overalls and frocks are now as universal as broadcloth used to be. 1833 J. HALL *Harpe's Head* 12 The fractures had been remedied . . . by a thong of buckskin. 1878 *Rep. Indian Affairs* 19 Buckskin is sold to the traders in heavy aggregate amounts, and is hauled to the railroad by the ton. 1891 *Century Mag.* March 652 He wore no clothing whatever save a narrow piece of calico or buckskin about the loins.

3. Garments or breeches made of buckskin. Usu. pl. {*a*1658-}

1832 KENNEDY *Swallow Barn* II. 97 Harry Davenport close at your heels, thrusting his long lance right at the seat of your yellow buckskins. 1843 'CARLTON' *New Purchase* II. 123 Never before had so much law been cased in a hunting shirt and buckskin. *a*1861 WINTHROP *John Brent* 55 Showers shrank his buckskins and soaked the macheers of his saddle to mere pulp. 1873 MILLER *Amongst Modocs* 28 My tattered clothes were replaced by soft brown buckskins.

+4. One who wears buckskin garments. Originally and usually, a Virginian.

1745 *Itinerant Observ.* 51 The Inhabitants on the *Western Shore* are supply'd . . . from this *Eastern Shore*, as they call them, by Way of Distinction; to whom they give, also, ironically, the epithet of *Buckskins*, alluding to their Leather Breeches, and the Jackets of some of the common People. 1774 FITHIAN *Journal* I. 242, I suppose . . . [she] has in a merry hour call'd him a Lubber, or a thick-Skull, or a Buckskin. 1797 PRIEST *Travels* 207 A prospect you Buck-skins can have no idea of. 1800 WEEMS *Washington* (1877) ii. 8 What! a buckskin! say they with a smile. George Washington a buckskin! pshaw! impossible! he was certainly an European. 1825 NEAL *Bro. Jonathan* I. 245 '*He*, a Yankee! he's a Buckskin, every inch of him, I know.' — The Virginians are called Buckskins. 1837 *S. Lit. Messenger* April 257/2 Common as this [use of *howsomever*] is said to be in England, it has no place among the Buckskins. 1885 EGGLESTON in *Century Mag.* April 890/2 Entire suits of deer-skin were worn on Sunday in the newer parts of the country, and backwoods rustics were familiarly known as 'buckskins.'

+b. *attrib.* Virginian or native American.

1776 J. LEACOCK *Fall Brit. Tyranny* III. vi, His jetty black hair, such as Buckskin saints wear. 1783 FRENEAU *Poems* (1786) 333 Why did not heaven . . . Teach me to take the true-born Buckskin side? 1800 J. BOUCHER *Glossary* p. 1, At dinner, let me that best buck-skin dish, Broth made of bacon, cream, and eke cat-fish, With toss 'em boys, and belly bacon see. 1809 WEEMS *Marion* (1833) 233 To be treated thus by buckskin girls, the rebel daughters of convict parents, was more than the British officers could put up with. 1841 H. PLAYFAIR *Papers* I. 33 'Sir, have you not slaves in Massachusetts?' asked Colonel Richard Wentworth, one of the buckskin gentlemen from Virginia. 1845 GREEN *Texian Exped.* 281 One of our buckskin Republicans, . . . threw the larieta over the head of the young Jesus.

+c. *Buckskin men* (see quotation).

1866 *Rep. Indian Affairs* 97 The haunts of the notorious 'buckskin men,' or kidnappers, in the small valleys or on the mountains would be under our control.

+5. *attrib.* Of a horse: Of the color of buckskin.

1874 *Vt. Bd. Agric. Rep.* II. 402 The buckskin McClellan was a regular hollow or sway back. 1899 T. HALL *Tales* 263 'Buckskin Nell,' they called her, because of the buckskin pony she rode with all the dash and skill of a cowboy. 1910 J. HART *Vigilante Girl* 195 The cowboys had with them a handsome buckskin mustang.

+b. A horse of this color.

1889 *Cent.* 1891 BUNNER *Zadoc Pine*, etc. 174 The man on the queer-looking buckskin . . . is McAlpine. 1894 *Outing* April 101/2 That Clip of hers . . . is a pretty mustang. He's a bright buckskin with a dark stripe. 1902 WHITE *Blazed Trail* xxxi. 205 The young fellow glanced solicitously at the splendid buckskins, the best horses in camp. 1916 H. TITUS *I Conquered* 83 The mares stirred. One, a bright buckskin, trotted up the rise a dozen yards.

+c. The color of buckskin.

1902 MCFAUL *Ike Glidden* 23 Only thing he has against him's his color; says he can't bear buckskin.

*6. Attrib. in sense: Made of buckskin; esp. with *breeches, glove, legging, pants, pantaloons, shirt*, etc.

Very common throughout the 19th century.

1723 *Weekly Mercury* 22-29 Aug. 2/2 He had on a grey Frys Coat, . . . a pair of Buck-skin Breeches and brownish Stockings. 1775 *Journals Cont. Congress.* III. 318 That . . . 3,000 pair of buckskin breeches . . . be immediately purchased. 1818 SCHOOLCRAFT *Journal* 30 The girls had buckskin frocks, [which] were abundantly greasy and dirty. 1824 DODDRIDGE *Notes* 129 The ladies dressed in Linsey petticoats . . . and buckskin gloves, if any. 1827 COOPER *Prairie* x, His lower limbs were protected by buckskin leggings. 1838 INGRAHAM *Burton* II. 217 The clippings and dust falling, as he worked, into a buckskin tray accurately fitted to the pillar of the vice. 1845 J. J. HOOPER *Taking Census* i. 155 The money was tied up in a buckskin pouch. 1847 HOWE *Hist. Coll. Ohio* 571 The rich and the poor dressed alike; the men generally wearing hunting shirts and buckskin pants. 1849 PARKMAN *Oregon Trail* 12 One or two French hunters from the mountains, with their long hair and buckskin dresses. 1851 A. O. HALL *Manhattaner* 20 The dirty man whose idiosyncrasy seems to lie in the manufacture and sale of buckskin purses and suspenders. 1870 KEIM *Sheridan's Troopers* 173 Their buckskin shirts are elaborately decorated with bead-work. 1871 *Harper's Mag.* Oct. 686 Others were clad in buckskin coats and uniform trowsers. 1873 BEADLE *Undevel. West* 725 The only instruments were a tin drum and what appeared to be a buckskin tambourine. 1880 G. INGHAM *Digging Gold* 290 His arms were securely tied behind him with a buckskin string. 1890 N. P. LANGFORD *Vigilante Days* ii. 38 Buckskin sacks, containing about eighty thousand dollars, were distributed. **1890** RYAN *Told in Hills* 26 A fair, fine-looking fellow, in a ranchman's buckskin suit. **1909** 'O. HENRY' *Options* 112 They wash the gold ... and then they pack it in buckskin sacks of one arroba each.

+**Bucksnatcher.** *Obs.* A river boat engaged in piratical undertakings. — **1830** *Western Mo. Review* III. 356 For night and secret work Plug had a fleet of Bucksnatchers with chosen crews, to row up and down the river [Ohio].

+**Bucktail,** ***Buck's tail.** [BUCK *n.*[1] 1.]

1. The tail of a male deer.

1775 FITHIAN *Journal* II. 24 Almost all have a cockade, & bucks-tale in their hats, to represent that they are hardy, resolute, & invincible natives. **1813** *Niles' Reg.* IV. 25/2 The society are requested to attend this morning, precisely at nine o'clock, with buck's tails in their hats. **1821** J. HOWISON *Recollections* 320, I observed the celebrated Tammanies, 'a motly crew,' with buck-tails in their hats. **1832** KENNEDY *Swallow Barn* II. 5 His black leather cap, with ... a white buck-tail set on one side, gave a martial fierceness to his ... face. **1836** *S. Lit. Messenger* II. 183 A round black hat, mounted with the bucks-tail for a cockade, crowned the figure and the man. **1879** B. F. TAYLOR *Summer-Savory* 54 Figuring in political history, the hat has been garnished with the black cockade and the bucktail. **1889** *Harper's Mag.* May 977/2 The citizens who march and sing nonsense, ... or wear a corn-skin or a buck-tail, are in deadly earnest. *transf.* **1825** NEAL *Bro. Jonathan* II. 394 Mistaking him for a person who had called his horse a buck-tail.

2. A member of the Tammany Society in New York City; a political opponent of DeWitt Clinton. Now hist.

1818 J. M. DUNCAN *Travels U.S.* II. 247 Tammany Hall is one of the public hotels, and noted for the public meetings of the democratic party, or Bucktails, as they are called. [*Note*], From their wearing the tail of a buck in their hats at an annual festivity. **1820** B. F. BUTLER in Mackenzie *Life Van Buren* 163 Education, habit, inclination and principle all conspire to make me a Bucktail. **1821** QUITMAN in *Life & Corr.* I. 57, I perceive that your ambitious colts, ... who are aiming at popularity, are Bucktails. **1842** J. D. HAMMOND *Hist. Polit. Parties* (1852) I. 451 The New York Bucktails ... formed an organized opposition. **1872** *Harper's Mag.* April 695/1 The 'Bucktails' (so called from a conspicuous feature in Tammany's Indian uniform).

b. Attrib. with *flag, paper, party*, etc.

1821 QUITMAN in *Life & Corr.* I. 57 We take the American, the most violent of the Bucktail papers. **1838** NOAH in Mackenzie *Life Van Buren* 198 You may remember when in 1817 we ran up the Bucktail flag we had but eighteen men with us in the Legislature. **1843** J. D. HAMMOND *Polit. Hist. N.Y.* I. 450 Hence the party opposed to the administration of Mr. Clinton were ... called the 'Bucktail Party.' **1846** MACKENZIE *Life Van Buren* 167 The Bucktail Council very unpopular. *Ib.* 188 In Feb. 1823, the bucktail legislature reappointed ... Marcy as Comptroller.

3. *pl.* A regiment of Pennsylvania troops in the Civil War. Also in *Bucktail Rifles.*

1862 FRÉMONT in Kettell *Hist. Rebellion* II. 512 The forty-fifth New York, the Bucktail Rifles, of General Bayard's and General Milroy's brigades. **1863** VICTOR *Hist. Southern Rebellion* II. 470/2 The Kentuckians first showed themselves, when the fiery Bucktails advanced upon them. **1864** *Congress. Globe* Jan. 172/2 General Crawford led the famous Pennsylvania Reserves, shouting to them, ... 'Don't let the Bucktails (another Pa. regiment) beat you.' **1876** *Southern H. S. Papers* I. 436 We awaited with beating hearts, the sure and steady approach of the 'Pennsylvania Bucktails.'

***Buckthorn.**

1. A shrub or tree belonging to the genus *Rhamnus*, of which several species are native in the United States.

1785 V. B. Howard *Heroes* (1932) 143 East 520 poles to an ash and buck thorn, then 575 West. **1818** NUTTALL *N. Amer. Plants* I. 152 *Rhamnus.* (Buck-thorn.) ... Small trees or shrubs. **1850** *New Eng. Farmer* II. 286 The best plants for hedges, in this county, are undoubtedly the Buckthorn and the Osage Orange. **1865** *Maine Bd. Agric. Rep.* X. 59 Brakes, hardhacks, buckthorn, &c., must be subdued. **1878** B. F. TAYLOR *Between Gates* 214 Beneath avenues of live-oaks, among the junipers, the buckeyes and the buckthorns.

attrib. **1857** *Lawrence* (Kansas) *Republican* 6 Aug. 1 It was a little nest of a cottage, ... enclosed with a low buckthorn hedge.

b. The juice of buckthorn berries used as a purgative.

1779 *Narrag. Hist. Reg.* I. 93 Made nails. Took buckthorn.

c. With specific terms: (see quotations).

1843 TORREY *Flora N.Y.* I. 143 *Rhamnus alnifolius*, ... Alder-leaved Buckthorn, ... [grows in] sphagnous swamps in the northern and western parts of the State. **1846** BROWNE *Trees Amer.* 175 *Rhamnus catharticus*, the Purging Buckthorn, ... is a deciduous shrub or low tree, growing, when wild, to a height of eight or ten feet.

2. Applied (usually with distinctive name) to trees or shrubs of various other genera: (see quotations).

1857 GRAY *Botany* 80 *Frangula.* Alder-Buckthorn. ... Leaves with nearly straight and parallel veins. Otherwise as in Rhamnus. *Ib.* 267 *Bumelia lycioides.* (Southern Buckthorn.) Moist ground, S. Kentucky and southward. **1869** *Amer. Naturalist* III. 400 A few of the prominent species worthy of mention are the Sweet Bay ... ; the Southern Buckthorn (*Frangula Caroliniana*), [etc.]. **1875** *Ib.* IX. 391 More rarely in the southern part of the state [of Ill. are] two small trees, the two species of *Bumelia* or southern buckthorn. **1883** HALE *Woods & Timbers N.C.* 109 Buckthorn [is] ... a small tree ... found from North Carolina to Louisiana. **1885** HAVARD *Flora W. & S. Texas* 508 *Zizyphus obtusifolius*, ... Texas Buckthorn, ... makes excellent hedges in dry pastures. **1892** APGAR *Trees Northern U.S.* 79 Carolina Buckthorn ... [is] a thornless shrub or small tree, 5 to 20 ft. high. *Ib.* 80 California Buckthorn. ... A spreading shrub ... from California. *Ib.* 118 *Bumelia lanuginosa*, (Woolly-Leaved Buckthorn) ... [grows in] the woods of southern Illinois and southward. **1901** MOHR *Plant Life Ala.* 664 *Bumelia lanuginosa*, ... False Buckthorn.

+**Buckwagon.** 'A buckboard wagon' (W. '64).

***Buckwheat.**

***1.** The plant *Fagopyrum esculentum*, the meal of which is used for buckwheat cakes.

1698 G. THOMAS *Acc. Pensilvania* 21 They have commonly two Harvests in the Year; First of English Wheat, and next of Buck (or French) Wheat. **1709** LAWSON *Carolina* 76 Buck-Wheat is of great Increase in Carolina; but we make no other use of it, than instead of Maiz, to feed Hogs, and Poultry. **1751** MACSPARRAN *Diary* 45 My two Negro's plowing in the Buckwheat as Manure for English wheat. **1797** IMLAY *Western Territory* (ed. 3) 242 Buck-wheat justly deserves to be here mentioned, as the most fattening grain to all animals, but especially hogs and poultry. **1840** DEWEY *Mass. Flowering Plants* 102 *Polygonum fagopyrum.* L. Buckwheat or properly Beechwheat. So called from the close resemblance of its seeds to the seed of the Beech tree. **1852** D. MITCHELL *Dream Life* 200 The staggering stalks of the buck-wheat grow red with ripeness. **1892** *Vt. Agric. Rep.* XII. 149 Our State leads the list, producing more ... buckwheat per acre than any other State in the Union.

2. *ellipt.* +**a.** =BUCKWHEAT CAKE.

1830 *Collegian* 41 For tea, [take] six muffins, a dozen buck-wheats, and 6 cups of shells. **1854** in E. T. Brewster *Life J. D. Whitney* 141 The twenty-five hot buckwheats with which you have been wont to plaster your stomach. **1880** *Harper's Mag.* Sept. 582 We'd hed buckwheats an' tree molasses for breakfast that day. **1900** E. A. DIX *Deacon Bradbury* 224 'Mandy came in with another plate of hot buckwheats.

b. Buckwheat flour or meal; buckwheat batter.

1881 W. O. STODDARD *E. Hardery* 63 A sack of flour and some corn-meal and some buckwheat and a load of shorts. **1904** GLASGOW *Deliverance* 225 On the table was the bowl of buckwheat which Cynthia had been preparing.

3. Attrib. with *batter, field, meadow, pancake*, etc.

*a*1793 FRENEAU *Poems* (1809) II. 205 The horse ... Not fed with oats, but filled with wind, And buckwheat straw. **1799** BROWN *A. Mervyn* xiii, He was traversing his buckwheat-field, and measuring, the harvest that was now nearly ripe. **1835** HOFFMAN *Winter in West* I. 18 A wooded ravine ... and undulating fields, some ruddy with buckwheat stubble, ... filled up the curves. **1851** *Knickerb.* XXXVIII. 393 Enter into an alliance with the kitchen, keep your eye upon the over-night buckwheat pot. **1856** M. THOMPSON *Plu-ri-bus-tah* 28 To his lips he raised the buckwheat Pancakes, dripping with molasses. **1877** *Harper's Mag.* Feb. 475/2 A quite extended chemical examination of the ashes of the hemp and buckwheat plants is reported by Dr. Peters. **1878** STOWE *Poganuc People* 108 She hurried down into the kitchen to find Nabby stirring up her buckwheat batter. **1883** *Harper's Mag.* Sept. 525/2 [On the way to the Salisbury house] we went past corn fields and buckwheat meadows. **1887** FREDERIC *Seth's Brother's Wife* 91 There were robins, too, in the juniper trees beyond the white-flowering buckwheat patch.

+**b.** Of musical notes: Angular or shaped.

1883 HOWE *Country Town* (1926) 17 He had a collection of religious songs preserved in a leather-bound book, the notes being written in buckwheat characters on blue paper. **1903** *Atlantic Mo.* July 80 Who had attended singing school and learned to read buckwheat notes.

+**Buckwheat cake.** A griddlecake made with buckwheat meal.

1774 J. ADAMS *Diary* 21 Sept. II. (1850) 381 Mrs. Yard entertained us with muffins, buckwheat cakes, and common toast. **1775** ROMANS *Nat. Hist. Florida* 125 It is well known that in Philadelphia buckwheat cakes are one of the articles of that city at their breakfast. **1797** F. BAILY *Tour* (1856) 201 [We had] tea and coffee and a boiled chicken for our breakfast, attended with buck-wheat cakes, which are common in this part of the country [=Ohio]. **1831** PECK *Guide* 152 Pancakes, baked on the griddle, are a fine substitute for the buck-wheat cakes of New Jersey. *c*1849 [PAIGE] *Dow's Sermons* I. 51 If you have any communications to make, hurry them up, hot and hasty, like buckwheat cakes at any of our cheap eating-houses. **1872** ROE *Barriers Burned Away* viii, He pretended to be perfectly aghast at Dennis's onslaught on the buckwheat cakes, and rolled up his eyes despairingly as each new plate was emptied. **1883** *Wheelman* I. 337 While at this camp the conversation very naturally turned on ... hot beefsteaks, and buckwheat cakes and honey, which our folks at home were enjoying.

+**Buckwheat coal.** *local.* (See quotations.) — **1881** RAYMOND *Mining Gloss.* s.v. *Coal*, Buckwheat-coal ... is the smallest size, and usually included in the dirt or culm. **1889** *Cent.* 707/1 *Buckwheat coal*, in the anthracite region of Pennsylvania, the smallest size of coal sent to market. It is sufficiently small to pass through a half-inch mesh.

+**Buckwheat flour.** Flour made from buckwheat. — **1805** PARKINSON *Tour* 223 A farmer's waggon in America, when she comes into market, is something like a pedlar's pack: it consists of . . . buckwheat-flour, rye-flour, chopped straw, &c. **1856** *Rep. Comm. Patents: Agric.* 205 Buckwheat flour, in limited quantities, sells for near the same price as that of wheat.

+**Buckwheat meal.** Meal from buckwheat. — **1768** FRANKLIN *Writings* V. 96, I have received also the Indian and buckwheat meal, that they brought from you. **1787** WASHINGTON *Diaries* III. 230 That Buck Wheat Meal made into a wash is most excellent to lay on fat upon hogs. **1804** J. ROBERTS *Penn. Farmer* 62 Potatoes boiled and mixed with a small quantity of Indian, pea, bean or buckwheat meal, is a good fattener for them.

+**Buckwheat-nose.** A nonvenomous species of snake; the blauser or blowing-snake. — **1842** *Nat. Hist. N.Y., Zoology* III. 52 The Hog-nosed Snake, *Heterodon platyrhinos*. . . . This well known species . . . is also called Deaf Adder, Spreading Adder, Hog-nose and Buckwheat-nose.

+**Buckwheat tree.** A southern evergreen, the *Cliftonia nitida*, or *C. monophylla*. — **1813** MUHLENBERG *Cat. Plants* 45 Buckwheat tree. *Mylocarium*. **1818** NUTTALL *N. A. Plants* 276 Buckwheat-tree (*Mylocarium ligustrinum*), a tall evergreen shrub . . . [which grows] on the margins of swamps in Ga. & Fla. **1897** SUDWORTH *Arborescent Flora* 277 *Cliftonia monophylla*, Titi. . . . Common names [include] Buckwheat-tree (Fla., La.).

+**Buckwheat worm.** A species of cutworm, *Agrotis*. — **1854** EMMONS *Agric. N.Y.* V. 261 Index, Buckwheatworms, 243.

+**Buckwood.** The buckeye or horse chestnut. — **1787** M. CUTLER in *Life*, etc. II. 397 The prevailing growth of timber and the more useful trees are maple or sugar-tree, . . . butternut, . . . buckwood. **1810** MORSE *Amer. Gazetteer* s.v. *Ohio*, Hickory, cherry, buckwood or horse chesnut, [etc.].

+**Bud,** *n.*[1] [Childish pronunciation of *brother*. Cf. BUDDY and BUB.] Brother, as a form of address, or as a designation. Also in extended use.

1851 *Polly Peablossom* 19 'An't you joking, bud?' asked Polly of her boy brother. **1889** *Harper's Mag.* Aug. 459/1 He said that his name was 'Bud' Lightwood. . . . 'It's brother,' he said, . . . '"bud" and "sis" you know.' **1891** RYAN *Pagan Alleghanies* 133 Folks call boys 'bud' sometimes jest like they call girls 'sis'—short fer 'brother,' I reckon. **1896** HARRIS *Sister Jane* 99 Just tell Mandy that Bud wants to see her. **1902** WISTER *Virginian* iii. 39 They called to him; 'This way, Budd!'

* **Bud,** *n.*[2] +A girl just entering society; a debutante.

1880 R. GRANT *Confessions of Frivolous Girl* 39 'This is your first party, I believe, Miss Palmer?' 'Yes, I am what is called a "bud".' **1889** *Harper's Mag.* Sept. 571/1 As dashing a belle as there was in the rooms—not a bud—a belle of some six or seven years standing. **1892** HOWELLS *Quality of Mercy* 58 It'll be an old dance, rather, as far as the girls are concerned, but I've asked two or three buds. **1906** 'O. HENRY' *Four Million* 222 To the society bud comes but one debut.

+**Bud,** *n.*[3] (See quotation.) — **1891** 'THANET' *Otto the Knight*, etc. 237 But what fur did he kill the feller? Why cudn't he of given him the bud an' taken the money back? *Ib. n.*, 'To give the bud' or 'give the hickory' is Arkansas for to thrash.

***Bud,** *v.* +*intr.* Of birds: To eat buds. — **1888** *Forest & Stream* XXVIII. 131 Last night I saw a number of grouse budding upon a neighboring apple tree.

+**Buddy.** [Cf. BUD *n.*[1] and BUBBY.] Brother; comrade, assistant.

1852 WHITMORE *Diary* 25 Dec., Wrote to my folks and took a Christmas dinner with my buddy. **1858** *Harper's Mag.* Jan. 284/2 'Look, sister, see; the sky's got the measles!' 'No, buddy,' said she, correcting him, 'it's only freckled.' **1892** HARRIS *On the Plantation* 44 'Bless your soul, buddy,' exclaimed Mr. Locke. **1896** *Dialect Notes* I. 413 We were always great buddies together. **1904** 'O. HENRY' *Heart of West* 99 'We'll try to make it comfortable for you, buddy,' said the cattleman gently. **1917** U. SINCLAIR *King Coal* 30 A man might sink to sleep as he lay at work, and if his 'buddy,' or helper, happened . . . to delay a minute too long, it would be all over with the man. **1922** R. PARRISH *Case & the Girl* 204 Lieutenant, this is Captain West, over across the pond with the Engineers; we were buddies for about two months.

Budge. [f. *budge* to move, stir.] +Nervous irritation; fidgetiness. — **1824** JEFFERSON in *Private Corr. D. Webster* (1857) I. 373 Madame Neckar . . . was not very pleasant in conversation, for she was subject to what in Virginia we call the 'Budge,' that is, she was very nervous and fidgety. **1904** GLASGOW *Deliverance* 102 Having unfortunately crossed her knees in the parlour after supper, she suffered untold tortures from 'budges' for three mortal hours rather than be seen to do anything so indelicate as to uncross them.

* **Budget.**

+**1.** A bag or wallet in which Indians carried their totem, weapons, etc. (Cf. PACK *n.*)

1788 WM. BIGGS *Captivity* 13 Three of the Indians got up, put on their budgets and started. **1820** *Western Rev.* II. 48 The war budget is then hung in front of the door of the person that carried it on the march against the enemy. **1833** FLINT *D. Boone* 143 Every war party has a small budget, called the war budget, which contains something belonging to each one of the party, generally representing some animal. **1842** *Amer. Pioneer* I. 333 They discovered nine or ten Indians, who threw down their budgets and fled.

+**b.** A totem.

1833 FLINT *D. Boone* 143 When an attack is to be made, the war budget is opened, and each man takes out his budget, or *totem*, and attaches it to . . . his body.

+**2.** *Budget-husband*, a bundle of clothes representing a deceased Indian husband.

1833 FLINT *D. Boone* 141 [The Indian widow] is allowed to cheer her depressed spirits with a double dram, that of her budget-husband and her own. After a full year of this penance with the budget-husband, she is allowed to exchange it for a living one.

+**Budgeted husband.** (See BUDGET 2.)

1833 FLINT *D. Boone* 141 Her budgetted husband is permitted, when drams are passing, to be considered as a living one.

+**Budworm.** A larva that feeds upon the buds of corn, tobacco, etc. — **1849** *Rep. Comm. Patents: Agric.* (1850) 459 With the bud-worm you must be more particular, as you are apt to destroy the bud of the plant in killing it. **1909** *Cent. Suppl.* 172/2 *Bud-worm*, . . . the larva of an American noctuid moth, *Chloridea virescens*, which affects the bud of the tobacco plant, frequently doing much damage.

+**Buff,** *n.*[1] Abbrev. of BUFFALO. — **1884** *Bismarck Tribune* Aug., The ball struck the unsuspecting animal in the thigh, inflicting a slight wound. But the old 'buff' took the fling as an insult.

***Buff,** *n.*[2] *pl.* Breeches (or other garments) made of buff leather. — **1853** SIMMS *Sword & Distaff* 305 Ef he had some new clothes now! His old buffs are mighty full of stains. 'Twont do to wash buff breeches in swamp water no how.

* **Buffalo.** Also †**buffelo, bufelo, bofelo; bufalo, buffaloe, buffalow.**

+**1.** A North American bison, *Bison americanus*.

(*a*) **1635** *Relat. Maryland* iii. 23 In the upper parts of the countrey there are Bufeloes, Elkes, Lions, Beares, Wolues, and Deare there are in great Store. **1666** ALSOP *Maryland* iv. (1902) 69 Furrs and Skins, as Beavers, . . . and Elke or Buffeloe, . . . which were first made vendible by the Indians of the Country, and sold to the Inhabitant, and by them to the Merchant, and so transported into England. **1743** CATESBY *Carolina* App. p. iv, To these shady thickets of Canes (in sultry weather) resort numerous herds of Buffelo's, where solacing in these limpid streams they enjoy a cool and secret retreat. **1775** W. A. Pusey *Road to Ky.* (1921) 49, [I] saw 4 Bofelos . . . being the first ever I saw.

(*b*) **1705** BEVERLEY *Virginia* II. 39 They had a better Way of killing the Elks, Buffaloes, Deer and greater Game, by a method which we call Fire-Hunting. **1742** in *Travels Amer. Col.* 219 We set forward, the Indians killing plenty of Deer and Turkeys for our Refreshment, also several Buffaloes. **1770** WASHINGTON *Diaries* I. 423 He . . . treated us with great kindness; giving us a Quarter of very fine Buffalo. **1788** J. MAY *Jour. & Lett.* 80 A herd of elk were seen up this river [in Ohio] a few days ago; and Mr. Williams tells me that not long since he saw a drove of buffaloes. **1824** G. W. Rauck *Boonesborough* 166 A number of buffaloes of all sizes . . . made off from the lick in every direction. **1847** RUXTON *Adv. Rocky Mts.* (1848) 256 To 'throw a buffalo in his tracks,' which is the phrase for making a clean shot, he must be struck but a few inches above the brisket. **1872** *Newton Kansan* 28 Nov. 3/2 The telegraph Tuesday announces several thousand buffalos in one herd. **1907** C. C. ANDREWS *Recoll.* 124 Buffaloes still feed on its western banks.

+**b.** With *the*, as a generic name.

1709 LAWSON *Carolina* 115 The Buffelo is a wild Beast of America, which has a Bunch on his Back. **1737** BRICKELL *N. Carolina* 107 The Buffelo, or wild Beef, is one of the largest wild Beasts that is yet known in these parts of America. **1743** CATESBY *Carolina* App. p. xxvii, The Bufalo. These Creatures, though not so tall, weigh more than our largest oxen. **1779** in Ramsey *Tennessee* (1853) 202 We are now without bread, and are compelled to hunt the buffalo to preserve life. **1831** PECK *Guide* 161 The buffalo is not found on this side of the Mississippi, nor within several hundred miles of St. Louis. **1856** *Spirit of Times* (N.Y.) 25 Oct. 126/1 In our happy and beautiful [Minn.] Territory, . . . there yet roam the buffalo and the elk, but they are gradually retiring before the avalanche of white settlers. **1881** *Rep. Indian Affairs* p. xxiii, It is but a question of short time when . . . the disappearance of the buffalo will necessitate the confinement of the Crows to their reservation.

+**c.** In collective use, or as a plural.

1765 G. CROGHAN *Journal* 132 The country hereabouts abounds with buffalo, bears [etc.]. **1804** CLARK in *Lewis & C. Exped.* (1904) I. 123 Numerous herds of buffalow were seen feeding in various directions. **1840** *Knickerb.* XVI. 258 The buffalo had gathered together, as if by universal understanding, and had crossed the Mississippi, never to return. **1857** *Lawrence* (Kansas) *Republican* 25 June 1 We passed through one continuous herd of buffalo for forty miles. **1895** C. KING *Fort Frayne* 260 A deep cleft in the foothills through which the buffalo in bygone days had made their way.

+**2.** *ellipt.* **a.** =BUFFALO MEAT.

1743 CATESBY *Carolina* App. p. xiii, Our Indians being loaded with skins, and barbacued buffalo. **1894** ROBLEY *Bourbon Co., Kansas* 38 And then again they had nothing to eat but jerked buffalo and Pawnee macarroni.

+**b.** =BUFFALO FISH.

1788 J. MAY *Jour. & Lett.* 32 The [Ohio] river abounds in fish, such as cat, perch, pike, buffalo, sturgeon, etc. **1789** MORSE *Amer. Geog.* 405 In the rivers are plenty of buffalo and catfish of uncommon size. **1800** B. HAWKINS *Sk. Creek Country* 41 They get fish plentifully in the spring season . . . ; they are rock, trout, buffaloe, red horse and perch. **1842** BUCKINGHAM *Slave States* I. 262 We met several persons coming up from the river with many fine large fish, called buffaloes, of which it was said upwards of 500 were caught, at a single haul. **1857** *Harper's Mag.* Aug. 422/1 The arm which had lately been extended to ensnare the greedy cat-fish or the lubberly 'buffalo' now lay relaxed. **1886** *Nat. Museum Proc.* VIII. 13 *Ictiobus bubalus*, Rafinesque. Sucker-mouth Buffalo.

+**c.** =BUFFALO ROBE. Also attrib.

1835 REED & MATHESON *Visit* I. 75 You shall have a good buffalo and *umbrel*, and nothing will hurt you. **1840** *Knickerb.* XV. 326 Don't forgit to put in as many seats as you can, and all your buffaloes. **1854** *Harper's Mag.* VIII. 419/1 The indignant Jehu, who delights to fold himself in a buffalo. **1860** *Ib.* March 572/1 Mounting into the cutter, he tucked in the 'buffaloes,' put on his mittens [etc.]. **1884** *Boston Journal* 3 Sept., Another . . . was asked by the groom if he would like a couple of buffaloes. 'No,' replied the [British] scientist, 'No, we would much prefer horses.'

+**d.** =BUFFALO GRASS.

1880 HAYES *New Colorado* 37 The ranchero well knows the tufts of buffalo and gramma growth, . . . and remembers that it grows afresh twice a year.

+**3.** *pl.* A political faction in the Loco-foco or Equal Rights party. *Obs.*

1842 F. BYRDSALL *History of Loco-Foco* 178 Hence the Equal Rights party became divided within itself; the majority for union called the opposing minority Rumps, and the latter called the majority Buffaloes.

+**4.** A North Carolinian who favored the Union cause in the Civil War.

1865 KELLOGG *Rebel Prisons* 243 The rebels were very bitter against these 'buffaloes,' as they called them, for many of them had been on their side, and left it for the service of the Union. **1867** W. L. GOSS *Soldier's Story* 61 The Buffaloes, as the North Carolina companies were called, escaped in some cases by swimming the river.

+**b.** *pl.* 'A nickname given to the dwellers on the coast of North Carolina' (*Cent.*).

+**5.** Attrib., esp. with parts or products of the body of the buffalo, as *bladder, bone, dung, fat, flesh, gall, grease, hair, ham, marrow, rib, sinew, skull, soup, thong.* (See also below.)

(1) **1775** ADAIR *Indians* 415 Buffalo flesh is nothing but beef of a coarser grain, though of a sweeter taste than the tame sort. **1783** W. FLEMING in *Travels Amer. Col.* 665 We picked up many petrified substances . . . , Buffalo dung turned to a perfect stone. **1805** LEWIS in *L. & Clark Exped.* (1904) II. 191 A bear came . . . last night and eat up about thirty weight of buffaloe suit which was hanging on a pole. **1808** PIKE *Sources Miss.* App. II. 11 Their dishes were generally boiled sweet corn in buffalo grease. **1822** FOWLER *Journal* 151 We maid fire of the Buffalow dung and cooked our dinner. **1833** CATLIN *Indians* I. 116 'Marrow-fat' is collected by the Indians from the buffalo bones which they break to pieces, yielding a prodigious quantity of marrow, which is boiled out and put into buffalo bladders. **1835** IRVING *Tour Prairies* xxii. 170 Tonish served up to us his promised regale of buffalo soup and buffalo beef. **1837** — *Bonneville* I. 42 At one place, they observed a field decorated with buffalo sculls. *Ib.* II. 37 A sumptuous supper of buffalo humps and ribs, and other choice bits. **1846** SAGE *Scenes Rocky Mts.* v, The stomach never rebels against buffalo-fat. *Ib.* xvi, With one pint of water mix one-fourth gill of buffalo-gall, and you will then have before you a wholesome . . . drink. **1848** PARKMAN in *Knickerb.* XXXI. 398 Reynal's squaw was hard at work with her awl and her buffalo sinews upon her new lodge. **1850** GARRARD *Wah-To-Yah* 87 The young men . . . trade for dollars and silver coin . . . which they flatten thin, and fasten to a braid of buffalo hair. **1852** STANSBURY *Gt. Salt Lake* 44 Buffalo-soup, buffalo-ribs, tender-loin, and marrow-bones roasted . . . made a meal which . . . we thought not entirely unworthy of the day. **1856** WHIPPLE *Explor. Ry. Route* I. 26 Sixteen miles brought us to a spring. . . . Buffalo bones are bleaching near it. **1860** GREELEY *Overland Journey* 76 We crossed many old buffalo-trails and buffalo-heads nearly reduced to the skeleton. **1873** *Newton Kansan* 9 Jan. 3/4 For the purpose of curing buffalo hams and preparing them for shipment east, several houses have been erected. **1886** Z. F. SMITH *Kentucky* 166 He complained of the hurt from the buffalo thongs.

(2) **1820** DEWEES *Lett. from Texas* 18 This buffalo trip . . . eventually proved of advantage to me. **1837** IRVING *Bonneville* II. xii. 126 Several admirable horsemen and bold hunters, who amused themselves with a grotesque kind of buffalo bait. *Ib.* II. xvi. 165 It was the lot of the voyagers, one night, to encamp at one of these buffalo landing-places, and exactly on the trail. **1844** LEE & FROST *Oregon* 53 The Snakes now determined on a hunting match on the buffalo prairies. **1846** THORPE *Myst. Backwoods* 92 On the confines of the buffalo hunting-grounds, migrated a family. **1847** D. COYNER *Lost Trappers* 32 Their horses too were . . . well trained in all those dexterous movements to be practised in a buffalo-battle. *Ib.* 76 It is very rash . . . for a single man to engage in a buffalo chase in a country infested with prowling bands of Indians. **1847** LONGFELLOW *Evangeline* II. 4 Over them wandered the buffalo herds, and the elk and the roebuck. **1849** *Pres. Mess. Congress* II. 1020 A plentiful buffalo year, however, makes them neglect their agriculture. **1852** MARCY *Explor. Red River* (1854) 104 [The Comanche warrior] never mounts him [=his war horse] except when going into battle, the buffalo chase, or upon state occasions. **1852** *S. Lit. Messenger* XVIII. 315/2, I now draw my old Harper's Ferry 'buffalo slayer,' and select a barren cow . . . and deliver my fire. **1860** *Harper's Mag.* Oct. 588/1 Into this [=a sash worn by half-breeds] are thrust the buffalo-knife behind, and the fire-bag at the right side. **a1861** WINTHROP *J. Brent* 117, I am astonished that more of you American gentlemen do not profit by this great buffalo-preserve and deer-park. **1875** *Chicago Tribune* 2 July 7/6 Reports from the buffalo lands, in the western part of this State.

+**b.** *Buffalo breed, cattle:* (see quotations).

1819 *Amer. Farmer* I. 315 The buffaloe breed of cattle, or those without horns, will not answer well for working. **1858** C. FLINT *Milch Cows*, etc. 78 Hornless cattle . . . have been crossed with the common stock . . . to produce hornless grades. . . . These are not unfrequently known under the name of buffalo cattle.

+**c.** Attrib. in sense: Made of or with buffalo skin, as *buffalo bag, cushion, overcoat*, etc. Also BUFFALO COAT, etc.

1845 J. W. NORRIS *Chicago Directory* 119 Retail Dealers in . . . Buffalo Robes, Buffalo Overshoes. **1858** *Lawrence* (Kansas) *Republican* 15 April (*Advt.*), Buffalo overcoats. **1863** MRS. WHITNEY *F. Gartney* xviii, Faith . . . was borne safely from her snowy pinnacle to the buffalo cushion. **1868** in Custer *Following Guidon* (1890) 15, I have a pair of buffalo overshoes, the hair inside. **1893** ROOSEVELT *Wilderness Hunter* 296 All night I had lain in my buffalo-bag, under the lea of a windbreak of branches.

+**6.** Comb. with *chaser, eater, fed* p.p.

1843 FRÉMONT *Exped.* 30, I was really surprised at the number of little fat buffalo-fed boys that were tumbling about the camp. **1850** GARRARD *Wah-To-Yah* i. 4 [The] horse . . . was a noted buffalo chaser. **1847** RUXTON *Adv. Rocky Mts.* (1848) 271 The little dusky buffalo-fed urchins who played about the corral of the fort. **1852** MARCY *Explor. Red River* (1854) 102 The Northern and Middle Comanches subsist almost entirely upon the flesh of the buffalo; they are known among the other Indians as 'buffalo-eaters.'

+**Buffalo beat.** (See quotation.) — **1805** T. M. HARRIS *State of Ohio* 179 There are found open cleared spots on the summit of hills, called 'Buffaloe beats,' because supposed to be occasioned by the resort of those animals thither in fly time.

+**Buffalo beef.** Meat of the buffalo.

1775 G. W. Rauck *Boonesborough* 192 We had nothing here to refresh ourselves with, but cold water and lean buffalo beef. **1805** SIBLEY in *Ann. 9th Congress* 2 Sess. 1083 The women cook their buffalo beef in a manner that would be grateful to an English squire. **1827** COOPER *Prairie* ix, The man who denies that buffalo-beef is good, should scorn to eat it! **1847** D. COYNER *Lost Trappers* p. xiii, Seated by his fire, in his camp, . . . feasting upon his buffalo tongue, or buffalo beef, or buffalo marrow bones.

+**Buffalo beetle.** The carpet beetle or buffalo bug, *Anthrenus scrophulariae.* — **1892** V. KELLOG *Kansas Insects* 109 Buffalo beetle. . . . Small, dark-colored, hairy creatures, infesting carpets.

+**Buffalo berry.**

1. The fruit of one or other of two spiny shrubs (*Shepherdia argentea* and *S. canadensis*) of western North America.

1805 *Massachusetts Spy* 17 July 2/3 (Th.), Scions of a newly discovered berry, called the buffaloe berry. **1825** *Missouri Intell.* 18 June 2/3 During this period he subsisted upon cherries that hung over the spring, and *grains de boeufs*, or buffalo berries that were within his reach. **1833** CATLIN *Indians* I. 115 A kind of paste or pudding . . . finely flavoured with the buffalo berries, which are collected in great quantities in this country, and used with divers dishes in cooking, as we in civilized countries use dried currants, which they very much resemble. **1846** SAGE *Scenes Rocky Mts.* xii, The valley gave abundant indication of wild fruit at the proper season,—such as plums, cherries, currants, goose and buffalo berries. **1852** STANSBURY *Gt. Salt Lake* 233 Black currants and buffalo-berries abound upon the bank of the river. **1887** *Harper's Mag.* Aug. 368/2 Plums, buffalo-berries, and choke-cherries make a large part of his [the grizzly bear's] diet. **1893** ROOSEVELT *Wilderness Hunter* 20 We also have jellies and jams, made from wild plums and buffalo berries.

b. Attrib. with *bush, tree; jelly.*

1846 BROWNE *Trees Amer.* 429 The silvery-leaved Shepherdia. . . . Buffalo berry-tree. **1864** DICKSON *Across Plains* 191 Along the stream were many clumps of buffalo berry bushes. **1887** I. R. *Lady's Ranche Life Mont.* 67 A haunch of venison with buffalo-berry jelly.

2. The small thorny tree or shrub bearing this berry.

1846 STEWART *Altowan* I. 114 On its right bank runs a low range of sandstone bluffs . . . , with thickets of buffalo berry and currant bushes. **1858** WARDER *Hedges & Evergreens* 32 The Buffalo Berry (*Sheperdia eleagnoides*), . . . grows on the Rocky Mountains, whence it was brought by the botanist Nuttall. **1870** *Amer. Naturalist* IV. 30 A fringe of willows is often found along the stream, and a mingled thicket of 'Buffalo berry' . . . , Roses . . . , and other shrubbery. **1905** *Bureau of Forestry Bul.* No. 66, 33 The . . . valley mahogany, western serviceberry, buffalo berry, and dwarf maple have, without doubt, come down from the Rocky Mountains.

+**Buffalo-berrying,** *vbl. n.* [f. prec.] The gathering of buffalo berries. — **1887** I. R. *Lady's Ranche Life Mont.* 20 Two afternoons we spent in buffalo-berrying and shooting combined.

+**Buffalo boat.** A boat made by stretching buffalo hides over a frame. — **1844** GREGG *Commerce on Prairies* I. 65 On some occasions caravans have been obliged to construct what is called a buffalo boat, which is done by stretching the hides of these animals over a frame of poles, or, what is still more common, over an empty wagon-body. [Hence in later accounts.]

+**Buffalo bug.** =BUFFALO BEETLE. — **1889** *Cent.* 239/3 A larger species, ... known as the carpet-beetle and buffalo-bug, ... is very destructive to carpets and other woolen fabrics.

+**Buffalo bull.** [Cf. BULL *n.*[1]] A male buffalo.

1821 FOWLER *Journal* 12 We found a large Buffelow Bull lying dead soposed to be killed by the Indeans. **1832** CATLIN *Indians* I. 24 The buffalo bull is one of the most formidable and frightful looking animals in the world when excited to resistance. **1835** *S. Lit. Messenger* I. 534, I recognized my horse standing all benumbed and shivering with cold in company with a few old buffalo bulls. **1848** PARKMAN in *Knickerb.* XXXII. 45 He would come and seat himself at our side ... telling apocryphal stories how he had killed a buffalo-bull with a knife. **1873** *Newton Kansan* 10 July 2/2 A young menagerie, consisting of a buffalo bull, two buffalo calves and a half dozen prairie dogs ... passed through that town. **1890** CUSTER *Following Guidon* 183 A herd of buffaloes passed near the ranch, ... the buffalo bulls guarding their families.

attrib. **1780** W. FLEMING in *Travels Amer. Col.* 641, I had lived for a constancy on poor dried Buffalo bull beef cured in the smaok. *a***1918** G. STUART *On Frontier* I. 181 Only poor buffalo bull meat and water to live on.

+**Buffalo bur.** The sandbur, *Solanum rostratum.* — **1894** *Amer. Folk-Lore* VII. 95.

+**Buffalo bush.** The bush bearing the buffalo berry. — **1833** CATLIN *Indians* I. 72 The buffalo bushes, which are peculiar to these northern regions, lined the banks of the river and defiles in the bluffs, sometimes for miles together. *Ib.* 73 Stopping our boat wherever we saw the finest groves of the buffalo bush, collecting the berries and expressing the juice. **1860** GREELEY *Overland Journey* 271 Half a dozen specimens of a large, worthless shrub, known as buffalo-bush or bull-berry, ... comprise the entire timber of this delectable stream.

+**Buffalo calf.** The young of the buffalo.

1775 ADAIR *Indians* 421 [Indians] change the regimen in nurturing their young females; these they lay on the skins of fawns or buffalo calves, because they are shy and timorous. **1805** CLARK in *Lewis & Clark Exped.* (1904) I. 342, I observed a Drove of Buffalow Cows & Calves. **1825** *Missouri Intell.* 18 June 2/3 He had, however, the good fortune to be in at the death of a buffalo calf. **1833** CATLIN *Indians* I. 255 The buffalo calf, during the first six months is red, and has so much the appearance of a red calf in cultivated fields, that it could easily be mingled and mistaken amongst them. **1890** CUSTER *Following Guidon* 183 The ranchmen devised a plan to capture buffalo calves.

attrib. **1873** F. M. A. ROE *Army Lett.* 98 We bought a beautiful buffalo-calf robe for a bed for him.

+**Buffalo calfskin.** The skin of a buffalo calf. — **1847** RUXTON *Adv. Rocky Mts.* (1848) 253 The wolf ... was soon tugging away at an apishamore or saddle-cloth of buffalo calfskin which lay on the ground. **1868** in Custer *Following Guidon* (1890) 15, I am to have a vest made from a dressed buffalo calf-skin, with the hair on.

+**Buffalo carp.** (See quotation.) — **1820** RAFINESQUE in *Western Rev.* II. 299 Buffalo Carp Sucker, *Catostomus anisopturus,* ... is found in the lower part of the Ohio, and is called Buffalo carp, Buffalo perch, Buffalo sucker, White Buffalo-fish, &c.... Very good to eat.

+**Buffalo chip.** A piece of dried buffalo dung. Usu. pl.

1840 *Picayune* 11 Oct. 2 We raised an extensive cloud of smoke from burning 'buffalo chips' to keep off the musquitos. **1848** E. BRYANT *California* 80 Our fuel for cooking is what is called 'buffalo chips,' ... burning with a lively blaze and producing a strong heat. **1852** MARCY *Expl. Red River* 18 The only substitute for fuel that could be had was the buffalo 'chips.' **1875** *Amer. Naturalist* IX. 148 Throughout a vast stretch of country in the northwest, gopher-holes and buffalo-chips are the most noticeable points about the landscape. **1903** WHITE *Forest* iv. 35, I once slept on a bed of prairie grass, before a fire of dried buffalo chips and mesquite.

+**Buffalo cider.** 'The ludicrous name given to the liquid in the stomach of a buffalo, which the thirsty hunter drinks, when he has killed his game at a great distance from water' (De Vere 367–8).

+**Buffalo clover.** One or other of various species of clover, as *Trifolium pennsylvanicum, T. reflexum, T. stoloniferum,* etc.

1785 WASHINGTON *Diaries* II. 426 Also sowed about a tablespoonful of the Buffalo or Kentucke Clover. **1788** CUTLER in *Life & Corr.* II. 285, I likewise wish particularly to know what you find the May-apple, Rick-weed, and Buffalo-clover to be. **1822** J. WOODS *English Prairie* 292 Buffalo-clover resembles white clover, but does not run on the ground. **1850** [S. F. COOPER] *Rural Hours* 126 The buffalo clover found in the western part of this State, and common still farther westward, is the only undoubtedly native variety we possess. **1891** COULTER *Bot. W. Texas* I. 74 *Trifolium reflexum* ... [is] the common 'buffalo clover' of the Atlantic States and extending into Texas, where its Western limit is unrecorded.

+**Buffalo coat.** A coat made of buffalo skin. — **1845** J. W. NORRIS *Chicago Directory* 119 Retail Dealers in Hats, Caps, Muffs, Boas, Buffalo Coats, Buffalo Robes. **1848** PARKMAN *Oregon Trail* 372 He made a figure worthy of a painter ... enveloped in a huge buffalo coat. **1860** HOLLAND *Miss Gilbert's Career* 117 With whip in hand and buffalo-coat still unbuttoned. **1922** A. BROWN *Old Crow* 71 He saw Jerry Slate there in the pung, enveloped in the buffalo coat he had worn through the winter months.

+**Buffalo cod.** The green cod, *Ophiodon elongatus.* — **1890** *Cent.* 4124 *O. elongatus,* a Californian species, attains a length of 5 feet and ... is known by various names, as ... green-cod, buffalo-cod, and codfish.

+**Buffalo country.** The plains of the West.

1833 CATLIN *Indians* I. 251 My visit to these parts of the 'Great Far West' has brought me into the heart of the buffalo country. **1839** Z. LEONARD *Adventures* (1904) 59 Here we ... packed up a sufficiency of provision, as we then thought; for our subsistance through the wilderness to what is called the Buffaloe country. **1850** G. HINES *Voyage* 409 For our support at leaving the Missouri settlements, until we should get into the buffalo country, we drove twelve head of cattle besides a milch cow. **1866** *Rep. Indian Affairs* 274 Immediately after the payment in September, last year, the Indians began to go into the buffalo country. **1873** BEADLE *Undevel. West* 436 We hurry on, and soon after noon enter the buffalo country.

+**Buffalo cow.**

1. A female buffalo.

1779 W. FLEMING in *Travels Amer. Col.* 619 Kild a Buffalo Cow very fat. **1807** GASS *Journal* 258 Some men went out and killed two fine fat buffaloe cows. **1834** A. PIKE *Sketches* 53 He assured us that there was an abundance of buffalo cows. **1848** E. BRYANT *California* 85 Messrs. Grayson and Boggs ... returned this morning with their horses loaded with the choice pieces of a buffalo cow.

attrib. **1853** BOND *Minnesota* 302 Our tents were pitched, horses staked, supper cooked of buffalo cow-steaks, etc.

2. A cow having no horns.

1850 *New Eng. Farmer* II. 52 The buffalo, or hornless cows, spoken of in Statement No. 1, ... are there considered as natives. **1902** CLAPIN 80 *Buffalo-cow,* a common expression, among colored people of Virginia, for a cow without horns, because its head somewhat resembles that of the female buffalo, whose horns are very short.

+**Buffalo crossing.** A place where buffalo cross a stream; a buffalo ford. — **1775** CRESSWELL *Journal* 80 Proceeded a little way up the River to a great Buffalo crossing. **1846** STEWART *Altowan* I. viii. 204 The willows ... were followed by a plain open space, where there was a buffalo crossing. **1856** WHIPPLE *Explor. Ry. Route* I. 24 Here, deep-furrowed trails show a regular buffalo crossing.

+**Buffalo currant.** The Missouri currant, *Ribes odoratum.* — **1863** GRAY *Botany* p. lii, Buffalo ... currant ... is planted for its bright-yellow spicy-scented flowers, ... berries blackish, useless. **1891** COULTER *Bot. W. Texas* I. 109 Buffalo currant [grows] in shady ravines in western Texas, chiefly beyond the Pecos. Often ... cultivated for ornament.

+**Buffalo dance.** A dance to attract buffalo practiced by Indians on the plains. — **1805** CLARK in *Lewis & C. Exped.* (1904) I. 245 A Buffalo Dance (or Medeson) for 3 nights passed in the 1st. Village, a curious Custom the old men arrange themselves in a circle & after smoke[ing] a pipe which is handed them by a young man dress[ed] up for the purpose.... All this is to cause the buffalow to come near so that they may kill them. **1833** CATLIN *Indians* I. 83 The head and horns of a buffalo ... [the Indian] uses as a mask when called upon by the chiefs, to join in the buffalo-dance. **1841** BUCKINGHAM *America* I. 76 The 'buffalo dance' of the Mandans, another tribe, consists of men dressing themselves in the skins of buffaloes, two men erect generally sustaining the skin of one buffalo.... They look at a distance like real buffaloes.

+**Buffalo dog.** A dog used in hunting buffalo. — **1867** in E. B. Custer *Tenting on Plains* (1889) 575 One of them accidentally shot his horse, and also a large buffalo-dog.

+**Buffalo fish.**

1. A fish belonging to any species of large suckers of the *Catostomidæ* family.

'The name was probably given on account of the protuberant or hump-like back, which rises highest near the front of the dorsal fin' (*Cent.*).

1781–2 JEFFERSON *Notes Va.* (1788) 6 This river yields turtle, ... catfish of 100 lb. weight, buffalo fish, and sturgeon. **1788** J. MAY *Jour. & Lett.* 74 Dined on buffalo fish, the weight of which when caught, was fourteen and three-fourth pounds. **1812** STODDARD *Sk. Louisiana* 163 It produces a kind of fresh water sheep-head, and likewise the carp or buffaloe fish, both of which are indifferent. **1820** RAFINESQUE in *Western Rev.* II. 299 Brown Buffalo-fish, *Catostomus bubalus,* ... is called every where Buffalo-fish, and Piconeau, by the French settlers of Louisiana. **1864** DICKSON *Across Plains* (1929) 28 These indians were now literally swarming over the water in their fleet dugouts, spearing buffalo fish during the run. **1885** *Amer. Naturalist* Sept. 922 The lamprey eel of Kansas [is] parasitic on the buffalo-fish. **1902** W. S. GORDON *Recoll. Lynchburg* 100 On either side of which stands a man 'gigging' buffalo fish as the current hurries them through the break.

2. (See quotation.)

1842 *Nat. Hist. N.Y., Zoology* IV. 272 The Buffalo Bony Pike, *Lepisosteus bison,* ... is frequently known under the name of Buffalo-fish, which suggested its specific name.

+**Buffalo fly.** =BUFFALO GNAT. — **1846** LYELL *Second Visit* (1849) II. 89 There were swarms of buffalo flies to torment his horses, and sand flies to sting him and his family. **1869** BREWER *Rocky Mt. Lett.* 21 Mosquitoes and buffalo flies made it most trying. *Ib.* 24 Our greatest annoyance here consists of buffalo flies, which annoy our stock (and us) almost beyond endurance. **1889** *Secy. of Agric. Rep.* 346 [The Horn Fly] ... has also been called the 'Texas Fly,' the 'Buffalo Fly,' and the 'Buffalo Gnat.'

+**Buffalo ford.** A place where buffalo habitually cross a stream; a buffalo crossing (q.v.). — *c***1836** CATLIN *Indians* II. 95, I at length ... came to an old buffalo ford, where the banks were graded down. **1837**

BIRD *Nick of Woods* II. 84 Crossing the river at the buffalo-ford above ... they made their way through the forest.

+**Buffalo fuel.** Buffalo chips. — **1848** ROBINSON *Santa Fé Exped.* 13 The men scattered themselves about to pick up ... buffalo-fuel.

+**Buffalo gnat.** A small black fly of the genus *Simulium.*

1822 J. WOODS *English Prairie* 278 As the first part of it [=summer] was so dry, we had no buffalo gnats, and but few prairie flies or musquetoes. **1837** IRVING *Bonneville* I. iii. 43 Skirting along the north fork for a day or two, excessively annoyed by musquitoes and buffalo gnats, they reached ... a small but beautiful grove. **1848** E. BRYANT *California* 121 Our mules as well as ourselves suffer much from the myriads of buffalo-gnats and mosquitoes. **1860** *Harper's Mag.* Aug. 308/1 Wood-ticks burrow into and under the skin, ... whereas these buffalo-gnats swarm in millions, and ... will fly into the eyes, ears, and nostrils by scores. **1863** *Boston Herald* 5 April 1/2 The buffalo gnats are said to be killing large numbers of government horses. **1884** *Rep. Commissioner Agric.* 340 For many years past one of the greatest pests the stock-raiser of the South and West has had to contend with has been the so-called 'Buffalo Gnat.' This insect is a small fly, closely related to the well-known 'Black Fly' of the Northwestern woods. **1902** W. S. GORDON *Recoll. Lynchburg* 102 He is familiarly known as the buffalo gnat, being about one-third the size of a house fly, and the object of his visit is to run horses, cows and sheep mad.

+**Buffalo grass.** Any of several low grasses very common on the western plains.

1784 FILSON *Kentucke* 24 Where no cane grows there is abundance of wild-rye, clover, and buffalo-grass, ... affording excellent food for cattle. **1792** IMLAY *Western Territory* 206 The buffalo grass is rather coarse. ... It has a broad leaf, and seems unworthy of cultivation. **1843** T. TALBOT *Journals* 16 The grass is short, crispy and very elastic to the tread, is known by the name of 'Buffalo grass.' It is so short that it takes a horse sometime to get enough, but when they learn how to eat it they are very fond of and prefer it to other grass. **1845** FRÉMONT *Exped.* 277 It is the short curly grass, on which the buffalo delight to feed, (whence its name of buffalo,) and which is still good when dry and apparently dead. **1851** *S. Lit. Messenger* XVII. 567/1 The buffalo grass ... extends to the Missouri river, and within eighty miles of the State boundary. **1852** MARCY *Explor. Red River* (1854) 43 The grass upon the Staked Plain is generally a very short variety of mezquite, called buffalo grass. **1860** GREELEY *Overland Journey* 84 The herbage hereabout is nearly all the short, strong grass known as the buffalo-grass, and is closely fed down. **1878** BEADLE *Western Wilds* 438 The border line between the soft grass of the Missouri Valley and the buffalo grass of the plains moves westward at the rate of five miles per year! **1892** *Scribner's Mag.* June 732/1 The fine, hair-like 'buffalo grass' that covers the prairies for four hundred miles east of the mountains ... is as nourishing in winter as in summer. *c*1908 F. M. CANTON *Frontier Trails* 9 We spread our blankets down on the thick buffalo grass and turned in.

attrib. **1888** *Harper's Mag.* July 244/2 The buffalo-grass sod which has covered these plains for centuries.

+**Buffalo grease bush.** ?The buffalo berry, *Shepherdia argentea.* — **1806** CLARK in *Lewis & C. Exped.* (1905) V. 302 The bottoms on the Stard. Side low and extencive and covered with timber such as ... Grapevines together with the red berry or Buffalow Grees bushes.

+**Buffalo ground.** A region where buffalo abound; buffalo country. — **1837** IRVING *Bonneville* I. 135 Their united force was not sufficient to venture upon the buffalo grounds, which were infested by bands of Blackfeet. **1846** THORPE *Myst. Backwoods* 87 Imagine a splendid fall morning in the southern part of the buffalo 'grounds.'

+**Buffalo hide.** The skin of a buffalo, used for various purposes.

1800 B. HAWKINS *Sk. Creek Country* 82 They made shields ... of Buffalo hides. **1807** GASS *Journal* 45 Their band of musick, or orchestra, was composed of about twelve persons beating on a buffaloe hide. **1867** DIXON *New America* I. 6 The strange beast proved to be the driver, coiled up, concealed, and snoring in a buffalo hide. **1890** CUSTER *Following Guidon* 7 An Indian shield ... is made of the thickest part of the buffalo-hide.

+**Buffalo horn.** The horn of a buffalo. Also attrib.

1783 W. FLEMING in *Travels Amer. Col.* 665 We picked up ... a petrified Buffalo horn which unfortunately broke into three pieces separating it from the rock. **1833** CATLIN *Indians* I. 103 A pair of beautifully polished buffalo horns. **1842** E. A. HITCHCOCK *Journal* 161 Sambo told me that the Comanches make drums by stretching a skin over a large buffalo horn and use it in their dance. **1866** MRS. WHITNEY *L. Goldthwaite* iii, The great round coil ... fastened with a buffalo-horn comb.

+**Buffalo horse.** A horse trained for hunting buffalo.

1832 CATLIN *Indians* I. 24 He leads the party, mounted on his favourite buffalo horse (*i.e.* the horse amongst his whole group which is best trained to run the buffalo). **1846** SAGE *Scenes Rocky Mts.* xii, Both of them were 'buffalo horses,' and the fleetest and most valuable in our possession. **1868** *Amer. Naturalist* June 215 The Indians offer a big price (a large buffalo horse) for the dog. **1870** KEIM *Sheridan's Troopers* 66 He talks about his 'buffalo horse' with more pride than he would [of] himself.

+**Buffalo hump.** Meat from the hump of a buffalo. — **1827** *Western Mo. Rev.* I. 281 It affords him a delightful theme to recount to his listening companions ... feasting on the smoking buffalo hump, on a winter evening. **1837** IRVING *Bonneville* II. iii. 37 They ... proceeded to prepare a sumptuous supper of buffalo humps and ribs, and other choice bits. **1855** J. E. COOKE *Ellie* 423 '[We are to dine] on the prairie!' said Mr. Sansoucy: 'on the prairie, and off of buffalo hump.'

+**Buffalo hunt.** A hunt for buffalo.

1808 PIKE *Sources Miss.* App. II. 34 Restricting (by edicts) the buffalo hunts to certain seasons. **1820** DEWEES *Lett. from Texas* 15, I joined a party of about thirty men, who were going up Red river to the cross timbers on a buffalo hunt. **1846** THORPE *Myst. Backwoods* 82 To the wild Indian the buffalo hunt awakens the soul as absorbingly as the defying yell on the war-path. **1866** *Rep. Indian Affairs* 123 A considerable number of these Indians ... have this season accompanied Washakee to the Wind River valley on his annual buffalo hunt. **1872** *Newton Kansan* 28 Nov. 3/2 Quite a number of the young men of this place with a four horse team ... are out on a buffalo hunt. **1916** C. A. EASTMAN *From Deep Woods* (1929) 80 We soon had a good imitation of the old time buffalo hunt.

+**Buffalo-hunter.** One skilled in hunting buffalo; a horse used in such hunting.

1843 FRÉMONT *Exped.* 116, I had here the satisfaction to meet our good buffalo hunter of 1842, Christopher Carson. **1846** THORPE *Myst. Backwoods* 83 The Cumanches in the south, and the Sioux in the north, are, from their numbers, warlike character, and wealth, among the aborigines, *the buffalo hunters.* **1873** *Winfield* (Kansas) *Courier* 11 Jan. 3/1 Three large parties of buffalo hunters passed through town this week, their teams loaded with game. **1873** ABBOTT *C. Carson* 78 'Your horses,' said he, 'would make excellent buffalo hunters with proper training.' **1882** *Century Mag.* Aug. 511/1 In place of the cow-boy we find the buffalo-hunter, who comes into the town in the spring with the spoils of his winter's work. **1895** REMINGTON *Pony Tracks* 80 Turning it [the steer] on its back, after the manner of the old buffalo-hunters, it was quickly disrobed and cut up into hundreds of small pieces.

+**Buffalo-hunting.** Pursuing and killing buffalo.

1821 FOWLER *Journal* 8 The Indeans are all gon a buffelow Hunting, and are not expected to return till in the winter. **1841** CATLIN *Indians* I. 4, I have brought home ... 200 other paintings in oil, containing views of ... their buffalo hunting, and other amusements. **1868** WOODRUFF *Trotting Horse* 246 Mr. Larkin went buffalo-hunting with some Indian braves. **1885** *Rep. Indian Affairs* 79 From one to a dozen savages, yelling, and firing their guns, reminding one of the early days when buffalo-hunting was their chief sport. **1890** CUSTER *Following Guidon* 6 The buffalo-hunting among the tribes was over for the year.

+**Buffalo-jerk.** Buffalo meat cut into thin strips and dried. — **1841** *S. Lit. Messenger* VII. 56/2 The author has conversed with a number of our prairy hunters, and Texan adventurers, all of whom bear the same testimony in behalf of buffalo jerks. **1847** L. COLLINS *Kentucky* 509 They spent several days ... curing buffalo jerk and tallow for their journey.

+**Buffalo lick.** A place to which buffalo resort to lick the soil for salt. — **1780** W. FLEMING in *Travels Amer. Col.* 652 The Buffalo lick in No 2 is a water lick at the foot of a hill. **1791** BARTRAM *Travels* 35 We sat off from Augusta, early in the morning, for the Great Buffalo Lick. **1815** *Niles' Reg.* VIII. 135/1 At the first settlement of this place [in Kanawha Co., W.Va.] there was a great *Buffalo Lick.* **1837** A. WETMORE *Gaz. Missouri* 59 The only indication of the existence of salt in Clinton county is in the old buffalo licks, on the surface of the earth.

+**Buffalo meat.** Meat obtained from the buffalo. (Cf. BUFFALO BEEF.)

1779 in Ramsey *Tennessee* (1853) 202 [We] procured some buffalo-meat; though poor it was palatable. **1823** JAMES *Exped.* I. 178 They danced for us, and after receiving bread, buffaloe meat and tobacco, departed well-pleased. **1836** IRVING *Astoria* II. xxx. 146 They belonged to a party of Snakes who had come across the mountains on their autumnal hunting excursion to provide buffalo meat for the winter. **1844** LEE & FROST *Oregon* 120 Some small trouts were caught here, and were a welcome exchange for dried buffalo meat, which had been our chief food many days. **1858** D. PETERS *Kit Carson* 27 He attempted to rival French pastry and English beef with American venison and Buffalo meat on the table. **1870** KEIM *Sheridan's Troopers* 63 In momentary anticipation of a rare display of buffalo-meat. **1878** BEADLE *Western Wilds* 63 Having started with but one day's supply of provisions, and that of dried buffalo meat, we soon suffered for food.

+**Buffalo moth.** The moth of the buffalo beetle. — **1892** V. KELLOG *Kansas Insects* 109 Small, dark-colored, hairy creatures, infesting carpets, ... known to housekeepers as 'fish moths,' 'buffalo moths,' etc.

+**Buffalonian,** *n.* An inhabitant of Buffalo, N.Y.

1836 *Knickerb.* VIII. 352 A magnificent thoroughfare, Old Main, as the Buffalonians call it, stretched for miles before my eye. **1850** *Ib.* XXXV. 365 He was a Buffalonian, who must be living now. **1863** MASSETT *Drifting About* 22 The English were denounced, and the Buffalonians were ripe for a fight with John Bull. **1885** *Harper's Mag.* July 202/1 Here the Buffalonian gets his one 'marine' view, and here, too, he has a perpetual reminder of the original owners of the soil.

+**Buffalonian,** *a.* [Cf. prec.] Of or pertaining to Buffalo, N.Y. — **1893** M. Philips *Making of a Newspaper* 81 The Buffalonian *mauvaise honte* of Mr. Cleveland.

+**Buffalo nut.** The elk-nut or oil-nut, *Pyrularia oleifera.* — **1857** GRAY *Botany* 382 Buffalo-nut ... [is] a low straggling shrub, with ... small greenish flowers. ... [It grows on] rich wooded banks, mountains of Penn. and southward throughout and near the Alleghanies. **1859** BARTLETT 53 *Buffalo nut,* ... oil nut. Western.

‖**Buffalo pack.** Prob. an error for BUFFALO PERCH 2. — **1838** KIRTLAND in *2nd Rep. Ohio Geol. Survey* 193 *C*[*atostomus*] *bubalus.* ... The buffalo is a tolerably good article of food. The young is called the buffalo pack.

+Buffalo path. A way or track made by buffalo.

1770 WASHINGTON *Diaries* I. 420 The Indians showed us a Buffalo Path, the Track of which we see [=saw]. **1779** W. FLEMING in *Travels Amer. Col.* 619 Our march about 8 miles went along a Buffalo path. **1831** *Illinois M. Mag.* 448 The 'buffaloe paths' . . . are to be seen in several parts of the state. **1836** J. HALL *Stat. West* 110 The traces of them [=buffalo herds] are still remaining in the 'buffalo paths,' which are to be seen in several parts of the new states. These are well beaten tracks, leading generally from the prairies in the interior to the margins of the large rivers. **1850** GARRARD *Wah-To-Yah* i. 13 The whole country was cut up with innumerable buffalo paths, intersecting one another at all possible angles. **1880** BURNETT *Old Pioneer* 108 These buffalo-paths constituted quite an obstruction to our wagons.

+Buffalo pecker. ?The cowbird, so called because it lights on the backs of buffalo. — **1806** LEWIS in *L. & Clark Exped.* (1905) V. 201 Killed a buffaloe pecker a beautifull bird.

+Buffalo perch. **1.** (See BUBBLER, quot. 1832.) **2.** A species of buffalo fish, *Catostomus* or *Ictiobus bubalus.* Cf. BUFFALO PACK. — **1845** KIRTLAND in *Boston Jrnl. Nat. Hist.* V. 266 Buffalo Sucker. Brown Buffalo. . . . The young is nearly elliptical in outline, and is often sold in the market as a distinct species, under the name of *Buffalo Perch.*

+Buffalo pike. (See quot. and BUFFALO FISH 2.) — **1842** *Nat. Hist. N.Y., Zoology* IV. 271 The Buffalo Bony Pike, *Lepisosteus bison,* . . . occurs in many of the small lakes of the Western district, and has been taken at Ogdensburgh three feet long.

+Buffalo-pistol. A pistol of large caliber used for shooting buffalo. — **1847** PARKMAN in *Knickerb.* XXIX. 509 He . . . jerked a huge buffalo-pistol from his holster, and set out at full speed after her.

+Buffalo plain. A plain frequented by buffalo. — **1781–2** JEFFERSON *Notes Va.* (1788) 8 The Kaskaskia is 100 yards wide at its entrance into the Missisippi [*sic*] and preserves that breadth to the Buffalo plains, 70 miles above. **1808** PIKE *Sources Miss.* App. II. 14 The ease with which they live on the buffalo plains . . . [has] probably been the cause of a degeneracy of manners.

+Buffalo platform. An anti-slavery platform or program adopted in Buffalo, N.Y., Aug. 9, 1848 at the time of the organization of the Free Soil party. — **1850** *Congress. Globe* App. 19 Feb. 160 Mr. Webster . . . congratulates them [=northern Whig Party] that the Buffalo platform, though having some rotten planks . . . [gives] a secure place to stand upon. *a***1859** *Providence Journal* (B.), The Free Soil party regard every plank and splinter of the Buffalo platform as a relic of untold value. **1863** *Congress. Globe* 20 Feb. 1154/1, I do not care whether that doctrine is in the Buffalo platform or anywhere else. **1864** *Ib.* App. 27 Feb. 49/2 Was he an unwilling advocate of emancipation who first unfurled that banner in Missouri on the Buffalo platform in 1848?

+Buffalo range. A region frequented by buffalo; a buffalo region or buffalo run.

1775 ADAIR *Indians* 118 Living very scantily, even in a buffalo range, under a strict rule, lest by luxury their hearts should grow evil. **1835** IRVING *Tour on Prairies* 48 Osage hunters had recently crossed the river, on their way to the buffalo range. **1843** N. BOONE *Journal* (1917) 29 May 199 They had killed 25 buffalo in and about their camp, so that we are now in the buffalo range. **1859** MARCY *Prairie Traveler* 161 It will be a wise precaution in passing through the buffalo range, to lay in a supply of jerked meat for future exigencies. **1878** BEADLE *Western Wilds* 443 The buffalo range is now only one-twelfth what it was in 1830, and about one-third what it was in 1870. **1891** [see BUFFALO WOLF].

+Buffalo ranger. A buffalo that has wandered from its herd. — **1859** A. JACKSON *MS. Diary* 10 Kit caught a buffalo ranger.

+Buffalo region. A buffalo range. — **1848** E. BRYANT *California* 75 Now that we have approached so near the buffalo region, . . . this practice has been discontinued. **1850** GARRARD *Wah-To-Yah* i. 12 For the first night or two after entering the buffalo region, we were serenaded by the coyote wolf. **1860** GREELEY *Overland Journey* 83 We are near the heart of the buffalo region.

+Buffalo road. A road made by buffalo; a buffalo path or buffalo trail.

1750 T. WALKER *Journal* 55 We went up Naked Creek to the head and had a plain Buffaloe Road most of the way. **1792** IMLAY *Western Territory* 120 The manner by which they [salt springs] are mostly found in uninhabited places is, by the large buffalo roads which lead to them. **1826** J. BRADFORD *Kentucky Notes* 12 It was but about one hundred yards from a large buffalo road. **1843** N. BOONE *Journal* (1917) App., Saw some Buffalo, and passed some of the largest buffalo roads bearing E.S.E. **1850** *Congress. Globe* Dec. 57 The wild animals . . . are the first engineers to lay out a road in a new country; the Indians follow them, and hence a buffalo road becomes a war-path.

+Buffalo robe. The skin of a buffalo dressed with, or without, the hair on, for use as a covering, carriage-rug, etc.

1804 CLARK in *Lewis & C. Exped.* (1904) I. 130 The [Sioux] Squars wore Peticoats & a white Buffalow roabe. **1817** FORDHAM *Narr. Travels* 145 We have two blankets and a buffalo robe on which we sleep with our feet to the fire. **1835** HOFFMAN *Winter in West* I. 166 The crate being filled with hay, and the driver well wrapped up in a buffalo robe, the turn-out is complete, and by no means uncomfortable. **1852** MARCY *Explor. Red River* (1854) 84 Both of these tribes [the Wacos & Witchitas] . . . wear the buffalo robes like the Comanches. **1855** MRS. ROBINSON *Kansas* (1856) 28, I . . . slept on comfortables and buffalo-robes on the floor in the attic. **1861** MRS. S. COWELL *Diary* 241 The cosy family sleigh . . . is built to hold 7 or 8 and is luxuriously fitted up with soft cushions, and multitudinous buffalo robes. **1886** ROOSEVELT in *Century Mag.* XXXVI. 47/2 We made the men take off their boots . . . and go to bed, all three lying on one buffalo robe. **1894** ROBLEY *Bourbon Co., Kansas* 68 They found that even at the best hotel the bed consisted of a straw tick and a buffalo robe. *c***1908** F. M. CANTON *Frontier Trails* 60 Eight Indians in this lodge [were] just rousing from sleep, two of them on one side by themselves, under a fine buffalo robe.

attrib. **1849** PARKMAN *Oregon Trail* 372 He made a figure worthy of a painter . . . enveloped in a huge buffalo-robe coat.

b. (See quotation.)

1776 A. HENRY *Travels* 265 We were obliged to wrap ourselves continually in beaver blankets, or at least in ox-skins, which the traders call buffalo-robes.

+Buffalo rug. A rug made of a buffalo skin. — **1805** in *Ann. 9th Congress* 2 Sess. 1082 The surplusage [of vegetables, etc.] they exchange with the Hietans for buffalo rugs, horses and mules. **1844** GREGG *Commerce of Prairies* II. 213 The annual 'export' of *buffalo rugs* from the Prairies and bordering 'buffalo range,' is about a hundred thousand. *Ib.* 293 To dress a buffalo rug, the first step is to 'flesh' the skin.

+Buffalo run. A buffalo range. — **1867** DIXON *New America* I. 31 They must keep the buffalo-runs of Kansas and Colorado (as the white men have begun to call the plains—on paper) free from intrusion of mail and train.

+Buffalo-runner. A horse trained in hunting buffalo. — *a***1849** RUXTON *Life Far West* 12 He had his horse, a regular buffalo-runner, picketed round the fire quite handy. **1860** *Harper's Mag.* Oct. 586/2 Since 1850 the Sioux have stolen from the people of St. Jo more than four hundred horses, many of them buffalo-runners.

+Buffalo-running. Hunting buffalo on horseback. — **1849** PARKMAN in *Knickerb.* XXXIII. 8 The hunter came trotting back to the party, disgusted with buffalo-running.

+Buffalo salt lick. *Obs.* =BUFFALO LICK. — **1806** in *Ann. 9th Congress* 2 Sess. 1115 This creek . . . has obtained its name from the many buffalo salt licks which have been discovered in its vicinity.

+Buffalo sign. Tracks or traces of the (former) presence of buffalo. — **1805–8** PIKE *Sources Miss.* 33, [I] discovered the first buffalo sign. *a***1847** in Howe *Hist. Coll. Ohio* 358 Buffalo signs were frequently met with; but the animals had entirely disappeared before the first white inhabitant came into the country. **1852** MARCY *Expl. Red River* (1854) 14 Our Delawares report that they have seen numerous fresh buffalo 'signs' and that we shall probably soon come upon the herds. **1888** *Forest & Stream* 15 March (F.), A great many elk were seen, a few sheep, and much old buffalo sign.

+Buffalo skin.

1. The skin of a buffalo.

1732 *S.C. Gazette* 25/1 Preparing Buffelo, Deer, Sheep, Goat or Kid-Skins in Oil, in Imitation of Chamois. **1778** CARVER *Travels* 84 They carry with them their dead for interment bound up in buffaloes skins. **1805** D. MCCLURE *Diary* (1899) 63 The King & his Council . . . sat on Buffalo skins. **1835** HOFFMAN *Winter in West* I. 197, I wrapped myself in a buffalo-skin, and placing my saddle under my head for a pillow, soon 'slept like a king.' **1852** STOWE *Uncle Tom* xvii, The seats were taken out of the wagon. The buffalo-skins, doubled in fours, were spread all along one side. **1866** *Rep. Indian Affairs* 185 The Indians of ordinary rank dwell in huts, or 'tepes,' made of buffalo-skins tanned as white as the drifting snow. **1886** BRET HARTE *Snow-bound* 111 A few bear and buffalo skins covered the floor. **1890** CUSTER *Following Guidon* 75 It was made of tanned buffalo skins sewed together with leather thongs.

2. A piece of skin from a buffalo.

1818 SCHOOLCRAFT *Journal* 19 With this we bathed the ankle and bound it up with flannel and buffaloe skin.

3. *attrib.* Made of, covered with, buffalo skin.

1807 GASS *Journal* 54 They had 12 buffaloe-skin canoes or boats laden with meat and skins. **1846** THORPE *Myst. Backwoods* 75 We have next in the list of backwoods craft, what is styled by the white man, the buffalo-skin boat. **1861** WINTHROP *Open Air* 269 Sibley's tent . . . is the Sioux buffalo-skin lodge, or *Tepee,* improved. **1873** BEADLE *Undevel. West* 482 Two mirrors and a buffalo-skin lounge adorn the sitting-room. **1881** *Harper's Mag.* May 875/1 Inwrapped in a buffalo-skin coat . . . the Reporter found himself perfectly comfortable with the thermometer . . . below zero.

+Buffalo soldiers. Colored soldiers serving in the West. — **1872** F. M. A. ROE *Army Lett.* 65 The officers say the negroes make good soldiers and fight like fiends. . . . The Indians call them 'buffalo soldiers,' because their woolly heads are so much like the matted cushion that is between the horns of the buffalo. **1889** *Century Mag.* April 912/2 They paused to gaze at us and doubtless wondered for what purpose the buffalo-soldiers were abroad in the land. **1916** C. A. EASTMAN *From Deep Woods* 101 The Indians with their quick wit called them [colored troopers, wearing buffalo overcoats and muskrat caps] buffalo soldiers.

+Buffalo stamp. (See quotations.) — **1873** BEADLE *Undevel. West* 205 'Buffalo stamps,' are tracts of hard blue soil. **1878** — *Western Wilds* 131 The rock lies . . . but a few inches below the surface, which is largely dotted with 'buffalo stamps.' These are said to have been caused by buffaloes crowding together, stamping and licking the ground, led thereto by a saline element in the soil.

+**Buffalo steak.** A steak obtained from a buffalo.

1770 J. Rowe *Diary* 200 Part of our Dinner was Buffalo Stakes which was very tender. **1846** Thorpe *Myst. Backwoods* 95 A real buffalo steak! eaten in the very grounds which the animal inhabits! **1860** *Harper's Mag.* Oct. 595/2 Presently dinner was served, and we sat down to fresh buffalo-steaks, hot bread, rice-pudding, [etc.]. **1886** Z. F. Smith *Kentucky* 690 [It] was probably commuted for . . . buffalo steak.

+**Buffalo street.** =Buffalo road. — **1837** Bird *Nick of Woods* I. 38 You've as . . . broad a trace before you as man and beast could make —a buffalo-street through the canes.

+**Buffalo tallow.** Tallow obtained from buffalo. — **1805** Clark in *Lewis & Clark Exped.* (1904) II. 190, I . . . set Chabonah to trying up the Buffalow tallow. **1825** *Missouri Intell.* 18 June 2/1 The ordinary food of a trapper is corn and buffalo tallow. **1848** E. Bryant *California* 83 The Mexican and the Indian were engaged in frying bread in buffalo tallow for dinner.

+**Buffalo tongue.** The tongue of a buffalo.

1792 Imlay *Western Territory* 153 Neats tongues, 6 d. each. Buffalo ditto, which are a most delicious morsel, 9 d. **1823** *Missouri Intell.* 7 Jan. 4/1 Can briny shad—can turbot vie With buff'lo's-tongue and venison pie? **1833** *Niles' Reg.* XLIV. 373/2 Even the traders were compelled to subsist on Buffalo tongues. **1848** E. Bryant *California* 70 We purchased of them some dried buffalo tongues and jerked meat. **1872** F. M. A. Roe *Army Lett.* 63 Old Findlay had pickled a choice buffalo tongue with much care and secrecy. *a***1918** G. Stuart *On Frontier* II. 103 We had dinner at Bull creek [in 1880], a fine dinner, bread, buffalo tongue, and coffee.

+**Buffalo trace.** A way or road made by the passage of buffalo. — **1823** *S.D. Hist. Coll.* I. 190 We had to pursue the intricate windings of a buffalo trace, among rocks, trees, &c. **1838** Drake *Tales & Sk.* 108 Early on the morning of the fourth day, they . . . commenced a slow retreat, along the buffalo trace leading to the Blue Licks. **1852** Watson *Nights in Block-House* 121 The Indians had followed the buffalo trace. **1886** Z. F. Smith *Kentucky* 22 The hardy explorers took one of these roads, or buffalo traces, as they are called and known even yet.

+**Buffalo track.** =Buffalo road, Buffalo trace. — **1806** T. Ashe *Travels in A.* 47 The best roads to the Onondargo from all parts, are the buffalo-tracks. **1840** *Knickerb.* XVI. 160 These [*i.e.*, paths] were called buffalo-tracks, and traversed Kentucky from end to end, like high-ways. **1852** Watson *Nights in Block-House* 128 Most of the foot left the great buffalo track.

+**Buffalo trail.** A buffalo road. — *c***1834** Catlin *Indians* II. 18 We will take that buffalo trail, where the traveling herds have slashed down the high grass. **1843** Frémont *Exped.* 21 In the buffalo trails and wallows, I remarked saline efflorescences. **1878** Beadle *Western Wilds* 66 We descended through a side gorge into the cañon of the Cimarron, winding along a buffalo trail.

+**Buffalo tree.** =Buffalo nut. — **1883** Hale *Woods & Timbers N.C.* 154 Oil-Nut, Buffalo Tree, (*Pyrularia oleifera*, Gray) [is] a bush 3 to 6 feet high, abundant through our mountain range, and reaching north to the mountains of Pennsylvania.

+**Buffalo tug.** A thong of buffalo hide. — **1832** J. A. McClung *Sks. Western Adventure* 165 [The Indian] pinioned his arms until the buffalo tug was buried in the flesh. **1844** Gregg *Commerce of Prairies* I. 104 The spokes of some were beginning to reel in the hubs, so that it became necessary to brace them with 'false spokes,' firmly bound with 'buffalo tug.' **1847** in *Hist. Coll. Ohio* 404 Slover was . . . conducted to an empty house, to an upper log of which he was fastened by a buffalo-tug tied around his neck. **1852** Mrs. Ellet *Pioneer Women* 57 They omitted the precaution of binding him closely one night, merely tying the buffalo tug around his wrists, and fastening it to their bodies.

+**Buffalo wallow.** A depression caused by the rolling or wallowing of buffalo.

1834 A. Pike *Sketches* 18 Traveled all day, and encamped again in the prairie, at a hole where buffalo had been rolling, called by hunters a buffalo wallow, and containing water. **1843** N. Boone *Journal* (1917) 195 Our three last days marches have been over prairie, abounding in old Buffalo wallows. **1846** W. Stewart *Altowan* I. viii. 212 Near him however, was a buffalo wallow. **1870** Keim *Sheridan's Troopers* 71 In many places the 'buffalo wallow' furnishes a supply of stagnant water. **1873** Beadle *Undevel. West* 83 They lost all their stock, and took refuge in a 'buffalo wallow' a few rods in circumference—a splendid natural earthwork. **1887** Roosevelt in *Cent. Mag.* March 658 They had come to an alkali mud-hole, an old buffalo-wallow, which had filled up. **1895** *Cent. Mag.* Sept. 694 The one [tent] nearest the opening of the Hoo-thu-ga had red spots painted on the tent-cover, representing the buffalo-wallow. **1901** White *Westerners* vii. 46 Drinking muddy water from buffalo wallows which providential rains had filled. **1923** J. H. Cook *On Old Frontier* 51 Not daring to rise out of the buffalow wallow wherein I was lying, . . . I took a pot shot at him as he passed me.

+**Buffalo wolf.** The common gray wolf of the western plains, *Canis lupus occidentalis.* — **1846** Sage *Scenes Rocky Mts.* vi, Of these [=wolves] there are five distinct classifications, viz: The big white, or buffalo wolf; the shaggy brown; the black; the gray, or prairie wolf; and the cayeute, (wa-chunka-monet,) or medicine-wolf of the Indians. **1877** J. S. Campion *On Frontier* 23 The light cavalry, . . . the gray-coated uhlans of the Plains—the buffalo-wolves—were upon us. **1891** *Cent.* 6959/2 The gray wolf is also called the *buffalo-wolf*, from its former abundance in the buffalo-range, and *timber-wolf*, as distinguished from the prairie-wolf or coyote.

+**Buffalo('s) wool.** Woollike hair obtained from buffalo.

1775 Romans *Nat. Hist. Florida* 85 Buffaloe's wool also furnishes them a material for a useful manufacture. **1814** Brackenridge *Views* 57 In the instruction to Iberville by the king of France, two things were considered of the first importance, the pearl fishery, and the buffaloe wool. **1824** Marshall *Kentucky* I. 124 The buffaloe wool [was] employed in the composition of cloth. **1887** *Harper's Mag.* June 54/2 These brought . . . the spinning-wheel with which coarse yarns were made from buffalo wool.

+**Buffalo wrapper.** A coat made out of buffalo skins. — **1846** E. Farnham *Prairie Land* 356 He had sat all day muffled in his buffalo wrapper, scarcely speaking.

Buff-breasted, *a.* Having a buff-colored breast. Used specifically in bird-names. — **1839** Peabody *Mass. Birds* 367 The Buff Breasted Sandpiper, *Tringa rufescens*, is not uncommon in the Boston market in August and September. **1844** *Nat. Hist. N.Y., Zoology* II. 318 Buff-breasted Sheldrake, *Mergus Merganser*. . . . Its geographical range extends from Mexico to 68° north latitude. *a***1862** Thoreau *Maine Woods* 322 Buff-breasted merganser or sheldrake.

Buffelhead, Buffel-headed, variants of Bufflehead, -headed.

+**Buffel's-head duck.** =Bufflehead. — **1731** Catesby *Carolina* I. 95 *Anas minor purpureo capite.* The Buffel's Head Duck. . . . These Birds frequent fresh waters, and appear in Carolina only in Winter. [Hence in Jefferson, etc.]

Buffer. *Obs.* (Meaning doubtful; cf. Buffing.) — **1787** *Amer. Museum* in *Md. Jrnl.* 21 Dec. (Th.), Good news, brother dealers in metre and prose, The world has turned buffer, and coming to blows.

Buffet.

1. A closet for holding cups, plates, etc., built into a recess or corner. {*a*1720-} Cf. Beaufet, Boffat.

1789 Bentley *Diary* I. 118 He found all the doors open, & the plate in the Buffet. **1859** Stowe *Minister's Wooing* ii, Right across the corner stands the 'buffet,' as it is called . . . wherein are displayed the solemn appurtenances of company tea-table. **1869** — *Oldtown Folks* xvii, The apparition . . . only appeared in a certain room . . . which had across one of its corners a closet called a buffet.

+**2.** A liquor-bar.

1890 *Voice* (N.Y.) 1 May, A curb-stone reporter avouches that Democratic drinkers no longer 'take a drink' . . . , but they patronize the 'buffet.' **1896** *Chicago Record* 1 Jan. 15/5 Want cigar store with buffet attachment, center of city. **1899** *Ib.* 11 Jan. 1/5 This man . . . operates the only buffet in the state house.

+**Buffet car.** A parlor or sleeping car having a small kitchen for preparing light meals. Also *buffet sleeping car.* — **1887** George *40 Yrs. on Rail* 248 Buffet, . . . dining and sleeping cars have all been added to meet the needs and tastes of this enterprising age. **1897** *Chicago Ev. Post* 15 May, Arrangements have been made by the Baltimore and Ohio Road . . . to put buffet sleeping cars on the night trains. **1910** E. S. Field *Sapphire Bracelet* 98 A young man . . . swung himself aboard, and entered the buffet car.

+**Buffet-kitchen.** The kitchen of a buffet car. — **1895** *Century Mag.* June 273/1 Her own order for breakfast was confined to a cup of coffee, which the porter was preparing in the buffet-kitchen.

Buffing, *ppl. a.* (Meaning doubtful: cf. Buffer.) — **1799** *Aurora* (Phila.) 23 Aug. (Th.), If we were as fond of fighting France as ever buffing Jackson, or big Ben, or the tinker of Cornwall were of entering the lists.

+**Bufflehead, Buffelhead.** =Buffle-headed duck. — **1858** Baird *Birds Pacific R.R.* 798 The name buffle head is a corruption of buffalo head, under which name it is mentioned by Bartram, in 1791. **1870** *Amer. Natualist* IV. 49 Buffel Head (*Bucephala albeola*). . . . Stay late in fall and come early in spring; but few . . . winter here. **1874** Long *Wild-Fowl* 16 With the canvas-back I shall treat of the red-head, . . . tufted duck, and buffle-head or butter ball.

+**Buffle-headed duck.** Also **buffel-.** [Eng. *buffle-headed* large-headed {1654-}.] A duck (*Bucephala albeola*) the head of which appears to be disproportionately large. — **1813** Wilson *Ornithology* VIII. 51 The Buffel-headed Duck, or rather as it has originally been, the Buffaloe-headed Duck, from the disproportionate size of its head, is fourteen inches long, and twenty-three inches in extent. **1823** James *Exped. Rocky Mts.* I. 267 *Anas albeola*, Buffle-headed duck. **1856** *Spirit of Times* (N.Y.) 13 Dec. 242/2 The dusky duck . . . prefers fresh waters and meadowy morasses; . . . so do the two varieties of teal, . . . and the little buffel-headed duck, or dipper. **1870** *Amer. Naturalist* IV. 548.

+**Buffler, Bufler.** *dial.* =Buffalo. — **1848** Ruxton *Far West* i. 30 A clever man was Bill Bent as I ever know'd trade a robe or throw a bufler in his tracks. **1850** Garrard *Wah-To-Yah* 51 Cutting a piece of dried 'buffler' to chew. **1860** *Harper's Mag.* March 446/2 Painter and buffler was thick in them diggings about that time. **1886** *Outing* June 323/2, I want ter show this 'ere young man where I got that big stand on buffler last fall.

+**Buffum.** A variety of pear. — **1853** Fowler *Home for All* 145 The Buffum, very prolific, and almost equal to Vergalue. **1857-8** *Ill. Agric. Soc. Trans.* III. 338 The Buffum is the only one that has entirely escaped the blight, both in the nursery and orchard. **1863** *Rep. Comm. Agric.* 182 The Buffum is a native of Rhode Island, a remarkably erect and vigorous grower, with reddish brown, short-jointed wood.

Bug, *n.*

1. Any kind of insect, beetle, etc. {1642-1710; now *dial.*}

1744 *Mass. H. S. Coll.* VII. 177 The filth . . . in the summer time, breeds an innumerable quantity of bugs, fleas, and vermin. **1785** WASHINGTON *Diaries* II. 404 Indeed some kind of fly, or bug, had begun to prey upon the leaves before I left home. **1800** BOUCHER *Glossary* p. l, Almost all insects in America are called *bugs;* excepting that particularly offensive insect, so noisome in beds, so called in London. **1805** PARKINSON *Tour* 364 There are hundreds of those sorts of reptiles, flies, and bugs, (all denominated bugs by the Americans,) too tedious to mention. **1843** 'CARLTON' *New Purchase* I. 18 It was like the sudden increase of bugs that wait for the darkness before they take wing! **1868** *Rep. Comm. Agric.* (1869) 305 If farmers in this country . . . were better acquainted with 'bugs,' as many term them, such knowledge would be the means of saving thousands of dollars. **1879** *Congress. Rec.* Feb. 1211/2 What an idea! Pay these scientific men to hunt bugs! **1897** BRODHEAD *Bound in Shallows* 175 Many of the . . . leaves of the thick coppice were white now . . . with the ravages of some worm or bug. **1904** STRATTON-PORTER *Freckles* 219 There's a lot of hard-backed bugs—beetles, I guess.

attrib. **1861** *Ill. Agric. Soc. Trans.* V. (1865) 442 It is the *Galgulus oculatus*, belonging to the Bug tribe.

b. In figurative or slang phrases.

1856 J. D. WHITNEY *Life & Lett.* 160 Shall I let the survey go to the bugs and return home immediately? **1885** *Congress. Rec.* Jan. 998/1, I know as well what the bug is under this chip as I know that the resolution is pending here. **1891** E. S. ELLIS *Check No. 2134* 261 'That beats the bugs!' exclaimed the operator. **1909** 'O. HENRY' *Options* 9 How about this write-up of the Atlanta, New Orleans, Nashville, and Savannah breweries? . . . What's the chip over the bug?

2. =BED-BUG. {1622–}

1705 BEVERLEY *Virginia* IV. 66 Chinches are a sort of flat Bug, which lurke in the Bedsteads and Bedding. **1737** BRICKELL *N. Carolina* 161 The Chinch Wall-louse, or Buggs; these are flat, red, and in shape and bigness like the Sheep-louse. **1774** FITHIAN *Journal* I. 170 For company . . . I had Bugs in every part of my Bed. **1820** *Columbian Centinel* 1 July 4/6 An effectual remedy against that disagreeable, . . . insect, the Bed Bug, may be found in Jones' effectual Bug Water. **1840** *Knickerb.* XV. 387 Landladies were seen killing the bugs in hotels, putting two sheets on the same bed, and water and other conveniences in the chambers of their lodgers. **1859** [see BUNK *v.* 2].

+3. *slang.* An individual obsessed by some idea or enthusiasm.

Also in recent use (1902–), a craze, a foolish fancy.

1841 *Congress. Globe* June 133 Mr. Alford of Georgia warned the 'tariff bugs' of the South that . . . he would read them out of church. **1885** 'CRADDOCK' *Prophet* 201 Them crazy bugs in N-N-Nashval sent him a book ev'y time they made a batch o' new laws.

+4. *slang.* A trick; a hoax.

1848 W. T. THOMPSON *Major Jones's Sk. Trav.* 126 (Th.), They say the people of Stunnington in Connecticut live on fish so much that they . . . have scales on their backs. This may be a bug what they put on me, but one thing I do know [etc.]. **1853** 'P. PAXTON' *Yankee in Texas* 96, I smell a bug. Dave and that ar strannger's only playin' possum.

+Bug, *v.*[1]

1. *tr.* To clear (plants) of insects.

1877 *Vt. Bd. Agric. Rep.* IV. 113 For several years this 'bugging the potatoes,' as it was frequently termed, was the only effectual mode of combatting these insects that was known. **1895** *Voice* (N.Y.) 8 Aug. 7/6 While 'bugging' potatoes this season, I came across a number of beetles . . . , that I have never seen any mention of.

2. *intr.* (See quotation.)

1889 *Cent.* 711/1 *Bug*, . . . to hunt for bugs; collect or destroy insects: chiefly in the present participle: as, to go *bugging*.

+Bug, *v.*[2] *intr.* Of the eyes: To stick *out*, to bulge, protrude. — **1877** 'MARK TWAIN' in *Atl. Mo.* XL. 446 His dead-lights were bugged out like tompions; and his mouth stood . . . wide open. **1889** — *H. Finn* xix, Jim's eyes bugged out, when he heard that: and I reckon mine did too. **1902** WISTER *Virginian* 408 Can't you tell a man what's making your eyes bug out so?

Bugaboo. An object of terror; a bogy, bugbear. {1827–; in 1740 *buggybow*}

1787 *Columbian Mag.* (Phila.) 464/2 The maid . . . threatens to leave them [=children] in the dark for the *bug-a-boos*, if they are not quiet. **1791** *Md. Hist. Mag.* VI. 355 That bugaboo of the Indians is quite removed out of the way. **1835** CROCKETT *Van Buren* 187 All they hear on this subject from Blair and Ritchie is nothing but the bugaboo of an old coat and breeches hung up to scare them. **1862** NORTON *Army Lett.* 41 Our President is . . . too much afraid of touching the rebels in their tender spot—their niggers. General Sherman, whom he has sent to South Carolina, is such another bugaboo. **1873** MILLER *Amongst Modocs* 107 Grandmothers never hold up before naughty children a bigger or more delusive bug-a-boo than this universal fear of Indians. **1893** *Congress. Rec.* Oct. 2231/1 The fear and cry of negro domination was fitly named by a gentleman from the south, who said it was a 'bugaboo.' **1911** LINCOLN *Cap. Warren's Wards* 197 You're always seeing bugaboos.

attrib. **1842** *Spirit of Times* (Phila.) 18 May (Th.), Bugaboo Hall. **1843** *Ib.* 17 Nov. (Th.), Diseased potatoes form the last bugaboo story for the newspapers. **1844** POE *Premature Burial* Wks. III. 231, I read no 'Night Thoughts'—no fustian about church-yards—no bugaboo tales, such as this. **1870** BEADLE *Utah* 344 Next to the long-hackneyed and bug-a-boo whisperings of polygism is another abomination.

Bugbane. Any of various plants having reputed value as destroyers of bugs. {1804–} — **1817–8** EATON *Botany* (1822) 347 *Macrotrys serpentaria*, bug-bane, blacksnake root, cohosh. **1847** DARLINGTON *Weeds & Plants* 33 *Cimicifuga*, Bugbane. **1877** *Field & Forest* III. 39 *Cimicifuga racemosa* (Bugbane) is very abundant all along the valleys and up the mountain side. **1893** DANA *Wild Flowers* 78 Bugbane. . . . A curious-looking plant it is, bearing aloft the feathery flowers which have such an unpleasant odor that even the insects are supposed to avoid them.

+Bug-eater. *colloq.*

1. A native of Nebraska.

1872 *Harper's Mag.* Jan. 318/1 Below will be found a careful compilation of the various nicknames given to the States and people of this republic. . . . Nebraska, Bug-Eaters. **1888** *Amer. Notes & Q.* I. 155 *Bug-Eaters*. . . . The term is applied derisively to inhabitants of Nebraska by travellers on account of the poverty-stricken appearance of many parts of the State.

2. (See quot. 1878.)

*a***1859** *Southern Sketches* 99 (B.), Congo is a scrouger; he's up a gum, and no bug-eater, I tell you. **1878** *Field & Forest* III. 132 Our old teamster informed us that in Rocky Mountain parlance, a worthless fellow is called a 'bug eater.'

+Bugeye. =BUCKEYE 4. — **1881** E. INGERSOLL *Oyster Industry* 242 *Bugeye*, a flat-bottomed, center-board schooner, of three to fifteen tons, built of heavy timbers without a frame. A bugeye is always decked over and has a cabin aft. (Chesapeake.) **1886** DORSEY *Midshipman Bob* II. xi. 223 They had a 'permit' to go sailing in a 'bug-eye'—a craft peculiar to the Chesapeake—and three or four of them were baling the boat. **1889** *Cent.* 705/2 **1894** *Columbus* (O.) *Dispatch* 17 Oct., A small skiff containing four men was coming to the wharf from the bugeye, . . . when a heavy sea caused it to capsize.

+Bugfish. The menhaden, *Brevoortia tyrannus.* — **1857** *Harper's Mag.* March 442/1 Other varieties [of refuse fish] are sometimes taken, and among them the bug-fish. . . . Its characteristic peculiarity is only discovered on opening the mouth, in which it carries a sort of parasitic bug. **1875** *Field & Forest* I. 53 *Brevoortia menhaden* [is] known . . . at the South as bug-fish, from the abundance of these parasites, attaching to the inside of the mouth. **1878** *U.S. Nat'l Museum Proc.* I. 384 *Brevoortia tyrannus.*—Fat Back; Yellow Tail; Bug Fish. Very abundant. **1888** [see BUG-HEAD].

Buggy, *n.* Also †**buggie.**

1. A light four-wheeled vehicle for two persons. {1773–1866}

1807 IRVING, etc. *Salmagundi* viii. 174 An honest cit packs up . . . in a buggy . . . and rattles away on Sunday. **1836** C. GILMAN *Recoll.* (1838) 85 Papa preferred a little buggie, in which he could cross and reconnoitre two or three fields on his way. **1843** *Knickerb.* XXI. 49 He has recently become sole proprietor of . . . a nondescript four-wheeled vehicle, dignified with the name of 'buggy.' **1866** MOORE *Women of War* 71 The mail-carrier had given her his seat in the buggy, and was walking beside the horse. **1880** 'MARK TWAIN' *Tramp Abroad* xxvi. 267 He . . . said a buggy was just the trick to skim along mushy, slushy early spring roads with. **1885** *Rep. Indian Affairs* 163 The Indians came in their wagons and buggies drawn by fine horses. **1900** E. BRUNCKEN *N. A. Forests* 93 Hickory, on the use of which the world-wide fame of American 'buggies' and other vehicles was based. **1905** *N.Y. Herald* 19 Aug. 4/3 From the back country also come daily an assemblage of . . . old fashioned carriages, carryalls, sidebar buggies, Portland buggies—bearing the country folk. **1920** C. R. COOPER *Under Big Top* 7 Men depart by rail, buggy and automobile for the 'country routes.'

+2. The caboose or kitchen car of a freight train.

1899 *Boston Globe* 18 March 12/2 During the first eight weeks of this year 31,271 freight cars passed through Concord, N.H. Estimating the total length of these cars, with the engines and buggies, we find [etc.]. **1904** *Ib.* 28 Feb. 40/6 The caboose, or as it is better known, the buggy, is . . . a peculiar little car, and is the home of the crew while on the rail. It has four bunks, two at either end; while in the center is a compartment of about a dozen feet square. In one corner is a stove, in another a sink, while in the center is a stairway, leading up the monitor.

3. (See quotations.)

1875 *Chicago Tribune* 11 Sept. 4/2 The yard men load little iron carts,—called 'buggies' . . . —, with the due proportions of ordinary pig and charcoal iron. **1883** *Harper's Mag.* LXVI. 939/2 The men who do this work [=on the Brooklyn bridge cables] go out for the purpose on the strand in a 'buggy' so called, which is a board slat slung by ropes from the axis of a grooved wheel fitting and travelling on the strand as bound together.

4. Attrib. with *collar, cushion, pole, shed, sleigh*, etc.; *ride, trip*.

(1) *a***1841** [W. HAWES] *Sporting Scenes* II. 81 The light of the lantern . . . now disclosing a hat . . . , now an umbrella, and now a buggy-cushion. **1842** HALE *If, Yes and Perhaps* (1868) 84 The dear girl . . . agreed to go to Mrs. Pollexfen's ball that evening, ready to leave it with me in my buggy sleigh. **1853** *Mich. Agric. Soc. Trans.* V. 53 Farm Implements [exhibited include] . . . 1 fine buggy collar. **1867** DIXON *New America* I. 174 Men who got up early that morning had seen his body dangling from a buggy-pole in Main Street. **1872** FLAGG *Good Investment* 549/1 At the nearest wagon-maker's shop two old buggy wheels were found. **1884** 'CRADDOCK' *Where Battle was Fought* 256 [A young acquaintance stood]

with one boot upon the hub of the buggy-wheel. **1888** *Scribner's Mag.* Jan. 27/1 He considered . . . college itself as a place where young men . . . spent their money in buggy-hire and billiards, unbeknown to their fathers. **1897** BRODHEAD *Bound in Shallows* 269 The light clangor of handfuls of rice tinkled on the buggy-top. **1899** CHESNUTT *Conjure Woman* 128, I'd take a buggy-trace ter 'im. **1902** HARBEN *Abner Daniel* 9 He toted it out to the buggy-shed.

(2) **1862** G. W. WILDER *MS. Diary* 16 Jan., The officers took a buggy ride; joy go with them. **1863** *Ill. Agric. Soc. Trans.* V. (1865) 255 The one on the gang plow would have a fine buggy ride. **1881** *Amer. Naturalist* XV. 76 While on a buggy trip from Statesville to Hickory, I discovered from my buggy a deposit of drift gravel. **1901** *Munsey's Mag.* XXV. 696/2 Wilbur Bailey and Mary Lake went buggy-riding.

+**Buggy,** *v.* [BUGGY *n.* 1.] *tr.* To drive (a person) in a buggy. — **1872** *Newton Kansan* 5 Sept. 3/2 Our whilom friend . . . buggied Mrs. S. over to Augusta.

+**Buggy harness.** [BUGGY *n.* 1.] Harness suitable for a horse that pulls a buggy. — **1840** *Boston Directory* 11 Coach, Gig, & Buggy Harnesses. **1857** *Mich. Agric. Soc. Trans.* IX. 316 We found no premium offered in the printed list for Buggy Harness. **1862** *Catal. Internat. Exhib. Brit.* No. 4743, Gig, carriage, and American buggy harness.

+**Buggy horse.** [BUGGY *n.* 1.] A horse that pulls a buggy. — **1858** GLISAN *Jrnl. Army Life* 398, I succeeded in purchasing a splendid saddle and buggy horse, known all over the Territory. **1862** *Rep. Comm. Patents: Agric.* 551 The tendency to overgrowth, common to prairie horses, . . . is objectionable in a roadster or buggy horse. **1874** *Vt. Bd. Agric. Rep.* II. 401 He had no more training than we give our common buggy horses. **1911** HARRISON *Queed* 174 In the grove stood carriages; buggy horses reined to the tall trees [etc.].

+**Buggy plow.** [BUGGY *n.* 1.] A plow having wheels and a seat for the driver; a riding plow. — **1875** KNIGHT 1743/1 This, perhaps, is the pioneer of sulky plows and buggy plows, as we of the West call them. **1876** *Congress. Rec.* 17 June 4656/1 We are developing our wheat interest . . . by the addition of . . . the turning plow, the gang plows, . . . the buggy plow, and so on.

+**Buggy-seat.** [BUGGY *n.* 1.] A seat of a buggy, or buggy plow. — **1863** *Ill. Agric. Soc. Trans.* V. (1865) 255 The old plow jogger will be mounted on his buggy seat. **1884** HOWELLS *Silas Lapham* i. 23 Lapham, gathering up the hitching-weight, slid it under the buggy-seat and mounted.

+**Buggy wagon.** [BUGGY *n.* 1.] A very light four-wheeled wagon. — **1844** *Mass. Statutes* lxxxv, [Toll for] buggy wagon, 12 cents . . . ; buggy wagon on elliptical springs without top, 12 cents. **1852** *Knickerb.* XL. 20 Once upon a time I happened to be travelling with a friend in a buggy-wagon. **1856** *Harper's Mag.* XIII. 443/1 A basket of provisions, a roll of blankets, and a buffalo robe for bedding, were put upon mine host's buggy wagon.

+**Buggy whip.** [BUGGY *n.* 1.] A long switchlike whip suitable for use in a buggy.

1873 *Winfield* (Kansas) *Courier* 10 July 3/2 Buggy whips, cattle whips and riding whips at Old Log Store. **1884** CABLE *Dr. Sevier* liii, He pointed down with his buggy-whip just off the roadside, first on one hand and then on the other. **1899** CHESNUTT *Wife of His Youth* 307 Some of the spectators wondered why there should be so much ado about convicting a negro of stealing a buggy-whip. **1904** 'O. HENRY' *Heart of West* 259 Dry Valley bought the heaviest buggy whip in the Santa Rosa store.

+**Bughead.** *local.* =BUGFISH. — **1888** GOODE *Amer. Fishes* 386 Virginia gives us 'Bug-fish,' 'Bug-head' and 'Bug-shad,' referring to the parasitic crustacean found in the mouths of all Southern Menhaden.

+**Bug-horns.** 'Horns curving inward' (Th.). — **1766** *Mass. Gazette* 23 Oct. 4/3 Strayed away from the Owner in Boston, . . . a small dark brown Cow, with bug Horns. **1769** *Ib.* 30 Nov. 4/1 Strayed from Daniel Gay . . . , a Pair of Steers, . . . also a Heifer . . . , brown and white, with short bug Horns. **1809** *Mass. Spy* 27 Sept. (Th.), A middling sized red cow, with bug horns. **1819** *Ib.* 2 June (Th.), A stray Cow, of a deep red colour, having 'bug horns' (so called). **1821** *Ib.* 22 Aug.

+**Bug-horned,** *a.* Having bug horns. — **1823** *Somerset* (Me.) *Jrnl.* 28 Nov. 1/1 (Th.), Came into the enclosure of the subscriber . . . a red Cow, with a white face and bug horned.

+**Bug-house, Bughouse,** *a. slang.* [BUG *n.* 3.] Crazy; insane. — **1895** 'JOSIAH FLYNT' in *Century Mag.* June 291/2 How's that for bein' bughouse (crazy), eh? **1896** G. ADE *Artie* 161 If I don't get mine inside of a week I'll go bug-house. **1900** J. FLYNT *Tramping* 383 Old Boston Mary was the originator of it. Sitting in her little shanty one day, . . . she exclaimed suddenly: 'Blokes, I'm bughouse.' Asked what she meant, she said: 'I'm losin' me brain.' **1904** 'O. HENRY' *Cabbages & Kings* 300 The old boy looked pretty bughouse when she first grappled him.

Bug hunter. An entomologist. {1851} — **1898** *Mo. So. Dakotan* I. 75 When the bug hunter was killed on the Little Cheyenne Captain Miner was acting field officer of the day.

+**Bug juice.** *slang.* [BUG *n.* 1.] Bad or inferior whisky. — *a*1877 *Osborne* (Kansas) *Farmer* (B.), We have taken . . . bug juice on subscriptions in our time. **1882** PECK *Sunshine* 263 He can never see a person with his keg full of bug juice without giving him a talking to. **1888** *Century Mag.* Dec. 300/1 He stepped to the door and called: 'Mountain dew, Mat, and bug juice for Mr. Doyle.' **1902** HARBEN *Abner Daniel* 73, I kin make bug-juice all the rest o' my life an' sell it without bein' ketched. **1903** LEWIS *Boss* 191 Just now he's steeped in bugjuice to th' eyes, an' has been for a week.

+**Bug lamp, lantern.** [*Lightning* BUG *n.*] A lamp or lantern giving a feeble light. — *c*1849 [PAIGE] *Dow's Sermons* I. 75 You may wander outside in the darkness of ignorance—guided by the bug-lamps of instinct. **1924** R. CUMMINS *Sky-High Corral* 104 He produced a candle and a can from his pack and made a 'bug' lantern by cutting a hole in the side of the can and poking the candle through it.

+**Bugle cranberry.** (See quotation.) — **1874** *Dept. Agric. Rep. 1873* 445 The American cranberry is divided by growers and writers into three different varieties, viz., the Bell cranberry . . . ; the Bugle cranberry, which somewhat resembles a bugle-head . . . ; the Cherry cranberry.

Bugler. One who sounds a bugle. {1840–} — **1855** SIMMS *Forayers* 236 As they appeared, the bugler of the corps . . . welcomed them with a plaintive German air. **1863** NORTON *Army Lett.* 133, I am chief bugler of the brigade. **1866** 'F. KIRKLAND' *Bk. Anecdotes* 622/1 Frank, the Pretty Female Bugler of the Eighth Michigan.

+**Bugleweed.** The herb *Lycopus Virginicus.* — **1817–8** EATON *Botany* (1822) 345. **1840** DEWEY *Mass. Flowering Plants* 174 *Lycopus Virginicus*, Bugleweed, and *Lycopus Europæus*, Water Horehound, . . . have considerable reputation as a remedy for bleeding at the lungs, or spitting blood. **1848** BARTLETT 52 Bugle-weed . . . is also known as the *Virginian Water-horehound.* *a*1862 THOREAU *Maine Woods* 309, 317.

+**Bug light.** [*Lightning* BUG *n.*] (See quotations and cf. BUG-LAMP.) — **1882** GODFREY *Nantucket* 217 The Cliff lights, sometimes called 'Bug lights,' . . . are situated on the beach northwest of Nantucket Harbor. These are two small pyramidal structures . . . , the front being fixed white, the rear fixed red. **1899** SUSAN HALE *Letters* 341 My room is called the 'Buglight' because it is a little house all by itself set upon four legs over a sort of piazza where we read and sew.

***Bugloss.** One or other of several plants of the borage family.

1709 LAWSON *Carolina* 77 Our Pot-herbs and others of use, which we already possess, are Angelica wild and tame, Balm, Buglos, Borage. **1818** *Mass. H. S. Coll.* 2 Ser. VIII. 170 In July the lover of plants is gratified with . . . the northern mint, the penny-royal, the bugloss [etc.]. **1840** DEWEY *Mass. Flowering Plants* 184 *Anchusa officinalis*, Bugloss; . . . introduced from Britain. *Ib.* 185 *Lycopsis arvensis*, . . . Small Bugloss. **1850** [S. F. COOPER] *Rural Hours* 106 It will be easy to name a number of these: . . . bugloss, or blue-weed, and the pigeon-weed of the grain-fields.

+**Bugologist.** *jocular.* A student of bugs or insects; an entomologist. — **1881** *National Republican* 24 Feb. 2/4 Mr. Riley, the eminent bugologist, has had an interview with General Garfield on the subject of agriculture. **1901** G. S. HALL *Confess. Psychol.* 110 The 'Bugologist' . . . has long been the stalking horse or awful example of . . . narrowness.

+**Bugology.** *jocular.* The science of bugs; entomology.

1843 'CARLTON' *New Purchase* II. 171 Chemistry, botany, anatomy, conchology, bugology. **1888** *Grass Valley* (Cal.) *Tidings* (F.), Entomology, or bugology. **1893** *Congress. Rec.* 18 Oct. 2667/2 He sent me two large and handsome volumes on what . . . we plain people call bugology. **1894** *Advance* (Chicago) 89/1 There are people who think one half crazy who takes an interest in bugology, as they call it. **1898** *Congress. Rec.* App. 22 April 455/2 Those of you who are acquainted with bugology know there is rather a disreputable bug that looks one way and rolls the other.

+**Bug poison.** [BUG *n.* 1.] =BUG JUICE. — **1888** *Texas Siftings* 7 July (F.), Nearly every character introduced by Charles Dickens into his numerous novels, was addicted to drinking . . . ; each and every individual took his bug-poison with surprising regularity and eminent satisfaction.

+**Bugshad.** *local.* (See BUGHEAD.)

+**Bug-sharp.** *slang.* [BUG *n.* 1.] An entomologist. — **1877** *Field & Forest* III. 94 One [*Amblychila cylindriformis*] . . . was viewed with emotions too deep for words by jostling crowds of bug-sharps.

+**Bug worm.** [BUG *n.* 1.] A larva or caterpillar. — **1803** *Mass. Spy* 29 June (Th.), The means of destroying the canker and bug worms.

Buhr, irreg. variant of BURR *n.*

***Build,** *v.*

***1.** *tr.* To make, construct, lay out, etc. Also with *up.*

In literary Eng. use from the 15th century, but more freely employed in U.S.

1845 COOPER *Satanstoe* xxii, In this manner it was thought we should . . . sooner 'build up a settlement,' as the phrase goes. In America, the reader should know everything is 'built.' The priest 'builds up' a flock; the speculator a fortune; the lawyer a reputation; and the landlord a settlement; sometimes with sufficient accuracy in language, he even builds a town. **1852** BRISTED *Upper Ten Th.* 125 (Th.), These cravats are built on the same principle. **1860** MRS. S. COWELL *Diary* 150 A Mr. Christian . . . also gave him a pair of gold sleeve studs, but . . . he says Sam is only to wear these until Saturday, when a new pair shall have been 'built' for him. **1873** 'MARK TWAIN' & WARNER *Gilded Age* xlii. 382, I have heard that Congressmen have sometimes hired literary grubs to build speeches for them. **1876** 'MARK TWAIN' *Tom Sawyer* i. 17 The old lady pulled her spectacles down . . . ; they were her state pair, the pride of her heart, and were built for 'style.' **1883** *Harper's Mag.* Nov. 939/1 About 550 miles of railroad had been built. **1886** Z. F. SMITH *Kentucky* 21 They secured their boats and proceeded to build a camp.

2. To prepare (a fire) by collecting and placing of materials. {1805}

1859 BARTLETT 54 *To build a fire*, instead of *to make a fire*, is a common phrase, originating, probably, in the backwoods, where large fires are made of logs piled one above the other. **1863** [C. C. HOPLEY] *Life in*

South I. 39 'Aunt Ailsey' again drives them off, sending one for wood and another for water, and a third is to tell somebody to come and 'build' a fire. **1864** NORTON *Army Lett.* 212, I shall get out on shore, build up a fire and wait an hour. **1871** EGGLESTON *Hoosier Schoolm.* xxi. 155 She had just built a fire in the stove, and she now stood at the door with unwashed face and uncombed hair.

Building, *vbl. n.* In various attributive uses.

(1) **1664** *Groton Rec.* 12 Mathias Farnworth shall have forty polle of land to be layd out agaynst his house next to James his Broke for a building place. **1832** R. C. SANDS *Writings* II. 316, I was appointed on the building committee. **1871** *Rep. Indian Affairs* (1872) 278 In consequence of the lack of building-room, one apartment in the house . . . has to be used as a blacksmith shop. **1872** BRACE *Dangerous Classes N.Y.* 113 A building-fund for the Newsboys' Lodging-House. **1901** MERWIN & WEBSTER *Calumet K* 16 By four o'clock [he] had seen . . . plans, specifications, building book, . . . and even the pay roll. **1912** *Indian Laws & Tr.* III. 540 For general repairs and improvements, including fencing of building grounds.

(2) **1835** HOFFMAN *Winter in West* I. 69 A species of yellow freestone found in the vicinity is coming into use, which, for elegance as a building material, is not surpassed by marble itself. **1844** *Knickerb.* XXIV. 39 The wise worthies of Gotham . . . sent a detachment of town-carts to haul brick-bats and building rubbish. **1857** *Mich. Agric. Soc. Trans.* IX. 316 A dozen Patent Building Blocks . . . are worthy of attention. **1878** F. M. A. ROE *Army Lett.* 206 It was . . . shaped precisely like an ordinary building brick. **1883** *Harper's Mag.* Nov. 822/2 A superior quality of the ordinary building limestone.

Building association. A mutual savings and investment society that lends money, esp. for building purposes. Hence *Building and loan(ing) association.*

1851 *New York Laws* 74 Sess. cxxii 234 An act for the incorporation of building, mutual loan and accumulating fund associations. **1876** *Scribner's Mo.* Feb. 482/1 Lenders and depositors on one side, borrowers for every known purpose on the other, the poor lending to the rich, the rich borrowing and lending. They call such an association as this a building and loaning association. **1888** H. S. ROSENTHAL *Manual for Bldg. & Loan Ass.* (1891) 20 The Building Association, therefore, while not necessarily a *Building* Association, is always a *Saving* Society. **1891** S. DEXTER *Co-op. Savings & Loan Ass.* 42 The first name given to them was 'Building Associations.' This was succeeded by 'Building and Loan Associations.' *Ib.*, The first building association in this country was organized in a suburb of the city of Philadelphia, called Frankford, January 3, 1831, and named the 'Oxford Provident Building Association.' **1897** *Conn. Comm. Bldg. & Loan Ass. Rep.* 4 Building and Loan Associations. The business of these associations has noticeably increased within the past year.

+**Building bee.** A gathering for erecting or raising a building. — **1848** RUXTON *Far West* (1849) 257 A buildin' bee or a raisin' bee is, when they want to set up the frame or the logs of a house or barn. **1880** *Scribner's Mo.* June 247/1 This is the time of logging and building 'bees,' and . . . of hard drinking and 'corduroy' roads.

Building loan. A loan made for erecting a building or buildings. — **1856** D. MACLEOD *F. Wood* 167, 6 per cent Building Loan Stock, No. 2, redeemable in 1855 and 1856.

+**Building lot.** A plot of land laid out as a building site.

1701 *Conn. Col. Rec.* IV. 357 On the west side of old Jacksons lotts (vizt,) pasture, building lott, and long lott. **1798** *Ann. 7th Congress* 2 Sess. 1307 Had they been divided into building lots, it would have been infinitely more beneficial to him. **1809** F. CUMING *Western Tour* 140 Two parallel streets, on the one of which fronting the Ohio, building lots of a quarter of an acre, now sell at fifty dollars each. **1835** HOFFMAN *Winter in West* I. 85 The rapid rise of property here [in Cleveland] . . . is almost incredible; building-lots in some places commanding now as many thousands as they did hundreds of dollars five years since. **1867** RICHARDSON *Beyond Miss.* 26 Building lots were selling at from three hundred to seven hundred dollars. **1881** W. O. STODDARD *E. Hardery* 15 In a quarter of the . . . city, where the high prices of all building lots rendered the dwellings built thereon securely aristocratic.

+**Building paper.** A thick paper used by builders for covering interior surfaces or as a lining between inner and outer boarding. — **1873** *Newton Kansan* 20 Feb. 3/4 Building paper, the best substitute for plastering, for sale by Lehman & Co. **1880** G. INGHAM *Digging Gold* 337 The hotel where we stopped was plastered with building paper, tacked to the walls.

+**Building rock.** Stone suitable for use as building material. — **1800** B. HAWKINS *Sk. Creek Country* 28 The hill sides fronting the river, exhibit this building rock. **1849** [CHAMBERLAIN] *Indiana Gazetteer* 191 Iron ore, marble, excellent building rock and hydraulic cement are found in abundance.

+**Building spot.** A site or location suitable for a building. — **1802** *Mass. H. S. Col.* VIII. 201 So many houses and works have been erected, . . . that building spots now sell at a high price. **1853** FOWLER *Home for All* 23 Those persons who would economize, have only to order those very shells which the oyster-man has to pay to have carted from his cellar, on to your building spot. **1872** *Ill. Dept. Agric. Trans.* 174 In the west part of the city . . . are the finest building spots in the world.

Building stone. Stone suitable for building.

1790 *Penna. Packet* 2 Jan. 4/4 For Sale By Isaac Hazlehurst & Co. . . . Bourdeaux rough hewn building stone. **1805** SIBLEY in *Ann. 9th Congress* 2 Sess. 1095 On the bank of one of them there is plenty of stone coal, and several quarries of tolerable good building stone. **1849** *Rep. Comm. Patents: Agric.* (1850) 94 There has been manufactured in this country . . . twenty-seven thousand dollars worth of building stone. **1881** STODDARD *E. Hardery* 188 There never was better building stone, and there's any quantity of it out, over by the old quarry. **1884** *Century Mag.* Aug. 522/1 We are beginning to feel how greatly beauty depends upon the proper size, surface finish, and arrangement of our building-stones.

Building timber. Timber suitable for use in erecting buildings.

1647 *Springfield Rec.* I. 188 No man shall hence forth transport out of the town to other places, any buildinge tymber, board loggs, or sawne boardes or planks. **1670** *New Plymouth Laws* 164 Forasmuch as severall Townes in this collonie are alreddy much straightened for building timber and through Gods Providence some other townes are well accomodated to afford them a supply [etc.]. **1839** *S. Lit. Messenger* V. 137/2 In a few years they have made a scarcity of good building timber in the country. **1843** N. BOONE *Journal* (1917) App. 233 There being a great scarcity . . . of building or rail timber.

Building trade. A trade or occupation concerned in the erection of buildings. — **1890** *Columbus* (Ohio) *Dispatch* 18 Nov., It has been decided by the Trades Council to take radical measures . . . to unionize all work in the building trades. **1903** *McClure's Mag.* Nov. 30 As one of the representatives of his union Sam Parks had a seat and a vote in the Board of Building Trades.

Building yard. *Obs.* An area in which boatbuilding is carried on. — **1701** *Boston Rec.* 10 In Ship Carpenters building yards, Sett work coopers, and Ropemakers works. **1706** SEWALL *Letter-book* I. 342 When I returned from England, I had some thoughts of carrying out the Wharf, so as to fit it for a Building yard. **1735** *Boston Selectmen* 278 Voted, That the Building-Yard . . . be let to Messrs. John Waters and Joseph Glidden.

***Built,** *p.p.* +*To be built (that way)*, to be so constituted or disposed. — **1868** *Mo. Republican* 25 Jan. (F.), 'Why didn't you roll down?' 'I wasn't built that way.' **1882** *Amer. Humorist* 12 May (F.), Even womankind is not built as she was a few brief years ago. **1889** FARMER 100/1 The expression is even extended to individuals, to be built being used with the meaning of formed. 'I was not built that way'; and hence in a still more idiomatic sense to express unwillingness to adopt a specified course or carry out any inconvenient plan.

+**Bulberry,** variant of BULLBERRY.

Bulge, *n.* {1741–} +*slang.* Advantage, upper hand, superiority over something or somebody.

1860 *Richmond Enquirer* 30 Nov. 4/5 (Th.), It is in this respect [of field products] that the South has 'the bulge' on the North. **1867** CRAWFORD *Mosby* 143 Smith threw himself at the head of his men, and ordered us to charge, so that we would have the bulge on the enemy. **1880** 'MARK TWAIN' *Tramp Abroad* iii. 40 Now I guess I've got the bulge on you by this time! **1882** PECK *Sunshine* 272 Bob Ingersoll has got the bulge on all the Christians now. **1886** C. D. WARNER *Their Pilgrimage* ii. 36 An Atlantic City man . . . said that Cape May used to be the boss, but that Atlantic City had got the bulge on it now. **1889** CUSTER *Tenting on Plains* 689 Such shooting as Andrews did, got the bulge on everybody. **1896** J. C. HARRIS *Sister Jane* 161 They hain't nobody under the sun can git the bulge on a mule 'ceptin' it's a nigger. **1906** 'O. HENRY' *Four Million* 115, I consider I have the bulge on him as far as you could chase a rabbit.

Bulge, *v. colloq.*[2]

+**1.** *intr.* To rush or dash.

1834 CROCKETT *Narr. Life* 96 My dogs . . . bulged in, and in an instant the bear followed them out. *Ib.* 105 As soon as we struck, I bulged for my hatchway. **1849** *Knickerb.* XXXIV. 407/1 The Hosiers . . . war a standin on the shores of the Big Drink, when long bulged the old 'Meteor,' a regular screamer, I tell ye. **1884** 'MARK TWAIN' *H. Finn* 372 Whilst we was a-standing there in the dimmish light, here comes a couple of the hounds bulging in from under Jim's bed.

+**2.** *tr.* To force at high speed.

1868 WOODRUFF *Trotting Horse* 207 Brooks and Harry Jones bulged them [the horses] off in the lead at such a rate that I was forced to let them take the pole on the turn.

+**Bulger.** *slang.* Anything uncommonly large or impressive. — **1835** CROCKETT *Tour* 37 We . . . soon came in sight of the great city of New York, and a bulger of a place it is. **1871** DE VERE 587 *Bulger*, . . . in the United States generally designates anything very large. 'That's a bulger of a story.'

***Bulk,** *n.*[1]

+**1.** A pile of tobacco made up to undergo sweating.

1678 *New Castle Court Rec.* 253 Tobacco which was struck & lay in bulke. **1724** JONES *Virginia* 40 When it is in proper Case, (as they call it) and the Air neither too moist, nor too dry, they *strike* it, or take it down, then cover it up in *Bulk*, or a great Heap. **1784** J. SMYTH *Tour U.S.* II. 135 When the tobacco house is quite full, and there is still more tobacco to bring in, all that is within the house is struck or taken down, and carefully placed in bulks, or regular rows one upon another. **1849** *Rep. Comm. Patents: Agric.* (1850) 322 The bulk, when carried up to a convenient height, should have a few sticks laid on the top to keep it in place. **1863** *Ill. Agric. Soc. Trans.* V. (1865) 668 Let the tobacco . . . be put in a winrow as it is termed, viz: laid straight in a bulk or pile. **1880** TOURGEE *Bricks* 359 The spicy odor of the 'bulks' of tobacco, which was stored there. **1902** *Farmers' Bul. No. 60* (Dept. Agric.) 14 Before the sweat is completed the bulk is pulled down and built up eight or ten times.

+**2.** *attrib.* Of commodities, etc.: Kept or sold, dealt with, in bulk or large quantities.

1693 *Virginia State P.* I. 48 An answer to a former message of yours relating to the Act for Ports & Bulke Tobacco. **1847** *Rep. Comm. Patents* (1848) 527 Bulk pork is that which is intended for immediate use or smoking. **1849** *Pres. Mess. Congress* II. 1029 In bulk payments . . . the claimants should . . . be required to submit their accounts or vouchers to the inspection of the agent. **1865–6** *Ill. Agric. Soc. Trans.* VI. 644 Bulk Meats—salt being struck off but not swept, one per cent. tare to be allowed. **1888** *Voice* (N.Y.) June, I have noticed that wherever baled hay is used it supersedes the use of bulk hay rapidly.

***Bulk,** *n.*[2] +A sleeping shelf; a bunk. — **1805–9** HENRY *Camp. Quebec* 144 There were four rooms below . . . all capacious and well supplied with births or bulks, in the common method of barracks.

Bulk, *v.* [Cf. BULK *n.*[1] 1.] +*tr.* To place (tobacco, wheat, etc.) in a heap; to pile up (tobacco) in the process of curing. {1822–, of fish}

1849 *Rep. Comm. Patents: Agric.* (1850) 322 To 'bulk' tobacco requires judgment and neatness. *Ib.*, The strippers . . . tie up the bundles and throw them separate for convenience in bulking. **1863** *Ill. Agric. Soc. Trans.* V. (1865) 669 Care must be taken that the tobacco does not . . . get too high in case before it is bulked. **1880** TOURGEE *Bricks* 138 'Den yer lets de fire go down an' opens der do' fer it ter come in order, so't yer kin bulk it [=tobacco] down.' 'What do you mean by "bulking it down"?' 'Put it in bulk, like dis yer,' said he, pointing to a pile of sticks laid crosswise of each other with the plants still on them. **1884** *Rep. Comm. Agric.* 350 The bulking of early-threshed wheat without separating the chaff. **1902** *Farmers' Bul. No. 60* (Dept. Agric.) 17 The leaves [of White Burley tobacco] . . . are tied into hands and bulked down for a short time, after which they are 'prized' into hogsheads.

Bulker. +One who places tobacco, etc., in bulk. — **1863** *Ill. Agric. Soc. Trans.* V. (1865) 668 This is done by lapping the bundles over each course similar to shingling a roof, the bulker having his knees upon the bulk.

Bulkhead. *N. Eng.* +An outside door or doorway leading to the cellar of a building. — **1854** THOREAU *Walden* iv. 132 Some trader among the Green Mountains, who . . . stands over his bulk-head and thinks of the last arrivals on the coast. *a*1862 — *Cape Cod* 73 An old woman came out and fastened the door of her bulkhead. **1890** *Dialect Notes* I. 9 The word *bulkhead* [is] used in New England of the covering of an opening into a cellar.

***Bull,** *n.*[1]

***1.** The male of the domestic bovine stock.

Properly the uncastrated animal, but in 19th cent. also used in the West for 'bullock' or 'ox.'

1640 *Watertown Rec.* 7 Onely Bulls to be herded with the Milch Cattle. *a*1649 WINTHROP *Hist.* I. 200 Cattle were grown to high rates;—a good cow, £25 or £30; a pair of bulls or oxen, £40. **1736** [see BULL-HOUSE]. **1847** RUXTON *Adv. Rocky Mts.* (1848) 264 The meat of the elk is strong flavored, and more like 'poor bull' than venison. **1851** CIST *Cincinnati* 102 To this 'drag,' by aid of a yoke, or wooden collar, he geared his bull. **1881** *Rep. Indian Affairs* 46 The cows and bulls furnished these Indians during the two preceding years . . . have been well cared for.

b. In phrases.

1836 CROCKETT *Adv.* 90 He belonged to that numerous class, that it is perfectly safe to trust (as far as a tailor can sling a bull by the tail). **1855** SIMMS *Forayers* 442, I sweated like a bull in fly-time. **1902** HARBEN *Abner Daniel* 15, I wouldn't trust that skunk no furder 'n I could fling a bull by the tail.

+**c.** A male buffalo.

1835 IRVING *Tour Prairies* 190 Tonish arrived, . . . his white horse hung all round with buffalo meat. According to his own account, he had laid low two mighty bulls. **1846** THORPE *Myst. Backwoods* 88 Far before you are the long dark lines of the buffalo. In the centre of the group feed the cows and calves. Upon the outside are the sturdy bulls. **1870** KEIM *Sheridan's Troopers* 305 They approached so near that the low bellow of the bulls could be distinctly heard.

+**d.** The male of the moose or elk.

1857 HAMMOND *Northern Scenes* 323 When I laid down, the old bull made a pass under the log, as if he expected me down there. **1882** BAILLIE-GROHMAN *Camps in Rockies* 112 Wapiti are called elk out West; and the stag is spoken of as a 'bull.' **1885** *Century Mag.* XXX. 224/1 It was a grand bull, with massive neck and twelve-tined antlers.

2. A speculator in stocks who tries to force up the price. {1714–}

1805 *Ann. 8th Congress* 2 Sess. 1103 As well may your buyers and sellers of stock, your bulls and your bears of the alley, require indemnification for their losses at the hands of the nation. **1828** PAULDING *New Mirror* 136 Banking capital can . . . put the bulls and bears on tiptoe. **1870** MEDBERRY *Men Wall St.* 187 He soon became one of the most conspicuous bulls in the street.

b. Attrib. with *clique, market, movement, operator,* etc. {1851–}

1870 MEDBERY *Men Wall St.* 82 Bull operators take a stock at its lowest, and attempt to toss it up as high as may be. **1879** *Boston Globe* 29 Aug., A bull movement might develop in Chicago Gas. **1887** *Courier-Journal* 20 Jan. 7/4 For nearly a week it has been talked that there was a bull clique in wheat, which was backed by the great Bank of Nevada. **1890** *Harper's Mag.* Oct. 705/2 The speculators of the 'bull' party joined in the cry. **1891** *Century Mag.* Jan. 426 No office of its size in the Street made so much money for its customers in a bull market. **1893** *Chicago Tribune* 26 April 5/5 The forced sale of a big block of stock that had been pledged as collateral for a loan, compelling a 'bull pool' to liquidate.

3. =BULLDOG.

1848 *Knickerb.* XVIII. 119 He was . . . a 'reg'lar thorough-bred bull.' **1855** SIMMS *Forayers* 79 An animal with a cross of the English bull upon the Irish wolf-dog. **1878** BEADLE *Western Wilds* 185 He went into the backyard and onloosed a regular old English bull. **1901** WHITE *Westerners* xxii. 207 Your bull wouldn't be ace high. Look at the teeth on him!

Bull, *n.*[2] [Cf. *bull* absurd statement {1640–}.] +Any absurd error or mistake. — **1855** 'P. PAXTON' *Capt. Priest* 226, I had committed a bull myself, by intruding where I evidently was *de trop.* **1902** LORIMER *Lett. Merchant* 70 Milligan just stood there like a dumb Irishman . . . before he told me that you were the fellow who had made the bull. **1911** HARRISON *Queed* 392 He had never once made a bull in 'Mr. Queed's copy' since the day of the famous fleas.

Bull, *v.*[1] [BULL *n.*[1] 2.]

1. *tr.* To raise or try to raise the price of (stocks, etc.). {*a*1842–}

1848 ARMSTRONG *Stocks* 19 This is perhaps the grand theatre for bulling and bearing stocks. **1869** 'MARK TWAIN' *Innocents Abroad* 368 Stocks are up . . . partly because buyers are too weak to bear the market, while sellers are amply prepared to bull it. **1870** MEDBERY *Men Wall St.* 190 In June, Erie was bulled by the same skilful hand. **1881** *Chicago Times* 4 June, If we succeed in bulling silver we shall also succeed in bearing gold to the same extent. **1887** *Courier-Journal* 13 Jan. 7/4 The New Yorkers appear to have abandoned yesterday their effort to bull wheat.

+**2.** *intr.* To push ahead boldly.

1884 'MARK TWAIN' *H. Finn* 144 Up-stream boats . . . bull right up the channel against the whole river. *Ib.* 276 It injured the frauds some; but the old fool he bulled right along, spite of all the duke could say or do.

Bull, *v.*[2] *slang.* [BULL *n.*[2]] +(See quotation.)—**1851** HALL *College Words* 25 *Bull,* at Dartmouth College, to recite badly.

***Bullace.** Also †**bullys** (as a pl.).

***1.** A wild plum larger than the sloe. Also attrib. with *plum* and *tree.*

1671 *S.C. Hist. Soc.* V. 308 Delightfull forrests . . . [are] full of diuers sorts of excellent fruits as strawberrys, mulberrys, . . . Bullys, Nutts, with a multitude besides. **1797** THOMAS *Newengland Farmer* 266 The black bullace, is a globular, tart fruit, of the size of grapes. **1846** EMERSON *Trees & Shrubs Mass.* 450 Wild Bullace Tree, *P[runus] insititia,* [is] a bush or small tree, found on the banks of Charles River, in Cambridge. **1892** APGAR *Trees Northern U.S.* 98 Bullace Plum.

+**2.** *Bullace (grape* or *vine),* the muscadine grape.

1862 *Rep. Comm. Patents: Agric.* 479 The Muscadine, Bullace, or Scuppernong grape, (*Vitis rotundifolia* of Michaux). **1892** HARRIS *On the Plantation* 71 He knew . . . where the muscadines, or as he called them, the 'bullaces,' were ripest. **1898** — *Tales of Home Folks* 362 Ef you could 'a' seed 'em a-swingin' in the bullace vine, . . . you wouldn't 'a thought Loorany was bothered much. **1901** MOHR *Plant Life Ala.* 101 The slender-stemmed bullace grape.

+**Bullbat.** The nighthawk, *Chordeiles virginianus.*

1851 GLISAN *Jrnl. Army Life* 89 Of the birds and animals not usually eatable, there are the . . . bull-bat, wren, yellow-bird, [etc.]. **1853** BALDWIN *Flush Times Ala.* 194 He did not have the chance of blowing a hole through his carcass with his 'Derringer' that 'a bull-bat could fly through without tetching airy wing.' **1866** C. H. SMITH *Bill Arp* 28 The world, the flesh, and the devil are looking to you to extend the aegis of freedom over all creation, . . . over bull bats and screech-owls, grub-worms and grindstones. **1883** *Macmillan's Mag.* XLVIII. 134/1 The 'bull-bats' or nighthawks, in the air above us are circling to and fro. **1904** 'O. HENRY' *Heart of West* 35 There was a kind of conspicuous hullabaloo going on in the bushes between the bullbats and the orioles and the jack-rabbits.

+**Bull bay.** The big laurel, *Magnolia grandiflora.* — **1883** SMITH *Geol. Survey Ala.* 292. **1884** SARGENT *Rep. Forests* 19.

***Bull beef.** The flesh of a bull. {–1785}

1635 R. MATHER *Journal* 20 The flesh of them was good meate . . . the leane like bull-beefe. **1848** BRYANT *California* 240 Their luxuries, such as bull-beef and horse-meat, they obtain by theft, or pay for in labor at exorbitant rates. *c*1849 [PAIGE] *Dow's Sermons* I. 138 He is strong, too; . . . stronger than a horse, and tougher than bull-beef. **1853** BALDWIN *Flush Times Ala.* 51 So scarce were provisions—bull-beef excepted, . . . that we were forced to eat green corn. **1877** BARTLETT 809 Cheaper than bull-beef at a penny a pound. **1887** *Nation* XLIV. 205/2 New Yorkers do not want stale sea-fish in a mountain country, or look on bull-beef and ham as luxuries.

+**Bullberry, Bulberry.** The buffalo berry, *Shepherdia argentea* or *S. canadensis.*

1861 *N.Y. Tribune* 5 July, A shrub of some size, known as buffalo-bush or bull-berry, grows somewhere near its [the Humboldt River's] course. **1876** BOURKE *Journal* 28 July–8 Sept., The fertility of the soil in this valley was attested by . . . the dense growth of grapevines, wild plums, and 'bull'-berries. **1883** *Rep. Indian Affairs* 28 The wild plum and grape are abundant, and the bull berry and wild cherry also are found in certain localities. **1885** CUSTER *Boots & Saddles* 71 Jelly made from the tart, wild 'bullberries' that grew near the river. *a***1918** G. STUART *On Frontier* II. 131 There are large patches of choke cherries on the creek and quantities of bull berries and red hawthorn bushes.

attrib. **1888** ROOSEVELT in *Century Mag.* XXXVI. 45/2 For supper we again had prairie fowl, having shot four from a great patch of bulberry bushes. **1896** *Advance* (Chicago) 22 Oct. 541/3 The pretty growth of timber and bushes and the clumps of bulberry trees altogether made a pleasant landscape.

+Bull boat. A boat made of buffalo or elk hides placed over a light wooden framework.

1832 N. WYETH *Journal* 160 Encamped 15 miles on Lewis River; we are now employed in making bull boats in order to cross it. [*Ib.* 209 This day went out to get Bull Hydes for boat. Got enough and employed the rest of the day in making a boat.] **1833** CATLIN *Indians* I. 195 One of the women . . . took upon her head a skin-canoe (more familiarly called in this country a bull-boat), made in the form of a large tub of a buffalo's skin. **1846** W. G. D. STEWART *Altowan* I. vi. 184 He could also distinctly see Tona employed in attempting to move a bull-boat hauled up on the beach. **1859** MARCY *Prairie Traveler* 83 Two men can easily build a bull-boat of three hides in two days which will carry ten men with perfect safety. **1873** in Custer *Boots & Saddles* 285 By stretching the hides over a kind of basket-frame prepared by the Crow guide, [I] made what are known among the Indians as bull-boats.

+Bull-brier. Any of various species of smilax, esp. *S. Pseudo-China* and *S. hispida.* — **1853** 'P. PAXTON' *Yankee in Texas* 22, [I aided] his rude attempts at road-making whenever a mass of bull-brier or bamboo-vines . . . called for action. **1859** BARTLETT 55 *Bull Briar*, a large briar in the alluvial bottoms of the South-west, the root of which contains a farinaceous substance from which the Indians make bread.

+Bull buffalo. A male buffalo. — **1750** T. WALKER *Journal* 63 We . . . met so impudent a Bull Buffaloe that we were obliged to shoot him, or he would have been amongst us. **1825** NEAL *Bro. Jonathan* III. 85 His raw militia, who were about as manageable then, as a herd of bull buffaloes—or negroes.

+Bull butter. *colloq.*[2] Oleomargarine. — **1887** *Courier-Journal* 1 May 12/4 As To Bull Butter. . . . The recent interview with Commissioner Colman on the subject of oleomargarine . . . has caused considerable excitement.

***Bull calf.** A male calf.

1640 *Mass. H. S. Coll.* 4 Ser. VI. 55 Of these there was the first yeare with Dillingham 9 calves, 5 cow calves, 4 bull calves. **1650** *Essex Probate Rec.* I. 125 Two bull Calfes of this yeare. *c***1800** FESSENDEN *Orig. Poems* (1806) 83 My father has a nice bull calf. **1858** FLINT *Milch Cows*, etc. 43 Bull-calves often run eight months with the cow. **1897** *Outing* XXX. 244/2 He was running frantically down the road . . . in a fashion much resembling the farmer trying to stop a fractious bull-calf.

+Bull chip. =BUFFALO CHIP. — **1870** BEADLE *Utah* 221 So we took to the plains and gathered the fuel known to plainsmen as 'bull-chips,' which made a very hot fire.

Bull dance. +1. =BUFFALO DANCE. **2.** A dance by men only. — (1) **1833** CATLIN *Indians* I. 165 On the first day, this 'bull-dance' is given once to each of the cardinal points. **(2) 1845** GREEN *Texian Exped.* 134 This [the turkey-buzzard dance] is performed somewhat after the manner of the bull-dance in old Virginia, a dance well known to the young men of that good old state at the conclusion of their balls, after the retirement of the ladies. *Ib.* 316 Next to the monte bank, some eight or ten were engaged in a 'bull-dance' being the only one we could perform in our 'jewelry.' **1859** BARTLETT 443 Stag-Dance, a dance performed by males only, in bar-rooms, etc.; also called a *bull-dance.*

***Bulldog,** *n.* A dog of the breed so named.

1809 *Deb. Congress* Jan. 1037 When vessels were loaded with sugar they [=American privateers] would fight like bull-dogs for it. **1850** GARRARD *Wah-To-Yah* i. 18 Their heads are short, bearing some resemblance to that of a young bulldog. **1865** *Atlantic Mo.* XV. 602 The force by which a bulldog holds on to an antagonist. **1873** *Newton Kansan* 3 April 1/5 The small bird held on with the tenacity of a bull-dog. **1877** F. M. A. ROE *Army Lett.* 162 He was not the hound that whipped the big bulldog at Monroe, Louisiana, two years ago.

+Bulldog, *v.* {1883–} *tr.* To attack or assail like a bull-dog; *spec.* to seize and throw (an animal).

1842 *Congress. Globe* 29 April 457/3 Mr. Whitney had not been 'dogged' to the door of the committee-room, but, when inside, he had been 'bull-dogged' with a vengeance. *Ib.* 4 May 478/1, I made the reply about bull-dogging for the gentleman from Virginia. *Ib.*, President, . . . Senators, Members of the House, and private individuals were bull-dogged—or fice-dogged, if the gentleman pleases. **1907** WHITE *Arizona Nights* 151 One of the men . . . reached well over the animal's back to get a slack of the loose hide next the belly, lifted strongly, and tripped. This is called 'bull-dogging.' **1920** HUNTER *Trail Drivers of Texas* I. 297 [The cowboy] 'bulldogs' them by twisting the neck. **1923** COOK *On Old Frontier* 151 This was my first and only experience at bulldogging an elk.

+Bulldog fly. The gadfly. — **1893** ROOSEVELT *Wilderness Hunter* 115 There was a spell of warm weather which brought out a few of the big bull-dog flies, which drive a horse — or indeed a man — nearly frantic.

+Bulldog Indian. A pure-blooded Indian. — **1870** O. LOGAN *Before Footlights* 286 There are lots of 'big Injuns' in Milwaukee. There is the unapproachable or Bull-dog Indian, who wears the aboriginal dress.

+Bulldoze, -dose, *n.* [Cf. the verb.] An application of bulldosing. — **1877** BARTLETT 77 Give him a bulldose meant give him a flogging,—a 'cowhiding.' **1881** *Harper's Mag.* Feb. 479/2 The old man secured the subsidy [for voting], remarking, 'ef you is comin' de bulldose on dis ole niggah, he weakens.'

+Bulldoze, -dose, *v. colloq.* [BULL *n.*[1] and *dose, doze* n. or v.] *tr.* To intimidate by violence or threats, orig. for political purposes.

Bartlett ('77) cites Dr. J. Dickson Bruns of New Orleans for the statement that the term originally applied to the flogging of Louisiana Negroes suspected of disloyalty to the 'Union Rights' Leagues; and this explanation is repeated by M. Lane in *America* (20 Sept. 1888) 16. In ordinary use, however, from the earliest occurrence of the word and its derivatives, there is no reference to actual flogging, nor is there any evidence that the noun preceded the verb.

1876 *N.Y. Tribune* 23 Dec. 6/4 If the State of Connecticut . . . had any apprehensions lest . . . their representatives . . . might be 'intimidated,' or 'bulldosed,' or 'terrorized' [etc.]. **1876–7** *N.Y. Herald* (B.), A man and a brother was bulldozed into buying a large number of small flags by a gang of street Arabs in City Hall Park. **1880** C. W. BERRY *Other Side* 155 They . . . pull him out of bed with a revolver to his head and force him to . . . open his own safe. That's called 'bull-dosing' a man. **1882** SWEET & KNOX *Texas Siftings* 43 What sort of a crowd is this, anyhow, that tries to bulldoze the press? **1884** — *Through Texas* 238 He knew he could . . . bulldoze the judge for nothing. **1887** *Courier-Journal* 1 May 16/2 That would have naturally aroused the combativeness of every brave man in the Legislature who could not be buldozed. **1902** *Munsey's Mag.* XXVI. 551/2, I don't like to be bulldozed and made to appear as if I was doing something mean. **1911** LINCOLN *Cap. Warren's Wards* 42 Whether he is or not [a lunatic], he sha'n't bulldoze me.

+Bulldozed, *ppl. a. slang.* [f. prec.] Intimidated; cowed. — **1877** *N.Y. Herald* 7 March 6/2 If he [Pres. Hayes] yields he will be only a nominal President; will not be even a peer of the party leaders, but only their bull-dozed vassal.

+Bulldozer, -doser. *slang.* [BULLDOZE *v.*]

1. One who practises bulldozing.

'The term "Bulldozers," which is so variously printed in the New Orleans despatches, is the name applied to an organization of armed white men, whose ostensible business it is to keep the Negroes from stealing the cotton crop. On election day, however, the "Bulldozers" go gunning for Negroes who manifest a disposition to vote the Republican ticket' (*N.Y. Tribune* cited in B. '77).

1876 in *Congress. Rec.* 9 Jan. (1877) 500/1 A band of bull-dozers came into Saint Francisville, and by their yelling and hallooing . . . put the entire inhabitants in a mortal terror. **1876** *N.Y. Tribune* 23 Dec. 1/5 Capt. Barrow didn't tell me the bulldozers would call upon me. **1877** H. C. DIBBLE *Why Reconstr. Failed* 21 Thousands of men . . . sought relief . . . through the agency of the Kukluk Klan, . . . Bull-dozers, and such kindred secret organizations. **1877** *N.Y. Herald* 7 March (B.), If he has strength of character and tact, the bull-dozers cannot subdue him. . . . If he gives up Mr. Evarts, . . . the bulldozers will dictate his cabinet. **1879** TOURGEE *Fool's Errand* 295 The Klan, and its more subtle and complete successors, under various and sundry names, 'Rifle-Clubs,' 'Sabre-Clubs,' 'Bull-dozers,' and so forth, had fully established themselves throughout the country. **1884** *Boston Journal* 25 Oct. 2/4 The New Orleans Times-Democrat is trying to incite the bulldozer by giving a fictitious account of the action of United States Marshals in Cincinnati. **1887** *Courier-Journal* 11 Jan. 1/4 Green Smith is a bulldozer with no nerve, and will weaken when the fight comes on.

2. A revolver.

1881 *Sat. Review* 9 July 40/2 A Californian bull-doser is a pistol which carries a bullet heavy enough to destroy human life with certainty. **1889** *Cent.* 715 *Bulldozer*, a revolver.

+Bulldozing, *vbl. n. slang.* [BULLDOZE *v.*] The act of forcing or compelling by intimidation.

1876 *N.Y. Tribune* Dec. (B.), There was a bad case of 'bulldozing' in Cincinnati on Monday night. . . . Mr. C. was in the chair, . . . and declared . . . that he was not to be 'intimidated.' *Ib.* 23 Dec. 1/5 (Headline), Bulldozing said not to be political. **1880** in J. W. Buel *Border Outlaws* (1881) 233 The only bulldozing I ever did was in making men who remained at home during the winter of '62 get wood for the women and children. **1884** *Lisbon* (Dakota) *Star* 22 Aug., It was an honest . . . expression of the wishes of the voters . . . without any bulldozing. **1888** *Century Mag.* Dec. 313/2 We should be rid at one stroke of the assessments upon candidates, of the bribing and bulldozing of voters [etc.].

attrib. **1877** *Providence Jrnl.* 31 Jan., The Russian fleet is not engaged in a bulldozing mission in American waters. **1887** *Courier-Journal* 12 Jan. 2/3 The Republicans are at their old tricks, and deliberately propose to steal, if it is possible, by any bulldozing process or cool, downright corruption, the Senatorships of Indiana, New Jersey and California.

+Bulldozing, *ppl. a. slang.* [BULLDOZE *v.*] Exercising intimidation. — **1900** *Engineering Mag.* XIX. 761/1 The cursing, bulldozing foreman . . . creates so much confusion about casting time that one-third of the work is likely to be lost.

+**Bull-driver.** A man engaged in driving cattle. — **1877** WM. WRIGHT *Big Bonanza* 114 The swearing heard in camp . . . would have furnished any ordinary bulldriver a stock of oaths. **1883** 'MARK TWAIN' *Life on Miss.* 394 'Five hundred better!' said the foolish bull-driver. **1891** GARLAND *Main-travelled Roads* (1922) 136, I know what manners are, if I am a bull-driver.

+**Bull elk.** [BULL *n.* 1 d.] A male elk. — **1886** *Outing* IX. 51/2 Down went the sun in his flaming field, and between me and it . . . stood the king of all deer, a great bull elk. **1918** ROOSEVELT in *Maine my State* 21, I remember once when we had a bull elk and several deer hanging up.

***Bullet.**

***1.** A small projectile, usually of lead, for use in firearms.

1632 *Mass. Bay Rec.* I. 98 Noe person whatsoeuer shall att any time charge any peece of service with bulletts or shott, other then for defence of their howses. **1638** UNDERHILL *Newes from A.* 6 They finding our bullets to outreach their arrows, they fled before us. **1726** PENHALLOW *Indian Wars* (1824) 22 So soon as the Indians fired, it was observed that their guns were charged with bullets. **1807** *Ann. 10th Congress* 1 Sess. I. 449 It was considered inglorious there [=Ky.] to kill a squirrel, or even ducks, with anything but bullets. **1870** KEIM *Sheridan's Troopers* 302 The bullets flew thick and fast.

b. Attrib. and comb. with *box, gun, machine, making,* etc.

1642 *Md. Archives* 196 Eight pound of pistoll or bullett shott. **1720** *Weekly Mercury* 21 July 3/1 Lately imported from England a choice parcell of very good fowling Peices, and chamber'd Bullet Gunns. **1777** *N.H. Comm. Safety Rec.* 115 Ordered . . . to pay . . . for 68 Bullet Boxes. **1823** COOPER *Pioneers* xvii, Bullet wounds are apt to weaken flesh. **1827** — *Prairie* xiii, Several among them remembered also to have seen the aforesaid private bullet-marks. **1842** *Niles' Nat. Reg.* 23 July 336/1 One of the private bills . . . purchases the patent right to a bullet machine. **1876** INGRAM *Centennial Exp.* 144 Bullet-making was also carried on.

2. The heavy ball used in a throwing or casting game.

1723 *Boston Rec.* 172 Throwing, rolling or flingin of the Bullet, commonly called throwing the Long Bullet, in the . . . Streets, Lanes or Allyes of the Town, is attended with diverse Inconveniences.

3. A weight used on a chain for keeping a gate closed.

1836 DUNLAP *Mem. Water Drinker* I. 12 A ricketty wooden pale-gate drawn back by a chain and bullet.

+4. A nugget of gold.

1889 MUNROE *Golden Days* 112 In the clay he was . . . likely to strike 'bullets,' lumps . . . or pockets of pure-gold.

+5. An ace in the game of brag.

1807–8 IRVING, etc. *Salmagundi* xix. 433 Presently one of them spread his hieroglyphics on the table and exclaimed triumphantly, 'Two bullets and a bragger!' **1889** BARRÈRE & LELAND *Dict. Slang, Bullets* (cards) in American brag, are aces. . . . The highest hand in the game is three white (or real) aces, the next highest is 'two bullets and a bragger.'

+6. A vote cast for a single candidate where several are to be elected.

1897 *Boston Ev. Rec.* 23 Dec. 1/7 In . . . Dixon's ward, between 500 and 600 voters cast 'bullet' votes. These were ballots on which the only name crossed for alderman was that of Dixon.

***Bullet-bag.** A bag for carrying bullets on the person. — **1805** PARKINSON *Tour* 111, I took . . . his hoppes, powder-horn, bullet-bag, together with the gun, and marched off. **1824** DODDRIDGE *Notes* 113 In cold weather the mittens, and sometimes the bullet-bag occupied the front part of it [a belt]. **1850** GARRARD *Wah-To-Yah* xix. 222 They was brought on a waiter, size of my bullet-bag.

+**Bullet button.** A round, bullet-shaped button.—**1816** in *Centennial West Point* I. 511 *Vest*, gray cloth for winter, single breasted, yellow gilt bullet buttons, and trimmed with black silk lace. **1823** COOPER *Pioneer* v, A frock of bottle-green with bullet buttons. **1844** *Guide Book to West Point* 65 Uniform. . . . The Cadets have a gray cloth coatee, . . . three rows of gilt bullet buttons in front, and also upon the skirts and sleeves. **1859** *West Point Life* 3 When you doze in bed . . . [you] Dream of bullet buttons.

+**Bullet-buttoned,** *a.* [Cf. prec.] Furnished with bullet buttons. — **1843** *Knickerb.* XXI. 49 He often . . . flourishes in a bullet-buttoned coat in which he once marched in the country's service.

+**Bullet grape.** =BULL GRAPE. — **1829** EATON *Botany* (ed. 5) 447 *Vitis rotundifolia*, bullet grape, . . . berries large. **1847** [see BULL-GRAPE].

+**Bullet hawk.** The pigeon hawk. — **1844** *Nat. Hist. N.Y., Zoology* II. 15 The Pigeon Hawk, *Falco Columbarius*, . . . has been termed the Bullet Hawk, in allusion to its swiftness.

Bulletin, *v.* {1838} +To display on a bulletin board. — **1871** *Scribner's Mo.* I. 412 It was bulletined at noon . . . in the Merchants' Exchange at Chicago. **1884** *Reading* (Pa.) *Herald* 3 April, Mr. L— has made arrangements to have all . . . championship games bulletined at the Casino during the season.

+**Bulletin board.** A board on which bulletins, notices, etc., are posted.

1852 *Knickerb.* XXXIX. 380 The bar-room door is the bulletin-board of the temporary notices of the day. **1869** 'MARK TWAIN' *Innocents Abroad* 333 They had a great public bulletin-board in Pompeii—a place where announcements for gladiatorial combats, elections, and such things, were posted. **1877** WM. WRIGHT *Big Bonanza* 403 Reports of sales . . . are placed . . . on the bulletin-boards of the various stock-brokers. **1879** *Diary of a Daly Débutante* 5 There is a list of names of those who are to sing on a bulletin-board in the greenroom. **1884** CABLE *Dr. Sevier* xliii, At the newspaper offices . . . he had to go out into the middle of the way to get around the crowd that surrounded the bulletin-boards. **1896** *Cosmopolitan* XX. 406/2 From the bulletin-board we learn of new rules and regulations. **1904** F. LYNDE *Grafters* 14 Train Number Three . . . was late . . . ; and pending the chalking-up of its arriving time on the bulletin board, the two men sat on an empty baggage truck and smoked.

Bullet mold, mould. A mold used in making bullets. {1677}

1644 *Essex Probate Rec.* I. 30, I give . . . unto my sonne Joseph 2 S bullett moulds. **1666** *Md. Archives* II. 19 Voted necessary that there be . . . two dozen Bullett molds, high coluver bore. **1756** in *Lett. to Washington* I. 363 About 1 dozen riffells 4. ft. Barrells, best Iron-Bullet Mould to each. **1777** *Vt. Hist. Soc. Coll.* I. 193 We are detained a good deal for want of Bullet Moals [*sic*] as there is but one pair in Town. **1826** BRADFORD *Ky. Notes* 10 All the surgical instruments I had, was a knife, a mockason awl, and a pair of bullet moulds. **1853** RAMSEY *Tennessee* 371 She inquired for the bullet moulds, and was engaged, busily, in melting the lead and running bullets for different guns. **1871** *Atlantic Mo.* Nov. 564 Professor Brewer, upon whom a constant toothache wore painfully,—my bullet-mould failing even upon the third trial to extract the unruly member.

Bullet patch. A piece of cloth, leather, etc., in which bullets for muzzle-loading rifles are wrapped in loading. — **1824** DODDRIDGE *Notes* 289 They went on with their work of carrying water and cutting bullet patches for the men. **1871** *Pat. Off. Rep.* II. 240/1 *Bullet-Patch.*—Alfred C. Hobbs, Bridgeport, Conn. *Claim.*—A patch for bullets composed of paper-pulp applied to the bullet.

Bullet pouch. A bag or pouch in which bullets are carried.

1757 *General Orders* 65 That the Commanding officer . . . supply the Deficiency of Powder Horns & Bullet Pouches with those Men's Accotrements that are unfit for Service. **1791** in Jillson *Dark & Bl. Ground* 111 Above it hangs the rifle, horn and bullet pouch. **1825** NEAL *Bro. Jonathan* I. 289 A rifle over one shoulder; a hunting net over the other; a powder horn here; and a bullet pouch there. **1843** *Amer. Pioneer* II. 251 The man who carried the rifle gun and ammunition was so careless as to lose the bullet-pouch. **1885** M. THOMPSON *Byways & Bird Notes* 23 My Cracker host . . . [slipped] his frowzy head through the suspension-strap of his powder-horn and bullet-pouch.

Bull-eyed, *a.* [BULL *n.*[1] 1.] +*Bull-eyed mackerel*, the fall mackerel. — **1814** MITCHILL *Fishes N.Y.* 422 Thimble eyed, bull eyed, or chub mackerel, *Scomber grex*, . . . comes occasionally in prodigious numbers to the coast of New-York, in autumn. **1842** *Nat. Hist. N.Y., Zoology* IV. 102.

Bull-face. {1795–} +A variety of tobacco. ?*Obs.* — **1800** BOUCHER *Glossary* p. l, In twist-bud, thick-joint, bull-face, leather-coat, I'd toil all day.

+**Bull fever.** =BUCK FEVER. — **1839** TOWNSEND *Narrative* 168 Just then I was attacked with the 'bull fever' so dreadfully, that for several minutes I could not shoot.

***Bullfinch, Bulfinch.** +One or other species of finch (as the house finch, *Fringilla frontalis*), or other bird resembling them.

'The name is applied locally to many very different birds' (*Cent. Suppl.*).

1709 LAWSON *Carolina* 144 Bulfinches, in America, differ something from those in Europe, in their Feathers, tho' not in their Bigness. I never knew any one tame. **c1730** CATESBY *Carolina* I. 68 *Rubicilla minor nigra.* The little black Bullfinch. . . . The whole Bird is black, except the shoulders of the wings [etc.]. **1810** WILSON *Ornithology* II. 36 *Fringilla erythrophthalma.* . . . In Virginia he is called the Bulfinch; in many places the Towhè-bird; in Pennsylvania the Chewink, and by others the Swamp Robin. **1825** BONAPARTE *Ornithology* I. 50 The Crimson-necked Bullfinch was procured by Long's party, near the Rocky Mountains.

***Bull-fly.** *Obs.* [BULL *n.*[1] 1.] The stag beetle. {–1706} — **1781** PETERS *Hist. Conn.* (1829) 195 The bull-fly is armed with a coat of mail.

+**Bullfrog.** A species of large frog, *Rana catesbiana.*

1698 G. THOMAS *Penna. & N.J.* 16 There are among other various sorts of Frogs, the Bull-Frog, which makes a roaring noise, hardly to be distinguished from that well known of the Beast, from whom it takes its Name. **1705** BEVERLEY *Virginia* IV. 63 In the Swamps and running Streams, they have Frogs of an incredible bigness, which are call'd Bullfrogs, from the roaring they make. **1738** CATESBY *Carolina* II. 72 *Rana maxima Americana Aquatica.* The Bull-Frog. . . . It is the general belief of the people in Virginia that they keep the springs clean, and purify the water. **1791** BARTRAM *Travels* 277 The bull frog being frequently eighteen inches in length. **1827** J. L. WILLIAMS *West Florida* 29 The bull-frog is numerous every where: a stranger would imagine, that he often strained his lungs, to imitate the voice of the lordly alligator. **a1862** THOREAU *Maine Woods* 281, I also heard the sound of bull-frogs. **1872** *Newton Kansan* 31 Oct. 1/7 The species called bull-frogs, or shad-frogs, are about the only kinds that are used for culinary purposes. **1904** GLASGOW *Deliverance* v, Here [in the abandoned ice-pond] the bullfrogs were still croaking hoarsely.

+**Bull(-gine).** *slang.* A locomotive. — **1889** FARMER 101 *Bull*, . . . a locomotive. **1900** GARLAND *Eagle's Heart* 150 That's the bull-gine on the Great Western; we got two railroads now.

+**Bull-grape.** The muscadine grape. — **1847** DARLINGTON *Weeds & Plants* 84 Vulpine or Foxy Vitis, Fox-Grape, of the Southern States; also called 'Muscadine,' and 'Bullet- or Bull-Grape.' **1893** *Amer. Folk-Lore* VI. 139 *Vitis vulpina*, bull grape. Ala.

Bull grass. +A variety of pasture grass. — **1894** *Amer. Folk-Lore* VII. 104 *Paspalum undulatum*, . . . bull-grass, Ala. **1901** MOHR *Plant Life Ala.* 135.

***Bullhead.**

+1. One or other of several fishes belonging to the genus *Cottus*, *Amiurus*, or *Uranidea;* esp. the cathead or horned pout (*Amiurus nebulosus*).

1674 JOSSELYN *Acc. 2 Voyages N.E.* 113 Blew-fish, Bull-head, Bur-fish. **1758** J. WILLIAMS *Hist. Captivity* 18 There seven of us supped on the Fish, called Bull-head or Pout, and did not eat it up, the Fish was so very large. **1814** MITCHILL *Fishes N.Y.* 380 Eighteen-spined Bullhead, *Cottus octodecem-spinosus.* **1842** *Nat. Hist. N.Y., Zoology* IV. 51 The Common Bull-Head, *Cottus Virginianus*, [is] . . . not a bad article of food. *Ib.* 187 *P[imelodus] xanthocephalus*, the small Black Bullhead of the northern streams and lakes. **1848** BARTLETT 67 [The] Catfish . . . is also called by the name of horned-pout, bull-head, mud-pout and minister. **1864** NORTON *Army Lett.* 212 Catfish just like our bullheads, weigh thirty pounds. **1884** GOODE *Nat. Hist. Aquatic Animals* 259 In the lakes and streams of the Northern States are numerous species of *Uranidea* and allied genera, known in some localities by the English name of 'Miller's Thumb,' also called 'Bull heads,' 'Goblins,' 'Blobs,' and 'Muffle-jaws.' **1886** *Leslie's Mo.* June 742/2 It is now a penal offence to place bull-heads, perch or pickerel in waters where they do not exist. **1897** *Outing* XXIX. 574/1 Just then . . . the men appeared, bearing a string of bull-heads and one immense pickerel.

+2. The golden plover.

1856 *Spirit of Times* (N.Y.) 27 Sept. 51/3 We didn't get a shot at those bull-heads after all. **1858** BAIRD *Birds Pacific R.R.* 690 This bird, well known throughout the United States as the Bull-head, Field Plover, or Golden Plover, appears to be one of the species that inhabit . . . the entire Continent of America.

3. A stupid or obstinate person. {1624; 1877- *dial.*}

1840 SIMMS *Border Beagles* 487 We've time enough to scud and run tonight, and to-morrow we can turn upon that bullhead, Rawlins.

4. Attrib. with *eel, lily, plover, snipe, whiting:* (see quotations).

1842 *Nat. Hist. N.Y., Zoology* IV. 313 The Bull Head Eel, *Anguilla macrocephala*, . . . inhabits Saratoga lake. Mr. Lesueur states that it is a good table fish. **1856** *Spirit of Times* (N.Y.) 27 Sept. 51/3 Hunting bull-head plover in a swamp. **1878** *U.S. Nat'l Museum Proc.* I. 440 *Ægialitis montana*, Mountain Plover, . . . [which is] known here [in Calif.] as the 'Bull-head Snipe,' usually arrives at Stockton and Marysville in November. **1889** *Cent.* 716/2 Bull-head whiting, a sciænoid fish, *Menticirrus alburnus;* the southern king-fish. (Florida.) **1891** *Amer. Folk-Lore* IV. 147 [In New Hampshire] *Nuphar advena* was Bullhead Lily.

+Bullheaded mouse. A local name for a variety of meadow mice. — **1857** *Rep. Comm. Patents: Agric.* 84 Where several species [of meadow-mice] are found in one locality, they are commonly considered by farmers as one animal, known under various names, as . . . 'Bear Mice,' 'Bull-headed Mice,' 'Ground Mice,' 'Bog Mice,' &c.

***Bullhide.** The hide of the domestic bull, +or male buffalo or elk. Also attrib. — **1842** *S. Lit. Messenger* VIII. 465/1 The Indians instantly scattered to avoid a shot from the corporal, one of them dropping his bull-hide shield. **1846** [W. G. D. STEWART] *Altowan* I. vi. 164 Two men, who had just landed from a small boat composed of raw bull-hide. **1848** PARKMAN in *Knickerb.* XXXI. 191 He had a heavy whip, with a handle of solid elk-horn, and a lash of knotted bull-hide.

Bull-hole. +A hole or depression in prairies frequented by buffalo. — **1887** *Harper's Mag.* Feb. 350/1 These little ponds are called 'bull-holes.' The traveller is told that they are started in this watery soil by the pawing of bulls.

Bull-house. A structure in which bulls are housed. {1807} — **1736** *Boston Rec.* 142 A Motion made by the Select Men; shewing that the House wherein the Bulls are kept . . . is insufficient . . . ; and desiring the Town would give direction for removing the said Bull-House.

***Bullion.**

***1.** Gold or silver in the mass.

1677 *Boston Rec.* 111 The mony stampt in the Colony may be made somethinge lesse that . . . the bringinge in of Bullion may be incouraged. **1688** SEWALL *Letter-Book* 78 Which [articles] bring home with you, and the remainder in good mony or Bullion. **1721** *Springfield Rec.* II. 39 Province Bills, . . . Cash, . . . Bullions, Dollars. **1792** *Ann. 2nd Congress* 72 It shall be lawful for any person or persons to bring to the said mint gold and silver bullion, in order to their being coined. **1812** *Ann. 12th Congress* 2 Sess. 150 The difficulty of obtaining bullion, except in a great commercial city. **1854** BENTON *30 Years' View* I. 446/1 All other foreign coins . . . have ceased to be a legal tender. . . . Their value is degraded to the mint price of bullion. **1865** *Atlantic Mo.* XV. 751 Davis had robbed the banks of Virginia a few days before, seizing the bullion in the name of the Confederacy. **1887** *Courier-Journal* 15 Feb. 4/1 The House . . . provides that the trade-dollar bullion shall be additional to those monthly purchases for coinage.

+b. (See quotations.)

1845 *Cincinnati Misc.* I. 240 Cents or Coppers are generally known in the West as 'Cincinnati Bullion.' **1892** W. S. WALSH *Literary Curiosities* 841 *Old Bullion*, a sobriquet of Colonel Thomas Hart Benton . . . given to him for his persistent advocacy of a gold and silver currency.

2. Attrib. and comb. with *buyer, market, product(ion), returns*, etc.

1833 *Congress. Deb.* App. 11 Jan. 100/1 The general tenor of the columns of relative value in table B, illustrates, also, this superior influence of the bullion market in London on the relative value of gold and silver. **1870** MEDBERY *Men Wall St.* 272 The delightful abandon which lurks beneath the hard exterior of the bullion-operators. **1871** RAYMOND *Mines* 510 My predecessor had presented estimates of bullion production, involving confessedly a large amount actually accounted for by . . . the bullion tax. **1872** 'MARK TWAIN' *Roughing It* xliii. 299 'Regulars' are permanent sources of news, like courts, bullion returns, 'clean-ups' at the quartz mills, and inquests. **1876** RAYMOND *8th Rep. Mines* 267 The principal ore and bullion buyers of Salt Lake City. **1878** *Nation* 22 Aug. 107/1 Certain enterprising characters commenced the importation of trade dollars from California, which they bought at their bullion value and sold to traders, manufacturers, and others.

Bullionist. One who favors a metallic currency. {1811-} Also humorous. — **1837** WEBSTER *Works* I. 374, I profess to be a *bullionist*, in the usual and acceptable sense of that word. I am for a solid specie basis for our circulation. **1862** *N.Y. Tribune* 1 Feb., In this state of affairs, bullionist though I am, I highly approve of this temporary issue of government notes, made a legal tender. **1876** *Scribner's Mo.* April 773/1 The salaries of the college officers were paid in terms of beef, pork, wheat, and Indian corn, a medium not so elastic as Continental paper, but seemingly preferred by these ancient bullionists.

+Bullion state. A nickname of Missouri. — **1848** *N.Y. Herald* 13 June (B.), In my own State in the Bullion State, they did not succeed in depreciating our majority. **1859** BARTLETT 55 *Bullion State*, the State of Missouri; so called in consequence of the exertions made by its Senator, Mr. Benton, in favor of a gold and silver currency.

+Bull meat. [BULL *n.*[1] 1 c.] Meat of male buffaloes. — **1843** FRÉMONT *Exped.* 24 Tired and hungry, with tough bull meat without salt, . . . we sat down in silence to our miserable fare. **1847** RUXTON *Adv. Rocky Mts.* (1848) 239 Geese . . . afforded an agreeable variety to our perpetual venison and tough-bull-meat. **1895** REMINGTON *Pony Tracks* 41 Our 'bull meat' is cooked in the primitive style.

+Bull moose. [BULL *n.*[1] 1 d.]

1. A male moose.

1839 HOFFMAN *Wild Scenes* 58 The Indians . . . celebrate the death of a bull-moose, when they are so fortunate as to kill one, with all the songs of triumph that they would raise over a conquered warrior. **1857** HAMMOND *Northern Scenes* 321 About the biggest bull moose I ever happened to see, came crashin' like a steam-engine. **1860** *Harper's Mag.* March 442/1 It is yet the early gray of the morning, and . . . the bellow of the bull moose is heard in the woods. **1895** *Outing* XXVII. 48/2 Just as we struck the opening of the trail to the little lake, we saw on the opposite shore a bull moose. **1901** *Munsey's Mag.* XXV. 378/2 A tall shadowy form stalks along the shadow, the bulk of a bull moose.

2. A nickname applied to Theodore Roosevelt and to his supporters during the political campaign of 1912. Also attrib.

'It arose from his remark: "I feel as fit as a bull moose"' (McLaughlin & Hart *Cycl. Amer. Govt.* I. 186).

1912 *Literary Digest* XLV. 769/1 The Wisconsin Senator . . . went on to say that the treatment of this disease [=growth of trusts] 'is no job for a Bull Moose,' nor for 'an amiable, easy-going man.' **1913** *Nation* XCVI. 170/3 (*caption*), The Bull Moose and the Courts. *Ib.* 404/2 Mr. Victor Berger is much more kindly disposed to Democratic tariff revision than so many non-revolutionary citizens of Republican and Bull Moose affiliations. *Ib.* XCVII. 251/1 The Bull Moose . . . have simply been flocking back to the Republican fold.

Bullneck. +(See quotation.) — **1709** LAWSON *Carolina* 150 Bull-Necks. These are a whitish fowl, about the bigness of a Brant; they come to us after Christmas, in very great flocks, in all our Rivers. **1743** CATESBY *Carolina* App. p. xxxvii, The following American Sea-Fowl also frequent the Coast of Virginia and Carolina in Winter, and are called . . . Whistlers, Bullneck, [etc.].

+Bull nettle. A coarse prickly weed, *Solanum carolinense.* — **1876** *Congress. Rec.* 18 May 3166/2 [He] beat down the wild-brier and bull-nettle, . . . felled the forest, and hewed out his humble home. **1894** *Amer. Folk-Lore* VII. 95 *Solanum Carolinense*, . . . sand-brier, radical, West Va.; bull-nettle, Perrysville, Ind.

+Bull nigger. =BUCK NEGRO. — **1828** *Yankee* May 175/1 [The traveler in the South] sees one solitary man—a great bull nigger, coming toward him. **1840** HALIBURTON *Clockmaker* 3 Ser. 46 If there was a thing on airth that Ahab hated like pyson, I do believe it was a great bull-nigger.

+Bullnose. (See quotations.) — **1857-8** *Ill. Agric. Soc. Trans.* III. 508 The squash, the bull nose, the sweet mountain and sweet Spanish are [good varieties of peppers] for pickling. **1881** E. INGERSOLL *Oyster Industry* 242 *Bull Nose*, an old, overgrown, heavy quahaug, unfit for food (Cape May).

+Bullnut. A species of hickory (*Carya tomentosa*); the nut of this. — **1859** BARTLETT 55 *Bull-nut*, a large kind of hickory-nut. **1884** SARGENT *Rep. Forests* 134 *Carya tomentosa*. . . . Mocker Nut. Black Hickory. Bull Nut.

***Bullock.** An ox.

1641 *Dedham Rec.* III. 79 Granted to John Kingsbury certaine land . . . for a pasture to stay his Bullocks. **1689** SEWALL *Diary* I. 301, I din'd alone at Colebrook with a Bullock's Cheek. **1748** ELIOT *Field-Husb.* i. 3 For sundry years . . . the common Price for a grown Bullock was Twenty Pounds Sterling. **1760** CROGHAN *Journal* 103 Capt. Brewer of the Rangers with a Party of forty Men set of[f] by Land with the Bullocks. **1840** *Picayune* 29 July 2/4 The printer's boy came with a roll of hand-bills . . . bearing the following inscription . . . 'No Humdrum—no Bullock's Liver!' **1858** WARDER *Hedges & Evergreens* 94 A fence against all but the most unruly animals, whether they be rabbits, boys, or bullocks. **1898** *Jrnl. Sch. Geog.* Oct. 316 It is no unusual experience for the load to slide down and the bullock to trip over it.

attrib. **1761** NILES *Indian Wars* II. 515 Our people had the good success, in this time, to save their bullock-guard, with a drove of cattle. **1802** ELLICOTT *Journal* 221 They threw down the contractor's bullock pen. **1847** *Rep. Comm. Patents* (1848) 207 At 6 A.M. each beast is supplied with about 40 to 45 lbs. of yellow bullock turnips sliced.

Bullock heart. ?*Obs.* A variety of cherry. — **1760** WASHINGTON *Diaries* I. 145 Grafted 40 Cherrys—viz: 12 Bullock Hearts. . . . Planted them as followeth: the Bullock Hearts in the first Row next the Quarter.

+**Bullock's oriole.** =BULLOCK'S TROUPIAL. — **1858** BAIRD *Birds Pacific R.R.* 549 *Icterus Bullockii*, Bullock's Oriole. . . . *Hab.*—High Central Plains to the Pacific; rare on upper Missouri; south into Mexico. **1874** COUES *Birds N.W.* 195 Bullock's Oriole. . . . Breeds in suitable places throughout its United States range.

+**Bullock's pippin.** A variety of apple. — **1817** W. COXE *Fruit Trees* 125 Bullocks Pippin, or Sheep Nose, . . . is one of the finest apples in New-Jersey. . . . It is sometimes called the Long Tom; it derives one of its names from the family of Bullock. **1859** ELLIOTT *W. Fruit Book* 68 Bullock's Pippin. [Also called] American Golden Russet, Sheepnose [etc.]. **1867** WARDER *Pomology* 714 Bullock's Pippin, synonym of American Golden Russet.

+**Bullock's troupial.** [Named after William *Bullock*, English naturalist, fl. *c*1827.] (See quotations and cf. BULLOCK'S ORIOLE.) — **1839** AUDUBON *Ornith. Biog.* V. 9 Bullock's Troopial, *Icterus Bullockii*, . . . resembles the Common Baltimore Bird, which it supersedes from the first great bifurcation of the Platte, to the shores of the Columbia. **1881** *Amer. Naturalist* XV. 216 The hooded troupial . . . and the Bullock's troupial . . . are the most common around Tucson.

+**Bull-outfit.** A number of wagons pulled by oxen. — **1888** [W. F. CODY] *Wild West* 432 The wagon-master, in the language of the plains, was called the 'bull-wagon boss'; . . . and the whole train was denominated a 'bull-outfit.'

+**Bull pen.**

1. An enclosure for bulls or bullfighting. Also transf. in quots. 1823, 1860.

1823 JAMES *Exped.* I. 464 This basin is surrounded by high and rugged mountains, except at the place where the North fork passes into the plains. . . . The diameter of the circumscribed valley, called the Bull-pen, is one day's travel, about twenty miles. **1848** ROBINSON *Santa Fé Exped.* 60 The bull pen also attracts the notice of every traveller. **1860** W. GILPIN *Central Gold Region* 66 Soon upon the eastern flank the Northern Parc, or Bull-pen, reveals itself. **1879** *Congress. Rec.* 27 May 1626/1 If you give him [=a government official] authority about the cow-yards and the bull-pens of the country [etc.].

2. A roughly built enclosure for prisoners, used in emergencies instead of a jail; (loosely) a jail.

1809 WEEMS *Marion* (1833) 225 The tories were all handcuffed two and two, and confined together under a centinel, in what was called a bull-pen made of pine trees, cut down so judgmatically, as to form by their fall, a pen or enclosure. **1845** SIMMS *Wigwam & Cabin* II. 93 It is a common place of safe keeping in the absence of gaols and proper officers. It is called technically a 'bull pen,' and consists of huge logs, roughly put together, forming a hollow square. **1865** *Nation* I. 15 After two days Mr. Hudson . . . was carried to a guardhouse . . . which appears to have gone by the name of the 'Bull-pen.' **1884** SWEET & KNOX *Through Texas* 595 We may be caught by the provost-guard, and put in the bull-pen. **1891** *Amer. Notes & Q.* VII. 104 During the war of 1861–65, those rude military prisons which were rather common in the field of operations were generally called 'bull-pens.' **1917** SINCLAIR *King Coal* 104 When the jails would hold no more, they kept some two hundred in an open stockade, called a 'bull-pen.' **1920** *Nation* 31 Jan. 137/1 From 130 to 140 men were herded into the police 'bull-pen,' a room built to hold petty offenders for not more than three or four hours.

3. A boys' ball game involving an area called the 'bull pen' outlined by players on corners who throw at those in the pen.

1871 EGGLESTON *Hoosier Schoolm.* iv. 48 He could not throw well enough to make his mark in that famous western game of bull-pen. **1873** — *Hoosier School-Boy* 25 What did a boy that had lived on Wildcat Creek, in the Indian Reserve, know about playing bull-pen?

+**Bull pine.** Any of several varieties of pine; esp. the yellow pine, *Pinus ponderosa.* — **1884** SARGENT *Rep. Forests* 193 *Pinus Jeffreyi*, . . . Bull pine, Black Pine. *Ib.*, *Pinus ponderosa*, . . . Yellow Pine. Bull pine. *Ib.* 195 *Pinus Sabiniana*, . . . Digger Pine, Bull Pine. **1894** COULTER *Bot. W. Texas* III. 554 *Pinus mitis*, . . . extending into eastern Texas from the Atlantic and Gulf states, 'Bull pine.' **1905** *Bureau of Forestry Bul. No. 66* 33 The rock pine (*Pinus ponderosa scopulorum*), commonly called bull pine or yellow pine, is a variety of the western yellow pine of the Rocky Mountains.

+**Bull plover.** The black-bellied plover, *Squatarola helvetica.* — **1844** *Nat. Hist. N.Y.*, *Zoology* II. 215 The large Whistling Plover, or Bull and Beetle-head Plover as it is called in its autumnal dress, appears with us from the south in May.

+**Bullpout.** The horned pout, *Amiurus nebulosus.*

1823 COOPER *Pioneer* xxiii, 'Away with you, you varmint!' said Billy Kirby, plucking a bull-pout from the rushes. **1840** EMMONS *Mass. Quadrupeds* 48 The otter . . . lives in holes in the banks of streams, and subsists on fish, as salmon, bull-pouts, clams, etc. **1850** [S. F. COOPER] *Rural Hours* 378 Besides these our fishermen take eels, dace or roach, suckers, cat-fish and bull-pouts. **1883** ZEIGLER & GROSSCUP *Alleghanies* 109 The trout . . . has no scales; nor does it require—like its scaleless brothers, the slimy cat-fish and bull-pout—hot water and a scraping knife. **1897** ROBINSON *Uncle Lisha* 91 Two hours later he appeared, . . . bringing a number of dressed bull pouts.

+**Bullpuncher.** *colloq.* [BULL *n.*[1] I.] A cowboy or an ox driver. — **1874** *Chambers's Jrnl.* 543/2 Commissariat beeves, guarded by the commissariat 'bull-punchers.' **1887** M. ROBERTS *Western Avernus* ii. 19 He followed the profession of a 'bull-puncher,' that is, he went in charge of the cattle destined for slaughter and canning in the distant North. **1893** *Scribner's Mag.* June 711/2 A young 'bull-puncher' in a Wisconsin logging camp became in middle life Congressman, then United States Senator.

+**Bullpunching.** *colloq.* =COWPUNCHING. — **1887** M. ROBERTS *Western Avernus* ii. 20, I found this bull-punching a very wearisome and dangerous business.

Bull sap, sapling. A variety of pine. — **1851** SPRINGER *Forest Life* 41 Of the White Pine there are varieties, which by some are attributed to peculiar characteristics of the various locations in which they grow. That variety called sapling Pine, bull sapling, &c., usually grows on high, hard-wood land. **1902** WHITE *Blazed Trail* viii. 59 In a moment Thorpe found himself waist-deep in the pitchy aromatic top of an old bull-sap.

Bull's-eye. [BULL *n.*[1] I.]

+**1.** A thick, round, bulging watch, with the case partly enclosing the glass. Also attrib. with *watch.*

1833 NEAL *Down-Easters* I. 78 Lugging out a heavy silver watch, . . . a genuine bull's-eye with a huge copper logging-chain, a bell-metal face. **1854** SHILLABER *Mrs Partington* 26 The hand of the old bull's-eye watch on the nail over the mantel-piece denoted the hour of nine. **1857** *Ill. Agric. Soc. Trans.* II. 461 You will not send your old 'bull's eye,' for repairs, to a kettle tinker. **1860** HOLMES *Professor* ii. 53 A friend of mine had a watch given him, . . . a 'bull's eye,' with a loose silver case that came off like an oyster-shell from its contents. **1881** *Harper's Mag.* June 88/1 Our fat old bull's eye watch said half past ten.

2. The oxeye daisy, *Chrysanthemum leucanthemum.* Also attrib. with *daisy.* {1884 *dial.*}

1848 J. S. ROBINSON *Santa Fé Exped.* 10 The vegetables growing here . . . are the common prairie grass, rosin weed, bull's eye, red root. **1892** *Amer. Folk-Lore* V. 98. **1894** *Ib.* VII. 91.

Bull's-foot. +A crowbar with an end which suggests the foot of a bull. — **1872** HUNTINGTON *Road-Master's Assistant* 76 There are a good many kinds of claw-bars, some of which work well; . . . and probably the old style of 'bull's-foot' claw is as good as any.

***Bullskin.** =BULLHIDE. — **1843** 'CARLTON' *New Purchase* I. 75 The incessant stamping of feet shod with bull-skin boots armed to the center of the sole with enormous heels.

+**Bull snake.** The pine snake, belonging to the genus *Pityophis.*

Variously said to derive its name from 'the remarkable sound it makes when blowing,' or 'from its blunt head and thick clumsy body.'

1784 FILSON *Kentucke* 27 Serpents are not numerous, and are such as are to be found in other parts of the continent, except the bull, the horned and the mockason snakes. **1791** BARTRAM *Travels* 276 The pine or bull snake is very large and inoffensive with respect to mankind. **1817** S. BROWN *Western Gaz.* 357 Palmetto flatts, fit only for the present occupants, gouffres, salemanders, and bull snakes. **1853** in Marcy *Explor. Red River* (1854) 211 The names of Bull, Pine, and Pilot snake, are commonly given to different species of this genus. **1873** BEADLE *Undevel. West* 231, I killed one of the species known as 'bull snake,' which was five feet three inches long. **1891** ROBERTS *Adrift Amer.* 239 The bull-snake is said to grow to an enormous size, and is a kind of North American python or boa. **1907** WHITE *Arizona Nights* 219, I mind when they catched the great-grandaddy of all the bull-snakes.

+**Bull-strong,** *a.* Of a fence: Strong enough to hold back a bull. — **1873** BEADLE *Undevel. West* 40 A 'lawful fence' required five [strands of wire], which, the local courts consider, will make it 'horse-high, bull-strong, and pig-tight.' **1883** *Harper's Mag.* Oct. 718/1 A fence here [in Lexington, Ky.], according to a saying of the section, must be 'mule-high, bull-strong, and pig-tight.'

+**Bull-tailing.** (See quotation.) — **1889** FARMER 102 Bull-tailing is a Mexican term in use in the Western prairies. Well-mounted horsemen chase the bulls, and when a favorable opportunity offers, seize them by the tails and turn them somersaults.

+**Bull team.** A team composed of oxen. — **1879** *Harper's Mag.* Nov. 878/1, I wonder what they'd 'a said if they'd had to ride in a bull team, or drag a hand-cart all the way. **1888** *San Fran. W. Examiner* 23 Feb. (F.), I gave instructions to the wagon boss, and the long bull-team moved away.

+**Bull thistle.** The common thistle, *Cnicus lanceolatus.* Also fig. — **1863** RANDALL *Pract. Shepherd* 271 The hay, however, came from a new field, and contained an excessive quantity of bull-thistle. **1874** B. F. TAYLOR *World on Wheels* 193 The terrible frown of a bear-skin cap . . . its jaunty feather . . . , springing out of the fur like the blossom of a magnified and glorified bull-thistle. **1875** CARLETON *Farm Legends* 66 For when you are feeling the safest, it very oft falls out You rush head-foremost into a big bull-thistle o' doubt. **1881** W. O. STODDARD *E. Hardery* 90 There was nothing higher or stronger than a mullein-stalk or a bull thistle to impede him. **1900** BACHELLER *E. Holden* 212 It'll be . . . nice, smooth land and no stun on it. . . . No bull thistles, no hard winters, [etc.].

+**Bull tongue,** *n.* A simple form of plow, so called from its shape. Orig. *bull-tongue plough* or *plow.*

(1) **1849** *Rep. Comm. Patents: Agric.* (1850) 310 Sixty bull-tongue ploughs, $262.00. **1858** *Texas Almanac 1859* 73 A common bull-tongue plough will answer to open the furrow for the seed. **1868** *Rep. Comm. Agric.* (1869) 414 The field was plowed with a turning plow, followed in the same furrow with a long bull-tongue plow. **1885** 'CRADDOCK' *Prophet* 2 They are of the bull-tongue variety, and are sometimes drawn by oxen. **1905** E. W. PRINGLE *Rice Planter* 162 Gibbie comes behind in the same furrow with Jack and Sambo and a bull tongue plough.

(2) **1860** *Ill. Agric. Soc. Trans.* IV. 223 [The seed was] dropped by hand and covered with double-shovel or 'bull-tongues.' **1866** W. REID *After the War* 368 The negroes, who were breaking up the cotton lands, did it with little 'bull tongues,' such as Northern farmers use to cultivate their corn. **1871–3** *Texas Almanac* 12 A stout bull-tongue drawn by two horses. **1883** SMITH *Geol. Survey Ala.* 544 As a rule, the bed or ridge is opened with a narrow plow (scooter or bull-tongue). **1892** J. L. ALLEN *Blue-Grass Region* 250 Ploughing is commonly done with a 'bull-tongue,' an implement hardly more than a sharpened stick with a metal rim.

+**Bull-tongue,** *v.* [f. prec.] To plow with a bull-tongue plow. — **1861** *Ill Agric. Soc. Trans.* IV. 248 Whether hoeing the small corn or rolling or bull-tonguing or hilling up.

+**Bull train.** A series of freight wagons drawn by bullocks. — **1864** DICKSON *Across Plains* 173 The streets were lined with bull-trains and pack animals. **1877** J. S. CAMPION *On Frontier* 99 A Kansas City 'bull-train,' lately come in, had passed an encampment of over six hundred tents. **1888** BILLINGS *Hardtack* 370 The captain spent all winter and the following spring in perfecting the 'Bull Train,' as it was called. **1902** A. ADAMS *Log Cowboy* 131 Put your freight on a bull train, and it always goes through on time.

+**Bullweed.** The knapweed; a plant of it. — **1888** 'CRADDOCK' *Broomsedge Cove* 35 A tall bull-weed, that swung, purple and burly, among the rocks, was dry.

+**Bullwhack,** *n. colloq.* A whip used in driving oxen. — **1885** *Mag. Amer. Hist.* XIII. 98 In Texas and western Louisiana the 'bull-whack' is a terrible whip with a long and very heavy lash and a short handle. It is used by drovers to intimidate refractory animals.

+**Bullwhack,** *v. colloq.* [Cf. prec.] *tr.* To drive (an ox-team) with a whip. — **1896** MCCLURE *Rocky Mts.* 102 You will often find some graduate of Yale 'bull-whacking' his own team from the river to his mines, looking as if he had seldom seen soap and water. **1906** *Dialect Notes* III. 129 'What's Jim doin'?' 'O, he's a bull-whackin'.'

+**Bullwhacker.** *colloq.*

1. The driver of a bullock train.

1859 *Alta California* 17 Aug (Th.), Gentile and Mormon, bull-whacker and Pike's Peaker, all seem to mingle freely. **1870** BEADLE *Utah* 226 The 'bull-whackers' have to drive very late, for which reason they never seem so social and lively as the drivers in mule trains. **1880** *Harper's Mag.* April 678/2 In Santa Fe one may see . . . dirt-begrimed bull-whackers, just in from Las Vegas. **1890** HASKINS *Argonauts Calif.* 52 We employed a Pike county bullwhacker who agreed to deliver us and our effects in Hangtown. **1903** A. CHAPMAN in *Reader* Sept. 341 The argot of the bull-whackers has almost entirely passed, for the reason that the bull-whackers themselves have yielded to the promoters of a swifter form of transportation.

attrib. **1873** *Winfield* (Kansas) *Courier* 7 Aug. 4/1 Cotemporary with that, was what might be called 'bull-whacker' literature, detailing the immense traffic of the plains. **1875** *Chicago Tribune* 6 Nov. 8/7 The bull-whacker element in the Texas Constitutional Convention, which thus far has defeated every proposition for the establishment of the free-school system [etc.].

2. =BULLWHACK *n.* Also attrib. with *whip.*

1889 CUSTER *Tenting on Plains* 229 There is no sound like the snap of the lash of a 'bull-whacker.' **1898** WISTER *Lin McLean* 271 Limber Jim called for another drink, and, with his cigar between his teeth, cracked his long bull-whacker whip. **1902** CLAPIN 83 *Bull-whacker,* a heavy whip used in the South-West, for driving cattle.

+**Bullwhacking.** *colloq.* The occupation of a bullwhacker. — **1870** J. WHITE *Sketches from A.* 259 The profession of 'bull-whacking' has, in ante-railway days, been one of the foremost in the West.

+**Bull wheel.** A wheel or windlass on which the rope is wound in mining or drilling. — **1874** RAYMOND *6th Rep. Mines* 415 By means of a bull-wheel, rope, car, and railroad, the slimes were delivered . . . directly to the pans. **1883** *Century Mag.* July 329/2 Attached to the derrick is also a big windlass, called the 'bull-wheel,' which hoists the drilling apparatus out of the [oil] well.

+**Bull-whip.** [BULL *n.*[1] 1.] A long heavy whip used by teamsters and cattle drivers. — **1852** *S. Lit. Messenger* XVIII. 749/2 If an overseer . . . omitted . . . laying down at once his bull-whip for the yard-stick. **1919** L. F. CODY *Buffalo Bill* 63 The teams were again hitched to their wagons; once more the bull-whips cracked in the air.

∗**Bully,** *n.* +A class officer at Yale. See BULLY-CLUB quot. 1847. — **1871** [L. H. BAGG] *At Yale* 501 Each class . . . chose as leader their largest and most muscular man, to whom they gave the name of 'Bully.'

Bully, *a. colloq.* {1681–} +Fine, capital, first-rate.

a. Of a boat or other vessel.

1844 *Scribblings & Sk.* 181 (Th.), A two day's race with bully-boats combines every sort of pleasing excitement. It were well to inform you that a bully-boat means a boat that beats everything on those [Mississippi] waters. *c*1845 *Big Bear Ark.*, etc. 106 (Title of story), A bully boat and a brag captain. **1846** *Spirit of Times* 16 May 133/1 Our 'bully' boat sped away like a bird, however. **1855** *Cairo City Times* (B.), The bully 'Crystal Palace' passed up to St. Louis on Monday. **1872** 'MARK TWAIN' *Roughing It* i, The captain said she was a 'bully' boat and all she wanted was more 'shear' and a bigger wheel.

b. In general use.

1847 FIELD *Drama in Pokerville*, etc. 43 Mr. Wilson's boat—he owned a steamboat as well as the store-shed—arrived, having made a 'bully trip.' **1855** W. CARLETON *Willy Reilly* v. The cook will give you a bully dinner. **1860** OLMSTEAD *Back Country* 171 Bigger'n New Orleans? It must be a bully city. **1867** RICHARDSON *Beyond Miss.* 55 We were now on my guide's farm, which he declared 'bully land.' **1872** 'MARK TWAIN' *Roughing It* xlvii. 333 Take him all round, pard, there never was a bullier man in the mines. **1875** *Chicago Tribune* 22 Nov. 7/5 That's bully! I wish you'd let me stay out of school so's to see you catch and maul him. **1883** 'S. BONNER' *Dialect Tales* 118 Well, old man, you had a bully chance to judge. **1893** POST *Harvard Stories* 2 Then you would stand over them and crack a whip and have a bully time. **1907** FIELD *Six-Cylinder Courtship* 127 It was a bully car, and I loved it.

c. Used as an exclamation.

1861 *Atlantic Mo.* VII. 745/1 'Bully for you!' alternated with benedictions, in the proportion of two 'bullies' to one blessing. **1864** *Sanitary Commiss. U.S. Army* 183 *n.*, Others would say 'good,' and others would use the very expressive phrase 'bully.' **1869** 'MARK TWAIN' *Innocents* 283 Vulgar young boys in the gallery . . . [manifest] approbation or dissatisfaction by such observations as 'Bully for the lion.' **1899** VAN DYKE *Fisherman's Luck* 201 Bully for us . . . we got him!

d. As *adv.* Splendidly.

1869 'MARK TWAIN' *Innocents* 40 Oh, I'm coming along bully! **1870** O. LOGAN *Before Footlights* 268 Sa-ay, Ma'am, can't I walk on my hands bully? **1873** *Newton Kansan* 10 July 3/3 The old man is doing bully. **1880** *Harper's Mag.* March 544/2, I can call de dances bully—you bet! **1888** CUSTER *Tenting on Plains* 680 All the boys done bully, but Corporal Johnson he blinked.

+**Bullyard.** An enclosure in which cattle are kept. — **1868** *Mich. Agric. Rep.* VII. 99 The manure in this experiment was all taken from the 'bull yard.'

+**Bully-club.** A club or stick formerly entrusted to an official of a class at Yale. — **1847** [J. MITCHELL] *Scenes & Characters* 216 Such is the history of the bully-club. It became the occasion of an annual election of a person to take charge of it, and to act as leader of the students in case of a quarrel between them and others. 'Bully' was the title of this chivalrous and high office. **1871** BAGG *At Yale* 153 The hall is reputed to be a sort of repository for old college mementos; like the 'first college bell,' the original 'bully-club,' [etc.]. *Ib.* 502 [The Major Bully of the Seniors] transferred the College Bully Club to his successor, the Bully of the junior class.

+**Bullyism.** **1.** The conduct characteristic of a bully. **2.** The system of bullies and bully-clubs at Yale. — **(1) 1845** POE in *Broadway Journal* 29 March, The Outises who practise this species of bullyism are, as a matter of course, anonymous. **1860** ABBOTT *South & North* 264 They will raise a howl, which will split the public ear, about the violation of the privileges of debate, Southern bullyism, etc. **1886** *All Year Round* 27 Feb. 35 The spirit of 'bullyism' . . . peculiarly prevalent in the Northern States. **(2) 1843** BELDEN *Sk. Yale College* 170 *Bullyism* had its origin, like everything else that is venerated, far back in antiquity. **1871** L. H. BAGG *At Yale* 501 It was from this feud [between townspeople and students] that the custom of 'Bullyism' arose.

+**Bullyship.** Formerly the office held by a student leader or 'bully' at Yale. — **1871** L. H. BAGG *At Yale* 501 As the collisions with the 'townies' grew less frequent, . . . the 'bullyships' came to be looked upon in the light of honors.

∗**Bulrush, Bullrush.** One or other of various tall, rush-like grasses growing in marshes.

1622 'MOURT' *Relation* 37 Without was sundry bundles of . . . Bull-rushes. **1658** *Southampton Rec.* I. 170 Also liberty [was granted to the Indians] to cut in the summer time flags, bullrushes, and such things as they make their mats of. **1704** *N. H. Probate Rec.* I. 514 There is a little branch goes out into a parcel of bulrushes. **1773** H. FINLAY *Journal* 7 We embarked on still transparent water cover'd with bullrushes. **1832** WILLIAMSON *Maine* I. 128 We have also the pond, meadow, fluted and bull

Rushes. **1840** DEWEY *Mass. Flowering Plants* 203 *Juncus effusus*, Bull Rush, grows in dense bunches in wet, marshy, situations. **1880** CABLE *Grandissimes* 42 Clouds of starlings... rose from the high bulrushes and settled again.

+Bum, *n.*[1] *slang.*

1. A drunken spree, debauch.

1871 L. H. BAGG *At Yale* 153 Aside from the annual convention on Commencement night, there are two other 'bums' held during the year ... which bring many graduates from out of town. *Ib.* 172 Thursday night is the favorite time for the more depraved Stones men to 'go off on a bum' together, and afterwards wake the echoes of the college yard with their discordant howlings. **1885** CUSTER *Boots & Saddles* xx. 193, I intend to celebrate their return by going on a tremendous 'bum.'

2. *On the bum*, in a disordered or bad condition.

1896 G. ADE *Artie* 28, I sized it up that the house was on the bum and she didn't want me to see it. **1903** A. H. LEWIS *Boss* 301 One honest man will put th' whole force on th' bum!

+Bum, *n.*[2] *slang.* [Cf. BUMMER.]

1. A loafer, tramp, vagrant. Also transf. and attrib.

1887 *Lippincott's Mag.* Oct. 573 In one [fraternity] you will find ... the sporting element, or, as they are proud to be termed, the 'bums,' whose first principle is to do no more work than is absolutely necessary to get through. **1888** *Detroit Free Press* (F.), Twenty per cent are chronic bums, who beg or steal the price of their lodgings. **1889** SALMONS *Burlington Strike* 137 The Simonds bum element was weeded out, and many of the old men came back and took their places. **1891** C. ROBERTS *Adrift Amer.* 139 Near to me came and sat down a couple of tramps, real bonâ fide '*bums*.' There was no mistake about them, for they were ragged and filthy beyond description. **1896** F. NORRIS *Stories & Sk.* (1931) 39 There was the dude, the chippy, ... the bum, the drunk, [etc.]. **1901** RYAN *Montana* 83, I've helped old bums all over the country, and never heard or wanted to hear of them again. **1907** WHITE *Arizona Nights* 246 The regular inhabitants 're a set of Mexican bums.

2. *On the bum*, tramping; wandering without goal or occupation, as a vagrant or bum.

1895 *Century Mag.* Oct. 941/2 Plans are made also for going 'on the bum' the moment they are free. **1909** 'O. HENRY' *Options* 246, I guess George, maybe, is on the bum, ... or maybe gone to the dogs on account of whiskey or the races.

+Bum, *a. colloq.* [BUM *n.*[2]] Of poor or inferior quality; bad.

1888 *Nation* 31 May 439/2 One of them ... heard B. called a 'bum actor.' **1896** G. ADE *Artie* 109 When he was staked to the office he didn't have a sou markee except what was tied up in a bum little grocery store. **1899** *Boston Journal* 23 Jan. 8/1 Some time ago this paper called the Golden Gate Dramatic Company the bummest organization of the kind that ever struck Dayton. **1908** LORIMER *J. Spurlock* 68 'Why haven't I ever met you before?' I demanded. ... It was a bum start.

+Bum, *v. slang.* [Cf. BUMMER.]

1. *intr.* To loaf or wander *around;* to idle about.

1863 *Boston Herald* 2 Aug. 2/5 They are just fit to stay in this city, vegetate in the back slums, read the News and Express, bum round rumshops [etc.]. **1872** *Chicago Tribune* 24 Dec. 2/1 Harry Sweetser, late General Manager of the Atlantic and Great Western Railway, is 'bumming' around town. **1883** C. S. KEENE in Layard *Life & Lett.* (1892) 350, I've been bumming around all day ... and haven't caught a darned fish. **1904** HARBEN *Georgians* 218 The first night I got to bed late, after bummin' round with a feller that I met on the train. **1908** 'YESLAH' *Tenderfoot S. Calif.* 30 One night when I was bumming around town I just naturally strolled into a jewelry auction.

2. To act as a bum; to go on the bum.

'*Bum*, to sponge on others for a living; lead an idle or dissolute life' (*Cent.*).

1872 BRACE *Dangerous Classes N.Y.* 102, I say, Jim, this is raything better an' bummin'—eh? **1890** L. C. D'OYLE *Notches* 168 Qualifications which eminently fitted a man to 'bum it' on such a community. *a***1906** 'O. HENRY' *Trimmed Lamp*, etc. 47 Off every night playing pool and bumming with the boys instead of staying home with her.

3. *tr.* To obtain (a ride, food, money, etc.,) by surreptitious means or by begging; to beg from (a person).

1896 *Pop. Science Jrnl.* L. 254 Several of the 'lads' had been 'pulled' at the Rapids for 'bumming the freights.' **1923** H. L. FOSTER *Beachcomber in Orient* 2 Then he bummed me for the price of a 'square meal.'

Bumble. A bumblebee. {1638, 1789} — **1876** WHITMAN *Specimen Days* (1892) 85 The great wild bee, the bumble-bee, or 'bumble,' as the children call him. *Ib.* 88 An occasional wasp, hornet, honey-bee or bumble. **1884** ROE *Nature's Story* 246 Of what use are bumble-bees?—I like to say *bumble* best, as I did when a boy.

***Bumblebee.** Also **†bomble bee.** A large hairy social bee of the genus *Bombus*.

1791 BARTRAM *Travels* p. xxx, The object of his wishes was a large fat bomble bee. **1806** LEWIS in *L. & Clark Exped.* (1905) V. 88 The honey bee is not found here. The bumble bee is. **1845** *Lowell Offering* V. 85 He could also spell the 'bumble-bee-with-his-tail-cut-off,' without missing a letter. **1899** CUSHMAN *Hist. Indians* 214, I have often seen little fellows stir up nests of bumble-bees. **1914** *Boston Transcript* 2 April 10/2 One bumble bee can break up an entire camp meeting.

Bumbo. *?Obs.* Also **bombo, bumboe.** A liquor made of rum, sugar, and water {1748–1867} Also *whisky bumbo.*

1733 BYRD *Journey to Eden* (1901) 77 When they [=people of N.C.] entertain their Friends bountifully, they fail not to set before them a capacious Bowl of Bombo, so call'd from the Admiral of that name. **1735** *Ga. Hist. Soc. Coll.* II. 44 He had nothing to drink but a little bumboe, which is rum, sugar, and water and some hominy and milk, and potatoes. **1744** *Mass. H. S. Coll.* VII. 172 Our liquor was sorry rum, mixed with water and sugar, which bears the heathenish name of bumbo. **1770** *Ann. S.W. Virginia* 65 For Bumbo with two gills of Rum to the quart, made with white sugar, one shilling per quart. ... For Whiskey Bumbo ... seven pence half penny per quart. **1819–27** J. BERNARD *Retrosp.* 150 Between twelve and one his throat would require another emulsion, and he would sip half a pint of some mystery termed bumbo, apple-toddy, or pumpkin flip.

Bumby(e), variant of BIMEBY *adv.* — **1786** *Boston Ex. Advertiser* 19 Oct. (Th.), Oh! he say, land dear now, bumbye buy him five dollars nacre. **1862** LOWELL *Biglow P.* II. ii. 188 'You'll see nex' time!' an' 'Look out bumby!' *Ib.* 216 She'll come out right bumby.

+Bummer. *slang.*

1. An idler, loafer, or sponger. (Cf. BUM *n.*[2])

In early use confined to San Francisco.

1856 *San Francisco Call* 25 Dec. (Th.), 'Pon my word I'm no bummer. I never ate a lunch in all my life without taking a square drink. **1857** *Ib.* 28 April (Th.), The irreclaimable town 'bummer' figured in the police court. **1868** M. H. SMITH *Sunshine & Shadow* 171 The bummers are brought from their cell and placed in the lower part of the long hallway **1872** 'MARK TWAIN' *Roughing It* xxiv. 183 The auctioneer ... never got a bid—at least never any but the eighteen-dollar one he hired a notoriously substanceless bummer to make. **1878** in *Harper's Mag.* (1891) Dec. 96/2 We remained the fifteen minutes, listening to some bummers discussing national politics. **1890** N. P. LANGFORD *Vigilante Days* I. 202 For years he has been a 'bummer' among men of his class. He has lived off his friends.

2. During the Civil War, a soldier who deserted the ranks and plundered promiscuously; loosely, a member of a raiding force.

1861 *Md. Hist. Mag.* V. 324 We have a fair sprinkling of bummers, but instead of demoralizing their betters by their presence, they are only laughed at. **1865** G. W. NICHOLS *Story Gt. March* 164 If it be asked what a bummer is, the reply is easy. He is a raider on his own account—a man who temporarily deserts his place in the ranks while the army is on the march, and starts out upon an independent foraging expedition. **1865** *Nation* I. 682 He went on to relate, in a good-humored way, many amusing stories of Sherman's army, and the impudence of the bummers. **1866** E. A. POLLARD *Southern Hist. War.* II. 449 This organization, known as that of 'Sherman's bummers,' often mixed up with the regular troops of the army, carried devastation, ruin and horror along the march. **1879** TOURGEE *Fool's Errand* 218 Sherman ... who had made the term 'bummer' expressive of the quintessence of all ignominy. **1888** GRIGSBY *Smoked Yank* xxvi. (1891) 234 Whether with them [Howard's scouts], or with the common 'bummers,' I was always at the head of one or other of the columns.

3. On the stock exchange: (see quot. 1870).

1869 BROWNE *Adv. Apache Country* 292 The newly-discovered silver regions, which were then making a prodigious stir among the bummers, bankers, and other men of enterprising genius on Montgomery Street. **1870** MEDBURY *Men Wall St.* 144 There are numerous workers in this rich mine, some with far less capital than assurance. These latter form an outlying fringe, to which the slang of the street has given the expressive term. borrowed from the army, of 'bummers.'

4. A political hanger-on or dependent.

1872 *Chicago Tribune* 24 Dec. 2/3 Without general acquaintance here [*sc.* Washington] and utterly unknown as a Congressional bummer. **1872** *Newton Kansan* 5 Sept. 4/1 The political bummers ... are rallying everywhere around the Greeley standard. **1875** *Chicago Tribune* 27 Sept. 4/3 The public sprees in which a large number of city and county officials indulge from time to time, assisted by political bummers and dead beats. **1888** BRYCE *Amer. Commonwealth* II. 470 So that the incumbent may freely 'bleed' for party use, or, what is the same thing, for the use of party 'bummers.' **1888** *America* 20 Sept. 16 *Bummer.* The name is now applied to party hangers on, who are of no value, but expect to be taken care of for doubtful services in the past. **1898** *Forum* Dec. 414 Ward heelers and slum 'bummers' were conspicuous factors in the Presidential campaign of 1876.

+Bummerish, *a.* Characteristic of a bummer or loafer. — **1872** C. KING *Sierra Nevada* 36 Indians, ... lying off with that peculiar bummerish ease, associated with natural mock dignity.

+Bummerism. The habits or ways of bummers; bummers as a class; the influence of bummers in politics. — **1870** *Philadelphia Press* 5 Jan., If deputy sheriffs might attend without scandal, if beautiful bummerism, feminine and fair. **1875** *Chicago Tribune* 30 Sept. 4/2 But we decline as hopeless any attempt to compete with the German organ of bummerism in the slang of gamblers and thieves. **1894** [see next]. **1898** *Forum* Dec. 426 We are so far beyond the age of low 'bummerism' in Federal office that we can afford to hesitate and ask questions.

+**Bummery.** =prec. — **1894** *Advance* (Chicago) 3 May 277/4 Petitions in Boots & Bummery. To some these straggling adventurers [=Coxey's followers and their imitators] have been a sort of . . . abnormal lesson in bummerism and vagabondage.

+**Bumming,** *vbl. n.*[1] *slang.* [BUM *n.*[1]] Carousing; going 'on a bum.' — **1860** *Yale Lit. Mag.* XXV. 398 (Th.), Another great shame connected with our social life is that of spreeing or 'bumming.'

+**Bumming,** *vbl. n.*[2] *slang.* [BUM *v.*] Living or acting like a bum; loafing or begging. — **1872** BRACE *Dangerous Classes N.Y.* 101 It could be no worse than 'bumming,' *i.e.*, sleeping out. **1891** C. ROBERTS *Adrift Amer.* 66 The idea of begging, or 'bumming,' as it is popularly called out there, went strongly against my stomach.

***Bump,** *v.* +To (cause to) touch a sandbank. — **1844** MRS. HOUSTON *Yacht Voy. Texas* II. 150 The extremely heavy swell on the bar, . . . materially increases the chance of a vessel's 'bumping'; a term the Americans use for touching on the sand banks. **1875** *Chicago Tribune* 14 July 5/1 He overheard the Captain and Mate talking about 'bumping her,' and that the vessel once struck, but floated off.

Bumper. [f. *bump* v.]

+**1.** A contrivance to lessen the shock of impact, ordinarily at the ends of cars; a buffer.

1839 *Jrnl. Franklin Inst.* XXIV. 156 The bumpers or elastic cushions are to be attached . . . to the front and rear draw-bar of the carriage bed of each car. **1846** *Rep. Comm. Patents* (1847) 81 Upon the same car other springs for bumpers, &c., are used. **1864** *Sanitary Comm. U.S. Army* 110 The bumper [of the hospital car] is surrounded by a stiff spring, which prevents the communication of the jar when the motion is suddenly stopped or applied. **1874** B. F. TAYLOR *World on Wheels* I. 152 [The caboose] gathers itself up like a salient goat, and bounces against the bumper of the next car. **1881** *Chicago Times* 30 April, In the fall he struck the bumpers, and . . . bounded away from the cars and alighted on the ground uninjured. **1901** *Law Times* 11 May 29/2 (*Amer. lett.*), An elevator car . . . passed downward until it struck the bumpers at the bottom of the shaft. **1903** LORIMER *Lett. Merchant* 255 When a fellow . . . has any sort of stuff in him, . . . he'll usually hustle for his car fare, rather than ride through life on the bumpers of a freight.

+**2.** A boxlike cradle or rocker used in gold mining.

1860 *Harper's Mag.* April 609/2 Our machine, which resembled the 'bumper,' or Virginia rocker, consisted of a wooden trough, . . . so hung as to be rocked to and fro by hand. **1885** M. A. LEESON *Hist. Montana* 231 The pan, the rocker, the bumper, the Long Tom, the sluice, and the hydraulic have succeeded each other in the order named.

||**3.** A device to give a jar or bump.

1871 *Ill. Agric. Soc. Trans.* VIII. 247 He uses the wheelbarrow curculio bumper, his own invention.

+**Bumwood.** A poisonous variety of sumac (*Rhus metopium*); burnwood. — **1884** SARGENT *Rep. Forests* 54 *Rhus Metopium* . . . Poison Wood. Coral Sumach. Mountain Manchineel. Bum Wood. **1897** SUDWORTH *Arborescent Flora* 274 *Rhus metopium.* Poisonwood. . . . Common names [include] . . . Bumwood, Hog Plum, Doctor Gum.

***Bun**[1]. A soft, round roll made by commercial bakeries.

1637 *Mass. Bay Rec.* I. 214 No person shall sell any cakes or buns, either in the markets or victualling houses. **1837** in Kittredge *Old Farmer* (1904) 93 Wheat loaves, gingerbread, hot buns and seedcakes—these are all very clever. **1870** *Scribner's Mo.* I. 123 Here a female Falstaff . . . vends . . . soggy yellow buns.

***Bun**[2]. A squirrel. {1587–1614} — **1837** EMERSON *Poems* 155 The mountain and the squirrel Had a quarrel; And the former called the latter 'Little Prig'; Bun replied, [etc.]. **1889** FARMER 104 *Bun* . . . is in America often applied to the squirrel.

***Bunch,** *n.*

***1.** A swelling or tumor. {–1598}

1857 *Lawrence* (Kansas) *Republican* 11 June 3 See that he [the ox] does not have a . . . Missouri stick . . . which will gall his neck, or produce a bunch. **1874** *Vt. Board Agric. Rep.* II. 428 Their bite is poisonous to a certain extent, as bunches can be felt around their bites. **1882** THAYER *From Log-Cabin* 207 'There's a hard bunch on my left side, and pain,' said James to his mother. 'That's the ague-cake,' replied his mother, on examining the spot.

+**b.** The hump on a bison. *Obs.*

1733 BYRD *Journey to Eden* (1901) 312 We had still a rarer Morsel, the Bunch riseing up between the Shoulders of this Animal [=the buffalo], which is very tender and very fat. **1748** *Phil. Trans.* XLV. 172 The Bunch on their Shoulders [*i.e.* of the American bison] is esteemed by the Indians the most delicate Part of them.

+**2.** A clump *of* trees.

1683 *Topsfield Rec.* 49 A bunch of mapels at the brooke. **1712** *Duxbury Rec.* 89 We began at a maple tree . . . and run from thence North sixty rods, to a bunch of maples. **1742** *N.H. Probate Rec.* III. 101 The pine . . . is the Bounds . . . at said Mote River by the Bunch of Burches. **1902** HARBEN *Abner Daniel* 89 It will take a quarter of a million investment to market a half-million-dollar bunch of timber.

+**b.** A cluster or group *of* huts.

1865 *Atlantic Mo.* XV. 441 A small space for a bunch of huts.

+**3. a.** A pile of boards; a bundle *of* shingles.

1845 COOPER *Chainbearer* xxiii, There lay what the millers call a bunch of cherry-wood boards at no great distance from the spot where the roof joined the plate of the building, and within this bunch I arranged my hiding-place. **1872** *Harper's Mag.* Nov. 950/1 The good people . . . contracted with him to have him deliver them a certain number of sermons at the price of a bunch (1000) of shingles for a sermon.

b. A quantity or number *of* something.

1831 AUDUBON *Ornith. Biog.* I. 355 A person likewise informed me, that, along the cliffs of the Kentucky, he had seen many *bunches*, as he termed them, of these nests attached to the naked, shelving rocks overhanging that river. **1854** 'O. OPTIC' *In Doors & Out* (1876) 197 She sent the Irish girl to the apothecary's shop for a bunch of 'Bagdad cigars.' **1898** WESTCOTT *D. Harum* 350, I owe ye quite a little bunch o' money, don't I? **1904** *Public Opinion* (Watertown, S.D.) 28 Dec. 1/3 A bunch of bills was allowed, covering hydrant rental from July to January.

4. a. A company of people. {1622–}

1840 HOFFMAN *Greyslaer* I. 92 You'll find them pretty much here and there, in bunches, helping one another. **1902** MCFAUL *Ike Glidden* 91 He met a bunch of railroad laborers on their way to their tent. **1913** STRATTON-PORTER *Laddie* viii. (1917) 148 But she said . . . with the bunch of us to educate yet, we'd need the money.

+**b.** A herd of cattle, horses, etc.

1864 DICKSON *Across Plains* (1929) 95 It was a bunch of hosses over on this side along the ravine. *Ib.* 139 When yoking up we would drive the bunch into the circle if we corraled. **1881** *Rep. Indian Affairs* 86, I have visited them at their camps a number of times and nearly always find them at home, looking after their little bunches of stock. **1887** I. R. *Lady's Ranche Life Mont.* 91 It is so nice riding to all the different bunches of horses which I see in the distance. **1889** *Harper's Mag.* May 874/1 In the mountains of Colorado last summer there were two bunches of mountain bison. **1898** CANFIELD *Maid of Frontier* 18 He's got a bunch o' scabby sheep an' proposes to stay there. **1903** A. ADAMS *Log Cowboy* 19 Our men held the cattle as they came out in order to bait the next bunch.

+**c.** A swarm *of* bees.

1782 J. H. ST. JOHN *Letters* 29 A bunch of bees . . . issued from one of the hives.

***Bunch,** *v.*

1. *tr.* +**a.** To collect or herd (cattle, horses, etc.,) in a compact group or within a small area. Also *absol.*, to combine two or more herds.

1869 MCCLURE *Rocky Mountains* 99 The horses not captured by the Indians have been 'bunched' at either end of the hostile country, and I doubt whether there will be regular coaches. **1869** *Overland Mo.* III. 126 Two men often 'bunch' on the march, *i.e.*, unite their herds for convenience in driving. **1884** SWEET & KNOX *Through Texas* 173 We . . . were in camp one night, with the cattle bunched out on the prairie, under guard. **1907** WHITE *Arizona Nights* 108 It was somewhere near noon by the time we had bunched and held the herd.

b. To collect or bring together (separate things) so as to form a bunch or group. {1883–}

1828 WEBSTER, *Bunch*, v. t., to form or tie in a bunch or bunches. **1877** WANAMAKER in Appel *Biography* (1930) 137 Why should not individual ownership be permitted to grow peaceably and equally with industries that are bunched into trusts? **1881** *Chicago Times* 16 April, When trees are bunched together . . . they are scrubs. **1886** ROOSEVELT in *Century Mag.* Nov. 77/1 Before election day, many thousands of complete sets of the party ticket are printed, folded, and put together, or, as it is called, 'bunched.' **1888** *Scribner's Mag.* III. 427 He will . . . find it difficult . . . to bring the lines together without bunching them awkwardly at the junction. **1916** 'MARK TWAIN' *Mysterious Stranger* 26 When he was bunching the most illustrious kings and conquerors and poets . . . together.

+**c.** In baseball, to secure (hits) in close succession.

1889 *Century Dict.* 720/2 To bunch the hits in a game of base-ball. **1898** *Boston Globe* 15 May 36/4 There are two kinds of salesmen, the 'pikers,' who grind away all the time, and the men who bunch their hits, to use a baseballism.

2. *intr.* To collect in a close group or mass. Also with *up.*

1873 BEADLE *Undevel. West* 60 Buffalo grass and gama grass take its place, and there show a tendency to bunch together, leaving large portions of the surface bare. **1874** LONG *Wild-Fowl* 261 Be prepared to take advantage of the instant of their bunching or crossing. **1887** F. FRANCIS *Saddle & Moccasin* 124, I knew at once that they had got scared, and had bunched up like a bevy of quail. **1888** *Century Mag.* Jan. 455 By the time the dumbfounded brutes had 'bunched,' . . . we were right in among them. **1916** BOWER *Phantom Herd* 11 He had intended swinging back through Arizona, where in certain parts cattle still were wild enough to bunch up at sight of a man afoot.

+**Bunch bean.** The dwarf kidney bean.

1805 PARKINSON *Tour* 341 What are termed Indian peas, are a sort of kidney-bean; the bunch-bean is the same, and produces abundantly. **1822** J. WOODS *English Prairie* 221 There are some dwarf ones, called bunch-beans. **1834** R. BAIRD *Valley Miss.* 269 In early stages it [*sc.* cotton] resembles, when seen at a little distance, what are called *bunch beans* growing in hills or rows. **1850** *New Eng. Farmer* II. 295 We are sure no lover of a good bean, who eats the *frejole* . . . once, but will be desirous to have another 'dig' at them. They are a bunch bean.

Bunchberry. {1825–, *dial.*} +The berry or shrub of the dwarf cornel, *Cornus canadensis.*

1845 JUDD *Margaret* I. xiv. 106 She came to the shadows of the woods . . . where she got boxberry flowers and fruit, bunch-berry and star-of-Bethlehem flowers. **1848** THOREAU *Maine Woods* 59 The cornel, or bunch-berries, were very abundant. **1863** 'G. HAMILTON' *Gala-Days* 183 Bunch-berry hung out its white banner. **1880** *Harper's Mag.* Sept. 501/1 The carpet was . . . more suggestive—though starred with scarlet bunch-berries—of death and decay even than the grave-yard on the slope. **1890** *Ib.* April 709/1 The creamy blossoms of the bunch berry lie close together among their leaves. **1897** *Outing* XXX. 584/2, I even embroidered bunches of red berries on white linen, in memory of the gay little bunchberries that grew all about us.

+**Bunch-cherry.** The black cherry, *Prunus serotina.* — **1825** W. COBBETT *Woodlands* 185 American Wild Black Cherry. . . . The Americans call it the Bunch-cherry, because its fruit hangs in long bunches, somewhat like grapes.

+**Bunch cotton.** Handfuls of cotton taken from bales. — **1872** *Harper's Mag.* Oct. 677/2 Stealing 'bunch cotton' from bales, . . . is guarded against.

+**Bunchflower.** A liliaceous plant (*Melanthium Virginicum*) with a panicle of small greenish flowers. — **1817–8** EATON *Botany* (1822) 350 *Melanthium racemosum*, bunch flower. **1845** LINCOLN *Botany* App. 127/1 *Melanthium hybridum*, bunch-flower. [Also in later botanies.]

+**Bunch grass.** Any one of various Western grasses growing in clusters or bunches.

1837 IRVING *Bonneville* I. xii. 129 Their horses . . . [grazed] upon the upland bunch grass, which grew in great abundance, and though dry, retained its nutritious properties. **1842** M. CRAWFORD *Journal* 18 The country over which we have traveled today is mostly covered with bunch grass which the horses are very fond of. **1848** BRYANT *California* viii. 121 Occasionally there are patches of bunch-grass, which is heavily seeded. **1858** D. PETERS *Kit Carson* 229 The bunch grass . . . is not confined to the mountains in New Mexico; . . . but, in the low lands, it is useless, being too tough for animals to masticate. **1877** WM. WRIGHT *Big Bonanza* 278 The bunch-grass is considered to be as good for horses as barley, as it bears a heavy crop of seeds. **1891** RYAN *Told in Hills* ii. 32 Where the 'bunch-grass' of the grazing levels bends even now under a chance wild stallion. **1907** WHITE *Arizona Nights* 271 The hardy cow-ponies sought out the sparse, but nutritious bunch-grass.

attrib. **1878** BEADLE *Western Wilds* 125 One may ride all day through good bunch-grass pasture and his horse be walking in sand all the time. **1885** *Century Mag.* April 839 All the Sound country, and much of British Columbia, get their beef supply from the bunch-grass plains east of the Cascades. **1899** *Scribner's Mag.* XXV. 114/1, I have never seen such luxuriant grass anywhere. . . . It is of the bunch-grass variety.

Bunching block. *Obs.* {To *bunch* hemp, 1601 and later dial.} A block for beating or bruising hemp. — **1677** *Dedham Rec.* V. 60 Liberty giuen to Ensi Fullar to fell and take timber to finish his Barn and a tree to make him a bunching blocke.

+**Bunch oysters.** (See quotation.) — **1881** E. INGERSOLL *Oyster Industry* 242 *Bunch Oysters*, those growing in clusters. (South.)

+**Bunch pink.** The sweet-william, *Dianthus barbatus.* — **1857** GRAY *Botany* 54 Sweet William or Bunch Pink. **1877** *Vt. Bd. Agric. Rep.* IV. 99 The quantity of . . . bunch pinks and candytufts coming from self-sown seeds is quite startling.

+**Bunch plum.** =BUNCHBERRY. — **1840** *S. Lit. Messenger* VI. 518/2 There were the fringed polygula, the butter-cup, wild geranium, bunch-plum, ivy-berry. **1892** *Amer. Folk-Lore* V. 97 *Cornus Canadensis*, bunch plums; pudding-berry. N.H.

+**Bunco, Bunko,** *n. slang.* [Attributed to Sp. *banca*, a card-game similar to monte.] A swindle perpetrated by means of card-sharping, a sham lottery, the confidence game or similar means. Commonly attrib. with *game, man*, etc. Also BUNCO STEERER, STEERING.

1872 *Chicago Tribune* 18 Oct. 8/4 A quintet of bunco thieves were tried by jury. . . . Such verdicts are powerless to inspire gamblers with the proper respect for the law. **1875** *Ib.* 8 Dec. 12/3 This marriage was merely a 'confidence' or 'bunko' game on both sides,—purely a Mormon affair. **1883** *Putnam Co. Journal* (Palatka, Fla.) 28 Jan. 3/1 Bunko men are with us. Give them a wide street. **1884** CABLE *Dr. Sevier* (1885) 205 The tenpin alleys, the chop-houses, the bunko shows, and shooting-galleries. **1888** *Congress. Rec.* Dec. 260/2 A bunco game is a sort of mysterious game that is played by certain sharpers to filch honest people out of their money. **1889** *Cent.* 721/3 *Bunko-joint*, a house or rendezvous to which strangers are allured, and in which they are victimized, by bunko-men. **1894** C. H. HOYT *Texas Steer* (1925) III. 39 You're a . . . bunco sharp. **1900** R. H. SAVAGE *Midnight Passenger* 153 Reporter Snooks of the *Earth* coldly bluffed Sears of the *Ledger* with a bet, 'Two to one on his skipping out; even money on a bunco.' **1902** LORIMER *Lett. Merchant* 87 The bunco men aren't all at the county fair, and they don't all operate with the little shells and the elusive pea.

+**Bunco, Bunko,** *v. slang.* [f. the noun.] *tr.* To swindle, cheat.

1875 *Chicago Tribune* 6 July 8/1 The fugitive is the same person who bunkoed a stranger out of $75 recently. **1883** *Phila. Times* No. 2892, 2 A Reading banker bunkoed. **1892** *Congress. Rec.* March 2651/2 The farmer is always buncoed by the three-card monte, green-goods protection shouter. **1899** J. L. WILLIAMS *Stolen Story*, etc. 114 Mrs. Wells is tired of having these shop-keepers bunco her all the time, and she thought she'd make an example of this shoemaker. **1904** *McClure's Mag.* Feb. 417 It costs a feller money to be bunkoed, an' then it costs him more to find out that he's been bunkoed. **1910** 'O. HENRY' *Strictly Business* 37 Do you know of any immediate system of buncoing the community out of a dollar or two?

+**Buncoer, Buncoist.** [BUNCO *n.* and *v.*] A swindler. — **1894** *Columbus* (O.) *Dispatch* 28 May, A noted buncoist, who attempted to turn a trick on Farmer Abel Comstock, of Wood county. **1904** *Bookman* XIX. 145 The great bankers became great buncoers and went into all manner of schemes during the boom.

+**Buncombe,** *n.* (Cf. the earlier BUNKUM.)

1. In the phrase 'to talk to (or for) Buncombe,' or variants of this: (see quotation 1848).

1846 J. G. SAXE *Progress* (1847) 24 Here, would-be Tullys pompously parade Their timid tropes for simple 'Buncombe' made. **1848** BARTLETT 55 The origin of the phrase, as I have read it, is somehow so: A tedious speaker in Congress being interrupted and told it was no use to go on, for the members were all leaving the house, replied, 'Never mind; I'm talking to Buncombe.' Buncombe, in North Carolina, was the place he represented. **1849** L. J. FRAZEE *Medical Student* 17 In the House of Representatives everything was confusion, . . . some reading newspapers, and not a few busy in fixing up Documents for 'Buncombe.' **1855** W. PHILLIPS *Speeches* (1863) 234 They sometimes talked for Buncombe. **1856** GOODRICH *Recoll.* I. 101 On every side the ear was saluted by . . . the cawing of congresses of crows, clamorous as if talking to Buncombe. **1862** *Mass. Hist. Soc. Proc.* V. 370 He made no speeches for *Buncombe*, and seldom addressed the House at much length.

2. Used with reference to legislative action designed merely to satisfy or impose upon public opinion.

1857 *Harper's Mag.* Aug. 290/2 A simple, earnest people, who . . . did not understand legislating for Buncombe, that world-famous county not having been then established. **1857** *N.Y. Tribune* 2 March (B.), The House of Representatives broke down upon the corruption committee's bill to protect the integrity of members of Congress, having first passed it for buncombe. **1859** *N.Y. Herald* 12 March, The bill was another bid for buncombe. **1863** *Rio Abajo Press* 24 Feb. 2 Our legislators have two sessions to consult in to ascertain . . . what other public benefit [can be] forgone; for a similar 'credit,' and as a contribution to 'buncombe.' **1885** *Century Mag.* April 829 Several score of preposterous measures . . . annually make their appearance purely for purposes of buncombe.

3. Nonsense; humbug.

1861 *Vanity Fair* 5 Jan. 5/2 How piquant to see Buncombe and bluster . . . suddenly ice-watered by being proved to be swindling in disguise. **1865** *Atlantic Mo.* XV. 344 It is however, very certain that he gave them no buncombe. **1866** C. H. SMITH *Bill Arp* 69 It's good Buncombe to have a scape-goat! Mr. Buncombe can go home and say 'Didn't I give them Quartermasters and Commissaries fits?' **1874** J. M. HART *German Universities* 143 Bismarck . . . and the other leaders of debate say very good things, and say them to the point, with a refreshing absence of 'buncombe.' **1890** *Buckskin Mose* 204 That righteous amount of Buncombe, which is . . . so gratifying to the average American mind. **1894** 'MARK TWAIN' *P. Wilson* xvii, He said that he believed that the reward offered for the lost knife was humbug and buncombe.

4. *attrib.* Applied to political speeches, politicians, etc., with allusion to senses 1 and 2.

1848 *Commercial* (Wilmington, N.C.) 16 May 2/3 (Th.), The Rhodeislanders have no notion of taxing the people for Buncombe speeches. **1849** *Ib.* 27 Jan. 2/2 (Th.), The Buncombe politicians—those who go for reëlection merely. **1871** EGGLESTON *Duffels* (1893) 98 Captain Oscar, the popular politician, . . . made a buncombe speech. **1880** G. A. PIERCE *Zachariah* 196 It was Saturday, a day known in House parlance as 'buncombe day,' when members who desire to get their speeches before their constituents, are permitted to repeat them on the floor, and have them taken down by the official reporters and printed in the official 'Record.' **1887** *Courier-Journal* 18 Jan. 3/2 We can form some estimate of computations made in buncombe Congressional speeches.

+**Buncombe,** *a.*, variant of BUNKUM *a.* — **1859** *Harper's Mag.* Oct. 712/1 'Was the fence alluded to a good strong fence?' . . . 'It was a Buncombe fence, Sir! . . . A Buncombe fence, Sir, is a fence that is bull strong, horse high, and pig tight!'

+**Buncombe,** *v.* [BUNCOMBE *n.*] *intr.* To talk buncombe. — **1855** *Herald of Freedom* (Kansas) 8 Sept. 2/4 (Th.), Now, when we want anything done we jist come together and do it right up . . . ; and when it's done 'tis done, without buncomin' and gassin' on't two or three days.

+**Bunco steerer.** *slang.* Also **bunko steerer.** [BUNCO *n.*] A swindler.

1875 *Chicago Tribune* 1 Oct. 4/3 A 'bunko-steerer' seems to be a subordinate confidence-man who . . . conducts them [=countrymen] into a back room of some large building where they are 'confidenced' of what money they may have about them. **1882** in *Nat. Geogr. Mag.* Aug. (1929) 247 Notice: to Thieves, Thugs, Fakirs and Bunko-Steerers. **1888** *Congress. Rec.* Dec. 346/1 That poor deluded victim of a bunco-steerer is not more certain to lose . . . than is the farmer as he struggles in the toils and meshes of Republican tariff legislation. **1893** GUNTER *Miss Divi-*

dends 84 They wiped out every desperado, cut-throat and bunco-steerer in that town. **1910** 'O. HENRY' *Strictly Business* 36 Who wears the diamonds in this town? Why, Winnie, the Wiretapper's wife, and Bella, the Buncosteerer's bride.

+**Bunco steering,** *n. slang.* [Cf. prec.] Swindling. — **1875** *Chicago Tribune* 30 Sept. 4/2 The criminal classes . . . proceeded to introduce the business of 'bunko-steering.' **1892** *Daily News* 1 Jan. 7/3 Obtaining a sum of money . . . in Albany, New York, by what at first appeared to be a variation of the confidence trick, locally known as 'bunco-steering.'

***Bundle,** *n.* +A handful or 'hand' of tobacco leaves. — **1784** SMYTH *Tour* II. 136 Every night the negroes are sent to the tobacco house to strip, that is to pull off the leaves from the stalk, and tie them up in hands or bundles. **1797** IMLAY *Western Territory* (ed. 3) 248 In moist giving weather, they strip the leaves from the stalk, till they have a handful of them, called a hand, or bundle of tobacco, which they tie up with another leaf.

* **Bundle,** *v.*

+**1.** *intr.* Of the two sexes: To sleep or lie together in bed without undressing. Also const. *with.*

1781 PETERS *Hist. Conn.* (1829) 238 Notwithstanding the great modesty of the females . . . it is thought but a piece of civility to ask her to *bundle;* a custom as old as the first settlement in 1634. **1801** *Sp. Farmers' Museum* 194 One night, on her observing, that it was the fashion in that town to *bundle,* I quitted her father's house and her with precipitation, and never after troubled my preceptor by keeping late hours. **1809** IRVING *Knickerb.* v. iv, Stopping occasionally to . . . dance at country frolicks, and bundle with the beauteous lasses of those parts [of Connecticut].

+**b.** To share a bed (*with* another).

1813 J. LAMBERT *Travels* II. 29 During the whole of my tour through the States I never had occasion to bundle, though I have been sometimes asked if I wished to have a single bed. **1838** *Lexington Observer* 9 June, He was compelled to 'bundle' with the negro.

+**2.** *tr.* To put (persons of both sexes) in the same bed.

1807 R. WILSON *Travels* 92 When a girl, that was old enough to be married, had a suitor who had been a few times to see her, the parents, if they approved of the connection, would—what they called—*bundle* them; which *bundling* implied, putting them to bed together, the lady with only her under-petticoat on, and her sweetheart nothing but his breeches. **1884** *Congress. Rec.* App. 25 June 343/1 Upon mattresses laid on the bare ground within this tent twenty-five of us were 'bundled' in true Knickerbocker style, without regard to sex, side by side.

+**Bundler.** [BUNDLE *v.* 1.] One who bundles. — **1774-5** JANET SHAW *Jrnl. Lady of Quality* (1923) 135 The Lady is a fair American. . . . None of your bundlers a' faith for me. **1784** ABIGAIL ADAMS *Letters* (1848) 161 We have curtains [on shipboard,] it is true, and we only in part undress, about as much as the Yankee bundlers. **1819-27** J. BERNARD *Retrosp.* 183 The doors [of the separate rooms in a 'wooing-hut'] were fastened upon them, when, like Pennsylvanian 'bundlers,' they passed the night in innocent conversation. **1825** PAULDING *J. Bull in Amer.* vi. 68 To make people thieves, murderers, gougers, bundlers, [etc.].

+**Bundle shingles.** Shingles in packs or bundles. — **1819** *Amer. Farmer* I. 142 North-Carolina, bundle Shingles, the run and average quality, retail, $16.

Bundling, *vbl. n.* [BUNDLE *v.* 1.] +The practice of unmarried couples' (partly undressed) occupying the same bed.

1781 PETERS *Hist. Conn.* (1829) 240 *Bundling* has prevailed 160 years in New-England. *Ib.*, Bundling takes place only in cold seasons of the year. **1807** J. R. SHAW *Life* (1903) 142, I learned a new mode of courting, which is generally styled bundling. **1813** PAULDING *Sc. Fiddle* (1814) 192 In the custom of *bundling,* where innocent young women accommodate chaste young men with a part of their bed. **1825** NEAL *Bro. Jonathan* I. 118. The very 'bundling' of the Dutch settlers; that mischievous, wicked habit, which is now spreading through the frontier settlements. **1828** *Yankee* Aug. 259/1 I have since made enquiries about bundling, and have learned that it is really the custom here [in Maine], and that they think no more harm of it, than we do our way of a young couple's sitting up together. **1833** *Ind. Q. Mag. Hist.* XV. 243 Being the first time I had ever been through the operation of bundling in this style, I must say I felt a little embarressment [*sic*]. **1888** *Jrnl. Amer. Folk-Lore* I. 1331 That curious custom of courting termed bundling still survives in a few isolated localities along the eastern foothills of the Blue Mountains.

attrib. **1840** *Knickerbocker* XV. 388 Ten irregular citizens are now born to the republic, for one in those days of 'bundling' simplicity.

Bundling, *ppl. a.* +Accustomed to bundle. — **1809** IRVING *Knickerb.* IV. iii, He swore that he would have nothing more to do with such a squatting, bundling, . . . notion-peddling crew. **1825** PAULDING *J. Bull in Amer.* i. 2, I also fully believed that the people were a bundling, gouging, drinking, spitting, impious race.

Bunglesome, *a.* Clumsy, awkward, inconvenient. — **1896** *Columbus* (O.) *Dispatch* June, At the two King avenue store rooms the articles taken stamp the burglars as bunglesome. **1897** *Congress Rec.* App. Feb. 55/1 An inexcusable and bunglesome fraud or mistake on the part of some one handling [the ballots.] **1915** STRATTON-PORTER *M. O'Halloran* 337 But this sheet is going to be rather bunglesome. Ma, could you do anything about it?

+**Bungo.** [Amer. Sp. *bongo.*]

1. A kind of boat or dugout used in Central America and California.

1842 *Diplom. Corr. Texas* (1911) III. 954, I have made a voyage to the Islands of Cozumel for which purpose I had occasion to charter a Bungo, and . . . the captain (owner) of the Bungo remarked, that he with several other Bungos went from Sisal to the Alacranes. **a1848** *Picayune* (B.), The most urgent steps were being taken to press every bungo and canoe to the immediate relief of the people along the coast. **1849** T. T. JOHNSON *Sights Gold Region* 88 We tumbled in among the stone ballast of a large bungo provided to convey us to the U.S.M. Steamer 'Oregon.'

2. (See quotations.)

1849 T. T. JOHNSON *Sights Gold Region* 18 Our party of four took possession of a light little canoe or dug-out, provided, as in all cases, with a bungo, or species of roof made of the branches and leaves of the palmetto. **1889** K. MUNROE *Golden Days* 16 In the stern . . . was a palm-thatched bungo, or shelter from the weather.

+**Bungtown.** [See below.]

1. *Bungtown copper,* 'a spurious coin, of base metal, a very clumsy counterfeit of the English halfpenny or copper' (B. '59).

'It derived its name from the place where it was first manufactured, then called *Bungtown,* now *Barneysville,* in the town of Rehoboth, Mass.' (*Ib.*).

1787 *Newport Mercury* 13 Aug. 3/2 By a Correspondent of good Intelligence we are informed—that all Coppers by law in New-York, except Bungtowns, are fixed at 160 for a Dollar. **1840** *Knickerb.* XV. 385 [He took] a five cent piece and two bungtown coppers out of the till. **1845** JUDD *Margaret* I. iv. 19 They [=flowers] wouldn't fetch a bungtown copper. **1848** *Wilmington* (N.C.) *Commercial* 29 Aug. 1/6 (Th.), The farmer took out what he called a Bungtown copper and dropped it into the hat. **1855** M. THOMPSON *Doesticks* 62 Trying to pay the fare for three on this novel craft, with a single piece of money (which I now know to have been a Bungtown copper). **a1862** THOREAU *Yankee in Canada* (1866) 22 Our robust cents were compelled to meet on even terms a crew of vile halfpenny tokens, and bung-town coppers.

b. *Bungtown cent, money.*

[**1835** H. C. TODD *Notes* 83 Spurious half dollars and base currency, are called, at Hamilton, *Bung-town* money, in which place a band of regular burglars from the old country have been just broken up.] **1853** *Weekly Oregonian* 13 Aug. (Th.), What is the currency of the U.S.? Coppers, bogus, Bungtown cents, . . . pistareens, and shinplasters.

2. (See quotation.)

1890 *Amer. Notes & Q.* VI. 76 *Bungtown Coppers.* . . . Among numismatists this term is often used to designate any battered or otherwise mutilated old coins, which on account of their poor condition have practically no value.

Bunk, *n.*[1] Also †**bonk.**

1. In nautical and military use, a place or arrangement serving as a bed. {1815-}

1758 L. LYON in *Mil. Jrnls.* (1855) 37 Our mes being all of duty we made us up 2 straw bunks for 4 of us to lay in. **1780** *Heath Papers* 28 The bunks and lineing of the bomb proof were taken out. **1780** *N.H. Hist. Soc. Coll.* IX. 229 The Brigades who hutt are to be allowed no more [boards] than are necessary for making Doores windowes and Bonks. **1809** *Ann. 11th Congress* II. 2448 Amount of disbursements made . . . in the medical and hospital department . . . 20 bunks at $3½ each. **1836** HILDRETH *Campaigns Rocky Mts.* I. 45 Their barrack-rooms were neither provided with bunks, or anything substituted for them. **1847** MELVILLE *Omoo* 21, I was inducted into a wretched 'bunk' or sleeping-box built over another. **1861** NORTON *Army Lett.* 37 We have bunks made so that we can sleep in one-half of the tent. **1894** 'MARK TWAIN' *P. Wilson* xvi, When she went to her foul steerage bunk at last, . . . it was not to sleep.

2. A bed or sleeping place in a cabin, house, railway car, etc. {1862-}

1819-27 J. BERNARD *Retrosp.* 203 One corner of the room would be occupied by a 'bunk,' containing the family bed. **1835** HOFFMAN *Winter in West* I. 235 A couple of wooden bunks, swung from the roof, falling to the lot of those who had come in first, I wrapped myself in a buffalo-skin, and . . . soon 'slept like a king.' **c1838** J. VAILL *Memoir* (1839) 25 His lodging was a box of boards, called a bunk, with a ticken filled with pine shavings. **1851** MRS. CLAPPE *Lett. from Calif.* 153 His bunk, as those queer shelves on which miners sleep, ranged one above another somewhat like the berths of a ship, are generally called. **1873** *Newton Kansan* 22 May 3/2 A bunk with a couple of blankets thereon has been placed in the calaboose. **1883** *Wheelman* I. 352 These fishing shanties . . . are furnished with bunks for sleeping and a small stove for cooking. **1904** *Boston Globe* 28 Feb. 40/6 The caboose . . . is the home of the crew while on the rail. It has four bunks, two at either end.

attrib. **1893** *Scribner's Mag.* June 704/2 A seat made of a thick hewn slab, for which the bunk-frames furnish a back.

+**Bunk,** *n.*[2] (See quotations.) — **1848** BARTLETT 55 *Bunk,* a piece of wood placed on a lumberman's sled to enable it to sustain the end of heavy pieces of timber.—*Maine.* **1889** *Cent.* 721/2 *Bunk,* a piece of timber placed across a sled to sustain a heavy weight.

+**Bunk,** *v.*[1] [Bunk *n.*[1]] *colloq.*

1. *intr.* To sleep or spend the night, esp. in a bunk.

1840 Dana *Two Years* viii, [We] petitioned the captain for leave to shift our berths . . . into the forecastle. This . . . was granted, and we turned in to *bunk* and mess with the crew forward. **1854** Hammond *Hills, Lakes,* etc. 74 The half-breed was gone. . . . Old Pete Meigs and I bunked in his cabin many a trip after that. **1873** Aldrich *Marj. Daw,* etc. 111 'You're to bunk in here,' said the lieutenant, speaking to some one outside. **1887** *Courier-Journal* 2 May 8/2 Those who did not stand guard duty had bunked in the Council chambers and the City Court room. **1906** H. Fitzgerald *Sam Steele's Adv.* 226 The mate offered his little room to the Major and bunked with the sailors in the forecastle.

2. To go to bed, esp. in a bunk. Usu. with *in.*

1846 *Knickerb.* XXVII. 512 When . . . night has closed in, the watch is set, and all hands start off 'to bunk.' **1848** *R.I. Words* (Bartlett MS.), *Bunk in,* the sea term for going to bed in common use. **1859** *Harper's Mag.* June 39/2 'Ain't afeared of bugs, be ye?' . . . 'Oh, bunk in, bunk in!' 'Tain't nothin' when ye git used to it.' **1880** N. Brooks *Fairport Nine* i. 5 Hi Hatch bunked in with them [=the boys] that night. **1898** Westcott *D. Harum* 203 If I had an empty hogpen I wouldn't let him sleep in't overnight, much less to bunk in with a decent hog.

+**Bunk,** *v.*[2] [Bunk *n.*[2]] 'Among lumbermen, to pile wood deceitfully so as to increase the apparent quantity in the survey' (B. '77).

+**Bunk car.** [Bunk *n.*[1] 2.] In railroading, a car in which workmen sleep. — **1896** P. L. Ford *P. Stirling* xl, By the light one of the superintendents found the bunk-cars gone. **1918** Sandburg *Cornhuskers* 80 Then they go to the bunk cars and eat mulligan and prune sauce.

+**Bunker.** [Cf. Mossbunker.] The menhaden, *Brevoortia tyrannus.*

1842 *Nat. Hist. N.Y., Zoology* iv. 260 The Mossbonker, *Alosa menhaden.* . . . At the east end of the island, they are called Skippangs or Bunkers. *a***1877** *Sag Harbor Express* (B.), The 'Greenport Times' states that large quantities of bunkers are taken in pounds, as high as 50,000 being secured in some of them at a single lift. **1888** Goode *Amer. Fishes* 386 New Jersey uses the New York name with its local variations, such as 'Bunker' and 'Marshbunker.' **1898** *N.Y. Journal* 26 July 14/7 Thousands of bunkers, otherwise known as 'Long Island herring,' floated lifeless on the surface of the water.

Bunker bed. *Obs.* =Bunk *n.*[1] — **1796** B. Hawkins *Letters* 44, I saw a few bunker beds and the cannon, the only remains of the French establishment.

+**Bunkhouse.** [Bunk *n.*[1] 2.] A temporary structure in which miners, cowboys, lumbermen, etc., sleep.

1876 Raymond *8th Rep. Mines* 332 Bunk-house [of the Little Annie Mill cost] . . . [$]228.00. **1880** G. Ingham *Digging Gold* 353 The 'Bon Ton' restaurant . . . was a tent . . . with a sawdust floor, like our bunk-house. **1893** *Atlantic Mo.* Feb. 199/2 One of the men . . . was arranging hair . . . by the aid of a small warped mirror hanging outside of the bunk-house. **1902** Wister *Virginian* xxv. 295 In the early dawn Shorty sat up among his blankets on the floor of the bunk house and saw the various sleepers coiled or sprawled in their beds. *c***1908** F. M.Canton *Frontier Trails* 117 We found our man in McCool's bunkhouse.

+**Bunk mate.** [Bunk *n.*[1] 2.] One who shares a bunk. — **1877** Habberton *Jericho Road* 16 Folding his blanket double and piling it over his bunk-mate, . . . the Parson stretched himself in his bunk with no covering whatever. **1902** White *Blazed Trail* viii. 58 Thorpe had assigned him as bunk mate the young fellow who assisted Tom Broadhead in the felling.

+**Bunkroom.** [Bunk *n.*[1]] A room containing a bunk or bunks. — **1855** M. Thompson *Doesticks* 95 Took up my quarters in the bunkroom, where I slept by night in a bed occupied in the day-time by a big yellow dog. **1924** Mulford *Rustlers' Valley* vi, The cook was busy in the bunk-room.

+**Bunkum,** *n.*[1], earlier (and latterly common) variant of Buncombe *n.*

1828 *Niles' Reg.* XXXV. 66/2 'Talking to Bunkum!' This is an old and common saying at Washington. **1847** J. S. Robb *Squatter Life* 17 To sum it up, it is a little of government—a great deal of 'bunkum,' sprinkled with a high seasoning of political juggling. **1888** *Nation* 5 Jan. 2/2 It is a plain, sensible, straightforward document, without any bunkum or demagogy in it.

attrib. **1860** Olmsted *Back Country* 467 The South sends more 'orators' to Washington than the North, and the nuisance of Washington is 'bunkum' oratory. **1862** *N.Y. Tribune* 11 Feb., The rebel Brigadier-General, H. H. Sibley, was within 30 miles of Fort Craig . . . and had issued a bunkum proclamation. **1871** *Rep. Indian Affairs* (1872) 195 The best policy would be to go in and make a 'bunkum' speech in order to keep peace. **1887** *Nation* 27 Oct. 333/2 Oratory, other than of the bunkum or maudlin style, has long been rare.

+**Bunkum,** *n.*[2] *slang.* [Cf. next.] *The real bunkum,* the real thing (in excellence). — **1836** *Knickerb.* VII. 19 'Ain't she [=a boat] the raal bunkum?' exclaimed Hal. . . . 'Keep her trim, my hearties; she goes it bravely.'

+**Bunkum,** *a. colloq.* [Of obscure origin. Cf. prec. and Buncombe *a.*] Fine; excellent; first-rate.

1848 *R.I. Words* (Bartlett MS), *Bunkum* is used as good—as 'bunkum dinner,' 'bunkum peaches.' *c***1849** Paige *Dow's Sermons* I. 133 Yet some of our moons are bunkum—first-rate, as is everything American. **1854** H. H. Riley *Puddleford* 157 My clients, Whistle & Sharp, are bunkum yet—allers stands up to the rack at the end of an execution. **1864** Nichols *Amer. Life* II. 181 'Who is nominated for President?' 'James K. Polk, of Tennessee!' 'Bunkum! First Rate!' **1865** *Prairie Chicken* (Tilton, Ill.). 1 June 3/2 When I ask him if my cake is good, he says, 'Bunkum.' **1880** *Harper's Mag.* XLI. 615/1, I had heard the word 'bunkum' often used by bumpkins, but always with reference to something of an edible character, as an apple being 'bunkum,' or a piece of cake or pie. **1904** *Dialect Notes* II. 395. **1910** *Ib.* III. 452.

+**Bunky, Bunkie.** [Bunk *n.*[1] 1, 2.] A bunk mate; a comrade. — **1858** Viele *Following the Drum* 218, I rewarded [his affection for the dog] by giving him Jack for his 'bunkie'! **1890** Custer *Following Guidon* 17 Blankets were so scarce that everybody took a 'bunkey,' officers and all, in order to double the bedding. **1899** Remington in *Success* 13 May 409/3 'Bunkie,' which means, in the army, 'comrade.' **1903** A. Adams *Log Cowboy* 24 The Rebel and I were bunkies.

Bunt, *n.*

1. A push, butt, thrust. {1875, *dial.*}

1767 *Boston Gaz.* 19 Jan. (Th.), [The black ram] will sometimes come behind a fine great Weather . . . and give him a paultry Bunt at unawares. **1846** *Knickerb.* XXVIII. 466 The goat had been taught, by playing frequently at 'bunt' with a negro-boy of the family, to 'run into' every body. **1884** *Bismarck* (Dakota) *Tribune* Aug., The buffalo struck the tree with terrible force. . . . As the animal backed up for another bunt, [etc.].

+**2.** In baseball, a mere blocking of the pitched ball with the bat. Also attrib.

1892 *Courier-Journal* 1 Oct. 4/5 The visitors only made two hits off his delivery, and one was a little bunt by Brown. **1904** *Charlotte Observer* 20 June 4 Base hits or even successful bunts are not to be despised by the leaders. **1906** *Spalding's Base Ball Guide* 116 A 'bunt' hit is made when the batsman simply holds the bat up to meet the thrown ball, thereby allowing the ball to rebound from the bat to the ground.

Bunt, *v.*

1. *tr.* and *intr.* To push, butt, thrust, strike. {1825–, *dial.*}

1828 Webster, *Bunt,* in popular language, to push with the horns. **1858** *Harper's Mag.* April 714/2 Young Nick [was] pinned to the fence with the horns of a cow, one on each side of him, and now and then she would let him out, but only to 'bunt' him back again. **1859** Bartlett 58 To *Bunt,* to push with the horns, to butt. **1865** Browne *A. Ward His Book* (1906) 130 We then vilently bunted our heads together for a few minits. **1867** Bushnell *Mor. Uses Dark Th.* 203 When the gusty shocks of broadside pressure bunt upon the house. **1887** *Outing* X. 117/2 They bunted rudely together, upsetting each horse and rider.

b. (See quotation.)

1892 *Amer. Folk-Lore* V. 146 When a boy throws himself upon a sled . . . he *bunts,* or *bumps,* or *plumps,* etc., upon it, according to the manner of speech in his locality. (Maine.)

+**2.** In baseball: To stop (the ball) with the bat without swinging the latter. Also *bunted* ppl. a., *bunting* vbl. n.

1889 *Reach's Base Ball Guide* 144 Bunted Ball. **1892** *Courier-Journal* 2 Oct. 13/5 There is not a man in his team that can bunt. **1896** *Spaulding's Base Ball Guide* 77 Real skill in batting is also shown by the 'bunting' of the ball, so as to cause it to drop to the ground almost dead. **1906** *Ib.* 116 If the attempt to bunt result in a foul not legally caught, a strike shall be called by the umpire. **1912** Mathewson *Pitching* 23 Doyle bunted and was safe, filling the bases.

+**Bunter.** [Bunt *v.*] **a.** The bumper or buffer of a railway car. **b.** A heavy obstruction arranged at the end of a railroad track to prevent cars from running off. — **(a) 1884** Knight *Suppl.* 147/1 *Bunter,* . . . the bar on the front end of the car, which strikes against a similar bar on an adjacent car in coupling. **(b) 1898** *Boston Herald* 12 Aug. 4/7 A number of passenger cars were shunted into the trainshed . . . and, for some reason . . . , the bunter received a terrific blow that splintered a part of the woodwork and severely wrenched two of the coaches.

***Bunting**[1]. One or other of a group of small birds allied to the larks.

Usually with distinguishing epithets. See also Cow-, Lark-, Rice-, Snow-, and Towhee-bunting.

1811 Wilson *Ornithology* III. 68 Painted Bunting. . . . This is one of the most numerous of the little summer birds of Lower Louisiana. **1839** Audubon *Ornith. Biog.* V. 91 That the Painted Bunting at times retires far southward, . . . is a fact for which I can vouch, having seen one on the shore of the Mississippi in December 1820. *a***1862** Thoreau *Cape Cod* 125, I heard—in the summer—the Black-throated Bunting (*Fringilla Americana*). **1869** *Amer. Naturalist* III. 76 Chestnut-colored Bunting (*Plectrophanes ornatus*). I found this species . . . on the plains near Fort Benton, where it evidently breeds. **1883** *Century Mag.* XXVI. 683/2 It is a big price to pay—two larks for a bunting.

Bunting[2].

1. Light woolen material from which flags are often made. {1742–}

1711 *Boston News-Letter* 22 Oct. 2/2 Sadlery, Bunting, Millenary Goods. **1714** *Ib.* 18 Oct. 2/2 Buntings, red, blew, and white. **1759** *Newport Mercury* 26 June 4/3 Crimson bunting. **1795** *Ann. 4th Congress* 2

Sess. 2576 Bunting for the colors [of a frigate] is on hand. **1865** *Chicago Tribune* 10 April 1 Burlaps, Twines & Bunting.

2. Flags or pennants made of bunting. {1832–}

1814 *Niles' Reg.* V. 330/2 A very large portion of the honest foreign trade of the United States, for some time past, has been carried on in Baltimore vessels, under the 'Striped bunting.' **1878** *Harper's Mag.* Jan. 232 On a gala day, when all the patriotic bunting is unfolded, the view is more brilliant and ragged than ever. **1895** M. A. Jackson *Memoirs* 638 At the Virginia Military Institute bunting and flags of all descriptions floated from every conspicuous place.

+**Buntlinism.** [f. 'Ned *Buntline*,' pen-name of Edward Z. C. Judson (1822–86), organizer in 1853 of the 'Know-Nothing' party.] The political and social doctrines of 'Ned Buntline.' — **1855** *Olympia* (W. T.) *Pioneer* 6 July (Th.), In these days of Buntlinism, it is a common thing to hear men boast that some fellow has 'seen Sam,' or is 'Right on the Goose.'

Bunty, *a.* and *n. dial.* (See quots.) — **1856** *Spirit of Times* (N.Y.) 25 Oct. 129/2 The ring-necked duck, *anas rufitorques*, goes by the euphonious but unmeaning term of 'Bunty,' in the vicinity of Cincinnati, Ohio. **1870** *Nation* July 57/1 [In Pennsylvania] to be 'bunty' was to be squat in stature. {1890–, *dial.*} **1871** De Vere 380 A tailless fowl is in Pennsylvania called a bunty. {1721, *Sc. dial.*}

∗**Buoy.** Also †**boy.** The floating contrivance used especially for indicating channels or the position of objects under water. Also attrib.

1663 *Boston Rec.* 16 If any belonging to any vessell . . . doe drop any ancor . . . upon the flatts or within the Coue and haue noe Boy theareunto, theay ar to pay tenn shillings. **1789** *Ann. 1st Congress* I. 659 The bill for the establishment and support of light-houses, beacons, and buoys. **1805** *Ann. 8th Congress* 2 Sess. 1673 For fixing buoys in Long Island sound. **1875** 'Mark Twain' *Old Times Miss.* xii. 81 A buoy is nothing but a board four or five feet long, with one end turned up; it is a reversed school-house bench, with one of the supports left and the other removed. **1881** E. Ingersoll *Oyster Industry* 242 To buoy or buoy-off a certain piece of water area, means, in Rhode Island, to seclude it from being fished as long as the authorities deem proper. The area so secluded is indicated by a limit-line of buoys. **1886** S. W. Mitchell *R. Blake* 217, I think he must be six foot four; and they do say, maarm, as he ken heft a buoy weight.

∗**Bur(r),** *n.*

1. The husk or seed vessel of the chestnut. {1684}

1692 Sewall *Diary* I. 366 Bring home some Chesnuts in the Burs to set. **1778** [see Buttonwood 1]. **1852** Mrs. Ellet *Pioneer Women* 207 The children here loaded their little pockets with chestnuts, and for a while forgot the pinching cold of the half frozen leaves and frost covered burrs among which they were scattered. **1874** Roe *Opening Chestnut Burr* xiii, Plucking out the chestnut [she] tossed the burr away.

+**2.** The seed-bearing cone of the pine tree.

1859 G. W. Perry *Turpentine Farming* 24 We shall find that where pines are situated so that they are not exposed, and are perfectly sound, they will drop their burs clear and regular every year. **1905** *Bureau of Forestry Bul.* No. 63, 6 The seed of the white pine is borne in a cone, sometimes called a 'bur.'

Bur, *v.* [Bur *n.*] *tr.* To remove burs from (wool, etc.), esp. by the use of a special machine. {1879} — **1849** *Rep. Comm. Patents* (1850) 159 Having thus described my improved mode of constructing a cylinder for burring, opening &c., cotton, wool, . . . I shall state my claim. **1858** *Ib.* (1859) I. 508 Improved Burring Machine. *Ib.* 658 Improvement in Operating the teeth of Cylinders for Burring Wool.

∗**Burbot.** A cusk, or fresh-water cod; a fish of the family *Gadidae.* — **1842** *Nat. Hist. N.Y., Zoology* iv. 285 The Compressed Burbot, *Lota compressa.* The Eel-pout. *Ib.* 283 The Plain Burbot, *Lota inornata. Ib.* 284 The Spotted Burbot, *Lota maculosa*, . . . is a poor article of food. **1869** *Amer. Naturalist* III. 18 In this country . . . we have three species, . . . the Plain Burbot (*Lota inornata*) which is rare, the Spotted Burbot (*Lota maculosa*) which is abundant in our lakes, and the Compressed Burbot (*Lota compressa*) which is very rare.

+**Bur clover.** One or other species of medic, esp. *Medicago arabica.* — **1871** *Comm. Agric. Rep. 1870* 419 Bur clover, (*Medicago lupulina*).—This common plant of Southern California produces abundance of seeds, which are much relished by the Indians and by cattle. **1889** Vasey *Agric. Grasses* 92 *Medicago denticulata* (Bur Clover) . . . was early introduced into California and has become widely distributed in that State, where it is considered of great value. **1901** Mohr *Plant Life Ala.* 135 Vetch . . . , cowpeas, and bur clover . . . will yield crops for soiling in the earliest days of spring. *Ib.* 560 *Medicago arabica*, . . . Spotted Bur Clover.

+**Burden car.** Also **burthen car.** *Obs.* A freight car. — **1835** *Essex Inst. Coll.* LIV. 199 As soon as Burthen (freight) Cars can be provided, notice will be given. **1836** P. H. Nicklin *Peregrination* 60 The goods destined to the West, are taken from the boats and placed in Burthen Cars which are to carry them over the mountains. **1843** *Knickerb.* XXII. 185 The wheels of the Juggernaut carrying a train of burden-cars. **1849** *Penn. R.R. Ann. Rep.* 49 To which should be added, for Warehouse, Shops, Locomotives, Passenger and Burthen Cars . . . $1,990,000.

+**Burden grass.** Redtop, a well-known pasture grass, *Agrostis stolonifera major.* — **1749** Franklin *Writings* ii. 386, I threw in the following seed, . . . a peck of Burden grass . . . and two Pints of Red Clover per acre.

∗**Burdock.** A coarse weed having burs and with leaves like those of the dock, *Arctium lappa.*

1676 Glover *Acc. Va.* in *Phil. Trans.* XI. 629 There grow wild in the woods, . . . yellow-dock, bur-dock [etc.]. **1709** Lawson *Carolina* 78 Monks rhubarb, burdock, asarum, wild in the woods. **1784** Cutler in *Mem. Academy* I. 476 *Arctium*, . . . Burdock. The young stems boiled, divested of the bark, are esteemed little inferior to asparagus. They are also eaten raw with oil and vinegar. **1797** Asbury *Journal* II. 347, I applied leaves of burdock, and then a plaster of mustard, which drew a desperate blister. **1840** Dewey *Mass. Flowering Plants* 117 Burdock. . . . Its leaves have been a common application . . . for draughts upon the feet, and the softening of some tumors. **1891** 'Thanet' *Otto the Knight*, etc. 182 Burdock and jimson weeds held a kind of squalid revelry over a heap of tin cans. **1906** Valentine *H. Sandwith* 65, I'm sure I'd never trust him after he nearly poisoned you all, mistaking poke-root for burdock.

attrib. **1731** J. Seccomb *Father Abbey's Will* x, Some Devil's weed, And burdock seed To season well your porridge. **1856** M. J. Holmes *Homestead on H.*, Thanksgiving P. ii, You had better begin at once to dose yourself with burdock or catnip tea. **1903** K. D. Wiggin *Rebecca* 74 Wee baskets and plates and cups made of burdock balls.

Bureau. Also †**buro.**

+**1.** An article of furniture for holding clothing, usually surmounted by an adjustable mirror; a chest of drawers.

In the earlier of the following examples the name may be used in the original sense of a writingdesk with drawers. {1742–}.

1751 *Boston Ev. Post* 29 July, Fashionable furniture, consisting of mahogany, India & stone tables, buroes [etc.]. **1779** Freneau *Poems* (1786) 112 Quick, move, and bring from yonder black bureau The sacred book. **1815** *Niles' Reg.* IX. 36/1 The principle [*sic*] manufactures in wood are the following:—sideboards, secretaries, bureaus, and other articles of cabinet furniture. **1819** *St. Louis Enquirer* 15 Sept. (Th.), Look in the bureaus and trunks of modern men of fashion, and see the number of coats, waistcoats, pantaloons, hats, and boots. **1841** A. Bache *Fire-Screen* 49 Look at her bureau, with all the drawers open, and the things hanging out. **1844** *Knickerb.* XXIII. 19 It occurred to him . . . that . . . the garment had gotten into the drawer of a bureau that stood in one corner. **1860** M. J. Holmes *Maude* xvi. 171 Maude's chamber was ready at last . . . with its . . . handsome bedstead, marble washstand, and mahogany bureau, on which were arranged various little articles for the toilet. **1872** *Harper's Mag.* Aug. 326/2 We appropriate a wash-stand and bureau which stand in a neighboring unoccupied room. **1883** *Century Mag.* Oct. 889/1 She sat down by her bureau and began to bang and crimp her hair with grim resolution. **1899** *Boston Transcript* 16 Sept. 1 The combination of wardrobe, chiffonniere and bureau makes what our clever French neighbors call a 'Dresser.' **1902** *Harper's Bazar* Sept. 768 She looked on the table, then on the bed and bureau in the bedroom.

+**b.** *transf.* (See quotation.)

1888 J. D. Billings *Hardtack* 319 Their course could have been followed by the well stuffed knapsacks—or 'bureaus,' as some of the old vets called them—that sprinkled the roadside.

+**c.** Attrib. with *cover, desk, scarf, top.*

1843 'Carlton' *New Purchase* I. 199 The bureau-top was consecrated to Bibles and Hymn Books. **1852** *Knickerb.* XL. 13 [There are] books on the Oxford reading-table; books on the bureau-cover; books on the sofa. **1854** Shillaber *Mrs. Partington* 36 Paul's epistles . . . are yet treasured in the old black bureau-desk in the corner. **1906** Freeman *By Light of the Soul* 347 She began embroidering a bureau-scarf and table-cover for Lily's room.

+**2.** A subdivision of a branch of the Federal Government.

1831 *Deb. Congress* 26 Feb. 318 [The growing cost of government] is easily accounted for by the increased expense in every department—by establishing new bureaus—by erecting new offices. **1842** *Congress. Globe* Aug. 971/1 It was proposed . . . to repeal the law creating the Board of Navy Commissioners, and to divide the force . . . into seven bureaus, each bureau to be responsible for that branch of the service intrusted to its care. **1861** *Army Regulations* 11 The chief of any military bureau of the War Department. **1863** *U.S. Statutes* 507 An Act to establish a Bureau for the Relief of Freedmen and Refugees. **1880** 'E. Kirke' *Garfield* 43 What can a bureau do with the whole weight of congressional influence pressing for the appointment of men because they are our friends?

+**b.** Used in the official name given such a subdivision.

1850 *New Eng. Farmer* II. 30 The establishment of a 'Bureau of Agriculture,' at Washington, is a subject that has received considerable attention for the year past. **1859** Bartlett 58 A subdivision of one of the government departments, as the 'Indian Bureau,' the 'Pension Bureau,' etc. **1865** J. D. Whitney *Life & Lett.* 243 The most profound interest of everything connected with the subject exists in the General Land Office and the Census Bureau. **1871** *Scribner's Mo.* I. 412 The foregoing bulletin was prepared by . . . the Chief of the Meteorological Bureau. **1884** *Century Mag.* March 652/1 Mammoth establishments like the Printing Office and Bureau of Engraving and Printing.

c. Attrib. with *office, officer, work.*

1846 M'Kenney *Memoirs* I. 24 To dismiss from office in those days without cause . . .—and especially the dismissal of a bureau officer or clerk . . . would have been deemed an outrage. **1872** *Congress. Globe* 13 March 1631/2 A bureau office is any department within a department that reports to a chief; whether it is called a bureau or anything else makes no difference. **1881-5** McClellan *Own Story* 71 He [was] doing some little bureau work, . . . while I performed the real military labor. *Ib.* In some respects a very good bureau officer and a fair disciplinarian.

3. An office for the transaction of public or other business. {1720-}

1856 D. Macleod *F. Wood* 173 The duties now performed by the Bureau of Assessments, should be done by the present Board of Tax Commissioners. **1880** Cable *Grandissimes* 311 It was . . . convenient to the court-rooms and municipal bureaus. **1916** W. A. Du Puy *Uncle Sam* 208 The employment bureau immediately supplied her demand.

Bureau drawer. [Bureau 1.] A drawer in a bureau. — **1853** B. F. Taylor *Jan. & June* (1871) 100 At our house, bureau-drawers tumbled out their treasures of flannels and linens. **1862** *Trial C. M. Jefferds* 34 'Now, where did you put that pistol . . . ?' 'In a bureau drawer, in my house.' **1877** Phelps *Story of Avis* 265 Bidding him find the wedding slippers in the bureau-drawer. **1893** Howells *Evening Dress* 23 You ought to fold your clothes and lay them in a bureau drawer.

+**Burfish.** A spiny swellfish of the family *Diodontidae;* porcupine fish. — **1674** Josselyn *Acc. Voy. New-Eng.* 113 Blew-fish, Bull-head, Bur-fish. **1884** Goode *Fisheries U.S.* I. 170 The Porcupine Fishes—*Diodontidæ.* . . . The best known is the Swell Fish of New England, *Chilomycterus geometricus.* These fishes are commonly known by such names as 'Burr Fish,' 'Ball Fish,' 'Swell Fish,' and 'Toad Fish.'

+**Burg.** [G. *burg.*] *slang.* A town, village, or city.

1845 Sol. Smith *Theatrical Apprent.* 189 You will have the greatest congregation ever assembled in this burg. **1846** *Spirit of Times* 16 May 133/2 There is no man in this 'burg' with a sufficiently steady head, to attempt so rash an act as wearing that Hat!! **1857** *Lawrence* (Kansas) *Republican* 11 June 2 The party . . . made a descent upon the cabin of Mr. Hyde, about one mile from the burg. **1873** Beadle *Undevel. West* 85 Now it is a quiet and moral burg of some fifteen hundred inhabitants. **1888** *Battle Creek Wk. Jrnl.* 8 Feb., If successful, it will make a lively burg in the next few years. **1901** Flynt *World of Graft* 71 Course this berg [*sic*] ain't Chi, an' t'ain't 'Frisco either, but I can hold it down all right. **1910** J. Hart *Vigilante Girl* 325 He looked around that squalid burg with an expression of distaste. It was a typical decaying mining camp.

Burgaire: see Bergère.

+**Burgall,** variant of Bergall. — **1859** Bartlett 58 Burgall, (*Ctenolabrus ceruleus*), a small fish, very common in New York; also found on the coast of New England, and as far south as Delaware Bay. The usual length is about six inches, though they are sometimes found twelve inches.

+**Burgaloo.** [Corruption of *Virgoulée,* a French village.] The white doyenne, a variety of pear. — **1848** Bartlett 84 *Burgaloo,* a kind of pear. **1871** De Vere 109 We call the fine pear *Virgalieu* by the more convenient name of *Burgaloo.*

Burgamot, Burgamy: see Bergamot, Bergamy.

Burgee. [Of obscure origin.] A small tapered flag, triangular or swallow-tailed, used by cutters, yachts, or similar vessels. {1848-} — **1750** *Boston Post Boy* 18 June 2/1 They unfortunately left their Burgee flying at their Mast-head. **a1859** *Southern Sketches* 73 (B.), A large burgee was streaming out from the topmast-head. **1890** *Harper's Mag.* Sept. 596/1 'The topmast truck where flew the burgee with the field of blue,' as the fo'c's'le poet tunefully sings.

* **Burgess.**

+**1.** Formerly a member of a state legislative body, esp. in Maryland and Virginia.

1619 *Va. Ho. of Burgesses* 3 Every man [should] . . . pay into the hands . . . of the burgess one pound of the best tobacco . . . to be distributed to the speaker. **1638** *Md. Archives* I. 6 The choice of Robert Philpott, Gent., to be one of the Burgesses for the freemen of that Iland. **1666** Alsop *Maryland* ii. (1902) 47 Burgesses, . . . commonly sit in Junto about six weeks, being for the most part good ordinary Householders of the several Counties. **1676** P. Ludwell in *Va. Mag.* I. 183 He . . . presently drawes up his men before the state house door where the Governor, Councell & Burgesses were sitting. **1748** Washington *Diaries* I. 6 We reached as far as Major Campbells one of there [= their] Burgesses about 25 Miles from Town. **1775** Fithian *Journal* II. 14 Before dinner, Col. Isaac Zane, burgess for this county, came to the store. **1788** Franklin *Autobiog.* 374 The citizens at large chose me a burgess to represent them in Assembly.

+**2.** A representative on a local governing body; a councilor or magistrate. *Chief burgess* (see quot. 1889).

a1821 C. Biddle *Autobiog.* 194 Being Chief Burgess of the borough, I attended, and rode near the prisoner, who marched with great firmness. **1842** *S. Lit. Messenger* VIII. 6/2 He [H. H. Brackenridge] yielded . . . on condition that he should be accompanied by four or five of the citizens, the Chief Burgess among the rest. **1889** *Cent.* 725/2 In Connecticut boroughs the *board of burgesses* corresponds to the township board or board of trustees in some other States, or to the common council of a city. The chief executive officer of a Pennsylvanian borough is called the *chief burgess.*

Burgh, +occas. variant of Burg. — **1845** Sol. Smith *Theatrical Apprent.* 151 It so happened that the stranger who had played poker with us, also disembarked at the same burgh. **1884** 'Craddock' *Where Battle Was Fought* 292 You haven't heard the news from our little burgh. **1901** Ryan *Montana* 114 Well, I think I'll rest my weary body in this 'burgh' for a few weeks to come.

Burgher, †Burger.

+**1.** One of the early Dutch inhabitants of New York.

1677 *N.Y. State Col. Hist.* XII. 576 The Court have ordered that the Burgers in gennerall bee called together. **1809** Irving *Knickerb.* vii. ix, The ancient burghers contended who should have the privilege of bearing the pall. **1830** Cooper *Water Witch* III. 69 Day had dawned on the industrious burghers of Manhattan.

* **2.** A citizen; a townsman.

1837 *S. Lit. Messenger* III. 412 Who have had the advantage to visit the land of the pilgrim fathers—and partake . . . of the elegant hospitality of the burghers of Boston. **1899** Tarkington *Gentleman Ind.* 263 This bald, middle-aged young man, not without elegance, yet a prosperous burgher for all that.

Burglar alarm.

1. A contrivance designed to make known the presence of a burglar. {1884-}

1840 in M. D. Leggett ed. *Index of Patents for Inventions* (1874) 173 Burglar-alarm, L. E. Denison, Saybrook, Conn., Oct. 22, 1840, 1,835. **1868** *Mich. Agric. Rep.* VII. 363 Geo. S. Aker, Kalamazoo, [exhibited] 1 burglar alarm. **1876** Ingram *Centennial Exp.* 297 An improved electric burglar alarm was . . . exhibited. **1902** MacGowan *Last Word* 73, I suppose they could only have . . . connected you with a fire and burglar alarm, and hoped for the best.

+**2.** An alarm of burglary conveyed to the police.

1899 T. Hall *Tales* 116, I am going to send the burglar-alarm and have you arrested.

+**Burglarize,** *v.*

1. *tr.* To steal by burglary.

1871 *Southern Mag.* April (De Vere), The Yankeeisms donated, collided, and burglarized, have been badly used up by an English magazine writer. **1872** *Sacramento Union* 24 Feb. (Hoppe), Ovens had a pair of boots burglarized from his residence the other evening.

2. To break into (a house, etc.) and rob.

1876 *Congress. Rec.* 6 July 4419/2 The house of a lady moving in good society had been burglarized and articles of the value of several hundred dollars stolen from her. **1884** *Milnor* (Dakota) *Teller* 13 June, The prisoner is Lyman C. Burke who helped burglarize the postoffice at Luverne, Minn., on the 16th inst. **1887** *Troy* (N.Y.) *Times* 19 March, Another daring crime by sacrilegious hands is reported in the burglarizing of St. Stephen's church. **1894** *Congress. Rec.* Aug. 8350/1 The gentleman is speaking of a case where the post office was burglarized. **1920** C. R. Cooper *Under Big Top* 127 Residents of the neighborhood began to complain that their houses were being burglarized.

3. *intr.* To practice burglary.

1888 *Merchant Traveler* (F.), 'What have you been doing for a living lately?' asked a very tough looking citizen of a man who looked as if he might be a boon companion. 'Burglarizing.'

+**Burglarizing,** *vbl. n.* [f. prec.] The practice of burglary. — **1871** De Vere 655 In like manner the burglar's occupation has been designated as burglarizing.

Burglarproof, *a.* Affording security against burglars. {1882-} — **1856** *Spirit of Times* (N.Y.) 13 Dec. 247/3 Also manufacturers of the Alarm Patent Fire and Burglar Proof Safes for stores and dwelling houses. **1859** *Programme* (N.Y.) 7 Feb. 4 Wilder's patent salamander safes, secured with the best patent powder and burglar-proof locks. **1861** *Chicago Tribune* 15 April 1 Fire and burglarproof safes. **1871** *Harper's Mag.* Oct. 657 They revel in . . . treating the 'patent, compound, burglar-proof padlocks' with infinite scorn.

Burgle, *v. colloq.*[2] [f. Burglar.] *tr.* and *intr.* To burglarize. {1872-} — **1870** *Philadelphia Press* 15 March, Robbed. The Waverly National Bank burgled. **1871** De Vere 587 *Burglarize* . . . has a dangerous rival in the shorter *burgle.* **1879** *Indian Daily Mail* 7 Oct., [A] business-like American on leaving the city . . . placed a placard just inside the hall-door, couched in the following language.—'To burglars or those intending to burgle.' **1882** Peck *Sunshine* 156 You would almost rather let her go ahead and burgle. **1887** *Courier-Journal* 16 Feb. 5/5 Cleveland Burglars Still Burgling.

* **Burgomaster.**

+**1.** The chief magistrate in New Amsterdam or other Dutch settlement. Also attrib.

1664 *Penna. Archives* I. 25 If the Fort [in N.Y.] be not capable of lodging all the soldiers then the Burgomaster by his Officers shall appoint some houses capable to receive them. **1665** *Doc. Hist. N.Y. State* (1849) I. 603, I have thought it necessary to revoke & discharge the fforme and Ceremony of Government of this his Ma[jes]ties Towne of New Yorke, under the name or names, . . . of Scout, Burgomasters & Schepens. **1809** Irving *Knickerb.* III. ii, The burgomasters, like our aldermen, were generally chosen by weight. **1858** Vielé *Following the Drum* 247 The impetuosity of his Creole blood contending with . . . the stolidity of his burgomaster ancestors. **1865** *Atlantic Mo.* XV. 76/1 Trade with the savages, . . . a seat among the burgomasters, the feast of St. Nicholas . . . , —these were the joys which allured the earliest New-Yorkers to the island [of Manhattan].

2. The glaucous gull, *Larus glaucus.* {1678-}

1858 BAIRD *Birds Pacific R.R.* 842 Burgomaster. . . . New York in winter, rarely. 1874 COUES *Birds N.W.* 620 Glaucous Gull; Burgomaster . . . [comes] south in winter on the Atlantic coast of North America to Long Island. 1884 C. THAXTER *Poems for children* 9 The little auk Brings tidings that benumbs, . . . 'The Burgomaster comes!'

Burgoo, Burgou(t).

1. A thick gruel or porridge of oatmeal, chiefly used at sea. {1750-}

1787 FRENEAU *Misc. Works* 426 If I had him at sea, . . . I'd burn out his guts with a bowl of burgoo! 1828 A. SHERBURNE *Memoirs* v. 112 We had a mess of what is called burgoo, or mush, (the Yankee would call it hasty pudding). 1835 COOPER *Monikins* xiii, He proceeded to make experiments on their abilities . . . in mixing the various compounds of burgoo, lobscouse, and dough.

+**2.** *S.* and *S.W.* A soup of meat and vegetables, highly seasoned and served very hot. Also attrib.

'Popular in Kentucky and other places, especially at barbecues, picnics, and other outdoor feasts' (*Cent.*).

1853 MCCONNEL *Western Char.* 363 Around a burgou pot, or along the trenches of an impromptu barbecue, he shone in meridian splendor. *Note.* A kind of soup, made by boiling all sorts of game with corn, onions, tomatoes, and a variety of other vegetables. When skilfully concocted and properly seasoned, not at all unsavory. So called from a soup made by seamen. 1882 *Congress. Rec.* 22 June 5229/2 The fatted calf—the Kentucky ox—was killed for the returning prodigals. They were feasted on Bourbon and burgoo. 1886 *Century Mag.* Nov. 32/2 The young State swarmed with politicians . . . ; around the burgoo-pot of the hunting party they discussed measures and candidates. 1892 ALLEN *Blue-Grass Region* 43 Woods where . . . the steaming kettles of burgoo lend their savor to the nose of the hungry political orator. 1906 PITTMAN *Belle of Blue Grass C.* 272 The old-timers smacked their lips as they scented, in fancy, the odor of the barbecued meats, and tasted the burgout—delights unknown for more than a decade of years.

+**b.** (See quotation.)

1885 *Mag. Amer. Hist.* Jan. 98/2 *Burgoo.*—A Southern and Southwestern term akin to barbecue (*q.v.*). The feast, however, was furnished by hunters and fishermen—everything, fish, flesh, and fowl, being compounded into a vast stew. After this was disposed of, speeches were made, if the meeting was to have a political character.

+**Burgoynade.** *Obs.* [Cf. next.] A capture or seizure like that of Burgoyne. — 1779 *S.C. Gazette* 3 March, Col. Campbell's expedition from Savannah to Augusta . . . has proved as unfortunate as Major Gardner's to Port Royal; to escape a Burgoynade he has made a very sudden and precipitate retreat down the country. 1780 in *Mag. Amer. Hist.* V. 379 Our affairs to the Southward look blue. So they did when you took the command before the Burgoynade.

Burgoyne, *v. Obs.* [From the name of Gen. John *Burgoyne*, captured at Saratoga in 1777.] *tr.* To capture; to take prisoner. — 1777 *N.J. Archives* 2 Ser. I. 531 Our army by this time, 'tis hoped have come up with them, and will either have him Burgoyned or driven off. 1780 in *Mag. Amer. Hist.* V. 137 With these troops he [Gen. Gates] intended to have Burgoyned us, according to his own term. 1782 TRUMBULL *M'Fingal* (1785) IV, The Briton's startled pride Sees . . . all his troops to fate consign'd, By instantaneous stroke Burgoyned. 1787 *New Haven Gazette* 8 March 22/3 (Th. S.), Help us to burgoyn Lincoln and his army. 1807 *N.Y. Weekly Inspector*, New Year's address (Th.), Brag if you please, but I'll be shot If you'll Burgoyne a Bernadott.'

Bur grass, Burr grass. Any grass of the species *Cenchrus;* hedgehog grass. {1834} — 1829 EATON *Botany* (ed. 5) 165. 1843 TORREY *Flora N.Y.* II. 431 *Cenchrus tribuloides*, . . . Bur-grass, Hedgehog Grass, . . . [is] a troublesome weed in some places, on account of the adhering prickly burs. 1847 DARLINGTON *Weeds & Plants* 406 Bur Grass, Hedgehog Grass, . . . is very abundant in sandy districts along the coast and around the great Lakes,—and has found its way to some of the slaty hills of Pennsylvania. 1871 *Amer. Naturalist* IV. 690 Bur-grass is to be found only beyond the limits of New England. 1894 COULTER *Bot. W. Texas* III. 510 *Cenchrus* (Bur-grass,) . . . [has] spines minutely barbed backward, causing the burs to stick to anything with which they come in contact.

+**Burial case.** A coffin made of metal.

1851 CIST *Cincinnati* 191 Foundery castings.—This . . . is carried on in every possible variety, in which iron can be cast, from a butt hinge to a burial case. 1853 *Mich. Agric. Soc. Trans.* IV. 108 Stevens & Tug, Detroit, two metallic burial cases, a valuable improvement. 1854 *Penna. Agric. Rep.* 422 The Metalic Burial Cases of all colors and sizes, attracted much notice, being a new article for sepulture that has been recently introduced by this very enterprising firm. *c*1870 'MARK TWAIN' *Sketches* Wks. XIX. 259, I am talking about your high-toned, silver mounted burial-case. 1875 *Chicago Tribune* 26 July 7/6 Patent Metallic Burial Cases and Caskets of Cast and Sheet Metal. 1891 *Harper's Mag.* Dec. 50/1, I was interested in a large concern for the manufacture of patent metallic burial cases.

+**Burial casket.** [Cf. CASKET.] A burial case or coffin. Also attrib. — 1866 *Comm. Patents Rep.* I. 676 Removing from the side of a coffin or burial casket . . . so much of its front side as is required to sufficiently expose the person of the corpse. 1892 *Vt. Agric. Rep.* XII. 114 At Bristol there is the largest burial casket manufactory in New England. 1892 *Harper's Mag.* March 506/2 A dog-cariole of the best pattern—a little suggestive of a burial casket, to be sure.

Burial ground. A place set apart for burial; a burying ground, cemetery. {1803-}

1775 C. MARSHALL *Diary* (1877) 49 Went . . . to attend the funeral of Peyton Randolph . . . then proceeded to Christ's Church . . . then to Church Burial Ground. 1808 *Ann. 10th Congress* 2 Sess. 501 A law . . . authorizing the petitioners to raise [$12,000 for] . . . the purchase of a burial ground. 1825 NEAL *Bro. Jonathan* I. 126 It had been, a nursery; it was now, a burial ground;—a place of common sepulture. 1838 HAWTHORNE *Note-Books* I. 71 A large, rusty-looking edifice of wood . . . standing on the banks of the river, close by the site of an old burial ground. 1843 *Knickerb.* XXI. 228, I never saw a more perfect picture of beautiful repose than that small church and burial-ground. 1851 *Harper's Mag.* July 276/2 No religious sect or teacher, as such, without express legislative permission can receive any gift or sale of land, except five acres for a Church, Parsonage, or burial-ground. 1865 *Atlantic Mo.* XV. 6 The swinging gate communicated with the burial-ground. 1875 *Scribner's Mo.* July 269/2 The new City Hall, on the site of the ancient burial-ground, will . . . cost at least five millions of dollars. 1898 PAGE *Red Rock* 65 A great plantation, with a big rock by a burial-ground, and a red stain on it, said to be an Indian's blood.

+**Burial lot.** A private plot in a cemetery. — 1833 *Knickerb.* II. 259 The whole of this extensive area is laid off in burial lots which were offered by the original proprietors for sale. 1915 *Kansas Stat.* §2270 [Cemetery corporations are] hereby empowered to acquire and hold lands for cemetery purposes . . . and to divide said lands into burial lots.

+**Burial permit.** A certificate issued by the proper authorities granting permission to bury. — 1888 *St. Louis Globe Democrat* (F.), Yesterday's Burial Permits. 1908 *Daily Chron.* 22 May 1/3 The case . . . has developed sensational features through the refusal of the authorities [at Brooklyn] to grant a burial permit. 1924 A. L. H. STREET *Amer. Funeral Law* 208 The local registrar . . . shall take up the transit and removal permit and issue a burial permit.

Burial place. A place for burial; a cemetery. {1633-}

1639 *Essex Inst. Coll.* IX. 86 It is ordered that John Horne shall desist from his inclosure in the buryall place. 1668 *Manchester Rec.* 9 Sum Ground that they make use of for a bureall place which was Samuell Friend owne land. 1686 SEWALL *Diary* I. 121 Snow very deep; so in the new burial place 3 paths [were made]. 1821 COOPER *Spy* xiv, The graveyard . . . was not, however, intended as a burial-place for any of his own family. 1872 *Atlantic Mo.* Feb. 185 The place was, long after, enclosed and made the burial-place of the Jeffersons. 1905 *Indian Laws & Tr.* III. 145 Lot numbered four [is] . . . reserved . . . as a perpetual burial place for the Mille Lac Indians.

Burial yard. A cemetery, burial ground. {1842} — 1815 *Mass. H. S. Coll.* 2 Ser. IV. 72 On the hill in Dover, upon which is the burial yard, and near it, a crack . . . was said to have been discovered soon after this earthquake. 1830 *Collegian* 119, I . . . snatched a short look at the beautiful burial-yard.

+**Burion.** The house finch. — 1858 BAIRD *Birds Pacific R.R.* 415. 1889 *Cent.* 832/1 The burion or house-finch of the southwestern United States is *Carpodacus frontalis.*

Burlesque. +A theatrical entertainment comprising various singing, dancing and dialogue turns and featuring women in tights and scanty costumes. Also attrib.

1870 O. LOGAN *Before Footlights* 563 There are numberless people . . . who are utterly unable to see any difference in decency between the dancing of a ballet-girl and the caperings of a jigging burlesque woman. 1895 *N.Y. Dramatic News* 12 Oct. 5/3 Mr. Jack has the only burlesque show in town [*sc.* Chicago]. 1896 *Ib.* 11 Jan. 4/1 The courts . . . gave up in despair attempting to decide whether this choice mosaic was a comic opera or a burlesque. *Ib.* 7/2 Ada Dare, as the burlesque queen, was very acceptable.

Burlesquer. +An actor in (a) burlesque. — 1870 O. LOGAN *Before Footlights* 535 Our blonde burlesquers make a pretense of respecting public opinion, and offer 'appeals to the public.' 1895 *N.Y. Dramatic News* 9 Nov. 13/1 Many of the most noted burlesquers have been given their first opportunity by Mr. Jack. 1896 *Ib.* 4 July 11/2 Belle Black, the shapely burlesquer, is due at the Pleasure Palace next week.

+**Burley.** A variety of tobacco grown in Kentucky and neighboring states. — 1881 in B. W. Arnold *Tobacco Ind.* (1897) 35 The White Burley produced in the West has now thoroughly substituted our dark grades. 1900 *Dept. Agric. Yearbook* 435 The White Burley is entirely air cured, except in exceedingly damp weather, when wood fires may be used. 1909 *Cent. Suppl.* 177/1 *Burley*, a well known American variety of tobacco, having two subvarieties, red and white.

Burlington. A city in New Jersey noted for various products. In various attrib. uses: (see quotations). — 1777 CRESSWELL *Journal* 264. The Jerseys . . . are famous for Hams, which go under the name of Burlington Hams and are esteemed the best in the world. 1817 W. COXE *Fruit Trees* 129 Jersey, or Rhode-Island Greening. Sometimes called the Burlington Greening. 1817 *Ib.* 126 Newton Spitzenberg. This apple is in some parts of this State called the English, or Burlington Spitzenberg: it was brought from Newton on Long-Island. 1818 *Amer. Mo. Mag.* II. 428/2 Table Apples [include] . . . 16. Burlington Greening, October and November.

Bur marigold. Beggar-ticks; a species of *Bidens* with conspicuous yellow flowers. {1879}

1817-8 EATON *Botany* (1822) 205 *Bidens frondosa*, burr-marygold. 1821 *Mass. H. S. Coll.* 2 Ser. IX. 147 *Bidens cernua*, Water-beggar-ticks.

[*B.*] *frondosa*, Burr-mary-gold. **1847** DARLINGTON *Weeds & Plants* 183 Bur-marigold . . . is apt to be quite abundant in gardens, Indian-corn fields, &c. and if permitted to mature its fruit, becomes very annoying. **1870** *Amer. Naturalist* IV. 43 Larger Bur-Marigold . . . [grows] to the prodigious height of from six to eight and two-thirds feet. **1882** *Wheelman* I. 113 A gleam of gold . . : proceeds from a group of bur-marigolds sometimes, though wrongly, called the dwarf sunflower. **1892** COULTER *Bot. W. Texas.* II. 223 Bur-Marigold . . . [grows in] wet grounds, from Canada to South America.

* **Burn,** *n.*

+**1.** A burning-up, conflagration.

1847 ROBB *Squatter Life* 149 Here's a whole account of how the world is going to be destroyed this April.—Every thing has been counted up by Father Miller, and the sum total's a general *burn!*

+**2.** An instance of burning the vegetation on land as a means of clearing it for cultivation.

1861 *Ill. Agric. Soc. Trans.* IV. 489, I considered two crops of small grain equal to a burn. **1872** *Vt. Bd. Agric. Rep.* I. 350 Mr. Hovey . . . spoke of the injury resulting from heavy burns in clearing land, which destroyed the soil. **1874** *Ib.* II. 455 This land is not very difficult to clear, although a good burn is rare.

+**3.** A place where the trees, brush, etc., have been burned; a clearing in the woods or on the prairie resulting from this.

1846 FARNHAM *Prairie Land* 170 The prairies faded from their rich green, save where here and there a 'late burn' showed the tender grass. **1868** *Amer. Naturalist* Oct. 468 They [*sc.* deer] resort always to a recent burn, when grass and weeds are just shooting again and are soft. **1885** *Century Mag.* April 835 These 'burns' are marked features of Cascade Mountain scenery. The name is applied to a strip of plateau or mountain-side where a fire has ravaged the forest. **1920** HUNTER *Trail Drivers of Texas* I. 274 We escaped by fleeing to a part of the plain which had been burned before, called 'a burn' by people of that section.

* **Burn,** *v.*

1. *tr.* To clear the surface of (ground) for cultivation by burning the grass, weeds, etc., growing on it. {1669–} Also absol.

1631 *Mass. Bay Rec.* I. 90 Noe person . . . shall burne any ground any yeare till the first of March. **1637** *Essex Inst. Coll.* IV. 115/1 Mr. Verrin shall have libertie to cutt 3 load of hay grasse . . . provided that he burne all the marshe thereabout. **1651** *Southampton Rec.* I. 78 It is ordered that for this present year men have liberty to burn their meadows, at any time henceforward. **1754** J. J. FRIIS *Diary* 22 May, I planted Indian Corn, & then I began to the 24th to burn in my Tobacco plantation. **1774** *N.H. Hist. Soc. Coll.* IX. 78 The Wett ever since last Winter . . . has wholly prevented the burning the Lands which I have cleard. **1864** [see BURNT LAND].

2. To obtain or produce (tar or lime) by the use of fire.

1652 *Springfield Rec.* I. 205 To the end that such Candlewood as lyeth neere the Towne may not be wasted, by such as burne Tarr. **1653** JOHNSON *Wonder-w. Providence* 194 The country affords no Lime, but what is burnt of Oyster-shels.

3. a. To clean (a cask) by the application of flame.

1701 *Boston Rec.* 10 No cooper or coopers within this Town shall fire or burn thier cask in any Shop, ware house, or other place, then in a sufficient Chimney made convenient for that use.

* **b.** To brand (a person) as a punishment.

1671 *Plymouth Laws* 249 If any person shall Forge any deed or conveyance, . . . he shall pay the party grieved double damages, and be fined himself so much to the Countries use, and if he cannot pay to be publickly whipt and burned in the face with a Roman F. **1705** *Boston News-Letter* 30 April 2/2 Upon full evidence he was found guilty [of stealing], & burnt in the left cheek near the nose with the letter T. **1784** *Conn. Acts & Laws* 8 Both of them [=adulterers] shall be . . . burnt on the Forehead with the Letter A, on a hot Iron.

+**c.** *To burn powder*, to use or expend ammunition; to fire shots.

1775 *Md. Hist. Mag.* V. 159 Atkinson said he intended to burn powder that day. **1785** in *Amer. Museum* V. 578/1 The principal officers . . . were employed in preparing and ordering an expensive entertainment, for spectators and officers, while the soldiers were left to burn powder to no purpose.

d. *dial.* To roast (coffee).

1842 *Lowell Offering* II. 137 What! going to burn coffee now? We shan't have breakfast today.

4. In passive with *out:* To be forced out of one's house or premises by a destructive fire. {1710} Also attrib.

'It is hardly proper to say, that such a man was ruined by being *burned up*; . . . it should be . . . "burned out" '(B. '59).

1711 *Boston News-Letter* 19 Nov. 2/2 Mr. John Kilby that kept Shop in Cornhill Boston, . . . was burnt out in the late Fire. **1727** J. COMER *Diary* (1923) 16 My mother was then burn[t] out and was like to have lost her life. **1759** *Essex Inst. Coll.* XLV. 348 Four Families were burnt out and but few of their Goods saved. **1851** CIST *Cincinnati* 250 Henry Albro, who was burnt out some months since, on Front street, has recently put up new veneer and saw mills. *a***1861** WINTHROP *J. Brent* 7 They had been burnt out, they had been cleaned out, they had been drowned out. **1872** *Chicago Tribune* 16 Oct. 3/3 The burned-out merchants are going to erect temporary shanties on their old sites, and resume business immediately. **1891** O'BEIRNE *Leaders Ind. Territory* 36/2 Three years afterwards he was burned out and moved to Perryville.

* **5.** *intr.* **a.** Of vegetation: To become withered or dried up from excessive heat or sun. Also with *off*, *up*. {–1750}

1770 *Md. Hist. Mag.* XII. 368 We want Rain for our Corn, tobacco & Pastures, the last begin to burn. **1861** *Ill. Agric. Soc. Trans.* IV. 456 The difficulty is 'damping off,' and this is oftener the trouble in experiments that have come under his notice, than 'burning off.' **1865** *Nation* I. 366 The blades [of the corn], in great quantities, were burning up on the stalk.

b. Of damp substances: To generate heat and be affected by it.

1873–4 *Vt. Bd. Agric. Rep.* II. 244, I use sheep manure. . . . Pile it up and let it heat well, but not so as to burn white.

6. *tr.* To swindle, cheat. {1808–, *Sc.*}

1844 *Spirit of Times* (Phila.) 19 Aug. (Th.), Two negro burners were arrested in the act of trying to burn two Pottsville boatmen with a plated chain worth about fifteen cents.

+**7.** *To have* (money, time, etc.) *to burn*, to have abundance of.

1897 *Congress. Rec.* 27 March 400/1 Mr. Simpson of Kansas. You have plenty of time. Mr. Payne. No; I have not got time 'to burn.' **1904** *Courier-Journal* 2 July 5 She has . . . already had literary experience to burn. **1911** QUICK *Yellowstone N.* 240 The gall of my swearing against these big men that had money to burn.

+**8.** *To burn the earth* or *wind*, to go at full speed.

1891 'THANET' *Otto the Knight*, etc. 219 An' we all ayfter 'im, hollerin' with all the power. . . . Didn't he burn the wind, though! **1903** ADAMS *Log Cowboy* 23, I was half a mile in the lead, burning the earth like a canned dog. **1910** RAINE *B. O'Connor* 57 When he finds out how the horse he's after is burning the wind, his suspicions grow stronger.

+**Burned piece.** [BURN *v.* 1.] A piece of ground cleared for cultivation by burning. — **1860** *Harper's Mag.* Feb. 290/2 Here was a fellow who had come . . . twenty miles to see the circus. He had left his 'burned-piece' just in the nick of time.

Burner. *slang.* [BURN *v.* 6] A swindler, pickpocket, thief. — **1838** *Lexington Observer* 3 Nov., He pulls out his pocket book, it is seized by the burner who makes off with it. **1842** *Spirit of Times* (Phila.) 15 Jan. (Th.), The burners make better plots than most of our dramatists. **1845** *Congress. Globe* App. 6 Jan. 118/1 The Empire Club of New York . . . consisted of gamblers, pickpockets, droppers, burners, thimble-riggers and the like. **1859** MATSELL *Vocabulum* 16 *Burners*, rogues who cheat countrymen with false cards or dice.

* **Burnet.** * **a.** The garden herb and forage plant (*Poterium sanguisorba*); common burnet. +**b.** The American species (*P. Canadense*); wild or Canadian burnet.

1709 LAWSON *Carolina* 77 Our pot-herbs and others of use . . . are . . . borage, burnet, clary, marigold [etc.]. **1784** CUTLER in *Mem. Academy* I. 410 *Sanguisorba* . . . American Burnet, Snakeweed. . . . Its growth is generally luxuriant, and makes good fodder for cattle. **1786** WASHINGTON *Diaries* III. 34 Began to plow a piece of grd. in the Neck for Burnet, Saint foin, and Rib grass. **1804** J. ROBERTS *Penn. Farmer* 50 Burnet is a hardy grass, and will stand the frost and severity of the winter. **1843** TORREY *Flora N.Y.* I. 205 *Sanguisorba Canadensis*. . . . American Great Burnet. . . . Wet meadows. Common. **1868** GRAY *Botany* 680 *Poterium Sanguisorba*, Garden Burnet, . . . [grows in] fields and rocks, near Baltimore.

attrib. **1770** *Md. Hist. Mag.* XII. 353, I suppose Coll Sharpe does not want any more Burnet seed. **1840** DEWEY *Mass. Flowering Plants* 53 Burnet Saxifrage . . . grows in wet meadows. **1855** BROWNE in *Trans. Amer. Inst. N.Y.* 620 Burnet Grass, or Pimprenelle, [is] . . . an annual from France, well suited for pasturage on poor dry soils.

* **Burning,** *vbl. n.*

* **1.** The process of obtaining tar by the distillation of pine timber.

1646 *Springfield Rec.* I. 187 Jno. Clarke or those that shall joyne with him in the burninge of tarr.

2. Preparing land by fire for the better growing of grass or for cultivation. {1669–}

1634 WOOD *New Eng. Prospect* I. 8 Where it was all blacke by reason of Winters burnings, in a fortnight there will be Grasse a foote high. **1825** J. LORAIN *Pract. Husbandry* 335 Wheat, or any other small grain, except oats, however, seldom prospers after corn or potatoes, when the grounds have been cleared by burning in the Yankee way. **1832** Z. ALLEN *Practical Tourist* I. 263 From the summit of some commanding hill, the smoke of a score of burnings, as they are termed, may be sometimes seen.

3. An area cleared of underbrush, debris, etc., by fire.

1830 J. F. WATSON *Philadelphia* 53 The 'clearings' and the 'burnings' of the 'brushwood' and 'undergrowth,' had begun to mark, in rude lines, the originals of the present paved and stately streets. **1902** WHITE *Blazed Trail* x. 77 Down in the swamp the covey of partridges were beginning to hope that in a few days more they might discover a bare spot in the burnings.

*Burning ague. A form of ague. — a1672 BRADSTREET *Poems* (1897) 334 For the Restoration of My Dear Husband from a Burning Ague, June, 1661. 1822 E. PETTIGREW *Let. to Ann Pettigrew* 10 Sept. (Pettigrew P.), My complaint is something of what they call the burning ague, every day alike.

Burning bush. {1866–}

+1. The spindle tree, *Euonymus americanus* or *E. atropurpureus.*

1785 MARSHALL *Amer. Grove* 45 Ever-green Spindle Tree. From their [=its fruit's] red appearance [it] obtained the name of the Burning Bush. 1817–8 EATON *Botany* (1822) 276 *Euonymus americanus*, burning bush. . . . Fruit red. Said to grow in New England. 1843 TORREY *Flora N.Y.* I. 141 Burning-bush, Indian arrow, . . . [grows in] moist woods and along rivers in the western part of the State. 1881 *Harper's Mag.* March 522/2 A mass of the euonymus or burning-bush with its scarlet autumn seed-vessels is a thing to be remembered. 1897 SUDWORTH *Arborescent Flora* 281 *Evonymus atropurpureus*, Waahoo, . . . common names [include] Burning Bush [in 18 states], . . . 'Moses in the Burning Bush' (N.J.).

+2. The bittersweet.

1893 M. A. OWEN *Old Rabbit*, etc. 71 He hid himself in a thicket of plums and burning bush (bittersweet).

Burning fluid. Camphine; purified oil of turpentine, freq. with added alcohol. — 1855 *Mass. Acts & Resolves* 903 Establishments for the manufacture of camphene or burning fluid. 1864 *U.S. Statutes* XIII. 272 Be it further enacted, that . . . malt, burning fluid, printers' ink [etc.] . . . shall be . . . exempt from duty. 1887 *Courier-Journal* 16 Jan. 14/2 We used 'burning fluid' and camphine lamps in those days.

+**Burning ground.** Among the Indians, a place where executions by burning took place. — 1847 in Howe *Hist. Coll. Ohio* 404 The burning-ground, in the suburbs of Grenadier Squawtown, represented in the map, was also situated on an elevated spot. . . . The burning-ground at Old Chillicothe was somewhat similar, being in full view of the burning-ground at Squawtown.

Burning mountain. A volcanic mountain. — 1805 LEWIS in *L. & Clark Exped.* (1905) VI. 163, I can hear of no burning mountain in the neighborhood of the Missouri or its Branches. *Ib.* 164 The tract of Country which furnishes the Pummice Stone seen floating down the Missouri, is rather burning or burnt plains than burning mountains. 1828 WEBSTER, *Volcano* . . . is vulgarly called 'a burning mountain.'

+**Burning spring.** A spring whose waters are so impregnated with inflammable gas or oil that they appear to burn when the gas is ignited. — 1819 SCHOOLCRAFT *Mo. Lead Mines* 216 A phenomenon . . . under the name of a *burning spring*, exists on one of the principal forks of Licking River, Kentucky. 1827 MCKENNEY *Tour to Lakes* 84, I had no time to stop and take a look at the burning springs, not far from Canandaigua. 1835 MARTIN *Descrip. Va.* 25 Among them [=Va. curiosities] may be enumerated: . . . The various medicinal springs already noticed;—and the burning springs of Kanawha. 1843 *Nat. Hist. N.Y., Geology* IV. 309 Sometimes the gas alone is the only product; and in others it is accompanied by petroleum, or liquid bitumen, which spreads over the surface of the water, and can be collected in considerable quantities. These are the 'burning springs.'

+**Burnside.** [Named after Gen. A. E. *Burnside* (1824–1881).] Used attrib. to denote: **a.** A kind of hat. **b.** (See quot. 1909.) Also ellipt. — (a) 1866 'F. KIRKLAND' *Bk. Anecdotes* 169 A stalwart descendant of the Nubian race, . . . his Burnside hat surmounted with a feeble plagiarism of the 'Prince's feather.' (b) 1900 J. C. HARRIS *On the Wing* 156 A tall man with Burnside whiskers. 1907 *Outing* L. 279 [The] rounded wooden blocks . . . were adorned with such various patterns of ornamental whiskers as the 'Piccadilly Weeper' (No. 2), the 'Burnside,' etc. 1909 *Cent. Suppl.* 177/3 *Burnsides*, . . . a style of beard such as that affected by General Burnside (1824–81), consisting of a mustache, whiskers, and a clean-shaven chin.

*Burnt, *ppl. a.* [BURN *v.* 1.] Of ground: Cleared by intentional or accidental burning. See also BURNT LAND.

1718 *N.H. Probate Rec.* II. 5, I give and bequeath to my sons John and Benjamin Green . . . my land in the burnt swamp. 1741 *Ib.* III. 48, I give . . . part of my Land at a place called Burnt Swamp. 1801 *Austin Papers* (1924) I. 70 At the lower end of the Burnt Woods you pass an Island. 1880 *Harper's Mag.* Aug. 344/2 Whatever had happened to justify it, the prefix 'burnt' was very common. He came now . . . to Burnt Thoroughfare, and presently . . . to Burnt Cove.

Burnt brandy. Brandy from which some of the alcohol has been removed by burning. {1880–} — 1829 J. MACTAGGART *Three Years* I. 213 They are often troubled with a kind of dysentery, for which they swallow burnt-brandy and pepper. 1836 CROCKETT *Adventures* 18 It must be done soon, or even burnt brandy wouldn't save me. 1868 CHANNING *Recoll. Newport* 250 There were a few persons . . .—who indulged, as they smoked, in drinking 'burnt brandy.'

Burnt cork. 1. A material used esp. for blacking the faces of 'negro' minstrels. +2. =BLACK-FACE 2. Chiefly attrib. — (1) 1880 E. JAMES *Negro Minstrel's Guide* 4 Prepared burnt cork, ready for use, 25 and 50 cents per box. (2) *Ib.* 10 A pair of legs such as Nelse Seymour had and Cool Burgess has are great attractions in a burnt-cork artist. 1895 *Century Mag.* May 156/2 If any one who is acquainted with the average Southern negro stops to analyze the unpleasant impressions which the burnt-cork minstrel and the humorous publications make upon him. 1895 *N.Y. Dramatic News* 20 July 5/3 In the vaudeville there are no more amusing . . . features than those introduced by . . . versatile burnt cork comedians. 1895 *Ib.* 26 Oct. 13/4 He seems to have abandoned burnt cork. 1896 *Chicago Record* 12 Feb. 1/6 Give a female minstrel show. . . . The ladies of West Chicago gave their long-talked-of and much-opposed 'burnt cork' entertainment to-night.

+**Burnt district.** The part of a city destroyed by fire. — 1869 'MARK TWAIN' *Innocents* 328 The broken pillars lying about, . . . and the crumbled tops of the wilderness of walls, were wonderfully suggestive of the 'burnt district' in one of our cities. 1883 — *Life on Miss.* xli. 297, I think one would be able to tell the 'burnt district' by the radical improvement in its architecture over the old forms. One can do this in Boston and Chicago. 1889 FARMER 107 So frequent and devastating have been large fires in many of the cities of the Union that the term *burnt district* . . . has become quite familiar. 1904 G. WELLS *Life Dr. Wilson* 63 What the Americans call, in Western phrase, 'a burnt district.'

Burnt land. Land over which fire has swept, or which has been cleared for cultivation by burning. — 1811 *Niles' Reg.* I. 101/2 The burnt lands of many neighbourhoods could be employed advantageously for sheep walks. 1848 THOREAU *Maine Woods* 56 We . . . travelled up the north side, through burnt lands, now partially overgrown with young aspens. *Ib.* 70 We were passing over 'Burnt Lands,' burnt by lightning, perchance. 1864 *Maine Agric. Soc. Ret.* 25 Very little wheat is raised except on burnt land.

Burnt tongue. (See quotation.) — 1820 *Plough Boy* I. 255 The disease called the Burnt Tongue has lately made its appearance among the cattle in Baltimore county, Md.

Burnt-wood. =BRULÉ. — 1827 COOPER *Prairie* iv, 'Am I a fool not to know a burnt-wood Teton?' demanded the trapper. *Ib.* vii, You think to escape the craft and hatred of the burnt-wood Indians. a1848 RUXTON *Far West* (1849) 111 The Indians trading at this time on the Platte were mostly of the Sioux nation, including the tribes of Burnt-woods, Yanka-taus, Pian-Kashas [etc.].

Burnwood. **a.** =BUMWOOD. **b.** (See quotation.) — (a) 1889 *Cent.* 4588/1 *Poisonwood*, a small poisonous tree, *Rhus Metopium*, of the West Indies and southern Florida . . . [which is] also called *burnwood.* (b) 1897 SUDWORTH *Arborescent Flora* 277 *Cyrilla racemiflora.* Ironwood. . . . Common names [include] . . . He Huckleberry (N.C., S.C.), Burnwood (N.C.), Burnwood Bark (S.C.).

+**Bur oak, Burr oak.**

1. The overcup or mossy-cup oak, *Quercus macrocarpa.*

(*a*) 1815 DRAKE *Cincinnati* 82 The most valuable timber trees are the . . . white, black, low-land chesnut and bur oaks. 1831 PECK *Guide* ii. 122 The growth of the bottom lands [of Ill.] consists of black walnut, . . . several oaks—as, over cup, bur oak, [etc.]. 1856 *33d Congress 2 Sess.* Ho. Ex. Doc. No. 91, III. II. 20 In some of the bottoms, 'where the trees were of a more luxuriant growth,' he found 'the bur-oak.' 1875 *Amer. Naturalist* IX. 390 The bur, swamp and post oaks, are common in some localities [of Illinois]. 1905 *Bureau of Forestry Bul.* No. 66, 36 The bur oak is hardy, and probably lives to a greater age than any other broadleaf tree mentioned in this report.

(*b*) 1834 PECK *Gaz. Illinois* 23 Of oaks there are several species, as overcup, burr oak, swamp or water oak [etc.]. 1835 HOFFMAN *Winter in West* I. 218 A pile of burr-oak, which makes a capital fire, flames up the enormous wooden chimney before me. 1852 *Mich. Agric. Soc. Trans.* III. 179 The burr oak and the wild cherry were indigenous. 1878 *Rep. Indian Affairs* 162 It is quite well supplied with timber of good quality, principally burr and post oak, pecan [etc.].

2. Attrib. with *barren, opening, plain, tree.*

1835 HOFFMAN *Winter in West* I. 154, I struck a burr-oak opening. 1840 in *Mich. Agric. Soc. Trans.* VI. 275 Marl was examined . . . in a dry burr oak plain. 1849 CHAMBERLAIN *Ind. Gazetteer* 285 Still farther south, are burr oak barrens. . . . The burr oak barrens are very little inferior to the prairies in respect to soil. 1859 A. VAN BUREN *Sojourn in South* 320 Why, we have got prairie Illinois scattered all over Michigan besides the rich burr-oak plains. 1874 COLLINS *Kentucky* I. 177 A burr oak tree, cut on the farm . . . , measured 70 feet in length.

*Burr[1]. The external meatus of the ear. {–1730} — 1674 Alvord & Bidgood *Trans-Allegheny Region* 217 [He] shot Mr. Needham neare the burr of the eare. 1856 P. CARTWRIGHT *Autob.* 91, I struck a sudden blow in the burr of the ear and dropped him to the earth. 1899 GREEN *Va. Word-Book* 74 Burr of the ear.

Burr[2], Buhr. Also †*pl.* **burze.**

1. =BURRMILLSTONE, BURRSTONE. {1721–}

1652 *Dedham Rec.* III. 210 Things tendered to be sold . . . the mill itselfe, the mill house, the burze bought to make a new millstone, the pulleyes & Rope [etc.]. 1792 IMLAY *Western Territory* 123 Mill-stones, of a very good quality, which have been reckoned equal to French burrs. 1808 *Ann. 10th Congress* 2 Sess. 90 The preparation of mill-stones . . . was encouraged by permitting unwrought burrs to be imported from . . . France, free from imposts. 1834 *Jrnl. Science* XXV. 233 Millstones equal to the best French buhrs. 1851 CIST *Cincinnati* 182 The burrs, of which the millstones are composed, are imported from France, in cubes of about twelve inches average. 1883 *Harper's Mag.* June 77/1 In the old mill . . . there stood upon one side the usual row of buhrs, in this case twenty in number.

attrib. 1845 in *Cincinnati Misc.* 175 The mill is a square frame with four stout pillars, on which the mill stones, which are of burr blocks, cemented as usual, rest. 1864 *Ohio Agric. Rep.* XVIII. 77 The grinding surface of the Conical Burr Mill is made of the best imported French Burr stone.

||**2.** Flour ground by burr millstones.

1773 WASHINGTON *Writings* (1931) III. 109, I have now a vessell waiting ... to take in flour.... perhaps there may be about 200 barr'ls of super fine burr; 50 of midling do.

Burrass. [F. *bourras.*] Very coarse hempen cloth. {1807-} — **1770** *Carroll P.* in *Md. Hist. Mag.* XIII. 66 Pray write for 6 strong matrasses ... strongly quilted & covered with Burras or a coarse strong canvass.

***Bur reed, Burr reed.** One or other species of *Sparganium* having narrow, reedlike leaves.

1821 *Mass. H. S. Coll.* 2 Ser. IX. 156 Plants, which are indigenous in the township of Middlebury, [Vt., include] ... *Sparganium ramosum*, Burreed. **1840** DEWEY *Mass. Flowering Plants* 219 Lake Burr Reed grows near New Bedford, in ponds. **1843** TORREY *Flora N.Y.* II. 248 Branching Bur-reed ... [grows in] ditches and borders of swamps; common. *Ib.* 249 Smaller Bur-reed ... [grows in] ponds, lakes, and slow flowing streams, in the interior of the State. **1845** LINCOLN *Botany* App. 172 Floating bur-reed ... grows in great abundance in the little lake on Catskill Mountain, near the Mountain House. **1869** FULLER *Flower Gatherers* 290 Charley ... continued his search amid the Burr-reeds and Cat-tails, some of them higher than his head.

+Burrflower. Any of various species of waterleaf (*Hydrophyllum*). — **1817-8** EATON *Botany* (1822) 311 *Hydrophyllum virginicum*, burr-flower.... The flowers have the appearance of a burr several weeks before they expand. **1839** in *Mich. Agric. Soc. Trans.* VII. 409 *Hydrophyllum canadense*, Rough burr-flower.

+Burrier's oak. The Bartram oak, *Quercus heterophylla.* — **1813** H. MUHLENBERG *Cat. Plants* 87 *Quercus heterophylla*, (Burrier's oak) various-leav'd oak. **1817-8** EATON *Botany* (1822) 418 Burrier's oak.... Pursh says there is but one individual of this species known in the world, which is now growing on the Bartram plantation near Philadelphia. **1897** SUDWORTH *Arborescent Flora* 178 Bartram oak.... Common names [include] ... Burriers Oak (Lit.).

+Burrism. *Obs.* The political views of Aaron Burr. — **1806** *Ann. 9th Congress* 1 Sess. 775, I will take gentlemen on another principle—on the principle of Burrism, as it is called. *Ib.* 776 Are we for administering the Government on principles of Burrism? **1808** *Ann. 10th Congress* 1 Sess. I. 1321 Mr. G[ardenier] was no advocate of Burrism; nor was he one of those opposed to General Wilkinson for putting down Burrism.

+Burrite. *Obs.* A political adherent of Aaron Burr (1756-1836). — **1802** *Balance* (Hudson, N.Y.) 10 Aug. 250 (Th.), Burrites! Clintonians! Democrats! hear me for my family. **1807** *Ann. 10th Congress* 1 Sess. I. 647, I have little doubt that, ere this, you will have set me down as a Burrite. **1824** Mackenzie *Life Van Buren* (1846) 169 It is not very serviceable to talk much of *Burrites, Lewisites*, or the *High minded.* **1841** FOOTE *Texas & Texans* I. 148 Blennerhasset's Journal ... asserts ... that they were both *Burrites.*

+Burr millstone. [BURR².] A millstone made of burr; a burrstone.

1771 WASHINGTON *Writings* (1931) III. 63 [Send] a pair of French burr millstones of John Cooper.... I must through you request this Cooper to be very particular in his choice of the stone that the whole may be of good and even quality. **1825** *Columbian Centinel* 5 Jan. 4/3 Burr Mill Stones, made in the best manner ... at the State Prison. **1834** R. BAIRD *Valley Miss.* 303 In the region of the Appalachicola, fine burr mill-stone is found. **1846** *Rep. Comm. Patents* (1847) 100 In shaping and dressing burr mill-stones, the fragments which are broken off have heretofore been regarded as useless. **1849** THOREAU *Week on Concord* Writings (1906) I. 105 We must expect to feel it [=the writing in certain works of genius] ... wash away our critical brains like burr millstones. **1851** CIST *Cincinnati* 182 James Bradford & Co.... manufacture yearly seventy-five pairs burr millstones.

attrib. and *comb.* **1813** *Niles' Reg.* V. Add. A. 9/1 At the house of Thomas Hetick, in Chambersburg, appeared George Roupe, burr-millstone-maker. **1820** FLINT *Lett. from Amer.* 214 There are ... ten street pavers; one burr millstone factory.

Burro. *S.W.* [Sp.] A donkey. {1800}

1844 GREGG *Commerce of Prairies* I. 187 The chief riding animal of the peasant is the *burro*, upon which saddle, bridle, or halter, is seldom used. **1845** GREEN *Texian Exped.* 166 The sick were permitted to ride upon 'burros' (jack-asses). **1850** GARRARD *Wah-To-Yah* xv. 180 It was amusing to see the diminutive, long-eared burros. **1869** BROWNE *Adv. Apache Country* 171 A moving pile of mesquit wood, with the legs of a small burro or donkey underneath, is now and then seen passing along the principal street. **1887** *Outing* April 4/1 Not far off lay his dog and *burro* or Mexican donkey, both dead. **1893** K. SANBORN *S. California* 152 Every one should own a horse or pony or burro here. **1901** WHITE *Claim Jumpers* xxii. 277 They put the men's clothes on wrong side before, and tied them facing the rear on three scrubby little burros.

attrib. **1884** *Century Mag.* Sept. 657/2 Pepe returned and withdrew his *burro*-train from the town. **1884** *Harper's Mag.* Oct. 750/2 Even pottery and singing-birds, are ... brought burro-back. **1895** REMINGTON *Pony Tracks* 110 Leaving the 'burro men' to haul and pull at their patient beasts as they bound on their loads, our outfit 'pulled out.' **1909** 'O. HENRY' *Options* 134 The sheet of paper ... described the hiding-place of ten burro-loads of gold and silver coin.

+Burr oak, variant of BUR OAK.

+Burro deer. The blacktail or mule deer, *Cariacus macrotis.* — **1895** REMINGTON *Pony Tracks* 130 After hunting down the valley for a few days for 'burro deer' and wild turkey, we found that the tobacco was promptly giving out.

+Burrowing owl. A prairie owl (*Speotyto hypogæa*) living in burrows in the ground.

1825 BONAPARTE *Ornithology* I. 69 In the trans-Mississippian territories of the United States, the Burrowing Owl resides exclusively in the villages of the Marmot, or Prairie Dog. **1852** STANSBURY *Gt. Salt Lake* 37 A little, white, burrowing owl also ... is frequently found taking up his abode in the same domicile; and this strange association of reptile [=rattlesnake], bird, and beast [=prairie-dog], seem to live together in perfect harmony and peace. **1869** *Amer. Naturalist* II. 585 The Burrowing Owls do not migrate. Where I lived they were as numerous in winter as in summer. **1874** COUES *Birds N.W.* 322 The Burrowing Owl is the only bird of its family inhabiting, in any numbers, the entirely treeless regions of the West. **1881** *Amer. Naturalist* XV. 210 The little burrowing owl ... is very abundant, inhabiting the deserted holes of the California ground squirrel. **1895** *Dept. Agric. Yearbook 1894* 225 The burrowing owl ... feeds more extensively on insects than any of the other species.

+Burrowing squirrel. (See quotations.) — **1805** LEWIS in *L. & Clark Exped.* (1904) II. 301 In the course of the day they passed some villages of burrowing squirrels. **1814** Biddle *Lewis & Clark Exped.* II. 369 Throughout the glades are great numbers of holes made by the whistling- or burrowing-squirrel. **1868** *Amer. Naturalist* II. 532 The 'burrowing squirrel' of Lewis and Clarke ... was undoubtedly ... founded on at least two distinct animals.

Burrowing wasp. A wasp that burrows in wood. — **1884** *Rep. Comm. Agric.* 400 Among the few insects that destroy the worms in this State, several species of burrowing wasps are quite conspicuous.

Burr potato. ?*Obs.* [?Personal name.] A variety of the cultivated potato. — **1839** COLEMAN *Mass. Agric. Rep.* 88 The first seven rows were planted with the Burr or flesh-coloured potatoes. **1849** EMMONS *Agric. N.Y.* II. 41 Flesh-color or Burr Potato.... It will be observed that this potato contains less starch than many others in common use.

Burr-, Buhrstone. [BURR².]

1. A millstone of coarse silicious rock imported from France or quarried locally in the United States; a piece of this rock used in making composite millstones. {1690-}

(*a*) **1805** SIBLEY in *Ann. 9th Congress* 2 Sess. 1076 They had erected a good flour mill, with burr stones brought from France. **1815** *Niles' Reg.* IX. 36/2 Four pair of six feet burr stones will be run. **1835** MARTIN *Descr. Va.* 127 The mills ... turn two pair of Corn, and the same number of Burr stones. **1847** HOWE *Hist. Coll. Ohio* 201 The stream is estimated ... to afford sufficient power for one hundred and five pair of burr stones.

(*b*) **1883** *Harper's Mag.* June 78/1 A piece of wire fell in between the buhr stones. **1884** B. H. Young *Jessamine Co., Ky.* (1898) 221 This mill ... had the first French buhr stones brought to Jessamine County.

2. The silicious rock used for such millstones.

(*a*) **1816** *Ann. 14th Congress* 1 Sess. 1874 The following articles shall be imported ... free of duties ... burr stones, unwrought. **1837** WILLIAMS *Terr. of Fla.* 9 North of the Uche creek, burrstone is found.... It seems a congeries of small tellina shells, quite entire, cemented together with a strong alluminous matter. **1849** *Rep. Comm. Patents: Agric.* (1850) 467 Specimens of Georgia burr-stone may be seen in the Agricultural Room of the Patent Office.

attrib. **1851** CIST *Cincinnati* 169 Portable French burr-stone mills.

(*b*) **1819** SCHOOLCRAFT *Mo. Lead Mines* 216 The stone appears ... to be a pretty compact variety of that kind of vesicular quartz, called *buhrstone.* **1827** WILLIAMS *West Florida* 7 Buhrstone of an excellent quality is found in large masses near the Alabama line. **1837** PECK *New Guide* 37 Buhr stone, of a superior quality, exists in the surrounding hills [in Arkansas]. **1883** SMITH *Geol. Survey Ala.* 235 The rugged hills of the Buhr-stone, and the gently undulating surface of the Southern pine belt.

+Burseed, Burrseed. (See quotations.) — **1847** WOOD *Botany* 435 *Echinospermum Lappula.*... Burr-seed, an erect herb, in dry soils, roadsides, N. States to Arc. Am. **1909** *Cent. Suppl.* 178/1 Burseed, a species of stickseed, *Lappula Lappula*, introduced into the United States from Europe.

+Bursom. *Mining.* (See quotation.) — **1853** *Harper's Mag.* VI. 580/2 At each stage of the process [=the extraction of copper] there is a quantity of refuse matter, or poor-stuff, which is wheeled off in barrows to the *bursom*, or waste pile. This is also the term for a similar deposit of poor-stuff from the mine.

***Burst,** *n.* A spree; a drunken debauch. {1861-} (Cf. BUST *n.* 2) — **1849** T. T. JOHNSON *Sights Gold Region* 181 Miners were continually coming in from different *diggins*, to expend a part or all of their gold on what they term 'a burst.' **1855** MARRYAT *Mts. & Molehills* xv. 272 Nearly every one makes a point of travelling thither on a Saturday, to have a 'burst' on Sunday, and return in penitence on Monday. **1889** K. MUNROE *Golden Days* 64 He'll ... scratch round for some more dust, to go on another burst with.

***Burst,** *v.* [See also BUST *v*]

The following, in addition to those occurring below, are examples of the p.t. and p.p. *bursted:* **1809** WEEMS *Marion* (1833) 52 The ball ... bursted through the side of the house. *a***1846** *Quarter Race Ky.*, etc. 88 When he bursted the hoops [of the barrel] and cum out he rared a few. **1856** COZZENS *Sparrowgrass P.* 82 Then out came a bursted package of water-melon seeds. **1871** DE VERE 587 *Bursted*, a false participle from *burst*, is often used in the South to give emphasis to the word. 'What has become of Dick Farish? He has bursted all to pieces.'

+**1. a.** *intr.* To fail financially; to go bankrupt. Also with *up.*

1833 W. J. SNELLING *Exposé of Gaming* 10 Two persons who had bursted were sitting vis a vis by the fire-place. **1834** *Congress. Deb.* 10 March 848 Men, I say, who . . . are 'hard run' to make ends meet, . . . when they receive the magic touch of the 'pressure,' they burst, like a bombshell. **1848** W. ARMSTRONG *Stocks* 9 If any firm or individual does not fulfill his obligations by that time, it is considered as evidence that he is unable to do so, or, in polite phrase, that he has 'burst up.' **1861** MRS. S. COWELL *Diary* 242 The Cooper Opera Troupe 'burst up' about 3 or 4 weeks ago. **1863** S. C. MASSETT *Drifting About* 240 A bank 'bursts,' and I lose my money. **1875** *Chicago Tribune* 2 Sept. 1/2 Interesting Interview with Ralston. . . . Why the Bank Bursted.

+**b.** *tr.* To reduce to insolvency; to break.

1850 RYAN *Adv. Calif.* II. 209 An experienced player from New Orleans . . . not only regained his former losses, but . . . bursted the bank. **1873** *Chicago Tribune* 30 June (F.), Four lank and bursted frontiersmen.

+**2.** *intr.* To fail to recite well. *slang.*

1851 HALL *College Words* 33 *Burst*, to fail in reciting; to make a bad recitation. This word is used in some of the Southern colleges.

+**3.** *tr.* (See quotation.)

1846 *Spirit of Times* 18 April 91/2 You often hear this or that acquaintance speak of the misfortune of having '*bursted a cap*' at a fine buck or other valuable game, meaning thereby, that the percussion cap on their gun exploded without igniting the powder in the barrel.

Burster. {1611–} *slang.*

+**1.** A dandy; a roisterer; a large specimen.

1833 E. T. COKE *Subaltern's Furlough* xxv, When our coachman saw his new passenger squeezing himself edge-ways out of his late conveyance, he exclaimed, . . . 'My eye! a'nt he a burster?' **1836** in Kittredge *Old Farmer* (1904) 157 He will rue the day that he ever fell among dandies. But so it was, for his cousins were altogether for being *bursters:* and Bob was initiated into a clan of these mutton-faced non-essentials.

+**2.** A spree, drinking bout; a 'bust.'

1850 W. COLTON *3 Years Calif.* 290 You had some trouble with me in Monterey; I was on a burster; you did your duty, and I respect you for it.

***Bursting,** *vbl. n.* [f. BURST *v.* 1.] +Financial insolvency; bankruptcy. — **1834** CLAY *Congress. Deb.* 27 Feb. 747 You must lend us $300,000, to prevent a general bursting.

+**Bursting heart.** The burning bush, *Euonymus americanus.* — **1866** *Land We Love* (Charlotte, N.C.) May 80 Bursting Heart. . . . The bright crimson berries of this plant, open their embossed covering into four leaves, and display within the smooth scarlet seeds, which gives it the name of bursting heart. **1883** HALE *Woods & Timbers N.C.* 165 Strawberry Bush . . . [is] a shrub 2 to 5 feet high, found in all the Districts, and known by the names of Burning Bush, Fish-wood, and Bursting Heart.

‖ **Burthenage.** *Obs.* An impost levied on transported goods. — **1725** G. CHICKEN in *Travels Amer. Col.* 128 The Traders are obliged to pay double burthenage for every Pack.

***Burthened,** *a. Obs.* +Of vessels: Having a capacity of, capable of carrying (so much cargo). — **1704** *Boston News-Letter* 22 May 2/2 Arrived here this Day the Sloop Mary, . . . from New-York, burthen'd about 40 Tuns. **1723** *Weekly Mercury* 19 Sept. 2/2 The ship Globe, . . . burthened about 150 tons. **1761** *Essex Inst. Coll.* XLVIII. 94 A Snow burthened about one hundred and seventy Tons.

+**Burthener.** *Obs.* One who carries a burden; a burden bearer. — **1725** G. CHICKEN in *Travels Amer. Col.* 105 This Opportunity happening by two Burtheners who are going to Mr. Hasford's Cowpen, I thought it would be proper to acquaint your Honour of my Arrival. *Ib.* 128, I am Sorry to hear that its so hard for our Traders to get Burtheners among you.

***Burthensome,** *a. Obs.* +Capable of carrying or transporting a fair cargo. — **1763** *Boston Ev. Post* 9 May (Th.), A very good and burthensome Schooner for sale. **1817** *Cape-Fear Recorder* 5 April, The good substantial and burthensome brig Hibernia, of 145 tons' burthen. **1835** HOFFMAN *Winter in West* II. 68 The burthensome steamboats from New-Orleans reach here at the lowest stage of the river.

***Bury,** *v.* +**1.** *tr. To bury the hatchet* or *tomahawk*, see these nouns. +**2.** *intr.* Of a vessel: To dip or submerge the bows. — **1886** *Outing* Nov. IX. 117/1 It was asserted that she [the keel schooner] was too fine forward, . . . that she would bury in driving hard.

* **Burying,** *vbl. n. dial.* Also †**buring.** [BURY *v.*] A burial, funeral. {1681–1787; still common *dial.*}

1759 *Essex Inst. Coll.* XLIX. 13 Cap. Dean buried and exceeding large Buring, above 400. **1850** O. A. ROTHERT *Muhlenberg Co.* 200 Delivered two addresses at the burying and a prayer. **1859** ELWYN *Glossary* 27 *Burying*, for a funeral; as, 'he is gone to a burying,' is heard often in New England. **1861** NEWELL *Orpheus C. Kerr* I. 17 The first time I took a notion to her was down to the old shingle meetin'-house, when Sam Spooner had a buryin'. **1889** 'THANET' in *Harper's Bazar* 4 May 331/1 You shall have de bigges' an' de nices' burryin' of ary cullud pusson in Hot Springs. **1917** H. T. COMSTOCK *Man* 111 The minister has gone to a burying back in the hills.

+**Burying cloth.** *Obs.* Also **buring cloth.** A cloth for covering the coffin at a funeral; a pall. — **1729** *Manchester Rec.* 176 It was voted that the present Select men shall provide a desant buring Cloth at the Charge of the town. **1768** *Essex Inst. Coll.* XXI. 236 Voted to bye a burying Cloth in the Parish. **1777** *Smithtown Rec.* 49, I also bequeath to the town of Setauket a burying cloth to be purchased for them by my executors.

Burying ground. =BURIAL GROUND. {1711–1854}

1759 *Newport Mercury* July, The Proprietors also propose to grant . . . one hundred Acres for a School-Lot, Burying-Ground, and Training-Field, in each Township. **1784** FILSON *Kentucke* 103 These have a church, a minister, and a regular burying ground. **1800** BROWN *A. Mervyn* xxx, I might wait till a carriage were provided to remove the body to a burying ground, belonging to a meeting-house. **1815** DRAKE *Cincinnati* 163 This society is without any burying ground. **1839** *Knickerb.* XIV. 154 There was a quiet-looking burying-ground, just at the foot of the hill. **1852** *Harper's Mag.* VI. 10 Not far from the Navy Yard is the Congressional Burying Ground where are many monuments inscribed with names familiar to us. **1871** *Ib.* June 158/1 When visiting a friend the other day I strolled out to the family burying-ground. **1881** MCLEAN *Cape Cod Folks* 220 When the procession was about to start for the burying-ground, the request was made to me that I would blow the horn. **1893** K. SANBORN *S. Calif.* 63, I must add that the hotel was built just over an old Indian burying-ground. **1899** CHESNUTT *Conjure Woman* 33, I kin lead de way right ter Henry's grave ober yander in de plantation buryin'-groun'.

+**Burying-lot.** =BURIAL LOT. — **1882** *Harper's Mag.* Dec. 129/2 One golden bright afternoon, quite a crowd was assembled around the little burying-lot in the orchard.

* **Burying place.** Also †**burring(e) place.**

* **1.** =BURIAL PLACE.

1622 'MOURT' *Relation* 49 Anone we found a great burying place. **1642** *Watertown Rec.* 8 [They] are appointed to set up a sufficient fence about the Burying Place. **1669** *Essex Inst. Coll.* VI. 176/1 That parcell of land . . . lying next our comon Burringe place. **1702** SEWALL *Diary* II. 62 Our dear sister, Mehitabel is the first buryed in this new Burying place. **1796** in Imlay *Western Territory* (ed. 3) 513 We seldom go more than five or six miles along the banks of Cumberland river, without finding a large burying-place, the evident remains of a considerable town. **1840** DANA *Two Years* xv. 130 Had it been a common burying-place, it would have been nothing.

+**2.** A storage place or cache for baggage, canoes, etc.

1807 GASS *Journal* 101 We finished the burying place, so that we will be ready to start as soon as Capt. Clarke returns. **1808** F. CUMING *Western Tour* 415 When we came to the falls of Sandusky, we buried our birch bark canoes . . . at a large burying place for that purpose.

+**Burying yard.** A place for burial; a cemetery, graveyard.

1698 *Conn. Probate Rec.* I. 545, I give to the Towne of Wethersfield the Land at the burying yard. **1757** *General Orders* 47 The Ground is marked out for the new Buriing Yard, & for the Future the Troops are not to dig Graves any where else. **1770** in *N.H. Hist. Soc. Coll.* IV. 127 The burying yard should be cleared, and fenced with a good and sufficient board fence. **1773** FITHIAN *Journal* I. 74 Only the lower part of People are at the Church [-yard]; for the Gentleman [*sic*] have private burying-yards. **1824** J. Q. ADAMS *Diary* (1929) 329, I walked in the burying-yard. **1836** *Knickerb.* VIII. 389 The spire . . . leaned with a weight of years, and the fish looked downward into the burying-yard, as if seeking a place of repose.

Bus, 'Bus. Also †**buss.** An omnibus. {1832–}

1848 N. AMES *Childe Harvard* 91, I dreamed I saw them in a Cambridge omnibus;—and then 'the buss' tipt over! **1869** ALCOTT *Little Women* II. xxiii. 337 They . . . forgot to hail a 'bus. **1879** R. J. BURDETTE *Hawkeyes* 63 Abou arose and girt his raiment about him and hastened down stairs and crept into the 'bus. **1897** BRODHEAD *Bound in Shallows* 206 The young man . . . elbowed his way to the 'buses and wagons drawn up behind the long depot. **1923** WATTS *L. Nichols* 15 She must leave the house at six o'clock in order to reach the Pike, a half-mile walk, and catch the station-'bus.

* **Bush,** *n.*

1. With *the:* Country more or less covered with forest or brushwood; the woods or uncleared land. {1837–}

In more limited use than in the British Colonies.

1827 *Western Mo. Rev.* I. 441 The following tale has come to hand from a friend, who lives in the bush. **1828** SCOTT *Tapestr. Chamber*, When I was in the Bush, as the Virginians call it. **1840** DANA *Two Years* xix, For the first two months we seldom went into 'the bush' [in Calif.] without one of our number starting some of them [=rattlesnakes]. **1841** W. KENNEDY *Texas* I. 66 Intermittent fever . . . is the general penalty attached to settlements in the 'bush,' from the St. Lawrence to the Sabine. **1845** MRS. KIRKLAND *Western Clearings* 213, I lik'd the bush, so I took my gun and set off afoot through the wilderness. **1859** BARTLETT 59 *Bush*, . . . the woods, a forest, or a thicket of trees or bushes. This term, which is much used in the Northern States and Canada, probably originated in New York. **1870** *Cheyenne Chron.* 17 Aug. (De Vere), The Indians disappeared in the bush, when they saw the troops approaching. **1890** RYAN *Told in Hills* 191 From their tones one would gather the impression that all the splendors of a metropolis were as nothing when compared with the luxuries of 'shack' life in the 'bush.'

b. In *pl.* in the same sense.
1879 TOURGEE *Fool's Errand* 130 That refuge of free thought at the South, the woods (or 'the bushes,' as the scraggly growth is more generally termed).

+**2.** A grove of sugar trees; a place in the forest where sugar making is carried on. (Cf. SUGARBUSH.)
1823 COOPER *Pioneer* II. i. 12 The underwood had been entirely removed from this grove, or bush, as, in conjunction with the simple arrangements for boiling, it was called. **1842** MRS. KIRKLAND *Forest Life* II. 210 Sugar-making is undertaken . . . by everybody indiscriminately, who can command a 'bush.' **1850** S. F. COOPER *Rural Hours* 25 As the sap is running . . . and the sugar is boiling all together, day and night, it is a busy moment at the 'bush.' **1854** H. H. RILEY *Puddleford* 243 These March days, were 'sugar days.' . . . Men, women, and children turned out with kettles and pans, into the 'bush.'

+**3.** In the colloq. phrases: *to take the rag off the bush, drag the bush up, bang the bush,* to surpass, excel, take first place.
1835–7 HALIBURTON *Clockmaker* 1 Ser. 52 That's a cap sheef that bangs the bush. **1843** STEPHENS *High Life N.Y.* I. 56 Wal, . . . if this don't take the rag off the bush!—Cousin Mary's got to gadding about so much, that she has to send round word when she is going to stay at hum one evening. **1845** J. J. HOOPER *Simon Sugg's Adv.* xii. 142 That uther picture . . . kums nigher draggin the bush up by the roots an a most enny thing I ever seed. **1848** W. E. BURTON *Waggeries* 70 It happifies me to say that we bang the bush. **1871** DE VERE 197 The fact that the improvised target is not unfrequently a rag hung on a bush, has suggested to Professor S. S. Haldeman the thought that the familiar phrase: 'That takes the rag off the bush,' may have likewise originated from the use of the rifle in the hands of the Western hunter.

4. *attrib.* **a.** Covered with bushes.
1694 *Conn. Prob. Rec.* 497 Orchards, Gardens and Yards, and a pasture, Plow Land and Bush Lott. **1855** SIMMS *Forayers* 544 Who would have thought of any fellow being such a bloody booby as to bring a bathing-tub and chamber crockery into a pond and bush country? **1857** HAMMOND *Northern Scenes* 147 On my father's farm was a bush field, a place that had been chopped and burned over, and then left to grow up with bushes. **1867** *Iowa Agric. Soc. Rep.* (1868) 167 The soil best adapted to wheat growing is the timber and bush-land.

b. Made of or with bushes.
1775 *R.I. Hist. Soc.* VI. 12 [We] even had not the satisfaction . . . to build ourselves . . . a bush hut to pass the tedious night in. **1805** LEWIS in *L. & Clark Exped.* (1905) III. 14 Late in the evening I made the men form a bush drag, and with it in about 2 hours they caught 528 very good fish. **1850** TYSON *Diary in Calif.* 76 We slept under a deserted bush-tent. **1857** HAMMOND *Northern Scenes* 169 Crop crept close alongside of me, in our bush-shanty.

c. In plant names, as *bush cranberry, dogwood, huckleberry,* etc.
See also BUSHBEAN, CLOVER, HONEYSUCKLE below.
1762 CLAYTON *Flora Virginica* 60 Vitis Idaea Euonymi folio splendente, fructu nigricante. Bush-whoitle-berry. **1817–8** EATON *Botany* (1822) 252 *Cornus paniculata,* bush dogwood. . . . Berries white. *Ib.* 299 *Hedysarum canadense,* bush trefoil. **1843** TORREY *Flora N.Y.* I. 307 *Viburnum opulus,* . . . Bush Cranberry or High Cranberry. . . . The acid fruit is sometimes used as a substitute for cranberries. **1883** HALE *Woods & Timbers N.C.* 124 Bush willow (*S. humilis*). . . . During summer the branches of this and No. 2 [=gray willow] have cone-like excrescences on their ends. **1897** R. M. STUART *Simpkinsville* 146 Reckon I'll plant bush-squash myself after this.

***Bush,** *v.*
1. *tr.* With *in.* To cover (seed) with a bush or bush harrow. ?*Obs.* {1787–}
1749 FRANKLIN *Writings* II. 386, I threw in the following grass seed, . . . a peck of Burden grass . . . and two Pints of Red Clover per acre . . . and bushed them in. **1788** WASHINGTON *Diaries* III. 335 The ground which had been sown with Barley and Row grass, . . . was forced to be bushed in to day, the Barley being sprouted.

2. With *it.* To make one's way through the bushes.
1780 ASBURY *Journal* I. 386 When he saw how I could bush it and sometimes force my way through a thicket, and make the young saplings bend before me, . . . he took courage.

+**3.** With *out.* To clear of bushes, render passable.
1851 SPRINGER *Forest Life* 91 A road was bushed out to the spot where the poor creature lay.

+**Bush arbor.** [BUSH *n.* 4 b.] A temporary shelter made of boughs, bushes, etc. Also attrib. — **1848** E. Bryant *California* 457 The hill-sides were thickly strewn with canvas tents and bush arbors. **1904** HARBEN *Georgians* 3 He raised a regular bedlam at the bush-arbor meetin' below town.

+**Bush bean.** A bean that does not climb; a dwarf or bunch bean. — **1836** LINCOLN *Botany* App. 124 *Phaseolus nanus,* (bush-bean, six-weeks-bean). **1857** *Texas Almanac* 21 Bush beans may now be planted. **1862** *Ill. Agric. Soc. Trans.* V. (1865) 518 We usually plant bush beans in garden drills. **1887** *Harper's Mag.* Jan. 307/2 Those who need much instruction in regard to bush-beans should remain in the city.

+**Bushbeater.** =BUSHWHACKER 1. — **1809** IRVING *Knickerb.* VI. iv, Such was the legion of sturdy bush-beaters that poured in at the grand gate of New-Amsterdam.

+**Bush clover.** One or other species of a genus of plants (*Lespedeza*) similar to the clovers. — **1817–8** EATON *Botany* (1822) 335 *Lespedeza sessiliflora,* bush clovers. . . . Var. *reticulata.* **1840** DEWEY *Mass. Flowering Plants* 67 *Lespedeza capitata,* Bush Clover, . . . flowers in rather clustered or head-like racemes; somewhat woody. **1847** WOOD *Botany* 233 *Lespedeza capitata,* . . . Bush Clover, . . . [is] an erect, hairy, half shrubby plant, in dry soils, Can. to Car. **1891** COULTER *Bot. W. Texas* I. 86 *Lespedeza.* Bush clover. Ours have flowers of two sorts, the larger (violet-purple) perfect but seldom fruitful.

+**Bushed,** *a.* Tired; worn out. — **1870** *Nation* July 57/1 To be 'bushed' was to be tired [in Penna.]. **1900** MUNN *Uncle Terry* 157 'Whar might ye be goin'? Ye look bushed.' 'I am,' answered Page, 'and badly bushed too.'

***Bushel,** *n.* Also †**booshel.** A measure of capacity for grain, fruit, etc., varying for different commodities and in different states.
1622 'MOURT' *Relation* 31 We had in all about ten Bushels [of 'corne']. **1644** *Wyllys Papers* 74 A bushell is as much with us as a strike with you. **1675** R. WILLIAMS *Letters* (1874) 376, I gave . . . a bushel of apples to his men. **1713** *Boston Rec.* 101 Voted: That five thousand bushalls of Indian Corn be purchaced and layd up on some convenient place or places. **1781** PETERS *Hist. Conn.* (1929) 200 The common price of . . . [wheat] is three shillings sterling per bushel. **1837** PECK *Gaz. Illinois* 64 It is expected that not less than one million of bushels of coal will be transported annually to the river. **1867** EDWARDS *Shelby* 229 Killed half a dozen fat hogs, baked bushels of meal into hoe-cakes, and made a delicious supper for men and horses. **1901** MERWIN & WEBSTER *Calumet K* i. 1 The contract for the two million bushel grain elevator, Calumet K, had been let to MacBride & Company.

+**Bushel,** *v.* [App. G. *böscheln,* dial. var. of *bosseln* to do small jobs. Cf. BUSHELER.] *tr.* To repair or renovate (garments). Also fig. with *up.* — **1877** BARTLETT 777 *To bushel,* . . . to repair garments. **1890** *Boston Transcript* 9 Sept., Returning from the country, you will find last winter's woollens . . . needing to be pressed, cleaned and repaired. Our Busheling Department employs twenty men who do nothing but attend to this class of work. **1893** in *Congress. Rec.* (1894) 8327/1 To allow [this building] to be 'busheled up' or repaired by a private purchaser would be to court inevitable disaster.

+**Bushel-bean.** *Obs.* An especially prolific variety of bean. — **1709** LAWSON *Carolina* 76 Of the Pulse-kind, we have many sorts. The first is the Bushel-Bean, which is a spontaneous Product. They are so called, because they bring a Bushel of Beans for one that is planted. . . . The Bean is white and mottled, with a purple Figure on each side it, like an Ear.

+**Busheler, -eller.** [Cf. BUSHEL *v.*] (See quotations.) — **1860** WORCESTER 184/2 *Busheller,* one who repairs garments for tailors. (Local, U.S.) *Dr. Gilman.* **1877** BARTLETT 777 *Busheler, Bushelman,* . . . a tailor's assistant, whose business it is to repair garments.

+**Busheling,** *vbl. n.* (See BUSHEL *v.*)

+**Bushelman.** =BUSHELER. — **1864** WEBSTER 177/3. **1877** [see BUSHELER]. **1909** 'O. HENRY' *Options* 109 You would say he had been brought up a bushelman in Essex Street. **1920** SANDBURG *Smoke & Steel* 102 Cutters or bushelmen, or armhole basters.

+**Bushelwoman.** [Cf. prec.] 'A woman who assists a tailor in repairing garments' (*Cent.*).

Bushfighter. [BUSH *n.* 1.] One who fights from behind trees, rocks, etc. {1760–} — **1824** W. N. BLANE *Excursion U.S.* 305 A whole host of pioneers could scarcely clear away this, even if they had plenty of time, and were not liable to be harassed by such accomplished 'Bush-fighters.' [*Note.*] This is a term made use of by the Americans, when in their battles with the Indians they are obliged to run from tree to tree, taking care as they advance, to cover themselves from the deadly aim of their enemies. **1825** NEAL *Bro. Jonathan* I. 1 The 'Battle of Lexington' [was] a sharp skirmish between the New England, or Yankee bush-fighters, and his majesty's troops. **1840** HOFFMAN *Greyslaer* I. 116 If it means an old bushfighter, there's no man in all Tryon county . . . , but must knock under to old Balt in expayrience.

Bushfighting. [BUSH *n.* 1.] Fighting in the bush, or from behind trees, rocks, etc. {1760–}
1758 *Essex Inst. Coll.* XVIII. 101 [I] improved this Day chiefly in the exercise of Bush Fiting. *Ib.* 187 The Rangers exercise in Scout Marches and Bush fighting. **1784** J. SMYTH *Tour U.S.* II. 169 Without a much greater share of discipline it is impossible to make them leave off that habit of bush-fighting, or keeping themselves covered by trees. **1805** PARKINSON *Tour* 156 He fought the English as the Indians had fought him when he was in British service—by what is termed bush-fighting. **1836** *S. Lit. Messenger* II. 118 Most of the book is occupied with the ambuscades, bush fighting, and swamp adventures of partisan warfare in South Carolina. **1837** IRVING *Bonneville* I. 79 The men being, especially, unused to bush-fighting and the use of the rifle, were at a loss how to proceed.
fig. **1860** HOLMES *Professor* ii. 45 A barren interchange of courtesies, or a bush-fighting argument.

+**Bush-fire.** The shots of bushfighters. — **1761** S. NILES *Indian Wars* II. 435 The enemy . . . were beaten back by the bush-fire of Lieutenant Stark and his party.

+**Bush-firing.** Interchange of shots by bushfighters. — **1779** *N.J. Archives* 2 Ser. III. 578 A constant bush-firing then commenced, in which capt. Tyler . . . was killed, and several privates wounded.

Bush harrow, *n.* A harrow made of or provided with bushes or branches. {1770–}

1785 WASHINGTON *Diaries* II. 365 The grass Seed was sowed and harrowed with a Bush harrow. **1839** J. BUEL *Farmer's Comp.* 205 The bush harrow is to be preferred. **1877** *Harper's Mag.* Jan. 215/2 Then scores of torn up trees swept over, as a bush-harrow jumps on clods of the field.

Bush-harrow, *v.* [f. prec.] *tr.* With *in.* To bury [seeds] by means of a bush-harrow. {1834–} — **1788** WASHINGTON *Diaries* III. 328 He was sowing Seeds with intention to bush harrow them in.

+**Bush honeysuckle.** A shrub of the genus *Diervilla,* nearly related to the common honeysuckle.

1817–8 EATON *Botany* (1822) 266 *Diervilla canadensis,* bush honeysuckle. . . . Variable in size, 1 foot to 6. **1832** WILLIAMSON *Maine* I. 130 Bush-honeysuckle (*Diervilla*) grows 2 feet in height. **1850** S. F. COOPER *Rural Hours* 183 Observed the yellow diervilla or bush-honeysuckle still in flower. *a***1862** THOREAU *Maine Woods* 310 The prevailing shrubs and small trees along the shore were: . . . *osier rouge* and alders; . . . *Diervilla trifida* (bush-honeysuckle). **1883** HALE *Woods & Timbers N.C.* 164 Bush honeysuckle . . . [is] a small, rather delicate shrub, . . . with pointed toothed leaves which are 3 or 4 inches long.

+**Bush hook.** A heavy scythelike hook or knife for clearing away underbrush; a billhook.

1834 C. A. DAVIS *Lett. J. Downing* 19 The crittur had just come out of his bush pasture, and had his bush-hook with him. **1847** HOWE *Hist. Coll. Ohio* 493 Their tools are usually coarse, among which is the German scythe, short and unwieldy as a bush-hook. **1863** MITCHELL *My Farm* 45 A convenient mossy cherry tree was hung over with last year's scythes and bush-hooks. **1884** ROE *Nature's Story* 3 The angular fields, . . . marked by trees and shrubs that, in their earlier life, ran the gauntlet of the bush-hook.

Bushhouse. +A shelter or ambush from which pigeons are shot. — **1834** C. A. DAVIS *Lett. J. Downing* 367 Saratogue, for politicians, is jist like the bush-houses for killing pigeons.

+**Bush knife.** A bush hook. — **1851** *Florida Plant. Rec.* 439 Rec'd 6 scooter Ploughs, three axes and one Bush knife . . . and eight turn ploughs.

+**Bush-light.** (See quotation.) — **1836** C. GILMAN *Recoll.* (1838) xi. 82 A bush-light was flaming near Jacque's habitation. [*Note.*] A fire of light wood kindled on a small mound of earth.

+**Bushloper.** Also †**busslooper.** [Du. *boschlooper,* a rendering or synonym of F. *coureur de bois.* Cf. BOSSELOPER.] A coureur de bois; one accustomed to scouring the woods. — **1694** in Munsell *Annals Albany* II. 128 [That] there may be a company of buss Loopers raised to scour the cost for schulking partyes of the enemy. **1752** *Importance of Friendship* 17 By this means a number of *Bush-lopers,* as the Dutch call them, and the French, who are indefatigable in this point, *Coureurs de bois,* are created; a set of men, who from their acquaintance with the woods and Indians are very useful.

+**Bush-meeting.** A meeting or gathering held in the forest; a camp meeting. — **1863** *Young Parson* 175 She jined the last camp-meetin' I had, or rather last *bush*-meetin'. *Ib.* 183, I was comin' down here just to cut up at a bush-meetin'. **1877** *S. Atlantic* (Wilmington, N.C.) I. 58 Their spiritual needs were partially ministered to by peregrinating preachers of different denominations, who, in a missionary spirit, travelled over the country, and held at various points what were called 'bush meetings,' similar to the camp-meetings of the present time, though the people attending came from much greater distances. **1877** BARTLETT 85 At the South among the Negroes, . . . there can be no more delightful frolic than a bush-meetin'.

+**Bush-pasture.** A pasture composed of uncleared woodland. — *a***1817** DWIGHT *Travels* II. 460 The proprietor is always ready to sell: for he loves this irregular . . . life, and hates the sober industry . . . by which his bush pasture is changed into a farm. **1834** [see BUSHHOOK]. **1844** *Knickerb.* XXIV. 300 It was a little Dutch cow, she was in our bush-pasture, and it was a very dry summer.

+**Bush-pond.** [BUSH *n.* 1.] A pond or pool in the bush or among bushes. — **1897** *Outing* XXX. 434/1 The crawfish . . . were very abundant in the shallow water at the river-banks, in the creeks, and in certain bush-ponds.

Bushranger. {1817–} +A frontiersman or borderer. — **1830** H. H. PORTER *Betrothed of Wyoming* 171 Joseph's small party of bush-rangers, as they were called, were stationed in a valley about a mile distant. **1869** PARKMAN *Discov. West* xxviii. 389 [Tonty's] little garrison of bush-rangers greeted them [=French voyageurs] with a salute of musketry. **1888** *Century Mag.* Nov. 87/2 They pushed ahead of the slow habitant, and held their rights above the rights of any bush-ranger.

+**Bush rat.** [BUSH *n.* 1.] A species of wood rat found in the West. — **1867** *Amer. Naturalist* I. 399 The Bush Rat (*Neotoma Mexicana*) is abundant throughout the Territory [Ariz.], and forms no small item in the economy of the Indians.

***Bush scythe.** A short scythe used for cutting bushes; a billhook or bush hook. {1552} — **1856** *Mich. Agric. Soc. Trans.* VII. 54 D. O. and W. W. Perry . . . [exhibited] three bush scythes. **1873–4** *Vt. Bd. Agric. Rep.* II. 194 Other bushes and shrubs will be constantly obtruding themselves, but it is possible to subdue them . . . by cutting them off near the ground with a bush-scythe.

‖**Bush sheep.** [BUSH *n.* 1.] (See quotation.) — **1867–8** *Ill. Agric. Soc. Trans.* VII. 457 Sheep shipped in for sale because they 'didn't flourish' on prairie grass. These 'bush sheep,' as they are called, have been in abundant supply.

+**Bush sparrow.** The song or field sparrow. — **1858** *Atlantic Mo.* Oct. 594/2 In several localities these two species [the song sparrow and vesper bird] are distinguished by the names of Bush-Sparrow and Ground-Sparrow, from their supposed different habits of placing their nests, one on a bush and the other on the ground. **1869** BURROUGHS in *Galaxy* Aug. 139/2 A favourite sparrow of my own . . . is the wood, or bush-sparrow, usually called *spizella pusilla.*

+**Bush titmouse.** A small bird of the genus *Psaltriparus.* — **1881** *Amer. Naturalist* XV. 213 At Colton, Cal., I first found the nest of that diminutive little bird, the least bush titmouse (*Psaltriparus minimus*).

+**Bushwhack,** *n.* An instrument for cutting bushes or shrubs; a bushwhacker. — **1865** *Atlantic Mo.* XV. 521 It is so far escaping from the axe and the bushwhack as to have opened communication with the forest and mountain beyond by straggling lines of Cedar, Laurel, and Blackberry.

+**Bushwhack,** *v.*

1. *intr.* To make a vigorous display of oratory.

1836 CROCKETT *Exploits* 17 So I mounted the stump that had been cut down for the occasion, and began to bushwhack in the most approved style.

2. To use 'bushwhacking' as a means of pulling a boat against the stream.

1861 WINTHROP *Open Air* 84 Bushwhacking thus for a league, we circumvented the peril, and came upon the river flowing fair and free.

3. *tr.* To fire upon or attack in the manner of bushwhackers.

1866 C. H. SMITH *Bill Arp* 116 The truth is, that Confederate cavalry can fight 'em and dog 'em, and dodge 'em, and bushwhack 'em, and bedevil 'em for a thousand years. **1867** CRAWFORD *Mosby & His Men* 306 Three miles from the town, Montjoy, being far ahead of his men, was bushwhacked, and received a mortal wound in the head. **1877** FLEMING *Mirage* III. 212 A good many men were missing, shot or bushwhacked, we did not know which. **1891** *Century Mag.* Jan. 414 The home guard . . . bushwhacked his men from every hedge, hill, or tree, when it could be done. **1918** MULFORD *Man fr. Bar-20* 193 Here he is over this end of th' trail an' givin' you a fine chance to sneak up an' bushwhack him.

b. To fire upon (game) from a point of vantage.

1874 LONG *Wild-Fowl* 133, I . . . jumped into a paddle-boat, paddled ashore, and proceeded to 'bushwhack' them [*sc.* ducks].

4. *intr.* To dwell in, to prowl or search among, the bushes or forest.

1868 *Putnam's Mag.* I. 22 An old Dutch Continental, Bushwhacked up there a spell. **1881** BUEL *Border Outlaws* 192 The three survivors bushwhacked about for some time, two of them eventually escaping. **1888** 'CRADDOCK' *Broomsedge Cove* 428, I b'lieve we sarched every squar' mile fur ten mile, a-bushwhackin' fur 'em. **1889** 'MARK TWAIN' *Conn. Yankee* xxv. 324 He knew something about . . . bushwhacking around for ogres.

+**Bushwhacker.** [BUSH *n.* 1.]

1. A dweller in the backwoods; a frontiersman; a rustic.

1809 IRVING *Knickerb.* VI. iv, They were gallant bushwhackers and hunters of raccoons. **1817** PAULDING *Lett. from South* I. 140 In a few years a race of lusty bushwhackers rewards the labours of the industrious pair. **1834** SIMMS *G. Rivers* 100, I belonged to Captain Williams's troop called the 'Bush-Whackers.' **1843** 'CARLTON' *New Purchase* II. 86 Do you, sir, think our Mr. C. . . . could have compelled young bushwhackers to wear coats and shoes in recitation rooms? **1879** *Harper's Mag.* June 73/1 The 'bush-whackers' or small farmers hover around the outskirts of the crowd of fishermen. **1885** *Ib.* Sept. 591/2 The General was a natural bushwhacker, in the sense of having an intuitive knowledge of country.

2. One who lurks in woods or thickets and carries on guerrilla warfare or engages in plundering.

A sense originating in the Civil War period, and in later use chiefly historical.

1861 *N.Y. Herald* 21 Nov. 4/2 Nineteen bushwhackers arrived at Cincinnati . . . as prisoners. **1863** *Rio Abajo Press* 10 Feb. 3 It is reported . . . that Marmaduke and a portion of his bushwhackers had been captured by General Herron, while they were retreating from Missouri into Arkansas. **1865** BOUDRYE *Fifth N.Y. Cavalry* 26 Some of our men, while bathing in the river near New Market, were attacked by bushwhackers. **1866** in *Rep. Jt. Comm. on Reconstruction* I. 93 The bushwhacker and guerilla can defeat the most respectable Union man for constable. **1869** in Fleming *Hist. Reconstruction* II. 40 One of Governor Clayton's agents is a rebel bushwhacker whom I captured and tried by a drumhead court-martial in 1864. **1871** *Nashville Banner* 7 March (De Vere), In Smith County the government officials . . . were fired upon by bushwhackers, but no one was injured. **1887** *Courier-Journal* 8 May 5/2 The whole country was full of rebel soldiers, scouts and bushwhackers. **1891** *Century Mag.* Jan. 405 The fierce bushwhackers . . . never gave quarter to Confederate soldier or Southern sympathizer.

b. *transf.* (See quotation.)

1885 *Mag. Amer. Hist.* Jan. 99/1 *Bushwhacker,* in politics, as in war, simply a 'free-lance.'

3. A bush hook or bushwhack. Also fig.

*c***1849** PAIGE *Dow's Sermons* I. (B.), I know not the victim soon destined to fall before the keen-edged bushwhacker of Time, or I would point him out. **1870** EMERSON *Soc. & Sol.* 81 He is a graduate of the plough, and the stub-hoe, and the bushwhacker.

+**Bushwhackerism.** The principles and practices of bushwhackers. — **1883** *American* VI. 356 The 'border ruffianism' and the 'bushwhackerism' which disgraced Missouri.

+**Bushwhacking,** *vbl. n.*

1. Pulling a boat against the current by grasping bushes along the bank. (Cf. BUSHWHACK *v.* 2.)

1826 T. FLINT *Recoll.* 86 We began to pull the boat up the stream, by a process, which in the technics of the boatmen [of the Miss. R.], is called bush-whacking. **1832** — *Hist. Miss. Valley* I. 151 Its [keel boat's] propelling power is by oars, sails, setting poles, the cordelle, and when the waters are high, and the boat runs on the margin of the bushes, bush-whacking, or pulling up by the bushes. **1833** HAWKS *Hist. Western States* (1844) 30 When the waters are high, and the boat can run along under bushes on the river-bank, pulling up by the bushes, this is called 'bush-whacking.'

2. Using underhand or unfair means in political contests. Also attrib.

1841 *Congress. Globe* 8 Jan. 91 He again thanked the Senator—they should now have a fair contest, and no 'bush whacking.' **1845** *Ib.* App. 3 Feb. 152/1 All he [Sen. Foster of Tenn.] asked for was a clear field and a fair fight—no *bush-whacking*, if he might be indulged in an expressive word, well understood in the border wars of the West; no masked batteries. **1889** *Century Mag.* Jan. 406/2 This system of party warfare known in the vernacular as 'bushwhacking,' required . . . great adroitness, considerable self-poise, and a glib tongue. **1911** *Springfield W. Republican* 24 Aug. 8 It has been altogether a confusing, disturbing, bushwhacking session—a playing for party position and issues in a political war to come.

3. Carrying on guerrilla warfare; marauding.

1845 [see sense 2]. **1862** *N.Y. Herald* 29 June (Ch.), We would be glad to meet any number of the Confederates in a fair fight; but this infernal bushwhacking shall not be practised on the men of my command, without [my] enforcing the severest penalties of military retaliation. **1865** *Missouri Constitution* art. 2 sec. 3 That description of marauding commonly known as bushwhacking. **1872** FLAGG *Good Investment* 46/2 This was very good generalship . . . and subject to only the one criticism, that it amounted to 'bush-whacking.' **1887** CUSTER *Tenting on Plains* 31, Texas . . . was unhappily unaware that the war was over, and continued a career of bush-whacking and lawlessness. **1891** 'CRADDOCK' in *Harper's Mag.* Feb. 368/1 He had been a brave soldier, although the flavor of bushwhacking clung to his war record.

+**Bushwhacking,** *a.* **a.** Backwoods, rustic. **b.** Practising guerrilla warfare. — **1813** *Mass. Spy* 27 Jan. (Th.), These bush-whacking Yankees won't do. **1875** *Chicago Tribune* 20 Aug. 7/3 These are the Indians that 'spoke out in meetin',' and they all told the same story,—i.e., if that bushwhacking interpreter told the truth. **1883** *American* VI. 92 The scouting, bushwhacking Unionist, Fortner.

***Bushy,** *a.* In specific names of plants. — **1784** CUTLER in *Mem. Academy* I. 481 Bushy aster. Florets in . . . the center yellow. By fences. September. **1843** TORREY *Flora N.Y.* II. 46 *Gerardia Pedicularia*, . . . Bushy Gerardia, . . . [is] rather common throughout the State. *Ib.* 144 *Amaranthus Græcizans*, . . . Bushy Amaranth, . . . [grows in] cultivated grounds, waste grounds, and road-sides; common.

Business.

1. A particular occupation, trade, or industry. {1775-}

1831 PECK *Guide* 134 In 1823, the late Col. James Johnson . . . made arrangements to prosecute the business of smelting. **1887** *Courier-Journal* 19 Feb. 8/1 The grotesque gymnasts, greatly amused the audience by their performance on the horizontal bar. . . . They are very clever in their business. **1888** *Cosmopolitan* Oct. 446/2 The 'black-list' was first made to reach those players who, by dissipation or other disreputable conduct, were injuring base-ball as a business. **1907** C. C. ANDREWS *Recoll.* 88 He thought in that vicinity raising stock would be the chief business.

b. Attendance at a theater; a 'house.'

1847 *Knickerb.* XXIX. 53 Both have been playing to what is technically termed a 'good business.' **1895** *N.Y. Dramatic News* 12 Oct. 5/2 Hanlon brothers' Superba has played to 'banner' business.

2. With defining terms: A form of occupation or activity.

1861 NEWELL *Orpheus C. Kerr* I. 172 This New-Year's-calls business. **1866** C. H. SMITH *Bill Arp* 47 Now let me advise you to sing low about this fighting business. **1869** BROWNE *Adv. Apache Country* 193 Ask him the simplest question, and the extent of his knowledge is *quien sabe?* His whole life is a *quien sabe* business, signifying nothing. **1875** 'MARK TWAIN' *Life on Miss.* (1876) xvii. 136 Pray observe some of the effects of this ditching business. **1901** *Munsey's Mag.* XXV. 403/2 Murray . . . had come out to the plains to learn the cattle business. **1902** LORIMER *Lett. Merchant* 3 That is where I'm a little skittish about this college business.

b. Similarly with the qualifying term understood.

1862 *N.Y. Tribune* 28 May 4/1 At the various armories of our city militia regiments yesterday, all was business. **1895** C. KING *Fort Frayne* 39 Two ranchmen, now eagerly fingering their Winchesters and getting ready for business. **1900** SMITHWICK *Evolution of State* 40 When we were ready to begin business [*sc.* dancing] it was found Mose had failed to come to time. **1915** G. M. WHITE *Rose o' Paradise* 287 The only friends you have 're out of business.

3. *To mean business*, to be seriously bent on action. {1857}

1875 G. P. BURNHAM *Three Years* 34 They knew he 'meant business,' though his words were few. **1885** HOWELLS *S. Lapham* v, He looked as if he 'meant business,' and I mean business too. **1890** *Buckskin Mose* xiv. 212 If he meant business, it would be a pity to balk good intentions.

4. Attrib. with many nouns, such as *block, call, circle, class, committee, directory*, etc. Also BUSINESS AGENT, etc.

The number of these becomes steadily larger after 1880. Among those of late appearance are *business deal, proposition, section.*

1899 *Mo. So. Dakotan* I. 184 That year he erected the fine business block in Watertown which bears his name. **1861** MCCLELLAN in *Own Story* 177 Gen. Banks dined with me. When he left I had several business calls. **1900** STOCKTON *Afield & Afloat* 287 In fact, you have a very poor commercial standing in business circles. **1883** *Century Mag.* July 471/2 The manners of the business classes themselves admit of no little improvement. **1838** W. L. GARRISON in *Life* (1885) II. 227 A business committee was then appointed. **1841** *Boston Almanac* 2 A complete business directory to the city of Boston. **1886** *Courier-Journal* 2 Feb. 8 (*advt.*), The Louisville, Ky., Business College. . . . Thorough, Practical Business Education. **1849** LANMAN *Alleghany Mts.* 85 He . . . proposed (first excusing himself on account of a business engagement) that I should visit the mountain. **1892** *Vt. Agric. Rep.* XII. 144 With railroads extending the entire length of the County, . . . good transportation as well as business facilities are afforded. **1866** RICHARDSON *Secret Service* 59, It is a business firm and not a political one. **1865** *Atlantic Mo.* XV. 268 Stealing a moment from his precious business hours. **1882** 'M. HARLAND' *Eve's Daughters* 165 The graduates who embark upon the hurrying tide of American business life. **1883** *Harper's Mag.* Sept. 534/1 The Kaaterskill Falls . . . are . . . completely under business management. **1897** F. NORRIS *Third Circle* (1909) 104 'Business opportunities' [in San Diego] lie in wait for the unfortunate at dark street-corners. **1865** *Atlantic Mo.* XV. 224 Now that the angel has become chief business-partner in an earthly working firm, relations are different. **1865** MRS. WHITNEY *Gayworthys* xii. 110 Mrs. Gair was ordinarily rather shy of proffering . . . this sort of hospitality, to 'business people.' **1854** BENTON *30 Years' View* I. 295/1 It was a plain business proceeding. **1832** *Congress. Deb.* 25 June 3757 A business profit . . . would raise them to seventy-two and three-fourths cents per yard. **1861** *Vanity Fair* 9 Feb. 62/1 Stuyvesant . . . read the missive indited on one of Primpenny & Co.'s business sheets, and enclosed in the envelope of the firm. **1922** *Hotel Monthly* XXX. 57/2 Around the lobby is the writing room, the ladies' lounge, cafe, lunch room, cigar stand, and business stores. **1838** E. EVERETT in *Mass. Resolves* 9 Jan. 628 A bank is an institution designed to facilitate the operations of trade, by short loans in aid of business transactions. **1832** *Congress. Deb.* 28 May 3149 This is . . . a strict business view of our condition. **1905** *Sears, Roebuck & Co. Cat.* No. 115, 934 We have woolens . . . for business wear.

Business agent. One who transacts business for another. — **1849** LANMAN *Alleghany Mts.* 85 Mr. William H. Thomas, who is the 'guide, counsellor, and friend' of the Indians, as well as their business agent. **1891** RYAN *Pagan of Alleghanies* 51 He had then in his pocket a letter addressed to the senior telling him to send a business agent. **1901** MERWIN & WEBSTER *Calumet K* 15 All that remained was to wait until the business agent made the next move.

Business card. A card on which is printed one's name, business, address, etc. {1865-}

1840 *Boston Almanac* 119 Business cards printed in the most expeditious manner. **1861** NEWELL *Orpheus C. Kerr* I. 280 What sensitive and delicately-nerved female would marry a man whose business-card read, 'Try Hobbs & Dobbs' Knobs?' **1873** HOLLAND *A. Bonnicastle* xxv, I shall be certain to send the first business-card I get printed to Henry, and solicit his patronage. **1901** CHURCHILL *Crisis* 38 'Name, please,' says he. Mr. Hopper whips out his business card.

Business center. A town or part of a town in which business is largely centered. — **1851** CIST *Cincinnati* 278 Cincinnati, being the business centre of an immense corn-growing and hog-raising region, is . . . the principal pork market in the United States. **1888** J. KIRKLAND *McVeys* 4 In the 'business centre' one might see an occasional tall, narrow, straight-sided brick structure.

+**Business college.** A school devoted to commercial studies; a secretarial school. — **1877** *Harper's Mag.* April 724 The academy and school libraries . . . include seminaries and institutes for both sexes, business colleges, normal schools [etc.]. **1893** 'THANET '*Stories* 69, I went to the business-college and learned book-keeping, and afterward I learned typewriting and shorthand. **1909** A. C. RICE *Mr. Opp* 26 The sole decoration . . . was a large advertisement for a business college.

+**Business end.** The effective or active part; the commercial aspect. — **1878** HOLBROOK *Hygiene Brain* 56 The business end of a carpet-tack. **1901** CHURCHILL *Crisis* 113 Just now they callate I'm about good enough to manage the business end of an affair like this here.

Business letter. A letter dealing with business affairs. — **1844** *Knickerb.* XXIV. 180 You find the thick, dumpy letter, the business-letter, the half-sheet sealed with a wafer [etc.]. **1853** *Harper's Mag.* VII.

276/1 A sharp 'business letter' that, in the eyes of that class . . . who think that there is nothing valuable but trade in this multifarious world of ours! **1866** RICHARDSON *Secret Service* 57 They were written like ordinary business letters, treating of trade and monetary affairs, and containing drafts upon supposititious persons. **1916** E. H. WEBSTER *English for Business* 280 A woman writing a business letter places her title . . . either . . . before her signature or below it.

Businesslike, *a.* Having the precise or practical character of business.

1860 HOLLAND *Miss Gilbert's Career* 164 He finished this brief and business-like production. **1865** *Atlantic Mo.* XV. 496 The tears came into her eyes; but her mother looked up, in her cool, business-like way, and said [etc.]. **1880** *Harper's Mag.* Sept. 6/1 [He] presided . . . over the old place, now sadly fallen from its former business-like character. **1891** O'BEIRNE *Leaders Ind. Territory* 165/2 He is an energetic, reliable and business like young man. **1911** *Harper's Wkly.* 29 April 22/1 There is no good resolution from which I gain so much pleasure as the resolve to be businesslike.

Businessman. A man engaged in business.

1832 *Congress. Deb.* 30 Jan. 1511 Having been in the practice of the law . . . and somewhat conversant with business men. **1834** H. BRACKENRIDGE *Recoll.* 178 He must be content to become a *business man,* and leave the rest to fortune. **1846** *Knickerb.* XXVII. 171 He . . . scuds like a business-man through crowded streets. **1865** *Atlantic Mo.* XV. 82 Two or three may be styled commuters' roads, running chiefly for the accommodation of city business-men with suburban residences. **1887** TOURGEE *Button's Inn* 329 He must have been a very good business man in his day. **1897** FLANDRAU *Harvard Episodes* 297 The business man from whom he seeks employment . . . amuses the family circle at dinner by telling of the call he had from a 'typical Harvard man.' **1903** *Harper's Weekly* XLVII. 1694 The successful business man sticks to business for the same reason the saints stuck to saintliness,—because it is his job and he likes it.

Business manager. One who looks after the business interests of a company or concern. — **1865** *Atlantic Mo.* XV. 226 Can a bird make a good business-manager? **1870** MRS. STEPHENS *Married in Haste* 324, I'm going to be the agent and business manager of this concern.

+**Business office.** A place of business, spec. the office in charge of financial transactions and bookkeeping for a firm or institution. — **1877** *Harper's Mag.* April 688/1 Outside of his own home and business office, Roderick was rather a nervous man. **1893** M. Philips *Making of a Newspaper* 18 In this partial survey of the process and cost of making a 'mammoth newspaper,' no account has been taken of the business office, the mailing room, the foundry, and the press-room.

Business street. A street on which business houses are located. — **1881** *Harper's Mag.* April 711/1 Its [Milwaukee's] broad, Nicholson-paved business streets are bounded for block after block with warehouses and offices. **1883** *Century Mag.* Nov. 40/1 After I had learned that Tchoupitoulas 'Road' was now a great business street.

Business suit. A suit such as a businessman usually wears. — **1880** 'MARK TWAIN' *Tramp Abroad* xlviii. 556 We saw eight or ten wooden dummies grouped together, clothed in woolen business suits and each marked with its price. **1905** *Sears, Roebuck & Co. Cat.* No. 115, 940/3 A neat fine wearing business suit, cut over the best fitting patterns.

+**Businesswoman.** A woman active in business; a practical, businesslike woman. — **1844** *S. Lit. Messenger* X. 486 [Mrs. Jowers had the] reputation of being a 'business woman.' **1863** 'G. HAMILTON' *Gala-Days* 65 Some of these were, I suppose, what Winthrop calls 'business-women.' **1891** BUNNER *Zadoc Pine* 73 She's a business-woman, and she's got a good, sound head.

Business world. That portion of society concerned with business interests. — **1837** *S. Lit. Messenger* III. 391 An extra-ordinary convulsion in the business-world prostrated his hopes. **1892** *Vt. Agric. Rep.* XII. 144 With electric communication, one town with another, [and] all with the business world, good transportation . . . facilities are afforded.

+**Busk.** [f. Creek *púskita.*] An annual harvest feast held by the Creeks. — **1772** D. TAITT in *Travels Amer. Col.* 549 Ordered two young men to go to the Cherokees and bring two of their head men to the Cowetas about the Time of their busk or Green Corn dance (which will be about the beginning of August). **1791** BARTRAM *Travels* 509 The busk, or feast of first fruits, is their principal festival. *Ib.*, Every town celebrates the busk separately, when their own harvest is ready. **1792** J. POPE *Tour S. & W.* 55 In the public Square . . . also they hold their War Dances, display their Trophies of War, and keep their annual Festival called the *Busk.* **1842** E. A. HITCHCOCK *Journal* 116 The fire at the Round House is kept alive throughout the Busk.

Bust, Bu'st, *n.* [Dial. var. of BURST *n.*]

+**1.** A failure; a bankruptcy.

1842 *Knickerb.* XX. 99 'A mistake!' exclaimed the other; 'not a bit of it! It's a reg'lar built bu'st!' **1902** HARBEN *Abner Daniel* 213 Ef I knowed he had made by the bu'st I'd talk different, but I don't know it!

+**2.** A drinking bout; a spree. Also fig.

*c***1844** R. H. COLLYER *Amer. Life* 23 Young and old 'were on a bust.' **1851** *Polly Peablossom* 67 Mike . . . concluded that he would go on a 'bust.' **1867** A. DALY *Legend of 'Norwood'* 35 The darned old thing [a clock] goes on a regular bust when it strikes. **1873** *Congress. Rec.* 19 Dec. 334/2 There are some men that seek their Christmas holiday for other purposes than 'busts' or 'sprees.' **1883** SHIELDS *S. S. Prentiss* 32 It seems to me as though the whole people is on a bust.

Bust, Bu'st, *v. dial.* and *colloq.*[2] (except in 3). Past tense and past part. **bust, busted.** [English dialect) variant of BURST *v.*]

1. *intr.* To undergo bursting or breaking.

1837 *Knickerb.* IX. 68 That was a scene! . . . the lightnings a-bustin' overhead, and hissing in the water. **1839** *S. Lit. Messenger* V. 328/2 A . . . number of us resolved . . . to go it or *bust:* in three words we played truant. **1845** HOOPER *Simon Sugg's Adv.* ii. 20, I do wish to God he'd bust wide open. *a***1861** WINTHROP *J. Brent* 276 Engineer had reported to Captain, that 'Kangaroo No. 5 would bust, if he didn't stop trying to make her lift herself over the damp country by her braces.' **1866** C. H. SMITH *Bill Arp* 44 One of the shipwrecked foreigners . . . used to travel over the country with a certificate that a volcano had busted and run all over him. **1876** 'MARK TWAIN' *Tom Sawyer* xxx, If she'll let up on some of the roughest things, I'll . . . crowd through or bust. **1885** JEWETT *Marsh Island* xi. 147, I thought I should bu'st if I had to keep it all to myself. **1902** LORIMER *Lett. Merchant* 161 The best you can hope is that it will swell up and bust; and then, of course, there's nothing left.

b. To break *in, loose, out, up,* etc.

1840 KENNEDY *Quodlibet* 167 'What's the fraction,' said Neal, 'that you're all a busting out in such a spell of a laugh about?' **1847** ROBB *Squatter Life* 60 'What d'ye think, boys,' busted in old Jack. **1850** LEWIS *La. Swamp Dr.* 173 Doc, you've hearn a bar bustin' threw a cane-brake, and know how near to a harrycane it is. **1854** M. J. HOLMES *Tempest & Sunshine* xv. 207 By John, if Sunshine goes, old Josh'll bust up and go too. **1857** *Lawrence* (Kansas) *Republican* 11 June 2 We hope it [the Union] will not 'bust up' just yet. **1870** 'F. FERN' *Ginger-Snaps* 141, I was in an omnibus alone, save one lady, when a meeting of some sort in one of our churches 'bust up,'—excuse the expression—'bust up.' **1871** *Harper's Mag.* Oct. 795 The soldiers have milked our cows, or stolen our chickens, or *busted* into the smoke-house. **1905** PHILLIPS *Social Secretary* 63 Never before did I have a best dress that I wasn't afraid to breathe in for fear I'd bust out, back or front.

c. To fail financially, become bankrupt. Also with *up.*

1837 *Knickerb.* X. 329 Can it truly be That 'Providence, which oft afflicts the just,' Has fore-ordain'd that all the banks should *bu'st?* **1843** *Ib.* March 236 It's ruinous! I shall bu'st if she an't well soon. *c***1845** W. J. PAULDING *Madmen All* 191, I was tarred and feathered once, and just because my bank bust up. **1870** MEDBERY *Men Wall St.* 180 Then we shall hear that you've 'busted.' **1880** *Harper's Mag.* Oct. 729/1 After the fate of the town, be it to 'boom' or 'bust,' has been decided. **1902** NORRIS *Pit* ix, You've got the ready money. I know what you can stand without busting. **1904** 'O. HENRY' *Cabbages & Kings* (1916) 146 'Twas the project of a private corporation, but it busted, and then the government took it up.

d. To go on 'busts'; to dissipate.

1866 C. H. SMITH *Bill Arp* 118 Ike was at home on a busting furlow. **1869** *Picayune* 14 Feb. (De Vere), Because I was a good-natured fellow, I had to go with them, frolicking, teaparting, excursioning, and busting generally.

2. *tr.* To cause to burst or break; to smash or shatter.

1806 LEWIS in *L. & Clark Exped.* (1905) V. 137 This morning Windsor busted his rifle near the muzzle. **1834** CARRUTHERS *Kentuckian* I. 218 That'll make them think somebody's busted their biler. **1843** 'CARLTON' *New Purchase* II. 180 Bust my rifle! we'll dog out the rats now. **1845** HOOPER *Taking Census* i. 163 The furr a flyin' every time she jumped, like you'd a busted a feather bed open! **1854** M. J. HOLMES *Tempest & Sunshine* 206, I was so feared Bill would bust his jacket open that I whispered to him not to take on so. **1877** WM. WRIGHT *Big Bonanza* 362 The Comstocker first 'busted' his egg on the top of the Piocher's head, and the feat was loudly applauded by all present. **1884** NYE *Baled Hay* 48 You are not blamed because the Republican party has busted your crust. **1918** MULFORD *Man fr. Bar-20* 30 If he sends the kid a shotgun, I'll come down and bust his neck.

b. To cause to break financially; to make bankrupt, reduce to bankruptcy.

1829 R. C. SANDS *Writings* II. 153 For the Aigle Bank was *bussted,* and the Cataract of Freedom was stopped. **1869** BROWNE *Adv. Apache Country* 507 But you see me and my pardner is bust. We must have capital. **1870** MEDBERY *Men Wall St.* 181 'Why,' responded Kelley, with a woful expression of countenance, 'our house is "busted."' **1871** BRET HARTE *Poems* 54 Briggs . . . busted hisself in White Pine, and blew out his brains down in 'Frisco. **1883** 'MARK TWAIN' *Life on Miss.* xliii. 438 And you take in a poor man, and if you work him right he'll bust himself on a single lay-out. **1900** SMITHWICK *Evolution of State* 148 It wasn't long till I had the game busted. **1902** NORRIS *Pit* ix, If they all began to sell to you at once they'd bust you. **1917** MCCUTCHEON *Green Fancy* 17 Busted. Up the flue. Showed last Saturday night in Hornville, . . . and immediately after the performance him and his whole troupe started to walk back to New York.

c. To break *up,* force *in* by breaking, etc.

1840 KENNEDY *Quodlibet* 91 Miss Porter ses . . . that if you ain't busted up, you will be before night. **1845** J. J. HOOPER *Simon Sugg's Adv.* i. 17 Nothin' a'n't trumps now, . . . but clubs was, when you came along and busted up the game. **1869** BROWNE *Adv. Apache Country* 311 On that occasion he broke several of his ribs, or as he expressed it to me, 'Bust his sides in.' **1873** in Custer *Boots & Saddles* 275 We must bust him up to-day. **1878** BEADLE *Western Wilds* 183 The boys soon busted them [*sc.* the Millerites] up.

d. To force out.

1854 M. J. HOLMES *Tempest & Sunshine* xii. 173 Couldn't you manage to bust a tear or two, just to make it seem more like a real buryin'?

+3. To break or render docile.

1891 *Harper's Mag.* July 210/1 Two rides will usually bust a bronco so that the average cow-puncher can use him. **1900** GARLAND *Eagle's Heart* 172 Rope him, and put a saddle on him and bust him. **1903** *Wide World Mag.* April 545 It is upon the cowboys that the task falls of breaking to the saddle, or busting, the almost intractable 'broncos' that are raised ... for the open market.

***Bustard.** +The Canada goose, *Branta canadensis.* — **1820** Morse *Rep. Indian Affairs* (1822) II. 32 The water fowl, throughout this north-western country, are ... the bustard, wild goose, ... and the gull.

Busted, *a. dial.* and *colloq.*[2] [BUST *v.*] Broken, burst, financially ruined.

1837 *Knickerb.* X. 170, I've hear'n tell since, that he was a busted man. **1860** *Harper's Mag.* July 278/2 Skaggins ... having lost all he had except a fifty-dollar bill on a 'busted' bank at a game of poker. **1865** 'MARK TWAIN' *Sketches* (1926) 196 If there was a horse-race, you'd find him flush or you'd find him busted at the end of it. **1870** W. F. RAE *Westward by Rail* 212 To-morrow hardly a soul will deign to notice the concern which, in the slang of the locality [=Nevada], is 'played out' or 'busted.' **1881** HAYES *New Colorado* 80 It was a regular amalgamation of busted people. **1885** *Lisbon* (Dakota) *Star* 18 Sept., There was a busted keg on the floor, and I was smoking my pipe. **1889** 'MARK TWAIN' *Conn. Yankee* xix. 235 Just a rubbish-pile of battered corpses and ... busted hardware. **1909** 'O. HENRY' *Roads of Destiny* vi. 97 Its well-known superiority in ... achievements with the precarious busted flush.

Buster. [BUST *v.*] {1839}

1. *slang.* **+a.** A person of unusual capacity, spirit, dash, or assertiveness.

1843 *S. Lit. Messenger* IX. 732/1 Applause; laughter, cheers and cries of 'go on,' 'go it, Smith,' and 'he's a buster, ain't he?' *c***1845** *Big Bear Ark.*, etc. 24, I was reckoned a buster, and allowed to be decidedly the best bar hunter in my district. **1846** *Spirit of Times* 16 May 134/2 Our word 'buster' ... is commonly understood to signify a fellow who 'busts' things sky-high—a stump orator for instance, who after ... knocking his opponent into a 'cocked hat' is called a 'buster.' **1852** STOWE *Uncle Tom* iv, Mas'r George, however, joined the offender in the laugh, and declared decidedly that Mose was a 'buster.' **1888** J. WEBB *Adventures* 162 We are the six busters, and our labors of this day ought to be printed in the papers. **1921** PAINE *Comr. Rolling Ocean* 282 Give him my compliments, and tell him he is a buster of a man.

b. An animal or thing of unusual size or quality. {*dial.*}

(1) **1845** in *Cincinnati Misc.* 134 Finally I see a countryman leading a black colt—wasn't he a buster! He had the greatest withers ever you see on a hoss, and a set of limbs that would bring tears into a man's eyes. *a***1846** *Quarter Race Ky.*, etc. 140 The bear was commented on as he rushed by; one said he was 'a buster.' **1876** BOURKE *Journal* July 28—Sept. 8 He handed me his willow branch rod, ... at same time telling me there was a fine big trout—'a regular buster' in the hole beyond. **1886** *Outing* IX. 104/2 Did you really kill a bear?' 'Yes, and a buster, too.' **1888** C. D. WARNER *On Horseback* 88 There was the skin of one [rattlesnake] hanging upon a tree ... a buster; he skinned him yesterday. (2) **1848** BARTLETT 57 We sometimes hear this word applied to a gale of wind, as, 'This is a buster,' i.e. a powerful or heavy wind. **1852** STOWE *Uncle Tom* x, 'Lor, Pete,' said Mose triumphantly, 'han't we got a buster of a breakfast!' **1854** M. J. HOLMES *Tempest & Sunshine* 314 We'll have a buster [of a house], ... marble mantle top, windows that come to the floor, Brussels carpets. **1865** 'MARK TWAIN' *Sketches* (1926) 159 He couldn't spell the words; he tackled some of them regular busters toward the middle, you know, and they throwed him. **1867** F. LUDLOW *Fleeing to Tarshish* 176 The rector's growing reputation for preaching busters, which is the Missourian for pulpit eloquence. **1904** G. STRATTON-PORTER *Freckles* 109 The Portland company cut this for elm butts last year. ... It was a buster!

+2. *slang.* A 'bust,' spree, drinking frolic.

1848 BARTLETT 57 They were on a buster, and were taken up by the police.

+3. (See quotations.)

1879 *St. Nicholas Mag.* Nov., He [=young crab] still keeps on eating and gets bigger still, and then cracks a little, and is called a 'Crack-buster.' He still grows till he is called a 'Buster,' and then sheds. **1890** *Cent.* 5749/2 A crab in the act of casting its shell is termed a *shedder, peeler,* or *buster;* when the new shell begins to harden, a *crackler.*

+4. One who breaks mustangs, broncos, etc.

1891 *Harper's Mag.* July 208/1 The bronco buster ... cannot stick it out very long, for the business is sure to end by busting the buster. **1897** *Outing* XXX. 480/2 Mebbe my Joe, the buster, can tell you more'n I can about 'em. **1903** *Wide World Mag.* April 545 On a large ranch which employs many cowboys, there is much rivalry among them as to who is the best rider, or buster.

+Busthead. [BUST *v.*] Whisky of an inferior quality. — **1863** 'E. KIRKE' *Southern Friends* 49 Thirsty natives, imbibing certain fluids known at the South as blue ruin, bust-head, red-eye, tangle-foot, rifle-whiskey, and devil's dye. **1866** 'F. KIRKLAND' *Bk. Anecdotes* 446 Clean them mules, and I'll give you a drink of busthead. **1883** *Congress. Rec.* 1 Feb. 1898/2 A man in this country can not take a drink of American whisky, be it the Cincinnati bust-head or the N. Carolina pine-top, however distilled, without paying 200 per cent on it.

+Bustic. [Of obscure origin.] A tropical American tree with heavy, hard, dark-brown wood. — **1884** SARGENT *Rep. Forests* 101 *Dipholis salicifolia.* ... Bustic. Cassada.

Busting, *vbl. n.* [BUST *v.* 3.] The breaking-in or taming of horses. — **1891** *Harper's Mag.* July 208/2 The whole secret of 'busting' ... lies in completely exhausting the bronco at the first lesson. **1895** REMINGTON *Pony Tracks* 66 Anything and everything is his work, from the negotiation for the sale of five thousand ... cattle to the 'busting' of a broncho which no one else can 'crawl.'

Busting, *a. colloq.*[2] Immense; splendid. — **1851** *Polly Peablossom* 151, I soon see thar was gwine to be the bustinest fight that ever was. **1859** *S. Lit. Messenger* XXVIII. 143/1 Turkey, thar's the biggest, bustinest pike in that hole you uvver seed.

Bustle. [Cf. BUSTLER.] A pad or cushion formerly worn by women beneath their skirts at the back. {1788-}

1786 A. ADAMS in *Letters* (1848) 294 Pray, does the fashion of merry thoughts, bustles, and protuberances prevail with you? **1787** DALRYMPLE *Journal* (1871) 55 She is very genteal and wears monstrous Bustles. **1846** CORCORAN *Pickings* 50 Her dress was faded, and so was her face; her forehead was wrinkled, and so was her fan; and we verily believe that she had no bustle. **1852** *Harper's Mag.* V. 271/1 It is not a very long time ago, that 'bustles' formed a very essential part of a fashionable lady's dress. **1854** RILEY *Puddleford* 25 Some of them had mounted a 'bustle' about the size of a bag of bran, and were waddling along under their load with great satisfaction. **1875** G. P. BURNHAM *Three Years* 219 Indeed, in the early days, when the 'bishop' or 'bustle' ... first came into vogue, Mrs. Roberts sported a tremendous ornament of this description. **1891** WELCH *Recoll. 1830-40* 176 How fortunate that hoops were not then in fashion, nor bustles; however, the bustles of to-day are but miniatures of those of 1846.

‖**Bustler.** *Obs.* =BUSTLE. [The article cited appears to be the sole authority for the statement that the word originated in the visit to London in 1783 of the German duchess of Bustledorfe.] — **1787** *Amer. Museum* II. 483 Wool, which might cover the legs of hundreds, is diverted from that use, and manufactured into odious *bustlers.*

Bust-up. *dial.* An unfortunate plight, dilemma, or breaking up; a bank failure. (Cf. BUST n. 1.) — **1846** *Knickerb.* XXVIII. 313 Well, this is the houdaciousest bust-up I ever seed, any how! **1902** HARBEN *Abner Daniel* 205, I wanted to talk to you about Alan an' that bank bu'st-up. *Ib.* 213 Fincher's his best friend sence his bu'st-up, an' they are mighty thick.

***Busy,** *v.* [f. *busy* a.] ‖*tr.* To answer, or put off, with 'busy.' — **1827** *Harvard Reg.* May 84 Poor Croak was almost annihilated by this summons, and clinging to the bed clothes in all the agony of despair, forgot to 'busy' his midnight visiter.

But. [Eng. *butt*, a sole, flounder, plaice, etc.] The plaice. — **1807** *Mass. H. S. Coll.* 2 Ser. III. 57 The but or plaice, which has its mouth on the same side as the halibut, is caught during the whole year.

* **Butcher,** *n.*

***1.** One who slaughters animals for the market; a store-keeper who deals in meat.

1642 *Suffolk Deeds* I. 35, I, Robert Nash of Charlestowne in New England, Butcher. **1685** SEWALL *Diary* I. 75 The cow was dead and by the Heels, meaning hang'd up by the Butcher. **1716** *Boston Selectmen* 11 John Edwards who ... desires to dwell in this Town & to occupy the trade of a Butcher, is now ... warned to depart. **1775** J. ANDREWS *Letters* 83 There was a general squabble between the Butchers in the market and a number of Soldiers. **1841** HAWTHORNE *Note-Books* II. 24 Then there are the cattle-people and butchers who supply the Boston market. **1871** HOWELLS *Wedding Journey* 21 A marketing mother of a family paused at a provision-store, ... looking weakly in at the white-aproned butcher among his meats and flies. **1901** DUNCAN & SCOTT *Allen & Woodson Co., Kansas* 248 He discovered an opening in his community for a country butcher and he fitted out a store-on-wheels and engaged in the business.

b. In possessive (sing. or pl.) compounds, with *beef, block, cart,* etc.

1802 JEFFERSON in *Harper's Mag.* March (1885) 539/2 A View of the Consumption of butchers meat. **1809** WEEMS *Marion* (1833) xii. 102 They are as strong and fierce as game cocks or butchers' bull dogs. **1819** *Amer. Farmer* I. 142 Butcher's Beef best pieces. **1837** HAWTHORNE in *Democratic Rev.* I. 33 The next object passing townward is a butcher's cart, canopied with its arch of snow-white cotton. *a***1846** *Quarter Race Ky.*, etc. 185 Just imagine a butcher's block five feet long and four feet through at the butt. **1846** *Rep. Comm. Patents* 222 The saponization of animal entrails or butchers' offals by the means of a strong caustic alkali. **1861** *Vanity Fair* 9 Feb. 62/1 You may send your butcher's bills to undersigned. **1865** *Atlantic Mo.* XV. 83 Receipts of Butchers' Animals in New York during 1863.

c. Attrib. with *business, shop, wagon,* etc.

1886 P. STAPLETON *Major's Christmas* 162 Turkeys hang before the butcher-shop. **1891** O'BEIRNE *Leaders Ind. Territory* 42/1 He opened in the butcher business in the same place and remained at it for several years. **1897** FLANDRAU *Harvard Episodes* 230 Haydock . . . picked his way . . . among the disabled butcher-waggons, by the black alley.

+**2.** A copyreader in a newspaper office, etc.

1867 HOLMES *Guardian Angel* 297 These are the manuscript poems that we receive, and the one sitting at the table is commonly spoken of among us as The Butcher. **1902** CLAPIN 88 *Butcher*, in newspaper jargon, a term applied to the copy-reader, who uses mercilessly the blue-pencil in cutting short reporters' stories.

+**3.** One who sells candy, fruits, etc., on a train.

*a***1889** *Detroit Free Press* (Barrère & Leland), On a Michigan Central train the other day as the butcher came into the car with a basket of oranges [etc.]. **1900** G. ADE *More Fables* 2 As he rode toward the Great City he smoked a Baby Mine Cigar, purchased of the Butcher. **1904** *Columbus Ev. Dispatch* 16 Aug. 3 The days of the 'butchers' are numbered, and their privileges have been so restricted that they are able to do little, if any, business.

***Butcher,** *v.*

+**1.** *tr.* To cut up or divide (an animal) into convenient portions after the manner of a butcher.

1822 J. FOWLER *Journal* 121 Robert and Taylor went Hunting; the formor killed two elk, and left the latter to butcher them. **1843** T. J. FARNHAM *Travels* I. 70 We butchered him [=buffalo] in the following manner: Having turned him upon his brisket, split the skin above the spine, and pared it off, [etc.]. **1848** RUXTON *Life Far West* (1849) 178 Killbuck . . . saw, to his astonishment, La Bonté in the act of butchering a buffalo within two hundred yards of camp. **1858** G. A. JACKSON *Diary* 520 All off for the elk grounds. . . . Tom and Black Hawk to butcher the kill of yesterday and I to follow the elk trail.

+**b.** To cut away (*off* or *out*) in a rough and ready manner.

1848 RUXTON *Life Far West* (1849) 16 'One of you quit this arrow out of my hump.' . . . His nearest neighbour . . . expressed his opinion that the offending weapon would have to be 'butchered' out. *Ib.* 118 The . . . body of one of the Indian squaws, with a large portion of the flesh butchered from it. *Ib.* 160 Bill . . . called to him . . . to butcher off a piece of meat and put it in the pot.

+**2.** *intr.* To do butchering.

1865 *Atlantic Mo.* XV. 454 'Thinkin,' Huldy, if it is n't about time to butcher: we butchered last year' [etc.]. **1868** BRACKETT *Farm Talk* 77, I see you've butchered. How much did your pigs weigh? **1896** *Scribner's Mag.* VI. 484/1 'Don't butcher next week. Friday is Christmas day.' . . . 'Well, we always butcher Christmas week, don't we?'

Butcherbird. The shrike, loggerhead, or nine-killer, *Lanius borealis* or *L. ludovicianus.* {1668–}

1743 CATESBY *Carolina* App. p. xxiii, European Land-Birds inhabiting America [include] The greater Butcher Bird. **1808** WILSON *Ornithology* I. 75 The Butcher-bird sticks his [surplus food] on thorns and bushes. **1844** *Nat. Hist. N.Y., Zoology* II. 127 This bold and ferocious little bird, which is usually known as the Butcher-bird, . . . is exceedingly destructive, waging war upon all birds. **1884** ROE *Nature's Story* 112, I shall not say one word in favor of the next bird that I mention, the great Northern shrike, or butcher-bird.

Butchering, *vbl. n.* {1604–}

1. The action of killing and cutting up animals for food. Also attrib.

1773 *Carrol P.* in *Md. Hist. Mag.* XV. 63, I expect one more steer from the Island; the last we had from thence was . . . miserably mangled in the butchering. **1850** GARRARD *Wah-To-Yah* i. 21 But finding myself a green hand, at least not an adept, in the mysteries of prairie butchering. **1865** BUSHNELL *Vicar. Sacr.* IV. 395 Every woman, every child, looked on at the butchering. **1885** *Rep. Indian Affairs* 178 A slaughter-house was built and the butchering is now done in a more cleanly . . . manner than was possible before. **1891** *Anthony's Photogr. Bull.* IV. 329 The butchering of a 'beef' with the bos'n in the rôle of a butcher. **1913** STRATTON-PORTER *Laddie* (1917) 146 She had big jars of lard she wouldn't need before butchering time came again. *Ib.* 152 When . . . the field corn was all husked, and the butchering done.

2. The occupation of a butcher. Also attrib. {1877, *dial.*}

1851 CIST *Cincinnati* 220 Two butchering and rendering establishments . . . tried out . . . sixty thousand sheep. **1860** HOLMES *E. Venner* iii, Abner Briggs, Junior, was a great, hulking fellow, who had been bred to butchering. **1866** *Internal Revenue Guide* 75 No license is required for butchering as such. Selling meat at retail . . . requires the seller to have license.

+**Butcher knife.** A large knife now used chiefly as a kitchen utensil.

1822 *Mass. Spy* 25 Dec. (Th.), Her foot slipt, and she fell upon a large butcher-knife which she had in her hand. **1858** BRYANT *California* 308 Dismounting from his horse, he then takes from his leggin the butcher-knife that he always carries with him. **1866** *Rep. Indian Affairs* 83 Many of the Indians have been compelled to cut their wheat with common butcher knives. **1890** *Century Mag.* Dec. 163 One giving a can of powder, another a bar of lead or a butcher-knife.

attrib. **1847** T. FORD *Hist. Illinois* 88 These 'butcher knife boys,' as they were called, made a kind of balance of power party. *Ib.*, Most of the elections in early times were made under 'butcher knife influence.'

***Butler.** +At Harvard and Yale, a former college officer having charge of the buttery and performing various other duties. — **1734** in Peirce *Hist. Harvard* (1833) App. 137 The butler shall take care that all fines imposed by the President . . . be fairly recorded in a book. **1797** R. TYLER *Algerine Captive* I. 54 With being butler's freshman, and ringing the bell the first year, waiter the three last, and keeping school in the vacations, I rubbed through. **1811** *Yale College Laws* 31 The Butler shall make up his bill against each Student, in which every article sized or taken up by him at the Buttery, shall be particularly charged. **1850** T. D. WOOLSEY *Hist. Disc. Yale* 43 The classes since 1817, when the office of butler was abolished, are probably but little aware of the meaning of that singular appendage to the College. **1876** *Scribner's Mo.* XI. 769/1 The College Butler [at Yale], a licensed monopolist, . . . dispensed to such as had money or credit 'cider, metheglin, strong beer, . . . pipes, tobacco, etc.'

Butment.

1. The support of an arch; an abutment. {1624–1773}

1688 *Essex Inst. Coll.* XXXV. 214 All the Carpenters work of the said mill and Damm and Butments to the same belonging. **1718** *Lancaster Rec.* 183 The Neck Bridge . . . should have 5 Trussells, & . . . be a foot higher than before, to make good buttments. **1806** PAINE *Yellow Fever* Writ. IV. (1896) 474 Arches joining each other lengthways serve as buttments to each other. **1865** *Atlantic Mo.* XV. 74 Beyond the Park, Haarlem Lane, Manhattanville, . . . take up the thread of civic population, and carry it . . . quite to the butment of High Bridge. **1888** C. D. WARNER *On Horseback* 135, It [=a bridge] was carried away three or four years ago, and its ragged butments stand as a monument of procrastination.

2. A boundary mark.

1704 *Derby* (Conn.) *Rec.* 362 The butments at each corner [of John Pringle's lot] are meer stones, with stones heapt or layd about them.

***Butt,** *n.*[1]

1. A large cask, in early use esp. for wine or other liquor.

1633 *New-Hampshire Doc. & Rec.* I. 78, 1 butt with 5 nets in it. *a***1649** WINTHROP *Hist.* 269 The last year the court had imposed ten shillings upon every butt of sack, etc. **1683** *N.H. Hist. Soc. Coll.* VIII. 150 Whereas . . . one butt and one quarter cask of Malaga wine . . . was lately seized for his Majesty. **1852** MRS. ELLET *Pioneer Women* 387 Every house should be provided with a butt of water for use in case of fire. **1886** *Leslie's Mo.* XXI. 222/2 The flakes are covered with drying cod which have been salted in these same hogsheads or 'butts.'

+**2.** 'In the tobacco-trade, a box 12 inches square, with a capacity of from 15 to 50 pounds' (*Dicts.*).

***Butt, But,** *n.*[2]

***1.** A mound of earth on which a target is placed; a mark for practice in shooting.

1647 *R.I. Col. Rec.* I. 187 Each Towne shall have a pair of Butts. **1653** *Boston Rec.* X. 7 There may be a good Butt or kinde of Bullwarke raised of earth. **1780** *Virginia St. P.* I. 372 Tho' we endeavour to save them in Butts, yet there is a very great loss [of bullets] every time. **1861** *Army Regulations* 17 To determine accuracy of aim in firing shot and shell, butts or targets will be used.

***2.** A terminal or boundary point of ground. {–1726} Also fig.

1730 *Boston Selectmen* 203 All which are more fully and perticulerly set forth with Butts and Bounds in the said lease. **1827** *Western Mo. Rev.* I. 281 Fences, butts, and bounds, and partition lines . . . were terms of unhappy omen in his ear. **1833** FLINT *D. Boone* p. v, He finds the butts and bounds of legal tenures restraining his free thoughts. **1868** CHANNING *Recoll. Newport* 121 He had a way . . . of mapping out his case with 'buts and bounds.' **1902** MCFAUL *Ike Glidden* 44 Have you any documents for reference in order to fix the butts and bounds?

***Butt,** *n.*[3] Also **but.**

1. The thick lower end of a tree trunk; the part just above the root. {1601–}

1695 *Cambridge Prop. Rec.* 220 The Bounds . . . shall run from the Butt of a tree blown up by the Roots. **1760** *Essex Inst. Coll.* XLVI. 256 A spar or piece of timber . . . measuring about 70 feet in length, and between 2 and 3 feet diameter at the Butt. **1823** COOPER *Pioneers* xxxix, You over-calculate your aim . . . if you think to shoot a man through a tree with a three-foot butt. **1841** in Jillson *Dark & Bl. Ground* 86 A burr oak, about 2 feet across at the butt. **1883** HALE *Woods & Timbers N.C.* 42 This stock did not retain its stated diameter (at the butt) to its upper extremity. **1892** *Vt. Agric. Rep.* XII. 124 The butt is sawed into boards, and shipped to Massachusetts.

2. The lower end of a straw, cane, etc.

1804 J. ROBERTS *Penn. Farmer* 101 Then take rye or wheat straw, cut to about two feet long, making the buts even. **1862** *Ill. Agric. Soc. Trans.* V. 161, I topped it, cut the canes in the middle, and boiled the juice of the butts by itself. **1863** *Rep. Comm. Agric.* 94 In building it [a wheat shock] the butts should be firmly placed on the ground in the stubble. **1894** *Vt. Agric. Rep.* XIV. 42 The corn . . . stalks are divided into . . . the butts, or main stem with ears, tops, and blades removed.

***3.** A buttock, rump, or rump piece. {–1601; now *dial.*}

1859 BARTLETT 60 *Butt*, . . . 2. The buttocks. The word is used in the West in such phrases as 'I fell on my butt,' 'He kick'd my butt.' **1884** *Harper's Mag.* July 299/1 Rump butts, strips, rounds, and canning beef.

4. The base of the wing, where it joins the body of a bird.
1806 Lewis in *L. and Clark Exped.* (1905) IV. 28. A third stripe . . . passes from the sides of the neck just above the butts of the wings across the croop in the form of a gorget.

5. 'The small pipe affixed to the hose of a fire-engine' (B. '59).

6. A butt end; a short piece.
1888 Billings *Hardtack* 89 Even those troops having nearly three years to serve would exclaim, . . . 'It's only two years and a but.'

Butt, *n.*[4] A butt-hinge. {1881–}
1788 *Kentucky Gazette* 27 Sept. 1/3 Selling very Cheap for Cash . . . Table butts and Wood Screws. **1816** *Austin Papers* (1924) I. 262, 6 p[ai]r 4½ inch Butts. **1819** *Missouri Intell.* 23 July 3/4 (*advt*)., Iron, Butts and Screws. **1838** Ellsworth *Valley of Wabash* 53 The doors are 'batton doors,' hung with butts or hinges. *a***1870** Chipman *Notes on Bartlett* 60 *Butt*, . . . a sort of flat and short hinge, that, folded, butts on itself. **1882** *Rep. Indian Affairs* 463 Hardware. Butts, brass, 1½ inch, narrow.

***Butt,** *v.*[1] Also †**but.** [Butt *n.*[2] 2.]

***1.** *intr.* To have the boundary or bounding line *on* or *upon, against* or *to* (other land, etc.); to abut or adjoin. {–1798; now *dial.*} Also without prep. (quot. 1806).
1637 *Watertown Rec.* 3 Ordered that there be no Land granted to any person butting upon another mans Land before he have notice of it. **1655** *Suffolk Deeds* II. 113 The other ende butts vpon the Lande that some tymes was mr Clarkes. **1681** *Charlestown Rec.* 192 The land on the South Side of Cambridge Road butting to the marshes. **1704** *Boston News-Letter* 10 July 2/2 A Farm . . . containing 430 Acres . . . butting upon the Road by the 7 mile River. **1719** *Southold Rec.* II. 483 Note the above mentioned lots that butt against the creeks run into the same creeks. **1746** *Georgia Col. Rec.* VI. 149 He desires three hundred Acres butting and bounding upon Lands belonging to Rowland Pritchet. **1806** Clark in *Lewis and C. Exped.* (1905) V. 267 A high rugid rocky hill buts the river imediately below a very good buffalow road. **1853** Strother *Blackwater Chron.* 6 A large spur—apparently the Backbone itself—keeps straight to the south, and butts down on the Cheat.

2. *tr.* ***a.** In p.p. *butted:* Having the bounds or limits as specified. Usually *butted and bounded.* {–1727}
1658 *Portsmouth Rec.* 350 A percell of land . . . bounded and butted as followith, . . . three Rod lyinge next to the fence of the sayd Gyles. **1684** *Duxbury Rec.* 44 On the westerly side butted by said brook, and bounded on the southerly or south west side, with a rock. **1748** *N.H. Probate Rec.* III. 549 To my Son Caleb forty accers of my Home Lot on the North Side bounded on David Woodwell, butted East on Samson Colbey. **1816** U. Brown *Journal* I. 361 This [40,000 acres] is butted & bounded and described directly as the grant is from the Commonwealth of Virginia.

b. To fix, or mark off, the limits of (land).
1673 *Penn. Archives* I. 31 Conteyning as it is to be surveyed, butted, and bounded by the Surveyor Gen[era]l, five hundred and forty acres, English measure. **1816** U. Brown *Journal* I. 367 He butted and bounded of the 2 first lines with our 70,000 Acre tract, & then made the Survey himself.

+**Butt,** *v.*[2] [Butt *n.*[3] 1.]

1. *tr.* To beat (another person) in cutting through a tree or log.
1840 Thompson *Green Mt. Boys* II. 364 Her eldest son, having at length been enabled to butt his mother, to use a chopper's phrase, that is to get off his cut first, in a trial of skill on the same log, she concluded to betake herself to household duties. **1884** E. Ingersoll *Country Cousins* i, I had an uncle . . . who was a famous chopper. . . . When he was past seventy, he had a man working for him . . . and my uncle offered to butt him.

2. (See quot. 1850.)
1850 Judd *R. Edney* 41 Richard took an axe and very neatly proceeded to 'butt' a log; that is, to cut the end of it square off. **1880** *Northw. Lumberman* Jan. 24 If we were buying the logs we should try to get enough off the scale to pay for the butting.

***Butt,** *adv.* [The stem of *butt*, to thrust, strike.] Used to denote direct impact against something, esp. *full butt.* {–1837} — **1807** Irving, etc. *Salmagundi* v. 103 The army accordingly wheeled and came full butt against it in the rear. **1848** Lowell *Biglow P.* I. viii. 170 Say you're assured I go full butt for Libbaty's diffusion. **1865** *Atlantic Mo.* XV. 286 Here the road ended, [and] ran butt against the wall of a huge roofless inclosure. **1886** *Outing* IX. 52/2, I'll run ye butt up agin the door, open it—walk in.

+**Butt cut.** [Butt *n.*[3] 1.] The first portion of a tree cut off above the stump. Also in humorous or derisive use.
1830 *Northern Watchman* (Troy, N.Y.) 19 Oct. (Th.), [He] weighs little short of 450 lbs. and is familiarly known as the But-cut. **1840** *N.Y. American* 24 Nov. 3/2 The overshadowing sycamore . . . was a scraggy affair whose butt-cut would hardly make a back-log for an Illinois cabin. **1840** Kennedy *Quodlibet* 172 Nebuchadnezzar couldn't beat him at a speech. He's the Butt cut of democracy. **1845** Hooper *Simon Sugg's Adv.* iii. 38 In two hours more he won't be able to step over the butt cut of a broom straw. **1873** Beadle *Undevel. West* 259 The 'butt cut' of the tree lies as it fell, the top reached by means of a ladder. **1888** Eggleston in *Century Mag.* XXXVI. 265/2 He came out and stood in the fresh air, on the 'butt-cut' of a tulip-tree, or 'flowering poplar.'

+**Butte.** Also †**bute.** [F. *butte* hillock, mound.] In the West, a conspicuous or isolated hill or mountain, rising abruptly above the surrounding level or country. Cf. 1843 and 1882 in (*b*).

The pronunciation, rhyming with *mute*, as indicated by the early spelling, shows an adaptation of the unfamiliar French *u* (ü).

(*a*) **1805** Clark in *Lewis & C. Exped.* (1904) II. 61, I walked out after dinner and assended a but [*sic*] a few miles (off) to view the countrey. **1838** Parker *Rocky Mts.* 70 Red Bute, which is a high bluff. **1839** Townsend *Narrative* 194 Beyond . . . is a wide and level prairie, interrupted only by some gigantic peaks of mountains and conical butes in the distance. **1843** T. Talbot *Journals* 13 We camped upon the banks of the Kansas just below the junction of its two principal forks. . . . Limestone is the principal formation, and it frequently girdles the butes in successive gradations. **1846** W. G. Stewart *Altowan* I. ii. 40 He saw a horse where the first range of rough *Butes*, lays a foundation for the stupendous structure above.

(*b*) *a***1842** O. Russel *Journal* (1921) 76 We were now in sight of the red buttes on the River Platte, which appeared about forty miles distant southeast. **1843** Frémont *Exped.* 161 The French word *butte* . . . is naturalized in the region of the Rocky mountains; and, even if desirable to render it in English, I know of no word which would be its precise equivalent. It is applied to the detached hills & ridges which rise abruptly, and reach too high to be called hills or ridges, and not high enough to be called mountains. **1856** Whipple *Explor. Ry. Route* II. 19 A few yards north of our camp were a few low 'buttes,' covered with dwarf plum-trees. **1882** *Century Mag.* Aug. 510/2 Back of these mud buttes (everything in the way of hill, rock, mountain, or clay-heap is called a butte in Montana) are immense stretches of grazing country. **1903** A. Adams *Log Cowboy* xxii. 347 We could see in that rarefied atmosphere the buttes, like sentinels on duty.

attrib. **1880** *Scribner's Mo.* XX. 454/1 [Wagons] broken down among the rocks of a stony bit of butte-road, were grimly labeled 'Busted, by Thunder!'

Buttelled, *p.p. Obs.* [f. *buttel* v. {1571–83}.] Butted. (See Butt *v.*[1] 2 a.) — **1637** *Dedham Rec.* 35 As it lyeth by the sayd Riuer buttelled & bownded betweene a litte brook & certeyne Rocks. **1655** *Suffolk Deeds* II. 200 To haue and to hold the aforesajd Premisses as before buttelled and bownded. **1669** *Boston Rec.* 151 [They sold] the above . . . parcell of land . . . with all the libertyes, priveledges and apurtenances, buttelled, bounded and declared in the said Deed.

***Butt end.** +The part of a tree trunk immediately above the ground. Also fig.
1642 T. Lechford *Plain Dealing* 51 They [the Indians] cut downe a tree with axes and hatchets . . . & bring in the butt-end into the wigwam, upon the hearth, and so burne it by degrees. **1677** Hubbard *Narr.* 66 He nimbly got behind the butt-end of a tree newly turned up by the roots. **1760** Winthrop in *Phil. Trans.* LII. 10 A great tree, 2½ feet in diameter at the butt-end. **1843** Stephens *High Life N.Y.* II. 62 But it would take a week of Sundays to tell you all. To give you the butt eend, she was married to the harnsome chap that run off with her. **1853** J. P. Kennedy *Backwater Chron.* 132 And but-ends of the burned wood-pile. **1858** Thoreau *Maine Woods* 154 In forming the rafts, they use the lower three feet of hardwood saplings, which have a crooked and knobbed butt-end. **1889** *Harper's Mag.* Jan. 230/2 The largest poles are perhaps as thick as a man's wrist, the butt ends sticking up in the air.

+**Butt-ender.** *Obs.* A rowdy. — **1841** *Arcturus* (N.Y.) I. 79 (Th.), Gentlemen assembling under the delicate designation of 'Butt-enders' in Brooklyn or Williamsburgh. **1845** *New York W. Tribune* 29 Nov. 5/5 Calling it [=a project for land reform] 'Agrarian' and its advocates 'Empire Club-men' and 'Butt-enders' . . . does not satisfy us.

***Butter**[1].

***1.** The fatty substance obtained by churning cream. In freq. attrib. use: **a.** With names of receptacles or implements, as *barrel, boat, cask, churn, cooler, dish*, etc. See also Butter knife, tub.
1644 *Conn. Public Rec.* I. 460 Tubbs, pales, churms, butter barrells. **1790** *Columbian Centinel* 15 Sept. 3/3 At One o'clock, will be sold by publick Vendue, . . . one pair elegant silver Butter-Boats. **1875** Stowe *We & Our Neighbors* 24 So the butter-cask is got up and opened. **1643** *Essex Inst. Coll.* L. 319 Alsoe I give to her my great butter churne. **1790** *Penna. Packet* 7 Dec. 3/3 Joseph Anthony, Junior, . . . has imported . . . Butter coolers and a-la-bases. **1642** *Md. Archives* IV. 96, 2. basons & 4. litle butter dishes. **1652** in *Mayflower Desc.* XI. 90, 2 butter firkins. **1886** *Outing* VIII. 168/2 We three managed to make him one [a banjo] out of a butter firkin. **1850** *Knickerb.* XXXVI. 105 Then the owl-eyed spectacles . . . go exploring among the butter-kids. **1858** C. Flint *Milch Cows*, etc. 322 The butter-moulds are generally made of linden-wood. **1854** *Penna. Agric. Rep.* 87 When churned and the milk worked out of it, which is done entirely with the butter paddle [etc.]. **1819** Peirce *Rebelliad* 55 Coffee-cups and butter plates . . . all chequer the fray. **1647** *Essex Probate Rec.* I. 78 A Butter Pott, 1s. **1878** *Field & Forest* III. 150, I use what is termed here a stone butter pot, a low, wide mouthed stoneware jar, with a cover, holding about a gallon. **1873–4** *Vt. Bd. Agric. Rep.* II. 72 The implements used . . . consist of a strainer pail, . . . butter

pounder and ladle. **1851** CARY *Clovernook* 289 Didn't I tell you as soon as you had . . . taken home the butter-print, to go straight to school? **1872** HOLMES *Poet* i. 2 As the market people run a butter-scoop through a firkin. **1836** *S. Lit. Messenger* II. 480/1 One [punishment] was to beat the collected ends of the fingers with an implement, sometimes made like a butter stick, at other times like a broad, flat rule. **1867** 'T. LACKLAND' *Homespun* II. 192 How many a hard-working mother, fresh from the butter-tray . . . , thinks that her son on that horse would surely look 'the foremost man of all the world'! **1867** *Rep. Comm. Patents* (1868) II. 1218/1 *Butter Tryer*. . . . The scraper fits the trough of the gouge to remove the butter therefrom.

b. With *biscuit, cake, cracker.*

1789 *Kentucky Gazette* 25 April 1/4 A Bake Shop in Lexington, . . . where may be had . . . the several kinds of bread, viz. loaf bread, Butter Biscuit, Cakes of different kinds [etc.]. **1828** E. LESLIE *Receipts* 64 Butter Biscuits. **1854** *Penna. Agric. Rep.* 363 Butter and Water crackers, . . . a good article. **1905** *N.Y. Ev. Post* 18 Nov. 4 That lineal descendant of the saleratus bread of the dyspeptic forties—the 'butter-cake.'

c. With names of plants, as *butter pear, print, squash, -weed,* etc. See also BUTTER BEAN.

1817–8 EATON *Botany* (1822) 417 *Pyrus communis*, pear . . . Var. *liquescens*, (butter-pear). **1836** LINCOLN *Botany* (1845) 141 *Pinguicula vulgaris*, (butter-wort). . . . Wet rocks. Rochester, N.Y. Canada. **1845** *Ib.* App. 166/1 *Senecio lobata*, butter-weed. **1849** EMMONS *Agric. N.Y.* II. 296 The Butter squash was less sweet than the Vegetable Marrow. **1872** *Ill. Dept. Agric. Trans. 1871* p. ix, The Indian Mallow (*Abutilon Avicennae*) [is] variously known as 'stamp weed,' 'velvet leaf,' 'butter print,' 'Mormon weed,' etc. **1892** *Amer. Folk-Lore* V. 93 *Abutilon Avicennæ*, butter-weed. Peoria, Ill.

‖**d.** *Adv. phr. Butter side up*, with the buttered side uppermost. Humorous.

1834 S. SMITH *Major Downing* 163 He gits along—and when he lets his slice fall, or some one nocks [*sic*] it out of his hand, it always somehow falls butter side up.

+**2.** A sweet spread made of various fruits, vegetables, etc., esp. fruit cooked to a butterlike consistency. (Cf. APPLE-BUTTER.)

1864 DICKINSON *Across Plains* 151 She set out choke-cherry 'butter' and plum jelly which she had made. **1882** MRS. OWENS *Cook Book* 273 [Recipe for] Plum Butter. **1884** *Ib.* (rev. ed.) 342 Tomato Butter . . . takes an entire day to cook properly. **1885** *Buckeye Cookery* 250 Egg Butter. Boil a pint of molasses slowly about fifteen or twenty minutes, . . . add three eggs well beaten. **1917** POWELL *Successful Canning & Preserving* 168 Lemon Butter.—Select four medium-sized lemons, [etc.].

+**Butter**[2]. [BUTT *v.*[2] 2.] **1.** One who butts a log. **2.** (See quotation.) —(1) **1850** JUDD *R. Edney* 98 He teazed a butter with it, making as if he would thrust it under his axe. (2) **1874** KNIGHT 414/1 *Butter*, . . . a machine for sawing off the ends of boards.

Butter and eggs. A popular name for various yellow flowers, as the toadflax (*Linaria vulgaris*) and some varieties of narcissus. {1776–} — **1847** DARLINGTON *Weeds & Plants* 225 Toad-flax. Ranstead-weed. Butter and Eggs. **1869** FULLER *Flower Gatherers* 258 The school children call it 'Butter and Egg,' on account of the colors; but he told us it was the *Linaria vulgaris* or common Toad-flax. **1893** DANA *Wild flowers* 146 Butter-And-Eggs. Like nearly all our common weeds, this plant has been utilized in various ways by the country people. It yielded what was considered at one time a valuable skin lotion, while its juice mingled with milk constitutes a fly-poison.

+**Butterback.** A kind of duck. — **1796** MORSE *Amer. Geog.* I. 213 Little Black and White Duck, called Butter Back, *Anas minor picta.*

+**Butterball.** The buffle-headed duck, spirit duck or dipper, *Bucephala albeola.* — **1813** WILSON *Ornithology* VIII. 51 Buffel-headed Duck. . . . This pretty little species, usually known by the name of the Butter-box, or Butter-ball, is common to the sea shores, rivers and lakes of the United States. **1859** BAIRD *Cat. N. A. Birds* 595. **1874** LONG *Wild-Fowl* 16 In the deep water varieties, with the canvas-back I shall treat of the . . . tufted duck, and buffle-head or butter ball. **1895** *Outing* XXVII. 212/1 Over me they went, so close that I could tell that they were butter balls. **1902** WHITE *Blazed Trail* xiii. 87 He followed the trail by the river. Butterballs and scoters paddled up at his approach.

+**Butter bean.** A variety of Lima bean, *Phaseolus lunatus.*

1841 *S. Lit. Messenger* VII. 37/1, I clambered up a frail ladder, to assist the young tendrils of the butter-bean to catch the threads loosely suspended from post to post. *c***1866** BAGBY *Old Va. Gentleman* 47 A true Virginian . . . must have . . . fried chicken, stewed chicken, broiled chicken, and chicken pie; old hare, butter-beans [etc.]. **1898** E. C. HALL *Aunt Jane* 171 Aunt Jane and I were sitting on the back porch, shelling butter-beans for the next day's market. **1911** R. D. SAUNDERS *Col. Todhunter* 29 The Missouri supper of fried chicken, egg-bread, butterbeans and corn on the ear.

*attrib. c***1866** BAGBY *Old Va. Gentleman* 45 The frost lies heavy on the palings, and tips with silver the tops of the butter-bean poles.

+**Butterbill.** A species of sea duck, as the American scoter, *Œdemia americana.* — **1844** *Nat. Hist. N.Y., Zoology* II. 329 *Fuligula albeola.* This little duck is known under the various popular names of . . . Butter-bill [etc.]. *Ib.* 336 *Fuligula Americana.* This duck, which is known . . . farther east by the name of Butter-bill, is described in the books under the name of American Scoter Duck.

+**Butterboat-bill.** (See quotation.) — **1844** *Nat. Hist. N.Y., Zoology* II. 335 *Fuligula Perspicillata*, . . . Black Sea Duck or Butterboat-bill, is very common on the coast of New-York during the winter.

Butterbox.

1. A box in which butter is kept. {1756–} Also applied to a vessel or vehicle suggestive of this.

1840 DANA *Two Years* ix. 76 The *Loriotte* . . . was a lump of a thing—what the sailors called a butter-box. **1851** MELVILLE *Moby Dick* xvi, You may have seen many a quaint craft in your day, . . . butter-box galliots, and what not. **1877** *Vt. Bd. Agric. Rep.* IV. 189 This gentleman also has invented a very neat butter box. **1909** *N.Y. Ev. Post* 28 Jan. (Th.), What New York youngster ever heard of a butter box? This is the name applied to the spring wagons of farmer and grocer, divested of wheels and set up on runners for the winter season.

+**2.** A popular name for the buffle-headed duck, *Bucephala albeola.*

1806 CLARK in *Lewis & C. Exped.* (1905) IV. 150, I take this to be the same species of duck common to the Ohio, as also the atlantic coast, and sometimes called the butterbox. **1813** WILSON *Ornithology* VIII. 51 [The] Buffel-Headed Duck, *Anas Albeola*, . . . [is] usually known by the name of the Butter-box, or Butter-ball. **1844** *Nat. Hist. N.Y., Zoology* II. 329 This little duck is known under the various popular names . . . Butter-box, and Spirit Duck. **1874** LONG *Wild-Fowl* 281 Local names [of the buffle-headed duck]: butter-box, butter-ball, and little whistler.

+**Butterbush.** =BUTTONBUSH. — **1843** TORREY *Flora N.Y.* I. 313 *Cephalanthus occidentalis*. . . . Butter-bush, or Pond-Dogwood. . . . Borders of ponds and rivers, and in swamps. **1861** *N.Y. Tribune* 24 July, [The] butter-bush . . . grows in swamps, and low, wet, marshy grounds.

Butter cow. A cow valuable for her butter-producing qualities. — **1877** *Vt. Bd. Agric. Rep.* IV. 46 We . . . believe that the Jersey as a butter-cow has the advantage of at least the average life time of man. **1896** *Ib.* XV. 29 She is a specially bred butter cow.

Buttercup. Butterflower or crowfoot, a species of *Ranunculus.* {1777–}

1784 CUTLER in *Mem. Academy* I. 458 *Ranunculus*. . . . Crowfoot, Buttercup. Goldilocks. **1817–8** EATON *Botany* (1822) 423 *Ranunculus acris*, crowfoot, butter cup. **1833** *Ib.* (ed. 6) 297 *Ranunculus hirsutus*, pale butter-cup. **1852** MITCHELL *Dream Life* 234 The grass was never so green, the butter-cups were never so plenty. **1883** *Harper's Mag.* Aug. 428/2 The American fields have been altered by the steady advance of imported weeds and flowers; the butter-cup, the dandelion, and the ox-eyed daisy displacing the anemone and violet.

+**Butter duck.** A black surf duck, *Œdemia perspicillata.* — **1857** J. G. SWAN *Northwest Coast* 357 The Colonel saw a 'butter-duck' in a shallow creek. . . . These ducks are the black surf-duck.

+**Butter factory.** A place where butter is made in large quantities. — **1868** *Mich. Agric. Rep.* VII. 228 It is, perhaps, not improbable that the system of 'butter-factories,' first organized in Orange county, N.Y., and subsequently adopted to some extent in other counties of that State, may be introduced into Michigan. **1888** *Vt. Agric. Rep.* X. 14 If a man has a cheese factory he better keep it, but other things being equal a butter factory is better.

Butterfish. Any one of various fishes or mollusks having a smooth oily surface. {1674–}

1842 *Nat. Hist. N.Y., Zoology* IV. 153 The American Butter-fish, *Gunnellus mucronatus*, . . . is frequently found among rocks along the seashore, and in the mud. **1873** THAXTER *Isle of Shoals* 88 Perch are found in inexhaustible quantities about the rocks, and lump or butter-fish are sometimes caught. **1881** E. INGERSOLL *Oyster Industry* 242 *Butter Fish*, the long neck clam, *Mya arenaria* (Virginia). **1884** GOODE *Aquatic Animals* 333 The Butter-fish . . . known . . . at Norfolk as the 'Star-fish.' **1889** *Cent.* 737/2.

***Butterfly.**

***1.** The well-known winged insect.

1737 BRICKELL *N. Carolina* 155 The Butter-flies . . . are very plenty all over this Province, and of several sorts: some large, and others small, and most beautifully mottled with variety of fine Colours. **1743** CATESBY *Carolina* II. 84 The four-eyed Night Butterfly. . . . These Flies are found in Virginia, Carolina, Maryland, and Philadelphia, &c. **1862** *Rep. Comm. Patents: Agric.* 587, I confined in a box half a dozen of the larvæ of our common black butterfly, (*Papilio asterias*). **1886** *Amer. Naturalist* XX. 976 During the fore part of June, 1886, unusual numbers of the Ajax butterfly . . . migrated through this city [Chicago]. **1892** TORREY *Foot-Path Way* 104 Even the splendid black-and-yellow butterfly (*Turnus*) which was often to be seen sucking honey from the fragrant orchids, did not disdain to sip also from the sandwort's cup.

b. *Black butterfly*, ?mood; spell of temper.

1895 A. BROWN *Meadow-Grass* 168 Mrs. Blair and Miss Dyer . . . had proved utterly incapable of living in peace with any available human being; and . . . neither could be isolated to fight her 'black butterflies' alone.

c. *Butterfly cape*, a scarf or cape suggestive in its shape or cut of a butterfly.

1893 *Chicago Tribune* 23 April 29/5 Fine Cloth Butterfly Capes—butterfly silk lined—ribbon and embroidery trimmed, at $8. *Ib.*, 25 April 4/6 The maiden spends her money for a butterfly cape.

2. A bow tie, the shape of which suggests that of a butterfly. (See also quot. 1877.) Also *butterfly-bow, (neck-)tie.*

1877 BARTLETT 777 *Butterfly*, a small bow of silk, satin, or other material, made for attachment to the collar-button, so as to serve the purpose of a cravat, without passing around the neck. **1889** CUSTER *Tenting on Plains* 502 It was then the fashion for men to wear a tiny neck-bow, called a butterfly tie. **1891** GARLAND *Main-travelled Roads* (1922) 328 McIlvaine . . . wove a paper collar and a butterfly necktie, as befitted a man of his station. **1910** 'O. HENRY' *Strictly Business* 42 He dressed himself in . . . frock coat, striped trousers, . . . rolled-brim derby and butterfly bow from Schonstein's.

+**Butterfly pea.** Any one of various species of wild pea of the genus *Clitoria.* — **1857** GRAY *Botany* 106 *Clitoria*, Butterfly Pea. . . . *Centrosema*, Spurred Butterfly Pea. **1889** *Cent.* 1050/2 *C[litoria] Mariana*, the butterfly-pea, is a native of the United States and Mexico.

+**Butterfly root.** The pleurisy root, *Asclepias tuberosa.* — **1789** *Trans. Philos. Soc.* III. xviii, The best among pleuretic remedies must be the *pleuresy-root.* . . . Another asclepias bears high value in Maryland; called also *butterfly root.* **1888** *Century Mag.* XXXVI. 768/1 'A brilliant yellow' may be obtained by pouring boiling water upon other component parts of 'sassafras, swamp bay, and butterfly root.'

+**Butterfly tree.** The Monterey pine, *Pinus radiata.* — **1881** *Amer. Naturalist* XV. 572, I have been to Monterey, and was fortunate enough to see the 'butterfly tree,' or trees, as there are three of them.

+**Butterfly weed.** The pleurisy root, butterfly root, *Asclepias tuberosa.*

1817-8 EATON *Botany* (1822) 185 *Asclepias tuberosa*, butterfly weed . . . cathartic, diaphoretic, expectorant. **1832** WILLIAMSON *Maine* I. 121 Another herb, still more rich, is the Butterfly-weed, Pleurisy-root or Swallow-wort, found in dry, sandy soils. **1869** FULLER *Flower Gatherers* 173 An immense cluster of those fiery yellow blossoms which we always called 'Butterfly-weed.' **1889** COOKE *Steadfast* 181 The cheerful and persistent glow of the 'butterfly weed' on our sandy hillsides. **1904** T. WATSON *Bethany* (1920) 21 The bannered butterflies hover over the flowers of the butterfly-weed.

Butterine. Artificial butter; oleomargarine. {1874-} Also attrib.

*a***1877** *Philadelphia Record* (B.), About $1,000,000 pounds of 'butterine,' formerly known as oleomargarine, have been shipped from Philadelphia during the last month. **1881** *Ill. Rev. Statutes* (1883) 372 No person shall mix oleomargarine, suine, butterine, . . . or any other foreign substance with any butter or cheese intended for human food. **1887** *Courier-Journal* 6 Jan. 2/6 The butterine factories . . . at Allegheny closed down to-day on account of the State law prohibiting the manufacture and sale of oleomargarine being declared constitutional. **1897** *Chicago Tribune* 2 Sept. 10/4 Six Chicago grocers were arrested yesterday afternoon charged with having violated the butterine law by selling the product in a form colored to appear like butter. **1902** LORIMER *Lett. Merchant* 62 You can smell the clover in our butterine.

Butter knife. A knife used for cutting butter at table.

1856 *Mich. Agric. Soc. Trans.* VII. 268 Eleven butter knives. **1870** 'FERN' *Ginger-Snaps* 54 Some houses contain only silver soup-ladles, others a superabundance of butter-knives. **1905** *Sears, Roebuck & Co. Cat. No. 115* 99 Sugar Shell and Butter Knife Combination. . . . Length of butter knife, 7 inches.

Buttermaker. One who makes butter. {1859-}

1815 in *Rep. Comm. Agric. 1884* 247 Milk cows, which are never fed with rye by our farmers or butter-makers, exhibited more violent symptoms than oxen or horses. *a***1858** in C. Flint *Milch Cows*, etc. 230 An excellent butter-maker lived on one farm. *a***1877** *N.Y. Tribune* (B., p. 439) The [N.Y.] Governor having signed the act for the protection of buttermakers, all imitations of butter are hereafter to be sold only under the name of oleomargarine.

+**Buttermilk land.** A variety of wet or marshy land. — **1843** 'CARLTON' *New Purchase* I. 58 They had been sufficiently fortunate as to get a taste of 'buttermilk land,'—'spouty land,'—and to learn the nature of 'mash land.'

+**Butternut.**

1. The white walnut, *Juglans cinerea.*

1741 P. COLLINSON in *Mem. Bartram* (1849) 148 The butter-nut . . . with the Medlar and Sagamore's head. **1781** S. PETERS *Hist. Conn.* (1829) 187 Sumach, maple, and butternut, are the chief timber trees of this province. **1817-8** EATON *Botany* (1822) 322 *Juglans cinerea*, butternut. . . . The bark is a strong cathartic. **1832** BROWNE *Sylva* 174 The black walnut and butternut, when young, resemble each other in their foliage, and in the rapidity of their growth. **1857-8** *Ill. Agric. Soc. Trans.* III. 479 The black walnut and white walnut or butternut flourish finely upon our prairies, and the value of their timber renders them very desirable in cultivation.

attrib. **1886** *Leslie's Mo.* XXI. 388/2 Butternut-wood being the favorite along the Hudson for runner-plank centre timber [etc.].

b. A single tree of this species.

1841 COOPER *Deerslayer* xii, I've seen all the oaks, . . . all the walnuts, . . . the butternuts. **1863** MRS. WHITNEY *F. Gartney* xiv, He appeared about to pass the gate,— . . . that he might place his horse and his companion under the shade of the butternuts beyond. **1887** *Outing* X. 260/1 The first decked canoe that was on the Atanahee waters was a dug-out butternut, made . . . in 1860. **1893** TORREY *Footpath-Way* 235, I once passed a lazy dreamy afternoon . . . where the lumbermen had left standing a few scattered butternuts.

2. The nut or fruit of the white walnut tree.

1753 Chambers *Cycl. Suppl.* s.v., *Butter-nut*, a fruit in New England, whose kernel yields a great quantity of sweet oil. **1795** WINTERBOTHAM *Hist. View* II. 6 There are the wild cherries, . . . walnuts, hazelnuts, chesnuts, butter-nuts, beech-nuts. **1818** *Jrnl. Science* I. 362 September 21. Butternuts beginning to fall from the tree. **1821** DWIGHT *Travels* I. 100 The hailstones which were at first small, increased ultimately to the size of a large butternut. **1838** HAWTHORNE *Note-Books* I. 150 There is an old man, selling the meats of butternuts under the stoop of the hotel. **1857** HAMMOND *Northern Scenes* 287, We gathered . . . hickory-nuts and butter-nuts by the bushel. **1884** BURROUGHS in *Century Mag.* Dec. 218 The red squirrels find your grain in the barn or steal the butternuts from your attic.

attrib. **1843** STEPHENS *High Life N.Y.* 101, I don't care the value of a butternut-shell how many names you've got.

3. The wood, bark, or hull of the tree or nut.

1820 *U.S. Pharmacopœia* 129 Extract of Butternut. **1843** T. TALBOT *Journals* 29 The following are external applications: . . . Star root, Rattlesnake plantain, Butternut, Daphne Mezereum, or Spurge Olive. **1886** *Leslie's Mo.* XXI. 388/2 One of the finest boats on the Hudson is built of butternut. **1902** S. G. FISHER *Amer. Revol.* 261 Many regiments [in the Revolutionary War] stained their hunting-shirts with butternut, which was used for a similar purpose by the Confederates of the Civil War.

comb. **1879** *Harper's Mag.* Sept. 514 Their clothing is rarely better than . . . butternut-dyed homespun. **1887** EGGLESTON *Graysons* x, McCord's herculean right knee was bare, having that morning forced itself through his much-be-patched trousers of butternut-dyed cotton cloth.

4. The color obtained by using the bark, roots, etc., of the butternut tree as a dye. Also the cloth or a garment so colored.

1810 *Mass. Spy* 21 Feb. (Th.), Two pair home-made pantaloons, the one dark-colored, the other light butternut. **1867** 'E. KIRKE' *On Border* 150, I must add that this angel wore seedy butternuts, chewed tobacco. **1875** HOWELLS *Foregone Conclusion* 245 He was riding out near the camp one morning in unusual spirits, when two men in butternut fired at him. **1887** *Harper's Mag.* June 162/2 Here the mother dragged forward a shame-faced youngster in 'butter-nut.' **1909** [see sense 6 a].

5. A Confederate soldier in the Civil War.

1862 *N.Y. Tribune* 28 May 3/1 Capital shots are many of these 'Butternuts'—long lank, loose-jointed Mississippians and Texans though they are. **1863** NORTON *Army Lett.* 140 Six months she was a prisoner among the chivalrous butternuts. **1866** 'F. KIRKLAND' *Bk. Anecdotes* 150 A Mississippi 'Butternut' . . . had been taken prisoner and brought into Federal custody. **1875** G. P. BURNHAM *Three Years* 28 'Who ar yer? Whar yer from?' asked the butternut, rudely.

b. One who sympathized with the South in the Civil War. Also attrib.

1862 *Independent* 27 March 1/6 The butternut gentry, . . . availing themselves of Government passes over railroads, have flocked to this Northern watering-place [=Chicago]. **1862** *Cleveland Herald* 16 Oct., A Democrat this morning . . . discovered that had the Democrats all through the district stuck to Phelps, he would have been elected. Our 'butternut' friend exclaimed: 'What a pity we lost that district.' **1862** *Crisis* 22 Oct., The *Ohio State Journal*, true to its instincts, denominates the Democrats of Ohio in its election tables, 'Butternuts.' **1863** *Ib.*, 25 Feb., It has been the custom of late, among a certain class of abolitionists, to call the Democrats by the name of 'Butternuts.' **1866** 'F. KIRKLAND' *Bk. Anecdotes* 28 'You are what they call around here a Copperhead, an't you?' 'Yes, yes,' said the Butternut, propitiatingly; 'that's what all my ngighbors call me.' **1885** *Mag. Amer. Hist.* Jan. 99/1 *Butternuts.*—Equivalent at the North to 'copperheads.'

6. Attrib., denoting the color derived from the nut: **a.** With *color, brown, gray.*

1802 *Mass. Spy* 17 Nov. 3/1 The stockings were changed . . . to a brown, or what is commonly called a butternut color. **1881** PIERSON *In the Brush* 29 They had long riding-skirts made of coarse cotton-factory cloth, dyed the inevitable butternut-color. **1879** TOURGEE *Fool's Errand* 139 He was clad now in 'butter-nut-gray' homespun. **1909** *Dialect Notes* III. 393 *Butternuts*, overalls of a butternut brown.

b. With *cloth, flannel, homespun*, etc.

1848 DRAKE in *Pioneer Life Ky.* 74 My equipments were a substantial suit of butternut-linsey, a wool hat. **1862** 'P. V. NASBY' *Struggles* 73 A full uniform uv butiful butternut cloth and a copperheded sword wuz presented me. **1863** 'E. KIRKE' *Southern Friends* viii. 106 He was dressed in a suit of 'butternut homespun.' **1881** PIERSON *In the Brush* 117 Her arms were colored to above her elbows, where she had had them in the dye tub, preparing the 'butternut-woolsey' for the family use. **1883** *Harper's Mag.* Sept. 626/2 A big young fellow in butternut flannel appeared.

c. With *breeches, clothes, coat, garment*, etc.

1862 *Crisis* 22 Oct., The Democrat who sent us that pair of butternut breeches is politely informed that we don't wear breeches; we have put on sackcloth. **1863** *Cincinnati Gazette* 5 Feb. 1/1 The 'Butternut' coat and pants, and the unbleached cotton and woollen shirts have, even when new, a dirty, untidy appearance. **1867** EDWARDS *Shelby* 390 An order . . . directing Leper to take eighty men, dress them in 'butternut' clothing, march with them to White river. **1879** BURDETTE *Hawkeyes* 98 The man with butternut overalls tucked into his boots. **1882** *Harper's Mag.* Dec. 104/2 He was attired in a coat of . . . black, with butternut trousers. **1886** Z. F. SMITH *Kentucky* 84 The dried leaves . . . were nearly the color of his butternut garments. **1887** *Courier-Journal* 8 May 5/2 A man in butternut clothes suddenly stepped out in front of me from behind a large tree.

+**Butternut bark.** Bark of the butternut tree. — **1838** *Harvardiana* IV. 374, I had . . . the best butternut bark. **1859** HILLHOUSE tr. Michaux's *Sylva* I. 112 The medicinal properties of Butternut bark have long since been proved. **1877** *Vt. Bd. Agric. Rep.* IV. 92 The wool was colored with butternut bark.

+**Butternut-colored,** *a.* Colored with, having the color of, butternut. — **1830** *Mass. Spy* 24 Feb. (Th.), His were the coarse butternut colored, snug-setting trousers, reaching only to the calf of his leg. **1856** G. H. DERBY *Phoenixiana* 46 A man in butternut-colored clothing driving the oxen. *Ib.* 217 A tall, yellow-haired, sun-burned Pike, in the butternut-colored hat, coat and so forths 'of the period,' entered. **1861** STOWE *Pearl Orr's Isl.* i, The old fisherman stood up in the wagon, his coarse butternut-coloured coat-flaps fluttering and snapping in the breeze. **1871** *Harper's Mag.* XLIII. 686/1 Some wore uniform coats and butternut-colored pants and vests.

+**Butternut jean(s).** Jean dyed with the bark, roots, etc., of the butternut tree; *pl.* clothes made of this.

1867 'E. KIRKE' *On Border* 310 He was dressed in the common butternut jean of the district. **1874** EGGLESTON *Circuit Rider* 142 A long lank man, in butternut-jeans, opened the door. **1881** PIERSON *In the Brush* 32 For leggins I bought a yard and a half of butternut jean, which was cut into two equal parts. **1891** 'THANET' *Otto the Knight*, etc. 48 A hollow-eyed man in butternut jeans was stirred to reminiscence. **1897** BRODHEAD *Bound in Shallows* 35 Three stray oak ties, patrolled by a frog and a man in butternut jeans, made a landing for the steamer.

attrib. **1890** *Harper's Mag.* Feb. 488/1 Finally a butternut jeans specimen dropped into my seat.

+**Butternut State.** ?Missouri. — **1863** *Rocky Mt. News* (Denver) 19 March (Th.), We expect ere long to stand on the banks of the 'Big Muddy,' and meet the hominy-fed lasses of the Butternut State.

+**Butternut suit.** A suit made of cloth dyed a butternut color. — **1859** MRS. DUNIWAY *Capt. Gray's Co.* 86 (Th.), A stout-looking individual, in a butternut suit and home-made straw hat, rode up. **1864** PITTENGER *Daring & Suffering* 280 The ragged guards around, clad in their miserable butternut suits, growled. **1889** *Century Mag.* XXXVII. 407/1 The driver, a tall, lank mountaineer in a butternut suit and a cap of skins, pulled up his team. **1891** F. H. SMITH *Col. Carter* 130 An elderly white-haired gentleman, in a butternut suit.

+**Butternut tree.** The white walnut tree, *Juglans cinerea.*

[**1770** FORSTER tr. Kalm's *Travels* I. 69 A species of Walnut tree . . . called by the Swedes Butternuttrae.] **1788** *Amer. Museum* IV. 435/2 The butternut tree . . . is sometimes so large as to measure ten feet in circumference. **1800** J. MAUDE *Niagara* 93 There is a Butter-nut Tree, on which Nature has ingrafted a Sugar Tree. **1845** JUDD *Margaret* I. iii. 12 Opposite the house . . . was a butternut tree,—the Butternut par excellence—having great extension of limb. **1882** *Wheelman* I. 208/1 He lived in a one-story house with two immense butternut trees in front shading the whole building. **1904** WALLER *Wood-carver* 114 She's getting too big to run barefoot like that and swing on the butternut tree when the stage goes by.

+**Butter sauce.** A spiced or a sweet sauce, a main ingredient of which is butter. — **1882** MRS. OWENS *Cook Book* 88 *Drawn Butter Sauce.* Half cup butter, dessertspoon of flour rubbed well together. . . . Season with salt and pepper. **1884** *Ib.* (rev. ed.) 199 *Butter Sauce.* 1 cup butter. 2 cups sugar. **1896** J. C. HARRIS *Sister Jane* 61 She was sweet as butter sauce.

***Butter tub.** A tub or container for butter.

1645 *Conn. Public Rec.* I. 473, 2 Indean baggs, a file, a butter tub. **1658** *Southold Rec.* I. 440 In the dyrie milk panns, churne, butter tubb. **1868** *Mich. Agric. Rep.* VII. 236 Good white-oak wood is best for butter-tubs. **1892** *Ib.* XII. 128 Montgomery may be considered the banner town of the County for the manufacture of butter tubs.

+**Butterworker.** An implement for kneading and pressing butter to free it from buttermilk. — **1853** *Rep. Comm. Patents* (1854) 247 Improvement in Butter Workers. **1858** C. FLINT *Milch Cows* 226 A part of this butter . . . is then worked by a butter-worker or brake . . . which perfectly and completely removes the butter milk. **1872** *Vt. Bd. Agric. Rep.* I. 152 Work [it] again in butter-worker, using a large sponge and a cloth to absorb all moisture that remains in the butter. **1882** *Maine Bd. Agric. Rep.* XXVI. 153 A good butter worker of some kind should be provided, and also a thermometer, if one expects to make a uniform article.

***Buttery.**

+**1.** At Harvard and Yale: A room in the college where liquors, fruit, etc., were kept for sale to the students.

*c***1640** *Harvard Rec.* I. 14 [The study is] in the corner west off the buttery. **1651** *Lancaster Rec.* 17 When Sr Phillips came from Nashaway he came into the buttery at the College in Cambridge. **1767** Peirce *Hist. Harvard* 226 That an authentic copy of all the Laws be likewise kept in the Buttery, for the inspection of all the Scholars. **1790** *Harvard Coll. Laws* 21 Every Scholar . . . shall enter his name at the Buttery. **1811** *Yale College Laws* 31 In which every article sized or taken up by him at the Buttery, shall be particularly charged. **1827** *Harvard Reg.* Sept. 212 After opening sundry doors which led into the 'cellar-way,' butteries, bedrooms, and closets. **1871** L. H. BAGG *4 Years at Yale* 247 Another old college institution . . . , which flourished for a century, . . . was the Buttery; abolished in 1817.

2. A storeroom in an ordinary house in which provisions are kept; a pantry or larder.

So also in Eng. dial. use, but obsolescent in various districts.

1654 *Essex Probate Rec.* I. 164 In the shop, kitching & buttery. **1863** 'G. HAMILTON' *Gala-Days* 64, I could pick you up a dozen girls straight along, right out of the pantries and the butteries. **1869** STOWE *Oldtown Folks* 138 The old soul ran to her buttery, and crammed a small splint basket with turnovers, doughnuts, and ample slices of rye bread and butter. **1877** *Harper's Mag.* March 604/1, I spent the next fortnight house-hunting with her. The great desideratum seemed to be the right kind of a 'buttery.' **1887** WILKINS *Humble Romance* 58 She dragged herself in her chair with one foot, hitching herself along, into the buttery, to the flour barrel.

transf. **1878** B. F. TAYLOR *Between Gates* 77 Brisk little two-wheelers . . . are flying butteries, laden with butter in rolls.

3. Attrib. with *bill, book, hatch, sizing* (sense 1); with *door, window* (sense 2).

1779 E. PARKMAN *Diary* 156 Deduct £64.8.4 which (with the) buttery bill added is £103.6.4. **1790** *Harvard Laws* 60 If any scholar shall neglect to discharge his buttery-bill, for the space of three months, . . . the butler shall notify his parent or guardian of such neglect. **1674** *Harvard Rec.* I. 62, 3 Desks, 1 Butterie book, 1 Brasse tapp. **1871** STOWE *Sam Lawson* 6 They shook and rattled the buttery-door and the sinkroom-door and the cellar-door and the chamber-door. **1667** *Harvard Rec.* I. 46 If any schollar or schollars . . . take away, or detaine, any Vessell . . . from the Hall, out of Doores, from the sight of the Butter(y) Hatch, . . . he or they shall be punished. **1779** E. PARKMAN *Diary* 156 Besides these Mr. Philips Paylons Buttery Sizing from Nov. 27, 1778 to July 14, 1779 £38.18.0 not paid. **1846–51** MRS. WHITCHER *Bedott P.* v. 57, I took the thin one that Melissy spilt over, and sot it in the buttry winder to cool.

Butt hinge. [Cf. BUTT *n.*[4]] A hinge for use on the butting portions of doors, windows, etc. — **1815** *Niles' Reg.* VIII. 141/1 There are in Pittsburgh, three large and extensive air-founderies, . . . and a small foundery for casting butt-hinges, buckles, &c. **1851** CIST *Cincinnati* 191 Every possible variety, in which iron can be cast from a butt hinge to a burial case. **1897** MOORE *How to Build* 98 All doors to be hung with loose-joint butt-hinges large enough to swing clear of the architraves.

+**Butting pole.** The log or pole against which the lower end of the first row of clapboards in the roof of a log cabin rest. — **1791** Jillson *Dark & Bl. Ground* (1930) 109 The eave bearers [of a log cabin] are the end logs which project over to receve the butting poles, against which the lower tier of clapboards rest in forming the roof.

+**Butt log.** [BUTT *n.*[3]] A log from the butt of a tree. — **1851** SPRINGER *Forest Life* 41 The butt log was so large that the stream did not float it in the spring, and when the drive was taken down we were obliged to leave it behind. **1902** WHITE *Blazed Trail* ii. 12 The teamster clamped the bite of his tongs to the end of the largest, or butt, log.

***Button,** *n.*

+**1.** A guessing game in which forfeits are exacted of those who guess wrong.

1773 FITHIAN *Journal* I. 64 We played Button, to get Pauns for Redemption; here I could join with them. **1799** J. COWLES *Diary* 20 We played button. I was mortified by a lad's handing me the button twice following. **1805** WHITEHOUSE in *Lewis and Clark Exped.* (1905) VII. 143 Some of them [Indians] play away whatever they git for their horses, at a game nearly like playing button only they keep Singing all the while and do all by motions. **1828** *Yankee* 16 July 227/2 When a select party have met together, and they play button—roll the plate—chase the lady, and many other romping-plays. **1843** *S. Lit. Messenger* IX. 440/2 He was agreeably relieved by seeing those around him form a circle with the chairs, for the purpose of playing the game of 'button,' which . . . allows one . . . to assume more liberties than *gaming* generally. **1860** *Harper's Mag.* Nov. 792/1 Some of the company . . . played 'Button' in the house.

+**2.** The hard bonelike structure at the end of the rattles of a rattlesnake.

1833 *Niles' Reg.* XLIV. 327/2 He [*i.e.* the rattlesnake] carried fifty-four rattles, and a button (the terminating rattle) measuring 12 inches in length. **1835** SIMMS *Yemassee* I. 178 The snake had thirteen rattles, and a button; . . . it acquires the button during its first year, and each succeeding year yields it a new rattle. **1845** — *Wigwam & Cabin* I. 83 A little way behind him lay a dead rattlesnake, one of the largest I ever did see, counting twenty-one rattles besides the button. **1850** H. C. LEWIS *La. Swamp Dr.* 65 As fine a specimen of the Rattlesnake as ever delighted the eye or ear of a naturalist; . . . twenty-three rattles and a button.

+**3.** A rounded mass of metal.

1869 *Kansas Pac. Ry. Gold Loan* 18 Buttons of silver of from 500 to 800 pounds each. **1873** *Harper's Mag.* XLVI. 478 The scoundrel had stolen a pewter faucet, and made his assay buttons out of that.

+4. (See quotation.)

1883 SMITH *Geol. Survey Ala.* 401 Occasionally, where the red ore and its accompanying sandstones form the summit of the hills, they have received the name of Button mountains, from the great abundance of the 'buttons' or segments of the stems of crinoids with which they are filled.

+5. A pin having a circular front, usually of celluloid, on which is some sort of political propaganda.

1900 *Daily News* 5 Nov. 7/1 Another feature of an American Presidential campaign is the lavish display of political 'buttons.' 3000000 buttons have been sent out from the Republican headquarters. **1903** *N.Y. Tribune* 27 Sept., McClellan buttons in varying sizes and colors are on thousands of loyal Tammany coat lapels.

***Button,** *v.* **+a.** (See quotation.) **+b.** *tr.* To buttonhole (a person). — (**a**) **1841** *Weeks in Wall St.* 47 Not a man could be found in Wall-street, who confessed the ownership of a share. . . . This is called 'buttoning up.' (**b**) **1862-3** HALE *If, Yes* (1868) 8 But, if the reader wishes to lengthen out this story, he may button the next silver-gray friend he meets.

+Buttonball. [From the form of the fruit.] The (or a) sycamore or plane tree, *Platanus occidentalis.* Also attrib. with *tree.*

(*a*) **1821** *Mass. H. S. Coll.* 2 Ser. IX. 153 [Trees indigenous at Middlebury, Vt.] Button-ball tree. **1859** [see BUTTON-TREE 1]. **1878** STOWE *Poganuc People* 114 On the highest top of the great button-ball tree opposite the house sat the little blue angel singing with all his might. **1906** *Springfield W. Republican* 22 Feb. 16 The large buttonball tree standing in front of the Field place at Northfield has recently been cut down.

(*b*) **1845** *Knickerb.* XXVI. 510 You are brought immediately in front of the Inn, under the branches of a clump of large overhanging Buttonballs and Beeches. **1849** WILLIS *Rural Letters* ii. 31 Is it that big buttonball you'll have cut down, sir? **1882** *Century Mag.* March 760/2 Reaching the house, I stopped beneath the huge button-ball at the gate.

+Buttonbush. [From the form of the flower.] The shrub *Cephalanthus occidentalis,* bearing white flowers in spherical heads.

1754 ELIOT *Field-Husb.* v. 124 There was not the same Success attending the cutting these Button Bushes as the other Sorts. **1784** CUTLER in *Mem. Academy* I. 409 *Cephalanthus* . . . Globe-Flower Shrub. Pond Dogwood. Button Bush. . . . Common in watery swamps and pond-holes. **1817-8** EATON *Botany* (1822) 231 *Cephalanthus occidentalis,* button bush. . . . Swamps. **1851** THOREAU *Journal* (1906) III. 16 The blue river, . . . bordered by willows and button-bushes. **1870** *Amer. Naturalist* IV. 216 The Button-bush . . . is odd, with its buttons of white flowers, and worthy of cultivation. **1885** *Outing* VII. 180/2 It is a most eërie place . . enclosed by a thick hedge of button-bush. **1895** A. BROWN *Meadow-Grass* 5 The button-bush hung out her balls.

*** Buttonhole.**

1. A form of catch for gold buttons. *Obs.* {1685}

1771 COPLEY in *Copley-Pelham Lett.* 118 You will find in one of the Draws of the Desk some gold Buttonholes. **1773** TRUMBULL *Progress of Dulness* III. 63 What going forth of [ladies'] hearts and souls Tow'rd glares of gilded button holes!

2. The buttonhole in the lapel of a coat, in which a flower is frequently inserted. {1848-}

1842 *Knickerb.* XIX. 44 It was a Miss and Mister of the fashionable cut, . . . he . . . [with] a bud and two leaves, twined by the fingers of the Graces, at his buttonhole. **1860** HOLMES *Professor* 230 Much obliged, he said, and put it gallantly in his button-hole. **1883** *Wheelman* I. 426 She fastened in his button hole . . . a magnificent crimson rose.

attrib. **1883** 'MARK TWAIN' *Life on Miss.* xliv, The ushers grow their button-hole bouquets on the premises. **1887** N. PERRY *Flock of Girls,* The assemblage looked like a grand class-day at old Cambridge, with . . . the display of white neckties and buttonhole bouquets.

3. (See quotation.)

1889 *Cent.* 739/2 *Buttonhole,* . . . the hart's-tongue fern, *Scolopendrium vulgare,* because its fructification in the young state resembles a buttonhole in form and appearance.

+Buttonhole twist. Tightly twisted leaf tobacco. — **1868** *Rep. Comm. Agric.* (1869) 289 Button-hole twist is the same, with a tighter twist.

Button maker. One who makes buttons. {a1613-}

1723 *New-Eng. Courant* 7-14 Jan. 2/2 A Servant Boy's Time for five Years to be disposed of, by Mr. Brown, Brass-Button maker at the South-End. **1807** IRVING, etc. *Salmagundi* xii, One of those . . . self-important 'gemmen' who bounce upon us, half beau, half button-maker. **1815** *Niles' Reg.* VIII. 141/2 There are three button makers, who make about 200 gross weekly.

+Button-nose mole. The star-nosed mole, *Condylura cristata.* — **1842** *Nat. Hist. N.Y., Zoology* I. 14 The Star-nose is abundant throughout New-York, where it is occasionally called the Button-nose Mole.

Button-pear. *Obs.* ?A small variety of pear. — **1687** SEWALL *Diary* I. 173 Grafted the Button-pear tree stock. **1713** *Charlestown Land Rec.* 211 From the corner of Deericks & Eades Land to the butten pare trees is 23 foot. **1759** *Newport Mercury* 8 May 1/1 Plough it in, and harrow it . . . with a Thorn-bush Harrow, or a Harrow made of Plumb Tree, or Button-pear Tree.

+Button (rattle)snakeroot. One or other species of eryngo, esp. *Eryngium yuccaefolium,* or of the blazing star (*Liatris,* al. *Lacinaria*). Also attrib.

1775 ADAIR *Indians* 156 A thick whip, . . . composed of plaited silk grass, and the fibres of the button snake-root stalks. *Ib.* 160 This purifying physic, is warm water highly imbittered with button-rattlesnake-root, which as hath been before observed, they apply only to religious purposes. **1800** HAWKINS *Sk. Creek Country* 79 Every new moon, he drinks for four days the posson, (button snakeroot) an emetic. **1817-8** EATON *Botany* (1822) 336 *Liatris spicata,* gay feather, button snakeroot. . . . Diuretic and tonic. **1829** *Ib.* (ed. 5) 212 *Eryngium aquaticum,* button snake root. **1843** TORREY *Flora N.Y.* I. 324 *Liatris cylindracea.* . . . Small Button-snakeroot. . . . Banks of the Niagara river, near the Falls, on the east side. **1870** *Amer. Naturalist* IV. 581 Other remarkable forms are . . . the Yucca-leaved rattlesnake master, or button snakeroot (*Eryngium yuccæfolium*). **1892** COULTER *Bot. W. Texas* II. 182 Button snakeroot, Blazing star, . . . [grows in] dry soil, extending into Texas from the Atlantic States.

Button tree. Now *rare* or *Obs.* {1725-}

+1. =BUTTONBALL, BUTTONWOOD 1.

1762 J. ADAMS *Diary* Wks. II. (1850) 137 Sometimes I am . . . removing button trees down to my house. **1775** FITHIAN *Journal* II. 56, I saw . . . in the Bottom near the bank of the river a Sycamore or Button-tree, which measured, eighteen inches from the ground, sixteen feet in circumference! **1781** PETERS *Hist. Conn.* (1829) 147 Elms and button-trees surround the centre square of Newhaven. **1859** BARTLETT 61 Buttonwood or button tree (*Platanus occidentalis*) [is] the popular name in New England, of the sycamore tree; so called from the balls it bears, the receptacle of the seed. . . . Sometimes called Button-ball tree.

+2. =BUTTONBUSH.

1785 MARSHALL *Amer. Grove* 30 *Cephalanthus occidentalis.* Button tree. This shrub grows pretty common by creek sides and ponds. **1815** DRAKE *Cincinnati* 76 The botanical resources of this . . . Forest of the Miami country [include] . . . *Cephalanthus occidentalis,* Button tree.

Buttonweed. (See quotations.) — **1817-8** EATON *Botany* (1822) 472 *Spermacoce diodina,* button weed. **1857** GRAY *Botany* 171 *Diodia,* Button-weed. **1889** *Cent.* 739/2 *Button-weed,* . . . a name given to several rubiaceous plants belonging to the genera *Spermacoce, Diodia,* and *Borreria.* **1892** *Amer. Folk-Lore* V. 93 *Abutilon Avicennæ,* . . . buttonweed. Chestertown, Md.

+Buttonwood.

1. The plane tree or sycamore, *Platanus occidentalis.* Cf. BUTTONBALL, BUTTON TREE.

1674 *Cal. State P., Amer. & W. I.* VII. 581 [In Maine] grow . . . alder, shumack, willow, button wood, poplar [etc.]. **1778** CARVER *Travels* 499 The Button Wood is a tree of the largest size, . . . covered with small hard burs which spring from the branches, that appear not unlike buttons. **1817-8** EATON *Botany* (1822) 394 *Platanus occidentalis,* button wood, american planetree, false sycamore. . . . Grows to a greater size than any other tree in America. Very frequently hollow. **1832** BROWNE *Sylva* 248 On the margin of the great rivers of the west, the button-wood is constantly found to be the loftiest and largest tree of the United States. **1858** HOLMES *Autocrat* 176 The buttonwood throws off its bark in large flakes, which one may find lying at its foot, pushed out and at last pushed off. **1900** E. BRUNCKEN *N. A. Forests* 9 You are fairly within the realm of the . . . gigantic sycamore, or buttonwood as they call it in the Eastern States.

b. A single tree of this species. Also collective.

1775 FITHIAN *Journal* II. 67 On the bank of this creek I walked among the white-walnut, ash, buttonwood, birch, hazles, etc. **1835** BIRD *Hawks of Hawk-H.* II. 136 The attorney . . . would have been drowned had he not been luckily dashed into the crotch of a low and twisted buttonwood. **1851** SPRINGER *Forest Life* 16 General Washington measured a Buttonwood growing on an island in the Ohio, and found its girth, at five feet from the ground, about forty feet. **1880** *Harper's Mag.* May 908/2 Just down there, beyond the crooked buttonwood, opposite Bung's coopershop! **1898** DELAND *Old Chester Tales* 177 The road . . . kept . . . up and over the hills, through the shadows of buttonwoods and chestnuts.

c. Attrib. with *bark, meetinghouse, seed, stake.*

1766 H. GORDON in *Travels Amer. Col.* 473 [They] drove a Number of Button Wood Short Stakes in the Slope. **1796** J. DABNEY *Address* 17 Elm, button wood seeds, &c. were sowed. **1799** *Aurora* (Phila.) 21 May (Th.), The old button-wood meeting-house in Philadelphia was made into a military riding-house. **1833** NEAL *Down-Easters* I. 81 Dont care how close a feller is—closer an' button-wood bark, all the better for me.

2. =BUTTONBUSH, BUTTON TREE 2.

1802 DRAYTON *S. Carolina* 62 Button wood. (*Cephalanthus Occidentalis.*) Grows in watery places: blossoms in June. A wash of the decoction of this plant, is said to be good for the palsey. **1813** MUHLENBERG *Cat. Plants* 15 Globe-flower shrub, (button wood, or pond dogwood).

+Buttonwood caterpillar. (See quotation.) — **1854** EMMONS *Agric. N.Y.* V. 261 Index, Buttonwood Caterpillar, 234. [233-4 *Dryocampa imperialis* . . . its caterpillar feeds upon the buttonwood, . . . oak, and sweetgum.]

+Buttonwood tree. =BUTTONWOOD 1 b.

1674 *Cambridge Rec.* 1 A button wood tree to make two beams of. **1680** *Hartford Land Distrib.* 472 Two Button wood trees, one by each river.

1719 SEWALL *Diary* III. 217 Planted 7. Button-wood Trees at Engs's Pasture . . . one at Elm-Pasture; one White Oak at home. 1779 *N.H. Hist. Soc. Coll.* VI. 320 Here are the finest buttonwood trees that I have seen in my travels, growing as tall and straight as any pine trees that I ever saw, and equally as large. 1818 *Mass. Spy* 14 Oct. (Th.), A piece of a large button-wood tree has been hollowed out and placed for a curb, to prevent people from falling into [the well]. 1835 BIRD *Hawks of Hawk-H.* II. 255 His adventure in the brook, with his ride on the back of the buttonwood-tree, has . . . travelled into an adjacent county. 1880 *Harper's Mag.* Aug. 333/1 The buttonwood trees that made a hedge on the other side must . . . have hidden me from sight.

+**Buy**, *n. colloq.* A bargain, purchase. — 1882 *Century Mag.* Aug. 540 Do you not think that 'Denver' has a future? . . . I think myself it is a first-rate buy. 1890 VAN DYKE *Millionaires of Day* 134 Get it [=a city lot] for you for fifty thousand. . . . Biggest buy in town. 1911 QUICK *Yellowstone N.* 191, I believe it's a good buy!

***Buyer.** A purchasing agent, esp. for a mercantile firm. {1884–} — 1887 *Courier-Journal* 5 Feb. 7/2 A good many wholesale buyers . . . have already completed their early purchases. 1913 FERBER *Roast Beef Medium* 96 Old Sulzberg sends his buyers to the New York market twice a year.

Buz(z). +=BUZZ SAW. — 1821 *Mass. Spy* 26 Sept. (Th.), A circular buz, of thin, soft sheet iron, six inches in diameter. 1823 *Mechanic's Mag.* No. 7. 108 The Shakers sometimes made use of what he called a buzz to cut iron. 1830 S. SMITH *Major Downing* 27, I met a man . . . that said they've got them are wheels going now like a buz.

***Buzzard.**

*1. A hawk of the genus *Buteo*.

1812 WILSON *Ornithology* VI. 78 [An] American Buzzard, or White-Breasted Hawk: *Falco leverianus?* . . . amused itself by . . . hopping from one end of the room to the other. 1828 BONAPARTE *Synopsis* 32 The Red-tailed Hawk, American Buzzard, White-breasted Hawk, *Falco borealis*, . . . inhabits throughout North America. 1839 PEABODY *Mass. Birds* 268 The Short-winged Buzzard, *Falco buteoides*. . . . In New York, it is said to commit depredations on the poultry. 1858 BAIRD *Birds Pacific R.R.* 21 *Buteo Bairdii*, Baird's Buzzard; . . . [inhabits] northern and western North America. *Ib.* 24 *Buteo Harlani*, . . . Harlan's Buzzard; Black Warrior. The specimens . . . were obtained . . . in New Mexico [and] California. 1874 COUES *Birds N.W.* 365 Granting the heavy Buzzards commensurate courage to act with all their force, they cannot, nevertheless, acquire the requisite speed. 1887 C. ABBOTT *Waste-Land Wanderings* ii. 35 The only one of them that is prone to cry out while circling overhead is the red-tailed buzzard or hen-hawk.

b. *Between hawk and buzzard*, between one thing (time, etc.) and another. {1636–62}

1832 KENNEDY *Swallow Barn* I. 6, I entered Richmond between hawk and buzzard—the very best hour, I maintain, out of the twenty-four, for a picturesque tourist. 1835 PAULDING *J. Bull & Br. Jon.* xix. 87 He . . . was between hawk and buzzard, as they say. 1853 SIMMS *Sword & Distaff* 455 He was still, as before—not to speak disparagingly of the sex in our comparisons—betwixt hawk and buzzard. 1855 — *Forayers* 62 They felt that their game was twixt hawk and buzzard. 1904 *Courier-Journal* 12 July 4 The intelligence of the Commonwealth found itself literally between hawk and buzzard. It hovered in the balance.

+2. The California condor or vulture.

1805 CLARK in *Lewis & C. Exped.* (1905) III. 174 Those Buzzards are much larger than any other of ther Spece or the largest Eagle, white under part of their wings. 1807 GASS *Journal* 168 They killed a remarkably large buzzard, of a species different from any I had seen. It was 9 feet across the wings, and 3 feet 10 inches from the bill to the tail.

+3. The turkey buzzard or vulture, *Cathartes aura*.

1824 DODDRIDGE *Notes* 69 The buzzards, or vultures, . . . were very numerous here in former times. *c*1830 GODMAN in *Waldie's Select Library* II. 86/3 Now and then the buzzard, or turkey vulture, may be seen wheeling in graceful circles in the higher regions of the air. 1844 *Knickerb.* XXIV. 188 Mistaking a buzzard for a turkey is also very pleasant while it lasts. 1850 E. P. BURKE *Reminisc. Ga.* 135 The most useful bird in all the South, is the buzzard, more properly called the vulture. 1869 BROWNE *Adv. Apache Country* 43 It was a grand carnival for the buzzards and coyotes. 1885 *Outing* VII. 70/2 The panther had . . . covered it with leaves to prevent the buzzards from finding it. 1902 WISTER *Virginian* 312 From somewhere . . . rose a buzzard and sailed on its black pinions into the air above them. 1910 J. HART *Vigilante Girl* 367 Those are vultures. . . . You can tell them by the white patches under their wings; they are earlier than the buzzards.

+**b.** A nickname for an inhabitant of Georgia.

1845 *Cincinnati Misc.* 240 The inhabitants of . . . Georgia [are called] Buzzards. 1913 RUOFF *Dict. Facts* 372 Names given to the inhabitants of the different States by popular use: . . . Georgia, buzzards.

+**c.** *(Harris's) buzzard:* (see quot. 1922).

*a*1888 in J. Phelan *Hist. Tenn.* 381 It's all over; there is Harris's infernal buzzard in the mail. 1922 MCCORMAC *Biog. Polk* 141 Harris had a spread-eagle woodcut prepared. . . . As its appearance in the *Union* was always accompanied by news of Democratic victory, the Whigs expressed their contempt by calling it 'Harris's buzzard.' *Ib.* 150 On August 1 [1839] Polk was elected by a majority of three thousand votes, and Harris got out his 'buzzard' to adorn the front page of the *Union*.

4. *slang.* ***a.** A stupid, cowardly, or contemptible person; a jealous or vindictive person. {–1822} Also attrib.

1807 IRVING *Salmagundi* xi, The great crowd of buzzards, puffers, and 'old continentals' of all parties, who throng to the polls, to persuade, to cheat, or to force the freeholders into the right way. 1883 *Harper's Mag.* LXVII. 970/2 A soldier, even if he fit agin me, would er been welcome, but I do hate a buzzard bummer worse than a rattlesnake. 1889 BARRÈRE & LELAND s.v., *Buzzard*, (American), an oppressive, arrogant person, jealous of rivalry, and vindictive. 1904 'O. HENRY' *Heart of West* 154 'He's a plumb buzzard,' said Buck. 'He won't work, and he's the low-downest passel of inhumanity I ever see.' 1909 WASON *Happy Hawkins* 55, I ain't never heard o' the buzzard himself since that day long, long ago.

b. 'A badly-spoiled piece of work' (De Vere).

1871 *Lancaster Intelligencer* 6 May (De Vere), Said the venerable Mr. G. to one of his jours: Sir, I pronounce that job an unmitigated buzzard.

+**Buzzard dollar.** The silver dollar coined under the Bland bill of 1878, having on the back the figure of an eagle, derisively called a buzzard. — 1878 *Nation* 19 Sept. 170/2 The 'buzzard dollar' [is] the designation applied by indignant holders of the trade-dollar to the now standard dollar. *a*1890 *Chicago Tribune* (B. & L.), The waiters . . . will take anything you give them, from a nickel up to a buzzard dollar, and look happy.

+**Buzzard sweep.** An extra large sweep for a plough. — 1854 *Florida Plant. Rec.* 575, 16 Buzzard Sweeps, old patern.

‖ **Buzzardy,** *a.* Resembling a turkey buzzard or vulture. — 1885 'CRADDOCK' *Prophet* 242, I don't want ter stay in jail, an' be tried, . . . an' mebbe hev them buzzardy lawyers fix suthin' on me ennyways.

+**Buzz saw,** *n.* [Cf. BUZZ *n.*] A circular saw.

1860 HOLLAND *Miss Gilbert* 350 If you'll take thunder and lightning and a steamboat and a buzz-saw and mix 'em up. 1875 *Chicago Tribune* 5 Oct. 5/6 The Buzz-Saw. . . . Andrew Strienz had his hand almost severed from the wrist by a circular saw. 1883 M. D. LANDON *Wit & Humor* 118 Uncle George had a controversy with a buzz-saw. 1907 *Springfield Republican* 13 May 10 John Hanson . . . had the thumb on his right hand severely lacerated Saturday while at work with a buzz saw.

fig. 1903 *Boston Ev. Transcript* 26 Sept., There are unpleasant indications . . . that the Democratic party is contemplating further experiments with political buzzsaws and other things that bite and tear.

b. *attrib.* Resembling in some respect a buzz saw.

1895 WILLIAMS *Princeton Stories* 69 All summer long she sat on the sand without a veil and was nice to two little boys in clean duck trousers and buzz-saw hats which blew off sometimes. 1897 'MARK TWAIN' *Following Equator* 313 One of those whizzing green Ballarat flies . . . with his stunning buzz-saw noise.

+**Buzz-saw,** *v. tr.* To cut with a buzz saw. Also fig. — 1883 M. D. LANDON *Wit & Humor* 118, I was buzz-sawed, sure.

***By,** *adv.* and *prep.*

+1. *adv.* At, in, or into another's house when passing. With verbs, esp. *call, come, go, stop*. Orig. *S.*

1816 PICKERING 98 In North Carolina, Mr. B. asked me to stop and dine with him when I was passing his house, by saying, 'Will you go by and dine with me?' 1827 SHERWOOD *Gaz. Georgia* 139 *Go by*, for call, or stop at. 1863 C. C. HOPLEY *Life in South* I. 58 The Southerners . . . deem it a thing impossible that a friend should pass the house and not come in; so that 'come by' implies 'take *our* road home, and of course come in.' *Ib.*, 'Won't you call by?' and 'do come by,' mean always 'be sure to stop.' 1871 DE VERE 605 In travelling through Virginia and most of the Southern States, nothing is more common than to be asked by the hospitable planters to *go by* and dine, or spend the night with them. 1896 *Dialect Notes* I. 371 Come by and stay to supper. 1905 *Ib.* III. 96, I believe I'll stop by and see Bud. *a*1906 'O. HENRY' *Trimmed Lamp*, etc. 220 Granger . . . would call by for Mary Adrian. 1928 F. N. HART *Bellamy Trial* v. 172 They were going to stop by for her.

2. *prep.* +**a.** At or into (another's house) on passing it.

1896 *Dialect Notes* I. 385 'Come by my house and stay all night' =not pass by, but stop at the house. 1923 *Ib.* V. 244 *Stop by*, to visit. 'Stop by my house.'

b. *By the name of:* (see NAME).

By and large. [Orig. a nautical phrase {1669–} ='to the wind (within six points) and off it.'] +On the whole; in a general way; generally speaking. Orig. and usually with *take, taken,* or *taking*.

(1) 1769 in *S. Lit. Messenger* XXVII. 183/2 Captain (Thompson) . . . hath made prize of the President's daughter, Miss Betsey, a charming frigate, that will do honour to our country, if you take her by and large, as the sailors say. 1823 COOPER *Pioneers* xxxiv, Taking it by and large, Master Bump-ho, 'tis but a small matter after all. 1845 JUDD *Margaret* II. 283 And take it by and large . . . she is the beater of all. 1875 'MARK TWAIN' *Life on Miss.* iii. 48 Taking you by and large, you do seem to be more different kinds of an ass than any creature I ever saw before. 1897 *Atlantic Mo.* Oct. 542 The social aspects of the town—the town taken by and large—will also continue for some years fairly to deserve the same characterization. 1901 *Harper's Mag.* Jan. 287/2 Taking them by and large, the French people have a wider command of their mother tongue . . . than have the American people in relation to the English language.

(2) **1845** C. MATHEWS *Writings* II. 159 (Th.), He had been speaking for four hours, ostensibly on the Panama mission, but actually travelled over everything by and large. **1878** B. F. TAYLOR *Between Gates* 281 Those who sail over the old parallels of latitude by-and-large believe in fair play. **1880** 'MARK TWAIN' *Tramp Abroad* l. 580, I . . . walked through Holland and Belgium, . . . and I had a tolerably good time of it 'by and large.' **1890** *Congress. Rec.* 9 May 4376/2 By and large all of us who live there [=Me.] . . . know the immense benefit that has been derived from it [*i.e.*, the prohibition law].

By-bet. ?*Obs.* A side bet. {*a*1627} — **1803** LEWIS in *Journals of L. & Ordway* 59 The Comdts horse lost the main rase, but won by six inches the by betts, the odds generally given against him in the by betts was 12 feet. **1829** T. FLINT *George Mason* 109 *By-bets*, as they were called, and increased bets, were continually forming. *Ib.* 110 Beside the purse, and the great bets, there were many by-bets, many beaver hats . . . suspended upon the two horses. **1856** *Spirit of Times* (N.Y.) 25 Oct. 132/1 Mr. Doswell discovered that his entry was lame in the right hind leg . . . and refused to start unless all by-bets on him were drawn.

By-bidder. A bidder at an auction in league with the seller to raise prices. {1863, *dial.*} — **1848** BARTLETT 59 *By-bidder*, a person employed at public auctions to bid on articles put up for sale, to obtain higher prices. **1860** S. MORDECAI *Virginia* 283 It may be presumed that there were by-bidders to set the ball in motion, or to give it an impulse when retarded. **1900** S. A. NELSON *A B C Wall St.* 131 *By-bidder*, a man who bids at auction in behalf of the owner for the purpose of advancing the price of the property.

Bye.[1] A side current or stream. {1877} — **1801** *Mass. Spy* 29 July 3/1 For fear of being drawn into a bye, he put to shore at a steep bank, where a large tree fell across his boat.

||**Bye.**[2] The goal used in the Indian game of ball. (See BALL-PLAY 1.) — *c***1836** CATLIN *Indians* II. 124 We . . . witnessed the ceremony of . . . erecting the 'byes' or goals which were to guide the play. Each party had their goal made with two upright posts, about 25 feet high and six feet apart, set firm in the ground, with a pole across at the top.

+**Byfield.** [?From *Byfield*, Mass.] A breed of hogs. — **1838** COLMAN *Mass. Agric. Rep.* 74 A cross with some of our small boned breed, such as the Byfield or the China. **1851** CIST *Cincinnati* 279 The hogs raised for this market, are generally a cross of Irish Grazier, Byfield, Berkshire, [etc.]. **1864** *Me. Agric. Rep.* 28 Mr. Haines gave an account of the old Newbury White breed. They were introduced . . . under the name of 'Byfield.' . . . They had small ears, short legs, and long bodies.

* **Bylaw.** Also †**buy law.** An ordinance made by a local authority, or having a local or restricted application; a regulation adopted by a corporation or society.

1695 *Boston Rec.* 221 The Persons underwritten being sumoned before the Select men to answer for their breach of Town orders or by Laws in building to the Inconveniences of the street. **1699** *Braintree Rec.* 40 Then voted that the Selectmen should draw up a buy Law against horses running unfettered. **1715** *Boston Rec.* 119 The proposal of Deacon John Marion for a Town Order or By-Law to prevent abuses by such as offer to Sale any Sort of perrished meat. **1740** *Ib.* 264 Voted, that the Select Men be desired to prepare a By-Law to present to the next General Town Meeting. **1790** *Ann. 1st Congress* II. 2049 A by-law of the corporation of the Bank of North America . . . evidently aims at such a mean [between giving equal votes to all stockholders and giving each share a vote]. **1851** CIST *Cincinnati* 110 J. B. Russell . . . and R. Buchanan were appointed a committee to prepare a constitution and by-laws of the [Horticultural] Society. **1859** *Huntington Rec.* III. 442 We have a standing By-Law of the said Town, that no person, other than a resident thereof, shall take or catch any oysters within the bounds of said Town. **1880** *Harper's Mag.* July 216/1 [At Great South Bay] there is a Master of the Hounds whose duty it is to enforce all the rules, regulations, and by-laws relative to hunting.

By-letter. *Obs.* ?A letter to be delivered by the way. — **1792** *Ann. 2nd Congress* 62 The deputy postmasters . . . shall . . . answer to him, for all by or way letters, and shall specify the same . . . in the post bill.

Bymeby, By 'nd by, *adv. colloq.* Also **by 'n by, by am by, bye'm by, by'm by(e), bym by, byme by, bamby, bomby.** [Careless pron. of * *by and by.*] By and by; presently. [Cf. BIMEBY, BUMBY.]

(*a*) **1708** *Deplorable State of New Eng.* 35 The Business was so managed . . . that altho' . . . one Day it was voted, That the Fort should be attack'd, it was by 'nd by, unvoted again. **1839** *Mass. H. S. Coll.* 3 Ser. IX. 97 For sometimes he loves his Indians very much; by 'nd by, he don't love 'em so much. **1865** MRS. WHITNEY *Gayworthys* 205 We may hurry in 't the large end 'o the horn, an' have to crawl out at the small one, by 'n by!

(*b*) **1825** NEAL *Brother Jonathan* I. 106 Bym by, naiteral enough, there they go! **1843** STEPHENS *High Life N.Y.* II. 63 But by-am-by out come a queer looking chap, as chirk as a catydid. **1857** HOLLAND *Bay Path* (1864) 334 Byme-by I looked up, and there stood the widow crying. **1863** 'MARK TWAIN' & WARNER *Gilded Age* ii. 32 But bymeby she roused up like, and looked around wild. **1884** *Harper's Mag.* Feb. 410/2 Byme-by he sort of gave up goin' to see the . . . girls.

(*c*) **1795** B. DEARBORN *Columbian Grammar* 134 Improprieties, commonly called Vulgarisms, . . . [include] 13. Bamby for By and by. **1898** WESTCOTT *D. Harum* 324 Bom-by she got so she couldn't keep a hired girl in the house.

+**Byo(e)**, obs. var. of BAYOU. (Cf. BIO.) — **1803** LEWIS in *Journals of L. & Ordway* 50 The island is formed by a byo which makes out nearly in the direction observed course of the river. **1804** WHITEHOUSE in *Lewis & Clark Exped.* (1905) VII. 36 Got in to a Byoe, at the End of sd. Byoe came to the main River.

* **By-place.** An out-of-the-way place. {-1714; now *dial.*}

1674 *Md. Archives* II. 346 A member of this house proposeth the Inconveniences of Multitudes of Ordinaries in by Places & from such Places where Courts are kept. **1832** KENNEDY *Swallow Barn* II. 59 This brings us into all the by-places of the neighbourhood, and makes me many acquaintances.

fig. **1830** HAWTHORNE *Old Woman's Tale* Works (1883) XII. 109 There are a thousand of her traditions lurking in the corners and by-places of my mind.

By-settlement. An out-of-the-way or back settlement. — **1780** R. PUTNAM in *Memoirs* 153 He saw no foot, but heard of small partys being out and plundering some bye settlements.

By-town. An outlying town. {1683} — **1853** *Knickerb.* XLII. 317 Mark S— was a very fair specimen of that class of pettifoggers who thrive in some of the by-towns.

By-trail. A side track; a bypath. — **1873** MILLER *Amongst Modocs* iii. 53, I remember . . . that I always took some by-trail, if possible.

C

∗**C.** The third letter of the alphabet.

+**1.** A hundred-dollar bill. Also *C-speck.*

1845 Sol. Smith *Theatr. Apprent.* 149 So there's my hundred—and as my pocket-book's out, and my hand's in, there's another C. *a***1846** *Quarter Race Ky.*, etc. 117 Sol. Lauflin matched his bay four year old colt . . . to run a quarter, in the lane near this place, for a C speck.

+**2.** Abbrev. of 'connection' or 'coherence.'

1848 N. Ames *Childe Harvard* 33 These last six stanzas, I suppose, may seem Rather out of place, and should be marked with 'C'; That is, 'want of connection' in 'the theme.'

+**3.** Used as a mark on a college exercise.

1889 *Harvard Faculty Rec.* in M. L. Smallwood *Exams. & Grading Systems* 59 Any member of the graduating class who has attained Grade C or a higher grade in eighteen courses . . . will be recommended for a degree. **1897** Flandrau *Harvard Episodes* 279 If . . . [the instructor] let the boy through,—gave him . . . the undeserved and highly respectable mark of C. *Ib.* 280 Thorn . . . entered the boy's midyear mark in the records as C.

+**Ca-.** In various onomatopoeic formations conveying the idea of impact or sound. Cf. Ker-.

1843 Stephens *High Life N.Y.* II. 63 It was lucky the [theatre-]curtain went down ca-smash as it did. *Ib.* 67 It [a bouquet] fell ca-swash right down to Miss Elssler's feet. **1844** J. C. Neal *Peter Ploddy* 179 In I jumps, ca-splash! **1845** Hooper *Simon Suggs' Adv.* (1928) 142 [The sticks of wood] hit pretty close by me 'casionally, ca-junk! strikin' end-foremost. **1851** — *Widow Rugby's Husband* 90 Presently Jim come to the ground *ca-whop!* **1859** Bartlett 63 *Cachunk*, a word like thump! describing the sound produced by the fall of a heavy body. Also written kerchunk! **1889** Farmer 113/2 *Cachunk! Kerchunk! Cashunk!*—This word belongs to a class of exclamations which are intended to convey an imitation of the sound of a body falling heavily, that is, with a noise or thump.

Cab.

1. A horse-drawn covered vehicle that may be hired. {1827–}

1840 *Niles' Nat. Reg.* 17 Oct. 112/1 Cabs. The first seen in Boston, made its appearance on the 6th instant. **1842** *Knickerb.* XIX. 46 The rumbling and ponderous omnibus and clattering cab . . . passed on. **1865** Mrs. Whitney *Gayworthys* 131 The train came into the station at dusk. . . . The Doctor caught a cab. **1886** *Century Mag.* XXXII. 545 As soon as the cab stopped, the owner of the head opened the door. **1899** *Boston Herald* 20 March 4/3 Cabs and hansoms seeking business—'crawlers,' as they are called—should not be permitted to pass up and down some of the principal streets.

+**2.** The covered compartment of a locomotive that houses the engineer and fireman.

1859 Worcester 187/1 *Cab*, a small structure on a locomotive engine serving as a shelter to the engineer. **1877** 'E. Martin' *Hist. Great Riots* 33 There were several soldiers in the cab, and ten in all on the train, to protect the engineer and fireman and the train. **1880** *Harper's Mag.* Feb. 389/1 He seemed to project half his length out of the window of the 'cab' as he rounded the curves in about half of schedule time. **1887** *Ib.* May 969 Shackley leaned out despairingly from the cab of his engine.

attrib. **1901** Merwin & Webster *Calumet K* 94 The fireman [was] leaning far out of the cab window, closely scanning the track for signs of an obstruction.

+**b.** A compartment used by a brakeman.

1887 C. B. George *40 Years on Rail* 31 The brakes of all cars were on top, and the brake-man sat in that elevated position in a little cab.

Caba. [F. *cabas* basket, pannier.] 'A flat basket . . . for figs, &c.; hence, a lady's flat work-basket or reticule' (W. '64). — **1885** *Boston Journal* 7 Sept., The origin of the word 'caba' applying to the small hand-bag or satchel. . . . The French *cabas*, a frail basket, hand basket &c. was used upon ladies' work-boxes imported thirty years ago. **1886** *N.Y. Ev. Post* Sept. (Th.), The Philadelphian to the manner born knows that 'caba' is only another name for hand-bag, but the average New Yorker never heard it used. **1898** Deland *Old Chester Tales* 317 So Lucy came, with . . . her little caba full of worsted work.

Cabalgada. *S.W.* [Sp.] A cavalcade. (Cf. next.) — **1849** Audubon *Western Journal* (1906) 95 Those intending to run off the 'cabalgada' of a travelling party, take a strong horse.

+**Caballada.** *S.W.* Also **caballado.** [Sp. *caballada*, from *caballo* horse. Cf. Cavallada.] A drove or herd of horses (or mules).

(*a*) **1844** Gregg *Commerce of Prairies* I. 27 And swinging their lazos over their heads, [the Indians] plunged among the stock with a furious yell, and drove off the entire *caballada* of near five hundred head of horses, mules, and asses. **1845** T. J. Green *Texian Exped.* 75 If we become loaded with gains . . . whether these gains be in the way of a caballada or baby-clothes, it increases a home desire. **1853** *Harper's Mag.* VII. 313/1 Their caballada contained not only horses and mules, but here and there a stray *burro* (Mexican jackass). *a***1861** Winthrop *J. Brent* 133 We shifted our little caballada to fresh grazing-spots sheltered by a brake. **1884** Sweet & Knox *Through Texas* 60 There was a *caballada* (herd of horses—Texaniz'ed pronunciation, kavey-yard) in a corral about three miles from town. **1900** Smithwick *Evolution of State* 22 He had his caballada driven in for us to choose from. **1910** J. Hart *Vigilante Girl* 159 When I take my ride this afternoon I must go forth with a complete caballada, and not alone?

(*b*) **1841** W. L. McCalla *Adventures in Texas* 57 (Bentley), A party of these daring Indians had . . . taken off about fifty or sixty horses from the neighbourhood, forty of which were from one caballado. **1884** Sweet & Knox *Through Texas* 499 It was only a caballado of horses grazing on the prairie. **1900** Smithwick *Evolution of State* 161 We found ourselves in the midst of a caballado which . . . sprang to their feet snorting and stamping.

+**Caballero.** *S.W.* [Sp. *caballero* knight, gentleman.] A horseman; a gentleman; a squire (to a lady).

1837 Irving *Astoria* iii. 85 (*headline*), A Californian caballero. **1840** Dana *Two Years* xxviii. 314 He began to see that there was no use in playing the *caballero* any longer, and came down into the forecastle, . . . threw off all his airs, and enjoyed the joke as much as any one. **1845** T. J. Green *Texian Exped.* 134 As the lady is thus relieved, her caballero, in compliment to her performance serves her with either coffee [or] chocolate. **1848** Bryant *California* 314 In the rear were two caballeros, riding fine spirited horses, with gaudy trappings. **1850** Colton *3 Yrs. in Calif.* 207 The pistols were reloaded, and señoritas and caballeros all dashed up for another shower of fire and lead. **1876** Bret Harte *G. Conroy* xix, She had given orders to her servants that the moment a stranger caballero appeared on the road she was to be apprised of the fact. **1898** Atherton *Californians* 8 A caballero . . . who will . . . lie in a hammock smoking cigaritos all day. **1910** J. Hart *Vigilante Girl* 198 Her escort of *vaqueros*—heeding not her new *caballero*, for they owed allegiance only to her.

+**Caballo.** *S.W.* [Sp. *caballo.*] A horse. — **1851** *Alta Californian* 3 Aug., Here in California . . . we bandy about the common nouns . . . 'caballo.' *a***1861** Winthrop *J. Brent* 14, I slipped quietly down from my little Mexican caballo, and . . . stood watching the splendid motions of this free steed of the prairie. **1904** 'O. Henry' *Heart of West* (1907) 198 Throw a pot of coffee together while I attend to the *caballo.*

Cabaret. **1.** A small establishment in which liquor is sold and consumed. {1655–} +**2.** A restaurant which provides entertainment by singers, dancers, etc. Also attrib. — **(1)** **1835** J. H. Ingraham *South-West* I. 92 Ten, out of seventeen successive shops, or *cabarets*, upon the shelves of which I could discover nothing but myriads of claret or Madeira bottles. **1837** *S. Lit. Messenger* III. 464 During our stay we strolled into the village cabaret. **1851** A. O. Hall *Manhattaner* 102 Picayune dram-houses (better known among Crescent citizens as cabarets) smoke each other (tobaccowise) at every few steps. **(2)** **1912** W. Irwin *Red Button* 42 He spends most of his extra money at pool parlors, Austrian villages and cabaret shows. **1913** *Nation* XCVI. 352/3 Mayor Gaynor's war upon the cabarets. *Ib.* 353/1 The cabaret influence in standardizing dress ideals, cosmetics, and the vocabulary and humor of the day needs no extended comment. *Ib.*, The cabaret singer has gone far beyond Richard Strauss.

+**Cabarista,** inexact variant of Cabestro. — **1847** S. Reid *Scouting Exped.* 34 We then untied our *cabaristas* or Mexican halters, which are about some twenty or thirty feet long.

∗**Cabbage,** *n.* Also †**cabidge, cabage.**

∗**1.** The vegetable so called.

1624 Smith *Virginia* vi. 220 Those that sow . . . Carrots, Cabidge, and such like. **1685** T. Budd *Penna. & N.J.* 31 Garden Fruits groweth well, as Cabbage. **1704** S. Knight *Journal* 15 The woman bro't in a twisted thing like a cable, . . . which . . . shee serv'd in a dish of Pork and Cabage. **1775** Fithian *Journal* II. 151 Large platters covered with meat of many sorts; Beef; Venison; Pork;—& with these potatoes, turnips, cabbage. **1805** Parkinson *Tour* 339 Cabbages are very much used. . . . The early York and May are cultivated, but not in the same perfection as in England. **1880** *Harper's Mag.* Aug. 337/2 Hope Island had a single poor house and barn, with a patch of cabbages near by. **1917** C. Mathewson *Sec. Base Sloan* 252 Say, I goin' to cook a big mess of pork an' cabbage the very firs' thing!

2. In phrases or allusive uses.

1828 A. Royall *Black Book* II. 243 It is flint to cabbage emphatically. **1870** 'Mark Twain' *My Watch* Writings VII. (1922) 1 All this human cabbage could see was that the watch was four minutes slow.

3. (See quotations.)
1879 BISHOP *4 Months in Sneak-Box* 298 With their venison these men served a very palatable dish made from the terminal bud of the palmetto known as the 'cabbage,' and from which the tree derives its name of 'cabbage-palm.' **1889** *Cent.* 747/1 The cabbage is the terminal leaf-bud, the removal of which, though often done, destroys the tree.

4. Attrib. with *garden, leaf, patch,* etc.
1742 HEMPSTEAD *Diary* 394, I was at home fenceing in a Cabage yard. **1751** ELIOT *Field-Husb.* iii. 51 Millet . . . is a small grain of a yellowish Colour, and of the bigness of Turnip or Cabbage Seed. **1778** *Essex Inst. Coll.* LII. 13 Another [shot] I saw tearing up the ground . . . & burying itself in a cabbage yard. **1834** *Knickerb.* IV. 221 He . . . lives entirely alone, and cultivates a small cabbage-garden, which supplies him with necessaries. **1843** *Ib.* XXII. 496 [J. W.] Jarvis . . . encountered the Doctor, with a pound of fresh butter upon a Cabbage-leaf. **1861** NEWELL *Orpheus C. Kerr* I. 227 How often does man, after making something his particular forte, discover at last that it is only a cabbage-patch. **1870** R. TOMES *Decorum* 193 Such was the toughness engendered by sour-krout, smoked sausage, and cabbage-soup!

Cabbage, *v. tr.* To obtain dishonestly. *colloq.* {1712–} Also with *on.* —**1846** CORCORAN *Pickings* 204, I aint agoin' to let my karacter be *cabbaged* away right before my face. **1856** M. THOMPSON *Plu-ri-bus-tah* 43 Shaking both her fists in anger At the 'Injun,' and at Henry Who had 'cabbaged' all her 'Injuns' For his song of Hiawatha. **1887** *Lippincott's Mag.* Sept. 382 The million I cabbaged has done me more good than it would have done Mayden. **1902** HARBEN *Abner Daniel* 238 They both got into deep water speculatin', an' Craig was tempted to cabbage on the twenty-five thousand dollars.

+**Cabbage bug.** 'The *Murgantia histrionica,* more fully called harlequin cabbage-bug, from its brilliant markings' (*Cent.*). — **1870** *Rep. Comm. Agric.* (1871) 90 The harlequin cabbage-bug . . . has been much complained of during the past year as doing great damage to the cabbage in North Carolina and elsewhere. **1884** *Ib.* 309 The Harlequin Cabbage-bug derives its name from the gay, theatrical, harlequin-like manner in which the black and orange-yellow colors are arranged upon its body. **1892** V. KELLOG *Kansas Insects* 58 Harlequin cabbage bug. . . . It is said that half a dozen adult insects will kill a cabbage in one day.

Cabbage butterfly. A butterfly of the genus *Pieris,* whose caterpillars feed on the leaves of the cabbage and related plants. {1816–} — **1854** EMMONS *Agric. N.Y.* V. 261 Index, Cabbage butterflies, 205. [*Ib.* 205 This butterfly . . . is injurious to garden plants.] **1870** *Rep. Comm. Agric.* (1871) 78 The common cabbage-butterfly of Europe . . . was probably introduced into Quebec in 1856 or 1857 from Europe, . . . and . . . in 1866 it had found its way into New Hampshire and Vermont, and in 1869 was said to have been found in Hudson City and Hoboken. **1884** *Ib.* 416 The European Cabbage Butterfly . . . destroyed a large proportion of the late varieties, both of cabbage and cauliflower.

Cabbage caterpillar. Any of various insect larvae that infest cabbages. — **1862** *Rep. Comm. Patents: Agric.* 592 The insects [beetles] . . . are esteemed particularly useful in cabbage patches in destroying the cabbage caterpillar, (*Pontia brassica*).

+**Cabbage hammock.** *S.* A hammock (or hummock) covered with a growth of cabbage palm. — **1837** J. L. WILLIAMS *Florida* 142 Occasionally cabbage hammocks of considerable extent, rise in the midst of these glades.

Cabbagehead.

1. A head of cabbage: *fig.* a large round head.
1834 PECK *Gaz. Illinois* 29 A cabbage head three feet in diameter . . . is no wonder on this soil. **1845** JUDD *Margaret* I. xiii. 99 Pluck, sitting on his hams near the fire, with his full-orbed cabbage-head swaying to and fro. *a***1861** WINTHROP *C. Dreeme* 201 Garish steady sunshine, may do to swell wheat and puff cabbage-heads. **1865** *Atlantic Mo.* XV. 172, I thus learned a great deal . . . planting the seeds and watching the growth of even a cabbage-head. **1912** MRS. WOODROW *Sally Salt* 80 The clear little artificial stream, its sides bordered with . . . wonderful blue-green cabbage heads.

2. *fig.* A stupid person. {1682–}
1865 *Nation* I. 369 We hear persons whose talents are rather of the solid than the brilliant order familiarly spoken of as 'cabbage heads.' **1866** LOWELL *Biglow P.* II. xi. 77 My feller kebbige-heads, who look so green.

Cabbage-headed, *a.* Having a large round head. — **1846** CORCORAN *Pickings* 10 A low, chubby, cabbage-headed Dutchman . . . entered the office.

+**Cabbage land.** *S.* Land covered with cabbage palm. — **1837** J. L. WILLIAMS *Florida* 54 The St. Johns . . . [is] separated from the waters that run south, into the Everglades, by a very crooked rise of cabbage land.

Cabbage palm. *S.* +The palmetto of the southern states. Cf. next. {1772–}
1835 C. J. LATROBE *Rambler in N.A.* II. 34 After a long and wearisome day's journey . . . through a wilderness of saw-palmetto, swamps, and groves of cabbage-palm. **1837** J. L. WILLIAMS *Florida* 84 Cabbage Palm. . . . The greatest ornament of our sea coast; they sometimes rise on a straight column eighty feet. **1869** *Amer. Naturalist* III. 352 The few tree Palmettos or Cabbage-palms . . . that we have already met indicate that we are approaching the Gulf. **1890** H. M. FIELD *Bright Skies* 57 The 'cabbage-palm,' so named from its cabbage-like head, . . . forms a striking figure in the landscape.

+**Cabbage palmetto.** *S.* The ordinary palmetto of the southern states, *Sabal palmetto.* Also attrib.
1802 J. DRAYTON *S. Carolina* 66 Cabbage palmetto. (*Corypha* palmetto.) Grows on the sea islands, and on lands adjacent to salt water rivers, a few miles from the sea. **1833** B. SILLIMAN *Sugar Cane* 19 [The hammocks are] characterized by the natural growth of large evergreen oaks, . . . magnolia and cabbage-palmetto. **1849** *Rep. Comm. Patents* (1850) 250 What I claim . . . is the application . . . of the branches of the cabbage palmetto tree to the manufacture of brooms. **1850** E. P. BURKE *Reminisc. Ga.* 186 A great curiosity . . . was the cabbage-tree, or more properly in botanical language, the 'cabbage palmetto.' **1894** COULTER *Bot. W. Texas* III. 452 Cabbage Palmetto . . . [grows] in sparse clumps, from the mouth of the Rio Grande to Edinburg.

‖**Cabbage pea.** A species of edible pea. — **1859** A. VAN BUREN *Sojourn in South* 155 The Cabbage Pea, with its large broad pod, makes a fine soup.

+**Cabbage plusia.** (See quotations.) — **1890** *Cent.* 4571 *P. brassicæ* of the United States is one of the worst enemies of the cabbage. . . . [It is] known as the *cabbage-plusia.* **1892** V. KELLOG *Kansas Insects* 61 Cabbage plusia (*Plusia brassicæ*). . . . The caterpillars have but five pairs of legs instead of eight pairs, as is the case with the Imported Cabbage-worms.

+**Cabbage radish.** (See quotation.) — **1806** in *Ann. 9th Congress* 2 Sess. 1127 This cabbage must be considered as indigenous to this sequestered quarter, and may be denominated as the cabbage radish of the Washita.

Cabbage tree. *S.* +The cabbage palmetto.
Applied earlier in English (1725) to the West Indian tree *Areca* or *Oreodoxa oleracea.*
1763 T. ROBINSON in Roberts *Nat. Hist. Florida* 96 Interspersed promiscuously, as mulberry, cedar, cocoa, vanilla, moho, and cabbage-trees, &c. **1765** J. BARTRAM *Jrnl.* 31 Dec. in Stork *Acc. E. Florida* (1766) 18 We came now to plenty of the tree palmetto, which the inhabitants call cabbage-tree. **1772** B. ROMANS in Phillips *Notes* (1924) 124 The Savages are not so well provided with Bread as the Spaniards. . . . But both are supplied with that Article in a very great Measure by the Cabbage Tree. **1783** E. DENNY *Journal* 81 Visit Fort Sullivan. . . . Curtains and embrasures faced with the cabbage tree—soft spongy wood, admirably calculated for this use. **1833** *Md. Hist. Mag.* XIII. 367 The island is a sand bank—covered with the Palmetto, formerly known as the Cabbage tree, and the chosen emblem of Nullification. **1847** W. S. HENRY *Campaign Sk.* 302 The cabbage-tree (or palmetto) made its appearance in all its beauty, and the grazing was most luxuriant. **1883** HALE *Woods & Timbers N.C.* 108 The inner portion of the young plant is very tender and palatable, somewhat resembling the Artichoke and Cabbage in taste (hence its name of *Cabbage Tree*).

Cabbage worm. {1688} Any of various larvae which feed on cabbages. — **1854** EMMONS *Agric. N.Y.* V. 261 Index, Cabbage worms, 243. [*Ib.* 243 The attacks of these larvae [*Agrotidae*] extend to many of our most useful cultivated plants, corn, cabbages, wheat, together with cultivated flowers.] **1886** P. STAPLETON *Major's Christmas* 163 They discussed the respective merits of the potato-bug and cabbage-worm lucidly and eloquently. **1892** V. KELLOG *Kansas Insects* 59 Imported cabbage-worm (*Pieris rapæ*). . . . Infesting cabbage; a naked, green caterpillar about 1½ inches long, with a yellowish stripe along the back. *Ib.* 69 Southern cabbage-worm (*Pieris protodice*). . . . A black-dotted, greenish-blue caterpillar.

Cabdriver. [CAB *n.* 1.] The driver of a cab. {1842–}
1842 *Knickerb.* XIX. 44 What a huddle of . . . waiters, cab-drivers, and blackguards about the hotels. **1854** CUMMINS *Lamplighter* iii, Trueman Flint . . . supported himself for many years by whatever employment he could obtain; having been, at different times, a newspaper carrier, a cab-driver, a porter [etc.]. **1906** 'O. HENRY' *Four Million* 88 His cab-driver was waiting for his fare.

+**Caberos.** *S.W.* [Var. of CABESTRO.] A rope or lasso made of hair. Cf. CABRAS. — **1853** 'P. PAXTON' *Yankee in Texas* 45 Having found a stake driven in the ground, he affixed to it one end of the caberos (hair rope) which was attached to his horse's neck. *Ib.* 117 A rope he [=the Texan] knows not; everything in that line is either a *larriat* or a *caberos,* the one being made of raw-hide twisted or plaited, and the latter spun by hand from the hair of horses or neat cattle. *a***1859** *N.Y. Spirit of Times* (B.), Bill Stone had his rifle for himself and a strong caberos for his horse.

+**Cabestro.** *S.W.* [Sp. *cabestro.*] A hair rope. Cf. prec. and CABRESTO. — **1869** *Overland Mo.* III. 126 He had a long coil of *cabestros* dangling from the pommel of his saddle, and was evidently in search of strays. **1902** CLAPIN 90 The *cabestro* is also employed for fastening animals to stakes or pegs driven into the ground.

‖**Cabeza.** *S.W.* [Sp. *cabeza* head.] Head. — **1877** WM. WRIGHT *Big Bonanza* 374 He's got more instink, that dog has, . . . right in that ugly old cabeza of his, nor can be found in the heds of a whole plaza full of eddicated town dogs—poodles and sich.

+**Cabezon.** The bighead; 'a Californian species of sculpin, *Scorpænichthys marmoratus,* a fish of the family *Cottidæ*' (*Cent.* 549/2).

***Cabin,** *n.* Also †cabbin.

***1.** A small house or dwelling of rude or simple construction. Cf. LOG CABIN.
(*a*) **1623–4** *Va. House of Burgesses* 31 A small Fort fenced with Palisadoes, in it one slight howse, a store and some few thatcht cabbins. **1707** *N.C. Col. Rec.* I. 658 Some of their straglers planted corn and built

cabbins on the Chowanacke old fields. **1737** *Md. Hist. Mag.* III. 49 This Deponent saw but a few Indian Cabbins and a little Hutt made of logs. **1778** *Ky. Petitions* 44 If the said negro had been suffered to remain within his Cabbin, he could not have been hurt. **1819** E. DANA *Geogr. Sk.* 117 Hanover is a little village two miles above the mouth of Laughry; the houses are mostly cabbins. **1836** in *Ill. Hist. Soc. Trans.* (1910) 182, I have on my farm 4 log houses or Cabbins as we call them here.

(*b*) **1676** GLOVER *Acc. Va.* in *Phil. Trans.* XI. 632 Their [the Indians'] habitations are Cabins, about nine or ten foot high. **1788** J. MAY *Jrnl. & Lett.* (1873) 73 Till then I intend to live on board ship, which I like better than the little cabins covered with walnut bark. **1814** BIDDLE *Lewis & Clark Exped.* I. 261 At the lower extremity of which is a grove of the same tree, where are several Indian cabins of sticks. **1831** PECK *Guide* 126 The first buildings put up are of logs, slightly hewn on two sides, and the corners notched together. . . . This description of building is called a 'Cabin.' **1877** JOHNSON *Anderson Co., Kansas* 18 When the first whites settled in Anderson county, . . . they found some of the Indian cabins [described above as bark shanties]. **1890** J. C. HARRIS in *Century Mag.* Dec. 287 They came in sight of a cabin, and the blue smoke curling from its short chimney was suggestive of hospitality.

||**2.** A seat; a bench.

1791 BARTRAM *Travels* 368 All around the inside of the building, betwixt the second range of pillars and the wall, is a range of cabins or sophas. *Ib.* 451 The aged chiefs and warriors are seated on their cabbins or sophas.

***Cabin,** *v.* [CABIN *n.* 1.] *intr.* To stay in a cabin. {1586–1611} — **1865** 'MARK TWAIN' *Sketches* (1926) 164, I had cabined with him a few nights in Esmeralda several years ago.

Cabin bell. A bell for use on board a vessel. — **1702** *Essex Inst. Coll.* XLII. 161 Inventory of ship . . . a Cabin bell. **1851** A. O. HALL *Manhattaner* 179 Another [Negro] of the same description will be summoning courage for the exertion of shaking the large cabin-bell, whose sound is intended to diminish a passenger's quota of sleep.

+**Cabin car.** A caboose. — **1879** *Scribner's Mo.* Nov. 23/2 This road has also cabin cars, with stove, bunks, etc. which it will switch off at any station. **1884** KNIGHT *Suppl.* 150/1 *Cabin Car*, a car carried at the rear of a freight-train to accommodate the conductor and train-hands.

Cabin door. [CABIN 1.] The door of a cabin.

1824 BRYANT *Indian Story* line 35 A good red deer from the forest shade, . . . at her cabin door shall lie. **1844** S. M. FULLER *Summer on Lakes* 166 The American Tract Society boasted of their agents' having exchanged, at a Western cabin door, tracts for the Devil on Two Sticks. **1870** MRS. STEPHENS *Married in Haste* 331 The cabin door was open.

Cabined, *p.p.* and *ppl. a.* [CABIN *n.* 1. Cf. CABIN *v.*] Lodged in a cabin or cabins. {1602–1745}

1837 W. JENKINS *Ohio Gaz.* 489 A few families of squatters were cabined in the immediate neighborhood. **1865** PARKMAN *Pioneers France* 298 The Basques . . . were busied in a brisk trade with bands of Indians cabined along the borders of the cove. **1895** J. WINSOR *Miss. Basin* 248 The Hurons cabined about Detroit fled.

||**Cabineer.** [CABIN *n.* 1.] One who lives in a cabin. — **1776** Z. F. Smith *Kentucky* (1886) 75 Not one has arrived except a few cabineers down the Ohio.

* **Cabinet.**

See also KITCHEN CABINET.

***1.** A cupboard, or chest of drawers, used to hold objects of various kinds, such as curios, china, etc.

1653 *Boston Rec.* 23, I . . . have full releases & discharges from them . . . in my white boxe . . . upon which my Cabenet stands. **1715** *Boston News-Letter* 2 May 2/2 Cabbinetts, Escrutoires, . . . done and sold by William Randle at the Sign of the Cabbinett. **1759** ELIOT *Field-Husb.* vi. 146 This Timber [=mulberry] may be very useful to the Joiner, for Cabinets. **1905** *Sears, Roebuck & Co. Cat.* No. 115, 703 This cabinet is an illustration of this wonderful saving to our customers.

+**2.** The President's council, composed of the heads of executive departments, the Secretary of State, Secretary of the Treasury, etc.

1801 *Ann. 6th Congress* 3 March 1077 The President of the United States was to take his Cabinet from among the people of the United States. **1836** *Diplom. Corr. Texas* (1908) I. 74 Will you please, in conjunction with the Cabinet, take this matter into consideration. **1854** BENTON *30 Years' View* I. 48/2 Mr. Adams would . . . from the necessity of the case, have to make up a mixed cabinet. **1861** MCCLELLAN in *Own Story* 169 There are some of the greatest geese in the cabinet I have ever seen. **1874** BANCROFT *Footprints of Time* 236 The members of the President's Cabinet are seven in number. **1890** C. MARTYN *W. Phillips* 325 He urged Lincoln to dismiss Seward from the Cabinet as a hopeless obstructive. **1914** McLaughlin & Hart *Cycl. Amer. Govt.* I. 199 The official council . . . can be discovered emerging as a separate group in 1791; and, in 1793, it takes on a distinct collegiate life. . . . At this season, the name 'Cabinet' began to be applied. **1925** BRYAN *Memoirs* 187 President-elect Wilson . . . invited me to become a member of his Cabinet.

b. *Cabinet council*, in the same sense. {1625–}

1830 *Deb. Congress* 15 March 256/2 From the first organization of the Government, the Heads of Departments have been . . . a cabinet council. **1839** *Diplom. Corr. Texas* (1908) I. 385 This matter was once agitated in Cabinet Council while I was a member.

c. Attrib. with *adviser, appointment, chamber, day, lady, meeting*, etc.

1834 *Deb. Congress.* 7 Feb. 497 We are . . . indebted to him [=Jackson] 'who shuns no responsibility,' and his duplicate cabinet advisers. **1858** LINCOLN in Logan *Great Conspiracy* 74 They have seen in his . . . face, Post-offices, Land-offices, Marshalships, and Cabinet appointments. **1886** LOGAN *Great Conspiracy* 530 That great soldier [U. S. Grant] . . . received his commission at the hands of President Lincoln, in the cabinet chamber of the White House. **1845** POLK *Diary* I. 144 On Tuesday morning last, being Cabinet day, . . . I had read the message containing this and other nominations to some members of the Cabinet. **1861** STANTON in McClellan *Own Story* 67 Will not . . . cabinet intrigues, and Republican interference thwart him at every step? **1892** M. A. JACKSON *Gen. Jackson* 93 Being 'Cabinet ladies,' we, of course, were invited to all the grand entertainments. **1814** *Ann. 13th Congress* 3rd Sess. App. 1568 Occasional conversations . . . prior to the Cabinet meeting on the first of July last. **1855** *S. Lit. Messenger* XXI. 14 His popularity . . . was fatally shaken by his acceptance of a cabinet office under John Quincy Adams. **1836** *Diplom. Corr. Texas* (1908) I. 77 If desired hold the freeest and fullest conversation with the President and cabinet officers. **1914** McLaughlin & Hart *Cycl. Amer. Govt.* I. 198 In 1829, the Post-Office was raised to the rank of a Cabinet portfolio. **1883** *Harper's Mag.* July 320/2 His [*i.e.* the new Postmaster General's] acceptance of a cabinet position has been much discussed. **1884** *Century Mag.* April 810/1 The President receives in the Cabinet Room. **1834** *Deb. Congress* 21 Feb. 631 If we were to ask, the Executive might tell us it was a cabinet secret. **1873** 'MARK TWAIN' & WARNER *Gilded Age* xxxii. 290 The first select reception took place at a Cabinet Minister's—or, rather a Cabinet Secretary's—Mansion.

3. A similar executive council in city, church, or other government.

1885 *Methodist Review* LXVII. 15 Nothing that he [Bishop Simpson] did was done more satisfactorily than his work in what has come to be known as the *cabinet*. **1914** McLaughlin & Hart *Cyclop. Amer. Govt.* I. 202 In several American cities an endeavor has been made to create, by calling together at regular intervals the heads of the more important administrative departments, a sort of 'mayor's cabinet.' **1921** *Girl Reserve Movt.* 93 These officers and chairmen together with the girls' work secretary and one adviser complete the executive council known as either the cabinet or the council.

+**Cabinet cherry.** The wild black cherry, *Prunus serotina.* — **1817–8** EATON *Botany* (1822) 411 *Prunus virginiana*, wild cherry, rum cherry, cabinet cherry. . . . The bark is an excellent tonic.

+**Cabinet factory.** [CABINET 1.] A factory in which cabinetwork is done. — **1832** WILLIAMSON *Maine* II. 609 Here is a cabinet factory worked by water power, where ten or twelve men are employed, who make 'annually from 8 to 10,000 chairs.'

Cabinet-founder. [CABINET 1.] A maker of metal cabinets. {1800} — **1789** *Boston Directory* 179 Caster, Thomas, brass and cabinet-founder.

+**Cabinet furniture.** [CABINET 1.] Furniture of the nature of cabinetwork. Also attrib. — **1815** *Niles' Reg.* IX. 36/1 The principle manufactures in wood are the following:—sideboards, secretaries, bureaus, and other articles of cabinet furniture. **1827** DRAKE & MANSF. *Cincinnati* 59 Our Steam Engines, Castings, Cabinet Furniture, Chairs, Hats, etc. etc. are sent to Kentucky, Alabama, Louisiana. *Ib.* 64 Thirteen Cabinet Furniture Shops.

Cabinetmaker. [CABINET 1 and 2.]

1. A maker of cabinets and other articles of a similar nature. {1681}

1681 *Boston Rec.* 71 William Taylor . . . and Eleakim Hutchinson became sureties to the town for John Clarke, cabinet maker. **1714** SEWALL *Diary* III. 13 The Cabinet-maker, takes down the closet that stands in the corner, to make way for the window. **1762** *Md. Hist. Mag.* XVIII. 166 As Robert Harsnip, a Cabinet maker, was standing under the Gallows, . . . it fell, and struck him upon the Head. **1828** A. SHERBURNE *Memoirs* i. 16 He had served his time at the cabinet-maker's business. *c***1870** BAGBY *Old Va. Gentleman* 258 The whole turnout, rider included, had that slick varnished look that things have when fresh from the hands of the cabinet-maker. **1876** HABBERTON *Jericho Road* 215 The coffin was as superb a thing as the rival cabinet-makers of Mount Zion could turn out between them.

+**2.** One who assists or seeks to assist in forming the president's cabinet.

1884 *Boston Journal* 22 Nov. 2/4 The New York Sun says that 'the Cabinet-makers, the office seekers, and the schemers who abound in Washington are busy in laying-out plans for the future.' **1888** *Battle Creek Journal* 12 Dec., The Cabinet Makers . . . are told by Gen. Harrison that no portfolio has yet been offered.

Cabinet minister. [CABINET 2.] +A member of the president's cabinet. — **1806** *Ann. 9th Congress* 1 Sess. 561 My answer was, (and from a Cabinet Minister too,) 'There is no longer any Cabinet.' **1856** EMERSON *Eng. Traits* 285 Thus challenged, I bethought myself neither of caucuses nor congress, neither of presidents nor of cabinet-ministers. **1873** 'MARK TWAIN' & WARNER *Gilded Age* xxxii. 290 The first select reception took place at a Cabinet Minister's . . . Mansion.

+**Cabinet shop.** [CABINET 1.] A cabinetmaker's shop.

1817 S. BROWN *Western Gaz.* 93 There are [in Lexington, Ky.] . . . five cabinet shops. **1850** *N.H. Hist. Soc. Coll.* VI. 221 There are . . . two cabinet shops . . . with workmen in each. **1877** JOHNSON *Anderson Co., Kansas* 65 Burns has built several buildings in the town, [and] opened the first cabinet shop.

‖**Cabinette.** [CABIN *n.* 1.] A small cabin. — **1879** *Scribner's Mo.* Oct. 822/2 Can I ever forget that low-cowled cabinette . . . up on the hill-side?

+**Cabinet ware.** Also † **wares.** [CABINET 1.] Articles of furniture of the nature of cabinets; woodwork of the finer kind, such as is made by cabinetmakers. Also attrib.

1778 CARVER *Travels* 504 The wood of the black cherry-tree is very useful, and works well into cabinet ware. **1792** *Ann. 2nd Congress* 1000 Several important branches [of manufacture] have grown up, . . . [among which are] ships, cabinet wares, and turnery. **1811** MEASE *Philadelphia* 76 The cabinet ware is elegant, and with the manufactory of wood generally, is very extensive. **1833** *Niles' Reg.* XLIV. 351/2 A fair of the American Institute exhibits . . . musical instruments of the finest tone, and other articles of cabinet ware, of the most exquisite workmanship. **1851** CIST *Cincinnati* 197 The ordinary cabinet-ware coffins. **1857** *Knickerb.* XLIX. 91 [He] was to take, in full of all demands, the cabinet-maker's note for forty dollars, . . . payable 'in cabinet ware.' **1874** *Vt. Bd. Agric. Rep.* II. 460 Some idea may be gained of the consumption of valuable wood in large manufactories of fine cabinet ware, where the amount required for the smallest article exceeds that for a musket stock.

‖**Cabinet wareroom.** A room used for the making of cabinet-ware. — **1858** *S. Lit. Messenger* XXVI. 82/1 We shall probably find that he forsook boot-making to become a saddle and harness maker . . . and that he has now a cabinet ware-room.

+**Cabinetwork.** [CABINET 1] =CABINET WARE.

1732 *S.C. Gazette* 104/2 [There] will continue to be sold all sorts of Cabinet Work. **1794** T. COXE *View U.S.* 25 Potters ware, mill-stones, and . . . cabinet work . . . are tending to greater perfection. **1818** FEARON *Sketches* 24 Mahogany is used for cupboards, doors, and banisters, and for all kinds of cabinet work. **1834** PECK *Gaz. Illinois* 24 The black walnut is much used for building materials and cabinet work. **1874** B. F. TAYLOR *World on Wheels* I. 31 Flocks and herds from a thousand hills and plains roll along on iron casters like pieces of heavy cabinet-work. **1883** HALE *Woods & Timbers N.C.* 175 Arbor Vitae, (*Thuja occidentalis*), . . . is used in building and for cabinet work.

+**Cabin-raising.** [CABIN *n.* 1.] A gathering to assist in the erection of a cabin. — **1845** *Ind. Mag. Hist.* 11 Between log-rollings and cabin-raisings, we were together several days in each week.

+**Cabin roof.** [CABIN *n.* 1.] A simple form of house roof. — **1822** *Missionary Herald* XVIII. 81 A large dwelling house, . . . covered by a cabin roof 90 feet by 40. **1834** H. BRACKENRIDGE *Recoll.* 41 Barracks built of logs, . . . with what is called a cabin roof, and wooden chimneys. **1847** in H. Howe *Hist. Coll. Ohio* 198 It [=a new jail] was a rough log building; two stories high, with a cabin roof.

***Cable.** =next. — **1892** S. HALE *Letters* 269 There are cables, and electrics. . . . I mounted a cable, took a transfer [etc.].

Cable car. The car used on a cable railroad. {1887-}

1888 S. HALE *Letters* 200 Two rival processions which encumbered the streets . . . almost prevented our getting there in the cable-car. **1891** ROBERTS *Adrift Amer.* 13 It was here that I first saw cable cars in operation. **1897** *Outing* XXX. 370/1 It seemed like a quiet country lane to me, after my experience of Broadway cable-cars and brewers' wagons. **1902** BANKS *Newspaper Girl* 254, I arrived in Washington . . . and took a cable car for Capitol Hill.

+**Cablegram.** A telegraphic message sent by cable.

'Colloq. and low' (W. '79). 'Colloq.' (*Cent.*).

1868 *Daily News* (London) 26 Sept., The new word *cablegram* is used by a New York contemporary to characterise a telegraphic despatch. **1877** Bartlett 89 Cablegrams received by the State Department indicate that there is no longer any possibility of averting war between Russia and Turkey. **1883** *Harper's Mag.* March 605/2 My suspense was . . . relieved by a telegram, or cablegram as some say. **1890** *Congress. Rec.* 4390/1 These are the latest quotations by cablegram.

+**Cable railroad.** A street or other railroad on which the cars are drawn by a cable. Also attrib. — **1889** *N.J. Laws* 332 Every cable railroad company . . . and every corporation owning, using or operating any cable, electric or horse railroad [etc.].

Cable road. A cable railroad. — **1883** *Harper's Mag.* XLVI. 824/1, I should consider the cable road [in San Francisco] one of the very foremost in the list of curiosities. . . . It is a peculiar kind of tramway . . . , invented expressly for the purpose of overcoming steep elevations. **1887** *Courier-Journal* 15 Jan. 4/7 A dynamite cartridge had been placed on the track of the Larkin-street branch line of the Sutter-street cable road. **1891** *Harper's Mag.* Dec. 162/1 It was along a street traversed by a cable road.

Cabless, *a.* [CAB 2.] +Of a locomotive engine: Not furnished with a cab. — **1887** C. B. GEORGE *40 Years on Rail* 24 We had a small cabless engine, weighing about five tons. *Ib.* 129 The cabless engines gave no shelter for engineer or fireman.

Cabman. [CAB 1.] A cabdriver. {1850-}

1840 *Picayune* 28 Oct. 2/5 'I beg your pardon,' replied the cabman. **1846** CORCORAN *Pickings* 135 When I drives up to the stand he gets all the old cabmen to jaw me, and call me the milk-and-water cabman. **1865** *Atlantic Mo.* XV. 386 Cabmen all assume a new ferocity of bearing. **1865** MRS. WHITNEY *Gayworthys* 131 The Doctor caught a cab, or the cabman caught the Doctor. **1897** FLANDRAU *Harvard Episodes* 302 Beverly . . . rang for the steward and asked him to telephone to Foster to send round . . . the cabman at once.

+**Caboodle.** *colloq.* Also **capoodle.** [Of obscure origin. Cf. CA- and BOODLE.] *The whole caboodle,* the whole lot, number, or crowd.

See also KA-, KE-, KERBOODLE; KIT AND CABOODLE. 'The word . . . is used in all the Northern States and New England' (B. '48).

*a***1848** *Ohio State Journal* (B.), The whole caboodle will act upon the recommendation of the Ohio Sun, and endeavour to secure a triumph. **1865** TROWBRIDGE *3 Scouts* 23 It's only a little squad of guerillas: stand our ground, and we'll capture the whole caboodle of 'em! **1873** BRET HARTE *Fiddletown* 3 She had more soul than the whole caboodle of them put together. **1880** *Harper's Mag.* Sept. 541/1 Thar's a whole caboodle of high-toned folks thar, they tell me. **1895** A. O. MYERS *Bosses & Boodle* 40 The word 'boodle' . . . was probably taken from the word 'caboodle,' or 'capoodle,' as used in some sections, and meaning an entire lot. **1904** W. H. SMITH *Promoters* 78 If I haven't sized 'em up for about what they are worth, the whole 'caboodle,' then . . . I've lived . . . in vain.

Caboose. Also †**cabouse, cabbouze, carpouse,** *pl.* **cabusses, cabbusses.** [Cf. CAMBOOSE.]

1. A protection for the chimney or fireplace on a vessel; the cooking range or kitchen on the deck of a merchant ship. {1769-}

1747 *Essex Inst. Coll.* XLVI. 91 They shipp'd a Sea which carried overboard . . . their Boat and Carpouse. *Ib.*, Another [heavy sea] carried away their boat, Cabbouze and one Carriage Gun. **1764** J. ROWE *Diary* (1903) 67 Oct. 31. This day . . . Capt. Dashwood's Brigg caught on fire occasioned by the tar boiling over the Caboose. **1766** *Boston Ev. Post* 10 Nov. (Th.), 'Twas imagined she took fire at sea, as her cabouse was burnt. **1789** *Boston Directory* 211 Chimnies and cabbusses for vessels, built at the shortest notice. **1791** JEFFERSON in *Ann. 2nd Congress* (1792) 1042 Converting salt water into fresh . . . may be performed on board of vessels at sea, by the common iron caboose (with small alteration,) by the same fire and in the same time which is used for cooking the ship's provisions. **1823** G. A. MCCALL *Lett. from Frontiers* (1868) 54 A thin cloud of smoke, that arose from the caboose, showed that the crew were already preparing their evening meal. **1848** BARTLETT 60 *Caboose*, the common pronunciation for *camboose* (Dutch *kombuis*), a ship's cooking-range or kitchen. **1850** H. C. LEWIS *La. Swamp Dr.* 30 The cook of the boat discovered me, and . . . took me into the caboose. **1865** MRS. WHITNEY *Gayworthys* xxvi. 238 They were knocked about amongst lee-scuppers and cabooses and things. **1882** *Harper's Mag.* Aug. 359/2 A practical man went at once to the convenient caboose where the cook was to be installed.

attrib. **1807** in *Index of Patents* (1874) III. 1465 Caboose cooking stove [patented by] G. Youle, New York, Apr. 1, 1807. **1840** *Picayune* 22 Aug. 2/2 Lost—near Rockett's, . . . two five cent pieces, a caboose house, a pair of duck trousers, a copper fastened schooner. **1890** J. JEFFERSON *Autobiog.* 18 We traveled part of the way in a fast-sailing packet-boat on the Erie Canal, the only smoke issuing from the caboose stove-pipe.

2. A cooking oven used on land.

1786 *Md. Journal* 23 June (Th.), For sale, One elegant patent caboose. **1792** *Ann. 2nd Congress* 1044 Mr. Isaacks fixed the pot of a small caboose, with a tin cap and straight tube of tin passing obliquely through a cask of cold water. **1805** *Columbian Centinel* 17 April 4/2, 40 cabooses, different sizes; stoves, etc. **1883** *Century Mag.* Aug. 550/2 The lawn is studded with cabooses, over one of which a Councillor may be seen carefully skimming the water covering his twelve-pound salmon.

+**3.** A hut.

1839 *Congress Globe* App. 15 Feb. 343/1 We have a postmaster in our own little village . . . and in his little caboose of a post office I have found electioneering interferences. **1874** *Opelika* (Ala.) *Times* 30 Sept., [Such] a colored man . . . should be preferred as tenant of our houses, cabooses on the farm, drayman upon the streets.

+**4.** =CABOOSE CAR.

1871 BARNUM *Struggles & Triumphs* 679 If you can stand it to ride to Fort Wayne in the caboose of a freight train. **1873** BEADLE *Undevel. West* 729 We jogged along at eight or ten miles an hour . . . which gave me fair time to look at the country from the caboose. **1878** C. COALE in *Ann. S.W. Virginia* (1929) 1620 In the conductor's caboose, I had the pleasure of jolting into Charlottesville. **1883** PECK *Bad Boy* 35 Pa sneezed all the way in the caboose [of a freight train]. **1891** ROBERTS *Adrift Amer.* 168 The hind brakesman stowed me away in the tool box under the caboose, as they call the brake van. **1903** E. JOHNSON *Railway Transportation* 46 The first railroad-coaches were not unlike the four-wheeled caboose of to-day.

attrib. **1903** *New York Ev. Post* 25 Aug., The rest of the crew . . . saw from the caboose windows the bodies . . . lying along the tracks.

+**5.** (See quotation.)

1920 HUNTER *Trail Drivers of Texas* I. 213 Under a camp wagon is usually suspended an old cowhide called the 'caboose,' and in that we throw stray pieces of wood, etc.

+**Caboose car.** [Cf. CABOOSE 4.] A car, having a stove in it, attached to a freight train and used as quarters for the train crew.

1862 *Ashcroft's Railway Directory* 76 No. of Caboose Cars [on Central Railroad of New-Jersey], 6. **1865** *Penna. R.R. 18th Rep.* 92 Eight-wheeled

Caboose Cars. **1873** *Harper's Mag.* XLVI. 311 A caboose car, part of a construction train, . . . was thrown down an embankment.

+**Cabras, Caboras,** abbreviated forms of CABRESTO. — **1805** SIBLEY in *Ann. 9th Congress* 2 Sess. 1082 Their horses they never turn loose to graze, but always keep them tied with a long cabras or halter. **1826** DEWEES *Lett. from Texas* 61 We look us out a spot free from snakes, which we entirely surround with a caboras or hair rope, which we carry always with us.

+**Cabresto, Cabresta,** inexact variants of CABESTRO. (Cf. Pg. *cabresto.*) — **1846** *Knickerb.* XXVII. 251 He felt himself violently seized from behind, his arms pinioned, his mouth filled with the end of a hair cabresta. **1848** EMORY *Military Reconn.* 387 We soon conquered them with the aid of the 'lazo' or cabriesto [*sic*], as it is often called—a rope of hair, or plaited hide. **1871** DE VERE 130 Texans twine or rope a horse, . . . and then stake him out with a stake-rope. This may be either a cabresto, when it is made of hair, or . . . a lariat, of rawhide twisted. **1892** *Dialect Notes* I. 245 *Cabestro* . . . [is] often pronounced *cabresto.*

+**Cabri, Cabree.** Also **cabrit, cabrie, caberey.** [F. *cabri,* Sp. *cabrito* kid.] The pronghorn antelope.

1805 LEWIS in *Ann. 9th Congress* 2 Sess. 1046 The skins of the Missouri antelope, (called cabri by the inhabitants of the Illinois). **1807–8** PIKE *Sources Miss.* 136 [I] killed one cabrie, two deer, two turkies. *Ib.* 159 A band of cabrie came up. **1812** J. CUTLER *Topog. Descr. Ohio* 166 There were a considerable number of elk, buffaloe, cabree or antelope, and deer. **1817** S. BROWN *Western Gaz.* 180 Many of these hills are so washed, and become so steep, that no animal can ascend them, except the cabree, and mountain ram. **1821** J. FOWLER *Journal* 32 Buffelow Elk deer Caberey and Wild Horses are in great nombers. **1822** *Ib.* 147 Ward killed one Cabery. **1889** *Cent.* 245/2 The cabrit, pronghorn, or so-called American antelope, *Antilocapra americana.*

‖**Cabrouet.** 'A kind of cart used on sugar-plantations in the southern United States' (*Cent.*).

Caccalobe. The sea grape, *Coccolobis uvifera.* — **1837** J. L. WILLIAMS *Florida* 114 The Caccalobe or sea grape ornaments all our southern coast with its abundant clusters.

+**Cache,** *n.* Also **câche, caché.** *W.* [F. *cache* hiding-place, f. *cacher* to hide.]

1. A place of hiding or deposit for the storage of provisions or other articles; the store of provisions, etc., so concealed.

The following quots. show the origin and application of the term: **1805** LEWIS in *L. & Clark Exped.* (1904) II. 134 These holes in the ground or deposits are called by the engages *caches* (*cachês*). **1829** *Va. Lit. Museum* 16 Dec. 419 *Cache,* a term used in the western country, for a hole dug in the ground for the purpose of preserving and concealing such provisions and commodities, as it may be inconvenient for the travellers to carry with them. **1833** CATLIN *Indians* I. 122 The remainder [of their crop] is . . . packed away in 'caches', holes dug in the ground, some six or seven feet deep, the insides of which are somewhat in the form of a jug, and tightly closed at the top. **1835** HOFFMAN *Winter in West* II. 96 The 'cachés,' in which the modern Indians secrete their corn beneath the earth. **1844** GREGG *Commerce of Prairies* I. 68 The term *cache,* meaning a place of concealment, was originally used by the Canadian French trappers and traders. **1860** *Harper's Mag.* May 743/2 A *cachê* is made by digging a hole in the ground, which is lined with sticks, grass, or any material which will protect the contents from the dampness of the earth. **1869** *Ib.* November 802 We stowed the canoes and their contents in a 'cache.' Cutting down some young alders we fastened them across the trees to form a frame-work. On this the provisions and other 'iktas' were laid and covered with matting, while the canoes are thrust underneath.

1817 BRADBURY *Travels* 118 The excessive rains had penetrated into their caches, and spoiled the whole of their reserved stock. **1823** JAMES *Exped. Rocky Mts.* I. 91 He observed a recent mound of earth, about eight feet in height, which he was induced to believe must be a cachè, or place of deposit, for the spoils which the party . . . had taken from an enemy. **1830** MRS. VICTOR *River of West* (1870) 80 A pit is dug to a depth of five or six feet. . . . The men then . . . excavate a room of considerable dimensions, in which the furs are deposited. . . . These caches are the only storehouses of the wilderness. **1835** FEATHERSTONHAUGH *Canoe Voyage* I. 323 We should have to put our lading in a *cache,* or hiding-place. **1839** TOWNSEND *Narrative* 357 Their winter store of dried fish is stowed away in little huts of mats and branches, closely interlaced, and also in *caches* under ground. **1844** LEE & FROST *Oregon* iii. 34 Mr. Hunt, with the remainder of the party, prepared *caches* in which they deposited their surplus baggage and merchandise. **1846** SAGE *Scenes Rocky Mts.* xviii, Among other articles left in câche, were arms and tools of various kinds. **1854** BARTLETT *Personal Narr.* II. 199 We opened a *cache* in the bank here, in which Dr. Webb had buried a quantity of things, when the party under his charge passed down the Gila in December last. **1859** MARCY *Prairie Traveler* 164 These caches will be more secure when made at some distance from roads or trails, and in places where Indians would not be likely to pass. **1862** DICKSON *Across Plains* 36 Then we brought the boat out of its cache and had a good ride on the lake. **1870** *Amer. Naturalist* IV. 225 The sight of the tall caches, like corncribs, which mark the position of the village for which we are bound, is not unwelcome. **1872** 'MARK TWAIN' *Roughing It* xxii, In a 'cache' among the rocks we found the provisions and the cooking-utensils. **1888** ROOSEVELT in *Century Mag.* XXXVI. 42/2 The plunderers of our cache were a pair of cougars. **1903** WHITE *Forest* xiii. 172 A cache in the forest country is simply a heavily constructed rustic platform on which provisions and clothing are laid and wrapped completely about in sheets of canoe bark. **1915** E. ATKINSON *Johnny Appleseed* 32 Johnny built a fire of driftwood and found a dry cache for the mail and seed bags in a hollow tree. **1923** J. H. COOK *On Old Frontier* 146 We tried to kill the pesky varmint that had tampered with our meat cache.

b. In the phrase *to make (a) cache.*

1846 SAGE *Scenes Rocky Mts.* (1859) 196 A company of traders . . . made câche of one hundred and sixty packs of robes, which they were compelled to leave. **1856** EMERSON *Eng. Traits* 120 The wolf . . . makes a *cache* of his prey.

2. (See quotation.)

1837 IRVING *Bonneville* II. xviii. 185 In the present game, the object hidden, or the *cache* as it is called by the trappers, is a small splint of wood, or other diminutive article, that may be concealed in the closed hand.

+**Cache,** *v.* Also **câche, cash.** [F. *cacher* to hide, or f. the noun.]

1. *tr.* To place in a cache; to hide for preservation.

1821 J. FOWLER *Journal* 9 We this morning berryed or cashed as the French call it 32 Bever traps. **1823** JAMES *Exped.* I. 212 They [=Indians] then proceed to *cache,* or conceal in the earth these acquisitions [=parts of slaughtered bison]. **1843** FARNHAM *Travels W. Prairies* I. 288 It was necessary to recover them [*sc.* horses], or *cache,* that is, bury in some secret place in the dry sand, their remaining property. **1844** GREGG *Commerce of Prairies* I. 69 In *caching,* a great deal of skill is often required to leave no signs whereby the cunning savage might discover the place of deposit. **1850** G. HINES *Voyage* 140 We concluded to 'cache' our canoe in the bushes. **1877** COUES *Animals* 51 When they [=wolverines] can eat no more, they continue to steal the baits and câche them. **1898** WISTER *Lin McLean* 62, I had found the cubs where the she-bear had them cached by the foot of a big boulder.

2. *intr.* and *refl.* To conceal oneself.

1846 W. STEWART *Altowan* I. vi. 174 He believed he had scared them very much, as he had cached within range. **1848** RUXTON *Far West* (1849) 23 [They] resolved to retreat and câche themselves until the danger was over. **1850** GARRARD *Wah-To-Yah* vii. 100 The close proximity of the horse stealers caused some trepidation in our village, and even we felt like *caching.*

+**Cached,** *ppl. a.* [f. prec.] Placed in hiding; hidden. — **1901** WHITE *Westerners* 47 Lone Wolf's band took up quarters within striking distance of the cached schooners. **a1906** 'O. HENRY' *Trimmed Lamp,* etc. 234 The Man from Nome, loyal to her who had resurrected his long cached heart, . . . followed her.

+**Cachucha.** Also (erron.) **cachuca.** A lively dance of Spanish origin. — **1840** *Knickerb.* XVI. 411 The 'cachucha' had n't then been introduced into American *salons.* **1840** *Picayune* 27 Sept. 2/1 He is teaching his wild, Tartarian courser to dance the cachuca. **1843** STEPHENS *High Life N.Y.* II. 66, She was doing up a cachuca. **1856** STOWE *Dred* I. 12 O, do you know we girls have been trying to learn the cachucha. **1893** K. SANBORN *S. Calif.* 174 Most effective of all the cachuca danced by a girl of pure Castilian blood. **1901** WHITE *Westerners* xxx. 284 The cachucha is a beautiful dance when rightly done.

Cachunk. (See CA- and cf. COCHUNK.)

Cachupin. (See GACHUPIN.)

***Cacique, Cazique.** Also †**cacico.** [Cf. CASSIQUE.]

+**1.** An Indian chief or king.

(*a*) **1609** HAKLUYT tr. *Conq. Florida* 25 The Cacique had done the same to learn his mind. **1787** BARLOW *Vision Columbus* III. 106 The Inca now his farther course descry'd, A young cazique attending as a guide. **1838** 'TEXIAN' *Mexico v. Texas* 82 A man in a hideous mask . . . rules the dance, and not infrequently applies the lash to the caciques and grandees. **1844** GREGG *Commerce of Prairies* I. 273 Each Pueblo is under the control of a *cacique* or *gobernadorcillo,* chosen from among their own sages, and commissioned by the governor of New Mexico. **1854** WHIPPLE *Prelim. Rep. Explor. Ry. Route* 22 The Caciques . . . delegated three of their best men to show us the excellent route.

(*b*) **1682** T. ASH *Carolina* 36 They are . . . governed by Reguli, or Petty Princes, which our English call Cacicoes.

2. (See quotation.)

1871 DE VERE 71 The West India term *Cacique* . . . is often most absurdly applied . . . to mayors of New Mexican towns, and any somewhat pompous and self-sufficient man is apt to be nicknamed the Cacique of his town.

+**Cack.** [Cf. CALK *n.*[1]] 'A small shoe; a shoe for a child.—Mass., [used in] 1820 *sq.*' (Chipman).

Cactus. Pl. **cacti.**

1. One or other of the prickly plants belonging to the Linnaean genus so called. {1767–}

(*a*) **1774** in J. L. Peyton *Adv. Grandfather* (1867) 68 We made the first day in the scorching sun twenty-six miles through a sandy desert, covered with cactus, endemis, yuccas, helianthoides and wormwood. **1821** NUTTALL *Travels Arkansa* 170 The highest grounds are thin and sandy, so much so, that occasionally the Cactus or prickly-pear makes its appearance. **1838** 'TEXIAN' *Mexico v. Texas* 10 Vineyards are defended from the inroads of wild animals, by thick set rows of cactus. **1851** WOODS *At Gold*

Diggings 23 The whole undergrowth was a thorny thicket, in which the prickly pear and the cactus predominated. **1869** Browne *Adv. Apache Country* 77 That peculiar and picturesque cactus so characteristic of the country, . . . recognized by botanists as the *Cereus grandeus.* **1870** Beadle *Utah* 232 The contrast is most pleasing to the eye wearied by miles of desert and mountain, with scant growth of sage-brush, grease wood, and desert cactus. **1888** Bret Harte *Argonauts* 102 He reached the cactus; its fantastic bulk stood plainly before him, but nothing more. **1889** Vasey *Agric. Grasses* 98 *Opuntia Engelmanni.* . . . The use of the above species of prickly pear, or cactus, for forage in the dry regions of Texas and westward is a matter of considerable importance.

attrib. **1854** Bartlett *Narr.* I. 254 The banks . . . present . . . a variety of plants of the cactus family. **1857** Gray *1st Less.* 95 In many Cactus-flowers . . . all the parts are very numerous. **c1868** in Custer *Following Guidon* 3 [The troops] marched over cactus-beds and through a deep ravine. **1878** Beadle *Western Wilds* 64 Despite the warning of the more experienced, some of them ventured to eat the cactus bulb. **1910** J. Hart *Vigilante Girl* 347 There were two corrals, also built of cactus poles; in these there was a large herd of horses.

(*b*) **1823** James *Exped.* I. 131 You distinguish also some cacti. **1838** 'Texian' *Mexico v. Texas* 69 There flourish in pernicious variety, the different species of *cacti.* **1843** Frémont *Exped.* 14 The bed of the little creek was perfectly dry, and on the adjacent sandy bottom *cacti*, for the first time, made their appearance. **1858** Vielé *Following Drum* 151 We were obliged to ride slowly on account of the . . . thickly growing briers and cacti which ran all over the ground. **1875** *Amer. Naturalist* IX. 20 Not least among the attractions of this flowering season are the Cacti. **1890** Custer *Following Guidon* 3 This was a dry camp, poor grass and plenty of cacti.

attrib. **1846** Sage *Scenes Rocky Mts.* xx, The immense quantities of *cacti* fruit found near the mountains, at the proper season. **1851** *Harper's Mag.* Sept. 482/1 Leading my horse silently up among the cacti plants, [I] tied him to one of their branches.

+**2.** The fleshy part of a cactus plant.

1858 Vielé *Following Drum* 186 Then came the dessert, dulcies of candied cactus and melons.

+**Cactus wren.** [Cactus 1.] A wren of the genus *Campylorhynchus*, frequenting cactus plants. — **1869** *Amer. Naturalist* III. 183 The Rock Wren and Cactus Wren . . . chirrup loudly from the tiled roof or dense thickets. **1881** *Ib.* XV. 211 The cactus wren, so called from its habit of nesting in the cactus whenever available, is stationary in its habitat. **1889** *Cent.* 751/2 The brown-headed cactus-wren is *C[ampylorhynchus] brunneicapillus;* the St. Lucas cactus-wren is *C. affinis.*

***Cadder.** [Eng. *caddow* (also *caddo, cadowe;* now dial. and rare), an Irish rug or coverlet, a rough woolen covering.] (See quot. 1843.) — **1789** Robert Carter *Letter* 8 Dec., The bearer . . . calles on you for . . . a pr. of Cadders or Blankets. **1843** *Amer. Pioneer* II. 446 We soon found, . . . that to make rag carpeting, such as sometimes covers kitchen floors now, and to sew two breadths of proper length together, was a good substitute for blankets. . . . These cadders (for so we called them,) were a great help in bed.

+**Caddo, Cado.** A member of a tribe of Indians formerly living in Louisiana, Arkansas, and eastern Texas. Also attrib. with *Indian, tribe.*

1818 Birkbeck *Letters fr. Illinois* 111 (Th.), [He has] returned from a trading expedition . . . among the Iotans, Cados, and Choctaws. **1821** Dewees *Lett. fr. Texas* 20 We chanced to fall in with a party of Caddo Indians, who were out on a hunting excursion. **1830** *Ib.* 131 An Indian of the Caddo tribe was taken prisoner. **1836** Crockett *Exploits* 122 A Caddo had been seized as a spy, and threatened with death, in order to compel him to deliver up his knife. **1844** *Congress. Globe* 377/1 [The House agreed to pay] expenses attending the holding a treaty with the Caddoes and other wandering tribes.

Cad(d)y. +A container for water; a box holding from 10 to 20 pounds of tobacco. — **1883** *Harper's Mag.* Jan. 201/1 He picks up from near where his coat and saw and water caddy are lying, two sticks. **1899** *Mo. So. Dakotan* I. 151 The father bought chewing tobacco by the cady.

Cadet. [F. *cadet* younger son, gentleman volunteer, etc.] A (young) military or naval officer in training; a student in a military or naval academy. {1775–}

1802 *Ann. 7th Congress* App. 1306 Each company to consist of one captain, one first lieutenant, one second lieutenant, two cadets, four sergeants. **1815** *Niles' Reg.* IX. 17/2 The table of the secretary of war was now crowded with applications for *cadet's warrants.* **1832** P. Hone *Diary* I. 57 The cadets from West Point who have just now graduated are ordered on this service. **1852** *Knickerb.* XXXIX. 171 It was in the summer of 1850 that I entered Camp Gaines with the corps of cadets. **1884** Roe *Nature's Story* 406 The long line of cadets shifted their guns from 'carry arms' to 'shoulder arms.' **1892** M. A. Jackson *Memoirs* 477 The remains were taken in charge by the corps of cadets of the Virginia Military Institute.

attrib. **1772** J. Rowe *Diary* 230 July 7. Colo. Hancock turned out this forenoon with the Cadet Company. **1851** Cist *Cincinnati* 303 In 1825, he applied for, and . . . obtained a cadet appointment at West Point. **1854** Benton *30 Years' View* I. 184/1 The cadet officers must naturally feel themselves independent of the people. **1864** 'Penniman' *Tanner-Boy* 63 Standing in the midst of the prairie the cadet-guard could feel how small a thing man is. **1884** Roe *Nature's Story* 60 An antidote against the cadet fever. *Ib.*, The cadet barracks. **1889** *Century Mag.* Jan. 469/2 Evans was wildly waving the cadet colors from the top of a caisson.

transf. **1902** G. C. Eggleston *D. South* 311 Fred, the cadet of the dining room, . . . was being trained under Polydore's tutelage to keep his nails clean and to offer dishes to the guests at their left hands.

+**Cadet cloth.** A grayish-blue woolen fabric freq. used in cadet uniforms. (Cf. next.) — **1879** F. Roe *Army Lett.* 221 A tight chamois skin waist underneath my cadet-cloth habit and a broad fur collar completes a riding costume. **1887** [see Cadet gray].

+**Cadet gray.** The grayish blue of uniforms worn by cadets of military academies and by postmen. — **1887** *Postal Laws* 266 For Winter Wear . . . a single-breasted sack coat of 'cadet gray,' or, technically, 'blue-mixed cadet cloth.' **1894** Cable *J. March* xvii, All Rosemonters were required to sit together at Sunday morning service, in a solid mass of cadet gray.

Cadetship. [Cadet.] The position or appointment of a cadet. {1845–} +Also comb. in *cadetship-peddler*, a congressman who sells cadetships. — **1870** *Nation* X. 147/1 Mr. Golladay, of Kentucky, resigned his seat in the House, to avoid expulsion, he having also been dealing in cadetships. **1870** *Clipping from periodical*, The Rev. Carpetbagging Thief and Cadetship-peddler has arrived in Washington, and has had a long interview with Ben Butler. **1873** 'Mark Twain' & Warner *Gilded Age* li. 467 Next they will try each other for various smaller irregularities, like the sale of appointments to West Point cadetships, and that sort of thing. **1892** M. A. Jackson *Memoirs* 30 His uncle told him of the opportunity to get a cadetship at West Point.

+**'Cadian.** =Acadian. (Cf. Cajian.) Also attrib. — **1880** Cable *Grandissimes* 220 Loth to resell him with the rest to some unappreciative 'Cadian. **1894** Chopin *Bayou Folk* 59 The little 'Cadians had already disappeared like rabbits. *Ib.* 80 Grégoire had known her at the 'Cadian balls that he sometimes had the hardihood to attend.

Cady. *slang.* A hat or cap. {1869–} — **1846** *Spirit of Times* 6 June 170/2, I may be able to discover my lost 'Cady.'

Café. [F. *café.*]

1. A coffeehouse or restaurant. {1815–}

1835 Ingraham *South-West* I. 112 We repaired to an adjoining café, *à la mode* New Orleans. **1845** *Knickerb.* XXVI. 81 A 'foreign-kept' café, not a thousand miles from Broadway. **1851** A. O. Hall *Manhattaner* 18 The appetite . . . will find a café or restaurateur on every block [in New Orleans] . . . which tolerably emulates its counterpart in world-renowned Paris. **1888** Cable in *Century Mag.* Dec. 255 The cathedral, the convent of the Ursulines, five or six cafés, and about a hundred houses were all of it [=New Orleans in 1795]. **1922** *Hotel Monthly* XXX. 57/2 Around the lobby is the writing room, the ladies' lounge, cafe, lunch room, cigar stand, and business stores.

attrib. **1891** *Harper's Mag.* Dec. 49/2, I was inspired with the idea of taking our guest off to a café concert over in the Bowery. **1907** Lillibridge *Trail* 56 Bud Smith [had] . . . a complexion prairie wind had made like a lobster display in a café window. **1921** *Plant-Restaurant Management* March 12/1 (*caption*), Advantages and Disadvantages of the Subsidized Cafe Plan.

+**2.** A barroom.

1893– in dicts. **1906** *Independent* LX. 508/2 On the East Side of New York the café is competing with the saloon and driving it from business. The café is partly of foreign origin, partly a natural outgrowth of the tea and coffee saloons found in such large numbers east of the Bowery. **1910** *Boston Ev. Transcript* 17 Nov. 1/6 The saloon has gone out of existence in Jersey City. . . . The word 'café' is hereafter to be substituted.

+**Café car.** A combination dining and lounge car. — **1897** *Boston Herald* 11 Aug. 8/3 Instead of dining cars, the Illinois Central has placed on all its western lines cafe cars, in which meals are served a la carte.

+**Cafeteria.** [Amer.-Sp. *cafeteria*, coffee shop.] A restaurant or lunchroom in which the patrons obtain the food from a counter, or series of counters, and carry it to the tables at which they eat it. Also attrib.

'Then [c1853] came the *cafeteria*, but the term was used with a different significance from that now in vogue. It was rather a place for drinking than for eating' (Newark *60 Years S. Calif.* 133).

1894 *Lakeside Directory Chicago* 2188 Cafetiria Catering Co. 45 Lake. **1895** *Ib.* 2231 'Cafetiria,' 46 Lake, 80 Adams, 108 Quincy and 93 Vanburen. **1896** *Chicago Tribune* 28 June 4/1 The four men held by the police . . . for cracking the safe of the Caféteria, No. 46 Lake street, prove to be members of one of the boldest . . . gangs that ever operated in Chicago. *Ib.*, Gerbach used to be a waiter in a West Side restaurant subsequent to his employment by the cafeteria company. **1912** *Jrnl. Home Economics* IV. 245 Why when exactly the same menu was served in a large college dining room and at the cafeteria did complaints follow in the one case and praises in the other? **1923** *Mod. Lang. Notes* March 188 Every one knows by this time that a cafeteria is a 'help-yourself' restaurant.

***Cag,** *n.* Also †**cagg, kag.** A keg.

1653 *Plymouth Col. Rec.* III. 28 Wee present Richard Templer, of Yarmouth, for stealing certaine caggs of oysters. **1725** T. Fitch in *Travels Amer. Col.* 184 The said Spanyard arived at the Cowweetaws and brought with them two Caggs of Spainish Brandy. **1748** C. Weiser *Journal* 32 George Croghan & myself staved an 8 gallon Cag of Liquor. **1781** *Md. Hist. Mag.* V. 124 Our cag had no water in it. **1884** 'Mark Twain' *H. Finn* xxviii. 282 It does seem most like setting down on a kag of powder and touching it off.

‖**Cag**, *v.* [f. prec.] *tr.* To put *up* in cags. — **1777** F. Moore *Songs of Amer. Rev.* (1856) 171, I . . . Will . . . spoil your feathering and your tarring; And cagg you up for pickled herring.

‖**Cag bread.** [?CAG *n.*] A variety of ship bread. — **1788** *Md. Journal* 7 March (Th.), The subscriber has just begun to bake Ship, Pilot, and Cag Bread.

* **Cage.**

* **1.** A place for the detention of prisoners; a lockup.

1636 *New Plymouth Laws* 41 In every Constablerick there [shall] be a paire of stocks erected. Also a Cage which shall be of competent strength to detain a prisoner. **1660** *Plymouth Col. Rec.* XI. 205 There shalbee in the seuerall towneships of this Jurisdiction a Cage erected especially att Sandwich, Duxburrow, Marshfield and Scittuate. **1694** *Boston Rec.* 218 Phillips shall have the ground where the cage and watch hous stand leased to him for 21 years. **1707** *Ib.* 62 The Justices . . . do agree that a Cage be erected to joyn with the Watch House. **1883** ZEIGLER & GROSSCUP *Alleghanies* 142 The dark interior of the 'cage' used for petty misdoers, can be seen under the front outside stairs.

2. (See quotations.)

1866 'F. KIRKLAND' *Bk. Anecdotes* 134/2 They had him in a small iron cage, a terrible affair. **1880** *Harper's Mag.* Sept. 536/2 The cage, which forms a part of every Carolina jail, was a square room of stout iron bars, built in the center of a larger one. **1893** J. AULD *Picturesque Burlington* 53 Within this octagon is a rotary jail—a round steel 'cage' containing ten cells for prisoners. This 'cage' is closely surrounded by a barred iron railing with only one opening. When a prisoner is to be placed in his cell the 'cage' is revolved till the proper cell fronts the door; then the prisoner is put in, the cage is turned, and he is secure.

+**3.** *Baseball.* A space enclosed with wire walls, used for practicing batting, pitching, etc.

1893 W. CAMP *College Sports* 194 Some of the best equipped of these gymnasiums have long, low alleys, completely bounded by two walls and a wire netting, in which throwing and batting can be practiced. These are known as 'cages.' **1893** *Chicago Tribune* 26 April 7/4 University of Pennsylvania has $3,000 subscribed toward its proposed baseball cage. **1898** *Outing* April 13/1 A temporary 'cage' was arranged in a building half a mile from the college grounds, in the absence of the regular gymnasium, which after this year will have all the needed facilities for training the baseball players.

+**Cahoo.** [F. *cahot.*] A pitchhole. — **1874** *Vt. Bd. Agric. Rep.* II. 659 The highways leading to our larger villages . . . are frequently so full of pitchholes or 'cahoos' as to render them totally unfit for travel. *Ib.* 661 Pitch holes or 'cahoos,' in winter roads, are a dangerous nuisance.

+**Cahoole**, *v.* (See quotation.) — **1851** HALL *College Words* 40 *Cahoole*, at the University of North Carolina, this word in its application is almost universal, but generally signifies to cajole, to wheedle, to deceive, to procure.

‖**Cahoop**, *v.* [Cf. CA- and HOOP *v.*] *intr.* To whoop. — **1758** *Essex Inst. Coll.* XLV. 343 They came within a mile & 1/2 of this Stockade, where lay in Ambush near 50 of the Enemy, who cahoop'd. *Ib.*, The Indian sprung out of the Road towards the Enemy, and cahoop'd likewise.

+**Cahoot**, *n.* [Of obscure origin. F. *cahute* (cabin) and *cohorte* (company) have been suggested, but there is no evidence for connection with either.]

1. *In cahoot* or *cahoots (with)*, in or into partnership, company, or league (with).

(*a*) **1829** S. KIRKHAM *Eng. Gram.* 207 Hese in cohoot with me. **1837** A. WETMORE *Gaz. Missouri* 310 This hint induced me to take a neighbour in *cahoot* with me. **1847** FIELD *Drama in Pokerville*, etc. 198 The hoosier . . . told him . . . that if he liked he would 'go in with him—in *cahoot!*' **1852** *Knickerb.* Dec. 548 A cracker . . . informed me that a neighbor who was in cahoot with him had honey-fackled him in the matter of a heap of logs. **1880** *Harper's Mag.* Sept. 539/2 A hev always been in cahoot with well-to-do folk before naw. **1885** M. THOMPSON *Byways & Bird Notes* 49 A country lad . . . informed me that a robin and a rain-crow had a nest 'in cahoot.' . . . 'In cahoot' is a common Western and Southern phrase for in partnership. **1899** *Boston Transcript* 1 June 6/1 Senseless opposition . . . may place his honor in cahoot with a reunited Democratic party.

(*b*) **1862** G. K. WILDER *MS. Diary* 14 May, M^c wished me to go in cahoots in a store. **1889** K. MUNROE *Golden Days* 26 Are you willing to work in cahoots with yours truly, until one or the other of us gets tired of the partnership? **1890** BRET HARTE *Waif of Plains* 93, I'm dark, young fel. We're in cahoots in this thing? **1892** HARRIS *On Plantation* 74, I speck, all de birds wuz in cahoots. **1899** G. ADE *Doc' Horne* 280, I have good reasons for thinking they were in cahoots. **1904** *N.Y. Tribune* 10 July, So I became the sly abettor of Mickus—in short, we were in cahoots.

b. Attrib. with *business* = a partnership.

1845 HOOPER *Simon Suggs' Adv.* 29 If . . . I could only get the township and range, I'd make a *cahoot* business with old man Doublejoy.

‖**2.** A confederate or associate.

1869 *Congress. Globe* 6 April 538/3 Fisk and his 'cahoots' have got at cross purposes, and he has been put out of bed.

+**Cahoot**, *v.* [f. prec.] *intr.* To go into partnership; to consort. — **1857** *N.Y. Herald* 20 May (B.), They all agree to cahoot with their claims against Nicaragua and Costa Rica. **1886** S. W. MITCHELL *R. Blake* 261 The women ken cohoot together down at the old house, and me and you, we'll go a'-fishin'.

* **Cain.** [App. the Biblical name.]

+**1.** *To raise Cain*, to make a disturbance. Also fig.

[**1840** *St. Louis Pennant* 2 May (Th.), Why have we every reason to believe that Adam and Eve were both rowdies? Because . . . they both raised Cain.] *c***1849** PAIGE *Dow's Sermons* I. 247 They will feel that they have been raising Cain and breaking things. **1852** STOWE *Uncle Tom* xx, Topsy . . . [was] singing and whistling . . . ; in short, as Miss Ophelia phrased it, 'raising Cain' generally. **1866** 'F. KIRKLAND' *Bk. Anecdotes* 34 It's easier—isn't it—to smash horseteal boddies wen we air able, than it is when they air able to raze Cain with us? **1874** J. D. WHITNEY *Life & Lett.* 287 The legislature is terrible, and they are 'raising Cain' with the railroads. **1884** 'MARK TWAIN' *H. Finn* vi. 37 Every time he got drunk he raised Cain around town. **1894** P. L. FORD *P. Sterling* 13 'Tis little Peter Stirling . . . is shouting drunk as usual, and raising Cain! **1909** WASON *Happy Hawkins* 16 'What'll the night riders do?' I asked. 'Oh, they'll raise Cain as usual.'

‖**2.** *By Cain*, as an expletive.

1839 J. S. JONES *People's Lawyer* II. ii, By Cain, I got lost this morning, or I should have been in to see you.

+**3.** *What in Cain?* what in creation? what on earth?

1854 M. J. HOLMES *Tempest & Sunshine* 172 It had been there two weeks, and he didn't know what in cain to do with it. **1855** *Knickerb.* XLVI. 83 What in Cain did you play that for?

Caious: see COWISH *n.*

+**Cajian**, *a.* and *n.* Also **Cajan, Cajun.** Colloquial forms of 'CADIAN, Acadian. — **1880** R. L. DANIELS in *Scribner's Mo.* Jan. 383 Among themselves they are *'Créole Français'*; and Acadian—or rather its corruption 'Cajun,' as they pronounce it—is regarded as implying contempt. **1887** R. H. DAVIS in *Harper's Mag.* 918/1, I am glad to have met you, to correct your false impressions of the lazy, wretched 'Cajans'! **1894** CHOPIN *Bayou Folk* 83 That's the way with them Cajuns, . . . ain't got sense enough to know a white man when they see one. *Ib.* 268 He jis' gone a-caperin' yonda to de Cajun ball. **1906** *Springfield W. Republican* 28 June 11 Mr. Broussard is what is known in Louisiana as a 'Cajian.' That is, he is an 'up state' man and a descendant of the French-Canadians who were driven out of Acadia and who then settled in Louisiana in the upper part of the state.

* **Cake**, *n.*

* **1.** One or other of various forms of fancy bread.

See also *fried-, plain, plumcake*, etc.

1693 *Harvard Rec.* I. 343 No Commencer or other Schollar shall have any such Cakes in their Studies or Chambers. **1784** CUTLER in *Mem. Academy* I. 415 The leaves [of common comfrey] give a grateful flavour to cakes and panadoes. **1840** *Picayune* 18 Aug. 2/3 Somebody sent the editor of the Baltimore Clipper a smoking hot ginger cake. **1868** MRS. WHITNEY *P. Strong* 44 She will stir up a pan of cake because she finds she has to wait a few minutes for the flat-irons. **1887** N. PERRY *Flock of Girls* 165 Margie insisted that it should be cake and not gingerbread. The cake should be plain, but it should be cake. **1909** 'O. HENRY' *Roads of Destiny* 53 We've got a paper bag of cakes and chocolates.

+**b.** In combinations, as *cake and beer wagon*, etc.

1787 TYLER *Contrast* (1790) v. ii, Why, half my visits are cake and candle visits; it won't do, you know, for you to go. **1800** ASBURY *Journal* II. 469 The people gathered around my carriage, as if I had had a cake and cider cart. **1845** *Knickerb.* XXVI. 367 A cake-and-peanut girl, with a clean, sweet face, came along. **1851** *Polly Peablossom* 45 'Cake and beer' wagons were doing a brisk business.

2. *ellipt.* A griddlecake or pancake. Usu. in pl. (cf. *hot cakes*).

1828 WEBSTER, *Griddle*, a pan, broad and shallow, for baking cakes. **1849** *New Eng. Farmer* I. 124 Griddle Cakes of Unbolted Wheat. . . . These are better and more healthful cakes than buckwheat. **1852** STOWE *Uncle Tom* xiii, Mary stood at the stove, baking griddle-cakes. . . . There was so much motherliness and full-heartedness even in the way she passed a plate of cakes [etc.]. **1878** — *Poganuc People* x. 110 Here, carry in this plate o' cakes, for they're eatin' breakfast. **1880** *Buckeye Cookery* (1885) 51 If the cakes stick, sprinkle on salt and rub with a coarse cloth before greasing.

3. In various colloquial phrases. * **a.** *One's cake is all dough*, one's design or affair is unsuccessful. {–1708; now *dial.*}

1830 S. SMITH *Major Downing* 66 Then up steps the Supreme Court again and tells 'em their cake is all dough; for they hadn't been duin constitutional. **1836** *Quarter Race Ky.* (1846) 15, I'm afraid our cake is all dough—that's old Grapevine, and I told you point blank to walk round her.

+**b.** *To take the cake* (†*cakes*), or variants of this: to take the prize. (Cf. CAKEWALK.)

*a***1846** *Quarter Race Ky.*, etc. 120 They got up a horse and fifty dollars in money on a side, . . . each one to start and ride his own horse, . . . the winning horse take the cakes. **1882** *Sheldon* (Iowa) *Mail* 26 Jan., Sprague's Original Georgia Minstrel performance, given in this city last night, is, as a fraud and humbug, entitled to the cake. **1884** *Lisbon* (Dakota) *Star* 25 July, Sheriff Moore takes the cake for the first wheat harvesting in Ransom county. **1888** C. D. FERGUSON *Exper. Forty-Niner* 101

For beef this poor little heifer took the cake. **1892** *Harper's Mag.* Jan. 250/2, I think Mr. Westgate will find that Boston takes the cake.

+**c.** *To hurry up the* (or *one's*) *cakes*, to hasten matters.

1848 BARTLETT 186 *Hurry up the cakes*, i.e. be quick; look alive. **1857** HAMMOND *Northern Scenes* 321 The way he hurried up Crop's cakes was a thing to be astonished at. **1871** DE VERE 610 *Hurry up the cakes, to*, a slang phrase, originating in the great partiality Americans have for hot cakes at breakfast. **1897** ROBINSON *Uncle Lisha* 68 Go ahade and hurry up yo' cakes, foh I'll be bound Baker and his man's thah with the boat foh now.

***4.** A piece of some substance in a flat form resembling a cake; also ellipt. =oil cake, cotton cake, etc.

1818 SCHOOLCRAFT *Journal* 6 Putting three or four large cakes of corn-bread in a sack, . . . he mounted his horse. **1833** *Niles' Reg.* XLIV. 222/1 The cake is the very best food for stock. **1835** INGRAHAM *South-West* II. 161 The 'cake' is in consistency very much like that of flax-seed. *a***1892** M. A. Jackson *Gen. Jackson* 393 General Jackson had received among his presents a cake of butter with a gallant chanticleer stamped upon it.

attrib. **1884** KNIGHT *Suppl.* I. 152 Cake Grinder, a machine for breaking linseed oil cake for food for stock.

5. Attrib. with *basket, bowl, box, cover, jar, machine, mould, pan*, etc.

1805 MRS. E. S. BOWNE *Life* 205, 1 plated Cake Basket silver rims, 18.00. **1874** MRS. WHITNEY *We Girls* ii. 43 A cake-bowl in one hand, and an egg-beater in the other. **1875** STOWE *We & Our Neighbors* 55 She looked into the flour barrel, the sugar barrel, the safe, the cake box, and took notes. **1854** *Penna. Agric. Rep.* 139 To Elizabeth Flowers, a premium of one dollar for one Tidy and two Cake Covers. **1850** S. F. COOPER *Rural Hours* 433 Cake-jars are filling up with crullers. **1884** KNIGHT *Suppl.* I. 152 Cake Machine . . . takes the dough previously prepared . . . and cuts it into cakes of the required size and shape. **1828** E. LESLIE *Receipts* 49 Butter a large tin pan, or a cake-mould. **1896** E. HIGGINSON *Tales* 44 'Well, I guess I'll manage to get my rights, somehow,' said Isaphene, beginning to butter the cakepan. **1866** MRS. WHITNEY *L. Goldthwaite* x, Cake-plates were garnished with wreathed oak-leaves. **1851** A. O. HALL *Manhattaner* 7 Coffee and cake stands, in a brace of deserted markets. **1884** KNIGHT *Suppl.* 152 Cake Steamer, a machine for *washing* cakes, snaps, and crackers. **1841** *Knickerb.* XVII. 434, I have a faint recollection of . . . overturning the cake-table of an old dame. **1836** C. GILMAN *Recoll.* (1838) 127 Titus was summoned to carry the cake-tray. **1866** GREGG *Life in Army* 139 Farther on, you come in contact with candy shops, peanut stands, cake wagons.

Cake, *v.* [CAKE *n.* 1.] *tr.* ‖To entertain with cake. — **1861** J. B. JONES *Rebel War Clerk's Diary* I. 33 [The ladies of Richmond] wine them and cake them—and they deserve it.

+**Cakea.** ?A Californian night bird. — **1873** MILLER *Amongst Modocs* xxx. 341, I heard the call of the *cakea*, or night bird. **1887** J. HAWTHORNE *Fort. Fool* xxii, The call of the cakea sounded by night from hill-side to hillside.

Cake cutter. 'A device for cutting sheets of dough into round or ornamental forms, as heart-shaped, etc.' (Knight). — **1879** MRS. WHITNEY *Just How* 226 Little strips of paste, cut with notched edges, by a wheel cake-cutter, may be laid across the tops.

Caked, *ppl. a.* [*Cake* v.] Formed into a cake {*a*1691}; hardened. — **1863** RANDALL *Pract. Shepherd* 158 A ewe that refuses thus to stand will sometimes be found to have a hot, hard, inflamed or 'caked' udder.

+**Cake sugar.** (See quot. 1835.) — **1835** AUDUBON *Ornith. Biog.* III. 440 It takes ten gallons of sap to produce a pound of fine-*grained sugar;* but an inferior kind in lumps, called *cake-sugar*, is obtained in greater quantity. **1844** GREGG *Commerce of Prairies* I. 173 When short of means they often support themselves upon only a *real* each per day, their usual food consisting of bread and a kind of coarse cake-sugar *piloncillo* to which is sometimes added a little crude ranchero cheese.

+**Cake-tobacco.** [CAKE *n.* 4.] Tobacco in the form of flat pieces. — **1852** *Knickerb.* XL. 191 Its [the store's] contents made a curious *mélange*. Printed calicoes crowded cake-tobacco. **1867** DIXON *New America* I. 157 He finds it pay better to sell . . . cake-tobacco for chewing at six dollars a pound.

+**Cake urchin.** [CAKE *n.* 4.] (See quotation.) — **1889** *Cent.* 757/1 A flat sea-urchin; a sand-dollar. . . . *Mellita quinquefora* and *Echinarachnius parma* are common United States cake-urchins.

+**Cakewalk,** *n.* [CAKE *n.* 1.]

1. A parade or walk-around of Negro origin in which the reward for the fanciest steps was a cake.

1879 *Harper's Mag.* Oct. 799/1 Reader, didst ever attend a cake walk given by the colored folks? **1889** FARMER 115 In certain sections of the country, cake walks are in vogue among the colored people. It is a walking contest, not in the matter of speed, but in style and elegance. **1893** R. M. STUART *Golden Wedding* 191 Finding himself allotted to walk with her at a cake walk. **1895** *N.Y. Dramatic News* 19 Oct. 16/1 On Thursday, Friday and Saturday nights a cake walk will take place in conjunction with the regular performance. **1915** B. MATTHEWS in *Scribner's Mag.* June 758/2 The general neglect of opportunities for a more accurate presentation of Negro characteristics is to be seen in the strange fact that the minstrels failed to . . . put the cake-walk on the stage.

fig. **1894** 'MARK TWAIN' in *Critic* 7 July 8/1 This Shelley biography . . . is a literary cake-walk. **1894** HOWELLS *Traveller from Altruria* 161 It is the man with the most money who now takes the prize in our national cake-walk.

attrib. **1898** F. H. SMITH *C. West* 314 'Dat's de tip-nist, top-nist git-up I done seen fur a coon's age,' detecting a certain—to him—cake-walk cut to the coat and white duck trousers. **1899** *Chicago Record* 11 Jan. 4/4 The 'coon song' has been distinct and individual, as its subject, its swinging tunes and its cake-walk adjuncts show.

2. A dance modeled on the cakewalk.

1902 BANKS *Newspaper Girl* 142 In the midst, doing an amateur 'cake-walk' was Dinah, hugging a blue tin can. **1902** HARBEN *A. Daniel* 53, I was doing the cake-walk with that fat Howard girl. **1905** F. YOUNG *Sands of Pleasure* II. ix, She spoke to several men she knew, and even danced the 'cakewalk' with one of them.

+**Cakewalk,** *v. intr.* To perform a cakewalk. — **1898** [see CAKE-WALKER]. *a***1909** 'O. HENRY' *Roads of Destiny* xx. 341 The plumed knights were cake-walking in the banquet-halls above.

+**Cakewalker.** A person who performs a cakewalk. — **1898** WILLIAMS & WALKER in J. W. Johnson *Black Manhattan* 105 We, the undersigned world-renowned cake-walkers, . . . hereby challenge you [=W. K. Vanderbilt] to compete with us in a cake-walking match.

Cake-woman. [CAKE *n.* 1.] A woman who sells cake or cakes. — **1775** FITHIAN *Journal* II. 128 Sept. 6: at York [paid] Barber /9d; Tavern, 3/4; Cake-woman, /2. **1836** *S. Lit. Messenger* II. 303 Planters and pettifoggers—constables and cake women—farmers and felons.

+**Cala.** *La.* [Of African origin.] A sweet rice cake flavored with nutmeg. — **1880** CABLE *Grandissimes* 133 Frowenfeld entered after him, *calas* in hand.

Calabash. Also †**calibash, callabash, -basch, callebash.** {1604-}

1. A vessel made from a gourd hollowed out and dried, used esp. as a bottle or dipper. {1657-}

1716 CHURCH *Philip's War* (1865) I. 81 Mr. Church pulled out his Callebash . . . and drank a good Swig. **1765** R. ROGERS *Acc. N. America* 102 There was then brought him a calabash of water, to wash his hands. **1800** BOUCHER *Glossary* p. xlix, *Calibash;* the rind, or shell, of a gourd, used by negroes for the drinking of water, as a gourd shell is thought to give a remarkably sweet flavour to water. **1834** SIMMS *G. Rivers* II. 102 Here, Nick Snell, . . . run down with the calibash to the branch. **1836** C. GILMAN *Recoll.* (1838) 147 One old woman . . . , dropping a courtesy, handed Anna a calibash of eggs. **1843** 'CARLTON' *New Purchase* I. 61 Crockery and calabashes shared the mantel. **1852** MRS. ELLET *Pioneer Women* 265 Treating the women from a calabash of muddy whiskey which they carried with them.

+**b.** *Obs. slang.* A person's head.

'A humorous name for the head, generally implying emptiness' (B. '59). 'By far the most frequent use made of the word is, as a cant term, for a weak and empty head' (De Vere 121).

1723 *Boston News-Letter* 27 June 2/2 You have in the cavity of your Callabash a viscid juice. **1837** J. C. NEAL *Charcoal Sk.* (1838) 97 A man in grief is like a wood-piler in a cellar—mind how you chuck, or you'll crack his calabash. **1846** *Knickerb.* XXVII. 120 A great many clear-headed and ingenious skulls have been buried here, each one of them worth a hundred calabashes of Lazy-Lane. **1856** C. WHITE *Oh, Hush!* 8 Come, no prevarication, or I'll smash dat calabash.

+**2.** A gourd used as a rattle, drum, etc., esp. by Indians.

1743 J. BARTRAM *Observations* (1751) 43 He [an Indian] carried in one hand a large staff, in the other a calabash with small stones in it, for a rattle. **1772** D. TAITT in *Travels Amer. Col.* 517 As they come round the men [Indians] ratle a small Callabash in their hands. **1810** WEEMS *Washington* (1927) 38 Every day, at play-time, with corn-stalks for muskets, and calabashes for drums, the two armies [of school-boys] would turn out. **1843** F. L. HAWKS *D. Boone* 89 In this left [hand] they carried a calabash, tied to a stick about a foot long, and with this continually beat their breasts.

3. The gourdlike fruit of the calabash tree; any gourd which could be used as a calabash (sense 1).

[**1764** C. G. REUTER *Wachau, Callabasch*, a kind of Gourd. All sorts of vessels can be made from them; the hunters use them for powder flasks.] **1846** THORPE *Myst. Backwoods* 77 The most ingenious and laborious workman . . . cannot possibly form a vessel so general in its use, so excellent in its ends, as the calibash. The Indian finds it suspended in profusion in every glade of his forest home. **1907** WHITE *Arizona Nights* 212 All they had was calabash—a sort of squash.

4. The bottle gourd or gourd plant, *Lagenaria vulgaris* (*Cucurbita lagenaria*).

1817-8 EATON *Botany* (1822) 257 *Cucurbita lagenaria*, gourd, calabash. **1836** LINCOLN *Botany* App. 92. **1840** DEWEY *Mass. Flowering Plants* 112 *Cucurbita lagenaria*, Gourd Calabash. From India. **1847** DARLINGTON *Weeds & Plants* (1860) 138 Common Lagenaria. Calabash. Bottle gourd. . . . Gardens and lots: cultivated. Native of the tropical regions. **1871** DE VERE 120 The *calabash* of the United States is . . . , when at all applied to a plant, the Gourd (*Cucurbita lagenaria*). **1901** MOHR *Plant Life Ala.* 747 *Lagenaria vulgaris* (L.) . . . Common Gourd Calabash . . . Carolinian and Louisianian areas. Regarded as introduced and naturalized in the South Atlantic and Gulf States, although cultivated by the aborigines at the arrival of the earliest settlers.

+**5.** *Calabash banjo, tureen,* one made of a calabash (sense 3).

1843 'CARLTON' *New Purchase* I. 200 The merry rascals were dancing away to a cornstalk fiddle and a calabash banjo. **1855** SIMMS *Forayers* 542 Scarcely had they been seated when four great calabash tureens were placed severally at the extremities.

+**Calabazilla, -cilla.** *S.W.* [Mex.-Sp., f. Sp. *calabaza* calabash.] A species of squash growing in California and Texas (see quots.) — **1885** HAVARD *Flora W. & S. Texas* 522 *Cucurbita perennis*, Gray. (Calabacilla.) . . . The pulp of the green fruit is used with soap to remove stains from clothing. **1889** *Cent.* 757/2 *Calabazilla*, . . . in southern California, the *Cucurbita perennis*, a native species of squash, with an exceedingly large root. *c***1892** *Dialect Notes* I. 188 (Texas), *Calabacilla:* a gourd with round fruit the color of an orange.

+**Calaboodle.** *slang.* =CABOODLE. — **1856** *Knickerb.* XLVII. 54 The whole caluboodle [*sic*] hover around me like swarms of mosquitoes. **1857** *Ib.* XLIX. 135 The whole calaboodle is a—damned humbug.

+**Calaboose,** *n.* Chiefly *S.*; elsewhere jocular. Also †**calaboos, calleboose, callibouse.** [Louisianian Fr., from Sp. *calabozo;* see CALABOZO.] A prison or lockup.

Illustrated by Thornton from 1797 to 1888.

1792 J. POPE *Tour S. & W.* 43 Their Fate will be confinement . . . in the Callibouse at Mobille. **1797** F. BAILY *Tour* 289 Threatening me with the horrors of the Callibouse if I any longer disputed his authority. **1805** SIBLEY in *Ann. 9th Congress* 2 Sess. 1094 Others . . . followed the merchants; after them the priests and commandant; then the church and jail (or calleboose,) and now nothing of the old town is left. **1823** DEWEES *Lett. from Texas* 33 He was . . . deposited in a calaboose to await further trial. **1840** *Picayune* 29 July 2/4 How long since you came out of the calaboose, madam? **1852** STOWE *Uncle Tom* xvi, Why, send them to the calaboose, or some of the other places, to be flogged. **1861** *Ill. Agric. Soc. Trans.* IV. 259 We have also a calaboose, and an officers' horse shed. **1875** *Chicago Tribune* 28 July 3/4 A drunken man, named Jack Collins, [was] picked up on the streets . . . and lodged in the city calaboose. **1888** C. D. FERGUSON *Exp. Forty-Niner* 223 The first thing was to visit the calaboose, and see how many poor victims had found lodgings there. **1907** WHITE *Riverman* iii. 32, I'll just get along and bail the boys out of that village calaboose.

attrib. **1835** CROCKETT *Tour* 146 Sam he got off to the boat, but the Calaboos men got Joe.

+**Calaboose,** *v. tr.* To imprison. — **1840** *Picayune* 30 Oct. 2/3 He calaboosed him— . . . Charley took him in. **1846** CORCORAN *Pickings* 155 Without listening to a word from them he calaboosed them. **1857** *Cincinnati Commercial* (B.), Col. Titus . . . was calaboosed on Tuesday for shooting at the porter of the Planters' House.

+**Calaboz.** Anglicized form of next. — **1889** C. F. LUMMIS *'Lo' Who Is Not Poor* 45 Not uncommonly a governor has to be thrown for a few days into the calaboz before he will accept the high office to which he has just been elected.

+**Calabozo, -boza.** *S.* [Sp. *calabozo,* dungeon.] =CALABOOSE *n.*

(*a*) **1826** FLINT *Recollections* 208 The commandant, a priest, a file of soldiers, and a calaboza made up the engine of government. **1834** *Visit to Texas* 132 The refractory lieutenant having been . . . thrown into the calaboza, the commissary informed the agents that they had better be prepared against attack. **1846–7** MAGOFFIN *Down Santa Fé Trail* 169 Dr. Conley, Mr. McMannus and brother James, who went on ahead to C. have been taken prisoners, the two former lodged in the calaboza (calabozo—jail). **1880** CABLE *Grandissimes* 249 In the midst of the ancient town, . . . stood the Calaboza. **1883** *Century Mag.* March 649/2 The terrors of the calaboza, with its chains and whips and branding irons, were condensed into the French tri-syllabic Calaboose.

(*b*) **1835** INGRAHAM *South-West* I. 111 Directly on quitting the omnibus we passed the famous Calaboos, or Calabozo, the city prison, so celebrated by all seamen who have made the voyage to New Orleans. **1840** DANA *Two Years* xxviii. 312 He staid with us till he gave himself up, and was dragged off to the calabozo. **1844** GREGG *Commerce of Prairies* I. 20 The luckless traders . . . were . . . thrown into the *calabozos* of Chihuahua. **1911** S. CODY *Heroes of Plains* (Bentley), They were occasionally threatened with imprisonment in the Calabozo of St. Louis.

***Calamanco.** Also **calla-, cali-, callimanco; cala-, caliminco.** Cf. CALLAMINK.

***1.** A glossy, woolen, satin-twilled fabric orig. manufactured in Flanders and much used in the 18th c.

1711 *Boston News-Letter* 22 Oct. 2/2 The following . . . are to be sold . . . Searges, Duroys, Calaminco's. **1762** *Boston Gazette* 2 Nov., It is thought that in a few Years they will be supply'd with Callimanco and other Stuffs manufactured in this Province. **1779** BLEECKER *Maria Kittle* (1797) 48 Mrs. Kittle immediately singled out a piece of black calimanco. **1811** *Niles' Reg.* I. 46/1 Callimancoes . . . can only be made of wool long enough to be combed. **1868** G. G. CHANNING *Recoll. Newport* 90 [He] wore, when on horseback, a robe of stuff called at the time calamanco, a glossy, woollen material, of green color.

2. Attrib. in sense: Made of calamanco, as *calamanco breeches,* etc. {1605–}

1693 *Conn. Probate Rec.* I. 508 A Broad Cloth Coat and a Caliminco Jacket & Breeches. **1723** *Weekly Mercury* 11–18 April 4/2 Run away . . . Richard Wooten, by Trade a House-Carpenter, . . . he wears a Horse-Hair Wigg, a dark coloured Coat, and black Caliminco Vest and Breeches. **1727** *New-Eng. W. Journal* 10 April, I have been frequently . . . represented as a Merchant, wrapt up in a Callimanco Night-Gown, and seated very conveniently in a Compting-House. **1742** *Md. Hist. Mag.* XX. 178 Three pair Callamanco shoes Women with Leather Heel, fives & Middleing for Breadth. **1754** *S.C. Gazette* 1 Jan. 2/3 Run away, . . . a negro wench named Nancy, had on a brown callimanco gown. **1879** *Harper's Mag.* Sept. 522 One should have seen her as she tripped by to the store, . . . her short-waisted calimanco dress held up from the dust so as to show a pretty foot.

***Calamity.** (In colloq. uses.)

+**1.** A crude wagon.

1891 *Amer. Notes & Q.* VIII. 64, I do not know that any of the dictionaries have the word calamity in the sense of a rude vehicle. In the State of Maine, or in some parts of it, a cheap, homemade wagon, often of the rudest description, is known as a calamity, probably from the idea of a tumble-down affair.

+**b.** (See quotation.)

1914 *Dialect Notes* IV. 153 *Calamity,* old stuff, such as is bought at an auction. (N.H.)

+**2.** *Calamity howler,* a noisy pessimist. *Calamity-howling,* noisy pessimism. *Calamity prophet,* a person prone to predict calamity. *Calamity shouter,* a 'calamity howler.'

1892 *Congress. Rec.* 2 March 1654/1 We had some 'calamity howlers' here in Washington as well as in Kansas. **1894** *Ib.* 22 January 1215/1 The country needs certainty as to our tariff policy and rest from croakers and calamity-howlers. **1904** *Boston Herald* 29 Oct. 6 Candidate Douglas seems to have got a handsome reception. . . . His eloquent assurance that he is no pessimist and no calamity howler touched them on the right rib. **1910** MULFORD *Hopalong Cassidy* viii. 60 'You're a calamity howler!' snapped Shaw. 'That desert has wore a saddle sore on yore nerves somethin' awful.' — **1905** D. G. PHILLIPS *Plum Tree* 264, I . . . sent Woodruff East to direct a campaign of calamity-howling in the eastern press. — **1892** in *Rep. Camp. Text Bk.* (1894) 229 The calamity prophets of both parties. **1911** LINCOLN *Cap. Warren's Wards* 3 The pair of calamity prophets broke off their lament. — **1892** *Congress. Rec.* 17 March 2160/2 [They] were of the stripe of calamity-shouters whose occupation is gone unless they can prove that calamity stalks abroad.

‖**Calamityite.** *colloq.* [CALAMITY *n.* 2.] One who apprehends or predicts calamity. — **1894** *Rep. Camp. Text Bk.* 229 Bad for calamityites.

***Calamus.**

***1.** The sweet flag, *Acorus calamus.*

1828 WEBSTER, *Acorus,* . . . aromatic Calamus, sweet flag, or sweet rush. **1843** TORREY *Flora N.Y.* II. 244 *Acorus Calamus.* . . . Common Calamus or Sweet Flag. . . . A well known medicinal plant. **1849** *Rep. Comm. Patents: Agric.* (1850) 293 The roots . . . resemble those of the calamus—each joint sending up a tuft of blades. **1876** WHITMAN *Specimen Days* (1882) 88 [There is] the pond itself, with the sword-shaped calamus. **1901** MOHR *Plant Life Ala.* 424 Sweet Flag. Calamus. . . . The root forms the 'sweet flag root' or 'Calamus' of the U.S. Pharmacopœia.

2. Attrib. with *grass, root.*

1842 *Nat. Hist. N.Y., Zoology* I. 76 The Musquash or Muskrat . . . is said to be particularly fond of the calamus root. **1849** E. SMITH *Journey thro' Texas* 26 The Calamus grass alone, or mixed with the wire, and other natural grasses, covers the prairies of the black soil.

Calash, *n.* Also †**collash.**

1. a. A light, four-wheeled carriage, usu. having a removable folding hood, and sometimes a removable front; a calèche. {1679–} *Obs.* +**b.** A one-horse, two-wheeled vehicle of the chaise type.

'The calash resembles very much an old-fashioned gig, though in general built with a greater degree of strength' (1818 J. M. DUNCAN *Travels U.S.* II. 145).

1687 in *Va. Mag. Hist.* II. 141 You had best bring in [from England] an ordinary Calash with you, & I will find you horses to draw it with. **1701** SEWALL *Diary* II. 46 Going in the Calash and benighted, I lodge at Hart's and go thence in the morning early. **1718** in Church *Philip's War* (1865) I. p. xl, To the Collash with the Horse Saddle & Brydle &c 12 00 00. **1775** *Essex Inst. Coll.* XIII. 207, I went yesterday with 2 Mrs. Folgers &c. in a Calash alias Horse Cart (which sort of riding is in taste here). **1811** ASBURY *Journal* III. 367 We . . . went from thence with brother Glassford, in his calash. **1863** 'G. HAMILTON' *Gala-Days* 133 Calashes also we meet,—a cumbrous, old-fashioned 'one-hoss shay,' . . . wheels with huge spokes and broad rims, and the driver sitting on the dash-board. **1892** J. E. COOKE *B. Hallam* 82 She chose this [riding] . . . in preference to the light calash.

+**2.** *local.* (See quotation.)

1909 *Cent. Suppl.* 186/1 *Calash,* a primitive one-horse springless cart of the island of Nantucket, Massachusetts, house-chairs being used for seats.

3. A hood having hoops like a calash top, and projecting beyond the face; formerly worn by women to protect the headdress. {1774–}

1809 FRENEAU *Poems* I. 158 They show their ribbons and the huge calash. **1825** COOPER *L. Lincoln* xii, Mrs. Lechmere [was] endeavoring to screen her pallid features, by drawing down her calash. **1846** E. FARNHAM *Prairie Land* 337 Her head was covered with the soiled remnant of an ancient green calash. **1852** HAWTHORNE *Blithedale* II. 212 Priscilla wore . . . a calash, which she had flung back from her head, leaving it suspended by the strings. **1853** FELT *Customs New Eng.* 162 The calash . . . was in vogue sixty years ago, and lasted fifteen years. **1879** B. F. TAYLOR *Summer-Savory* 116, I see green calashes and vandykes and hats of beaver.

4. Attrib. and comb. with *bonnet* (in sense 3), *coach* (see quot. 1909), *hire, top, -topped* (in sense 1).

1722 *New-Eng. Courant* 19–26 March 1/2 To Coach and Calash Hire at several Times 064 09 03. **1830** J. F. WATSON *Philadelphia* 176 'A calash bonnet' was always formed of green silk; it was worn abroad, covering the head, but when in rooms it could fall back in folds like the springs of a calash or gig top. **1874** B. F. TAYLOR *World on Wheels* I. 16 And the next wheeled wonder was a calash-topped chaise. **1909** *Cent. Suppl.* 186/1 *Calash coach,* a coach having a bow top over the rear seat. The doors are in two parts, hinged separately. It can be converted from a closed into an open carriage.

‖**Calash,** *v. intr.* To drive in a calash. — **1732** B. LYNDE *Diary* 29 Dined at Justice Gardner's, and afterward rode and calash'd to Mr. Jas. Coffin's.

‖**Calashed,** *a.* [CALASH *n.* 3.] Provided with a hooped hood. — **1807–8** IRVING, etc. *Salmagundi* ii. 40 Our ladies in stays . . . well calash'd without, and well bolster'd within, . . . were shaped like a pail.

Calavance, Callavance. {1620–} A species of pulse, as *Dolichos barbadensis* or *D. sinensis.*

1682 ASH *Carolina* 14 Pulse they have of great Variety, not only of what Europe yield, viz. Beans, Pease, Callavance, Figdlaes, and Bonavist, &c. but many other kinds. **1772** D. TAITT in *Travels Amer. Col.* 515 We had black drink and afterwards bears meat and Callavances drest in Oil. **1775** *Rhode Isl. Commerce* II. 5, I suppose the same allowance of Callavances as of Pease allowed to the men.

***Calculate,** *v.* Also *dial.* **calkilate, calkerlate, calk'-late,** etc.; see also CALLATE.

+**1.** *tr.* To suppose, expect, believe after consideration; to judge. (Usu. with clause as object.)

'*Calculate,* used frequently in an improper sense, as reckon, guess' (1815 HUMPHREYS *Yankey* 104). 'The Yankee *calculates,* and pretty shrewdly also, while the Southron *allows*' (1853 'P. PAXTON' *Yankee in Texas* 116).

1805 PIKE *Sources Miss.* II. 152 We had reason to calculate, that they had good guides. **1810** LAMBERT *Travels* II. 506 (Pick.), 'The crops are progressing,' says Nathan, 'though I calculate as how this is a propitious weedy soil.' **1836** C. GILMAN *Recoll.* (1838) 36, I calculate it's pretty difficult to git edication down at Charleston. **1846** FARNHAM *Prairie Land* 37 Why, yes; I calculate 'tain't of much account to have a woman if she ain't of no use. **1850** N. KINGSLEY *Diary* 158 Mr. Edwin Ayer . . . brought no letter for me which was different from what I calculated. **1857** *Mich. Agric. Soc. Trans.* VIII. 459 Being about the oldest Yankees of whom we have record, they would probably have 'calculated' or 'guessed' that they would remain where they were. **1873** S. WARNER *Queechy* I. 271 Your aunt sets two tables, I calculate, don't she? **1882** *Maine Bd. Agric. Rep.* XXVI. 36 A common crop, . . . which we calculate lies at the foundation of successful agriculture, is English hay. **1898** CANFIELD *Maid of Frontier* 21 How many men . . . do you calk'late that Harriott has got now? **1917** *Dialect Notes* IV. 389, I ca'c'late he'll be here tomorrow.

+**2.** *intr.* To purpose or intend *to* do something; to expect.

1816 PICKERING 54, To expect; suppose. . . . I calculate to leave town to-morrow. **1822** J. WOODS *English Prairie* 345 Times are dull; I calculated to sell my creature there. **1845** COOPER *Chainbearer* vii, My children I calkerlate to bring up on pork. **1851** CIST *Cincinnati* 236 They calculate to occupy every available spot upon this vast space. **1867** 'T. LACKLAND' *Homespun* II. 157 He [the New Englander] does no talking so thoroughly as this to which he 'calculates' to devote himself on town-meeting day. **1880** 'MARK TWAIN' *Tramp Abroad* xx. 193 The thing I calculate to do . . . is to just sit down and forget it. **1884** *Harper's Mag.* Feb. 413/1 Calkilate to stop round here a spell? **1895** JEWETT *Nancy* 6, I don't calculate to get into Boston more'n once a week. **1917** *Dialect Notes* IV. 390 *Cowc'late* [is] . . . used by people who would recognize ca'clate as illiterate. . . . 'I cowc'late to be there.'

+**b.** *To calculate on* or *upon,* to intend or plan upon (doing something).

1836 R. WESTON *Visit* 59, 'I calculate upon doing so' is used by a Yankee, while we say 'I intend to do so.' **1847** ELIZA ROBBINS *MS. Letter* 22 May, Miss Sedgwick . . . said she should be much pleased to go to Roslyn on Saturday and should calculate upon it.

+**3.** To make due allowance *for,* depend upon, something.

1825 *Austin Papers* (1924) II. 1201 One of the Boats that I calculated for the Trip I found on examination was worm eaten. **1878** MRS. STOWE *Poganuc People* 186 Ye hain't calkerlated for the heft o' them fellers; governors and colonels and ministers weighs putty heavy.

***Calculation.** +Judgment. — **1870** *Putnam's Mag.* V. 80/2 You all know, though neighbor Vale has the best heart in the world, he haint a mite of kalkerlation; and none of the Vales never had, as ever I heerd on.

+**Cale, Caleb.** The grizzly bear. — **1833** CATLIN *Indians* I. 71 All eyes were turned at once upon *Caleb* (as the grizzly bear is familiarly called by the trappers in the Rocky Mountains—or more often 'Cale,' for brevity's sake).

Calèche. [F.]

1. =CALASH *n.* I. {1666–}

1776 C. CARROLL *Jrnl.* (1845) 73 We found our *calèches* ready to receive us. **1814** J. Q. ADAMS *Diary* (1929) 120 He had entered [the city] in an open caleche. **1832** R. COX *Adv. Columbia R.* 305 After some delay we procured a *calèche* sufficiently large to hold Wentzel, M'Neill, and myself. **1880** *Scribner's Mo.* Jan. 384/2 The *calèche* is . . . two-wheeled, hoodless, and springless; the body is of wood, rudely fashioned after the pattern of the old-time gig, and the seats are apparently intended for two persons, but on emergency they develop a capacity for accommodating a dozen. **1888** CABLE *Bonaventure* 11 Zoséphine and Bonaventure sat on a back seat contrived for them in the family calèche.

+**2.** =CALASH *n.* 3. *Obs.*

1839 *S. Lit. Messenger* V. 755/1 Betsy . . . screened her head in a large dove-colored caleche. **1891** S. M. WELCH *Recoll. 1830–40* 174 A green silk calèche . . . of whalebone or reeds, to fold and fall back on the back of the neck at will, or stretch forward over the face, . . . was an almost indispensable head gear.

***Calendar.**

1. A list of causes set for trial at a particular session of a court. {1764–, of criminal cases}

'In some of the American States; the [English sense of the] term is extended to embrace civil causes, as arranged for trial' (W. '47).

1839 *Knickerb.* XIII. 2 The calendar was made up as usual in four classes, thus: First class, of bills taken as confessed, fifty-two causes; second, of pleas and demurrers, thirteen [etc.]. **1894** P. L. FORD *P. Stirling* 45 When the courts opened, Peter kept track of the calendars. **1906** *Indian Laws & Tr.* III. 234 Said cause shall be advanced on the calendar of said court. **1910** J. HART *Vigilante Girl* 310 Almost from the moment that the case was called on the calendar, the gossips sat up with delighted looks.

b. Attrib. with *fee.*

1839 *Knickerb.* XIII. 7 Our circuit judge's annual income may . . . be safely estimated thus: His salary, eighteen hundred dollars; calendar fees, five thousand to six thousand dollars.

+**2.** (See quot. 1914.) Also attrib.

1839 *Congress. Globe* 25 Jan. 146/2 On the first and third [changed to fourth] Friday of each month, the calendar of private bills shall be called over. **1879** *46th Cong. 2d Sess.* H. Repr. Rep. No. 24, 34 There shall be three calendars of business reported from committees, viz.: . . . A calendar of the Committee of the Whole House on the state of the Union . . . , a House calendar . . . , a calendar of the Committee of the Whole House [for private bills]. **1890** *51st Cong. 1st Sess.* H. Repr. Rep. No. 23, 9 All reports of committees . . . shall be delivered to the Clerk for printing and reference to the proper calendar. **1914** McLaughlin & Hart *Cycl. Amer. Govt.* I. 202 A calendar is a register containing a list of the bills which have been reported from committees and which are ready to be considered in their turn. . . . The state legislatures all have their calendars, the number and kind varying among the different states. *Ib.*, Calendar Wednesday is the day set apart . . . for the consideration of public bills, excepting those that are privileged under the rules.

Calenture. A form of fever due to exposure to extreme heat. {1605–}

1623–4 *Va. House of Burgesses* 30 His people suddenly falling generally into most pestilent diseases of Callentures and feavors, not lesse then one hundred & fifty of them died within few moneths after. **1649** W. BULLOCK *Virginia* 11 Being over-heated he is struck with a Calenture or Feaver, and so perisheth. **1876** BOURKE *Journal* July 20 A few cases of diarrhoea and mild forms of calenture prevail. **1882** *Harper's Mag.* Dec. 68/1 The robust Englishman . . . was just the material for the Calentures which infested the low river-lands.

***Calf.**

***1.** The young of the cow.

1635 *Boston Rec.* 3 All barren cattell whatsoever . . . and weaned caulves 20 Weekes ould . . . shalbe kept abroad from off the neck. **a1649** WINTHROP *Hist.* I. 53 The wolves killed six calves at Salem. **1758** *Essex Inst. Coll.* XVIII. 93 Six men . . . put under Guard on suspicion of killing a young Beef and 2 Calves. **1806** in *Ann. 9th Congress* 2 Sess. 1116 Sheep and calves are frequently his [=the bear's] prey. **1896** *Vt. Agric. Rep.* XV. 26 The calves are nearly all sent to market for veal.

+**2.** =BUFFALO CALF.

1824 G. W. Rauck *Boonesborough* 166 A number of buffaloes . . . made off, . . . others loping slowly and carelessly, with young calves playing, skipping and bounding through the plain. **1867** in Custer *Tenting on Plains* (1889) 564 The first member of the buffalo family that I saw was a calf about four weeks old.

3. Attrib. with *corral, crop, herd.*

1652 *Southampton Rec.* I. 84 The calf herd shall be kept for the ensueing year at Sagaponack. **a1918** G. STUART *On Frontier* I. 184 Laid foundation for calf corral. *Ib.* II. 230 The cattle were in fine condition and the 'calf crop' unusually large.

+**b.** Attrib. in sense: Immature, crude, as *calf college, preacher.*

1851 *Harper's Mag.* June 37/1 He's a calf preacher—a young bottle-nosed Gospeller. **1909** WASON *Happy Hawkins* 203 A prep-school is a sort of a calf college.

+**Calf-keeper.** One who tends calves. — **1657** *Hempstead Rec.* I. 17 All men in this towne that will have Calves kept by the Calfe keeper to give in thare number. **1662** *Ib.* I. 126 The Calfe-keeper went forth with the Calfe heird.

+**Calfkill. 1.** The lambkill or sheep laurel, *Kalmia angustifolia.* **2.** Applied to other species of plants (see quotations). — **(1) 1859** BARTLETT 64 Calf-kill . . . [is] so called from its poisonous properties. **1871** DE VERE 413 Calfkill is the absurd name given in the North to one of the most beautiful flowering shrubs of North America. **(2) 1909** *Cent. Suppl.* 188/1 *Calf-kill*, . . . 2. *Leucothoë Catesbæi*, a shrub of the southern Alleghanies, poisonous to cattle and sheep. . . . 3. The velvet-grass, *Holcus lanatus.*

Calf-kneed, *a.* Knock-kneed. — **1894** *Vt. Agric. Rep.* XIV. 119 The chest should be full, . . . forearms long, . . . knees strong, neither calf-kneed nor sprung.

+**Calf pasture.** A pasture for calves.

[**1639** *Boston Rec.* 1 Two Accres . . . of Broken up ground in the Calues pasture.] **1656** *Suffolk Deeds* III. 255 The Land in the Orchard And Calfe Pasture, together with the meadow & other Land belonging therevnto. **1665** *East-Hampton Rec.* I. 241 Jeremy Mecham shall have all the land in the point beyond the calfe paster in leue of addition land that he wants. **1736** *Ib.* IV. 30 By virtue of his fathers grant to him of any meadow land in the place called the calf-pasture. **1775** FITHIAN *Journal* II. 144 Mrs. Brown . . . rode with us three miles on our way to the calf-pasture. **1867** *Atlantic Mo.* Jan. 105/1 It'll make a good calf-pastur'. **1897** *Outing* XXX. 245/2 Mounting, we left her far behind as we sped down the Calf Pasture.

Calf-pen. A pen for confining a calf or calves. {1856}

1667 *Rowley* (Mass.) *Rec.* 170 Andrew Headen should have halfe an acer of meddow laid out to him upon that river nere the old calfe pen. **1857** *Harper's Mag.* Sept. 570/1 Our worthy clergyman pictured him [the elder brother] as coming in from the corn-field and stopping to look in at the calf-pen. **1882** *Maine Bd. Agric. Rep.* XXVI. 163 The waste of the dairy, whether sour milk or whey, can be profitably utilized in the piggery or calf pen.

transf. **1851** *Knickerb.* XXXVIII. 184 They have built a kind of calf-pen for smokers, at the foot of Boston Common.

Calf's-head. +The pitcher plant (*Chrysamphora californica*) of California. — **1889** *Cent.* 764/1 Calf's-head [is so called] . . . in allusion to the ventricose hood at the summit of the leaf.

+**Calf-wrestler.** *W.* One who throws calves for branding. — **1888** ROOSEVELT in *Century Mag.* April 861/2 The calf-wrestlers, grimy with blood, dust, and sweat, work like beavers.

+**Calhounery.** (See quot. and cf. next.) — **1858** *Missouri Democrat* in *N.Y. Tribune* 12 July 6/4 Certain crimes unknown to the common law, and which we know by the general title of Calhounery. These crimes are stuffing ballot boxes, giving false returns, and permitting illegal votes to be cast.

+**Calhounism.** [See next.] The political principles of the Calhounites. — **1839** *N.Y. Express* 14 Dec. 2/4 Mr. Rhett has escaped from a Lethonian fog,—or from a denser darkness, the mistifications of Calhounisms. **1878** *N. Amer. Rev.* CXXVII. 98 The wires of Calhounism and Garrisonism were joined and the war began.

+**Calhounite.** A supporter of J. C. Calhoun (Democratic statesman, 1782–1850) and his political principles. Also attrib. — **1824** J. Q. ADAMS *Diary* (1929) 319 A Calhounite transferred to Jackson. **1858** *N.Y. Tribune* 6 Feb. 3 Calhounite Fleeing. . . . With one exception, every member of the Calhoun Constitutional Convention has fled from the Territory. *Ib.* 2 March 3 Frank Marshall, the Calhounite Governor. *a***1882** WHITMAN *Specimen Days*, etc. 261 A resolute and arrogant determination on the part of the extreme slaveholders, the Calhounites, to carry the states rights' portion of the constitutional compact to its farthest verge.

+**Calibogus.** Also **cala-, callibogus.** A mixed drink of rum, spruce beer, and molasses.

[**1758** N. AMES in *Dedham Hist. Reg.* I. 16 Calabogus Club begun.] **1785** GROSE *Dict. Vulgar Tongue, Calibogus*, rum and spruce beer, American beverage. **1792** G. CARTWRIGHT *Jrnl. Labrador* I. Gloss. p. ix, *Callibogus*, a mixture of spruce-beer and rum. **1832** J. M'GREGOR *British America* I. 221 Spirits are frequently mixed with spruce beer, to make the drink named Callibogus. **1841** H. PLAYFAIR *Papers* I. 122 *Callibogus*, a mixed drink, consisting of rum, molasses, and spruce beer.

***Calico,** *n.* Also †**callico, calicho.**

***1.** A cotton cloth, sometimes figured, orig. imported from India.

1644 [see 7]. **1687** SEWALL *Letter-Bk.* I. 45 Half a duz peices of coloured callico. **1716** *Mass. Bay Currency Tracts* 175 It will rather Encourage the working upon *Linen* or upon *Cotton* which with suitable Encouragement, is capable of a vast Improvement here, by making Sheeting, Shirting, & Callicoes. **1794** *Mass. H. S. Coll.* III. 280 Since the peace, calico has become the general fashion of our countrywomen.

+**2.** A cotton cloth printed on one side.

1779 *R.I. Commerce* II. 82 Good handsome purple and white Calicho to make her two Gowns. **1828** WEBSTER s.v., In the United States, calico is printed cotton cloth, having not more than two colors. I have never heard this name given to the unprinted cloth. **1830** S. H. COLLINS *Emigrant's Guide* 176 Calico is called muslin, and prints are called calicoes here. **1856** WHIPPLE *Explor. Ry. Route* I. 112 After an explanation the spirit of trade was restored [with the Mojaves], and calico being established as currency, became as popular as beads had been. **1865** MRS. WHITNEY *Gayworthys* xxxiii, Mrs. Hopeley's adverbs . . . effected a certain point and dazzle by their recurrence, like skilful dashes upon printed calico. **1873** 'MARK TWAIN' & WARNER *Gilded Age* I. 19 Such coats and vests . . . were rather picturesque than otherwise, for they were made of tolerably fanciful patterns of calico. **1882** *Rep. Indian Affairs* 412 Cotton Goods [include] . . . Calico, standard print.

+**3.** A dress or garment made of calico.

1856 M. J. HOLMES *Homestead* 159 Mrs. Welsh, donning a pink calico. **1867** *Nation* 3 Jan. 2/2 Thousands of dollars . . . he has stolen from poor women who really need new calicoes to their backs. **1870** *Scribner's Mo.* I. 61 She was not like the raw-boned women he knew, in their sleazy pink calicoes. **1886** P. STAPLETON *Major's Christmas* 266 A tall woman . . . clad in a brown calico, with white collar and apron.

+**b.** A woman. *slang.*

[**1861** 'A. WARD' in *Vanity Fair* 23 Feb. 95/1 The gals among you, sum of which air as slick pieces of caliker as I ever sot eyes on.] *c***1895** *Dialect Notes* I. 414 'Look at the calico comin!' Parker Co., Tex. **1902** CLAPIN 93 *Calico.* A slang term, especially among students, for a woman, individually as companion to a man, or collectively wherever sex plays a part in social life.

attrib. **1902** CLAPIN 93 'A calico course' [is] a course frequented by women students. **1916** *Dialect Notes* IV. 313 *Calico-side, on the*, 'a-courting.'

+**4.** A member of the Calico Club.

1743 *Boston News-Letter* 14 July 2/2 This is to inform the most worthy and hospitable Society of Calico's . . . that there will be a Meeting of said Society at the Bunch of Grapes on Tuesday. . . . [Signed] Calico.

+**5.** *ellipt.* **a.** (See quot. 1842.)

1842 *Nat. Hist. N.Y., Zoology* IV. 304 The New York Sole, *Achirus mollis*, . . . is common in our waters. . . . They abound on the shallow flats on the Jersey shore opposite New York, where they are called Calico and Coverclip. **1871** DE VERE 384 *Coverclip* is the curious name by which the sole is known in the waters of New York; but even more mysterious is that of *Calico*, which may be heard as frequently.

+**b.** A calico horse or mare.

*a***1861** WINTHROP *Canoe & Saddle* 203 A hundred horses, roans, calicos, . . . blacks, and whites.

+**6.** *Conn.* A destructive disease in tobacco, distinguished by yellow spots on the leaves. (1909– in Dicts.)

***7.** *attrib.* or *adj.* **a.** In sense: Made of calico, as *calico apron, cap, cloak, curtain, dress*, etc.

1644 *Essex Probate Rec.* I. 36, 2 Callico approns lased about. **1720** *Weekly Mercury* 17 Nov. 3/2 Run away . . . a Servant Man named John Corbett . . . little or no hair, a Callicoe Cap. **1787** *Md. Gazette* 1 June 4/3 Very often [she] has on a callico cloak with red flowers. **1842** E. A. HITCHCOCK *Journal* 76 They gave me a good bed (feather) with calico curtains. **1852** MITCHELL *Dream Life* 210 She wears a sky blue calico dress. **1867** A. D. RICHARDSON *Beyond Miss.* 95 A stolid squaw in a bright red calico frock. **1843** *Lowell Offering* III. 92 Cousin Mary would sit and wait for him . . . with her pink calico gown on. **1847** *Knickerb.* XXX. 207 No more pineboard and calico-gown religion would be done by Mrs. Wiggins. **1841** COOPER *Deerslayer* x, The girl . . . was dressed in a calico mantle. **1833** WATSON *Hist. Tales Phila.* 117 In the summer season, men very often wore calico morning-gowns at all times of the day. **1692** BULKELEY *Will & Doom* 206 His finger accidentally catch'd in the constable's old calico neck-cloth. **1756** in *Lett. to Washington* II. 26, 1 Let. Calicoe Patrens. **1711** *Boston News-Letter* 17 Sept. 2 A speckled callico Pettycoat. **1880** *Harper's Mag.* Aug. 354/2 His daughter drapes her calico polonaise by the latest fashion in the *Bazar.* *a***1842** *Ind. Q. Mag. Hist.* XV. 225 They had taken the prisoner's shirt off of him and gave him a calico shirt instead. **1847** ROBB *Squatter Life* 119 In her hand she held a faded calico sun-bonnet. **1891** WILKINS *New Eng. Nun* 83 He wore a calico tier . . . and showed in front his little calico trousers. **1825** NEAL *Bro. Jonathan* I. 142 Four of his brothers . . . each with a flaming calico waistcoat on, gorgeous with many colors. **1879** *Scribner's Mo.* Oct. 822/1 As to interiors, there are all the grades from a mud floor and rough-rock fireplace, . . . to the elaborate structure with muslin ceiling and calico walls, . . . Brussels carpet, piano, and St. Louis furniture. **1873** E. S. PHELPS *Trotty's Wedding* xviii, If I don't make some calico wrappers before long, I shall have to tie myself into a pillow-case.

+**b.** In sense: Of the color or pattern of calico.

1807–8 IRVING *Salmagundi* xviii. 413 They display their singular drollery in bantering nature . . . representing her tricked out in . . . calico rocks. **1835** MARTIN *Descr. Virginia* 27 The carved or calico rock of Kanawha. **1893** *Stand.* 1079/3 Marble is variously distinguished by special names: (1) from its structural features or resemblances; as, bird's-eye marble, black-and-gold m[arble], . . . calico-m[arble].

+**c.** Of animals (esp. horses): Having a skin resembling printed calico; piebald; spotted.

1809 IRVING *Knickerb.* VII. iii, His doughty trumpeter Van Corlear, mounted on a broken winded, wall eyed, calico mare. **1818** *Amer. Mo. Mag.* II. 326/1 Calico Angler—*Lophius calico.* **1878** B. F. TAYLOR *Between Gates* 207 There would be scant room for the calico horses to canter. **1878** I. L. BIRD *Rocky Mts.* 263 On Mr. K. going out, he found, instead of our 'calico' cow, a brindled one. **1891** GARLAND *Main-travelled Roads* (1922) 283 The stranger drove a jaded-looking pair of calico ponies. **1892** BRET HARTE *Col. Starbottle's Client* 250 The man she most despised . . . mounted on a 'calico' mustang . . . dashed among them. **1899** *Ani-*

mal & Plant Lore 40 The bite of the 'calico spider,' a large yellow and black species, is supposed to be deadly poison. Eastern Mass.

+**Calico,** *v. slang.* [CALICO *n.* 3 b.] *intr.* To court the ladies. — **1887** *Lippincott's Mag.* July 102 For it very frequently happens that the best students do a good deal of 'calicoing.' **1915** *Dialect Notes* IV. 181 He's out a *calicoin'* every Sunday. (Va.)

+**Calicoback.** [CALICO *n.* 7 c.] **1.** *East. local.* The turnstone, *Strepsilas interpres.* **2.** The cabbage bug, *Murgantia histrionica.* — **(1) 1872** COUES *Key* 246 *Strepsilas.* . . . Turnstone. Brant Bird. Calico back. **1877** C. HALLOCK *Sportsman's Gaz.* 164 [The name] Calico-back [has reference] to the curiously variegated plumage of the upper parts. **(2) 1890** WEBSTER 204/3 *Calicoback,* . . . an hemipterous insect (*Murgantia histrionica*) which injures the cabbage and other garden plants. **1895** COMSTOCK *Man. Insects* (1923) 145 The Harlequin Cabbage-bug or Calico-back . . . is very destructive to cabbages, radishes, and turnips in the Southern States.

+**Calico ball.** [CALICO *n.* 3.] A ball at which ladies wear calico gowns. — **1859** A. VAN BUREN *Sojourn in South* 192 [They] came home late this evening from the 'calico ball,' given in Yazoo City. In this ball the ladies all wore calico dresses. **1876** WARNER *Gold of Chickaree* 328 It might be a calico ball, you know. **1889** FARMER 116/1 The popular *calico-balls* [are] now as well known here [=England] as across the water [=U.S.], whence they were introduced.

+**Calico bass.** [CALICO *n.* 7 c.] The barfish or strawberry bass, *Pomoxys sparoides.* — **1884** GOODE *Nat. Hist. Aquatic Animals* 406 The Calico Bass, *Pomoxys sparoides.* **1888** — *Amer. Fishes* 69 In Lake Michigan the name 'Bar-fish' is in general use, giving place in Illinois to the name 'Calico Bass.'

Calico-betty. *Obs.* A card game. — **1775** FITHIAN *Journal* II. 126 In our dining room companies at cards, Five & forty, Whist, Alfours, Callico-Betty etc.

+**Calico bird.** [CALICO *n.* 7 c.] =CALICOBACK 1. — **1891** *Cent.* 6543/1.

+**Calico bug.** [Cf. prec.] =CALICOBACK 2. — **1890** WEBSTER 204/3 *Calicoback,* . . . [is] called also calico bug and harlequin cabbage bug.

+**Calico bush.** [CALICO *n.* 7 b.] The mountain laurel, *Kalmia latifolia.* (Cf. CALICO FLOWER and CALICO TREE.)

1814 PURSH *Flora Amer.* I. 297 *Kalmia latifolia,* . . . a shrub from three to eight feet high, very elegant when in flower; called Laurel or in the mountains Callico-bush. **1832** WILLIAMSON *Maine* I. 116 Lamb-kill . . . has been called mountain Laurel, . . . Ivy and Calico Bush. Its wood is dense and hard. **1850** *New Eng. Farmer* II. 109 The Mountain Laurel, or Calico Bush, is a fine evergreen shrub, found in Gloucester. **1869** FULLER *Flower Gatherers* 137 This first one is a *Kalmia latifolia* sometimes called the 'Calico-Bush,' on account of its richly variegated bloom. **1883** HALE *Woods & Timbers N.C.* 20 The beautiful Calico Bush, or Ivy, [is] rarely found but in rocky regions. **1901** MOHR *Plant Life Ala.* 654 Calico Bush, Poison Ivy of the Southern States. . . . The leaves, known as 'poison ivy,' are used medicinally.

+**Calico Club.** (See quotation and cf. CALICO *n.* 4.) — **1761** N. AMES in *Dedham Hist. Reg.* I. 145 White, Hunt, Bliss & Honyman rusticated from College for being in the Calico Club, Comm[encemen]t Night.

+**Calico corn.** [CALICO *n.* 7 b.] (See quotations.) — **1849** EMMONS *Agric. N.Y.* II. 264 Calico corn. Color remarkably variegated. . . . It is cultivated mostly as a curiosity, or for popping. **1892** *Amer. Folk-Lore* V. 105 *Zea mays,* . . . yellow kernels, striped with red; calico corn. Ill.

+**Calico counter.** [CALICO *n.* 1, 2.] A store counter at which calicoes are sold. — **1869** ALCOTT *Little Women* II. 332 She . . . covered herself with confusion by asking for lavender ribbon at the calico counter.

+**Calico flower.** [CALICO *n.* 7 b.] =CALICO BUSH.

1802 J. DRAYTON *S. Carolina* 69 Calico flower, wild ivy, or laurel . . . is a beautiful flowering ever green; whose flowers of red and white, grow in such large clusters together; as to give the whole plant at a small distance, the appearance of having a bit of calico thrown over it. **1814** PURSH *Flora* II. 688 (Index), *Kalmia latifolia;* Calico-flower. **1839** *Monthly Chron.* III. 513 The Kalmias are called by the Americans Calico flowers, a name admirably adapted to express the peculiar appearance of the flower. **1897** SUDWORTH *Arborescent Flora* 315 Mountain Laurel. . . . Common names [include] . . . Calico Bush, . . . Calico-tree (Tenn.), Calico Flower (Tenn.).

+**Calico hop.** =CALICO BALL. — **1875** *Chicago Tribune* 21 Nov. 3/2 The Skinner Club . . . held a calico hop Tuesday.

‖**Calicoist.** *slang.* (See quotation and cf. CALICO *n.* 3 b and *v.*) — **1887** *Lippincott's Mag.* July 102 He soon makes the acquaintance of most of the young ladies in the neighborhood, if he is a 'calicoist' (which implies a greater lover of the fair sex than of his studies).

+**Calico jacket.** =CALICOBACK 1. — **1891** *Cent.* 6543/1.

+**Calico party.** [Cf. CALICO BALL.] A party at which ladies wear calico dresses. — **1855** *Harper's Mag.* X. 554/1 You can not make a Calico Party, in a time of public want, beautiful nor interesting because you give away the gowns afterward. **1855** M. THOMPSON *Doesticks* xvi. 131 Twice I have been invited to 'calico' parties.

Calico printer. [CALICO *n.* 2.] One occupied or engaged in the printing of calicoes. {1706–}

1796 *Boston Directory* 275 Prentiss, Appleton, calico printer, house Cambridge street. **1822** *Ann. 17th Congress* 1 Sess. I. 204 Mr. Rodney presented the petition of Issachar Thorp, and others, Cotton manufacturers and Calico Printers. **1855** PRAY *Mem. J. G. Bennet* 93 They conceived the plan of turning the water power of New England to good account, and by the year 1820 had introduced calico printers from the old country. **1881** *Harper's Mag.* Jan. 187/2 In the year 1797 Archibald Hamilton Rowan . . . established himself as a Calico printer and dyer on the banks of the Brandywine.

Calico printing. [See prec.] The printing of calico. {1753–} Also attrib.

1828 A. ROYALL *Black Book* II. 338 Calico-printing is done here. **1832** CLAY *American System* Speeches (1842) 184 The introduction of calico printing into the United States constitutes an important era in our manufacturing industry. **1842** *Niles' Nat. Reg.* 16 July 311/3 A discovery has lately been made in calico printing which will probably cause a reduction in the price of that article. **1884** KNIGHT *Suppl.* 153/1 *Calico-printing machine,* a machine for printing tissues. It was originally designed for cotton prints or calicoes, but has more lately been applied to a very great variety of fabrics of wool, linen, silk, and other materials.

+**Calico tree.** [CALICO *n.* 7 b.] The calico bush (q.v.).

1810 MICHAUX *Arbres* I. 35 Mountain laurel, . . . Sheep laurel, . . . [or] Callicoe tree, dans quelques parties des Etats méridionaux. **1814** PURSH *Flora* II. 698 (Index), Calico-tree, *Kalmia latifolia.* **1832** BROWNE *Sylva* 191 The Mountain Laurel . . . indifferently bears the names of Mountain Laurel, Laurel, and Calico Tree. **1897** [see CALICO FLOWER].

+**Calico wood.** The silver-bell tree, *Mohrodendron carolinum.* — **1884** SARGENT *Rep. Forests* 106 *Halesia tetraptera.* . . . Rattlebox. Snow-drop Tree. Silver-bell Tree. Calico Wood. **1889** *Cent.* 765/1 *Calico-wood,* the snowdrop-tree . . . of the southern United States, having a soft, compact, light-brown wood. **1897** SUDWORTH *Arborescent Flora* 323 Silverbell-tree. . . . Common names [include] . . . Calicowood (Tex., Ill.).

California. [Name of a state on the Pacific coast.]

1. Used attrib. (esp. with names of products) usually in sense: Of, belonging to, or produced in California.

1840 DANA *Two Years* xiii. 98 [Mexicans] at Monterey . . . have no circulating medium but silver and hides—which the sailors call 'California bank notes.' **1848** *Calif. Claims* (Sen. Rep. 23 Feb.) 8 Do you know whether any considerable number of the American emigrants to Sacramento joined the California battalion? **1878** I. L. BIRD *Rocky Mts.* 25 A luxurious bed . . . with . . . costly California blankets. **1890** *Century Mag.* XLI. 171/2 At this time there was not in California any vehicle except a rude California cart. **1889** *Cent.* 917/2 Effervescent wine, wherever made: as, Swiss champagne; California champagne. **1854** SIMMS *Southward Ho* 439 The sails of a California clipper. **1850** GARRARD *Wah-to-Yah* xx. 247 Lieutenant Talbot, California Battalion, and several men dressed in California costume. **1840** DANA *Two Years* xvi. 146 The dishes contained baked meats, frijoles stewed with peppers and onions, boiled eggs, and California flour baked into a kind of macaroni. **1862** DICKSON *Across Plains* 53 The forty-niner, caught by the lure of California gold. **1879** *Scribner's Mo.* May 21/2 California honey is white and delicate and highly perfumed. **1884** KNIGHT *Suppl.* 154 *California Sight,* a hind sight for a gun; capable . . . of adjustment for ranges of varying distance. **1876** CROFUTT *Trans-Continental Tourist* 53 The best [saddle of the plains] now in use is made with what is known as the 'California Tree.' **1854** BOYNTON & MASON *Journey through Kansas* 29 Having provided ourselves with two horses and a light California wagon, in which we could sleep, if necessary, we crossed the Missouri.

2. Frequent in the specific names of animals, plants, etc. (see quots. and cf. CALIFORNIAN *a.* 2).

A large number of other examples are given in special works, as Sargent *Rep. Forests* (1884), Sudworth *Arborescent Flora* (1897), and the larger dictionaries.

1889 *Cent.* 1176/2 California condor, the large vulture of California, *Cathartes* or *Pseudogryphus californianus.* **1881** *Amer. Naturalist* XV. 364 Along the shores of San Francisco bay . . . one may find . . . the bones of the common California deer. **1862** *Rep. Comm. Patents: Agric.* 479 The California grape (*Vitis Californica* of Bentham) completes the list of species of grape which are known to be natives of North America north of Mexico. **1858** BAIRD *Birds Pacific R.R.* 896 *Podiceps Californicus,* Heermann. The California Grebe. *Ib.* 846 *Larus Californicus,* Lawrence. The California Gull. **1869** *Amer. Naturalist* III. 518 California Hawk. *Buteo Cooperii.* **1884** SARGENT *Rep. Forests* 84 *Heteromeles arbutifolia.* . . . California Holly. **1858** BAIRD *Birds Pacific R.R.* 584 *Cyanocitta Californica,* . . . California Jay. **1882** *Century Mag.* June 227/2 Up through the forest region, to a height of about nine thousand feet above sea-level, there are . . . five or six species of ceanothus, called deer-brush or California lilac. **1873** MILLER *Amongst Modocs* 2 Silver rivers . . . wind among the rocks and mossy roots, with California lilies. **1886** BRET HARTE *Snow-bound* 160 That shabby, overgrown cat you call a California lion. **1892** APGAR *Trees Northern U.S.* 86 *Acer macrophyllum,* Large-leaved or California Maple. **1858** BAIRD *Birds Pacific R.R.* 378 *Sitta Pygmaea,* California nuthatch. **1883** RATHBUN in *U.S. Museum Bulletin 27* 117 The California Prawns (*Pandalus Danæ* and *P. sp.*). **1849** *Congr. Ex. Doc.* 64, 52 The California quail, with a long plume from the top of its head. **1878** *U.S. Nat'l Museum Proc.* I. 69 *Oncorhynchus Quinnat* . . . California Salmon. **1884** GOODE *Nat. Hist. Aquatic Anim.* 569 The California Sardine—*Clupea sagax.* **1883** RATHBUN in *U.S. Museum Bulletin 27* 117 The California Shrimp (*Crangon franciscorum*). **1889** *Secy. of Agric. Rep.* 340 Our correspondents have also referred to it, however, as the 'Leaf-mite,' the 'Spider,' the 'California Spider,' the 'Red-spotted Mite,' and the 'Red Spider.' **1874** COUES *Birds N.W.* 366 This bird is known as the 'California Squirrel Hawk' in some localities, but it is not to be inferred that they often capture the agile arboreal *Sciuri.*

1862 *Rep. Comm. Patents: Agric.* 190 *Fragaria lucida*, California strawberry. **1889** VASEY *Agric. Grasses* 39 *Phalaris intermedia*, . . . California Timothy Grass, . . . grows in South Carolina and the Gulf States, extending to Texas. **1882** *Century Mag.* Aug. 521/2 The vultures follow, represented by two species: the turkey-buzzard and the great California Vulture. **1849** EMMONS *Agric. N.Y.* II. 141 California Wheat . . . has not met with much favor. **1891** *Cent.* 6921/1 The green-headed widgeon [is] also called locally . . . southern widgeon, California widgeon, [etc.].

b. Designating a breed of horses developed in California.

1862 *Rep. Comm. Patents: Agric.* 164 The California horse excels the generality of what we know here as the American horse, in the particular that he excels the latter in being enabled to perform a greater amount of work . . . with less subsistence. **1868** W. E. WATERS *Life among Mormons* 51 The California horse, or the Indian horse, which is a native of the plains or mountains. **1876** CROFUTT *Trans-Continental Tourist* 91 Terms heard on the Plains: . . . 'Bronco,' California or Spanish pony. **1877** J. S. CAMPION *On Frontier* 304 We set out . . . well-mounted on unshod California nags. **1891** *Harper's Mag.* June 4/2 The California horse is small—fourteen and a half to fifteen hands. *a***1918** G. STUART *On Frontier* I. 150 The horses used were California mustangs, noted for their surefootedness, speed, and endurance.

3. *California fashion, plan:* (see quotations).

1840 DANA *Two Years* xiv. 109 The captain made it harder for us, by telling us that it was 'California fashion' to carry two [*sc.* hides] on the head at a time. **1888** J. D. BILLINGS *Hardtack* 301 The hospital tents in the Army of the Potomac were heated, for the most part, by what was called, for some reason, the *California Plan.* This consisted of a pit, dug just outside of the hospital door, two and a half feet deep, from which a trench passed through the tent [etc.].

+**California fever.** [Cf. FEVER.]

1. Laziness. *Obs.*

1840 DANA *Two Years* xxi. 216 Their children are brought up Spaniards, in every respect, and if the 'California fever' (laziness) spares the first generation, it always attacks the second.

2. (See quotation.)

1849 WIERZBICKI *California* 83 The diseases that may be said to be incident to the climate, are tractable, and we had the good fortune to lose not a single case . . . be it diarrhoea . . . or what may be called California fever—a confused type of all fevers.

3. Extreme desire to go to California.

1849 CHARLES WELFORD *MS. Let.* 28 June (J. C. Brown Library), The California Fever is rather up again. **1863** S. C. MASSETT *Drifting About* 103 The California fever raged high. I . . . caught the complaint, and accordingly . . . bid goodby to my friends in New York. **1882** E. K. GODFREY *Nantucket* 207 In 1849 an epidemic appeared here which . . . seemed as if it would depopulate the town. It was called the 'California fever.'

‖**California gridiron.** *jocular.* (See quotation.) — **1850** W. RYAN *Adv. Calif.* I. 129 The 'California Gridiron' now came into active and general use. It is a straight stick cut from a tree, stripped of its bark, and whittled to a sharp point. Several pieces of beef are 'speared' upon this.

+**California hat.** A sombrero or slouch hat. — **1853** FELT *Customs New Eng.* 119 They were at first called sombreros, the Spanish for hats, slouches, and California hats.

+**Californiaized,** *ppl. a.* Rendered Californian in sentiment or character. — **1873** BEADLE *Undevel. West* 156 Most of the business men were 'Californiaized Jews,'—an improved variety of the race.

+**California Jack.** A card-game resembling seven up or all fours. — **1889** *Cent.* 3209/1 *California jack* . . . is esteemed one of the best [games] for two players. **1921** MULFORD *Bar-20 Three* 39 For two hours they sat and played California Jack in plain sight of the street.

Californian, *n.*

1. A native or inhabitant of California of aboriginal or Spanish extraction.

1789 MORSE *Amer. Geog.* 479 The characteristics of the Californians, are stupidity and insensibility. **1840** DANA *Two Years* xii. 93 Add to this the never-failing cloak, and you have the dress of the Californian. **1848** E. BRYANT *California* 453 The religion of the Californians is the Roman Catholic, . . . and they appear to be devotedly attached to the forms of their religion. **1873** ABBOTT *C. Carson* 77 The idea of the Californians generally, as well as other Mexicans, that the Americans are too shrewd for them, is true enough.

+**2.** A resident of California not of aboriginal or Spanish origin.

1840 DANA *Two Years* xxvi. 281 A newly begun settlement, mostly of Yankee Californians, called Yerba Buena, . . . promises well. **1852** *Harper's Mag.* V. 403/2 A few days previous a party of five Californians were all killed by Mexicans near San Fernando. **1852** *Knickerb.* XXXIX. 155 A blushing young man, who was said to be a returned Californian, with lots of gold. **1870** W. F. RAE *Westward by Rail* 333 Nothing so strikingly illustrates the comparative isolation in which the inhabitants of California have lived, as the way in which they speak of themselves, not as Americans, but as Californians. **1893** K. SANBORN *S. Calif.* 18 Some one says that Californians 'irrigate, cultivate, and exaggerate.'

+**3.** One emigrating to California.

1849 AUDUBON *Western Journal* (1906) 69 Whether Don Francisco was taking a midnight walk to see the fate of the 'Californians,' or watching what others might be doing to them, we could never find out.

4. *pl.* 'Generic for gold pieces' (F.).

Californian, *a.*

1. Pertaining or belonging to California.

1784 CUTLER in *Mem. Academy* I. 400 The Spaniards are said to have procured from the Californian Indians, the art of dyeing the best black ever yet known. **1837** IRVING *Bonneville* II. 190 One of the captain's men, who had been in the Californian expedition. **1843** FRÉMONT *Exped.* 129, I have heard it [the river] called by Indian refugees from the Californian settlements the Rio Colorado. **1848** POLK in *Pres. Mess. & P.* IV. 599 By the possession of the safe and capacious harbors on the Californian coast we shall have great advantages. **1856** D. MACLEOD *F. Wood* 58 In September of the next year, 1848, he received . . . news of the first Californian gold. **1870** EMERSON *Society & Solitude* 222 In Californian mountains A hunter bold was he. **1875** *Scribner's Mo.* July 270/1 He will find Corinthian, Gothic, Doric, Byzantine huddled together, . . . an architectural kinship that is essentially Californian. **1889** MUNROE *Golden Days* 2 The steamer was . . . of the newly established Californian line.

+**2.** In specific names: see quots. and cf. CALIFORNIA 2.

1878 *U.S. Nat. Museum Proc.* I. 402 *Thryomanes bewicki*, [var.] *spilurus.* —Californian Bewick's Wren. *Ib.* 398 The Californian Bluebird is a common constant resident of the valleys and foothills. **1833** BONAPARTE *Ornithology* IV. 15 The wings are three feet nine inches long . . . as in the closely related species the Californian Condor. **1850** B. TAYLOR *Eldorado* I. vii. 47 A few miles west of the Pueblo there is a large forest of redwood, or Californian cypress. **1848** BRYANT *California* 304, I tasted here, for the first time, *aguardiênte*, or brandy distilled from the Californian grape. **1874** COUES *Birds N.W.* 634 *Larus californicus*, . . . Californian Gull. **1891** *Cent.* 6409/2 *Toyon*, the Californian holly, *Heteromeles arbutifolia.* **1878** *U.S. Nat. Museum Proc.* I. 413 *Carpodacus frontalis*, [var.] *rhodocolpus*, . . . Californian House Finch, . . . is an abundant constant resident of the valleys and foot-hills of this region [= Central Calif.]. **1894** *Amer. Folk-Lore* VII. 99 *Quercus chrysolepis*, . . . Californian live oak. **1873** *Amer. Naturalist* VII. 327 Next, we have the Californian Mocking-Thrush (*Harporhynchus redivivus*). **1869** *Ib.* III. 477 My inquiries about the Californian Opossum found along the Mexican boundary did not indicate its existence in this valley. **1878** *U.S. Nat. Museum Proc.* I. 404 *Helminthophaga celata*, [var.] *lutescens*, Californian Orange-crowned Warbler, . . . is a common summer resident of Big Trees. **1839** AUDUBON *Ornith. Biog.* V. 152 Californian Partridge, *Perdix Californica*, . . . was discovered in the course of the voyage of *La Perouse.* **1890** *Cent.* 4515/2 The Californian pitcher-plant [is] sometimes called *calf's head.* **1845** FRÉMONT *Exped.* 245 We . . . hurried on; . . . some of the banks being absolutely golden with the Californian poppy, (*eschscholtzia crocea*). **1878** *U.S. Nat. Museum Proc.* I. 413 *Carpodacus purpureus*, [var.] *Californicus*, Californian Purple Finch. **1897** SUDWORTH *Arborescent Flora* 203 *Umbellularia californica.* . . . Californian Sassafras. **1889** FARMER 120 Canary Grass (*Phalaris intermedia*), also known as . . . Gilbert's Relief Grass, and Californian Timothy, . . . is a native of the Southern and some of the Western States. **1878** *U.S. Nat. Museum Proc.* I. 422 *Aphelocoma californica*, Californian Valley Jay, . . . is a common constant resident of the valleys and foot-hills. **1839** AUDUBON *Ornith. Biog.* V. 240 Californian Vulture, *Cathartes Californianus*, . . . inhabits the valleys and plains of the western slope of the continent, and has not been observed to the eastward of the Rocky Mountains. **1891** *Cent.* 6795/3 *Californian vulture*, the Californian condor. **1878** *U.S. Nat. Museum Proc.* I. 403 *Troglodytes hyemalis*, [var.] *pacificus*, Californian Winter Wren. *Ib.* 430 *Melanerpes formicivorus*, Californian Woodpecker.

+**3.** *Californian herring:* a red or hard-dried herring. *C. horse:* see CALIFORNIA 2 b. *C. pancake:* (see quotation).

1873 *Cassell's Mag.* Jan. 245 About the time of Gold discoveries some one applied the term Californian to these. The word was appropriate and Californian such highly-coloured herrings are called to this day. — **1869** BREWER *Rocky Mt. Lett.* 18 Hoffman rode beside me, each of us with a barometer, as of old, and as if to complete the illusion, he rode a Californian horse. — **1851** *Birmingham & Midl. Gard. Mag.* Oct. 176 He did recommend Mr. Cole to produce a Californian pancake, by tying the plant to a hurdle.

+**California prayer book.** *jocular.* A deck of cards. — **1852** W. KELLEY *Diggings of Calif.* 47 But by far the greater number were engaged in the study of the 'California prayer-book.'

+**California quail.** The valley quail (*Lophortyx californicus*) of California. — **1846** in Emory *Military Reconn.* 575 The crane, the duck, the plover, the deer, and the California quail. The latter differs from the quail of the United States. **1858** BAIRD *Birds Pacific R.R.* 644 *Lophortyx Californicus*, California Quail. . . . This species supplies in western California and Oregon the place of the Bob White of the eastern States. **1871** *Kansas Laws* 281 It shall be unlawful for any person or persons to net, entrap, shoot, or in any manner capture or kill a bird known as the California quail. **1902** *Harper's Mag.* Feb. 488 She saw thirteen as fine, lusty California quail as the fondest of mothers ever looked upon.

+**California saddle.** An elaborate type of saddle favored in California. (Cf. *Mexican saddle.*) — **1849** WIERZBICKI *California* 69 The materials entering into the construction and trimming of a California saddle, are as few and as simple as possible. *a***1861** WINTHROP *J. Brent* 222 The heavy California saddle, with its macheers and roll of blankets, fell to the ground. **1871** *Scribner's Mo.* II. 2 Each man was supplied with a strong horse, well equipped with California saddle, bridle, and cantinas.

+**California toothpick.** [Cf. ARKANSAS TOOTHPICK.] A bowie knife. — **1856** SIMMS *Eutaw* xiii. 142 His . . . hunter-knife . . . [was] a most formidable weapon only inferior in size and weight to the modern 'California toothpick.'

+**California widow.** *colloq.* A married woman whose husband deserts her for an extended period. — *c*1873 DE VERE *MS. Notes* 481 *Grass widows.* . . . Also Cal. widow. **1877** BARTLETT 261 'California widow' . . . came into use during the rush to California, 1850 to 1860, when the new-found treasures of that country separated so many husbands from their wives.

+**Caliker,** dialect form of CALICO. — **1850** LEWIS *La. Swamp Dr.* 51 Thar war Mam, fust on one side, then on t'other, her new caliker swelled up round her like a bear with the dropsy. **1862** *N.Y. Tribune* 21 March, The commonest ten years' antiquated 'caliker' (their [the Virginians'] own pronunciation) is brisk at 40 cents per yard—other dry goods in proportion. **1884** WILKINS in *Harper's Mag.* July 302/1 Thar's Mis' Bliss's pieces in the brown kaliker bag.

+**Calinda.** *S.* (See quot. 1891.) — **1880** CABLE *Grandissimes* 121 There our lately met *marchande* . . . led the ancient Calinda dance. **1886** *Century Mag.* Feb. 527 The true Calinda was bad enough. . . . Its song was always a grossly personal satirical ballad. . . . To dance it publicly is not allowed this side the West Indies. **1891** *Amer. Folk-Lore* IV. 70 *Calinda* . . . is the name of a song or dance still remembered in Louisiana, where it has been practiced by negroes. **1894** CHOPIN *Bayou Folk* 286 Le beau Mézor . . . was sold away into Georgia, . . . where he would no longer hear his Creole tongue spoken, nor dance calinda.

Calipash. {1689-} Also **callipash, calapash.** The fatty, gelatinous, greenish substance belonging to the upper shield of the turtle. — **1800** BOUCHER *Glossary* p. xlix, *Calibash.* . . . It is from this gourd, that the back of a turtle, the shell of which, when emptied, forms a bowl, has been called the calapash; as the belly shell, or part, is in like manner called the calipee; all of them Indian terms. **1805** *Independent Chronicle* 26 Dec. 3/1 Callipee and callipash, clams and oysters, . . . custards, and other sweat meats. **1846** WORCESTER 98/2 *Callipash,* . . . (Cookery) the part of a turtle which forms the upper shield of the animal. *W. Ency.*

Calipee. Also †**callipee, callope.** The light-yellow gelatinous substance next to the lower shell of the turtle. {1657-} — **1682** T. ASH *Carolina* 29 The Belly, which they call the Callope of the Turtle, . . . is an excellent Dish. **1800-1805** [see prec.]. **1846** WORCESTER 98/2 *Callipee,* . . . (Cookery) a part of a turtle which belongs to the lower shield. *W. Ency.*

+**Calisthenium.** [E. *calisthenics* (*a*1846 in Worc.), *callisthenics* {1847-}] A place for exercising in calisthenics. — **1871** *Scribner's Mo.* II. 344 Besides the College [at Vassar] we find the Calisthenium. **1878** *Harper's Mag.* April 677/1 The Normal College of New York City . . . contains . . . a library, a calisthenium, two drying-rooms. **1883** *N.Y. Tribune* 25 Dec., After the play the calisthenium was thrown open and the girls danced until supper-time.

***Calk,** *n.*[1] Also †**caulk.**

+**1.** An iron device with sharp points worn on the heel or sole of a boot or shoe to prevent slipping.

[**1805** *Naval Chron.* XIII. 113 In Canada it is customary during the winter season . . . to wear on the feet a sort of patten, called *caulks.*] **1874** KNIGHT 430/1 The calk . . . attached to a boot consists of a plate with spurs, which project a little below the heel. **1889** *Cent.* 766/1 *Calk,* . . . worn . . . to prevent slipping on the ice or to make it [=the shoe] wear longer: also worn by lumbermen in the woods, and especially on the drive.

***2.** A calkin. (Cf. CORK *n.*)

1828 WEBSTER, *Calk,* . . . in New-England, a sharp pointed piece of iron on a shoe for a horse . . . used to prevent the animal from slipping. **1858** *Rep. Comm. Patents* (1859) I. 525 The described horse shoe, the calks and shoe being of one piece of metal, formed by drawing down the shoe.

+**Calk,** *n.*[2] *slang.* **1.** (See quotation.) **2.** *W.* A person; a man. — **(1) 1851** HALL *College Words* 85 *Cork* [or] *Calk.* In some of the Southern Colleges, this word, with a derived meaning, signifies a ***complete stopper.*** Used in the sense of an entire failure in reciting. — **(2) 1865** 'MARK TWAIN' *Sketches* (1926) 193 Such is the touching story of Uncle Lige. It may not be quite so sick as Dan's, but there is every bit as much reasonable material in it for a big calk like either of us to cry over.

Calk, *v.* Also **caulk, cawk.** {1624-} *tr.* To provide (a horse or ox) with shoes having calks. Cf. CORK *v.*

1752 J. MACSPARRAN *Amer. Dissected* 39 With a Horse well caulk'd and frosted, 'tis fine Travelling for one that can sometimes 'light and run, to bring the Blood into his feet. **1828** WEBSTER, *Calk,* . . . in some parts of America, to set upon a horse or ox shoes armed with sharp points of iron, to prevent their slipping on ice. **1859** ELWYN *Glossary* 92 To have one's horses cawked, is the common expression in New England.

***Calker, Caulker.** One who calks; esp. one whose occupation is calking vessels.

1653 *Suffolk Deeds* I. 298 Indenture . . . betweene George Dell of Boston Marriner . . . and Thomas Rider of the same shipp Caulker. **1716** HEMPSTEAD *Diary* 56, I went to Preston to get a Caulker. **1762** *Essex Inst. Coll.* XLVIII. 357 A Negro Man named Norton Minors, is by Trade a Caulker and Ship Carpenter. **1817** *Ann. 14th Congress* 2 Sess. 780 Before she is launched, a different set of men, the caulkers, perform their parts. **1822** *Ann. 17th Congress* 1 Sess. I. 279 Armorers, reemers, Caulkers, and other laborers. **1889** BRAYLEY *Boston Fire Dept.* 368 He is a calker by trade.

***Call,** *n.*

1. An invitation to a minister to become the pastor of a church. {1666-}

***a*1649** WINTHROP *Hist.* II. 22 They gave him [=Rev. J. Burr] a call to office, which he deferring to accept [etc.]. **1717** F. Endicott *Stoughton & Canton Rec.* (1896) 4 It was put to vote whether the Congregation in this precinct would renew there Call to the revrend mr Josip Morse. **1771** CUTLER in *Life & Corr.* I. 29, I refused to comply with the request, which was that I should preach six more Sabbaths in order to have a call. **1830** J. FERGUSON *Memoir of Samuel Hopkins* 33 As their call [*i.e.*, from a congregation] was not unanimous, he declined accepting it. **1883** *Harper's Mag.* Sept. 623/1 He'll wait a long time for a call in our Synod if they suspect he's an abolitionist.

2. An inward prompting or urge. {1650-}

1704 S. KNIGHT *Journal* 19 The Reflections, as in the afternoon of the day that my Call was very Questionable, w[hi]ch till then I had not so prudently as I ought considered. **1856** GOODRICH *Recoll.* I. 38 A man who had a call for plowing, mowing, carting manure, &c., in summer, and for teaching school in the winter. **1888** *Critic* 14 April 181/1 Perhaps no one has any right to expect to make a success of authorship unless he has a 'call.' **1910** C. HARRIS *Eve's Husband* 239 He gets a profound 'call' to turn the country upside down.

3. A need, right, occasion. *colloq.* {*a*1674-}

1810 ADAMS *Lect. on Rhetoric* I. 254 He has no call to act upon the will of his hearers. **1861** LOWELL *Biglow P.* II. i. 27 A Southuner'd allow I'd . . . Some call to shake. **1885** 'CRADDOCK' *Prophet* 7, I hev no call ter spen' words 'bout sech ez that. **1891** WILKINS *New Eng. Nun* 194 There ain't no call for you to say sech things as that. **1909** WASON *Happy Hawkins* 11, I didn't have much call to go anywhere.

4. A calling device used by hunters for decoying wild turkeys; a yelper. {1654-}

1846 THORPE *Myst. Backwoods* 62 The implements of the turkey-hunter are few and simple; the 'call,' generally made of the large bone of the turkey's wing, and a sure rifle complete the list. **1891** *Cent.* 7017/3 A whistle or call used by sportsmen to imitate the cry of the wild turkey hen.

+**b.** A horn or buglelike contrivance for decoying moose.

1860 *Harper's Mag.* March 442/1 'Tom, can you call moose?' . . . Stripping a sheet of bark from a birch-tree, Jenks quickly fashions a 'call,' and . . . raises the bark to his lips.

+**5.** *Poker.* A demand that the hand of a player or players be shown.

1850 LEWIS *La. Swamp Dr.* 123 A gambler who has staked his whole pile, and found at the call that he has been bluffing up against a greenhorn with 'three white aces.' **1887** *Courier-Journal* 24 Jan. 2/4 Then they [the poker players] put up their railway shares in good-sized blocks, until when the call was made a controlling interest in each railroad was represented in the pot.

fig. **1884** *Century Mag.* Dec. 194 Gentlemen, let Judge Neversweat politely inform you, on the first call of his hand, that this yar camp aint lost no goat.

6. *Stock exchange.* The right to demand a certain amount of stock, grain, etc., at a stipulated time or price. {*a*1860-}

1857 *Hunt's Merchants' Mag.* XXXVII. 136 Curb-stone brokers [in Wall-street] . . . are particularly fond of operating in puts and calls. **1870** MEDBERY *Men Wall St.* 100 The feature of this speculation was the employment of calls instead of buyer's options. **1885** *Harper's Mag.* Nov. 844/1 A 'call' is the privilege of calling for or buying a certain stock at a specified price within a given time. **1886** *Ib.* July 213/1 Calls may also be made of one cent per bushel above or below current quotation. **1900** [see CALL *v.* 7].

+**7.** (See quotation.)

1864 WEBSTER 186/2 *Call,* . . . [in] Land Law, an object, course, distance, or other matter of description in a survey or grant requiring or calling for a corresponding object, &c., on the land.

8. *Phrases.* +*On* (*upon*) *call,* on demand; immediately available.

1870 *Nation* 10 Feb. 86/1 These [three per cent.] certificates, in reality, simply represent money borrowed by the Government of the banks, *on call,* that is, money that the Treasury might be called upon to repay at a moment's notice. **1889** 'MARK TWAIN' *Conn. Yankee* xlii. 532 He bought about twice as much more [stock], deliverable upon call.

b. *To have the call,* to be the favorite; to have the advantage. {1840-}

***a*1846** *Quarter Race Ky.*, etc. 117 As the colt was known to be a sharp one, and his owner 'one of the b'hoys' for a quarter race, . . . he had the call in the betting at six to four. **1868** WOODRUFF *Trotting Horse* 266 The attendance at the course was large, and the mare had a trifle the call at the betting. **1887** *Courier-Journal* 5 May 5/2 In the last, a selling race at six furlongs, Brambleton had the call in the betting. **1912** RAINE *Brand Blotters* 267 Boone nodded sulkily. 'I said you had the call, didn't I?'

***Call,** *v.*

***1.** *tr.* To give an official invitation to the pastorate of a church.

1846 LYELL *Second Visit* (1849) II. 25 The clergyman had been recently 'called' to a larger church. **1888** *Brooklyn Daily Eagle,* It is quite likely that the First Baptist Church in Pierrepont Street will call a pastor within the next two months.

transf. **1891** O'BEIRNE *Leaders Ind. Territory* 135 In 1890 he was called to the senate, which office he now holds.

2. +**a.** To decoy (turkeys) by imitating their cry.

1846 THORPE *Myst. Backwoods* 63, I hunted the gobbler always in the same 'range,' . . . and he got so, at last, that when I 'called,' he would run from me. **1877** JOHNSON *Anderson Co., Kansas* 152 Two neighbors . . . were hunting turkeys in the timber on the creek in the early morning, neither knowing that the other was near him, each calling turkeys and crawling through the brush, expecting to see his game.

+**b.** To decoy (moose) by imitating their call.

1860 [see CALL *n.* 4 b.] **1893** ROOSEVELT *Wilderness Hunter* 218 In the Northeast a favorite method of hunting the moose is by 'calling' the bulls in the rutting season, . . . the caller imitating their cries through a birch-bark trumpet.

+**3.** (See quotation.)

1864 WEBSTER 186/1 *Call*, . . . to require, as objects, courses, or distances, to answer or correspond with a description in a survey, or grant, of land.

+**4.** *Poker.* To ask for a show of hands after putting into the pool a sum equal to the largest bet made by any preceding player. Also *intr.*

1844 J. COWELL *Thirty Years* 94 The young lawyer . . . looked at the money staked, and then his hand again, and lingeringly put his wallet on the table and called. **1846** *Spirit of Times* 18 April 88/3 'I have bet twenty thousand,' said the young man, firmly, 'you can call it or not, just as you choose.' **1872** 'MARK TWAIN' *Roughing It* xlvii, I reckon I can't call that hand. **1889** — *Conn. Yankee* xxxix. 507 Forty-nine times out of fifty nobody dares to 'call.' **1921** MULFORD *Bar-20 Three* vii. 87 He pushed the money out onto the table. 'I calls,' he grunted.

fig. **1898** PAGE *Red Rock* 493 'Called your hand, rather, didn't he?'

+**b.** With personal object.

1845 SOL. SMITH *Theatrical Apprent.* 150, I go it—and—call you. **1887** S. CUMBERLAND *Queen's Highway* 284 Thinking as he staked the equivalent what a rich haul I should have when he did venture to call me.

fig. **1876** MILLER *First Families* 94 Even the head man of the company . . . jumped a first-class poker game . . . to come in and weigh out dust enough to 'call' the Parson and Sandy. **1896** *Congress. Rec.* 23 May 5634/1 Mr. Milliken. . . . I do not know how great the amount of our saving might be, if . . . [Mr. Cummings] should consult all of his . . . colleagues on this floor. Mr. Cannon. . . . Do you think we had better 'call' him?

+**5.** *Baseball.* Officially: **a.** To start a ball game. **b.** To declare a game ended. **c.** To pronounce a pitched ball a 'strike' or a 'ball.' **d.** To rule that a runner is 'out' or 'safe.' **e.** To decide a close play for or against one side. **f.** To pronounce a struck ball a 'fair hit' or a 'foul.' **g.** To determine when a pitcher's motions constitute a balk.

(**a**) **1875** *Chicago Tribune* 6 July 5/1 The game . . . was called at 3 o'clock. **1897** *Boston Journal* 8 June 4/5 Just before yesterday's game was called a man . . . stepped up to Capt. Anson. (**b**) **1868** CHADWICK *Base Ball* 58 When the umpire 'calls' a game, it shall end. **1880** N. BROOKS *Fairport Nine* ii. 32 But the umpire . . . called the game, which was accordingly postponed until next day. (**c**) **1868** CHADWICK *Base Ball* 39 The umpire is empowered to call balls on the pitcher every time a ball is so bowled. **1888** *Outing* May 119/1 Mills called a ball before it had passed the home-plate, and on this called ball being hit a base was run. **1912** MATHEWSON *Pitching* 63 Two strikes were gathered on Cooley, one at which he swung and the other called. *Ib.* 178 He called more bad ones on me that day than he ever had in his life before. (**d**) **1912** MATHEWSON *Pitching* 194 The Chicago team at last won the game when Clarke was called out at third base on a close play, late in the contest. (**e**) **1912** MATHEWSON *Pitching* 174 Most clubs try to keep an umpire from feeling hostile toward the team because . . . he is likely to call a close one against his enemies, not intending to be dishonest. (**f–g**) **1868** CHADWICK *Base Ball* 61 [The umpire] must call foul balls and balks without being asked.

+**6.** To name, by way of direction, the figures in a dance.

1873 BEADLE *Undevel. West* 455 They never have the set 'called,' as in the States. **1880** *Harper's Mag.* March 544/2, I can call de dances bully—you bet! **1886** *Outing* IX. 232/2 In accordance with frontier custom the dances were *called*, and not twice alike. **1898** CANFIELD *Maid of Frontier* 165 The band, in addition to furnishing the music, called the figures.

7. *Stock exchange.* To demand delivery at a stipulated time and price.

1900 NELSON *ABC Wall St.* 54 You could have 'called' 100 Third Avenue at 112, and received the difference between the price of your 'call' and the market price, 112.

8. *Phrases.* +**a.** *To call one's* (or *the*) *bluff*, to accept one's challenge or dare; to demand a 'showdown.' Also with personal object. (Cf. sense 4 and 4 b.) *colloq.*

1876 BRET HARTE *Two Men of Sandy Bar* 17 But suppose that he sees that little bluff, and calls ye. **1893** *Congress Rec.* 13 Oct. 2493/1 The Republican Senate saw their bluff, called them, and made them show down. **1896** *Congress. Rec.* 26 March 3248 Where shall we be when the bluff is called? **1920** MULFORD *J. Nelson* 62 'What you think yo're doin'?' he demanded. 'Callin' yore bluff.' **1923** B. M. BOWER *Parowan Bonanza* 70 We'll call you on that breakfast bluff.

+**b.** *To call to the book*, to take to task; to call to account.

1867 *Congress. Globe* 16 March 138/2 We are calling to the book men who have been in arms against us.

9. With adverbs. **a.** *To call down*, +to reprimand severely; to take issue with. *colloq.*

1897 *Chicago Tribune* 25 July 15/2 Mrs. Lease recently called down Queen Victoria. **1901** MCCUTCHEON *Graustark* 52, I intended to call him down, as you Americans say. *a***1906** 'O. HENRY' *Trimmed Lamp*, etc. 77, I didn't think I'd have to call you down. **1923** R. HERRICK *Lilla* 74 She boxed this boy's ears when he was impudent, 'called down' a snippy upper class girl, [etc.].

b. *To call in*, to collect debts, fines, etc. {1701, 1713}

1666 *Conn. Public Rec.* II. 37 This Court doth impower Capt. Talcot and Lt. John Allyn to call in John Scots fine. **1898** PAGE *Red Rock* 223, I advise calling in all the debts at once.

c. *To call off*, + to count; to announce. Cf. CALL *v.* 6.

1840 COOPER *Pathfinder* xii, Name them? It is no easy matter to call off the stars, for the simple reason that they are so numerous. **1879** *Harper's Mag.* Oct. 799/1 Recently one of these heel-and-toe affairs was held in Lawrence, Kansas, and . . . the colored fiddler 'called off' the cotillion. **1903** K. D. WIGGIN *Rebecca* 24 He played the violin, and 'called off' at dances.

d. *To call out.* +*a.* To single out an actor or actress for special applause. +*b.* To summon members of a labor union to strike. +*c.* (See quotation.)

(*a*) **1870** O. LOGAN *Before Footlights* 306 It has been the custom when an actor or actress was 'called out' as the phrase is, that they should come out before the curtains. (*b*) **1895** ROBINSON *Men Born Equal* 284 Ugly threats, moreover, were being made by the strikers that the members of other labor organizations would be 'called out.' (*c*) **1916** *Dialect Notes* IV. 268 *Call out*, . . . at a carnival ball, when one is masked, to invite (a lady) to dance. (New Orleans.)

Calla. [mod. L. (Linnæus).]

+**1.** The water arum, *Calla palustris.*

1834 MRS. SIGOURNEY *Poems* 95 Magnificent Calla, with mantle like milk. **1847** WOOD *Botany* 520 *C. Palustris.* Northern Calla. **1869** BRACE *New West* 18 The callas and exquisite water-flowers in the pools. **1883** *Harper's Mag.* March 606/2 [In Florida] the most lovely flora was brought to view . . . lilies, callas, and other water-plants.

2. The calla lily, *Zantedeschia aethiopica.*

1845 *Lowell Offering* V. 257 Her callow [is] in a broken pitcher, and this great thing she says is her 'chrystianthum.' **1883** 'MARK TWAIN' *Life on Miss.* ix. 583 Callas are blooming out-of-doors, and the people are complaining of the warm weather.

attrib. **1893** K. SANBORN *S. California* 67, I remember, in contrast, solitary calla plants that I have nursed with care all winter in hopes of one blossom for Easter.

3. *Ethiopian calla* =2. {1829–}

1847 WOOD *Botany* 520 *Calla Æthiopica*, Ethiopian Calla. . . . A magnificent plant from Cape Good Hope, often met with in green-houses and parlors. **1863** GRAY *Botany* p. lxxx, Egyptian or Æthiopian Calla, . . . [is] largely cultivated for its ample sagittate green leaves and showy white one-leaved spathe.

+**4.** *Wild calla* (see quotation).

1885 *Outing* VII. 178/2 An interesting plant is the wild calla (*Peltandra sagittifolia*), growing in cold, wet places.

+**Calla lily.**

1. =CALLA 2.

1872 'MARK TWAIN' *Roughing It* lvi. 411 Calla lilies, all sorts of geraniums, passion flowers, moss roses—I do not know the names of a tenth part of them. **1884** ROE *Nature's Story* 68 Nor should moisture ever stand under the pots, unless the plants are semi-aquatic, like this calla-lily. **1893** K. SANBORN *S. California* 67, I am glad that I have lived to see hedges of heliotrope, of geraniums and calla-lilies. **1899** M. GOING *Flowers* 117 The lily's tribe is described by the ponderous term 'Monocotyledons,' and includes palms, rushes, sedges, grasses, the Calla-lily and her kin.

2. *Wild calla lily* (see quotation and cf. CALLA 4).

1901 MOHR *Plant Life Ala.* 425 *Peltandra sagittifolia* . . . White Arrow-Arum, Wild Calla Lily. . . . North Carolina to Florida, along the Gulf coast to Mississippi.

+**Callalou.** [Cf. W. Ind. *calalou* soup; Costa Rican *calalú* poke; etc. See W. A. Read *La. French*, 119 f.] (See quotation.) — **1892** HARRIS *On the Plantation* 122 Then there was callalou—a mixture of collards, poke salad, and turnip greens.

+**Calla-, Callemink.** *dial.* [Du. *kalamink.*] =CALAMANCO. — **1795** B. DEARBORN *Columbian Grammar* 134 Improprieties, commonly called Vulgarisms, [include] . . . Callemink for Calamanco. **1901** JEWETT *Tory Lover* xii. 106, I dove into my pockets an' come upon this old piece o' calamink I'd wrapped up some 'baccy in.

+**Callate, Cal'late,** dialect reduction of CALCULATE *v.*

1846 LOWELL *Biglow P.* I. i. 13 The sarjunt . . . cal'lated to hook him in, but Hosy woodn't take none o' his sarse. **1851** *Knickerb.* XXXVIII.

372 We call it 'meetin'-seed,' 'cause we cal'late it [=caraway-seed] keeps us awake in meetin'. **1865** 'MARK TWAIN' *Sk., Jumping Frog,* He ketched a frog one day and . . . said he cal'lated to educate him. **1870** 'O. OPTIC' *Field & Forest* 43, I cal'late they mean mischief. **1884** JEWETT *Country Doctor* ii. 14, I cal'lated I could make up a good lively blaze. **1898** WESTCOTT *D. Harum* 191, I was cal'latin' to rob the old lady. **1911** LINCOLN *Cap'n Warren's Wards* 57 Abie seemed to cal'late that [etc.].

+**Call box.** A post-office box from which mail can be withdrawn only by the postmaster or his assistant. — **1887** *Courier-Journal* 23 Jan. 12/5 The post-office there [Corinth, Miss.] is not provided with lock-boxes, but uses what are known as call-boxes, with ordinary glass fronts. **1900** E. DIX *Deacon Bradbury* 40 The plain glass of the call-boxes.

Callboy.

1. *Theatr.* A boy who notifies actors to be ready to go on stage. {1794-}

1844 J. COWELL *Thirty Years* 65 Bob Maywood, on his benefit night, . . . mistaking the noise made by the call-boy . . . for the commencement of the performance. **1863** MASSETT *Drifting About* 51, I proceeded to the 'Greenroom' awaiting the dread word of the 'call boy.' **1887** *Courier-Journal* 13 Feb. 16/4 The prompter and the call-boy have carefully searched the manuscripts and have 'taken out' their 'plots.'

2. A boy who answers a call bell; a bellboy. {1863-}

1871 HOWELLS *Wedding Journey* v. 100 Abjectly I take my key, and creep off up-stairs after the call-boy. **1880** 'MARK TWAIN' *Tramp Abroad* II. App. A. 253 So the landlord-apprentice serves as call-boy; then as under-waiter.

‖**Call court.** *Obs.* A 'called' or summoned court. — **1779** in L. Summers *Ann. S.W. Virginia* (1929) 730 To the Sheriff for summoning a Call Court on Robert Carr.

Called, *ppl. a.*

+**1.** Of meetings: Specially summoned.

1849 CHAMBERLAIN *Ind. Gazetteer* 52 At a called meeting of the Board, . . . the Central Medical College of Indiana was made a part of the University. **1857** in Johnson *Anderson Co., Kansas* (1877) 78 The board of county commissioners met this 28th day of November, 1857 . . . (a called meeting). **1889** *Cent.* 766/2 *Called session,* a special session of a legislative body summoned by the executive.

+**2.** In baseball: Applied to a pitched ball ruled by the umpire a 'ball' or a 'strike.'

1868 CHADWICK *Base Ball* 129 Smith . . . getting round to his third on passed balls, came in on the three called balls. **1887** *Outing* January 406/1 The batsman is now decided out when the ball after the third called strike is not struck at or hit. **1887** *Courier-Journal* 26 May 2/6 He . . . held the big batter of the Brooklyn Club down to five small hits, two of which were bases on called balls.

***Caller.** +**a.** A head waiter. **b.** One who calls offers of sale in the produce exchange; an auctioneer. **c.** (See quotation.) **d.** One who calls moose with a moosecall. **e.** *Railroad.* One who calls men to report for work. **f.** An official who announces the result of a vote in the legislature.

(a) 1842 *Knickerb.* XX. 6 The head-waiter . . . or 'Caller' as he was designated. **(b) 1886** *Harper's Mag.* LXXIII. 213/1 William L. Eichell, caller of grain, presides. **(c) 1893** M. PHILIPS *Making of a Newspaper* 212 No reporter . . . can watch a field of six or more horses through a race, and then from memory write a correct account of it. . . . He does not trust his memory, but summons to his aid an assistant, who is known as a 'caller.' **(d) 1893** [see CALL *v.* 2 b]. **(e) 1898** HAMBLEN *Gen. Manager's Story* 72 When it became known that Joe's fireman was sick, all the others made it a point to be away from home when the caller made his rounds with orders to call the first man he found off duty. **(f) 1911** *Okla. Session Laws* 3 Legisl. 227 When callers announce a vote, the enumerators shall call the numbers aloud, keeping check on each other.

Caller-out. [CALL *v.* 6.] +One who announces the changes in steps in a dance. — **1882** *Century Mag.* Oct. 878/2 The 'caller-out,' though of less importance than the fiddler, is second to no other. He not only calls out the figures, but explains them at length to the ignorant, sometimes accompanying them through the performance.

Calling. Social visiting.

1861 NEWELL *Orpheus C. Kerr* I. 172 This New-Year's-calls business is not a sensible calling, and simply amounts to a caravan of monkeys attending a menagerie of trained crinoline. **1880** *Harper's Mag.* March 621/1 The old Dutch custom of universal calling, which was long peculiar to New York, formerly made the day [=New Year's Day] especially a New York day.

attrib. **1865** STOWE *House & Home P.* 37 In our bedroom . . . they sit all day long, except at calling-hours, and then Sophie dresses herself and comes down. **1877** PHELPS *Story of Avis* 397 Lest society strike him from her calling-list. **1898** DUNBAR *Folks from Dixie* 239 The next day being Sunday, and universal calling-day in Miltonville, Eli Thompson's house . . . was filled with guests. **1898** ATHERTON *Californians* 187 A calling-frock of fawn-coloured camel's hair and silk. **1905** PHILLIPS *Social Secretary* 39 There's the Calling-Book. Already I've got down more than a thousand names. The obscurer the women are . . . the greater the necessity for keeping the calling account straight. **1905** *N.Y. Times* 7 Feb. 5 We'll execute calling cards to your order in conformity with the very latest requirements of fashion.

+**Calliope.** [Name of ninth Greek muse.] A harsh-sounding musical instrument consisting of a series of steam whistles operated by a keyboard; a steam organ.

'A musical instrument of recent invention' (Worc. '60).

1858 *Harper's Mag.* Dec. 138/1 Some time in the spring of '57 the steamer *St. Nicholas* 'opened' in this [Southern] city with a caliope — the first one ever heard in these parts. **1866** RICHARDSON *Secret Service* 98 Our calliope saluted her with lively music. **1888** F. M. A. ROE *Army Lett.* 366, I heard the shrill notes of a calliope that reminded me that Forepaugh's circus was to be in town that day. **1899** TARKINGTON *Gentl. Indiana* 109 Last of all came the tooting calliope, followed by swarms of boys. **1909** A. C. RICE *Mr. Opp* 97 The last show boat that was here had a calliope. **1923** WATTS *L. Nichols* 164 The excursion-steamer standing upchannel for Lowery's Beach with the calliope blatantly discoursing 'The Holy City.'

+**Calliope hummingbird.** A hummingbird which inhabits the western states. — **1878** *U.S. Nat. Museum Proc.* I. 426 *Stellula calliope.* —Calliope Humming-bird.

+**Callithump,** *n.* [See CALLITHUMPIAN *n.*, quot. *a*1870.] A noisy band of miscellaneous instruments, as horns, tin pans, etc. — **1856** HALL *College Words* (ed. 2) 342 The band [=Pandowdy, noise-making band of Bowdoin] corresponds to the *Calliathump* [*sic*] of Yale. **1871** DE VERE 589 *Callithump* . . . represents the French *charivari,* the German *Katzenmusik.*

+**Callithump,** *v.* **1.** *intr.* 'To caterwaul; to produce discordant "musical" sounds by means of instruments, either incongruous in themselves or in conjunction—such as tin kettles, bells, rattles, etc.' (F.). **2.** *tr.* 'To treat to a callithumpian concert' (*Cent. Suppl.*).

+**Callithumpian,** *a.* and *n.* Also **callia-, cally-, cali-, calthumpian.** [See CALLITHUMP *n.*]

1. *adj.* Designating a band of discordant instruments (see first quotation).

1848 BARTLETT 61 *Callithumpians.* It is a common practice in New York, as well as other parts of the country, on New Year's eve, for persons to assemble with tin horns, bells, rattles, and similar instruments, and parade the streets making all the noise and discord possible. This party is called the *Callithumpians* or the *Callithumpian Band.* **1863** *Young Parson* 93 You know they get out what they calls a Callythumpian band; some people calls it an ox band. They have tin horns, and buckets, and cow-bells, and what's worse, a horse-fiddle. **1886** GREELY *3 Yrs. Arctic Service* I. 177 A concert from a well-organized calthumpian band, in which the tinware of the expedition played an important part. **1904** *N.Y. Times* 25 May 1 The calithumpian band had kept up the music without interruption all night.

b. Of or pertaining to such a band.

1865 *Atlantic Mo.* XV. 300 There was never a tutor's windows to be broken in, or a callithumpian frolic, (which were in vogue in those days). **1886** *Harper's Mag.* July 213/2 The call [on the exchange] lasts ten or fifteen minutes, and occasionally has the accompaniment of callithumpian discord. **1889** *Cent.* 931/3 *Charivari.* . . . Serenades of this sort . . . are still occasionally heard in the United States, where they are also known as callithumpian concerts. *a***1897** *Phil. Hartmann & the Boys* (B. & L.), Hartmann's neighbours thought it would be a bright thing to give him a calliathumpian serenade.

2. *n.* A member of a callithumpian band.

1848 [see sense 1]. *a***1870** CHIPMAN *Notes on Bartlett* 65 Callithumpians, an allusion to *Calliope* &, as well, to *thumping.* **1881** *Reinbeck* (Iowa) *Times* 30 June 3/1 All who wish to join the calithumpians are requested to meet at Cremer's blacksmith shop Friday night. **1889** *Cent.* 769/1.

Call loan. A loan of money repayable on call or demand. Also attrib. {1882}

*a***1859** *N.Y. Herald* (B.), To speculate in fancy stocks on call loans is simply to put your hand in the lion's mouth. **1859** *Bankers' Mag.* (N.Y.) XIV. 77 So many brokers suffered loss and inconvenience from the late sharp turn in the money market that they are now refusing again to try the 'call loan' system. **1870** MEDBERY *Men Wall St.* 73 Call-loans were four per cent. **1882** *Nation* 7 Sept. 190/2 Call-loan rate on stocks advanced to 6 and 7 per cent. **1891** EGGLESTON in *Century Mag.* Feb. 552 He was accustomed to make call loans to a large amount on collateral security. *a***1906** 'O. HENRY' *Trimmed Lamp,* etc. 61 He was backed by money in hand that would have stayed off a call loan at Rothschilds'.

fig. **1870** *Nation* 10 Feb. 86/2 To the minds of all thoughtful financiers, this enormous call-loan, these forty-five millions of three per cent. certificates [etc.].

+**Call number.** A number assigned to a library book, to be used in calling or borrowing it. — **1876** *Public Libraries U.S.* (Bureau of Educ.) I. 626 Users of the [decimal] scheme . . . will find it of great practical utility . . . in determining the character of any book simply from its call number. **1888** *Library Jrnl.* XIII. 321/1, I always feel outraged when I make up a long list of call numbers in order to make sure of a book. **1915** FAY & EATON *Use of Books* 108 This number distinguishes the book from other books in the library. It is known as the 'call number' of the book.

+**Call room.** [CALL *n.* 6.] A room in a stock exchange where 'calls' are made. — **1886** *Harper's Mag.* July 213/1 The Call Room daily presents an impressive spectacle of the traffic in grain.

+**Call slip.** A slip for noting the number, title, etc., of a library book desired by a borrower. — **1881** *A. L. A. Papers* 4/1 All books are to be asked for on call-slips made out from the catalog. **1888** *Library Jrnl.* XIII. 321/1 In connection with Mr. Tyler's new call slip I would like to ask [etc.]. **1909** *Library Bureau Catalog L1009* 104 The borrower presents his card together with call slip . . . giving number of the book wanted.

‖**Call spring.** A spring at which travelers plan a stop. — **1786** *Md. Hist. Mag.* XIX. 267 He has seen Wm. Rogers and Nicholas Gay surveyor of the Country run a line of Eagers Land and stopped at the call spring now called Cloppers Spring.

***Calm.** +A stretch of calm water. — **1728** *Md. Hist. Mag.* XVIII. 12 Luke Stansbury appointed overseer to clear a road according to law from the long calm of Gunpowder Falls to Edward Reston's plantation. **1730** *Ib.* 13 Ordered, that the Road formerly cleared from the long Calm to Mr. Gist's be continued into the road . . . called the Old Indian Road.

Calomel. Mercurous chloride, a heavy, white, tasteless compound used esp. as a purgative. {1676–}

1727 *Md. Hist. Mag.* XVIII. 229 To be had of Silvanus Beven in Plough Court in Lumbard Street. Vid. . . . lb ss Calomell. **1802** ELLICOTT *Journal* 292 Each of these pills was composed of two grains of calomel, with half a grain of gamboge. **1837** PECK *New Guide* 87 Whenever nausea of the stomach, pains in the limbs, and yawning, or a chill, indicate the approach of a disease, a dose of calomel is taken at night in a little apple, honey, [etc.]. **1852** *Florida Plant. Rec.* 80 It seames like Nothing will brake the Fever hear except Calomel, Ippecac and Qinine. **1872** *Atlantic Mo.* May 536 An abiding confidence in all acute cases, in calomel and quinine. **1882** THAYER *From Log-Cabin* xiv. 206 In severe cases [of the ague] a physician was called in to administer calomel—that was considered a specific at that time—until salivation was produced.

attrib. **1872** EGGLESTON *End of World* 208 Every morning Dr. Dibrell, a calomel-doctor . . . rode by the house. **1901** HEGAN *Mrs. Wiggs* 48 This here is a calomel pill. . . . I jes' rolled the calomel in with some soft, light bread.

+**Calopogon.** [mod. L. (from Gr., 'beautiful beard,' with reference to its bearded lip).] A small wild orchid of the genus *Limodorum*, growing in moist places. — **1857** GRAY *Botany* 450 Calopogon, *C. pulchellus*, . . . [grows in] bogs; common. July. Flowers 1' broad, pink-purple, fragrant. **1894** TORREY *Fla. Sketch-Book* 125 Here I picked a goodly number of novelties . . . [among which was] a calopogon, quite as pretty as our Northern *pulchellus*. **1901** MOHR *Plant Life Ala.* 459 *Limodorum.* Four species, perennials, Atlantic North America: . . . grass-pink; . . . pale-flowered calopogon; . . . small-flowered calopogon; . . . many-flowered calopogon.

* **Caltrop.** A four-spiked iron ball formerly placed on the ground to obstruct the advance of an enemy.

1823 J. THACHER *Military Jrnl.* 51, I observed a prodigious number of little military engines called caltrops, or crow feet, scattered over the ground in the vicinity of the works to impede the march of our troops in case of an attack. The implement consists of an iron ball armed with four sharp points about one inch in length, so formed that which way soever it may fall one point still lies upwards to pierce the feet of horses or men. *a***1861** WINTHROP *Canoe & Saddle* 103 Every inch of the surface was planted with laming caltrops.

+**Calumet.** Also †**calamet, calumate, calamut, calmute.** [Norman-Fr. *calumet* (Fr. *chalumeau*), applied by the Canadian French to 'plants of which the stems serve as pipe-tubes, and to the Indian pipe' (O.E.D.).]

1. The ceremonial pipe used by North American Indians.

1705 Beverley *Virginia* III. 21 This Calumet is the most mysterious thing in the World, among the savages . . . ; for it is used in all their important transactions. However, it is nothing else but a large Tobacco pipe, made of red, black or white Marble. **1727** C. COLDEN *Hist. 5 Indian Nations* 82 *n.*, The Calumet is . . . shaped some-what in the form of a Hatchet, and adorned with large Feathers of several Colours. **1760** R. ROGERS *Jrnls.* 214 That evening we smoaked the calamet, or pipe of peace, all the officers and Indians smoaking by turns out of the same pipe. **1829** WEEMS *Franklin* 184 He sent around among them the Calumet, or pipe of peace, inviting them to a friendly talk. **1836** IRVING *Astoria* I. 195 The principal warriors . . . lighted a fire, seated themselves in a semicircle round it, and, displaying the calumet, invited the party to land. **1855** LONGFELLOW *Hiawatha* i, Smoke the calumet together, And as brothers live henceforward! **1869** *Amer. Naturalist* II. 645 They [=Indians] must make their calumets from the soft stone, and smoke them in their councils. **1880** CABLE *Grandissimes* 21 The father . . . had so . . . outsmoked —their 'Great Sun,' as to find himself, as he finally knocked the ashes from his successful calumet, possessor of a wife.

transf. **1808** PIKE *Sources of Miss.* I. App. 22 We may make peace with them, being assured of their pacific disposition when we shall see the calumet marked on the trees.

attrib. **1842** *S. Lit. Messenger* VIII. 462/2 A calumet party of about twenty Grand Pawnees paid them a visit in their villages.

b. Freq. in *calumet of peace*, or the like.

[**1751** (see sense 3).] **1831** PECK *Guide* 270 The calumet of peace was now smoked. **1844** *Knickerb.* XXIV. 242 The Oneidas will reproduce the calumet of perpetual union and friendship. **1879** H. PHILLIPS *Coins* 2 A Quaker seated on the ground is receiving from an Indian the calumet of peace. **1884** SWEET & KNOX *Through Texas* 54 The Muscogees sitting on a decayed log, smoking the calumet of peace.

2. Short for *calumet dance* (see sense 4).

1823 *Niles' Reg.* XXIII. Suppl. 64/2 A part of my nation . . . came to my village three times . . . to dance the *calumet*, (make presents), and triumph at the expense of the whites whom they plundered.

3. *Calumet pipe* = sense 1.

1751 GIST *Journals* 50 We might smoak the Calumet Pipe of Peace with them. **1752** W. TRENT *Journal* The Twightwees have sent one Thomas Burney, express, who brought me . . . a calmute pipe (being an emblem of peace with those they send it to).

4. *Calumet dance*, among some of the American Indians, esp. in the West, a ceremonial dance of an invocatory nature in which calumets were conspicuously displayed and used.

1778 CARVER *Travels* 268 The Indians have several kinds of dances which they use on different occasions, as the Pipe or Calumate Dance. **1791** J. LONG *Voyages* 35 The dances among the Indians are many and various, and to each of them there is a particular whoop. 1. The calumet dance. **1809** KENDALL *Travels* II. 295 The calumet-dance is a sacred rite.

5. *Calumet eagle*, any eagle (as the golden eagle and bald eagle at certain stages) having black and white tail feathers used or suitable for adorning the Indian calumet.

1806 CLARK in *Lewis & C. Exped.* (1905) IV. 158 The Calumet Eagle is sometimes found on this side of the Rocky Mountains. **1826** *N. Amer. Rev.* Jan. 118 The bird itself is called the Calumet Eagle. . . . They are very rare, and killed with difficulty. **1833** CATLIN *Indians* I. 68 This bird has often been called the calumet eagle . . . from the fact, that the Indians almost invariably ornament their calumets or pipes of peace with its quills.

6. *Calumet bird*, the calumet eagle.

1805 LEWIS in Biddle *Lewis & Clark Exped.* (1814) II. 504 The beautiful eagle or calumet-bird, so called from the circumstance of the natives decorating their pipe-stems with its plumage. **1814** BIDDLE *Ib.* I. 112 Our chief tells us that the calumet-bird lives in the holes formed by the filtration of the water from the top of these hills through the sides.

‖**Calumeting,** *vbl. n.* [CALUMET 1.] (See quotation.) — **1808** T. ASHE *Travels* 272, I learned from Adario [an Indian chief] that he was going a *calumeting*. That is a practice of gallantry among the Indians. . . . The lover . . . lights his calumet, enters the cabin of his mistress, and gently presents it to her. If she extinguishes it, she admits him to her arms.

Calvinistic Baptist. A Baptist accepting the doctrines of Calvin. The sect was founded in London in 1633. — **1823** *Baptist Mag.* IV. 32 In March, 1818, agreeably to the request of the Calvinistic Baptist church and society in this place, I came to reside with them. **1835** in H. Martineau *Society* (1837) III. 272 The Episcopalian Methodists are the most numerous sect: then the Catholics, Calvinistic Baptists, Presbyterians, Congregationalists, [etc.].

Calycanthus. +Carolina allspice or strawberry shrub, *C. floridus* (al. *Butneria florida*), or related species. Also attrib.

1814 MITCHILL in *Mineral. Journal* I. 213 The persimmon, the pape-flora, the calycanthus, and the papaw, strike their roots through the sands of the shore. **1851** LINCOLN *Botany* 262 *Calycanthaceæ*, the Calycanthus Tribe. **1892** ALLEN *Blue-Grass Region* 242 Along the streams in the lowlands blooms the wild calacanthus [*sic*], filling the air with fragrance. **1901** MOHR *Plant Life Ala.* 518 *Butneria fertilis* (Walt.) . . . Smooth Calycanthus. Mountain Spice-wood. *Ib.*, *Butneria florida* (L.) . . . Calycanthus. Carolina Allspice.

+**Calzoneros,** *n. pl.* Also **calzonera(s).** [Mex.-Sp.] Trousers buttoned at the sides. — **1844** GREGG *Commerce of Prairies* I. 211 A curiously shaped article called *calzoneras*, intended for pantaloons, with the outer part of the legs open. **1848** BRYANT *California* 314 They were dressed in steeple-crowned glazed *sombreros*, *serapes* of fiery colors, velvet (cotton) *calzoneros*. **1850** B. TAYLOR *Eldorado* (1862) xiii. 122 A handsome young Californian, dressed in blue calzoneros. **1910** J. HART *Vigilante Girl* 196 She had replaced their calzonera, or riding-breeches, with a divided skirt of doeskin.

Camanche, -chee, -she, etc. *Obs.* See COMANCHE.

+**Camas, Comas.** Also **camash, camass, cammas, cammass, commas(s).** Cf. KAMAS. [Chinook jargon, ultimately from '*chamas*, signifying "sweet" in the Nootka language of Vancouver' (Hodge *Handbook* I. 196).]

1. The quamash, *Camassia esculenta*, or related species, whose sweet, nutritious bulbs are eaten by Indians of the Northwest and of western Canada.

1805 ORDWAY in *Journals of Lewis & O.* 290 These natives have a large quantity of this root bread which they call commass. The roots grow in these plains. **1807** GASS *Journal* 141 Their bread is made of roots which they call comas, and which resemble onions in shape, but are of a sweet taste. *Ib.* 223 The commas grows in great abundance on this plain, and at this time looks beautiful, being in full bloom with flowers of a pale blue colour. **1838** S. PARKER *Tour Rocky Mts.* 204 The cammas, a tunicated root, is one of great importance to the Indians. . . . It is roasted, pounded, and made into loaves like bread. **1845** DE SMET *Oregon Missions* (1847) 117 The women arm themselves with long, crooked sticks, to go in search of the camash. **1847** J. PALMER *Rocky Mts.* 105 There is a root here found in great abundance, and known as the *camas*, which is held in high repute by the Indians for some medicinal qualities. **1873** MILLER *Amongst Modocs* 22 This camas . . . is prepared for food by roasting in the ground. . . . Sometimes it is kneaded into cakes and dried. **1905** G. E. COLE *Early Oregon* 48 A drove of hogs which we were taking to the Rogue river valley to feed on camas, the feed for hogs at that season of the year.

2. Attrib. with *blossom, bulb, flat, ground, meadow, plant, prairie.* (Cf. CAMAS ROOT.)

1884 MILLER *Memorie & Rime* 83 The camas blossom . . . purples all Oregon in the early spring. **1891** *Century Mag.* March 645 Two Pi-Ute women engaged in digging camass bulbs. **1806** ORDWAY in *Journals of Lewis & O.* 414 A number of Indians went across this commass flat on horseback to another prarie or flat to the north. **1880** BURNETT *Old Pioneer* 150 Every succeeding fall they found . . . our settlements . . . encroaching more and more upon their pasture and camas-grounds. **1884** *Cent. Mag.* May 139 We encamped in a prairie dotted with clumps of cottonwood trees and camas meadows. **1868** W. F. RAYNOLDS *Explor. Yellowstone* 97 The camas plant also abounds in the vicinity. **1885** *Century Mag.* Jan. 448 There are many camas prairies in Montana and Idaho, but the largest is in the Flathead nation.

+**Camas rat.** The pocket gopher, *Thomomys talpoides* of the northwestern states, or *T. bulbivorus* of the Pacific slope. — **1868** WOOD *Homes without Hands* 35 The Camas Rat (*Pseudostoma borealis*). . . . The name is derived from its food, which consists chiefly of quamash root. **1893** COUES in *Lewis & Clark's Exped.* 994 *n.*, The pocket-gopher of this region, a species of *Thomomys* known as the camass-rat from its fondness for the bulbs of the camass.

+**Camas root.** The esculent root of the camas (q.v.).

1837 IRVING *Bonneville* II. 57 The Indians . . . likewise come to it in the summer time to dig the camash root. . . . When this plant is in blossom, the whole valley is tinted by its blue flowers, and looks like the ocean when overcast by a cloud. **1845** DE SMET *Oregon Missions* (1847) 117, I cannot pass over in silence the camash root, and the peculiar manner in which it is prepared. **1873** MILLER *Amongst Modocs* 22 The camp was . . . pitched here for the purpose of gathering and drying a sort of mountain camas root from the low marshy springs of this region. **1878** *Rep. Indian Affairs* 88 A large prairie in the vicinity of their village furnishes them with camas and bitter-root. **1897** *Chicago Tribune* 2 July 5/1 Camass root, a blue-flowered bulb whose sweet taste is much coveted by the Indians.

Camblet, obsolete variant of CAMLET.

Cambletee. Also **cambleteen.** *Obs.* An imitation camlet; a kind of worsted camlet. {1730, 1753} — **1754** *S.C. Gazette* 29 Jan. 3/1 William Taylor . . . has just imported . . . cambletees [etc.]. **1776** *N.J. Archives* 2 Ser. I. 196 An assortment of dry goods . . . among which are . . . plain and striped camblets, camblettees, [etc.]. **1790** *Columbian Centinel* 2 Oct. 23/4 Imported in the Boston-Packet . . . and now ready for sale. . . . Shalloons, Cambleteens, &c. &c. **1845** JUDD *Margaret* II. xi. 358 Margaret . . . wore a black beaver hat, and a dress of cambleteen.

Camboose. [F. *cambuse* (Du. *kombuis*), 'apparently introduced into the navy about the middle of the 18th century' (Littré).] =CABOOSE 1, 2. Also attrib. with *factory.*

1779 *Remembrancer* VIII. 297 [Invoice of stores found at Kempe's Landing, Va., includes] 2 cambouses, (1 large and 1 small). **1790** *Penna. Packet* 8 Nov. 1/4 For Sale by Benjamin Morgan, . . . Ship's Cambooses of different sizes. **1814** BIDDLE *Lewis & Clark Exped.* 159 When the blacksmith cut up an old cambouse of metal, we obtained, for every piece of four inches square, seven or eight gallons of corn from the Indians. **1839** C. F. BRIGGS *H. Franco* II. 71 A coppersmith's shop, . . . and a camboose factory. **1882** *Harper's Mag.* Feb. 331 Outside are 'cambooses' for preparing fish in the open air.

***Cambric.** Also †**cambrick, camrick.**

***1.** A thin, fine, white linen, originally manufactured at Cambray in Flanders; in later use, also an imitation of this made of hard-twisted cotton yarn.

1693 SEWALL *Letter-Book* 137 Two p[iece]s of fine 3/4 Cambrick. **1729** *Md. Hist. Mag.* XVIII. 335 A peece of Cambric of about 5 shil[ling]s a yard. **1780** *R.I. Commerce* II. 87 Five peices of Cambrick were staind. **1866** MRS. WHITNEY *L. Goldthwaite* i, The perfectly gloved hand that upheld a bit of extravagance in Valenciennes lace and cambric. **1877** *Harper's Mag.* March 557/2 The infantile surroundings of cambric and cradle.

+**b.** A dress or a handkerchief of this material.

1838 HAWTHORNE *Note-Books* I. 156 Well-dressed ladies were in the meeting-house in silks and cambrics. **1852** STOWE *Uncle Tom* xvi, I wish some of your Northern servants could look at her closets of dresses,—silks and muslins, and one real linen cambric, she has hanging there. **1856** M. J. HOLMES *L. Rivers* x. 122 Her linen cambric went up to her forehead as if trying to smooth out the scowl.

2. Attrib. with *bonnet, dress, handkerchief,* etc.

1742 *Md. Hist. Mag.* XX. 177 A Suit of Camrick head Cloths. **1757** E. Singleton *Social N.Y.* 173, I was . . . in the winter relieved again with a single cambric neckcloth. **1759** *Boston Gazette* 13 Aug., Cotton, Cambrick and Scotch Threads. **1778** *Journ. Cont. Congress* X. 11 Six cambrick or muslin Stocks. **1841** *Lowell Offering* I. 2 She had begun to fear that she must always wear the same brown cambric bonnet. **1842** *Ib.* II. 237 Her muslin robe is exchanged for her cambric night dress. **1852** STOWE *Uncle Tom* xvi, Cologne and cambric handkerchiefs. **1856** M. J. HOLMES *L. Rivers* xix. 213 Her rich cashmere gown flowing open, so as to reveal the flounced cambric skirt. **1892** WILKINS *Jane Field* viii, Flora wore a bright blue cambric dress and a brown straw hat.

3. *Cambric muslin* (see quot. 1889). *Cambric needle,* a fine needle for sewing cambric.

1813 *Niles' Reg.* IV. 295/1 To James Hall, of Baltimore, for manufacturing ten pieces of 1800 cambric muslin. . . . A piece of plate or its value, fifty dollars. **1889** *Cent.* 776/1 *Cambric muslin,* . . . 1. Fine cotton cloth made in imitation of linen cambric. 2. A somewhat coarser cotton cloth, finished with a glaze, much used for linings. — **1827** *Hallowell* (Maine) *Gaz.* 20 June 3/3 *Commercial Advertiser* offers to bet Pompey's pillar against a cambric needle that it is not so. **1843** STEPHENS *High Life N.Y.* II. 101 His eyes [are] as . . . sharp as a hull paper of cambric needles. **1869** STOWE *Oldtown Folks* i. 2 Israel Cran's store, where everything was sold, from hoe-handles up to cambric needles. **1882** PECK *Sunshine* 82 His head is about as big as a graham gem, and runs down to a point not bigger than a cambric needle.

+**Cambric tea.** [See quot. 1891.] A drink of milk and sugar mixed with hot water, freq. given to children instead of tea. — **1888** *Union Signal* (Chicago) 21 Jan. 3 [She] offered me tea, cambric tea to be sure, but in a beautiful cup. **1891** *Amer. Notes & Q.* VI. 174 Cambric Tea . . . is so called because it is thin, white and weak. **1903** BURNHAM *Jewel* 225 'Is there going to be some cambric tea for this baby?' inquired Dr. Ballard.

+**Cambridge platform.** A code of rules for church government, comprised in seventeen chapters, adopted by New England Puritans in 1648.

'A synod assembled at Cambridge, September 30, 1648, . . . framed, agreed and published, "the Platform of Church-discipline" ' (C. Mather *Magnalia* v. i.).

1770 STILES *Lit. Diary* (1901) I. 59 Here I saw the original MS. of the Cambridge Platform in the writing of Mr. Rd. Mather, the principal compiler. **1784** BELKNAP *Hist. N.H.* I. 81 The principle on which this power [of the magistrates] is grounded is expressed in the Cambridge Platform in terms as soft as possible. **1832** WILLIAMSON *Maine* I. 379 A code of ecclesiastical rules, or articles of discipline, among the churches, which . . . consisted of 17 chapters, and have been denominated 'The Cambridge Platform';—being subsequently the ecclesiastical constitutions throughout the New-England churches. **1845** M. Blake *Mendon Association* (1853) 56 We agreed that a reassertion of the principles of the Cambridge Platform . . . is very desirable. **1848** LOWELL *Biglow P.* I. ii, It would be wise to fill our bombshells with alternate copies of the Cambridge Platform and the Thirty-nine Articles, which would produce a mixture of the highest explosive power.

***Camel.**

***1.** The ruminant quadruped so called, native to western Asia and northern Africa, and introduced experimentally in the southwestern states. Also attrib.

1789 *Salem Mercury* 4 Aug., Two Camels, Male and Female, imported from Arabia. **1855–65** WHITMAN *Amer. Primer* (1894) 15 If success and breed follow the camels and dromedaries, that are now just introduced into Texas, to be used for travel and traffic over the vast wilds between the lower Mississippi and the Pacific, [etc.]. **1857** *Harper's Mag.* Oct. 688/1 The camel experiment upon the plains is pronounced to be entirely successful. **1884** *Amer. Naturalist* XVIII. 221 The camels now running wild in Arizona were bought by the United States Government in Asia Minor. . . . They were first employed in packing between Fort Tejon and Albuquerque. **1884** SWEET & KNOX *Through Texas* 637 In a pasture near Austin we saw about twenty camels. In our journeyings through Texas we had seen many strange things, but nothing so strange and foreign as a camel-rancho.

+**2.** (See quot. 1903.) Also *camel-back.*

1877 'E. MARTIN' *Hist. Great Riots* 337 The strikers were quiet and orderly at first, the only violence being the throwing of a man from a camel-back engine for attempting to start the fires. **1903** E. JOHNSON *Railway Transportation* 44 Ross Winans . . . brought out the first 'camel' type of engine, so named because the engine-driver's cab is placed above the middle part of the boiler.

+**Camel cricket.** The praying mantis or 'rearhorse,' *Phasmomantis carolina.* — **1859** BARTLETT 356 *Rear Horse,* the vulgar name, at the South, for the orthopterous insect called the Mantis, Camel Cricket, or Johnny Cock-Horse. **1889** *Harper's Mag.* June 45/2 The camel-cricket is another active destroyer of injurious insects.

***Cameleon.** Also **camelion.** [Older E. *cameleon.*] + Any of various American species of lizard, esp. of the family *Anolidæ* or *Iguanidæ,* able to change color. Also attrib. with *lizard.* (See also CHAMELEON.)

1796 MORSE *Amer. Geog.* I. 218 We have . . . the green lizard, or little green cameleon of Carolina . . . ; [it] has the faculty of changing its colour. **1821** ROYALL *Lett. from Ala.* 138 The Camelion is also a native of this place. **1821** NUTTALL *Travels Arkansa* 241 Among the more common reptiles of this country [=La.] . . . I know of none more curious, than a kind of Cameleon lizard. **1848** J. S. ROBINSON *Santa Fé Exped.* 11 Here are . . . thousands of little lizards or cameleons, horned frogs, prairie dogs, &c.

Camellia. A plant or flower of the genus *Camellia* of evergreen shrubs belonging to the tea family; esp. the common cultivated variety, *C. Japonica.* {1753–} Also attrib.

1847 *Horticulturist* I. 432/2 Mr. Becar's taste leads him to devote his range of glass almost wholly to Camellias. *Ib.* 433/1 A detailed account of the gems of this fine camellia house. **1858** WARDER *Hedges & Evergreens* 272 The Camellia is characterized by the remarkable beauty of its flowers, which occur during Winter. **1863** 'M. HARLAND' *Husks* 13 Then the abundant hair, . . . a camellia, a rosebud, or a pearl hairpin, its sole adornment. **1886** B. P. POORE *Reminisc.* I. 469 Carriages and camelias were thenceforth in demand.

Camel's-hair. {1611–} *attrib.* **a.** Made of the hair of the camel. +**b.** Of shawls: Made of cashmere.

(*a*) [**1678** *New Castle Court Rec.* 361 A Camell haire Rugg.] **1854** M. CUMMINS *Lamplighter* 178 That boy . . . has sent you home a camel's hair scarf. **1865** *Atlantic Mo.* XV. 10 Cotton-bales, bound in striped camel's-hair cloth.

(*b*) **1823** COOPER *Pioneers* xxvi, In twelve months from this day you may make an umbrella for your daughter of her camel's hair shawl. **1870** 'M. HARLAND' *For Better, For Worse* 338 She vows that she must and will have . . . a camel's hair shawl. **1883** C. F. WILDER *Sister Ridnour* 163 Mrs. Lincoln . . . had on an elegant camel's-hair shawl. **1902** FITCH *Capt. Jinks* (1915) I. 252 Give me my camel's-hair shawl.

(*c*) *ellipt.* **1876** WARNER *Gold of Chickaree* 295 He indulged himself and Primrose with a delicate gray camel's hair at last.

+**Camerist.** [From *camera.*] A photographer. — **1890** *Internat. Ann., Anthony's Photogr. Bul.* III. 19 Theoretically, all camerists believe in a good negative. **1891** *Ib.* IV. 88 The true camerist is constantly revising his methods and tools. **1900** *Boston Ev. Transcript* 23 Feb. 12/6 When a high wind is encountered, the cloth at one end can be buttoned . . . around the head or face of the camerist.

+**Camino real.** *S.W.* [Sp., 'royal road, highway'.] A main road or highway. — **1840** D. TURNBULL *Travel in West* 176 In traveling along the neglected highway or Camino real . . . I thought I had observed . . . indications of coal. **1844** G. W. KENDALL *Texan Santa Fé Exped.* I. 271 After having obtained directions as to our course toward the Camino real, or principal road, we proceeded on our way.

Camisa. *S.W.* [Sp.] A shirt or chemise. {1690, 1796} — **1845** GREEN *Texian Exped.* 320 Any sergeant's wife in the castle would trust him for the washing of his camisa. **1846–7** MAGOFFIN *Down Santa Fé Trail* (1926) 93 The women were clad in *camisas* (chemises) and petticoats only.

* **Camlet.** Also †**camlett, -lit; camblet.**

* **1.** A strong woven fabric, of variable nature and quality, but usually of hair or wool, or both. Cf. quot. 1889.

1713 SEWALL *Letter-Book* II. 12 Send a pattern for a cloak of good black hair camlet. **1762** in H. M. Brooks *Gleanings* 37 Strip'd and plain Camblets, strip'd Swanskins. **1811** *Niles' Reg.* I. 46/1 Callimancoes, shalloons, . . . camblets, . . . and other useful goods, can only be made of wool long enough to be combed. **1889** *Cent.* 778/3 *Camlet*, . . . a very durable plain cloth used for cloaks and the like; a water-proof material in common use before the introduction of india-rubber.

b. A cloak or other garment made of this material. {1613–}

1830 J. F. WATSON *Philadelphia* App. 52 As a defence from rain, the men wore 'rain coats,' and the women, 'camblets.' **1843** 'CARLTON' *New Purchase* I. 177, I raps up in the ole-camlit, and laid down.

2. Attrib. with names of garments, etc., in sense: Made of camlet, as *camlet breeches, cloak,* etc.

1686 *Narrag. Hist. Reg.* III. 104 A pair of Camlett britches. *Ib.*, A camlet cote. . . . A camlet cloke. **1708** *Boston News-Letter* April 2/2 Ranaway from Her Majesties Garison . . . Michael Welden . . . [wearing] a sort of blew Camlet Wastcoat. **1725** *New-Eng. Courant* 8–15 March 2/2 A blue Camblet Riding-Hood . . . was taken out of a House in Town. **1726** *N.H. Probate Rec.* II. 290, I alsoe give unto my said son Sam . . . my feather Bed, my Camlet Curtains, Blankets, [etc.]. **1768** *Essex Inst. Coll.* LIV. 251 A red Camblet Jacket, trim'd with Silver. **1779** E. PARKMAN *Diary* 106 My Camlet gown, lined with Green Baise. *c***1845** W. T. THOMPSON *Chron. Pineville* 18 A professional looking camblet wrapper, constituted his usual costume. **1851** J. H. ROSS *In New York* 45 There she sat . . . with an old brown camblet cloak . . . drawn around her. **1898** I. H. HARPER *S. B. Anthony* I. 20 A camlet cloak with a big cape . . . affording the best protection for the long, cold rides he had to take.

* **Camomile.**

* **1.** The aromatic creeping herb *Anthemis nobilis*, also named CHAMOMILE. Also attrib.

1737 BRICKELL *N. Carolina* 22 Camomil thrives well here, but it must be planted under a Shade. **1835** LONGSTREET *Ga. Scenes* 211, I had nothin' but dried yerbs, sich as camomile, sage, pennyryal. **1839** *S. Lit. Messenger* V. 752/1 Neighboring cats . . . would scratch and scramble over her favorite beds of violets and camomile. **1877** *Harper's Mag.* March 605/1 Wildly I hurled my cigar into the camomile bed. **1880** *Ib.* Sept. 500/2 There were hollyhocks, camomile, and dahlias in some of the small dooryards.

2. With qualifying terms (see quotations).

1845 LINCOLN *Botany* App. 82/2 *Baltonia glastifolia* (false camomile). **1901** MOHR *Plant Life Ala.* 813 *Anthemis arvensis.* . . . Field Camomile. . . . Adventive in several localities on the Atlantic coast. *Ib.*, *Matricaria inodora maritima.* . . . Seaside Wild Camomile. . . . Alabama: Adventive from Europe with ballast.

* **Camp,** *n.*

* **1.** The place or ground occupied by a body of troops, with tents, huts, or other temporary structures erected as shelters.

*a***1649** WINTHROP *Hist.* I. 91 There was a camp pitched at Boston in the night, to exercise the soldiers against need might be. **1711** *Boston News-Letter* 23 July 2/2 On Tuesday . . . the whole Forces were under Arms at the Camp and a General review was made of them by General Hill. **1775** *Jrnls. Cont. Congress* III. 265 Resolved, That a committee of three members of this Congress be appointed to repair immediately to the camp at Cambridge. **1864** J. N. EDWARDS *Shelby* 470 Even his camp had no sentinels or efficient police. **1874** GLISAN *Jrnl. Army Life* 443 When a permanent camp or military post is about to be established [etc.].

* **b.** Temporary quarters used esp. by men on the march or trail, or when hunting, etc.

[**1700** in *Md. Hist. Mag.* XIX. 358 Beales Camp.] **1789** in Cist *Cincinnati* (1841) 204 We raised what in this country is called a camp, by setting two forks of saplings in the ground, a ridge-pole across, and leaning boat-boards . . . one end on the ground and the other against the ridge pole. **1836** IRVING *Astoria* 205 At length the jovial cry was given of 'an Indian camp!' **1850** S. F. COOPER *Rural Hours* 177 Later in the day we went to their camp, as they always call their halting-place. **1878** H. H. JACKSON *Travel at Home* 340 A half-mile farther on we came upon the camp of the men who were building the road. 'Camp' is an elastic word. In this case, it meant merely a small pine grove, two big fires, and some piles of blankets. **1904** STRATTON-PORTER *Freckles* 3 He turned into the newly made road and followed it to the camp.

+**c.** A sugar camp (q.v.).

1823 COOPER *Pioneers* xx, The sugar-boiler . . . was busy in his 'camp.' **1848** in Drake *Pioneer Life Ky.* 85 There were but few sugar trees on father's land, and he rented a 'camp,' as the grove was called. **1898** N. E. JONES *Squirrel Hunters of Ohio* 18 There are a few of the older crop of sugar trees still remaining; but the great 'camps' that furnished sweets in abundance have, with other varieties of timber, fallen victims to the woodman's ax.

+**d.** A group of buildings erected as living quarters for people engaged in lumbering, mining, etc.; freq., a town that has sprung up around or near a mine or group of mines.

1839 F. A. KEMBLE *Journal* 18 There are four settlements or villages (or, as the negroes call them, camps) on the island, consisting of from ten to twenty houses. **1855** F. S. MARRYAT *Mts. & Molehills* 241, I did not see a woman in the [mining] 'camp.' **1856** *Mich. Agric. Soc. Trans.* VII. 828 The companies proceed to the pineries, . . . building their shanties and forming 'camps' in the immediate vicinity of the timber. **1868** HARTE *Luck of Roaring Camp*, The camp lay in a triangular valley between the hills and a river. **1877** WM. WRIGHT *Big Bonanza* 27 This was a little hamlet of a dozen houses of all kinds. . . . In this little town or 'Camp,' as such places are usually styled in mining countries.

+**e.** One or more buildings, freq. situated near a lake or in the woods or mountains, forming a temporary residence, esp. in summer.

1881 *Harper's Mag.* May 873/1 An Adirondack Camp may seem cut off from the busy world. **1906** *N.Y. Ev. Post* 16 June, Resort Sec. 4 The word 'camp' is ambiguous as applied to abodes in the Adirondack forest, for it may be used to designate a snug little cabin, with its modest half-acre of territory, or it may apply to an extensive establishment that represents the outlay of thousands of dollars, standing in the midst of a royal estate of 50,000 acres. **1921** *Rural Organization* 14 We have a little camp of our own two or three miles out from the town of Oregon.

+**2.** *To make camp*, to camp or encamp. *To take into camp*, to kill or defeat.

1850 GARRARD *Wah-To-Yah* xxi. 256 We made camp in a bottom opposite the mouth of the Purgatoire. **1895** *Outing* XXVII. 47/1 About dusk we made camp at the portal of the forest primeval. **1900** DRANNAN *Plains & Mts.* 558 The third day out we made camp early on account of water. — **1877** 'MARK TWAIN' in *Atl. Mo.* XL. 723/1 One night the trap took Mrs. Jones's principal tomcat into camp, and finished him up. **1889** — *Conn. Yankee* xix. 235 He had six [sons] left for Sir Marhaus and me to take into camp.

+**3.** A stage of a march or journey.

1837 IRVING *Bonneville* I. xvii. 176 He turned his back upon the swamp and its muskrat houses, and followed on at 'long camps,' which, in trapper's language, is equivalent to long stages.

+**4.** A place for the holding of open-air meetings by religious bodies, political parties, etc.

1843 'CARLTON' *New Purchase* II. 136 The camp was furnished with several stands for preaching, exhorting, jumping, and jerking. **1888** 'CRADDOCK' *Broomsedge Cove* 37, I hev seen ye, a-many-a-time—at preachin', . . . at the church-house, and at camp, too. **1911** C. HARRIS *Eve's Husband* 175 Some friends of Clancy Drew's pitched what they called a 'camp' two miles from town and invited every colored voter . . . to come and have a good time.

+**5.** A lodge or other local division of a society or organization.

1880 TOURGEE *Invisible Empire* 415 Sometimes several 'camps' or 'dens' [of the Ku-Klux Klan] would . . . direct a warning to be sent to the same individual. **1885** [see CANTON *n.* 3]. **1904** HARBEN *Georgians* 132 The general is invited to address nearly all the veteran camps over the State when the badges of honor are presented once a year. **1909** WEBSTER 316/1 A lodge or local division of certain patriotic societies connected with past wars; as, a *camp* of the Sons of Veterans. *U.S.*

6. Attrib. with *arrangements, baggage, basket, bed, bedstead, cabin,* etc.

1836 SIMMS *Mellichampe* xii, Having made camp arrangements for the night, Barsfield left Clayton in command of the troop. **1853** — *Sword & Distaff* 173 Tom's world of kitchen and camp baggage was fairly divided among the negroes. **1869** W. MURRAY *Adventures* 116 Before I had gone fifty rods, the camp-basket weighed one hundred and twenty pounds. **1759** J. ROWE *Letters* 335, I endeavored to get a Camp Bed to send but in short did not know where to send it. **1849** *Rep. Comm. Patents* (1850) 480 A portable cot-bedstead has been patented, designed to be used as a camp bedstead. **1886** Z. F. SMITH *Kentucky* 4 The ends of the poles . . . rested against, or on top of, the fallen tree, thus forming a frame-work for the side of the camp-cabin. **1852** *Harper's Mag.* VI. 8 The camp-chest and a part of the wardrobe of Washington. **1897** C. A. DANA *Recoll. Civil War* 188, I had got into my camp clothes, had borrowed a pistol. **1878** M. PARLOA (*title*), Camp Cookery; or, How to live in Camp. **1887** *Courier-Journal* 8 May 18/5 This young fellow . . . had this morning heroically deserted his camp-cot as early as 9 o'clock. **1878** I. L. BIRD *Rocky Mts.* 47 Consumptives . . . trying the 'camp cure' for three or four months. *Ib.* 161 People . . . came from the east to try the 'camp cure' now so fashionable. **1808** PIKE *Sources Miss.* 204 Up the river . . . the Spanish officers had made a camp deposit. **1861** MRS. S. COWELL *Diary* 398 This force . . . had not received either camp or garrison equipments. **1900** DRANNAN *Plains & Mts.* 423 Convinced that the reds might get their camp fixings mixed with ours. **1879** STOCKTON *Rudder Grange* xi, Having locked up the smaller articles of camp-furniture, we . . . started off home. **1849** T. T. JOHNSON *Sights Gold Region* 123 Carrying ashore our tent, blankets, hammocks, camp hamper, &c. **1761** S. NILES *Indian Wars* II. 481 They carried off five or six of the camp-horses. **1885** CUSTER *Boots & Saddles* 167, I have seen the leaves come out on the logs that . . . were in use as the frame-work of our camp-huts. **1850** H. C. WATSON *Camp-Fires Revol.* 107 Here and there is found among their posterity, a letter, a camp-journal, or a written narrative. **1847** *Knickerb.* XXIX. 199 The following impromptu lines . . . written by camp-light, near Camargo. **1865** *Atlantic Mo.* XV. 66/1 We have now a good regimental hospital, . . . a fine well of our digging, within the camp-lines. **1758** *Essex Inst. Coll.* XVIII. 106 This Day was ful of Camp News. **1890** H. Palmer *Stories Base Ball Field* 215 Camping and Camp Outfits. A Manual of Instruction for Young and Old Sportsmen. **1866** 'F. KIRKLAND' *Bk. Anecdotes* 507 Savory pork steaks were frying in many a camp pan. **1916** EASTMAN *From Deep Woods* 106 The teacher of a new camp school. **1869** W. MURRAY *Adventures* 27 The 'essentials' [are a] . . . pair of common winter boots and camp shoes. **1871** *Atlantic Mo.* Nov. 565 You seem to have a pleasant camp-spot here. **1886** S. W. MITCHELL *R. Blake* 127 Seated on two rough camp-stools, the friends chatted gaily of home and the war. **1869** BROWNE *Adv. Apache Country* 273 This is a well-authenticated incident, and has long been a favorite camp-story in Arizona. **1861** NORTON *Army Lett.* 21 Some say he expects to have us there on the Fourth, but I think that's all camp talk.

b. With names of persons functioning or staying in a camp, as *camp boss, boy, bully, cook,* etc.

*a***1904** WHITE *Blazed Trail Stories* ii. 22 Especially is it true of the camp boss, the foreman. **1846** WORCESTER 99/2 *Camp-Boy*, a boy performing service in a camp. **1837** IRVING *Bonneville* I. vii. 94 The camp bullies and prime trappers of the party began to ruffle up. **1903** 'O. HENRY' in *McClure's Mag.* Dec. 130, I crawled out near the grub wagon, and reclined helpless under the conversational fire of Judson Odom, the camp cook. **1905** *Forestry Bureau Bul.* No. 61 *Camp inspector*, a lazy lumberjack, who goes from one logging camp to another working only a short time. *a***1842** O. RUSSEL *Journal* (1921) 43 Heaps of ashes might be seen with the fire burning on the summit and an independent looking individual, who is termed a camp-kicker, sitting with a 'two-year-old club' in his hand watching the pile. **1917** SINCLAIR *King Coal* 20 This would enable the camp-marshal to keep him from straying. **1855** SIMMS *Forayers* 531 Their camp-master had no idea of what was the duty to be done. **1845** *Knickerb.* XXV. 198 He had assisted in the cure, by holding the sufferers during the operations of the camp-surgeon. **1913** W. C. BARNES *Western Grazing Grounds* 380 Among stockmen . . . 'Camp Tender, Camp Rustler' [is] a man who accompanies the sheep herd, looks after the packs, locates camp and relieves the herder from such matters.

***Camp,** *v.*[1]

***1.** *intr.* To make or pitch one's camp; to live in a camp. Also with *it.*

1725 in G. Sheldon *Hist. Deerfield* (1895) I. 446 We . . . then struck over the Mountain 6 miles further & then we camped. **1740** *S.C. Hist. Soc. Coll.* IV. 150 General Oglethorpe passed into Florida, campt upon the Spanish side of the River St. John's, [etc.]. **1841** COOPER *Deerslayer* xxxii, That night, the three 'camped' on the head-waters of their own river. **1852** *Harper's Mag.* V. 267/2 The sportsman who now camps it by Long Lake, or shoots coot by Moniment Point. **1895** *Outing* XXVII. 44/1 He was at home and invited us to camp there, but we preferred a wilder site.

+**b.** (See quotation and CAMP *n.* 1 c.)

1852 MRS. ELLET *Pioneer Women* 164 Large parties of old and young, male and female, . . . assembled and bivouacked, or 'camped,' to use their own phrase, in the woods near the grove of [sugar-]maples, which were soon notched and pierced.

+**c.** *To camp on the trail of*, to follow persistently.

1882 BAILLIE-GROHMAN *Camps in Rockies* p. v, I shall have to ask him to camp, to use another Western expression, on the trails of all sorts of beasts and uncouth characters.

+**2.** *To camp down:* **a.** To form a camp; to settle down for a time.

1781 in G. Powers *Hist. Sk. of Coos* (1841) 197 Camped down on the River Lamoille this night. **1788** J. MAY *Jour. & Lett.* 49 On the field we found a spring of delightful water, at which we camped down. *c***1835** S. FOBES *Arnold's Exped.* 11 At night we went ashore . . . and camped down, as we called it. **1840** HOFFMAN *Greyslaer* III. 222 They therefore tethered their steeds and 'camped down,' as it is called in our hunter phrase. *a***1889** *Spirit of Times* (F.), They . . . when day broke took to the bush, camped down a smart piece off the trail.

+**b.** To lie down; also, to sit down.

1850 W. COLTON *3 Years Calif.* 310, I have seen this *savan* camp down and snore soundly through the night. **1852** STOWE *Uncle Tom* xxxii, I's jest gwine to camp down, and sleep while I ken. **1869** ALCOTT *Little Women* II. 100, I'll be hanged if I camp down before her table afterward.

+**3.** *To camp out*, to live or spend the night in the open or in a tent or camp. {1867}

1748 WASHINGTON *Writings* I. 3 We camped out in the field this night. **1803** L. DOW *Travels* Wks. 1806 I. 229, I missed the trail, and was necessitated to camp out without any company, (except my horse). **1817** M. BIRKBECK *Journey in A.* 95 Our rear party . . . were benighted . . . and . . . compelled to make our first experiment of 'camping out.' **1835** BIRD *Hawks of Hawk-H.* II. 253 Several rude huts . . . such as the hunters make, when they 'camp out' in the wilderness. **1848** COOPER *Oak Openings* I. xiii. 194 Peter was as well content to remain in his canoe, as to 'camp out' in the openings. **1871** BAGG *At Yale* 531 Seniors, in the interval between Presentation and Commencement, often 'camp out' for a week or two upon one of the Thimble Islands. **1885** *Outing* VII. 74/1 But you don't expect to camp out by yourself?

transf. **1835** LONGSTREET *Georgia Scenes* 9 The old gentleman and his lady had consented to *camp out* for a day. **1852** BRISTED *Upper Ten Th.* 103 There seemed a strong probability of their having to 'camp out' on the portico.

***Camp,** *v.*[2] *New Eng. tr.* To kick (a ball, etc.), esp. so as 'to raise it in the air' (B. '77). — **1859** HALE *If, Yes, & Perhaps* (1868) 193 In the world's great football match, the ball by chance found him loitering on the outside of the field; he closed with it, 'camped' it, charged it home. **1877** BARTLETT 94 *Camp*, . . . to kick with the foot, . . . [is current in] Eastern Massachusetts.

Campaign, *n.* {1628–}

1. The operations of an army during a single season, in a particular region, or in a definite enterprise. {1647–}

1776 *N.Y. Packet* 13 June, [The patriot] burns for a part in the next brave campaign. *Ib.*, The ensuing campaign. *Ib.*, This glorious campaign. **1806** JEFFERSON *Writings* (1894) VIII. 456, I presume however it [*sc.* a citadel] will be surrendered at the end of this campaign. **1838** *Diplom. Corr. Texas* (1911) III. 850 The stock . . . had been dispersed during the campaign of 1836, across the Rio Grande. **1862** NORTON *Army Lett.* 117 Thus, I apprehend, ends the campaign on the Peninsula. **1895** M. A. Jackson *Memoirs* 492 The movements of his troops and the plans and progress of campaigns, were prohibited topics. **1901** WHITE *Westerners* xxxv. 328 Sitting Bull . . . had a good time until he began ghost-dancing and was killed in the Wounded Knee campaign.

+**2.** Political activity before an election, marked by organized action in influencing the voters.

'*Campaign*, (U.S. Politics) the season of excitement and effort preceding an election' (W. '79). 'Its specific application to politics appears to be mainly American, though this usage has been to some extent adopted in England' (Norton *Polit. Americanisms* 26).

1809 *Steele Papers* II. 601 The electioneering campaign having become much warmer than I had anticipated. **1836** *Diplom. Corr. Texas* (1908) I. 119 The electioneering campaign has opened with Some activity and will probably be conducted with a good deal of Spirit. **1844** *Lexington Observer* 1 June 2/4 The commencement of another great political campaign has at length arrived. **1852** *Harper's Mag.* V. 832/1 The fall campaign has opened with vigor. **1857** S. BOWLES *Let. to H. L. Dawes* 16 Feb., We should get those amendments out of the way before we strike out for the summer campaign. **1877** JOHNSON *Anderson Co., Kansas* 130 Both parties entered the campaign sanguine of success in the election. **1884** *Century Mag.* Nov. 149 The present [Presidential campaign] has come to be . . . a campaign having largely to do with the record, character, and fitness of the principal candidates. **1893** *Forum* XV. 150 The law operated very well so far as giving publicity to the sums expended . . . in the campaigns was concerned. **1912** *Literary Digest* XLV. 357/1 Is this the campaign of 1912 or that of 1904?

+**3.** *College slang.* The period in which new members are sought and pledged by college organizations. Also attrib.

1871 BAGG *At Yale* 72 The . . . members of the initiation committee are also chosen on the night of the campaign. . . . Besides attending to the initiation when it comes, they are supposed to take the lead beforehand in electioneering, and pledging sub-Freshmen to the society. Gamma Nu elects a . . . 'campaign committee.' **1887** *Lippincott's Mag.* Nov. 741 The most able and influential men are chosen for societies . . . and the 'campaign' as the annual struggle for recruits is called, often becomes very exciting. . . . As a rule . . . election is the result of work at 'campaign' time.

+**4.** The period during which a furnace is in continuous operation.

1871 *Amer. Inst. Mining Eng. Trans.* I. 98 By their corrosive action on the lining . . . they shorten a campaign or run to a few days. **1874** RAYMOND *6th Rep. Mines* 393 A campaign lasts six months; but the men are changed frequently, as . . . the work is . . . very unhealthy.

5. Attrib. **a.** In sense: (Such as is) worn or used during a (military) campaign, as *campaign hat, shoe*, etc. {1677–}

1873 F. M. A. ROE *Army Lett.* 130, I recognized him instantly by the long light-blue overcoat and big campaign hat with brim turned up. **1744** *Md. Hist. Mag.* XXI. 245 A pair of mens Campaign Shoes good strong soals. **1866** MOORE *Women of War* 162 The old campaign stove had grown cool for the first time. **1715** *Boston News-Letter* 17 Oct. 2/2 A tall slim, thin favoured Fellow, . . . wears a black Campaign Wigg.

+**b.** In sense: Of or pertaining to a political campaign, as *campaign biography, book, button, club*, etc. (Cf. CAMPAIGN DOCUMENT.)

1879 H. JAMES *Hawthorne* 136 The 'campaign biography' . . . consists of an attempt, more or less successful, to persuade the many-headed monster of universal suffrage that the gentleman on whose behalf it is addressed is a paragon of wisdom and virtue. **1904** *Omaha Bee* 16 Aug. 4 The republican campaign book stands upon . . . a record of promises made good. **1900** *Congress. Rec.* 8 March 2670/2 A social condition that dictates to a man what kind of a button he shall wear . . . makes a man want to stick campaign buttons all over him. **1892** W. S. WALSH *Literary Curiosities* 651 In the Presidential campaign of 1860 . . . campaign clubs were organized. **1884** *Savannah News* Aug., It would be much better for General Butler if he would turn one of his barrels over to the Democratic campaign committee. **1894** *Congress. Rec.* 12 Jan. 774/1 In 1888, an enormous campaign contribution was levied upon the sugar trust. **1899** TARKINGTON *Gentleman from Ind.* i, Everybody read the campaign editorials, and found them interesting. **1851** CIST *Cincinnati* 337 While the Presidential struggle of 1844 was raging, Mr. Longworth was applied to for a contribution of one hundred dollars for campaign expenses. **1905** D. G. PHILLIPS *Plum Tree* 187 A big campaign fund properly distributed in the doubtful states. **1900** HOWELLS *Literary Friends* 33 This house had published in the East the campaign life of Lincoln which I had lately written. **1894** P. L. FORD *P. Stirling* 281 They've flooded it [*sc.* the ward] with campaign literature, which has served to light fires. **1882** *Nation* 21 Dec. 522/3 Garfield seems to have reposed great confidence in Dorsey as a campaign manager. **1873** BAILEY *Life in Danbury* 179 They are making campaign medals now. **1903** *Evanston* (Ill.) *Press* 11 April, Campaign Meetings: John T. Barker for Mayor. **1896** *Boston Journal* 21 Nov. 6/5 At first you thought it to be the final argument of a campaign orator. **1855** *S. Lit. Messenger* XXI. 2 A new campaign-paper was established at Jackson, called the True Issue. **1906** PITTMAN *Belle of Blue Grass C.* 248 This was the opening of the campaign season. **1881** *Harper's Mag.* Jan. 197/2 Horace Greeley . . . was then editor of the *Log-Cabin*, a General Harrison Campaign sheet. **1880** *Ib.* Dec. 144 The New York writer holds that in our political contests the 'Campaign speech' is . . . intended . . . merely to stimulate and encourage friends. **1914** McLaughlin & Hart *Cycl. Amer. Govt.* I. 363/1 The Spanish American War created an entirely unexpected situation which the congressional committee met in its campaign text book.

Campaign, *v.* {1701–}

+**1.** *tr.* To operate, exploit.

1888 *Boston Wk. Globe* 28 March (F.), The new owner sold the steed for 800 dollars to James Gray . . . , who after campaigning him on the track for a couple of years, . . . sold him to Bonner.

+**2.** *intr.* To conduct a political campaign.

1896 *Columbus* (Ohio) *Dispatch* 11 July 1/7 Bryan . . . campaigned for election to the United States senate. **1905** D. G. PHILLIPS *Plum Tree* 276 The exigencies of campaigning, the necessity of rousing the party spirit. **1912** W. IRWIN *Red Button* 367 Martin . . . comes up for reelection in November—fact is we're campaigning now. **1923** R. HERRICK *Lilla* 181 Gordon made various short tours in the state giving addresses. . . . All this was indirect campaigning.

+**Campaign document.** [CAMPAIGN *n.* 2.] A document distributed by a party during a political campaign.

1871 *Congress. Rec.* 2 June 3543/1 It is said that we get all our campaign documents from the public printer. **1876** *Harper's Mag.* Dec. 145/2 The newspaper will not supersede the orator, nor the 'campaign document' the stump speaker. **1884** SWEET & KNOX *Through Texas* 612 He paid in advance for two hundred copies, intending to circulate them as a campaign document. **1904** *N.Y. Ev. Post* 1 Nov. 3 It does not appear that any effort will be made to prevent the distribution of the pamphlet as a campaign document.

+**Campaigning suit.** (See quotation and CAMPAIGN *n.* 1.) — **1845** *Knickerb.* XXVI. 517 He put on an old campaigning suit of his, which he had long before received as a present from a Cayuga chief.

+**Campbellism.** The doctrines or religious principles of the Campbellites (see next). — **1844** *Knickerb.* XXIV. 587 This whole region [= Ky.] has hitherto been overrun with Campbellism. **1856** P. CARTWRIGHT *Autobiog.* 357 He was so confused by fishing in the muddy waters of Campbellism, that he lost his mental balance. **1872** MORRELL *Flowers & Fruits* 272 Campbellism and the anti-mission element gave us the principal troubles up to this time.

+**Campbellite.**

1. A member of a religious denomination founded by Rev. Alexander Campbell (1788–1866), a Baptist minister of Bethany, Va., in 1827; a Disciple of Christ or 'New Light.'

1834 PECK *Gaz. Illinois* 91 The Cambellites, or 'Reformers' . . . have several traveling, and a number of stationary preachers. **1847** DAVIDSON *Presbyterian Ch. Ky.* 216 The new sect were commonly known as Campbellites. **1867** W. H. DIXON *New America* II. 308 In a very short time, this body [Baptists] was divided into Old School Baptists . . . , Sabbatarians, Campbellites, [etc.]. **1871** EGGLESTON *Hoosier Schoolm.* xii. 101 Squire Hawkins . . . had become a member of the 'Reformers' . . . who now call themselves 'Disciples,' but whom the profane will persist in calling 'Campbellites.' **1881** THAYER *From Log-Cabin* ii, Abram Garfield and his noble wife . . . united with a comparatively new sect, called Disciples, though Campbellites was a name by which they were sometimes known. **1881** PIERSON *In the Brush* 161 A theological discussion between the Rev. Alexander Campbell, the founder of the sect popularly known as 'Campbellites,' and the Rev. Dr. N. L. Rice. **1907** 'E. C. HALL' *Aunt Jane of Ky.* 162 (Th.), Campbell was jest as good a man as Wesley . . . but you can't make a Campbellite madder than to call him a Campbellite.

b. Attrib. with *Baptist, leader, preacher; church*, etc.

(*a*) **1830** *Mass. Spy* 22 Dec. (Th.), Elder Rigdon . . . is described as having been 'a Campbelite leader of some notoriety.' **1843** 'CARLTON' *New Purchase* II. 139 A Campbellite Baptist . . . was holding forth against all Doctors. **1848** *S. Lit. Messenger* XIV. 652/1 Brockman . . . was a blacksmith by trade—a Campbellite preacher by choice. **1858** *Harper's Mag.* Jan. 282/2 Attending an Association of Campbellite Baptists in the southwestern part of this State [Virginia]. **1872** *Ib.* July 315/2 A doctor and a Campbellite preacher [were] riding along together in the outskirts of Kingston, Missouri.

(*b*) **1844** FEATHERSTONHAUGH *Slave States* 55 The party was given to a lady on her marriage to a preacher of the Campbellite persuasion. **1892** *Congress. Rec.* 30 Jan. 695/1 Garfield was preaching in Campbellite churches after driving mules upon the towpath of an Ohio canal.

2. The crappie or 'new-light' (*Pomoxis annularis*) of the Mississippi valley.

'The names new-light and Campbellite are due to the fact that it became abundant and the subject of observation when the religious denomination bearing those names originated' (1885 *Stand. Nat. Hist.* III. 235).

1872 *Harper's Mag.* July 315/2 'What do you call those fish?' 'Campbellites,' promptly responded the boy. **1884** GOODE *Nat. Hist. Aquatic Animals* 407 The Crappie. . . . Other names are . . . 'New Light' and 'Campbellite' in Kentucky and Indiana.

+**Camp chair.** A form of folding chair suitable for use when camping. — **1861** *Rep. Comm. Patents* (1863) I. 467 Peter J. Hardy, of New York, N.Y., Improved Camp Chair. **1885** *Harper's Mag.* 631/1 Winthrop found a camp chair, and placed it near her.

+**Camp distemper.** *Obs.* Camp fever. — **1779** E. PARKMAN *Diary* 145 He is ill of bilious Fever and Camp Distemper. **1798** I. ALLEN *Hist. Vermont* 71 The small-pox and a camp distemper raged in the army which was in a bad state of health and spirits.

+**Campeachy hat.** [*Campeachy* or *Campeche*, Mexico.] A type of hat having a broad brim for wear in hot climates. — **1858** *Texas Almanac* (*advt.*), We are constantly receiving a general assortment of . . . campeachy hats. **1888** CABLE *Bonaventure* 11 Broad-brimmed Campeachy hat of Sosthène.

+**Camp equipage.** The equipment of a camp. {=E. 'camp equipment' (1811)}

1775 J. ADAMS in *Warren-Adams Lett.* I. 118 The accounts I mean are of Ammunition; such as Powder, Ball, . . . Camp Equipage, [etc.]. **1777** *Jrnls. Cont. Congress* IX. 912/2 Every State shall . . . constantly have ready for use . . . a proper quantity of arms, ammunition and camp equipage. **1812** *Niles' Reg.* I. 373/1 The bill authorizing the purchase of . . camp equipage. **1828** A. SHERBURNE *Memoirs* 192 We were each of us heavily loaded with our camp equipage. **1846** SAGE *Scenes Rocky Mts.* xiii, Two pack mules for the conveyance of provisions and camp-equipage. **1858** VIELÉ *Following Drum* 210 Canales drinking out of a silver flagon . . . which at that time formed part of the camp equipage. **1862** F. Moore *Rebellion Rec.* V. II. 5 Wounding many, and capturing some prisoners, their camp equipage, etc. **1871** *Harper's Mag.* XLIII. 670/2 The Indians . . . had with them their families and camp equipage. **1881–5** MCCLELLAN *Own Story* 42 The governors . . . at once took steps to obtain . . . the requisite arms, . . . camp equipage, etc.

Camper. {1631–}

+**1.** One who attends a camp meeting.

1805 L. Dow *Travels* Wks. 1806 II. 61 We held Quarterly-meeting on Clarke's creek; some supposed I would get no campers. **1883** *Advance* 16 Aug., At the Sabbath services none but the regular campers were in attendance—the gates being closed to outsiders.

2. One who lives or lodges in a camp or tent. {1869–}

1861 *Ill. Agric. Soc. Trans.* IV. 22 The President was authorized . . . to grant permits to campers about the grounds. **1880** *Harper's Mag.* March 552/2 With the approach of cold weather the camper sells his outfit. **1883** *American* VII. 169 A true and circumstantial delineation of the camper's life in the Maine forests. **1900** DRANNAN *Plains & Mts.* 289 For the first time I saw Denver, there being then as I supposed about fifty tents and campers' houses in the place.

+**3.** *Camper out*, one who 'camps out.'

1856 KANE *Arctic Explor.* II. ix. 92 As ingeniously . . . crowded together as the campers-out in a buffalo-bag. **1880** *Atlantic Mo.* XLVI. 195/2 Berries, be they red, blue, or black, seem like a special providence to the camper-out. **1881** *Harper's Mag.* May 869/1 It also presumes . . . that the Camper-out is an invalid. **1891** *Fur, Fin, & Feather* March 207 Not one sportsman in a hundred, old camper out though he may be.

Camp fever. An epidemic fever incident to life in a camp; esp. typhus or typhoid fever. {1753–}

1758 C. REA *Journal* 15 Some with intermittents, very few or none with the regular symptoms of the Camp Fever. **1775** J. ANDREWS *Letters* 90 Ned Hill . . . is dead of the camp fever. **1778** in *S. Lit. Messenger* XXVII. 331/2 The danger of the Small Pox and camp fever is more alarming to many, than any danger they apprehend from the arms of the Enemy. **1825** NEAL *Bro. Jonathan* III. 43 Raw country people; terror struck; yielding, by droves, to the camp fever. **1848** E. BRYANT *California* 128 The fatal febrile complaint known among them as 'camp-fever.' **1879** *Diseases of Swine* 216 An army generates camp-fever, measles, and other diseases, no matter how strictly every sanitary regulation may be enforced. **1920** HUNTER *Trail Drivers of Texas* I. 252 Young Potter was seized with an attack of 'camp fever.'

Campfire.

1. A fire lit in an encampment for cooking or for warmth. (Freq. from *c*1845.) {1837–}

1675 *N.Y. State Col. Hist.* XII. 541 He hath beene . . . [with the] Indians & lay at their Campfires. **1818** SCHOOLCRAFT *Journal* 5 We find it necessary to gain a knowledge of things . . . [as] the best way of building a camp-fire. **1835** J. HALL *Sk. of West* II. 131 They effected the latter object [*i.e.* concealing their numbers] . . . by using but few camp-fires. **1840** *Knickerb.* XVI. 213 The generous camp-fire of blazing pine, which the men kindled. **1855** SIMMS *Forayers* 236 By the failing camp-fires and the slowly-rising moon, the picturesque of the bivouac was greatly enlivened and increased. **1872** 'MARK TWAIN' *Roughing It* iii. 34 Camp-fires and hot suppers in the deserts would be impossible but for the friendly sage-brush. **1884** CABLE *Dr. Sevier* liii, Off in the direction of the main fork the sky was all aglow with camp-fires. **1897** *Outing* XXX. 326/2 Through the lower gloom camp-fires glowed like red eyes from jutting points and scattered islands.

transf. **1850** GARRARD *Wah-To-Yah* 247 There are numbers of mountain men . . . whose prowess in scalptaking and beaver-trapping is the theme of many campfires.

b. Attrib. with *circle, coffee, meal, smoke.*

*c***1837** CATLIN *Indians* II. 198 The camp-fire circle and the wigwam fireside, gave silent audience to the whispered narratives of the 'travelled Indian.' **1852** J. W. BOND *Minnesota* 259 A little boiled ham, salt, and hard bread . . . added additional zest to the camp-fire meal. **1881** *Harper's Mag.* March 549/1 The Indians squatted on the floor . . . with a smell of camp-fire smoke . . . about them. **1887** *Century Mag.* March 738/1 The suppers of bacon and freshly caught trout, and the late lingering over the camp-fire coffee.

+**2.** A social gathering of members of a post or posts of the Grand Army of the Republic, as if around a campfire.

1884 *Boston Journal* 6 Sept., Edwin-Humphrey Post No. 104 G.A.R. of this town celebrated its fifteenth anniversary by a camp-fire Friday evening. **1885** *Boston Herald* 1 July, The fourth annual reunion of the Lake Sunapee G.A.R. Association opened to-day. . . . A camp fire was held this evening.

Camp follower. One other than a soldier who follows a camp or an army. {1810–} — **1858** GLISAN *Jrnl. Army Life* 413 Two hundred Camp followers, packers, wagoners, etc. were to leave Walla Walla. **1864** J. N. EDWARDS *Shelby* 467 Numerous camp-followers, dead-heads and stragglers . . . incontinently fled . . . with shouts of terror. **1865** GRIGSBY *Smoked Yank* (1891) 187 Guess she isn't much of a lady after all. Believe she is a kind of a camp-follower. **1879** TOURGEE *Fool's Errand* 161 At the North [a] carpet-bagger [was] a man without means, character, or occupation, an adventurer, a camp-follower, 'a bummer.' **1889** *Century Mag.* Jan. 470/1 The camp-followers had made away with nearly all our haversacks and blankets. *a***1918** G. STUART *On Frontier* I. 147 We then went to Camp Floyd . . . selling our horses to the soldiers and camp followers.

Camp furniture. The light, folding, or other portable furniture of a camp or encampment. {1857} — **1781** *Va. St. Papers* I. 449 No more clothing, camp furniture etc. is in future to be furnished the Gentlemen of the army from the public Store. **1837** IRVING *Bonneville* I. 234 A breast-work was thrown up of saddles, baggage, and camp furniture. **1865–6** *Ill. Agric. Soc. Trans.* VI. 40 Best Set of Folding Camp Furniture: [by] H. H. Palmer.

+**Campground.**

1. The site of a camp meeting.

1805 L. Dow *Travels* Wks. 1806 II. 94, I viewed the Camp-ground, and preparations making for the meeting. **1820** DEWEES *Lett. from Texas* 16 There were at the camp ground, three ministers and a considerable congregation. **1856** STOWE *Dred* I. 279 A fatted coon [was] to serve as the basis of a savory stew on the camp-ground. **1900** C. WINCHESTER *W. Castle* 103 Pastor Castle . . . started for the camp ground, with a one-horse load of baggage and provisions.

2. A camping ground.

1816 U. BROWN *Journal* II. 360 Their Pilot mist his way, & never could find their Camp ground. **1828** A. SHERBURNE *Memoirs* 248, I passed over Gen. Washington's camp ground. **1837** PECK *New Guide* 182 Let the reader imagine an extensive Camp-ground, a mile in circumference. **1848** E. BRYANT *California* 163 Our camp-ground, we conjecture, is the same that was occupied by captain Fremont last year. **1852** *S. Lit. Messenger* XVIII. 48/2 This afternoon, as we approached a beautiful camp-ground, on Ash Creek, a large herd came rushing by our front. **1888** GRIGSBY *Smoked Yank* i. 16 Perhaps some old soldier . . . may let it lead him back to the old camp ground. **1900** DRANNAN *Plains & Mts.* 422 We saw a band of Indians . . . evidently bound for the same camp ground that the soldiers were. **1923** J. H. COOK *On Old Frontier* 40 Roberts pointed out the course . . . and then rode ahead to select our first camp ground.

Camphene. Also **camphine.** [From CAMPHOR.]

1. Rectified spirits of turpentine, esp. used as a fuel for lamps. Also attrib. with *oil.* {1839–}

1843 *Niles' Nat. Reg.* 19 Aug. 400 This is the forty-seventh death which has been caused by the accidental explosion of the camphine oil. **1852** *Harper's Mag.* Jan. 281/1 The picture . . . seemed more beautiful by daylight than it had appeared by the midnight camphene. **1863** B. TAYLOR *H. Thurston* 340 Mrs. Waldo rustled about in a dark-green silk (turned, and with spots carefully erased by camphene). **1870** 'O. OPTIC' *Field & Forest* 16 They took that jug of whiskey, but it's jest like camphene. 'Taint fit to drink no more'n pizen. **1889** BRAYLEY *Boston Fire Dept.* 293 The manufacture, storage, and sale of petroleum, camphene, and burning-fluids.

2. Attrib. and comb., as *camphene(-fed) burner, lamp*, etc.

1845 *Knickerb.* XXV. 178 The 'black snow-storm' that was falling silently from the chimney of our camphine reading-lamp. **1849** *Rep. Comm. Patents* (1850) 72 Improvement in Camphine Lamps. **1861** *Vanity Fair* 5 Jan. 11/1 We once saw a combustible old woman, upon whom conflagration had unexpectedly come through a crack in a camphene lamp. **1873** E. S. PHELPS *Trotty's Wedding* xviii, We never thought of the camphene-burner. **1880** *Scribner's Mo.* Oct. 856/1 The red, camphene-fed lamp of the venders' torches flare and flicker.

Camphor. Also *dial.* **camphir(e), cam(p)fire.** {1553–, *camphire*; 1605–, *camphor.*}

1. The whitish, translucent, volatile substance so called.

(*a*) **1729** *Md. Hist. Mag.* XVIII. 333 To be had of Eyre & Beecher Druggists . . . 16 B. Camphir, £0 . . 4 . . 0. **1834** C. A. DAVIS *Lett. J. Downing* 261 When it gits hold, kamfire and lodnum stand no chance with it! **1869** STOWE *Oldtown Folks* 87 She's fainted clean away. . . . I must jest run for the camphire.

(*b*) **1790** *Penna. Packet* 1 Jan. 4/1 Doctor Amos Gregg . . . has just imported . . . a fresh and general Assortment of Drugs and Medicines; among which are . . . Ipecacuana, Camphor, Rhubarb. **1851** A. CARY *Clovernook* 192 A small bottle of camphor [was] Mrs. Claverell's infallible remedy for all disease. **1857** C. VAUX *Villas* 85 One almost expects to see the lady of the house walk in with a bottle of camphor in her hand, to prevent infection. **1873** BAILEY *Life in Danbury* 42 He was shrieking camphor and profanity at every leap.

2. Attrib. with *bag, ball, bottle; chest, trunk.*

1852 STOWE *Uncle Tom* xxix, Marie sobbed, . . . and called Mammy . . . to bring her the camphor-bottle, and to bathe her head. **1861** — *Pearl Orr's Isl.* I. 59 That ar shawl your mother keeps in her campfire chist. **1869** — *Oldtown Folks* 34 Mrs. Major had a real *Ingy* shawl up in her 'camphire' trunk. **1877** *Harper's Mag.* Jan. 287/2 If it isn't typhoid, it's consumption, or rheumatics, or something worse. I never catch it. I always wear a camphor bag. **1902** L. BELL *Hope Loring* 98 The odour of sanctity is so strong in our house that I carry camphor balls in my pockets to counteract it.

+**Camphor ice.** A cerate having camphor as an ingredient. — **1881** A. A. HAYES *New Colorado* 197 In alkali regions, glycerine, or what is called 'camphor ice,' should be used on face and hands.

Camphorwood. The wood of the camphor tree, freq. used for making chests or trunks. Used attrib. — **1859** STOWE *Minister's Wooing* xii, Mrs. Katy, Mary, and . . . the dressmaker, might have been observed sitting in solemn senate around the camphor-wood trunk.

Camp hospital. The hospital of a military encampment. — **1867** J. M. CRAWFORD *Mosby* 28 The dangers of the battle-field and . . . sickness in a camp hospital, were no drawback to their ardor. **1885** *Century Mag.* XXX. 461/1 A field . . . was occupied by a camp hospital. The field was filled with hospital tents.

+**Camp house.** A cabin or house at a camp, esp. at a summer camp. — **1897** *Outing* XXX. 374/2 The permanent camp . . . , of course, is more of a house than a camp, and may be roughly built of large logs [etc.]. . . . This style of camp-house has proved thoroughly useful for its purpose and has many friends.

+**Camp hunt.** A hunt of several days' duration. — *a***1846** *Quarter Race Ky.*, etc. 44 You see a passel uv us fellers made up a camp-hunt betwixt us. **1889** *Congress. Rec.* 19 Jan. 1010/2 The 'camp hunts' for deer, . . . in his day, as now, were in vogue in Louisiana.

* **Camping,** *vbl. n.*

* **1.** Living in a camp or camps; accommodation for forming a camp; settling down in a camp or for a halt.

1846 W. STEWART *Altowan* I. viii. 201 There is good grass and camping to the very base. **1888** *Century Mag.* Jan. 448/1 Tracks seen . . . just before camping, had shown that wild horses were in the vicinity. **1890** BRET HARTE *Waif of Plains* 86 Why, on'y the week afore we kem up to you, that thar hoss bolted with me at camping!

2. Attrib. with *cap, expedition, fire, outfit, party*, etc.

1832 *Louisville Directory* 108 There must be a spring near the spot, and marks of an old camping fire. **1844** GREGG *Commerce of Prairies* II. 74 Robledo, a camping-site upon the river. **1850** W. COLTON *3 Years Calif.* 317 A few gray hairs strayed from under his camping-cap. **1861** *Army Regulations* 87 When the camping-party precedes the regiment [etc.]. **1880** *Harper's Mag.* Aug. 397 If the camping outfit is dispensed with . . . great speed [may be] attained. **1902** A. MACGOWAN *Last Word* 395 Camping expeditions—nights on the bald prairie. **1923** C. J. DUTTON *Shadow on Glass* 116 We were going on a little camping trip in a few days.

Camping ground. Ground forming the site of a camp; a campground or camping place. {1867}

1837 IRVING *Bonneville* I. xvi. 165 Most of these kind of disasters to traders and trappers arise from . . . the position of their camping ground. **1844** FRÉMONT *Expl. Exped.* (1845) 264 We had a very poor camping-ground, a swampy, salty spot, with a little long unwholesome grass. **1850** L. SAWYER *Way Sketches* 24 Found good camping grounds today, about every five miles. **1888** P. H. SHERIDAN *Memoirs* I. 167 This section of our country . . . had many advantages in the way of better camping-grounds. **1902** WISTER *Virginian* xxvi. 314 There was no telling how wide this pine strip might extend . . . before they could . . . reach another suitable camping-ground.

fig. **1888** *N.Y. Examiner* Aug. (F.), They say that he will soon go to the Eternal Camping Ground to join the many jolly campers who have gone before.

+**Camping out,** *vbl. n.* [CAMP *v.*[1] 3.] The action or an occasion of living in the open in a camp or tent.

1834 *Western Mo. Mag.* II. 664 All the taverns and houses of entertainment are crowded with strangers of another class— . . . families who are not accustomed to 'camping out.' **1837** H. MARTINEAU *Society* I. 293 The 'camping out' is usually done in a sheltered, dry spot in the woods, not far from some little stream, where the kettle may be filled. **1848** COOPER *Oak Openings* II. i. 4 A place of encampment, or for 'camping out' as it is termed in the language of the west. **1869** 'MARK TWAIN' *Innocents* 436 If you call this camping-out, all right—but it isn't the style I am used to. **1901** WHITE *Claim Jumpers* xvi. 189 Reminiscences of the old home in 'Illinoy' and trophies of the new camping-out on the frontier.

attrib. **1873** BAILEY *Life in Danbury* 218 It is here the picnic and camping-out parties gather. **1887** J. BURROUGHS in *Century Mag.* XXXIV. 323 You meet in a walk, . . . or get acquainted on a fishing or camping-out expedition. **1891** *Fur, Fin, & Feather* March 188 [A] sportsman tells us how a camping-out party can have a good time.

Camping place. A campground or camping ground. {1616–}

1748 WASHINGTON *Writings* I. 4 We then . . . returned to our camping place at Stumps. **1775** ADAIR *Indians* 323 They came to the Choktah camping place. **1835** IRVING *Tour on Prairies* xxxiv. 259 We resumed our march about one o'clock . . . : it was late before we found a good camping place. **1883** 'MARK TWAIN' *Life on Miss.* lxviii, We passed Prairie du Chien, another of Father Marquette's camping-places. **1885** *Outing* Oct. 19/1 Five miles up and down mountains . . . led to a fine camping-place.

+**Camping spot.** A camping place. — *a***1861** WINTHROP *J. Brent* 61 The night's camping spot was near. **1890** RYAN *Told in Hills* 70 Remembering the camping-spot they were making for, she gave Betty rein. **1893** CHITTENDEN *Ranch Verses* 57 Hit's not my campin' spot.

* **Campion.** The popular name of various plants belonging to the genera *Lychnis* and *Silene* of the pink family (see quotations).

Also with other terms, as BLADDER CAMPION, etc. (q.v.).

1791 MUHLENBERG *Index Florae* 169 *Cucubalus stellatus.* Campion. **1832** HALE *Flora* 23 Bachelor's Button. *Lychnis, dioica.* White field campion. Flowers in June. **1840** DEWEY *Mass. Flowering Plants* 86 *Lychnis chalcedonica.* Scarlet Lychnis or Campion. A native of Russia, cultivated for its beauty. **1847** WOOD *Botany* 190 *Silene Acaulis.* Stemless Campion. . . . On the White Mts., N.H., and throughout Arctic America. **1857** GRAY *Botany* 55 *Silene Stellata.* (Starry Campion). . . . Wooded banks. **1901** MOHR *Plant Life Ala.* 496 *Silene ovata.* . . . Southern Campion. *Silene rotundifolia.* . . . Round-leaved Campion.

+**Camp-keeper.** One who tends a camp. — **1825** *Austin P.* (1924) II. 1206 Mr. Dixon . . . undertook surveying on the Brazos and Kilpatrick accompanied him as Campkeeper. **1837** IRVING *Bonneville* I. xviii. 190 Camp-keepers . . . cook, pack, and unpack; set up the tents, take care of the horses, and do all other duties usually assigned by the Indians to their women. *a***1842** O. RUSSEL *Journal* (1921) xii. 55 The camp keepers' business in winter quarters is to guard the horses, cook and keep fires. **1846** W. STEWART *Altowan* I. vi. 174 He was camp-keeper to some of the boys.

‖**Camp-keeping.** The care of a camp. — **1837** IRVING *Bonneville* I. vii. 91 In return for this protection, and for their camp keeping, they [=free trappers] are bound to dispose of all the beaver they take, to the trader who commands the camp, at a certain rate per skin.

Camp kettle. A type of pot adapted for use in camp. {1805–}

1755 in *Lett. to Washington* I. 112 Have sent to New York for some Camp Kettles. **1775** *S.C. Hist. Soc. Coll.* II. 29 The following articles were immediately wanted, viz.: bayonets, . . . camp kettles, [etc.]. **1784** WASHINGTON *Diaries* II. 299 The Camp Kettles are under a lock. **1792** IMLAY *Western Territory* 143 By having two or three camp kettles, . . . and by kindling a fire they may soon dress their food. **1812** *Niles' Reg.* II. 131/1 The purveyor of public supplies advertises for . . . 5000 iron camp kettles. **1846** SAGE *Scenes Rocky Mts.* xiii, Filling a large camp-kettle with portions of the 'fleece' and ribs, we allowed it to boil. **1861** NORTON *Army Lett.* 28 Our cooking is done in the open air, by swinging our camp kettles on poles over the fire. **1885** *Harper's Mag.* July 189/1 The black face of the negro cook . . . is bent over the camp kettle, filled to the brim with steaming coffee for the men's breakfast.

+**Camp kit.** (See quotations.) — **1864** *Rep. Comm. Patents* (1866) I. 992 Camp Kit.—December 20, 1864.—This invention consists in the arrangement of two plates forming a case, in which the cooking and eating utensils for a soldier or traveller may be conveniently packed and carried. **1874** KNIGHT 435/1 *Camp-kit,* a box, with its contents, for containing soldiers' cooking and mess utensils, such as the camp-kettle, plates, etc. **1880** *Harper's Mag.* Aug. 400/2 The camp kit . . . must be compact as well as light.

+**Camp meeting.**

1. 'A meeting held in the wood or field for religious purposes, where the assemblage encamp and remain several days. These meetings are generally held by the Methodists' (B. '59). Cf. WOOD MEETING.

'The practice of holding such meetings originated in the United States in 1799, and is still common, especially in the Methodist denomination' (*Cent.* '89). In very frequent use from *c*1805 to *c*1885.

1803 L. DOW *Travels* Wks. 1806 II. 21 We went on to the camp-meeting which I had appointed last August. **1804** in C. Janson *Stranger in A.* (1807) 107 The public is hereby informed, that a Camp-Meeting will be held near Mr. Minard Farley's. *a***1808** in J. Lambert *Travels* (1813) II. 271 Camp meetings are held in the open fields. **1810** J. LEE *Short Hist. Methodists* 279 About this time [1801] Camp Meetings were first introduced. But I never could learn whether they began in the upper parts of South-Carolina, in Tennessee, or in Kentucky. **1822** J. WOODS *English Prairie* 216 We passed a wood on the east side of the mountains, where a camp-meeting had recently been held; these meetings often continue four or five days. **1836** W. O'BRYAN *Travels* 37 In the summer, or about Autumn, the Methodists hold their protracted meetings sometimes in the open air, where the people erect tents (generally in a wood) this is called a Camp-meeting. **1843** 'CARLTON' *New Purchase* II. 130 How'd do! Mr. Carlton—come, won't you go to camp meetin? **1847** R. DAVIDSON *Presbyterian Ch. in Ky.* 134 The first regular Camp-Meeting was held in the vicinity of Gasper river church, in July, 1800. **1865** 'MARK TWAIN' *Sk., Jumping Frog,* If there was a camp-meeting he would be there reglar to bet on Parson Walker, which he judged to be the best exhorter about here. **1875** *Chicago Tribune* 2 July 8/2 The yearly camp-meeting of the M.E. churches in this district commenced yesterday on the old rendezvous at Desplaines. **1883** *Harper's Mag.* Jan. 283/1 The great festivals of Western life are camp-meetings, barbecues, and log-rollings. **1886** *Century Mag.* Nov. 29/2 The camp-meeting may be said, with no irreverent intention, to have been their [*i.e.* of Ill. pioneers] principal means of intellectual excitement. **1901** DUNCAN & SCOTT *Allen & Woodson Co., Kansas* 59 The 'Camp Meeting' was one of the most important features of church work for the first twenty years of the County's history. . . . A large and well shaded grove on the banks of some stream, . . . was selected, and there the people would come in covered wagons with tents, and spend two or three and sometimes four weeks.

2. a. Attrib. with *day, district, enclosure*, etc.

1804 *Phila. Gazette* 28 Sept. 3/2, 38 carts were counted on the camp-meeting ground on Sunday last. **1837** *S. Lit. Messenger* III. 658 There were beauty and poetry in the minds which originated these camp-meeting gatherings. **1851** *Polly Peablossom* 71 As I was er sayin', camp meetin' day it came. **1853** BALDWIN *Flush Times Ala.* 108 The camp-meeting standard of elocution. **1866** MOORE *Women of War* 133 A large camp-meeting supply tent, where barrels of goods were stored. *c***1866** 'MARK TWAIN' *Scriptural Panoramist* Works VII. (1922) 360 He [=a pianist] was to fit it [a picture] to a dot with a piece of music that would . . . warm them [=the audience] up like a camp-meeting revival. **1882** *N.Y. Tribune* 7 Aug. 4/3 The camp-meeting season has set in with vigor so far as the crowds in attendance are concerned. **1900** C. WINCHESTER *W. Castle* 105 Returning to the camp meeting enclosure, he entered a tent where a prayer meeting was being held. **1910** J. HART *Vigilante Girl* 121 Those chronic backsliders in the camp-meeting districts.

b. *Camp-meeting ditty, hymn, song*, one composed for or sung at a camp meeting.

1863 B. TAYLOR *H. Thurston* 286 Melinda . . . strode away, . . . muttering fragments of camp-meeting hymns. **1872** EGGLESTON *End of World* 270 They had passed to an excited shouting of the old camp-meeting ditty. **1902** BANKS *Newspaper Girl* 153 In an ecstasy of religious fervour she sang the camp-meeting hymns. **1912** MRS. WOODROW *Sally Salt* 80 Sally was . . . crooning camp-meeting songs under her breath.

+**Campoody, -ie.** [Piute, from Sp. *campo* 'camp,' etc.] **a.** An Indian village. **b.** An Indian hut. — **1850** JACKSON *Forty-niner* (1920) 10 There is an Indian campoody up on the ridge above Brush Creek, where about two hundred Digger Indians are camped. **1869** 'MARK TWAIN' *Innocents* li. 541 Endor . . . is worse than an Indian *campoodie*. **1887** *Rep. Indian Affairs* 11 Many live in comfortable board or log houses, and others in 'campoodies' (huts) made of puncheons, pieces of boards &c.

+**Camp out.** [CAMP *v.*[1] 3.] An occasion of camping out. — **1879** STOCKTON *Rudder Grange* 120 If it gives you a good camp out, I don't mind.

+**Camp preacher.** One who preaches at a camp meeting. — **1845** JUDD *Margaret* I. xvi. 152 In the midst of all . . . might be heard the voice of the Camp-preacher. **1851** *Harper's Mag.* July 218/2 A camp preacher . . . thundered forth the evil consequences of not listening to what he was saying with reverence.

+**Camp-stove.** A light, portable, sheet-iron stove, 'adapted for heating a tent or hut, and for cooking purposes' (Knight).

1862 T. J. JACKSON in *Memoirs* (1892) 363 Last night was very cold, but . . . McGuire secured a camp-stove for me. **1870** KEIM *Sheridan's Troopers* (1885) 108 The camp-stove was too heavy to be hauled just at that moment. **1879** *Scribner's Mo.* Oct. 832/2 After placing a well-filled tea-kettle upon the roaring camp-stove, W—— . . . sought a convenient spot to carve the mutton. **1897** *Outing* XXX. 584/1 We had no cots or camp-stoves.

+**Campus.** [L., 'field.']

1. The principal grounds of a university, college, or school; the open space between or around the buildings. (Cf. COLLEGE YARD.)

First used at Princeton, and probably introduced by Witherspoon. A monograph on the use of the word, by Albert Matthews, appeared in the *Publications of the Colonial Society of Mass.* III. 431–7.

1774 in J. F. Hageman *Hist. Princeton* (1879) I. 102 Having made a fire in the Campus, we there burnt near a dozen pounds [of tea]. **1787** *Ib.* II. 316 A play . . . much practiced . . . by the grammar scholars with balls and sticks, in the back campus of the college. **1807** J. MacLean *Hist. College N.J.* (1877) II. 80 That part of the road to the eastward of the middle gate of the front campus. **1821** LaBorde *Hist. S.C. College* (1874) 123 That he be required to construe . . . twenty lines of Virgil's Æneid, and not be seen out of the Campus until he had done so. **1835** *Niles' Reg.* XLIX. 89 The large marquee, erected . . . in the campus of the college [at Princeton]. **1866** *Yale Lit. Mag.* XXXI. 146 (Th.), The students retreated hastily to the College Campus (after the riot of 1854). **1890** *Science* 12 Sept. 141/1 The main buildings [at Cornell U.] are principally at the north extremity of the campus. **1897** *Scribner's Mag.* XXII. 23/1 Groups of men begin to thicken about the [Yale] campus. **1910** O. JOHNSON *Varmint* 20 The school bell, ringing a hundred laggards across the budding campus to hard seats and blackboarded walls. **1921** PAINE *Comr. Rolling Ocean* 10 There are more kinds of education than you dig out of a college campus.

2. A field for athletic sports.

1887 *Lippincott's Mag.* Sept. 453 The Campus, or play-ground, is several miles off. **1897** A. MATTHEWS in *Publ. Col. Soc. Mass.* III. 433 At twenty of these [colleges] . . . Campus is applied to an athletic field alone. **1902** CLAPIN 94 *Campus*, a student's word meaning the college grounds; also, the athletic field.

Camp-woman. A female camp follower; a soldier's wife who accompanies an expedition.

1759 *Essex Inst. Coll.* XIX. 187 There was 2 Campwomen sent back from Crown point they was not allowd to follow the army. **1847** in H. Howe *Hist. Coll. Ohio* 434 Many of Wayne's soldiers and camp-women settled in the town, so that it for a time became a town of drunkards and a sink of corruption. **1874** GLISAN *Jrnl. Army Life* 453 The wives of the private soldiers and non-commissioned officers are called camp-women.

***Can,** *n.* Also †**cann, canne.**

***1.** A metal vessel for holding liquids, etc., usu. of small size and cylindrical form.

1639 *Md. Archives* IV. 78 A silver canne bruised. *a***1656** BRADFORD *Hist.* 196 One in his sicknes desiring but a small cann of beere. **1725** SEWALL *Letter-Book* II. 189 Large porringer with a Cover. One small Cann. **1750** WALKER *Journal* 11 June, We lost a Tomohawk and a Cann by the Flood. **1781** *Salem Gazette* 3 July, All kinds of turned Work, in Silver, such as Tankards, Cans, &c. **1820** *Columbian Centinel* 5 Jan. 3 George Andews [*sic*] . . . will offer for sale . . . gold burnished China Tea Sets, Cups, Cans, Saucers &c.' **1895** *Chicago Tribune* 6 April 1 A fight growing out of a dispute about a can of beer.

b. A large metal container in which milk is sent to the market.

1856 *Rep. Comm. Patents: Agric. 1855* 29 Vessels, called 'cans,' or 'kettles,' used for conveying it [milk], are made of tin, commonly containing 40 quarts each. **1878** *Vt. Bd. Agric. Rep.* 78 That evening I was at every can of milk as soon as the cover was raised.

+**2.** A small metal container in which meats, fruits, vegetables, etc., are hermetically sealed for preservation. {=E. *tin*}

1867 RICHARDSON *Beyond Miss.* 147 Mitchell . . . was fined two cans of oysters for contempt. **1870** *Rep. Comm. Agric. 1869* 451, 2,400,000 cans of sweet corn have been put up in Maine the past season. **1874** *Harper's Weekly* XVIII. 799/2 Salmon . . . pickled, smoked, and put up in cans. **1891** B. MATTHEWS in *Harper's Mag.* July 219 An Englishman calls for a *tin* of condensed milk, when an American would ask for a *can*. **1902** LORIMER *Lett. Merchant* 32 When we get through with a hog nowadays, he's scattered through a hundred different cans and packages. **1916** E. PORTER *David* 147 One [of the boys] had an old tomato can with a string tied to it.

comb. **1888** *Ann. Cyclop. 1887* 743 Baltimore, Md.—May 3, 1886. Canmakers strike for eight-hour system.

+**b.** A glass jar in which fruits, vegetables, etc., are 'put up' in the home.

1884 MRS. OWENS *Cook Book* 319 Fill your cans, as many as will stand in your wash boiler. . . . Put cold water in the boiler, nearly to the top of the jars.

+**Can,** *v.*

1. *tr.* To put or seal up (meats, fruits, or vegetables) in metal cans or glass jars for preservation. Also absol.

1861 *Ill. Agric. Soc. Trans.* IV. 511 Good fruit . . . is always marketable in large cities . . . and much will be dried, or canned, for export. **1876** M. F. HENDERSON *Cooking* 245 The manner of canning one kind of fruit or vegetable applies to all kinds, except corn. **1883** *U.S. Museum Bul. 27* 110 The process of canning Crabs is somewhat similar to that for lobsters, as practiced on the New England coast. **1902** LORIMER *Lett. Merchant* 24 The boys drive a bunch of steers toward him, or cows maybe, if we're canning. **1913** STRATTON-PORTER *Laddie* iii. (1917) 55 If we found one [peach] on the ground, we had to carry it to her, because it *might* be sound enough to can or spice for a fair.

transf. **1865** *Atlantic Mo.* XV. 395/1 The copper vessel wherein Solomon had so cunningly 'canned' the rebellious Afrit.

2. *slang.* To dismiss from a position or situation; to expel from a college or school.

1905 *Dialect Notes* III. 73 Jim was up before the faculty and got canned for two weeks. **1912** *Ib.* 572 *Can*, v.t. To dismiss one summarily. . . . Can in this sense, it should be noted, does not mean 'to put into a can,' as is frequently supposed, but 'to tie a can to,' which expression is also used. [Western Ind.] **1914** ATHERTON *Perch of Devil* 269 They would merely be made scapegoats or canned—I beg pardon, fired. **1921** PAINE *Comr. Rolling Ocean* 99 He had trouble in prep school and was canned.

Canack. (See CANUCK *a.* and *n.*)

Canada. [Name of the Dominion lying north of the U.S.]

1. *attrib.* Belonging or native to Canada; made or grown in Canada.

1726 PENHALLOW *Indian Wars* (1824) 33 They took Monsieur Lafebure, and his two sons, with a Canada Indian. *c***1729** CATESBY *Carolina* I. 23 A Canada Indian . . . told me he had seen them [='pigeons of passage'] . . . far north of the river St. Lawrence. **1776** *Vt. Hist. Soc. Coll.* I. 16 That part of America being situated south of Canada line, . . . commonly called . . . the New Hampshire Grants. **1811** *Niles' Reg.* I. 168/2 The timber . . . was principally of Canada oak. **1829** R. C. SANDS *Writings* II. 152 A gentleman in a Canada fur cap. **1839** W. SCOTT *Let. to J. Monroe* 12 March, If I could have come by Washington instead of proceeding . . . to the Canada border. **1859** *Harper's Mag.* Sept. 504/1 Canada straw hats for Ben and Peter. **1869** W. MURRAY *Adventures* 28 Canada fly . . . [is] an excellent fly. **1874** HOWELLS *Chance Acquaintance* 57 Fortified against the winter by a huge Canada stove of cast-iron.

+**b.** In specific names, as *Canada blueberry, blue grass, crane, distemper*, etc.: see quotations and cf. CANADIAN 4. (See also CANADA BALSAM, CORN, etc.)

1858 THOREAU *Maine Woods* 95 Many plants . . . grew abundantly between the rails,—as Labrador tea, Kalmia glauca, Canada blueberry. *a***1862** *Ib.* 311 At camps and carries [I saw]: raspberry, *Vaccinium Canadense* (Canada blueberry). **1901** MOHR *Plant Life Ala.* 826 *Poa compressa*, Canada Blue Grass. Prairie region and north, [cultivated] for pasture. **1844** *Nat. Hist. N.Y., Zoology* II. 218 Wilson long ago supposed the Brown or Canada crane to be the young of the great white Whooping Crane. . . . Dr. Bachman has since conclusively demonstrated the identity of the two. **1802** J. DRAYTON *S. Carolina* 63 A malignant fever called the Yellow Water, Canada distemper, &c. . . . has carried off numbers of the horses in the United States. **1907** W. LILLIBRIDGE *Trail* 126 The swelling, diminishing note . . . of the grey Canada honker. **1897** SUDWORTH *Arborescent Flora* 30 *Pinus divaricata*, . . . Jack Pine, . . . Canada Horn-cone Pine (Cal. lit[erature]). **1821** *Jrnl. Science* III. 278 Floral . . . Calendar for Plainfield, Mass. . . . July 8. Roundleaved hypericum, Canada or narrowleaved hypericum . . . [are] beginning to ripen. **1894** Coulter *Bot. W. Texas* III. 550 *Elymus Canadensis* (Canada Lyme-grass) . . . [grows on] river banks, Texas and northward. **1815** J. Hutton *Fashionable Follies* I. ii, I'll bilk old Perry—get a pair of Canada ponies for the mammoth curricle. **1849** Emmons *Agric. N.Y.* II. 265 Canada pop-corn, Egyptian corn. . . . There are several varieties . . . used only for popping. **1826** J. Godman *Nat. Hist.* II. 150 The Canada Porcupine. *Hystrix Dorsata.* . . . In some parts of the Western states, . . . they are found in great abundance, and are highly prized by the aboriginals, both for the sake of their flesh and their quills. **1848** Bartlett 62 Canada Rice. (*Zizania aquatica.*) A plant which grows in deep water along the edges of ponds and sluggish streams, in the Northern States and Canada. **1844** *Nat. Hist. N.Y., Zoology* II. 44 This well known bird [*Bombycilla Carolinensis*] has various popular names. . . . In Massachusetts, it is called Canada Robin.

+2. *absol.* The Canada goose.

[**1871** Lewis *Poultry Book* 90 The America Wild Goose is identical with the Canada.] **1894** *Outing* XXIV. 74/2 We see four old Canadas winging their way diagonally toward us.

+**Cañada.** *S.W.* [Sp.] A narrow valley between mountains; a small canyon; a ravine.

1836 C. J. Latrobe *Rambler in Mexico* 64 We considered the scenery of the Cañada superior to any we had ever seen. **1838** 'Texian' *Mexico v. Texas* 58 It is a sequestered *canada,* (id est, glen) on the Eastern side of the Sierra madre. **1844** Gregg *Commerce of Prairies* II. 146 A water-course, at the distance of a hard day's ride, which he designated as a *cañada* or valley. **1848** Bryant *California* 148 The mountains on either side of the Canada or gorge are precipitous. **1850** W. Colton *3 Years in Calif.* 320 A gush of waters from the rocks, which beetled over a cañada. **1874** Raymond *6th Rep. Mines* 332 On the opposite side of the cañada . . . is another ledge. **1877** Harte *Story of Mine,* etc. 410 A keen wind . . . was already creeping from the cañada as from the mouth of a funnel. **1893** — *Susy* 2 The San Leandro turnpike . . . [rises] from this cañada into the upper plains again.

Canada balsam.

1. A transparent aromatic liquid resin exuded from the balsam fir, *Abies balsamea.*

1818 *Mass. H. S. Coll.* 2 Ser. VIII. 170 We have . . . spruce, hemlock, and silver fir, from the last of which the Canada balsam is obtained. **1858** Warder *Hedges & Evergreens* 256 *Picea balsamea* . . . abounds in resinous matter which is collected and known as Canada Balsam. **1859** Bartlett 20 The blisters under the bark [of the Balsam fir] furnish the well-known 'Canada Balsam.' **1869** *Amer. Naturalist* III. 165 The Diatomaceæ, after . . . boiling in acid can be mounted in Canada balsam.

2. *attrib.* (with *fir*) or *ellipt.* The balsam fir.

1859 Bartlett 20 Balsam Fir . . . is also called Canada Balsam and Gilead Fir. **1897** Sudworth *Arborescent Flora* 51 *Abies balsamea.* . . . Common names . . . [include] Canada Balsam (N.C.).

+**Canada corn.** A species of corn associated with Canada. — **1837** Colman *Mass. Agric. Rep.* (1838) 82 This is what we call Canada corn; a kind I never planted here before. **1850** *New Eng. Farmer* II. 175 The Canada corn, and the small cap corn, will bear near planting. **1851** J. F. W. Johnston *Notes N. Amer.* I. 152 In some the horny part is large, as in the varieties known by the names of brown, Canada, rice, and pop corns.

+**Canada flycatcher.** The Canadian fly-catching warbler, *Myiodioctes canadensis,* Aud., abundant in the eastern states. — **1811** Wilson *Ornithology* III. 100 [The] Canada Flycatcher, *Muscicapa Canadensis,* . . . is a solitary, and in the lower parts of Pennsylvania, rather a rare species. **1828** Bonaparte *Synopsis* 79 The Canada Flycatcher . . . inhabits throughout the United States during summer: rare especially in the Atlantic States. **1839** Peabody *Mass. Birds* 297 The Canada Flycatcher . . . is not now uncommon in this state. **1858** Baird *Birds Pacific R.R.* 294 Canada Flycatcher . . . [inhabits] eastern United States to the Mississippi.

Canada goose. The common wild goose (*Bernicla canadensis*) of North America.

[**1676** Willoughby *Ornithology* 276 *Anser Canadensis:* The Canada Goose. . . . Locum titulus indicat.] **1731** Catesby *Carolina* I. 92 The Canada Goose. . . . In Winter they come from the Northern parts of America to Carolina, &c. **1813** Wilson *Ornithology* VIII. 53 [The] Canada Goose, *Anas Canadensis,* . . . is the common Wild Goose of the United States, universally known over the whole country. *Ib.* 7 The Canada Goose is now domesticated in numerous quarters of the country. **1835** Audubon *Ornith. Biog.* III. 1 The Canada Goose. . . . The number of individuals that remain at all seasons in the milder latitudes . . . fully entitles this bird to be looked upon as a permanent resident there. **1856** *Spirit of Times* (N.Y.) 13 Dec. 242/1 The Canada goose and Hutchins' goose make their migratory journeys over land. **1874** Coues *Birds N.W.* 553 Canada Goose; Common Wild Goose. . . . It nests in various parts of the Upper Missouri and Yellowstone regions, *in trees.*

+**Canada grouse.** The spotted grouse (*Canace* or *Dendragapus canadensis*) of the northern and Canadian forests. — **1839** Audubon *Ornith. Biog.* V. 563 Spotted or Canada Grous, *Tetrao Canadensis,* . . . is also plentiful on the Rocky Mountains and the plains of the Columbia. **1844** *Nat. Hist. N.Y., Zoology* II. 207 The Spruce or Spotted Grouse, or Canada Grouse, or Spruce Partridge as it is called in this State, is yet common in the northern counties. **1874** Coues *Birds N.W.* 395 The Canada Grouse is chiefly a boreal bird, reaching but a little way over our border.

+**Canada jay.** The whisky-jack, *Perisoreus canadensis.*

1811 Wilson *Ornithology* III. 33 [The] Canada Jay, *Corvus Canadensis,* . . . inhabits the country extending from Hudson's bay . . . to the river St. Lawrence. *Ib.,* [The] Canada Jay . . . feeds on black moss, worms, and even flesh. **1839** Audubon *Ornith. Biog.* V. 208 Now, to my eye, the Canada Jay is as elegant in its movements . . . as any other of our Jays, although its apparel is certainly very homely. **1850** S. F. Cooper *Rural Hours* 310 The Canada jay—sometimes seen in this State [N.Y.]; . . . is not so fine a bird as the common sort. **1872** *Amer. Naturalist* VI. 398 The Canada jays were of frequent occurrence in the mountains. **1892** Torrey *Foot-Path Way* 100, I happened to espy a Canada Jay. . . . I was . . . desirous to hear his voice, the loud, harsh scream with which the books credit him. **1901** White *Westerners* 126 Occasionally she threw a remnant to the few silent Canada jays.

+**Canada lynx.** The loup-cervier (*Lynx canadensis*), a large, robust species of lynx. — **1840** Emmons *Mass. Quadrupeds* 33 The Northern or Canada Lynx presents a very striking resemblance to the cat. **a1862** Thoreau *Maine Woods* 188 Loup cervier (or Canada lynx) were plenty yet in burnt grounds.

+**Canada nettle.** The wood nettle, *Urtica canadensis.* — **1817–8** Eaton *Botany* (1822) 500. **1821** *Mass. H. S. Coll.* 2 Ser. IX. 157 Plants, which are indigenous in the township of Middlebury, [Vt., include] . . . *Urtica dioica,* Common nettle; *U. procera,* Great nettle; . . . *U. canadensis,* Canada nettle. **1859** Bartlett 5 *Albany Hemp,* . . . Canada nettle, so called from the use made of its fibrous bark.

+**Canada owl.** The American hawk owl, *Strix canadensis.* — **1792** Brackenridge *Adv. Capt. Farrago* 27 It is doubtless . . . the great Canada owl, that comes from the lakes.

+**Canada patriot.** (See quot. 1846.) — **c1845** Paulding *Madmen All* 192 Green-horns, Canada Patriots, Loafers. **1846** Mansfield *Winfield Scott* 287 The flame of insurrection was kindled in Canada. . . . The frontier inhabitants of the United States . . . enrolled themselves as Canada patriots or sympathizers . . . capable of bearing arms, . . . professed friends and abettors of the Canadian movement.

+**Canada plum.** The wild plum, *Prunus nigra.* — **1848** *Knickerb.* XXXI. 31 We add the Hawthorn, Poplar, . . . Larch and Canada-Plum. **1851** Barry *Fruit Garden* 120 The Canada or Wild Plum . . . abounds in Ohio, Michigan, and other western states. **1897** Sudworth *Arborescent Flora* 236 Canada Plum [is the common name in] Mass., N.Y., Mich., Ont.

+**Canada snakeroot.** The wild ginger, *Asarum canadense.* — **1832** Williamson *Maine* I. 122 Canada Snakeroot. . . . The aromatic flavour of its root has rendered it a fit and wholesome substitute for ginger. **1847** Darlington *Weeds & Plants* 269 The Canada Snake-root . . . is common in rich woodlands.

+**Canada sparrow.** The Canadian or tree sparrow, *Spizella monticola.* — **1869** Burroughs in *Galaxy* VIII. 173 The fox-sparrow . . . comes to us in the fall, from the North, where it breeds. Likewise the tree or Canada-sparrow. **1884** — in *Century Mag.* Dec. 220 In winter, especially, they sweep by me and around me in flocks,—the Canada sparrow, . . . the shore-lark, . . . the red-poll, the cedar-bird.

+**Canada thistle.** The cursed thistle, *Cnicus* (*Carduus*) *arvensis.*

'Canada Thistle. . . . First appeared in Canada, where it was probably introduced from France, as it is common in Normandy, and also in England' (B. '77). 'Within the memory of men now living, this plant came into the northern part of Vermont and New York, and has since spread to the south part of New England and New York' (Dewey *Mass. Flowering Plants* 122).

1799 *Mass. Spy* 31 July (Th.), A torvous, stubborn, and vexatious weed, known by the name of the Canada thistle. **1818** *Mass. H. S. Coll.* 2 Ser. VIII. 170 In July the lover of plants is gratified with . . . Canada and spear thistles. **1842** Mrs. Kirkland *Forest Life* I. v. 42 A passing flock of sheep . . . sowed it [a public square] thickly with Canada thistles, with which their fleeces were abundantly stored. **1847** Darlington *Weeds & Plants* 197 Canada Thistle . . . is, perhaps, the most execrable weed that has yet invaded the farms of our country. **1873** *Ill. Dept. Agric. Trans.* X. 208 'An act concerning Canada Thistles,' approved and in force March 15, 1872. **1897** *Chicago Tribune* 6 July 12/1 You are hereby notified . . . to cause all Canada thistles to be cut down.

+**Canada violet.** A species of violet (*Viola canadensis*) common along the Alleghanies and northward. — **1821** *Jrnl. Science* III. 274 Floral . . . calendar for Plainfield, Mass. . . . May 3. Lombardy poplar and Canada violet in blossom. **1857** Gray *Botany* 44 Canada Violet . . . [grows in] rich woods; common northward and along the Alleghanies. **1882** *Century Mag.* May 153/2 Our Canada violet . . . has a sweet perfume.

+**Canada warbler.** (**a**) The Canadian fly-catching warbler. (**b**) The black-throated blue warbler. — **1844** *Nat. Hist. N.Y., Zoology* II. 91 The Spotted Canada Warbler, *Sylvicola pardalina,* . . . is occasionally very rare in New York, or at least in its southern portions. **1865** *Atlantic Mo.* May 521/1 Those birds of the deep Northern forests, that, like the Speckled Canada Warbler . . . , only the privileged hear. **1868** *Amer. Naturalist* II. 176 The Canada Warbler (*Myiodioctes Canadensis*) . . . arrives about the middle of May. **1892** Torrey *Foot-Path Way* 16 In climbing the mountain path . . . [I] heard only twelve kinds of birds: red starts, Canada warblers [etc.].

***Canadian,** *n.* and *a.*

***1.** *n.* A native or inhabitant of Canada; in earlier use, a French inhabitant of Canada (cf. FRENCH CANADIAN).

1705 *Boston News-Letter* 14 May 1/2 Our Harbour was beset with . . . French Souldiers, . . . some Accadians, . . . and Cannadians. **1759** Brooks *Days of Spinning-Wheel* (1886) 11 The virtues of the plant . . . were first discovered by the Aborigines, and from them the Canadians learned them. **1784** CUTLER in *Mem. Academy* I. 454 The powdered root [of water avens] will cure tertian agues, and . . . is much used by the Canadians for that purpose. **1809** A. HENRY *Travels* 128 (*note*), *Populus nigra*, called, by the Canadians, *liard*. **1882** *Nation* 7 Sept. 203/1 The Canadians disliked Imperial copyright because it produced 'dear books.'

+2. A Canadian horse. (Cf. sense 3 b.)

1856 *Rep. Comm. Patents: Agric.* 43 We have blood animals, 'Morgans,' 'Lions,' 'Canadians,' and a very fine 'Norman' diligence horse. **1876** *Vt. Bd. Agric. Rep.* III. 132 The result of the cross of the Morgan upon this Canadian has been a great improvement to the Canadian.

3. *adj.* Of or pertaining to Canada; native to or residing in Canada. {*c*1789-}

1757 *Army Orders* 121 Two Canadian Prisoners . . . confined in the Fort at Albany. **1796** *Ann. 4th Congress* 2 Sess. 1670 The petition of the Canadian and Nova Scotia refugees. **1806** LEWIS in *L. & Clark Exped.* (1905) V. 114 One of our party . . . had previously made him a present of a pair of Canadian shoes or shoe-packs. **1807** IRVING *Salmagundi* xii. 272 Particular account of the Canadian Indians. **1813** *Niles' Reg.* IV. 10/2 They came down the Canadian side from Malden to fort George. **1835** HOFFMAN *Winter in West* II. 10 A room heated to suffocation by a large Canadian stove. **1842** CHANNING *Works* 624/1 Did such a state of things exist on the Canadian frontier? **1846** PARKMAN *Oregon Trail* (1849) 152 A shrivelled little figure, wrapped . . . in a dingy white Canadian capote. **1846** SAGE *Scenes Rocky Mts.* iii, We were further increased by the accession of two Canadian *voyageurs*—French of course. **1857** T. B. GUNN *N.Y. Boarding-Houses* 44 An old major who had been in the Canadian army. **1876** BANCROFT *Hist. U.S.* III. xiii. 193 The Canadian war-parties were on the alert.

+b. Denoting a breed of horses raised in Canada.

1816 'SCENE PAINTER' *Emigrant's Guide* 23 Canadian horses (a small but hardy race). **1831** PECK *Guide* 164 Wild horses, . . . of the Indian or Canadian breed. **1834** BRACKENRIDGE *Recoll.* 126 A youth . . . on a stout Canadian poney, issuing from the busy town. **1841** *S. Lit. Messenger* VII. 219/1 The vivacity of a little rough-coated, bob-tailed chunk of a Canadian poney. **1882** *Wheelman* I. 14/1 Like a racking Canadian horse, with his head down and forward, he rocked from side to side.

+4. In specific names: *Canadian balsam, barberry, blueberry, cherry tree, dogwood, elder,* etc.: see quots. and cf. under CANADA 1 b.

1806 LEWIS in *L. & Clark Exped.* (1905) IV. 46 This [fir] tree affords considerable quantities of a fine clear arromatic balsam in appearance and taste like the Canadian balsam. **1846** BROWNE *Trees Amer.* 37 The Canadian Berberry is a low shrub, not exceeding five feet in height. **1847** WOOD *Botany* 370 *Vaccinium Canadense.* . . . Canadian Blueberry . . . not uncommon in rocky fields and thickets, N.H. Me. **1813** MUHLENBERG *Cat. Plants* 48 *Prunus Canadensis*, Canadian Cherry Tree, *Habitat.* Pens. *Ib.* 17 *C[ornus] Canadensis*, Canadian Dogwood. **1802** J. DRAYTON *S. Carolina* 66 Canadian elder . . . grows near fences on high land. **1892** TORREY *Foot-Path Way* 16 A hurried search showed black polls . . . [and] one Canadian flycatcher (singing lustily). **1874** COUES *Birds N.W.* 80 *Myiodioctes Canadensis.* . . . Canadian Fly-catching Warbler. . . . *Hab.* . . . West to the Lower Missouri. **1836** LINCOLN *Botany* App. 140 *Solidago canadensis*, (Canadian golden-rod). **1847** WOOD *Botany* 331 *S[olidago] Canadensis*, Canadian Goldenrod, . . . [grows in] old fields, hedges, U.S. and Brit. Am. **1806** LEWIS in *L. & Clark Exped.* (1905) IV. 143 The common Canadian or wild goose. **1897** SUDWORTH *Arborescent Flora* 42 *Tsuga canadensis.* . . . Common names . . . [include] Canadian Hemlock. **1901** MOHR *Plant Life Ala.* 674 *Apocynum cannabinum* . . . Canadian Hemp. . . . The root is the 'Canadian hemp root' . . . of the United States Pharmacopœia. **1785** MARSHALL *Amer. Grove* 64 *Ilex canadensis.* Canadian, or Hedge-hog Holly. **1845** LINCOLN *Botany* App. 131/2 *Nemopanthes canadensis*, wild holly, Canadian holly. . . . Berries deep red. **1847** WOOD *Botany* 381 Canadian Holly . . . [grows in] damp or rocky woods, Can., New Eng. to Mich. **1878** Killebrew *Tennessee Grasses* 224 *Elymus Canadensis*, Canadian Lyme Grass. . . . Perennial, common, flowering in July. **1785** MARSHALL *Amer. Grove* 86 *Menispermum canadense.* Canadian Moonseed. **1843** TORREY *Flora N.Y.* II. 222 *Urtica Canadensis.* . . . Canadian Nettle. . . . Moist shady soils, particularly along rivers. **1854** *Penna. Agric. Rep.* 75 The next best oats, called Canadian. **1803** LAMBERT *Descr. Genus Pinus* 50 Canadian Pine, *P. Canadensis*, bears a great resemblance to the Common Yew. **1813** MUHLENBERG *Cat. Plants* 92 *Populus monilifera*, . . . Canadian Poplar. **1802** J. DRAYTON *View of South-Carolina* 72 Canadian puccoon. (*Sanguinaria Canadensis.*) . . . The root dies a bright red, with which the Indians used to paint themselves. **1822** *Jrnl. Science* IV. 183 A small quadruped . . . which I immediately knew to be the Canadian Rat, with large pouches on the sides of his neck. **1791** *Amer. Philos. Soc.* III. 114 *Sanicula canadensis* (Canadian Sanicle). **1874** COUES *Birds N.W.* 146 *Spizella Monticola*, . . . Canadian, or Tree Sparrow. . . . *Hab.*—North America at large, excepting, probably, the Gulf States. **1785** MARSHALL *Amer. Grove* 146 *Spiraea hypericifolia.* Canadian Spiraea. . . . This makes a very good appearance when in flower. **1795** WINTERBOTHAM *Hist. View* III. 392 Flowering Trees, Shrubs, &c., . . . [include] Canadian spiræa. **1836** R. WESTON *Visit* 102 What are called Canadian thistles . . . emigrate to the Southern States in great numbers. **a1862** THOREAU *Maine Woods* 320 *Desmodium Canadense* (Canadian tick-trefoil). **1843** TORREY *Flora N.Y.* I. 75 *Viola Canadensis.* . . . Canadian Violet . . . [grows in] shady woods in rich soil. **1839** AUDUBON *Ornith. Biog.* V. 188 Canadian Woodpecker. *Picus Canadensis* . . . is more plentiful . . . in the State of New York. **1785** MARSHALL *Amer. Grove* 151 *Taxus canadensis.* Canadian Yew-Tree . . . is a beautiful evergreen shrub, capable of being formed into any shape. **1860** *Ill. Agric. Soc. Trans.* IV. 462 An Evergreen Vine on the Fox River. . . . Mr. Edwards believes it the Canadian Yew.

Canadian French, *a.* and *n.* **1.** *adj.* Of or belonging to the native French stock of Canada; French Canadian. **2.** *n.* The variety of French spoken by natives of Canada. — **(1) 1853** *Harper's Mag.* VI. 582/2 The laborers are Canadian-French, and are giving loose to all the merriment which to them is constitutional. **(2) 1846** M'KENNEY *Memoirs* I. 62 These dexterous Canadians . . . enlivening the scene . . . with their boat songs, and a jabbering of their Canadian French. **1847** LANMAN *Summer in Wilderness* 146 They [the songs of the voyageurs] are invariably sung in Canadian French.

Canadian-Frenchman. A Canadian of French descent; a French Canadian. — [**1817** E. P. FORDHAM *Personal Narrative* 144 The owner is a Canadian Frenchman.] **1850** GARRARD *Wah-To-Yah* i. 4 Canadian Frenchmen . . . composing part of our company, as drivers of the teams. **1878** R. T. COOKE *Happy Dodd* 82 Father was a Canadian Frenchman, a charcoal burner.

+Canaigre. *S.W.* [Mex. Sp.] A species of dock (*Rumex hymenosepalus*) having roots rich in tannin; the tannin obtained from these. {1884-} Also attrib. with *plant, root.* — **1878** *Rep. Comm. Agric.* 119 In many respects cañaigre root resembled rhubarb. **1894** H. TRIMBLE *Tannins* II. 106 The use of canaigre in tanning has passed the experimental stage. *Ib.* 107 The Canaigre plant is from one to three feet in height. **1894** *Nation* 6 Sept. 176/3 Canaigre is . . . a kind of dock (*Rumex hymenosepalus*, Torrey), which in general appearance is much like the 'yellow dock.'

***Canal,** *n.* Also †**canol, canawl.**

1. A navigable waterway constructed to connect two bodies or stretches of water. {1673-}

1732 BYRD *Progress to Mines* (1901) 335 We rode down to the mouth of the canal. **1789** MACLAY *Deb. Senate* 146 Maryland would suffer a canal to be dug between the bays of Chesapeake and Delaware. **1798** I. ALLEN *Hist. Vermont* 254 A canal . . . is now nearly completed from navigable waters in Hudson's River [to Lake Champlain]. **1809** *Ann. 10th Congress* 2 Sess. 326 The bill . . . to defray the expense of deepening, and extending to the river Mississippi, the canal of Carondelet; was read. **1835** H. C. TODD *Notes* 64 The Erie canal—here called *canol*—was at first attempted to be laughed down, under the cognomen of The Big, and Clinton's Ditch. **1843** *Niles' Nat. Reg.* 22 July 336 The quantity shipped at Pittsburg through the Pennsylvania canal. **1854** BENTON 30 *Years' View* I. 22/1 The Cumberland road, and the Chesapeake and Ohio Canal, were the two prominent objects discussed. **1865** *Atlantic Mo.* XV. 693 The two great branches of internal trade . . . consisted of the trade of the Lake and the canals leading from them.

2. Attrib. with *barge, boy, craft, extra, fleet,* etc.

1865 *Atlantic Mo.* XV. 242/1 Some canal-barge is moored at the crazy Virginian wharf. **1872** BRACE *Dangerous Classes N.Y.* 89 'Canawl-boys' . . . seem to drift into the city every winter, and live a vagabond life. **1843** *Niles' Nat. Reg.* 16/1 The line boat Cincinnati, one of the new class of canal craft. **1847** ROBB *Squatter Life* 90 'Take it cool, gentlemen,' shouted a westerner, from a top berth, 'these are the canal extras [=extra services].' **1878** PINKERTON *Strikers* 205 Troops were able to remove the embargo and put the canal fleet once more in motion. **1849** CHAMBERLAIN *Ind. Gazetteer* 204, 50,000 acres of the vacant land were selected for the canal grant. **1833** *Niles' Reg.* XLIV. 353/1 The canal hands . . . are now . . . clear of the disease. **a1861** Canal horn [see CANAL-BOATMAN]. **1854** HAMMOND *Hills, Lakes,* etc. 60 At West Troy I hired a canal-horse and a wagon, and started for Albany. **1836** *Ind. Q. Mag. Hist.* IX. 270 The great dam . . . will be put under contract at the canal letting on the 23rd inst. **1843** *Niles' Nat. Reg.* 144/2 The progress made towards negotiating the Illinois canal loan. **1874** *Ill. Rev. Statutes* (1883) 183 Said commissioners . . . shall have authority . . . to lease from time to time any of the canal lands or lots owned by the state. **1811** *Ann. 12th Congress* 1 Sess. II. 2166 Aid in making a canal navigation between the Great Lakes and Hudson river. **1827** DRAKE & MANSF. *Cincinnati* 14 In February, 1825, the Legislature . . . adopted what is now denominated the Canal Policy. **1879** BAGBY *Old Va. Gentleman* 244 New names and new faces, from the canal region of New York . . . were seen and heard. **1883** *Harper's Mag.* Aug. 328/2 The Portage Railroad . . . received travelers by the canal route . . . and conveyed them over the mountain. **1844** *Ind. Senate J.* 85 Treasury notes and canal scrip. **1877** 'E. MARTIN' *Hist. Great Riots* 74 These men are charged with the specific crime of burning a canal steamer. **1824** MARSHALL *Kentucky* II. 372 It did not succeed very well; 'canal stock' commanding but little cash. **1881** *Nation* 10 March 160/2 The suits brought by the State against the 'canal thieves.' *Ib.* 161/1 How the chief lesson of the suits against the canal thieves could have been taught by Confucius . . . , Mr. Conkling did not explain. **1838** *Niles' Nat. Reg.* 10 Nov. 176/2 The Albany Argus . . . in publishing a statement of the [N.Y.] canal tolls . . . says [etc.]. **1840** *Ib.* 4 July 288/1

Canal transportation: . . . It is expected that the expense . . . will be reduced one half. **1879** BAGBY *Old Va. Gentleman* 234, I had . . . yet to have my first experience of canal travelling. **1837** W. JENKINS *Ohio Gaz.* 118 Five canal warehouses, through which extensive commercial dealings are transacted.

+Canal, *v.*

1. *tr.* To cut a canal through or across (land); to dig a canal around (falls).

1819 E. DANA *Geog. Sks.* 20 The operation of canalling and locking the falls has lately been commenced. **1829** D. HOSACK *Dewitt Clinton* 331 Valuable improvements could be made by canalling the portages. **1829** A. ROYALL *Pennsylvania* I. 123, I am pleased to hear they are canaling and rail-roading the whole country. **1870** EMERSON *Society & Sol.* 144 What of the grand tools with which we engineer, . . . canalling the American Isthmus?

2. *intr.* To construct a canal or canals. (Cf. CANALLING 1.)

1828 *Deb. Congress* 9 April 2251 To canal across lofty mountains must be considered as a physical impossibility.

Canalboat. A comparatively long, narrow boat or barge, chiefly used on canals, for conveying goods and passengers. {1843-}

1818 *Jrnl. Science* I. 164 The canal-boat has her wheel in the stern. **1824** *New Bedford Mercury* 28 May (Th.), It is not uncommon to see thirty or forty women and children comfortably stowed away in one of the large covered canal boats. **1837** *S. Lit. Messenger* III. 684 Travellers . . . can proceed on without . . . delay in the stages or canal boats. **1848** W. E. BURTON *Waggeries* 87 Cato joined a knot of the passengers on the deck or roof of the canal boat. **1865** *Atlantic Mo.* XV. 81 A series of tows, each of these being a rope-bound fleet, averaging perhaps fifty canal-boats and barges. **1879** *Scribner's Mo.* May 37/1 An elevator alongside raised the grain from a canal-boat, and then sent it down a spout. **1900** STOCKTON *Afield & Afloat* 25 My idea is to hitch on to a canal-boat and be towed to the lake.

attrib. **1839** MRS. KIRKLAND *New Home* (1840) 21, I called to mind some canal-boat experiences. **1883** *Wheelman* I. 374 Canal-boat rides of 4 miles on the Erie . . . may be added.

Canal boatman. One who operates a canalboat. — *a***1861** WINTHROP *J. Brent* 92 A canal-boatman hails the locks with a canal horn. [**1863** 'G. HAMILTON' *Gala-Days* 70 We . . . watched the canal-boats and boatmen go down.] **1877** BARTLETT 620 *Snub up* [is] an expression used by canal-boatmen.

+Canal commissioner. A state official concerned with the construction or regulation of a canal or canals. — **1838** *Ind. Ho. Rep. J.* 27 According to the rule agreed on . . . between our then canal commissioners and the commissioner of the General Land Office. **1850** *Harper's Mag.* II. 122/1 Mr. Mather (Dem.) [was nominated] for Canal Commissioner [of N.Y.]. **1874** *Ill. Rev. Statutes* (1883) 182, I do solemnly swear . . . that I will faithfully discharge the duties of the office of canal commissioner according to the best of my ability.

Canal company. A company that constructs and operates a canal. — **1808** in *Niles' Reg.* XV. 50/2 Contracts . . . tie the canal company to the original construction of the work, and forbid further improvement. **1811** *Ann. 12th Congress* 1 Sess. II. 2160 The canal companies were left to languish. **1819** *N. Amer. Rev.* VIII. 4 Documents relative to the . . . Appomattox Canal, Potomac Canal, and James River Canal, companies. **1834** C. A. DAVIS *Lett. J. Downing* 180 We charter'd this Bank for twenty years, and so we do Canal Companies, and Railroad Companies.

+Canal driver. One who drives canalboat horses. — **1840** *Niles' Nat. Reg.* 29 Aug. 404/1, 18 dead bodies [were found, including] . . . James Van Buren, . . . a canal driver. **1855** M. THOMPSON *Doesticks* 22 Every man, woman, child, canal driver, . . . will be provided with a copy. **1882** THAYER *From Log-Cabin* 187 Jim, you've too good a head on you to be . . . a canal driver.

+Canal land. Land ceded to the states or set aside by them for canal purposes. — **1845** *Ill. Rev. Statutes* 108 Purchasers of school or canal lands or town lots, may . . . transfer and assign all right and title to the lands or lots purchased. **1848** *Ind. Gen. Ass. Doc.* I. 185 The expenses of canal land office within the Vincennes district. **1849** CHAMBERLAIN *Ind. Gazetteer* 251 Of the county [=Howard] . . . 34,000 acres are canal lands. **1874** [see CANAL *n.* 2].

+Canaller. Also **canaler.**

1. One who works or lives on a canalboat.

1864 NICHOLS *Amer. Life* I. 133 Steamboat men, sailors, canallers, . . . mingled with some of the wilder young clerks from the forwarding houses. **1875** G. P. BURNHAM *Three Years* 85 At an early age he associated with canallers at Albany and Troy. **1884** *San Fran. Chron.* Aug., These clusters of canal-boats are substantially floating villages. The 'canaler's' family is seen on deck.

2. A canalboat.

1887 *Century Mag.* Aug. 487 Near the bow of each canaler was a lantern of uncertain hue.

Canalling, *vbl. n.* Also **canaling.**

1. The construction of a canal or canals. {1834}

1813 *N.H. Gazette* 19 Jan. 1/4 The subject of Canalling is revived in Philadelphia. The Canal there between the Delaware and Chesapeake would be extremely important. **1818** in *N.E. Hist. & Gen. Reg.* XXIV. 293 Various surveys . . . were made many years since, when the business of canalling was less understood. **1826** Peck *Guide* (1831) 214 The spirit of improvement throughout the United States, especially evidenced in canalling. **1837** PECK *New Guide* 108 Those from the latter [Ireland] are more generally found about our large towns and cities, and along the lines of canalling.

2. Travel or transportation by canalboat.

1834 *Boston Post* 8 Aug. 2/3 Canalling Extraordinary. . . . A small boat containing a family of 12 souls . . . passed through . . . on the Erie Canal. **1837** *S. Lit. Messenger* III. 740/1 It is about the same length as the other [tunnel], and saves five miles of canalling. **1885** *Harper's Mag.* May 858/2 The journey . . . is made up of twenty miles of . . . canalling. **1885** *Graceville* (Minn.) *Transcript* 3 Jan. 11/1 They say the days of canaling are over. . . . The railroads . . . have taken all that business. **1889** K. MUNROE *Golden Days* 85 For leisurely travelling this beat canalling all hollow.

Canal lock. A lock forming the connection between an upper and lower level of a canal. Also attrib. with *company, gate.* — **1844** *Ind. Senate Jrnl.* 239 The petition of the stockholders in the Williamsport canal lock company. **1874** KNIGHT 440/1 The hinged doors at each end of a canal-lock . . . are opened and closed to admit the passage of vessels. **1875** *Ib.* 1419/1 Meeting-post . . . [is] that stile of a canal-lock gate which meets . . . the other gate at the midwidth of the bay.

Canalman. One who works on a canal or a canalboat. — **1878** PINKERTON *Strikers* 199 The canal-men . . . were also on a strike. **1886** P. STAPLETON *Major's Christmas* 296 The Myer house became a low boarding house for the canal men.

+Canal packet. A packet boat used on canals. — **1837** *S. Lit. Messenger* III. 740 The arrangements for sleeping . . . on board the New York canal packets. **1852** *Harper's Mag.* Jan. 183/2 A crowd composed . . . of persons about to depart by a canal-packet for Buffalo. **1857** *Knickerb.* XLIX. 93 A burlesque account . . . of the first passage of an old scow-built, basswood-bottomed canal-packet. **1864** T. L. NICHOLS *Amer. Life* I. 116 There were two modes of reaching Buffalo — the mail-coaches and the canal-packets.

***Canary.** [Name of a group of islands off Morocco.]

***1.** =CANARY WINE.

1686 *Conn. Public Rec.* III. 408 Every butt or pipe of Sherry, Sack, Malaga, Canary, Muscells, Tent and Alicant, twenty shillings. **1704** *Boston News-Letter* 21 Aug. 2/2 At Mr. Joseph Hiller's House near the Mill-bridge in Boston, there's . . . to be sold . . . right Canary by the quarter Cask or smaller quantities, at reasonable prices. **1715** in *Mass. H. S. Coll.* 6 Ser. V. 311, I sent the jugg of Canary last week.

2. *ellipt.* =CANARY GRASS.

1791 MUHLENBERG *Index Florae* 160 *Phalaris*, Canary.

3. The canary bird (see next). {1655-}

1843 *Lowell Offering* III. 45 Your little canaries she has fed until they are both sick. **1865** *Atlantic Mo.* XV. 523/2 The Canary . . . displays different degrees of proficiency in the exercise of his musical gifts. **1873** *Amer. Naturalist* VII. 313 One of our canaries had a bad cold. **1906** *Dept. Agric. Yearbook* 172 The position of the canary among cage-birds is unique . . . because of its widespread popularity.

***Canary bird.**

***1.** A cage bird of the finch family, orig. introduced from the Canary Islands; valued as a songster.

1759 E. Singleton *Social N.Y.* 395 [James Bernard, . . . at King's Bridge, had] a large collection of Canary Birds. **1787** BENTLEY *Diary* I. 70, I received of Mrs. Hodges a present of a canary Bird, bred in her own house. *a***1800** T. TWINING *Visit* 358, I found on board . . . an extraordinary number of canary birds. . . . I afterwards understood that a considerable profit was obtained on the sale of these birds in the southern parts of the Union. **1840** [see CANARY GRASS 1]. **1858** HOLMES *Autocrat* iv. 96, I bought me a canary-bird, and hung him up in a cage at my window. **1863** A. D. WHITNEY *F. Gartney* viii, Not even a cat or a canary-bird had she for companionship.

2. *Canary-bird flower, seed:* (see quotations).

1821 NUTTALL *Travels Arkansa* 158 The principal grasses which prevail are . . . *Phalaris canariensis* (Canary bird-seed) [etc.]. **1863** GRAY *Botany* p. xl, *Tropæolum peregrinum.* Canary-bird flower. Annual, climbing high.

Canary grass.

1. The grass *Phalaris canariensis*, indigenous to the Canary Islands, and yielding the seed used to feed canaries. {1668-}

1817-8 EATON *Botany* (1822) 386 *Phalaris canariensis*, canary grass. Introduced. **1840** DEWEY *Mass. Flowering Plants* 236 Canary Grass. From Britain, cultivated, as the Canary bird is very fond of its seed. It is a handsome grass in the gardens. **1850** S. F. COOPER *Rural Hours* 124 The timothy is also an imported grass . . . ; and the canary-grass, which yields a seed for birds. **1901** MOHR *Plant Life Ala.* 364 *Phalaris canariensis*, . . . Canary Grass, . . . [is] valuable for its seeds.

2. With qualifying terms (see quotations).

1817-8 EATON *Botany* (1822) 386 *Phalaris americana*, ribbon grass, wild canary grass. **1843** TORREY *Flora N.Y.* II. 418 *Phalaris arundinacea.* . . . Reed Canary Grass. . . . Swamps and wet borders of streams. **1889** VASEY *Agric. Grasses* 38 Reed Canary Grass [is] a perennial grass . . . growing . . . usually in low or wet ground. **1889** FARMER 120 Canary Grass

(*Phalaris intermedia*).—Also known as Red Canary Grass, Stewart's Canary Grass, Gilbert's Relief Grass, and Californian Timothy. It is a native of the Southern and some of the Western States. **1894** COULTER *Bot. W. Texas* III. 512 *P*[*halaris*] *intermedia*, Southern canary grass, . . . [is] cultivated as a winter forage plant.

+**Canary slip.** An official form used by the federal Pension Office. — **1894** *Congress. Rec.* App. 3 March 624 The slips . . . instead of giving [the applicant's] military history, gave simply the date of enlistment, muster in, and the date of discharge. . . . These slips have an office nomenclature. They are called 'canary slips,' in distinction from full record slips.

Canary wine. [CANARY I.] A light sweet wine made in the Canary Islands, and formerly in demand. {1620, 1670} — **1687** *Doc. Hist. N.Y. State* (1849) I. 163 For every pipe of Madera, . . . Canary, Malaga, Sherry & all sweet wines the summ of forty shillings [duty]. **1714** *Boston News-Letter* 7 June 2/2 Spanish Iron, . . . Jamaica Sugar . . . , and new Canary Wine just arriv'd. **1769** *Boston Chronicle* 1 June, Wine to be sold . . . , viz. . . . Port, Canary, Malaga, Tent, sweet and other Wines.

Cancan. [F.] A dance of French origin formerly considered improper. {1848} — [**1869** 'MARK TWAIN' *Innocents* 136 Twenty sets . . . were dancing the renowned '*Can-can.*' *Ib.*, I moved aside and took a general view of the *can-can.*] **1882** SWEET & KNOX *Texas Siftings* 36 He usually compromises by dancing the Can-can. **1894** CHOPIN *Bayou Folk* 66 The everlasting *can-cans!* when will they have done with them?

Cancer. *College slang.* +*To catch a cancer* (in rowing), to catch a 'crab.' — *a***1860** *Songs of Yale* 25 Catch a 'cancer' if you dare, And of 'swallows,' too, beware.

+**Cancerroot.** The squawroot, *Conopholis* (*Orobanche*) *americana*, or closely related species.

1714 *Phil. Trans.* XXIX. 64 To this [=boar thistle] they add a Root, call'd the Cancer Root. **1817–8** EATON *Botany* (1822) 272 *Epiphegus virginianus*, beech drops, cancer-root. . . . The whole plant is yellowish-white . . . and of a naked appearance. **1840** DEWEY *Mass. Flowering Plants* 156 Cancer Root . . . has been used as a remedy for this dreadful disease. . . . [It is] common in woods of beech. *Ib.*, *Orobanche uniflora*, Small Cancer Root, . . . [grows in] woods; June. **1857** GRAY *Botany* 280–1 *Orobanchaceæ* (Brown-rape family) . . . [includes] Beech-drops, Cancer-root, . . . *Epiphegus Virginiana*; . . . *Aphyllon uniflorum*, Torr. & Gr., One-flowered Cancer-root. **1859** BARTLETT 441 Squaw-Root (*Conopholis americana*), a medicinal plant put up by the Shakers, also called Cancer-Root. **1901** MOHR *Plant Life Ala.* 731 *Thalesia uniflora*. . . . One-flowered Cancer Root. . . . Mountain region. Dry gravelly hillsides.

+**Cancerweed.** A weed or plant popularly believed to be remedial in cancer. — (1) **1802** DRAYTON *S. Carolina* 60 Cancer weed. (*Salvia Lyrata, et Mexicana.*) **1806** LEWIS in *L. & Clark Exped.* (1905) V. 108, I observe here . . . cansar weed. **1847** WOOD *Botany* 418 Wild or Meadow Sage. Cancer-Weed. . . . Native of shady woods. May, June. — (2) **1889** *Cent.* 786/3 *Cancer-weed*, the rattlesnake-root, *Prenanthes alba*, of the United States, a milky-juiced composite having an intensely bitter root, which is used as a domestic tonic.

Canchalagua, variant of CONCHALAGUA.

Candidacy. Candidature; candidateship. {*Q. Rev.* (Worc. '60)}

[**1852** MITCHELL *Battle Summer* 129 He . . . avows his own candidatecy.] **1861** *N.Y. Tribune* 22 Nov., Mr. Opdyke . . . by the unprecedentedly brilliant and energetic canvass made under his candidacy, carried the party with vast prestige. **1864** FRÉMONT in *Daily Tel.* (London) 21 June, In accepting the candidacy you propose to me. **1884** *Boston Jrnl.* 7 Nov. 7 Mr. Morse's candidacy has corrupted every city and town in the district. **1906** L. STEFFENS in *McClure's Mag.* Feb. 431 Colby opened with an announcement of his candidacy, backed by a statement of his program.

Candidate, *n.* {1600– (Stanford)}

1. An aspirant for the ministry or for a charge. {1704–}

1726 C. MATHER (*title*), Manuductio ad Ministerium. Directions for a Candidate of the Ministry. **1747** *N.H. Hist. Soc. Coll.* IX. 4 We agree not to encourage . . . any as Candidates for the Ministry till they are recommended by some Association. **1775** Fithian *Journal* II. 2 The Presbytery . . . recommend him as a candidate of good standing. **1800** CUTLER in *Life & Corr.* II. 36 [The men] whom I proposed for examination as candidates for the ministry . . . were examined and approbated. **1828** WEBSTER, s.v., *Candidate*, a man who is qualified, according to the rules of the church, to preach the gospel, and take the charge of a parish or religious society, and proposes to settle in the ministry. **1844** Rupp *Relig. Denominations* 586 Candidates for the Ministry — The controversy among the members of the synod. **1868** W. M. BAKER *New Timothy* (1870) 155 All the . . . miserable feelings of one about making his appearance in the pulpit as a candidate on exhibition. **1888** *Century Mag.* Oct. 957/2 'We cannot allow a man to preach as a candidate here,' said the shrewd deacon of a New England church. **1892** M. A. JACKSON *Gen. Jackson* 341 Hugh White was . . . a candidate for the ministry.

2. A contestant for an elective office. {1613–}

1755 in *Lett. to Washington* I. 158 It would have been far better to have acquainted me with your Intention of standing Candidate for Frederick. **1821** *Ann. 17th Congress* 1 Sess. I. 31 A candidate then will attract consideration only by his distinguished character for talents and patriotism. **1848** LOWELL *Biglow P.* I. viii. 109 There ain't no kin' o' quality in can'idates, it's said, So useful ez a wooden leg. **1865** KELLOGG *Rebel Prisons* 329, I never remember hearing this candidate [McClellan] spoken of in any other terms than those of the warmest commendation. **1884** R. GRANT *Average Man* xi, Woodbury . . . was a candidate for the Assembly again, and there were some who were opposed to his reëlection. **1907** C. C. ANDREWS *Recoll.* 96 A resolution was passed . . . declaring it inexpedient to nominate a candidate for Congress.

+**Candidate,** *v.* [f. prec.] *intr.* To be a candidate (for an office, position, etc.); to stand or act as a candidate.

1848 LOWELL *Biglow P.* I. viii. 108 The can'idatin' line, you know, 'ould suit me to a T. . . . So I'll set up ez can'idate fer any kin' o'office. **1870** *Congregationalist* 6 Jan., Setting him to candidating in season. **1884** *Century Mag.* June 308 Let him put the question to some [choir-singers] who every spring have to candidate for a situation. **1887** *N.Y. Evangelist* 17 Nov., But the church refuses to call without a hearing. 'Thanks,' says Mr. Man; 'I am quite happy here, and do not care to candidate.' **1888** *Century Mag.* XXXVI. 957/2 The business of 'candidating' is admirably adapted to strike terror to the heart of a minister of ordinarily sensitive nerves. **1903** K. D. WIGGIN *Rebecca* 192 Mr. Burch . . . stayed here once when he was candidatin'.

* **Candle.** A cylinder of tallow, wax, or the like, containing a wick and used to furnish light.

Also in early use (quots. 1630, 1701) a piece of resinous wood burning with a bright flame. (Cf. CANDLEWOOD.)

1630 F. HIGGINSON *New-England* 16 Yea our Pine-Trees . . . doth allow vs plentie of Candles, which are verie vsefull in a House. *a***1649** WINTHROP *Hist.* II. 264 The negligence of a servant who fell on sleep leaving a candle burning. **1701** C. WOLLEY *Jrnl. in N.Y.* (1860) 53 They make their Candles of the same wood that the Masts of Ships are made of, which they call *Woss-ra-neck.* **1771** FRANKLIN *Autobiog.* 233, I was employed in cutting wick for the candles, filling . . . the molds for cast candles. **1821** COOPER *Spy* x, The black . . . held a long, lank candle of yellow tallow, in such a manner as to throw its feeble light on the volume. **1880** CABLE *Grandissimes* 93 A small piece of candle of the kind made from the fragrant green wax of the candleberry myrtle.

b. (*By*) *inch of candle* (see quots. 1677 and 1828.) {1652–}

1654 *New Haven Col. Rec.* II. 74 It is ordered that the vessell and tackling . . . should be sould at Millford on Tuesday . . . by an inch of a candell. **1677** *Oyster Bay Rec.* I. 242 They . . . led him [a horse] to Oyster-bay to sell, . . . setting a inch of candle that he that biddeth most for him before it was burnt out was to have him. **1682** *Huntington Rec.* I. 339 The Hassokey swamp . . . shall be sold at a vandue by the burning of an inch of candle. **1704** *Boston News-Letter* 12 June 2/2 [To] be Exposed to sale by Inch of Candle, the Sloop *Tryal.* **1828** WEBSTER s.v., *Sale by inch of candle*, is an auction in which persons are allowed to bid, only till a small piece of candle burns out.

+**Candle alder.** The smooth alder, *Alnus serrulata.* — **1847** DARLINGTON *Weeds & Plants* 328 Common Alder. Candle Alder. . . . [Grows in] swamps and margins of rivulets: throughout the United States. . . . This shrub is of little or no value.

+**Candleberry. 1.** The fruit of the bayberry or wax myrtle, which yields a kind of wax used for candles. **2.** A shrub of the genus *Myrica;* esp. the bayberry myrtle, *M. cerifera.* **3.** Used attrib. with *bush, shrub, wax.* — (1) **1738** BYRD *Dividing Line* 27 In that moist Soil . . . grew that kind of myrtle which bears the candle-berries. **1901** MOHR *Plant Life Ala.* 464 *Myrica inodora.* . . . Bartram's Wax Myrtle. . . . The berries, called 'candle berries,' yield wax. (2) **1892** *Amer. Folk-Lore* V. 103 *Myrica cerifera*, candle-berry, Worcester Co., Mass. **1901** MOHR *Plant Life Ala.* 464 *Myrica cerifera* L. . . . Southern Wax Myrtle. Candle Berry. . . . The berries yield wax. *Ib.*, *Myrica caroliniensis.* . . . Bayberry. Candle Berry. Flowers in March. (3) **1871** *Rep. Comm. Agric. 1870* 204 Candleberry or myrtle wax . . . is yielded by the genus *Myrica.* **1891** *Amer. Notes & Q.* VI. 210 Allusion has been made . . . to the candleberry shrub, bayberry, or wax-myrtle. **1912** *Comrade* 6 Jan. 3 Our grandmothers used to make candles out of these bayberries, and thus it has its name, candleberry bush.

+**Candleberry myrtle.** The bayberry myrtle or wax myrtle, *Myrica cerifera*, whose berries have a coating of wax used in making candles.

*c***1730** CATESBY *Carolina* I. 13 The broad-leaved Candle-berry Myrtle. *Ib.* 69 The narrow-leaved Candle-berry Myrtle. **1766** W. STORK in J. Bartram *Jrnl.* 15 *n.*, This is a dwarf kind of the . . . Candleberry-myrtle, of such importance to the people of North America, by supplying them with excellent wax. **1785** MARSHALL *Amer. Grove* 94 Candleberry Myrtle [has] . . . roundish berries, . . . affording a kind of green wax which is sometimes used in making candles. **1789** *Amer. Philos. Soc.* III. p. xxi, Two kinds of *Myrica*, Candle berry myrtle, are known. **1801** *Hist. Review & Directory* I. 148 Plants and Vegetables . . . [include] Candleberry myrtle. **1861** WOOD *Botany* 650 Candleberry Myrtle. . . . Drupe [is] . . . covered with . . . wax. **1880** CABLE *Grandissimes* 34 The northern shore of Biloxi Bay was rich in candleberry-myrtle.

+**Candleberry tree.** The candleberry myrtle.

1753 *Chambers' Cycl.* Suppl., *Candle berry tree*, . . . an aromatic evergreen . . . also called the Virginia myrtle. **1770** FORSTER tr. *Kalm's Trav.* I. 192 Candleberry Tree, Bayberry-bush, [or] Tallow shrub. **1828** WEBSTER, *Candle-berry tree*, the . . . wax-bearing myrtle; a shrub common in North America, from the berries of which a kind of wax or oil is procured, of which candles are made. **1901** MOHR *Plant Life Ala.* 15 The fragrance of the common wax or candleberry tree.

*** Candlebox.**

***1.** A box for holding a stock of candles.

1775 J. ANDREWS *Letters* 88 Last Saturday evening a load of cartridges were seized pack'd in candle boxes. **1806** in Commons, etc. *Doc. Hist.* III. 77 He should not even make candle boxes for Case, his employer. **1845** *Knickerb.* XXVI. 416 There he sits on an upturned candle-box, with a cutting-board on his lap. **1871** HARTE *Luck of Roaring Camp* 5 On this a candle-box was placed, and within it . . . lay the last arrival at Roaring Camp. **1902** 'MARK TWAIN' in *Harper's Mag.* Jan. 266 A tin can of blasting-powder, which they placed upon the candle-box.

+2. *Candlebox returns,* fraudulent election reports.

1858 *Congress. Globe* 15 March 1122/1 Cincinnati directories and candle box returns have been infinitely more potent than the real votes of the inhabitants.

+Candle-dipper. A device or machine for making candles by dipping. — **1874** KNIGHT 442 The candle-dipper shown is intended to give a determinate weight to any number of candles. **1911** FERBER *Dawn O'Hara* 207 The simple woman told the story of each precious relic, from the battered candle-dipper on the shelf, to the great mahogany folding table.

+Candle factor. One who makes or vends candles. — **1864** 'MARK TWAIN' *Sketches* (1926) 122 John Smith, Soap Boiler and Candle Factor. **1865** STOWE *House & Home P.* 222 We buy . . . candles of the candle-factor.

Candle factory. A factory where candles are made. — **1839** *Ind. Ho. Rep. Jrnl.* 281 A communication . . . on the subject of becoming a partner of the State in the candle factory. **1873** *Iowa Agric. Soc. Rep.* 175 The panacea for all these ills is to be found in tanneries, . . . butter factories, candle factories, [etc.].

+Candlefish. The beshow or horse mackerel (*Anoplopoma fimbria*) of the Pacific coast. — **1884** GOODE *Fisheries of U.S.* I. 268 Black Candle-fish (*Anoplopoma fimbria*). . . . At San Francisco it is usually called 'Candle-fish.' **1899** *Boston Transcript* 2 Sept. 24/4 Candlefish . . . get their name from the fact that when dried they will light and burn like candles. In fact, they are thus used for illuminating purposes to a considerable extent.

*** Candlelight.** The time towards evening when candles are lighted; dusk. {1663–} Freq. in *at (early) candlelight.*

'An expression much used in places or regions where no correct standard of time is easily accessible' (*Cent.*).

(1) **1710** SEWALL *Diary* II. 283 Twas Candle-light before Col. Nicholson got to the Council Chamber. **1774** FITHIAN *Journal* I. 79 When we returned about Candle-light, we found . . . the Colonel in the Parlour tuning his Guitar. **1854** S. SMITH *'Way Down East* 37 By early candle-light, the company began to drop in. **1884** *Boston Jrnl.* 26 Sept. 2/2 His wife did not get her silk dress, but he got a piece of her mind that reached from nearly candle-light to breakfast time. **1896** WILKINS *Madelon* 22 The two young men . . . were hurrying to finish the decorations before candle-light. **1905** VALENTINE *H. Sandwith* 75, I'll be out this evening by early candle-light. **1921** C. GREER-PETRIE *Angeline at Seelbach* 16 Along about early candle-light, we hit the train and hulled out.

(2) **1730** J. COMER *Diary* 110 So yt candle light an alarm was beat. **1791** ASBURY *Journal* II. 106 [I] preached to them at candle-light. **1809** WEEMS *Letters* II. 404 The Rev. Mason L. Weems, will deliver a discourse, this Evening, . . . at early candle light. **1899** GREEN *Va. Word-Book* 77 The evening service will begin at 'candle-light.'

*** Candlelighting.** {Th.S.} 'Time of, or near the time of, lighting candles' (B. '77). Cf. prec.

1696 SEWALL *Diary* I. 439 Just about Candle-lighting the news of it is brought to Town. **1708** *Boston News-Letter* 15–22 March 2/2 Before Candle lighting if no Post be come in; The same is to be seen . . . at the Post-Office Window. **1784** *Maryland Jrnl.* 17 Sept. (Th.), Said School to begin at Candle-lighting, and continue till Nine o'Clock, P.M. **1804** CUTLER *Life & Corr.* II. 157 At length, just at candle-lighting, a motion for adjournment . . . was barely carried. **1846** *Knickerb.* XXVIII. 144 There'll be time to look at it before early candle-lightin'. **1896** *Dialect Notes* I. 385 Evenin' meetin' took up at early candle-lightin'.

Candle manufacturer. One who manufactures candles. — **1841** CIST *Cincinnati* (*advt.*), Soap and candle manufacturers, and starch factors.

*** Candle mold, mould.** A mold for casting candles.

1775 *Ann. S. W. Virginia* 644 The Sheriff . . . had attached one dark bay horse . . . four candle moulds [etc.]. **1806** *Austin P.* (1924) I. 102 Candle Moulds, $0.80. **1874** KNIGHT 442/2 At the present day, candle-molds are usually made of pewter or tin; in some cases glass has been employed. **1882** *Rep. Indian Affairs* 454 Candle molds, stand of 8 molds.

Candle-rod. A rod used in making dipped candles. — **1714** *Boston News-Letter* 1–8 Feb. 2/2 A convenient work-House, fit to make Candles and Sope, with a Press, two Coppers, Candle-Rods, Moulds [etc.]. **1878** STOWE *Poganuc People* 230 A frame was placed quite across the kitchen to sustain candle-rods, with a train of boards underneath to catch the drippings.

Candle shade. A cover or shield used to protect a candle from wind, etc. {1780–} — **1810** *Columbian Centinel* 13 Jan. 4/2 William McIlhenney . . . has just opened, a splendid collection of . . . cut glass Candle Shades, with plated stands.

*** Candle snuffer.**

1. An attendant in a theatre who had charge of the candles or lamps. {1711–}

1812 PAULDING *Beaut. Bull-us* 93 One of the *candle-snuffers* to the New-York theatre. **1817** *Amer. Mo. Mag.* II. 63 It would be unfair to charge him with having turned in his scene shifters, candle snuffers, and supernumeraries to break that peace which the civil authority was charged with preserving. **1828** *Yankee* June 199/1 The three rounds of applause with which the candle-snuffers, the green curtain, and the growl of the trombone were received. **1840** SIMMS *Border Beagles* 62 Tilton, I know him — a mere candle-snuffer.

transf. **1877** WM. WRIGHT *Big Bonanza* 361 Half a dozen men went one night to a pistol gallery to practice. To snuff a candle with a pistol or rifle has always been a great feat. . . . The man who held the candle got a bullet through his left hand. . . . [A second shooter] put a bullet through his friend's arm. . . . They concluded that they were not candle-snuffers.

***2.** An instrument for snuffing candles.

1858 *Rep. Comm. Patents 1857* II. 392 Improvement in Candle Snuffers. —Patent dated November 24, 1857. **1870** *Rep. Comm. Agric. 1869* 324 In this invention [*i.e.*, a hand planter] there are provided two legs, pivoted together like the divisions of a candle-snuffer.

+Candlestand. A small table used as a rest for a candlestick. — **1828** WEBSTER, *Stand*, . . . a small table; as a candle-stand. **1829** A. ROYALL *Pennsylvania* II. 181 Her Bible . . . lay on a candle-stand before her. **1840** *Ind. Q. Mag. Hist.* XVI. 305 Between the tables was a small mahogany candle stand . . . bearing the Brides cake. **1856** *Harper's Mag.* Dec. 67/1 A candle-stand is drawn conveniently near the yellow pillow. *c*1870 BAGBY *Old Va. Gentleman* 13 The graceful candle-stand; the gilt mirror, with its three compartments [etc.].

Candle stool. *Obs.* A candlestand. — **1757** *MS. Acc. Bk. Ol. Smith* (Hadley, Mass.), Mending a candle stool for Samuel Gaylord, 3/–. **1766** *Ib.*, Candle stool for Mabel, 30/–.

+Candle tree. 'The *Catalpa bignonioides*, from its long round pods' (*Cent.*).

Candlewood. {1712–}

+1. A resinous wood, as pitch pine, the splinters of which are burned to provide light, make tar, etc.

1634 WOOD *New Eng. Prospect* I. v. 17 Out of these Pines is gotten the candlewood that is so much spoken of, . . . but I cannot commend it for singular good. **1652** *Springfield Rec.* I. 205 No person shall have liberty . . . to burne any Candlewood for the making of Tarr, Pitch, or Coale. **1694** *Mass. Prov. Laws* VII. 414 Our best pine wood alias candlewood. **1700** *Springfield Rec.* II. 357 No Stranger or any that are not proper Inhabitants of the Town shal . . . draw any Candell wood for Tarr from tyme to tyme. **1746** *N.H. Hist. Soc. Coll.* IX. 139, [I] sent John with my team for a load of candlewood. **1857** HOLLAND *Bay Path* 12 The meal had but just been cleared away, and the candle-wood set blazing on the hearth. *Ib.* 15 The fitful light of the burning candle-wood [flashed] full upon his tawny face. **1875** TEMPLE & SHELDON *Hist. Northfield 22* 161 Every family would gather in the fall enough candle wood for use in the winter evenings. This was the hard pine. **1885** E. EGGLESTON in *Century Mag.* April 880/2 For light our ancestors learned to burn, on the hearth or in a torch, the bright-blazing pitch-pine, called 'candlewood' in New England and lightwood at the South.

+2. The ocotillo (*Fouquieria splendens*) of the southwestern states.

1889 *Cent.* 789/1.

Candleworks. A candle factory. — **1807** *Mass. H. S. Coll.* 2 Ser. III. 26 [Nantucket] contains . . . a great number of shops, beside candle works, rope walks, &c.

*** Candy.**

1. A confection made of sugar, with the addition of flavoring matter, and possibly nuts, chocolate, etc. {1808–}

Used more extensively and in a wider sense in the U.S. than in England

1838 HAWTHORNE *Note-Books* I. 138 They dispatch him with two or three cents to buy candy and nuts and raisins. **1840** *Picayune* 19 Sept. 2/1 Southern and Western agent in the sale of celebrated Pease Horehound Candy. **1850** JUDD *R. Edney* viii. 117 At the Confectioners', glass globes of candies and lozenges, . . . stood a-row. **1860** M. J. HOLMES *Maude* ii. 26 The darkey . . . crammed her with ginger-bread, raisins, and candy, bidding her eat all she wanted at once. **1865** MRS. WHITNEY *Gayworthys* xi, There are nuts and funny little shiny cakes and candies. **1886** *Harper's Mag.* June 94/1 Clear candy is not kneaded or pulled. Flat candy is run into pans, and a knife is run across. **1904** *Delineator* Aug. 298 The digestion must not be impaired by . . . nibbling candy, eating pastry or drinking soda-water. **1920** R. L. ALSAKER *Eating for Health* 449 Sweet fruits are better than candies for adults.

2. Attrib. and comb. with *bag, box, company,* etc.

*c*1849 [PAIGE] *Dow's Sermons* (B. '77), To leave stains as conspicuous as the traces of candy about the handles of a young candy-sucker's mug. **1863** B. TAYLOR *H. Thurston* 234 Rows of glass jars full of candy-sticks. **1886** P. STAPLETON *Major's Christmas* 133 In the middle of the room is a large tree with tiny candles all over it, gay candy bags, and toys and books. **1891** CHASE & CLOW *Industry* II. 140 You remember the name, G. W. Peppers, that has smiled down at us . . . from the charmed ends of candy boxes? **1895** *Denver Times* 5 March 8/4 The I. X. L. Candy company is situated at 1024 Eighth street. **1911** H. P. FAIRCHILD *Greek Immigration* 127 The line in which the Greeks have made their greatest success is the fruit stores, candy kitchens and ice cream parlors.

b. *Candy boy, girl, merchant, peddler, seller,* one who sells candies. Also with *force.*

1853 BRACE *Dangerous Classes N.Y.* (1872) 91 The girls . . . are the crosswalk sweepers, the little apple-peddlers, and candy-sellers of our city. **1855** M. THOMPSON *Doesticks* 78 A company . . . composed entirely of . . . stagedrivers, candy-peddlers, pop-corn men. **1863** MRS. WHITNEY *F. Gartney* xxxvi, The shivering little candy-girl, threading her way . . . among the throng. **1863** M. COLES *Louie's Last Term* 168 The candy-woman did not make any thing of the dough-balls at all. **1870** 'FERN' *Ginger-Snaps* 61 To the delight of these youngsters and the candy-merchants. **1870** *Nation* 20 Jan. 45/1 Maid-servants, trundling babies, candy pedlars, [etc.] . . . furnish the objects of interest. **1872** *Harper's Mag.* Jan. 319/1 A candy-boy, passing through a car, meets a cross old gentleman, and says, 'Pop-corn! pop-corn!' **1920** C. R. COOPER *Under Big Top* 109 The menagerie and candy force hurries to the cookhouse for the noonday meal.

||**Candy braid.** A braid or twist of candy. — **1870** EMERSON *Society & Sol.* vii. 143 Why need I speak of steam, . . . which . . . can twist beams of iron like candy-braids?

+**Candy factory.** An establishment where candy is made on a large scale for sale. — **1851** CIST *Cincinnati* 260 [Cincinnati industries include] sarsaparilla, cough candy factories, 1. **1895** *Denver Times* 5 March 8/4 A Candy Factory [was the scene of a] scrap of the secretary with his partner.

+**Candy grass.** The skunk grass or stink grass, *Eragrostis major.* — **1894** *Amer. Folk-Lore* VII. 104 *Eragrostis major* . . . candy-grass; Central Neb. **1901** MOHR *Plant Life Ala.* 380 Candy Grass . . . [is] a frequent garden weed.

Candymaker. +One who makes candies; a confectioner. — **1880** (*title*), The Candy-maker, or Confectioner's Handbook. 137 recipes and other valuable matter. **1896** *Godey's Mag.* Feb. 145/2 Why do you haunt me with your supernatural toothaches? Go haunt the candy-maker, or the cook.

+**Candy party.** A party at which candy is made; a candy pull. — **1845** *Lowell Offering* V. 268 We used to have sewing parties, tea parties, candy parties. **1876** *Wide Awake* 279/2 Well enough, Nan, for you to give your invitations for that candy-party.

+**Candy pull.** ['From the process of pulling required in making the candy' (*Cent.*)] A social gathering of young people for the purpose of making candy, esp. molasses candy. — **1877** PHELPS *Story of Avis* 31 Once I went to see my grandmother in the country, and everybody had a candy-pull. There were twenty-five candy-pulls and taffy-bakes in that town that winter. **1887** *Boston Jrnl.* 20 Aug. 5/3 The candies suggest pleasant winter evenings, and 'candy pulls' at the beach in summer. *c***1897** *Brooklyn Eagle* (B. & L.), The good old-fashioned amusement known as a candy-pull has had more or less of a revival in society this season.

+**Candy pulling.** A candy pull. — **1854** SHILLABER *Mrs. Partington* 20 Candy pullings, with their customary consequences to broad shirt-collars and cheeks sweeter than molasses. **1867** 'MARK TWAIN' *Jim Wolfe & the Cats,* Cousin Mary . . . gave what they called a candy pulling, in those days, in the West. **1887** *Courier-Journal* 13 Jan. 6/4 A candy-pulling will be given at the Walnut street Baptist Church, Friday. **1899** CHESNUTT *Conjure Woman* 123 So one night I cotch 'im down by de swamp on his way ter a candy-pullin'.

+**Candy shop.** A candy store. Also attrib. — **1845** *Knickerb.* XXV. 424 Candy-shop keepers, washer-women and tailors, all have a harvest to reap. **1866** GREGG *Life in Army* 139 Here are eating booths; . . . and farther on, you come in contact with candy shops, peanut stands, cake wagons. **1884** *Philadelphia Times* Sept. The proprietor of a fashionable candy shop. **1903** C. L. BURNHAM *Jewel* 103 Next door was a candy shop with alluring windows.

+**Candy stew.** A candy pull or candy party. — *c***1870** BAGBY *Old Va. Gentleman* 11 Of parties of all kinds, from candy-stews and 'infairs' up to the regular country balls at the county seat. **1887** *Courier-Journal* 30 Jan. 13/3 A supper in addition to a 'candy-stew' was an unheard-of luxury.

+**Candy store.** A store in which candies are sold. — **1884** *N.Y. Herald* 27 Oct. 7/6 Girl to learn to attend bakery, lunch room or candy store. **1890** J. JEFFERSON *Autobiog.* 11, I was in a state of insolvency, being heavily in debt at the candy-store. **1924** *Scribner's Mag.* Dec. 636/2 Young men and boys . . . loafing . . . in the pool-rooms, the candy stores, and the 'hang-outs.'

Candytuft. {1664-} A species of the genus *Iberis* of herbaceous plants or shrubs.

1817-8 EATON *Botany* (1822) 317. **1836** LINCOLN *Botany* App. 106 *Iberis umbellata,* purple candy-tuft. . . . [*I.*] *amara,* white candy-tuft. **1840** DEWEY *Mass. Flowering Plants* 38 Candy Tuft. A species with whitish flowers has been long cultivated as edging for aisles in gardens and walks. Another beautiful variety, with purple flowers, is becoming common. **1889** *Cent.* 2964/3 Several species [of *Iberis*] are cultivated in gardens, under the name of *candytuft.*

***Cane.**

***1.** The slender, flexible, woody stalk or stem of various reeds and grasses; esp. that of a tall woody grass of the genus *Arundinaria,* abundant in the South, and freq. forming canebrakes. Also (in sing.) as the name of this grass.

1674 in Alvord & Bidgood *Trans-Allegheny Region* 212 The slashes are full of very great canes. **1674** in Jillson *Dark & Bl. Ground* 16 [They] tied Gabriell Arthur to a stake and laid heaps of combustible canes about him to burne him. **1709** LAWSON *Carolina* 101 Of Canes and Reeds we have many sorts. The hollow Reed, or Cane, such as Angling-Rods are made of, and Weavers use, we have great Plenty of. **1743** CATESBY *Carolina* App. p. iv, Brooks and Rivulets of clear water, whose banks are covered with spacious tracts of Canes, which retaining their leaves the year round, are an excellent food for Horses and Cattle. **1791** W. BARTRAM *Travels* (1792) 232 The Canes are ten or twelve feet in height, and as thick as an ordinary walking staff; they grow so close together, there is no penetrating them without previously cutting a road. **1802** ELLICOTT *Journal* 184 The soil . . . is very fertile, and covered either with the large cane . . . or the small cane or reed, (*arundo tecta*). **1815** DRAKE *Cincinnati* 83 The cane (*arunda gigantea*) seems not to have at any time grown north of the Ohio. **1853** RAMSEY *Annals of Tennessee* 475 At that time canes and weeds grew up so luxuriantly, in all parts of the country, that two or three men . . . could not pass through without leaving a discernible trace. **1856** P. CARTWRIGHT *Autobiog.* i. 21 What perilous times the first settlers had to reach that new and beautiful country of 'canes and turkeys' [=Kentucky]. **1901** MOHR *Plant Life Ala.* 58 Other plants of Southern distribution that are only rarely met farther north, as, . . . long-leaf pine (*Pinus palustris*), and cane (*Arundinaria macrosperma*).

b. In collective sing. A field, expanse, or growth of canes.

1784 FILSON *Kentucke* 18 This great tract is beautifully situated, covered with cane, wild rye, and clover. **1812** MARSHALL *Kentucky* 64 A large party of Indians, till then concealed in the thick cane. **1819** SCHOOLCRAFT *Mo. Lead Mines* 249 The cane . . . affords a nutritious food for cows, horses, and hogs, who . . . may feed upon it all winter. **1836** J. HALL *Stat. West* 27 The inhabitants drive their cattle to the cane in the autumn.

2. A walking stick made of a cane stem; hence, a slender walking stick of any wood. {1662-}

1683 *N.H. Hist. Soc. Coll.* VIII. 119 Capt. Barefoot, with his cane, struck him on the fingers. **1714** *Boston News-Letter* 24-31 May 2/2 On Monday the 17th instant was lost . . . on the Road between Charlstown and Lewisses at Lynn, a handsome clouded Cane. **1723** *Boston Rec.* 174 No Indian Negro or Molatto Servant . . . shall be suffered to wear or carry about him any manner of . . . Stave, Cane or knives. **1855** SIMMS *Forayers* 108 His gold-headed cane lay on the table, convenient to his grasp. **1886** P. STAPLETON *Major's Christmas* 225 Miss Ham waved him aside with her gold headed cane. **1905** *N.Y. Ev. Post* 30 Dec., The heavy cane in his right hand thumps the flag-stones monotonously.

3. The (or a) sugar cane. {1781-}

[**1724** *New-Eng. Courant* 7-14 Dec. 2/2 The Planters [in Barbadoes] . . . are no small Sharers in this unhappy Accident; . . . their Canes in many Places levelled, and in some carried away with the Mold.] **1796** B. HAWKINS *Letters* 14 In the neighborhood of this line there is plenty of young cane and provisions. **1816** *Niles' Reg.* X. 28/2 The cane is then totally covered with earth, say 2 inches deep—one thousand cane will plant an acre of land in this manner. **1833** B. SILLIMAN *Man. Sugar Cane* 11 In describing this process, . . . [we will] begin our account with the period when the canes are ripe. **1874** *Dept. Agric. Rep. 1873* 109 A yield of 10,000 pounds per acre furnishes cane for the mill at half a cent per pound. **1925** TILGHMAN *Dugout* 91 George secured men to plow, and put in a crop of kafir and cane.

4. The (or a) stalk of sorghum, or the plant itself.

1882 *Comm. Agric. Rep.* 463 By mixing in the immature canes [of sorghum] we really obtain only about one-fourth the sugar which the one ton of good cane would have yielded. **1889** *Secy. of Agric. Rep.* 150 At Kenner a prolonged drought . . . greatly injured the sorghum, making it small and spindling. When the rains began on last of June it produced suckers, greatly to the detriment of the cane. **1917** *Dialect Notes* IV. 409 *Cane,* . . . sorghum. (N.C.) Also Kan., Ky.

5. The stalk or stem of the raspberry, blackberry, or the like. {1861-}

1880 HOWELLS *Undis. Country* xiii. 189 The canes of the blackberries and raspberries in the garden were tufted with dark green. **1880** *Scribner's Mo.* March 762/2 The canes are stocky and strong, and unless growing thickly together, are branching.

6. Attrib. with *fishing rod, hut, rocker, splinter, stick,* in sense: Made of a cane or canes.

1848 COOPER *Oak Openings* I. 131 The bee-hunter had . . . a fragment of the larger end of a cane fishing-rod, which he used as a sort of wand. **1889** K. MUNROE *Golden Days* 13 Cane huts . . . formed the village of Chagres. **1900** E. A. DIX *Deacon Bradbury* 5 The deacon dropped into his large cane rocker, and put on his glasses. **1775** ADAIR *Indians* 407 When the flour is stirred, and dried by the heat of the sun or fire, they sift it with a sieve of different sizes, curiously made of the coarser or finer cane-splinters. **1846** CORCORAN *Pickings* 16 He held in his hand a cane stick.

b. Attrib. and comb. (in sense 3) with *crop, cutting, fodder, ground, growing,* etc.

1853 *Harper's Mag.* Nov. 755/1 The cane crop would sicken and die. **1887** *Century Mag.* Nov. 115/2 The cane-cutting season begins the 1st of October. **1851** *Florida Plant. Rec.* 422, 1 [slave] hawling Cain [*sic*] fodder in the Lot. **1856** *Magnolia Place Jrnl.* 1 Oct. (N.C. Univ. MS.), 6 Plows breaking up Cane Ground. **1887** *Century Mag.* Nov. 105/2 Cane-growing is not a forced and unnatural industry. **1850** S. F. COOPER *Rural Hours* 29 A very great proportion comes from the cane plantations of Louisiana. **1887** *Century Mag.* Nov. 104/1 It is true that cane planting and grinding require a stricter and more systematic labor organization than raising cotton or rice. **1884** *Rep. Comm. Agric.* 25 Undertook experiments with cane-raising in this locality. **1862** *Rep. Comm. Patents: Agric.* 302 The cane ricks may extend fifty or more feet each way. **1853** *Harper's Mag.* Nov. 756/2 Some few planters . . . plant their cane rows ten feet apart, and plow the 'trash' under the earth in the centre of the rows. **1856** *Spirit of Times* (N.Y.) 15 Nov. 182/2 My cane-seed was planted about the 20th of May. **1833** SILLIMAN *Man. Sugar Cane* 12 Every joint sends up cane shoots. **1876** KNIGHT 2444/2 The cane-slips are placed in the chute and delivered into the furrow made by the first plow. **1858** *Texas Almanac 1859* 76 The three soils mentioned above, namely, stiff black, peach, and cane-soils, are the principal soils in this portion of the country. **1835** INGRAHAM *South-West* I. 241 The cane-song—which is improvised by one of the gang [of sugar-cane workmen]. *Ib.* 239 The *baggasse* or cane-trash . . . is received into carts and conveyed to a distance from the sugar-house to be burnt as soon as may be. **1853** *Harper's Mag.* VII. 761/1 The stalks . . . on the ground [are] soon . . . placed in the cane-wagons which, with their four gigantic mule-teams, have just come rattling on to the scene of action. **1862** *Rep. Comm. Patents: Agric.* 302, I should say two acres would be sufficient for cane-yard and sheds. The mill should be situated at one end of the cane-yard.

Cane-back(ed), *a.* Also **caned-back.** Having a back made of cane. — **1778** *Essex Inst. Coll.* XLIX. 106 Sold . . . caned back chairs, at 7s 6d. **1810** *Columbian Centinel* 10 Jan. 3/4 (*advt.*), A Variety of Household Furniture . . . comprising . . . pembroke Tables, . . . cane-back Chairs. **1851** A. O. HALL *Manhattaner* 58 The mosquitoes . . . know a cane-backed chair a room's length off.

‖**Cane-barrel.** [CANE 1.] A section of a canestalk. — **1883** SHIELDS *S. S. Prentiss* 63 The bursting of the pent-up air from the cane-barrels [as the cane burned] sounded like the rattle of musketry upon a battle-field.

+Cane bottom.

1. A stretch of low land, generally along a river, upon which cane is growing. Also attrib. with *land.*

1819 E. DANA *Geogr. Sk.* 188 The river cane bottom land . . . may average in width a half or three-quarters of a mile. **1833** in *Life Benj. Lundy* (1847) 37 The land here [on the Brazos River] is cane-bottom. **1837** A. WETMORE *Gaz. Missouri* 289 Joplin reached his old haunts, in a cane-bottom on Flat Creek.

2. *attrib.* Of chairs, etc. = CANE-BOTTOMED.

1843 *Knickerb.* XXI. 150 His apartments . . . were adorned with . . . a sufficient allowance of cane-bottom chairs. **1883** HAY *Bread-Winners* 103 There were a dozen or so of cane-bottom chairs. **1894** C. HOYT *Texas Steer* (1925) III. 39, I was seated alone in my own room, sir, seated in a cane-bottom chair, when this devilish fusillade began beneath me.

Cane-bottomed, *a.* Having a bottom or seat made of cane. {1877} — **1841** E. A. HITCHCOCK *Journal* 44 His furniture [includes] elegant, cane bottomed chairs, of high finish. **1847** ROBB *Squatter Life* 88 A couple of long cane-bottomed settees . . . occupied the centre of the cabin. **1855** M. THOMPSON *Doesticks* 69 She . . . sat down in a cane-bottomed chair, and asked me what my name was. **1882** J. HAWTHORNE *Fortune's Fool* I. xix, I'll get you a cane-bottomed chair and put it by the window. **1909** A. C. RICE *Mr. Opp* 37 In a high-backed, cane-bottomed chair, slept an old negress.

+Canebrake, -break. *S.*

1. A stretch of land overgrown with canes (esp. *Arundinaria macrosperma*); a thicket of canes.

(*a*) **1775** W. A. Pusey *Road to Ky.* (1921) 42 [We] lodged this night at Clinch by a large cainbrake & cuckt our Suppers. **1784** J. FILSON *Kentucke* 24 There are many cane brakes so thick and tall that it is difficult to pass through them. **1809** F. CUMING *Western Tour* 157 He said that the whole country was then an entire cane brake, which sometimes grew to forty feet high. **1827** *Western Mo. Rev.* I. 210 It is an amusement of high holiday for the negroes to fire a cane brake so prepared. **1837** BIRD *Nick of Woods* I. 15 The Shawanee and the Wyandot still hunted the bear and buffalo in the cane-brake. **1866** C. H. SMITH *Bill Arp* 36 Horses hid in the cane-brake. **1876** *Ill. Dept. Agric. Trans.* XIII. 311 Cane-brakes were found in which buffalo, deer, horses and other animals were completely housed and sheltered, and I may add fed, during the winter storms. **1903** *N.Y. Sun* 29 Nov. 29 The Louisiana negroes from the region of canebrakes and ricefields.

(*b*) **1790** D. FANNING *Narrative* 3 About 300 of our Men . . . encamped at the Big Cane Break. **1812** MARSHALL *Kentucky* 38 They were suddenly met, on the side of a Cane Breake, . . . by a superior party of Indians. **1835** *Knickerb.* V. 50 The swamps, the embankments, the cane-breaks of the Father of Waters . . . were far behind him. **1870** KEIM *Sheridan's Troopers* 299 We found great difficulty in crossing several lagoons, covered with thick cane-break.

b. A region abounding in canebrakes.

1883 Smith *Geol. Survey Ala.* 472 The chief crops in the Canebrake are cotton and corn.

2. Attrib. with *cheese, country, creek,* etc.

1809 F. CUMING *Western Tour* 321 Some of the cane brake hills, not being exceeded for richness in the world. **1831** M. A. HOLLEY *Texas* (1833) 57 The cane-brakes are of immense extent, particularly on Cane-brake creek. **1836** EDWARD *Hist. Texas* 35 We first find . . . a low, woody, cane-brake country. **1869** *Overland Mo.* III. 129 When you see a man . . . get a cold boiled sweet potato . . . and a piece of cane-brake cheese . . . you may be certain he is a North Carolinian. **1883** SMITH *Geol. Survey Ala.* 268 The Black Belt or Cane-brake Region. **1905** N. DAVIS *Northerner* 78 Billy is a cane-brake nigger.

+Canebrake land. *S.* Land abounding in canebrakes.

1796 B. HAWKINS *Letters* 41 Here commence large swamps and between them and the river are some rich flat canebrake land. **1809** F. CUMING *Western Tour* 322 The climate becomes much more salubrious — that will however never draw inhabitants to it [=pine woods] while a foot of cane brake land or river bottom remains to be settled. **1849** *Rep. Comm. Patents: Agric.* (1850) 310 The cost . . . of making 128,000 pounds [of cotton] upon the 'cane-brake lands of Alabama' last year was $6,676.80. **1883** SMITH *Geol. Survey Ala.* 466 Some of the best of the canebrake lands of the State are situated in Hale county.

+Cane branch. A stream running through a canebrake or cane-brakes. — **1772** D. TAITT in *Travels Amer. Col.* 497 We encamped at a Cane branch runing NW by W into Weoka or Little Scambia. **1772** B. ROMANS in Phillips *Notes on Romans* (1924) 122 A Cane Branch which falls into the Weeocca. **1775** ADAIR *Indians* 266 When they came to a boggy cane-branch, they strove to persuade him to alight.

+Cane brush. ?Tops and leaves of canes. — **1848** *Rep. Comm. Patents 1847* 454 Cane brush is the best for them [silkworms] to wind in.

+Cane carrier. *S.* (See quotations and cf. next.) — **1833** SILLIMAN *Man. Sugar Cane* 31 The canes are brought up to the mill by means of a machine called the Cane carrier. **1835** INGRAHAM *South-West* 239 The cane, . . . as soon as it is harvested, . . . is placed upon a cane-carrier, so called, which conveys it to the mill.

+Cane cart. *S.* A cart for hauling sugar cane. — **1858** *Texas Almanac* (*advt.*), Axles, suitable for Cane carts. **1883** *Century Mag.* July 421/2 The huge, ungainly cane-carts . . . come lumbering from the sugar-house yard with loads of *bagasse.* **1887** *Ib.* Nov. 108/2 The great cane-carts carrying the plant cane to the freshly tilled fields.

Cane chair. A chair made of canework. {1696} — **1714** *Boston News-Letter* 19–26 April 2/2 To be sold by Mr. James Oliver at his Ware-house . . . Cane Chairs, . . . Cheshire Cheese, and sundry European Goods. **1727** *Md. Hist. Mag.* XVIII. 226 Send me the contents of the inclosed invoice: . . . half a Dozen Cane Chairs. **1880** *Harper's Mag.* June 30/1 In the city or suburbs [of N.Y.] we find women employed . . . in making willow-ware and cane chairs.

+Cane country. Land marked by thick growth of canes. — **1800** W. TATHAM *Agriculture & Commerce* 65 In the cane countries and poccosins it is equally so in the winter. **1824** G. W. Rauck *Boonesborough* 163 We arrived at the commencement of a cane country, traveled about thirty miles through thick cane and reed.

+Cane cutter. *S.* **a.** One who reaps or cuts sugar cane. **b.** A machine which cuts up sugar cane. — **(a) 1850** LEWIS *La. Swamp Dr.* 200 The cane that would conceal my bones would be falling before the knife of the cane-cutter. **(b) 1843** in *Index of Patents* (1874) I. 198 Cane-cutter [invented by] J. P. Bryan [of] Princeton, Ky. July 8, 1843. **1884** *Rep. Comm. Agric.* 46 The Cane-Cutter . . . consists of a cast-iron disk, conical in shape, and carrying three knives shaped like the bit of a carpenter's plane. **1886** *Harper's Mag.* June 80/2 Cane-cutters first slice the cane diagonally . . . in pieces three or four inches long [in making sugar].

Canee. *Obs.* (Affected var. of CANE *n.* 2.) — **1795** *Tablet* (Bost.) 18 Such gentlemen as carry small canes, in modish language termed *canees*, ought to put them in a horizontal position under their right arm. **1815** in Kittredge *Old Farmer* (1904) 220 [To] brandish a canee, . . . and smoke segars, are not the most essential qualifications for a schoolmaster.

+Cane field. *S.* A field of sugar cane.

1833 SILLIMAN *Man. Sugar Cane* 16 A cane field planted in the open manner. **1850** B. TAYLOR *Eldorado* (1862) i. 5 The night-air came heavy with the scent of cane-fields, orange groves and flowers. **1862** F. Moore *Rebellion Rec.* V. II. 611 The main body were posted back in the cane-fields to the west. **1883** *Century Mag.* Nov. 47/1 The river . . . is ever gnawing the levee to get at the fat cane-fields. **1916** W. A. DU PUY *Uncle Sam* 83 The handling of the raw sugar that came from the canefields of Louisiana.

+Cane grass. The cane *Arundinaria macrosperma*, forming cane-brakes in certain southern states. — **1827** *Western Mo. Rev.* I. 209 Wild rice . . . very accurately resembles the cane grass of the vast swamps and savannahs on the gulf of Mexico. **1835** E. J. HOOPER *Address Lit. Soc. Pittsborough,* Are any of you, my audience, acquainted with the cane grass? **1845** SIMMS *Wigwam & Cabin* 1 Ser. 15 A swamp-bottom, the growth of which consisted of . . . dense thickets of low stunted shrubbery, cane grass, and dwarf willows.

Cane juice. The juice of the sugar cane. {1750–}

1828 WEBSTER s.v. *Spirit,* In America, *spirit* . . . signifies the liquor distilled from cane-juice, or rum. **1829** *Va. Lit. Museum* 180/2 The lime . . . neutralizes the acids of the cane juice. **1835** in Ingraham *South-West* I. 240 They drink freely of cane-juice and the sickly among them revive and become robust. **1856** *Spirit of Times* (N.Y.) 15 Nov. 172/3 Four boys were ladling out or skimming off the cane juice, bubbling in the right hand row of sugar kettles. **1867** *Atlantic Mo.* March 275/2 No one is justified in drinking whiskey, while he can get cane-juice. **1874** KNIGHT 443 Cane-juice Bleacher [is] an apparatus for decolorizing cane-juice by means of sulphurous acid vapor. **1888** CABLE *Bonaventure* 14 She was as sweet as the last dip of cane-juice from the boiling battery.

+**Cane knife.** A knife for cutting cane. — **1798** A. Ellicott in *Life & Lett.* 159 [The country] could only be explored by using the cane knife and hatchet. **1887** *Harper's Mag.* July 272/1 The children . . . squabbling for the possession of the one cane-knife to split kindlers.

+**Cane land.** *S.* Land upon which cane grows in abundance. — **1786** in *Mag. Amer. Hist.* I. 312 On the North Fork of Licking, where we passed, is some fine Cane land. **1814** *Niles' Reg.* V. 322/1 Hundreds of buffaloe . . . living on the high cane lands during the season of inundations. **1831** Holley *Tex. Lett.* (1833) 51 When a colonist wishes to describe his land as first rate, he says it is all peach and cane land. **1886** Z. F. Smith *Kentucky* 59 The old yearning for the 'caneland' came over them.

Cane leaf. The leaf of the cane, used for various purposes. — **1837** Bird *Nick of Woods* II. 83 Nathan had . . . added a new stock of cane-leaves for his own bed. **1850** Lewis *La. Swamp Dr.* 196 With the saddle and cane-leaves [I] made me a couch. **1856** *Florida Plant. Rec.* 455, 6 with Wagon ox and Mul Cart hauling Cane leave [*sic*] in lot.

Cane maker. [Cane 2.] One who makes canes or walking sticks. — *a***1821** C. Biddle *Autobiog.* 227 There was a grand Federal procession [July 4, 1788] in which all classes of citizens joined . . . coopers, plane-makers, whip and canemakers [etc.].

+**Cane marsh.** A marsh having a thick growth of canes. — **1790** *N.C. Gazette* 13 Dec., It is computed that one third of this Tract is of valuable Tide swamp, or cane marsh and meadow.

+**Cane meadow.** *S.E.* A canebrake. — **1791** Bartram *Travels* 233 Cane meadows, so called by the inhabitants of Carolina, &c. *Ib.* 377 There are extensive cane brakes or cane meadows spread abroad round about.

Cane mill. 'A machine for grinding sugar-cane or sorghum-stalks' (Knight). — **1833** Silliman *Man. Sugar Cane* 30 The Cane mill consists of three cast iron cylinders. **1863** *Horticulturist* June 1 Manufacturers of Hedge's & Clark's celebrated Cane Mills. **1884** *Rep. Comm. Agric.* 46 Cane-mills are a constant source of trouble.

+**Cane pole.** Also **canepole.** A cane stem; a pole, esp. a fishing pole, made of cane. — **1816** *Niles' Reg.* X. 225/2 More mud is added, until a surface is formed above the water, and then a growth of canepoles spring up. **1883** *Century Mag.* July 378/2 Luke rigged up a stout line the length of his big cane pole. **1888** Grigsby *Smoked Yank* xii. (1891) 100, I saw some starving men with long willow or cane poles . . . trying to kill food, swallows [etc.].

+**Cane rack.** A game popular at fairs, carnivals, etc., in which walking canes serve as prizes. Also attrib. — **1896** *Chicago Rec.* 14 Feb. 1/4 Delegate Hutchinson . . . defended the cane rack and declared that the agriculturists and fair officials of his county had decided that it was a game of skill and not of chance. *Ib.*, The cane-rack scheme he [=Arthur Babbitt] attacked with great violence. **1916** *Dept. Agric. Yearbook* 239 Various forms of amusements, such as 'merry-go-rounds' and 'cane racks,' . . . turn the evenings into a continual festival.

‖**Cane-raised,** *a. S.* Raised on cane fodder. — **1853** 'Paxton' *Yankee in Texas* 121, I rode an all fired chunk of a pony—real Creole, cane raised.

+**Cane region, ridge.** (See quots. and cf. Cane land.) — **1852** J. Reynolds *Hist. Illinois* 195 Above the cane region, the rushes grew on the sandy margins of the Mississippi. — **1850** Lewis *La. Swamp Dr.* 112 The land between the tillable or cane ridges, was low swamp, almost quagmire, never thoroughly dry.

+**Cane rush.** [Cane 2.] (See quotation 1902 from Clapin.) — **1890** *Cent.* 5277/3 *Cane-rush,* a rush between the freshmen and sophomores of an American college or academy for the possession of a cane, carried in defiance of custom by one of the freshmen. **1902** Clapin 95 *Cane-rush,* in college slang, a contest for class supremacy, which consists in trying to get and retain control, by force, of a stick or cane held at the start by members of each class. **1902** L. Bell *Hope Loring* 109 Brewster, of our class, who saved the day for us in the cane rush.

+**Cane-seat.** Attrib. in sense: Cane-seated. Also absol. — **1851** Cist *Cincinnati* 205 Cane-seat and rocking-chairs, are made to a considerable extent. **1873** Bailey *Life in Danbury* 116 He never could sit on a 'cane seat.' A wooden chair was at once offered him. **1868** *Mich. Agric. Rep.* VII. 353 Detroit Chair Factory . . . [had a] display of cane seat chairs. **1885** *Century Mag.* May 12/2 The graceful bent-wood, cane-seat furniture . . . is now exactly imitated by a factory in Sheboygan, Wisconsin. **1887** *Courier-Journal* 20 Feb. 3/7 At Auction. . . . Cane-seat chairs and Rockers.

Cane-seated, *a.* Having a seat of cane; cane-bottomed. {1881} — **1869** W. Murray *Adventures* 224 An old cane-seated chair stood in one corner. **1873** *Winfield* (Kansas) *Courier* 24 July 2/3 Better to use the old cane-seated chairs . . . than to tremble at the bills sent him from the upholsterers. **1876** Ingram *Centennial Expos.* 619 A wide hall . . . furnished with matting, cane-seated chairs and benches, tables and a piano.

Cane settee, sofa. One made of or with cane. — **1847** Robb *Squatter Life* 91 By making a bridge of the cane settees, the ladies were safely conducted from their watery quarters [in a sunken canal boat]. **1886** Harte *Snow-bound* 55 Half reclining on a cane sofa was the wounded man.

+**Cane spree.** At Princeton University: =Cane rush Also *cane-spreeing.* — **1879** *Princeton Book* 384 [The] cane-spree, that annual expression of the . . . superiority of Sophomores to Freshmen. **1894** Wallace *Princeton Sk.* 176 After the rush comes the pasting of the 'procs,' and then the cane-spree. **1898** Alexander *Princeton* 31 In 1896 the old custom of having three cane sprees held at night was permitted to be revived, as a mark of favor from the Faculty. — **1895** Williams *Princeton Stories* 13 'Now, that is cane-spreeing,' said the junior casually.

Canestalk. The stalk or stem of a cane. — **1797** F. Baily *Tour* 367 Transverse poles proceeding from each post, on which is supported a layer of cane-stalks, which serves for a bed. **1829** T. Flint *G. Mason* 31 The noise of the bursting cane-stalks was like the report of a thousand guns. **1862** *Rep. Comm. Patents: Agric.* 306 The amount of bagasse, or pressed cane-stalks, in a large manufactory is very great.

Cane sugar. Sugar present in or obtained from sugar cane; also, a sugar of the saccharose group. {1855-}

1863 *Rep. Comm. Agric.* 540 If . . . the juice is rich in cane sugar and poor in grape sugar. **1880** *Vt. Agric. Rep.* VI. 110 In 1860 the total consumption of cane sugar in this country was 415,281 tons. **1887** *Century Mag.* Nov. 102/1 The Louisiana product of cane sugar is practically the national product.

attrib. **1868** *Rep. Comm. Agric.* 8 The present depressed condition of the cane-sugar interest at the south.

+**Cane swamp.** *S.* A stretch of swampy land overgrown with canes.

1709 Lawson *Carolina* 10 Some Sewee Indians [were] firing the Canes Swamps, which drives out the Game. **1735** *New Voyage to Ga.* 57 We came to a large cane swamp, about half a mile through. **1741** *Ga. Hist. Soc. Coll.* II. 250 Cane swamps are the best feeding for all sorts of cattle. **1772** D. Taitt in *Travels Amer. Col.* 500 We encamped on the north east side of the Creek in a large Cane Swamp. **1775** Adair *Indians* 299 Two sprightly young fellows came through the cane-swamp. **1800** B. Hawkins *Sk. Creek Country* 23 The Alabama is margined with cane swamps.

+**Cane top.** The top of the cane, esp. the sugar cane, used for various purposes. — **1826** J. Bradford *Ky. Notes* 11, I ordered Jamie to make us a shelter, which he did by erecting forks and poles, and covering them with cane tops, like a fodder house. **1836** Simms *Mellichampe* xix, Steeds . . . browsed upon the luxuriant cane-tops. *a***1846** *Quarter Race Ky.*, etc. 134 Few [beds] can be better than a good supply of cane tops, covered with a blanket. **1853** *Harper's Mag.* Nov. 756/1 These leaves and cane-tops really form a large proportion of the gross vegetation of the annual product of the soil.

Canework. Interwoven strips of cane used for the backs and seats of chairs, etc. — **1858** Vielé *Following Drum* 53 Divans of cane-work and rocking-chairs seem to be the principal articles of furniture. **1875** *Scribner's Mo.* Nov. 109/2 All the world prefers crimson velvet and will not pay for cool cane-work.

Caney. (Variant of Cany *a.*)

Can hook. a. A short rope having hooks at each end for hoisting casks or barrels. {1626-} +**b.** (See quotation.) — **(a)** *c***1728** *MS. Inv. Nixson's Estate, Bertie Co.* (N.C.H.C.), One pair Can Hooks. **1781** *Md. Hist. Mag.* VI. 312 Invoice of Schooner Nautilus's Materials . . . [includes] 3 Buckets, 1 Canhook. **1849** *Rep. Comm. Patents* (1850) 314 Improvement in Can Hooks. **(b) 1859** Bartlett 66 *Cant-hook* . . . [is] sometimes called Can-hook.

Canker. Noma (*Cancrum oris*). — **1743** Hempstead *Diary* 418 A child of Ann Fords died . . . [of] Canker. **1753** *Ib.* 604 A child . . . died yesterday with the hooping Cough first, then Canker. **1895** [see next].

+**Canker lettuce.** (See quotations.) — **1890** *Cent.* 4875 *Pyrola rotundifolia,* the larger wintergreen, . . . has been called Indian lettuce and canker-lettuce. *c***1895** *Dialect Notes* I. 385 *Canker lettuce* . . . [is] said to be a cure for 'canker.' Mass. w.

+**Canker rash.** 'The disease called Scarlatina' (B. '59). — **1828** Webster, *Scarlatina,* the scarlet fever; called in popular language, the 'canker rash.' **1831** A. Sherburne *Memoirs* xii. 280 Her sickness . . . was the canker-rash. **1840** *Niles' Nat. Reg.* 30 May 194/2 A distemper . . . has prevailed . . . this season among children—a disease commonly known as the canker rash. **1854** Thoreau *Walden* 173 If some eruption would break out there soon—either scarlatina or canker-rash.

***Cankerworm.**

***1.** A name applied to various caterpillars that are destructive to trees (esp. fruit and shade trees) and their fruits; esp. the larva of the winter moth, *Geometra brumata.*

'In America, this name is given to a worm that, in some years, destroys the leaves and fruit of apple trees. This animal springs from an egg deposited by a miller, that issues from the ground' (W. '28).

*c***1680** J. Hull *Diary Occurr.* 203 The canker-worm hath, for the four years, devoured most of the apples in Boston. **1750** Hempstead *Diary* 550 They [pigeons] are very plenty in Rodgers's orchard eating the Canker worms who have eat the Trees bare. **1793** *N.Y. State Soc. Arts* I. 187 The canker-worm, only destroys the leaves and fruit for the season. **1815** *Mass. H. S. Coll.* 2 Ser. III. 166 There are several old orchards remaining, infested by the canker-worm. **1833** *Niles' Reg.* XLIV. 313/2 The canker worm has spread devastation over this whole tract of country. **1841** Emerson *Miscell.* 230 The canker-worms have crawled to the topmost bough of the wild elm, and swing down from that. **1863** Longfellow *Wayside Inn, Poet's Tale* xxv, From the trees spun down the canker-worms upon the passers-by. **1882** *Vt. Agric. Rep.* VII. 69 [The English sparrow] had, however, freed the trees from the canker worm.

attrib. **1884** Packard in *Amer. Naturalist* XVIII. 292 We noticed . . . two of these Platygasters upon two bunches of freshly laid eggs of the canker-worm moth, probably *Anisopteryx pometaria.*

+**2.** *Fall, spring cankerworm:* (see quotations).

1889 *Cent.* 791/3 The spring canker-worm, *Anisopteryx vernata,* is found . . . from Maine to Texas. **1892** V. Kellog *Kansas Insects* 76 Spring canker-worm. . . . When in large numbers, this pest may so completely defoliate an orchard as to leave the trees as if swept by fire. — **1890** *Vt. Agric. Rep.* 242 The Fall Canker Worm, *Anisopteryx pometaria*, Harr., is found, not only in the fall, but throughout the season in one form or another.

Canmaker. {1623} One who makes cans. — **1765** *Boston Gazette* 29 April 3/2 We have . . . tub, kegg and can makers. **1887** *Appleton's Ann. Cycl.* 743/2 Can-makers strike for eight-hour system.

+**Cann.** A variety of winter apple. Also attrib. with *apple.* — **1817** W. COXE *Fruit Trees* 132 Cann Apple . . . is cultivated in West-Jersey as a fine cider fruit. **1859** ELLIOTT *Western Fruit Book* 129 Cann. American. Fruit . . . 'very good.' October to December.

Canna. One of a genus of tropical plants of the family *Cannaceae* much cultivated in gardens. {1883} — **1863** GRAY *Botany* p. lxxx, [Of the] Canna or Arrowroot Family . . . two are cultivated for ornament: 1. *Canna Indica,* Indian Shot. . . . 2. *Maranta zebrina.* **1877** *Harper's Mag.* Feb. 448/1 The rest [of the hens] . . . are picking and scratching down among the cannas. **1908** LORIMER *J. Spurlock* xii. 297 A bed of elephant's ears on one side of the drive and one of cannas on the other. **1923** WATTS *L. Nichols* 166 There's a ghastly sameness about the bodies [of our cities]. Trolley-cars, department stores, . . . beds of cannas.

+**Cannacker.** [Cf. CANUCK.] A Canadian. — **1846** W. G. STEWART *Altowan* I. vii. 191 The Cannackers, as they were commonly called, set themselves quietly about reviving their fire.

+**Canned,** *ppl. a.*

1. Of foodstuffs: Put up and sealed in a can for preservation. {=E. 'tinned.'}

'*Canned goods,* a general name for fruit, vegetables, meat, or fish, preserved in air-tight cans' (W. '79).

1859 R. B. MARCY *Prairie Traveler* 31 Canned vegetables are very good for campaigning. **1863** in *Century Mag.* Sept. (1885) 775 The townsfolk continued to dash through the streets with their arms full, canned goods predominating. **1871** F. M. A. ROE *Army Lett.* 28 The post trader sends to St. Louis for turkeys, celery, canned oysters, and other things. **1879** *Scribner's Mo.* July 378/2 All their money [*i.e.* of Negroes] goes . . . for bright calicoes, . . . and all sorts of canned fruit. **1882** HOWELLS *Modern Instance* x, He also opened a few canned goods, as he called some very exclusive sardines and peaches. **1890** C. KING *Sunset Pass* 51 Condensed milk, canned corned beef, potted ham, canned corn and tomatoes, . . . were placed close to the ambulance. **1904** 'O. HENRY' *Heart of West* 289 An old empty case that had once contained canned corn. **1916** WILSON *Red Gap* 7 Had to send out for canned milk that morning.

transf. **1904** 'O. HENRY' *Cabbages & Kings* vi. 94 'The Latin races,' says Henry, . . . 'are peculiarly adapted to be victims of the phonograph.' . . . 'Then,' says I, 'we'll export canned music to the Latins.'

b. *slang.* Artificially built up or protected.

1893 *Harper's Mag.* LXXXVI. 969/2 Many 'canned' reputations have been destroyed, and many maligned characters have been uplifted to honour.

2. Having a can tied to the tail.

1903 A. ADAMS *Log Cowboy* iii. 37, I was half a mile in the lead, burning the earth like a canned dog.

Cannel coal. A grade of compact bituminous coal, used esp. in fireplaces. {1610–}

1840 *Picayune* 29 July 1/5, 800 bbls. superior Cannel Coal, . . . for sale. **1847** COLLINS *Kentucky* 491 The cannel or English coal, of a very superior quality, is also found in great abundance along the banks of these rivers. **1867** *Atlantic Mo.* Feb. 156/2 The Cannel coal burned and flashed more fiercely in the open grate. **1886** WINCHELL *Walks & Talks* 138 From cannel coal and coaly shales oil is spontaneously evolved.

+**Canner.**

1. One employed or engaged in the canning of meat, fish, fruit, etc.

1878 BISHOP *Voy. Paper Canoe* 120 The canners take a large portion. **1881** *Amer. Naturalist* XV. 179 The canners think . . . that salmon which would not have run till later, are brought up by the contact with the cold water. **1894** *Secy. of Agric. Rep.* 197 Canners will be more careful in the character of the tins which are used. **1899** *Bulletin U.S. Fish. Comm.* XVIII. 6 In the opinions of the canners . . . the coho should rank next after the king salmon in food value.

2. An animal fit only for canning.

1892 *Pall Mall Gaz.* 8 Dec. 2/1 'Canners,' which is the designation of all animals collected at the Chicago and other markets that are refused by the butchers as unfit for their trade. **1902** LORIMER *Lett. Merchant* 94 A big drought happened along in Texas and began driving the canners in to the packing-house quicker than we could tuck them away in tin. **1911** QUICK *Yellowstone N.* 303 A collection of skips an' culls an' canners that was sure a fraud on the Injuns.

+**Cannery.** An establishment or factory where meats, fruits, or other foodstuffs are canned.

1870 *Dept. Agric. Rep. 1869* 600 Aside from the canneries about one hundred men are engaged in salmon fishing, . . . who have their own nets, [etc.]. **1880** *Libr. Univ. Knowl.* XI. 47 The first cannery [for salmon in Oregon] was established in 1868 by Mr Hume, of Maine. . . . There were, in 1878, 28 large canneries upon the Columbia. **1883** R. RATHBUN in *U.S. Nat. Museum Bul. No. 27* 115 In 1880, there were twenty-three canneries in Maine, . . . giving employment to about 650 factory hands and 2,000 fishermen. **1888** *San Fran. W. Chron.* 26 July (F.), A petition . . . to allow the school children to assist in the cannery at the most important time. **1911** JENKS & LAUCK *Immigration Problem* 219 During the year 1909 some 3,000 of the Chinese were employed in the salmon canneries in Oregon, Washington and Alaska.

+**Canning,** *vbl. n.*

1. The process or business of putting up and sealing meats, fish, fruit, or vegetables in cans or glass jars for preservation.

1876 M. F. HENDERSON *Cooking* 245, I also advise the canning of sweetmeats of every kind. **1879** *Harper's Mag.* June 66/1 When canning is introduced . . . business will receive a new impetus. **1891** CHASE & CLOW *Industry* II. 111 In Chicago is an establishment where 200,000 head of cattle are slaughtered every year and 'canning' is carried on to a great extent

2. Attrib. with *industry, room, season.*

1879 *Dept. Agric. Rep. 1878* 582 Baltimore . . . employs, during the canning season, great numbers of men, women, and children. **1883** R. RATHBUN in *U.S. Nat. Museum Bul. No. 27* 115 The canning industry was first started about 1840, at Eastport, Maine. **1902** LORIMER *Lett. Merchant* 133 The matter will be reported to . . . the boss of the canning-room.

b. *Canning establishment, factory, house,* a cannery.

1875 *Dept. Agric. Rep. 1874* 279 In 1873 there were in Maine thirty-three canning-factories. *Ib.*, The canning establishment of Mr. William Archdeacon . . . occupies 13 acres of land. **1884** *Harper's Mag.* July 297/2 The inferior quality passes from the killing to the canning house. **1890** JEWETT in *Harper's Mag.* Dec. 101/2 The lights went out in the canning factory. **1916** WILSON *Red Gap* 188 The canning factory closed down the fall before.

attrib. **1890** JEWETT in *Harper's Mag.* Dec. 102/1 A white handkerchief fluttered at one of the canning factory windows.

***Cannon.** Also †**canon.**

***1.** A large mounted piece of artillery; a heavy gun. Freq. collective.

1644 R. WILLIAMS *Bloudy Tenent* (1867) 148 But to take a strong hold, men bring Canons, Culverins, [etc.]. **1685** SEWALL *Diary* I. 70 Three Volleys and then Canon fired. **1776** C. LEE in Sparks *Corr. Rev.* (1853) I. 153 Inclosed I send you a return of the good and indifferent pieces of cannon. **1794** *Ann. 3rd Congress* 1448 It shall not be lawful to export from the United States any cannon, muskets, pistols. **1815** *Niles' Reg.* VIII. 141/1 There are in Pittsburgh, three large and extensive air-founderies, where are cast . . . cannons, cannon balls, [etc.]. **1863** KETTELL *Hist. Rebellion* II. 430 Steel cannon were introduced in the United States in 1861. **1867** EDWARDS *Shelby* 74 The cannon were taken, retaken, and taken a second time by the Confederates. **1887** CUSTER *Tenting on Plains* 34 The cannon were fired.

+**b.** A pistol. *slang.*

1901 FLYNT *World of Graft* 137 The thief had him covered with his 'cannon' before he could do any damage.

2. Attrib. with *foundry, shot.*

1756 in *Lett. to Washington* II. 7 It is . . . overlooked by several Hills within cannon-shot. **1774** J. ANDREWS *Letters* 56 Joseph Scott having sold a large quantity of Cannon Shot . . . for the use of the Army. **1811** *Agric. Museum* I. 25 A Cannon Foundary and Paper Mill near Georgetown. **1850** *Ann. of Sci. Discovery* 48 A new method has been resorted to at the cannon-foundry near Pittsburg, for the production of guns.

Cannon ball. A ball to be shot from a cannon. {1663–}

1775 *Essex Inst. Coll.* XLVIII. 46 The grap shot and canon bauls com so thik that we retreted back to the rode. **c1790** COXE *View U.S.* 62 The produce, manufactures, and exports of Pennsylvania . . . [include] rolled iron tire, . . . cannon balls. **1815** [see CANNON 1]. **1886** LOGAN *Great Conspiracy* 325 A Rebel cannon-ball, and an unfortunate charge of our own Cavalry, scatters most of the 5th Maine.

b. Attrib. in sense: Fast, rapid, or speedy.

1888 *Chicago Weekly Inter-Ocean* 3 Jan. 1/5 The north and south bound cannon-ball trains on the Cincinnati Southern Railroad collided to-day. **1904** A. DALE *Wanted, a Cook* 86 The wreck occurred on the Illinois Central Cannon Ball Train, eighty-three miles from New Orleans. **1920** TILDEN *Lawn Tennis* 146 A fast cannon-ball smash.

+**Cannon cracker.** A large firecracker. — **1871** BAGG *At Yale* 297 A party of carousers insist upon . . . firing off cannon-crackers in the entries. **1912** DREISER *Financier* 26 Uncle Seneca . . . brought some great cannon-crackers out on the evening of July the Fourth.

***Cannoneer, -ier.** One who serves a cannon; an artilleryman or gunner.

1634 *Mass. Bay Rec.* I. 125 Mr. John Samford is chosen cannoneere for the ffort att Boston. **1640** *Boston Rec.* 48 There is granted 500 Acrs of Land . . . for the use of the Canoneere of Boston. **1701** *Ib.* 17 Ordered, That there be annually . . . chosen in the Moneth of March . . . a person who shall be stiled a Canonneer. **1862** Rothert *Muhlenberg Co.* 269 We took . . . six cannon from the enemy, bayonetting the cannoneers at their post. **1884** *Century Mag.* Nov. 112 The dead cannoniers lay with the rammers of the guns . . . still in their hands. **1910** J. HART *Vigilante Girl* 259 The infantrymen were standing at 'place rest'; the cannoneers had loaded their pieces and then stood in place.

Cannon-mouthed, *a. Naut.* (See quotation.) — **1813** PAULDING *J. Bull & Br. Jon.* (ed. 2) xix. 98 A pair of tow linen trowsers; . . . what they wanted in length they made up in breadth, being of that individual sort called by sailors cannon-mouthed.

Cannon stove. 'A cast-iron stove, somewhat cannon-shaped, the lower portion, or bosh, forming the fire-pot, and the upper a radiating surface' (Knight). — **1764** *Penna. Gazette* 26 April 3/3 The esteemed Cannon-stoves are yet sold by him.

***Canoe,** *n.* Also †**canoa, canow(e),** etc. [Sp. (f. Haytian) *canoa*, obs. F. *canoe* (1600). The forms *canow, cannow*, etc., appear in English use in the 16–17th c.]

***1.** A boat made of a hollowed tree trunk, or consisting of a framework covered with hide or bark.

To paddle one's own canoe: see PADDLE *v.*

1608 SMITH *Newes from Va.* Wks. (1884) 28 Captain Nuport returned, . . . leauing me and Maister Scriuener a shore, to follow in Canowes. **c1618** *Mass. H. S. Coll.* 4 Ser. I. 243 In the morning there came a canoa unto them, and in her a Sagamo and four salvages. **1622** 'MOURT' *Relation* 30 We saw the Canow lie on the dry ground. **1623** *Plymouth Col. Rec.* XI. 3 No man . . . [shall] sell or transport any manner of works as frames for houses, . . . cannoos or whatsoever may tend to the distruction of timber. **1630** *Mass. Bay Rec.* I. 74 Noe person shall vse or take away any boate or cannoe without leave from the owner. **1631** T. DUDLEY in *N.H. Hist. Soc. Coll.* IV. 235 Complaintes were received against him . . . for not bringing a Cannowe unto him to cross a river withall. **1640** *R.I. Col. Rec.* I. 108 No Indian shall take any Cannew from the English, neyther from their Boatside or shoreside. **1677** *N.H. Hist. Soc. Coll.* III. 100 He went to breck his conow that they might not have ani ues of it. **1697** in *Mayflower Desc.* X. 14 To Canowes and Cart Rope, [£]01 18[s]. **1727** J. COMER *Diary* 36 Two men drowned . . . the connue in which they were sinking under them. **1740** *S.C. Hist. Soc. Coll.* IV. 76 [I] therefore have sent you . . . 2 Boats of 10 oars, . . . besides several Cannous of a smaller size. **1742** in *Travels Amer. Col.* 219 The Packhorse Man got his Things over in a Leather Canoe. **1748** *N.H. Hist. Soc. Coll.* V. 209 March'd down the lake; . . . discovered a large cannoo with sails . . . with six Indians in it. **1795** J. SULLIVAN *Hist. Maine* 104 The canoes used by the North Americans are made of the bark of birch trees, peeled with a great deal of art, and sewed on ribs . . . formed from ash wood. **1836** IRVING *Astoria* I. xx. 212 [The] fleet . . . consisted of a number of canoes, each made of a single buffalo hide stretched on sticks, so as to form a kind of circular trough. **1845** HOOPER *Daddy Bigg's Scrape* 193 He must a' had a kunnoo to fasten it whar he did. **1880** CABLE *Grandissimes* 26 Two overbold young Frenchmen . . . ventured away from their canoes on the bank of the Mississippi. **1899** CHAMPLIN & BOSTWICK *Young Folks' Cycl.* (ed. 2) 134/1 Pleasure canoes, in general, are of two kinds: paddling canoes and sailing canoes.

fig. **1845** HOOPER *Simon Sugg's Adv.* iv, Prudence is the stob I fasten the grape-vine of my cunno to.

+2. In specific use (see quotation).

1880 *Harper's Mag.* Aug. 396 'A canoe,' according to a recent official and technical definition, 'is a boat sharp at both ends, not more than thirty-six inches beam' [etc.].

+b. *Big canoe*, an Indian name for a ship.

1813 *Niles' Reg.* V. 78/2 The Indians . . . being determined to see which of the *big canoes* had the command of the lake. **c1833** CATLIN *Indians* I. 88 This object is in form of a large hogshead, . . . religiously preserved unhacked or scratched, as a symbol of the 'Big Canoe,' as they [Mandan Indians] call it. [**1846** MELVILLE *Typee* 31 When the inhabitants of some sequestered island first descry the 'big Canoe' of the European rolling through the blue waters toward their shores.]

3. Attrib. and comb. with *bark, boat, bottom, boy*, etc.

1903 WHITE *Forest* xiii. 172 [In a cache] provisions and clothing are . . . wrapped completely about in sheets of canoe bark. **1863** *Boston Sunday Herald* 16 Aug. 3/3 Oil Creek, bearing on its bosom such freights of oil in long canoe boats, thus making the scene more picturesque. **1894** 'MARK TWAIN' *P. Wilson* iv, So he came down on his head in the canoe-bottom. **a1918** G. STUART *On Frontier* I. 30 We soon became expert canoe boys and fearlessly went everywhere in it. **1858** THOREAU *Maine Woods* 153, I made a faithful study of canoe-building. **1807** GASS *Jrnl.* They had got to the canoe-deposit on the 8th instant. **1841** COOPER *Deerslayer* vi, These three [canoes] we have with us here; one being fastened in the canoe-dock beneath the house. **1844** S. M. FULLER *Summer on Lakes* 250 S. and I had a mind for a canoe excursion. **1902** WHITE *Conjuror's House* xii. 168 At noon the squaws set out to gather canoe gum on the mainland. **a1861** T. WINTHROP *Canoe & Saddle* ii. 20 The tariff of canoe-hire on Whulge is equally simple,—a blanket for the boat, and one for each paddler. **1895** REMINGTON *Pony Tracks* 135 My 'canoe kit' is the best arranged and the most perfect in the world. **1843** FRÉMONT *Exped.* 190 The delay it frequently occasions to the canoe navigation. **1873** EGGLESTON *Myst. Metr.* 168 It was rowing against Niagara with a canoe-paddle. **1773** *Cincinnati Misc.* 265 Pawpawwood . . . is used chiefly for canoe poles. **c1837** CATLIN *Indians* II. 162 One of their [= Chippeways'] favourite amusements . . . [is] an Indian regatta or canoe race. **1884** *Century Mag.* Aug. 555/1 Thousands [at Lake George] . . . give themselves up to pleasure of every healthful sort . . . , boat-racing, canoe-racing, [etc.]. **1902** WHITE *Conjuror's House* ii. 16 At first the men sang their canoe songs. **1749** W. DOUGLASS *Summary* I. 461 Some ferries . . . consisting of a large scow or flat, to carry passengers, cattle, and goods with a canoe-tender. **1843** FRÉMONT *Exped.* 190 Cape Horn . . . appears to form a serious obstacle to canoe travelling. **1879** BISHOP *4 Months in Sneak-Box* 21 He would need a canoe light enough to be easily carried upon the shoulders of one man, with the aid of the canoeist's indispensable assistant—the canoe-yoke.

+Canoe, *v.* [f. prec. Cf. CANOEING *vbl. n.*]

1. *tr.* To transport or convey in a canoe.

1794 ASBURY *Journal* II. 229, I got two men to canoe me across the river. **1841** COOPER *Deerslayer* vi, Just canoe yourself off into the middle of the lake. **1850** *Knickerb.* XXXV. 21 We descended their tortuous slope to 'South Bay,' across which we were canoed.

2. *intr.* (or with *it*). To paddle a canoe; to make a journey in a canoe.

1841 COOPER *Deerslayer* xix, Shall you or I canoe it? **1870** MRS. STEPHENS *Married in Haste* 253, I have just been rocking, . . . that is canoeing in the river. **1883** *Harper's Mag.* April 692/2 Many enterprising souls . . . would have . . . bicycled, or canoed. **1884** 'MARK TWAIN' *H. Finn* Wks. (1923) XIII. xli. 385 Come along, let Sid foot it home, or canoe it, when he got done fooling around.

+Canoeable, *a.* [CANOE *n.* 1 or *v.* 2.] Affording passage for canoes. — **1755** L. EVANS *Anal. Map Colonies* 28 [The branch] is canoable about twenty miles farther. **1756** J. MAURY in Winsor *Miss. Basin* 216 The navigable, or rather canoeable parts of the rivers which empty themselves into the sea.

+Canoe birch. [CANOE *n.* 1.] The paper birch (*Betula papyrifera*), the bark of which is used in making canoes.

1810 MICHAUX *Arbres* I. 25 Canoe birch (*Bouleau à canot*). **1814** PURSH *Flora Amer.* II. 621 A large tree, highly useful to the natives for constructing their large portable canoes, from which circumstance it is known by the name of Canoe Birch. **1832** BROWNE *Sylva* 122 The canoe birch attains its largest size . . . on the declivity of hills and in the bottom of fertile valleys. **1843** TORREY *Flora N.Y.* II. 199 Canoe Birch. . . . The bark is used by the northern Indians for making their canoes. **1861** WINTHROP *Open Air* 49 The white-birch, paper birch, canoe-birch, grows large in moist spots near the stream where it is needed. **1892** APGAR *Trees Northern U.S.* 145 Paper or Canoe Birch . . . [is] a large tree, 60 to 75 ft. high, with white bark splitting freely into very thin, tough layers.

+Canoe cedar. *N.W.* [CANOE *n.* 1.] The Pacific arborvitæ, *Thuja plicata.* — **1884** SARGENT *Rep. Forests* 177 *Thuya gigantea.* . . . Red Cedar. Canoe Cedar. **1899** SUDWORTH *Arborescent Flora* 71 Pacific Arborvitæ. . . . Common Names . . . [include] Canoe Cedar (Oreg., Wash.).

+Canoe club. An organization of canoeists. — **1872** *Scribner's Mo.* Aug. 479/2 From the model of the third Nautilus built by the inventor [Baden-Powell], the New York Canoe Club has built, with slight modifications, . . . its entire fleet. **1880** *Harper's Mag.* Aug. 396/1 The introduction of canoeing in the United States may be said to have taken place in 1870, when the New York Canoe Club was founded by William L. Alden.

+Canoeing, *vbl. n.* [CANOE *n.* 1. Cf. CANOE *v.* 2.] Paddling, or journeying in, a canoe. Also attrib.

1752 P. STEVENS in *Travels Amer. Col.* 306, [I] lodged at the canoeing place from said lake to the drowned land. **1840** COOPER *Pathfinder* iii, I call all hands to witness . . . that I do not look on this affair as any thing more than canoeing in the woods. **1880** [see CANOE CLUB]. **1897** *Outing* June 227/1 The occasional sailor . . . is apt to adopt that method of canoeing which affords him the most fun at the least expenditure of effort.

Canoeist. [CANOE *n.* 1.] One who practices canoeing. {1865–}

1879 BISHOP *4 Months in Sneak-box* 21 He would need a [light] canoe . . . with the aid of the canoeist's indispensable assistant—the canoe-yoke. **1880** *Harper's Mag.* Aug. 396 Twenty-five miles to the northward of Quebec the exploring canoeist is beyond the bounds of civilization. **1882–6** (*N.Y. magazine title*), American Canoeist. **1885** *Harper's Mag.* LXX. 226/2 All this country [about Charlotte Harbor] lies within the reach of the canoeist. **1897** *Outing* June 226/1 There are two schools of canoeists. *Ib.* 230/1

+Canoeload. [CANOE *n.* 1.] The amount which can be carried in a canoe.

1691 Munsell *Annals Albany* II. 115. The def[endan]t accused him of stealing 1/2 canoe load of water millions. **1753** WASHINGTON *Diaries* I. 46 They were sent from New-Orleans with . . . 8 Canoe-Loads of Provisions. **1791** BARTRAM *Travels* 303 A feast of Water mellons and Oranges, the Indians having brought a canoe load of them to the trading-house. **1807** GASS *Journal* 197, 3 canoe loads of them were setting out for the falls to fish. **1835** HOFFMAN *Winter in West* II. 15 Of ducks.. . . it is easy to kill a canoe-load, when they begin to fly along the Mississippi. **1880** *Harper's Mag.* Dec. 31 Indians brought in canoe-loads of fine full jacketed potatoes.

Canoe maker. [CANOE *n.* 1.] One who makes canoes. — **1805** PIKE *Sources Miss.* (1810) 36 Killed a number of pheasants and ducks, while visiting my canoe-maker.

+Canoeman. [CANOE *n.* 1.] One who operates a canoe. {1834}

1755 L. EVANS *Anal. Map Colonies* 17 The River is full of Falls and Rifts for forty Leagues, where the Canoe Men are often obliged to carry over Land, and to trade in several Places. **1774** D. JONES *Journal* (1865) 59 Two of our canoe-men lay under the hands of an old *squaw*, having had their feet badly frozen. **1809** A. HENRY *Travels* 109 The goods . . . would have been saved, if the canoe-men had called them French property. **1832** R. Cox *Adv. Columbia R.* iv. 54 Here are found . . . ninety artisans and canoe-men, or, as they are commonly called in the Indian country, *voyageurs.* **c1838** CATLIN *Indians* II. 214 The Sacs and Foxes, like all other Indians, . . . are expert swimmers and skillful canoemen. **1897** *Outing* June 228/1 The ability to carry sail in such a light contrivance, depends entirely upon the skill of the canoeman.

+Canoe place. *Obs.* [CANOE *n.* 1.] A place at which canoes are kept or can be used.

1653 *Southampton Rec.* I. 94 John Cooper Sen shall send forth men to . . . bring to the towne what cattell they can meete with beyond the cannoo place. **1662** *Ib.* 167 The lawful bounds of Southampton . . . begin at the canoe place otherwise Niamuck. **1724** in Temple & Sheldon *Hist. Northfield, Mass.* (1875) 207 The third scout . . . steering east came to the canoe place. **1754** *Virginia St. Papers* I. 250 We intend to meet at our Canoe place. **1766** in W. Smith *Bouquet's Exped.* (1868) 145 *n.*, To the canoe place, 6 miles.

+Canoer. [CANOE *n.* 1.] A canoeist. — **1898** *Outing* June 269/1 Not so long ago the Adirondacks and New England were almost unthought of as fields for the summer camper, canoer and angler.

+Canoe tree. [CANOE *n.* 1.] A tree out of which a canoe can be made. — **1638** *Springfield Rec.* I. 164 It shall be lawfull for any inhabitant to fell any Cannoe trees and work them for his owne use. **1640** *Ib.* 167 No man shall fall any Cannoe tree that shall be within the bounds of the Plantation.

‖**Canoeuver.** *slang.* App. a humorous variant of *manoeuver.* — **1837** J. C. NEAL *Charcoal Sk.* (1838) 98 Tisn't every man that . . . has studied the nature of a pig, so as to beat him at canoeuvering, and make him surrender.

+Canoewood. The tulip tree or whitewood, *Liriodendron tulipifera.* Also attrib.

1762 CLAYTON *Flora Virginica* 83 *Polyandria Polygynia. Liriodendrum.* . . . White-wood & Canoe-wood-tree nostratibus. **1813** MUHLENBERG *Cat. Plants* 53 Tulip tree, poplar, white wood, canoe wood. **1832** BROWNE *Sylva* 202 In Connecticut, New York and New Jersey, it is known by the name of White Wood, and of Canoe Wood. **1883** HALE *Woods & Timbers N.C.* 128 Tulip Tree, or Poplar (*Liriodendron Tulipifera*, Linn.) . . . in some of the Northern States . . . is called White Wood and Canoe Wood.

+Cañon, *n.* [Mex.-Sp. (Sp. 'tube, pipe, conduit,' etc.).]

1. A deep, comparatively narrow gorge or ravine, usu. having very steep sides. (See CANYON.) Orig. and chiefly *S.W.*

Well illustrated by Thornton from 1834 to 1869.

' "Cañon," (pronounced *kanyon,*) . . . in this country, has been adopted to describe the passage of a river between perpendicular rocks of great height' (1843 Frémont *Exped.* 73). 'The word cañon is most generally applied to a deep and narrow valley, enclosed on either side by escarpments. It sometimes, however, means a shallow valley' (1849 *31st Cong. 1 Sess.* Sen. Doc. 64, 61). 'Cañons [are] . . . gorges or channels, which separate spurs or buttresses of mountains' (1857 *Harper's Mag.* Nov. 818/1). '*Canon* . . . is a Spanish word, meaning a valley or a pass in the mountains, and is universally used throughout the far West' (1868 W. E. Waters *Life among Mormons* 32).

1834 PIKE *Sketches* 20 Between these three points two cañons ran up into the bosom of the ridge. **1843** TALBOT *Journals* 53 Snake River, . . . in the parlance of the country, is said to run through a 'canon.' **1854** BARTLETT *Personal Narrative* II. xxvi. 123 We now entered a cañon, or mountain pass. **1866** *Rep. Indian Affairs* 109 The deep and dismal but sublime chasms and cañons of the upper Colorado. **1883** *Rep. Indian Affairs* 139 The cañons on the outskirts of the reservation produce plenty of wood and timber. **1890** CUSTER *Following Guidon* 70 We came . . . suddenly . . . upon cañons that were sharp fissures in the earth extending for many miles. **1902** WISTER *Virginian* vi. 67, I would . . . ride up toward the entrance of the cañon.

comb. **1886** ROOSEVELT in *Outing* July 387 Across some of the steep canon-like gullies, the wagon had to be brought.

2. Attrib. with *bed, country, gap, side.*

1845 FRÉMONT *Exped.* 147 A cañon gap in the mountains. *Ib.* 280 The country lower down on the Colorado, to which the trappers usually apply the name of a cañon-country. *Ib.*, He could watch . . . the sheeted rain drive along the cañon-sides. **1907** WHITE *Arizona Nights* ii. 18 Our way led first through a canon-bed filled with round boulders.

‖**Cañon,** *v. W.* [From the noun.] *intr.* To enter, or flow in, a canyon. — **1851** MAYNE REID *Scalp-Hunters* v, I soon came to a bend, where the stream, after running parallel to the ridge, swept round and cañoned through it. **1853** — *Rifle Rangers* xlv, We had struck the water at a point where the stream cañoned!

+Cañoned, *a. S.W.* [CAÑON *n.*]

1. Enclosed or confined in a cañon.

1846 in W. H. Emory *Notes Mil. Reconnoissance* (1848) 443 We reached the 'Ocate'; as it is a [*sic*] cañoned, that is, is enclosed with high rocky walls, we were forced to go two miles up stream in order to reach the crossing. **1848** BRYANT *California* xxii. 275 The river is *cañoned* between high mountains and precipices. **1849** *31st Congress 1 Sess.* Sen. Ex. Doc. No. 64, 137 The Colorado is so deeply cañoned from its mouth upward.

2. Cut by cañons.

1848 BRYANT *California* 342 On the southern side the shore is hilly, and *cañoned* in some places. **1886** J. S. DILLER in *8th Ann. Rep. Geol. Survey* I. 426 The long, gentle slope . . . is . . . deeply cañoned by numerous streams.

+Cañon finch, towhee, warbler, wren. *S.W.* (See quotations.)

1881 *Amer. Naturalist* XV. 212 There are two other species of the same genus . . . which I afterwards found breeding in Arizona, the Abert's finch (*Pipilo aberti*) and the cañon finch (*Pipilo mesoleucus*). — **1872** COUES *Key to Birds* 152 Brown Towhee, Cañon Towhee, . . . [is found in] New Mexico, Arizona, and southward. **1873** *Amer. Naturalist* VII. 324 Abert's Towhee (*Pipilo Abertii*) and the Cañon Towhee (*Pipilo fuscus* of Swainson . . . [var. *mesoleucus*]) are two large species related to our chewink. — **1918** RIDEOUT *Key of Fields* 311 A cañon warbler lavished his melody as if he could go on forever. — **1878** *U.S. Nat. Museum Proc.* I. 402 *Catherpes mexicanus*, [var.] *conspersus.*—Cañon Wren. **1882** COUES *Key to Birds* (ed. 2) 276 *Catherpes.* . . . Cañon Wrens. . . . *C. mexicanus.* Mexican Cañon Wren.

+Canoodle, *v. slang.* Also **conoodle. 1.** *intr.* To indulge in caresses or endearments. **2.** *tr.* To coax or blandish by caresses or endearments. **3.** *intr.* (See CANOODLER.) — **(1) 1859** G. A. SALA *Twice round Clock* 112 A variety of harmless endearing blandishments, known to our American cousins . . . under the generic name of 'conoodling.' **1898** HARTE *Stories in Light & Shadow* 189 The children still admired her as one who had undoubtedly 'canoodled' with a man 'a-going to be hung.' **(2) 1864** SALA in *Temple Bar* Dec. 40 (F.), He is an adept in that branch of persuasive dialects known as conoodling. He will conoodle the ladies . . . into the acquisition of whole packages of gimcrack merchandise. **1897** HARTE *Three Partners* 134 He'd have been called another victim of the brute Horncastle, and been as petted and canoodled as you.

+Canoodler. *slang.* (See quotation.) — **a1897** *Green Room Jokes* (B. & L.), 'Pray, good sir, what is a canoodler?' 'Tell you, mum, queer business, mum, but prosperous, money—heaps of it, mum, for you and me. . . . I'm an original thinker, mum. Invent business opportunities. Share 'm with actors, and then we *canoodle*—divvy the profits.'

+Can opener. An implement for cutting or prying open cans of preserved meats, fruits, etc.

1874 KNIGHT 452 Can-opener. . . . The illustration shows several forms. **1877** BARTLETT 97. **1890** H. O. WILLS *Twice Born* 76, I was selling a can-opener—the first in the market. **1902** LORIMER *Lett. Merchant* 74 Used to brag around about . . . how his sin was the original brand, direct from Adam, put up in cans to keep, and the can-opener lost.

***Canopy.** +*Under the* (or *God's*) *canopy* (esp. as an intensive), 'on earth,' 'in the world.'

1845 *Knickerb.* XXV. 443, I was again at home, and overwhelmed with questions about 'everything under the canopy.' **1862** *Congress. Globe* 23 May 2309/3, I do not suppose that any one under God's canopy would make any such decision. **1869** STOWE *Oldtown Folks* xi. 131 What under the canopy are you up to now, making such a litter on my kitchen floor? **1883** *Harper's Mag.* Jan. 212/1 What else under the canopy I'm makin' the trip for I can't see. **1904** *Hartford Courant* 2 Dec. 8 What under the canopy does little, poverty-stricken Greece want with an outfit of warships?

***Cant.** +A squared log. — **1877** *Lumberman's Gaz.* 24 May, A cant or square-edged timber. **1879** *Ib.* 5 Nov., The cheapest and most effective means yet devised for holding the cant in place.

Cantab. {1750–} +Colloq. abbreviation of CANTABRIGIAN. — **1834** *Knickerb.* III. 301 Nick was made a cantab at Harvard.

Cantabrigian. {c1645–} **+1.** *n.* A person belonging to Cambridge, Mass., or to Harvard University. **+2.** *adj.* Pertaining or belonging to Cambridge or Harvard. — **(1) 1887** *Harper's Mag.* March 589/1 Mrs. Saintsbury was Boston-born, . . . and was a Cantabrigian by marriage. **(2) 1893** W. K. POST *Harvard Stories* 26 The New Haven men struggled to the Cantabrigian twenty-yard line.

+Cantac. (See quot.) — **1806** in *Ann. 9th Congress* 2 Sess. 1107 *n.*, The cantac, occasionally used by the hunters [of the Black River region, La.] for food, . . . has a bulbous root, ten times the size of a man's fist.

+Cantalope, Cantelope. [Representing a prevalent pronunciation.] =CANTALOUPE. Also attrib.

1789 J. MORSE *Amer. Geog.* 53 Cantalopes . . . are a species of the muskmelon, but much superior in richness and flavor. **1792** IMLAY *Western Territory* 92 The cantilope [*sic*] melon is only to be equalled by those in Persia. **1797** BENTLEY *Diary* II. 239 A Friend gave me as I passed, a Cantelope, a species of Melon for the first time cultivated among us. **a1817** DWIGHT *Travels* I. 45 Cantelopes, particularly the Green Cantelope, the Persian, Minorca, Nutmeg, Citron, and Cretan melons are exquisitely fine. **1833** 'ELMWOOD' *Yankee among Nullifiers* 92 She inscribed the letter I on the rind of a cantalope. **1856** COZZENS *Sparrowgrass P.* x. 134 You call all kinds of melons 'cantelopes' in Philadelphia. **1883** F. M. CRAWFORD *Dr. Claudius* xiv, Cantelopes are American melons, small and of sickly appearance.

Cantaloupe. Also †-eleup. [Fr. *cantaloup*, from the Italian place name *Cantalupo*.]

1. A variety of muskmelon, of delicate flavor; occas. any muskmelon. {1763–}

[**1790** DEANE *New-Eng. Farmer* 171/2 Of all the kinds of melons, Mr. Miller greatly prefers the cantaloupe, a native of America [*sic*]. But I have not heard whether it has yet found its way into this country.] **1809** CUT-

LER in *Life & Corr.* II. 341 Went to Mr. Lyman's—ate cantaloupes. **1840** DEWEY *Mass. Flowering Plants* 113 One variety of the muskmelon is commonly called canteleup, or, as often written, cantelope, a very delicious fruit. **1856** *Harper's Mag.* XII. 857/2 Some rascal had got into his garden and carried off his cantaloupes. **c1862** BAGBY *Old Va. Gentleman* 84 Those copious crops of watermelons, muskmelons, and cantaloupes for which Mountain View is famous. **1899** G. ADE *Fables in Slang* (1902) 2 A tall, rangy Person with a Head in the shape of a Rocky Ford Cantaloupe. **1902** *Harper's Mag.* March 623/2 A fine question whether he should take them between the cantaloupe and the broiled chicken.

2. Attrib. with *melon.* {1739-}

1798 B. HAWKINS *Letters* 322, [I] planted shallots and canteloup melons. **1876** M. F. HENDERSON *Cooking* 337 Cantaloupe Melons [should be] put ... into the refrigerator until just before serving. **1893** 'THANET' *Stories* 43 Cavendish, whose memory is honored by lovers of the cantaloupe melon.

Cant dog. {1847} +A cant hook.

1850 JUDD *R. Edney* iv. 51 Silver seized the cant-dog, and aimed at the head-stock man. **1851** J. S. SPRINGER *Forest Life* 156 All hands are ... lifting with heavy pries, hand-spikes, and cant-dogs, to roll these massive sticks into the brook channel. **1885** *Boston Journal,* In the United States there are only two establishments for the manufacture of cant-dogs. **1902** *Boston Globe* 4 May 14 Cant dogs ... slipped from the hands of careless drivers.

Canteen. Also **-tine.**

1. A small vessel of metal (or occas. wood) used by soldiers, workmen, etc., esp. for holding water, liquor, or liquid food. {1744-}

1756 in *Lett. to Washington* I. 165 The Blanketts, Camp Kettles, Canteens, Spare Shoes & Stockins & Shirts. **1805** CLARK in *Lewis & C. Exped.* (1904) II. 199, I caused her as also the others of the party to take a little spirits, which my servent had in a canteen. **1848** PARKMAN in *Knickerb.* XXXII. 318 His squaw ... was giving him a draught of water out of a canteen purchased or plundered from some volunteer soldier. **1899** *Mo. So. Dakotan* I. 172 Thus by mutual consent we became pards, ... and as it were drank from the same canteen.

2. A shop or store where liquor and various other commodities are sold; esp. in military use. {1744-}

1845 *Knickerb.* XXV. 320 They soon became great friends, formed a partnership in hunting, and were boon companions at the *cantines* or grog-shops. **1899** *Boston Transcript* 21 June 1/7 Canteen or beer-room. No distilled liquors are sold there. **1923** R. HERRICK *Lilla* 234 There is more responsible work for me to do than running a soldier's canteen.

***Canterbury bell(s).** A species of campanula or bellflower, *Campanula medium.* — **1833** EATON *Botany* (ed. 6) 65 *Campanula medium,* canterbury bells; ... stem erect, leafy: flowers erect. **1857** GRAY *Botany* 244 The Canterbury Bells, and some other species, are common in gardens. **1898** E. C. HALL *Aunt Jane* 256, I watched the quick, luxuriant growth of ... the Canterbury-bell, so like a prim, pretty maiden.

+Cant hook.

1. (See first quot. and cf. CANT DOG.)

1848 BARTLETT 62 *Cant-hook,* a wooden lever, with an iron hook at one end, with which heavy articles of merchandise or timber are canted over. **1883** *Harper's Mag.* Jan. 206/2 Chinese laborers easily roll them [=logs] ... down upon the cars, aiding themselves with cant-hooks. **1900** E. BRUNCKEN *N. Amer. Forests* 79 As the logs come floating down the stream men armed with long 'cant hooks' guide each into the compartment where it belongs. **1903** W. D. HULBERT in *Outlook* 7 Nov. 591 Jimmy was working hard with his cant-hook at a log that had twisted around.

b. *Cant-hook man,* a lumberman who uses a cant hook.

1902 *Munsey's Mag.* XXV. 389/1 The log must ascend evenly. To that the two cant-hook men below attend. **a1904** WHITE *Blazed Trail Stories* ii. 30 The rollways became choked with the logs.... The cant-hook men became discouraged.

2. 'A sling with hooks for raising and tilting casks, to empty them' (Knight). Cf. CAN HOOK.

+Canticoy, *n.* Also **-ico, -ica.** *Obs.* [See KENTICOY *n.*]

1. Among Indians, a ceremonial dancing match.

1670 D. DENTON *Descr. N.-Y.* (1902) 50 At their Cantica's or dancing Matches, where all persons that come are freely entertain'd, it being a Festival time. **1683** PENN *Works* (1782) IV. 309 Their worship consists of two parts, sacrifice and cantico. *Ib.,* The other part is their cantico, performed by round dances, sometimes words, sometimes songs, then shouts.

b. An occasion of frolic, as 'a dancing assembly' (B. '48), or 'social gathering' (B. '59).

1848 BARTLETT 62-3 *Canticoy,* or *Cantica,* an Indian word, ... still used by aged people in New York and on Long Island. **1871** DE VERE 45 At the North, the thrifty farmer, no longer able to enjoy the *Canticos,* as his fathers called their frolics ..., invites his neighbors, far and near, to help him.

2. 'A noisy conversation' (B. '48).

+Canticoy, *v. Obs.* [See prec.] *intr.* =KENTICOY *v.* — **1867** H. C. MURPHY tr. J. Danker's *Voyage to New Netherland* (1679) in *L.I. Hist. Soc. Mem.* I. 275 These Indians had *canticoyed* (*gekintekayt*) there to-day, that is, conjured the devil, and liberated a woman among them, who was possessed by him, as they said.

+Cantina. *S.W.* [Sp., 'cellar,' 'case,' etc.]

1. A form of saddlebag.

1844 GREGG *Commerce of Prairies* II. 99 A pack-mule to carry his *cantinas* (a pair of large wallets or leathern boxes). **1871** *Scribner's Mo.* II. 2 Each man was supplied with a strong horse, well equipped with California saddle, bridle, and cantinas. **1874** CODMAN *Mormon Country* 63 My cantinas, containing clothes and pistol-holster, and my blankets and overcoat, ... were as much as one horse ought to carry. **1890** N. P. LANGFORD *Vigilante Days* II. 38 Buckskin sacks, containing about eighty thousand dollars, were distributed in cantinas through the entire pack train. **1913** G. D. BRADLEY *Story of Pony Express* 58-9 The *mochila* had four pockets called *cantinas* in each of its corners—one in front and one behind each of the rider's legs. These *cantinas* held the mail.

2. A saloon where liquor is sold. (Cf. CANTEEN 2.)

c1893 *Dialect Notes* I. 245 *Cantina,* bar-room. Of frequent use [in Texas]. Often found on signs of Mexican bar-rooms. **1923** W. SMITH *Little Tigress* 153 (Bentley), In a few steps they were at the cantina called the Spring of the Golden Dreams.

***Cantle.** Also **cantel.**

***1.** The hind bow of a saddle.

1835 J. P. KENNEDY *Horse Shoe Robinson* II. xxv. 225 A long sweep from the pommel to the cantle—it is a saddle worth riding on! **1850** GLISAN *Jrnl. Army Life* 10 The high cantel of the dragoon saddle added greatly to the difficulty of gaining my seat. **1886** ROOSEVELT in *Century Mag.* July 340/1 A cowboy ... sitting forked well down between his high pommel and cantle. **1897** *Outing* XXX. 101/2 These [strips of leather] are woven between a steel pommel attachment and a bent hickory cantle. **1920** MULFORD *J. Nelson* xxv. 284 The cantle of the saddle, striking the barrel of the Winchester, tore the weapon from its owner's hands.

b. Attrib. with *string.*

1903 A. ADAMS *Log Cowboy* ii. 15 The indispensable slicker [waterproof] ... securely tied to our cantle strings.

***2.** A thick slice of pie, melon, or the like. {-1737; 1804- dial.}

1880 *Harper's Mag.* Dec. 94/2 He ... loved a bit of good eating—[as] a cantle of chicken pie. **1891** *Ib.* Sept. 573/2 Lucy gave him a huge cantle [of melon].

***Canton,** *n.*[1]

+1. A nation or tribe of Indians. *Obs.*

1688 *Penna. Archives* I. 104 The late attempt ... made by the French upon the five Nations or Cantons of Indians. **1764** T. HUTCHINSON *Hist. Mass.* (1765) I. 471 They had grand fishings at the several falls of the rivers, at most of which a canton or company of Indians had their chief residence. **1820** *Amer. Antiq. Soc. Coll.* I. 64 We desired them to give notice to the five cantons of their nation.

2. A division of a county; a small district. *Obs.*

1715 *Virginia St. Papers* I. 199, I think it necessary that you give immediate Orders to the Commanding Officers of the Militia in the Several Cantons of the Countys under your Command. **1796** JEFFERSON *Writings* IX. 355 In the retired canton where I am, I learn little of what is passing.

+3. A division or unit of a friendly society.

1885 *Revised Odd-Fellowship* (1891) 282 The name of the Degree is changed to 'Patriarchs Militant,' and the name of Canton substituted for Uniform Camp, as a unit of organization. **1906** *Springfield Republican* 7 Feb. 10 Lieut.-Col. E. E. Gilson of Canton Athol has been elected colonel of the 5th regiment of Odd Fellows, department of Massachusetts. This regiment includes a number of cantons in the middle and western part of the state.

Canton, *n.*[2] Denoting various textiles, originally or still manufactured in Canton, China. Usu. attrib. with *crape, flannel, matting,* etc.

1709 *Essex Inst. Coll.* VIII. 19 In a pine chist. 6 peses of Canton qt 31 anns. **1852** STOWE *Uncle Tom* xx, Miss Ophelia found Topsy with her very best scarlet India Canton crape shawl wound around her head for a turban. **1860** *Texas Almanac* 244 Shirts, Carpets, Canton-Matting, shoes. **1869** *Atlantic Mo.* July 74/2 My small Canton flannel knee-pants. **1881** *Art Interchange* (N.Y.) 27 Oct. 93/1 Mantel scarfs ... could be of double-faced Canton flannel. **1896** E. HIGGINSON *Tales* 217 She bent over the canton flannel night-shirt she was making for Mr. Wincoop.

***Canton,** *v.*

1. *tr.* 'To allocate separate quarters to each regiment of an army or body of troops' (W. '28). {1700-1755}

1752 MACSPARRAN *America Dissected* (1753) 20 Four Independent Companies ... are cantoned in York, Albany, Schenectady, ... to watch the Motions of their Neighbours the French. **1787** in M. Cutler *Life & Corr.* (1888) I. 248 The capture of a large detachment of Hessian troops cantoned in this town. **1806** CLARK in *Lewis & C. Exped.* (1905) V. 375, 300 of the american Troops had been cantuned on the Missouri a fiew miles above it's mouth. **1826** EVERETT *Orations* (1850) I. 116 O, the disciplined, the paid, the honored mob; ... marching ... to lay waste a feebler state; or cantoned at home among an overawed and broken-spirited people! **1857** E. STONE *Life of Howland* iii. 69 A part of the third regiment . . . fled to Bordentown, where we should have accounted for them with the rest of the division cantoned at that place. **1867** EDWARDS *Shelby* vii. 107 He . . . cantoned his infantry in unhealthy localities until they died by regiments and brigades. **1876** BANCROFT *Hist. U.S.* VI. lv. 432 Washington and the eastern army were cantoned for the winter in their old positions around New York.

+**b.** To settle (Indians) in cantons or districts.

1867 PARKMAN *Jesuits in N. Amer.* p. liv, The Iroquois . . . separated into five distinct nations, cantoned from east to west along the centre of New York.

2. *intr.* Of soldiers: To take up quarters. {1697–}

1861 *Army Regulations* 81 When cavalry and infantry canton together, the latter furnish the guards by night, and the former by day.

Cantonment.

1. The separate quarters of a regiment or other division of an army. {1756–}

1777 W. HEATH in Sparks *Corr. Rev.* (1853) I. 338 Every purpose . . . has been answered, by the troops in their present cantonment. **1802** *Ann. 7th Congress* 154 Small parcels of land . . . have been purchased . . . for cantonments and other military purposes. **1813** *Niles' Reg.* V. 107/1 This cantonment (called Mount Vernon) was very ill calculated for defence. *c***1834** CATLIN *Indians* II. 15 In this delightful Cantonment [*sc.* Fort Leavenworth] there are generally stationed six or seven companies of infantry. **1870** KEIM *Sheridan's Troopers* (1885) xxiii. 165 The camp had the appearance of a regular winter cantonment. **1881** *Rep. Indian Affairs* 20, I notified the commanding officer at the cantonment. **1917** *Lit. Digest* 27 Oct. 51/2 Colonel Littell . . . is the man in charge of the construction of the cantonments for the training of America's selective army.

+**2.** A place of occupation; quarters. {1875}

1837 IRVING *Bonneville* I. ix. 106 All hands now set to work to prepare a winter cantonment. *Ib.* 107 Rarely could the inmates of the cantonment boast of having made a full meal.

‖**Cantsloper.** (Meaning uncertain.) — **1788** MAY *Jrnl. & Lett.* (1873) 54 At 11 A.M. paid the visit to our Governor, wrapped in my cantsloper. **1876** *N.E. Hist. & Geneal. Reg.* Jan. 44 'Cantsloper' . . . is found again in [the Journal] . . . of '89 and also in a copy of the Journal made by the original writer's oldest daughter, Abby; but it is spelled . . . "*Kentsloper, khansloper.*"

‖**Cantum.** *slang. Obs.* [From *cant* n. or v.] (See quotation.) — **1781** S. PETERS *Hist. Conn.* 280 Some travellers have called the fanatical sects of Connecticut . . . Pumguntums, Cantums, &c. because they groan and sing with a melancholy voice their prayers, sermons, and hymns.

+**Canuck,** *n.* and *a.* Also **Canack.** (Cf. KANUCK and CANNACKER.)

1. *n.* A native or inhabitant of Canada, spec. French Canada; a Canadian.

'Colloquial and in all newspapers' (Chipman). 'In Canada the nickname of French Canadians; in the United States a nickname for all Canadians' (1890 Norton *Polit. Americanisms* 26).

1855 *Knickerb.* XLV. 341 [Giving] our donkey into the keeping of a lively *Canuck*, . . . we commenced the slow ascent [of Mt. Holyoke]. **1871** DE VERE 589 *Canacks, Canucks*, and even *K'nucks*, are slang terms by which the Canadians are known in the United States. **1873** BEADLE *Undevel. West* xxxiii. 711 The Yankee shudders as he thinks of the hard fate of the 'Canucks' and 'Blue-noses' of British America. **1895** *Century Mag.* Sept. 674/2 That would be convenient over the line among the Canucks. **1897** HOWELLS *Landlord at Lion's Head* (1908) vii. 30 'What's that?' 'It's that Canuck chopping in Whitwell's clearing.' **1907** *N.Y. Ev. Post* 22 April 6 Polacks and Canucks have taken the places of most of the old-time American woodsmen in the Adirondacks. **1917** C. MATHEWSON *Sec. Base Sloan* xviii. 243 La Croix was a thick-set, hook-nosed Canuck.

2. A Canadian horse.

1888 C. D. FERGUSON *Exp. Forty-niner* ii. 23 No frontier town ever saw a grander sight than those four Canucks.

3. *adj.* Of or pertaining to Canada; Canadian.

1862 *Congress. Globe* 29 April 1867/3 They went . . . from St. Louis to Canada to buy the little Canuck ponies at $130 apiece.

***Canvas,** *n.* Also †**canvass.**

***1.** A strong, heavy, closely woven cloth of hemp, flax, or cotton, used for making tents, sails, etc.

1640 *Conn. Public Rec.* I. 449 An Inventory of the goods . . . of James Olmestead . . . [includes] 27 yards of course Canuas. **1754** *S.C. Gazette* 21–28 May 3/2 Samuel Peronneau has just imported . . . White Sarsnet, Cruels and Canvas. **1770** *Carroll P.* in *Md. Hist. Mag.* XIII. 66 Pray write for 6 strong matrasses . . . covered with Burras or a coarse strong Canvass. **1818** *Niles' Reg.* XV. 112/1 A fair test has been made of the comparative durability of American and Russian canvass. **1897** *Outing* XXIX. 476/2 He reached out dumbly to where his sword stood a-prop against the canvas that shut him from the sun.

2. Attrib. in sense: Made of canvas, as *canvas arrangement, awning, bag, boat*, etc.

1857 *Phila. Bulletin* 25 May (B. '59), The bags containing the nicks were neat little canvas arrangements. **1880** CABLE *Grandissimes* 132 It was a long, narrowing perspective . . . of canvas awnings with fluttering borders. **1661** *Md. Council Proc.* 412 He found . . . a Canvas bagg all bloody and an english paire of shoes. **1862** BARNARD in McClellan *Own Story* 248 The canvas boats will answer for crossing the creeks. **1841** COOPER *Deerslayer* xx, A canvas cap . . . was forced so low on his head as to conceal his face. **1622** 'MOURT' *Relation* 33 It was bound vp in a Saylers canvas Casacke. **1841** J. B. JONES *Wild Western Scenes* (1856) 9 The interrogator . . . reclined musingly in a wagon, the canvas covering of which served . . . to protect him from the wind and rain. **1880** *Harper's Mag.* Aug. 398 The canvas craft — a pretty and most serviceable boat. **1639** *Md. Archives* IV. 80, 3 paire of Canvas drawers at 12l a paire. **1677** SEWALL *Diary* I. 43 There came in a female Quaker, in a Canvas Frock. **1871** RAYMOND *3d Rep. Mines* 63 Canvas hose was first brought into general use in 1853. **1877** WM. WRIGHT *Big Bonanza* 24 As early as 1851, there were erected a few temporary structures, principally canvas houses. **1885** *Rep. Indian Affairs* 33 A large portion of them is still living in canvas lodges instead of permanent habitations. **1887** *Outing* X. 5/2 Another man whose feet were sore from footing it among rocks and stones in canvas shoes. **1858** in Glisan *Jrnl. Army Life* 397 Our military friends . . . are perhaps barely sheltered under canvas tents on the snow-covered plains of Utah. **1688** SEWALL *Diary* I. 228, I goe with Mr. Newgate in the rain to Hogg-Island, having a canvas Tilt. **1840** BIRD *Robin Day* 26 He was a . . . middle-aged man, . . . [with] a new blue cloth jacket, and old canvass trousers.

b. *Canvasman*, a circus man who erects and takes down the tent.

1910 MCCUTCHEON *Rose in Ring* 63 You have certainly felt . . . servile in contact with a boss canvasman.

***Canvas,** *v. tr.* To cover (a ham) with canvas. — **1840** *Picayune* 17 Oct. 2, 500 'Washington's' superior Canvassed Hams. **1851** CIST *Cincinnati* 230 In the third and attic stories are done the canvasing, coloring, decorating etc., of the hams. **1902** LORIMER *Lett. Merchant* 119 We were carrying a couple of canvased hams where our hands ought to be.

Canvasback. {1605–} Also †**canvassback.**

+**1.** A species of wild duck, *Aythya (Fuligula) vallisneria*, so named from the color of its back feathers, and much esteemed as an article of food.

1782 JEFFERSON *Virginia* vi. 77 Besides these [birds], we have The . . . Widgeon, Sheldrach, or Canvas back. **1796** F. BAILY *Tour* 109 The canvass-back, a most delicious bird, frequents this river [Susquehanna]. **1805** PARKINSON *Tour* 300 Wild ducks are plentiful, of different kinds. The sort called canvas-backs is the most delicious I ever tasted. . . . They are only to be found in the Potowmac and Susquehanna rivers. **1813** WILSON *Ornith.* VIII. 86 The Canvass backs and Widgeons . . . live in a state of perpetual contention. **1836** M. A. HOLLEY *Texas* v. 100 Large . . . flocks of . . . teal—canvass-back, and summer duck—and other water fowl, frequent the rivers and sea shore. **1856** *Spirit of Times* (N.Y.) 13 Dec. 242/2 The widgeon . . . on the Chesapeake . . . feeds on wild celery with the canvass backs. **1898** *Boston Transcr.* 19 Nov. 24/4 Sometimes a poodle-dog is employed to run along the shore, off which the canvas-backs are feeding, and 'tole' them within range by exciting their curiosity. **1907** LILLIBRIDGE *Trail* 35 The teal, the mallard, the widgeon, the shoveller, the canvasback—all mingled in the loud-voiced throng that arose before the leader's approach.

+**b.** In collective singular.

1852 *Harper's Mag.* V. 534/1 The man . . . had followed a large flock of canvas-back until they entered a cove. **1857** *Spirit of Times* (N.Y.) 3 Jan. 290/2 The *Spirit*, still, will treat . . . of canvas-back, of curlew, [etc.].

+**c.** One of these ducks, or the flesh of one, as used for food.

1845 POE *Secrets Prison-House* Wks. IX. 289 Five-and-twenty dollars . . . to be spent generously in canvas-backs and champagne. **1860** HOLMES *Professor* vii. 211 The class of people who grumble if they don't get canvas-backs and woodcocks every day. **1878** *Harper's Mag.* March 495/2 Washington, with its venison, wild turkeys, canvas-backs, . . . etc., furnished better viands than Paris. **1899** T. HALL *Tales* 174 He had just finished a dinner of canvasback.

+**2.** *Canvas-back duck* = sense 1.

1796 T. TWINING *Travels Amer.* (1894) 79 Its waters were said to afford . . the celebrated canvas-back ducks. **1799** WELD *Travels* 73 One duck in particular . . . surpasses all others: it is called the white or canvass-back duck, from the feathers between the wings being somewhat of the colour of canvass. **1827** *Mass. Spy* 26 Dec. (Th.), Providence River and Bristol Bay have been thronged with canvass back ducks this fall. **1829** B. HALL *Travels in N.A.* III. 68 Down the muddy Potomac . . . myriads of canvass-back ducks . . . literally blackened the surface of the water. **1844** *Nat. Hist. N.Y., Zoology* II. 321 The Canvass-back Duck breeds on the Rocky mountains and in high northern latitudes. **1862** A. TROLLOPE *N. Amer.* I. 466 Canvas-back ducks and terrapins are the great glories of Baltimore. **1884** NYE *Baled Hay* 73 The bird is constructed of an eagle's head, a canvas back duck's bust and feet.

+**b.** =sense 1 c.

1791 MACLAY *Deb. Senate* 282 Canvass back ducks, ham, and chickens, . . . all amazingly fine, were his constant themes. **1802** CUTLER in *Life & Corr.* II. 55 We supped on canvas-back ducks. **1830** R. C. SANDS *Writings* II. 164 Are your famous canvas-back ducks now in season? **1887** W. R. HOUSTON, etc. *Rules Etiquette* (ed. 11) 94 Skill in cooking is as readily shown in a baked potato or johnny-cake as in a canvas-back duck. **1897** *Outing* April 456/1 Talk of . . . canvasback duck fed on Maryland wild celery.

Canvas-backed, *a.* +**1.** Of ducks: (see CANVASBACK). +**2.** Of wagons: Canvas-covered. — (1) **1841** H. PLAYFAIR *Papers* I. 289 The roasted fowls, and canvass-backed ducks, were all admirable. **1870** *Amer. Naturalist* III. 639 Canvas-backed Duck . . . is much less common in New England than several authors represent. (2) **1856** N. H. PARKER *Iowa As It Is* 56 Our ferry is busy all hours in passing over the large canvas-backed wagons, densely populated with becoming Iowaians.

Canvas-covered, *a.* Of wagons or boats: Having a covering of canvas. — **1879** *Harper's Mag.* June 71/1 Passing one or two canvas-covered wagons laden with fish. **1882** *Century Mag.* Sept. 771/1 Many people were living in little A tents or in their canvas-covered wagons. **1888** SHERIDAN *Memoirs* I. 417 Enough canvas-covered boats for a small pontoon-bridge were also provided. **1894** CHOPIN *Bayou Folk* 147 [Désirée] had been purposely left by a party of Texans, whose canvas-covered wagon . . . had crossed the ferry.

+**Canvas duck.** A canvas-back duck. — **1814** PAULDING *Sc. Fiddle* v. 102 Twelve canvas ducks, at morning play, By that discharge all found their grave.

Canvass, *n.* {1611–}

1. A campaign for election to governmental office. {1691–}

1792 TROUP in Jay *Corr.* III. 426 If a fair canvass takes place we are all very sanguine in our expectations that we shall prevail. **1825** CLAY *Speeches* (1860) I. 214 The irritating circumstances which attended the preceding canvass. **1846** M'KENNEY *Memoirs* I. 27 The canvass . . . resulted in the election of General Harrison to the Presidency. **1857** *Harper's Mag.* Sept. 561/1, I went into the canvass, and stumped my native State for Buchanan. **1886** ROOSEVELT in *Century Mag.* Nov. 77/2 To pay for the extravagant methods by which our canvasses are conducted. **1892** *Courier-Journal* 3 Oct. 1/7 An exceedingly active canvass is going on.

b. The personal solicitation of votes prior to an election.

1875 *Chicago Tribune* 2 July 7/6 Gov. Kirkwood will make a thorough canvass of the State. **1879** *Scribner's Mo.* Aug. 608/2 Uncle Clif volunteered to assist him in managing his canvass. **1887** *Courier-Journal* 11 Jan. 2/5 Mrs. Lowe . . . was greatly assisted in her canvass by her niece. **1925** BRYAN *Memoirs* 160 Some of my prominent political friends . . . made an active canvass of Nebraska.

+**c.** A survey to determine the sentiment for or against a candidate or a cause. (Cf. CANVASS *v.* 3 b.)

1898 *Kansas City Star* 18 Dec. 4/2 The efforts of the advocates of an extra session of the Fifty-sixth Congress . . . have not been fruitful. The canvass of the House . . . has been far from satisfactory. **1914** McLaughlin & Hart *Cycl. Amer. Govt.* II. 772 A preliminary canvass is often made . . . to determine the advisability of entering the lists.

+**2.** An official scrutiny of votes in an election.

1778 *N.Y. Laws* 27 March, As soon as they shall be able to determine upon such canvas and estimate, [etc.]. **1848** *Knickerb.* XVIII. 518 When the canvass took place, it was declared that Brief and Carbuncle were nominated. **1877** JOHNSON *Anderson Co., Kansas* 78 On the canvass of the vote the probate judge threw out all the returns except the Shannon precinct. **1888** BRYCE *Amer. Commonw.* II. App. 682 If all the returns have not been received, the canvass must be postponed. **1903** *N.Y. Sun* 20 Nov. 5 The official canvass of the vote in the borough of Brooklyn was practically finished yesterday.

3. Personal solicitation of a district for custom or sale.

1887 *Courier-Journal* 8 May 10/6 Mr. A. H. Perry . . . is now making a canvass of this city, and the demand for this remarkable book will doubtless be very great.

* **Canvass,** *v.*

1. *intr.* To solicit or go about soliciting votes or support for a person or thing. {a1626–} Hence *Canvassing* vbl. n.

1792 Jay *Correspondence* III. 427 The canvassing has proceeded. **1828** WEBSTER s.v., To canvass for an office, or preferment; to canvass for a friend. **1865** *Atlantic Mo.* XV. 556 There was not even canvassing for favorite candidates. **1879** *Harper's Mag.* LIX. 76/2 He . . . had, no doubt, been selected . . . to canvass for free lecturers.

fig. **1883** 'MARK TWAIN' *Life on Miss.* xxxiv, He had seen them [mosquitoes] around the polls 'canvassing.'

+**2.** *tr.* In an election, to examine or scrutinize (votes) officially, as by recounting; to test (a return of votes) in this way. (Cf. CANVASS *n.* 2.)

1778 *N.Y. Laws* 27 March, The joint Committee . . . [shall] canvas and estimate the votes. **1792** in Jay *Corr.* III. 430 Jacob Morris . . . claims . . . , as a matter of right, that the votes be canvassed. **1847** WEBSTER 171/1 To canvass the votes for senators. **1860** *Ohio Rev. Statutes* I. 549 (*margin*), It shall be the duty of the governor, auditor and secretary of state, to canvass the votes cast at the annual election. **1872** *Ill. Revised Statutes* (1883) 510 The county clerk or his deputy . . . shall proceed to open, canvass and publish the return from each precinct or election district. **1891** *Harper's Mag.* Aug. 486/1 Mr. Hooks, you will please canvass the vote, and report the result.

3. To go about (an election district, etc.) soliciting votes or support. {1812–}

1847 WEBSTER 171/1 To canvass a district for votes. **1871** DE VERE 270 Generally he [*i.e.* the candidate] begins canvassing the county or the State. **1907** C. C. ANDREWS *Recoll.* 153 He canvassed the state . . . to secure his election.

+**b.** To test or determine by a survey the prevailing sentiment. (Cf. CANVASS *n.* 1 c.)

1859 STOWE *Minister's Wooing* xiv. 182 D—— must canvass the Senate thoroughly.

4. To solicit (a district) for custom or sale. Also *vbl. n.*

1887 *Courier-Journal* 22 Jan. 4/5 Yesterday he canvassed the city in the interest of the Provident Savings Life Assurance Society of New York. . . . Maj. Norman told him he would have to . . . have him fined $50 . . . , then, after obtaining the proper license, [he could] proceed with his canvassing.

* **Canvasser.**

+**1.** One who officially examines the return of votes at an election.

1792 in Jay *Correspondence* III. 428 This reference was understood by us all as intended to procure a cloak for the canvassers to cover their villainy in rejecting the votes of Otsego. **1829** R. C. SANDS *Writings* II. 136, I suppose you know that the canvassers rejected six hundred votes. **1860** *Ohio Revised Statutes* I. 542 (*margin*), When canvassers may adjourn. **1877** *Colo. General Laws* 377 The state board of canvassers shall meet at the office of the secretary of state. **1904** *Newark Ev. News* 25 Nov. 5 Governor Murphy has appointed . . . the State Board of Canvassers. . . . The board will . . . officially determine the number of votes which were cast for the different candidates.

2. One who canvasses for orders for goods, subscriptions, etc. {1865–}

1856 *Spirit of Times* (N.Y.) 27 Sept. 57/3 City Distribution — Chance for Canvassers. **1880** *Scribner's Mo.* July 354/2 The foot of West Twenty-third street is the place of departure for boats . . . and all have canvassers warmly devoted to their interests waiting on the docks.

3. One who canvasses a district for the purpose of urging citizens to register as voters.

1892 *Boston Jrnl.* 7 Nov. 7/4 In all the alleged cases noted in this ward we have personal knowledge that the parties are legally entitled to a vote, and that no money whatever was paid to any canvasser beyond a day's pay.

+**Canvassing board.** A board which certifies the results of an election. — **1875** *Chicago Tribune* 11 Nov. 5/3 The Canvassing Board continued their operations yesterday afternoon in the County Building. **1883** *Century Mag.* July 397 There was a canvassing board, sitting with closed doors in the City Hall, which changed the totals. **1906** *Indian Laws & Tr.* III. 187 An election commissioner . . . shall distribute all ballots and election supplies, . . . and deliver the same to the canvassing board herein named.

Canvas-topped, *a.* Of wagons: Having a canopy of canvas. — **1877** HALE *G. T. T.* 155 She found simply a long canvas-topped wagon, lightly sprung. **1880** *Harper's Mag.* July 192/2 Instead of . . . long lines of canvas-topped wagons I saw farms and school-houses. **1889** K. MUNROE *Golden Days* ix. 95 They sold the great canvas-topped wagon that had been their home for months.

Cany, Caney, *a.* {1667} +Abounding with canes; marked by growths of canebrakes. Freq. in place names: (see quot. 1859.) — **1797** MORSE *Amer. Gazetteer* s.v., Cany Fork, in the state of Tennessee, is a short navigable river. **1831** M. A. HOLLEY *Texas* (1833) vi. 57 Cane-brake creek or Caney, as it is usually called, winds its way through this tract. **1859** BARTLETT 66 *Caney Fork* or *Branch* is a frequent name for streams in Kentucky and Tennessee, undoubtedly from canes having grown there formerly.

+**Canyon,** *n.* [Anglicized form of CAÑON.] = CAÑON *n.*

'As the word "Canyon" will occur several times, I may now . . . defend the form of spelling which I have adopted. . . . Some persons write the word in its Spanish form; others spell it "Kanyon," while the most general method of spelling it is "Canyon" '(1870 W. F. Rae *Westward by Rail* 94).

*a*1842 O. RUSSEL *Journal* (1921) xv. 65 This stream ran through a tremendous mountain in a deep, narrow canyon of rocks. *Ib.*, After leaving the canyon we encamped at a small spring. **1850** GARRARD *Wah-To-Yah* xiii. 171 On emerging from the canyon, the view expanded. **1867** LATHAM *Black & White* 81 Great ravines called Canyons . . . have been cut through the hard lava and granite to a depth of from 2,000 to 3,000 feet. **1884** NYE *Baled Hay* 78 Adown the canyons and gulches of the Rocky mountains comes the melodious cadences of the poet of the Greeley Eye. **1899** *Boston Transcr.* 8 Aug. 24/1 The canyons of the Rio Grande are a series of gigantic roofless tunnels carved by the river through range after range of mountains. **1905** G. E. COLE *Early Oregon* iv. 53 We were but a short distance from Hardy Eiliff's at the south end of the canyon.

attrib. **1872** 'MARK TWAIN' *Roughing It* xii. 101 The simple rivulet . . . plodding its patient way down the mountainsides, and canyon-beds. **1901** *Science* n.s. XIII. 950/2 Mother-Lode (Cal., Ransome) exhibits parts of the uplifted and dissected peneplain of the Sierra Nevada; . . . it is now trenched by canyon-valleys. **1902** *Ib.* n.s. XV. 86/1 These may be called 'canyon springs,' a new term introduced in the classification of springs.

+**Canyon,** *v. S.W.* [f. prec.] **1.** *intr.* To flow in a cañon. **2.** *tr.* To cut or form into cañons. — (1) **1870** BEADLE *Utah* 441 Bear River . . . forms a great U in Idaho, then turning southwest 'canyons' downward three miles. (2) **1878** I. L. BIRD *Rocky Mts.* 195 Below them lay broken ravines of fantastic rocks, cleft and canyoned by the river.

***Cap,** *n.*

***1.** A close-fitting head covering of soft material, worn by men and boys.

a1649 WINTHROP *Hist.* 12 He came in his worst clothes, . . . in a foul linen cap pulled close to his eyes. **1723** *Weekly Mercury* 20–27 June 2/2 He has a mill'd Cap on his head without a Hatt. **1820** *Columbian Centinel* 1 Jan. 1/1 Thomas Whitmarsh . . . has on hand . . . traveling Caps and Sacks; . . . Washington Caps for children. **1823** COOPER *Pioneer* (1869) i. 4 A cap of martin skins . . . the sides of which . . . were fastened beneath his chin. **1840** DANA *Two Years* x. 79 We had on oilcloth suits, and southwester caps. **1861** in Logan *Great Conspiracy* 142 Mr. Wigfall . . . alluding to Mr. Lincoln . . . [as] 'a man who disguises himself in a soldier's cloak and a Scotch cap.' **1866** 'F. KIRKLAND' *Bk. Anecdotes* 327 Confederate officers, . . . attired in a coarse, but neat-fitting suit of gray clothes, with a blue military cap. **1898** WESTCOTT *D. Harum* 121 Seating himself, he took off his cap and dropped it with his gloves on the floor.

***2.** A head covering or headdress for women.

1711 *Boston News-Letter* 13 Aug. 2/2 A Carolina Indian Maid-Servant . . . has carried away . . . several pair of Stockings, & several Lace Caps. **c1762** E. Singleton *Social N.Y.* 217 Elizabeth Colville . . . has now by her a fashionable assortment of Caps, Ruffs, Handkerchiefs. **1847** LONGFELLOW *Evangeline* I. 20 Matrons and maidens sat in snow-white caps and in kirtles. **1879** *Scribner's Mo.* July 350/2 The golden ripples, silver now, are hidden under a 'round-eared cap.' **1898** T. N. PAGE *Red Rock* 179 The evening of the ride on which Blair lost her cap and Middleton recovered it for her.

3. 'The lintel of a door or window-frame' (Knight). {1688}

1696 *Boston Rec.* 136 A Window Stoole and capp fitt for windows. **1718** *Lancaster Rec.* 183 The posts . . . are to be of sound oak & so the Caps and braces. **1761** S. NILES *Indian Wars* II. 513 One of the spars of the house was carried into a neighbor's house . . . and struck off the cap of his door. **1851** C. CIST *Cincinnati* 153 The coping to the walls, caps and sills to windows, &c., are of Dayton stone.

4. *Mining.* (See first quotation.)

1871 RAYMOND [*3d Rep.*] *Mines* 313 The 'cap,' a term usually employed to express the impoverished condition of the vein, may be due either to the pinching together of the walls of the fissure, or . . . to the filling of the vein with barren rock. **1884** KNIGHT *Suppl.* s.v., A vein is 'in the cap' when it is much contracted.

+5. (See quot. 1888.)

1872 W. J. FLAGG *Good Investment* xv. 722/1 He was pretending to be at work arranging a 'cap' to shed a coming rain. **1888** J. D. BILLINGS *Hardtack* 47 A small piece of canvas, called a *cap*, to which were attached two long guys, covered the opening at the top [of a Sibley tent] in stormy weather.

+6. *colloq.* The crowning point. (Cf. CAP *v.* 3 a.)

1826 *Mass. Spy* 7 June (Th.), Having gradually advanced towards the cap of his climax. **1829** T. FLINT *G. Mason* 163 The family . . . was precisely the cap of the climax of the ancient German grandees in the country.

7. Attrib. with *ribbon, string.*

1841 *Knickerb.* XVII. 109 Widow Quaintley rushed in, . . . her cap-strings fluttering in the breeze. **1859** STOWE *Minister's Wooing* i, You commonly see her . . . at her shady parlor-window . . . hemming muslin cap-strings. **1860** HOLMES *Professor* ix. 260 The Landlady . . . adjusted her cap-ribbon with an unconscious movement. **1865** MRS. WHITNEY *Gayworthys* 324 She hurriedly settled her cap-ribbon with the other [hand].

+Cap, reduced form of CAPTAIN. — **1886** HARTE *Snow-bound* 90, I reckoned I had the right to a little fun on my own account, cap. **1900** DRANNAN *Plains & Mts.* 408 If everything is favorable, Cap and I can take care of the Indians.

Cap, *v.* [CAP *n.*]

+1. *tr.* To provide with a 'cap' or lintel. (Cf. CAP *n.* 3.)

1771 H. PELHAM in *Copley-Pelham Lett.* 170 The lower Windows must be capped and Cornished.

2. To put a cap on (the nipple of a gun). Also absol. {1872}

1851 *Harper's Mag.* June 101/1 After capping afresh, hanging the bridle on the bow of the saddle, and stoking my mule, I followed the trail. **1856** KANE *Arctic Exp.* I. xxix. 387 While the men were loading and capping anew. **1862** O. W. NORTON *Army Lett.* 91 A ball struck my gun . . . as I was capping it, and cut it in two.

b. To remove the cap from (a shell or cartridge).

1874 LONG *Wild-Fowl* 35 By capping the shells before filling, which should always be done, all positive danger from accidental explosion is avoided.

3. *colloq.* **+a.** *To cap the climax*, to beat or surpass everything.

Well illustrated by Thornton, 1804–1861 (Suppl., 1814–1879).

(1) **1804** *Lancaster* (Pa.) *Intelligencer* 21 Feb. (Th.), Your correspondent caps the climax of Misrepresentation. **1811** *Mass. Spy* 18 Sept. (Th.), It caps the climax of French arrogance and turpitude. **1819** *Ib.* 28 April (Th.), To cap the climax of his villany, True forced Mr. Buswell to swallow a large quantity of pearl-ash and red-pepper. **1835** R. M. BIRD *Hawks of Hawk H.* II. 34 He had capped the climax of effrontery by taking part in the jubilee of liberty. **1857** *Lawrence* (Kansas) *Republican* 2 July 2 To cap the climax of outrage [he] takes both the *Governor* and the *Secretary* from the South. **1879** *Congress. Rec.* 5 April 261/2 To cap the climax of absolutions, . . . the votes of those States were stolen.

(2) **1837** *Knickerb.* X. 329 Their lips are thick; their cheeks display no roses: And then, to cap the climax, oh! what noses! **1847** LANMAN *Summer in Wilderness* 23 To cap the climax, an occasional flock of ducks might be seen. **1872** EGGLESTON *End of World* xxxvii. 254 She capped her climax . . . by asking God to convert her daughter. **1891** F. H. SMITH *Col. Carter* 130 To cap the climax . . . here come a gang of fire-eaters.

‖**b.** *To cap the vortex* = prec.

1901 'O. HENRY' *Heart of West* 52 To-day he caps the vortex.

+4. To free (strawberries, etc.) of hulls.

1906 H. D. PITTMAN *Belle of Blue Grass C.* ix. 129 Close beside her sat a great basket of fresh strawberries which must be capped before she could set out for church.

+5. *slang.* To act as decoy or tout for a confidence or gambling game, or in an auction or sale. (Cf. CAPPER.)

1903 G. ADE *In Babel* 72 Now you say there're all out cappin' for this fellow.

Capbox. 1. A box for holding percussion caps. **2.** A box for holding ladies' caps. {1798–} — (1) **1843** T. J. FARNHAM *Trav. Gt. Western Prairies* I. 2 Bullets were moulded; powder-horns and cap-boxes filled. **1866** 'F. KIRKLAND' *Bk. Anecdotes* 212 His cap box had slipped from his belt plate. (2) **1856** STOWE *Dred* II. 113 In the same carriage . . . sat Aunt Nesbit also, and her cap-boxes. **1868** MRS. WHITNEY *P. Strong* 172 Where is my second-best cap-box?

+Cap corn. A variety of corn. — **1850** *New Eng. Farmer* II. 175 The Canada corn, and the small cap corn, will bear near planting.

***Cape.**[1]

***1.** A point of land jutting into a body of water.

In New England, usu. with specific reference to Cape Cod.

1602 *Mass. H. S. Coll.* 3 Ser. VIII. 74 Near this cape we came to anchor in fifteen fathoms, where we took great store of codfish, for which we altered the name, and called it Cape Cod. **c1618** STRACHEY *Virginia* 28 The north foreland of this bay . . . we call Cape Charles, in honor of our now prince. **1622** 'MOURT' *Relation* 2 Purposing to goe to a Riuer ten leagues to the South of the Cape. **1705** *Boston News-Letter* 12 Feb. 2/2 The Chanel that was cut for the passage of Vessels out of the Harbour of Glocester into Ipswich Bay, to save going about the Cape, is quite filled up. **1778** CARVER *Travels* 138 On the south side of it [the lake] is a remarkable point or cape, of about sixty miles in length. **1809** E. A. KENDALL *Travels* II. 128 The harbour . . . is accounted the second-best on the peninsula, commonly called the *cape.* **1815** DRAKE *Cincinnati* 64 It [a limestone region] extends . . . from the shores of Lake Erie . . . probably to the cape of East Florida. **1828** COOPER *Notions* I. 42 [Large ships] are obliged to pass within musket shot of the point, Cape, or *Hook*, as it is here called. **1906** *Springfield W. Republican* 19 July 15 The army worm has attacked the cranberry bogs of the Cape, after an absence of several years.

+b. Attrib. with *fishing.*

1673 *Plymouth Laws* 167 One halfe of the excise due to the Country on the Mackerell to be caught att the Cape bee . . . abated; . . . except any shall come in before the next Court and rent the said privilidge of Cape fishing. **1689** *Ib.* 216 Ordered . . . that the magistrates of the County of Barnstable or any two of them be a Committee to dispose and manage the Cape fishing.

+c. *The capes:* (*a*) Cape Charles and Cape Henry, Va. (*b*) Cape Ann and Cape Cod, Mass.

(*a*) **1636** *Md. Council Proc.* 40 Neyther was presumption the cause of so hastye a choice before Sir John Harvey was out of the Capes. **1705** *Boston News-Letter* 2 July 2/1 A Sloop from Virginia that arrived [in Phila.] on Sunday last, who came out of the Capes the Wednesday before, . . . saw 4 or 5 large Ships standing in for Virginia. **1784** J. SMYTH *Tour U.S.* I. 25 We anchored . . . about an hundred and thirty miles within land, from the Capes of Virginia. **1815** *N.Y. Lit. & Phil. Soc. Trans.* I. 335 The gale had so far moderated, as to enable them . . . to steer for the capes of Virginia. **a1913** Bleyer *Newspaper Writing* 263 A run from the southern drill grounds, outside the capes, to Hampton Roads. (*b*) **1715** *Boston News-Letter* 11 April 2/2 About half way between the Two Capes, Thomas Trevie of Marblehead, Master of a Fishing Shallop, . . . took up a small Boat.

+2. A piece of land (as timberland) projecting into a plain or the like.

1831 PECK *Guide for Emigrants* 110 The traveller is surrounded by timber; his eye never loses sight of the deep green outlines, throwing out its capes and headlands. **1836** J. HALL *Statistics of West* vi. 83 The forest has pushed long capes or points into the prairie.

***Cape.**[2] A circular sleeveless covering for the shoulders.

1676 B. TOMPSON *New Englands Crisis* 5 Deep-skirted doublets, puritanick capes Which now would render men like upright Apes. **1837** HAWTHORNE *Twice-told T.* (1851) II. xii. 190 To see the stream of ladies, gliding along the slippery sidewalks, with . . . quilted hoods, boas, and sable capes. **1852** *Harper's Mag.* V. 487/2 The children . . . were tying their warm capes close about their necks. **1875** STOWE *We & Our Neighbors* 35 We embroidered our own capes and collars. **1892** M. A. JACKSON *Mem-*

oirs xxii. 434 The thoughtful young man then detached the large cape of the garment and spread it over his general.

+**Cape Ann.** [Name of a cape in Mass.] *In the Cape Ann stage* (see second quot.). *C. A. turkey*, a 'Cape Cod turkey' (q.v.). *colloq.* — **1844** *Knickerb.* XXIV. 470, I had left a *real* gobbler at home, to come here and dine on a 'Cape-Ann turkey'! Of all articles tolerated . . . I most abominate boiled salt fish. **a1856** *Burlington Sentinel* in Hall *Coll. Words* (ed. 2) 460–1 Various words and phrases which have been in use . . . to signify some stage of inebriation: Over the bay, . . . a passenger in the Cape Ann stage, [etc.].

+**Capeau.** Incorr. spelling of CAPOT after F. *chapeau.* Cf. CAPPO. — **1821** [see BLANKET CAPEAU]. **1839** TOWNSEND *Narrative* iv. 182 Towards mid-day . . . our large blanket *capeaus* . . . were drawn tightly around us. **1844** LEE & FROST *Oregon* xviii. 204 Of the crew . . . one has a pair of good cotton corduroy pants . . . and another has an old capean [*sic*], which he wears wrong side out.

+**Cape bonnet.** [CAPE.[2]] A fashion of ladies' bonnet with a projecting front.

[**1799** WELD *Travels* 89 There is a kind of bonnet very commonly worn [in Va.], which, in particular, disfigures them amazingly; it is made with a caul, fitting close on the back part of the head, and a front stiffened with small pieces of cane, which projects nearly two feet from the head in a horizontal direction.] **1836** C. GILMAN *Recoll.* (1838) xix. 131, I perceived . . . a young girl . . . dressed in homespun, with a *cracker*, or cape bonnet of the same material. **1854** M. CUMMINS *Lamplighter* xxvii. 239 She's got on that white cape-bonnet of hers; and that checked gingham dress! **1865** MRS. WHITNEY *Gayworthys* iv. 43 She swung by the strings, as she spoke, her muslin cape-bonnet, needless since the summer sun went down. **1896** POOL *In Buncombe County* 21 A woman in a very deep cape bonnet, a bonnet which makes a face look as if it were at the far end of a cavern, —pushed her way up.

Cape cloth. *Obs.* ?Cloth from which capes are made. Also attrib. — **1705** *Boston News-Letter* 10 Dec. 4/2 David Thomas Souldier . . . hath on a new white Cape cloth Watch Coat. **1718** *N.H. Hist. Soc. Coll.* IX. 422 Shipped [out] by the Grace of God in good order and well conditioned, . . . two ps. Cape Cloth.

Cape coat. [CAPE.[2]] A coat furnished with a cape. {1691} — **1752** *N.C. Gazette* (Newbern) 13 March, Three Coats, . . . one a Bear-skin Cape-coat. **1848** *Knickerb.* XXXII. 85 Well do we remember him . . . with his blue cape-coat and big silver-headed cane. **1887** *Lippincott's Mag.* Aug. 290 A young man emerges, . . . clad in a fashionable cape coat and English hunting-cap.

+**Cape Cod.** [Name of peninsula in s.e. Mass.] *Cape Cod clergyman*, the sculpin. *colloq. Cape Cod cottage, measure, protection, trousers*, (see quots.). *Cape Cod turkey*, salt codfish. *colloq.*

1846 LOWELL *Biglow P.* I. Ser. ii. 30 They might have been permitted . . . to take some few sculpins, . . . known in the rude dialect of our mariners as Cape Cod Clergymen. **1923** W. NUTTING *Massachusetts* 22 The Cape Cod cottage has achieved the distinction of receiving this specific name. . . . This cottage is . . . uniformly found at the Cape. **1881** MCLEAN *Cape Cod Folks* i, We call it four miles, more or less. That's Cape Cod measure—means most anythin' lineal measure. **1844** *Lexington Observer* 27 Nov. 1/3 A raw boned yankee made his appearance with a knife and a pine stick in one hand, and a Cape Cod protection, alias a cake of gingerbread in the other. **1804** W. AUSTIN *Lett. from London* 68 After thinking a moment what would be least likely in New England to find its way to Rag Fair, I asked for a pair of *Cape Cod trowsers*. **1865** C. NORDHOFF *Let.* 1 May (F. & H.), A salted cod fish is known in American ships as a Cape Cod turkey. **1890** *N.Y. Herald* 3 June (F. & H.), Factories have been established for the production of Cape Cod turkeys; i.e. salted cod fish. **1901** GREENOUGH & KITTREDGE *Words & Their Ways* 331 'Welsh rabbit' is merely a joke, like 'Cape Cod turkey' for codfish.

+**Cape Coder.** One that belongs to Cape Cod. — **1825** J. NEAL *Bro. Jonathan* III. 281 Tongues an' sounds! that's a Cape Cod-er, you know. **1883** S. RICH *Truro* 189 A genuine Cape Coder is never in love with lakes and rivers that have no tide and no clams.

+**Cape fever.** [CAPE.[1]] (See quot.) — **1856** OLMSTED *Slave States* 200 So among sailors and soldiers, when men suddenly find themselves ill and unable to do their duty in times of peculiar danger, or when unusual labor is required, they are humorously said to be suffering under an attack of the powder-fever, the cape-fever, the ice-fever.

+**Cape grape.** [CAPE.[1]] (See quot. 1854.) — **1826** FLINT *Recoll.* 60 They . . . cultivated a blue grape which, I think, they called the 'cape grape.' **1854** ELLIOTT *Fruit Book* 247 Schuylkill . . . [also called] Cape Grape. . . . Its value is only as wine grape.

+**Cape Horner.** A vessel on a voyage round Cape Horn. — **1840** DANA *Two Years* xxxv. 444 No merchant vessel looks better than an Indiaman, or a Cape Horn-er, after a long voyage. **1851** MELVILLE *Moby Dick* iii. 12 The picture represents a Cape-Horner in a great hurricane.

Cape jasmine. *S.* The Cape jessamine. {1760}

1835 J. H. INGRAHAM *South-West* I. 243 The delicately leaved Cape-jasmine. **1859** A. VAN BUREN *Sojourn in South* 133 The cape jasmine, with its rich polished foliage spangled all over with white starry blossoms. **1865** CUMMING *Hospital Life* (1866) 193/2 As we entered the town we were greeted by the perfume of the cape jasmine, which filled the air. **1881** *Harper's Mag.* April 731/1 The village . . . [was] a collection of low, scattered houses hedged with oleanders and Cape jasmines.

Cape jessamine. [*Cape* of Good Hope.]

1. A variety of jasmine, *Gardenia florida*, cultivated esp. in the South for its fragrant white flowers.

1826 FLINT *Recoll.* 300 The houses are . . . in the midst of orange groves and pretty gardens, in which are . . . delicious cape jessamine, a flowering shrub, . . . and a great variety of vines. **1852** STOWE *Uncle Tom* xvi, There sat Tom, . . . every one of his button-holes stuck full of cape-jessamines. **1901** MOHR *Plant Life Ala.* 137 The fragrant pittosporum . . . , jessamines, cape jessamine (*Gardenia*) are perfectly hardy.

2. Attrib. with *hedge, shrub.*

1829 *Western Monthly Rev.* III. 57 Cape Jessamine shrubs, and other splendid flowering plants adorn the garden. **1858** VIELÉ *Following the Drum* 58 Cape jessamine hedges, . . . and passion flowers, in profusion.

+**Capelin, Caplin.** Also †**capline, -ling.** [F. *capelan, caplan.*]

1. A small fish (*Mallotus villosus*) belonging to the smelt family, and valued as bait.

[**1620** JOHN MASON *Briefe Discourse Nevv-found-land* (1887) 151 June hath Capline, a fish much resembling Smeltes in forme and eating.] **1824** *Salem Observer* 29 May (Th.), In the capling season, the codfish are such epicures that they will not taste anything but capling. **1871** *Amer. Naturalist* V. 119 The Capelin . . . is well known as a bait for cod-fish. **1879** *Scribner's Mo.* Nov. 18/2 Grayling, wherever found, are spring spawners, as also are the smelt and the capelin.

2. *Conn.* The green smelt, *Menidia notata.*

1884 GOODE *Nat. Hist. Aquatic Animals* 456 The Green Smelt of the Connecticut coast *Menidia notata*, also called . . . by the boys about Boston the 'Capelin.'

+**Capellina.** [Sp.] (See quotation.) — **1874** KNIGHT 455 *Capellina*, the *bell* or cover of the pile of amalgam bricks in the Spanish process of separating the mercury from the metal. **1889** *Cent.* 803/1 *Capellina* [is used] in the western mining districts of the United States. . . . *H. W. Halleck.*

+**Cape May.** [The most southerly point of N.J.]

1. *Cape May goody*, the spot or lafayette, *Leiostomus xanthurus.*

1855 S. F. BAIRD in *9th Rep. Smithsonian Inst.* 329 The 'Cape May Goody' of the Jersey coast, so called from its great abundance at Cape Island, is very rarely taken in winter. **1859** BARTLETT 235 Lafayette Fish . . . appears in the summer in great abundance at Cape Island on the Jersey coast, and is hence called the Cape May Goody. **1884–5** *Riverside Nat. Hist.* (1888) III. 218 One of its common names, 'Cape May goodie,' embodies this favorable opinion of its merits.

2. *Cape May warbler*, the wood warbler, *Dendroica tigrina* (*Sylvia maritima*).

1812 WILSON *Ornith.* VI. 99 [The] Cape-May Warbler, *Sylvia Maritima*, . . . was discovered in a maple swamp, in Cape May county. **1825** BONAPARTE *Ornith.* I. 33 The female Cape-May warbler may be very easily mistaken for an imperfect *Sylvia coronata.* **1844** *Nat. Hist. N.Y., Zoology* II. 104 The Cape-May Warbler. . . . Little or nothing is known of this beautiful species: its shy and solitary habits may have contributed to elude our observation. **1868** *Amer. Naturalist* II. 175 One of the rarest of all [warblers] is the Cape May Warbler (*D. tigrina*). **1891** *Cent.* 6819/3 [The] Cape May warbler . . . in full plumage . . . is one of the handsomest of the wood-warblers.

3. *Cape May diamond*, (see quotation).

1866 W. REID *After the War* 81 Others [of the negroes] . . . were dressed in broadcloth, with flashy scarfs and gaudy pins, containing paste, or Cape May diamonds.

Cape pigeon. [CAPE.[1]] The damier or pintado petrel, *Daption capense.* {1844} — **c1830** GODMAN in *Waldie's Select Library* II. 94/2 The Cape pigeon, some of the gulls and other marine fowls, . . . are constantly soaring by thousands over every sea. **1858** BAIRD *Birds Pacific R.R.* 828 The Cape Pigeon. Hab.—Off the coast of California.

Caper.[1] *Obs.* [Du. *kaper.*] A privateer. {1657–93} — **1672** J. HULL *Diary* 161 This winter, the ships that went home to London were many of them taken by the Dutch capers. **1690** *Mass. H. S. Coll.* 4 Ser. V. 243 Besides our being much exposed to the incursions of the French capers by sea. **1704** *Boston News-Letter* 28 Aug. 1/1 Several Swedish Ships taken by our Capers, going for France with Counterband Goods. **1708** *Ib.* 20–27 Dec. 2/2 Yesterday came in . . . a Dutch Caper with two Prizes.

*****Caper.**[2] +*slang.* 'A device, idea, performance, or occupation' (F. 1891). — **1840** HOFFMAN *Greyslaer* I. 84 The bizness is a bad one, any how you can fix it, capting; but I think I understand the caper on't. **a1889** *Boston Herald* (B. & L.) Mind-reading is now the proper caper. **a1889** *N.Y. Morn. Jrnl.* (B. & L.) This trap caper knocks the newspaper friends silly.

+**Cape-race.** [*Cape Race*, Newfoundland, where it is often seen.] The red-throated loon, *Colymbus septentrionalis.* — **1875** *Fur, Fin, & Feather* 119 The smaller species of loon I have heard variously called the spike-bill, the cape-race, [etc.].

‖**Caper juice.** *slang.* Whisky. — **1888** *Portland Transcript* 29 Feb. (F.), Say, fellers, let's take a leetle mo' uv the caper juice.

Caper sauce. A sauce containing capers. {1791} — **1853** A. BUM *Old Eng. & New Eng.* 38 Revere House Bill of Fare. . . . Leg of Mutton, Caper Sauce. **1870** 'F. FERN' *Ginger-Snaps* 11 Better is a leg of Mutton and Caper-sauce. **1878** *Amer. Home Cook Book* 34 Pour caper sauce over it, and serve.

Caper tree. {1609} +(See quots.) — **1897** SUDWORTH *Arborescent Flora* 204 *Capparis jamaicensis.* Florida Caper; Caper Tree. **1899** *Animal & Plant Lore* 119 'Caper-tree,' or 'mole-tree' (*Euphorbia Lathyris*) is supposed to keep moles out of flower-beds if planted there [Ohio].

+**Cape wheat.** [CAPE.[1]] A variety of wheat. — (1) **1786** WASHINGTON *Diaries* III. 4 The Cape Wheat which (on the 30th of November) was cut. **1787** *Ib.* 210 The Cape wheat at Dogue run is forwarder than the common Wheat. (2) **1855** BROWNE in *Trans. Amer. Inst. N.Y.* 590 Cape wheat, from the Cape of Good Hope, . . . doubtless produces an excellent flour. It will probably do much better in the South than in the North, if sown in autumn.

**Capias, n.* A judicial writ issued to a sheriff or other officer ordering him to take into custody the person of the one named in it.

1630 *Mass. Bay Rec.* I. 74 The next p[ro]cesse to be a capias or distringas, att the discrec[i]on of the Court. **1674** *Md. Archives* II. 366 The Writ of Capias . . . upon w[hi]ch the s[ai]d Jo. Balley was arrested doth not appeare upon Record. **1716** *N.C. Col. Rec.* II. 266 Orderd, that a capias go out against Jno. Molton Sen[io]r for contempt in not appearing as an evidence in the case. **1867** 'T. LACKLAND' *Homespun* II. 243 Writs, summons, capiases, . . . and the whole of that sort of legal paper-work, fly from hand to hand like ballots at a tight election. **1880** TOURGEE *Bricks* 270 Here's a *capias* for you, too. . . . It seems there's a bill of indictment against you.

‖**Capias,** *v. tr.* To take into custody on a writ of capias. — **1868** *N.Y. Trib.* 17 July 2/4 It appeared that Bright was indebted . . . and it became desirable to get Bright into the state of Illinois to *capias* him. . . . As soon as he arrived in Chicago he was *capiased* and thrust into jail on the debt.

Capillaire. {1754; from Fr.} +The maidenhair fern, *Adiantum pedatum.* — **1806** in *Ann. 9th Congress* 2 Sess. 1142 Poke, fern, capillaire, honeysuckle, mosses, petu to make ropes with.

Capital.

1. The city or town chosen as the official seat of government of the country, a state, county, etc. {1667–}

1732 *N. J. Archives* 1 Ser. V. 316 The gentlemen of his Majesties Councill live verry remote from each other and most of them from either of the capitals (which consist of about two hundred houses). **1797** MORSE *Amer. Gaz., Hartford City,* the capital of Connecticut, lies on the west bank of Connecticut river. **1841** LYELL *Trav. N.A.* (1845) I. 107 It is far more usual to place the capital, as it is called, in the centre of the State, often in some small village or town of no importance. **1865** *Nation* I. 451 At Grove Hill, the capital [of the county], he received promises of aid from several gentlemen of standing. **1884** BLAINE *20 Years of Congress* I. 268 Meanwhile a body of men had assembled in the National Capital.

2. The amount of money invested in any particular business; accumulated wealth, esp. as available for investment in commerce, industry, etc.; a capital stock or fund. {1630–}

1789 *Ann. 1st Congress* I. 214 The capital employed in this business of distillation amounts, at least, to half a million of dollars. **1792** *Ann. 2nd Congress* 972 Nothing can afford so advantageous an employment for capital and labor, as the conversion of this extensive wilderness into cultivated farms. **1824** *Congress. Deb.* 2179 The production of a country must depend on its capital and labor. **1857** *Lawrence* (Kansas) *Republican* 9 July 3 Gov. Walker goes to Kansas 'backed up by a large amount of Wall street capital.' **1893** M. HOWE *Honor* 284 His vast capital became more and more potent an influence in the land. **1925** BRYAN *Memoirs* 217 The age-long question between capital and labor.

+**b.** *colloq.* Information, influence, or the like, that one may use to personal advantage. *To make (political) capital of,* to use for private (or party) advantage. {1855–}

'*Political capital* [is] a term purely American in its origin, though long since transplanted to England, and naturalized there in the political slang dictionary' (De Vere 266).

1842 H. MANN *Boston Oration* 4 July 78 In common and expressive phrase, this is called 'making political capital' out of a thing; and the art of making 'capital' seems now to be incorporated into the regular tactics of party leaders. **1857** *N.Y. Times* 14 Oct. (B. '59), All . . . who are not disposed to turn every thing into political capital, must feel rejoiced over the result in Kansas. **1882** *Nation* 6 July 6/1 Sometimes his father and mother . . . seem to join in trying to 'make capital,' to use a slang phrase, out of his [=a condemned prisoner's] situation. **1889** FARMER 429 Incidents which tell in a man's favor constitute part of the political capital of his supporters.

Capital city. {1667} =CAPITAL 1. — **1887** H. FREDERIC *Seth's Brother's Wife* 9 'Society,' in whose giddy mazes he had mingled while on a visit to his legislative sire at the Capital City. **1910** J. HART *Vigilante Girl* 239 Gone? . . . Where? Why? Down to the capital city.

Capitalism. [CAPITAL 2.] The concentration of wealth in the hands of a few; the power or influence of large or concentrated capital; a system which favors this. {1854–}

1886 *N. Amer. Rev.* CXLIII. 312 The working-men find the journals out of sympathy with their aims and aspirations, and have learnt to regard them as hopelessly subservient to what they call 'capitalism.' **1910** C. W. ELIOT (*title*), The Future of Trades-Unionism & Capitalism in a Democracy. **1918** H. CAHN *Collapse of Capitalism* 8 A small number of socialists . . . saw in this world war . . . an act of suicide on the part of capitalism.

Capitalist. A man of wealth which is or may be invested in industry, commerce, or other business enterprise. {1792–} Also attrib.

1791 WASHINGTON *Writings* XII. 66 The immediate proposers . . . alledged . . . that they were supported by others who could be deemed Capitalists equal to the undertaking. **1820** CLAY *Speeches* (1842) 114 Do capitalists give too low wages? **1842** TYLER in *Pres. Mess. & P.* IV. 182 The loan would be eagerly sought after and taken up by capitalists. **1853** *Harper's Mag.* VI. 550 A company, embracing the wealthiest of New York capitalists, to construct a trans-continental railroad. **1872** *Ib.* XLIV. 493/1 Mr. Dallas inspired such a degree of confidence among the capitalists of the country that the public credit was at once restored. **1896** *The Voice* (N.Y.) 12 March 3/2 Let the capitalist alone. His very selfishness is a blessing, since he can not multiply his capital unless he parts with it. **1904** GRAFTON *Treasury* Oct. 7/2 In America the three great powers are the capitalists, the professional politicians, and, subordinately, the Press. **1918** H. CAHN *Collapse of Capitalism* 21 Modern imperialism aims at the political control of all backward countries by the great capitalist governments.

+**Capitalistic,** *a.* Of or belonging to capitalists or capitalism.

1873 in Commons, etc. *Doc. Hist. Amer. Indust. Soc.* (1910) IX. 371 The growth of capitalistic association and monetary institutions. **1877** A. DOUAI *Better Times!* 8 Let no small farmer imagine that he can stand any competition with great Capitalistic farming. **1889** D. A. WELLS *Recent Econ. Changes* 399 The natural and necessary growth of what has been termed the 'capitalistic system.' **1910** C. W. ELIOT *Future of Trades-Unionism* 3 The invention of the corporation with limited liability . . . was . . . the starting point of the tremendous expansion of capitalistic association.

Capitalization. {1860} +The using of capital letters in printing or writing. — **1864** WEBSTER 194/2. **1913** SLATER *Freshman Rhetoric* 2 Strict obedience . . . to custom, in all matters of spelling, . . . capitalization, and other formal details.

Capitalize, *v.* [CAPITAL.] {1856–}

+**1.** *tr.* To begin (a word) with a capital letter; also, to print in capitals.

1764 *Acct. College N.J.* 25 All these compositions . . . are critically examined with respect to the language, orthography, pointing, capitalizing, with other minutiae. **1809** W. CUNNINGHAM *Corr.* (1823) 165, I capitalized the prophetic parts of the letter, . . . and italicized the Latin. **1848** WHIPPLE in *N. Amer. Rev.* LXVI. 82 Sheridan's attempts at serious imagery rarely reached beyond capitalizing the names of abstract qualities. **1893** *Nation* LVI. 255 Duché capitalizes his nouns. **1911** HERRICK & DAMON *Comp. & Rhet.* 180 A writer may capitalize all the words.

2. To invest (money, capital, etc.) for profit. Also fig. and absol. {1868–}

1878 *N. Amer. Rev.* Sept. 241 They should teach us to capitalize our philanthropy to the utmost, and fund it freely in deeds of active beneficence. **1880** *Atlantic Mo.* Dec. 848/2 Capital, labor, and capitalizing cover all the necessary forms of wealth and individual activity in so far as we can define social life in material terms.

+**3.** To turn into a source of private profit or capital.

1869 *Kansas Hist. Coll.* (1900) VI. 164 Its only purpose [opening the Cherokee Strip] seems to have been to capitalize this land in the hands of speculators.

+**4.** To combine, establish, or incorporate on a basis of capital. Also *ppl. a.*

1870 MEDBERY *Men Wall St.* 11 The variations of its [=Wall St.'s] share market affect the whole volume of capitalized indebtedness the country through. **1895** *Denver Times* 5 March 8/4 The I. X. L. Candy company . . . is capitalized, and has 100 shares of stock. **1903** E. JOHNSON *Railway Transportation* 91 Different views obtain as to the proper basis for capitalizing a railroad. **1905** D. G. PHILLIPS *Plum Tree* 173 As my clients were bonded and capitalized on the basis of no expense either for taxes or for franchises, the governor's suggestion . . . foreshadowed ruin. **1909** A. S. JOHNSON *Intro. Economics* 248 Monopoly profits may be capitalized in the same way as other permanent incomes from property.

+**Capitalizer.** [From prec.] One who invests capital for increase; a capitalist. — **1880** *Atlantic Mo.* Dec. 848/2 The administrator of capital and labor is not a mere middleman; he is a capitalizer. **1882** W. B. WEEDEN *Soc. Law Labor* 28 Small farmers . . . are almost always capitalizers.

Capitan. *S.W.* {1755–; from Sp.} +A captain, esp., the chief leader, of a Mexican band or an Indian band or tribe. Also transf.

'Once commonly used on the Spanish American frontiers' (Bentley).

1844 GREGG *Commerce of Prairies* II. 37 Three of our visitors left us for the purpose of going to bring all the 'capitanes' of their tribe. **1853** BREWERTON *With Kit Carson* (1930) 137 He inquired for the 'capitan.' **1877** WM. WRIGHT *Big Bonanza* 272 We had with us a Piute guide known as Captain or 'Capitan' Juan. **1884** *Century Mag.* Sept. 662/2 The sentinel smiled as he dispatched a messenger with her request, and thought what a lucky fellow the *capitan* Pedro was. **1895** REMINGTON *Pony Tracks* 79 Mr. Johnnie Bell, the *capitan* in charge, was walking about in his heavy *chaparras*. **1919** J. S. CHASE *Calif. Desert Trails* 173 Arrived at Toro, I sought an interview with the *capitan*.

Capitation tax. A poll tax. {1776–}

1787 *Constitution* I. ix. § 4 No capitation . . . tax shall be laid. **1796** *Ann. 4th Congress* 2 Sess. 2705 Capitation taxes tend to increase the price of labor. **1802** *Ann. 7th Congress* 181 Suppose, for instance, that a capitation tax . . . were imposed. **1837** *S. Lit. Messenger* III. 644 The white mechanic and laborer would be very glad to pay ten times the amount paid by the free negro as a capitation tax. **1865** Fleming *Hist. Reconstruction* I. 285 It . . . is hereby made the duty of the county police . . . to levy a poll or capitation tax on each and every freedman, [etc.]. **1884** BLAINE *20 Years of Congress* I. 188 He was earnestly opposed to 'a capitation-tax.' **1890** *Cent.* 4598/2 A capitation-tax . . . [is] still levied in some of the United States.

* **Capitol.**

+**1.** 'In some states, the State-house, or house in which the legislature holds its sessions; a government house' (W. '28).

'Of the public buildings, the most important are the State House, or Capitol—as all the legislative halls are here called' (1842 Buckingham *E. & W. States* I. 121).

1699 *Va. Assembly Acts* (1727) I. 205 An act directing the Building the Capitol and the City of Williamsburgh. **1699** *Va. Statutes* III. 420 The said building [the statehouse] shall forever hereafter be called and known by the name of the *Capitol*. **1705** BEVERLEY *Virginia* IV. 53 The College and Capitol are both built of Brick. **1772** WASHINGTON *Diaries* II. 57 Spent the Evening at the Burgesses' Ball in the Capitol. **1819** *Plough Boy* I. 167 The Court of Errors . . . will convene at the Capitol in Albany. **1834** C. D. ARFWEDSON *United States* I. 318, I visited one day the Capitol, as it is called, or Statehouse occupied by the Legislature of the State. **1838** *S. Lit. Messenger* IV. 28/2 Louisville is a fine flourishing place. . . . The Capitol is a handsome edifice. **1843** 'CARLTON' *New Purchase* I. 101 On an eminence between the others . . . stood the primitive and patriarchal cabin—the capitol. **1865** TROWBRIDGE *Three Scouts* i. 7 A few miles distant . . . was the city of Nashville, . . . its lofty capitol gilded with faint gold. **1884** *Century Mag.* May 63 The Albany Capitol stands at the top of the high hill which dominates the town.

+**2.** The edifice or building occupied by Congress at Washington.

Usually with initial capital letter.

1793 JEFFERSON *Writings* IX. 18 Dr. Thornton's plan of a capitol has . . . captivated the eyes and the judgments of all. **1795** J. SCOTT *Gazetteer* s.v. *Washington*, The capitol is now building and is situated upon a beautiful eminence. **1819** *Niles' Reg.* XVI. 430/2 The capitol at Washington, is nearly ready for the reception of congress. **1842** F. WOOD in MacLeod *Biog.* 104 How long do the majority intend to keep us at the Capitol? **1888** *Harper's Mag.* June 50/1 The part of the Capitol which is completed (Senate Chamber, House of Representatives, Library, Historical Society, etc.). **1902** BANKS *Newspaper Girl* 254, I arrived in Washington. . . . I had learned that at the Capitol I would find the eminent personage.

+**3.** Attrib. with *building, commission, grounds*, etc.

1752 J. BLAIR in *Dinwiddie Papers* (1883) I. 146, I laid the last top Brick on the Capitol Wall [Williamsburg], and so it is now ready to receive the roof. **1781** in *Virginia Mag.* I. 10 Dined with some Militia officers at the Capitol landing. **1835** *S. Lit. Messenger* I. 258 A superb monument to the memory of Washington on the capitol square. **1860** CLAIBORNE *Sam. Dale* xi. 181, I was strolling, at sunrise, in the Capitol grounds. **1869** S. BOWLES *Our New West* iv. 89 On the bluff . . . the capitol buildings and the fine residences will all be located. **1884** *Century Mag.* March 645/1 The lots on Capitol Hill were all bought up by speculators. **1910** *Okla. Session Laws* 3 Legisl. 8 The Executive Mansion shall be located in the vicinity of the said capitol grounds on a site consisting of one-half block, the same to be selected by the Capitol Commission. *Ib.* 11 When any person, firm or corporation shall provide and furnish to the State of Oklahoma a free Capitol site.

* **Capmaker.** One who makes caps.

1789 *Boston Directory*, Dyer, John, Sadler and Cap-maker. **1851** CIST *Cincinnati* 49 Occupations [include] . . . Cap makers, 15 [people]. **1865** *Atlantic Mo.* XV. 616 The Cap-makers constitute a numerous body, whose wages average three dollars.

Cap'n. *colloq.* Also **capen, cappen, cap'in, cappin.** [Reduction of CAPTAIN.] A captain. {Cf. Cornwall & Devon dial. (1880–2) *cappen, -un.*}

1829 *Yankee* April 120/3 Cap'n Jessamine had got kicked out o' bed by his wife. **1837** J. C. NEAL *Charcoal Sk.* (1838) 216 The cap'ins might flourish the brush, and the corpulars carry the bucket. **1840** *Crockett Almanac* 18, I stepped up to the cappin and doused my peak. **1846** E. FARNHAM *Prairie Land* 17 Cappen, please to come hyur. **1863** LOWELL *Biglow P.* II. vii. 181 But this 'ere histin', creak, creak, creak, Your cappen's heart up with a derrick. **1866** 'F. KIRKLAND' *Bk. Anecdotes* 408/2, I pulled my hat over my eyes and jogged along on the Cap'ns horse. **1884** *Century Mag.* June 284/2 They had looked at the relics of Cap'n Poinsett's voyages to the Orient. **1886** P. STAPLETON *Major's Christmas* 280 We've jest been talkin' of ye, Capen. **1905** A. H. RICE *Sandy* 14, I guess the cap'n will be wantin' to see you [=a stowaway].

Cap of Liberty. =LIBERTY CAP. {1709–} Also fig. — **1802** ELLICOTT *Journal* 141 The cap of liberty but ill becomes you, who opposed in arms the independence of the United States. *a***1821** C. BIDDLE *Autobiog.* iv. 225 The Cap of Liberty (was) carried by John Nixon, Esquire.

* **Capon.** A castrated cock; the flesh of one.

1640 *Md. Council Proc.* 95 Our will is that from such tenants you demand no more . . . then the said two Capons for every Year that the Rent hath been behind. **1705** BEVERLEY *Virginia* IV. 55 Their Capons [are sold] at eight-pence or nine-pence a-piece. **1738** BYRD *Dividing Line* (1901) 63 Some good women . . . brought their children to be baptiz'd, but brought no capons along with them to make the solemnity cheerful. **1850** BROWNE *Poultry Yard* 119 Some persons . . . train capons to act as nurses to their broods of chickens. **1911** *Dept. Agric. Farmers' Bul. No. 452* 6 A large flock of capons may be kept together. *Ib.*, Capon in season brings 18 to 25 cents and often more a pound.

Caporal.** [Sp., 'corporal'] +An overseer or foreman. *S.W.* — *c1892** *Dialect Notes* I. 245 (Texas words), *Caporál:* overseer, man who directs the work, but does not pay the laborers. **1913** W. C. BARNES *Western Grazing Grounds* 380 Expressions in common use among stockmen . . . [include] Caporal, . . . the foreman in charge of a sheep outfit. **1923** J. H. COOK *On Old Frontier* 7 Meeting . . . one of Ben Slaughter's Caporals or foremen, I secured employment from him.

Capot. [F., now only naut.] =CAPOTE 1. {1775} (Cf. CAPEAU, CAPPO.)

1805 PIKE *Sources Miss.* (1810) 31 Found a small red capot hung upon a tree; this my interpreter informed me was a sacrifice by some Indian to the *bon Dieu*. **1814** BRACKENRIDGE *Views of La.* 137 We still see a few of both sexes in their ancient habiliments; capots, moccasins, blue handkerchiefs on the head. **1832** R. COX *Adv. Columbia R.* xxix. 307 The dress of a *voyageur* generally consists of a capot made out of a blanket [etc.]. **1847** T. FORD *Hist. Illinois* (1854) 36 For an upper covering of the body the men wore a blanket garment, called a 'capot' (pronounced cappo) with a cap to it at the back of the neck. **1852** JOHN REYNOLDS *Hist. Illinois* 51 The *capot* made of white blanket, was the universal dress for the laboring class of people.

Capote. Also †**capotte.** [F.]

1. A long coarse coat or cloak, properly having a hood, and esp. worn by travellers. {1812–}

1814 BRACKENRIDGE *Views of La.* 137 The men wore a blanket coat, of coarse cloth or coating, with a cape behind, which could be drawn over the head; from which circumstance it was called a *capote*. **1827** MCKENNEY *Tour to Lakes* 296 She took from her head the hood of her *capote*, . . . and shewed me where she had been scalped. **1834** A. PIKE *Sketches* 102 He demanded to see some cloth for a capote. **1838** INGRAHAM *Burton* I. 144 The guide was seated in front wrapped up in a capote of bearskin. **1847** PARKMAN in *Knickerb.* XXX. 27 Their hard, weather-beaten faces and bushy moustaches looked out from beneath the hoods of their white capotes with a bad and brutish expression. **1852** WATSON *Nights in Block-House* 439 Suddenly, one of the warriors drew from beneath the skirts of his capôte a keen, bright tomahawk. **1888** ROOSEVELT in *Century Mag.* XXXVI. 834/2 The fourth member of our party . . . wore a gayly colored capote, or blanket-coat. **1902** WHITE *Conjuror's House* i. 5 Everywhere was gay color, . . . the capotes of the brigade.

2. A fashion of bonnet worn by women. {1882–}

1851 *Harper's Mag.* II. 864/1 *Capotes* or bonnets of satin are also worn.

+**3.** 'The hood or top of a wagon, as of a buggy, or any similar protection for a vehicle' (*Cent.*).

* **Capper.**

+**1.** *slang.* The confederate or decoy of a cardsharper.

1870 W. F. RAE *Westward by Rail* 188 A 'capper' with whom I conversed supplied me with what he deemed a defence of the 'institution.' **1871** DE VERE 319 Cappers they ['strikers'] are called, when the game is the famous Three-Card Monte. **1873** J. H. BEADLE *Undevel. West* iv. 93 The horny-handed miner, and the dapper, conservative looking gentleman, are 'cappers.' **1908** WHITE *Riverman* vii. 62 They were using him as a capper to draw the crowd into their game. **1913** MULFORD *Coming of Cassidy* vii. 177 He glanced around swiftly, trying to locate the cappers, but they were not to be seen.

+**b.** A tout for a gambling house.

1897 *Chicago Tribune* 1 Aug. 3/5 Many of the resorts . . . had 'cappers' at work among the crowds on the street, . . . directing them to the game if they wanted to play.

+**2.** A dummy bidder at an auction or purchaser at a sale.

1877 BARTLETT 98. **1893** *Harper's Mag.* LXXXVI. 712/2 Professional 'boomers,' with a retinue of surveyors and cappers and strikers, invaded the State. **1925** J. BLACK *You Can't Win* xiii. 184 His 'cappers,' 'boosters,' and 'shills' fought with the yokels for a chance to get something for nothing.

+**Cap-piece.** A piece acting as the cap of a structure. — **1795** *Essex Inst. Coll.* LIV. 100 That the highth of the bridge be at least one foot higher than the cap piece. **1796** MORSE *Amer. Geog.* I. 405 Each pier is composed of seven sticks of oak timber, united by a cap-piece, strong braces and girts. **1889** *Cent.* 807/3.

+**Cappo, Capo.** Spelling variants of Fr. *capot.* =CAPOT. (Cf. CAPEAU.) Also attrib. — **1799** JAMES SMITH *Acc. Captivity* 10 They gave me . . . a tinsel laced cappo. **1806** CLARK in *Lewis & C. Exped.* IV. 119 Kuskalaw brought a dog which Peter Crusat had purchased with his capo which this fellow had on. *Ib.* V. 88 They lost three blankets and a Blanket Cappo. **1847** in H. Howe *Ohio Hist. Coll.* 131 On the day of the battle, St. Clair ... wore a coarse cappo coat and a three-cornered hat.

+**Cap-rock.** *Mining.* (See quot. 1881.) — **1874** RAYMOND *6th Rep. Mines* 317 The barren, or 'cap rock,' now met with at the water-line in that mine. **1881** — *Mining Gloss., Cap* or *Cap-rock*, barren vein matter, or a pinch in a vein, supposed to overlie ore. **1889** *Cent.* 809/2.

Capsheaf.

1. The sheaf placed on top of a shock. Also in fig. context. {1846–, *dial.*}

1782 S. BALDWIN in *Life & Lett.* 106 The whole was crown'd with a capshief of Albany politeness. **1859** A. CARY *Country Life* i. 13 Having laid this cap-sheaf upon the stack of his previous eloquence. **1863** *Rep. Comm. Agric.* 94 Not more than one dozen sheaves should be put in a single shock—ten in the body of it, and two used as cap sheaves.

+**2.** The highest or extreme degree (of anything); the climax or limit.

1815 *Mass. Spy* 31 May (Th.), This is the crowner, the cap-sheaf. **1817** *Niles' Reg.* XIII. 128/2 The following article, the 'cap sheaf' of impudence. **1823** *Ib.* XXIV. 323 Really, this is the 'cap-sheaf' of presumption! **1838** *Lexington Observer* 7 July, The following trick ... is the 'cap sheaf' of all the pieces of impudence we have heard of lately. **1847** WHITCHER *Widow Bedott P.* ix. 88 Of all the strains ever I heerd of I should think that was the cap sheef. **1859** S. COX *In Congress* (1865) 79 When it came to the cap-sheaf—when there was a fair opportunity of extending the last vote of welcome to the expected sister State [=Oregon] ... he was not there! **1867** 'T. LACKLAND' *Homespun* III. 316 In time, courtship leads to marriage.... This event, in the family, is the cap-sheaf of all others.

+**b.** Said of persons.

1800 *Aurora* (Phila.) 8 April (Th.), Goodrich a cap-sheaf, won't be led. [**1838** HALIBURTON *Clockmaker* 2 Ser. 40 If there's any man you don't like, ... abuse him like old Scratch.... Do this, and you'll be ... the truckle-head and cap-sheave.] **1864** *Boston Commonw.* 19 Feb., When Gov. Johnson says ... 'I am for the liberty of the negro, but I am for a white man's government,' he ... is the capsheaf. **1865** TROWBRIDGE *Three Scouts* vi. 63 If you ain't the capsheaf of all the complainin' women! **1873** M. HOLLEY *Betsy Bobbet* 337 Of all the painted, ... and humped-up, and laced-down critters I ever see, she was the cap sheaf.

+**3.** *To put the capsheaf on* (or *to*), to add the finishing touch (to a matter).

1840 J. P. KENNEDY *Quodlibet* 26 The commissioners come this way and put the cap-sheaf on Michael's worldly fortune. **1867** *Congress. Globe* 15 March 117/3 Building the foundation upon the voice of the people, and putting the superstructure up with that voice, and putting the very capsheet [*sic*] to the structure with that same voice. **1871** STOWE *Sam Lawson* 185 That put the cap-sheaf on for Bill.

Capsicum. Cayenne or red pepper (*Capsicum annuum*), freq. cultivated in gardens, and bearing a berry used as a condiment. {1725–} Also transf. — **1822** J. WOODS *Eng. Prairie* 224 Capsicum is cultivated for seasoning soups, &c. **1845** C. M. KIRKLAND *Western Clearings* 83 Her husband, whose capsicum was completely roused, began pummelling Ashburn as high as he could reach. **1847** DARLINGTON *Weeds & Plants* 255 Annual Capsicum ... [grows in] gardens and lots; cultivated. **1867** COZZENS *Sayings* iii. 15 Our own gardens, Sir, furnish capsicum.

+**Capsill.** Also †**cap-sell, -shall, -cell.** The topmost horizontal beam in the frame (of a wharf, etc.).

1681 *Boston Rec.* 144 The lower capshall of said Vyall's wharfe was one inch within said Berryes ground. *Ib.*, The line is to run down upon the flatts from the said Inch, within said Vyall Capsell and the said 2 foote without said Berrys Corner post. **1711** *Boston Selectmen* 154 The circular line as it crosses the cap-cell of the south side of the new wharfe. **1736** *Boston Rec.* 149 The Committee ... have taken a Survey of the North Battery Wharf, and find ... [it] in pretty good Repair, only wanting of good Cap-Sills. **1821** *Boston Selectmen* 226 The cap-sill of Hancocks wharf having gone to decay [etc.]. **1889** *Cent.* 810/1.

***Captain.**

***1.** An officer who commands a company or body of men.

1622 'MOURT' *Relation* 80 We chose Miles Standish our Captaine. **1643** *Plymouth Rec.* 15 Nathaniell Souther and Thomas Southwood shalbe captaines or masters of the watch. **1757** *General Orders* 98 The Capt. of the Main Guard is to Send a Searjt. **1788** FRANKLIN *Autobiog.* 414 The inhabitants ... formed themselves into companies, and chose their captains. **1821** COOPER *Spy* xviii. (1831) 208 The soldier returned with his prizes, and offered them to the acceptance of his captain. **1846** CORCORAN *Pickings* 16 'Where did you find this man?' said the Recorder, addressing the captain of the guard. **1878** J. H. BEADLE *Western Wilds* xxxiii. 532 He served on the staff of General Phil. Kearney, and ... was made full captain and aid-de-camp of General McClellan.

+**b.** *Captain of the caravan*, the leader of a company migrating to the west. Now hist.

1844 GREGG *Commerce of Prairies* I. 45 A gentleman by the name of Stanley ... was unanimously proclaimed 'Captain of the Caravan.' **1880** A. A. HAYES in *Harper's Mag.* LXI. 187/2 In such a caravan there would be, perhaps, one hundred wagons, and a 'captain of the caravan' would divide them into four divisions, with a lieutenant to each. **1918** CONNELLEY *Hist. Kansas* I. 140 When the traders had all arrived at Council Grove ... there was elected a Captain of the Caravan, whose duty it was to direct the order of travel and select the camping-places.

+**c.** In transf. use: A minor party official, responsible for keeping an election district in line.

1914 McLaughlin & Hart *Cycl. Amer. Govt.* I. 229 The captain wields a good deal of power in his small district.

2. The master or commander of a ship or other vessel. {1704–}

*a*1649 WINTHROP *Hist.* I. 32 Our captain set our children and young men to some harmless exercises. **1776** *Journals Cont. Cong.* IV. 106 The captain & mates of the transport Blue Mountain Valley. **1840** DANA *Two Years* xxxiii. 425 The captain came forward, and also began to give orders. **1886** P. STAPLETON *Major's Christmas* 282 The weather had been foul, ... and the Captain was surly and fault-finding.

+**b.** The master of a small boat.

1807 C. SCHULTZ *Travels* I. 167 Here the master of every boat, should she even be no larger than a canoe, is always a 'captain.' **1818** J. PALMER *Travels U.S.* 56 Our conveyance was one of the long Kentucky boats. ... After pulling out in the stream, our Captain, as they styled him, let the boat drift with the current. **1822** J. FLINT *Lett. Amer.* 144 The persons who take charge of keel-boats are also Captains.

+**c.** In transf. use: One in charge of any other means of transportation.

1835 P. SHIRREFF *Tour* 49 Captain is the general title for stage drivers. **1874** B. F. TAYLOR *World on Wheels* 72 The conductor is a 'captain.' **1889** FARMER 123 The conductor or guard of a train. This official, on whom devolves the chief responsibility for the safety ... of a train, is, in America, often addressed as *captain*.

+**3.** As a courtesy title.

'I found, both in the States and Upper Canada, that military titles of high sounding were often used as nicknames' (1835 Shirreff *Tour* 49).

1746 *London Mag.* XV. 324 Wherever you travel in Maryland (as also in Virginia and Carolina) your Ears are constantly astonished at the number of Colonels, Majors, and Captains, that you hear mentioned. **1805** PARKINSON *Tour* I. 272 Of the company then present, there will not be one out of ten who is not either Esquire, General, Colonel, Captain, or Doctor. **1845** SOL. SMITH *Theatr. Apprent.* xi. 77, I say, capt'n, and Jack, let's have eighteen pence worth of stars. **1873** 'MARK TWAIN' & WARNER *Gilded Age* lvii. 515 When we first came here, I was *Mr.* Sellers, and *Major* Sellers, and *Captain* Sellers, ... but the minute our bill went through the House, I was *Colonel* Sellers every time.

+**b.** *slang.* One who excels.

1917 *Dialect Notes* IV. 409 'He's a *captain* on the floor to dance.' 'He's a *captain* to tell a tale.' (N.C.) Also Kan., Ky.

+**4.** The chief or leader of a tribe of Indians. (Cf. CAPITAN.)

1634 WOOD *New Eng. Prospect* II. xiii. 84 The Indians ... use no other weapons in warre than bowes and arrowes, saving that their Captaines have long speares. **1716** CHURCH *Philip's War* (1865) I. 76 He appointed him to notifie Awashonks, her Son Peter, their Chief Captain, ... to meet him two dayes after. **1803** J. DAVIS *Travels* 299 A young Mingo War Captain. **1838** *Mass. H. S. Coll.* 3 Ser. IX. 71 Francis, the first captain, is the most intelligent, and speaks English the best, of any in the tribe.

+**5.** A leader *of* industry. Also attrib.

1887 *Harper's Mag.* May 973/2 The modern captain of industry guides and protects the productive forces of society. **1908** G. H. LORIMER *J. Spurlock* i. 6 He ... had had his Sunday-school-superintendent whiskers trimmed down to the captain-of-industry length. *Ib.* 20, I assured him that the idea of my ever becoming a captain of industry was preposterous.

+**6.** *Captain Lynch*, in allusive use: (see LYNCH LAW).

1841 FOOTE *Texas* II. 16 Being cut off from all opportunity of bringing the offender to justice through the regular legal tribunals ... they resolved to have recourse ... to that well-known arbiter vulgarly yclept Captain Lynch.

+**7. a.** *Captain's beat*, the residential limits of a military company. *S.*

1859 BARTLETT 68 *Captain's Beat*, the limits within which the members of a military company reside.... Southern.

+**b.** *Captain's clerk*, the clerk of a sea captain.

1794 *Ann. 3rd Congress* 1426 The following petty officers ... shall be appointed by the captains of the ships: ... two master's mates, one captain's clerk. **1796** *Ann. 4th Congress* 2 Sess. 2786 Pay of the officers, seamen, and marines [per month]: ... 2 Captain's Clerks, $13.

***Captain general.**

+**1.** The chief commander of the militia of a colony or state.

1653 *Va. House of Burgesses* 86 Lieut. Coll. Cornelius Loyd and ... his General meaning the Governor who is stiled Captain General of Virginia. **1686** *N.H. Hist. Soc. Coll.* VIII. 273 We do ... grant unto you ... to do and execute all and every other thing which to a captain-general doth or ought of right to belong. **1733** *Boston Rec.* 54 Represent the decaying Circumstances of the Fortifications of this Town, to the Capt General. **1747** *N.J. Archives* 1 Ser. VII. 11 The Council then administered to his Excellency ... the usual oath for the due Execution of his Office of Captain General and Governor of this province. **1828** WEBSTER s.v., The governor of a state is Captain-General of the militia. **1889** *Cent.* 811/1 The governor of Rhode Island is by title captain-general and commander-in-chief of the military and naval forces of the State.

*2. A commander of an army; the commander in chief of the army.

1826 COOPER *Mohicans* xx, The grand Frencher [=Montcalm], he who is Captain-General of the Canadas. **1852** BANCROFT *Hist. U.S.* IV. 168 [In 1754] the direction and conduct of American affairs was left entirely to the Duke of Cumberland, then the captain-general of the British army. **1881** *Harper's Mag.* Feb. 476/1 Among its recommendations to Congress were the following: To create the office of Captain-General of the Army for General Grant.

‖**Captainize,** *v.* [CAPTAIN 1.] *intr.* To act as captain. — **1840** *Bentley's Misc.* VII. 625 Shall I captainise over my troops one day, and put up with such a 'tarnal confounded insult as this the day after?

Captain-lieutenancy. *Obs.* The rank of captain with lieutenant's pay. — **1777** A. HAMILTON *Wks.* (1886) VII. 477, I should beg leave to recommend to your notice, as far as a captain-lieutenancy, Mr. Thompson.

Captain lieutenant. *Obs.* (See prec.) — **1775** *Jrnls. Cont. Congress* II. 220 *Resolved,* . . . That in the artillery, the pay of captain be 26 2/3 dollars per month. Captain lieutenant, 20. **1778** *Ib.* XI. 539 The lieutenant of the colonel's company, [is] to have the rank of Captain lieutenant. **1828** WEBSTER s.v., Thus the colonel of a regiment being the captain of the first company, that company is commanded by a Captain-Lieutenant.

+**Capting.** Dial. variant of CAPTAIN. — **1840** C. F. HOFFMAN *Greyslaer* I. vii. 84 The bizness is a bad one, any how you can fix it, capting. **1867** LOWELL *Biglow P.* II. p. xxv, Capting, for instance, I never heard save in jest, the habitual form being *kepp'n.*

***Caption,** *n.*

+1. The heading or title of a document, section, chapter, etc.

'*Caption* is often used in the U.S. in the sense of preamble, or head of a chapter or discourse' (Worc. '46); 'but this use is not sanctioned by good writers' (*Ib.* '60).

1789 J. MADISON *Writings* (1904) V. 355 In the Caption of the address . . . we have pruned the ordinary stile of the degrading appendages of Excellency, Esqr. &c. **1799** W. W. HENING *New Va. Justice* 259 The caption of an indictment . . . runs thus. **1821** *Mass. Spy* 24 Oct. (Th.), [The statute] is under the caption of 'Fees in the Secretary's Office.' **1846** *Rep. Comm. Patents* (1847) 26 The discovery patented under this caption presented itself as one of extensive moment. *a***1869** in *Report Ku-Klux Conspiracy* XIII. 36 The Grand Dragon . . . shall keep . . . a list of the names (without any caption) of the Grand Titans of the different dominions of his realm. **1888** *Congress. Rec.* 14 July 6295/1, I send to the clerk's desk a letter which I ask that he will read, including the printed caption at its head.

+2. The title or heading of an article, story, etc. {1854–}

'This legal term is used in the newspapers in cases where an Englishman would say *title, head,* or *heading*' (B. '59). 'In this sense, the word is an Americanism, but is not used by our best writers' (W. '64).

1823 G. A. MCCALL *Lett.* (1868) 124 The caption of the article was in large capitals and in these words. **1838** *Yale Lit. Mag.* III. 157 Nothing is more confusing than to begin with a magnificent caption, and then find one's self unable to proceed. **1879** PRESCOTT *Sp. Telephone* 111 A short article . . . appeared in . . . this journal under the caption 'Galvanic Music.' **1884** *N.Y. Herald* 7 June, The Herald will say editorially, under the caption, 'Worse than a Crime' [etc.]. **1903** *N.Y. Ev. Post.* 16 Sept., The stories have appeared in a running series under the caption of 'The Adventures of Brigadier Gerard.' **1919** H. L. WILSON *Ma Pettengill* ii. 43 The caption says of Vida Sommers: 'Her Love Has Turned to Hate.'

+b. A legend or title; a designation.

*a***1904** WHITE *Blazed Trail Stories* iv. 58 Under each [picture] was an appropriate caption, such as Surprise, Grief. **1904** A. DALE *Wanted, a Cook* 64 Under the caption of 'man' we had not recognized Arthur Tamworth.

+**Caption,** *v. tr.* To furnish with a title or caption. — **1901** *Science* XIV. 808/1 An effective poem . . . captioned 'The Song of the Innuit.' **1909** *N.Y. Herald* 28 Sept. 1/6 The Washington Times in an editorial captioned 'Commander Peary appears in a Bad Light,' today says [etc.]. **1912** LONDON *Son of Sun* vii. 246 It means the feathers of the sun. Thus does the base interloper caption himself.

***Captivate,** *v.*

*1. *tr.* To seize by force; to take captive; to capture. *Obs.* {*c*1555–1750}

In very frequent use from *c*1705 to *c*1815.

'The word [captivate] (in this sense) was . . . new to me. . . . I have not yet, indeed, met with it in any of our newspapers, but to my great surprise, I have lately found it in the works of two or three of our authors' (1784 Belknap *Hist. N.H.* I. p. x). '*Captivate,* for *take,* in its literal use, is nearly obsolete' (1817 Webster *Lett. to Pickering* 13). '*To captivate* . . . cannot be said to be in use among writers at the present day' (B. '48).

1666 *R.I. Col. Rec.* II. 156 The said Indians . . . molesting, captivating, and fineing, your Majesties leige people here liveing. **1677** W. HUBBARD *Indian Wars* (1865) II. 49 His Corn, Cattel, Barns all burned, his Family captivated. **1709** *N.H. Hist. Soc. Coll.* III. 46 The enemy fell upon Groton about day break, killed 22 persons, and captivated 13. **1734** *Mass. Ho. Rep. Jrnl.* 57 The grievous misfortunes he has undergone by being captivated by the Indian Enemy. **1776** JEFFERSON *Declar. Independence* (orig. draft), He has waged cruel War against human Nature itself, violating its most sacred Rights . . . in the Persons of a distant People . . . , captivating and carrying them into Slavery in another Hemisphere. **1793** *Mass. H. S. Coll.* III. 8 They . . . surprised the unwary inhabitants . . . killing about seventy-five and captivating as many more. **1805** PARKINSON *Tour* 101 The Indian camp . . . was about a half mile from the place, where we were captivated. **1825** J. NEAL *Bro. Jonathan* III. 86 The flower or pride of their force . . . captured, or 'captivated,' four successive patrols. **1840** HOFFMAN *Greyslaer* I. 114 We can captivate those chaps complete, I tell ye, if they only move a little further down stream. **1842** *Amer. Pioneer* I. 169 He was returned to the two masters who captivated him at his house. **1855** SIMMS *Forayers* 361 You see how easy it was to captivate you. **1873** BAILEY *Life in Danbury* 137 Captivating coons is not a very easy task.

+2. To hold as a captive.

1674 in Jillson *Dark & Bl. Ground* 15 My poore man Gabriell Artheur all this while ecaptivated [*sic*] . . . in a strange land. **1884** 'MARK TWAIN' *Huckleberry Finn* xxxv, When he wants to send any little common ordinary mysterious message to let the world know where he's captivated.

***Captive,** *n.* and *a.*

*1. A person taken prisoner, esp. in conflict or war.

1622 'MOURT' *Relation* 91 Squanto . . . was one of the twentie Captiues that by Hunt were carried away. **1711** *Boston News-Letter* No. 369, 14 May 2/2 A small Company of Indians . . . took Humphrey Fols, but upon firing of the Guns, some of the Fore Horses return'd, who rescued the Captive. **1821** *Ann. 16th Congress* 2 Sess. 939 An act relating to the ransom of American captives of the late war. **1870** KEIM *Sheridan's Troopers* (1885) xxiii. 164 Frequently fifty or a hundred chiefs and warriors entered our camp to visit the captives.

*2. Appositive or as adj. with *girl, Negro, woman.*

1676 I. MATHER *Brief Hist.* 177 A Captive Negro . . . escaped from Philip. **1678** *East-Hampton Rec.* I. 412, I Samuell Rodgers . . . Doe sell . . . unto the said James Loper . . . one Indian Captive girle. **1707** C. MATHER *Diary* I. 598 Many months ago, I sent you, by a Captive-woman . . . a Number of Little Books.

+b. *Captive lines,* (see quotation). *Obs.*

1754 *N.H. Hist. Soc. Coll.* I. 279 There was next to their skin tied a number of small metump lines, . . . a collar of a length about sufficient to go round a man's neck, . . . what is called captive lines.

***Captivity.** The state or fact of being held a captive, esp. by Indians.

1641 *Mass. Liberties* 231 There shall never be any bond slaverie, villinage or Captivitie amongst us unles it be lawfull Captives taken in just warres. **1684** I. MATHER *Providences* II. 28 The account which one lately belonging to Deerfield . . . hath drawn up respecting his own captivity and redemption. **1695** *Maine Wills* 109 Unto my Dear Daughter now in Captivity with the Indians . . . I will and give the sum of five pounds. **1748** J. NORTON (*title*), The Redeemed Captive; Being a Narrative of the Taking and carrying into Captivity [of] The Rev. Mr. John Norton. **1806** PIKE *Sources Miss.* II. 111 These Indians have been redeemed from captivity among the Potowatomies. **1844** GREGG *Commerce of Prairies* II. 314 War parties have frequently penetrated to the very heart of the settlements, . . . bearing away into captivity numerous women and children. **1885** A. GARDNER SHARP (*title*), History of the Spirit Lake Massacre and Captivity of Miss Abbie Gardner.

Capture, *v.* {1795–} **1.** *tr.* To run away with; to steal. Also fig. +**2.** To secure (a legislator) in one's interests. — **(1) 1832** CATLIN *Indians* I. 46 The Crows . . . call this *capturing,* where they sometimes run off a Trader's horses and make their boast of it. **1897** *Advance* (Chicago) 29 April 542/1 They will capture streets . . . , will say to urbanites and suburbanites, 'Stand and deliver—your fare.' **(2) 1887** *Courier-Journal* 15 Jan. 5/1 He feared one of the Democratic members of the Legislature had been captured by Republican boodle. **1888** BRYCE *Amer. Commonwealth* III. 404 The [railway] companies might succeed in 'capturing' individual legislators or committees of either or both Houses.

***Capuchin(e).** *Obs.* A hooded cloak formerly worn by women, and 'made in imitation of the dress of the capuchin friars' (Johnson). Also attrib. {1749–52 (1859).} — **1754** *S.C. Gazette* 15–22 Jan. 3/1 Robert & Wm. Brisbane have imported . . . bombazines, alapines, . . . tammies, . . . capuchines. *Ib.* 21–28 May 3/1 Samuel Kynaston has just imported from London, a large and choice Assortment of Ribbons . . . ,—Capuchine Silk and Cock's Comb. **1757** E. Singleton *Social N.Y.* 237 Mary Wallace and Clementia Ferguson intend to follow the business of . . . making . . . roman cloaks, cardinals, capuchins. **1761** *Essex Inst. Coll.* XLVII. 358 A variety of black figured silk for capuchins and cardinals. **1770** in Chalkley *Scotch-Irish Settlement Va.* I. 160 Attached—a piece of Sagathy, one capuchin.

+**Capulin.** *S.W.* Also **capul.** [Sp. *capuli(n).*] **1.** The Mexican or wild cherry, *Prunus capuli.* Also attrib. **2.** The ground cherry, *Physalis pubescens.* — **(1) 1806** WEBSTER 43/1 Capulin, *n.* The Mexican cherry. *c***1893** *Dialect Notes* I. 245 (Texas words), *Capul, -es,* a tree or shrub of southwestern Texas, not identified, with small, blackish-red or deep yellow edible berries, called *capules.* **(2) 1893** *Stand.* 282/3 *Capulin,* . . . a species of ground-cherry (*Physalis pubescens*); strawberry-tomato.

+**Cap wire.** ?Wire to make frames for caps. — **1711** *Springfield Rec.* II. 41 A peice of smal cap wire, 1 shilling. **1775** E. Singleton *Social N.Y.* 247 Henry Wilmot, in Hanover Square, sells . . . cloak trimmings, skeleton and cap wires. **1784** *Mass. Centinel* 26 June 3/3 For Sale, a Variety of Goods, by wholesale, amongst which are . . . Cap Wire, Pile Beavers, Washing Buff, Herring Bone, [etc.].

***Car.**

+1. a. A railroad car, esp. a boxcar, for the conveyance of freight; a freight car. {=truck, wagon, van}

1826 *Mass. Statutes* 4 March, The conveyance of stone and other property in their cars and vehicles on said railways. **1830** *Baltimore Amer.* 20 May, A car was loaded with double the weight. **1873** Poor *Manual Railroads 1873–74* 90 Cars [owned by the Connecticut Western Railroad] —passenger, 10; . . . freight, . . . 195—total cars, 207. **1903** E. Johnson *Railway Transportation* 123 The conductor of the freight train by which the car is moved. **1917** C. Mathewson *Sec. Base Sloan* 3 An hour ago they had been rudely awakened from their sleep in a box car. . . . They had lain undisturbed in the car ever since the middle of the previous afternoon.

+b. A coach or carriage of a railroad train. (Also *passenger car, railroad car.*)

1830 *Baltimore Amer.* 24 May, A brigade of cars will run three times a day each way from Baltimore to Ellicott's Mills—Damage 25 cents. **1835** Ingraham *South-West* I. xvi. 172 The cars for passengers . . . were standing in a line under a long roof, which covers the end of the rail-way. **1840** *Picayune* 30 July 2/2 The Directors of the Providence Railroad have voted to allow colored gentlemen to take seats by the side of the wives and daughters of white men, in the cars on their road. **1851** J. F. W. Johnston *Notes N. Amer.* I. 132 If . . . all classes were indiscriminately mixed up in large carriages—cars, as they call them here— . . . I doubt if Old England passengers would, as a whole, behave as well as those of New England do. **1864** T. L. Nichols *Amer. Life* I. 241 The cars, as the Americans designate their railway carriages, . . . are among the nicest I have ever seen. **1879** Harlan *Eyesight* viii. 109 Straining the accommodative apparatus of the eye . . . by reading in a car or carriage. **1885** E. B. Custer *Boots & Saddles* ii. 17 After so many days in the car . . . , we were glad to stop on an open plain. **1901** White *Westerners* xxi. 220 Little did those three tenderfeet realize, as they dutifully changed cars at Grand Island, . . . how much their holiday jaunt . . . meant to a whole community.

+c. *The cars*, a railroad train. *To take the cars*, to set off on a railroad journey.

In very frequent use *c*1845–*c*1875.

1831 *Niles' Reg.* XLI. 21 The cars now leave Schenectady at a little after 12 M. **1835** *Ib.* 28 Nov. XLIX. 210 The cars on the Lowell rail road made the trip from Boston to Lowell on Tuesday afternoon in *fifty-five minutes.* **1838** *N.Y. Advertiser & Exp.* 5 May 1/5 One third of the city was laid in ashes at the departure of the cars this morning at six o'clock. **1849** E. Davies *Amer. Scenes* 186 We set off by railway, or (as the Americans would say) 'by the cars,' to Baltimore. **1850** Glisan *Jrnl. Army Life* 11 At Harrisburg we took the cars for Huntington. **1866** Mrs. Whitney *L. Goldthwaite* ii. 30 It was about as cheap comin' by the cars as it would ha' ben to hire a passage any other way. **1875** G. P. Burnham *Three Years* 51, I was also aware there was risk in jumping from the cars, when the train was flying along at such a rate. **1888** Stockton *Dusantes* 104 You kin send telegraphs all along the line to one station an' another for conductors to give to him in the cars. **1906** *N.Y. Ev. Post* 7 Sept. 6 The San Francisco business man steps on the cars for New York, as if he were going to a nearby suburb.

2. A streetcar or tramway car. {Also E.}

1862 *Trial C. M. Jefferds* 23 What is your business? A. Conductor on the Fourth avenue cars. **1875** *Chicago Tribune* 15 Oct. 8/1 It is to be decided whether the Company's special policemen . . . have a right to enter cars of the bobtail pattern and eject non-paying passengers. **1895** *Chicago Strike of 1894* 401 The crowd would run ahead of them about six blocks and tip over another car. **1902** Harben *Abner Daniel* 26 At the first corner he saw a car which would take him to his brother's. *Ib.*, Reaching it, the planter left the car.

b. An automobile or motorcar. {Also E.}

1910 E. S. Field *Sapphire Bracelet* 47 He would get his bag from his car, and tidy up a bit before dinner. **1911** L. J. Vance *Cynthia* 61 A man that buys one of them cars and pays for its keep's a fool. **1923** R. Herrick *Lilla* 135 Gordon . . . had his heart set upon owning a car and talked motors all winter.

+3. The cage of an elevator.

1889 *Cent.* 1876 *Elevator*, a car or cage for lifting and lowering [etc.]. **1904** *N.Y. Ev. Post* 2 Feb. 2 The car made a sheer drop from the fourth story to the basement. **1916** W. A. Du Puy *Uncle Sam* 204 The operator . . . obeyed instantly and some excuse was made to the passengers on the car.

‖4. (See quotation.)

*a***1870** Chipman *Notes on Bartlett* 69 *Car*, . . . a square box in which, floating, are preserved live fish.—New England and Middle States.

+5. A carload.

1867–8 *Ill. Agric. Soc. Trans.* VII. 446 A farmer had far better send . . . one car of good sheep in the twelve months, than six cars . . . of bad breed. **1879** *Lumberman's Gazette* Dec. 3 Ten cars of dressed lumber have been shipped from Gowen . . . to parties in Nebraska. **1902** Lorimer *Lett. Merchant* 133 The last car of lard was so strong that it came back of its own accord from every retailer they shipped it to. **1905** A. H. Rice *Sandy* 41 A car of live stock . . . was on its way to a great exposition in a neighboring city.

+6. Attrib. and comb. with *cap, cleaner, folks*, etc.

1890 H. Frederic *Lawton Girl* 3 Then he . . . pocketed his thin car-cap, adjusted his glossy silk hat carefully, and proceeded to tug out his own valise. **1887** C. B. George *40 Yrs. on Rail* 27 In those days the baggage-master . . . had to keep his own car clean, inside and out, as car cleaners were then unknown. **1873** Marietta Holley *My Opinions* (1891) 268, I see that all the car folks felt friendly towards me. **1907** M. H. Norris *Veil* v. 38 A car-horse, sore-footed and generally weather-beaten, . . . completed this part of his purchase. **1878** Pinkerton *Strikers*, etc. 318 These trains were intercepted . . . by men jumping upon them, . . . uncoupling the cars, and throwing car-links and pins away. **1903** E. Johnson *Railway Transportation* 174 If each car carrying the mails be taken as a unit, the 'annual travel' or car mileage aggregated 302,613,325. **1848** W. E. Burton *Waggeries* 177 When we arrived at the car office, he dragged his box from the dray. **1907** W. Lillibridge *Trail* 194 As at that first meeting on the car platform, the girl had turned facing them. **1883** *Harper's Mag.* Aug. 331/2 'Pitchburg,' as, with unconscious sarcasm, a darky car-porter called it. **1874** Knight 478/1 *Car-register.* (*Railway.*) A device for keeping account of all persons entering a car, so as to fōrm a check on the receipt of fare by the conductor. *Ib.*, *Car-replacer.* (*Railway.*) An instrument or means for restoring to the rails a car which has run off the track. **1902** Harben *Abner Daniel* 25 Now I have a long car-ride before me, and it's growing late. **1892** 'Mark Twain' *£1,000,000 Bank-Note* (1893) 261 The car-routes are marvellously intricate, and often the drivers get lost and are not heard of for years. **1886** *Starry Flag* (San Francisco) May 4/2 We would be willing to wager a battered nickel against a wooden car ticket. **1920** C. R. Cooper *Under Big Top* 44 There were dogs in the streets, in the alleys and on the car tracks. **1883** *Century Mag.* Sept. 650/2 You see them from the car windows.

Carabineer. See Carbineer.

+Caracara eagle. Also **carra-carra.** [From its call.] The Mexican eagle, *Polyborus tharus* var. *auduboni.* {1838} Also ellipt.

1839 Audubon *Ornith. Biog.* V. 351 Caracara Eagle. *Polyborus Braziliensis.* Nests of the Caracara found in the Floridas . . . were placed on the highest branches . . . in the pine barrens. **1849** — *Western Journal* (1906) 139 There were the Carra Carra Eagles in great number. **1858** Baird *Birds Pacific R.R.* 45 The Caracara Eagle. . . . *Hab.*—Southern North America. Florida. Texas. Mexico. *a***1874** Coues *Birds N.W.* 372 The carrion of an ox was covered with Turkey Buzzards, and one specimen of the Caracara Eagle was among them. **1874** *Ib.*, This statement in respect of the nidification of the Caracara is confirmed by other naturalists. **1895** *Yearbook Dept. Agric. 1894* 211 Among the birds may be mentioned the white-crowned pigeon, Zenaida dove, . . . and caracara eagle.

+Carajo, Caraho, *n. S.W.* [Sp. *carajo* virile member.] **1.** A base person; a low fellow. **2.** *Carajo pole*, an ox goad. — (1) **1844** Gregg *Commerce of Prairies* I. 298 Then you shall die first, carajo! **1850** Garrard *Wah-To-Yah* iv. 64 He became so independent, and so regardless of justice, in his condescension toward the *Carahos.* (2) **1901** *Kansas Hist. Coll.* (1902) VII. 52, I hurried him [an ox] along by repeated punches with my *carajo* pole.

+Carajo, Caraho, *v. S.W.* [Carajo *n.*] *intr.* To shout 'carajo.' — **1846** *Knickerb.* XXVIII. 246 All the Mexicans cursing and swearing and threatening and carrahooing [*sic*] at once. **1850** Garrard *Wah-To-Yah* iv. 65 At other times, he *sacre*-ed in French, *caraho*-ed in Spanish-Mexican. **1900** Smithwick *Evolution of State* 53 They gave chase, *carajoing* and firing their carbines.

+Caramba. *S.W.* [Sp. (colloq.) 'ha.'] In Mexican Spanish use: An exclamation of astonishment, dismay, etc. — **1853** Brewerton *With Kit Carson* (1930) 32 Parties of sauntering Californians . . . smoking their eternal *cigarritos* . . . or uttering an occasional *caramba.* *a***1861** Winthrop *J. Brent* ii. 21 He gave me a Mexican's sulky stare, muttered a caramba at my rashness.

Caramel, *v.* {1727–} +*intr.* To be converted into caramel. — **1887** *Century Mag.* Nov. 114/1 The chief sugar-maker . . . seeks to keep the temperature down to 130°. If it is too high some of the sucrose will 'invert' or caramel into glucose. **1897** *Yearbk. U.S. Dept. Agric.* 515 The sugar in the milk caramels in baking and browns the crust.

+Carau. *Fla.* The crying bird or limpkin, *Aramus giganteus.* — **1858** Baird *Birds Pacific R.R.* 657 *Aramus Giganteus*, . . . Carau; Crying Bird; Courlan. **1889** *Cent.* 1311/1 *Courlan*, . . . also called *carau, crying-bird*, and *limpkin.*

***Caravan.**

+1. A body or company of traders, emigrants, or other travelers on a journey, with their wagons, pack horses, and mules.

Captain of the caravan: see Captain *n.* 1 b.

1743 Catesby *Carolina* App. p. iv, Canes . . . are an excellent food for Horses and Cattle, and are of great benefit particularly to Indian Traders, whose Caravans travel these uninhabited Countries. **1791** Bartram *Travels* 374 Our caravan consisting of about twenty men and sixty horses, we made a formidable appearance. **1807** in Pike *Sources Miss.* III. 231 Passed the encampment of the caravan, going with about 15,000 sheep for the other provinces. **1842** *S. Lit. Messenger* VIII. 146/1 The frontier traders have been in the habit of collecting in large caravans, and traversing . . . the great American desert. **1854** PIERCE in *Pres. Mess. & P.* V. 282 A piratical resort of outlaws or a camp of savages depredating on emigrant trains or caravans and the frontier settlements of civilized states. **1871** DE VERE 105 In former days *caravans* furnished the only means of communication between the new settlements and the Eastern cities. **1897** J. L. ALLEN *Choir Invisible* ii. 14 A company of travellers with pack-horses—one of the caravans across the desert of the Western woods.

+**b.** A train *of* wagons.

1817 S. BROWN *Western Gaz.* 77 General Harrison . . . was accompanied in his march through the wilderness by a caravan of waggons! **1819** *Niles' Reg.* XVI. 238/2 A *caravan*, consisting of eleven covered waggons, drawn by two, three, or four horses each, . . . [bound] for the state of Illinois.

+**c.** A string *of* pack mules.

1905 VALENTINE *H. Sandwith* 3 Caravans of pack-mules followed lone Indian trails.

2. A large wagon for travel or transport; a van. {1674–}

1819 F. WRIGHT *Views* (1821) 228, I remember, when taking a cross cut in a queer sort of caravan, . . . observing, with no small surprise, the operations of our charioteer. **1832** CATLIN *Indians* I. 63 And that keel-boat, that Mackinaw boat, and that formidable caravan, all of which are richly laden with goods, . . . are outfits starting for the *West.*

b. A covered vehicle of a menagerie or travelling show.

1824 IRVING *T. Trav.* I. 272 Several caravans, containing wild beasts, and other spectacles. **1873** W. MATHEWS *Getting on in World* xiii. 179 Lumbering caravans with ear-stunning bands of music. **1876** MILLER *First Families* xv. 135 Yours to take and go home, . . . and . . . not live here like a wild beast in a caravan.

c. A show or circus which travels in a caravan.

1845 SOL. SMITH *Theatr. Apprent.* 176 He is one person today and another to-morrow— . . . some people say he is as good as a caravan! **1851** HAWTHORNE *Twice-told T.* I. 248 The immense showbill of a wandering caravan.

3. Attrib. and comb. with *animal, keeper, life, trail, trader.*

1841 COOPER *Deerslayer* xiv, The Otsego is a favorite place for the caravan-keepers to let their elephants bathe. **1844** GREGG *Commerce of Prairies* I. 74 In accordance with the habitual carelessness of caravan traders, a great portion of the men were unprepared for the emergency. **1846** SAGE *Scenes Rocky Mts.* ii, The caravan animals, securely picketed, . . . occupied an area of several acres. *a***1861** WINTHROP *J. Brent* xi. 120, I must wait for some artist . . . who can perceive the poetry of American caravan-life. *c***1908** F. M. CANTON *Frontier Trails* 169 We started out on an old caravan trail.

Caravanserai, -sary. {1712–} +An inn. *W.* — **1826** FLINT *Recoll.* 211, I have seen two of the latter [handsome houses] which were not content with the title of 'hotel,' . . . but which carried on their signs the still more fashionable term 'caravanserai.' *a***1861** WINTHROP *Canoe & Saddle* 312 They sleep in an Americanized caravansary. **1888** *Kansas Hist. Coll.* (1890) IV. 246 Lawrence, a rude town of some forty or fifty log and rough board cabins with a 'caravansary' for immigrants, built of sod walls and cloth roof.

***Caraway.**

***1.** A biennial plant, *Carum carui*, valued for its fruit or seeds: (see next).

1709 LAWSON *Carolina* 78 The more Physical [herbs], are . . . Dill, Carawa, Cummin, Anise. **1832** WILLIAMSON *Maine* I. 122 Caraway is indigenous and flourishes luxuriantly. **1865** *Atlantic Mo.* XV. 150 Having despatched all the edible matter upon a stalk of caraway. **1891** BUNNER *Zadoc Pine* 144 She holds her hymn-book and a spray of caraway in one hand.

***2.** *Caraway seed(s)*, the seed(s) or fruit of the caraway, valued for flavoring cakes, etc.

1720 *Weekly Mercury* 9 June 2/2 To be sold by Edward Horne . . . very good new *Caraway* Seed at Reasonable Rates. **1852** MITCHELL *Dream Life* 97 Cookies, spiced with caraway seeds. **1881** *Harper's Mag.* May 855/2 She is even there tonight, caraway seeds, malice and all.

3. *Caraway cake, cooky*, etc., one flavored with caraway seeds.

1805 *Pocumtuc Housewife* (1906) 33 [Recipes for] Caraway Cookies . . . Doughnuts . . . Rye Doughnuts. **1832** L. M. CHILD *Frugal Housewife* 73 Caraway Cakes. Take one pound of flour [etc.]. **1898** I. H. HARPER *S. B. Anthony* I. 14 Doughnuts, caraway cakes and other toothsome things which little ones love.

+**Carbarn.** [CAR 1, 2.] A building for housing street- or railroad cars. — **1882** *Chicago Tribune*, In case the street car conductors get up another strike, you had better . . . head for the car barns. **1909** *Springfield Republican* 25 Feb. 16 A fire . . . burned the central car barn and repair shop of the Blue Hill street railway company. **1923** WATTS *L. Nichols* 51 The time he nearly got caught in the turntable pit at the East St. Louis car-barns.

+**Car-bell.** [CAR 2.] The bell of a streetcar. — **1863** 'M. HARLAND' *Husks* 20 The tinkle of the car-bell, three blocks off, arose to her window. **1896** *Godey's Mag.* Feb. 171/1 Then silence fell; the sound of the car-bells in the street came distinctly to them. **1902** HARBEN *Abner Daniel* 297 We git our pay for our land in bein' glad an' heerin' car-bells an' steam-whistles in the middle o' the night.

Carbine, Carabine. [Fr. *carabine.*] A short musket or rifle. {1605–}

(*a*) **1636** in Winthrop *Hist.* I. 473 Put my brother Stephen in mind to send me my carbine. *a***1656** BRADFORD *Hist. Plym. Plant.* 242 He . . . with a carbine . . . had thought to have shot Captaine Standish. **1744** *N.J. Archives* 1 Ser. VI. 193 [Each] shall keep at the place of his abode . . . a well fix'd carbine. **1842** *Niles' Nat. Reg.* 5 Feb. 368/2 Small fire arms manufactured at Harper's Ferry and Springfield . . . [include] muskets, . . . rifles and carbines. **1867** J. N. EDWARDS *Shelby* iv. 72 Who will fire a flint-lock musket, when Sharpe's best carbine may be had for the asking? **1888** P. H. SHERIDAN *Memoirs* I. 383 This concealed line opened a destructive fire with repeating carbines. **1900** [see CARAJO *v.*].

(*b*) **1666** *Md. Archives* II. 19 Voted necessary that there be . . . Carabines for Horsemen. **1809** BARLOW *Columbiad* VI. line 499 Unwearied Francis still prolonged the strife, Till a chance carabine attain'd his head. **1827** COOPER *Prairie* I. iv. 65 Each man laid aside the light fowling-piece which, under the name of a carabine, he carried in virtue of his rank. **1840** POE *Journal J. Rodman* iii. Wks. V. 312 The savages had no fire-arms . . . , except an old carabine carried by one of the chiefs.

Carbineer, -ier. Also **carabineer.** [f. CARBINE.] One (esp. a horseman) armed with a carbine. {1672–} — **1803** in *Ann. 8th Congress* 2 Sess. 1509 Carabineers, or privileged companies of horse, two companies of 70 each. **1845** DE SMET *Oregon Missions* (1847) 134 Polk and Peel . . . are as unknown to our carbineer [=a trapper], as the two greatest powers of the moon. **1847** EMORY *Military Reconn.* 119 We moved to the river in our habitual order of march, . . . a company of volunteer carbiniers in the rear. **1866** MOORE *Women of War* 56 The carbineers . . . being deployed as skirmishers in the skirt of the pine woods.

Carbonado,** *v. tr.* To broil or grill. — *a1870** CHIPMAN *Notes on Bartlett* 69 Carbonado, v.t. To broil; to cook upon coals.—Southern U.S.

Carbonate. {1794–} +'The common term in the West for ores containing a considerable proportion of carbonate of lead. They are sometimes earthy or ochreous (soft carbonates), sometimes granular and comparatively free from iron (sand carbonates) and sometimes compact (hard carbonates).'—Raymond *Mining Glossary.*

+**Carbonated warbler.** A warbler, *Sylvia carbonata*, reported by Audubon. — **1831** AUDUBON *Ornith. Biog.* I. 308 The Carbonated Warbler[s], *Sylvia Carbonata*, . . . were both busily engaged in searching for insects along the branches and amongst the leaves of a Dog-wood tree. **1858** BAIRD *Birds Pacific R.R.* 288 The Carbonated Warbler is known only by the description and figure of Mr. Audubon, taken from two specimens killed at Henderson, Kentucky, in 1811.

+**Carborundum.** [f. *carbo(n), (co)rundum.*] Silicon carbide, used for polishing and scouring. Also attrib. — **1892** *Official Gazette U.S. Patents* LIX. 1914/1 [Trade-mark registered by] The Carborundum Company, Monongahela City, Pa. *Ib.*, Trade-marks registered June 21, 1892 [include] Carborundum. **1893** *Amer. Jrnl. Sci.* 3 Ser. XLVI. 472 While examining the hardness of 'carborundum,' a carbide of silicon, made by Mr. Acheson of Pittsburg, it was found that it readily scratched red, blue, white, pink, and yellow corundum in the form of fine gems.

+**Carbuilder.** [Cf. next.] A workman who builds cars. — **1883** J. D. FULTON *Sam Hobart* 165 Car Builders' Dictionary. **1894** CARWARDINE *Pullman Strike* 81 Car builder . . . $13.00.

+**Carbuilding.** [CAR. Cf. prec.] The building or making of cars. — **1853** *Knickerb.* XLII. 541 He held . . . the position of general superintendent of the department of car-building. **1876** INGRAM *Centennial Expos.* 631 Notable among . . . [the resources and industries of Delaware] are the agricultural, mechanical, and those of iron ship-building, morocco manufacturing and car-building. **1883** *Harper's Mag.* Aug. 328/1 Mr. John P. Levan . . . was the first apprentice of the company, at a time when the car building force comprised only thirty-six men.

‖**Carcage.** [Sp. *carcaj, -cax.*] A quiver. — **1844** GREGG *Comm. Prairies* I. 90 Swung upon the shoulder of each [buffalo hunter] hangs his *carcage* or quiver of bow and arrows.

+**Carcajou.** Also **carcagieu, -gue; corcajou,** etc. [Fr. (18th c.), of unknown (prob. Amer. Indian) origin.]

1. The North American variety of wolverine or glutton, *Gulo luscus.*

[**1744** A. DOBBS *Hudson's Bay* 40 The Beavers have three Enemies, Man, Otters, and the Carcajon [*sic*], or Queequehatch. **1761** CHARLEVOIX *Voyage to N. Am.* I. vii. 201 The elk has other enemies. . . . The most terrible of all these is the *Carcajou* or *Quincajou.*] **1778** CARVER *Travels* 450 The Carcajou. This creature, which is of the cat kind, is a terrible enemy to the preceding four species of beasts [i.e. deer, elk, moose, caribou]. **1804–6** *Lewis & Clark Exped.* (1905) VI. 107 Carkajous wolverine or Beaver Eaters. **1832** WILLIAMSON *Maine* I. 133 The Wolverine, (Carcajou,) is as large as a wolf and of like colour. **1846** SAGE *Scenes Rocky Mts.* xv. 126 The 'carcague' is a native of the Rocky Mountains, . . . partaking the mixed nature of the wolf and bear. **1859** G. A. JACKSON *Diary* 521 Corcajou came into camp while I was at fire; dogs killed him after I had broken his back with belt axe. **1904** WHITE *Silent Places* v. 38 The travellers were to be forced . . . , just as are the wolves, the eagles, the hawks, the carcajous, . . . to give their first thoughts to the day's sustenance.

2. The American badger, *Taxidea americana.*

1864 WEBSTER 197/1 *Carcajou*, . . . the American badger (*Meles Labradorica*), found in the sandy plains or prairies of North America. **1877** BARTLETT 100 *Carcajou*, a name now appropriated to the American

Badger (*Meles Labradorica*, a species so named, apparently, because *not found* in Labrador).

‖**Car-carriage.** =CAR *n.* 1 b. — **1854** *S. Lit. Messenger* XX. 725/1 An easy and commodius car-carriage whirls the Baltimorian through in half a day.

Carcel lamp. [f. B. G. *Carcel* (d. 1812), French inventor.] A lamp in which oil is supplied to the wick by clockwork. {1845–} Also ellipt. as n. — **1845** *Knickerb.* XXVI. 470 The Carcel lamps were first introduced into this country by Augustus Deacon. *Ib.*, Gradually, the 'Carcels' have made their way into all our principal hotels. **1857** YOUMANS *Household Science* 114 In the Carcel lamp, . . . clockwork is applied to pump up the oil. **1874** KNIGHT 466/1 Carcel-lamp . . . [is] a mechanical lamp, used in lighthouses, where the wick is overflowed with oil as a measure of equality of supply.

Car conductor. One in charge of a horse- or other streetcar. — **1876** *Scribner's Mo.* April 911/2 There were addresses . . . relating to the . . . car-conductor. **1876** in Bartlett 79 Unable to earn an honest living, without brains for any position higher than that of a car conductor, he lives by lobbying.

+**Car coupling.** 'A device for connecting the cars in a train. In the United States this is usually a form of shackle' (Knight). Also attrib. — **1847** *Index to Patents* (1874) I. 210 Car-coupling [patented by] W. C. Bussey, Rockgrove, Ill., July 17, 1847. **1872** HUNTINGTON *Road-Master's Assistant* 123 There are other accidents . . . which may also be classed as unavoidable, such as the breaking of car-couplings. **1883** J. D. FULTON *Sam Hobart* 170 A Division Superintendent came into our rooms, who was interested in a car-coupling arrangement. I suppose there are hundreds of different kinds of car-couplings.

* **Card,** *n.*[1]

* **1.** An instrument provided with wire or iron teeth for smoothing out the fibers of wool, cotton, etc. Also attrib.

1660 *East-Hampton Rec.* I. 180 The Estate of John Hand [consists of] . . . The woll yarne wheles & cards [etc.]. **1706** *Boston News-Letter* 28 Jan. 2/2 On Thursday . . . will be exposed to Sale . . . a Parcel of old Woollen Cards, [etc.]. **1768** J. ROWE *Diary* 154 We will not for one year send for any European Commodities excepting . . . Card Wire. **1807** C. JANSON *Stranger in A.* 29 The principal manufactures of Boston are, sail-cloth, cordage, hats, wool and cotton cards. **1840** *Picayune* 28 July 4/1 The following compose a part [of the merchandise], viz.:— . . . Whittemore's cotton cards. **1885** *Harper's Mag.* July 249/1 'Cards,' or combs with wire teeth, comb out the dirt . . . and short fibre.

+**2.** A currycomb.

1820 *Columbian Centinel* 8 Jan. 4/3 Wool, Cotton, and Cattle Cards. **1858** *Rep. Comm. Patents* (1859) I. 346 Improvement in Cards for currying Cattle. **1860** OLMSTED *Back Country* 246 He picked up a piece of corn cob and began scraping him. 'Hadn't he got a curry comb or card?' I asked. **1864** WEBSTER 197/2.

* **Card,** *n.*[2]

* **1.** A playing card.

1630–1 *Mass. Bay Rec.* I. 84 All p[er]sons whatsoeuer that haue cards, dice, or tables in their howses, shall make away with them before the nexte Court. **1699** SEWALL *Diary* I. 498 A Pack of Cards are found strawed over my fore-yard. **1818** BIRKBECK *Lett. Illinois* 116 With these cobs . . . , structures are raised by the little half-Indian brats, very much like our houses of cards. **1894** HAMILTON *Mod. Scientific Whist* 18 The five highest cards . . . can be arranged 120 different ways. **1922** *Science* LVI. 418/2 Deal at random 25 cards from a pack of 52 playing cards.

attrib. and *comb.* **1851** HALL *Manhattaner* 182 There is little card-fleecing nowaday on the Mississippi first-class packets. **1900** C. C. MUNN *Uncle Terry* 119 Albert . . . seldom entered into any card games.

* **b.** *pl.* A game played with these.

1643 WILLIAMS *Key* (1866) 194 A Game like unto the English Cards. **1656** *Plymouth Laws* 101 Whosoever shall . . . suffer any to play att Cards . . . shalbee fined the sume of forty shillings. **1734** *Harvard Rec.* I. 142 If any Undergraduate shall play at Cards or Dice, he shall be punished by fine. **1809** F. CUMING *Western Tour* 166 There are four billiard tables in Lexington, and cards are a good deal played at taverns. **1861** *Army Regulations* 148 If any disbursing officer shall bet at cards or any game of hazard. **1902** WISTER *Virginian* xxiii. 272 But there was nights I made a heap more at cyards.

c. *transf.* A person having some outstanding quality, often of eccentricity; a drawing card. Esp. with adjs., as *sure card*, *queer card*, etc. {1836–}

1840 KENNEDY *Quodlibet* 42 Consider me a sure card in that line. **1862** LOWELL *Biglow P.* II. iv. 126 Mason *wuz* F. F. V., though a cheap card to win on. **1864** T. L. NICHOLS *Amer. Life* I. 67 Let a man write a popular book . . . and the curiosity to see him makes him a good card for lecture-committees. **1869** BARNUM *Struggles & Triumphs* 142 Dr. Valentine . . . gave imitations and delineations of eccentric characters. He was quite a card at the Museum when I first purchased that establishment. **1924** R. CUMMINS *Sky-high Corral* 116 Jim Harvey's a queer card.

+**2.** 'A note published by some one in the papers, containing a brief statement, explanation, request, &c.' (W. '47).

This usage is well illustrated by Thornton from 1769 to 1813.

1769 *Boston News-Letter* 2 Feb. (Th.), A Card from the London and British Merchants to the American Merchants. **1779** *Boston Gazette* 8 March 2/2 A Card: A friend to Liberty presents his cplmts to the Gen. Court. **1801** *Mass. Spy* 1 July (Th.), A Card, concerning Kine Pox, from Dr. Waterhouse. **1819** *Plough Boy* I. 107 A Card: E. Watson presents his respects to Presidents of Agricultural Societies. **1846** *Knickerb.* XXVII. 364 A dentist . . . assures the public in a 'card' that 'he will spare no pains in extracting the teeth of those who will favor him with a call.' **1851** *Harper's Mag.* III. 129 The principal Catholic laity and the clergy published a card in which they express their unqualified condemnation of the conduct of the rioters. **1884** SWEET & KNOX *Through Texas* xxxvi. 505 If the Indians ever . . . publish a card, they, too, will have something to say on the subject of wicked partners. **1891** S. M. WELCH *Recoll. 1830–40* 397 Reports . . . annoyed Mr. Cashier Shearman and caused him to publish a card in which he stated that the bank was as strong and firm as the 'Rock of Ages.'

transf. **1839** 'M. PENCIL' *White Sulphur P.* 40 A corn-doctor's card has been posted up for several days.

+**b.** *colloq.* An effective advertisement.

1887 *Courier-Journal* 1 May 12/1 The festival of last year was quite a card for Louisville.

3. A calling card. {1795–}

1779 S. HOLTEN in *Essex Inst. Coll.* LVI. 31 The Chevalier paid us a visit by leaving a card. **1881–5** MCCLELLAN *Own Story* 551, I left my card, with P. P. C. written upon it, at the White House. **1893** HOWELLS *Coast of Bohemia* 20 He took a card from his pocketbook, and gave it to the mother.

comb. **1883** HOWELLS *Woman's Reason* viii, A card inscribed with The Misses Amy in the neat penciling of a professional card-writer.

4. An invitation written or printed on a card or heavy note paper. {1771–}

1787 TYLER *Contrast* (1790) II. i, Instead of freezing me with a cold card of compliment to dine with him ten days hence, he . . . asked me to dine with him today. **1789** MACLAY *Deb. Senate* 133 Had a card to dine with the Vice President on Friday. **1853** F. S. COZZENS *Prismatics* 80 Rowley's mother at this time issued cards of invitation for a small party. **1891** S. M. WELCH *Recoll. 1830–40* 384 Mrs. Coe sent out cards to all her friends, inviting them to a series of three balls or dancing receptions.

+**5.** A flat cake (or 'sheet') of gingerbread; a 'pan' of biscuit, etc. Also attrib.

1823 COOPER *Pioneers* ix, With 'cards of gingerbread.' **1846** FARNHAM *Prairie Land* 31 He had just purchased two large cards of gingerbread. **1853** J. G. BALDWIN *Flush Times Ala.* 103 He distributed a piece of calico here, a plug of tobacco there, or a card of *iown* gingerbread to the little snow-balls. **1867** 'T. LACKLAND' *Homespun* III. 322 He makes lavish investments in card-gingerbread and spruce beer. **1871** *Atlantic Mo.* Nov. 574 Through clouds of smoke and steam . . . sprang the cooks . . . dropping a card of biscuits and picking them up again in their fists. **1881** R. T. COOKE *Somebody's Neighbors* 393 Cards of yellow gingerbread.

6. A card on which a special entry is made for reference, as in library usage. Also (railroad) *card waybill*.

1849 [see CARD INDEX]. **1854** *Boston Doc. 74* 12 [The card catalogue] contains a full title of each book on a separate card, with short alphabetical references on other cards to each word of the title under which the book is likely to be called for. **1903** E. JOHNSON *Railway Transportation* 123 This way-bill either accompanies the freight or is forwarded by mail. In the latter case the agent makes out a 'card way-bill,' which is given to the conductor of the freight train.

+**7.** A number of matches, candies, etc., attached to or arranged on a card of pasteboard.

1870 'O. OPTIC' *Field & Forest* 65 Mr. Mellowtone gave me a card of matches. **1899** WILKINS *Colonial Times* 107, I'll buy you a whole card of peppermints. **1904** MACKAYE *Panchronicon* 342 She found again her card of matches, and breaking off one of them, soon had a tiny taper.

+**8.** (See quotation.)

1884 PHIN *Dict. Apiculture* 20 *Card*, a frame filled with honeycomb, a sheet of honeycomb.

+**9.** *To give cards and spades*, to give or concede an advantage. *colloq.*

[**1888** *Grip* (Toronto) May (F.), He found a Chinaman . . . who could give him cards and spades and beat him out.] **1898** *N.Y. World* 3 Sept. 2/5-6 The calentura can give cards and spades to yellow fever in the game of death.

10. A large pasteboard placard.

1897 *Boston Herald* 9 Sept. 8/4 The railroad committee of the association sent out with each circular cards furnished by the traffic departments . . . and requested that same be hung in shipping offices and be used in routing freight.

* **Card,** *v.*[1]

* **1.** *tr.* To comb or smooth (wool, flax, cotton, etc.) with cards. Also absol.

1749 ELIOT *Field-Husb.* ii. 43 The Wool might have time to acquire its primitive Oileness drawn from the Sheeps Body, which made it stronger and better to Card. **1837** W. JENKINS *Ohio Gaz.* 370 It contained . . . one carding machine for carding wool. **1872** *Atlantic Mo.* May 535 She could card and spin and weave, and her nimble fingers made up many a suit of homespun and plaid cotton. **1885** *Rep. Indian Affairs* 156 They card this wool by hand.

+**2.** To dress or curry (a horse, ox, etc.) with a currycomb or card. (Cf. CARD *n.*[1] 2.) Also absol.

1851 J. S. SPRINGER *Forest Life* 82 In the morning, ... his faithful visits are repeated to hay ... and card, and yoke up. **1884** *Vt. Agric. Rep.* VIII. 18 [He] was ... in favor of stanchions, but would card the cows regularly. **1888** *Ib.* X. 35 [He] spoke favorably of carding heifers and cows, and thinks it will pay.

Card, *v.*[2]

‖**1.** *tr.* To announce or designate by means of a card.

1844 POE *Oblong Box* Works III. 233, I observed that his name was carded upon *three* state-rooms.

+**2.** To send a message to (a person) on a postal card. *colloq.*

1875 in *Newspaper*, Fulcitus carded almost daily his friend Ruisseaux. **1880** (*from a letter*), Will you card for me here an answer to my friend the professor's question?

+**3.** To provide a book with record cards.

1893 *Stand.* 284/3 In library usage, the carding of books is distinguished from 'cataloguing,' which includes the determination of the form of entry and all necessary bibliographic details.

Card-basket. A basket or receptacle for calling cards. — **1841** A. BACHE *Fire-Screen* viii, To this treasury does the tasteful disposer of drawing-room decorations consign her antiquated card-baskets. **1852** *Knickerb.* XXXIX. 166 The names in your card-basket are fashionable names. **1854** B. F. TAYLOR *Jan. & June* 45 It was, as if one should invert a huge shell card-basket.

Cardboard. {1858–} +A railroad pass. — **1887** *Courier-Jrnl.* 8 May 15 People who have life passes over the railroads seem to be numerous. Most of them want to know if the Interstate Commission can ... force the railroads to honor their own cardboard.

Cardcase. A case for holding calling cards. {1835–} — **1851** BUSHNELL *Work & Play* (1864) 380 Two [ladies] ... calling back and forth with a card-case in their hand. **1871** *Harper's Mag.* June 57 He took from his pocket a heavy silver card-case. **1897** FLANDRAU *Harvard Episodes* 141 Haydock answered by unbuttoning Wolcott's coat and finding ten dollars in his card-case.

+**Card catalog(ue).** A catalogue, usually of the books in a library, made out on cards.

1854 *Boston City Doc. No. 74* 12 The Alphabetical Card Catalogue, which contains a full title of each book on a separate card. **1878** H. STEVENS (*title*), Photo-Bibliography; or, A Word on Printed Card Catalogues of Old, Rare, and Costly Books. **1895** *Century Mag.* June 266/1 The Boston Public Library depends in this way upon its enormous card catalogue. **1908** *A. L. A. Catalog Rules* 62 In a written card catalog abbreviations may be used more frequently than is desirable for printed cards. **1911** DEWEY *Decimal Classification* 20 In the card catalog of subjects the classification is mapt out above the cards by projecting guides.

+**Card end.** (See quotation.) {1864–} — **1841** PARK *Pantology* 475 The cotton, after being picked or batted into a light, uniform mass, and then twice carded, ... comes ... in continuous rolls, called card ends.

***Carder.** One who cards wool, etc. — **1837** W. JENKINS *Ohio Gaz.* 318, 24 clerks, 6 painters, 8 blacksmiths, 1 carder, 1 turner, [etc.]. **1844** *Lowell Offering* IV. 48 The spinners, carders, dressers, warpers, &c.... have much spare time. **1851** CIST *Cincinnati* 49 Occupations [include] ... carders, 8 [people].

Cardigan. A close-fitting woolen jacket. {1868–} Freq. *cardigan jacket.* — **1867** in Custer *Tenting on Plains* (1887) xviii. 552, I have worn the worsted cardigan. **1887** C. B. GEORGE *40 Years on Rail* viii. 160 Mr. Beecher in his cardigan jacket, a silk hat on his head. **1898** E. N. WESTCOTT *D. Harum* 107 His most conspicuous garment ... was a cardigan jacket of a frowsiness beyond compare.

* **Cardinal.**

1. A hooded cloak formerly worn by women. {1745–}

1757 E. Singleton *Social N.Y.* 237 Ladies and gentlemen ... reasonably served in making ... roman cloaks, cardinals, capuchins, dauphnesses, [etc.]. **1761** *Essex Inst. Coll.* XLVII. 358 A variety of black figured silk for capuchins and cardinals. **1842** *Knickerb.* XX. 438 Glancing ... at the tantalizing folds of a new satin cardinal. **1848** BARTLETT 65 The cardinal worn by ladies at the present day is a short cloak usually made of velvet, satin, or other rich material. [Not in eds. 1859, 1877.] **1875** R. T. COOKE in *Galaxy* XIX. 40/2 The lavender silk, the cardinal, the big bonnet, had been worn to church year after year.

2. The redbird or cardinal grosbeak.

[**1756** P. BROWNE *Jamaica* 467 The Cardinal. This bird is frequently imported from South Carolina.] **1858** BAIRD *Birds Pacific R.R.* 509 *Cardinalis Virginianus*, ... Red Bird; Cardinal. **1874** COUES *Birds N.W.* 173 The Cardinal lays rather a peculiar egg, some specimens reminding one of a Night-Hawk's. **1885** M. THOMPSON *Byways & Bird Notes* 159 In the region of Tallulah Falls I met with an old man whose chief business was snaring red-birds (cardinals) for the sake of their skins.

+**3.** =CARDINAL FLOWER.

1838 *S. Lit. Messenger* IV. 318/2 The little noisy brook ... steals off among the flowers it nourishes, the brilliant cardinals and snow-white clematis. **1842** HAWTHORNE *Note-Books* II. 85 The flowers, ... even the golden-rod and the gorgeous cardinals, ... have this gentle sadness amid their pomp. **1881** *Harper's Mag.* Sept. 585/1 The fragrant clethra, whose prim fingers of creamy bloom made a good foil to the cardinals.

Cardinal bird. The cardinal grosbeak or redbird, *Richmondena cardinalis.* {1678} — **1786** FRANKLIN *Writ.* IX. 503 It is rare that we see the Cardinal Bird so far north as Pennsylvania. **1864** WEBSTER 197/3 *Cardinal-bird*, ... having a fine scarlet plumage, and a high, pointed crest on its head. **1889** *Cent.* 820/2 *Cardinal-bird*, ... is sometimes called the *Virginia nightingale*, on account of its song. **1917** *Birds of Amer.* III. 63 Cardinal.... Other names [include] ... Virginia Cardinal; Kentucky Cardinal; Cardinal Bird.

Cardinal flower.

1. The scarlet lobelia (*Lobelia cardinalis*) or its showy red flower.

[**1629** PARKINSON *Paradisus* 356 The rich crimson Cardinals flower. This braue plant, from a white roote spreading diuers wayes vnder ground, sendeth forth many greene leaues.] **1705** BEVERLEY *Virginia* II. 24 The Cardinal-Flower, so much extoll'd for its Scarlet Colour, is almost in every Branch. **1835** HOFFMAN *Winter in West* I. 145 The purple fleur-de-lis bloomed along the wet marshes, where the splendid cardinal-flower tossed its scarlet blossoms in the breeze. **1840** DEWEY *Mass. Flowering Plants* 110 *Lobelia cardinalis.* L. Cardinal Flower ... is a splendid plant when in flower, and is found over much of the United States. **1858** *Harper's Mag.* May 841/2 A shrewd boy knows ... along what winding, bowery stream the cardinal-flowers stand in gorgeous state. **1865** *Nation* I. 367 In the low grounds ... the cardinal-flower forces itself upon the eye. **1913** STRATTON-PORTER *Laddie* i, On either side of the entrance he had planted a cluster of cardinal flower that was in full bloom.

+**2.** (*Blue*) *cardinal flower*, the large blue-flowered lobelia, *L. syphilitica.*

1828 WEBSTER, *Cardinal-flower*.... The natives of this country use a decoction of one species, the siphilitica, as a remedy in the venereal disease. **1847** WOOD *Botany* 364 *L. syphilitica.* Blue Cardinal Flower. ... A fine, showy plant, but inferior in beauty to *L. cardinalis*, growing in wet meadows and along streams. **1869** J. G. FULLER *Flower Gatherers* 238 Blue Cardinal Flower is a very handsome species, common in wet meadows. **1889** *Cent.* 820/2.

Cardinal grosbeak. The Virginia nightingale or cardinal, *Richmondena cardinalis.*

[**1802** BINGLEY *Anim. Biog.* (1813) II. 161 The Cardinal Grosbeak ... is an inhabitant of several parts of North America.] **1810** WILSON *Ornith.* II. 38 [The] Cardinal Grosbeak, *Loxia Cardinalis*, ... is one of our most common cage birds. **1839** PEABODY *Mass. Birds* 329 The Cardinal Grosbeak, *Fringilla cardinalis*.... Wherever the celebrated red-bird appears, it attracts attention, not only by its splendid plumage, but its bold and beautiful song. **1849** LONGFELLOW *Kavanagh* xv. Pr. Wks. (1886) II. 338 He resumed his labor of stuffing a cardinal grossbeak. **1876** J. BURROUGHS *Winter Sunshine* I. 28 Now and then ... there was a dash of scarlet—the cardinal grossbeak. **1885** *Century Mag.* March 682 The brown thrushes, the cardinal grosbeaks, and the cat-birds were singing in the hedges.

+**Cardinal plant.** The cardinal flower. — **1869** *Amer. Naturalist* III. 211 Many of the fern-like mosses ... do perfectly well if planted in a very small quantity of soil upon this top stone.... The red cardinal plant (*Lobelia cardinalis*), seem[s] especially adapted for this purpose.

+**Cardinal redbird.** =CARDINAL GROSBEAK. — **1889** *Cent.* 820/2 The cardinal, cardinal grosbeak, or cardinal redbird ... is common in many parts of the United States, especially in the south.

+**Cardinal tanager. a.** The scarlet tanager, *Piranga rubra.* **b.** The summer redbird, *P. æstiva.* — **1889** *Cent.* 820/1.

+**Card index.** An alphabetical index formed by entries on cards. Also attrib. and fig.

1849 *Rep. Comm. Patents* (1850) 344, I also claim the card index formed with the shoulder *b*, to suspend the card in the slit of the plate or false bottom *a*. **1900** *Engineering Mag.* XIX. 767 Those who desire to clip the items for card-index purposes. **1911** H. S. HARRISON *Queed* vi. 67 She had touched the spring of the automatic card-index system, known as his memory. **1918** M. B. OWEN *Typewriting Speed* 120 In this the filing is done by numerals and you have the safeguard of a card index to make the filing more secure.

Carding machine. A machine provided with cylinders set with cards for combing wool or cotton. {1830–; carding engine, 1776}

1788 *Salem Mercury* 25 Nov., A Providence paper informs, that the Carding and Spinning Machines used in England in manufacturing cotton stuffs, are introducing into that town by some publick spirited gentlemen. **1817** PAULDING *Lett. from South* II. 121 A younger [daughter] ... was tending a carding-machine in a little shed near the house. **1845** C. M. KIRKLAND *Western Clearings* 195 He paced the bank of the noisy little 'privilege' that turned the grist-mill, the carding machine and the trip hammer. **1874** KNIGHT 470 The first carding-machines built in America were made for Mr. Orr, of East Bridgewater, Mass., in 1786. **1880** *Harper's Mag.* Nov. 862/2 The carding-machine is gone, and has given place to a rustic cider-press.

Carding mill. A mill for carding wool, cotton, etc. — **1816** U. BROWN *Journ.* I. 273 He has a Merchant Mill, a Saw Mill, a Carding Mill all on the Waters of Bath. **1823** *New Eng. Farmer* II. 103 The Grist, Chocolate, and Carding Mills, of Major Foster, at Danvers, were unfortunately consumed by fire. **1880** *Harper's Mag.* Nov. 861 Here we are, on the road to that carding mill.

***Cardmaker.** [CARD *n.*[1] 1.] One who makes cards.
1649 *Suffolk Deeds* I. 111 Francis Smith of Boston Cardmaker. **1708** *Boston News-Letter* 5–12 Jan. 2/2 A Good large striking Watch to be Seen and Sold at Mr. Adam Baeth, Cardmaker, his House. **1789** *Boston Directory*, Grubb William, card-maker. **1812** *Niles' Reg.* I. 390/2 The art of making emery . . . has been discovered by Pliny Earle and Brothers, card makers. **1851** CIST *Cincinnati* 49 Occupations [include] . . . card maker, 1 [person].

Card manufactory. A factory for making cards. — **1789** WASHINGTON *Diaries* IV. 38, I went to the Card Manufactory, where I was informed . . . all kinds of Cards are made. **1837** *S. Lit. Messenger* III. 688 Some enterprising Yankee had a card manufactory worked by the river.

Card manufacturer. A cardmaker. — **1796** *Boston Directory* 277 Richards, Mark, card manufacturer.

Card party. A social gathering for the purpose of playing cards. {1777–}
1796 A. BARTON *Disappointment* II. i, Remember the many hours we . . . have passed together . . . in visiting, in card-parties. **1839** *S. Lit. Messenger* V. 140/1 But another card party, among whom no bets occurred, excited my attention. **1894** P. L. FORD *P. Stirling* 379 She told Peter the first evening that she was going to a card-party. **1912** W. IRWIN *Red Button* 108 Also, he makes the Welsh rabbits with which, at her suggestion, they finish off the card-parties.

Card plate. A plate for holding calling cards. — **1875** STOWE *We & Our Neighbors* 60, 'I see you have cards there for Mrs. Wat Sydney's receptions this winter,' said Aunt Maria, turning her attention to the card plate.

***Card playing.** The playing at games of cards.
1687 JEWALL *Diary* I. 169 Mr. Mather . . . speaks sharply against Health-drinking, Card-playing, Drunkenness. **1717** in Quincy *Hist. Harvard* (1840) I. 443 He had been before publicly admonished for card-playing. **1770** R. HALE in *Biogr. N. Hale* 148 Shun all vice especially card Playing. **1803** *Lit. Mag.* (Phila.) Dec. 171 Hamburgh, or Carter's-town [Pa.] . . . seems to carry on a brisk trade in card-playing and horse-racing. **1890** HARTE *Waif of Plains* 84 To precocious habits of drinking, smoking, chewing, and card-playing this overgrown youth added a strong tendency to exaggeration of statement.
attrib. **1839** *S. Lit. Messenger* V. 140/2 The frequent pronunciation of the . . . terms of the card playing vocabulary, kept me awake.

Card press. A small press for printing cards. — **1851** CIST *Cincinnati* 232 This establishment has also just completed a new and improved card press.

Card rack.
1. A receptacle or container for holding cards, especially calling cards. {1826–}
1790 *Penna. Packet* 11 Dec. 3/2 Imported . . . by William Poyntell, . . . Card racks or containers. **1841** A. BACHE *Fire-Screen* 169 To these were now added . . . a pair of tarnished card-racks, a few soiled pencil drawings, and myself. **1850** JUDD *R. Edney* ii. 25 Above it was suspended a shell card-rack.
‖**2.** Formerly, a box, container, etc., for letters and messages, put up in a coffeehouse or other public place.
1871 *Harper's Mag.* Oct. 646 There was kept up the 'card-rack,' sticking full of letters and business notices.
+**3.** 'A small shelf or case on the outside of a freight-car, used to hold the shipping directions' (*Cent.*).

+**Card receiver.** A card tray. — **1861** *Vanity Fair* 16 March 129/1 She undertook this morning to wash my Sèvres card receiver and vases. **1868** *Mich. Agric. Rep.* VII. 355 [An] exhibition of silver or plated ware, 1 silver soup ladle, and 1 silver filligree card receiver. **1875** STOWE *We & Our Neighbors* ii. 27 My card-receiver is full of most fashionable names. **c1903** *Sears, Roebuck & Co. Cat. No. 113* 98 Card Receiver, very fancy.

Car driver. One who drives a car. — **1865** *Atlantic Mo.* XV. 82/2 She licenses twenty-two hundred car- and omnibus-drivers to . . . carry them over twenty-nine different stage-routes and horse-rail-roads. **1876** *Scribner's Mo.* Apr. 911/2 There were addresses . . . relating to the . . . car-driver.

Cardroom. A room in which card playing is carried on. {1876}
1802 MRS. E. S. BOWNE *Life* 93 At one we left dancing and went to the card-room. **1835** LONGSTREET *Georgia Scenes* 129 This would be a great improvement . . . could the married men only *manage* to keep out of the card-room. **1874** PINKERTON *Expressman & Detective* 33 McGibony . . . passed with him into the card-room at Patterson's. **1887** C. B. GEORGE *40 Years on Rail* xi. 223 President Vanderbilt's private car . . . contains a state room, card-room, sitting and dining-room. **1905** N. DAVIS *Northerner* 210 In the . . . card-rooms, every head was turned toward the little group of four.

+**Cardsharp.** {Cf. *sharp*, 1797–} A cardsharper. — **1884** HARTE *On the Frontier* 273 We ain't takin' this step to make a card sharp out of him. **1904** *Phila. Ev. Telegraph* 1 Aug. 8 A professional card sharp. **1909** R. A. WASON *Happy Hawkins* 336 You sneakin' card sharp.

Card table. A table at which cards are played. {1713–}
1767 (*title* in H. M. Brooks *Gleanings* 2), An Address to Persons of Fashion, concerning frequenting of Plays, Balls, Assemblies, Card-Tables, &c. **1839** *S. Lit. Messenger* V. 140/1 A party at a card table played a few games for money. **1891** WILKINS *New Eng. Nun* 140 The entry was small and square and unfurnished, except for a well-rubbed old card-table against the back wall.
transf. **1843** N. BOONE *Journal* (1917) App., On our left were a singular range of ridges, called by Capt. Boone the Devil's Card Table.

***Career.** ‖*To make the career*, to make a success, become famous. — **1888** *Detroit Free Press* (F.), Minnie Palmer has made the career rapidly. She is now both rich and famous, and not a line of her early beauty has been obliterated.

Carefree, *a.* Cheerful; happy; free from care. {1919–} — **1854** B. TAYLOR *Life & Landsc. Egypt* vii. 96 As happy and care-free as two Adams in a Paradise without Eves. **1880** 'MARK TWAIN' *Tramp Abroad* xxvii. 275, I was interrupted by a young and care-free voice. **1901** *Scribner's Mag.* XXIX. 426/2 Snatches of strange song fell from him . . . expressing his care-free mood.

+**Careless,** *n.* Any one of several plants of the genus *Amaranthus.* Also attrib. — **1843** J. S. WILLIAMS *Amer. Pioneer* II. 451 Grass, careless, lambs-quarter, and Spanish needles were reserved to pester the better prepared farmer. **1883** SMITH *Geol. Survey Ala.* 295 As weeds . . . the following are common: . . . *Amarantus spinosus* (careless weeds).

+**Carette.** 'A street-car consisting essentially of the body of an ordinary street-car mounted on wooden spoke-wheels, with crank-axles. It is low, runs easily, and does not require rails' (*Cent.* '09). — **1896** *Columbus* (O.) *Dispatch* 1 July 9/5 The carette rumbling on its way to the north side was half-filled. **1899** A. THOMAS *Arizona* 24 Bonita prances comically up to the carette.

+**Carey's sedge.** *local.* A variety of sedge grass. — **1843** TORREY *Flora N.Y.* II. 409 *Carex Careyana.* . . . Carey's Sedge. . . . Shady dry woods, Auburn (*J. Carey, Esq.*) . . . This handsome species has been found also in Ohio.

***Carf.** The place at which a tree is cut. — **1636** *Dedham Records* (1892) III. 25 Yf any man henceforth from this day shall fell any Tree of sixe inches thicknes in the Carfe. **1897** HOWELLS *Landlord Lion's Head* vii. 31 He lifted his axe, and struck it into the carf on the tree.

+**Carfare.** The sum paid for riding on a streetcar or similar conveyance.
1870 'F. FERN' *Ginger-Snaps* 182 What troubles me most is, whether I am to pay six cents for car-fare and ten cents for omnibus, or six cents for car and five for omnibus. **1883** C. F. WILDER *Sister Ridnour* 110, I paid Evangeline's car-fare. **1891** RYAN *Pagan* 59, I am not sure I have quite money enough left to pay car-fare in any direction. **1904** STRATTON-PORTER *Freckles* 67 One of the superintendents gave me car-fare. **1925** *Scribner's Mag.* July 96/2 Your only chance for car-fare out of town.

+**Car ferry.** A boat used for transporting railroad cars across rivers, lakes, etc. Also attrib. — **1880** H. HALL *Census of 1880* VIII. 221 Side-wheel car-ferry Transport, iron, of 1,595 tons and 2,000 nominal horse-power . . . with three railroad tracks on deck. **1911** *Chicago Daily News Almanac* 345/2 The Pere Marquette car ferry steamer No. 18 . . . sank in Lake Michigan. . . . Thirty-three persons were rescued by car ferry No. 17. **1914** *Ib.* 140/2 The largest car ferry in the world is the Contra Costa, built in 1913 for the Southern Pacific railroad.

Carga. *S.W.* [Sp.] A load or weight varying according to locality, but usu. consisting of 300 lbs. avoirdupois. {1622–1753} — **1844** GREGG *Commerce of Prairies* I. 181 The *carga*, if a single package, is laid across the mule's back. **1854** BARTLETT *Personal Narrative* II. xxiv. 63 The weighing is also necessary; as the company pays so much a carga for bringing it . . . to the surface. **1876** RAYMOND *8th Rep. Mines* (1877) 7 A carga is a Mexican load of cleaned ore, ready for the furnaces, weighing 300 pounds avoirdupois.

+**Cargador(e).** *W.* [Sp., freighter, loader, etc.]
1. A porter or carrier.
1844 GREGG *Commerce of Prairies* II. 103 The *cargadores* who were carrying my packages were no doubt as much frightened as myself. **1844** G. W. KENDALL *Santa Fé Exped.* II. xix. 362 Cargadores, with their leather trousers rolled up. **1849** T. T. JOHNSON *Sights Gold Region* viii. 73 This would often bring a poor lean little horse upon his knees, or induce a cargodore after a violent jabbering to consider his pilgrimage over.
2. (See quotations.)
c1893 *Dialect Notes* I. 245 *Cargador*, the man in charge of the packs, in a pack train. **1923** J. H. COOK *On Old Frontier* 153 One of these was Arthur Sparhawk, an expert cargador or mule-packer.

Cargo, *n.*
1. The freight of a ship or other vessel; a shipload or boatload. {1657–}
a1649 WINTHROP *Hist.* II. 252 His ship and cargo [were] bound over to the said Keyser his mate. **1704** *Boston News-Letter* 12 June 1/1 'Tis hoped her Cargo will be saved. **1765** *Rhode Isl. Commerce* I. 134 A Cargoe of Flour, Bread, and some Barr Iron. **1808** *Austin Papers* (1924) I. 148, I have inclosed to you a Bill of loading for a cargo of shott and Lead. **1846** *Niles' Reg.* 14 March 32/3 The barque Elizabeth Hall was cleared at this port on Thursday . . . with a cargo of 3,350 bbls. flour. **1880** CABLE *Grandissimes* xxvi. 199 Just abreast of them lay a 'flat-boat,' emptied of its cargo and moored to the levee.
2. A load or burden. {1714–1845}
1827 *Boston Advertiser* 5 Feb. 2/4 Twenty large American sleighs, with what they call cargoes, will return. . . . The cargoes will consist of fresh fish. **1849** AUDUBON *Western Journal* (1906) 85 We met some French traders with a long train of mules and their 'cargoes.' **1900** DRANNAN

Plains & Mts. 301 Before supper I went to our cargo and got three rings and three strings of beads.

+3. =CARGA.

1849 AUDUBON *Western Journal* (1906) 108 Here we bought . . . abundance of corn for two dollars and fifty cents per cargo (six bushels).

4. Attrib. and comb. with *beef, can, mule, port,* etc.

1792 Roosevelt *Amer. Backlogs* (1928) 50 Michael Turner . . . was then separated from the crew for having broke open & stole Gin out of the Cargo Cans. **1800** *Columbian Centinel* 22 Jan. 1/2 Let all common Ox and Cow Beef . . . be packed and branded 'Cargo Beef.' **1875** 'MARK TWAIN' *Life on Miss.* vi, I was carrying about as many short answers as my cargo-room would admit of. **1891** *Century Mag.* April 930, I set out, keeping all the while a sharp eye on my muleteers and the cargo mule. **1901** *N. Amer. Rev.* Feb. 289 The subsidies will chiefly accrue to cargo-carrying ships. **1911** L. J. VANCE *Cynthia* 299 She saw the head and shoulders of her guide . . . visible through an open cargo port.

+Cargo, *v. tr.* To load or supply with a cargo. Also fig. — **1892** *Congress. Rec.* 18 March 2188/1 Pelts and pelfries, and anything else the teamster may be cargoed with. **1909** WASON *Happy Hawkins* 253 He slouched into the office purty consid'able cargoed up with conflictin' emotions.

+Car hook. An iron hook used by the driver of a horsecar. 'The hook with which the whiffle-trees are let up and down by the driver' (1871 *N.Y. Tribune* 23 May). Also attrib. — **1873** *N.Y. Tribune* 29 Jan. 1/2 The last duty of the courts with regard to the car-hook murderer, Wm. Foster, was performed on Friday. **1876** *Congress. Rec.* 5 Aug. 5209/1 Is it fair to charge crime upon the whole people of N.Y.: of the Nathan murder or the car-hook murder? **1876** 'MARK TWAIN' & WARNER *Gilded Age* liv. 489 The indictment . . . charged Laura Hawkins . . . with killing him with a slung-shot, a bludgeon, carving knife, . . . car hook, dagger [etc.].

+Carhouse. A train shed.

1839 *Boston Almanac* 72 From the Car House in Boston to the Car House in Salem. *Ib.*, The proposed Car House in Newburyport. **1850** *Knickerb.* XXXVI. 290 Two minutes more, involving . . . a rumbling into the car-house, and we are passing along the pleasant streets. **1852** *Harper's Mag.* V. 393/1 It was in the immense car-house, or dépôt, at Syracuse. **1872** HUNTINGTON *Road-Master's Assistant* 32 Notice the kegs and barrels full of bent and broken spikes . . . around every car-house, shop or depot.

+Caribou. Also **caribo, carraboo, carriboo,** etc. [F., from Algonquian source.] The native North American reindeer. (Cf. BUCCAREBOU.)

[**1610** in *Jesuit Relations & Allied Doc.* I. 82 Ilz pechent les Castors, dont ilz vivēt, & d'autres chasse, comme Ellans, Caribous, Cerfs, [etc.].] **1672** JOSSELYN *New Eng. Rarities* 20 The *Maccarib, Caribo,* or *Pohano,* a kind of Deer, as big as a Stag. **1778** CARVER *Travels* 110 Buffaloes, carraboo, and moose deer, are numerous in these parts. **1838** *Knickerb.* XII. 293 Carriboo and dun-deer bound across our way, with startling sound. **1848** THOREAU *Maine Woods* 81 Such is the home of the moose, the bear, the caribou, . . . and the Indian. **1888** ROOSEVELT in *Century Mag.* XXXVI. 202/2 There are many kinds of game to be found in the least known . . . parts of this wooded mountain wilderness—caribou, elk, ungainly moose. **1896** *Harper's Mag.* April 729/1 No sign of life, no vegetation, save . . . the gray moss and lichens upon which the musk-ox and caribou feed.

pl. **1703** tr. *La Hontan's Voy. N. Amer.* I. 59 Harts and Caribous are kill'd both in Summer and Winter. **1744** A. DOBBS *Hudson's Bay* 19 They have . . . a kind of Deer they call *Cariboux* (Rain-Deer). **1778** CARVER *Travels* 72, I observed here many deer and carraboes, some elk, [etc.]. **1832** R. COX *Adv. Columbia R.* xviii. 193 We have no buffalo or deer, except the *cariboux* (reindeer); and not many even of those.

attrib. **1779** *Essex Inst. Coll.* XLIX. 112 Sold . . . 82 caribou skins, at £6.10. 0. **1895** *Outing* XXVII. 218/1 Here we found the caribou roads at least six inches deep, and evidently used daily to and from water. **1902** WHITE *Conjuror's House* viii. 94 She felt . . . the hunger that yet could not stomach . . . the hairy, black caribou meat.

+Caribou shanks. *pl.* (See quot. 1888.) — **1887** *Harper's Mag.* Feb. 458/2 The hunter . . . covers his feet with . . . a pair of moose or caribou shanks, with the hair outside. **1888** *Ib.* Sept. 510/2 The skin from the hind legs of some caribou . . . worn with the hair outside, are 'caribou shanks.'

Cariole, Carriole. [Fr. *carriole.*] Cf. CARRYALL.

1. A light vehicle drawn usually by one horse. {1834–}

1767 *Boston Gazette* 9 Feb., John Malcom . . . was going from Town to his Country-House in a Cariole. **1770** *Carroll P.* in *Md. Hist. Mag.* XIII. 55 Nothing is done to y[ou]r Carriele, because the wheelright is more usefully employed. **1812** HENRY *Camp. Quebec* 98 [The landholder] shall with his horses and cariole, retrace the road. **1833** E. T. COKE *Subaltern's Furlough* xvii, We saw several of them with their squaws riding to town on horseback, and in the common American carriole, or carry all. **1868** HAWTHORNE *Note-Books* II. 36 The last I saw of her was her vivacious face peeping through the curtain of the cariole. **1871** *Scribner's Mo.* II. 458 The light cariole carries pleasant parties.

+2. A light sleigh, frequently drawn by dogs.

1806–8 PIKE *Sources Miss.* 71 He presented me with his dogs and cariole, valued in this country at two hundred dollars. **1809** H. HENRY *Travels* 9, I discerned a *cariole,* or sledge, moving our way. **1835** HOFFMAN *Winter in West* I. 203 A muffled-up Frenchman, driving furiously in his cariole on the river.

attrib. **1835** HOFFMAN *Winter in West* I. 102 Their highest ambition is to turn out the fastest trotting pony when the carriole races commence on the ice at mid-winter.

+Carioling, *vbl. n.* Riding in a cariole or sleigh. {1884} — **1806** T. ASHE *Travels in A.* 30 In winter, carioling or sleying predominates.

+Carlicue, Carlacue. [Variant of CURLICUE.] (See quot. 1848.) — **1840** C. F. HOFFMAN *Greyslaer* II. 27, I soon saw, by the way in which the white man's track doubled and doubled again . . . that the fellow could not be cutting such carlicues for nothing. **1848** BARTLETT 394 *Carlacue,* a caper; a boyish trick. 'To cut up carlacues,' is a common expression, equivalent to 'cutting up didoes.' Used in New York. *c***1850** Dow *Serm.* III. 48 (B.), It is generally supposed that nature is perfect in all her works,—except when she gets odd freaks in her head, and cuts up carlicues by way of experiment.

+Car line. A line of railroad over which cars, especially streetcars, are operated.

1890 H. Palmer *Stories Base Ball Field* 222 Cincinnati, Hamilton & Dayton R.R. [is] . . . the favorite Through Car Line Cincinnati to St. Louis. **1901** CHURCHILL *Crisis* 335 They started to walk toward the car line. **1911** H. S. HARRISON *Queed* xvii. 200 The schedules of even electric car-lines are inexorable.

b. A company operating such a line.

1894 P. L. FORD *P. Stirling* 365 All the car lines took off their cars.

+Carload.

1. A load for a car, esp. a freight car. Also attrib.

1854 THOREAU *Walden* 130 This car-load of torn sails is more legible and interesting now than if they should be wrought into paper and printed books. **1867–8** *Ill. Agric. Soc. Trans.* VII. 446 A farmer had far better send into market one car-load of good, well-matured cattle. **1887** *Nation* 29 Dec. 516/1 Several car-loads of flour had been consigned to the Philadelphia Grain Elevator Company. **1903** E. JOHNSON *Railway Transportation* 114 The majority of commodities is placed in a different class when shipped in car-load quantities than when offered to the railroad in less than car-load lots. **1917** SINCLAIR *King Coal* 96 He had taken out over forty car-loads of rock.

b. As a unit of measurement or weight: (see quots.).

1875 *Chicago Tribune* 16 Sept. 8/7 Nominally a car-load is 20,000 pounds. **1889** *Cent.* 826/1 *Car-load,* . . . a customary unit of measure in the United States, equal to 70 barrels of salt, 90 barrels of flour, 9,000 feet of boards, 340 bushels of wheat, 430 bushels of potatoes, etc. **1893** *Stand.* 287/2 [A] car-load . . . varies on different railroads . . . , and . . . also with different substances.

2. *fig.* Enough to fill a car; a large number or quantity; a great deal.

1882 SWEET & KNOX *Texas Siftings* 16 It is estimated that one first-class conductor has more sense than a car-load of legislators. **1885** *Outing* VII. 152/1 Yo'll hab jes' a cah-load ob fun. **1902** HARBEN *Abner Daniel* 57 No parental objection, everything smooth, and a car-load of silverware. **1915** D. R. CAMPBELL *Proving Virginia* 132 She could learn a whole carload from her!

***Carman.**

***1.** The driver of a car or cart; a carter.

1686 *Ann. Albany* (1850) II. 94 No carman or other person shall henceforth . . . digg any sand on the north side of the Shennechtady path. **1760** *N.J. Archives* XX. 442 Tuesday last was given to a Negro, by a Carman, . . . a Letter. **1790** *Broadside Verse* (1930) 211/1 A carman with a load of wood draws nigh. **1832** J. F. WATSON *Hist. Tales N.Y.* 84 All the carmen of the city . . . are ordered to be enrolled, and to draw for 6d. an ordinary load. **1857** T. B. GUNN *N.Y. Boarding-Houses* 264 On pushing your way through the crowd of immigrants, 'runners,' carmen, 'dock-loafers,' and blackguards generally. **1873** BAILEY *Life in Danbury* 126 One of our carmen who stables his horse in an up-town barn, was at the place Sunday. **1877** WM. WRIGHT *Big Bonanza* 187 The only men in the works were the engineer and the car-man. Two miners were at work at the bottom of the shaft.

‖**2.** *Carman load,* the load carried by a car or cart.

1850 *Huntington Rec.* III. 404 Resolved that six cents a carman load be hereafter charged for sand sold on Eaton's Neck Beach.

‖**Car mate.** A fellow passenger on a car. — **1898** *N.Y. Journal* 29 June 14/1 My car mate . . . answered, in every detail of dress and manner, to this conception of the mysterious woman arail.

***Carnation.**[1]

***1.** Some variety of the clove pink, *Dianthus caryophyllus.*

1682 ASH *Carolina* 13 Their [planters'] Gardens also begin to be beautified and adorned with . . . the Rose, Tulip, Carnation and Lilly, &c. **1836** LINCOLN *Botany* App. 93 *Dianthus caryophyllus,* (carnation or pink). **1916** WILSON *Red Gap* 277 He picked all my pink carnations to make a mat on the table.

2. *Carnation pink,* =sense 1.

1818 *Jrnl. Science* I. 370 June 21. Carnation pink . . . in flower.

b. The color of this flower.

1844 *Knickerb.* XXIII. 23 At this [she] looked a carnation pink, and commenced fanning herself violently.

Carnation.[2] Usu. attrib. Pertaining to or denoting a variety of cherry. {1664–}

1760 WASHINGTON *Diaries* I. 145 Grafted 40 Cherrys . . . 10 Carnation Cherry. The Carnation finishing the Row. **1786** *Ib.* III. 25 Three trees are from Stratford, given to me by Colo. Henry Lee, . . . the 3d the Carnation cherry. **1859** ELLIOTT *Western Fruit Bk.* 207 Carnation . . . [is] a variety of the Morello, that from its hardiness has been pretty largely disseminated through our Western and Southwestern States. **1867–8** *Ill. Agric. Soc. Trans.* VII. 509 The Carnation Morello has failed with me.

***Carob tree.** An evergreen tree (*Ceratonia siliqua*) introduced from the East. — **1846** BROWNE *Trees Amer.* 211 The Carob-tree, (*Ceratonia siliqua,*) which is generally considered as the locust-tree mentioned in the Bible. **1855** — in *Trans. Amer. Inst. N.Y.* 622 The Carob Tree, or St. John's Bread . . . is unquestionably of eastern origin. . . . The seeds were procured for the office from Alicante, in Spain.

Carolina. [From *Carol-us,* =Charles II.]

'We . . . do . . . ordain the same into a Province, and call it the Province of Carolina' (*First Carolina Charter,* 1663, clause 5).

1. *pl.* An inclusive term for North and South Carolina.

1809 FRENEAU *Poems* II. 205 *n.*, A shrub leaf very commonly used in the Carolinas, as a substitute for tea. **1835** SIMMS *Yemassee* II. 27 Did it include the Indian nations generally—twenty-eight of which, at that time, occupied the Carolinas? **1840** EMMONS *Mass. Quadrupeds* 44 The Mink . . . ranges from the Carolinas to 69° North latitude. **1893** POST *Harvard Stories* 15 If the governors of the Carolinas had been with them, those celebrated dignitaries, I suspect, would have experienced none of their proverbial trouble.

2. *attrib.* **a.** Of, from, or pertaining to these states.

1741 *S.C. Hist. Soc. Coll.* IV. 44 A violent Shower of Rain fell, and . . . the Carolina Arms in particular, being exposed, were rendered unfit for action. **1846** *Georgia Messenger* 24 Dec., Forcing into circulation the *paper credits* of the Carolina banks. **1853** SIMMS *Sword & Distaff* 515 The month of March . . . is considered a tolerably cool one, even in a Carolina climate. **1788** FRANKLIN *Autobiog.* 428 The Carolina fleet was detain'd near three months longer. **1845** SIMMS *Wigwam & Cabin* Ser. I. 7 But you aint said, . . . who was your Carolina gineral. **1840** HALIBURTON *Clockmaker* 3 Ser. ix, Regular built bruisers too; claw your eyes right out, like a Carolina gouger. **1707** *Boston News-Letter* 31 March 2/2 A Pretty Carolina Indian Boy aged about 12 years, to be Sold. **1709** SEWALL *Diary* II. 248 Mr. Bridgham buried a Carolina Indian Man last Monday. **1707** *Boston News-Letter* 15 Sept. 2/2 Ran-away from her Master, . . . a Tall Lusty Carolina Indian Woman named Sarah. **1780** *N.J. Archives* 2 Ser. IV. 635 The subscriber . . . has on hand Carolina indigo in tierces and barrels, and by retail. **1705** *Boston News-Letter* 12 March 2/2 The New-York man . . . is gone with her, and his own Vessel in Company of the Carolina Privateer. **1907** F. W. Hodge *Handb. Amer. Indians* I. 150/1 Black drink ('Carolina tea' Catawba yaupon).

b. In the names of (*a*) plants, trees, (*b*) animals, birds, etc.

(*a*) **1785** MARSHALL *Amer. Grove* 50 *Fraxinus americana.* Carolina or Red Ash. **1843** TORREY *Flora N.Y.* II. 513 *Azolla Caroliniana.* . . . Carolina Azolla. . . . In slowly flowing waters, island of New-York. **1829** EATON *Botany* (ed. 5) 326 *Phaseolus lunatus,* Carolina bean, lima bean. **1861** WOOD *Botany* 495 Carolina Beech-drops, . . . *Schweinitzia odorata,* Ell. [grows in] rich shady soils, Md. to N.Car. **1901** MOHR *Plant Life Ala.* 46 Carolina black gum (*Nyssa biflora*). **1813** H. MUHLENBERG *Cat. Plants* 18 Carolina boxthorn (red berry). **1745** FRANKLIN *Writings* II. 286 It is a siphon made of two large joints of Carolina cane. **1789** BENTLEY *Diary* I. 115 Letters from W. Mason with Gazettes, & specimens of Carolina cotton. **1870** *Rep. Comm. Agric. 1869* 181 Spiry topped and conical forms are seen in the larches, Carolina cypress, Lombardy and other poplars. **1762** CLAYTON *Flora Virginica* 17 Carolina globe tree. **1792** IMLAY *Western Territory* 212 The Carolina ground-nut grows low down on the Mississippi. **1905** *Bureau Forestry Bul. No. 60* 16 The typical trees are red spruce, Fraser fir, and Carolina hemlock. **1813** H. MUHLENBERG *Cat. Plants* 25 Clustered cyrilla or Carolina Ironwood. **1795** WINTERBOTHAM *Hist. View* III. 391 Carolina iron-wood tree. **1821** NUTTALL *Trav. Arkansa* 65, I found it to be the plant which I have called *Wisteria speciosa* . . . the Carolina kidney-bean tree. **1842** *Nat. Hist. N.Y., Zoology* IV. 114 The Carolina Lichia, *Lichia carolina,* . . . is exceedingly rare on this coast. **1810** J. LAMBERT *Travels thro' U.S.* III. 9 The Carolina live oak is interspersed among the pines in different parts of the country. **1835** INGRAHAM *South-West* II. 16 The long black moss, well known at the north as the 'Carolina moss,' hangs in immense fringes. **1821** W. P. C. BARTON *Flora N. Amer.* I. 86 *Solanum Carolinense.* Carolina Nightshade. Horse-nettle. **1901** MOHR *Plant Life Ala.* 603 *Ilex caroliniana.* . . . Carolina Privet. . . . North Carolina to Florida, west to Louisiana. **1795** WINTERBOTHAM *Hist. View* III. 391 Carolina red-bud. **1775** ROMANS *Nat. Hist. Florida* 19 Carolina red oak, prickly when young. **1787** JEFFERSON *Writings* VI. 194 The objection to the Carolina rice then, being, that it crumbles in certain forms of preparation. **1901** MOHR *Plant Life Ala.* 89 The Carolina silverbell tree (*Mohrodendron* (*Halesia*) *carolinum*) also makes its appearance here. **1832** HALE *Flora* 174 Carolina Syringa, *Philadelphus inodorus.* . . . This species of the mock Orange is native of the Southern States. **1815** *Mass. H. S. Coll.* 2 Ser. IV. 270 A fine specimen of the Carolina walnut tree of delicate foliage may be noticed opposite this house. **1843** TORREY *Flora N.Y.* I. 62 *Draba Caroliniana* . . . Carolina Whitlow-grass. . . . Sandy fields on the island of New York.

ellipt. **1870** *Rep. Comm. Agric. 1869* 184 Summer Apples. . . . Aromatic Carolina. Origin, South Carolina; fruit, full medium size.

(*b*) [**1774** GOLDSM. *Hist. Earth* (1822) III. 143 The Carolina black squirrel. **1815** STEPHENS in Shaw *Gen. Zool.* IX. I. 93 Carolina Cuckow.] **1859** BAIRD *Catal. N. Amer. Birds* 709 Carolina grebe. **1743** CATESBY *Carolina* II. 86 The largest Carolina Moth . . . is a native of Carolina, and other provinces more north. **1874** COUES *Birds N.W.* 296 *Conurus Carolinensis,* . . . Carolina Parroquet. **1842** *Nat. Hist. N.Y., Zoology* I. 21 The Carolina Shrew. *Sorex Carolinensis.* **1879** *Scribner's Mo.* July 396/1 The larva of the Carolina sphinx. **1857** *Rep. Comm. Patents: Agric.* 59 The fox-squirrel, with the migratory and Carolina squirrels, . . . buries large quantities of nuts and acorns under the leaves in autumn. **1844** *Nat. Hist. N.Y., Zoology* II. 61 [Mr. Bell] succeeded recently in obtaining a specimen . . . which proved to be the Carolina Tit. It . . . is more shy than the Chickadee. **1839** AUDUBON *Ornith. Biog.* V. 474 Carolina Titmouse . . . reaches eastward as far as the State of New Jersey. **1835** SIMMS *Yemassee* II. 170 The Carolina whippoorwill, broke fitfully upon the silence, to which it gave an added solemnity. *c***1733** CATESBY *Carolina* II. 12 *Alburnus Americanus.* The Carolina Whiting. . . . The market at Charles-town in Carolina is plentifully supplied with these Fish. [**1815** STEPHENS in Shaw *Gen. Zool.* IX. I. 182 Carolina Woodpecker.]

+**Carolina allspice.** The strawberry shrub, *Euonymus americanus.* — **1789** *Amer. Philos. Soc.* III. p. xxi, The barks of young Sassafras, and of *Calycanthus Floridus* . . . called Carolina allspice much resemble cinnamon. **1832** S. J. HALE *Flora* 30 Carolina Allspice . . . [has] flowers at first dark brown, . . . changing entirely to olive green, scented like ripe apples. **1839** AUDUBON *Ornith. Biog.* V. 44 The plant represented [in the plate] . . . , the Carolina alespice [*sic*], . . . abounds in the Southern States. **1847** DARLINGTON *Weeds & Plants* (1860) 135 *Calycanthus.* . . . Carolina-allspice. Sweet-scented Shrub. Strawberry-bush. **1889** *Cent.* 773/1.

+**Carolina bat.** A native American bat, *Vespertilio carolinensis.* — **1823** JAMES *Exped. Rocky Mts.* I. 261 *Vespertilio Carolinus,* Carolina bat. **1826** GODMAN *Nat. Hist.* I. 67 Carolina Bat . . . is a native of Carolina, where it is found in the vicinity of Charleston. **1842** *Nat. Hist. N.Y., Zoology* I. 10 The Carolina Bat is found along the Atlantic States from Georgia to Connecticut.

+**Carolina buckthorn.** An American shrub of the genus *Rhamnus.* — **1813** H. MUHLENBERG *Cat. Plants* 24 *Rhamnus Carolinianus,* Carolina Buckthorn. **1860** Hale *Woods & Timbers N.C.* 150 Carolina buckthorn (*Frangula Caroliniana*) A thornless shrub . . . the berry is blackish, of the size of a small pea. **1901** MOHR *Plant Life Ala.* 133 The lime-loving Carolina buckthorn.

+**Carolina dove.** The mourning dove. — **1874** COUES *Birds N.W.* 389 *Zenædura Carolinensis,* . . . Carolina Dove; Common Dove. **1883** *Century Mag.* Sept. 653/2 The Carolina or turtle-dove is common on the Cape. **1894** B. TORREY *Fla. Sketch-Book* 147 Herons in the usual variety were present, with ospreys, an eagle, kingfishers, ground doves, Carolina doves, [etc.].

+**Carolina jasmine.** =next. — **1890** *Cent.* 2478/3 The plant . . . known in the United States as the wild, yellow, or Carolina jasmine.

+**Carolina jessamine.** The yellow jessamine. — **1831** AUDUBON *Ornith. Biog.* I. 114 It [Florida jessamine] is also named *Carolina Jessamine* and *Yellow Jessamine.* **1866** *Land We Love* (Charlotte, N.C.) May 80 Carolina Jessamine (*Gelsemium sempervirens*). **1883** HALE *Woods & Timbers N.C.* 190 Carolina jessamine. . . . Most of the plant, especially the root, taken internally, is narcotic and poisonous.

+**Carolina laurel.** *S.* **1.** The red bay, *Persea* (*Laurus*) *carolinensis.* **2.** The cherry laurel or wild orange, *Prunus caroliniana.* — (1) **1846** BROWNE *Trees Amer.* 415 *Laurus carolinensis,* the Carolina Laurel, . . . rarely exhibits a regular form. **1858** WARDER *Hedges & Evergreens* 279 The *L. carolinensis,* or Carolina Laurel, is a native evergreen, found from Virginia to Louisiana. (2) **1852** *Horticulturist* VII. 52 The Wild Orange or Carolina Laurel . . . should be called the Carolina laurel—as it has no affinity with the orange.

+**Carolina parrot.** The Carolina parakeet, a native American parrot. — **1811** WILSON *Ornith.* III. 97 The Carolina, or Illinois Parrot (for it has been described under both these appellations) is thirteen inches long. **1828** BONAPARTE *Synopsis* 41 The Carolina Parrot. *Psittacus carolinensis.* **1857** *Rep. Comm. Agric. 1856* 147 The Carolina parrot, or parrakeet, is . . . exceedingly annoying to the farmers.

+**Carolina pigeon.** =CAROLINA DOVE, q.v. — **1812** WILSON *Ornith.* V. 91 Carolina Pigeon, or Turtle Dove: *Columba Carolinensis.* **1828** BONAPARTE *Synopsis* 119 The Carolina Pigeon. . . . Inhabits the United states during summer; common; wintering chiefly in the southern states.

+**Carolina pink.** The American wormroot, an herb of the genus *Spigelia.*

1789 *Amer. Philos. Soc.* III. p. xviii, Carolina pink; a southern plant: it will destroy the worms; but caution in the dose is requisite. **1820** *Pharmacopoeia of U.S.* 155 Infusion of Carolina Pink. **1840** DEWEY *Mass. Flowering Plants* 150 *Spigelia Marylandica.* L. Pink Root. . . . It is a well-known vermifuge, under the name of Carolina Pink. **1859** BARTLETT 323 *Pink Root* . . . [is] remarkable for its beautiful flowers. It is also known as the Carolina Pink.

+**Carolina pinkroot.** =CAROLINA PINK. — **1779** *N.J. Archives* 2 Ser. IV. 21 To be sold, . . . Carolina pink root. **1791** MUHLENBERG *Index Florae* 163 *Spigelia marilandica,* Carolina Pink-root. **1841** PARK *Pantology* 414 Among the anthelmintics, are Carolina pink root; and cowhage.

+**Carolina poplar.** The cottonwood, *Populus deltoides.* — **1860** in Hale *Woods & Timbers N.C.* 120 Carolina poplar (*Populus angulata*). . . .

The wood does not appear to be used. **1892** APGAR *Trees Northern U.S.* 169 Cottonwood. Carolina Poplar. Necklace-Poplar. . . . Common in the Mississippi valley, but found in western New England. **1905** *Bureau Forestry Bul. No. 65* 36 On bottomlands, cottonwood—the horticultural variety known as Carolina poplar—will grow most rapidly.

+**Carolina potato.** The common sweet potato. Also ellipt.

1775 ROMANS *Nat. Hist. Florida* 123 The varieties, in an ascending scale for goodness, [are] 1st. Spanish, . . . 2d. Carolina, little superior to the first. 3d. Brimstone. **1819** SCHOOLCRAFT *Mo. Lead Mines* 34 The sweet, or Carolina potatoe was raised last year in considerable perfection. **1833** J. BOARDMAN *America* 89 Two of the favourite vegetables for the table are the Carolina or sweet potato, and maize or Indian corn. **1848** LOWELL *Biglow P.* 1. ix. 138 Till I hed gut his corn an' his Carliny taters in. **1859** *Harper's Mag.* Feb. 420/1 The conversation fell upon sweet or Carolina potatoes, and their similarity of taste, when raw, to chestnuts. **1884** *Century Mag.* XXVII. 442/1 The sweet potato was adopted from the aborigines in all the Southern colonies, and it is yet known in the market as the 'Carolina.'

‖**Carolina race-horse.** *humorous.* A razor-back hog. — **1862** 'E. KIRKE' *Among Pines* 212 We call them Carolina race-horses, said the Colonel, as he finished an account of their peculiarities.

+**Carolina rail.** A variety of sora, *Porzana carolina.* — **1831** WILSON & BONAPARTE *Amer. Ornith.* III. 110 *Rallus Carolinus*, Linnaeus and Wilson,—Carolina Rail. **1869** *Amer. Naturalist* III. 231 In the marshes and low swampy islands near the coast, occur in more or less abundance the Common Sora or Carolina Rail, the Virginia Rail, [etc.]. **1874** COUES *Birds N.W.* 538 *Porzana Carolina*, . . . Carolina Rail.

+**Carolina rose.** A variety of climbing rose; the Cherokee rose. — **1802** J. DRAYTON *S. Carolina* 72 Carolina rose. (*Rosa Caroliniana.*) Grows on clayey soils, near water: and adjacent ditches. **1832** HALE *Flora* 141 Carolina Rose. . . . Flowers crimson, large. *a*1858 Warder *Hedges & Evergreens* 33 A great many shrubs and trees have been used for the formation of hedges, but none is better adapted to this purpose than the Cherokee or Carolina Rose.

+**Carolina turtledove.** The mourning dove; CAROLINA DOVE. Also *Carolina turtle.* — **1812** [see CAROLINA PIGEON]. **1831** AUDUBON *Ornith. Biog.* I. 91 The Carolina Turtle Dove. *Columba Carolinensis.* . . . The roosting places which the Carolina Turtles prefer are among the long grasses found growing in abandoned fields. **1839** PEABODY *Mass. Birds* 350 The Carolina Turtle Dove . . . is . . . called the Mourning Dove, from the plaintiveness of its call. . . . The flesh is pronounced equal to that of the woodcock. **1844** *Nat. Hist. N.Y., Zoology* II. 197 The Carolina Turtle Dove. *Ectopistes carolinensis.* **1867** *Amer. Naturalist* I. 54 Carolina Turtle Doves.

+**Carolina waxwing.** The cedar waxwing or cherry bird. — **1874** COUES *Birds N.W.* 93 *Ampelis Cedrorum*, . . . Cedar Bird; Cherry Bird; Carolina Waxwing. **1884** ROE *Nature's Story* iv, I won't speak of the Carolina wax-wing.

+**Carolina wren.** A large wren, *Thryothorus ludovicianus.*

1810 WILSON *Ornith.* II. 61 [The] Great Carolina Wren, *Certhia Caroliniana*, . . . is frequently seen, early in May, along the shores of the Delaware. **1831** AUDUBON *Ornith. Biog.* I. 399 The Great Carolina Wren. *Troglodytes Ludovicianus. Ib.*, I shall give you the history and life of the Great Carolina Wren, as studied in the State of Louisiana, where that bird is a constant resident. **1858** BAIRD *Birds Pacific R.R.* 361 Great Carolina Wren. **1872** COUES *N. Amer. Birds* 151 Its rolling notes recall those of the Carolina wren, but are stronger. **1884** *Amer. Naturalist* XVIII. 23 My Carolina wrens do not mimic.

Caroline. [f. CAROLINA.] +Occasional variant of Carolina, esp. in names of birds. — **1823** James *Exped. Rocky Mts.* I. 265 *Columba Carolinensis*—Caroline pigeon or dove. *Ib.*, *Psittacus Carolinensis*—Caroline perroquet.

+**Carolinian,** *n.* A native of North or South Carolina.

1707 J. ARCHDALE *Descr. of Carolina* 15 After a very mature Deliberation, and by the Encouragments of several Carolinians then in England my Going was concluded for. **1765** TIMBERLAKE *Mem.* 91 Ostenaco told me . . . that the Carolinians had renewed the war before they had well concluded a peace. **1775** ADAIR *Indians* 226 The eastern, or lower parts of this country, are sharp and cold to a Carolinian in winter, and yet agreeable. **1809** WEEMS *Marion* (1833) 61 This colonel Laurens . . . was a very extraordinary young Carolinian. **1845** SIMMS *Wigwam & Cabin* 1 Ser. 56 Many persons living still remember that terrible war, and how the Carolinians humbled them at last. **1889** *Century Mag.* XXXVII. 579/2 The favorite, Madge Dillon, an enthusiastic young Carolinian.

Carolinian, *a.* [f. CAROLINA.]

+**1.** Of or pertaining to North or South Carolina. See also CAROLINA 2.

1706 PENN in *Penn-Logan Corr.* (1872) II. 105 Lord Cornbury had but £600 pr. ann. . . . for salary, . . . and for Colonel Dudley, . . . they have not allowed him more, or very little, and the Carolinian Lords, not so much. **1775** ROMANS *Hist. Florida* 174 In the article of beef, cattle can hardly yield profit where the *Carolinian* or *Georgian* method of killing at two, three, and four years old obtains. **1835** SIMMS *Yemassee* II. 197 The Carolinian woodman knew enough of the savages to know that they were no opponents, generally speaking, to be feared. **1851** *S. Lit. Messenger* XVII. 26/1, I determined to try my fortune among the . . . stirring pursuits of the Carolinian gold country. **1901** MOHR *Plant Life Ala.* 89 The line of demarcation between the mountain region and this part of the Carolinian area.

2. Esp. in names of plants, trees, insects, etc.

1785 MARSHALL *Amer. Grove* 24 *Calycanthus floridus.* Carolinian Allspice. This delightful sweet-scented shrub, grows naturally in Carolina. **1810** MICHAUX *Arbres* I. 35 *Carolinian ash* (*Fraxinus platicarpa*), nom donné par moi. **1785** MARSHALL *Amer. Grove* 73 *Laurus Borbonia:* Red-stalked Carolinian Bay-Tree. *Ib.* 114 Carolinian Evergreen Bay-Tree. **1802** J. DRAYTON *S. Carolina* 70 Carolinian catchfly. (*Silene Caroliniana.*) Grows on the declivity of hills in the lower country, adjacent to swamps. **1785** MARSHALL *Amer. Grove* 71 *Juniperus caroliniana.* Red Carolinian Cedar. **1846** BROWNE *Trees Amer.* 272 *Cerasus caroliniana*, the Carolinian Cherry-tree. **1843** TORREY *Flora N.Y.* I. 120 *Geranium Carolinianum* . . . Carolinian Cranesbill. **1785** MARSHALL *Amer. Grove* 47 *Fothergilla Gardeni.* Carolinian Fothergilla. **1802** J. DRAYTON *S. Carolina* 65 Carolinian Glasswort or prickly salt wort. . . . Jerusalem oak. (*Chenopodium Anthelminticum.*) A noxious weed, growing in dry grounds. **1785** MARSHALL *Amer. Grove* 64 *Ilex Cassine.* Dahoon, or Carolinian Holly. This grows naturally in Carolina. *Ib.* 9 *Andromeda plumata.* Plumed Andromeda, or Carolinian Iron-wood Tree. . . . The flowers are produced at the extremity of the branches. *Ib.* 153 *Tilia caroliniana.* Carolinian oblique-leaved Lime-Tree. *Ib.* 8 *Andromeda nitida*, Evergreen shining-leaved Andromeda, or Carolinian Red-buds. This shrub grows naturally in Carolina and Florida. *Ib.* 80 *Lonicera caroliniana.* Carolinian scarlet Trumpet-flowered Honeysuckle. *Ib.* 22 *Callicarpa americana.* Carolinian Shrubby Callicarpa. *Ib.* 10 *Annona glabra.* Carolinian Smooth-barked Annona. **1795** WINTERBOTHAM *Hist. View* III. 392 Carolinian syrianga, . . . Sorbus tree. **1846** WOOD *Botany* 220 *V. Caroliniana.* Carolinian Vetch. **1785** MARSHALL *Amer. Grove* 164 *Vitis arborea.* Carolinian Vine, or Pepper Tree.

+**Carolinian cherry.** The Carolina laurel cherry, *Prunus caroliniana.* Also attrib. with *tree.* — **1846** BROWNE *Trees Amer.* 272 *Cerasus caroliniana*, The Carolinian Cherry-Tree. . . . The wood of the Carolinian cherry is fine-grained. **1897** SUDWORTH *Arborescent Flora* 247 *Prunus caroliniana.* . . . Common names [include] . . . Carolinian Cherry (lit.).

Carolinian poplar. =CAROLINA POPLAR. — [**1810** MICHAUX *Arbres* I. 40 *Carolinian poplar*, nom donné à cet arbre en Europe.] **1832** BROWNE *Sylva* 251 The Carolinian poplar blooms in March or April. **1859** A. L. HILLHOUSE tr. Michaux *Sylva* II. 163 In the 'North American Flora,' my father has confounded the Carolinian Poplar and the Cotton Wood.

‖**Carolinite.** A native of Carolina. — **1775** *N.C. Gazette* (Newbern) 24 March, Now it came to pass that the Carolinites of the North . . . had heard all these sayings.

Carolus doubloon. (See quotation.) — **1891** S. M. WELCH *Recoll. 1830–40* 168 The gold coins most popular in circulation [in upper New York] were the 'Carolus Doubloons,' standard value $16.

+**Carom,** *v.* [*carom*, a stroke in billiards.] *intr.* To glance, rebound. Also fig.

1860 HOLMES *Professor* iii. 88 She glanced from every human contact, and 'caromed' from one relation to another. **1869** 'MARK TWAIN' *Innocents* lxi. 645 Croquet . . . is a game where you don't pocket any balls and don't carom on any thing of any consequence. **1873** BAILEY *Life in Danbury* 187, I detected on their faces the ripple of a smile as the stage caromed on the new-formed clods. **1884** JOAQUIN MILLER *Mem. & Rime* 113 This Chinook wind . . . caroms from mountain-top to mountain-top. **1904** *N.Y. Ev. Post* 29 Oct., A well-dressed man caromed against me on his way to the elevator. **1911** MULFORD *Bar-20 Days* iv. 45 The table skidded through the door on one leg and caromed off the bar at a graceful angle.

***Carp. a.** Any one of several varieties of fish of the family *Cyprinidae.* **b.** A carp sucker.

1637 MORTON *New Canaan* 62 There are in the rivers, and ponds, very excellent Trouts, Carpes, Breames, Pikes. **1709** LAWSON *Carolina* 160 We have the same Carp as you have in England. **1772** ROMANS in Phillips *Notes* (1924) 123 Black and Red Drum, this Last miscalled in this Country the Carp. **1846** THORPE *Myst. Backwoods* 36 The carp is a fish known to all anglers. . . . In these lakes they vary in weight from five to thirty pounds. **1856** *Spirit of Times* (N.Y.) 18 Oct. 113/2 The Carp must be angled for . . . in the vicinity of banks of weeds, water-lilies, or river-grass. **1889** *Cent.* 832/2 Carp-sucker[s] . . . superficially resemble the European carp, and are sometimes called *carp;* they are also known as *buffalo-fish.*

***Carpenter.** An artisan who does the heavier or more solid kinds of woodwork.

'In New-England, a distinction is often made between the man who frames, and the man who executes the interior wood-work of a house. The framer is the *carpenter*, and the finisher is called a *joiner*. . . . In New York, the term *carpenter* includes both the framer and the joiner' (W. '28).

1622 *Va. House of Burgesses* 17 You would be pleased to send ouer some . . . Carpenters Brickmakers and Bricklayers. **1641** *Conn. Public Rec.* I. 65 Sufficient able Carpenters, Plow writs, . . . and Coopers, shall not take aboue 20d. for a dayes worke. **1709** LAWSON *Carolina* 167 All sorts of Handicrafts, as Carpenters, Joiners, . . . and most others, may . . . thrive very well in this Place. **1823** COOPER *Pioneers* xxix, One is Hiram Doolittle; a carpenter by trade, as you know. **1872** *Atlantic Mo.* Jan. 21 He saw his father patiently drilling negroes, not long from their native Africa, into carpenters, millers, wheelwrights, shoemakers, and farmers.

1902 LORIMER *Lett. Merchant* 262, I sent some carpenters over to knock together a long frame pavilion.

Carpenter bee. {1844–} +An American species of solitary bee, *Xylocopa virginica.* — **1867** *Amer. Naturalist* I. 157, I send specimens in alcohol of the pupa of *Xylocopa virginica*, the Carpenter Bee.

+Carpenter bird. The California woodpecker. — **1858** *Atlantic Mo.* Dec. 870/1 The little Hair-Bird . . . is called the 'Chipping-Sparrow,' as if he were in the habit of making chips, like the Carpenter-Bird.

+Carpenter shop. The workshop of a carpenter; a shop in which carpentry work is carried on.

1866 *Rep. Indian Affairs* 83 The carpenter shop is not sufficiently large for the repairing of large wagon beds. **1876** *Fur, Fin, & Feather* Sept. 111 Mr. Michael Gross's carpenter-shop. **1882** THAYER *From Log-Cabin* ix. 127 James' job at Treat's carpenter-shop introduced him into further business. **1898** ATHERTON *Californians* 119 The stable-boy . . . conducted Trennahan through the dairy, granary, carpenter shop, and various other outbuildings. **1909** A. C. RICE *Mr. Opp* 12 He bought a whole printin' outfit, and set it up in Pete Aker's old carpenter shop.

Carpenter's rule. A folding rule, suitable for carrying in the pocket. — **1815** *Niles' Reg.* IX. 94/2 Carpenter's rules [were manufactured]. **1864** T. L. NICHOLS *Amer. Life* I. 207 No doubt they have some way of folding themselves up like carpenters' rules.

Carpenter's shop. =CARPENTER SHOP. {1841} — **1773** J. ROWE *Diary* 238 A Fire . . . consumed . . . Mr. Calfs' Tanhouse & a Carpenter's shop. **1848** J. S. ROBINSON *Santa Fe Exped.* 14 The buildings are a blacksmith's shop, carpenter's shop, [etc.].

+Carpenter weed. *N.H.* Selfheal, or heal-all, *Prunella vulgaris.* — **1891** *Amer. Folk-Lore* IV. 148 Carpenter Weed was our only name for *Brunella vulgaris.* **1892** *Ib.* V. 102.

***Carpet.**

***1.** A thick heavy fabric used as a floor covering.

1649 *Conn. Public Rec.* I. 496, 2 small carpets, . . . a window cushion. [etc.]. **1686** *Narrag. Hist. Reg.* III. 105, 2 tables, 1 carpit, 6 chairs. **1830** J. F. WATSON *Philadelphia* 185 The rarity of carpets, now deemed so indispensable to comfort, may be judged of by the fact, that T. Matlack, Esq. now aged 95, told me he had a distinct recollection of meeting with the first carpet he had ever seen, about the year 1750. **1856** GOODRICH *Recoll.* I. 74 Carpets were then [Conn., early 19th cent.] only known in a few families, and were confined to the keeping-room and parlor. **1892** M. A. JACKSON *Memoirs* xvii. 363 All his carpets were sent to the army as covering for the suffering soldiers.

b. Attrib. and comb. with *cleaning machine, establishment, fastener, hive, lining,* etc.

1874 KNIGHT 476 *Carpet-cleaning Machine*, a brushing-machine for carpets. **1850** *Annual of Sci. Discovery* 53 Besides this large carpet-establishment, there is in this village a factory . . . for the manufacture of knit shirts. **1874** KNIGHT 477 *Carpet-fastener*, a screw-knob and screw-socket inserted in the floor with the carpet between them. **1870** *Rep. Comm. Agric. 1869* 332 The carpet hive was patented in 1868, and is composed of a skeleton frame or trellis, from which the textile covering is to be removed during warm weather. . . . As the weather grows cold the carpet is to be thrown over the trellis. **1874** KNIGHT 477 *Carpet-lining*, a material for placing beneath a carpet, to . . . decrease the wear. **1850** *Annual of Sci. Discovery* 53 Mr. James M'Kenzie of Schenectady, N.Y., has made some improvements on the carpet-loom. *Ib.* (*subtitle*), The Carpet-Manufacture in America. **1865** *Atlantic Mo.* XV. 534 The linen and carpet-mats in that house you're in now come down from the time before Washington. *Ib.* 736 She can take up carpet-nails with an iron spoon. **1866** MRS. WHITNEY *L. Goldthwaite* xvi, They had improvised a pretty bit of scenery at the back, with a few sticks, some paint, brown carpet-paper. **1889** BRAYLEY *Boston Fire Dept.* 592 He came to Boston twenty-one years ago and learned the carpet-printer's trade. **1870** O. LOGAN *Before Footlights* 195 Uncle Joe excels any gentleman of my acquaintance in the accomplishments of whitewashing and carpet shaking. **1835** HOFFMAN *Winter in West* I. 255, I was travelling with a simple furred wrapper as an overcoat and a pair of carpet socks over my boots. **1874** KNIGHT 477 *Carpet-stretcher*, a toggle-jointed frame to stretch carpets on floors preliminary to tacking down.

c. Attrib., with implication of dilettantism or shirking: **c. knight*, +a member of the State or National Guard; *c. poet*, one who does not face practical issues.

1862 in McClellan *Own Story* 281 There is a prodigious cry of 'On to Richmond!' among the carpet-knights of our city, who will not shed their blood to get there. **1880** *Harper's Mag.* May 916/2 These 'carpet knights,' as they were called, spent [days of terrible suspense] in building bridges. — **1875** EMERSON *Lett. & Social Aims* 55 None of your parlor or piano verse,—none of your carpet poets, who are content to amuse.

2. *On the carpet*, under discussion; in contemplation. {1726–1773}

1779 S. ADAMS in *Warren-Adams Lett.* II. 100 We have had on the Carpet Questions relating to our Ministers abroad. **1785** JEFFERSON *Writings* V. 216 They have on the carpet a contract for live oak from the southern States. **1845** in *Cincinnati Misc.* I. 177 When he had no work among Indians on the carpet, [Wetzel] ranged the town for a few days. **1854** KANE *Arctic Explor.* (1856) I. 215 A journey on the carpet; and the crew busy with the little details of their outfit.

+b. Under investigation; undergoing scolding or reprimanding. {Cf. *carpet* v., 1840–}

1902 LORIMER *Lett. Merchant* 134 You must . . . say that . . . the boss of the canning-room [will be] called up on the carpet and made to promise that it never will happen again. **1910** E. A. WALCOTT *Open Door* xxiii. 287 I'm here and he's on the carpet. **1920** OSTRANDER *How Many Cards?* 145, I had him up on the carpet for three hours but no amount of grilling will get out of him where he was.

+c. *To come on the carpet*, to put in an appearance. *colloq.*

1888 *Century Mag.* XXXVI. 552/2 She certain' have been more dressy and pink in the face since—since you come on the carpet.

Carpetbag, *n.*

1. A traveling bag, originally one made of carpet. {1844–}

1830 *Boston Directory* 28 *advt.* **1848** W. E. BURTON *Waggeries* 171, I crammed a change of clothing into a carpet bag. **1852** BRISTED *Upper Ten Th.* ii. 43 This important personage brought over . . . carpet bags full of boots. **1879** R. J. BURDETTE *Hawkeyes* 101 And the man . . . who always carries an old-fashioned, oil-cloth carpet-bag with him. **1921** C. GREER-PETRIE *Angeline at Seelbach* 3 He . . . was a-rechin' fur my kyarpet bag, when I let him know I'd tote thatar bag myself.

+2. Attrib. and comb. **a.** *Carpetbag gentry, emigration,* with reference to those having little or no baggage.

1846 *Georgia Messenger* 24 Dec., [It] may be traced to some of those carpet-bag gentry, who are wandering through upper Georgia. **1857** *Herald of Freedom* (Lawrence, Kansas) 19 Sept. (Th.), Early in the spring several thousand excellent young men came to Kansas. This was jokingly called the carpet-bag emigration.

+b. *Carpetbag member, state,* etc. Cf. CARPETBAGGER.

1870 *Nation* 6 Jan. 6/1 No one expects high political morality from carpet-bag senators. **1870** in Tourgee *Invisible Empire* (1880) xii. 504 As to the carpet-bag members of the Convention . . . they were thirteen in number. **1873** BEADLE *Undevel. West* xxiii. 471 If a State, this would be a most complete 'rotten borough'—the worst 'carpet-bag' State in the Union. **1884** *Century Mag.* April 862/1 The methods which overturned the carpet-bag and negro dynasties find their justification . . . in the instinct of self-preservation. **1886** Z. F. SMITH *Kentucky* 795 Instead of the twelve years of carpet-bag corruption and spoliation, . . . there might have been . . . a reconstruction. **1887** *Courier-Journal* 29 Jan. 5/5 During the carpet-bag days he was the friend of the South. **1888** *Chicago Inter-Ocean* (F.), One of the most vulnerable men who figured in Southern politics in the carpet-bag era. **1895** CHAMBLISS *Diary* 300 These rowdies are not Mississippians. They belong to the carpet-bag element. **1904** PAGE in *McClure's Mag.* April 623 The eight years of Negro domination under carpet-bag leaders had passed.

+c. *Carpetbag government*, political rule by carpetbaggers.

1871 *Congress. Globe* App. 3 March 273 The favorite name applied to our southern governments by our Democratic friends is that of 'carpet-bag governments.' **1872** *N.Y. Herald* 22 Aug. (F. & H.), City plunderers, and carpet-bag State Governments. *Ib.*, The present wholesale plunder of the carpet-bag governments in the South, [etc.]. *a*1877 *New York World* (B.), The carpet-bag governments of the Southern States . . . have rolled up an aggregate debt . . . of $194,000,000. **1885** *Outing* VII. 200/2 This infernal Yankee carpet-bag gov'ment will never do for South Carolina. **1898** *Mo. So. Dakotan* I. 108 It was, however, the plan of the administration at that period to bestow upon the territories carpet-bag government.

+Carpetbag, *v. intr.* To travel with very little baggage; also see quot. 1889. — **1872** *Ill. Dept. Agric.* 266 Almost the entire force of our common schools tends to . . . send [our young men] . . . 'carpet bagging,' down South. **1882** *Nation* 17 Aug. 121/1 They had served in Congress together, and had lived not far from each other before Dorsey 'carpet-bagged' from Ohio to Arkansas. **1889** *Cent.* 830/3 *Carpet-bag*, to act or live in the manner of a carpet-bagger. **1890** *Congress. Rec.* 4 June 5598/2 Mr. McDuffie carpet-bagged from somewhere down into Alabama.

+Carpetbagged, *a.* Having a carpetbag; ruled or dominated by carpetbaggers. — **1857** *Harper's Mag.* Sept. 558/1 Brown and Rogers, carpet-bagged and duster-clad, . . . set foot once more . . . upon the solid pavement. **1872** *Chicago Tribune* 10 Oct. 4/6 Repudiation there, and in other carpet-bagged States, is, we fear, but a question of time.

+Carpetbagger.

1. One of the Northern adventurers who went South to profit by the social and political upheaval following the Civil War.

'*Carpet-bagger.*—After the Civil War, numbers of Northerners went South, some with honest intent, others with hope of profit from irregular means. . . . Originally, however, a carpet-bagger was a "wild-cat banker" in the West. A banker, that is, who had no local abiding place, and could not be found when wanted' (1885 *Mag. Amer. Hist.* Jan. 99/1). See also sense 2, quot. 1879.

1868 *U.S. Public Docs. No. 1367* 196, I would sooner trust him [the Negro] than the white scalawag or carpet-bagger. **1868** *Nation* VI. 123 A good deal of bitterness of feeling has been shown in all the conventions in regard to the presence, and great prominence as members, of what the Louisiana people call 'carpet-baggers'—men, that is, who are new-comers in the country. **1875** *Chicago Tribune* 12 July 4/6 The plundering of some of the Southern States by carpet-baggers. **1879** BISHOP *4 Months in Sneak-Box* 182 The Carpet-baggers from up north has filled their heads with all kinds of stuff. **1886** B. P. POORE *Reminisc.* II. 272 The 'carpet-baggers' from the South were gradually being replaced. **1911** Rolt-Wheeler *Boy with Census* 46 The Freedman's Bureau an' the carpet-baggers made trouble right an' lef'.

2. A term of contempt or humor applied to a transient, stranger, foreigner, etc. (Cf. Carpetbag *n.* 2.)

1869 *Republican Daily Jrnl.* (Lawrence, Kans.) 3 Nov., Fifty loaded teams between Burlington and Emporia . . . [included] coaches heavily loaded with passengers, besides several *carpet-baggers* on foot. **1872** *Kansas Mag.* 11 Nov. 475, I fell in with a party of 'carpet-baggers,' numbering ten, who had just arrived from the 'hub.' **1873** *Newton* (Kansas) *Kansan* 12 June 3/4 Adam and Eve . . . were ready to be entertained by any carpet bagger that came along. **1879** Tourgee *Fool's Errand* xxvi. 158 An organization . . . putting their notes in circulation by means of agents, who carried the bills about the country in carpet-bags, and were hence denominated 'Carpet-baggers.' *Ib.* 161 Carpet-bagger.—A man without means, character, or occupation, an adventurer, a camp follower, a 'bummer.' **1901** Churchill *Crisis* ii. xviii. 279 There's lots of those military carpet-baggers hanging around for good jobs now. **1905** *Springfield W. Republican* 28 July 6 Porto Rico's grievance is the lack of home rule. They complain that they are governed by a lot of carpet-baggers from the U.S. **1914** McLaughlin & Hart *Cycl. Amer. Govt.* I. 230/2 *Carpet-bagger.* . . . By extension the term was often applied to any unpopular northerner living in the south.

+**Carpetbaggery.** Corrupt political rule by nonresident demagogues. — **1874** in Fleming *Hist. Reconstruction* II. 146 The real author of carpetbaggery (Uncle Sam) stepped upon the stage. **1884** *Milnor* (Dakota) *Teller* 30 July, My talk on Dakota before the house committee on territories . . . led to the introduction of a bill by Mr. Tillman of South Carolina, to abolish this infamous system of territorial carpet-baggery.

+**Carpetbagging,** *vbl. n.* **1.** Traveling with no baggage other than a carpetbag. **2.** The practice of carpetbaggery. Also attrib. — **(1) 1869** *Atlantic Mo.* XXIII. 747 After three weeks' delightful Carpet-Bagging. **(2) 1888** Bryce *Amer. Commw.* II. 621 Negro suffrage produced, during the few years of 'carpet-bagging' and military government which followed the war, incredible mischief. **1904** *N.Y. Ev. Post* 1 Feb., The infernal 'carpet-bagging' system at present in vogue should be done away with.

+**Carpetbagging,** *ppl. a.* Traveling with a carpetbag or other light baggage. — **1870** *Clipping from periodical,* The Rev. Carpetbagging Thief and Cadetship-peddler has arrived in Washington, and has had a long interview with Ben Butler.

+**Carpetbag(g)ism.** The principles and practices of carpetbaggers.

*a***1870** Chipman *Notes on Bartlett* 69 *Carpet-bagism.* Political rule, &c. of carpet-baggers. **1872** *N.Y. Herald* 16 Dec. 5/1 Carpet-Bagism in Alabama and in New Orleans. **1881** *Phila. Record No. 3459* 2 The 'solid South' is a protest against carpet-bagism. **1887** *Courier-Journal* 27 Jan. 1/5 Carpet-Bagism in Texas. **1911** H. S. Harrison *Queed* iv. 45 The morning *Post* . . . had crucified carpet-baggism.

‖**Carpet-ball.** A large soft ball designed as a child's plaything. — **1832** Cincinnati correspondent in *Mirror* (London) 26 May (Th.), Egg-plants are here brought to market; some of them . . . are as large as a child's carpet-ball.

Carpet beetle. 'A popular name of *Anthrenus scrophulariæ*, . . . so called from its destructiveness to carpets and other woolen fabrics. It was brought into the United States from Europe at a recent period' (*Cent.*).

+**Carpet chair.** A folding chair with back (and seat) of carpet. — **1882** Howells *Modern Instance* xx, She had done what could be done with folding carpet chairs to give the little room a specious air of luxury. **1886** Susan Hale *Letters* 164 It shuts up flat when not in use, like carpet chairs. **1886** Howells *Minister's Charge* 152 There were bright folding carpet-chairs.

‖**Carpet cress.** Swine's cress. — **1861** Wood *Botany* 239 *Senebiera,* Poir. Carpet Cress. Swine Cress.

Carpet factory. A place where carpets are manufactured. — **1834** in *Atlantic Mo.* XXVI. 744, I did not hear of any but a carpet-factory. **1872** *Newton* (Kansas) *Kansan* 19 Sept. 2/5 It is claimed that the only carpet factory west of Philadelphia is in Kansas. **1880** *Harper's Mag.* June 33/1 Others are engaged as designers in carpet factories, wall-paper factories [etc.].

+**Carpet fly.** (See quotation.) — **1869** *Amer. Naturalist* II. 592 The Carpet-fly, *Scenopinus pallipes,* . . . in the larva state, is found under carpets, on which it is said to feed.

Carpet grass. {1756} +A species of pasture grass, *Axonopus compressus.* — **1882** A. M. Macy in E. K. Godfrey *Nantucket* 36 The carpet-grass and the orange-grass . . . were eagerly sought for at that period. **1894** Coulter *Bot. W. Texas* iii. 500 Carpet Grass. . . . Moist meadow land, . . . eastern Texas to Virginia. **1901** Mohr *Plant Life Ala.* 120 Carpet grass (*Paspalum compressum*), a West Indian species most probably introduced.

Carpet house. A store that specializes in the sale of carpets. — **1867** *Atlantic Mo.* March 338/2 Now it is a gorgeous and enormous carpet-house that arrests his attention; now a huge dry-goods store, or vast depot of groceries. **1887** *Courier-Journal* 7 May 3/6 This supplies a long-felt want of this city—an exclusive Carpet House at popular prices.

Carpet rags, *pl.* Rags for making up into carpets.

1845 *Knickerb.* XXV. 448, I was . . . up in the garret, beholding rolls of wool, balls of carpet-rags, skeins of yarn. **1865** *Atlantic Mo.* XV. 474 When entirely past service, they were cut up into carpet-rags. **1883** 'S. Bonner' *Dialect Tales* 86 'That ain't the pint at all,' says Sister Sweet, 'whether 'twas carpet-rags, or . . . satin robes for the rich.' **1898** Dunbar *Folks from Dixie* 87, I was jes' settin' hyeah sawtin' my cyahpet rags.

+**Carpet sack.** A traveling bag; a carpetbag.

1855 *Herald of Freedom* 30 June 2/6 Risking our precious bodies, trunks, carpet-sacks, and 'hoss pistols,' without insurance, on the . . . Missouri river. **1857** *Harper's Mag.* Sept. 443/1 Several hospitable carpet-sacks were opened, and bread, butter, pickles, and ham were proffered. **1866** 'P. V. Nasby' *Struggles* 333, I opened the carpet sack on the train. **1874** Pinkerton *Expressman & Detective* 85, I provided him with a carpet-sack and the necessary tools. **1896** J. C. Harris *Sister Jane* 78 He took . . . what little of his belongings that he had left and packed 'em all up in a carpet-sack. **1901** Churchill *Crisis* 402 He had contrived to be rid of the carpet-sack in which certain precious letters were carried.

‖**Carpet satchel.** =Carpet sack. — **1856** Cozzens *Sparrowgr. Papers* xiii. 183, I found them with their new carpet-satchels all ready.

+**Carpet shell.** An edible clam of the genus *Tapes,* found on the Pacific coast. — **1893** *Stand.* 289/1 *Carpet-shell,* a small clam (*Tapes staminea*) extensively used as food in California.

+**Carpet store.** A store in which carpets are sold. — **1865** Stowe *House & Home P.* 85 They proceed to the carpet-stores, and there are thrown at their feet by obsequious clerks velvet and Axminsters. **1868** Mrs. Whitney *P. Strong* 128, I . . . ran up into the carpet store.

+**Carpet sweeper.** (See quotations.) — **1859** *Rep. Comm. Patents 1858* II. 444 This invention has reference to that description of carpet or floor sweepers in which a revolving brush . . . is made to take up and deposit the sweepings in a case covering the brush. **1874** Knight 477 *Carpet-sweeper,* a mechanical broom for sweeping carpets and collecting the dust and dirt in trays. **1877** Bartlett 778 *Carpet-Sweeper,* a roller to which hog's bristles are affixed for sweeping carpets.

Carpet weaver. A person who weaves or makes carpets. — **1827** Drake & Mansf. *Cincinnati* viii. 66, 4 Carpet and Stocking Weavers. **1871** W. M. Grosvenor *Protection* 314 Carpet-weavers about Philadelphia were on strike for some time.

+**Carpetweed.** A native North American weed, *Mollugo verticillata;* Indian chickweed.

1784 Cutler in *Mem. Academy* I. 407 Carpet-weed. . . . Blossoms greenish white. **1817–8** Eaton *Botany* (1822) 355 *Mollugo verticillata,* carpet weed, generally grows in gardens among purslain. **1840** Dewey *Mass. Flowering Plants* 90 Carpet Weed. . . . A native of this country. **1891** Coulter *Bot. W. Texas* i. 138 Carpet-weed. Sandy river banks.

Carpet wool. (See first quotation.) — **1889** *Secy. of Agric. Rep.* 245 About seven-tenths of the entire importation of the last ten years has been admitted under the third class as 'carpet wools,' a designation very inexact, as it includes the wool of all the races of sheep in the world, improved and unimproved, merino and English only excepted. *Ib.* 247 A wide belt of the country, from the Atlantic to the Pacific, was long the home of sheep producing carpet wools. **1899** *Dept. Agric. Yearbook 1898* 706.

Carpouse. (Obs. form of Caboose.)

+**Carp sucker.** A large sucker of the genus *Carpiodes,* as the carp (*C. carpio*) of the Ohio and lower Mississippi Rivers; a buffalo fish.—**1884** Goode *Fisheries* i. 615 The different species . . . known as 'Carp,' 'Carp Suckers,' . . . etc., abound in all the larger bodies of water south and west of New York.

+**Carrel(l).** An early variant of Corral *n.* — **1847** J. Palmer *Rocky Mts.* 28 On the eastern side is an additional wall, . . . enclosing ground for stables and *carrell.* **1850** W. Miles *Journal* (1916) 15 Our mules and cattle . . . might . . . be made secure within this *carrel* or yard.

+**Carreta.** *W.* and *S.W.* [Sp.] A light wagon or cart.

1844 Gregg *Commerce of Prairies* I. 176 A great many years ago, a firm causeway was thrown up . . . [through one of the salt lakes] upon which the *carretas* and mules are driven. **1848** E. Bryant *California* 314 We met this morning a Californian *carreta,* or travelling-cart, freighted with women and children. **1863** *Rio Abajo Press* 6 Oct. 3 Juan José Jaramillo . . . loaded his musket, . . . placed it in his carreta, [etc.]. **1883** Sweet & Knox *Mex. Mustang through Texas* 367 All the goods . . . were hauled up from the coast on uncouth vehicles called *carretas.* **1903** *N.Y. Herald* 8 March, The bed of the carreta is made of open cross sections of mesquite wood. **1923** H. G. Wilson *Early Transp. Arizona* (Bentley), On these creaky, wabbly carretas, fruit panoche, and zarapes were brought.

+**Carretela, -atel(l)a.** *S.W.* [Sp.] A small cart or wagon. — **1846** Magoffin *Down Santa Fe Trail* (1926) 86 He is eternally singing, even when he is driving *la carratela* (carriage) over the worst kind of . . . roads. **1854** Bartlett *Personal Narrative* II. xxxvi. 375 As my carratella (little wagon) was quite light. **1856** Whipple *Explor. Ry. Route* I. 30 The carretela which carries the [surveying] instruments was again upset.

***Carriage.**

***1.** Transportation, conveyance.

1622 in Winthrop *Hist.* I. 405 Except one send by some friend, the carriage and custom cost so much, as there will be little saved. **1705** Beverley *Virginia* iv. 54 The Slate, which will hardly be made use of, till the Carriage there becomes cheaper, and more common. **1754** in *Lett. to Washington* I. 6 The Carradge on horses is so expensive that sum Method must be thought of to mend the Roads. **1818** Flint *Lett. from Amer.* 81 At present the carriage of goods from Baltimore to Wheeling is cheaper than from Philadelphia to Pittsburg. **1834** Peck *Gaz. Illinois* 38 A large proportion of the land carriage is by means of large wagons.

*2. A wheeled vehicle, a wagon, a surrey.

a1656 BRADFORD *Hist. Plym. Plant.* I. 377 For want of boats and carriages. **1738** *Boston Rec.* 204 Mark the carriages on their return as aforesaid. **1790** BENTLEY *Diary* I. 205 Mr. Burrell's Child's Funeral was the first in the Boston fashion of four wheel carriages. **1849** PARKMAN in *Knickerb.* XXXIII. 10 The close black carriages in which the traders travel and sleep. **1869** STOWE *Oldtown Folks* 22 She might have been Mrs. Captain Shawmut, and had her carriage and horses. **1909** 'O. HENRY' *Options* 71 Nevada, . . . watching the carriages and autos roll by in the street, took the envelope.

3. *Railroad.* A passenger coach or car. {*a* 1824–}

1829 J. MACAULEY *Hist. N.Y.* I. 190 On some [railroads] the carriages are moved by horses, and on others by steam. **1871** BRYANT (in an unpublished letter) 27 May, I found the two ladies in a stateroom at the end of the Pullman carriage in which I was.

*4. A gun carriage.

1642 *Plymouth Rec.* 11 Richard Church shall speedyly make the carriage for another piece of ordinance. **1796** *Ann. 4th Congress* 2 Sess. 2786, The cannon . . . are ready for mounting on the carriages. **1861** *Army Regulations* 16 A post-book of record will be kept . . . in which will be duly entered the number of each mounted gun . . . [and] the description of its carriage.

attrib. **1761** in H. M. Brooks *Gleanings* 10 She has 10 Carriage and 6 Swivel Guns, belonging to her.

5. =AUTOMOBILE *n.* 1. Also attrib.

1901 *Outing* XXXVII. 550/2 The electric and steam carriages as known at present are to all intents and purposes new commodities. *Ib.* 552/1 The Electric Vehicle Company's gasoline carriage supports the engine . . . entirely on the running gear, leaving the carriage box free for other purposes.

6. Attrib. and comb. with *axle, beast, blanket, bolt,* etc.

1858 *Rep. Comm. Patents* (1859) I. 503 Improved machine for upsetting carriage axles. **1772** *Mass. Gazette* 30 Jan. (Th.), [A mare is described as] a ganty lofty carriage Beast. **1864** WEBSTER 28/1 *Afghan*, . . . a kind of carriage blanket. **1874** KNIGHT 479/2 *Carriage-bolt*, a screw-bolt, . . . for use in carriage-making. *Ib.*, *Carriage-brake*, a retarding arrangement for carriages when descending a hill. **1868** *Rep. Comm. Patents 1867* II. 1194/2 Carriage Circle. . . . The dowel pin engages in the corresponding groove on the upper side of the lower sections of the circle. **1875** *Chicago Tribune* 21 Nov. 3/4 Even elaborate carriage costumes are rarely seen before January. **1884** HOWELLS *S. Lapham* xx. 363 Mrs. Lapham fell back against the carriage cushions. **1863** 'M. HARLAND' *Husks* 9 The butler—on carriage days, the footman—checked his flirtation with the plump and laughing chambermaid. **1902** LORIMER *Lett. Merchant* 53, I take just as much pride in it as the fellow who . . . can't find any place to put it, except on his carriage door and his letter-head. **1838** COOPER *Home as Found* i. (1873) 12 She was in a carriage dress. **1835** LONGSTREET *Georgia Scenes* 108 Mrs. Smith added to the donation, her own cook and carriage-driver. **1798** *Ann. 5th Congress* I. 1068 The committee had received certain information on the subject of the carriage duty. **1827** DRAKE & MANSF. *Cincinnati* viii. 65 Eight Carriage and Wagon Factories. **1864** *Ohio Agric. Rep.* XVIII. 50 Entries in Matched Horses and Mares . . . 1 pair carriage geldings. **1880** CABLE *Grandissimes* lii. 394 Honoré led the doctor through the cool, high, tesselated carriage-hall. **1817** *Ann. 14th Congress* 2 Sess. 993 The carriage-holders and a large proportion of the retailers have already paid for the full term of the current year. **1874** KNIGHT 480/1 *Carriage-jack*, a lever-jack, made in various ways, designed to lift an axle. **1876** WARNER *Gold of Chickaree* 376, I have brought a carriage load of books with me. **1889** *Advance* (Chicago) 21 March 229 Carpentry, blacksmithery, and carriage making are also chief industries for the Indian on the plain. **c1858** *Mich. Agric. Soc. Trans.* IX. 162 The Irish hunter is . . . sprung from a thorough-bred sire and a roadster or carriage-mare. **1815** *Niles' Reg.* IX. 35/2 Plated saddlery and carriage mounting of all kinds . . . are manufactured. **1896** *N.Y. Dramatic News* 4 July 7/4 We already owed manager Savage $42.50 fares and $8 carriage parade. **1870** 'M. HARLAND' *For Better, for Worse* 332 The wife's refusal to be one of the carriage-party. **1878** *Decorum* 135 A carriage-robe to protect it [a lady's dress] entirely from the mud. **1881** W. O. STODDARD *E. Hardery* 145 Professor Nain . . . leaned . . . almost perilously forward from his carriage seat to exclaim [etc.]. **1874** KNIGHT 480/2 *Carriage-shackle*, . . . which connects the axle-clip to the thill or shaft. **1854** W. BROMWELL *Locomotive Sk.* 37 The most prominent . . . is the barn . . . around which are scattered wagon and carriage-sheds, corncribs, [etc.]. **1858** *Rep. Comm. Patents* (1859) I. 577 Improvement in Upsetting Carriage Tire. **1845** *Knickerb.* XXVI. 509 It usually contained only one narrow well-beaten carriage-track in the centre of the sward. **1858** *Texas Alm.* (*advt.*), Carriage Trimmings, Oil and Varnish. *Ib.*, Carriage Trimming done at the shortest notice. **1923** E. F. WYATT *Invis. Gods* III. iii. 119 He threw out the carriage weight [from the buggy] and started toward the house. **1898** PAGE *Red Rock* 174 A man standing in the crowd had a carriage-whip in his hand.

Carriage block. A block of stone or other material used in mounting into or alighting from a carriage. — **1890** FREDERIC *Lawton Girl* 99 Father ought to set out a hitching-post and a carriage-block, so that we can receive our callers in style. **1898** ATHERTON *Californians* 157 But she . . . sat still and erect until he reached the carriage block, when she went to the head of the steps to meet him.

Carriage body. The enclosed part for passengers in a carriage, railroad car, etc. Also transf. — **1812** *Index to Patents* (1874) I. 252 Carriage-body [invented by] H. Dunlap [of] Georgetown, D.C. [patented] Aug. 27, 1812. **1869** 'MARK TWAIN' *Innocents* 229 We sit in the cushioned carriage-body of a cabin [of a Venetian gondola]. **1874** KNIGHT 399/1 The third form [of spring on a railroad carriage] has a central buffer with a shaft acting upon a spiral spring beneath the carriage-body.

Carriage boot. +1. A waterproof cover or apron to protect the driver of a carriage from rain and mud. 2. A boot or shoe made especially for wear in a carriage. — (1) **1868** *Rep. Comm. Patents 1867* I. 481/2 Carriage Boot.—[patented] January 15, 1867. The apron is combined with a dash cover. (2) **1907** M. C. HARRIS *Tents of Wickedness* III. iv. 266 When she was ready, carriage-boots and all, she went drearily out of the door.

Carriage box. The box or bed of a carriage. — **1802** *Index to Patents* (1874) I. 252 Carriage-box [invented by] T. B. Whitlock [patented] Feb. 23, 1802. **1901** [see CARRIAGE 5].

Carriage builder. A carriage maker. {1887–} — **1888** *Vt. Agric. Rep.* X. 41 As they needed carriages, carriage builders made their appearance. **1903** E. JOHNSON *Railway Transportation* 46 Carriage-builders in making vehicles for the railroad followed the designs with which they were familiar.

Carriage hire. Charge for the use of a carriage; the hiring of one. — **1846** S. SMITH *Theat. Appr.* 55 Hoping to raise a sufficient sum to pay our carriage-hire, we consented. **1855** THOMPSON *Doesticks* 138 If there is any money left after paying expenses and the Committee don't spend it in carriage-hire. **1875** MRS. STOWE *We & Neighbors* ii. 27 Carriage-hire costs money.

***Carriage horse.** A horse that draws a carriage or coach. — **1831** PECK *Guide for Emigrants* 165 Carriage horses . . . cost about seventy-five or eighty dollars. **1893** M. HOWE *Honor* 206 You are not fit to touch anything but . . . the manes of her fat pigs of carriage-horses.

+**Carriage house.** A building in which a carriage is kept when not in use.

1803 *Steele Papers* I. 395 A Carriage House 16 feet square. **1845** DOUGLASS *Life* 16 His stable and carriage-house presented the appearance of some of our large city livery establishments. **1863** CUMMING *Hospital Life* (1866) 107/1 One of the wards, called the carriage ward (as it had been a carriage house), has about fifty patients. **1883** C. F. WILDER *Sister Ridnour* 21 The barn and carriage house would have to be altered for a new carriage and horse. **1900** C. WINCHESTER *W. Castle* v. 90 On the table stood a lighted lantern, ready to guide his steps to the carriage-house and stable.

Carriage maker. A carriage builder; one who makes carriages.

1819 M'MURTRIE *Sk. Louisville* 137 There are at this moment, in Louisville, . . . six saddlers and harness makers, two carriage makers. **1848** E. BRYANT *California* vi. 77 Mr. Eddy, a carriage-maker by trade, was soon as busily at work . . . as if he had been in his own shop. **1876** INGRAM *Centennial Expos.* 235 Besides all the varieties of screws used by carpenters, carriage-makers, [etc.]. **1887** *Courier-Journal* 8 May 12/7 His father, a carriage-maker, earning good wages, and his stepmother . . . were all the time living in comfortable quarters.

Carriage-place. *Obs.* A portage. — **1775** J. MELVIN *Jrnl.* (1857) 10 The carriage-place is about a mile in length.

Carriage porch. A porch under which a carriage may conveniently be stopped. — **1857** C. VAUX *Villas* 303 A carriage porch leads to a vestibule and octangular hall. **1861** WINTHROP *Open Air* 268 The old villa serves us for head-quarters. . . . Four granite pillars . . . make a carriage-porch.

+**Carriage shop.** A carriage maker's shop. — **1847** H. HOWE *Hist. Coll. Ohio* 126 Chagrin Falls contains . . . 1 carriage, 2 tin, 3 harness and 3 cabinet shops. **1887** *Trial H. K. Goodwin* 49 There is a harness shop and then a carriage shop.

Carriage tax. A tax on owning and operating carriages. {1887} — **1813** *Ann. 13th Congress* 1 Sess. I. 364 On the 28th of May, 1796, the President's signature was affixed to a carriage tax. **1816** *Ann. 14th Congress* 2 Sess. 269 Some observations to show the severity of the operation of the carriage tax on that description of carriages, (light wagons, &c.) used by farmers and people in moderate circumstances. **1832** JACKSON *Speeches* (ed. Thorpe) 236 The excise law in Pennsylvania, the embargo and nonintercourse law in the Eastern States, the carriage tax in Virginia, were all deemed unconstitutional.

Carriageway. A road or part of a road suitable for carriages. {1833–}

1807 *Ann. 10th Congress* 1 Sess. II. 2823 A way for foot passengers . . . shall be separated from the carriage-way by a good and sufficient railing. **1830** S. BRECK in *Recollections* (1877) iv. 187 It was of modern construction, . . . with a carriage-way into Filbert Street. **1869** STOWE *Oldtown Folks* 194 A few moments after, we were in the grounds of the place, and struck into what had formerly been the carriage way.

b. A driveway or entrance way.

1880 CABLE *Grandissimes* 376 One entered a high, covered carriage-way with a tesselated pavement and green plastered walls.

***Carrier.**

*1. One who transports commodities for hire.

1662 *Plymouth Laws* 136 In case any master Carrier or waggoner shall have cause to suspect any . . . goods may bee concealled [etc.]. **1753** *Md. Hist. Mag.* XVIII. 28 One John Dobbs, a carrier found drowned. **1792** [see 3]. **1847** in Drake *Pion. Life Ky.* 13 Father . . . was afterward a miller, and now a wagoner, or common carrier on the highway. **1866** *Internal Revenue Guide* 78 Express carriers and agents shall pay ten dollars.

b. A group, company, association, etc., engaged in transportation.

1887 *Courier-Journal* 8 May 12/5 The rights of passengers and the duty of drivers or agents of street-cars or other common carriers. **1903** E. JOHNSON *Railway Transportation* 124 A copy of the bill must be sent to each of the railroads . . . and to any freight association of which the carrier may be a member.

**2.* One who carries.

1769 WASHINGTON *Diaries* I. 337 The Wheat was thinner, which enabled the Rakers and carryors to keep up better. **1904** STRATTON-PORTER *Freckles* 348 She told the men to ask every able-bodied man they met to join them so that they could change carriers often and make good time.

3. One engaged in transporting or delivering the mail. Also attrib. {1621–}

1792 *Ann. 2nd Congress* 62 It shall be lawful for . . . carriers of goods by carts or wagons, to be carriers and deliverers of all such letters or packets. **1825** *P. O. Laws & Reg.* (1843) I. 22 No additional allowance shall be made, by the Postmaster General, to the contractor or carrier of any mail. **1887** *Postal Laws* 262 Broken street letter boxes and worn-out carrier satchels should, as far as practicable, be utilized by using the good parts of some to repair others. **1923** C. J. DUTTON *Shadow on Glass* 170 The letter . . . had been picked up by a carrier who had the eastern section of the town for his route.

+b. One employed to deliver a newspaper.

1845 SOL. SMITH *Theatr. Apprent.* ii. 27, I was carrier of the 'Herald.' **1854** CUMMINS *Lamplighter* iii, Having been, at different times, a newspaper carrier, a cab-driver, a porter, [etc.].

4. *Mech.* A device or contrivance for conveying various articles. {1858–} Also attrib.

1853 *Harper's Mag.* VII. 761/1 In the mean while the cut cane is accumulating in the carrier shed. *Ib.* 763/2 Attached to the mill is an ingenious contrivance known as the carrier. This consists of a never-ending band, . . . that runs upon rollers, and is used to bring the cane from the outside of the building up and into the mill. **1903** G. ADE *In Babel* 18 An overhead cash-carrier of the kind used in retail stores.

+5. (See quotation.)

1881 E. INGERSOLL *Oyster Industry* 242 *Carrier*, an oyster which will endure transportation well (Trade term).

Carrion beetle. {1815–} (See quots.) — **1854** EMMONS *Agric. N.Y.* V. 261 Index. **1889** *Cent.* 834 *Carrion-beetle*, . . . a necrophagous coleopter; a beetle that feeds upon or deposits its eggs in carrion.

Carrion bird. =CANADA JAY. — **1844** *Nat. Hist. N.Y., Zoology* II. 130 The Canada Jay. *Garrulus Canadensis.* . . . Its food consists of berries, caterpillars, eggs of other birds, and even carrion, from whence it derives one of its popular names of Carrion Bird.

***Carrion crow.** The black vulture, *Coragyps atratus.* {1699–}

1791 BARTRAM *Travels* 152 The other species may very properly be called the coped vulture, and is by the inhabitants called the carrion crow. **1813** WILSON *Ornith.* IX. 104 In the towns and villages of the southern states, . . . the carrion-crows may be seen . . . sauntering about the streets. **1837** J. L. WILLIAMS *Florida* 73 There are many birds in Florida. . . . Turkey Buzzard. . . . Carion Crow. . . . Raven. **1858** BAIRD *Birds Pacific R.R.* 5 *Cathartes Atratus*, . . . The Black Vulture—The Carrion Crow. **1894** B. TORREY *Fla. Sketch-Book* 191 The air was full of vultures (carrion crows).

Carrion flower. {1855–} +A species of cat brier whose flowers have an offensive smell. — **1843** TORREY *Flora New York* II. 303 *Smilax herbacea.* . . . Carrion-flower. . . . Meadows, thickets, & borders of woods. *a*1852 THOREAU *Summer* (1884) 123 Carrion flower, a rank green vine. **1857** GRAY *Botany* 463 Carrion-Flower [grows in] moist meadows and river-banks. **1894** COULTER *Bot. W. Texas* III. 432 Carrion flower. . . . Common in the Atlantic States extending into Texas.

***Carrot.**

**1.* A well-known garden plant, *Daucus carota*, or its root.

1610 *Estate of Va.* 31 What should I speake of cucumbers, muske melons, pompions, potatoes, parsneps, carrets, turn vps. **1630** F. HIGGINSON *New-Eng.* 9 Our Turnips, Parsnips and Carrots are here both bigger and sweeter then is ordinarily to be found in England. **1709** LAWSON *Carolina* 77 The Garden-Roots that thrive well in Carolina, are Carrots, Leeks, Parsnips. **1781–2** JEFFERSON *Notes Va.* (1788) 40 We cultivate also potatoes, both the long and the round, turnips, carrots, [etc.]. **1831** PECK *Guide for Emigrants* 143 April 7 . . . carrots . . . planted. **1885** *Rep. Indian Affairs* 52 Approximate figures can therefore only be given, . . . as follows: . . . rutabagas, carrots, beets, etc. 12,160 bushels.

fig. **1846** FARNHAM *Prairie Land* 29 There'd be more sense in giving that ruffled carrot yonder a taste of a live man's fists.

attrib. and *comb.* **1832** CHILD *Frugal Housewife* 67 Carrot pies are made like squash pies. **1843** N. BOONE *Journal* (1917) 31 May 201 The indians near Camp dug a quantity of a sort of carrot shaped root. **1865** *Atlantic Mo.* XV. 668 She tended the calf, . . . gave it . . . apple-parings and carrot-tops. **1873–4** *Vt. Board Agric. Rep.* II. 92 Mr. D. said he had used carrots for coloring, and thought those who used them should have a regular carrot grater. **1890** S. HALE *Letters* 253 It [the snow] clogs the carrot-slice wheels of the four-wheelers.

+2. A roll of leaf tobacco.

1772 D. TAITT in *Travels Amer. Col.* 537 Others took the Cock off his riffle and Sixteen carrots of Tobacco. **1775** ROMANS *Nat. Hist. Florida* 149 The uppermost leaves being the best tobacco and the lower the worst; they are then made up into very close packed bundles called in Florida Carrots. **1788** WM. BIGGS *Captivity* 33, I bought him a carrot of tobacco; it weighted about three pounds. **1805–8** PIKE *Sources Miss.* 26, I sent a flag and two carrots of tobacco. **1857** *Ill. Agric. Soc. Trans.* II. 360 The Creoles manufactured the tobacco into carrots, as they were called. A carrot is a roll of tobacco twelve or fifteen inches long. **1890** *Congress. Rec.* 27 Aug. 9213/2, I have here some carots [*sic*] of Cuban tobacco.

Carrot seed. The seed of the carrot. {1832–}

1772 *Carroll P.* in *Md. Hist. Mag.* XIV. 362 Turnbull has little or no Carrot seed. **1787** WASHINGTON *Diaries* III. 187 The 20 acre cut designed (if Carrot Seed can be obtained) for Carrots. **1856** *Rep. Comm. Patents: Agric.* 260 Carrot-seed, of all others, requires a very damp, fine soil to vegetate.

Carry, *n.*

+1. The carrying or transporting of canoes, goods, etc., around falls or shoals in a river or from one navigable stream to another; a portage.

1861 WINTHROP *Open Air* 28 A *bateau* cannot climb through breakers over boulders. We must make a 'carry,' an actual portage. **1867** LOWELL *Biglow P.* II. p. lviii, A few phrases not in Mr. Bartlett's book which I have heard [include] . . . *Carry:* a *portage.* **1879** *Scribner's Mo.* Nov. 20/1 By a short 'carry' one can pass from the head-waters of the Manistee to those of the Au Sable. **1887** A. W. TOURGEE *Button's Inn* 6 The sharp precipitous cañon made the carry especially tedious. **1899** JEWETT *Queen's Twin* i. 5 It belonged to the up-country Indians when they had to make a carry to the landing here to get to the out' islands.

attrib. **1858** THOREAU *Maine Woods* 96 The carryman called this about one hundred and forty miles above Bangor. *a*1862 *Ib.* 287 The carry-paths themselves were more than usually indistinct.

+2. The route, way, or road over which such a portage is performed.

1848 THOREAU *Maine Woods* 29 This portage probably followed the trail of an ancient Indian carry round these falls. **1857** *Knickerb.* L. 494 From this place we were to walk over a 'carry,' stated to be about a mile and a half. **1876** *Fur, Fin, & Feather* Sept. 163 One can . . . catch more bass than one can 'tote across the carry.' **1886** *Harper's Mag.* Aug. 423/1 She could not walk around the 'carry'; she must go by the direct road.

Carry, *v.*

1. *tr.* To transport (a canoe, boat, etc.) over a portage or 'carry.'

1725 in G. Sheldon *Hist. Deerfield* (1895) I. 445 We . . . came to ye Great Falls & carried our canoes across. **1748** J. NORTON *Redeemed Captive* (1870) 31 We sailed down the river between thirty and forty miles, and then carried over our canoes and packs across the land to the St. Lawrence. **1894** J. WINSOR *Cartier to Frontenac* 258 The party began to carry the material . . . along the portage track for twelve miles.

+b. Absol. in same sense.

1759 *New American Mag.* Aug. 577 [At] the great carrying-place between the Mohawks river and Wood-Creek . . . they carry four or five miles according to the season to Wood-Creek. **1848** THOREAU *Maine Woods* 31 The most skilful boatman anywhere else would here be obliged to take out his boat and carry round a hundred times. **1869** W. MURRAY *Adventures* 10, I have boated up and down that [=Adirondack] wilderness, going ashore only to 'carry' around a fall.

2.* *tr. S.* and *dial.* To convey, guide, or escort: **a. Persons. {Now *dial.*}

1622 'MOURT' *Relation* 89 We carried them [the Indians] . . . to the place where they left their Bowes and Arrowes. **1700** *Essex Inst. Coll.* VIII. 217, I carryed my mother to Boston by Winny Simmit. **1827** *Md. Hist. Mag.* XVII. 260 He afterwards carried me to see the Academy of Arts. *a*1846 *Quarter Race Kentucky*, etc. 46 The sheriff nabbed him an carried him too the Cort-house. **1896** M. E. WILKINS *Madelon* 131 My son shall hitch up and carry you home. **1917** *Dialect Notes* IV. 409 He carried her to church.

b. Cattle or horses.

1667 *Plymouth Rec.* 89 Cattle shall not be put turned or Carryed to the salthouse beach. **1715** *Essex Inst. Coll.* XXXVI. 329, I went to Wenham and caryed home my fathers horse. **1350** H. C. LEWIS *La. Swamp Doctor* 182 A servant relieved him of the task by carrying the steed to the stable. **1857** *Harper's Mag.* Nov. 735/2 They might even carry the horses a mile further if they wished.

c. Wagons or boats.

1756 in *Lett. to Washington* I. 167 Waggons have been carried that way already. **1840** COOPER *Pathfinder* vi, Jasper himself can carry a boat safely through it, in the dark.

+3. To set in motion; to operate.

1831 PECK *Guide for Emigts.* 199 There is a spinning machine [etc.] . . . of one hundred and sixty spindles, and one . . . of one hundred and twenty-six spindles. They are carried by ox power on an inclined plane. **1837** — *Gaz. Illinois* I. 32 Factories for spinning cotton . . . are carried by animal power on the inclined plane.

+**4.** To hold (stock) without selling, in expectation of a rise; to keep (merchandise) on hand or in stock.

1848 W. Armstrong *Stocks* 10 It is nominally considered that the stock is meanwhile 'carried' or possessed by the seller. **1870** Medbery *Men of Wall St.* 77 When a broker agrees to 'carry' stock, he says, 'Seven per cent, unless the market tightens.' **1885** *Harper's Mag.* Nov. 841/1 A broker or operator is 'long of stocks' when 'carrying' or holding them for a rise. **1900** S. A. Nelson *A B C Wall St.* 133 *Carrying stock,* to hold stock with the expectation of selling it at an advance. **1905** *N.Y. Ev. Post* 1 Sept. 7 One house in this city carries twelve hundred designs in picture post cards. **1907** *Pearson's Mag.* Jan. (*advt.*), [Book-cases] carried in stock by agents in over 1,200 cities.

+**5.** (See quotation.)

1859 *Harper's Mag.* Nov. 729/1 The beautiful grain [rice] falls.... The reaper usually 'carries' or takes a sweep of three rows at a time.

6. To win the approval or endorsement of. {1868-}

1843 *Knickerb.* XXI. 375 Seldom ... has a public lecturer 'carried the town with him' more unanimously. **1898** T. N. Page *Red Rock* 436 There wasn't a man in the State could carry a jury like Mr. Bagby.

+**7.** *Polit.* To gain the support of (the country, a state, etc.) in an election; to succeed or win in (an election).

1848 Lowell *Biglow P.* I. ix. 124, I thought our ticket would ha' caird the country with a resh. **1864** — *Study Windows* 157 The Republicans had carried the country. **1875** *Chicago Tribune* 6 Nov. 5/6, I never before saw such determination to carry an election. **1882** *Nation* 231/2 The money Dorsey is supposed to have spent in 'carrying Indiana.' **1905** Phillips *Plum Tree* 122 We, our party, carried the state, as usual. **1911** *Amer. Yr. Bk. 1910,* 50 The insurgents carried the Republican primaries in Kansas.

+**8.** To take a leading or guiding part in (singing); to bear or sustain (a part or melody).

1868 G. G. Channing *Recoll. Newport* 73 Four of the congregation, with the leader already referred to, volunteered as a *quintette* to '*carry* the singing.' **1890** *Harper's Mag.* Dec. 147/1, I carried the toon. Peleg sung a real sweet second. **1903** Wiggin *Rebecca* 27 She 'carried' the alto by the ear.

+**9.** To maintain or keep up with financial support.

1883 *Harper's Mag.* Nov. 877/2 The men of business ... have for years carried the New York Academy of Music. **1901** Norris *Octopus* 57 Derrick had practically been obliged to 'carry' Hooven and some of the others.

+**10.** To tease or joke (one).

1887 E. B. Custer *Tenting on Plains* v. 169 He used to carry me high and dry about the little roads leading off to folks he said I was a-feedin'.

+**11.** Phrases. **a.** *To carry guts to a bear:* (see quotation).

1877 Bartlett 103 'He ain't fit *to carry guts to a bear*' is a phrase that expresses a degree of worthlessness impossible to be equalled.

b. *To carry down,* to go through with or perform (a set dance).

1810 Weems *Washington* (ed. 10) 9 This I have from one who tells me that he has carried down many a sett dance with her.

c. *To carry on:* **1.** *tr.* To proceed with, continue, keep up. {1606-} **2.** *intr.* To go on, get along. **3.** To behave uproariously, conspicuously, or scandalously. *colloq.* {1856-}

(1) **1746** in *Penn. Col. Rec.* V. 36 This Province hath at many times been at great Expence ... for carrying on Treaties with them [Indians]. **1758** in *Lett. to Washington* II. 371 With this number I am ordered to Carry on the Well and cover the Barracks. **1823** James *Exped.* I. 59 The circumstance ... leads us to believe that even a limited commerce was carried on between them. **1891** O'Beirne *Leaders Ind. Territory* 170/1 He again engaged in the Mercantile business with his son-in-law ... which business they are still carrying on.

(2) **1825** J. Neal *Bro. Jonathan* II. 152 Mr. Ashley ... asked him, cheerfully, how they 'carried on, to home?' **1854** M. J. Holmes *Tempest & Sunshine* xix. 264 The dogs had howled, the death watches had ticked in the wall, and everything had carried on t'other side up ever since she'd been gone.

(3) **1828** Royall *Black Book* II. 27 They romped and squalled, and to use a Yankee phrase, 'carried on at such a rate that he and Mrs. C. were greatly annoyed.' **1832** Kennedy *Swallow Barn* I. xviii. 187 Old Virginny's not going to let Congress carry on in her day! *c*1869 'Mark Twain' *Sk., How the Author Was Sold in Newark,* What made you carry on so towards the last? **1883** Peck *Bad Boy* 192, I guess her conscience hurt her for the way she had been carrying on in Chicago. **1891** Wilkins *New Eng. Nun* 187 If you don't stop carryin' on so I'll go in the spare bedroom.

d. *tr. To carry up,* to present or deliver officially. *Obs.*

1717 *Mass. H. Rep. Jrnls.* I. 213 Which were cerried [*sic*] up by the said Committee. **1721** *Ib.* III. 33 A Committee to Carry up the Votes of this House for Civil Officers.

+**Carryall.** Also **carry-al(l).** [Popular alteration of Cariole.] Orig. a light vehicle or carriage, capable of being drawn by one horse, but later a large heavy carriage as well.

1714 J. Stoddard *Jrnl.* in *N.E. Hist. & Gen. Reg.* V. 27 Mr. Longuille sent a carryall for us, which carried us to Montreal. **1775** *Mass. H. S. Coll.* 2 Ser. II. 288, I rode out in a Carry'al with my Landlord. **1797** M. Austin in *Amer. Hist. Review* (1900) V. 540 Being furnished with a Carry all and Two Horses I left St Genevieve. **1811** *Colonial Centinel* 5 June 3/1 For sale a Carryall, that is very convenient to carry five or six persons to their places of visitation. **1820** A. Hodgson *Lett. from N. America* (1824) I. 119 They travelled in a little Jersey waggon (or dearborn, or carry-al). **1826** A. Royall *Sketches* 130 To remedy this inconvenience, the proprietors of the line have provided a large vehicle, something like a stage coach; it is called a carry-all, and would carry twenty persons. **1833** E. T. Coke *Subaltern's Furlough* I. 210 One of the four-wheeled carriages known at Philadelphia as a 'dearborn,' in the eastern States as a 'carryall,' and in Utica as a 'wagon.' **1841** Hawthorne *Amer. Notebook* (1932) 83 The last thing I saw of her was her vivacious face, peeping through the curtain of the carryall. **1851** *Polly Peabl. Wedding* 132 In the old-fashioned, but strong 'carry-all,' ... he journeyed some forty miles. **1868** *Congress. Globe* 1 June 2756/1 Whether she can ... swear that her old carryall is not worth $300. **1876** *Vt. Board Agric. Rep.* III. 167 It is a settled fact that we cannot raise large horses for the team and carryall. **1886** H. James *Bostonians* 346 Six or eight men ... projected themselves upon the solitary rickety carry-all.

***Carrying,** *vbl. n.* +The process of transporting over a carry. Also attrib. — **1756** R. Rogers *Jrnls.* 17 Next morning [we] marched to the Indian carrying-path, that leads from Lake George to Lake Champlain. **1857** *Knickerb.* L. 495 This was my first experience in 'carrying,' the generic word for this sort of business.

Carrying horse. A baggage horse, pack horse. — **1758** in *Lett. to Washington* II. 351, I suppose that you may provide them w[i]th the necessary Carrying Horses for their Tents. **1788** Franklin *Autobiog.* 398 With two hundred and fifty-nine carrying horses, [they] were on their march for the camp.

+**Carrying place.** A place where canoes, goods, etc., have to be carried overland around barriers in a stream or from one stream to another.

1689 *Mass. H. S. Coll.* 4 Ser. V. 221 Then we marched down to ... several of the carrying-places. *c*1707 in G. Sheldon *Hist. Deerfield* (1895) I. 361 They followed them till Saturday Night, at which time they had got to the last carrying place. **1736** J. Gyles *Mem. Captivity* 6 A Carrying-Place is a Path or Track in which they pass from one River or part of a River or Pond to another. **1775** Benedict Arnold in J. H. Smith *Arnold's March* (1903) 480 Entered on the great carrying Place into Chaudiere Pond. **1797** Imlay *Western Territory* (ed. 3) 329 The carrying-place is three quarters of a mile long. **1832** Williamson *Maine* I. 47 Here was the Indian carrying place between Casco and Merry-Meeting bays. **1900** *Jrnl. Sch. Geog.* April 132 A number [of forts] were built ... in the vicinity of the Oneida carrying-place.

attrib. **1832** Williamson *Maine* I. 48 It then passes the 'carrying place rips,' half a mile in length.

Carrying trade. A branch of commerce involving the transporting of goods from one place or country to another. {1776-}

1789 *Ann. 1st Congress* I. 242 Can it be good policy, then, to destroy a competition among foreigners for the remainder of our carrying trade? **1806** *Ann. 9th Congress* 1 Sess. 619 What is called with us the carrying trade, and the direct trade, cannot easily be separated. **1812** *Niles' Reg.* II. 5/1 They have now 1 schooner ... and about 12 fishing boats and smacks, mostly employed in the carrying trade, viz. that of clams, oysters, [etc.]. **1871** W. M. Grosvenor *Protection* 17 A vast carrying-trade fell into our hands.

+**Carry-log.** A set of wheels used for transporting heavy objects, esp. logs.

1781 *Virginia St. Papers* I. 569 [Capt. Allen] is in want of waggons and a carry-log. *a*1859 *N.Y. Spirit of Times* (B.), I was drivin' 'long, settin' straddle of a stock on my carry-log, when ... the durned log come unfastened. **1862** *N.Y. Tribune* 27 Feb. (Chipman), The only carry-log we could obtain broke in attempting to transport the first gun.

+**Car seat.** (See quot. 1874.) Also attrib.

1852 *Rep. Comm. Patents 1851* 158 What we claim as new ... is the mode ... of reversing the back of car seats. **1866** 'F. Kirkland' *Bk. Anecdotes* 107 Mr. Ford sat on one of the car seats, with his child wrapped closely in his arms. **1874** Knight 481/2 *Car-seat,* a seat in a railway-car. The back is usually reversible, so as to adapt it for passengers in either direction of motion of the car.... Car-seats are also made reclining. *Ib.* 482/1 *Car-seat Arm-lock.* (*Railway.*) A lock attached to the bar of a seat-back, to prevent its being reversed by unauthorized persons. **1876** Ingram *Centen. Expos.* 179 The back of the settee reversed like a car seat.

+**Car shed.** A structure under which railroad cars or trains are protected from the weather.

1883 J. D. Fulton *Sam Hobart* 117 The machine-shop, elevators, car-sheds filled with freight cars, ... were on fire. **1889** Brayley *Boston Fire Dept.* 506 The West End Railway Company have at the Point three large stables and car-sheds. **1902** Harben *Abner Daniel* 26 It was near the ancient-looking brick car-shed under which the trains of two main lines ran. **1908** *Dialect Notes* III. 296 *Car-shed,* a large depot or station where the trains are under cover.

+**Carshop.** A place where cars are made or repaired.

1872 *Harper's Mag.* XLIV. 875/1 The Pullman Company ... in its new car-shops will employ one thousand more [persons]. **1878** Pinkerton *Strikers* 242 The car-shops consisted of a large main building, [etc.]. **1889**

BRAYLEY *Boston Fire Dept.* 506 Two large sugar refineries . . . are located here, . . . also Railroad machine and car shops. **1903** *Sci. Amer. Suppl.* LV. 22934/1 The following general classification of railway shops may be made: First, machine, erecting, and car shops; second, paint shops; third, round houses.

Car starter. 1. (See quots.) **2.** An employee who gives the signal at which cars start. — **(1) 1874** KNIGHT 484/1 *Car-starter. (Railway.)* A device to assist in starting a street-car from the dead stop. **1889** *Cent.* 835/3 *Car-starter*, . . . a device by which the momentum of a street-car is utilized in overcoming its inertia in starting again. **(2) 1876** *Scribner's Mo.* Apr. 911/2 The stockholders and directors, the 'car-starters' and 'spotters,' . . . were all embalmed in verse. **1889** *Cent.* 835/3 *Car-starter*, . . . a car- or train-dispatcher.

+**Car step(s).** The steps leading into a railroad car or streetcar.— **1863** 'G. HAMILTON' *Gala-Days* 44 A court of justice was improvised on the car-steps. **1901** MCCUTCHEON *Graustark* 41 He reached her side in time to assist her in mounting the car steps.

* **Cart,** *n.*

* **1.** A strong two-wheeled vehicle.

1637 *Plymouth Col. Rec.* I. 58 The heigh wayes, both for horse, cart, and foote, shalbe as followeth. **1676** SEWALL *Diary* I. 22 Daniel Goble is drawn in a Cart upon bed cloaths to Execution. **1715** *Boston News-Letter* 31 Oct. 2/2 Two Carts, a Slade and Trucks, four Horses, and a Negro Man a Carter, to be Sold. **1818** DARBY *Emigrant's Guide* 258 Waggons, carts, and drays . . . are made in this city [Pittsburgh]. **1854** BARTLETT *Personal Narrative* I. xii. 293 By sawing the box in two, the vehicle was converted into a cart. **1890** *Century Mag.* Dec. 171 These carts were always drawn by oxen.

2. Attrib. with *axle, clevy, cover, dung, frame,* etc.

1852 J. W. BOND *Minnesota* 257 Our French-Canadians and half-breeds, . . . have been . . . making new cart-axles. **1686** *Huntington Rec.* I. 435 An Inventore and aprizment of the Estate of John Core deceased, . . . Cart yoak and Cart clevey. **1843** FRÉMONT *Exped.* 12 The men were kept busy in drying the provisions, painting the cart-covers, and otherwise completing our equipage. **1749** ELIOT *Field-Husb.* ii. 23 [Farmers] without any concern to amend their Land, except a little helped by the Fold and Cart-dung. **1899** CHESNUTT *Wife of His Youth* 157 Needham and John took their seats on opposite sides of the cart-frame, with their feet dangling down. **1641** *New Haven Col. Rec.* 52 The hyer . . . for a horse or mare 16d, for cart furniture and man 6d. **1642** *Doc. & Rec. New-Hampshire* I. 144 James Wall shall have allowed to him 3 bushels of corn . . . to be paid by John Bursley for leaving open a cart gapp. **1647** *R.I. Col. Rec.* I. 175 He that shall malitiously and vnlawfully burne or spoile a cartheap of wood prepared for coals . . . shall pay to the partie agrieved his costs. **1653** *New Haven Rec.* 164 To maintayne a good Cart high way before their dores. **1706** *Derby* (Conn.) *Rec.* 238 Then it runns with a cart line 8 rods & three foot to a heap of stones and a little walnut bush. **1845** C. M. KIRKLAND *Western Clearings* 99 Oh! the pleasures of the cart ride! **1864** *N.Y. Herald* 7 April, The man . . . was struck on the head with a cart rung. **1825** WOODWORTH *Forest Rose* I. i, Did you say the houses all joined together? . . . To be sure they do, Harriet, just like our corn-house and cart-shed.

* **Cart,** *v. tr.* To convey in a cart or similar vehicle.

1640 *New Haven Col. Rec.* 38 So putt in that when carted from the water side . . . the hogshead may yet remaine full. **1713** *Southold Rec.* II. 260 There is a way through the land of Joseph Conkelyne to the mill meadows . . . for to cart hay or otherwise. **1832** *Congress. Deb.* 16 June 3636 Nor can they do this any more than an infant or an idiot could consent that his neighbor might . . . cart chip stone from his quarry on to his garden. **1881** *Harper's Mag.* Jan. 317/2, I'll cart her off in a wheelbarrow 'fore I'll pay such a price . . . to hev her put underground.

fig. **1909** R. A. WASON *Happy Hawkins* 241 We knew that Barbie carted around at all times what they call a spirit of combativity.

* **Cartage.** The act or process of conveying in a cart; the charge for this.

1757 W. SMITH *Hist. N.Y.* 187 Such is . . . the Situation of the Houses, that the mean Cartage from one Part to another, does not exceed one Quarter of a Mile. **1770** *Md. Hist. Mag.* XII. 353 Considering the Cartage of my Corn & wheat & the weakness of my Teams . . . I cannot Doe more. **1880** *Harper's Mag.* May 878/1 The receipts from this source did not pay cartage and other expenses.

* **Cart body.** The bed or box of a cart, in which the load is carried.

1662 *Essex Probate Rec.* I. 379 A stone cart & sleid & a ould cart body. **1779** *Narrag. Hist. Reg.* I. 93 Went to Tower hill for a cart body. **1834** SIMMS *Guy Rivers* 414 The conflagration . . . destroyed his cart-body and calicoes. **1868** G. G. CHANNING *Recoll. Newport* 19 The pin intended to hold the cart-body in its place got loose.

Cart box. *Obs.* A metal thimble or skein for use on the axle of a cart.

1688 *Huntington Rec.* II. 4 New cart and new wheels with a good sett of cart boxes. **1738** in *Letter Book J. Browne* (1929) 52 Latt the hollow wair be sorttable . . . sum scilets sum Cart Boxis two or three pair of andiorns. **1761** *N.J. Archives* XX. 529 To be sold . . . a large quantity of old refuse cast Iron, such as Cart-boxes, Sash-weights, [etc.]. **1790** *Penna. Packet* 2 Jan. 3/3 The Subscriber hath for Sale at his House . . . cart and waggon boxes of all sizes.

Cart bridge. *Obs.* A bridge over which carts may be driven.

1633 *Mass. Bay Rec.* I. 107 It is agreed, that there shalbe a sufficient cartbridge made in some convenient place over Muddy River. **1696** *Conn. Col. Rec.* IV. 188 That a sluice and cart bridge might be built upon the river. **1710** *Duxbury Rec.* 86 A stake, at or near the brook near the old cart bridge. **1734** *Mass. Ho. Repr. Jrnls.* XII. 131 A Grant of some Money, . . . to enable them to build a good Cart or Horse Bridge over Suncook River.

Cart driver. One who drives a cart. {1611} — **1891** *Century Mag.* March 759 The party was well armed and mounted, with the exception of the eight cart-drivers. **1898** PAGE *Red Rock* 3 The overseer's son . . . envied every cart-driver and stable-boy on the place.

* **Cartel,** *n.*

1. *Mil.* A written agreement for the exchange of prisoners; an exchange thus effected. {1692–}

1716 CHURCH *Philip's War* (1867) II. 179 There were several Gentlemen sent down from Canada to concert with our Governor about the settling of a Cartile for the Exchange of Prisoners. **1776** *Jrnls. Cont. Congress* V. 420 Three [letters] from Brigadier General Arnold . . . enclosing cartel . . . for exchange of prisoners. **1780** *Va. St. Papers* I. 385 Resolved, That he be and hereby is authorised to negotiate from time to time a Cartel or exchange of prisoners. **1884** GRANT in *Century Mag.* XII. 617 There was a cartel in existence at that time which required either party to exchange or parole all prisoners. **1891** *Ib.* April 852/1 A cartel had been agreed upon and a draft of five hundred prisoners was ordered for exchange.

attrib. **1796** *Captivity of Mrs. Johnson* 131 [He had] taken passage in a cartel ship for Halifax.

2. A ship used in exchanging prisoners. {1769–}

1812 *Niles' Reg.* II. 381/1 A cartel has arrived at Salem from Halifax, with fourteen or fifteen American prisoners. **1836** J. HALL *Stat. West* xii. 231 The *Enterprise* . . . made one voyage to the gulf of Mexico as a cartel.

* **Cartel,** *v. tr.* To exchange prisoners of war. — **1798** I. ALLEN *Hist. Vermont* 232 The Governor . . . directed a spirited officer . . . to take the prisoners out of confinement, and march them to the frontiers, for the purpose of being carteled.

* **Carter.**[1] The driver of a cart.

1658 *Boston Rec.* 147 Many children and others are exposed to many dangers . . . by the Carters riding through the towne in their Carts. **1724** *New-Eng. Courant* 20–27 April 2/2 A certain Person wants to hire a good Carter, or to sell his Team. **1790** BENTLEY *Diary* I. 210 He was 66 years old, a noted Carter. **1825** NEAL *Bro. Jonathan* II. 109 The stranger wore . . . a sort of gabardine, or carter's dress. **1851** CIST *Cincinnati* 49 Occupations [include] . . . carters, . . . 54 [people].

Carter.[2] +A variety of potato. Also attrib. with *potato.* — **1847** *Rep. Comm. Patents* (1848) 356 The mercers and carters, two favorite varieties, suffered most. **1849** EMMONS *Agric. N.Y.* II. 45 Carter Potato. . . . This is esteemed as a rich variety. **1855** *Amer. Inst. N.Y. Trans.* 209 One member . . . raised last year 300 bushels of carter potatoes on an acre.

* **Cart gate.** A wide gate through which a cart may be driven. — **1654** *Springfield Rec.* I. 230 The proprietors of the field in the long meddow shall make a sufficient Cart gate at the Bridge over the long medo brook. **1716** *Providence Rec.* XIII. 4 The s[ai]d Capt. Scott shall haue Liberty to fence the highway that was the Country Roade ouer Pautucket Riuer prouided he make conueniant Carte Gates in the Roade.

* **Cart horse.** A horse of a kind commonly used for drawing a cart.

1711 *Boston News-Letter* 15 Oct. 2/2 Two good Cart Horses, Trucks and Tackling to be sold. **1786** WASHINGTON *Diaries* III. 4, I also directed that . . . my Waggon and Cart Horses should be fed with chopped Rye. **1833** NEAL *Down-Easters* I. 123 His coal-black hair streaming over his shoulders like the mane of a cart-horse. **1876** INGRAM *Centennial Expos.* 673 They were mostly heavy cart horses, some of them magnificent animals. **1912** MRS. WOODROW *Sally Salt* 308 Old Anthony is as tame as a cart horse in comparison.

Carthouse. +A variety of apple. — **1818** *Amer. Mo. Mag.* II. 428/2 Table Apples [include] . . . Carthouse, December. **1851** BARRY *Fruit Garden* 289 [Winter apples] *Carthouse* (Gilpin, Red Romanite) . . . cultivated rather extensively in some parts of the south.

+**Car ticket.** A ticket entitling the holder to ride on the cars. — **1867** *Atlantic Mo.* Feb. 202/1, I was tearing a strip of Neck car-tickets in two, one day, to give Jenny half. **1885** CABLE in *Century Mag.* April 919/2 Instead of five-cent pieces we had car-tickets.

+**Car time.** The time at which a streetcar or train is due. — **1854** M. J. HOLMES *Tempest & Sunshine* xvii. 245 Ask anything you please; only be quick, for it is almost car time. **1868** MRS. WHITNEY *P. Strong* 126 This went through my mind, standing in the village waiting for the cars. There was little stir except what car-time made.

* **Carting.** Hauling or conveying in a cart. Also attrib.

1644 *Harvard Rec.* I. 6 Expense . . . carting . . . 3[s]–8[d]. *c***1650** *Lancaster Rec.* 260 The high way that lyes between the Carting place in the north River. **1716** *Wyllys Papers* 387 A List of Persons who have kindly promised me to give a days Carting to fetch home the Timber for my House. **1853** FOWLER *Home for All* 21 This will save even the carting of the materials. **1881** W. O. STODDARD *E. Hardery* 202 Perhaps he wanted to complete his manure carting first.

Cart irons. Iron parts used in making a cart. — **1647** *Essex Prob. Rec.* I. 83 A plow & cart Irons. **1725** Kidder *Exped. Lovewell* (1865) 93 [Inventory] Item, Cart Irons.

Cartman. A man who drives a cart. {1719–}

1807 IRVING, etc. *Salmagundi* xii. 273 They frightened a cartman's horse, who ran away. **1829** R. C. SANDS *Writings* II. 203 Two other persons came in: the one a plain-looking citizen, the other in a cartman's frock. **1879** *Scribner's Mo.* May 43/1 They have their social distinctions, too, for the cartmen who collect the refuse consider themselves immeasurably superior to the pickers. **1887** *Courier-Journal* 8 May 12/4 Thomas Ahearn, a cart man, has been indicted.

+**Cart neap.** The tongue or pole of a cart. — **1828** WEBSTER, *Clevis*, an iron bent to the form of an ox bow, with two ends perforated to receive a pin, used on the end of a cart-neap to hold the chain of the forward horse or oxen. **1884** *Harper's Mag.* Sept. 613/1 They had . . . perched themselves on a cart neap.

Cartoon, *n.* A picture or drawing, usually comic, caricaturing a subject or person. {1863–} — **1873** Paine *Thomas Nast* (1904) 280 [My eyes were] gladdened . . . at beholding your two cartoons. **1900** *Bookman* XII. 117/2 The best cartoons . . . are to be found, not in the weekly periodicals, . . . but in the daily newspapers. **1923** *Lit. Digest* 5 May 27/2 The moving cartoons now familiar at the picture shows are made with the aid of transparent sheets of pyralin.

Cartoon, *v.* +*tr.* To portray or caricature in a cartoon. — **1884** A. A. PUTNAM *10 Years Police Judge* 194 They make bold to cartoon . . . the goodly profession of the law. **1911** R. D. SAUNDERS *Col. Todhunter* 130 It's you they ought to cartoon, if they've got to cartoon somebody.

Cartoonist. One who draws cartoons. {1880–} — **1888** F. M. A. ROE *Army Lett.* 374 Mrs. Ord pulled up and pinned up her serge skirt in a way that would have brought in a small fortune to a cartoonist. **1904** A. B. PAINE *Thomas Nast* 268 Concerning the Credit Mobilier, the cartoonist had been eager to do precisely what they [opposition journals] demanded, having been withheld by his publishers.

Cartouche. Also †**carduce.** *Obs. Mil.* A cartridge. {1611–} Also attrib. with *belt* and *box*, or ellipt. for this (quot. 1808).

1678 *Plymouth Col. Rec.* X. 478 Powder bags, horns, carduce boxes, flints. **1689** *New Plymouth Laws* 215 Each man to be provided with . . . a horne or cartouch box suitable amunition & a snapsack. **1702** *Essex Inst. Coll.* XLII. 160 Inventory of ship: . . . Six catouch boxes. **1758** in *Lett. to Washington* II. 263, I likewise sent up to Capt. Dickinson . . . ten Muskets with Bayonets & Cartouches. **1777** *Md. Hist. Mag.* V. 208, I enclose you a Return of Cartouches wanting for the use of fort Mifflin. **1808** BARLOW *Columbiad* VII. 595 No cramm'd cartouch their belted back attires. **1813** *Niles' Reg.* III. 295/2 [List of military supplies includes] cartouche boxes and belts. *c***1836** CATLIN *Indians* II. 142 His musket levelled upon them—his bayonet fixed—his cartouch box slung.

Cart passage. A way or road suitable for a cart. — **1646** *Dedham Rec.* 112 Sufficient space for a convenient cart passage from the said p[ar]cell [of land] to the Streete. **1647** *Ib.* 151 To make a water course 4 foote wide & a sufficient cart passag ouer it is left to the care of Joh Kingsbery. **1683** *Providence Rec.* XVII. 22 Allowing to the Townes use a Cart passage.

+**Cart path.** An unmade way or road over which a cart may be driven.

1652 *Suffolk Deeds* I. 289 [The] land abutteth . . . vpon the Cart Path leading towards Muddey Riuer meadow towards the South. **1705** *Waterbury Rec.* 63 The hollow where his cart path goes up. **1724** *Cambridge Prop. Rec.* 288 Where the ancient cart path is now. **1833** *Trial E. K. Avery* 21 He was standing still in the cart path. **1854** THOREAU *Walden* 184, I was obliged to conduct him to the cart-path in the rear of the house. **1863** S. HALE *Letters* 14 Such a wood-road, narrow cart-path, grassy, and hung with raspberry bushes. **1870** 'O. OPTIC' *Field & Forest* 91, I gazed at her with curiosity and interest, as she walked up the cart path towards the castle. **1883** *Century Mag.* Sept. 651/1 There are numberless wagon roads that began existence merely as unofficial cart-paths. **1896** WILKINS *Madelon* 2 At times the road was no more than a cart-path through the forest.

+**Car track.** Usu. *pl.* The tracks or rails of a railroad, streetcar, or other car line.

1875 *Field & Forest* I. 36 One can hardly fail to notice the thrifty young trees . . . as they line each side of the car tracks. **1877** WM. WRIGHT *Big Bonanza* 308 A car-track—a railroad track in miniature—is laid through the floor in the centre of the station. **1882** C. KING *Rep. Prec. Metals* 639 The kind of car track employed can be allowed to control the grade within certain limits. **1897** FLANDRAU *Harvard Episodes* 223 He fell off when we went over the car-tracks. **1908** 'YESLAH' *Tenderfoot S. Calif.* 32 You have to follow the car tracks to find your way home. **1923** C. J. DUTTON *Shadow on Glass* 11 Then down a hill, crossing the electric car tracks.

Cart rail. A rail or bar of a cart frame or cart ladder. — **1823** COOPER *Pioneers* xxxv, Unable to distinguish . . . the hard visage that was just peering over the cart-rails. **1896** S. HALE *Letters* 298 After wrangling at cart-rails till I was nearly wild, . . . I shrieked to Francis, 'Let's get out of this!'

+**Car train.** *Obs.* A railroad train made up of engine and passenger cars. — **1855** *Amer. Inst. N.Y.* 164 Who does not fail to see, from the car trains in their daily and weekly transit, . . . all the low places? **1886** LOGAN *Great Conspiracy* 84 What with special car trains, and weighty deputations, and imposing processions, . . . his [Douglas's] political journey through Illinois had been more like a Royal Progress than anything the Country had yet seen.

***Cartridge.** Also †**catteridge, cattrage.**

***1.** A case or envelope of heavy paper, cardboard, or metal, containing the powder or powder and shot for firearms or cannon.

(a) **1716** CHURCH *Philip's War* 15 Mr. Church's Men having their Catteridges fix'd, were soon ready to obey his order. **1805** CLARK in *Lewis & C. Exped.* (1904) II. 190 Cattrages a few small lumbersom articles Capt. Lewis Desk and some books & small articles in it. **1848** J. S. ROBINSON *Santa Fé Exped.* 29 The people were very anxious to obtain cartridges. **1925** TILGHMAN *Dugout* 75 She snatched Ira's rifle and box of cartridges.
(b) **1766** *Essex Inst. Coll.* LII. 143 Some imprudent Persons firing Cannon, in ramming down the Charge before one of the Guns was well spunged, the Cartridge took Fire. **1867** EDWARDS *Shelby* iv. 61 The ramming home of each cartridge thrilled through every bosom upon the boat.

2. Attrib. with *bag, block*, etc.

1874 LONG *Wild-Fowl* 152 Hang up your cartridge-bag on a branch of the buck-brush. **1781** *Va. St. Papers* I. 496 The Cartridge Blocks at Mr. Moody's shop as well as those at the store have all been burned by the Enemy. **1778** *Jrnls. Cont. Congress* X. 271 In case in any State they have quantities of tin, instead of the cartouch boxes, an equal number of tin cartridge canisters be furnished. **1702** *Essex Inst. Coll.* XLII. 160 Inventory of ship . . . Eight Cartridge Cases. **1911** ROLT-WHEELER *Boy with Census* 92 They test the trigger pull, the cartridge ejection, the fall of the hammer . . . and all such points. **1868** *Rep. Munitions War* 47 The cartridge-extractor E in the act of drawing the empty cartridge C. *Ib.* 16 The recent fatal explosion in the Cartridge Factory at Woolwich.

Cartridge belt. A belt provided with loops for cartridges. — **1874** KNIGHT 487/2. **1884** *Century Mag.* May 140 Our men . . . groped about for shoes and cartridge-belts. **1891** *Scribner's Mag.* X. 219 Each man [was] girded with a cartridge-belt, and armed with a Winchester rifle. **1905** N. DAVIS *Northerner* 237 The soldiers, . . . with hands in their empty cartridge-belts, strolled into the yelling crowd.

Cartridge box.

1. A box or container for cartridges. {1699–}

1701 *N.H. Probate Rec.* I. 473, I also bequeath the sword, belt, Cartridg-Box, & Silver-headed Cane. **1787** *Ky. Gazette* 18 Aug., Every non commission officer and private, is by law directed to furnish himself with . . . a cartridge box, properly made, to contain and secure twenty cartridges. **1833** E. T. COOKE *Subaltern's Furlough* vii, The American light troops carry powder and ball flasks suspended across their shoulders in place of a cartridge-box. **1884** *Century Mag.* Nov. 109 Our dress consisted of a belt around the body, which held a cartridge-box and bayonet, [etc.]. **1888** P. H. SHERIDAN *Memoirs* I. 176 Every man had grabbed his rifle and cartridge-box at the first alarm.

||**2.** = CARTRIDGE BELT.

1846 EMORY *Military Reconn.* 61 Most were furnished with the Mexican cartridge-box, which consists of a strap round the waist, with cylinders inserted for the cartridges.

Cartridge paper. Heavy coarse paper formerly used in making cartridges. {1712–}

1678 *New Castle Court Rec.* 241, 3 quiers of Cartridge paper. **1792** *Ann. 2nd Congress* 1031 In the enumeration of the several kinds, made subject to that duty, sheeting and cartridge paper have been omitted. **1865** *Atlantic Mo.* XV. 649 Bishops . . . who convert old sermons upon the divine sanction of slavery into cartridge-paper. **1910** 'O. HENRY' *Strictly Business* 245 The artist gazed dreamily at the cartridge paper on the wall.

Cartridge shell. The shell or container for the powder and bullet of a cartridge. — **1868** *Rep. Munitions War* 284 A slight pressure of the thumb applied to the operating lever of this gun, exerts a considerable and ample force to . . . withdraw a tightly expanded cartridge-shell from the bore of the barrel. **1870** KEIM *Sheridan's Troopers* xxi. 146 The grass, where they lay, was much trodden, and a number of cartridge-shells, scattered on the ground, testified to the valor of the defence.

Cart road. A road over which a cart may be driven. {1868–}

1700 *Duxbury Rec.* 71 From said pine tree by the same line, a range of trees marked, until we come to a cart road. **1844** GREGG *Commerce of Prairies* II. 53 A point from whence there was a cart-road to Santa Fé. **1856** *Spirit of Times* (N.Y.) 27 Dec. 277/3 A plan is before the Common Council to cut a cart road from Beekman-street across the old Park. **1883** *Harper's Mag.* Oct. 711/2 The 'pine-hen,' with a loud, horrified cluck, . . . flopped across the cart-road.

***Cart's tail, Cart tail.** The back or hind part of a cart.

In former use, as in Eng., commonly mentioned in connection with the punishment described in the quotations.

1686 in Munsell *Annals Albany* (1850) II. 91 The court have ordered the s[ai]d neger Hercules to be whipt throw the towne att the cart tale by the hands of the hangman. **1723** *Weekly Mercury* 29 Aug.–5 Sept. 2/2 They . . . received Sentance . . . to be tied to a Carts-Tail, and receive 30 lashes through the Town. **1750** A. M. Earle *Curious Punishments* 80 David Smith . . . was sentenced to be whipped at the Carts Tail round this Town. **1764** HUTCHINSON *Hist. Mass.* (1795) I. i. 187 They were sentenced to be whipped at the cart's tail in Boston. **1839** C. F. BRIGGS *Harry Franco* II. i. 2 Three or four cartmen . . . were seated on their cart tails, each of them studying a penny paper. **1870** WHITTIER *Spiritual Manifestation* line 35 Scourged at one cart-tail, each denied The hope of every other.

attrib. **1843** WHITTIER *Cassandra Southwick* 39 Sore from their cart-tail scourgings, and from the pillory lame, Rejoicing in their wretchedness, and glorying in their shame.

***Cartway.** A road or way over which carts are driven.

1634 *Essex Inst. Coll.* IV. 89/2 They doe promise to make a suffitient cart way. **1661** *Manchester Town Rec.* 10 The Cart way that now is shall be left soe for the use of the Plantation. **1711** in *Mass. H. S. Coll.* 6 Ser. V. 239 You must get some good pilate that knows the cart-ways well. **1767** in *Mayflower Desc.* XI. 133 A convenient cartway out of the neck on the upland. **1876** *Wide Awake* 175/1 The cart-way led round the foot of a . . . mountain. **1897** BRODHEAD *Bound in Shallows* 5 This stony, deeply rutted cart-way, twisting past the station platform, made a final rise to the level of the bluff.

***Cart wheel.**

***1.** The wheel of a cart.

1653 *Conn. Public Rec.* I. 241 Will: Waller is to deliuer unto John Clarke Junior . . . a pair of carte-wheels. **1769** *Md. Hist. Mag.* XII. 281, I can not possibly tell when Buckly will finish the cart wheels. **1865** MRS. WHITNEY *Gayworthys* iii. 33 All the way from a cart-wheel to a tea-plate.

2. *colloq.* A large coin, esp. a silver dollar. Also attrib. {a five-shilling piece 1867–}

[**1855** BARNUM *Life* 21 Talk of 'cart wheels,' there was never one half so large as that dollar looked to me.] **1873** MILLER *Amongst Modocs* 38, I gave you a whole cart-wheel, did I not? a clean twenty dollar, and told you to keep the change. **1899** T. HALL *Tales* 242 My buckskin cayuse agin two hundred an' fifty cart-wheels. **1904** *Boston Herald* 7 July 6 Small bills grow scarcer and scarcer west of the Mississippi river, cartwheel dollars taking their place. **1910** *N.Y. Ev. Post* 8 Dec. 8 We have detected little popular enthusiasm for anything smaller than a 'cart-wheel.'

‖**Cartwrighting.** The work of a cartwright. — **1845** F. DOUGLASS *Life* 12 The blacksmithing, cart-wrighting, coopering, and grain-grinding, were all performed by slaves.

***Carver.**

***1.** A wood carver.

1630 SMITH *True Trav.* 35 Gold-smiths, Plummers, Carvers, and Polishers of stone. **1682** *Boston Rec.* 72 David Edwards became surety to the town for Richard Knight, carver. **1714** *Boston News-Letter* 13–20 Sept. 2/2 With Smiths work, Blockmakers, Joyners, Carvers work. **1800** BENTLEY *Diary* II. 328 John Skillings, an eminent Carver in Boston, died suddenly. **1879** *Scribner's Mo.* May 46/1, I found also a figure-head carver making a woman for a new vessel.

2. One who splits fish in preparing them for market.

1765 R. ROGERS *Acc. N. America* 21 The carver, with a single-edged knife, six or eight inches long, . . . splits the fish open.

3. A carving knife. {1840–}

1816 *Austin Papers* (1924) I. 262, I Carver and Fork. **1853** SIMMS *Sword & Distaff* 355 The carver was as frequently the broadsword as the knife, and the fingers supplied all deficiency of forks.

+4. (See quotation.)

1913 W. C. BARNES *Western Grazing Grounds* 381 Cutting Horse.—A horse used especially for the work of cutting out; a 'carver,' a 'chopper,' chopping horse.

Car wheel. +The wheel of a railroad car.

1845 *Index to Patents* (1874) I. 231 Car-wheel [invented by] G. W. Eddy [of] Waterford, N.Y. [patented] Dec. 26, 1845. **1858** *Rep. Comm. Patents* (1859) I. 509 Improvement in Casting Car Wheels. **1878** PINKERTON *Strikers* 248 A detachment of soldiers . . . rolled several car-wheels upon the tracks to prevent the passage of the cars. **1883** 'MARK TWAIN' *Life on Miss.* xlviii, A man whom the spirits . . . were teaching how to contrive an improved railway car-wheel. **1887** C. B. GEORGE *40 Yrs. on Rail* iv. 67 Richard Norton Allen, the inventor of the famous paper car-wheel called by his name.

Car window. +A window in a railroad car.

1854 M. J. HOLMES *Tempest & Sunshine* xvii. 239 From the car windows Fanny watched the long blue line of hills. **1868** A. B. CONDICT *P. Eckert* 171 A lady, speaking from a car window to a young man. **1873** J. H. BEADLE *Undevel. West* ii. 53 From a car window one may note a curious though very gradual and almost imperceptible change in soil and climate. **1905** N. DAVIS *Northerner* 138 From the car-window, as the long trip back to Alabama neared its end, Falls marked its icy smile with bitter eyes.

+**Car works.** A factory for making cars or wagons. — **1884** HOWELLS *S. Lapham* xx, The Great Lacustrine & Polar Railroad . . . 's going to build car-works right by those mills.

+**Casa.** *S.W.* [Sp.] A dwelling house.

1848 BRYANT *California* 336 They [the insects] do not disturb the inmates of those casas where cleanliness prevails. **1851** *Alta Californian* 3 Aug., Here in California . . . we bandy about the common nouns . . . casa, [etc.]. **1853** BREWERTON *With Kit Carson* 151 In the *casa* of a New Mexican *rico* stands, or rather hangs, a picture which I was requested to examine. **1871** HARTE *Luck Roaring Camp*, etc. 213 That white building you see yonder is the *casa.* **1895** REMINGTON *Pony Tracks* 91 The men repair to the *casa* and indulge in games and pranks.

Cascade. Also †**casquade. a.** A small waterfall. {1684–} **b.** *pl.* A stretch of river in which there are such falls.

1738 BYRD *Dividing Line* (1901) 166 A Ledge of Rocks, which reacht across the river, and made a natural casquade. **1781–2** JEFFERSON *Notes Va.* (1788) ii. 27 The only remarkable cascade in this country, is that of the Falling spring in Augusta. **a1817** [see CATARACT]. **1884** *Cent. Mag.* Feb. 497 He was stationed in Washington Territory, and while there was engaged in defending the Cascades of the Columbia River against Indians.

transf. **1835** IRVING *Tour on Prairies* xxxv. 272 Sundry great morsels of beef, with a regiment of turnips tumbling after them, and a rich cascade of broth, overflowing the whole.

***Case,** *n.*[1]

1. Physical condition or state. {1640–}

1634 *Maine Doc. Hist.* III. 31 They [the pigs] kept themselves in very good Case. **1729** J. HEMPSTEAD *Diary* 210 Thos. is not well. Somthing out of case yesterday. **1745** *Essex Inst. Coll.* XLVIII. 299, I was still out of Case but keept about. **1807** GASS *Journal* vi. 68 In the day time they are permitted to run out and gather what they can; . . . and in this way are kept in tolerable case. **1834** *Visit to Texas* xxi. 195 As for my little horse, he also had returned in better case.

+2. The condition of leaf tobacco when soft and pliant.

1640 *Md. Archives* 98 Bad Tobacco shall be judged ground leafes Second Crops leafs notably brused . . . frost bitten . . . in the house sooty wett or in too high Case. **1661** *Md. Hist. Mag.* VIII. 7 [Two hogsheads] struck in too high case and in a rotting condition. **1724** JONES *Virginia* 40 When it [=tobacco] is in proper Case, (as they call it), . . . they *strike* it, or take it down. **1800** W. TATHAM *Tobacco* 37 *Case* is a technical term made use of by the planters to signify a specific condition of the plants. **1864** *Maine Agric. Soc. Ret.* 162 The fires should be suffered to go out and the tobacco be suffered to come in case, or get soft again. **1903** *Dialect Notes* II. 308 When hung in a barn the leaves become dry and brittle. Toward spring the leaves soften and when quite pliable are said to be 'in *case.*'

***3.** *Law.* A cause or suit brought up for trial.

1649 *R.I. Court Rec.* I. 7 Such cases as are presented to this Court & putt of untill the next courte if the Pll: [etc.]. **1767** CUTLER in *Life & Corr.* I. 19 [I] was employed in two cases at the Bar. **1840** *Niles' Nat. Reg.* 4 April 80/3 The case has terminated, the jury finding a verdict of not guilty, on the ground of insanity. **1925** BRYAN *Memoirs* 18, I used to go down to the courthouse . . . and listen to the trial of cases.

+4. *colloq.* A person peculiar or remarkable in some way. Frequently with a qualification as *bad* case, *hard* case, etc.

1840 HALIBURTON *Clockm.* 3 Ser. 112 Indeed, among our ministers he is actilly at the top of the pot. He is quite 'a case,' I do assure you. **1853** F. W. THOMAS *J. Randolph* 123 He's tall in a good many ways; he's what we call a 'case.' **1856** STOWE *Dred* I. xv. 203, This sister of mine is a pretty rapid little case, I can tell you, as you saw by the way she circumvented us this morning. **1870** W. M. BAKER *New Timothy* 115 The General will tell you . . . what a terrible hard case I've been. **1873** ALDRICH *Marj. Daw*, etc. 79 Mr. O'Rouke was a very bad case indeed; . . . he was almost constantly drunk. **1890** *Harper's Mag.* May 894/1 The hardest-looking case I had ever seen came to the door.

***Case,** *n.*[2]

***1.** A receptacle or container.

1640 *Conn. Public Rec.* I. 449 An Inventory of the goods and Cattell of James Olmestead . . . one case of bottells. **1678** *Ib.* III. 12 Others shall be provided wth a good and serviceable horss, sword, case of pistolls and holsters. **1855** SIMMS *Forayers* 384 There he produces a little tin case which might contain a dozen sheets of paper folded compactly.

***2.** *Printing.* A shallow tray for type, having compartments or sections for the various letters, figures, etc.

1725 *New-Eng. Courant* 4 Jan. 1/2 You Letter-picking Juglers at the Case. **1771** FRANKLIN *Autobiog.* 257 And now he had got another pair of cases, and a pamphlet to reprint. **1841** *Knickerb.* XVII. 34 A single mould candle . . . shed an uncertain light over the forms, cases, and cabalistic instruments of art. **1870** MAVERICK *Raymond & N.Y. Press* 233 Each man stood at his 'case' 'stick' in hand.

+3. *Faro.* The last card of any denomination remaining in the dealing box.

1856 *Harper's Mag.* Dec. 69/1 He has no great faith in 'cases,' but believes in betting on three cards at a time.

+b. *To keep cases,* to note the cards as they come from the dealing-box. Also transf.

1896 G. ADE *Artie* iii. 24, I could see that a Johnny-on-the-spot with a big badge marked 'Committee' was tryin' to keep cases on her. **1903** A. ADAMS *Log Cowboy* xiii. 199 We found Quince Forrest and Wyatt Roundtree playing the faro bank, the former keeping cases. **a1906** 'O. HENRY' *Trimmed Lamp*, etc. 216, I've been keeping cases on you. **1916** H. L. WILSON *Somewhere in Red Gap* vii. 290, I don't know what her notion was, keeping cases on the orchestra that way. **1920** MULFORD *J. Nelson* xiv. 144, I'm keepin' cases on these cattle.

Case, *n.*[3] *Obs.* [E. Anglian dialect.] Cause. — **1667** *Topsfield Rec.* 8 Vntel such time as the Towne see Case to alter it. **1675** EASTON *Indian*

War 30 We have Case to think that was the great Case of the war against them.

‖**Case,** *n.*[4] =CACHE *n.* — **1807** GASS *Journal* viii. 97 It was thought adviseable to leave . . . part of the stores and baggage, and some of the men were engaged in digging a case to bury them in.

***Case,** *v. tr.* To remove or strip off (the skin of an animal) entire. {1601–1796}

1806 LEWIS in *L. & Clark Exped.* (1905) IV. 245 The deerskins which we have had cased for the purpose of containing our dryed meat. **1821** J. FOWLER *Journal* 44 The Hunters killed two deer, [and] cased the skins for Baggs. **1900** SMITHWICK *Evolution of State* 178 The vessels for carrying water were made of deerskins cased—stripped off whole.

Case comb. A comb carried in a case. {1654; *Sc.* cais camb, 1575} — **1870** 'F. FERN' *Ginger-Snaps* 26 He can draw from another pocket a case-comb, and put those fine touches to his hair.

Case knife. {1704–} An ordinary table knife. (Originally, one furnished with a sheath.)

1714 *Boston News-Letter* 12–19 April 2 To be Sold by Publick Vendue or Outcry . . . Broad Cloths, Case Knives and Forks. **1764** *Mass. Gazette* 28 June 4/2 Samuel Franklin . . . has just imported from London a good assortment of case knives and Forks. **1835** LONGSTREET *Georgia Scenes* 227 The stock of Soap-stick seemed to have been made with a case knife. **1902** HARBEN *Abner Daniel* 243 She turned over the pone with the aid of a case-knife.

+b. *Case-knife bean:* (see quotation). *Obs.*

1790 S. DEANE *New-Eng. Farmer* 20/1 The case-knife bean is so called, because the pod is shaped like that instrument.

Casemate, *v. tr.* To cover or provide with a casemate. — **1717** *Mass. H. Repr. Journals* I. 253 That all the Repairs mentioned therein be proceeded in as soon as conveniently may be, excepting the second Article relating to the Casemeting the Cover'd way. **1741** *S.C. Hist. Soc. Coll.* IV. 11 The Castle . . . [is] a square Fort . . . with four Bastions; . . . the Rampart twenty feet high, casemated underneath for Lodgings. **1763** W. ROBERTS *Nat. Hist. Florida* 24 It is a square building . . . and it is cazemated.

***Cash,** *n.*

***1.** Money; financial resources.

1654 JOHNSON *Wonder-w. Prov.* 182 A chargeable war with the naked Natives, that have neither plunder, nor cash to bear the charge of it. **1704** *Boston News-Letter* 29 May 2 [He] lodg'd his Cash with our Merchants here to remit to England. **1771** FRANKLIN *Autobiog.* 254 My whole stock of cash consisted of a Dutch dollar, and about a shilling in copper. **1887** C. B. GEORGE *40 Years on Rail* ii. 35 Tickets . . . were at first sold only to through passengers, while the 'locals' had to pay cash. **1902** WISTER *Virginian* xxv. 290 Alter your plans for spending cash in town, and make a little money instead.

b. Attrib. and comb. with *balance, basis, capital,* etc.

1882 SWEET & KNOX *Texas Siftings* 101 He neglects to reduce his cash balance by subscribing the $2 in advance. **1883** 'MARK TWAIN' *Life on Miss.* xxxiii, The purpose [of a cotton-growing syndicate] is to work on a cash basis. **1861** *Chicago Tribune* 19 July 1/8 Wanted—A Partner with a small cash capital, to take half interest in a light and profitable business. **1903** [see CARRIER 4]. **1837** J. C. NEAL *Charcoal Sk.* (1838) 65 These Timpkinses . . . won't lend me any money, because I can't pay—and they're persimmony and sour about cash concerns. **1902** *Harper's Mag.* May 965/1 He . . . refurnished it, keeping only the tables, the partition, the small cash-counter by the door, and the cooking-range. **1868** *Dept. Agric. Rep.* (1869) 18 Wheat is a cash crop, and demands a small outlay of labor. **1847** *Knickerb.* XXX. 281 Mrs. — . . . is always a cash customer. **1889** *Cent.* 843/2 *Cash-day,* . . . a day on which cash is regularly paid; a pay-day or settling-day. **1844** A. LAWRENCE *Diary & Corr.* 187, I have derived . . . as much comfort and enjoyment from it as I ordinarily should from a cash dividend on my shares. **1887** C. B. GEORGE *40 Years on Rail* xii. 243 There was not a single cash fare in the train of seven cars. **1889** *Century Mag.* XXXVII. 557/2 Mr. Chase went in person to New York to try the effect of the sale of 'cash gold' upon the trade in phantom gold. **1853** J. W. BOND *Minnesota* 166 All the products of the soil find a ready cash market. **1887** H. FREDERIC *Seth's Brother's Wife* 235 He's standing out for a cash payment. **1781** *Va. St. Papers* I. 438 The articles were furnished at cash prices. **1865** *Atlantic Mo.* XV. 86 There were 101 joint-stock companies for the underwriting of fire-risks, with . . . net cash receipts from premiums amounting to $10,181,031. **1878** *Sci. Amer.* 16 Feb. 95/1 The new 'cash recorder' certainly offers a very simple mode of keeping forcibly accurate records. *Ib.,* The Cash Recording Machine. We illustrate herewith a new machine for making people honest. **1892** *Vt. Agric. Rep.* XII. 153 [Sheep raising] was the *one* source upon which the farmer depended for cash returns. **1872** *Harper's Mag.* XLIV. 498/1 In the north wing [of the Treasury building] is the celebrated marble 'cash-room,' the walls, floors, doors, and window-frames of which are of solid marble. **1863** MRS. WHITNEY *F. Gartney* xi, Noting down against each the cash valuation. **1862** *Trial C. M. Jefferds* 48 Charles then came up to the cash window and threw a fifty-cent piece in.

+2. *Financial.* (See quot. 1870.) Also attrib. indicating immediate delivery.

1870 MEDBERY *Men of Wall St.* 49 Cash, in broker's language, means that the contract entered upon shall be fulfilled by payment and delivery of stock, at or before 2.15 P.M. of the day of sale. **1875** *Chicago Tribune* 13 Sept. 6/1 A large Premium on Cash Pork, Wheat and Corn. **1900** S. A. NELSON *A B C Wall St.* 133 Cash grain. Grain for immediate delivery, or to be delivered during the current month. **1902** NORRIS *Pit* (1922) ix, Jadwin sold, . . . a tremendous load of 'cash' wheat at a dollar and sixty cents a bushel.

+3. *Cash down,* in ready money; cash paid down.

1839 J. S. JONES *People's Lawyer* II, ii, This umbrella—what is it worth; cash down? **1870** MRS. STEPHENS *Married in Haste* xxxvi. 195 One thousand cash down, and it is yours. **1879** TOURGEE *Fool's Errand* x. 45, I bought this property, paid for it cash down. **1890** M. E. RYAN *Told in Hills* 97 He wants the money cash down for this lay-out. **1907** WHITE *Arizona Nights* ii. 33, 'I'll pay you next time I come down.' 'Cash down,' growls Pete. **1911** L. J. VANCE *Cynthia* 222 They bought this vessel . . . for a song, paying part cash down.

+b. *Equal to cash:* (see quot. 1889).

1836 HALIBURTON *Clockm.* 1 Ser. xvi, Though I say it, that shouldn't say it, they [the U.S. Americans] fairly take the shine off creation—they are actilly equal to cash. **1889** FARMER 126 Equal to Cash—Of undoubted merit. An idiom, no doubt allusive to the fact that paper currency is largely the medium of exchange.

+c. *Cash on the nail,* ready money; 'spot cash.' Also *cash down on the nail.*

1855 HALIBURTON *Nat. & Hum. Nat.* II. 111 What's the price . . . cash down on the nail? **1883** 'MARK TWAIN' *Life on Miss.* xxii, He sold unaccountable cords of it every year for cash on the nail.

comb. **1892** A. C. GUNTER *Miss Nobody of Nowhere* xvi. 185 These horse dealers are cash-on-the-nail chaps, so I gave 'em my check.

Cash, *v.*

1. *tr.* To exchange (a note, check, order, etc.) for cash; to obtain or give cash for. {1811–}

1828 H. FINN, etc. *Whimwhams* 18 Her owner's notes would not At Boston banks be cashed. **1840** DANA *Two Years* xxix. 341 At the same time he cashed the order, which was endorsed to him. **1889** *Cent.* 843/1 The paying teller of a bank cashes notes when presented.

+2. *intr. To cash down, over, up,* to supply cash, to pay or settle at once. *colloq.*

1854 M. J. HOLMES *Tempest & Sunshine* xvi. 227 Tempest is in a desput hurry to know whether I'm goin' to cash over and send her to market in New Orleans. **1882** SWEET & KNOX *Texas Siftings* 41 Cash down, quick, or I'll bounce you off at the next station we come to. **1890** *Buckskin Mose* xvii. 246 He might run to Tom Long's, and inform him of our use of the contents of his cellar, without cashing up.

+3. *tr. To cash in,* in poker, faro, etc., to hand in (one's checks, chips, etc.) and get cash for; to convert into cash. Also absol. *colloq.*

1899 G. ADE *Doc' Horne* xxi. 232, I lost back to $2,500 and cashed in. *a***1906** 'O. HENRY' *Trimmed Lamp* 233 With his gold dust cashed in to the merry air of a hundred thousand. **1916** WILSON *Red Gap* 265 Then he watches Sandy Sawtelle cashing in his chips.

fig. **1896** G. ADE *Artie* v. 46 If you're stuck on him I'll cash in right here and drop out of the game. *a***1904** WHITE *Blazed Trail Stories* viii. 146, I don't stack up very high in th' blue chips when it comes to cashin' in with th' gentle sex. *Ib.* xii. 224 By all the rules of the game, Peter should have failed long since, should have 'cashed in and quit' some five years back.

b. *tr.* and *intr.* To pass away, to die. Also without *in. colloq.*

1888 *Amer. Humorist* 11 Aug. (F., p. 134), Do you and each of you solemnly sw'ar that you will . . . cling to each other through life till death calls upon you to cash in your earthly checks? **1908** MULFORD *Orphan* xix. 250 The Orphan not only saved me but also some of them, for I'd a gotten some of them before I cashed. **1909** R. A. WASON *Happy Hawkins* 287 She was welcome to take my life any way she wanted . . . or if she selected that I cash it in the next hour, my only regret would be that I hadn't but one life to give her. *Ib.* 318 Just at this time ol' Pizarro cashed in. **1911** L. J. VANCE *Cynthia* 49 They hadn't lived together for twenty years when he cashed in. **1920** C. E. MULFORD *J. Nelson* xx. 220 He's been follerin' me around steady since Wolf cashed in. **1922** Z. GREY *Last Man* ix. 210, I'm goin' to cash. I feel it heah.

+Cash article. An article or commodity for which money may be readily obtained. — **1835** *S. Lit. Messenger* I. 339 A man was a cash article there. **1847** *Knickerb.* XXIX. 200 Cotton . . . has the advantage of always being a cash article. **1858** HOLMES *Autocrat* ii. 29 You are wasting merchantable literature, a cash article.

Cashaw. Variant of CUSHAW.

Cashbox. A box in which cash is kept. {1864–}

1855 *Harvard Mag.* I. 452 Millions of grateful sixpences flowed into that worthy's cash-box. **1870** 'F. FERN' *Ginger-Snaps* 60, I should nail up a cash-box at the foot of the stairs, and people should drop in whatever they liked. **1894** 'MARK TWAIN' *P. Wilson* xix, A lamp was burning low, and by it stood the old man's small tin cash-box, closed.

Cashboy. An errand boy in a store who takes cash or change to the clerks or customers.

*a***1872** BRACE *Dangerous Classes N.Y.* 355 They . . . are cash-boys, light porters. **1872** ROE *Barriers Burned Away* iv, Applying at a large dry-goods store, he was told that they wanted a cash boy. **1882** *Century Mag.*

Oct. 956/1 Some means of conveying small parcels and packages from one part of the store or building to another without the aid of 'cash' or elevator boys. **1899** G. ADE *Fables in Slang* (1902) 186 In a Department Store, while waiting for the Cash Boy to come back with the Change, he would find out the Girl's Name.

Cashgirl. A girl who performs duties similar to those of a cashboy. — **1880** *Harper's Mag.* June 37/1 The cash-girls are paid a dollar and a half a week. *a***1906** 'O. HENRY' *Trimmed Lamp*, etc. 78, I was a cash girl and a wrapper and then a shop girl until I was grown.

***Cashier.** An employee, officer, or official of a bank or other business establishment who has charge of money.

1796 *Boston Directory* 231 Burroughs, George, cashier of Union bank, Pitt's lane. **1834** C. A. DAVIS *Lett. J. Downing* 165–66 All the presidents and cashiers, and clerks, and money counters, about the crib. **1892** GUNTER *Miss Dividends* 111 Can I see the cashier or the president?

transf. **1729** FRANKLIN *Writings* II. 145 The Banks are the general Cashiers of all Gentlemen.

Cashiership. The position held by a cashier. {1884–} — **1820** *Niles' Reg.* XVII. 440/2 Jonathan Smith has resigned the cashiership of the U.S. bank. **1891** EGGLESTON in *Century Mag.* Feb. 551 What would become of the cashiership?

Cashmere. Also †**cachmere.**

1. A cashmere shawl. {1822–}

1833 NEAL *Down-Easters* I. 143 Every pulse fluttering at the sight of her cashmere. **1865** STOWE *House & Home P.* 179 We don't of course, expect to get a fifteen-hundred-dollar Cashmere.

2. The fabric of which these shawls are made; also a fine woolen cloth resembling this.

1851 *Harper's Mag.* May 864/1 Boots of pale violet cachmere and morocco. **1887** N. PERRY *Flock of Girls* 270 She held up to the light a long polonaise of gray cashmere. **1901** CHURCHILL *Crisis* 40 She wore a long Talma of crimson cashmere.

3. A garment made of cashmere.

1886 H. D. BROWN *Two College Girls* 174, I heard her again behind that hedge. My embroidered cashmere was the subject, if you please. **1887** N. PERRY *Flock of Girls* 273, I shall give Joe my foulard and the gray cashmere. **1897** E. W. BRODHEAD *Bound in Shallows* 56 Mrs. Bohun dragged her festal black cashmere from the room.

4. Attrib. with *scarf, shawl*, etc.

1844 S. M. FULLER *Woman in 19th C.* (1862) 27 Every article of luxury from jewels and cashmere shawls down to artificial flowers. **1854** M. CUMMINS *Lamplighter* xxvii. 238 She sat there, attired in a blue cashmere morning-dress. **1891** WILKINS *New Eng. Nun* 141 She wore a gay cashmere-patterned calico dress with her mourning-bonnet. *Ib.* 174 Old Jonas . . . had his wife's cashmere scarf wound twice around his neck.

+**Cash register.** A mechanical device for recording cash receipts. Also attrib. — **1879** *U.S. Patents Off. Gazette* XVI. 847/1 [Patent No.] 221,360. Cash Register and Indicator. . . . Filed Mar. 26, 1879. *c***1895** F. NORRIS *Vandover* (1914) 43 Behind it was a huge, plate-glass mirror, balanced on one side by the cash-register and on the other by a statuette. **1905** *Cassier's Mag.* XXVIII. 353/2 The normal courses in the art of selling cash registers cover six weeks. **1915** *Literary Digest* L. 678/1 Editors commenting on the quashing of the National Cash-Register Company convictions.

+**Cash sale.** A sale for cash; a deal or transaction involving cash payment.

1808 *Steele Papers* II. 558 A cash sale at present I found to be totally impracticable. **1820** *Niles' Reg.* XVIII. 25/1 It changes the mode of disposing of the public lands from credit to cash sales. **1865** *Atlantic Mo.* XV. 86 This measure of metropolitan influence is based on statistics attainable mainly outside of cash sales. **1902** HARBEN *Abner Daniel* 278 That's the only thing that now stands between you and a cash sale. **1911** R. D. SAUNDERS *Col. Todhunter* 109 Quit settin' there lookin' like a poor man at a cash sale.

+**Cash store.** A store in which articles are sold for ready money. Also attrib.

1830 PAULDING *Chron. Gotham* 156 The Honourable Peleg Peshell, cash-store keeper at Peshellville. *Ib.* 159 Passing a unanimous resolution, not to buy anything at his cash-store. **1849** WILLIS *Rural Lett.* xviii. 156 You do injustice to the 'cash stores' of Owego. **1873** 'G. HAMILTON' *Twelve Miles* x. 171 There is a warning spurt and sputter of Chinese crackers about the stoop of the 'cheap cash store.'

+**Cash system.** A system of conducting an enterprise without allowing credit. — **1841** CIST *Cincinnati* 93 The last two [periodicals] . . . are published on the cash system. **1842** *Diplom. Corr. Texas* (1908) I. 579 Countries forced from necessity to carry their produce through the United States ports, must have been greatly crippled and impoverished under the Cash System of duties now adopted by this Government. **1854** BENTON *30 Years' View* I. 12/1 The principle of the relief was to change all future sales from the credit to the cash system.

Casing. {1791–}

+**1.** The framework about a door or window.

1873 F. ROE *Army Lett.* 143 We draped them from the casing of one window to the casing of the next. **1887** A. W. TOURGEE *Button's Inn* 203 A hand touched the casing, and a footstep fell upon the floor. **1913** STRATTON-PORTER *Laddie* (1917) 38 All the casings were oiled wood, and the walls had just a little yellow.

+**2.** *Mining.* (See quot. 1881.)

1869 J. R. BROWNE *Adv. Apache Country* 525 They are all true fissure veins, with well-defined casings. **1872** 'MARK TWAIN' *Roughing It* xl. 218 It's a blind lead for a million!—hanging wall—foot wall—clay casings—everything complete! **1881** RAYMOND *Mining Gloss.* 18 Pac[ific slope]. Casings are zones of material altered by vein-action, and lying between the unaltered country rock and the vein.

attrib. **1872** 'MARK TWAIN' *Roughing It* xxix. 160 The wall or ledge of rock . . . maintained a nearly uniform thickness . . . away down into the bowels of the earth, and was perfectly distinct from the casing rock on each side of it.

+**3.** An iron pipe or tubing, esp. as used in oil and gas wells.

1875 *Chicago Tribune* 6 Nov. 2/5 The gas was flowing through a 5⅝ inch casing, the full size of the well, at a pressure of 100 pounds to the square inch. **1883** *Century Mag.* July 330/1 The 'casing,' a six-inch iron tube, is put in to keep the water from veins in the rock from getting into the well. **1901** *Munsey's Mag.* XXV. 747/2 The hole is gradually reduced to five and five eighths inches in diameter. Then a tube of this size, technically called a 'casing,' . . . is put down and ground into the tapering portion of the hole.

b. A watertight jacket around a gun barrel.

1888 *Century Mag.* XXXVI. 889/1 By means of this casing, or water-jacket, it is impossible to overheat the gun by firing.

+**4.** The outer rubber covering of an automobile tire.

1902 *Sci. Amer.* 1 March 150/1 The inner tube is protected by an outer tube or casing having a U-shaped cross-section and made of interlaid rubber and fabric.

+**5.** Usu. *pl.* Intestines of cattle, hogs, etc., prepared for use as containers for sausage.

1904 *Encycl. Amer.* s. v. *Packing Industry*, The intestines are cleansed and salted and used for sausage casings in their own sausage factories.

***Cask,** *n.*

***1.** A cylindrical wooden container made with staves and hoops; a barrel or keg. Also collective.

1622 'MOURT' *Relation* 141 Let your Cask for Beere and Water be Ironbound. **1701** *Boston Rec.* 10 No cooper or coopers within this town Shall Fire or burn thier cask in any Shop ware house or other place, then in a Sufficient Chimney made convenient for that use. **1755** in *Lett. to Washington* I. 106 The Coopers . . . ask extravagant Rates for Casks to wit 4/ a bar[re]l. **1891** C. ROBERTS *Adrift Amer.* 21 There is some water in that cask (pointing out a barrel that stood at the side of the house).

attrib. **1683** *Huntington Rec.* I. 360 At a towne meeting Legally warned . . . John Wood was chosen caske gager. **1818** *Niles' Reg.* XV. 106/2, 398,340 lbs. of cask hoop iron. **1761** E. Singleton *Social N.Y.* 364 To be sold, wholesale and retail, by William Keen, grocer and confectioner on Rotten Row: . . . Jarr Raisins and Cask ditto. **1856** KANE *Arct. Exp.* I. xvii. 209 Enriching them in return with . . . a treasure of old cask-staves. **1772** *Carroll P.* in *Md. Hist. Mag.* XIV. 140, I desier Mr. Deards may pack 10 or 12 Dzn. of the Cask Wine th[a]t came from France.

2. A container of this kind in which tobacco was formerly packed.

1636 *Va. House of Burgesses* 126 Be yt allso Enacted . . . that his Fee and allowance be two pence per cask for the Tobacco. **1655** *Md. Council Proc.* 314 Eleven hundred and fiftie pounds of Tobacco in Caske without Ground Leaves.

+**3.** The weight formerly allowed or estimated for the cask or hogshead in which tobacco was marketed.

1642 *Md. Archives* I. 123 Every freeman or freewoman & every Servant . . . shall pay the said Tobacco with Cask (or allow for Cask after the rate of 10l p hundred). **1650** *Ib.* 297 That Georg Manners be allowed 200 of Tob: and Caske for his Corroners ffee. **1705** *N.C. Col. Rec.* I. 617 A Plea of Debt for Four Hundred Forty and Three pounds of good Merchantable Tobacco & Cask. **1731** *Md. Hist. Mag.* XIX. 285, I have never received the Acct. Sales you mention of three hogshead & Cask.

***Cask,** *v.* +*tr.* To put or pack (tobacco) in a cask. — **1639** *Md. Archives* I. 70 Tobaccos shall be struck and casked. **1644** *Ib.* IV. 270, 200 lb. tob for 2. tonne of cask provided & used by him for the casking of the said tobacco.

+**Casked,** *ppl. a.* [f. prec.] — **1650** *Md. Archives* I. 321 Hee demanded twelve thowsand pounds of Casked Tobacco. **1666** *Ib.* II. 132 Upon the penalty or forfeiture of tenn thousand pounds of Casked Tobacco. **1669** *Ib.* 220 Two thousand pounds of Casked Tobacco.

***Casket.** +A coffin.

1863 HAWTHORNE *Our Old Home* (1879) 101 'Caskets'!—a vile modern phrase, which compels a person . . . to shrink . . . from the idea of being buried at all. **1874** *Congress. Rec.* 13 March 2143/2 The casket containing Mr. Sumner's remains having been removed [etc.]. **1888** *N.Y. Life* 21 Jan. 26/2 The pall-bearers placed the casket before the chancel. **1892** M. A. JACKSON *Gen. Jackson* 474 The casket, enveloped in the Confederate flag, . . . was placed in the centre of the reception-room in the Executive Mansion. **1908** C. H. PARKHURST *Little Lower than Angels* 264 We stand by the side of the casket.

+**Casket girl.** *Hist.* One of the girls who were sent out by the French authorities in 1727 to become wives of the early French settlers in the Louisiana area. — **1880** CABLE *Grandissimes* iv. 30 Clotilde, the Casket-

Girl, . . . was one of an heroic sort. **1895** J. WINSOR *Miss. Basin* 260 An occasional arrival of 'casket girls' stirred the domestic passions.

Caspian tern. The largest species of tern, *Sterna caspia.* — **1858** BAIRD *Birds Pacific R.R.* 859 *Sterna Caspia,* Pallas. The Caspian Tern. *Hab.*—Coast of New Jersey northward. **1874** COUES *Birds N.W.* 667.

Casse tête. [F.] (See quotations.) — **1778** CARVER *Travels* 294 Those . . . who have not an opportunity of purchasing these kinds of weapons, use bows and arrows, and also the cassé Tête or war club. **1812** in J. Cutler *Topog. Descr. Ohio* 195 The men were armed with the *Casoetite* [*sic*], or war club.

***Cassia.** Any one of various North American plants of the senna family. — [**1824** LONDON *Encycl. Plants* 348 *Cassia nictitans* Virginian Cassia.] **1847** DARLINGTON *Weeds & Plants* 109 *Cassia Marilandica,* L. . . . Maryland Cassia. Wild, or American Senna. **1856** *Rep. Comm. Patents: Agric.* 65 The caterpillar of the . . . *Zanthidia niceppe,* . . . sometimes devours the Maryland cassia.

Cassimere.

1. A twilled smooth woolen cloth used for men's clothing. {1774–}

1789 WASHINGTON *Diaries* IV. 27 Their Broad-cloths are not of the first quality, as yet, but they are good; as are their Coatings, Cassimeres, Serges and Everlastings. **1812** *Niles' Reg.* II. 9/1 Leaving the soft fine shorter wool for good coat cloths, and cassimeres. **1873** *Winfield* (Kansas) *Courier* 15 May 3/2 Stacks and Piles of cottonades, tweeds, cassimeres, . . . and all new, nobby and cheap, at Old Log Store. **1888** W. LAWRENCE *A. A. Lawrence* 30 He opened his own counting-room in a corner of the Phillips Building near Liberty Square, and for three years was a commission merchant for broadcloths, cassimeres, and silks.

attrib. **1845** *Lowell Offering* V. 97 The 'cassimere weaving-room,' where all kinds of cloth are woven from plain to almost exquisite fancy.

2. *pl.* A pair of trousers made from this cloth.

1882 PECK *Sunshine* 26 He had to put on a pair of nankeen pants and hide his cassimeres in the boat house.

+**Cassin.** [John *Cassin,* 1813–69, Amer. ornithologist.] Used in the names of various birds: (see quotations).

1858 BAIRD *Birds Pacific R.R.* 174 Cassin's Flycatcher . . . Valley of Gila, eastward to Pecos river, Texas. *Ib.* 340 Cassin's Vireo. . . . Fort Tejon, Cal. **1869** *Amer. Naturalist* III. 184 The first specimen collected was a Cassin's Kingbird (*Tyrannus vociferans*). **1874** COUES *Birds N.W.* 106 *Carpodacus Cassini* . . . Cassin's Purple Finch. *Ib.* 140 *Pencœa Cassini* . . . Cassin's Pine Finch. *Ib.* 209 Blue Crow; Cassin's Jay; Maximilian's Jay. *Ib.* 238 *Tyrannus vociferans,* . . . Cassin's Flycatcher.

+**Cassine, Cassena.** Also **casseena, cusseena,** etc. [F. and Sp. fr. Amer. Indian.]

1. A species of southern holly, *Ilex vomitoria;* the leaves of this used for preparing a drink.

(*a*) **1587** HAKLUYT tr. Laudonnière *Notable Hist. Fla.* in *Voyages* III. (1600) 307 Baskets full of the leaues of Cassine, wherewith they make their drinks. **1682** ASH *Carolina* 16 The famous Cassiny . . . is the Leaves of a certain Tree, which boyl'd in Water (as we do Thea) wonderfully enliven and envigorate the Heart. **1785** MARSHALL *Amer. Grove* 26 *Cassine.* Cassine, or South-Sea Tea-Tree. **1792** J. POPE *Tour S. & W.* 95 The Cassine is a low umbrageous Tree. . . . 'Tis from the Leaves of this Tree . . . the Creeks make their Black Drink.

(*b*) **1699** DICKENSON *God's Protecting Providence* 29 Having a Pott on the Fire wherein he was making a Drink of the Leaves of a Shrubb (which We understood afterwards . . . , is called Casseena). **1709** LAWSON *Carolina* 90 This Yaupon, call'd by the South-Carolina Indians, Cassena, is a Bush, that grows chiefly on the Sand-Banks and Islands, bordering on the Sea of Carolina. **1745** *Itinerant Observ.* 32 The settlers make use of prodigious Quantities [of persimmon] to sweeten a Beer, which they brew of *Cassena* and divers Herbs. **1775** ADAIR *Indians* 361 The Yopon, or Cusseena, is very plenty, as far as the salt air reaches over the low lands. **1838** *S. Lit. Messenger* IV. 800/2 The popular designation of this species of Holly [south-sea tea] is Yaupon or Yopon, a name of Indian origin. It is also sometimes called Cassena. **1857** GRAY *Botany* 263 *Ilex Cassine,* Cassena, Yaupon. . . . Leaves used for tea, as they were to make the celebrated *black drink* of the North Carolina Indians.

2. A drink prepared from this plant.

(*a*) **1587** HAKLUYT tr. Laudonniere's *Notable Hist. Fla.* in *Voyages* III. (1600) 307 The King . . . commaundeth Cassine to be brewed, which is a drinke made of the leaues of a certaine tree: They [=Fla. Indians] drinke this Cassine very hotte. **1791** W. BARTRAM *Travels* 236 The king conversed, drank Cassine and associated familiarly with his people and with us.

(*b*) **1699** DICKENSON *God's Protecting Providence* 31 [They] went to drinking Casseena. **1775** ADAIR *Indians* 167 They drink of the Cusseena, using such invocations as haue been mentioned. **1896** *Gard. & For.* IX. 253 Cassena—from *cassine,* . . . a name in the language of the Timucua Indians (a family long ago extinct) for an exhilarating beverage prepared from the leaf of the plant. The word has the appearance . . . of having been modified by a prefix & suffix, from the Muscogee name âssi, 'leaves,' abbreviated from *âssi lupûtski,* 'little leaves.'

3. Attrib., esp. with *yaupon* (*yupon, yapon*).

1699 *God's Protecting Providence* 68 Also they gave us some Casseena-drink. **1797** in *Ga. Hist. Soc. Coll.* III. i. 7, I have bought some Aus-ce (Cassine Yupon) for you. **1800** B. HAWKINS *Sk. Creek Country* 30 They haue but a few plum trees, and several clumps of cassine yupon. **1806** in *Ann. 9th Congress* 2 Sess. 1128 The cassina yapon . . . grows here along the banks of this stony creek. **1861** WOOD *Botany* 497 *Ilex Cassena* Walt. Cassena Tea. A shining, evergreen, bushy shrub, common in S. States near the coast.

+**Cassinet.** Also **casinitte, casinet.** A light mixed cloth having a cotton warp and a filling of fine wool or wool and silk.

1813 *Austin Papers* (1924) I. 231, 3 yds. Casinitte. **1817** S. BROWN *Western Gaz.* 94 The articles manufactured consist of . . . chambrays, cassinets, sattinets. **1838** *S. Lit. Messenger* IV. 59/2 His pantaloons and vest were of white—the former of the finest cassinet. **1850** GARRARD *Wah-To-Yah* ix. 123 His pantaloons, of gray cassinet, were threadbare. **1863** *Rio Abajo Press* 17 Feb. 2 Most of the raw-material which is now exported, may be more profitably manufactured at home into flannels, blankets, casinets, carpets, etc.

attrib. **1846** *Indiana Mag. Hist.* XXIII. 447, I have known him . . . wear . . . cassinet pantaloons. **1863** DICEY *6 Mo. Federal States* I. 255 Casinet pants, and yellow gauntlet gloves.

Cassique. *Obs.* exc. hist. Also **cassick, casseka.** [Variant of CACIQUE.] {*a*1618}

+**1.** A chief or leader among the Indians.

1670 *N. C. Col. Rec.* I. 208, I there contracted a leauge with the Emp[ero]r & all those petty Cassekas. **1674** in *S.C. Hist. & Geneal. Mag.* (1910) XI. 84 Wee the Cassiques naturell Born Hears & Sole owners & proprietors of great & lesser Cussoe. **1763** W. ROBERTS *Nat. Hist. Fla.* 6 Then the cassique carries round a kind of liquor, like our tea.

+**2.** Formerly a member of an order of nobility in Carolina provided for by John Locke's scheme of government.

1669 *S.C. Hist. Soc. Coll.* V. 121 Each Square that shall be taken up by a Landgrave or Cassique is to be a Barrony. **1702** *S.C. Statutes* I. 42 The upper house, consisting of the Landgraves and Casiques, . . . are . . . a middle state between Lords and Commons. **1738** BYRD *Dividing Line* (1901) 77 Neither Land-graves nor Cassicks can procure one drop for their wives. **1911** *S.C. Hist. & Geneal. Mag.* XII. 111 On 1st April, 1686, Sir Nathaniel Johnson was created a Cassique by the Lords Proprietors of Carolina.

***Caster.** {1676–81}

+**1.** A cruet stand; = CASTOR *n.*[2]

1881 *Harper's Mag.* May 853/2 This caster . . . held instead of the ordinary pepper and mustard, various liquids and spices of mysterious nature. **1883** 'MARK TWAIN' *Life on Miss.* xxv, A bright new edifice, picturesquely and peculiarly towered and pinnacled—a sort of gigantic casters, with the cruets all complete. **1897** C. A. DANA *Recoll. Civil War* 49 The table is a chest with a double cover, . . . the dishes, knives and forks, and caster are inside.

attrib. **1906** 'O. HENRY' *Four Million* 251 On each table is a caster-stand containing cruets of condiments and seasons.

+**2.** One who fishes with rod and reel.

1885 *Harper's Mag.* April 776/1 The caster stands on a platform. **1903** *Forest & Stream* LX. 150/3, The big fish is what we are all after, and the caster gets them if anyone does.

***Casting.**

***1.** The process of pouring molten metal into molds; founding.

1841 PARK *Pantology* 530 The *casting,* or founding, of statues, is most frequently executed in bronze. **1875** *Chicago Tribune* 11 Sept. 4/1 We are fortunate to reach the place just at eleven o'clock, when a casting is to take place.

attrib. **1849** N. KINGSLEY *Diary* 30 Our sugar is black enough for casting sand. **1875** *Chicago Tribune* 11 Sept. 4/6 Foundrymen regard their casting-brushes . . . as indispensable.

2. An article made by this process. {1869–}

1788 in *Rep. Comm. Patents* (1850) 532 His application . . . for castings for a steam engine, is insinuated to have been in October. **1815** *Niles' Reg.* VIII. 141/1 Three large and extensive air-founderies, where are cast all kinds of hollow-ware, castings, cannons, cannon balls, [etc.]. **1889** 'MARK TWAIN' *Conn. Yankee* ix. 112 He went rattling and clanking out like a crate of loose castings.

+**b.** *slang.* A piece of money; a coin.

1846 CORCORAN *Pickings* 18 He slipped a Mexican casting into the hand of Fournier. **1851** *Polly Peabl. Wedding* 41 A substantial farmer, . . . by years of toil, had accumulated a tolerable pretty pile of castings.

3. The throwing of a line in fishing.

1885 *Harper's Mag.* April 776/2 A considerable degree of flexibility is necessary to efficient . . . casting. **1888** *Outing* July 307 In the minnow casting (½ oz. sinker) for black bass, the record was beaten fearfully.

attrib. **1869** W. MURRAY *Adventures* 29 To every fly-fisher my advice is, be sure and take plenty of casting-lines. **1885** *Harper's Mag.* April 779/2 The casting elbow is to be held quite close to the side.

Casting net. In fishing, a net designed for throwing out and drawing in immediately. {*a*1680–}

1644 *Essex Inst. Hist. Coll.* L. 335 One rugg two Coverlets: two blanketts: my casting nett. **1645** *Essex Probate Rec.* I. 48 One casting nett. **1884** KNIGHT *Suppl.* 177/2 *Casting Net,* . . . a net in extensive use in the West Indies, Florida, and elsewhere on the southern coast.

Casting voice. *Obs.* =next. {1622-}

1638 *Conn. Public Rec.* I. 25 The Gouernour or Moderator shall haue . . . the casting voice. **1641** *Mass. Liberties* 228 The Governor shall have a casting voice whensoever an Equi vote shall fall out in the Court of Assistants. **1650** *Harvard Laws* (1812) 7 The said President having a casting voice. *a***1817** DWIGHT *Travels* I. 271 The Speaker has a casting voice.

Casting vote. A deciding vote given by a chairman or president when the voting is equal; the right to give such a vote. {1692-}

1678 *Springfield Rec.* II. 137 Nath: Burt had a casting vote. **1789** J. MORSE *Amer. Geog.* 298 The governor . . . has a casting vote in their debates. **1846** POLK *Diary* (1929) 129 The Senate would be equally divided and that would enable the Vice-President to give his Casting vote for the bill. **1852** *Harper's Mag.* V. 693/1 A bill was also passed . . . in the House of Representatives . . . by the casting vote of the Speaker. **1886** ALTON *Among Law-Makers* 15 The Vice-President . . . can vote only in the event of a tie; in that case he may determine the question by his 'casting-vote.'

Cast iron, Cast-iron.

1. Iron that has been shaped or cast in molds. {1664-}

1744 FRANKLIN *Account Fire-Places* 14 These are all of Cast Iron. **1805** in R. H. Collins *Kentucky* (1874) I. 408 Tobacco, flour, beef, pork, tallow, hog's lard, hemp, cordage, whisky, or cast iron will be taken in payment for the land. **1851** CIST *Cincinnati* 298 The front will be of brick, finished with cast-iron, painted in imitation of free-stone. **1875** KNIGHT 1198/1 A process for decarbonizing molten cast-iron . .-. was invented by C. Shunk.

2. Attrib. **a.** With *boot-jack, case, pillar,* etc.

1839 *Amer. Phil. Soc. Proc.* I. 71 This cast-iron pipe has on its exterior a lead pipe. **1851** CIST *Cincinnati* 194 The upper mill-stone is inclosed in a *cast iron* case of suitable weight. **1855** M. THOMPSON *Doesticks* vii. 52 My frantic eye caught sight of my cast-iron boot-jack. **1876** J. S. INGRAM *Centen. Expos.* xi. 355 A railroad supported on one side by heavy cast-iron pillars . . . carries a travelling platform. **1883** *Harper's Mag.* Oct. 716/1 The residence . . . is disfigured . . . by tawdry modern cast-iron work, sanded to represent stone. **1894** ROBLEY *Bourbon Co., Kansas* 26 Their cooking utensils consisted of a big cast-iron skillet, . . . iron spoons and knives and forks.

b. In figurative uses. {1830-}

1850 JUDD *R. Edney* ii. 25 That well-meaning but stupid creature, with a cast-iron face, has undertaken to perform for us the office of warmth and sociability. **1852** S. S. COX *Buckeye Abroad* 12, I would advise every one who thinks of crossing the sea, to provide a cast-iron stomach. **1863** 'E. KIRKE' *Southern Friends* ii. 26 Two dull, cast-iron sermons at the old meeting-house. **1883** 'MARK TWAIN' *Life on Miss.* xxxi, I opened up in cast iron German.

+**Cast-iron dog.** *colloq.* The Mexican hairless dog. — **1853** BREWERTON *With Kit Carson* (1930) 208 One of those hairless, rat-tailed New Mexican curs, which the Americans are in the habit of designating as 'cast-iron dogs.' **1882** SWEET & KNOX *Texas Siftings* 60 The stranger . . . calls him a cast-iron dog.

* **Castle.**

* **1.** A building or structure fortified against attack.

1643 *New Eng. First Fruits* II. v, [We have] planted 50 Townes and Villages built 30. or 40. Churches, and more Ministers houses; a Castle, a Colledge, Prisons, Forts. **1705** *Boston News-Letter* 5 Nov. 2/1 All Officers of Customs, Naval and Impost Officers, and Commanders of Castles and Forts within this Province. **1776** *Jrnls. Cont. Congress.* IV. 15 The seizing & securing the barracks & Castle of St. Augustine will greatly contribute to the safety of these colonies.

attrib. **1655** *Essex Inst. Coll.* IX. 188 Benjamin ffelton beeinge spoken to by the Select men to gather his part of the Castle Rate.

+**2.** The chief place of defense or refuge for Indians.

*a***1649** WINTHROP *History* I. 3 When we came before the town, the castle put forth a flag. **1666** *State N.Y. Doc. Hist.* (1849) I. 72 The Governor . . . by the mistake of his guides hapned to fall short of the castles of the Mauhaukes. **1696** *Ib.* 346 The Five Indian Nations . . . have been driven by the French from their wooden castles and are returned. **1721** *Mass. H. S. Coll.* 2 Ser. VIII. 244 The Mohawks have two castles; the nearest to Albany is about 40. miles distant. **1794** S. WILLIAMS *Hist. Vt.* 142 The Indians . . . have no other fortification but an irregular kind of fortress, which they call a castle. **1826** COOPER *Mohicans* v. 25 Every Indian who speaks a foreign tongue is an Iroquois, whether the castle of his tribe be in Canada, or be in York.

+**Cast net.** A casting net. — **1855** 'P. PAXTON' *Capt. Priest* 143 Whether the fish be taken by rod and reel, or by drop-line, by drag-net or cast-net. **1883** RATHBUN in *U.S. Museum Bulletin 27* 119 Cast nets measuring from 10 to 15 feet in diameter are preferred to the seines.

* **Castor.**[1]

1. Originally a hat made of beaver fur but later a hat made in imitation of this. {1640-}

1651 *Suffolk Deeds* I. 190 Seventy pounds to be pajd in felts & castors . . . and thirty pounds to be pajd in bevors. **1667** P. SANFORD *Letter Book* 46 Please to sent [*sic*] me a good hatt Case with two very good Castors in it for my owne Ware. **1691** SEWALL *Letter-Book* I. 118 Send me a couple of good Castors for my own wearing. **1739** FRANKLIN *Poor Richard* (1740) 18 He also makes and sells all Sorts of Hats, Beavers, Castors and Felts. **1826** COOPER *Mohicans* ii, The stranger, making diligent use of his triangular castor, to produce a circulation in the close air of the woods. **1850** LEWIS *La. Swamp Dr.* 22 Gazing at our graceful castors [we] remember the identical hollow tree in which we caught the coon that forms its fair lines and symmetrical proportions. *a***1918** G. STUART *On Frontier* II. 24 'Con' Orem . . . deposited his castor over the ropes.

+**2.** The gland or musk bag of the beaver.

1765 R. ROGERS *Acc. N. America* 255 The musk bags or castor taken from these animals [beavers] is of great use among druggists. **1806** LEWIS in *L. & Clark Exped.* (1905) III. 319 The male beaver has six stones, two of which contain a substance much like finely pulverized bark of a pale yellow colour . . . these are called the *bark stones* or castors.

3. An odorous substance made of the dried perineal glands of the beaver. {1601-}

1778 CARVER *Travels* 460 Castor, which is useful in medicine, is produced from the body of this creature [the beaver]. **1815** *Niles' Reg.* IX. 94/2 Oils, of mint, sassafras, worm and penyroyal and castor, . . . are to be found in our druggists' shops. **1833** CATLIN *Indians* I. 115 A piece of the 'castor,' which it is customary amongst these folks to carry in their tobacco-sack to give it a flavour. **1834** A. PIKE *Sketches* 33 You then dip a little twig in your bait (that is, in dissolved castor). **1888** *Dispensatory U.S.* (ed. 16) 1746 The virtues of castor are impaired by age.

Castor.[2] +(See quot. and cf. CASTER 1.) — **1853** FELT *Customs N.E.* 21 Castor.—as a frame of wood or metal, it holds small bottles with various condiments. . . . Now it is seen in most families with comfortable means of support.

‖**Castor.**[3] (See quotation.) — **1892** *Harper's Mag.* March 496/2 An Indian who came in with furs threw them down, and when they were counted received the right number of castors—little pieces of wood which served as money.

+**Castor bean.** The seed of the castor-oil plant; the plant itself.

1829 *Va. Lit. Museum* 221 It is the palma chrysti, called by them, castor bean. **1850** *New Eng. Farmer* II. 64 The castor bean is a common production in parts of Southern Illinois. **1872** *Illinois Dept. Agric. Trans.* 159 The crops are corn, wheat, oats, grass and castor-beans. **1883** *Rep. Indian Affairs* 80 Winter wheat, corn, oats, rye, broom-corn, sorghum, castor beans, . . . are successfully grown. **1901** MOHR *Plant Life Ala.* 56 *Ricinus communis* (castor bean).

* **Castoreum.** =CASTOR[1] 3.

1701 C. WOLLEY *Jrnl. in N.Y.* (1860) 40 The bladders containing the Castoreum are distinct from the Testicles or Stones. **1778** CARVER *Travels* 461 A soft resinous adhesive matter, mixed with small fibres, greyish without, and yellow within, of a strong disagreeable and penetrating scent, and very inflammable. This is the true castoreum; it . . . becomes brown, brittle, and friable. *a***1842** O. RUSSEL *Journal* (1921) xxvi. 106, I had bathed my wounds in salt water and made a salve of beaver's oil and castorium.

Castor hat. =CASTOR[1] 1. {1680-}

1655 *Essex Probate Rec.* I. 202 Caster hatt. **1708** *Boston News-Letter* 15-22 March 2/2 A Person . . . described to be of a middle Stature, to have a brown friese Coat, a black Castor Hat. **1778** *Jrnls. Cont. Congress* X. 11 Every regimental commissioned officer in the Army of the United States shall during the war be entitled to draw annually . . . a fine castor Hatt. **1811** *Niles' Reg.* I. 292/1 Philip J. Hahn, makes . . . rorum, castor, or common fur hats. **1857** E. STONE *Life of Howland* v. 99, I . . . asked him the price of a castor hat.

Castor oil. Oil obtained from the seed of the castor-oil bean. {1746-}

1812 *Niles' Reg.* II. 86/2 *Sweet and castor oil* is made in great abundance on the sea coast of Georgia. **1823** W. H. KEATING *Narr.* 49 Raising the Palma Christi, and manufacturing from it castor oil. **1841** *Niles' Nat. Reg.* 21 Aug. 400/1 A western paper states that castor oil is manufactured to a large extent in Illinois. **1867** COZZENS *Sayings* iii. 19 What has become of the castor-oil I gave you to put away?

attrib. **1834** PECK *Gaz. Illinois* 47 There are five or six castor oil presses in the state. *Ib.* 164 [Brighton] has two stores, a castor oil factory, and a dozen families.

Castor-oil bean. The tropical plant or shrub palma Christi, *Ricinus communis;* =CASTOR BEAN.

1814 PURSH *Flora Amer.* II. 603 Ricinus communis. . . . Frequent in old plantations in Virginia and Carolina. . . . Known by the name of Castor-oil Bean. **1831** PECK *Guide* 158 The *Palma christi,* or castor oil bean, is produced in large quantities. **1840** DEWEY *Mass. Flowering Plants* 72 Castor-oil Bean . . . is the plant whose fruit yields the castor-oil. **1847** WOOD *Botany* 488 Castor-oil Bean . . . is a tall, smooth plant of a light bluish-green color. **1901** C. MOHR *Plant Life Ala.* 594 *Ricinus communis,* Castor Oil Bean.

Castor-oil plant. The palma Christi or castor-oil bean. {1845-}

1836 LINCOLN *Botany* App. 133 *Ricinus communis,* castor oil plant, palma christi. **1848** E. SMITH *Journey thro' Texas* 32 We saw the Castor Oil Plant and the Sarsaparilla Plant growing luxuriantly. **1863** C. C. HOPLEY *Life in South* II. 306 The castor-oil plant is indigenous in Louisiana, Alabama, and Florida. **1874** *Rep. Comm. Agric.* (1875) 152 The seeds of the castor-oil plant . . . have not been very extensively produced in this country until within a few years. **1895** *Dept. Agric. Yearbook* (1896) 192 Castor-oil plants have been cultivated to some extent in the United States for over twenty years.

+**Castor tree.** A species of magnolia. — **1871** DE VERE 208 The Beaver-tree (Magnolia glauca) is so called in the West, while elsewhere it is more generally known as Castor-tree.

+**Castor wood.** =CASTOR TREE. — **1859** BARTLETT 27 *Beaver-tree, . . .* called also Beaver-wood, and sometimes Castor-wood.

Cast steel, Cast-steel. Steel made by a process involving fusion. {1800–}

1807 IRVING, etc. *Salmagundi* xii, His learned distinctions between wrought scissors, and those of cast-steel. **1843** *Niles' Nat. Reg.* 6 May 160/2 The manufacture of cast steel by Messrs. Shoenberger, is now in full and successful operation. **1876** KNIGHT 2364/2 This is essentially the process yet followed in making fine cast-steel, suitable for cutlery.

attrib. **1847** EMORY *Military Reconn.* 132 Their implements of husbandry are the wooden plough, the harrow, and the cast-steel axe. **1876** INGRAM *Cent. Expos.* 191 Galvanized cast-steel wires. *Ib.* 242 They exhibited bars of cemented steel, blooms and cast-steel ingots.

∗ **Cat,** *n.*

∗ **1.** =WILDCAT *n.*

1685 T. BUDD *Penna. & N.J.* 38 The commodities fit to send to England . . . are the skins of the several wild Beasts that are in the Country, as . . . Mink, Cat, &c. **1709** LAWSON *Carolina* 118 Wild Cat. This Cat is quite different from those in Europe; being more nimble and fierce, and larger. **1846** T. B. THORPE *Myst. Backwoods* 179 As an animal of sport, the cat in many respects is preferable to the fox.

2. Short for CATFISH. {1796}

Also *brown cat, channel cat, mud cat,* etc.: see these words.

1705 BEVERLEY *Virginia* II. 32 Conger-Eels, Perch, and Cats, &c. **1760** WASHINGTON *Diaries* I. 149 Hauld the Sein again, catchd 2 or 3 White Fish . . . and a great Number of Cats. **1784** *Ib.* II. 312 The large Cats and other fish of the Ohio are to be met with in great abundance in the River above them. **1846** T. B. THORPE *Myst. Backwoods* 131 A cat would come along and swallow the trout, and perhaps, on the Mississippi, the alligators use up the cat, and so on to the end of the row. **1889** RILEY *Pipes o' Pan* 171 A sunfish, or a 'chub,' or 'cat'—A 'silver-side'—yea, even that!

attrib. **1850** LEWIS *La. Swamp Dr.* 112 Whenever the levees proved insufficient, or happened to break, chickens and garden-tools fell to a discount, and ducks and cat-hooks rose to a premium.

+**3.** (See quotations.)

1893 EGGLESTON *Duffels* 189, I broke into my stock of school-boy stories of the jokes about the 'cat,' or roll pudding we had twice a week. **1899** *Boston Transcript* 14 Jan. 12/2 The word cat is still applied to the first rough coat in plastering which fills the space between the laths.

4. Any one of various games played with a ball, or a ball and bat, stick, etc. {1626–}

1812 in *Niles' Reg.* IV. 329/1, How much time I wasted when a boy in playing cat and fives and steal-clothes. **1850** *Knickerb.* XXXV. 84 We . . . never indulged in a game of chance of any sort in the world, save the 'bass-ball,' 'one' and 'two-hole-cat,' and 'barn-ball' of our boyhood. **1894** P. L. FORD *P. Stirling* 49 Here 'cat' and 'one old cat' render bearable many a wilting hour for the little urchins.

∗ **b.** A small stick or peg used in the game of tipcat.

1864 WEBSTER 1387/3 *Tipcat,* a game in which a small piece of wood, called a *cat,* is tipped or struck with a club or bat. **1891** *Amer. Folk-Lore* IV. 233 The 'cat' is whittled from a piece of wood, and is usually about six inches in length by an inch in diameter. . . . The pitcher throws the cat toward the circle.

5. In faro: (see quotation).

1889 *Cent.* 852/3 *Cat,* . . . the occurrence of two cards of the same denomination out of the last three in the deck.

6. Phrases. **a.** *How* or *which way the cat jumps,* how affairs turn out. {1827–}

1825 WOODWORTH *Forest Rose* I. ii, You'll find yourself mistaken, for I know how the cat jumps. **1830** S. SMITH *Major Downing* 6 In these politics there's never any telling which way the cat will jump. **1859** BARTLETT 146 *Fence-riding,* the practice of 'sitting on the fence,' or remaining neutral in a political contest until it can be seen 'which way the cat is going to jump.'

+**b.** *Like a cat in a strange garret,* frightened, amazed, excessively timid.

1824 *Woodstock* (Vt.) *Observer* 16 March (Th.), 'What was King Caucus like?' said an old gentleman. 'Why, like a cat in a strange garret, frightened at every step it took.' **1848** J. MITCHELL *Nantucketisms* 42 'Like a cat in a strange garret.' Amazed. **1886** P. STAPLETON *Major's Christmas* 102, I'd be a cat in a strange garret. **1900** C. C. MUNN *Uncle Terry* 110 When . . . he arrived in Boston, he felt . . . like a cat in a strange garret.

+**c.** *Dog* (*on*) *my cat*(*s*), hang it, darn it. *colloq.* Cf. DOGGONE.

1853 'P. PAXTON' *Yankee in Texas* 18 Dog on my cat! ef thar hain't been bar about, ye can take my hat! **1871** HAY *Pike Co. Ballads* 22 Now dog my cats ef I kin see, . . . What you've got to do with the question Ef Tim shill go or stay. **1893** 'MARK TWAIN' *P. Wilson* iii, Dog my cats if it ain't all I kin do to tell t'other fum which.

d. *Like a singed cat:* (see quotations). {1721–, (Kelly *Scottish Proverbs* 382)}

1837 NEAL *Charcoal Sketches* (1838) 48 His new friend, however, proved . . . to be like a singed cat, much better than he looked. **1848** J. MITCHELL *Nantucketisms* 42 'Like a singed cat,' better than she looks. Better than appearance indicates. **1876** 'MARK TWAIN' *Tom Sawyer* i, I reckon you're a kind of singed cat, as the saying is—better'n you look.

e. *To let the cat out of the bag,* to divulge or reveal that which should be kept secret. {1760–}

1809 WEEMS *Marion* (1833) 30 On the morrow they came, and 'let the cat out of the bag.' *c***1840** NEAL *Beedle's Sleigh Ride* 11 The cat was soon out of the bag. **1894** *Outing* XXV. 57 The cat was out of the bag, and there was no object in further concealment.

+**f.** *Cat in the meal* (*tub*), something hidden or kept secret.

1839 *Diplom. Corr. Texas* (1908) I. 412 They say there is a cat in [the] meal, by his retirement. **1878** *Congress. Rec.* 8 April 2350/1 When I find republicans . . . voting solidly for an Irish Catholic democrat, then I know there is a cat in the meal-tub. **1880** *Ib.* 10 May 3193/1 Is this the cat in the meal-tub of refunding?

g. *Cats and dogs:* +(see quotations).

1900 S. A. NELSON *A B C Wall St.* 133 Cats and dogs. Worthless securities. **1912** THORNTON *Glossary* 153 'To pay in cats and dogs' is to pay, not in cash, but in inconvenient or useless commodities.

+**h.** *As high as a cat's back,* exceedingly, excessively. *colloq.*[2]

1848 J. MITCHELL *Nantucketisms* 42 'Dust as high as a cat's back.' Quite a row. **1903** ADAMS *Log Cowboy* 269 Old Paul is playing them as high as a cat's back.

+**i.** *Spry as a cat,* active, nimble.

1822 'Yankee Phrases' in *N.J. Almanac 1823,* I late was *as fat as a doe,* And playsome and *spry as a cat.*

+**j.** *That cat won't fight,* that plan will not work.

Cf. E. *that cock won't fight* {1850–} in same sense.

1869 'MARK TWAIN' *Innocents* iv, First I thought I would leave France out and start fresh. But . . . the governor would say, 'Hello, here—didn't see anything in France?' *That* cat wouldn't fight, you know.

+**k.** *To poke a dead cat at somebody,* to insult or revile some one.

*a***1846** *Quarter Race Ky.,* etc. 87, I only thought he might be a pokin his dead cat at somebody what lives in this holler.

+**l.** *To look like the cat after it had eaten the canary,* to look smug, satisfied, eminently pleased.

1871 F. ROE *Army Lett.* 26, I . . . forced myself to be halfway pleasant to the four men who were there, each one looking precisely like the cat after it had eaten the canary!

Cat, *v.* +*intr.* To fish for catfish. — **1834** CARRUTHERS *Kentuckian* II. 217, I'm jist now like I've been at times when I've been out catting. **1859** BARTLETT 72 *Catting,* fishing for 'cat.' Thus, a story is told of an old negro, who while fishing was seen to keep only the catfish and throw all others, even of the better kinds, back into the water. On being asked the reason, he replied, 'Lilly massa, when I goes a cattin, I goes a cattin.'

Cataded, -did, variants of KATYDID. — **1827** *Western Mo. Rev.* I. 451 Not the slightest noise was heard, but the never ending creakings of the catadeds. **1829** T. FLINT *George Mason* 11 The measured creaking of the crickets and catadeds. **1832** KENNEDY *Swallow Barn* I. 311 The little catadid pierced the air with his shrill music.

∗**Catalan.** (See quotation.) — **1805** *Amer. Pioneer* II. 231 The retail groceries are generally kept by Spaniards, who are called Catalans, (from Catalonia, I suppose).

+**Catalo.** Also **cattelo.** [See quot. 1899.] A hybrid or cross between the American buffalo or bison and domestic cattle. — **1899** C. J. JONES in H. Inman *Buffalo Jones' 40 Yrs. Adv.* 243 To these crossbreeds I have given the name 'Catalo,' from the first syllable of *cattle* and the last three letters of *buffalo.* **1903** *Science* 6 March 386 'The Goodnight Herd of Buffaloes and Cataloes in Texas' . . . comprised fifty buffaloes and about seventy Cataloes, or crosses between the buffalo and domesticated cattle. **1906** *Harper's Mo.* April 798 [The buffaloes] are now reduced to a few scattered remnants, and captives sinking to slow extinction in the hybrid cattelo with his mongrel name.

∗ **Catalogue.**

+**1. a.** A list of college or university students, officers, alumni, etc. **b.** A volume or booklet issued by a college or university containing regulations, announcements, etc.

1682 *Mass. H. S. Coll.* 4 Ser. VIII. 311, I lately received . . . a catalogue of Harvard's sons. **1702** MATHER *Magnalia* IV. 136 Our Catalogue is now, without any further Ceremony to be produced; A Catalogue of Christian Students. **1727** *Harvard Coll. Rec.* II. 553 In case that any after they have recieved their Degree, shall presume to make any of the forbidden Provisions, their names shall be left or ras'd out of the Catalogue of Graduates. **1786** in J. Maclean *Hist. Coll. N.J.* (1877) I. 344 Ordered, That a complete catalogue of the graduates of this college be prepared and published at the expense of the present Senior Class. **1832** *N.H. Hist. Soc. Coll.* III. 102 Levi Frisbie, A.M., the first named graduate on the catalogue of Dartmouth College, was a native of Branford, Connecticut. **1838** *S. Lit. Messenger* IV. 480/2 Catalogue of the Officers and Students of William and Mary College. **1844** *Yale Lit. Mag.* IX. 432 The Triennial Catalogue of the College has been published in its usual neat style. **1850** HALE *M. Percival in Amer.* 140 The prospect of securing . . . the position of 'assistant principal,' as, in the barbarous patois of the catalogue, it was called, did not seem very encouraging. **1873** BEADLE *Undevel. West* 686 The 'University of Deseret' puts forth a pretentious catalogue, with a lengthy list of professors. **1899** HALE *Lowell & Friends* 170 In 1856 . . . Lowell's name first appears as a professor in the Harvard catalogue.

2. A systematic list of the books in a library, giving the authors, titles, etc. {1667–}

1702 *Boston Rec.* 26 Ordered that Mr. John Barnerd junr be desired to make a Cattalogue of all the bookes belonging to the Towns Liberary. **1790** *Harvard Laws* 41 A written catalogue of all the books . . . shall be placed therein; and an alphabetical catalogue of the whole library . . . shall be printed. **1801** *Ann. 7th Congress* 2 Sess. 1292 To procure for their own use, and the use of both Houses of Congress, printed catalogues of all the books, with the labelled number of each. **1900** *N.Y. Pub. Library Bul.* IV. 329 At the end of June, 1900, the index catalogue at the Astor Building contained 693,600 cards.

attrib. **1877** *Harper's Mag.* April 726/2 To perform the varied duties necessarily implied in so large a business there is an ample staff, consisting of the superintendent, . . . the catalogue department, [etc.].

+Catalpa. [Amer. Indian.] Either of two well-known trees of the genus *Catalpa* (*C. bignonioides* and *C. speciosa*), bearing large leaves and showy flowers, and cultivated as ornamental and shade trees. (Cf. CATAWBA 3.)

1785 WASHINGTON *Diaries* II. 347 Planted . . . two catalpas (large) west of the Garden House. **1806** T. ASHE *Travels* vii. 62 The virtues of the magnolia, calalpa [*sic*], and spice-wood . . . are not sufficiently ascertained. **1836** J. HALL *Stat. West* 27 The catalpa is a small graceful tree, remarkable for the beauty of its flowers. **1869** *Overland Mo.* III. 13 The tall catalpas proudly display their violet-white panicles, the China trees, their sweet wealth of lilac flowers. **1876** *Field & Forest* II. 27 Can anybody living in southeast Illinois render account concerning the above considerable quantity of Catalpas split for rails? **1901** MOHR *Plant Life Ala.* 61 Catalpa . . . and dogwood . . . follow the rich slopes fronting the streams.

b. Attrib., esp. with *tree*.

*c***1730** CATESBY *Carolina* I. 49 The Catalpa Tree . . . was unknown to the inhabited parts of Carolina, till I brought the seeds from the remoter parts of the country. **1770** *Carroll P.* in *Md. Hist. Mag.* XIII. 72 You may get . . . Catalpa seeds in y[ou]r owne Garden. **1785** WASHINGTON *Diaries* II. 384 The Catalpa Trees were pretty generally displaying their Blossoms. **1836** C. GILMAN *Recoll.* (1838) 72, I suppose you would stop the mouth of the mocking-bird that is singing his every-day song on the catalpa-tree. **1860** S. MORDECAI *Virginia* vii. 86 The very humble edifice, yet standing, shaded by an old Catalpa tree, . . . was the office of the Commissioner. **1897** R. M. STUART *Simpkinsville* 185 An' that ol' catalpa-tree that was there a'ready, I was a-fixin' to chop it out.

Catamaran.

1. A crude raft consisting of a few logs lashed together. {Stanford 1673–}

1758 *Newport Mercury* 5 Dec. 1/2 The 27th, one Brass 24 Pounder was lost in twelve Fathom water, by slipping of the Catamaran, as they were coming from the Ship to land it. **1854** HAMMOND *Hills, Lakes* 49 We left our shantee on the shore, and our catamaran in the water, for any who should come after us.

+b. (See quotation.)

1905 *Forestry Bureau Bul.* No. 61, 33 *Catamaran*, a small raft carrying a windlass and grapple, used to recover sunken logs.

+2. A vessel having twin hulls placed parallel to each other.

1848 COOPER *Oak Openings* II. xiv. 202 It only remained to get sail on the catamaran . . . in order to keep ahead of the sea. **1884** KNIGHT *Suppl.* 178/1 *Catamaran.* . . . The name has been applied to other craft, especially used on the Hudson River, and in New York harbor. These vessels have twin hulls united, and carry a cloud of canvas, being remarkably staunch. **1886** *Outing* IX. 17/2 The Providence entry was the famous catamaran *Amaryllis*.

3. A quarrelsome or cantankerous person. *colloq.* {Stanford 1779–}

Probably by association with *cat* or *catamount*.

1835–7 HALIBURTON *Clockmaker* 1 Ser. 268 Did you ever see, said Mr. Slick, such a catamaran as that? **1857** *Knickerb.* L. 36 You pitiful catamaran, you're too all-fired mean to kill. **1887** H. FREDERIC *Seth's Brother's Wife* 87 You can go back . . . to your old catamaran of a sister and your young sneak of a son. **1911** R. D. SAUNDERS *Col. Todhunter* 101 You've let that old catamaran see that you're skeered of her.

+Catamingo. (See quot. 1842.) — **1842** *Nat. Hist. N.Y., Zoology* I. 37 The New-York Ermine . . . is called, in some parts of the State, the Catamingo, and the White Weasel. **1850** S. F. COOPER *Rural Hours* 500 The Ermine of New York is a small creature. . . . Our people sometimes call it the Catamingo.

Catamount. {1664–} **+a.** A wildcat or lynx. **b.** A cougar, puma, or mountain lion.

1698 *Springfield Rec.* II. 348 Voted to allow Wm. Mackeranny twenty shillings outt of the Rates for his killing four Cattamounts. **1713** *Conn. Public Rec.* V. 406 If any person shall kill and destroy any grown wolf or wolves, cattamount or panther, within the bounds of any town or plantation in this Colony, he shall have forty shillings. **1765** R. ROGERS *Acc. N. America* 261 The Catamounts and Wild-Cats are great enemies to the elk. **1832** WILLIAMSON *Maine* I. 134 The Catamount (the Indian Lunkson, or evil devil,) is a most ferocious and violent creature. **1840** EMMONS *Mass. Quadrupeds* 37 It is quite doubtful whether I have delineated the entire species, and it is still a question whether the southern animal known as the Panther or Catamount, is the same as the northern. **1850** S. F. COOPER *Rural Hours* 404 A man was killed by a 'catamount,' in this country, some fifty years ago. **1890** C. KING *Sunset Pass* 130 That's no panther; they have a tawny hide; but it's the biggest catamount or wildcat I ever set eyes on. **1922** A. BROWN *Old Crow* 92 Is that what you were yelling about? I thought you were a catamount, at least.

transf. and *attrib.* **1835–7** HALIBURTON *Clockmaker* 1 Ser. 97 She was a dreadful cross-grained woman, a real catamount, as savage as a she bear that has cubs. **1847** ROBB *Squatter Life* 137, I . . . went into him all-fours, catamount fashion.

***Catamountain.** [Abbreviated from CAT OF THE MOUNTAIN.] =prec. — **1763** W. ROBERTS *Nat. Hist. of Florida* 4 The wild animals found in this country are the panther, bear, catamountain, stag, goat. **1853** B. F. TAYLOR *Jan. & June* 132 You . . . 'played' you were a 'painter' or a catamountain.

*** Cat and clay.** Sticks or straw mixed with clay to form a simple building or chinking material; (see also quot. 1847). {1561–, *Sc.*}

1842 *Amer. Pioneer* I. 47 Our cabin . . . consisted of a single room with a French made chimney of cat-and-clay. **1847** in Drake *Pioneer Life Ky.* 20 These 'cats and clay' were pieces of small poles, well imbedded in mortar. **1852** MRS. ELLET *Pioneer Women* 232 The fire-place was usually very large, built up on three sides six or eight feet with stone, and then topped with 'cat and clay,' as it was termed. **1883** SHIELDS *S. S. Prentiss* 18 The school-house was a hewn-log house, chinked and daubed with cat and clay.

attrib. **1869** A. REDFORD *Hist. Methodism Ky.* II. 238 The first house of worship [in Lewis Co., Ky.] . . . had also what was familiarly known in those times as a 'cut [*sic*] and clay chimney.'

*** Cataract.** A waterfall.

1797 MORSE *Amer. Geog.* s.v. *Niagara*, Niagara Fort . . . is about 9 miles below the cataract. **1809** KENDALL *Travels* III. 42 On each arm of the [Saco] river there is a cataract or fall. *a***1817** DWIGHT *Travels* II. 109 It [*i.e.*, the descent of the Waterquechee R.] presents very little of the force and grandeur of a cataract, but all the beauties of a widespread and most elegant cascade. **1866** MRS. WHITNEY *L. Goldthwaite* 107 The hot water was let on to make the starch; and down it rushed, a cataract like Niagara. **1915** J. G. FLETCHER *Irradiations* xxxvi. 1 Like cataracts that crash from a crumbling crag Into the dull-blue smoldering gulf of a lake below.

+Catawampously, -ptiously, *adv. colloq.*[2] Savagely, fiercely, eagerly. — **1846** Northall *Yankee Hill* 103 On the bloody ground on which our fathers catawampously poured out their claret free as ile, [etc.]. **1857** F. DOUGLASS *Speech* (B.), Where is the wealth and power that should make us fourteen millions take to our heels . . . for fear of being catawamptiously chawed up?

+Catawampus, *n.* A person of a spiteful or malicious nature; a bogy, sprite, or hobgoblin. — **1843** 'CARLTON' *New Purchase* I. 265 The tother one what got most sker'd, is a sort of catawampus. **1866** C. H. SMITH *Bill Arp* 54 It is a thing that plots and plans and schemes for a few weeks and then suddenly pokes its head out like a catawampus and says 'Booh!'

+Catawampus, *a. colloq.* Spiteful or resentful; cater-cornered, not in line, askew, wrong. — [**1844** DICKENS *Martin Chuzzlewit* xxi, There air some catawampous chawers in the small way too, as graze upon a human pretty strong.] **1884** 'CRADDOCK' *Tenn. Mts.* 3 It sets me plumb catawampus ter hev ter listen to them blacksmiths. **1885** — *Prophet* 153 She got me plumb catawampus, so ez I didn't rightly know what I wanted ter do myself.

‖**Catawampussed,** *a.* Confused, perplexed, bewildered. — **1880** P. DEMING *Adirondack Stories* 31 May I be cat-a-wampussed if he won't swaller all the soap that old coot is a mind to give him!

+Catawba. Also **Cattaba, Katahba,** etc. [Amer. Indian.]

1. =CATAWBA INDIAN.

1716 *N.C. Col. Rec.* II. 252 The false Representation of the Virginians in England . . . wherein is asserted that the Cattabas are in their Government. **1725** G. CHICKEN in *Travels Amer. Col.* 104 The said Milikin arrived here from the Catawabaws [*sic*]. **1775** ADAIR *Indians* 223, I begin with the Katahba, because their country is the most contiguous to Charles-Town in South-Carolina. **1854** *S. Lit. Messenger* XX. 396 The Catawbas, . . . at this day, can scarcely be said to exist at all. **1858** *S.C. Hist. Soc.* II. 335 A regular conjugation may be made which is intelligible to the Catawbas themselves. **1895** *Cent. Cycl. of Names* 563 *Kataba* or *Catawba*. . . . The few survivors of this people are on the Kataba reservation in York County, South Carolina.

2. The language or dialect used by the Catawba Indians.

1858 *S.C. Hist. Soc.* II. 327 The difficulty of the Catawba is increased by the fact, that . . . many words are lost.

3. =CATALPA.

1842 BUCKINGHAM *Slave States* I. 476 The catawba, or catalpa, . . . grows to a large size. **1884** SARGENT *Rep. Forests* 115 *Catalpa bignonioides.* . . . Catalpa, Catawba, Bean Tree, Cigar Tree, Indian Bean. **1894** *Amer. Folk-Lore* VII. 96 *Catalpa Bignonioides*, . . . catawba, West Va.

4. =CATAWBA GRAPE.

1846 *Knickerb.* XXVII. 419 A trellis . . . with a snaky-looking vine trailed over it, from which glorious bunches of catawbas and Isabellas may be gathered. **1855** *Rep. Comm. Patents: Agric.* 305 The 'Catawba,' as an open vineyard grape, is not so well adapted to this locality [=northern Ohio]. **1863** *Rep. Comm. Agric.* 123 The Catawba is a native of the Catawba River, in N. Carolina. . . . For many years it has been regarded as the best wine grape in the country. **1871** *Harper's Mag.* July 207/1 The Catawba, driven by disease from the neighborhood of Cincinnati, thrives luxuriantly [at Put-in-Bay], and never fails to reward the cultivator with ripened clusters. **1884** ROE *Nature's Story* 284 The season insured the perfect ripening of those fine old kinds, the Isabella and Catawba, that too often are frost-bitten before they become fit for the table.

5. Wine made from these grapes.

1851 CIST *Cincinnati* 256 Good Catawba commands six dollars per dozen bottles. **1852** *Harper's Mag.* V. 267/2 We . . . will stew a trout in Longworth's Catawba. **1870** *Harper's Mag.* XLI. 112 Sparkling Catawba . . . is fully equal to the average quality of the Champagne we import.

6. Attrib. with *cobbler, dialect, warrior, wine.* See also CATAWBA GRAPE, etc.

1809 *Steele Papers* II. 589 The Lord's prayer in the Catawba dialect w[oul]d be useful to me. *c*1854 LONGFELLOW (*title of poem*), Catawba Wine. **1863** SIMMS *Mellichampe* xxi, This bow and these arrows . . . were the gift of a Catawba warrior to my father. **1876** M. F. HENDERSON *Cooking* 341 (*recipe*), Sherry, Claret, or Catawba Cobblers.

+Catawba grape. A variety of native grape first cultivated along the Catawba River in South Carolina.

1832 VIGNE *6 Mo. in Amer.* I. 148 'Tokay' . . . is made from the 'Catawba' grape. **1851** CIST *Cincinnati* 266 From our native Catawba grape, excellent wines can be made. **1854** *Ohio Agric. Rep.* XVIII. 25 A premium of $20 shall be offered for the best three samples of pure Ohio wine, made from the Catawba, Virginia Seedling or Delaware grape. **1898** E. C. HALL *Aunt Jane* 171 Concord and Catawba grapes loaded the vines on the rickety old arbor.

+Catawba Indian. An Indian of a Siouan tribe formerly occupying a part of the Carolinas. — **1715** *Virginia St. P.* I. 178 Two of our Traders . . . were among the Catawba Indians at the breaking out of this War. **1775** *S.C. Hist. Soc.* II. 31 Two Catawba Indians . . . said, they were come to have the news. **1785** *Narr. of J. Marrant* 29, I next visited the Catawar [*sic*] Indians. **1858** *S.C. Hist. Soc.* II. 327, I had as a camp servant, a Catawba Indian.

+Catawba nation. The tribe or 'nation' of Catawba Indians. — **1775** ADAIR *Indians* 223 (*caption*), An Account of the Katahba Nation. **1775** *S.C. Hist. Soc.* II. 31 Resolved, that a proper letter, or talk, be prepared to be sent to the Catawba nation. **1858** *Ib.* 327 It is known that the Catawba nation at present numbers but fifty human beings, men, women and children.

+Catawba rhododendron, rosebay. A species of rosebay (see quotations). — **1813** MUHLENBERG *Cat. Plants* 43 Catawba Rosebay. **1868** GRAY *Field Botany* 216 *R. Catawbiense*, Catawba Rose-bay. High Alleghanies from Virginia s[outhward]. **1890** *Cent.* 5157/1 The ordinary species of American outdoor plantations is *Rhododendron Catawbiense*, the Catawba or Carolina rhododendron.

+Catawba tree. =CATALPA TREE. — **1832** BROWNE *Sylva* 126 In the Carolinas and in Georgia the Catalpa is called Catawbaw Tree, from a tribe of Indians by that name who inhabited that part of the country. **1848** W. E. BURTON *Waggeries* 122 On a small bluff, delicately carpeted with the finest grass, and shaded by a few catawba and dogwood trees, the Waddiloves had pitched their tent.

Cat-ball. A well-known game played with a bat and ball. — **1888** *Cosmop. Mag.* Oct. 443 Primitive 'base-ball' . . . was simply 'cat-ball' played by 'sides,' with a feature introduced as a measure of skill.

+Catbird. A mocking-thrush, *Mimus carolinensis.*

1709 LAWSON *Carolina* 143 The Cat-Bird . . . makes a Noise exactly like young Cats. **1796** WANSEY *Excursion U.S.* 194 Of some kinds of birds they have great plenty, such as robins, swallows, cat birds, and king birds. *a*1817 DWIGHT *Travels* I. 54 The Cat-Bird, and the Thrush, have native notes in an almost endless variety. **1839** HOFFMAN *Wild Scenes* 173 The cat-bird from the brier-thicket replied in mocking notes. **1842** L. M. CHILD *Lett. N.Y.* xvii. 191 A cat-bird (our New England mocking-bird) perched near, and began to imitate the notes [of the bobolink]. **1853** BALDWIN *Flush Times Ala.* 37 He is like a cat-bird—the only intolerable discord she makes being her own notes. **1880** *Harper's Mag.* June 70 The pert cat-bird in his Quaker garb is here, and with a flippant jerk of tail and impertinent mew bustles about among the arbor vitæs. **1910** *Outlook* 25 June 438 The catbird shouts all he knows or guesses about everybody's pet songs. **1913** STRATTON-PORTER *Laddie* (1917) 57 The orchard was alive with doves, thrushes, catbirds, bluebirds, vireos and orioles.

Catboat. A sailboat having a large mast and a single large sail. {1887–} — **1878** *Harper's Mag.* Feb. 324/2 By thrifty living the best of these have acquired the proprietorship of small cat-boats or sloops. **1882** *Century Mag.* July 357/2 George Steers made his first hit with the cat-boat *Manhattan.* **1909** 'O. HENRY' *Options* (1916) 236, I'll buy a catboat and a rowboat.

+Cat brier, briar. Any of several species of greenbriers or smilax.

1839 *S. Lit. Messenger* V. 375/2 On the left was a large bay-gall . . . thickly beset with cat-briers and undergrowth. **1843** TORREY *Flora N.Y.* II. 302 *Smilax rotundifolia.* . . . Common Greenbrier or Cat-brier. . . . Moist thickets and woods: very common. *c*1845 *Big Bear Ark.*, etc. 44 We . . . kept on about a mile, . . . wading through mud-holes, tearing through cat briers, and stumbling among bogs. **1856** *Spirit of Times* (N.Y.) 27 Sept. 51/3 Cat-briars caught in our clothes. **1899** VAN DYKE *Fisherman's Luck* 188 Blackberry bushes . . . and cat-briers trailed and twisted themselves in an incredible tangle.

attrib. **1888** *Outing* XII. 483/2 The first rattle of the ox-cart may start them [=quail] from the stubble-field to the shelter . . . of the cat-brier coppice.

***Catch,** *n.*

+1. A place where something is obtained or caught.

1850 MITCHELL *Lorgnette* 1 Ser. 81 Went the other night to take supper at Dobson's—a very scholarly sort of a catch. **1920** HUNTER *Trail Drivers of Texas* I. 98 Our camp was the catch and cut-out for all the other bosses.

2. A person of either sex (but esp. of the male) regarded as a desirable matrimonial prospect. {1837–}

1856 M. J. HOLMES *L. Rivers* viii. 83 Altogether he was, she thought, a 'decided catch.' **1863** 'M. HARLAND' *Husks* 121 If Sarah Hunt allows such a catch as this to slip through her fingers, she shall hear a piece of my mind! **1881** M. J. HOLMES *Madeline* 192 Those who interested themselves most in the matter never said anything worse of her and Mr. Guy than . . . . insinuating that it would be a great catch for Grandfather Markham's child. **1896** J. C. HARRIS *Sister Jane* 127 They were regarded as 'good catches' by the mothers of marriageable daughters.

3. An act of catching fish; the number or amount of fish caught at one time. {1799–}

*a*1859 *N.Y. Courier & Enquirer* (B.), The catch of blue fish in the inlet and river is greater than ever known. **1868** B. J. LOSSING *Hudson* 248 These fishermen . . . generally have a 'catch' twice a day when the tide is 'slack.' **1884** ROE *Nature's Story* 127 Burt . . . explained that the 'catch' was small at present.

+4. *Agric.* A stand of small grain, grass, or clover sufficient to obviate the necessity of replanting. (Cf. CATCH *v.* 3.)

1868 G. BRACKETT *Farm Talk* 128 'Seed this down this year?' 'Yes, that's one reason why I sowed the field to barley,—so as to get a good catch.' **1872** *Vt. Bd. Agric. Rep.* I. 126 A moderately wet season is more favorable to a good 'catch' of grass than a dry one. **1888** *Vt. Agric. Rep.* X. 48 Wheat gives a good catch, barley next, and oats poorest of all. **1898** *L. H. Bailey's Princ. Agric.* 81 On hard and poor lands, it is often difficult to secure a 'catch' of clover.

5. The act of catching a ball, as in baseball or football. {1770–}

1868 CHADWICK *Base Ball* 111 Total Foul Bound Catches. **1886** *Outing* Aug. 587/1 There were fourteen innings, marked by great stops, throws, and catches. **1893** W. K. POST *Harvard Stories* 22 The Yale full-back retreated for a catch.

6. In rowing, the act of beginning a stroke. {1881–}

1897 *Outing* XXX. 237/2 A long reach and swing forward, a sharp and hard catch or beginning, a clean finish, . . .—these are the principles lying at the foundation of the system now in vogue at Harvard.

***Catch,** *v.* Also *dial.* **ketch.**

I. *1. *tr.* To take, capture, apprehend.

1646 *R.I. Col. Rec.* I. 84 The reason of this order is, that the wolves the more readily come to bayte that they may be catched for the general good of the Island. **1675** EASTON *Indian War* 22 The English Army cote an old Indian and tormented him. **1748** WASHINGTON *Diaries* I. 6 We cleaned ourselves (to get rid of the Game we had catched the Night before). **1902** HARBEN *A. Daniel* 73, I kin make bug-juice all the rest o' my life an' sell it without being ketched.

+2. *Baseball. intr.* To occupy the position of catcher; to catch (the delivery of) a pitcher; to act as catcher (during) a game.

1887 *Courier-Journal* 26 May 2/6 Young Love Cross caught Ramsey in fine style, and Greer also handled Porter's delivery as well as could be desired. *Ib.* 27 May 2/4 O'Brien caught a poor game, and his six passed balls were all costly. **1890** W. CARLETON *City Legends* 37 'An' will you pitch or catch?' Says I, 'I'll catch, if so desired.' **1901** *Outing* XXXVIII. 600/1 Durfee of Williams, another Freshman, catches well and is a good hitter.

+3. To germinate or sprout. (Cf. CATCH *n.* 4.)

1868 G. BRACKETT *Farm Talk* 128 Sow oats thin, and fix the ground as well as for barley, and grass will catch well enough. **1868** *Rep. Comm. Agric. 1867* 238 In dry seasons seeding [of oats and corn] is surer to 'catch.'

+**4.** To catch on. (Cf. 7b.)

1896 *Godey's Mag.* April 406/2, I am a child myself. Do you catch? We ought all to be children.

II. *Phrases.* +**5.** *To catch goss,* to receive a severe scolding or punishment.

1844 *Cincinnati Misc.* 13, I incurred ... the displeasure of the proprietors of that house, and was informed ... that I should catch goss, on the first suitable opportunity.

+**6.** *To catch napping:* (see quotation).

1868 CHADWICK *Base Ball* 39 A player is said to be caught napping when he is touched with the ball when off a base he was previously standing upon; or, when caught between two bases obliging him to run backward and forward to escape being touched. He is regarded, too, as being caught napping when he is outwitted in a point of play by his opponent.

7. *To catch on,* to grasp, seize, hold on. Also fig.

1873 BAILEY *Life in Danbury* 129 'Catching on behind' is the crowning enjoyment now for boys. *Ib.* 130 Catching on behind ... requires a great deal of adroitness and decision. **1884** *Lisbon* (Dakota) *Star* 27 June, Now is the time to catch on in order to keep up with the procession.

+**b.** To understand or comprehend. *colloq.*

1883 PECK *Bad Boy* 62 Don't he ever catch on, and find out you have deceived him? **1887** *Courier-Journal* 9 May 1/3 Mr. Barnum ... was guilty of his old fault of leaking, and the Nutmeg boys caught onto the racket. **1891** *Harper's Mag.* July 208/1 The best English rider fights shy of ground which the cowboy will gallop over until he 'catches on to it.' **1899** A. H. QUINN *Penna. Stories* 147 You look like him, and you've been to enough of the rehearsals to fake it through without anyone catching on. **1904** W. H. SMITH *Promoters* 10, I was afraid you wouldn't catch on to start with. **1922** R. PARRISH *Case & Girl* 312 You never did catch on to me until I got into the wrong clothes, did you, old dear?

+**c.** (See quot. 1889.)

1888 *Peabody Reporter* (F.), The managers of the *Boston Globe* ... have a faculty of catching on, ... and when there is no opportunity open to them they make an opportunity. **1889** FARMER 128 To *catch on* has likewise come to signify a capacity to quickly grasp an opportunity and turn it to advantage.

+**8.** *To catch on the fly:* (see FLY *n.*).

9. *To catch out,* in ball-playing, to put a batter out by catching the ball. {1850-}

1858 A. G. SPALDING *Base Ball* (1911) 61 Our first man took the bat; tipped out.... Next man got scared; caught out. **1883** EGGLESTON *Hoosier School-Boy* 12 He gave up his bat to the one who had caught him out.

fig. **1894** 'MARK TWAIN' *Those Twins* v, There was a fine outburst of laughter, but as the judge was caught out himself, his reprimand was not very vigorous.

+**b.** In *passive:* To be overtaken by darkness, rain, snow, etc., at a place remote from shelter.

1873 BEADLE *Undevel. West* 727 There is less snow in northern Minnesota ...; but the little there is blows worse, and it is more dangerous to be 'caught out.'

+**10.** *To catch the larks,* to prosper. *slang.*

1857 *Spirit of Times* (N.Y.) 3 Jan. 294/1 Your farm kingdom must not, if you would *catch the larks,* be limited to one, two, or three products.

11. *To catch up,* to overtake. {1855-}

1829 *Va. Lit. Museum* 16 Dec. 419 To *catch up.* To overtake—Kentucky. *c***1870** 'MARK TWAIN' *Sk., My Watch,* The watch ... would keep on slowing down ... until all the clocks it had left behind caught up again.

+**b.** To catch and harness horses, oxen, etc., preparatory to beginning a journey.

1843 T. J. FARNHAM *Travels Prairies* I. 57 After this, we 'caught up' and went on with the intention of encamping with the Santa Féäns. **1844** GREGG *Commerce of Prairies* I. 50 The familiar note of preparation, 'Catch up! catch up! was now sounded. **1847** PARKMAN in *Knickerb.* XXIX. 396 Shaw lay in the shade, under the cart, to rest for awhile, before the word should be given to 'catch up.' **1848** BRYANT *California* 32 The scene of 'catching up' as the yoking and attaching of the oxen to the wagons is called in emigrant phraseology, is one of great bustle and confusion. **1853** *Harper's Mag.* VII. 315/1 When the hour for our departure from camp had nearly arrived, Kid would rise from his blanket and cry 'Catch up.' **1888** J. J. WEBB *Adventures* 47 As soon as possible after daylight we 'catched up' and drove out.

+**12.** *To catch up with,* to detect and bring to justice; to be entirely through with. *colloq.*

1902 HARBEN *Abner Daniel* 73 You are a-axin' that beca'se you think I'll be ketched up with, ... but I tell you the' ain't no man on the face o' the earth that could find my still now. **1924** *Scribner's Mag.* Dec. 649/2 I'm all caught up with this army. Get me? I'm through, resigned, quit.

+**Catchall.** Also *dial.* **ketch-all.**

1. A box, bag, closet, nook, etc., used as a receptacle for various articles.

1841 *Knickerb.* XVII. 327 It is as much as I can do to keep things clean that are in sight, without cleaning out every dirty hole. There must be some *catch-all.* **1851** *Ib.* XXXVIII. 88 A light wagon, one of those old-fashioned vehicles with a box, a kind of 'catch-all,' behind. **1876** MRS. WHITNEY *Sights & Insights* I. 23 One ['sea-pocket'] has an oiled silk sponge-bag, and one a beautiful deep catch-all at the bottom. **1916** BOWER *Phantom Herd* 157 He looked under the squat adobe cabin which held all the odds and ends ... and which he called the 'ketch-all.' **1924** MULFORD *Rustlers' Valley* 62 The gallery leading from the ranchhouse to the summer kitchen was far from being the customary catch-all of riding gear and general miscellany.

attrib. **1874** HOWELLS *Foregone Conclusion* xviii. 246 They hunted out Ferris's property from a catch-all closet in the studio of a sculptor with whom he had left them. **1916** BOWER *Phantom Herd* 236 The boys ... trailed off to bed, in the ketch-all cabin.

fig. and *transf.* **1838** *Congress Globe* App. 16 April 275 [The party includes] old Federalists, ... Antimasons, and Abolitionists. They have, sirs, been a kind of catch-all, or omnium gatherum. **1859** STOWE *Minister's Wooing* viii, All but this dead grind, and the dollars that come through the mill, is by them thrown into one waste 'catch-all' and labeled romance. **1865** *Atlantic Mo.* XV. 355, I can't have my study made the general catch-all and menagerie for Rover and Jennie, and her baskets and balls. **1892** *Harper's Mag.* Feb. 373/2 This is the mere catch-all for the furs got at posts farther up the coast.

2. (See quotation.)

1884 KNIGHT *Suppl.* 178/2 *Catch-all,* a tool ... for withdrawing from drilled wells broken tools or bars which may have fallen in.

Catch basin.

1. (See quotations.)

1874 KNIGHT 503/1 *Catch-basin,* a cistern at the point of discharge into a sewer, to catch heavy and bulky matters which would not readily pass through the sewers, but which are removed from time to time. **1877** BARTLETT 778 *Catch-basin,* the receptacle beneath the grating of a sewer, to catch the dirt that is washed in.

2. A reservoir for collecting or impounding the surface water of an extensive area.

1884 *Science* III. 372/1 It may fairly be questioned ... whether any extension of forests, or system of catch-basins or reservoirs, could possibly retain or mitigate to any considerable extent such general and overwhelming floods. **1889** *Secy. of Agric. Rep.* 268 The building of numerous catch-basins throughout the plains to save the rain-fall which is wasted ... will add greatly to the supply.

Catch-bolt. A form of bolt used in fastening a door, window, etc.— **1858** *Rep. Comm. Patents* (1859) I. 537 The levers or arms are designed to force back the catch-bolt and lock-bolt. **1874** KNIGHT 503/1 *Catch-bolt,* a cupboard or door bolt which yields to the pressure in closing and then springs into the keeper in the jamb. [It is] usually retracted by a small knob.

‖**Catch crumb.** *slang.* An admirer, enamorata. — *c***1837** CATLIN *Indians* II. 198 One of his little fair enamoratas, or 'catch crumbs,' ... fixed her eyes and her affections upon his beautiful silk braces.

Catch-dog. *colloq.* A dog that will attack and seize his quarry. — **1860** *Congress. Globe* App. 16 June 436/3 God forbid that the heart of a single freeman ... should prostitute his body in the service of those [=slave-hunters] who, at home, perform the same labor with well-trained blood-hounds and catch-dogs.

***Catcher.**

***1.** One who or that which catches.

1853 SIMMS *Sword & Distaff* 482 They were old followers of Porgy;—the one Doctor Oakenburg, a culler of simples and catcher of snakes. **1864** *Ohio Agric. Rep.* XVIII. App. 29 A catcher in the form of a light frame with muslin stretched on it being first spread under the tree, on to which the insects drop, and from which they are transferred to a pail of scalding water. **1884** *Century Mag.* Feb. 519/1 The catcher ... must be alert and with a sheep ready for each shearer as wanted.

+**2.** A mail catcher or mail-bag catcher. Also attrib.

1875 *Chicago Tribune* 18 Sept. 5/3 The 'catcher' is known as Ward's patent. **1887** *Postal Laws* 253 'Catcher' pouches must not under any circumstances be sent out upon any stage or horseback routes, or used for any other purpose than to exchange mails where trains do not stop. *Ib.,* Postmasters at post-offices ... which are supplied by 'catcher service,' will comply with the following instructions.

+**3.** *Baseball.* A player stationed behind the home-plate to catch the balls thrown by the pitcher. {1774- in cricket}

1856 *Spirit of Times* (N.Y.) 27 Dec. 276/3 The two best players upon each side—first and second mates, as they were called, by common consent—were catcher and thrower. **1868** CHADWICK *Base Ball* 31 The catcher of a nine must be qualified for his position according to the style of pitching he has to face. **1871** EMERSON *Plutarch* Wks. (Cent. ed.) X, 309 They are like the baseball players, to whom the pitcher, the bat, the catcher and the scout are equally important. **1886** *Outing* March 697/2 The only weak position seems to be that of catcher. **1894** 'MARK TWAIN' *Those Twins* v, Rogers bent himself ... in the modern attitude of the catcher at a baseball match.

***Catchfly.** A popular name for various plants of the genus *Silene* that secrete a viscid fluid. — **1791** MUHLENBERG *Index Florae* 169. **1832** HALE *Flora* 34 Catchfly, *Silene....* One of the most splendid species, flowers bright scarlet, is found in Ohio and Lower Louisiana. **1847** EMERSON *Poems* 62 Clover, catchfly, adder's tongue. **1868** GRAY *Field Botany* 66 *Silene* ... [includes] night-flowering catchfly, ... sweetwilliam c., . . . sleepy c., . . . Pennsylvanian c. or wild pink, . . . Virginian c. or fire pink, . . . royal c.

+**Catchfly grass.** 'A marsh grass (*Leersia lenticularis*) of the southern United States' (W. '34). — **1829** EATON *Botany* (ed. 5) 273 *Leersia lenticularis*, catch-fly grass. **1845** LINCOLN *Botany* App. 118/2. **1894** COULTER *Bot. W. Texas* III. 512 *H[omalocenchrus] lenticularis*. (Catch-fly grass.)—Not yet reported from Texas, but it may be expected in the eastern half of the State.

Catching, *a.* Of weather: Variable, uncertain, unexpected. {*c*1611–1832} — **1868** BRACKETT *Farm Talk* 124 'How do you get along hay-ing?' 'Pretty fair; though the weather has been catching last week. I got some nice English [hay] wet in the shower.' **1876** *Vt. Bd. Agric. Rep.* III. 481 The 'catching' rains of harvest time . . . will always fetch a lugubrious wail from any farmer.

Catching out. In ball-playing, the action of putting a player out by catching the ball. — **1882** G. C. EGGLESTON *Wreck of Red Bird* 130 The third throw went wide of the mark, and so I missed, but it didn't matter, for there was no catching out to be done in that game.

+**Catch phrase.** A phrase that attracts attention. — *a***1850** CALHOUN *Works* (1874) IV. 206 The whole scheme, with all its plausible catch-phrases. **1856** LINCOLN in *Century Mag.* XII. 110/1 The President . . . adopts the 'Enquirer's' catch-phrase.

+**Catch-up.** The command or signal to prepare teams for beginning a journey. (Cf. CATCH *v.* 11 b.) — **1844** GREGG *Commerce of Prairies* I. 50 (*chap. heading*), The 'Catch up'—Breaking up of the Encampment [etc.]. **1846** G. STEWART *Altowan* I. iii. 109 The sunset came, and the '*catch up*' sounded on the camp.

Catchwater drain. {1861–} +A small stream or rivulet. — **1817** *Ann. 14th Congress* 2 Sess. 1008 The Pungo branch of North river is the nearest body of water to it, (except mere catchwater drains).

+**Catclaw.** *W.* A prickly plant, as *Acacia Greggii* and *A. Wrighti*; =CAT'S-CLAW.

1898 CANFIELD *Maid of Frontier* 204 The catclaw flowered into white after each infrequent rain. **1904** 'O. HENRY' *Heart of the West* 250 A little brown rabbit skipped around a bunch of catclaw. **1913** BARNES *Western Grazing Grounds* 43 In the foothills there are several varieties of edible bushes like Mountain mahogany (*Cercocarpus*) and the catclaw.

‖**Cat-cry.** A hiss, call, or cry expressive of impatience, disapproval, etc.; a catcall. — **1898** DELAND *Old Chester Tales* 53 The audience came stamping and scuffling in, . . . [with] much loud, good-natured raillery, and some cat-cries.

‖**Cat-doze.** A cat nap. — **1847** in H. Howe *Hist. Coll. Ohio* 199 [He] slept cat-dozes in an upright position.

***Catechise.** *dial.* The catechism. {–1715; now *dial.*} — **1825** NEAL *Bro. Jonathan* III. 150 After the fashion of your 'nat'ral born' Yankee, when he is . . . teaching the 'catechise.' **1833** WHITTIER *Lays of Home* 122 All seeming to his knowing eyes Familiar as his 'catechize.'

Cater-cornered, Catacornered, *a.* and *adv. colloq.* Diagonal(ly), askew, out of adjustment. Also *cater-cornered-like.* {1828–, *dial.*}

1843 'CARLTON' *New Purchase* I. 261 Two panes were . . . bestowed on our friend . . . with directions how to . . . paste them on the sash, and to secure, by two strings diagonally fastened, or as he better understood it—'katterkorner'd-like.' *a***1846** *Quarter Race Ky.*, etc. 190 When he got putty cloast he walked 'round catecornered-like. **1853** FOWLER *Home for All* 75 The raftering, boarding, shingling, uniting the eight sheets of roof at their catercornered junctions, so as to prevent their leaking. **1871** DE VERE 450 *Cater-cornered*, a very common term in Virginia and the South. **1893** *Harper's Mag.* June 112/1 He leaned against the wall, eying me catacornered, but innocent. **1895** *Century Mag.* Aug. 541/1 There was one brook . . . that came out of the woods about half a mile away from the hotel, and ran down cater-cornered through a sloping meadow. **1906** DELAND in *Harper's Mo.* July 252 You do leave things so catacornered!

+**Cater-, Catter-, Catecornering,** *a. colloq.* Crosswise; diagonally slanting.

1843 STEPHENS *High Life N.Y.* II. 124 It aint easy work, this ere, of talking when a feller's mouth cuts through his face catecornering as mine does. **1885** *Century Mag.* XXXI. 64/1 He just takes them records . . . and brings his side line down catercornerin'—that way. **1888** J. KIRKLAND *McVeys* 59 Now, suppose the railroad runs diagonally across a field, 'cater-cornering,' as he says. **1913** A. B. EMERSON *R. Fielding at Snow Camp* 3 They had climbed the steep bank now and started across the pasture in what Tom called 'a catter-cornering' direction.

***Caterpillar.** The wormlike larva of various insects. Also transf.

1645 *Boston Rec.* 189 Innumerable armys of Catterpillers filled the Country. *c***1680** J. HULL *Diary Occurr.* 218 This summer, multitudes of flying caterpillars arose out of the ground and from roots of corn, making such a noise in the air that travellers must speak loud to hear one another. **1737** BRICKELL *N. Carolina* 167 The Caterpillar, Palmer or Cankerworm, is the same in Carolina as . . . in Ireland. . . . These Insects are very destructive to Herbs and Corn. **1856** *Rep. Comm. Patents: Agric.* 77 Another insect . . . often found in cotton fields, and mistaken for the real cotton-caterpillar, is commonly known by the trivial name of the 'grass-worm,' or 'caterpillar.' **1878** *Rep. Indian Affairs* 9 Second planting was devoured by caterpillars as soon as it was a few inches high.

attrib. **1881** *Harper's Mag.* Jan. 254/2 The sluggish river winds through tracts of salt-meadow, . . . now creeping under 'caterpillar bridges.'

Catesby's lily. [Mark *Catesby*, d. 1749, Eng. naturalist.] The southern red lily. — **1869** FULLER *Flower Gatherers* 176 He bade us look also in his American Herbarium for another lily, called 'Catesby's Lily,' which was one of the finest American species.

+**Catface.** (See quot. 1905.) — **1879** *Lumberman's Gazette* 3 Dec. (Th.S.), Logs that have cat faces or burnt places. **1905** *Forestry Bureau Bul.* No. 61 *Catface*, a partly healed over fire scar on the stem of a tree.

Catfish. {1620–} +Any of various common fresh-water fishes of N.A. having some fancied resemblance to a cat. (Cf. CAT *n.* 2.)

1612 SMITH *Virginia* 15 Of fish we were best acquainted with . . . Rock-fish, Eeles, Lampreyes, Catfish, Shades. **1682** in *S.C. Hist. Coll.* II. 75 Cat-fish, whose Head and glaring Eyes resemble a Cat; it's esteem'd a very good Fish. **1770** WASHINGTON *Diaries* I. 419 At this place . . . we found a Cat fish of the size of our largest River Cats. **1788** J. MAY *Diary* 69 Williams caught a catfish today which weighed fifty-nine and a half pounds. **1864** NORTON *Army Lett.* 212 Catfish just like our bullheads, weigh thirty pounds. **1898** *Mo. So. Dakotan* I. 79 Our piscatorial friends are just at the present time enjoying rare sport in hauling out catfish, perch, wall-eyed pike, &c., from the Big Sioux. **1901** CHURCHILL *Crisis* 27 He reflected that Stephen must feel as strange in St. Louis as a cod might amongst the cat-fish in the Mississippi.

attrib. and *comb.* **1840** HALIBURTON *Clockm.* 3 Ser. xi, Them white-livered, catfish-mouthed, dipt-candle lookin' scoundrels the Brunswickers. **1840** *Picayune* 17 Sept. 2/3 Thomas Cunniff . . . had all the appearance of one who sleeps in the market at night and patronizes the catfish hotel by day.

+**Catfish soup.** A soup of which the chief ingredient is catfish. — **1834** BRACKENRIDGE *Recoll.* 21 Coarse black bread, a kind of catfish soup, hot with pepper, and seasoned with garlick, was almost the only food they gave me. **1857** D. H. STROTHER *Virginia* 14 Mr. Penn . . . copied at length a recipe for making cat-fish soup. **1878** *Amer. Home Cook Book* 28 (*recipe*), Cat-fish Soup.

Catfoot. A short high foot with arching toes, resembling that of a cat. — **1889** *Cent.* 861/3. **1897** *Outing* XXIX. 486/1 The feet [of English setters] may be either what is termed 'harefoot,' or 'catfoot,' so long as there is plenty of hair between the toes.

***Catgut.**

***1.** A violin string made from the intestines of sheep. Also attrib.

1768 FRENEAU *Poems* (1795) 10 Rosin and catgut strings for fiddling wights. **1807** IRVING *Salmagundi* ii, His very bowels seem to sympathise at every twang of the catgut, as if he heard at that moment the wailings of the helpless animal that had been sacrificed to harmony. **1841** EMERSON *Ess., Spiritual Laws* 116 Paganini can extract rapture from a catgut.

2. A heavy cloth made of thick cord. *Obs.* {1731–}

1767 *Boston Gazette* 19 Oct., Several Ladies have signified of having a desire to learn that most ingenious art of Painting on Gauze and Catgut. **1793** *Mass. Spy* 19 Sept. 4/3 (*advt.*), John Nazro . . . has . . . ready for Sale . . . Catguts, Men's and women's cotton and thread Hose, Tiffanies, [etc.].

attrib. **1773** TRUMBULL *Progress of Dulness* III. 52 Work'd catgut hand-kerchiefs, whose flaws Display the neck, as well as gauze.

+**3.** A trailing herb, *Tephrosia virginiana.*

1840 DEWEY *Mass. Flowering Plants* 65 Goat's Rue . . . popularly called catgut . . . appears to be spread widely over the United States and Canada. **1843** TORREY *Flora N.Y.* I. 167 Catgut [grows in] . . . dry sandy soils; often on hill-sides. **1868** GRAY *Field Botany* 106 *Tephrosia Virginiana*, called Catgut, from the very tough, long and slender roots.

Cat ham. A ham or thigh that is thin and flat. — **1856** *Rep. Comm. Patents: Agric.* 23 Our old race of cattle . . . had hollow backs, cat hams, and lopped horns.

+**Cat-haul,** *n.* (See quotation.) — **1824** 'SINGLETON' *Lett. South & West* 79 The cat-haul . . . is, to fasten a slave down flatwise . . . and then to take a huge fierce tom-cat by the tail backward, and haul him down along the . . . bare back, with his claws clinging into the quick all the way.

+**Cat-haul,** *v.* [f. prec.] *tr.* To subject to this punishment. — **1840** *Congress. Globe* App. 12 Jan. 99 The Anti-Slavery Almanac for 1840 is filled up with pictures, such as white people of the South branding slaves, —hunting slaves with dogs and guns,—cat-hauling slaves, &c. **1847** *Chambers' Misc.* XVII. 17, I saw a slave punished by cat-hauling.

fig. **1881** *Congress. Rec.* 28 Feb. 2202/2 You . . . begin to ransack and examine and cat-haul the whole Navy, big and little, with a view to disposing of it.

+**Cat-hauling.** *fig.* A severe scolding or tongue-lashing. — **1867** D. R. LOCKE *Swingin' Round* 118 Let me ketch yoo at it, . . . and I'll give you sich a cat-haulin ez yoo never—.

Cathead, †Catshead.

+**1.** A catfish.

1683 PENN *Works* (1782) IV. 303 Of fish, there is the sturgeon, herring, rock, shad, catshead, sheepshead, [etc.]. **1778** CARVER *Travels* 171 There is also [in Lake Ontario] a sort called the Cat-head or Pout, which are in general very large, some of them weighing eight or ten pounds. **1809** A. HENRY *Travels* 252 We took trout, cat-fish, or cat-heads, of six pounds weight.

2. (See quot. 1817.) {cat's-head, 1617–1767, now *dial.;* cat head, *dial.*}

1817 W. Coxe *Fruit Trees* 133 Cathead. This is a very large round apple; flattened at the ends. **1856** *Rep. Comm. Patents: Agric.* 295 The autumn varieties [of apples] are the 'Gravenstein,' . . . 'Belle-fleur,' 'Fall Pippin,' 'Cat Head,' and 'Pound.'

Cat-headed, *a.* Having a head resembling that of a cat. — **1845** Judd *Margaret* I. v. 24 She saw a brown cat-headed owl asleep.

Catherine pear. A variety of small early pear. {1641–} — **1786** Washington *Diaries* III. 24 In the No. Et. square of this garden . . . [are] 7 Row, 3 Bell Pears East and 1 Catherine Ditto.

***Cat-hole.**

***1.** A hole or opening through which a cat may pass. {1536 *Sc.*}

1845 *Knickerb.* XXV. 444 A venerable pussy ran out of the cat-hole in the linter-door. **1852** J. Reynolds *Hist. Illinois* 286 Teel went to the door . . . and stood with his foot near the *cat hole.* **1867** *Amer. Naturalist* I. 255 She brushes against a lid which hangs from above, not unlike an old-fashioned swinging door of a cat-hole, as sometimes seen about barns or corn-cribs.

+2. A hole in a stream or swamp such as catfish might frequent.

1857 *Mich. Agric. Trans.* IX. 578 The very important work of draining our swamps, marshes and 'cat holes,' has been fairly commenced. **1883** *Century Mag.* July 378/2 He . . . seated himself on a log at the edge of a deep pool, or 'cat-hole,' and began fishing.

***Catholic,** *n.* A Roman Catholic; a member of the Roman Catholic church.

1778 Anburey *Travels* II. 285 Among the numerous sects of religion with which this province [*i.e.*, Pennsylvania] abounds . . . [are] Lutherans, Catholics, Methodists. **1846** *Niles' Nat. Reg.* 4 April 80/2 Catholics in Texas—Bishop Odin has embarked 27 Catholic priests at Havre, for his diocese in Texas. **1855** Hambleton *H. A. Wise* 334 Why are Northern Abolitionists and Know Nothings persecuting and proscribing foreigners and Catholics?

***Catholic,** *a.* Belonging or pertaining to the Roman Catholic Church.

1635 Wm. Smith in *Md. Archives* IV. 16 And further I professe that I die a member of the Catholique Romane Church, out of wch there is no salvation. **1685** *Md. Wills* I. 159 To brothers Anthony and William, of Catholic brotherhood at St. Inigoes, [etc.]. **1819** Morse *Rep. Indian Affairs* (1822) ii. 91 A few converts were made by them [=Presbyterians], who were put to death by the Catholic Indians, on account of their religion. **1840** *Niles' Nat. Reg.* 4 July 278/2 The Catholic ladies of the city of Washington, held a fair a few days since for the benefit of the St. Vincent's Orphan asylum. **1847** L. Collins *Kentucky* 140 The first Catholic emigrants to Kentucky. **1866** *Rep. Indian Affairs* 298, I enclose herewith request of the Catholic Indians on the Bad River reservation for permission to build a Catholic church on said reservation.

+Catline. A variety of apple. — **1817** W. Coxe *Fruit Trees* 114 The Catline is an apple rather below the middling size. **1818** *Amer. Mo. Mag.* II. 428/2 Table Apples [include] 1. Junating, ripens in June and July. . . . 10. Catline, September.

+Catlinite. [From George *Catlin,* an American traveler.] A variety of red clay found in the Upper Missouri region. — **1857** Dana *Mineralogy* 358 The Pipestone of the North American Indians was in part a red claystone or compacted clay from the Coteau de Prairies. It has been named *catlinite.* **1895** *Century Mag.* Sept. 694/1 Each [tribal pipe] had a bowl of red catlinite.

‖**Cat-luck.** The luck of falling or landing on one's feet. — **1716** Church *Philip's War* (1867) II. 160 The said Edee turning him over, generally had Cat luck falling on his feet.

***Catmint.** =Catnip.

1737 Brickell *N. Carolina* 20 The Pot-Herbs . . . are . . . Derg, red and white, Nep or Cat-mint. **1795** Winterbotham *Hist. View* III. 398 Among the native and uncultivated plants of New-England, the following have been employed for medical purposes: . . . Germander, . . . Catmint, or catnip. **1832** Williamson *Maine* I. 121 Those [herbs] of less importance are the Celandine; the Comfrey; the Catmint, or Catnip, (*Nepeta*) whose appearance and virtues are well known.

attrib. **1835** Longstreet *Georgia Scenes* 211, I had nothin' but dried yerbs, . . . so I put a hot rock to his feet, and made him a large bowl o' catmint tea.

+Cat nap, Cat's-nap. *colloq.* A short nap or doze while sitting up.

1823 Cooper *Pioneers* xxxii, I just closed my eyes in order to think the better with myself. . . . It was only some such matter as a cat's nap. **1866** 'Mark Twain' in *Harper's Mag.* XXXIV. 105 The Captain also got a few good cat-naps. **1873** Beadle *Undevel. West* 448 My head pitches forward and back in involuntary 'cat-naps' of a minute each. **1899** T. Hall *Tales* 107 We get but a cat nap, however, and are soon moving again, this time in a direction at right angles to the road.

transf. **1899** *Atlantic Mo.* LXXXIII. 753/1 This submissive aspect was only a little folding of the hands in sleep, merely a cat nap before a fierce awakening.

+Catnip. [f. *cat* and *nip* (var. of *nep*).]

1. A common aromatic weed (*Nepeta cataria*) of the mint family; catmint.

1712 *Essex Inst. Coll.* X. 94 He boiled tansey, sage, hysop, and catnip in some of the best wort. **1832** J. K. Paulding *Westward Ho!* I. 122 Well, some of us called it summer-savory, some catnip, some sweet basil. **1858** Holmes *Autocrat* iv. 87, I open a certain closet. . . . On its shelves used to lie bundles of sweet-marjoram and penny-royal and lavender and mint and catnip. **1875** Stowe *We & Our Neighbors* 20 There were closets smelling of elderblow, catnip, feverfew, and dried rose leaves. **1891** S. M. Welch *Recoll. 1830–40* 119 The old squaws would bring the various green herbs, catnip, summer savory, sorrel, water cresses. **1896** J. C. Harris *Sister Jane* 46, I reckon Mandy's got catnip on her clothes.

2. *ellipt.* =Catnip tea.

1809 Irving *Knickerb.* vii. x, A whole army of old women . . . were bent upon driving the enemy out of his bowels . . . with catnip and penny royal. **1852** Mitchell *Dream Life* 100 He thinks that a dose of catnip, under Providence, will effect a cure. **1856** M. J. Holmes *Homestead on H.* 229 Miss Lucy . . . was much given to drinking catnip.

+Catnip tea. Tea made from the leaves of catnip.

1837 J. C. Neal *Charcoal Sk.* (1838) 160, I go about doing little jobs for a fip or a levy, so's to get my catnip tea and bitters regular. **1854** Shillaber *Mrs. Partington* 19 Here speaking the consoling word, and there dispensing comfort, mingled with catnip tea. **1861** Stowe *Pearl Orr's Isl.* I. 20 A mongrel species of snub-nosed tea-pot which fumed strongly of catnip tea. **1863** Mrs. Whitney *F. Gartney* viii, Any old woman can make gruel, and feed a baby with catnip tea. **1871** Eggleston *Hoosier Schoolm.* xxii. 158, I don't see any sense in a minister of the gospel calling prayer-meeting a lower ordinance than feeding catnip-tea to Mrs. Brown's last baby.

+Catogan. [F.] (See quots. 1885 and 1888.) Also attrib. — **1885** *N.Y. Wk. Sun* 29 April 3 To dress the hair on the top of the head and form it into a catogan loop in the nape of the neck, as ultra-fashionable women are arranging their coiffure at this moment. **1888** Cable in *Century Mag.* Dec. 258/1 For driving or for evening they [=ladies of New Orleans] placed on top of the high, powdered hair what they called a *catogan,* a little bonnet of gauze or lace trimmed with ribbons. **1923** Wyatt *Invisible Gods* ii. i. 38 Her hair neatly arranged in what was called a 'Catogan queue,' and tied with white hair ribbons.

Cat-o'-nine-tails.

1. A whip having nine lashes. {1695–}

1703 *N.C. Col. Rec.* I. 594 Him the s[ai]d Wm Hudson did then & there with a certain Weapon comonly called or known by the name of Catt of Nine tayles . . . beat wound & kill. **1762** A. M. Earle *Curious Punishments* 122 Robert McKnight to receive 800 lashes on his naked back with cat-o'-nine tails. **1837** *Diplom. Corr. Texas* (1908) i. 271 Hogan and Campo received one hundred lashes on the bare back with a cat o' nine tails. **1884** *Boston Journal* 25 Nov. 2/3 A curious scene was witnessed in New Castle, Del., last week. The old fashioned punishment of placing the culprit in the pillory and inflicting a castigation with the cat-o-nine tails, was performed.

fig. **1911** L. J. Vance *Cynthia* 83 Madame Savaran could tear the English language into strips and lash Sidonie with the cat-o-nine-tails so extemporised.

+2. ? A catfish.

1791 J. Brevard *MS. Diary* 18 July (N.C. Univ.), The Fish called the Cat o' nine Tails.

+3. The common cattail, *Typha latifolia.*

1858 Holmes *Autocrat* xii. 330 The spire . . . swayed back and forward like a stalk of rye or a cat-o'nine-tails (bulrush) with a bobolink on it. **1876** Ingram *Centennial Expos.* 310 [He] is seen veering to the right of a group of cat-o'-nine-tails, which he is as loth to disturb. **1883** *Harper's Mag.* Dec. 100/1 A mossy bank with overhanging ferns and cat-o'-nine-tails. **1895** *Outing* XXVII. 76/2 We came to higher ground, where the cat-o'-nine-tails took the place of reeds and vines.

‖**Cat-o'-sixty-nine-tails.** Fanciful variation of the preceding. — **a1841** W. Hawkes *Sporting Scenes* II. 54 What a husband she would have had in that usher, with his cat-o'-sixty-nine-tails swinging from his long, lean, foul-nailed fingers!

***Cat o(f) the mountain.** A wild cat or catamount.

1666 Alsop *Maryland* (1902) i. 37 The Elke, the Cat of the Mountain, the Rackoon, . . . and several others . . . inhabit here in Mary-Land in several droves and troops, ranging the Woods. **1778** Carver *Travels* 445 The Cat of the mountain . . . is in shape like a cat, only much larger. **1800** D. R. D'Eres *Memoirs* 164 Cat of the Mountain, or Wild Cat, in shape much resembles our common house Cat. **1825** Neal *Bro. Jonathan* III. 392 Some say 'twas a Mohawk Injunn— . . . some, a cat o' the mountain. **1826** Cooper *Mohicans* xii, These knavish Maquas cling to life like so many cats-o'-the-mountain.

+Caton chimney. A cat-and-clay or stick-and-dirt chimney having tobacco stalks substituted for the wooden sticks. — **1899** *Boston Transcript* 14 Jan. 12/2 The 'Caton chimney' of Kentucky is doubtless an emigrant from the Atlantic coast, with tobacco stalks substituted for cat-sticks.

+Cat owl. A large owl whose head has a fancied resemblance to that of a cat, esp. the great horned owl, *Bubo virginianus.*

1792 IMLAY *Western Territory* 225 [Birds in south central U.S. include] night hawk, cat owl, screech owl, [etc.]. **1835** *Knickerb.* VI. 184 The very owls that made that night vocal, were not the large vulgar cat-owls, that coarsely whoop. **1839** PEABODY *Mass. Birds* 223 The Great Horned or Cat Owl, *Strix Virginiana*, . . . is one of those which rear their young in Massachusetts. **1844** *Nat. Hist. N.Y., Zoology* II. 24 The Great Horned Owl, *Bubo Virginianus*, . . . is often called the Cat Owl, and builds in trees. **1854** THOREAU *Walden* 139 A hare or woodchuck under the house, a screech-owl or cat-owl behind it. **1857** *Rep. Comm. Patents: Agric.* 121 The large-horned owl, or cat-owl, may be met with from Hudson's Bay to Florida. **a1862** THOREAU *Maine Woods* 200 Just below this, a cat-owl flew heavily over the stream.

+**Cat pine.** *local.* A variety of white spruce. — **1894** *Amer. Folk-Lore* VII. 99 *Picea alba*, . . . cat-pine, Buckfield, Me.

+**Cat-rig.** (See quot. 1877.) Also attrib. — **1867** F. LUDLOW *Little Bro.* 96 The cat-rig boat . . . carries a main-sail only and is a favourite on the Shrewsbury river. **1877** BARTLETT 106 *Cat-Rig*, a boat-rig with one mast near the bow with only one sail, and that one a boom-sail.

+**Cat-rigged,** *a.* Having only one sail extended by a long boom. — **1882** GODFREY *Nantucket* 360 Nantucket can boast of a very fine fleet of small yachts. The majority of them are cat-rigged, and are usually sailed by their owners. **1883** *Harper's Mag.* Aug. 453/1 There is no greater abomination than the cat-rigged boat. **1886** *Outing* IX. 14/1 The building of open yachts, sloop and cat-rigged, was immensely stimulated by the action of the Centennial Commission.

Cat's-claw. *S.W.* +(See quots. and cf. CATCLAW.) — **1849** AUDUBON *Western Jrnl.* (1906) 73 Every tree, shrub and plant is thorny to a degree no one can imagine until they have tried a thicket of 'tear-blanket' or 'cat's claw.' **1884** SARGENT *Rep. Forests* 63 *Acacia Wrighti.* . . . Cat's Claw. **1889** *Cent.* 865/2 *Cat's claw*, in western Texas, several species of *Acacia* with hooked thorns, as *A. Greggi* and *A. Wrighti.*

***Cat's-foot.** **1.** Any one of various plants having in some respects a fancied resemblance to the foot of a cat. +**2.** (See quotation.) — **(1) 1784** CUTLER in *Mem. Academy* I. 480 *Gnaphalium*. . . . Cats foot. Wooly Mouse-Ear. Blossoms yellowish white. Road sides. **1791** MUHLENBERG *Index Florae* 178 *Filago germanica monogamia*, Cats-foot. **(2) 1877** BARTLETT 778 *Cat's Foot!* An exclamation of disbelief. New England.

Cat show. A show or exhibition of cats. (Cf. DOG-SHOW.) — **1883** E. M. BACON *Dict. Boston, Mass.* 304 All sorts of public meetings, balls, cat-shows, dog-shows, foot-races, walking-matches, and wrestling-matches.

‖**Catskillian.** An inhabitant or native of the Catskill region, New York. — **1883** *Harper's Mag.* Sept. 524/1 The lore which all old Catskillians cling to, and which . . . no congregation of the 'summer boarder,' can ever take away.

Catskin, Cat's-skin. {1600–} The skin or pelt of a wild or tame cat. {1692–}

1634 WOOD *New Eng. Prospect* II. 65 Most of them [*sc.* Indians] in the Winter having his deepe furr'd Cat skinne, like a long large muffe, which hee shifts to that arme which lieth most exposed to the winde. **1647** *Conn. Probate Records* I. 11 The Goods . . . [include] 1 coate made of Catte skins, 1 coate made of Racoone skins. **1701** C. WOLLEY *Journal N. Y.* 39 A Cat's-skin [is worth] half a Crown. **1790** *Penna. Packet* 1 Jan. 4/1 E. Dutilh & Wachsmuth . . . have for Sale . . . Beaver, racoon, fox, cat, and bear skins.

b. Attrib. in sense: (1) Made of catskin. (2) Wearing a cap of catskin.

(1) 1840 C. MATHEWS *Politicians* I. i, I must borrow that catskin cap of yours, that's moth eaten. **1845** T. J. GREEN *Texian Exped.* 105, I . . . found . . . two or three officers counting their catskin and tiger-tailed pouches. **(2) 1847** ROBB *Squatter Life* 85 Gus . . . made a wry face at his cat-skin observer.

+**Cat sleep.** A cat-nap, short sleep. — **1837** SEDGWICK *Live & Let Live* (1876) 63 Roused from her cat-sleep by the unwonted noise.

+**Cat spruce.** *local.* The black or the hemlock spruce. — **1894** *Amer. Folk-Lore* VII. 100 *Picea nigra*, . . . cat-spruce, Penobscot Co., Me., yew-pine, spruce-pine, West Va. **1897** SUDWORTH *Arborescent Flora* 37 *Picea canadensis*. . . . Common names [include] . . . Cat Spruce (Me.).

Cat squirrel. {1788–, *dial.*}

+**1.** A gray or reddish variety of the fox-squirrel.

1826 J. GODMAN *Nat. Hist.* II. 129 The Cat-Squirrel, *Sciurus Cinereus*, . . . is found in great abundance throughout the oak and chestnut forests of this country. **1834** M'MURTRIE *Cuvier's Animal Kingdom* 80 The Cat Squirrel (*Sc. cinereus*, Lin.) of America is cinereous above, white beneath. **1855** M. REID *Hunters' Feast* xix, The cat squirrel . . . prefers concealing itself behind the trunk, dodging round the tree as the hunter advances upon it. **1890** *Cent.* 5882 Fox- or cat-squirrels are several large red, gray, or black species of North America.

+**2.** *S.* The common gray squirrel.

1884 J. C. HARRIS *Mingo* 171 The cat-squirrels . . . occasionally scamper across the crumbling shingles. **1908** *Dialect Notes* III. 297 *Cat-Squirrel*. . . . The gray squirrel in distinction from the red or fox-squirrel.

3. *S.W.* The ring-tailed bassaris or mountain-cat, *Bassaris astuta*. (*Cent.*)

***Cat's-tail.** **a.** =CATTAIL. **b.** A tall perennial grass, *Phleum pratense.* — **1791** MUHLENBERG *Index Florae* 179 *Typha latifolia.* Cats-tail. **1837** IRVING *Bonneville* II. 131 Their lives are past in the great sand plains and along the adjacent rivers; they subsist sometimes on fish, at other times on roots and the seeds of a plant, called the cat's-tail. **1863** *Ill. Agric. Soc. Trans.* V. 862 Timothy grass, or Cat's Tail, or as it is called in New England, Herd's Grass.

attrib. **1651** in *Mayflower Desc.* X. 201 An old Catts tayle bed and pillow . . . 4 [shillings]. **1796** MORSE *Univ. Geog.* I. 187 Timothy, or bulbus cat's tail grass.

Catstick. **a.** A stick or bat used in playing ball. {a1626–} **b.** A small piece of wood or kindling.

1836 CROCKETT *Yaller Flower Almanac* 12 Put dat catstick on de top and saw dem boat togedder. **1848** BARTLETT 67 *Catstick*, a bat or cudgel used by boys in a game at ball. It is known by the same name in England, though used for a different play. I have never heard the word here except in Rhode Island. **1867** LOWELL *Fitz Adam's Story* xvii, And more to abate the price, his gimlet eye Would pierce to catsticks that none else could spy. **1889** FARMER 127 *Cat-stick*, a small stick; or in Pennsylvania, Massachusetts, Maryland, and further South the term is applied to firewood. **1899** [see CATON CHIMNEY].

+**Catstitching.** Ornamenting or decorating with catstitches. — **1871** STOWE *Pink & White Tyranny* 40 There were all sorts of . . . cat-stitching and hem-stitching going on.

+**Cat-swamp.** ? A small swamp having no outlet. — **1704** *Providence Rec.* IV. 178 Bounded . . . on the southeasterne Corner with a white oake tree marked, standing a little way in the cat swamp.

* **Cattail.** A tall marsh or aquatic plant having furry spikes, *Typha latifolia.*

1816 U. BROWN *Journal* II. 148, I should call them abominable Swamps with high rough grass Bushes & Cat tails in abundance. **1868** *Rep. Comm. Agric.* 177 'Cat-tails' . . . should, of course, be carefully pulled up by the roots. **1899** *Mo. So. Dakotan* I. 143 The sitting room of the little brown house was decorated with . . . furry brown cat-tails. **1913** STRATTON-PORTER *Laddie* (1917) 313 A big blacksnake darted its head through sweet grass and cattails, and caught a frog.

attrib. **c1730** *MS. Inv. D. Magee's Estate, Bertie Co.* (N.C.H.C.), One Cattail Bed. **1834** PECK *Gaz. Illinois* 205 Cat Tail Swamp, is in the south part of Jo Daviess County. **1857** *Mich. Agric. Soc. Trans.* VIII. 649 Upon land which . . . was originally a cat-tail swamp, we saw a field of corn.

Cattail flag. =CATTAIL. — **1805** LEWIS in *L. & Clark Exped.* (1904) II. 290 The bull rush & Cat-tail flag grow in great abundance in the moist parts of the bottoms. **1872** *Amer. Naturalist* VI. 77 Those are certainly the long strap-shaped leaves, and the dark cylindrical spikes of *Typha latifolia!* the veritable Cat-tail Flag. **1899** M. GOING *Flowers* 144 The cat-tail flag is like a calla, . . . with its creamy leaf torn away.

+**Cattail millet.** Any of several varieties of sorghum. — **1889** VASEY *Agric. Grasses* 30 *Pennisetum spicatum*, . . . (Pearl Millet; Cat-tail Millet; Egyptian Millet), . . . is best adapted for cultivation in the South. **1901** MOHR *Plant Life Ala.* 135 Cattail millet, Hungarian grass and the so-called Johnson grass . . . furnish green forage and hay crops throughout the summer.

Catted, *a.* +Of a chimney: Furnished with cat-sticks or with a clay filling. — **1665** *Southampton Rec.* I. 154 Post is agreed with to build a watch house of 15 foot square, 7 foot gice over it, a chimney catted and fit for daubing. **1889** *Cent.* 853/1 A chimney well catted.

+**Catted chimney.** A stick-and-dirt or cat-and-clay chimney. — **1639** in J. B. Felt *Annals of Salem* 119 He is to build a meeting house, . . . one catted Chimney of 12 feet long and 4 feet in height. **1684** I. MATHER *Providences* pref. 15 A violent flash . . . of Lightning . . . broke and shivered one of the Needles of the katted or wooden Chimney. **1899** *Boston Transcript* 14 Jan. 12/2 The 'catted chimney' was quickly and easily made of cat-sticks and clay.

+**Cat-thrasher.** (See quot. 1889.) — **1888** GOODE *Amer. Fishes* 394 Around the Gulf of Maine this species is also known by the names 'Kyack' or 'Kyauk,' 'Saw-belly,' and 'Cat-thrasher.' **1889** *Cent.* 865/3 *Cat-thrasher*, a clupeoid fish, *Clupea æstivalis.* (Maine, U.S.)

* **Cattle.**

* **1.** A collective designation for domestic live stock.

1630 *Plymouth Laws* It shall be lawfull . . . to transporte cattle of all kinds. **1632** *Plymouth Col. Rec.* I. 6 Such damage or losse as fell upon any to be made good by the owners of the same cattle trespassing. **1634** WOOD *New Eng. Prospect* I. 41 The inhabitants use to put their Cattle in these [islands] for safety, viz. their Rammes, Goates, and Swine, when their Corne is on the ground. **1775** BURNABY *Travels* 80 It [Penna.] yields likewise flax-seed, hemp, cattle of different kinds, and various other articles.

* **2.** Animals of the ox family.

1635 *Boston Rec.* 3 All barren cattell whatsoever . . . shalbe kept abroad from off the neck. **a1656** BRADFORD *Hist.* 189 Mr. Winslow . . . brought 3 heifers & a bull, the first begining of any catle of that kind in the land. **c1790** T. COXE *View U.S.* 63 The produce, manufactures, and exports of Pennsylvania are . . . working and pleasurable carriages, horses, horned cattle, [etc.]. **1840** *Niles' Nat. Reg.* 8 Aug. 368/1 A great sale of Durham cattle took place at Lexington, Kentucky, recently. **1896** *Va. Agric. Rep.* XV. 26 In nearly all the eastern states there are scarcely any cattle raised except for cows. **a1918** G. STUART *On Frontier* II. 175 Herds of from two thousand to five thousand head of cattle were being gathered in Texas and New Mexico.

3. Applied to horses. {a1680–}

1684 I. MATHER *Providences* (1856) 55 He made a shift with the use of one leg to get to his cattle (being an horse and two oxen). **1825** Neal *Bro. Jonathan* II. 63 The two remaining horses . . . were able to free themselves and come out over the backs of the 'cattle,' whose feet . . . would hardly reach the slippery clay at which they were pawing. **1846** *Knickerb.* XXVII. 14 Having made free use of the pump at which their cattle also had been refreshed, [they] came into the parlour. **1867** Holmes *Guardian Angel* 109 All my cattle's out but this critter, 'n' I don't jestly want to have nobody drive her that ain't pretty car'ful. **1877** Hale *G. T. T.* 163 Dustin only spoke to his 'cattle' and the girls said no word to each other or to him.

***4.** Men and women, in contemptuous use.

1821 Doddridge *Backwoodsman & Dandy* 44 If you mean squires, and preachers, and lawyers, and judges, and sheriffs, we had no such cattle among us for many years. **1842** *Amer. Pioneer* I. 183, I wanted to see what kind of cattle they were, and I found them a little set of fellows not fit to fight with us. *c*1871 'Mark Twain' *Sk., Journalism in Tenn.*, Do you suppose I am going to speak of those cattle [=rival editors] that way? **1885** 'Craddock' *Prophet* 202 The rest of us hyar in the Big Smoky hev worked on till sech c-c-cattle ez 'Cajah Green an' his buzzardy dep'ty hain't got no sort'n c-chance o' breakin' thar necks over the rocks an' sech.

5. Attrib. and comb. with *association, breeding, bug, business*, etc.

1893 G. W. Curtis *Horses* 142 We give the following standard description, . . . which has been formally adopted by the Dutch-Belted Cattle Association of America. **1898** Canfield *Maid of Frontier* 128 He knew nothing of cattle-breeding, but was willing to learn. **1889** Farmer 99/2 *Cattle-bugs*, that is, wealthy stock-raisers. **1880** *Harper's Mag.* Oct. 798/1 Mr. Hayes's book embraces interesting descriptions of . . . the cattle and sheep business. **1891** *Century Mag.* Jan. 421 We assumed the character of cattle-buyers. **1820** *Columbian Centinel* 8 Jan. 4/3 W. & G. Tuckerman . . . offer for sale . . . Wool, Cotton, and Cattle Cards. **1903** A. Adams *Log Cowboy* 210 We were frequently forced to resort to the old bed grounds of a year or two previous for cattle chips. **1897** *Outing* XXIX. 548/1 The . . . scow headed for one of the cattle-chutes that straddle the dreary shore of Lakeside. **1868** *Mich. Agric. Rep.* VII. 449 The cattle-commissioners of the State of New York, have made very important investigations. **1635** *Boston Rec.* 5 Mr. William Brenton shall sett pryces upon all cattell comodities. **1850** G. Hines *Voyage* 21 A meeting was immediately called at the mission house, for the purpose of forming a California Cattle Company. **1887** *Courier-Journal* 27 Jan. 7/7 Cattle Corn. Z. T. Smith, Ballard county, first [prize]. **1877** *Rep. Indian Affairs* 62 A cattle-corral, 150 by 300 feet, has been built by the agency employes. **1873** *Newton Kansan* 24 April 3/2 Some of them report double the sales now to that of any time during the Texas cattle days. **1865** *Atlantic Mo.* XV. 667 Steve Kenyon being the present master . . . of his father's tavern, a great resort for horse-jockeys, cattle-dealers. **1912** Raine *Brand Blotters* 53 Norris . . . was the cattle detective of the association and for a year now the rustlers had outgeneraled him. **1869** *Dept. Agric. Rep.* (1870) 16 The investigation [was] instituted to develop the character and cause of the 'Texas cattle disease.' *Ib.* 433 An American cattle farm [is owned by] J. T. Alexander, of Morgan County, Illinois. **1839** J. Buel *Farmer's Comp.* 64 Many a farmer . . . is scrupulously economical of his cattle-feed. **1868** *Rep. Comm. Agric.* 337 An experienced cattle-feeder could not so easily fatten stock on grass raised on newly seeded grounds. **1669** *Watertown Rec.* 96 The acount of catle and hogge fines. **1892** V. Kellog *Kansas Insects* 116 The cattle pest from Europe that bids fair to extend itself over the whole United States, and be as troublesome as its nearly related pest, the well-known Stable Fly, or Cattle Fly. **1898** Canfield *Maid of Frontier* 153 No disease blighted the herds, and the hearts of the honest cattle-folk were happy. **1889** *Secy. of Agric. Rep.* 182 Cotton-seed meal is destined to be a cattle food of great importance. **1867–9** *Ill. Agric. Soc. Trans.* VII. 257, I made it a point to inquire diligently among all these drovers, cattle-holders, etc. **1786** *Columbian Mag.* (1787) I. 36/1 The barn, cattle-houses, sheds, stacks, &c. are so disposed round the farm yard, as to afford the best winter shelter for live stock. **1887** *Courier-Journal* 2 Feb. 1/3 The cattle interest of Mississippi is growing rapidly. **1825** J. Lorain *Pract. Husbandry* 419 The cattle jockey when the market is full of the best and most approved breeds, will be compelled to receive a moderate profit. **1848** Bartlett 373 *Vacher*, (French,) the stock or cattle keeper on the prairies of the South-west. **1888** Roosevelt in *Century Mag.* Feb. 504/1 When the game was gone, they [criminals and roughs] . . . naturally took to horse-stealing, cattle-killing, and high-way robbery. **1902** Wister *Virginian* 282 Days look alike, and often lose their very names in the quiet depths of Cattle Land. **1887** *Harper's Mag.* Feb. 349/1 Large blocks of it [salt] are sent to the Western Plains for 'cattle licks.' **1898** Canfield *Maid of Frontier* 134 Chick Haralson, himself a partially reformed cattle-lifter. **1846** in Claiborne *Life & Corr. Quitman* I. 284 Rancho Nogales appears to be more of a place for cattle-minders and goatherds than a regular rancho. **1879** *Scribner's Mo.* Nov. 139/2 You visit these frontier cattle-pastures. **1892** V. Kellog *Kansas Insects* 113 The Horn Fly of Cattle (*Hæmatobia serrata*). . . . This cattle pest has not yet made its way into Kansas. **1879** *Diseases of Swine* 48 No cure has ever been found for glanders, anthrax, and cattle-plague. **1887** R. H. Davis in *Harper's Mag.* 918/2 Landry . . . is a shrewd, money-making fellow, overseer on a great cattle plantation. **1892** *Scribner's Mag.* June 732/2 Stock was neglected as valueless. Men were 'cattle-poor,' and it was a time of discouragement. **1912** Raine *Brand Blotters* 188 You've made a mistake. We're not holding a cattle rustlers' convention. **1900** Drannan *Plains & Mts.* 394 Three days' ride from the fort I struck plenty of cattle sign. **1903** A. Adams *Log of Cowboy* 201, 'I'll not ship any more cattle to your town,' said Pierce to a cattle solicitor. **1868** *Rep. Comm. Agric.* 289 Between the cattle stalls in the south wing . . . there is a passage way ten feet wide. **1892** W. S. Walsh *Literary Curiosities* 949 The Spanish *rancho* . . . also meant a cattle-station or a hunting-lodge far away from the haunts of men. **1910** J. Hart *Vigilante Girl* 114 They do execute cattle-stealers, but only in the grazing districts. **1898** Canfield *Maid of Frontier* 181, I've killed, and as for cattle-stealin' I've seen things knocked, but I never did half of what was laid to me. **1867** J. N. Edwards *Shelby* 385 Telegraph poles, wires, cattle-stops, bridges, trestle-work, . . . and heavy timbers were given to the flames. **1867** 'Lackland' *Homespun* II. 181 At the Tavern were consummated cattle swaps and horse trades uncounted. **1902** A. MacGowan *Last Word* 431 Jim's Panhandle cattle-ranch lies near the headquarters of the Texas Cattle Syndicate. **1880** *Scribner's Mo.* March 768/1 New Sharon . . . was known out West as 'a cattle-town.' **1858** Vielé *Following Drum* 150 It was a beaten cattle-track, cut through the chapparal. **1873** *Newton Kansan* 29 May 2 The company will also secure another favorable point in the cattle trade. **1682** *Groton Rec.* 72 [They] ar to order the goeng out of thar hard both for time and wai of ther Catel walkse.

+Cattle barn. A barn for housing cattle. — **1850** *New Eng. Farmer* II. 46 The most fitting place to keep laying hens over winter is in the stable, or cattle-barn. **1874** *Vt. Bd. Agric. Rep.* II. 514 In 1868 I built me a large and commodious cattle barn. **1920** *3rd Nat. Country Life Conf. Proc.* 155 No argument is necessary to justify . . . cattle barns.

+Cattle baron. A wealthy cattle raiser; a cattle king. — **1898** Canfield *Maid of Frontier* 129 Having been used to the cattle baron or his immediate underling, they would have gone far and fared hard for him. **1902** A. MacGowan *Last Word* 382 Mr. Lord was a cattle baron in the Texas Panhandle.

Cattle breeder. One engaged in the breeding and raising of cattle. {1827–}

1862 *Rep. Comm. Patents: Agric.* 136 Compare the advantages of the sheep-grower over the cattle-breeder. **1864** *Ohio Agric. Rep.* XVIII. 397 If cattle breeders generally were to avail themselves . . . of using thoroughbred breeds, the improvement would soon be universal. **1884** *Dept. Agric. Rep.* 203 Reliable . . . information having been received by the cattle-breeders of this section of the State [of Ky.] that . . . pleuro-pneumonia was now affecting the herd of Frisbie & Lake. **1889** W. Warfield *Cattle-Breeding* 85 One of the first problems which presents itself to the Cattle-breeder is, What definite plan shall be followed in order to secure the best results?

+Cattle broker. (See quot. 1866.) — **1866** *Internal Revenue Guide* 69 Cattle brokers, whose annual sales do not exceed ten thousand dollars, shall pay ten dollars. . . . Any person whose business it is to buy or sell, or deal in cattle, hogs, or sheep, shall be considered as a cattle broker. **1870** Beadle *Utah* 520 No license was taken out by any of them as cattle brokers.

+Cattle car. A railroad car designed for transporting cattle.

1867 Goss *Soldier's Story* 23 We were packed into filthy cattle cars, the sick and wounded crowded together, and sent into Richmond. **1881** *Chicago Times* 30 April, The first parlor cattle-car left to-night for New York. **1884** Knight *Suppl.* 179/1 *Cattle Car*, . . . a car for live stock. . . . Among the various kinds may be mentioned: . . . combined cattle and box car, . . . Box cattle-car, . . . Slat cattle-car. **1891** 'Thanet' *Otto the Knight*, etc. 241 They sent me, with a dozen other fellows, in a cattle-car to Arkansas River, to make a corduroy-road. **1909** 'O. Henry' *Roads of Destiny* 313 He hoped to rejoin a pal known as 'Slick,' this adventurous pilgrim having preceded him by one day in a cattle-car into which a loose slat had enticed him.

+Cattle country. An extensive area in which cattle raising is the principal industry.

1886 Roosevelt in *Century Mag.* July 340/1, I had to leave the East in the midst of the hunting season to join a round-up in the cattle country of western Dakota. **1888** *Ib.* Feb. 497 [Picture depicting] An Episode in the Opening up of a Cattle Country. **1916** B. M. Bower *Phantom Herd* 307, I have watched the 'long shadow' fall across God's own cattle country.

attrib. **1902** A. MacGowan *Last Word* 47 The drawings . . . are for Hexter's new cattle-country book. **1907** White *Arizona Nights* 110 The ponies stood where we left them, 'tied to the ground' in the cattle-country fashion.

Cattle driver. One engaged in driving cattle. — **1856** Whipple *Explor. Ry. Route* I. 42 Our cattle drivers yesterday took the wrong road from Sheep springs, and travelled towards Las Vegas. **1880** *Harper's Mag.* Sept. 609 Here . . . nightly sat . . . cattle-drivers, peddlers, or mysterious strangers.

Cattle driving. The driving of cattle in large herds or droves. Also attrib. {1878–} — **1834** *Visit to Texas* xiii. 121 He had had experience in cattle-driving long before I had ever seen Texas or a wild ox. **1863** 'E. Kirke' *Southern Friends* 301 He embarked largely in 'cattle driving.' **1879** *Harper's Mag.* Oct. 715 The margin in the cattle-driving business is now considered . . . close.

Cattle drover. One who drives herds or droves of cattle. — **1838** Hawthorne *Note-books* I. 163 In the evening there was a strange fellow in the bar-room,—a sort of mock Methodist,—a cattle-drover. **1866** A. D. Richardson *Secret Service* 28 My querist was a cattle drover, who spent most of his time in traveling through Alabama, Mississippi and Louisiana.

1872 *Atlantic Mo.* May 550 The stentorian 'Hi! hi!' of the cattle-drovers and the shrill 'Yap! yap!' of the ungentle shepherds.

Cattle fair. A cattle show or exhibition of live stock. — **1819** C. B. JOHNSON *Letters fr. Penna.* 76, I saw an account of a cattle fair, in one of the states to the north of this. **1819** *Plough Boy* I. 149 Cattle Shows and Fairs. The approaching Agricultural Fairs . . . will be held at the times and places following. **1830** J. F. WATSON *Philadelphia* 43 A Cattle Fair, was established to be held annually on the 15th Oct. . . . beginning from the year 1641.

+**Cattle growing.** Cattle raising. Also attrib. — **1860** GREELEY *Overland Journey* 327 Cattle-growing was the chief employment of the Californians of other days. **1862** *Rep. Comm. Patents: Agric.* 444 We mention this importation . . . as being the first step in an improved agriculture that was to revolutionize our large cattle-growing districts.

+**Cattle guard.**

1. One or more persons who watch over cattle.

1842 *S. Lit. Messenger* VIII. 455/2 The company to my left had met the cattle-guard, and they were saved. **1848** BRYANT *California* 75 The morning cattle-guard is summoned to drive the oxen into the corral.

2. A device, consisting essentially of a deep pit, to prevent hogs, cattle, etc., from passing into or out of a field or pasture through which a railroad track passes.

1843 in Edwards *Chancery Cases* III. 489 The first cattle guards he saw were in one thousand eight hundred and thirty six. **1872** HUNTINGTON *Road-Master's Asst.* 39 The most effective cattle-guard is a deep pit left entirely open, without even cross-sleepers, as they make a trap similar to slats. **1879** BURDETTE *Hawkeyes* 208, I halted at a cattle guard. **1881** *Chicago Times* 14 May, The night was . . . dark, and in groping along the track the negro fell into a cattle-guard. **1897** C. A. DANA *Recoll. Civil War* 130 A tie had been inserted in a cattle guard to throw the train down an embankment. **1900** S. A. NELSON *A B C Wall St.* 152 Repairs and renewals of bridges, culverts, fences, crossings, signs, cattle-guards, stations, . . . and telegraph.

Cattle herd. a. A herder, one in charge of a herd of cattle. **b.** A herd of cattle. — **(a) 1844** M. FULLER *Woman in 19th Cent.* (1862) 45 Penelope is no more meant for a baker or a weaver solely than Ulysses for a cattle-herd. **(b) 1877** *Rep. Indian Affairs* 47 What beef is issued to the Indians is furnished by cattle-herd.

+**Cattle herder.** One in charge of a herd of cattle.

1847 RUXTON *Adv. Rocky Mts.* (1848) 184 Near a new settlement of San Antonio [is] a little hamlet of ten or twelve log-huts, inhabited by pastores and vaqueros—shepherds and cattle-herders. **1873** *Newton Kansan* 24 July 3/2 The bartender [in Dodge City] . . . was last Sunday night shot . . . by a cattle herder. *a***1877** *Chicago Tribune* (B.), The cowboy is the cattle-herder and drover. **1883** ZEIGLER & GROSSCUP *Alleghanies* 315 A huge flat rock near the summit of the mountain, whereon the cattle-herders used formerly to place the salt brought by them to the stock which range the summit meadows.

Cattle herding. The herding of or caring for cattle. — **1891** C. ROBERTS *Adrift Amer.* 178 We sat up some time round the camp fire and told yarns . . . about western life, cattle-herding, Indian fighting, and such things.

Cattle hunt. A hunt or search for cattle. — **1850** GARRARD *Wah-To-Yah* xi. 151 After chuck, and some horridly pronounced Spanish with the *rancheros*, we remounted for a grand cattle hunt. **1878** I. L. BIRD *Rocky Mts.* 145 We were to have had a grand cattle-hunt yesterday, beginning at 6.30, but the horses were all lost.

+**Cattle hunter.** One accustomed to hunt for cattle. — **1708** *Boston News-Letter* 17–24 May 2/2 We shall have . . . 1000 good Negroes that knows [*sic*] the Swamps and Woods, most of them Cattle-hunters. **1740** *S.C. Hist. Soc.* IV. 148 A troop of Rangers or Cattle Hunters, if they can be got time enough. **1740** W. STEPHENS *Proc. Georgia* 613 Seven or eight of our most expert Cattle-Hunters were sent out on Horseback to scout about.

Cattle hunting. Searching for cattle. — **1739** W. STEPHENS *Proc. Georgia* 314 Among others, the Affair of Cattle-hunting . . . was thought by the General deserving his consideration. **1853** 'P. PAXTON' *Yankee in Texas* 124 [He] picked up a pocketful of rocks when cattle-huntin' wer in season. **1878** I. L. BIRD *Rocky Mts.* 129 We're going cattle-hunting, will you come?

+**Cattle king.** A wealthy owner of ranches and large herds of cattle.

1878 I. L. BIRD *Rocky Mts.* 172 The 'Cattle King' of the State is Mr. Iliff, of South Platte, who owns nine ranches, with runs of 15,000 acres, and 35,000 cattle. **1882** *Century Mag.* Sept. 774/2 One hears a great deal said in the Territory of the wealth of the 'cattle-kings,' and how they began their careers a few years ago with only a few hundred dollars. **1886** *Leslie's Mo.* XXI. 705/1 Victor Shirlaw went . . . for an interview with the cattle-king. **1887** F. FRANCIS *Saddle & Moccasin* 159 A one-idea man, whose heart and soul were wrapped up in cattle, and whose gods were the cattle-kings of California. **1888** ROOSEVELT in *Century Mag.* Feb. 500 Anything more foolish than the demagogic outcry against 'cattle-kings' it would be difficult to imagine. **1892** in *So. Dak. Hist. Coll.* I. 72 The laws of association ranchmen, based on a common sense of rights, afford to a cowboy the chance to become a 'cattle king' by fairness and wise investment. **1902** WISTER *Virginian* 501 But you cannot all be—what is the name?—Cattle Kings. **1921** MULFORD *Bar-20 Three* 106 Soon a bundle of handbills was on its way to the office of the cattle king.

Cattleman. {1878–} +A ranch owner; one engaged in raising cattle on a large scale.

1864 *Ohio Agric. Rep.* XVIII. 150 Our 'cattle men' have not been derelict in endeavoring to improve the character of their herds. **1881** *Harper's Mag.* April 767/1 In the spring of the year the cattle-men of the plains have a grand 'round up.' **1888** ROOSEVELT in *Century Mag.* Feb. 500 Wealthy cattle-men, like miners who have done well, always spend their money freely. **1901** S. E. WHITE *Claim Jumpers* (1916) 173 'What's next? What's next?' she called excitedly to a tall young cattleman. **1905** *Bureau of Forestry Bul.* No. 62, 8 The sheepmen and cattlemen are in frequent collision because of incursions upon each other's domain. **1913** W. C. BARNES *Western Grazing Grounds* 29 It came from the cattlemen at first, and for several years the sheepmen have refused to admit its value. **1924** R. CUMMINS *Sky-High Corral* 66 His cattle were . . . his all, and the loss of them would be almost worse than the loss of his own life to the old cattleman.

+**Cattle mark.** A brand or mark of ownership placed upon cattle. — **1731** *Braintree Rec.* 143 The keeping of Bulls and Boars, description of cattle marks, and laying out of Town ways &c. **1889** FARMER 129 *Cattle-mark*, a proprietor's brand placed upon cattle.

Cattle market. A place where cattle are bought and sold. {1838–} — **1850** *Snow's Pathfinder* Jan. 55 A cattle train leaves Wells River and Montpelier each Tuesday morning for Brighton cattle-market. **1883** J. D. FULTON *Sam Hobart* 21 Brighton is the cattle-market of Boston. *Ib.*, To the South cattle and mules were driven, and Brighton was the cattle-market most widely known.

Cattle owner. One who owns cattle. — **1877** JOHNSON *Anderson Co., Kansas* 55 These cattle owners were not long before they advocated the opening of the roads to Kansas City. **1877** BARTLETT 386 Many years ago, a large cattle-owner named Maverick neglected to brand his yearlings. **1881** *Rep. Indian Affairs* p. xv, There has been for the past two years . . . an increasing feeling of hostility on the part of cattle-owners and settlers. **1889** *Secy. of Agric. Rep.* 64 Trusted agents of the Bureau . . . were sent into the field to gather the most accurate figures possible from the cattle-owners' organizations.

+**Cattle path.** A path made by cattle.

1838 HAWTHORNE *Note-Books* I. 194 Turning off towards the south village, followed a cattle-path till I came to a cottage. **1852** WATSON *Nights in Block-House* 84 He was sauntering along at his ease, in an obscure cattle-path. **1862** F. Moore *Rebellion Rec.* V. II. 299 Finding no trace of the presence of the enemy, he took a cattle-path through the woods. **1872** *Harper's Mag.* Sept. 505/2 In brief, their only highways [*i.e.*, of people living in the Alleghany Mts.] are sled tracks and cattle paths. **1887** *Outing* X. 117/2 The bank was worn away on the other side by a cattle-path just wide enough for one.

Cattle pen. An inclosure for cattle. {1837–}

1841 HAWTHORNE *Note-Books* II. 25 All these, and other varieties of man-kind . . . walked about among the cattle-pens, looking with knowing eyes at the horned people. **1844** GREGG *Commerce of Prairies* I. 62 Not to embarrass this cattle-pen, the camp fires are all lighted outside of the wagons. **1855** SIMMS *Forayers* 79, I took the opposite woods, . . . and came down by Henderson's old cattle-pen. **1883** J. D. FULTON *Sam Hobart* 28 From the stock-yard and cattle-pen Sam passed to the machine-shop. **1893** HOWELLS *Coast of Bohemia* 4 The men occasionally stopped at the cattle-pens. **1909** 'O. HENRY' *Roads of Destiny* 148 A cattle pen and chute stood on one side of the track.

+**Cattle queen.** A wealthy woman engaged in cattle raising. (Cf. CATTLE KING.) — **1886** *Harper's Mag.* Nov. 883/1 Women . . . who now rejoice in the sobriquet of 'cattle queens.' **1893** CHITTENDEN *Ranch Verses* 133 (*title of poem*), Texas Types—The Cattle Queen. **1904** 'O. HENRY' *Heart of West* 5 When the old man died they commenced to call Santa the 'cattle queen.'

+**Cattle raiser.** One who engages in raising cattle on a large scale; also (quot. 1853) one who steals cattle.

1853 'P. PAXTON' *Yankee in Texas* 122 He lived on the frontier among the Ingens, and cattle-raisers. **1870** MEDBERY *Men Wall St.* 2 The heavy cattle-raisers of Texas, . . are not merely subject to fluctuations in the prices of their products. **1877** JOHNSON *Anderson Co., Kansas* 194 Its cause was made a matter of investigation by cattle raisers and scientific men. **1889** *Secy. of Agric. Rep.* 73 The removal of the restrictions would be of the very greatest advantage to American cattle-raisers.

+**Cattle raising,** *vbl. n.* The raising of cattle: used attrib. — **1878** I. L. BIRD *Rocky Mts.* 170 Perry's Park is one of the great cattle-raising ranches in Colorado. **1882** SWEET & KNOX *Texas Siftings* 21 Jacob played sharp tricks on Laban, his partner in the cattle-raising business.

+**Cattle ranch.** In western U.S., an extensive tract of prairie country, provided with houses, corrals, etc., on which cattle are raised.

1857 OLMSTEAD *Journey through Texas* 160 Some live upon the produce of farms and cattle-ranches owned in the neighborhood. **1869** J. R. BROWNE *Adv. Apache Country* 396 Several fine valleys, now used as hay and cattle ranches, lie between Aurora and Bodie. **1878** *Ill. Dept. Agric. Trans.* XIV. 105 The cattle ranches of Texas have almost destroyed whatever profit there was in raising native stock. **1883** *Century Mag.* Oct. 805/2 The California cattle ranch in which either milk or butter could be found was an exception to the rule. **1887** WILKINS *Humble Romance* 228 He was reported to be running a cattle ranch in one of those distant territories. **1902** MCFAUL *Ike Glidden* 31 The estate of Jonathan Wiggins, consisting of immense mining properties and cattle ranches in the West. **1906** L. BELL *C. Lee* 189 'Better go West on a cattle ranch,' she thought, with bitter passion. **1923** R. HERRICK *Lilla* 273, I tramped down the state until I found a job on a cattle ranch.

+**Cattle ranching.** The carrying on of the business or affairs of a cattle ranch. — **1888** ROOSEVELT in *Century Mag.* Feb. 500 Cattle-ranching can only be carried on in its present form while the population is scanty. **1923** J. H. COOK *On Old Frontier* 32 Cattle ranching soon grew to be a lucrative and attractive business over the entire grazing ground of the territory lying north of Texas.

+**Cattle range.** An unsettled or sparsely settled region over which cattle graze, used esp. of the prairie regions of the west.

1640 *Essex Inst. Coll.* V. 170/1 Ordered that none of the land within the cattle range shall be granted . . . to any man. **1835** HOFFMAN *Winter in West* II. 206 The 'cattle ranges,' however, are generally the steep hill-sides. **1857** D. BRAMAN *Texas* 29 This county has good cattle and hog ranges. **1869** J. R. BROWNE *Adv. Apache Country* 261 Embracing over twenty square leagues of mountain and valley, it [a ranch] comprises . . . some of the best silver and copper lodes and cattle-ranges in the country. **1881** *Rep. Indian Affairs* p. xiv, A journey of about twenty-five days through a country now practically destitute of game, but occupied by settlers and for cattle-ranges. **1895** *Yearbook Dept. Agric. 1894* 118 How can we tell the isolated overseers of cattle ranges in Wyoming of the approach of a blizzard? **1905** *Bureau of Forestry Bul.* No. 62, 8 Land which for years has been regarded as exclusively cattle range may be infringed upon by large bands of sheep. *a***1918** G. STUART *On Frontier* I. 194 My handsomely beaded buckskin suit . . . was stolen from my cabin on the cattle range.

b. (See quotations.)

1835 HOFFMAN *Winter in West* II. 130 We entered at once upon a large and beautiful park or chase. [*Note*] Called 'a cattle-range,' if I mistake not, in Kentucky. **1848** BARTLETT 68 *Cattle-range*, in Kentucky, a park. **1889** FARMER 129/1 *Cattle-range.* Parks, even those attached to country residences, are so called in Kentucky; this State is famous for its pasture and grazing lands.

Cattle scales. Platform scales suitable for weighing cattle. Also attrib. — **1854** *Penna. Agric. Rep.* 395 Best Hay and Cattle Scales. **1871** *Rep. Indian Affairs* (1872) 473, I have had Cattle-scales erected at a suitable distance from the Agency. **1881** *Ib.* 121 Agency Buildings at Poplar River are agent's house, . . . cattle-scales house.

Cattle shed. A shelter or covered area for cattle. — **1845** *Lowell Offering* V. 254 Directly in front [of the house] . . . is a huge barn, with all the appurtenances of cow-yard, watering trough, cattle-shed, [etc.]. **1868** BEECHER *Norwood* 535 Besides the barn proper, there were lean-tos, sheds, sheep-barns, straw-barns, cattle-sheds, a horse-barn, and colt-pens. **1871** *Rep. Indian Affairs* (1872) 278 There is also a farm-house, a tolerable good log barn, with comfortable cattle-sheds.

Cattle ship. A ship for transporting cattle. {1891-} — [*a***1649** WINTHROP *History* I. 29 One Mr. Weatherell, whose father was master of one of the cattle ships.] **1891** *Scribner's Mag.* X. 610 The loading of cattle-ships is interesting.

Cattle show. A public gathering or fair where fine cattle are exhibited.

1815 *N. Amer. Rev.* II. 136 The Cattle show, and exhibition of domestick manufactures at Pittsfield, is stated to have been very fully attended this season. **1823** *New Eng. Farmer* II. 47 The annual Cattle Show for Worcester County is announced in the Worcester papers. **1850** S. F. COOPER *Rural Hours* 311 The cattle-show is said to be respectable; the ploughing match and speech were also pronounced creditable. **1872** HOLMES *Poet* x. 320 A small riding-whip is the most popular article with the miscellaneous New-Englander at all great gatherings, cattle-shows, and Fourth-of-July celebrations. **1887** *Lippincott's Mag.* Oct. 574 Commencement . . . was then [in 1838] celebrated in much the same way as the modern country cattle-show. **1895** *Dept. Agric. Yearbook 1894* 85 This 'cattle show' was quite successful, and before many years the annual exhibit became a permanent and popular institution in Massachusetts.

+**Cattle thief.** One who steals cattle; a rustler.

1871 *Rep. Indian Affairs* (1872) 326 The stock is increasing yearly . . . and this despite the cattle-thieves, who infest the adjacent country. **1885** *Ib.* 74 Horse and cattle thieves could have been arrested and punished. **1903** A. ADAMS *Log Cowboy* 100 The biggest cattle thief ever born in Medina County. **1909** 'O. HENRY' *Roads of Destiny* 151 Bud King's band of desperadoes, outlaws and horse and cattle thieves were in camp at a secluded spot on the bank of the Frio. **1916** C. A. EASTMAN *From Deep Woods* 117/2 This was a golden opportunity for the white horse and cattle thieves in the surrounding country.

+**Cattle tick.** A species of cow-tick or fever tick. — **1869** *Amer. Naturalist* III. 51 The Cattle Tick[s] . . . drop from the cattle in the woods, and more frequently along the cattle paths. **1909** *Cent. Suppl.* 213/1 *Southern Cattle-tick*, an American ixodid, *Boöphilus bovis*, that carries the blood-inhabiting parasite of Texas fever from Texas cattle to non-immune cattle in northern states.

+**Cattle trail.** *W.* A route or way along which great herds of cattle are driven.

1873 *Winfield* (Kansas) *Courier* 27 March 3/1 Mr. Collins of Arkansas City passed through town this week on his way home from Washington, where he has been spending the winter in the interest of the Cattle Trail, Post Road, &c., across the Indian Territory. **1878** BEADLE *Western Wilds* 437 Each owner selects those [cattle] bearing his own mark, and thence they set out on the long drive northward through the Indian Territory, along the famous cattle trails. **1886** ROOSEVELT in *Outing* April 3 Antelope Shooting on the Cattle Trail. **1912** RAINE *Brand Blotters* 18 A swift zigzagged across the cattle trail he was following.

Cattle train. A train carrying cattle.

1850 *Snow's Pathfinder* Jan. 55 A cattle train leaves Wells River and Montpelier each Tuesday morning for Brighton cattle-market. **1877** 'E. MARTIN' *Hist. Great Riots* 22 At noon a cattle train bound for Baltimore attempted to start, whereupon the rioters flocked on board. **1883** *Harper's Mag.* Nov. 968/2 Occasionally persons who belong in the cattle train get into a passenger car. **1902** A. MACGOWAN *Last Word* 14 This unhappy conductor of a train through West Texas rebelled. 'This ain't a cattle train,' he objected.

Cattle yard. An inclosure or pen for cattle. Also attrib.

1825 J. LORAIN *Pract. Husbandry* 357 The back of them forms the cattle yard fence. **1837** COLMAN *Mass. Agric. Rep.* (1838) 55 [Manures] should be turned over and thrown into heaps in the cattle yards in the spring. **1868** BEECHER *Norwood* 535 There was water for each cattle-yard, for the sheep-yard, for the colt-yard. **1881** *Rep. Indian Affairs* 330 M. R. Evans claims 1,280 acres of land just above the agency, . . . has a small house and cattle-yard thereon. **1889** *Secy. of Agric. Rep.* 237 The Missouri River cattle-yards promise to rank above Chicago.

Catty. {*dial.*} += CATFISH.

1837 J. C. NEAL *Charcoal Sk.* (1838) 98 If you don't trot, . . . boss will be down upon you and fetch you up like a catty on a cork-line—jerk! **1847** ROBB *Squatter Life* 146 The old man might as well try to catch a Massissippi [*sic*] *catty* with a thread line, as git his fingers on me. **1850** *Knickerb.* XXXVI. 105 There he will squat under a big, projecting rock . . . ; now soberly hauling up an eel, now a 'catty.' **1856** *Spirit of Times* (N.Y.) 4 Oct. 71/2 Up came Biljones' line, with a fine catty, of course.

+**Catty-cornered,** *a.* Cater-cornered; slantwise; not regular. Also *Catty-cornedest.* — **1837** J. C. NEAL *Charcoal Sk.* 196 One of that class . . . who, when compelled to share their bed with another, lie in that engrossing posture called 'catty-cornered.' **1882** S. HALE *Letters* 135 One, a big *salon* of a catty-cornered description, with windows looking all sorts of ways. — *c***1875** BAGBY *Old Va. Gentleman* 301 Rubenstein . . . had the blamedest, biggest, catty cornedest pianner you ever laid eyes on.

+**Catty-cornering.** A diagonal movement. — *a***1854** PAIGE *Dow's Sermons* IV. 79 (Th.), All the cris-crossings, meanderings, trianglings, and catty-cornerings (of a dance).

+**Catydid.** Variant of CATADID, KATYDID.

1825 PAULDING *J. Bull. in Amer.* iii. 35 The catydids caty-didded it. **1838** FLAGG *Far West* II. 214 Even until the morning dawned did a concert of whippoorwills and catydids keep up their infernal orations. **1859** A. CARY *Country Life* iv. 92 The caty-dids . . . were noisily welcoming the early autumn.

+**Caucus,** *n.* Also †**corkus.** [Of obscure origin.]

An Indian origin from Algonquian *caucauasu* 'one who advises, urges,' appears more plausible than Pickering's suggestion (1816) that it is a corruption of *caulkers'* (meeting). The use of West-Corcus as a place name in the first example given below may also be significant.

1. A meeting of political leaders for making plans, agreeing upon candidates, etc. {1878-} Cf. CONGRESSIONAL CAUCUS.

[**1745** *Boston Ev. Post Suppl.* 19 Aug. 1/1 Whereas the Association of Lay-Brethren, lately convened at Boston, to take into their serious Consideration the Conduct of those reverend Clergymen, who have encouraged the Itineration of Mr. George Whitefield, whereby the Liberties of the Laity have been invaded, [etc.]. . . . It is accordingly proposed, that there be such a general Meeting, and that it be held . . . at West-Corcus in Boston.] **1773** J. ADAMS *Works* IX. 334 This no doubt, was concerted last Saturday, at Neponset Hill, where Brattle and Russel dined, by way of caucus, I suppose. **1809** KENDALL *Travels* I. 173 The meeting to which I allude is in use in all parts of the United States, and is denominated a *caucus*—but why so denominated, I have found many to inquire, but none to teach. **1827** *Hallowell* (Me.) *Gaz.* 20 June 2/3 A caucus for the nomination of state officers should in the first place never be composed of members of the assembly. **1862** S. COX *In Congress* (1865) 232 They can deploy around a convention or caucus, and fire their political thunder from the batteries of a demagogue, masked with the negro. **1888** M. LANE in *America* 27 Sept. 15 *Caucus*, a meeting, either private or public, of citizens, either to select candidates for office, or to consider public measures. **1904** A. B. HART in *Nation* 14 April 289 The term 'caucus' is habitually used in Mass., and presumably throughout New England, for precisely the form of assembly which in other parts of the country is called 'primary meeting' or 'primary convention.'

transf. **1886** H. D. BROWN *Two College Girls* 80 The meeting instantly dissolved itself into whispering caucuses.

b. Attrib. with *army, club, committee, convention*, etc.

1762 *Mass. H. S. Proc.* XX. 48 We daily see many of your predictions accomplished respecting the connections & discords of our politicians, corkusmen, plebeian tribunes, &ca. **1763** J. ADAMS *Diary* Wks. II. 144 This day learned that the Caucus Club meets, at certain times, in the garret of Tom Dawes, the Adjutant of the Boston Regiment. **1800** WEEMS *Washington* (1810) 52 General Forbes, with a caucus squad of his officers were actually in deep debate. **1809** *Ann. 10th Congress* 2 Sess. 1421

We are to meet to-morrow here to attend the registering of the election of a caucus President; we are to have a caucus army, I understand, a caucus non-intercourse, a caucus loan of ten millions. **1816** *Ann. 14th Congress* 2 Sess. 354 Each district, insulated and unsupported, will become the victim of caucus influence, State intrigue, and Executive patronage. **1824** *Niles' Reg.* XXV. 353 It seems the caucus-party have resolved to hold one [caucus] at any rate. **1820** *Columbian Centinel* 29 Jan. 1/2 Having a perfect knowledge of all the facts relating to the caucus proceedings of 1816, we assert, that the above is a gross misrepresentation. **1842** H. MANN *Boston Oration* 10 Our National Songs, our Fourth of July Orations, and Caucus Speeches. **1859** J. B. JONES *Southern Scenes* 60, I offers a likely sound fellow ob de Caucus tribe, to the highest bidder. **1882** *Nation* 7 Dec. 478/3 The Caucus Committee was instructed to confer with the Democratic caucus for the purpose of filling the committee vacancies . . . and also to decide upon a permanent chairman. **1888** *Chicago Inter-Ocean* 3 Jan. 6/4 The following named Senators bolted the caucus convention.

2. (See quotations.)

1828 COOPER *Notions* II. 35 Directly under the dome [of the Capitol at Washington] is a gloomyvaulted hall, that I have heard called the 'caucus'; more, I believe, from its fancied fitness for the political meetings that are thus termed, than from the fact that it has ever actually been appropriated to such an use. **1835** H. C. TODD *Notes* 33 Under the dome is a gloomy vaulted hall, called the *Caucus;* the soubriquet of an electioneering committee, being a corruption of calker-meeting, which originated amongst the shipping interest of Boston. **1837** COOPER *Gleanings in Eng.* II. 48 The room . . . reminded me of the apartment beneath the rotunda of the Capitol; that which is called the *caucus.*

+Caucus, *v. intr.* To meet or assemble as a caucus.

1811– [see the vbl. n.]. [**1816** *Mass. Spy* 1 May (Th.), It is said that a caucus at Washington is to be counter-caucussed.] **1822** *Amer. Beacon* (Norfolk, Va.) 11 July 3/2 (Th.S.), It is the next Congress that is to Caucus and nominate candidates for the Presidency and Vice-Presidency. **1824** *Mass. Spy* 14 Jan. (Th.), A tavern is a little republic, where you may caucus and nominate, and vote for yourself without a dissenting voice. **1837** WHITTIER in Pickard *Life* I. 199 We have caucussed in season and out of season. **1887** *Courier-Journal* 6 Feb. 2/2 Republicans in the Senate caucussing on Revenue Reduction. **1894** ROBLEY *Bourbon Co., Kansas* 180 Political meetings and conventions caucused and pulled wires. **1904** *N.Y. Ev. Post* 5 July 1 The Michigan delegation [to the National Dem. Convention] which came here uninstructed, will caucus late this afternoon to decide whom it shall support. **1906** *Nation* LXXXII. 110 The Republicans have never fallen so low as to caucus on a treaty. . . . The Republicans in the Senate may not caucus, but they get the practical result just as if they did.

+Caucus candidate. A political candidate selected or nominated by a caucus. — **1816** *Ann. 14th Congress* 2 Sess. 352 They were pledged before they were chosen to vote for the caucus candidate, and no man doubts they have redeemed the pledge. **1854** BENTON *30 Years' View* I. 49/1 All joined in opposing the 'caucus candidate,' as Mr. Crawford was called.

+Caucus nomination. A political nomination made or agreed upon in a caucus, formerly esp. one for the office of President or Vice-President made by the members of Congress belonging to a particular party.

1816 *Ann. 14th Congress* 2 Sess. 352 In Virginia the legitimacy of caucus nomination has been fully sanctioned. **1824** B. F. BUTLER in Mackenzie *Life Van Buren* (1846) 169 They may yet be induced to give a warm support to the Electoral Law, if they become satisfied . . . that their candidates have no chance of a Caucus Nomination. **1847** T. FORD *Hist. Illinois* (1854) 64 Many people believing caucus nominations by members of Congress to be utterly corrupt and corrupting, a powerful party was formed to break up the usage. **1854** BENTON *30 Years' View* I. 49/1 They succeeded . . . in rendering these Congress caucus nominations odious to the people. **1888** *Chicago Inter-Ocean* 3 Jan. 6/4 In the lower house all the caucus nominations were confirmed without a scratch.

+Caucusser. One who takes part in a caucus. — **1823** *Niles' Reg.* XXV. 101 The danger of a choice in the house of representatives would not be dreaded, even by Messrs. Gales and Seaton, the great caucussers of the day.

+Caucussing, *vbl. n.* The holding by political leaders of preliminary meetings for formulating plans.

1811 *Mass. Spy* 18 Dec. (Th.), The electioneering caucussing will be over, and Mr. Madison still the man of the people. **1816** *Ann. 14th Congress* 2 Sess. 354 Will it prevent future caucussing? **1820** *St. Louis Enquirer* 19 July (Th.), The libel on the Convention, which charged them with caucusing for the principal offices of the State. **1823** *Niles' Reg.* XXV. 49 If caucussing . . . be necessary among parties, to secure unity of action, would it not be expedient to devise some more equitable method than the present? *Ib.* 101 The choice would not come before the house, if caucussing had *legitimate* caucussing power. **1872** 'MARK TWAIN' *Sk., Cannibalism in Cars,* A recess of half an hour was then taken and some little caucusing followed.

transf. **1821** *Mass. Spy* 17 Jan. (Th.), [Our cousin's] bandboxes and wardrobes have been the subject of much curiosity and secret caucussing among my girls.

+Caucus system. A method of political control or management by caucuses. — **1846** MACKENZIE *Life Van Buren* 186 Because he differed a little from Van Buren's party caucus system, the senate rejected Governor Yates's nomination. **1854** BENTON *30 Years' View* I. 122/1 The convention system, now more unfair and irresponsible than the exploded congress caucus system, must eventually share the same fate.

Caudle lecture. [fr. *Mrs. Caudle's Curtain Lectures* by D. Jerrold.] A scolding lecture given by a wife to her husband. — **1856** M. J. HOLMES *L. Rivers* x. 121 Poor Mr. Graham . . . was almost constantly provoking the green-eyed monster by his attentions to some one of the fair sex. In spite of his nightly 'Caudle' lectures, he would transgress again and again. **1889** CUSTER *Tenting on Plains* 226 There seemed to be no sort of provision for 'Caudle lectures.' **1890** — *Following Guidon* 82 A government that deprives a man of the luxury of a Caudle lecture may have male supporters in plenty.

Caul fat. Fat obtained from the intestines or omentum of the bear. {1882–} — **1799** JAS. SMITH *Acc. Captivity* 21 [We] wrapped some of the caul fat round and put it on a wooden spit. *a***1846** *Quarter Race Ky.*, etc. 144 Bob Herring, while the dressing of the bear was going on, took the skin, and on its inside surface . . . deposited the caul fat, that looked like drifted snow.

***Cauliflower.** Also **†colli-, colly-.** A well-known variety of cabbage, *Brassica oleracea,* with a large white edible inflorescence.

1676 GLOVER *Acc. Va.* in *Phil. Trans.* XI. 629 Their Gardens have all sorts of English Pot-herbs, and sallets; they have Cabbages, Colworts, Colly-flowers, Parsnips, [etc.]. **1743** MACSPARRAN *Diary* 2 Stepney payed 3d per Plant for the Colliflowers. **1884** ROE *Nature's Story* 340 Turnips were thinned out, winter cabbages and cauliflowers cultivated, and the . . . celery earthed up.

attrib. **1724** *New-Eng. Courant* 2–9 March 2/2 Extraordinary good Italian Colly-flower Seed, to be sold by James Sterling. **1757** *Md. Hist. Mag.* VI. 234 They generally discover many wants more—Imprimis, some Colly Flower Plants, some off-setts of white Currants. **1849** EMMONS *Agric. N.Y.* II. 292 Analysis of the Cauliflower cabbage (sub-var. *botrytis*). **1850** C. MATHEWS *Moneypenny* 79 Then it was a young grapevine in the infancy of its tendrils—then something looking like a cauliflower-bush with the blossoms half developed. **1910** C. HARRIS *Eve's Husband* 138 Henceforth you have a model husband, a cauliflower-saint.

***Causeway,** *n.* A somewhat elevated road through a marsh, swamp, etc.

1640 *New Haven Col. Rec.* I. 44 The causway to the neck shall be made forthwith. **1704** S. KNIGHT *Journal* 69 In going over the Causeway at Dedham . . . I very narrowly escaped falling over into the river Hors and all. **1800** *Mass. H. S. Coll.* 1 Ser. VI. 216 The causeway between the neck and Winter island now forms two coves. **1830** J. F. WATSON *Philadelphia* 54 A cluster of black walnut trees . . . formed a 'cause-way' along the line of Front street. **1835** HOFFMAN *Winter in West* I. 44 Worse than any artificial road I ever travelled, except perhaps the log causeways among the new settlements in northern New-York. **1891** *Century Mag.* March 645 Crook conceived the idea of building a causeway of rock across the narrow neck.

Causeway, *v.* {1740–} *tr.* To form a road across (a low, swampy, or marshy place); to raise or make passable by means of a causeway. Also absol.

1702 *Cambridge Prop. Rec.* 230 Those Barrs that lead into the said Meadow on the easterly Side where it is caswayed with Gravel & timber. **1740** *Ga. Col. Rec.* IV. 667 There are some bad Places which ought to be causewayed and made good. **1791** W. BARTRAM *Travels* 10 On the verges of the canals, where the road was causewayed, stood the *Cupressus disticha.* **1802** ELLICOTT *Journal* 183 The swamps were numerous, and many of them so deep, that . . . we had to causeway. **1868** *Comm. Agric. Rep.* (1869) 351 The roads of all the States . . . [are] sufficiently cleared of trees, rocks, and stumps to be passable with the worst marshes causewayed.

***Causey,** *n. Obs.* Also **causye, cassey.** A causeway.

1637 *Dedham Rec.* I. 35 Mr. Dalton [and others are] . . . chosen to view & estimate the Making of a Causey & bridge over the little River. **1665** *Boston Rec.* 26 Being desirous to paue the causye . . . they haue libertye to sett vp posts. **1716** CHURCH *Philip's War* 5 He would go and fetch his Horse back, which was going off the Cassey. **1784** WASHINGTON *Diaries* II. 309 Some Causeys in the richest and deepest parts of the Glades will enable a common team to draw twenty hundred with ease. *a***1817** DWIGHT *Travels* II. 125 In this township we began to find the bridges, and causeys, made of round sticks, and logs. **1869** LOWELL *Under the Willows* 19 The dusty Tramp, Seeing the treeless causey burn beyond, Halts.

Causey,** *v. tr. Obs.* To bridge or make passable by means of a causeway. Also *Causeying* vbl. n. — **1740** *S.C. Hist. Soc.* IV. 171 In a narrow Path full of Palmetto Roots, so causeyed, by rough marching in the Night . . . [we] came over a fine run of water, where the Regiment halted. *a1817** DWIGHT *Travels* II. 298 The swamps they could not causey. *Ib.* 478 About three miles of the road are causeyed with logs. — **1784** WASHINGTON *Diaries* II. 307 The ground would admit an exceedingly good Waggon Road with a little causeying of some parts of the Glades.

***Caution.**

***1.** *Law.* Security or bail given for the performance of a stipulated obligation. *Obs.*

1793 *Addison's Reports* (1800) 59 This coin . . . should be delivered to them . . . they giving caution for the performance of the trust reposed in them. **1798** *Dallas' Reports* II. 122 A Court of Admiralty . . . can take a caution or stipulation; which is usually for appearance, or to perform a decree.

+**2.** (See quotation.)

1857 T. H. Gladstone *Englishman in Kansas* 171 On a piece of paper nailed to a tree, appear the words, . . . 'This is Jim Barton's claim; and he'll shoot the first fellow as comes within a mile of it.' Such an announcement is technically called a 'caution.'

+**3.** *colloq.* A person or thing that provokes admiration or astonishment.

Orig., something serving as a caveat or warning. Cf. quot. 1834 in next. **1835** Hoffman *Winter in West* I. 197 The way in which the icy blast would come down the bleak shore of the lake 'was a caution.' **1839** Marryat *Diary* I. 236 The way in which they kill pigs here is, to use a Yankee phrase, quite a caution. **1849** W. Brown *America* 21 He is, as his neighbours say, a 'caution.' **1870** M. Collins *Vivian* III. ii. 26 His wife was what the Yankees call a 'caution.'

+**b.** In phrase *a caution to* (a person, group, or thing).

1834 *Knickerb.* III. 35 The way I'll lick you will be a caution to the balance of your family. **1838** Drake *Tales & Sketches* 84 He did not hesitate to declare . . . that the way in which he would 'use up' his opponent, would be a 'caution' to yankee pedagogues in all coming time. **1842** *Knickerb.* XX. 359 The quantities he used, not knowing the strength of Scotch powder, were, as the phrase goes 'a caution to new beginners.' **1848** *Wilmington* (N.C.) *Commercial* 14 Oct. 2/2 The way locofocoism was done up by the orator was a caution to political sinners. **1850** H. C. Watson *Camp-Fires Revol.* 161 The way we marched over that five miles of rough ground was a caution to Continentallers. **1861** Newell *Orpheus C. Kerr* I. 230 The way that gal squealed when we struck a rut, was a caution to screech owls. **1888** *Battle Creek Moon* 21 Jan. 88 The way he [a drummer] ravels sweet nothing in the ears of the girls is a caution to a tin-can serenade. *a***1904** S. E. White *Blazed Trail Stories* 206 The way he [=a horse] climbed up through that dark gorge was a caution to thoroughbreds.

+**Cavallada.** [Sp. *caballada.*] 'The name universally given in Texas and along the Mexican frontier to a drove of horses or mules' (B. '77). — **1844** Kendall *Sante Fé Exped.* I. 97 Nothing can exceed the grandeur of the scene when a large *cavallada*, or drove of horses, takes a 'scare.' **1857** *Harper's Mag.* Oct. 642/2 This was only a ruse . . . and while it partially succeeded, others made a concerted attack upon the *cavallada.*

Cavallard. *S.W.* Also †**cavalyard.** = Cavallada.

1836 Dewees *Lett. from Texas* 208 Several persons . . . went round calling themselves press-masters, and by this means soon obtained a fine cavalyard of horses. **1846** Sage *Scenes Rocky Mts.* 80 Stealing our whole *cavallard*, consisting of ten heads of horses and mules. **1850** W. R. Ryan *Upper & Lower Calif.* I. 291 We perceived several waggons in advance. They appeared to belong to a numerous party and were accompanied by a large cavallard. **1878** Beadle *Western Wilds* 69 All hands sprang up only to witness our noble *cavallard* under full headway before a body of Mexican horsemen.

Cavallo,[1] **-ally.** Also **cavalli.** [Sp. *caballa;* It. *cavallo,* pl. *cavalli.*] Any of several fish of the genus *Carangus* or related genera. {1634-}

1624 Smith *Virginia* v. 172 Some of them yet knowne to the Americans, as the Purgoose, the Cauallo, the Gar-fish, Flying-fish and Moreraves. **1709** Lawson *Carolina* 155 Cavallies are taken in the same places [*sc.* inlets]. They are of a brownish colour, have exceedingly small scales, and a very thick skin. **1743** Catesby *Carolina* App. p. xxxii, Common Names of . . . Sea Fish [of Carolina include] . . . Cavally, Blue-fish, [etc.]. **1772** Romans in Phillips *Notes on B. Romans* (1924) 123 It abounds here [=Fla.] in fish of all kinds, . . . Rays and Species of Turbot, Cavallos, Dolphins, . . . besides prawns and many others. **1802** Ellicott *Journal* 255 Along the Florida Reef, and among the Keys, a great abundance and variety of fish may be taken: such as . . . cavallos. **1892** *Dialect Notes* I. 189 *Cavalli*, a species of fish found in the Gulf of Mexico.

+**Cavallo.**[2] *S.W.* [Sp. *caballo* Caballo.] A horse. — **1845** T. J. Green *Texian Exped.* 205 How, then, . . . do you catch your cavallos and chickens? **1907** White *Arizona Nights* 23 Get your cavallos and follow me. *Ib.* 261 That cavallo of his is a heap sight better than the Shorty horse.

‖**Cavalrist.** A cavalryman. — **1898** *Boston Herald* 19 June 17/1 He leads the life alternately of a cavalrist, infantrist, engineer, artillerist and staff officer.

***Cavalry.**

***1.** *Mil.* Mounted troops or warriors.

1715 *Boston News-Letter* 22 August 2/2 The Indians Cavalry consists of a 100 Horse and about a thousand Foot; they set their Horse into the Fields of Rice and Corn to destroy it. **1838** *Diplom. Corr. Texas* (1911) III. 1211 After a severe and bloody battle fought in the open prairie without artillery and without cavalry. **1892** M. A. Jackson *Memoirs* 349 The next morning Jackson's cavalry reached Martinsburg, where the people, equally astonished and delighted, greeted him with a glad welcome.

2. Attrib. with *blanket, brigade, bugle,* etc.

1861 *Army Regulations* 389 Cavalry blankets. Artillery blankets. **1884** *Century Mag.* XXVII. 498/1 The Second Cavalry Brigade of the Army of the Mississippi. **1872** F. M. Roe *Army Lett.* 75 The 'long roll' was beaten on the infantry drums, and 'boots and saddles' sounded by the cavalry bugles. **1813** *Niles' Reg.* III. 295/2 [A list of military supplies includes] Cavalry cloaks . . . 1,000. **1881-5** McClellan *Own Story* 224, I threw forward Sumner with two divisions and Stoneman with a cavalry command to proceed as far as the Rapidan. **1867** J. N. Edwards *Shelby* 443 He had been their cavalry commander, almost without intermission, since they had been in the service. **1884** *Century Mag.* April 815/1 In the war-period, when Lincoln rode out to his summer residence on the hills near the city, he was attended by a cavalry detachment. **1873** *Newton Kansan* 10 July 3/5 As one . . . saw the stars and stripes unfurled to the breeze . . . it reminded him of a cavalry encampment. **1867** J. N. Edwards *Shelby* 381 He adopted the cavalry expedition. **1898** Page *Red Rock* 52 They used to call him 'The baby'; but after a sharp cavalry fight on a hill-top one afternoon they stopped this. **1901** Churchill *Crisis* 339 The Captain took off his cavalry gauntlet and knocked at the door, more gently than usual. **1897** Dana *Recoll. Civil War* 188, I have a cavalry guard ready and a good horse myself. **1890** Custer *Following Guidon* p. xiii, The present cavalry guidon is a small United States flag sharply swallow-tailed, and mounted on a standard with a metal point. **1862** O. W. Norton *Army Lett.* 106 The cavalry horses are harvesting the wheat. **1895** Remington *Pony Tracks* 7, I go away on the arms of some 'cavalry kids' (as young lieutenants are called) to a hole in the ground (a dugout) where they are quartered. **1861** Newell *Orpheus C. Kerr* I. 135 The President said that, with the exception of the horses and the men, it was one of the finest cavalry mobs he ever saw. **1865** *Atlantic Mo.* XV. 674 Prices paid at our arsenal . . . Cavalry Pantaloons, 60 [cents]. **1862** McClellan in *Own Story* 178, I have sent out cavalry patrols that may bring in intelligence of value. **1862** F. Moore *Rebellion Rec.* V. II. 365 One of our cavalry regiments . . . charged over a regiment of rebel infantry, dispersing them and driving them into the woods. **1909** 'O. Henry' *Roads of Destiny* 195 Opposite hung the major's old cavalry sabre that he had carried at Shiloh. **1862** McClellan in *Own Story* 514, I propose . . . to push cavalry scouts to Vienna *via* Freedom Hill and Hunter's Lane. **1891** *Harper's Mag.* June 6/1 Our cavalry seat in its best form is perhaps as good as can be. **1880** Cable *Grandissimes* 220 There was a green parade-ground, . . . and cavalry stables. **1897** Dana *Recoll. Civil War* 243 The dispatch . . . was placed between two thicknesses of the pair of re-enforced cavalry trousers which the messenger wore. **1898** Page *Red Rock* 118 Steve . . . wore his old cavalry uniform, the only suit he possessed.

Cavalry boot. A boot such as a cavalryman wears. — **1867** J. M. Crawford *Mosby* 114 The most acceptable of all was one hundred and seventy-five pairs of fine cavalry boots. **1867** J. N. Edwards *Shelby* 337 From his feet there were cast away the rough cavalry boots. **1892** M. A. Jackson *Gen. Jackson* 109 With a pair of india-rubber cavalry boots and a heavy army overcoat he was independent of the weather.

Cavault. (See Cavort *v.*)

Cavayard. Variant of Cavy-yard.

***Cave,** *n.*[1] (See quotation.) — **1814** Brackenridge *Views La.* 148 Leads (or loads) are the smaller fissures that connect with the larger, which are called by the miners, *caves.*

+**Cave,** *n.*[2] A falling in of earth; a cave-in.

1876 Harte *G. Conroy* VI. viii, Gabriel was amazed to find that during the earthquake a 'cave' had taken place in the drift. **1876** Raymond *8th Rep. Mines* 319 A very serious cave occurred about 170 feet from the entrance of the drift. **1887** Farrell *How He Died* 164 A 'cave' had happened in a mine.

fig. **1862** *N.Y. Tribune* 6 March, The great subterranean phenomenon [the great cavern] in Edmonson County, Ky., the giving up [by the Rebels], of Clarksville, and the surrender of Nashville are three mammoth caves. **1862** *Ib.* 31 March, I do not believe that there will be a speedy general cave of all Secession sympathies.

Cave, *v.* {1830- dial.; also *calve,* 1755-}

1. *intr. To cave in.* Of earth, banks, etc.: To slide, slip, or shelve off; to give way and fall in.

1707 Sewall *Diary* II. 186 Grave was caved in. **1726** S. Penhallow *Indian Wars* (1824) 91 Upon the falling of much rain, the trenches caved in. **1764** *Boston Ev. Post* 30 Jan. (Th.), Nor was he missed till he had been buried an Hour, when the People found the Well caved in. **1820** Irving *Sketch Bk.* vii. 65 As some labourers were digging to make an adjoining vault, the earth caved in, so as to leave a vacant space almost like an arch. **1832** Williamson *Maine* II. 115 The heavy rains caused the banks of the trenches to cave in upon them. **1856** *Mich. Agric. Soc. Trans.* VII. 155 From the effects of heavy rain the sides had 'caved in' and caused much injury to the shape of the drains. **1864** T. L. Nichols *Amer. Life* I. 169 They would not cave in and be washed away, as whole villages sometimes are. **1865** *Atlantic Mo.* XV. 3 Like a miner sinking his shaft and running a hideous peril of the earth caving in above him. **1896** J. C. Harris *Sister Jane* 81 Mandy, I wish you'd . . . see if any of the walls has caved in.

fig. and *transf.* **1852** H. V. Huntley *California* (1856) I. 15 He had not brass enough to carry it out, and the attempt 'caved in.' **1869** J. R. Browne *Adv. Apache Country* 462 The Union army triumphant everywhere. The rebellion caving in. **1875** Stowe *We & Our Neighbors* 326 How often has the ground caved in and let the victim down into dungeons of despair that never open! **1898** Hamblen *Gen. Manager's Story* 32, I was caught between the corners of the cars . . . and heard my ribs cave in. **1921** Paine *Comr. Rolling Ocean* 91 Battered and unkempt she looked, . . . rails twisted, ventilators caved in like an old hat.

b. Similarly without *in.*

1848 Thoreau in *Atlantic Mo.* LXIX. 744 He dug his cellar for the new part too near the old house . . . and it has caved and let one end of the house down. **1873** BEADLE *Undevel. West* 69 He had dug two wells, one seventy feet deep and got no water, but struck sand which 'caved so he could not curb.' **1882** C. KING *Rep. Prec. Metals* 639 Wherever the rock in the tunnel has a tendency to cave, slide, or swell, it must be timbered.

2. *tr. To cave down* or *in*, to undermine; to cause to collapse.

1761 S. NILES *Indian Wars* II. 340 But Providence prevented them by sending a great rain, and caved down the sides of their trench. **1851** CIST *Cincinnati* 344, I obtained permission to open a sand-pit, which had long been closed for fear of caving down a house, by further excavation. **1809** CUMING *Western Tour* 194 Water street . . . would be a fine street, had not the river floods caved in the bank in one place near the middle.

3. *intr.* To fall *away*, to drop *off*. Also fig.

1819 *Niles' Reg.* XVII. 244/1 A piece of land of upwards of two acres . . . instantaneously caved away and sunk about twenty feet from its former level. **1874** 'MARK TWAIN' *Sk., True Story*, Well, I jist march' on dem niggers—so, lookin' like a gen'l—an' dey jist cave' away befo' me an' out at de do'. **1880** — *Tramp Abroad* xlii. 486 We frequently came across spots where this masonry had caved off and left dangerous gaps for mules to get over.

4. (With or without *in*.) Of persons: To give up; to confess guilt; to admit defeat. *colloq.*[2]

(1) **1846** G. A. MCCALL *Lett. from Frontiers* (1868) 370 The regiment has been principally on fatigue duty ever since we came here, patching and repairing; . . . and when we prop them up at the end, they cave in in the middle. **1855** J. HOLBROOK *Among Mail Bags* 188 The old gentleman . . . hated to yield; but, when I showed him the documents, he caved in and made the best of it. **1858** *N.Y. Tribune* 27 Jan. 7/4 The last time he 'caved in' and said he was one of them [a gang of counterfeiters]. **1866** GREGG *Life in Army* xxiv. 200 Both resources failed them, and they ignominiously fled, thinking it best to cave in, and capitulate. **1908** S. E. WHITE *Riverman* iii. 20 'Now, listen,' said Orde, . . . 'when that sheriff comes, . . . I want you to go peaceably. Understand?' 'Cave in? Not much!' cried Purdy.

(2) **1855** 'PAXTON' *Capt. Priest* 64 We'll have a supper together, said he, and the one who 'caves' first shall pay the shot. **1858** *N.Y. Tribune* 1 May 4/2 One . . . of the six South American opponents of Lecompton caved; the others stood firm. **1860** HOLLAND *Miss Gilbert* 390, I tell you when a man gets in front of him Sunday, he catches it—no use dodging—might as well cave. **1875** BURNHAM *Three Years* iv, *Cave*, to yield, give in, come down at last. To own up. **1876** G. H. TRIPP *Student-Life* 436 Enough fellows would stand aloof to spoil everything, and you would have to cave at last, Charley. **1878** PINKERTON *Strikers* 64 He [a tramp] may manage to beg his way perhaps two weeks more, but . . . he has become desperate and will make his mark upon something before he 'caves.' **1904** STRATTON-PORTER *Freckles* 393 When he found out about them, and it wasn't anything so terrible, he just caved!

5. *tr.* To beat, knock, or 'bash' *in*.

1857 *Knickerbocker* XLIX. 278 He would feel like caving my head in if he knew that I ever made an allusion to the subject. **1864** 'MARK TWAIN' *Sketches* (1926) 156 At the same time he let go with his right [fist] and caved the side of my head in. **1873** HARTE *Mrs. Skagg's Husbands*, etc. 61 Reckon she's caved in his head the first lick!

***Caveat.** +Formerly a notice filed at the Patent Office by an inventor to prevent the possible granting of a patent to another for the same invention. — **1847** WEBSTER 184/2 [A] caveat . . . [is] lodged in the office before the patent right is taken out. **1879** G. PRESCOTT *Sp. Telephone* 256 A caveat, describing his invention, was filed by Gray. **1881** [see next].

Caveator. [Cf. prec.] +One who secures a caveat. — **1881** *Sci. Amer. Circular*, After a Caveat has been filed the Patent Office will not issue a patent for the same invention to any other person without giving notice to the Caveator.

+Cave-in. [CAVE *v.*] A falling in or collapsing as of a mine, well, etc.

1860 *Harper's Mag.* April 616/1 [The miner] works, on a single day, huge caverns into the hill-side with his 'water-batteries,' until by certain indications he knows that a 'cave in' is about to take place. **1883** *Ib.* June 156/2, April 10—Eight men buried by a cave-in at the Red Bridge Mine, in Michigan. **1887** *Century Mag.* XXXIV. 698/1 The muskrats have done it. Here's a 'cave-in' as deep as a well. **1890** RYAN *Told in Hills* 323, I found a 'cave-in' of rock and gravel right at the end of the tunnel. **1896** J. C. HARRIS *Sister Jane* 82, I know there must have been a cave-in somewhere. **1902** *Sci. Amer. Suppl.* 6 Dec. 22512 The chamber . . . will thus become unworkable because of these cracks and threatened cave-ins.

Cavendish. Choice leaf tobacco pressed into plugs or cakes. {1839–}.

1842 'UNCLE SAM' *Peculiarities* I. 209 He will imagine one man leaning against the wall, whittling (cutting up) a stick for amusement; another chopping up cavendish (flat cake) tobacco into small pieces. **1843** J. LUMSDEN *Amer. Mem.* 14 Full details of the methods adopted by the Virginian planters in the manufacturing of the . . . cavendish, plug, pigtail. **1848** W. E. BURTON *Waggeries* 13 The sailors ashore . . . chawed them right up like a piece o' sweet cavendish. **1860** *Harper's Mag.* Oct. 715/2 Uncle Miley fortified himself with an immense piece of cavendish.

attrib. **1849** A. MACKAY *Western World* I. 253, I witnessed all the processes which the weed underwent in its passage from dry leaves to the marketable shape of Cavendish tobacco.

+Cavern limestone. 'The carboniferous limestone of Kentucky, so called from the innumerable caves which its hard strata contain' (B. '59).

Caviard. Variant of CAVY-YARD.

+Caving, *vbl. n.* The falling *in* of the sides or tops of excavations.

(1) **1809** *Mass. Spy* 25 Oct. (Th.), Mr. Benanuel Bucklin was killed by the caving in of a fountain which he was stoning. **1836** EDWARD *Hist. Texas* 22 Of course there are no cut-offs, and but rarely such a thing as caving in. **1842** BUCKINGHAM *E. & W. States* III. 439 The ground has given way there by repeated underminings or cavings-in, as they are called, of the soil. **1853** *Harper's Mag.* VII. 707/2 How hard they had labored, night and day, to sink a shaft, often interrupted by 'caving-in,' and rising water from the bottom. **1879** *Scribner's Mo.* Nov. 54/2 The channel . . . is enlarging very rapidly by caving in.

fig. **1852** *Congress. Globe* 17 May 1385/3 The result . . . will be a universal 'caving in'. upon the part of Southern Whigs. **1860** in J. Redpath *Life of John Brown* 387, I remarked . . . that the question was frequently asked, 'Whether there was any caving in on his [Brown's] part,' and his reply was, that there was no caving in about him.

attrib. **1859** T. B. GUNN *N.Y. Boarding Houses* 98 An especially uncomfortable chair with a caving-in seat and rickety back was assigned to us.

(2) **1857** R. TOMES *Amer. in Japan* xiv. 330 Stakes or palisades are driven in along the cuttings to prevent the earth from caving. **1876** RAYMOND *8th Rep. Mines* 179 A very extensive caving of the soft ore and gangue (brown oxide of iron) soon after destroyed the usefulness of the discovery. **1887** *Courier-Journal* 21 June 1/1 At Erie, Pa., yesterday, by the caving of a bank, John Elsie and Jacob Fehrenback were killed.

+Caving, *ppl. a.* [CAVE *v.*] Falling in, through being hollowed out underneath. — **1846** T. B. THORPE *Myst. Backwoods* 154 The high waters of the spring, bearing within their bosom the sediment of almost unlimited caving shores, deposited in time at the mouth of the 'cut off' the solid earth. **1873** 'MARK TWAIN' & WARNER *Gilded Age* I. 35 A deep silence pervaded the air and was emphasized, at intervals, rather than broken, by the hooting of an owl . . . or the muffled crash of a caving bank in the distance. **1882** *Harper's Mag.* Jan. 166/2 When a . . . caving bank . . . extinguishes a light, a mighty growl goes up from the fraternity of the tiller-rope. **1891** *Ib.* Nov. 890/1 Invalidism of a more serious nature is not infrequent where men work . . . beneath caving earth.

Caviya. (See CAVY-YARD.)

+Cavort, *v. colloq.*[2] Also **cavault, covault, cauvaut, cavoort.** [Origin unknown.] *intr.* To act up; to prance, caper, cut up didos or shines. Also fig.

The precise relationship of quots. 1829 and 1830 to the verb is not clear.

1793 *Steele Papers* I. 106 The Hon. J—e 'cauvauted,' don't laugh at the expression, it suits the idea I meant to convey. [**1829** *Va. Lit. Museum* 16 Dec. 419 *Cavault* or *Cavort*, ranting, highflying.—West. **1830** ROYALL *Lett. fr. Ala.* 122 *Covault* is of Tennessee birth. . . . It signifies an unruly or ungovernable man; also an untame horse, or anything that cannot be controuled.] **1830** *Illinois Mo. Mag.* 71 The most amusing individuals, were some two or three, who were *cavorting*. Now, if any lady or gentleman is so ignorant of the American language as not to know what cavorting is, . . . it expresses the conduct of an individual who fancies himself the smartest and best man in the world. **1840** *S. Lit. Messenger* VI. 506/2 You can't win my soul nor my heart nuther, so its no use to come snorting and cavorting about me in this fashion. **1854** RILEY *Puddleford* 108 At one time, while Wiggins was 'cavorting in the upper regions,' . . . Sile Bates . . . started to his feet. **1868** W. BAKER *New Timothy* (1870) 134 Tell him . . . to think of another proud animal . . . a-cavorting an' loping along to ruin. **1873** BAILEY *Life in Danbury* 97, I could no more get hold of the fearful agony that was cavorting around in me, [etc.]. **1880** *Congress. Rec.* 22 Jan. 483/2, [I concluded] that it was not wise to allow the wild colt of the prairies to cavort around without a curb. **1888** STOCKTON *Dusantes* 144, I'd do anythin' in the world to make 'em content to live on dry land . . . instid of cavoortin' about on the pitchin' ocean. **1899** VAN DYKE *Fisherman's Luck* 39 The fish . . . went wallowing through the pool and cavorting along the rapid like a playful hippopotamus. **1903** G. ADE *In Babel* 251 Well, to see 'em cavortin' around town here in their cowboy hats . . . you'd think, by cracky, that every one of 'em had chawed up a thousand o' them Spanish generals.

+Cavorter. *colloq.*[2] One who cavorts. — **1835** LONGSTREET *Ga. Scenes* 21, I could see nothing in it [the crowd] that seemed to have anything to do with the cavorter.

+Cavorting, *vbl. n. colloq.*[2] Kicking, rearing, plunging; ranting, extravagant, or flamboyant behavior or conduct.

1840 *Daily Pennant* (St. Louis) 18 June (Th.), That ar man he tooks up a dornick, and made a heap of cavortins. **1845** J. J. HOOPER *Simon Sugg's Adv.* iii. 31 Of all the kickin', snortin', hollerin', and cavortin' that ever was seen, they'll do it. **1848** *Knickerb.* XVIII. 499 The Scorpion filly . . . indulged herself in *cavorting;* which in Georgia parlance means a series of kicks and plunges.

+Cavorting, *ppl. a.* That cavorts. — **1839** HOFFMAN *Wild Scenes* 30, I had . . . expected of course to see one of those roystering, 'cavorting,' rifle-shirted blades that I have seen upon our western frontier. a**1909** 'O. HENRY' *Roads of Destiny* 103 Did Hot Tamales fancy he saw a steer, red and cavorting, that should be headed off and driven back to herd?

||**Cavortish,** *a. colloq.*[2] Inclined or given to cavorting. — **1835** LONGSTREET *Ga. Scenes* 28 Bullet became more and more cavortish: insomuch that, when the blanket came off, he had reached the kicking point in good earnest.

+**Cavy-yard.** *W.* Also **cavayard, caviard,** etc. [Var. of CAVALLARD.] A drove or herd of horses.

(*a*) **1824** DEWEES *Lett. from Texas* 54 He stated that he was traveling in the employ of a gentleman, by the name of Corasco, who was driving a large cavyyard of horses and mules to Louisiana. **1836** EDWARD *Hist. Texas* 107 When this powerful tribe wishes to raise the wind, as the saying is, they will carry back a Mexican cavy-yard. **1843** T. J. FARNHAM *Travels West. Prairies* I. 187 The Indians . . . make an annual levy upon the cavy-yard of the fortress. **1847** DEWEES *Lett. from Texas* 301 Two hundred dollars would be sufficient to purchase a cavayard of twenty [mares]. **1850** GARRARD *Wah-To-Yah* xviii. 214 'Now, hobble your cavyard,' said Louy, relaxing in a smile at . . . calling Garmon's one mule a whole cavyard, 'an drink coffee with us.' **1874** J. C. McCOY *Cattle Trade of West* 86 The extra horses not under the saddle are called the cavvieyard, and are driven behind the camp wagon. **1913** W. C. BARNES *Western Grazing Grounds* 380 Following is a list of definitions of words and expressions in common use among stockmen: . . . Cavvyard, Cavvy. (Spanish.) A bunch of horses.

(*b*) **1825** *Austin Papers* (1924) II. 1013 The Indians are very troublesome; they do a grate deal of mischief, killing people and taking of Caviards. **1853** 'P. PAXTON' *Yankee in Texas* 97 Two or three more [darkies] were mounted, and sent into the prairie in search of the 'caviarde' of horses—and we went in to dinner.

(*c*) **1908** MULFORD *Orphan* 24 He was soon able to count seven warriors who were driving another 'cavvieyeh' of horses. **1908** — *J. Nelson* 267 The caviya of a hundred and thirty saddle horses.

+**Cawcawwassough.** [Algonquian.] One who advises or encourages. (See note under CAUCUS *n.*) — **1612** SMITH *Virginia* 5 In all these places is a severall commander, which they call Werowance, except the Chickhamanians, who are governed by the Priests and their Assistants of [*read* or] their Elders called Caw-cawwassoughes.

Cayenne. *C. pepper* (or *capsicum*), the well-known condiment or seasoning agent, red pepper. {1756-} Also ellipt. {1774-}

(1) **1785** WASHINGTON *Diaries* II. 383 Sowed the following Nuts and Seeds: . . . two rows of the Bird pepper; then one row of the Cayan pepper. **1802** ELLICOTT *Journal* 289 The dysentery . . . was thought to be owing to the profuse use of stimulants, such as cayenne pepper. **1846** CORCORAN *Pickings* 52, I then steamed him strong, administered bayberry tea, cayenne capiscum [*sic*], lobelia, pepsinay, and No. 2 and No. 6. c**1849** PAIGE *Dow's Sermons* I. 9 Stick to a salt diet—make free with cayenne pepper. **1906** *Dept. Agric. Yearbook* 174 It was discovered that by feeding young canaries freely on cayenne pepper the yellow could be deepened into a rich orange.

(2) **1809** IRVING *Knickerb.* III. iii, Hideous crimes, that like Cayenne in cookery, do give a pungency and flavour, to the dull detail of history. **1878** *Amer. Home Cook Book* 13 Seasoning of salt and pepper to taste; add cayenne.

+**Cayenne tern.** A large tern, *Sterna maxima.* — **1828** BONAPARTE *Synopsis* 353 The Cayenne Tern. *Sterna cayana.* . . . Inhabits the tropical seas of America: common on the coasts of the southern states. **1835** AUDUBON *Ornith. Biog.* III. 505 We found it necessary to use large shot, the Cayenne Tern being a strong and tough bird, the largest of the genus met with on our Atlantic coasts. **1844** *Nat. Hist. N.Y., Zoology* II. 299 The Cayenne Tern . . . occurs sparingly on the seacoast of New-York. It resembles . . . the smaller Gulls. **1891** *Cent.* 6244 Cayenne tern . . . is common along the Atlantic coast of the United States.

+**Cayeute.** Also **cayote, cayotah.** Variants of COYOTE.

(*a*) **1846** SAGE *Scenes Rocky Mts.* vi, The buffalo range affords every variety of wolves . . . the gray or prairie wolf; and the cayeute . . . or medicine wolf of the Indians. a**1849** RUXTON *Life Far West* iii, Round the camp, during the night, the cayeute keeps unremitting watch.

(*b*) **1852** *Knickerb.* XXXIX. 225 The carcass of a mule, upon which a horde of cayotes had been regaling. **1860** GREELEY *Overland Journey* 109 The bark of the cayote is heard. a**1861** WINTHROP *J. Brent* 207 Now in the broken country, a cayote or two scuttled away as we passed. a**1861** — *Canoe & Saddle* 197 Many a cayote had appropriated them [=moccasins] after they were thrown away as defunct.

(*c*)**1858** *N.Y. Tribune* 9 March 6/3 The bones were very much bleached, and had been scattered by the cayotah, or prairie wolves, that had picked them.

b. *Mining.* Used attrib. (see quotations).

1854 A. DELANO *Life on Prairies* 374 At Nevada some of the shafts of deep placer (or, as they are termed in California mining parlance, *cayote*) diggings, are eighty feet deep. **1871** RAYMOND [*3rd Rep.*] *Mines* 78 This ridge had been broken away . . . , leaving a sugar-loaf-shaped mound between, and at this point drifts, then called 'cayote holes,' were run to develop the channel.

+**Cayuga.** An Indian of an Iroquoian tribe formerly occupying the region around Cayuga Lake, N.Y. — **1792** *Affecting Hist. F. Manheim* 34 A number of . . . Cayugas will commence hostilities. **1823** COOPER *Pioneers* vii, [The Iroquois] consisted of the tribes . . . of the Mohawks, the Oneidas, the Onondagas, Cayugas, and Senecas; who ranked, in the confederation, in the order in which they are named. **1840** VAN BUREN in *Pres. Mess. & P.* III. 562 There are special money provisions for the Cayugas, the Onondagas, the Oneidas of New York, [etc.]. **1894** ROBLEY *Bourbon Co., Kansas* 7 These various tribes of New York Indians, consisting of the remnants of the Senecas, Onondagas, Cayugas, Tuscaroras, [etc.] . . . were called the 'Six Nations.'

+**Cayuse.** *N.W.* Also †**kiyuse.** ['From the name of a Waiilatpuan tribe' (Hodge).]

1. An Indian pony.

1869 McCLURE *Rocky Mts.* 302 Twice our kiyuse broke nearly out of the harness. . . . The kiyuse is never perfectly tamed. **1885** *Harper's Mag.* LXXI. 190/2 With one last wicked shake of the head the wiry 'cayuse' breaks into his easy lope. **1889** *Century Mag.* XXXVII. 340/1 The cayuse is generally roan in color, with always a tendency this way, no matter how slight. **1909** C. H. STERNBERG *Life of Fossil Hunter* 151 We heard the jingling bells of a pack horse or Indian cayuse, and soon a boy hove in sight, driving a couple of pack ponies.

2. In depreciatory or jocular use: Any horse, esp. one of little value.

1889 FARMER 131 Cayuse has now come to be used in a depreciative sense, being applied to any poor broken-down jade. **1892** *Harper's Mag.* Dec. 136 How many miles per hour do you figure that cayuse of yourn can travel? **1901** WHITE *Claim Jumpers* 82 'He is shore a fine cayuse,' he asserted with extreme impressiveness. **1910** MULFORD *Hopalong Cassidy* 121 Some people say cayuses ain't got no sense.

3. Attrib. with *bell, horse, pony.*

1857 *Oregon Wkly. Times* Jan. (Th.), All manner of wrought and cast work . . . down to Shoeing a 'Cultus' Cayuse Horse. **1864** 'MARK TWAIN' *Sketches Sixties* (1926) 127 When we got pretty close to it, the island shrunk into a fish . . . and the mastodon dwindled down to a Cayuse pony. **1873** MILLER *Amongst Modocs* 10, I had ridden my little spotted Cayuse pony. **1885** *Century Mag.* Jan. 453 The incongruity of a sober farm-wagon, made in Jackson, Michigan, drawn by a pair of Cayuse ponies and filled with a motley company of barbarians. **1901** M. E. RYAN *Montana* 27 The 'cayuse' bell sounded nearer and nearer, and directly from the dense forest a packhorse came stepping with care over the fallen logs. a**1918** G. STUART *On Frontier* I. 158 In the fall of 1860, Frank L. Worden and Captain C. P. Higgins came up from Fort Walla Walla with a pack train of cayuse horses.

||**Cayuseship.** *jocular.* The quality or state of being a cayuse. — **1894** *Outing* XXIV. 150/2 The only method of procedure on the part of his cayuseship consisted in a series of mad plunges ahead.

Cazique. (Variant of CACIQUE.)

Ceanothus. One or other species of the genus *Ceanothus* of the buckthorn family, occas. cultivated for ornament; a shrub of this genus. — **1785** MARSHALL *Amer. Grove* 27 American Ceanothus, or New-Jersey Tea-Tree. **1843** TORREY *Flora N.Y.* I. 145 *Ceanothus ovalis,* . . . Narrow-leaved Ceanothus, . . . [grows in] barren rocky places; western shore of Lake Champlain. **1871** HARTE *Luck of Roaring Camp* 172 The azaleas were already budding, the ceanothus getting ready its lilac livery for spring. **1882** *Century Mag.* June 227/2 Up through the forest region, to a height of about nine thousand feet above sea-level, there are . . . five or six species of ceanothus, called deer-brush or California lilac.

Cecropia. {1833-} +A large silkworm moth, *Attacus cecropia.* Also attrib. — **1868** *Amer. Naturalist* II. 313 It is not a soft, flossy cocoon, like that of *Cecropia.* **1881** *Ib.* XV. 241 The staunch cocoon of the Cecropia. **1909** STRATTON-PORTER *Girl of Limberlost* 157 Big gray Cecropias come from this kind.

attrib. **1884** *Amer. Naturalist* XVIII. 1046 Poison Glands in the skin of the Cecropia caterpillar. **1885** *Ib.* XIX. 1142 The anatomy of the Cecropia moth.

***Cedar.** Also †**ceder, seder,** etc.

1.+**a.** One or other of various evergreen pinaceous trees of the genera *Juniperus, Chamaecyparis, Libocedrus,* and *Thuja;* a single tree of these kinds.

1637 MORTON *New Canaan* I. xviii, If he would endeavor to finde out any goodly Cedars, hee must . . . make his inquest for them in the vallies of the Salvages. **1656** *Dedham Rec.* I. 140 Granted to Daniell Morse two Seders to make Clabbord. **1711** *Boston News-Letter* 26 Feb. 2/2 The Trees [were] so prodigious thick, that sometimes they could hardly get passage through, they being mostly Spruce and Cedar. **1779** FRENEAU *Poems* (1786) 104 There cedars dark, the osier, and the pine, Shorn tamarisks, and weeping willows grew. **1841** WHITTIER *Funeral Tree of Sokokis* line 15 Yet green are Saco's banks below, And belts of spruce and cedar show. **1884** ROE *Nature's Story* 357 They all grouped themselves in the shade of a clump of cedars. **1905** N. DAVIS *Northerner* 311 In the dark wall of the cedars a redbird flashed in and out.

+**b.** With distinguishing epithets: (see quotations). See also RED CEDAR, WHITE CEDAR.

a**1817** DWIGHT *Travels* II. 436 On the road from Berlin to Williamstown, we saw the species of cedar, which I have named *mongrel cedar.* **1848** THOREAU *Maine Woods* 54 While he . . . lopt off the smallest twigs of the flat-leaved cedar, the arbor-vitae of the gardens, we gathered them up. **1866** GRAY *First Less. Bot.* 152 Over twelve hundred layers have actually been counted on the stump of an aged tree, such as the Giant Cedar or

Redwood of California. **1884** SARGENT *Rep. Forests* 186 *Torreya taxifolia*. . . . Stinking Cedar. Savin.

c. *Cedar of Lebanon*, the evergreen tree, *Cedrus Libani*. (Cf. LEBANON CEDAR.)

1847 DARLINGTON *Weeds & Plants* 339 Cedar of Lebanon . . . has been recently introduced, and bids fair to become common in cultivation. **1863** GRAY *Botany* p. lxxx, Cedar of Lebanon, with dark green foliage, horizontal side-branches, and terminal shoot, erect. **1892** APGAR *Trees Northern U.S.* 189 Cedar of Lebanon . . . [is] a cultivated tree . . . somewhat tender when young in the Middle States, but forming a grand tree in proper positions.

2. The wood of one or other of these trees.

1610 *Estate of Va.* 54 The country yieldeth abundance of wood, as . . . Ashe, Sarsafrase, liue oake, greene all the years, Cedar and Firre. *a***1649** WINTHROP *Hist.* I. 185 One of his pinnaces was about forty tons, of cedar, built at Barbathes. **1682** ASH *Carolina* 5 The Dust and Shavings of Cedar, laid amongst Linnen or Woollen, destroys the Moth and all Verminous Insects. **1709** LAWSON *Carolina* 4 The Inhabitants of Carolina . . . build a considerable Number of Vessels of Cedar, and other Wood. **1752** FRANKLIN *Elec. Experiments* (1753) 106 Make a small cross of two light strips of cedar. **1848** THOREAU *Maine Woods* 17 These camps were about twenty feet long by fifteen wide, built of logs,—hemlock, cedar, spruce, or yellow birch.

3. Attrib. and comb. with *barren, beam, board*, etc.

1824 *Catawba Journal* 26 Oct., A residence on cedar or pine barrens during the summer, has been efficacious in pulmonary cases. **1854** WHIPPLE *Prelim. Explor. Ry. Route* 19 Among the ancient ruins of fortifications, upon Pueblo creek and elsewhere, erected previous to the conquest of Mexico by Cortez, were found cedar beams on ties which remain nearly perfect. *c***1638** *Harvard Rec.* I. 172 For 250 Cedar boards . . . [£]10. 10[s]. **1869** W. MURRAY *Adventures* 154 Two men sit bareheaded and erect at either end of their cedar boat. **1807** GASS *Journal* 42 We again went on, having . . . a cedar bottom on the south side. **1836** *S. Lit. Messenger* II. 733, I was as restive . . . as my horse is under a cedar broom. **1805** SIBLEY in *Ann. 9th Congress* 2 Sess. 1103 Some small, cultivated fields, fenced round with small cedar and moscheto brush. **1836** IRVING *Astoria* I. 103 They had constructed a cedar canoe, the same in which they had reached Astoria. **1883** *Harper's Mag.* Oct. 710/2 We returned to the lodge, and the ashes of a cedar-charcoal fire. **1870** STEPHENS *Married in Haste* 140 A strong aromatic smell of camphor, cedar-chips, and sandal-wood came up from the chest. **1690** SEWALL *Letter-Book* I. 113 Their Meetinghouse [was] well finish'd in the inside with Cedar Clapboards. **1805–8** PIKE *Sources Miss.* 2 About 3 o'clock P.M. [we] passed Buffaloe, or riviere au Bœuf, above which, about 5 miles, commences a beautiful cedar cliff. **1883** *Harper's Mag.* Oct. 710/1 From the Utah Lake southward . . . nearly every river bend, willow bush, cedar clump, or isolated rock marks the scene of some tragic encounter. **1858** *Texas Almanac* 74 Cedar fences are more common. **1901** MOHR *Plant Life Ala.* 82 Large supplies of the valuable timber of the cedar . . . are drawn every year from the cedar glades. **1800** BROWN *A. Mervyn* xlviii, At five o'clock; the sun will then be risen; in the cedar-grove under the bank. **1901** MOHR *Plant Life Ala.* 102 These cedar hammocks once formed detached tracts extending over many square miles. **1814** J. TAYLOR *Arator* 199 Clipping will make cedar hedges extremely thick. No animal will injure them by browsing. **1708** E. COOK *Sot-Weed Factor* 19 In an antient Cedar House Dwelt my new Friend a Cockerouse. **1774** in Phillips *Notes on B. Romans* (1924) 19 No Beach is to be seen excepting at two high Cedar Keys. **1850** LONGFELLOW *Building of Ship* line 59 The knarred and crooked cedar knees. **1899** *Animal & Plant Lore* 99 Lumbermen carry cedar knots in their pockets as a cure for rheumatism. Michigan. **1813** *Mass. Spy* 14 April 4/4 To be sold . . . two Cedar Lots, lying in the Great Cedar Swamp. **1836** C. GILMAN *Recoll.* (1838) 10 When the moon rises over the cleared fields, . . . the cedar-mound stands out in full relief. **1906** F. LYNDE *Quickening* 18 Thomas Jefferson only ground his face deeper into the thick mat of cedar needles and begged to be let alone. **1869** 'MARK TWAIN' *Innocents* 398 It seems to come as natural . . . as it is to put your friend's cedar pencil in your pocket. **1893** in *So. Dak. Hist. Coll.* I. 301 In this are set cedar pickets fifteen feet long, which leave them twelve feet above the ground. **1872** W. J. FLAGG *Good Investment* 99/1 There's the cedar piggin business, and canning fruit, which I understand perfectly. **1780** E. PARKMAN *Diary* 286 Mr. Harrington with my Team fetches me a Cedar pole for my west Stanchells. **1805–9** HENRY *Camp. Quebec* 42 The cedar root was in plenty under our feet. **1848** THOREAU *Maine Woods* 26 We got here a draught of beer . . . , clear and thin, but strong and stringent as the cedar-sap. **1897** *Outing* XXX. 240/1 Among minor features of the year are, the increased use of cedar shells [etc.] **1797** *Spirit Farmer's Mus.* (1801) 92 A few cedar slabs stop the leaks over head. **1848** THOREAU *Maine Woods* 22 In the night we were entertained by the sound of rain-drops on the cedar-splints which covered the roof. **1865** *Atlantic Mo.* XV. 514 Presently I . . . perceive a troop . . . of Ruby-Crowned Wrens, . . . hanging like jewels on the Cedar sprays. **1726** *Boston Selectmen* 26 March, We drove down a large Cedar Stake in the Place & mark't it M.B.C. **1827** WILLIAMS *West Florida* 7 Peat is sometimes found there in extensive beds, with abundance of cypress and cedar stumps, standing far beneath the sand. **1848** THOREAU *Maine Woods* 55 This night we had a dish of arbor-vitae or cedar-tea, which the lumberer sometimes uses when other herbs fail. **1656** *Dedham Rec.* III. 140 No other part [of the swamp shall] . . . be layed out but only such as shall be useful for Cedar timber. **1839** HOFFMAN *Wild Scenes* 173 The oriole, perched upon a cedar-top, whistled as usual. **1723** *Narrag. Hist. Reg.* V. 156 Churn, Cedar Tubs, Cider in Cellar. **1848** THOREAU *Maine Woods* 54 We accompanied Tom into the woods to cut cedar-twigs for our bed. **1748** *N.H. Hist. Soc. Coll.* V. 36 [Fire] first broke out in the deal or cedar wainscot passage between the doors of the chambers. **1824** DODDRIDGE *Notes* 145 The ceder ware by having alternatly a white and red stave, was then thought beautiful.

+**Cedar apple.** A fungous parasite of the genus *Gymnosporangium* which grows upon cedar trees. — **1846** LYELL *Second Visit* (1849) II. 244 The cedar . . . is often covered at this season with what is termed here the cedar apple . . . supposed by many of the inhabitants to be the flower or fruit of the tree itself. **1876** WHITMAN *Specimen Days* (1882) 87 These cedar-apples last only a little while, however, and soon crumble and fade.

+**Cedar ball.** =prec. — **1889** *Cent.* 875/3 Cedar-apple . . . [is] also called *cedar-ball*. **1909** *Dialect Notes* III. 297.

Cedar bark. The bark of the cedar tree. — **1805** CLARK in *Lewis & C. Exped.* (1905) III. 206 The womens Peticoat is . . . made of *arbervita* or the white Cedar bark wove to a string and hanging down in tossles. **1844** LEE & FROST *Oregon* 229 We . . . calked the largest cracks in the canoe with cedar bark. **1858** THOREAU *Maine Woods* 136 The two ends [of the poles] were tied with cedar-bark, their usual string. **1919** KIDDER & GUERNSEY *Archæol. Explor. Arizona* 175 Cedar bark was . . . used for making cradles, sandals, torches, and as padding in bed nets and baby carriers.

+**Cedar-beer.** (See quotation.) — **1737** BRICKELL *N. Carolina* 38 The following are made in Country, viz. Cyder, Persimon-Beer, made of the Fruit of that Tree, Ceder-Beer, made of Ceder-Berries.

+**Cedar-berry.** The juniper-berry or fruit of the red cedar, *Juniperus virginiana*.

[**1709** LAWSON *Carolina* 90 The Cedar-Berries are infused, and made Beer of, by the Bermudians.] **1737** [see CEDAR-BEER]. **1787** WASHINGTON *Diaries* III. 278 The other hands . . . were employed in getting the Cedar Berries. **1847** LOWELL *Indian-Summer Reverie* line 37 The sobered robin, hunger-silent now, Seeks cedar-berries blue, his autumn cheer. **1884** BURROUGHS in *Century Mag.* Dec. 220 In winter, especially, they [wild birds] sweep by me and around me in flocks, . . . feeding upon frozen apples in the orchard, upon cedar-berries, [etc.].

+**Cedar-bird.** The American or cedar waxwing, *Ampelis cedrorum* or *Bombycilla carolinensis* (cf. CAROLINA WAXWING).

1791 BARTRAM *Travels* 288 *Ampelis garrulus*, crown bird or cedar bird. These birds feed on various sorts of succulent fruit. **1818** IRVING *Leg. Sleepy-Hollow*, There was . . . the cedar-bird, with its red-tipt wings and yellow-tipt tail, and its little monteiro cap of feathers. **1872** *Vt. Bd. Agric. Rep.* I. 328 A bird quite as much disliked by fruit growers as the Robin is the Cedar Bird, or Cherry Bird. **1892** TORREY *Foot-Path Way* 33, I saw that the ground was already preëmpted by a company of cedar birds.

+**Cedar bluff.** A cliff covered or crowned with cedars. — **1779** in Ramsey *Tennessee* (1853) 202 We have found a few log cabins which have been built on a cedar bluff above the Lick. **1807** GASS *Journal* 30 We passed cedar bluffs on the north side, a part of which were burning.

+**Cedar brake.** *S.* An area, freq. a swamp, overgrown with cedar.

1830 DEWEES *Lett. from Texas* 124 The night was very dark, and our course lay over mountains of rock and through cedar brake. **1889** FARMER 131/2 The Cedar swamps of the South, unlike the mere swampy marshes of the North, are low-lying grounds mainly under water; these are also called Cedar brakes. **1909** 'O. HENRY' *Options* 137 Across the river were a dozen little mountains densely covered by cedar-brakes.

+**Cedar-bush.** A young cedar tree; a dwarf cedar, cedar shrub, etc.

1663 *Plymouth Rec.* I. 62 Lott [1] is ffoggland bound with a well or spring and a Cedar bush on the north beach therof. **1838** *Knickerb.* XII. 199 They spent their time in swinging on the cedar bushes, throwing stones at the birds, [etc.]. **1855** WILLIS *Convalescent* 41 There was also a considerate road laid out across the river to Garrison's dock, the safe line between the air-holes indicated by cedar bushes stuck in the snow. **1878** STOWE *Poganuc People* 363, I ran away, over to the church, and got asleep under a great cedar-bush, listening to the Christmas music.

+**Cedar chest.** A box made of or lined with cedar for the protection of clothing, etc., from moths and other insects. — **1864** WEBSTER 209. **1881** *Harper's Mag.* April 732 Dulcie was waiting with . . . blankets and shawls from the cedar chest. **1896** WILKINS *Madelon* 245 Madelon . . . was folding up her own wedding-silk and putting it away in the cedar chest, until she should want it. **1910** J. HART *Vigilante Girl* 219 What would you say if I were to give you a locked chest—a mysterious chest—a cedar chest full of finery made for a carnival dance?

+**Cedar closet.** A closet lined with cedar. — **1860** in *Diary of Mrs. S. Cowell* 69 We notice a . . . cedar closet, lined with shelves, wherein to keep clothing free from moths. **1866** HALE *If, Yes & Perhaps* (1868) 256, I was up in the cedar closet one day, looking for an old parade cap of mine.

+**Cedar cooper.** (See quotation.) — **1832** BROWNE *Sylva* 148 The superior fitness of this wood [white cedar] for various household utensils, has given rise, in Philadelphia, to a distinct class of mechanics called cedar coopers.

+**Cedar elm.** A variety of elm, *Ulmus crassifolia*. — **1884** SARGENT *Rep. Forests* 122 *Ulmus crassifolia*. . . . Cedar Elm. **1897** SUDWORTH *Arborescent Flora* 180.

+**Cedar knob.** A mound or hill covered with cedar-trees. — **1805** SIBLEY in *Ann. 9th Congress* 2 Sess. 1104 From the Panis towns to Santa Fe, . . . all the country [is] prairie, a few scattering cedar knobs excepted. **1838** DRAKE *Tales & Sk.* 33 He was a full grown Kentuckian, born on the cedar knobs of the Blue Licks.

+**Cedar log.** A log of cedar.

1749 FRANKLIN in *Jrnl. Science* IV. 365 A deer park five miles round, fenced with cedar logs, five logs high, with chocks of wood between. **1854** *Oregonian* 28 Oct., A deep chasm had, reaching across it, a small ancient looking cedar log, which had either to be walked or cooned. **1896** WILKINS 119 An ox-team drawing a sled laden with cedar logs.

+**Cedar pail.** A bucket made of cedar wood.

1772 *Rhode Isl. Commerce* I. 420 Here is also a parcel of Cedar pails. **1852** *Harper's Mag.* V. 854/2 We finally settled down upon a cedar-pail or bucket for the elder of two boys, and a miniature hoe for the younger. **1863** KEMBLE *Residence in Ga.* 52 A very small cedar pail—a piggin as they termed it.

+**Cedar pine.** One or the other of two varieties of pine: (**a**) The spruce pine (*Pinus glabra*). (**b**) The scrub pine (*P. virginiana*). — (**a**) **1884** SARGENT *Rep. Forests* 201. **1894** COULTER *Bot. W. Texas* III. 554 *Pinus glabra*. A tree 24 to 30 m. high. . . . Extending into Eastern Texas from the Gulf states. 'Cedar pine.' (**b**) **1897** SUDWORTH *Arborescent Flora* 27 *Pinus virginiana*. Scrub Pine. Common names [include] . . . Short-leaved Pine (N.C.), Cedar Pine (N.C.).

+**Cedar post.** A fence-post of cedar wood.

1779 *N.J. Archives* 2 Ser. IV. 76 To be sold, a number of Cedar Posts and Rails. **1807** *Norfolk* (Va.) *Gazette* 13 Nov. 4/3 For Sale, 2000 Cedar and Chinquepin Posts. **1885** *Rep. Indian Affairs* 185 Sixty rods of new fence, of cedar posts and fencing lumber, were built around the stock corral. **1904** E. W. PRINGLE *Rice Planter* 77, I have already bought the wire . . . and had the cedar posts got out, so that it will not cost so much to get the fence put up.

+**Cedar rail.** A rail for fencing made of cedar. Also transf.

1751 HEMPSTEAD *Diary* 568, I was mending fence. . . . 4 Cedar Railes &c, Cheesnut. **1779** [see prec.] **1843** *Knickerb.* XXI. 256 He soon entered into friendly intercourse on the subject of cedar rails. **1856** OLMSTEAD *Slave States* 151 A great many rough poles of the juniper, under the name of 'cedar-rails,' are sent to New York.

+**Cedar shingle.** A shingle made of cedar.

*c***1680** J. HULL *Diary Occurr.* 233 The wind carried broad flakes of fire, being cedar-shingles and clap-boards, over a great many houses. **1744** *Mass. Stat.* 22 March 5 Each shingle to bear . . . not less than three inches broad exclusive of sap, except cedar shingles only. **1811** MEASE *Philadelphia* 25 In general, the houses are covered with cedar shingles. **1884** 'CRADDOCK' *Where Battle Was Fought* 100 A moment later the cedar shingles that roofed the gin-house were blazing timorously.

+**Cedar swamp.** A swamp in which cedar is the prevailing growth.

1636–7 *Plymouth Col. Rec.* I. 51 A parcell of land is graunted vnto Mr Thomas Prence, lyinge betweene the two cedar swamps at Iland Creeke Pond. **1643** *Suffolk Deeds* I. 51 Six acres of Ground at Muddy River bownded with Georg Beamslye his Lott on the Sowth wth the Seader Swampe on the West. **1677** HUBBARD *Narr.* 53 Those that were left alive [were] forced to hide themselves in a Cedar Swamp. **1726** *Southampton Rec.* III. 110, [I] grant and confirm to said trustees [of Southampton] all my rights to ye seder swamp at Ocabog. **1789** MORSE *Amer. Geog.* 143 One species generally predominating in each soil, has originated the descriptive names of maple, ash, and cedar swamps. **1832** J. M'GREGOR *British America* II. 591 Cedar Swamps, are deep mossy bogs, soft and spongy below, with a coating sufficiently firm to uphold smaller cedar or fir-trees, or shrubs. Such lands are more difficult to reclaim than any of our bogs in the United Kingdom. **1847** ROBB *Squatter Life* 71 By all means be careful not to let him get into that cussed cedar swamp! *a***1904** WHITE *Blazed Trail Stories* vi. 87 The high beech-ridge . . . ended in a narrow cedar-swamp.

attrib. **1695** *Conn. Col. Rec.* IV. 153 A cart path which is caled the ceder swamp path.

+**Cedar thicket.** A cedar brake. — **1850** GARRARD *Wah-To-Yah* xviii. 212 A fatiguing walk of half an hour brought me to—to greater aspen groves, and almost impenetrable cedar thickets. **1863** MRS. WHITNEY *F. Gartney* xviii, Down under Grover's Peak, with the river on one side, and the white-robed cedar thickets rising on the other. **1923** J. H. COOK *On Old Frontier* 45 The country was rough and broken, and here and there were large cedar thickets or brakes.

* **Cedar tree.** +A tree belonging to one or other American species of cedar. (See CEDAR 1.)

1634 WOOD *New Eng. Prospect* I. v. 17 The Cedar tree is a tree of no great growth, not bearing above a foot and a halfe square at the most, neither is it very high. **1669** *R.I. Col. Rec.* II. 275 He sent for them [Indians] . . . to come and help him in that business of barking cedar trees. **1750** T. WALKER *Journal* 48 Small Cedar Trees are very plenty on the flat ground nigh the River. **1865** *Atlantic Mo.* XV. 21, I see The mock-grape's blood red banner Hung out on the cedar tree. **1896** WILKINS *Madelon* 70 The smell of wounded cedar-trees was strong about him.

attrib. **1649** *Description Va.* 5 Choice Walnut-tree-wood, Ceader-tree-timber and the like, is transported by them [=masters of ships] if Tobacco is not their full lading.

+**Cedar waxwing.** =CEDAR-BIRD. — **1844** *Nat. Hist. N.Y., Zoology* II. 44. **1878** *U.S. Nat. Museum Proc.* I. 411 *Ampelis cedrorum.*—Cedar Waxwing. The Cedar-bird is sometimes found in the extensive orchards of Marysville, and may also visit those of Stockton. **1918** *Outing* LXXII. 243/1 No bird has ever accorded me a more intimate glimpse into its family ways than the cedar waxwing.

Cedar wood.

+**1.** Wood obtained from the cedar tree (q.v.).

*a***1649** WINTHROP *Hist.* II. 272 They were frigates of cedar wood of about sixty and eighty tons. **1707** *N.C. Col. Rec.* I. 664 [There is] Tarr pitch Clapborde Cedarwood and all provision in such extraordinary plenty that they are able to furnish all at the Island plantations with victuals.

+**2.** A forest or grove of cedar trees. Also collect. =cedar trees.

1855 *Knickerb.* XLVI. 224 The white dreamy waste of sand-hills, contrasted with the black foliage of the cedar-woods. **1857** W. CHANDLESS *Visit Salt Lake* I. 64 Cedar-wood is sprinkled thinly over the bluffs. **1884** *Century Mag.* Oct. 843/1 Sitting down in the cedar woods of a gulch and imagining how much gold there may be under twenty feet of gravel, is not a short cut to wealth. **1890** RYAN *Told in Hills* 112 All the cedar wood was in the drip, drip of tears that follow tempests.

Cede, *v.* {1633–} *tr.* To surrender or give up (land or territory) to another country, state, or people by formal grant. {1798–}

1784 in *S. Lit. Messenger* XXVIII. 34/2 Virginia ought to cede all westward of the great Kanawha. **1792** *Ann. 2nd Congress* 1048 The whole of the said twenty thousand dollars . . . is to be applied solely to the purpose of extinguishing the Indian claims to the lands they have already ceded to the United States. **1822** *Ann. 17th Congress* 1 Sess. I. 161 Virginia ceded all her vacant and unappropriated lands . . . to the United States. **1845** POLK in *Pres. Mess. & P.* IV. 379 Texas was once a part of our country—was unwisely ceded away to a foreign power. *a***1918** G. STUART *On Frontier* II. 74 They were not being driven from their homes or ceding large tracts of territory to the whites.

Ceded, *ppl. a.* Given up; transferred. {1844–}—**1803** *Ann. 8th Congress* 1 Sess. 54 The inhabitants of the ceded territory shall be incorporated into the Union of the United States, and admitted . . . to the enjoyment of all the rights . . . of citizens of the United States. **1848** POLK in *Pres. Mess. & P.* IV. 600 These great advantages, far more than the simple value of the public lands in the ceded territory, 'constitute our indemnity for the past.' **1878** BEADLE *Western Wilds* 25 The Osage Ceded Lands . . . were now dotted with neat villages flanked by well cultivated farms. **1909** *Indian Laws & Tr.* III. 397 Compensation shall be paid . . . out of any money in the Treasury arising from the sale of said ceded lands.

+**Ceja.** *S.W.* [Sp.] **a.** A ridge or brow terminating an upland plain. **b.** (See quot. 1893.) — (**a**) **1834** A. PIKE *Sketches* 44 In the course of fourteen days we should arrive at a descent, or falling off of the prairie to the east, and . . . there (rising out of this ceja, or eyebrow, as they called it) we should find the rivers. **1844** GREGG *Commerce of Prairies* II. 48 The basis of the plain not having been sufficiently firm to resist the action of the waters, these have washed and cut the bordering *cejas* or brows into all the shapes they now present. **1909** *Cent. Suppl.* 215/1 *Ceja*, . . . in phys. geog., the brow or cliffed margin of a mesa or upland. (Southwestern U.S.) (**b**) **1893** *Dialect Notes* I. 245 *Ceja*, eyebrow. In Texas, a long and narrow strip of *chaparral.*

* **Celandine.** A perennial herb of the poppy family, *Chelidonium majus.*

1784 CUTLER in *Mem. Academy* I. 455 Celandine . . . is very acrimonious. The juice destroys warts and cures ringworms. **1792** IMLAY *Western Territory* 208 Of herbs, &c. we have of the wild sort . . . celandine, jew's-ear, horse-mint. **1843** TORREY *Flora N.Y.* I. 44 Common celandine . . . [is] a common plant along fences and in waste places: doubtless introduced from Europe. **1868** GRAY *Field Botany* 49 Celandine . . . [grows] in all gardens and in moist waste places; . . . small yellow flowers in a sort of umbel, all summer. **1891** [see CELANDINE POPPY].

b. *local.* The jewel-weed, *Impatiens fulva.*

1893 *Amer. Folk-Lore* VI. 139 *Impatiens fulva,* celandine. Buckfield, Me.; Ferrisburgh, Vt.

+**Celandine poppy.** The yellow poppy, *Stylophorum diphyllum.* — **1857** GRAY *Botany* 25 *Stylophorum.* Celandine Poppy. . . . Perennial herb, with . . . pinnately divided leaves like Celandine. **1891** *Cent.* 6013/2 *Stylophorum diphyllum* is the celandine poppy or yellow poppy of the central United States. . . . Its light green leaves resemble those of the celandine, and, like it, contain a yellow juice.

Celery. A cultivated plant (*Apium graveolens*) the stalks of which are blanched for table use. {1664–}

1737 BRICKELL *N. Carolina* 19 Asparagus, thrives in this Province. . . . As likewise Selery and Clary. **1842** C. M. KIRKLAND *Forest Life* I. 52 Lilacs and lilies, and even cauliflower and celery are mere superfluities. **1875** STOWE *We & Our Neighbors* 275 The celery's not enough, we shall want two or three more bunches. **1907** *Dept. Agric. Farmer's Bul.* No. 282, 7 The culture of celery on an extensive scale is limited to comparatively recent years.

attrib. **1863** MRS. WHITNEY *F. Gartney* xiv, Your father has driven over to Sedgely about some celery and tomato plants, and won't be home till tea-time. **1882** F. E. OWENS *Cook Book* 88 [Recipe for] celery sauce for boiled fowls.

+Celery(-leafed, -leaved) crowfoot. A variety of the crowfoot, *Ranunculus sceleratus.*

1817-8 EATON *Botany* (1822) 424 *Ranunculus sceleratus*, celery crowfoot. **1840** DEWEY *Mass. Flowering Plants* 26 Celery-leafed Crowfoot . . . grows in wet places, and flowers in June. **1901** MOHR *Plant Life Ala.* 514 Celery-leaved or Cursed Crowfoot . . . [grows] throughout Atlantic North America west to British Columbia and Arizona.

***Celestial,** *n.*

+1. A term popularly applied to natives of the Chinese Empire.

1843 *Knickerb.* XXI. 192 The Chinese have so many millions to disburse to the English, in payment of expenses incurred in killing off the Celestials. **1849** T. T. JOHNSON *Sights Gold Region* 238 The Canton Cafe was kept by Chinamen, who were real celestials. **1867** COZZENS *Sayings* 2 Our ladies must thank the Celestials for their tea-pots. **1886** Z. F. SMITH *Kentucky* 505 The appearance of the pig-tailed Celestials was the occasion of irrepressible merriment. **1910** J. HART *Vigilante Girl* 376 What strain there was on Sing's nerves and temper was not apparent outside the celestial's kitchen.

‖**2.** An inhabitant of Los Angeles, California.

1848 E. BRYANT *California* 394 We had now arrived at the abode of the *celestials.*

***Celestial,** *a.* Pertaining to the Chinese Empire or to the Chinese. {1824-} — **1840** *Knickerb.* XVI. 447 We have seen a Chinese map of the world, in which the celestial country occupies the entire space, with the exception of a few island-like circles. **1855** MARRYAT *Mts. & Molehills* 331 The Chinese are a strong contrast to the thriftless Mexicans and joyous Gauls. The Celestial digger . . . is up with the dawn and at work. **1872** 'MARK TWAIN' *Roughing It* 396 We ate chow-chow with chop-sticks in the celestial restaurants.

***Cellar.** Also †**cellor, seller.**

***1.** A place of storage; now usu. an underground room or rooms beneath a house or other building.

*c***1638** *Harvard Rec.* I. 172 The frame in the Colledge yard & digging the cellar, carriage & setting it up, [£]120. **1639** *Portsmouth Rec.* 5 Land at the Common seller on the neck. **1643** *Conn. Public Rec.* I. 455 Inuentory of the goods of Tho: Scott. . . . In the seller, vessells & seurall goods. . . . In the seller without dores, dyet vessels. **1705** *Charlestown Land Rec.* 172 Digg and sufficiently ston a Conveinent seller under said house, and . . . build and carry up A Double Stack of Brick Chimneys. **1790** *Columbian Centinel* 22 Sept. 12/4 *To Be Let*, Two large dry Cellars, under the Meeting-House. **1853** FOWLER *Home for All* 32 Nor should the cellar be a little pit hole under one corner of your house, . . . for the entire cellar story can be made most useful for one purpose or another. **1907** C. C. ANDREWS *Recoll.* (1928) 42, I continued to room at Mr. Woodbury's and had the use of their kitchen stove and cellar.

2. Attrib. and comb., as *cellar basement, bin, boss, bridge,* etc. (See also CELLAR-CASE, KITCHEN, etc.)

1883 *Century Mag.* Sept. 730/1 There is a large cellar-basement, . . . but the 'laboratory' proper is . . . entered from the ground. **1875** WHITTIER *Mabel Martin* line 2 It was the pleasant harvest time, When cellar-bins are closely stowed. **1902** LORIMER *Lett. Merchant* 108 One of those fellows . . . who goes around and makes the boys give up their lunch money to buy flowers for the deceased aunt of the cellar boss' wife. **1861** *Vanity Fair* 13 April 172/1 The unsuspicious pedestrian is very angry at being stopped by what is called a 'jam' at the commencement of one of the temporary platform cellar-bridges. **1851** CIST *Cincinnati* 49 Occupations [include] . . . Cellar diggers, 20 [people]. **1845** in *Cincinnati Misc.* 198 The man is still living, and in the full possession of his faculties, bodily and mental, who stood by surveying the first cellar-digging in Cincinnati. **1888** *Forum* Sept. 103 The saloon, the cellar-dive and the bar-room usurped the place formerly held by the inn. *a***1649** WINTHROP *Hist.* II. 277 The said impost was forced to break open the cellar doors where their wines lay. **1712** *Boston Selectmen* 15 March 158 Liberty is granted to William Sutton to digg up the H. way in Comon Street for the repairing his Cellar drayn there. **1693** SEWALL *Diary* I. 379 John Barnard lays our Cellar Floor. **1854** THOREAU *Walden* 276 Cato's half-obliterated cellar hole . . . is now filled with the smooth sumach. **1665** *Hempstead Rec.* I. 162, I the a fors'd John Smith have sold on to my soninlaw Samuell Denton the afore saide seller and seller lotte. **1655** *Suffolk Deeds* II. 205 To haue and to hold . . . the vpland . . . digged for a cellar place with the well and orchard & fruite trees growing therein. **1865** STOWE *House & Home P.* 268 'O, Bob!' exclaims Marianne, 'there are the kitchen-pantries! you ruin them,—and no place for the cellar-stairs!' **1853** Cellar story [see sense 1]. **1875** STOWE *We & Our Neighbors* 54 There was a cellar table that she had been intending this very morning to revise. **1828** NEAL *R. Dyer* 126 [They] being employed by the prisoner to take down her cellar-wall. **1681** *Springfield Rec.* I. 327 To Jose: Leonard for a Cellar window.

Cellar-case. 1. ?A box or other receptacle for holding bottles. **+2.** *New Hamp.* (See quot. 1890.) — **(1) 1654** *Essex Probate Rec.* I. 165 A Cellar Case, firken, forme & halfe tub. **(2) 1890** *Dialect Notes* I. 18 *Cellar-case*, outside entrance to a cellar, with a sloping door. In Eastern Massachusetts 'bulkhead' is invariably used. **1895** A. BROWN *Meadow-Grass* 161 Caleb saw that she had prepared for her return by leaving the doors of the cellar-case open, and laying down a board over the steps.

+Cellar kitchen. A basement kitchen. — **1830** J. F. WATSON *Philadelphia* 202 Cellar Kitchens, now so general, are but of modern use. **1846** CHILD *Fact & Fiction* 247 She was mostly confined to the cellar kitchen, from which she looked out upon stone-steps and a brick wall. **1856** *Rep. Comm. Patents: Agric.* 223 My place of keeping [sweet potatoes] is a cellar-kitchen.

Cellar way. An entrance or passage-way to or through a cellar.

1761 S. NILES *Indian Wars* II. 512 Two or three were found lying on that part of the floor which was left, and in the cellar-way. **1845** S. SMITH *J. Downing's Lett.* 54 Jimmy, you didn't bring that grid-iron and poker, that stood in the cellar-way, now. **1863** S. C. MASSETT *Drifting About* 50 The stage entrance was through a cellar-way in Broadway. **1897** 'THANET' *Missionary Sheriff* 172 She had the ill-hap to fall down her cellar-way injuring her spine. **1922** R. PARRISH *Case & Girl* 181 His fingers explored the edge of this opening cautiously, revealing a cellar-way, leading down into the basement.

+Celluloid. An artificial substance with a cellulose base used in place of ivory, coral, etc., in the manufacture of many small objects. Also attrib. {1871-}

1871 *Amer. Dental Ass. Trans.* XI. 152 We have many so-called cheap materials . . . : rubber, celluloid, pyroxyline, porcelain base, aluminum, and the alloys of tin. **1873** *Official Gaz. U.S. Patents* III. 38/2 [Trademark No.] 1,102.—Compound of Pyroxyline.—Celluloid Manufacturing Company, Albany, N.Y. **1882** SWEET & KNOX *Texas Siftings* 9 He is usually swung to a satchel containing a comb and brush, . . . a clean celluloid collar, and a newspaper. **1887** *Courier-Journal* 16 Jan. 16/7 Celluloid is a comparatively recent invention, in appearance closely resembling ivory. **1889** 'MARK TWAIN' *Conn. Yankee* xv. 184 Celluloid teeth, nine dollars a set. **1895** *N.Y. Dramatic News* 14 Dec. 4/4 The clams were made of celluloid, and are used every time the town celebrates. **1903** *Evanston* (Ill.) *Press* 11 April (*advt.*), Celluloid Card Counters—each 10c.

***Cemetery.** Also †**cemetry, cimetery.** A place of burial; a graveyard. Also attrib.

1686 SEWALL *Diary* I. 126 Father Porter laid in the Old Cemetery; is acknowledged by all to have been a great Man in Prayer. **1835** *S. Lit. Messenger* I. 276 The tomb of *Spurzheim*, in the cemetery of Mount Auburn, near Boston. **1871** DE VERE 183 The judge held 'that . . . the conveyance of a cemetery-lot was allowable.' **1873** *Newton Kansan* 3 July 3/2 [A] forty acre piece of school land . . . for a city cemetry [*sic*]. **1881** *Harper's Mag.* Jan. 207/1 The comptroller of the Cemetery Association . . . lent them his help. **1909** *Indian Laws & Tr.* III. 419 The same [land] shall not be subject to taxation so long as the same may be used for cemetery purposes.

***Censor.**

***1.** An officer having supervision of public conduct and morals. *Obs.*

1654 JOHNSON *Wonder-w. Prov.* v. 8 These and the like your civill Censors shall reach unto that the people of, and under your Government, may live a quiet and peaceable life. **1790** *Ann. Congress* I. 3 Feb. 1153 We should add censors, and banish the immoral from amongst us.

+2. *Council of censors:* (see quotations). Now hist.

1776 *Penna. Constitution* § 47 There shall be chosen . . . two persons in each city and county . . . , to be called the Council of Censors. **1777** *Vt. Constitution* ii. § 44 There shall be chosen . . . thirteen persons . . . to be called the Council of Censors. **1794** S. WILLIAMS *Vermont* 349 A council of censors, to consist of thirteen persons to be elected by the people every seventh year. The duty assigned to them is to inquire whether the constitution has been preserved inviolate. **1841** *Niles' Nat. Reg.* 19 June 256/3 The council of censors of this state [Vermont] are in session, and propose several amendments to the constitution. **1873** *Harper's Mag.* XLVI. 575 The septennial Council of Censors, which until recently existed under the Constitution of Vermont (and which was borrowed from the first Constitution of Pennsylvania), [etc.].

+3. A person engaged in making an official enumeration of the inhabitants of a city, state, etc.; a census taker. *Obs.*

1837 *Mass. Statutes* 12 April, The said census shall be taken in the several cities by censors appointed by the mayor and alderman.

4. An officer who in time of war examines private correspondence, telegrams, etc. {1914-}

1898 *Review of Rev.* XVIII. 540/2 Scores of untried young men . . . evolved the most elaborate schemes for evading censors . . . and sent to the newspapers that employed them graphic, thorough, and immediate accounts of the notable actions of the war. **1901** *Forum* XXXI. 467 The censor [at Manila] had irregular office hours, and did not understand that a civilian might want to send a cable message when the censor did not choose to be available. **1917** *Nation* CV. 81/1 It is always the simplest cablegrams which the hardened censor suspects most.

attrib. **1917** *Nation* CV. 81/1 Will every . . . [cabled] communication be paraphrased by the censor office in order to insure against a secret code?

Censored, *ppl. a.* Having been examined by a censor; dominated by a censor. — **1899** *N.Y. Journal* 10 Aug. 14/4 The people of the United States don't know about the fatalities as yet. How can they, with all press reports censored as they are? **1902** *Nation* LXXV. 296 After a censored war, a censored inquiry into it. That was the case with our Philippine war. **1914** *Current Opinion* LVI. 298/3 The New York *Evening Post*

. . . speaks sarcastically of . . . censored writers. **1917** *Lit. Digest* 19 May 1502/1 The editor of the censored *Nation* (London) . . . would not be expected to take kindly to his truncated circulation.

***Censorship.** A system of military surveillance providing for censors; the position of a censor in such a system. — **1899** *Atlantic Mo.* LXXXIII. 425/2 With . . . the establishment of censorship at Santiago, Key West, and New York, the efforts of the enemy . . . became most energetic. *Ib.* 428/2 A supplement to this news [of the destruction of Cervera's fleet] which was one of the most impressive and interesting incidents of my censorship. **1901** *Forum* XXXI. 463 A military censorship over the American people was maintained until after the second election of Mr. McKinley. **1918** H. C. LODGE in *N. Amer. Rev.* CCVIII. 704 The Associated Press and all other news agencies serving American newspapers have agreed to submit to censorship.

Censurate. {1803} =CENSORSHIP. — **1898** *Boston Globe* 24 April 8/4 The censurate of the press is now stricter than ever.

Census. {1613–} An official enumeration of population, usually including information about social and economic conditions. {1846–}

1777 *N.Y. Constit.* § 5 A census of the electors and inhabitants of this state shall be taken, under the direction of the legislature. **1787** *Constitution* i. § 9 No capitation or other direct tax shall be laid unless in proportion to the census or enumeration hereinbefore directed to be taken. **1815** DRAKE *Cincinnati* i. 33 The proportion of inhabitants above forty-five years of age . . . was, by the last census, in Ohio, as nine to one hundred. **1877** JOHNSON *Anderson Co., Kansas* 23 On the 22nd day of January, 1855, Gov. Reeder issued precepts to certain persons to take a census of the Territory. **1906** *Indian Laws & Tr.* III. 180 All municipalities . . . having a population of over two thousand to be determined by the last census taken under any provision of law or ordinance of the council of such municipality, [etc.].

b. Attrib. with *board, bureau, office,* etc.

1849 TAYLOR in *Pres. Mess. & P.* V. 23 The duties enjoined upon the census board thus established having been performed, [etc.]. **1891** *Atlantic Mo.* June 810/1 The Census Bureau at Washington has the material for making these comparisons in the different states. **1883** SMITH *Geol. Survey Ala.* p. v, The Superintendent of the Census . . . placed at my disposal for the use of the State, the maps and wood cuts engraved for the Census Office. **1865** *Atlantic Mo.* XV. 372 The champions of insurrection come from figures of the Census Report. **1852** *Harper's Mag.* IV. 552/2 The subject of printing the census returns has engaged a good deal of attention. **1890** *Ib.* December 160/1 The half-dozen suitors might . . . diminish the population of Boomopolis by at least five of her leading citizens, which operation would result in considerable loss of prestige for the town, particularly in a census year.

+**Census marshal.** A census taker. — **1890** *Cent.* 3639/2 The officers who take the State census in certain States are called *marshals* or *census marshals.*

+**Census taker.** One who collects data for a census.

1840 *Picayune* 25 Aug. 2/2 The following took place between a census taker and a married lady. **1871** STOWE *Pink & White Tyranny* 103 Who should walk into the parlor . . . but that terror of American democracy, the Census-taker. **1890** *Harper's Mag.* Oct. 807/1 The writer met recently, in the Colorado desert of Arizona, a forlorn census-taker . . . roaming over the alkali-plains. **1911** ROLT-WHEELER *Boy with Census* 1 Since I'm going to be a census-taker, I think I'd like to apply for this district.

***Cent.**

+**1.** A coin made partially or entirely of copper and having a value of one hundredth of a dollar. (Cf. RED CENT.)

1782 MORRIS in Sparks *Life G. Morris* (1832) I. 275 One hundred [units] would be the lowest silver coin, and might be called a *Cent.* **1786** *Jrnls. Cont. Congress* 8 Aug. 504 The two copper coins shall be as follows: One equal to the one hundredth part of the federal dollar, to be called *a cent:* And one equal to the two-hundredth part of the federal dollar to be called *A half cent.* **1789** *Ann. 1st Congress* I. 121 He used the term cents because it was a denomination of national coin, fixed by the late Congress, ten of which make a *dime* and ten *dimes* one dollar. **1810** M. V. H. DWIGHT *Journey* 16, I believe at least 50 dutchmen have been here to day to smoke, drink, swear, pitch cents, [etc.]. **1857** *Harper's Mag.* March 549/2 A new cent has been prepared to take the place of that now issued. **1889** 'MARK TWAIN' *Conn. Yankee* xiv. 166 In a week or two now, cents, nickels, . . . and half-dollars . . . would be trickling in thin but steady streams through the commercial veins of the kingdom.

attrib. **1848** THOREAU *Maine Woods* 16 One of the party commenced distributing a store of small cent picture-books among the children. **1856** *Spirit of Times* (N.Y.), Nov. 150/1 The new cent piece recently finished at the United States Mint, Philadelphia, is the size of the old half cent.

+**2.** Fig. in sense: The smallest amount.

1803 J. DAVIS *Travels* 389 But I never wronged Master of a cent. **1812** *Ann. 12th Congress* 1 Sess. II. 1518 You will of course lay a tax of ten millions of dollars . . . without benefitting the Treasury a single cent. **1830** S. SMITH *Major Downing* 21 Uncle Joshua did well to carry his 'puckery apple-sauce' to Boston. He couldn't get a cent for't here. **1856** GOODRICH *Recoll.* I. 142, 'I would not give a penny for it,' was genteel; 'I would not give a cent for it,' was plebeian. **1865** MRS. WHITNEY *Gayworthys* xl, I will never touch a cent of hers. **1872** EGGLESTON *End of World* 11, I don't believe that you'd care a cent if she did marry a Dutchman! **1889** 'MARK TWAIN' *Conn. Yankee* xxxvi. 418 My master stuck stubbornly to it—twenty-two dollars. He wouldn't bate a cent. **1900** DRANNAN *Plains & Mts.* 144, I haven't a scout in my entire command that is worth a cent to scout for Indians.

+**b.** In adv. phrase *not . . . worth a cent,* not well, not at all. *colloq.*

1830 S. SMITH *Major Downing* 23 They don't seem to rip up worth a cent. **1867** J. N. EDWARDS *Shelby* 393 The enemy, largely reinforced, 'would not drive worth a cent,' as poor Shanks afterward expressed it.

***Centaury.** One or other species of plants of the genus *Erythræa* or *Centaurea,* +or of the genus *Sabbatia:* (see quotations and cf. AMERICAN CENTAURY).

1791 MUHLENBERG *Index Florae* 178 *Centaurea Cyanus benedicta,* Centaury. **1815** DRAKE *Cincinnati* ii. 85 *Chironia angularis*—centaury, the herb [is a tonic]. **1843** TORREY *Flora N.Y.* II. 111 *Erythrea Centaurium.* . . . Common Centaury. . . . Fields near the old French fort, Oswego. *Ib.* 113 *Sabbatia stellaris.* . . . Salt-marsh Centaury. . . . Brackish marshes in the neighborhood of New-York and on Long Island. **1886** S. W. MITCHELL *R. Blake* 219 The plumy golden-rods were thick on the dikes, with asters and centaury, while around every brown pool the salt-wort or samphire began to wear its autumn lake-tints.

Centennial, *n.* +A celebration upon the one-hundredth anniversary of an event; spec. the exposition held in Philadephia in 1876 in commemoration of the signing of the Declaration of Independence.

1876 HOWELLS in *Atlantic Mo.* July 92/1 The Centennial is what every one calls the great fair now open at Philadelphia. **1876** INGRAM *Centennial Expos.* 725 While it [=a tiny steam engine] remained on exhibition at the Centennial, it stood on the platform of the great Corliss engine. and rested on a gold twenty-five-cent piece. **1880** *Harper's Mag.* July 318/2 Looking at the water-works at Fairmount, . . . during the Centennial, an Irishman said [etc.]. **1883** *Ib.* Oct. 791/1 This month of October will see at Newburgh upon the Hudson the last of the Revolutionary centennials. **1885** *Century Mag.* May 7/1 The Philadelphia Centennial, . . . three years in preparation, . . . was strongly supported by the United States Government.

Centennial, *a.* Pertaining to, connected with, a hundredth anniversary {*a*1797–}; +commemorating the hundredth anniversary of the Declaration of Independence.

(*a*) **1833** *Amer. Almanac 1834* 325 [Feb. 12, 1833:] Centennial celebration of the settlement of Georgia at Savannah. **1859** *Celebration of 100th Ann. of Westminster, Mass.* 3 We respectfully request a copy of the Address prepared by you for our Centennial Celebration, that it may be published. **1873–4** *Vt. Bd. Agric. Rep.* 221 If this is not satisfactory, since this is a day of tea parties and centennial celebrations, go back with me a hundred years.

(*b*) **1873** *Dept. Agric. Rep.* (1874) 10 The approaching Centennial Exposition affords an additional argument for the preparation of such a collection of our forest specimens. **1876** WHITTIER (*title*), Centennial Hymn. **1876** INGRAM *Centennial Expos.* 722 Albums of the photographs and autographs of the most prominent of the Centennial officers, governors of States and other leading men. **1876** Raymond *8th Rep. Mines* 375 What more fitting celebration of the centennial year of American Independence could be possibly suggested or devised? **1877** *Harper's Mag.* Jan. 303/1 The trains in every direction were full of visitors going to or coming from the Centennial Exhibition. **1878** BEADLE *Western Wilds* 478 Colorado . . . at last succeeded in becoming a State, just in time to aid in the election of a centennial president. **1886** Centennial Commission [see CATRIGGED].

+**Centennialism.** The practice of holding centennials. — **1874** *N.Y. Tribune* 14 Sept. 7/1 Centennialism is the order of the day, and if anything has the least twang of a dead century, it is pretty sure to succeed.

+**Centennial State.** Colorado. — **1878** BEADLE *Western Wilds* 489 Whether in material or moral greatness, we may be justly proud of our Centennial State. **1882** J. F. GRAFF (*title*), Graybeard's Colorado; or, Notes on the Centennial State, 1881–82. **1889** *Secy. of Agric. Rep.* 265 The settler . . . is growing a better crop of maize in all the eastern counties of the Centennial State than is the farmer of Michigan. **1895** *Cent. Cycl. of Names* 268/3 Colorado . . . was admitted as a State in 1876. Called the Centennial State.

***Center, Centre,** *n.*

1. A place or region centrally located, or ranking first in population, industry, social influence, etc.

1729 in *N.H. Hist. Soc. Coll.* VII. 351 It was decided that 'ye place called ye centre' should be the place for the meeting house. **1788** *N.H. Town Papers* XI. 276 The lands aforesaid are . . . so remote from the Centers of the respective towns to which they belong that we have hitherto found the greatest inconvenience in attending public worship and ordinary Town meeting. **1829** *Va. Lit. Museum* 137/1 A very simple and plausible method of finding the centre of population . . . consists in determining the position of two lines, each of which shall bisect the population of the district in question. **1866** *Rep. Indian Affairs* 136 This reservation, on the Pecos river, comprises forty square miles, with Fort Sumner as a centre. **1894** ROBLEY *Bourbon Co., Kansas* 62 Already foundations for future cities were being laid, which in the near future were to become . . . 'manufacturing and railroad centers.'

attrib. **1860** HOLLAND *Miss Gilbert* 125 A fit person to take charge of the centre school.

b. In place names.

1791 *N.H. State P.* XXII. 206 The fourth [post route] from Portsmouth to . . . Sandwich Center harbour Plymouth. **1844** in S. F. Smith *Hist. Newton* 491 A new road, wide and nearly level, . . . leads from the West Newton Centre direct to Watertown Bridge. **1857** E. A. CHARLTON *New Hampshire* (ed. 2) 201 South of the Shaker Village . . . are three flourishing villages, known as 'North End,' 'Enfield Centre,' and 'Fish Market.' **1881** G. J. VARNEY *Gazetteer Me.* 246 North Fryeburg and Fryeburg Centre are small villages. **1889** R. T. COOKE *Steadfast* 292 Tempy Hopkins had come down in the chaise with Parson Dyer from Pickering Centre.

attrib. **1846** *Knickerb.* XXVII. 560 Where was the Ellington Center School, that day?

2. A player occupying a central position on a football or basketball team. (Cf. CENTER RUSH, RUSHER.)

1894 *Outing* XXV. 57/2 Yale commenced to pound through the center and the tackle, and . . . finally secured a touchdown. **1902** L. BELL *Hope Loring* 109 There were [in the room tonight] Glendenning, the captain of the football team, Van Tassel, the halfback, and Loring, the centre. **1916** BANCROFT & PULVERMACHER *Handbk. Ath. Games* 92 The center should be a very tall man, who is able to jump and reach high in the air.

3. In various phrases.

+*To set on centers,* in building, to place posts, rafters, etc., at a given distance from center to center. +*fig. To catch on center,* to stop where neither a backward nor forward impulse can be effective; to be on dead center. +*To come to the center,* to come out openly, take a prominent position. *colloq.*[2]

1897 FRANCIS C. MOORE *How to Build a House* ii. 21 The extra cost of using timber three inches thick and twelve inches wide for floor-beams, set sixteen inches on centers (i.e., sixteen inches from center to center or thirteen inches apart) will be fully justified by the stiffness of the floor. — **1869** 'MARK TWAIN' *Innocents* iv. 45 He had no one to blame but himself when his voice caught on the centre occasionally, and gave him the lockjaw. — **1873** MILLER *Amongst Modocs* 38 Haven't got the tin. Can't come to the centre! Haven't got the dust. *Ib.* 75 Whenever my man comes to the centre, I will call him, see if I don't.

Center, *a.* Central; occupying or marking the center. {1791-}

c1703 *Essex Inst. Coll.* XLII. 362 A Ston in the middel of the plaien . . . is the Sentar Stoen for the fouer devesions of land in that plaien. **1709** *Braintree Rec.* 73 From thence on each side the center trees in the said line a Rodd wide unto a Walnut Center Tree. **1744** *Ga. Col. Rec.* VI. 96 The Re-Survey . . . which Avery took from the original Center Stake yet standing in the Front of the Village. **1872** HUNTINGTON *Road-Master's Asst.* 16 It is only necessary to set one grade-stake opposite each center-stake. **1916** E. PORTER *David* 100 The church was . . . only a quarter of a mile away; and in due time David . . . was following Mr. and Mrs. Holly down its long center aisle.

+**Centerboard, Centreboard.** A keel that may be raised or lowered as occasion demands.

1849 *Rep. Comm. Patents* 221 What I claim . . . as my invention . . . is suspending in a jointed frame a centre board composed of one or more pieces capable of being turned with either their edges or sides to the bottom of the vessel. **1855** *U.S. Nautical Mag.* Nov. 96 The invention of the centre-board is due to the genius of a Philadelphia mechanic, and was first applied on small sail vessels and pleasure boats. **1882** G. C. EGGLESTON *Wreck of Red Bird* 61 This boat with her centre-board down, is seaworthy; but as she isn't beachworthy—and no vessel is that—I don't want to get her upon a beach. **1885** *Century Mag.* XXX. 503/1 A vast majority [of the canoes at the meet of the Amer. Canoe Ass.] now seem alike to the uneducated eye, being decked canoes . . . with center-board and rudder worked with tiller outside and steering foot-yoke within. **1895** *Outing* XXVI. 488/1 The result is a very speedy boat with plate centre-board.

attrib. **1880** *Harper's Mag.* Aug. 401 Centre-board canoes are a novelty in the United States. **1886** *Outing* IX. 13/2 The *Mayflower* and *Puritan,* center-board sloops, . . . are superior to anything in the New York Yacht Club. **1892** *Boston Journal* 17 Dec. 3/4 The Wyer G. Sargent was a centreboard schooner, built at Sedgwick, Me., in 1883.

+**Centerboarder.** A vessel having a centerboard. — **1886** *Outing* VIII. 58/1 The boats are necessarily of light draught and center-boarders. **1897** *Ib.* XXX. 337/1 The slippery bilge of an eggshell centreboarder.

+**Center field, Centre field.** *Baseball.* That portion of the outfield contiguous to second base.

1868 CHADWICK *Base Ball* 64 In recording the center field, however, we use M instead of C, recording it as middle field, as C is used for catcher. **1875** *Chicago Tribune* 15 July 5/5 George . . . sent a fly to a lucky place in short centre-field. **1887** *Courier-Journal* 26 May 2/6 Kerins next posted a beautiful two-bagger past center field. **1897** *Boston Journal* 8 June 4/5 Put Callahan in centrefield and let Lange hold down third base.

+**Center fielder.** *Baseball.* A player covering center field. — **1868** CHADWICK *Base Ball* 16 He hit the ball over the center fielder's head. **1886** *Outing* May 238/2 Bryan, manager and center fielder of the Charleston club, broke his kneecap. **1893** W. K. POST *Harvard Stories* 86 He . . . ran to congratulate the centre-fielder.

+**Center-fire, Centre-fire.** (See quots. 1874 and 1907.) Also transf. Usu. attrib.

1874 KNIGHT 510/2 Center-fire cartridge, one in which the fulminate occupies an axial position, instead of being around the periphery of the flanged capsule. **1907** WHITE *Arizona Nights* III. 288 A sidesaddle had arrived. . . . It was 'Centre fire,' which is to say it had but the single horsehair cinch. **1909** 'O. HENRY' *Options* (1916) 67 These centre-fire buttons are a nuisance. I'd rather wear buckskins. . . . It'll be midnight before I get these gloves off! **1923** J. H. COOK *On Old Frontier* 112 The California rider used a center-fire or broad single cinch, hung center from the rigging of his saddle.

Center pole. A pole occupying a central position, as in a tent. — **1896** J. C. HARRIS *Sister Jane* 99 In the big vacant lot behind the tavern I could see the tops of the centre-pole and the smaller poles [of the circus tent]. **1901** *Munsey's Mag.* XXV. 662/1 A circular pit is paved with hard rock. In the middle of this is planted a stout round center pole. **1920** C. R. COOPER *Under Big Top* 185 So that they may be laced into place about the bale-rings of the center poles.

+**Center rush.** The center or snapper-back on a football team. — **1887** *Century Mag.* XXXIV. 891/1 The 'center rush,' kicks the ball backward, or 'snaps it back,' to the quarter-back. **1905** *McClure's Mag.* June 121 Greene . . . returned to Philadelphia with two promising Exeter football players, Henry R. Bankart, the centre-rush, and Edward J. Hart, a half-back.

Center rusher. = CENTER RUSH. — **1890** *Cent.* 5726/3 *Snap-back,* in foot-ball, the act of a center rusher in putting the ball in play by pushing it with his foot [etc.]. **1893** W. CAMP *College Sports* 99 As he usually stood in the middle, he was called the center-rusher. This name has since given place almost entirely to 'snap-back.'

+**Center shot.** A marksman capable of hitting the center of a target.

1842 *Amer. Pioneer* I. 225 And as to the use of the rifle, he was said to be one of the quickest and surest centre shots to be found. **1850** GARRARD *Wah-To-Yah* xxiii. 288 'Our hearts are big,' and we are all center shots. **1883** ZEIGLER & GROSSCUP *Alleghanies* 218 Their fame as 'center shots,' with the rifle, was well known to the British regulars, who feared to meet them.

b. A shot that hits the center of a target. In quot. fig.

1853 'P. PAXTON' *Yankee in Texas* 120 They give me some stuff that tasted like iron hoops stewd down, but 'twouldn't make a center shot nither.

Center table, Centre table. A parlor table often occupying the center of the room. {1868-}

1833 *Knickerb.* I. 158 What in the world can one do in the way of getting up a scene, while the whole family are collected around the centre table? **1866** A. D. RICHARDSON *Secret Service* 263 He relieved himself by leaping two or three times over a center-table! **1870** 'F. FERN' *Ginger-Snaps* 248 A woollen cloth on the centre-table, approachable only by a pair of tongs. **1887** *Courier-Journal* 2 May 5/2 They [novels] lie on your center table to curse your children. **1910** C. HARRIS *Eve's Husband* 116 He . . . vowed it before the center table in the parlor, then recorded the vow in the Bible, which always rested there for this purpose.

Centillion. {1852} +'The hundredth power of 1000' (*Cent.*).

Centipede. Any one of various invertebrates having long wormlike bodies each segment of which is provided with a pair of jointed legs. {1835-}

[**1789** MORSE *Amer. Geog.* 62 Of the astonishing variety of Insects found in America, we will mention . . . Forty Legs or Centipes, Caterpillar, [etc.].] **1853** 'P. PAXTON' *Yankee in Texas* 163 The musquitoes, snakes, scorpions, centipedes, red bugs, and tarantulas, are impartially distributed. **1880** CABLE *Grandissimes* 237 What surroundings! Owls and bats, racoons, opossums, rats, centipedes and creatures of like vileness.

+**Central,** *n.*

1. A telephone exchange; an operator employed in such an exchange.

1889 'MARK TWAIN' *Conn. Yankee* xv. 184, I used to wake . . . and say 'Hello, Central!' just to hear her dear voice. **1902** *Scientific Amer.* LXXXVII. 238/2 All the subscribers' lines terminate at central in similar terminals. *Ib.,* The machine at central is provided with a series of rods. **1912** W. IRWIN *Red Button* 339 While they waited for the police central to get the number, neither spoke.

2. A large grinding and boiling plant where sugar is made from cane grown in the region.

1904 *Nation* LXXVIII. 29 The excursion on the Mississippi, with stops at Chalmette and at a great sugar 'central.'

Central, *a.*

1. Being near or at the center of an area or district; occupying the chief or leading position in a system. {1647-}

1877 MINTURN *Travels West* 20 We were then shown the future Central Depot. **1887** *Courier-Journal* 3 May 1/3 The Controller of the Currency to-day designated Chicago as a central reserve city under the provisions of the act passed at the last session. **1887** *Trial H. K. Goodwin* 26 He was calling the central office or the exchange office. **1894** *Forum* July 594 The ninth generation from 1622, pilgrimaging westward now-adays and settling on the central plains, could not afford to send their daughters 'back east' to school.

2. In proper names.

1851 CIST *Cincinnati* 55 One [building] is used for the Central School, and the other is the Orphan Asylum. **1866** MOORE *Women of War* 251 The New York Woman's Central Relief Association sent for Mr. and Mrs. Barker to engage in a special home service.

+**Central committee.** *Political.* A committee that looks after party interests.

1840 *Niles' Nat. Reg.* 4 July 295/1 We are requested by the central committee of the democratic party of Virginia [etc.]. **1845** POLK *Diary* 7 Mr. O'Sullivan read a paper, the object of which was to form a central committee at Washington. **1854** HAMBLETON *H. A. Wise* 59 Indeed, so indignant was the Whig Central Committee at Washington with the Democratic party . . . that it burst forth . . . in the following tirade [etc.]. **1892** *Courier-Journal* 1 Oct. 8/1 (*caption*), Democratic State Central Committee Prepared for a Red-Hot Canvass From Now On.

+**Centralism.** = CENTRALIZATION.

1831 *Congress. Deb.* 2 Feb. 51 A system of centralism, hostile to the federative principle of our Union, encroaching upon the wealth and power of the States. **1839** *Diplom. Corr. Texas* I. 387 This is his master stroke, to quell home dissentions and fasten permanently centralism on the people of Mexico. **1841** FOOTE *Texas & Texans* II. 150 The people know that the government is changed—that centralism is established. **1871** *Congress. Globe* 13 April 651/1 Nor am I deterred from this conclusion by any cry of centralism, or it may be of imperialism.

Centralization. The practice or system of centralizing the powers of government. {1801–} Also transf.

1864 WEBSTER 211 The centralization of power in the general government. **1872** *Harper's Mag.* XLVI. 150 The tendency toward centralization in the government and in the great moneyed interests of the country is a manifestation of this characteristic feature of the age. **1885** *Mag. Amer. Hist.* Jan. 99/1 *Centralization*, the political creed which favors large powers for the general government as opposed to the limitations of State rights. **1886** *Harper's Mag.* Nov. 829/2 New York does not pretend to dictate centralization in the republic of letters.

Centralizer. One who believes in centralization. {1857–} — **1857** *Dem. Rev.* XL. 207 The Centralizers were ready to sacrifice the entire internal system of the State, in order to gain a temporary victory over the city [=New York] proper. *Ib.* 210 The struggle of Whigs, Federalists, Centralizers, and Abolitionists, generally . . . has been to extend and apply to State purposes the powers of the Federal government. **1886** *American* XII. 277 The victory of the centralizers at Cleveland merely transferred the struggle to another arena.

+**Central State.** The state of Kansas. — **1888** *Harper's Mag.* June 39/1 When they think of . . . her geographical situation, then Kansas is the 'Central State.' **1907** *Boston Transcript* 9 Nov.

+**Central states.** The states now or formerly regarded as being in the center of the U.S. — **1809** W. TATHAM *Agric. & Commerce* 45 To what Circumstance is it owing, that eight Bushels of Wheat . . . are a profitable Crop in the central States? **1861** *Harper's Mag.* May 721/2 Our Central States (the mighty land of Hubbabub that lies between the Federal Capital and Albany). **1876** CROFUTT *Trans-continental Tourist* 33 Nebraska, so lately opened up to the world, and so lately considered one portion of the 'wild West,' forms now one of our central States.

Centrical, *a.* Central; located at the center. {1741–}

1756 WASHINGTON *Writings* I. 267 This [Winchester, Va.] is the place generally fixed upon, as it has a free and open communication with all the country, from its centrical situation. **1763** in Roberts *Nat. Hist. Fla.* 97 From the excellent and centrical position of this fine port, it carries a good trade. **1766** W. SMITH *Bouquet's Exped.* (1868) 14 The principal and centrical stage between Carlisle and Fort-Pitt. **1871** DE VERE 450 *Centrical* has, in Virginia especially, maintained itself in spite of its more popular rival 'central,' which has elsewhere completely usurped its place.

+**Centrifugal. 1.** A centrifugal machine, or a drum in such a machine, for drying sugar. **2.** Sugar freed from molasses by a centrifugal machine. — **(1) 1883** 'MARK TWAIN' *Life on Miss.* xlviii, You heave your cane into the centrifugals and grind out the juice. **1887** *Century Mag.* XXXV. 114/2 Next the 'masse cuite' falls into the 'centrifugals,' which are small drums holding about 120 pounds of sugar. **(2) 1887** *Ib.* 119/1 Centrifugals [ranged in price] from 4⅝ for 'seconds' to 6¼ cents.

+**Cent shop.** A small shop in which articles are sold for a cent. — **1851** HAWTHORNE *House 7 Gables* ii, Reduced now, in that very house, to be the huckstress of a cent-shop! *Ib.* iii, The business of keeping cent-shops is overdone.

Centurial, *a.* Pertaining to a period of one hundred years. {1877–} — **1817** *Mass. Col. Soc. Publ.* XXVI. 418 'The Blessed Reformation.' A Sermon preached in St. Paul's Church, in the City of New York, on . . . the Third Centurial Jubilee. **1853** M. BLAKE (*title*), A Centurial History of the Mendon Association. **1864** LOWELL *Fireside Trav.* 71 Quadrangles mossy with centurial associations.

‖**Centurially,** *adv.* By centuries. — **1799** in *Historical Mag.* (1858) Jan., In reckoning centurially we adopt a different phraseology from that which is used in all other accounts of time.

***Centurion.** +One who has made a ride of one hundred miles on a bicycle. — **1897** *Outing* XXX. 346/1 There are long-distance riders, too, galore in the N.Y.A.C. and not a few centurions. **1898** *N.Y. Journal* 15 Aug. 8/3 Walter McGrath, the boy champion centurion of Philadelphia, . . . has a record of more than a score of one hundred mile rides.

***Century,** *n.* +A hundred-mile ride on a bicycle. Also attrib. — **1897** *Outing* XXX. 349/1 The more enthusiastic indulge in century runs. **1898** *N.Y. Journal* 8 Sept. 11/1 His wonderful one hundred mile ride of today . . . completed two hundred and fifty consecutive centuries.

Century, *a.* and *adv.*

1. Pertaining to a period of one hundred years; centennial. {1626–}

1729 *New Eng. Wkly. Jrnl.* 18 Aug. 2 On Wednesday the 6th of this Instant, was celebrated here, the 1st Century Lecture in the Meeting House. **1814** CUTLER in *Life & Corr.* II. 349 Proposed to the people a meeting on Thursday afternoon at 2 o'clock, with a view of delivering a century sermon, being 100 years since the foundation of this church and society. **1829** *Mass. Col. Soc. Publ.* XXVI. 419 [In 1829 Rev. Charles W. Upham published at Salem] Principles of Congregationalism. The Second Century Lecture of the First Church.

2. *Century-blooming*, flowering or blooming every century, a supposed characteristic of the century plant.

1846 CHILD *Fact & Fiction* 60 The century-blooming aloe is luxuriantly growing. **1865** MRS. WHITNEY *Gayworthys* xxiii. 219 Say . . . would not have been a palm or an aloe, or a cereus, or any grand and solitary, century-blooming thing, if she had known of such.

+**Century plant.** A species of agave, *A. americana*.

1847 WOOD *Botany* 539 *Agave Americana.* American Aloe. Century Plant. . . . It is a popular notion that it flowers but once in a hundred years. **1856** *Rep. Comm. Patents: Agric.* 243 'Great American aloes,' or 'Century plant,' . . . the fibre of which is manufactured into cordage and various other articles of use. **1869** C. L. BRACE *New West* 299 Near the landing, in a gentleman's garden, is a beautiful product of the south of California—the Century Plant, or Agave Americana. **1893** SANBORN *S. Calif.* 116 There are many century plants about the grounds; they blossom in this climate after twelve years, and die after the tall homely flower has come to maturity. **1899** M. GOING *Flowers* 113 The century plant does double duty.

Ceonosa. ?A shrub of the genus *Ceanothus;* the mountain lilac. — **1861** *Harper's Mag.* June 13/1 The air is fragrant with the scent of wild roses, honey-suckle and ceonosa.

Cereal, *n.*

1. Any of various grasses that produce grains used for food. {1868–}

1851 *Knickerb.* XXXVIII. 178 Nature is getting ready to publish her 'cereals.' **1877** *Rep. Indian Affairs* 44 Sufficient cereals could be annually produced to support the whole Ute nation. **1892** *Vt. Agric. Rep.* XII. 148 It will be shown that in the product of cereals our State leads the list.

+**2.** A breakfast food made from some cereal.

1900 F. NORRIS *Man's Woman* iv. 86 The agent of a patented cereal (who sought the man of the hour for an endorsement of his article). **1906** R. W. CHAMBERS *Fighting Chance* 163 To breakfast all alone was delicious; . . . to loiter over cream-jug and cereal.

Cereal, *a.* Consisting of edible grain. {1818–} — **1862** S. B. RUGGLES *Rep. Enlargement of Canals* 50 The cereal wealth yearly floated on these waters [*i.e.*, the Great Lakes] now exceeds one hundred millions of bushels.

***Cerne.** [F.] +In hunting buffalo, an encircling of the entire herd. — **1839** C. A. MURRAY *Travels* I. 336 A 'cerne' or 'surround,' in this part of the wilderness, requires a great deal of arrangement to render it successful. **1843** FRÉMONT *Exped.* 29 It had been a large herd when the cerne commenced, probably three or four hundred in number.

+**Cero.** [Sp. *sierra* saw.] A scombroid fish related to the Spanish mackerel. — **1884** GOODE *Nat. Hist. Aquat. Animals* 307 The Spotted Cero, or King Cero, *Scomberomorus regalis*, has seventeen dorsal spines.

+**Ceroon.** A seroon; a package or bundle covered with hides. — **1824** *Shipping & Commercial List* 31 July (Pettigrew P.), A sale of 30 ceroons of Cuba [tobacco], was made, by auction, at 13½ a 14¼ cents, 60 days. **1832** *Louisville Pub. Adv.* 3 March, 8 puncheons Jamaica rum; 2 ceroons indigo. *a*1861 T. WINTHROP 'Chitrés,' *Isthmiana*, A young ragamuffin . . . had come into town on a nag between two hide ceroons, full of mami apples.

Cerro. [Sp.] (See quot. 1843.) — **1843** FRÉMONT *Exped.* 161 The French word *butte* . . . is applied to the detached hills and ridges which rise abruptly, and reach too high to be called hills or ridges, and not high enough to be called mountains. . . . Cerro is the Spanish term. **1855** *Knickerb.* XLVI. 280 Almost at the same moment Colonel Ransom died at the van of his regiment, the Ninth, but not until he had attained the crest of the cerro.

***Certificate,** *n.*

***1.** A formal or legal written statement of fact.

1643 *Plymouth Laws* 312 Vpon the Certyficate of one Majestrate in the Jurisdiccon out of which the said servant fled . . . the said servant shalbe deliuered . . . to his Master. **1705** BEVERLEY *Virginia* IV. 45 The Governor thereupon administers [an oath of allegiance] and immediately makes certificate of it under the Seal of the Colony. **1898** PAGE *Red Rock* 341 What I want is not advice, but a certificate of the state of those titles. **1904** WALLER *Wood-Carver* 285 There was . . . Twiddie's baptismal certificate with her name, Theodora.

+**2.** A title to land or a statement about ownership.

1694 *N.C. Col. Rec.* I. 405 Ordered that a certificate thereto be made to the Secretary's office. **1780** W. FLEMING in *Travels Amer. Col.* 631 The Court having finished the buisness rose at nine Oclock in the Evening, having in the course of this buisness granted certificates for 1,096,650 acres. **1872** *Rep. Indian Affairs 1871* 171 The Omahas [on a reservation in Nebraska] have received certificates—a kind of possessory title—which secures the land to them and their heirs.

3. A written or printed acknowledgment of indebtedness; a note.

1780 *Va. State P.* I. 380 We are become the Hated Beasts of a whole people by Pressing horses, Boats etc. Killing Cattle etc. . . . , for which no valuable consideration is given: even many not a certificate, which is hear looked on as next to nothing. **1798** *Ann. 5th Congress* 485 An act providing for the payment of the interest on a certificate due to General Kosciusko. **1865** *Atlantic Mo.* XV. 190 In Connecticut, mobs collected to prevent the army officers from receiving the certificates for the five years' pay. **1870** *Nation* 10 Feb. 86/1 It was decided, in the summer of 1867, to allow the Secretary to issue, for the use of the national banks only, certain certificates bearing three per cent. interest, and hence called three per cent. certificates. **1889** *Cent.* 901/3 *Gold and silver certificates*, certificates issued by the United States government, circulating as money. . . . The smallest denomination of the former is twenty dollars, and of the latter one dollar.

attrib. **1843** 'CARLTON' *New Purchase* I. 236 He naturally lies down on the puncheons with his certificate wallet for a bolster.

4. A written testimonial of fitness or competence.

1857 M. J. HOLMES *Meadow-Brook* iv, I was as sure of my certificate then as I was fifteen minutes afterwards, when a little slip of paper was given me, declaring me competent to teach a common school. **1883** HOWELLS *Woman's Reason* xv, Some of 'em . . . go into the hospitals and learn to be professional nurses—that takes you about two years before you can get a certificate. **1903** *Columbia Univ. Q.* Sept. 438 The lax enforcement of published requirements for admission, together with the very general acceptance of certificates from uninspected and unvisited schools, has demoralized college standards very generally.

5. In various phrases, as *certificate of character, damage, debenture*, etc.

1830 COOPER *Water Witch* II. x. 266, I send my certificate of character as an avant courier. **1864** *U.S. Statutes* XIII. 299 Any certificate of damage . . . [is subject to a stamp duty of] twenty-five cents. **1794** *Ann. 3rd Congress* 1309 Resolved, That after the —— day of ——, there be paid the following stamp duties: . . . Certificates of debentures for drawbacks, 20 cents. **1864** *U.S. Statutes* XIII. 299 Certificate of deposit of any sums of money in any bank or trust company, . . . for a sum not exceeding one hundred dollars [is subject to a stamp duty of] two cents. **1824** MARSHALL *Kentucky* I. 125 The state . . . proposed to issue a new species of bill of credit—called, certificates of depreciation—which would pay taxes. **1861** *Army Regulations* 30 No enlisted man shall be discharged . . . except . . . by the commander of the Department or of an army in the field, on certificate of disability. **a1817** DWIGHT *Travels* I. 267 At 9 o'clock the Representatives assemble, exhibit their certificates of election, and form themselves into a House, by choosing their Speaker and Clerks. **1865** *Atlantic Mo.* XV. 752/2 There was . . . a collapse, a shrivelling up, like a parched scroll, of the entire Confederacy, which, like its bonds, notes, and certificates of indebtedness, was old rags! **1869** TOURGEE *Toinette* xxvii, The original deed of manumission . . . had the certificate of probate and registration upon it, and she did not doubt its genuineness. **1842** *Cultivator* X. 37 The purchaser receives a certificate of purchase, and afterwards obtains a patent from the President. **1705** BEVERLEY *Virginia* IV. 42 This Survey being made, a Copy thereof is carried, with a Certificate of Rights to the Secretaries Office. **1848** W. ARMSTRONG *Stocks* 5 An individual wishing to invest $10,000, in the undertaking does so by purchasing one hundred shares, and receives a certificate to that effect from the officers of the company, which is termed a 'Certificate of Stock.' **1898** *Kansas City Star* 18 Dec. 4/2 All school children and all school teachers in Lincoln county must have a certificate of vaccination before attending school Monday morning.

Certificate, *v.* {1818–} +(See quotation.) — **1828** WEBSTER, *Certificate, v. t.* or *i.*, to give a certificate; to lodge a certificate with the proper officer, for the purpose of being exempted from the payment of taxes to support the ministry, in a parish or ecclesiastical society. *New England.*

***Certification.** +The act of guaranteeing the payment of a check. — **1870** MEDBERY *Men of Wall St.* 263 Whispers . . . of certifications of checks to the amount of twenty-five millions by one bank alone . . . lent color to the rumor.

+**Certified check.** (See quot. 1880.) Also transf. — **1880** WEBSTER *Suppl.* 1548/2 *Certified check*, a bank-check, the validity of which is certified by the bank on which it is drawn. **1883** *Century Mag.* July 334/1 When a producer . . . wants to use his oil in store as collateral to borrow money upon . . . he gets what is called an acceptance, which is virtually a certified check. **1887** *Courier-Journal* 2 Feb. 3/6 Bidders will be required to make a deposit of money or certified check with each bid. **1902** WHITE *Blazed Trail* xxiii. 158, I suppose you have cash or a certified cheque; that's all they'll take here. **1906** 'O. HENRY' *Four Million* 198 The bride is the certified cheque among the wedding presents that the gods send in when man is married to mortality.

* **Certify,** *v.*

+**1.** *tr.* To transfer or deed (land).

1845 HOOPER *Simon Sugg's Adv.* vi. 71 He told his wife that her father must 'certify' his land to him.

+**2.** (See quotation.)

1864 SALA in *Daily Tel.* (Lond.) 16 July, There is a process known as 'certifying' a check. The teller puts his initials in one corner, thus warranting the genuineness of the instrument and the fact of the drawer having sufficient funds in the hands of the bank to meet it. **1892** VAN SCHAACK *Law of Bank Checks* 88 If the bank only accepts or certifies the check, the holder can demand its payment at any time thereafter.

Certifying, *ppl. a.* Making certification. — **1845** HOOPER *Simon Sugg's Adv.* vi. 71 The certifying agent saw a thousand silver dollars paid to the Indian.

+**Cerulean warbler.** A warbler having distinctive blue and white markings, *Dendroica cerulea.* — **1828** BONAPARTE *Synopsis* 85 The Caerulean Warbler, *Sylvia caerulea*, . . . inhabits the northern and middle states in summer: rare in the Atlantic states: common in the Western.

* **Cession.** {of territory 1678–} +The granting or ceding of land or territory to the United States.

1783 R. PUTNAM in *Memoirs* 217 The cession of so grate a tract of Teritory to the United States, in the Western World, . . . [is] a very happy circumstance. **1792** *Ann. 2nd Congress* 1036 Within these triangles, however, are the following claims of citizens, reserved by the deed of cession. **1806–8** PIKE *Sources Miss.* 267 Father M'Guire, . . . on the cession of Louisiana, . . . followed the standard of the 'king, his master,' who never suffers an old servant to be neglected. **1819** SCHOOLCRAFT *Mo. Lead Mines* 21 The emigration to Louisiana, which had partially commenced under the Spanish government, took a more decided character after the cession of the country to the United States. **1853** RAMSEY *Tennessee* 117 Before the Indians had agreed to make the cession, one of the Cherokee orators . . . rose and delivered a very animated and pathetic speech. **1885** in Thoburn *Hist. Oklahoma* xviii. 799 They involve not only a cession of large tracts of valuable lands, . . . but a thorough, sweeping, and radical change in the political relations between the Indians and the government of the United States.

attrib. **1790** MACLAY *Deb. Senate* 189 April 1, 1790. This day, in Senate, two bills were signed: The Carolina cession act and the bill for giving effect to the State inspection laws. *Ib.* 188 Message from the Representatives, with cession bill agreed to.

+**Chachalac.** *Texas.* (Variant of next.) — **1878** *U.S. Nat. Museum Proc.* I. 159 The Chachalac, as the present species is called on the Lower Rio Grande, is one of the most characteristic birds of that region.

+**Chachalaca.** *Texas.* [Nahuatl.] The Texan guan, *Ortalis vetula maccalli.* — **1858** BAIRD *Birds Pacific R.R.* 611 Chiacalacca. . . . Body above dark greenish olive. **1889** *Cent.* 906/3 [The] chachalaca . . . is easily domesticated, and is said to be sometimes used as a game-fowl.

***Chadlock.** Variant of CHARLOCK. — **1751** ELIOT *Field-Husb.* iii. 61 The Land should be very free from Chadlock, Tares, Chess. **1900** S. HALE *Letters* 364 Cornelia came down yesterday and brought me a mess of greens (chadlocks, spinach, milk-weed, dandelions).

Chafery. ?*Obs.* One of the forges in an ironwork. {1663–} — **1742** *Penna. Gazette* 11 Jan. 3 To be sold, . . . a large Forge with good Brick and Stone Chimneys, well compleated for two Finerys and one Chastery [*read* Chaffery]. **1758** *N.J. Archives* XX. 184 To be sold . . . one new Chasery [*sic*], with the Utensils thereto belonging. **1881** RAYMOND *Mining Glossary, Chafery*, a forge fire for reheating.

Chaff-bed. A bed the mattress of which is stuffed with chaff. {1683}

1684 *Hempstead Rec.* I. 431 Two chaff beds and two boulsters. **1769** in Chalkley *Scotch-Irish Settlement Va.* I. 155 Attached: One chaff bed. **1784** J. SMYTH *Tour* I. 76 A miserable thin chaff-bed somewhat raised from the floor, in a corner of the room. **1841** A. BACHE *Fire-Screen* 170 Here, a chaff bed, stained and torn; there, a pair of elegant glass shades.

Chaffed, *ppl.a.* Of hay: Cut small for use as fodder. {1883–} — **1868** *Mich. Agric. Rep.* VII. 47 'Chaffed' hay was fed in each pen, so that each sheep had all it would eat. *Ib.*, In addition to the chaffed hay, each pen was supplied with a fixed ration of other feed.

Chaffing, *vbl. n.* The process of freeing grain from chaff. — **1819** *Niles' Reg.* XVI. 165/1 The mere act of '*chaffing*' can be performed by *winnowing*, the mode practised by our ancestors long before the invention of fans, and still in use by the great majority of the farmers of every country.

+**Chaffseed.** A perennial herb (*Schwalbea americana*) of the eastern United States. — **1817–8** EATON *Botany* (1822) 450 *Schwalbea americana*, chaff-seed. **1857** GRAY *Botany* 294 Chaff-Seed, . . . [an] upright herb, with leafy simple stems, terminated by a loose spike of rather large dull purplish-yellow flowers.

* **Chafing dish.** Also †**chaffing, -in, chafen, cheafen.**

* **1.** A portable utensil to hold ignited fuel for keeping food warm or for other purposes.

1638 *Md. Archives* IV. 86, 2 broken chafing dishes. **1644** *Essex Probate Rec.* I. 46 Two paire of hinges & too hookes & a cheafendish. **1720** SEWALL *Letter-Book* II. 106 Six small strong brass chafing-dishes, about four shillings a-piece. **1833** in Kittredge *Old Farmer* 249 Take a few hot coals on a shovel or chafingdish, and burn some brown sugar in your bedrooms and parlors, and you effectually destroy the musquetoe for the night. **1853** FELT *Customs New Eng.* 21 Since the introduction of furnaces and stoves, the chafing dish has been scarcely known, and seldom seen.

+**2.** A portable alcohol stove used for cooking.

1893 POST *Harvard Stories* 99 You get your chafing-dish, Dick. **1904** L. BELL *At Home with Jardines* 123 Mary appeared bearing the chafing-dish full of blazing, flaming peaches.

attrib. **1909** STRATTON-PORTER *Girl of Limberlost* 451 They . . . made chafing-dish tea.

***Chain,** *n.*

1. The instrument used for measuring land, consisting of a hundred short iron links, each 7.92 inches in length. {1610–}

1651 *Watertown Rec.* 26 John Sherman shall measure . . . his proportion of land. . . . Power is hereby given . . . to call forth such a Company of persons . . . to carry the chain [etc.]. **1694** *N.C. Col. Rec.* I. 410 Ordered that the dividing line . . . shall begin about the length of a chaine up the swamp. **1777** FRANKLIN *Autobiog.* 295 He . . . carri'd the chain for surveyors, who taught him surveying. **1852** MARCY *Explor. Red River* (1854) 121 The distance from Fort Smith to Santa Fé, as measured with the chain, is eight hundred and twenty miles.

b. The length of a surveyor's chain; a distance of 66 feet. {1661–}

1706 *Jamaica* (L.I.) *Rec.* I. 408 [His land] runs north 15 chains to a stump . . . , thence west 2 chains & 08 links to a stak. **1792** *Ann. 2nd Congress* 1040 This . . . runs due north on that boundary 1,306 chains and 25 links. **1832** WILLIAMSON *Maine* I. 15 They appointed an exploring party to survey the highlands . . . and to return a plan of 80 chains to an inch. **1909** *Indian Laws & Tr.* III. 418 A strip of land ten chains wide . . . is reserved for cemetery purposes.

***2.** A chain stretched across a river to obstruct the passage.

1777 *Journals Cont. Congress* IX. 866 A number of gallies, gunboats, fire-rafts, chains, . . . to be provided . . . for obstructing and keeping possession of the North River. **1864** PARTON *Gen. Butler in New Orleans* 222 The chain broke at length, and the whole structure, cable, logs, anchor, buoys, and trees, were swept down by the current.

+3. *Chain and ball:* see BALL AND CHAIN.

1872 E. B. TUTTLE *Boy's Bk. Indians* (1882) 127 The fellow while in limbo sawed off the chain and ball from his leg and escaped. **1887** F. FRANCIS *Saddle & Moccasin* 62 A chain-and-ball gang of convicts slowly advanced, sweeping the dusty road.

4. A range or series *of* places, mountains, lakes, etc. Also ellipt. {1695–}

1795 *Ann. 3rd Congress* 1169 With respect to the amount of force necessary for the defence of the chain of posts and other necessary purposes. **1807** GASS *Journal* 69 It is presumed, no part of the great chain of Rocky Mountains comes as near as 90 miles to fort Mandan. **1857** HAMMOND *Northern Scenes* 124 We started early the next morning up Bog River, intending to reach the 'first chain of ponds,' some twenty miles deeper in the wilderness. **1892** M. A. JACKSON *Memoirs* 204 The beauty and grandeur of the scenery [of the Shenandoah Valley], with its chains of mountains [etc.].

+b. *spec.* A chain of rocks in a river.

1823 JAMES *Exped.* I. 44 The Ohio would also admit of a bridge at the chains. **1828** *Western Mo. Rev.* I. 512 The circumstances, that change the aspect and current of the river, are denominated, in the vocabulary of the watermen, chutes, races, chains, sawyers . . . and cypress bends.

+5. A connected or associated number *of* banks, etc.

1846 MACKENZIE *Van Buren* 208 Is it not evident that Throop was secretly selected . . . as a convenient instrument for regulating future state elections through a chain of banks, controlled by county juntos of greedy politicians? **1895** *N.Y. Dramatic News* 14 Dec. 6/2 A chain of eleven theatres to be run in connection with the Bijou circuit. **1917** J. F. DALY *A. Daly* 195 Theatrical management is in the hands . . . of a commercial concern with a 'chain of theatres.'

+6. *To brighten the chain,* to renew friendship. *fig.*

1754 [see CHAIN BELT]. **1846** *Spirit of Times* 18 April 96/2 At Petersburg, he had brightened the chain with his old friend Dr. Minge, one of nature's noblemen.

***Chain,** *v.* [CHAIN *n.* 1.] *intr.* and *tr.* To measure, or lay *out,* with a surveyor's chain. {1610}

1743 *N.J. Archives* 1 Ser. VI. 155 You are to chain eastward upon the main land. **1816** U. BROWN *Journal* II. 224 [But for the rain] I should certainly have caused this line on the river to have been correctly run & chain'd. **1845** COOPER *Chainbearer* xxv, You're welcome to chain out just as much of this part of the patent as you see fit.

+Chain bearer. [CHAIN *n.* 1.] One who carries the measuring chain in surveying operations; a chain carrier or chainman.

1736 *Va. State P.* I. 226 Take three Chain-bearers, to be duly sworn according to the Laws of this Country. **1775** ROMANS *Nat. Hist. Fla.* 195 These same two men serve as chain-bearers. **1837** PECK *New Guide* 135 Deputy-surveyors are employed to do the work . . . [and they] employ chain-bearers, an axe and flag man and a camp-keeper. **1845** COOPER *Chainbearer* v, 'How can a mere chainbearer contract for a full survey?' asked Tom Bayard. **1869** *Overland Mo.* III. 248 The only way for the chain-men to work along these cliffs . . . was by being suspended by ropes from above, the chain-bearers signaling to those holding the ropes.

+Chain belt. A belt symbolizing a 'covenant chain.' — **1754** *Mass. H. S. Coll.* 3 Ser. V. 41 We return you all our grateful acknowledgements for renewing and brightening the covenant chain. This chain belt is of very great importance to our United Nations.

Chain bridge. A bridge suspended by chains. {1818–}

1809 F. CUMING *Western Tour* 171 A calculation of the expence of the chain bridge about to be thrown over the Kentucky river at Frankfort. **1829** A. ROYAL *Pennsylvania* I. 100 That over the Lehigh is a chain bridge. **1843** *Amer. Pioneer* II. 60 One . . . was a chain bridge, of the kind patented by the Hon. James Finley. **1873** *Harper's Mag.* XLVI. 274 They fought just over the Chain Bridge, beyond Georgetown. **1897** *Outing* XXX. 287/1 Portsmouth is twenty-two miles beyond . . . via the 'chain bridge.'

+Chain carrier. [CHAIN *n.* 1.] = CHAIN BEARER.

1702–3 *Penn-Logan Corr.* (1870) I. 174 Neither surveyors nor chain-carriers will go thither. **1733** BYRD *Journey to Eden* (1901) 302 We could advance no further than 8 Miles, and the Chain Carryer's thought that a great way. **1785** in *Life & Corr. Cutler* II. 431 Each surveyor shall be allowed . . . two dollars for every mile, . . . including the wages of chain-carriers. **1798** B. HAWKINS *Letters* 286 He informs me that the surveyor and chain carriers would set out from Tugalo the 4th of this month. **1810** *Steele Papers* II. 635 The Surveyor's Fees are abt. 2 . . . Dolls. a Day . . . & the Chain-carriers abt: half a Dollr. a day. **1838** *S. Lit. Messenger* IV. 307 The surveyor and two of his chain-carriers were killed. **1867** G. W. HARRIS *Sut Lovingood* 98 While yu am waitin' fur yer chain-kerriers.

+Chain carrying, *vbl. n.* [CHAIN *n.* 1.] The carrying of a surveyor's chain.

1798 in *Ann. 10th Congress* 1 Sess. II. 2739 The surveying at present is done by Mr. Gillespie, the chain-carrying by Mr. Ellicott and Mr. Walker. **a1909** 'O. HENRY' *Roads of Destiny* 93, I'll . . . go back to chain-carrying for the county surveyor.

Chained lightning. = CHAIN LIGHTNING. — **1859** BARTLETT, *Chained Lightning,* Western, for forked lightning. **1871** DE VERE 451 Chain-lightning . . . is generally . . . changed into chained-lightning. In both forms it is constantly applied to inferior whiskey. **1908** WHITE *Riverman* xvii. 159 He's quick as chained lightning.

Chain gang. A number of prisoners chained to each other while working. {1858}

1835 INGRAHAM *South-West* II. 185 This galley-looking procession . . . was what is very appropriately termed the 'Chain gang.' **1850** TYSON *Diary in Calif.* 28 The streets are all paved, a duty performed by what is termed the 'chain-gang,' composed of those who have committed offenses against the laws. **1873** BEADLE *Undevel. West* 742 The Church . . . takes all his money and puts him on the chain-gang a month. **1891** *Atlantic Mo.* June 805/1 The convicts in the chain gang in the New Orleans Parish prison and the Birmingham mines. **1904** *Buffalo Express* 7 July 4 A negro girl is said to have died from cruel treatment administered by the brute in charge of the chaingang to which she had been sentenced.

Chain guard. A number of guards posted at close intervals. — **1888** GRIGSBY *Smoked Yank* (1891) 28 We were . . . formed in line and roll called before camping, and then a chain guard was placed around the camp to keep us from getting out.

Chain harrow. (See quotation.) — **1870** *Rep. Comm. Agric. 1869* 322 Only one patent was taken out during the year of the class known as 'chain' harrows, *i.e.,* composed entirely of iron chains, no beams whatever being employed.

Chain horse. An extra horse harnessed with chains for use over rough road or up hills. {1899–} — **1878** H. H. JACKSON *Travel At Home* 46 The turns are so sharp that you often lose sight of the leaders and of the heads of the chain-horses.

Chaining, *vbl. n.* [CHAIN *v.*] Measuring land with the chain. — **1743** *N.J. Archives* 1 Ser. VI. 154 You are to direct the chainbearers in chaining to hold the stick . . . in the same hand with the chain.

+Chain lightning.

1. Forked lightning: fig. or in fig. context.

1834 C. A. DAVIS *Lett. J. Downing* 37, I'm goin there like a streek [*sic*] of chain-lightning. **1843** *S. Lit. Messenger* IX. 651/1 Good! it flashed upon me like chain lightning! the distinguished strangers! **1852** E. BENNET *Mike Fink* 28/2, I'll jump right straight down yer throats, quicker nor a streak o' greased chain-lightning can down a nigger's! **1879** B. F. TAYLOR *Summer-Savory* 109 One of those darting spiders that outlines chain-lightning has you by the nape of the neck. **1882** HOWELLS *Modern Instance* xxx, Those of his following considered him as smart as chain-lightning and bound to rise. **1902** 'MARK TWAIN' in *Harper's Mag.* Feb. 433 By jiminy, but he's chain-lightning. **1918** MULFORD *Man from Bar-20* 141 He's dangerous, chain-lightnin' with his guns.

2. *slang.* Inferior whisky. Also attrib.

1843 HALIBURTON *Attaché* 1 Ser. xv, The drinks ain't good here [=in England]; they hante no variety in them nother: no white-nose, apple-jack, stone-wall, chain-lightning, rail-road [etc.]. **1861** LOWELL *Biglow P.* II. i, I know the smell of ole chain-lightnin' whiskey. **1865** 'MARK TWAIN' *Sketches* (1926) 163 Our reserve (whom we . . . had kept out of sight and full of chain-lightning . . .) came filing down the street as drunk as loons. **1871** DE VERE 217 The worst of lickers . . . is called Chain-lightning, from its terrible strength and stunning effect. **1890** D'OYLE *Notches* 8 'Fine Old Rye Whiskey' . . . was the . . . title which Old Hank was wont to affix to his bottles of 'Chain-lightning.'

+Chainman. [CHAIN *n.* 1.] = CHAIN BEARER, CARRIER.

1714 in *Mass. H. S. Coll.* 6 Ser. V. 299 The survayer and chainmen being under oath. **1721** *Mass. Ho. Repr. Jrnls.* III. 103 Mr. David Freeman, proposed that . . . a Surveyor and Chain-men be appointed to measure the Land. **1754** *Harvard Rec.* I. 279 A piece of Salt-Marsh [was] . . . laid down; . . . Chainmen, Mr. John Robinson & Mr. Saml How. **1810**

Repertory (Boston) 6 April (Th.), Chadwick was acting as chainman. **1843** *Amer. Pioneer* II. 379 In running the back line of the survey, . . . I was about one hundred yards in advance of the chainmen and marker. **1880** G. INGRAHAM *Digging Gold* 427 It is said that a chain-man, while assisting in the survey of one of those claims, discovered the little vacant lot.

Chain pump. A device for raising water consisting of an endless chain with disks or buckets attached. {*a*1618–1830, *naut.*} — **1866** 'F. KIRKLAND' *Bk. Anecdotes* 591 Joe Baxter, what staid in the Perkins settlement, . . . a sellin' chain-pumps. **1873** HOWELLS *Chance Acquaintance* xii. 230 It's better even than the water from the old chain-pump in the back yard at Eriecreek. **1882** *Century Mag.* May 158/2 The chain-pumps, so extensively used in some parts of the country.

+**Chain snake.** A harmless snake common in the U.S., so called from the distribution of its black and white markings.

1736 CATESBY *Carolina* II. 52 As it wanted a Name, the best I could think of was, that of *Chain-Snake.* **1789** MORSE *Amer. Geog.* 61 The Snakes which infest the United States, are the following, viz. The Rattle Snake, . . . Chain do. **1842** *Nat. Hist. N.Y., Zoology* III. 37 The Chain Snake. *Coluber getulus.* . . . Their northern and eastern range does not extend beyond New York, and they are found as far south as Louisiana. **1853** BAIRD & GIRARD *Cat. N. A. Reptiles* I. 86 *Ophibolus getulus.* . . . Thunder Snake; King Snake; Chain Snake. **1875** *Field & Forest* I. 31 Careful measurements show the length of the Chain snake to be 27 inches, with a maximum circumference of 1¾ inches.

Chain traces. Harness traces made of chain. — **1744** *Md. Hist. Mag.* XXI. 244, 12 pair chain traces. **1772** *Carroll P. Ib.* XIV. 141 If Deards had Considered the Invoice Book He would Have seen Chain Traces almost Constantly wrote for.

***Chair.**

1. A sedan chair. *Obs.* {1634–1777}

1740 *Boston Selectmen* 227 A Motion . . . for putting into Repair, a Sedan, or Chair.

2. A light two-wheeled vehicle drawn by one horse and commonly for one person. *Obs.* {1753–1821}

Originally in New England use, but latterly southern. Properly different from a *chaise,* but sometimes identified with it. 'In the *Southern* States this name is given to that kind of one-horse pleasure-carriage, which in the *Northern* States is generally called by the old English name, *chaise*' (Pickering).

1737 PARKMAN *Diary* 40 Mr. Jarvis came up last night in a chair. **1760** WASHINGTON *Diaries* I. 156 Abt. 11 o' broke my chair and had to walk to Port Tob[acc]o. **1797** *MS. Receipt for Chair-tax* (Pettigrew P.), A two wheel Carriage called a chair, owned by him, without a top on wooden Springs, to be drawn by one horse, for the conveyance of one person. **1809** ASBURY *Journal* III. 308 My horse twice attempted to run away with my chair. **1816** SINGLETON *Lett. South & West* 64 The Virginians . . . instead of a chaise . . . use a chair, which is very light, but unsocial, as they are usually single. **1836** C. GILMAN *Recoll.* (1838) 41 Jim, go to the stable and harness the horse and chair.

attrib. **1747** *Harvard Rec.* II. 769 The Profits of horse & Chair Hire &c. . . . are very much increased.

3. The office or person of a chairman of a meeting {1659–}; +*spec.* the speakership or speaker of the House of Representatives.

1766 in *S. Lit. Messenger* XXVII. 118/1, I cannot help felicitating myself on a resolution of our Assembly for separating the Chair and Treasury. **1840** *Niles' Nat. Reg.* 4 April 78/2 The main question being on sustaining the decision of the chair, it was carried without a count. **1884** BLAINE *20 Yrs. Congress* I. 497 Schuyler Colfax was especially fitted for the duties of the Chair.

Chair back. +A tidy or antimacassar. — **1880** *Harper's Mag.* Oct. 656/1 She . . . carries home an embroidered 'Chair-back'—the more dignified name that she gives nowadays to her 'tidy.' **1881** *Art Interchange* (N.Y.) 27 Oct. 90/1 Coverings for sofa cushions, . . . chair-backs with lace falling from the edges.

Chair board. A board fixed along the wall of a room to prevent injury to it by the backs of chairs pushed against it. {chair rail, 1842} — **1854** *S. Lit. Messenger* XX. 559/2 The wainscoting [is] of walnut, and extending unbroken around the whole apartment to the height of what is called the chair-board.

+**Chair bottom.** The seat of a chair. — **1807** IRVING, etc. *Salmagundi* ii. 35 All the chair-bottoms in the house teem with his productions. **1842** BUCKINGHAM *E. & W. States* I. 156 From the fibres of its inner bark are wrought bed-cordings and chair-bottoms. **1875** STOWE *We & Our Neighbors* 7 Jack . . . planted his toe nails . . . in the embroidered chair bottom.

+**Chair bottoming.** The process of putting seats in chairs. — **1872** BRACE *Dangerous Classes N.Y.* 400 The kind of work . . . is generally some . . . easy trade-work, like shoe-pegging, or chair-bottoming. **1887** *Century Mag.* XXXIV. 858/2 The mysteries of broom-making, chair-bottoming, and the cobbling of shoes.

Chair box. *Obs.* [CHAIR 2.] A receptacle in the body of a 'chair.' — **1775** in *Amer. Museum* III. 120/1 The little trunk was . . . tied behind the chair, and the chair-box moreover crammed with trumpery.

+**Chair car.** A railroad car having separate chairs for seats; a parlor car. — **1895** *Chicago Strike of 1894* 420, I mean those palace cars in which seats are sold at an extra price?—Ans. That would be a chair car. **1903** *Atlantic Mo.* Sept. 369 He had half slunk into a day coach, fearing to go into the chair car lest he should meet some one he knew. **1910** 'O. HENRY' *Options* (1916) 210 My chair-car was profitably well filled with people of the kind one usually sees on chair-cars.

Chair factory. A factory in which chairs are made. — **1827** DRAKE & MANSF. *Cincinnati* 65 Six Chair Factories [employ] 38 hands. **1868** *Mich. Agric. Rep.* VII. 353 Detroit Chair Factory, [exhibited] 1 set cane seat parlor chairs. **1909** F. CALHOUN *Miss Minerva* 153 He's just got Him a baby factory in Heaven like the chair factory and the canning factory.

Chair horse. *Obs.* [CHAIR 2.] A horse suitable for drawing a 'chair.' — **1758** *Huntington Rec.* II. 438, I . . . bequeath unto my loving wife: my riding chair and chair horse. **1797** *Wilmington* (N.C.) *Gaz.* 2 March, A large likely well broken chair Horse, and a neat Sulkey with Harness.

Chair house. *Obs.* [CHAIR 2.] A carriage house for a 'chair.' — **1753** E. Singleton *Social N.Y.* 41 An estate at Whitestone . . . consisting of a good dwelling-house, stable, chair-house, &c. **1754** *S.C. Gazette* 1 Jan. 4/1 The house wherein I live, containing 6 rooms, with a chair-house and stable adjoining in the yard. **1762** *Newport Mercury* 10 Aug. 4/1 A Large handsome well-finished House, . . . together with a Shad, Chair House, Wharf, and Store.

Chairmaker. One who makes chairs. {1813–}

1684 *Boston Rec.* 76 Thomas Stapleford, Chayre maker, became surety . . . for Thomas Mallet. **1734** *N.H. Probate Rec.* II. 517 Bond of Elizabeth Hammet, . . . with Abraham Senter, sail-maker and John Gains, chair-maker as sureties. **1785** *Md. Hist. Mag.* XX. 51 He became apprentice to James Kelly . . . being a Chairmaker by trade. **1815** *View N.Y. State Prison* 33 Many of the chair-makers in the city are supplied from the prison with their materials. **1847** L. COLLINS *Kentucky* 232 [In] Christian County . . . there are . . . four cabinet and chair makers. **1851** J. H. Ross *In New York* 91 My worthy guide . . . I found to be by trade a chair-maker.

Chairmaker's rush. A variety of club rush (*Scirpus americanus*), used in making chair bottoms. — **1843** TORREY *Flora N.Y.* II. 352 *Scirpus triqueter.* . . . Chairmaker's Rush. . . . Swamps and wet meadows, both salt and fresh: common. **1847** DARLINGTON *Weeds & Plants* 361 Sharp-pointed Scirpus. Chair-maker's Rush.

Chairman. Also †**cheerman.** One appointed to preside at a meeting or to act as the leading person in a committee, etc. {1654–}

1650 *Md. Archives* I. 280 Committee all assembled with Mr. Greene, & Capt. Price of the Vpper howse, Mr. ffenwick appoynted Cheerman. **1775** *Vt. Hist. Soc. Coll.* I. 11 To choose a Moderator or Chairman for said meeting. **1829** *Va. Lit. Museum* 214 *Chearman.* This pronunciation is common not only in this State but others of the Union. **1895** M. A. Jackson *Memoirs* 645 One of his letters written to me as chairman of the Military Committee of the Confederate House of Representatives. **1900** E. A. DIX *Deacon Bradbury* 236 Mr. Clark . . . was unofficial chairman of the committee.

Chair palankan. *Obs.* ?A palankeen. — **1802** *Essex Inst. Coll.* LIII. 210 There was a hansome Carrage and four Horses for the Children, and Two Chair Palankans for him and his Lady.

Chair porter. An attendant who pushes or rolls a wheel chair. — **1877** *Harper's Mag.* April 692/1 The chair porter was stupid; . . . he seemed as if he were just leaning against the chair and following it.

Chair post. One of the upright posts of a chair. — **1788** *Amer. Museum* IV. 519/1 The snake was . . . about the thickness of a common chair-post. **1872** *Congress. Globe* App. 578/2 They went out and got big long brushes, as big as these chair posts. **1911** *Roxboro* (N.C.) *Courier* Nov., The snake was as large around as a chair post.

+**Chair road.** *Obs.* [CHAIR 2.] A road suitable for light wheeled traffic. — **1781** *Royal Ga. Gaz.* 4 Jan. (Th.), There is a good chair road from Savannah.

Chair saddle. *Obs.* [CHAIR 2.] The saddle for a chair horse. — **1779** *N.J. Archives* 2 Ser. III. 164 Was stolen out of the barn of the subscriber . . . a chair saddle almost new.

Chair wheel. *Obs.* [CHAIR 2.] One of the wheels of a 'chair.' — **1770** *Carroll P.* in *Md. Hist. Mag.* XIII. 55, I Believe my old Chair wheels will Carry downe yr Carriele. **1830** J. F. WATSON *Philadelphia* 617 You saw the exposed coffins on chair-wheels.

Chairwoman. [After CHAIRMAN.] A woman who acts as a chairman. {1699–} — **1833** NEAL *Down-Easters* I. 153 She who has the readiest tongue . . . is made chair-woman, . . . Lady president if you please. **1845** Commons, etc. *Doc. Hist.* VIII. 228 The Chairwoman [of the Female Industry Assn., N.Y.] observed that it was opened to all who were . . . oppressed.

Chaise. Also †**chase.**

1. A light open or closed carriage, originally with two wheels and drawn by one horse, latterly also four-wheeled and with two or four horses. {1701–}

1724 JONES *Virginia* 32 Most Families of any Note having a Coach, Chariot, Berlin, or Chaise. **1794** *Ann. 3rd Congress* 1309 Every person . . . shall pay, annually, . . . For a chaise, or other two-wheeled carriage, 2 dollars. **1802** *Ann. 7th Congress* 1027 The clergy . . . generally kept a horse and chaise. **1883** *Wheelman* I. 422 His poverty was one reason . . . for his riding a bicycle instead of driving the orthodox and decorous horse and chaise.

b. Used as a plural. (Cf. SHAY.) *Obs.*

[**1750** BURNABY in E. Singleton *Social N.Y.* 350 Thirty or forty gentlemen meet to dine together, . . . and then return home in Italian chaise.] **1794** C. Prentiss *Fugitive Ess.* (1797) 103 Coaches and sulkeys, hacks and chaise, A running round a hundred ways.

2. *Chaise-and-four*, a chaise drawn by four horses.

1835 J. TODD *Student's Manual* 264 The man that makes the road smoke under his chaise-and-four.

3. Attrib. with *horse, nail, step, top, whip.*

1725 *New-Eng. Courant* 10–17 July 2/2 A Chase and an extraordinary good Chase-Horse, to be sold, either together or apart. **1759** *Newport Mercury* 26 June 4/3 To be sold by Jacob Richardson, . . . Brass Chaise Nails. **1863** MRS. WHITNEY *F. Gartney* xiv, Faith's foot was instantly on the chaise step, and she sprang to the ground. *Ib.* xxxvi, A tall . . . woman, with . . . a bonnet that . . . looked like a chaise top flattened back at the first spring. **1781** *Salem Gazette* 3 July, Isaac Greenwood . . . makes Flutes, Fifes, Hoboys, Clarinets, Chaise-Whips.

Chaise house. A carriage house for a chaise. {1812}

1746 *Boston Ev. Post* 10 Feb. 4/2 To be Lett, A Chaise-House, and Room to keep a Horse. **1789** BENTLEY *Diary* I. 128 Capt. Allen . . . has raised a building contiguous to his house . . . covering the Pump, & fitted for a Chaisehouse. **1845** *Lowell Offering* V. 254 A huge barn, with . . . cowyard, watering-trough, cattle-shed, chaise-house, 'and all.' **1898** N. BROOKS *Boys of Fairport* xiii. 178 Joyfully Ned Martin rushed into the chaise-house.

Chaise maker. A builder of chaises.

1759 in H. M. Brooks *Gleanings* 34 Adino Paddock, Chaise-Maker, near the Granary, has six second-hand Chaises to sell. **1785** MARSHALL *Amer. Grove* 51 The timber of this [American white ash] is used much by wheelwrights, chaise-makers &c. **1816** *Mass. H. S. Coll.* 2 Ser. VII. 119 These tacks are chiefly used by saddlers, chaise-makers, trunk-makers, . . . &c. **1845** *Knickerb.* XXVI. 508 His vehicle [had] a thorough . . . examination from the chaise-maker and wheelwright of the parish.

Chaise-trimmer. One employed in adding the finishing and decorative touches to a chaise. — **1819** *Mass. Spy* 12 May (Th.), Wanted, a Journeyman Chaise-Trimmer.

Chaldron. A measure of coal, varying in different ports, but usually containing about 35 bushels. {1615–}

1714 *Boston News-Letter* 26 April 2 To be Sold by Publick Vendue [or] Outcry . . . ten Chaldron of the best new Castle Coal. **1784** *Mass. Centinel* 24 July 3/3 Will be sold . . . about 50 Chaldrons Sea-Coal. **1818** DARBY *Emigrant's Guide* 259 The medium price, six and a quarter cents per bushel, or two dollars and twenty-five cents per chaldron. **1839** BUEL *Farmer's Companion* 287 A chaldron of coals is 58⅔ cubic feet. **1889** *Cent.* 912/3 *Chaldron.* . . . In American ports the weight is very various, but the ordinary weight in the United States is 26¼ hundredweight.

***Chalk,** *n.*

***1. a.** The soft white rock consisting mainly of carbonate of lime; one or other deposit resembling this. Also attrib. **b.** A piece of this used for marking or writing.

1631 in Winthrop *Hist.* (1853) I. 458 Store of . . . chalk and chalk-line. **1637** MORTON *New Canaan* 57 Chalke stones there are neere Squantos Chappell. **1740** *Ga. Col. Rec.* IV. 670 The Hill Country is very different, there being Marble, Chalk, Gravel, Rocks, and all the same Variety of Soil that is in Europe. **1792** IMLAY *Western Territory* 124 Marle, chalk, gypsum, and ochres, are found in various parts. **1826** FLINT *Recoll.* 174 Some of the most perfect have been dug from what are called the 'chalk banks,' below the mouth of the Ohio. **1865** in *Amer. Naturalist* I. 53 Chalk has at last been found in this country—genuine chalk. . . . Smoky Hill, Colorado, is an outlying mass of chalk. **1883** SMITH *Geol. Survey Ala.* 531 The surface . . . is generally covered with fragments of sandstone and claystone (the latter usually called *chalk*). **1902** G. M. MARTIN *Emmy Lou* 86 Emmy Lou took the chalk and stood on her toes to reach the board. **1909** 'O. HENRY' *Options* 132 Not a chalk-mark on the gate-post nor a post-card in the post-office to give us a clew.

b. *The* (*clear*) *chalk*, the real or proper thing. *Obs. slang.*

1840 HALIBURTON *Clockm.* 3 Ser. 203, I have had liberal offers from the sect here, for whatever is the go to Europe will soon be the chalk here. **1843** STEPHENS *High Life N.Y.* II. 202, I tell you what, it was the clear chalk, the ginuine thing.

+2. A quarter of a dollar. *Obs.*

1796 B. HAWKINS *Letters* 451, I gave the account to Mr. Barnard to show you; it amounts to 130 chalks. **1798** *Ib.* 304 Christian Russel . . . is willing to give 200 chalks and a rifle gun for the negro. **1805** Dow *Jrnl.* 10 Jan., A girl . . . asked one dollar, and three quarters, which they call seven chalks.

3. a. *To come up to* (*the*) *chalk*, to come up to the mark, be quite satisfactory. *slang.*

1839 *Congress. Globe* App. 21 Dec. 187/2 Cases have happened in which some have not come 'up to the chalk' . . . , —have not followed in the footsteps of the party leaders. **1843** STEPHENS *High Life N.Y.* I. 215 If any on 'em see anything that don't come right up to the chalk, in the way of gentility, they may be sartin it aint mine. **1871** DE VERE 318 The President, in whom he is disappointed for one reason or another, does not *come up to chalk.*

b. *To walk one's chalks* or (*the*) *chalk*, to make off, to hasten away. *colloq.* {1857–}

1835 LONGSTREET *Ga. Scenes* 6 Oh, wake snakes, and walk your chalks. **1840** HALIBURTON *Clockmaker* 3 Ser. 148 The way she walks her chalks ain't no matter. She is a regilar fore-and-after. **1871** DE VERE 318 When he dismisses an official, he is made to *walk the chalk.* c**1874** 'MARK TWAIN' *Sketches* (1875) 204 If anybody come meddlin' wid you, you jist make 'em walk chalk.

‖**c.** *Chalk and water*, nonsense.

1834 C. A. DAVIS *Lett. J. Downing* 179 Some on you say it ain't right to pay interest to foreigners. . . . Well, that's all chalk and water.

***Chalk,** *v.*

+1. *tr.* To mark with chalk, in special senses: **a.** To mark (one's hat) as a sign of leave to travel free of charge. *colloq.*

1823 QUITMAN *Life & Corr.* 78, I shall be able to say, 'Come and see me,' and I will 'chalk your hat' for the journey. **1881** HAYES *New Colorado* 149 Twenty-five seedy, second-class ruffians, who proposed to travel, as they say in the West, 'with their hats chalked,' or free. **1887** *Nation* 21 April 329/1 All railway officers and most railway employees have their 'hats chalked' all over the U.S.

b. To mark as an indication that the object has been passed or directed officially.

1866 MRS. WHITNEY *L. Goldthwaite* iii, Stooping to examine the trunk . . . [he said,] 'These things is chalked all right for Littleton.' **1873** MILLER *Amongst Modocs* 38 A tall fine-looking man stepped ashore, . . . and said, 'chalk that.' **1892** 'MARK TWAIN' *£1,000,000 Bank-Note*, etc. 258 He was going to try to bribe the postman to chalk it through.

c. *slang.* (See quotation.)

1857 *Boston Post* 5 March (F. & H.), Chalking the lamp post. The term for bribery in Philadelphia.

+2. To set *down;* to estimate, figure on.

1835 BIRD *Hawks of Hawk-H.* II. 78 He chalked me down like a fool, me and Tom Staples. **1874** *Vt. Bd. Agric. Rep.* II. 618 The farmers on that committee were outwitted, for while they chalked from $25,000 to $30,000, others chalked from $150,000 to $200,000.

+3. *To chalk up.* **a.** With *it:* To mark *up* or raise the price of.

1834 C. A. DAVIS *Lett. J. Downing* 83 Tell the folks Kolery is comin, and they go at it mixin Paragoric and Kamfire, and chalk it up like gold dust. **1837** COOPER *Gleanings in Eng.* II. 83 The language of the shop, such as . . . 'chalking up,' 'selling out,' and other Pearl-street terms, frequently find their way into the leading articles of a New York paper.

b. *intr.* To add or mount *up.*

1878 STOWE *Poganuc People* 36 But who's going to pay for it all? These 'ere sort of things chalk up, ye know.

4. *To chalk on a barn-door*, to calculate roughly.

1880 *Congress. Rec.* 19 April 2478/2 [The Geneva arbitrators] took the two statements, . . . went up into a mountain and chalked on a barn door, and split the difference.

+Chalked hat. [CHALK *v.* 1 a.] A hat marked with chalk as an indication of a free pass; a person wearing a hat so marked. (See CHALK *v.* 1.) — **1846** *Spirit of Times* 16 May 133/1 The chalked hats were 'numerous' on the occasion. *Ib.* 4 July 217/3, I would also take this opportunity of hinting to the directors of some Rail Roads and Steamboats . . . when a gentleman calls on them, by request, for a 'chalked hat' [etc.].

***Chalk line.**

1. A cord covered with powdered chalk or similar material for making a guideline to be followed in sawing or hewing.

1631 in Winthrop *Hist.* (1853) I. 458 Store of shoemakers' thread and hobnails; chalk and chalk-line. **1633** *N.H. Doc. & Rec.* I. 77, 4 knotts chalke line. **1771** *Carroll P.* in *Md. Hist. Mag.* XIII. 173 Prey desier Mr Deards to send me by him two Drumlines. . . . I want them to Plant out my Lucern, the Chalk Lines are too weak & small. **1881** *Harper's Mag.* Sept. 556/2 It was a common saying among the boys that Old Hobson had more girl than chalk-line.

2. A line drawn with chalk as a guide in quilting.

1825 NEAL *Bro. Jonathan* I. 55 Eight or ten young women at work; not one of whom stayed her needle, or chalk-line, for a single moment.

b. *fig.* A straight line, as if drawn with chalk.

1878 B. F. TAYLOR *Between Gates* 227, I watched an apparently perpendicular rock a thousand feet in the air, and saw a chalk-line.

+3. The small green heron.

1844 *Nat. Hist. N.Y., Zoology* II. 224 The Poke, Chalk-line, Fly-up-the-creek . . . is a southern species.

+Chalk rag. A duster for a blackboard. — **1854** M. J. HOLMES *Tempest & Sunshine* 29 Then she would resolve . . . not to pin any more chalk rags to the boys' coats.

Chalk-talk. A talk or lecture which the speaker illustrates by means of a blackboard and chalk. {1881} Also *chalk-talker.* — **1888** *St. Paul & Mpls. Pioneer Press* 22 July (F.), Rolo Byron, the celebrated chalk-talker, entertained a fair-sized audience this evening on prohibition. **1891** *Boston Transcript* 8 May 5/2 Bert Poole gave a 'chalk talk.'

***Challenge,** *n.* +(See quot. 1847.) — **1829** *Ill. Rev. Laws* (1833) 246 (*marginal note*), Challenges. **1847** WEBSTER 190/1 *Challenge*, . . . in elections, an exception to a person as not legally qualified to vote. (United

States.) **1889** *Mich. Gen. Statutes* III. 2827 [If] the challenge is not withdrawn, one of the inspectors shall tender to him . . . one of the following oaths.

*****Challenge,** *v.* +*tr.* 'In elections, to object to a person as not qualified to vote' (W. '47). See also CHALLENGER. — **1829** *Ill. Rev. Laws* (1833) 246 If his vote shall be challenged by any elector . . . , the judges of the election shall tender to such person an oath. **1851** *Iowa Code* 46 Any person offering to vote may be challenged, as unqualified. **1889** *Mich. Gen. Statutes* III. 2827 If any person offering to vote shall be challenged as unqualified by any inspector . . . , the chairman of the board of inspectors shall declare to the person challenged the constitutional qualifications [etc.].

‖**Challenge bell.** A bell on a Mississippi riverboat conveying a racing challenge. — **1847** ROBB *Squatter Life* 143 Her laugh rung like a challenge bell on a 'fast trip.'

Challenge cup. A cup, usually of silver, offered as a reward for winning a race or competition. — **1897** *Outing* XXX. 89/1 In 1878 Mr. Hermann Oelrichs presented a challenge cup, to be competed for annually.

*****Challenger.** [CHALLENGE *v.*] +One who challenges the right of another to vote. — **1853** *Knickerb.* XLII. 653 He was shrewdly suspected of not being 'right' by a man who winked at a 'challenger,' who 'thus then' interposed: 'Are you naturalized?' **1875** *Chicago Tribune* 12 Nov. 7/4 The officials peremptorily refused to allow the number of Republican challengers claimed. **1889** *Mich. Gen. Statutes* III. 2827 At every election, each of the political parties shall have the right to designate and keep a challenger at each place of voting. **1911** *Okla. Sess. Laws* 3 Legisl. 78 Every person desiring to vote at such special election, after having passed the challengers [etc.].

+**Chally, Challie.** [Variant of *challis* {1849–} taken as a pl. or as French.] The light wool and silk, all-wool, or cotton material known as challis. Also attrib., esp. with *dress*. — **1838** Buckingham *Amer., N. States* (1841) II. 209 They carried off an entire coat of fresh paint from the gallery, regardless of the cost of silks and challys. **1842** *Knickerb.* XIX. 527 [She] presented herself in her ball-room finery, including . . . a new challey dress. **1862** CUMMING *Hospital Life* (1866) 40/2, I bought a very pretty chally dress for fifty cents per yard. **1893** *Chicago Tribune* 23 April 29/6 Javanaise Challie Sale—Another invoice of French Printed Javanaise Challies. **1903** C. L. BURNHAM *Jewel* 197 She ran to the closet where hung her dotted challie dress.

*** Chamber,** *n.*

1. An upper room in a dwelling house, usually serving as a bedroom. {1684–, *dial.*}

Originally distinct from a garret or attic, but in later use sometimes synonymous with this.

*a***1649** WINTHROP *Hist.* I. 311 Briscoe . . . came in and went up to his chamber. **1694** *Mass. H. S. Coll.* 4 Ser. I. 105 The houses are built generally low; but very few of them have an upright chamber. **1742** *N.H. Probate Rec.* III. 98 The use of the Stairs in the Said Entry to pass up & Down to the Chamber & Garret of the Said Eastern End. **1761** S. NILES *Indian Wars* II. 459 The Indians fired into the loft, or chamber, and soon were joined by other Indians. **1809** *Steele Papers* II. 579 The upstairs par(t) is divided into four chambers, of these . . . my family constantly occupy two. **1889** HOWELLS *Hazard of Fortunes* I. 59 She had conformed to a law for the necessity of turning round in each room, and had folding-beds in the chambers.

+**b.** An upper floor used for storage.

1644 *Essex Inst. Coll.* L. 320 Corne upon the ground, 3li.; corne upon the chamber, 18s. **1657** *East-Hampton Rec.* I. 120 Mary & I had brought the corne into the chamber. **1864** *Me. Agric. Soc. Ret.* 25 He harvested & carried into his chamber a good crop of sound corn.

+**c.** *Up chamber,* to an upper room, upstairs.

1774 FITHIAN *Journal* I. 209 She then retired up chamber. **1833** S. SMITH *Major Downing* 162 Then when they come up chamber, in the Cabinet Room.

+**d.** *S.E.* (See quotations.)

1863 HOPLEY *Life in South* I. 204 The lady led me into the 'chamber,' as the family sitting-room of a Virginia house is called. *c***1870** BAGBY *Old Va. Gentleman* 12 There was, of course, a large hall or passage, a parlor and dining-room, 'the chamber' proper for the old lady and for everybody. **1902** G. C. EGGLESTON *D. South* 292 The chamber, in an old plantation house, was that room on the ground floor in which the master of the plantation, whether married or unmarried, slept.

2. A room or suite of rooms occupied by a student or other resident in a college. Also attrib. with *fellow, lecture.*

1643 *New Eng. First Fruits* II. i, Their Chambers and studies also fitted for, and possessed by the Students. **1654** JOHNSON *Wonder-w. Prov.* 163 Young Students could make but a poor progress in learning, by looking on the bare walls of their chambers. **1729** SEWALL *Letter-Book* II. 274 He and I were Chamber fellows and Bed-fellows in Harvard-College Two years. **1776** *N.J. Archives* 2 Ser. I. 217 On Wednesday the 6th the Chambers will be fixed and assigned, so that those who do not appear that day will lose all claim from their former possession. **1780** STILES *Lit. Diary* II. 486, I held a theological Chamber Lecture this afternoon for a select number of Seniors & pious Graduates. **1790** *Harvard Laws* 20 If his [*sc.* an undergraduate's] absence shall exceed three months, his chamber shall be taken away. **1871** BAGG *At Yale* 19 'A chamber' usually comprises—in addition to the main sitting room . . . —two bed rooms, a coal closet, a clothes press . . . , a wash room, etc.

3. *Chamber of commerce,* a board organized to protect the interests of commerce. {1727–}

1797 *Ann. 4th Congress* 2 Sess. 2076 The petition of the Chamber of Commerce of Boston, praying for the placing of certain buoys in the harbor of Boston. **1811** MEASE *Philadelphia* 67 An association of persons, concerned in trade, was formed in the year 1801, 'for the purposes of aiding the trade of the city of Philadelphia . . . ,' by the name of 'The Chamber of Commerce.' **1822** *Ann. 17th Congress* 1 Sess. I. 65 Mr. Lloyd presented the memorial of the Chamber of Commerce of the City of Baltimore. **1837** *Niles' Nat. Reg.* 28 Jan. 352/3 The Philadelphia chamber of commerce has recommended a repeal of the laws on usury. **1911** *Okla. Sess. Laws* 3 Legisl. 126 Any commercial club, chamber of commerce, . . . shall be permitted to lease or purchase land from the Commissioners of the Land Office.

+**4.** A lock on a canal; a confined part of a stream.

1829 A. ROYALL *Pennsylvania* I. 151 The Union canal is eight feet wide, . . . and the locks or chambers, as they are called, are very long and narrow. **1872** FLAGG *Good Investment* iv. 222/1 He entered the chamber of Lower Twin, and followed that in its descent. **1890** *Cent.* 3497/2 When a vessel is descending, water is let into the chamber of the lock till it is on a level with the higher water.

5. Attrib. in sense 1 with *bedroom, bellows, door,* etc.

1729 COMER *Diary* (1923) 94 My mother [was] in the forenoon about 10 of ye clock in ye chamber bedroom. **1720** SEWALL *Letter-Book* II. 106 One pair of chamber bellows with brass noses. **1682** *Witchcraft Cases* (1698) 64 The biggest stone . . . that had burst open my Chamber Door. **1738** *N.H. Probate Rec.* II. 281 The entry of the said dwelling house and the chamber entry shall still remain undivided. **1657** *Essex Inst. Coll.* VII. 39/2 To smooth the boards of one of the chamber flowres. **1855** SIMMS *Forayers* 550 Having a taste for baths, warming-pans, and chamber-furniture. **1852** *Harper's Mag.* VI. 143 A chamber gown of *hongroise* (a new tissue of wool and silk ribbon like reps). **1638** *Md. Archives* IV. 48, 1. old pewter chamberpott. **1886** *Harper's Mag.* June 61/1 Often there is a puncheon floor and no chamber roof. **1856** OLMSTEAD *Slave States* 49 The chamber-servants are negroes, and are accomplished in their business. **1871** STOWE *Sam Lawson* 131 He'd . . . call down the chamber-stairs to Miry to go to bed. **1868** *Mich. Agric. Rep.* VII. 349 D. Kellogg, Detroit, [exhibited the] best parlor and chamber stove. **1780** PARKMAN *Diary* 210 A valuable, tho old fashioned chamber Table, with large slate in ye Middle. **1722** *New-Eng. Courant* 2–9 April 1/2 She first throws open her Chamber Window.

*****Chamber,** *v.* +**1.** *tr.* Of a firearm: To receive in the chamber. +**2.** To try (buckshot) in order to secure a size suitable to the gauge of the gun. **b.** *intr.* To suit the gauge. +**3.** *intr.* Of a mining vein: To spread out. — (1) **1839** *S. Lit. Messenger* V. 97/2 My father's big gun . . . would chamber five buckshot. **1902** WHITE *Blazed Trail* xx. 141 Wallace's rifle chambered the .38 Winchester cartridge. (2) **1884** *Forest & Stream* XXII. 225 'W. J.' should be very careful to . . . chamber buckshot at muzzle of gun, . . . and to choose that size shot that most nearly chambers. (3) **1873** BEADLE *Undevel. West* 335 The miner starts with a vein a foot or more wide . . . ; then it suddenly 'chambers' to some size, then 'pinches' to the thickness of a knife blade.

Chamberlain. (See first quot.) — **1889** *Cent.* 916/1 *Chamberlain.* . . . The name is given in some of the larger cities and towns both of Great Britain and of the United States to the treasurer or officer who has charge of the moneys of the municipal corporations. **1897** *Charter for Greater New York* 25 The money . . . deposited shall be placed to the account of the chamberlain, and he shall keep a bank book, in which shall be entered his account. **1905** KEENAN *N.Y. City Chamberlain Ann. Rep.* 8 The Chamberlain has also paid to the Sinking Fund Redemption Account the interest received from the deposits of city moneys.

*** Chambermaid.**

*** 1.** A maid who attends especially to the bedrooms of a house or hotel. Also attrib.

1803 E. S. BOWNE *Life* 184, I am half crazed with Sempstresses, waiters, chambermaids, and everything else. **1870** 'F. FERN' *Ginger-Snaps* 16 Chamber-maid . . . left suddenly because she was requested not to use the cologne. **1906** *N.Y. Herald* 5 March 14 A neat young girl as chambermaid and waitress in small private family. **1917** J. F. DALY *A. Daly* 189 [A] young actress of what, in the old 'lines of business,' were called 'Chambermaid' parts.

*** 2.** A lady's maid. *Obs.* {–1719}

1722 *New-Eng. Courant* 19–26 March 1/1 They ['journeyman gentlewomen'] must have a Chamber-Maid to wait on themselves.

‖**Chamberman.** A sleeping-car attendant on a train. — **1878** H. H. JACKSON *Travels at Home* 5 'Make your beds now, ladies?' said the chamberman.

Chamber mate. [CHAMBER *n.* 2.] A student who shares a room with another. {1886}

Cf. the earlier *chamber fellow* (quot. 1729 under CHAMBER *n.* 2).

1766 *Mass. H. S. Coll.* 3 Ser. V. 182, I became chamber-mate, the first year, to a senior and a junior sophister. **1814** *Harvard Laws* 38 The president and tutors shall charge such delinquent . . . the full proportion, which sum shall be paid to his chamber mate. **1851** HALL *College Words* 41 *Chamber-mate,* One who inhabits the same room or chamber with another.

+**Chamber set.** A suite of bedroom furniture. — **1851** CIST *Cincinnati* 204 Burley & Lyford . . . manufacture chamber sets. **1858** *Texas Almanac (advt.)*, Parlor and chamber sets. **1892** *Vt. Agric. Rep.* XII. 124 What we do want is men . . . to manufacture our millions of hard wood into every thing that is made of wood, from a tooth pick to a polished chamber set.

Chamberwork. +The housework necessary to keep a chamber in order; the work of a chambermaid. — **1870** 'F. FERN' *Ginger-Snaps* 20 Having done chamberwork or cooking, for such a number of years in New York, they don't need any lady to instruct them how! **1873** E. S. PHELPS *Trotty's Wedding* xviii, She . . . manifests no intention of taking any responsibility as to the chamberwork. **1885** *Rep. Indian Affairs* 161 The girls also take great interest in the household duties, such as sewing, cooking, chamber-work, etc.

+**Chambray.** [Fr. *Cambrai*, France.] 'A kind of gingham; plain colors, linen finish, ladies' dress-goods' (Knight). Also attrib.

1814 *Niles' Reg.* V. 317/2 Twenty-four cases cotton and woollen goods, cloths, ginghams, chambrays, shirtings, threads, &c. **1817** S. BROWN *Western Gaz.* 94 The articles manufactured consist of . . . chambrays, cassinets, sattinets, woolen cords, &c. **1914** *Sears, Roebuck & Co. Cat.* No. 128, 38 No better wearing chambray is to be had at any price. *Ib.*, Low priced plain color chambray ginghams.

***Chameleon.** +**1.** =CAMELEON 1. +**2.** The horned toad. — **(1)** **1827** J. L. WILLIAMS *W. Florida* 28 The chameleon is the least ugly of the species; he is very frequently seen. **1836** HOLLEY *Texas* v. 102 Lizards, . . . and that singular and beautiful animal, the chameleon, are to be found every where. **1881** [see AMERICAN CHAMELEON]. **(2)** **1844** GREGG *Commerce of Prairie* I. 195 Another indigenous reptile is the horned-frog of the Prairies, known here by the name of *camaleon* (or chameleon), of which it is probably a species, as its color has been observed to vary a little in accordance with the character of the soil it inhabits.

+**Chamisal.** Also **chemisal, -izal.** [Mexican Sp., f. *chamiso.*] A dense growth or thicket of chamiso. — **1853** *Ho. of Repr. Ex. Doc.* 91 (Bentley), Traveling . . . is rendered very trying by . . . patches of dense masses of shrubbery known as the chemizal. **1891** *Century Mag.* Jan. 401 Our way had taken us . . . through tangled chemisal and underbrush. **1897** *Outing* XXX. 551/2 The roadway of Eel River, [with] its lofty walls smoothed out of jagged feature by sweeps of forest and chemisal. **1902** *Bureau Plant Industry Bul.* No. 12, 31 These chaparral areas . . . have become landmarks, the word chamisal, sometimes corrupted into chemisal, . . . being adopted as a local name.

+**Chamiso.** Also **chamiza, -isa, -ise.** [Mexican Sp.] A Californian evergreen shrub, *Adenostoma fasciculatum.* Also attrib. with *brush.* — **1846** EMORY *Military Reconn.* 77 In one view could be seen clustered, the . . . green wood acacia, chamiza, . . . and a new variety of sedge. **1856** WHIPPLE *Explor. Ry. Route* I. 74 Dry twigs of chamisa have been the only fuel available for camp fires. **1893** *Amer. Folk-Lore* VI. 141 *Adenostoma fasciculatum*, chamise; chamise brush. So. Barbara Co., Cal. **1904** *N.Y. Tribune* 17 July, One afternoon they located a grizzly, and ran him into a field of chamiso brush.

***Chamlet.** Obs. variant of CAMLET. — **1651** in *Mayflower Desc.* X. 163, I give unto my Daughter . . . a Chamlett gowne and a fayer red petticoate. **1678** *New Castle Court Rec.* 362 A dublet & briches and A old Chamblet Cloake. **1689** SEWALL *Diary* I. 282 My new cloath-colour'd suit with the chamlet cloak.

Chamoiser. [Cf. Eng. *chamoiz'd* (1620), *chamoising* (1727).] A dresser of chamois leather. — **1732** *S.C. Gazette* 25/2 The Skins are then return'd from the Mill to the Chamoiser, to be scour'd.

Chamomile. Variant of CAMOMILE. Also attrib. with *tea.*

1791 MUHLENBERG *Index Florae* 177. **1818** EASTBURN *Yamoyden* (1834) 247 Like the meek chamomile, it grew. **1857** GRAY *Botany* 225 *A[nthemis] arvensis*, L. (Corn Chamomile). **1893** DANA *Wild Flowers* 71 Mayweed. Chamomile. . . . The country-folk brew 'chamomile tea' from these leaves, and through their agency raise painfully effective blisters in an emergency. **1898** *N.Y. Journal* 16 Sept. 11/6 Each contained . . . chamomile and peppermint teas.

Champagne.

1. The sparkling wine made in the province of Champagne in France. {1664-}

1806 WEBSTER 47/2 *Champaign*, a flat open country, a kind of wine. **1837** J. C. NEAL *Charcoal Sk.* (1838) 10 Drinking fairy Champagne and eating canvass-back ducks in air-drawn places. **1857** M. J. HOLMES *Meadow-Brook* xi, Regularly on her dinner table appeared either porter, champagne, or madeira. **1898** PAGE *Red Rock* 449, I've found champagne make its way to a man's heart when you couldn't get at it through his pocket.

2. Attrib. with *basket, bottle, cork*, etc.

1869 *Atlantic Mo.* July 76/2 He contented himself, therefore, with two champagne-baskets. **1870** TOMES *Decorum* 136 He will be sure to detect the Newark cider in your Champagne bottle. **1855** *Harvard Mag.* I. 5 Your armories, too, whose walls have so often echoed . . . the pop of the champagne-cork. **1842** *Spirit of the Times* 30 Aug. (Th.), The editor . . . crows over a champagne julep to which he has been treated. **1909** 'O. HENRY' *Options* 291 There are champagne pails set about. **1892** A. DALY *Test Case* (1893) 36, I'll make one of my famous champagne punches. **1841** W. KENNEDY *Texas* I. xl, Shortly before I quitted Houston, I was invited to a 'champagne supper.'

* **Champaign.** Also **champagne.**

* **1.** Flat, open country.

In later use only literary.

*a***1610** Bradford *Hist.* (1912) I. 154 We trended the coast southerly, which was all champaign and full of grass. *a***1649** WINTHROP *Hist.* I. 138 The country on the west of the Bay of Naragansett is all champaign for many miles. **1787** BARLOW *Vision* I. 14 His freshening waves . . . isles and champaigns hide. **1844** EMERSON *Lect., Young American*, These rising grounds which command the champaign below.

2. Attrib. with *country, land*, etc.: Level and open; forming an extensive plain.

1792 IMLAY *Western Territory* 38 We will suppose ourselves at Limestone, where the champaign country on the eastern side of the river begins. **1835** HOFFMAN *Winter in West* I. 22 The chief part of the town [Harrisburg, Pa.] lies on a piece of champaign land. **1792** IMLAY *Western Territory* 123 The champaign part of this country has no stone on its surface. **1819** E. DANA *Geogr. Sk.* 90 A young growth of various kinds of trees now covers this champaign space.

b. Pertaining to, characteristic of, a champaign.

1841 FOOTE *Texas & Texans* II. 379 The open champagne character of the country . . . may be set down as [a cause] of this healthfulness.

Champian, -ion.** Obs. variants of CHAMPAIGN. {Freq. in 17th c.} — *c1622** PORY *Plymouth & New Eng.* (1918) 50 Up the river . . . there is a place of even champian countrie. **1634** WOOD *New Englands Prospect* (1898) I. v. 16 There is scarce a bush or bramble, or any combersome underwood to bee seene in the more champion ground.

+**Champlain.** The name of the lake lying between the states of New York and Vermont, used attrib. with *black oak, minnow, pickering, willow.* — **1801** MICHAUX *Histoire des Chênes* 7 Chêne quercitron à feuilles anguleuse. *Great Black Oak*, or *Champlain Black Oak.* **1842** *Nat. Hist. N.Y., Zoology* IV. 220 The Champlain Minnow. *Hydrargira atricada.* **1842** *Ib.* 16 The Champlain Pickering. *Pileoma semifasciatum.* **1810** MICHAUX *Arbres* I. 41 *Champlain willow*, nom donné par moi.

* **Chance.** In colloquial uses.

In early Maryland land records (1667–1700) also frequent with personal names to denote a person's 'lot' of land, as James Chance, Oglesbyes Chance, Dixsons Chance, Hollis his Chance, etc. See the *Md. Hist. Mag.* XIX–XXI.

+**1.** A quantity or number (*of* something).

Used with various adjs., esp. *smart, right smart, powerful, mighty*, or *fine*, to denote a (fairly or very) large number, quantity, etc. Similarly in senses 2 and 3.

(1) **1819** D. THOMAS *Travels* 230 (Th.), A considerable quantity is expressed by a smart chance; and our hostess at Madison said there was a smart chance of Yankees in that village. **1827** SHERWOOD *Gaz. Georgia* 139 *Smart chance*, for good deal, large quantity, large company, great number. **1834** SIMMS *G. Rivers* 99 He did have a power of money and a smart chance of lands and field-niggers. **1840** *Crockett Almanac* 29, I had a smart chance of small shot in my rifle. **1847** FIELD *Drama in Pokerville*, etc. 198 The confidential hoosier . . . told him that there was a 'smart chance of a pile' on one of the tables. **1855** SIMMS *Forayers* 61 Don't we know you've been selling a smart chaince of corn and fodder?

(2) **1829** *Va. Lit. Museum* 16 Dec. 419 *Chance.* A supply, a quantity—'he lost a right smart *chance* of blood'—vulgarism of the Southern States. **1832** S. A. FARRELL *Ramble* 87 Our host told us that there was 'a pretty smart chance of deer' in the neighbourhood. **1846** *Knickerb.* XXVIII. 86 There was . . . for a few moments 'a considerable smart chance of a scramble.' **1856** S. T. L. ROBINSON *Kansas* 27 They say, 'a right smart chance of calicoes.' **1867** A. D. RICHARDSON *Beyond Miss.* 132, I have fed a heap [of corn] to my cattle and got a right smart chance left. **1888** 'CRADDOCK' *Broomsedge Cove* 250, I've been huntin' guinea-hens' aigs. . . . I fund a right smart chance of 'em.

(3) **1822** J. WOODS *Eng. Prairie* 345 You have a powerful chance of plunder on your creature. What are you going to do with it? **1830** ROYALL *Lett. from Ala.* 121 There was some monstrous purty gals there—and a powerful chance of apples and cyder. **1835** LONGSTREET *Ga. Scenes* 211 They gin' her a powerful chance o' truck.

(4) **1834** CROCKETT *Narr. Life* 89 We found a fine chance of potatoes in it. **1840** HALIBURTON *Clockmaker* 3 Ser. xvii. 238 There had fallen a little chance of snow in the night. **1842** *Knickerb.* XX. 491 There's a mighty chance of lawyers' lies in the papers. **1843** STEPHENS *High Life N.Y.* II. 155 They got up a small chance of a cheer. *Ib.* 171 If this ere leetle chance of music sets her feet a goin so. **1873** BEADLE *Undevel. West* 433 Fine chance o' corn planted an' doin' well. **1913** MORLEY *Carolina Mts.* 175 'Yes, I've a nice chance of flowers,' a woman modestly admits when you admire her little garden.

+**2.** A sample or specimen; a show.

1830 ROYALL *Southern Tour* I. 62 The Postmaster—is a poor *chance*, a rough course looking creature. **1830** — *Lett. from Ala.* 190 Honorable Mr. Mitchell is a poor *chance* as we say in the West. *a***1846** *Quarter Race Ky.*, etc. 55 You have got a mighty small chance of legs there. **1849** *Knickerb.* XXXIV. 113 He strode a 'right smart chance of a critter,' that couldn't be beat in 'them diggins.' **1855** *Herald of Freedom* 16 June 3/3 Kansas City is, as they say out here [in Fort Leavenworth], a 'right smart chance of a place.' **1888** *Kansas Hist. Coll.* IV. 245 We found Chicago then, as I first heard the expression—'a right smart chance of a place.'

||**3. a.** A distance. **b.** A space of time.

(a) 1840 SIMMS *Border Beagles* 98, I can't tell you [how far it is to Benton]—it's on the other road, and a smart roundabout chance to get to it. **(b) 1845** — *Wigwam & Cabin* I. 45 There I stood a pretty considerable chance.

*** Chancellor.**

+1. The chief judge in the court of equity or chancery in certain states.

1789 *Ann. 1st Congress* I. 26 The oath . . . would be administered by the Chancellor of the State of New York. **1794** *Amer. Calendar* 120 Court of Chancery. Robert R. Livingston, chancellor. **a1817** DWIGHT *Travels* III. 277 The Governour, Chancellor, and Judges of the Supreme Court [of New York] . . . are constituted a Council. **1831** *Amer. Almanac* 214 The chancellor and judges [of Md.] are nominated by the governor. **1838** *Dem. Review* I. 362 He became . . . a student of law, in the office of Mr. Desaussure, afterwards chancellor of South Carolina. **1849** *Knickerb.* XXXIII. 462 A man . . . who in the course of time attained the high position of chancellor.

+2. A judge of a court of equity or chancery.

1856 *Harper's Mag.* XIII. 844/1 The Convention created upward of sixty chancellors, or judges, with the full attributes of that office. **1889** *Cent.* 919/2 *Chancellor*. . . . In Delaware, New Jersey, and some others of the United States, a judge of the Court of Chancery or Equity. In Alabama, Mississippi, and Tennessee there are district chancellors chosen by popular vote.

+Chancer, *v. Obs.* [Reduced from CHANCERY *v.*] *tr.* To adjust or settle equitably, after the manner of a court of chancery; to bring *down* in amount in this way.

1692 *Mass. Acts* I. 75 The justices . . . are impowred to chancer the same [bond] unto the just debt and damages. *Ib.* 356 The justices of the said courts . . . are hereby impowred and authorized . . . to chancer the forfeiture. **1709** *R.I. Col. Rec.* IV. 26 Judgment was given for the appellee, in that the bond should be chancer'd. **1742** *N.H. Prov. Papers* V. 159 Ascertain the vallue of money & Exch[ange] for Chancering the vallue of the bills of Credit. **1768** *Ib.* XIII. 110 The same is hereby Chancered and abated down to the sum of twenty pounds lawful money only. **1798** ROOT *Law Rep.* I. 114 The Court is of opinion that the case is within the statute and that said note be chancered to £3. 15. 3.

+Chancerable, *a. Obs.* [f. prec.] Capable of judicial adjustment. — **1726** *Conn. Col. Rec.* VII. 74 It is resolved, that the aforesaid note is chancerable.

+Chancering, *vbl. n. Obs.* [f. CHANCER *v.*] The action of adjusting judicially. — **1684** *Mass. Court of Assist. Rec.* I. 261 The plaintiff and defend[an]ts pleas as to the Chancering of the bond. **1740** W. DOUGLASS *Discourse* 7 England, France and Holland have tacitly allowed their several American Colonies . . . by Chancerings in their Courts of Judicature . . . to depreciate . . . the value of their original Denominations.

+Chancerize, *v. Obs. tr.* = CHANCER *v.* — **1707** *R.I. Col. Rec.* IV. 26 This Assembly . . . do order and enact, that the said bonds be by the Governor and Council truly chancerized. **1722** *Ib.* 320 This assembly do adjudge and decree that the judgment . . . is hereby chancerized down to twenty shillings.

*** Chancery,** *n.*

***1.** A court of equity. Usually *court of chancery.*

1694 SEWALL *Diary* I. 388 Council Day for Chusing Commissioners for the Chancery. **1705** *N.C. Col. Rec.* I. 627 In Barr of all further proceedings the Def[enden]t prays an Appeal in to the next Hon[ora]ble Court of Chancery. **1728** *N.J. Archives* 1 Ser. V. 225 Courts of Chancery . . . are known to be necessary in many cases to correct the severity of the common law. **1789** MACLAY *Deb. Senate* 94 The gentlemen of the bar, in the House, seemed to have made a common cause of it, to push the power of Chancery as far as possible. **1805** *Huntington Rec.* III. 231 A certain Cause pending in the Court of Chancery of the State of New York. **a1817** DWIGHT *Travels* I. 273 The Circuit Court is also a Court of Chancery, in any case, in equity. **1849** COOPER *Sea Lions* v, The deacon . . . might be even called on to give some sort of an account, in a court of chancery, of the information obtained from the deceased. **1887** *Mich. Gen. Statutes* III. 3693 Either party to a cause in chancery shall have the right to an examination of all the witnesses in the case.

+2. Adjustment of a sum or matter in dispute as by a court of chancery. *Obs.*

1679 *Mass. Court of Assist. Rec.* I. 154 After ye Court had heard ye partjes pleas (for?) a chancery of ye bond they Judged it meet [etc.] **1699** SEWALL *Diary* I. 495 The Jury brings in their verdict for Madam Usher. Mr. Leverett and Newton crave a Chancery. **1706** *Ib.* II. 167 Mr. Blagrove is cast, Asks a Chancery in writing.

3. Attrib. with *bill, cause, court, district, paper, relief, rule, suit.*

1685 SEWALL *Diary* I. 81 This day the Chancery Bill is passed. **1819** Mackenzie *Life Van Buren* (1846) 154, I shall endeavor as soon as possible to send you some papers in these Chancery causes. **1892** M. A. JACKSON *Gen. Jackson* 11 Jonathan was a successful lawyer, especially as a pleader in the chancery courts. **1866** 'F. KIRKLAND' *Bk. Anecdotes* 64 This person was elected Judge of the Chancery District. **1898** PAGE *Red Rock* 309 He was . . . examining a bundle of old Chancery papers. **1835** *S. Lit. Messenger* I. 423 *Chancery* or *equitable relief* is rarely sought in the Massachusetts courts. **1822** *Ann. 17th Congress* 1st Sess. I. 110 The common law or chancery rule, may apply to all such cases. **1707** J. LOGAN in *Penna. Hist. Soc. Mem.* X. 209 A Chancery suit is to be dreaded.

+Chancery, *v. Obs.* [f. prec.] *tr.* = CHANCER *v.* — **1674** *Mass. Court of Assist. Rec.* I. 21 The Court . . . chanceried the dammage additional to 40 s. only. **1684** *Ib.* 261 The plaintiff desired his bond might be chanceried. The Court . . . did chancery it to sixty-eight pounds.

*** Chandler.** One who makes or sells candles as a trade. (Cf. TALLOW CHANDLER.)

1680 *Boston Rec.* 69 William Porter, Chandler. **1720** *Ib.* 140 John Clark, Chandler. **1741** W. STEPHENS *Proc. Georgia* II. 114 His Wife, at the same Time, kept a Chandler's Shop. **1855** *Amer. Inst. N.Y. Trans.* 268 Fatty matter, such as chandlers' greaves, may be fed to swine.

*** Change.**

***1.** A place where merchants, brokers, etc., meet to transact business; an exchange.

The spelling *'change* is due to the erroneous idea that the form is an abbreviation of *exchange.*

1717 SEWALL *Diary* III. 131 Governour gave the Staves on the Change by reason of the wet Weather. Mr. Jona. Belcher speaks to me on Change. **1768** J. ROWE *Diary* 170 He engaged to meet them on the Change this day. **1842** L. M. CHILD *Lett. N.Y.* 161 The merchant seeks his moral standard on 'Change—a fitting name for a thing so fluctuating. **1886** A. DALY *After Business Hours* 28 We'll buy all the South American Electric Elevated we can get. . . . We can get all we want on 'Change.

2. Conversion to a religious frame of mind. Also *change of heart.*

c1847 F. M. WHITCHER *Widow Bedott P.* xi. 108 'Do you mean to insiniwate that ye've met with a change?' said the Widow Bedott to Jim Clarke, the peddler. **1885** *Harper's Mag.* Sept. 645/2 All colored people claim the fraternal relation, . . . if they are members of the same church, or have 'experienced a change.' **1901** HARBEN *Westerfelt* 296 Sister's gone an' had a change o' heart.

+3. *Change pitcher,* in baseball, an alternate or relief pitcher. *Obs.*

1868 CHADWICK *Base Ball* 36 Your change pitcher should occupy the position of short-stop. *Ib.* 160 Of the Atlantics, Zettlein occupies the regular position, with Pratt as change pitcher. **1886** *Outing* VII. 697/2 Vian, '88, will probably be change pitcher.

4. *Change of base,* removal to a new scene of operations; a departure or retreat. (Cf. BASE *n.*[1] 2.)

1870 O. LOGAN *Before Footlights* 219 [The room had] recently been occupied by an officer of rank whose brother officers . . . required the most minute explanation in regard to his sudden change of base. **1888–96** [see BASE *n.*[1] 2]. **1897** C. S. DANA *Recoll. Civil War* 222 A far more brilliant evolution than McClellan's 'change of base.'

+Changeable hare. The American varying hare, *Lepus americanus.* — **1814** BRACKENRIDGE *Views* 57 The changeable hare (*lepus variabilis*) a beautiful animal, gray in summer, and white in winter is seen in this country [=La. Territory].

Change bill. *Obs.* A bill of exchange. — **1682** *Mass. Bay Currency Tracts* 10 Payments on Change-bills.

*** Channel.** The bed in which a river runs; the deep part of a stream, estuary, or other stretch of water; a (natural or artificial) watercourse or waterway.

1622 'MOURT' *Relation* 113 We . . . sent our two Interpreters to speake with them, the channell being betweene them. **1670** *Derby* (Conn.) *Rec.* 15 Bounded . . . with the chanel of Potatuck River westt. **1722** *Providence Rec.* XVI. 204 The Thach beds . . . Lieing on the South side of the Channel. **1786** *Md. Hist. Mag.* XIX. 270 There was a Channel through which Jones's falls disembogued its waters. **1823** JAMES *Exped.* I. 36 No places of anchorage for boats of heavy burden are to be found, except in the main channel of the river. **1886** DORSEY *Midshipman Bob* I. 72 There's channel enough in the Chesapeake to float heavy ships up to the sea-wall of the Academy.

+Channel bass. The redfish, *Sciæna ocellata.* — **1889** *Cent.* 921/3. **1897** *Outing* XXIX. 231/2 The channel-bass, or 'redfish,' which sometimes attains a weight of fifty pounds.

+Channel cat, cat-fish. One or other of several species of catfish found in the channels of rivers, esp. of the genus *Ictalurus.*

1836 KIRTLAND in *Ohio Geol. Survey* 169 *Pimelobus pallidus*, . . . Channel cat-fish. **1855** BAIRD in *Smithsonian Rep.* 341 The sea-cat or channel-cat was occasionally taken with the hook in the channel of the river. **1883** *Century Mag.* July 382/2 He succeeded in getting . . . a Channel Cat-fish, weighing fully ten pounds. **1897** *Outing* XXX. 439/1 What the boys called 'channel-cats' were taken from midstream by long hand-lines. **1912** I. COBB *Back Home* 5 [From a negro fishhouse] came the smell and sounds of perch and channel cat frying on spitting-hot skillets.

***Channelled,** *ppl. a.* Of pumps: Having a grooved sole. *Obs.* — **1754** *N.J. Archives* XIX. 379 [He] had on when he went away . . . leather breeches, with brass buttons, blue stockings, with single channell'd pumps.

Channel pump. *Obs.* A shoe having a groove in the sole along which it is stitched to the upper. — **1758** in *Lett. to Washington* II. 278 Six pair of the very neatest shoes (viz.) 2 pr. double Channel Pumps—2 pair turned Ditto. **1769** *Md. Hist. Mag.* XII. 280 Sam is particularly ordered to get off 2 Hours before Day with what you ordered Viz . . . 1 pre. Double Channell pumps & your Stretchers.

Channel shoe. =CHANNEL PUMP.

1762 in Chalkley *Scotch-Irish Settlement Va.* I. 328 The plaintiff was possessed of . . . one pair double channel shoes @ 15 shillings. **1874** *Harper's Wkly.* 26 Sept. 803 She wore English channel shoes. **1874** *Leslie's Illust. Newsp.* 10 Oct. 74 (Hoppe), What are English channel-shoes? Sewed shoes have the seam that unites the sole and upper sunk into a channel cut in the sole.

Channelway. A channel affording passage to a stream or to boats, etc. — **1833** *Niles' Reg.* XLIV. 394/2, I have seen channel ways of 12 and 14 feet deep, passing through these islands. **1855** BAIRD in *Smithsonian Rep.* 340 The tautog, smooth black fishes, or chub, . . . are caught off the steep banks, in the channel ways and the thoroughfares. **1862** F. Moore *Rebellion Rec.* V. II. 121 The Monitor had orders to fall back into fair channel-way. **1890** *Harper's Mag.* Sept. 598/1 Clear of the channelway the royal masts of a sloop of war tower above the loftiest of the pleasure craft.

+**Chaparajos, Chaperajos.** *S.W.* [Mexican Sp.] =CHAPARRERAS. — **1887** *Outing* X. 115/1 We had all discarded our *Chaparajos*, and the horses were lightly blanketed. **1888** ROOSEVELT in *Century Mag.* Feb. 505/2 The broad hat, huge blunt spurs, and leather *chaperajos* of the riders. **1891** *Harper's Mag.* July 204/2 The most striking part of the cowboy's rig is the chaperajos, or huge leathern overalls, he is apt to wear.

+**Chaparral.** Orig. *S.W.* Also **chaparal, chapparral, -aral, -eral, -oral, -ural; chapparrel, -arel, -erell, chaperelle.** [Sp. *chaparral*, grove of evergreen oaks, thicket, f. *chaparro, chaparra*, evergreen oak, thorny bush, etc.]

1. A dense thicket of low thorny shrubs; a piece of ground covered by brushwood.

(*a*) **1847** W. S. HENRY *Campaign Sk.* 26 We here met with the chaparrel, . . . which here means an almost impenetrable thicket of small bushes, so interlaced with a thick undergrowth, covered with thorns, that a passage through it is next to impossible. **1851** CLAPPE *Lett. from Calif.* 28 Sometimes we were compelled to cross broad plains, acres in extent, called chaparrals, covered with low shrubs. **1879** *Harper's Mag.* June 92/2 In the close chaparral the heat was intense. **1888** J. J. WEBB *Adventures* 236 He crawled into the chaparral and as soon as he was satisfied the Indians had left the vicinity, he made the best time he could for camp. **1907** MULFORD *Bar-20* 50 Half a mile beyond the point of separation was a chaparral, which was an important factor to them.

(*b*) **1845** QUITMAN *Life & Corr.* 225 We are inured to the summer sun. We have no dread of chapparals or yellow fever. **1851** *Alta Californian* 16 Nov., It was then deemed futile to enter the chapparral with so few men. **1854** BARTLETT *Personal Narr.* I. 256 The road first entered a thick chapporal of mezquit. **1873** BEADLE *Undevel. West* 819 He climbed the wall, got down outside into a ditch, reached the *chappural* [etc.].

(*c*) **1878** E. B. TUTTLE *Border Tales* 33 The most timid dropped on the ground, or ran into the chapperell to hide away, if possible, from the dreaded disaster. **1890** *Buckskin Mose* viii. 124 Pushing through the chapparel and heavy timber I had wandered on.

fig. **1870** 'MARK TWAIN' *Sketches* (1875) 153 Her hair was frizzled into a tangled chapparel. **1878** *Congress. Rec.* App. 15 June 453/2 They see in every democratic Representative upon this floor a Mexican bandit skulking in the political chaparral.

2. Close-growing, tangled or thorny shrubs such as form a chaparral.

1850 B. TAYLOR *Eldorado* (1862) x. 94 The road passed between low hills, covered with patches of chapparal. **1853** *Harper's Mag.* VII. 333/2 Get the mules together, and drive them up to that little patch of chapperal, while we follow with the Indian. **1857** *Recoll. West. Texas* 51 The mule . . . thrust his head into a cluster of chaperelle that grew in the centre of the level and interminable solitude. **1868** I. SAXON *5 Years* 105 The Road . . . crosses continuous undulating sandhills, partially covered with 'chapparel,' of which poison-oak forms a principal shrub. **1873** MILLER *Amongst Modocs* 273 The ground was . . . covered with a thick growth of black stiff chaparral. **1881** *Rep. Indians Affairs* 161 The tribes under my supervision [are] . . . located at the extreme northwest point of the United States, . . . with an almost impenetrable barrier of timber and chaparral on the east and south. **1910** J. HART *Vigilante Girl* 325 On the mountains was a scanty growth of greasewood, scrub, and chaparral.

b. With defining terms.

1854 BARTLETT *Personal Narr.* II. 350 We returned while we could see to find our way back through the thick mezquit chapporal. **1872** 'MARK TWAIN' *Roughing It* xxiii, In a minute and a half the fire seized upon a dense growth of dry manzanita chapparal six or eight feet high.

3. Attrib. and comb. with *berry, bush, leaf, thicket; -crested, -walled.*

1920 HUNTER *Trail Drivers Texas* I. 134, I walked all day with nothing to eat but chapparal berries. **1887** CUSTER *Tenting on Plains* vi. 204 The chapparral bushes defeated us frequently, by making such good hiding-places for the hare. **1904** 'O. HENRY' *Heart of West* 190 A few kids walked the top of it [=a brush corral], nibbling the chaparral leaves. **1897** *Outing* XXX. 243/2 Sometimes the chapparal thickets made a wall of green on each side. — **1871** HARTE *Luck of Roaring Camp* 60 The going down of the sun behind the chaparral-crested mountain. **1883** *Century Mag.* Oct. 819/1 The soft, chaparral-walled cañons would, in some lights, press them hard for supremacy of place.

+**Chaparral cock.** [CHAPARRAL.] A species of cuckoo (*Geococcyx californianus*) native in the Southwest.

1858 BAIRD *Birds Pacific R. R.* 73 A single species known as the Paisano, Chapparal Cock, or sometimes Road Runner, on account of its frequenting public highways. **1881** *Amer. Naturalist* XV. 218 Another bird peculiar to this fauna is the chapparal cock or road-runner. **1898** H. S. CANFIELD *Maid of Frontier* 93 The chaparral cock, with tufted head, darted uneasily in and out of the undergrowth. **1907** MULFORD *Bar-20* 226 A chaparral cock strutted from its decapitated enemy, a rattlesnake, and disappeared in the chaparral. **1917** *Birds of Amer.* II. 126 Road-runner, *Geococcyx californianus*. Other names [include] Ground Cuckoo; Chaparral Cock; Snake Killer; [etc.].

+**Chaparral tea.** (See quotation.) — **1885** HAVARD *Flora W. & S. Texas* 514 Encenilla; Chaparral Tea. . . . An infusion of the flowering tops, either green or dried, makes excellent tea.

+**Chaparras, -arros,** reduced forms of CHAPARRERAS. — **1889** FARMER 133/1 *Chaparajos* or *Chaparro[s]*, trousers made of stout leather [etc.]. **1895** REMINGTON *Pony Tracks* 79 Mr. Johnnie Bell . . . was walking about in his heavy *chaparras*, a slouch hat, and a white 'biled' shirt.

+**Chaparreras.** *S.W.* Also **-araras, -ar(r)eros.** [Mexican Sp. *chaparreras*, f. *chaparro:* see CHAPARRAS and cf. CHAPARAJOS.] Leather trousers worn to protect the legs while riding through chaparral. — **1865** *Atlantic Mo.* XV. 61 Don had insisted on my assuming . . . Mexican riding-costume: cool linen drawers, cut Turkish fashion; over these . . . the leathern chapareros or overalls. **1902** WISTER *Virginian* xi. 130 The fringed leathern chaparreros, the cartridge belt, the flannel shirt . . . were now an old story to her. **a1909** 'O. HENRY' *Roads of Destiny* 95 Lonny is one of them, a knight of stirrup and chaparreras.

Chapbook. A small popular book of the kind sold by itinerant chapmen. {1824-} Also attrib. — **1798** WEEMS *Letters* II. 96 By Guthrie's Geography alone you might have made more in twelve months, than you will clear in five years peddling with shabby almanacs & chap Books. **1809** *Ib.* 412 In consequence of your suffering nearly the whole of the Children & Chap book business to be monopoliz'd by Friend Johnson, he is now underselling all the Trade.

***Chapel.**

***1.** A place of worship, usually of small size, and belonging to a particular religious denomination.

1705 BEVERLEY *Virginia* IV. 26 In these Chappels the Minister preaches alternately. **1765** R. ROGERS *Acc. N. America* 46 The town of Portsmouth . . . contains . . . four meeting-houses and a chapel. **1883** *Century Mag.* Aug. 519/2 The Catholic priest . . . goes there three or four Sundays in a year, to hold service in a little adobe chapel. **1905** E. W. PRINGLE *Rice Planter* 178 Our little chapel, Prince Frederick's Pee Dee, is beautifully wreathed with wild flowers and vines.

***b.** *Chapel of ease*, a chapel built for the use of those living at a distance from the parish church. *Obs.* {Still in use}

1701 *N.C. Col. Rec.* I. 544 Ordered that the Inhabitants of the So West Shore, build a Chappel of Ease on their Shore. **1708** *Ib.* 681 The people . . . have resolved forthwith to build a church and two chapels of ease. **1726** *Md. Hist. Mag.* VII. 282 Motioned to this Vestry . . . that a Chappell of Ease be Carried on. **1757** in Chalkley *Scotch-Irish Settlement Va.* II. 445 [It is] unnecessary to build a chapel of ease there.

c. *King's* or *Queen's Chapel:* (see quotations). *Obs.*

1712 *N.J. Archives* 1 Ser. IV. 162 The Representer . . . persists in his former opinion to call the Queens Chapel in the Fort . . . by that hard name. **1728** *Mass. H. S. Coll.* 4 Ser. II. 179, A letter concerning some late divisions we have had in our church called the King's chapel.

***2.** The building, hall, or room in a university, college, or school, in which religious services are held; also, the service itself.

1790 *Harvard Laws* 12 If any Undergraduate shall come unseasonably to any of the public lectures in the chapel, he shall be fined two pence. **1818** *N. Amer. Rev.* March 426 The members of the College attend prayers and the reading of the Scriptures in the Chapel every morning and evening. **1827** *Harvard Reg.* Sept. 202 We hurry to the Chapel, and then crowd to the recitation room. **1835** B. D. WINSLOW *[Harvard] Class Poem* 10 For this behold him some ten minutes wait To come to Commons Hall or Chapel late. **1871** BAGG *At Yale* 43 *Chapel*, religious services which must be attended in that building. **1902** G. M. MARTIN *Emmy Lou* 196 At Grammar School, classes attend chapel.

***3.** A room in a house set apart for worship.

1867 PEYTON *Adv. Grandfather* 171 In every old Virginian mansion, a room was fitted up for private devotion, called the chapel.

4. Attrib. with *bell, church, exercise, expense, goer, house.*

1836 *Harvardiana* II. 199 The cracked chapel bell . . . was summoning him . . . to his morning devotions. **1877** PHELPS *Avis* 298 Once I went to the chapel-church to see you. **1902** G. M. MARTIN *Emmy Lou* 197 The Principal who conducted Chapel Exercises called him William. **1803** in *Ann. 8th Congress* 2 Sess. 1519 Those salaries, except that of the bishop, together with an allowance for sacristans and chapel expenses, are paid by the Treasury at New Orleans. **1893** W. K. POST *Harvard Stories* 84 Blathers always got out with the nine o'clock lecture men and chapel goers. **1643** *Md. Archives* IV. 263 The Leiuten[an]t grall . . . tendred to Capt. Tho Cornwaleys the chappell house w[i]th appurtenances.

∗ **Chaplain.**

∗ **1.** A clergyman discharging religious duties in the household of an official or other person. *Obs.*

1686 SEWALL *Diary* I. 139 A great Wedding from Milton, and are married by Mr. Randolph's Chaplain. **1697** *Ib.* 461 Mr. Saml Mather is the Chaplain.

2. A clergyman appointed to conduct religious services, or discharge other clerical functions, in the army, navy, an institution, legislative body, etc. {1727–}

1704 *Boston News-Letter* 31 July 2/2 On the 22d. the Rd. Mr. Mott, Chaplain to the Forces here died. **1789** *Ann. 1st Congress* I. 19 The committee . . . reported: That two Chaplains, of different denominations, be appointed to Congress for the present session. **1827** *Western Mo. Rev.* I. 503 The senate of Kentucky, in its present session, has voted to elect a chaplain. **1874** GLISAN *Jrnl. Army Life* 461 The majority of frontier posts have no Chaplain. **1892** M. A. JACKSON *Memoirs* 49 The chaplain of the garrison was Rev. Mr. Parks.

Chaplaincy. The office of chaplain. {*a*1745–} — **1824** *Baptist Mag.* IV. 394 He was afterwards promoted to a brigade chaplaincy on the continental establishment. **1846** POLK *Diary* (1929) 157 Mr. Leiper, giving him a good character and recommending him for a Chaplaincy.

∗ **Chapman.**

∗ **1.** A buyer or purchaser; a customer. *Obs.* {–1807}

1634 J. ENDECOTT in *Winthrop P.* 131 Thomas Read . . . is now in England to finde out a chapman if hee can. **1664** *Springfield Rec.* II. 55 No Inhabitant shall sell . . . his house lott or any part of it . . . before he hath made the Select Townsmen acquaynted who his Chapman is. **1704** J. LOGAN in *Penna. Hist. Soc. Mem.* IX. 290 Of the manor we may reserve a piece, unless some chapman would buy the whole. **1792** BRACKENRIDGE *Adv. Capt. Farrago* xv. 69, I have sent for you to give you a hint of this chapman, that you may have a knowledge of his wish to possess the property. **1830** COOPER *Water Witch* I. xi, The Yankees will find others than the Mohawks for chapmen. **1845** JUDD *Margaret* II. xii. 380 When multitudes deserted the city, he became chapman of their estates.

∗ **2.** An itinerant vendor; a peddler.

1771 FRANKLIN *Autobiog.* 238 They were small chapmen's books, and cheap. **1775** *Amherst Rec.* 67 A Resolve of the Provincial Congress . . . to suppress all Pedlars & Petty Chapmen.

+**Chapote.** *S.W.* [Mex. Sp. *sapote, zapote,* Nahuatl *tzapotl.*] The black persimmon. — **1884** SARGENT *Rep. Forests* 105 *Diospyros Texana.* . . . Black Persimmon. Mexican Persimmon. Chapote. **1885** HAVARD *Flora W. & S. Texas* 523 Mexican Persimmon; the Chapote of the Mexicans. Shrub or small tree 10 to 20 feet high.

+**Chaps.** Colloq. abbreviation of CHAPARAJOS or CHAPARRERAS. (See also SHAPS.)

1884 NYE *Baled Hay* 139 'Chaps,' as they are vulgarly called, . . . are made of leather with fronts of dog-skin with the hair on. . . . The seat of the garment has been postponed *sine die.* **1887** *Scribner's Mag.* Oct. 511 When they ride through a country hedged with impenetrable thicket . . . it is necessary to don their *chaps* . . . , which are trousers made of stout leather, and stitched with leather cording. **1891** *Harper's Mag.* Dec. 36/1 It was still possible for me to see in some tents the squaws at work . . . making bead-work for moccasins, pouches, 'chaps,' and the rest. **1908** MULFORD *Orphan* 18 He wore . . . the indispensable chaps, which were of angora goatskin.

∗ **Chapter.** +A branch of an organization or society, esp. of a college fraternity.

1815 DRAKE *Cincinnati* 166 A Chapter of Royal Arch Masons was established in this place. **1847** *Cat. Harvard Chapter ΦBK* (1912) 168 A petition . . . presented from certain members of the graduating class at Amherst College, praying for the establishment of a Chapter of the ΦBK Society in that institution. **1871** BAGG *At Yale* 55 Sigma Eps at Yale, calling itself the 'Kappa' chapter, established a branch 'Alpha' chapter at Amherst. **1882** *Alpha Delta Phi* p. xxv, This meeting [in 1836] after formally adopting the word 'Chapter,' and disapproving of the words 'club' and 'branch,' passed a series of resolutions. **1887** *Lippincott's Mag.* Nov. 739 These are houses owned by the Amherst chapters of the various Greek fraternities. **1905** N. DAVIS *Northerner* 4 The Daughters of the Confederacy, the local chapter, are to present what they call 'The Southern Cross of Honor.'

attrib. **1851** CIST *Cincinnati* 160 The furniture of the chapter room is of mahogany.

Chaptered, *a.* [f. prec.] +Having chapters in different localities. — **1871** BAGG *At Yale* 110 There are other important chaptered fraternities existing in American colleges.

∗**Chapter house.** +The building or room used as a meeting place or clubhouse by a college fraternity. — **1888** *Century Mag.* XXXVI. 755/1 The wealthy chapter-houses of the East are furnished with all the luxury and refined taste of the highest modern art. **1899** QUINN *Penna. Stories* 177 He could come back at any time . . . to his Chapter-house.

Char. {1662–} +The brook trout (*Salvelinus fontinalis*) or other species related to the European char. — **1805** CLARK in *Lewis & C. Exped.* (1904) III. 215 Five Indians came down in a canoe loaded with fish of salmon spes. called *Red Charr.* **1839** TOWNSEND *Narrative* 199 Trout, grayling, and a kind of char are very abundant here. **1842** *Nat. Hist. N.Y., Zoology* IV. 235 The Brook Trout. *Salmo fontinalis.* New York Char. **1889** *Cent.* 926/3 The American char nearest the European is known as the Rangeley lake (in Maine) trout, *Salvelinus oquassa.*

∗ **Character.**

1. A person or personage, esp. one of some distinction. *Obs.* {1749–, with adjs.}

1666 *Md. Archives* II. 16 There is a Law . . . that whosoever shall kill a Man shall dye for it, & so for other agreements either with red or white Characters. **1786** JEFFERSON *Writings* V. 328 The first character among the American merchants in Scotland. **1793** B. LINCOLN in *Mass. H. S. Coll.* 3 Ser. V. 120 They lost, among others, ten or twelve of their chiefs or first characters. **1809** *Ann. 10th Congress* 2 Sess. 1372 The gentleman from Connecticut, a Revolutionary character, . . . called upon us.

2. An odd or peculiar person; one of an unusual or original type. {1773–}

1831 PECK *Guide* 66 The most of the intemperance to be found [in New Orleans] . . . is to be found among the half horse, half alligator characters that come down the river. **1848** *Knickerb.* XXXI. 178 We stumbled on 'a character'; one of those geniuses that hang about stables. **1868** I. SAXON *5 Years* 145 The 'character' in question was an individual known by the familiar title of 'Uncle Freddy.' **1888** *Harper's Mag.* Oct. 678/1 Among the latter were many of the so-called 'characters' who . . . made for the West its popular reputation.

∗ **Charcoal.** Also †**charcole.**

1. The black substance left as a solid residue after the imperfect combustion of wood, bones, or similar matter.

1650 *Conn. Public Rec.* I. 526 Whosoeuer shall wittingly and willingly burne or destroy any . . . heapes of wood, charcoale, . . . pitch or tarr, hee shall pay double dammages. **1673** *York Deeds* III. 92 John Lambs Landing place where hee burned Char Coales. **1701** *Boston Rec.* 10 This order shall not be understood . . . to debarr . . . any tradesmen or others from kindling charcole in a pot or pan out of doors. **1805** LEWIS in *L. & Clark Exped.* (1904) II. 212, I then set a couple of men to pounding of charcoal to form a composition with some beeswax which we have and buffaloe tallow. **1863** CUMMING *Hospital Life* (1866) 118/1 We are using a great deal of charcoal on the wounds. **1881** *Rep. Indian Affairs* 81 The Indians have also manufactured all the charcoal used in the blacksmith shop.

+**b.** *fig.* (See quotations.)

*a*1862 *Exchange Paper* (B., p. 397), The members of the [Missouri] Legislature are divided into Charcoals, Clay-banks, White-legs, [etc.]. . . . The 'Charcoal' believes slavery a moral enormity. **1915** W. B. STEVENS *Missouri* I. 40 The Union men of Missouri divided sharply in 1862 upon the question of freeing the slaves. . . . The Charcoals were for immediate emancipation.

2. Attrib. with *bloom, cart, fire, furnace,* etc.

1886 Z. F. SMITH *Kentucky* 505 These became well known . . . for the superior charcoal bloom of the latter [furnace]. **1850** C. MATHEWS *Moneypenny* 72 A horse can pick up any thing worth knowing . . . in a charcoal cart. **1723** *New-Eng. Courant* 22–29 April 2/1 Two Men and a Boy . . . made some Charcoal Fires in the Hold to dry it. **1851** CIST *Cincinnati* 193 They also make . . . charcoal furnaces. **1836** *Knickerb.* VIII. 71 Speaking of the last trumpet, makes me remember the reply of a veteran old charcoal man. **1873** BAILEY *Life in Danbury* 244 A demure-looking chap hailed a charcoal pedler. **1869** J. R. BROWNE *Adv. Apache Country* 203 The smoke of many charcoal pits filled the air. **1898** *Voice* (N.Y.) 6 Jan. 5/2 Three or four antiseptic charcoal tablets, taken after each meal.

Charcoal basket. *Obs.* A basket used as a recognized measure in selling charcoal. — **1772** *Boston Selectmen* 7 Sept. 143 Orders . . . [were] given to mr. Ephraim Vaux . . . for the examining of Charcoal Baskets. **1813** *Ib.* 20 Jan. 82 Mr. Nathaniel Brewer was appointed to measure charcoal baskets used in this Town by the sellers of that article.

Charcoal burner. One who makes charcoal. {1841–}

1825 NEAL *Bro. Jonathan* II. 71, I mistook them at first for charcoal-burners. **1839** HOFFMAN *Wild Scenes* 28 The demolition of the pine forests . . . will rapidly . . . convert the lumber-men and charcoal-burners into farmers. **1875** *Amer. Naturalist* IX. 9 Old charcoal burners in the Pines entertain the belief that the pinesnake destroys the rattlesnake. **1880** *Harper's Mag.* Aug. 355/2 They rode up the nearly perpendicular wagon-trails left by charcoal-burners. **1905** VALENTINE *H. Sandwith* 178 Work among the wood-cutters and charcoal-burners . . . took him on rides.

Charcoal iron. Iron containing a certain percentage of carbon. {1858} Also in combination. — **1871** W. M. GROSVENOR *Protection* 214 The quantity of charcoal-iron . . . then declined, so that the aggregate production of 1848 cannot have been materially greater. *Ib.* 224 In the States of Pennsylvania, Virginia, Maryland, and New Jersey, charcoal-iron makers were prostrated.

Charcoalman. {1697–} A charcoal peddler. — **1876** *Wide Awake* 85/1 Once in five minutes or so, the charcoal-man would cry out, 'Charcoal!'

+**Charcoal road.** A road made of pieces of wood covered with dirt and straw and fired. — **1850** *New Eng. Farmer* n. s. II. 240/2 We had an opportunity last week of passing over a portion of the charcoal road between this place and Oconomowoc.

Charge, *v. Library.* +*tr.* To make a record of (the lending of a book). — **1893** *Library Bureau Catalog* 95 Call Slips. Plain manilla, white or colored paper, cut into small slips, . . . used for charging loans, memo., etc. **1910** A. E. BOSTWICK *Amer. Pub. Library* 41 Having chosen his books, . . . the user next presents them at the desk to be charged.

1925 Arnett *Elements of Library Methods* 165 This method of charging books is known as the Newark system.

Chargé. (Ellipt. for next.) — 1857 Olmsted *Texas* (1861) 17 As we left, we met Mr. James Clay, once *chargé* to Portugal. 1876 Bancroft *Hist.* (rev. ed.) IV. 328 Garnier, 'the extremely intelligent' French chargé.

Chargé d'affaires. Also †**des affaires.** [F.] A member of the diplomatic service at a foreign court who directs affairs in the absence of the ambassador or minister; a diplomatic representative sent to a country in place of one of higher rank. {1768–}

(*a*) 1783 J. Adams *Wks.* (1853) VIII. 130 In conversation yesterday with M. d'Asp, the *chargé des affaires* in Sweden. 1789 *Ann. 1st Congress* I. 94 They confirmed the appointment of William Carmichael, as Chargé des Affaires from the United States of America to the Court of Spain. 1819 *U.S. Statutes* III. 501 The chargé des affaires at London, the Hague and Stockholm.

(*b*) 1789 Maclay *Deb. Senate* 84 Some of them were entangled about the secretary of the legation and the chargé d'affaires, not knowing a distinction. 1832 Jackson in *Mess. & P.* II. 564 My ratification having been exchanged in due form . . . by our chargé d'affaires at Constantinople. 1845 Polk *Diary* (1929) 11 Andrew J. Donelson, Esquire, late chargé d'affaires to Texas, visited the President today. 1854 Benton *30 Years' View* I. 569/2 The President had . . . instructed the United States' *chargé d'affaires* to demand the money. 1915 *Statutes at Large* 805 For such time as any secretary of embassy . . . shall be . . . authorized to act as chargé d'affaires ad interim . . . , he shall be entitled to receive . . . compensation.

* **Charger. a.** An attachment to a powder flask, or a separate device, for measuring the charge of powder for a fire arm. {*a*1711–}. **b.** 'A device for dropping into the base of a fowling-piece from a shot-belt or pouch a gaged quantity of shot' (Knight).

1837 A. Wetmore *Gaz. Missouri* 325 We made a few powder-horns, and highly-finished 'chargers,' and new wiping-sticks. 1841 Cooper *Deerslayer* vii, With a hunter's habits, his hands were mechanically feeling for the powder-horn and charger. 1855 Simms *Forayers* 170 First you put in the powder, you know—there's the little charger—then the wadding, and then the bullet. 1868 W. Baker *New Timothy* (1870) 119 Beneath the heavy tangle of shot-pouches, and powder-flask, and dangling chargers of antelope-horn, and the like. 1874 Long *Wild-Fowl* 37 A quick-loading flask, *i.e.*, one having a large feed-hole to the charger, should also be used.

+**Chargéship.** [Chargé.] The office or appointment of chargé d'affaires.

1830 Mackenzie *Life Van Buren* (1846) 260 A Senator high in his confidence pressed me to accept the Charge-ship to Sweden at Somerville's death. 1855 Hawthorne in H. Bridge *Personal Recoll.* (1893) 148 The office [is still] . . . a mere chargé-ship with only $4500 salary. 1858 Lincoln in Logan *Great Conspiracy* 74 They have seen in his round . . . face, . . . Marshalships, and Cabinet appointments, Chargéships and Foreign Missions.

* **Chariot.**

1. A light four-wheeled carriage with only back seats. {1661–1838} Also transf.

1708 Sewall *Diary* II. 229 The Gov[erno]r met me at my Sons Gate and carried me in his Chariot to Cambridge. 1760 Washington *Diaries* I. 107 Mrs. Barnes . . . yesterday returned home in my Chariot, the weather being too bad to travel in an open Carriage. 1836 *S. Lit. Messenger* I. 542 In a short time the Chalgrave chariot . . . brought the glad tidings of my return to the home of my fathers. 1893 Post *Harvard Stories* 55 Riley . . . had his chariot at the door of Rattleton's staircase.

b. Attrib. with *horse.*

1783 *Essex Inst. Coll.* III. 163, I also give her my Chariot and two Chariot Horses. 1786 Washington *Diaries* III. 3, I also directed my Chariot Horses . . . to be fed with Bran and chopped Hay. 1836 *S. Lit. Messenger* II. 161 The chariot horses Mass Charles sent to the court house.

***2.** A conveyance for transporting goods. {–1693}

1849 *Pres. Mess. Congress* II. 460 [The copper ore] is sent down on a chariot which runs upon a tram-road to the platform.

+**Chariotee.** [Chariot 1.] A light four-wheeled carriage having two seats and a top. — 1825 *Catawba Journal* 17 May, A coachee, chariotee, phaeton, panneled and stick gigs [etc.]. 1867 'Lackland' *Homespun* I. 50 An open wagon, set on the old-fashion 'thorough-braces,' comes as near to a coupé, chariotee, or barouche as you can ordinarily discover.

Charioteer. {1667–} The driver of a chariot (in sense 1). *Obs.* — 1719 Sewall *Diary* III. 230 Gave Judith Hale, Mary Elithrop, the Negro Main, and Negro Charioteer 5s each.

* **Charitable,** *a.* Founded or organized for charitable purposes {1655–}, esp. +*charitable society.*

1792 N. Webster in Ford *Notes* I. 362 Forming a Constitution for a Charitable Society. *Ib.*, At evening a number of Gentlemen convened at the Court House & formed themselves into a 'Charitable Society.' 1796 *Ann. 4th Congress* 2 Sess. 2696 Property belonging to religious or charitable societies, cities, or free schools, is altogether exempted. 1820 Flint *Lett. from Amer.* 214 Cincinnati has . . . two Bible societies; two tract societies, . . . and three charitable societies. 1823 *Amer. Baptist Mag.* IV. 180/1 Massachusetts Baptist Charitable Society, for the relief of the Widows and children of deceased Baptist Ministers. 1839 A. Lawrence *Diary & Corr.* 172, I will give to the Charitable Mechanic Association ten thousand dollars. 1865 *Atlantic Mo.* XV. 613 Any charitable institutions where orphan children are taken in and cared for. 1898 Page *Red Rock* 271 She has had some correspondence with him on behalf of her charitable society for the freedmen.

* **Charity.** Used attrib. in sense: Connected with, devoted to, or supported by charity. {1711–}

The following are early examples of this use, which becomes common after 1860.

1724 *Essex Inst. Coll.* XXXVI. 333 Charity Meeting at night. 1766 *Harvard Rec.* II. 858 The Money in & belonging to my charity Bag, I wou'd have dispos'd of, to Charitable Uses. 1775 *N.H. Hist. Soc. Coll.* IX. 86 The College Improvements here will hence forward . . . Support 30 Charity Schollars excepting their Cloathing. 1787 Washington *Diaries* III. 217 Accompanied Mrs. and some other ladies to hear a Mrs. O'Connell read (a charity affair). 1793 Bentley *Diary* II. 5 There was provision made in the Charity house [at Salem] for a good dinner of excellent chosen beef & plumb puddings. 1822 *Missionary Herald* XVIII. 19 Donations. . . . A charity student, avails of labour, $1.44. *Ib.* 51 From a charity box . . . 5.00. 1852 *Knickerb.* XL. 202 They are just now going to dispose of last night's dead from the charity-hospital.

Charity school. A school established or maintained for the purpose of providing free or cheap education for poor children. {1682–}

1710 C. Mather *Diary* II. 24, I would sett up a Charity-School, and make it a precious opportunity of good unto many children. *Ib.* 379 A Charity-School, for Negros in evenings. 1712 *Boston Rec.* 94 The gentlemen that are about to erect a Charity School, or Hospitall for poor children. 1752 *Penna. Gazette* 26 Oct. 1/3 The Charity-school, opened by the Trustees in the Academy, now teaches Reading, Writing and Arithmetic to a Hundred poor children. 1767 *N.H. Hist. Soc. Coll.* IX. 72, I received £54 Lawful money from your Hand as a Charitable Donation to the Indian Charity School. 1817 *N. Amer. Rev.* V. 314 New Bedford . . . contains also . . . a charity school for the education of eighty two children. 1833 *Niles' Reg.* XLIV. 3/1 The whole number of students . . . [in] charity (English) schools [of the University of Pa. was] 164. 1887 'Pansy' *Little Fishers* viii, 'I have heard of them,' said Lorena Barstow. 'They are sort of charity schools, are they not?'

Charivari, *n.* Also **chara-.** [F.] A disorderly demonstration, accompanied by discordant music, esp. as an expression of popular disapproval of some person or persons, or on the occasion of a wedding. {1735–}

Also in various popular forms, as *sherrivarrie, chivaree, shiveree.*

1843 *Knickerb.* XXI. 45 There is a pleasant custom . . . that is nowhere more duly observed than at Idleberg. I refer to the *charavari.* *a*1851 in Hall *College Words* 317 The wildest of the College boys . . . are always on hand when a wedding is to take place, and join in a most tremendous Charivari. 1879 Cable *Creole Days* (1903) 203 There is a respectable difference . . . between a mob and a charivari. 1889 *Amer. Notes & Q.* IV. 81 The neighbor was engaged in giving him what is called in the despatches a 'charivari,' but is more idiomatically known in some of the rural parts of our country as a 'horning.'

‖**Charivari,** *v.* [f. prec.] *tr.* To annoy with a charivari. — 1900 Smithwick *Evol. State* 72 The boys went . . . to *charivari* them. 1910 J. Hart *Vigilante Girl* 326 The head of the procession . . . was a drabbled and weeping trollop who was being 'chivareed' out of town.

+**Charlestonian.** A native of Charleston, S.C.

1835 H. C. Todd *Notes* 12 The Charlestonians . . . neither encouraged, nor ever forgave this new species of traffic. 1854 Simms *Southward Ho* 5 You Charlestonians are such braggers. 1857 *Harper's Mag.* June 3/1 It is a present project with the Charlestonians . . . to dredge this channel. 1888 *Century Mag.* XXXVI. 279/1, I assure you he does not use the stately anathemas of the Charlestonian or Savannese. 1905 N. Davis *Northerner* 56 Nothing short of the old Charlestonians, and the angels right next the throne were included within that sacred pale.

Charley. *Obs. slang.* A night watchman. {1812–56} — 1805 *Mass. Spy* 20 Feb. (Th.), I will be upon the spot As punctual as 'Charley.' 1840 *Picayune* 23 Sept. 2/2 The Charlies . . . [are] the d—dest kind of fellows for nabbing chaps like you wot stay out late at night. 1846 Corcoran *Pickings* 50 One Yankee looking policeman . . . was making a rough draft, with his pencil, of a 'Charley on duty.'

***Charlock.** [Cf. Chadlock.] The wild mustard or wild radish. — 1754 Eliot *Field-Husb.* v. 104 Charlock, commonly called Terrify, . . . may be effectually conquered. 1817–8 Eaton *Botany* (1822) 425 *Raphanus raphanistrum*, wild raddish, charlock. . . . It may have been introduced; but it is now growing wild in all the middle and southern towns of the western counties of Massachusetts. 1884 *Dept. Agric. Rep.* 317 The Cabbage Aphis occurs commonly on the turnip, radish, field cress . . . , shepherd's purse . . . , and charlock.

Charlotte russe. A dish made up of custard or whipped cream inclosed in spongecake. {1855–} — 1856 *Spirit of Times* 6 Dec. 224/3 One [man] was to be eating a Charlotte Russe. 1861 *Vanity Fair* 16 Feb. 73/1 Mrs. Blummerie . . . always gives me sponge-cake, and Charlotte-russe and chocolate-ice. 1893 Crane *Maggie* (1896) 122 [He] insisted upon her having a charlotte russe and a glass of beer.

Charret. Obs. variant of CHARIOT. — **1712** SEWALL *Diary* II. 361 Proceeded and waited on Madam Dudley in her Charret to Brooklin.

***Charter,** *n.*

1. One or other of the formal documents by which the British sovereigns granted certain rights and privileges to the American colonies.

[**1647** in Winthrop *Hist.* II. 337 Shaomett, and the other parts of that tract of land, which is mentioned in a charter of civil incorporation heretofore granted them by us.] **1669** *Md. Archives* II. 159 Then was sent to the lower howse the coppy of the lord Prop[rieto]rs Charter. **1707** SEWALL *Diary* II. 207 The governour . . . Reads a Letter of Mr. Bridger complaining of Trees cut contrary to Charter. **1776** *Declar. Independence,* For taking away our charters, abolishing our most valuable laws, and altering fundamentally the forms of our governments.

***2.** A formal document or deed, issued by a competent authority, incorporating, or embodying the constitution of, a borough, college, company, etc.

1708 *Boston Rec.* 55 The said Selectmen do therefore propose that this Town do now Chuse a Committee . . . to draw up a Scheme or draught of a Charter of Incorporation. **1759** *N.H. Hist. Soc. Coll.* IX. 39 A Committee chosen last year to prefer a Petition to His Excellency the Governor, for a Charter of a College in this Province. **1816** *Ann. 14th Congress* 2 Sess. 346 A bill to extend the charters of certain banks in the District of Columbia. **1831** BENTON *30 Years' View* (1854) I. 195/2, I recur to a provision contained in two different clauses in the bank charter. **1888** BRYCE *Amer. Commw.* II. II. 263 *n.*, The constitution or frame of government of a city, which is always given by a State statute, general or special, is called its charter.

3. Attrib. with *claim, government, governor, privilege, right, time.*

1781 PETERS *Conn.* (1829) 46 The prevarications of the Colonists themselves in regard to their charter-claim, sufficiently exploded it. **1706** *N.C. Col. Rec.* I. 631 In most of these Proprietary and Charter (vizt. Connecticut and Rhode Island) Governments the Governors have not applyed themselves to your Majesty. **1767** HUTCHINSON *Hist. Mass.* (1768) II. 13 Thereupon the venerable charter governor Bradstreet resigned the chair. **1721** *Boston Rec.* 157 Be not deterred by any frowns or threats from maintaining what in you lyes our Charter Priviledges. **1774** J. T. Buckingham *Newspaper Lit.* I. 194, I will, as much as in me lies, maintain the Charter Rights and Liberties of this Province. **1832** WILLIAMSON *Maine* II. 11 He is not known to have been a member of the Board [of Assistants] after his charter-time expired.

Charter, *v.*

1. *tr.* To furnish with, establish by, a charter. {1800–}

1841 F. WOOD in MacLeod *Biog.* 91 Go on—pass this bill—charter your bank—fasten this iniquity upon the country. **1851** CIST *Cincinnati* 112 Medical College of Ohio. This Institution was first chartered, and placed in the hands of a Board of Trustees, in 1819. **1852** A. LAWRENCE *Diary & Corr.* 328 The seceders from Williams College petitioned to be chartered as Amherst College.

2. To hire or engage (a vehicle). {1869–}

1842 BUCKINGHAM *Slave States* I. 187 We had to take the stage-coach, and were fortunately able to engage the whole of it for our party, or to 'charter' it, as the expression is here [in Ga.]. **1847** FIELD *Drama in Pokerville,* etc. 73 Every horse and every vehicle was chartered for the afternoon.

Chartered, *ppl. a.* [CHARTER *v.*]

1. Established or guaranteed by charter. {1780–}

1775 TRUMBULL *M'Fingal* (1785) I. 43 Affirm'd he never wrote a line Your charter'd rights to undermine. **1788** *Steele Papers* I. 21 Lands allotted to them for hunting grounds within the chartered limits of this State. **1816** U. BROWN *Journal* II. 357 No paper can be received except Virginia Charter'd paper unless Pennsylvania & Maryland Chartered paper at 10 pr Cent Discount. **1850** *Western Journal* IV. 217 Our present banking law is an improvement upon the old, or the chartered bank system.

‖**2.** (See quotation.)

1853 *Weekly Advertiser* (Fredericksburg, Va.) 12 Feb. 1/2 The half-breeds, loafers and 'chartered fighters,' as they called themselves, held a caucus.

+Charter election. [CHARTER *n.* 2.] An election held in accordance with the charter of a city or borough.

1834 P. HONE *Diary* I. 94 Our only hope lies in the elections in New York and Pennsylvania, particularly our charter election. **1834** *Knickerb.* IV. 119 Ladies in New-York, at the time of the late charter election, . . . were not allowed to vote. **1838** *N.Y. Advertiser & Exp.* 7 April 2/1 'The Charter Election' in the city of Schenectady, resulted yesterday, in a glorious triumph for the Whigs. **1855** F. WOOD in MacLeod *Biog.* 200, I look upon spring charter elections as essential to the well-being of this city [New York]. **1900** C. WINCHESTER *W. Castle* 209 At the next charter election, after the revival, a live Christian man was elected Mayor.

+Charter Oak.

1. The oak at Hartford, Conn., in which the charter of the Colony of Connecticut was believed to have been hidden in 1687. Hence *Charter Oak City,* Hartford.

1836 REED & MATHESON *Visit* I. 316 There is shown here as a great curiosity what is called the Charter Oak. **1868** BEECHER *Norwood* 327 What of that famous Boston Common Elm, which is to Massachusetts what the Charter Oak was to Connecticut? **1871** DE VERE 663 Hartford . . . derives the name of Charter Oak City, from a large oak-tree, now no longer in existence [etc.].

2. *Charter Oak grape:* (see quot. 1856).

1849 *New Eng. Farmer* I. 320 Any information from Mr. C., concerning the Charter Oak grape, will be very acceptable. **1852** *Horticulturist* VII. 417 On the narrow bottoms . . . grow thousands of wild grapes . . . with pulp as hard and indigestible as bullets; and this new 'Charter Oak' grape . . . is one of the same unadulterated type. **1856** *Rep. Comm. Patents: Agric.* 308 Several gentlemen, of this vicinity, have vines of the 'Charter Oak' grape, said to be a native of Connecticut, the fruit of which grows almost as large as a plum.

***Charter party.** The indenture made between the merchant and the owner for the hire of a ship.

*a***1656** BRADFORD *Hist.* 343 The bills of sale, or charterparties, were taken in their owne names. **1709** *Boston News-Letter* 28 March 2/2 Bonds, Bills, Indentures, Charter-parties, &c. are Drawn; and Youth Boarded, in Cross-street, Boston. **1796** *State P.* (1819) III. 48 The demand of the freight, agreeable to the charter party signed by Mr. Fauchet, has been long since, and remains, with the commission of commerce. **1839** *Diplom. Corr. Texas* (1908) I. 433 The goods delivered to sd Maynard all in good order, according to the tenor of the charter party. **1848** E. BRYANT *California* 340 Demurrage at the rate of twenty-five cents per hour for all delays ordered by the charter-party. **1889** *Cent.* 933/3 [A] charter-party . . . usually contains stipulations concerning the places of loading and delivering, and the rate of demurrage.

Chase lane. *Obs.* Also **chasse, chast.** [E. Anglian and Essex dial. *chase* (1804), Norman F. dial. *chasse.*] A narrow lane or byroad. — **1639** *Conn. Hist. Soc. Coll.* XIV. 331 A Chasse lane leading from the litle Riuer to the meeting house [at Hartford]. **1685** *Ib.* XIV. 366 The chase lane leading from the Meeting house to the litle riuer. **1692** *Ib.* XIV. 355 Sayd parcell of land containeth three acres . . . & abutteth . . . on the east by a Chast lane or alley.

Chase way. *Obs.* Also **cheace, chas.** =CHASE LANE. — *c***1640** *Conn. Hist. Soc. Coll.* XIV. 393 Abuting on the . . . Cheace way alley to the metting house. **1664** *Ib.* 108 From the chasway that leadeth to ye long meadow down to the great River.

Chasm. (See BLOODY *a.* 3 b.)

Chat. {1697–} +A passerine bird of the genus *Icteris,* of which two varieties (the yellow-breasted and long-tailed) have been commonly recognized.

1731 CATESBY *Carolina* I. 50 The yellow brested Chat. . . . They frequent the Banks of great Rivers. **1808** WILSON *Ornithology* I. 92 While the female of the Chat is sitting, the cries of the male are still more loud and incessant. **1869** *Amer. Naturalist* III. 295, I obtained there also . . . [the nest] of the Chat (*Icteria viridis*), with four eggs. **1894** B. TORREY *Fla. Sketch-Book* 226 A white-eyed vireo . . . seems a pretty clever substitute for the chat in the chat's absence.

***Chattel.** Also **†chattle, -ell, -well; chatle.**

***1.** An article of movable property. Usually in plural and in the phrase *goods and chattels.*

Common in records of the 17th century. In later use literary and legal.

(1) [**1626** Bradford *Hist.* 254 To sell . . . all & every the stocks, shares, lands, marchandise, and chatles, what soever, to the said adventurers.] **1671** *R.I. Col. Rec.* II. 416 An exact inventory of the personal estate of each inhabitant, consisting either of house, household stuff, goods, cattle, horse kinde, or any other chattells whatever. **1782** FRENEAU *Poems* (1786) 249 My chessmen and tables, and other such chattels I give to Cornwallis renowned in battles. **1855** SIMMS *Forayers* 274 If the British triumphed, he contemplated the valuable lands and chattels of certain estates, the confiscation of which was certain.

(2) **1632** *New Plymouth Laws* 30 To be levied out of the goods or chattles of the said person. **1701** *Essex Inst. Coll.* XXXVIII. 253 The goods and chattwells of Captain George Corwin. **1847** RUXTON *Adv. Rocky Mts.* (1848) 265 Often charging furiously into a camp, and playing all sorts of pranks on the goods and chattels of the mountaineers. **1852** *Harper's Mag.* May 722/2 As soon as he had put his goods and chattels back in his pockets, he . . . set out to run as fast as he could over the bridge.

2. A person as an article of property; a slave. {1649–}

1852 STOWE *Uncle Tom* xi, This same gentleman . . . took a ride over to the factory, to see what this intelligent *chattel* had been about. **1852** A. LAWRENCE *Diary & Corr.* 318 The old Slave States will feel compelled to send their chattels away to save themselves from bankruptcy. **1858** *Harper's Mag.* Sept. 569/1 The Colonel was possessed of two chattels called Cæsar and John.

b. *Chattel real* (incorrectly used).

1869 TOURGEE *Toinette* (1881) 17 The girl 'Toinette,' with sundry other 'chattels-real,' passed into the hands of the young master. **1880** — *Bricks* 120 According to the former law, the slave was a sort of chattel-real.

+Chatteldom. [CHATTEL 2.] The institution or condition of slavery. — **1858** *N.Y. Tribune* 12 April 3/2, I insisted upon the propriety of placing the hand of chattledom on 'small farmers and greasy mechanics,' to prevent the impertinence of their wanting to associate with gentlemen's body-servants.

Chattelhood. [CHATTEL 2.] The state of being a chattel or slave. {1871} — **1870** *Congress. Globe* 25 Feb. 1561/3 When a race has been elevated from chattelhood to all the rights of humanity.

+**Chattelism.** [CHATTEL 2.] The system of holding human beings as chattels or slaves. — **1865** W. PHILLIPS in *Commonwealth* (Boston) 18 Feb., To grind the negro without restoring chattelism. **1875** *Scribner's Mo.* Dec. 275/2 The system of human Chattelism does not enter here. **1879** TOURGEE *Fool's Errand* 336 That transition period which comes between Chattelism . . . and absolute individual autonomy.

+**Chattelization.** [CHATTEL 2.] The action of converting (persons) into chattels. — **1854** A. L. STONE *Boston Oration* 4 July 25 A system of human chattelization.

+**Chattelized,** *ppl. a.* [Cf. prec.] Converted into chattels. — **1878** *N. Amer. Rev.* CXXVII. 251 This system of chattelized humanity rested upon that false relation . . . which is the life of every form of oppression.

+**Chattelizing,** *ppl. a.* [Cf. prec.] Reducing persons to the state of chattels. — **1863** in Logan *Great Conspiracy* 530 This Amendment . . . would . . . 'obliterate the last lingering vestiges of the Slave System; its chattelizing, degrading, and bloody codes.'

+**Chattel mortgage.** [CHATTEL 1.] A mortgage effected upon the chattels (in contrast to the real estate) of the mortgagee. — **1860** M. J. HOLMES *Maude* xxi. 213 There was a heavy mortgage upon the farm, and even a chattel-mortgage upon the furniture. **1874** *Florida Plant. Rec.* 582 A Chattel Mortgage by a Negro Tenant. **1889** in *Michigan Statutes* III. (1890) 3805 *n.*, An act to provide punishment for the fraudulent removal . . . of personal property under chattel mortgage.

* **Chatterer.** +**a.** The cedarbird of Carolina. **b.** The Bohemian waxwing. {1768-}

(a) *c*1730 CATESBY *Carolina* I. 46 *Garrulus Carolinensis.* The Chatterer. **1743** *Ib.* App. p. xxxvi, The Chatterer of Carolina. **1808** WILSON *Ornithology* I. 107 Notwithstanding the name *Chatterers* given to them, they are perhaps the most silent species we have; making only a feeble, lisping sound. **1864** BAIRD in *Webster* 220/2 *Chatterer;* . . . the common American species, called also cedar-bird, is the *Ampelis Carolinensis.* **(b) 1839** PEABODY *Mass. Birds* 290 The Waxen Chatterer, *Bombycilla garrula,* is . . . a visiter in our State though probably accidental. **1858-66** [see BOHEMIAN CHATTERER]. **1889** *Cent.* 181/3 The Carolina waxwing (*A. cedrorum*), the Bohemian waxwing (*A. garrulus*), and the Japanese waxwing (*A. phœnicopterus*) . . . are also called chatterers.

* **Chattering,** *ppl. a.* +Used as the distinctive epithet of a species of plover (the killdee) and flycatcher. — *c*1730 CATESBY *Carolina* I. 71 *Pluvialis vociferus.* The Chattering Plover. This is about the size of the larger Snipe. **1794** *Amer. Philos. Soc.* IV. 102 The chattering plover, and the whip-poor-will take advantage of a hollow place in the ground. **1858** BAIRD *Birds Pacific R.R.* 248 Yellow Breasted Chat. . . . Chattering flycatcher. . . . Eastern United States to the Missouri.

+**Chautauqua.**

1. The name of a county and lake in the western part of New York state, used attrib. to designate the religious and educational meetings held in summer at Lake Chautauqua (from 1871), the organization arising from these, and activities, etc., connected with this.

1873 (*title*), The Chautauqua Lake Journal, published for the Chautauqua Lake Camp-Meeting Association. **1879** *Harper's Mag.* Aug. 357/2 By far the most valuable fruit of the Chautauqua plan . . . will come from the Chautauqua Literary and Scientific Circle. **1886** J. H. VINCENT (*title*), The Chautauqua Movement. *Ib.* 278 The 'Chautauqua Salute' was introduced for the first time [in 1877].

2. An assembly or organization imitating that established at Lake Chautauqua.

1884 *Dakota Mission Conf. of M. E. Ch.* 5 Session 64½ Religious Summer Resort, The Great Chautauqua of the West, Big Stone Lake, Dakota. **1886** J. H. VINCENT *Chautauqua Movement* 40 From Chautauqua came other Chautauquas. These were in some cases new meetings called from the beginning 'Assemblies.' **1892** in *So. Dak. Hist. Coll.* I. 79 They have not lacked men and women of skillful leadership to organize movements in behalf of popular intelligence on the 'chautauqua' plan. **1901** DUNCAN & SCOTT *Allen & Woodson Co., Kansas* 59 The earlier and cruder forerunner of the Chautauqua Assemblies which are now held annually in many parts of the country, combining religious worship and spiritual culture with rest, recreation and social enjoyment. **1903** *Boston Ev. Transcript* 26 Sept., The Methodist camp-meeting is no longer an evangelistic force, but the chautauquas and summer conferences are multiplying.

+**Chautauquan.** A member of the Chautauqua 'circle.' — **1878** J. H. Vincent *Chautauqua Movement* 80 Now, let every Chautauquan present and absent read Dr. Vincent's lecture. **1886** *Ib.* 48 Chautauquans believe in wealth when honesty wins it, prudence protects it, and benevolence uses it.

* **Chaw,** *v.*

+**1.** With *up.* **a.** To chew completely; to reduce to pieces as if by chewing. Usu. in fig. context. *colloq.*[2]

1837-40 HALIBURTON *Clockmaker* (B. & L.), I felt as if I could chaw him right up, I was so mad. **1846** THORPE *Myst. Backwoods* 180 [The pack] pounce upon him [a cat], and in a few moments the 'nine lives' of the 'varmint' are literally chawed-up. **1853** *Harper's Mag.* VI. 584/2 The Indian succeeded in slaying his adversary by means of his knife, but it was at the expense of being mutilated, and horribly 'chawed up,' as my informant stated.

+**b.** *fig.* To demolish, defeat or discomfit completely, 'do for.' *slang.*

1839 *Knickerb.* XIII. 65 Sometimes it is used with reference to the discomfiture of individuals, as thus: 'I will chaw you up'; a threat involving defeat. **1846** THORPE *Myst. Backwoods* 28 (B.), Miss Patience said she was gratified to hear Mr. Cash was a musician. . . . Whereupon Cash fell into a chair, as he afterwards observed, chawed up. **1846** ROBB *Squatter Life* 63, I heerd Tom Jones swar he'd 'chaw me up, ef an inch big of me was found in them diggins in the mornin.' **1873** BEADLE *Undevel. West* 787 A 'half-horse, half-alligator' sort of a being, . . . seeking somebody whom he may 'chaw up.' **1884** SWEET & KNOX *Through Texas* 247 His tale of the many Indians he had chawed up soon gave him a prominent position among the boys. **1901** WHITE *Westerners* xxxiii. 305 They agreed that they'd be tee-totally chawed up.

+**2.** (See quotations and cf. 1 b.) *slang.*

1842 *Dartmouth* IV. 117 Yesterday, a Junior cracked a joke on me, when all standing round, shouted in great glee, 'Chawed! Freshman chawed!' . . . I didn't understand, when a fellow is used up, he is said to be chawed. **1909** *Dialect Notes* III. 298 *Chaw,* v. tr., . . . to hack or guy one.

+**3.** To think *over,* meditate on. *slang.*

1843 STEPHENS *High Life N.Y.* II. 39 So I . . . cut across towards the *Express Office,* detarmined to du up my chores in that quarter without chawing over the matter any longer. **1884** 'MARK TWAIN' *H. Finn* xxxv. 363, I couldn't see no advantage in my representing a prisoner if I got to set down and chaw over a lot of gold-leaf distinctions like that.

+**Chawed rock.** (See quotations.) — **1843** *Nat. Hist. N.Y., Geology* IV. 162 The calcareous matter is soon dissolved out from weathering, leaving the hornstone in jagged and irregular projecting points, from which it receives the local name of 'chawed rock.' **1846** EMMONS *Agric. N.Y.* I. 182 It weathers out into extremely rough masses, so that persons who have occasion to work the rock generally call it chawed rock.

‖**Chawing gum.** Colloq. variant of CHEWING GUM. — **1867** 'MARK TWAIN' *Advice for Good Little Girls,* You ought never to take your little brother's 'chawing-gum' away from him by main force.

+**Chaw tobacco.** ?*Obs. colloq.*[2] Chewing tobacco. — **1834** CARRUTHERS *Kentuckian* I. 103, I'll be bound you'd look at some body else's pretty cheeks more nor you would at the parson's chaw-tobacco.

Chean. Obs. variant of CHEYENNE.

* **Cheap,** *a.* Contemptible, low, mean. *colloq.* {-1799}

1827 COOPER *Prairie* xi, Why should I go to my grave with so cheap a lie in my mouth. **1867** HARTE *Condensed Novels* 280 To have let 'bigger things go by, and to be taken in by this cheap trick . . . is what gets me!' **1887** *Harper's Mag.* Jan. 327/1 The Pharaoh who wrote 3887 may have had some conceit in the figures, but it was a cheap pride. **1907** M. C. HARRIS *Tents of Wickedness* III. 250 He has a pretty cheap opinion of me, and I don't blame him, considering the people I go with generally.

Cheap-John. *colloq.* A peddler of cheap wares. {1826-}. Also attrib. — **1869** *Overland Mo.* III. 64 Auctioneers were yelling forth at the top of their lungs the merits of the Cheap John clothing. **1872** 'MARK TWAIN' *Roughing It* xlvi, None of your cheap-John turnouts for me. I'm here to have a good time. **1880** *Harper's Mag.* Aug. 348/1 Outside stood Isaacson—a travelling cheap-John who had opened a stock of second hand garments for ladies and gentlemen in a disused fish-house on the wharf.

Cheat.[1] **a.** A species of brome grass (*Bromus secalinus*), an annual weed growing among wheat; also called *chess.* **b.** Darnel. {1856-, *dial.*}

1784 J. SMYTH *Tour* II. 121 By this means all my fields consisted entirely of fine healthful clean wheat, without a single head of darnel or cheat to be discovered by the closest examination. **1786** WASHINGTON *Diaries* III. 71 The first [*sc.* wheat], besides having a small head generally, was mixed exceedingly with cheat. **1847** *Rep. Comm. Patents* (1848) 102 In July the wheat fields of Ohio are said to abound in cheat or chess. **1889** VASEY *Agric. Grasses* 73 (Chess; cheat.) It is an old tradition which some farmers still cling to that chess is a degenerated wheat.

‖**Cheat.**[2] *local.* ?*Obs.* A form of dance. — **1886** B. P. POORE *Reminisc.* I. 74 The 'basket dance,' and, on exceptional occasions, the exhilarating 'cheat,' formed the staple for saltatorial performance.

+**Chebacco boat.** [From *Chebacco,* 'Indian name of what is now the township of Essex, Essex Co., Mass.' (Chipman).] A type of vessel formerly used in the Newfoundland cod-fisheries. — **1835** INGRAHAM *South-West* I. 27 Those short, stump-masted *non-de-scripts* . . . sometimes denominated fishing smacks, but oftener and more euphoniously, 'Chebacco boats.' **1859** *Congress. Globe* 22 Feb. 1210, I recollect a little stream in the county of Essex, in Massachusetts, where, some fifty years ago, they used to manufacture a sort of little boat, called chebacco boat. **1886** *Leslie's Mo.* XXI. 223/1 Squam was in its ascendency in the days of the old pinkies and of the still earlier chebacco-boats.

+**Chebaccoman.** =CHEBACCO BOAT. — **1823** COOPER *Pilot* I. i. 13, I was born on board a chebacco-man.

+**Chechinquamin.** *Obs.* [Algonquian.] =CHINQUAPIN. — **1612** SMITH *Virginia* 11 They haue a small fruit growing on little-trees, husked like a Chesnut, but the fruit most like a very small acorne. This they [=Va. Indians] call Chechinquamins, which they esteeme a great daintie. *c*1618 STRACHEY *Virginia* 72 They plant their fields and sett their corne, and live after those monthes most of acrons [*sic*], walnutts, chesnutts, chechinquarnins [*sic*], and fish.

*Check, *n.*[1]

1. A fabric so woven or printed as to present a checked pattern. {1614–}

1711 *Boston News-Letter* 22 Oct. 2/2 Printed linnen, . . . ticking, checks, plush [etc.]. **1727** *Ib.* 29 June 2/2 Galloons, callamincos, . . . checks. **1778** *N.H. Hist. Soc. Coll.* IX. 287 All kinds of Woollen & linnin goods & checks, suitable for the Army. **1830** E. A. HITCHCOCK *Journal* 23 Her little girl about 10, also neatly dressed in check.

b. *attrib.* Having a checked pattern; made of checked cloth.

(*1*) **1758** *Newport Mercury* 26 Dec. 3/1 A check linen shirt. **1835** *Knickerb.* III. 182 She instantly withdrew, and wiped dry her fair hands upon her check-linen apron. **1856** COZZENS *Sparrowgrass P.* 103 His fine, intelligent face, under a check-cloth cap.

(*2*) **1754** *S.C. Gazette* 1 Jan. 4/2 The goods in hand consist in . . . check mantuas and Irish stuffs, everlastings, [etc.]. **1830** J. F. WATSON *Philadelphia* 177 Very decent women went abroad and to churches with check aprons. **1830** E. A. HITCHCOCK *Journal* 23 His wife, . . . neatly dressed in a check frock. **1843** *Knickerb.* XXI. 257 First he hauled out an ear of red corn, then a check-handkerchief. **1847** ROBB *Squatter Life* 167 Sir George was dressed in check pants and a snuff-colored coat. **1850** C. MATHEWS *Moneypenny* 35 He had . . . check gaiters, and an olive coat. **1865** *Atlantic Mo.* XV. 545 She would be asleep now, . . . her wan limbs curled up under her check nightgown.

+**2.** *Agric.* The point at which furrows at right angles to each other cross; a square marked off by such furrows.

1787 WASHINGTON *Diaries* III. 194 In each of these checks or crosses, a root, when it was large and looked well, was put. **1857** *Ill. Agric. Soc. Trans.* III. 62, I lay off my ground with a corn-marker . . . into checks of three feet three inches square. **1863** *Ib.* V. 666 A small hill [is to be] made in or on the check as may be preferred, for the reception of the plant.

+**3.** A square section of land. ?*Obs.*

1795 J. SULLIVAN *Hist. Maine* 195 The method of regular settlement by lots, checks, and ranges, is quite a modern contrivance in the District.

*Check, *n.*[2]

***1.** A means of limiting or counteracting administrative power when this might be carried to excess. +Chiefly in the phrase *checks and balances*, used to denote a constitutional principle. (Cf. BALANCE *n.* 1.)

1787 J. ADAMS *Def. Const. U.S.* (1794) I. p. i, The checks and balances of republican governments have been in some degree adopted by the courts of princes. **1794** S. WILLIAMS *Hist. Vermont* 140 No mutual checks and ballances, accountability and responsibility. **1802** *Ann. 7th Congress* 1 Sess. 532, I will agree that there are times when checks and balances are useful. **1842** TYLER in *Pres. Mess. & P.* IV. 193 A proceeding tending to the utter destruction of the checks and balances of the Constitution. **1860** *36th Cong. 1 Sess.* H. Repr. Rep. 249, 97 What is your opinion of the establishment of a government printing office, with proper checks and balances? **1877** *Harper's Mag.* Feb. 462/2 The 'checks and balances' which are held to be the glory of our institutions.

2. A form by which a bank is authorized to pay money to a specified person or party. {1774–1845. Now *cheque.*}

Certified check, marketed check: see the adjs.

1798 J. JAY *Corr.* IV. 251 Pay them as they become due by checks on the bank. **1838** *N.Y. Advertiser & Exp.* 10 Jan. 2/1 The Yarmouth Register states that the Cape Cod and Cape Ann Fishermen have been compelled to take their bounty . . . in *'rags,'* called 'checks,' on certain 'Rag Factories' in the city of Boston. **1855** J. HOLBROOK *Among Mail Bags* 133 In this desk was found about $40,000 in bank drafts, checks, &c. **1916** E. PORTER *David* 229 Any money would do the job— . . . gold, or silver, or greenbacks, or—or a check, if it had the dough behind it.

‖**3.** A check list (of voters).

1792 *Ann. 2nd Congress* 464 The superintending officers at elections are empowered to appoint three clerks . . . to keep three rolls or checks.

4. A ticket or token, or substitute for this, entitling one to readmission to a theatre, etc., or to a seat in a railroad car, etc. {1812–}

1835 INGRAHAM *South-West* I. 223 A shouting of 'Your check, sir! your check!—Give me your check—Please give me your check!' **1851** *Knickerb.* XXXVIII. 602 'Jim, do you want a check?' said a red-shirted vagabond to a long, round-shouldered, over-grown boy. **1892** *Harper's Mag.* Feb. 437/1 She took the velvet chair her check called for.

+**5.** =BAGGAGE-CHECK.

1848 *Major Jones's Sk. Trav.* 58 (Th.), Sir, give me yer checks for yer baggage, and I'll take ye to the Exchange Hotel. **1863** 'G. HAMILTON' *Gala-Days* 45 'Well,' says the Baggage-man, . . . 'you let me take your check, and I'll send the trunk on by express.' **1871** HOWELLS *Wedding Journey* vii. 173 The young Canadian who took charge of the trunks for the boat . . . did not give checks for the pieces, but marked them with the name of their destination. **1879** BURDETTE *Hawkeyes* 123, I saw my baggage re-checked, and got the checks in my hand. **1913** STRATTON-PORTER *Laddie* viii, So one afternoon father took her trunk to the depot and bought the tickets and got the checks.

+**6.** A bill at a restaurant or dining room.

1868 A. D. WHITNEY *P. Strong* 128, I let her settle for the dinner checks at Vinton's, while I finished my ice-cream. **1886–7** STOCKTON *Hundredth Man* ix, Tossing to each diner his pasteboard check with an accuracy of aim which was sure to deposit it upon some retentive article of food. **1910** 'O. HENRY' *Strictly Business* 192 Through an arched opening at the bottom you thrust your waiter's check and the money.

+**7.** A counter or chip used in playing certain games.

1845 HOOPER *Simon Sugg's Adv.* v. 57 He called for 'Twenty, five-dollar checks. . . .' The dealer handed him the red checks. **1848** JUDSON *Mysteries N.Y.* I. 20 Heaps of red and white ivory checks . . . are changed for money . . . and are redeemable for cash at the bank—the faro bank. **1856** *Harper's Mag.* Dec. 68/2 His delight is to be seated over against a grim . . . faro-dealer—to have bets of 'red checks' all over the table.

+**b.** *To pass* (or *hand*) *in one's checks*, to die. Also, to give in, to surrender. *colloq.* (Cf. CASH *v.* 3 b.)

(1) **1869** *Overland Mo.* III. 31 Three or four miners and axemen sat whittling on the logs as the doctor came out; and Hy Fender asked: 'Well, now; has he passed in his checks?' **1870** NOWLAND *Indianapolis* 164 He has closed his game and handed in his checks several years since. **1871** HAY *Pike Co. Ballads* 17 Jimmy Bludso passed in his checks The night of the Prairie Belle. **1876** MILLER *First Families* 108 Some poor idiot will pass in his checks tonight, if he don't come back pretty soon. **1901** *Scribner's Mag.* April 409/2 You and Lave were blown clean across the yard, and how you missed passing in your checks, nobody knows.

(2) **1876** HARTE *G. Conroy* VI. iv, The game's up, and we might as well pass in our checks now. **1873** MILLER *Amongst Modocs* 193 Hands up, gentlemen! hands up! . . . You are the one we want. Pass in your checks!

8. *ellipt.* A checkrein.

1868 WOODRUFF *Trotting Horse* 202 In order to prevent him from throwing down his head . . . the well-known Kemble-Jackson check . . . was invented. **1887** TOURGEE *Button's Inn* 122 Throw me off that rein, if you please. . . . Just shift those inside checks, won't you?

Check, *n.*[3] *local.* A slight meal. {1826– Sc. (and N. Irel.), usually *chack*, 1818–}

1775 FITHIAN *Journal* II. 6 This is an Irish settlement—they speak in a shrill, acute, Accent, & have many odd Phrases. . . . 'Will you just take a Check?'—She meant a late Dinner. **1817** U. BROWN *Journal* II. 368 Thence 15 Miles to the half way house, fed & took a Check. **1839** MARRYAT *Diary in A.* II. 228 'Will you have a *feed* or a *check?*'—A dinner, or a luncheon? **1871** DE VERE 452 *Check* is in Pennsylvania the name of an impromptu meal of cold provisions. (S. S. Haldeman.)

Check, *n.*[4] *local.* [Eng. dial.] (See quotations.) — **1774** FITHIAN *Journal* I. 252 Often [the girls play] at a small game with Peach-stones which they call checks. **1909** *Dialect Notes* III. 298 *Checks*, an indoor game with marbles, being a series of movements of catching and placing the marbles (usually five) in various combinations, forms, etc.

*Check, *v.*[1]

+**1.** *tr.* To mark out (ground) in squares for planting. (Cf. CHECK *n.*[1] 2 and CHEQUER *v.*)

1768 WASHINGTON *Diaries* I. 265 At the first and last of which [plantations I] just began to check Corn G(roun)d. **1871** *Ill. Agric. Soc. Trans.* VIII. 239 After the field has been thoroughly prepared . . . proceed to check it off from east to west with a three-rowed marker.

+**2.** *intr.* To split without breaking apart.

1880 *Harper's Mag.* Aug. 398 The streaks of the clinker-built canoe rarely check, the wood being generally well seasoned. **1903** *Geol. Survey: Contribs. to Econ. Geol. 1902* 277 The coal is not crushed, but can be obtained in large pieces which 'check' but do not break up readily on exposure to the air.

+**Check,** *v.*[2] [CHECK *n.*[2] 2, etc.]

1. *intr.* To write or draw checks (*for* an amount, *on* a bank, etc.).

1809 *Ann. 10th Congress* 2 Sess. 416 The money . . . is deposited in the Treasury as in a bank, to be checked for, whenever that commerce . . . shall be again reopened. **1843** POE *Murders Rue M.* Wks. I. 190 [She] had checked for nothing until the third day before her death, when she took out in person the sum of 4000 francs. **1863** in C. C. Hopley *Life in South* I. 323 Dr. Charles E. Everett . . . had authorized the Governor to check upon him for $500, and to repeat the check . . . one hundred times. **1869** *Atlantic Mo.* Sept. 376/1 This gentleman can check for much more than fifteen millions. **1902** HARBEN *A. Daniel* 163 It'll take a day or two to collect it, but he'd let me check on it right now fer any reasonable amount. **1912** MULFORD *Buck Peters* 320 That beastly German had the check to get away with the money after all. He checked against the blessed lot yesterday forenoon.

b. *tr.* To draw *out* by a check.

1879 B. F. TAYLOR *Summer-Savory* 210, I am not quite sure it would not be a luxury to put a dollar into some bank just for the sake of checking it out. **1916** DU PUY *Uncle Sam* 28 In this way a depositor who never had a thousand dollars in the bank eventually checked out $50,000.

2. *tr.* To consign (baggage) on a railroad, etc., receiving an identification check therefor; to send on or *through* in this way.

1846 *Daily Ev. Traveller* (Boston) 16 July 3/2 Passengers . . . will consult their comfort and convenience by being particular to have their Baggage 'checked.' **1857** *Harper's Mag.* Sept. 434/2 The baggage was checked for the Washington Junction. **1860** *Congress. Globe* 21 Dec. 177/2

It is a great convenience to the traveling public to be able to check baggage through. **1871** HOWELLS *Wedding Journey* i. 6 Basil would have eked out the business of checking the trunks into an affair of some length, but the baggage-master did his duty with pitiless celerity. **1897** *Outing* XXX. 628/2 These attendants will be found in the several waiting-rooms at Grand Central Station, for the free assistance of patrons in checking baggage and carrying hand-bags. **1907** M. C. HARRIS *Tents of Wickedness* I. 89 She felt vaguely comforted that she should not have to buy the tickets nor to check her trunk.

fig. **1860** *Richmond Enquirer* 6 Nov. 1/5 (Th.), Douglas men, will you follow Little Sandy Rives into Black Republicanism, for he has taken his ticket and checked his baggage through. **1871** HAY *Pike Co. Ballads* 22 He kin check his trunks to a warmer clime Than he'll find in Illanoy. **1884** SWEET & KNOX *Through Texas* 16 Phil Parker was pointed out to strangers as a gambler, and a man who had checked several of his acquaintances through to the other world.

b. To leave (articles) in charge in return for a check.

1897 *Westminster Gaz.* 25 Feb. 10/2 Here are some . . . extracts from the programmes of the Chicago theatres. . . . 'Remove your hats during the performance. You can check them with the maid.' **1908** LORIMER *J. Spurlock* 263 Your clothes came from the East Shore this morning, and are checked downstairs.

3. To take and give a check for (articles left in charge).

1871 HOWELLS *Wedding Journey* i. 8 The ticket-seller was there, and the lady who checked packages left in her charge. **1888** *Amer. Humorist* 21 July (F.), Turning to the man who checks umbrellas and canes.

Checkbook. [CHECK *n.*²] **a.** A book in which business transactions are recorded. *Obs.* **b.** A book containing blank checks on a bank. {=cheque-book, 1848–}

(a) 1777 J. ADAMS *Wks.* (1854) IX. 452 The certificates and check-books for the loan office. **1778** *Journals Cont. Congress* 29 Sept. 966 The check books of the loan office certificates, which he had issued to lenders. **1801** in *N.H. Hist. Soc. Coll.* V. 58 From the manner in which the grants were made, the check books being all lost, a great difficulty will oppose the renewing issue of warrants for those lands. **(b) 1817** *Boston Commercial Gaz.* 30 June (*advt.*), Among them are . . . Bills of Lading, Bank Checks, Check Books. **1823** M'Kenney *Memoirs* I. (1846) App. 296 Was it not the rule of the office to write in the body of each check, and on the margin of the check-book, what each check was for, and to whom paid? **1854** 'O. OPTIC' *In Doors & Out* (1876) 105 The young merchant took down his check book, and examined the state of his bank account. **1860** HOLMES *Professor* i. 28 A check came back to me at last with these two words on it, *No funds.* My check book was a volume of waste-paper. **1868** A. D. WHITNEY *P. Strong* 104 An account, . . . with a deposit of three thousand dollars, . . . and a cheque-book, to draw the money out with. **1907** M. C. HARRIS *Tents of Wickedness* I. 29 It is surprising the education contained in one's first check book.

+**Check clerk.** [CHECK *v.*²] (See quotations.) — **1889** *Cent.* 940/3 *Check-clerk*, a clerk whose business it is to check the accounts of others, their time of attendance at work, etc. **1889** FARMER 134/1 *Check clerk*, the clerk in charge of a cloak-room, or one employed in the office at hotels, to allot rooms to visitors, and to book their names in the hotel register.

*****Checked,** *a.* [CHECK *n.*¹] Of garments: Made of cloth woven or printed in checks. — **1825** NEAL *Bro. Jonathan* III. 236 A checked shirt, a drab coat, and a drab hat. **1840** DANA *Two Years* i. 6 The loose duck trowsers, checked shirt and tarpaulin hat of a sailor. **1856** M. J. HOLMES *L. Rivers* iii. 25 Wiping her fingers upon the corner of her checked apron.

Checked, *ppl. a.* [CHECK *v.*²] Kept in check. (Cf. CHECK *n.*² 1.) — **1796** *Gazette U.S.* 5 Nov. (Th.), The checked and balanced government that Mr. Adams so much admires.

+**Checker.** *slang.* [?f. CHECKERS.] *The checker*, the very thing. — *c*1850 WHITCHER *Widow Bedott P.* 324 'That's the checker,' said Teeters. **1854** M. J. HOLMES *Tempest & Sunshine* ix. 122 'By Jupiter!' said Mr. Middleton, 'that's just the checker. No wonder I like you so well.' **1911** H. QUICK *Yellowstone N.* 97 When I hadn't but four sections I thought 'twas about the checker f'r a man with three sons.

+**Checkerberry.** [Cf. Eng. dial. *checkers* {1649–}, the fruit of the wild service-tree. See also CHICKERBERRY.] One or other of several red berries or the plants bearing these: **a.** The foxberry or bearberry. ?*Obs.* **b.** The partridge-berry (*Mitchella repens*). **c.** The creeping wintergreen (*Gaultheria procumbens*).

1784 CUTLER in *Mem. Academy* I. 444 *Arbutus.* . . . Foxberry. Checkerberry. . . . The berries are rather of an agreeable taste and are sometimes eaten by children in milk. **1843** *Amer. Pioneer* II. 125 The vivid green leaves and bright scarlet berries of the 'Partridge bush,' or 'Checkerberry.' **1856** M. J. HOLMES *L. Rivers* xxi. 231 Wouldn't Lena stare when she saw him so much improved from what he was when they picked checkerberries together? **1869** FULLER *Flower Gatherers* 99 It has berries on the end of the stem, . . . red as checkerberries, but not sweet and spicy like them. **1892** TORREY *Footpath-Way* 59, I made myself young again by putting a few checkerberries into my mouth.

attrib. **1852** STOWE *Uncle Tom* xvii, Chewing some checkerberry-leaves as he spoke. *a*1862 THOREAU *Maine Woods* 211 It had a slight checkerberry flavor, and . . . was really better than the black tea which we had brought. *Ib.* 280 We called this . . . Checkerberry-tea Camp. **1905** *N.Y. Ev. Post* 4 Aug. 7 The introduction of peppermint and checkerberry essences has almost resulted in driving carraway seeds out of the pharmacopoeia of the family.

Checkerboard. [See CHECKERS and cf. CHEQUERBOARD.] The board upon which the game of checkers is played. {1779} Also fig.

1775 *Essex Inst. Coll.* XIII. 186, 1 frying pan, 1 checker Board. **1816** PICKERING 58 The board is also called a *checker*-board in those parts of the country where the game is called checkers. **1860** M. J. HOLMES *Maude* xxi. 222 Married life is just like a checker-board. **1879** B. F. TAYLOR *Summer-Savory* 115 That old meeting-house . . . was as angular as an elbow, and as square as a checker-board. **1906** *Harper's Mag.* Feb. 422 Fleets of barges lay upon the river like the black squares of some huge checker-board.

attrib. **1850** C. MATHEWS *Moneypenny* 35 He . . . wore a checker-board straw hat.

+**Checkered adder.** Also **chequered.** The spotted adder or milk snake, *Lampropeltis triangulum.* — **1839** STORER *Mass. Reptiles* 227 *Coluber eximius.* Chicken snake; milk snake; and chequered adder. **1843** STEPHENS *High Life N.Y.* II. 172, I say, par, did you ever see a checkered adder a charmin a bird?

+**Checkermen.** =CHECKERS 2. — **1883** E. E. HALE in *Harper's Mag.* Jan. 278/2 He had built up a little tower of checkermen.

Checker-playing. Playing at checkers. — **1879** STOCKTON *Rudder Grange* 26 The kettle had been put on to boil during the checker-playing.

Checkers. Also †**checkerds, -ards.** [Plural of earlier Eng. *checker* (*chequer*) chessman, chessboard.]

1. The game of draughts.

1712 SEWALL *Letter-Book* I. 417 When your neighbor Joshua Brown gave you trouble with his wiggleing Whip-Rows; you us'd to Huff him, and humble him at a game of Checkers. **1786** A. ELLICOTT in *Life & Lett.* 59 Our Amusements such as Cards, and Draughts, commonly called checkards. **1794** *Ib.* 119 We amuse ourselves with playing checkerds. **1825** NEAL *Bro. Jonathan* I. 7 Peters had beaten him . . . at fox and geese; then at checkers, or draughts. **1865** BOUDRYE *Fifth N.Y. Cavalry* 91 While in camp checkers and cards afford a pastime to many. **1904** HARBEN *Georgians* 1 The clerk of the court . . . sat playing checkers with Jim Carden.

2. The pieces used in the game of draughts.

1864 WEBSTER 221/1. **1870** EMERSON *Soc. & Solitude* 94 Out of blocks thread-spools, cards, and checkers, he will build his pyramid. **1887** *Lippincott's Mag.* Sept. 350 If your checkers are jumped off the board so fast, you won't get any in the king-row. **1904** HARBEN *Georgians* 3 He put the checkers into a cardboard box.

Checking, *vbl. n.* +The consigning of baggage in return for a check. (See CHECK *v.*² 2.) — **1870** RAE *Westward by Rail* 77 Excited passengers are rushing about in quest of the luggage which, despite the system of 'checking,' is often going astray or getting out of sight. **1886** B. P. POORE *Reminisc.* I. 41 Baggage checks and the checking of baggage were then unknown.

Check letter. [CHECK *v.*²] A letter of the alphabet serving as a mark of identification or control. — **1776** *Journals Cont. Congress* 15 Nov. 955 That each denomination [of the certificates] have a check letter corresponding with a letter in the margin to be left in the book. **1851** *Ann. 5th Congress* 708 There was also a check-letter in the books and on the certificates which rendered forgery almost impossible.

+**Check list.** [CHECK *v.*²]

1. A list of names, titles, etc., so arranged as to form a ready means of reference, comparison, or verification.

1853 (*title*), Check list of periodical publications received in the reading-room of the Smithsonian Institution. **1873** J. ROBINSON (*title*), Check List of the Ferns of North America north of Mexico. **1874** COUES (*title*), Check List of North American Birds.

2. A list of qualified voters on which the names of these may be checked as they vote at an election. (Cf. CHECK *n.*² 3.)

1885 *Boston Journal* 9 March 1/8 Croydon's check-list has 205 names, the largest number in many years. **1888** BRYCE *Amer. Commw.* II. II. xii. 433 The composition of a primary is determined by the roll or 'check list,' as it is called, of ward voters entitled to appear in it.

+**Check-master.** [CHECK *n.*² or *v.*²] A railroad official having charge of baggage. — **1874** B. F. TAYLOR *World on Wheels* I. 63 The tremendous voice of the check-master tolls like a bell, '4689 Cleveland!' . . . and the baggage-car is as lively with all sorts of baggage as corn in a corn-popper.

Checkrein. A rein that prevents a horse from lowering his head; =CHECK *n.*² 8. Also fig.

1849 WILLIS *Rural Lett.* 61 Easing off the check reins a couple of holes . . . we struck into the traveller's trot. **1873** HOLLAND *A. Bonnicastle* 14 He had a little boy . . . who could exactly reach the check-rein of his leading horse. **1875** STOWE *We & Our Neighbors* 11 Mrs. Betsey . . . had been accustomed to these sudden pullings-up of the moral check-rein from Miss Dorcas. **1903** C. L. BURNHAM *Jewel* 12 Unfasten the check-rein. . . . I only hope there's a purgatory for the folks that use too short check-reins on their horses.

+**Checkrow,** *n.* [CHECK *n.*¹ 2.] One of the rows in a cultivated field so arranged as to form a check pattern. Also attrib.

1858 *Rep. Comm. Patents* (1859) I. 474 The seed may . . . be distributed from either hopper, and sown either in drills or check-rows. **1861** *Ill. Agric. Soc. Trans.* IV. 209 In spring, it will be harrowed thoroughly, planted by hands in check rows three feet ten inches apart each way. *Ib.* 312 Most of the corn is now planted with drills, or check row machines. **1888** *Vt. Agric. Rep.* X. 26 He puts the crop in check rows, to be able to cultivate thoroughly both ways.

+**Checkrowed,** *ppl. a.* [f. prec.] Planted in checkrows. — **1888** *Sci. Amer.* n. s. LVIII. 298/1 Particularly for use on growing check-rowed and listed corn.

+**Checkrower.** (See prec. and quotation.) — **1884** KNIGHT *Suppl.* s.v., *Check Rower.* 1. A corn planter. 2. An attachment to a corn planter by which it is made automatically to drop the seed corn at regular intervals of distance across a field [etc.]

+**Check-set.** [CHECK *n.*[1] 2.] =CHECKROWER 2. — **1861** *Ill. Agric. Soc. Trans.* IV. 248 He must have a boy to tend the check-set of the corn-planter.

+**Check stand.** [CHECK *v.*[2] 2.] A place used for checking baggage. — **1886** E. W. HOWE *Moonlight Boy* 102 My friend left his own baggage at a check stand. **1904** F. LYNDE *Grafters* 31 The train was in, and the porter had fetched Loring's hand-bag from the check-stand.

Checkstrap. {1833–} +A strap controlling the bit in a horse's mouth; a strap to be pulled as a signal for stopping a vehicle. — **1887** *Scribner's Mag.* Oct. 508/1 'I'll put a check-strap on him, if he won't do it!' a little chap exclaimed, . . . using a phrase drawn from the training of horses; for the 'check-strap' in cow-boy parlance, controls the bit in the horse's mouth. **1906** F. LYNDE *Quickening* 130 At the Woodlawn gates she pulled the old-fashioned, check-strap signal, and Scipio reined in his horses.

Check-will's-widow. (See CHUCK-WILL'S-WIDOW.)

+**Checkword.** [CHECK *v.*[2]] The keyword of a cipher. — **1807** *Ann. 10th Congress* 1 Sess. I. 561, Take the following for the catchword or checkword, and you may very readily decipher the figures.

Cheddar (cheese). {1684–} A kind of cheese similar to that made at Cheddar, England. — **1858** FLINT *Milch Cows* 266 American cheese . . . is made of almost every conceivable variety and quality, from the richest Cheddar or Cheshire to the poorest skim-milk cheese. **1887** *Courier-Journal* 20 Jan. 7/2 Cheese—Sheboygan twin cheddar, 13 @ 13½c.

Cheeger. Variant of *chegre, chigre,* CHIGOE.

* **Cheese.**

***1.** The curd of milk pressed into a mold and allowed to harden; a single mass of this in a distinctive form.

1622 'MOURT' *Relation* 17 Our victuals was onely Bisket and Holland cheese. **a1649** WINTHROP *Hist.* I. 74 This place they called Cheese Rock, because, when they went to eat somewhat, they had only cheese. **1715** *Boston News-Letter* 2 May 2/2 At the store-house No. 5 . . . [is] to be sold . . . Cheshire cheese very good. **1775** *Essex Inst. Coll.* XLVIII. 54 This morning there was won whipt for steling a chese. **1805** SIBLEY in *Ann. 9th Congress* 2 Sess. 1097 [The people of Bayou Pierre] supply us with our cheese entirely, and of tolerable quality. **1896** *Vt. Agric. Rep.* XV. 23 The . . . cheese factory . . . at Antwerp [N.Y.] . . . turns out over 200,000 fancy cheeses yearly.

fig. **1848** W. E. BURTON *Waggeries* 12 But what took my cheese was the parson's tellin' us abeout tew fellows as got up the biggest chunk of a fight.

***2.** One of the round flat seeds of the common mallow.

1878 B. F. TAYLOR *Between Gates* 137 The mallows . . . whence you used to gather the little green 'cheeses.' **1898** DELAND *Old Chester Tales* 192 The little whity-green seeds of the mallow, which are 'cheeses.'

3. Attrib. and comb. (in sense 1) with *cask, curd, dairy,* etc.

1835 LONGSTREET *Georgia Scenes* 11 If she like . . . the shape of a cheese-cask for her body; what is all that to me? **1865** A. D. WHITNEY *Gayworthys* 63 She was cutting up a pure white mass of cheese-curd. **1847** *Rep. Comm. Patents* (1848) 206 Three-fifths [of the cows milked in N.Y.] . . . were for butter dairies and the remainder for cheese dairies. **1872** in *N.Y. Agric. Soc. Trans.* XXXI. 442 It must at any rate require a larger expansion of the cheese dairying interests of the country, to meet the wants of that year [1900]. **1868** BEECHER *Norwood* 94 It was the cheese-day, and Aunt Rachel's cheeses . . . admitted of no rivalry. **1874** *Vt. Bd. Agric. Rep.* II. 107 The cheese fly, whose larvæ are deposited in the cells of a cheese, is a trouble unknown to butter makers. **1868** *Mich. Agric. Rep.* VII. 252 You know better than I can tell you whether your cheese-houses are encumbered to any extent with surplus or unsaleable stock. **1863** *Rep. Comm. Agric.* 49 The plan . . . of establishing a cheese manufactory . . . possesses many advantages. **1868** *Mich. Agric. Rep.* VII. 251 John M. Webb, of New York, gave an address reviewing the cheese market of 1868. **1778** *Essex Inst. Coll.* XLIX. 106 Sold . . . 6 pewter cheese plates, at 2s. 1d. **1877** *Harper's Mag.* March 604/2 There was a cheese-press, and I don't know but a cider mill. **1874** HOWELLS *Chance Acquaintance* ii. 65 Then the oil-regions gracefully withdrew and left the cheese-regions and grape-regions to come back and take possession. **1776** *Essex Inst. Coll.* XLIX. 101 Cheese toaster. **1870** *Rep. Comm. Agric. 1869* 441 The Chicago Tribune states that at the opening of 1869 there were in that city three firms engaged exclusively in the cheese trade.

+**Cheese apple.** A southern variety of flat apple. — **1709** LAWSON *Carolina* 109 We have . . . the long Apple, . . . Flattings, Grigsons, Cheese-Apples, and a great number of names. **1867** WARDER *Pomology* 467 Flat Apples. . . . Cheese. This fruit was received from . . . Grass Hills, Gallatin County, Kentucky.

+**Cheesebox.**

1. A round box in which cheese is kept.

1855 *Knickerb.* XLV. 14 A cheese-box, used as a tanning-vat. **1863** KETTELL *Hist. Rebellion* II. 466 Her singular and diminutive appearance . . . was described by the enemy as that of a 'cheese-box upon a plank.' **1878** TUTTLE *Border Tales* 17 One of the redskins . . . manufactured a drum by stretching a deerskin over the rim of a cheesebox.

2. One of the Federal gunboats, of the monitor type, used during the Civil War. Also attrib. (See prec. 1863.)

1862 *N.Y. Tribune* 10 June, Where is the Monitor? We have not heard a word of the little cheese-box since the repulse in James River until yesterday. **1866** POLLARD *Southern Hist. War* I. 278 Here, there, and everywhere, was the black 'cheese box.' **1871** DE VERE 335 Irreverent Confederates called the hideous-looking vessels cheese-boxes. **1871** *Harper's Mag.* XLIII. 482/1 Ericsson's 'cheese-box' monitors.

Cheesebread. *Obs.* 'A board to press curd for cheese, somewhat less in circumference than the vat.' {1629} — **1647** *Essex Probate Rec.* I. 89, 3 cheese mootes & two cheese breads.

* **Cheesecake.**

1. A fancy cake, originally containing cheese or curd, now made with a variety of ingredients.

1783 *Broadside Verse* (1930) 193/1 Chesecakes, cold hams, plumb-puddings, and mince-pies! **1805** *Pocumtuc Housewife* (1906) 25 [Recipe for making] Cheese Cakes. **1828** E. LESLIE *Receipts* 20 You may bake it either in a soup-plate, or in two small tin patty-pans, which, for cheese-cakes, should be of a square shape. **1842** *Life in West* 255 His wife soon spread out her store of good things before us . . . prairie-hen, . . . cheese-cakes, cherry-pie. **1884** F. E. OWENS *Cook Book* 284 [Recipe for] Lemon-Cheese Cakes. Prepare mixture as for cheese cakes from curd.

2. =CHEESE 2. (*Cent.*)

Cheesecloth. a. A cloth in which the curds are pressed in cheese-making, or in which cheese is wrapped. {1741–} **b.** A cotton cloth of open texture used for various purposes. Also attrib.

1657 *Mass. H. S. Coll.* 4 Ser. VII. 83 Your maid likewise wants vessells for to sett milke in, & some chesse clothes. **1892** V. KELLOG *Kansas Insects* 65 Wires thrust in the ground so as to form two crossing arches, . . . and covered with cheese cloth or netting, do well. **1909** 'O. HENRY' *Options* 39 There's certain things in life that are naturally intended to fit and belong together. One is pink cheese-cloth and green roses. **1923** WATTS *L. Nichols* 235 He marched off and marched back collecting a pan, a sieve of archaic pattern lined with a cheese-cloth rag, [etc.]

+**Cheesedom.** 'A name facetiously applied to the cheese-producing part of the Western Reserve' (Th. S.). — **1867** *Congress. Globe* 14 Feb. 1253/3, I am very sorry that my colleague and friend is not here to defend his butter and cheese, representing as he does what in Ohio we call 'Cheesedom.'

+**Cheese factory.** An establishment in which milk is received or collected and cheese manufactured on a large scale.

1868 *Mich. Agric. Rep.* VII. 228 The cheese factory of Rufus Baker & Son . . . received the past season the milk of 600 cows. **1878** *Ill. Dept. Agric. Trans.* XIV. 293 Cheese-factories all over the country could be bought for fifty cents on the dollar. **1888** *Vt. Agric. Rep.* X. 14 If a man has a cheese factory he better keep it, but other things being equal a butter factory is better. **1896** *Ib.* XV. 23 We believe the dairymen of Vermont are making a mistake in not establishing more cheese factories.

***Cheesefat.** *Obs.* The vessel or mould in which cheese is made. {–1741; later *cheese-vat.*} — **1650** in *Mayflower Desc.* X. 173 One cherne, 3 cheesfatts. **1651** *Ib.* 161, 3 cheesfatts with theire boards. **1655** *Essex Probate Rec.* I. 206 Ten milk trayes & 3 cheesfats.

Cheese hoop. A broad wooden or metal ring in which the curds are pressed in cheese making. — **1849** *Rep. Comm. Patents* (1850) 257 Improvement in Machines for cutting and slitting Cheese Hoops, &c. **1858** *Ib.* (1859) I. 546 Improvement in casting metallic cheese hoops. **1889** *Cent.* 944/2 The curds are placed in a cheese-hoop and this is put in the [cheese] press.

Cheese knife. A knife with a broad curved blade used for cutting cheese. {1833} — **1804** J. ROBERTS *Penna. Farmer* 193 One [scoop] resembles the half of a bullet mould, another a cheeseknife. **1861** NEWELL *Orpheus C. Kerr* I. 233 The critter screamed like a rantankerous tom-cat with his tail under a cheese-knife.

Cheese maker. One who makes cheese. — **1868** *Mich. Agric. Rep.* VII. 237 The cheese-maker watching all the conditions, and standing ready at any time to check the curds when the proper changes are developed. **1874** *Dept. Agric. Rep. 1873* 242 Tainted milk seems to be susceptible of better control by skillful cheese-makers than we had once supposed.

Cheese making. The making of cheese. {1846} — **1831** PECK *Guide* 171 The most important arrangement for the dairy business in Illinois, and especially for cheese-making. **1856** *Rep. Comm. Patents: Agric.* 28 The greater portion of our farmers make more or less butter for sale, and a few are engaged in cheese-making. **1868** *Mich. Agric. Rep.*

VII. 227 As cheese-making is advanced, the tendency must be to enhance the price of butter.

***Cheesemonger.** A seller of, or dealer in, cheese. — **1838** DRAKE *Tales & Sketches* 29 This cheese-monger had been watching the game from the beginning.

Cheesemot, -moot. *Obs.* =CHEESEFAT. {1617–29} — **1635** *Essex Probate Rec.* I. 5, 6 chesemots, 2 jugs, 3 pans, one tray. **1647** [see CHEESE-BREAD].

*** Cheese press.** A press used in making cheese.

1640 *Conn. Public Rec.* I. 448 One chese presse, old hogsheads & a pype. **1673** *Essex Inst. Coll.* L. 28 In the Little chamber . . . a trough a syder presse a cheese press. **1731** HEMPSTEAD *Diary* 237, I was at home all day. I fitted a Cheesepress. **1842** *Lowell Offering* II. 134 Well, I've made more [cheese] than I did a year afore—thirty in my largest hoop. . . . Our cheese press is terribly out of order, now. **1867** 'LACKLAND' *Homespun* II. 192 How many a hard-working mother, fresh from . . . the cheese-press, thinks [etc.].

Cheese tub.

1. A tub in which the curd is prepared for cheese making. {1629–}

1651 in *Mayflower Desc.* X. 161 Item, 2 beere vessells & one Cheestubb. **1812** Kittredge *Old Farmer* (1904) 272 You look to your cheese-tubs, I'll see to the hogs. **1858** FLINT *Milch Cow*, etc. 252 The cheese-tub should be so graduated that it may be correctly known what quantity of milk is used.

2. =CHEESEBOX 2.

1867 HEADLEY *Farragut & Nav. Commanders* 519 Worden in his 'cheese-tub,' as the rebels called her, was crowding all steam to overtake his powerful adversary.

Cheeweeh. *Obs.* =CHEWINK. — **1796** MORSE *Amer. Geog.* I. 210 [Birds of the United States include] Towhe Bird, Pewee, Cheeweeh. **1832** WILLIAMSON *Maine* I. 143 The Pewit, or Cheeweeh, lives in the summer months about barns and out buildings.

Chelone. [Mod. L. (from Greek) =tortoise.] +A perennial plant having a corolla resembling the head of a tortoise; the snake-head or turtle-head. — **1784** CUTLER in *Mem. Academy* I. 464 *Chelone.* . . . Chelone. Fish-head. Snake-head. Blossoms in spikes; white. **1818** *Mass. H. S. Coll.* 2 Ser. VIII. 170 In August the eye is gratified with the flowers of . . . the beautiful chelone or snake-head. **1875** *Amer. Naturalist* IX. 388 With these charming plants are found . . . white chelone [etc.].

Chemisal, -izal. Variants of CHAMISAL.

+Chemise brush. See CHAMISO. — **1897** *Outing* XXX. 552/1 The deer's favorite browse is chemisal—'chemise brush' it is commonly called.

***Chemist.** A retailer of medicines or drugs. *rare.* {1745–} — **1683** *N.H. Hist. Soc. Coll.* VIII. 152 Your orator, having lent one Abraham Lee, . . . chemist, . . . several sums of money. **1795** *Ann. 3rd Congress* 1456 Nothing herein contained shall be construed to extend . . . to physicians, apothecaries, surgeons, or chemists.

Chenango. ?*Obs.* A variety of potato. — **1838** COLMAN *Mass. Agric. Rep.* 34 The Chenango, sometime called the Mercer, or Pennsylvania Blue.

Chenanekin, -anigan. Variants of SHENANIGAN.

Chenook. Variant of CHINOOK.

Cheque. Occasional variant of CHECK.

Chequer, †Checquer,** *v.* +*tr.* To mark out (land) with the plow in squares for planting. (Cf. CHECK *v.*[1]). — **1788** WASHINGTON *Diaries* III. 378 At Muddy hole, One plow . . . was employed in checquering . . . the three feet ridges which had been plowed for Pease. **1800** TATHAM *Agric. & Commerce* 56 It is also to be remembered, that a crop of maize is constantly ploughed and hoed, from the time of breaking up the ground, and *checquering* it. *c1836** CATLIN *Indians* II. 158, I have seen the rich Louisianian chequering out his cotton and sugar plantations.

Chequerboard. Variant of CHECKERBOARD. Also fig.

1732 FRANKLIN *Writings* II. 189 Mr. Crownhim . . . is always dreaming over the Chequer-Board. **1830** *Collegian* 128 Riding, walking, sailing, conversing, and the chequer-board, were our only resources. **1849** WILLIS *Rural Lett.* 74 It was the design of William Penn at Philadelphia, and think what a binding it would have been to his chequer-board.

fig. **1870** 'F. FERN' *Ginger-Snaps* 79 When some clerical big-gun is supposed to make a false move on the sacerdotal chequer-board.

Chequered, *a.* and *adv.* (See quotations.) — **1675** JOSSELYN *Two Voyages* 112 The Checkquered snake, having as many colours within the checkquers shadowing one another, as there are in a Rainbow. **1827** J. L. WILLIAMS *West Florida* 29 The garter, riband, green, chequered, and glass snakes, make up the account of this species, in West Florida. **1852** BRISTED *Upper Ten Th.* i. 33 The team are greys and chestnuts . . . driven *chequered:* that is, the horses of the same color diagonally.

+Cherk. Variant of CHIRK *a.* — **1878** COOKE *Happy Dodd* 286, I didn't feel real cherk this week. *Ib.* 354, I expect we all feel cherker and powerfuller in new clean clothes. **1891** — *Huckleberries* (1896) 163, I spose 'tis more cherk up there.

+Chermany. [Origin obscure.] (See quot. 1889.) — **1889** *Cent.* 948/3 *Chermany*, . . . in the southern United States, a variety of the game of base-ball. **1904** M. D. CONWAY *Autobiog.* I. 35 Our recess games were chiefly chermany and bandy.

+Cherokee. Also **†Cherackee, -ekee, -ikee, -ookee, Charokee, Cheerake.** ['Their national name is derived from *cheera*, 'fire,' which is their reputed lower heaven' (Adair). 'The tribal name is a corruption of Tsálăgĭ or Tsárăgĭ, the name by which they commonly called themselves' (Hodge).]

I. 1. *pl.* An Indian tribe of Iroquoian stock, formerly inhabiting the Carolinas and latterly settled in Oklahoma.

1721 *N.C. Col. Rec.* II. 422 The remaining 3800 Indians are the Cherokees, a Warlike Nation. **1724** H. JONES *Virginia* 5 The Senecaa Indians in their War Dress may appear as terrible as any of the Sons of Anak. The Usherees, Shuterees, and Cherackees are full as formidable. **1765** TIMBERLAKE *Mem.* 49 The Cherokees are of a middle stature, of an olive colour, tho' generally painted, and their skins stained with gun-powder, pricked into it in very pretty figures. **1789** *Ann. 1st Congress* I. 66 The Cherokees reside principally within the territory claimed by North Carolina. **1821** NUTTALL *Trav. Arkansa* 123 Along either bank the lands are . . . pretty thickly scattered with the cabins and farms of the Cherokees, this being the land allotted to them by congress, in exchange for others in the Mississippi Territory, where the principal part of the nation still remain. **1854** BENTON *30 Years' View* I. 166/1 The State of Georgia was seeking to subjugate and destroy the liberties both of the Creeks and the Cherokees. **1894** ROBLEY *Bourbon Co., Kansas* 5 In 1828 a treaty was made with the Cherokees, of Georgia, by which they were given the territory known as the Cherokee Nation.

b. *sing.* An Indian belonging to this tribe. *White Cherokee:* (see quot. 1873).

1836 HILDRETH *Campaigns Rocky Mts.* I. 97 Near to our encampment is the dwelling of an old Cherokee, named Rodger. **1873** BEADLE *Undevel. West* 358 The phrase 'White Cherokee' is generally applied to those of less than half Indian blood. **1878** — *Western Wilds* 43, I was let in under their law as bein' married to a Cherokee that had head-rights.

c. A Cherokee pony. (See sense 7.)

1839 *Knickerb.* XIII. 245 Never do I feel more vividly the pride of existence, than when . . . mounted on my swift-footed Cherokee.

2. a. Cherokee ways or customs. **b.** The language of the Cherokees, sometimes used as a symbol of remote learning or of something unintelligible.

(**a**) **1834** CARRUTHERS *Kentuckian* I. 220 We might show them fellers a little of the real Cherokee. (**b**) **1835** B. D. WINSLOW [*Harvard*] *Class Poem* 14 He peruses Persian, Hebrew, Greek Or dips for pleasure into Cherokee. *c***1849** PAIGE *Dow's Sermons* I. 155 There are all kinds of gibberish, from Cherokee up to Chaldee—but I consider the old English the best of any agoing. **1852** *Harper's Mag.* V. 395/2 The boys listened in silent awe to the eloquent appeal of the 'Luminary of the West,' but it was all Cherokee to Billy.

II. Attrib. or as adj.

3. Relating, pertaining, or belonging to, connected with, or characteristic of, the Cherokees.

1716 *N.C. Col. Rec.* II. 256 For an encouragement to the officers who shall command the said soldiers in the said Cherokee expedition. **1725** G. CHICKEN in *Travels Amer. Col.* 139 The Slav's that are now come up talk good English as well as the Cherokee Language. **1757** in *Lett. to Washington* II. 80 Rec[eive]d the above Goods . . . together with 13½ li. of Cherokee Beads. **1765** J. HABERSHAM *Letters* 36 Our clear Creek Leather is now rather esteemed better than Cherokee. **1778** *Va. State P.* I. 306 This deponent says, that he does not understand the Cherokee Tongue. **1800** B. HAWKINS *Sk. Creek Country* 44 He has employed an active girl of Georgia, . . . who was in the Cherokee department. **1821** NUTTALL *Trav. Arkansa* 130, I had again the pleasure of seeing the brother of the late governor Lewis, now Cherokee agent. **1867** W. H. DIXON *New America* II. 96 These people say, they want no Cherokee medicines, no plantation bitters, no Bourbon cocktails.

4. Of persons: Pertaining to the tribe of the Cherokees; esp. *Cherokee Indian, nation.*

(1) **1725** G. CHICKEN in *Travels Amer. Col.* 97 The place I ordered the Cherokee Indians (then down) to go to from my house. **1741** *Ga. Col. Rec.* III. 389 Horsemen can now ride from this Town to Savannah, as likewise to the Cherokee Indians. **1776** in Ramsey *Tennessee* (1853) 135 About six years ago, Col. Donelson . . . held a Treaty with the Cherokee Indians. **1847** D. COYNER *Lost Trappers* 142 Two days journey from these falls [in the Ark. River] they overtook eight Cherokee Indians going down to one of their villages.

(2) **1741** *S.C. Hist. Soc. Coll.* IV. 20 The General acquainted his Hon[o]r . . . that he had sent up an officer into the Cherokee Nation. **1775** ADAIR *Indians* 3 He went round an hundred miles, towarde the Cheerake nation, with his family, and the head warriors. **1787** *Steele Papers* I. 19 Hostilities may have commenced or are on the eve of commencing between the State of No. Carolina and the Cherokee nation of Indians. **1854** BENTON *30 Years' View* I. 625/1 Mr. Clay presented a memorial and protest against it from the 'Cherokee nation.' **1894** [see sense 1].

(3) **1725** G. CHICKEN in *Travels Amer. Col.* 103 The French Indians had killed . . . two Cherokee women. *Ib.* 120 The Cherokee woman. **1765** TIMBERLAKE *Mem.* 14 A party of seven or eight Cherokee hunters. **1853** RAMSEY *Tennessee* 301 To lose his horse, his tomahawk or his rifle, is equivalent, in the Cherokee warrior's code, to the loss of consequence and of honor.

5. Constituting, or connected with, the area occupied by the Cherokees; esp. *Cherokee country, strip.*

(1) **1756** *N.C. Col. Rec.* V. 635 Major Lewis is return'd from the Cherokee Country. **1765** TIMBERLAKE *Mem.* 9 We began our march towards the Cherokee country. **1775** *S.C. Hist. Soc. Coll.* II. 34 We will go into the Cherokee country—we never will make peace with them. **1854** BENTON *30 Years' View* I. 164/2 The legislature of the state laid off the Cherokee country into counties. **1873** BEADLE *Undevel. West* 355 This portion of the Cherokee country is but little settled.

(2) **1788** Marshall *Kentucky* (1812) 354 In case congress shall find it necessary to order troops to the Cherokee towns to enforce a due observance of the said treaty. **1789** *Steele Papers* I. 40 The Cherokee Claim within the limits of North Carolina was . . . from the River Tennessee to a line which had been fixed (I believe by Governor Tryon). **1797** B. HAWKINS *Letters* 92, I have judged proper to postpone the runing of the Creek line till we run the Cherokee line. **1847** D. COYNER *Lost Trappers* 142 They drew near a Cherokee village. **1849** LANMAN *Alleghany Mts.* 12 The State Legislature had divided the Cherokee Purchase into lots and regularly numbered them. **1888** *Congress. Globe* 24 July 6757/2 That is the issue . . . —whether . . . the Cherokee Outlet . . . shall be opened up . . . to settlement by white people.

(3) **1869** *Congress. Globe* 8 Dec. 29/2 Settlers on certain lands within the State of Kansas known as the 'Cherokee Strip.' **1871** *Ib.* 18 March 152/3 Mr. Pomeroy . . . obtained leave to introduce a bill . . . to provide for the sale of certain Indian lands in Kansas known as the 'Cherokee strip.' **1872** *Newton Kansan* 22 Aug. 2/4 Instructions for the entry of the Cherokee strip have been received at the Independence land office. **1888** *Congress. Globe* 24 July 6756 A debate which took place touching the Cherokee Strip.

fig. **1905** *Baltimore American* 7 March 4 On the boundary of what is known as the 'Cherokee Strip,' or, in other words, the section on the Democratic side occupied by Republican Senators who cannot find desks on the Republican side.

6. a. *Cherokee plum*, a species of wild plum.

1781–2 JEFFERSON *Notes Va.* (1788) 36 Cherokee plumb. *Prunus sylvestris fructu majori.* **1786** WASHINGTON *Diaries* III. 32 Hoed the ground behind the Garden again and planted therein, in three rows, 177 of the wild, or Cherokee plumb. **1842** BUCKINGHAM *Slave States* I. 180 The Cherokee plum, now putting forth its blossoms, was like the blackthorn of England in May, and produces a small, round, harsh, and sour fruit, like the sloe.

b. *Cherokee rose*, a Chinese climbing rose, with fragrant white flowers, naturalized in the southern states.

1829 EATON *Botany* (ed. 5) 368 *Rosa laevigata*, Cherokee rose. **1833** J. STUART *3 Years N.A.* II. 158 There were hedges of the Cherokee rose. **1846** THORPE *Myst. Backwoods* 158 A rough Virginia fence, over which the Cherokee rose had entwined itself. **1896** J. C. HARRIS *Sister Jane* 19 The Cherokee rose was rapidly covering the broken-down fences with its glistening green shield. **1901** MOHR *Plant Life Ala.* 54 The Cherokee rose . . . , also at home in eastern Asia, is said to have been found by the whites on their first arrival at the villages of the Cherokees and Creeks.

c. *Cherokee (rose) hedge*, a hedge composed of Cherokee roses.

1836 GILMAN *Recoll.* (1838) 53 [He] asked me some questions about the Cherokee rose-hedge, and other objects in view. *Ib.* 89 It was his delight to . . . enter the avenue where the Cherokee hedge shut out the view. **1888** *Harper's Mag.* May 867/1 Their only exit lay at the end of the Cherokee hedge.

7. *Cherokee cattle, pony* (cf. 1c), *turkey*, (see quotations).

1834 SIMMS *Guy Rivers* II. 138 The reader has already heard something of the Cherokee pony. . . . They are a small, but compactly made and hardy creature. **1868** *Ill. Agric. Soc. Trans.* VII. 142 The long-horned or Cherokee cattle passing through North Carolina and Virginia on their way to the Northern markets. **1893** *Columbus* (O.) *Dispatch* 30 Nov., We . . . beg leave to present you with the accompanying 'Cherokee turkey,' alias bald eagle, in time for the approaching Thanksgiving festival.

‖**Cherokeed,** *a.* (See quotation.) — **1771** *Mass. Spy* 21 March (Th.), An old fashioned lady, with a foretop of hair Cherokeed, to imitate the Indian dress.

Cheroot. A cigar with both ends cut flat. {1759–} — **1856** *Spirit of Times* 25 Oct. 130/2 By the aid of this [=punch], and a dozen cheroots, . . . the evening passed quickly. **1902** WHITE *Conjuror's House* vii. 83 The doctor, lighting a cheroot, took his way across to his infirmary.

Cherri-, Cherryderry. *Obs.* Also **Cherrederry, Cheridary.** [Of obscure origin.] A make of cloth used for garments. Chiefly attrib. — **1712** *Boston News-Letter* 11–18 Aug. 2/2 A Spanish Indian man . . . [wearing] a Cheridary Wastcoat. **1723** HEMPSTEAD *Diary* 132 Cuz Fox made my Cherryderry breeches. **1724** *New-Eng. Courant* 6–13 July 2/2 He took with him an old Cherriderry Jacket and Breeches. **1728** *Boston News-Letter* 15–22 Aug. 2/2 She . . . has on a narrow stript Cherrederry Gown. **1732** *S.C. Gazette* 135/2 Lately imported, and to be sold . . . Seersuckers, Cherryderrys, china Ware [etc.].

***Cherry.**

***1.** The fruit of various wild or cultivated species of *Cerasus* or American species of *Prunus*.

'Our wild plums are like cherries in having the leaves folded before expansion, . . . thus confounding the distinction' (Gray).

1612 SMITH *Virginia* 11 They have Cherries, and those are much like a Damsen; but for their tastes and colour, we called them Cherries. **1634** WOOD *New Eng. Prospect* I. v. 18 The Cherrie trees yeeld great store of Cherries, which grow on clusters like Grapes. **1685** SEWALL *Diary* I. 83 Carried my Wife to Dorchester to eat Cherries, Rasberries, [etc.]. **1760** in E. Singleton *Social N.Y.* 42 A garden . . . filled with a choice collection of English fruit, such as . . . plums, cherries, [etc.]. **1815** DRAKE *Cincinnati* 55 Pears, cherries and plumbs, of different kinds, are common. **1899** *Mo. So. Dakotan* I. 139 About twenty bushels of cherries on a baker's dozen of trees.

2. One or other of the trees bearing this fruit. {1626–} Freq. in collective or generic sense.

1709 LAWSON *Carolina* 104 The Cherries of the Woods grow to be very large Trees. **1789** E. DENNY *Journal* 132 A great deal of poplar, walnut, locust, cherry, shellbark hickory and black oak. **1807** GASS *Journal* 195 The timber is mostly of the fir kind, with some cherry. **1883** ZEIGLER & GROSSCUP *Alleghanies* 49 We noticed several cherries measuring four and a half feet through, and towering . . . . 79 feet before shooting out a limb. **1906** PITTMAN *Belle of Blue Grass C.* 3 The cherries and the pears and apples were all abloom.

3. The wood of the cherry tree. {1793}

1879 B. F. TAYLOR *Summer-Savory* 79 In that shadow on a summer's day stood a tea-table, with a coffin of cherry upon it. **1888** *Amer. Humorist* 5 May 8/2 The reading room is 18 by 25 feet, finished in polished cherry.

4. *ellipt.* A cordial made of the juice of cherries (esp. wild cherries) and spirits, sweetened and diluted.

1828 WEBSTER s. v., Cherry . . . is moderately bitter and astringent.

5. The characteristic color of a red cherry.

1875 STOWE *We & Our Neighbors* 44, I can judge . . . better than he can settle the difference between . . . cherry and solferino in curtains.

6. *attrib.* **a.** In sense 1, with *bitters, draught, dumpling, pudding*, etc.

1843 'CARLTON' *New Purchase* II. 16 Mr. James Jimmey will take strange students . . . to board . . . and—give them their dog-wood and cherry-bitters every morning into the bargain. **1867** *Common Sense Cook Book* 110 [Recipe for] Cherry Draught. **1832** CHILD *Frugal Housewife* 63 Cherry Pudding. For cherry dumpling, make a paste about as rich as you make short-cake. **1845** F. DOUGLASS *Narrative* i, I do not remember to have ever met a slave who could tell of his birthday. They seldom come nearer to it than . . . cherry-time, spring-time, harvest-time, or fall-time. **1867** W. H. DIXON *New America* II. 101 The ladies at Mt. Lebanon . . . make rose-water, cherry-water, peach-water.

b. In sense 2, with *blow, bud, bush*, etc.

1887 WILKINS *Humble Romance* 193 Silas kept talking to himself or rather murmuring, . . . 'apple-blows and cherry-blows and daffodils.' **1775** WASHINGTON *Diaries* II. 179 The cherry buds were a good deal swell'd. **1832** in Kennedy *Texas* (1841) I. 185 Undergrowth [consists of] plum, cherry, and currant bushes, with much grape-vine. **1760** WASHINGTON *Diaries* I. 146 Transplanted to the Corner of the Borders by Garden House a Cherry Graft. **1783** FLEMING in *Travels Amer. Col.* 663 Travelling through poor indiferent green cherry land. **1764** WASHINGTON *Diaries* I. 199 To the end of the Row are Cherry Scions for Grafting upon another year. **1879** *Scribner's Mo.* Nov. 35/2 Some twig . . . has been grafted or budded on the ordinary cherry stock.

c. In sense 3, with *furniture, plate.*

1886 *Harper's Mag.* July 194/2 The Library . . . amply provided with leather-covered cherry furniture. **1845** S. JUDD *Margaret* I. ii. 10 Margaret . . . had a cherry plate [ed. 1851 cherry-wood plate] with a wolf's bone knife and fork.

d. In names of insects, etc., infesting cherries.

1892 V. KELLOG *Kansas Insects* 90 Cherry aphis (*Myzus cerasi*). . . . I have seen young cherry trees with large portions of their fresh leaves . . . blackened by these insects. **1854** EMMONS *Agric. N.Y.* V. 79 The rosebug, or cherrybug, as it is called, is very destructive. **1865–6** *Ill. Agric. Soc. Trans.* VI. 398 The cherry slug, the most disgusting insect of its size I know of.

+Cherry birch. The sweet or black birch, *Betula lenta*.

1810 MICHAUX *Arbres* I. 26 (*Betula lenta*). Black birch, cherry birch. **1850** S. F. COOPER *Rural Hours* 385 The cherry birch, or black birch, is also a northern variety, and very common here; it is used for cabinet work. **1857** GRAY *Botany* 411 Cherry Birch. . . . A rather large tree, . . . timber rose-colored, fine-grained, valuable for cabinet-work. **1901** MOHR *Plant Life Ala.* 72 In this valley the hemlock is accompanied by the sweet or cherry birch, . . . at home in the same northern life zone.

+Cherry bird. The cedarbird or Carolina waxwing, *Bombycilla cedrorum*.

1808 WILSON *Ornithology* I. 112 In some parts of the country they are called Crown-birds; in others Cherry-birds, from their fondness for that fruit. They also feed on ripe persimmons. **1850** *New Eng. Farmer* II. 213 The cedar or cherry bird was first noticed west of the Genesee River in 1828. **1872** *Vt. Bd. Agric. Rep.* I. 328 A bird quite as much disliked by the fruit growers as the Robin is the Cedar Bird, or Cherry Bird. **1884** *Harper's Mag.* March 616/1, I won't speak of the Carolina wax-wing, alias cedar or cherry bird, now.

Cherry bounce. An alcoholic liquor flavored with cherries. {1798–; cherry-bouncer, 1693}

1784 WASHINGTON *Diaries* II. 299 In my equipage Trunk and the Canteens—were Madeira and Port Wine—Cherry Bounce—Oyl [etc.]

1810 M. V. DWIGHT *Journey* 54 They gave us a great many apples & some cherry bounce. 1836 W. O'BRYAN *Travels* 70 On the road had a cordial new to me then, called Cherry Bounce, made of Cider, Whiskey, and Cherries. 1889 S. HALE *Letters* 212 The last thing was home-made cherry bounce.

Cherry brandy. Brandy in which cherries have been steeped. {1728–}

1686 DUNTON *Lett. New Eng.* (1867) 33 My Dearest Love . . . had laid out about £8 in Sweet-meats, . . . Cherry-Brandy, and the like Knick-knacks. 1866 MOORE *Women of War* 133 On the other [side were] boxes of tea, coffee, . . tamarinds, cherry brandy, &c. 1883 BAGBY *Old Va. Gentleman* 141 In a little store at the station they had discovered a lot of delicious cherry brandy, which they were dispatching with thoughtless haste.

+**Cherry cranberry.** (See quotation.) — 1874 *Dept. Agric. Rep. 1873* 445 The American cranberry is divided by growers and writers into three different varieties, viz., the Bell cranberry, . . . the Bugle cranberry, . . . the Cherry cranberry, which is similar in size, shape, and color to the cherry.

+**Cherry currant.** (See first quot.) — 1855 *Chicago Times* 19 July 4/3 We were shown on Saturday a noble specimen of fruit called the 'cherry currant.' . . . Except for its transparency, the fruit might pass for grapes. It is a new variety. 1868 *Mich. Agric. Rep.* VII. 429 Currants—Red Dutch, Cherry, White Grape, and Black Naples.

Cherrying. Gathering cherries. — 1716 CHURCH *Philip's War* 26 Mr. Church . . . rid out with his Wife and some of his friends . . . under a pretence of Cherrying.

Cherry pie. A pie made with cherries.

1832 CHILD *Frugal Housewife* 67 Cherry pies should be baked in a deep plate. 1842 [see CHEESECAKE]. 1867 *Iowa Agric. Soc. Rep.* (1868) 190 A cherry pie in Christmas times is a luxury. 1912 N. WOODROW *Sally Salt* 22 There are berries and melons and cherry pie.

+**Cherry rum.** Rum made with cherries. — 1793 in *Harper's Mag.* (1877) Feb. 479/2 Charlestown, April 6, 1793. This day Recd. of Benja[min] Wright one Glass of Cherry Rum. *a*1848 in Northall *Yankee Hill* 118 Our folks at hum would have all come to this meeting, but they've been busy making cherry rum. 1855 BARNUM *Life* 21 My stock . . . comprised 'ginger bread,' cookies, . . . and cherry rum.

+**Cherry-stone clam.** A small round species of clam or quahog. — 1880 'MARK TWAIN' *Tramp Abroad* xlix. 574, I have selected a few dishes, and made out a little bill of fare . . . as follows: . . . Cherry-stone clams.

+**Cherry table.** A table made of cherrywood. — 1855 *S. Lit. Messenger* XXI. 515/2 A score of little cherry tables upon which to serve whiskey punch and lager beer. 1857 *Quinland* I. 19 Still another gets out, from one corner of the room, the 'cherry table,'—a table that is never used, except upon state occasions, in Peter Quinland's house. 1889 R. T. COOKE *Steadfast* 13 A small cherry table with two leaves.

+**Cherry tomato.** A variety of tomato having a small fruit. — 1847 DARLINGTON *Weeds & Plants* 251 The small round kind, known as 'Cherry Tomato,' is probably *L. Cerasiforme.* 1892 COULTER *Bot. W. Texas* II. 297 *Lycopersicum esculentum.* (Cherry tomato.) . . . Introduced from tropical America.

* **Cherry tree, Cherry-tree.** Also †**cheri-, chirrie.**

* **1.** A tree of the genus *Cerasus* or of American species of *Prunus.*

1622 'MOURT' *Relation* 62 Vines euery where. Cherry trees, Plum-trees, and many other which we know not. 1676 GLOVER *Acc. Va.* in *Phil. Trans.* XI. 628 The Cherry-Trees grow more large generally than they do in England, and bear more plentifully without any pains-taking of digging about them, or pruning them. 1737 WESLEY *Journal* I. (1910) 402 In the moistest part of this land some persimmon-trees grow . . . , and a few mulberry and cherry-trees. 1873 PHELPS *Trotty's Wedding* xiii, I knew the cherry-trees in the garden must be shaking and tossing. 1881 M. J. HOLMES *Madeline* v. 82 On a rustic bench, built for Maddy beneath the cherry-trees, Grandpa Markham sat down to rest.

fig. 1830 PAULDING *Chron. Gotham* 252 '*You* will!' cried her ladyship, contemptuously, 'your will is in the cherry-tree.'

2. Attrib. with *bluff, hollow, table, worm.*

1754 *Ga. Col. Rec.* VI. 429 He prayed for two hundred Acres of Land, situated at a Place known by the Name of Cherry Tree Bluff. 1659 *Hempstead Town Rec.* I. 75 There is Granted vnto Josias Forman, the wallnut hollow, and the cherry-tree hollow. 1825 NEAL *Bro. Jonathan* I. 10 Edith had rubbed with her own little hands, a fine old cherry-tree table. 1854 EMMONS *Agric. N.Y.* V. 261 Index, Cherrytree worms.

Cherry wine. A fermented liquor made from cherry juice. {*a* 1648} — 1781 PETERS *Conn.* (1829) 186 The inhabitants [of Connecticut] . . . make . . . grape, cherry, and currant wines. 1854 *Penna. Agric. Rep.* 176 Cherry Wine, first premium to Mrs. Miller Fox.

Cherrywood. The wood of the cherry tree. Also attrib. — 1821 *Jrnl. Science* III. 167 In staining cherry wood, cabinet-makers generally employ some kind of red paint. 1840 HOFFMAN *Greyslaer* II. 96 A small cherry-wood table and a few rush-bottomed chairs. 1889 R. T. COOKE *Steadfast* 119 A tall piece of old cherry-wood furniture on four slender claw-footed legs.

+**Cheshire.** A breed of white hogs, originating in N.Y. *c*1850. — 1890 *Cent.* 6113/2 Cheshires and Victorias are white swine, originating in New York State, which do not represent distinct breeds. 1893 G. W. CURTIS *Horses*, etc. 314 Mr. R. D. Button, a leading breeder of Cheshires. *Ib.*, Breeding, selling, and exhibiting Cheshire swine.

* **Chess.**[1] The game of that name.

1788 FRANKLIN *Autobiog.* 347 An acquaintance, who was also learning it, us'd often to tempt me to play chess with him. 1827 DEWEES *Lett. Texas* 70 Here is a game of chess, and there a game of roulette. 1883 *Wheelman* I. 352 On other tables were cards, chess, etc.—for the club. 1907 C. C. ANDREWS *Recoll.* (1928) 28 One rainy forenoon, Fred Curtis and I were playing chess in my office.

Chess.[2] One or other species of brome grass growing as a weed, esp. in wheat fields. {1736–} Cf. CHEAT.

1751 ELIOT *Field-Husb.* iii. 61 Otherwise Tares, Cockle, Chess, and the like . . . will increase from year to year. 1805 *Balance* (Hudson, N.Y.) 15 Oct. 332 (Th.), None of them came up, except three small blades just before winter, which I suppose are chess. 1835 P. SHIRREFF *Tour* 83, I had observed the wheat crops of America abounding with a species of grass passing by the name of chess, which I imagine to be the *Bromus secalinus* of botanists. 1898 *Congress. Rec.* App. 13 Jan. 463/1 A sample of seeds . . . sold to a New Hampshire farmer . . . was composed entirely of chess—one of the most vile weeds known to the farmer.

attrib. 1849 *Rep. Comm. Patents: Agric.* (1850) 455, I am prepared to say that chess-seed will grow, and that wheat will not turn to chess. 1863 *Rep. Comm. Agric.* 103 If he sows chess seed with his wheat, he will be quite likely to harvest a mixture of wheat and chess.

* **Chessman.** [CHESS.[1]] A piece used in playing the game of chess.

1781 *Salem Gazette* 3 July, Isaac Greenwood . . . makes Flutes, . . . Back-Gammon Boxes Men and Dies, Chess Men, Billiard-Balls [etc.]. 1836 J. D. WHITNEY *Life & Lett.* 16, I have received two bundles from home, one containing Chessmen, etc. and the other a pair of pantaloons. 1912 N. WOODROW *Sally Salt* 41, [I] noticed the chessmen on the what-not looking kind of lonesome and dusty.

Chessy, *a.* [CHESS.[2]] Full of chess. — 1842 C. M. KIRKLAND *Forest Life* I. 153 My wheat was unaccountable chessy, though I turned water upon it and kept it moist all summer.

Chessy cat. Also **chesse.** [Alteration of *Cheshire cat* {*a*1800–}.] *To grin like a chessy cat,* to grin broadly. — 1830 *Collegian* 193 Sherry, contrary to his wont, grinning like a chesse-cat. 1849 *Knickerb.* XXXIV. 339/1 First he grinned like a chessy cat, and then laughed right eoüt. 1889 *Amer. Notes & Q.* IV. 23 Fifty years ago, in New England, we used to hear the expression, 'Grinning like a *Chessy* cat.'

* **Chest.** Also **chist** (now *dial.*), †**cheast.**

* **1.** A box with a lid and usually a lock, in which personal property or other articles are kept for safety or easy transport.

1643 R. WILLIAMS *Key* (1866) 68 Many of them [=Indians] begin to be furnished with English Chests. 1674 *Harvard Rec.* I. 60 Only the plate [is] to be brought to the presidents house and lodged in the Colledg desks or chest there. 1712 HEMPSTEAD *Diary* 8, I was at home . . . making a Cheast for Christopher Darro. 1775 *Essex Inst. Coll.* XLVIII. 50, I went to work for John Barker a making him a Chist. 1827 J. HOWE *Journal* 32 On the top of the chest and on each box, were old bedclothes. 1861 *Army Regulations* 164 The regimental and company desk . . . will be transported; . . . and for medical officers, their medical chest. 1891 WILKINS *New Eng. Nun* 90 There I had a whole house, with . . . beddin' packed away in chists, an' bureau drawers full of things.

2. A box in which certain articles, as tea, are commonly packed.

1773 J. ANDREWS *Letters* 324 Hall and Bruce arriv'd Saturday evening with each an hundred and odd chests of the detested Tea.

* **3.** A simple form of coffin. {now *dial.*}

1676 SEWALL *Diary* I. 20, I holp carry her part of the way to the grave. Put in a wooden Chest.

4. *Chest of drawers,* an article of furniture consisting of several drawers fitted within a substantial casing. {1677–}

1649 *Conn. Public Rec.* I. 501 An Inventory of the estate of Mr. Thomas Hooker . . . [lists] a clock, a safe, . . . a chest of drawers. 1714 *Boston News-Letter* 10–17 May 2/2 To be Sold . . . new Fashioned Chests of Drawers, Walnut-Tree, and Wainscot Desks. 1807 IRVING, etc. *Salmagundi* xiv, Every chest of drawers . . is decorated with enormous china punch-bowls. 1896 WILKINS *Madelon* 28 There was a tall chest of drawers that reached the ceiling.

b. *Chest upon chest,* an article of furniture so constructed as to resemble two chests of drawers placed one upon the other.

1819 NOAH *She would be a Soldier* I. i, I had put my house in such nice order—painted my walls—got a new chest upon chest.

5. Attrib. with *draw, hinge, key, lock.*

1648 *Conn. Public Rec.* I. 492 A chest lock. 1718 *N.H. Probate Rec.* II. 74, I give all my Plate to my four daughters . . . with all my wife's linnen in the Chest Draws. 1778 *Essex Inst. Coll.* XLIX. 106 Sold by order of Capt. William Pickman: . . . H hinges, chest hinges, shirt buttons [etc.]. 1853 STOWE *Key* II. 236 It was proved on the trial that Carroll, a white man, . . . had in his possession . . . the chest-keys of the deceased.

+**Chester White.** [See quot. 1893.] A breed of swine; a pig of this breed. Also attrib. with *boar, pig.*

1856 *Rep. Comm. Patents: Agric.* 61 The best breed of swine which we rear is the 'Chester White.' **1880** *Harper's Mag.* Nov. 927/1 One of his parishioners . . . had presented him with a Chester White pig. **1885** in G. W. Curtis *Horses* (1893) 307 Mr. S. H. Todd . . . in 1867 began crossing these animals with pure Chester-Whites, . . . finally producing what is now known as Todd's Improved Chester-White. **1893** *Ib.* 305 Chester-Whites. The breed derives its name from the place of its origin—Chester county, Pennsylvania. **1925** BRYAN *Memoirs* 34 My first experience with hogs was with a Chester White boar.

Chest founder. [Cf. next.] A rheumatic affection of the muscles of the chest in horses. — **1791** WASHINGTON *Diaries* IV. 150 The lame horse . . . as soon as he stopped, discovered a stiffness in all his limbs, which indicated some painful disorder. I fear a Chest founder.

Chest-foundered, *a.* Affected with chest founder. {1703} — *a*1846 *Quarter Race Ky.*, etc. 96 'Chest foundered' and hairless, And 'sprung' though she be, She's an eye-sore to others, A good 'un to me.

***Chestnut, †Chesnut.** Also †**chestnutt, chessnut(t).**

***1.** The nut or seed of a species of *Castanea* (see sense 2), of which two or three are inclosed in a round prickly bur.

1588 T. HARRIOT *Briefe & True Report Virginia* ii, Chestnuts, there are in diuers places great store: some they vse to eate rawe. **1681** *Penna. Mag.* VI. 175 The Hoggs eat the *Chesnuts*, as they do the Acorns. **1709** LAWSON *Carolina* 53 Here is plenty of Chesnuts, which are rarely found in Carolina, and never near the Sea, or Salt-Water. **1761** NILES *Indian Wars* II. 410 She made her escape, and was 14 days in the woods, . . . and lived on chestnuts. **1852** MITCHELL *Dream Life* 201 The squirrels . . . gnaw off the full-grown burs of the chestnuts. **1880** *Harper's Mag.* Aug. 355/2 There are enough chestnuts . . . to feed all famishing India.

***2.** The large handsome tree *Castanea vesca*, esp. the American variety of this, native in the area east of the Mississippi.

1616 SMITH *New England* 16 Oke, is the chiefe wood; . . . walnut—chesnut, birch . . . and many other sorts. **1637** MORTON *New Canaan* II. ii, Chestnut: of this sorte there is very greate plenty, the tymber whereof is excellent for building. **1643** R. WILLIAMS *Key* (1866) 42 They set no corne, but live on the bark of Chestnut and Walnut, and other fine trees. **1755** L. EVANS *Anal. Map Colonies* 28 This has fine Land, while extended Meadows, lofty Timber; . . . Walnut, Chestnut and Poplar [fitted] for domestic Services. **1824** BRYANT *Summer Wind* line 30 Among the nearer groves, chestnut and oak Are tossing their green boughs about. **1865** *Atlantic Mo.* XV. 521 The ground is mainly occupied with Cedar and Chestnut.

3. A single tree of this species.

1612 SMITH *Virginia* 11 In some parts, were found some Chestnuts whose wild fruit equalize the best in France, Spaine, Germany, or Italy. **1668** *Boston Rec.* 42 The first tree . . . is . . . a chestnutt by the ash swampe. **1788** J. MAY *Journal & Lett.* 69, I have . . . not seen any chestnuts, nor any birch or alders. **1865** *Atlantic Mo.* XV. 514, I go out in the woods, and am attracted by a faint piping and lisping in the tops of the Oaks and Chestnuts. **1891** RYAN *Pagan* 187 Krin . . . leaned breathless against the young chestnut she had been working to bring down.

4. The horse chestnut or buckeye. {1832–}

1775 BURNABY *Travels* 12 They are likewise adorned and beautified with . . . scarlet-flowering chesnuts, fringe-trees, flowering poplars.

5. The wood of the chestnut tree. {1823}

1728 *Boston Rec.* 222 We are of opinion that no popler, chestnut, pine, . . . or ceder shall be corded up or exposed to sale with . . . any firewood.

6. A chestnut-brown horse. {1840–}

1760 WASHINGTON *Diaries* I. 161, I . . . was told that my great Chestnut folded [*sic*] a Horse Colt. **1855** BRISTED in *Cambridge Ess.* 64 The Americans also used the word chesnut, but with a limited signification, applying it only to the dark chesnut, what the French call *alezan brulé.* **1868** WOODRUFF *Trotting Horse* 82 The horse who got the little bay out of her was a pacer,—a chestnut. **1894** *Vt. Agric. Rep.* XIV. 96 She is a handsome chestnut.

+**7.** An old or stale joke or story. *colloq.*

The numerous accounts of the origin of this use offered from 1886 onward are mutually exclusive and all incapable of proof. A writer in *Notes & Queries* (1889, VII. 52) stated: 'I first heard the word in 1882, in a theatrical chop-house (Brown's) in New York.'

1886 *Boston Herald* June, One of the peculiar tidal waves of popularity having brought the term 'chestnut,' as applied to everything jocular and antediluvian, into prominence, its origin is being discussed. **1886** *Detroit Free Press* 25 Sept., One of the latest slang terms is the word 'chestnut.' *Ib.*, While they rung off their old chestnuts on me, they were sweltering in laundried shirts. **1887** *Harper's Mag.* May 942/1 'Well, you know *Punch's* advice to those about to marry?' 'I know—chestnuts.' **1888** *Congress. Rec.* 11 July 6147/1 Those remarks were uttered in years past, and are the oldest kind of chestnut.

8. *attrib.* **a.** With *bark, bloom, blossom,* etc.

1643 R. WILLIAMS *Key* (1866) 61 Burching barke, and Chestnut barke which they dress finely, and make a Summer covering for their houses. **1880** *Harper's Mag.* LXI. 184/2 Delicious vistas opened . . . of the Cheat winding through hills white with Chestnut blooms. *Ib.* 355 The endless lines of hills . . . were fawn-colored with early chestnut blossoms. **1865** *Atlantic Mo.* XV. 514 Presently I perceive a troop of . . . Ruby-Crowned Wrens flashing through the Chestnut-Branches. **1840** *Knickerb.* XVI. 164 Bob Tarleton, a strapping fellow, with a head like a chestnut-burr, . . . stepped up. **1733** *Providence Rec.* IX. 67 E: 52 P to a Chestnut bush. **1691** *Derby* (Conn.) *Rec.* 152 Marked . . . from thence Eastward with a Chestnut stub. **1683** *Jamaica* (L.I.) *Rec.* I. 271 [A line] runing to the great chesnut stump by his house. **1831** PECK *Guide* 124 It is reported that in some of the northern portions of the state, some chestnut timber is found.

b. With *country, hill, land, ridge.*

1817 U. BROWN *Journal* II. 372 Thence 21 Miles through a poor thin Chestnut Country without farmers. **1693** *Waterbury Prop. Rec.* 38 Two acers of land one the sid of chesnut hill. **1755** L. EVANS *Anal. Map Colonies* 28 Consisting in general of low dry Ridges of White-Oak and Chestnut Land. **1754** in Chalkley *Scotch-Irish Settlement Va.* III. 323, 155 acres on a chestnut ridge in Beverley Manor.

c. With *bell* (sense 7).

1886 *Detroit Free Press* 25 September, The now well-known chestnut bell. This is a little gong attached to the vest, and when an old story is told the silver tone of the gong takes the place of the words 'chestnut' or 'rats.'

9. *comb.* In specific names: (see quotations).

1874 COUES *Birds N.W.* 22 Chestnut-backed Chickadee. . . . The centre of abundance of this species appears to be in Washington Territory. **1858** BAIRD *Birds Pacific R.R.* 435 Chestnut-collared bunting. . . . A chestnut band on the back of the neck extending round on the sides. **1874** COUES *Birds N.W.* 192 Chestnut Hangnest . . . is abundant in the eastern portions of the Missouri, and of common occurrence along the wooded streams of the mountains. **1885** *Amer. Naturalist* Sept. 923 The lamprey eel of Kansas, parasitic on the buffalo-fish, etc., proves to be usually the chestnut lamprey. **1785** MARSHALL *Amer. Grove* 125 *Quercus Prinus.* Chesnut-leaved Oak. . . . The timber somewhat approaches toward that of Chesnut in appearance.

+**Chestnut coal.** Anthracite coal in small pieces of about an inch in size: (see also quotation 1924). — **1858** *Rep. Comm. Patents* (1859) I. 105 The next screen contains the 'nut' and its successor the 'chestnut' size. **1889** *Cent.* 951 Chestnut coal . . . is known in the trade as No. 5 coal. **1924** SHURICK *Coal Industry* 149 Anthracite coal is separated into seven common sizes, which have been standardized as follows: . . . chestnut, $\frac{3}{4}$ to $1\frac{3}{8}$ inches; stove, $1\frac{3}{8}$ to 2 inches [etc.].

+**Chestnut oak.** Also †**chesnut.**

1. One or other American species of oak having leaves resembling those of the chestnut; esp. the common southern species, *Quercus prinus.*

Other species are commonly distinguished by specific names, as *dwarf, mountain, rock, yellow chestnut oak.*

1709 LAWSON *Carolina* 91 Chesnut-Oak, is a very lofty Tree, . . . the largest Oaks we have, yielding the fairest Plank. **1785** MARSHALL *Amer. Grove* 119 Our swine are often wholly fatted upon the several kinds of acorns, but for these [of the white oak] and Chesnut Oak they seek most diligently. **1815** DRAKE *Cincinnati* 82 The most valuable timber trees are the . . . white, black, low-land, chestnut and bur oaks. **1901** MOHR *Plant Life Ala.* 91 On the outcrops of the subcarboniferous limestone the chestnut oak (*Quercus acuminata*), here in its best development, is not infrequent.

attrib. **1703** *Providence Rec.* V. 176 The Northwest Corner is a Chessnut Oake Tree. **1847** in H. Howe *Ohio Hist. Coll.* 27 They . . . collect the chestnut-oak bark from the neighboring hill tops.

2. A single tree belonging to one of these species.

1708 SEWALL *Diary* II. 222 By the Stump grows up a fine little Chestnut Oak. **1787** SARGENT in *Mem. Academy* II. I. 156 White, and Chestnut Oaks, from eighteen inches to six feet diameter. **1816** U. BROWN *Journal* I. 221 [We] found on our right 4 or 5 poles a Chestnut Oak. **1884** 'CRADDOCK' *Tenn. Mts.* 60 Now and again the forest quiet was broken by the patter of acorns from the chestnut-oaks.

+**Chestnut rail.** A fence rail made from the chestnut tree.

1783 *Huntington Rec.* III. 99, 1300 Chestnut Rails which fenced the above Trees at 3s per 100. **1820** *Niles' Reg.* XVIII. 256/1 At 97 he went into the woods and split 100 chesnut rails in less than a day. **1876** WHITMAN *Specimen Days* (1882) 83 As every man has his hobby-liking, mine is for a real farm-lane fenced by old chestnut-rails.

attrib. **1854** EMMONS *Agric. N.Y.* V. 261 Index, Chestnut-rail worm. [*Ib.* 118 *Clytus campestris.* . . . The larva is injurious to fallen chestnut timber, damaging it for rails.]

+**Chestnut-sided,** *a.* Having chestnut-colored sides; the specific epithet of a species of warbler (*Dendroica pennsylvanica*). Also ellipt.

1810 WILSON *Ornithology* II. 99 [The] Chesnut-Sided warbler, *Sylvia Pennsylvanica,* . . . is one of those transient visitors. **1839** PEABODY *Mass. Birds* 309 The Chestnut-sided Warbler . . . in 1837, [was] quite common near Connecticut river. **1844** *Nat. Hist. N.Y., Zoology* II. 102 The Chestnut-Sided Warbler, *Sylvicola icterocephala,* . . . winters in Mexico and does not appear to advance much farther north than Massachusetts. **1865** *Atlantic Mo.* XV. 521, I miss in the woods . . . the Chestnut-Sided Warbler, the Blue-Backed Warbler, [etc.]. **1895** *Outing* April 69/2, I made out the blue yellow-back, the Nashville, the chestnut-sided, the magnolia, the blackpoll and the black-throated green.

Chestnut-sorrel, *a. Obs.* Of a bright chestnut color. Also as *n.*, a horse of this color. — **1738** *Va. Gazette* 29 Dec., Strayed away . . . a Chestnut Sorrel Stallion, branded on the near Buttock, with a V V. **1751** *Ib.* 28 Feb., They stole two horses . . . one a middle-siz'd dull Bay, the other a Chestnut Sorrel.

+**Chestnutting,** *vbl. n.* and *pres. pple.* Also †**-nuting, chesnut(t)ing.** Gathering chestnuts.

1775 S. HAWS in *Mil. Journals* (1855) 77, I went a chesnuting with a number of respectable gentlemen that belonged to the army. . . . I went a chesnuting up to Neutown. **1854** THOREAU *Walden* 211, I went a-chestnutting there in the fall. **1875** STOWE *We & Our Neighbors* 314 Reminiscences of boys and girls going chestnutting. **1884** ROE *Nature's Story* (1885) 370 She had that very morning broached the subject of a chestnutting party. **1907** M. C. HARRIS *Tents of Wickedness* II. 113, I know I would apostatise for a chestnutting in Frost's woods on a mellow September afternoon.

* **Chestnut tree.** Also †**chesnut, chessnut(t).**

* **1.** = CHESTNUT 3.

1622 'MOURT' *Relation* 105 There is much good Timber both Oake, Walnut-tree, Firre, Beech, and exceeding great Chessnut-trees. **1679** *Conn. Public Rec.* III. 27 Neer Haddum bownds we marked two chessnutt trees which grew on one roote close by a great rock. **1703** *Providence Rec.* V. 53 A Chesnut Tree Marked, the which is a Southerne Corner bound of said percell of land. **1782** J. ST. JOHN *Letters* 81 A New-England man . . . shewed us how to split them [=shingles] out of chestnut-trees. **1838** HAWTHORNE *Note-Books* I. 151 He had one hundred chestnut-trees on his own land. **1882** *Wheelman* I. 13 The riders . . . , dismounting, walked away into a pasture in search of a group of prehistoric chestnut trees.

2. = CHESTNUT 2.

1676 GLOVER *Acc. Va.* in *Phil. Trans.* XI. 629, I lately made mention of the Chesnut, Walnut and Hasel-Tree, which all of them bear their several Nuts. **1785** MARSHALL *Amer. Grove* 46 *Fagus castanea dentata.* American Chesnut Tree. . . . The timber is used for rails. **1805** PARKINSON *Tour* 374 The chesnut-tree is very handsome, and its fruit pleasant. **1851** SPRINGER *Forest Life* 30 The Chestnut-tree . . . is distinguished by the rapidity of its growth.

+**Chestnut weevil.** (See quotations.) — **1862** *Rep. Comm. Patents: Agric.* 604 The 'chestnut weevil,' found abundantly upon chestnut and chincapin trees, about the time the burs break out and expose the fruit in early autumn. **1891** *Cent.* 6870/2 Chestnut weevil, *Balaninus caryatripes,* a very long-nosed weevil whose larva is the common chestnut-grub of the United States.

+**Chestnut white oak.** The swamp white oak (*Quercus platanoides*) of the eastern states. — **1708** SEWALL *Diary* II. 222 Southward of the Swamp is a small Chestnut White-Oak. **1814** PURSH *Flora Amer.* II. 633 This large and useful tree is known by the name of Chesnut White Oak, Swamp Chesnut Oak, and, to the south, White Oak. **1859** A. L. HILLHOUSE *Michaux's Sylva* I. 44 In Pennsylvania this species . . . is called Chestnut White Oak, Swamp Chestnut Oak, [etc.].

+**Chestnutty,** *a. colloq.* [CHESTNUT 7.] Of the nature of a chestnut; old and well known. — **1884** *Detroit Free Press* 14 May 2/1 Excitement about it soon dies away, and references to it are regarded as chestnutty in the press and in the pulpit.

+**Chevals.** (Reduced form of SHERRYVALLIES, riding breeches.) — **1803** L. DOW *Journal* 28 Oct., My pantaloons were worn out; my riding chevals were worn through in several places.

Chevaux-de-frise. [Plural, but also used as a singular.] {1688–}

1. A military defensive appliance, properly consisting of heavy timbers with projecting stakes.

1776 HEATH in Sparks *Corr. Rev.* I. 333 It is surrounded by *chevaux-de-frise,* hooked together; yet I think it might have been taken, if we had had a few Continental troops. **1869** PARKMAN *Disc. Gt. West* (1875) xiv. 168 Its declivities were . . . guarded by *chevaux-de-frise.*

2. A similar device used to block a channel against enemy vessels.

1777 *N.J. Archives* 2 Ser. I. 492 While the enemy were attacking the fort, the Augusta of sixty-four guns, . . . the Merlin of eighteen, and their large galley, came thro' the lower chevaux de frize, and kept up a great firing. **1783** FRENEAU *Poems* (1786) 321 Let us sink in our channel some *Chevaux de frise*—And then let 'em come. **1825** NEAL *Bro. Jonathan* III. 45 To hinder this enterprise, the North River was crowded with chevaux-de-frise; heavy timber, chains, &c.

3. *transf.* A device or object presenting an array of points or stakes.

1827 COOPER *Prairie* iv, The *chevaux de frise* of branches now lay within reach of his arm. **1837** IRVING *Bonneville* II. 186 In wide parts of the river, also, they place a sort of chevauxdefrise, or fence, or poles interwoven with withes. **1883** *Harper's Mag.* July 172/2 An unsightly fence with *chevaux-de-frise* of nails.

***Cheven.** The chub. (Cf. CHIVEN.) — **1792** *Mass. H. S. Coll.* I. 239 At all times the ponds and rivers are well supplied with perch, . . . suckers, and cheven.

* **Chew,** *v.* (Cf. CHAW *v.*)

+**1.** *intr.* To chew tobacco.

1704 S. KNIGHT *Journal* 43 They seldom loose their Cudd, but keep Chewing and Spitting as long as they'r eyes are open. **1832** *New England Mag.* III. 221, I snuffed and smoked and chewed. **1852** A. LAWRENCE *Diary & Corr.* 319 From that time to this [I] have never chewed, smoked, or snuffed.

* **2.** *tr.* To consider, think over. {–1696}

1843 STEPHENS *High Life N.Y.* I. 51, I gin Judy White the sack right off the reel, without stopping to chew the matter a bit.

3. *intr.* With *at* or *on:* To ruminate, meditate. {–1823}

1883 'MARK TWAIN' *Life on Miss.* liii. 378 When you come to look at it all around, and chew at it and think it over, don't it just bang anything you ever heard of? **1911** LINCOLN *Cap'n Warren's Wards* 340 As for goin' to work, you let me chew on that for a few days.

+**Chewallop,** *adv.* [Imitative.] With a flop or splash. — **1836** *Public Ledger* 27 July (Th.), Down I came chewhallop right on Deb's bonnet and her fixups, and overset the chair. **1840** HALIBURTON *Clockmaker* 3 Ser. ii, I was on the edge of a wharf, and only one step more [and I] was over head and ears chewallop in the water.

Chewer. [CHEW *v.* 1.] One who chews tobacco. {1871} — **1863** BOUDRYE *Fifth N.Y. Cavalry* (1868) 362 If the chewer be careful to use the spittoon, he annoys or injures no one but himself. **1888** J. ELLIS *New Christianity* 24 Compare the children . . . of smokers and chewers . . . with the children of those who totally shun this poison.

+**Chewing gum.** A preparation of chicle gum or other plastic substance, usually flavored, which is held in the mouth and chewed. Also fig.

1850 *Chicago Democrat* 25 Oct. (*advt.*), Chewing Gum! A new and superior preparation of Spruce Gum. **1876** 'MARK TWAIN' *Tom Sawyer* vii, What I like is chewing-gum. **1884** NYE *Baled Hay* 122 Chewing-gum is rapidly advancing in price, and the demand is far beyond the supply. **1888** *Scribner's Mag.* Jan. 23/1 The foul-smelling paraffine was made into chewing-gum 'for young misses.' **1893** POST *Harvard Stories* 159 He will also distribute, gratis, tops and marbles to the boys and chewing-gum to the ladies. **1904** WALLER *Wood-carver* 87 You lived near a big spruce wood, where you can find the real spruce gum. I'm so tired of the stick chewing-gum.

fig. **1882** *Advance* (Chicago) 6 April 219 [The novels] are the 'chewing-gum of literature, offering neither savor nor nutriment, only subserving the mechanical process of mastication.'

Chewing tobacco. [Cf. CHEW *v.* 1.] Tobacco adapted for chewing.

1792 *Ann. 2nd Congress* 1000 [Among branches of manufacture are] Snuff, chewing and smoking tobacco. **1835** MARTIN *Descr. Virginia* 175 A dark greyish soil . . . which produces the best chewing tobacco in the state. **1853** *Mich. Agric. Soc. Trans.* (1854) 73 Miscellaneous Articles [include] . . . specimens of fine cut chewing tobacco. **1891** S. M. WELCH *Recoll. 1830–40* 183 The use of chewing tobacco was rare excepting among sailors. **1909** 'O. HENRY' *Options* 200 Before you go, which one of you has got any chewing-tobacco?

+**Chewink, Cheewink.** [Imitative of the note uttered by it.] The towhee bunting or ground robin (*Pipilo erythrophthalmus*). Cf. CHEEWFEH.

1794 *Trans. Philos. Soc.* IV. 110 This bird was the chewink, or ground-robin. **1810** WILSON *Ornithology* II. 36 In Virginia he is called the Bulfinch; in many places the Towhè-bird; in Pennsylvania the Chewink. **1844** *Nat. Hist. N.Y., Zoology* II. 172 This beautiful and unobtrusive little species is familiarly known in this State (where it breeds) under the name of Chewink, from its peculiar note. **1867** 'LACKLAND' *Homespun* I. 99 The homely chewink advertised us of her brisk where-abouts, by her musical monotone in the neighboring thicket of birches. **1877** BURROUGHS *Birds & Poets* 114 Across the fields in the early morning I hear some of the rare April birds—the cheewink and the brown thrasher. **1903** *N.Y. Ev. Post* 12 Sept., Still another shy visitor, yet more timid than the catbird, was the cheewink. **1908** WHITE *Riverman* xii. 108 More circumspect chewinks, catbirds, and finches hopping down from above.

+**Cheyenne.** Also †**Chian,** †**Chean.** [Sioux *Shahíyena,* one who speaks a strange language.] One of a warlike tribe of Indians formerly inhabiting S. Dakota, Wyoming, and Colorado. Usually in pl. or attrib.

1821 J. FOWLER *Journal* 59 We have heare now about seven hundred lodges . . . with the addicion of the Cheans—about two hundred lodges. **1853** *S. Lit. Messenger* XIX. 307/2 After marching about seven miles we saw Chian lodges before us on a level meadow of the stream. **1867** DIXON *New America* I. 12 He has no objection to our being damned, as we certainly shall be after making unpleasant acquaintance with a Cheyenne knife. **1886** STAPLETON *Major's Christmas* 31, I've faced the Utes, the Cheyennes and the rest of them, and I guess a preacher won't scare me. **1888** ROOSEVELT in *Century Mag.* XXXVI. 39/1 It was the last great Indian hunting-ground across which Grosventres, . . . Sioux and Cheyennes . . . wandered in chase of game.

+**Chicagoan.** A native or inhabitant of Chicago, Ill. — **1882** *Advance* (Chicago) 27 July, A nervous, brain-weary Yankee or Chicagoan. **1917** *Harper's Mag.* June 80/1 The final insult to a Chicagoan is to recognize his town after any absence from it.

‖**Chicagoese,** *a.* Characteristic of, spoken in, Chicago. — **1855** *Knickerb.* XLVI. 315 Anything that offers a speculation is called in the Chicagoese language 'a good thing.'

+Chicagonese. =CHICAGOAN. (In quots. as pl.) — **1867** *Atlantic Mo.* March 335/2 The inconvenience to which they [draw-bridges] subject the busy 'Chicagonese' . . . must be seen to be understood. **1886** *Harper's Mag.* July 217/1 This bold statement . . . gave no small offense to the Chicagonese.

‖**Chichado.** =CHICKADEE. — **1850** LEWIS *La. Swamp Dr.* 98 Not even a frog or a chichado was to be heard.

+Chichico(u)e, -iqua. A rattle made from a gourd, used by Indians as a musical instrument. — **1778** CARVER *Travels* 268 The music of the drums and chichicoues, make an agreeable harmony. **1818** EASTBURN *Yamoyden* (1834) IV. xiv. 266 With a rattling chichicoe he led Or swift, or slow, their measured tread. **1840** *Knickerb.* XV. 405 The drum beat, the chichiqua rattled, and the song rose in the Mandan village.

+Chickadee, Chicadee. [Imitative of the note.] The American black-capped titmouse (*Penthestes atricapillus*) or related species.

1839 AUDUBON *Synopsis* 79 *Parus atracapillus*, . . . Black-cap Tit.—Black-cap Titmouse, or Chicadee. . . . Never [seen] in the southern parts. **1845** *Knickerb.* XXV. 200 There was no sound but the note of the little 'chick-a-dee-dee,' so familiar to the pine woods in winter. **1863** A. D. WHITNEY *F. Gartney* xvii, This [crashing of icicles], with now and then a chickadee's note, was all the winter music of the woods. **1872** *Vt. Bd. Agric. Rep.* I. 322 The Chicadee or Black-capped Titmouse is one of our winter birds. **1881** *Harper's Mag.* April 645/2 A chicadee . . . was the only visitant of the bird world that had come out on this piercing morning. **1904** WALLER *Wood-Carver* 73 The chicadees are fairly singing somersaults over one another.

fig. **1860** HOLLAND *Miss Gilbert* 62 When a feller gets tied to a wife and has a lot of little chickadees around him.

+Chickaree, †Chickeree. [Imitative of the cry.] The American red squirrel, *Sciurus hudsonius.*

Cf. the earlier CHIPAREE.

1829 J. RICHARDSON *Fauna Bor. Amer.* I. 187 *Sciurus Hudsonius* (Pennant). The Chickaree. **1850** S. F. COOPER *Rural Hours* 286 Presently a beautiful red squirrel made his appearance. . . . He paused every few steps to utter the peculiar cry which has given them the name of chickaree. **1857** *Rep. Comm. Patents: Agric.* 59 With the exception of the little 'Chickaree,' no true squirrel that I have observed ever collects food for winter in hollow trees. **1868** *Amer. Naturalist* II. 530 Squirrels . . . came down . . . and scolded with the same fearlessness shown by the Chickaree. **1888** ROOSEVELT in *Century Mag.* June 211 Occasionally a chickaree or chipmunk scurried out from among the trunks of the great pines.

+Chickasaw. Also † **Chickesaw, -esau, -isaw, Chicasa(w), Chick-, Chikkasah, Chigasaw, Chicksha.**

1. *pl.* A tribe of Indians formerly inhabiting Mississippi and the northern part of Alabama.

1725 [see CHOCTAW 1]. **1741** *Ga. Coll. Rec.* III. 398 The Chickesaws were to send their Deputies. **1743** CATESBY *Carolina* App. p. x, I have seen amongst the Chigasaws very sharp salt in cristalline lumps. **1764** J. HABERSHAM *Letters* 19 If the Cherokees, Chickesaws and Chactaws could be induced to annoy the Creeks at the same time, . . . they would soon comply with our just and reasonable demands. **1775** ADAIR *Indians* 3 In the year 1747, I headed a company of the cheerful, brave Chikkasah, with the eagles tails, to the camp of the Shawano Indians. **1788** *Steele Papers* I. 29 Not to say anything positive to him respecting a Treaty with the Creeks nor Chickasaws. **1854** *S. Lit. Messenger* XX. 396 Among the red men . . . the [brave] Chickasahs . . . feared nothing, fled from nothing, and made themselves feared whenever they came in anger. **1880** CABLE *Grandissimes* 228 The overseer would sooner have intercepted a score of painted Chickasaws than that one lover. **1899** CUSHMAN *Hist. Indians* 459 It was twenty-one miles southwest of the famous great village of the Chickasaws.

2. Attrib. with *country, horse, Indian, nation,* etc.

1775 ADAIR *Indians* 2 The Shawano Indians . . . were passing . . . within fifty miles of the Chikkasah country. **1784** J. SMYTH *Tour* I. 139 A beautiful Chickasaw horse, named so from a nation of Indians who are very careful in preserving a fine breed of Spanish horses they have long possessed. **1726** PENHALLOW *Indian Wars* (1824) 79 Col. Gibs . . . commissioned . . . Capt. Welch, with the assistance of the Chicksha Indians, to fall on them in several parts. **1737** W. STEPHENS *Proc. Georgia* 47 These Indians were a vagrant Branch of the Chickasaw Nation. **1840** *Niles' Nat. Reg.* 14 March 26/3 The approved value of the 16th section in the Chickasaw purchase. **1899** CUSHMAN *Hist. Indians* 459 Bienville secured the aid of 600 Choctaw warriors and promised rewards for each and every Chickasaw scalp. **1846** POLK in *Pres. Mess. & P.* IV. 436 A report of the Secretary of War . . . relating to certain claims of the Chickasaw tribe of Indians.

3. a. *Chickasaw plum,* a native American plum (*Prunus angustifolia*) of the southern states, bearing a red or yellow fruit. Also attrib. with *tree.*

1775 ADAIR *Indians* 360 They have a large sort of plums, which their ancestors brought with them from South America, and which are now become plenty in our colonies, called Chikkasah plums. **1785** MARSHALL *Amer. Grove* 111 *Prunus angustifolia.* Chicasaw Plumb. . . . There are varieties of this with yellow and crimson coloured fruit. **1791** BARTRAM *Travels* 38 The Chicasaw plumb I think must be excepted, for though certainly a native of America, yet I never saw it wild in the forests. **1821** NUTTALL *Trav. Arkansa* 100 The land on the Indian side, contiguous to the river, abounded with thickets of Chicasaw plum-trees. **1827** *Western Mo. Rev.* I. 323 The Chickasaw plum is common from 34° to the gulf of Mexico. **1841** E. R. STEELE *Summer Journey* 205 We also observed the Chickasaw plum, the pawpaw, and cotton tree. **1852** MARCY *Explor. Red River* (1854) 20 The plums also grow upon small bushes from two to six feet high . . . ; they are the Chickasaw-plum.

b. *Chickasaw rose,* a variety of small climbing rose.

1835 C. J. LATROBE *Rambler in N.A.* II. 8 The Chickasaw-rose, a beautiful briar with snow-white expanded flowers and yellow stamina, was abundant near the plantations. **1835** INGRAHAM *South-West* II. 108 The 'chickasaw rose,' which is a beautiful hedge thorn, grows luxuriantly [in Miss.]. **1865** *Atlantic Mo.* XV. 424 The deserted house was embowered in great blossoming shrubs, . . . among which predominated that of the little Chickasaw roses. **1887** *Harper's Mag.* Feb. 350/1 Along one side of his home . . . runs a superb hedge of Chickasaw roses.

c. *Chickasaw tea,* the bignonia. *Chickasaw pea,* a variety of pea. Also ellipt. for a variety of cultivated grapes.

1813 MUHLENBERG *Cat. Plants* 59 Chicasa tea. *Bignonia capreolata.* — **1837** J. L. WILLIAMS *Florida* 112 The cow pea, lady pea, and chickasaw pea, produce excellent crops during the heat of summer. — **1861** *Ill. Agric. Soc. Trans.* IV. 97 A new seedling which is called the Chickasaw, which is a very delicious grape.

+Chickberry. *local.* =CHECKERBERRY. — **1859** BARTLETT 76 Chequer berry, . . . also called Chickberry. **1871** DE VERE 402 It is also known as *chequer*-berry, and in New England occasionally as *chick*-berry.

***Chicken.**

***1.** A barnyard hen or cock, esp. one less than a year old.

1677 SEWALL *Diary* I. 44 Giving my chickens meat, it came to my mind that I gave them nothing save Indian corn and water. **1722** *New-Eng. Courant* 19–26 March 1/2 To 275 Turkeys, and 205 Doz. Chickens, &c. **1805** PARKINSON *Tour* 223 A farmer's waggon in America, when she comes into market, is something like a pedlar's pack: it consists of . . . turnips, cucumbers, chickens, ducks, geese. **1839** BIRD *Robin Day* 47 Chickens to fight, and chickens to eat. **1864** *Southern Hist. Soc. P.* I. 379, I sent him off to cook a chicken and some biscuits. **1888** *Boston Journal* 20 Oct. 2/4 Wolves . . . invade farm yards and depredate upon chickens and calves.

+2. The prairie chicken or pinnated grouse. Also attrib. and comb.

1876 *Fur, Fin & Feather* Sept. 95 You can always find good 'chicken dogs' wherever there are chickens. *Ib.* 96 The season for chicken shooting commences from the first to the twentieth of August. **1895** *Outing* XXVII. 42/1 Quickly the heavy sound of chickens' wings notified us that game had been found. **1901** WHITE *Westerners* xx. 189 The careful attention necessary for the destruction of the wily 'chicken' or experienced squirrel.

3. *fig.* (See quotations.)

1888 J. D. BILLINGS *Hardtack* 52 A Marblehead man called his chum his 'chicken,' more especially if the latter was a young soldier. **1890** *Congress. Rec.* 21 April 3637/1 In the hospital I saw an admirable illustration of the affection which a sailor will lavish on a ship's boy to whom he takes a fancy, and makes his 'chicken,' as the phrase is.

+b. (See BLUE HEN'S CHICKENS.)

4. *attrib.* **a.** With *cholera, farm, fit,* etc.

1879 *Diseases of Swine* 200 Chicken-cholera . . . prevails to a fearful extent, and sometimes carries off as high as nine-tenths of the crop. **1895** *Outing* XXVI. 452/1 Wilson . . . owned a prosperous chicken farm. **1845** HOOPER *Simon Sugg's Adv.* iii. 31 Won't they roll over the floor, and have chicken-fits a dozen at a time! **1876** *Fur, Fin & Feather* Sept. 96 The best chicken ground is undoubtedly to be found in Iowa. **1819** *Amer. Farmer* I. 46 Respecting the cleansing of poultry-houses from vermin, or chicken-lice.

b. With *broth, dinner, pasty,* etc.

1733 BYRD *Journey to Eden* (1901) 282, I prescribed him a Gallon or two of Chicken Broth. **1896** I. H. HARPER *S. B. Anthony* I. 7 The fame of her coffee and biscuits, apple dumplings and chicken dinners, spread far and wide. **1893** POST *Harvard Stories* 43 Bring us some of that chicken pasty. **1850** *New Eng. Farmer* II. 385 Chicken Pot-Pie. **1888** B. P. POORE *Reminisc.* I. 524 At the supper-tables . . . chicken and lobster salads . . . were furnished in profusion. **1816** U. BROWN *Journal* II. 350, [I] gets them to make some chicken soop, . . . & after a little gets better. **1863** MASSETT *Drifting About* 133 Did anything ever taste quite as nice as that chicken-stew? **1879** A. D. WHITNEY *Just How* 138 Put the chicken-tea into the pork fat.

5. *comb.* With *lifter, stealer.*

1852 *Knickerb.* XXXIX. 562 They came pouring into the village by hundreds, . . . to get a sight of the greatest chicken-stealer ever known since the creation of fowls. **1875** G. P. BURNHAM *Three Years* 196 He learned for the first time that Applegate . . . was a first-class chicken stealer. **1877** HARTE *Story of a Mine* 305 Ye ain't one of them chicken-lifters that raided Henderson's ranch?

+Chickenberry. *local.* The partridgeberry (*Mitchella repens*). — **1832** WILLIAMSON *Maine* I. 130.

+Chicken cock. A domestic cock; a rooster. — **1859** BARTLETT 524 Head and tail up, like chicken-cocks in laying-time. **1865** 'MARK TWAIN'

Jumping Frog, Smiley had rat-terriers, and chicken cocks, and tom-cats and all of them kind of things.

Chicken coop. A coop in which chickens or fowls are kept. {1789-}

1828 ROYALL *Black Book* II. 71 These barns are a burlesque on the home; no more like the great mossy stone barns of Pennsylvania, than a chicken coop. **1867** J. M. CRAWFORD *Mosby* 307 Nothing was left on the plantation but the spring-house. They even applied the torch to the chicken-coops. **1891** RYAN *Pagan* 234 Jake was listening . . . from behind the chicken-coop. **1901** WHITE *Claim Jumpers* (1916) 22 The Holy Smoke mine . . . he found to consist of a hole in the ground, of unsounded depth, two log structures, and a chicken coop.

+**Chicken corn.** The common sorghum growing out of cultivation. — **1856** *Congress. Globe* 17 April 960/2 Chinese sugar cane is nothing more than what we call chicken corn down in Georgia, and is of no sort of value. **1901** MOHR *Plant Life Ala.* 339 *Sorghum vulgare.* . . . Chicken Corn. . . . Escaped from cultivation, becoming a pernicious weed in many parts of the Southern States.

+**Chicken dance.** A kind of dance performed by Indians. — **1899** CUSHMAN *Hist. Indians* 499 Then followed the fun-making dances, such as chicken dance, horse dance.

+**Chicken feed.** Food for poultry. Also transf., food suggestive of this. — **1865** R. H. KELLOGG *Rebel Prisons* 109 The rations . . . were slightly varied in the shape of two buckets of mush for ninety men. 'Chicken feed,' the boys called it. **1879** STOCKTON *Rudder Grange* 173 The houses scattered a long ways apart, like stingy chicken-feed. **1886** *Century Mag.* May 44/1 All the refuse [of the wheat] is sold for chicken-feed.

+**Chicken fight, fighter.** A cockfight; one who patronizes cockfighting. — **1845** HOOPER *Simon Sugg's Adv.* ii. 21 Don't you know that all . . . chicken-fighters . . . go to hell? **1865** 'MARK TWAIN' *Jumping Frog,* If there was a chicken-fight, he'd bet on it.

+**Chicken fixings.** *colloq.* Also **fixins, fixens.** Chicken or fowl prepared for eating; also, unusual or elaborately prepared food.

1838 FLAGG *Far West* II. 72 [It is said] that the first inquiry made of the guest by the [Illinois] village landlord is: 'Well, stran-ger, what'll ye take? wheat-bread and chicken fixens, or corn-bread and common doins?' **1842** *S. Lit. Messenger* VIII. 64/2 An old ranger like me seldom depends wholly upon the corn-bread and 'chicken fixins' of the squatter farms. **1843** 'CARLTON' *New Purchase* I. 63 The good woman . . . placed the 'chicken fixins' on a large dinner-plate. **1846** *Knickerb.* XXVIII. 308 Coffee kettles were bubbling; 'chicken fixens' were smoking. **1874** EGGLESTON *Circuit Rider* 20 The strife has given them vigorous relish for Mrs. Lumsden's 'chicken fixin's.' **1885** 'CRADDOCK' *Prophet* 178 Brother Jake Tobin sets mo' store on chicken fixin's than on grace.

fig. **1854** M. J. HOLMES *Tempest & Sunshine* v. 78 We don't have any of your chicken fixins nor little three-cornered handkerchiefs laid out at each plate. **1886** PROCTOR in *Knowledge* 1 April 179/1 Chicken-fixings, . . . now applied sometimes to any particularly fine arrangements as distinguished from 'common doings.' **1914** *Dialect Notes* IV. 70 *Chicken-fixin's,* . . . anything fancy, in food, dress, or otherwise. 'With all the little chicken-fixin's on.'

+**Chicken gaffs.** {*Gaffs,* spurs for cocks, 1688-} An artificial spur for a fighting cock. — **1834** H. J. NOTT *Novellettes* I. 19 He brought forth a dice-box, several dice, a pair of chicken gaffs, and various other utensils.

+**Chicken grape.** The winter or frost grape, *Vitis cordifolia;* also, the riverside grape, *Vitis vulpina.*

1814 PURSH *Flora Amer.* I. 169 *Vitis cordifolia* . . . commonly called Winter-grape or Chicken-grape. **1836** HOLLEY *Texas* 87 Almost every variety of grape is native in Texas from the large fox-grape down to what is called the chicken-grape. **1859** BARTLETT 77 *Chicken grape,* the River Grape, or *Vitis riparia.* . . . The sterile vine is cultivated for its sweet-scented blossoms. **1871** DE VERE 412 The Bermuda Vine (*Vitis riparia*) is the Chicken Grape of Southern States, famous for its fragrant blossoms, but bearing no fruit. **1886** MITCHELL *R. Blake* 260 Mrs. Ludlam says she is 'waitin' for them chicken-grapes to git a little more sun.' **1891** COULTER *Bot. W. Texas* I. 62 Frost or Chicken grape [is] a common grape of the Atlantic States.

+**Chicken gumbo.** Chicken soup in which gumbo is an ingredient. Also attrib.

1867 *Common Sense Cook Book* 61 [Recipe for] chicken gumbo. **1880** SALA in *Daily Tel.* (Lond.) 26 Feb. 5/6 The once affluent Southerners . . . who once delighted to entertain their guests on chicken gumbo, venison, [etc.]. **1894** CHOPIN *Bayou Folk* 269 Alcée reached the ball . . . too late for the chicken gumbo which had been served at midnight. **1908** LORIMER *J. Spurlock* 207 First there was a chicken gumbo soup, and then cold boiled Virginia ham.

Chicken hawk. {1890, *dial.*} Any of various hawks that prey on chickens.

1827 J. L. WILLIAMS *West Florida* 30 Of Eagles, *Falco,* we have . . . Hen Hawk. *F. gallinareus.* Chicken Hawk. *F. pullenarius.* **1837** — *Florida* 73 There are many birds in Florida. . . . Fishing Eagle, . . . Hen Hawk, . . . Chicken Hawk, [etc.]. **1844** *Nat. Hist. N.Y., Zoology* II. 14 The Duck Hawk, *Falco Anatum,* . . . is . . . known under the various popular names of Hen Hawk, Chicken Hawk and Pigeon Hawk. **1894** CABLE *J. Marsh* xix, That man's afraid o' me—jess as 'fraid as a chicken-hawk is of a gun. **1895** *Dept. Agric. Yearbook 1894* 231 Cooper's hawk is preeminently a 'chicken hawk.'

phr. **1835** LONGSTREET *Ga. Scenes* 62 'What you think he's made of?' 'Steel-springs and chicken-hawk, God bless you.' **1843** HALIBURTON *Attaché* II. 248 She actilly did seem as if she was made out of steel springs and chicken-hawk.

+**Chicken house.** A house for poultry; a hen house.

1853 *Harper's Mag.* VII. 753/1 You notice that the 'chicken-house' seems to be in excellent condition; its inhabitants are thrifty and well-conditioned. **1875** G. P. BURNHAM *Three Years* 193 They should go together, on the following night, and rob Aaron Gaskill's chicken-house. **1896** HARRIS *Sister Jane* 63 One time when I was in my chicken-house, . . . a settin' hen flew in my face. **1901** WHITE *Westerners* xxiv. 222 The chicken house is beyond th' blacksmith's shop.

+**Chicken man. a.** *humorous.* A counter of chickens; a census taker. **b.** A rearer of, a dealer in, chickens. — **1845** HOOPER *Taking Census* i. 149 The excitement against the unfortunate officers—who were known as '*chicken-men*'—made it almost dangerous for them to proceed with the business of taking the census. **1890** *Harper's Mag.* Feb. 353/2, I am a-goin' to see Pete Jones, the chicken man.

+**Chicken money.** *colloq.* Small money; money involved in buying or selling chickens. — **1853** SIMMS *Sword & Distaff* 266 Did you suppose that the widow . . . would go to the country and take no money with her—even if it were only a stocking full of shillings for chicken money. **1856** STOWE *Dred* II. 156 Drinking up all my chicken-money down to 'Bijah Skinflint's.

+**Chicken pie.** A pie having chicken as the principal ingredient.

1733 BYRD *Journey to Eden* (1901) 324 After our bounteous Landlady had cherisht us with Roast beef and Chicken-Pye, we thankfully took Leave. **1775** E. Singleton *Social N.Y.* 367 Chicken Pies ready for Supper every night. **1809** F. CUMING *Western Tour* 198 A most excellent breakfast of good coffee, roast fowls, chicken pie, potatoes, etc. **1835** LONGSTREET *Ga. Scenes* 47 My wife is very sick, and is longing for chicken pie. **1847** BRIGGS *Tom Pepper* I. 270 We don't eat a lobster salad every night, nor boiled crabs, nor a cold chicken pie. **1869** STOWE *Oldtown Folks* 346 Chicken pies, which might possibly be overdoing in the ovens at home. **1886** B. P. POORE *Reminisc.* I. 43 Colonel E., will you help to that chicken-pie before you? **1896** HARRIS *Sister Jane* 166 Aunt Sally a dishin' out the chicken pie at her house.

fig. **1871** DE VERE 264 A curious term has, of late, sprung up in the South, to designate the necessary expenses for purchasing legislative votes and newspaper influence. . . . These are called Chicken-pie.

+**Chicken plover.** *local.* A ploverlike shore bird of the genus *Arenaria.* — **1870** *Mass. Acts & Resolves* 224 Nothing in this section shall be held to apply to Wilson's snipe . . . or chicken plover.

+**Chicken ranch.** A poultry farm. — **1887** I. R. *Lady's Ranche Life Mont.* 55, I hope we may do pretty well with the chickens— . . . as Jem says this is a very good chicken ranche.

+**Chicken shad.** *local.* A young male shad. — **a1873** *Dept. Agric. Rep. 1873* 452 The 'chicken-shad,' as they are called among the pound-fishermen, instead of being a distinct species are the yearlings of the *præstabilis.* **1884** ROE *Nature's Story* (1885) 197 The males will come back next spring, and these young males are called 'chicken shad' on the Connecticut.

+**Chicken snake.** One or other of several snakes which eat chickens and eggs.

1709 LAWSON *Carolina* 134 The Egg or Chicken-Snake is so call'd, because it is frequent about the Hen-Yard, and eats Eggs and Chickens. **1744** F. MOORE *Voy. Georgia* 120 Besides the rattle snake . . . there are also many others, as the black, the red, and the chicken snake. **1791** BARTRAM *Travels* 275 The chicken snake is a large, strong and swift serpent. **1835** A. PARKER *Trip to Texas* 152 The large black snake . . . is here called the 'chicken snake,' because it sometimes robs hen's nests. **1842** *Nat. Hist. N.Y., Zoology* III. 39 In this State, its most usual popular name is Milk Snake, although it has various other appellations. It is called Chicken Snake, Thunder and Lightning Snake, House Snake, and Chequered Adder. **1855** SIMMS *Forayers* 549 The chicken-snake is of unexceptionable tenderness; . . . but, unless near a hencoop, or a corncrib, it is not easy to find the chicken-snake. **1890** *Cent.* 3763/1 [The] milk-snake, . . . *Ophibolus eximius,* . . . is also called *chicken-snake.*

+**Chicken thief. a.** A river trading-boat, so called because its presence encouraged Negroes to steal chickens, etc. **b.** One who steals chickens.

(a) 1819 DEWEES *Lett. from Texas* 11 The vessels upon this river consist . . . mostly of upper country flat boats, (generally called broad-horns,) and chicken thieves. **1828** FLINT *Geogr. Miss. Valley* I. 237 The . . . singular looking Spanish and French trading retail boats commonly called chicken thieves. **1853** 'P. PAXTON' *Yankee in Texas* 233 A host of smaller craft, enjoying the beautiful appellation of 'Chicken-thieves,' . . . run up and down the Bay, . . . driving a profitable trade in wood and charcoal, butter, poultry, and eggs. **1856** OLMSTED *Slave States* 675 He had lately caught one of his own negroes going towards one of the 'chicken thieves,' (so the traders' boats are called) with a piece of machinery. **(b) 1883** *Harper's Mag.* June 162/2 Dar's moah den forty chicken thieves in Austin.

+**Chicken yard.** An enclosed area in which chickens are kept. — **1853** *Harper's Mag.* VII. 759/1 Every one [of the Negroes] has his pigs and his poultry; for all adults have not only the chicken-yard, but also their garden. **1879** *Scribner's Mo.* May 50/1 The board fence ... shut out a neighbor's chicken yard and sundry other unsightly objects. **1923** R. HERRICK *Lilla* 257 Down beyond the new barn ... were the chicken yards.

+**Chickerberry.** =CHECKERBERRY. — **1821** COOPER *Spy* xxix, 'They will not think of such a thing,' returned the pedler, picking the chicker-berries that grew on the thin soil where he sat. **1823** — *Pioneer* ix, Is the poor devil to ... put them in his pocket, ... as you would a handful of chestnuts, or a bunch of chicker-berries?

∗ **Chickweed.**

∗**1.** One or other of various small-leaved weeds or plants (esp. *Stellaria media*), the leaves and seeds of which are relished by small birds.

1784 CUTLER in *Mem. Academy* I. 431 *Alsine*. ... Chickweed. If it be boiled when young, it can hardly be distinguished from spring spinach. **1832** CHILD *Frugal Housewife* 29 A poultice made of ginger or of common chickweed, that grows about one's door in the country, has given great relief to the tooth-ache. **1849** *Rep. Comm. Patents: Agric.* (1850) 157 Chick-weed, ... of which cows are very fond. **1899** F. NORRIS *McTeague* 75 The lunch baskets were emptied. ... There were huge loaves of rye bread full of grains of chickweed. There were wienerwurst and frankfurter sausages.

∗**2.** With distinguishing terms.

See also *mouse-ear, sea,* and *water chickweed.*

1832 WILLIAMSON *Maine* I. 122 Red chick-weed is a beautiful low plant procumbent on the ground. **1840** DEWEY *Mass. Flowering Plants* 95 *Queria Canadensis,* Forked Chickweed; ... blossoms in July. **1843** TORREY *Flora N.Y.* I. 100 *Cerastium nutans*. ... Nodding Chickweed. ... Low moist and rather shady places. *Ib.* 105 *Anychia dichotoma*. ... Common Forked Chickweed. ... Dry woods and hill-sides. **1845** LINCOLN *Botany* App. 88/1 *Cerastium viscosum,* (sticky chickweed).

+**Chick(weed) wintergreen.** The starflower, *Trientalis americana.*

(*a*) **1821** *Mass. H. S. Coll.* 2 Ser. IX. 157 Plants, which are indigenous in the township of Middlebury [Vt., include] ... Chick wintergreen. **1840** *S. Lit. Messenger* VI. 518/2 There were ... the beautiful varieties of Solomon's seal, chick-wintergreen, strawberry, ... all within reach of my eye. **1850** S. F. COOPER *Rural Hours* 85 Some persons call this [=the may-star] chick wintergreen, a name which is an insult to the plant.

(*b*) **1843** TORREY *Flora N.Y.* II. 11 *Trientalis Americana*. ... Chick-weed Wintergreen. ... Low shady woods, and in sphagnous swamps. **1868** GRAY *Field Botany* 224 *Trientalis Americana,* American Chickweed-wintergreen or Star-flower. In open low woods; ... a pretty plant.

+**Chickwit.** *local.* The squeteague or weakfish. — **a1870** CHIPMAN *Notes on Bartlett* 37 [The Weak-fish, or Squeteague] or Chickwhit. **1884** GOODE *Aquatic Animals* 362 The Squeteague—*Cynoscion regale*. ... 'Squitee,' and 'Chickwit' are doubtless variations of this name in different ancient and modern dialects.

∗**Chicory.** Also †**chiccory. a.** A blue-flowered plant, cultivated esp. for its fleshy root. **b.** The root of this used as an adulterant of coffee; hence, the drink itself. — **(a) 1847** DARLINGTON *Weeds & Plants* 200 *Cichorium Intybus*. ... Wild Succory. Chiccory. **1889** *Cent.* 955/3 Chicory is also cultivated as feed for cattle, and the blanched leaves are sometimes used as a salad. **(b) 1874** HOWELLS *Chance Acquaintance* 62 To see the havoc he's making in the ham and eggs and chicory is to be convinced that there is no appetiser like regret. **1880** 'MARK TWAIN' *Tramp Abroad* xlix. 576 Continue the boiling and evaporation until the flavor and aroma of the coffee and chiccory has been diminished to a proper degree.

∗ **Chief.**

+**1.** The recognized head, or one of the heads, of an Indian tribe or section of one.

1637 R. WILLIAMS *Lett.* (1874) 36 Some of the chiefs at Connecticut are almost adverse from killing women and children. **1655** *Southampton Rec.* I. 114 There came up an Indian whom the sachem had appointed chief among our Indians with his squa. **1711** *Boston News-Letter* 26 March 1/2 The Indian promis'd to go to the Chiefs among them, and return in ten days with those who would gladly make peace with us. **1792** *Mass. H. S. Coll.* 1 Ser. I. 287 The leading men of these Six Nations, or what they call Chiefs, were on the road with me. **1807** GASS *Journal* 26 Captain Lewis and Captain Clarke held a council with the Indians. ... Six of them were made chiefs, three Otos and three Missouris. **1834** PECK *Gaz. Illinois* 53 In all probability some of these embankments enclosed their villages, others the residence of their chiefs or head men. **1877** *Rep. Indian Affairs* 13 Besides the loss of their horses, they lost seventeen killed, including Looking-Glass and Joseph's brother and three other chiefs. **1888** P. H. SHERIDAN *Memoirs* I. 81 The chief and head-men said they had nothing to do with the capture of the Cascades.

+**b.** (See quotation.)

1877 WRIGHT *Big Bonanza* 131 Not a few noted and well-known desperadoes arrived and walked the streets and presided in the saloons as 'chiefs.'

2. +**a.** *Chief of police,* the head of a police force.

1851 J. H. ROSS *In New York* 28 The 'Chief of Police' has his office at the City Hall. **1851** W. K. NORTHALL *Curtain* 131 Mr. Niblo ... sought the Chief of Police. **1901** *World's Work* II. 1315/1 The chief of police ought to be a man with a keen sense of honor.

b. *Chief of staff,* the chief officer of a military staff. {1863- (Kinglake *Crimea*)}

1865 *Atlantic Mo.* XV. 763 That very moment was chosen by the trusted chief of staff of the Lieutenant-General to go over to the enemy. **1885** *Century Mag.* XXX. 295/1 Another peculiarity of Jackson's was to select for his chief-of-staff, not a military man, but a Presbyterian clergyman. **1888** P. H. SHERIDAN *Memoirs* I. 234 A solid shot carried away the head of Colonel Garesche, the chief-of-staff, and killed or wounded two or three orderlies.

∗**3.** The greatest, main, or principal part. *Obs.* {-1607}

1704 *Penn. Col. Rec.* II. 133 It shall be the chief of my study. **1758** *Lett. to Washington* II. 307 The Rest of the Indians ran away and left the horses and the Chief of the Plunder they had Stolen. **1778** HOLTEN in *Essex Inst. Coll.* LV. 165 Attended in Congress and the chief of the day was taken up in Disputing on the Articles of Confederation. **1786** JAY in Sparks *Corr. Rev.* IV. 128 Commendation ... borrows the chief of its worth from the merit of those who bestow it.

Chief clerk. The clerk holding the leading position in an office staff. {1700- (J. Chamberlayne *Pres. State Eng.*)}

1789 MACLAY *Deb. Senate* 107 This Chief Clerk, on the removal of the Secretary, will become the principal in the office, and so may remain during the Presidency. **1837** *Diplom. Corr. Texas* (1908) I. 236 Mr. Forsyth, the Secretary of State, being absent, the courtesies of the Department devolved upon his Chief Clerk. **1841** *Ib.* III. 1330, I was at the time ... as at present, Chief Clerk of the Treasury Department. **1909** G. F. PARKER *G. Cleveland* 31 He began as chief clerk with the modest salary of $600, which was increased year by year.

Chief cook. A head cook. (In colloq. or figurative phrase.) — **1844** P. HONE *Diary* II. 224 And then, the idea of running Silas Wright subordinate to General Jackson's chief cook and bottle-washer. **1877** J. S. CAMPION *On Frontier* 3 He offered himself for the post of what he inelegantly called, 'chief cook and bottle-washer to the outfit.'

Chiefess. A female chief. {1862-} — **1778** J. CARVER *Travels* 41 This heroine was ever after treated by her nation as their deliverer, and made a chiefess.

Chief Executive. +The President of the United States.

1842 TYLER in *Pres. Mess. & P.* IV. 192, I have been clothed with the high powers which they have seen fit to confide to their Chief Executive. **1876** GARFIELD in Kirke *Life* 30/2 Our great military chieftain [=Grant] ... had command as chief executive during eight years of ... eventful administration. **1903** *N.Y. Times* 17 Sept., The President's programme was carried out under conditions that are probably unprecedented in the history of the official visits of the Chief Executive.

+**b.** The governor of a state.

1873 BEADLE *Undevel. West* 805 My first duty was to call upon the Chief Executive, Governor E. Y. Davis. **1903** *N.Y. Ev. Post* 17 Sept. 1 Governor Murphy, the Chief Executive of the State.

Chief hare. One or other species of the pika or calling hare (genus *Ochotona*) of the western states; esp. the little chief hare, *O. princeps.* — **1875** *Amer. Naturalist* IX. 150 They stretch clear away to the Rocky Mountains ... ; but a day's march ... from the rocky haunts of the little chief hare (*Logomys princeps*). **1905** *Field Columbian Mus. Publ.* Zool. ser. VI. 337.

∗ **Chief justice.** The justice or judge holding the position of official head of a court.

'The presiding judge ... of the Supreme Court of the United States' (W. '47).

1692 SEWALL *Diary* I. 370 After Lecture, the Governour delivers Mr. Stoughton his Commission as Chief Justice of the Superior Court. **1703** *Ib.* II. 82 The Secretary alleged that through decay of his health, he was unable to sustain the place of Chief-Justice any longer. **1787** *Constitution* I. iii. § 6 When [on impeachment] the president of the United States is tried, the chief justice shall preside. **1816** *Ann. 14th Congress* 2 Sess. 357 Chief Justice and Associate Justices of the Supreme Court of the United States shall cease to be Judges of the Circuit Courts of the United States. **1865** *Atlantic Mo.* XV. 506 He couldn't have found a Chief Justice in the world to uphold him in it at that time. **1888** CABLE in *Century Mag.* XXXVII. 110/2, I appealed to a former chief-justice of the State.

Chief magistracy. +The office of President of the United States. — **1790** *Steele Papers* I. 60 The vice-President by virtue of his present appointment would take the chief Magistracy untill the 4th. March 1793. **1835** BENTON *30 Years' View* (1854) I. 527 [If] the gentleman meant that he [Calhoun] ... was anxious to see any particular man elevated to the Chief Magistracy, he did him great injustice. **1842** TYLER in *Pres. Mess. & P.* IV. 192 The succession of the Vice-President to the Chief Magistracy has never occurred before.

Chief magistrate.

1. The highest official charged with the administration of civil affairs in a community.

1640 *R.I. Col. Rec.* I. 100 It is ordered, that the Chiefe Magistrate of the Island shall be called Governour, and the next Deputie Governour. **1673** F. B. Hough *Nantucket P.* (1856) 55, I have thought fitt to ... Appoint Mr. Richard Gardner ... to be Chiefe Magistrate of the said Islands of Nantuckett and Tuckanuckett. **1845** P. HONE *Diary* II. 266 Our sister city of the Bay State has been without a chief magistrate for some time past.

+2. The President of the United States.

Often (and more properly) with initial capitals. Cf. CHIEF EXECUTIVE. **1788** A. HAMILTON *Federalist* No. 68, 14 March, The chief magistrate of the United States. **1791** in White *Ga. Hist. Coll.* (1855) 622 Long may you [Washington] remain to fill the exalted station of Chief Magistrate of the American Republic. **1813** *Ann. 12th Congress* 2 Sess. 565 Without their support, the re-election of the present Chief Magistrate was hopeless. **1843** *Knickerb.* XXII. 49, I have . . . had the opportunity of seeing a great deal of our Chief Magistrate. **1884** CURTIS in *Century Mag.* Nov. 128 The very men from among whom the Presidential electors ought to select a chief magistrate for the nation. **1888** BRYCE *Amer. Commonw.* I. xi. 145 Congress has other means of muzzling an ambitious chief magistrate.

*** Chieftain.** +An Indian chief.

1684 I. MATHER *Providences* (1856) 254 The chieftans amongst them were all cut off. **1775** ADAIR *Indians* 1 The English traders . . . are often very glad to be allowed to pass muster with the Indian chieftains, as fellow-brethren of the human species. **1818** EASTBURN & SANDS *Yamoyden* I. 12 And the chieftains, in turn to the pile as they go, In each brand saw a warrior. **1838** FLAGG *Far West* II. 210 Our . . . moralizing upon the destinies of the Indians had been indulged upon a very fitting spot—the grave of one of its chieftains. **1853** RAMSEY *Tennessee* 1 He recollects to have seen his chieftain . . . perpetuating the annals of his tribe in rude hieroglyphics upon the mountain granite.

Chieftainship. {1771–} +The position or office of an Indian chief. — **1820** MORSE *Rep. Indian Affairs* (1822) II. 32 The Chieftainship descends from father to son, and the line becomes extinct by the death of the last male. **1840** *S. Lit. Messenger* VI. 191/1 All the tribes look to certain families, as having the hereditary right to the chieftainship.

‖**Chienté.** Incorrect variant of SHANTY, by association with F. *chien* dog. — **1841** COOPER *Deerslayer* xix, There isn't a jail in the colony that has a more lock-up look about it than old Tom's *chiente.* **1848** — *Oak Openings* I. ii. 33 The supper was finished, . . . the whole party left the chienté, to enjoy their pipes.

Chigoe, Chigger. Also **chego, chigre, cheeger,** etc. [Of West Indian origin. {1708–}]

1. A species of flea (*Sarcopsylla penetrans*), the female of which burrows under the human skin, esp. of the feet.

(*a*) **1743** CATESBY *Carolina* App. p. xxxvii, The particular genus's I observed in Carolina [include] . . . Fleas. Chego. The Louse. **1780** ASBURY *Journal* I. 384, I cannot go into the woods, there are so many ticks, chiegoes, and such insects at this season upon the ground. **1869** *Amer. Naturalist* II. 644 The Chigoe lays about sixty eggs, depositing them in a sort of sac on each side of the external opening of the oviduct. **1902** W. S. GORDON *Recoll. Lynchburg* 141 In roaming over the fields he was beset with chigoes.

(*b*) **1848** BARTLETT 73 *Chigres* (commonly called *jiggers*), sand-fleas, which penetrate under the skin of the feet, but particularly the toes. **1851** *Polly Peablossom* 68 The etarnalest . . . place for . . . cheegers. **1859** A. VAN BUREN *Sojourn in South* 198 The chegre, an infinitesimal gnat, . . . I have felt but little of, though his sting awakens one to the memory of hornets or yellow-jackets. **1872** MORRELL *Flowers & Fruits* 381 Next to these is the chegre, a malicious insect, a little larger than the red bugs that used to annoy us greatly. **1887** CUSTER *Tenting on Plains* 139 What was most aggravating were two pests of that region, the seed-tick and the chigger. **1915** *Dept. Agric., Farmer's Bull.* No 671, 1 'Chiggers' usually enter the skin near the shoe tops or at points below the knees.

+2. *Chigger flower, -weed,* (see quotations).

1899 *Animal & Plant Lore* 117 *Anthemis cotula* is called 'chigger-weed' because it is supposed to harbor chiggers. Indiana. *Ib.* 118 *Asclepias tuberosa,* the butterfly milkweed, is called 'chigger flower,' from the belief that insects known as chiggers harbor in it. Southwestern Missouri.

*** Child.**

+1. *This child* (used by a speaker to denote himself or herself), I, me. *local.*

1842 *Spirit of Times* (Phila.) 11 Oct. (Th.), Says I, 'Mr. Coon,' and then he smiled, 'You can't quite come it over this child.' **1844** *S. Lit. Messenger* X. 486/2 I'll be hanged ef I didn't always know that I'd get all when I got married,—ketch this child asleep. *a***1849** RUXTON *Life Far West* 28 Thar plans is plain to this child as beaver sign. **1857** *Harper's Mag.* Oct. 643/1 You can't come no such game as that on *this* child—for he's seen such doing afore, *he* has. **1860** HOLLAND *Miss Gilbert* 239 You always had favors enough for you know who, but nothing for this child. **1871** *Harper's Mag.* Dec. 157/2, I haven't pascience to write eny more but dont you never go back on this child.

2. *Child of the forest,* an Indian.

1823 COOPER *Pioneers* vii, As this child of the forest approached them, the whole party stood aside. **1850** GLISAN *Jrnl. Army Life* 19 Such interviews on the part of these children of the forest with the government officers at all the frontier stations are numerous.

+Child board. The board to which a young Indian child is strapped when carried on the back of the parent. — **1823** KEATING *Narr.* 182 At the time he approached us he had a child-board on his back.

+Children's warbler. (See quotations.) — **1831** AUDUBON *Ornith. Biog.* I. 180 Children's Warbler. *Sylvia Childrenii.* . . . I have named it after my most esteemed friend, J. G. Children, Esq. of the British Museum. **1891** *Cent.* 6819/3 *Children's warbler,* the female or young summer yellow-bird, *Dendrœca æstiva.*

Chile, Chili. Also **chilly.**

1. Red or cayenne pepper; the pod yielding this. {1662–}

(*a*) **1836** PARKER *Trip to Texas* 271 (Bentley), You will have for a holiday dinner . . . soup with meat balls and chile in it, chicken with chile, fried beans with more chile. **1865** *Atlantic Mo.* XV. 60 We had . . . an infinity of Mexican hashes and stews seasoned with chiles or red-pepper pods.

(*b*) **1854** BARTLETT *Narrative* I. 440 Its use . . . is almost wholly confined to the production of corn, wheat, beans, pumpkins, and chili. **1856** G. W. WEBBER *Tale of South Border* 41 (Bentley), Our frontier meal of beef . . . seasoned to scalding heat with 'chili.' **1874** BOURKE *Journal* 13 Oct., Chili is also one of their vegetables.

+b. *ellipt.* A dish or sauce seasoned with chile. (Cf. sense 3 and CHILI SAUCE.)

1846 in Emory *Milit. Reconn.* (1848) 40 Chile the Mexicans consider the chef-d'oevre of the cuisine. . . . It was red pepper, stuffed with minced meat. **1891** [see CHILI SAUCE].

+2. *Chile colorado,* =sense 1.

(*a*) **1844** KENDALL *Santa Fé Exped.* II. 160 Seated upon the ground, a female might be seen with a few chiles colorados, or red peppers, for sale. **1848** BRYANT *California* 305 Our breakfast consisted of . . . stewed beef, seasoned with *chile colorado,* a species of red pepper. **1863** *Rio Abajo Press* 24 Feb. 2 Congress takes fifty thousand dollars out of the pockets of the people of the United States to make us good roads for intercommunication and the transportation of Chile Colorado to market.

(*b*) **1900** SMITHWICK *Evolution of State* 46 They finally emerged . . . dry and shrunken as so many pods of chili colorado. **1910** 'O. HENRY' *Strictly Business* 25 There [=El Refugio] only will you find a fish . . . baked after the Spanish method. . . . Chili colorado bestows upon it zest, originality and fervour.

+b. A dish seasoned with chile, as chile con carne (q.v.).

1869 BROWNE *Adv. Apache Country* 78 We had Chili colorado and onions and eggs, and wound up with preserves and a peach-cobbler. **1888** J. J. WEBB *Adventures* 66 Our bill of fare was the usual dishes of Chili Colorado, beans, atole, tortillas, &c.

+3. *Chile con carne,* a Mexican dish containing meat and kidney beans flavored with chile.

1895 *Outing* XXVI. 28/2, I went to a little Mexican restaurant . . . and, sitting there eating my *frijoles* and *chile con carne,* [etc]. **1897** A. H. LEWIS *Wolfville* 72 She jest shoves them . . . [their] chile con carne. **1918** FARMER *Cook Book* 246 [Recipe for] Chili con carne.

Chilian clover. (See quotation.) — **1855** BROWNE in *Trans. Amer. Inst. N.Y.* 618 Chilian Clover, or Alfalfa . . . , from Chili, a perennial variety of lucerne, which succeeds well in our middle and southern States.

+Chili sauce. A sauce the principal ingredients of which are tomatoes, onions and peppers. — **1882** F. E. OWENS *Cook Book* 90. **1885** *Buckeye Cookery* (rev. ed.) 132 This Chili sauce is excellent and much better and more healthful than catsups. **1891** *Amer. Notes & Q.* VII. 299 *Chile,* or *Chilly,* as the name of a sauce, and a very familiar word at this season, is in none of the dictionaries. . . . I find 'Chile Sauce' in a cooking book published at San Francisco in 1879. **1918** FARMER *Cook Book* 590.

*** Chill.** A sudden or severe cooling of the body, causing illness. +*The chills,* or *chill(s) and fever:* an intermittent fever; fever and ague.

(1) **1773** *Penna. Mag. Hist.* V. 198 To-day very unwell with a chill and fever. **1834** R. BAIRD *Valley Miss.* 85 These maladies are intermitting and remitting bilious fevers . . . which . . . have received the names of 'Ague,' 'dumb ague,' and 'chill and fever.' **1838** *Democratic Rev.* I. 60 My son . . . was very suddenly attacked by that vile disease called chills and fever. **1845** *Knickerb.* XXV. 238 Chills-and-fever was so general, that the exempts were looked upon as having a 'charm.' **1861** LOWELL *Biglow P.* 2 Ser. i. 212 'T ain't the chills 'n' fever Thet makes my writin' seem to squirm. **1887** *Century Mag.* March 738/2 Hunters told us stories about bears in the neighboring hills—not very near us, for bears are like chills and fever. **1907** C. C. ANDREWS *Recoll.* 103 Malaria had been unusually prevalent, and I had already begun to feel indications of chills and fever.

(2) **1835** LONGSTREET *Ga. Scenes* 191 The chills ran from my head to my toes, like ague-fits. **1865** HARTE *Dow's Flat* 33 Then the bar petered out, . . . And the chills got about, And his wife fell away. **1879** B. F. TAYLOR *Summer-Savory* 11 If it [the sun] could only spend an autumn or two in Indiana, and get the 'chills' and have an intermittent fever, instead of the steady, unwinking blaze! **1884** SWEET & KNOX *Through Texas* 97 The old woman is down with the chills.

comb. **1883** 'MARK TWAIN' *Life on Miss.* xxxv, Crazy rail fences . . . with one or two jeans-clad, chills-racked, yellow-faced male miserables roosting on the top rail.

+Chill-day. The day on which one has (or expects to have) a recurrent chill. — **1879** STOCKTON *Rudder Grange* 166 It was his chill-day, an' he didn't take his quinine. **1884** SWEET & KNOX *Through Texas* 102 'Can't do it,' said Bud; 'to-morrow is my chill day.'

***Chilly,** *a.* +In the colloq. phr. *a chilly day,* 'a facetious way of expressing extreme infrequency of occurrence' (Th. S.). — **1893** *Congress. Rec.* 16 Dec. 290/1 'Under the present low temperature in the Pension Office'; it is a chilly day when a Congressman goes to the Pension Office.

‖**Chimisal.** (Irreg. variant of CHAMISAL.) — **1867** HARTE *Condensed Novels* 244 Except the occasional pattering of a squirrel, or a rustling in the chimisal bushes, there were no signs of life. **1876** — *G. Conroy* xiii,

The Chimisal began to yield to their weight. **1879** — *Drift from 2 Shores* 117 We toiled on in silence, the buckeye giving way to chimisal.

***Chiml(e)y, Chimbl(e)y.** *dial.* [Sc. *chymlay* (1540–), *chimbley* (1626–), *chimbly* (1653). Eng. dial. *chimly, chimbly,* etc.] = CHIMNEY.

1675 *Hempstead Rec.* I. 299 It is allso ordered that every man in this townd that hath a defective chimly shall . . . make it sofishant an good. **1706** *N.H. Probate Rec.* I. 574 My will further is that . . . my two son[s] . . . build two Chimlys of Brick in the middle of sayd House. **1795** B. DEARBORN *Columbian Grammar* 134 Improprieties, commonly called Vulgarisms, . . . [include] Chimbley for Chimney. **1854** M. J. HOLMES *Tempest & Sunshine* 12 The mightiest mean-looking house you ever seen, I reckon; one chimbley tumbled down, and t'other trying to. **1889** 'MARK TWAIN' *H. Finn* vi, I couldn't get up the chimbly; it was too narrow.

***Chimney.** Also †**chimneye, -ny, chymny.**

***1.** The ordinary vertical opening or structure serving to carry off the smoke from a fireplace.

[**1622** 'MOURT' *Relation* 35 The chimney was a wide open hole at the top.] **1637** *Mass. H. S. Coll.* 4 Ser. VII. 119, I would have wood chimneys at each end, the frames of the chimnyes to be stronger then ordinary. **1662** *Boston Rec.* 12 Each man fined 5s a pes for thear chymnyes fyringe. **1663** *Jamaica* (L.I.) *Rec.* I. 27 That every inhabitant shall sweep his Chimney once a Month till May next. **1716** *Boston Selectmen* 12 John Reed Black smith doth Ocupie a chimny in mr Butlers Rents . . . , which is dangerous . . . to that Neighbourhood. **1823** JAMES *Exped.* I. 167 The stone quarry, which supplied limestone for building chimnies for camp Missouri. **1898** PAGE *Red Rock* 517 In his terror he ran to the chimney and attempted to climb up in it.

b. The similar structure on a steamboat, etc. {1825–}

1789 *Boston Rec.* 211 Chimnies and cabbusses for vessels, built at the shortest notice. **1832** *Louisville Directory* 165 Steam-boilers, chimnies, britches, etc. for steam boats made and repaired at shortest notice. **1851** *Polly Peablossom* 194 Some struck the wheel-house, while others glanced upon the iron chimneys, causing them to ring and vibrate.

+**2.** A natural rock formation suggestive of a chimney.

1837 IRVING *Bonneville* I. 45 Opposite to the camp at this place, was a singular phenomenon, which is among the curiosities of the country [of western Neb.]. It is called the chimney. **1839** TOWNSEND *Narrative* 178 This pillar is known to the hunters and trappers who traverse these regions, by the name of the 'chimney.' **1858** D. K. BENNETT *Chronology N.C.* 84 Winding our way along the margin of this most wild and restless foaming river, we reach . . . what are called the 'chimneys.'

+**3.** *Mining.* 'A body of ore, usually of elongated form, extending downward within a vein' (Raymond).

1873 BEADLE *Undevel. West* 334 It may be a 'chimney' from some lode ten thousand feet away through solid rock. **1880** G. INGHAM *Digging Gold* 259 Crossing the ledge . . . a body, or chimney of rich quartz, about four feet wide, paid eighty dollars per ton. **1882** C. KING *Rep. Prec. Metals* 471 The common run is regarded as satisfactory in quality, but rich chimneys are reported as existing.

Chimney back. The back of a fireplace. {1764}

1698 CHAMBERLAIN *Lithobolia* (1914) 65 Also a pressing-Iron lying on the ledge of the Chimney back, was convey'd invisibly into the Yard. **1709** SEWALL *Diary* II. 258 The plaistered Wall is mark'd by the Fire so as to resemble a Chimney back. **1790** *Penna. Packet* 8 Nov. 1/4 Cast iron hollow ware, . . . Chimney backs and jambs. **1839** *S. Lit. Messenger* V. 314/1 The materials . . . are now to be traced in many a hovel in the shape of '*chimney backs*' and hearth stones. **1878** STOWE *Poganuc People* 89 The widow paused and gazed reflectively on the sparks at the chimney-back.

+**Chimney cap.** A rotating top or cowl for a chimney. — **1846** *Rep. Comm. Patents* (1847) 221 What I claim, therefore, as my invention . . . is a ventilator or chimney cap. **1847** *Ib.* (1848) 42 Several patents have been granted for chimney caps professing superiority over other known forms. **1889** *Cent.* 961/3.

+**Chimney cloth.** *Obs.* A valance placed round a chimney piece as a decoration, or to retain the smoke. — **1744** FRANKLIN *Fire-Places* 7 A Chimney-cloth was look'd upon as essential to a Chimney. **1885** EGGLESTON in *Century Mag.* April 879/2 But fire-places so open did not always draw well, on which account a 'chimney-cloth' had to be used at times to close the upper part of the fire-place and keep the smoke from escaping into the room.

***Chimney corner.** The corner beside an open fireplace, an ordinary place for a seat, esp. for aged persons.

1654 JOHNSON *Wonder-w. Prov.* 171 Every Northwest wind that blew, they crept into some odd chimney-corner or other. **1704** S. KNIGHT *Journal* 53 The House where the Vendue was, had Chimney Corners like ours, and they and the hearths were laid with the finest tile that I ever see. **1851** *Polly Peablossom* 165 The boys . . . posted an old fiddler at the chimney corner. **1885** 'CRADDOCK' *Prophet* iii, A fat young person . . . sat in the chimney-corner in a little wooden chair.

attrib. **1796** ASBURY *Journal* II. 288 The Continental officers . . . were not chimney-corner whigs. **1807** IRVING, etc. *Salmagundi* iii, When the ladies do not go abroad of a morning, the usual chimney-corner dress is a dotted, spotted, striped, or cross-barred gown. **1871** STOWE *Sam Lawson* 2 Hence, in those days, chimney-corner story-telling became an art and an accomplishment.

Chimney glass. A mirror placed over the chimney piece. {1809–39} — **1715** *Boston News-Letter* 16 May 2/2 New Fashion Looking-Glasses and Chimney-Glasses. **1775** *Essex Inst. Coll.* XIII. 185 Wax Work and Chimney Glass each with its Branches.

Chimney hook. A hook fixed in a chimney or fireplace to serve as a means of support for fire irons, etc. — **1759** *Newport Mercury* 26 June 4/3 Brass and Steel Chimney-hooks. **1790** *Penna. Packet* 1 March 1/1 Brass pullies and sconces, chimney hooks. **1889** *Cent.* 961/3.

Chimney jamb. The side of a fireplace, usually of stone or brick. {1726} — **1814** *Mineral. Journal* I. 93 A considerable quantity of it [marble] is manufactured for various purposes; such as chimney-jams, grave-stones, etc. **1887** TOURGEE *Button's Inn* 253, 'I don't know, sir,' she responded, setting the spider in its place by the chimney-jamb. **1896** HARRIS *Sister Jane* 77 If you've ever heard of it, jest let me know an' I'll up an make a black mark on the chimney-jam there.

Chimney piece. a. An ornamental superstructure (and surround) for an open fireplace. **b.** The shelf or ledge above a fireplace; a mantelshelf. {1680–}

1670 *N.Y. State Col. Hist.* XII. 476 If you can conveniently send me what Walnutt Beames you can for my Chimney pieces. **1789** MACLAY *Deb. Senate* 53 He got rid of this small distress by laying the spectacle case on the chimney-piece. **1815** *Niles' Reg.* IX. 35/2 Chimney pieces . . . are executed with neatness and taste. **1900** STOCKTON *Afield & Afloat* 375, I pointed to the portrait of the lady near the chimney-piece.

+**Chimney place.** An open fireplace.

1800 *Raleigh* (N.C.) *Register* 18 March, Having left fire burning in the chimney place. **1834** *S. Lit. Messenger* I. 183 [The man] was ushered . . . into an apartment where a single chump was burning feebly in the chimney place. **1850** C. MATHEWS *Moneypenny* 225 There was but one old woman present; she . . . had fallen, drunk, asleep by the chimney-place. **1880** *Harper's Mag.* Nov. 893/1 A fire was crackling and rolling up the big chimney-place.

+**Chimney rock. 1.** *Geol.* An isolated column of rock resulting from weathering. **2.** Rock or stone suitable for building chimneys. — (1) **1850** *Western Journal* IV. 359 The sides of these buttes are . . . covered with grass. This is the formation of which . . . the Chimney rocks of the Platte river are composed. (2) **1870** *Congress. Globe* App. 26 March 225/2 The marbles of our western border have heretofore served as 'chimney rock' for the cabin of the luxurious border farmer.

‖**Chimney shelf.** A mantelshelf. — **1881** McLEAN *Cape Cod Folks* 293 The bare, shining floor, the unpainted table, the chimney-shelf.

Chimney stack. A brick or stone structure enclosing one chimney or several. {1840–} — **1852** MITCHELL *Dream Life* 220 Your rambling . . . vision . . . traces the familiar chimney-stacks. **1867** 'E KIRKE' *On Border* 23 It had . . . two enormous chimney-stacks rising at either gable. **1883** *Harper's Mag.* Sept. 536/2 At the first appearance of British troops Major Dies would betake himself to the garret, where he hid in the hollow of the chimney-stack.

Chimney swallow. {1775–} +A species of swift (*Chætura pelagica*) which builds its nest within chimneys.

1789 MORSE *Amer. Geog.* 60 [Birds of the United States include:] The . . . Red winged Starling, Swallow, Chimney do., Snow bird [etc.]. **1812** WILSON *Ornithology* V. 48 One of the first settlers in the state of Kentucky . . . cut down a large hollow beech tree which contained forty or fifty nests of the Chimney Swallow. **1838** HAWTHORNE *Note-Books* I. 69 There having been a heavy rain yesterday, a nest of chimney-swallows was washed down the chimney into the fire place. **1850** S. F. COOPER *Rural Hours* 56 The chimney-swallows have come in their usual large numbers, and our summer flock of swallows is now complete. **1863** *Century Mag.* XXX. 771 A pair of chimney-swallows have built in the parlor chimney. **1885** *Ib.* 730/1 Sometimes a nest of young chimney-swallows, loosened by the rain, would fall upon the hearth.

Chimney sweep. =next. {1727–} — **1780** *N.J. Archives* 2 Ser. IV. 200 Wanted immediately, One or two Chimney-Sweeps, of small stature. *c***1849** PAIGE *Dow's Sermons* I. 20 The mantle of religion is torn into more rags and tatters than the most disunanimous blanket you ever saw upon the back of a chimney-sweep.

***Chimney sweeper.**

***1.** One who makes a business of removing the soot from chimneys.

1687 *Boston Rec.* 191 Voted, That the Select men apoynt Chimney sweepers. **1720** SEWALL *Diary* III. 241 This day a Negro Chimney-sweeper falls down dead in the Governour's house. **1725** [see CHIMNEY-SWEEPING]. **1786** Brooks *Days of Spinning Wheel* (1886) 81 The Select-men . . . have approbated a number of Chimney-Sweepers, who are furnished with badges agreeable to the By-Laws. **1840** HAWTHORNE *Note-Books* I. 211 Methinks my profession is somewhat akin to that of a chimney-sweeper.

+**2.** (See quotation.)

1849 *Rep. Comm. Patents: Agric.* (1850) 393 The sooty powder on the flowering parts of corn-plants, called smut, chimney-sweepers, and dust-brand, is formed of the spores of another uredo.

***Chimney sweeping.** The removal of soot from chimneys by sweeping. Also attrib.

1725 *New-Eng. Courant* 15–22 Feb. 1/1 Another thing that bespeaks the Town's consideration, is the business of *Chimney-Sweeping:* there having several Fires almost happened of late for want of Chimney-Sweepers.

1762 *Newport Mercury* 17 Aug. 3/3 There is a young Man late from London, that has been regularly brought up to the Art of Chimney-Sweeping. **1819** *Plough Boy* I. 47 The Humane Society of New-York have recommended Evrard's chimney sweeping machine. **1868** G. G. CHANNING *Recoll. Newport* 22 Records were kept with reference to the regular chimney-sweepings.

+Chimney swift. =CHIMNEY SWALLOW.

1867 *Amer. Naturalist* I. 110 [April] 25th to 30th. The Chewink or Towhee Bunting, Barn Swallow, Chimney Swift, ... begin to arrive. **1868** A. D. WHITNEY *P. Strong* 61 The chimney-swifts were flying about in their quick, graceful circles. **1892** TORREY *Foot-Path Way* 110 The chimney swifts darted hither and thither with their merry, breathless cacklings. **1894** — *Fla. Sketch-Book* 209 Noting by the way the advent of the chimney swifts, which I had not found elsewhere.

+Chimney viewer. *Obs.* An inspector of chimneys. — **1684** *Conn. Hist. Soc. Coll.* VI. 211 The Chimney veiwers ... shall make presentments of what defects they find in chimneys & want of ladders, to the next authority to be fined.

***Chin,** *v.* {1599; 1869–}

+1. *intr.* To talk, chatter, discourse. *slang.*

1883 HAY *Bread-Winners* 161 You haven't done a — thing but lay around on the grass and eat peanuts and hear Bott chin. **1888** WHITMAN *Nov. Boughs* 80 I find this incident in my notes (I suppose from 'chinning' in hospital with some sick or wounded soldier). **1908** MULFORD *Orphan* 40 Why in h—l don't you quit chinning and get started? **1920** LEWIS *Main Street* 247 Lots of folks dropping in to chin with Bea and me now.

+2. *tr.* To address or talk to (a person). *slang.*

1893 GUNTER *Miss Dividends* 247, I heard one of them call another 'Constable,' and the other chinned him as 'Sheriff.' **1898** CANFIELD *Maid of Frontier* 7 He chinned the barkeep mos' to death. **1911** HARRISON *Queed* 85 [I've] been up chinning your sporting editor.

China.[1] Also †**cheny, cheyney.** [Orig. shortened from CHINAWARE.]

1. Earthenware of a fine quality; porcelain. {1653–}

'One of the earliest mentions of china in America is in the inventory of the estate of President Davenport of Harvard College, in 1648—"Cheyny £4"' (*Scribner's Mag.* X. 345). See also quot. 1647 in sense 2 a.

1731 E. Singleton *Social N.Y.* 381 The Petitioners shall collect among themselves as much Money as will buy a set of China. **1749–51** FRANKLIN *Electr. Exper.* 59 China left in the air unsupported will fall and break. **1809** IRVING *Knickerb.* VII. iv, Another [man] throws looking glasses and china out of the window, by way of saving them from the flames. **1898** PAGE *Red Rock* 284 The China was old and cracked.

fig. **1904** *N.Y. Times* 8 March 3 The statement has been freely made that when the facts came out they would break as much china for the Democrats as for the Republicans.

2. *attrib.* and *comb.* **a.** In sense: Made of china. With *basin, bowl, cup, plate,* etc.

1707 *N.H. Probate Rec.* I. 553 My sillver scallup dish and my white codell pote and cheny basan. **1773** *Mass. Col. Soc. Publ.* VI. 116 The Person who received a very large China Bowl from Capt. Barrett's House ... shall be handsomely Treated if he will return it. **1741** W. STEPHENS *Proc. Georgia* II. 169, I thought it as transparent as our ordinary strong China Cups commonly are. **1647** in *Scribner's Mag.* X. 345/2 One parcel cheyney plates and saucers. **1852** STOWE *Uncle Tom* viii, She found ... two gilded china-saucers with some pomade in them. **1787** *Amer. Museum* I. 12 A looking-glass, china tea-geer, and a hundred other things. **1775** *Essex Inst. Coll.* XIII. 185, 2 China Vases. a Japan Plate Tripod.

b. With *shelf, shop, store.*

1773 E. Singleton *Social N.Y.* 83 [Joseph Cox from London] makes ... clothes presses and chests, china shelves, ... brackets for lustres and busts. **1855** HAMBLETON *H. A. Wise* 147 The long coffin-like garret of Stebbins' china-shop, in this city. **1860** S. MORDECAI *Virginia* xxii. 247 An occasional appendage to the Swan was a house nearly opposite to it, ... where a large China store now stands.

China.[2] *Obs.* [Variant of *cheyney* (1668).] A kind of woolen stuff. Also attrib. — **1747** in Chalkley *Scotch-Irish Settlement Va.* I. 529 They were robbed of ... one orange-colored sitting gown, a pale china gown. **1762** H. M. Brooks *Gleanings* 37 Crimson and green China, 7–8th, yard wide.

***China.**[3] **+a.** =CHINAROOT. **b.** =CHINA TREE 1. **c.** *Wild china,* = CHINA TREE 2. — **(a) 1682** ASH *Carolina* 11 The China grows plentifully there, whose Root infus'd, yields us that pleasant Drink, which we know by the Name of China Ale in England. **(b) 1847** *Knickerb.* XXIX. 197 The China is the favorite shade-tree of this and many of the southern towns. **1848** *Ib.* XXXI. 545 One long winding street, flanked by rows of stately poplar and button-wood trees, with a sprinkling of sycamores and chinas. **(c) 1852** MARCY *Explor. Red River* (1854) 6 The timber, consisting of overcup, white-oak, elm, hackberry, and wild china, is large and abundant. *Ib.* 8, 14. **1884** SARGENT *Rep. Forests* 44 *Sapindus marginatus.* ... Wild China. Soapberry.

+China.[4] =POLAND CHINA. Also attrib.

1838 H. COLMAN *Mass. Agric. Rep.* 74 A cross with some of our small boned breed, such as the Byfield or the China. **1851** CIST *Cincinnati* 279 The hogs raised for this market, are generally a cross of Irish Grazier, Byfield, ... and China. **1856** *Rep. Comm. Patents: Agric.* 63 [In Beaver county, Penn.] the 'China' breed is the most prevalent, though some keep the 'Russian.' **1871** EGGLESTON *Hoosier Schoolm.* xxvi. 180 You can't make nothin' else out of him, no more nor you can make a china hog into a Berkshire.

China aster. An annual flowering plant (*Callistephus chinensis*), allied to the asters proper and extensively cultivated in gardens. {1794–}

1817–8 EATON *Botany* (1822) 193 *Aster chinensis,* China aster. ... A variety has very full flowers, various-coloured. ... Cultivated. **1845** KIRKLAND *Western Clearings* 76 Beds ... were filled to overflowing with dahlias, China-asters and marigolds. **1861** *Harper's Mag.* June 63/2 The mahogany table was garnished with china asters and colored grasses falling from a blue vase. **1873** 'G. HAMILTON' *12 Miles* 181, I may as well look into the garden, to see what the sun is doing for my one China-aster. **1889** *Cent.* 768/3 The China aster ... is much prized as a hardy annual, remaining long in flower.

Chinaberry. +The wild china or soapberry. Also attrib. with *tree.*

1890 *Harper's Mag.* Dec. 106 The high gray towers ... were crowned with ornaments like the berries of the chinaberry-trees. **1894** CHOPIN *Bayou Folk* 180 Groups of men and maidens ... were gayly matching their Easter-eggs under the shade of the China-berry trees. **1897** SUDWORTH *Arborescent Flora* 295 *Sapindus marginatus.* ... Common Names: Soapberry, ... Chinaberry.

+China brier, briar. [Cf. CHINA.[3]] A species of smilax (*S. pseudo-china* or *S. hispida*); the bullbrier.

1745 *Itinerant Observ.* 14 The good Indians regaled us, and for greens, boiled us the Tops of China-Briars, which eat almost as well as Asparagus. **1800** B. HAWKINS *Sk. Creek Country* 21 The China briar is in the flat, rich, sandy margins of streams. **1806** in *Ann. 9th Congress* 2 Sess. 1121 With a scattering undergrowth of whortleberry, hawthorn, china briar, and a variety of small vines. **1819** E. DANA *Geogr. Sk.* 190 The undergrowth is reed and cane, palmettos, rattan, grape vines and china brier. **1837** J. L. WILLIAMS *Florida* 79 Briar, China. Smilax China—grows every where, but best in damp soils, near streams. **1899** CUSHMAN *Hist. Indians* 371 They made a palatable jelly from the pounded roots of the China brier, strained through baskets.

China closet. A closet in which household china is kept. {1807–} — **1771** in *Copley-Pelham Lett.* 137 You see I have Drawn the Chinea Clossit Store Room in the east piaza. **1837** *S. Lit. Messenger* III. 591, I sprung through it, not into the passage, but into Miss Deborah's china closet. **1875** STOWE *We & Our Neighbors* 300 After putting in my turkey, I went on inspecting my China-Closet.

+Chinadom. The Chinese community or quarter in a city. — **1872** 'MARK TWAIN' *Roughing It* lxiii. 456 The combined stenches of Chinadom and Brannan Street slaughter houses. **1883** *Harper's Mag.* May 831/1 The cemetery seemed to me the most curious of all the sights connected with Chinadom in San Francisco.

Chinaman. +A man of Chinese birth or ancestry.

1849 JOHNSON *Sights Gold Region* 238 The Canton Cafe was kept by Chinamen. **1852** *Harper's Mag.* V. 403 The whole number of Chinamen who had arrived at San Francisco ... was 11,953. **1853** *Ib.* VI. 262 It is stated that the Chinamen are beginning to return in great numbers to their own country. **1883** *Ib.* LXVI. 831/2, I will say that I have not found parsimony a vice of the Chinaman, though he lives upon so little. **1898** ATHERTON *Californians* 295 One was almost afraid to break the silence; even the soft-footed Chinaman walked on his toes.

+Chinaroot. The root of an American species of smilax (*Smilax pseudo-china*), or the plant producing this.

[**1673** in H. R. Fox Bourne *Life of J. Locke* (1876) I. vi. 326 By the last fleet I sent you a parcel of Carolina china-root.] *c*1730 CATESBY *Carolina* I. 52 Of these Roots the Inhabitants of Carolina make a Diet-Drink, attributing great virtues to it in cleansing the blood, &c. ... 'Tis called there China Root. **1766** STORK *Acc. East Fla.* 48 The senna shrub, sarsaparilla, China-root, wild indigo, ... are indigenous plants of East-Florida. **1817** S. BROWN *Western Gaz.* 146 The China root and passion flower are abundant on the rich grounds. **1899** CUSHMAN *Hist. Indians* 229 To produce a copious perspiration, a hot decoction of the China root swallowed had the desired effect.

attrib. **1806** in *Ann. 9th Congress* 2 Sess. 1142 The saw briar, single rose briar, and china root briar.

China silk. Silk from China. — **1858** HOLMES *Autocrat* 314, I own perhaps I might desire ... Some marrowy crapes of China silk, Like wrinkled skins on scalded milk. **1887** *Courier Journal* 20 Feb. 1/6 Very fine line China Silks. **1893** *Chicago Tribune* 26 April 8/6 All black figured China Silks—seasonable fabrics—fair value $1.25—at $1.00.

+Chinatown. The Chinese quarter of a city or town; a place inhabited by Chinese immigrants.

1877 WM. WRIGHT *Hist. of Big Bonanza* 28 A large number of Chinamen being at work at the mouth of the Cañon, ... that place finally became known as 'Chinatown,' a name which it long retained. **1880** *Harper's Mag.* Dec. 70 The strong local prejudice against our Asiatic immigrants, and the proverbial procrastination ... unite to keep 'Chinatown' practically a sealed book. **1886** *Starry Flag* (San Francisco) May 2/1, I had long been wishing to explore the mysteries of Chinatown. **1898** ATHERTON *Californians* 51 Helena had been escorted through Chinatown by her adoring parent and a policeman.

China trade. Commerce with China. — **1788** FRENEAU *Misc. Works* 149 He doubts, and frets, and seems afraid The States will lose by China trade, Since dollars for their tea are paid. **1830** COOPER *Water Witch* II. x, The China trade will come to something in time. **1884** *Harper's Mag.* Jan. 223/1 The first clipper . . . was the Rainbow, . . . built about the year 1843 . . . for the China trade.

+China tree.

1. The pride of China, or pride of India (*Melia azederach*), extensively planted as a shade tree in the southern states.

1819 E. EVANS *Pedestrious Tour* 315 Here grew the China tree, of a beautiful appearance, and bearing fruit of an inviting aspect, but of an unpleasant taste. **1827** A. SHERWOOD *Gaz. Georgia* 97 The town is regularly laid out, the streets wide and ornamented with the China tree. **1834** R. BAIRD *Valley Miss.* 43 The china tree is a beautiful shade tree and is the ornamental tree of the towns and villages in the southern part of the valley. **1856** *Rep. Comm. Patents: Agric.* 67 Many planters in the Southern States recommend the berries of the 'China-tree,' . . . 'Pride of China,' . . . to be put around cabbage-plants, in order to prevent the attack of the cut-worm. **1859** A. VAN BUREN *Sojourn in South* 135 There is the umbrageous China-tree, in all its rich, feathery foliage.

b. A single tree of this kind.

1827 A. SHERWOOD *Gaz. Georgia* 22 China trees were killed. **1838** *S. Lit. Messenger* IV. 96/1 China trees, with their bright green leaves and yellow berries, were scattered in groups over the large yard. **1869** *Overland Mo.* III. 13 The tall catalpas proudly display their violet-white panicles; the China trees, their sweet wealth of lilac flowers. **1896** HARRIS *Sister Jane* 191 The bird . . . flew wildly to the top of the big China tree on the sidewalk.

2. *Wild China tree*, the soapberry; CHINABERRY.

1885 HAVARD *Flora W. & S. Texas* 458 To a closely allied order [of the maple] belongs the Wild China-tree or Soapberry (*Sapindus marginatus*).

Chinaware. = CHINA[1] 1. {1634 *cheney ware;* 1699–}

1741 W. STEPHENS *Proc. Georgia* II. 154 It began to be currently reported about Town, that Mr. Duchee, the Potter, had now accomplish'd his Intention of making China Ware. **1767** H. M. Brooks *Gleanings* 32 A Variety of Stone, China, and Glass Ware, which will be sold very low at his Shop. **1819** *Niles' Reg.* XVI. 24/2 The manufacture of China ware, or porcelain, equal in firmness to the French, has been commenced in New-York. **1891** HOLMES *Over Teacups* 81, I suppose he has often been . . . made to feel as we may suppose a cracked piece of china-ware feels when it is clinked in the company of sound bits of porcelain.

+China wheat. 'A spring wheat grown in the United States, said to have been derived from a grain found in a tea-chest' (*Cent.* 6888).

+Chinawoman. A Chinese woman. — **1872** 'MARK TWAIN' *Roughing It* liv. 392 There are few white servants and no Chinawomen so employed. **1883** *Harper's Mag.* May 831/2 They bore freights of Chinamen and Chinawomen and curiously assorted provisions.

+Chincapin. (Variant of CHINQUAPIN.)

Chinch, Chinche. Also †**chince, cinch.** The common bedbug. {1665–1730}

1675 JOSSELYN *Two Voyages* 117 If you chance to break one of the Bugs it will stink odiously: they call them *Chinches* or *Wood-lice.* **1708** E. COOK *Sot-Weed Factor* (1865) 19 But Heat and Chinces rais'd the Sinner, Most opportunely for his Dinner. **1797** J. PETTIGREW *MS. Let.* 22 March (N.C. Univ.), I very much dread the approach of warm weather on account of the chinches which are innumerable. **1835** P. H. NICKLIN *Va. Springs* 28 The stinking chinch does not like sulphur water. **1853** BREWERTON *Ride with Kit Carson* (1930) 199 It may be that the *chinches* (in plain English—bed-bugs), which swarm . . . in this favored land, were too numerous for comfort. **1903** S. W. NORTH *Mother of Calif.* 114 (Bentley), Fortunately, the 'pestivorous' little chinche and the jigger . . . do not infest the Peninsula.

+Chinch bug. (See also CHINTZ BUG.)

1. A small hemipterous insect of the genus *Blissus*, destructive to wheat and corn in the southern and western states.

1786 WASHINGTON *Diaries* III. 97 Examined the low and sickly looking corn in several parts of this field and discovered more or less of the Chinch bug on every stalk between the lower blades and it. **1790** *Penna. Packet* 30 March 1/4 For the best information . . . for preventing damage to crops by insects; especially the Hessian-fly, the wheat-fly, . . . and the corn chinch bug or fly. **1854** EMMONS *Agric. N.Y.* V. 169 To this family belongs the chinch-bug, which figured so largely in Wisconsin in 1845. **1884** *Comm. Agric. Rep.* 399 About ten days before harvest or during the early part of July the Chinch-Bug began to appear in grain fields in great numbers. **1892** V. KELLOG *Kansas Insects* 14 The Chinch-bug is unfortunately a familiar object to Kansas farmers.

2. A bedbug; a chinch.

1819 *Plough Boy* I. 79, I will inform her, as a good housewife, how she can keep her beds and bed-rooms clear of vermin, vulgarly called chinch bugs.

+Chincomen tree. [Amer. Indian, prob. Algonquin *chinqua* 'large,' 'great,' *min* 'fruit,' 'seed.'] Early form, probably nearer original, of CHINQUAPIN. — **1615** R. HAMOR *True Discourse Virginia* 23, I know no one Country yeelding without art or industry so manie fruites, . . . many groues of *Chincomen trees* with a huske like vnto a Chesnut, rawe or boyled, luscious and harty meate.

+Chincopin. (Variant of CHINQUAPIN.)

+Chinee. *colloq.*[2] [From CHINESE taken as a plural.] A Chinaman. Also attrib.

1871 R. SOMERS *Southern States* 163 The Chinée, who struts even here with a celestial sort of air, must have his tent all nicely fixed up and provided for him. **1910** MULFORD *Hopalong Cassidy* 142 That cross between a nigger an' a Chinee is in Davy Jones' locker, is he? **1910** J. HART *Vigilante Girl* 375 Think of feeding two train-loads all to once—with one force of girls and one Chiney [*sic*] cook.

b. *Heathen Chinee*, as a humorous term.

1870 HARTE *Plain Language* line 5 For tricks that are vain, The heathen Chinee is peculiar. **1871** — in *Every Saturday* 27 July 117 The 'Heathen Chinee' in the South. **1877** *Congress. Rec.* 8 Nov. 296/1 [The army is maintained] to put down the 'heathen Chinee.' **1881** STODDARD *E. Hardery* 133 Vote for him, sir? Never, sir! Why, the man's an infidel, sir. . . . I'd as soon vote for a heathen Chinee.

Chinese, *n.* {1606–}

+1. A form of ornamental railing. *Obs.*

1771 in *Copley-Pelham Lett.* 130 A pattern of Chinese for the Top of the house I will send you. **1771** *Ib.* 170, I don't think the Chinese you sent by Smith is so hansome as Mr. Vassell's.

2. A native of China; a person of Chinese birth or descent. Usually *pl.* {1606–}

1845 *Knickerb.* XXV. 445 Set out on the circular table . . . [were] the blue plates, 'Chineses,' with umbrellas crossing a bridge. **1852** *Harper's Mag.* V. 257/1 Measures have been taken in several of the mining localities to exclude the Chinese from them. **1889** FARMER 138/1 The Chinese must go.—An expression which has recently acquired new significance in that the prejudice against the Chinese has come to a head.

Chinese, *a.* Of or belonging to, derived or brought from, or associated with, China. {1647–}

1. In the specific names of various trees and plants: see quotations and cf. CHINA.

Many other examples of this common use of the term may be found in botany books, etc.

1858 WARDER *Hedges & Evergreens* 270 The Chinese Juniper, is a shrub of three feet in height, with twisted and very spreading branches. **1880** *Harper's Mag.* Dec. 72 At nearly every window was . . . a dish of the favorite Chinese lily, the narcissus in full bloom. **1832** BROWNE *Sylva* 218 Silk worms . . . feed with advantage only on the smooth, thin and tender foliage of the white and Chinese mulberry. **1856** *Rep. Comm. Patents: Agric.* 258 The 'Chinese' pea, from its size and color, could not be distinguished from the Oregon pea. **1849** *New Eng. Farmer* I. 220 It is equally effective for Sweet Williams, Chinese pinks, and indeed for the whole genus. **1868** *Rep. Comm. Agric.* 306 The Chinese rose . . . blooms perpetually when cultivated in the conservatory. **1880** *Vt. Agric. Rep.* VI. 222 The first varieties introduced were from China and were called Chinese sorghums. **1855** BROWNE in *Trans. Amer. Inst. N.Y.* 599 Chinese Yam (*Dioscorea batatas*), proposed as a substitute for the common potato, and appears to be particularly worthy of a place in the kitchen garden.

2. In various applications, as *Chinese box, cracker, lantern*, etc.

1829 R. C. SANDS *Writings* II. 57 Unless they patronized some of the members . . . thus compacted like Chinese boxes. **1841** *Knickerb.* XVII. 276 The first sign of the dawning of this virtue is discoverable in the *penchant* of our younglings for Chinese crackers, and indeed gunpowder in any form. **1865** *Chicago Tribune* 10 April 1 Fire works and Chinese lanterns, for illuminations. **1904** *Grand Rapids Press* 25 Nov. 5 Men raided Chinese Laundry. **1846** *Knickerb.* XXVII. 51 It is harder than a Chinese puzzle to put your finger on a bit of territory, . . . where Yankee-Doodle is not. **1844** KENDALL *Santa Fé Exped.* II. 98, I have little doubt he was very officious among [such fireworks as] squibs, India crackers, Chinese wheels.

+Chinese (sugar) cane. A sweet variety of sorghum, *Sorghum saccharatum.*

(*a*) **1856** *Spirit of Times* 29 Nov. 214/2 The farmers of Ohio . . . can make their own sugar cheaper . . . by cultivating the Chinese sugar-cane. **1874** *Dept. Agric. Rep. 1873* 108 The Chinese sugar-cane (*Sorghum saccharatum*) was introduced into this country from France in 1854. **1901** MOHR *Plant Life Ala.* 68.

(*b*) **1856** *Spirit of Times* 15 Nov. 182/2 The chief advantages of the Chinese cane as a sugar-plant . . . is the facility of its cultivation and the easy treatment of its juice. **1863** *Rep. Comm. Agric.* 131 The Chinese cane has a very lofty and well-proportioned stalk.

+Chin fly. A botfly (*Gastrophilus nasalis*) which infects horses. — **1867** in Carpenter *6 Mo. at White House* 129 You were brought up on a farm, were you not? . . . Then you know what a *chin fly* is. *Ib.* 130 If Mr. — has a presidential chin fly biting him, I'm not going to knock him off. **1909** *Cent. Suppl.* 236/2 *Chin-fly* a horse bot-fly, *Gastrophilus nasalis*, possibly so called because its eggs are laid about the horse's mouth.

***Chink,** *n.*[1] A small aperture in a solid surface, +esp., a crevice between logs in a log house.

1659 Roosevelt *American Backlogs* (1928) I. 3 The bird vanished as they conceived through the chink of a joynted-board. **1788** J. MAY *Jour. &*

Lett. 27 The buildings are made of hewn logs, the chinks filled in with stones, and plastered over with lime-mortar. **1839** *Knickerb.* XIV. 141 A clumsy, ill-shapen log hut, with interstices, or, to speak more classically, 'chinks,' wide enough to throw a sizeable bear through. **1851** GLISAN *Jrnl. Army Life* 51 The chinks, or spaces between the logs, are filled in with strips of wood. **1871** *Scribner's Mo.* II. 588 A few glances through the chinks of the casement.

transf. and *fig.* **1830** Perrin *Ky. Pioneer Press* (1888) 77 A half a hundred of mortar would scarcely fill up the chinks of the skulls that were broken. **1872** 'MARK TWAIN' *Roughing It* xli. 285 He would groan and wail and howl with the anguish, and fill up the odd chinks with the most elaborate profanity that strong convictions and a fine fancy could contrive.

b. *Chink(s) and daubing,* (cf. CHINK *v.* 1 and 2).

1804 ORDWAY in *Journals of Lewis & O.* 166 We raised the roof of the meat & Smoak house bringing it up with Timber cross drawing in, So as to answer with chinks & dobbing. **1881** H. PIERSON *In the Brush* 51 The large openings between the logs had been filled with 'chink and daubing.'

+**Chink,** *n.*[2] *local.* The wintergreen or checkerberry, *Gaultheria procumbens.* — **1892** *Amer. Folk-Lore* V. 100 *Gaultheria procumbens,* . . . jinks or chinks. N.H.; Mass.

Chink, *n.*[3] *colloq.* A Chinaman. Also transf.

1901 *Munsey's Mag.* XXIV. 536 The leader suggested the 'chink,' and to the one Chinese laundry . . . the little band departed. **1904** *Grand Rapids Ev. Press* 25 Nov. 5 Robbed the Chink. Hold-up Men Raided Chinese Laundry. **1907** MULFORD *Bar-20* 123 Yu white-washed Chink yu! **1910** RAINE *B. O'Connor* 41 Chinks, greasers, and several other kinds of citizens driftin' that way. **1912** MULFORD & CLAY *Buck Peters* 11 And no one had been able to convince her that sympathy was wasted on a 'Chink.' **1925** FRASER & GIBBONS *Soldier & Sailor Words* 54 Chink is an old pre-War name for a Chinaman, long current in the East-End of London and the Chinese quarters of Liverpool, Cardiff, etc., and in America.

* **Chink,** *v.*

+**1.** *tr.* To close up (the logs in a log house, a wall, etc.) by filling in the chinks. {1822–}

1748 in Chalkley *Scotch-Irish Settlement Va.* I. 35 Presentment vs. Court House, . . . built of logs, chinked with mud, but cracks 4 to 5 inches wide. **1791** Jillson *Dark & Bl. Ground* 111 The walls . . . are chinked with white clay. **1805** CLARK in *Lewis & C. Exped.* (1905) III. 284 All hands at work about the huts Chinking them. **1841** *Knickerb.* XVII. 209 Aware of the dangers to which he was exposed, Mr. Hart had 'chinked' the logs, before open and admitting of being fired through by the musketry or rifles of an enemy. **1878** BIRD *Lady's Life in Rocky Mts.* 289 The house was chinked, and the rooms felt quite warm.

b. To fill in (chinks or openings).

1843 'CARLTON' *New Purchase* I. 60 The interstices of the log-wall were 'chinked.' **1859** A. DUNIWAY *Capt. Gray's Co.* 19 The crevices between the logs were chinked with pieces of split wood. **1904** STRATTON-PORTER *Freckles* 203 Big Duncan . . . worked early and late to chink every crack about the cabin. **1920** HUNTER *Trail Drivers of Texas* I. 376 Most of our houses were built of logs . . . and the cracks 'chinked' with sticks and muds.

c. *intr.* and *fig.*

*a***1859** *Spirit of Times* (B.), Perhaps you would like to have it to use for chinking in among your election returns.

+**2.** *To chink and daub,* to make close or weather-tight by inserting pieces of wood, stone, etc., and plastering with clay or mud.

1829 T. FLINT *G. Mason* 10 They knew infinitely better than he did how to 'daub and chink' a log cabin. **1831** PECK *Guide* 127 The interstices between the logs of both the cabin and log house are chinked with strips of wood, and daubed with . . . [mud or clay] mortar. **1844** KENDALL *Santa Fé Exped.* I. 25 Our log-house quarters, however, were closely 'chinked and daubed.' **1867** RICHARDSON *Beyond Miss.* 55 It had a huge fireplace, and was neatly 'chinked' and 'daubed'; (the cracks between the logs filled with bits of wood and plastered with mud). **1883** SHIELDS *S. S. Prentiss* 18 The school-house was a hewn-log house, chinked and daubed with cat and clay.

+**Chinkapin.** Variant of CHINQUAPIN.

***Chinked,** *ppl. a.* +Of crevices between logs in a log house: Filled with twigs, clay, plaster, etc. (See CHINK *v.*) — **1880** BURNETT *Recoll.* 29 A log cabin about eighteen by twenty feet, with chinked cracks, clapboard roof, and puncheon floor. **1895** *Outing* XXVI. 36/1 A shanty built of logs chinked with mud.

***Chinker.** +An object suitable for stopping up a crevice or gap. — **1857** *Spirit of Times* 3 Jan. 294/2 The farmer calls the pebbles used to fill these spaces between the big blocks, 'chinkers.'

* **Chinking.**

+**1.** The material used to fill crevices in a log house.

1791 Jillson *Dark & Bl. Ground* 107 It has a dirt floor pounded hard and no chinking in the walls. **1829** T. FLINT *G. Mason* 10 The intervals between the logs were tightly closed with chinking. **1856** S. T. ROBINSON *Kansas* 308 He knocked the chinking out of the walls and took possession. **1887** 'CRADDOCK' *Keedon Bluffs* 210 Be thar enny draught thar in the chinkin'? **1912** WASON *Friar Tuck* 175 We had hard work thawin' out the clay for chinkin', an' we didn't get the cabin as tight as we'd a' liked.

+**b.** *transf.* Padding or filling.

1835 LONGSTREET *Ga. Scenes* 197 [In dressing up as Daniel Lambert] Billy required the aid of at least eight pillows, with some extra chinking, as we say in Georgia. **1888** *Amer. Missionary* April 108 She wore one of the smallest thimbles with a bit of cloth inside for 'chinking' to keep it on.

+**2.** The process of filling the crevices in a log house.

1824 W. N. BLANE *Excursion through U.S.* 181 This operation is called *chinking;* and before it has been performed, the cabin, in winter, would be uninhabited from the cold, were it not for the great fire that is kept up. **1888** P. H. SHERIDAN *Memoirs* I. 26 With the aid of some old condemned paulins obtained from the quartermaster, the walls were covered and the necessity for chinking obviated.

Chin music. *slang.* Chatter; idle talk. {1877–, *dial.*}

1836 HILDRETH *Campaigns Rocky Mts.* I. 26 He was . . . a thorough-bred Kentuckian, full of chin music, as the species of loquacity which he possessed is termed. **1843** STEPHENS *High Life N.Y.* II. 108, I thought it wouldn't do no harm to give 'em a short specimen of Weathersfield chin music. [**1857** *Jrnl. Discourses* V. 101 (Th.), Whenever he attempts to amuse them with his chin-music, they expect that he will say something funny.] **1873** 'MARK TWAIN' & WARNER *Gilded Age* xxix. 267 Thereupon a young sprig . . . began to sass the conductor with his chin music. **1881** M. ALEXANDER *Going West* 170 Some of the crew laughed, and said, 'Bill Johnson, you had better learn to keep your chin-music to yourself.' **1909** 'O. HENRY' *Roads of Destiny* 80 Of course, I'm awfully obliged to you for making that chin-music to her of evenings.

Chinning. *colloq.* Talk, chatter, reassuring words. — **1890** CUSTER *Following Guidon* 308 Men called out to each other very pointed remarks about snoring, or too much 'chinning,' as they said, when they wanted to sleep. **1892** GUNTER *Miss Dividends* (1893) 232 She needs chinning, she does. I have had to step into your shoes and comfort her! **1920** LEWIS *Main Street* 42 'Great fellow for chinning, He'll talk your arm off, about religion or books or anything.'

+**Chinny,** *a. colloq.*[2] Much given to talking. — **1883** HAY *Bread-Winners* 81 He hated these 'chinny bummers,' as he called them, who talked about 'State help and self-help' over their beer. *Ib.* 100, I forgot about the old lady, though she was more chinny than the young one.

+**Chinook.** Also †**Chenook,** etc. [Amer. Indian]

1. *attrib.* Belonging to a well-known Indian tribe of the Chinookan family, situated near the mouth of the Columbia River.

1805 CLARK in *Lewis & C. Exped.* (1905) III. 294 The Chin-nook womin are lude. **1806** LEWIS *Ib.* IV. 170 We were visited this afternoon by Delashshelwilt a Chinnook Chief his wife and six women of his nation. *c***1836** CATLIN *Indians* II. 110 Plate 209, is the portrait of a Chinook boy, of fifteen or eighteen years of age. **1843** FRÉMONT *Exped.* 197 A Chinook Indian, a lad of nineteen, who was extremely desirous to 'see the Whites,' . . . was received into the party. **1848** *Calif. Claims* (Senate Rep. 23 Feb.) 52 The other eight were . . . William Chinook, an Indian lad of the Chinook tribe, John Stevens, a French creole by name of Durand, [etc.].

2. A member of this tribe; also *pl.* or *collect.*, the tribe or group as a whole.

1831 R. COX *Adv. Columbia R.* I. 299 He was rescued when in a state of great exhaustion by two Chinooks. *c***1836** CATLIN *Indians* II. 110 The Chinooks, Inhabiting the lower parts of the Columbia, are a small tribe, and correctly come under the name of Flat Heads. **1842** PRICHARD *Nat. Hist. Man* 414 To the Nootka-Columbia family belong the tribes known by the names of *Chenooks* [etc.]. **1844** LEE & FROST *Oregon* 99 The Chenooks inhabit the north side of the Columbia. **1907** HODGE *Indians* I. 272 The Chinook were first described by Lewis and Clark, who visited them in 1805, though they had been known to traders for at least 12 years previously.

3. The language spoken by the Chinook Indians. Also attrib. with *language.*

1836 IRVING *Astoria* II. 88 The tribes, both north and south of the Columbia, . . . all speak the Chinook language, and probably originated from the same stock. **1850** G. HINES *Voyage* 31 Mr. Perkins, in addition to learning the Chenook, applied himself to the acquirement of the Walla-Walla. **1890** RYAN *Told in Hills* 171 'Learn some Indian songs,' advised that little conspirator impressively; 'in the Kootenai country you must sing Chinook if you want to be appreciated.'

4. A trade language or jargon in use in the Pacific northwest, composed of elements from Chinook proper, Nootka, English, French, and other sources. Freq. attrib. with *jargon.*

1855 H. R. SCHOOLCRAFT *History of Indian Tribes* V. 548 A jargon of Indian words in Oregon and Washington mixed with English, French, and Spanish, . . . called the Chinook Jargon. *a***1861** T. WINTHROP *Canoe & Saddle* ii, A grotesque jargon called Chinook is the lingua-franca of the whites and Indians of the North-west. **1886** B. P. POORE *Reminisc.* II. 110 Finally an officer who had served on the Pacific coast recognized it as 'Chinook,' a compound of the English, Chinese, and Indian languages used by the whites in trading with the Chinook Indians. **1888** *Puget Sound Gazetteer* July 9/1 There is a common jargon of limited vocabulary, called Chinook, which seems to supply the wants of these taciturn and uncommercial peoples. *a***1918** G. STUART *On Frontier* I. 91 We called to them in Chinook jargon, which is understood by all Indians from here up to Russian America (now Alaska).

5. A warm, moist wind off the ocean, blowing over the Pacific northwest; also a warm, dry wind of the Rocky Mt. region.

So called orig. by the Hudson Bay Company's traders in Astoria because it blew from the direction of an encampment of Chinook Indians.

1878 F. ROE *Army Lett.* 190 The weather had been bitter cold, but during the night a chinook had blown up, and the air was warm and balmy. **1884** W. SHEPHERD *Prairie Exper.* 116 A chinook or warm wind had produced a thaw, and the floods had washed out the line. **1889** *Secy. of Agric. Rep.* 307 In Denver a chinook has been known to induce a rise in temperature of 57° Fahr. in twenty-four hours. **1899** *Mo. So. Dakotan* I. 197 Spring . . . was near at hand. There was a balmy suggestion in the caress of the stealing chinook which confirmed this conviction. **1911** QUICK *Yellowstone N.* 128 Every little snow was followed by a chinook.

6. Attrib. with *cloud, liquorice, wind.* (See also 1, 3, 4.)

*a***1918** G. STUART *On Frontier* II. 149 On the evening of the seventeenth, I noticed flat pancake chinook clouds in the western sky. **1893** *Amer. Folk-Lore* VI. 140 *Lupinus littoralis,* Chinook liquorice. Washington, D.C. **1884** *Boston Journal* 6 March, Our cold weather is not of long duration, and is tempered by the Chinook wind from the Pacific coast.

+**Chinook salmon.** The common salmon of the Columbia river, tyee salmon or quinnat, *Oncorhynchus tschawytscha.*

1881 *Amer. Naturalist* XV. 177 Quinnat. . . . Chinook salmon, Columbia River salmon, Sacramento salmon. **1884** GOODE *Aquatic Animals* 479 On the Columbia River the name 'Chinook Salmon' is in universal use. **1892** *Courier-Journal* 2 Oct. 17/8 My brother . . . hooked and landed a twenty-pound Chinook salmon. **1912** F. J. HASKIN *Amer. Govt.* 151 The bureau of fisheries . . . has tried to establish the chinook salmon in Atlantic coast waters.

+**Chinquapin.** Also **chinquepin, chinkapin, chinkopen,** etc. [Amer. Indian. See CHINCOMEN TREE.]

1. The small, sweet nut of the dwarf chestnut: (see next).

1676 GLOVER *Acc. Va.* in *Phil. Trans.* XI. 629 Beside these [nuts], here is another called a Chincopine, which is like a Chesnut, with a Burry husk, but lesse by far. **1696–8** *Mass. H. S. Coll.* V. 126 The woods also bringing good store of chesnuts, walnuts, hickory nuts, chincopins. **1710** *N.C. Col. Rec.* I. 740 The Nottoway Indian old men being gone to gather Chinkopens We deferred the taking their Examinacions till our Return. **1836** C. GILMAN *Recoll.* (1838) vi. 47 Look at Cornelia's face! It is as brown as a chinquapin. **1861** NORTON *Army Lett.* 26 In the woods near us we found any quantity of grapes and chinquapins. **1886** *Leslie's Mo.* XXI. 150/1 A mess of chinkapins and hickory nuts. **1904** E. GLASGOW *Deliverance* 91 He had saved every stray penny from his sales of hogs and cider, of water-melons and chinkapins.

2. The dwarf chestnut (*Castanea pumila*), a shrub or small tree native to the South.

1692 in *Phil. Trans.* XVII. 619 The Flowring Beech of Virginia, and . . . the Chinquapin of the same place. **1709** LAWSON *Carolina* 99 Chinkapin is a sort of Chesnut, whose Nuts are most commonly very plentiful; insomuch that the Hogs get fat with them. **1724** JONES *Virginia* 130 Upon the Leaves of the Chinckapin . . . I have frequently found a very large Worm not much unlike the Silk-Worm. *c***1728** CATESBY *Carolina* I. 9 The Chinkapin . . . is a Shrub which seldom grows higher than sixteen feet, and usually not above eight or ten. **1819** E. DANA *Geogr. Sk.* 171 The soil is . . . thickly covered with timber; such as various species of . . . hornbeam, chincapin, wildberry. **1832** BROWNE *Sylva* 130 In the south of the United States the chinquapin fructifies on the most arid lands: its perfect development requires a cool and fertile soil. **1859** A. L. HILLHOUSE tr. *Michaux's Sylva* III. 17 The nuts of the Chincapin are brought into the markets, and are eaten raw by children.

3. a. *ellipt.* = CHINQUAPIN OAK.

1829 EATON *Botany* (ed. 5) *Quercus chinquapin,* dwarf chestnut oak, Chinquapin. . . . A low shrub. . . . *S.*

b. The goldenleaf or western chinquapin, *Castanopsis chrysophylla.*

1889 *Cent.* 964/1 *Chinkapin, chincapin,* . . . a tree or shrub of the Sierra Nevada and Cascade mountains. **1897** SUDWORTH *Arborescent Flora* 149 Goldenleaf Chinquapin. . . . Common names [include] Chinquapin (Cal., Oreg.), . . . Western Chinquapin.

c. The water chinquapin or wankapin, *Nelumbo lutea.*

1892 *Amer. Folk-Lore* V. 91 *Nelumbium luteum,* chinquapine. Carroll Co., Mo.

4. Attrib. with *bush, log, nut,* etc.

1762 CLAYTON *Flora Virginica* 150 Chinquapin-bush. **1881** HARRIS *Uncle Remus* 27 En way up de hill he see Brer Rabbit settin' cross-legged on a chinkapin log koamin' de pitch outen his har wid a chip. **1709** LAWSON *Carolina* 28 We found here good Store of Chinkapin-Nuts, which they gather in Winter. **1791** *Lower Norfolk Co., Va., Antiquary* I. 30 William Willoughby . . . agreed to inclose the academy . . . with good sawed pine railes and pales and Chinquipin posts. **1839** *S. Lit. Messenger* V. 378/2 Master Billy . . . continued tapping his right leg with the chinquepin switch he held in his hand. **1845** THOMPSON *Chron. Pineville* 65 If that one on this side didn't have whiskers, I hope I may never see chinkapin time agin, dadfetch me! **1682** ASH *Carolina* 7 The Chincopin Tree bears a Nut not unlike the Hazle, the shell is softer. Of the Kernel is made Chocolate, not much inferior to that made of the Cacoa.

+**Chinquapin oak.** One or other variety of scrub oak, *Quercus acuminata* or *Q. prinoides.*

1785 MARSHALL *Amer. Grove* 125 *Quercus Prinus humilis.* Dwarf Chesnut or Chinquepin Oak. This generally rises with several shrubby, spreading stalks, to the height of two or three feet. **1810** MICHAUX *Arbres* I. 23 *Chincapin oak,* . . . dans la partie haute des Carolines et de la Georgia. **1821** NUTTALL *Trav. Ark.* 205 We found the small chinquapin oak by acres, running along the ground as in New Jersey. **1843** TORREY *Flora N.Y.* II. 193 *Quercus prinoides.* . . . Chinquapin Oak. . . . Sandy woods. . . . This species . . . is often called Dwarf Chestnut Oak. **1860** CURTIS *Woody Plants N.C.* 60 Chinquapin oak . . : is a mere shrub, 2 to 4 feet high, of no value. **1907** HODGE *Indians* I. 275 Two species of oak (*Quercus acuminata* and *Q. prinoides*) are named Chinquapin oak and dwarf chinquapin oak, respectively.

+**Chinquapin perch.** (See quotations.) — **1884** GOODE *Aquatic Animals* 407 The Crappie—*Pomoxys annularis* . . . [is] called . . . 'Chinquapin Perch' in the Lower Mississippi. **1907** Hodge *Indians* I. 275 A species of perch (*Pomoxys annularis*), known also as crappie, is called Chinquapin or Chinkapin perch.

Chinquoimine. (Cf. CHINCOMEN TREE.) — **1799** *Farmer's Reg.* (Greensburg, Pa.) 30 Nov. (Th.), She remembered chinquoimines, chesnuts, walnuts, &c., where the principal buildings in Philadelphia now stand.

Chintz.[1] Also †**chince,** †**chints.**

1. Cotton cloth printed with colored designs and usually glazed. {1614–}

1726 *New-Eng. Courant* 5–12 March 2/2 Edward Carter, Silk-Dyer and Scowerer, . . . Dyes and scowers, . . . Needle-Work and Embroidery, . . . fine Chinces and Callicoes. **1775** Singleton *Social N.Y.* 247 Henry Wilmot, in Hanover Square, sells . . . cambrices clear, flowered and long lawns, dark ground and other calicoes and chintzes. **1825** J. NEAL *Bro. Jonathan* I. 54 Edith had been slily tacking little bits of chintz together, for a year or two. **1832** CLAY *Sp., American System* (1842) 185 Are the fine graceful forms of our fair country-women less lovely when enveloped in the chintses and calicoes produced by native industry? **1850** HAWTHORNE *Note-Books* II. 164 [She wore] a dark gown (chintz, I suppose the women call it) a good, homely dress. **1878** R. T. COOKE *Happy Dodd* 324 One or two cushions of dingy chintz [were] recovered with gay patchwork. **1904** GLASGOW *Deliverance* 358 She was standing by the window, holding aside the curtain of flowered chintz.

2. Attrib. in sense: **a.** Of the character of chintz; made of chintz. **b.** Covered with chintz.

(**a**) **1859** STOWE *Minister's Wooing* iv, Aunt Katy . . . sat in full flowing chintz petticoat and spotless dimity short-gown. **1863** A. D. WHITNEY *F. Gartney* xiv, Here, in the old doctor's 'one-hoss shay,' and with her round straw hat and chintz wrapper on, [etc.]. **1865** *Atlantic Mo.* XV. 299/1, I have put charming blue chintz curtains in the spare chamber. **1881** *Harper's Mag.* LXII. 528/1 Chintz calico formed the curtains.

(**b**) **1860** S. WARNER *Say & Seal* 540 This one [room] was . . . furnished with the simplest of chintz furniture. **1869** STOWE *Oldtown Folks* 205 A wide, ample-bosomed chintz sofa and a great chintz-covered easy-chair.

+**Chintz.**[2] [Variant of CHINCH.] A chinch or bedbug. — **1807** C. W. JANSON *Stranger in Amer.* 58 The inhabitants called bed-bugs, *chintzes.* **1832** TROLLOPE *Domestic Manners* I. 221 Possible! do you pretend you don't know what chintzes are? Why the nasty little stinking blood-suckers that all the beds in London are full of. **1882** SALA *America Revisited* II. 296 The most efficacious poison for 'chintzes' or bed-bugs.

+**Chintz bug.** = CHINCH BUG 1.

1785 in *S. Lit. Messenger* XXVIII. 38/1 The devastation of the Chintz bug, which since harvest have infested the Indian Corn. **1786** WASHINGTON *Diaries* III. 96 An Overseer of mine (at the ferry) informed that the chintz bug was discovered in his Corn. **1867** *Iowa Agric. Soc. Rep.* (1868) 143 The great enemy to spring wheat has been the chintz bug. **1873** BEADLE *Undevel. West* 225 The fly is a little troublesome to wheat, but its principal enemy is the chintz bug, so-called here. **1910** *Omaha Bee* March (Th.), The scales of American prices . . . are so delicate that the yell of a crop killer who has discovered a chintz bug down in Texas will swing the balances in Chicago.

Chintzed, *a.* Decorated, covered, or furnished with chintz. — **1882** HOWELLS *Woman's Reason* 384 The pretty chintzed and muslined room in which she seemed to drowse her life away.

+**Chin whiskers.** Whiskers growing from the chin. — **1882** HOWELLS *Woman's Reason* 322 One was a gentleman in what he would have called chin-whiskers, with his hair gathered in a puff over his forehead. **1883** R. G. WHITE in *Atlantic Mo.* LII. 101/1 That adornment known at the West as 'chin-whiskers.' **1897** STUART *Simpkinsville* 159 Eben is a handsome man, even here, with his hen-pecked face an' chin whiskers on.

‖**Chiota.** (Var. of COYOTE.) — **1850** KINGSLEY *Diary* 153 We saw . . . any quantity of chiotas or praira [*sic*] wolf, which are very impudent.

***Chip,** *n.*

1. A small fragment chipped from a block, log, etc., and used as kindling wood.

More freq. in U.S. than in England. Also in allusive use: cf. BASKET 2b, and *chip-basket* in sense 8.

1800 *The Nightingale, or Rural Songster* 77 A basket of chips. 1875 HOWELLS *Lady of Aroostook* xxiii, She looks as blooming . . . as a basket of chips. 1885 *Congress. Rec.* Jan. 998/1, I know as well what the bug is under this chip as I know that the resolution is pending here. 1887 I. ALDEN *Little Fishers* ii, Then came a visit to the back-yard in search of chips; both children following close at her heels, saying nothing, but watching every movement with wide-open wondering eyes. Back again to the kitchen, and the fire was made up.

2. A trade or craft. (Cf. BROTHER-CHIP.)

1820 *Western Carolinian* 29 Aug., P.S. Some of our chip ask 25 per cent. on their own notes; I will shave my own, (if due,) at 10 per cent.

3. A counter in poker and other games of chance.

1856 *Harper's Mag.* Dec. 68/2 The Editor's . . . great delight is to be seated over against a . . . faro-dealer—to have . . . half a dozen 'piddlers' of 'white chips' to be leaning over his shoulder and admiring his nerve. 1872 'MARK TWAIN' *Roughing It* xlvii. 336 Don't put up another chip till I look at my hand. 1884 'CRADDOCK' *Where Battle Was Fought* 35 The slow, cumbrous fellow . . . laid his cards, face downward on the table in front of him, with a single chip upon them to hold them in place. 1899 *Boston Transcript* 21 Aug. 10/6 A complete fantan layout and dominoes, cards, chips and dice cup were seized by the liquor squad in a raid. 1909 'O. HENRY' *Options* 114 How did you get in the game? I didn't see you buy any chips.

fig. 1903 A. H. LEWIS *Boss* 205 There was a saw-bones here, . . . pawin' me over for a life-insurance game that I thought I'd buy chips in.

+b. *pl.* Money. *slang.*

1857 *San. Fran. Call* in *Thornton* II. 971 All the browns his uncle lent him, All the chips and dust and clinkers.

+4. A dried buffalo dropping. Usu. in plural. (Cf. BUFFALO CHIP.)

1848 BRYANT *California* 80 The 'chips' are an excellent substitute for wood. 1857 CHANDLESS *Visit Salt Lake* I. 61 Buffalo were looked for; a solitary 'chip' . . . found one evening caused quite an excitement in camp. 1862 COLT *Went to Kansas* 53 Made a fire on the top of chips, laying stones on to the chips, to keep them confined so as to serve my use. 1903 ADAMS *Log Cowboy* 210 We had begun to feel the scarcity of wood for cooking purposes. . . . These chips were a poor substitute.

5. =CHIP HAT. {1784}

1880 *Harper's Mag.* March 576/2 A nice black chip suited Aunt Beulah well. 1883 *Boston Visitor's Guide* 24 Oct. (*advt.*), A new Bonnet can be made of an Old One. . . . Bring your old Beaver, Felt, Straw or Chip.

+6. An item of news in a newspaper. *slang.*

1889 BARRÈRE & LELAND *Slang* 244/2 (American journalism). Local items in newspapers are called *chips*, and sometimes the term is applied to the reporter who collects them.

7. In various phrases. **+a.** *To carry* or *go about with* (etc.) *a chip on one's shoulder*, to display combativeness by daring others to offend one. Also *to knock a chip from* or *off (someone's) shoulder*, to give offense to someone by a defiant attitude.

1840 *Daily Pennant* (St. Louis) 9 May (Th.), Jonathan's blood is 'pretty considerable riz' anyhow, and it wouldn't take so much as knocking a chip off a boy's shoulder to make it a darnationed sight riz-er. 1849 *Knickerb.* XXXIV. 336/2 They have knocked the chip off of one another's shoulder, and Professor Hart [is] a-doing all he can to stay the commotion. 1857 *Harper's Mag.* XV. 640/2 A provocation to a fight, after the fashion of some 'shoulder-hitters' in placing a chip upon a man's shoulder and daring another to knock it off. 1870 *Boston Daily Times* 10 Aug., England won't stand still long after the chip is knocked from her shoulder. 1887 *Harper's Mag.* Oct. 658/1 The way that dog went about with a chip on his shoulder . . . was enough to spoil the sweetest temper. 1891 *Ib.* July 211/2 A Yankee boy would carry a chip on his shoulder. 1925 MULFORD *Cottonwood Gulch* 178 A chip on each flannel-shirted shoulder.

+b. *fig.* (in sense 3). *To pass in (one's) chips*, to die. *colloq.*

1888 *Century Mag.* Dec. 215/2 The folks over there will keep hold of her until Jack has passed in his chips, as he would phrase it. 1891 WELCH *Recoll. 1830–40* 156 Bill Lockwood, a noted horse plunger, who quite recently 'passed in his chips.' 1907 MULFORD *Bar-20* 130 He passed in his chips last night.

8. Attrib., as *chip-basket*, a basket for fragments of wood resulting from chopping (fig. in ex.); *chip bridge*, ?a flimsy wooden bridge, a toy bridge; *chip-fire*, a fire of small thin bits of wood; *chip manure*, manure mixed with rotten chips of wood and soil; *chip pile*, a pile of bits of wood resulting from cutting or chopping; *chip stone*, fragments of stone broken off in chipping; *chip-stuff*, =CHOP *n.*[1] 2.

1856 STOWE *Dred* I. 22 [She] throws you into her chip-basket of beaux and goes on dancing and flirting as before. 1669 *Essex Inst. Coll.* V. 274/1 A popler tree . . . standing by a way through a swampe or bridge called the chip bridge. 1870 EMERSON *Society & Sol.* 34 From his [=a child's] first pile of toys or chip bridge to the masonry of Minot Rock Light-house of the Pacific Railroad. 1903 BEACH in *McClure's Mag.* Nov. 93/1 The silver ball of amalgam sizzled and fried on the shovel over the little chip-fire. 1821 *Mass. H. S. Coll.* 2 Ser. IX. 139, [I] filled up the cavity, around the roots, with chip manure. 1857–8 *Ill. Agric. Soc. Trans.* III. 472 Because a man is a farmer, or a countryman, is no reason why . . . the back yard or grounds around the back door [should be] filled with rags, bones, chip piles, broken hoe handles, [etc.]. 1832 *Congress. Deb.* 16 June 3636 Nor can they do this any more than an infant or an idiot could consent that his neighbor might . . . cart chip stone from his quarry on to his garden. 1849 *Rep. Comm. Patents: Agric.* (1850) 102 These cows are fed with shorts or chip-stuff, together with roots and slops from the kitchen.

* **Chip,** *v.*[1] (In various colloq. phrases, usually with *in.*)

+1. *intr.* In poker, to place a chip or counter in the pool. In quots. fig.

1876 HARTE *G. Conroy* VI. ii, You've jest cut up thet rough with my higher emotions thet there ain't enough left to chip in on a ten-cent ante. 1904 W. H. SMITH *Promoters* 101 If he got a rake-off on the game he'd have to chip into the play.

+2. To contribute money, usually to a charitable purpose or for a common need. Also *tr.*

1861 *Winsted* (Conn.) *Herald* 22 Nov., An idea seems very generally to prevail that the printer should 'chip in' to every charitable and religious operation. 1877 HARTE *Story of Mine*, etc. 221 Thar isn't a time that I couldn't and wouldn't hev chipped in and paid 'em for ye. 1878 BEADLE *Western Wilds* 41 At Angell's Camp we chipped in together and hired regular guards. 1886 *Harper's Mag.* Dec. 36 'Here's a dollar.' 'Here's another.' And they all chipped in their share. 1887 *Courier-Journal* 8 May 8/3 The shake-purse didn't count up over $40. The hat was passed to me, but I declined to chip. 1904 HARBEN *Georgians* 67 Me 'n George 'll have to chip in an' buy you another [coat], Christmas. 1917 SINCLAIR *King Coal* 17 We got our own preacher—you chip in fifty cents a month for him out of your wages. 1925 BRYAN *Memoirs* 170 The signers, chipping in, as they say, to pay the expense of the telegram.

3. To join in a conversation; *tr.* to throw *in* (a remark.) {1888}

1869 HARTE *In the Tunnel* line 44 Just you chip in, Say you knew Flynn. 1872 'MARK TWAIN' *Roughing It* xlvii, Pard, he was a great loss to this town. It would please the boys if you could chip in something like that and do him justice. 1883 — *Life on Miss.* iii, Next the Child of Calamity chipped in again, bigger than ever. 1891 RYAN *Told in Hills* 173 'Better fight shy o' that territory,' advised Andrews, chipping in with a cowboy's brief say-so. 1894 *Congress. Rec.* 26 Feb. 2437 The gentleman from Maine. [Thos. B. Reed] . . . is in the habit of 'chipping in' in everybody's time. 1902 HARBEN *A. Daniel* 154 They must not chip in with that sort of talk before Wilson. 1903 A. H. LEWIS *Boss* 271 Madam, let me chip in a word.

4. To unite with others in an enterprise.

1872 'MARK TWAIN' *Roughing It* l. 356 Mind you, I don't object to trying him, if it's got to be done to give satisfaction; and I'll be there and chip in and help, too. 1888 HARTE *Argonauts* 143 Ef the — fools keep quiet they won't be hurt, for our men will be ready to chip in the moment of the attack.

Chip, *v.*[2] *intr.* To cheep; of a bird, to make a chirping note; *transf.*, to make a remark or sound. {*dial.*} — 1885 THOMPSON *Byways & Bird Notes* 155, I heard the mother-bird 'chipping' dolefully. 1887 FRANCIS *Saddle & Moccasin* 124 Now, you let me do the talking when they begin to sing 'Indians'; don't you chip! 1902 LORIMER *Lett. Merchant* 118 At the church sociables he used to hop around among them, chipping and chirping like a dicky-bird.

+Chiparee. (Early form of CHICKAREE.) — 1804 *Md. Hist. Mag.* IV. 9 These squirrels are exceedingly active and the mountaineers call them the Chiparee squirrel.

+Chip bird. A chipping sparrow or hairbird; the tree sparrow.

1824 *Mass. Yeoman* 28 April (Th.), The destruction of a robin, chip, blue, or black bird is not all. 1844 *Nat. Hist. N.Y., Zoology* II. 159 The Chip-Bird, *Emberiza Socialis*. . . . The familiar Chipping-bird is known to all. 1869 LOWELL *Study Windows* (1871) 15 The only bird I have ever heard sing in the night has been the chip-bird. 1872 COUES *N. A. Birds* 142 Chipping Sparrow. Chipbird or Chippy. Hairbird.

+Chip bonnet. A bonnet or headdress made of chip-hat palm or similar material. — 1820 BRECK in *Recoll.* (1877) App. 298 She has gone on, . . . bedecking herself in merino shawls, chip bonnets, etc. 1845 NOAH *Gleanings* 65 On her little head she wore a good sized chip bonnet, decorated with artificial flowers. 1856 DERBY *Phoenixiana* 147 All imaginable styles of colors—white hats, red shawls, chip bonnets, green aprons, and pink colored boots.

+Chip-day. *Obs.* (See quot. 1847.) — 1847 WELLS & DAVIS *Sk. Williams Coll.* 79 They give us, near the close of the second term what is called 'chip day,' when we put the grounds in order, and remove the ruins caused by the winter's siege on the wood-piles. 1854 *Boston Ev. Trav.* 12 July, '*Chip day*,' at the close of the spring term, is still observed in the old-fashioned way [at Williams College]. 1873 CHAPIN in Tyler *Hist. Amherst Coll.* (1895) 79 Each spring we had our 'chip day,' when the students in mass turned out to scrape and clear up the grounds near the buildings.

+Chip-dirt. Earth mixed with decayed and partly decayed chips of wood; soil scraped from a chipyard.

1849 *Rep. Comm. Patents: Agric.* 103 Shallow ploughings given annually, liquid manure, chip-dirt, road scrapings, . . . have been turned in with marked advantage. **1864** *Maine Agric. Rep.* 136 The plum . . . thrives best . . . if planted near accumulations of chip dirt. **1867** *Iowa Agric. Soc. Rep.* 190 Sub-soiling, chip-dirt, well-rotted manure will always help this fruit. **1873–4** *Vt. Bd. Agric. Rep.* II. 271 If the ground has settled so that any of the trees stand too shallow, more soil, (chip dirt is best) should be . . . placed around them.

Chip hat. A hat made of chip or chip-hat palm, *Thrinax microcarpa.* {1771–}

1759 *Newport Mercury* 26 June 4/3 Imported . . . and to be sold by Jacob Richardson, . . . silver'd Paper, chip and black Satten Hats, [etc.] **1784** *Mass. Spy* 22 April 1/2 S. & S. Salisbury . . . have imported . . . a general assortment of English goods, viz. . . . muffs and tippets, chip hats, [etc.]. **1788** in Brooks *Gleanings* 59 Large and small Bibles—Chip Hats—Watch Chains—Bottled Mustard—Playing Cards. **1840** HOFFMAN *Greyslaer* I. 128 The dress of this man, which was . . . shoes without buckles, and a broad-leaved chip hat, . . . marked him. **1847** ROBB *Squatter Life* 119 An old chip hat surmounted his figure, and in his right hand he held the sceptre of the pioneer—a rifle! **1877** *Harper's Mag.* April 686/1 She had lost her chip hat when thrown from the boat. **1889** R. T. COOKE *Steadfast* 58 The tiny rose-wreathed chip hat, set aslant on her high-heaped dark hair. **1906** 'O. HENRY' *Four Million* 58 Her relatives chipped in enough in her chip hat for her to go 'North' and 'finish.'

+**Chipmunk.** Also **chipmuck.** [Of Algonquian origin.] A small striped rodent of the genus *Tamias;* a ground squirrel.

(*a*) **1841** COOPER *Deerslayer* xix, Have you discovered a chip-munk in a tree? **1861** LOWELL *Biglow P.* II. i. 26 Here I be ez lively ez a chipmunk on a wall. **1882** *Wheelman* I. 113 A comical little chipmunk, or ground squirrel, races along before me . . . and sits up . . . chattering away as if he resented this intrusion upon his domain. **1903** COMSTOCK in *Chautauquan* Nov. 285 The red squirrel . . . keeps his keen eye on chipmunks and mice hoping to find where they store their food.

(*b*) **1841** *Knickerb.* XVII. 365 The very herd boy looks cautiously . . . before he ventures the stone, twice aimed, at the unoffending chip-muck. **1850** S. F. COOPER *Rural Hours* 103 The chipmucks, or ground-squirrels, are also very mischievous in the maize-fields. **1857** *Rep. Comm. Patents: Agric.* 71 The chipmuck exists through the Eastern, Middle, as well as in some of the Western States. **1871** *Scribner's Mo.* II. 664 We were sure of a run after a chip-muk [*sic*] or a squirrel as he scampered along the rail-fence to or from a clump of oaks in the clearing. **1880** HOWELLS *Undiscovered Country* 204 From the first of the strawberries to the last of the blackberries, the birds and chipmucks feasted.

***Chipped.** +Of meat, usu. beef: Smoked and cut in very thin slices.

1819 *Mass. Spy* 18 Aug. (Th.), No vapid tea, or cold toast, and greasy butter, and chipped meat. **1833** HALL *Harpe's Head* 214 A little farther up were venison steaks, then fried ham; then there was cold ham, and chipped beef, and sausages. **1850** S. F. COOPER *Rural Hours* 430 Or it may be corned pork, for dinner; and chipped smoked beef, or tongue, for tea. **1859** *Knickerb.* LIV. 406 Such waffles, chipped beef, sweetmeats, melon.

Chipper, *n.* Chirping, twittering. {*dial.*} — [**1865** BURRITT *Walk to Land's End* 314 They made a mirthful chipper and laugh under the song of the soaring larks.] **1884** BURROUGHS *Fresh Fields* 136 Our chimney swallow, with his incessant, silvery, rattling chipper.

Chipper, *a.* Cheerful, lively. {1875–, Sussex dial.}

1838 HALIBURTON *Clockmaker* 2 Ser. ix. 139 There sot Katey by the fire, lookin' as bloomin' as a rose, and as chipper as a canary bird. **1843** STEPHENS *High Life N.Y.* I. 177 Harnsome gals and spruce looking fellers . . . talked and laughed as chipper as could be. **1852** STOWE *Uncle Tom* xxxi, You's got to look chipper, I tell you. **1871** HAY *Little Breeches* 13 Peart, and chipper, and sassy, always ready to swear and fight. **1880** 'MARK TWAIN' *Tramp Abroad* 627 Sometimes, in place of the criticism, the first-class daily gives you what it thinks is a gay and chipper essay. **1899** A. THOMAS *Arizona* 11 She's been here a whole week, and I never saw her chipperer in her life. **1908** WHITE *Riverman* vi. 55 The rivermen . . . turned up at noon chipper as larks.

b. In good order; neat, spruce, dapper.

1878 BEADLE *Western Wilds* 42 Got home . . . an' found every thing chipper. **1880** 'MARK TWAIN' *Tramp Abroad* xlii. 489 The landlady, the portier, the waitress, and the chambermaid, were not separate persons but were all contained in one neat and chipper suit of spotless muslin. **1887** *Courier-Journal* 5 May 1/4 Henry Dixon, looking very chipper in a light, new, well-fitting suit.

Chipper, *v.* [Prob. of imitative origin.]

1. *intr.* Of birds: To chirp or twitter. {E. Anglian dial. *a*1825–}

1712 SEWALL *Diary* II. 343, I saw Six Swallows together flying and chippering very rapturously. **1716** *Ib.* III. 78 This day I first saw the Swallows; I think I had heard some chipper before. **1861** STOWE *Pearl Orr's Isl.* I. 77 The little one picked it up and with much chippering . . . at last succeeded in making him taste it.

+**2.** Of persons: To chatter, prattle. *colloq.*

1858 *Harper's Mag.* June 46/2, I saw about three-quarters of a yard of dimity whisk by the hall-door, and I heard 'em smiling and chipering behind the door. **1875** STOWE *We & Our Neighbors* 106 She chippered to them in various little persuasive intonations. **1891** R. T. COOKE *Huckleberries* (1896) 70 He sot right down 'longside of Lane and chippered away real brisk. **1900** *Congress. Rec.* App. 28 Feb. 114/1 Men can harp about the Constitution and chipper about the flag.

+**3.** *tr.* and *intr. To chipper up,* to make or become cheerful. *colloq.*

1873 A. D. WHITNEY *Other Girls* 235 There was nothing that chippered you up so, as being real driving busy. **1884** 'MARK TWAIN' *H. Finn* xxi. 204 After they'd jumped overboard and took a swim it chippered them up a good deal. **1886** *Harper's Mag.* Sept. 583/1 She'd chipper up and fix up what she could. **1889** *Ib.* Nov. 965/1 The point of view of modern English criticism, which likes to be melted, and horrified, and astonished, and blood-curdled, and goose-fleshed, no less than to be 'chippered up' in fiction. **1904** LORIMER *Old Gorgon Graham* 129 'Young man, I've decided to help you out of this hole,' he began. Percy chippered right up.

‖**Chipperness.** The state of being lively or gay. — **1894** 'MARK TWAIN' *P. Wilson* viii, Then he worked up . . . a hollow chipperness of manner.

+**Chippewa, Chippeway.** Also **Chippawa,** etc. [Variant of OJIBWAY.] A member of a large Algonquian tribe of Indians found in the Great Lakes region.

[**1671** in *N.Y. State Col. Hist.* IX. 803 St Mary of the Falls, the place where . . . the Indian nations called Chipoës, Malamechs, Noquets and others do actually resided [*sic*].] **1754** WASHINGTON *Writings* I. 51 We are informed that six hundred Chippewas and Ottawas are marching down Scioto Creek, to join the French, who are coming up the Ohio. **1805** PIKE *Sources Miss.* App. I. 10 If the Chipeways are obstinate, and continue to kill the Indians who bear our flags, . . . we would take them in hand. **1835** HOFFMAN *Winter in West* I. 215 The driver was also accompanied on the box by a well-made young half-blood Chippeway . . . who had come down from Mackinaw to seek employment. **1841** TYLER in *Pres. Mess. & P.* IV. 61 Of the Chippewas and Ottawas now in the northern part of Michigan it is believed there are over 5,000 under treaty obligations to remove to the Southwest. **1880** *Harper's Mag.* Dec. 43 The guttural ejaculations of the Chippewas who came to her door.

b. Attrib. with *friend, ground, language,* etc.

1853 *Harper's Mag.* April 585/1 They were then favored by their Chippeway friends with a war-dance. **1840** *Niles' Nat. Reg.* 8 Aug. 356/2 A war party of the Sioux Indians (400 strong) had assembled, and taken up their march for the Chippewa grounds. **1860** *Harper's Mag.* Sept. 568/2 The Rev. Mr. Seymour . . . selected a good-natured, . . . old fellow, . . . who spoke the Chippewa language well. *a***1862** THOREAU *Maine Woods* 173, I have once heard a Chippewa lecture. **1789** *Ann. 1st Congress* I. 41 The treaties of Fort Harmar, on the 9th of January, 1789, . . . with the sachems and warriors of the Wyandot, . . . Chippawa, Pattiwatima, and Sac nations.

+**Chippewan, Chippewayan,** *a.* Used with *Mountains* as an early name for the Rocky Mountains. *Obs.* — **1815** DRAKE *Cincinnati* 91 North America is traversed by two ranges of high mountains—the Allegheny and Chippewan. **1829** *Va. Lit. Museum* 146/1 A slope, or inclined plane, extending from the rocky or Chippewayan mountains, towards the Pacific Ocean. **1831** PECK *Guide* 10 The Rocky, or Chippewan Mountains, which separate the waters of the Atlantic from those of the Pacific ocean. **1837** — *New Guide* 25 The melting snows on the Chippewan Mountains pour their contents into the Missouri.

+**Chippewayan,** *n. absol.* The language of the Chippewa Indians. — **1861** *Ladies' Repository* XXI. 354/1 It was in monotonous Chippewayan, and to our ears the burden of the song is lost.

***Chipping,** *n.* +The scarified surface made on a pine in securing turpentine from it. — **1832** BROWNE *Sylva* 232 The chippings extend the first year a foot above the box. **1859** PERRY *Turpentine Farming* 61 Consequently, I commenced with five chippings.

Chipping, *ppl. a.* Also **chippin, -en.**

1. Used in bird names; esp. of the hairbird or chip bird (*Spizella passerina*).

(*a*) **1791** BARTRAM *Travels* (1792) 289 *Passer domesticus;* the little house sparrow or chipping bird. **1810** WILSON *Ornithology* II. 127 The Chipping-bird builds his nest most commonly in a cedar bush. **1832** WILLIAMSON *Maine* I. 143 The Spring Bird is larger than a chipping bird, and is one of the very first to sing the vernal song. *c***1845** *Big Bear Ark.,* etc. 16 Game, indeed, that's what city folks call it; and with them it means chippen-birds and shite-pokes. **1855** *Knickerb.* XLVI. 22 The small house-sparrow, or, as he is generally known, the 'chippin-bird' comes to our very doors. **1861** STOWE *Pearl Orr's Isl.* I. 58, I've seen 'em big as chippin-birds' eggs. **1869** BURROUGHS in *Galaxy Mag.* Aug. 139/2 The social-sparrow, . . . *alias* 'red-headed chipping-bird,' is the smallest of the sparrows. **1871** — *Wake-Robin* 60 The snow-bird, or 'black chipping-bird,' . . . is the finest architect of any of the ground-builders known to me.

(*b*) **1844** GIRAUD *Birds Long Island* 106 *Emberiza socialis.* . . . Chipping Bunting. . . . This . . . is very generally known by the name of 'Chipping Bird.' **1844** *Nat. Hist. N.Y., Zoology* II. 159.

(*c*) **1810** WILSON *Ornithology* II. 127 [The] Chipping Sparrow . . . inhabits, during summer, the city, in common with man, . . . gleaning up crumbs from our yards. **1839** AUDUBON *Ornith. Biog.* V. 517 The Chipping Sparrow is almost as abundant in our country, as the Domestic Sparrow is in Europe. **1867** *Amer. Naturalist* I. 402 The Chipping Sparrow awakes, and is soon heard chanting his simple cricket-like song from the garden and lawn. **1892** TORREY *Foot-Path Way* 179 One cannot go far now without finding the road full of chipping sparrows. **1904** WALLER *Wood-*

Carver 144, I bethought me of the little chipping-sparrow's nest in a spruce tree.

+**2.** *Chipping squirrel*, the chipmunk. Also attrib.

1800 *Raleigh* (N.C.) *Register* 1 July, An Advertisement was lately published in several papers, offering a generous price for 10,000 chipping squirrel skins, for exportation. **1849** THOREAU *Week Concord Riv.* Tues. 205 The chipping or striped squirrel. **1857** *Rep. Comm. Patents: Agric.* 71 It is well known . . . under the name of 'Striped Ground Squirrel,' 'Chipping Squirrel,' or 'Chipmuck.' **1889** *Cent.* 965/1 The hackee or chipping-squirrel of the United States, *Tamias striatus*.

+**Chippy.** Any one of various small birds characterized by a low chirping note; esp. the chipping sparrow or hairbird.

1864 WEBSTER *Chipping-bird*, . . . also *chippy*. **1872** [see CHIP BIRD]. **1880** *Harper's Mag.* June 76 [The] dear little eggs of chippies in their horse-hair bed. **1891** WILKINS *New Eng. Nun* 172, I dunno but what bein' a missionary to robins an' starvin' chippies an' little deaf-an'-dumb children is jest as good as some other kinds. **1900** *Congress. Rec.* 30 April 4872/2 The ground chippy darted under the fences and had its nest in the tall grass.

attrib. **1913** STRATTON-PORTER *Laddie* iii, In the hollow of a rotten rail a little chippy bird always built a hair nest. **1898** S. HALE *Letters* 338, I must tell you of our little chippy sparrows that had their nest in the trellis.

+**Chip-squirrel.** A chipmunk. — **1843** STEPHENS *High Life N.Y.* II. 220, I could feel the leetle hand a movin on the pillar agin my back, like a chip squirrel in its nest. **1875** STOWE *Deacon Pitkin* 35 The very chip squirrels in the stone-walls . . . were rushing about with chops incredibly distended.

+**Chipyard.** An area in which wood is cut and which consequently is filled with chips of wood.

1850 *Knickerb.* XXXVI. 73, I first let down her bars, crossed her chip-yard, and stood before her habitation. **1862** *Constitution* (Middletown, Conn.) 30 April, If the soil around the body of the trees should become too stiff, it may be carefully removed and its place supplied by coarse stable manure, or the scrapings of the chipyard. **1863** A. D. WHITNEY *F. Gartney* xiv, The spicy smell of the chip-yard round the corner, where the scraps of pine lay . . . under the summer sun. **1891** RYAN *Pagan* 232 After awhile, two men . . . halted out at the chip-yard.

attrib. **1879** B. F. TAYLOR *Summer-Savory* 110 Thus a number of residents of La Porte, Indiana, went and camped out for a week in plain sight of the city! It was a sort of Chipyard picnic.

‖**Chirivaris.** Irreg. variant of CHARIVARI. — **1852** REYNOLDS *Hist. Illinois* 145 The Americans became enamored with the French custom of *chirivaris*, and practiced it sometimes right, but more often wrong. *Ib.*, The chirivaris party was composed of old and young, and generally conducted by some orderly and aged man.

+**Chirk,** *a. dial.* [Cf. CHIRK *v.*] Cheerful; lively; in good spirits. (See also CHERK.)

'It should be remembered, that the adjective *chirk* is used only in the interior of New England; and even there, I think, only by the illiterate. It is never heard in the sea-port towns' (Pick.).

1789 WEBSTER *Diss. Engl. Lang.* 387 This word is wholly lost except in New England. It is there used for *comfortably, bravely, cheerful*, as when one inquires about a sick person, it is said, he is chirk. **1815** HUMPHREYS *Yankey in Eng.* 29 'How fare you?' 'Cleverly. Stiddy, pretty stiddy, and quite chirk again.' **1834** C. A. DAVIS *Lett. J. Downing* 20 The Gineral looked as chirk and lively as a skipper. **1843** [see CHIRK *v.* 1]. **1850** JUDD *R. Edney* 55 You would buzz around your little Arbor, as chirk and bobbish as a fly in springtime. **1869** STOWE *Oldtown Folks* xlii. 526 'Sam, are the folks all well?' 'O lordy massy, yes! Chirk and chipper as can be!'

+**Chirk,** *v.*

1. *tr.* Usually with *up.* To make (one) lively or comfortable; to cheer *up.*

Possibly a survival of obs. E. *cherk* to incite by chirruping (1486, 1601).

1843 *Yale Lit. Mag.* I. 26 (Th.), All our folks appear more chirkier than they really feel, in order to chirk her up. *c***1847** WHITCHER *Bedott P.* 76 It'll chirk you up and dew you good to go out into socierty. **1878** R. T. COOKE *Happy Dodd* 122 Ef there's a mortal thing I can do to help ye, or chirk ye up, I want to do it right off. **1889** 'THANET' in *Harper's Bazar* 4 May 331/1 Chana might be 'chirked up a bit' to know what a nice funeral she would have. **1907** *Springfield W. Republ.* 17 Jan. 2 Dr. Osler's correction of a certain depressing statement attributed to him chirks one up. **1912** W. IRWIN *Red Button* 40 The thought chirked me a lot.

2. *intr.* Usually with *up.* To become cheerful. *dial.*

1843 STEPHENS *High Life N.Y.* I. 231 All I could do she wouldn't chirk up. **1858** *Harper's Mag.* Sept. 487/2 All she had to do was to chirk up again, and look as sweet and perty as might be, and so to be married. **1860** HOLLAND *Miss Gilbert* 134 Well, well, dear, you must chirk up, or you won't enjoy your flapjacks. **1884** WILKINS in *Harper's Mag.* June 28 P'rhaps nothin' awful's goin' to happen. . . . Chirk up an' give us a kiss. **1894** 'MARK TWAIN' *P. Wilson* xxi, The house burst into volleys of relieving and refreshing laughter, and Tom chirked and joined in the fun himself. **1898** WESTCOTT *D. Harum* 325, I begun to chirk up some.

Chiropodist. One whose profession it is to treat ailments of the feet. {1785–} — **1879** BURDETTE *Hawkeyes* 211 All the vaunted skill of the chiropodist cannot keep the ache out of the feet of a young man whose boots are smaller than his socks. **1886** JAMES *Bostonians* 204 It was exactly as if she, Mrs. Luna, had struck up an intimacy with the daughter of her chiropodist.

+**Chiropractic,** *a.* [See note.] Designating or pertaining to a drugless curative system based on manipulation of the spine.

'The name chiropractic was suggested for the new science by the Rev. Samuel H. Weed of Bloomington, Ill., an early patient. The name (Greek *cheir*, hand, and *praktikos*, efficient) was freely translated by Palmer as "done by hand"' (*Dict. Amer. Biog.* XIV. 177/1).

1898 *Stone's Davenport* (Iowa) *City Directory* 384 Dr. Palmer Chiropractic School & Cure, Daniel D. Palmer propr. **1911** B. J. PALMER (*title*), The philosophy and principles of chiropractic adjustments. **1914** *Boston Journal* 3 April 7/6 International chiropractic association. **1924** *Calif. Bd. of Chiropractic Examiners Ann. Rep.* 9 Those [applicants for license] . . . had graduated from chiropractic institutions.

+**Chirp,** *a.* Cheery, chirk, as if given to chirping. — **1824** *New Bedford Mercury* 28 May (Th.), As chirp as a flock of blackbirds. **1850** JUDD *R. Edney* 320 She was always chirp. **1863** 'G. HAMILTON' *Gala-Days* 233 We walk away as 'chirp as a cricket.'

Chirp, *v.* +**a.** *tr.* To encourage (one) by chirrups or cheerful remarks. **b.** *intr.* To grow cheerful; to chirk or cheer *up.* — (**a**) **1865** A. D. WHITNEY *Gayworthys* 247 She's to chirp us all up Boar-back [Mt.] next Saturday. (**b**) **1897** R. M. STUART *Simpkinsville* 35 Mis' Meredith is chirpin' up a' ready.

+**Chirpiness.** The state of being given to chirps or of being cheery. — **1867** HOWELLS *Italian Journeys* 248 He saluted us with a cricket-like chirpiness of manner.

‖**Chirpling.** A young bird. — **1888** *Advance* (Chicago) 26 April 257 For the joy that our chirplings will give us!

Chirpy, *a.* Lively, merry. *colloq.* {1859–}

1837 in Gilman *Recoll.* vi. 53, I have writ a much longer letter than I thought on; but somehow it makes me chirpy to think of Roseland. **1878** R. T. COOKE *Happy Dodd* 331 [She] was yet so cheerful, so content, and as chirpy as a cricket. **1885** *Harper's Mag.* April 724 The captain was as chirpy as a bird. **1898** PAGE *Red Rock* 573 Andy Stamper was chirpy and facetious, and had a look of deeper mystery than he was wont to wear.

***Chirurgeon.** *Obs.* A surgeon.

1638 UNDERHILL *Newes from A.* 26 A chirurgeon we wanted; our chirurgeon, not accustomed to war, durst not hazard himself where we ventured our lives. **1642** *Plymouth Laws* 72 If any children . . . shalbe sent . . . to a Phisician or Chirurgeon . . . they shalbe releeved . . . by the Townships whence they came. **1698** *Boston Rec.* 230 Mary Lee a poor Widdow of the Town, hauing [a child] . . . sorely afflicted with the Stone, . . . [was] advised by the Chyrurgion that the said Child should be Cutt. **1711** *N.C. Col. Rec.* I. 824 Read the petition of Edmund Ellis praying to be admitted Chyrurgeon for the expedition against the Tusqueroras. **1721** *Mass. Ho. Rep. Jrnls.* III. 18 A Petition of Francis Gathman, Chyururgeon, Praying, that this House would make him some allowance, for the time he was in their service.

***Chisel,** *n.* Also †**chessill,** †**chizel(l),** etc.

***1.** A metal tool with a sharp cutting edge at the end of a blade beveled on one or both sides.

1638 *Md. Archives* IV. 74 Owing from Anthony Cotton 3. chessills & other tooles. **1678** *New Castle Court Rec.* 362, 20 Chizells & goudges. **1744** HEMPSTEAD *Diary* 435 Joshua Cut his Shin very much with a Chizel. **1812** *Niles' Reg.* I. 390/1 The subscriber . . . can furnish . . . hay knives, straw knives, chissels, [etc.]. **1881** INGERSOLL *Oyster Industry* 242 The lignum vitae conical block, having an iron chisel fixed in its top, upon which oysters are broken before being opened. **1883** *Century Mag.* Sept. 742/1 Then he . . enjoyed himself in a rational way with his files and chisels and screw-drivers.

+**2.** In the adv. phrase *full chisel:* At headlong speed; impetuously. *colloq.*

1835 S. SMITH *Major Downing* 125 We are coming on full chisel . . . When we've been on the road I couldn't catch my breath . . . we kept flying so fast. **1840** HALIBURTON *Clockmaker* 3 Ser. iii, I . . . was a-posten away as hard as I could leg it, full chisel down by the Mall in Boston to a tea. **1850** *Knickerb.* XXXVI. 333 So I out with my ramrod, and with the small end rammed away at the piece of silk till I rammed it home, and then started again 'full chisel.' **1871** STOWE *Sam Lawson* 69 Wal, arter dark, Parson Carrul he driv into the yard, full chizel, with his pig. **1878** — *Poganuc People* 98 He'd turn and run up the narrow way, full chisel.

***Chisel,** *v.* Also **chizzle, chizzell,** etc. *tr.* To cheat (one) *out of* money or property; to swindle. *colloq.*[2] {1808 in Scots; 1821–, E. colloq.}

'A Western word' (B. '48).

1834 C. A. DAVIS *Lett. J. Downing* 181 If you can chizzle them out of their property . . . without turnin as red as a beet when you meet 'em, I for one say I can't, and I won't. *a***1846** *Quarter Race Ky.*, etc. 160, I ain't a goin to be chizzelled out of my fees for making the arrest, that way. **1858** *Savannah Republ.* 17 May (De Vere), The stockholders would be chiselled out of a pretty considerable sum. **1874** EGGLESTON *Circuit Rider* iv. 47 He will chisel you out of every thing you've got before you're of age. **1882** SWEET & KNOX *Texas Siftings* 201 He chisels all the other boys out of their marbles.

Chispa. *S.W.* or *W.* [Sp. 'spark' or 'bit of fire,' hence 'small diamond.'] A speck of gold. — **1877** W. WRIGHT *Big Bonanza* 541 He was washing it down, stopping once in a while . . . in the expectation of seeing a 'chispa' or a 'nugget.'

Chit.

1. The germinal end of a grain of wheat or corn. {1601 of dates; 1725– of barley, etc.}

1849 EMMONS *Agric. N.Y.* II. 192 [The maize] was strongly glazed at this time, and filled all the spaces upon the cob; but the chit shrank some on drying. **1856** *Rep. Comm. Patents: Agric.* 238 The phosphates . . . in wheat, concentrate wholly about the germs, in their mucilage, or 'chits.' **1886** *Century Mag.* May 41/2 At one end of the [wheat] berry is a tuft of fine vegetable hairs, called the brush, and at the other is the chit, or germ, which contains the germinal principle.

‖**2.** 'The small end of a cigar. Very uncommon' (Th.).

1846 *Yale Lit. Mag.* XII. 71 (Th.), But, Doctor, you have not bitten off the chit.

+**3.** *pl.* A grade of rice, consisting of small grains.

1856 OLMSTED *Slave States* 477 In the Carolina mills the product is divided into 'prime,' 'middling' (broken), 'small' or 'chits,' and 'flour' or 'douse.'

Chitlings. Also **chetlins,** etc. [Reduction of CHITTERLINGS.]

1. The smaller intestines of swine, esp. when prepared like tripe. {1854–, *dial.*}

1880 'MARK TWAIN' *Tramp Abroad* xlix. 575 Hot corn-pone, with chitlings, Southern style. **1887** *Boston Jrnl.* 31 Dec. 2/4 A dish of smoking sausages was flanked by a dish of chitlins. **1890** *Amer. Notes & Q.* V. 6 *Chetlins* (that is, chitterlings) are a favorite article of food in that district of the country [*i.e.* in eastern Kentucky]. **1898** DUNBAR *Folks from Dixie* 103 There was hog jole and cold cabbage, ham and Kentucky oysters, more widely known as chittlings. **1909** F. B. CALHOUN *Miss Minerva* 23 Me an' Wilkes Booth Lincoln been eatin' chitlins . . . an' Brunswick stew ever sence we's born.

+**2.** *fig.* Shreds, tatters.

1845 HOOPER *Simon Sugg's Adv.* ii. 29, I only wish 'twas full of . . . blue vitrul, so as 'twould cut your interls into chitlins! **1847** ROBB *Squatter Life* 135 While I was . . . rolling in clover, . . . they wur tarin' my character all to *chitlins* up at home. [**1855** HALIBURTON *Nature & Human N.* (1859) 344 They did all they could to tear my reputation to chitlins.]

Chittagong. [Place name in Bengal, India.] A breed of poultry; the Malay, or a variety of this. {1816– (Moubray *Poultry*)} — **1871** LEWIS *Poultry Book* 34 The Chittagongs as a breed is quite leggy, in many instances, the cock standing twenty-six inches high.

+**Chittamwood.** [A Choctaw origin has been suggested (W. 1934). Cf. SHITTIMWOOD.] The American smoke tree, *Cotinus americanus.*

1843 N. BOONE *Journal* 4 July (App.), Marched 4 miles E. S. E. and encamped on a pretty grove of Elm, hackberry, Tallow tree, and chittim (wood) with good grass and water. **1884** SARGENT *Rep. Forests* 52 *Rhus cotinoides.* . . . Chittam Wood. **1897** SUDWORTH *Arborescent Flora* 274 American Smoke-tree. . . . Common names [include] Chittamwood (Ala.). **1901** MOHR *Plant Life Ala.* 34 The American smoketree or chittamwood (*Cotinus cotinoides*) in its isolated localities in north Alabama and southwestern Missouri.

Chittediddle. Var. of KATYDID, representing a different appreciation of the sound. — **1804** LEWIS in *L. & Clark Exped.* VI. 127 The green insect known in the U' States by the name of the sawyer or chittediddle, was first heard to cry on the 27th. of July.

Chitter, *n.* {*chitter* v., to twitter; 1789–, *dial.*} The twittering of birds. — **1859** STOWE *Minister's Wooing* iii, An ever-gentle rustle and whirr of branches and blossoms, a chitter of birds, and an indefinite whispering motion. **1869** A. D. WHITNEY *Hitherto* 147 The faint chitter of birds.

* **Chitter,** *v.*

+**1.** *intr.* To be busy or engaged; to potter about. *colloq.*

1714 SEWALL *Diary* III. 32 Genl Nicholson, who kept Satterday, was this Lord's Day Rummaging and Chittering with Wheelbarrows &c., to get aboard at the long Wharf.

+**2.** *tr.* (See quotation.)

1889 FARMER 141 *Chitter, To,* to call in question one's right to a thing; as 'If any man in these hills considers to *chitter* him, etc.,' *i.e.* stops to question his right.

* **Chitterling.**

* **1.** A frill or pleating on the front of a shirt. *Obs.*

1776 *N.J. Archives* 2 Ser. I. 125 Run away from the subscriber . . . a negroe man . . .; when he went away, had on . . . a swanskin jacket, [and] fine shirt with chitterlings on the bosom. **1777** *Ib.* 467 Thomas Riggon . . . had on when he escaped . . . a half wore Holland shirt with chitterlins at the bosom. **1783** R. W. Griswold *Republican Court* (1856) 25 [The handkerchief is] made to set out before like the chitterling of a man's shirt. **1807** IRVING, etc. *Salmagundi* (1824) 116 Your five inch chitterlings and nine inch ruffs!

* **2.** *pl.* The small intestines of swine prepared as food. (Cf. CHITLINGS.)

1841 *S. Lit. Messenger* VII. 39/2, I have never yet learned to relish chitterlings. **1859** VAN BUREN *Sojourn in South* 157 He eats . . .the brains, harslet, milt, lights and chitterlings. **1884** L. BALDWIN *Yankee School Teacher in Va.* 43 Chitterlings is a mighty good dish! . . . It's hog's insides, that's all; biled soft and salvy.

transf. **1835** LONGSTREET *Ga. Scenes* 6 My soul, if I don't jump down his throat and gallop every chitterling out of him, before you can say 'quit'! **1848** W. E. BURTON *Waggeries* 50 If my *sow*-licitude is hurtin' yer chitterlings, why be smashed into a hog's pudding.

+**Chiv.** (See quot. 1860.) — **1860** B. TAYLOR *At Home & Abroad* 3 Ser. (1888) 322 How long, I wondered, before these *Chivs* (the California term for Southerners—an abbreviation of Chivalry) start the exciting topic [slavery]. **1910** J. HART *Vigilante Girl* 293 These Chivs have been bullying us Northern Democrats long enough.

* **Chivalry.** +The aristocratic, slaveholding element in the South.

' "The Southern Chivalry" was a common phrase before and during the civil war. It was claimed as a proud title by Southerners and their friends, but has always been heard and used at the North with a shade of contempt' (*Mag. Amer. Hist.* XIII. 99).

1849 *S. Lit. Messenger* June (De Vere), The Chivalry of the South differs from the Yankee precisely as the Cavalier differed from the Puritan. **1851** *N.Y. Tribune* 10 April (B.), Had the Free States been manly enough . . . to enact the Wilmot Proviso . . . we should have had just about the same didoes cut up by the chivalry. **1862** *Harvard Mem. Biog.* (1866) I. 411 This iron howitzer is the one the negroes fired when the place became too hot for the chivalry. **1862** 'E. KIRKE' *Among Pines* 228 A crowd of drunken chivalry, through whom the Colonel with great difficulty elbowed his way to the counter. **1866** *Congress. Globe* 5 June 2960/2 This man Jackson is a clerk in the Second Auditor's office, one of the 'chivalry.' **1876** GARFIELD in *ib.* 4 Aug. 5184/1 [The Democrats] made you believe that the war would begin in the streets of our northern cities; that we were a community of shopkeepers, or sordid money-getters, and could not stand against your chivalry.

* **Chive.** Usu. *pl.* A plant (*Allium schoenoprasum*), related to the onion, used to flavor soups, stews, etc.

1840 DEWEY *Mass. Flowering Plants* 210 Chives or Cives. From Britain; grows in handsome tufts. **1847** DARLINGTON *Weeds & Plants* 357 Chives, or Cives. . . . Cultivated as a culinary herb; and often used as a kind of medicinal food for young poultry. **1857** GRAY *Botany* 470 Chives [grow on the] shore of Lakes Huron, Superior, and northward. **1879** *Harper's Mag.* Dec. 24/1 Mushrooms, sweet herbs, okras, chives, cresses, and other products of mother earth claimed successive attention.

***Chiven, -in.** The chub. (Cf. CHEVIN.) — **a1862** THOREAU *Me. Woods* 187 Many fishes, apparently chivin, came close up to us. **1888** GOODE *Amer. Fishes* 428 In Massachusetts it is often called . . . the 'Chiven' from its resemblance to the English Chub or Cheven.

***Chock,** *v.* [Var. of CHUCK.] With *up.* To break down or fail. — **1888** *St. Paul & Minneapolis Pioneer Press* 22 July (F.), That duffer chocked up after going six furlongs. **1889** FARMER 141/2 *Chock-up* . . . [is] used in the sense of to collapse; or 'to go to pieces.'

Chock, *adv.* Completely, fully (as an intensive). *colloq.* {1834–}

1825 NEAL *Bro. Jonathan* I. 106 He *outs* with a knife; and he *ins* with it, into Bald Eagle, chock up to the hilt. **1832** KENNEDY *Swallow Barn* I. 150 It's only the big wheel stopped as chock as a tombstone. **1837** BIRD *Nick of Woods* I. 94 The road . . . leads you, chock up, right on the Upper Ford. **1846** *Spirit of Times* 16 May 133/2 We were shooting down the Ohio, under a head of steam 'chock up' to 54 40! **1894** HARTE *Bell-Ringer,* etc. 146, I've been filled chock up by Simpson over there.

* **Chock-full,** *a.* Completely filled; often transf., of the emotions, deeply imbued.

'The American lexicographers have *chock-full* as the standard form, with *choke-full* as a cross-reference; and this appears to agree with literary usage in U.S. *Choke-full* appears to be rather the more frequent in literary use in England' (*O.E.D.*).

1787 TYLER *Contrast* (1790) v. ii, I feel chock-full of fight. **1809** WEEMS *Letters* II. 420, I am chock-full of zeal burning with the Book fever. **1822** *N.J. Almanac 1823,* As sound as a nut, o'er the plain I of late whistled, chock full of glee. **1837** MARTINEAU *Society* I. 98, I was told by a leading nullifier that the ladies were 'chock full of fight.' **1885** 'CRADDOCK' *Prophet* 8 That man hev got his mouth stuffed chock full o' words.

Chocolate. Also **†chocho-, chockalatte, chuchaletto, chocolatta, choco-, chokolatto.**

1. An edible substance made from the cacao bean; a beverage made from this; candy made of or covered with this. {1604–}

(*a*) **1676** B. TOMPSON *Poet. Wks.* 50 Twas ere a Barge had made so rich a fraight As Chocholatte, dust-gold, and bitts of eight. **1697** SEWALL *Diary* I. 462 Breakfast together on Venison and Chockalatte. **1724** JONES *Virginia* 52 Here is likewise used a great deal of Chocolate, Tea, and Coffee. **1775** FITHIAN *Journal* II. 145 The inhabitants . . . have not, it is true, coffee, chocolate, nor many other of what is allow'd to be needful in polite life. **1807** C. JANSON *Stranger in A.* 29 The principal manufactures of Boston are . . . loaf sugar, tobacco, chocolate, and an immense quantity of playing cards. **1830** *Collegian* 41 For breakfast take 4 bowls of chocolate, 2 fourpenny biscuits, and a pound of beef-steak. **1882** *Wheelman* I. 56 If going on a journey, take some refreshment in your bag or basket—biscuit, eating chocolate, and cold tea, with plenty of milk are the best. **1897** BRODHEAD *Bound in Shallows* 30, She *has* got a lot of ribbon on, hasn't she?—tied up like a box of chocolates.

(*b*) **1671** *Boston Rec.* 58 Mrs. . . . Jones . . . is approued of to keepe a house of publique Entertainment for the sellinge of Coffee & Chuchaletto. **1682** *Ib.* 156 John Sparry to sell Coffee Chocolatto & Sydr. **1687** SEWALL *Letter-Book* I. 46, I received not yours of the 23 December till March 11 then came safe by the Katherine Jno. Pullin Commander with the . . . 21 balls chokolatto. **1699** J. DICKENSON *God's Protecting Providence* 75 We . . . had Chocolatta for breakfast.

+**2.** (See quotation.)

1682 ASH *Carolina* 7 The Chincopin Tree bears a Nut not unlike the Hazle, the shell is softer: Of the Kernel is made Chocolate, not much inferiour to that made of the Cacoa.

3. *Indian chocolate,* (see CHOCOLATE ROOT).

4. Attrib. and comb. with *bean, flour,* etc.

1827 DEWEES *Lett. Texas* 66 Oranges, . . . chocolate beans, granathas, and plantains are to be found here in great quantities. **1718** *Mass. H. S. Coll.* 6 Ser. V. 383, I intended to have sent you some chocolatt flower. **1904** DERVILLE *Other Side of Story* 277 Cool off for the night with 'chocolate Fridays,' 'strawberry Sundays,' and other popular concoctions. **1867** *Common Sense Cook Book* 96 [Recipe for] chocolate iceing for cakes. **1780** *N.J. Archives* 2 Ser. IV. 367 Peter Low Begs leave to inform the public that he has lately erected a Chocolate Manufactory in New Brunswick. **1796** *Boston Directory* 291 Welsh, Jonas, chocolate manufacturer, house Prince street. **1845** KIRKLAND *Western Clearings* 178 'Where is the silver chocolate-pot, Anna?' Mrs. Clifford inquired one morning at breakfast. **1814** *Niles' Reg.* 15 Jan. 330/1, 2 lbs. coffee, 2 lbs. chocolate shells, 1 doz. cabbages.

b. Used to denote soils of a specific color or texture.

1819 E. DANA *Geogr. Sk.* 188 Next to the river swamp . . . we enter upon an extensive body of level, rich land, of fine black or chocolate-coloured soil. **1821** NUTTALL *Travels Arkansa* 99 Everywhere I observed the chocolate or reddish-brown clay of the salt formation, deposited by southern freshets. **1827** A. SHERWOOD *Gaz. Georgia* 87 This has been one of the most fertile counties in the State; the real chocolate soil. **1858** *Texas Almanac* 56 The soil is chocolate loam. **1869** *Overland Mo.* III. 130 Texas is notable for the number of its soils. . . . There is the 'chocolate' prairie, and the 'mulatto.'

Chocolate cake. A cake in which chocolate is an important ingredient. — **1876** M. F. HENDERSON *Cooking* 299 Chocolate-cake. Make a cup-cake with the following ingredients: One cupful of butter, [etc.]. **1895** WILLIAMS *Princeton Stories* 272 Beaten biscuit and chocolate cake and fruit cake, or black cake, as they call it in the South. **1901** *Harper's Mag.* Dec. 230 At one end of the table in a silver dish there would be a chocolate cake, for Lizzie-in-the-kitchen had baked one that afternoon.

+**Chocolate corn.** A variety of millet. — **1856** *Rep. Comm. Patents: Agric.* 284 A species of millet known as 'Chocolate Corn,' in Lower Virginia. **1865** *Ill. Agric. Soc. Trans.* V. 567 This remark also applies to what is called 'chocolate corn.' **1890** *Cent.* 3765/3 Indian millet [or] African millet, . . . *Sorghum vulgare,* . . . is sometimes called coffee- or chocolate-corn, because of its attempted use as a substitute for coffee.

Chocolate cream. A confection consisting of a fondant center covered with chocolate. — **1865** *Atlantic Mo.* XV. 386 Miselle discovered but two points of superiority . . . and these were chocolate-creams and policemen. **1909** 'O. HENRY' *Roads of Destiny* 146 The boy . . . liked chocolate creams best.

Chocolate drop. A chocolate cream of a somewhat pyramidal shape. {1827- (Jarrin *Ital. Confec.*)} — **1869** ALCOTT *Little Women* II. 324 'Tisn't in mine head, it's in mine mouf,' answered literal Demi, putting out his tongue with a chocolate-drop on it. **1870** R. TOMES *Decorum* 193 That fastidious dame . . . will on the sly swallow . . . caramels and chocolate-drops by the pound's weight. **1898** *Kansas City Star* 18 Dec. 3/7 (*advt.*), Hand Made Chocolate Drops, lb. 12½ c.

+**Chocolate flower.** *local.* A species of geranium. — **1892** *Amer. Folk-Lore* V. 93 *Geranium maculatum,* chocolate-flower. Stratham, N.H.

Chocolate grinder. One whose occupation is to grind chocolate.

1725 *New-Eng. Courant* 13–20 Nov. 2/2 James Lubbuck Chocolate Grinder, . . . sells the best Chocolate. **1769** *Mass. Col. Soc. Pub.* VI. 14 Thomas Bodkin of Boston in the County of Suffolk Chocolate Grinder. **1789** *Boston Directory* 204 Welch, Jonas, miller and chocolate grinder, Prince-street. **1794** *Mass. H. S. Coll.* III. 273 Riggers, joiners, . . . chocolate grinders, &c. should not occupy wooden shops or sheds within the vicinity of dwelling houses.

Chocolate mill. A mill in which cacao beans are ground in the preparation of chocolate.

1785 *Mass. Stat.* 30 June, Chocolate mills and machines for roasting cocoa have been erected in the town of Boston. **1794** *Mass. H. S. Coll.* III. 247 Three mills more are constructed, viz. a grist mill, a saw mill, and a chocolate mill. *a***1817** DWIGHT *Travels* I. 417 On these waters are erected eight Grist-mills, six saw-mills, two oil-mills, two chocolate mills, [etc.]. **1823** *New Eng. Farmer* II. 103 The Grist, Chocolate, and Carding Mills, of Major Foster, at Danvers, were unfortunately consumed by fire. **1889** BRAYLEY *Boston Fire Dept.* 88 The chocolate mill occupied by Mr. Welch . . . was burnt with all its stock on April 15.

+**Chocolate plant.** *New Eng.* The water avens, *Geum rivale.* Also ellipt. — **1832** WILLIAMSON *Maine* I. 121 The Chocolate plant . . . flourishes luxuriantly in woods. . . . Its root, when boiled, makes a drink in taste and goodness like chocolate. **1893** *Amer. Folk-Lore* VI. 141 *Geum rivale,* chocolate. Buckfield, Me.; Franconia, N.H.

+**Chocolate-root.** (See quotation and cf. prec.) — **1890** *Cent.* 2504/3 The roots of . . . the water-avens, *Geum rivale,* . . . from their reddish-brown color are sometimes known by the names of chocolate-root and Indian chocolate.

+**Chocorua plague.** [A mountain in New Hampshire; allegedly named after an Indian.] (See quotation.) — **1877** *Vt. Dairym. Ass. Rep.* V. 51 The 'Chocorua Plague' or 'cripple ail,' which prevails in New Hampshire near the foot of the White Mountains, arises from this cause [=lack of phosphate].

+**Choctaw.** Also **Shacktau, Choktah.** ['Possibly a corruption of the Sp. *chato,* 'flat' or 'flattened,' alluding to the custom of these Indians of flattening the head' (Hodge *Indians* I. 288).]

1. An Indian of a tribe of the Muskhogean stock, formerly located east of the lower Mississippi River.

[**1700** IBERVILLE in Margry *Déc.* IV. 463 Je crois que vous pourrés . . . destacher . . . quatre hommes, pour aller dans le dedans du pays et jusqu' aux Chaqueta, et voir ce que c'est que cette nation, dont les autres Sauvages parlent tant.] **1725** G. CHICKEN in *Travels Amer. Col.* 122 The Chickesaws have made a peace with the Choctaws. **1726** PENHALLOW *Indian Wars* (1824) 79 Another tribe called the Shacktaus, made many incursions on Carolina. **1741** *Ga. Col. Rec.* III. 398 The Choctaws (who are upon the Frontiers between the English and French Settlements) and the Chickesaws were to send their Deputies. **1775** ADAIR *Indians* 2 The Creeks . . . took this opportunity to chide the Choktahs. **1805** *Ann. 10th Congress* 1 Sess. I. 646, I had some expectation of procuring . . . a tract of land for my young Choctaw. **1882** *Amer. Naturalist* XVI. 222 The two thousand Choctaws still living in their ancestral homes in Mississippi, retain, in all their pristine vigor, many of the usages of their ancestors. **1885** *Century Mag.* XXX. 602 The Choctaws appear to understand trading and money-making better than any of their brethren. **1891** O'BEIRNE *Leaders Ind. Territory* 68/1 Mr. Lowery's father was a white man and his mother a quadroon Choctaw.

2. The language of the Choctaw Indians.

1880 CABLE *Grandissimes* 60, I speak it [=English], but I also speak Choctaw.

b. Taken as a type of unknown, difficult language.

1873 EGGLESTON *Myst. Metrop.* 34 Charlton . . . was slipping into an attachment for a woman to whom both words were Choctaw. **1880** 'MARK TWAIN' *Tramp Abroad* xviii. 163, I spoke in the purest German, but I might as well have spoken in the purest Choctaw for all the good it did. **1912** RAINE *Brand Blotters* 262 'Doesn't she understand English?' 'No more'n you do Choctaw, miss.'

3. Attrib. with *boy, chief, horse, Indian,* etc.

1805 *Ann. 10th Congress* 1 Sess. I. 645, I have had some talk . . . about securing a tract of land to a Choctaw boy. **1867** DIXON *New America* II. 13 The Choctaw chief may invoke the Big Father, whom white men call for him the Great Spirit. **1775** ADAIR *Indians* 411 He rode a young Choktah horse, which had been used only to a rope round his neck. **1738** W. STEPHENS *Proc. Georgia* 82 The Choctaw Indians in the French Interest, had . . . come in a great body. **1796** MORSE *Amer. Geog.* I. 669 The Chicasaw and Choctaw languages. **1860** CLAIBORNE *Sam. Dale* 104 Captain Cassity certified that he received similar information from John Walker, a white man residing in the Choctaw nation. **1898** CUSHMAN *Hist. Indians* 144 The property of the mission . . . had been there deposited to await the arrival of the Choctaw packet to carry it to Elliot. **1852** MARCY *Explor. Red River* (1854) 19 The point where the line dividing the Choctaw territory from the State of Texas crosses Red river. **1805** *Ann. 10th Congress* 1 Sess. I. 646 The Choctaw treaty, I fear, will fall through this season. **1834** JACKSON in *Pres. Mess. & P.* III. 50 The sales of the public lands in the district of country acquired from the Choctaw tribe of Indians. **1775** ADAIR *Indians* 2 A large body of the English Indian traders, on their way to the Choktah country, were escorted by a body of Creek and Choktah warriors.

+**Chogset.** Also **chaugset.** [Amer. Indian.] The burgall or blue perch, *Tautogolabrus adspersus.* — **1842** *Nat. Hist. N.Y., Zoology* IV. 173 The Bergall has various popular names [including] . . . Chogset, a name derived from the Mohegan dialect, but its purport unknown. **1871** DE VERE 66 More generally known is the Chogset, . . . frequently called Burgall or Blue Fish, and found on the whole Eastern coast under a variety of designations. **1888** GOODE *Amer. Fishes* 93 Chogset, squeteague, [etc.,] . . . are among the best of them. **1899** *Animal & Plant Lore* 62 Chaugset (Indian), for the cunner, *Tautogolabrus adspersus.* Buz zard's Bay.

* **Choice,** *n.* +A place picked out for settlement; frequent in place names.

1667 *Md. Hist. Mag.* XX. 24 Phillips Choice. **1673** *Ib.* XXI. 355 Maidens Choice. **1707** *Ib.* I. 7 A town should be erected on a tract on the same River belonging to Anne Felks and called Taylor's Choice. **1834** H. BRACKENRIDGE *Recoll.* 19 In ten days we reached the encampment of General Wayne, at a place called Hopson's choice, now a part of the city of Cincinnati.

* **Choice,** *a.* Careful *of,* valuing highly, fond *of.* Now *colloq.* {1875–, *dial.*}

1775 A. ADAMS *Familiar Lett.* (1876) 128, I received . . . the other articles you sent. . . . I shall be very choice of them. **1805** *Lewis & Clark Exped.* (1905) VII. 162 They have buffaloe robes but are verry choice of them. **1840** DANA *Two Years* xxix, They [=the crew of the *California*] had many of the latest sailor songs, . . . which they were very choice of. **1859** TOMLINSON *Kansas in 1858* 99 While living here in Kansas he was very choice of her, scarcely allowing her to stir out. **1872** *Vt. Board Agric. Rep.* I. 78 Men are as choice of a little scrub apple tree . . . as [of] . . . the most favorite varieties of the day. **1906** *Harper's Mo.* Oct. 765 She was all her mother had, and her mother was dreadful choice of her.

* **Choke,** *v.* With adverbs.

1. *tr. To choke down,* +to conquer or subdue by choking.

1833 CATLIN *Indians* I. 253 The laso is . . . used chiefly to catch the wild horse, which is done by throwing over their necks a noose which is made at the end of the laso with which they are 'choked down.'

b. To keep under control or force back. {1888–}

1856 KANE *Arctic Explor.* I. 85 The deck blazed . . . but . . . I choked it down till water could be passed from above. **1866** BRYANT *Death of Slavery* iii, Choked down, unuttered, the rebellious thought.

2. *To choke off,* to force to relinquish or prevent from carrying out a purpose; to prevent from continuing talk or discussion. {1818–}

1841 *Congress. Globe* 23 Dec. 55 (Th.), When did modern Democracy ever give up an office? When she was choked off, and not otherwise. **1846** COOPER *Redskins* pref., This is not a tax for revenue . . . ; but a tax to 'choke off' landlords, to use a common American phrase. **1848** BARTLETT 76 [To] stop a public speaker when addressing an audience, is called *choking him off.* This is done by shuffling the feet. **1864** *Congress. Globe* 19 April 1735/3 If we are to be choked off from argument, I hope that the House will choke down the bill. **1872** J. D. WHITNEY *Life & Lett.* 282 An attempt was made to 'choke me off.'

b. To put a stop to, to block (discussion, etc.).

1884 *Congress. Rec.* 18 June 5309/2 An attempt to pass any bill . . . under the whip and spur, and with an idea of choking off a full, fair, and free discussion of the merits, . . . does not do credit to the intelligence of this House. **1903** *N.Y. Times* 2 Oct. 1 This [speech] was greeted with hisses and shouts of 'Sit down!' and 'Choke it off!' **1910** *N.Y. Ev. Post* 21 March (Th.), Had the effort to choke off Mr. Burleson's motion for the deposition of Speaker Cannon succeeded [etc.].

3. *To choke out,* to utter as if with difficulty.

1848 C. PICKERING in *U.S. Exploring Exped.* IX. 23 The Chinooks . . . seemed to choke out their words.

4. *To choke up,* to shut up, stop speaking. *slang.*

1907 MULFORD *Bar-20* 105 'Why, about eight years ago I had business—' 'Choke up,' interposed Red.

+**Chokeberry.** Also †**choak berry.**

1. A shrub of the apple family (*Aronia arbutifolia*); the fruit of this.

1778 CARVER *Travels* 511 The Choak Berry. The shrub thus termed by the natives grows about five or six feet high, and bears a berry about the size of a sloe, of a jet black. **1821** *Jrnl. Science* III. 276 June 4. Visited the bog in Goshen [Mass.], where I found the black chokeberry. **1847** J. PALMER *Rocky Mts.* 111 The banks of the stream are lined with cottonwood, balm of gilead, choke berries and every variety of bushes. **1867** 'LACKLAND' *Homespun* I. 115 The choke-berries, in their long and clustering spikes, display red, or black. **1871** DE VERE 403 Very different is the so-called choke-berry, in reality the fruit of a low apple-tree. **1901** MOHR *Plant Life Ala.* 71 The chokeberry, which is here of arborescent habit, presents a beautiful sight when loaded with its bright scarlet fruit.

2. =CHOKECHERRY 1.

1832 WILLIAMSON *Maine* I. 117 The Prune genus embraces . . . the Choke-cherry, or as some may call it the choke-berry, of two varieties. **a1862** THOREAU *Maine Woods* 310 The prevailing shrubs and small trees along the shore were: . . . choke berry, [etc.].

‖**Choke bow.** 'A word of doubtful meaning' (Th.). — **1811** *Mass. Spy* 26 June (Th.), Strayed, a Bay Mare; . . . had on a Choke Bow, tied with a string.

+**Chokecherry.** Also †**choak-cherry.**

1. The wild cherry, either *Padus virginiana* or *P. demissa.*

1784 CUTLER in *Mem. Academy* I. 449 Choke Cherry. A low shrub. . . . The Red Choke Cherry. A shrub. **1785** MARSHALL *Amer. Grove* 113 Fruit . . . greatly corrugating the mouth and throat, so as to obtain the name of choak-cherry. **1793** I. ALLEN *Hist. Vermont* 9 Apples . . . damascenes, red, black, and choke cherries . . . rise to great perfection in open fields and gardens. **1805** LEWIS in *L. & Clark Exped.* (1904) II. 28 The choke-cherry also grows here in the hollows and at the heads of the gullies . . . this growth has frequently made it's appearance on the Missouri from the neighbourhood of the Bald pated Prarie, to this place. **1822** J. FOWLER *Journal* 143 In the bottoms along the cricks cotten wood black alder and willows with the chock cherry black curren [etc.].

a1918 G. STUART *On Frontier* I. 129 The menu consisted of buffalo meat, boiled smoked tongue, bread, dried fruit, a preserve made from choke-cherries and coffee.

attrib. **1834** A. PIKE *Sketches* 28, I found I was freezing, and stopped in a cliff of rocks, and made a little fire of choke-cherry bushes. **1906** *Springfield W. Republican* 7 June 7 Where a friendly choke-cherry tree throws its shadow on a hot morning.

2. In colloq. contexts, with reference to the sharp astringency of the berries.

1857 HOLLAND *Bay Path* 281 Slap goes the man right down in the middle of the road, all curled up as if he was full of choke cherries. **1900** C. WINCHESTER *W. Castle* 152 The first time he preached upon the subject of holiness the congregation looked as though they had been eating choke-cherries. **1916** E. PORTER *David* 274 You know what she is—sour as a lemon an' puckery as a chokecherry.

Choke-dog. {*dial.*} +**1.** A coarse kind of drink or liquor. +**2.** A twining or trailing plant of the genus *Gonolobus.* — **(1) 1821** COOPER *Spy* xxi, Replenishing the mug with a large addition of the article known to the soldiery by the name of 'choke-dog,' she held it towards the peddler. **(2) 1845** LINCOLN *Botany* App. 107/2 *Gonolobus obliquus,* false choak-dog.

* **Choke pear.**

***1.** A pear with a sharp, astringent taste; a kind of wild pear. {–1672}

1839 BUEL *Farmer's Companion* 269 It is as easy to cultivate the vergaleu as it is the choke pear. **1851** *Knickerb.* XXXVII. 376 Friend, school-mate, dost remember the old tree, ('Choke-pears' it bore,) which oft we'd climb with glee. **1857–8** *Ill. Agric. Soc. Trans.* III. 353 Those parties have again been subdivided into advocates of certain stocks [of pears]. . . . The Native Thorn, the Apple, the Choke Pear, and our best Table Pear. **1872** *Vt. Bd. Agric. Rep.* I. 107 Man, by his industry, skill and perseverance applied to the wild choke pear of our fields, . . . has transformed it.

+**2.** =CHOKEBERRY 1. *local.*

1892 *Amer. Folk-Lore* V. 95 *Pyrus arbutifolia,* . . . choke-pear. Washington Co., Me.

***Choke plum.** A rough, astringent kind of plum. {1556 only} — **1800** *Mass. H. S. Coll.* VII. 245 Whortle-berries, choak-plums, and a few cranberries, are found on Hog and Haley's isles.

* **Choker.**

1. a. A neckerchief worn high around the throat. *Obs.* {1848–} **b.** *White choker,* a white tie worn with evening dress or by clergymen.

1863 'G. HAMILTON' *Gala-Days* 113 The chieftain yonder, in white choker, . . . bears Atlas on his shoulders. **1870** R. TOMES *Decorum* 209 Some invited person . . . may by chance have neglected to put on the swallow-tail and white choker *de rigueur.* **1874** McNeal *When Kansas Was Young* (1922) 52 His presence brought up to the proper clerical standard by the addition of a white choker and shad belly coat. **1880** P. DEMING *Adirondack Stories* 32 While Farmer Fernwell toiled in the field throughout the summer, the elder stuck it out, in black clothes and white choker, in the parlor. **1894** E. S. PHELPS *Singular Life* 135 He ain't no dummy in a minister's choker.

2. One who wears a choker, as a preacher.

1875 G. P. BURNHAM *Three Years* iv, Choker, a dominie, a white cravat. A 'parson,' also.

+**Choketater.** An edible tuber of the Jerusalem artichoke, *Helianthus tuberosus.* — **1893** *Voodoo Tales* 145 The choke-taters or artichokes, (not the green vegetable rosettes served to 'white folks,' but the tubers of the great 'Jerusalem sunflowers' . . .) were buried in the ashes.

+**Choke whortleberry.** A variety of whortleberry. — **1784** CUTLER in *Mem. Acad.* I. 439 The Choke Whortleberry.

+**Choking-snake.** (See quotation.) — **1795** in S. Williams *Nat. Hist. Vt.* (ed. 2) I. App. 485 In a field in Connecticut . . . I approached with caution within twenty feet of a black snake, about seven feet long, having a white throat, and of the kind which the people there call runners or choking snakes.

* **Cholera.**

1. =CHOLERA MORBUS. {1601–}

1827 DRAKE & MANSFIELD *Cincinnati* 52 Every summer and autumn, however, Cincinnati . . . is, to a certain extent, affected with cholera and bilious fever. **1900** STOCKTON *Afield & Afloat* 321, I've got the cholery.

2. The Asiatic cholera, a disease that spread from India in various epidemics, the worst in America being in 1832. {1819–}

1832 *Congress. Deb.* 30 June 3833 A general fast in reference to a deliverance from . . . a prevalence of the Asiatic cholera. **1833** *Foreign Miss. Chron.* (Pittsburgh) I. 46 There was considerable sickness among them [immigrants in Arkansas] and many deaths by cholera. **1836** *Niles' Nat. Reg.* 22 Oct. 128/2 The cholera has been severe on some of the plantations in the vicinity of Charleston. **1841** TRUMBULL *Autobiog.* 288 The cholera made its appearance in New York, soon after I commenced, and was peculiarly fatal in the sixth ward, in which I lived. **1850** R. GLISAN *Jrnl. Army Life* 12 The cholera is quite prevalent along the Ohio and Mississippi Rivers.

+3. A disease of swine, highly contagious and fatal. (Cf. HOG CHOLERA.)

1879 *Diseases of Swine* 178 Cholera in Kansas and Nebraska seems to attack preferably the Berkshire.

4. Attrib. with *epidemic, hospital, year.*

1833 E. T. COKE *Subaltern's Furlough* ix, A rough stone prison . . . and a building . . . used as a cholera hospital . . . occupy one side of the park. **1856** *Spirit of Times* 22 Nov. 192/1 The great 20 mile race . . . came off over the Union Course, L. I., in 1832, 'the cholera year.' **1883** *Harper's Mag.* Sept. 647/1 During the cholera epidemic of 1873 in Kentucky, Lancaster suffered more than any of the other interior towns.

+Cholera infantum. A disease of children that occurs in summer and is characterized by vomiting and diarrhea. — **1829** B. HALL *Travels in N.A.* III. 389 Our researches . . . were all cut short . . . by the illness of our little girl, whose long exposure to the noxious air of the great rivers, had given her a complaint very fatal to children in that country, and called by the ominous name of Cholera Infantum. **1882** 'M. HARLAND' *Eve's Daughters* 35 Both babies had a stormy infancy. What with teething, convulsions, cholera-infantum, and . . . epileptic fits, [etc.]. **1895** *Outing* XXVI. 405/2 You are forced to wish that cholera-infantum had been more prevalent sixty years ago.

Cholera morbus. An acute disease occurring in hot weather and characterized by severe vomiting, diarrhea, cramps, etc. {(Stanford) 1673–}

1823 J. THACHER *Military Journal* 248 Cholera morbus, dysentery and remittent fevers, are the prevailing complaints, which demand all my attention. **1832** CHILD *Frugal Housewife* 29 A spoonful of ashes stirred in cider is good to prevent sickness at the stomach. Physicians frequently order it in cases of cholera-morbus. **1877** BURDETTE *Rise of Mustache* 300 In two hours he was writhing in a premature and unseasonable attack of cholera morbus. **1882** 'M. HARLAND' *Eve's Daughters* 53 An attack of cholera morbus usually sets all right again if the indulgence is carried too far.

+Cholla. *S.W.* [Sp. 'a head.'] One or other of several species of spiny cacti, esp. *Opuntia cholla.*

1883 *Harper's Mag.* March 502/2 The cholla is one mass of spines, barbed on the fish-hook principle. **1907** WHITE *Arizona Nights* xii. 186 The hill I had to climb was steep and covered with chollas. **1919** J. S. CHASE *Calif. Desert Trails* 79 Even the hateful cholla has a fruit that is said to be agreeable.

b. Attrib. with *cactus, spine.*

1891 *Century Mag.* March 659 Their knees were full of the thorns of the cholla cactus. **1907** WHITE *Arizona Nights* xii. 186, I . . . slipped down the bluff, getting pretty well stuck up with the cholla spines.

Chonk, *v. colloq.* [Imitative; cf. E. *champ, chomp.*] To chew vigorously; to 'chomp.' — **1843** STEPHENS *High Life N.Y.* I. 50 But there sot the old man a chonking an apple. **1908** *Dialect Notes* III. 298 You chonk like a horse.

‖**Chonking.** *colloq.* A small piece or fragment nibbled away or pared off. — **1882** *Century Mag.* XXV. 299/1 The ground . . . [was] covered with the 'chonkings' of the frozen apples, the work of the squirrels in getting at the seed. [**1895** *Dialect Notes* I. 385 *Chankings*, parings of apples and other fruits, or the core and other rejected parts of an apple. Me., Vt., Mass., Conn.]

***Choose,** *v.*

***1.** *tr.* To elect as a representative or official.

1683 *Penna. Col. Rec.* I. 58 Upon the whole matter the Assembly went to chuse a Speaker. **1708** *Manchester Rec.* 118 Voted to chus our town offiser for the year. **1721** *Mass. Ho. Rep. Jrnl.* III. 7 Ordered, That a Precept be sent to the Town of Cambridge, to Chuse another Representative. **1788** FRANKLIN *Autobiog.* 362 The officers of the companies composing the Philadelphia regiment, being met, chose me for their colonel. **1822** *Ann. 17th Congress* 1 Sess. I. 85 The Legislatures have heretofore regulated the manner of choosing electors for President. **1890** *Cent.* 4706/1 The President of the United States is chosen once in four years by presidential electors.

2. *colloq.* To wish to have or to occupy.

1829 *Va. Lit. Museum* 85/2 The old woman remarked she 'expected' he 'chose bed,' . . . pointing to one which stood in a corner of the room. **1871** DE VERE 453 A dish offered at table is declined with the words, 'I don't choose any.' **1908** *Dialect Notes* III. 298 'Will you have some butter?' 'No, I thank you, I wouldn't choose any.'

***Chop,** *n.*[1]

+1. A cut, notch, or gash made in a tree.

1662 *Va. Statutes* II. 101 The surveighors being for the most part careles of seeing the trees marked, . . . in a small time the chopps being growne up, or the trees fallen, the bounds become as uncertaine as at first. **1685** *Duxbury Rec.* 59 Several trees marked with three chops in every tree. **1750** T. WALKER *Journal* 54 Besides several Trees blazed Several ways with 3 Chops over each blaze. **1832** *Louisville Directory* 106 Jacob Sodowsky . . . was the first man who shewed a method of identifying the chops which were made on the line and corner trees of old surveys.

+2. a. (See quot. 1830.) **b.** *Chop feed*, feed for horses or cattle, consisting of chopped hay or straw, etc. {chop, *dial.* 1868–}

1830 S. H. COLLINS *Emigrant's Guide* 132 When it [rye] is ground only (as it is used for bread in England) they here call it 'chop,' and give it to cattle. **1852** *Mich. Agric. Soc. Trans.* III. 151 Chop feed is good for them in small quantities, say half a pint to a sheep. **1871** *Rep. Indian Affairs* 529, I have added . . . a hay-cutter for preparing 'chop-feed.'

Chop, *n.*[2] The entrance or mouth of a river; a rapid part of a channel. {chops of the channel, 1692–} — **1765** R. ROGERS *Journals* (1883) 180 Having passed both, . . . we entered the chops of a river, called by the Indians the Grace of Man. **1795** J. SULLIVAN *Maine* 27 The Chops of Merry Meeting Bay. . . . The Chops is a strait where the ebbing and flowing tides are alike rapid and hazardous to navigation.

Chop, *n.*[3] [Hind. *chhāp* stamp, brand.] *First chop*, in commercial use, superior or first-rate quality. {1823–} Also attrib.

1810 *Columbian Centinel* 17 Jan. 4/3 Real first chop Madras Hankerchiefs . . . for sale by Asa Dow. **1820** *Ib.* 22 Jan. 3/3 For sale—7000 pieces short Yellow Nankins, of first chop. **1852** STOWE *Uncle Tom* i, 'I've seen over a thousand, in my day, paid down for gals not a bit handsomer.' . . . 'Capital, sir—first chop!' said the trader.

b. Of persons as well as articles in non-commercial use. {1848} Also adverbial.

1810 M. DWIGHT *Journey to Ohio* 49 He thinks himself a gentleman of the first chop, & takes the liberty of coining words for himself. **1825** NEAL *Bro. Jonathan* II. 80 'Ye hain't gut sich a thing . . . as a chaw o' pig tail, have yer!' . . . 'I ruther guess I have, such as 'tis—tain't fuss chop.' **1860** *Harper's Mag.* March 442/1 'Let's try our luck in the woods. . . . Tom, can you call moose?' 'Well, I can, fust chop, and no mistake.' *a***1861** T. WINTHROP *Canoe & Saddle* 171 Need I say that the grouse were admirable, that everything was delicious, and the Confucian weed first chop? **1881** HOWELLS *Modern Instance* xix. 236 But I hate to live in a town where I'm not first chop in everything.

***Chop,** *v.*

+1. *tr.* To begin clearing (land) by felling and trimming the timber. (See quot. 1868.)

1821 W. DALTON *Travels U.S.* 82 Farms are called improved, when the settler, having chopped a few acres, has piled up into the form of a dwelling-house, a number of logs. **1846** *Knickerb.* XXVIII. 338 The two men . . . having chopped five acres of land according to their engagement, returned home. **1868** S. SMITH *Autobiog.* 10 My brother Josiah chopped twelve acres for a Mr. Wildman, his compensation being a yoke of oxen. 'Chopping' consists of felling the trees, cutting them into logs 12 feet long, and piling the brush!

2. To cut down or clear away (weeds, etc.); to break up (land).

1770 WASHINGTON *Diaries* I. 394 The Ground here was tolerably clean and in Good Order, the Grass and Weeds being Choped over. **1859** *Harper's Mag.* Nov. 727/1 Just before planting [rice] the ground is first chopped or broken rudely.

b. *To chop in*, to plant (small grain) by hoeing it into the soil.

1787 WASHINGTON *Diaries* III. 198 Women putting up the New fence but ordered them to chop in Oats in the low parts w[hi]ch had been hoed.

+3. *To chop (out) cotton*, to thin out young cotton plants. 'Cotton-seed is drilled in and comes up in a row; the cotton-chopper straddles the row and chops wide gaps, leaving the plants in hills' (Knight I. 543/2).

1820 in *Henderson's N.C. Almanack* (1823) 25 The hands may begin to thin by chopping out the cotton with their hoes. **1852** *Florida Plant. Rec.* 65, I have choped out a Little Cotton. **1856** *Ib.* 476 Stoped chopen cotton on account of frost, went to worke the groun peas. **1899** CHESNUTT *Conjure Woman* 30 Mars Dugal' 'cluded he would'n sell Henry 'tel he git de crop in en de cotton chop'.

Chophouse. A restaurant. {*c*1690–*a*1861}

1819 NOAH *She would be a Soldier* II. i, The honourable captain Pendragon, who never ate anything more gross than a cutlet at Molly's chophouse! **1840** BIRD *Robin Day* 31, I summoned courage enough to enter a little tavern or chophouse. **1873** MILLER *Amongst Modocs* 340 The food was cold refuse of some low chop-house. **1877** WRIGHT *Big Bonanza* 356 A Comstocker who dropped in at a chop-house where about a dozen newcomers had just settled in a flock, at two or three adjoining tables. **1907** FIELD *Six-Cylinder Courtship* 74 A moment later we drew up in front of a well-known chop-house.

***Chopped,** *ppl. a.*

***1.** Of grains, hay, etc.: Ground, broken, or reduced to fragments by chopping.

1786 WASHINGTON *Diaries* III. 4 My Chariot Horses . . . to be fed with Bran and chopped Hay. **1800** *Steele Papers* I. 185 He has every advantage there, a Green lott, . . . hommany, oats & Chopt rye & Cut Straw. **1805** PARKINSON *Tour* 223 A farmer's waggon in America, when she comes into market, is something like a pedlar's pack: it consists of . . . buckwheat-flour, rye-flour, chopped straw, &c. **1856** *Rep. Comm. Patents: Agric.* 220 Potatoes . . . are cooked and mixed with wheat that has been 'chopped.' . . . A bushel of cooked potatoes, with a bushel of chopped wheat, is worth more than 2 bushels of wheat fed dry. **1865** *Nation* I. 240 My horse could have some chopped oats.

+**2.** Of waves: Choppy.

1849 N. KINGSLEY *Diary* 26 Oweing to the winds shifting, and causeing heavy chopped seas, many of them come aboard of us. **1860** ABBOTT *South & North* 61 A stern norther rose in the night, blowing . . . and raising that short, chopped sea, as the sailors term it. **1880** WALLACE *Ben-Hur* 12 Here chopped waves, there long swells.

*** **Chopper.**

+**1.** A wood chopper; one who cuts down trees, either as a pioneer or as a lumberman.

1785 A. ELLICOTT in *Life & Lett.* 44 My Brother Joseph at Present runs the guide Line for the Choppers. **1805** CLARK in *Lewis & C. Exped.* (1904) II. 222, I Set out with Serjt. Pryor four Choppers two Invaleds & one man to hunt. **1824** DODDRIDGE *Notes* 134 The fatigue party consisted of choppers, whose business it was to fell the trees and cut them off at proper lengths. **1846** *Knickerb.* XXVIII. 337 On the second day of our journey we (myself, a teamster and two 'choppers,') had left behind us all marks of civilization. **1851** J. S. SPRINGER *Forest Life* 92 First, then, come the 'boss,' or the principal in charge. Then the choppers, meaning those who select, fell, and cut the logs, one of whom is master chopper. **1888** GRIGSBY *Smoked Yank* (1891) 180, I had never chopped a cord of wood in my life, but wanted to be in the fresh air, so I managed to get taken out as a chopper. **1918** ROOSEVELT in *Maine My State* (1919) 20, I became acquainted with a quiet, resolute-looking man, named Brown, one of the choppers.

+**2.** One who operates a ticket box at a subway station.

1899 *N.Y. Journal* 7 Feb. 4/2 The ticket agents and 'choppers' are shivering in their shoes. At several of the down stations where the traffic is light at night, the services of both the old agents and 'choppers' have been dispensed with. **1904** *N.Y. Ev. Post* 26 Nov., I asked policemen, ticket-sellers and choppers if they had seen a lady in a gray dress with two valises pass through.

*** **Chopping.**

+**1.** A tract on which the trees have been (or are being) felled, but which has not been cleared of logs, brush, etc.

1817 *Mass. Spy* 11 June (Th.), A. S., in a piece of chopping that he was clearing, fell a tree across a stump. **1846** *Knickerb.* XXVIII. 343, I succeeded . . . to get the whole of my 'chopping' logged and cleared.

2. The felling of trees.

In quots. *a-chopping:* See A prep.[1] 3.

1846 *Knickerb.* XXVII. 276, I was in the woods a-chopping. **1870** 'O. OPTIC' *Field & Forest* 279, I took to the river for a livin'. I worked a choppin', a flat boatin' and firin' on a steamboat.

3. The loud barking of a dog.

1897 *Outing* XXX. 127/1 Of a sudden the character of the baying changed from the noisy yapping of a lot of playful puppies to the persistent chopping of the driving hound—the fox was up.

4. Attrib. with *ax, block, board,* etc.

1779 *Penobscot Exped. Proc.* (1780) 5 Such number of camp kettles, spades, shovels, pick-axes, and chopping-axes, as the Commanding-Officer . . . may think proper. **1833** 'ELMWOOD' *Yankee among Nullifiers* 84 They saw my man Tom with the two axes and the chopping-block. **1848** PARKMAN in *Knickerb.* XXXII. 42 Hand me Papin's chopping-board, or give it to that Indian, and let him cut the mixture [of tobacco]. **1873** 'G. HAMILTON' *12 Miles* 51 Think of finding your chopping-bowl under the garret-eaves doing duty as a nail-box. **1638** *Md. Archives* IV. 86 A chopping knife, a measuring barrell, a quilt. **1837** W. JENKINS *Ohio Gaz.* 338 It contains . . . a large merchant grist mill, with 5 runs of burrs, and 1 pair of chopping stones, in which there can be manufactured from 80 to 100 bbls. flour per day. **1875** KNIGHT 1074/1 *Hatchet,* . . . a one-handed chopping-tool. **1904** WALLER *Wood-Carver* 75 Having placed the wooden chopping-tray of quartered apples on the work-bench.

+**Chopping bee.** A gathering of neighbors to assist an individual in clearing land. Also *chopping frolic.*

1809 *Mass. Spy* 12 July (Th.), At Bristol (Vt.), June 7, at a chopping bee, a limb of one of the falling trees struck one of the men. **1853** RAMSEY *Tennessee* 720 Weddings, military trainings, house-raisings, chopping frolics, were often followed with the fiddle, and dancing, and rural sports. **1860** *Harper's Mag.* April 712/2 One of his neighbors had a 'chopping-bee' on Christmas day. . . . The axes flew rapidly, . . . making the woods ring with the joyous music. **1868** *Western Mag.* Jan. (De Vere), The inhabitants within a radius of ten miles were invited to a chopping-bee.

+**Chop sea.** A rough, choppy sea. — **1854** SHILLABER *Mrs. Partington* 317 Here comes Jim Sly through the wet, pitching like a mackerel-catcher in a chop sea. **1883** *Century Mag.* XXVI. 472 An hour later, the ship has entered a chop sea. **1883** *Harper's Mag.* Aug. 375/1 The wind kicks up a chop sea of the worst description.

*** **Choral,** *a.* Designating groups interested in music. — [**1865** *Atlantic Mo.* XV. 181 Choral societies [in Europe grow] . . . under the powerful impulse given them by the state.] **1881** *Harper's Mag.* May 812/2 The organists attached to several of the larger churches have established choral associations. **1883** C. F. WILDER *Sister Ridnour* 35 If she sings in the choir she must go to Choral Union, Monday evenings.

Chore, *n.* A small job or routine task in a household, on a farm, etc. {1746–, *s.w. dial.*}

1751 MACSPARRAN *Diary* 56 He sent with Peter his black Boy Calais to do chores for a few Days. **1758** J. ADAMS *Works* (1850) II. 37 Chores, chat, tobacco, tea, steal away time. **1789** WEBSTER *Diss. Engl. Lang.* 112 *Chore* . . . is an English word. . . . It signifies small domestic jobs of work, and its place cannot be supplied by any other single word in the language. **1835** HOFFMAN *Winter in West* I. 118 The good woman is engaged doing some 'chores' at the farther end of the apartment. **1869** STOWE *Oldtown Folks* 261 It was resolved . . . [that we should] share between us certain family tasks or 'chores.' **1872** W. W. FLAGG *Good Investment* xii, The hewing of wood and drawing of water, commonly called 'chores,' had been done by Robert. **1925** BRYAN *Memoirs* 35, I . . . learned to milk and care for the stock and do the general chores.

transf. **1845** C. KIRKLAND *Western Clearings* 173 Girl-hunting is certainly among our most formidable 'chores.' **1848** *Ladies' Repository* VIII. 127 Having several little chores to do up with our correspondents, on this page, we conclude to dispatch them in the beginning.

b. Attrib. and comb. with *gal, girl, man, woman.*

*c*1848 WHITCHER *Bedott P.* xiv. 142 Nobody in the house but a little chore-gal. **1858** WHITTIER *Telling the Bees* x, Forward and back, Went drearily singing the chore-girl small. **1872** BRACE *Dangerous Classes N.Y.* 159 One old red-faced tippler, Mrs. McK., . . . was the best chore-woman on the Hill when sober. **1874** A. D. WHITNEY *We Girls* vi. 134 William, the chore-man. **1903** E. O. WHITE *L. Chilton* 36, I was talking of a hypothetical chorewoman. **1906** *Atlantic Mo.* Dec. 861 Watching curiously while the choreman and the scrubwoman pursued their reckless path through the . . . upper shelves.

Chore, *v.*

1. *intr.* To perform chores. {1746–, *s.w. dial.*}

1788 J. MAY *Jrnl. & Lett.* 88 Five hands at work on the house. Two playing the whipsaw, and the rest choring in the woods, such as felling trees from three to five feet through. **1867** 'LACKLAND' *Homespun* I. 139 It is the lad's work to go about home choring; getting in the wood . . . , tending the sheep [etc.]. **1874** A. D. WHITNEY *We Girls* vi. 127 The man came who 'chored' for us. **1900** S. HALE *Letters* 363, I was engaged with Robert B., pursuing our agreement that he 'chore' for me one hour a day.

b. With *about, around, round.*

1839 C. KIRKLAND *New Home* (1840) 80, I was obliged to employ Mrs. J. to 'chore round,' to borrow her own expression. **1869** CHIPMAN *Notes on Bartlett* 81 *To chore,* Anglice, *char.* 'My wife was choring [working], when I left home.' 'To chore about.' Conn. **1909** *Forward* 25 December 423 He learned more oldfashioned wisdom than farming from Uncle Allen during the two years he 'chored' around the Tetlow farm.

‖**2.** *tr.* To burden (a person) with chores.

1898 WESTCOTT *D. Harum* 173 Polly . . . bein' the youngest girl, was chored most to death herself.

+**Chore boy.**

1. A boy who does chores.

1848 *Knickerb.* XXXII. 230, I afterwards saw Betty . . . laughing with the gardener and 'chore-boy.' **1856** *Ib.* XLVII. 102 He entered the employ of the Chief Justice of the Province, Sewall, as a chore-boy. **1871** EGGLESTON *Hoosier Schoolm.* xxii. 157 Ralph had come to live as a chore-boy at his uncle's. **1884** *Century Mag.* July 477/2 Knitting is the maid o' the kitchen, Milly, Doing nothing, sits the chore-boy, Billy. **1918** C. WELLS *Vicky Van* iii. 38, I believe the laundress and chore boy come by the day.

2. On a ranch or in a lumber camp, a cook's helper or camp keeper.

1893 *Scribner's Mag.* June 711/2 For a crew of sixty men, the cook has a helper, called in camp parlance the 'cookee,' and a 'chore-boy' to fetch wood and water and help wait on table. **1902** WHITE *Blazed Trail* xxviii. 198 You would have to be chore-boy in a lumber camp. *a*1904 — *Blazed Trail Stories* i. 12 A fat cook . . . and a chore 'boy' of seventy-odd summers were the only human beings in sight. **1905** *Forestry Bureau Bul.* No. 61 s.v., *Chore boy,* one who cleans up the sleeping quarters and stable of a logging camp, cuts firewood, builds fires, and carries water. **1907** *N.Y. Ev. Post* (semi-w. ed.) 18 July 5 The shanty-keeper himself is often an expert at meats and potatoes, while the assistant and the chore boy do the cleaning and dishwashing. **1924** R. CUMMINS *Sky-high Corral* 11 'Stub,' the wizenfaced chore boy, carrying wood to the kitchen, kept one eye upon the road.

Choring. Performing chores. {1746–, *s.w. dial.*} — **1885** THAYER *From Tannery* 67 Teaming, farming, choring, . . . was preferable to tanning leather. **1889** BUTLER *Recoll.* 315 Father had not done any heavy work for two years, but he still did much light work, and choring.

*** **Chorister.** +One who leads the congregation of a church, or a choir, in singing.

1769 *Plymouth Church Rec.* I. 332 To choose one or more Persons (since our dear Brother John May is taken from us by death who was our former Chorister) to lead in singing in the publick Worship. **1777** *Ib.* 353 Deacon Crombie, our former Chorister, had left ye usual Singer's Seat. **1779** E. PARKMAN *Diary* 89, I replyed with Consent, provided they would acquaint ye appointed Choristers with it. **1841** *Knickerb.* XVII. 33 A New-Hampshire Yankee . . . wants to set up a singin'-school in Tinnecum, where I have been chorister for these ten years past. **1846** *Ib.* XXVII. 55 Their very psalm-tunes languish, unless the chorister is a-shaking.

Chowchow. A dish composed of several ingredients cut up and mixed; with reference to Chinese cookery often mixed preserved fruits; mixed pickles. {1857–} Also attrib.

1850 B. TAYLOR *Eldorado* (1862) xii. 117 The grave Celestials serve up their chow-chow and curry, besides many genuine English dishes. **1876** M. F. HENDERSON *Cooking* 258 Chowchow Pickle. **1878** BEADLE *Western Wilds* 187 The dog that started it all [was] so chawed up a Chinaman couldn't 'a made him over into chow-chow. **1880** *Scribner's Mo.* July 357/2 The Ferguson family . . . drink cold coffee in tumblers from what was once a chow-chow bottle. **1898** *Kansas City Star* 18 Dec. 5/2, 1,200 bottles Chow-Chow, mixed or plain pickles, very fine, indeed, per bottle, 7¢.

fig. **1883** WILDER *Sister Ridnour* 234 Did you ever think what sort of a 'chow-chow' a woman's life is?

+Chowder, *n.* Also †**chouder.** [F. *chaudière* kettle, pot.]

1. A stew or thick soup composed of fish (or clams), onions, potatoes, crackers, milk, etc. {1762}

1751 *Boston Ev. Post* 23 Sept., Directions for making a Chouder. First lay some Onions to keep the Pork from burning, Because in Chouder there can be no turning [etc.]. **1802** *New Eng. Palladium* 28 Dec. 2 Our Sucktash and our Chowder:—May they never be supplanted by the *soup-meagre* of France. **1832** WILLIAMSON *Maine* I. 153 The Cusk . . . makes good 'chowder,' and no dry fish is better, especially when it is three years old. **1838** HAWTHORNE in *Democratic Rev.* I. 197 The smoke . . . brings with it a savory smell from a pan of fried fish, and a black kettle of chowder. **1840** *Knickerb.* XVI. 26, I never thought that any idea connected with a pot of chowder [etc.]. **1846** *Spirit of Times* 11 July 231/2 As to your Chowders, whether of Codfish or tautog, we don't believe in them. **1851** MELVILLE *Moby Dick* xv. 71 The landlord . . . had assured us that cousin Hosea, as he called him, was famous for his chowder. **1883** *Harper's Mag.* Aug. 463/1, I should like mutton broth and gumbo every day when I didn't have oyster stew or chowder. **1886** POORE *Reminisc.* I 384 She could make a regal Cape Cod chowder. **1904** *Delineator* Aug. 290 Cream soups, bouillons or chowders are made in the morning and warmed for dinner.

transf. **1870** *Congress. Globe* 22 Dec. 281 This bill may be called a 'chowder' of rare and varied ingredients. **1918** in *Liberty* 11 Aug. (1928) 8/2 Battery D found the straw pile first, and that led to a tired cat and dog fight. We won, and retired in a variety of straw chowder.

2. A chowder feast or party.

1848 BARTLETT 82 Nearly 10,000 persons assembled [at a political mass-meeting] in Rhode Island, for whom a clambake and chowder were prepared. **1884** *Century Mag.* XXVIII. 555/2 A chowder was given a few nights ago at the head of our little bay. **1896** *N.Y. Dramatic News* 4 July 10/4 The epic description of the return of the Tim Sullivan association from a chowder. **1906** *N.Y. Ev. Post* 6 Nov. 8 The Bowery . . . went about the business . . . with as much good nature as if it were 'Big Tim's' annual 'chowder.'

3. Attrib. and comb. with *builder, excursion,* etc.

1840 *Knickerb.* XVI. 26 The chowder-builder and the poet must alike be born, each to his 'art unteachable, untaught.' **1889** FARMER 143/2 *Chowder excursion.* . . . This almost national dish . . . has given a distinctive name to some of these jaunts, in that a chowder forms the *pièce de resistance.* **1874** *Atlantic Mo.* Sept. 309/2 All keeping beach hotels, . . . with the collateral occupation of 'running a chowder mill,' as the phrase goes here [at Coney Island]. **1857** WILLIS *Convalescent* 250 We found it was still an hour to 'chowder-time.'

+Chowder, *v. tr.* (See quotations.) — **1806** WEBSTER, *Chowder, v. t.* to make a chowder. **1889** *Cent.* 983/3 To chowder fish.

Chowderhead. {chowderheaded 1819.} (See quot. 1867.) — **1833** NEAL *Down-Easters* I. 119 That's our Amos! if taint I'm a chowderhead. **1867** LOWELL *Biglow P.* II. p. lviii, A few phrases not in Mr. Bartlett's book which I have heard [include]. . . . *Chowder-head:* a muddle-brain [etc.].

+Chowder party. A social gathering or picnic at which chowder is made and eaten. — **1826** FLINT *Recoll.* 354 We had public chowder-parties, where sixty people sat down under grape-vine arbours, to other good things beside fish. **1848** *Yale Lit. Mag.* XVI. 380 (Th.), We hate chowder-parties, we do. **1853** BALDWIN *Flush Times Ala.* 80 In the science of getting up . . . a picnic or chowder party, or fish fry, the Virginian . . . was first.

Christadelphian. [Gr. *Christ-os* Christ and *adelph-os* brother.] One of a sect (founded by John Thomas about 1850) which, though denying the Trinity, believe that Christ saves from sin; a Thomasite. {1873–} Also attrib. — **1882** *Amer. Univ. Cycl.* III. 826 *Christadelphians,* a recently organized religious sect in America. . . . The adherents of this sect are few. **1894** A. H. NEWMAN *Baptist Churches U.S.* 503 Most Plymouth Brethren and Christadelphians . . . agree with Baptists in rejecting infant baptism. **1919** *Census of Religious Bodies: 1916* II. 189/2 In polity the Christadelphians are thoroughly congregational.

***Christian,** *n.*

+1. A white person, or colonist, as distinguished from an Indian. *Obs.*

1658 *Hempstead Rec.* I. 44 In case an Indian doe wrong a Christian eyther in person or estate . . . hee shall make full sattisfaction. **1671** *N.Y. State Col. Hist.* XII. 484 The Occasion of the Present Meeting is . . . the Murder of two Christians (Dutch Men) killed by some Indyans. **1678** *N.Y. State Doc. Hist.* (1849) I. 90 Commodityes imported are all sorts of English manufacture for Christians & blancketts, Duffells &c. for Indians. **1711** *Boston News-Letter* 10 Sept. 2/2 All our Forces were gone from thence towards Canada; . . . There are about 1000 Indians besides Christians. **1723** *N.Y. State Doc. Hist.* (1849) I. 717 The Language of those Indians is not understood by any Christian among us. **1732** *Ib.* 383 The Indian names of Brooks, Rivulets . . . &c which were and still are known to very few Christians. **1737** BRICKELL *Nat. Hist. N.C.* 402 An honest and substantial Planter . . . was afflicted with a strange and lingering distemper, not usual among the Christians. **1838** *S. Lit. Messenger* IV. 800/2 Cassena . . . is still used by the 'Christians' or whites wherever it grows.

+2. A member of the religious sect known as Christian Connection (q.v.).

A new formation, pronounced with long *i* as in *Christ;* hence the italics and hyphen in the earlier examples.

1805 E. SMITH (ed.) The Christian's Magazine, Reviewer, and Religious Intelligencer. **1815** in Mills & Smith *Missionary Tour* 19 There was even a man of the New England sect of *Christ*-ians [Footnote: The sect of Elias Smith] preaching . . . in this [=Missouri] and the adjacent Territory. **1827** SHERWOOD *Gaz. Ga.* 18 There are also in the state Episcopalians, Roman Catholics, *Christ*-ians and Jews. **1831** PECK *Guide* 308 Ellison prairie . . . is sometimes called the Christian settlement, from a large society of the sect usually called Christ-ians, who located themselves here. **1844** Rupp *Relig. Denominations* 167 Within about one half century, a very considerable body of religionists have arisen in the United States, who, rejecting all names, appellations, and badges of distinctive party among the followers of Christ, simply call themselves Christians. **1859** BARTLETT 81 Christian, . . . a name assumed by a sect which arose from the great revival in 1801.

+3. =CAMPBELLITE, DISCIPLE OF CHRIST.

1849 CHAMBERLAIN *Indiana Gazetteer* 175 Presbyterians, Methodists, United Brethren, Christian, (or Campbellite), [etc.]. **1880** WEBSTER *Suppl.* 1549/1 *Christian,* . . . one of a sect of Baptists; called also *Disciples of Christ.* **1898** NICHOLAS *Idyl of Wabash* 7 The religious sect variously known as 'Disciples,' 'Christians' and Campbellites.

***Christian,** *a.* **a.** Used in designating a group or division of the Reformed Presbyterian Church in the U.S. usually known as New Lights. **b.** (See quot. 1853.) — **(a) 1824** R. H. BISHOP *Hist. Church Ky.* 130 They have assumed to themselves the exclusive name of 'The Christian Church.' They have usually been called 'New Lights, or Stoneites.' **1837** PECK *New Guide* 364 Christian Sect, or Newlights, have become to a considerable extent, amalgamated with the 'Reformers' or 'Campbellites.' **(b) 1853** J. R. DIX *Transatlantic Tracings* 247 The societies of communist celibate ascetics, calling themselves 'Christian Friends,' but commonly designated 'Shakers.'

+Christian Connection. A religious sect that arose in the U.S. early in the 19th century. — **1844** RUPP *Relig. Denominations* 167 Sometimes in speaking of themselves as a body, they use the term Christian Connexion. **1889** P. BUTLER *Recoll.* 210 Geo. W. Hutchinson had been a preacher in what was known as the 'Christian Connection' in the New England States.

***Christianize,** *v. tr.* To convert (Indians) to Christianity.

1676 I. MATHER *Brief Hist.* (1862) 48 He was Christianized and baptiz'd and was a Preacher amongst the Indians. **1702** C. MATHER *Magnalia* (1853) I. 78 One of the Princes in the Massachusetts-Bay seemed hopefully to be christianized before he dyed. **1767** HUTCHINSON *Hist. Mass.* II. 137 The intelligence was brought . . . by some of the praying or christianized Mohawks. **1835** FEATHERSTONHAUGH *Canoe Voyage* I. 11 He told me that he proposed to 'christianize' all the Indians.

+Christian Science.

1. The religion founded by Mary Baker Eddy in 1866 and represented by the Church of Christ, Scientist.

The term was used, in a different connection, as early as 1850. (Cf. L. P. Powell *M. B. Eddy* 106.)

*c*1867 EDDY *Science of Man* (MS) 10 Jehovah cannot be understood so as to demonstrate Christian Science when interpreted through a belief or doctrine. **1875** — in *Lynn* (Mass.) *Transcript* 10 July, Christian Science, whereby the sick are healed. **1885** S. FOWLER in *Homilet. Rev.* X. 135/1 At the present time, in Boston and many other places, the so-called 'Christian Science,' or 'Metaphysical Healing,' is taking a strong hold in the communities. **1886** EDDY *Science & Health* (ed. 16) 11 In the year 1866 I discovered metaphysical healing, and named it Christian Science. **1890** *Ib.* (ed. 50) p. ix, Her first pamphlet on Christian Science was copyrighted in 1870; but it did not appear in print until 1876. **1906** L. BELL *C. Lee* 86, I don't think I care to investigate Christian Science.

2. Attrib. with *church, doctor, faith,* etc.

1895 *Outlook* 19 Jan., A great Christian Science church was dedicated in Boston on Sunday, the 6th inst. **1906** L. BELL *C. Lee* 123 Christian Science doctors just as selfless and single-minded as you. **1897** *Chicago Record* 13 Nov. 5/2 E. A. Kimball . . . will . . . read a paper, written by Mrs. N. [=M.] Eddy, founder of the Christian science faith. **1903** C. L. BURNHAM *Jewel* 183 It looks to me as if there was something those Christian Science folks know that the rest of us don't. **1889** A. DALY *Great Unknown* 31 She wants me to take her to a Christian Science matinée to-morrow. **1899** *Christian Science Jrnl.* XVII. 516 Finally a Christian Science practitioner was employed, and I was completely healed. *Ib.* 370, I received Christian Science treatment from one of Mrs. Eddy's students.

+Christian Scientist. An adherent to the teachings of Christian Science. — **1886** EDDY *Science & Health* (ed. 16) 107 A Christian Scientist dealing with the sick or the sinful and not improving the health of the one or the morals of the other is at fault. **1895** in L. P. Powell *M. B.*

Eddy 149 [Mr. Eddy was] the first individual who put onto a sign the words Christian Scientist. **1897** *Chicago Record* 13 Nov. 5/2 It is expected that over 2,000 Christian Scientists from other cities will attend the dedication. **1903** C. L. BURNHAM *Jewel* 155, I began to read out loud from 'Science and Health' to Anna Belle. She's a Christian Scientist, too.

∗ **Christmas.**

∗ **1.** The annual festival on December 25, commemorating the birth of Christ; December 25. See also quot. 1881.

1684 I. MATHER *Providences* (1890) ii. 40, I came in at Christmass, and went thence May 2d. **1839** LONGFELLOW *Hyperion* I. 14 It all happened . . . four years ago, come Christmas. **1881** TOURGEE *'Zouri's Christmas* i, The use of the word Christmas at the South is curiously contradistinguished from the same word at the North. At the North it means the twenty-fifth of December. At the South it may either mean that particular day or include the week succeeding.

+**b.** *ellipt.* 'A Christmas gift' (*Dial. Notes* I. 386).

2. Attrib. and comb. with *cake, fund,* etc.

1854 S. SMITH *Down East* 33 There was baking of pound cake, and plum cake, and sponge cake, and Christmas cake. **1898** *Kansas City Star* 18 December 2/4 Contributions to the Christmas fund for the children of St. Joseph's Female Orphan home . . . may be left at Altman's store. **1875** STOWE *We & Our Neighbors* 350 The brief, sudden little passage between Mr. St. John and Angelique among the Christmas-greens was . . . equivalent to an engagement. **1773** FITHIAN *Journal* I. 75 Ben staid last Night at Mr. Turburville's & got Home today about twelve from his Christmas Jaunt. **1685** SEWALL *Diary* I. 115 [There] was less Christmas-keeping than last year. **1854** S. SMITH *Down East* 49 These two cakes have each of 'em a Christmas ring in them; and whichever gets the slice that has the ring in it, will be married before the year is out. **1905** N. DAVIS *Northerner* 190 Men, busy with their Christmas shopping, paused, listened, edged away, and passed on. **1886** H. D. BROWN *2 College Girls* 237 You know you are coming to see me in the Christmas vacation.

+**Christmas berry.** *local.* An evergreen shrub having bright red berries (*Heteromeles arbutifolia*); the toyon or tollon. — **1897** SUDWORTH *Arborescent Flora* 235 *Heteromeles arbutifolia*. . . . Common names [include] . . . Christmas Berry (Cal.), Chamiso (Cal.), [etc.].

Christmas box. {1611–} A Christmas present.

1810 WEEMS *Letters* III. 29 Liberal allowance made to those . . . who take several copies of Washington and Marion for Christmas Boxes to their young relations. **1823** COOPER *Pioneers* xvi, So said my father when he gave me this packet to offer you as a Christmas-box.

Christmas gift.

1. A present given or received at Christmas.

1826 *Nat. Intelligencer* 23 Dec. 3/5 (*advt.*), Elegant Christmas Gifts. . . . Elegant miniature editions of Standard Works, . . . and a great variety of other new and interesting publications, suitable for Christmas and New Year's Gifts. **1856** M. J. HOLMES *L. Rivers* v. 49 Then came a bedstead, which Mrs. Livingston had designed as a Christmas gift to one of the negroes. **1869** TOURGEE *Toinette* (1881) 31 'A Christmas gift to Geoffrey Hunter!' said Mabel incredulously. **1881** — *'Zouri's Christmas* i, Marse Santy Claus allers comes roun' 'bout Christmas-time, wid a whole cartful ob Christmas gifs. **1898** *Kansas City Star* 18 Dec. 4/7 (*advt.*), Crown and Pinaud's [soaps], in fancy boxes, suitable for Christmas gifts.

+**2.** A form of greeting used on Christmas morning by those desiring presents.

[**1844** *Knickerb.* XXIII. 16 Threatening to catch him for a Christmas gift next morning, [she] disappeared up the stairs.] **1860** *Harper's Mag.* Dec. 133/1 We were aroused from our slumbers by the usual Christmas-morning salutation of 'Christmas gift, massa!' 'Christmas gift, mistis!' **1908** *Dialect Notes* III. 298 *Christmas gift*, a greeting on Christmas morning. The person who is caught, i.e., who is greeted first, is expected to give a present to the one who catches him. The custom is passing away.

‖**Christmas-gifting.** The practice of giving presents at Christmas. — **1853** KANE *Grinnell Exped.* 270 But even here that kindly custom of Christmas-gifting was not forgotten.

Christmas tree. A small evergreen tree set up at Christmas and decorated with candles or other lights, presents, etc. {1835–}

1865 *Atlantic Mo.* XV. 353 [They] held high festival around a wonderful Christmas-tree. **1875** STOWE *We & Our Neighbors* 359 She's going to be there when we get the Christmas-tree ready and tie on the things. **1900** E. A. DIX *Deacon Bradbury* 227 Of course we get Christmas trees up there. **1907** ANDREWS *Recoll.* 215 Christmas, as with us, was observed generally with presents and Christmas trees. **1916** EASTMAN *From Deep Woods* 105 It was planned to keep the Christmas tree standing in the chapel for a week.

‖**Chromatograph,** *v. tr.* To represent or do in colors. — **1859** HOLMES *Professor* viii, Having been photographed, and stereographed, and chromatographed, or done in colors.

+**Chromo,** *n.* [f. *chromo*lithograph {1860–}.] A picture printed in colors. Also attrib.

'It is claimed that the word "chromo" was coined in Boston, in 1864, by our honored fellow-citizen, Mr. Louis Prang' (*Bostonian Soc. Proc.* XVI. 26).

1869 *Republican Jrnl.* (Lawrence, Kans.) 20 March, Chromos, paintings, engravings and everything which adds to the ornamenting of a parlor are to be found at their store. **1870** *Scribner's Mo.* I. 46 Maps, charts, pretty chromos and lithographs, adorn the walls. **1880** *Harper's Mag.* Aug. 334/1 We . . . composed a jocose catalogue of chromos that decorated her walls. *Ib.* Dec. 144/2 A chromo copy of a great picture does not supersede painting. **1883** *Ib.* Aug. 482/1 Glancing around on the chromos, the new carpets, and the glittering white walls. **1886** HOWELLS *Minister's Charge* 152 There was a mirror on the wall, . . . a family-group photograph . . . and two chromos. **1889** 'MARK TWAIN' *Conn. Yankee* vii. 84, I had been used to chromos for years. *Ib.*, In East Hartford . . . you couldn't go into a room but you would find an insurance-chromo, or at least a three-color God-Bless-Our-Home over the door. **1890** E. B. CUSTER *Following Guidon* 253 Even in those days if we had chromos we were glad for . . . a poor picture even took away a little of the bare look. **1909** 'O. HENRY' *Roads of Destiny* 91, I'm no art critic, but it . . . looks like the worst kind of a chromo to me.

b. *To take* (or *contest*) *the chromo*, to 'take the cake'; to vie *with. colloq.*

1893 'MARK TWAIN' *£1,000,000 Bank-Note*, etc. 93 The full name . . . will be Mrs. Ambulinia Valeer Elfonzo. It takes the chromo. *Ib.* 255 With Chicago it contests the chromo for flatness of surface.

‖**Chromo,** *v. tr.* To reproduce in a chromo. — **1877** HARTE *Story of Mine* ix. 111 Something that could be afterwards lithographed, or chromoed.

Chronic, *n.* A chronic invalid, drunkard, etc. {1886–} — **1866** C. H. SMITH *Bill Arp* 33 But it give 'em a powerful scare and developed more rheumatics and chronics than was thought possible to exist in a limestone country. **1897** R. M. STUART *Simpkinsville* 96 Ef it wasn't for the chronics, I reckon you an' I'd have to give up practisin' an' go to makin' soap.

‖**Chronicle song.** A ballad on a historical subject. — **1853** BALDWIN *Flush Times Ala.* 149 He was the merriest . . . feller . . . and can sing more chronicle songs than one of these show fellers.

‖**Chrono-thermalist.** A medical practitioner whose system was based on time and heat. — **1864** T. L. NICHOLS *Amer. Life* I. 364 There are also physicians of every school. There are . . . hydropaths mild and heroic; chrono-thermalists, Thompsonians, [etc.].

∗ **Chrysanthemum.** Any one of various plants of the genus *Chrysanthemum* having large showy flowers; the flower of such a plant. {1798–} Also attrib.

1804 CUTLER in *Life & Corr.* II. 169 At Holt's Garden, procured a Chrysanthemum root for 12½ cents. **1852** *Horticulturist* VII. 54/2 This being the show night for Chrysanthemums, there were eight collections presented, in which were many of the choicest kinds. **1878** R. T. COOKE *Happy Dodd* 98 Sheaves of chrysanthemums shed their refined odor of bitter sweetness on the shelf in either room. **1899** GOING *Flowers* 39 That flower-aristocrat, the dishevelled and expensive chrysanthemum. **1902** L. RICHARDS *Mrs. Tree* 142 Here were plenty of flowers still, marigolds, coreopsis, and chrysanthemums.

∗ **Chub.**

∗ **1.** One of various river fishes of the cyprinoid or carp family.

1778 CARVER *Travels* 478 The Carp and Chub are much the same as those in England. **1814** MITCHILL *Fishes N.Y.* 459 Chub of New York. *Cyprinus oblongus*. . . . Lives in fresh streams and lakes like the sucker. **1857** HAMMOND *Northern Scenes* 147 The stream swarmed with chub and dace, a rare circumstance with the streams of this region [=upper New York]. *a***1862** THOREAU *Excursions* 31 The chub is a soft fish, and tastes like brown paper salted. **1884** in GOODE *Fisheries* I. 616 The species of this family known as 'Minnows,' 'Chubs,' 'Shiners,' and 'Dace' literally swarm in all of the fresh waters of the United States. **1889** *Cent.* 2129/1 *Fall-fish*, a cyprinoid fish, *Semotilus bullaris*, . . . also called *chub* and *silver chub*.

2. *local.* One of various other U.S. fish species, as the tautog or blackfish, the spot, and the black bass.

1842 [see CHUB SUCKER]. **1855** BAIRD in *Smithsonian Rep.* 340 The tautog, smooth black fish, or chub, . . . [is] caught off the steep banks, in the channel-ways and the thoroughfares. **1884** *Century Mag.* April 908/1 A black bass . . . becomes a 'chub' in Virginia. **1884** in Goode *Fisheries* I. 269 In New Jersey [the tautog is called] also 'Black-fish' . . . or 'Chub'; at the mouth of the Chesapeake 'Salt-water Chub.' *Ib.* 370 The Lafayette, or 'Spot,' *Liostomus xanthurus*, . . . is known . . . at Charleston, South Carolina, as the 'Chub.' *Ib.* 401 The Large-mouth [Black Bass is called] . . . in the Southern States, generally, 'Trout,' though on the Tar River of North Carolina it is called 'Chub.' **1890** MCALLISTER *Society* xxiii. 311 Menu of an old-fashioned Southern dinner: . . . Boiled fresh water Trout (known with us at the North as Chub).

+**3.** A Texan. *colloq.*

1869 *Overland Mo.* III. 129 For the Texan soubriquet 'Chub' I know of no explanation, unless it be found in the size of the Eastern Texans.

‖**4.** (See quotation.)

*a***1870** CHIPMAN *Notes on Bartlett* 81 *Chub*, . . . a round squash. Conn.

‖**Chubby.** A fresh water fish of the genus *Semotilus*. — **1820** RAFINESQUE in *Western Rev.* II. 239 Bigback Chubby. *Semotilus dorsalis*. . . . It is found in the Kentucky, and several other rivers.

+Chub eel. *local.* The American burbot, *Lota maculosa.* — **1884** GOODE *Fisheries* I. 236 The burbot . . . is called 'Chub-eel' . . . in Mohawk River, New York. *Ib.*, 'Chub-eel' is a mere off-hand name given to the species by a fisherman who supposed it to be a hybrid between an eel and a catfish.

+Chub mackerel. A small sea mackerel, *Pneumatophorus grex.* — **1814** MITCHILL *Fishes N.Y.* 422 Thimble eyed, bull eyed, or chub mackerel. *Scomber grex.* . . . Comes occasionally in prodigious numbers to the coast of New-York, in autumn. **1842** *Nat. Hist. N.Y., Zoology* IV. 102 The Fall Mackerel. . . . Thimble-eyed, Bull eyed or Chub Mackerel. **1884** GOODE *Fisheries* I. 303 The Chub Mackerel . . . closely resembles in general appearance the common Mackerel.

+Chub sucker. A fish belonging to one or other variety of sucker common in the eastern part of the U.S.; esp. the sweet sucker or creekfish, *Erimyzon sucetta.*

1817 C. A. LE SUEUR in *Acad. Nat. Sc. Phila. Jrnl.* 1 Ser. I. 93 *C[atostomus] gibbosus.* . . . This species I discovered in the river Connecticut, near Northampton, where it is named Chub Sucker. **1842** *Nat. Hist. N.Y., Zoology* IV. 193 The Brilliant Chubsucker, *Labeo oblongus*, . . . is a fish of much beauty. . . . It is familiarly known under the name of Chub, and Chubsucker. **1855** BAIRD in *Smithsonian Rep.* 341 The Horned Sucker, Chubsucker. . . . These . . . constitute almost the only cyprinoids of the fresh waters on our coast. **1859** BARTLETT 81 *Chub Sucker*, a seafish, otherwise called the Horned Sucker. **1884** in Goode *Fisheries U.S.* I. 614 The 'Chub Sucker' . . . is one of the most abundant and widely diffused of the Suckers.

+Chuck.[1] =WOODCHUCK. Also *Chuck of the wood.*

1781 PETERS *Hist. Conn.* (1829) 189 The woodchuck . . . when eating makes a noise like a hog, whence he is named Woodchuck, or chuck of the wood. **1809** *Mass. Spy* 8 Nov. (Th. p. 952), Then if to go further I was put in doubt By a Chuck at the mouth of a hole. *c*1845 PAULDING *Madmen All* 196 All out doors was full of . . . 'chucks, bear-meat, skunks, and other varmints. **1880** *Harper's Mag.* Sept. 586 'Hullo! there's a 'chuck,' shouted Mandy, and off he went . . . to wage war with a sober old woodchuck.

Chuck.[2] *slang.*

1. Food, provisions. {(Hotten) 1864–, *slang* and *dial.*}

1873 *Winfield* (Kansas) *Courier* 7 Aug. 3/1 Best 'chuck' at the Bradish House. **1883** 'MARK TWAIN' *Life on Miss.* lii, I wish i was nere you so i could send you chuck (refreshments) on holidays. **1901** *Munsey's Mag.* XXIV. 450/2 Nowadays the cowboy's knife is used principally for cutting 'chuck.' **1903** A. ADAMS *Log Cowboy* vii. 86 My peelers and I are . . . lining our flues with Lovell's good chuck. **1920** MULFORD *J. Nelson* 93 While I'm washin', you rustle th' chuck. **1920** HUNTER *Trail Drivers Texas* I. 51 The outfit consisted of a wagon loaded with chuck.

attrib. **1903** A. ADAMS *Log Cowboy* xviii. 280 He was riding the chuckline all right. **1905** — *Outlet* 16 A carpenter was then at work building chuck-boxes for each of the six commissaries.

+2. A meal or mealtime.

1890 RYAN *Told in Hills* 302 'Past chuck?' On being informed that the midday meal had been ended two hours before, [etc.]. **1901** — *Montana* 25 After 'chuck,' we'll go over and give you a nearer view of the tribe on the other shore. **1907** WHITE *Arizona Nights* 112 When the last man had returned from chuck, Homer made the dispositions for the cut.

+Chuck-a-luck. Also **chutter-luck, chuckle-luck, chuck-luck.** [Origin obscure.] A game played with three dice, the players betting on the numbers that will turn up.

1836 *Quarter Race Ky.* (1846) 24, I thought I'd make a rise on chuck-a-luck, but you prehaps never saw such a run of luck. **1843** J. H. GREEN *Exposure of Gambling* 90 Chutter-luck. This game is sometimes called sweat-cloth. . . . This game is played with three dice . . . and a box to throw them from. **1856** *Liberator* XXVI. 12 Leper and Doolin got into a quarrel over a game called 'chuckle luck.' **1865** T. KNOX *Camp-Fire* 489 At the other end of the table a party of gamblers, with twenty or thirty spectators, were indulging in 'Chuck-a-Luck.' **1882** *Century Mag.* April 884/2 He had the faculty of losing his money, and other people's money, . . . at all games of chance, from chuck-a-luck to brag. **1887** *Courier-Journal* 23 Jan. 16/4 'What is Chuck-a-luck?' 'Mercy alive! Didn't you ever see a lot of fellows mark off numbers 1–2–3–4–5–6, put the money on the numbers and throw dice, and the fellow's numbers turned up take the pot?' **1888** GRIGSBY *Smoked Yank* (1891) 106 Chuck-luck, faro, poker, . . . tricks and games of every variety were played and carried on openly. **1907** WHITE *Arizona Nights* x. 165 A man's so sick of himself by the time he gets this far that he'd play chuck-a-luck. **1916** WILSON *Red Gap* 246 There was chuck-a-luck and a crap game going.

attrib. **1845** HOOPER *Simon Sugg's Adv.* ix, An endless series of games of 'old sledge'; as well as the occasional exhibition of a chuck-a-luck table. **1873** BEADLE *Undevel. West* 94 We walk down to the 'chuck-a-luck' board. **1925** MULFORD *Cottonwood Gulch* 57 Chuck-a-luck gamblers.

‖**Chuckaway.** =CHUCK.[2] — **1873** *Newton Kansan* 20 Feb. 3/4 An Indian scout . . . asked first for chuckaway.

Chucker. **a.** *pl.* A game in which coins or objects shaped like them are tossed at a hole. **b.** (See quotation.) — **(a)** **1811** A. GRAYDON *Memoirs* (1846) 55, I never could boast my winning at marbles or chuckers. **(b)** **1830** J. F. WATSON *Philadelphia* 240 They pitched also 'chuckers'—a kind of pewter pennies cast by the boys themselves.

Chuck-full, *a.* Variant of CHOCK-FULL; entirely full. *colloq.* {1770–}

1834 C. A. DAVIS *Lett. J. Downing* 276 There were so many Committee folks in Washington, every tavern was chuck full. **1843** 'CARLTON' *New Purchase* I. 181 The sole labour of the attendants being to keep the plates 'chuckfull' of something. **1859** ELWYN *Glossary* 31 *Chuck* full, or, as it is more generally pronounced, *chock* full, . . . is also common there [=New Eng.]. **1886** STAPLETON *Major's Xmas* 24, I've got a mine chuck full of gold. **1902** HARBEN *Abner Daniel* 17 He believed it [the land] was chuck-full o' iron ore, soapstone, black marble, an' water-power. **1915** D. R. CAMPBELL *Proving Virginia* 37 The Jordans are so chuck full of the real thing they never have to think about it.

Chuck hole. A mudhole, rut, or depression in a road. {chock-hole *dial.* 1877–}

1847 WEBSTER 203/3 *Chuck-hole*, a steep hole in a wagon rut. *local.* **1860** GREELEY *Overland Journey* 272 It certainly is not a pleasure to ride, night and day, along such a stream with . . . the roads all gullied, and ground into chuck-holes. **1872** *Harper's Mag.* July 166/1 'Is the road any better beyond here?' . . . 'Wa'al there air some pretty bad chuck-holes, but I guess you can squeeze through.' **1883** BEADLE *Western Wilds* 589 Every new road that the stage company makes to avoid the dust and chuck holes is almost immediately appropriated by the freighters. **1887** J. KIRKLAND *Zury* 2 'Chuck-holes' is the expressive Western name for the short, sharp depressions which use makes in unworked country roads. **1909** STERNBERG *Life Fossil Hunter* 63 If we dozed off for a moment, a sudden lurch of the coach into a chuck-hole would break our heads against a post or a neighbor's head.

Chucklehead. {1731–} ‖A variety of clover. — **1784** *Mem. Academy* I. 473 *Trifolium.* . . . The indigenous species of this genus [include] . . . the woolly-headed clover, or chuckle-head.

+Chuck wagon. *W.* A wagon carrying provisions, cooking equipment, etc., for cowboys, harvest hands, etc.

1890 D'OYLE *Notches* 26 The sun blistered the paint upon the 'mess-box' behind the 'chuck-waggon.' **1907** WHITE *Arizona Nights* v. 91 We picked us each a tin cup and a tin plate from the box at the rear of the chuck wagon. **1913** BARNES *Western Grazing Grounds* 116 One can still find the old-time 'chuck wagon' and the great mess box with its hospitable lid and cranky cook. **1918** *Dialect Notes* V. 23 *Chuck-wagon*, a cooking-wagon that follows a gang of harvest hands about a great ranch. **1920** HUNTER *Trail Drivers Texas* I. 44 We drowned a horse hitched to the chuck wagon. **1923** J. H. COOK *On Old Frontier* 115 The simple life led on the range . . . away from chuckhouses and fancy chuck-wagons loaded with canned goods, [etc.].

‖**b.** A dining car or diner. *slang.*

1910 RAINE *B. O'Connor* 76, I see the chuck-wagon is toddling along behind us.

+Chuck-will's-widow. [Imitative.] A goatsucker found in the southern part of the U.S., *Antrostomus carolinensis.*

1791 BARTRAM *Travels* 154 (*note*), *Caprimulgus rufus* called chuck-will's-widow, from a fancied resemblance of his note to these words. **1812** WILSON *Ornithology* V. 65 Three species only, of this genus, are found within the United States; the Chuck-will's-widow, the Whip-poor-will, and the Night-hawk. **1831** AUDUBON *Ornith. Biog.* I. 274 The flight of the Chuck-will's-widow is as light as that of its relative, the well-known Whip-poor-will. **1867** *Atlantic Mo.* March 276/1 The strange 'chuck-will's-widow' droning his ominous note above my head. **1872** COUES *N.A. Birds* 180 Chuck-will's-widow. Singularly variegated with black, white, brown, tawny and rufous. **1884** CABLE *Dr. Sevier* liii, Now they heard the distant baying of house-dogs, now the doleful call of the chuck-will's-widow. **1894** B. TORREY *Fla. Sketch-Book* 96 Listening to the strange low chant of the chuck-will's-widow.

+Chufa. [Sp.] The earth almond, a cultivated species of sedge (*Cyperus esculentus*), producing small edible tubers; also, one of these tubers.

1856 BROWNE in *Trans. Amer. Inst. N.Y.* 605 Earth Almond, or Chufa, . . . from the south of Spain. . . . The tubers resemble in taste a delicious chestnut or cocoa nut, and like them; may be eaten raw or cooked. **1856** *Rep. Comm. Patents: Agric.* 259 Last season, I raised a patch of the 'Earth Almond,' or 'Chufa,' . . . each plant of which produced over one hundred tubers. **1874** *Dept. Agric. Rep. 1873* 281 He has found the chufa to be highly relished by hogs. **1879** *Home & Farm* (Louisville, Ky.) 15 My hogs had no corn. They had abundance of chufas with the run of potato pinder & pea fields.

+Chug, *n.* [Onomatopoeic.] A sudden dull or muffled sound. — **1894** *Outing* XXIV. 56/2 One weapon after another struck 'chug—chug—chug—chug,' while a flying furrow on the surface told [etc.]. **1897** *Ib.* XXX. 175/1, I accidentally cast myself into the pool with a sounding chug. **1902** *PMLA* XIX. 257 The 'chug' of the arrow as it buries itself in the target. **1904** E. RICKERT *Reaper* 335 No sound about him except the chug and splash of his own oars.

+Chug, *v. colloq.*

1. *tr.* To spur *up* or urge (a horse) forward.

1887 CUSTER *Tenting on Plains* 384 Come on, old lady! Chug up that old plug of yours; I've got one orderly.

2. *intr.* To go with a puffing or explosive noise.

1907 FIELD *Six-Cylinder Courtship* 59 An automobile chugged up to the station-house and stopped before the door. **1910** — *Sapphire Bracelet* 129 The little car chugged up to the hotel. **1921** PAINE *Comr. Rolling Ocean* 4 A small automobile came chugging along.

+Chum, *n.* [Origin obscure.]

1. The remains of menhaden after the oil has been pressed out.

1859 *Me. Bd. Agric. Rep.* IV. 182 Pogies will be caught for the chum and not for the oil. **1861** *Ib.* VI. 44 The chum . . . contains nearly the whole fertilizing portions of the fish. **1875** *Chicago Tribune* 27 Sept. 315 The chum, as that which remains after the oil is extracted is called, is sold for a fertilizer. **1879** *Bureau of Fisheries Rep.* V. 219 The fish-refuse enters our markets in several conditions. The following have come under my observation: 1. 'Crude stock,' 'green scrape,' 'chum,' [etc.].

2. Fish chopped up and used as bait or a means of attracting fish.

1872 T. LYMAN *6th Rep.* [*Mass.*] *Comm. Inland Fisheries* 25 When mackerel were cheap, the younger ones . . . were laboriously chopped up with a hatchet and thrown over as 'chum.' **1876** [see CHUM *v.* and CHUMMER *n.*]. **1889** *Cent.* 993/2 *Chum*, a bait, consisting usually of pieces of some oily fish, as the menhaden, commonly employed in the capture of bluefish.

attrib. **1876** *Fur, Fin, & Feather* Sept. 131 He carries a basket with . . . a 'chum-thrower' which may be described as a shovel with all the edges turned up.

+Chum, *v. intr.* To fish with chum; to attract fish by means of chum. — **1876** *Fur, Fin, & Feather* Sept. 131 The chummer's principal duty is to 'chum.' This performance consists in throwing out quantities of chum from the stand to the particular spot in the water where the fisherman will cast his line. **1897** *Outing* XXX. 259/1 His object now was to chum or draw the fish around us. *Ib.* 546/1 The captain and I have trolled and chummed for bluefish.

‖**Chummer.** One who uses chum in fishing. — **1876** *Fur, Fin & Feather* Sept. 131 The chummer cuts up bait . . . and thus manufactures the chum.

+Chumming. Taking fish with chum. — **1882** *Forest & Stream* XIX. 363 Chumming is much more sport, the fish then being captured with rod and reel. **1888** GOODE *Amer. Fishes* 106 Chumming in the Cuttyhunk and Newport style would doubtless be very effective.

+Chumpa. *S.* [?Amer. Indian.] A small bundle of pine kindling wood. — **1851** E. S. WORTLEY *Travels in U.S.* 136 We . . . saw numbers of the chumpa girls returning from the pine woods . . . so laden with the chumpa(pine) that they could hardly move. **1857** A. B. MEEK *Romantic Passages* 322 All are familiar with the soft quick, petitionary voice in which they exclaim 'chumpa,' as they offer their cheap burdens for sale.

+Chumpa girl. (See quot. 1851.) — **1851** E. S. WORTLEY *Travels in U.S.* 131 This morning we had a visit from two Indian chumpa girls. They are called so from carrying little fagots of pine-wood for sale. **1857** A. B. MEEK *Romantic Passages* 330 Let who will hereafter experiment upon Choctaw character, to discover whether these Chumpa-girls have not like affections with other people.

Chunk, *n.* [App. variant of *Chuck* in the same sense.]

1. A short, thick billet of wood. *colloq.* {1691, *dial.*}

1781 WITHERSPOON *Druid Papers* No. 7, *Chunks*, that is brands, half burnt wood. This is customary in the middle colonies. **1804** CLARK in *Lewis & C. Exped.* (1904) I. 56, I threw chunks and drove this snake off Several times. **1843** 'CARLTON' *New Purchase* I. 202 The seats were long benches with very ricketty limbs, . . . and double planks resting on rude chunks. **1879** *Harper's Mag.* July 205 Taking a seat on one of the driest of the fallen logs he took a large 'chunk' upright between his knees. **1898** CUSHMAN *Hist. Indians* 308 Then a huge pile of logs and chunks, previously prepared, were set on fire.

b. *transf.* and *fig.* A lump; a substantial piece, amount, or quantity *of* something.

1843 STEPHENS *High Life N.Y.* I. 14 There was long chunks o' glass hanging down. *Ib.* II. 58 She had on a short petticoat that showed a . . . considerable chunk of understandings. **1849** FOSTER *New York in Slices* 101 Now and then a small chunk of sentiment or patriotism or philanthropy is thrown in awkwardly among the crudities and immoralities of the scene. **1857** T. H. GLADSTONE *Englishman in Kansas* 46 If there's a dog-gauned Abolitionist aboard, . . . I'm the man to put a chunk o' lead into his wooly head, right off. **1873** BEADLE *Undevel. West* 334 Do we encounter silica, ochre, or small brittle chunks of galena? **1883** 'MARK TWAIN' *Life on Miss.* iii, Why, they hove it overboard, and it sunk like a chunk of lead. **1884** *Harper's Mag.* Aug. 389/2 Instead of almost shapeless chunks of mud . . . regular unburned bricks are made. **1887** *Ib.* Feb. 451/1 Having wrenched a chunk of greater or less length from its bed, he withdraws his head. **1897** S. HALE *Letters* 325 The weather was perfect, . . . fluffy white clouds with chunks of blue between. **1907** *Chicago Tribune* 8 May 7 (*advt.*), It's really ridiculous the way we've knocked chunks off these Spring overcoat prices.

+c. *Chunk of fire*, a small firebrand.

1834 A. PIKE *Sketches* 30, I threw away my chunk of fire. **1837** *S. Lit. Messenger* III. 86 One brought a chunk of fire. **1851** *Polly Peablossom* 16 After calling out for a chunk of fire . . . he dashed at once over into Alabama. **1856** P. CARTWRIGHT *Autobiog.* 215 He threw down his chunk of fire. **1876** 'MARK TWAIN' *Tom Sawyer* vi. 63 Mary, get me a silk thread, and a chunk of fire out of the kitchen. **1898** CUSHMAN *Hist. Indians* 273 A blazing chunk of fire.

ellipt. and *fig.* **1852** 'MARK TWAIN' in *Hannibal* (Mo.) *Journal* 16 Sept., [Man] contemplates Suicide. . . . He resolves to 'extinguish his chunk' by feeding his carcass to the fishes of Bear Creek. **1904** 'O. HENRY' *Heart of West* 148 You'll be a rich man, Ranse, when my chunk goes out.

+2. A strong, stocky horse. Also attrib.

1829 T. FLINT *G. Mason* 111 (Th.), Away scamper chunks, donkeys, mules, and negroes. *Ib.*, After an hour's prelude, in which these matters were settled, and a dozen chunk-races run. **1829** *Western Mo. Rev.* III. 180 It is a usage, not wholly disallowed, for the candidate to ride a race on a Kentucky 'chunk' for the amusement of the spectators. **1887** *Boston Herald* 12 Aug. (*Cent.*), For sale, 4 Morgan chunks. **1906** *Springfield Republican* 7 Feb. 2 (*advt.*), Pair gray farm chunks, 9 years, 2350 lbs. **1909** *Cent. Suppl.* 248/1 *Chunk*, specifically, a range-bred horse of the western United States, suitable for draft purposes.

3. A large clumsy piece of meat, bread, etc.

1833 CATLIN *Indians* I. 116 Chunks of this marrow-fat are cut off. **1837** PECK *New Guide* 122 The bosom of this dress sometimes serves as a wallet for a 'chunk' of bread. **1839** F. A. KEMBLE *Journal* 149 The consequence of this is, that four lumps or chunks are all that a whole sheep ever furnishes to our table. **1884** *Harper's Mag.* Dec. 95/1 Chunks of meat went sailing in all directions. **1888** *Milnor* (Dak.) *Teller* 18 May 6/5 Wait until the wedding-trip is over, and the last dismal chunk of bride's-cake has vanished from mortal view. **1904** 'O. HENRY' *Heart of West* 111 'Say,' interrupted Pete, rising with a chunk of corn bread in each hand, 'that was a dirty shame.'

transf. **1863** NORTON *Army Lett.* 137 The devils [camp lice] amuse themselves nights by biting out chunks and throwing them away.

+4. In the colloq. phrase *chunk of a. . . .* **a.** With *boy, lawyer, Negro.* A well-grown or promising specimen; a fair sample.

1821 DODDRIDGE *Backwoodsman & Dandy*, I was then a thumpin chunk of a boy, may be ten or a dozen years old. **1866** C. H. SMITH *Bill Arp* 115, I want to buy a nigger, and I had just as lief buy a chunk of a free nigger as any other sort. **1881** PIERSON *In the Brush* 240 One often meets . . . a 'chunk of a boy,' as his father called him. **1887** GEORGE *40 Years on Rail* 22 You're a pretty good chunk of a boy to be riding for half [fare]. **1894** *Congress. Rec.* 13 July 7445/1 'You are a lawyer.' . . . 'Yes, a chunk of a lawyer.'

b. With *horse, pony.* A thickset, compact horse. (Cf. 2.)

1827 *Western Mo. Rev.* I. 386 Himself ambling by her side upon a 'chunk' of a poney. **1841** *S. Lit. Messenger* VII. 219/1 Miranda, curbed in the vivacity of a little rough-coated, bob-tailed chunk of a Canadian poney. **1845** SIMMS *Wigwam & Cabin* 2 Ser. 83 He was . . . riding a short, heavy chunk of a horse. **a1846** *Quarter Race Ky.*, etc. 95, I can beat any man what wars har, for a mighty nice chunk of a poney, at any game of short cards. **1853** 'P. PAXTON' *Yankee in Texas* 44 Got a smart chunk of a pony thar. **1865** *Nation* I. 396, I'll get a piece of ground and a chunk of a hoss. **1871** DE VERE 454 'A tolerable chunk of a pony,' means in Southern and Western parlance, a cob.

c. With *fight.* A considerable encounter; a fray.

1833 J. HALL *Leg. West* 50 If a man got into a chunk of a fight with his neighbour, a lawyer would clear him for half a dozen muskrat skins. **1844** *Lexington Obs.* 29 May 2 We had a right smart 'little chunk' of a street fight this morning, between two of our 'tape and calico' gentry. **1848** W. E. BURTON *Waggeries* 12 But what took my cheese was the parson's tellin' us abeout tew fellows as got up the biggest chunk of a fight.

d. (See quotations.)

1822 J. WOODS *English Prairie* 185 A hog of two hundred lbs. weight is here called a fine chunk of a fellow. **1883** ZEIGLER & GROSSCUP *Alleghanies* 88 He lives in a poor chunk of a cabin over in them woods.

+Chunk, *v. colloq.*

1. *tr.* =CHINK *v.* Also with *up.*

1782 L. Summers *Ann. S.W. Va.* (1929) 761 Ordered that the Clerk of this Court hire some persons to chunk and daub the Courthouse. **1817** FORDHAM *Narr. Travels* 143 They [= cabins] are to be chunked, doors to be cut out. **1818** M. BIRKBECK *Lett. Illinois* 34 (Th.), The intervals between the logs 'chunked,' that is, filled in with slips of wood. **1824** DODDRIDGE *Notes* 137 They made billets for chunking up the cracks between the logs of the cabin.

2. *fig.* To cut or break into chunks.

1834 C. A. DAVIS *Lett. J. Downing* 166, I'll give you my notions . . . and leave you to slice it or chunk it as best suits you.

3. To throw at or pelt, esp. with chunks of wood; to knock *down* or *out* by pelting or striking with something hard.

1835 SIMMS *Partisan* 425 His dog stole my bacon . . . and when I chunked the varmint, the nigga gin me sass. **1841** *S. Lit. Messenger* VII. 40/2 Uncle Daniel, there's Louis chunking down the haws. **1853** 'P. PAXTON' *Yankee in Texas* 116 When man or boy, biped or quadruped, bird or beast is pelted, the unfortunate recipient of projectile favors is said to be rocked, unless indeed wood be put in requisition, and then he is chuncked. **1856** *Harper's Mag.* XII. 161/2 She handed her entrapped escort a stone. 'Here, Sammy, chunk your foot out with this!' **1871** DE VERE 188 In the South . . . they say: 'I'll chunk him,' meaning that they will throw a clod of earth or a stick of wood at some animal. **1886** J. C. HARRIS in *Century Mag.* Jan. 426/1 What could 'a' possessed you to be a-chunkin' ole Blue that away? **1898** — *Tales of Home Folks* 11 Why, honey, . . . you've let the niggers chunk my dogs till they are no manner account.

1906 F. LYNDE *Quickening* 253, I didn't believe hit that night when he r'ared and took on so to me and 'lowed to chunk me with a rock.

4. To feed (a fire) with chunks of wood; to mend, to rake *up* or bring together the embers of (a fire).

1840 *S. Lit. Messenger* VI. 398/2 Chunk the fire, Charles, and see if you cannot make it burn better. **1850** GARRARD *Wah-To-Yah* iv. 65 Smith kept the squaws of the lodge 'chunking' up the fire. **1902** A. MACGOWAN *Last Word* 15 The fire in the engine was, in Southern parlance, 'chunked up.'

5. (See quotation.)

1905 *Forestry Bureau Bull.* No. 61, 33 *Chunk*, to clear the ground with engine or horses, of obstructions which can not be removed by hand. *To chunk up*, to collect and pile for burning the slash left after logging.

Chunk, *adv.* [Imitative.] With a sound suggestive of the syllable *chunk*. — **1843** STEPHENS *High Life N.Y.* I. 40 The Dutch feller kept a opening his mouth, and once in a while a word would come out full chunk, right in t'other's face. **1850** NORTHALL *Yankee Hill* 40 The door flew in and I flew out, all dripping with custard, bang agin Nance, chunk agin Sal Barton. **1852** STOWE *Uncle Tom* viii, The ice went crack! c'wallop! cracking! chunk!

+**Chunk bottle.** *S.* A stout, squat bottle. — **1845** SIMMS *Wigwam & Cabin* 2 Ser. 146 Returning towards nightfall to the camp, Mingo brought with him a 'chunk-bottle' of whiskey. **1852** *Florida Plant. Rec.* 70 Poor of a Chunck bottle full of the solution and drench your Mule with it While it is warm.

Chunk cherry. ?Variant of CHOKECHERRY. — **1886** ROOSEVELT in *Outing* May 134 We descended . . . into a smooth open valley, through whose bottom extended a dry water course, filled up with a dense growth of wild plums, ash and chunk cherries.

+**Chunked,** *a. colloq.*

1. Plump, thickset, chunky.

1843 STEPHENS *High Life N.Y.* I. 115 She had on a great loose . . . gown, that made her seem twice as chunked as she used to. *Ib.* II. 96 She held up her two chunked hands. **1847** HOWE *Ohio Hist. Coll.* 432 He was a small 'chunked' man, quick and restless in his motions and conversation. **1883** HARTE *Poetical Wks.* 294 For you know I am 'chunkèd' and clumsy, as she says are all boys of my size. **1906** H. FITZGERALD *Sam Steele's Adv.* 220, I was gettin' altogether too chunked and fat.

2. Impudent. *S.W.*

1853 'P. PAXTON' *Yankee in Texas* 227 By Ned, says he, if it aint that owdacious critter of Miss Mash's, a helpin' hisself in broad daylight; . . . that's putty chunked. **1859** BARTLETT 82 Any person who is impudent or bold, at the South-west, is said to be chunked.

3. Plastered, daubed, chinked.

1857 D. H. STROTHER *Virginia Illust.* 206 The old homestead, with its chunked and daubed walls.

+**Chunker.** (See quot. 1887.) — **1887** *Century Mag.* XXXIV. 488/1 The majority were empty coal-boats,—'chunkers' from Mauch Chunk, or 'Skukers' from 'Schuylkill Haven.' **1893** *Dial. Notes* I. 329 *Chunker*, coal boat used on the canal.

+**Chunkey.** Also **chunké, -kee, chungke.** [App. of Ind. origin.] (See quot. 1907.)

1775 ROMANS *Nat. Hist. Florida* 77 When growing up, they use wrestling, running, heaving and lifting great weights, the playing with the ball two different ways, and their favourite game of *chunké*, all very violent exercises. **1775** ADAIR *Indians* 401 The warriors have another favourite game, called *Chungke;* which, with propriety of language, may be called 'Running hard labour.' . . . Only one, or two on a side, play at this ancient game. **1871** DE VERE 27 Later researches have led to the discovery that Chunkee was the Indian name of a game played with a flat, round stone and a pole about eight feet long. **1907** HODGE *Indians* I. 298/1 *Chunkey*, the name commonly used by the early traders to designate a man's game formerly popular among the Gulf tribes and probably general in the S., E. of the Mississippi. It was played with a stone disk and a pole which had a crook at one end. The disk was rolled ahead, and the object was to slide the pole after it in such a way that the disk would rest in the curve of the crook when both came to a stop.

Chunkhead. =COPPERHEAD 1. —**1818** *Science* I. 84 *Scytalus cupreus* or Copper-head Snake . . . is known by a variety of names in different parts of the State of New-York: . . . *copper-head, copper-snake, chunk-head*, [etc.]. **1842** *Nat. Hist. N.Y., Zoology* III. 54 The Copper-head. . . . In other districts, it is called Copper-belly, Red Viper, Deaf Adder, and Chunk-head.

Chunky, *a.* Also **chunkey.** *colloq.* [f. CHUNK *n.*] Thickset; stocky in build. Also *chunky made.* {1856, *dial.*}

Orig. and still chiefly applied to persons. App. first widely used in descriptions of runaway slaves and bond servants.

1751 *N.J. Archives* XIX. 95 A short, chunkey, well set fellow, of a red complexion. **1754** *Penna. Gaz.* 8 Aug. 3/1 Run away. . . . A native Irish servant girl, . . . chunky and well-set, short legs, and pretty thick. **1775** *Ib.* 27 Sept. 3/3 Run away, . . . an Irish servant Girl, . . . of a short chunky stature. **1776** *Md. Journal* 21 Aug. (Th.), Deserted: . . . Matthew Murray, a well set chunkey fellow. **1779** *N.J. Archives* 2 Ser. III. 73 The other named Mark, about 5 feet 5 inches high, 24 years old yellow and chuncky. **1807** *Republican* (Savannah, Ga.) 10 March 4/1 He is full-faced, fat, and chunky. **1830** R. C. SANDS *Writings* II. 221 She was, as to person, what is called chunky. **1833** J. HALL *Leg. West* 12 (Th.), Dennie . . . once amused himself by criticising an advertisement of a man who had stolen 'a chunky horse'; and with such a lesson before our eyes we should hardly venture upon a chunky young man for a hero. **1841** *S. Lit. Messenger* VII. 525/1 He was a low, chunky, hardy looking person. **1858** *N.Y. Tribune* 2 March 2/5 Her pony, a chunky piece of Delaware horse flesh. **1860** GREELEY *Overland Journey* 94 On this ant-hill sits the proprietor—a chunky little fellow. **1890** *Harper's Mag.* Dec. 146/2 Right on top I was goin' to put Pely's little chunky, leather cover Bible. **1917** MATHEWSON *Sec. Base Sloan* 17 The proprietor was a short chunky youth. — **1783** *Md. Gaz.* 29 Aug. 4/1 Ran away . . . a Negro Wench named Jenny, she is . . . chunky made, a yellow cast. **1787** *Md. Journal* 21 Dec. (Th.), Ran away: . . . Negro Jupiter . . . thick and chunky made.

+**Chunk yard.** A square enclosure in which Indians played chunkey. Also transf. — **1791** BARTRAM *Travels* 520 Chunk yard, a term given by the white traders, to the oblong four square yards, adjoining the high mounts and rotundas of the modern Indians. **1860** THOREAU *Letters* (1865) 189 That memorable stone 'chunk yard.'

* **Church,** *n.*

* **1.** An organized group of Christian believers of the same faith and practice.

For the distinction between *church* and *congregation* mentioned in quot. 1685 see the latter word.

1631 *Mass. Bay Rec.* I. 87 Noe man shalbe admitted to the freedome of this body polliticke, but such as are members of some of the churches within the lymitts of the same. **1640** J. ENDECOTT in *Winthrop P.* 145, I think the church & all that heard mee will cleare mee of the things layd to my chardge. **1670** J. ELIOT *Brief Narrative* 3 There was a meeting at Maktapog . . . to gather a Church among the Indians. **1685** SEWALL *Diary* I. 94 This day, Augt. 28 is a Church meeting at which tis consented that persons may be taken in, the Church only being present, and not the Congregation. **1791** *N. Eng. Hist. & Gen. Reg.* XXVII. 398 Now Ch[urc]h[e]s in N.E. are not bodies corporate, therefore can have no poor. **1831** J. FOWLER *Tour New York* 67 The body of professors assembling, and not the building, is usually understood by the term church here. **1864** NICHOLS *Amer. Life* I. 64 In America, every town of five or six thousand people is likely to have five or six different religious societies, called churches.

* **2.** A building in which religious services are regularly held; a meetinghouse.

Church in the U.S. has been from early times applied to all places of worship despite some efforts to restrict it to those of the Episcopalians.

1640 *Bay Psalm Book* (*title-page*), The necessity of the heavenly Ordinance of singing Scripture Psalmes in the Churches of God. **1643** *New Eng. First Fruits* II. v. 21 [We have] built 30. or 40. Churches, and more Ministers houses. **1749–51** FRANKLIN *Elec. Exper.* 62 May not the knowledge . . . be of use to mankind, in preserving houses, churches, ships, &c.? **1810** J. LAMBERT *Travels thro' U.S.* III. 95 In the cities, those [places] appropriated to the episcopal form of worship are always called churches. **1816** PICKERING 60 *Church.* This word . . . is generally used in New England, to denote the places of worship of the *Episcopalians*, as they are here called. **1830** *Mass. Spy* 20 Oct. (Th.), 'The editor . . . dislikes the practice of calling meeting-houses churches.' We never call them so. **1835** H. C. TODD *Notes* 39 All places of public worship, in New York state, are called churches, but in most others, meeting-houses or chapels. **1841** BUCKINGHAM *Amer., N. States* I. 46 The Episcopalian churches, and the chapels of other denominations, (though all are called churches here,) are the same in this respect. **1846** E. WAYLEN *Reminiscences* 49 The old New England 'meeting houses' . . . or 'churches' as they are beginning to be called in the cities and towns of America, though the term as applied to buildings was repudiated by the congregationalists till lately. **1856** GOODRICH *Recoll.* I. 193 It is not till within the last ten years that the word church has been popularly applied to all places of worship. **1870** NOWLAND *Indianapolis* 176 'Churches,' said the man; 'do you mean meeting houses?'

* **3.** Religious services held in church.

1724 *New-Eng. Courant* 23–30 March 1/2, I can speak for my self and most of my Faculty, that we are of a Catholick Spirit, and can attend upon our Employers either to Church or Meeting. **1865** A. D. WHITNEY *Gayworthys* xli, Say came round in the rain, when church was over. **1898** PAGE *Red Rock* 137 To which proposal, made in the aisle after church, when the weekly levee was held, [etc.].

4. Attrib. and comb. with *aisle, bell, Bible, book*, etc.

1843 *Knickerb.* XXI. 327 It is an interesting spectacle to witness the air he assumes when taking the lead up the church aisle. **1702** SEWALL *Diary* II. 70 Heard the church [Kings Chapel] Bell ring for Capt. Crofts. **1703** *N.C. Col. Rec.* I. 570 There being three church Bibles intended for this Country one whereof belongs to this precinct. **1791** *Wheeley's Baptist Ch. Min.* July (N.C. Univ. MSS.), A refferance being on the Church Book Concerning Brother John Morpheys Neglect of Meeting, he appear'd and gave Sattisfaction. **1862** NORTON *Army Lett.* 81 There are calls 'To Strike Tents,' 'To Assemble,' . . . 'Officers Call,' 'Church Call,' etc. **1648** *Platform Church-Discipline* (1772) 5 We refer ourselves to the platform of church-discipline, agreed upon by this present assembly. **1865** *Atlantic Mo.* XV. 681 That was for my church-dress, first communion, you know. **1881** STODDARD *E. Hardery* 268 There was no peril of the widow becoming an object of 'church help.' **1639** *Mass. H. S. Coll.* 4 Ser. VI. 101 Synce my last I haue nothing to certifye you but what fell out the last day of the last weeke in our congregation at a church-meeting. **1639** *New Haven Col. Rec.* 17 Church members onely shall be free burgesses. **1781** PETERS *Hist. Conn.* (1829) 48 The Minister should be the judge of the qualifications for church-membership. **1833** *Trial E. K. Avery* 28 My impression was that Rev. Mr. Avery, in Bristol, was a Church minister (Episcopal,) not a Methodist clergyman. **1832** WILLIAMSON *Maine* II. 687 Church Organs and even Pianos, were rare instruments, till within a short period prior to the Separation. **1898** WESTCOTT *D. Harum* 298 Mrs. Bixbee perused, with rather perfunctory diligence, the columns of her weekly church paper. **1666** *Conn. Public Rec.* II. 55 Vnto whom shal such persons repaire that are greiued at any Church process or censure, or whether they must acquiesce in the Churches sentence. **1883** *Harper's Mag.* Sept. 634/2 Half a dozen different church relief societies are relieving hundreds of the same persons at the same time. **1644** R. WILLIAMS *Bloudy Tenent* (1867) 91 Therefore at last also this Rejecting ... of him from their Church-societie. **1868** *Amer. Naturalist* II. 489 We have captured the 'Barn Owl' ... in a high church steeple. **1900** DIX *Deacon Bradbury* 13 His pa's been church treasurer f'r more 'n twenty year. *Ib.* 44, 'I wonder what he was there for?' 'Can't imagine. Church-trustee business, I reckon.' **1722** *New-Eng. Courant* 15–22 Oct. 1/2 Whether this Gentleman ought not to be out of Charity with his Wife for turning Church-Woman, who was a profess'd Dissenter.

* **Church,** *v.* +*tr.* To subject to church discipline.

1829 *Western Mo. Rev.* III. 114 It is notorious, that a woman was churched there [N.E.], for cutting off the ends of the fingers of her gloves, and exposing the tips of her dainty and delicate fingers. **1843** STEPHENS *High Life N.Y.* I. 55 Jest tell him, the next time he threatens to church you for what I'm doing down here in York, ... you'll 'stop his supplies.' **1901** HARBEN *Westerfelt* x. 136 He ... said some'n about folks bein' churched in his settlement fer the mistreatment o' widows. **1902** WILSON *Spenders* xii. 132 Only I hope the First M.E. Church of Montana City never hears of her outrageous cuttin's-up. ... They'd have her up and church her, sure.

‖**Church-burner.** App. a humorous variant of BARN-BURNER. — **1856** *Congress. Globe* 9 Jan. 187/1 We see the good-natured gentleman from Philadelphia voting ... with those whom he has called 'Church-burners.'

Church covenant. *Obs.* {*c*1640} A statement of the doctrines, practices, etc., which the members of a particular church agree to hold; faithfulness or devotion to it.

1636 *Springfield Rec.* I. 156 We purpose to Joyne in Church Covenant to walke in all the ways of Christ. **1646** T. E. EDWARDS *Gangræna* 99 Mr. E. ... brought in the Covenant of Abraham and Asa 2 Chron. 15. Ezek. 16. to prove his Church-Covenant. **1654** JOHNSON *Wonder-w. Prov.* 178 It is the duty of the Magistrates ... to be present ... to prevent the disturbance might follow in the Commonwealth by any, who under pretence of Church-Covenant, might bring in againe those cursed opinions that caused such commotion. **1670** I. MATHER *Life R. Mather* 85 The Discourse about the Church-Covenant ... Mr. Mather was the sole Author of.

+**Churchers.** 'A body of Indians living E. and N.E. of the white settlements in New England in 1634. ... Not the Praying Indians, as the period is too early' (Hodge *Indians* I. 299/1). — **1634** WOOD *New Eng. Prospect* II. i. 56 The Indians to the East and North east, bearing the name of Churchers, and Tarrenteenes.

+**Church fair.** A festival at which articles are sold for the benefit of a church.

1872 *Newton Kansan* 5 Sept. 4/1 At a certain church-fair, a set of Cooper's works was promised to the individual who should answer a set of conundrums. **1890** *Congress. Rec.* 8 May 4343/2 Certain entertainments and church fairs, which I have attended, when the admission was free. **1907** MULFORD *Bar-20* 63 All kinds of excitement except revival meetings and church fairs.

Churchgoer. One who attends church. {1687–}

1859 STOWE *Minister's Wooing* iv, Mrs. Jones was a church-member, a regular church-goer. **1872** *Newton Kansan* 5 Dec. 3/5 We have read a story of a steady old church-goer. **1883** *Harper's Mag.* Sept. 645/2 Colonel W— was not much of a church-goer. **1898** WESTCOTT *D. Harum* 282, I wa'n't a very reg'lar churchgoer.

* **Churchgoing,** *n.* Attendance at church.

1840 COOPER *Pathfinder* ix, You think the gal will consent to quit all her beloved settlement usages, and her visitin's, and her church-goin's. **1865** *Atlantic Mo.* XV. 252 A regular calling in the week and customary church-going on Sunday. **1882** HOWELLS *Modern Instance* iii, The habit of church-going was ... strong and universal in Equity.

Churchgoing, *a.* Given to attending church. {1712–} — **1844** *Lowell Offering* IV. 148 Yes, Lowell is a church-going place. **1848** *Knickerb.* XVIII. 309 Mrs. Miranda Meeks and several other church-going 'ceruleans of the second sex' had a tea-party. **1891** WILKINS *New Eng. Nun* 107 They had all been church-going people.

***Church house.** ‖**a.** A parsonage. +**b.** (See quotation.) — **(a)** **1881** *Harper's Mag.* Jan. 225/1 Let us stop at the church-house a moment and see Miss Lois. **(b)** **1889** *Cent.* 995/1 *Church-house,* ... a building in which to rest, keep warm, eat lunch, etc., between the services of the church on Sunday; a Sabbath-day house. (U.S.)

+**Church lot.** A lot owned by a church.

1646 *Suffolk Deeds* II. 147 Sayd lot & parcell of land lyeth betweene the Church lot yt was once Mr. Tillyes [etc.]. **1754** *Ga. Col. Rec.* VI. 436 The Lotts will be One hundred and twenty by eighty Feet, except ... the Church Lotts, which will be One Hundred and eighty by two-hundred feet. **1846** WILEY in *Indiana Mag. Hist.* XXIII. 327 A valuable addition to the church lot for a site on which to build a parsonage. **1857** C. VAUX *Villas* 302 The bay-window in the library ... would give a desirable relief to the straight, uninteresting wall adjoining the church lot.

+**Church-maul,** *v. tr.* (See quotations.) — *a***1870** CHIPMAN *Notes on Bartlett* 83 *Church-maul,* To.—To call to account, to discipline, by ecclesiastical methods.—N. E., vulgar.

+**Church session.** [Cf. Sc. *kirk-session,* 1717–.] (See quots. 1789, 1832.) — **1789** MORSE *Amer. Geog.* 268 The church session ... consists of the minister or ministers and elders of a particular congregation. **1832** WILLIAMSON *Maine* II. 694 There are four ecclesiastical bodies in the polity of this denomination [Presbyterians]. The first and lowest is the Church-session, which consists of the minister and twelve select members, denominated ruling elders or deacons. **1851** *Knickerb.* XXXVII. 70/1 Set me down for two more bottles ... and charge it to the church-session, and send the bottles, postage free.

+**Church sociable, social.** A social gathering of church members and their friends.

(a) **1876** 'MARK TWAIN' *Tom Sawyer* v, At church 'sociables' he was always called upon to read poetry. **1883** *Century Mag.* May 156/1 The leading 'ladies' of such towns, even if their leadership has more to do with church sociables [etc.] **1889** *Harper's Mag.* April 747/2 One would be in another world, and forget ... church sociables, and the wiggling village gossip. **1898** DELAND *Old Chester Tales* 48 He went to church, and slept heavily during the service; but he never went to the church sociables. **1902** LORIMER *Lett. Merchant* 118 At the church sociables he used to hop around among them.

(b) **1882** *Harper's Mag.* Jan. 318/2 At a church 'social' ... the faithful shepherd of the flock observed ... some simple devices for the entertainment of the young people present. **1888** *Milnor* (Dak.) *Teller* 18 May, [To] tackle a wash-tub as quickly as a church-social. **1891** EGGLESTON in *Century Mag.* Feb. 556 Hilbrough was left in doubt as to whether all the contempt was intended for the church socials in Degraw street. **1925** BRYAN *Memoirs* 450, I find his diversions to have been ... an occasional church social.

* **Churchwarden.** An officer (usu. of an episcopal church) who has charge of the finances of a church and other temporal matters.

1619 *Va. House of Burgesses* 13 The Ministers and Church wardens shall seeke to prevente all ungodly disorders. **1671** *Brookhaven Rec.* 40 William Satterly is to be in the place of a church warden for this present yere, for to see the minister's Raetes be brought in an paied. **1705** BEVERLEY *Virginia* IV. 28 The Busness of these Church-Wardens, is to see the Orders, and Agreements of the Vestry perform'd; to collect all the Parish Tobacco's, and distribute it to the several Claimers. **1773** *Ann. S. W. Virginia* 187 Ord[ered] that the church wardens bind out John Simpson, orphan of Andw. Simpson. **1875** STOWE *We & Neighbors* 117 The gorgeous, many-colored lights streamed silently the while through the stained windows, turning the bald head of one ancient church-warden yellow. **1887** EGGLESTON in *Century Mag.* April 909/1 We find the Goose Creek parish church in South Carolina [*c*1774] setting apart in perpetuity the front pews of the middle row for the church-wardens and vestrymen and their successors forever.

Church watch. *Obs.* Spiritual oversight exercised by a church. — **1648** *Platform Church-Discipline* (1772) 47 These church members that were so born, or received in their childhood, ... are also under church-watch. **1666** *Conn. Pub. Rec.* II. 54 Whether the adult seed of visible beleiuers not cast out be not true members and the subjects of Church watch. **1702** MATHER *Magnalia* (1853) I. 241 They did more generally ... take in their children, as under the churchwatch with themselves.

* **Churchyard.** A yard or enclosure surrounding, or adjacent to, a church, commonly used as a place of burial.

1622 'MOURT' *Relation* 49 One part ... was incompassed with a large Palazado, like a Church-yard. **1745** J. MACSPARRAN *Dairy* 24, I preached his Funeral Sermon to a great Assembly of negro's in the ch. & interred him in ye ch. yard. **1825** NEAL *Bro. Jonathan* III. 142 When he first appeared before Olive Montgomery, in the church-yard. **1848** E. JUDSON *Mysteries N.Y.* IV. 53 Bury her and me in the lower corner, back from the street, of — church yard. *a***1886** E. DICKINSON *Works* (1924) 185 A bird broke forth and sang, ... And shook his throat Till all the churchyard rang.

* **Churn.** Also †**churne, cherne.** A household vessel in which milk or cream is churned to make butter.

1641 *Conn. Rec.* I. 444 A Inuentory of the goods of Richard Lyman deceased [includes] ... a Churne & meat in it. **1650** [see CHEESEFAT]. **1783** E. PARKMAN *Diary* 300 A Meal Chest & churn. **1850** S. WARNER *Wide, Wide World* xxxv, He was ordered to take the churn and bring the butter. **1883** WILDER *Sister Ridnour* 117 When we were little, we naturally delighted in caring for our dolls, ... tea-set, ... and enjoyed even the wash-tub, dust-pan, and churn.

attrib. **1788** FRENEAU *Misc. Works* 371 She would have killed the parish schoolmaster with the churn-stick. **1887** FREDERIC *Seth's Brother's Wife* 319, I think it's a pesky shame ... to make a girl wag this old churn-dash till her arms are ready to drop off.

Churn-dasher. The dasher which agitates the milk in a churn. Also fig. {churn-dash, 1870–}

1845 C. M. KIRKLAND *Western Clearings* 101 Yet their hands had handled the churn-dasher too often to be very satiny in the palm. *c*1850

WHITCHER *Bedott P.* xxiv. 291 Here the churn-dasher come down with such a vengeance, that the cream spirted up. **1873** *Winfield* (Kansas) *Courier* 17 July 1/4 Every time I think of you my heart flops up and down like a churn dasher. **1910** C. HARRIS *Eve's Husband* 196 Once you . . . become the noble churn-dasher of the multitude.

Churning day. The day on which a housewife regularly churns. — **1891** CHASE & CLOW *Industry* II. 103 When all the cream has been skimmed off, and enough of it taken for breakfast and tea, and home use, the rest is put aside until 'churning day.' **1900** DIX *Deacon Bradbury* 16, I'd ought t' help 'Mandy with th' dishes. . . . It's churnin'-day.

+**Churro.** *S.W.* [Sp.] The coarse-wooled sheep of Mexico. — **1889** *Cent.* 996/3 [The] *churro*, . . . used extensively in crossing with the merino, in Texas, northern Mexico, California, etc.

+**Chute,** *n.* Also †**chutte.** [F.]

In U.S. this form is widely used in place of Eng. *shoot*.

1. A fall or rapid in a river; a narrow, rocky, or precipitous channel or passage. Also transf.

1806 DUNBAR & HUNTER *Observ. Voy.* in *Mess. & Rep.* 141 About four miles below the 'chuttes,' (falls) they, from a good observation, found the latitude. *Ib.* 142 Immediately above the chuttes, the current of the water is slow. **1832** *Louisville Directory* 92 Here, on an island in the midst of the rapids of the river (or chutes, as they are termed, from the French), . . . the few adventurous families who accompanied Clarke, made their first crop of corn. **1836** J. HALL *Stat. West* 40 The bars of the second class are composed of fine gravel . . . and occur . . . at the lower junction of the chutes formed by the islands. **1847** LONGFELLOW *Evangeline* II. 90 Now through rushing chutes . . . they swept with the current. **1852** E. BENNETT *Mike Fink* 13 'All clear now, Deb,' said Mike. 'Take the chute and run her through.' **1864** *Congress. Globe* 19 April 1735/2 The draws are to be constructed at the head of two chutes and there is only one chute through which boats can be passed under [ordinary] circumstances. **1864** NICHOLS *Amer. Life* I. 172 Many of these bends may be avoided at high water, by taking the cross cuts, called 'running a *chute*,' when the whole country for twenty miles on each side is submerged. **1882** *Harper's Mag.* Aug. 329/1 In its [*sc.* the Wisconsin River's] northern portion, too, it is remarkable for its beauty, . . . pouring in its downward passage over chutes and falls of gneiss and granite. **1908** WHITE *Riverman* iv. 30 Immediately below Reed's dam ran a long chute strewn with boulders, which was alternately a shallow or a stretch of white water according as the stream rose or fell.

b. A road, path, or way.

1834 *S. Lit. Messenger* I. 142, I can tell you a chute that's a heap shorter than the road you talk of taking. **1873** BEADLE *Undevel. West* 564 On the steepest part he took the wrong chute, pulling up his burro just in time to avoid his plunging head first into a ravine.

fig. **1860** *Baltimore Patriot* Sept., The Douglas and Breckinridge men . . . are rushing to Lincoln with a perfect stampede. Besides this, the Bell men are also taking the same chute every day.

2. A sluice, trough, or flume by means of which logs are passed through a dam or down a precipitous descent.

1878 *Lumberman's Gazette* 18 Dec. 426 The gates [of the dam] . . . are opened, the logs are run through the chute, and sufficient water is furnished to carry them below. **1897** BRODHEAD *Bound in Shallows* 154 No hauling or such; the river just waiting to freight the sticks to your chute. **1903** WHITE *Forest* viii. 95, A dozen rivermen, one after the other, would often go through a chute of a dam standing upright on single logs.

b. A structure enabling fish to pass a dam in a stream.

1871 *Ohio Laws* LXVIII. 15 An act to provide for the erection and maintenance of 'chutes' for the passage of fish over the dams. **1875** KNIGHT 874/2 It may consist of a chute with a sinuous track for diminishing the velocity and assisting the passage of the fish to the level above the dam.

3. An inclined plane, trough, or slide used in conveying grain, ore, etc., to a lower level.

1872 'MARK TWAIN' *Roughing It* lii. 380 Under the bins are rows of waggons loading from chutes and trap-doors in the bins. **1876** RAYMOND *8th Rep. Mines* 447 From the ore-breaker the ore went through a chute to the first set of steel rolls below. **1888** *Boston Journal* 20 Oct. 2/4 The cars are loaded through chutes connected with the wheat bins. **1903** E. JOHNSON *Railway Transportation* 51 Cars are filled with coal, coke, and ore from 'pockets' or chutes, which discharge their contents into the cars by the force of gravity. **1910** J. HART *Vigilante Girl* 15 The passengers were descending from the steamer, and the cabin luggage was sliding out of the chutes.

4. *Mining.* A vein or body of ore.

1882 C. KING *Rep. Prec. Metals* 111 The chute exposed is 20 feet, but neither end had been reached.

5. A branding chute; a narrow passageway by which cattle are driven on cars.

1881 *Rep. Indian Affairs* 8 The contractor puts the cattle . . . in a chute, where they are branded. **1882** SWEET & KNOX *Texas Siftings* 34 The less common way is to drive the animal into a narrow chute. **1916** BOWER *Phantom Herd* 307 The big four-year-old steer prodded up the chutes into the shipping cars. **1920** MULFORD *J. Nelson* 259 You can build a chute that'll hold eight head [of cattle].

comb. **1911** MULFORD *Bar-20 Days* 197 Chute-branding robbed them of the excitement . . . which they always took from open or corral branding.

6. In amusement places, a descent down which one slides or rides with great rapidity.

1895 *N.Y. Dramatic News* 30 Nov. 17/4 Shooting the Chutes, the latest craze that has struck the town, is . . . drawing large crowds. **1896** *Ib.* 4 July 14/2 A large chute is being built which will run into the water. **1906** 'O. HENRY' *Four Million* 3 To Coney me and Tobin went, thinking that a turn at the chutes . . . might raise the heart in his bosom.

+**Chute,** *v. tr.* To send through a chute; to enclose or confine in a chute. — **1884** *Harper's Mag.* May 872/1 Logs . . . are often chuted down from the lofty ridges. **1920** MULFORD *J. Nelson* 234 Anybody knows that chutin' 'em [cattle] and stampin' on th' brand is easier.

+**Chutter-luck.** Obs. variant of CHUCK-A-LUCK.

+**Cibola.** [Sp. f. Amer. Indian 'buffalo.'] An ancient region in New Mexico now identified with the pueblos of the Zuñis. Cf. SEVEN CITIES. — [**1540** CORONADO *Letter* 3 Aug.] **1873** S. W. COZZENS *Marvellous Country* 30 The treasure came from a country known as Cibola. **1889** BANCROFT *Works* XVII. 31 Hides and other articles from Cíbola were plentiful.

***Cicada.** One or other species of large homopterous insects capable of producing a shrill sound; commonly called a locust.

1748 CATESBY *Carolina* App. p. xxxvii, The particular genus's [of insects] I observed in Carolina [include] . . . The Cicada, or Locust, the Grasshopper. **1854** EMMONS *Agric. N.Y.* V. 151 *Cicada septendecim*. . . . The Cicada lays between four and five hundred eggs. **1884** *Boston Journal* 11 Oct. 2/4 Billions of insects have been killed by the electric lights in the Capitol. . . . They comprise . . . hornets, butterflies, moths, cicadas, froghoppers. **1898** CANFIELD *Maid of Frontier* 93 The rain-crow on either hand was hoarsely calling, and the monotonous iteration and reiteration of the cicada was on the air. **1912** N. M. WOODROW *Sally Salt* 38 She shrilled on complainingly, monotonously as a cicada at noontide.

Cicala. [It.] A cicada. {1821-} — **1871** HAY *Pike Co. Ballads* 96 The hot cicala's sultry cry, The murmurous dream of bees. **1892** HARTE *Col. Starbottle's Client* 10 The click of billiard balls, languidly played, came at intervals like the dry notes of cicale in the bushes.

***Cicely.** +An umbelliferous perennial herb: (see quot. 1857). — **1847** WEBSTER 204/3 The sweet cicely of New England is *Osmorrhiza longistylis*. **1857** GRAY *Botany* 158 *Osmorrhiza longistylis*, Smoother Sweet Cicely. . . . Rich moist woods, commonest northward. *Ib.*, *O. brevistylis*, Hairy Sweet Cicely.

***Cider.** Also †**cyder, sider, sydar.**

***1.** A well-known drink made from apples.

1659 *Conn. Pub. Rec.* I. 330 This Court hath remitted a third part of the fine . . . for giueing Cider to Indians. **1660** R. WILLIAMS *Letters* (1874) 306 Your loving lines in this cold, dead season, were as a cup of your Connecticut cider. **1709** LAWSON *Carolina* 108 Long-stalk is a large apple, with a long stalk, and makes good Summer Cider. **1795** WINTERBOTHAM *Hist. View* III. 37 The apples of this State [Md.] are large, but mealy; the peaches plenty and good: from these the inhabitants distil cyder and peach brandy. **1871** A. C. DAY *Knickerb. Life* (1897) 213 The Yankee Thanksgiving, with its turkey, cranberry sauce, mince, pumpkin, apple pie, and cider, found favor with the dames of Knickerbocker proclivities. **1892** M. A. JACKSON *Memoirs* 13 Cummins Jackson was . . . noted for his herculean strength which . . . he proved by lifting a barrel of cider.

+**2.** In the phrase: *All talk and no cider*, much talk but no results, 'much cry and little wool.' Hence *more cider and less talk. colloq.*

1807 IRVING, etc. *Salmagundi* vii. 79 The people, in fact, seem to be somewhat conscious of this propensity to talk, by which they are characterized, and have a favorite proverb on the subject, viz. 'all talk and no cider.' **1833** A. GREENE *Life Dr. Duckworth* 71, I think it's all talk and no cider. **1835-7** HALIBURTON *Clockmaker* 1 Ser. xxi, Its an expensive kind of honour that bein Governor, and no great thanks neither; great cry and little wool, all talk and no cider. **1849** N. KINGSLEY *Diary* 50 Fine stories are cold comfort, when it is as they say 'All talk and no cider.' **1862** BROWNE *A. Ward His Book* (F.), What we want is more cider and less talk.

3. Attrib. and comb. with *barrel, beggar, brandy*, etc.

1703 *N.H. Probate Rec.* I. 502, I give unto Mary my Beloved Wife, my best Bed, . . . Bible, warming Pan, thre Cyder Barrels [etc.]. **1851** *Knickerb.* XXXVII. 557 In olden times there was a distinct class of itinerants in New-England, who were called 'cider-beggars.' **1800** *Columbian Centinel* 22 Jan. 4/4 For Sale, A quantity of Cider-Brandy and Gin. **1832** CHILD *Frugal Housewife* 71 Cider cake is very good, to be baked in small loaves. **1877** *Southern H. S. Papers* III. 17 The passage of a cider-cart (a barrel on wheels) was a rare and exciting occurrence. **1703** *N.H. Probate Rec.* I. 504, I give to my beloved Son Josiah . . . in this my will, Cyder Cask [etc.]. **1715** *Boston News-Letter* 30 May 2/2 (*advt.*), There is fine bottl'd Sydar Sold . . . either at the House of James Pitson . . . or at his Sydar Cellar in Queen Street. **1809** KENDALL *Travels* III. 110 The apple thrives in a remarkable manner, and promise [*sic*] to render Maine a cider country. **1835** HOFFMAN *Winter in West* II. 125 While I joined the cider-drinker in his thin potations, the landlord soon returned. **1835** *Rep. Indian Affairs* 159 There is a great deal of cider-drinking among the Indians on all the reservations. **1848** BURTON *Waggeries* 10 He was gettin' his cider fixins ready in the fall. **1844** *S. Lit. Messenger* X. 529/2 A 'cider frolic,' in which the Green Mountain boys especially delight. **1869** Stowe *Oldtown Folks* v. 49 The leader of our music was old Mump Morse, a giant of a man, in form not unlike a cider-hogshead. **1857** *Quinland* I. 28 Peter Quinland placed before him the cider-jug and the silver cup. *c***1790** *Mem. Academy* II. I. 112 But permit it to be supposed that the cider-maker has been cautious enough to catch the first fining above mentioned. **1871** Stowe *Sam Lawson* 157 You see, along in October, jest in the cider-makin' time, Abel Flint he was took down with dysentery and died. **1708** *Essex Inst. Coll.* I. 172/2 The same sloop took the following . . . items: . . . forty Eightt sider pails, two barrils. **1855** *Harvard Mag.* I. 64 We filled the cider-pitcher, and then both carried it up stairs. **1843** Stephens *High Life N.Y.* I. 6 Jest as we pick out our apples in cider time. **1898** I. Harper *S. B. Anthony* I. 15 The pride of the children's lives was to eat cider toast out of them [*sc.* porringers]. **1885** *Rep. Indian Affairs* 159 The cider traffic is demoralizing . . . to the Indians. **1809** Irving *Knickerb.* IV. ii, [A bill ordering] his trusty . . . subjects . . . to buy none of their pacing horses, meazly pork, apple brandy, Yankee rum, cyder water, apple sweetmeats. *Ib.* iii, A squatting, . . . pumpkin-eating, molasses-daubing, shingle-splitting, cider-watering, horse-jockeying, notion-peddling crew. **1780** *N.J. Archives* 2 Ser. IV. 606 There is on said farm . . . new cyder works compleat, smokehouse, [etc.].

Cider apple. An apple suitable for use in making cider. {1875–} — **1880** *Harper's Mag.* Oct. 683 In October . . . you can find some cold little cider apples. **1901** *Ib.* Dec. 48 There were a few knurly little yellow cider-apples on the mossy twigs.

Cider house. *Obs.* A house in which cider is kept.

1697 *Conn. H. S. Coll.* VI. 248 The Town have Granted libertye to mr Jno Ollcott for the Standing of a Sider house. **1771** *Carroll P.* in *Md. Hist. Mag.* XIII. 263, I am in hopes of Having my Cyder House & Mill ready in time. **1777** *N.J. Archives* 2 Ser. I. 298 The improvements thereon consist of a good frame house with four rooms, . . . a cyder-house, barracks, [etc.]. **1779** *Ib.* III. 600 There is on the place . . . a good barn, cyder house, and cyder-mill.

‖**Ciderish,** *a.* Somewhat like cider in flavor. — **1854** Thoreau *Walden* 277 There where grow still the apple-trees, . . . their fruit still wild and ciderish to my taste.

Cider mill. A mill for crushing apples in making cider. {1688–}

1703 *N.H. Probate Rec.* I. 504, I give to my beloved Son . . . Barn, orchard, out houses, . . . cellars, cyder mill, press. **1764** *N.H. Hist. Soc. Coll.* IX. 147 [I] sold my quarter of ye cider mill for 8 days work. **1825** Woodworth *Forest Rose* II. ii, Even the old cider-mill, is in being yet. **1862** *Rep. Comm. Patents: Agric.* 520 The mill we use in our establishment for mashing the grapes is a well-constructed combined cider-mill. **1863** Mitchell *My Farm* 45 There was the cider mill with its old casks, and press. **1877** *Harper's Mag.* March 604/2 There was a cheese-press, and I don't know but a cider mill.

attrib. **1752** Hempstead *Diary* 596, I got Mr. Taber to mend the Cyder-Mill beam Screw. **1900** Winchester *W. Castle* 118 The next morning the cider-mill man knocked at the door of the old yellow parsonage. **1764** *N.H. Hist. Soc. Coll.* IX. 163, [I] brot cider mill sweep from Rattlesnake Hill.

+**Cider oil.** = Cider royal.

1792 Brackenridge *Adv. Capt. Farrago* xxiii. 115 She ordered him a pint tumbler of cider oil, with powdered ginger, to warm his stomach. **1809** F. Cuming *Western Tour* 86 We stopped at Wm. Croxton's tavern . . . and got a bowl of excellent cider-oil. This is stronger than Madeira and is obtained from the cider by suffering it to freeze in the cask during the winter, and then drawing off and barrelling up the spiritous part which remains liquid, while the aqueous is quickly congealed by the frost. **1816** *Henderson's N.C. Almanack*, To make Cider-Oil. This liquor is a very favourite drink with a large portion of our German citizens. **1816** 'Scene Painter' *Emigrant's Guide* 30 Cider is made an intoxicating drink by boiling and reducing the quantity one-half; it is then called cider-oil. **1836** W. O'Bryan *Travels* 70 On the road had a cordial new to me then, called . . . Cider Oil. **1859** Bartlett 83 *Cider Oil*, cider concentrated by boiling, to which honey is subsequently added.

+**Cider pap.** (See quotation.) — **1708** E. Cook *Sot-Weed Factor* 5 Homine and Syder-pap, (Which scarce a hungry dog wou'd lap). . . . Syder-pap is a sort of Food made of Syder and small Homine, like our Oatmeal.

Cider press. A press used in cider making for crushing the apples. {1676–}

1673 *Essex Inst. Coll.* L. 28 In the Little chamber a great Tray a trough a syder presse. **1796** H. Wansey *Excursion U.S.* 105 [In New Jersey] I observed many cyder-presses. **1827** *Md. Hist. Mag.* IV. 315 Riding one way and looking another, the horse run him under a cider press. **1856** A. Cary *Married* 389 Fruits were ripe, cider-presses busy, and barns full. **1879** Burdette *Hawkeyes* 70 So that the sound of the cider press ceased not from morning even unto the night.

+**Cider royal.** Cider that has been concentrated by boiling or freezing. (Cf. Cider oil.)

1758 *Lett. to Washington* II. 399 To 8 Q[uar]ts Cyder Roy[a]l @ 1/6, 12s. **1811** *Niles' Reg.* 7 Sept. 10/2 [There] passed the falls of Ohio, from October 5, 1810, to May 5, 1811, . . . Cider-royal, barrels, 1,350. **1826** Flint *Recollections* 103 Some have loads of cider, and what they call 'cider royal,' or cider that has been strengthened by boiling or freezing. **1837** A. Wetmore *Gaz. Missouri* 290 The disturber known in . . . Pennsylvania [as] . . . 'cider royal,' and by the Indians appropriately named 'fire-water,' . . . was happily beyond their reach.

Cider screw. A wooden screw forming part of a cider press or mill. — **1751** MacSparran *Diary* 53 Harry and I . . . went and searched . . . for timber for ye Cyder Skrews. [**1752** Cf. Cider mill.]

Cider vinegar. Vinegar made from cider. {1858–} — **1851** Cist *Cincinnati* 251 But there is a good deal of cider vinegar made. **1860** Holmes *E. Venner* xxv, His voice was at that moment heard above the rest,—sharp, but thin, like bad cider-vinegar.

+**Cienaga, Cienega.** *S.W.* [Sp. *ciénaga*, f. *cieno* mud.] A marsh or swamp.

(*a*) **1863** *38th Congress Sp. Sess.* Sen. Ex. Doc. No. 1, 22 A good road can be found *via* Urias ranch, . . . coming into the Arivaca cienaga, and avoiding the worst part of the entire route. **1869** J. R. Browne *Adv. Apache Country* 246 In summer-time the remainder [of the water] never finds its way to the Gulf, but forms a lake, or cienaga. **1913** W. C. Barnes *Western Grazing Grounds* 380 *Cienaga.*— . . . A wet, swampy place with many springs. **1919** J. S. Chase *Calif. Desert Trails* 149 [I] found pasturage for Kaweah in a little *ciénaga*, or marshy spot.

(*b*) **1877** Cozzens *Young Trail Hunters* (1907) 200 Our route next day, passed through a fertile cienega; thence over an alkali plain. **1886** H. H. McLane *Irene Viesca* 274 This mission was founded in the year 1703 in the *cienega* of the Rio Grande. **1887** F. Francis *Saddle & Moccasin* 132 We passed the Clanton Cienega. [*Ib.* 152 'Where did you kill the antelope?' . . . 'In the big draw, back of Clanton's ciniky.']

Cigar.

1. A small roll of tobacco for smoking. {1777–} Also attrib. (See also Segar.)

1798 Fessenden *Orig. Poems* (1806) 53 We quaff the bumper, smoke çigar, Nor heed the howl of Indian war. **1809** *Monthly Anthology* 253 We agree with Mr. Webster in spelling *cigar.* **1840** *Picayune* 11 Aug. 2/4 You smoked a dozen cigars, didn't you? **1884** Harte *In Carquinez Woods* 174 Brace . . . took off his coat, leaned against a tree, and lit a cigar. **1911** Vance *Cynthia* 65 The Inventor of Occupations studied the ash of his cigar thoughtfully.

+**2.** The seed pod of the catalpa or Indian bean.

1876 *Field & Forest* II. 51, I verily believe that some boys . . . took their first lesson, in smoking, by using the 'beans' or 'cigars' of the Catalpa.

3. Attrib. and comb. with *drummer, emporium, factory,* etc.

1909 'O. Henry' *Options* 69 A manner . . . that not even a cigar-drummer would intrude upon. **1869** J. R. Browne *Adv. Apache Country* 350 Posters . . . displaying to the public eye the prodigious assortments of Regalias, Principes, Cheroots, etc., . . . to be had within the limits of their cigar and tobacco emporium. **1893** M. Philips *Making of a Newspaper* 96 Patrolman Blucher had finished his nap in the entry-way leading to Eckstein's cigar factory. **1898** Westcott *D. Harum* 62 Mr. Lenox reached over for the cigar-lamp. **1863** *Ill. Agric. Soc. Trans.* V. 669 Tobacco of this description should be . . . prized lightly in the casks so as to admit of a free and open leaf, such being mostly required for cigar leaf. **1865** *Atlantic Mo.* XV. 616 At the repulsive business of cigar-making . . . many hundred women earn their bread. **1863** Massett *Drifting About* 35 It ended in our . . . going in to John Anderson's cigar shop next the hospital, and getting one shilling's worth of cigars. **1895** *N.Y. Dramatic News* 30 Nov. 3/2 In the next act Gaylor prevents a murder by masquerading as a cigar-sign Indian. **1850** Lewis *La. Swamp Dr.* 196 Fortunately, being a cigar-smoker, I had a box of matches in my pocket. **1835** *S. Lit. Messenger* IV. 90/2 Its toleration of that disgusting nuisance —cigar-smoking. **1861** *Vanity Fair* 9 Feb. 63/1 The senior Mr. Primpenny then hailed a stage passing up the true Broadway, Mr. Kineboy remarking . . . he thought it was a yaller soda-water or cigar wagon.

Cigar box. A box in which cigars are kept.

1846 *Knickerb.* XXVII. 89 A dark-looking foreigner, bearing under his arm a small red-cedar cigar-box. **1876** Tourgee *Toinette* i. 8 Several shorter editions of the same [=pipes] were stuck in an open cigar-box upon the mantle. **1877** Hale *G. T. T.* 76 Effie . . . broke to pieces a nice large cigar-box. **1920** Hunter *Trail Drivers of Texas* I. 257 They passed an empty cigar box and all 'chipped in.'

fig. **1878** B. F. Taylor *Between Gates* 252 We have been circling about that cigar-box of a town.

Cigar case. 1. A holder or case in which cigars are carried. {*a*1863–} **2.** A glass show case in which cigars are displayed. — (1) **1846** *Boston Almanac* 163/1 Boynton & Woodford . . . [sell] Goggles; Cigar Cases; Wallets; Pocket Books. **1871** *Harper's Mag.* XLIII. 268/2 He . . . took a cigar-case from his pocket, and soothed himself with a smoke. (2) **1897** Brodhead *Bound in Shallows* 14 Alexa inclined herself idly against the rim of the small cigar-case. **1900** G. Ade *More Fables* 6 Next Morning, at the Hotel he spotted a stylish little chunk of a Woman who kept the Cigar Case.

Cigarette. {1842–} A small quantity of finely cut tobacco in a cylindrical envelope (usually of thin paper) open at both ends.

1864 Webster 230/2 *Cigarette*, a little cigar; a little fine tobacco rolled in paper for smoking. **1874** Knight 553/1 [The tobacco] is supplied at one end of the machine, while the finished cigarettes emerge at the other end. **1879** Cable *Old Creole Days* (1883) 189 Manuel Mazaro . . . had the hands of a woman, save that the nails were stained with the smoke of cigarettes. **1883** HOWELLS *Woman's Reason* xxi, He allowed her to vent [her vexation] freely, before he answered her a word, chewing the end of his cigarette. **1891** E. S. ELLIS *Check No. 2134* 34 The abominable habit of smoking cigarettes. **1911** LINCOLN *Cap'n Warren's Wards* 134 His cigarette had gone out, and he threw the stump savagely into the waste-paper basket.

attrib. and *comb.* **1874** KNIGHT 553/1 Cigarette-filler, a little implement for introducing the finely cut tobacco into the paper envelope. **1884** *Century Mag.* Nov. 154 Knowing, *blasé*, young gentlemen . . . contrived somehow, in intervals of gambling and cigarette-puffing, to get well up on most modern literatures. **1903** A. H. LEWIS *Boss* 173 Young Morton, still with the empty smile, brought forth a cigarette case. **1912** *Dept. Agric. Yearbook 1911* 231 The bright cigarette tobacco produces 500 to 1,200 pounds per acre of high-grade leaf.

+**Cigar fish.** *local.* A small tropical fish whose shape suggests that of a cigar. — **1888** GOODE *Amer. Fishes* 230 The Round Robin, *Decapterus punctatus*, called at Pensacola 'Cigar-fish.'

Cigarito. Variant of CIGARRITO.

+**Cigar lighter. a.** A twist of paper used to light a cigar. **b.** (See quot. from Knight.)

*c***1845** W. THOMPSON *Chron. Pineville* 49 'Cigar-lighter,' added a mischievous fellow on the opposite side, with a wink to the crowd. **1870** O. LOGAN *Before Footlights* 219 Mrs. Woolt—(the rest burnt off for a cigar lighter) would be happy to see him at dinner next Sunday at half-past three precisely. **1874** B. F. TAYLOR *World on Wheels* II. ii. 200 Ticket 104,163 was worth—well—about a twist for a cigar-lighter! **1874** KNIGHT 553/1 *Cigar-lighter*, a little gas-jet suspended by an elastic tube.

Cigar maker. One whose occupation is making cigars.

1856 MACLEOD *F. Wood* 47 He . . . became a journeyman cigar-maker—for small enough wages, we may be sure. **1873** BEADLE *Undevel. West* 769 They are porters, . . . cigar-makers, and some few artisans of other sorts. **1898** *Mo. So. Dakotan* I. 106 What would the dear people think of a law saying how much a printer, or painter, or cigarmaker, . . . shall receive for doing certain labors? **1909** 'O. HENRY' *Roads of Destiny* 303 Denver got a Cuban cigar-maker to fix up a little cipher code with English and Spanish words.

Cigar manufactory. A place or establishment where cigars are made. — **1858** VIELÉ *Following Drum* 65 We visited a cigar manufactory and saw 'the weed' in every variety of form. **1881** *Harper's Mag.* May 814/2 The upper stories [were turned] into tenements and cigar manufactories.

+**Cigar(r)ito.** *W.* [Sp. *cigarrito*, dim. of *cigarro* cigar.] Also **cigarita.** A cigarette.

(*a*) **1838** 'TEXIAN' *Mexico v. Texas* 177 He [the general] lay himself, half reclining, on his camp bed, smoking a cigarrito. **1844** KENDALL *Narrative* I. 276 A bundle of cigarritos, . . . small cigars, in N. Mexico made of punche, a species of tobacco, covered with corn-husks or shucks. **1850** *Western Journal* IV. 235 He was then probably using my most important papers to cover cigarritos. **1869** J. R. BROWNE *Adv. Apache Country* 193 A genuine native of this region sits shivering all day long over three twigs of mesquit, . . . the inevitable cigarrito in his mouth. **1879** HARTE *Drift from 2 Shores* 130 Jack began to twist a cigarrito. **1884** *Century Mag.* Sept. 666 Tobalito sat before his door and smoked incessantly his corn-husk cigarritos.

(*b*) **1848** BRYANT *California* 329 The *cigarita* is freely used by the señoras and señoritas, and they puff it with much gusto while threading the mazes of the cotillon or swinging in the waltz. **1853** *Harper's Mag.* VII. 306/1 Sauntering Californians . . . watched our movements with a sort of idle curiosity, smoking their eternal 'cigaritos.' **1858** VIELÉ *Following Drum* 187, I had heard a great deal of the grace with which these donnas handled their cigarritos. **1876** HARTE *G. Conroy* xvi, Don Pedro shrugged his shoulders, and rolled a fresh cigarito. **1889** K. MUNROE *Golden Days* 17 The patrone . . . passed his time in smoking corn-husk cigaritos. **1898** ATHERTON *Californians* 8 'A caballero!' she cried: 'who will . . . lie in a hammock smoking cigaritos all day.' **1910** J. HART *Vigilante Girl* 348 But there was no sign of activity; the bandits were lolling around their fire, smoking cigaritos.

+**Cigar stand.** A stall or counter where cigars, cigarettes, etc., are sold. — **1887** *Courier-Journal* 20 Feb. 1/3 Direct Importer of Havana Cigars, . . . 638 W. Main St., and Galt House Cigar Stand. **1910** MCCUTCHEON *Rose in Ring* 381 We could open the nicest kind of a cigar stand with that, and live like honest, respectable men ever afterward.

+**Cigar store.** A shop specializing in the sale of cigars and smoking accessories.

1848 E. JUDSON *Mysteries N.Y.* II. 23 Are you going back to that hateful cigar store? **1869** J. W. BROWNE *Adv. Apache Country* 350 A cigar store not much bigger than a dry goods box must have its mammoth posters out over the town and hill-sides. **1883** *Century Mag.* Nov. 41/1 American life is invading the thoroughfare, . . . multiplying flashy saloons and cheap restaurants, cigar stores and oyster-rooms. **1909** 'O. HENRY' *Roads of Destiny* 299 Is he going to revive the Georgia Minstrels or open a cigar store?

attrib. **1878** A. DALY in *Life* (1917) 254 The little blue tickets hang in alluring hundreds on strings in every cigar store window. **1904** 'O. HENRY' *Heart of West* 87 At the depot I telegraphed a cigar-store man I knew in New York to meet me .

+**Cigar tree.** *local.* [CIGAR 2.] The catalpa. — **1884** SARGENT *Rep. Forests* 115 *Catalpa bignonioides*. . . . Catalpa. Catawba. . . . Bean Tree. Cigar Tree. Indian Bean. **1897** SUDWORTH *Arborescent Flora* 335 *Catalpa speciosa*. . . . Common Names [include] . . . Cigartree (Mo., Iowa).

Cimlin = CYMLING.

+**Cimline.** *local.* (See quotation.) — **1880** BURROUGHS in *Scribner's Mo.* Aug. 492/2 The top cord or line of the [drift] net is called a 'cimline' [in N.Y.].

+**Cimmaron.** *S.W.* [Sp.] The bighorn or Rocky Mountain sheep. Also attrib. with *sheep*. — **1857** M. REID *Scalp Hunters* 299 We can recognise the horns and frontlets of the elk, the cimmaron, and the grim bison. **1884** *Century Mag.* June 218/1 The mountain sheep, or cimarron, the most difficult to capture of all four-footed animals, whose gigantic curved horns are the best trophy of skill and enterprise that a hunter can bring home with him. **1888** ROOSEVELT *Ranch Life* 155 The big-horn or cimarron sheep, as the Mexicans call it, is the sole American representative of the different kinds of mountain sheep that are found in the Old World. **1897** A. H. LEWIS *Wolfville* 81 First we-alls knows, these yere Britons would be runnin' cimmaron in the hills.

+**Cinch,** *n.*[1] Also †**sinch(e).** [Sp. *cincha.*]

1. A strong girth for a saddle, often of braided horsehair. Also attrib. *W.*

1859 G. A. JACKSON *Diary* 521, [I] nailed shoes on Old Chief to-day, and Black Hawk and I made Hackamore and sinche. **1878** E. TUTTLE *Border Tales* 35 The whole is fastened by a broad 'belly-band' termed a *sinch*, which by a method of drawing up loops of rope . . . known as sinching, is tightened until a load of three hundred pounds may be piled high on top. **1889** *Amer. Notes & Q.* III. 47 There are no buckles on the belly-band, and their place is supplied by two rings through which is passed the cinch-strap, which is tied by the cinch-knot. **1899** A. THOMAS *Arizona* 107 We can't stop. . . . This is simply a halt to water, and tighten cinches. **1907** MULFORD *Bar-20* 43 He grasped the end of the cinch strap in such a way that when the pony jumped forward in its last desperate effort the buckle slipped and the cinch became unfastened. **1923** J. H. COOK *On Old Frontier* 9 When I tightened the cinch the pony jumped into the air and tried to turn cartwheels.

b. *fig.* A strong or sure hold.

1888 *Chicago Inter-Ocean* 2 Feb. (F.), Black and Blue thinks the Dwyers have a cinch on both the great events. **1899** A. THOMAS *Arizona* 9 A woman that's married to a fellow has a pretty tight cinch on him—that is, if he likes her. **1899** QUINN *Penna. Stories* 198, I'd give twenty Scholarships if I had the cinch on the shot that you have on the quarter. *a***1906** 'O. HENRY' *Trimmed Lamp* 256 The devil seems to have a cinch on all the business in New York.

2. A sure thing; a dead certainty. *colloq.*[2]

1898 *Chicago Record* 1 Apr. 4 The word 'cinch' . . . means 'absolutely sure of attaining one's purpose, or succeeding in what one is about to undertake.' **1901** MERWIN & WEBSTER *Calumet 'K'* 264 The surest way to get left is to begin now telling ourselves that this is easy and it's a cinch. **1904** *Phila. Ev. Telegraph* 1 June 6 After remaining single for eighty years a Jersey woman has decided to marry. It is a cinch that she is taking the matrimonial step without her parents' consent. **1924** MULFORD *Rustlers' Valley* 146 It's a dead shore cinch there won't be no tracks to tell 'em anythin'.

b. An easy, pleasant experience.

1907 MULFORD *Bar-20* 60 Yu won't have no cinch ridin' home with that leg.

+**Cinch,** *n.*[2] Also **sinch.** [Origin obscure.] A card game resembling seven-up. — **1889** (Amer. newspaper,) I found that sinch is the great Northwestern game of cards, a recent invention, and played everywhere and by everybody. . . . It is a variation of High, Low, Jack. **1897** BRODHEAD *Bound in Shallows* 79 'Hardly,' signified Dillon, loosening the ash from his cigar; 'not when the game is cinch.' **1901** WHITE *Claim Jumpers* (1916) 121 They had a dreary game of 'cinch.'

attrib. **1895** CHAMBLISS *Diary* 172, This poker 'income tax' is based upon the strength of the winner's 'hand'. . . . I suppose the Parvenucracy would consider it 'bad form' if I were to call this a 'cinch game.'

+**Cinch,** *v.*[1] [f. CINCH *n.*[1]]

1. *tr.* To fasten (a saddle) by a cinch; to make (a saddle) secure by means of a cinch or girth. *W.*

1873 BEADLE *Undevel. West* 273 With all set and everything tightly 'cinched,' we took the start. **1893** K. SANBORN *S. Calif.* 178 The girth, which passes under the horse's belly and cinches the saddle in place, is woven of hair from horses' manes by a native artisan. **1905** A. ADAMS *Outlet* 310 Saddles were shaken out of gunny-sacks and cinched on waiting horses. **1910** J. HART *Vigilante Girl* 141 When wearied of this elevated post, he would descend and seat himself in the riding-saddle cinched on the back of the near wheeler.

fig. **1902** *Harper's Mag.* 468, I spoke awful good English to him most of the time. . . . I can, yu' know, when I cinch my attention tight on to it.

b. *intr.* To tighten or fasten the girth of a saddle. *W.*

1887 *St. Nicholas* XIV. 732 At Giles's ranch, on the divide, the party halted to cinch up. **1913** MULFORD *Coming of Cassidy* 35 Cinching deftly [he] slung himself up by the stirrup.

2. *tr.* To bring into a fix or tight place; to put severe pressure upon; to squeeze. *colloq.*[2]

1875 *Scribner's Mo.* X. 277/1 [At San Francisco] a man who is hurt in a mining transaction is 'cinched.' **1881** *N.Y. Times* 18 Dec. 4/3 It is unfairly said that the Northern Pacific Company intends to 'cinch' the settlers by exacting large prices for its lands. **a1889** *Denver Republ.* (B. & L.), My father is wealthy, and I think I can cinch him for five hundred dollars. **1899** G. ADE *Doc' Horne* 85, I called him in a minute, and I had him cinched, too, becuz I seen 'em down there. **1910** ROOSEVELT in *Outlook* 3 Sept. 2/1 If the rich man strives to use his wealth to destroy others, I will cinch him if I can.

3. To make sure of, to render certain.

1910 RAINE *B. O'Connor* 25 That extra hour and a half cinches our escape. **1911** LINCOLN *Cap'n Warren's Wards* 286 He said that there was such a man and that he had the estate cinched.

+**Cinch,** *v.*[2] Also †**sinch.** [f. CINCH *n.*[2]] *tr.* In the game of cinch, to prevent an opponent from making his points. — **1889** (Amer. newspaper,) Prevent him from making as many points as he has agreed to make. If he fails to make good his offer, he is 'sinched.'

+**Cincha.** *W.* [Sp.] The cinch or girth of a saddle; = CINCH *n.*[1] 1. Also attrib.

1883 E. INGERSOLL *Knocking Round Rockies* 21 The crupper is gained, and the first hand pull made upon the cincha (as the girth is termed). **1887** *Outing* X. 118/1 We rode up the 'draw' about a quarter of a mile and stopped for Johnnie to fix a *cincha.* **1891** *Harper's Mag.* July 204/2 The cowboy's saddle is held in place by one very wide or two narrower cinchas, though the single cincha is more a Californian habit. **1895** REMINGTON *Pony Tracks* 122 A little fire is built, and one side of a cincha ring is heated red-hot, with which a rawhide artist paints HF in the sizzling flesh.

transf. **1876** BOURKE *Journal* 27 Feb., This is made double in the middle of its length by a 'cincha,' or belt of canvas passing around the girth. **1884** NYE *Baled Hay* 138 The full . . . swell and broad cincha of the chaparajo have given place to the tight pantaletts.

+**Cinch bill.** [Cf. CINCH *v.*[1]] A legislative bill aimed at companies or corporations who, it is hoped, will bribe the legislators to kill the bill. — **1887** *San Francisco News Letter* 29 Jan. 20/2 The 'cinch' bill which is aimed at the gas companies . . . is a measure of such a bare-faced nature that no one can plead ignorance in regard to it.

+**Cincinnati.**[1] [f. *Cincinnatus*, Roman dictator.]

'An organization composed largely of the soldiers of the Revolutionary War. It was formed very soon after the disbandment of the army, and held very much such a relation to the country as the Grand Army of the Republic does at the present time' (1888 Lane *Pol. Catch-words*).

1783 *N.H. Hist. Soc. Coll.* VI. 279 The officers of the American Army . . . possess high veneration for the character of that illustrious Roman, Lucius Quintus Cincinnatus, and being resolved to follow his example . . . they think they may with propriety denominate themselves The Society of the Cincinnati. **1787** M. CUTLER in *Life & Corr.* I. 294 Every gentleman at table was of the Cincinnati except myself. **1789** WASHINGTON *Diaries* IV. 37 At 11 went to an Oratorio—and between that and 3 o'clock rec'd the Addresses of the Governor . . . and of the Cincinnati of the State. **1798** J. ADAMS *Wks.* IX. 223 When the Cincinnati of South Carolina pledge their lives, their fortunes, and their sacred honor, I believe no man will doubt their integrity. **a1821** C. BIDDLE *Autobiog.* 334 All moneys received will be forwarded or handed over to Charles Biddle, Esq., Treasurer of the Cincinnati of Pennsylvania. **1883** *Harper's Mag.* Aug. 470/2 The innocent company of elderly gentlemen were . . . the members of the Cincinnati. **1906** J. HARRISON *G. Washington* 378 A great outcry arose over the country, when it was found that the 'Cincinnati' formed a kind of secret Masonic society.

attrib. **1838** *S. Lit. Messenger* IV. 792/1 It is therefore our purpose to make 'The Cincinnati Oration' one of the standing exercises at the college commencements.

+**Cincinnati.**[2] [f. prec., named in 1790.]

1. Whisky made at Cincinnati, Ohio. *Obs.*

1847 ROBB *Squatter Life* 57 What'll you take Missus? shall I sweeten you a little of about the best Cincinnati rectified that ever was toted into these 'ere parts? **1858** *Nat. Intelligencer* 10 July (B.), A citizen of St. Paul . . . says a barrel of the 'pure Cincinnati' . . . is a sufficient basis upon which to manufacture one hundred barrels of 'good Indian liquor!'

2. *attrib.* Of or pertaining to Cincinnati, Ohio.

1858 LINCOLN in Logan *Great Conspiracy* 79 That decision, I repeat, is repudiated in the Cincinnati platform. **1881** *Harper's Mag.* May 836/1 In her specialty, which may be called Cincinnati faience, Miss McLaughlin has been constantly at work. *Ib.* 839/2 The various kinds of work mentioned, . . . except a few pieces of overglaze-work on European porcelain, are all done in Ohio clays from Cincinnati potteries. **1888** CABLE *Bonaventure* 190 They've got the schoolhouse, . . . and Cincinnati furniture, . . . and they've caught the spirit of progress!

b. In humorous or slang use: (see quotations).

1845 *Cincinnati Misc.* I. 240 Cents or Coppers are generally known in the West as, 'Cincinnati Bullion.' **1877** BARTLETT 121 *Cincinnati Oysters*, pigs' feet. **1889** BARRÈRE & LELAND 252/2 *Cincinnati Olives* (American), pigs because a large quantity of olive oil is manufactured out of Cincinnati lard.

c. *Geol.* Pertaining to a division of the lower Silurian series. (Cf. CINCINNATIAN *a.*)

1889 *Cent.* s.v. *Group.*

+**Cincinnatian,** *n.* Usu. in *pl.* A citizen of Cincinnati, Ohio.

1832 *N.Y. Observer* X. 66/5 As for the poor Cincinnatians, on whom especially Mrs. Trollope has wreaked her vengeance, how they will ever rise from the blighting of her hand, I know not. **1835** HOFFMAN *Winter in West* II. 112 It is therefore in the highest degree absurd to speak of the Cincinnatians as a provincial people in their manners. **1846** *Knickerb.* XXVII. 79 The Cincinnatians, like all other enlightened people, love to ride on an excitement. **1870** O. LOGAN *Before Footlights* 200 This brave young soldier, a Cincinnatian, was killed at the battle of Chickamauga. **1885** *Harper's Mag.* March 530/1 The original was sold for $3000 to a wealthy Cincinnatian. **1899** *Commercial Tribune* (Cincinnati) 5 Aug. 12/5 Cincinnatians who go East hear of him frequently.

+**Cincinnatian,** *a. Geol.* Pertaining to formations of the lower Silurian age. — **1899** *Science* X. 877 Probably in no other region is the succession of these [Lorraine and Richmond] faunas so complete as about Cincinnati, and this fact justifies the recognition of the term Cincinnatian. **1906** CHAMBERLIN & SALISBURY *Geol.* II. 310 Cincinnatian (Neo-Champlainic): Richmond beds, Lorraine beds, Utica shales.

Cincinnati Society. = CINCINNATI.[1] — **1838** *S. Lit. Messenger* IV. 792/1 One declared object of the Cincinnati Society, was 'to preserve the memory of the American Revolution.' **1865** *Atlantic Mo.* XV. 190 A great clamor was raised against the Cincinnati Society.

Cincinnatus. [Name of a Roman dictator.] *Order of Cincinnatus*, = CINCINNATI.[1] — **1784** J. ADAMS *Wks.* IX. 524, I am sorry you have any marks of an order of Cincinnatus, which is the first step taken to deface the beauty of our temple of liberty.

***Cinder.** Used with *path, road*, to designate a way or path laid or dressed with cinders. (Cf. CINDER TRACK.)

1861 *Atlantic Mo.* April 447/1 He never was to go down that old cinder-road again. **1882** *Wheelman* I. 33 The cinder path between the rails had been decided on for the first two miles. **1883** *Harper's Mag.* Nov. 907/2 St. Paul's School . . . has . . . a quarter-mile cinder path. **1884** *Century Mag.* June 286/2 Horace buttoned his light overcoat, and tramped down the cinder-path between the tracks. **1897** *Outing* July 344/1 Bringing out racing 'cracks' on the cinder path.

Cinderella. [Name of the heroine of a well-known fairy story.] +*Cinderella slipper*, (see quotation). — **1810** *Columbian Centinel* 17 Jan. 3/1 Thomas Wiley . . . has just received a specimen of the new invented Gold and silver Cinderrella Slippers, designed for Balls and Assemblies. [**1874** ALDRICH *P. Palfrey* xvii, Sitting . . . with her feet thrust into a pair of satin slippers of the Cinderella family.]

+**Cinder hole.** (See quot. 1852.) — **1852** *Harper's Mag.* V. 151/2 A cinder hole is a small cavity left in the iron at the time of the manufacture of it. **1861** *Army Regulations* 469 Musket barrels . . . [are] rejected for defects [like]: . . . Interior cinder-holes, . . . Exterior cinder-holes.

Cinder track. A running track finished off with fine, closely packed cinders. {1887-} — **1893** POST *Harvard Stories* 148 Is it to be on a cinder track, or over an ordinary road? **1893** *Outing* XXI. 135/2 There is a sharp line dividing cinder-track athletes from cross-country runners. **1898** *Outing* April 11/1 There are fine cinder tracks at both fields. **1917** MATHEWSON *Sec. Base Sloan* 143 It had . . . a cinder track one-eighth mile in circumference.

Cinereous, *a.* Used in designating various birds having ashen or dark plumage. {1661-}

1828 BONAPARTE *Synopsis* 436 The Cinereous Owl, *Strix cinerea*, . . . [is] an accidental winter visitant of the north-western territory. *Ib.* 370 The Cinereous Petrel, *Puffinus cinereus*, . . . [is] common between the banks of Newfoundland and the United States. **1839** PEABODY *Mass. Birds* 375 The Cinereous Coot, *Fulica americana*, is found in almost every part of North America. **1839** AUDUBON *Ornith. Biog.* V. 434 Great Cinereous Shrike. *Lanius excubitor.*

***Cinnabar.** Red mercuric sulphide, a well-known ore of mercury.

1848 BRYANT *California* App. 463 The ore (cinnabar) occurs in a large vein, dipping at a strong angle to the horizon. **1872** DANA *Mineralogy* 288 Cinnabar is the ore from which the principal part of the mercury of commerce is obtained. . . . A large mine has been discovered in Upper California.

b. Attrib. and comb. with *bearing, lode, mine.*

1876 RAYMOND *8th Rep. Mines* 57 A high grade of ore has been cross-cut, which occurs in alternate bands of sulphurets of iron and cinnabar-bearing quartz. **1873** HARTE *Mrs. Skagg's Husbands*, etc. 29 The finding of a cinnabar lode at Angel's absorbed all collateral facts or subsequent details. **1876** RAYMOND *8th Rep. Mines* 462 The total receipts at the tide-water from all the cinnabar-mines of the State [of California] exceed 50,000 flasks.

***Cinnamon.**

***1.** An aromatic spice of a reddish-brown color, chiefly used for flavoring.

1636 *Essex Probate Rec.* I. 5, 2 steels & Cinamon, . . . a carde of lace. **1759** *Newport Mercury* 26 June 4/3 Imported . . . and to be sold by Jacob Richardson, . . . new Raisins, Nutmegs, Cinnamon, Cloves and Mace. **1781** *R.I. Commerce* II. 119 Nutmegs [are sold at] 5 dollars, Cinnamon 6. **1891** WILKINS *New Eng. Nun* 198 She sprinkled in various spices too, then sniffed at the mixture daintily. 'Needs a little more cinnamon,' she murmured.

+**2.** *ellipt.* = CINNAMON BEAR.

1855 MARRYAT *Mts. & Molehills* 253 The cinnamon's weight was quoted at 400 lbs. **1891** *Fur, Fin, & Feather* March 170 They were a big party of cinnamons harvesting their way back toward the mountains. **1903** A. ADAMS *Log Cowboy* 367 Pressure of duty held those of us who had fastened on to the old cinnamon.

3. Attrib. and comb. with *bark, candy*, etc.

1852 E. ELLET *Pioneer Women* 37 It was usual with her to keep a supply of maple-sugar and cinnamon-bark in her spice-box. **1894** CABLE *J. March* ii, I wish double-O-K would mean firecrackers; firecrackers and cinnamon candy! **1836** O'BRYAN *Travels* 70, I stopped at a store and had a cordial, called cinnamon cordial at two cents a glass. **1875** STOWE *Deacon Pitkin* vii. 81 She came in arter some cinnamon sticks.

b. Of the color of cinnamon.

1872 *Harper's Magazine* LXVI. 20 The sportsman looks to his rifle as he sees the monstrous tracks of the cinnamon grizzly. **1873** MILLER *Amongst Modocs* 63 On the little shelf . . . lay a brace of pistols . . . within hand's reach of the cinnamon-haired bar-keeper. **1876** — *First Families* xiii. 114 The cinnamon-headed man behind the bar dodged down behind his barricade. **1874** COUES *Birds N.W.* 568 The Cinnamon Teal was found breeding in Idaho.

+**Cinnamon bear.** A cinnamon-colored variety of the American black bear.

1829 J. RICHARDSON *Fauna Boreali-Amer.* I. 15 The Cinnamon Bear of the Fur Traders is considered by the Indians to be an accidental variety of this species (*Ursus americanus*). **1855** MARRYAT *Mts. & Molehills* 253 A long-expected fight had come off between a grizzly bear and a cinnamon bear. **1873** BEADLE *Undevel. West* 676 A day . . . will bring one to the range of larger game, such as cinnamon bears, mountain lions and big-horn sheep. **1880** INGHAM *Digging Gold* 383 Some parties in a neighboring camp killed a cinnamon bear. **1909** 'O. HENRY' *Roads of Destiny* 309 He was dancing like a cinnamon bear.

+**Cinnamon(-colored) fern.** A species of fern (*Osmunda cinnamomea*), in which the fertile fronds bear cinnamon-colored spores. — **1847** WOOD *Botany* 634 Cinnamon-colored Fern. . . . This is among the largest of our ferns, growing in swamps and low grounds. **1857** GRAY *Botany* 601 *Osmunda cinnamomea*, L. (Cinnamon-Fern.) **1869** *Amer. Naturalist* II. 522 We have two others, the Cinnamon Fern, and the Interrupted leaved Fern, well known to young botanists in the spring.

+**Cinnamon honeysuckle.** *local.* The swamp azalea, *Azalea viscosa.* — **1894** *Jrnl. Amer. Folk-Lore* VII. 93 *Rhododendron viscosum.* . . . Gray, cinnamon honeysuckle, West Va. **1901** MOHR *Plant Life Ala.* 653 *Azalea viscosa glauca.* . . . Cinnamon Honeysuckle. . . . Mountain region. Rocky banks of brooks.

Cinnamon rose. A highly fragrant variety of rose. {1664-} Also ellipt.

1817-8 EATON *Botany* (1822) 433 *Rosa cinnamomea*, cinnamon rose. . . . Stem brown-cinnamon colour. **1834** *S. Lit. Messenger* I. 98 Clusters of full blown peonies, or large double damask and cinnamon roses. **1871** *Scribner's Mo.* II. 626/1, I wanted some of the blessed old cinnamons, . . . so I ran down into the vegetable-garden whither Tom had banished them. **1892** TORREY *Foot-Path Way* 32, I wished also to say something of sundry minor enjoyments: of the cinnamon roses, for example.

* **Cinquefoil.** *Bot.* One or other species of *Potentilla*, a rosaceous plant having compound leaves of five leaflets.

1778 CARVER *Travels* 515 Balm, Nettles, Cinque Foil, Eyebright, Sanicle, [etc.]. **1785** MARSHALL *Amer. Grove* 109 *Potentilla fruticosa americana.* American Shrubby Cinquefoil. **1836** EDWARD *Hist. Texas* ii. 42 Examples [of the herb varieties] are the balm of Gilead, the cinque-foil, [etc.]. *a***1862** THOREAU *Maine Woods* 181 The plants which chiefly attracted our attention were the mountain cinquefoil, . . . very beautiful hare-bells overhanging the precipice, etc. **1891** 'THANET' *Otto the Knight*, etc. 15 The levee was . . . not altogether green, because the spring had bespattered it with blue and yellow-white from violets, cinquefoil, and oxalis.

***Cipher,** *n.* +The zero mark on a thermometer. — **1796** MORSE *Amer. Geog.* I. 475 The range of the quicksilver . . . is between the 24th degree below, and the 105th degree above cypher. **1815** DRAKE *Cincinnati* 94 From nine years observations, at Cincinnati, it appears that the thermometer falls below cypher twice every winter.

* **Cipher,** *v.* Also †**cypher.**

+**1.** *To cipher out*, to work out (as if) by calculating; to make out by study; to think out. *colloq.*

1825 NEAL *Bro. Jonathan* I. 172 Let each man [figuratively] take a slate and cipher it out. **1842** *Niles' Nat. Reg.* 6 Aug. 368/2 The Millerites held a convention at Concord New Hampshire last week, to consider the fulfillment of prophecies and the 'end of the world,' which they have cyphered out. **1847** ROBB *Squatter Life* 108, I . . . was jest tryin' to cypher out some way of gittin' to shore. **1872** 'MARK TWAIN' *Roughing It* xv. 85 Every time a woman wants to do well by her darling, she puzzles her brain to cipher out some scheme for getting it into my hands. **1891** 'THANET' *Otto the Knight*, etc. 6 Waal, I cayn't cipher it out, nohow. **1898** WESTCOTT *D. Harum* 154 S'posen you come 'round to my place tomorro' 'bout 'leven o'clock, an' mebbe we c'n cipher this thing out.

+**2.** (See quotation.)

1889 *Cent.* 1005/3 *Cipher, v.* 2. In fox-hunting, to hunt carefully about in search of a lost trail; said of a dog. (New Eng.) 3. To run on three legs: said of a dog. (Kentucky).

Ciphering, *ppl. a.* [f. CIPHER *v.* 1.] +Designing, calculating, *colloq.* — **1825** J. NEAL *Bro. Jonathan* I. 154 A . . . cool, keen, cyphering, thrifty temper.

Circassian. A light twilled fabric of wool and cotton. {1853-} — **1845** *Lowell Offering* V. 255 If cold, her gown is of 'green circassian.' **1846** *Knickerb.* XXVIII. 304 She wore a dark brown dress of coarse circassian.

* **Circle.**

1. (See quot. 1889.)

1862 BROWNE *A. Ward His Book* (1865) 33 Sperretooul Sircles is held nitely & 4 or 5 long hared fellers has settled here and gone into the sperret bizniss excloosively. *Ib.* 36 When the Sircle stopt they axed me what I thawt of it. **1868** *Spiritual Age* (Boston) 3 Oct. (De Vere), A few evenings since, as a private Circle of Spiritualists were receiving communications from the other world, [etc.]. **1871** DE VERE 245 Their papers . . . advertise sedulously, that 'a Circle is held for Medium Developments and Spiritual Manifestations at Bloomfield-street every Sunday.' **1889** FARMER 147/2 *Circle*, a spiritualist's term for a gathering of people assembled for the purpose of holding communication with spirits. Among the more elementary phenomena are table tipping and rapping, and as for convenience sake, a round table was, in the early days of the movement, frequently used, those present naturally sat round it in a circle. Later on, the term circle was enlarged in meaning to include all meetings at which spirit communion was practised.

2. A society of women or girls who meet periodically, esp. to sew for charity.

1887 I. ALDEN *Little Fishers* xxiv, Nettie's room . . . is a lovely room; I was in it once when the circle met there. **1890** *Century Mag.* XL. 563 A circle sews, not for the poor, for there are none, but for some public object like an organ for the Sunday meeting or a library for the Sunday school.

3. *Swinging round the circle*, (see SWING *v.*).

+**4.** Attrib. with reference to brands used on cattle ranches.

1903 A. ADAMS *Log Cowboy* ii. 12 We were in honor bound to accept everything bearing the 'circle dot' on the left hip. **1910** RAINE *B. O'Connor* 219 We're after them for rustling a bunch of Circle 33 cows.

+**Circle rider.** A cowboy engaged in rounding up cattle by circle riding. — **1888** ROOSEVELT in *Century Mag.* April 860/1 As soon as . . . the last circle-riders have come in . . . we begin to work the herd. *a***1918** G. STUART *On Frontier* II. 179 The circle riders started out together in every direction and drove to the corral all the cattle that they could find.

+**Circle riding.** (See quotation.) — **1888** ROOSEVELT in *Century Mag.* April 857/2 This morning work is called circle riding. . . .As the band goes out, the leader from time to time detaches one or two men to ride, . . . making the shorter, or what are called inside, circles, while he keeps on; and finally . . . makes the longest or outside circle himself.

***Circling.** +(See quotation.) — **1878** BEADLE *Western Wilds* 536 The savages attacked in the manner known as 'circling'—that is, riding round and round the whites, hanging on the opposite side of their horse so as to be shielded.

* **Circuit.**

* **1.** A judicial district through which a judge travels at definite intervals to hold court.

1719 *Mass. Bay Currency Tracts* 193 Ministers, School-Masters, Judges of the Circuit, President & Tutors at Colledge, Widows and Orphans, &c. are pincht and hurt more than any. **1801** GADSDEN in J. Adams *Wks.* IX. 579 Many of our new-comers, . . . especially in the circuits, have brought on a strange renversement in our State. **1820** QUITMAN in *Life & Corr.* I. 55 Mr. Brush is mostly absent on circuit; the duties of the land-office fall upon me. **1835** LONGSTREET *Ga. Scenes* 98 He was at the second Court of the Circuit and had been from home nearly a fortnight. **1839** *Knickerb.* XIII. 2 In this city [New York] alone, are three law courts; a superior court with three justices; a court of common pleas, with five, and a circuit judge of the first circuit. **1870** *Nation* 10 March 147/1 The chief topics in the Senate have been the Funding Bill, the bill to compensate Southern loyalists, and the bill to alter the judicial circuits. **1871** *Scribner's Mo.* I. 423 The lawyer was off on circuit.

b. *ellipt.* =CIRCUIT COURT.

1748 *N.J. Archives* 1 Ser. VII. 107 You may remember what Mr. Kearny said relating to the Rioters and Holding the circuit in Essex. **1812** *Ann. 12th Congress* 1 Sess. 1275 This circuit is a court of ***original*** as well as ***appellate*** jurisdiction.

2. In the Methodist church, a number of congregations forming a part of a district. {1766-}

1776 [see 3]. **1832** WILLIAMSON *Maine* II. 698 Each annual conference is divided into Districts . . . [which] are divided into Circuits. **1844** Rupp *Relig. Denominations* 463 No minister or preacher to be stationed longer than three years, successively, in the same circuit. **1851** *Polly Peablossom* 80 Circuits were assigned to the different preachers. **1872** EGGLESTON *End of World* 243 The quarterly meeting for the circuit was held at the village of Brayville. **1874** — *Circuit-Rider* xx, On his two circuits he had reported extraordinary revivals.

b. The church membership included in a circuit.

1846 *Indiana Mag. Hist.* XXIII. 213 The circuit increased this year from six hundred and sixty-two to eight hundred and forty-five, after making allowance for those detached to Greenville circuit.

3. *To ride the circuit,* to make the rounds of a circuit as a minister, judge, or lawyer.

1718 SEWALL *Letter-Book* II. 90 By reason of the inability of the late hon[ora]ble Chief Justice Winthrop to ride the remoter circuits, I have frequently presided. **1776** ASBURY *Journal* I. 159 They now [1774] began to ride the circuit, and to take care of the societies already formed. **1846** *Knickerb.* XXVIII. 360 The lawyers in travelling round from court to court with the judges, perform what a Methodist minister denominates 'riding the circuit.' **1870** W. W. HOLDEN *Proclamations* 31 The life of the Judge whose duty it is to ride the circuit . . . has not been safe.

4. An association of baseball teams from various cities that play among themselves for the league championship.

1898 *Kansas City Star* 18 Dec. 3/1 Little was heard to-day of changes in the league circuit, the prime movers in the scheme preferring to work in the dark. *Ib.*, The advocates of a reduced circuit have little intention of buying any one out at lofty prices.

5. Attrib. (in senses 1 and 2) with *attorney, meeting,* etc.

1845 *Indiana Mag. Hist.* XXIII. 54, I attended it [the fourth quarterly meeting], having been made one of the circuit stewards. **1852** *Knickerb.* XL. 93, I attended a circuit-meeting the other day, where a 'powerful' preacher held forth. **1859** *Ladies' Repository* XIX. 511/2 Does not the objector see that this lies against the circuit system, rather than against itinerancy? *Ib.* 318/2 The ministerial labor is chiefly circuit-work. **1904** *N.Y. Ev. Post* 11 April 6 He began his work in St. Louis as Circuit Attorney—the office corresponds to that of district attorney here.

Circuit breaker. *Elec.* A device which breaks or interrupts a circuit.

1872 *U.S. Patents Official Gazette* II. 140/1 Claim . . . [includes] the combination of two batteries with a circuit and a circuit-breaker. **1874** KNIGHT 554/1 The simplest and first form of rheotome or circuit-breaker was a file connected to one wire of a battery, [etc.]. **1876** INGRAM *Centennial Expos.* 122 Its motion is communicated by a cord running over a pulley to the circuit-breaker of an electro-magnet. **1879** G. PRESCOTT *Speaking Telephone* 251 A delicate circuit-breaker, attached to the membrane, was arranged to break the circuit of a telegraph line at the vibration.

Circuit clerk. The clerk of a circuit court. — **1848** *S. Lit. Messenger* XIV. 648/1 One of the proprietors went immediately to the circuit clerk, and complained on oath against the authors of, and actors in, this riot. **1891** O'BEIRNE *Leaders Ind. Territory* 51/2 In 1879 he was appointed circuit clerk under Judge Loring Folsom.

Circuit court. {1679–, *Sc.* (*D.O.S.T.*)}

+1. A Federal court having jurisdiction superior to that of a district court. Abolished in 1911.

1789 *Statutes at Large* I. 93 All writs and processes issuing from a supreme or a circuit court. **1797** *Ann. 5th Congress* 478 A letter from the Judges of the Supreme Court of the United States, representing the inconvenience arising from altering the time of holding the Circuit Court for the State of Delaware, from April to June. **1807** *Ann. 10th Congress* 1 Sess. I. 424 The annexed statement . . . as given in the circuit court of the United States for the fifth circuit and Virginia district, [etc.]. **1813** *Ann. 12th Congress* 2 Sess. 90 A bill to alter the times and places of holding the circuit court for the sixth circuit of the United States. **1903** *Chicago Chronicle* 11 April 2/1 The decision of the circuit court . . . destroys the last legal device for the suppression of competition.

+2. A state court presided over by a circuit judge.

*a***1817** DWIGHT *Travels* I. 273 The Circuit Court [of Conn.] is also a Court of Chancery. **1838** *Ind. Ho. Rep. Jrnl.* 146 An act establishing circuit courts, and defining their power and duties. **1840** *Niles' Nat. Reg.* 1 Aug. 347/1 The supreme court of Illinois . . . affirmed the judgment of the circuit court. **1854** BENTON *30 Years' View* I. 130/1 He was well occupied where he was—clerk of the lucrative office of the State Circuit Court. **1910** J. HART *Vigilante Girl* 308 Mark my words, Yarrow, if this case gets into the circuit court somebody is going to get hurt.

attrib. **1877** *Mich. Gen. Statutes* (1882–3) I. 93 There shall be published of the volume containing the public acts of each session . . . a sufficient number of copies to supply the following persons: . . . prosecuting attorneys, circuit court commissioners, sheriffs, [etc.]. **1879** *Ib.* 552 Such securities as shall be approved by any circuit judge, or by any circuit court commissioner of the county.

+3. *Circuit court of appeals,* an appellate Federal court immediately below the Supreme Court, established in 1891.

1891 *U.S. Session Laws* XXVI. 827 There is hereby created in each circuit a circuit court of appeals. **1905** *Indian Laws & Tr.* III. 158 Hereafter all appeals and writs of error shall be taken from the United States courts in the Indian Territory to the United States circuit court of appeals for the eighth circuit.

Circuit judge. {1773–, *Sc.* (Erskine *Institutes*)} A judge who presides over a circuit court.

1801 *Ann. 6th Congress* 9 Jan. 902 His travelling expenses were trifling compared with those of the Circuit Judges. **1816** *Ann. 14th Congress* 2 Sess. 357 There shall be appointed . . . a Judge to be called a Circuit Judge, who shall . . . hold the circuit courts in the respective districts. **1818** FORDHAM *Narr. Travels* 155 He is an associate Judge and sits on the bench with the circuit or law judge. **1830** *Amer. Almanac 1831* 197 The eight circuit judges [for New York State] are vice-chancellors for their respective circuits. **1846** MACKENZIE *Van Buren* 203 Governor Clinton could not have nominated Herman J. Redfield as circuit judge of the western district. **1847** COLLINS *Kentucky* 203 Bledsoe . . . was appointed by Gov. Adair, a circuit judge in the Lexington district. **1904** LYNDE *Grafters* 303 Will you take . . . MacFarlane's job as circuit judge?

+Circuit preacher. A minister having charge of one or more churches in a circuit; a circuit rider.

1834 PECK *Gaz. Illinois* 89 The Illinois conference (of the Methodist Episcopal denomination), . . . has five districts, fifty-six circuit preachers. **1846** *Indiana Mag. Hist.* XXIII. 243 Although the local preachers were not equal to the White Water circuit preachers in number, talents, zeal, and usefulness, there were some excellent and useful men among them. **1850** *Knickerb.* XXXV. 172 On one occasion a 'circuit-preacher' in Alabama took his text from the Epistle to the Hebrews. **1850** LEWIS *La. Swamp Dr.* 48 Last Saturday, who should cum ridin' up but the new cirkut preacher. **1872** EGGLESTON *End of World* 245 Then he stepped to the door and called in the circuit preacher.

+Circuit rider. A minister serving churches in a circuit.

1838 FLAGG *Far West* II. 61 [He] forthwith announced himself a 'Baptist circuit-rider!' **1845** *Indiana Mag. Hist.* XXIII. 24 A Methodist circuit rider, as the traveling preachers were then called, was a new thing among us Indianians. **1850** LEWIS *La. Swamp Dr.* 43 At one moment she would be heard discussing whether the new 'circus rider,' (as she always called him,) was as affecting in Timothy as the old one was pathetic in Paul. **1858** *Harper's Mag.* May 852/2 The Doctor was presiding elder of the district in which he lived, and as such was often obliged to entertain the 'circuit-riders' as guests. **1872** *Newton Kansan* 3 Oct. 2/3 His first services were as 'circuit rider' in the frontier districts of Virginia, Kentucky and Tennessee. **1881** PIERSON *In the Brush* 142 On one of these journeys the Bishop found at a mountain-inn a Methodist circuit-rider, class-leader, steward, and local preacher, assembled for an 'official meeting.' **1898** CANFIELD *Maid of Frontier* 17 At the earnest solicitation of the circuit-rider—who came twice a year, and when he did, got away as soon as possible. **1909** *N.Y. Ev. Post* (semi-wkly. ed.) 23 Sept. 5 A last survival was he of the old circuit rider of early Methodism. **1910** C. HARRIS (*title*), A Circuit Rider's Wife.

Circular. A communication printed or reproduced in large numbers for wide distribution. {1818–}

1789 *Ann. 1st Congress* I. 16 It was agreed that a circular should be written to the absent members, requesting their immediate attendance. **1796** *Steele Papers* I. 144 A rough of a letter which may at some future period compose part of a circular to the Collectors on the same subject. **1825** NEAL *Bro. Jonathan* I. 134 It was a printed circular from the 'Brotherhood of Safety'; informing all the ministers . . . that a petition from the colonies . . . had been treated . . . with contempt and laughter. **1887** *Postal Laws* 151 The term 'circular' is defined to be a printed letter, which, according to internal evidence, is being sent in identical terms to several persons.

Circular cloak. A long, full, loose-fitting cloak. Also ellipt. — **1837** *S. Lit. Messenger* III. 225 A huge umbrella under . . . which was an . . . urchin . . . carrying home some gentleman's new circular cloak. **1883** PECK *Bad Boy* 125 Ma . . . got the doctor to prescribe a fur lined circular.

Circular saw. A thin steel disk provided with teeth on its periphery, which is used as a saw by being made to revolve rapidly on its axis. {1852–} Also attrib.

1817 *Niles' Reg.* XII. 336/2 At the steam saw mill there is a circular saw, about four feet in diameter, chiefly calculated for cutting veneers. **1821** *Mass. Spy* 26 Sept. (Th.), The circular saw is a recent invention. The Shakers, at their village in Watervliet, near Albany, have this in very excellent use and great perfection. **1851** J. ROSS *In New York* 211 Their circular saws were splendid. **1853** J. W. BOND *Minnesota* 125 The mill near the upper landing runs one upright and one circular saw. **1858** THOREAU *Maine Woods* 154 We visited Veazie's mills, . . . where were sixteen sets of saws,—some gang saws, sixteen in a gang, not to mention circular saws. **1865** 'MARK TWAIN' *Sk., Jumping Frog,* Greeley always come out winner on that pup till he harnessed a dog once that didn't have no hind legs, because they'd been sawed off in a circular saw. **1868** *Mich. Agric. Rep.* VII. 361 Lane & Bodley, Cincinnati, [exhibited] 1 portable circular saw mill and engine. **1898** *Mo. So. Dakotan* I. 48 The signal of danger was produced by beating upon a circular saw.

ellipt. **1909** WHITE *Rules of Game* I. iv, We cut with 'circulars' instead of band-saws. *Ib.* vii, Band saws. No circulars here.

Circulate,** *v.* +*intr.* To travel or go about. *colloq.* — *a1859** Bartlett 83 Arriving in Maryland, a slave State, he circulates at a cost of from three to five cents a mile. **1907** MULFORD *Bar-20* 83 Shore, go home. I'll just circulate around some for exercise.

Circulating library. A library whose books circulate among the subscribers or the general public. {1742–}

1793 *Md. Hist. Mag.* XII. 298 It is a circumstance to be regretted, that a town like this, containing upwards of fifteen thousand inhabitants, does not afford a circulating library. **1809** KENDALL *Travels* I. 136 This is not a circulating library, of which the property is private. **1842** DICKENS *Amer. Notes* 28 Nearly all these young ladies subscribe to circulating libraries. **1877** *Harper's Mag.* April 724/2 The first circulating library, established by John Mein, at Boston, in 1765. **1896** *Godey's Mag.* Feb. 118/2 Those sharp-witted folk should find a whole circulating library in the study of the freaks of nature.

Circumferentor. Also †**-enter.**

1. An instrument for taking horizontal angles and bearings in surveying. {1610–}

1674 *Md. Archives* II. 393 For every resurvey being made with a Chaine Circumferenter with Sights and other Instruments for that purpose necessary the surveyor Generall . . . may aske . . . double the fees before in this Act provided. **1744** *Md. Hist. Mag.* XXI. 252 One Light Circumferrenter for Surveying Land with a Staff and Two pr. Chains. **1790** *Penna. Packet* 10 May 4/3 John Sparhawk . . . has for Sale, . . . plotting instruments, circumferenters, two-pole chains, . . . miniature cases and frames. **1805** LEWIS in *L. & Clark Exped.* (1904) II. 197 S[h]arbono lost his gun, . . . Capt. Clark his Umbrella and compass or circumferenter. **1848** THOMPSON *L. Amsden* 146 One blunder . . . was his mention of 'circumflutors,' meaning, probably, to have hit on circumferentors, of which he might have heard from some students.

+**2.** An instrument for measuring the circumference of a tire or wheel.

1874 KNIGHT 556/2.

* **Circumstance.**

+**1.** In various negative expressions, *e.g.* 'not a circumstance to': nothing in comparison with, not to be compared with. *colloq.*

1836 *Crockett's Yaller Flower Almanac* 19 Orson the wild man of the woods, is nothing to him—not a circumstance. **1843** STEPHENS *High Life N.Y.* I. 86, I thought the table, when I eat dinner at cousin John's, took the shine off from every thing that I'd ever seen . . . but it wasn't a circumstance to this. **1845** JUDD *Margaret* II. v. 284 O, it an't a circumstance to what it used to be. **1857** HAMMOND *Wild Northern Scenes* 62, I've travelled on the cars in my day, . . . but that kind o' goin' wasn't a circumstance to the way we tore along. **1863** NORTON *Army Letters* 173 The scorn and disgust the revolutionary tories met won't be a circumstance to what is waiting for them [=northern rebels]. **1878** BEADLE *Western Wilds* 615 Job's luck wasn't a circumstance. **1893** *Congress. Rec.* 2 Oct. 2044/1 The affection of Damon and Pythias or that of David and Jonathan is not a circumstance to the love of the white Republican for the negro while the ballots are going in. **1903** *Nation* 1 Oct. 258 Undigested securities are not a circumstance to undigested political principles.

+**2.** *Mere* (or *remote*) *circumstance*, a person or thing of little or no consequence. *colloq.*

1838 FLAGG *Far West* I. 145 The race of John Gilpin or of Alderman Purdy were, either or both of them, mere circumstances to ours. *c***1840** Florida newspaper (Th. 969), I'm a small specimen, as you see, a remote circumstance, a mere yearling; but cuss me if I ain't of the true imported breed. **1840** *Knickerb.* XVI. 154 My uncle was a little wiffet of a man; one that in Kentucky we would not call even an 'individual'; nothing more than a 'remote circumstance.' **1840** SIMMS *Border Beagles* I. vi. 90 Five thousand dollars will swallow me and all my substance, and you must rub that down to a mere circumstance. **1856** — *Eutaw* 394 'To be beaten by such a mere circumstance of a gal-child,' as he himself phrased it, was a circumstance of mortification.

+**3.** (See quotation.)

1889 FARMER 148 To *Whip* (something) *into a Circumstance* . . . means that the thing whipped is thrown into the shade; or compares unfavorably with the object of comparison. Thus a newspaper correspondent writes, that the streets of Georgetown, Demerara, 'are broad, smooth, and well laid out. Georgetown could give points to New York in its roads and whip it into a circumstance.'

* **Circus,** *n.*

1. =AMPHITHEATER I.

1810 *Columbian Centinel* 10 Jan. 3/3 Mr. D[avis] has erected a convenient Stage, with appropriate Scenery in the Circus, purposely for this Comedy. **1845** SMITH *Theatr. Apprent.* 94 We took up our summer quarters in Utica, where we converted a circus into a theatre. **1855** WOOD *Recoll. Stage* 239 A lease was offered by the proprietors of the Walnut street theatre (or rather circus).

2. A traveling company which gives performances, usu. in a tent, consisting largely of animal acts, acrobatic feats, etc.; also one of the performances. {1791–}

1833 E. COKE *Subaltern's Furlough* viii, A band of music was playing upon Camp Hill at the entrance of the town, where the tents of an itinerant circus were pitched. **1865** *Atlantic Mo.* XV. 146 No traveling circus, . . . no progressive young men. **1878** J. F. Daly *Life A. Daly* (1917) 253, I have been travelling with old John Robinson's Circus and Menagerie. **1882** *Wheelman* I. 100 'Going to the circus, are you?' said Grandmother. **1920** C. R. COOPER *Under Big Top* 141 It was in the winter quarters of a western circus.

+**3.** A noisy dispute, row, uproar; an exhibition of rough sport; a lively time. *colloq.*

1885 *N.Y. Mercury* 23 May (Ware), Coghill found out that he had paid Lafayette just three times too much for the Louisiana lands. . . . Then there was a circus. **1891** *Scribner's Mag.* Oct. 454/1 In Western vernacular, 'we had a circus' packing those skins on my horse. **1895** C. KING *Fort Frayne* 69 We'll have a circus with him. **1903** A. ADAMS *Log Cowboy* ii. 22 Yes, you'll get all the circus there is.

+**4.** *To play circus*, to go around in circles. *colloq.*

1867 *Atlantic Mo.* May 589/1, I believe we are playing circus here. **1876** HABBERTON *Jericho Road* 11 The West wasn't made fur blunderin' shadders to play circus in.

+**b.** *To see the circus*, to face trouble or difficulty; to 'see the sights.' *colloq.*

1891 'THANET' *Otto the Knight*, etc. 106 But Billy says, 'No, sir; it has been Atherton and Temple too long, for that; we'll see the circus together.' **1898** ATHERTON *Californians* 13 He was persuaded by Polk to take a trip into the San Joaquin valley to 'see the circus,' as the Yankee phrased it.

5. Attrib. and comb. with *actor*, *bill*, *catch*, etc.

1839 *Knickerb.* XIII. 76 A company of circus-actors . . . were attacked by the town-officers, and sent packing. **1891** 'THANET' *Otto the Knight*, etc. 218 Witness the flaming circus-bills plastered over Jerry Milligan's saloon. **1893** *Chicago Tribune* 28 April 7/3 The infield executed three neat double plays, while Halliday made one of his circus catches in center field. **1896** HARRIS *Sister Jane* 95 The pillars of the church . . . began a crusade against the sin of circus-going. **1873** BAILEY *Life in Danbury* 103 Mr. Luce was among the first on the circus grounds, Saturday. **1920** C. R. COOPER *Under Big Top* 2 To circus makers the next season begins at the same time. **1886** JAMES *Bostonians* 205 She will run off with some lion-tamer; she will marry a circus-man! **1901** WHITE *Westerners* xx. 186 Peter was making enough noise for a circus parade. **1882** 'MARK TWAIN' *Stolen White Elephant* i. 25 Barnum . . . wants to paste circus-posters on him. **1857** *Spirit of Times* 3 Jan. 295/1 (*advt.*), Great sale of circus property, at auction. **1855** W. B. WOOD *Recoll. Stage* 249 The house having been originally constructed only with a view to circus purposes. **1857** M. J. HOLMES *Meadow-Brook* iii, But circus riding was not Sorrel's forte. **1855** M. THOMPSON *Doesticks* 41 Hereafter you may not mistake a Grand Street stage for a perambulating Circus wagon.

‖**Circus,** *v.* **1.** *intr.* To go in circles. *colloq.* (Cf. CIRCUS *n.* 4.) **2.** To pretend that one is performing in a circus. — **(1) 1872** 'MARK TWAIN' *Roughing It* xxxi. 228 Boys, these are our own tracks, and we've actually been circussing round and round in a circle for more than two hours out here in this blind desert! **(2) 1876** — *Tom Sawyer* xxii. 178 The boys played circus for three days afterward in tents made of rag carpeting—admission, three pins for the boys, two for the girls—and circusing was abandoned.

+**Circus day.** The day on which a circus performs in a town or community. — **1860** *Harper's Mag.* Feb. 290/2 It was circus day in the shire town. Joe Pentland was coming, and all was bustle and excitement. **1882** PECK *Sunshine* 179 If a boy knows that there will be no school on the afternoon of circus day, he will study like a white-head all the forenoon. **1911** HARRISON *Queed* 257 Circus day in a small town was not a dot upon the atmosphere of thrilled expectancy so all-pervasive here.

Circus rider. One who performs equestrian feats in a circus. {1876–}

1839 *S. Lit. Messenger* V. 802/2 The man . . . asked, if we were circus riders. **1840** *Picayune* 21 Aug. 2/1 George Sweet, a circus rider, threw himself from the third story of the Eagle Tavern, Buffalo, N.Y. **1848** PARKMAN in *Knickerb.* XXXII. 45 He had been a circus-rider at St. Louis. **1860** S. COWELL *Diary* 136 Sam, Sidney and I went to Nikla's to see the Circus riders. **1883** 'MARK TWAIN' *Life on Miss.* xlviii, It is not every circus-rider that could stay on it.

+**Cisatlantic,** *a.* Of or pertaining to this side of the Atlantic.

1782 JEFFERSON *Notes Va.* 118, I only mean to suggest a doubt, . . . whether nature has enlisted herself as a Cis- or Trans-Atlantic partisan. **1818** FESSENDEN *Ladies Monitor* 96 Select their jewels [*i.e.*, of the British classics] and unite to those Some cis-atlantic works in verse and prose. **1827** COOPER *Prairie* vi, Obed Bat, . . . M.D., and fellow of several cisatlantic learned societies. **1838** — *Homeward B.* v, Her associations abroad had unavoidably imparted greater reserve to her ordinary deportment than the simplicity of cis-Atlantic usages would have rendered indispensable in the most fastidious circles. **1848** LOWELL *Biglow P.* I. p. vii, I have included the names of several Cisatlantic societies. **1865** *Atlantic Mo.* XV. 376 He came to owning a Cisatlantic birth. **1879** HOLMES *Motley* xvii. 107 What can I say to you of cis-Atlantic things?

+**Cisco.** [Amer. Indian.] (See quots. 1848, 1902.)

1848 BARTLETT 81 *Cisco*, the popular name of a fish of the herring kind which abounds in Lake Ontario. **1872** *Fur, Fin & Feather* 200 Ciscoes are caught mostly on shore, although many take them . . . from boats. **1884** JORDAN in Goode *Aquatic Animals* 541 The Moon-eye or 'Cisco' of Lake Michigan . . . is the smallest of our White-fish, rarely weighing over half a pound. **1888** GOODE *Amer. Fishes* 464 The cisco, *Coregonus Hoyi*, a well-known fish closely resembling the white-fish. **1902** *Amer. Folk-Lore* 243 *Cisco* (*sisco*). A name applied to certain species of fish found in the Great Lakes and adjoining waters: (1) The lake 'moon-eye' (*Coregonus hoyi*); (2) the lake herring (*Coregonus artedi*). The word is probably derived from one of the Algonkian dialects of this region. **1903** *N.Y. Sun* 1 Nov., In the same warehouse are trout, ciscoes, bluefish, weakfish, porgies, and so on.

+**Ciscoette, Ciscovet.** =SISCOWET. — **1847** LANMAN *Summer in Wilderness* 159 A fish called ciscovet, is unquestionably of the trout genus, but much more delicious. **1902** *Amer. Folk-Lore* 243 *Ciscoëtte*, a name of the lake herring. Apparently a derivative, with French diminutive suffix, from *Cisco* (q.v.), but rather a corruption of *Siskowit.*

||**Ciscoist.** One who fishes for cisco. — **1872** *Fur, Fin & Feather* 200 The lucky ciscoist is he (or she) who brings to this classic shore a sixteen-foot rod.

***Cistern.** Also **†cestern.**

***1.** An artificial reservoir for storing up water.

1685 *Boston Rec.* 172 The s[ai]d select men were willing to grant them the libertie . . . to bring s[ai]d water into a Cisterne. **1702** *Ib.* 26 Liberty is granted unto Elder Joseph Bridgham to Newmake and repaire the Cestern. **1792** BENTLEY *Diary* I. 405 Last Saturday evening in preparing the cistern at the Western end, the dirt caved in, & put an end to the existance of a man. **1827** DRAKE & MANSFIELD *Cincinnati* 31 They were bound . . . to fill all such cisterns or reservoirs, free of expense. **1851** CIST *Cincinnati* 168 There are eighty-three public cisterns, and seventy-nine fire-plugs, employed for the extinguishment of fires exclusively. **1881** *Harper's Mag.* Jan. 197/1 Finally we found a cistern near the barn and used that.

+2. A large receptacle for maple sap or molasses.

*a***1797** in Imlay *Western Territory* (ed. 3) 149 The sap flows into wooden troughs, from which it is carried and poured into store troughs, or large cisterns, in the shape of a canoe, or large manger. **1835** Ingraham *South-West* I. 240 All the molasses is removed from the cistern.

3. Attrib. and comb. with *building, house, maker*, etc.

1851 CIST *Cincinnati* 184 Jos. S. Cook has been several years engaged in cistern-building. **1849** Commons, etc. *Doc. Hist.* I. 253 With . . . all the improvements, viz: . . . Cistern House, Smoke House, [etc.]. **1789** *Boston Directory* 175 Bradley Nathaniel,—cistern-maker. **1874** KNIGHT 558/2 *Cistern-pump*, a small pump, lift or force, for pumping water from the moderate depth of a cistern. **1835** Ingraham *South-West* I. 240 When all the molasses is removed from the cistern, an inferior kind of sugar is re-manufactured, which is called cistern-sugar, and sold at a lower price.

Cistern bottom. +(See quot. 1833.) — **1833** SILLIMAN *Man. Sugar Cane* 41 On draining off the molasses cisterns, a quarter or less deposit of sugar, called cistern bottoms, is found in these vessels. **1856** *Rep. Comm. Patents: Agric.* 278 Some of our planters have not, perhaps, made so much molasses of late years, while others have made a greater quantity than they did last season, more particularly those who rolled a good portion of their crop into syrup or molasses, which, I am satisfied, must give them a larger quantity of cistern bottoms.

Cistern water. Water, esp. rain water, stored up in a cistern.

1858 *Texas Almanac* 82 Cistern water is used for culinary purposes. **1863** E. KIRKE *My Southern Friends* 49 New England rum, and cistern water. **1872** *Newton Kansan* 17 Oct. 4/4 It is well known, however, that cistern-water becomes impure. **1884** SWEET & KNOX *Through Texas* 636 Some thought it was thunder, and thousands of respectable people went out for the purpose of fixing the pipes to catch cistern-water.

***Cistus.** Any one of various plants of the natural order *Cistaceæ*. — **1784** CUTLER in *Mem. Academy* I. 457 *Cistus*, . . . American Cistus. Little Sunflower. . . . In dry pastures. June. **1785** MARSHALL *Amer. Grove* 75 *Ledum thymifolium.* Thyme leaved Marsh Cistus. This grows naturally in the Jerseys, in low, moist places. **1791** MUHLENBERG *Index Florae* 171 *Cistus tomentosus.* Cistus.

Citess. {1685} +(See quot. 1816.) *Obs.* — **1796** *British Critic* VII. 367 The Americans have coined the term *Citess*, which is better [than Citizeness]. **1816** PICKERING 61 *Citess.* This word, as well as citizenness, was used in America during the first years of the French Revolution, as a translation of the Revolutionary title *Citoyenne;* but it has for several years been wholly disused.

+Citified, *a.* Also **cityfied.** *colloq.* Having the manners of one accustomed to the city; suggestive of the city.

1855 M. THOMPSON *Doesticks* xvi. 132 Being so far cityfied in my habits that I desired to combine amusement with charity. **1876** 'MARK TWAIN' *Tom Sawyer* i. 22 He had shoes on—and it was only Friday. He even wore a necktie. . . . He had a citified air about him that ate into Tom's vitals. **1886** *Century Mag.* XXXII. 207/2 Our . . . summer homes . . . must not have a 'citified' look. **1888** *Ib.* XXXVI. 194/2 How admirably it fitted and complete my whole toilet looked. **1902** HARBEN *Abner Daniel* 254, I reckon you've got too citified for us.

+Citify, *v. colloq. tr.* To make citylike or more refined. — **1865** *Atlantic Mo.* XV. 501, I'd take n' citify my English.

***Citizen.**

***1.** A person entitled to enjoy the rights and required to perform the duties prescribed by law.

1684 I. MATHER *Providences* (1856) iv. 90 The citizens had like to have lost their lives by the prevailing drought. **1787** *Constitution* i. § 2 No person shall be a Representative who shall not have . . . been seven years a citizen of the United States. **1836** *Diplom. Corr. Texas* (1908) I. 164 In framing such an act great care should be taken in order to secure all of the rights of Texas and its citizens. **1868** *Constitution* Amend. 14 All persons born or naturalized in the United States, and subject to the jurisdiction thereof, are citizens of the United States and of the state wherein they reside. **1907** ANDREWS *Recoll.* 41 Many prominent Boston citizens were on the platform.

+b. In a sarcastic or derogatory sense: A fellow, 'guy,' bad character. *colloq.*

1897 CLOVER *Paul Travers' Adv.* 67 Paul was left in inky darkness with two presumably tough citizens. **1910** RAINE *B. O'Connor* 41 Chinks, greasers, and several other kinds of citizens driftin' that way.

2. A civilian; one not a soldier, policeman, etc. {1607–}

1790 *Ann. 1st Congress* II. 1225 The public faith . . . was pledged to the soldiery and to citizens who furnished supplies. **1843** N. BOONE *Journal* (1917) 209 Supposing the crossing to be near as the indians had represented and also the citizens we had in Camp, the camp was broken up. **1887** CUSTER *Tenting on Plains* 260 How difficult it was for an officer in command of a division to act in perfect justice to citizen, soldier and negro. **1894** CABLE *J. March* i, One of the most influential, and yet meekest, among the 'citizens'—men not in the army— . . . was Judge Powhatan March. **1910** *N.Y. Ev. Post* 24 Dec. 6 Happily, in this city the situation has improved as between the citizen and the policeman.

3. *attrib.* **a.** Composed of or designed for citizens in general. **b.** Pertaining to or characteristic of civilians as opposed to soldiers.

(a) 1871 *Rep. Indian Affairs* (1872) 513 There is much feeling on the part of the 'citizen party,' as they are called. **1906** *Indian Laws & Tr.* III. 232 He is hereby, authorized, . . . to allot the lands covered thereby to some member or members of the Citizen Band.

(b) 1871 F. ROE *Army Lett.* 17, I wore one of Fae's citizen caps, with tabs tied down over my ears, . . . in keeping with the dressing of the officers, who had on buckskin shirts, handkerchiefs, [etc.]. **1907** ANDREWS *Recoll.* 180 While we were resting and lunching, a scout brought to me a citizen physician who appeared to be a candid and honest man.

||**Citizening.** Admitting to citizenship. — **1890** *Home Missionary* (N.Y.) April 528 The citizening of the five tribes [in Indian Territory, U.S.] and statehood are inevitable.

***Citizenize,** *v. tr.* To invest with the rights of a citizen.

*c***1811** T. PICKERING (W. '28), Talleyrand was citizenized in Pennsylvania, when there in the form of an emigrant. **1835** INGRAHAM *South-West* I. 179 The residue are citizenized northerners, and individuals from other states. **1869** *N.Y. Evangelist* 25 March (*Cent.*), In 1843 Congress passed a law declaring them [Stockbridge Indians] civilized, Christianized, and citizenized. **1883** *WestChester* (Pa.) *News* XIII. 4 Resolved that the American Indian should be citizenized. **1885** *Advance* (Chicago) 1 Oct. 641 A hundred Sioux Christian families, citizenized.

+Citizen soldier. A civilian who in an emergency serves as a soldier.

1843 PRESCOTT *Mexico* (1850) II. 310 The citizen-soldiers of Villa Rica. **1844** *S. Lit. Messenger* X. 490/1 Colonels were strutting with valiant pomp, while the 'citizen soldiers' were drawn up in crooked array to 'bask in the sunshine.' **1844** 'UNCLE SAM' *Peculiarities* II. 34 Such were a few of the remarks made in La Grange Place, Philadelphia, by the undressed citizen-soldiers. **1865** *Atlantic Mo.* XV. 247/2 Five hundred thousand hearts following . . . his fortunes . . . : what is all this but weaving a strong network of alliance between the citizen at home and the citizen soldier? **1907** ANDREWS *Recoll.* 152 He said he would make no distinction between officers and men, but would address them all as citizen soldiers and gentlemen.

+Citizen soldiery. A military force of citizen soldiers; a militia. — **1837** *S. Lit. Messenger* III. 643 In addition to the ordinary engine, hose and axe companies there is a detachment of citizen soldiery . . . always on what is called alarm duty. **1851** NORTHALL *Curtain* 144 Dispositions were made on Thursday to meet any emergency, by detailing a body of three hundred men to the Opera House, and ordering two regiments of citizen soldiery to be under arms. **1876** INGRAM *Centennial Expos.* 658 One of the largest, most imposing, and, in all respects, most complete displays of the citizen-soldiery of Pennsylvania.

+Citizens' ticket. (See quot. 1888.) — **1873** *Newton Kansan* 10 April 3/3 The Citizens' Ticket did not make its appearance generally until Sunday morning. **1888** BRYCE *Amer. Commonw.* II. II. I. 269 When both the great parties put forward questionable men, a non-partisan list, or so-called 'citizens' ticket,' may be run by a combination of respectable men of both parties.

***Citron.**

***1.** The citron tree (*Citrus medica*) or its fruit. Also attrib.

1766 J. BARTRAM *Descr. East-Florida* (1769) 11 This was the fatal night that destroyed the lime, citron and banana-trees in Augustine. **1775** BURNABY *Travels* 99 In the gardens [of N. Jersey] is a very large collection of citrons, oranges, limes, . . . and other tropical plants. **1812** STODDARD *Sk. Louisiana* 168 The Delta produces various kinds of excellent fruit; such as . . . limes, citrons, and shaddock. **1849** WIERZBICKI *California* 11 The grape, the pomegranate, the citron, the orange . . . are found here. **1883** *Century Mag.* Oct. 807/1 The lemon, lime, and citron ripen and hang, like the orange.

2. The preserved rind of citron fruit.

1873 *Harper's Mag.* XLVI. 275 The young ladies of the family and myself were in the dining-room stoning raisins, blanching almonds, and cutting citron for the big cake. **1889** *Secy. of Agric. Rep.* 439 The citron . . . has a very thick sweet rind, from which is prepared the article known by grocers and cooks as 'preserved citron.'

+3. (See quotation.)

1877 BARTLETT 122 *Citron*, sweetmeats made from a melon, so as to closely resemble that made from the fruit of the citron-tree.

+Citron melon. A kind of watermelon having a hard thick rind. — **1806** CLARK in *Lewis & C. Exped.* (1905) IV. 175 The substance is about the consistancy of the rind of the citron Mellon and 3/4 of an inch thick, yellow celindrick, and regularly tapering. **1877** BARTLETT 122 *Citron melon*, the sort of melon employed for the purpose [of making imitation citron].

Citrus. A tree of the genus *Citrus.* {1865–} Usually attrib. — **1878** *Comm. Agric. Rep.* 206 In time the nomenclature of the Citrus family will become quite as accurate as that of pears and apples. **1902** *Harper's Mag.* May 875 The sun, . . . dazzled here and there against the young shoots of the citrus-grove. **1916** *Dept. Agric. Yearbook* 38 The citrus industry of California . . . owes its present magnitude . . . in large measure to the . . . Washington navel orange.

+**Citrus fair.** An exhibition of citrus fruits. — **1883** *Century Mag.* Oct. 810/1 At a citrus fair in the Riverside colony in March, 1882, in a building . . . built of redwood planks. **1893** K. SANBORN *S. Calif.* 61 Los Angeles is the place to go to see a new play, or marvel at the display of fruits seen at a citrus fair.

+**Citrus fruit.** Fruit obtained from any tree of the genus *Citrus.* — **1882** *Harper's Mag.* Dec. 59/2 The lands suitable for the cultivation of the 'citrus fruits,' too, are limited in extent. **1883** *Century Mag.* Oct. 804/1 The citrus fruits thrive, but need irrigation. **1891** *Harper's Mag.* Jan. 169/2 The lands with water are very much alike in their producing power, but some, for climatic reasons, are better adapted to citrus fruits. **1916** *Dept. Agric. Yearbook* 38 The results of several years of systematic study of citrus fruits in California show that important bud variations exist.

Cits. {1644–} +Civilian clothes. — **1895** KING *Ft. Frayne* 86 Will was . . . vaguely longing to get out and air his new 'cits.' **1907** *Chicago Tribune* 8 May 2 They were in full dress uniform. Later they were joined by Maj. . . . Judson of the engineers in 'cits.'

***City.**

***1.** In general, an inhabited place larger than a town; an incorporated municipality. (See quots. 1888, 1903.)

1654 JOHNSON *Wonder-w. Prov.* 209 Our Maritan Towns began to encrease roundly, especially Boston, the which of a poor country village, in twice seven years is become like unto a small City. **1675** *Penna. Mag.* VI. 87 There being also a place Chosen and set out for a Town or City to be Built. **1747** *N.J. Archives* 1 Ser. VII. 59, I have made a short visit to New York and another to Philadelphia which are pretty little cities for North America. **1837** *Diplom. Corr. Texas* (1911) III. 828, I arrived in this City on the 9th instant. **1855** GLISAN *Jrnl. Army Life* 222 Port Arford . . . was thought to be an admirable spot for a large city. **1888** S. Low in Bryce *Amer. Commonw.* II. II. lii. 296 In the United States a city is a place which has received a charter as a city from the legislature of its State. . . . Whenever in the United States one enters a place that is presided over by a mayor, he may understand, without further inquiry, that he is in a city. **1895** M. A. Jackson *Memoirs* 587 There was nothing to prevent a small force of cavalry riding into the city. **1899** E. E. HALE *Lowell & Friends* 17 From a New England town, . . . he changed it [Boston] into a 'city,' as America calls it, ruled by an intricate system of mayor, aldermen, council, school committee, and overseers of the poor. **1903** A. B. HART *Actual Govt.* 181 In the statistical publications of the U.S. government, a city is defined as an aggregate of 8,000 persons living in one territorial unit and under one local government.

+**2.** A grandiose or anticipatory designation for a mere hamlet or village.

'It is strange that the name of city should be given to an unfinished log-house, but such is the case in Texas. . . . This city mania is a very extraordinary disease in the United States' (1843 Marryat *Travels M. Violet* xxxii).

1747 *N.J. Archives* 1 Ser. VII. 66 After weighing all things I have pitcht upon this City (as call'd tho' but a village of 170 houses) for the place of my residence. **1819** *Niles' Reg.* XVI. 431/1 This *city* commenced 6 months ago. **1840** THOMPSON *Green Mt. Boys* I. 63 That fine and fertile swell of land, now occupied as the site of a pleasant and flourishing village, to which, as before mentioned, the more dignified name of city has long since been legally applied. **1856** *Harper's Mag.* XIII. 598/1 To the right lay the little town of Empire City—every collection of dwellings in Oregon and California is a city. **1862** *N. Amer. Rev.* July 200 Most of the settlements in these counties are so small, that one might pass near them without seeing them, and half a dozen houses are sufficient to secure the name of 'city.' **1867** DIXON *New America* I. 36 In two or three more [hours] we are at Junction City; a city of six wooden shanties. **1883** J. LAWRENCE *Silverland* 68 We reached Alta city—all mining camps are cities hereabouts.

+**3.** Frequent in designations of cities, as *C. of the Angels*, Los Angeles, Calif.; *C. of Brotherly Love*, (see BROTHERLY *a.* 1); *C. of Elms*, New Haven, Conn.; *C. of Magnificent Distances*, Washington, D.C.; *C. of Notions*, Boston, Mass.

1846 STOCKTON in E. Bryant *California* (1848) 298 We entered the 'City of the Angels,' the capital of California, on the 13th of August, and hoisted the North American flag. **1843** *Yale Lit. Mag.* VIII. 328 Some inconsiderate hard-hearted beauty, that was supposed to reside somewhere in the 'City of Elms.' **1842** DICKENS *Amer. Notes* 45 It is sometimes called the City of Magnificent Distances, but it might with greater propriety be termed the City of Magnificent Intentions. **1846** *Spirit of Times* 9 May 132/3 Boston, April 13. . . . Dear Sir: The last 'Spirit' has caused quite a sensation in our 'City of Notions.'

4. Attrib. and comb.: Of or pertaining to the government of a city; owned or administered by a city.

1905 N. DAVIS *Northerner* 111 Are we boys playing marbles—or is this a city administration? **1807** IRVING, etc. *Salmagundi* xii. 304 Wholesale merchants—have the privilege of going to the city assembly! **1835** GARRISON in *Life* (1885) II. 29 At the earnest solicitation of the city authorities, . . . I deemed it proper to leave the city for a few days. **1873** *Newton Kansan* 3 April 3/2 City election takes place next Monday. **1856** D. MACLEOD *F. Wood* 163 The amount raised by tax for the support of the city government. **1865** CUMMING *Hospital Life* 164/2 It was the city hospital, and part of it is still reserved for the use of the sick citizens. **1870** 'M. HARLAND' *For Better, for Worse* 347 The prisoner was sentenced to three months' imprisonment in the city jail. **1822** *Boston Selectmen* 13 March, Lists of the qualified voters . . . printed for the use of the wards at the election of city officers. **1873** *Newton Kansan* 8 May 3/2 Two new city ordinances in this paper. **1904** STRATTON-PORTER *Freckles* 20 The restricted life of a great city orphanage was the other extreme of the world. **1889** Salmons *Burlington Strike* 355 The mob was dispersed by the arrival of a platoon of city police. **1883** *Harper's Mag.* Sept. 611/2 Demoralization . . . prevails in State as well as city politics. **1827** DRAKE & MANSFIELD *Cincinnati* 50 The Council have power . . . to erect a City prison. **1855** F. WOOD in MacLeod *Biog.* 243 You draw from the City Treasury as pay, in the aggregate nearly one million of dollars per annum. **1788** FRANKLIN *Autobiog.* 352 The city watch was one of the first things that I conceiv'd to want regulation.

b. In titles of officials of a city.

1887 *Courier-Journal* 2 Feb. 3/2 Mr. William Baird, the well-known city attorney, . . . is lying in a most critical condition. **1909** G. PARKER *G. Cleveland* 46 Remissness in the duties of the City Auditor's office. **1871** *Mich. Gen. Statutes* I. 116 The city clerk shall cause the proper register to be placed in the hands of the inspectors of election. **1891** 'THANET' *Otto the Knight* 113 Temple used to . . . get directions about the mill and store. He had the city clerk do the same. **1885** *Cent. Mag.* Oct. 916 A giant pine which had survived the cruelties of the city engineer and . . . one lightning stroke was chopped down. **1856** MACLEOD *F. Wood* 170 The City Inspector's Department attends to the removing of nuisances, carrying off dead horses, and other animals, and has general charge of every thing relating to the streets, which affect their sanitary condition. **1855** F. WOOD *ib.* 246 You have been selected by the Mayor, the Recorder, and the City Judge . . . as worthy to be intrusted with delicate and important duties. **1865** RICHARDSON *Secret Service* 143 After the disbanding of the Committee of Safety I was brought before the City Recorder. **1887** *Courier-Journal* 1 Feb. 8/4 The City Treasurer paid off yesterday coupons on the bonded debt of the city.

c. With reference to organizations, institutions, etc., located in a city.

1855 *Harper's Mag.* XI. 256/2 Mayor Dow . . . recently purchased $1600 worth of liquor for the city agency. **1852** *Ib.* V. 267/2 The City market on the corner of Spring-street. **1853** M. BLAKE *Mendon Association* 186 In 1841, he [=Rev. A. A. Phelps] entered upon the Agency for City Missions.

d. Of or pertaining to a city.

1845 KIRKLAND *Western Clearings* 38 We see the managers of a city ball admit the daughters of wholesale merchants. **1923** R. HERRICK *Lilla* 80 In spite of the disfiguring lumps of 'city improvements.' **1856** SIMMS *Charlemont* 216 The active wants and duties of a large city-practice. **1912** N. M. WOODROW *Sally Salt* 104 But of all the summer folks that's ever taken their meals with me, no one has ever paid me the prices that Grissom has. City prices, Jake, city prices! **1784** *Mass. Centinel* 27 March 3/1 Several towns have been incorporated with City Privileges. **1865** *Atlantic Mo.* XV. 83 As an item of city property, Central Park is at present valued at six million dollars. **1887** *Courier-Journal* 20 Feb. 3/6 Wanted—A Young Man—To drum City Trade.

e. Pertaining to a newspaper published in a city.

1877 *Harper's Mag.* Dec. 47/1 But the local work of the day begins in the City Department, which includes the city editors and reporters. **1889** *Cent.* 1020/1 *City item*, in American newspapers, an item of local or city news. **1899** J. L. WILLIAMS *Stolen Story*, etc. 106 But the moment he [a reporter] left the hot exciting atmosphere of the City Room, it seemed a very different business.

+**City block.** [BLOCK *n.* 1.] A regular division of a city bounded by streets; the distance along one side of this, or an equivalent distance.

1884 *Century Mag.* May 64/2 It was no easy task to take such a site—only a city block—and yet secure such ample accommodation and illumination. *Ib.* July 326/2 He was given . . . only a single city block to build upon. **1891** *Harper's Mag.* Dec. 38/1 The medicine-men . . . sat in a row with their backs to the dancers a city block away. **1907** LILLIBRIDGE *Trail* 131 He was within half the distance of a city block of the latter [sentinel].

City charter. A written instrument incorporating and setting forth the powers, duties, etc., of a municipality.

1839 *Indiana Ho. Rep. Jrnl.* 597 An act granting to the citizens of Madison and the town of Lawrenceburgh a city charter. **1855** F. WOOD in MacLeod *Biog.* 198 In relation to the proposed City Charter, I can express a favorable opinion of its leading features. **1869** J. R. BROWNE *Adv. Apache Country* 498 The city charter was passed with due solemnity in April, 1864. **1903** *McClure's Mag.* Nov. 31/1 When Mr. Steffens went to Philadelphia they showed him with pride their magnificent city charter.

+**City collector.** A tax collector for a city. — *c***1870** BAGBY *Old Va. Gentleman* 263 'Well,' said I, 'if you will turn a city collector into a courting man, I can't help it.' **1875** *Chicago Tribune* 21 Sept. 8/2 The City Collector announces that delinquents on city taxes have but a few more days of grace. **1897** *Ib.* 14 July 5/3 The City Collector . . . estimates there are 300,000 bicycles in [Chicago].

+**City council.** The legislative branch of a city government, now usually a single elective chamber.

1789 MORSE *Amer. Geog.* 428 The intendant and wardens form the city council. **1822** *Ann. 17th Congress* 1st Sess. I. 163 Authorizing the City Council of Charleston to impose and collect a duty. **1827** DRAKE & MANSFIELD *Cincinnati* 50 This instrument vests the municipal power of the city in a City Council, which is to consist of three Trustees. **1841** CIST *Cincinnati* 46 A board of trustees . . . usually known by the name of the City Council. **1872** *Newton Kansan* 24 Oct. 3/2 There is an ordinance in force passed by our city council. **1888** *Chicago Inter-Ocean* 3 Jan. 1/1 Atlanta's new City Council, five Prohibitionists and ten Anti-Prohibitionists, . . . reduced the liquor license to $1,000. **1894** ROBLEY *Bourbon Co., Kansas* 184 Public sentiment may have found vent . . . in the action of the City Council. **1911** *Okla. Session Laws* 3 Legisl. 129 The mayor and city council of the city of Durant, are hereby empowered to issue and sell bonds of the said city of Durant.

City court. The municipal court of a city.

1786 *Penna. Col. Rec.* XIV. 667 The appointment of a Clerk of the City Court and Orphans' Court for the City and County of Philadelphia. **1796** MORSE *Amer. Geog.* I. 552 A city court is held by the mayor, recorder, and aldermen [of Philadelphia] four times a year. **1809** KENDALL *Travels* I. 85 The act of incorporation further establishes a city-court. *a***1817** DWIGHT *Travels* I. 196 The City Court is formed by the Mayor and two Aldermen; and has jurisdiction in all civil causes. **1827** DRAKE & MANSFIELD *Cincinnati* 48 There are three Courts, . . . these are the Supreme Court, the Court of Common Pleas, and the City Court. **1877** *Ga. Constitution* Art. 6 § 9 The jurisdiction, powers, . . . and practice of all courts or officers invested with judicial powers (except city courts), of the same grade or class, . . . shall be uniform. **1899** *Kansas City Star* 12 Jan. 2/2 The state senate two years ago passed a bill creating two city courts for Kansas City, Kas. **1904** *Ga. Sup. Ct. Rep.* CXXI. 593 The city court of Sylvester is not a constitutional city court, and . . . no writ of error lies . . . to the Supreme Court.

attrib. **1789** MORSE *Amer. Geog.* 331 The other public buildings in the city [of Philadelphia] . . . are the following, viz. A state house and Offices, A city court house, A county court house, [etc.]. **1827** DRAKE & MANSFIELD *Cincinnati* 50 The City Court Room, and Mayor's office, are in a brick building on the north side of Third street.

City debt. A debt incurred by a city. — **1831** A. LAWRENCE *Diary & Corr.* 170, I should personally sooner vote to sell ten acres of the Common, in front of my house, to pay the city debt (of Boston), than vote to sell the ten acres on Bunker Hill. **1856** D. MACLEOD *F. Wood* 167 Interest on city debts. **1888** *Boston Journal* 10 Dec., An increasing city debt and extravagant expenditures for jobs and junkets are bad for the poor man as well as for the rich.

City directory. A book containing the names and addresses of those living in a city. Also attrib.

1815 (*title*), Longworth's American Almanac, New-York Register and City Directory for the Fortieth Year of American Independence. **1846** *Spirit of Times* 4 July 217/1 They [bores] swell the City Directory half its bulk. **1893** M. Philips *Making of Newspaper* 52 Two men expert in the use of a city directory and well acquainted with Boston were able to decide what numbers the houses bore. **1904** A. DALE *Wanted, a Cook* 251 We believed in the home, not as a mere place to sleep in, or a city-directory address for the reception of letters, [etc.]. **1922** PARRISH *Case & the Girl* 129 Bring me up a City directory, will you?

City editor. +The editor in charge of collecting and editing local news in a city newspaper. Also *city editor in chief.*

1870 MAVERICK *Raymond & N.Y. Press* 326 The City Editor, directs the work performed by the reporters, whose duty is to gather all the local intelligence of the day. **1877** *Harper's Mag.* Dec. 52/1 The city editor-in-chief divides his staff into five or six squads. **1887** FREDERIC *Seth's Brother's Wife* 120, I'm the City Editor. I and my gang are downstairs. **1892** *Harper's Weekly* 9 Jan. 42/4 It probably never happened that the city editor could get all of the space he desired. **1899** J. L. WILLIAMS *Stolen Story*, etc. 128 But he soon found that each reporter was sent for a particular piece of news, the existence of which was determined in some mysterious way by the city editor. **1903** SHUMAN *Practical Journalism* 18 Under the managing editor are the city editor, who collects the local news; the telegraph or news editor, [etc.]. **1910** WALCOTT *Open Door* 242 It's written up already, and the copy is in the City Editor's hands.

City fathers. *pl.* The officials in charge of the government of a city.

1853 *Harper's Mag.* VI. 705/2 Such City Fathers as rob us not only of our pence, but of our pride, and of all our self-respect? **1857** *Lawrence* (Kansas) *Republican* 25 June 1 The reporter . . . hits off such of our worthy city fathers as were among the guests. **1861** *Vanity Fair* 13 April 172/2 Had his Worship the Mayor, or one of the City Fathers been distributed into the cellarage when that block fell, our report of the accident would have been fuller. **1876** *Wide Awake* 103/1, I wish they'd elect me one of the Common Council! City Fathers! Just so; rightly named! **1883** E. M. BACON *Dict. Boston* 359 Money spent in junketing by the city-fathers and their favourites.

+**City folks.** *pl.* Those who reside in a city. — **1789** S. LOW *Politician Outwitted* III. i, It's spelt . . . con-sti-tu-ti-on, but your city folks calls it constitushon. *c***1845** *Big Bear Ark.* 16 Game, indeed, that's what city folks call it; and with them it means chippen-birds and shite-pokes. **1885** *Harper's Mag.* Aug. 353/1 In the eyes of a discreet scribe and pilgrim, the 'city folks' there are all 'nice.'

+**City hall.** A building in which the principal officials of a city have their offices.

1675 ANDROS in Easton *Indian War* 106 There was at the City Hall an Order of the last Gen[er]all Court of Assizes. **1754** E. Singleton *Social N.Y.* 339 The books . . . are placed for the present, by leave of the Corporation, in their library room in the City Hall. **1807** IRVING, etc. *Salmagundi* v, A pair of colors were presented at the City Hall. **1833** COKE *Subaltern's Furlough* iv, Of the public buildings, the City Hall, containing the supreme court, mayor's court, and various public offices, . . . is the most remarkable. **1882** *Wheelman* I. 73 Meanwhile the election of officers took place in the City Hall. **1889** BRAYLEY *Boston Fire Dept.* 183 The old State-House, or City Hall, as it was then called, was badly damaged. **1920** C. R. COOPER *Under Big Top* 46 Permission to salute him . . . on the steps of the city hall.

attrib. **1872** BRACE *Dangerous Classes N.Y.* 28 These youthful ruffians . . . live on . . . City-Hall places and pot-houses. **1877** *Harper's Mag.* Dec. 43/1 Two gentlemen crossed the breezy interspace of City Hall Park.

+**City limits.** *pl.* The boundaries of a city.

1861 *Atlantic Mo.* April 433/1 The mill to which she was going lay on the river, a mile below the city-limits. **1865** *Ib.* XV. 84 Large numbers of uncounted sheep are consumed within the city limits. **1870** *Scribner's Mo.* I. 36 A shabby village street . . . made it easier to realize that . . . we were still within city limits. **1907** ANDREWS *Recoll.* 144 Its city limits extended into the forest over two miles. **1911** *Okla. Session Laws* 3 Legisl. 127 The council may purchase or condemn and hold for the city, within or outside of the city limits, all necessary lands for hospital purposes and waterworks.

+**City lot.** A piece or portion of land within a city or a proposed city.

1683 W. PENN *Works* IV. 316 The city-lot [is conveniently posted] for a dock. **1788** R. PUTNAM in *Life & Corr. Cutler* I. 379 The City lots will be ready to draw by the first Wednesday of July. **1829** R. C. SANDS *Writings* II. 169 The latter sat pensive and silent, while Miss Violet discoursed . . . about western lands and city lots. **1844** LEE & FROST *Oregon* vi. 79 The above-mentioned gentleman . . . was selling off small city lots at one hundred dollars a piece. **1863** MASSETT *Drifting About* 131, I was always the auctioneer selected by them whenever they put any of their city lots 'into the market.' **1879** *Scribner's Mo.* May 155/2 The shape and size of these city lots have not proved specially inconvenient. **1923** R. HERRICK *Lilla* 19 'Put it into city lots around Chicago,' he replied superiorly.

City marshall. {1632–} +A city official having charge of the police force. — **1840** *Picayune* 27 Sept. 2/2 Mr. John C. Cohen was yesterday elected City Marshal by the Boards of Mayor and Aldermen and Common Council. **1867** A. D. RICHARDSON *Beyond Miss.* 67 The mob picked up the city marshal and police as if they had been children. **1873** *Newton Kansan* 1 May 3/2 David Rosure has been appointed city marshal.

+**City park.** A park within a city and under the management of city officials. — **1885** *Century Mag.* Oct. 911 It would seem that the primary purpose of a city park . . . is to furnish a free bath of fresh air for lungs doomed to inhale some fluid which is not always fresh nor over cleanly. **1904** *Mass. Col. Soc. Publ.* VIII. 397 It should perhaps be added that in addition to National Parks, there are in the United States various State Parks, City Parks, and, in Massachusetts at least, Metropolitan Parks. *c***1908** Dale & Rader *Okla. Hist.* (1930) 726 A barbecue was planned to be given at the city park to feed the hungry multitude.

+**City school.** A public school maintained by a city. Also attrib. — **1849** CHAMBERLAIN *Ind. Gazetteer* 298 The public buildings in the City are the Court House . . . [and] two fine buildings for City Schools. **1852** *Boston City Doc.* No. 32, 19 Graduates from the city schools. **1904** *Forum* Oct. 257 The most comprehensive and in many ways the best all-around American city school exhibit.

+**City scrip.** *collective.* Certificates of indebtedness issued by a city. — **1873** *Winfield* (Kansas) *Courier* 18 Sept. 2/3 City Scrip is selling for 80 cents, County Scrip 80 cents, and School Bonds at 90 cents. **1875** *Chicago Tribune* 12 July 4/5 The tax-payers . . . began to buy up city scrip and turn it into the Treasury in payment of city taxes. **1916** THOBURN *Hist. Okla.* II. lxxii. 782 The alley . . . was vacated, with forty feet off of the lots on either side, at a cost of $16,000, which sum was paid in city scrip.

***Cive.** Usu. *pl.* A perennial plant resembling the onion. (Cf. CHIVE.) — **1709** LAWSON *Carolina* 77 The Garden-Roots that thrive well in Carolina, are . . . Garlick, Cives, and the Wild-Onions. **1737** BRICKELL *N. Carolina* 18 The Garden Roots that thrive here are . . . Shallots, Cives, Garlick. **1817–8** EATON *Botany* (1822) 167 *Allium schoenoprasum*, cives. E[xotic]. **1847** WOOD *Botany* 551.

Civet cat. +The mountain cat or cacomistle, *Bassariscus astutus.* — **1853** MARCY *Explor. Red River* (1854) 200 *Bassaris Astuta.* Licht. Civet cat. [Found at] cross-timbers.

+Civics. The science of the rights and duties of citizenship.

'In 1885 he [=Henry R. Waite] founded the American institute of civics, of which he has since been president. He was the first to employ the term "civics" to designate those branches of science that pertain to the elevation of citizenship' (1889 *Appleton's Cycl. Biog.* VI. 318).

1886 *Citizen* (Boston) Dec. 5 Shall Civics be taught in the public schools? **1888** *Boston Journal* 13 Oct. 3/5 The meeting then considered the question of the day, viz.: 'The End to be Kept in View in Teaching Civics.' **1896** *Peterson Mag.* VI. 313/1 Mrs. Talcott Williams . . . has made her mark in the past two years by some very able and almost masculine articles upon civics. **1904** *Education* Oct. 106 The word 'civics' is only about fifteen years old, and the thing 'civics'—if it can yet be called a thing—is not even so old as that.

***Civil,** *a.*

***1.** Secular; not ecclesiastical. Now arch. or obs.

*a***1649** WINTHROP *Hist.* II. 15 The elders had moved at a general court before, that the distinction between the two jurisdictions might be set down, that the churches might know their power, and the civil magistrate his. **1654** JOHNSON *Wonder-w. Prov.* 133 Yet seeing the benefit that would accrew to the Churches of Christ and Civil Government, by the Lords blessings, upon learning, they began to erect a Colledge. **1658** *New Plymouth Laws* 107 Wee hold and doe afeirme that both Courts of Justice and Magistrates, who are the minnesters of the Lawe are essentially Civill.

***2.** *Law.* Not criminal; pertaining to legal proceedings between individuals.

1676 *Conn. Pub. Rec.* II. 276 Lnt Joseph Orton is by this Court appoynted . . . to grant warrants in ciuill actions. **1822** *Ann. 17th Congress* 1st Sess. I. 84 A pretext would be furnished for usurping jurisdiction in all criminal as well as civil cases arising under that prohibition. **1839** *Knickerb.* XIII. 1 We do not now purpose to allude to criminal, nor to minor civil courts. **1877** JOHNSON *Anderson Co., Kansas* 89 The Territorial Legislature, in 1855, attempted to confer civil and criminal jurisdiction on the probate court, concurrent with the district courts. **1911** *Okla. Session Laws* 3 Legisl. 264 The county court . . . shall likewise transfer all civil causes within the jurisdiction of the superior court upon motion of plaintiff.

3. Not military; civilian. {1612–}

1775 FITHIAN *Journal* II. 135 The Civil Law is abolished through this colony, & the Law Martial declared to be in force! **1816** *Ann. 14th Congress* 2 Sess. 273 That no writ or civil process, issuing from any court of the United States, shall be served upon any militia man. **1865** *Atlantic Mo.* XV. 247/1 Will they [Civil War soldiers] find content . . . in the workshops, in the tranquil labors of civil life? Can they in short, put off the harness of the soldier? **1874** GLISAN *Jrnl. Army Life* 455 Social games of chess and cards are probably oftener resorted to in garrison than in civil life. **1907** ANDREWS *Recoll.* 218 But I thought that as American diplomatic officers as a rule wore civil dress I would waive the privilege of wearing my uniform.

Civil engineer. One who designs and supervises the construction of roads, bridges, tunnels, etc. {*a*1792–}

1819 *N. Amer. Rev.* VIII. 13 The profession of a civil engineer is scarcely known among us. **1840** *Diplom. Corr. Texas* (1908) I. 453 As a draughtsman, civil engineer, and agriculturalist, I believe he is unsurpassed. **1871** RAYMOND *3rd Rep. Mines* 128 Mr. Uren, of Dutch Flat, a civil engineer and surveyor, has made a reconnaissance of the country between Bear River and the North Fork of the American River. **1894** P. L. FORD *P. Stirling* 37 Peter called on his friend, the civil engineer.

Civilize, *v.* {1601–} *+tr.* (See quot. 1864.) *S.* — *c***1845** *Big Bear Ark.*, etc. 98 Arter howd'ying and civerlizin' each other I sot down. **1864** NICHOLS *Amer. Life* I. 387 When people salute each other at meeting, he [the Southerner] says they are howdyin' and civilizin' each other.

+Civilizee. One who is civilized. — **1848** *N.Y. Observer* (B.), The barbarian likes his seraglio; the civilizee admires the institution of marriage. The barbarian likes a roving, wandering life; the civilizee likes his home and fireside. **1883** *Century Mag.* XXVI. 933/2 The 'song' of Hiawatha has the epic quality that pertains to early ballads, the highest enjoyment of which belongs to later ages and to the creature that Whitman terms the civilizee. **1897** *New Eng. Mag.* Dec. 407 The members [of Brook Farm, *c*1837] looked upon the outside world as in some degree barbarian, and spoke of its people with a tone of contempt as civilizees.

Civil list. A list of charges for the civilian or nonmilitary establishments of government. *Obs.* {1712–} Also attrib.

1788 T. Speed *Danville Polit. Club, Ky.* (1894) 143 Civil list warrants would be better perhaps than paper currency. **1790** MACLAY *Deb. Senate* 207 So large an annual interest would be due to Pennsylvania that she would draw money enough from the Continent to pay her whole civil list, make her roads, build her bridges, open her canal. **1802** *Ann. 7th Congress* 1322 The sum of one hundred thousand dollars . . . is appropriated towards defraying the expenditure of the civil list. **1802** *Steele Papers* I. 262 The house have passed a partial appropriation bill for the civil list. **1822** *Ann. 17th Congress* 1 Sess. I. 148 If we propose to reduce the army, the friends of the army oppose; . . . if the officers of the civil list, their friends oppose it.

Civil right.

1. Usu. *pl.* The rights possessed in common by all citizens; +spec. the rights contemplated in the 13th and 14th Amendments to the Constitution.

1721 *Boston Rec.* 154 That they Indeavor to maintain all our Civel Rights and Properties against any Incrochments upon them. **1865** *Atlantic Mo.* XV. 160 Avowedly he was ready to lay the time-honored principles of civil right and the ancient law at the feet of the Slave Power. **1874** Fleming *Hist. Reconstruction* II. 201 The mere mention of civil (negro) Rights has almost destroyed the public schools and colleges in some of the Southern States. **1875** *Statutes at Large* XVIII. 335 An Act to protect all citizens in their civil and legal rights.

+2. *Civil rights bill*, a bill passed by Congress in 1866 designed to protect the civil rights of Negroes; also applied to a supplementary bill passed in 1875.

1866 A. JOHNSON in Fleming *Hist. Reconstruction* I. 225 The Civil Rights bill was more enormous than the other. **1867** *Ib.* II. 15 Who gave us the Civil Rights Bill? **1875** *43d Congress 2 Sess.* H. R. Rep. No. 262, 1262 [The carpetbaggers have sided with the Negroes] regardless of the . . . consequences to ensue from the passage of said odious civil-rights bill. **1876** *Congress. Rec.* 14 Jan. 421/1 The civil-rights bill . . . was designed to give the rights of manhood to the colored members.

Civil service.

1. That branch of the public service carried on by civilians. {*c*1785– in India; *a*1863–}

1871 *Statutes at Large* XVI. 514 The President of the United States [is] . . . authorized to prescribe . . . rules and regulations for the admission of persons into the civil service of the United States. **1872** *Atlantic Mo.* Feb. 253 Those who do not agree with Mr. Morton that we have the best civil service in the world. **1873** *Newton Kansan* 9 Jan. 2/1 Reforms . . . can hardly fail to purge our civil service of many abuses. **1883** *Century Mag.* July 469/2 The questions of most immediate importance in our public affairs to-day are those relating to the tariff, the civil service, and the government of corporations. **1888** LOWELL *Lit. & Polit. Addresses* 214 Our first aim should be . . . the reform of our civil service, for that is the fruitful mother of all our ills. **1893** 'THANET' *Stories* 118 Tommy talked of the civil service in the tone of Harry himself.

b. Attrib. with *abuse, appointee, bill, board,* etc.

1882 *Nation* Nov. 372/1 General Grant . . . was, when he left the Presidential chair, a very active perpetrator of most of the civil-service abuses. **1904** DERVILLE *Other Side of Story* 170 Foisting upon the Departments a lot of civil service appointees in place of political allies appointed by influence alone. **1871** *Harper's Mag.* XLIII. 19/1 Dreamers may talk of 'civil service bills,' where merit alone is to keep and command the patronage of the government. **1882** *Nation* 14 Dec. 498/1 A Civil-Service Board . . . shall have cognizance of all cases of complaints for removal. **1887** *Courier-Journal* 6 Feb. 2/2 A Brace Game With Civil-service Cards, in Which the Democrat is Fleeced. **1904** DERVILLE *Other Side of Story* 173 Many things published in newspapers and magazines regarding the civil service clerk. **1882** *Nation* 31 Aug. 165/1 The civil-service doctrines of the President's Message. **1883** *Harper's Mag.* Oct. 805/2 [He] instantly answered, as if he had been in a civil service examination. **1873** *Newton Kansan* 24 April 4/2 The new administration would carry out the civil service rules. **1873** *Winfield* (Kansas) *Courier* 10 April 2/1 The Civil Service system that was to have been adopted by the general government and enforced by Grant's new administration seems to have been abandoned already.

+2. *Civil Service Commission*, a board having charge of examinations, admissions, promotions, etc., in the civil service.

1872 *Atlantic Mo.* Feb. 254 The report of the Civil-Service Commission was immediately sent to Congress. **1878** *N. Amer. Rev.* CXXVI. 272 He had already appointed an able Civil-Service Commission. **1883** *Century Mag.* May 153/2 The general supervision of the system would be intrusted to the Civil Service Commission. **1916** *Amer. Academy Annals* LXIV. 155 Private business has much to learn from civil service commissions in selecting employees fit to do particular jobs.

+3. *Civil service reform*, (see quot. 1885).

1872 *Atlantic Mo.* March 384 The President had three times declared himself in favor of civil service reform. **1873** *Newton Kansan* 1 May 1/5 A much needed Civil Service Reform—Putting civil men in office. **1880** *Harper's Mag.* May 898/2 A short-lived attempt was made to apply the essential principles of civil service reform to the administration of the Custom house in the city of New York. **1883** *Century Mag.* July 469/2 In regard to civil service reform, there is not much disagreement among the rank and file. **1884** *Ib.* Nov. 128 If we ever reach the condition that is aimed at in what is called Civil Service Reform, an administration of any vigor can always find means to prevent inferior officers of the civil service from acting improperly against its public policy. **1885** *Mag. Amer. Hist.* Jan 99/2 *Civil Service Reform.*—The correction of abuses in the public service, or more specifically, the adoption of a system which shall not permit the removal of good and faithful officers for partisan reasons, and which shall prevent appointment to office as a reward for partisan services. **1887** *Courier-Journal* 6 May 2/2 We favor honest civil service reform. **1909** *Forum* XLI. 402 It seems peculiarly appropriate to give . . . at this time a review of the progress of civil service reform.

attrib. **1882** *Nation* 2 Nov. 370/3 A Civil-Service Reform Association with a membership of over 200 was formed in Rochester, N.Y., on Thursday night. *Ib.* 12 Oct. 300/1 Many are impatient about the slow progress of the civil-service reform movement.

* **Civil War.** +With reference to the war between the North and South in the U.S. **a.** Generic sense: Civil strife, internal war, a war between the states.

1819 *Ann. 15th Congress* 2 Sess. I. 1203 Sir, if a dissolution of the Union must take place, let it be so! If civil war, which gentlemen so much threaten, must come, ... let it come! **1861** J. DAVIS *Letters* (1923) V. 31 If you desire at this last moment to avert civil war, so be it; it is better so. **1861** *Congress. Globe* 19 July 209/2 Resolved ..., That the present deplorable civil war has been forced upon the country by the disunionists of the southern States now in revolt. **1861** W. PHILLIPS in *Harper's Mag.* LXXXIX. 141/1 Civil war is a momentous evil. It needs the soundest, the most solemn justification. **1863** LINCOLN *Gettysburg Address* 19 Nov., Now we are engaged in a great civil war, testing whether that nation, or any nation so conceived and so dedicated, can long endure. **1864** J. R. GIDDINGS *Hist. Rebell.* 457 Georgia, Alabama, Florida, and Louisiana, now followed these examples of secession which were rapidly precipitating the nation into civil war.

b. Spec. the war between the Southern Confederacy and the Federal government (1861–1865).

1862 LONGFELLOW in *Life* (1886) II. 382 Of the Civil War I say only this. It is not a revolution.... It is Slavery against Freedom. **1863** J. T. HEADLEY (*title*), The Great Rebellion; a History of the Civil War in the United States. **1886** A. L. Long *Memoirs R. E. Lee* 33 This fine old mansion was seized by the Federal Government at the commencement of the Civil War. **1894** *Harper's Mag.* LXXXVIII. 273/1 The economic changes produced in the country by the civil war ... have attracted little attention compared with the social, financial, and political changes.

Clabber, *n.* [Ir. Gael. *clabar.*] Milk that has coagulated or curdled; bonny-clabber.

1828 WEBSTER, *Clabber* or *Bonny-clabber*, milk turned, become thick or inspissated. **1836** C. GILMAN *Recoll.* (1838) 52 When I told Aunt Patty that the Southern folks ate clabber, she rolled up her eyes. **1840** *S. Lit. Messenger* VI. 510/2 The center was filled with pans of clabber, sweet milk, cheese, and various kinds of cornbread. **1884** SWEET & KNOX *Through Texas* 152 The reticent man failed to reply to this; as he was engaged in warehousing a bowl of clabber. **1894** 'MARK TWAIN' *P. Wilson* iv, Chambers got mush and milk, and clabber without sugar.

+**Clabber,** *v. intr.* (See quot. 1880.) — **1880** WEBSTER *Suppl.* 1549 *Clabber*, ... to turn thick in the process of souring—said of milk. **1920** ALSAKER *Eating for Health* 47 Clabbered milk and buttermilk are easily digested.

Clabbo(a)rd, Clabo(a)rd. Variants of CLAPBOARD.

‖**Clacker,** *v. tr.* To utter noisily. — **1851** S. JUDD *Margaret* III. (ed. 2) 345 Mounting a rock she harangued the people, or, rather, clackered her own merit.

+**Claco.** [Mex. Sp. *claco, tlaco.*] A minor coin formerly current in Mexico and the Southwest and worth about three cents. — **1844** KENDALL *Santa Fé Exped.* II. 216 A crowd of poor wretches ... [called] upon every saint in the Mexican calendar to shower down prayers ... if we would but give them a solitary claco. **1844** GREGG *Commerce of Prairies* 220 By casting a few clacos into his [a beggar's] outstretched hand. **1845** GREEN *Texian Exped.* 399 The little fellow would dance either for *clacos* or *aguardiente*, of both of which he was very fond.

* **Claim,** *n.*

***1.** A demand for something regarded as a right or as due.

1638 *Md. Archives* I. 4 Then was proclaymed, that all freemen omitted in the Writts of Summons, that would clayme a voyce in this generall assembly, should come and make their claim. **1660** BERKELEY in Neill *Virginia Carolorum* 273 Your titles, and claims to land in this northern part of America. **1744** *Ga. Col. Rec.* VI. 109 Mr. Dobell ... had no Book wherein he had registered the Claims of any Person whatever.... The Original Draft of Persons Claims which he had lately sent to the honourable Trustees he had by him only on broken Pieces of Paper. **1797** *Ann. 4th Congress* 2 Sess. 1820 A return from the Accountant of the Treasury, on certain claims not admitted to be valid. **1891** O'BEIRNE *Leaders Ind. Territory* 26/2 The most important event of the past twelve months was the appropriation and payment of the 'Net Proceeds Claim,' the distribution of which threw a large sum of money into general circulation.

attrib. **1870** 'MARK TWAIN' *Great Beef Contract* 105, I got through the Claims Department. **1882** *Nation* 14 Sept. 215/2 The notion of the Attorney-General's office of each State being converted into a 'claim agency' appears to us to be a mere bugbear. **1884** *Century Mag.* March 654/2 The Southern gentleman is disposed of by sending him off to Mexico as counsel for some sort of claims commission.

b. Phrases. *Court of claims* {1691}, +*committee of claims*, a court or committee before whom claims are presented for adjustment. (See also quot. 1889.)

1738 W. STEPHENS *Proc. Georgia* 246 He ordered the Court of Claims to be put off farther to the 27th Instant. **1775** *Jrnls. Cont. Congress* III. 315 The committee of claims reported that there is due ... 133 3/10 dollars. **1797** *Ann. 4th Congress* 2 Sess. 1820 The House went into a Committee of the Whole on the report of the Committee of Claims, ... on a return from the Accountant of the Treasury. **1889** *Cent.* 1313 *Court of Claims.* (*a*) A United States court, sitting in Washington, for the investigation of claims against the government. (*b*) In some States, a county court charged with the financial business of the county. **1891** O'BEIRNE *Leaders Ind. Territory* 161/2 He was commissioned as a member of the committee on the court of claims.

+**2.** A tract or body of government land petitioned for or claimed by a prospective settler.

1792 *Ann. 2nd Congress* 1036 Within these triangles, however, are the following claims of citizens, reserved by the deed of cession, and consequently forming exceptions to the rights of the United States. **1839** PLUMBE *Sk. Iowa* 40 We made inquiries about vacant lands, if claims could be got reasonable, &c. **1842** *Cultivator* IX. 194 Improved land can now be bought for a lower price than used to be paid a few years since for the bare 'claim.' **1847** ROBB *Squatter Life* 124 The Land Agent ... informed the unsuspecting squatter, that the stranger had, indeed, entered the claim his cabin was upon. **1851** *Polly Peablossom* 157 He would give his 'claim' and all the 'truck' on it, if his 'darter' could have such a 'cupboard!' **1857** *Lawrence* (Kansas) *Republican* 28 May 2 A settler ... had purchased a claim with a house on it. **a1861** WINTHROP *Canoe & Saddle* 86 These two [Yankee settlers] had taken this pretty prairie as their 'claim,' hoping to become the vanguard of colonization. **1879** *Scribner's Mo.* Nov. 137/2 The 'claims' are small, few exceeding forty acres. **a1918** G. STUART *On Frontier* I. 24 In 1838 my parents also moved across the river and took up a claim.

fig. **a1861** WINTHROP *J. Brent* 18 If he throws me and breaks my neck I get a claim in Paradise at once. **1884** NYE *Baled Hay* 55 The servant girl ... has 'a claim' in the promised land.

+**b.** An area over which the Indians claimed or exercised ownership: see INDIAN CLAIM.

+**3.** A piece of land staked out by a miner in accordance with mining law.

1850 KINGSLEY *Diary* 144 We got the claim ready to go to work on to morrow with a quicksilver machine. **1855** MARRYAT *Mts. & Molehills* 240 It is customary to leave your mining tools in your claim, to indicate to all new comers that it is occupied. **1861** HITTELL *Mining in Pacific States* 181 Any man entitled to mine may take up a claim for himself or for a company. **1869** BREWER *Rocky Mt. Lett.* 43 'Claims' were staked for miles along the line of its supposed site. **1876** RAYMOND *8th Rep. Mines* 44 Small-size garnets are found ... in this claim. **1881** HAYES *New Colorado* 82 He will seek a 'claim,' and fondly see a bonanza in the smallest and shallowest of his 'prospect holes.' **1883** E. LORD *Control Mining* 98 The first locators were entitled to the exclusive possession of the section of the ledge included in their claim. **1891** *Century Mag.* Feb. 533 This auriferous region ... [has] the richest ravines, the most remarkable river claims. **1897** *McClure's Mag.* Sept. 963 Claims run about ten to the mile and are limited practically only by the width of the ground between the two 'benches' or sides of the hills, that close in the stream. **1904** *Churchman* 22 Oct. 711 The white miners had come back to the towns from the scattered claims upon which they had been working.

4. Attrib. and comb. with *holder, locator, notice*, etc.

1860 *Harper's Mag.* Aug. 299/2 Claim-stakes and claim-shanties speck the road from one end of the [Sauk] river to the other. **1872** *Ib.* Dec. 24 Either the claim owners effect a consolidation—a mining company being formed—or the capitalist steps in and purchases the whole. **1889** *Cent.* 1023/2 *Claim-notice*, ... a notification posted by a miner or other settler upon a piece of public land [etc.]. **1891** GARLAND *Main-travelled Roads* (1922) 137 He was of German parentage, a middle-sized, cheery, wide-awake, good-looking young fellow—a typical claim-holder. **1898** *Mo. So. Dakotan* I. 14 During the stay of the Holman party at Yankton, they opened a regular claim record book, in which were recorded the names of claimants, and a description of the land claimed by prospective residents. **1899** *Ib.* 154 The only companionable human beings within the range of the eye are the claim locators, more commonly styled land sharks. **1901** A. C. THOMAS *History of U.S.* 443 At midday crowds of eager claim-seekers rushed across the line. **1916** BOWER *Phantom Herd* 149 We learned our little lessons when we were building claim-shacks for ourselves. **1923** — *Parowan Bonanza* 57 He's a durrty claim-robber.

* **Claim,** *v.*

+**1.** *tr.* To take up or enter upon (public land). Also transf.

1835 *Ind. Mag. Hist.* IV. 70 He will perhaps lay the foundation of a cabin, is 'claimed' or located, and no person will interfere or presume to settle upon it without first purchasing the first claimant's right. **1889** K. MUNROE *Golden Days* 291 The thirsty travellers ... dared not drink ... without first obtaining permission of the man who had thus 'claimed' [the spring].

+**2.** To maintain, contend, or assert *that* (something is so); also, to make a claim *to be* (something).

1864 NORTON *Army Lett.* 204, I don't claim that they fought well, only as well as they could. **1869** 'MARK TWAIN' *Innocents* 539 Though they have been ruled out of our Modern Bible, it is claimed that they were accepted gospel twelve or fifteen centuries ago. **1883** — *Life on Miss.* xli. 427 New Orleans claims to be ... one of the healthiest cities in the Union. **1903** ELY *Evol. Industrial Soc.* 277 The constitutionality of the law was contested because among other things it was claimed that the tax was a direct tax on property. **1913** MORLEY *Carolina Mts.* 175 Here we 'aim' to do a thing, and 'claim' that we have done it.

+Claim agent. Also **claims agent.** An attorney or representative who handles claims.

[**1873** *Winfield* (Kansas) *Courier* 26 June 1/7 An Indian Claim Agent. . . . If there is anything that an Indian agent will not do, it is that he will not treat his clients, the Indians, honestly.] **1886** *Stand. Guide of Washington* 110 Business Houses of Washington, D.C. [include] . . . claim agents, collecting agents, patent agents. **1903** E. JOHNSON *Railway Transportation* 189 Some companies have a chief claim agent subordinate only to the traffic manager and those above him. **1903** *N.Y. Ev. Post* 6 Oct. 6 Our pension policy has furnished an enormous incentive to claims agents and Congressmen.

***Claimer.** One who makes a claim; +spec., one who preëmpts land. *Obs.* — **1680** *Charlestown Land Rec.* 188 That a Committee may be Chosen for the heareing & proveing & confirming of the Titles of Clajmers to the respective Commons. **1769** *Mass. Col. Soc. Publ.* VI. 30 . . . He never knew of any of the Inhabitents . . . being Disturbed by any Claimer whatsoever. **1780** W. FLEMING in *Travels Amer. Col.* 645 Each claimer [is] to make his entries according to the number drawn to his name.

+Claim jumper. [CLAIM *n.* 2, 3, JUMP *v.*] One who takes unlawful possession of another's claim.

1859 BARTLETT 84 *Claim-jumper*, one who violently seizes on another's land claim. **1873** *Winfield* (Kansas) *Courier* 22 May 3/1 To Claim Jumpers.—Our efficient County Surveyor . . . started yesterday to Floral to lay out a cemetery for the good people of that locality. Those who want claims of that kind can jump one without risk of contest. **1882** BAILLIE-GROHMAN *Camps in Rockies* 366, I imagined this possibly might be a new way of demonstrating ownership to would-be 'claim-jumpers.' **1889** *Harper's Mag.* Aug. 484/2 This was in western Kansas, the Elysium where flourished . . . the claim-jumper. **1905** *Bureau of Forestry Bul.* No. 67, 60 He is always at the mercy of the claim jumper. **1922** MULFORD *Tex* 237 An' he needs us to keep our eyes on them blasted claim jumpers.

+Claim jumping. (See quotation 1859.) — **1859** BARTLETT 84 *Claim-jumping*, violently seizing on another's claim. **1877** WRIGHT *Big Bonanza* 409 Men were out in the night staking off ground and posting notices, and there was a good deal of claim-jumping, with some fights, going on. **1909** GREELY *Handbook Alaska* (1925) 29 Thus ended claim-jumping by mass meeting.

+Claim shanty. A hut, often very flimsy, erected on a land claim in order to fulfil legal requirements.

1860 [see CLAIM *n.* 4]. **1873** EGGLESTON *Myst. Metrop.* 23 Here and there Charlton noticed the little claim-shanties. **1885** *Lisbon* (Dakota) *Star* 27 March 5/7 (*advt.*), Claim Shanties built and delivered to any part of the County. **1888** *Harper's Mag.* March 568/1 The country is now taken up and dotted with claim shanties. **1902** *Kansas Hist. Coll.* VII. 425 At last the claim shanty on the Marais des Cygnes is reached—a journey that took at least a month.

***Clam,** *n.* Also †**clamm.** (Cf. CLAMP.)

+1. A bivalve shellfish, either the hard clam (*Venus mercenaria*) or the soft clam (*Mya arenaria*).

Also locally, or with specific names, applied to various other species of mollusks.

1637 MORTON *New Canaan* 61 Clames is a shellfish. . . . These our swine feede upon. *a***1649** WINTHROP *Hist.* II. 91 Corn was very scarce all over the country, so . . . many families in most towns had none to eat, but were forced to live of clams, muscles, cataos, dry fish, etc. **1699** J. DICKENSON *God's Protecting Providence* 30 He gave her a Parcell of Shelfish, which are known by the name of Clamms. **1716** CHURCH *Philip's War* 27 There were a great many Indians gone down to Wepoiset to eat Clams. **1796** *Smithtown Rec.* 129 Any person not an inhabitant . . . taking Soft shelled clams within the limits of said Town shall pay six pence for every bushel. **1832** WILLIAMSON *Maine* I. 167 Clams . . . are often made an article of food, especially by the Indians. **1851** J. F. JOHNSTON *Notes N. Amer.* II. 464 The clam, (*Mya arenaria*,) or long clam, as it is often called, to distinguish it from the round clam, . . . is a most valuable gift of the sea to the inhabitants of the coast of New England and New York. **1880** *Harper's Mag.* Aug. 343/1 The landlord . . . was seen . . . afar on the mud flats of the cove . . . digging what he called 'a mess o' clams.' **1889** *Pall Mall Gaz.* 30 Nov. 7/1 There are two distinct varieties of clam in America, the hard and soft shelled. The latter are never eaten raw, but they make a most delicious and nutritious soup. **1903** *Atlantic Mo.* Sept. 326 A shrewd Yankee came and saw the abundance of clams in the long stretches of beach at low tide, and began shipping them away by barrowfuls to Boston and New York.

b. *Happy as a clam* (*at high water* or *tide*), well pleased, contented.

1834 *Harvardiana* I. 121 He could not even enjoy that peculiar degree of satisfaction, usually denoted by the phrase 'as happy as a clam.' **1838** *Knickerb.* XI. 208 'Happy as a clam,' is an old adage. *a***1870** CHIPMAN *Notes on Bartlett* 523 *Happy as a clam* (*in the mud at high water*). Both forms are used. The latter form is a learned appendix added kindly from condescension to wits somewhat dull. **1875** HOLLAND *Sevenoaks* 436 The two fellers . . . as happy as two clams in high water. **1907** *N.Y. Ev. Post* (semi-weekly ed.) 20 June 5 Now I'm in business and happy as a clam at high tide. **1911** LINCOLN *Cap'n Warren's Wards* 244, I was as happy as a clam at highwater

||**c.** *fig. To sell a clam*, to have even the slightest success. *colloq.*

1872 'MARK TWAIN' *Roughing It* xlvii. 334 Just go in and toot your horn, if you don't sell a clam.

+2. The fresh-water mussel.

1849 DANA *Geology* 27 The fresh-water clam (*Unionidæ*). **1857** HAMMOND *Northern Scenes* 142 The bottom . . . is of clean yellow sand, in which are imbedded millions of clams, resembling, in every respect, those of the ocean beach.

+3. A close-mouthed, taciturn person. Contemptuously, a dull, stupid person.

1866 'MARK TWAIN' *Screamers*, 'Travelling Show' 150 That lets you out, you know, you chowder-headed old clam! **1889** — *Conn. Yankee* xii. 155 These innumerable clams had permitted it so long that they had come . . . to accept it as a truth. **1889** *Pall Mall Gaz.* 30 Nov. 7/1 What is meant by the expression, 'Don't be a clam'? . . . —Oh, well, it's just a sort of slang phrase. It means much the same as 'dumb as an oyster.' It is said of people who won't learn any new thing, won't take advice, [etc.].

+4. The mouth. *slang.* (Cf. CLAMSHELL 2.)

1825 NEAL *Bro. Jonathan* I. 143 Shet your clam, our David.

5. Attrib. with *bag*, *bed*, *bluff*, etc. Also (sense 3) with *critic*, and *opening* (see quotation).

1827 *Harvard Reg.* May 83 A blue cotton handkerchief, . . . [which] never was intended as a clam-bag, for it was hardly a foot square. **1854** SIMMS *Southward Ho* 25 The gigantic bulk of Jones went over, like a thousand of brick, shaking the clam-beds for sixty miles along the shore. **1841** *S. Lit. Messenger* VII. 854/2 Its boundaries . . . run thus: . . . in a direct line along shore over the clam bluff as it stood before the tide washed it away. **1851** *Knickerb.* XXXVIII. 555 He started life as a clam-boy, and the old clam-boat to which he belonged used to be stationed near Washington-market. **1896** *N.Y. Dramatic News* 4 July 3/2 He had eaten nothing but beef tea and clam broth for two weeks. **1889** BARRÈRE & LELAND I. 253/2 *Clam butcher* (American), a man who opens clams. **1838** *N.Y. Advertiser & Exp.* 14 Feb. 3/5 A couple of long shorers . . . hitched an old broken winded horse . . . to the skeleton of a vehicle which they distinguished by the appellation of 'clam cart.' **1889** *Phila. Times* 15 July, Don't bother about clam critics. **1870** *Scribner's Mo.* I. 60 His oyster and clam farms, in which he had at last become master and director of other men. **1825** *Mass. Statutes* 15 Feb., An Act to prevent the destruction of the lobster and clam fishery in the town of Truro. **1802** *Mass. H. S. Coll.* VIII. 194 It is as necessary to stir the clam ground frequently, as it is to hoe a field of potatoes. **1880** LUDLOW *Dramatic Life* 680 It was 'a clam opening,' which meant, in the theatrical slang, that he opened and closed on the same night. **1852** *Knickerb.* XXXIX. 573 The captain espied a clam-pedlar. **1870** *Scribner's Mo.* I. 167 When she was gone he would sink back into Dick Dort, clam and oyster trader.

+Clam, *v. intr.* To dig for or collect clams.

[**1636** Cf. CLAMMING.] **1676** *Mass. H. S. Coll.* 3 Ser. I. 71 His father and mother were taken by the Pequts and Monhiggins about ten weeks ago, as they were clamming . . . at Courwesit. **1716** CHURCH *Philip's War* 29 They came near the bank, and saw a vast company of Indians, . . . some catching Eels & Flat-fish in the water, some Clamming. **1769** *Huntington Rec.* II. 505 Liberty to Hunt Gun fish or clam within the Limmits of ye s[ai]d Town.

b. Of hogs: To root for clams. *Obs.*

1641 *Dorchester* (Mass.) *Rec.* 1 Jan., If there be any Liuinge neare vnto any Clam bankes where they would haue their hogges to Clam.

+Clam bait. Fish bait made of clams. Hence *Clam-baited* a. — **1838** *Mass. Stat.* 17 April, An Act to regulate the Inspection of Clam Bait. **1851** J. F. JOHNSTON *Notes N. Amer.* II. 465 Seven bushels of clams are required to fill one barrel, and of these 5000, under the name of *clam bait*, are put up every year along this coast, and sold at six or seven dollars a barrel. **1871** DE VERE 69 When salted for the fisheries it takes the name of *clam-bait*. — **1894** *Outing* XXIV. 263/1 Then we cast forth our clam-baited hooks and waited.

+Clambake. A social gathering at which clams are baked and eaten. Also attrib.

A full description is given by Bartlett, with mention of one held on the 4th of July, 1840.

1842 *Spirit of Times* (*Phila.*) 3 Sept. (Th.), The Great Clam Bake the other day in Rhode Island went off with immense eclat. **1855** THOMPSON *Doesticks* 71 She judged I should break my neck coming home from a clam-bake. **1871** BARNUM *Struggles & Triumphs* 657 Several times we had delightful sails, dinners, and clam-bakes at Charles Island. **1890** MCALLISTER *Society* 186 All pronounced this kind of clambake picnic a species of *fête* not to be indulged in knowingly a second time. **1906** *Springfield W. Republican* 19 July 16 The annual clambake of the Hartford business men's association was held Friday, some 200 arriving in special cars. **1911** LINCOLN *Cap'n Warren's Wards* 342 They could make a crew hop 'round like a sand-flea in a clam bake.

+Clam bank. Also †**clamm bank.** A bank upon which clams abound.

1634 WOOD *New Eng. Prospect* I. ix. 35 When the tide ebs and flowes, a man running over these Clamm bankes will presently be made all wet, by their spouting of water out of those small holes. **1726** S. PENHALLOW *Hist. Indian Wars* 70 Colonel Walton was again preparing to traverse the eastern shore with an hundred and seventy men, being the usual season of visiting their clam banks. **1746** *N.H. Probate Rec.* III. 362 He is to have . . . my Piece of salt marsh at the Clam Banks so called. **1849** *Knickerb.* XXXIV. 153/2 Mr. Dumbidikes followed in an elaborate essay on the clam-banks of Long-Island, with an allusion to clamb-aches. **1871** DE VERE 69 The clam of Boston is the *Mya arenaria* of the clam-banks.

+**Clam boat.** A boat used in gathering clams. Also attrib. — **1808** in Thornton *Glossary* II. 982 A lilliputian king Towing his clam-boat navy with a string. **1851** [see Clamboy s.v. CLAM *n.* 4]. **1856** THOMPSON *Plu-ri-bus-tah* 71 Put him in a Jersey clam boat.

+**Clam catcher.**

1. One whose occupation is catching clams.

1851 *Knickerb.* XXXVIII. 555 They were by profession fish-catchers (we are not aware that they were clam-catchers or fish speculators). **1855** *Ib.* XLVI. 222 In the sounds, 'hard-shell' clam-catchers, fishermen, and oyster-men steadily ply their different callings.

2. A native or resident of New Jersey. *colloq.*

1845 *Cincinnati Misc.* I. 240 The inhabitants of . . . New Jersey [are called] Clam-catchers. **1872** *Harper's Mag.* Jan. 318/1 Nicknames given to the States and people of this republic: . . . New Jersey, . . . Clam-Catchers. **1888** WHITMAN *Nov. Boughs* 70 Those [soldiers] from . . . New Jersey . . . [were called] Clam Catchers.

+**Clam chowder.**

1. A chowder in which clams are an ingredient.

1836 *Harvardiana* III. 36 A dish of untasted clam-chowder. **1846** *Yale Lit. Mag.* XI. 235 (Th.), Such affectionate mention of clam-chowder, roast-veal, and baked-beans! **1883** W. H. HILLS *Students' Songs* 23 Oh! all ye fellers that have California clam chowder and oysters on the half-shell, and give your neighbor none. **1886** *Harper's Mag.* July 178/2 A sign informing the reckless that they can obtain there clam chowder and ice-cream. **1888** KIRK *Queen Money* 144 They could have eaten the clam chowder sold at the stalls on the beach with a relish.

2. A social gathering at which this dish is served.

1898 HAMBLEN *Gen. Manager's Story* 131 The engineers had a clam chowder.

+**Clam cod.** (See quot. 1889.) — **1888** GOODE *Amer. Fishes* 339 These are called 'Shoal-water Cod,' . . . 'Worm-cod,' 'Clam-Cod.' **1889** *Cent.* 1082/2 *Clam-cod*, inshore cod which feed on clams.

+**Clamcracker.** *local.* (See quotation.) — **1881** INGERSOLL *Oyster Industry* 242 *Clam cracker*, a fish, a species of ray, *Rhinoptera quadriloba*, which molests the oyster beds (Savannah).

+**Clam digger.** One who digs clams. — **1855** WHITMAN *Leaves* 18 The boatmen and clamdiggers arose early. **1870** *Scribner's Mo.* I. 166, I am a clam-digger to you, that's all! **1881** MCLEAN *Cape Cod Folks* 208, I could watch the ocean on one side and the clam-diggers on the other. **1903** *Atlantic Mo.* Sept. 327 He became far and away the best among the clam-diggers.

+**Clam digging.** The digging of clams. — **1838** *Knickerb.* XI. 207 Sam's trade was clam-digging. **1860** S. WARNER *Say & Seal* 146 Faith . . . was certainly 'spry' in getting ready for the clam-digging.

+**Clam fisher.** One who fishes for clams. — **1838** *Knickerb.* XI. 207 She shone down upon the lonely clam-fisher so benignantly. **1865** *Atlantic Mo.* XV. 534 'And the people in the hamlet?' questioned Mary. . . . 'Clam-fishers, the maist o' them.'

+**Clam fritter.** A fritter made with clams.

1867 *Common Sense Cook Book* 10 [Recipe for making] Soft Clam Fritters. Clean your clams, and envelope them in the batter, which must be stiffer than for ordinary fritters. **1879** *Harper's Mag.* July 217 Mary . . . had surpassed herself in the chowder and clam fritters. **1886** MITCHELL *R. Blake* 228 Breakfast for ten people,—fish, and clam fritters and oysters, and 'cranberry sass,' and split chickens. *c*1895 NORRIS *Vandover* (1914) 44 Underneath it was the lunch counter, where clam-fritters, the specialty of the place, could be had.

+**Clammer.**

1. One who gathers clams.

1883 GOODE *Fish. Indust.* 47 The fishery is not an expensive one, the whole outfit of the 'clammer' not requiring an expenditure of over $150. **1897** *Outing* XXX. 213/1 [Picture of] The little clammers.

2. A boat used in the collecting of clams; a clam boat.

1882 *Harper's Mag.* Aug. 359/1, I tell you, to face a yacht in a clammer is an awful come-down. **1888** *Cambridge* (Mass.) *Press* 15 Sept. 1/7 Clammers call in daily at the Neck, on their way up to Ipswich.

+**Clamming.** [Cf. CLAM *v.*] The gathering of clams.

1636 *Dorchester* (Mass.) *Rec.* 5 July, Provided they leave stiles and gates for persons and cattle, when persons are disposed to travell or drive Cattle or swine that way to Clamming. **1675** *Wyllys Papers* 217 A party of Ninecrafts men sent out in Canooes to keepe ye enemy from fishing & claming. **1774** *Huntington Rec.* II. 526, I will Not Hinder any Person whatsoever from fishing oystering claming or guning anywhere in the mill pond. **1838** *Knickerb.* XI. 207 But Sam evidently looked upon clamming as an important and mysterious thing. **1871** BARNUM *Struggles & Triumphs* 760 A narrow lane reaching down to the shore enabled parties to drive near to the water for the purpose of clamming. **1880** *Harper's Mag.* July 206/2 Clamming is the inherent right and occupation of every South-Sider, be he rich or poor. **1894** *Youth's Companion* 22 Nov. 562/3 The bulk of the eeling and quahaug clamming as well as the lobstering was done in its vicinity.

attrib. **1883** GOODE *Fish. Indust.* 46 All along the southern shore of the sound are prolific clamming grounds.

***Clammy,** *a.* +Particularizing certain plants, as *clammy cherry, locust, rice,* etc.: (see quotations).

1802 DRAYTON *S. Carolina* 127 A third kind was called clammy rice, as adhering, when boiled, into one glutinous mass. **1817-8** EATON *Botany* (1822) 342 *Lychnis viscaria*, clammy lichnis. E[xotic]. *Ib.* 431 *Robinia viscosa*, clammy locust; . . . flowers approaching from white to red. Cultivated. **1860** *N.C. Geol. Survey: Botany* 98 Clammy Honeysuckle (*A*[*zalea*] *viscosa*). . . . The flowers are white or flesh-colored and very fragrant. **1889** *Cent.* 949 Clammy cherry, *Cordia Collococca.* **1892** APGAR *Trees Northern U.S.* 94 Clammy Locust. . . . A small tree, 30 to 40 ft. high; native south, and has been quite extensively cultivated north.

Clamp. **1.** =CLAM *n.* 1. *Obs.* +**2.** A toothbrush made of a small twig. *Obs.* ‖**3.** (See quotation.) — **(1)** **1616** SMITH *New England* 30 You shall scarce finde any Baye, shallow shore, or Coue of sand, where you may not take many Clampes. **1634** WOOD *New Eng. Prospect* I. ix. 35 Clamms or Clamps is a shel-fish not much unlike a cockle. **1672** JOSSELYN *New Eng. Rarities* 153 Clam, or Clamp, a kind of Shell Fish, a white Muscle. **1676** THOMPSON *Poet. Works* 49 The dainty Indian Maize was eat with Clamp-shells. *Ib.* 91 Some grope for Lobsters, some to clamp banks run. **(2)** **1774** FITHIAN *Journal* I. 252 Sometimes they get sticks & splinter one end of them for Brushes, or as they call them here *Clamps*, & spitting on part of the floor, they scrub away with great vigor. [In Virginia, referring to the way the children in their play did what their parents did.] **(3)** **1855** WILLIS *Convalescent* 56 The children [were] on skates, . . . and myself on a pair of neighbor Ward's 'clamps'—the sharpened shoe-points with which he goes near the edges of the floating ice-slabs, in drawing his winter nets.

+**Clam rake.** A rake used in gathering clams. — **1837** *Harvardiana* IV. 156 And now he sleeps in coral cave, . . . His clam-rake by his side. **1860** WHITMAN *Songs of Joy* line 36, I come with my clam-rake and spade, I come with my eel-spear. **1879** *Scribner's Mo.* Sept. 647/1 We found . . . a collection of fishing gear, including nets, eel-pots, and clam-rakes.

Clam ranch. *To take up a clam ranch,* (see quotation). — **1882** *Standard* 26 Sept. 2/1 'To take up a clam-ranch' is a proverbial expression [in Oregon] to express the last stage of hard fortune.

***Clamshell.**

+**1.** The shell of a clam.

1668 *Huntington Rec.* I. 129 The second Division of meadow Bounded on the east side with the Creeke as far as the Clamsheals. **1791** J. LONG *Voyages & Travels* 46 Wampum is of several colours, but the white and black are chiefly used; the former is made of the inside of the conque, or clam shell, the latter of the muscle. **1825** LORAIN *Pract. Husbandry* 114 Fresh oyster or clam shells, when broken into pieces are a very valuable manure. **1832** WILLIAMSON *Maine* I. 80 On several projections of land hereabouts, are beds of clam-shells, from one to two acres in extent. **1869** STOWE *Oldtown Folks* 157 Offering a large, clean clam-shell to each of the children, she invited them to help themselves. **1914** *McClure's Mag.* XLII. 113 Millions of dollars' worth of buttons were destined to come from the clam-shells that had lain so long unnoticed at their feet.

fig. **1856** KANE *Arctic Explor.* I. 335 A dome, or . . . a great outspread clam-shell of ice. **1861** STOWE *Pearl Orr's Isl.* II. 128 A pattern [for a quilt] commonly denominated in those parts clam-shell. **1867** *Carmina Yalensia* 13/2 Give us but our rum to sip; We don't care a clam-shell.

+**2.** *slang.* (Orig. in *pl.*) The jaws or mouth.

1834 C. A. DAVIS *Lett. J. Downing* 104, Shut up your clack, or I'll knock your clam-shells together pretty quick. **1850** WATSON *Camp-Fires Revol.* 159 If you will only shut up your etarnal clam-shells, I'll tell ye all about it. **1860** HOLLAND *Miss Gilbert* 95 All those opposed will shut their clam-shells. **1861** LOWELL *Biglow P.* 2 Ser. i, You don't feel much like speakin', When, ef you let your clamshells gape, a quart o' tar will leak in. **1880** BROOKS *Fairport Nine* 156 Fishing is the business just now, so you may shut up your clamshell about Major Boffin and his tall grass.

+**3.** Attrib. with *padlock, pattern, ring,* etc.

1859 BARTLETT 85 The padlock now used on the United States mail-bags is called the 'Clam-shell padlock.' **1861** NORTON *Army Lett.* 18 A good many of them [boys] are making clam-shell rings. **1861** STOWE *Pearl Orr's Isl.* II. 130 She stuck a decisive needle into the first clam-shell pattern.

+**Clam soup.** Soup made with clams.

1836 *Harvardiana* III. 36 He found it . . . illegible by the spilling of some clam-soup. **1840** MAXWELL *Run thro' U.S.* II. 53 A thrill of admiration shakes my pen as it traces the short, the unobtrusive, the humble-looking words, Clam soup! **1846** COOPER *Redskins* i, Clam-soup, sir, well made, is one of the most delicious soups in the world. **1850** HONE *Diary* II. 379, I dined with my friend Giraud on Wednesday, on capital clam soup. **1851** J. F. JOHNSTON *Notes N. Amer.* II. 464, I enjoyed a very comfortable dinner, in which the chief novelty was clam soup. **1884** F. OWENS *Cook Book* 14 Clam soup. Take 50 large clams and chop fine, [etc.].

+**Clam tongs.** A large forcepslike tool used in gathering clams. — **1881** Ingersoll *Oyster Industry* 242 Clam Tongs.—'Differs from oyster tongs only in the width of the head, which averages 3½ feet.' **1883** RATHBUN in *U.S. Museum Bul.* No. 27, 110 Seines, hoop-nets, baited with meat, and clam-tongs are also occasionally employed for catching Crabs.

+**Clam trap.** [Cf. CLAM *n.* 4.] The mouth. — **1800** *Aurora* (Phila.) 8 April (Th.), Otis shut up his clam trap.

***Clan.** +Among American Indians, an intratribal group or gens actually or theoretically related by blood.

1797 B. HAWKINS *Letters* 62 The chiefs after consultation in the square, determined that the murderer should suffer death, and they directed two of his clan to carry the determination into execution. **1808** in Beadle *Undevel. West* (1873) 410 The blood of him or them shall not be required . . . from the clan the person so killed belonged to. **1819** *Niles' Reg.* XVI. Suppl. 101/1 The Cherokee people are divided into seven different clans, each having a distinct name. **1844** LEE & FROST *Oregon* 99 Farther up the river we meet with a remnant of a clan called the Ne Coniaks. **1849** M. EASTMAN *Dahcotah* p. xix, Each clan takes a root for its medicine, known only to those initiated into the mysteries of the clan. **1898** CUSHMAN *Hist. Indians* 26 May not the Choctaw words Hishi Itih, the name of one of their ancient Iksas (clans), be itself a corruption of the word Hittite?

***Clapboard,** *n.* Also **cla(b)bo(a)rd,** etc.

***1.** Boards (or a) board split from oak and used for making barrels, casks, etc. *Obs.*

It is possible that some of the following quotations refer to sense 2.

(*a*) **1612** SIMMONDS *Proceedings* 86 For their exercise, they made clapboard, wainscot, and cut down trees against the ships comming. **1624** *Va. House of Burgesses* 28 [We] weare . . . wholly imployed in cuttinge downe of masts, cedar, black wallnutt, clapboarde. **1640** *Mass. H. S. Coll.* 4 Ser. VI. 143 And the towne agreed not to cutt any great tymber which is fitt for shipping planckes or knees &c. nor any for clapboard within twoe miles of the towne eury way. **a1656** BRADFORD *Hist.* 130 This ship (caled the Fortune) was speedily dispatcht away, being laden with good clapboard as full as she could stowe, and 2. hoggsheads of beaver and otter skins. **1724** H. JONES *Virginia* 60 Here may likewise be found as good Clapboards, and Pipe-Staves, Deals, Masts, Yards, Planks, &c. for Shipping, as we are supplied with.

(*b*) **1640** *Mass. H. S. Coll.* 4 Ser. VI. 90 Wee are bold to intreat your furtherance in counsell and other helpe for the suppressing pipe staff riuers and clabords in our towne. **1714** *Mass. H. S. Coll.* 6 Ser. V. 287 The bellows, with the other things I wrote you, are on bord. . . . There is a smale cask of nayles, 3m of bord, 4m of clabord.

+2. A riven board, often thinner at one edge, used in making the sides, roof, etc., of a house. Also collect.

1637 [see CLAPBOARD *v.*] **a1649** WINTHROP *Hist.* I. 90 Mr. Oldham had a small house . . . made all of clapboards, burnt down by making a fire in it when it had no chimney. **1656** *Dedham Rec.* 140 Granted to Daniell Morse two Seders to make clabbord. **1672** *N.J. Archives* 1 Ser. I. 85, I . . . looked out and saw the said Robert Moss and Mr. Crayne beating down the claboards of Richard Michells house. **1688** SEWALL *Letter-Book* I. 85 If it be not well filled between the clapboards and the cieling, I doubt the House will be cold. **1705** *Boston News-Letter* 12 March 2/2 The Meeting-house was built of Timber 60 Foot long, 25 Foot wide, & 18 Foot studd ceiled with Clapboards. **1739** STEPHENS *Proc. Georgia* 480 They would add a convenient Enlargement with Clapboards in a few Days more. **1756** HEMPSTEAD *Diary* 678 In the foren[oon] I was at Daughter Starr's puting in some Clabords in ye Leantoo Chamber. **1789** MORSE *Amer. Geog.* 314 Clapboards . . . are a kind of coarse shingles, split out of short oak logs. **1791** Jillson *Dark & Bl. Ground* 109 Butting poles, against which the lower tier of clapboards rest in forming the roof. **1800** TATHAM *Tobacco* 32 Clap-boards are thin pieces of four feet long, riven generally out of white oak, and one edge thicker than the other. **1834** R. BAIRD *Valley Miss.* 231 They must erect cabins, . . . with roofs made of clap-boards, that is, of large undressed shingles, not nailed on, but kept in their places by large saplings or pieces of timber laid on them. **1843** 'CARLTON' *New Purchase* I. 60 The roof was thick ricketty shingles, called clapboards. **1851** CARY *Clovernook* 192 A little way off, beneath a shed of clapboards, his mother was baking currant pies. **1874** EGGLESTON *Circuit Rider* 94 The roof of rough shingles which Western people call 'clapboards.' **1903** *Atlantic Mo.* Sept. 384 Even the stark meeting-houses tell, by their falling clapboards and faded wooden shutters, a tale of long neglect.

3. Attrib. and comb. with *bolt, cleaver, hut, river,* etc.

1639 *Portsmouth Rec.* 10 For men to gett a shippload of . . . pipe stauffes & clabboard boults. **1637** *Essex Inst. Coll.* IX. 31 Noe sawyer clapboord cleaver . . . shall cutt downe saw or cleave any boards or tymber within our lymits. **1739** *Ga. Col. Rec.* IV. 677 A certain Number of other Soldiers were employ'd in building Clap-board Huts. **1633** *Mass. Bay Rec.* I. 109 It is ordered, that maister carpenters, sawers, masons, clapboard-ryvers, brickelayers, . . . &c., shall not take aboue 2s a day. **1869** BROWNE *Adv. Apache Country* 402 Rough clap-board shelves heaped with books, hardware, crockery, and groceries abound at convenient intervals. **1843** 'CARLTON' *New Purchase* I. 108 [The] window . . . being occasionally shut at first with a blanket, afterwards with a clapboard shutter. **1900** SMITHWICK *Evolution of State* 38 We sat on stools around a clapboard table. **1764** *N.H. Hist. Soc. Coll.* IX. 145 [I] went . . . to find clapboard timber.

+Clapboard, *v.* Also **†clabboard, clabord,** etc. *tr.* To cover with clapboards.

1637 *Plymouth Col. Rec.* XII. 26 The house to be . . . clap boarded within . . . and a partition to be made of clap board. **1642** *Boston Rec.* 6 Aug., The walls claboarded tight from the injury of rayne. **1682** *Topsfield Rec.* 38 They will give Zacheus Curties senr Clabords & shingels for to Clabor[d] & shingell his house. **1705** *Charlestown Land Rec.* 172 [To] board or clabboard the outside of said house. **1721** *Harvard College Rec.* II. 457 Voted, That . . . the s[ai]d College be Clap-boarded on the East Side. **1764** *Ib.* 757 This Corporation will consent to pay for the Windows in Their Gallery & clapboard the upper part of the Front of the Meeting-house. **1825** NEAL *Bro. Jonathan* III. 382 Sheds . . . with more windows than glass—and more holes than windows; one part, half clap-boarded. **1840** DANA *Two Years* xxii. 223 The sides of the between-decks were clap-boarded. **1853** SIMMS *Sword & Distaff* 215 Originally, the house had been clap-boarded (a large, coarse, and inferior shingle) with split pine.

+Clapboarded, *a.* Covered with or formed of clapboards.

1835 *Southern Literary Messenger* II. 53 We behold the low log-cabin of a school-house—the clap-boarded roof but indifferently tight. **1839** *Knickerb.* XIII. 345 This brought us to the door of an old clap-boarded, dingy, long, one-story building. **1846** BUSHNELL *Work & Play* (1864) 258 An oblong clapboarded box, with a gable to the street. **1871** *Rep. Indian Affairs* 580 The confiscated property consists of a round log store-room, with a rough shingle clapboarded shed and end attached. **1884** *Century Mag.* XXVIII. 11 It is a plain clapboarded structure of small size. **1897** BRODHEAD *Bound in Shallows* 11 The settlement was indeed only a scattering of poor sheds, all of them sunken in the pervasive dog-fennel of the lowlands, and with clapboarded roofs.

+Clapboard house. A house made with clapboards. — **1640** *Suffolk Deeds* I. 16 The litle Claboard howse. **1654** *Rowley Rec.* 91 All thached houses shall be swept that day fornight and ol clapboard houses that day month. **1757** *Lett. to Washington* II. 174 The rest of the Town is indifferently improved, many very bad low clapboard Houses upon their Principal Streets which are in general narrow & confined.

+Clapboarding. Also **†cla(b)bo(a)rding.**

1. The putting on of clapboards.

1637 *Dedham Rec.* III. 32 It is agreed concerning Clapboarding of houses yt it shalbe at liberty vntill midsomer day next. **1651** *Watertown Rec.* 29 About the scoolehouse . . . Clabording and shingling.

2. A facing, or other part of a structure, made of clapboards.

1767 *Boston Ev. Post* 15 June (Th.), The lightning fell in a perpendicular direction, ripping the clapboarding and plaistering as it fell. **1872** *Vt. Bd. Agric. Rep.* I. 309 Paper . . . can be advantageously used between floors and between boarding and clapboarding on the walls. **1905** H. GARLAND *Tyranny of Dark* 59 The paint was blistering and peeling from the clapboarding on the sunny side of the main building.

+Clapboard roof. A roof made of clapboards.

1770 Summers *Ann. S. W. Virginia* (1929) 77 A log cabin . . . with a clapbord roof. **1843** 'CARLTON' *New Purchase* I. 108 Our cabin . . . had . . . [a] rude puncheon floor, a clapboard roof, and a clapboard door. **1872** *Harper's Mag.* June 21/2 A log-cabin with clapboard roof and mud chimney. **1880** BURNETT *Recoll. Old Pioneer* 29 (Th.), A log cabin . . . with chinked cracks, clapboard roof, and puncheon floor.

+Clapboard tree. A tree whose timber can be split into clapboards. — **1646** *Cambridge Rec.* 8 June, To fell two clapboard trees. **1658** *Manchester Rec.* 8 For a clabbord tree . . . 1 [shilling]. **1676** *Jamaica* (L.I.) *Rec.* I. 182 They are to have Liberty to take any timber . . . in our commons exsept Clappborde trees and Rayle trees under eightene inches.

+Clape. [Of unknown origin.] The golden-winged woodpecker, *Colaptes auratus.*

1844 *Nat. Hist. N.Y., Zoology* II. 192 The Clape, or Golden-Winged Woodpecker, *Picus Auratus,* . . . is called High-hole, Yucker, Flicker, [etc.]. **1848** BARTLETT 83 *Clape,* the common name of the golden-winged woodpecker in the State of New York. **1850** COOPER *Rural Hours* 99 A handsome Clape, or golden-winged woodpecker, a pretty wood-pewee, and a very delicate little black-poll warbler. *Ib.* 300 A pair of golden-winged woodpeckers, or clapes, as many persons call them, have been on the lawn all the afternoon.

+Clapmatch. [Du. *klapmuts.*] 'A kind of woman's cap' (B. '77).

+Clapper rail. A small wading bird of the species *Rallus crepitans;* the mud hen.

1813 WILSON *Ornithology* VII. 112 The Clapper Rail, or, as it is generally called, the Mud Hen, soon announces its arrival in the salt marshes, by its loud, harsh and incessant cackling. **1844** *Nat. Hist. N.Y., Zoology* II. 259 The Saltwater Meadow-Hen, *Rallus crepitans,* . . . the Clapper Rail, Mud-hen, or Meadow-hen. **1858** BAIRD *Birds Pacific R.R.* 747 Clapper rail [or] mud hen . . . is . . . an inhabitant of the seacoast. **1870** *Amer. Naturalist* III. 48 Off the coast of Cape Charles, Va., I found the nest of the Clapper-rail . . . built in a bush.

b. *Lesser clapper rail,* the Virginia rail, *Rallus virginianus.*

1890 *Cent.* 4941/1 The Virginia rail is . . . also called *red rail,* . . . *lesser clapper-rail, small mud-hen,* etc.

‖**Clarifier.** A tonic; medicine to clarify the system. — **1881** McLEAN *Cape Cod Folks* 140 As Grandpa and I daily refused our food, she affirmed, . . . that the one need of our deranged systems was a clarifier.

+Clarkia. [Wm. *Clark,* Amer. explorer.] A genus of plants, natural order *Onagraceae,* natives of the United States west of the Rocky Mountains. — **1863** *Horticulturist* XVIII 155 The Clarkia grows about two feet high. The color is mostly rosy red. It is a very pretty plant for the border. **1882** *Century Mag.* June 223/1 Here were bahia, madia, . . . etc., . . . blending finely with the purples of clarkia, orthocarpus, and oenothera. **1885** *Ib.* Jan. 447 Upon the swelling green slopes . . . were . . . dense growths of the clarkia, the peculiar, ragged little flower named for Captain Clark, the explorer.

+Clark's crow. [Wm. *Clark*, Amer. explorer.] The American nutcracker (*Nucifraga columbiana*), found in mountainous regions.

1811 WILSON *Ornithology* III. 29 Clark's Crow, *Corvus columbianus*, . . . inhabits the shores of the Columbia, and the adjacent country, . . . frequenting the rivers and sea shore, probably feeding on fish. **1828** BONAPARTE *Synopsis* 57 [The] Clark's Crow . . . inhabits the shores of the Oregan. **1858** BAIRD *Birds Pacific R.R.* 573 Clarke's Crow. . . . There is considerable variation in the size of this species, as well as a striking difference in the length of the bill. **1893** ROOSEVELT *Wilderness Hunter* 173 The Clarke's crow, an ash-colored bird with black wings and white tail and forehead, is as common as it is characteristic.

*** Class.**

+1. The students of a college who are of the same scholastic rank, *i.e.*, who normally enter in the same year. They are designated by the year of graduation, *e.g.*, the class of 1900 entered in 1896.

1671 SEWALL *Letter-Book* I. 19 Remember me kindly to all our Class; jointly and severally named. **1684** *Harvard Rec.* I. 77 Mr. Samuel Mitchell was . . . desired to undertake ye charge of ye class of ye Sophimores untill further order. **1702** C. MATHER *Magnalia* (1820) II. 9 The Fellows [of Harvard] resident on the place, became Tutors, to the several classes. **1766** CLAP *Ann. Yale College* 81 Undergraduate Students . . . are divided into four Classes; according to the respective Years in which they were admitted. Each Class is under the immediate Instruction of a particular Tutor. **1837** *Harvard Laws* 30 Each member of the Senior and Junior Classes. **1877** *Harper's Mag.* Feb. 464/1 At the new university . . . is an abolition of 'the class' of this or that year, and a consequent sacrifice of class pride and fellowship. **1882** THAYER *From Log-Cabin* 396 Whatever may happen to me in the future, I shall feel that I can always fall back upon the shoulders and hearts of the class of '56. **1899** E. E. HALE *Lowell & Friends* 180 The class of youngsters who entered Harvard College in 1856, when Lowell began his work there, graduated in 1860.

2. a. A rank or grade of society. {1772-} **b.** The system of such divisions in society. {1845-}

1789 WEBSTER *Diss. Engl. Lang.* 119 *Rome* is very frequently pronounced *Room*, and that by people of every class. **1830** COOPER *Water Witch* III. x, Those of the more fortunate class resembled men who retained a recollection of serious evils that were past. **1886** *Harper's Mag.* Nov. 957/1 It is one advantage of a society of class that wealth cannot buy its way beyond its caste. **1889** 'MARK TWAIN' *Conn. Yankee* xxviii. 366 There are wise people who talk ever so knowingly and complacently about 'the working classes.' **1917** SINCLAIR *King Coal* 235 How do you come to know so much about the psychology of the leisure class?

3. In Methodist usage, a group who meet for religious purposes; also a meeting of such a group. {1742-}

1832 WILLIAMSON *Maine* II. 697 A *Class* is a voluntary association of twelve or more, at whose head is a class-leader chosen by themselves, who is next below an exhorter; and the third part of a class is called a *Band*. **1844** Rupp *Relig. Denominations* 446 The classes . . . meet together weekly for mutual edification, in singing, prayer, and exhortation. **1845** *Ind. Mag. Hist.* XXIII. 24 The few members about there went to class at a brother Finley's near Hardingsburg.

4. Attrib. (in sense 1) with *album, cane, cap*, etc.

1871 BAGG *At Yale* 476 Lithographic title-pages of various designs, for the class albums are issued every year. **1856** HALL *College Words* (ed. 2) 67 At Union College, as a mark of distinction, a class cane was for a time carried by the members of the Junior Class. **1851** *Ib.* (ed. 1) 45 At Hamilton College, it is customary for the Sophomores to appear in a class cap on the Junior Exhibition day. **1851** *Ib., Class committee*, at Harvard College a committee of two persons . . . whose duty it is, after the class has graduated, during their lives to call class meetings. **1895** WILLIAMS *Princeton Stories* 195 If you would like to see a college campus as it really is, . . . do not come to Princeton for one of the class dances. **1871** BAGG *At Yale* 44 *Class election*, an after-choice to a secret society by one's own classmates, who themselves enjoyed the greater honor of being chosen by the class above them. **1895** WILLIAMS *Princeton Stories* 94 Yes, he's a mighty fine fellow. He played on his class eleven in his freshman year. **1871** BAGG *At Yale* 279 A 'class history' is nothing unless 'funny.' **1895** WILLIAMS *Princeton Stories* 255 With the dark green of many class-ivies for a background. **1856** HALL *College Words* (ed. 2) 77 In many colleges in the United States, a class marshal is chosen by the Senior Class from their own number, for the purpose of regulating the procession on the day of Commencement. **1895** J. L. WILLIAMS *Princeton Stories* 283 Other honors, such as . . . the class oratorship on Class Day. **1903** WIGGIN *Rebecca* 243 Did he offer to lend you his class-pin, or has it been so long since he graduated that he's left off wearing it? **1893** POST *Harvard Stories* 6 Gray would have wrecked the Varsity crew to a certainty. I watched him in the class races last year. **1906** *Springfield W. Republican* 28 June 10 Among the class reunions which are being held [at Yale], the most interesting is that of the class of '56. **1895** KING *Fort Frayne* 309 Of course it wasn't my class ring. **1895** WILLIAMS *Princeton Stories* 12 He had missed the class rush about the cannon, where freshmen are so closely pressed together that they never after get quite apart. **1887** *Lippincott's Mag.* Oct. 577 But the return of spring brings the halcyon period of college life; for this is the season of out-door sports, of class-sings, class-suppers, and the longed-for Commencement. **1855** *Knickerb.* XLV. 194 He sends us an original 'class-song,' . . . written by Oliver Wendell Holmes. **1902** MARTIN *Emmy Lou* 252 'Thinking it over,' said Hattie, 'I'll join; one owes something to class-spirit.' **1871** BAGG *At Yale* 476 An enlarged representation of the 'class stamp.' **1851** HALL *College Words* 50 *Class supper.* In American colleges, a supper attended only by the members of a collegiate class. **1879** *Scribner's Mo.* Dec. 202/1 The abolition of the traditional class system enables a young man to take the position . . . in that branch [of study which] fits him. **1856** HALL *College Words* (ed. 2) 79 *Class trees.* At Bowdoin College, 'immediately after the annual examination of each class, . . . the members that compose it are accustomed to form a ring round a tree, and then, not dance, but run around it.'

Class book. {1831} +(See quots.) — **1838** *Harvardiana* IV. 368 The 'Class Book' is a large volume, in which autobiographical sketches of the members of each graduating class are recorded. **1851** HALL *College Words* 44 Every graduating class [at Harvard] procures a beautiful and substantial folio of many hundred pages, called the Class Book, and lettered with the year of the graduation of the class.

+Class crew. A rowing crew composed of students who are members of the same class. — **1893** POST *Harvard Stories* 6, I should think he did, ejaculated Randolph, who had rowed in his class crew. **1897** *Outing* XXX. 239/2 Class crews, as well as the 'varsity crew at Harvard, have been given the best coaching.

+Class cup. (See quot. 1856.) — **1854** *Presentation Day Songs* (Yale) 14 June, Each man's mind was made up To obtain the 'Class Cup.' **1856** HALL *College Words* (ed. 2) 68 *Class cup.* It is a theory at Yale College, that each class appropriates at graduating a certain amount of money for the purchase of a silver cup, to be given . . . to the first member to whom a child shall be born.

+Class day. A day set aside by a class shortly before its graduation for social and memorial functions.

1851 HALL *College Words* 186 Class day [is] . . the day on which the members of that class finish their collegiate studies, and retire to make preparations for the ensuing Commencement. **1855** WILLARD *Mem., Youth & Manhood* II. 320 The leave-taking of the College by my class, on the 21st of June, 1798,—Class-day, as it is now called. **1860** *Harvard Orders & Regul.* xix, No entertainments by members of the College are allowed on Exhibition or Class Days without permission of the President. **1863** 'HAMILTON' *Gala-Days* 353 Class-Day is the peculiar institution of the Senior Class. **1904** *N.Y. Tribune* 5 June, Perhaps the only person who does not enjoy class day is the senior president of Columbia.

attrib. **1885** HOWELLS *S. Lapham* v, Before he knew it his son had him out to his class-day spread at Harvard. **1887** *Harper's Mag.* Feb. 385/1 He . . . wore with elegance the evening dress which Class Day custom prescribes for the Seniors. **1896** MOE *Hist. Harvard* 61 The Class Day exercises . . . had been begun in 1760. **1897** FLANDRAU *Harvard Episodes* 12 The . . . eloquent conventionality of the Class Day Orators.

‖Classhood. The condition of having social classes. — **1878** *Congress. Rec.* 7 March 1551/2 [Free labor in America] eliminated classhood in society and made opportunities for advancement socially, politically, and financially equal among men.

+Classic city. A term formerly applied to Boston, Mass. — **1859** *Ladies' Repository* XIX. 51/1 Boston is the 'Classic City,' the 'Modern Athens,' and the 'Literary Emporium,' from its acknowledged pre-eminence in the literary and fine-art pursuits. **1871** DEVERE 662 Boston, in Massachusetts, . . . is called the Classic City, in appreciation of the high culture of her inhabitants.

+Classified (civil) service. That part of the public service which has been classified or graded under civil service rules. — **1897** *Amer. Academy Annals* IX. 292 The most important extensions [of the civil service rules in Massachusetts] made during the present year . . . include in the classified service, messengers in city service, [etc.]. **1912** *Statutes at Large* XXXVII. 555 No person in the classified civil service of the United States shall be removed therefrom except for such cause as will promote the efficiency of said service. **1920** *Civil Service Comm. 37th Rep. 14 (caption)*, Statutes affecting the classified service.

*** Classis.** [Latin.]

+1. =CLASS 1. *Obs.*

1643 *New Englands First Fruits* II. iv, The Students of the first Classis that have beene these foure yeeres trained up in University-Learning. **1673** *Harvard Rec.* I. 56 Mr Daniell Gookin . . . is forthwith to take upon him the charg of a classis. **1723** *Ib.* 483 After his taking the Care of the Classis to the End of this Year. **1851** HALL *College Words* 49 *Classis.* Same meaning as Class.

***2.** A presbytery or inferior judicatory body of elders and pastors in a Presbyterian church. Also in use in certain Reformed churches.

1781 PETERS *Hist. Conn.* 234 The Dutch presbyterians in New-York were held in subordination to the classis of Amsterdam, till, a few years since, they . . . erected a classis for the ordination of ministers, in defiance of the ecclesiastical judicatory at Amsterdam. **1796** MORSE *Amer. Geog.* I. 273 The Dutch Reformed churches . . . [constitute] six classes, which form one synod. Each classis delegates two ministers and an elder to represent them in synod. **1832** SANDS *Writings* II. 316 Last year the classis met, and recommended to the congregation to build a new church.

Class leader. In Methodist usage, the directing member of a class (sense 3). {1857}

1832 [see CLASS 3]. **1838** GILMAN *Recoll.* 269 *n.*, It is the office of a class-leader to assemble those under his charge once or twice a week, usually on the Sabbath, . . . and instruct them in their Christian duties. **1844** Rupp *Relig. Denominations* 447 The class leader . . . has charge of a class, and it is his duty to see each member of his class once a week to inquire how his soul prospers. **1856** P. CARTWRIGHT *Autobiog.* 183, I found a large society, a fine class-leader, and a very pious . . . preacher. **1881** PIERSON *In the Brush* 142 On one of these journeys the Bishop found at a mountain-inn a Methodist circuit-rider, class-leader, steward, and local preacher, assembled for an 'official meeting.' **1896** HARRIS *Sister Jane* 10 He was a class-leader in his church. **1900** WINCHESTER *W. Castle* 162 A trustee and class-leader who, it was generally believed, was accustomed to go from the Sunday morning service to a neighboring saloon and get a drink of beer.

+**Classmate.** A student who is in the same class with another; a fellow student.

1713 SEWALL *Diary* 5 June, He had spoken for my Classmate Capt. Saml. Phipps to the Gov[erno]r. **1727** *Ib.* 22 Dec., I have now been at the Interment of 4 of my Class-mates. **1773** Fithian *Journal* I. 35 There are a number of our friends and class-mates getting into business as fast as possible. **1813** *Niles' Reg.* IV. 11/2 A captain Elliott, who had been a class-mate with him at Princeton College, waited on Captain Hart. **1827** *Harvard Reg.* Sept. 202 The day is wound up with a scene of careless laughter and merriment, among a dozen of joke-loving classmates. **1856** M. J. HOLMES *Homestead on Hillside* 18 Mr. Hamilton would have gone almost anywhere for the sake of hearing from his classmates. **1895** WILLIAMS *Princeton Stories* 81, I thought I was coming to my own room— . . . I mean my classmate's room. **1899** TARKINGTON *Gentl. Indiana* 64 The dozen or so emblazoned classmates (it was the time of brilliant flannels) who suddenly sent up a volley of college cheers in his honor. **1916** EASTMAN *From Deep Woods* 68 Some of my classmates who had failed to prepare their relation.

‖**Classmating.** The seeking of favors from, or sponging on, one's classmates. — **1774** J. ADAMS in *Fam. Lett.* (1876) 10 You know I never get or save anything by cozening or classmating.

+**Class meeting.**

1. A meeting for business or pleasure of students who are in the same class.

1790 *Harvard Laws* 35 No Class-meetings shall be held, but with the special licence of the President; nor more than four for each Class in a year. **1837** *Harvardiana* III. 314 Arrangements were made for calling a class-meeting. **1851** HALL *College Words* 49 *Class meeting*, a meeting where all the class are assembled for the purpose of carrying out some measure. **1871** BAGG *At Yale* 165 The neutral editor refused to obey, and called a class meeting which voted to sustain him. **1895** WILLIAMS *Princeton Stories* 12 He had missed the class meeting, where freshmen get a first sight of one another which lasts always. **1916** EASTMAN *From Deep Woods* 67 On the evening of our first class meeting, lo! I was appointed football captain.

2. In the Methodist Church, a meeting of a group or class for religious instruction and improvement.

1798 MANNING *Key of Liberty* 68 The Class Meetings may be formed by a grater or less number just as their situation, circumstances, or inclinations Sute. **1843** *Knickerb.* XXI. 41 The exercises were conducted by one of the colored leaders of the class-meetings. **1846** *Ind. Mag. Hist.* XXIII. 330 The people did not expect more than preaching and class meeting. **1871** EGGLESTON *Hoosier Schoolm.* 170 She could get happy in class meeting . . . and could witness a good experience in the quarterly love-feast. **1883** WILDER *Sister Ridnour* 58 These same Church members will . . . think it too much trouble to open their kitchen, dining-room, or parlor door for a feeble class-meeting. **1900** WINCHESTER *W. Castle* 196 You have a lot of people among you who do not love the prayer meeting and the class-meeting.

+**Class poem.** A poem commemorating events in the history of a college class. — **1835** B. WINSLOW (*title*), Class Poem, delivered in the University Chapel, July 14, at the Valedictory Exercises of the Class of 1835. **1897** FLANDRAU *Harvard Episodes* 181, I was thinking of all the horrible Class Poems and Odes and Baccalaureate Sermons and ghastly Memorial Day orators that are allowed to go on.

+**Class secretary.** The secretary of a college class. — **1851** HALL *College Words* 44 The book [Class Book] is then deposited in the hands of the Class Secretary, whose duty it is to keep a faithful record of the marriage, birth of children, and death of each of his classmates. **1871** BAGG *At Yale* 536 One of these [on the committee] is chosen 'class secretary,' and on him the greater part of the burden falls.

+**Class tutor.** (See quot. 1856.) — **1856** HALL *Coll. Words* (ed. 2) 466 *Class Tutor.* At some of the colleges in the United States, each of the four classes is assigned to the care of a particular tutor, who acts as the ordinary medium of communication between the members of the class and the Faculty. **1860** *Harvard Orders & Regul.* ii, The Class Tutors grant leave of absence from church and from town on Sunday.

‖**Clatterwacking.** [Imitative.] A rattling, clattering noise. — **1851** *Polly Peablossom* 148, I hearn the darndest clatter-wacking and noise.

+**Claw balk.** (See quotation.) — **1884** *Century Mag.* XXIX. 280 Each two men carrying a claw-balk, or timbers fitted with a claw, one of which held the gunwale of the boat, the other the shore abutment.

+**Claw bar.** (See quotation 1874.) — **1872** HUNTINGTON *Road-Master's Asst.* 75 As claw-bars are usually made, it is impossible to draw a spike without spoiling it for future use. **1874** KNIGHT 562 *Claw-bar*, a lever or crow-bar with a bent bifurcated claw for drawing spikes.

Claw-foot, *a.* = CLAW-FOOTED *a.* — **1881** *Harper's Mag.* March 528/1 About 1700 the claw-foot side-boards, sofas and tables were generally used.

Claw-footed, *a.* {1667} Of furniture: Having the feet carved to look like claws.

1847 PARKMAN in *Knickerb.* XXX. 229 On the Platte one may sometimes see the shattered wrecks of ancient claw-footed tables. **1871** STOWE *Pink & White Tyranny* 22 The heavy claw-footed, mahogany chairs . . . all spoke of days past. **1875** STOWE *We & Neighbors* 88 She had made Eva sit down in an old fashioned claw-footed arm-chair in the warmest corner. **1889** COOKE *Steadfast* 167 A claw-footed table, round, and shining with beeswax and rubbing.

+**b.** *fig.* Out of fashion, stodgy, heavily ornate. (With reference to out-of-date claw-footed furniture.)

1851 MELVILLE *Moby Dick* xvi, With an old-fashioned claw-footed look about her.

Claw hammer.

1. A hammer having one end of its head slit for use in extracting nails, tacks, etc. {1769–}

1827 SHERWOOD *Gaz. Georgia* 185 Near a fort an iron claw hammer was found. **1878** TAYLOR *Between Gates* 27 A youthful descendant of Ham, with a heel like the head of a clawhammer.

+**2.** Attrib. with *coat:* A swallowtail coat for formal evening dress. †Also with *jacket.*

1845 *Knickerb.* XXV. 424 The young man had a new blue claw-hammer jacket manufactured. **1865** WHITMAN *Specimen Days* (1882) 64, I saw Mr. Lincoln, drest all in black, with white kid gloves and a claw-hammer coat. **1887** *Courier-Journal* 15 Feb. 4/3 It takes more than a claw-hammer coat to make a good Envoy Extraordinary. **1895** CHAMBLISS *Diary* 392 In all parts of the civilized world except California, the term 'Evening Dress' means 'swallow-tailed' or 'claw-hammer' coats for gentlemen. **1902** HARBEN *Abner Daniel* 191, I don't know but I'd move down to Atlanta an' live alongside o' Bill, an' wear a claw-hammer coat an' a dicky cravat fer a change.

+**b.** *ellipt.* A swallowtail coat.

1881 *Harper's Mag.* Sept. 556/2 Adoniram's coat was made in the style then called straight-bodied, now known as dress-coat, and by the facetious called claw-hammer, etc. **1888** *N.Y. Sun* 29 Sept. (F.), Don't . . . call a dress-coat a swallow-tail, or a claw-hammer. **1889** FARMER 152/2 *Claw-Hammer*, American for the coat worn in 'evening dress.' **1895** *Outing* XXVI. 434/2, I'd . . . sow the dark woods with fragments of claw-hammer and patent leathers.

+**Claw-toed,** *a.* = CLAW-FOOTED *a.* — **1886** MITCHELL *R. Blake* 58 Claw-toed chairs with carved scroll and shell work backs.

***Clay.**

***1.** A viscous earth consisting of decomposed rock.

Also BLUE CLAY (1778–).

1622 'MOURT' *Relation* 62 We found heere . . . excellent clay. **a1649** WINTHROP *Hist.* I. 69 There came so violent a storm of rain, . . . as (it [the building] being not finished, and laid with clay for want of lime) two sides of it were washed down to the ground. **1705** BEVERLEY *Virginia* IV. 54 Tho' they have Slate enough . . . and as strong Clay as can be desired for making of Tile, yet they have few tiled Houses. **1792** IMLAY *Western Territory* 124 Clay is very common in every part of this country which is proper for bricks. **a1817** DWIGHT *Travels* I. 35 Clay, of the kind fitted for the manufacture of bricks, and of coarse earthen ware, abounds in almost all parts of New-England. **1881** *Rep. Indian Affairs* p. xxi, Soil, loam, and clay; and will grow well and abundantly all kinds of cereals.

***2.** *attrib.* Pertaining to or made of clay; clayey.

1749 ELIOT *Field-Husb.* ii. 41 The next sort of Manure . . . is Clay Ashes. **1897** *Outing* XXX. 392/1 In addition to the various track and field contests, there were several clay-bird matches. **1884** 'CRADDOCK' *Tennessee Mts.* 40 A little log house surmounted the slope. . . . Its clay chimney had a leaning tendency. **1821** *Jrnl. Science* III. 2 The Clay country is so called because clay predominates. **1843** *Knickerb.* XXII. 4 In the up country [of South Carolina] every shade of greenness is lost in the interminable red clay-fields which spread out every where around you. **1878** *Ill. Dept. Agric. Trans.* XIV. 173 The intermediate 'clay flats' . . . are found to produce wheat of fair yield and superior quality. **1791** BARTRAM *Travels* 183 A loose, . . . sandy loam, on a clay or marley foundation. **1772** D. TAITT in *Travels Amer. Col.* 499 We Encamped in a strong clay ground having very little mould on its surface. **1677** *Boston Rec.* 113 Libertie was granted . . . to set vp a Lime kilne vpon the clay hill. **1751** BARTRAM *Observations* 30 So far we had pale clay land from the wilderness. **1888** ROOSEVELT in *Century Mag.* XXXVI. 209/1 These clay licks were mere holes in the banks. **1849** CHAMBERLAIN *Ind. Gazetteer* 297 The soil is various, though mostly a clay loam, with a mixture of sand, and very productive. **1839** BUEL *Farmer's Companion* 47 Hence the advantage of applying lime to clayey, and clay-marl to sandy lands. **1837** COLMAN *Mass. Agric. Rep.* 78 This drain is four feet wide at the top, and goes down some small depth into the clay pan. **1880** *Vt. Agric. Rep.* VI. 25 This deterioration is especially observable in the clay pastures of the Champlain Valley. **1854** *Penna. Agric. Rep.* 425 Silver Medal for best stone, clay and coal picks. **1860** GREELEY *Overland Journey* 231 Crossing, just west of the city, . . . we are . . . once more on a parched clay plain. **1853** SIMMS *Sword & Distaff* 491 Through chinks between the logs, from which the clay-plastering had fallen out. **1796** *Mass. H. S. Coll.* V. 108

The one who chased me, endeavouring to cut me off, got into a clay pond, near where the new tavern is now built. **1855** Hambleton *H. A. Wise* 421 'Clay' poultices [were applied] to the abdomen. **1860** Greeley *Overland Journey* 176 A range of such precipitous clay-rock bluffs as I have tried to describe. **1869** Browne *Adv. Apache Country* 525 The clay seam between the quartz and the casings renders the excavation of the ores comparatively easy. **1882** Worthen *Econ. Geol. Ill.* II. 10 It is underlaid by fire-clay, or clay shale, twenty inches thick. *Ib.* 18 This coal-seam is subject to some irregularities, such as 'clay slips' or 'horse-backs,' sometimes called 'faults' by the miners. **1804** J. Roberts *Penna. Farmer* 11 (*caption*), Clay Soils. **1637** *Ipswich Hist. Soc. Pub.* IX. 25, I think it best to have the walls without all clap boarded besides the clay walls. **1860** Greeley *Overland Journey* 198 Black's Fork, which, a few miles below, runs whitish with the clay-wash of the desert, is here a clear, sparkling mountain torrent.

Clayball. A mass or globule of clay. — **1843** *Nat. Hist. N.Y., Geology* IV. 231 'Clay-balls,' or concretions in ordinary clay, which, however, rarely attain more than a few inches in diameter. **1849** *Amer. Phil. Soc. Proc.* V. 708 Clay-balls placed in the fire increased the amount of heat.

Claybank.

1. A bank of clay.

1839 Buel *Farmer's Companion* 42 We are enabled to obtain it from the clay-banks in Albany. **a1846** *Quarter Race Ky.*, etc. 174 Jist get rite up from that table! . . . Jist hist, and take yourself off to that clay bank down thar! **1878** Jackson *Travel at Home* 92 After breaking against the yellow clay-bank, it fell turbid and thick, in masses of gamboge-colored foam. **1890** *Lordsburg Californian* 8 May 7/2 Go out into some secluded canyon and kick your own shadow into the clay-bank. **1897** *Outing* XXX. 330/1, I was told to follow the stream for about a mile to some clay-banks where was a runway.

2. A yellowish color.

1851 Reid *Scalp Hunters* xxiii, [A mare] of that dun-yellowish colour known as 'clay-bank.' **1869** *Overland Mo.* III. 126 'Clay-bank' is a yellowish dun.

+3. A horse of a yellowish-brown color resembling that of clay. (Cf. 5.)

1858 *Kansas Hist. Coll.* V. 540 Stolen, . . . one yearling, a claybank, with white and flaxen mane and tail. **1882** Baillie-Grohman *Camps in Rockies* 91 Among the half-dozen horses that were running loose behind the long string of huge waggons was the 'claybank' Bibleback. **1884** Sweet & Knox *Through Texas* 63 One of the ponies was of a pale dun color . . . ; the other what is known as a 'claybank,' the name being suggested by the natural color of the animal. **1885** 'Craddock' *Prophet* 108 The mountain colt, a clay-bank, . . . reared violently under the surprise of the lash. **1886** *Outing* IX. 104/2 The 'clay-banks' were put to their speed. **1891** 'Thanet' *Otto the Knight*, etc. 26 She laid out t' cyar' Boo, but she rode the claybank, and he's sicher ill hoss, she dassent. **1896** Pool *In Buncombe County* 40 The steed was a 'clay bank.'

+4. *pl.* A nickname for the members of one faction of the Missouri legislature.

1864 *Century Mag.* (1889) Sept. 697/1 'The Clay Banks,' as the Conservatives were called, wished the radicals to declare for Lincoln. **a1877** in Bartlett 397 The Missourians have quite a penchant for curious characterization. The members of the Legislature are divided into Charcoals, Clay-Banks, White-legs, [etc.].

+5. *attrib.* Of the color of clay. Also comb. with *colored.*

1855 *Putnam's Mag.* Feb. 188, I mounted a claybank colored nag and rode to the hunt. **1869** *Overland Mo.* Aug. 126, I met a man, with a pinched face and a yellow beard, who was mounted on a clay-bank horse. **1871** Eggleston *Hoosier Schoolm.* 102 Ralph found that he was to ride the 'clay-bank mare.' **1884** 'Craddock' *Tenn. Mts.* 101 A yoke of oxen, a clay-bank filly, ten hogs. **1906** 'O. Henry' *Rolling Stones* (1912) 30 An elegant gentleman of a slightly claybank complexion sitting in an upholstered chair. **1909** — *Roads of Destiny* 81 Fergus was at the other end of the room trying to break away from two maroons and a claybank girl. **1910** — *Strictly Business* 68 'Keep that awhile for me, mister,' he said, chewing at the end of a virulent claybank cigar.

+Clay bluff. A bluff composed largely of clay. — **1804** Clark in *Lewis & C. Exped.* (1904) I. 48 We passed a high land, & clay bluff on the S.S. called the Snake bluff. **1833** Catlin *Indians* I. 69 We stopped at the base of some huge clay bluffs. *Ib.*, This group of clay bluffs, which line the [Missouri] river for many miles.

+Clay-colored bunting. =next. — **1889** *Cent.* 722/2 Clay-colored bunting . . . [is] a small bird closely resembling the chipping-sparrow. **1890** *Ib.* 5845/2.

+Clay-colored sparrow. A bunting (*Spizella pallida*), closely related to the chipping sparrow — **1869** *Amer. Naturalist* III. 299, I saw . . . the Clay-colored Sparrow. **1874** Coues *Birds N.W.* 148 The Clay-colored Sparrows nest abundantly in Dakota, and especially along the Red River.

+Clay dog. *local.* A concretion found in clay. — **1892** *N.J. State Geologist Rep.* 138 The low plain [south of Morristown is] . . . equally rich in concretions, which are locally known as 'clay-stones,' 'clay-dogs,' 'stone-dogs,' etc.

+Clay eater. One who eats clay; spec. a low-class white person of the South.

See Bartlett '59; also Dirt eater.

1841 Simms *Kinsmen* xiv, He was a little, dried up, withered atomy,—a jaundiced 'sand-lapper' or 'clay-eater' from the Wassamasaw country. **c1845** Thompson *Chron. Pineville* 41 Then, too, might be seen the torpid clay-eater, . . . as he closed in with his antagonist, and showed by his performances that he could eat clay as well in its animate as in its inanimate form. **1863** 'E. Kirke' *Southern Friends* 43 A woman whose dress and appearance designated her as one of the species of 'white trash' known in North Carolina as 'clay-eaters.' **1865** Andrews *South since War* 177, I am certain that there can be no lower class of people than the North Carolina 'clay-eaters,'—this being the local name of the poor whites. **1896** Harris *Sister Jane* 31 The men . . . were as lanky and as lousy-looking a set as I had ever seen—pale, cadaverous, and careworn—veritable 'clay eaters.' **1897** Barton *Sim Galloway* 33 His wife was a clay-eater.

+Clay-eating, *a.* Characterized by the eating of clay. — **1863** 'E. Kirke' *Southern Friends* 47 It was fortunate for the clay-eating feminine that her conversation had disgusted us. **1888** *Fort Smith Tribune* Feb. (F.), He came originally from the clay-eating and turpentine district of South Carolina.

+Clay gall. A spot of clayey soil that has been rendered barren by erosion. — **1898** Harris *Tales of Home Folks* 25 Where the ridge and the hunt entered the woods there was what is known as a 'clay gall,' a barren spot, above two acres in extent.

Clay hole. A hole from which clay has been dug. — **1844** S. M. Fuller *Summer on Lakes* 215 He drowned himself after . . . in a broad shallow clay hole. **1860** Cox *Recoll. Wabash Valley* 10 One of the Indian women, after remaining in the water in the clay-hole amongst the dead bodies of her slaughtered relatives for two days and nights, was taken out alive.

‖**Clayism.** The political principles of Henry Clay. — **1832** *Louisville Pub. Advert.* 10 Nov. (*caption*), Clayism Against Anti-Masonry. **1842** [see Coonism].

+Clayite. A supporter of Henry Clay. — **1832** *Louisville Public Advert.* 27 March, A Clayite—has introduced a bill. **1833** Coke *Subaltern's Furlough* xxvii, A cabin full of fiery, hot-headed Clayites and Jacksonmen, each espousing the cause of his favourite candidate. **a1859** *N.Y. Herald* (B., 39) Horace Greeley, and a train of real blue light Clayites from your State, have arrived this morning.

+Clayman. A supporter of Henry Clay. — **1832** *Louisville Pub. Advert.* 17 Oct., Claymen, antimasons, and bankites, where are you? **1833** Coke *Subaltern's Furlough* xxvii, A tall broad-shouldered Kentuckian . . . dispersed the entire conclave, by saying to a little Clayman, 'You are a pretty sample of a white man.' **c1849** Paige *Dow's Sermons* I. 130 My unfortunate accomplices in political rascality, the Clay-men, are hopping about like peas upon a hot shovel.

+Clay mortar. Clay used as mortar to fill crevices. — **1829** Flint *George Mason* 10 It was made of clefts, plastered with clay-mortar. **1831** Peck *Guide* 126 [The chimney is] built of sticks of wood . . . laid up with . . . clay mortar.

+Clay pan. A layer of clay in the soil. — **1837** Colman *Mass. Agric. Rep.* (1838) 78 This drain is four feet wide at the top, and goes down some small depth into the clay pan.

Clay pigeon. A clay target sprung into the air from a trap. Also attrib. — **1888** *Outing* Sept. 501 Doubtless he had broken innumerable glass balls and 'clay pigeons' at a trap. **1893** Post *Harvard Stories* 16 Next morning the clay-pigeon match came off, as usual.

Clay pipe. A tobacco pipe made of clay. {1836–, (Dickens *Pickwick Papers*)}

1845 *Knickerb.* XXV. 445 My grand-father took down his long clay-pipe. **1865** *Atlantic Mo.* XV. 392/1 [The driver's] less placid wife sat upon a throne of oil-barrels, . . . alternately smoking a clay pipe and shouting profane instructions to her husband. **1879** Taylor *Summer-Savory* 139 Here [in a country store] clouds of smoke from clay pipes float up among the bed-cords and brooms. **1890** *Century Mag.* Nov. 66 Three clay pipes with reed stems, and a buckskin bag of tobacco. **1902** Gordon *Recoll. Lynchburg* 14 The smoke rose languidly from the ancient clay pipe.

***Clay pit.** A pit from which clay is dug.

1637 *Dedham Rec.* I. 35, 9. acres more or lesse as it lyeth betweene the medowe & hill . . . & abutteth vpon ye Claypitts towards the West. **1641** *New Haven Col. Rec.* 52 The clay pitts shalbe layd out as como[n], as itt was first intended. **1646** *Ib.* 209 Mr. Davenport . . . may fence crosse the way to the clay-pitts, makeing a gate & hanging a lock vppon it. **1706** *Cambridge Prop. Rec.* 227 Near the Clay pitts on ye Rhoad. **1760** *Md. Hist. Mag.* XVIII. 157 She fell into a Clay pit and the log fell on her and killed her. **1834** Hawthorne in *New Eng. Mag.* VII. 456 The schoolboys . . . found plenty of ammunition [for pelting] in the neighboring clay-pits and mud-holes.

attrib. **1687** *Southampton Rec.* II. 55 Layd out . . . a piece of land unto Iecamiah Scott lying and being on the east side of Samuel Clarkes clay pit close. **1685** *Portsmouth Rec.* 295 An Indi[an] who . . . was found Dead in or near the Clay pitt field lands in the Town of Portsmouth.

Clay road. An unimproved road passing over clayey ground. — **1856** Olmsted *Slave States* 63 We picked our way . . . through a deeply corrugated clay-road. **1891** *Century Mag.* Feb. 483 Flung as if by chance beside a red clay road, . . . a settlement appears.

Clay slate. A sedimentary rock composed of indurated clay. {1837–}

1815 Drake *Cincinnati* 65 [The limestone] is in strata from one to eighteen inches thick, which alternate with layers of clay-slate, the *argilla* *fissilis* of Turton. **1822** J. WOODS *English Prairie* 273 The soil found in digging wells, is, first, a vegetable mould, next loamy clay, then sandstone, and lastly clay-slate. **1831** PECK *Guide* 311 The basis rock in all the counties on the Wabash is sandstone, resting . . . on clay slate. **1892** *Vt. Agric. Rep.* XII. 143 Through Roxbury . . . and Woodbury extends a broad belt of clay slate.

Clay stone. +(See CLAY DOG.)

Claytonia. The spring beauty (*Claytonia virginica* and *caroliniana*), a perennial herb of temperate regions. — **1818** *Mass. H. S. Coll.* 2 Ser. VIII. 168 Among our herbaceous wild plants, the first that appear are the delicate claytonia, the graceful three-lobed hepatica, [etc.]. **1870** JACKSON *Verses* 85 Violets stir, . . . Claytonia's rosy bells unfold. **1880** *Scribner's Mo.* May 101/2 A good sample of our native purslane is the Claytonia, or spring beauty.

+**Clay Whig.** A Whig who gave his political support to Henry Clay. — **1855** Hambleton *H. A. Wise* 264 How can the old Clay Whigs give in their adhesion to a new party? **1900** [see CONSTITUTIONAL 5].

***Clean,** *a.*

‖**1.** Not stained by bloodshed; free from strife.

1802 DRAYTON *S. Carolina* 14 The path over this mountain has been crooked and straight, bloody and clean; (according to the Indian talks).

2. Perfect, complete, pure.

1843 STEPHENS *High Life N.Y.* II. 160, I whistled the colt up tu us, and pinted out his harnsome head and chist, and the clean notion that he has got of flingin out his legs. **1857** *Quinland* I. 4 You've got Bill off to that ere expensive college, where he's likely to make a pretty clean go of it. **1877** HARTE *Story of a Mine*, etc. 421 He's clean gold on the bed rock after all! **1895** REMINGTON *Pony Tracks* 164 Between the Doctor, who explained, expostulated, and swore, and a great many 'clean misses' [in duck-shooting], I wore onto the high-school stage. **1903** A. ADAMS *Log Cowboy* xviii, He wouldn't do it. He was clean strain—I'm not talking.

+**3.** (See quot. 1859.)

1859 BARTLETT 86 *Clean Ticket*, the entire regularly nominated ticket at an election; a ticket without any erasures. 'He went the clean ticket on the Whig Nominations.' **1871** DE VERE 269 Only when a man adopts the whole list as made up by his party is it called a clean or straight ticket.

+**4.** Of cotton: Ginned. (Cf. CLEAN *v.* 1.)

1857 D. BRAMAN *Texas* 24 The land is quite fertile, producing, on an average, one bale, or 500 lbs. clean cotton per acre.

+**5.** Clear, actual. *colloq.*

1855 *Knickerb.* XLVI. 97, I think . . . if all my debts were paid I should be worth three hundred dollars clean cash! **1863** 'E. KIRKE' *Southern Friends* 235 Made a clean forty thousand on the rosin speculation. **1875** *Chicago Tribune* 21 Nov. 2/6 'In clean cash, right in the savings-bank,' answered Jim.

+**6.** Free; not infringed upon; clear.

1886–7 STOCKTON *Hundredth Man* xii, He's to have a clean two weeks to begin with, to come down into the country to see his mother and me.

7. Unencumbered.

1898 PAGE *Red Rock* 337 Leech, it was reported, had come up from town, given a clean title and prepared a deed which was to be delivered on a certain day.

+**8.** *Baseball.* Free from error.

1893 *Chicago Tribune* 28 April 7/3 The fielding of the Washingtons was clean and effective.

+**b.** *Clean hit*, a hit that enables the batter to reach a base without the aid of an error.

1868 CHADWICK *Base Ball* 67 Pike secured his base four times by clean hits. **1875** *Chicago Tribune* 4 Sept. 'A'/3 The Athletics utterly failed to hit him, making only five clean hits in the game. *Ib.* 30 Sept. 2/4 'Cuthy' somewhat regained his old reputation, as he made three clean hits with telling effect. **1887** *Courier-Journal* 26 May 2/6 Collins then stepped to the plate and drove a clean hit to left field.

+**c.** *Clean home run*, (see quotation).

1868 CHADWICK *Base Ball* 39 A 'clean home run' is only made when the batsman hits a ball far enough out of the reach of the out-fielders as to enable him to run around to home base.

+**9.** *The clean thing*, the honest or proper course of action.

1835 CROCKETT *Tour* 193, I don't like it. It isn't the clean thing. **1849** KINGSLEY *Diary* 69 The Directors are doing the clean thing, and for the first time have taken their proper position in this company. **1850** LEWIS *La. Swamp Dr.* 52 The old woman commenced strippin' to lighten, till it wouldn't bin the clean thing for her to have taken off one dud more. **1871** *Washington Patriot* 3 April (De Vere), It would have been the clean thing to say at once that no debate would be allowed. **1873** *Newton Kansan* 19 June 3/2 Let patriots everywhere . . . prepare to do the clean thing by Uncle Sam.

Clean, *v.*

+**1.** *tr.* To gin (cotton); to free (wheat) from chaff.

1827 SHERWOOD *Gaz. Georgia* 116 At three or four gin-houses much of the cotton raised in the vicinity, and in Burke, was cleaned. **1860** T. D. PRICE *MS. Diary* 17 Aug., Threshed out wheat with horses, tramped out 15 doz. for seed, cleaned through mill once. **1870** *Ib.* 9 Feb., P. Glynn . . . borrowed windmill to clean wheat.

2. *To clean out*, to free from trash or rubbish, to clear. {1844–}

1812 *Niles' Reg.* II. 9/2 Hammers are also used to clean out and smooth the holes. **1840** DANA *Two Years* 168 By the regulations of the ship, the forecastle was cleaned out every morning.

+**b.** To drive out by force; to overcome, defeat, or 'use up' (an opponent). (Cf. 3 f.) Also without *out*. *slang.*

1867 CRAWFORD *Mosby* 285 Captain Brasher, alias Blazer, whom the authorities at Washington had selected from their whole army for his bravery and daring, and sent . . . to 'clean out Mosby.' **1869** Dumont *Benedict's Songster* 49, I can beat old Uncle Snow, the best way he can go, I will clean the whole caboodle, then ye people watch my step. **1872** 'MARK TWAIN' *Roughing It* xlvii. 334 When some roughs jumped the Catholic boneyard and started in to stake out town lots in it he went for 'em! And he cleaned 'em, too! **1889** MUNROE *Golden Days* 118 We'd . . . have to clean 'em out, and I'm that tender-hearted that I don't hanker after killing no human. **1891** *Harper's Mag.* Nov. 883/2 He usually gave one warning to evil-doers, and if they did not heed that he 'cleaned them out.' **1909** 'O. HENRY' *Roads of Destiny* 92 The man who cleaned out the horse thieves.

+**c.** To empty or rid (a place) of the occupants or one's adversaries. *colloq.*

1868 HARTE *Society upon Stanislaus* line 20 On several occasions he had cleaned out the town. **1890** CUSTER *Following Guidon* 155 Even the sober, law-abiding ones would set out the next night to 'clean out the town.' **1901** RYAN *Montana* 97 They . . . would proceed to 'clean out' any establishment where their own peculiar set was ignored. **1902** WHITE *Blazed Trail* 175 He invaded the enemy's camp, attempted to clean out the saloon with a billard cue single handed.

d. To leave (one) entirely without money. Freq. in passive. {1812–}

1840 DANA *Two Years* xxviii, He was 'cleaned out' to the last real, and completely 'used up.' **1871** HARTE *Luck Roaring Camp*, etc. 95, I'm cleaned out again, Jack. . . . Can't you help me with a hundred till to-morrow's clean-up?

e. To pick or gather (berries, fruit, etc.) completely.

1891 *Fur, Fin, & Feather* March 169 They are regular berrying parties, and they reckons to clean out the ripest fruit and berries as they works their way gradually down stream.

+**3.** *To clean up.* **a.** To obtain, acquire, 'net.' *colloq.*

1831 PECK *Guide* 147 He gave a friend one measured acre . . . and cleaned up thirty-five bushels and eight quarts [of wheat]. **1851** JACKSON *Forty-niner* 51, I hope to clean up about ten thousand dollars. **1860** GREELEY *Overland Journey* 146 Another Indiana company . . . on the 11th had three sluices in operation for the first, and cleaned up $1,009 . . . from the product of that day's labor of twelve men. **1897** *Chicago Tribune* 5 September 4 Ohio man cleans up $240,000 [in the Klondike region]. **1905** R. BEACH *Pardners* 25 When the river broke we cleaned up one hundred and eighty-seven dollars' worth of lovely, yellow dust. **1908** WHITE *Riverman* 254 We ought to clean up five dollars a thousand on our mill. **1913** MULFORD *Coming of Cassidy* 136 If he had the cattle he could clean up a fortune for his ranch.

+**b.** To free (land) of trash, litter, etc., preparatory to cultivation.

1839 Bassett *Plantation Overseer* 117, I have got my cotton land the half of it cleaned up and is running four plows. **1896** HARRIS *Sister Jane* 218, I could begin the job of cleanin' up the new groun', for it jest had to be cleaned up.

+**c.** *Mining.* (See quotations.) Cf. CLEAN-UP *n.* 1.

1851 JACKSON *Forty-niner* 84 Last week was an off week, but we are going now to put in steady work until we clean up our ground. **1872** 'MARK TWAIN' *Roughing It* xxxvi. 255 At the end of the week the machinery was stopped and we 'cleaned up.' That is to say, we got the pulp out of the pans and batteries and washed the mud patiently away till nothing was left but the long-accumulating mass of quicksilver, with its imprisoned treasures. **1889** MUNROE *Golden Days* 186 They were obliged to 'clean up' or remove what was lodged against the riffle-bars at least four times a day. **1910** HART *Vigilante Girl* 51 What a life to lead! . . . To 'clean up' on Saturday a few ounces of gold dust, to take their dust to the town on Saturday night and spend it for whiskey.

+**d.** To beat, vanquish, overcome. (Cf. 2 b.)

1888 SHERIDAN *Memoirs* I. 47 As the regular troops up there were of no account, the citizens . . . intended cleaning up the hostiles. **1922** H. L. FOSTER *Adv. Tropical Tramp* 184, I haven't seen Red since we beat it out of Iquique that night we cleaned up the police force.

+**e.** (See quotation.)

1888 ROOSEVELT in *Century Mag.* April 860/1 He becomes a good brand reader and is able to really 'clean up a herd'—that is, be sure he has left nothing of his own in it.

+**f.** To free or rid of undesirable characters. *slang.*

1925 MULFORD *Cottonwood Gulch* 188 Colonel Hutton will make a good judge, an' our friend Dangerfield [sheriff] will clean up this cursed country like a new broom.

Cleaning up.

+**1.** *Mining.* Collecting the products of value that have accumulated over a given period in a stamp mill, mine, etc.

1872 PLAYER-FROWD *Six Mo. Calif.* 88 At the end of this fortnight or month, called a 'run,' comes the cleaning up. No more dirt is thrown in, and the water is allowed to flow till it runs out of the end quite clear. *a*1891 J. LAWRENCE *Silverland* 176 (Hoppe), The cleaning up . . . consists in removing the pavement and blocks from the bed of the sluice, gathering the precious compost, and replacing or renewing the blocks or stones of the pavement.

+2. The act of reforming a bad or scandalous state of things.

1916 DUPUY *Uncle Sam* 170 The cleaning up of the customs scandals in the port of New York was a most complicated task. **1924** MULFORD *Rustler's Valley* 235 That town needs cleanin' up.

+**Clean-out.** An appliance for cleaning drains. — **1888** (Boston newspaper advt.) Patent Traps and cleanouts for drains.

+**Clean-up.**

1. In mining, the process of periodically separating the valuable mineral from the gravel and rock which has collected in the sluices or at the stamping mill.

1866 *Congress. Globe* 18 June 3231/1 When what they technically call in mining the clean-up comes, very often the clean-up exhibits the lofty sum of nothing, while thousands have been expended in the effort. **1871** [see CLEAN *v.* 2 d]. **1871** R. W. RAYMOND *3rd Rep. Mines* (1872) 70 They . . . made their first 'run' in 1869, since which time the following 'clean-ups' have been made. **1876** BOURKE *Journal* 8 Sept. 22 In speaking of the 'clean-up,' the Deadwooders always said so many 'pounds,' in other 'diggings,' the word 'ounces' is used. **1880** INGHAM *Digging Gold* 77 Once or twice a month, . . . according to the richness of the bars or banks being washed, occurs . . . 'the clean-up.' **1897** F. NORRIS *Third Circle* (1909) 96 He found out . . . that the superintendent of the Little Bear [mine] amalgamated and reported the cleanup on Sundays.

2. An exceptional financial success; a big 'haul.' *colloq.*[2]

1907 WHITE *Arizona Nights* 181 He and Simpson had made a pretty good clean-up, just enough to make them want to get rich. **1910** HART *Vigilante Girl* 28 Where he made his biggest clean-up was in buying some mud-flats. **1923** BOWER *Parowan Bonanza* 134, I want you to meet a friend of mine who is just down from Alaska, after his own little clean-up. **1924** CUMMINS *Sky-high Corral* 71 His great plans for making a clean-up . . . had not panned out.

***Clear,** *n.* ||The area above the tree line. — **1784** CUTLER in *Life & Corr.* I. 102 This kind of walking did not extend above sixty or seventy rods before we came into the clear, as it is called, which is above the trees.

***Clear,** *a.*

1. Of land: Free from trees and undergrowth. {1694–}

1634 WILLIAM WOOD *New Englands Prospect* (1865) 17 And whereas it is generally conceived, that the woods grow so thicke, that there is no more clere ground than is hewed out by labour of men; it is nothing so; in many places, divers Acres being cleare. **1704** *Boston News-Letter* 8 May 2/2 There is . . . to be Let or Sold, . . . a Plantation, having on it . . . a young Orchard, and 20 Acres clear Land. **1711** *N.C. Col. Rec.* I. 764, I have about a dozen Acres of clear ground. **1753** *Brookhaven Rec.* 167 Several tracts or persels of land, wood land, clear land. **1776** *N.J. Archives* 2 Ser. I. 138 A large number of Tories in Monmouth county, New Jersey, . . . have encamped in a clear swamp near that place. **1836** *S. Lit. Messenger* II. 354 These are either clear prairies, totally destitute of trees, or oak openings. **1838** *Ib.* IV. 27 A clear prairie looks like an expanse of water.

+2. Full-blooded; not of mixed breed; pure.

1797 *Mass. H. S. Coll.* V. 264 All the Indians, both clear and mixed, in all New-England, do not probably exceed one thousand. **1834** C. A. DAVIS *Lett. J. Downing* 25 Though I tell'd 'em down south my father was an Irishman, and my mother, too, I am as clear a Yankee . . . as the Major himself.

+3. Unadulterated, real, pure. *slang.*

1834 THOMPSON *Adv. T. Peacock* 91 'These Dutch minxes,' coolly observed the latter, 'are clear pepper-pots for grit.' **1840** HALIBURTON *Clockmaker* 3 Ser. xii, But is it [a piece of land] refuge or superfine, clear stuff, or only marchantable? **1843** — *Attaché* 1 Ser. II. 126 Is all these forks and spoons . . . rael genuwine solid silver, the clear thing, and no mistake?

b. (See quot. 1889 and cf. CLEAR PORK.)

1851 CIST *Cincinnati* 214 Pig-iron, and one thousand tons Tennessee clear blooms. **1889** *Cent.* 1037/2 Without admixture, adulteration, or dilution: as, a fabric of clear silk; clear brandy; clear tea.

+4. Of lumber: Free from knots or other imperfections.

1832 *N.H. Hist. Soc. Coll.* III. 204 Great quantities of excellent clear boards have been sawed at the several mills in town. **1865–6** *Ill. Agric. Soc. Trans.* VI. 645 Clear flooring, rejected on account of thickness, shall be classed with common flooring. **1867** LOWELL *Biglow P.* II. p. lxv, The parson . . . annoyed him by looking into his workshop every morning, and cautioning him to be very sure to pick out 'clear mahogany without any knots in it.' **1900** BRUNCKEN *N. Amer. Forests* 80 The various grades [of lumber] are known by technical names, such as clear, select, culls, and the like.

b. (See quotation.)

1905 *Forestry Bureau Bull.* No. 61 s.v., *Clear length* is in some cases used to designate that portion of the stem entirely free from branches, in others that portion free from dead branches, or from growing branches of a given size. Syn[onym]: *clear trunk.*

***Clear,** *v.*

1. *tr.* To fell and remove timber or underbrush from (land intended for cultivation). {1697–}

1634 WOOD *N. Eng. Prospect* 40 This place is called Massachusetts fields where the greatest Sagamore in the countrey lived, before the Plague, who caused it to be cleared for himselfe. **1640** *Boston Rec.* 53 Natha: Willis is spared from Cleareing half an acre of his ground . . . in regard his servant did scald his legg. **1704** S. KNIGHT *Journal* 58 Abundance of land well fined and Cleerd all along as wee passed. **1788** J. MAY *Jour. & Lett.* 61 My people employed in clearing land. **1797** THOMAS *Newengland Farmer* 168 What need has the man who possesses three hundred acres to destroy the wood, or clear the land, as they call it, any faster than he can make use of the soil? **1890** *Century Mag.* Dec. 166 He first went to a friend in Indiana . . . helping to clear land.

b. With *up.*

1896 HARRIS *Sister Jane* 216 He was telling of an experience he had in clearing up a new ground.

c. To chop out or open a road through the wood.

1758 *Lett. to Washington* II. 355 The woods are open here, but as I have orders to make the road wide, I find it very difficult to clear the timber being all large. . . . We only cleared half a mile the day before yesterday. **1876** BANCROFT *Hist. U.S.* III. 435 Virginia volunteers formed the advance guard, the axemen followed to clear three paths.

2. a. To free (a vessel) for sailing by satisfying custom and harbor dues and regulations. {1703–} **b.** *intr.* Of a ship: To comply with these regulations so as to obtain permission to leave port. {1807–}

1705 *Boston News-Letter* 15 Jan. 2/2 There is . . . cleared from hence, Hubbert for Madera's. **1775** *Jrnls. Cont. Congress* III. 372 Many vessels which had cleared at the respective custom houses . . . have been seized. **1817** *Niles' Reg.* XIII. 290/2 The brig, with provisions and lumber for the winter quarters of the slaves, attempted to clear to day. **1865** *Atlantic Mo.* XV. 81 In 1861, 965 vessels entered New York from foreign ports and 966 cleared for foreign ports.

+3. *intr.* To depart, leave, make off. *colloq.* (See also 5 b and 6 b.)

1839 KIRKLAND *New Home* 102 Mr. Mazard had absconded; or, in Western language, 'cleared.' **1844** 'UNCLE SAM' *Peculiarities* II. 37 My name is Robinson, captain. Please tick me off, and let me clear. **1845** *Cincinnati Misc.* I. 179 The negro laughed, his neighbors laughed, and finally the whole table was in a roar, and he cleared for the bar-room. **1886** *Knowledge* 1 April 179/1 *Clear out*, to get away. Sometimes used without the preposition. 'Gentlemen, will you please clear' is American for 'get out.'

refl. **1805** ORDWAY in *Journals of Lewis & O.* 255 The rest all mounted their horses and cleared themselves as they do not wish to fite. **1827** *Western Mo. Rev.* I. 283 Boone . . . was allowed to take his own range, with so little restraint, that finally, in the language of the west, 'he cleared himself.'

+4. *tr.* To try or otherwise dispose of (the cases awaiting court action). Also with *up.*

1842 Buckingham *E. & W. States* II. 23 This, however, being the last day of the court, and the judges being obliged to 'clear their docket,' sufficient time could not be found to determine the matter. **1899** TARKINGTON *Gentleman from Ind.* ii, The court had cleared up the docket by sitting to unseemly hours of the night.

fig. **1866** LOWELL *Biglow P.* 2 Ser. xi. 236 Did he put thru the rebbles, clear the docket, An' pay th' expenses out of his own pocket?

5. *intr. To clear off*, of the weather, to become bright, free from clouds, fogs, etc. {1854–}

1807 GASS *Journal* 164 This morning the weather appeared to settle and clear off. **1840** DANA *Two Years* xi, On the sixth day it cleared off, and the sun came out bright. **1843** N. BOONE *Journal* 210 Cleared off about 11 o'clock, still a very heavy black cloud in the S. with thunder.

+**b.** To depart, go away. (Cf. 3.)

1816 U. BROWN *Journal* II. 365 Called to her & flatter'd her to Come back, She would not; Clear'd off & left me.

6. *To clear out.* **a.** *Naut.* To clear (sense 2 above); to depart or leave a harbor. {1758–}

1704 *Boston News-Letter* 15 May 2/1 Cleared out this Week, Mountford for North Carolina. **1708** *Ib.* 12–19 Jan. 2/2 We have had no Vessels either Entered Inwards or Outward Bound Last week, nor Cleared Out except John Scot in the Brigt. William for Jamaica. **1719** *Weekly Mercury* 22 Dec. 2/2 Nicholas and Web for Barbados, cleared out. **1795** *State P.* (1819) II. 375, I beg leave to inform you, in regard of the schooner Rose, that she cleared out at the customhouse. **1817** *Ann. 14th Congress* 2 Sess. 147 The bill authorizing vessels departing from . . . the basin of the Canal de Carondelet, for foreign ports, to clear out at the customhouse, in the city of New Orleans.

+**b.** To depart, leave, be off. (Cf. 3, 5 b.)

1792 *Ann. 2nd Congress* 1127 The Indians were clearing out as fast as possible. **1805** CLARK in *Lewis & C. Exped.* (1905) III. 55 In the course of the night the horse broke loose & cleared out. **1816** U. BROWN *Journal* II. 231, I had got my horse ready to mount & Clear out for Baltimore. **1842** *Amer. Pioneer* I. 206 He executed a deed to the winner, and then cleared out to the south. a**1846** *Quarter Race Ky.*, etc. 27 By this time, the sharks had all cleared out, and the black fish were biting again. **1925** MULFORD *Cottonwood Gulch* 142 This is one time you ain't goin' to clear out. Yo're goin' to stay right here on this ranch.

+**c.** *tr.* To drive out, send packing. (Cf. CLEAN *v.* 2 c.)

1877 HARTE *Story of Mine*, etc. 338, I reckon he'll clear out that yar Sacramento counter-jumper. **1888** — *Argonauts N. Liberty* 198, I'll push on and clear him out.

+**7.** *intr. To clear outward(s). Naut.* = 2 a, 6 a. *Obs.*

1708 *Boston News-Letter* 11–18 Oct. 4/2 Cleared Outward *Downing, Presbury* and *Walter* for Connecticut. **1715** *Ib.* 3–10 January 2/2 Cleared Outwards Jacob Parker for Piscataqua. **1719** *Weekly Mercury* 22 Dec. 2/2 Cleared Outwards, Dan. Wait, Jos. Jackson, and Tho. Miller for Piscataqua.

Clear, *adv. Clear through*, right through; entirely, wholly. — **1842** KIRKLAND *Forest Life* II. 97 The most I could accomplish . . . was the breaking of needles, and the pricking of my fingers, in the vain attempt to do as I was bid, and take my stitches 'clear through.' **1855** THOMPSON *Doesticks* 274 A police Justice must gamble a little, . . . and get drunk 'clear through' every Saturday night. **1901** RYAN *Montana* 130 They'd all think I was bad clear through.

* **Clearance.**

1. a. A certificate showing that a ship has complied with customs or port regulations. {1755–}

1727 *Penna. Col. Rec.* III. 283 Four hundred persons, were imported into this Province . . . from Dover, as by Clearance from the Officers of his Majesties Customs there. **1775** *Jrnls. Cont. Congress* III. 495 The Continent should run the risk of sending vessels without clearances. **1792** *Ann. 2nd Congress* 1045 Let the clearance for every vessel sailing from the ports of the United States be printed on paper. **1846** *Knickerb.* XXVIII. 67 Nearly three weeks had elapsed after the arrival of the Mary C— before her 'clearance' was made out from the Rio customhouse. **1887** *Postal Laws* 289 Every collector, or other officer of the port empowered to grant clearances, shall require [etc.].

b. Attrib. with *papers.*

1845 *Knickerb.* XXVI. 208 He hadn't his clearance-papers all made out. **1893** M. Philips *Making of Newspaper* 166, I had not only provided myself with a passport, but had taken out regular clearance-papers for the vessel. **1916** DU PUY *Uncle Sam* 54 Delivered in thirty days—Brooklyn —how can you get clearance papers?

+**2.** (See quotation.)

1900 NELSON *A B C Wall St.* 134 *Clearances*, freight shipped by water for interior or coast ports.

+**3.** A clearing; an area from which the trees and undergrowth have been removed.

1800 J. MAUDE *Niagara* 100 Passed three clearances; . . . Soil excellent. **1846** CORCORAN *Pickings* 49 At making a 'clearance,' chopping wood, or working a flat-boat, . . . he could beat a dozen of them [=Irishmen]. **1846** LEVINGE *Echoes fr. Backwoods* II. 226 After a drive of a couple of hours, arrived at some small 'clearances,' amidst a great tract of forest. **1857** GLADSTONE *Englishman in Kansas* 170 Often, in riding over the prairie, the traveller meets with a small clearance, sufficient, at least, to show that some one has been there.

* **Cleared,** *a.* +Of land: Having the trees and undergrowth cut away.

1642 *Va. Statutes* I. 244 Ev'rie planter shall make a sufficient fence about his cleared ground. **1677** *Doc. Hist. N.Y. State* I. 12 The town is newly settled, double stockadoed, but little cleared ground. **1698** *East-Hampton Rec.* II. 429 John Buckland . . . sold . . . a certain tract or parcell of cleared land. **1790** DEANE *New-Eng. Farmer* 180/1 A New-England farmer is not content, unless he yearly mows over the greater part of his cleared land. **1832** WATSON *Hist. Tales N.Y.* 45 The burnt stumps of the 'cleared lands' . . . are still every where visible along the public highways. **1862** MCCLELLAN in *Own Story* 234 The country now alluded to is much more favorable for offensive operations: . . . more cleared land, the woods less dense, [etc.]. **1891** RYAN *Pagan* 51 Don was struck as never before with the meagerness of the life that is wrested from the bit of cleared ground. *Ib.* 186 The only sound that now broke the quiet of those heights was the ring of an ax out in the edge of the cleared space.

+**Clear grit.** [Cf. GRIT.] Sound or genuine material; the real thing; fearless courage. Freq. in predicative use: Of solid, genuine character or indomitable spirit.

1825 NEAL *Bro. Jonathan* II. 14 A chap, who was clear grit for a tussle, any time. **1835–7** HALIBURTON *Clockmaker* 1 Ser. xxiv, Them are the folk who do mischief. They show such clear grit it fairly frightens me. **1844** — *Attaché* 2 Ser. iii, I always used to think champagne no better nor mean cider, and p'r'aps the imertation stuff we make to New York ain't, but if you get the clear grit there is no mistake in it. **1867** LOWELL *Biglow P.* II. p. lxxviii, He was six foot o' man, A1, Clear grit an' human natur'. **1873** ALDRICH *Marj. Daw*, etc. 117 That fellow Quite So is clear grit, and . . . he'll do something devilish. **1880** BROOKS *Fairport Nine* 12 Little Sam was 'clear grit,' as his brother proudly remarked. **1890** HASKINS *Argonauts Calif.* 335 Wasn't that little Providence chap, Dicks Arnold, clear grit, though?

attrib. **1861** *N.Y. Tribune* 10 Oct., Nor do we think the matter much mended by a clear-grit Republican convention putting one or two Democrats on the foot of their ticket.

* **Clearing.**

+**1.** The process of removing trees and undergrowth from land.

1623–4 *Va. House of Burgesses* 28 There were some few poore howses built, & entrance made in cleeringe of grounde. **1643** *Portsmouth Rec.* 25 Fencinge Cleeringe . . . of ground. **1740** STEPHENS *Proc. Georgia* II. 51 Planting and clearing of Land, he has an utter Aversion to. **1759** Commons, etc. *Doc. Hist.* I. 110 By this practise steadily pursued a convenient quantity of land may be provided at Moss's neck without clearing. **1842** C. M. KIRKLAND *Forest Life* I. 43 'Clearing' is his daily thought and nightly dream; and so literally does he act . . . that not one tree, and not so much as a bush of natural growth must be suffered to cumber the ground. c**1845** *Big Bear Ark.*, etc. 95 It's that drotted three day agur I cotch'd last fall a clearin' in the new grouns. **1879** *Scribner's Mo.* Dec. 240/2 The crops . . . will amply repay for the extra labor of clearing.

+**2.** A piece of forest land cleared of trees for cultivation; a home, settlement, or village in such an area.

1817 M. BIRKBECK *Journey* (1818) 123, I could judge of the extent of the 'clearing' if I saw the people. **1820** J. HALL *Lett. fr. West* 191 (Th.), Immediately below us is a clearing which seems to have been made some years ago, and near it another of more recent origin. **1834** *Knickerb.* III. 31 The few clearings which I had passed, indicated contentment rather than wealth. **1841** COOPER *Deerslayer* xv, What comfort can a man look for in a clearin', that he can't find in double quantities in the forest. **1866** *Rep. Indian Affairs* 289 Some of the bands have . . . opened clearings in the timber. **1880** *Scribner's Mo.* June 249/1 They unload the piano . . . and kitchen gear, among the stumps and blackened logs in the clearing, and the new life begins. **1888** WHITNEY *Names and Places* 203 A glade is also an 'opening' or 'clearing' in the forest, and this word may be applied either to a space naturally destitute of trees, or to one where they have been removed by the hand of man. **1906** *Harper's Mag.* Oct. 707 She had lived alone in this little clearing, backed by pine woods, for over thirty years.

3. *Clearing certificate, papers*, = CLEARANCE 1.

1719 *Essex Inst. Coll.* XLIV. 152 A Pyrat . . . stript ye Brigg of what Suted them tooke away my Clearing Certificats and other papers. **1893** *Harper's Mag.* Jan. 228/1 There were clearing-papers to sign and a crew to choose.

+**4.** *Mining.* = CLEAN-UP.

1851 KINGSLEY *Diary* 168 We kept the machine running on the top dirt in the last clearing and got 13 ounces 11 dollars in amalgam. *Ib.* 172 This begins to pay as we anticipated the whole clearing would.

Clearing house.

1. An institution at which the bankers of a city or region exchange their claims on one another and settle the balance. {1832–}

1859 BARTLETT 86 *Clearing House*, an establishment recently organized in the city of New York. **1865** *Atlantic Mo.* XV. 85 The total amount of business transactions managed by the New York banks in connection with the Clearing House during the past two years. **1870** MEDBERY *Men Wall St.* 237 He sells $100,000 at 130 cash, and supplements the statement to the Clearing-House with a check for $4,625. **1912** DREISER *Financier* 61 The clearing-house had only recently been thought of in New York.

transf. **1870** MEDBERY *Men Wall St.* 66 Our great financial centre is rapidly acquiring the function of a National clearing-house. **1883** *Harper's Mag.* Sept. 634/2 The Charity Organization Society is a central exchange or clearing-house for all the single relief associations of every denomination and kind. **1903** E. JOHNSON *Railway Transportation* 130 There is no railway clearing-house through which the accounts of all the railroads of the United States are settled. **1916** *N.Y. Times Mag.* 9 Jan. 19 We will build up a clearing house for information. . . . We will acquire information invaluable in the work of crime prevention.

2. Attrib., esp. with *certificate:* (see quot. 1907).

1864 *Statutes at Large* XIII. 109 Clearing-house certificates, representing specie or lawful money specially deposited for the purpose of any clearing house association, shall be deemed to be lawful money. **1907** *Springfield W. Republican* 31 Oct. 2 The clearing-house certificate, as a form of emergency currency for use among associated banks, was first resorted to in New York during the civil war. **1908** MCGAFFEY *Show-Girl* 38 It was a check. . . . To me, and in my real name, for one hundred cold, hard Clearing House certificates. **1908** *Quart. Jrnl. Econ.* XXII. 501 Resort was made by the banks to clearing-house loan certificates, clearing-house checks, cashiers' checks . . . , or other substitutes for legal money.

+**Clear-nosed ray.** A species of skate, *Raia eglanteria*, with semi-transparent snout. — **1814** MITCHILL *Fishes N.Y.* 478 Clear-nosed Ray. *Raja diaphanes.* The snout . . . is semi-transparent almost to the eyes. **1842** *Nat. Hist. N.Y., Zoology* IV. 366 Clear-nosed Ray . . . [is] caught along with codfish, and . . . [is] eaten by the poorer classes.

+**Clear pork.** Pork freed from bones. — **1848** THOREAU *Maine Woods* 25 A couple of blankets, . . . fifteen pounds of hard bread, ten pounds of 'clear' pork, and a little tea, made up 'Uncle George's' pack. **1851** CIST *Cincinnati* 281 The inspection laws require that clear pork hall be put up of the sides, with the ribs out. **1874** *Dept. Agric. Rep. 1873*

133 From the winter packing of 1873–'74 resulted . . . 75 barrels of clear pork.

+**Clear swing.** Free range; unhampered space. — **a1859** *N.Y. Tribune* (B.), We expect to see our cities purged of rowdyism, incentives to vice abated, and a clear swing and ample reward granted to labor and intelligence. **1908** *Dialect Notes* III. 299 Give him a clear swing, and he'll beat you every time.

+**Clearweed.** Richweed, *Pilea pumila*, a low-growing herb of the nettle family, with shining pellucid stems.

1821 *Mass. H. S. Coll.* 2 Ser. IX. 157 Plants, which are indigenous in the township of Middlebury, [Vt., include] . . . Great nettle, . . . Clearweed, Canada nettle. **1833** EATON *Botany* (ed. 6) 377 *Urtica pumila*, stingless nettle, rich-weed, clear weed. . . . Stem smooth and shining. **1857** GRAY *Botany* 399. **1871** DE VERE 406 A nettle with succulent, semi-transparent stems is called Clearweed. **1901** MOHR *Plant Life Ala.* 478 *Adicea*, . . . Clear Weed. . . . Light, shaded ground. July, August.

Cleavelandite. [Parker *Cleaveland*, Amer. mineralogist.] (See quotation.) {1823} — **1837** DANA *Mineralogy* 297 The variety [of Albite] from Chesterfield [Mass.] was denominated Cleavelandite, in compliment to Prof. Cleaveland, by Mr. Brooke, who supposed at the time that it was a distinct species.

***Cleaver.** An instrument for cleaving, esp. a butcher's chopper.

1642 *Md. Archives* IV. 97, 2 sawes, a cleaver. **1643** *Conn. Public Rec.* I. 455, 4 hows, 4 axes, 1 bill, 2 cleuers, 1 mattoke. **1651** *Mayflower Desc.* X. 161 One Cliver & a Driing box. **1674** *Harvard Rec.* I. 61 Kitchins Utensils . . . 1 clever. **1838** *Knickerb.* XII. 331 He carried in his arms a cleaver and a block, having fully made up his mind to cut off the animal's tail. **1869** E. PUTNAM *Receipt Book* 318 It is quite . . . necessary to have . . . a cleaver. **1881** *Rep. Indian Affairs* 419 Cleavers, 8-inch, butchers'.

***Cleavers.** Also †**clivers.** Goose grass, *Galium aparine*, or other species of *Galium*.

1781–2 JEFFERSON *Notes Va.* (1788) 35 Clivers, or goose-grass, *Galium spurium*. **1836** LINCOLN *Botany* App. 99 *Galium tinctorium*, (dier's cleavers, w. Ju.) stem diffuse, smoothish; leaves linear. . . . Used as a red die. **1847** WOOD *Botany* 304 Common Cleavers . . . [is found] in wet thickets, Can. and Northern States to Ia. . . . The herbage is valued as a domestic remedy. **1863** *Rep. Comm. Agric.* 159 We were near passing over the Madderwort family with its 'cleavers,' and 'bedstraws,' and 'wadders.'

***Cleft,** *a.* *Cleft stick*, a split stick to be fastened on the tongue as a punishment for speaking ill. *Obs.*

1640–1 *Mass. Bay Rec.* I. 313 Samuell Haukes . . . was censured to . . . have a clefte stick on his tongue while the Court thinks meete. **a1649** WINTHROP *Hist.* I. 296 She had a cleft stick put on her tongue half an hour, for reproaching the elders. **1651** *East-Hampton Rec.* I. 21 It is ordered that Goody Edwards shal pay 3 £ or have her tonge in a cleft sticke for the Contempt of a warent in sainge she would not come. **1651** *Southampton Rec.* I. 80 Sara Veale . . . was . . . sentenced by the magistrates for exorbitant words of imprecations to stand with her tongue in a cleft stick soe long as the offence committed by her was read and declared.

***Clematis.** One or other of various species (native or cultivated) of a genus of plants, mostly woody climbers, of which the common wild species is the Virgin's Bower (*C. Virginiana*).

1818 *Mass. H. S. Coll.* 2 Ser. VIII. 170 In August the eye is gratified with the flowers of the graceful clematis, the downy leaved spiraea, or hardhack, [etc.]. **1838** *S. Lit. Messenger* IV. 318/2 The little noisy brook . . . steals off among the flowers it nourishes, the brilliant cardinals and snow-white clematis. **1904** STRATTON-PORTER *Freckles* 83 About the case he planted wild clematis, bitter-sweet, and wild grapevines.

b. Attrib. with *bloom, vine.*

1869 FULLER *Flower Gatherers* 304 The Clematis vines by the brook-side looked like fleeces of silken down. **1879** *Scribner's Mo.* May 56/1 Clematis vines, Jackmanni, viticella, Hellêne and *Azurea grandiflora*, bearing purple, pink, or white flowers. **1885** H. H. JACKSON *Zeph* ii, Two women entered, bringing . . . a large sheaf of white clematis blooms.

***Clergy.** Ordained ministers; those in ecclesiastical orders. — **1717** WISE *Vindication* (1772) 64 His [Arius'] heresy continued and prevailed, and especially amongst the clergy. **1743** CHAUNCY *Seasonable Thoughts* 358 This I take to have been the great Fault of the Clergy, in these Days. **1835** REED & MATHESON *Visit* II. 76 The Presbyterian church gives officially the style of bishops to her pastors; all ordained ministers are the clergy. **1900** DIX *Deacon Bradbury* 153, I know not if in this I am in accord with the views of my brother clergy. **1904** *Churchman* 28 May 659 There was a constant stream of people from the city and diocese, including the clergy of all denominations.

***Clergyman.** An ordained minister. {In Eng. commonly with reference to the Established Church.}

1771 FRANKLIN *Autobiog.* 238, I . . . have since often regretted that . . . more proper books had not fallen in my way, since it was now resolved I should not be a clergyman. **1796** *Ann. 4th Congress* 2 Sess. 2694 A like tax has been imposed on every hundred pounds of stock . . . ; clergymen, mechanics, schoolmasters, and schoolmistresses excepted. **1870** *Nation* 27 Jan. 59/1 In Maine, at the end of 1868 there were forty Universalist clergymen. **1903** *N.Y. Ev. Post* 30 Sept. 7 The young Congregationalist clergyman who headed the Jackson ticket was Socialistic in his views.

***Clerk,** *n.* Also †**clark.**

***1.** A minor official of a governing body, usually with clerical duties. Cf. TOWN CLERK.

1634, etc. [see TOWN CLERK]. **1646** *Plymouth Laws* 85 There shalbe in every Towne . . . a Clark . . . to keep a Register. **1666** *Maryland Laws* 1 May, An Act prohibiting the Office of Clerke and Sheriffs to be officiated at the same time, by one and the same Person. **1792** *Boston Selectmen* 186 The Clerk [was] directed to deliver Mr. Nazro his Bonds as Clerk of the Market. **c1845** *Big Bear Ark.*, etc. 160, I 'ave my . . . deed record in de clerk's office. **1884** *Century Mag.* Feb. 582/2 The visitor looks with pleased interest at the statistical records of the clerk's office.

b. In phrases showing specific application.

1665 *Huntington Rec.* I. 79 Richard Charlton Clerk of the Assizes. **1786** *Penna. Col. Rec.* XIV. 667 Council this day proceeded to the appointment of a Clerk of the City Court and Orphans' Court for the City and County of Philadelphia. **1911** *Okla. Session Laws* 3 Legisl. 133 The clerk of the county court, the registrar of deeds, and the treasurer shall each have the power to appoint one or more deputies. **1636** *New Plymouth Laws* 37 That a clarke of the court also be chosen for the yeare. **1654** JOHNSON *Wonder-w. Providence* 110 Mr. William Torry, a good penman and skild in the Latine tongue, usually Clerke of the Deputies. **1875** *Chicago Tribune* 2 Nov. 4/3 Every challenger . . . must watch the clerks of election. **1789** *Ann. 1st Congress* I. 122 The Clerk of the House shall take an oath for the true and faithful discharge of the duties of his office. **1659** *Md. Council Proc.* 365 Upon Information given by Richard Pight Clerke of the Irons in the Mint, . . . Ordered, that a Warrant be issued. **1640** *Essex Inst. Coll.* IX. 104 Jeffery Mascey is Chosen Clarke of the Market for this year next insuinge. **1757** *Penna. Col. Rec.* VII. 501 Mr. James Humphreys having petition'd the governor to be appointed to the Office of Clerk of the Orphans' Court. **1729** *Boston Rec.* 11 Voted For a County Treasurer were 162 votes which were Sealed up by Constable Russell, and by Him were Delivered to the Clerke of the Peace. **1811** MEASE *Philadelphia* 58 These brands are to be registered with the clerk of the Quarter Sessions of the County. **1846** POLK *Diary* 149 Mr. Trist, chief clerk of the State Department, . . . came in to deliver to me some despatches received by the last steamer. **1869** TOURGEE *Toinette* xxi, Hunter went to the office of the Clerk of the Superior Court for the County of Cold Spring. **1690** *Braintree Rec.* 27 James Brackitt chosen clerke or sealer of weights & measures. **1645** *N.H. Doc. & Rec.* I. 179 We do likewise humbly request that John Legat may be established clark of the writes.

***2.** The recording secretary of a meeting.

1686 *Charlestown Land Rec.* 204 Then was the wor. James Russell Esqr. Chosen moderator in the Sd. Assembly or meeting, And Jno. Newell Clerk to them. **1721** *Mass. Ho. Repr. Jrnls.* III. 4 The House proceeded to the Election of a Clerk by written votes. **1789** *Hist. Congress* 16 When a motion is made, and seconded, . . . it shall be . . . read aloud by the clerk.

***3.** One who keeps books and accounts in a business office, public or private.

1714 *Mass. Bay Currency Tracts* 76 One Head Clerk, and one Under Clerk or more if need be; each of whom . . . shall be Obliged to keep two setts of Books for the Affairs of this Partnership. **1796** *Boston Directory* 247 Furness, John, clerk in loan office, Federal street. **1886** MITCHELL *R. Blake* 200 Records of small commercial failures or of defalcations and breaches of trust on the part of clerks or petty bank-officers.

+**b.** An employee of a fur company at a trading post.

1878 BEADLE *Western Wilds* 252 Mr. Thomas V. Keams, Agency Clerk, was acting in place of Miller, deceased.

4. *Mil.* One who performs clerical duties for the commanding officer of a trainband or company. *Obs.*

1642 *Conn. Public Rec.* 75 The Clarke of the Band in euery Plantation wthin these Libertyes, shall giue in to the deputyes of their seurall Townes, an exacte list of all the Trayne men. **1645** ENDECOTT in *Winthrop P.* 150 If the Clarke of the band were sent for. **1656** *Portsmouth Rec.* 70 The Constable and the Clarke of the band. **1721** *New-Eng. Courant* 2–9 Oct. 2/2 By Direction of the Select Men of the Town of Boston, . . . the several Clerks of the Train-Bands made a Strict Enquiry at all the Houses within their respective Beats. **1757** *General Orders* 28 It is Gen[era]ll Lyman's Orders that ye Clerke of Each Company Do it [*sc.* make a return] with out Fail.

+**5.** An assistant to a storekeeper; one who waits on customers in a store.

1771 FRANKLIN *Autobiog.* 286 He propos'd to take me over as his clerk, to keep his books, in which he would instruct me, copy his letters, and attend the store. **1835** HAWTHORNE *Note-Books* I. 5 They seemed to be merely Sunday gentlemen,—mostly young fellows, clerks in dry-goods stores being the aristocracy of them. **1853** *S. Lit. Messenger* XIX. 69/2 The influence of his father procured for Simon a situation . . . as clerk or assistant in a store for retailing spirituous liquors. **1860** HOLMES *E. Venner* xii, There were a few 'clerks,'—that is, young men who attended shops, commonly called 'stores.' **1867** — *Guardian Angel* 197 He became what they call a 'clerk' in what they call a 'store' up in the huckleberry districts. **1880** ALDRICH *Stillwater Tragedy* 53 There's the Union store, if they happen to want a clerk. **1903** CURTIS *True A. Lincoln* 33 He . . . became a clerk in the store, . . . measuring calico, weighing out sugar and nails, [etc.]. **1905** COLE *Early Orgon* 19, I returned in the morning to the store at which Hovey was a clerk.

+**6.** One who acts as purser on a steamboat.

1849 E. DAVIS *Amer. Scenes* 82 The dimensions, as given me by the 'clerk' or purser, are—length of keel 182 feet, breadth of beam 26 feet. **1850** R. BAIRD *Impressions N. Amer.* 188 An office where the 'clerk of the boat' takes fares and issues tickets. **1864** CUMMING *Hospital Life* 157/1, I had a little girl with me, for whom the clerk of the boat had charged full price.

+**7.** In hotels, an employee who assigns rooms to guests and attends to their comfort. (Cf. HOTEL CLERK.)

1888 STOCKTON *Dusantes* 98, I shall leave the jar, suitably packed, in the care of the clerk of this hotel. **1891** HOWELLS *Imperative Duty* ix, He made her . . . come with him to the hotel parlour. He went to arrange the business with the clerk.

8. A postal employee. {1866–} Also attrib.

1887 *Courier-Journal* 6 Feb. 16/6 Many seek appointment under the impression that the position of railway postal clerk is a 'soft snap.' **1887** *Postal Laws* 16 The Office of the First Assistant Postmaster-General. To this office is assigned . . . the consideration of allowances for clerk-hire, rent, fuel, light, [etc.].

9. *Clerk of the weather*, +'in the United States, a popular name for the head of the meteorological department of the Signal Service' (*Cent.*).

* **Clerk,** *v.*

+**1.** *intr.* To work as a salesman or saleswoman in a store.

*a*1849 RUXTON *Life Far West* 17 Young Sublette comes up, and he'd been clerking down to the fort on Platte, so he know'd something. **1872** 'MARK TWAIN' *Roughing It* xlii. 230, I had clerked in a drug store part of a summer. **1887** *Courier-Journal* 7 May 4/7 He had formerly clerked in the store and knew where the pistol was kept. **1888** *Pall Mall Gaz.* 5 Nov. 11/2 Some years ago she came here from Green Bay and clerked in Chapman's store. **1891** O'BEIRNE *Leaders Ind. Territory* 27/1 From thence he moved to Caddo, where he clerked for a few years for Major Harlan. **1904** *Omaha Daily Bee* 14 Aug., I clerked in a country store for five years.

+**2.** *To clerk it*, in same sense.

1862 BROWNE *A. Ward His Book* 231 Sarah's father use to keep a little grosery store in our town, and she used to clerk it for him in busy times. **1871** DE VERE 303 A man . . . has nothing left but to clerk it, that is, engage himself as clerk . . . to some more fortunate man, who owns a store. **1886** *Harper's Mag.* Sept. 580/1 He come here about a year ago, and hez been clerkin' it ever since. **1889** *Ib.* July 314/1 He . . . then 'clerked it' in a drug-store.

Clerking, *vbl. n.* **a.** The business of serving as a bookkeeper. {1679–} +**b.** The action of working in a store as a salesman or saleswoman. — (**a**) **1821** QUITMAN in *Life & Corr.* 61, I mean to live by the practice of law, not by clerking in a land-office. **1849** *N.Y. Tribune* 19 April (B.), Teaching, clerking, law, etc. are . . . precarious except to men of established reputation and business. — (**b**) **1887** *Harper's Mag.* Jan. 220/2 Ef she was in your place and wanted to go to clerking, she'd believe she'd go further from home.

+**Clerk-hire.** Money devoted to the payment of wages to a clerk or clerks.

1793 *Statutes at Large* I. 323 The money, thus paid, . . . shall pass to the account of clerk-hire in that office. **1794** *Ib.* 343 For stationery and clerk-hire. **1802** *Ann. 7th Congress* 1305 The accounting officers of the Treasury Department . . . are hereby authorized . . . to make the following allowance for clerk hire. **1817** *Ann. 14th Congress* 2 Sess. 849 Strangers . . . who are at no expense, either of house-keeping, store-rent, or clerk-hire; . . . are enabled to monopolize our money and our markets. **1834** *Knickerb.* XXII. 238 Barely enough to pay the cost of transportation, clerk-hire, and store rent. **1887** [see CLERK *n.* 8].

* **Clerkship.**

+**1.** The position of a clerk or secretary in a court.

1790 *Steele P.* I. 59 Mr. M. Stokes has bartered for the Superior Court clerkship with Martin.

‖**2.** An entire group or staff of clerks.

1812 *Niles' Reg.* II. 131/1 The whole of this business has been done without any material addition to the ordinary clerkship.

3. The position of one who performs clerical duties in an office.

1819 Mackenzie *Van Buren* 155, I considered it absolutely impossible for him to confine himself to so irksome an employment as a clerkship in a law office. **1898** WESTCOTT *D. Harum* 23 He had thought it rather fine of himself to undertake a clerkship in the office of Rush & Co. **1909** PARKER *G. Cleveland* 38, I had just graduated from Yale and made application for and was admitted to a clerkship in the office of Laning, Cleveland and Folsom.

+**4.** A secretarial position with the U.S. government.

1880 *Harper's Mag.* May 901/1 For clerkships at a salary of $1200, they are more difficult. **1883** *Century Mag.* Aug. 576/2 She had for a long time thought of trying to obtain a clerkship at Washington. **1884** *Boston Journal* 13 Sept., The character of the men at Washington in the Government clerkships does not compare favorably with that of the women.

+**5.** A position as clerk in a store.

1891 O'BEIRNE *Leaders Ind. Territory* 137/2 After his marriage Alonzo started stock-raising and farming, and took a clerkship with John D. Hardin, a merchant of Atoka.

Clethra. [Gr.] A genus of plants; a tree or shrub of this genus, which includes the white alder or sweet pepper bush. Also attrib.

1785 MARSHALL *Amer. Grove* 34 *Clethra alnifolia.* Alder leaved Clethra. This shrub grows common in Maryland, Virginia, and Carolina, in moist ground and by rivulets. **1850** *New Eng. Farmer* II. 109 The Clethra is found on the margin of ponds, and exhibits its raceme of white fragrant flowers in August. **1866** WHITTIER *Maids of Attitash* 911 Hardhack, and virgin's-bower, And white-spiked clethra-flower. **1882** *Harper's Mag.* June 71 We find . . . the fragrant clethra, and azaleas and lovely orchids.

* **Clever,** *a.*

1. Of horses, etc.: Well made; clean-limbed; well trained.

1776 *Battle of Brooklyn* (1873) 27 My letter tells me they are clever horses. **1816** PICKERING 62 In speaking of any thing but man we use the word much as the English do. We say a clever horse, &c. **1839** *S. Lit. Messenger* V. 432/1 He . . . looked as big as a clever young ox. **1907** *Springfield W. Republican* 13 May 2 (*advt.*), For sale, one bay horse, weight 1200, good chunk, true, clever in harness.

2. Good-natured, liberal, accommodating. *colloq.* {*c*1682–, *dial.*}

1758 *Essex Inst. Coll.* XII. 148 This afternoon secured a place to have ye Small Pox in, with a very clever family. **1776** Duane *Lett. to B. Franklin* 72 They said they had all been very clever, and said there had been but one or two disagreeable things had happened. **1814** *Steele P.* II. 727 Tho' I dont know the Gentleman, I hope & doubt not, he is a clever Man and will make her happy. **1883** *Academy* 2 June 379/2 No one who has travelled from the Eastern to the Far Western States but must have noticed how the adjective 'clever' alters its meaning, from being translateable by 'smart' in New England to being considered in Oregon akin to a term of disrespect—for there it is equivalent to soft, good-natured, and anything but smart. **1891** *Harper's Mag.* July 220/2 It is an Americanism to call him clever whom we deem good-natured only. **1904** DARROW *Farmington* 233 City people may not know that in Farmington we used the word 'clever' to mean kind or obliging.

3. Honest, conscientious, trustworthy. *colloq.* {1860–, *dial.*}

1804 W. AUSTIN *Lett. from London* 68 *Clever*, in New England, means, honest, conscientious; but we do not use the word as defined in the dictionaries. **1818** FLINT *Lett. from Amer.* 77 Where a family seem to be poor and clever, he does not charge any thing for their sleeping on the floor. (By clever, he meant honest, or of a good disposition.) **1820** *Ib.* 264 These I must call Americanisms, and will subjoin some examples, a[s] . . . *Clever*, —Honest, or of good disposition.

4. Well. *colloq.* {1841–, *dial.*} (Cf. CLEVERLY *a.*)

1815 *Mass. Spy* 14 June (Th.), I somehow did not feel quite clever, but hoped for the best.

Clever, *adv.* In a good-natured or accommodating manner; amiably. — **1769** J. ROWE *Diary* 182 Last night I was awakened by the cry of Fire. . . . The Officers & Army behaved extremely clever on this occasion. **1822** *Mass. Spy* 5 June (*Th.*), [Court of Oyer and Terminer, Philadelphia.] Question, Why, Sir, have you a prejudice against me? Ans. Because neither you nor the other counsel have acted Clever towards the Jury.

+**Cleverly,** *a. local.* In health, well. — **1784** A. ADAMS *Letters* 210 She is cleverly now, although she had a severe turn for a week. **1816** PICKERING 63 In answer to the common salutation, How do you do, we often hear [in New Eng.], I am cleverly. **1834** C. A. DAVIS *Lett. J. Downing* 82, I've been amost sick for a week. . . . But I'm getting cleverly now.

***Cleverly,** *adv.* Fairly; entirely. *dial.* {1696–, now *dial.*} — **1788** JEFFERSON *Writ.* VII. 113 While our second revolution is just brought to a happy end with you, yours here is but cleverly under way. **1841** POE *Tales of Mystery* (1852) 68 We had let our sails go by the run, before it [=a hurricane] cleverly took us. **1843** HALIBURTON *Attaché* viii, Mister landlord . . . comes to me, as soon as I was cleverly up this mornin'. **1884** 'CRADDOCK' *Where Battle Was Fought* 78 It'll be cleverly dark by the time Mirandy gits ter her house.

+**Clew hitch.** A kind of knot. — **1811** *Trial of Ed. Tinker at Carteret*, A rope was bound round the body, and two stones fastened to it with a small cord by means of a knot, called by the sailors a clew hitch.

***Click,** *v.* ‖*intr.* To walk pertly or sprightly. *local.* — **1824** Ford *Notes N. Webster* II. 271 You wou'd smile to see how alert I am, with a little quilted hood on my head—*clicking* (to use an Amherst expression) over the green, & back again before the girls have miss'd me.

Click beetle. A beetle of the family *Elateridae*, which makes a clicking sound when it springs upward from its back. {1881} — **1861–4** *Ill. Agric. Soc. Trans.* V. 416 There is scarcely an individual . . . unacquainted with the 'Spring-beetles' or . . . 'Click-beetles.' **1862** *Rep. Comm. Patents: Agric.* 609 It is the brown 'click beetle,' or *Cratonyclus brevicalis* of Herbst. The length is about five-eighths of an inch, and the color of a chestnut brown.

* **Cliff.** Also †**cleft, clift.** A steep face of rock; an escarpment.

1622 'MOURT' *Relation* 125 There we found many Lobsters that had beene gathered together by the Saluages, which we made ready vnder a cliffe. **1668** *East-Hampton Rec.* I. 274 The tree soe marked is one A cleft one the north side commonly caled the Clay Cleft. **1690** *Manchester Rec.* 40 A white oak standing on the southerdly end of a high cliff of rocks. **1702** *Conn. Col. Rec.* IV. 380 A young chestnut tree . . . stands within a rod of said pond under a clift of rocks. **1789** *Ky. Petitions* 132 They experience many Inconveniences . . . owing to . . . the difficulty in descending the Clifts down to the river Kentucky. **1831** PECK *Guide* 124 The clifts that overhang the bottoms. **1834** PIKE *Sketches* 28 [I] stopped in a cliff of rocks, and made a little fire. **1888** FERGUSON *Exp. Forty-niner* 127 The Armstrongs used to bring up cattle . . . and herd them down by a little bend . . . perfectly hemmed in by high clifts of rocks. **1901** *Scientific Amer.* LXXXIV. 297/3 Long steep slopes of débris . . . merge into a succession of steeps and slopes, culminating above in a series of lofty cliffs.

attrib. **1865** *Atlantic Mo.* XV. 43 In the distance, however, and as a variety in this unswarded cliff-coast, it was sweet. **1886** *Outing* VIII. 135/1, I crept out on the face of a great cliff shoulder.

Cliff brake. One or other species of fern of the genus *Pellaea*, esp. *P. atropurpurea.* — **1867** GRAY *Lessons in Bot.* 659 *Pellæ.* Cliff-brake. . . . *P. atropurpurea.* . . . [Grows on] dry calcareous rocks: not common, but of wide range. **1901** MOHR *Plant Life Ala.* 313 Cliff Brake. . . . Eleven species North American, chiefly from the arid table-lands west of the Mississippi to the Pacific. *Ib., Pellaea atropurpurea,* . . . purple cliffbrake.

+**Cliff city.** A group or city of cliff dwellings. — **1873** BEADLE *Undevel. West* 517 Farther west are the 'Cliff cities' of Cañon de Chelley. **1878** — *Western Wilds* 257 We should reach the celebrated 'cliff cities' which have made this cañon so famous.

+**Cliff dweller.** *S.W.* An Indian belonging to one or the other of the tribes that made their homes in caves or upon ledges in canyon walls.

1881 *Rep. Indian Affairs* 137 The peach trees are supposed to have been originally planted by a superior race or by ancient explorers, possibly by the cliff-dwellers. **1899** S. D. PEET *Cliff Dwellers & Pueblos* 55 The relative age of the Pueblos and Cliff-dwellers is a mere matter of conjecture. **1907** *Old West* XXVI. 494 There is no more interesting architecture . . . than that of the so-called Cliff Dwellers of New Mexico, Arizona, and the adjacent portions of Colorado, Utah and Nevada.

b. *transf.* One who lives in a city apartment house.

1893 FULLER *Cliff-Dwellers* 5 It will be unnecessary for us to go afield either far or frequently during the present simple succession of brief episodes in the lives of cliff-dwellers.

+**Cliff dwelling.** *S.W.* A habitation built on a rocky ledge or dug out of the face of a cliff by the Indians. — **1888** *Science* XI. 258/1 Some cliff-dwellings in Walnut Cañon, about twelve miles southeast of Flagstaff, Arizona, were examined. **1896** *Harper's Mag.* XCIII. 548/2 Probably there is no other district . . . more rich in these communal Cliff dwellings than a great plateau . . . in the Ute Indian Reservation. **1901** *Scientific Amer.* LXXXIV. 298/1 A type closely related to the cliff dwelling proper is the cave dwelling. **1917** *Sunset* April 62/2 Jesse L. Nusbaum . . . [has] restored the crumbling and almost inaccessible cliff dwellings of Colorado.

+**Cliff limestone.** Limestone rock of Silurian and Devonian age outcropping in cliffs in the Mississippi Valley. *Obs.* — **1840** *Mich. Agric. Soc.* V. 289 Its place is higher in the series than the blue limestone . . . and without doubt is equivalent in position to the 'cliff limestone' of Indiana. **1841** CIST *Cincinnati* 68 The name, cliff-limestone, has been applied by the inhabitants of some parts of Ohio to this rock, from its peculiar disposition to form massive abrupt cliffs and precipices. **1857** DANA *Mineralogy* 278 They abound in what has been called 'cliff limestone,' in the states of Missouri, Illinois, Iowa, and Wisconsin.

+**Cliff plum.** (See quotation.) — **1819** *Western Rev.* I. 93 Plants peculiar to this region [=Ky.] and giving a decided character to its vegetation [include]: . . . *Prunus pendula,* Cliff plumb.

Cliff stone. +=CLIFF LIMESTONE. *Obs.* — **1851** CIST *Cincinnati* 20 The superincumbent cliff-stone . . . is developed into a stratum of six-hundred feet in height.

+**Cliff swallow.** The eaves swallow or mud swallow, or other species of the genus *Petrochelidon.*

1825 BONAPARTE *Ornithology* I. 65 The Cliff Swallow advances from the extreme western regions, annually invading a new territory farther to the eastward. **1831** AUDUBON *Ornith. Biog.* I. 353 The Republican or Cliff Swallow. *Hirundo Fulva.* **1858** BAIRD *Birds Pacific R.R.* 309 *Hirundo Lunifrons.* . . . Cliff Swallow. . . . *Hab.* North America from Atlantic to Pacific. **1874** COUES *Birds N.W.* 89 Cliff Swallow is, and always has been, amenable to the ordinary laws of migration, and spread over nearly all of North America, the South Atlantic States perhaps excepted. **1891** H. HERRMANN *His Angel* 7 Wood-peckers, cliff-swallows, and king-fishers chattered winging from tree to tree.

Clift. Variant of CLIFF.

+**Climate, 'Climate,** *v. tr.* To acclimatize. — **1849** KINGSLEY *Diary* 92 Relinquishing the idea of going to the diggings this winter [to] get ourselves climated ready for spring. **1852** STOWE *Uncle Tom* x, If he stands the fever, and 'climating, he'll have a berth good as any nigger ought ter ask for. **1863** 'E. KIRKE' *Southern Friends* 61 It gits a feller's stumac used to Tophet 'fore the rest on him is 'climated.

+**Climate-struck,** *a.* (See quotation.) — **1724** JONES *Virginia* 48 This easy Way of Living, and the Heat of the Summer makes some very lazy, who are then said to be Climate-struck.

* **Climber.**

+**1.** One who seeks to advance himself unduly in society or in business.

1833 *Knickerb.* I. 179 But with all her meanness as a climber, what a glorious leader of fashion she'd make. **1901** C. FITCH (*title*), The Climbers. **1902** *Harper's Mag.* April 690 There are more 'climbers' in Washington than in any other city. **1908** HORNBLOW *Profligate* 27 He was a climber, and his one ambition was to possess great wealth. **1920** OSTRANDER *How Many Cards?* 89 If by the Fords you mean Lonsdale Ford and his wife, they're climbers; never heard of until a few years ago.

attrib. **1911** HARRISON *Queed* 301 He was of the climber type, a self-made man in the earlier and less inspiring stages of the making.

+**2.** An iron spur strapped to the leg or boot, used in climbing telegraph poles, trees, etc.; the boot with such a spur attached.

1874 KNIGHT 566 *Climber,* a boot provided with spurs, by which a person is enabled to climb telegraph-poles to make repairs or additions to the wires or insulators. **1894** *Outing* XXIII. 355/2 A pair of such steel climbers as linemen fasten to their feet when about to climb telegraph poles. **1903** 'O. HENRY' *Rolling Stones* (1912) 35 All he wants is . . . a pair of Western Union climbers to go up the bread-fruit tree. **1911** QUICK *Yellowstone N.* 29 He began with a pair of pliers, a pair of climbers, a lineman's belt and a vast store of obstinacy.

***Climbing,** *n.* +*College slang.* (See quotation.) — **1851** HALL *College Words* 50 It was customary [at Dartmouth] for each one of these four [best scholars] to treat his classmates, which was called 'Climbing,' from the effect which the liquor would have in elevating the class to an equality with the first scholars.

* **Climbing,** *a.* Designating various plants of a clambering or prehensile nature. {1670–}

1840 DEWEY *Mass. Flowering Plants* 102 *Polygonum cilinode.* Climbing Bindweed. Less common, . . . climbing on and over other plants. **1847** DARLINGTON *Weeds & Plants* 86 *Celastrus scandens.* . . . Climbing Celastrus. Wax-work. Climbing Bitter-sweet. **1817–8** EATON *Botany* (1822) 402 *Polygonum scandens,* climbing buckwheat. **1868** *Rep. Comm. Agric.* 205 Climbing Annuals for Summer Decoration. Climbing cobæa, (*Cobæa scandens*). **1817–8** EATON *Botany* (1822) 253 *Corydalis fungosa,* climbing colic-weed. **1857** GRAY *Botany* 375 *Polygonum dumetorum.* (Climbing false buckwheat.) . . . Moist thickets. **1843** TORREY *Flora N.Y.* I. 47 *Adlumia cirrhosa.* . . . Climbing Fumitory. **1857** GRAY *Botany* 188 *Mikania.* Climbing hemp-weed. **1785** MARSHALL *Amer. Grove* 28 *Celastrus scandens.* American Climbing Staff-tree. **1817–8** EATON *Botany* (1822) 354 *Mikania scandens,* climbing thoroughwort. . . . Damp or wet. **1785** MARSHALL *Amer. Grove* 21 *Bignonia radicans,* Climbing Trumpet-Flower, . . . shaped somewhat like a trumpet, and . . . of an orange colour.

+**Climbing fern.** The Hartford fern, *Lygodium palmatum.*

1817–8 EATON *Botany* (1822) 345 [The] climbing fern . . . generally climbs to the height of about 3 or 4 feet. **1843** TORREY *Flora N.Y.* II. 504 Climbing-fern. . . . Western part of the State. **1857** GRAY *Botany* 600 Climbing Fern . . . [grows in] shaded or moist grassy places, Massachusetts to Virginia, Kentucky, and sparingly southward; rare. July. **1871** *Amer. Naturalist* V. 115 The beautiful Climbing Fern . . . flourishes in its wild state within the borders of 'old Essex.' **1899** GOING *Flowers* 262 The Hartford climbing-fern, the common sensitive-fern and a few others.

Climbing rose. Any of various clambering roses.

1836 EATON *Botany* (ed. 7) 489 *Rosa rubifolia,* climbing rose. **1845** LINCOLN *Bot.* App. 156/2. **1865** *Atlantic Mo.* XV. 614 To admire the remarkable blending of the climbing rose, the honeysuckle, and the grape. **1894** *Outing* XXIV. 101/1 She held herself like a climbin' rose above them. **1891** COULTER *Bot. W. Texas* I. 106 *Rosa setigera.* Climbing or Prairie rose. A common eastern species extending into northern Texas.

attrib. **1877** *Harper's Mag.* April 659/1 In a climbing rose-bush trained against the house was another nest.

Clinch, *n.* {1627–} +**1.** A 'rough and tumble.' Also attrib. ‖**2.** Grasp or clutch. — **(1) 1849** LANMAN *Alleghany Mts.* 50 He found the wolf alive, when a 'clinch fight' ensued, and the hunter's knife completely severed the heart of the animal. **1860** HOLMES *Professor* iii. 64 Both rolled down together, and the conflict terminated in one of those inglorious and inevitable Yankee clinches. **(2) 1850** C. MATHEWS *Moneypenny* 10 Somehow or another we never could get our clinches on you.

+**Clinch,** *v. intr.* In fighting or wrestling, to grapple and struggle at close grips.

The general sense occurs in early modern English (1652) but the modern technical use is American: see quot. 1863.

1828 *Yankee* May 174/3 A native Yankee . . . would never be the first to strike a blow, nor hardly ever the first to clinch, as he calls it. **1860** HOLMES *Elsie Venner* iii, The rough-and-tumble fighters all *clinch,* as everybody knows. [**1863** in Miles *Pugilistica* (1906) III. 516 The Yankee again 'clinching'—we must borrow an Americanism which expresses more than our word 'closing'—succeeded in once more putting on the 'hug' and throwing King heavily.] **1869** 'MARK TWAIN' *Siamese Twins,* Chang knocked Eng down, and then . . . both clinched and began to beat and gouge each other without mercy. **1887** *Courier-Journal* 17 Jan. 5/2 Glass returned with a blow on Bowen's neck. The men then clinched.

+**Cling.** A clingstone peach.
1845 DOWNING *Fruits Amer.* 494 The Catherine cling is a very fine, old English variety. **1867–8** *Ill. Agric. Soc. Trans.* VII. 510 We have a late, large peach which we call the Allman Cling. **1904** 'O. HENRY' *Heart of West* 140 'Open me some yellow clings,' ordered Poky Rodgers. **1913** STRATTON-PORTER *Laddie* iii, One [peach] was a white cling, and one was yellow.
attrib. **1872** *San Francisco W. Bulletin* 27 Sept. (Hoppe), Cling peaches are moderately plentiful. **1913** STRATTON-PORTER *Laddie* iv, I led her straight to our best cling peach tree.

+**Clingjohn.** (See quotation.) — **1866** LOWELL *Biglow P.* 2 Ser. p. lviii, I subjoin a few phrases not in Mr. Bartlett's book which I have heard: . . . *Cling-john:* a soft cake of rye.

+**Clingstone.** A variety of peach in which the flesh adheres closely to the stone. {1840–} Cf. CLING.
1705 BEVERLEY *Virginia* IV. 78 The best sort of these [=peaches and nectarines] cling to the Stone, and will not come off clear, which they call Plum-Nectarines, and Plum-Peaches, or Cling-Stones. **1839** *Knickerb.* XIII. 54 The peach, particularly called the cling-stone, was scarcely digestible. **1849** *Rep. Comm, Patents: Agric.* 434 'Hoosier peaches,' to wit: small, . . . late varieties, principally cling-stones. **1856** *Ib.* 298 We are provided with good peaches for more than two months in the season; . . . the 'Golden Drop' and 'Old-mixon Clingstone,' which are ripe in September.
attrib. **1837** WILLIAMS *Florida* 98 The clusters of fruit [of the Sea Grape] taste much like a clingstone Peach. **1852** *Mich. Agric. Soc. Trans.* III. 487 Four cling stone peaches, cultivated.

+**Clinician.** A physician, esp. one who works in or has charge of a clinic. — **1878** H. WOOD *Therap.* (1879) 526 The chief interest of the clinician in . . . muriate of ammonia centres in its effects when given continuously for some time. **1887** *Nation* 24 Feb. 173/1 A well-known American clinician is not cited at all. **1897** *Amer. Pediatric Soc. Trans.* IX. 112 Clinicians to Children's Clinic. Medical College of Ohio, Cincinnati, O.

Clinker.** Used attrib. of a type of building or construction in which the upper plank or clapboard overlaps the lower one. — **1807** *Ann. 10th Congress* 1 Sess. 457 Bissel told me to get six men, with the Clinker boat, to take him down the [Ohio] river. *a1860** *Songs of Yale* 26 As within our 'clinker' cottage We devour our homely pottage.

+**Clinton.** A choice species of eastern grape. — **1849** *Rep. Comm. Patents: Agric.* 188 We have put down both the Isabella and the Clinton in cotton-batting, and kept them fresh until February. **1860** *Ill. Agric. Soc. Trans.* IV. 474 The Clinton and Concord are hardy, and consequently better adapted to vineyard culture here. **1868** *Rep. Comm. Agric. 1867* 155 Not even the Clinton . . . will make a good wine unless allowed to hang late.

+**Clintonia.** [fr. De Witt *Clinton.*] A genus of plants of the lily-of-the-valley family. Also attrib. — **1843** TORREY *Flora N.Y.* II. 301 *Clintonia umbellata.* . . . Small-flowered Clintonia. . . . Jamestown, Chautauqua county. **1857** GRAY *Botany* 468 Clintonia. . . . *C. borealis.* . . . Cold moist woods, Massachusetts to Wisconsin and northward, and southward in the Alleghanies. June. . . . *C. umbellata.* . . . Rich woods, S.W. New York, and southward along the Alleghanies.

+**Clintonian,** *n.* A political supporter of George Clinton (1739–1812) or of De Witt Clinton (1769–1828). Now hist.
1792 JEFFERSON *Writings* VI. (1895) 89 The Clintonians again tell strange tales about these votes of Otsego. **1804** *N.Y. Herald* 28 April 1/4 In behalf of the Federalists, we present our best compliments to our friends, the Clintonians. **1807** IRVING, etc. *Salmagundi* x, I have just heard of the loss of three thousand votes at least to the Clintonians. **1819** *Niles' Reg.* XVI. 224/1 In the house of representatives, [there are] 'republicans' 43, federalists 43, 'Clintonians' 34. **1829** VAN BUREN in Mackenzie *Life* 206 The only personal objection that was made to Mr. Butler, was his conduct last winter in regard to the Clinton Bill, and I believe that every Clintonian in both houses voted against him. **1872** *Harper's Mag.* XLIV. 842/2 The Bucktails began to denounce the Clintonians as lukewarm in the cause of public works.

+**Clintonian,** *a.* [Cf. prec.] Adhering politically to De Witt Clinton. — **1802** *Balance* (Hudson, N.Y.) 10 Aug. 250 (Th.), [Parody by] a Clintonian Burrite. . . . Burrites! Clintonians! Democrats! hear me for my family. **1812** *Mass. Spy* 23 Nov. 3/3 The Madisonian ranks at Washington are thrown into utter consternation by the certain information that the Clintonian electoral ticket had prevailed in Ohio, by a majority of 547. **1846** J. S. JENKINS *Hist. Polit. Parties N.Y.* 231 After the adjournment of the Legislature [in 1820] a meeting of the Clintonian members of the Assembly was held.

+**Clintonianism.** *Obs.* The political philosophy of the Clintonians. — **1812** *Mass. Spy* 2 Dec. 3 Federalism, weak of itself, has called disaffection and Clintonianism to its aid.

+**Clintonite.** [See quot. 1843.] A mineral belonging to the brittle mica group; seybertite. — **1831** *Science* XIX. 159 Dr. Torrey presented bronzite (Clintonite) from Orange Co. **1843** L. C. BECK *Min. N.Y.* 362 The name clintonite was given it by the discoverers in honor of De Witt Clinton. **1868** DANA *Mineralogy* (1872) 149 Clintonite. . . . Occurs in limestone with serpentine at Amity, N.Y. . . . It has also been called *Seybertite.*

+**Clinton's ditch.** A derisive nickname for the Erie canal. — **1835** H. C. TODD *Notes* 64 The Erie canal—here called *canol*—was at first attempted to be laughed down, under the cognomen of The Big, and Clinton's Ditch. **1879** *Congress. Rec.* 22 Jan. 629/2 Clinton's ditch, as it used to be called, was sneered at when it was an experiment.

Clip, *n.* {1681–}

1. The quantity of wool sheared on an occasion or during a period. {*a* 1825–}
1840 *Niles' Nat. Reg.* 25 April 128/3 Allowing the estimate at three pounds per head, the clip of 1839 would be 45,000,000, pounds of wool. **1852** *Mich. Agric. Soc. Trans.* III. 149 We never received a clip of wool . . . equal to yours. **1892** *Vt. Agric. Rep.* XII. 142 Our annual clip of wool is 130,000 pounds. **1904** 'O. HENRY' *Heart of West* 233 The sheep sheared six pounds all round this fall; and I'm going to get Marilla an instrument if it takes the price of the whole clip to do it.

2. A sharp blow. {1830–}
1828 *Yankee* May 174/3 If you give him [a Yankee] a heavy clip—one is enough. **1840** SIMMS *Border Beagles* 71 Now, he says that if I had only let Watson give me the first clip, he could defend me very well. **1856** — *Charlemont* 442, I'd give all I'm worth to have a fair shot or clip at that rascal Stevens. **1902** LORIMER *Lett. Merchant* 271 Some man . . . fetching him a clip on the ear for having come back and put the laugh on him.

+**3.** A single stroke or time; a 'fell swoop.' *colloq.*
1801 Brooks *Gleanings* 64 Twenty per Cent was struck off at one clip, from those kind of Shoes, which are mostly worn. It is fifteen months since the Shoe War commenced. **1853** *S. Lit. Messenger* XIX 218/1 Why, for contempt at ten dollars a clip—that was old Ramkat's tariff. **1902** WISTER *Virginian* xxiii. 270 It looks like it did too wholesale a business to turn out an article up to standard every clip. **1909** WASON *Happy Hawkins* 12 A man can drink an' fight an' carry on for a year at a clip an' then all of a sudden feel a hurtin' somewhere inside.

4. A fast rate, gait, or pace. {1877, *dial.*}
1868 WOODRUFF *Trotting Horse* 79 A thoroughbred colt . . . can go a four-minute clip, and that without the least education. **1902** MCFAUL *Ike Glidden* 201 The horse was holding steady up to his clip, but it could be easily seen that he was 'all in.' **1922** MULFORD *Black Buttes* 32 At dawn the herd went on again at a twenty-mile-a-day clip, the dust soaring high into the heated air.

* **Clip,** *v.*

***1. a.** *tr.* To lessen (coins) in size and value by cutting off part of the edge. Also absol. (Cf. CLIPPING 1.)
1705 *Boston News-Letter* 30 April 2/1 On the 17th Currant was Emitted by his Excellency . . . a Proclamation, Prohibiting the Importation of any clipt Money of Bitts or double Bitts into this Colony. **1738** STEPHENS *Proc. Georgia* 82 One Smith—paying away a few Spanish Bits, the Receiver observed them to be fresh clipped. **1838** INGRAHAM *Burton* II. 215, I will then clip; 'tis three months since I have clipped, and times are getting harder.

b. To cut or cut *off* (ears) as a penalty. *Obs.*
1729 J. COMER *Diary* 65 Nicholas Octis stood in ye pillory, and had his ears clipt for making money. **1775** ADAIR *Indians* 144 (*note*), The Muskohge lately clipt off the ears of two white men for supposed adultery.

***c.** To shear (sheep or their fleece). Also, to yield when sheared.
1849 *Rep. Comm. Patents: Agric.* 16 The census of 1850 will give no information as to the number of fleeces clipped in the United States. **1852** *Mich. Agric. Soc. Trans.* III. 150 My flock . . . clips an annual average of . . . two and three quarter pounds of pure wool. **1870** *Rep. Comm. Agric. 1869* 373 Many sheep . . . are ready for market as soon as the wool can be clipped.

d. To cut out (a passage) from a newspaper. Also absol. {1873–}
1872 *Harper's Bazaar* 6 Jan. 11 The following marriage notice is clipped from a Texas paper. **1904** *N.Y. Ev. Post* 10 Sept. 4 A suggestion for a college girl's vacation that should be clipped and pasted for reference next June. **1914** *Boston Herald* 20 June 10/5 Mr. Allen A. Brown of this city has clipped for many years.

2. To strike with a sharp blow. {1880 *dial.*}
1857 E. STONE *Life of Howland* 57 Jones . . . drew his long sword and swore he would clip any man who dared approach him. **1871** DE VERE 455 *Clip,* to, in the sense of to give a blow; and the noun, a *clip,* meaning a blow, must be looked upon as Americanisms.

* **Clipper.**

+**1.** A sailing vessel designed primarily for speed, first built at Baltimore (see BALTIMORE 3). {1830–} Also fig.
1823 COOPER *Pilot* I. 26, I have seen a little clipper, in disguise, outsail an old man-of-war's-man in a hard chase. **1841** DANA *Two Years* 26 Clippers are fastest *on* the wind. **1860** MORDECAI *Virginia* 324 Some enterprising men . . . relied on the fleetness of their clippers and the dangers of the coast, to carry on trade with Cuba. **1891** *Scribner's Mag.* X. 267 In 1845 the American clippers, long, low, of good beam, . . . set a greater spread of canvas in proportion to their tonnage than any ship hitherto sailed.

2. A fast horse. {1840–}
1835–7 HALIBURTON *Clockmaker* 1 Ser. xv, I raised a four year old colt once, . . . a genuine clipper, could gallop like the wind.

+**3.** A kind of clam.
1832 WATSON *Hist. Tales N.Y.* 36 Their most frequent diet was clams, called clippers.

4. A likeable or attractive girl. *colloq.* {1848–}

1835–7 HALIBURTON *Clockmaker* 1 Ser. xx, She was a real handsum looking gall; . . . a real clipper, and as full of fun and frolic as a kitten. **1888** A. DALY *Lottery of Love* 19 Oh, she's a clipper. **1904** DERVILLE *Other Side of Story* 186 What a clipper she was! Here was genuine beauty in genuine distress.

+5. Attrib. (in sense 1) with *barque, craft*, etc.

1854 *Monthly Nautical Mag.* Nov. 140 A superior clipper barque, of about 500 tons, intended for a freighter. **1851** *Knickerb.* XXXVIII. 180 Oh! for a sail this very day on its broad silver bosom in the clipper craft named of 'Old Knick.' **1891** *Scribner's Mag.* X. 105 If we have no very bad weather I could almost take a race with one of the clipper packets.

b. In transf. sense, with *mill, plow, sled.*

1879 TAYLOR *Summer-Savory* 125 The clipper mill on the top of the woodshed that runs at the wind's will. **1861–4** *Ill. Agric. Soc. Trans.* V. 507 With our clipper plows, two-horse cultivators and iron rollers. **1883** *Harper's Mag.* Dec. 146/2 A large . . . sled . . . twice as wide and twice as long as your clipper-sled.

+Clipper-built, *a.* Of ships: Built on sharp, rakish lines conducive to fast sailing.

1835 SIMMS *Yemassee* I. 116 Immediately before him, . . . in the broadest part of the stream, rested motionless as the hill upon which he stood, the sharp clipper-built vessel. **1840** DANA *Two Years* iv. 25 Looking astern, we saw a small clipper-built brig with a black hull heading directly after us. **1861** *Chicago Tribune* 26 May 1/5 This beautiful clipper-built craft, of 300 tons burden, which was seized by Assistant-Marshal Thompson, . . . is now lying at Atlantic Docks. **1886** *Leslie's Mo.* XXI. 303/1 [A] more clipper-built craft never left Gloucester Harbor.

transf. **1873** BEADLE *Undevel. West* 70, I then observed . . . a peculiar sort of clipper-built fly. **1878** — *Western Wilds* 443 These people . . . are of florid complexion, leathery aspect, and 'clipper built' as to limbs.

+Clipper schooner. A clipper-built schooner. — **1842** HALE *If, Yes, & Perhaps* 97 He immediately took measures for the charter of two little clipper schooners. **1853** *Traveler* 18 Aug. 1/5 The new clipper schooner . . . will stow about 500 barrels. **1883** in *Diary & Lett. T. Hutchinson* I. 480 [I was] recently put ashore somewhere near Long Wharf, out of one of those clipper schooners, . . . of which I had become proprieter for nine Massachusetts pence.

+Clipper ship. A fast sailing vessel; a clipper.

1856 PARKER *Boston Oration* 4 July 28 In the game for the peaceful harvest of the seas she [*sc.* America] ruffles out the snowy plumage of her clipper ships. **1860** ABBOTT *South & North* 319 But will they [the slaves] build clipper ships, and construct imperial locomotives? **1866** 'MARK TWAIN' in *Harper's Mag.* XXXIV. 104/1 The superb clipper-ship *Hornet*, Captain Josiah Mitchell, sailed out of New York harbor. **1869** DANA *Two Years* (new ed.) 440 The Presidio . . . has a noble situation, and I saw from it a clipper ship of the very largest class, coming through the Gate, under her fore-and-aft sails.

attrib. **1887** *Courier-Journal* 8 May 12/7 For the first time in a quarter of a century there is to be a clipper-ship race between two famous vessels from this city around Cape Horn to San Francisco.

***Clipping.**

***1.** The fraudulent cutting or trimming of the edges of coins.

1705 *Boston News-Letter* 25 June 2/2, I am of Opinion it will be necessary to pass an Act to prevent the Clipping and Defacing the Foreign Coyn which has currency in this Province. **1797** *Annals 5th Congress* 2 Sess. I. 718 They knew the silver coin circulated by tale, the gold weight; the value of the latter had actually diminished by various means, such as sweating, plugging, clipping, &c.

+2. A piece cut from a newspaper or magazine.

1838 *Diplom. Corr. Texas* I. 338 A newspaper clipping containing Van Buren's proclamation of the treaty. **1872** *San Francisco W. Bulletin* 27 Sept. (Hoppe), A thousand thanks for your letter and clippings. **1894** *N.Y.P.O.* 10 July, Press clippings . . . are mailable at the third class rate of postage. **1902** LORIMER *Lett. Merchant* 259, I note the enclosed clippings. **1925** BRYAN *Memoirs* 273, I found a yellowed newspaper clipping with a date of 27 years ago.

3. The shearing of sheep.

1898 CANFIELD *Maid of Frontier* 188 Near by was the sheep pen . . . crowded with sheep waiting for the morrow's clipping.

Clique. {1711–} +A group of businessmen who attempt to regulate the price of stocks or commodities. — **1865** *Atlantic Mo.* XV. 575 The impresario and his agents, the broker and his clique cry out. **1870** MEDBERY *Men Wall St.* 168 The clique went short in the stock, and then suddenly annulled the agreement. **1901** MERWIN & WEBSTER *Calumet 'K'* 285 The Clique of speculators who held the floor were buying, buying, buying.

attrib. **1887** *Courier-Journal* 3 May 7/6 The clique houses did pay for the cash wheat to-day—the most important move so far made in a deal which has amazed the crowd.

Cliqued, *ppl. a.* {1884} ‖Manipulated by a business 'ring.' — **1885** *Graceville* (Minn.) *Transcript* 3 Jan. 6/3 Indian corn has been higher, under cliqued holding of light stocks.

Clitchy. (See quotation.) {*dial.*} — **1816** PICKERING 63 *Clitchy.* Clammy, sticky, glutinous. I have heard this word used in a few instances by old people in New England; but it is very rarely heard.

Cloakroom. {*c*1825– (T. Moore)} +A rest or lounging room, used by members of Congress, in the Capitol at Washington, D.C.

1876 *N. Amer. Rev.* CXXIII. 317 Politicians of national standing . . . filled the air of cloak-rooms at the Capitol and of private apartments with mean insinuations. **1886** ALTON *Among Law-Makers* 51 [The Senators] always do retire to the cloak-rooms when they wish to smoke. **1913** LA FOLLETTE *Autobiog.* 72, I found him waiting for me near the cloak-room.

attrib. **1880** LAMPHERE *U.S. Govt.* 265/1 Appointed by the doorkeeper: . . . pages, laborers, and cloak-room men. **1906** *N.Y. Ev. Post* 26 May 4 Without giving credence to a word of cloak-room gossip, there is abundant warrant for the feeling . . . against the special conference rule.

***Clock.** Used in comb. with names of various occupations as *cleaner, keeper*, etc.

1749 *Harvard Rec.* II. 804 (*marginal note*), Clock-keeper re-chosen. **1835** *Knickerb.* V. 275 The drawing propensity had never slumbered in our clock-cleaner. **1851** *Ib.* XXXVIII. 470 Several actions of H—, a clock-vender, came on for trial. **1856** GOODRICH *G. Go-Ahead* 119 The sailors left the ship, and the clock-merchant left it also. *Ib.*, After a time, the poor clock-seller heard of all this, and so he went to the great city and claimed his property.

+Clock factory. A place where clocks are made. — **1820** FLINT *Lett. from Amer.* 213 Ivory and wood clock factory, [employs] 14 [men]. **1827** DRAKE & MANSFIELD *Cincinnati* 57 [Manufactured products of] One Clock Factory, 18 hands, [in 1826 were valued at] $20,000. **1902** *Harper's Mag.* May 991 The great centre of clock-manufacture was then in Thomaston and Bristol, Connecticut, where are still some of the largest clock factories.

***Clock-maker.** One who makes clocks. — **1683** *Boston Rec.* 73 David Edwards, mariner, became surety for William Davis, Clockmaker. **1708** *Boston News-Letter* 5 April 2/2 Isaac Webb Watch-maker and Clock-maker, that formerly Liv'd the next Door to the Royal-Exchange Tavern. **1812** MELISH *Travels* II. 55 The following enumeration of the professions exercised in Pittsburgh will show the rapid progress that society has made here. . . . Lock-smiths, screw and hinge-makers, clock and watch-makers.

+Clockmutch. (See quotation.) — **1848** BARTLET 86 *Clockmutch.* (Dutch, *klapmuts*, a night-cap.) A woman's cap composed of three pieces,—a straight centre one, from the forehead to the neck, with two side pieces. A New York term.

+Clock-peddler, -pedlar. One who travels about selling clocks.— **1833** *Trial E. K. Avery* 64 A clock pedlar took tea that night. **1837** *Knickerb.* X. 167 He was accosted, somewhat abruptly, by a clock-pedlar. **1849** LANMAN *Alleghany Mts.* 15, I came into this Southern country twenty-four years ago as a clock-pedler.

+Clock-peddling. The selling of clocks by a peddler. — **1853** *Harper's Mag.* VII. 708/2 He first tried clock-peddling; but his instruments . . . were returned. **1883** EGGLESTON *Hoosier School-Boy* 99 Ignorant and pretentious men, wanderers from New England, who had grown tired of clock-peddling.

Clod-breaker. {1818–} +A machine for crushing clods. — **1849** *Rep. Comm. Patents* 523 There is no difficulty in combining the effect of the plough, harrow and pulverizer, or clod-breaker, in the same machine.

***Clog.**

***1.** An implement to be attached to a horse or other animal to prevent it from leaping fences or running away.

1669 *Watertown Rec.* 95 Horses that goe in Commons . . . sum with Clogs. **1790** DEANE *New-Eng. Farmer* 58/2 *Clog*, a wooden instrument fastened to the neck or leg of a beast, to prevent his leaping over or breaking fences. **1923** COOK *On Old Frontier* 66 The horses were lassoed by the feet and thrown down, and either strong rawhide hobbles or clogs were placed on their front legs.

***2.** A heavy, clumsy shoe or overshoe. Usually *pl.*

1733 *S.C. Gazette* 20 Jan. (*advt.*), Womens cloggs, rice sieves, reap hooks. **1770** *Carroll P.* in *Md. Hist. Mag.* XIII. 69 Things sent by the wagon: . . . 3 Casks of fine Flour, . . . 1 pair of clogs for Mr. Deards. **1794** *Ann. 3rd Congress* 1472 There shall be levied . . . on shoes and slippers for men and women, and on clogs and goloshoes, per pair, five cents. **1832** WATSON *Hist. Tales N.Y.* 145 In the miry times of winter they wore clogs, gala shoes, or pattens.

+3. *ellipt.* = CLOG DANCE. Also attrib.

1869 *Atlantic Mo.* July 74/1 This was, I think, the first introduction of clogs as a drawing-room entertainment. **1880** E. JAMES *Negro Minstrel's Guide* 6 Except for the clog or jig, the costumes may be made by any lady relation or friend. **1887** *Courier-Journal* 19 Feb. 8/1 The clog led by Mr. Willis Pickett is a novelty, and is very finely done, Mr. Pickett himself holding the championship as a clog dancer. His clog solo was much applauded.

Clog dance. A clattering dance performed with (or as if with) clogs. {1881–} — **1869** *Atlantic Mo.* July 72/1, I mention this kindly old gentleman, because he suffered a great deal from my early penchant to perform the clog-dance on the thin deck above his stateroom. **1893** HOWELLS *Coast of Bohemia* 37, He danced a little clog-dance in her parlor.

Clog-dancer. One who performs clog dances.

1873 BAILEY *Life in Danbury* 266 A landlady . . . writes to learn how long it requires for a middle-aged man to become an accomplished clog dancer. **1882** PECK *Sunshine* 120 After handing down a few of the female clog dancers a cloud appeared on the horizon. **1890** CUSTER *Following*

Guidon 77 There were the clog-dancers, who were the idols of our regiment. **1896** *N.Y. Dramatic News* 4 July 7/2 On Wednesday evening the following artists will appear: . . . Kusel and Laughlin, in a new sketch; Bertha Waring, champion clog dancer of the world.

* **Close,** *n.* An inclosed piece of land. Now legal only.

1638 *Charlestown Land Rec.* 32 Three acres of meaddow . . . scituate in the south meade . . . bounded on the west by Bakers close. **1653** *Conn. Prob. Rec.* 125 The Close of Upland in ye Close by the Barn. **1667** *Charlestown Land Rec.* 165 Nine pole and three foote . . . reaches to the trayning close. **1835** *Ind. Mag. Hist.* XXII. 435 This was an action by the plaintiff for entering his close, cutting timber and making a road to a toll bridge. **1893** *Mass. Supreme Ct. Rep.* CLX. 34 The second count was for forcibly entering the plaintiff's close in Springfield.

* **Close,** *a.*

1. *fig.* Leaving a very small margin. *colloq.*[2]

1832 KENNEDY *Swallow Barn* II. 91 She as much as signified . . . that she didn't wish to make my acquaintance: and so, I took the hint and was off:—wa'nt that close grazing, Ralph? **1877** WRIGHT *Big Bonanza* 94 When them boys finally got convalescent and riz up and come for me, it was close papers for a time. **1887** *Courier-Journal* 8 May 8/6 We are in the field armed to the teeth with closest prices ever given to the world.

+**2.** Almost equally divided in political strength. {of a contest, 1855–}

1828 WEBSTER, *Close election*, an election in which the votes for the different candidates are nearly equal. **1844** *Lexington Obs. & Rep.* 14 Aug. 3 It is believed that the race [for election] has been a close one. **1874** *Congress. Rec.* Jan. 1042 In 1870 it gave 30 democratic majority. It is considered a very close parish. **1887** *Ib.* 20 Jan. App. 50/1 Mr. Goff: What do you mean by doubtful counties? Mr. Grosvenor: Close counties, like some of those in the State of my friend from West Virginia. **1904** *Forum* July 17 In the last Congressional election there were comparatively few close districts.

* **Close,** *v.*

1. *intr. Stock exchange.* To be worth at the end of a trading period. {1860– (*Times*)}

1875 *Chicago Tribune* 18 Nov. 6/1 Panama opened at 126, fell off to 125, advanced to 129, and closed at 128 @ 128¼. **1899** *Kansas City Star* 21 Jan. 6/1 Mixed corn sold slowly and closed ¼c lower than yesterday.

2. *To close down.* +**a.** To come down upon, suppress. +**b.** =sense 3 b.

(**a**) **1869** 'MARK TWAIN' *Innocents* xxiv. 254 They have set a gun-boat to watch the vessel night and day, with orders to close down on any revolutionary movement in a twinkling. (**b**) **1883** —*Life on Miss.* 536 The night presently closed down.

***3.** *To close in.* **a.** To come to terms *with.* {–1742} +**b.** Of night: To approach, draw on.

(**a**) **1838** MCDONALD *Biog. Sk.* 31 His proffered terms were soon closed in with. — (**b**) **1829** IRVING *Granada* (1850) 88 As the night closed in, they reached the chain of little valleys and hamlets. **1867** PARKMAN *Jesuits N. Amer.* (1875) 77 Night was fast closing in.

+**4.** *To close on,* in baseball, to catch.

1880 BROOKS *Fairport Nine* 184 Jake Coombs and Eph Mullett hit high balls to Pat Adams, at third base, and he closed on them, and umpire Dunbar declared them out. *Ib.* 187 Bill closed on the ball, doubling himself together in his anxiety to keep it.

5. *To close out,* +to sell off (goods), wind up (a business), finish (a transaction). Also absol.

1852 J. M. LETTS *California* 159 We offered him [a mule] to Mr. Priest for six dollars. . . . He offered two, at which we 'closed him out.' **1884** NYE *Baled Hay* 101 It will be closed out very cheap. **1888** *St. Paul Globe* 22 Jan. (*advt.*), I shall also close out absolutely my Instruments of all kinds. **1891** O'BEIRNE *Leaders Ind. Territory* 59/1 In 1879 he opened business in Audubon, Wise county, but closed out in 1883, arriving in Caddo the following year. **1898** BATES *Clothing Bk.* No. 2502 There is no excuse for this with summer clothing at the prices at which we are closing out. **1898** WESTCOTT *D. Harum* 355 It was not until August, however, that the deal was finally closed out. **1907** *Methodist Rev.* Nov. 958 One of the platform agitators who had stirred the people to riot has been deported and two of the native papers threatened with being closed out. **1910** WHITE *Rules of Game* 234, I should advise closing out the business by killing the fowl.

b. *fig.* With personal object.

1869 'MARK TWAIN' *Innocents Abroad* xxxvii. 402, I was equal to the emergency. I said we had eighty thousand convicts employed on the railways in America. . . . That closed *him* out. **1880** — *Tramp Abroad* xlvi. 538 The fall would have been only one hundred feet, but it would have closed me out as effectually as one thousand.

***6.** *To close up.* +**a.** To wind up, finish off.

1898 WESTCOTT *D. Harum* 137, I guess 't won't take him long to close up his matters. **1903** *N.Y. Post* 28 Dec. 1 The preparations going on for closing up the affairs of the legation. **1923** HERRICK *Lilla* 39 The Porters, the Lawndale addition having finally been 'closed up' at a handsome profit, had planned a trip to Europe.

b. To cease talking. *slang.*

1856 *Spirit of Times* 6 Sept. 4/1 If they didn't 'close-up' there'd be another 'clam-cart' after them.

+**Close call.** A narrow escape from some danger or misfortune. *colloq.* (See also CLOSE FIT and CLOSE SHAVE.)

1881 *Harper's Mag.* LXIII. 118/1 My! but that was a close call, 's Mr. M. used to say. **1898** NICHOLAS *Idyl of Wabash* 171, 'I had one or two close calls,' he said lightly. **1903** *N.Y. Sun* 27 Nov. 2 Private Oldberg had a close call. One bullet knocked his hat off and another threw dust on his shoes. **1920** MULFORD *J. Nelson* 123 Just th' same, I'm sayin' we had a close call.

Close carriage. A carriage in which the occupants are enclosed on all sides. — **1845** SOL. SMITH *Theatr. Apprent.* 64 My friend came to the door, with a close carriage, into which we got. **1872** *Atlantic Mo.* June 702 McCandless drove up in a handsome new close carriage. **1898** PAGE *Red Rock* 562 The next moment a close carriage, with a good pair of horses, drove quickly by them in a cloud of dust.

Close communion. In the Baptist church, communion in the Lord's Supper restricted to members of that denomination. — **1824** *Baptist Mag.* IV. 411 With these views of catholicism we do not see that the practice of close communion at all interferes. **1828** SHERBURNE *Memoirs* 181 In respect to close communion . . . I could not but question whether any had a right to partake of the Lord's supper. **1856** P. CARTWRIGHT *Autobiog.* 110 A great many of their members gave up . . . close communion.

attrib. **1880** *Harper's Mag.* Aug. 346 The Concerns of the meeting-houses —Seventh-day Baptist, Close-Communion Baptist, and Adventist . . . were among their strongest preoccupations.

+**Close cut.** A short cut; a way more direct that the usual one. — **1845** SIMMS *Wigwam & Cabin* 2 Ser. 79, I was busy in adjusting my foot in the stirrup . . . to find my way by a close cut.

Closed gentian. A species of gentian (*Dasystephana andrewsii*) with non-opening blue flowers. — **1857** GRAY *Botany* 346 *Gentiana Andrewsii.* . . . Closed Gentian. . . . [Grows in] moist rich soil; common, especially northward. **1901** H. ROBERTSON *Inlander* 157 Ah! it's—why, it's closed gentian, isn't it?

+**Close-down.** The stopping of work in a factory. — **1889** *Voice* (N.Y.) 5 Sept., Interfere with the unrestricted manufacturing interests of our country by forced 'close-downs,' lockouts, &c.

+**Close fit.** A danger point or crisis; a 'pinch.' *colloq.*[2] (See also CLOSE CALL, CLOSE SHAVE.) — **1884** 'MARK TWAIN' *H. Finn* xxix. 305 Stead of being fixed so I could take my own time—and have Mary Jane at my back to save me and set me free when the close-fit come, here was nothing in the world betwixt me and sudden death.

+**Close-herd,** *v.* (See quot. 1887.) Also fig. Hence *close-herding* vbl. n. — **1887** *Scribner's Mag.* Oct. 508/2 A friend tells me he has heard a sheriff talk of 'close-herding' several prisoners in his charge. On the plains it means the difficult art of keeping cattle in a compact body, close together. **1923** BOWER *Parowan Bonanza* 264 He stopped at Tommy's Place and told Tommy that he wouldn't be needed, close herding anybody. **1925** MULFORD *Cottonwood Gulch* 148 We've got to round-up, loose herd durin' the day, an' close herd nights.

+**Close-mouthed,** *a.* Taciturn, silent, uncommunicative. *colloq.*

1881 MCLEAN *Cape Cod Folks* 270 He was held somewhat in awe among the Wallencampers, and regarded generally as a 'close-mouthed' fellow. **1892** HOWELLS *Quality of Mercy* 109 Well, he's a kind of close-mouthed man. **1901** WILKINS *Parson Lord*, etc. 222 He's as close-mouthed as a rock. **1917** FREEMAN & KINGSLEY *Alabaster Box* 79 Well, I do hope she won't be so close-mouthed with you girls.

‖**Closer-on.** One who joins or sews together the pieces forming the upper leather of a shoe. — **1885** *Harper's Mag.* Jan. 280/2 A small cut on the front of the lining is the only guide by which an experienced 'closer-on' knows where to begin her work.

+**Close shave.** A narrow margin of success; a narrow escape, a close call. *colloq.* (See also CLOSE FIT.)

[**1856** KANE *Arctic Explor.* I. 73 We passed clear; but it was a close shave.] **1892** *Courier-Journal* 2 Oct. 5 Had one of them been different the local team might have won the game. As it was the Colonels got there by a very close shave. **1893** *Chicago Tribune* 19 April 1/1 Candidates for other offices fought shy of expressing any preference for Mayor. It was a close shave for everybody. **1902** WHITLOCK *13th District* 20 Well, . . . it was a close shave, after all. **1907** HARRIS *Tents of Wickedness* I. 26 'It was a rather close shave,' he said; the fact of being so near a tragedy had shaken him out of his sulks. **1908** WHITE *Riverman* 40 'That was a close shave,' said he to the last man ashore.

+**Close sleigh.** *Obs.* A sleigh closed in on all sides. — **1767** *Mass. Gaz.* 12 Feb. 4 A close sleigh or booby-hutch, to go with either one or two horses. **1779** *Boston Gaz.* 13 Dec. 3/3 A second-hand Chariot with harness compleat, . . . two neat close sleys.

* **Clot bur, Clottbur.** One or other species of *Xanthium*, a genus of weeds bearing rough burs.

1817–8 EATON *Botany* (1822) 517 *Xanthium strumarium*, clott-burr. . . . Has a little the habit of a burdock. **1821** *Mass. H. S. Coll.* 2 Ser. IX. 158 Plants, which are indigenous in the township of Middlebury, [Vt., include] . . . Clott-bur, Twinberry, [etc.]. **1840** DEWEY *Mass. Flowering Plants* 143 Sea Burdock. Clott Burr: . . . grows on beaches near salt water. **1857** GRAY *Botany* 212 Clotbur. . . . Coarse and vile weeds, with annual roots. **1870** *Rep. Comm. Agric. 1869* 504 The thorny clotbur, (*Xanthium spinosum,*) justly stigmatized by Darlington as an 'execrable weed,' within a few years has been creeping into the grass lands of Maine.

***Cloth.**

1. A burial cloth or pall.

1702 *Boston Rec.* 26 It being proposed . . . that there be a Moderation in the prizes of Coffins, . . . And also that there be two or three black cloaths provided at the Town charge.

+2. Phr. *Out of whole cloth,* used of a statement that is entirely false. *colloq.*

1840 HALIBURTON *Clockmaker* 3 Ser. iii, All that talk about her temper was made out of whole cloth, and got up a-purpose. *Ib.* xx, What a fib! . . . it's all made out of whole cloth. **1843** C. MATHEWS *Writings* 68 Isn't this entire story about your Jersey grandmother made out of whole cloth? **1863** *Boston Herald* 8 Feb. 1/3 It is a lie manufactured out of whole cloth. **1896** *Boston Journal* 29 Dec. 2/2 This report is positively denied in official circles, who affirm that nothing of the kind occurred, but that the story is made out of whole cloth.

3. Comb. with names of occupations.

1840 C. MATHEWS *Politicians* I. ii, That gives us the tailors . . . and might have its effect with the cloth-dealers. **1831** PECK *Guide* 300 In this county [Morgan, Ill.] are . . . twelve tailors, one cloth dresser, [etc.].

Cloth-colored, *a. Obs.* {cloth-colour *n.* 1681, 1704} Having the color of cloth, perhaps drab or of a natural color. — **1725** SEWALL *Letter-Book* II. 188 *Imprimis,* . . . One full Suit of Striped Satin lined with Cloth-colourd Lutestring, One Silk Night-Gown, and three pairs of Stays. **1770** *Md. Hist. Mag.* XII. 365, I Have two pair of Woven Cloath Coloured silk Britches. **1775** *Narrag. Hist. Reg.* III. 263 A cloth-colored surtout, half worn; cloth-colored coat, velvet jacket.

***Clothes.**

‖1. The covering or blanket for a horse.

a1846 *Quarter Race Ky.,* etc. 121 The old man, supposing they would steal his horse that night, and run him, had put Dick's clothes on another horse of the same colour and marks, and about the same size.

2. Attrib. with reference to wearing apparel.

1861 WINTHROP *Open Air* 310 He took a clothes-broom and selected two straws. **1857** OLMSTED *Journey thro' Texas* 160 A dog or a cat on or under the bed, or on the clothes-chest. **1876** WARNER *Gold of Chickaree* 318 If you want needles, Josephine, or a thimble—or a sewing-bird, . . . or a clotheshamper, help yourself! **1853** FOWLER *Home for All* 113 Four dozen clothes-hooks put up in the bedrooms and closets, as the owner may direct. **1857** STROTHER *Virginia* 46 He . . . strode out, upsetting the water-bucket and knocking over the clothes-rack in his progress. **1892** *Boston Journal* 19 Dec. 1/7 (*advt.*), Our English Oak Clothes-Tree . . . keeps your clothing from all wrinkles, dries and ventilates it, and preserves it from being 'mussed.' **1835** *Stimpson's Boston Directory* 12 (*advt.*), Shepherd Simonds, Clothes Warehouse. . . . All kinds of clothing at the lowest prices.

Clothes-bag. {1879–} A bag used by sailors in place of a suit case or valise. — **1834** *Knickerb.* III. 81 The crew were disposed in various groups about the deck . . . ; some with their clothes-bags beside them. **1864** NICHOLS *Amer. Life* I. 232 He went forward on deck again, and stowed the package of bank-notes at the bottom of his clothes-bag. **1883** *Century Mag.* XXVI. 947, I bent a small line to the becket of the clothes-bag.

Clothes-boiler. A large container in which clothes are boiled. — **1868** *Mich. Agric. Rep.* VII. 348 Shepley & Irwin, White House, [exhibited] 1 herculean clothes-washer and boiler. **1872** FLAGG *Good Investment* 547/2 The household labor was further alleviated by introducing the latest-contrived clothes boiler, washer, and wringer.

Clothes-cleaner. One who cleans clothes. — **1846** *Knickerb.* XXVII. 279 Some of the ultra-reformers of the day are well typified by an indefatigable clothes-cleaner, who officiates daily in Wall-street.

Clothes closet. A closet in which clothing is kept. — **1825** PETTIGREW *Let.* 31 Jan. (Pettigrew P.), Please to get her to look for my receits in the close closet in a ban box. **1882** 'M. HARLAND' *Eve's Daughters* 73 Jack and Willy are pretty certain to have savings-banks on the mantel of their bedroom, or hidden away at the back of the top-shelf of their clothes-closet. **1912** IRWIN *Red Button* 188 She took refuge in her own big clothes-closet—which . . . was sound-proof.

Clothes-drier. A frame or device upon or in which clothes may be dried. — **1868** *Mich. Agric. Rep.* VII. 348 Henry P. Crouse, Hartland, [manufactured] 1 clothes dryer for hotel. **1882** *Century Mag.* Oct. 829/2 Going out of doors, they inspected the revolving clothes-drier, which David, with a seaman's instinct, had already rigged with four little sloops, to sail about on the ends of the projecting arms.

Clotheshorse. A wooden framework on which clothes may be hung to dry. {1806–} — **1775** *Essex Inst. Coll.* XIII. 187 Cellar [contains] a Cloath's Horse. **1855** COOKE *Ellie* 227 Aunt Phillis . . . was regarding from time to time a clothes-horse, upon which hung a very, very few clothes. **1884** *Harper's Mag.* Nov. 888/2 They . . . contented themselves with hanging [them] over the clothes-horse.

fig. **1889** 'MARK TWAIN' *Conn. Yankee* xxxiii. 420, I . . . could see her [*sc.* England's] erect statues . . . to her unspeakable Georges and other royal and noble clothes-horses.

Clothesmoth. A moth (of one or other species of the genus *Tinea*) that attacks woolen and other fabrics. Also attrib. {1753–} — **1832** *Encycl. Amer.* IX. 69 The clothes-moth itself is perfectly innocuous. **1867** *Amer. Naturalist* I. 110 The housewife must now guard against the intrusion of Clothes' moths. **1885** McCOOK *Tenants Old Farm* 87 *Pellionella,* the only 'clothes-moth' known in the United States. **1892** V. KELLOG *Kansas Insects* 3 The larvae of moths and butterflies are the voracious caterpillars, as those of the Codlin Moth, the Tomato-worm, . . . and the Clothes-moth Worm.

Clothespin. A forked peg or clamp used to fasten clothes on a line. — **1852** *Harper's Mag.* March 444/2 Hugh, on a bench in the corner, occupied himself with making clothes-pins. **1858** VIELÉ *Following Drum* 223 They sat on their horses like a parcel of clothes-pins. **1869** 'MARK TWAIN' *Sk., Niagara,* She had just carved out a wooden chief that had a strong family resemblance to a clothespin. **1898** M. LEONARD *Big Front Door* 2 He assented meekly, adding, 'and Sallie's clothes-pin.'

attrib. **1881** STODDARD *E. Hardery* 404 He owns a bank and the best part of a city, out west, and a gold mine, and a coal mine, and an iron mine, and a clothes-pin factory.

Clothespole. A pole for propping up a clothesline. — **1865** *Atlantic Mo.* XV. 659 She never conjectures to what base uses a clothes-pole may come. **1866** A. D. WHITNEY *L. Goldthwaite* iv, She . . . lifted her elbows, like clothes-poles, to raise her draperies.

Clothespress. {1713–} A press or closet in which clothes may be kept; +also, a wardrobe or chest.

1773 in E. Singleton *Social N.Y.* 83 [Joseph Cox from London] makes . . . clothes presses and chests, china shelves, [etc.]. **1847** LONGFELLOW *Evangeline* I. iii, Simple that chamber was, with its curtains of white, and its clothes-press Ample and high. **1868** *Rep. Comm. Patents* (1870) 462/1 *Clothes Press.* . . . A series of winged or swinging bars is enclosed in a frame provided with a door, and having a cloth covering in front and rear. **1876** *Scribner's Mo.* April 814/1 The wardrobes, or clothes-presses, as they were called, . . . were often extremely handsome. **1908** *Dialect Notes* III. 299 *Clothes-press,* wardrobe. The common term.

+Clothes room. A room in which clothes are kept. — **1857** VAUX *Villas* 137 In the attic . . . a space for lumber is marked on the plan; but this might be used as a clothes-room. **1865** A. D. WHITNEY *Gayworthys* xviii. 176 She vanished up the end staircase, and hid herself away in the old clothes-room.

‖Clothes slice. A clothes stick, battling stick. — **1899** A. BROWN *Tiverton Tales* 6 With two russets for balls and the clothes-slice for a mallet . . . Della . . . played her first game [of croquet].

Clothes stick. A stick used in handling clothes while washing them; a battling stick. — **1854** SHILLABER *Mrs. Partington* 157 Ike, who was busy in transforming the old lady's new clothes-stick into a bat, did n't say a word. **1896** *Cosmopolitan* XX. 432/1 The clothes on the stove boiled, and the suds splashed over and sizzled on the hot iron. Mrs. Sherman . . . rammed them down with the clothes-stick.

Clothes-wringer. A device consisting of rollers between which washed clothes are run in order to press out the water.

1861 *Chicago Tribune* 15 April 1 The Universal Clothes Wringer. Effective, Cheap and Durable. Fits any wash tub. **1863** *Horticulturist* March 7 (*advt.*), The Universal Clothes Wringer will finish work that . . . other . . . wringers have left undone. **1865** *Nation* I. 828 Universal Clothes Wringer with cog-wheels. . . . We also warrant it the best and most durable Wringer made. **1882** PECK *Sunshine* 49 If any gentleman present has got a cow here with him, and I can borrow a clothes-wringer, I will show you whether I can milk a cow or not. **1893** M. Philips *Making of Newspaper* 98 The clerk ran the despatch through a copying-press resembling a clothes-wringer.

+Clothes yard. A plot of ground devoted to the drying of clothes.

1856 M. J. HOLMES *Rice Corner* vi, I suspected nothing when Sally's white dress was bleached on the grass in the clothesyard for nearly a week. **1859** STOWE *Minister's Wooing* xxv, Mrs. Scudder was . . . sprinkling some linen, which was laid out to bleach on the green turf of the clothesyard. **1866** A. D. WHITNEY *L. Goldthwaite* iii, The windows looked out from one side into a village street, and from the other into stable and clothes yards!

***Clothier.**

***1.** One who makes cloth. *Obs.*

1707–8 *Boston Rec.* 48 The Land of Daniel Eppes of Boston aforesaid Clothier. **1714** *Boston News-Letter* 1 Feb. 2/2 Jeremiah Jackson Cloathier and Stuffe Weaver has set up his Trade of Weaving, Dying, and Pressing. **1780** *N.J. Archives* 2 Ser. IV. 554 Wool-combing is performed at the clothiers shop of Abraham Fairchild.

+2. A fuller; one whose occupation is to cleanse and thicken cloth. *Obs.*

1751 Chalkley *Scotch-Irish Settlement Va.* I. 45 Joseph Love, clothier, has leave to build a fulling mill on Roan Oak. **1806** WEBSTER 54/1 *Clothier,* one who fulls and scours cloths. **1816** PICKERING 64 Although we use *clothier* for *fuller,* yet the place, where the cloth is cleansed and dressed, is called a fulling-mill.

+3. *Clothier general,* formerly an officer in the Continental and U.S. Army, a quartermaster general. Hence *Clothier's department.*

1777 *Jrnls. Cont. Congress* VIII. 426 *Resolved,* That the clothier general furnish each non-commissioned officer and soldier . . . with the articles of cloathing enumerated by a resolution of Congress. **1778** *Ib.* X. 23 *Resolved,* That the cloathier general be directed to deliver . . . as much linen and as many blankets as can be spared. — **1797** *Ann. 5th Congress* 704 All persons having unliquidated claims against the United States, pertaining to the . . . Hospital, Clothier's, or Marine Department, should exhibit particular abstracts of such claims.

***Clothing.** Also **†cloathing.** Attrib. with *card, contract, department*, etc.

1863 Moore *Women of War* 442 When a soldier brings me a clothing card, I refer him to the agent of his division. **1877** *Rep. Indian Affairs* 5 So that competitors for clothing-contracts might know in advance precisely what kinds of garments would be wanted for the Indian service. **1778** *Jrnls. Cont. Congress* X. 10 The committee on the Cloathing Department beg Leave further to report. **1866** RICHARDSON *Secret Service* 365 At that early hour, the clothing dépôt of the Confederate government was surrounded. **1861** *Vanity Fair* 9 March 120/1 Everybody is rushing to the Apollo Clothing Emporium, 2006 Broadway. **1874** PINKERTON *Expressman & Detective* 136 Here she went into a large building occupied by an extensive wholesale clothing establishment. **1835** LONGSTREET *Ga. Scenes* 13 Davy Moore, went [*i.e.*, danced] like a suit of clothes upon a clothing line on a windy day. **1867** *Atlantic Mo.* May 530/1 He placed his little engine in one of the rooms of the Quincy Hall Clothing Manufactory, and . . . offered to sew up any seam that might be brought to him. **1847** H. HOWE *Hist. Coll. Ohio* 238 Findlay . . . contains . . . 1 clothing, 1 flouring and 1 grist mill. **1865** *Atlantic Mo.* XV. 176 Clothing-shops and other establishments went into operation. **1869** *Rep. Comm. Agric.* 7 A sufficiency of most grades of clothing wools has been produced at home and sold at lower prices than . . . foreign wools.

Clothing dummy. A figure on which clothing is displayed. — **1887** *Courier-Journal* 11 Feb. 6/6 Kleinhaus & Simonson Fined Twenty Dollars For Obstructing the Sidewalk With Clothing Dummies.

Clothing house. A place where clothing is made or sold. Also attrib. — **1883** HOWELLS *Woman's Reason* xxi, Kimball found a place as night watchman in a large clothing-house, where he distinguished himself . . . by quelling a panic among the sewing-girls. **1887** *Courier-Journal* 6 Feb. 5/3 The following notice has been posted in the offices and cutting-rooms of the clothing-houses. **1912** IRWIN *Red Button* 6 That fellow would do for a clothing house ad.

+Clothing store. An establishment at which clothes are retailed or made.

1829 B. HALL *Travels in N.A.* I. 18, I amused myself one morning by noting down a few of the signs over the shop doors. . . . Flour and feed store—Cheap Store—Clothing Store—[etc.]. **1837** *S. Lit. Messenger* III. 687 Detroit has an over proportion of clothing stores. **1865** *Atlantic Mo.* XV. 616 The clothing-store . . . paying so little that every tailor's working woman seeks . . . opportunity of changing her employment. **1873** BAILEY *Life in Danbury* 242 If a new clothing store doesn't soon make its appearance we fear some of our citizens will become naked. **1880** 'MARK TWAIN' *Tramp Abroad* xlviii. 556 In the vestibule of what seemed to be a clothing store, we saw eight or ten wooden dummies grouped together. **1898** CAHAN *Imported Bridegroom* 48 He did not go directly to his residence, but first took his importation into a large 'clothing and gents' furnishing store' on Broadway.

attrib. **1869** 'MARK TWAIN' *Innocents* xxvi. 278 The clothing-store merchant wished to consume the corner-grocery man with envy.

***Cloth-worker.** One who makes or dresses cloth. — **1681** *Boston Rec.* 71 Stephen Feilder, tallow-chandler, became surety to the town for John Hickes, cloth worker. **1891** CHASE & CLOW *Industry* II. 41 Teazels befriend the cloth-workers, who would be at a standstill without them.

Clotweed. The clotbur. {1804-} — **1791** MUHLENBERG *Index Florae* 180 *Xanthium strumarium*, Clott-weed. **1861** WOOD *Botany* 444 Clot-weed. . . . Sterile, in globous heads; scales distinct, in one row.

***Cloud,** *n.*

+1. *fig.* The shadow of war, strife, or violence.

1777 *Virginia State P.* I. 292 The Dragging Canoe in some part of the Treaty said . . . that there was a dark cloud over that country. **1778** *Ib.* I. 315 What did you understand by the Expression of the Indians at the Treaty 'that a black cloud hung over the Country they were selling said Henderson.' *Ib.*, Was the Metaphor Black Cloud ever interpreted to relate to the Cherokees' right to the soil in that Country? Answer, No.

2. A light knitted shawl or scarf. {*a*1877-}

1875 STOWE *We & Neighbors* 87 Eva . . . snatched from the hat-tree a shawl and a little morsel of white, fleecy worsted, which the initiated surname 'a cloud,' and tied it over her head. **1879** TAYLOR *Summer-Savory* 212 You have seen that apron flung over its owner's head like 'the knitted cloud' of modern times, when she went to the next neighbors. **1922** A. BROWN *Old Crow* 207 Charlotte appeared, done up in an old-fashioned shawl and . . . a nondescript knitted thing, old-fashioned when he was a child. 'A cloud,' he said to himself. 'That's what they called the thing.'

***Cloud,** *v.*

+1. *To cloud over*, to become overcast or cloudy. Also fig.

1758 *Essex Inst. Coll.* XVIII. 187 A very pleasant morn but Clouds over after noon. **1807** GASS *Journal* 171 In the evening it clouded over and rained again. **1885** JEWETT *Marsh Island* ii. 13, I thought it seemed clouded over a while ago. **1909** WARE *Passing English* 80/1 *Clouded over* (American), overwhelmed by misfortune.

+2. *To cloud up*, to become cloudy.

1758 *Essex Inst. Coll.* XVIII. 101 At Night [it] Clouded up. **1775** *Ib.* XLVIII. 52 It clouded up and it rained som. **1804** CLARK in *Lewis & C. Exped.* (1904) I. 205 Wind Shifted to the S.W. about 11 o Clock and blew hard until 3 o Clk. clouded up. **1848** BRYANT *Calif.* (1849) 29 Although the morning was fine and pleasant, it clouded up before eight o'clock and commenced raining. **1883** 'MARK TWAIN' *Life on Miss.* iii, It begun to cloud up again.

***Cloudberry.** The knotberry or mountain bramble. — **1781-2** JEFFERSON *Notes Va.* (1788) 37 Cloudberries. *Rubus chamaemorus.* **1801** *Hist. Review & Directory* I. 147 Plants and Vegetables, with . . . the popular Names . . . [include] Cloud-berries, *Rubus chamœmorus.* **1894** TORREY *Fla. Sketch-Book* 29 The cloudberry, which once . . . I had found on the summit of Mount Clinton, in New Hampshire, and refused to believe a *Rubus.*

+Cloudburst. A violent and heavy fall of rain.

[*a*1817 DWIGHT *Travels* III. 249 This deluge, which they call the bursting of a cloud, took place in Oct. 1784.] **1872** *Amer. Naturalist* VI. 71 In the mountains there are 'cloud bursts,' when the rains fall in a cataract, and filling the gulches sweep every thing before them. **1886** *Amer. Meteor. Jrnl.* II. 556 The following is an account of an Oregon cloud-burst. **1890** CUSTER *Following Guidon* 297 Fearing another cloud-burst, tents were sent . . . to the divide that sloped gradually from the stream, and we slept there. **1905** *N.Y. Ev. Post* 4 Sept. 1 A cloudburst occurred in that village last night. Water flowed in the streets to the depth of four feet.

Clouting diaper. *Obs.* Cloth for making babies' diapers. — **1733** *S.C. Gazette* 282/1 Just Imported, and to be Sold . . . , platillas and clouting diaper. **1754** *Ib.* 20-27 June 2/2 Archibald & Richard Park Stobo Have just imported . . . napkining and clouting diapers, fringed diaper and damask table cloths.

+Clove. *local.* [Du. *klove.*] A ravine, cleft, gap, etc.

1777 *N.J. Archives* 2 Ser. I. 433 The other Part [of Washington's army is] to be commanded by Mr. Green, at the Clove, and Parts adjacent. **1828** WEBSTER, *Clove.* . . . This word, though properly an appellative, is not often used as such in English; but it is appropriated to particular places, that are real clefts, or which appear as such; as the Clove of Kaaterskill, in the state of New-York, and the Stony Clove. It is properly a Dutch word. **1883** *Harper's Mag.* Sept. 528 The Cloves are many [in the Catskills], and I think that known as the Platterkill is the wildest. . . . Eighteen water-falls may be counted in a walk up this Clove. **1896** *Dialect Notes* I. 414 *Clove*, a narrow gap or valley, =*notch* in N.E. **1911** *N.Y. Ev. Post* 15 March 6 The village of Winnesook, with its clove and cross-clove, suggests a hamlet at the foot of the Catskills.

attrib. **1821** *Niles' Reg.* XXI. 29 The Falls [in the Catskill Mts.], the Clove Passage, the view from the Pine Orchard, . . . are objects worthy of regard. **1884** ROOSEVELT *Amer. Backlogs* 16 Twenty long miles lay between us and our destination, including . . . passing through a steep and precipitous canyon, or 'clove-road' as it was called in the vernacular.

+Clove currant. *local.* A sweet-scented, ornamental currant, *Ribes odoratum.* — **1892** *Amer. Folk-Lore* V. 96 *Ribes aureum*, flowering currant. General. Clove currant. Cambridge, Mass.

Clove pink. A pink (*Dianthus caryophyllus*), having flowers that smell like cloves. {1837-} — **1857** GRAY *Botany* 54 *Dianthus Caryophyllus* is the original of the Clove-Pink or Carnation, &c. of the gardens. **1880** ALDRICH *Stillwater Tragedy* 90 An empty camphor vial on Richard's desk had always a clove pink . . . stuck into it. **1883** *Century Mag.* July 419/2 Here sit the flower *marchandes*, making bouquets of jasmines and roses, clove-pinks, violets, and lady-slippers.

***Clover.**

***1.** A low herb of the genus *Trifolium*, of which there are many native and cultivated species (the former chiefly west of the Rocky Mountains, the latter introduced from Europe), valuable as forage plants. (Cf. ALSIKE, BUFFALO CLOVER, etc.)

1724 JONES *Virginia* 41 The Blades and Tops [of Indian corn] are excellent Fodder, when well cured, which is commonly used though many raise good clover and Oats. **1804** J. ROBERTS *Penna. Farmer* 11 Green crops of turnips, buckwheat, clover or any other succulent grasses, . . . greatly enrich such soils. **1863** [see sense 2]. **1898** HALL *Aunt Jane* 4 For it was June in Kentucky, and clover and blue-grass were running sweet riot over the face of the earth.

2. Attrib. and comb. with *bloom, bottom, chaff, crop*, etc.

1856 WHITTIER *Last Walk in Autumn* 46 What airs outblown from ferny dells, And clover-bloom and sweet-brier smells. **1751** GIST *Journals* 42 All the Way from Licking Creek to this Place is fine rich level Land, with large Meadows, fine Clover Bottoms & spacious Plains. **1863** RANDALL *Pract. Shepherd* 244 Clover chaff . . . is, what is left of clover after thrashing or hulling—a black, unpromising looking mass. **1862** *Rep. Comm. Patents: Agric.* 271 The clover crop should be pastured but lightly. **1840** EMERSON *Woodnotes* I. 102 The wind . . . may blow north, it still is warm; . . . Or east, it smells like a clover-farm. **1871** WHITTIER *Singer* 20 A memory haunted all her words Of clover-fields and singing birds. **1870** *Rep. Comm. Agric. 1869* 37 Such restorative agencies as clover-growing, green-manuring, fertilizing. **1862** *Rep. Comm. Patents: Agric. 1861* 642 Harvesters, Clover, [invented by] David Hinkle, New Pittsburg, Ohio. **1771** *Carroll P.* in *Md. Hist. Mag.* XIV. 132 The Clover Lay at Heesons about 24[a] which is all the Wheat ground w[hic]h Remains to be sowed. **1882** *Amer. Naturalist* XVI. 248 Further notes on the imported Clover-leaf Weevil (*Phytonomus punctatus*). **1883** MACON *Uncle Gabe Tucker* 58 When you kick up a bumler-bee nes' in de clover-paster, . . . you better . . . take de nighes' paf to de woods. **1904** LOVETT *R. Gresham* 17 Seen the old bumblers goin' into Stacy's Clover patch last summer, 'n folleyed 'em to their stump. **1852** *Mich. Agric. Soc. Trans.* III. 170 The field lay in clover sod. **1862** *Rep. Comm. Patents: Agric.* 639 Clover-stripper and Hay-rake, Combined [invented by] R. H. Blair and A. W. Beatty, Saltsburg, Pa. **1856** *Ib.* 172 The best method of cultivating clover-stubble, or sod-land, is to break it in the fall or winter, and cross-plough in the spring. *Ib.* 179 A Timothy or clover sward, which has been mown for several successive years, is selected. **1791** J. BREVARD *MS. Diary* 16 Aug. (N.C. Univ.), A pretty even sloping piece of ground improved with gravel & clover walks. **1868** *Rep. Comm. Agric.* 73 Mr. Riley also gives an account and figures of the clover worm, *Asopia costalis.*

+**Clover-eater.** *S.W.* A Virginian. — **1869** *Overland Mo.* III. 129 For no particular reason that I am aware of, a Virginian is styled a 'Clover-eater.'

Clover field. A field in which clover grows.

1848 IRVING *Knickerb.* (rev. ed.) IV. i, As some sleek ox, sunk in the rich repose of a clover-field, . . . will bear repeated blows before it raises itself, [etc.]. **1863** MITCHELL *My Farm* 232 [The young farmer] has hardly seen his lime dumped upon his clover-field. **1907** ANDREWS *Recoll.* 149 By Tuesday we were in camp . . . on a clover field five miles south of Louisville. **1912** N. M. WOODROW *Sally Salt* 30 They started together across a clover-field.

Clover hay. Hay made of clover.

1748 ELIOT *Field-Husb.* i. 12 He that raiseth Clover Hay, need not be afraid of the expense of Seed. **1843** 'CARLTON' *New Purchase* I. 27 The tea, was a perfect imitation of a decoction of clover hay, with which in boyhood we nursed the tender little calves. **1847** *Rep. Comm. Patents* 376 Our farmers . . . secure large crops of clover hay. **1888** *Vt. Agric. Rep.* X. 51 Roots should . . . be fed . . . with good early-cut or clover hay.

Clover hay worm. 'The larva of the pyralid moth, *Asopia costalis* (Fabricius). It occurs all over the United States . . . , and was probably brought from Europe' (*Cent.*).

Cloverhead. The bloom of the clover plant. — **1842** *Knickerb.* XIX. 433 The mower reaps the tall clover-heads in the meadow. **1859** STOWE *Minister's Wooing* xxxiv, Cerinthy turned quickly away, and began reaching passionately after clover-heads. **1867** EDWARDS *Shelby* 149 Over the cloverheads dewy and sheen . . . the weird waltzers held their voluptuous carnival.

+**Clover-huller.** A machine for freeing clover seed from the hull. — **1841** C. CIST *Cincinnati* (*advt.*), Agricultural Machinery, . . . including . . . Clover Hullers. **1853** *Mich. Agric. Soc. Trans.* IV. 35 A. O. Holmes, Tecumseh, clover huller. **1854** *Penna. Agric. Rep.* 80 William Kirkpatrick, Lancaster city, . . . 1 clover huller and cleaner.

Clover seed. The seed of the clover plant. — **1723** *Weekly Mercury* 7 March 2/2 Very good Red Clover-Seed, at 12*d.* per Pound, or 10*s.* per Dozen. **1868** *Mich. Agric. Rep.* VII. 271 More nitrogen is left after clover-seed than after hay, which accounts for wheat yielding a better crop after clover-seed than after hay.

attrib. Ib. 346 W. A. Pettingill, Inkster, [exhibited a] combined clover seed thresher and separator.

+**Clover tea.** (See quotation.) — **1841** CIST *Cincinnati* 166 Clover tea, . . . under the name of Pouchong, &c. is now the fashionable article of modern times.

* **Club,** *n.*

1. An Indian tomahawk or war club.

1634 *Relation Md.* 37 They also use in Warres, a short club of a cubite long, which they call a Tomahawk. **1684** *N.H. Hist. Soc. Coll.* VIII. 220 One of the company did strike him with a club over the head. **1819** *Amer. Antiq. Soc. Coll.* I. 280 War is always determined on by the head warriour of the town. . . . He lifts the war hatchet or club. **1856** GLISAN *Jrnl. Army Life* 342 The Indians here (who have no guns) were to pitch in with their knives and clubs.

2. A knot in which men's hair was worn in the late 18th c. {1785–}

1791 *Mass. Mag.* III. 221 What would become of the ladies' bishops and cushions, and of the clubs and tight breeches of our bucks? **1828** NEAL *R. Dyer* 167 He shook his black hair loose, and parted it on his forehead and twisted it into a club, and bound it up hastily after the fashion of the tribe. **1856** R. W. GRISWOLD *Republican Court* 53 His hair is turned back from his forehead, powdered, and collected in a club behind. **1889** CABLE in *Century Mag.* Feb. 513/2 Although it was impossible for us to work up a club and pigeon wings . . . we arranged a very fine queue wrapped with a black ribbon.

3. An association for social or cultural purposes. {1648–} See also BOOK-CLUB.

1689 SEWALL *Diary* I. 265 Treated John Rawson at the Clubb to day. **1722** *New-England Courant* 22 Jan., The young wretch . . . calls those who wrote the several pieces in the Courant the Hell-Fire Club of Boston. **1865** *Nation* I. 12 Our other chief cities are following the lead of New York, and the club may now be considered a recognized feature of American town life. **1883** *Century Mag.* May 156/1 It has had for ten years or more its Shakspere Club, under most competent leadership.

b. A group interested in some form of athletics. {cricket club, 1755–}

1833 *Knickerb.* I. 147 Like one of the young gentlemen of the boat club. **1855** (*title*), Atlantic Base Ball Club, Jamaica, N.Y. **1868** CHADWICK *Base Ball* 105, I would suggest to clubs making tours in the West to give Chicago a wide berth. **1873** BAILEY *Life in Danbury* 143 It afterward transpired that the grand cripple was the captain of a champion base-ball club. **1895** *Outing* XXVI. 474/1 The officers of the 4th Cavalry, stationed at Fort Walla Walla, Washington, will be honored in future histories of polo as the founders of the first regular regimental club. **1897** *Ib.* XXX. 346/2 The New York Athletic Club, and similar institutions, might satisfy the needs of the metropolitan cyclers. **1912** MATHEWSON *Pitching* 25 Why can certain pitchers always beat certain clubs and why do they look like bush leaguers against others?

+**4.** The bill for the beverages of a meal, as distinct from the food. *Obs.*

1793 *Mass. H. S. Coll.* 3 Ser. V. 111 Care is also taken to keep out of your way small beer and cider, so that your club at dinner amounts to more than the dinner itself. **1799** BROWN *A. Mervyn* iii, 'Tis our custom to charge dinner and club; but, as you drank nothing, we'll let the club go.

+**5.** A clump (of trees).

1836 EDWARD *Hist. Texas* 36 We find . . . one solid prairie . . . intersected . . . with variegated clubs of timber.

6. Attrib. (esp. in senses 3 and 3 b) with *bill, boat, cane, day,* etc.

1904 *McClure's Mag.* Feb. 381/2 'Winning girls' hearts isn't as much fun then?' she said. 'Well, you can't spend them,' I said. 'They won't pay your club bills.' **1838** *N.Y. Advertiser & Exp.* 28 March 3/1 The houses were occupied . . . by Mr. Seaman, the well known builder of club boats. **1790** MACLAY *Deb. Senate* 231 This was mess or club day. I went and stayed till the fumigation began, *alias* smoking of cigars. **1883** *Wheelman* I. 476/2 The first thing on the programme was a club-drill, well executed by eight members of the club. **1883** *Harper's Mag.* Sept. 632/1 The elderly club dude may lament the decay of the good old code of honor. **1880** *Ib.* July 212/2 It was thought useless to dig for water on the club grounds. **1898** P. L. FORD *Tattle-Tales* 87 He is charming, of course, but—well —he is such a club habitué. **1883** *Wheelman* I. 412 Club-life, in our modern society, is, apparently, a necessary element. **1868** CHADWICK *Base Ball* 42 Out-fielders.—There are three out-fielders in a club nine, viz., the left, center, and right fielders. **1898** *Kansas City Star* 18 Dec. 3/1 Chicago is willing to give Dahlen in exchange, a proposition acceptable to the Gotham club owner. **1883** *Wheelman* I. 352 The club quartette sang our club songs. **1883** *Ib.* 294 The fixture committee of the Boston Bicycle Club arranged for a hundred-mile club-run. **1923** WATTS *L. Nichols* 20 Club-stewards bought so liberally, it was wise to 'throw off' for them. **1887** *Lippincott's Mag.* Aug. 290 The boys are going to their eating-clubs to get breakfast. As there is no 'Memorial Hall' or college dining-room at Yale, the 'club system' is maintained by most of the students, rather from necessity than from choice.

* **Club,** *v.*

1. *tr.* To grasp or use a pistol, musket, etc., as a club. {1843–}

1758 *Essex Inst. Coll.* XVIII. 113 Ye Reg[imen]t of Royal Hunters Clubbed Muskets and were marching out of ye Camp. **1792** *Affecting Hist. F. Manheim* 5 He . . . clubbed his firelock. **1824** MARSHALL *Kentucky* II. 134 Logsdon then clubbed his empty gun, and gave the Indian a blow, which occasioned him to retreat. **1860** CLAIBORNE *Sam. Dale* 123 As quick as lightning, he clubbed it [a rifle], and aimed at me a furious blow.

+**2.** (See quotation.) *Obs.*

*a***1752** W. DOUGLASS *Brit. Settlem. N. Amer.* (1755) II. 280 People [were] forceably turned out of the possession of their lands, this they call clubing them out.

3. *To club together*, to combine resources. {1889–}

1840 DANA *Two Years* xxvi, Several of us clubbed together and bought a large piece of twilled cotton. **1855** BARNUM *Life* 107 We frequently clubbed together and bid off a lot which being divided between us, gave each about the quantity he desired. **1860** MORDECAI *Virginia* 232 As the fee for such a composition was equal to several days' pay, two or more members from counties remote from each other would club together for a circular. **1870** 'MARK TWAIN' *Sk., Widow's Protest*, They clubbed together and fixed him up as a sutler. **1879** *Scribner's Mo.* Nov. 135/1 The smaller farmers secure all these advantages readily by clubbing together.

Clubbing. +Subscription to a periodical by each of a group of people, or to a group of magazines by a single subscriber, at a reduced rate. Also attrib. — **1856** G. H. DERBY *Phoenixiana* 123 Inducements For Clubbing. Twenty copies furnished for one year, for fifty cents. **1880** *Boston Journal Chem.* (*O.E.D.*), The clubbing price of any American or foreign periodical not on the list will be furnished on application. **1907** *Pearson's Mag.* Jan. Contents-page, The face value of a subscription bill may be applied to any combination or clubbing offer advertised.

Club dinner. A dinner for, or at, a club. {1855–} — **1830** S. BRECK in *Recollections* 208 He ordered that respectable innkeeper to have an extra club-dinner for the next Thursday. **1837–48** B. D. WALSH *Aristoph.* 114 (*note*), A club-dinner, it appears, was an ordinary affair. **1883** *Century Mag.* July 397 The club dinners, the drives, . . . were dependent on his services to the Ring. **1892** *Harper's Mag.* Dec. 162 A big club dinner, with . . . every . . . Christmas dish known to culinary science.

Clubhouse. A house occupied by a club. {*a*1845–}

1865 *Atlantic Mo.* XV. 366 In the larger cities of the East . . . the exhibition, the club-house, the social assembly, . . . take from the lecture audiences the class that furnishes the best material in the smaller cities. **1884** 'CRADDOCK' *Where Battle Was Fought* 28 Marston boasted no club-houses. **1892** *Courier-Journal* 2 Oct. 2/2 At Miller's club-house, . . . Charles Johnson . . . shot and instantly killed Jacob App. **1901** *N. Amer.*

Rev. Feb. 2 (*advt.*), The building of the club-house was a victory over financial obstacles. **1925** *Scribner's Mag.* Oct. 358/2 The Charlotte Cushman Club in Philadelphia has a club-house for young actresses which, in a single year, accommodates over twelve hundred girls.
attrib. **1894** *Vt. Agric. Rep.* XIV. 25 The 'club house' cheese is purely an American production.

* **Club moss.** Any of several species of the genus *Lycopodium*, properly *L. clavatum*, which has upright clublike spikes of spore cases.
1791 MUHLENBERG *Index Florae* 183 *Lycopodium.* Club-moss. **1843** TORREY *Flora N.Y.* II. 510 *Lycopodium clavatum.* ... Common clubmoss. ... Dry woods: frequent in the interior of the State, but rare near New-York. **1894** CLARK *On Cloud Mt.* 64 Behind some rocks where she knew a tiny spring welled forth and thick club-mosses grew. **1905** *Bureau of Forestry Bul.* No. 60, 14 The ground cover is chiefly partridge berry, club moss, wood sorrel, ferns, and mosses.

Club-raiser. One who induces a group or club to subscribe to a newspaper or magazine. — **1872** *Newton Kansan* 26 Sept. 4/5 If agents and club-raisers want to make it 'pay,' try this. **1887** *Courier-Journal* 2 Feb. 3/6 Weekly, to clubs of eight, with extra copy to club-raiser (nine copies one year). ... $8.00.

Club-room. A room in which the members of a club meet. {*c*1712– (*Spectator*)} Also attrib.
1727 Buckingham *Newspaper Lit.* I. 98 Dr. H— R. ... has attained to a considerable Perfection in the Art of Painting, ... Having obliged our Club-Room, with the Draught of a Beau, a clown and a Coquet. **1788** FRENEAU *Misc. Works* 100 An exact and minute map of the town is ordered to be ... hung up in the club room for the use of the members in general. **1850** MITCHELL *Lorgnette* I. 224 Merit is reckoned by the club-room babble and the newspaper 'item.' **1868** CHANNING *Recoll. Newport* 211 An attack upon their club room was instantly agreed upon. **1872** *Harper's Mag.* XLVI. 95 Many of these establishments had club-rooms attached, where members of Congress and others amused themselves with brag, vingt-et-un, and whist. **1905** DAVIS *Northerner* 53 Falls's manager had sent in bills to the various guilds and church societies for lighting the churches and club-rooms, and meeting-halls of all kinds.

Club rush. A plant of the genus *Scirpus;* a bulrush. {1677–} — **1817–8** EATON *Botany* (1822) 450 *Scirpus tenuis,* Club-rush, ... [grows] in wet places. **1843** TORREY *Flora N.Y.* II. 355 *Scirpus atrovirens.* ... Dark Green Clubrush. ... Wet meadows and swamps: common. **1857** GRAY *Botany* 498 *Scirpus.* Bulrush. Club-Rush. *Ib.* 500 *S. maritimus.* (Sea Club-Rush.) ... Salt marshes; common on the coast. *Ib., S. fluviatilis.* (River Club-Rush.) ... Borders of lakes and large streams, W. New York to Wisconsin and Illinois.

+**Club shoe.** A coarse, heavy shoe. — **1830** ROYALL *Lett. from Ala.* 175 [They] come running into the Rotunda with their muddy club shoes.

+**Club skates.** [?N.Y. *Club* skate.] Skates that may be fastened to ordinary shoes; clamp skates. — **1868** *Mich. Agric. Rep.* VII. 356 E. T. Barnum, Detroit, [exhibited a] display of club skates. **1887** *Courier-Journal* 5 Jan. 6/3 As to the ponds, they are filled with people from the type of grace and beauty displayed in the cut above, fitted out with seal-skin cap and the latest club skates, to the urchin who ties his runners on with a string.

+**Club squash.** A kind of squash. — **1817–8** EATON *Botany* (1822) 257 *Cucurbita verrucosa,* club squash. E[xotic]. **1840** DEWEY *Mass. Flowering Plants* 112 Club Squash. From the Levant. **1854** *Penna. Agric. Rep.* 206 David S. Hoffman, for one club squash.

+**Clubtail.** *local.* (See quotation.) — **1842** *Nat. Hist. N.Y., Zoology* IV. 257 The American Shad. *Alosa praestabilis.* ... On the coast of Carolina, the fatter ones have the tail swollen, and are called Club-tails.

+**Club wheat.** A variety of wheat having short, thick spikes, *Triticum compactum.* — **1849** EMMONS *Agric. N.Y.* II. 142 Club wheat, Pennsylvania Wheat. ... Heads short. **1849** *Rep. Comm. Pat.: Agric.* 181 The club wheat, which has a remarkably stiff straw. **1861** *Ill. Agric. Soc. Trans.* IV. 317 A neighbor tried shrunk club wheat for seed.

+**Club woman.** A woman who is a member of a club; esp. one who is active in club work. — **1895** S. HALE *Letters* 294 She ... is a 'club-woman,'—and she early secured me to 'attend a meeting' of her club. **1906** *New Eng. Mag.* n.s. XXXIV. 627 If the American club woman is wicked, she knows it.

Cluck, *n.* {1703–} A sharp sucking sound formed between the tongue and palate. Also transf.
1846 THORPE *Myst. Backwoods* 65 [The turkey-hunter] takes his 'call,' and gives one solitary cluck, so exquisitely, that it chimes in with the running brook and the rustling leaf. **1878** TAYLOR *Between Gates* 213 With a little cluck of satisfaction she munched a sandwich. **1880** TOURGEE *Invisible Empire* 397 The peculiar clucks which were used by them [the Ku-Klux-Klan] as a signal. **1897** *Outing* XXX. 112/2 The team [of horses], if properly trained, will start without a 'cluck,' or any such phrase as 'Come up,' 'Pull up,' etc. **1904** GLASGOW *Deliverance* 5 He gave an insinuating cluck to the horses.

Cluck, *v. intr.* To utter a cluck as encouragement to a horse. — **1896** O. READ *Jucklins* 24 'You are a stranger in North Caroliny,' he said when he had clucked to his horses. **1898** WESTCOTT *D. Harum* 11, I clucked an' gitapp'd, an' finely took the gad to him a little.

* **Clump.**

+**1.** A group *of* houses.
1870 HAWTHORNE *Eng. Note-Books* I. 121 The clump of village houses. **1898** PAGE *Red Rock* 519 The two rescuers ... dismounted behind a clump of buildings.

2. A heavy, cumbrous ship or vessel. Hence *clump-built.* Also attrib.
1808 *Columbian Centinel* 17 Feb. 3/1 A clump black looking brig, ashore, with her foremast gone, was seen 9th inst. **1830** S. BRECK in *Recollections* 139 Our brig was a clump, and made but small way. — **1809** IRVING *Knickerb.* VI. v, The mariners are busily prepared, hoisting the sails of yon top sail schooner, and those two clump built Albany sloops.

Clumpers. Coarse heavy shoes. {1830–54, *dial.*} — **1845** *Knickerb.* XXVI. 417 Stilton made me ten pairs of 'clumpers.' **1859** ELWYN *Glossary* 32 *Clumpers,* very thick and heavy shoes. We used the word, as boys, in the above sense. Shoes with thick soles we called a 'real pair of clumpers.

+**Clumsy-cleat.** (See quotation.) — **1874** C. M. SCAMMON *Marine Mammals* 224 About three feet from the stern is the 'clumsy-cleet,' a stout thwart with a rounded notch on the after side, in which the officer or boat-steerer braces himself by one leg against the violent motion of the boat, caused by ... the efforts of the whale while being 'worked upon.'

‖**Clunce,** *v.* (See quotation.) — **1781** *Md. Hist. Mag.* V. 124 We took it in, but not being acquainted with carrying that article [corn], never 'clunced the ceiling,' that is stopped the cracks to prevent the corn from getting to the pumps.

Cluster, *n.* A group of buildings or huts. — **1827** SHERWOOD *Gaz. Georgia* 31 Bedford [is] a cluster of houses 3 miles N.W. [of] Augusta. **1842** HITCHCOCK *Journal* 104 Riding back with Mr. Hill he showed me a cluster of log huts where he said a family of Natchez Indians lived.

* **Cluster,** *a.*

1. In names of plants having bunched fruit, flowers, etc.
1765 J. BARTRAM *Journal* 9 'Tis diverting to observe the ... live oaks, chinqua-pines and cluster-berry all of an uncommon size. **1867** J. MELINE *Santa Fé & Back* 45 On one side, miles of the diminutive sunflower thickly intermingled with the cluster-lily, making a combination of purple and gold. **1835** HOFFMAN *Winter in West* I. 144, I thought of ... the clumps of cluster-roses that here [in Mich. Territory] grow wild and cover whole acres.

+**2.** With *diamond, pin, ring,* in sense: Having precious stones set in a cluster.
1872 'MARK TWAIN' *Roughing It* xlviii. 339 The cheapest and easiest way to become an influential man ... was to stand behind a bar, wear a cluster-diamond pin, [etc.]. **1873** 'MARK TWAIN' & WARNER *Gilded Age* 301 He wore a diamond cluster-pin and he parted his hair behind. *a*1906 'O. HENRY' *Trimmed Lamp,* etc. 173 She wore a cluster ring of huge imitation rubies.

Clustered millet grass. Any of various grasses of the genus *Milium.* — **1829** EATON *Botany* (ed. 5) 331 *Piptatherum racemosum,* clustered millet-grass. **1839** *Mich. Agric. Soc. Trans.* VII. 414 *Piptatherum nigrum,* Clustered millet-grass.

Cluster grape. A small wild grape that grows in clusters. {1664–} — **1737** WESLEY *Journal* I. 402 The cluster-grape is of a harsh taste too, and about the size of a white currant. **1765** R. ROGERS *Acc. N. America* 138 On these lands are found the black mulberry, the American cherry, fox and cluster grapes, as they are called by the inhabitants [of South Carolina]. **1800** HAWKINS *Sk. Creek Country* 24 The small cluster grapes of the hills is destroyed by fire.

Clutter, *n.* Disorder; litter. *colloq.* {1694–} — **1859** ELWYN *Glossary* 33 *Clutter,* for *confusion.* The things are all in a clutter. **1893** S. HALE *Letters* 284 Oh! those mornings! ... making myself the coffee, sweeping the red room, in a royal clutter. **1924** *Scribner's Mag.* Dec. 635/2 The necessity of living 'all in a clutter' makes a self-respecting family unwilling to have strangers come into the home.
transf. **1891** *Harper's Mag.* Nov. 881/2 A tiny clutter of frame houses and tents. **1912** COBB *Back Home* 263 They passed a clutter of negro cabins clustering about a little doggery.

Clutter, *v. tr.* To throw into confusion; to fill (a place) with odds and ends. Freq. with *up.* {1674–}
1832 PAULDING *Westward Ho!* I. 185 The Garbroth people are cluttering up the country. **1859** BARTLETT 89 To *Clutter up,* to crowd together in disorder, to fill with things in confusion; as, 'to clutter up a room.' **1888** *Sturdy Oak* (Boston) May (F.), There's plenty of room; but if this gentleman be hunting minerals, there'll be a nice pair to clutter up.
fig. **1888** *Detroit Free Press,* I've seed strange things in my time, but this clutters me!

‖**Clutterbuck.** A term of derision or contempt. — **1887** *Courier-Journal* 24 Jan. 4/3 The difference between a wide-awake city at the head of the procession and a sleepy-headed old clutter buck which stumbles along at the tail end.

Cluttered, *ppl. a.* Crowded, full of confusion, choked up. *colloq.* {1685–}
1854 THOREAU *Walden* 99 The nation itself ... is just such an unwieldy and overgrown establishment, cluttered with furniture. **1865** *Commonwealth* (Boston) 11 March, A little dingy room, cluttered with pots, kettles, tables and chairs. **1867–8** *Ill. Agric. Soc. Trans.* VII. 573 The slovenly, cluttered up appearance that characterizes Western habitations. **1922** TITUS *Timber* 75 At a cluttered desk sat an old man.

Clydes(dale). [*Clydesdale,* Scotland.] A breed of horses suitable for drawing heavy loads. {1831–} — **1893** CURTIS *Horses* 24 Description ... of Modern Clydesdale: Color, either bay, brown or black, with usually a white strip in the face, [etc.]. **1894** *Vt. Agric. Rep.* XIV. 100 The

Percherons . . . are . . . quicker than the Clydes and have not so much hair on the legs.

Co. Abbreviation of COMPANY. Also in phrases *in Co., and Co.*

This abbrev. is often spoken [ko] in England, but the word is generally pronounced in full in America.

1789 *Boston Directory* 200 Thomas, Isaiah, and Co. printers & booksellers. **1816** U. BROWN *Journal* II. 228 Lemuel Howard . . . or any of their Lovely Fraternity & Co. **1838** 'TEXIAN' *Mexico v. Texas* 11 Two foreign physicians, the one a Frenchman, the other an American, exercised the healing art in Co. **1850** KINGSLEY *Diary* 130 The Co worked some at floating down logs for the dam. **1865** R. H. KELLOGG *Rebel Prisons* 198 He belonged to Co. A, of the 52d N.Y. Reg't. **1888** *Nation* 5 July 3/2 In the case of Newfoundland Messrs. Frye, Tugalls & Co. consider the claim presumptuous.

* **Coach.**

* **1.** A large carriage.

[**1613** *N.E. Hist. & Gen. Reg.* XXII. 83 There is no remedy but my Lady must coacht: she can not go to church to serve God without a coach.] **1785** FRENEAU *Poems* (1786) 376 But your market-day mornings we cannot forget, Without your coaches to lend, and your horses to let. **1891** WILKINS *New Eng. Nun* 95 An' she had a coach with lamps on the sides, an' blue satin cushings, to ride in, an' four horses to draw it, an' a man to drive.

b. *Coach-and-four*, a coach drawn by four horses. {*c*1720- (Swift)}

1774 J. ANDREWS *Letters* 26 Robert Treat Paine, who set out with the Committee for the Congress this morning; . . . in a coach and four preceded by two white servants. **1851** *Harper's Mag.* Sept. 452/1 [He] kept a coach-and-four.

2. A stagecoach.

1686 SEWALL *Diary* I. 137 Mr. Randolph . . . takes Coach for Roxbury. **1833** E. T. COKE *Subaltern's Furlough* xii, I took the coach and proceeded through the village of Portsmouth. **1857** *Lawrence* (Kansas) *Republican* 4 June, On this line there plies a good daily line of coaches. **1862** COLT *Went to Kansas* 41 Our slow coaches have come 18 miles today. **1869** BRACE *New West* 204 There was a woman and child inside the coach who commenced bucking so, and there ain't none of them passengers as ever have pistols. **1901** DUNCAN & SCOTT *Allen & Woodson Co., Kansas* 17 Afterwards the [mail] service was made tri-weekly, and the little mule gave way to a two horse hack, then a jerky, or two horse stage, and finally an imposing Overland coach.

+**3.** A railroad passenger car.

1870 RAE *Westward by Rail* 50 This company build and run their own elegant sleeping coaches and palace day cars. **1874** TAYLOR *World on Wheels* I. 71 They call a sixty-soul car a coach now. **1884** *Lisbon* (Dakota) *Star* 22 Aug., The Fargo Southern is equipped with the latest and most improved coaches and locomotives. **1885** *Outing* VII. 150/2, I took my seat in a railway car—'coach' the rail-road men say.

4. One who instructs and directs athletes in preparation for, and during, games, contests, etc.

[**1871** BAGG *At Yale* 386 Yale's trainers, or 'coaches' as the English call them, have been professional characters from New York City. William Wood . . . 'coached' the winning '70 freshman crew.] **1882** *Nation* 6 July 9/2 In settling the final arrangements at the meeting of the 'coaches' of the two crews last night, a serious question arose as to the manner in which the two boats should be lined at starting. **1899** QUINN *Penna. Stories* 24 But the coaches on the side lines were not so jubilant.

5. Attrib. with *car, factory, fare*, etc.

1873 *Newton Kansan* 27 Feb. 3/2 About twenty couple . . . chartered a coach car and special engine and attended Grand Masonic and Odd Fellows ball. **1856** Summers *Hist. S.W. Virginia* (1903) 646 It broke out in the extensive coach factory. **1856** M. J. HOLMES *L. Rivers* xxxiv. 362 Altogether too stingy to pay the coach fare, his own horse had carried him out. **1891** CHASE & CLOW *Industry* II. 69 Fine morocco, for coach furniture and cabinet work, is made from the skin of the goats. **1889** *Century Mag.* April 840/2 Mrs. Herbert of Alexandria was often asked . . . to fetch a coach-load of her offspring for a 'staying-visit' to the Washingtons. **1856** Summers *Hist. S.W. Virginia* (1903) 646 The inflammable contents of the large, well-filled coach shop. **1787** *Md. Gazette* 1 June 3/2 Runaway . . . , a certain Morris Quill, about twenty-two years of age, . . . by trade a blacksmith, or coach spring-maker. **1863** 'G. HAMILTON' *Gala-Days* 98 We disembarked and posted ourselves on the coach-top for a six-mile ride to Champlain. **1852** STOWE *Uncle Tom* xvi, Eva . . . was merrily laughing at various things which she saw from the coach-windows, as it rattled along.

Coachee. +A carriage resembling a coach but lighter in construction and longer. *Obs.* — **1790** *Penna. Packet* 11 Oct. 4/2 A light Waggon or Cochee to be sold. Very elegant, and as good as new. **1803** J. DAVIS *Travels* 107 Here [in Charleston, S.C.] was to be perceived a Coachee, without a glass to exclude the dust, driven by a black fellow. **1832** Va. Act in *Statutes at Large* IV. 657 For every chariot, coach, coachee, stage, or phaeton with two horses, [a toll of] twelve and a half cents [shall be collected].

Coacher. =COACH 4. Also, in baseball games, one who from the side lines directs runners. — **1886** *Outing* March 697/2 Mr. Mutrie was unanimously chosen as coacher of the team for three months prior to the opening of the season. **1887** *Courier-Journal* 25 Jan. 8/4 Cline . . . is a capital coacher, and would strengthen almost any team. **1895** WILLIAMS *Princeton Stories* 180 He paid very little attention to anything except the scrub captain's orders and the admonitions of the coachers.

Coach gun. *Obs.* A gun of a type supplied for the defense of a coach. — **1774** *Mass. Gazette* 3/3 A few . . . coach guns or blunderbusses.

***Coach horse.** A horse used in drawing a coach. — **1688** SEWALL *Diary* I. 234 Mr. Hutchinson's Coach-Horses also plung'd. **1725** *Ib.* III. 365, I . . . had difficulty and danger in getting over the Ferry, by reason of . . . two Coach-Horses in the Boat. **1896** WILKINS *Madelon* 117 He was watering the coach-horses for the next relay.

Coach house. 1. A building in which a carriage is kept. {1679-} **2.** (See quotation.) — **(1) 1687** *Boston Rec.* 193 Anthony Howard had set upon the towne ground . . . pte. of a coach house. **1728** [see COACH-MAKER]. **1771** *Carroll P.* in *Md. Hist. Mag.* XIV. 127 Carry a shed the whole length of the Old & New Coach House. **1857** C. VAUX *Villas* 308 The vignette illustrates a design for the coach-house and stable, which was erected at some little distance from the house. **(2) 1838** COOPER *Homeward Bound* 12 Mr. Effingham led his daughter into the hurricane-house—or, as the packet-men quaintly term it, the coach-house.

Coach lace. Lace used by coach trimmers in fitting out the interiors of coaches. Also attrib. — **1805** *Columbian Centinel* 1/1 (*advt.*), Coach lace manufactory. *a***1817** DWIGHT *Travels* IV. 480 Webbing, Coach laces, Table clothes. **1846** *Rep. Comm. Patents* 74 An old and well known patent for a loom for weaving coach lace, Brussels carpeting, &c., has been reissued.

***Coach-maker.** One whose business is to build coaches. — **1678** *Boston Rec.* 123 Ordered . . . to be returned to the Countie Court, George Wardnr. Coatch maker not admitted into ye Colony. **1728** SEWALL *Letter-Book* II. 241 Made a Lease of the Coach-House and Stable to John Lucas, Coach-Maker, from March 25, 1728, for Five years. **1843** CHILD *Lett. N.Y.* ii. 8 Toward the close [of a procession], came two barouches, containing . . . a carpenter, a coach-maker, a tailor, [etc.]. **1891** O'BEIRNE *Leaders Ind. Territory* 114/1 The subject of this sketch was . . . the fourth son of Joseph Ward, . . . a coach-maker by trade.

* **Coachman.** One who drives a coach.

1720 *Weekly Mercury* 5 Jan. 2/2 Run away from his Master . . . his Coach-man A Mallato named Johney. **1796** WEEMS *Letters* II. 9 My Coz. Polly says that she will distribute (by her Coachman I suppose) these 13 or 14 copies. **1835** HOFFMAN *Winter in West* II. 28 The driver . . . was a forward two-third witted fellow, grafting the impudence of a New-York hackney coachman upon the not disagreeable freedom of western character. **1883** *Century Mag.* XXVII. 130/2 Our party consisted of Mrs. Davis, Miss Howell (her sister), the four children, Ellen (the mulatto maid-servant), and James Jones (the mulatto coachman).

Coach office. A business office of a stagecoach line. {1833-} — **1818** FLINT *Lett. from Amer.* 41 On the morning of the 20th of September, I went to the Coach-Office in Philadelphia to take my seat. **1837** *S. Lit. Messenger* III. 226/1, I had been much amused with the various specimens of human nature who had visited a coach office opposite the church. **1853** *Harper's Mag.* VI. 838/2 He walked straight to the coach-office.

Coach-painter. One whose business is to paint coaches. — **1814** *Mineral. Journal* I. 87 The blue earth has been used in arts as a pigment, . . . and is said to be durable. I am informed that a piece was tried by a coach-painter in Germantown. *a***1821** C. BIDDLE *Autobiog.* 227 Then followed [in 1788] . . . other trades and professions . . . cordwainers, coach-painters, [etc.]. **1851** CIST *Cincinnati* 9 Occupations [include] . . . coach painters, 3 [people].

Coach-trimmer. One who finishes the interior of coaches with lace and other trimmings. — **1840** *Picayune* 28 July 1/2 Materials and tools for saddlers and coach trimmers, together with a fine assortment of Saddlery ware. **1851** CIST *Cincinnati* 9 Occupations [include] . . . coach trimmers, 29 [people]. **1886** *Boston Directory* 259 Jacobs, David, coach-trimmer.

+**Coachwhip snake.** A long, slender snake of the genus *Masticophis.*

1736 CATESBY *Carolina* II. 54 *Anguis flagelliformis*. The Coach-whip Snake. This is a very long slender Snake, particularly the hind Part, . . . and from the Resemblance of a Coach-Whip has received its Name. **1791** BARTRAM *Travels* 219 The coach-whip snake is . . . very slender, and from the abdomen tapers away in the manner of a small switch or coach-whip. **1835** A. PARKER *Trip to Texas* 152 There are other snakes, not venomous, such as the coach-whip snake, the large black snake, [etc.]. **1890** *Cent.* 3653/2.

b. Also ellipt.

1827 WILLIAMS *West Florida* 29 The coach-whip is most frequently seen in the pine barrens; he resembles a coach-whip, with a black handle; but is very innocent. **1836** HOLLEY *Texas* 104 Land and water moccasin, coach whip, and copper heads are the only venomous snakes, besides the rattlers fround in Texas. **1887** *Sci. Amer.* n.s. LVII. 7 A 'coachwhip,' a snake much like the common black snakes in form, but in color a very dark brown. **1899** *Animal & Plant Lore* 87.

+**Coakum.** Also **cocum.** [Orig. obscure.] The pokeweed, *Phytolacca decandra.* — **1814** BIGELOW *Florula Bostoniensis* 112 Poke. Cocum. . . . One of the most common and conspicuous plants in waste grounds, by road sides, &c. **1832** WILLIAMSON *Maine* I. 127 Poke, an abbreviation of Pocum, is frequently called Cocum, and erroneously, Garget. **1896** *Garden & Forest* IX. 262/2 Coakum, . . . with its variants Cocum and Cunicum, is a word of Indian (Tarascan) origin, but not of Indian application. ... The colonists of Massachusetts ... formed the word through a corruption of Mechoacan.

***Coal.**

***1.** A hard black mineral consisting of carbonized vegetable matter, used for fuel.

a1649 WINTHROP *Hist.* II. 137 The pinnace went up John's river some 20 leagues and loaded with coal. **1739** *Boston Selectmen* 12 March, Selling coal in baskets commonly called two bushel baskets. **1831** PECK *Guide* 193 There are a number of beds of coal in this county, and equally good. **1899** *Boston Globe* 22 Aug. 36/6 'Trimmers' pass the coal from the bunkers to the furnace door.

***b.** In the pl.; rare in U.S. since the 18th c., except in the sense of embers.

'Coal: the English generally use the plural *coals;* and we as generally use the singular collectively. *Coals* with us mean charcoal, in England, never' (B. '59). 'In America *coal* is put on the grate in the singular, while in England *coals* are put in the grate in the plural' (B. Matthews in *Harper's Mag.* LXXXIII. 220/2).

1637 *Mass. Bay Rec.* I. 206 Abraham Shawe is graunted haulfe of the benefit of coles or yron stone, w[hi]ch shalbee found in any common ground. **1645** *Essex Inst. Coll.* IX. 139 Ordered that there shall be layd out 4 bushells of wheate for 8 bushells of coales. **1674** *Cal. State Papers Amer. & W. I.* VII. 581 [In] Maine ... the bowels of the earth are enriched with plenty of iron ore, tin, copper, lead, coals, [etc.]. **1763** *Boston Post-Boy* 19 Dec., Just Imported And To Be Sold ... Newcastle Coals, Lisbon and Salterduda Salt. **1778** in Benton *30 Years' View* (1854) I. 490/2 These merchandises which follow shall not be reckoned among contraband or prohibited goods; ... tin, iron, latten, ... coals. **1848** [see COAL HOD]. **1880** DANA *Mineralogy* 754 Bituminous Coals ... [burn] in the fire with a yellow, smoky flame. **1886** [see COAL OIL *n.*].

2. In attrib. use: **a.** In sense of charcoal, with *basket, brand,* etc.

1771 *Boston Selectmen* 19 June, William Barret appointed to measure Coal Baskets. **1783** *Ib.* 24 Nov., The four Constables of the Watch are appointed to examine all Coal Baskets and prosecute offenders ... as the Law directs. **1780** *Narrag. Hist. Reg.* I. 170 George brought home a load of coal brands. **1658** *Southold Rec.* I. 449 An Inventorie of the personall estate whereof Elizabeth Payne widdow dyed [includes]: ... a frame of a Table—an iron colerack.

b. In sense 1: Dealing in or involving transactions in coal, with *agent, dealer,* etc.

1859 *35th Cong. 2 Sess.* Ho. Repr. Rep. No. 184, 29 Question. What is the proper business of the coal agent? **1840** *Niles' Nat. Reg.* 31 Oct. 132/1 Within a few days, the coal dealers [of Boston] had a meeting, and agreed to raise the prices of coal. **1859** *35th Cong. 2 Sess.* H. R. Rep. No. 184, 29 One coal inspector could not attend to the whole. **1887** *Courier-Journal* 20 Jan. 4/3 If the correspondent will look around Washington, ... he will find plenty of kings—lumber kings, coal kings, iron kings, etc. **1917** SINCLAIR *King Coal* 63 There had not been a damage suit filed against any coal-operator in that county for twenty-three years! **1839** J. D. WHITNEY *Life & Lett.* 33 Every sweep and coal-seller and newsboy in the city seems to redouble his exertions as he comes under my window. **1882** *Harper's Mag.* Jan. 162/2 This capriciousness of the Ohio ... renders the experiences of the coal-shipper unique.

c. In sense 1 with *bucket, camp, cellar, claim,* etc.

1887 *Courier-Journal* 25 Jan. 3/7 At Auction, ... 1 elegant French-Plate Pier Mirror; ... 20 dozen new Coal buckets and Vases. **1917** SINCLAIR *King Coal* 3 The town of Pedro stood on the edge of the mountain country; a straggling assemblage of stores and saloons from which a number of branch railroads ran up into the canyons, feeding the coal-camps. **1857** VAUX *Villas* 266 In the basement will be found a servants' entrance, ... provision-cellar, coal-cellar, and furnace-room. **1891** O'BEIRNE *Leaders Ind. Territory* 75/2 He has also a good coal claim. **1808** *Niles' Reg.* XV. 52/1 The Chickahominy, a river rising in the coal country, ... offers a means of carrying down the coal destined for distant exportation. **1917** SINCLAIR *King Coal* 116 We'll show 'em a trick from the coal-counties! **1847** L. COLLINS *Kentucky* 158 The coal district of Kentucky. **1882** *Nation* 21 Dec. 526/3 There are great new piers, storehouses, and coal-dumps at Newport News. **1887** *Courier-Journal* 6 May 6/4 An ordinance was passed granting to the Winefrede Coal Company the right to erect a coal elevator on a piece of land belonging to the city. **1842** *Nat. Hist. N.Y., Geology* II. 169 Two great basins, ... one to the north in the coal-field of New-Brunswick, the other to the south in the coal-fields of Pennsylvania. **1809** F. CUMING *Western Tour* 58 On entering Habach's tavern, I was no little surprised to see a fine coal fire. **1880** *Harper's Mag.* Dec. 54 The tide ... taken at the flood leads the coal fleet to Southern and Western markets. **1887** *Courier-Journal* 1 Feb. 3/1 Charles Romberg ... was living temporarily on a coal-float at the foot of Floyd street. **1845** *Knickerb.* XXVI. 432 He cast a new set of 'Blackstone' ... into the lighted coal-grate before him. **1882** HOWELLS *Modern Instance* xxxix, The coal-grime blackened even the sheathing from which the young leaves were unfolding their vivid green. **1863** MITCHELL *My Farm* 300 There were ... four or five disorderly buildings about the farm-house—sheds, shops, coal-houses, smoke-houses—built up of odds and ends of lumber. **1833** B. SILLIMAN *Man. Sugar Cane* 90 Their [*sc.* copper buckets] form is not unlike that of a common coal kettle. **1878** PINKERTON *Strikers* 318 All the coal shipped by the Philadelphia and Reading Coal and Iron Company, and also by the 'coal laterals,' is forwarded through Reading to the great markets of the East. **1854** *Penna. Agric. Rep.* 425 Silver Medal for best stone, clay and coal picks. **1885** *Harper's Mag.* July 194/2 The river ... [whose] margins [were] now lined with elevators, floaters, lumber-yards, coal pockets, chutes, and trestles. **1917** SINCLAIR *King Coal* 134 A difficulty had occurred to him for the first time—that he did not know anything about the working of coal-scales. **1868** *Rep. Comm. Agric.* 361 All the small stones ... on the middle of the road-bed ... may be rapidly gathered by the use of the malleable cast-iron coal-scoop. **1853** FOWLER *Home for All* 177 It can be plastered on the outside with common mortar, or an addition of coal screenings, or left rough, as the builder can afford. **1850** *Annual of Sci. Discovery* 272 One of the most remarkable features of these coal-seams is their prodigious bulk. **1835** HOFFMAN *Winter in West* I. 53 The tall cliffs of the Monongahela, ... pierced in various points with the deep coal-shafts that feed their fires, frowned. **1881** *Harper's Mag.* March 603/1 The fireman had stepped over to the blacksmith's for a coal shovel. **1902** WISTER *Virginian* ii. 13 Medicine Bow was my first [frontier town], and I took its dimensions, twenty-nine buildings in all,—one coal shute, one water tank, [etc.]. **1858** *Rep. Comm. Patents* I. 745 Improvement in Coal or Ashes Sifters. **1917** SINCLAIR *King Coal* 384 There was never a strike more investigated than the Colorado coal-strike. **1846** *Niles' Nat. Reg.* 4 April 80/2 Coal Tax. A bill is before the legislature of Pennsylvania, and has passed the house of representatives, ... taxing anthracite coal mined in said state, 10 cents per ton. **1909** 'O. HENRY' *Roads of Destiny* 305 We get the heelers out with the crackly two-spots, and coal-tickets, and orders for groceries. **1882** *Harper's Mag.* Jan. 173/1 A coal tow will measure from 500 to 800 feet by 200. **1850** *Annual of Sci. Discovery* 272 There are several detached tracts of anthracite in Eastern Pennsylvania, which form some of the most remarkable coal-tracts in the world. **1855** COOKE *Ellie* 21 Her basket was nearly full of the coal 'trash.' **1834** *S. Lit. Messenger* I. 91/2 The Rev. Mr. Conybeare, ... speaking of the coal veins (or coal measures, as they are there [=England] called) of his country, thus expresses himself. **1840** HAWTHORNE *Note-Books* I. 216 On the deck of a Yankee coal vessel. **1889** BRAYLEY *Boston Fire Dept.* 251 A small house for the storage of coal-wagons and spare ladders was erected in the yard.

+Coal bank. An exposed seam of coal.

1805 Collins *Kentucky* I. 408 A coal bank is within three hundred yards. There are also five valuable coal banks near the river. **1831** PECK *Guide* 193 Mr. Nielson has opened a very extensive coal bank about four miles above Brownsville. **1849** CHAMBERLAIN *Ind. Gazetteer* 197 The best coal bank that has been found in the State is near the mouth of this stream [=Coal Creek]. **1877** 'E. MARTIN' *Hist. Great Riots* 144 The city was again thrown into a tumult of excitement by a report that almost one thousand miners from the coal banks of the Monongahela river had arrived. **1886** *Harper's Mag.* June 62/2 A gentleman who wanted a coal bank opened engaged for the work a man passing along the road.

Coal barge. A flatboat used to carry coal. {1827}

a1861 T. WINTHROP *Canoe & Saddle* 188 Bruin, hearing hoofs, lurched on like a coal-barge in a tide bobbery. **1861** *Atlantic Mo.* April 430/1 The river ... drags itself sluggishly along, tired of the heavy weight of boats and coal-barges. **1883** 'MARK TWAIN' *Life on Miss.* xxxv, Coal-barges from Pittsburg, little trading scows from everywhere. **1885** *Century Mag.* XXX. 326/1 The barges used were coal-barges, about eighty feet long and twenty wide, scow-shaped with both ends alike.

+Coal baron. The owner of a rich coal mine or mines. — **1887** *Harper's Mag.* April 822/1 The great 'coal barons' ... deliberately combine to put up the price of coal. **1888** *Boston Globe* (F.), The Coal barons who imagined that the strike would be settled so easily are mistaken. **1904** [see COAL REGION].

Coal bed. A seam or stratum of coal. {1802–} — **1821** NUTTALL *Trav. Arkansa* 19 The coal basin, or rather bed [near Pittsburgh] ... is almost horizontal. **1840** *Knickerb.* XV. 103 The coal-beds, however, are found to extend beyond the valley of Wyoming. **1903** *Geol. Survey Bul.* No. 213, 277 Wherever they have been opened the coal beds of the Washington Creek Basin show no evidence of faulting.

+Coalbin. A boxlike receptacle or space for coal.

1864 WEBSTER 133. **1865** *Atlantic Mo.* XV. 505 To have seen whether he came up by the coal-bin or the meat-safe. **1869** ALCOTT *Little Women* II. 10 The kitchen stairs seemed built for the express purpose of precipitating both servants and china pell-mell into the coal bin. **1883** PECK *Bad Boy* 20, I want to see you there by the coal bin for a minute or two.

Coal boat. A coal barge.

1818 *Niles' Reg.* XV. 16/2 The annual tolls raised on fourteen thousand tons of country produce, and on two thousand coal boats, have amounted to 16,750 dollars. **1833** C. MINER in *Life* (1916) 64 We ... were making preparations to build coal boats to carry about ten tons each. **1880** *U.S. Census* VIII. 183 For coal boats, or broad-horns, the standard size is 170 feet in length. **1884** SARGENT *Rep. Forests* 574 Formerly large numbers of coal-boats and salt-boats were built upon the Elk river.

attrib. **1880** *Harper's Mag.* Dec. 53 The Magic Wand which ... transforms the river-front of Pittsburgh ... is the sudden advent of a 'coal-boat' stage of water, *i.e.,* anything over eight feet. **1887** *Courier-Journal* 1 Feb. 3/5 The towboat John Moren ... was the first to arrive at this port with a tow on the coalboat water of 1887.

Coal-breaker. +A machine, structure, or building for the breaking of coal. — **1871** *Harper's Mag.* June 151 The next day the rioters, increased in numbers, prevented all working at the mines, and burned two coal-breakers. **1881** RAYMOND *Mining Glossary, Coal-breaker,* a building containing the machinery for breaking coal with toothed rolls, sizing it with sieves, and cleaning it for market. **1887** *Courier-Journal* 3 May 1/3 An Immense Coal Breaker Burns at Wilkesbarre, Pa. **1889** *Cent.* 1068/1 Coal-breakers were first used in the Pennsylvania anthracite region in 1843.

Coal bunker. A receptacle for coal on a ship.

1840 *Monthly Chron.* (Boston) July 240 The engines, boilers and coal-bunkers [of S.S. 'Britannia'] occupy a space of 70 feet, the width of the vessel. **1863** F. Moore *Rebellion Rec.* V. I. 71 One eleven-inch shell went through her side a foot above the water-line, and lodged in the 'coal-bunkers.' **1886** *Harper's Mag.* June 4/2 The capacity of her coal-bunkers is 630 tons.

+**Coal car.** A railway car designed to carry coal.

1858 *Penna. R.R. Rep.* 14 The rolling Stock . . . consisted . . . of . . . 92 Four-wheeled Coal Cars. **1876** *Ib.* 27 During the year, 222 eight-wheeled coal cars were purchased. **1873** 'Mark Twain' & Warner *Gilded Age* lxiii. 569 Long trains of coal cars, laden and unladen, stood upon sidings. **1883** Fulton *Sam Hobart* 222 Four heavily loaded coal cars belonging to a train ahead had by accident become detached and had begun the descent from the summit toward Johnstown.

b. A car used in hauling coal in or from a mine.

1906 Lynde *Quickening* 99 When he . . . had handled the levers of the great steam-hoist that shot the coal-cars from the mine to the coal-yard bins.

Coal cart. A cart for carrying coal. — **1839** *Boston Herald* 17 Dec. 1/6 His horse shied at a coal-cart. **1872** Brace *Dangerous Classes N.Y.* 152 The village ['Dutch Hill,' N.Y.C.] is filled with snarling dogs, which aid in drawing the swill or coal carts. **1873** 'Mark Twain' & Warner *Gilded Age* xii. 120, I don't know an engine from a coal cart.

attrib. **1887** *Courier-Journal* 1 May 4/2 On their way they met a colored letter-carrier who said that the name on the coal-cart ticket was Scott Parker.

Coal company. A company engaged in coal mining; a business firm that deals in coal. — **1852** *Knickerbocker* XXXIX. 167 Mr. Fudge needs no dividends. Coal companies generally pay no dividends. **1878** Pinkerton *Strikers* 205 The Hampshire . . . and Piedmont coal companies were busily engaged bringing coal to the surface. **1905** Valentine *H. Sandwith* 48 Wentworth was attorney for the Snow Shoe Coal Company.

attrib. **1917** Sinclair *King Coal* 222 There was a living to be made sitting on the bench, while one's partner appeared before the bench as coal-company counsel.

+**Coal-digging.** A place where coal is dug. — **1882** Worthen *Econ. Geol. Ill.* II. 173 Shelton's coal-digging . . . supplies the country for miles around with its blacksmith coal.

Coal dish. *Obs.* A receptacle for holding burning charcoal. — **1640** *Conn. Rec.* I. 448 An Inventory of the goods . . . of James Olmestead [includes] . . . 2 perre of cobirons, 1 fier pan, 1 cole dishe and a perre of bellowes. **1641** *Conn. Probate Rec.* I. 39 An Inventory of all . . . goods, belonging to Joyce Ward, wydow, [includes] . . . one brasse coal dish.

Coalfish. The pollack (*Pollachius virens* or *carbonarius*), related to the cod, found in northern waters. {1603–} — **1839** Storer *Mass. Fishes* 129 *Merlangus carbonarius.* The Coal Fish. It is often met with in our market in considerable quantities, and . . . is called, by our fishermen, the 'pollack.' **1871** *Amer. Naturalist* V. 400 Young Pollock or Coal-fish . . . pursue the same species in large schools.

+**Coal flat.** A coal barge. — **1851** *Knickerb.* XXXVII. 182 The river is dark as night; but we see, every now and then, 'broad-horns' and coal-flats, with a twinkling light. **1883** 'Mark Twain' *Life on Miss.* iii, He took a berth on a Pittsburg coal-flat, or on a pine-raft. **1887** *Courier-Journal* 1 May 14/6 The current was so swift at this point that their boat was thrown in between two coal-flats, and while trying to get clear of them, the skiff was upset.

Coal formation. *Geol.* A stratum in which coal predominates. — **1823** James *Exped.* I. 10 The sandstones of the coal formation begin to appear alternating with narrow beds of bituminous clay-slate. **1843** *Nat. Hist. N.Y., Geology* III. 12 In this report the term New-York System will be used, and will include all from the Potsdam sandstone, inclusive, to the 'Coal formation.'

+**Coal-handler.** One who loads or unloads coal. — **1887** *Evening Standard* 27 Jan. 2/5 The strike of the coal-handler [in New York]. **1887** *Courier-Journal* 31 Jan. 1/7 Matters were comparatively quiet among the striking coal-handlers and longshoremen to-day. **1888** *Nation* 12 Jan. 22/1 There had been a similar difficulty brewing for some time among the coal-handlers at Port Richmond . . . regarding 'scab coal' from the Lehigh region.

Coal-heaver. A coal-handler. {1763–}

1840 Hawthorne *Note-Books* I. 213, I was not half frozen by the bitter blast, nor tormented by those grimy coal-heavers. **1850** C. Mathews *Moneypenny* 109 There was a negro cooper in the cellar . . . who made baskets for the coal-heavers. **1887** *Courier-Journal* 3 Feb. 3/3 The railroad men and coal heavers were very reticent as to what action they would take.

Coal hill. A hill composed of or containing coal.

1781–2 Jefferson *Notes Va.* (1788) 27 Another coal-hill on the Pike run of Monongahela has been a-fire ten years; yet it has burnt away about twenty yards only. **1818** Darby *Emigrant's Guide* 257 There is but one point of approach [to Pittsburgh] that affords a good view of the place; that is the apex of the coal hill, in the road from Washington in Pennsylvania. **1891** *Century Mag.* March 738 This is the marsh and that is the coal hill.

Coal hod. A coal scuttle. {1825–, *dial.*}

1848 Bartlett 87 *Coal-hod*, a kettle for carrying coals to the fire. More frequently called, as in England, a coal-scuttle. **1855** Thompson *Doesticks* 37 Endeavoring to . . . get out doors to see what the matter was, and in the attempt falling over the stove and knocking my teeth out against the coal-hod. **1859** *Harper's Mag.* Feb. 342/1 The rooms [were] placed in an unusual state of tidiness—the hearth freshly swept—the coal-hod searched for the largest lump. **1873** Bailey *Life in Danbury* 24, I took that animal out to exercise him. . . . He leaned forward a little, and hoisted both hind legs, and threw about two coal hods of mud over a line full of clothes. **1895** *Dial. Notes* I. 396 In the stove and hardware trade *coal hod* is universal, and this form is more common in cities.

Coalhole.

1. A recess for storing coal. {1661–}

1846 Melville *Typee* vii, And what, in the name of caves and coal-holes, do you expect to find at the bottom of that gulf but a broken neck? **1886** Stapleton *Major's Christmas* 250 Mr. Funk by stratagem had escaped, minus coat, through the coal hole in the shed, which had been recently whitewashed.

+**2.** A hole in a sidewalk, covered by a lid, leading into a coalbin or coal cellar.

1854 Shillaber *Mrs. Partington* 56 When you look up, . . . avoid the coal-holes and cellar-ways that are open for your unwary feet. **1895** *N.Y. Dramatic News* 23 Nov. 4/3 Some of the dramatis personæ disappear as quickly as if they had fallen through a coal hole.

Coaling.

1. The making of charcoal. {1602–}

1772 *Carroll P.* in *Md. Hist. Mag.* XIV. 287 The Smiths being out a Coaling. **1898** Parmenter *Hist. Pelham* (Mass.) 245 The burning of wood into charcoal or 'coaling' as the business was termed, has been carried on . . . for many years.

2. The action of loading with coal. {1887}

1855 Glisan *Jrnl. Army Life* 196 The agent had promised us transportation to that place in time to regain the steamer before she should finish coaling. **1869** *Causes Reduct. Tonnage* 201 Without frequent coaling.

3. A place where charcoal is burned.

1905 Valentine *H. Sandwith* 268 Dave . . . drove off with him as far as Custard's, a lonely inn not far from the coalings.

4. Attrib. with *center*, *ground*.

1786 *Ann. S.W. Virginia* 417 Road ordered established from the Brunswick Iron Works to the Sinking Spring Coaling Ground. **1883** 'Mark Twain' *Life on Miss.* xxv, Grand Tower was a great coaling center and a prospering place.

Coaling station. A place where boats or trains may get coal. {1870} — **1853** *Harper's Mag.* VI. 260 The very general application of steam to navigation demands new coaling-stations. **1881** *Century Mag.* Dec. 303/1 While stopping at a coaling station, I think in Delaware, we gave him a bath. **1898** *McClure's Mag.* X. 362 We . . . had to stop at the freight coaling-station and coal up.

***Coal kiln.** A kiln for making charcoal. {1533; *obs.*} — **1776** Fithian *Journal* II. 162 A fog of smoke rises from off it as from a coal kiln. **1836** *Huntington Rec.* III. 361 All the wood that remains on the land after that time to belong to Said town No Coalkill to be burned on the premises. **1847** *Florida Plant. Rec.* 318, 2 work on the mill, 3 make Coal kill.

+**Coal land.** Land on which there are coal deposits.

1750 Walker *Journal* 21 June, Deer are very scarce on the Coal Land. **1840** *Knickerb.* XV. 103 A large district of coal land having been purchased, a canal was constructed. **1847** Howe *Hist. Coll. Ohio* 350 In 1833, Mr. Pomeroy having purchased most of the coal land on the river for four miles, formed a company. **1886** Mitchell *R. Blake* 278 There are those coal-lands in Kanawha: . . . something might be made out of them. **1904** *Indian Laws & Tr.* III. 100 Said lands shall be sold as other leased coal and asphalt lands in Choctaw and Chickasaw Nations in the Indian Territory are sold.

***Coal man. a.** One who sells or delivers coal. {1707–} +**b.** One who owns coal property. — **1848** *Knickerb.* XXXI. 221 The coal-man's bill, the flour-man's bill, the house rent, were all quickly settled. **1855** Whitman *Leaves of Grass* 24, I am . . . Comrade of raftmen and coalmen. **1917** Sinclair *King Coal* 250 'Billy' Harris, son of another 'coal man.'

Coal merchant. One who sells coal. {1677–} — **1722** *New-Eng. Courant* 3 Sept. 2/1 Some are Orange-Merchants, others Coal-Merchants, and some very good Gentlemen are contented to be called Rag-Merchants. **1853** *Harper's Mag.* VI. 566/2 'Coal is *coal* now,' said a city coal-merchant to a man who was remonstrating with him upon its high price. **1872** *Newton Kansan* 12 Dec. 3/2 Our coal merchants are complaining bitterly of a lack of cars.

Coal mine. A mine from which coal is taken. {1613–}

1709 Lawson *Carolina* 83 There has been a Coal-Mine lately found near the Mannakin Town, above the Falls of James-River in Virginia. **1789** Morse *Amer. Geog.* 265 Lead and coal mines are found in this state [N.Y.]. Also petrified wood, . . . asbestos, and several other fossils. **1804** Clark in *Lewis & C. Exped.* (1904) I. 58 At 3 Miles passed a Coal-Mine, or Bank of stone Coal, . . . this bank appears to Contain great quantity of fine Coal. **1833** Coke *Subaltern's Furlough* v, Since wood fuel has become more scarce, a great trade has been carried on, up the Schuylkill and Lehigh rivers, with the coal mines. **1840** *Knickerb.* XV. 103 The coal mines of the Lackawana, equal in extent and importance to any other in Pennsylvania, are situated in the village of Carbondale. **1906** LYNDE *Quickening* 299 We'll consolidate the two plants and the coal-mine, if it's agreeable all around.

+Coal oil, *n.* Petroleum or oil refined from it, esp. kerosene.

1858 *Rep. Comm. Patents* I. 126 This lamp . . . is more especially designed for burning coal oil and similar substances that are rich in carbon. **1860** *Penna. R.R. Rep.* 103 Oil (coal) shipped from Pittsburgh to Philadelphia. **1877** 'E. MARTIN' *Hist. Great Riots* 68 A train of coal oil numbering thirty-seven cars was fired by means of cotton waste saturated with coal oil and matches, which were placed in each car and then lighted. **1883** *Century Mag.* July 326/1 The 'coal oil,' as it was then generally called, taking the name before applied to kerosene distilled from coal, did not compare . . . with the refined oil of the present day. **1886** WINCHELL *Walks & Talks* 152 Cannel Coals . . . were used in the earliest manufacture of illuminating gas and kerosene, or 'coal oil.' **1900** HOWELLS *Literary Friends* 20 A manufactory where they did something with coal-oil (which I now [c1860] heard for the first time called kerosene) refused itself to me. *c***1908** F. M. CANTON *Frontier Trails* 166 Even our coal oil would freeze partially.

attrib. **1858** *U.S. Patent* 25 May, Coal oil and other lamps. **1865** RICHARDSON *Secret Service* 175 At Cannelton, a hundred slaves were employed in the coal-oil works. **1877** 'E. MARTIN' *Hist. Great Riots* 152 The train consisted of ten coal-oil cars. **1879** BISHOP *4 Months in Sneak-Box* 39 During this part of my journey particularly, the need of a small coal-oil stove was felt. **1886** B. P. POORE *Reminisc.* II. 183 Booth squandered the money received by him in coal-oil speculations. **1888** *Century Mag.* Nov. 151/1 The unsavory coal-oil torch . . . and the campaign banners unite in a general procession. **1891** 'THANET' *Otto the Knight*, etc. 65 Need the shelf holding the coal-oil can have broken down the only night when the crock of mince-meat stood underneath?

‖**Coal-oil,** *v.* To pour coal oil on (a person). — **1894** *Congress. Rec.* 5 Feb. 1862/1 The colored people . . . are tortured; they are coal-oiled and burned—and this in a land of pretended civilization.

+Coal-passer. One who passes coal from a coalbin to a furnace.

1869 'MARK TWAIN' *Innocents* 405 The coal-passers moved to their duties in the profound depths of the ship. **1880** LAMPHERE *U.S. Govt.* 64/2 Petty officers and seamen: . . . Fireman, . . . Coal-passer. **1886** *Harper's Mag.* July 206/1 Specific tasks, graduated in importance from those of Superintendent William E. Fletcher, down to those of assistant-porters, coal-passers, and closet attendants. **1887** *Courier-Journal* 15 Feb. 2/5 An attempt to cause trouble among the firemen and coal-passers on some of the coastwise lines . . . proved a failure.

Coal pile. A heap of coal. — **1845** *Knickerb.* XXVI. 410 Coal-piles lie where wood-piles generally lie in ordinary villages. **1898** An American in *London D. News* 15 June 6/3, I pledge you my word that the grains [of powder] is bigger than the lumps in a coalpile.

***Coalpit.**

***1.** =COAL MINE.

1802 ELLICOTT *Journal* 6 A few paces within the coal-pit, the temperature of the water was 51°. **1878** *Harper's Mag.* LVI. 521/1 We're all going to hide in the coal-pit. **1882** WORTHEN *Econ. Geol. Ill.* 176 Its depth [*i.e.*, of a coal bed] . . . would not be greater than that of many coal-pits in other countries.

***2.** A kiln where charcoal is made. {–1577}

1828 WEBSTER, *Coal-pit*, . . . in America, a place where charcoal is made. **1852** *Harper's Mag.* VI. 8 He remembered that when a boy, he had seen a heavy iron chain melted when by accident exposed to the heat of a coal-pit. **1853** 'P. PAXTON' *Yankee in Texas* 278 He started a brick-kiln, burnt a coal-pit, cut cord-wood, bought a market-boat, and tried trading upon the bayou. *a***1918** STUART *On Frontier* I. 240 Reece Anderson and I hauled wood for a coal pit and while he set up the pit, I tried to fix the meat-house so it would be fly proof.

3. (See quotation.)

1828 *Yankee* July 227/1 Then they all repair to the house, or the refreshment is brought out to them, where a motherly quantity of lusty pumpkin and coalpit or two-story apple platter pies are provided.

Coal region. An area in which coal is mined extensively.

1827 DRAKE & MANSFIELD *Cincinnati* 11 The nearest localities to Cincinnati, of this important mineral, are where the western line of the great eastern coal region crosses the Ohio. **1833** *Niles' Reg.* XLIV. 409/2 We were pleased to notice the return . . . of professor Ducatel and the gentlemen who accompanied him on the late expedition to the Alleghany coal region. **1850** *Annual of Sci. Discovery* 272 In 1847 the anthracite coal regions of Pennsylvania furnished 3,000,000 tons. **1904** *McClure's Mag.* Feb. 366/1 The Pennsylvania coal regions, in which miner and coal baron are equally well organized.

Coal scuttle.

1. A strong metal pail or bucket, or scooplike container, in which coal for domestic use is carried. {*a*1825–}

1833 *Knickerb.* I. 157 Just imagine . . . John entering with the coal-scuttle. **1889** S. HALE *Letters* 229, I hear the gentle stir of the poker, and the softly falling coal-scuttle. **1895** *Dial. Notes* I. 396 In the usage of country families in central N.Y. *coal scuttle* seems to predominate.

2. *Coal-scuttle bonnet*, a woman's bonnet shaped somewhat like a coal scuttle. Also ellipt. {1839–}

1848 W. E. BURTON *Waggeries* 37 A full-grown girl in a short-waisted spencer and an Angouleme straw bonnet, as big as a modern coal-scuttle. **1865** *Atlantic Mo.* XV. 56 Venture to preach against coal-scuttle bonnets—until the ladies have really taken to wearing them.

Coal seam. A bed or stratum of coal. {1850–} — **1849** CHAMBERLAIN *Ind. Gazetteer* 183 The section of the coal seam at Cannelton increases in thickness in the interior. **1873** 'MARK TWAIN' & WARNER *Gilded Age* I. 461 The timber is worth more than the mortgage; and if that coal seam does run there, it's a magnificent fortune. **1882** WORTHEN *Econ. Geol. Ill.* II. 55 The coal-seam is underlaid by limestone.

Coal stove. A stove designed for burning coal rather than wood.

[**1834** *23d Congress* 1 *Sess.* H. R. Doc. No. 58, 30 Stove, anthracite coal, combination [patented by] James Atwater, New Haven, Conn.] **1854** *Penna. Agric. Rep.* 100 Three parlor cottage Franklin stoves, two cook stoves, and one coal stove. **1880** *Harper's Mag.* Aug. 373 In the corner near the old lady's chair was a little coal stove with a bright fire in it. **1881** McLEAN *Cape Cod Folks* 20 One was a man, . . . who sat gazing into the coal-stove.

attrib. **1858** *Rep. Comm. Patents* I. 758 Improved Construction of Coal-Stove Lining.

Coal trade. a. The mining and distribution of coal. {1655–} **b.** Coal merchants.

1808 *Niles' Reg.* XV. 52/1, I have dwelt specially on the coal trade to which this canal is subservient. **1827** DRAKE & MANSFIELD *Cincinnati* 70 When the coal trade is made a regular and certain business [etc.]. **1842** *Niles' Nat. Reg.* 22 Jan. 336/3 The Pennsylvania Coal Trade. A table is published in the Miners' Journal showing the quantity of anthracite coal sent to market from the different regions in Pennsylvania. **1859** *35th Cong. 2 Sess.* Ho. Repr. Rep. No. 184, 18 So far back as 1845 . . . the coal trade in Philadelphia . . . felt desirous of introducing a better article.

Coal train. A train loaded with coal.

1861 *Chicago Tribune* 26 May 1/6 Governor Letcher has detained the coal trains and hands belonging to them. **1877** *Harper's Mag.* Jan. 315/2 A coal train ran into a passenger train, on the Delaware, Lackawanna, and Western Railroad. **1878** PINKERTON *Strikers* 318 The passage through Reading of coal trains is the great feature of railroad business at that point. **1885** *Century Mag.* XXX. 285/2 These coal trains passed Harper's Ferry at all hours.

Coal wood. Wood to be burned for charcoal. {1691–} — **1788** WASHINGTON *Diaries* III. 293 The Men were cutting the Tops of the Trees which had been fallen for Rails into Coal-wood. **1847** *Florida Plant. Rec.* 210, 1 [slave] geting cole wood.

Coalyard. A place where coal is stored.

1805 R. H. COLLINS *Hist. Kentucky* (1874) I. 408 There are also . . . a coal yard and boat yard; and, it is said, several saltpetre caves. **1840** *Picayune* 28 July 3/5 He has established a Coal Yard in Lafayette, where he will be always ready to deliver the best of Pittsburg and other Coal. **1843** *Knickerb.* XXII. 144 They were Irishmen employed in coal-yards. **1851** A. O. HALL *Manhattaner* 6 The much talked of flat boats, mere floating granaries and coal-yards, secure in their timber fragility. **1854** CUMMINS *Lamplighter* ii. 10 Back of the building where Nan Grant lived, was a large wood and coal yard. **1871** BAGG *At Yale* 312 The Sophs of '69 have the discredit of introducing the practice of burning the College 'coal-yard.' **1884** *Century Mag.* April 832/2 He has filled some places under the Maryland and Baltimore political governments, and now keeps a coal, wood, and feed yard in North Baltimore. **1893** *Harper's Mag.* Jan. 283/1, I did hear at the coal-yard, on the way round, that the new folks are literary.

attrib. **1906** [see COAL CAR b].

Coarse, *a.* +In gold mining, applied to gold or quartz. **1882** C. KING *Rep. Prec. Metals* 79 The gold is a coarse-quartz gold, very little washed, and often connected with its original quartz matrix. The sources from which this quartz comes are evidently ledges in the immediate vicinity. **1910** HART *Vigilante Girl* 142 What quantities of golddust, of 'coarse-gold,' of amalgam, . . . were brought down from mines and mills to assay-offices and mint.

Coarsehand. +A large kind of handwriting. — **1845** KIRKLAND *Western Clearings* 154 'What should I want coarse-hand for?' said the disciple [in penmanship] with great contempt. **1884** 'MARK TWAIN' *H. Finn* xviii. 169 She asked me if I could read writing, and I told her 'no, only coarse-hand.'

***Coast,** *n.*

+1. The fertile land along the lower Mississippi.

1814 BRACKENRIDGE *Views La.* 175 The dwellings on the Coast are generally frame, of one story in height. The Coast may be said to begin at Pointe Coupée. From this to La Fourche, two-thirds of the banks are perfectly cleared. **1826** FLINT *Recoll.* 297 Were it not for these mounds, this rich, beautiful, and productive strip of soil [about 150 miles above New Orleans], called 'the coast,' would be annually inundated. **1835** INGRAHAM *South-West* II. 24 *note*, The banks of the Mississippi are termed 'the coast' as far up the river as Baton Rouge. **1853** *Harper's Mag.* VII. 752/2 Upon the banks of the Mississippi, which are termed by the inhabitants the coast, may be seen the appliances of plantation life in their perfection. **1883** 'MARK TWAIN' *Life on Mississippi* xl, Twenty-one years ago everything was trim and trig and bright along the 'coast,' just as it had been in 1827. **1888** CABLE *Bonaventure* 119 Mr. Tarbox . . . was travelling on horseback and touching from house to house of the great sugar-estates of the river 'coast,' seeing the country and people.

attrib. **1887** *Century Mag.* March 673/1 There would not be . . . so many strapping youths sent, all unlettered, to the sugar-kettles of the coast plantations.

+**b.** (See quot. 1867.)

1852 STANSBURY *Gt. Salt Lake* 29 A range of small hills of a sandy reddish clay, with a sharp outline toward the river, forming the 'coast of the Nebraska.' **1867** J. MELINE *Santa Fé & Back* 18 It is the summit of the dunes or sand-hills. . . . These sand-hills form a line of bluffs sometimes called 'Coast of the Nebraska.'

+**2.** A slope down which one may coast on a sled; also, an act of sliding or gliding down.

1775 *Mass. Hist. Soc. Proc.* VIII. 398–9 Some of our school lads—who as formerly in this season improv'd the Coast from Sherburn's hill down to School street. General Haldimand, improving the house that belongs to Old Cook, his servant took it upon him to cut up their coast and fling ashes upon it. **1872** ALCOTT *Old-fash. Girl* 36 'Let's run,' said Polly as they came into the path after the last coast. **1881** *Harper's Mag.* April 786/2 The buck darting down an icy slope is almost resistless, but on an ordinary 'coast' it is readily manageable. **1883** E. BACON *Dict. Boston* 19 The boys of Boston are as fond as the boys of the Revolutionary days of the coast on the Common. **1889** *Boston Journal* 5 Feb. 2/3 During a racing contest at a coast in Albany . . . a loaded bob-sled came in contact with some ice hummocks, breaking the steering apparatus.

transf. **1897** *Outing* Feb. 461/1 The road outside the town afforded a most delightful coast, and down we flew [on bicycles] without any exertion.

+**3.** Phr. *On the coast*, near at hand. *local.*

1848 MITCHELL *Nantucketisms* 40 'On the coast.' Near. **1859** BARTLETT 303 *On the coast*, near, close at hand. A nautical expression, in common use in Nantucket. **1871** DE VERE 341 A gallant lover will assure his lady-love that if she will only fix the day, 'he'll be sure to be on the coast with the parson.'

* **Coast,** *v.*

+**1.** *intr.* To glide down a snow-covered slope on a sled.

1836 *Boston Pearl* 9 Jan. (Th.), Skate, if you like; 'coast,' if you are boy enough. **1843** HALIBURTON *Attaché* II. 254 The moment she found herself a coasting of it that way, flounder fashion, she hung on by her . . . ten fingers and her ten toes. **1854** *Springfield Republican* (Th.), Adown thy hills, when I's [*sic*] a boy, O how I used to coast. **1860** Hitchcock *Remin. Amherst Coll.* (1863) 259 And here upon their hand-sleds These ancient creatures sat, And coasted down the hill-side, And many a bump they 'gat.' **1888** STOCKTON *Dusantes* 59 If I'm to go coastin' at all, . . . I'd as lief do it with strangers as friends. **1888** *Amer. Folk-Lore* I. 78 *Coast*, to descend a hill over the snow, on a sled, in winter. The word, in this sense, . . . is even now not familiar in parts of New England, where the usual expression is to *slide*. **1913** STRATTON-PORTER *Laddie* iii. 57 The east end ran along the brow of a hill so steep we coasted down it on the big meat board all winter.

b. (See quotation.)

1889 *Amer. Folk-Lore* II. March 64 *Coast*, . . . the word was common in my boyhood,—passed in Wayne and neighboring counties of New York State,—though the sense was usually the riding over fences, etc., upon the hard crust formed upon the surface of snow.

c. To glide by momentum on a bicycle or other vehicle. Said also of birds on the wing.

1889 *Cent.* 1070/2. **1897** *Outing* Feb. 463/2 We were once more coasting. **1904** *Scientific Amer. Suppl.* LVII. 23663/3 When the wings are motionless, the great birds are 'coasting.' . . . That coasting in the air . . . is possible is readily proved.

+**2.** (See quotation.)

1894 EGGLESTON in *Century Mag.* XLVII. 856 To 'coast' in flat-boatman's phrase is to peddle a cargo to the French planters on the lower Mississippi.

+**3.** To walk about aimlessly.

1889 JEWETT *Betty Leicester* 21, I do' know but I'll coast round up into the town a little.

* **Coaster.**

1. A vagabond, idler, or loafer. *Obs.*

Probably an alteration of the earlier Eng. *common cursetor* (1567) or *coursiter* (1581), a vagrant beggar.

1633 *Mass. Col. Rec.* I. 109 It is further ordered, that noe p[er]son . . . shall spend his time idlely . . . and for this end it is ordered, that the constable of eu[er]y place shall vse speciall care & deligence to take knowledge of offenders in this kinde, espetially of common coasters, unprofittable fowlers, & tobacco takers. **1650** *Conn. Rec.* I. 528 [same as prec.].

***2.** One who engages in traffic along a coast.

1677 HUBBARD *Indian Wars* II. 165 Most of those that were upon the Island, were Strangers, Coasters, and such as came from the Mayne. **1684** *Mass. H. S. Coll.* 4 Ser. V. 123 It's commonly said by coasters, that there are in Virginia far greater boys than this of Narroganset. **1713** *Boston Rec.* 183 Voted. That Mr George Thomas be desired to take into his Custody, the Townes halfe bushells . . . to be applyed for the use of Coasters or others who Shall deliver graine at ye Dock. **1819** E. DANA *Geogr. Sk.* 174 Two miles below is the Grand Gulf, which though it inspires inexperienced boatmen with terror, is slightly regarded by old coasters. **1837** IRVING *Bonneville* I. 73 A New England coaster and his neighbors will coolly launch forth on a voyage to the Black sea, or a whaling cruise to the Pacific. **1850** COLTON *3 Yrs. Calif.* 402 Her [=California's] geography, the habits of her citizens, and her resources, when little known beyond the furtive glances of the coaster, [etc.].

3. A ship that trades along a coast. {1687–}

1704 *Boston News-Letter* 15 May 2/1 Our private Man of War-Sloop came over Nantucket Sholes with about 16 Sail of Coasters. **1739** *Boston Rec.* 233 Our Fishery, and Coasters (on which great part of Our Food and Firing depends) will be Expos'd. **1793** ASBURY *Journal* II. 184 The printed list of vessels in the harbor sets forth, fifty-three ships, fifty-five brigs, . . . besides pilot-boats and coasters. **1879** *Harper's Mag.* July 164 Next . . . come the dim outlines of Block Island . . . swarming with coasters. **1900** MUNN *Uncle Terry* 295 Both her husband an' son went down in a coaster one winter's night.

+**4.** An animal of the ox kind bred on the coast.

1901–2 *Kansas State Bd. Agric. Rep.* 154 Fine specimens have been . . . landed in the hands of the Philistines, with dire results to the offspring—bodies that could not make a shadow, and horns of the old Texas coaster—all from the lack of decent care.

+**5.** A sled for coasting down a snow-covered slope.

1881 *Harper's Mag.* Jan. 222/2 [The] slippery road-track was hardly used at all during the winter, save by coasters. **1888** *Battle Creek Moon* 2 Jan., The Deadly Coaster. Pittsburgh, Pa. . . . A bob-sled on which a party of half a dozen young men were coasting struck a carriage. **1911** WHITE *Bobby Orde* 195 The centre of the street was entirely given over to the coasters darting down.

+**b.** A footrest on a bicycle for use in coasting.

1897 *Outing* Feb. 463/2 Having gleefully perched my feet up on the coasters, I . . . shot forward like an arrow.

+**6.** One who is sliding on a sled.

1887 *Courier-Journal* 13 Jan. 2/7 A Little 'Coaster' Injured.

+**Coast fever.** A fever found along a coast; also in humorous sense (see quot. 1856). — **1841** DANA *Two Years* 247 A captain . . . murdered a lad from Boston who went out with him before the mast to Sumatra, by keeping him hard at work while ill of the coast fever, and obliging him to sleep in the close steerage. **1856** OLMSTED *Slave States* 200 So among sailors and soldiers, when men suddenly find themselves ill and unable to do their duty in times of peculiar danger, or when unusual labor is required, they are humorously said to be suffering under an attack of the powder-fever, the cape-fever, the ice-fever, the coast-fever, or the reefing-fever.

+**Coast fox.** A fox found along the southern California coast. — **1870** *Amer. Naturalist* III. 186 The Coast Fox (*Vulpes littoralis*), if really distinct from the gray, does not occur northward. **1890** *Cent.* 2355/2 [The] genus *Urocyon* . . . , to which the coast-fox of California (*U. littoralis*) also belongs.

Coasting. {1621–}

+**1.** The sport of sliding down a snow-covered slope.

1775 J. Eliot in *Belknap P.* III. 77 The General at first did not understand what they meant by the term coasting. When informed of its meaning, he . . . ordered [his servant] to go & throw water on the place sufficient to rectify the damage caus'd by the ashes. **1832** GOODRICH *Syst. Univ. Geog.* 201 Coasting is another winter pastime, in which, as in many other games, the labor seems to be at least equal to the pleasure. **1881** *Harper's Mag.* April 786 [The] victory of this season was the general adoption of the word 'coasting' to describe sliding down hill. **1886** *Boston Journal* Nov., Coasting will probably be the leading sport this winter. **1909** *N.Y. Ev. Post* 28 Jan. (Th.), Coasting is fun for everybody. . . . In the frosty night, grown men and women fill the flying 'bobs' that go whizzing down the icy incline.

+**2.** Of a bicycle, railroad car, or other vehicle: The action of gliding from the force of gravity.

1883 *Wheelman* I. 337 No pedalling was necessary, for on such a road, with a brisk wind, . . . no additional motive power was required, and, this being the case, 'coasting' was indulged in for a number of miles. **1909** *Cent. Suppl.* 265/1 *Coasting*, in railroading, the act of allowing a train or a car to run upon a down grade by its own gravity, without steam or electric power (U.S.).

+**3.** Attrib. with *accident*, *ground*, *path*, etc.

1775 J. ELIOT in *Belknap P.* III. 77 One of his servants . . . had spoiled their sport by tossing a quantity of ashes over a spot of ground which they & their fathers before them had taken possession of for a coasting-place. **1872** *Congress. Globe* 7 Feb. 869/2 The sidewalk, the plankway, and the brickway were given up entirely as a coasting-ground. **1881** *Harper's Mag.* April 786/2 Even the New York newspapers did not disdain to recount 'coasting accidents,' not meaning marine disasters to coasters, but tragedies of the hill-side. **1882** *Ib.* May 859/2 The old farm coasting path is near by upon the long knoll slope. **1909** *N.Y. Ev. Post* 18 Feb. (Th.), As a consequence of a coasting accident, six professors and students were injured.

Coasting coat. *Obs.* A heavy coat. — **1677** *New Castle Court Rec.* 104 Hee . . . did by force . . . detayne from Mr Thomas Morse, one sandy browne Coasting Coate to ye vallue of fyve lb then in his Custodie. *Ib.* 105 About ten weekes sence hee missed this same Coasting Coate now found in the house of Symon Gibson. **1678** *Ib.* 350, 1 Coasting Coat.

Coasting schooner. A schooner used in the coasting trade.

1775 *S.C. Hist. Soc. Coll.* III. 84 Capt. Alex. Wylly, master of a coasting schooner which had been seized about five weeks ago, had come up to town last night. **1872** *Atlantic Mo.* April 399 [Lieut. Dudington] adopted the system of boarding everything that floated—packets, market-boats, ferry-boats, coasting schooners, Indiamen, [etc.]. **1885** *Outing* VII. 206/1 A large fleet of coasting schooners and sloops came up through Hell Gate. **1899** M. ROBERTSON *Where Angels Fear*, etc. (1921) 139 An outward-bound coasting-schooner, resenting this lawlessness on one occasion, attempted to assert her rights.

Coasting sloop. A sloop engaged in the coasting trade. — **1712** *Conn. Public Rec.* V. 307 The masters of the coasting sloops now lying in this harbour, prefered to this board a petition. **1730** *N.H. Hist. Soc. Coll.* I. 229 The coasting sloops from Boston, carry from hence thither in fish and timber, about five thousand pounds per annum. **1812** *Niles' Reg.* II. 5/1 They have now 1 schooner in the W. I. trade, 3 coasting sloops, and about 12 fishing boats. **1885** [see COASTING SCHOONER].

Coasting smack. A coasting vessel. — **1876** *Harper's Mag.* Dec. 147/2 His mouth fairly watered at the luxury of the forecastle and galley of a half-starved coasting smack.

Coasting trade. The shipping business along a coast. {1745}

1802 ELLICOTT *Journal* 126 The coast being too shoal for any other than the coasting trade. **1832** WILLIAMSON *Maine* II. 202 A vessel, the Snow, was likewise built, for the protection of the coasting and truck trade. **1870** *Causes Reduction Tonnage* 150 You think that the coasting trade should be relieved by the remission of duties and taxation? **1882** *Nation* 10 Aug. 102/1 Those who favor the admission of 'foreign-built ships to American registry' desire to 'break down what they call the odious monopoly of the coasting-trade.' **1892** *Courier-Journal* 1 Oct. 3/4 Bituminous coal, which is afterward used for fuel in American steam vessels engaged in the coasting trade.

Coasting vessel. A ship that plies along a coast. {1702–}

1794 T. COXE *View U. S.* 9 The coasting vessels, entered at the custom-house of Philadelphia in the year 1785 were 567 sail. **1817** *Ann. 14th Congress* 2 Sess. 842 There shall be paid a duty of fifty cents per ton upon every ship or vessel of the United States . . . except . . . it be a coasting vessel going from Long Island . . . to the State of Rhode Island. **1870** *Causes Reduction Tonnage* p. xiii, Coasting vessels. **1883** *Century Mag.* Sept. 651/2 It is quite common for the crews of coasting vessels hauled up in the winter to turn to felling wood.

+**Coast live oak.** California live oak. — **1884** SARGENT *Rep. Forests* 147 Enceno. Coast Live Oak. **1897** SUDWORTH *Arborescent Flora* 405 *Quercus agrifolia*. . . . Common names [include] Coast Live Oak (Cal.).

Coast range. +A range of mountains along the Pacific coast of the U.S. Also attrib.

1844 FRÉMONT *Exped.* 252 The Indians . . . make frequent descents upon the settlements west of the Coast Range. *Ib.* 255 The Cascade Range of Oregon, between which and the ocean there is still another and a lower range, . . . which may be called the Coast Range. *c***1856** *Kit Carson's Life* 68 Got a few animals and crossed the coast range to see if we could hear anything of our party. **1883** *Century Mag.* Aug. 526/1 It lies about twenty-five miles east of San Luis, among broken spurs of the coast range. **1890** *Ib.* December 163 The first settlement . . . was located in the eastern foothills of the Coast Range Mountains.

+**Coast survey.** A survey of a coastal region.

1832 *Congress. Deb.* 30 May 3187 The coast survey . . . will not be completed . . . under sixty years. **1837** *25th Congress 2 Sess.* H. R. Ex. Doc. No. 14, 1, I . . . transmit to you . . . the report made to this Department by Professor Hassler, superintendent of the coast survey. **1851** CIST *Cincinnati* 145 The survey was commenced by Dr. John Locke, upon the system of triangulations, adopted in the United States coast survey. **1890** *Cent.* 6088/3 The Superintendent of the Coast and Geodetic Survey.

attrib. **1860** *36th Cong. 1 Sess.*, H. R. Rep. 249, 66 Question. The Coast Survey Report, too? **1866** HALE *If, Yes, & Perhaps* (1868) 266 A neat parcel of coast-survey maps of Georgia. **1883** *Wheelman* April 2/1 The United States coast-survey charts show that the channel of the river . . . averages a depth of ten fathoms. **1883** *Century Mag.* Sept. 731/2 The Coast Survey steamer Blake.

Coast-surveying, *a.* Engaged in a coast survey. — **1852** *Harper's Mag.* VI. 121 The Coast Surveying party continues its operations.

Coast trade. Commerce among ports situated along one coast. — **1741** W. STEPHENS *Proceedings in Georgia* II. 75 The Sloop was designed to be employed in the Coast-Trade. **1851** CIST *Cincinnati* 282 Flat-boats . . . take down more or less bacon for the coast trade.

Coastwise, *a.* Situated, carried on, plying, etc., along the coast. {1885–}

1817 *Ann. 14th Congress* 2 Sess. 1008 This route . . . has appeared to be the most eligible for the 'coastwise canal.' **1821** *Ann. 16th Congress* App. 1726 The forts . . . satisfy one or more of the following conditions: . . . 5. To cover the coastwise and interior navigation. **1857** *Lawrence* (Kansas) *Republican* 11 June 1 The inter-State and the Coast-wise traffic in human beings . . . shall be broken up. **1886** *Harper's Mag.* Nov. 922/2 By such exceptional experience their officers become trained and skilled in coastwise cruising. **1892** *Congress. Rec.* 19 May 4414 What coastwise States on the Atlantic Coast have abandoned the compulsory pilotage system? **1913** *Boston Globe* 16 Nov. 25/2 Coastwise steamers . . . have their . . . pilot house on the upper passenger deck.

Coat beaver. *Obs.* Beaver skins suitable for making coats. — *a***1656** BRADFORD *Hist.* 375 They [the colonists] sent in beaver 3366 li[ber] waight, and much of it coat beaver, which yeeled 20s. per pound.

+**Coatee.** Also †**coatie.**

1. *Mil.* A short close-fitting coat.

1757 *N.Y. Mercury* 31 Jan. 3/1 My coat, when coatees flourished, was reduced to the size of a dwarf's, and then again increased to the longitude of a surtout. **1775** in *Harper's Mag.* LXVII. 546 Every officer to provide himself with a blue cloath Coatie faced and cuffed with scarlet cloath, and lined with scarlet; white buttons, and white Waistcoat and Breeches. **1816** *Cent. Hist. U.S. Mil. Acad.* I. 511 A coatee of gray satinette, single-breasted, three rows of eight yellow gilt buttons in front. **1880** LAMPHERE *U.S. Govt.* 163/1 Each Cadet must keep himself supplied with the following-mentioned articles, viz: One gray cloth coatee, [etc.]. **1889** *Century Mag.* Jan. 462/1 Several years before I had seen those wonderful coatees with their forty-four buttons of shining brass. **1895** C. KING *Fort Frayne* 267 Barely arrived by man's estate, not yet a year out of the cadet coatee.

2. A civilian garment resembling this.

1800 *Lancaster* (Pa.) *Journal* 20 Sept. (Th.), A Negro Man named Isaac . . . took with him a home-made lincy coattee. **1803** J. DAVIS *Travels* 346 Coatee is the American for a short coat. **1835** KENNEDY *Horse Shoe Robinson* I. 20 A spherical crowned hat with a broad brim, a coarse grey coatee of mixed cotton and wool. **1848** *Knickerb.* XXXII. 77 They [the 'sisters' at a meeting-house] wore short linsey-woolsey 'coatees.'

Coating. Coarse stuff from which coats may be made. {1802–}

Cf. the earlier BEAVER COATING (1759–1784).

1768 FRENEAU *Poems* (1795) 10 Shelves pil'd with lawns and linens, . . . Coatings and stuffs, and cloths, and scarlets red. **1775** N. HALE in *Biog. & Mem.* 172 He had no Scarlet Coating. **1792** *Ann. 2nd Congress* 1000 Great quantities of . . . coatings . . . are made in the household way. **1814** BRACKENRIDGE *Views* 137 The men wore a blanket coat, of coarse cloth or coating, with a cape behind.

attrib. **1787** *Maryland Gaz.* 1 June 3/2 [He] had on when he went away, a dark brown coating coat. **1805** D. MCCLURE *Diary* 160 He had no shirt on & was wrapped in a coating great coat.

***Coat money.** *Obs.* Money furnished to a soldier for buying a coat. {–*a*1662; *hist.*} — **1776** *N.H. Comm. Safety Rec.* 39 Their wages, exclusive of Coat Money. *Ib.* 55 Cheating Soldiers out of their Coat Money.

Coatroom. A cloakroom.

1870 KEIM *Sheridan's Troopers* 10 [He] made his appearance through the window looking into the coat-room. **1876** INGRAM *Centennial Expos.* 701 It contained one very large room, ladies' parlor, coat and baggage room, [etc.]. **1883** *Boston Advertiser* 9 Nov., Each guest before reaching the reception room has run the gauntlet of a dozen or more 'boots' in the Algonquin livery, before reaching the coatroom. **1902** LORIMER *Lett. Merchant* 98 The kid wandered off to the coat-room.

* **Coat tail.** The tail of a coat.

*c***1845** THOMPSON *Chron. Pineville* 49 The legs of his trowsers split clear up to the waistband and his coat-tail crapt close off. **1891** *Century Mag.* Feb. 543 He found himself at dinner with more cloth in the tail of his coat than there was in the coat-tails of his neighbors. *a***1918** G. STUART *On Frontier* I. 28 James did the skating and I just squatted down and held to his coat tail.

‖**b.** *fig.* A hurried departure, with coattails flying. *colloq.*

1834 CARRUTHERS *Kentuckian* I. 95, I'm for making a straight coat-tail out of this place, and that in a hurry, for . . . I'm keen to be among the Yorkers.

* **Cob,** *n.*[1]

+**1.** The central spine or axis on which the kernels of an ear of corn grow in rows.

1684 I. MATHER *Providences* 159 Then Nicholas Desborough . . . was strangely molested by stones, pieces of earth, cobs of Indian corn, &c. **1767** *Boston Gaz.* 19 Jan. (Th.), I take a cobb every morning and a basket full of Ears, and go out and shell 'em to the Sheep. **1784** SMYTH *Tour* I. 293 In the middle is a hard substance called a cob, on which the grains grow close together. **1818** J. TAYLOR *Arator* 104 But the quality of every part of the corn offal is better as manure than the wheat offal. The cob is said to be a valuable food reduced to meal. **1847** DRAKE *Pioneer Life Ky.* 54 The green glass quart whiskey bottle, stopped with a cob, was handed to everyone. **1865** *Atlantic Mo.* XV. 288 His rations were eight ounces of Indian meal, cob and kernel ground together.

b. *To confess the cob*, to admit a charge, imputation, etc. (Cf. CORN *n.* 2 b.)

1853 PAIGE *Dow's Sermons* IV. 127 (Th.), He might as well have confessed the cob.

c. Attrib. and comb. with *grinder, mill, tenement.*

1854 *Penna. Agric. Rep.* 363 Corn and cob grinder, Thomas H. Wilson, a good article. **1859** BARTLETT 99 *Corn and cob mill*, a mill for grinding the entire ear of Indian corn. **1851** *Knickerb.* XXXVII. 496 Suddenly they perceived a light through the cracks of the cob-tenement.

2. A thickset, stocky horse. {1818–}

'In the United States the standard for a cob is somewhat larger than in

England, a typical cob standing about 15 hands high and weighing from 1,000 to 1,050 pounds' (*Cent. Suppl.*).

1857 *Spirit of Times* 294/2 Two or three great hulking colts to . . . give the farmer a serviceable cob to ride round. **1867** 'T. LACKLAND' *Homespun* II. 167 You will see a whole caravan of old cobs about the premises, some with bob-tails and some with switch. **1892** J. E. COOKE *B. Hallam* 82 The good-humored old fellow yielded at once, and mounting a stout cob, . . . they set forth. **1897** *Outing* XXX. 318/1 He [sat] with his eyes fixed on the upright ears of the hurrying cob.

Cob, *n.*[2] A blow in paddling. {1790–, *dial.*} — **1828** *Cherokee Phœnix* 10 April (B.), Should any negro be found vending spirituous liquors, without permission from his owner, such negro so offending shall receive fifteen cobbs or paddles for every such offence. **1859** BARTLETT 89 [citing prec.] *Cobb*, a blow on the buttock.

Cob, *v.* +*tr.* (See quot. 1874.) — **1874** KNIGHT 582 *Cŏb.* (*Mining.*) To break ore with a hammer, to reduce its size, to enable its separation from portions of the gangue, and its assortment into grades of quality. **1880** G. INGHAM *Digging Gold* 37 Balbach & Sons informed them that if the rock had been properly 'cobbed,' as it should have been, they would have had in that sum the product of about four tons of ore, or . . . eighty-six dollars per ton.

Cobalt. A metallic element resembling nickel. Also attrib. {1683–} **1785** *Deane Papers* 215 You have herewith a Small Box of Ore from the Cobalt Mine Near Middletown. *a***1817** DWIGHT *Travels* I. 35 A mine of Cobalt has been discovered in Chatham. **1867** *Atlantic Mo.* June 665/2 Within one hundred miles of St. Louis, the following metals and minerals are found in quantities that will repay working: gold, iron, lead, zinc, . . . cobalt, coal, [etc.].

***Cobble.** +'A rounded hill' (*Cent.*). — **1890** M. TOWNSEND *U.S.* 135 *Cobble.* From the German, *koble*, meaning 'rocks.' Name applied to a hill or other moderate elevation whose sides have a covering of loose or cobble-stones. *Cobble Hill* (Adirondacks), N.Y., *Cobbleskill*, N.Y. (In the Catskills.) The word is local with Massachusetts and New York.

*Cobbler. Also †cobler.

***1.** One whose business is mending shoes.

1640 *Conn. Public Rec.* I. 55 The goods of the Cobler deceased. **1788** FRENEAU *Misc. Works* 79 Not far from thence a cobler's son Stood by his hides. **1895** M. A. JACKSON *Memoirs* 445 In the case of a cobbler, or the tailor, for instance, religion will produce more care in promising work.

+2. A drink composed of wine, sugar, fruit juices and crushed ice. Cf. SHERRY COBBLER.

1846 *Spirit of Times* 6 June 170/1, I made 'julaps' and 'coblers' for them in the early part of the evening. **1852** *Harper's Mag.* V. 334/1 There is nothing else to see or do there, but to look at the falls, eat dinner, drink cobblers, and smoke. **1857** *Ib.* February 348/2 [This] piece of intelligence . . . greatly enlarged the demand for slings and cobblers. **1876** G. H. TRIPP *Student-Life* 54 To Kent's they had repaired, however, at his invitation, with a mighty thirst for 'cobblers.' **1887** WHITMAN *Nov. Boughs* (1888) 437 My recollection of the 'cobblers' (with strawberries and snow on top of the large tumblers,) . . . help[s] the regretful reminiscence of my New Orleans experiences.

+3. A fruit pie, now usu. made in a deep pan with crust only on the top.

1859 BARTLETT 90 *Cobbler*, . . . a sort of pie, baked in a pot lined with dough of great thickness, upon which the fruit is placed; according to the fruit, it is an apple or a peach cobbler. Western. **1880** 'MARK TWAIN' *Tramp Abroad* xlix. 575, I have . . . made out a little bill of fare . . . as follows: . . . Peach cobbler, Southern style. **1884** F. OWENS *Cook Book* 187 Apple Cobbler. Fill an earthen pudding-dish 2/3 full of tart, juicy apples, peeled, quartered, and cored [etc.]. . . . Peach cobblers are made similarly. **1888** L. HARGIS *Graded Cook Book* 270 Puddings. Without eggs. Apricot or Peach Cobbler for Winter. **1904** DERVILLE *Other Side of Story* 71, I often dream of peach cobblers and blackberry pies.

+**Cob-crusher.** A machine for crushing corncobs. — **1850** *New Eng. Farmer* II. 363 Beal's Patent Corn-Cracker and Cob-Crusher. This machine is used for cracking cobs and corn previous to passing through the millstones. **1852** *Mich. Agric. Soc. Trans.* III. 29 Best corn and Cob crusher, by horse power.

Cob dollar. [cob, etym. unknown, 1672–.] A Spanish dollar. {1745} — **1786** *New Haven Gaz.* 6 April 63/2 [The robbers found] some small pieces of coin, and a cobb dollar. **1786** *Md. Jrnl.* 14 March (Th.), In one of the Desks they found Thirteen milled Dollars, . . . and a Cobb Dollar; the latter being a Counterfeit was thrown on the Floor. **1880** BROOKS *Fairport Nine* 124, Some folks call them cob dollars, I don't know why, unless Gen. Cobb first dug 'em up.

+**Cob fashion.** A method of arranging logs, etc., having the ends interlocked, as in a child's cob house. — *a***1862** THOREAU *Maine Woods* 193 They had got a young moose, . . . confined in a sort of cage of logs piled up cob-fashion. **1888** BILLINGS *Hardtack* 49 By far the most common way of logging up a tent was to build the walls 'cob-fashion,' notching them together at the corners.

Cob gold. Gold, in coined or uncoined form, purporting to be of Spanish origin. (See COB DOLLAR, MONEY). — **1789** *Md. Jrnl.* 2 Jan. (Th.), The public are hereby cautioned against taking a certain kind of cob-gold, which is now in circulation. **1860** S. MORDECAI *Virginia* 276 Also a portion of Cob gold and silver in irregular uncoined pieces.

+Cob house.

1. A toy house built of cobs; a structure of sticks or other material laid criss-cross.

1774 J. BELKNAP in *Life* 68 They have a neat poultry house, built of sawed strips of wood, in the form of a cob-house, with four apartments. **1776** J. ADAMS in *Fam. Lett.* (1876) 195 They are erecting governments as fast as children build cob-houses. **1818** BIRKBECK *Lett. Illinois* 116 In this country they build 'cob houses'; . . . with these cobs . . . structures are raised by the little half Indian brats, very much like our 'houses of cards.' **1830** *Mass. Spy* 21 July (Th.), The [Negro] victim is chained to a stake, and a pile of combustible wood built up around him, in the form of a cob-house. **1856** M. J. HOLMES *L. Rivers* 53 Knocking down a cob-house, which 'Thomas Jefferson' had been all day building, he mounted his favorite 'Firelock.' **1881** *Harper's Mag.* Nov. 824 George builds a cob house of chips and is soon rewarded with a blaze. **1886** *Century Mag.* Sept. 789/1, I have often found their [cranes'] nests, and always in the shallow water in the slough, built out of sticks, much as the children build cob-houses.

attrib. **1859** *Harper's Mag.* March 485/1 Long golden bars of 'diet-bread' piled up, cob-house fashion. **1882** THAYER *From Log-Cabin* i. 20 It was twenty by thirty feet, made of unhewn logs, notched and laid one upon another, in what boys call the 'cob-house' style.

2. *fig.* An insecure, unstable scheme; a 'house of cards.'

1854 HAMMOND *Hills, Lakes* 261 The fifteen or sixteen States went on increasin' to twenty, and then twenty-five, and so on till Texas came in, and then there was a talk about the cob-house goin' down agin. **1913** *N.Y. Ev. Post* 5 June 6/3 (Th. S.), Mayor Gaynor made a statement comparing the 'Curran Scandal committee' to a 'cobhouse of sensationalism, lying, and scandal. All cobhouses [he added] fall down at the first jar.'

attrib. **1834** *Congress. Deb.* 26 Feb. 736 With the first shock in the commerce or credit of the country, the whole cob-house fabric must tumble.

+**Cobia.** The sergeant fish, *Elacate canada.* — **1884** GOODE *Aquatic Animals* 444 The Cobia or crab-eater, *Elacate canada*, . . . is considered one of the most important food-fishes of Maryland and Virginia.

‖**Cobish meal.** (See quotation.) — **1824** *New Eng. Farmer* II. 262 By 'cobish meal,' we believe our correspondent means the produce of Indian corn ground or broken with the cob, without shelling it before it was submitted to the operation of the mill.

+**Cob meal.** A meal consisting of ground corn and corncobs. (Cf. prec.) — **1837** COLMAN *Mass. Agric. Rep.* (1838) 83 Beef animals fattening . . . on boiled potatoes, apples, and cob meal. **1868** *Comm. Agric. Rep.* (1869) 439 Poor pastures, poor meadows, hay, and a few shorts or cob-meal. *c***1872** *Dept. Agric. Rep. 1873* 414 He gives each cow four quarts of a mixture of shorts and cob-meal per day.

+**Cob money.** Early Spanish American coins, usually of silver. (See COB DOLLAR, GOLD.) — **1793** *Mass. H. S. Coll.* III. 120 At times to this day, there are King William and Queen Mary's coppers picked up, and pieces of silver, called cob money. *a***1862** THOREAU *Cape Cod* 148 Pieces of silver called cob-money. **1868** LOSSING *Hudson* 80 The old silver coins occasionally found at Fort Edward are called 'cob-money' by the people.

+**Cob pipe.** A tobacco pipe whose bowl is made from a section of a corncob.

1847 in Drake *Pioneer Life Ky.* 63 Father [was] meanwhile quietly smoking a cob pipe in the corner. **1868** W. BAKER *New Timothy* 186 Doc. Meggar has placed the stem of his cob pipe firmly between his teeth. **1895** L. BELL *Little Sister* 16 His shriveled wife . . . leaned forward on the front seat, with her elbows on her knees, smoking a cob-pipe. **1902** LORIMER *Lett. Merchant* 147 [He] usually kept a chew in one cheek and a cob pipe in the other.

Cobweb muslin. A fine grade of cotton cloth. — **1807** IRVING, etc. *Salmagundi* v, Will thundered down the dance like a coach-and-six, . . . making sad inroads into ladies' cobweb muslins and spangled tails. **1807** *Salem Gazette* 3 April, Constantly for Salem, American, French, English, Italian, Dutch and India manufactures, from the coarse Tow Cloth to the fine Cobweb Muslin. **1820** *Columbian Centinel* 1 Jan. 1/1 The subscriber . . . will sell at wholesale or retail . . . white Jeans, . . . Cobweb muslins.

+**Cobwork.** Articles laid in the manner of the cobs in a child's cob house. — **1845** JUDD *Margaret* I. xvii. 158 A great fire, composed of a huge green back-log, a large green forestick, and a high cob-work of crooked and knotty refuse-wood.

+**Cocash.** [Amer. Indian.] (See quots. 1828 and 1907.) — **1828** RAFINESQUE *Medical Flora* I. 167 They [*sc.* plants of the genus *Erigeron*] were known to the Northern Indians by the name of Cocash or Squaw-weed. **1896** *Garden & For.* IX. 262 Cocash (*Aster puniceus*). — From Natick (Algonkin) *kokoshki*, 'it is very rough,' a name referring to the hispid character of the stems, which has given the plants one of its common names—'rough-stemmed aster.' **1907** Hodge *Indians* I. 316 Cocash. A name of the red-stalk or purple-stem aster (*Aster puniceus*), known also as swan-weed, early purple aster, etc.

+**Coch.** Ellipt. for COCHLEAUREATUS. Hence *Cochship.* — **1871** BAGG *At Yale* 131 The Delta Phi men attended the class meeting, and voted for the three Cochs and two Editors whom they had—without hope of success—nominated in the usual way. *Ib.* 407 At first, when all the non-appointment men were called Cochleaureati, the Cochs were expected to be mostly chosen from their number. — *Ib.* 422 It was announced that DKE had ordered that none of its members should accept cochships.

Cochin. *ellipt.* =next. {1853–} — **1871** [see next]. **1876** INGRAM *Centennial Expos.* 679 Of the large Cochins there were several varieties, some of them large pure white, others pure black. **1877** *Harper's Mag.* Feb. 447/1 Somebody dropped over the fence a pair of big black Cochins, that stalked about as if the earth was too good to tread on. **1894** *Vt. Agric. Rep.* XIV. 173 But you ask what breed shall I select? . . . If for roasters, then select the Brahma Cochin, Langshan, or Plymouth Rocks.

Cochin China. A variety of domestic fowl, originally imported from Cochin China. {1853–}

1850 BROWNE *Poultry Yard* 36 In the United States, there are numerous individuals who possess large fowls bearing the name of 'Cochin-China,' which have been crossed with the Dorking and other large breeds. **1853** B. F. TAYLOR *Jan. & June* 81 The pears and the apples are coming on; the setting Bantams and Cochin Chinas are coming off. **1854** *Penna. Agric. Rep.* 78 Cochin Chinas. Best pair to Robert Purvis . . . $2.00. **1871** LEWIS *Poultry Book* 36 Although called Cochin Chinas, the Buff Cochins are the real Shanghaes. **1912** N. M. WOODROW *Sally Salt* 40 A great flock of industriously pecking chickens, snow-white Leghorns, gray speckled Plymouth Rocks, buff cochin-chinas, [etc.].

attrib. **1850** BROWNE *Poultry Yard* 34 The Cochin-China cock has a large, upright, single, deeply-indented comb. *Ib.* 35 [Illustration of the] Cochin-China Hen. *Ib.* 33 *Gallus giganteus* (var.?), of Temminck; Cochin-China Fowl, Ostrich Fowl, of the English and Anglo-Americans. **1870** MEDBERY *Men Wall St.* 313 There were hen-brokers in New Orleans, Boston, and London. A pair of Cochin China fowl were valued at $700.

*** Cochineal.** Also †**cochineel, -nele.**

***1.** A dyestuff made from the bodies of an insect (*Coccus cacti*) that feeds on cactus.

[**1705** *Boston News-Letter* 9 July 1/1 A French Ship, homeward bound from Martinico, which had on Board . . . Indico, Cochineel, &c.] **1819** E. DANA *Geogr. Sk.* 203 Rice, indigo and cochineal, are also produced in this country [Florida]. **1836** EDWARD *Hist. Texas* 132 Cocoa, maguey, vanilla and cochineal are also perennial staples. **1863** C. C. HOPLEY *Life in South* II. 306 Cochineal is found in South Carolina, Georgia, and Alabama.

b. The color of this dye.

*a***1886** E. DICKINSON *Works* (1924) 19 Can blaze be done in cochineal?

***2.** The insect *Coccus cacti* used in making this dye.

1690 J. EDWARDS *Demonstration* (1696) II. 215 Whether the cochinele is to be numbred among the volatile insects I am not certain. **1827** DEWEES *Lett. Texas* 64 Upon the leaf of the prickly pear grows a small red insect, called cochineal. When this cochineal is dried, it bears a strong resemblance to a little bug, and is very valuable for dyeing. **1836** M. A. HOLLEY *Texas* 84 The fruit [of the nopal] is not permitted to grow on the plants designed for the cochineal, as the nourishment necessary for the insects would thus be diminished.

3. Attrib. with *fly, insect, plant.*

1739 *Ga. Hist. Soc. Coll.* I. 188 Taking the flies off though green upon the shrub, and squeezing them, they dye the fingers with a deep red, . . . which this deponent verily believes to be the cochineal fly. **1801** *Hist. Review & Directory* I. 12 The Cochineal insect is found in great plenty. **1805** LEWIS in *L. & Clark Exped.* (1904) II. 272 There is another species of the prickly pear . . . with the flat leaf, like the Cocheneel plant.

+Cochleaureatus. [L. *cochlea*, a snail shell or spoon, after *laureat-us*, crowned with laurel.] Pl. **cochleaureati.** (See quotations.) *Yale college use.* (Cf. WOODEN SPOON.) — **1853** *Songs of Yale* 37 Now give in honor of the spoon, Three cheers, long, loud, and hearty, And three for every honored June In *coch-le-au-re-a-ti.* **1856** HALL *College Words* (ed. 2) 81 At Yale College, the wooden spoon is given to the one whose name comes last on the list of appointees for the Junior Exhibition. The recipient of this honor is designated *cochleaureatus.* **1871** [see COCH].

Cochmelies. (See COJINILLO.)

+Cochranism, Cochranite. The beliefs and practices of a religious sect in New England; a member of the sect. — **1819** Brooks *Gleanings* 103 (*advt.*), Cochranism Delineated, Or a description of, and specific for, a religious Hydrophobia, which has spread & is spreading in . . . the counties of York and Cumberland, . . . Maine. [**1853** *Maine H. S. Coll.* III. 165 In 1816 the religious movement under Jacob Cochran commenced in this town [Scarborough], and some of those concerned in it remain at the present time amongst his followers.] **1871** DE VERE 242 The *Cochranites* of the New England States held public exhibitions of so gross a character that the civil authorities were more than once compelled to intervene, for the vindication of public decency.

+Cochuck, *adv.* [Echoic.] =COCHUNK. — **1857** *Knickerb.* XLIX. 41 He came out most all-sufficiently strong, co-chuck up to the hub in slashergaff style.

+Cochunk, *adv.* An echoic formation designating the sound made when a heavy body hits an object. (Cf. CA- and KERCHUNK.) Also *colloq.* as an intensive. — **1847** *Chunkey's Fight* 128 Co chunk! went Jem into the middle of the floor. **1847** ROBB *Squatter Life* 31 We 'spect you to be right co-'chunk up to the hub on them thar questions. **1850** LEWIS *La. Swamp Dr.* 50 Preacher tried to pass Colt, and cowollop, crosh, cochunk! we all cum down like 'simmons arter frost.

+Cocina. *S.W.* [Sp.] Also **cochina.** A kitchen. — **1844** KENDALL *Santa Fé Exped.* II. 148 At the cocina, or kitchen, amid the steams of rank and highly-seasoned stews, he may esteem himself lucky if he can purchase a bowl of mutton broth. [**1846** MAGOFFIN *Down Santa Fé Trail* 103 We have four rooms including *la cochina* (the kitchen).]

+Cocinera, -o. *S.W.* [Sp.] A cook. — **1844** GREGG *Commerce of Prairies* I. 242 Respecting *fandangos*, . . . from the grandest *señora* to the *cocinera*—all partake of this exhilarating amusement. **1845** GREEN *Texian Exped.* 258 When not presiding as chief cocinero (cook) much of my time was employed at the desk.

*** Cock.**[1]

1. A male turkey; a gobbler.

1636 *Winthrop P.* 515, I have but one turky, which . . . proves to be a cocke. **1870** KEIM *Sheridan's Troopers* 154 Towards sunset, about fifty fine birds, headed, as usual, by a noble cock, appeared on the bluff overlooking the camp.

2. A comrade or familiar friend. *colloq.*[2] {1639–}

1835 LONGSTREET *Ga. Scenes* 22 Well, fetch up your nag, my old cock; you're jist the lark I wanted to get hold of. **1879** STOCKTON *Rudder Grange* 34 Certainly, my high old cock!

3. Phrase. *That cock won't fight*, that will not do; that scheme will not work. *colloq.*[2] {1850–}

1836 CROCKETT *Exploits* 99 The captain of the boat, a determined fellow, went ashore in the hope of persuading them to refund—but that cock wouldn't fight. **1860** HARTE *Luck of Roaring Camp*, etc. (1870) 179 Want her yourself, do you? That cock won't fight here, young man!

***4.** In phrases *cock of the company, of the loft, of the roost, of the walk*, etc., chief person, leader.

1785 *Md. Hist. Mag.* XXI. 36 My back is no sooner turned than you whip down, who but you, and are the Cock of the Company. **1832** PAULDING *Westward Ho!* II. 56 He was getting to be cock of the wood. **1835** HOFFMAN *Winter in West* I. 259 Bill was too much a cock of the walk to mind it. **1906** 'O. HENRY' *Four Million* 165 The cock-of-the-roost sits aloft like Jupiter on an unsharable seat, holding your fate between two thongs of inconstant leather. **1907** ANDREWS *Recoll.* 166 'We're cock of the loft here,' and similar expressions.

*** Cock.**[2] A conical heap of hay, carrots, etc.

'When hay is dry and rolled together for carting, the heaps are not generally called *cocks*, at least not in New England. A large conical pile is called a stack' (W. '28).

1684 I. MATHER *Providences* (1856) v. 116 Several cocks of English-hay, mowed near the house, were taken and hung upon trees. **1735** HEMPSTEAD *Diary* 306, I dryed about a L[oa]d of hay yt was in Cock not Cured & Stacked it back Side of the Lot with the boys help. **1804** J. ROBERTS *Penna. Farmer* 177 They [carrots] should be dug in dry days in October, and, the tops being cut off, put up in small covered cocks of ten bushels each. **1839** BUEL *Farmer's Companion* 218 The advantage of curing clover in the cock is this, that when cured by being spread, the leaves and blossome are dry long before the stems are cured. **1904** E. W. PRINGLE *Rice Planter* 121 Monday's cutting is tied up and put in little cocks in the field.

Cockade. A badge of ribbons worn on the hat. (Cf. BLACK COCKADE.) {1709–}

1774 *N.H. Hist. Soc. Coll.* IX. 193 [The officers to wear] white Stockings —Cockades—Sashes and white Gorgets. **1823** THACHER *Military Jrnl.* 185 He entered his pulpit with his sword and cockade. **1860** MORDECAI *Virginia* 78, I have a faint recollection of seeing cockades mounted in the hats of many gentlemen, toward the close of Washington's administration. **1887** *Century Mag.* April 848/1 [During the Civil War], some of the young men, though they wore the blue cockade, did not align themselves with the minute-men.

transf. **1890–3** E. M. TABER *Stowe Notes* 34 It was somewhat difficult to tell these latter . . . from the sumach cockades, off which I noticed them feeding.

+Cockarouse. Also **caucorouse, cockoroose, coccorous,** etc. *Obs.* [f. Amer. Indian.] A chief or leader among the Indians.

Also transf. (quots. 1651, 1708). '*Cockarouse* . . . [was] used by the English settlers as a term for a person of consequence' (B. '59).

1624 SMITH *Virginia* II. 38 They haue . . . few occasions to vse any officers more then one commander, which commonly they call Werowance, or Caucorouse, which is Captaine. **1634** *Relat. Md.* v. 33 They have also Cockorooses that are their Captains in time of war, to whom they are very obedient. **1651** *Discovery of New Brittaine* 28 Aug. (Th. S.), There was a Wainoake Indian told him that there was an Englishman a Cockarous hard by Captaine Floods. **1705** BEVERLEY *Virginia* II. 33 That man was counted a Cockarouse, or brave Fellow, [who would not lose his hold of a Sturgeon]. **1708** E. COOK *Sot-Weed Factor* 19 E'er long we lighted at the Gate: Where in an antient Cedar House, Dwelt my new Friend a Cockerouse. **1743** CATESBY *Carolina* App. p. xi, The Indians [of Carolina deem] . . . it ignominious for a *Coccorous*, that is a war-captain, or good hunter, to do mechanick works, except what relates to war or hunting.

+Cockbill, *v. tr.* To hang (the anchor) from the cathead ready for dropping. — **1840** DANA *Two Years* xxxvi. 137 The pilot gave orders to cockbill the anchor.

*** Cockcrowing.** The crowing of a cock; early dawn, when cocks crow. {–1642}

1643 R. WILLIAMS *Key* 67 Chouoeatch, [Indian term, meaning] About Cockcrowing. **1843** *Knickerb.* XXII. 1 A fine old planter . . . amused me until nearly cockcrowing with his long stories of revolutionary days. **1844** EMERSON *Nature Addresses, Young Amer.*, All this drudgery, from cockcrowing to starlight. **1878** *N. Amer. Rev.* CXXVII. 59 Like the cock-crowing that sounded in the ears of Peter.

Cocked, ***ppl. a.*** {1650–}

+1. *fig.* Prepared, ready.

1832 *Congress. Deb.* 3 May 2725 We would say $20,000 is necessary. He would then be cocked and primed for his report.

+2. Intoxicated, drunk. *slang.* {Cf. Australian slang, *half-cocked*, 1888}

a1856 Hall *College Words* (ed. 2) 461 Words and phrases which have been in use . . . to signify some stage of inebriation: Over the bay, half seas over, hot, high, corned, cut, cocked, [etc.]. **1859** Elwyn *Glossary* 103 He is confounded slewed, means very intoxicated. . . . 'Cocked' is a synonym.

+3. *Cocked joint,* (see quotation).

1872 Huntington *Road-Master's Asst.* 15 Otherwise the joint-tie will be likely to roll somewhat to one side, and thus form a 'cocked joint.'

Cocked hat.

1. A hat with the brim turned up; the three-cornered hat fashionable in the late 18th c. {1673–}

1787 *Maryland Gaz.* 1 June 3/2 [He] had on a good drab-coloured coat, cocked hat, boots, his other clothes unnoticed. **1837** *Knickerb.* X. 378 The cocked-hat is obsolete. **1892** J. E. Cooke *B. Hallam* 22 His broad, fine brow, full of intelligence and grace, is covered by an old cocked hat.

comb. **1855** Thompson *Doesticks* vi. 42, [I] afterwards visited (by particular desire) the cocked-hat shaped Sahara known as the 'City Hall Square.'

+2. *To knock into a cocked hat,* to beat badly, to ruin or demolish entirely. *colloq.* {1873–}

1833 Paulding *Banks of Ohio* I. 217 (Th.), I told Tom I'd knock him into a cocked hat if he said another word. **1834** Crockett *Narr. Life* 36, I didn't know how soon I should be knocked into a cocked hat. **1838** Drake *Tales Queen City* 92 Many were trampled under foot, some gouged . . . and not a few knocked clear into a cocked hat. **1840** *Congress. Globe* 20 July 545/3 Why pummel and beat over again that which is already beaten to a jelly, jammed into a cocked hat, and flung into the middle of next week? **1846** Corcoran *Pickings* 148 With hair dishevelled, bonnet knocked into a 'cocked hat,' and dress draggled and in disorder, she appeared as though she had been enacting antics under the joint influence of rum and romance. **1866** Pollard *Lost Cause* (De Vere), Although it took little more to knock Fort Sumter into a cocked hat, [etc.]. **1907** in Bryan *Memoirs* 332 Would that we could do something . . . to knock Mr. Bryan once for all into a cocked hat.

+3. 'A variety of the game of bowls in which but three pins, placed at the angles of a triangle, are used' (*Cent.*).

1858 *S. Lit. Messenger* XXVII. 351/1 His great strength compelled him to use the largest balls, even when playing 'Cocked-Hat.'

Cockeye. [? Ellipt. for *woodcock eye.*] A snap hook on the end of a trace. — **1849** *Rep. Comm. Patents* 266 The combination of the loop of the trace with a sectional cross piece, (B,) and a cockeye, (A,) whereby the trace is secured to a swivel cockeye. **1874** Knight 582 *Cock-eye,* . . . an iron loop on the end of a single-tree. **1883** *Rep. Indian Affairs* 386.

*** Cockfight,** ***n.*** A match in which cocks are set to fight each other.

1774 Fithian *Journal* I. 144, I was before Dinner very strongly urged . . . to attend a Cock-Fight, where 25 Cocks are to fight, & large Sums are betted. **1812** *Amer. Rev. Hist.* Oct. 370 Let there be a horse race, or a cock fight, . . . and notice the multitudes of able bodied individuals who attend them. **c1845** *Big Bear Ark.*, etc. 33 He was a general referee . . . whether it was a horse swap, a race, a rifle match, or a cock fight. **1861** *Vanity Fair* 9 Feb. 65/2 The President of the Board, with several of his colleagues, had gone to a cock-fight. **a1918** G. Stuart *On Frontier* I. 69 Every Sunday there were horse racing, cock fights and dog fights.

+Cockfight, ***v. intr.*** To hold or conduct a cockfight. — **1815** *Wheeley's Baptist Ch. Min.* June (N.C. Univ. MSS.), Report Says Brother Wheely is in the habit of Selling Spirits to Negroes on the Lords day . . . & also alowing the Liberty for people to Cockfight there.

Cock-fighter. One who patronizes the sport of cock-fighting. {1721–} — **1845** *N.Y. Herald* 7 May 2/2 The potential agencies to which . . . Mr. Polk owes his election [are] . . . 'pocket book droppers,' 'brothel-owners and bullies,' 'cock-fighters,' 'dog stealers.'

***Cock-fighting.** The practice of setting cocks to fight each other. — **1724** H. Jones *Virginia* 48 The common Planters leading easy Lives don't much admire Labour, or any manly Exercise, except Horse-Racing, nor Diversion, except Cock-Fighting, in which some greatly delight. **1784** J. Smyth *Tour U.S.* I. 67 That most barbarous of all diversions, that peculiar species of cruelty, Cock-fighting. **1840** Dana *Two Years* xiii, Monterey is a great place for cock-fighting, . . . fandangos [etc.].

‖**Cock-gaff.** A metal spur for a fighting cock. (See Chicken gaff.) — **1759** *Newport Mercury* 26 June 4/3 Imported . . . and to be sold by Jacob Richardson, . . . Cock-gaffs, Money-purses, &c.

Cocking main. =Cock main. — **1883** 'Mark Twain' *Life on Miss.* xlv. 458 The 'cocking-main' is an unhuman sort of entertainment; . . . still, it seems a much more respectable and far less cruel sport than fox-hunting. **1887** *Courier-Journal* 20 Feb. 4/2 A lively cocking main took place last night at a farm-house, on the Preston-street road, at which about fifty leading cock-fanciers were present. **1898** *Kansas City Star* 20 Dec. 3/2 A big interstate cocking main has been arranged.

*** Cockle.**[1]

***1.** A bivalve mollusk, esp. the edible *Cardium edule.*

1612 Smith *Virginia* 15 Of fish we were best acquainted with . . . Pearch of 3 sorts, Crabs, Shrimps, Creuises, Oysters, Cocles, and Muscles. **1698** G. Thomas *Acc. Pensilvania* 14 As also the large sort of Fish, as . . . Cockles, (some as big as Stewing Oysters of which are made a Choice Soupe or Broth). **1805** Parkinson *Tour* 316 At New-York, there are salmon, cod-fish, lobsters, clams (by some called cockles), &c. **1868** *Amer. Naturalist* II. 242 The common Cockle (*Purpura lapillus*) . . . is another very common species on our coast.

+2. A small boat (from the shape like a cockleshell).

1829 *Va. Lit. Museum* 438 Why as I crept off t'other shore there was a bubble of a sea a-running enough to fill the old cockle. **1868** Lossing *Hudson* 308 Two or three duck-hunters, in their little cockles.

+3. A piece of candy accompanied by a motto or verse.

1851 Hawthorne *Twice-told T.* I. viii. 149 And those little cockles . . . much prized by children for their sweetness, and more for their mottoes. **1893** Hale *New Eng. Boyhood* 159 She frosted it [a cake] herself, and dressed it with what in those days they used to call 'cockles' of sugar. These cockles generally had little scraps of poor verses, which were supposed to be entertaining.

***Cockle.**[2] The corn cockle (*Lychnis Githago*), a weed that infests grainfields. — **1792** *N.Y. State Soc. Arts* I. 25 Cockle, drips and sorrel often mingle their seeds with the crop. **1863** *Rep. Comm. Agric.* 90 Nothing but wheat should be allowed to mature; cockle, cheat, and smut should be carefully weeded out of it. **1886** *Century Mag.* May 44/1 There still remains an objectionable element in the grain [=wheat] which must be gotten rid of—the seeds of cockle and other weeds.

+Cocklebur(r). Also **cuckle-burr.**

1. A coarse annual weed of the genus *Xanthium.* {1866–}

1815 Drake *Cincinnati* 119 The wide alluvial vallies of these rivers . . . abound in . . . cockle burr (*Xanthium strumarium*). **1831** Audubon *Ornith. Biog.* I. 135 These birds [Carolina parrots] are represented feeding on the plant commonly named the Cockle-bur. **1871** *Ill. Agric. Soc. Trans.* VIII. 241 The cockle-burr and rag-weeds are great enemies to the farmers. **1918** Rideout *Key of Fields* 234 Bolders looked cautiously through his weeds, a mass of cockleburs and greasewood, withered brown.

2. An involucre of this plant, with a rough, spiny covering.

1845 Hooper *Daddy Biggs' Scrape* 196 They was as thick all round me, as cuckle-burrs in a colt's tail. **1876** Habberton *Jericho Road* 128 One of them attempted to create a diversion by throwing a cockle-burr upon the bald pate of a kneeling person. **1896** Harris *Sister Jane* 14 She brought back . . . none of those airs that seem to stick like cockle-burrs on a sheep, to many young ladies. **1925** Tilghman *Dugout* 7 And we put a cockle-bur under old Sam's crupper.

3. Used as an exclamation.

1850 Lewis *La. Swamp Dr.* 45 Murder! Hingins! h—l and kuckle-burs! Oh! Lordy!

Cock main. A series of cockfights. {main of cocks, 1760–} — **1813** *Raleigh* (N.C.) *Minerva* 30 April, On Thursday, the 18th next month a Cock Main, for a considerable sum. **1890** H. Frederic *Lawton Girl* 33, I've seen dog-fights and cock-mains in England. **1896** Harris *Sister Jane* 303 But think of a Virginian gentleman talking about nothing but racing events, cock mains, and driving all over the country to see them!

*** Cockney.** A townsman; an effeminate, uncultivated, but forward person. Also attrib. or as *adj.*: Having these characteristics. {–1826; *Obs.*}

1830 Cooper *Water Witch* II. i, The night-air has taut'ned the cordage of that flying-jib-boom, fellows, until it begins to lift its nose like a squeamish cockney when he holds it over saltwater! **1835** Hoffman *Winter in West* I. 165, I take a singular pleasure in surveying these beauties, as yet . . . unprofaned by the cockney eyes of city tourists. **1844** *Knickerb.* XXIII. 443 None of your reed-birds and meadow-larks, such as cockney sportsmen frighten away from the fields of Jersey or Long Island. **1846** Cooper *Redskins* iv, As for comparing the bay of New York with that of Naples on the score of beauty, I shall no more be guilty of any such folly, to gratify the cockney feelings of Broadway and Bond Street. **1851** *Knickerb.* XXXVIII. 642 The country church is a square old building of wood . . . of that genuine Puritanic stamp which is now fast giving way to Greek porticos and cockney towers. **1904** *N.Y. Tribune* 17 July 8 Now even many rural districts are as dependent on the beef packer, the vegetable canner, . . . as the veriest cockney.

+Cock of the plains. The sage cock (*Centrocercus urophasianus*), a large kind of grouse.

1805 Lewis in *L. & Clark Exped.* (1904) II. 384 Capt. C. killed a cock of the plains or mountain cock. It was of a dark brown colour with a long and pointed tail. **1828** Bonaparte *Ornithology* III. 56 The name of Cock of the Plains was given by Lewis and Clark [who] . . . first met with this bird on their journey westward near the fountain of the Missouri. **1852** Baird in Stansbury *Gt. Salt Lake* 319 *Tetrao urophasianus*, Bp.—Cock of the Plains, or Prairie Cock; Sage Cock. **1886** *Stand. Nat. Hist.* (1888) IV. 209 The sage-cock, or cock-of-the-plains, . . . is the largest grouse found in America. **1917** *Birds of Amer.* II. 29 [The] Cock of the Plains . . . exceeds all other Grouse in size, with the possible exception of the Great Black Grouse . . . of Europe, and its peculiar nuptial performances go far to establish it as one of the wonders of animated nature.

Cockroach. A beetlelike insect of the genus *Blatta*, that infests kitchens, ships, etc. (*B. occidentalis, germanica*, etc.). {1624– in West Indies.}

1737 BRICKELL *N. Carolina* 161 The Cock-roch, is a kind of Beetle, something larger than a Cricket, and of a dark brown Colour. **1789** MORSE *Amer. Geog.* 62 Of the astonishing variety of Insects found in America, we will mention . . . Cock Roche, [etc.]. **1800** BOUCHER *Glossary* p. xlix, *Cockroaches;* inoffensive beetles, that much infest dwelling houses. **1836** R. WESTON *Visit* 77 Besides my old enemies the bugs and fleas, I now discovered a new one called a cock-roach. **1847** *Knickerb.* XXX. 394 At twilight a score of gentlemen cock-roaches enter the sitting-room. **1854** EMMONS *Agric. N.Y.* V. 141 We have several species of cockroach, which either inhabit fields or woody places. The common domestic one (*Blatta orientalis*) is an imported kind. **1865** *Atlantic Mo.* XV. 16, I made many inquires about these terrible *persicas*, and finally discovered that they were neither more nor less than—cock-roaches. **1892** V. KELLOG *Kansas Insects* 108 Cockroach. (*Periplaneta orientalis* and *Blatta germanica*) . . . The roaches attack provisions of all kinds.

+**Cock-robin duck.** The hooded merganser, *Lophodytes cucullatus.* — **1856** *Spirit of Times* 13 Dec. 242/2 Of the mergansers and goosanders, known as shell-drakes, and, in some places, as 'Cock-robin ducks,' we do not deign to speak. **1889** *Cent.* 1789/1 *Cock-robin duck*, the hooded merganser. (New Jersey, U.S.)

***Cockscomb.** Also **coxcomb.** One or other of several plants, esp. certain species of amaranth. (See quotations.) {1741–}

1791 MUHLENBERG *Index Florae* 164 *Celosia castrensis*, Cocks-comb. **1836** LINCOLN *Botany* App. 74 *Amaranthus albus*, white coxcomb. . . . Common garden weed. **1899** GOING *Flowers* 354 Some species of amaranth are cultivated in old fashioned gardens, and called 'cockscomb,' 'love-lies-bleeding,' and 'prince's feather.' **1901** *Harper's Mag.* Dec. 211 They had their own yards, . . . brave with hollyhocks and cock's-comb around the fountain.

Cocksfoot (grass). a. A well-known hay and pasture grass, *Dactylis glomerata;* orchard grass. {1697–} **b.** Cockspur grass.

1791 MUHLENBERG *Index Florae* 161 *Dactylis glomerata*, Cock's foot-grass. **1795** WINTERBOTHAM *Hist. View* III. 401 Besides the cultivated grasses, the States of New-England abound with a great variety which are found growing in their native soils and situations. . . . Most common are the following. . . . Cock's foot grass, . . . Millet, [etc.]. **1839** BUEL *Farmer's Companion* 228 American Cock's-foot and Orchard-grass are different names given to the *Dactylis glomerata* of botanists. *Ib.*, American Cock's-foot . . . may be known by its . . . seed-glumes resembling a cock's-foot. **1849** EMMONS *Agric. N.Y.* II. 81 *Panicum Crus-galli* (Cocksfoot grass). Grown in the yard of the old State House. **1889** VASEY *Agric. Grasses* 14 Pastures consisting largely of early, strong-growing grasses, particularly cock's foot (orchard grass).

***Cockspur.** +COCKSPUR THORN. — **1792** IMLAY *Western Territory* 213. **1858** WARDER *Hedges & Evergreens* 25 The Cockspur . .. is a native of our Middle States, and is truly beautiful, with its deep green and highly-foliated leaves.

Cockspur grass. Barnyard grass, *Panicum crus-galli.* — **1861** WOOD *Botany* 787 *Oplismenus* Beauv. Cock-spur Grass. **1901** MOHR *Plant Life Ala.* 357 Barnyard Grass, Cockspur Grass. . . . Low wet ground, cultivated places, border of marshes; annual.

Cockspur hawthorn. The cockspur, or cockspur thorn. {1741–} — **1781–2** JEFFERSON *Notes Va.* (1788) 38 Cockspur hawthorn. *Crataegus coccinea.* **1795** WINTERBOTHAM *Hist. View* III. 392 Flowering Trees, Shrubs, [include] . . . Holly, . . . Cockspur hawthorn. **1897** SUDWORTH *Arborescent Flora* 216 *Cratægus crus-galli.* . . . Cockspur Hawthorn (Pa.).

Cockspur thorn. A handsome North American species of hawthorn, *Crataegus crus-galli.* {1825–}

1833 EATON *Botany* (ed. 6) 111. **1837** COLMAN *Mass. Rep. Agric.* 123 There is a native shrub abundant in this vicinity most admirably adapted for fences; the common Cockspur Thorn. **1846** BROWNE *Trees Amer.* 278. [**1850** S. F. COOPER *Rural Hours* 121 During the war of the Revolution the long spines of the thorn were occasionally used by the American women for pins, none of which were manufactured in the country; probably it was the cockspur variety, which bears the longest and most slender spines.] **1892** APGAR *Trees Northern U.S.* 104 Cockspur Thorn. . . . A small tree with a flat, bushy head. . . . Wild and common throughout, and often planted.

Cocktail. {1808–}

+**1.** A mixed drink composed of spirit, sugar, bitters, etc.

1806 *Balance* (Hudson, N.Y.) 13 May 146 (Th.), Cock-tail is a stimulating liquor, composed of spirits of any kind, sugar, water, and bitters. **1833** J. ALEXANDER *Transatlantic Sk.* II. 299 *Cocktail* is composed of water, with the addition of rum, gin, or brandy, as one chooses—a third of the spirit to two-thirds of the water; add bitters, and enrich with sugar and nutmeg. **1840** *Picayune* 25 Oct. 2/5 The Baltimore Clipper suggests that cock-tails should henceforth be called rooster's shirts! **1862** LOWELL *Biglow P.* II. iv. 119 With our heels on the backs o' Napoleon's new chairs, An' princes a-mixin' our cocktails an' slings. **1869** 'MARK TWAIN' *Innocents* 148 Well, if you don't know what that is, give us a champagne cocktail. **1897** FLANDRAU *Harvard Episodes* 216 What do you expect the college to do anyhow? Supply wet-nurses for all the silly little boys who make themselves sick on cocktails at the Adams House? **1902** HOWELLS in *Harper's Mag.* March 627 Then he felt that he had in a manner retrieved himself, and could retire from the five-o'clock cocktails with honor.

2. Attrib. and comb. with *mixer, powder*, etc.

1865 *Reader* 8 July 30 Advertisements of quack medicines, patent skirts, cock-tail powders, plantation bitters. **1893** *San Francisco Chron.* in *Voice* (N.Y.) 20 July, Patrons of the 'cocktail' route know that the ladies' entrance is more disastrous to morals . . . than any other vice. **1904** 'O. HENRY' *Cabbages & Kings* 47 A bullet-headed man Smith was, with an oblique, dead eye and the moustache of a cocktail-mixer. **1910** HART *Vigilante Girl* 305 In the cocktail window, Yarrow and Judge McCarrew were discussing the case.

Cocktailed, *a.* {1769–} ||Under the influence of cocktails. — **1856** *Harper's Mag.* Dec. 66/1 Cocktailed past the point of nervousness and remorse, he dresses himself.

+**Coco, Cocoa.** [f. COCONUT.] A person's head. *slang.* — **1837** NEAL *Charcoal Sk.* (1838) 37 Your cocoa is very near a sledge-hammer. If it isn't hard, it may get cracked. **1916** DU PUY *Uncle Sam* 154 If he could make a scratch shot and land on the coco of Mr. Goliath he would win. **1922** R. PARRISH *Case & Girl* 185 We'll slip out and leave Mike to explain how he got his coco cracked.

Cocoa. Also †**cocao, coco.**

1. The seed of the cacao, *Theobroma cacao* {1707–}, or the powder obtained by grinding this. {1788–}

1704 *Boston News-Letter* 14 Aug. 1/2 Two Dutch Privateers have brought in here two French Prizes of 16 Guns each, laden with Sugar, Coco, Indigo and Cotton. **1711** *Ib.* 17 Sept. 2/2 The Loading of the Ship Success Galley consisting of Anchors, . . . Patteraroes, Muskets, Cocoa, &c. **1732** *S.C. Gazette* 12 Aug., Good Cocao to be sold. **1785** *Mass. Stat.* 30 June, Whereas chocolate mills and machines for roasting cocoa have been erected in the town of Boston. **1836** EDWARD *Hist. Texas* 132 Cocoa, maguey, vanilla and cochineal are also perennial staples. **1847** *Knickerb.* XXIX. 257, I see there has been a cargo of cocoa landed.

attrib. **1820** *Columbian Centinel* 5 Jan. 4/2 David Harding . . . keeps constantly for sale . . . American Cocoa Shells, of first quality. **1854** BARTLETT *Narr.* I. xii. 285 It [chocolate] is usually prepared in families from the cocoa-nut.

2. A beverage made from the pulverized seed of the cocoa bean or its husk. {1798–}

1815 *View N.Y. State Prison* 36 Usually the convicts breakfast on Cocoa made from the shell, sweetened with molasses. **1884** F. ADAMS *Cook Book* 309 Breakfast cocoa. Put a teaspoon of the powder into a breakfast cup, add a tablespoon of boiling water, [etc.].

+**3.** =COCO GRASS. Also attrib.

1873 *Dept. Agric. Rep.* (1874) 269 Even the hardy and noxious gramineal plant, commonly called 'coco' in Louisiana, is destroyed after two seasons of broadcast cultivation. **1897** STUART *Simpkinsville* 43 A heavy dew . . . hung in glistening gems upon the blades of bright green cocoa spears that had shot up between the drier clods.

+**Coco grass.** Also **cocoa grass.** *S.* Any of several widely distributed sedges of the genus *Cyperus*, esp. the nut grass, *C. rotundus.*

1837 Commons, etc. *Doc. Hist.* I. 221 Cutting coco grass on the 22d. **1846** in Darlington *Weeds & Plants* 360, I send you inclosed a spear or shoot of the vilest of all pests, the Coco-grass,—which has taken possession of, and caused to be abandoned, some of the best Sugar estates in Louisiana. **1855** *Amer. Inst. N.Y. Trans.* 168 In Louisiana and Mississippi a species known as coco grass is a great trouble to cotton planters. **1894** *Congress. Rec.* 17 July 7587/1 In my State [=Miss.] . . . there is a grass that is as damaging to the land as the thistle can be to the people of the other part of the country, and that is the cocoa grass. **1902** GORDON *Recoll. Lynchburg* 111 The floods, the irrepressible cocoa-grass, the poisonous vegetable exhalations are in his way.

Coconut, Cocoanut. Also †**cokernut, cocco'nut.**

1. The nut of the coco palm, *Cocos nucifera.* {1613–}

1678 *New Castle Court Rec.* 352 A Parcell of Cokernutts. **1787** *Steele Papers* I. 16 If I can prevail on the waggoner, or rather if I can see him. I will send you a cocco'nut. **1898** *Dept. Agric. Yearbook 1897* 340 The domestic production of cocoanuts, which is confined to the coast region of lower Florida, is unimportant.

fig. **1737** *Penna. Gazette* 6–13 Jan. 2 He's eat the Cocoa Nut [=he is inebriated].

b. The edible part of this shredded or prepared as a confection.

1878 *Amer. Home Cook Book* 167 Stir them gradually into the milk, alternately with the cocoa-nut and sugar. **1887** N. PERRY *Flock of Girls* 260 Margie Gaines became absorbed in tasting a piece of candied cocoanut.

2. =COCONUT PALM. {1852–}

1837 WILLIAMS *Florida* 19 The cocoanut and sugar apple grow wild at Cape Sable. **1850** J. L. TYSON *Diary in Calif.* 20 The pomegranate, the tamarind, the date, the plantain, the banana, the cocoanut, the orange, . . . were scattered around in rich profusion. **1862** *Rep. Comm. Patents: Agric. 1861* 403 In this locality [=Fort Myers, Fla.] the cocoa-nut, date, . . . cassava, ginger, and coffee, are all growing, and might be successfully cultivated to supply to the States of a colder latitude. **1868** *Rep. Comm. Agric.* 147 The Cocoa-nut, (*Cocos nucifera,*) and Brazil nut, (*Bertholletia excelsa,*) attain their highest degree of perfection [in Florida].

3. A person's head. *slang.* {1873–}

1834 CARRUTHERS *Kentuckian* I. 66, I rather suspicion he thought a two year old colt's heel had got a taste of his cocoanut. **1854** *Knickerb.* XLIII. 432 Do you remember breaking an ear of corn one night at a husking-bee, over the old 'cocoa-nut' of that 'cross-patch,' old J. **1883** HAY *Bread-Winners* 250 The first thing I did with that hammer, I'd crack Art Farnham's cocoa-nut.

+**4.** A variety of squash.

1857–8 *Ill. Agric. Soc. Trans.* III. 509 The Lima cocoanut, long and blue, is excellent.

5. Attrib. with *cake, candy, pudding.*

1891 CHASE & CLOW *Industry* II. 145 There were tiers of cocoanut cakes, some baked to a delicate brown. **1877** *Harper's Mag.* April 693/1 He didn't get me any cocoa-nut candy. **1828** E. LESLIE *Receipts* 17 Cocoa-nut Pudding.

Coconut palm, Cocoanut palm. The palm tree *Cocos nucifera* which bears the coconut. {1852–} Also *cocoa palm.*

1886 H. G. WARNER *Fla. Fruits* (rev. ed.) 232 The cocoa-nut palm requires the vicinity of the sea to reach its highest perfection, and this requisite is everywhere present in . . . Florida. **1898** *Dept. Agric. Yearbk. 1897* 200 Cocoanut palm (*Cocoa nucifera*).—About twenty years ago a consignment of cocoanuts was received from Central America . . . [and] distributed. . . . Of late years . . . more attention has been given to this fruit in southern Florida. **1911** *Ib. 1910* 53 An extensive study has been made of the bud-rot of the coconut palm, which has caused enormous losses. — **1893** *Harper's Mag.* March 507 Here the cocoa-palm flourishes, and every landscape is far more tropic in appearance than those of northern Florida.

Cocoon, *v.* **1.** *tr.* To wrap or swathe as in a cocoon. **2.** *intr.* To make or form a cocoon. — **(1) 1880** 'MARK TWAIN' *Tramp Abroad* xxviii. 296 We . . . cocooned ourselves in the proper red blankets. **(2) 1884** *Science* III. 685 The whole operation of the lycosid when cocooning. *Ib.* 686 The cocooning habits of Lycosa.

+**Cocoonery.** A place where silkworms are bred and form their cocoons.

1839 *S. Lit. Messenger* V. 753/1 She . . . even went to the expense of having a neat little cocoonery erected in the centre of the lot. **1840** *Niles' Nat. Reg.* 18 July 320/3 There are about twelve millions of worms now feeding at Mr. Physic's Highfield cocoonery. **1842** *Amer. Pioneer* I. 147 Connected with the factory are thirty acres covered with the mulberry tree, and three cocooneries. **1860** MORDECAI *Virginia* 293 A few cocooneries were formed, but not skillfully managed. **1876** *Wide Awake* 271/1 Fortunately there was a large basket of leaves in the cocoonery, collected by the girls that morning in removing the litter from the tables where the silkworms lay. **1885** *Boston Jrnl.* 7 Sept. 2/4 A cocoonery that will protect a million worms.

Coco plum, Cocoa plum. A tropical tree or shrub, *Chrysobalanus icaco.* {1676–}

1775 ROMANS *Hist. Florida* App. 19 This island affords . . . cocoplumbs and palm cabbage. **1848** *S. Lit. Messenger* XIV. 530/2 In reaching the boats, through a dense border of cocoplumbs, custard apples, and dwarf cypress, . . . myriads of birds . . . were frightened from their coverts. **1861** WOOD *Botany* 326 Cocoa Plum. . . . *Chrysobalanus oblongifolius.* . . . Pine barrens, Ga., Ala. and Fla. **1897** SUDWORTH *Arborescent Flora* 236 *Chrysobalanus icaco.* . . . Common Names [include] Cocoa Plum (Fla.).

Cocum. (See COAKUM.)

+**C.O.D.** Abbrev. of 'collect on delivery,' directing payment to be made to carrier on receipt of goods. Also fig.

'This plan of shortening the sentence "collect on delivery" originated in the New York office of the Adams Express Company' (Tucker *Waifs* 110).

1863 *Rocky Mt. News* 12 March (Th.), When does your creditor consider you fishy? When he puts C.O.D. on your bill. **1866** *Congress. Globe* 19 Dec. 204/1 They informed me that . . . many hundred pardons had been sent by this express company . . . ; that each one had marked upon it 'C.O.D. $300'—'C.O.D.' meaning, I believe, 'collect on delivery.' **1886** *Knowledge* 1 April 179/1 *C.O.D.* Collect on delivery. Often used as a colloquial expression. **1904** *Grand Rapids Press* 24 May 4 According to later returns it appears that instead of having carried Michigan Mr. Hearst has merely arranged to have it sent C.O.D. **1916** DU PUY *Uncle Sam* 227 In New York it was found that the excess trunk had been sent on to North Philadelphia with the charge C.O.D.

***Cod.** =CODFISH 1.

1616 SMITH *New England* 17 In March, Aprill, May, and halfe Iune, here is Cod in abundance. **1702** SEWALL *Diary* III. 398 No-Man's-Land and the Gay-head are the only certain places for Fishing for Cod. **1807** *Mass. H. S. Coll.* 2 Ser. III. 56 Cod and haddock are caught in the spring: the first is good; but the last is poor and small. **1878** *Amer. Home Cook Book* 7 Cod should be judged by the redness of the gills.

attrib. **1851** MELVILLE *Moby Dick* xv. 73 A fine cod-chowder was placed before us. **1877** *Fish Comm. Rep.* (1879) 541 The 'fishing grounds,' 'cod-meadows,' have an extent of about 200 geographical miles in length, and 67 miles in breadth.

+**Codder.** A person or vessel engaged in codfishing. — **1846** *Knickerb.* XXVII. 513 There's a school of 'em, as sure as I'm a living codder. **1893** *Harper's Mag.* April 726/2 'We should lie in the track of some ships,' said the captain. . . . 'There's the codders and the herring-busses.'

+**Codding.** (See quot. 1859.) Also attrib. — **1859** BARTLETT 90 *Codding*, fishing for codfish. A common term in New England seaports, where vessels are fitted out for the purpose. **1891** CHASE & CLOW *Industry* II. 122 The grandest codding station in the world is Newfoundland.

***Codfish.**

***1.** A sea fish of the North Atlantic, *Gadus morrhua.*

1630 HIGGINSON *New-England* 11, I saw great store of Whales, and Crampusse, . . . likewise Cod-Fish [in] aboundance on the Coast. **1650** *Suffolk Deeds* II. 124 Wee . . . Accknowlidg our selues to be indebted . . . ye full some of fiue hundred fourty & seauen pownds tenn shillings to be paid . . . in good marchantable drye Codd fish at ye price Currant of ye Countrey, And to be deluered Vpon ye Rock. **1789** MORSE *Amer. Geog.* 149 Codfish . . . are still exported in large quantities. **1814** *Portsmouth* (N.H.) *Oracle* 9 April 1/5 *Kentuckian.* . . . Let us stand by each other—keep up a good democratic party in the North, and we have nothing to fear from the land of Codfish and Onions [=New Eng.]. **1870** *Amer. Naturalist* IV. 519 Nearly all the codfish obtained on our coast are brought to market in an unsalted condition, but they form only a small portion of the number in Massachusetts.

fig. **1911** *Washington Times* 27 Jan. 8 The man who threatened the Bank of England is declared insane. Now, what must be thought of a reciprocity agreement which threatens the Sacred Codfish?

b. =BUFFALO COD.

1884 Goode *Fisheries* I. 267 Cultus Cod (*Ophidion elongatus* Girard).—This species is universally called 'Cod-fish' where the true cod is unknown.

+**2.** *Codfish aristocracy*, originally, in Massachusetts, a class made wealthy by the codfisheries; in later use, the newly rich. Also *C. gentility.*

*c***1850** WHITCHER *Bedott P.* 305, I've noticed that yer codfish gentility always dew [feel uneasy]. **1850** *Congress. Globe* App. 9 July 1248 We should regard it as somewhat strange if we should require a codfish aristocracy to keep us in order. **1851** *Knickerb.* XXXVIII. 555 As wealth increased, he found himself at the head of the 'cod-fish aristocracy.' **1876** *Congress. Rec.* 19 May 3221/1 In the Statehouse at Boston . . . there hangs, swimming in air, the well-mounted effigy of an enormous codfish, suggesting the origin and giving a typical representation of what is called there 'the codfish aristocracy.' **1897** *Ib.* 7 July 2444/1 Just the other day England was the richest nation. To-day Uncle Sam could buy the whole of the tight little island . . . and hold it as a summer resort for our codfish aristocracy.

3. Attrib. with *chowder, craft, hash, man.*

1840 *Knickerb.* XV. 186 No one who has ever eaten fried tongues and 'sounds' at Siasconset, can ever long for any other dish, unless it be a codfish chowder, served up at the same place. *a***1841** W. HAWES *Sporting Scenes* I. 53 Who? a codfish craft off o' Newfoundland, I expect. **1866** MOORE *Women of War* 137 We varied our dinners with custard and baked rice puddings, scrambled eggs, codfish hash, [etc.]. **1902** E. BANKS *Newspaper Girl* 143, I'll tell him he may call to-morrow afternoon, and if he's not the codfish man at all, I'll cough very loud.

+**Codfish ball.** Codfish and potato molded into a small sphere and fried. — **1845** *Knickerb.* XXVI. 462 Wonder if they had any 'codfish-balls' or 'bread-puddings?' **1876** HENDERSON *Cooking* 110 Cod-fish Balls. Cut the cod-fish in pieces; soak them about an hour in luke-warm water, [etc.]. **1881** *Harper's Mag.* Jan. 227/1 Cod-fish balls for breakfast on Sunday morning . . . and fried hasty pudding.

Codfisherman. One whose business is fishing for codfish. {Newfoundland, 1883–} — **1885** *American* X. 78 The pollack is regarded by the codfisherman as practically worthless. **1896** *Boston Transcript* 21 Nov. 20/1 The fish are then dipped out with great scoop nets, and are sold to the cod fishermen!

Codfishery. The business of catching codfish; an organization for carrying on such fishing. {1753}

1735 *Boston Rec.* 120 Our Cod Fishery, which for many Years past have Employ'd abundance of Men and Vessels, . . . remains under such discouragement, that it's much to be feared that there will not be, the Year ensuing, near Two Thirds, of the Fishery kept up. **1791** *Ann. 2nd Congress* 1 Sess. Dec. 51 A bill for the encouragement of the bank and other codfisheries. **1804** *Ann. 8th Congress* 2 Sess. 1591 Agreeable to the report made to the last congress on this subject, there were employed in the cod fishery in 1800, twenty-five thousand tons of shipping. **1864** NICHOLS *Amer. Life* I. 71 They had a suitable regard to the 'wealth of seas' in a productive and profitable cod-fishery. **1891** CHASE & CLOW *Industry* II. 122 There are also important cod-fisheries on the coasts of New England.

Codfishing. Fishing for cod. Also attrib.

1637 MORTON *New Canaan* II. vii, The Codd fishing is much used in America . . . in so much as 300 sayle of shipps, from divers parts, have used to be imployed yearely in that trade. **1846** *Spirit of Times* 4 July 218/2, I have caught cat-fish in the Mississippi, but 'tis not such sport as cod-fishing. **1876** *N.Y. Herald* 16 March 7/4 Rice is a bachelor of expensive habits living in Washington. He must have his codfishing in summer and his trip to Florida in winter. **1881** *Amer. Naturalist* XV. 367, I had the opportunity of spending three months on a cod fishing schooner.

Cod hook. Also †**cod huck.** A hook used in catching codfish.

1634 WOOD *New Eng. Prospect* I. xii. 52 Here likewise must not be forgotten all vtensils for the Sea, as Barbels, splitting-knives, Leads, and Cod-hookes, and Lines [etc.]. **1686** SEWALL *Letter-Book* I. 34 Please to send 20 Duz. of middling cod hooks, 50 Duz. large codd hooks; the last you sent are complained off, as not well seasoned and dear. **1709** *Essex Inst. Coll.* VII. 20 To 7 gross of Cod Hucks. **1893** *Outing* XXII. 95/1 Each man was provided with a large, soft-laid, cotton line about thirty yards long, to one end of which was attached the largest-sized cod-hook, while the other end was made fast in the boat.

Codlin. (See CODLING *n.*[2])

Cod line. A line used in fishing for cod. {1794}

1634 WOOD *New Eng. Prospect* I. ix. 34 The Fisherman taking a Cod-line, . . . throwes it into the Sea, the fish biting at it as he pulls her to him. **1663** *Essex Probate Rec.* I. 419, 4 codlines, 2 pr. of shoes & portugall cap. **1686** SEWALL *Letter-Book* I. 34 Please to send . . . 20 Duz. of English cod Lines sound and strong. **1793** BENTLEY *Diary* II. 10 There was found a stone formed with a head resembling the leads fastened to cod lines as used by the Indians. **1846** *Knickerb.* XXVII. 511 Some of them Beverly men are lazy as the d—l; snore half the time, with the cod-line in their hands. **1884** *Century Mag.* May 103/1 The cod-lines were brought out and dropped over the side.

***Codling.**[1] +A fish of the genus *Phycis;* a hake. — **1814** MITCHILL *Fishes N.Y.* 372 Codling. *Gadus longipes.* . . . Weighs sometimes as heavy as eighteen pounds. . . . This is the hake of the New-York fishermen. **1842** *Nat. Hist. N.Y., Zoology* IV. 291 The American Codling. *Phycis americanus.* . . . American Hake. Storer. *Ib.* 292 The Spotted Codling. *Phycis punctatus.* . . . This is an exceedingly rare but distinct species. It occurs from the coast of New York to the gulf of St. Lawrence.

***Codling.**[2] Also **codlin.** A variety of apple. Also attrib. with *cider.*

1709 LAWSON *Carolina* 108 The Juniting is early ripe, and soon gone, in these warm countries. Codlin; no better and fairer fruit in the world; yet the tree suffers the same distemper, as the Pearmains, or rather worse. *Ib.* 109 We beat the first of our Codlin Cider, against reaping our wheat, which is from the tenth of June, to the five and twentieth. **1817** W. COXE *Fruit Trees* 105 The Codling, called also the English Codling, is a very fine fruit. **1849** *Rep. Comm. Patents: Agric.* 438 Of all early fruits, that not over-good sort, the Keswick Codlin, is the most early, uniform, and enormous bearer.

Codling moth. Also **codlin, coddling moth.** A moth (*Carpocapsa pomonella*) whose larvae infest apples. {1749– (B. Wilkes *Eng. Moths*)}

1861 *Mass. Bd. Agric. Rep.* II. 91 The apple worm, or coddling-moth, . . . is what the orchardist must contend against. **1867** *Amer. Naturalist* I. 110 Many other species of minute moths . . . will be flying about orchards and gardens just as the buds are beginning to unfold; especially the Coddling Moth. **1868** *Mich. Agric. Rep.* VII. 168 The larvae of the codling moth . . . [have] been quite a nuisance during the past season. **1887** *Amer. Naturalist* XXI. 481 About seventy-five per cent. of the apples exposed to injury by the codlin-moth were saved. **1892** V. KELLOG *Kansas Insects* 80 [The] Codlin moth . . . has spread all over North America, and is, perhaps, our most destructive apple pest.

Cod-liver oil. Oil extracted from the liver of codfish. {1783 –} — **1851** MELVILLE *Moby Dick* xxv, Certainly it cannot be olive oil, castor oil, . . . nor cod-liver oil. **1854** *Corr. R. W. Griswold* (1898) 296 Stick to cod-liver oil. I know several cases where it has done wonders. **1881** *Harper's Mag.* May 868/1 Cod-liver oil and quinine had done as much and as little for him as for others.

+**Co-ed.** *colloq.* (See quot. 1900.) — **1893-** in dicts. **1900** *Dialect Notes* II. 28 *Co-ed*, a woman studying at a coeducational college or university. Used generally. **1907** *Independent* LXIII. 873 The fellows in a body may laugh at the co-eds yet they rarely fail to open or close a door for them. **1912** *Collier's* XLVIII. 23, I sat with a coed who is nearing her graduation.

+**Coeducate,** *v.* [Back formation from COEDUCATION.] *tr.* and *intr.* To educate (students of both sexes) together. — **1855** *Penna. School Jrnl.* III. 201 Another enumerates the great number of schools where the sexes are coeducated. **1894** *Forum* July 585 The men who have been 'co-educated' bear the marks of it through life, I believe, in their attitude towards women. **1923** [See COEDUCATION].

+**Coeducation.** The education of male and female students jointly at one institution.

1852 *Penna. School Jrnl.* I. 9 Co-Education of the Sexes. The instruction of males and females in the same room and in the same class, is supposed by many to be an evil. **1854** *Ib.* II. 214 The Executive Committee suggested the following topics for reports at the next meeting: . . . 2. The co-education of the sexes. *Ib.* III. 121 My worthy and esteemed friend, the writer, was now, or had lately been at the head of an Institution for the co-education of the sexes. **1867-8** *Ill. Agric. Soc. Trans.* VII. 511 Co-education of the Sexes. . . . Resolved, That it is the sense of this Society, that in the admission of students to the Industrial University, both sexes be placed upon an equal footing. **1868** *Amer. Jrnl. Educ.* (*title*), The Coeducation of the Sexes. **1880** *Harper's Mag.* Dec. 101 The college is still unknown which, having made a fair trial of co-education, has excluded women. **1894** *Forum* July 583, I believe in co-education just as I believe in co-nursing, co-feeding, co-living in general. **1898** HARPER *S. B. Anthony* I. 156 The woman who advocated co-education in those days was indeed in a 'bold and conspicuous position.' **1923** *Forum* LXX. 2050 This sympathetic attitude [of thoughtful people toward coeducation] is naturally based on the belief that coeducation coeducates.

+**Coeducational,** *a.* Permitting the attendance of students of both sexes in the same classes.

1881 *Williamsport* (Pa.) *Sun & Banner* VIII. No. 3. 1 It is a co-educational school. **1887** *Nation* 12 May 404/1 Since the opening of Bryn Mawr College two years ago, the twelve fellowships that have been awarded have without exception been given to graduates of coeducational colleges. **1894** *Forum* July 586, I think the incentive to manliness and womanliness is stronger—other things being equal—in co-educational institutions. **1910** C. HARRIS *Eve's Husband* 242 Girls . . . have frisked sometimes entirely through a coeducational institution at the head of the class.

+**Coeducationist.** One who favors coeducation of the sexes. — **1855** *Penna. School Jrnl.* III. 202 The term child no longer exists with the co-educationist. *Ib.* 214 The co-educationist complains that no Yale or Harvard opens its doors to females. Let us imagine that a change has come over society. That the co-educationists have triumphed.

‖**Coetus.** [L.] The governing body of the Dutch and German Reformed Churches in America during the latter half of the eighteenth century. — **1781** PETERS *Hist. Conn.* 235 Upon which a majority of the ministers, in their coetus, erected a classis for the ordination of ministers.

* **Coffee,** *n.*

***1.** A beverage decocted from the coffee bean.

1671 *Boston Rec.* 58 Mrs. . . . Jones . . . is approued of to keepe a house of publique Entertainment for the sellinge of Coffee & Chuchaletto. **1775** FITHIAN *Journal* II. 77, I drank coffee last evening at Mr. Read's. They appear to be a sociable, kind, neat family. **1796** F. BAILY *Tour* 103 Their breakfasts consist of . . . eggs, coffee and tea, and a dish, or rather a cake, peculiar to the southern states, made out of the meal of Indian corn, and called hoe-cake. **1822** *Missionary Herald* XVIII. 152, I often smiled to find myself sitting over a cup of coffee between a Chickasaw and a Choctaw. **1876** WARNER *Gold of Chickaree* 15 Wych Hazel heard Mr. Falkirk's announcement and poured out his 'after-dinner coffee' with a steady hand. **1911** VANCE *Cynthia* 269 The dishes Acklin set before her she left untouched; even coffee threatened to choke her.

+**b.** A substitute beverage for coffee, made of beans, peas, etc.

1806 T. ASHE *Travels in A.* 20 My breakfast consisted of Indian bread, wild pigeons, and coffee made of native peas. **1817** *N. Amer. Rev.* IV. 177 [We] drank coffee made of parched beans, and black pepper.

c. The drinking of coffee; the time or occasion of this.

1774 FITHIAN *Journal* I. 213 Only just before the Sun went Down Ben & I had our Horses & rode to . . . the Corn-field. . . . We returned to Coffee. **1776** E. DRINKER *Journal* 41 Crossed ye Ferry at Dunks, dined at Andersons' at ye Red Lion; stopped at A. J.'s Frankford, and came home to Coffee.

2. Coffee beans, freq. collective as a merchantable product; also, the beans when roasted and ground ready for use. {1626–}

1719 *Mass. Bay Currency Tracts* 187 Other things . . . have been Imported and Spent in greater Quantities, than has been for our good, Such as Wine, Rum, Brandy, (not to mention Tea, Coffee, Chacolet). **1841** *Diplom. Corr. Texas* (1908) I. 482 The coffee, Sugar, cigars, Tobacco fruit Etc, of Cuba could be furnished Texas at reduced rates. **1857** YOUMANS *Household Science* 297 Ground coffee is very extensively adulterated. Various substances are employed for this purpose, as roasted peas, beans, and corn, and dried and roasted roots, such as turnips, carrots, potatoes, &c. But the most common adulterant is Chiccory. **1881** *Rep. Indian Affairs* p. v, We agree to give them so many pounds of beef, flour, coffee, sugar. **1908** HANDSAKER *Pioneer Life* 20 We 'browned' our own coffee and in the absence of a mill would place the berries in a cloth and pound them.

3. The seeds of the Kentucky coffee tree.

1784 J. FILSON *Kentucke* 23 The coffee-tree greatly resembles the black oak, . . . and also bears a pod, in which is enclosed good coffee.

b. *California coffee,* 'the somewhat coffee-like fruit of *Rhamnus Californica*' (Cent.).

4. In attrib. uses: **a.** In sense 1, with *cart, cup,* etc.

1880 *Chicago Tribune* 23 Dec., The coffee cart made its appearance at Clark and Twelfth streets—a location selected by the promoters for the first trial of their enterprise. **1819** A. PEIRCE *Rebelliad* 15 The coffee-cups and saucers rattle. **1846** *Knickerb.* XXVIII. 308 A few tidy maidens were sweeping the stand . . . ; coffee kettles were bubbling. **1865** A. D. WHITNEY *Gayworthys* xxviii. 282 She found . . . the table cleared, except of . . . a quaint little coffee mug. **1880** *Scribner's Mo.* May 129/1 Oh, what a trial it was, after one particularly hard day's work . . . to have the steaming and fragrant coffee-pail kicked over by a clumsy foot. **1871** *Rep. Indian Affairs* 469 Early in the twelfth month I began to issue the usual annuity goods, which consisted, last year, of . . . 40 dozen Coffee-pans. **1900** R. H. SAVAGE *Midnight Passenger* 224 'Coffee parlors,' museums, cheap theaters, and music halls, . . . were thronged with those pitiless-eyed Devil's Children, the women of the night side of New York. **1867** *Rep. Comm. Patents 1865* II. 1012 [Patent] No. 51,741.—[Issued to] James H. Mason, Franklin, Mass.—[For] Coffee Percolator. **1833** *Niles' Reg.* XLIV. 178/1 A coffee room or *restaurat* will be established on the

Third street front of the building. **1872** Brace *Dangerous Classes N.Y.* 291 The necessary sums were raised to open a 'Coffee and Reading Room' in the worst district of the city—the Fourth Ward. **1887** Custer *Tenting on Plains* 231 The colored boy rushed around and gathered everybody's coffee-saucer. **1863** Whitney *F. Gartney* i, She glanced over the table whereon shone a silver coffee-service. **1856** Stowe *Dred* I. 18 A small table, which displayed an antique coffee-set of silver. **1902** E. Banks *Newspaper Girl* 288 There were four kittens . . . and I was . . . feeding them with the milk, each in its turn, from an after-dinner coffee-spoon. **1869** 'Mark Twain' *Innocents* xxxviii. 404 A table-cloth mottled with grease-spots and coffee-stains. **1847** C. F. Briggs *Tom Pepper* I. 58 Not the least attractive of all the pleasant things in this noisy locality, were the hot coffee stands, at one of which I breakfasted on hot dough nuts. **1863** *Rep. Comm. Patents 1861* I. 265 [Patent] No. 31,910.—[Issued to] Rufus S. Sanborn, of Sycamore, Ill.—[For] Improved Coffee-Steeper. **1847** *Knickerb.* XXX. 240 Martha arranged the furniture and carried the coffee-tray. **1860** M. J. Holmes *Maude* x. 116 Hannah carried the coffee-urn to the dining-room.

b. In senses 2 and 3, with *bag, box,* etc.

1853 'P. Paxton' *Yankee in Texas* 401 A hundred more or less, huge boats all lie with their bows . . . pointing to the . . . unwieldy sugar puncheons or countless coffee bags which they are about to engulf. **1881** *Harper's Mag.* April 735/2 Then crushing them [= grains of coffee] between two stones, she flung them into her coffee bag. **1864** Trowbridge *Cudjo's Cave* 222 'Him stay wid us now till he chirk up again,' said Cudjo, running to his coffee-box. **1861** H. Jacobs *Life Slave Girl* 106 You are . . . tossing coffee-grounds with some wicked fortuneteller. **1797** Imlay *Western Territory* (ed. 3) 275 Drying floors, intended to take all benefit of the fine drying weather during the coffee harvest. **1822** *Ann. 17th Congress* 1 Sess. I. 292 The East-Florida Coffee-Land Association. **1858** *Harper's Mag.* June 45/1 In addition to the proper paraphernalia of a sportsman, there was a small frying-pan, a tin case filled with fat pork, a coffee-machine, and various other necessaries for camp life. **1873** *U.S. Patents Official Gaz.* IV. 225/1 The coffee-package A, made of paper, lined with tin-foil, [etc.]. **1884** *Penna. School Jrnl.* XXXII. 382 A skinful of moist coffee-paste. **1851** Cist *Cincinnati* 258 [Industries include] Coffee roasters. **1850** Garrard *Wah-To-Yah* xxiii. 272 We carried charcoal from the pit to the intended 'shop.' With coffeesacks on our shoulders, we lifted until our appearance would have well vied with that of a city *charbonnier.*

+**Coffee,** *v.* **1.** *intr.* To drink coffee. {recent colloq.} **2.** *tr.* To serve (a person) with coffee. — **(1) 1851** Curtis *Nile Notes* xiii. 100 He coffeed and smoked, and would leave a duck for dinner, gave us all the last news, &c. **1885** W. T. Hornaday *2 Years in Jungle* 277 Rose very early, coffeed in haste, and . . . set out. **(2) 1868** S. Hale *Letters* 48 The Colonel, who coffeed us the day before.

Coffee bean (tree). +=Coffee tree.

1821 Nuttall *Trav. Arkansa* 41 Among the trees, we still continue to observe the coffee-bean (*Gymnocladus canadensis*). *Ib.* 178 In this elevated alluvion I still observed the Coffee-bean tree. **1848** *Cultivator* n.s. V. 213, I will remark . . . that . . . two young coffee bean trees are in a thrifty condition. **1897** Sudworth *Arborescent Flora* 255 *Gymnocladus dioicus.* . . . Common names [include] . . . Coffee Bean (Ill., Kans., Nebr.). Coffee Bean Tree (Ky., Ark.).

Coffee berry. 1. The fruit of the shrub *Coffea arabica.* {1662–} +**2.** The Kentucky coffee tree. — **(1) 1884** *Century Mag.* Jan. 434/2 Neither Lane nor Wiggins . . . succeeded in finding an important agricultural commodity suited to the New England sandy coasts and rocky hillsides; and this, notwithstanding . . . the coffee-berries sown by Harvard students in 1723, and by other students in 1748. **(2) 1822** J. Woods *English Prairie* 224 On the creek bottoms, [there grow] coffee-berry, poplar, pecon, white walnut, [etc.].

+**Coffee-boiler.** A vessel in which coffee is boiled.

1851 A. O. Hall *Manhattaner* 18 Bachelor bread-toasters, coffee-boilers, and the like, are soon picked up from neighboring shops. **1866** Moore *Women of War* 589 Her coffee-boiler stoutly replies to all drafts made upon it. **1881** *Rep. Indian Affairs* p. xxxv, This year the Carlisle school has shipped to forty-two Indian agencies 8,929 tin cups, coffee-boilers, [etc.]. **1904** Glasgow *Deliverance* 58 Here a cheerful blaze made merry about an ancient crane, on which a coffee-boiler swung slowly back and forth.

+**Coffee-cooler.** One who idles, esp. an inactive or old soldier.

For other examples (1890–1896) see Th. S.

1886 S. W. Mitchell *R. Blake* 294 'He is nothing but an old coffee-cooler, Mr. Pennell.' 'And what is a coffee-cooler?' 'A man who blows his coffee while the brigade is going by into action.' **1890** *Congress. Rec.* 17 July 7344/2 There the Indians went in their savage state, before they became mere coffee-coolers, wards of the Government, to procure their supplies. **1895** *Ib.* 18 Jan. 1129/2, I am opposed to . . . giving bounties and pensions to deserters, and 'coffee-coolers,' and bounty jumpers, and camp followers.

+**Coffee corn.** (See quotations.) — **1817–8** Eaton *Botany* (1822) 471 *Sorghum vulgare,* indian millet, coffee corn. . . . Var. *bicolor.* **1840** Dewey *Mass. Flowering Plants* 252 Coffee Corn. Grand Millet. Sometimes cultivated in gardens as a curiosity, or for feeding hens, etc.; not considered of great value. . . . Its tops are used also for brooms.

Coffeehouse. A house where coffee and other refreshments were obtained and where people often gathered to learn and exchange news. Latterly (see quots. of 19th c.) a dramshop or saloon. {1615–}

1687 Sewall *Diary* I. 197 Mr. Palmer at the Coffee-House said Connecticut had received letters from their Agent by Prentice. **1715** *Boston News-Letter* 3 Jan. 2/2 Gentlemen . . . may be faithfully served and accommodated with a large Room and other conveniences fit for such Business, by Mr. Daniel Stevens at his Coffee-House in Ann Street, Boston, where all Persons may have Lodging and Dyet. **1772** Washington *Diaries* II. 82 Dined at the Coffee House with the Jocky Club. **1809** F. Cuming *Western Tour* 166 There is a coffee house here, where is a reading room for the benefit of subscribers and strangers. **1837** Featherstonhaugh *Canoe Voyage* II. 168, I saw the words 'coffee-house,' painted at almost every tenth house, which I was told were all low, gambling dramshops, frequented only by the most profligate and desperate. **1866** Gregg *Life in Army* 184 All the whiskey shops, even down to the lowest hell-hole, adopt the decent name and character of a 'Coffee-house.' **1871** *Harper's Mag.* XLIII. 646/2 New York city kept up the custom. The coffee-houses maintained their popularity. **1891** S. M. Welch *Recoll. 1830–40* 337 The town had an abundance of 'Restaurants,' 'Recesses' and 'Coffee Houses,' as they were variously called.

Coffee mill.

1. A hand mill for grinding coffee beans. {1691–}

1759 *Newport Mercury* 26 June 4/3 Imported . . . and to be sold by Jacob Richardson, . . . Sieve-bottoms, Iron and Wood Coffee-mills, Flat-irons, [etc.]. **1838** Hawthorne *Note-Books* I. 163 There was a clock without a case . . . and a coffee-mill fixed against the wall. **1845** *Knickerb.* XXV. 106 He was about proposing, when Miss Bachelor said, in a voice to which a coffee-mill would have been music: 'I declare, I feel quite chilly!' **1894** *Outing* XXIV. 87/1 A stock of canned fruits and vegetables, . . . coffee (which we were compelled to crush, lacking of a coffee mill) and such condiments as sugar, pepper, salt, etc., completed the commissariat.

+**2.** (See quotation.)

1887 H. L. Williams *Buffalo Bill* 10 One of the old-pattern Colts, with the barrels revolving, the ancient 'coffee-mill' or 'pepperbox,' laughed at all over the West in the present day.

+**Coffee nut.**

1. =Coffee tree.

1804 Clark in *Lewis & C. Exped.* (1904) I. 95 The Groves contain Hickory, Walnut, coffee nut & Oake in addition. **1815** Drake *Cincinnati* 82 The most valuable timber trees [near Cincinnati, Ohio] are the . . . honey locust, shell-bark hickory, coffee nut and beech. **1836** Hildreth *Campaigns Rocky Mts.* I. 100 Sycamores interspersed with the cotton-wood, the coffee-nut and pekaun. **1857** *Lawrence* (Kansas) *Republican* 2 July 3 There is the best timber I have seen in Kansas, consisting of walnut, burr oak, hackberry, coffeenut, ash, hickory and mulberry. **1884** Sargent *Rep. Forests* 58 *Gymnocladus Canadensis.* . . . Kentucky Coffee Tree. Coffee Nut.

attrib. **1817** Brown *Western Gaz.* 25 Sugar maple, . . . coffee-nut tree, and sycamore, are found in their congenial soils [in Ill.]. **1820** *Amer. Farmer* I. 398, I send you a pod of the 'Coffee Nut Tree,' sometimes called pea locust. The coffee nut is a common tree growing in the forests of this country [*i.e.*, Ky.].

2. The fruit of the coffee tree.

1872 Eggleston *End of World* 195, I wouldn't a pulled that greeny's coffee-nuts out of the fire, and I won't hold the hot things for you. **1883** — *Hoosier School-Boy* ix. 65 It might be coffee-nuts, which would explode harmlessly.

Coffee pea. The chick-pea (*Cicer arietinum*), allied to the vetch. — **1816** *Gales's N.C. Almanack* 25 There is a kind of pea . . . much covered with a fine downy or hairy substance. It is known by various names, but mostly by the name of *Coffee Pea.* **1847** Darlington *Weeds & Plants* 103 Coffee-pea . . . is sometimes cultivated for the seeds—which are said to be a tolerable substitute for coffee. **1868** Gray *Field Botany* 111 Common Chick-Pea, . . . [is] called Coffee-Pea at the West, there cultivated for its seeds, which are used for coffee.

Coffee plant. a. A single plant of the true coffee shrub. +**b.** The cascara buckthorn. +**c.** The evening primrose. — **(a) 1889** *Sec. Agric. Rep.* 123 In southern Florida, below 27½ degrees north latitude, coffee plants withstand the climate in ordinary seasons and occasionally produce ripe berries. **(b) 1890** *Congress. Rec.* 12 June 5992 An indigenous plant found on that coast, the common name of which is 'coffee plant.' **(c) 1893** *Amer. Folk-Lore* VI. 142 *Oenothera biennis,* scurvish. Franconia, N.H. fever-plant; coffee-plant. Eastern States.

Coffeepot. A vessel with a cover and a spout, in which coffee is made or served. {1705–}

1711 *Boston News-Letter* 19 Feb. 2/2 One pair of Scales and a small set of Troy weights, two Coffee Pots, several peices of Plate. **1759** *Newport Mercury* 26 June 4/3 Imported . . . and to be sold by Jacob Richardson, . . . Brass Kettles and Skillets, Warming Pans, Tea-kettles, Coffee-pots, Sauce-pans. **1806** Lewis in *L. & Clark Exped.* (1905) III. 328 This traffic on the part of the whites consists in vending, guns, (principally old british or American musquits) powder, . . . brass tea-kettles and coffee pots. **1815** *Niles' Reg.* VIII. 141/2 A Pottery . . . [in] Philadelphia, where are made pitchers, coffee and tea pots, and cups. **1850** Glisan *Jrnl. Army Life* 37, I had failed to have anything in the culinary line except a tin coffee-pot and frying-pan. **1894** Robley *Bourbon Co., Kansas* 26 The coffee pot is on, some 'rashers' are cut from the 'flitch' of bacon and the grease tried out. **1898** *Outing* April 17/2 The tin pail, which was to do duty as coffee-pot and canteen, he was forced to dangle from his handle-bars.

+**Coffee shell.** A gastropod (*Melampus coffea*) found on the Florida coast. — **1870** *Amer. Naturalist* III. 403 Many snails . . . can be collected and the Coffee-Shell . . . is close at hand.

+**Coffee tree.** The Kentucky coffee tree (*Gymnocladus canadensis*), indigenous in the upper Miss. valley.

1784 FILSON *Kentucke* 23 The coffee-tree greatly resembles the black oak, grows large, and also bears a pod, in which is enclosed good coffee. **1785** MARSHALL *Amer. Grove* 56, I have lately received several seeds from Kentucky, supposed to be of this tree, where it is said to grow plenty, and is called the Coffee or Mahogany tree. **1843** TORREY *Flora N.Y.* I. 191 Coffee-tree. . . . On Seneca Lake. . . . The wood . . . is fit for cabinet-making. . . . Much esteemed as an ornamental tree. **1860** CURTIS *Woody Plants N.C.* 50 Kentucky Coffee Tree. . . . Occasionally cultivated about houses as a handsome shade tree. **1905** *Bureau of Forestry Bul.* No. 66, 38 The coffeetree (*Gymnocladus dioicos*) is found occasionally in Kansas.

b. A species of buckthorn, *Rhamnus californicus.*

1890 *Cent.* 5147 The California coffee-tree yields an unimportant coffee-substitute.

* **Coffin.** Also †**coffen, cophen.**

* **1.** A box or boxlike receptacle in which a corpse is buried.

1645 *Conn. Public Rec.* I. 464 Tho: Kirkman shall haue 20s. for makeing my Coffen. **1678** *Boston Rec.* 124 Complaint is made to the Select men that there is lately taken vp a custome in this towne, of diggine graues & makeinge Coffins vpon the Lords day without any vrgent occasion or necessitie thereof. **1711** HEMPSTEAD *Diary* 5, I came to town to get my tools to make a Coffin. **1764** *MS. Acc. Book El. Smith* (Hadley, Mass.), Cophen for Sarah with a door to it, 50/. **1840** DANA *Two Years* xviii, The little coffin was borne by eight girls. **1892** M. A. JACKSON *Memoirs* 189 A number of soldiers were busily engaged in making coffins for their dead comrades.

+**2.** A large shoe. *jocular* or *slang.* Also comb.

1851 HALL *College Words* 51 *Coffin*, at the University of Vermont, a boot, especially a large one. **1880** 'MARK TWAIN' *Tramp Abroad* xlvii. 547 In the seat thus pirated, sat two Americans, greatly incommoded by that woman's majestic coffin-clad feet.

3. Attrib. with *box, flower, furniture*, etc.

1876 HABBERTON *Jericho Road* 26 The first shovel full of dirt fell upon the coffin-box. **1876** *Wide Awake* 357/1, I felt as if the gifts were coffin-flowers; they were meant for long, long good-byes, I know. **1790** *Penna. Packet* 3 Feb. 2/4 Ironmongery. . . . Will be sold, . . . A quantity of hinges, locks of all sorts, . . . coffin furniture, [etc.]. **1866** 'F. KIRKLAND' *Bk. Anecdotes* 384 To express her appreciation of his patriotism by sending him—what?—a set of expensive coffin-handles! **1858** L. Wilmer *Press Gang* (1859) 359 In the coffin-house, behind the women's hospital, there were twenty or thirty coffins. **1856** M. J. HOLMES *L. Rivers* xxvii. 305 He knew that he had helped to break the heart now lying cold and still beneath the coffin lid. **1851** CIST *Cincinnati* 49 Occupations [include] . . . Coffin makers, 3 [people]. **1889** RILEY *Pipes o' Pan* 14 The countryman from 'Jessup's Crossing,' with the cornstalk coffin-measure, loped into town. **1837** BIRD *Nick of Woods* II. 105 He ar'n't much hurt to speak on, for all his looking so much like coffin-meat at the first jump. **1835** *Harvardiana* II. 24 He . . . looks on the coffin-plate to ascertain his age. **1855** *S. Lit. Messenger* XXI. 3 The coffin processions of the Jackson Presidential campaign, emblematic of the general, and habitual cruelty and recklessness of human life. **1872** *Rep. Comm. Patents 1871* II. 903/1 The within-described coffin-receptacle [is] composed of the body A, [etc.]. **1884** CABLE *Dr. Sevier* (1885) 99 And the sawing and hammering in the coffin-shop across the inner court ceased not day or night. **1833** T. HAMILTON *Men & Manners* I. 17 'Coffin Warehouse,' however, was sufficiently explanatory of the nature of the commerce carried on within.

+**Coffin boat.** (See quotations.) — **1851** E. J. LEWIS *Hints to Sportsmen* 189 The Surface-boat, Coffin boat, or Battery.—The use of the old-fashioned dug-outs has been pretty much superseded . . . by the introduction of the surface-boats that we are about describing.

+**Coffin canoe.** A canoe shaped like a coffin. (Cf. COFFIN BOAT.) — **1851** MELVILLE *Moby Dick* cx, He desired a canoe like those of Nantucket, all the more congenial to him, being a whaleman, that like a whaleboat these coffin-canoes were without a keel.

+**Coffin-carrier.** [From its black back, conceived as mourning.] The great black-backed gull, *Larus marinus.* — **1872** COUES *N. Amer. Birds* 312 Great Black-backed Gull. Saddle-back. Coffin-carrier. **1917** *Birds of Amer.* I. 41.

Coffin handbill. *Hist.* A circular bordered with woodcuts of coffins issued during the presidential campaign of 1828 by the Adams forces in an attack upon Andrew Jackson for his harshness in executing deserters during the Florida campaign of 1818. — *c*1828 in Pray *Mem. J. G. Bennett* 97 They print cheap tracts, circulate cheap pamphlets, get up cheap coffin-hand bills, scrape together cheap barbecues, and all to put down Jackson. **1846** M'KENNEY *Memoirs* I. 202, I am told . . . that you took an active part in distributing under the frank of your office, the 'coffin hand-bills.'

Coffle, *n.* A gang of Negro slaves chained together. {1799-}

1842 CHANNING *Works* 610/1 It is even reported that the slave-coffle is sometimes headed by the flag of the United States. **1856** STOWE *Dred* I. 302 'There's into him!' said a Georgia trader, who, having camped with a coffle of negroes in the neighborhood, had come up to the camp meeting. **1865** *Atlantic Mo.* XV. 510 His wife and child . . . were on their way to Tallahassee in a coffle which had been made up as a speculation on the cheerful Bourse of Jacksonville. **1877** *Reminisc. of Abolitionist* i. 11 The coffle of slaves came first, chained in couples on each side of a long chain which extended between them. *Ib.* 13 A slave dealer had arrived with a coffle of slaves. **1901** CHURCHILL *Crisis* 2 Eliphalet . . . had bid the overseer good-by at Cairo, and had seen the pitiful coffle piled aboard a steamer for New Orleans.

attrib. **1865** *Atlantic Mo.* XV. 751 The coffle-gang was made up in the jail-yard, within a stone's throw of the Monumental Church. **1892** *Ib.* March 368/1 [Many a lesson] I spelled out from the . . . tracts published by the American Antislavery Society, illustrated by rude woodcuts of . . . coffle-gangs.

+**Coffle,** *v. tr.* To fasten (slaves, etc.) together with chains. Also *ppl. a.* — **1859** J. DOY *Narr.* (1860) 128 Berkeley was afterwards sold for jail fees, and his new owner started with him for the Southern market. He was coffled with a huge $1200 chattel. **1865** *Atlantic Mo.* XV. 752 Millions now of Confederate promises to pay, which the hurrying multitude and that coffled gang were treading under foot.

Cog mill. A mill in which cogs form an important part of the machinery. — **1802** J. DRAYTON *S. Carolina* 121 Three kinds of rice mills, called pecker, cog, and water mills, are used in this state. **1837** PECK *New Guide* 127 A cog-mill is formed by constructing a rim, with cogs upon the shafts, and a trundle head to correspond. Each person furnishes his own horses to turn the mill.

Cognac. Also †**coniac.** A kind of French brandy. {1755-}

1763 W. Roberts *Nat. Hist. Fla.* 97 In my humble opinion, here may be made excellent wine: tho' its generally turning sour has been hitherto no small discouragement, yet it might be remedied, by falling upon some simple ingredient, such as the *solium Indicum*, or by alcaline salt, coniac, and sugar. **1851** *Polly Peablossom* 178 The landlord had, in a joke, placed in the side pockets of his overcoat a bottle of good old Bourbon whiskey, and one of 'Cognac.' **1895** M. A. Jackson *Memoirs* 523 This was done, but he commended to my own use a rundlet of cognac, as being much too good to be staved.

attrib. **1778** *Penna. Packet* 28 July 3/3 To Be Sold . . . A few pipes of coniac brandy. **1834** H. J. NOTT *Novellettes* I. 12 He made Cognac brandy, Jamaica rum, Scheidam, [etc.].

Cog railway. A railway equipped with a cogged center rail to enable a locomotive with a cogwheel to go up steep grades. — **1896** *Vt. Agric. Rep.* XVI. 126 We cannot boast of a Mt. Washington with its cog-railway.

+**Cohee.** An inhabitant of the mountains of western Virginia and Pennsylvania. Usu. *pl.* Also attrib.

1817 PAULDING *Lett. from South* I. 112 The people of whom I am now writing, call those east of the mountain Tuckahoes, and their country Old Virginia. They themselves are the Cohees, and their country New Virginia. **1834** CARRUTHERS *Kentuckian* II. 192 In Virginia, the inhabitants east of the Blue Ridge are called Tuckahoes, and those on the west Cohees; as some allege, from the Scotch-Irish phrase 'quo'he' (quoth he). **1853** *S. Lit. Messenger* XIX. 40/1 In Western Virginia, . . . even about Lexington, the Cohee Athens—your Petitioner is well nigh discarded. **1860** *Harper's Mag.* Aug. 350/1 My father often declared that this rough raking from the old Cohee, . . . finally determined him to execute a scheme, . . . of throwing up his commission. **1866** LOWELL *Biglow P.* 2 Ser. p. lviii, Cohees': applied to the people of certain settlements in Western Pennsylvania.

Coho. A salmon (*Oncorhynchus kisutch*) found in the northern Pacific. — **1898** *Fish Comm. Bul.* No. 18, 6 In the opinions of the canners . . . the coho should rank next after the king salmon in food value.

+**Cohoes.** *New Eng.* Also **cohas, cohoze, coos, cowass, kohass,** etc. [Of Indian origin; see quot. 1888.]

1. A bend in a river, or land adjacent thereto.

1781 PETERS *Hist. Conn.* 110 In its [the river's] northern parts are three great bendings, called cohosses. **1888** J. Q. BITTINGER *Hist. Haverhill, N.H.* 363 The Indian names which were given to the territory of Haverhill and its rivers have been retained in part. The country was known in earliest times as Cowass, Kohass and Cohas or Cohos. . . . . *Cohos* it is said means *crooked*, and was borrowed from the Cohasaukes, a part of the St. Francis tribe, *uck* or *auke* meaning *river* or *place*, and was applied to the territory of Haverhill, on account of the crooked course of the river and the consequent large bends of the land.

2. A fall of water, or a cascade.

1798 MORSE *Amer. Gaz.* 106 Cohoez, or the *Falls* in Mohawk R. between 2 and 3 miles from its mouth, and ten miles northward of Albany, are a very great natural curiosity. **1804** C. B. BROWN tr. Volney's *View* 95 This name, Cohoez, appears to be an imitative sound, borrowed from the Indians; and it is very remarkable, that the same name is bestowed upon a small cascade, nine miles from Spa. **1828** WEBSTER, *Cohoes*, or *Cohoze*, a fall of water, or falls; a word of Indian origin in America.

3. A tract of land, esp. one overgrown with pines.

1809 KENDALL *Travels* III. 191 Above and below the Fifteen-mile Falls, in the Connecticut, are tracts of country, called respectively the Upper and the Lower *Coos* or *Cohoss*,—which term implies, according to some, a fall in a river; according to others, a Bend in a river; and according to a third party, a parcel of meadow-land. But the true interpretation is *pine land.* *a*1817 DWIGHT *Travels* II. 135 Lancaster and Northumberland in New Hampshire, and the towns opposite to them in Vermont, compose a tract, long known in New England by the name of the *Upper Coos.* **1881** *Amer. Naturalist* XV. 426 The country [in N.E. Vermont] . . . was called by the Indians 'Coos,' which word in the Abenaqui language is said to signify 'the Pines.'

Cohog. Also **cohag.** =QUAHAUG. Also attrib. — **1788** CUTLER in *Life & Corr.* I. 416 Went into the water; found a great number of clam cohag shells, some very large. **1867** LOWELL *Biglow P.* II. p. xli. **1871** DE VERE 29 The more costly beads came from the largest shells of the Quahaug or Cohog, a welk, known in the Middle and Southern States as the Round Clam, and belonging to the genus *Venus mercenaria,* which is so called on account of their being used as currency.

+**Cohogle,** *v.* (See quot. 1829); also, to associate. *jocular.* — **1829** *Va. Lit. Museum* 16 Dec. 419 To *cohogle.* 'To bamboozle.' Kentucky. **1855** *Olympia* (W. T.) *Pioneer* 6 July (Th.), Now the question is, will it pay to cohogle with these owls any longer?

+**Cohonk.** Also †**cohunk.** [Echoic; cf. HONK.]

1. The Indian name of a kind of wild goose.

1724 JONES *Virginia* 12 They [the Indians in Va.] count their Time by Days, or by the Return of the Moon, and Cohonks, a sort of wild Geese. **1738** BYRD *Dividing Line* 146 The Indians call this fowl cohunks.

2. A winter or year (as an Indian measurement of time).

1705 BEVERLEY *Virginia* III. 43 They reckon the Years by the Winters, or *Cohonks,* as they call them; which is a Name taken from the Note of the Wild Geese. **1800** J. BOUCHER *Glossary* p. xlix, *Cohonc:* a year: so called from wild-geese, which in their flight during their annual migrations, constantly utter a cry, resembling *Cohonc.* **1841** *S. Lit. Messenger* VII. 219/1 Cohonk. . . . Indian term for Winter.

+**Cohosh.** Also **cohush.** [An Algonkin dial. word meaning 'bristly,' 'rough.']

1. The baneberry (*Actaea alba* and *A. rubra*). (Cf. BLACK COHOSH and BLUE COHOSH.)

'Black cohosh is black snakeroot, or bugbane (*Cimifuga racemosa*); blue cohosh is squawroot (*Caulophyllum thalictroides*); white cohosh is white baneberry (*Actæa alba*); red cohosh is red baneberry (*A. ruba*)' (Hodge *Indians* I. 321).

1796 MORSE *Amer. Univ. Geog.* I. 189 Among the native . . . plants of New England, the following have been employed for medicinal purposes: . . . Cohush (*Actæa spicata*). This is a valuable plant. **1814** PURSH *Flora Amer.* II. 367 *Actaea alba.* . . . Known by the name of Red and White Cohosh, and considered by the natives as a valuable medicine. **1843** TORREY *Flora N.Y.* I. 22 White Cohosh. . . . Rocky woods; common . . . in the southern counties. . . . A mild astringent and tonic. **1845** JUDD *Margaret* I. xvi. 143 She gathered the . . . red cohosh, purple bush-trefoil, . . . and other flowers. **1855** *Mich. Agric. Soc. Trans.* VI. 149 In the low grounds are skunk cabbage, birth root, . . . cahush [*sic*], . . . and spikenard. **1891** *Amer. Folk-Lore* IV. 147 [In New Hampshire] *Actaea alba* was Cohush.

2. Black snakeroot.

1817–8 EATON *Botany* (1822) 347 *Macrotys serpentaria,* bugbane, black snakeroot, cohosh. . . . In woods.

3. *False cohosh,* (see quot. 1840).

1840 DEWEY *Mass. Flowering Plants* 41 *Leontice thalictroides,* Poppoose Root, and False Cohosh, . . . blossoms in April and May. **1845** LINCOLN *Botany* App. 119/1.

***Coinage.** The system of coins in a country; the minting of coins; the product of a mint.

1792 *Ann. 2nd Congress* 69 Be it enacted. . . . That a mint for the purpose of a national coinage, be, and the same is, established, to be situate and carried on at the seat of the Government of the United States. **1833** *Niles' Reg.* XLIV. 392/1 Up to that period it [*i.e.* gold] had been received at the mint only from North Carolina, from which quarter gold was first transmitted for coinage in the year 1804. **1836** *Niles' Nat. Reg.* 19 Nov. 192/2 The U.S. mint is about to issue fifty cent pieces of a new and beautiful coinage. **1840** *Ib.* 23 May 178/3 The coinage in the years 1838 and 1839 at the branch mint at New Orleans was, gold, $23,490; silver, $280,403. **1897** [see BIMETALLISM]. **1925** BRYAN *Memoirs* 239 In his second term Mr. Bryan . . . favored the free coinage of silver.

***Coiner.** One who makes coins, a minter; also, a counterfeiter.

1704 *Boston News-Letter* 21 Aug. 2/2, We have lately discovered a number of ill men, Coyners of Money, & Forgers of our Bills of Credit, which are in Prison to answer. **1748** *N.J. Archives* 1 Ser. VII. 201 They do not effectually strengthen the hands of the Government, to bring the Traitors & Rioters, Coiners & Counterfeiters to justice. **1792** *Ann. 2nd Congress* 69 The chief coiner shall cause to be coined all metals which shall be received by him. **1793** *Lady's Mag. & Repos.* (Phila.) Feb. 151 Mr. Henry Voight, of this city, is appointed by the President . . . principal coiner to the mint of the United States. **1851** *Harper's Mag.* July 277/1 Large sums of money have been issued by private coiners.

***Coining.** The minting of coins. Used attrib. with *press, room.* — **1795** *Ann. 3rd Congress* 1408 The three coining presses, when complete, will strike from eight to twelve thousand of the smaller kinds of coin per day. **1880** LAMPHERE *U.S. Govt.* 70/2, 1 foreman coining-room [receives] per diem $4.50.

+**Coin notes.** Government notes to be paid in coin. — **1876** *Congress. Rec.* 25 July 4866/1 The first section of this bill requires coin-notes to be paid out, and consequently it involves the . . . necessity of redeeming those coin-notes.

Cojinillo, Coginillo. [Sp., diminutive of *cojin,* saddle pad.] A saddlebag or pocket in the pillion. — **1808** PIKE *Sources Miss.* (1810) III. 218, I soon found that the old soldier . . . was fond of a drop of the cheering liquor, as his boy carried a bottle in his cochmelies [*sic*] (a small leather case attached to the saddle for the purpose of carrying small articles). **1844** GREGG *Commerce of Prairies* I. 214 The *corazas* [=covers] of travelling saddles are also provided with several pockets called *coginillos*—a most excellent contrivance for carrying a lunch or bottle.

Coke. A form of carbon made from coal by distilling the volatile substances. Used attrib. and comb. with *breeze, burner, furnace, kiln,* etc. {1669–}

1884 *Harper's Mag.* April 777/1 Coke breeze (the refuse of gas-works). **1883** *Ib.* Aug. 335/1 The single file fires of the coke-burners . . . continue the long chain of labor stretching from Pittsburgh to Altoona. **1879** WHITMAN *Specimen Days* (1882) 139 Pretty good view of the city and Birmingham—fog and damp, smoke, coke-furnaces, flames, &c. **1905** VALENTINE *H. Sandwith* 420 So he has turned the Hecla into a coke furnace, with the new appliances that permit of making iron in much larger quantities at a much cheaper rate. **1835** HOFFMAN *Winter in West* I. 75 Dismounting on a small platform some two hundred feet above the river, from which a railway empties the coal into the coke-kilns upon its bank, [etc.]. *Ib.* 76 At the mouth of the glen we paused to look at a salt factory; and then . . . we passed by a steel factory and several coke-kilns. **1851** CIST *Cincinnati* 49 Occupations [include] . . . Coke maker, 1 [person]. **1880** *Harper's Mag.* Dec. 54, 5000 coke ovens blacken the fair land and sky with their dense smoke. **1891** RYAN *Pagan* 135 Them blamed coke-ovens on the other side . . . do send unearthly belches o' smoke up this way sometimes. **1887** *Courier-Journal* 4 Feb. 2/6 The coke-workers throughout the Connellsville region have demanded an advance in wages. **1865** *Atlantic Mo.* XV. 617 They labor in the coke-works and coal-pits. **1906** LYNDE *Quickening* 321 The pipe-line running from the coke-yard tank up to the barrel-spring on high Lebanon.

Coking. The making of coke. {1791–} Also attrib. with *coal.*

1833 CLAY *Speeches* (1842) 271 The successful introduction of the process of coking would have great effect. **1889** *Harper's Mag.* Jan. 264/2 This discovery of coking coal adds greatly to the value of the iron ores in northeastern Kentucky. **1906** LYNDE *Quickening* 76 He saw . . . an accessible vein of coal, second only to Pocahontas for coking.

***Cold,** *n.* Phr. *to leave out in the cold,* to neglect, to ignore, to deprive of advantages. (In fig. context.) {1879–}

1861 *N.Y. Tribune* July (B.), The 'Assents' continue to come in freely at the Erie Railroad office; and the appearances are that at the closing of the books . . . there will be few shares or bonds left out in the cold. **1880** G. INGHAM *Digging Gold* 411 The Denver and Rio Grande Railway extended their line to this point, making it the terminus, thus leaving the . . . town of Cleora two miles south 'out in the cold.' **1883** 'MARK TWAIN' *Life on Miss.* xxvii. 304 There's been a cut-off in that section, and Vicksburg is left out in the cold. **1886** ALTON *Among Law-Makers* 135 When an amendment not permitted by the rules is offered, . . . a member has merely to make the 'point of order' . . . and the amendment is left out in the cold. **1887** *Courier-Journal* 21 Jan. 2/6 The two young ladies she adopted are, of course, left out in the cold. **1897** C. A. DANA *Recoll. Civil War* 2 Several of the Republican leaders of New York . . . had begun to fear that they would be left out in the cold in the distribution of the offices.

***Cold,** *a.* and *adv.*

+**1.** Phr. *cold as a wagon tire.*

1832 J. HALL *Legends of West* (1885) 264 Here's the Speckled Snake as cold as a wagon tire. **1836** *Quarter Race Ky.* (1846) 18 Oh! my Grapevine! tear the hind sights off him!—you'll lay him out cold as a wagon-tire.

***2.** *Hunting.* Of a scent: Old and faint; weak.

1773 WASHINGTON *Diaries* II. 100 Touched now and then upon a Cold Scent till we came into Colo. Fairfax's Neck. **1786** *Ib.* III. 9 Found a Fox . . . and run him sometimes hard and sometimes as cold hunting from 11 oclock till near two.

transf. **1846** THORPE *Myst. Backwoods* 147 That man is the greatest chief, who follows the coldest trail, and leaves none behind by his own footsteps. **1853** *Knickerb.* XLII. 537 Hammond had satisfied himself that he was pursuing a 'cold trail,' and in his turn to speak, told the sovereign public that . . . he had determined to retire from the canvass.

+**b.** *Cold-nose,* of a dog, able to follow a faint scent.

1836 C. GILMAN *Recoll.* (1838) 210 After driving about for sometime, Bounce, a cold-nose dog, struck a trail. **1892** HARRIS *On the Plantation* 35 He had what is called a 'cold nose,' which is a short way of saying that he could follow a scent thirty-six hours old.

c. In children's games: (see quot. *a*1870). {common}

*a***1870** CHIPMAN *Notes on Bartlett* 91 Cold, *adj.* . . . Distant. Said of the one who, in play-hunting to find the thing concealed, is remote from it. **1876** 'MARK TWAIN' *Tom Sawyer* ix. 89 Now they're stuck. Can't find it. Here they come again. Now they're hot. Cold again. **1887** A. DALY *Railroad of Love* 17 You are nowhere near it. As the children say in their game—you're 'cold.'

+3. Without animation because of a severe blow or shock.
*a***1846** *Quarter Race Ky.*, etc. 45 He picked up an ole axe helve an gin me a wipe aside the hed that laid me cole fur a while I tell you. **1905** Rex Beach *Pardners* v. 127 Some Polack . . . laid out the quartermaster cold.
fig. **1847** Field *Drama in Pokerville*, etc. 93 It is 'bound' to lay every thing in the way of architecture west of the Alleghanies 'out cold,' and no mistake!

***4.** Of soil: Not well suited to cultivation, because of excess moisture or clayey consistency.
1634 Wood *New Eng. Prospect* (1865) 11 The Soyle is for the generall a warme kinde of earth, there being little cold-spewing land. **1846** Emmons *Agric. N.Y.* I. 253 What are called cold lands are not uncommon in this district. . . . This condition is produced by the agency of many springs. **1863** Mitchell *My Farm* 238, I doan't like myself to turn up much o' the yaller; it's a kind o' cold sile.

+5. Stale.
1889 Farmer 158 Cold bread is stale bread.

6. Special combs.: (see quotations).
1816 *Mass. H. S. Coll.* 2 Ser. VII. 119 *Cold Tacks*, so termed from the manner in which they are made, have become an article of important manufacture in this town [Abington, Mass.]. **1878** *Decorum* 310 Those [freckles] which are constitutional and permanent are called 'cold freckles.' **1885** *Harper's Mag.* Jan. 274/2 Some tanners then place them in the vats, and cover them up to take a 'warm sweat' or a 'cold sweat,' the pungent moisture from the hides loosening the hair and scurf. **1888** W. Lawrence *A. A. Lawrence* 218 The description of Nahant society by his near neighbor Mr. Thomas G. Appleton, 'cold roast Boston,' was to Mr. Lawrence its chief recommendation.

***Cold,** *v. tr.* With *off.* To make cold. *local.* — **1891** Wilkins *New Eng. Nun* 257 You'd better shut your door or you'll cold your house all off. **1897** — *Jerome* 389 You're coldin' of the shop off, Belindy. **1922** Brown *Old Crow* 398 What you openin' winders for, a day like this, coldin' off the room?

Cold-air. Used attrib. with *box, pipe* in sense: Containing or conducting air of a low temperature. — **1865** Stowe *House & Home P.* 285 Good, fresh, out-door air from a cold-air pipe. **1897** Moore *How to Build* 55 The Cold-Air Box which supplies the furnace should be of metal.

+Cold deck. In card games, a prepared deck, a pack of cards arranged to benefit one player. — **1868** *All Year Round* 31 Oct. 490/1 He's got everything all set to ring a 'cold deck.' **1870** 'Mark Twain' *History Repeats Itself*, I never have gambled from that day to this—never once—without a 'cold deck' in my pocket. **1887** F. Francis *Saddle & Moccasin* 225 Between them they put up a cold deck in a faro-box. **1914** J. H. Keate *Destruction Mephisto's Web* 212 It was no trouble to ring in the 'cold deck,' as everything was going along smoothly and Fowler had no suspicion of anything wrong.
fig. **1876** Harte *G. Conroy* vi. ii, You've been . . . playin' it very low down on my moral and religious nature, generally ringin' in a cold deck on my spiritual condition for the last five years.

Cold feet.

+1. Phr. *to get* or *have cold feet*, to lose one's desire or courage. *colloq.*[2]
1896 Ade *Artie* 108 He's one o' them boys that never has cold feet. **1903** *McClure's Mag.* Nov 37/2 President Bahlhorn himself began, as a labor leader expressed it, 'to have cold feet.' **1904** E. Robins *Magnetic North* 1 Instead of 'getting cold feet,' as the phrase for discouragement ran, and turning back, they determined to cover as many as possible of the seventeen hundred miles. **1909** 'O. Henry' *Roads of Destiny* 64 She got cold feet.

+2. The loss of courage; one who has lost his spirit.
1900 *Kansas Hist. Coll.* VI. 136 The regiment developed but two or three cowards, two or three pairs of weak knees—two or three pairs of 'cold feet,' as the soldiers expressively term the complaint. **1916** *Boston Journal* 5 April 8/1 Hot-heads and cold-feet (—rioters and cowards).

+Cold flour. A kind of corn meal. (See Nocake and Pinole.) — **1859** Bartlett 91 *Cold Flour*, a preparation made of Indian corn (maize) parched and pulverized, mixed with one third its quantity of sugar. Two or three teaspoonfuls of this compound stirred in a glass of water will answer for a meal when food is scarce. **1871** De Vere 207 Cold flour . . . is a delicacy . . . ; a few spoonfuls are stirred in a tin cup with water, and make a good meal when other food is not to be had. **1916** Thoburn *Hist. Oklahoma* I. xxxiv. 262 Corn was also prepared for use on . . . long journeys by being carefully parched and then ground into a fine powder, which was called 'cold flour.'

Cold frame. A boxlike structure with glass at the top, in which plants are protected. — **1857–8** *Ill. Agric. Soc. Trans.* III. 503 The seed for early summer cabbages can be planted in a cold frame early in September. **1877** *Field & Forest* II. 164 These insects had all gathered along the Northern and Eastern margin (inside) of a 'cold frame,' in his garden. **1885** *N.H. Forestry Comm. Rep.* June 82 The common cold frame used by market gardeners—six feet wide, and as long as may be desired—will be found convenient.

Cold lead. {1771 (a coffin)} +A bullet or bullets. *colloq.*
1809 Fessendon *Pills Poetical* 32 Our spouting democrats . . . , When they can't reason with a Fed, In logick substitute cold lead. **1841** *S. Lit. Messenger* VII. 225/2, I will give him a piece of cold lead, . . . if he will stand long enough. **1846** *Knickerb.* XXVII. 560 Instead of gold and silver, you took it in cold lead! **1873** *Newton Kansan* 22 May 3/2 The Marshall administered cold lead to eight dogs last Tuesday.

+Cold plague. A kind of ague. *Obs.*
1819 E. Dana *Geogr. Sk.* 35 The diseases vulgarly called the *spotted fever*, and *cold plague*, which in the severest seasons of winter cold, at the northwest, have occasionally made dreadful ravages. **1819** *Plough Boy* I. 94 The Nashville Register makes mention of an effectual remedy for the disorder which is there called the *influenza*, or *cold plague*. **1826** in Peck *Guide* (1831) 203 The disease which a few years since prevailed in Kentucky and elsewhere, called the cold plague. **1828** *Western Mo. Rev.* I. 582 The dreadful malady, so well known by the name 'cold plague,' was chilling the blood in his young veins. **1828** *Free Press* (Tarboro, N.C.) 12 Sept., After four days illness of a disease, designated by his physicians, the cold plague. **1853** A. Lawrence *Diary & Corr.* 41 The distemper was variously named, cold plague, spotted fever, and malignant remittent fever.

‖**Cold scald.** 'A double misfortune, as of a person who should be at once frozen and scalded' (B. '77).

Cold setting. In dairying, the process of cooling milk preparatory to removing the cream. — **1888** *Vt. Agric. Rep.* X. 14 Mr. Parker, of Georgia, who runs two cream separators at Westford, cold setting at Georgia and also at Jeffersonville, thought there was but little difference in quantity of milk to pound of butter. *Ib.* 15 When cream was raised in a large can by deep cold setting more inches of cream would be indicated at the end of four hours.

+Cold shut. (See quotation.) — **1887** *Scribner's Mag.* II. 304/2 Out West the same [bear-]trap is used, but instead of pinning it to the ground a long chain is attached, and the end of this chain is made fast around a log, with a 'cold-shut' or split-ring, such as you put your pocket-keys on, and which can be fastened by hammering.

+Cold snap. A spell of sharp weather.
1776 T. Smith *Jrnl.* (1849) 279 A dismal cold snap of weather. **1835** C. Mathews *Memoirs* (1839) IV. 342 Since my last letter we have had what is called by the Americans 'a cold snap!' again. **1851** *Knickerb.* XXXVII. 392 The night grew chilly, and brought along one of those cold snaps, as they are not inaptly termed in New-England. **1865** S. Andrews *South since War* 288 The landlord said . . . that he reckoned he would have to get a stove into the office of the hotel pretty soon if this cold snap continued. **1885** *Harper's Mag.* April 697/2 An early cold snap found many growers with their vines uncovered. **1899** *Mo. So. Dakotan* I. 155 The 'cold snap' was anything but a snap, so prolonged was it and so intense. **1903** *N.Y. Ev. Post* 23 Sept., The damage done by the late cold snap.

***Cold water.** +In attrib. use with *army, man*, etc., with reference to the cause of total abstinence.
1830 *Congress. Deb.* 25 Feb. 584 It may be expedient to make our sailors cold water drinkers. **1832** (*title*), The Cold-water Man; or a Pocket Companion for the Temperate. **1840** *Niles' Nat. Reg.* 18 July 320/3 A cold water army, as it was denominated, assembled at Salem. **1843** *Knickerb.* XXI. 377 He was instantly seized with a desire to join the cold-water army. **1848** W. E. Burton *Waggeries* 20 You oughter be the commodore of all them cold water clubs, and perpetual president of all temp'rance teetotallers. **1906** *Springfield Republican* 16 Aug. 1 Another [case in point] comes in the action of the prohibition state executive committee in Pennsylvania. . . . The cold water convention there nominated William H. Berry.

b. *Cold-water régime*, the administration of President Hayes (1877–1881), who served no spirits at his table.
1884 *Century Mag.* April 807/2 The cold-water régime lasted four years, and has left behind an interesting souvenir in the fine portrait of Mrs. Hayes, by Huntington, which stands in the Green Room.

Cold wave. A spell of cold weather, traveling in a certain direction. Also attrib.
1884 *Science* III. 149/2 A cold wave does not travel in a well-defined curve. **1886** Z. F. Smith *Kentucky* 737 North-west winds bring the 'cold waves' and the bitter 'blizzards' of midwinter. **1887** *Courier-Journal* 30 Jan. 7/7 The Signal-service department here received instructions to hoist the cold-wave flag, and a decided fall in temperature is promised. **1889** *Scribner's Mag.* Aug. 159/2 Heat causes them [=fish] to run in from the Gulf to cruise along the coast, . . . but a 'norther,' or 'cold wave,' drives them back into deep water.
fig. **1885** Howells *S. Lapham* xxi, I guess there's a cold wave comin'; but you can't generally 'most always tell, . . . where the old man's concerned.

+Coleslaw. Also **cold slaw.** [ad. Dutch *koolsla*, from *kool*, cabbage, *sla*, a reduced form of *salade.*] A salad made of sliced cabbage with condiments.
(*a*) **1794** *Mass. Spy* 12 Nov. 412 A piece of sliced cabbage, by Dutchmen ycleped cold slaw. **1821** Cooper *Spy* xiii. 156 Potatoes, onions, beets, cold slaw, rice, and all the other minutiae of a goodly dinner. **1842** *Knickerb.* XX. 355 The table was soon spread and garnished, from pepper-castor to cold-slaw. **1876** M. F. Henderson *Cooking* 225 Cold slaw is especially nice served with fried oysters. **1896** E. Higginson *Tales* 50 The cabbage was chopped finely for the cold-slaw. . . . Then Mrs. Bridges 'set' the table.
(*b*) **1842** *S. Lit. Messenger* VIII. 202/1 Does not this mean *separated*, just as the fibres of the dried Calamus are separated, . . . like the *cole-slaw* of

the table, cut into vermicular tortuosity. **1889**– *Cent.* and dicts. **1918** Farmer *Cook Book* 288 Cole-slaw.

***Colewort, †Colwort.** A kind of cabbage. (Cf. Collard.)

1676 Glover *Acc. Va.* in *Phil. Trans.* XI. 629 Their Gardens . . . have Cabbages, Colworts, . . . Potatoes, and Yams. **1682** Ash *Carolina* 13 Their [planters'] Gardens begin to be supplied with such European Plants and Herbs as are necessary for the Kitchen, viz. Potatoes, Lettice, Coleworts, . . . and Reddish. **1751** Eliot *Field-Husb.* iii. 56 There is another Advantage to be had by Sowing Cole-worts. **1796** B. Hawkins *Letters* 31 There is 30 acres in the farm, the product, corn, cotton, rice, . . . pumpkins, watermelons, colewarts. **1896** Harris *Sister Jane* 8 We planted asparagus and bachelor's buttons on his ground, and he had planted his favorite coleworts . . . on ours.

attrib. **1751** J. Eliot *Cont. Field-Husbandry* 9, I would Propose the Sowing of Cole-wort Seed. This Plant is of the Cabbage-kind; it is sometimes called Cale. **1840** Hoffman *Greyslaer* II. 8 The Indian girl . . . had bound up the contusion with a fillet of colewort leaves.

+Colicroot.

1. Butterfly weed.

1833 Eaton *Botany* (ed. 6) 33 *Asclepias tuberosa*, butterfly-weed, colicroot, pleurisy-root, white root. . . . Cathartic, diaphoretic, expectorant.

2. A low herb (*Aletris farinosa* and *aurea*) found along the Atlantic coast, reputed to have medicinal properties.

1840 Dewey *Mass. Flowering Plants* 208 *Aletris farinosa.* False Aloe. Colic Root. . . . The root is very bitter, and in small quantities used as a tonic and stomachic. **1843** Torrey *Flora N.Y.* II. 310 Star-grass. Colicroot. . . . Dry woods and thickets, sometimes in dry swamps. **1889** *Cent.* 136/3 The two species, *A. farinosa* and *A. aurea*, . . . are called colic-root from their medicinal reputation.

3. The wild ginger (*Asarum canadense*), and closely related plants.

1894 *Amer. Folk-Lore* VII. 97 *Asarum canadense*, . . . coltsfoot, N.Y. Colic-root, West Va. **1901** Mohr *Plant Life Ala.* 481 Colic Root [grows in] Alleghenian and Carolinian areas.

+Colicweed. An herb of the genus *Corydalis.*

1817–8 Eaton *Botany* (1822) 253 *Corydalis cucullaria*, colic weed. **1821** *Mass. H. S. Coll.* 2 Ser. IX. 149 Plants, which are indigenous in the township of Middlebury, [Vt., include] . . . *Corydalis . . . glauca*, Colic-weed. **1840** Dewey *Mass. Flowering Plants* 40 Colic Weed . . . blooms in May, along hedges and light woods.

+Colin. [Mexican Sp. *colín.*] The American quail or bob-white.

[**1678** Ray tr. *Willughby's Ornith.* 393 Those of New Spain call Quails *Colin.* **1753** Chambers *Cycl. Suppl.*, *Colin*, . . . the name of an American bird, called by most authors a quail.] **1806**– Webster and dicts. **1871** *Mich. Gen. Statutes* (1882–3) I. 583 No person shall kill or destroy, or attempt to kill or destroy, any colin or quail, [etc.]. **1881** *Ib.* 585 The People of the State of Michigan enact, That no person or corporation or company shall, at any time, kill . . . any deer, ruffed grouse, colin or quail, [etc.].

‖**Collah.** (See quotation.) — **1822** *Amer. Beacon* 5 Sept. 214 (Th. S.), Put into your mouth this crab claw, and you can't be wounded. . . . He said, give me back my corn, and collah (that is, crab's claw).

Collapse, *v.* {1732–}

+1. *tr. To collapse a flue*, of a steamboat, to undergo the collapsing of a boiler-flue. Also fig.

1833 E. T. Coke *Subaltern's Furlough* v, I . . . used often to imagine what a hurry and scuffle there would be in the cabin, if the vessel 'collapsed its flue.' **1847** Robb *Squatter Life* 146, I do feel as ef I wur about to collapse a flue, or bust my biler, for the fact of the marter is, Marie, . . . ef I git caught here thar'll be suthin' broke. **1855** Glisan *Jrnl. Army Life* 264 Rumor has it that she [a ship] collapsed a flue. **1883** 'Mark Twain' *Life on Miss.* xxv, We burnt a boiler; broke a shaft; collapsed a flue; and went into Cairo with nine feet of water in the hold.

+2. To break down.

1902 S. G. Fisher *True Hist. Amer. Rev.* 200 Such complete destruction and devastation of the country as would collapse the patriot party.

+3. To cause (a thing) to fall into a looser form or smaller compass.

1921 Mulford *Bar-20 Three* 229 Far back . . . a Mexican collapsed his telescope.

‖**Collapsity.** A collapsed condition. — *a***1859** *Boston Post* (B.), Many emigrants, arriving in that state of collapsity termed *flat broke*, staid at Los Angeles because they couldn't go on.

***Collar.**

1. An iron band placed around the neck of a Negro slave.

1819 *La. Acts* 6 March 64 If any person or persons . . . shall cut or break any iron chain or collar which any master of slaves should have used in order to prevent the running away . . . of any such slave [etc.]. **1839** Weld *Slavery as It Is* 22 A heavy iron collar, with three long prongs projecting from it, was placed round her neck. **1853** Stowe *Key* 89 *n.*, The iron collar was also in vogue in North Carolina.

+2. *Polit.* Used attrib. with *man*, *press*, etc., to indicate abject subservience to party or party interests. *Obs.*

1833 *Niles' Reg.* XLIV. 146/2 Almost every generally accepted principle laid down in the proclamation may be clearly traced in Mr. Webster's 'federal,' or 'blue light' speech, as many of the 'collar presses' bawled out that it was. **1834** *Louisville Pub. Advertiser* 7 June, 'Collar-men,' 'collar presses' and 'collar-representatives' are terms very much used by the opposition. **1840** *Log Cabin Song Book* 49 Van Buren's collar men . . . , They soon will fly their courses. **1841** *Congress. Globe* 12 July 185/1 These electioneering speeches . . . were [insulting] . . . to the majority, whose mildest form of designation was 'collar men,' and other epithets equally degrading.

+b. *To wear* or *take (someone's) collar*, to follow a party or party leader slavishly. *Obs.*

1834 *Boston Transcript* 5 April 2/1 Dennis Doyle . . . handed round a paper to obtain signatures to denounce the patriot Macneven, for refusing to wear a collar! **1836** *Congress. Globe* App. 9 May 337/1 Sir, I . . . am proud to wear the collar of such a man as Andrew Jackson, whose collar is the collar of Democracy. **1862** *Ib.* 23 Jan. 452, I belong to no party. I am too old; my remaining years on earth are too few for me ever to expect to wear another party collar. **1866** *Ib.* 6 April 1802/2 The Senator from O. has suggested that I have taken upon myself the collar of the President of the U.S.

‖**3.** *To fill (one's) collar*, to perform (one's) duties adequately. *colloq.*

1898 Westcott *D. Harum* 195, I seen right off that you was goin' to fill your collar, fur's the work was concerned.

Collar box. A box for holding collars. {1881} — **1852** Stowe *Uncle Tom* xv, My tape and needle box is four; and my bandbox, five; and my collar-box, six; and that little hair trunk, seven. **1868** *Mich. Agric. Rep.* VII. 363 Henry Fowler, Detroit, [exhibited] . . . 1 dozen muff and collar boxes, combined in one. **1886** Stapleton *Major's Christmas* 130 Bobby handed it over, a collar box with a round hole cut in the top.

Collar button. +A detachable buttonlike device used to fasten a collar on a shirt. — **1886** Stapleton *Major's Christmas* 253 Poor old Funk, he never has anything—a silver fruit knife and a collar button. They were all he had. **1887** *Courier-Journal* 6 Feb. 5/6, 1,000 best Rolled Gold Lever Collar Buttons at 10c each. **1909** 'O. Henry' *Roads of Destiny* 163 There on the floor was still Ben Price's collar-button that had been torn from that eminent detective's shirt-band.

Collard. [Phonetic development of Colewort.] A kind of cabbage that does not head. {1755 collart; 1807 collard; now *dial.*}

1791 Imlay *Western Territory* (ed. 3) 477 He likewise makes a small garden for peas, beans, collards, and other vegetables. **1854** Simms *Southward Ho!* xv. 320 His cabbage invariably turns out a collard. **1869** *Overland Mo.* Aug. 130 'Collard' (probably corrupted from *colewort*) is the kind of cabbage found everywhere in the South, whose leaves, not heads, furnish the greens for the inevitable dish of bacon and greens. **1898** *Congress. Rec.* 15 March 2830/2, I must say that a dinner of hog jowl and sweet Georgia collards . . . is better than all the pork and beans . . . that can be spread on any table in New England.

+Collar dog. See Collar 2. — **1836** *Congress. Deb.* 9 May 3552, Those who compose the Jackson party are denounced by the new-born whigs, as 'collar dogs.' . . . Sir, I am a party man, and one of the true collar dogs.

***Collar-maker.** One whose business is to make collars. — **1722** *Boston Selectmen* 96 Sam[ue]ll Deming Late of Boston Collermaker dyed yesterday. **1770** *Carroll P.* in *Md. Hist. Mag.* XIII. 75 Cash Expended. Nov. 26. By pd Kirbie Collar Maker, £5: 5: 0. **1865** *Atlantic Mo.* XV. 474 The collar-maker had complained of being in everybody's way.

+Collar paper. Paper used for the manufacture of collars. Also attrib. — **1867** *Atlantic Mo.* March 370/2 They learned that Columbia wears about her neck annually nearly as many reams of paper as she uses to write upon, and that this collar-paper may be made of stock much inferior to that employed for letter-paper. *Ib.*, In the Collar-paper Manufactory, . . . the pulp, when first drawn from the stuff-chest, is carried into a large trough.

***Collateral,** *a. Collateral security*, something pledged to make good the fulfilment of an obligation. {1777–}

1720 *Mass. Bay Currency Tracts* 368 That the whole profits . . . remain in the Bank as a Fund, or colateral Security, until the profits amount unto the original Sum Emitted. **1857** *Harper's Mag.* Feb. 404/2 The forged paper was used mainly as collateral security for the purpose of raising money. **1862** *Huntington Rec.* III. 473 To pledge any of the bonds and mortgages or other vouchers belonging to the Town of Huntington, as collateral security for the payment of said loan. **1904** A. K. Fiske *Modern Bank* 141 Whether a loan on collateral security is on time or at call, it has to be passed upon by an authorized officer of the bank.

+b. Also ellipt. as noun.

1832 *Congress. Deb.* App. 62/2 May 13, 15 days $20,000 collateral. **1858** *Knickerb.* LI. 24 Collaterals of stocks and bonds had depreciated, and currency had run short. **1869** *Congress. Globe* 25 March 273/2 When we want money to move our wheat we understand we can go down there and borrow it. If we have got the collaterals to put up we get it. **1902** Banks *Newspaper Girl* 306, I am not willing to trust you without collateral. I notice that you have a ring on your finger. I am willing to take that as collateral and give you a receipt for it. **1911** Saunders *Col. Todhunter* 112 The Todhunter farm is as pretty a piece of collateral for a three-thousand-dollar loan as old Shylock himself would have the heart to ask.

***Collect,** *n.* +A place where something, esp. water, collects.

Since this sense is found in the region of Dutch influence, Bartlett suggested as an etymol. Dutch *kolk*, a pit, a lake.

1839 in *Mich. Agric. Soc. Trans.* VII. 386 These sinks derive their name from the fact of their being collects for the waters of the surrounding region. *c***1870** CHIPMAN *Notes on Bartlett, Collect*, a pond supplied by rain; a water puddle—Dutch settlers in New York. **1877** BARTLETT 133 That portion of the city of New York now occupied by the 'Tombs,' the 'Five Points,' and vicinity, was formerly known as 'The Collect.'

Collect, *v.*

1. *tr.* To obtain payment of (an account) by personal, or persistent, application.

1838 HAWTHORNE *Note-Books* I. 70 Fellow-passenger, a Boston dry-goods dealer, travelling to collect bills. **1864** SALA in *Daily Tel.* 12 Aug., In this country [U.S.A.], to dun a debtor for a bill is called 'collecting an account.' **1887** *Postal Laws & Regul.* 268 Carriers are required to collect . . . all postage due on any matter entrusted to them for delivery.

+**2.** *intr.* or *absol.* (See quotations.) Cf. C.O.D.

1889 FARMER 159/1 To *Collect*, a contraction for 'to collect payments.'

+**3.** To take or pick up. *colloq.*

1875 C. JAMES *Yoke of Freedom* 53 Jack went down the great marble staircase, . . . collected his hat and cloak, [etc.].

+**4.** Used adverbially or as adj. to indicate that something sent, esp. a telegram, is to be paid for on delivery.

1901 MERWIN & WEBSTER *Calumet 'K'* 47 As the last click sounded, Bannon handed his message to the operator. 'Send it collect,' he said. *Ib.* 226, I'll give Brown one more warning—a long 'collect' telegram, about forty words. **1917** McCUTCHEON *Green Fancy* 275 They had the insolence to send the telegrams collect. **1922** H. L. FOSTER *Adv. Trop. Tramp* 186 He sends it [a telegram] to us 'collect.'

***Collection.** The gathering of taxes, bills, etc. Used attrib.

(*a*) **1789** MACLAY *Deb. Senate* 63 The *collection bill* is at last reported. **1802** *Ann. 7th Congress* App. 1313 The collectors in each district shall prepare and transmit to their respective supervisors, correct lists of all lands within their respective collection districts. **1843** *P. O. Laws & Reg.* II. 45 A draft office may be required to deposite, or to pay on a collection order, or a collection office to deposite or to pay on a draft. **1903** A. B. HART *Actual Govt.* 7 The coast of the ocean fronts and the Great Lakes is divided into 120 tariff collection districts; the interior and the coast together are divided into 63 internal-revenue collection districts.

(*b*) **1887** *Courier-Journal* 6 Feb. 5/4, I saw Tom Dalton go into Mrs. Polk's house several times with a collection book. **1903** *Chicago Chronicle* 11 April 1/1 That office was leased and furnished by me under an arrangement with another man, . . . to do a collection business.

***Collector.**

1. One who collects customs at a port.

1648 *Portsmouth* (R.I.) *Rec.* 38 Mr. Boston is Chosen Collector for the Port. **1679** *N.C. Col. Rec.* I. 245 [They] have factiously made one Mr Culpeper . . . the Collector of his Ma[jes]ty's Customes. **1723** *Weekly Mercury* 22–29 Jan. 2/2 Lost or strayed away . . . a large and dark coloured Mare, formerly belonging to Mr. Robert King, Collector of Amboy. **1761** *Descr. S. Carolina* 33 There is a Comptroller of the Customs; Three Collectors, one at each Port. **1808** *Ann. 10th Congress* 1 Sess. I. 107 That complaint having been made to the collector of the port of Nantucket, he had noted his intention to seize the vessel and cargo. **1852** FILLMORE in *Pres. Mess. & P.* V. 148 The appointment of George C. Laurason as collector of the customs for the district of New Orleans. **1887** CUSTER *Tenting on Plains* vi. 189 Besides visiting at the house of the collector of the port, . . . we have been hospitably treated by some people to whom Armstrong was able to be of use.

2. One who receives the tax money of a town, county, state, or federal district.

See also CITY COLLECTOR.

*c***1636** *Dedham Rec.* I. 23 Samuell Morse chosen Collector for money to be . . . payd out according to such seu[e]rall occasions as shall (arise) of & conc[e]rneing our sayd Towne. **1684** *Huntington Rec.* I. 393 There should be a collector to gather all Rates that is to say ye County Rate ye ministers fifty pound a year and all towne Rats. **1704–5** *Boston Rec.* 33 It being proposed to the Town whether they would chuse a Collecto[r] to gether the rates, . . . the same was voted in the negative. **1794** *Ann. 4th Congress* 2 Sess. 2852 The opposition broke out in an act of violence upon the person and property of Robert Johnson, collector of the revenue for the counties of Allegany and Washington. **1802** [see COLLECTION (a)]. **1873** *Harper's Mag.* XLVI. 469 The only important bill passed in both Houses during the session is that abolishing the offices of assessors . . . and transferring their duties to collectors. **1883** *Ib.* Aug. 486/1 Hon. A. L. Pridemore . . . introduced a bill for the relief of the sureties of H. G. Wax, who was a collector of taxes. **1903** *Evanston* (Ill.) *Press* 11 April, The action taken by this meeting in relation to compensation to the town collectors is . . . illegal.

3. One authorized to demand payment of debts; also one who collects fares.

1851 CIST *Cincinnati* 49 Occupations [include] . . . collectors, 27 [people]. **1862** *Trial C. M. Jefferds* 25 What is your business? A. Collector on the South Ferry. Q. What is called a ferrymaster? A. Yes, sir. **1902** LORIMER *Lett. Merchant* 186 Another time I had a collector that I set a heap of store by.

Collectorate. {1825–} A district and its organization under the control of a collector of revenue. — **1791** WASHINGTON *Writings* XII. 42 If your collectorate cannot furnish money to defray your expenses, in which you will observe due economy, . . . you will supply yourself from the collector of Savannah.

***Collectorship.** The office of collector. — **1793** *Steele Papers* I. 101 Will you inform me . . . whether you would move to any of the Towns at a distance from your present residence for any Collectorship, the loan office, etc, if they should become vacant. **1857** *Harper's Mag.* Sept. 561/1 My evil genius tempted me in the form of a Collectorship. It was vacant, for the incumbent died just about the time of the election. **1889** *Phila. Times* 15 July, John Cadwalader retires from the Collectorship of the Port to-day and will be succeeded by Senator Cooper.

***College.** Also †**colledg(e).**

***1.** An institution at which instruction is given in the higher branches of learning.

In England the word generally refers to a self-governing corporation that forms part of a university; 'in U.S. "college" has been the general term, and is still usually applied to a small university (or degree-giving educational institution) having a single curriculum of study' (O.E.D.).

Under pioneer conditions the word has been sometimes applied to institutions (degree-giving or not) with rather restricted facilities for instruction.

1636 *Harvard Rec.* I. 171 The Court voted for the erecting a publick Schooll or Colledge in Cambridge. **1643** *New Eng. First Fruits* II. i, The Colledge was, by common consent, appointed to be at Cambridge, . . . and is called (according to the name of its first founder) Harvard Colledge. **1705** BEVERLEY *Virginia* IV. 31 Their Majesties granted a Power to certain Gentlemen . . . to build and establish the College by the Name of *William* and *Mary* College. **1751** *N. J. Archives* 1 Ser. VII. 580 When I consider the poverty of this little Province . . . I almost despair of any help here towards the building and support of our college. **1758** *N.H. Hist. Soc. Coll.* IX. 37 We may be able in a little Time to raise a Sufficient Fund for erecting & carrying on an Academy or College. **1780** *N.J. Archives* 2 Ser. IV. 223 The college and grammar-school in this place are now beginning to recover from the desolation they have suffered in consequence of the war. **1846** T. H. JAMES *Rambles U.S.* 66 The numerous little boys' schools scattered over the country, where the dirty-nosed urchins are whipped, or ought to be, once a week, are all designated *colleges*. Thus there are more colleges and universities, so called, in America, than throughout Europe. **1883** *Century Mag.* Aug. 633/2 He had no papers, save an honorary degree of master of arts conferred on him before his downfall by a too-confiding college. **1884** *Critic* 10 May 216/2 A college is understood nowadays to be the undergraduate department alone, shorn of all the sister schools, such as law, medicine, etc. But the usage in America is loose. Some of our universities, so called, have not the full complement of faculties; and some that call themselves colleges have very nearly the full number of a university. **1925** BRYAN *Memoirs* 21 He had intended to attend a Baptist college.

b. Without the article; often in the phr. *to go to college.*

1764 S. DEANE *Journal* 302 The General Court came up to College. The President opened the assembly by mentioning the occasion of the present meeting, and requested the Governor to give a name to the new house. **1772** TRUMBULL *Progress of Dulness* I. 5 How he went to college, and what he learned there. **1799** WASHINGTON *Writings* XIV. 165, I do not think it will be a very reconcilable matter to Gentlemen of more respectable ages . . . to have a young man fresh from College placed over their heads. **1840** DANA *Two Years* vi. 49 You think, 'cause you been to college you know better than anybody. **1892** M. A. JACKSON *Memoirs* 90 The girls were old enough to be sent to boarding-school and the boys to college.

***2.** The building or set of buildings occupied by the institution.

*a***1649** WINTHROP *Hist.* II. 139 There was an assembly at Cambridge of all the elders in the country. . . . They sat in the college, and had their diet there. **1684** I. MATHER *Providences* (1856) iii. 59 In the year 1678, on the 29th of June, at Cambridge in New-England, a thunder-clap with lightning broke into the next house to the colledge. **1712** *Dialect Notes* II. 99 Wee are of Opinion wth respect to the Old College, That the best way is to take off the Roof. **1795** FRENEAU *Poems* 374 On the Demolition of a Log-College. **1807** IRVING, etc. *Salmagundi* iv, Princeton . . . —students famous for their love of a jest—set the college on fire, and burnt out the professors: an excellent joke, but not worth repeating.

+**3.** One of a group of buildings occupied by a college.

On this sense see O. F. Emerson in *Nation* LXI. 293 ff., *Dial. Notes* IV. 299–300; and A. Matthews in *Dial. Notes* II. 91–114 and *Mass. Col. Soc. Publ.* XV. cxxviii–cxxxi.

1654 *Harvard Inventory* in *Nation* LXI. 346/1 Another house called Goffes colledge, & was purchased of Edw. Goffe. conteyning five chambers. **1676** in T. Hutchinson *Coll. Orig. Papers* 501 There are three colledges built in Cambridge, one with timber at the charge of Mr. Harvard and bears his name; [etc.]. **1781** *Boston Gazette* 31 Dec. 1/1 In the evening, the Students to confess their Joy upon the occasion, by the leave of their Instructors, illuminated the Colleges. **1821** *New-Eng. Hist. Register* XXX. 189 Rode up to N. Haven, took a view of the town, the Colleges all in a range, the Churches and the extensive burying-ground.

1871 *Ib.* XXV. 231 The first object of any interest in approaching the colleges from Boston . . . is a large imposing structure . . . commonly known as the head-quarters of General Putnam. **1893** E. E. HALE *New Eng. Boyhood* (1900) 189 This made a company of two or three hundred ladies and gentlemen, who came out to 'see the colleges' on those particular days. **1916** *Dial. Notes* IV. 300, I remember especially the night of the tornado which blew down the buildings of the college near our time of graduation,—the first report along the street was 'the colleges are down.'

+**4.** A divisional unit in some universities.

1870 *Rep. Comm. Agric. 1869* 455 The university embraces a college of science, literature, and art; an agricultural and mechanical college, a college of the Bible; a normal college; a college of law; and a college of medicine. **1899** *Univ. of Chicago Reg. 1898–99* 37/1 The Faculties of the Schools of Arts, Literature, and Science have been organized as follows: (1) The Faculty of the Junior Colleges; (2) The Faculty of the Senior Colleges; [etc.].

+**5.** =ELECTORAL COLLEGE.

1837 *Democratic Rev.* I. 24 He was chosen to act as elector of President and Vice President of the United States . . . and repaired to Raleigh, where he presided over the deliberations of the college of electors. **1877** *Harper's Mag.* Feb. 476/2 The electoral vote in all the colleges was cast December 6. **1903** R. L. ASHLEY *Amer. Govt.* 273 Each State is entitled to as many electors in the 'college' which elects the President as it has senators and representatives in Congress.

+**6.** (See quotation.) *slang.*

1844 FEATHERSTONHAUGH *Slave States* 98 Adjourning when they had drunk to the warehouse up stairs, which they called 'the college,' and which was converted into a gambling room for faro and rouge et noir.

7. Attrib. and comb. in various significations: **a.** Employed by a college.

1684–5 SEWALL *Diary* I. 67 He had been College Cook a long time. **1848** N. AMES *Childe Harvard* 141, I do conjure you, that ye suffer not Contempt of College Faculty to go Unpunished! **1848** *Ib.* 170 With trembling step in presses An Under College Officer,—and thus addresses. **1657** in Peirce *Hist. Harvard* App. 14 When the Corporation shall hold a meeting for agreeing with College servants. **1734** *Harvard Rec.* I. 135 None shall be admitted Fellow Commoner, unless he first pay, one hundred pounds, to the College Treasurer, for the time being.

b. With reference to expenses in college.

1828 *Yankee* Oct. 323/3 The college bills, that is, the amount paid to the treasurer each term, for tuition, room-rent, etc. are the same to every student. **1818** *N. Amer. Rev.* March 426 The College charges are made in four quarter bills.

c. Pertaining to the founding or administering of a college.

1696 SEWALL *Diary* I. 441 [Several] give in a paper . . . shewing their dislike of our draught for the Colledge Charter. **1702** C. MATHER *Magnalia* (1853) II. 12 Fellows . . . signed a copy of the Colledge laws. **1708** SEWALL *Diary* II. 209 The Books of the College Records, Charter, Seal and Keys were laid upon a Table running parallel with that next the Entry.

d. Having reference to the routine education program carried on by a college.

1877 *Harper's Mag.* April 695/1 The number of names on a college catalogue affords . . . no means of estimate of the actual character of the instruction given by its authority. **1883** *Ib.* September 635/1 The college Commencement season excites more public attention every year. **1880** *Ib.* July 257/2 It seems impossible that the requirements for admission to the college department should be raised. **1836** *S. Lit. Messenger* II. 614 The belief, that the matters usually taught in schools, such as will enable the pupils to get a college diploma, comprehend the whole of . . . education. **1827** *Harvard Reg.* July 133 Themes, forensics, declamations, and all the rest of the tribe of college exercises. **1856** HALL *College Words* (ed. 2) 11 *Appointee*, one who receives an appointment at a college exhibition or commencement. **1836** *Harvardiana* II. 272 He will contemn beyond measure college honors. **1883** *Harper's Mag.* Aug. 479/1 The Messrs. Harper have published a new edition of the late Professor Orton's excellent high school and college manual of the science of Comparative Zoology. **1770** FITHIAN *Journal* I. 7 Mr. Hunter and myself, were admitted into the junior-Class . . . after a previous Examination by the president . . . : Which was about three Weeks after the College-Orders began. **1883** *Harper's Mag.* Sept. 635/2 [J. F. Adams'] criticism is not a vague general assault upon college studies. **1842** *Knickerb.* XIX. 430 There is an increasing disposition to give up one of the most valuable parts of college training. **1707** SEWALL *Diary* II. 193, I acquainted the Govr and council that Mr. Willard was not capable of doing the College work, another year. **1865** A. D. WHITNEY *Gayworthys* xvii. 157 He would have been nearly through a college year, by this time.

e. Owned or operated by a college or forming part of its equipment or surroundings.

1827 *Harvard Reg.* Nov. 286 The College-bath was erected in 1801. *Ib.* May 84 How in days of yore his Satanic Majesty rung the college bell at midnight, when some students were 'hooking' chickens. **1877** PHELPS *Story of Avis* 37 This pretty young thing peeped shyly . . . at the congregation in the college chapel. **1871** BAGG *At Yale* 287 It is in sophomore year that the undergraduates in considerable numbers begin to occupy the college dormitories. **1789** MORSE *Amer. Geog.* 384 The college edifice is a huge misshapen pile. **1874** *Dept. Agric. Rep. 1873* 307 Professor Goessman . . . gives the results of experiments made in 1872 on the college farm and in various localities in New York. **1876** G. H. TRIPP *Student-Life* 147 No water ever runs off the college grounds. **1827** *Harvard Reg.* Nov. 286 The College-house stands without the college yard. **1852** *Harper's Mag.* V. 334/2, I shall always see the gathering groups of students and alumni upon the college lawn. **1871** BAGG *At Yale* 534 The 'College lot' is quite near the entrance of the same [New Haven Cemetery], and many tutors as well as undergraduates of all classes have been laid there side by side. **1796** MORSE *Univ. Geog.* I. 759 The [Yale] college museum . . . contains many natural curiosities. **1877** PHELPS *Story of Avis* 159 He wouldn't let him go to those hot college-rooms. **1790** *Harvard Laws* 42 A print of the college seal . . . shall be pasted in the beginning or end of every book. **1715** *Harvard Rec.* II. 427 Mr John White . . . is impowered and directed to take the College-Stock, and all things thereunto belonging into his Custody and care. **1850** THAXTER *Poem before Iadma* 19 Arrived at Harvard, straightway he adopts the bulletin's advice, And buys his books at the College Store.

f. Enrolled in or attending college.

1882 HOWELLS *Modern Instance* iii, These college-belles . . . were inferior to Marcia Gaylord, too, in looks and style. **1880** *Harper's Mag.* Sept. 539/2, I wish I could send all the college-lads and worked-out business men . . . on such an expedition. **1779** *N. J. Archives* 2 Ser. III. 672 Though the number of proper college members last summer did not exceed ten, yet one or other of the instructors was constantly upon the spot. **1847** A. LAWRENCE *Diary & Corr.* 245 The government or the proper authorities of the college are authorized to fill the vacancy or vacancies from their own college pupils.

g. With reference to things or activities conducted, participated in, or originated by students in college.

1871 BAGG *At Yale* 302 'Glee Clubs' are often organized, sometimes as class, sometimes as college affairs. **1883** *Harper's Mag.* Sept. 503/2 'Wentworth!' cried the man . . . in the same deep accents with which he had given voice to the college air. **1893** POST *Harvard Stories* 23 Dignified men . . . acted as they never do on any other occasion except a college boat-race. **1895** WILLIAMS *Princeton Stories* 204 The amount of patience and ubiquity required to 'run' three girls' cards at a college dance. **1897** BRODHEAD *Bound in Shallows* 86 'Ma,' she expostulated, 'how you go on! Just because Mr. Dillon gets me to play him college glees now and again.' **1836** *Harvardiana* III. 163 Embarrassments [are] to be met in conducting a College Magazine. **1836** *Ib.* II. 387 Evidently, a college periodical has . . . higher pretensions. **1845** *Knickerbocker* XXVI. 583 We count it no small pleasure to have been favored . . . with the perusal of portions of a prospective college-poem. **1909** WEBSTER 438/1 *College settlement*, a social settlement in charge of an organization of college students or graduates. **1904** GLASGOW *Deliverance* 317 He stood impatiently uprooting a tuft of grass as he whistled a college song in unsteady tones. **1923** WYATT *Invis. Gods* 62 To Louise Marshfield, Will Halliday seemed more and more the zenith of manly perfection . . . in college yells.

h. Known or associated with in college.

1846 POLK *Diary* I. 370 He was my College associate and personal friend. **1898** PAGE *Red Rock* 33 The same invitation should be extended to his college chum. **1877** *Harper's Mag.* Dec. 110/1 Mr. Daly was a college classmate of mine. **1865** *Atlantic Mo.* XV. 591 The parson, with the letter in his hand, asked if she remembered an old college friend, Maverick.

i. Made up or composed of college students.

1871 BAGG *At Yale* 243 The college club . . . was started in the summer term of 1866, . . . for the purpose of furnishing a cheap but respectable board at its cost price. **1889** *Century Mag.* March 799/2 An article on 'College Fraternities' in the *Century* for September, 1888. **1882** *Nation* 30 Nov. 458/2 All the 'athletic sport' that the great majority of the students get consists in the payment of money to the 'College eight,' or 'College nine,' as the case may be. **1854** *Harper's Mag.* IX. 555/1 That summons . . . was not to a solemn Commencement, nor to a College Society, . . . but to the parting celebration of the Class.

j. Worn by students in college.

1905 A. H. RICE *Sandy* 117 Bright-flowered hats flashed among college caps. **1872** *Atlantic Mo.* Jan. 27 The very day that they [the Indians] rejoined their tribe they threw off their college clothes, resumed their old costumes and weapons, and ran whooping into the forest, irreclaimable savages. *Ib.* 384 The college colors are liberally and often tastefully displayed in the costumes of the lady dancers.

+**College Bible.** A book containing the college regulations. — **1850** THAXTER *Poem before Iadma* 14 The Student cons the College Bible with eager, longing eyes. **1851** HALL *College Words* 52 The laws of a college are sometimes significantly called *the College Bible.* **1855** *Harvard Mag.* I. 414 Whatever the College Bible tells us to do,—if we except nine tenths of it which is a dead letter,—that we usually do with all our might.

+**College boy.** A young man attending a college.

*a*1851 in Hall *College Words* 317 The wildest of the College boys [etc.]. **1872** HOLMES *Poet* ix. 295 That sounds a little like what we college-boys used to call a 'squirt.' **1877** PHELPS *Story of Avis* 25 The attack of universal scepticism which she had successfully weathered at eighteen, in common with the existing senior class of college-boys in her father's lecture-room. **1882** *Nation* 13 July 22/3 College boys and college girls fresh from their books could stand a better examination than people who had practical experience. **1925** Bryan *Memoirs* 97, I was still a college boy in 1880.

College-bred, *a.* Having had a college education; having attended college.

1842 *Knickerb.* XIX. 429 Many mechanics and merchants are as well educated as many college-bred men. **1844** Emerson *New Eng. Reformers* Wks. III. (1903) 260 The most conservative circles of Boston and New York had quite forgotten who of their gownsmen was college-bred, and who was not. **1883** *Century Mag.* Sept. 784/2 Some remarks in these columns . . . have been taken as unwarrantably prejudiced in favor of 'college-bred' statesmen. **1893** 'Mark Twain' *P. Wilson* i, He was twenty-five years old, college-bred, and had finished a post-college course. **1902** *Harper's Mag.* May 963/2 Will Van Dorn, college-bred and diplomaed as a lawyer, [etc.].

College building. A building in which a college is housed. {1875}

1655 *Harvard Rec.* I. p. lxxv, The Colledge building . . . in a very ruinous condition. **1749** *Ib.* p. cxxvi, The College-Building consists of a Court built on three Sides. **1817** Worcester *Gazetteer* s.v. *Princeton,* The College building is a handsome stone edifice. **1895** *Century Mag.* Sept. 795/1 Shall we fill the college campus and college buildings with the roar of an athletic boom?

+**College campus.** The main grounds of a college.

1834 Simms *Guy Rivers* I. xv. 219 Ralph . . . acted . . . precisely as he might have done in the College Campus, with all the benefits of a fair field and a plentiful crowd of backers. **1866** *Yale Lit. Mag.* XXXI. 146 (Th.), The students retreated hastily to the College Campus. **1900** Winchester *W. Castle* 11 He had just returned . . . from walking around the twenty-acre college campus. **1915** Campbell *Proving Virginia* 113 Elizabeth caught up with Virginia on the college campus.

***College church.** +**1.** A church connected with a college. +**2.** A collegiate church. (See Collegiate *a.* 2.) — **1889** *Cent.* 1102/3.

College course. The curriculum of study to be followed at a college.

1818 *N. Amer. Rev.* March 422 Persons may be admitted to advanced standing at any part of the College course. **1839** J. D. Whitney *Life & Lett.* 25 Three years in Yale had done for Josiah Whitney what a college course in his day was intended to do. **1856** M. J. Holmes *Homestead on Hillside* ii, She would be thrown in the way of Walter Hamilton, who was about finishing his college course. **1883** *Harper's Mag.* Sept. 635/2 The youth sees that the college course which his own age demands is of less actual honorable distinction in the college than the studies of an earlier time.

College dues. The payment required for attendance at a college; tuition and other fees.

1670 *Harvard Rec.* I. 52 The Treasurer is ordered to accept his proposall, or . . . to require the Colledge dues from him forthwith. **1694** *Ib.* 347 Such as Shall be admitted into Colledge, upon Admission Shall bring Security to the Steward for the paying all Colledge dues as they Shall arise. **1734** *Ib.* 134 His Parent . . . [shall] give Bond to the Steward . . . to pay College dues Quarterly as they are charged. **1818** *N. Amer. Rev.* March 422 A bond is to be given . . . for the payment of College dues, with two satisfactory sureties.

College education. An education of the kind acquired through attendance at a college.

1771 Franklin *Autobiog.* 233 But my father, in the meantime, from a view of the expense of a college education, which having so large a family he could not well afford, [etc.]. **1794** *Mass. H. S. Coll.* III. 200 Only four persons from Truro have had a college education. **1868** Beecher *Norwood* 181 There is almost a superstitious reverence for a 'college education.' **1877** *Harper's Mag.* April 695/2 College education, if it is to be of real value, must not take into view the difference of sex. **1880** *Ib.* July 257/2 The writer would thus separate distinctly college education and university education. Their methods and aims are different. **1902** *Ib.* May 882/2 A brother-in-law like that will be worth a college education to you any day.

+**College girl.** A young woman attending a college. — **1882** [see College boy]. **1904** *N.Y. Ev. Post* 10 Sept. 4 A suggestion for a college girl's vacation that should be clipped and pasted for reference next June.

College green. A piece of grassy land on which college buildings are situated. {1736– in Dublin (Swift)}

1814 *N.Y. Herald* 17 Aug. 3/5 The Students of Columbia College . . . are requested to meet at the College Green, on Tuesday. **1860** M. J. Holmes *Maude* xviii. 193, I walked with him upon the College Green. **1871** Bagg *At Yale* 28 The ground had hardly been staked out . . . when a cry was raised in the newspapers that the beauty of the college green —the pride of the city—would be ruined thereby. **1893** J. Auld *Picturesque Burlington* 116 The old 'College Green' itself deserves more than passing mention.

College hall. An assembly or dining hall used by a college.

1643 *New Eng. First Fruits* II. i, Their publique declamations . . . and Disputations . . . (besides their ordinary Exercises in the Colledge-Hall). **1765** Peirce *Hist. Harvard* 260 The company returning to the College Hall were entertained with an handsome dinner. **1767** E. Singleton *Social N.Y.* 313 Many Gentlemen of Distinction honoured the Governors of the College with their Company in the College Hall at Dinner. **1815** *Salem Gazette* 28 Feb. 2/3 An elegant dinner was served up in the college hall.

b. *transf.* In the plural: The college as a seat of learning. Cf. Halls (of learning).

1788 Freneau *Misc. Works* 70 Why (he cry'd) did I forsake . . . the limpid lake For musty books and college halls? **1883** *Century Mag.* July 457/2, I hope persecution does not, indeed, light his fires in your college halls.

+**College Indian.** An Indian that has attended the schools provided by the white man. — **1724** Jones *Virginia* 19 The Northern and Southern Nations might be managed by Missionaries from the Society, and the College Indians.

College land. Land owned by a college. — **1660** *New Haven Col. Rec.* II. 372 Under the name & title of colledg land. **1775** *N.H. Hist. Soc. Coll.* IX. 91, I have lately agreed with one of this Town to prepare, Sow with Wheat & Fence fifty Acres of the College Land. **1838** Colton *Ind. Delineated* 31 Indiana College is located on the College lands, adjacent to Bloomington.

College library. The book collection of a college; the building that houses it.

1693 Sewall *Letter Book* 139 Bestow the Skeleton in Colledg Library. **1701** — *Diary* II. 28 Gave to the College-Library Dr. Owens two last Volumes on the Hebrews. **1796** Morse *Univ. Geog.* I. 527 The college library [at Princeton] was almost wholly destroyed during the late war. **1836** *Harvardiana* II. 174, I [was] . . . wandering through the alcoves of the college library. **1877** *Harper's Mag.* Jan. 240/2, I was glancing, in the college library, at an old volume of one of the earlier historians of Virginia.

College life. The experiences and occurrences during attendance at college.

1836 *Harvardiana* II. 268 There is nothing which will give to your college life such a pleasurable excitement. **1842** *Knickerb.* XIX. 430 The object of college life has been overrated. **1848** S. A. Eliot *Sk. Hist. Harvard* 19 The only Indian, who ever passed through the four years of College life. **1856** M. J. Holmes *L. Rivers* i. 10 A wealthy young southerner, who, just freed from the restraints of college life, found it vastly agreeable making love to the fair Helena. **1877** *Harper's Mag.* April 696/2 They [=women graduates] will come back from their college life to their homes with a broader appreciation of the value of those homes. **1916** C. A. Eastman *From Deep Woods* 67, I must confess that western college life is quiet compared with that of the tumultuous East.

College man. A man who has attended college. {1611–} — **1825** Neal *Bro. Jonathan* I. 385 There's a college-man over at Mr. Colonel Chowder-head's tavern. **1898** Page *Red Rock* 22 The freemasonry which exists among young college-men. **1903** *Atlantic Mo.* July 36 The college men of America need no help and no pity from any source.

***College mate.** One who attends, or once attended, the same college with another. {1590} — **1877** *Harper's Mag.* Dec. 109/1 [He] was employed . . . in the office of his friend Benjamin, a college mate. **1890** H. Bunner *Short Sixes* 112 He discussed the situation with his foreman, who was also his confidant, his best friend and his old college mate. **1898** Page *Red Rock* 522 So Dr. Cary sat down in prison and wrote a letter to his old college-mate.

+**College president.** The academic and administrative head of a college. — **1845** *Knickerb.* XXV. 182 The writer gives the reply of a fellow-student to a question of a college president. **1876** *Harper's Mag.* Dec. 144/1 The Easy Chair has heard from the lips of an accomplished college president the same glowing praises of a political and social system of superiors and inferiors. **1883** *Century Mag.* July 467/1 A college president is a purely American institution.

+**College pump.** A water pump situated on college grounds. — **1764** Peirce *Hist. Harvard* 283 Two of the College pumps being then rendered useless. **1848** N. Ames *Childe Harvard* 10 How Childe Harvard . . . Screamed under the college pump, I sing. **1871** Bagg *At Yale* 293 Each man must . . . draw his own water at the college pump, or hydrant or cistern.

***Colleger.** +A student at a college. — **1827** *Harvard Reg.* (1828) 214, I guess as how, if we get fore-handed enough we'll send him to be a Colledger, and make a Parson of him. **1836** *Harvardiana* III. 9 We stood like veteran collegers the next day's screw. **1851** Hall *College Words* 53 *Colleger,* a member of a college. . . . (Little used.) [**1927** J. Freeman *When West Was Young* 345 You don't need to git rough, you young colleger!]

+**College scrip.** 'A species of land scrip issued and sold in order to establish colleges' (Th. S.). — **1869** *Congress. Globe* 4 Feb. 874/2 The proposition of the Senator from New York is to give to this college scrip a very considerable increased value. **1873** *Harper's Mag.* XLVI. 469 Located with college scrip, 693,613.37 [acres]. **1880** Lamphere *U.S. Govt.* 199/2 A homestead settler may . . . pay for it with cash, warrants, or college scrip, or private land scrip.

+**College town.** A town in which a college is located. — **1852** *Harper's Mag.* V. 334/2 It was in one of those quiet college towns which are the pleasantest spots in New England. **1865** *Atlantic Mo.* XV. 505 Preaching in a New England college town and ticket-agency on the Underground Railroad.

+**College widow.** A young woman who stays about a college year after year in order to associate with the men students.

1871 BAGG *At Yale* 523 A 'college widow' is the unfortunate young woman, who, having been the pet of several college generations without making a single permanent capture, at last finds herself deserted of admirers, and with faded charms falls out of sight and memory. **1887** *Lippincott's Mag.* Aug. 298 That class of young ladies known among the students as 'college widows,' and commonly supposed to have the acquaintance of several generations of collegians. **1904** ADE (*title*), The College Widow. **1907** *Nation* 26 Dec. 591/1 The professor's wife of this type is, we suppose, almost as well recognized in such an atmosphere as the 'college widow.'

+**College yard.** A plot of ground, usually enclosed by a fence, etc., on which college buildings are situated. (Principally at Harvard and other northeastern universities.)

1639 *Harvard Rec.* I. 172 Imprimis. The frame in the Colledge yard & digging the cellar, carriage & setting it up, [£] 120. **1659** *Ib.* 44 Neither do we allow that any the said Watchmen should lay violent hands on any of the students, being found with in the precincts of the College yard. **1702** SEWALL *Diary* II. 67 Goe with the Govr about 2 p.m. Dine; into the College yard. *c***1764** in Woolsey *Hist. Disc. Yale* (1850) 55 The Freshmen are forbidden to wear their hats in College-yard . . . until May vacation. **1770** J. MADISON *Writings* I. 4 Their letter to the merchants in Philadelphia, requesting their concurrence, was lately burnt by the students of this place [Princeton] in the college yard. **1830** *Collegian* 96 He had been heard ranting in the College yard, and finishing the definition of his Critic, to the great nuisance of the soporific Sophs. **1850** *Knickerb.* XXXVI. 575 It appears that the professor had an old horse that used to roam about the college-yard. **1897** *Outing* XXX. 408/1 It takes boldness and nerve to put on a top-hat, and ride a brute like that through the college yard.

* **Collegian.** One who attends or has attended a college; a college student.

1722 *New-Eng. Courant* 15–22 Jan. 1/1 A young babbling Collegian, who has just Learning enough to make a Fool of himself. **1818** *N. Amer. Rev.* VII. 118 If a collegian, he commits Euclid and Locke to memory without understanding them. **1852** MITCHELL *Dream Life* 150 Very few individuals in the world, possess that happy consciousness of their own prowess, which belongs to the newly graduated Collegian. **1882** 'M. HARLAND' *Eve's Daughters* 331 A young collegian of whom I have lately heard;—a semi-idiot upon most subjects and utterly deficient in common sense. **1903** ADE *People You Know* 58, 'I swiped those,' replied the Collegian.

Collegiate, *n.* A student at a college. {1609–1818} — **1843** E. P. BELDEN *Sk. Yale College* 161 He enters strangely enough into familiar talk with the recently admitted collegiate. **1851** HALL *College Words Collegiate*, a member of a college. **1854** M. J. HOLMES *Tempest & Sunshine* 109 Miss Warner keeping a watchful eye upon her pupils, lest some lawless collegiate should relieve her from the trouble of seeing them safely home.

* **Collegiate,** *a.*

* **1.** Pertaining to an educational institution whose students are of a rank above high school or academy.

1831 PECK *Guide* 244 The facilities for common schools in the more populous portions of the state, and even for an academical or collegiate course, will be equal to most of the states in the union. **1837** — *New Guide* 347 Number of students in collegiate, academical and primary departments [of Augusta College, Ky.], about 200. **1851** CIST *Cincinnati* 298 The style of architecture is what is called the Collegiate Gothic. **1870** *Rep. Comm. Agric. 1869* 461 A department to be called 'the collegiate department,' in which the student will be suitably prepared to enter any of the higher departments of the university. **1882** 'M. HARLAND' *Eve's Daughters* 162 If you do not say . . . that a man can plow nearer to a stump without grazing it for having had a collegiate education, [etc.]. **1900** MUNN *Uncle Terry* 18 Albert's mother had . . . given him a collegiate education.

+**2.** *Ecclesiastical.* (See quotations.)

1818 J. BRISTED *Resources U.S.* 413 There is, however, in some of our cities, a custom, which diminishes their usefulness; namely, the collegiate system which makes three or four churches common to as many, or more clergymen. . . . The essence of the collegiate system is, not to suffer the same clergyman to preach twice successively in the same church. **1864** WEBSTER 251 *Collegiate church*, . . . a church which is united with others under the joint pastorate of several ministers. (U.S.)

+**3.** *Collegiate school*, an early name for Yale College.

1707 *Boston News-Letter* 17 March 2/1 Mr. Abraham Pierson Minister of the Gospel in this Town, & Rector of the Collegiate School in Connecticut. **1712** *Conn. Public Rec.* V. 353 The collegiate school at Seybrook, for maintaining a rector and tutors, . . . shall receive this present year out of the Colony treasury the sum of one hundred pounds in money or bills of credit of this Colony. **1717** *Mass. Col. Soc. Pub.* VI. 183 To the Hon[ora]bl[e] The Gov[e]r[nor] and Compa[ny] for Setling ye disputes concerning ye place of ye Collegiate School & dependencys thereof.

4. Pertaining to a united body of colleagues. {1625–}

1914 McLaughlin & Hart *Cycl. Amer. Govt.* I. 192 The essential characteristic of a cabinet government is the union in a collegiate ministry of the supreme direction of both legislation and administration. *Ib.* 201 In the second year of the Civil War, the collegiate Cabinet was not sufficiently in evidence to satisfy certain leaders.

Collegiately, *adv.* {1624–} In the manner of a college. — **1812** *Niles' Reg.* II. 53/1 There appears in the United States a redundancy of young men, collegiately educated in the arts and sciences.

Colleging, *vbl. n.* The receiving of a college education. — **1848** LOWELL *Indian Summer Reverie* xxxviii, I am glad That here what colleging was mine I had.

Collegious, *a. Obs.* = COLLEGIATE *a.*— **1718** MATHER in Quincy *Hist. Harvard* (1840) I. 525 The Colony of Connecticut, having for some years had a College at Saybrook without a collegious way of living for it, have lately begun to erect a large edifice for it in the town of New Haven.

Collide, *v.* {1621–} *intr.* Of vessels, vehicles, etc.: To strike against each other; to come into collision (with something). {1886–}

When this word was first used of ships and trains *c*1860–70 it was regarded by some writers as being an Americanism. See *Notes and Queries* 4 Ser. IX. 409; XII. 15.

1868 *Notes & Q.* 4 Ser. I. 293 In this country [U.S.], instead of saying that two vessels came into collision together, it is usual to say that they *collided* with each other. This word seems needed, and is formed from *collision* by analogy with *collude* and *collusion.* **1869** *Supreme Court Cases* VIII. 305 The mate . . . believed . . . the vessels . . . might collide. **1871** *Ib.* XIV. 171 She had collided with a steamer which mistook her for another steamer. **1889** FARMER 159 *Collide, to*, to come in collision with. Formerly confined to railway phraseology, but now anything that comes into violent contact with another object is said to *collide* with it. In spite of the objections raised to the use of this word, it has forced its way afresh into the dictionaries, for in reality *collide* is an instance of a word falling into disuse, and after the lapse of time again making its way into popular favor.

* **Collier.**

* **1.** One who makes charcoal. {–1608}

1777 *N.J. Archives* 2 Ser. I. 409 Wanted at Batso and Mountholly Iron-Works a number of labourers, colliers, nailers, and two or three experienced forgemen. **1894** *Dial. Notes* I. 329 *Collier*, charcoal-burner. (S[outh New] J[ersey]).

* **2.** A coal-miner.

*a***1821** C. BIDDLE *Autobiog.* 263 He mentions his being consulted by one Fergus Ferguson, collier, who was taken up as an insurgent. **1849** CHAMBERLAIN *Ind. Gazetteer* 184 One town was first laid out in 1835, and settled by colliers under the supervision of Rhodes and McLane. **1905** VALENTINE *H. Sandwith* 148 Hain't I ben a master-collier all me days an' don't I know?

3. The dolphin-fly, *Aphis fabae*. Also attrib. {1744–1784}

1849 *Rep. Comm. Patents: Agric.* 339 Another species, which, from their sooty color, are called the black-flies, black dolphins, or colliers. **1889** *Cent.* 1726 *Dolphin-fly* . . . [is] also called, from its black color, the collier-aphis.

+**Collins ax.** A small ax. — **1869** BROWNE *Adv. Apache Country* 63 One [Indian] went with a necklace of mattocks around his neck and three Collins axes in his girdle.

+**Collinsia.** [From Zaccheus *Collins* (1764–1831), a botanist of Philadelphia.] An annual plant (*Collinsia verna*, etc.), native to the United States. — **1821** NUTTALL *Trav. Arkansa* 127 The acclivity, through a scanty thicket, rather than the usual sombre forest, was already adorned with violets, and occasional clusters of the parti-coloured Collinsia. **1843** TORREY *Flora N.Y.* II. 33 *Collinsia verna*. . . . Early Particolored Collinsia. **1857** GRAY *Botany* 285 Collinsia. . . . Rich shady places, W. New York to Wisconsin and Kentucky. May, June.

‖**Collise,** *v.* [Back formation from *collision.*] *intr.* To collide. — **1793** *Gaz. U.S.* 11 May (Th.), But if these little globes collise, Adieu to amity and peace.

+**Colloquian.** One who engages in a colloquy. — **1871** G. R. CUTTING *Student Life at Amherst Coll.* 40 For the Exhibition, four orators are now chosen in each society from the Senior class, instead of three as formerly, and the colloquians of each society unite in the composition of an original 'colloquy.'

* **Colloquy,** *n.* +A college exercise consisting of a prepared conversation. Also attrib. — **1860** *Yale Lit. Mag.* XXV. 399 (Th.), Some cue that will enable colloquy men to save an inglorious fizzle. **1861** *Ib.* XXVI. 80 (Th.), [He] has just succeeded in getting a Colloquy appointment. **1871** [see COLLOQUIAN].

+**Colloquy,** *v. intr.* To converse; to engage in a colloquy. — **1868** HAWTHORNE *Note-Books* I. 135 Then they colloquied at much length about the various peculiarities and merits of the new invention. **1871** *Congress. Globe* 16 March 126/1, I saw the Speaker colloquying with the Democrats.

* **Cologne.** +A toilet water composed of alcohol and aromatic oils; *eau de Cologne.*

1832 KENNEDY *Swallow Barn* I. 125 She would like to have some Cologne of a particular kind. **1840** *Knickerb.* XVI. 34 Reclining rashly under the hemlock, perfumed 'as to our locks' with the bay-rum or fragrant cologne, we will eat pic-nics upon the green turf. **1870** A. S. STEPHENS *Married in Haste* 301 She snatched a flask of cologne . . . and dashed its contents over her handkerchief. **1903** WIGGIN *Rebecca* 276, I had it [an idea] while I was putting cologne on your head. **1911** VANCE *Cynthia* 194 Take some handkerchiefs for bandages, cologne, peroxide.

attrib. **1847** FIELD *Drama in Pokerville*, etc. 172 Ah, a Cologne wipe, delightful! and now for a *champoo*—never mind those fellows waiting! **1851** A. O. HALL *Manhattaner* 56 His cologne bottle and flesh brush will find active employment in the duties of the toilet.

+**Cologne water.** = COLOGNE.

1838 HAWTHORNE *Note-Books* I. 119 Cologne-water is among the essences manufactured though the bottles have foreign labels on them. **1839** BRIGGS *H. Franco* II. 44, I bathed my temples in cologne water. **1845** M. M. NOAH *Gleanings* 193 Her flesh begins to creep, and then they wash their temples with cologne water, to recover from the shock. **1852** STOWE *Uncle Tom* xvi, I put his magnificence upon an allowance of cologne-water, and actually was so cruel as to restrict him to one dozen of my cambric handkerchiefs. **1897** *Outing* XXX. 320/1 Mrs. Holland shook her head, while searching for the salts and cologne-water.

* **Colonel.** Also †**coronel, kernel,** etc. Abbreviated *Col.*, †*Coll.*

***1.** The chief officer of a regiment, in rank directly below a general officer.

(*a*) **1654** *Suffolk Deeds* III. 487 On the South lyeth the sajd Colonells house. **1704** Church *Hist. Philip's War* II. 137, I do . . . Appoint you to be Colonel of all the Forces raised. **1777** *Jrnls. Cont. Congress.* IX. 913/2 When land forces are raised by any State, for the common defense, all officers of or under the rank of colonel shall be appointed by the legislature of each State respectively. **1806** *Ann. 9th Congress* 1 Sess. 1250 The colonel or commanding officer of the regiment or garrison. **1866** *Land We Love* (Charlotte, N.C.) May 69 Presently a little tallow-greased Colonel stepped in front.

(*b*) **1745** *Essex Inst. Coll.* XLVIII. 294 This Day our Corronoll ordered us ashore on ye aforesaid Island.

b. Used attrib. as a title.

1688 *Conn. Public Rec.* III. 455 Pray my humble service to all our friends and acquaintance especially to our good brother Coronel Pynchyon. **1705** *Boston News-Letter* 16 July 2/2 We have heard nothing of Coll. Peartree since he went last out in pursuit of the French Privateer. **1846** POLK *Diary* 86 Col. Benton called before General Cass left. **1895** in M. A. Jackson *Memoirs* 471 A number of Federal surgeons were quartered in a room adjoining Colonel Munford's.

+**2.** As a title of respect, officially or unofficially given, but without military associations.

1744 ALEXANDER HAMILTON *Itinerarium* (1907) 94 Had it been a rattlesnake I should have been entitled to a colonel's commission for it is a common saying here [along the Hudson] that a man has no title to that dignity until he has killed a rattlesnake. **1746** E. KIMBER *Itinerant Observ.* 36 Wherever you travel in Maryland (as also in Virginia and Carolina) your Ears are constantly astonished by the number of Colonels, Majors, and Captains, that you hear mentioned. **1831** ROYALL *Southern Tour* II. 119 The next best fellow . . . was one Cushing, a Judge, a Colonel, a black-smith, and a Justice of the Peace. **1873** 'MARK TWAIN' & WARNER *Gilded Age* v. 57 This morning my wife says, 'Colonel'—she will call me Colonel spite of everything I can do. **1886** HARTE *Snow-bound* 17 I'm Rawlins, of Frisco. Heerd of ye afore, Kernel. **1896** HARRIS *Sister Jane* 11 His title of colonel . . . was purely a title of respect, a mark of the esteem in which he was held by his friends and neighbors, a tribute to his moral and business qualities.

Colonelcy. The office or commission of a colonel. {1797–}

1855 SIMMS *Forayers* 521, I will reserve Major Sinclair, whom I design to advance to a colonelcy in the state line, for a separate duty. **1858** *Texas Almanac* 115 Sherman was solicited to run for the colonelcy of it. **1865** *Atlantic Mo.* XV. 507 Lee has since cashiered [him] from his colonelcy for selling the commissions in his regiment. **1884** *Century Mag.* Feb. 498/1 Shortly afterward the colonelcy of one of the Michigan regiments fell vacant.

Colonial, *a.* {1796–}

+**1.** Pertaining to the period in American history before 1776, when independence was declared.

1776 *Boston Rec.* 240 How many Persons belonging to this Family are now in the Service? Is it Continental, or Coloniel? Is it by Sea, or by Land? *Ib.* 242 The Question [was] accordingly put—Whether holding any military Commission in the Continental or Colonial Army is not incompatable [*sic*] with holding any Civil Trust? **1807** J. BARLOW *Columbiad* VII. 258 While in his march athwart the wide domain, Colonial dastards join his splendid train. **1836** *S. Lit. Messenger* II. 284 The Colonial Legislature claimed the supreme power as residing within itself. **1860** MORDECAI *Virginia* 74 This stove, a work of note, bears the old Virginia colonial arms and other embellishments in relief. **1871** *Scribner's Mo.* I. 498 Possibly it was built in colonial times. **1884** *Century Mag.* March 677/2 The public buildings of colonial and immediately post-colonial times. **1891** *Advance* 5 Nov., Upon the basis of the old colonial Stock . . . there will be coming on still higher attainments of character. **1918** [see COLONIAL DAMES OF AMERICA].

+**2.** Pertaining to settlers in Texas. (See COLONIST 1 b.)

1842 *Diplom. Corr. Texas* (1911) III. 951 This indeed our Colonial interests already foresee, which is the main cause of the efforts now making to villify [*sic*] the country.

+**b.** Relating to efforts to colonize the West.

1872 TICE *Over Plains* 143 Colorado seems to be regarded as a favorable ground for trying colonial experiments.

+**3.** Of a kind characteristic of the colonial period; antique; time-honored.

1831 P. HONE *Diary* I. 34, I . . . got very good colonial quarters, near the bath-house. **1885** *Century Mag.* April 825 It is in this class [of educated men] that what has been recently most aptly termed the 'colonial' spirit still survives. There sometimes crops out among our educated men in politics the same curious feeling of dependence upon foreign opinion. **1903** WISTER *Philosophy Four* 23 Bertie and Billy had colonial names (Rogers, I think, and Schuyler), but the tutor's name was Oscar Maironi. **1903** *Boston Herald* 19 Aug., They are especially appropriate for colonial teas, Thanksgiving celebrations and other occasions which seek to recall the early history of New England. **1904** *Methodist Rev.* Jan. 101 Sometimes we wonder whether personal reminiscences will ever become colonial. Will people some day search for them as they do for old china?

+**4.** (See quotation.)

1903 *Dial* 16 Jan. 43 'Colonial' and 'Imperial' are among the terms extensively used, in recent years, in referring to the relations newly assumed by the United States. The first of these adjectives is wrongly applied to the dependencies of our republic.

+**Colonial Dames of America.** A society or organization of American women of colonial descent, for the purpose of collecting and preserving early American documents, relics, etc. — **1897** (*title*), Officers and Members of the Massachusetts Society of the Colonial Dames of America. **1905** *Mass. Soc. Col. Dames America Reg.* 13 The Society of Colonial Dames of America has been formed . . . to do honor to the virtues of their forefathers, [etc.]. **1918** *Encycl. Amer.* VII. 286/2 Colonial Dames of America, The National Society of. An ancestral and patriotic organization of American women, founded 19 May 1892, and composed of one Colonial Society from each of the 13 original States, one society from the District of Columbia and one associate society from each of the non-colonial States.

Colonialism. {1864–} **1.** A condition or attitude of dependency felt by a community toward its parent state. **2.** A condition characteristic of the colonial period in American history. — **(1) 1884** *Boston Journal* 30 Dec. 2/4 The Anglomaniacs are delighting their small souls with this remnant of the spirit of colonialism. **1887** *Nation* 24 Feb. 172 It is a sign of enfranchisement from colonialism, of a genuine culture spreading in the community, when conviction and purpose of this sort are found in a work of the secondary class. **1891** *Harper's Mag.* July 215/2 The last tie of colonialism which bound us to the mother country is broken. **(2) 1904** *N.Y. Times* 9 May 9 Through the southern part of Maryland to the Potomac, a region of old families, old prejudices, sleepy Colonialism, and the colored brother.

‖**Coloniarch.** One who founds or rules a colony. — **1807** J. BARLOW *Columbiad* IV. 517 That great coloniarch, . . . at a courtier's shrine His plans relinquish, and his life resign.

+**Colonist.** {1774–}

1. A member of a colony; often, *spec.*, a settler in America before 1776.

1701 LOGAN in *Penna. Hist. Soc. Mem.* IX. 68 If good colonists were brought into them, . . . there might be raised some thousands of pounds. **1764** T. HUTCHINSON *Hist. Mass.* I. 323 [The people of Mass.] are sensible that they are colonists, and therefore subject to the controul of the parent state. **1791** BARTRAM *Travels* 487 The British colonists of Georgia and South Carolina. **1823** COOPER *Pioneers* ii, Mr. Effingham had, from the commencement of the disputes between the colonists and the crown, warmly maintained what he believed to be the just prerogatives of his prince. **1836** IRVING *Astoria* II. ix. 78 The colonists had at times suffered considerably for want of provisions. **1853** in Winthrop *Hist.* (1853) I. 1 *note*, Endicot and the first colonists of Massachusetts demand our gratitude for the Abigail.

b. A settler from the United States in Texas, principally before its admission into the Union in 1845.

1838 C. NEWELL *Revol. Texas* 203 A large portion of our population, usually denominated 'the Colonists,' and composed of Anglo-Americans, have been greatly calumniated before the Mexican government. **1860** *Texas Almanac* 41 The native Mexicans, causing or permitting its [*i.e.*, San Antonio's] annihilation, the Colonists were exonerated from all obligation to sustain it.

c. An early settler in the western part of the U.S.

1872 TICE *Over the Plains & Mts.* 144 [Greeley, Colo.,] started with seventeen stores and no customers except the colonists. **1877** JOHNSON *Anderson Co., Kansas* 209 Spriggs and Heflin opened a store at a little town . . . where they kept such articles as were most needed by the colonists. **1901** DUNCAN & SCOTT *Allen & Woodson Co., Kansas* 69 His sympathies were against the Abolition Colonists, and as he had the reputation of backing his opinion with his revolver, he was a terror to the 'Yankee Colonists.'

+**d.** One who takes up government land with the intention of transferring it to another individual or company (cf. COLONIZE 1 b).

1910 WHITE *Rules of Game* 534 'The "colonists,"' said Bob, 'took up this land merely for the purpose of turning it over to the company.'

2. A person who moves temporarily into a polling district to vote for a political party. (Cf. COLONIZE *v.* 4.)

1868 *Nation* VI. 282 When every town and city in the United States is voting on the same day, and 'colonists' and 'repeaters' are needed at home, and each State is reduced for its voters to its own citizens.

3. A member of a group united by a common bond of cultural, political, or other interests. (Cf. COLONY 3.)

1893 J. AULD *Picturesque Burlington* 32 Wilcox and his disciples . . . entered into their socialistic scheme under the name of Dawn Valcour Community. The colony was hardly settled before dissensions arose and the colonists divided themselves into two camps, one on either end of the island.

4. A member of a summer colony; a resident at a summer resort.

1903 *N.Y. Tribune* 27 Sept., The younger colonists [at Tuxedo] joined in a paper chase through the park this afternoon on horseback.

Colonization.

1. The establishment of a colony; the settling of an uninhabited or partly inhabited region. {1770–}

1781 PETERS *Hist. Conn.* (1829) 31 Thus far had colinization [*sic*] taken place in the neighboring country, when [etc.]. **1848** CALHOUN *Works* IV. (1854) 460 The word 'colonization' has a specific meaning. It means the establishment of a settlement by emigrants from the parent country in a territory either uninhabited, or from which the inhabitants have been partially or wholly expelled. **1853** *Harper's Mag.* VI. 549 A fortnight after, that gentleman supported his views by an elaborate speech upon the broad topic of foreign colonization in America. **1870** *Rep. Comm. Agric. 1869* 411 Charles K. Landis, who had some previous experience in colonization, and had recently been through the West with the view of founding a new colony, first visited the place in February, 1861.

attrib. **1829** DEWEES *Lett. Texas* 118 By the terms of the colonization law, all the titles issued by the Empresarios, whose contracts are quoted above are good to the holders. **1848** *Calif. Claims* (Senate Rep. 23 Feb.) 14 There is good reason to believe . . . that the revolutionary movement . . . prevented the completion of the colonization grant of three thousand square leagues of Macnamara. **1852** *Harper's Mag.* V. 834/1 The grant . . . can only be transferable so far as regards the colonization part.

attrib. **1872** TICE *Over Plains* 146 There is scarcely a State east of the Mississippi but has colonization schemes.

+2. The sending of Negroes away into colonies in Africa or elsewhere. (Cf. COLONIZATIONISM.)

1816 *Niles' Reg.* XI. 296/2 Colonization of the free blacks. The senate of Virginia has agreed to the proposition of the house respecting this matter. **1834** *S. Lit. Messenger* I. 88 The abolitionists find fault with colonization, because say they, its aim is to postpone or prevent emancipation. **1852** A. LAWRENCE *Diary & Corr.* 318, I have never countenanced these abolition movements at the North; and have lately lent a hand to the cause of Colonization. **1862** LINCOLN in Logan *Great Conspiracy* 402 Room in South America for colonization can be obtained cheaply and in abundance. **1883** *Harper's Mag.* Nov. 961/1 The movement for African colonization under the auspices of the Colonization society.

+b. Attrib. with *cause, company*, etc. (See also COLONIZATION SOCIETY.)

1818 J. BRISTED *Resources U.S.* 150 The intention, at present, on the part of the Colonization Company, is to settle as many free blacks as they can induce to go. **1833** in *Century Mag.* XXX. 784/2 [Wm. Lloyd Garrison] has only since 1830 turned against the Colonization cause. **1834** MINOR *Diary* in *Atl. Mo.* XXVI. 746 He announced a Colonization Meeting for next Saturday.

+3. The sending of Indian tribes into reservations established for them.

1856 PIERCE in *Pres. Mess. & P.* V. 410 The suggestions in this report in regard to . . . the colonization of Indian tribes.

+4. The placing of political supporters where their votes may influence the result of a closely contested election.

1842 *Congress. Globe* App. 31 May 471/2 Could it even be hoped, while the street of a compact city should be made the boundary between congressional districts, that 'colonization' and 'pipe-laying' would be effectually prevented? **1892** *Boston Journal* 7 Nov. 7/4 My attention was directed to the alleged cases of false registration or colonization in this morning's Herald. **1897** *Atlantic Mo.* LXXX. 535/2 [The Civic Federation of Chicago's] committee on political action has dealt through its own secret service department with fraudulent naturalization, colonization, and registration. **1914** McLaughlin & Hart *Cycl. Amer. Govt.* III. 629 In crowded city wards colonization of voters is sometimes attempted. Groups of voters transferred from a 'safe' precinct to a 'doubtful' one get a show of legal residence for the few days necessary before the election. . . . More often illegal colonization is practiced.

+Colonizationism. The policy of ameliorating the condition of the Negroes by sending them into colonies elsewhere, chiefly in Africa. — **1831** *Liberator* I. 174/1 It is the intention of the writer of this article to discuss the subject with some fair and able . . . advocate of Colonisation-ism. **1832** in Garrison *W. L. Garrison* I. 327 Here I am now in the hot-bed of Colonizationism.

+Colonizationist. An advocate of colonizationism.

1831 W. L. GARRISON in Garrison *Life* I. 261, I am truly rejoiced to learn that you are no colonizationist. **1831** *Liberator* I. 174/1 Why do Colonizationists generally shrink from a fair contest on the merits of their system? **1836** CROCKETT *Exploits* 52, I am neither an abolitionist nor a colonizationist. **1839** BRIGGS *H. Franco* I. 150 'Are you not the abolitionist?' 'No, sir.' 'Are you not mistaken? I am pretty certain I saw it in the papers. Are you a colonizationist?' **1852** STOWE *Uncle Tom* xv, The doctor, who was a staunch colonizationist, inclined to the opinion that Miss Ophelia ought to go, to show the Orleans people that we don't think hardly of them. **1856** J. MCNAMARA *3 Years on Kansas Border* 48 Mr. S. then went on to say . . . that he was a colonizationist in principle.

attrib. **1854** in C. Robinson *Kansas Conflict* (1892) 94 So it is with the colonizationist societies and their dupes they send to abolitionize Kansas.

+Colonization Society. A society devoted to the colonizing of free Negroes in Africa or elsewhere.

1817 *Niles' Reg.* XIII. 82/2 It is contemplated, by the present plan of the American colonization society, to find each colonist with food for one year, after his arrival in Africa. **1818** *Ann. 15th Congress* 1 Sess. II. 1772 The auxiliary Colonization Societies which are daily springing up in other quarters of the United States. **1823** *Amer. Baptist Mag.* IV. 181/1 A part of the proceeds is for the Colonization Society. **1828** *Yankee* July 231/1 The Colonization Society with the best intention in the world, cannot of themselves cope with such a destructive increase. **1841** PARK *Pantology* 217 The American Colonization Society, was formed in 1816; to colonize in Africa the free colored people of the United States. **1844** *Niles' Nat. Reg.* 10 Feb. 384/2 The Colonization Society, is to send off a vessel from New York about the middle of March with emigrants for Africa. **1860** BUCHANAN in *Pres. Mess. & P.* V. 594, I entered into an agreement with the Colonization Society . . . to receive the Africans which had been captured on the slaver *Echo* from the agent of the United States in Liberia. **1865** *Nation* I. 229 And, on the other hand, the Colonization Society tempted them with lands and political equality. **1869** in *Century Mag.* XXX. 780 In that the condition of the colored people, both slaves and free, was truthfully portrayed, the double-dealing and manifest deception of the Colonization Society were faithfully exposed. **1883** *Ib.* May 154/2 Dr. Bacon early in life fell into the toils of the Colonization Society. **1914** McLaughlin & Hart *Cycl. Amer. Govt.* I. 323 The American Colonization Society is still in existence and occasionally sends a cargo of negroes to Liberia.

Colonize, *v.*

1. *tr.* To settle (parts of a country) with groups of people; to occupy land as a bona fide settler. {*c*1645–}

1682 ASH *Carolina* 2 The most Able and Ingenious Planters, who have had their Residence on the place from its first being Coloniz'd. **1760** FRANKLIN *Works* (1887) III. 127 The 'pejorate,' and the 'colonize,' since they are not in common use here [England], I give up as bad; for certainly in writings intended for persuasion and for general information, one cannot be too clear. **1846** BUSHNELL *Work & Play* (1864) 248 Whatever man . . . removes to any new country . . . makes a large remove also towards barbarism; for this necessary incident belongs to emigration, or a newly colonized state. **1885** *Century Mag.* Aug. 603/2 An organized movement, known as 'the Oklahoma boom,' has been made to seize and colonize a large body of the territorial lands.

+b. To secure (land) in excess of the government maximum by paying others to take out individual claims. Also *vbl. n.* (Cf. COLONIST 1 d.)

1910 WHITE *Rules of Game* 366 'This bunch of prospectors files on the claims, and gets them patented. Then it's nobody's business what they do with their own property. So they just sell it to me.' 'That's colonizing,' objected Bob. *Ib.* 534 It appears as though the lands were 'colonized.' *Ib.* 559 They believe that we did actually colonize the lands.

+2. To transport (Negroes) into colonies in Africa or elsewhere.

1817 *Ann. 14th Congress* 2 Sess. 939 Mr. Pickering . . . made a report on the petition of the President and Board of Managers of the American society for colonizing the free people of color of the United States. **1832** KENNEDY *Swallow Barn* I. 47 She . . . is supposed to have pensioned out several poor families; besides being a stirring advocate of the scheme for colonizing the negroes. **1862** LINCOLN in Logan *Great Conspiracy* 438 The effort to colonize Persons of African descent . . . upon this continent. **1863** KETTELL *Hist. Rebellion* II. 641 The President alluded to the efforts he had made in relation to emancipation, and also in relation to colonizing the emancipated blacks.

+3. To establish (the Indians) in homes on special tracts of land.

1853 *Harper's Mag.* VIII. 121/2 The Indians were pleased with the plan of colonizing them on the government lands, which seemed to be the only mode of preserving permanent peace among them. **1858** *Ib.* Feb. 399/2 The President . . . recommends that the present system of making valuable presents to the Indian tribes should be discontinued, and that the policy should be adopted of colonizing them in suitable localities.

+4. To place (political supporters) in voting districts where they may decide a closely contested election. Also *absol.*

1885 *Century Mag.* Feb. 636 All the political rascality of the country stands ready to contribute its services. . . . Arrangements are made for colonizing voters from the neighboring States. **1886** LOGAN *Great Conspiracy* 43 On March 30, 1855, a Territorial Legislature was similarly chosen by Pro-Slavery voters 'colonized' from Missouri. **1903** *N.Y. Tribune* 13 Sept., The attempt to colonize in the Third Ward by a faction of the Democratic party was frustrated to-day.

‖**5.** With *out:* To place in lodgings separate from the main hotel or lodging house.

1854 CUMMINS *Lamplighter* 354 The houses is pretty considerable full just now, to be sure, but maybe you can get colonized out. *Ib.*, 'One room, in the next street!' cried the doctor. 'Ah, that's being colonized out, is it?'

+**6.** *intr.* To settle in a previously unoccupied region; to 'homestead.'

1873 *Newton Kansan* 9 Jan. 2/3 Twenty-three Kentucky families have colonized and taken up homesteads in McPherson County.

Colonizer. One who colonizes (in its various senses). {1817–}

1781 PETERS *Hist. Conn.* 25, I have given the Reader some idea of the first colonizers in Connecticut. **1876** BANCROFT *Hist. U.S.* VI. 92 The oldest colonizers of the Delaware were Swedes. **1892** *Nation* LV. 274/3 With the New York cheats, bullies, receivers, colonizers, . . . he can have but a very slight acquaintance. **1904** *N.Y. Ev. Post* 7 Nov. 1 The superintendent of elections is authority for the statement that there are gangs of colonizers and repeaters in the city.

Colonizing. {1622–}

1. The action or process of establishing a settlement. Also attrib.

1764 HUTCHINSON *Hist. Mass.* I. 2 Both English and French continued their voyages to the coast. . . . There was no spirit in the people of either nation for colonizing. **1781** PETERS *Hist. Conn.* 6 They . . . cast off the allegiance of their English Governor, and proceeded in their colonising pursuits under one of their own nation. **1795** J. SULLIVAN *Hist. Maine* 53 The spirit of colonising became faint.

+**2.** The placing of political supporters in voting districts for the purpose of carrying an election.

1842 *Congress. Globe* App. 31 May 471/1 So far as he was informed, the practice of colonizing had its origin, as connected with the elections of the people in our country, in the city of New York.

+**3.** (See COLONIZE *v.* 1 b.)

* **Colony.** Also †**colonye, collony(e), col(l)oney.**

***1.** A community of settlers in a previously unoccupied region, retaining their allegiance to the mother country. In America the reference is chiefly to the settlements before 1776, from the early plantations to the later thirteen governments among which the land was distributed.

'The governments of the early plantation colonies had in them the elements of both local and general control, managing as they did the actual interests of single small settlements and yet holding the powers necessary for governing the whole region in which a settlement lay. . . . When settlements multiplied, the extensive powers of the several executives, which had been possessed from the beginning, were utilized to enforce political unity. The change brought no break in the sequence of colonial administration. The word 'colony' merely took on a broader meaning than before, while 'plantation' remained what it had been, a local community subject to colonial government' (*Amer. Hist. Rev.* VIII. 267–8).

1609 in J. Smith *Works* (1910) p. xcviii, I am bold to write the truth of some late accidentes, be falne his Maiesties Virginia Collonye. **1619** *Va. House of Burgesses* 8 You are bounde to accepte of the Tobacco of the Colony, either for commodities or upon bills at three shillings the best. **1623–4** *Ib.* 28 The first Plantation in Virginia consisted of one hundred persons, so slenderly provided for that before they had remained halfe a yeare in this new Collony they fell into extreame want. **1693** C. MATHER *Wond. Invis. World* 11 The first Planters of these Colonies were a chosen Generation of Men. **1758** *Newport Mercury* 19 Dec. 2/2 Skill and Industry are only wanting to make this little colony as famous and as rich as any would desire from our own Productions. **1776** *Jrnls. Cont. Congress* IV. 2 That it be recommended to all the United Colonies . . . to cultivate, cherish and increase the present happy and necessary union. **1789** MACLAY *Deb. Senate* 21, I admitted that the people of the Colonies (now States) had enjoyed formerly great happiness under that species of government. **1830** COOPER *Water Witch* I. i, The colony has reason to regret the services of a governor who can quit his bed so soon. **1869** STOWE *Oldtown Folks* 336 Life itself is the greatest possible amusement to people . . . who have that intense sense of what can be brought to pass by human effort, that was characteristic of the New England colonies.

b. Settlements dependent upon the United States, or those of foreign powers on the American continent.

1817 PAULDING *Lett. from South* 60 The time, I hope, is not far distant, when not an inch of this great continent will be tributary to any other quarter of the globe; and when, if we choose to extend our ambition so far, we may have colonies in Europe, as Europe has so long had in America. **1817** *Niles' Reg.* XIII. 76/1 But she [Great Britain] has no danger to fear on that score—she may rest satisfied that the United States have no thought of possessing colonies. **1839** *Diplom. Corr. Texas* (1908) I. 423 The fatal effect of the tardy and illjudged course of Spain toward her revolted colonies who had so gallantly won their independence. **1845** POLK *Diary* 16 He would maintain all our rights, . . . and reaffirm Mr. Monroe's ground against permitting any European power to plant or establish any new colony on the North American continent. **1886** LOGAN *Great Conspiracy* 8 Meanwhile the vast territory included within the Valley of the Mississippi and known at that day as the 'Colony of Louisiana,' was, in 1803, acquired to the United States. **1903** *Dial* 16 Jan. 43 This nation has no 'colonies' in the proper meaning of that word, and never has had any.

2. The territory that colonists occupy. (See quot. 1672 for a special sense.) {1612–}

1636 *Md. Council Proc.* 40 Sir John Harvey had expressed his Intent to the Councell heere of departing the Colonye. **1641–2** *Va. House of Burgesses* 67 All the commodities raised in the colony shall be parted with, exchanged or vended at such rates and prices as they set down. **1665** *Conn. Col. Rec.* II. 27 Each Town in this Colony . . . shal haue a towne brand for horses. **1672** *S.C. Hist. Soc. Coll.* V. 391 It is advised . . . that warrants be forthwith issued out to the Surveyor Generall for the laying out of three Colonies or Squares of twelve thousand acres.

3. A group of people who have a unity as of race or occupation, living in one locality. {1711–}

'In Am. this use of the word is considerably extended' (Horwill *Dict. Mod. Amer. Usage* 74).

1852 *Harper's Mag.* V. 835/1 His [Ole Bull's] Norwegian colony in Northern Pennsylvania is flourishing. **1867** in *41st Congress 2 Sess.* H. R. Rep. No. 121, 486 General Howard wishes one of your own agents to inform himself of the conduct and condition of General Ely's colony, . . . and to see that the freed people are properly protected and cared for. **1883** HOWELLS *Woman's Reason* xvi, We are quite an aesthetic colony here, under Mrs. Hewitt's hospitable roof—with Miss Root's art-work and your literature and my journalism. **1893** J. AULD *Picturesque Burlington* 32 The Colony finally succumbed and scattered, and the attempt to found a new Utopia in the Champlain valley was ended. **1906** *Springfield W. Republican* 25 Oct. 1 He [Clemenceau] lived in New York for four years when a young man, and as a physician actually started a substantial practice in the French colony there.

4. A group of people, of the same town or district, who move together to another place; also, the settlement of such a group.

1838 C. NEWELL *Revol. Texas* 13 The establishment of a colony in Texas by Stephen F. Austin, in 1821–2 . . . was establishing the Anglo-American one remove farther to the South and West. **1860** EMERSON *Cond. of Life* 49 Import into any stationary district . . . a colony of hardy Yankees, with seething brains, heads full of steam-hammer, pulley, crank, and toothed wheel,—and everything begins to shine with valves. **1877** JOHNSON *Anderson Co., Kansas* 62 The company at once made arrangements for sending a colony from Louisville to the new town. **1883** *Century Mag.* Aug. 523/1 One of the colony schemes, so common now in California, has been formed for the opening up and settling of the San Jacinto valley. This Indian village will be in the colony's way.

+**5.** (See quotation.)

1900 FLYNT *Notes Itinerant Policeman* 192 [Tramps] are collected into colonies by unscrupulous electioneering specialists, and paid to vote as they are told.

+**6.** *Old Colony*, (see quots. 1809 and 1907).

1809 KENDALL *Travels* II. 36 To the south-east of Boston, distant about forty miles, is Plymouth, the oldest of the settlements in New England, and hence, in Boston, commonly known by the name of the *Old Colony.* **1823** J. THACHER *Military Jrnl.* 14 He has been, for many years, the leading law character in the Old Colony. **1882** *Nation* 20 July 50/2 We of the old colony feel much honored . . . that your journal should devote so much attention to the discussion of the true landing date of the Pilgrims at Plymouth. **1903** K. M. ABBOTT *Old Paths & Legends New Eng.* 357 All roads lead to Plymouth—you will remark that at the very beginning of your pilgrimage through the Old Colony. **1907** *Boston Transcript* 9 Nov., A list of the popular names of the States [includes] . . . Old Colony—That part of Massachusetts which from 1620 to 1692 was Plymouth Colony.

attrib. **1858** LONGFELLOW *Courtship M. Standish* I. 1 In the Old Colony days, in Plymouth the land of the Pilgrims, [etc.]. **1883** WILDER *Sister Ridnour* 136 At Boston I had to change cars, and waited a few dreary hours at the then 'Old' Colony Depot.

7. In attrib. use. **a.** In sense 1, with *agent* (cf. AGENT), *bill, coaster, law*, etc. (See also COLONY LINE, SEAL.)

1774 *Jrnls. Cont. Congress* I. 104 Resolved, That the address to the King, be enclosed to the several colony agents. **1775** *Ib.* II. 24 The inclosed Packet, containing . . . a Letter to our Colony Agent, Benjamin Franklin, Esqr. [etc.]. **1740** W. DOUGLASS *Discourse* 7 Some are . . . in Paper Money called Colony or Province Bills of public Credit. **1832** WILLIAMSON *Maine* I. 317 At one time d'Aulney pressed an English colony-coaster into his service, and compelled the master to go with him to St. John's. **1767** HUTCHINSON *Hist. Mass.* II. 52 The old colony law, which makes witchcraft a capital offence, was revived, with the other local laws, as they were called, and made a law of the province. **1661** *Providence Rec.* II. 138 It is ordered that the prisoner . . . shall be sent downe into New-port to the Colloney prison, There to be Kept until his.

Tyme of Triall. **1678** *Portsmouth Rec.* 198 To pay as their part and Share of A colony Rate of three hundred pounds. **1853** in Winthrop *Hist.* (1853) I. 1 *note*, The unfailing accuracy of Prince led him beyond Hubbard to original private manuscripts and the Colony Records, for the exact spelling. **1637** MORTON *New Canaan* 342 Like the Colony servant in Virginia, that, before hee should goe to the gallows, called to his wife to set on the loblolly pot. **1733** *Conn. Col. Rec.* VII. 461 This Assembly allows Capt. John Marsh and Ensign James Church the sum of twenty shillings out of the Colony treasury.

b. In sense: Belonging or going back to the colonial period.

1857 E. STONE *Life of Howland* 33 Repairs of bridges on the great colony road. *Ib.*, The distinction of colony roads and town roads should cease. **1883** *Century Mag.* Oct. 934/1 Nor does the Plymouth idyl show much sympathy . . . but chiefly a cavalier perception of what romance and grace there might have been in the good old Colony time.

c. In sense 4 with *agent, excursion, scheme.*

1878 BEADLE *Western Wilds* 388 [Duluth] was lively with immigrants, colony agents, real estate speculators, travelers and freighters. **1889** *Whitewater* (Wis.) *Reg.* 25 Oct., Ho! For California. All who desire can join the colony excursions going there and get homes and wealth in that mild and healthful climate. **1883** *Century Mag.* Aug. 524/1 The colony scheme has been completed; the [San Jacinto] valley has been divided up.

‖**Colonyite.** A member of a colony. — **1873** *Newton Kansan* 12 June 2/3 The Syracuse colonyites are stampeding for Barton county.

Colony line. The boundary line of a colony, usually that between two colonies. — **1690** *Conn. Col. Rec.* IV. 40 Neer the northeast corner of the Colony line. **1705** *Providence Rec.* XVII. 201 The which tree is in the Collony line, & also is a bound Marke betweene the s[ai]d two Plantations of s[ai]d Providence & Warwick. **1816** *Mass. H. S. Coll.* 2 Ser. VII. 118 Some of the water of the great pond in Weymouth, will flow southerly, which shews that the colony line is, in this part of it, on the height of land.

Colony seal. The official seal of a colony. — **1652** *Va. State P.* I. 1 All pattents shall hereafter be signed under the Governers hand, . . . & shal be accompted authentique vallid in law, untill a Collony Seal shal be provided. **1673** *Conn. Public Rec.* II. 201 This Court orders that the impression of the Coloney Seale shall be affixed in the begining of euery law booke. **1776** in Ramsey *Tennessee* 136 We have admitted common proof against ourselves, on accounts, &c., from the colonies, without pretending a right to require the Colony Seal.

* **Color.** Also **colour, †culler.**

***1.** An ensign or flag. **a.** Of a military regiment or other unit. Sometimes fig. (as in quot. 1689) for the group of men.

1634 *Mass. Bay Rec.* I. 133 Ensigne Damford shalbe sent for by war[ran]t with commaund to bring his col[o]rs with him to the nexte Court. **1662** *Md. Council Proc.* 455 Hee was to buy Drumm and Cullers and other necessarys for the vse of the Company. **1689** *Mass. H. S. Coll.* 4 Ser. V. 190 The country coming in that morning,—six companies or colors over Charles Ferry, and four over Boston Neck. **1783** Durrett *Louisville* (1893) 147 [Military stores include]: 1 Stand of old Colours. **1826** COOPER *Mohicans* xvi, The garrison to retain their arms, their colors, and their baggage. **1861** MCCLELLAN in *Own Story* 87, I deprived the 79th of their colors, and have them downstairs, not to be returned to them until they have earned them again by good behavior. **1892** M. A. JACKSON *Gen. Jackson* 40 As they . . . marched in perfect order, with martial music and colors flying.

attrib. **1861** *Army Regulations* 54 The company officers and the color-rank advance four paces. **1862** NORTON *Army Letters* 64 Our color guard leaped the ditch and planted the flag of the Eighty-third on the fortifications. **1863** in Logan *Great Conspiracy* 502 The color-sergeant of the 1st Louisiana, on being mortally wounded . . . , hugged the colors to his breast, when a struggle ensued between the two color-corporals on each side of him, as to who should have the honor of bearing the sacred standard. **1901** CHURCHILL *Crisis* 428 Three times the besiegers charged, sank their color staffs into the redoubts, [etc.].

b. Of a ship.

1654 JOHNSON *Wonder-w. Prov.* 71 All of a sudden they spy two tall Ships, whose colours shewed them to be some forrein Nation. **1707** *Boston News-Letter* 21 July 2/2 Capt. Burton . . . was Chased by a great Flyboat without any Colours. **1836** *Diplom. Corr. Texas* (1908) I. 115 She is, to be sure, to sail under American Colors.

2. *People of color*, people of the African race; Negroes. {1796– (W. Indies)}

Sometimes applied to mulattoes as distinct from full-blooded Negroes.

1792 *Md. Hist. Mag.* XII. 188 Whereas it has hitherto been a practice amongst the poorer class of people, and people of color, to Bury their deceased relations . . . in several of the different Streets and Allies of this town. **1824** R. H. BISHOP *Hist. Church Ky.* 232 He also regularly attended a meeting-house on the lands of General Levi Todd, which had been appropriated by the General for the use of the Methodist and Baptist people of colour. **1832** T. HAMILTON *Men & Manners* I. 12 But for the number of blacks and people of colour, one encounters in the streets, there is certainly little to remind a traveller that the breadth of an ocean divides him from Great Britain. **1837** *S. Lit. Messenger* III. 644 We are told . . . that in South Carolina, there is a tax on free people of color.

b. *Man, person,* etc. *of color,* a Negro. {1803– (W. Indies)}

(1) **1792** *Md. Hist. Mag.* XII. 315, I conceive that justice and equity will excite you to choose one Man of Color to represent so many hundreds of poor Blacks as inhabit this town. **1820** *Hillsborough* (N.C.) *Recorder* 18 Oct., Mason Scott, who had . . . been convicted of murder, on the body of a man of colour, was sentenced on Saturday last. **1885** *Century Mag.* Jan. 415 We allow the man of color to go and come at will, only let him sit apart in a place marked off for him.

(2) **1817** *Ann. 14th Congress* 2 Sess. 90 The bill respecting the transportation of persons of color for sale . . . was read. **1840** *Niles' Nat. Reg.* 22 Aug. 387/1 President Lamar has issued a proclamation commanding all free persons of color, now in the republic of Texas to remove therefrom before the 1st day of January, 1842. **1844** *McDonogh Papers* 77 You inform me that there is an admirable school and college in the north part of your state where persons of color can be received. **1888** BRYCE *Amer. Commonwealth* II. 54 Suffrage . . . often excludes free persons of colour.

(3) **1788** *Mass. Centinel* 30 July 155/3 'It is a very dark night,' says Cato to one of his brethren of colour, as they both were staggering home from a frolick on a thanksgiving eve. **1833** in *Century Mag.* XXX. 782 Her School will be opened for the reception of young Ladies and little Misses of color. **1880** CABLE *Grandissimes* xlviii. 374 By morning the gentlemen of color will know their places better than they do to-day. **1794** *N.C. Gen. Assem. Public Acts* II. 53 And every person who shall knowingly sell, buy or hire such slave or indented servant of colour, shall in like manner forfeit and pay the sum of one hundred pounds for each and every slave or servant of colour so sold, bought or hired. **1840** *Picayune* 15 Oct. 2/6 Servants of color for sale and hire at the above establishment.

3. The hue of the skin; race, esp. with reference to Negroes. {1798–}

1870 *15th Amendment to Const.* §1 The right of citizens of the United States to vote shall not be denied or abridged by the United States, or by any state, on account of race, color, or previous condition of servitude. **1870** O. LOGAN *Before Footlights* 42 Observing the child carefully, she detected her color. **1875** [see COLORED *a.* b]. **1886** *Boston Jrnl.* 20 Oct. 6/6 A colored Congregational preacher . . . was politely but firmly informed that he could not be served on account of his color.

+**4.** *Western mining.* A trace of metallic gold. (With or without the def. article.)

1851 L. A. CLAPPE *Lett. from Calif.* 92 There is a deep pit in front of our cabin, and another at the side of it, though they are not worked, as, when 'prospected,' they did not 'yield the color.' **1873** G. A. LAWRENCE *Silverland* 181 In this [residuum] you must look for 'colour'—the miner's term for presence of gold. **1876** BOURKE *Journal* 3 July, They had proceeded six or eight miles down stream, washed sand in frying pan and found 'color.' **1889** K. MUNROE *Golden Days* 175 They . . . moved along the shore, washing a little earth here and there, sometimes finding the 'color' a little more plentiful than at others. **1910** J. HART *Vigilante Girl* 51 Sometimes riffles would be clogged with coarse gold; . . . often there was nothing in them but 'the color'—ghostly flakes of gold set in black sand.

fig. and *transf.* **1868** HARTE *Luck of Roaring Camp*, 'Is that him?' 'mighty small specimen;' 'hasn't mor'n got the color.' **1873** MILLER *Amongst Modocs* 43 'Are you really dead-broke?' 'Skinned clean down to the bedrock. Haven't got the colour.'

b. In *pl.*, or with *a*, where 'a color' is conceived of as a particle of gold.

1859 G. A. JACKSON *Diary* 5 Jan., Panned out two cups, nothing but fine colors. **1874** RAYMOND *9th Rep. Mines* 18 Each sample or pan so taken showed one or more 'colors' to the pan. In no case was there a failure to obtain a color. **1880** INGHAM *Digging Gold* 309 Miners began to prospect for gold. Panning out some of the earth along the streams they found colors. **1886** *Leslie's Mo.* XXI. 424/2 A prospector handy with the pan will seldom fail to bring to light a fine streak of 'colors' with every pan of dirt from the salted claim. **1904** E. ROBINS *Magn. North* 148 Mining up here's an awful gamble. Colours pretty well everywhere, and a few flakes of flour gold, just enough to send the average cheechalko crazy. **1905** BEACH *Pardners* i. 22 We cross-cut in three places, and never raised a colour, but we kept gophering around till March, in hopes.

***5.** A pigment or paint substance.

1711 *Boston News-Letter* 12 March 2/2 Good new Lancers, and most sorts of Painters Colours. *a***1817** DWIGHT *Travels* I. 154 An act was passed, imposing a duty, to be collected in the Colonies, on tea, paper, glass and painters' colours. **1899** *U.S. Gen. Appraisers* 22 June, The merchandise would appear to be dutiable as a color, crude or otherwise.

attrib. **1841** EMERSON *Essays* 1 Ser. 'Art,' They . . . console themselves with colour-bags and blocks of marble. **1891** CHASE & CLOW *Industry* II. 29 The color house at the print-works is an important place.

+**6.** The flag of the U.S. Occas. *colors.*

1861 *Army Regulations* 475 Each regiment of Artillery shall have two silken colors. The first, or the national color, of stars and stripes. . . . Each color [is] to be six feet six inches fly. **1891** H. PATTERSON *Illustr. Naut. Dict.* 352 *Colors*, the national ensign. In port colors are made at 8 a.m. and hauled down at sunset. *c***1916** *Army Regulations 1913* 100 While the flag is being lowered . . . the field music will sound 'To the Color.' **1917** J. A. MOSS *Officers' Manual* 65 Officers and enlisted men passing the uncased color will render honors.

7. *Off color*, not quite up to normal or usual (in health, temper, quality, etc.). {1885–}

1876 HARTE *G. Conroy* xxvi, For some weeks Mr. Hamlin had not been well, or, as he more happily expressed it, had been 'off color.' **1891** *Har-*

per's Mag. Sept. 575/2 How was yesterday for one of the days off-color? **1901** HARTE *Ib.* CIV. 66/1 'The Kernel seems a little off color to-day,' said the barkeeper.

+**b.** Of questionable standing or taste; not in good repute.

1875 HOLLAND *Sevenoaks* 114 Everybody invited her, and yet everybody, without any definite reason, considered her a little 'off color.' **1886** *Harper's Mag.* June 116/1 It's a little off color to walk much on the cliffs; you lose caste if you bathe in the surf. **1891** *Century Mag.* April 937 That she was . . . a sharer in this off-color part of his existence made a sort of community of feeling between him and her. **1900** R. H. SAVAGE *Midnight Passenger* 21 All the 'off color' men and women of New York's 'fly' circles knew and feared the steady eyes gleaming through the cerulean lenses.

+**Coloradan,** *n.* Also **Coloradoan.** A native or resident of Colorado. — **1879** TAYLOR *Summer-Savory* 44 Soon night came up, for in the mountain it never comes down. Had Homer . . . been a Coloradan, he would never have said the god 'came down like night.' **1880** INGHAM *Digging Gold* 331 To Eastern people it is a grand sight; to Coloradoans it is but tame compared to . . . grander cañons in the State.

+**Coloradan,** *a.* Pertaining to, or characteristic of, Colorado. — **1879** TAYLOR *Summer-Savory* 33 There is yet another cough, which may be called the cough colloquial and Coloradan.

+**Colorado.** A river and state in western United States.

1. a. Used attrib. in plant names: (see quotations).

1894 *Amer. Folk-Lore* VII. 103 *Agropyrum glaucum,* . . . slough-grass, pond-grass, Colorado blue-grass. **1897** SUDWORTH *Arborescent Flora* 40 *Picea pungens.* . . . Common names [include] . . . Colorado Blue Spruce (Colo.). **1894** COULTER *Bot. W. Texas* III. 549 *Agropyron repens.*—(Colorado Blue-stem.) . . . High plains, western Texas and northward. **1898** *Kansas City Star* 18 Dec. 317 (*advt.*), Choice Colorado Cabbage. . . . 200 sacks extra fine Colorado Potatoes. **1889** VASEY *Agric. Grasses* 25 *Panicum Texanum* (Texas Millet). . . . It is frequently called Colorado grass, from its abundance along the Colorado River in that State. **1897** SUDWORTH *Arborescent Flora* 55 *Abies concolor.* . . . Common names [include] . . . Colorado White Fir (Col. lit.).

b. In the names of certain animals and fish: (see quotations).

1858 BAIRD *Birds Pacific R.R.* 563 *Corvus Cacolotl,* Wagler, Colorado Raven. *Ib.* 564 The general appearance is that of the Colorado raven. *Ib.* 682 *Tantalus loculator,* Linn. Wood ibis . . . is said to be abundant on the Colorado river, especially about Fort Yuma, and to be there called Colorado turkey.

2. *Colorado beetle, bug,* or *potato beetle,* the potato bug (*Doryphora decemlineata*), a pest that destroys potato vines.

(1) **1868** *Mich. Agric. Rep.* VII. 181 A plant, . . . of the night-shade family, . . . was well covered with the Colorado beetle and its slugs. **1869** *Amer. Naturalist* III. 92 It would be better for the entire North-west, so far as the Colorado Beetle has extended, to abstain from planting potatoes for one year. **1879** WEBSTER *Suppl.* 1550 *Colorado Beetle,* . . . a yellow beetle . . . about three eighths of an inch in length, with ten longitudinal black stripes upon its back. **1882** *Maine Bd. Agric. Rep.* XXVI. 11 Before the days of the potato rot and the Colorado beetle, growing potatoes, it seems to me, must have represented the extreme of unskilled farm labor. **1888** BILLINGS *Hardtack* 82 What the Colorado beetle is to the potato crop they ['graybacks'] were to the soldiers of both armies.

(2) **1867** *Mich. Agric. Rep.* VI. 72 The Colorado bug is a native of Colorado, and . . . was confined there till the potato was brought thither, which, suiting its taste better than its original food, it commenced its fearful ravages, moving eastward sixty miles a year, destroying the entire potato crop in its course. **1868** *Rep. Comm. Agric.* 64 Specimens of . . . the 'Colorado bug' have reached the Department, and prove to be merely varieties of the *Cantharis,* or potato bug of the eastern States.

(3) **1868** *Mich. Agric. Rep.* VII. 165 In the report of 1867, quite a lengthy account was given of the Colorado potato beetle—(*Doryphora* 10=*lineata*) of Say. **1871** *Ill. Agric. Soc. Trans.* VIII. 174 The same remedy that answers for destroying the Colorado Potato-beetle (Paris Green) would probably destroy the Currant worm. **1874** *Mich. Agric. Rep.* XIII. 106 Colorado potato beetle . . . is a native of Colorado, . . . and from thence spread rapidly eastward till it now has actually gained our Atlantic coast, where it only awaits opportunity to take passage for Europe. **1884** *Rep. Comm. Agric.* 416 The Colorado Potato-beetle . . . appeared in greater numbers than it has done since 1881.

+**Color-bearer.** A soldier who carries the flag or colors.

1861 *Army Regulations* 55 The color-bearer will remain in the ranks while passing and saluting. **1862** in *Harvard Mem. Biog.* I. 111 The color-bearer fell, but before the flag reached the ground some one else seized and put it up again. **1866** 'F. KIRKLAND' *Bk. Anecdotes* 228 He went on to say how the dead enemy was the color-bearer of a rebel regiment. **1888** SHERIDAN *Memoirs* I. 311 There seemed to be a rivalry as to which color should be farthest to the front; . . . the color-bearers vying with one another as to who should be foremost, etc.

* **Colored,** *a.* Also **coloured.**

1. Of a dark-skinned African race. {1760–}

'In census-tables, etc., the term is often used to include Indians, Chinese, etc.' (*Cent.*).

a. *Colored people.*

1780 *M.E. Church Ann. Conf. Minutes* (1840) I. 12/2 Ought not the assistant to meet the colored people himself? **1819–27** J. BERNARD *Retrosp.* 299 The greatest amusement I had in Boston was derived from the colored people, as they call the free blacks. **1830** WATSON *Philadelphia* 479 Once they submitted to the appellation of servants, blacks, or negroes, but now they require to be called coloured people. **1858** *N.Y. Tribune* 25 Sept. 7/4 Colored People in the City Cars. . . . The conductor . . . told the man that he must get off, and wait for one of the cars set apart by the Company for colored people. **1865** *Nation* I. 137 The colored people appear good-natured. **1886** STOCKTON *Mrs. Lecks* 36 We both put on black stockin's. I've read that sharks never bite colored people. **1898** B. H. YOUNG *Jessamine Co., Ky.* 185 The population of the village is . . . about 200, mostly colored people.

b. *Colored man.*

1818 FEARON *Sketches* 59 Now, my boss, I guess, ordered me to turn out every coloured man from the store right away, and if I did not he would send me off slick; for the slimmest gentleman in New York would not come to his store if coloured men were let in. **1845** F. DOUGLASS *Narrative* 18 He met a colored man and addressed him in the usual manner of speaking to colored people on the public highway of the south. **1875** *Congress. Rec.* 8 Jan. 342/1, I will show him colored men who . . . vote the democratic ticket, notwithstanding the terror in which they stand of their own color. **1880** *Harper's Mag.* Dec. 157 In a Mississippi court a colored man sued a neighbor for damages for killing his dog. **1903** *N.Y. Ev. Post* 22 Dec. 6 It is proposed [in Maryland] to remodel the Constitution so as to exclude colored men from voting. **1907** ANDREWS *Recoll.* 160 The afternoon, before, on going to town, I had met a colored man with chickens to sell.

c. With other designations referring to members of the African races.

1836 C. GILMAN *Recoll.* (1838) 163 The younger passengers, scattered in various parties. . . . Followed by their coloured attendants, they sang and danced. **1854** M. J. HOLMES *Tempest & Sunshine* xxvi. 371 Even Judy, who had predicted all manner of evil for her colored brethren, . . . now changed her mind. **1854** *Harper's Mag.* IX. 851/1 A dusty-looking 'colored child,' about 40 years of age, was passing under the scaffolding of the building. **1836** W. L. GARRISON in Garrison *W. L. Garrison* II. 104 In Massachusetts, a colored citizen stands on the same equality with the Governor of the State. **1852** STOWE *Uncle Tom* ix, His wife, and their only colored domestic, old Aunt Dinah, were busily engaged in restorative measures. **1842** *Spirit of Times* (Phila.) 18 April (Th.), The most prominent object was a 'long nine' with a fierce looking buck of a colored fellow hanging to the end of it. **1825** NEAL *Bro. Jonathan* III. 236 [They] were enjoying the society of 'brother Joseph,' the 'coloured frind,' as if he were truly inspired. **1880** *Harper's Mag.* Dec. 157 Colonel M— . . . called Sam Parker, a colored gent, to prove that the dog was a worthless cur. **1846** COOPER *Redskins* viii, Jaaf belonged to a school by which the term of 'colored gentlemen' was never used. **1833** *Knickerb.* I. 205 The shining face of the colored girl before mentioned, was dimly seen, as she opened the door. **1865** *Nation* I. 174 On the railroad the colored laborers when employed in cutting cord-wood are expected to cut what a white man usually cuts. **1823** QUITMAN in *Life & Corr.* I. 84 The 'colored ladies' are invariably Miss Joneses, Miss Smiths, or some such title. **1846** LOWELL *Biglow P.* I. i. 10 Hain't they sold your coloured seamen? **1898** B. H. YOUNG *Jessamine Co., Ky.* 137 The following is a list of the colored soldiers who served in the United States Army. **1885** GARRISON *W. L. Garrison* I. 456 The Whig party the colored voters 'should dread more than any other.' **1870** O. LOGAN *Before Footlights* 42 She . . . inquired who her mother was. The reply was that her mother was a colored woman.

d. Postpositive.

1845 F. DOUGLASS *Narrative* 2 She was the daughter of Isaac and Betsey Bailey, both colored, and quite dark. **1862** F. MOORE *Rebellion Rec.* V. II. 208 We then proceeded up the river, guided by William, (colored and free,) who had joined the boat voluntarily the previous night. **1882** *Nation* 2 Nov. 370/1 Arthur Payne, colored, one of the four men for whose arrest warrants were issued, . . . was arrested in Washington on Wednesday. **1911** M. W. OVINGTON *Half a Man* 181 In the United States . . . there are but two groups, white and colored, or as the latter is now more frequently designated, Negro, the term thus losing its original meaning, and becoming a designation for a race.

+**2.** *Colored school,* a school for Negro students.

1829 *Yankee* April 127/2 The primary schools—colored schools— . . . are now so good in themselves, [etc.]. **1833** in *Century Mag.* XXX. 786 The Deputy Sheriff of Windham County, in behalf of those zealous patrons of colored schools, . . . presented me with five indictments for a panegyric upon their virtuous and magnanimous actions. **1865** *Nation* I. 194 The colored schools in Richmond have closed for the season. **1878** C. COALE in *Ann. S.W. Va.* (1929) 1558 We have three banks, . . . a photograph gallery, two barber shops, and the biggest sort of a colored school. **1898** PAGE *Red Rock* 398 Colored schools were not a novelty in the County.

+**3.** With things which pertain to, or communities, etc., which are composed of, members of the Negro race.

1877 *Harper's Mag.* April 706/2 The darky owner of a horse of any kind ranks among the colored aristocracy. **1898** B. H. YOUNG *Jessamine Co., Ky.* 184 A colored church, with forty members, completes the list of houses of worship. **1852** STOWE *Uncle Tom* xviii, The style under which he moved, among the coloured circles of New Orleans, was that of Mr.

St. Clare. **1872** in Fleming *Hist. Reconstruction* II. 48 Northern men who ... excite the animosity of the colored class against their old masters. **1872** *Newton Kansan* 3 Oct. 2/2 A colored colony lost very heavily, and many others. **1880** *Harper's Mag.* Dec. 158 When Brother Bledso was pastor of a colored congregation in Texas, [etc.]. **1845** *Niles' Reg.* 6 Sept. 16/2 A colored convention was held at Syracuse, N.Y. **1854** BENTON *30 Years' View* I. 9/2 The clause in her constitution relative to the free colored emigration into the State. **1864** B. H. Young *Jessamine Co., Ky.* (1898) 186 J. C. Randolph Deputy Marshal and Superintendent of Colored Enlistment at Camp Nelson. **1887** *Courier-Journal* 8 May 11/2 The National Colored League season was formally opened yesterday at the Louisville Base Ball Park. **1881** *Harper's Mag.* Feb. 479/1 The poems of 'Uncle Remus' are among the best, if not the best, that the South has contributed to our 'cullud' literature since the war. **1837** *S. Lit. Messenger* III. 644 She dwells upon the hatred entertained by the white towards the colored population. **1862** LINCOLN in Logan *Great Conspiracy* 425 Without the institution of Slavery, and the Colored race as a basis, the War could not have an existence. **1864** *Nat. Almanac* (Phila.) 476/2 The 1st South Carolina colored regiment. **1899** CHESNUTT *Wife of His Youth* 109 He was well known and well received in good colored society. **1887** *Courier-Journal* 19 Feb. 8/1 The 'Colored Society Ball' introduced a song and dance that is much more refined than most of those exhibitions are. **1878** *N. Amer. Rev.* CXXVI. 387 State governments are opposed to colored suffrage. **1865** *Atlantic Mo.* XV. 637 In the few passages relating to the colored troops, [etc.].

+4. With things which are designated for the Negro race.

1885 *Century Mag.* XXX. 685/1 The 'ladies' car' of the morning trip became the 'colored car' of the return, afternoon, trip. **1851** *Polly Peablossom* 104 The yellow tickets are for parquette and boxes, the blue ones for third tier, and the white for the coloured gallery. **1861** *Independent* 19 Dec., The new colored quarters, [for colored persons,] near the fort. **1898** DUNBAR *Folks from Dixie* 44 The minister knew instantly that he now beheld the colored saloon which was the frequenting-place of his hostess's son 'Lias.

+5. Of a dark-skinned Indian.

1798 ALLEN *Hist. Vermont* 65 Colonel Allen ... seized the young coloured officer, a small man, and kept him as a target between himself and the Indians.

Color guard. A guard of honor which carries or accompanies the colors of a military unit or organization. {1823–} — **1862** in F. Moore *Rebellion Rec.* V. II. 417 All the color-guards were killed.

Color line.

+1. *Military.* A line of stacked rifles at which the colors rest.

1861 *Army Regulations* 75 The colors are then planted at the centre of the color line, and the arms are stacked on the line. **1862** NORTON *Army Letters* 80 The buglers of each regiment as quickly as possible assemble on the color line, give their regimental call and repeat the reveille. **1888** BILLINGS *Hardtack* 73 Each company of a regiment should pitch its tents in two files ... at right angles with the color-line of the regiment.

+2. The line of social and political distinctions between the Negro race and the white race.

For other examples see Thornton *Suppl.*

1876 in *Congress. Rec.* App. Jan. 21/2 We are in favor of the color line as a principle, a necessity, and a policy. **1882** *Nation* 13 July 24/3 North Carolina Democrats ... in their platform made the color-line the keynote of the campaign. **1884** *Century Mag.* July 462/1 Peace and happiness never could come to the South so long as the political lines were coexistent with the color lines, with the blacks in the ascendancy. **1887** *Courier-Journal* 20 Feb. 5/3 The managers of the Freedmen's Aid Society of the Methodist Episcopal Church are to meet next Tuesday for a conference, very likely a fight, over the color line. **1897** HOWELLS *Open-eyed Conspiracy* xi, I was glad to find that the good taste and the correct fashion were without a color-line; there were some mulatto ladies present as stylish as their white sisters, or step-sisters.

+b. Esp. in *to cross* or *draw the color line.*

1894 CABLE *J. March* xxii, 'I'd marry you ef you wuz pyowhite!' ... 'You wouldn' be afeared evm to cross de color line?' **1896** *Chicago Record* 1 Feb. 1/4 He declines to speak on the subject if the meeting of the club is held in a hotel in which the color line is drawn. **1917** MATHEWSON *Sec. Base Sloan* 214 The Bemis House drew no colour line.

‖**Color person.** A colored person. — **1835** *Knickerb.* V. 300 A very attentive 'color person' answered my call.

+Colorphobia. Dislike of Negroes. — **1847** W. L. GARRISON in Garrison *W. L. Garrison* III. 200 A genuine specimen of American democratic, Christian colorphobia. **1862** *Congress. Globe* 3 July 3100/1 There was a democratic colorphobia—as I believe it is described in some of our abolition prints. **1886** *Boston Jrnl.* 23 Oct. 6 Colorphobia in Chicago. A colored Congregational preacher ... began suit to-day for $5000 against Robert J. Mossop, a restaurant keeper on West Madison street, and his head waiter James Hughes. The charge against the defendants is that they refused to allow Smith to take a meal in the restaurant.

Colory. {1853–} +Designating a grade of tobacco. Also comb. — **1887** *Courier-Journal* 7 Feb. 7/1 The differences, which are not more than one or two bids, include colory smokers. **1900** *Dept. Agric. Yearbook* 435 These tobaccos are used exclusively for pipe-smoking and cigarettes, the following grades being made by the packers: Fine yellow, medium bright, good ordinary 'colory,' fine red.

Colportage. The business of the colporteur. — **1846** WORCESTER 138 *Colportage,* ... the trade or business of a colporter, hawker, or pedler. **1851** CIST *Cincinnati* 157 This City was selected, ten years ago, as a central point for the supervision of colportage in the west and south-west, and for the reshipment of books to colporteurs.

Colporteur. Also **colporter.** A hawker or pedler; spec., a person who distributes Bibles, tracts, or other religious works free or at a low price. {1796–}

1838 DRAKE *Tales & Sketches* 49 He ..., taking another scrutinizing survey of Mr. Slow and his wares, ... muttered, 'yankee colporteur.' **1844** R. BAIRD *Religion* IV. xx. 376 Sensible, pious, and zealous *colporteurs,* or hawkers, ... are sent into the 'Far West' to carry books and tracts to the frontier people. **1846** WORCESTER 138 *Colporter,* ... a hawker; a pedler; a pedler of books. **1861** *Harper's Mag.* Jan. 280/2 The colporter of Louisa County called on an old lady in his regular rounds, and introduced himself as a colporter. **1867** L. BAKER *U.S. Secret Service* 53 My next questioner was a woman, assuming the calling of a colporteur, or tract distributor. **1881** PIERSON *In the Brush* 18, I traveled several miles to see an old man who had been recommended for a colporteur. **1904** *Boston Transcript* 13 Feb. 24/6 Hence the employment by the American Bible and tract societies of that cosmopolitan figure, the colporter.

***Colt.** A young horse.

'In America, *colt* is equally applied to the male or female, and this is unquestionably correct' (W. '28).

1651 *Conn. Rec.* I. 226 They were judged to pay for a colte. **1656** *Plymouth Laws* 100 None shall sell any horse or mare coult or foale to any Indian. **1778** *Maryland Jrnl.* 24 March, Strayed, a black colt, three years old. **1790** BENTLEY *Diary* I. 290 A colt was put into a pasture upon Nahant Head to wean from the Mare. **1858** HOLMES *Autocrat* xi. 297 Colts grew horses, beards turned gray, ... But there stood the stout old one-hoss shay. **1868** H. WOODRUFF *Trotting Horse* 63 All the fast colts that they have shown there have not, however, been equally fortunate with Cora. **1878** *Rep. Indian Affairs* 21 At an inspection of the horses in possession of the Indians made in February last, 248 head, including colts, were found to be unbranded. **1898** WESTCOTT *D. Harum* 276 This day we'd got a piece out into the country an' I had the brown colts.

Colter. (See COULTER.)

+Colt's. With *firearms, pistol, revolver,* etc. Firearms of a type invented by Samuel Colt (1814–1862).

1846 MACKENZIE *Van Buren* 172 The rest of the letter is about Colt's fire-arms. **1854** BARTLETT *Narrative* I. 19 All were provided with rifles or carbines, and many of the cavalry with Colt's revolvers, or six shooters. **1873** MILLER *Amongst Modocs* 40 The man was richly dressed, ... a rich, red sash around his waist, where swung a pair of Colt's new patent. *a*1918 G. STUART *On Frontier* I. 102 We were armed with muzzle loading rifles, (Colt's navy cap and ball revolvers had not been invented then).

b. Also ellipt. *Colt('s).*

1852 *Knickerb.* XXXIX. 561 When they thought of the little Colt which he carried in his pocket, their courage caved in. **1855** J. HOLBROOK *Among Mail Bags* 198 The 'pale face' ... fired his 'Colt,' and saw the blood spirt from the naked breast of the Indian. **1866** 'F. KIRKLAND' *Bk. Anecdotes* 487 She rode boldly up to the men, presented a persuader in the shape of a 'Colt,' and made known her intention of riding her mule no longer. **1869** 'MARK TWAIN' *Innocents* 125 Presently I found a revolving pistol several hundred years old which looked strangely like a modern Colt. **1901** NORRIS *Octopus* 256 The puncher flourished his teaser, an army Colt's. **1913** MUMFORD *Coming of Cassidy* 119 A still-smoking Colt covered them.

***Coltsfoot,** *n.* Also **colt('s) foot.**

***1.** A weed (*Tussilago farfara*), naturalized in America.

1784 CUTLER in *Mem. Academy* I. 481 *Tussilago.* ... Colt's Foot. ... They [=the leaves] have been much used in coughs and consumptive complaints. **1795** WINTERBOTHAM *Hist. View* III. 399 Among the native and uncultivated plants of New-England, the following have been employed for medical purposes: ... Colts foot, *Tussilago farfara.* **1840** DEWEY *Mass. Flowering Plants* 128 *Tussilago farfara.* Garden Colt's Foot. ... Expectorant; its leaves were smoked in ancient times as a cure for diseases of the lungs.

2. As a local name for other plants: (see quotations).

1762 CLAYTON *Flora Virginica* 72 *Asarum aquaticum.* ... Nostratibus errore Coltsfoot. **1806** LEWIS in *L. & Clark Exped.* (1905) V. 108, I observe here [on the Clearwater River] ... coltsfoot. **1843** TORREY *Flora N.Y.* II. 131 *Asarum Canadense.* ... Wild Ginger. Coltsfoot. ... Shady woods, in rich soil. ... The root is a popular medicine. It is aromatic and has somewhat the taste of ginger. **1867** *Amer. Naturalist* I. 406 In Sweet Coltsfoot (*Nardosmia*), a rare plant of this order growing north of this latitude, some of the little flowers are sterile. **1891** *Amer. Folk-Lore* IV. 148 *Asarum Canadense* was Snakeroot: father said, 'Colt's-foot Snakeroot' ... (New Hampshire). **1892** *Ib.* V. 91 *Caltha palustris,* May-blobs. Salem, Mass. ... Coltsfoot, Stratham, N.H. **1894** *Ib.* VII. 94 *Galax aphylla,* ... coltsfoot, Banner Elk, N.C.

‖**Coltsfoot,** *v. intr.* To engage in gathering coltsfoot. — **1895** A. BROWN *Meadow-Grass* 72, I used to go in to see if she'd go coltsfootin' with me, or plummin'; but she never'd make me no answer.

Colt's-tail. {1735–} **+1.** (See quotation.) **2.** The butterweed or horseweed. — **(1) 1829** *Mass. Spy* 13 May (Th.), It has been the uniform custom, at our courts, to break in the new members of every

Grand Jury, by requiring them to pay what is called a colt's tail—or in other words a treat. (2) **1833** EATON *Botany* (ed. 6) 135 *Erigeron canadense*, colts tail, flea-bane, pride-weed.

Colt yard. A yard or enclosure for colts. — **1868** BEECHER *Norwood* 535 There was water for each cattle-yard, for the sheep-yard, for the colt-yard.

+**Columbia.** [*Columbus*, the Latinized name of the discoverer of America.]

1. A poetical or oratorical name of the United States.

1781 *Independent Ledger* 24 Dec., Come all Continentals, who Washington love, The pride of Columbia, the fav'rite of Jove. **1789** *Salem Mercury* 3 March, Yeoman and Tradesmen, pillars of each state, On whose decision hangs Columbia's fate. **1798** W. DUNLAP *André* II. ii, Three thousand miles the Atlantic wave rolls on, Which bathed Columbia's shores. **1802** J. SANSOM *Lett. from Europe* II. 464 A true Son of Columbia will feel a patriotic affection for every branch of the Union, from New Hampshire to Georgia. **1823** I. HOLMES *Account* 10 In many parts of the United States, the appellation 'Columbia,' is not unknown. **1852** L. A. CLAPPE *Lett. from Calif.* 257 They think that it is the grand characteristic of Columbia's children to be prejudiced. **1861** NEWELL *Orpheus C. Kerr* I. 269 Though Columbia did not rule the wave, her champions would see to it that she never waived the rule. **1875** *Chambers's Journal* 13 March 172/1 The entire continent itself is Old Stars and Stripes, Uncle Sam, the New World, or Columbia. **1910** 'O. HENRY' *Strictly Business* 28, I don't know where this country of yours is, but I'm for it. I guess it must be a branch of the United States, though, for the poetry guys and the schoolmarms call us Columbia, too, sometimes.

2. With names of animals: *Columbia jay, partridge.* Also *Columbia root*, by mistake for COLUMBO ROOT.

1831 AUDUBON *Ornith. Biog.* I. 483 The Columbia Jay. *Corvus Bullockii.* **1819** E. DANA *Geogr. Sk.* 53 The plumage of the Columbia Partridge is very beautiful. **1822** J. WOODS *English Prairie* 219 The following trees and herbs are used in medicine— . . . Columbia-root, and sumach, and sassafras trees.

+**Columbiad.** [f. mod. L. *Columbia:* see prec.] A kind of cannon formerly used by the U.S. army.

Named from *The Columbiad* (1807), epic poem by Joel Barlow.

'About 1812, Colonel Bomford, U.S.A., introduced a chambered gun called by him the Columbiad. These were made thicker at the breech and thinner at the muzzle than was then customary' (Knight 447).

1818 J. M. DUNCAN *Travels U.S.* I. 36 Fulton also intended that she should carry upon her upper deck four Columbiads, as they are called, enormous guns capable of discharging a ball of a hundred pounds weight. **1861** WINTHROP *Open Air* 230 We were absolutely in doubt whether a seemingly inoffensive knot of rustics . . . might not . . . unmask a battery of giant columbiads, and belch blazes at us, raking our line. **1862** KETTELL *Hist. Rebellion* I. 96 On Sullivan's Island were Fort Moultrie and a new battery of heavy columbiads and ten-inch mortars. **1867** 'MARK TWAIN' *Sk. N. & O.* (1875) lxiii. 303 A sheet soaked in icewater was wound around me until I resembled a swab for a Columbiad. **1880** *Harper's Mag.* Dec. 68/1 The Fort Pitt Cannon Foundry . . . furnished, during the Civil War, two thousand cannon, from the twenty-inch Columbiad to the six-pounder or field piece.

attrib. **1862** LOWELL *Biglow P.* 2 Ser. v. 145 The spunk jes' to mount Constitootion an' Court With Columbiad guns.

fig. **1865** 'HAMILTON' *Skirmishes* vii. 84 They looked upon them [preachers] all as a kind of ecclesiastical columbiad. **1872** *Newton Kansan* 3 Oct. 3/2 A Republican columbiad was fired at Newton last night.

+**Columbian,** *n.* [COLUMBIA I.] A native of America.

1789 S. LOW *Politician Outwitted* II. ii, As the East is to the West . . . or the Aborigines of America to the Columbians of this generation, so is that line to this line. *a***1793** FRENEAU *Poems* (1809) I. 256 Where Irish and English, Columbians and Dutch Had agreed to lie down, without quarrels or feuds. **1797** *Spirit Farmer's Mus.* (1801) 75 Bid each Columbian's mind, First love its country, then embrace mankind. **1798** W. DUNLAP *André* III. iii, And tho' Columbians Will lament his fall, they will lament in blood. **1815** W. THORNTON *Outlines Const. for Columbia* 1, I was born in America, between the tropics, and being a Carib by birth, I feel an unspeakable attachment to the whole race of the Columbians.

+**Columbian,** *a.*

1. Of Columbia; pertaining to or characteristic of America.

1784 FRENEAU *Poems* (1809) II. 197 Who would be sad, to leave a sultry clime, Where true Columbian virtue is a crime. **1786** *Broadside Verse* (1930) 195 Succeeding ages will your virtues tell, . . . Columbian Daughters' skill extends so wide. **1797** C. PRENTISS *Fugitive Ess.* 49 The Columbian muse is leading her sons to the pinnacle of poetical excellence. **1813** *Niles' Reg.* IV. 25/2 (*caption*), Tammany Society or Columbian Order. **1818** FESSENDEN *Ladies Monitor* 116 'Tis said indeed among Columbian fair, A lady-gambler is extremely rare.

2. With names of birds characteristically American. Also ellipt.

1839 AUDUBON *Ornith. Biog.* V. 271 Little Columbian Owl. *Strix Passerinoides.* **1849** — *Western Journal* (1906) 128 The Ultramarine takes its [*sc.* Stellar's Jay's] place, and I hope in a few days to see the Columbian; a few ravens are to be seen.

3. Pertaining to or commemorative of Christopher Columbus.

1890 HARRISON in *Pres. Mess. & Papers* IX. 140, I do hereby invite all the nations of the earth to take part in . . . the World's Columbian Exposition. **1893** *Harper's Mag.* July 316/1 The World's Columbian Exposition in Chicago was formally opened on the 1st of May; 300,000 people were present at the opening. **1894** *Ib.* Jan. 317/1 The World's Columbian Exposition at Chicago closed on October 31st. The total number of paid admissions was 21,477,212. **1898** *Forum* Feb. 677 Now, all the people of America, at the date of their discovery by Europeans in the Columbian epoch, were organized into tribes. **1904** *Amer. Almanac* 291/2 The Columbian Exposition, held in Chicago in 1893, to commemorate the 400th anniversary of the discovery of America, was another magnificent enterprise.

* **Columbine.** A common flowering plant of the genus *Aquilegia.*

[**1640** PARKINSON *Theater of Plants* 1367 One [columbine] out of Virginia with a single flower, which Master John Tradescant brought from thence [is] *Aquilegia Virginiana flore rubescente præcox*, The early red Columbine of Virginia.] **1709** LAWSON *Carolina* 78 Our pot herbs and others of use . . . are . . . summer and winter Savory, Columbines, Tansey, Wormwood, [etc.]. **1784** CUTLER in *Mem. Academy* I. 457 *Aquilegia.* . . . Columbine. Honey Horns. **1832** WILLIAMSON *Maine* I. 121 The Columbine . . . is an annual plant, and grows 12 inches high. **1872** *Harper's Mag.* XLVI. 28 Idaho, named from the 'purple flower' of the Utes—a rich, wild columbine here growing in profusion—is a quiet little village. **1904** STRATTON-PORTER *Freckles* 82 He planted harebells; violets, blue, white, and yellow; wild geranium, cardinal-flower, columbine, [etc.].

+**Columbine worm.** (See quotation.) — **1854** EMMONS *Agric. N.Y.* V. 261 Index, Columbine-worm, 243. [243 Another *Goetynia* attacks the roots of columbine, and has been named by Dr. Harris *leucostigma.*]

Columbo. {1789–} Also **columba.** =AMERICAN COLUMBO. Also attrib. with *root.*

1803 *Lewis & Clark Exped.* (1905) VII. 244, ½lb. Columbo Rad. [$]1. **1814** *Niles' Reg.* VI. 210/1 There are also many plants of great interest, such as the ginseng, columbo, &c. **1819** E. DANA *Geogr. Sk.* 85 Of the Herbaceous Indigenous productions, trees and shrubberies of natural growth, divers species may be collected from the forests, which are useful in medicine and the arts; such as . . . sassafras, spice wood, gensang, prickly ash, columbo. **1821** A. ROYALL *Lett. from Ala.* (1830) 138 This is the region of . . . the Columba root. The Columba root has several broad leaves near the ground in the shape like a hound's tongue, of a yellowish green, the leaf thick and furzy. **1852** *Mich. Agric. Soc. Trans.* III. 189 The Columbo root grew spontaneous, and other flowers in great abundance. **1855** *Ib.* VI. 149 The plants on the uplands are columbo, sundial, indigo root.

Columbus. *attrib.* +Designating a celebration or day in honor of Christopher Columbus. — **1892** *Lit. Digest* V. 668/2 This complete and fervid American sentiment . . . at this Columbus celebration . . . is even more striking. **1893** *New-Eng. Hist. & Gen. Reg.* XLVII. 164 The following paper is a portion of an article which was prepared by the author, apropos of the approach of Columbus day.

* **Column.** *Military.* A formation of troops consisting of a single line or of several lines marching abreast. {1704–}

1758 *Essex Inst. Coll.* XLV. 344 They march'd off in 5 Paths or Columns towards South Bay. **1792** *Ann. 2nd Congress* 1138 The detachment marched in three columns. **1846** *Amer. Review* IV. 173/2 Our Army was immediately formed in column of attack. . . . The column was then deployed into line, except the 8th infantry, which still stood in column.

b. A group of soldiers that march in column formation; a detachment of soldiers. {1746– (Home *Hist. Rebell.* 1745)}

1843 N. BOONE *Journal* 202 The Column started about ½ past 5, and after searching the sand hills . . . for indians, proceeded. **1861** *Army Regulations* 96 The advance guard is not always at the head of the column; in a march to a flank, it takes such positions as cover the movement. **1861** MCCLELLAN in *Own Story* 210 The main point to which I desire to call your attention is the necessity of entering Eastern Tennessee as soon as it can be done, . . . and I hope that you will, with the least possible delay, organize a column for that purpose. **1869** BROWNE *Adv. Apache Country* 111 In 1861 they sold to Mr. White [a government buyer] 300,000 pounds of wheat, . . . and a large amount of dried and fresh pumpkins, which was all intended for the supply of the California column. **1881–5** MCCLELLAN *Own Story* 215, I . . . constantly urged Buell to send a column to that region. **1898** *McClure's Mag.* X. 350/1, I [C. A. Dana] urged Mr. Stanton . . . to push as strong a column as possible eastward.

transf. Ib. 331 A little before reaching the dam by which he had crossed I met the column of prisoners whom he had just taken.

+**Comadre.** *S.W.* [Sp., the name by which a mother and godmother address each other; a gossip.] A godmother; a close woman friend of a family. — **1834** A. PIKE *Sketches* 105 We have been brought up together; our mothers are comadres, (sponsors) and you can never know me better than you do now. **1846–7** MAGOFFIN *Down Santa Fé Trail* 154 It pleased her so much she called me 'comadre' (godmother) all the time. **1863** *Rio Abajo Press* 28 April 1 But he did not find her, and his search for her among comadres, relatives, and friends had no satisfactory result.

+**Comal, Comalli.** *S.W.* [Mex. Sp. *comalli*, < Nahuatl *comalli.*] (See quotations.) — **1844** GREGG *Commerce of Prairies* I. 153 This is afterwards spread on a small sheet of iron or copper, called *comal* (*co-*

malli, by the Indians), and placed over a fire. **1844** KENDALL *Santa Fé Exped.* II. 150 Light round cakes, which are afterward toasted on a smooth plate, called the comalli (comal they call it in Mexico). **1892** *Dial. Notes* I. 189 *Comál*, a slightly hollow utensil of stone or earthenware on which *tortillas* are cooked or baked.

+**Comanche,** *n.* Also **Camanche, -chee, Cumanche.**

1. *pl.* An Indian tribe of Shoshonean stock, originally living in northern Texas.

1806 WILKINSON in Pike *Sources Miss.* 109 You will also receive a . . . large one [=belt] for the Tetaus or Camanches. **1838** 'TEXIAN' *Mexico v. Texas* 124 The Comanches . . . are the best horsemen in the world. **1888** *Congress. Rec.* 4810/2 A day-school among the Comanches . . . would not be any better than having a school of blue-jays.

2. A member of this tribe.

1836 CROCKETT *Exploits* 157, I beheld in the distance about fifty mounted Cumanches, . . . dashing toward the spot where I stood. **1843** N. BOONE *Journal* 202 This gave a hint of the presence of Comanches and a turn of opinion as to the true horse thieves. **1860** *Harper's Mag.* Feb. 426/1 A numerous band of Camanches, mounted on their fleet chargers, were descried. **1923** J. H. COOK *On Old Frontier* 44 The Indians who were hovering about us were Comanches.

3. Used, esp. in comparisons, as an equivalent of: **a.** An uncivilized person; also attrib. **b.** A superlative horseman (cf. sense 1 quot. 1838).

(a) 1831 HOLLEY *Texas* 90 To denote the greatest degree of degradation, they [the Mexicans] call a person a Comanche. **1874** B. F. TAYLOR *World on Wheels* 76 The two engines are neck and neck. They scream at each other like Camanches. **1883** 'MARK TWAIN' *Life on Miss.* xix. 231 [He] ordered me out of the pilot house with more than Comanche bluster. **1889** — *Conn. Yankee* iv. 56 Many of the terms . . . would have made a Comanche blush. **1897** *Outing* XXX. 275/1 You're yelling like a wild Comanche Indian, and they must be half-way up the second flight by this time. **1902** MACGOWAN *Last Word* 6 The boys give one look, an' then yelled like Comanches.

(b) 1836 EDWARD *Hist. Texas* 109 To pass the highest praise on an American's horsemanship, is to say, he rides like a Comanche!

4. Attrib. with *brave, country, horse* (fig.), etc.

1884 SWEET & KNOX *Through Texas* iii. 38 We were attired in a costume that seemed to be a cross between a second-class tramp's undress uniform and the habiliments of a Comanche brave. **1847** RUXTON *Adv. Rocky Mts.* (1848) 277 We were now in the outskirt of the Pawnee and Comanche country. **1832** in Kennedy *Texas* (1841) I. 189 We this day . . . met with a Comanche Indian, who informed us they were encamped on a small creek to the N. **a1846** *Quarter Race Ky.* etc. 66 The old man was a perfect Cumanche horse at any game whar tha was curds [cards]. **1923** J. H. COOK *On Old Frontier* 5, I had purchased a fine Comanche pony at Fort Harker for $15 and a good second-hand Texas saddle for $5. **c1835** CATLIN *Indians* II. 89 A noble animal of the Camanchee wild breed.

‖**Comanche,** *v. pass.* To be attacked by the Comanches. — **1887** E. B. Custer *Tenting on Plains* 446 'Injuns!' replied Brigham, who knew by many an experience how wagons were Apached, Comanchied, or otherwise aboriginated.

Comas. Variant of CAMAS.

* **Comb,** *n.*

***1.** A toothed instrument for disentangling or cleaning hair or hairlike material.

1649 *Conn. Public Rec.* I. 497 An Inventory of the Estate of Mr. William Whiting . . . thimbles, boxes, kniues, sissers, combs, Jewes harps. **1718** HEMPSTEAD *Diary* 77, I Lent my combs pad and pipe in good order to Culver. **1812** *Emporium Arts & Sci.* (Phila.) May 73 The combs, for instance, which Connecticut prepares annually for market, are estimated at $70,000. **1852** *Harper's Mag.* V. 533/2 A present . . . proved to be a fine-tooth comb! **1903** C. L. BURNHAM *Jewel* 182 Her parting looked as though a saw had been substituted for a comb.

b. Often ornamental, used to hold a woman's hair in place.

1838 HAWTHORNE *Note-Books* I. 182 A pedler, with girls' silk neckerchiefs, . . . red bandannas, and a variety of horn combs, trying to trade with the servant-girls of the house. **1860** ABBOTT *South & North* 322 We might continue these questions in regard to . . . every article of male or female dress from the hat or the comb upon the crown of the head. **1865** *Atlantic Mo.* XV. 336 For I remember a high comb in her hair. **1891** 'THANET' *Otto the Knight*, etc. 318 The widow . . . always wore her hair looped smoothly over her ears and fastened behind with a 'tuckin' comb.'

2. The ridge of a roof. {*dial.* 1886–}

1824 in Z. F. Smith *Kentucky* 394 The roof was formed by making the end logs shorter, until a single log formed the comb of the roof. **1845** HOOPER *Taking Census* i. 161 They'd come and set on the comb of the house. **1869** 'MARK TWAIN' *Innocents* 174 From the eaves to the comb of the roof stretched in endless succession great curved marble beams. **1880** — *Tramp Abroad* iii. 40 He just had strength enough to crawl up on to the comb and lean his back agin the chimbly. **1908** *Dialect Notes* III. 300 On the comb of the house.

attrib. **1911** JENKS & LAUCK *Immigration Problem* 173 The houses occupied by the laborers on construction work throughout the South usually have a comb roof of about four feet pitch, which gives more air space than the flat tops which are more rarely found.

3. A steep-sided ridge or escarpment. {1808–, chiefly in Sc. forms}

1862 in *N.Y. Herald* 24 May 7/4 The bluff is a high ridge or comb. **1885** *Century Mag.* Jan. 454 There is no trouble about getting up to the ridge or comb on a stout horse.

***4.** *To have (one's) comb cut:* (see quot. 1877).

1877 BARTLETT 779 'To have one's comb cut' is to undergo mortification as a sequel to excessive pride. **1902** G. C. EGGLESTON *D. South* 187 She was pleased, too, with Madison Peyton's discomfiture. 'He needed to have his comb cut,' she reflected in homely metaphor. 'It may teach him better manners.'

5. Attrib. and comb. in sense 1, with *brush, factor*, etc.

1678 *New Castle Court Rec.* 362, 5 Combe brushes. **1853** FOWLER *Home for All* 146 My trees . . . fruit so early, . . . [due] to two causes—throwing several horns, obtained of tanners and comb-factors, . . . into the holes, under the trees, [etc.]. **1873** *U.S. Patents Official Gaz.* IV. 483/2 Comb-Holder. . . . Application filed September 26, 1873. **1837** COLMAN *Rep. Agric. Mass.* 58 The refuse of comb manufactories, horn tips and horn shavings, are greatly valued as manures. **1922** F. COURTENAY *Physical Beauty* 42 If you want that 'marcelled' look, there are comb sets (mounted on springs) which will give it.

* **Comb,** *v.*

+**1.** *intr.* Of a wave: To roll over and break with a foamy crest.

'App. of U.S. origin' (*O.E.D.*).

1807 J. BARLOW *Columbiad* I. 412 The stream ungovernable foams with ire, Climbs, combs tempestuous. **1828** WEBSTER, *Comb.* . . . In the language of seamen, to roll over, as the top of a wave; or to break with a white foam. **1838** POE *A. G. Pym* Wks. (1902) III. 9 Still the wind was increasing fearfully; and whenever we rose from a plunge forward, the sea behind fell combing over our counter, and deluged us with water.

2. (See quotation.)

1854 THOREAU *Walden* 321 Ice has its grain as well as wood, and when a cake begins to rot or 'comb,' that is, assume the appearance of honeycomb, . . . the air cells are at right angles with what was the water surface.

+**3.** *To comb up*, to make oneself neat by combing one's hair.

1884 'MARK TWAIN' *H. Finn* vi. 38, I didn't see how I'd ever got to like it so well at the widow's, where you had to wash, and eat on a plate, and comb up, and go to bed and get up regular.

+**4.** *tr.* To search closely, to examine, as with a fine-toothed comb.

1904 'O. HENRY' *Cabbages & Kings* iv. 80 In Coralio Señor Goodwin himself led the searching party which combed that town as carefully as a woman combs her hair; but the money was not found. **1912** RAINE *Brand Blotters* 209 Flatray . . . knew this country well; for he had run cattle here, and combed the draws and ridges on the annual spring and fall round-ups. **1920** MULFORD *J. Nelson* 188 There they are, . . . ridin' off to comb th' range. **1922** PARRISH *Case & the Girl* 330 Say I combed that pier, believe me, West, and finally I ran across a kid who put me wise.

***Comb case.** A case in which a comb or combs are kept. {–1663} — **1678** *New Castle Court Rec.* 362, 3 Combe Cases. **1838** INGRAHAM *Burton* II. 194 An oilcloth-covered combcase on one side of the little glass, . . . in keeping with the pin and needle cushion on the other. **1843** *Amer. Pioneer* II. 444 A small eight by ten looking-glass sloped from the wall over a large towel and combcase.

Comber.

1. One whose business is to comb (wool). {1646–}

See WOOL-COMBER, WORSTED-COMBER.

+**2.** A wave that breaks with a foamy crest; a breaker.

1840 DANA *Two Years* ix. 71 The heavy swell of the Pacific was setting in, and breaking in loud and high 'combers' upon the beach. **1884** *Boston Journal* 10 Nov. 2/3 Oil . . . has no effect on these turbulent 'combers.' **1885** *Harper's Mag.* Jan. 223/1 There were reefs . . . , over which good combers tumbled. **1897** *Outing* XXX. 246/1 In an instant, we were struggling in the combers. **1921** PAINE *Comr. Rolling Ocean* 84 A thundering comber fell on deck forward with a crash of splintered woodwork.

+**3.** (See quotation.)

1874 KNIGHT 597/2 *Comber*, a ledge around the well or passenger portion of a sail-boat to keep back spray and waves which 'comb' over the deck.

Comb factory. A manufactory of combs. — **1827** DRAKE & MANSFIELD *Cincinnati* 65 Two Comb factories. **1836** *Niles' Nat. Reg.* 29 Oct. 144/3 A comb factory has been recently established at Pittsburg. **1847** H. HOWE *Hist. Coll. Ohio* 476 It contains . . . 3 comb and 1 fire engine factory.

Comb foundation. A thin strip of beeswax placed or left in the frames and sections of a bee hive to promote uniformity in the building of the honeycomb. — **1880** *Harper's Mag.* Oct. 778/1 Comb foundation has another and far greater merit than that of saving labor to the bee: it secures a perfectly even, straight comb for each frame.

Comb grain. A kind of grain in pine. *attrib.* — **1897** MOORE *How To Build* 21 Where comb-grain pine is specified (so named because the grain is straight and in appearance like the artificial graining done by the grainer's comb) the best results may be secured as to wear and appearance.

*** Combination.**

***1.** An agreement or compact for mutual defense, government, etc. *Obs.*

1624 WINSLOW *Good Newes* (1897) 527 Having heard many rumours of the French, and not knowing whether there were any combination between the savages and them; the Governor told the Indians, [etc.]. **1636** *Plymouth Laws* 36 We finde a solemne and binding combinačon, as also L[ette]rs Patents derivatory from his Ma[jes]tie of Eng. . . . for the ordering of a body politick within the severall limits of this patent. **1654** *East-Hampton Rec.* I. 59 It is ordered that there shalbe a copie of the coneticut combinacon . . . Drawen forth as it is convenient for us. **a1656** BRADFORD *Hist.* 109, I shall . . . begine with a combination made by them before they came ashore, being the first foundation of their govermente in this place.

b. The union arising out of such an agreement. *Obs.*

1639 *Conn. Rec.* I. 30 Consult with Mr. Fenwicke about a treaty of combinacon w[hi]ch is desired againe to be on foott with the Bay. **1644** *Ib.* 104 Agitate such businesses as shall fall out to be attended in behalfe of the Combination.

***2.** A union of merchants, politicians, laborers, etc., for common action or mutual advantage.

1748 *N.J. Archives* 1 Ser. VII. 224 By this deposition also appears, some of the means that the rioters use, to bring & keep people into their combinations. **1819** *Amer. Farmer* I. 38 They are a source of perplexity and of considerable fault finding amongst the planters of Maryland, many of whom attribute it to occasional combinations amongst the purchasers here. **1823** in M'Kenney *Memoirs* I. App. 297 Did you not assign as a reason why the goods were sacrificed at Detroit, that of a combination among the purchasers? . . . Combinations existed, I believe, among the merchants. **1846** POLK *Diary* I. 253 Senator Haywood . . . said there was a combination between Mr. Calhoun and a few Democratic Senators with the body of Whig Senators to take the subject out of the hands of the Executive. **1906** F. LYNDE *Quickening* 182 There is that contract with the combination, for example.

+b. A union of corporations in order to establish a monopoly. Also attrib.

1883 *Harper's Mag.* Nov. 938/1 By combinations and traffic agreements forced on other companies they [=the Union Pacific and Central Pacific railroads] have come to control the traffic of the State [of California]. *Ib.* 942/2 Combinations and consolidations, though tending to form monopolies, are not unmixed evils. **1887** *Courier-Journal* 8 Jan. 4/1 In the last sixteen years the combination coal roads have sustained the rate of transportation at 1¾ cents per ton per mile. **1893** *Harper's Mag.* Feb. 384/1 There are four refineries in and out of the great sugar combination, and all are kept running by night and by day. **1903** *Chicago Chronicle* 11 April 2 Attorney General Knox is already preparing to bring suit against a number of combinations which he considers unlawful as being in restraint of trade.

***3.** A conspiracy; a confederacy for antisocial or nefarious ends. *Obs.*

1642 *Conn. Rec.* I. 73 It is Ordered, that there shall be a letter writt from the Courte . . . to preuent their mischeuous plotte in their late Combination. **1689** SEWALL *Diary* I. 310 Some in the Council thought Hawkins, because he got out of the Combination before Pease was killed, might live as well as Coward. **1693** C. MATHER *Wonders Invis. World* 83 In such extravagant ways have these Wretches propounded, the Dragooning of as many as they can, in their own Combination, and the Destroying of others. **1704** *Boston News-Letter* 31 July 2/1 And forasmuch as there must necessarily be a Combination of divers Persons in the said wicked Design of Forgery and Deceit. **1715** *Boston Rec.* 221 For the more effectual discovery of the Combination or Knotts of Robbers . . . Voted. That the Sume of Twenty five pounds Shall be given and paid out of ye Town Treasury.

+b. In college life: (see quot. 1851.)

1798 *Harvard Laws* 27 If any combination or agreement, to do any unlawful act, or to forbear a compliance with any injunction from lawful authority [etc.]. *Ib.* 39 All class meetings, held without license, shall be considered and punished as unlawful combinations. **1851** HALL *College Words* 54 An agreement entered into by students to resist or disobey the Faculty of the College, or to do any unlawful act, is a *combination.* **1859** M. LABORDE *Hist. S.C. College* 90 But the highest crime of the year, and the highest crime known to the law, was perpetrated near its close; I mean the crime of combination.

+4. A theatrical company which travels with one or more set plays, or which offers mixed vaudeville and dramatic performances. Also attrib.

1866 *Charleston Courier* 10 May, The Hibernian Hall. The Southern Combination Troupe: Comic, Irish Singing, Fancy Dresses, and Negro Performances. Barry Carter, Stg. Mgr. **1872** *Chicago Tribune* 31 March, The Seldon-Irvin combination will play in *Everybody's Friend.* **1875** *Ib.* 13 Sept. 7/5 Academy of Music, . . . the Marion Taylor combination. The most complete organization in America. **1895** *N.Y. Dramatic News* 19 Oct. 14/1 A comparatively new departure in continuous vaudeville is the engagement of entire combinations which help to fill out the bill. *Ib.* 16 Nov. 13/2 The return of the Fourteenth street theatre to the ranks of the combination houses again demonstrates the fact that the Western idea of drama and vaudeville combined is not acceptable to Eastern patrons. *Ib.* 23 Nov. 17/1 Out of the combinations, Nat Goodwin has been the only one that has drawn good houses. **1896** *Ib.* 4 July 17/3 Proctor's Leland Opera House, Albany, N.Y. Open Time For Stars And Combinations.

transf. **1868** *Charleston Courier* 28 Dec., Stone and Murray's Combination Circus, starring John Henry, Equestrian and Thaumaturgic Artiste, at The Citadel Green.

+5. A railroad coach with a section for baggage and one for passengers. Also attrib.

1896 *N.Y. Tribune* 7 Sept. 1/3 The baggage-car, a combination and a passenger coach were overturned [in the wreck]. **1901** MERWIN & WEBSTER *Calumet 'K'* 202 There was an engine and three box cars . . . and a combination—that's baggage and passenger. **1903** C. T. BRADY *Bishop* xv. 277 We were the only passengers in the combination-car—half-baggage, half-passenger.

+6. Attrib. with *lock* (also *bolt, knob,* etc.) designating a lock (or parts of this, etc.) which can only be opened by a series of movements of a knob or dial.

1845 *Cincinnati Misc.* 194 The locks which are on the combination principle, not only defy picking, but cannot be opened, even by their own keys, unless in the owner or maker's own hands. **1851** CIST *Cincinnati* 215 Combination and detector bank lock. **1858** *Report Comm. Patents* (1859) I. 540 Improvement in Combination Locks. **1869** *Ib.* (1871) II. 715/2 Combination-Padlock.—December 7, 1869. **1902** HARBEN *Abner Daniel* 272 Wilson . . . then reluctantly turned to the big iron safe against the wall. . . . With his fat, pink hand on the silver-plated combination-bolt he turned to Miller again. **1909** 'O. HENRY' *Roads of Destiny* 164 That's Dandy Jim Valentine's autograph. He's resumed business. Look at that combination knob—jerked out as easy as pulling up a radish in wet weather.

+b. *ellipt.* A lock of this kind, or the series of movements required to open it.

1875 *Chicago Tribune* 29 July 2/2 They [robbers] succeeded in getting the hinges off and partly removing the combination [of the bank door]. **1880** 'MARK TWAIN' in *Atlantic Mo.* XLVI. 228/2 They commanded him to reveal the 'combination,' so that they could get into the safe. **1909** 'O. HENRY' *Roads of Destiny* x. 170 She had then shot the bolts and turned the knob of the combination as she had seen Mr. Adams do.

fig. **1906** L. BELL *C. Lee* 271 What did you do about praying while changing your idea of a personal, corporeal God to one of spirit? Why, Carolina, I've lost the combination!

+7. A number of magazines which may be subscribed for together at a reduced rate.

1907 *Pearson's Mag.* Jan. Contents-page, The face value of a subscription bill may be applied to any combination or clubbing offer advertised.

+Combination report. A summary of news items from various parts of the country, published and distributed to subscribers by a central news bureau. — **1877** *Harper's Mag.* Dec. 57/2 Each of these Southern cities is interested in the news of the others, and to supply them with it a summary of all that has been received at Washington is included in the combination report, which, being delivered at all points, gives back to each city some of its own news.

+Combination store. A general store, where every kind of commodity is sold. — **1897** *Outing* XXIX. 583/2 There was a little 'combination-store'; hats and calico on one side, canned goods and coffee on the other, and a post-office at the back.

Combine. {1610} +A combination or alliance of persons to further personal interests, often by fraudulent means.

'Colloq. and recent; first publicly used in the trial of an alderman for bribery in New York in 1886' (*Cent.*).

Other quotations, 1890–1896, are given by Thornton in his *Suppl.*

1887 *Courier-Journal* 3 May 4/3 Chicago's 'combines' are of a far-reaching kind. While the late May deal in wheat was pending parties at various points in the country sold the May option in Chicago against wheat actually in their possession. **1888** *N.Y. Ev. Post* 6 March 4 An anti-Platt combine composed of seven Senators. **1889** 'MARK TWAIN' *Conn. Yankee* xxxiii. 428 They're a 'combine'—a trade union, . . . who band themselves together to force their lowly brother to take what they choose to give. **1889** *N.Y. Times* 8 Sept., The investigation by the Senatorial commission into the dressed-beef combine was resumed here to-day. . . . Should the combine get a hold on the local business it would ruin the butchers of the town. **1892** A. DALY *Little Miss Million* (1893) 72 Well, since you won't either of you give in, I tell you what you do. Make a 'combine' and buy the stuff together! **1904** L. STEFFENS in *McClure's Mag.* April 591 The 'combine' was only the chief instrument of the lobby and was made up of dishonest legislators. . . . The honest legislator . . . may want to vote against the 'combine,' but the lobby serves the party as well as business. **1917** J. F. DALY *Life A. Daly* 82 The citizen in question . . . had been engaged in a campaign for municipal reform in his town, and had conceived the ingenious idea of representing the wicked 'combine' of the local 'boodlers' on the stage.

b. An alliance of corporations.

1887 *Courier-Journal* 8 Jan. 4/1 A writer in the *North American Review* shows how the Pennsylvania coal monopoly illustrates the public benefits of 'monopolistic combines.' **1888** *Boston Herald* 22 Aug. 8/3 Louisville, Ky., Aug. 22, 1888. The gentlemen representing the principal coal companies of Kentucky and Virginia met at the Galt House yesterday afternoon, and formed a combine. **1898** N. E. JONES *Squirrel Hunters of Ohio* 164 The 'money power,' with its 'trusts,' 'combines,' . . . may smile at the success. **1905** D. G. PHILLIPS *Plum Tree* 74 A secret, absolutely secret combine of a dozen of the big corporations of my state.

∗**Combing,** *vbl. n.*

1. Wool that has been combed.

1779 E. PARKMAN *Diary* 143 Miss P. has rid unto ye South of ye Town to procure Worsted Combings.

2. Attrib. with *wool:* Suitable for combing.

1867–8 *Ill. Agric. Soc. Trans.* VII. 455 The demand for combing wools has long since been far ahead of the ability to provide for it. **1874** *Vt. Bd. Agric. Rep.* II. 418 There is a growing demand for good combing wool, and the manufacturers assure me that if there were many times as much first quality combing wool raised in this country as there now is it would be as high as now.

+**3.** The action of crested waves.

1848 COOPER *Oak Openings* II. 202 Among breakers, or amid the combing of seas.

Combing, *ppl. a.*

1. That which combs.

1812 *Niles' Reg.* II. 9/1 This wool has another peculiar value. Much of it will do for the hand comb or for the combing machine.

+**2.** Of the sea: Characterized by crested waves. {1857–1867}

1838 COOPER *Homeward B.* xiii, Combing seas, with which the ship was still racing. **1851** MELVILLE *Moby Dick* cxxxv, Two of them clutched the gunwale again, and rising to its level on a combing wave, hurled themselves bodily inboard again. **1883** 'MARK TWAIN' *Life on Miss.* li. 502 Far-reaching ranks of combing whitecaps.

Combing down. A severe reprimand. — **1865** *Atlantic Mo.* XV. 595/2 Reuben . . . receives such a combing down . . . as he remembers for a month thereafter.

∗**Comb-maker.** One whose business is making combs. — **1796** *Boston Directory* 279 Sadler, John, comb maker, Charter street. **1845** J. COFFIN *Hist. Newbury* 225 Enoch Noyes . . . employed William Cleland, a deserter from Burgoyne's army, a comb-maker by profession. **1855** BARNUM *Life* 16 He brought the comb-maker four fine-looking ox horns.

Comb pot. A charcoal pot formerly used for heating wool-combs. Now a small stove for the same purpose. {1782, 1888} — **1723** *New-Eng. Courant* 15–22 July 2/2 'Tis suppos'd the Fire was occasion'd by some Coals being blown out of a Comb-Pot, where a Fire had been made the Day before. **1874** KNIGHT 598/1 A stove at which the combs are warmed in the operation of preparing long-stapled wool for *worsted.*

+**Comb thistle.** An herb (*Carduus pectinatus*) that resembles a thistle. Also *comb-tooth thistle.* — **1833** EATON *Botany* (ed. 6) 67 *Carduus pectinatus,* comb thistle, meadow thistle. **1836** LINCOLN *Botany* App. 182 Comb-tooth thistle. Cardu[us]. **1840** DEWEY *Mass. Flowering Plants* 123 *Carduus pectinatus.* Comb Thistle. . . . Rarely cultivated in gardens.

∗**COME,** *v.*

I. *Quasi-tr.* in various colloquial and slang phrasal uses.

1. *To come it* (or *that*), to succeed in an undertaking. Usu. with negative. {*dial.* 1888–}

(*a*) **a1846** *Quarter Race Ky.*, etc. 119 But he can't quite come it—'H.'s horse is too smart, and can beat him every inch of the road.' **1848** BARTLETT 62 *Can't come it,* is a vulgar expression for cannot do it. **1848** G. E. ELLIS *Let.* (Bartlett MS.) *You can't come it*—is heard all over the Union. **1849** LANMAN *Alleghany Mts.* 89 The fellers laughed at me and said I couldn't come it. **c1850** WHITCHER *Bedott P.* xxiv. 285 It takes you to come it, Aunt Lucy. **1866** GREGG *Life in Army* 141 Feeling secure from their voracious bills, as they hum around your room, and try to 'come it,' but find an abatis in their way. **1909** *Dialect Notes* III. 300 He tried hard, but he couldn't quite come it.

(*b*) **1859** BARTLETT 67 *Old Gent.* Let me take you on my lap. *Woman.* No, you can't come that, old chap. **1908** WHITE *Riverman* 137, 'I intended that seat for this lady,' said Orde, touching him on the shoulder. The youth looked up coolly. 'You don't come that!' said he.

2. *To come a game on* (someone), to trick, deceive, or hoax.

a1846 *Quarter Race Ky.*, etc. 181 You want to come that same old game on me, do you? **1869** 'MARK TWAIN' *Innocents* 189 *Tout les jours* you are coming some fresh game or other on me. **1884** — *H. Finn* vi. 40 He said he would like to see the widow get me. He said he would watch out, and if they tried to come any such game on him he knowed of a place six or seven mile off to stow me in. **1886** HOWELLS *Minister's Charge* 43 Any them beats 'round here been trying to come their games on you?

b. *To come the moral on,* to appeal to the moral feelings of (a person).

1862 BROWNE *A. Ward His Book* 18 We must work on their feelins. Cum the moral on 'em strong.

3. *To come it over,* to get the upper hand of; to overcome by guile, deceit, trickery, etc.

1842 *Spirit of Times* (Phila.) 11 Oct. (Th.), Says I, 'Mr. Coon,' and then he smiled, 'You can't quite come it over this child.' **1847** ROBB *Squatter Life* 163 Tom had 'come it' over him for so many odd dinners, without a shadow of prospect for pay, that he would stand it no longer. **1852** STOWE *Uncle Tom* viii, Don't you think to come it over me. **1854** M. J. HOLMES *Tempest & Sunshine* 98, I didn't know but Tempest had come it over you with her pretty face. **1860** ABBOTT *South & North* 93 God Almighty never yet made a nigger that could come it over me! **1871** STOWE *Sam Lawson* 78 'Why, Parson Carryl,' says Mis' Deakin Blodgett, 'how you've come it over us.' **1876** 'MARK TWAIN' *Tom Sawyer* vii. 74, I'll go the other way and come it over 'em the same way. **1881** *Harper's Mag.* Dec. 106/2 'They think they're comin' it over me, down there to Washington,' Sam observed. **1889** K. MUNROE *Golden Days* 172 Some galoot stood ready to figger out how he could come it over the owner.

b. With *giraffe, gum, gum game, hoax,* etc., as the direct object. {1785–}

1846 CORCORAN *Pickings* 31 'No you don't,' said the watchman, 'you don't come the giraffe over me that a way.' **1847** ROBB *Squatter Life* 74 'No!' shouted Tom, with mock surprise, 'you ain't comin' a hoax over a fellar?—you raally are the sure enough Jedge?' **1848** J. MITCHELL *Nantucketisms* 40 'He tried to cum the gum over him, but, By Golla! Lijah was up & dressed.' Ready—not to be taken in. **1853** BALDWIN *Flush Times Ala.* 275 He had lost in trying to come the old soldier over another man. **1859** BARTLETT 185 Opossums and raccoons . . . will fly for refuge to the Sweet Gum tree. . . . This is called 'coming the gum game' over the hunter. **1862** 'E. KIRKE' *Among Pines* 189 He seems well enough, sir; I believe he's coming the possum over mother. **1863** — *Southern Friends* 79 You can't intend to come the Yankee over me! **1869** *Kansas City Advertiser* 7 May (F.), You can't come that gum game over me any more; I've been to the land-office and know all about the place. **1887** H. FREDERIC *Seth's Brother's Wife* 344, I suspected all along that he intended to come some game over us about the farm.

4. *To come it round* (a person), to circumvent, 'get round.'

1871 STOWE *Sam Lawson* 43 Wal, that was the reason why Jeff Sullivan couldn't come it round Ruth tho' he was silkier than a milkweed-pod. **1875** — *We & Neighbors* 100 They don't come it round Jim, I tell you. Any boy that don't toe the crack gets it.

II. With prepositions.

5. *To come around* (a person), to circumvent. (Cf. 4.) {come round, 1830–}

a1859 *Wedding at Nutmegville* (B.), They've come around that young man, they've come around him. **1887** *Atlantic Mo.* Feb. 279/2 From earliest infancy girls appear to know by intuition how to circumvent (which is, being translated, come around) the male dwellers in the abode.

6. *To come at,* +to imply, to mean.

1872 'MARK TWAIN' *Roughing It* xxviii. 156 Here—what you mean? What are you coming at? Is there any mystery behind all this? *Ib.* xxxi. 172 Is that your idea? Is that what you're coming at? **1894** WILKINS *Pembroke* 52 What I was comin' at was—I'd been kind of wrong in my reasonin'.

∗**7.** *To come over,* +to say over, repeat.

1846 *Spirit of Times* 18 April 88/1 He never spoke of her, or gave an order without 'coming over' her name.

∗**8.** *To come to,* +to be due or owed to (one).

1793 *Md. Hist. Mag.* VI. 356, I am satisfied that there is something considerable comming to me in the Limekills account. **1891** *Harper's Mag.* Nov. 888/2 He decides upon his own responsibility whether they have sufficient money coming to them to meet the accommodation. **a1904** WHITE *Blazed Trail Stories* 31 Three hundred men each with four months' pay coming to him. **1909** 'O. HENRY' *Roads of Destiny* 265 There was some land, or a pension, coming to him from the state that he never would ask for. **1911** SAUNDERS *Col. Todhunter* 77 Don't you worry about their not getting what's coming to them. **1914** ATHERTON *Perch of Devil* 91, I do believe in a woman . . . gettin' all the admiration that's comin' to her. **1921** PAINE *Comr. Rolling Ocean* 44 You had it coming to you.

III. With adverbs.

∗**9.** *To come again,* +to make a second effort; to keep on trying.

1868 WOODRUFF *Trotting Horse* 267 She was then, and remained to the last, a wonderful mare to 'come again.'

∗**10.** *To come back,* +to respond or reply in kind; to start up.

1896 G. ADE *Artie* vi. 54 Did you ever get the worst of it in such a way that you couldn't come back at the time? **1912** WASON *Friar Tuck* 22 Touch him up on a ticklish subject, an' he just had to come back at ya, same as a rattler.

11. *To come down.* **a.** With *to:* To think or act on the same level with.

1880 *Harper's Mag.* May 936/2 Now such an editor does not 'come down' to his public.

b. To become ill *with* (a disease).

1911 LINCOLN *Cap'n Warren* 147 The housekeeper felt sure he was coming down' with some disease or other.

∗**12.** *To come in.* **a.** To calve. {1886, *s.w. dial.*}

1838 H. COLMAN *Mass. Rep. Agric.* 60 He gives an opinion, . . . that heifers which 'come in' with their first calf at two years old, do better than when their coming in is delayed until three years old. **1857** *Ill. Agric. Soc. Trans.* II. 381 The coming in of the cows should be regulated to occur in early spring. **1874** *Vt. Board Agric. Rep.* II. 93 He . . . has his cows come in usually in April. *Ib.* 384 There is much variance of opinion and discussion as to the time a heifer should first come in. **1878** *Ill. Dept. Agric. Trans.* XIV. 282 Of this family [of shorthorns], nine out of ten come in at two years old, in which case one is worth as much as two to come in older. **1882** *Maine Bd. Agric. Rep.* XXVI. 22 The best cows we ever buy are those which happen to come in . . . in the late fall or early winter. **1884** *Vt. Agric. Rep.* VIII. 25 [He] would have some of the cows come in in the fall. **1896** T. D. PRICE *MS. Diary* 27 Nov., Spotted Maholm cow came in.

b. To spring or grow up. (See also quot. 1855.)

1831 PECK *Guide* 161 The white clover comes in naturally where the ground has been cultivated, and thrown by, or along the sides of old roads and paths. **1855** *Trans. Amer. Inst. N.Y.* 493 This change in the case of hemlock timber is continually going on in this country, where land, once cleared of it, 'comes in,' as the expression is, to a hard wood growth.

+**c.** In poker: To enter the game by accepting a hand after the deal; also, to join a group of persons already playing.

1887 KELLER *Draw Poker* 23 If he comes in, he must make good the ante and deposit in the pool a sum equal to the raise, if there be any, of the preceding player. **1913** MULFORD *Coming of Cassidy* 215 Baxter walked over to watch the play. 'I'm comin' in next game. Who's winnin' now?' **1922** T. A. MCNEAL *When Kansas was Young* 187 'That need not stand in the way of a pleasant evening,' remarked the Major, 'you have plenty of cattle. Suppose we make the ante a steer and two steers to "come in."'

fig. **1901** NORRIS *Octopus* 59 He had turned rancher and had 'come in' on the new tracts of wheat land just thrown open by the railroad.

d. Of cattle: To be entering on (a specified age).

1746 *N.H. Probate Rec.* III. 419, I also Give to my s[ai]d Wife all my Stock of Cattle Sheep & Swine, Excepting one Yoke of Steers, now Coming in four Years of Age.

***13.** *To come off.* **a.** To happen. {1825–}

1847 FIELD *Drama in Pokerville*, etc. 114 In the evening, the house was crowded, sure enough; everybody going from a vague idea that something was to 'come off.' **1853** *Alta Californian* 15 Feb., A shooting affair came off here today.

+**b.** To change one's actions or attitude; to shut up; usu. imperative.

1892 *N.Y. Mercury* Feb. (Ware), 'How much does yez ax for this book?' 'Six dollars' replied the smiling clerk. 'Six dollars! Oh, come off!' **1904** W. H. SMITH *Promoters* 293 '[It] makes one conscious of his own superiority to call some one else down.' 'Oh, come off!' Goldsby replied.

***14.** *To come out.* **a.** To leave, depart from a port or foreign country; to go or come abroad.

1704 *Boston News-Letter* 26 June 2/1 On the 19. Instant arrived Moses Butterworth in a Sloop from Barbadoes, 22. days passage, came out in Company with the Blackwall man of War. *Ib.* 17 July 2/2 Capt. Jenkins came out in Company with a Fleet of about 200 Sail. **1705** *Ib.* 23 July 1/2 On the 18th Currant arrived here the *Deptford* . . . with whom came out for Boston Capt. Rymes in a Ship. **1899** JEWETT *Queen's Twin* 100 Before ever I thought of coming out [to America].

b. To speak or act in a frank or bold manner. {1850}

1788 in *Mem. T. Parsons* (1859) 462 The Governor . . . has come out, and tells us, that two very respectable States, Virginia and New York, propose a convention to consider amendments. **1832** *Niles' Reg.* XLI. 337/2 Mr. Clay 'came out' decidedly and manfully respecting the American System.

c. To announce oneself for public office.

1835 LONGSTREET *Georgia Scenes* 234 If ever you come out for any thing, Lyman, jist let the boys of Upper Hogthief know it, and they'll go for you.

d. To emerge from an undertaking or contest; to fare; to turn out. {1868–}

1859 BARTLETT 92 'How did you come out?' means, how did you fare in your undertaking? *Come off* would be more agreeable to English usage. **1863** NORTON *Army Letters* 192 Next day I was put on as 'officer of the guard' and my letter writing and everything of the kind are coming out slim. **1905** *N.Y. Ev. Post* 12 Jan. 6 They avoid those controversies over exact facts in which he has invariably come out second-best.

+**e.** To profess religion.

*c***1847** WHITCHER *Bedott P.* 108, I experienced religion . . . at one o' brother Armstrong's protracted meetin's. . . . Them special efforts is great things—ever sence I come out I've felt like a new critter. **1871** DE VERE 231 A person proposing to join a church is expected first openly to come out, that is to say, to profess his religion.

+**15.** *To come through.* **a.** To experience and announce a religious conversion.

1881 PIERSON *In the Brush* 172 They could scarcely speak for hoarseness—enjoyed seeing them 'come through.' **1898** DUNBAR *Folks from Dixie* 15 The congregation redoubled its exertions, but all to no effect, Anner 'Lizer wouldn't 'come thoo.' **1905** A. H. RICE *Sandy* 310 Aunt Melvy, after seeking religion for nearly sixty years, had chosen this inopportune time to 'come th'u.' **1913** STRATTON-PORTER *Laddie* xii. 220 Leon said our house reminded him of the mourners' bench before anyone had 'come through.' *Ib.* xv. 305 Pretty soon it began to look like she was going to come through as Amos Hurd did when he was redeemed.

b. To be successful in overcoming obstacles.

1886 A. EDWARDS *Playwright's Daugh.* xvi, You will do as I tell you, and, please God, shall come through without a singe. **1912** MATHEWSON *Pitching* 33, I have been told that Clarke was the most relieved man in seven counties when O'Toole came through with that victory in Boston.

***16.** *To come up*, +of a playing card, to turn up as the card just dealt.

*a***1846** *Quarter Race Ky.*, etc. 79, I took the two dollars up and let him make another turn when I replaced the bet, and the queen came up in my favour.

17. *To come up with* {1678–}, to outwit, get the better of.

1856 *Harper's Mag.* XII. 710/1 One of our smart young lawyers was well come up with the other day. **1871** STOWE *Sam Lawson* 126 The way he got come up with by Miry was too funny for anything. **1873** S. HALE *Letters* 123 She gets come up with occasionally, and then I'm delighted. **1887** WILKINS *Humble Romance* 425, I'd like to see Lawrence Thayer come up with. **1901** WHITE *Westerners* 78 Revenge with him seemed to be . . . in the victim's realization that he was being come up with.

18. In various colloquial phrases: *to come down to it*, to get to fundamental principles; *to come out of that*, to cease meddling with; *to come up missing*, to be absent.

1891 BUNNER *Zadoc Pine* 74 'Oh, Popper Leete,' remonstrated his wife, ''tain't so bad as that!' 'Well,' Mr. Leete insisted, . . . 'tain't much better, when you come right down to it.' **1869** 'MARK TWAIN' *Innocents* iii. 35, I saw a long spy-glass on a desk . . . and reached after it. . . . 'Ah, Ah, hands off! Come out of that!' **1900** DRANNAN *Plains & Mts.* 503 The young man who had been riding in the middle, also four mules and their packs, as the saying is, 'came up missing.'

+**Come-again,** *a.* Recuperative, persevering. — **1868** WOODRUFF *Trotting Horse* 299 People forget the wonderful constitution and come-again qualities of Flora.

+**Come-as-you-come.** — 'The name of a popular fireside amusement, wherein one person gives the others present the initial letter or letters of some object there visible, by which to guess to what object he refers' (B. '77, p. 779).

‖**Come-at-able.** *colloq.* Anything that is readily accessible. — **1840** SIMMS *Border Beagles* I. 125, I donned my first come atables, and rammed the rest in dad's old saddle-bags.

+**Come-back.** *colloq.*

1. A retaliatory measure.

1896 G. ADE *Artie* 59, I never will be able to give him the right kind of a hot come-back for what he done to me. **1921** MULFORD *Bar-20 Three* 184 Nobody can buffalo me an' chuck me into jail without a come-back.

2. A retort; a (prompt or effective) reply.

1899 G. ADE *Fables in Slang* (1902) 132 And all rattled, he told her his Name, instead of giving her the scorching Come-Back that he composed next Day, when it was Too Late. **1908** MULFORD *Orphan* 168 He didn't have no come-back to that, but just looked sort of funny. **1909** WASON *Happy Hawkins* 66 A feller was a fool to argue with that little witch. She allus had a come-back. **1912** — *Friar Tuck* 152 The only come-back Horace made was to start to sing with his mouth full o' cornbread an' bacon. **1916** BOWER *Phantom Herd* 124, I can talk business without any come-back from Mart.

3. A recovery; a return to a former state of health, prosperity, etc.

1908 K. MCGAFFEY *Show-Girl* 224 But it is a good thing to have a bank account to flash, so that the boob will think he will get a comeback if he does lose. **1912** MATHEWSON *Pitching* 34 Then I knew he was all right. He was there with the 'come-back.' **1924** A. J. SMALL *Frozen Gold* 90 It looks as though I'm in time to congratulate you on a real come-back.

***Comedian.** An actor or stage-player; esp., in later use, one who plays comic parts. {1601–}

1750 in E. Singleton *Social N.Y.* 272 Last week arrived here a company of comedians from Philadelphia, . . . where they intend to perform as long as the season lasts. **1752** *Virginia Gazette* 30 April 3/2 The Company of Comedians, from the new Theatre at Williamsburg, propose playing Hobbs's-Hole, from the 10th of May to the 24th. **1768** in *S. Lit. Messenger* XXIII. 37 By the Virginia Company of Comedians. On Friday the 3d of June will be presented The Beggar's Opera. **1885** *Century Mag.* Jan. 464 To play in comedy . . . these things are elemental, the very ABC of the society primer, and yet how few of our young 'comedians,' as they are called, evince the slightest acquaintance with them. **1898** *N.Y. Journal* 19 Nov. 2/1 Wearing spats, front crease in trousers and throwing out one's chest is the receipt followed by Dan Daly, the comedian, to gain height.

***Come-down.** {In phr. *Castle Come-down*} +A drop in social esteem or in position.

1840 DANA *Two Years* xxviii, This was indeed a come-down, from the highest seat in the synagogue to a seat in the galley. **1877** BARTLETT 779 'A great *come down*,' a remarkable fall of pride. **1879** WEBSTER *Suppl.*, *Come-down*, . . . a downfall; a sudden descent from a higher position. (*Colloq.*) **1887** H. H. JACKSON *Between Whiles* 18 It was a sad come-down from his old air-castles for her and for himself. **1903** H. HAPGOOD *Autobiog. of Thief* 175 What a come-down for a man who could throw his whole city for any state or national candidate at election time, to be compelled to apologize . . . to the lowest element in prison.

Come-off. {1634–} +An excuse; a false explanation; a subterfuge. {1849–}

1722 *New-Eng. Courant* 3 Dec. 1/2 Quoth she, This is a nice Come-off, Like hiding broken Wind b' a Cough. **1800** *Aurora* (Phila.) 19 May (Th.), He replied that he was not at liberty to say—we had a sedition law—which will soon be done away—then I can explain. A very good come-off this! **1845** SIMMS *Wigwam and Cabin* I. 93, I began to think that what he said was only a sort of come-off. *Ib.*, I thought his offer to stake diamonds that he couldn't show was pretty much like a come-off. **1870** EMERSON *Soc. & Solitude* 103 To give money to a sufferer is only a come-off.

+**Come-out.** Capacity for improvement, development, etc.

1853 *S. Lit. Messenger* XIX. 669/2 It is astonishing, Frank, what come-out there is in men! **1869** TOURGEE *Toinette* ii. 26 He was simply speculating on the probable future value of his newly acquired possession, as the jockey calculates the 'come out' of a colt. *Ib.* xxi. 235 'Ah!' said the old clerk, looking after him, 'there's a heap of come-out in the Hunter stock yet.' **1882** THAYER *From Log-Cabin* xii. 186 Jim, I hear there is some come-out to you, and if you have no objections I would like to make up my own mind in regard to it.

+**Come-outer.** One who separates himself from an established organization. Originally one opposed to ecclesiastical organizations; later a social or political reformer.

1840 LONGFELLOW in *Life* (1891) I. 373 Not long after, came up from Cape Cod a new sect called the 'Come-outers,' who formed a holy alliance with the Transcendentalists. **1840** *Niles' Nat. Reg.* 5 Dec. 224/1 The 'Come Outers' ... are a sect recently sprung up on Cape Cod. Their leading or sectarian views are said to be: 1. Opposition to a regular ministry, [etc.]. **1845** *Knickerb.* XXV. 259 The 'Old Fellows,' the 'Rechabites,' the 'Come-Outers,' and the 'Transcendentalists,' lay claim to only a few of its advantages. **1864** NICHOLS *Amer. Life* II. 45 These ultras, who were anti-everything, were called, and perhaps called themselves, come-outers. **1880** *Scribner's Mo.* Oct. 913/1, I am inclined to agree with Governor Andrew that in politics as well as in religion the 'stay-inners' can do better service than the 'come-outers.' **1880** *Harper's Mag.* Jan. 182/2 Mr. Parker ... walked thirty miles ... to attend a convention called by Second Adventists and 'Come-outers.' **1903** *Atlantic Mo.* Sept. 352 Dr. Holmes was rather a believer in existing institutions than a come-outer. **1914** *Cycl. Amer. Govt.* I. 330 *Comeouter.* The name originally applied to certain religious dissenters. ... Such a group flourished in New England, about 1840, including that group of non-resistance Abolitionists.

b. An inactive member of the Mormon Church. Also, one who has left the Mormon Church.

1860 GREELEY *Overland Journey* 187 We met several wagon-loads of come-outers from Mormonism on their way to the states. **1870** BEADLE *Utah* 392 He properly belonged to the class known as 'hickory Mormons' or 'Come-outers.' **1871** *N.Y. Tribune* 2 May 4/6 With plenty of 'gentiles' to keep them in countenance, trade with them, pray with them, protect them, the 'come-outers' will increase rapidly.

+**Come-outerism.** The beliefs or system of thought of the come-outers. — **1847** W. L. GARRISON in *Life* (1889) III. 202 A good deal of prejudice is cherished against me on account of my 'infidelity' and 'come-outerism.' **1869** J. H. BROWNE *Great Metropolis* 636 She is a thorough come-outer, in the strictest sense of come-outerism. **1896** LEONARD *Cent. of Congregationalism in Ohio* 47 Comeouterism then [1840–50] flourished, which called upon the elect [ultra-abolitionists] ... to break loose from the Laodicean churches.

||**Come-out-ness.** Emergence. — **1891** *Harper's Mag.* Dec. 158/1 It is an act of consecration, of rigid, simple come-out-ness into the light of truth.

***Comer.** +An animal or person that shows promise of development.

1879 *St. Nicholas Mag.* Nov. 84/2, I don't know what a crab is usually called at first, whether a soft or hard crab. We say he is a 'Buckler.' A buckler is always very poor to begin with; but he eats everything he gets hold of, which, of course, fattens him up some. Then he is called a 'comer.' **1890** H. PALMER *Stories of Base Ball Field* 91 He piled up error after error, but Dan said he was a 'comer.' **1901–2** *Kansas State Bd. Agric. Rep.* 202 He ... still shows that remarkable looseness and elasticity of hide that indicates a 'comer' when he is put next to the feed-box.

+**Comer-out.** = COME-OUTER. — **1841** EMERSON *Miscell.* (1855) 267 Mysticism ... forms the sole thoughts of some poor Perfectionist or 'Comer out.'

+**Come-uppance.** [Cf. COME-UPPINGS.] (One's) just deserts.

1859 *Harper's Mag.* Jan. 277/1 Dennis once got his 'come-up-ance.' **1885** HOWELLS *Silas Lapham* xx. 366 But I guess he'll find he's got his come-uppance. **1893** M. A. OWEN *Voodoo Tales* 29 Den dey [*sc.* geesel git dey come-uppunce des lak folks. **1896** E. HIGGINSON *Tales* 155, I can give him his come-up'ans if he goes to foolin' around. **1912** W. L. PHELPS *Teaching in School & College* 59, I thereafter learned that Aristides got his come-uppance six lines from the bottom of the left-hand page. **1923** BOWER *Parowan Bonanza* 70 'An' that's where he got 'is come-uppance,' he gloated.

Come-uppings. *pl.* = COME-UPPANCE. {*dial.* 1880–} — **1896** E. HIGGINSON *Tales* 230, I'll give her her come-uppings! **1897** HOWELLS *Landlord at Lion's Head* 153 That [flirt] ... had merely got her come-uppings.

***Comfort.** Also †**comfit.** +A thick quilted counterpane; a wadded quilt; = COMFORTER 2.

1834 *S. Lit. Messenger* I. 168 A lady of our party ... aptly compared it to a Yankee comfort. **1844** *Rep. Comm. Patents* (1847) 35 It [cotton] has already been employed in what are variously called 'comforts' and 'comfortables.' **1855** J. E. COOKE *Ellie* 430 Covering her face with her great white snow-ball ornamented comfort, she held it securely. **1863** CUMMING *Hospital Life* (1866) 82/2 There is also a place for dyeing comforts, as the latter are made out of cotton in its pure state. ... Then there is a quilting-room, where these comforts are made, after being dyed. **1880** INGHAM *Digging Gold* 352 The beds consisted of loose hay, thrown upon the boards; ... blankets and comfits were used for covers. **1898** WESTCOTT *D. Harum* 164 She bustled out of the room, returning in a minute or two with an armful of comforts. **1913** STRATTON-PORTER *Laddie* xi. 211 Laddie had filled the kitchen oven with bricks and hung up a comfort at four o'clock to keep the Princess warm.

Comfortable.

1. Anything which makes for comfort. {1650–75}

1786 CUTLER in *Life & Corr.* II. 247 He appeared much pleased, and proposes to provide well in comfortables for the journey.

+**2.** = COMFORTER 2.

1842 in Buckingham *E. & W. States* III. 434 Still Mr. Van Buren was not content; he longed for the 'Turkish divan' and the 'French comfortable.' **1844** [see COMFORT]. **1845** KIRKLAND *Western Clearings* 68 Let 'em make comfortables out o' their old gowns, and if that don't do, let 'em sleep in their day-clothes, as I do! **1856** S. T. L. ROBINSON *Kansas* 28, I gave up my room to some of the new comers, and slept on comfortables and buffalo-robes on the floor in the attic. **1878** R. T. COOKE *Happy Dodd* 42 Mrs. Dodd made a bed for them out of her winter comfortables in the little attic. **1906** FREEMAN *By Light of Soul* 437 She did not get into bed, but took a silk comfortable off, and wrapped it around her.

+**Comfort-bag.** A bag in which soldiers keep small articles. — **1866** MOORE *Women of War* 586 The little child diligently sewing with tiny fingers upon the soldiers' comfort-bag.

***Comforter.**

1. A heavy woolen scarf. {1833–}

1840 DANA *Two Years* xxv. 263 This added to guernsey frocks, striped comforters about the neck, ... and a strong, oily smell, ... will complete the description. **1847** *Knickerb.* XXIX. 9 His countenance was entirely concealed by the voluminous folds of a red woollen comforter. **1852** BRISTED *Upper Ten Th.* 20 His neck is defended by a blue worsted comforter. **1888** STOCKTON *Dusantes* 37 This head was wrapped ... in a brown woolen comforter. **1899** A. BROWN *Tiverton Tales* 64 The little group marched away, swathed in comforters.

+**2.** A heavy quilt; a comfort.

1832 S. G. GOODRICH *Univ. Geog.* 107 The females also have similar meetings called 'quilting bees,' when many assemble to work for one, in padding or quilting bed coverings or comforters. **1840** *Boston Almanac* 126 Theodore Baker ... has for sale ... Quilts, Counterpanes, Comforters, Bockings. **1850** *Knickerb.* XXXV. 76 The bed-clothes being removed and the pillows properly arranged, a comforter is first spread out upon the mattress. **1865** TROWBRIDGE *Three Scouts* 63 There ain't a feather, nor even a straw tick, to spare, say nothing of pillers and comforters! **1890** *Century Mag.* Dec. 303 There was an old lounge in the room, home-made, covered with a calico comforter and a dyed brown shawl. **1913** A. B. EMERSON *R. Fielding at Snow Camp* 28 Later Aunt Alvirah made up the couch with plenty of blankets and thick, downy 'comforters.'

3. A thing that gives physical comfort.

1835 AUDUBON *Ornith. Biog.* III. 145 The fishermen and eggers often use their [=guillemots'] skins with the feathers on as 'comforters' round their wrists. **1837** IRVING *Bonneville* II. 69 He had about him ... a trusty plaid; an old and valued travelling companion and comforter.

***Comfrey.** Also †**comfery.**

***1.** A plant of the genus *Symphytum*, whose root is used medicinally. Also attrib. with *root.*

Quot. 1737 may refer to wild comfrey: see sense 2.

1737 BRICKELL *N. Carolina* 20 In these Parts [are found] ... Comfery, Monks-Rhubarb, Burdock. **1773** FITHIAN *Journal* I. 61 The Hostler, when we had led him to the Stable, applied Spirits of Turpentine, and in the Evening is to fill it with Comfrey Roots pounded Soft. **1784** CUTLER in *Mem. Academy* I. 414 *Symphytum.* ... Comfrey. ... The roots are much used by the common people for sprains. **1817–8** EATON *Botany* (1822) 482 *Symphitum officinale*, comfrey. ... Dr. Cutler says the leaves give a grateful flavor to cakes. **1861** WOOD *Botany* 560 Comfrey [is] a large, coarse-looking mucilaginous plant, in gardens and low grounds. **1889** *Cent.* 1123 The root of the common comfrey, *S. officinale*, ... is used in decoction in dysentery, chronic diarrhea, etc.

+**2.** *Wild comfrey*, a plant (*Cynoglossum virginicum*) closely related to hound's tongue.

1857 GRAY *Botany* 325 *C. Virginicum*, L. (Wild Comfrey.) ... Rich woods, Vermont to Virginia along the mountains, and westward. **1889** *Cent.* 1123/3. **1901** MOHR *Plant Life Ala.* 690 Wild comfrey [grows in] New England west to Minnesota, Ohio Valley to Missouri, Kansas, and Arkansas, south along the mountains from New York to Tennessee and North Carolina.

+**Comida.** *S.W. colloq.* [Sp., 'food,' 'dressed victuals.'] (See quotation.) — **1898** CANFIELD *Maid of Frontier* 212 Pancho's mother . . . had 'comida,' too, which is bread stewed in rich goat's milk with pepper.

***Coming,** *ppl. a.*

1. *Coming appetite,* a developing desire for food. Also fig. {*c. stomach,* 1694–1708}

1853 BALDWIN *Flush Times Ala.* 3 He lied with a coming appetite, growing with what it fed on.

+**2.** Likely to attain prominence; growing in importance.

1865 *Atlantic Mo.* XV. 635 The job was the taking of Charleston and the 'coming man' was Brigadier-General . . . Gillmore. **1868** WOODRUFF *Trotting Horse* 282 Many thought then Lancet was the 'coming horse.' **1869** BOWLES *Our New West* 261, I can discover no successor to Brigham Young. He has men of ability . . . but I see no 'coming man' for his place.

Coming out. [Cf. *come out* v., 1782–] A formal entrance into society. Often attrib. (hyphened) with *ball, party,* etc.

1850 MITCHELL *Lorgnette* I Ser. 198 Her coming out will be a very taking card. **1877** JEWETT *Deephaven* xiii. 280 Miss Sally told us a long story about her friends and about her 'coming-out party.' **1883** *Harper's Mag.* Oct. 726/1 [A horse's] first race is an occasion for which he is prepared with as much pains as a young girl for her coming-out party. **1901** CHURCHILL *Crisis* 91 Miss Carvel's coming-out party was the chief topic. **1909** 'O. HENRY' *Roads of Destiny* 62 Then Aunt Maggie says she is going to give me a coming-out banquet in the Bonton. **1915** D. R. CAMPBELL *Proving Virginia* 51 My aunt in New York gave me a coming-out ball.

+**Commandancia.** *S.W.* [Sp.] The commandancy; the power of a commandant. — **1848** BRYANT *California* (1849) 283 The village of Branciforte, . . . on account of the smallness of its population, is subject to the commandancia of Monterey.

Commandant. The commanding officer at a post. {1687–}

1798 MORSE *Amer. Gazetteer* 172/1 All the settlers in these districts [= Florida Terr.] are under the immediate orders of the military commandants. **1823** J. THACHER *Military Jrnl.* 354 The commandant of the garrison . . . assured him that this would never be required. **1838** FLAGG *Far West* II. 165 Each district had its commandant, and each village its syndic. **1843** F. L. HAWKS *D. Boone* 131 [Boone] was appointed by the Spanish commandant the commandant over the district of St. Charles. **1847** FRÉMONT in *30th Congress 1 Sess.* Senate Rep. No. 75, 3 In the discharge of my official relations in California, as military commandant and governor of that territory, I incurred liabilities. **1865** R. H. KELLOGG *Rebel Prisons* 378 A subordinate asked the post commandant, Maj. John H. Gee, 'Shall I give the prisoners full rations?' **1867** GOSS *Soldier's Story* 163 The commandant of the prison had full knowledge of all its details.

+**Com(m)andante.** *S.W.* [Sp.] = COMMANDANT.

1844 KENDALL *Santa Fé Exped.* II. 119 Colonel Velasco . . . took his leave, at the same time introducing the commandante of our new guard. **1846** SAGE *Scenes Rocky Mts.* xx, The Mexicans seized their arms for resistance, and the commandante advancing demanded of the nearest assailant [etc.]. **1897** *Outing* XXX. 74/2 In the old adobe . . . Resánoff dined with the comandante. **1900** SMITHWICK *Evol. of State* 30 The Comandante offered to . . . get an outfit. **1904** 'O. HENRY' *Cabbages & Kings* 12 The *comandante* . . . wrote in his secret memorandum book the accusive fact that Señor Goodwin had on that momentous date received a telegram.

Commandant-general. The principal officer at a post. {1827}

1803 in *Ann. 8th Congress* 2 Sess. 1500 In the Illinois there are commandants at New Madrid, St. Genevieve . . . and St. Andrew's, all subordinate to the commandant-general. **1807** in Pike *Exped.* (1810) III. App. 62 Presented to the commandant-general in a blanket cappot. **1846** POLK *Diary* 142 Col. Frémont with his men had been attacked near San Francisco by Castro, the Commandant General of Mexico in California. **1848** BRYANT *California* (1849) 279 Upper California . . . takes the character of territory, the government of which is under the charge of a commandant-general.

***Commander.**

***1.** One who commands a ship; latterly as the title of a naval officer.

1622 'MOURT' *Relation* 83 He . . . knew by name the most of the Captaines, Commanders, & Masters that vsually come. **1653** *Suffolk Deeds* I. 4 Robert Cannon of London master and Commander of the good shipp called the charitie of Boston of the burthen of sixty Tunnes. **1685** SEWALL *Letter-Book* I. 2 Invoice of goods shipped on Board the America Mr Heugh Sampson Commander Bound for London. **1711** *Boston News-Letter* 9 July 2/2 Capt. Tho. Butler late Commander of Her Majesty's Ship the Dunkirk. **1867** EDWARDS *Shelby* 485 The Westfield . . . was blown up, and with her, Commander Renshaw, Lieutenant Zimmerman and all her crew.

***2.** An officer who commands a military force.

1654 JOHNSON *Wonder-w. Prov.* 191 The Government is divided into four Counties, . . . each containing a Regiment, over whom the chief Commander is only a Serjeant-Major. **1676** *N.Y. State Col. Hist.* XII. 556, I do hereby . . . appoint you, Capt. John Collyer, to be Commander in Delaware River and Bay . . . And the officers and Souldiers thereof are required to obey you as their Commander. **1720** *Mass. Ho. Repr. Jrnls.* II. 309 It has been accustomary, for the commander of Castle William, to have Three Servants. **1846** POLK *Diary* 175 A more permanent government should be provided by Congress over the conquered provinces than the temporary governments which had been established by our naval and military commanders. **1861** *Army Regulations* 3 Nothing contrary to the tenor of these Regulations will be enjoined in any part of the forces of the United States by any commander whatsoever. **1862** in Kettell *Hist. Rebellion* II. 588 Army corps commanders will immediately establish mounted patrols under charge of commissioned officers. **1867** EDWARDS *Shelby* 504 [He] at last rejoined his old commander Shelby upon his ranch at Cordova. **1886** LOGAN *Great Conspiracy* 474 The Rebels themselves . . . brought the Thirty-seventh Congress, as well as the Military Commanders, and the President, to an early consideration of the Slavery question.

+**b.** An Indian chief. *Obs.*

1622 'MOURT' *Relation* 98 Massasoyt, the greatest Commander amongst the Savages. **1654** *N.C. Col. Rec.* I. 18 They found the great commander of those parts with his Indians a-hunting.

+**3.** A military governor.

During reconstruction in the South after the Civil War, the military governors were called commanders, as in later quots.

1637 *Md. Archives* I. 2 Capt: Robert Evelin, gent, Commander of the Ile of Kent. **1865** in Fleming *Hist. Reconstruction* I. 204 Commanders of Districts will circulate this order at once after receiving it. **1867** *Ib.* 430 Commanders in each of the States comprised in this military district are authorized to appoint one or more general supervisors. **1898** PAGE *Red Rock* 81 It reached the ears of Colonel Krafton, the new commander of that district.

+**4.** An overseer of slaves. *Obs.*

1842 *McDonogh Papers* 65, I was in the habit of never retiring to rest at night until seeing my commander, and knowing that the people had come in from their work.

Commander in chief. {1654–}

+**1.** The officer in command of the military forces of an American colony, often the civilian governor.

1684 *Plymouth Laws* 203 It shall be felony for any person . . . to serve in America in an hostile manner under . . . any . . . forreigne prince . . . without speciall licence for so doing, under ye hand and seal of ye Gov[erno]r or Comaunder in chiefe of this Colony. **1705** *Boston News-Letter* 25 June 2/2 No Governour, Lieut. Governour or Commander in Chief of this Province shall receive any Gift or Present from the Country. **1709** *N.C. Col. Rec.* I. 703 We humbly offer, that your Majesties Royal Letters Mandatory, be sent to the Governor or Commander in Chief of the said Colony of Virginia. **1721** *Mass. Ho. Repr. Jrnls.* III. 9 Payment of Money either to you the Governour, or to the Commander in Chief, or to any of His Majesties Council. *Ib.* 76 The Power of Adjourning the Great and General Court is wholly Vested in their Governour or Commander in Chief. **1723** *New-Eng. Courant* 7–14 Jan. 2/2 *Quære,* Whether . . . the Ministers of this Province, ought now to pray for Samuel Shute Esq.; as our immediate Governour, and at the same time pray for the Lieut. Governour as Commander in Chief? **1744** *N.J. Archives* 1 Ser. VI. 192 The Captain General or Commander in Chief may order one or two troops of horse.

+**2.** The highest officer in the Armies of the Revolution, namely George Washington (1775–1783).

1775 *Journals Cont. Congress* II. 100 To George Washington, Esq. This Congress having appointed you to be General and Commander in chief of the Army of the united Colonies. **1783** WASHINGTON *Writings* X. 163, The public interest might be benefited if the Commander-in-Chief of the Army were let more into the political and pecuniary state of our affairs than he is. *Ib.* 330 It only remains for the Commander-in-chief to address himself once more, and that for the last time, to the armies of the United States. **1790** R. PUTNAM in *Memoirs* 243 The utility and policy of . . . forming settlements that should extend from the Ohio to Lake Erie was clearly pointed out in a letter from the Commander in Cheif. **1823** J. THACHER *Military Jrnl.* 349 Our Commander in Chief fairly out generaled Sir Henry Clinton.

+**3.** The military officer at the head of the nation's armed forces. (Unofficial since the adoption of the Constitution. See 4.)

'The title is often unofficially applied to the acting general officer of highest rank (*i.e.,* the senior major-general)' (*O.E.D.*).

1777 *Jrnls. Cont. Congress* IX. 922/2 The United States . . . shall never engage in a war, . . . nor appoint a commander in chief of the army or navy, unless nine states assent to the same. **1807** JEFFERSON in *Ann. 10th Congress* 1 Sess. I. 17, I informed Congress . . . of the enterprises against the public peace . . . by Aaron Burr and his associates, . . . defeated by the fidelity of the Army and energy of the Commander-in-Chief. **1868** COPPÉE *U.S. Grant* 258 On the 2d of March, 1864, Grant was confirmed by the United States Senate . . . as Lieutenant-General in the Army of the United States. This put him over all our other generals, but did not, without a special order, make him commander-in-chief of our armies.

b. Applied, semiofficially, to the various commanders of the military forces during the Civil War. (Cf. 4.)

1868 COPPÉE *U.S. Grant* 259 There were the President and his entire cabinet; General Halleck, the retiring commander-in-chief. *Ib.* 263 Such

. . . was the man . . . who had come to Washington, on his own merits, . . . to be made lieutenant-general and commander-in-chief. **1887** A. L. LONG *Memoirs Lee* 401 One of these [events] was the appointment of General Lee, on February 6, 1865, as commander-in-chief of all the Confederate armies. **1895** M. A. JACKSON *Memoirs* 324 General Lee, having arrived with Longstreet upon the scene of action, the morning of the 30th found the commander-in-chief at the head of his army.

c. Often used to designate the head of an army in the field, or of a state militia; also the senior officer of a naval station.

1819 *McDonogh Papers* 32 The commander-in-chief of our army, General Andrew Jackson, dispatched a flag of truce to the British fleet with three gentlemen. **1862** *Mich. Gen. Statutes* (1882–3) I. 282 The commander-in-chief may order out, by draft, voluntary enlistment, or otherwise, the whole, or so much of the militia of this state as the public necessity demands. **1865** *Atlantic Mo.* XV. 717, [I] was duly . . . rewarded by being offered the honorary and honorable title of A. D. C. to the commander-in-chief of Virginia. **1873** *Newton Kansan* 26 June 1/4 There dwelt Commodore Chauncey, Commander-in-Chief of the Naval Station, New York. *fig.* **1890** RYAN *Told in Hills* 35 You are going to Hardy's camp to act as commander-in-chief of the eastern tramps in it.

+**4.** According to the Constitution, the President.

1787 *Constitution* ii. §2 The President shall be commander in chief of the army and navy of the United States, and of the militia of the several States, when called into the actual service of the United States. **1808** *Ann. 10th Congress* 1 Sess. I. 335 The President of the United States is Commander-in-chief of the Army and Navy. **1858** *S. Lit. Messenger* XXVI. 87/2 The Constitution tells us that the Commander-in-Chief of the Army and Navy is the President of the United States.

b. According to the Constitution of the Confederacy, the President of the Confederacy.

1861 *Constitution of the Confederacy* ii. § 2 The President shall be Commander in Chief of the Army and Navy of the Confederate States. **1868** F. H. ALFRED *Life J. Davis* 370 It is true that the President did not delegate to these officers his constitutional functions as commander-in-chief.

***Commandery.** +(See quot. 1874.) — **1867** *Mich. Gen. Statutes* (1882–3) I. 1147 Any ten or more residents of this state being members either of any commandery of knights templars, council, chapter of royal arch masons, [etc.]. *Ib.*, The name and location of the commandery, council or chapter of which they are members. **1874** MACKEY *Encycl. Freemasonry* 175/2 In the United States all regular assemblies of Knights Templars are called Commanderies. . . . These Commanderies derive their warrants of Constitution from a Grand Commandery, or . . . from the Grand Encampment of the United States.

+**Command-in-chief,** *v. tr.* To have chief command of (a military force). — **1759** in Franklin *Writings* (1840) III. 290 All [regiments were] to be commanded in chief by a general officer of rank. **1846** QUITMAN in *Life & Corr.* I. 269 Col. Davis, of the Mississippi Riflemen, on the part of Maj. Gen. Taylor, commanding-in-chief the United States forces; . . . and Señor Manuel M. Llano, . . . on the part of Señor Don Pedro Ampudia, commanding-in-chief the army of the North of Mexico.

***Commanding,** *a.* With *general* or (usually) *officer:* In command.

1720 *Mass. Ho. Repr. Jrnls.* II. 307 If any do not appear, the Commanding officer [is] to give the reason of such absent Men. **1776** *Jrnls. Cont. Congress* V. 437 The commanding officer of the riffle batallion of associators in this city [=Lewistown]. **1804** CLARK in *Lewis & C. Exped.* (1904) I. 19 The evidences aduced against William Warner & Hugh Hall . . . for speaking in a language . . . tending to bring into disrespect the orders of the Commanding officer. **1885** *Century Mag.* XXX. 323/1 The commanding-general heard full reports. **1907** *Indian Laws & Tr.* III. 268 The powers conferred by section twenty-one hundred and forty of the Revised Statutes upon . . . commanding officers of military posts are hereby conferred upon the special agent of the Indian Bureau.

‖**Commandment sin.** An immoral act, contrary to one of the Ten Commandments. — **1900** DIX *Deacon Bradbury* 29 As the deacon would afterward constantly say to his wife, it was no 'Commandment sin.'

Commelina. The dayflower (of the genus *Commelina*). — [**1846** EMORY *Military Reconn.* 13 We find in the bottoms . . . commelina angustifolia.] **1901** MOHR *Plant Life Ala.* 431 Hirtellous Commelina [grows in] Pennsylvania and New Jersey to Florida; Ohio Valley west to Missouri.

***Commence,** *v. intr.* To take an academic degree. Often with the complement of the name of the degree. *Obs.*

Adopted at Harvard from the usage of Cambridge University, England. **a1649** WINTHROP *Hist.* II. 84 Nine bachelors commenced at Cambridge. **1674** *Harvard Rec.* I. 60 Ordered that the four persons that commenced Masters in the year 1674 they having first paid their detriments unto the Colledg; shall . . . be rebated forty shillings a peece. **1683** *Mass. H. S. Coll.* 4 Ser. VIII. 510, I was much pleased to see the names of those who commenced in your college. **1690** SEWALL *Diary* I. 324 Mr. Rogers and Emmerson should have Commenc'd last year, but were hindred by Sickness. **1766** CLAP *Ann. Yale-Coll.* 20 Four Senior Sophisters . . . received the Degree of Batchelor of Arts, and several others commenced Masters. **1787** CUTLER in *Life & Corr.* I. 210, I have not seen him . . . since we commenced at college twenty-two years ago. **1812** in W. Emerson *1st Church Boston* 211 Charles Chauncy . . . was . . . sent to the university of Cambridge, where he commenced bachelor of divinity. **1820** in *Princeton Book* (1879) 169 Thirty-one commenced in the class before mine, and the same number in the class to which I belonged. These were the largest classes that had commenced at that time. **1879** *Ib.*, Even among ourselves the verb 'to commence,' in the sense of taking the first degree in the arts, has utterly disappeared from the parlance of college technicalities.

***Commencement.**

***1.** The exercises of prize giving, degree taking, etc., at the end of the academic year.

1643 *New Eng. First Fruits* II. iv, So have they [*sc.* students] lately kept two solemne Acts for their Commencement. **1670** *Mass. H. S. Coll.* 4 Ser. I. 13 August 2. Was printed our theses for ye commencement. **1798** A. HOLMES *E. Stiles* 14 At that period, the candidates for the first degree had no higher exercise at Commencement, except a salutatory oration. **1812** MELISH *Travels* I. 71 A friend, with whom she was to live during *commencement.* **1851** *Harper's Mag.* III. 415/2 During the past month have been celebrated the Annual Commencements of a number of the colleges of the country. **1877** *Ib.* March 580/1 At Antioch they act a play the night before Commencement. **1887** *Ib.* Jan. 315/2 There is something of the same feeling in the melody of college songs heard at a little distance on awakening in the night before Commencement. **1902** *Ib.* May 878/2 Olivia with Lois was to start for Europe immediately after Commencement.

2. Attrib. with *anniversary, ball, cake,* etc.

1843 *Yale Lit. Mag.* VIII. 116 The week of the commencement anniversary of Raravan College. **1814** *S.C. Statutes* (1839) V. 725 Hereafter the students of the South Carolina College shall be . . . prohibited from holding their commencement ball in the State House. **1707** SEWALL *Diary* II. 192, I gave Mr. Stoddard for Madam Stoddard two half pounds of Chockalot, instead of Commencement Cake. **1851** HALL *College Words* 70 *Commencement card.* At Union College, there is issued annually at Commencement a card containing a programme of the exercises of the day. . . . To be 'on the Commencement card' is esteemed an honor, and is eagerly sought for. **1691** *Harvard Rec.* II. 830 The Steward's allowance for providing and cooking the Commencement Dinner. **1778** STILES *Lit. Diary* (1901) II. 312, 1777 Sept. 10. No Commenc[emen]t Exercises. **1683** *Harvard Rec.* I. 73 Inventory . . . Commencement Linnen 5 Diaper Table cloethes. **1871** BAGG *At Yale* 150 Below the society cut is the date . . . of Commencement night. **1867** *Atlantic Mo.* Jan. 121/1 It is the thirst of his immortal nature,—as a young gentleman not long since said in a pretty Commencement poem. **1854** *Harper's Mag.* IX. 555/2 Sing on undauntedly, occasional Commencement poets! **1798** *Harvard Laws* 6 The parents, or guardians of those who have been accepted . . . shall . . . give bond to the President . . . to repair their chambers or studies, should any damage be done to them during the Commencement season. **1850** *Knickerb.* XXXVI. 526 The exaggeration of language and sentiment which are almost proverbially the characteristics of commencement speeches. **1895** WILLIAMS *Princeton Stories* 42 He bade fair to graduate a typical poler with a bad breath and an eye on Commencement stage and special honors. **1759** *Essex Inst. Coll.* XLIX. 12 Cloudy but excessive Hot. Commencement weather. **1734** in Peirce *Hist. Harvard* App. 142 No other scholars . . . shall continue in the College from and after the Commencement week.

Commencement day. The day when commencement exercises are held. {1606–} — **1676** SEWALL *Diary* I. 15 Commencement day. **1698** — *Letter-Book* 203 Writt a Letter . . . enclosing what I spoke at the Desk at Cambridg Augt. 11, 1674, on the Commencment day. **1858** HOLMES *Autocrat* 107 'Commencement day' always reminds me of the start for the 'Derby.' **1900** H. ROBERTSON *Red Blood & Blue* 289 The assemblage reminded Outcault of the old Commencement Day gatherings, always the largest known in Ferne Run.

Commencer. {1655–} A college student who is about to be graduated. (See quot. 1851.) *Obs.*

1643 *New Englands First Fruits* 17 A Copie of the Questions given and maintained by the Commencers in their publick Acts, printed in Cambridge in New England. **1681** *Harvard Rec.* I. 240 The reverend . . . is to begin the day with prayer & give the Commencers their degrees. **1688** SEWALL *Letter-Book* I. 85, I inclosed the Commencers theses. **1693** in S. A. Eliot *Hist. Harvard Coll.* (1848) 33 The custom taken up in the College . . . for the commencers to have plumb-cake, is dishonorable to the College. **1734** *Harvard Rec.* I. 148 No commencer shall have at his Chamber any Plumb cake, plain cake or Pyes, or hot meats of any sort except what is left of the dinner in the Hall. **1851** HALL *College Words* 70 *Commencer*, in American colleges, a member of the Senior Class, after the examination for degrees.

***Commerce.** Used attrib. and in phrases: *Commerce Clause, Commerce Commission, Department of Commerce,* etc.

See also *Chamber of Commerce* (CHAMBER *n.* 3) and *Committee of Commerce and Manufactures* (COMMITTEE 3).

1898 PRENTICE & EGAN *Commerce Clause* 15 The judicial construction of the commerce clause by the Supreme Court of the United States begins with the case of *Gibbons v. Ogden.* **1914** McLaughlin & Hart *Cycl. Amer. Govt.* I. 334 *Commerce Clause.* The Constitution of the United States gives Congress power 'to regulate commerce with the foreign nations, and among the several states, and with the Indian tribes.' **1900** *Independent* LII. 412/2 The transfer of these [bureaus] and various other related bureaus to the Department of Commerce would greatly relieve . . . the Treasury and Interior Departments. **1913** *Rev. of Reviews* XLVII. 397/2 The new Department of Labor . . . will have its Bureau of Information, which ought to do many things for industrial labor . . . that the Department of Commerce does for importers and exporters. **1900** *Independent* LII. 412/1 The different commercial and industrial organizations of this country have recognized the need of a new department of the Government whose function and service would be well described by the title, 'The Department of Commerce and Industries.' **1914** McLaughlin & Hart *Cycl. Amer. Govt.* I. 333 *Commerce and Labor, Department of*, an executive department of the Federal Government, established in 1903. **1903** *N.Y. Herald* 5 June 7/1 Among the interesting announcements was a donation of $10,000 to endow a professorship in the School of Commerce in memory of the late Dean Haskins. **1903** *Outlook* LXXIII. 471/2 The special interest which has attached to the anti-trust legislation, and the powers conferred by it upon the new Secretary of Commerce. **1914** McLaughlin & Hart *Cycl. Amer. Govt.* I. 333 Following is a list of the Secretaries of Commerce and Labor from . . . 1903 to . . . 1913.

Commerce destroyer. A cruiser designed to destroy the merchant ships of the enemy. — **1886** *Harper's Mag.* June 20/1 She could also be of service as a commerce destroyer. **1889** Mahan *Influence Sea Power* 31 Commerce-destroyers scatter, that they may see and seize more prey.

Commercial, *a.* {1687–}

1. Of commerce: Pertaining to business transactions or the carrying on of trade.

1789 *Ann. 1st Congress* I. 234 It is said we should enable those nations, with whom we have commercial treaties, to participate more largely of our trade. *Ib.* 205 We soon shall be in a condition, we now are in a condition, to wage a commercial warfare with that nation [G. Britain]. **1791** Bartram *Travels* 477 [Within ten years] arose a flourishing commercial town, the seat of government of the county. **1828** *Yankee* May 145/2 Of most of our large papers, seven eighths are made up either of advertisements or of ship-news, and commercial-news, price-currents, etc. **1840** *Picayune* 16 Aug. 2/6 State of Louisiana—Commercial Court of New Orleans.—The creditors of John Wiley are hereby notified to appear. **1841** *S. Lit. Messenger* VII. 5/2 Our Commercial Marine keeps in constant training seamen more than enough to man all the ships that this nation will ever build. **1843** *P. O. Laws & Reg.* II. 21 The Price Currents, etc., printed at stated intervals, and sent by great Banking and Commercial houses to their customers, are not newspapers. **1860** Mordecai *Virginia* 43 These 'Commercial Conventions,' as they are called, composed more of planters, lawyers and politicans than merchants, assemble to discuss subjects of which few of them have any practical knowledge. **1866** *Internal Revenue Guide* 70 Salaried clerks or men hired by the month . . . should not be required to take licenses as commercial brokers. **1866** Richardson *Secret Service* 57 My dispatches . . . were addressed alternately to half a dozen banking and commercial firms in New York. **1881** *Chicago Times* 12 March, It is said that the initiative in the competitive cutting of tariffs was taken by the Commercial Express Fast Freight line. **1882** *Century Mag.* April 884/1 Our domestic jocosity, . . . reserving for its most palpable hits the bully, the visionary speculator, the gamester, and the commercial agent. **1887** *Courier-Journal* 8 Feb. 3/4 The highest compliment that can be paid Mr. Lane is to say that those who have seen commercial tourists en route will recognize him at a glance. **1911** *Okla. Session Laws* 3 Legisl. 126 Any commercial club . . . shall be permitted to lease or purchase land from the Commissioners of the Land Office.

2. Phrases. *Commercial emporium*, a place of extensive business. *C. fertilizer*, a fertilizer of the kinds placed on the general market. *C. high school*, a high school in which commercial subjects are taught. *C. note paper* (see quotation). *C. states*, the states whose chief business is non-agricultural. (See also Commercial college, paper, etc.)

1835 Hoffman *Winter in West* II. 65 The ancient city of St. Louis, the capital and metropolis, though not yet the commercial emporium, of the grand valley of the Mississippi. **1837** *S. Lit. Messenger* III. 178 The way I looked down on the 'aristocracy of wealth' . . . as I strutted through the Broadway of the 'Commercial Emporium' . . . was truly 'a sin.' *Ib.* 659, I am on my way to the great commercial emporium New York. — **1888** *Vt. Agric. Rep.* X. 32 If half the money spent each year for commercial fertilizer was spent annually in preventing the waste of the valuable properties of manure, . . . the crops would increase in value. **1896** *Ib.* XV. 46 That our Crops are deficient in fertility is shown . . . by the large quantities of commercial fertilizers that are annually bought. **1904** T. Watson *Bethany* 11 No commercial fertilizers were bought in those days. — **1914** McLaughlin & Hart *Cycl. Amer. Govt.* III. 259 *Schools, High, Commercial.* The leading cities in the United States are providing special high school courses, and even special high schools, for boys and girls who intend to enter business. — **1879** Webster *Suppl.* 1550 *Commercial note-paper*, a small size of writing-paper, usually about 5 by 7½ or 8 inches. — **1781** *N.H. Comm. Safety Rec.* 247 Money has never been so plenty here as in the Commercial States. **1789** *Ann. 1st Congress* I. 211 The impost must come from the commercial States.

+Commercial college. A school specializing in commercial techniques; a business college.

1858 *Hunt's Merchant's Mag.* XXXIX. 412 Commercial colleges . . . are peculiar institutions, which have sprung but lately into vigorous life in response to a general and widely-felt want. **1870** *Rep. Comm. Educ.* (1875) 75, 26 commercial colleges have been reported to the Bureau. **1877** *Harper's Mag.* March 604/1 By virtue of the handsome figures I learned to make at Commercial College, I proved to her it would be cheapest to hire the car. **1887** *N. Amer. Rev.* CXLIV. 465 The merchant's clerk who has been educated in a commercial college [is] superior to one who has merely picked up his knowledge at random.

Commercial paper. Negotiable paper, such as bills of exchange, promissory notes, etc.

1836 in Mackenzie *Van Buren* (1846) 176 The demolition of the Usury laws, in relation to commercial paper, . . . is probably desirable. **1846** *Mich. Gen. Statutes* (1882–3) I. 459 It shall be lawful for all parties loaning money in this state, to take, reserve, or discount interest upon any note, bond, bill, draft, acceptance, or other commercial paper. **1875** *Chicago Tribune* 2 July 3/4 Commercial Paper and Mortgages bought and sold; loans made on real estate. **1900** Nelson *A B C Wall St.* 134 *Commercial paper*, negotiable notes drawn against the buyer of merchandise.

Commercial travel(l)er. A traveling salesman for a wholesale business firm. {1855–}

[**1830** N. S. Wheaton *Jrnl.* 497, I found a number of commercial travellers.] **1870** O. Logan *Before Footlights* 261 On the sea everybody is sick as a general thing, and the favored few who are not, are, for the most part, the ubiquitous commercial traveler, the . . . man who writes his 'voyage round the world,' [etc.]. **1880** *Harper's Mag.* Aug. 373 He became a commercial traveller, and was away from the city for months at a time. **1884** Sweet & Knox *Through Texas* 343 One of the parties was a consumptive from Connecticut; the other, a commercial traveller from New York. **1887** C. B. George *40 Yrs. on Rail* 178 Commercial travelers with their heavy sample trunks did not exist as in these later times. **1896** *N.Y. Tribune* 7 Sept. 1/3 A meeting of the Chicago division of the Commercial Travellers' Home Association was held last evening. **1900** Goodlander *Fort Scott* 92 In 1862 was about the first advent of the drummer, or commercial traveler visiting Fort Scott.

Commissariat.

1. The department of the military service that provides food and other supplies. {1799– C. James *Regimental Companion* 30}

1776 *Jrnls. Cont. Congress* V. 752 Mr. Trumbull's appointment to the commissariat. **1779** Jefferson *Writings* IV. 51 Wagonage, indeed, seems to the commissariat an article not worth economising. **1849** Quitman in *Life & Corr.* II. 20 No officer . . . contributed more to our success in Mexico by his admirable administration of the commissariat.

transf. **1865** *Atlantic Mo.* XV. 559 We despatched . . . some of our best pedestrians, as commissariat of the party.

2. Food supply or provisions. {1861–}

1856 Kane *Arctic Explor.* I. 56 [It] has prevented our rifles from contributing any material aid to our commissariat. *Ib.* 126 He saw seven reindeer. . . . This looks promising for our winter commissariat. **1867** Edwards *Shelby* 271 He must replenish his commissariat from the surrounding country. **1870** Keim *Sheridan's Troopers* 68 They constitute the commissariat of the Indian, and govern frequently his ability for war or control his desire for peace. **1900** in I. Richey *When Love is King* 3 Where the Indian and his commissariat, the buffalo, wandered when these vast plains were first opened up to the white race for homes, in 1854.

3. Attrib. with *article*, *department*.

1780 Jos. Reed *Life & Corr.* (1847) II. 227 We have quartered the whole number of wagons and horses on the counties, as well as the commissariat articles. **1821** *Ann. 17th Congress* 1 Sess. I. 28 One third of the expense of the late war would have been saved to this nation if we had had at its commencement well organized commissariat and Quartermaster's Departments. **1875** Stowe *We & Neighbors* 24, I am head marshal of the commisariat department—committee of one on supplies, and all that.

*** Commissary.**

*** 1.** A military officer in charge of food and other supplies.

1671 *N.Y. State Col. Hist.* XII. 487 That the Places, where the Towneships upon the River shall bee kept, bee appointed & Agreed upon by the Schout, Commissaryes and the rest of the offic[e]rs there. **1676** *Conn. Rec.* II. 298 Such persons shall address themselues to the Commissary, who is ordered to deliuer unto them out of the country gunns in the Treasurer's hand. **1712** *N.C. Col. Rec.* I. 879, I have likewise appointed Mr. Furnifold Green, Commissary to impress and supply the army. **1776** *Battle of Brooklyn* I. i, If he has credit enough with the Commissary, to get his canteens filled with rum. **1848** Parkman in *Knickerb.* XXXII. 312 He told Coates, the master-wagoner, that the commissary at the fort had given him an order for sick-rations. **1895** M. A. Jackson *Memoirs* 514 He had a pet commissary, General Banks.

b. Used in designating officers of specified duties.

1757 in *Lett. to Washington* II. 79, I prevailed on him to accompany me, under expectation of an appointment as Commissary of Musters, added to some other Commission. **1775** J. Adams in *Warren-Adams Lett.* I. 86, I have laboured with my Colleagues to agree upon proper Persons to recommend for a Quarter Master General, a Commissary of Musters and a Commissary of Artillery—but in vain. **1776** *Jrnls. Cont. Congress* VI. 858 *Resolved*, . . . That a commissary of cloathing be appointed for each of the armies of the United States, whose duty shall be to make constant returns to the assemblies or conventions of the respective states. **1852** Glisan *Jrnl. Army Life* 10 July, The Commissary of Subsistence gave to the Indians a beef upon which they feasted to their hearts' content.

*2. The representative of a bishop; an officer in church government. Now hist.

[**1654** JOHNSON *Wonder-w. Prov.* 101 The poore people of Christ ... began to deeme themselves in a more dolorous condition then when they were in the Commissaries Court, and Prelates Prisons.] **1743** MACSPARRAN *Diary* 1 Many secret Doings to obtrude ministers on Places without their Privity or the Privity of Commissary. **1875** *Scribner's Mo.* Nov. 6/2 The presidents were the 'commissaries' or representatives of the bishops in the colony.

+3. Food supplies; = COMMISSARIAT 2.

1883 *Century Mag.* Sept. 672 This enforced idleness reduced our commissary to an alarming minimum. **1895** REMINGTON *Pony Tracks* 180 Our appetites had been sharpened by a nine hours' fast, when a soldier called us to the 'commissaries' which were spread out on a pack canvas.

+4. A food store, sometimes containing general merchandise also.

1882 *Rep. Indian Affairs* 1 Sept. 151 Two new buildings ... have been constructed; a commissary with offices, and a council-house with guard rooms. **1898** PAGE *Red Rock* 37 He is a clerk in old Bolter's commissary. **1902** GORDON *Recoll. Lynchburg* 106 Even these expenses are often 'booked' at the commissary. **1905** *Forestry Bureau Bul.* No. 61, 33 *Commissary*, a general store for supplying lumbermen.

b. A commissary wagon.

1905 A. ADAMS *Outlet* 245 A wagon-way could be easily cut in the bank and the commissaries lowered to the river's edge with a rope to the rear axle.

5. Attrib. with *building, bureau, butter*, etc.

1851 GLISAN *Jrnl. Army Life* 81 The buildings will be arranged into ... a parallelogram ... —the commissary and quartermaster buildings at one end. **1892** *Harper's Weekly* 9 Jan. 42/1 General Meigs's plan of reorganization for the Quartermaster's Department was also adopted in the Commissary Bureau. **1873** BEADLE *Undevel. West* 528 For the last three days we lived on Navajo bread, coffee, and 'commissary butter,' straight. **1792** *Ann. 2nd Congress* 1141 He ... never heard an individual ... point out any defects, except in the commissary and pack-horse departments. **1872** *Atlantic Mo.* Jan. 27 One of the commissary-presidents of the college ... could not proceed against the clergy for drunkenness, because he was himself a drunkard. **1895** *Outing* XXVII. 255/2 The non-commissioned staff comprises a sergeant-major, a quarter-master-sergeant, a commissary-sergeant, and a hospital steward. **1780** R. PUTNAM in *Memoirs* 154 Either a commesary store should be keept here or some extra provition should be lodged here for the supply of such small parties.

***Commissary general.** The military official in charge of the commissary service.

1776 J. HANCOCK in Sparks *Corr. Rev.* (1853) I. 236 The cost of a ration, as furnished by the Commissary-General. **1777** *Jrnls. Cont. Congress* VII. 12 *Resolved*, That the treasurer be directed to pay to Joseph Trumbull, Esq. commissary general, the sum of three hundred thousand dollars. **1861** *Army Regulations* 241 Whenever subsistence stores are purchased, the advertisements and bids, ... will be forwarded by the purchasing officer to the Commissary-General. **1892** M. A. JACKSON *Gen. Jackson* 285 Lee is out of rations again, and Jackson is detailed to call on the 'commissary-general.'

b. In phrases: *Commissary general of purchases, of stores and provisions.*

1778 *Jrnls. Cont. Congress* X. 48 The commissary general of purchases is invested with powers adequate to, and sufficient for, the purpose of importing salt for the use of the army. **1775** *Ib.* II. 94 *Resolved* ... That there be one Commissary general of stores and provisions, and that his pay be eighty dollars per month.

***Commissaryship.** The position of commissary. {-1726} — **1811** J. ADAMS *Works* IX. 633 All applications ... for commissions and promotions in the army, and for contracts, commissaryships, quartermasterships, &c., were committed to me.

+**Commissary wagon.** A vehicle which carries food and other provisions. — **1848** J. S. ROBINSON *Santa Fé Exped.* 10 If we cannot overtake the commissary wagons we shall have nothing to eat. **1865** BOUDRYE *Fifth N.Y. Cavalry* 92 Long trains of forage and commissary wagons may be seen passing to and fro.

***Commission.**

*1. A charge or set of instructions given by an authority; an appointment to perform certain functions, e.g., of a particular office.

1624 J. SMITH *Virginia* IV. 163 Being enioyned by our Commission not to vnplant nor wrong the Saluages. **1642** *Plymouth Laws* 307 Their Commission is as followeth. **1685** *Penna. Col. Rec.* I. 142 To make Voyd all other Commissions if any be. **1771** FRANKLIN *Autobiog.* 286 He would promote me by sending me with a cargo of flour and bread, etc., to the West Indies, and procure me commissions from others which would be profitable. **1777** *Jrnls. Cont. Congress* IX. 913/2 Nor shall any State grant commissions to any ships or vessels of war, nor letters of marque or reprisal, except it be after a declaration of war by the United States. **1804** *Lewis & Clark Exped.* (1905) VII. 47 He gave 3 of the head chiefs a Meaddle Each; and the other three Commissions in the Name of the president of the U.S. **1857** in Johnson *Anderson Co., Kansas* (1877) 79 Therefore I call upon your excellency ... to issue the commissions for the respective officers as was [*sic*] elected.

*b. *Commission of the peace*, authority vested in persons to act as justices of the peace; also the group of persons with such authority.

1701 *Penna. Archives* I. 142 With this comes a new Com[miss]ion of ye Peace for ye County of Newcastle. **1707** *N.J. Archives* 1 Ser. III. 200 My Lord ... had already put him ... and Anthony Woodward in the Commission of the Peace. **1788** FRANKLIN *Autobiog.* 374 The governor put me into the commission of the peace.

c. An appointment as officer in the army or navy. {1643-}

1811 [see COMMISSARYSHIP]. **1865** *Atlantic Mo.* XV. 507 A boy ... cashiered from his colonelcy for selling the commissions in his regiment. **1865** KELLOGG *Rebel Prisons* 230 Quite a large number of Sergeants, holding officers' commissions, ... were ... told by the rebels they were destined to our lines for exchange. **1870** O. LOGAN *Before Footlights* 251 Get a commission! Is that the way to serve your country?

*2. The warrant or written instrument setting forth the charge or appointment to an office.

1636 *Md. Council Proc.* 40 After Sir John Harvey had expressed his Intent to the Councell heere of departing the Colonye, we opened his Maj[es]ties Commission. **1692** SEWALL *Diary* I. 370 After Lecture, the Governour delivers Mr. Stoughton his Commission as Chief Justice of the Superior Court. **1777** *Jrnls. Cont. Congress* VII. 8 *Ordered*, That the Committee of Secret Correspondence prepare a commission for doct. Franklin. **1845** POLK *Diary* 26, I signed the commission of Hon. John Slidell as Envoy Extraordinary.

b. *Commission of bankrupt*, an instrument declaring bankruptcy. *Obs.* {1707-}

1714 *Boston News-Letter* 14-21 June 2/2 Whereas there is a Commission of Bankrupt Issued out against Thomas Givin of Boston. *Ib.* 4-11 Oct. 2/2 These are to give Notice that the Commissioners in a Commission of Bankrupt awarded against Louis Boucher of Boston ... intend to meet at the Great Britain Coffee-House.

*3. A group of persons charged with special duties; a body of commissioners.

1854 BARTLETT *Narrative* I. 3 The day on which the joint Commission was to meet, agreeably to the adjournment in the preceding February. **1870** KEIM *Sheridan's Troopers* 29 The Board was known as the Peace Commission. **1883** *Harper's Mag.* Sept. 609/1 The Legislature of the State [N.Y.] made provision for the appointment of a commission to reduce them [=confused laws] into a consistent and symmetrical whole. **1889** *Cent.* 1030/1 Commission of Appeals, in some States, [is] a court organized for a limited time to hear and determine appeals, when the permanent court is overburdened with business. **1897** C. A. DANA *Recoll. Civil War* 164 If Watson could have had his way, the guilty parties ... would have been tried by military commission and sternly dealt with. **1920** *3rd Nat. Country Life Conf. Proc.* 109 By far the most effective remedy in this connection has been the creation of the county commission.

4. The fees or profit that an agent takes in a business transaction. {1725-}

1764 J. HABERSHAM *Letters* 16 If Mr. Harris can do them, He will charge them to H. & W. whereby we shall save a Commission of 2 ... pct. **1865** *Atlantic Mo.* XV. 320 We paid the teacher for the privilege of learning ... and the manufacturers paid her a commission for all that she disposed of. **1900** [see sense 5, commission book].

5. Attrib. and phrasal uses: **a.** In sense 4, with *agent, book, broker*, etc.

1839 BRIGGS *H. Franco* II. 23 No, I warn't even a jobber, ... I was only a commission agent for a New England concern. **1900** NELSON *A B C Wall St.* 35 The loan book contains a record of all stock loans, and the commission book a record of all commissions. **1848** W. ARMSTRONG *Stocks* 7 They both speculate upon their own account, and act as Commission Brokers for all who may wish to employ them. **1837** PECK *Gaz. Illinois* 153 [Beardstown] has thirteen stores, four of which do commission and forwarding business. **1863** RANDALL *Pract. Shepherd* 177 The wool depot system ... was conducted on the same general principles with the ordinary commission establishments. **1877** *Vt. Bd. Agric. Rep.* IV. 55 The cheese [was] being returned to the commission men. **1888** *Vt. Agric. Rep.* X. 24 The commission plan of selling butter is not the best. **1867-8** *Ill. Agric. Soc. Trans.* VII. 451 Even our commission salesmen, who are the most painstaking set of business men we have ever met with, ... are beginning to regard the trade ... as a bore. **1820** FLINT *Lett. from Amer.* 212 The enumeration of houses, made in March, 1819, was as follows: ... Auction and commission stores, 5. **1829** S. CUMINGS *Western Pilot* 15 It contains ... a large number of stores, and commission ware houses.

+b. In sense 3: *Commission form of government, Commission government*, city government controlled and administered by a commission.

1908 H. B. RICE *Commission Form of Govt.* 1 The subject of my discussion is the commission form of government in Houston, Texas, and how it works. **1911** *Annals Amer. Academy* XXXVIII. 726 Commission government originated, has been in operation longest, and has reached its highest degree of perfection in the West. **1914** McLaughlin & Hart *Cycl. Amer. Govt.* I. 346 Advocates and sponsors of commission government point out that the management of a city's affairs is not government but business. **1914** *World Almanac* 188 Commission government of cities in

United States . . . instead of by a Mayor and other city officials, was first instituted in Galveston, Tex., in 1901.

c. *Out of commission,* out of service or good running order.

1904 STRATTON-PORTER *Freckles* 181, I'll play and you'll sing, and we'll put the birds out of commission. **1907** M. C. HARRIS *Tents of Wickedness* IV. 342 From those [houses] . . . there came little light; there was . . . a general look of being out of commission.

Commissioned officer. {1685–} A military officer holding a commission.

1704 SEWALL *Diary* II. 98 Chuse Capt. Checkley and me to join Comiss[ione]d officers to acquaint him with it. **1777** *Essex Inst. Coll.* XIII. 118 The Commissioned Officers of Each Company. **1792** *Ann. 2nd Congress* 80 Three additional regiments of infantry, each of which, exclusively of the commissioned officers, shall consist of nine hundred and twelve non-commissioned officers, privates, and musicians. **1840** COOPER *Pathfinder* xv, The particular duty on which he was now sent should have been confided to a commissioned officer. **1890** *Cent.* 4092/1 Commissioned officers . . . in the United States army . . . hold their commissions from the President, the lowest grade being that of second lieutenant.

* **Commissioner.**

* **1.** One who is deputed to carry out a special piece of work; a member of a commission.

1631 *Mass. Bay Rec.* I. 92 This to be done with all convenient speede by theis 5 commission[e]rs. **1684** *Papers Relating to Pemaquid* 28 April, To bee Justices of the Peace for the County of Cornwall and Commissioners for the settling his Royall Highnesses Territoryes. **1704** *Boston News-Letter* 3 Nov. 2/1 On Fryday night the 3d Currant returned from Albany, the Honourable Colonel Penn Townsend, and John Leveret Esqrs. Commissioners for a Treaty with the 5 Nations. **1777** *Jrnls. Cont. Congress* VII. 8 Congress proceeded to the election of Commissioners to the courts of Vienna, Spain &c. **1861** BUCHANAN in *Pres. Mess. & P.* V. 664, I deemed it a duty to transmit to Congress with my message of the 8th of January the correspondence which occurred in December last between the 'commissioners' of South Carolina and myself. **1881** *Harper's Mag.* Jan. 197/2 The commissioners of the exhibition had notified the owners to remove them [=statues] before the fire started.

b. An officer in an ecclesiastical organization.

1832 WILLIAMSON *Maine* II. 695 The highest court of appeals in the last resort, is the General Assembly;—and it consists of Commissioners from all the Presbyteries associated. It sits annually in Philadelphia.

2. Before the Revolution: +**a.** A legislative and semi-judicial officer of a colony or town; a member of a general court.

1636 *Plymouth Laws* 45 It is agreed upon by the Commissioners that it shalbe but one pound of powder and foure pounds of bullets, with match foure fathome for eich matchcock peece. **1652** *Portsmouth Rec.* 18 Mr. Ambrose Landre and James Johnson are chosen Commishioners [unto] the nexte Courte at boston. **1708** SEWALL *Diary* II. 219, [I] made two fair Copies of the Original, and had them Subscrib'd by the Commissioners attesting their examination and Allowance of them.

b. An agent of the Crown sent to treat with the colonies.

1671 ELIOT *Brief Narr.* 19 To the right worshipful the commissioners under his majesties great-seal. **1776** J. ADAMS in *Fam. Lett.* (1876) 158 We are waiting, it is said, for Commissioners; a messiah that will never come.

3. An administrative officer of the government in various capacities (see quotations), usually appointed rather than elected. (Cf. also COUNTY COMMISSIONER).

1747 *Penna. Col. Rec.* V. 61 It is thought equitable that the value of the Sand . . . should be paid by the Commissioners of the County. **1796** WASHINGTON *Writings* XIII. 227, I should view the residence of the Commissioners . . . as a nest egg (pardon the expression) which will attract others. *a***1846** *Quarter Race Ky.* etc. 82 He's a squire, a school comishoner, overlooker of a mile of Nob road that leads towards Roody's still-house. **1873** *Harper's Mag.* XLVI. 629 New York has a school commissioner for each Assembly district, making 113 for the State. His salary is $800 a year. **1898** *Kansas City Star* 18 Dec. 4/3 Mr. Stanley is disposed to favor the election of railroad commissioners by the people. **1913** STRATTON-PORTER *Laddie* xiii. 247 Father was one of the commissioners, and as long as he filled that office, every road in the county would be just as fine as the law would allow him to make it.

b. *Commissioner for small causes,* a judicial official in early Massachusetts. *Obs.*

1641 in Coffin *Hist. Newbury* 34 Mr. John Woodbridge, Mr. Edward Woodman, and Mr. Edward Rawson, appointed commissioners for small causes in Newbury. **1643** *Mass. Rec.* III. 357 As the three commissioners for small causes . . . have great power of judicature.

c. *Commissioners' Court,* a body of men with judicial functions.

1684 SEWALL *Diary* I. 50 May 6, Commissioners Court. **1844** *Ind. Senate Jrnl.* 107 The petition of . . . citizens of the county of Randolph, praying for the passage of an act to extend the time of holding the commissioners' court in said county. **1857** in Johnson *Anderson Co., Kansas* (1877) 38 In consequence of insurrection throughout Kansas Territory . . . the probate and commissioners' court were unable to hold their regular or adjourned court.

d. In the titles of officials having specific duties.

1717 *Mass. Ho. Repr. Jrnls.* I. 194 Ordered, That the Committee which Audited the Treasurer's Accompts, be a Committee to Examine and Audit the Accompts of the Commissioner of Imposts. **1721** *Ib.* III. 49 Whereas the above-named A. B. is Appointed Commissioner of Excise for said County. **1722** *New-Eng. Courant* 2 July 2/1 The General Assembly of this Province beg you to receive their Humble and Hearty Thanks, for Communicating to them the Letter from the Commissioners of the Indian Affairs at Albany. **1794** *Ann. 3rd Congress* 763 An act authorizing a settlement of certain expenses of the Commissioner of Loans. **1802** *Ann. 7th Congress* App. 1338 There shall be appointed by the President of the United States . . . as many general commissioners of bankruptcy . . . as he may deem necessary. **1818** *Niles' Reg.* XIII. 362/2 Otis was basely assassinated in a coffee-house, in the night, by a well-dressed banditti, with a commissioner of the customs at their head. **1822** *Ann. 17th Congress* 1 Sess. I. 445 The House have passed a bill, entitled . . . An act fixing the compensation of the Commissioner of the Public Buildings. **1840** *Niles' Nat. Reg.* 7 March 13/1 Mr. Jones, of Virginia, indicating his intention to move that the house proceed to the consideration of the bill continuing the office of commissioner of pensions. **1840** *Ib.* 4 April LVIII. 69 From the annual report of the commissioner of the general land office it appears . . . the quantity of public land sold amounted to 3,414,907 acres. **1846** POLK *Diary* (1910) II. 108 Mr. Buchanan . . . seemed to be deeply concerned at the removal of a clerk . . . by Mr. Piper, the acting commissioner of the Public Lands. **1846** *Ib.* (1929) 178 He said he had seen Mr. Burke, the Commissioner of Patents. **1866** *Statutes at Large* XIV. 133 The commissioner of internal revenue . . . may prescribe . . . regulations for the inspection . . . of cigars, cheroots, and cigarettes. **1872** BRACE *Dangerous Classes N.Y.* 60 The success of . . . the Commissioners of Emigration in their 'Labor Exchange,' indicate what might be accomplished. **1888** *Chicago Inter-Ocean* 2 Jan. 1/4 In the former [saloon] was the Hon. Pat Mealey, Commissioner of Police of this city, the Hon. N. D. Wallace, [etc.]. **1891** O'BEIRNE *Leaders Ind. Territory* 56/2 Later, in 1872, he was appointed deputy warden of the National Penitentiary, and in the same year commissioner of the quarantine district. **1898** *Kansas City Star* 18 Dec. 2/2 Addresses will be made by Samuel Gompers, president of the American Federation of Labor; . . . S. J. Kent, commissioner of labor of Nebraska, [etc.]. **1910** *Okla. Session Laws* 3 Legisl. 4 The salary of the Commissioner of Charities and Corrections of the State of Oklahoma shall be two thousand five hundred ($2,500.00) dollars per annum. **1911** *Ib.* 242 The Commissioners of the School Land Office shall cause the land to be appraised by three disinterested freeholders of the state.

e. As a title applied to one who holds a post as commissioner.

1898 *Boston Herald* 21 April 9/5 Commissioner Goodwin inquired if it was the intention to have all the closed cars vestibuled.

4. *Board of commissioners,* a commission; commissioners acting as a group.

1789 *Ann. 1st Congress* I. 60 A person is to be appointed to fill the vacant seat at the Board of Commissioners for settling the accounts between the United States and individual States. *Ib.* 389 The heads of the Treasury Department, the Board of Commissioners, I do not believe have closed their accounts to this very day. *a***1817** DWIGHT *Travels* I. 154 After this, a custom house and a board of commissioners, were established in the Colonies. **1823** *Baptist Mag.* IV. 23 The Ordination of three Missionaries, . . . who were to be sent by the American Board of Commissioners for Foreign Missions to propagate the gospel among the heathen. **1866** *Rep. Indian Affairs* 133 None of these claims should be audited until they shall have been most thoroughly and critically examined by an experienced board of commissioners. **1873** *Newton Kansan* 26 June 3/4 A petition will be presented to the Board of commissioners.

Commissioner-General. A chief commissioner. — **1885** *Century Mag.* May 6/1 Mr. Morehead was made Commissioner-General to travel and interest State governments, manufacturing firms, and foreign nations in making displays.

+**Commission house.** A business firm which deals for its customers in return for a percentage of the profits.

1840 *Picayune* 26 Aug. 2/5 A Warehouseman . . . wants employment. To a Commission and Forwarding house, having their own warehouse, his services would be valuable. **1847** HOWE *Hist. Coll. Ohio* 331 Toledo has . . . 9 forwarding and commission houses. **1861** *Chicago Tribune* 15 April 1 M. S. Nichols & Co. have opened at 188 South Water street, Chicago, a General Commission House, for the purchase and sale of Grain, Flour, Provisions, &c., and solicit consignments and orders. **1871** *Ill. Agric. Soc. Trans.* VIII. 183 Many of these commission houses are conducted by men as honest and upright as any the country affords. **1922** T. A. MCNEAL *When Kansas Was Young* 187 The Major had established his commission house at Kansas City, in the early eighties.

Commission merchant. A merchant who does business on commission.

1812 *Ann. 12th Congress* 2 Sess. 1270 The subscribers, commission merchants, and auctioneers, of the city of New York. **1822** A. ROYALL *Lett. from Ala.* 152 [Huntsville, Ala.,] has now . . . several commission merchants; auctioneer; a land office, and various other public offices. **1856**

Spirit of Times 25 Oct. 133/3 The commission merchants ... should make them [retail butchers] pay high prices for the sake of credit. **1871** *Ill. Agric. Soc. Trans.* VIII. 13 Some of the commission merchants of Chicago ... brand, and sell as New York cheese, cheese manufactured in this vicinity. **1881** *Harper's Mag.* Oct. 720/2 [The cotton farms] are passing, one after the other, into the hands of the commission merchants. **1910** J. HART *Vigilante Girl* 22 Making a corner in salt beef, and thereby ruining a rival commission merchant, would not give me an extra pulse-beat.

Commission officer. *Obs.* {1650–1708} = COMMISSIONED OFFICER.

1662 *Plymouth Laws* 139 Liberty is granted unto the major to admitt of soe many volunteers into the troop of horse as will make up the number forty eight; the Commission officers excepted. **1690** *Mass. H. S. Coll.* 4 Ser. V. 262 We have three commission officers for our county. **1724** *New-Eng. Courant* 14–21 Sept. 1/2 There is indeed some faint Shadow of Honour and Profit attending the inferior Commission Officers. **1776** *Jrnls. Cont. Congress* VI. 858 That the commanding officer of each regiment be directed ... to send a commission officer to visit the sick ... in the general hospital.

Commitment. {1611–} A pledge or promise (implied or explicit) to take a course of action. {1871–} — **1789** WASHINGTON *Diaries* IV. 17 If Mr. Gouv'r Morris was employed in this business, it would be a commitment for his appointment as Minister. **1793** JEFFERSON *Writings* IX. 225 Urge one [an answer] as much as you can without commitment. **1900** S. A. NELSON *A B C Wall St.* 135 *Commitment*, an act of engagement or pledging.

***Committee.**

1. A group of persons, usually appointed, to whom some function or business is given. {1621–}

1698 *Boston Rec.* 231 It being proposed ... that a compatent number of p[er]son[s] of the principle Gent[le]men of this town be chosen to be a Commettee to inquire into & consult, the most Proper methods to be taken [etc.]. **1721** *Mass. Ho. Repr. Jrnls.* III. 16 The Committee which carried up the Vote ... prepare an Answer. **1776** TRUMBULL *M'Fingal* I. 21 Addresses signed, then chose Committees, To stop all drinking of Bohea-teas. **1846** POLK *Diary* 58 The Secretary of War and Secretary of Navy had with my concurrence made communications with the Military and Naval Committees of both houses of Congress. **1925** BRYAN *Memoirs* 466 The Legislative Committee of the Anti-Saloon League.

attrib. **1789** MACLAY *Deb. Senate* 148 The York Senators and representatives were in the committee-room. **1886** ALTON *Among Law-Makers* 16 Committee-service is irksome as well as important. **1886** H. D. BROWN *Two College Girls* 80 The fourth was chosen because, though inexperienced, she might 'work up' into a good committee woman. **1900** DIX *Deacon Bradbury* 228, I'll jest slip down-town an' fix up a committee meetin' f'r after dinner.

2. In the names of various (legislative) committees of a more or less institutional nature: **a.** *Committee of safety*, a committee whose purpose is to safeguard the welfare of a town, colony, etc. {1659}

1740 W. STEPHENS *Proc. Georgia* 482 These Proceedings being well known to be the Result of our Committee of Safety. **1775** in *Amer. Hist. Review* I. 304, I recd. from the Continental Treasury the 1000 Dollars lately advanced to our Com[mitt]ee of Safety. **1775** in *N.H. Hist. Soc. Coll.* VII. p. iv, Resolved, ... that the time of their inlistment continue to the last day of December, unless the Committee of Safety should judge it proper that a part or the whole be discharged sooner. **1776** *Jrnls. Cont. Congress* IV. 106 Resolved, That ... the convention, or committee of safety of New Jersey, do get the arms already ordered. **1861** in Logan *Great Conspiracy* 250 A Conspiracy for the overthrow of the Government through the military organizations, the dangerous secret order, the 'Knights of the Golden Circle,' 'Committees of Safety,' Southern leagues, [etc.].

+b. *Committee of correspondence*, during the Revolutionary period, a committee appointed by a town or colony to communicate and co-ordinate the measures variously taken toward redress of grievances.

1766 in Franklin *Works* (1847) VII. 318 On the 10th we had the pleasure of finding that thou hadst wrote a letter to the Committee of Correspondence, which at once stopped the virulence of the proprietary party. **1772** *Boston Rec.* 93 It was then moved by Mr. Samuel Adams, That a Committee of Correspondence be appointed to consist of twenty one Persons —to state the Rights of the Colonists and of this Province in particular; ... to communicate and publish the same to the several Towns in this Province and to the World. **1776** *N.E. Hist. & Gen. Reg.* XXX. 381/2 *Resolved*, That the several Towns in the Colony [Mass.] ... choose ... a number of Freeholders ... whose Principles are known to be friendly to the Rights and Liberties of America, to serve as a Committee of Correspondence. **1823** TUDOR *Otis* 22 He [Gen. Warren] was the author of the scheme for forming Committees of Correspondence, which he communicated to Samuel Adams, in 1773, who was making him a visit. **1863** *N.H. Hist. Soc. Coll.* VII. p. iii, During this session [of May, 1774] ... the House of Representatives ... appointed a Committee of Correspondence for the purpose of interchanging important information with Committees in other colonies appointed ... for similar duties.

+c. *Committee of the whole*, the whole of a legislative or other body sitting informally to consider the details of a measure. {committee of the whole house, 1685– (*Jrnl. Ho. Comm.* IX. 759)}

1775 *Jrnls. Cont. Congress* III. 307 The Congress resolved itself into a Com[mitt]ee of the whole, to take into their farther consideration the state of the trade of the confederated Colonies. **1783** J. JONES *Letters* 121 The letter of the delegates and the report of the committee respecting the cession has been read and referred to a Committee of the Whole. **1798** *Ann. 5th Congress* II. 1973 The House again resolved itself into a Committee of the Whole, on the bill concerning aliens. **1811** CLAY *Speeches* I. 15 It was the pleasure of the House not to deliberate on it in Committee of the Whole. **1844** *Ind. Senate Jrnl.* 211 Mr. Lane moved to refer the joint resolution to the committee of the whole. **1891** WELCH *Recoll. 1830–40* 211 The Society resolved itself into what might be called the committee of the whole.

d. *Committee of Ways and Means*, a committee (usually in a legislative body) to whom financial matters are referred. {1737–}

1776 *Jrnls. Cont. Congress* 562 *Resolved*, That Thursday morning be assigned for ... the report of the committee of ways and means. **1797** *Ann. 5th Congress* I. 680 *Resolved*, That the Committee of Ways and Means be instructed to prepare ... a plan for raising a sum [etc.]. **1802** CUTLER in *Life & Corr.* II. 70 Attempts to instruct the Committee of Ways and Means to make particular inquiry whether it be expedient, or not, to reduce the duty [etc.]. **1846** POLK *Diary* 85 Mr. McKay of North Carolina, Chairman of the Committee of Ways and Means of the House of Representatives. **1870** *Nation* 24 Feb. 118/1 Any idea which is fit to live will live, ... and if it have no root in human nature, or in the order of the universe, the Committee of Ways and Means can never save it.

+e. *Committee of the States*, under the Articles of Confederation, a committee with a semblance of executive power when Congress was not in session.

1777 *Jrnls. Cont. Congress* IX. 923/1 The committee of the States, or any nine of them, shall be authorized to execute in the recess of Congress, such of the powers of Congress as the United States in Congress ... shall ... think expedient.

3. In the names of various bodies performing a specified task or routine subsidiary duties.

(a) 1724 JONES *Virginia* 30 At the other End are several Chambers for the Committees of Claims, Privileges & Elections. **1789** *Ann. 1st Congress* I. 231 Ordered, That the said petitions be referred to the Committee of Elections. **1798** *Ann. 5th Congress* I. 656 The Committee of Commerce and Manufactures are of opinion that this case must be considered as one for which no provision had been made by law. *Ib.* 692 The report of the Committee of Revisal and Unfinished Business. *Ib.* 955 It was moved that this resolution be referred to a committee to be denominated a Committee of Privileges. **1804** CUTLER in *Life & Corr.* II. 165 The Committee of Inquisition is nearly ready to report. **1830** S. BRECK in *Recoll.* 195 He kept it a secret from them, and went to the committee of health ... to have the man removed. **1846** POLK *Diary* 136 It was agreed that he as Secretary of State should address a letter ... to the chairman of the committee of finance in the Senate.

(b) 1744 *Boston Selectmen* 30 April, Requiring them [=constables] to consider the Reports of the Town's Committees on Several Affairs. **1774** *Boston Rec.* 169 The further Consideration [was] referred, till the Report of the Committee on the State of the Granary be laid before the Town. **1832** *Congress. Deb.* 2 July 1161 Mr. Grundy ... put a question to the Committee on Public Lands, if they intended to push the question through. **1839** *Diplom. Corr. Texas* (1908) I. 374 The Committee on Foreign affairs in the United States Congress. **1843** *Niles' Nat. Reg.* LXIV. 123/3 The committee on commerce, to whom were referred sundry memorials asking congress to make an appropriation to improve the navigation of the Mississippi river and its principal tributaries. **1846** *Niles' Nat. Reg.* 20 June 256/1 Chairman of the U.S. Senate's Committee on Foreign Relations. **1854** BENTON *30 Years' View* I. 34/1 It was then ... referred to the committee on manufactures. **1881** *Harper's Mag.* LXII. 669/2 The house Committee on Indian Affairs ... urged that the government had made treaty stipulations specially providing for education with nomadic tribes. **1920** *3rd Nat. Country Life Conf. Proc.* 192 We recommend that the Executive Committee or the Committee on Public Information ... take under advisement the possibility of the publication of a rural life journal. **1925** BRYAN *Memoirs* 107 It would have been impossible for me to be chairman of the Committee on Resolutions.

+4. *Committee of one, C. of two*, one or two (persons). *humorous.*

1880 *Harper's Mag.* Dec. 91 She slept in that 'grand committee of two' which is the strength and comfort of a happy marriage. *a***1889** FARMER 161 To use an American expression he was an investigating committee of one, that had to be continually lubricated.

Committeeman. {1654–} A member of, or a representative on, a committee; a deputy; a commissioner.

1686 *Huntington Rec.* I. 470 At a towne meeting Thomas Powell was chossen commitieman for this present year. **1728** *Lunenburg* (Mass.) *Proprietors' Rec.* 173 Voted that Capt Josiah Willard be the first Committee man to Make up a Book of Records. **1752** *Duxbury Rec.* 310 The said town chose Mr. George Partridge their committee man for to join with the church committee, in procuring a Minister. **1809** E. A. KENDALL *Travels* I. 27 The deputies are now frequently denominated representatives. They were anciently called committeemen. **1843** *Knickerb.* XXII. 232 To the Whig committee-man who called to ask his support for that party, he propounded first the question, [etc.]. **1901** ADE *40 Modern Fables* 25 The Committeemen said they would need a little Money right away to get out some Printing.

Commode.

1. An elaborate headdress with a wire framework, of French origin. {a1688–1730}

*c*1781 in *Harper's Mag.* LIX. 500/1 [Benoni Peckham] informs his customers that he has furnished himself with a new supply of Hair, and is now ready to furnish ladies with braids, commodes, cushions, and curls in the newest fashion. **1838** 'TEXIAN' *Mexico v. Texas* 85 The men . . . wrap round their head, a white linen handkerchief, or some piece of showy silk. You may even, sometimes, see priests . . . decorated with this strange kind of commode.

2. An article of furniture with drawers, such as a dresser in a bedroom or a sideboard in a dining room. {1760–(Stanford)} Also attrib.

1773 E. Singleton *Social N.Y.* 83 [Joseph Cox from London] makes . . . commode dressing and toilet-tables. **1845** *Lowell Offering* V. 254 Do they have commodes, and workstands, and spoolstands, and tape-measures, and finger-nail brushes? **1890** *Boston Journal* 25 Feb. 1/3 To-day we place on sale a Bedroom Suit. . . . It has the wide French bureau and the 1890 English commode.

3. A small stand equipped with a closet. {1851–}

1887 *Nation* XLIV. 205/2 In place of the odorous 'commode,' a big can of water, a tin tub, and twice the usual supply of towels, will bring in . . . a clear addition of at least two dollars a week.

Commodore. {1694–} A naval officer ranking below a rear admiral and above a captain. {1695–}

The office was created officially in the U.S. in 1862, but the term had been used for the commander of a squadron. Colloq., the word is applied to a person connected with the sea or with watercraft.

1777 *Md. Hist. Mag.* V. 207 A Flag just appears from Ld. Cornwallis demanding to know why the Commodore wishes to fire on the defenceless Inhabitants. **1827** G. MELLEN *Chronicle of '26* 20 And so the patriots won the commodore—They promised too, to make him Admiral. **1840** *Niles' Nat. Reg.* 2 May 134/1 The rank of commodore is now almost exclusively American, we believe, and only means a post-captain in command of a squadron. **1842** *S. Lit. Messenger* VIII. 91/1 Even his [the American Commander's] title of Commodore is a matter of courtesy, tolerated as a convenience, in spite of a positive order from the Navy Department. **1859** *Harper's Mag.* Aug. 319/2 The commodore builds most of our lake craft. . . . It would go mighty hard with him to be beat! **1898** *Congress. Rec.* 9 May 4725 This resolution, tendering the thanks of . . . the American people to the gallant commodore in chief . . . for achieving . . . one of the most marvelous, brilliant victories in the annals of naval warfare. **1909** I. BACHELLER in *American Mag.* LXVII. 467/2 The Commodore was now leaning over the map and looking down upon it.

* **Common,** *n.*

* **1.** Undeveloped land owned in common by members of a town or township, especially in New England, and set aside for common pasturage, timber cutting, etc. Frequently *pl.*

(*a*) **1634** *Watertown Rec.* 1 No man shall fell or cut down any timber trees upon the Common. **1635** *Ib.* 2 There is a dayly abuse in felling of Timber upon the Common. **1657** *Portsmouth Rec.* 78 The remainder of land then undesposed of to be a perpetual Common to the towne ffor Ever. **1713** *Duxbury Rec.* 219 Provided he will grant as much of his land to the town of Duxbury, adjacent to the meeting house, to be a perpetual Common for a training field &c. **1834** PECK *Gaz. Illinois* 198 A *common* is a tract of land granted to the town for wood and pasturage, in which each owner of a village lot has a *common*, but not an individual right. In some cases this tract embraced several thousand acres. The 'common' attached to Cahokia, extends up the prairie opposite St. Louis. **1841** H. PLAYFAIR *Papers* I. 119 *Common*, in America, or lands attached for common purposes to a town, is often covered with the original forest. **1876** *Scribner's Mo.* March 744/2 Sods for this purpose are, as a rule, cut from some worn-out pasture, neglected public 'common,' or may be the roadside.

(*b*) **1640** *Conn. Hist. Soc. Coll.* XIV. 162 Abutting on a hyway leadding from the Towne in to the Commones. **1658** *Portsmouth* (R.I.) *Rec.* 84 A towne meettinge . . . Concerninge Stentinge the Commons. **1676** *R. I. Col. Rec.* II. 533 Each family soe wanting a libertye shall have a cow kept upon the commons. **1703** *Conn. Hist. Soc. Coll.* VI. 271 No person or persons do or Shall Cutt Stadle wood upon ye Commons. **1791** BARTRAM *Travels* 396 Here are very extensive old fields, the abandoned plantations and commons of the old town. *a*1821 C. BIDDLE *Autobiog.* 41 Immense pieces of walls were carried from the seaside to the commons back of the town. **1836** J. HALL *Statistics of West* 132 The blue grass grows spontaneously wherever the soil has been trodden hard; it skirts the road-sides, and covers the commons around our towns.

b. *pl.* The pasturage or timber belonging to a person's share in such land. *Obs.*

1638 *Charlestown Land Rec.* 24 [The possessions of Ralph Moussell include] Commones for foure milch Cowes and A haulf. **1658** *Ib.* 76 No man shall sell his wood or commons but to the Inhabitants of Charletowne, upon forfeiture of twelve pence, p. load of eyther wood or Tymber.

c. *To lay into* (or *down to*) *common*, to set aside for pasturage, woodcutting, etc. *Obs.*

1649 *New Haven Col. Rec.* I. 507 The planters w[hi]ch hire oystershellfeild doe laye it into common w[i]th the quarters next it. **1684** *Providence Rec.* XVII. 71 To fence in a part of ye Comon upon ye playne above ye mill and plant and sooe it for three yeers and then lay it Downe to Comon againe. **1704** *Ib.* IV. 184 The which said Twenty acres of land hath since been Relinquished . . . & againe laid downe into Comon. **1710** *Ib.* XI. 144 He may lay downe to Common Twenty acres of land . . . & to take it up againe in some other Place of ye Townes Common.

d. *Right of commons*, the right to use the common land owned by a community. *Obs.* {1711–1853}

1733 J. HEMPSTEAD *Diary* 260, I bot of Love Manwaring her Right of Commons & p[ai]d her £4. *Ib.* 264, I wrote a Deed & sent to Norwalk by Mr. Fitch for the Right of Comons belonging to Sam[ue]ll Raymond to give £20 to be p[ai]d next Spring.

+**e.** With esp. reference to Boston Common, now a public park.

1678 *Boston Rec.* 120 The Buryinge Place in ye common is leased out to Mr. John Woodmansey for ye pasture of it. **1723** *New-Eng. Courant* 2 Sept. 2/2 [The Indians] kill'd an Ox with their Bows and Arrows, and boil'd him in the Common. **1732** SEWALL *Letter-Book* II. 288 Part of his real Estate Viz. Ten Rods Front of his Pasture called Elm-Pasture, at the Lower End of the Common in said Town. **1829** B. HALL *Travels in N. A.* II. 126 There was, moreover, a fine Mall, or public promenade, called the Common, laid out in grass fields, surrounded and intersected by broad gravel walks. **1889** BRAYLEY *Boston Fire Dept.* 47 The keeper of the powder-house on the Common, informed the selectmen.

+**2.** In *pl.* Pasture lands or pasturage.

1857 *Lawrence Republican* 18 June 1 Two-thirds of her [Virginia's] soil that was formerly fertile and productive has been exhausted and much of it thrown into commons. **1857** D. BRAMAN *Texas* iii. 51 The rich prairies of this county afford free commons to any number of herdsmen.

+**3.** A vacant lot.

1865 *Atlantic Mo.* XV. 474/1 There lay numerous open lots or commons, all of which afforded abundant evidence of the extent to which this public wastefulness was carried. **1871** EGGLESTON *Duffels* viii. 161 The cows [grazed] on the 'commons,' as the open lots were called. **1880** CABLE *Grandissimes* xlviii. 369 None dreamed of looking for him . . . on the lonely suburban commons. **1901** H. ROBERTSON *Inlander* 26 The three [boys] . . . became . . . friendly with the young barbarians on the commons.

* **Common,** *a.*

* **1.** Of or belonging to the whole community; public.

1638 *R.I. Col. Rec.* I. 54 The neck of Land by Th. Esson's house shall be sufficiently fenced in with five rayles . . . for to lye as a common field belonging to the towne. **1640** *Conn. Hist. Soc. Coll.* VI. 25 [If the fence viewers] hear or knowe of anny beast or swine in anny Comon Cornefeild one this side the great River [etc.]. **1642** *Ib.* VI. 61 Remove the Comon gate leading into the north meadow. **1644** *New Haven Col. Rec.* I. 148 Richard Miles, Jasper Craine, . . . were chosen to be constant surveyers . . . of all the comon high wayes aboute the towne and the bridges allso. **1649** *Charlestown Land Rec.* 111, I . . . have sould . . . A House, . . . which House stands nere the Comon fery. **1652** *Plymouth Col. Rec.* III. 6 Wee further present the towne of Taunton for not hauing a common stock of powder & shott, according to order. **1664** *Conn. Col. Rec.* I. 418 The bounds between ye said plantations shall be where the common passage over Manunketesek River is. **1673** *Conn. Public Rec.* II. 213 Moween . . . was secured in the common goale upon suspition of murthering a Pequit girle. **1710** *Boston Selectmen* 113 The Proprietors of the dreine or Common-Shore in Prince Street have liberty to digg or break up the Highway. **1839** [see CONFEDERATED *ppl. a.* 2]. **1884** BLAINE *20 Years of Congress* I. 249 The state of Louisiana was . . . paid for . . . by the United States out of the common treasury of the whole people.

+**b.** Particularly applied to schools or education. (Cf. COMMON SCHOOL.)

1831 PECK *Guide* 244 The influx of emigrants . . . is producing a rapid change in common education. **1837** H. MARTINEAU *Society* III. 335 A fund was also accumulating, which was to be applied whenever its income would support a common free-school in every district of the State, for two months in the year. **1849** CHAMBERLAIN *Ind. Gazetteer* 204 Common English schools are kept from three to six months in the year, but no higher branches are taught. *Ib.* 262 Many private and common district schools are also to be found in most parts of the city.

* **2.** Of ordinary rank or qualities; pertaining to or performed by ordinary persons.

1636 *Plymouth Laws* 48 For measuring of land according to the distance & trouble of the same and his paines therein not to be valued with comon labor. **1704** *Boston News-Letter* 27 Nov. 2/2 There was 2 Seargents, 1 Gunner & 7 common Souldiers. **1831** PECK *Guide* 189 Common laborers have ten dollars per month, or fifty cents per day. **1841** E. A. HITCHCOCK *Journal* 39 The seats were split logs or hewn logs supported by pins like a common farmers stool. **1848** *Ib.* 30 The payment of money to the 'common people' only made them dissipated. **1869** Tourgee *Toinette* ix. 100 Her parents and forebears had been 'common livers,' who had never owned slaves. **1877** *Rep. Indian Affairs* 41 There are several good carpenters capable of doing any kind of common work.

b. Unpretentious, democratic. *local.*

1913 M. W. Morley *Carolina Mts.* 175 When you hear one of your friends spoken of by a highlander as being 'common' you are puzzled, to say the least, until you learn that the word is the most complimentary possible, retaining its original meaning as understood when we speak of the 'common people,' the 'common good.'

3. Used absol. in phrase *for common*, customarily, for ordinary usage.

1792 Brackenridge *Adv. Capt. Farrago* xxiii. 113 You are welcome, Sir, if you wish to stop, and can put up with such as we have; though, since my old man's time, we don't take in strangers for common. **1854** H. H. Riley *Puddleford* 92 Longbow had bo't a bran new carpet for downstairs, and used sales-molasses for common, every, most every day.

***4.** Of the most familiar or most widespread kind or species of anything: **a.** Of animals.

1813 Wilson *Ornithology* IX. 61 [The] Common Coot, *Fulica Atra*, ... is known in Pennsylvania by the name of the Mud-hen. **1839** Peabody *Mass. Birds* 331 The Common Crossbill, *Loxia curvirostra*, belongs to northern regions, and comes to us during the winter, in search of food. **1858** Baird *Birds Pacific R.R.* 566 *Corvus Americanus*, Common Crow. **1825** Bonaparte *Ornithology* I. 42 Female Common Crow-Blackbird. *Quiscalus Versicolor.* **1858** Baird *Birds Pacific R.R.* 604 *Zenaidura Carolinensis*, Carolina, or Common Dove. **1821** Nuttall *Trav. Arkansa* 154 We found in this country [at the head of the Red R.] two poisonous species of Coluber, or common snake.

b. Of plants.

1785 Marshall *Amer. Grove* 20 *Betula-Alnus rubra.* Common Alder. **1815** Drake *Cincinnati* 77 The botanical resources of this ... Forest of the Miami country [include] ... *Æsculus flava*, Common or fœtid buckeye. **1897** Sudworth *Arborescent Flora* 334 *Catalpa catalpa*, ... Common Catalpa. **1784** Cutler in *Mem. Academy* I. 469 *Geranium.* ... Common Cranesbill. The root is astringent, and frequently used in gargles for cankerous sores in the mouth. **1813** Muhlenberg *Cat. Plants* 17 *Cornus sanguinea*, Common dogwood. **1823** James *Exped.* I. 66 The shore was lined with common elder. **1814** Pursh *Flora Amer.* II. 638 *Juglans tomentosa.* ... This is known under the name of Mocker Nut, White-heart Hickory or Common Hickory. **1897** Sudworth *Arborescent Flora* 99 *Juniperus communis.* Common Juniper. **1813** Muhlenberg *Cat. Plants* 2 *Syringa vulgaris*, Common lilac (pipe tree). **1823** James *Exped.* I. 66 The cleared fields were yellow with the flowers of the common mullein. **1846** Browne *Trees Amer.* 287 The Common Pear-tree, in a wild state, has a pyramidal shaped head, with thorny branches. **1822** J. Woods *English Prairie* 220, I have seen no sweet potatoes; but Irish, or common potatoes, grow tolerably in a wet season. **1843** T. Talbot *Journals* 29 To be taken internally, ... White Horehound, Black Currant, Solidago or Golden Rod, Common Saffron. **1846** Browne *Trees Amer.* 366 *Halesia tetraptera*, the Common Snowdrop Tree. **1802** Ellicott *Journal* 286 Common swamp gum, (*nyssa integrifolia*,) ... [is] in great abundance in some parts of the Mississippi Territory. **1897** Sudworth *Arborescent Flora* 275 *Rhus copallina.* ... Common Sumach (S.C.). *Ib.* 230 *Cratægus tomentosa.* ... Black Haw. Common names [include] ... Common Thorn (Pa.).

c. Of inanimate things.

1891 Wilkins *New Eng. Nun* 2 Their daily tables were laid with common crockery. **1650** *Conn. Public Rec.* I. 214 By theire rooting vpp and wronging otherwise the common feed of cattle. **1831** Peck *Guide* 46 Common quartz, limped quartz, mica, and novaculite ... abound in the vicinity of the springs. **1812** *Niles' Reg.* II. 131/1, 300 hospital, horsemen's and common tents ... have been bought or made. **1832** *Louisville Pub. Adver.* 3 March, O'Beirne, Baldwin & Co. offer for sale ... 150 bbls. rectified and common whiskey. **1872** *Florida Plant. Rec.* 198 Perhaps it would pay to get some common whiskey for the nigs.

***Common,** *adv.* {–1798} Commonly, usually. *colloq.*

1784 Washington *Diaries* II. 297 The Land is leveller than is common to be met with in this part of the Country. **1817** E. Pettigrew *Let. to Ann Pettigrew* 22 March (Pettigrew P.), She is as well as common. **1834** A. Pike *Sketches* 115 'Busy as common, comadre!' said Lopez as he entered. **1884** Sweet & Knox *Through Texas* 44 He had sort o' aggravated me more than common that morning. **1897** Brodhead *Bound in Shallows* 256 'It seems nearer than common,' said Alexa. **1901** Harben *Westerfelt* 41 'Oh, I reckon I'm all right. ... How's Luke?' 'As well as common.' **1916** E. Porter *David* 75 We don't use this room common, little boy, nor the bedroom there, either.

Commonage. {1610–} Now rare, except hist.

1. Land held in common; a common or commons. {1771–}

1635 *Watertown Rec.* 2 Agreed ... that no Foreainer comming into the Towne ... shall have any benefit either of Commonage or Land undivided. **1653** *Norwalk* (Conn.) *Rec.* 42 If there shall be any timber felled in any of the commonage belonging to the Town of Norwake [etc.]. **1681** *Dedham Rec.* V. 118 The motion made by ... Mr. Adams for adding mor commonage to his Lott is Left to consideration [etc.]. **1752** MacSparran *America Dissected* 13 The Climate is benign, and their Outlets or Commonages large. **1807** *Huntington Rec.* III. 241 Any of the Inhabitants of said Town may Cut Pine Timber on the Commonage belonging thereto.

2. *Right of commonage*, the right to pasture animals on land held in common.

1646 *Boston Rec.* 88 It is ordered that all who shall after the dat herof come to be an inhabitant in the towne of Boston, shall not have right of Commonage, unless he hier it of them that are Commoners. **1655** *Portsmouth Records* 69 Philip Tabor ... hath equall right of Comonage with the rest of the inhabitants. **1708** *Boston News-Letter* 7 June 2/2 There is to be Sold a Farm Scituate ... at the Head of Bristol Neck towards Swanzey, ... with Rights of Commonage in both said Towns. **1719** *Providence Rec.* XVI. 127 A Right of Commonage within the Seaven mile Line.

b. Ellipt. in same sense.

1653 *Suffolk Deeds* III. 232 All ye aboue mentioned lands houses outhouses mills yards gardens grasse ground commonage of pasture woods vnderwoods [etc.]. **1665** *Oyster Bay Rec.* I. 19, [I] doe by these pr[e]sents Absolutely sell ... A sertaine dwelling house and house lott ... togeather w[i]th all Comonege & other Lands Liberties previllages, [etc.].

3. A share in the common land. Freq. in pl.

1651 *Southold Rec.* II. 17 His Commonage in the Town bounds is a fourth lott. **1661** *Rowley Rec.* 119 A Survay of The Severall Gates or Commonages belonging unto The Severall Inhabbitants of The Towne of Rowley. **1704** *N.H. Probate Rec.* I. 527, I Give & bequeath ... with all Rights to Lands or Commonages What Soever unto her my Said Daughter. **1713** *Harvard Rec.* II. 407 The Town of Rowley having Entred upon the whole of the Gates or Comonages belonging to the Estate of Mr. Ezekiel Rogers. **1735** *Harvard Rec.* I. 295 [There are] also four freehold rights or Commonages in Mill Swamp pasture in the lower Commons.

4. The condition of land held in common. {1808–}

1669 *Huntington Rec.* I. 133 The Reare with the woods in Comonadge the frunt with the street or high waye. **1773** *Amherst Rec.* (1884) 62/2 Timothey Green Shall have Liberty to ... Improve all the town way ... for the space of two year and then fling it up to Commonage weell [*sic*] seeded to grass.

***Commonalty, Commonality.** The general body of the community.

1631 J. Smith *Advertisements* 23 Make your plantations so neere and great as you can; ... nor impose too much upon the commonalty either by your maggazines ... nor any other too hard imposition for present gaine. **1635** *N.H. Probate Rec.* I. 5 Ye said Mayor and Cominalitye their Successors or Assignes. **1641–2** *Va. House of Burgesses* 68 We ... do declare from ourselves and all the commonalty of this colony that it was never desired [etc.]. **1691** *Penna. Archives* I. 114, I doe hereby grant to the said Bailiffe, Burgesses and Comonalty of German Towne, [etc.]. **1703** *Southampton Rec.* II. 180 Wee ... Indian Sachems ... Doe hereby acknowledge to have Received ye sum of twenty pounds ... of and from ye trustees of ye Comonalty of Southampton. **1736** *East-Hampton Rec.* IV. 35 We the trustees of the freeholders and commonalty of the town of East-Hampton. **1830** J. F. Watson *Philadelphia* 237 Hipesaws and jigs were the common dances of the commonalty. **1883** *Harper's Mag.* Sept. 613/2 The expenditure of from twenty to thirty millions of the money of the Mayor and Commonalty of New York.

***Common council.** The legislative body in a city government.

1686 Munsell *Ann. Albany* II. 71 The mayor and any three or more of the aldermen, and any three or more of the assistants ... shall be called the common council of the said city. **1701** Penn *Charter of Phila.*, The inhabitants ... [may] build wharves so far out into the river there, as the mayor, aldermen and common council ... shall see meet. **1810** *Columbian Centinel* 20 Jan. 2/3 The Common Council have passed a severe ordinance against the exhibition of Masquerades, or Masqued Balls. **1822** *Mass. Laws* 23 Feb. VIII. 739 The citizens of each ward ... shall be called upon to give their votes for four able and discreet men ... to be members of the Common Council. **1844** *Indiana Senate Jrnl.* 130 A bill to ratify the proceedings of the common council of the city of Fort Wayne. **1884** *Century Mag.* April 866/1 The Common Council appropriated twenty-five thousand dollars ... and appointed a building committee.

b. A meeting of this body.

1723 *Weekly Mercury* 19–26 Sept. 2/2 At a Common Council held at the City Hall ... [there were] Present Robert Walter Esq; Mayor, &c.

Common councilman. {*a*1637–} A member of a common council.

1683 *N.Y. Hist. Soc. Coll.* XVIII. 46 The Freemen in each ward doe once every yeare elect their own Officers that is to say Aldermen, Common Councilmen, [etc.]. **1701** Penn *Charter of Phila.*, The said mayor, recorder, aldermen and common council men ... shall be ... one body corporate and politic in deed. **1784** *Mass. Centinel* 15 May 3/1 Twenty four Common councilmen, to be chosen annually. **1844** 'Uncle Sam' *Peculiarities* II. 201 They wanted to make it [the village] into a city, so that there might be the little aristocracy of mayor and common-councilmen. [**1873** Ruskin in *Contemp. Rev.* XXI. 934 Mr. Greg's ... philosophy of Expenditure was expressed with great precision by the Common Councilmen of New York.]

+Common doings. Plain or ordinary fare.

1838 FLAGG *Far West* II. 72 What'll ye take: wheat-bread and chicken fixens, or corn-bread and common doins? by the latter being signified bacon. **1839** MARRYAT *Diary in A.* II. 228 In the West, when you stop at an inn, they say—'What will you have? Brown meal and common doings, or white wheat and chicken fixings.' **1846** LEVINGE *Echoes fr. Backwoods* II. 46 We were, therefore, obliged to content ourselves with 'common doings,' instead of 'chicken fixens'—the southern mode of expressing the difference between an *en famille* manner of feeding and the preparation for a guest.

***Commoner.**

***1.** One who has a joint interest in land held in common. *Obs.* {-1613, 1839}

1646 [see COMMONAGE 2]. **1669** *Groton Rec.* 25 Th[ey shall be] and now ar free Commoners for wood and timber. **1735** *Harvard Rec.* I. 295 The said several Lots being butted and bounded as in the Commoners Book of Records. **1760** *Essex Inst. Coll.* XXI. 225 Chosen, a Committee to Go to the Commoners to ask for a burying Place. **1800** *Mass. H. S. Coll.* VI. 235 The cottagers would not agree with the commoners.

2. In certain colleges, a student who boards in the college. {1613-}

1807 *Union Coll. Laws* 34 The steward shall keep an accurate list of the commoners. **1856** HALL *College Words* (ed. 2) 112 *Commoner*, . . . one who boards in commons. **1856** KANE *Arctic Explor.* I. 419 They [=Eskimos] truly sit down, . . . knife in hand, . . . and . . . falling to like college commoners after grace [etc.].

3. *Great Commoner*, a title popularly used to honor political leaders supposed to possess the virtues of the common people, +esp. Henry Clay (1777-1852), Thaddeus Stevens (1792-1868), R. P. Bland (1835-1899), and W. J. Bryan (1860-1925).

No doubt suggested by the application of the name to the elder William Pitt, as a prominent member of the House of Commons.

1844 E. SARGENT *H. Clay* 6/2 Mr. Clay . . was soon regarded as the leading spirit of the opposition party; and it was about this time [=*c*1800] that the title of 'The Great Commoner' was bestowed upon him. **1852** *Harper's Mag.* V. 392/2 We have just returned from . . . witnessing the long procession, . . . that accompanied the remains of the 'Great Commoner' and great statesman, Henry Clay. **1868** *Congress. Globe* 17 Dec. 131/1 With his own supporters . . . 'Old Thad' was a phrase of endearment; while even his foes spoke of him with pride as the 'great Commoner.' *Ib.* 18 Dec. 147/2 Mr. Stevens was in the latter part of his career sometimes pleasantly called 'the great Commoner.' **1900** *Congress. Rec.* 17 Feb. 1901/2 Here is the gentleman from N.Y. [Mr. Sulzer] who was created to look like the great commoner, Mr. Clay. *Ib.* 3896/1 He [= Bland] was justly termed the 'Great Commoner.' His tastes and habits were simple and unostentatious. He was a modest man. **1906** *Rev. of Reviews* XXXIV. 259/1 Most of these anti-Bryan leaders have fallen into line and are loudly proclaiming their allegiance to the 'Great Commoner.'

+b. *Old Commoner*, Thaddeus Stevens.

1882 *Congress. Rec.* 10 April 2733/1 The grandest man I have ever met in the American Congress—the 'Old Commoner' of Pennsylvania, Thaddeus Stevens. **1886** LOGAN *Great Conspiracy* 608 As he [Thaddeus Stevens] said these words, the crowded floors and galleries broke out into involuntary applause for the grand 'Old Commoner.'

***Commoning,** *vbl. n. Obs.* The possession, or exercise, of rights in common land. Also attrib.

1661 *Providence Rec.* I. 82 A ffull Right of Commoning in all the Lands aforsaid. **1674** *Ib.* VI. 14, I doe give vnto my Daughter . . . All my Right of Comonaninge on ye East side of ye Seaven mile Line. *Ib.* XIV. 104 Ye said houseing, landes, Meaddowes & Comoning. **1683** *Ib.* V. 50 Lands, meadowes & Comoning, lieing in the aforesd Towne of Providence, betwixt the seven mile line & ye foure mile line. **1704** *Waterbury Town Rec.* 12 Dec. 61 No man shall . . . baight cattell after ye first of Aprill till commoning time.

***Common pleas.** Ellipt. for COURT OF COMMON PLEAS. — **1885** HOWELLS *S. Lapham* i, He's one of their leading lawyers, out Dubuque way; been judge of the Common Pleas once or twice.

***Commons.** (See also COMMON *n.* 1.)

***1.** The citizens of a town. *Obs.*

1631 *Mass. Bay Rec.* I. 87 It was ordered nowe, with full consent of the commons then present, that . . . a Generall Court shalbe holden. *a***1649** WINTHROP *Hist.* I. 63 All the freemen of the commons were sworn to this government.

***2.** A meal or meals served in certain colleges.

1643 *New Eng. First Fruits* II. i, Harvard Colledge . . . having in it a spacious Hall (where they daily meet at Commons, Lectures, and Exercises) and a large Library with some Bookes to it. *a***1649** WINTHROP *Hist.* II. 139 They sat in the college, and had their diet there after the manners of scholars' commons, but somewhat better. **1653** *Boston Rec.* 13 This gift may continue . . . for an addition or an inlargement to the comons of the poorer sort of schollrs which I have often heard is too short & bare for them. **1667** *Harvard Rec.* I. 47 The Butler & Cooke, shall not deliver at meale-tymes, save in case of sickness, . . . any Commons to any schollars. **1852** *Harper's Mag.* V. 276/1 Before commons were abolished at Yale College, it used to be customary for the steward to provide turkeys for the Thanksgiving dinner. **1863** 'G. HAMILTON' *Gala-Days* 376 That commons be of better quality, have more variety, clean table cloths . . . and that plates be allowed.

b. The place where such meals are served; also, the arrangement for eating such meals.

1790 *Harvard Laws* 37 Undergraduates . . . shall constantly be in commons. *Ib.* 38 No graduate shall put himself out of commons, unless he be going out of town, for more than a day. **1836** *Harvardiana* II. 273 You board in commons. **1871** BAGG *At Yale* 44 Commons, the college boarding house. **1871** *Scribner's Mo.* II. 522 Irregularities and roughnesses so often complained of in college commons.

transf. **1845** S. JUDD *Margaret* I. 11 The house was divided by the chimney into two principal apartments, one being the kitchen or commons, the other a work-shop.

attrib. **1827** *Harvard Reg.* Oct. 254 The summons of the Commons-bell. **1835** B. D. WINSLOW [*Harvard*] *Class Poem* 10 For this behold him some ten minutes wait To come to Commons Hall or Chapel late.

+c. A college eating club.

1871 BAGG *At Yale* 243 The college club—usually called the 'Commons,' though it bears no resemblance to the obsolete institution of that name—was started in the summer term of 1866 . . . for the purpose of furnishing a cheap but respectable board at its cost price.

+Common school.

1. An elementary or secondary public school, supported wholly or in part by taxation.

1795 in R. Boese *Public Educ. in City of N.Y.* (1869) 21 The establishment of Common Schools throughout the state is happily calculated to remedy this inconvenience. **1818** *Conn. Educational Docs.* (1853) 147 The School Fund, shall remain a perpetual fund, the interest of which shall be inviolably appropriated to the support . . . of the public or common schools throughout the State. **1820** W. TUDOR *Lett. Eastern States* 120 Next to these common schools, come the grammar schools, which are maintained in the more populous towns, and the scale of tuition in these is higher. **1825** *Conn. Educational Docs.* (1853) 151 Between our common schools, and an academic education in our colleges, our laws recognize an intermediate grade. **1832** WILLIAMSON *Maine* II. 686 By an ordinance of 1647, all towns were required to support free and common schools; and also grammar-schools, when the towns were so large as to contain 100 families. **1851** *Mich. Constitution* vi, The general assembly shall . . . secure a thorough and efficient system of common schools throughout the state. **1857** *Quinland* I. 273 To-day I have been before the School Commissioners to be examined and get my certificate of qualification for teaching a common school. **1883** *Century Mag.* Aug. 572/1 Miss Windom remained but a few months at the common school, and then left it for the high school. **1886** Z. F. SMITH *Kentucky* 713 An effort . . . to revive the university and place it at the head of our system of rising common schools failed to meet the approval of the Legislature. **1902** *Rep. Comm. Education* p. x, A comparative summary showing the increase in what are called common schools, including under this designation schools of the elementary and secondary grades supported from public funds.

2. The building in which an elementary public school is accommodated.

1835 J. MARTIN *Description of Va.* 153 It contains several dwelling houses, . . . a mercantile store, and a common school.

3. *attrib.* **a.** *Common-school education*, the learning and training to be derived from the common schools; also, the process or systematic instruction by which such learning and training are inculcated.

1818 *Boston Daily Advertiser* 21 April, Have they not a right to a good bringing up, and to a common school education? **1837** *S. Lit. Messenger* III. 161 The introduction of too specific and practical branches . . . into common school education is nugatory. **1837** MARTINEAU *Society* III. 337 New Jersey.—A fund of 222,000 dollars being realised, a system of Common School education was about to be put in action. **1842** *Niles' Nat. Reg.* 29 Jan. 352/3 This [contribution] is purely voluntary, and exhibits the growing interests of the people on the subject of common school education. **1872** *Atlantic Mo.* June 704 It was inculcated . . . that a common-school education included all the moral virtues. **1885** *Rep. Indian Affairs* 199 The common-school education of white children is very different from that required by Indian children. **1905** G. E. COLE *Early Oregon* 22 [They] had never had the benefit of a common school education and of course were but beginners.

b. *Common-school system*, the organization of common schools into a unified plan or scheme.

1831 PECK *Guide* 245 A complete common school system must . . . be organized. **1835** *S. Lit. Messenger* II. 18 The Common-school system of New York . . . has been in operation since the year 1816. **1871** in Fleming *Hist. Reconstruction* II. 203 The sparseness of our population is the greatest drawback to a common-school system. **1871** *Rep. Indian Affairs* 489 The common school-system, the great bulwark of civilization, can be best applied here, of course subject to such modifications as may be necessary. **1877** *Harper's Mag.* April 722/2 Our common school system . . . and public libraries . . . constitute a new and powerful force. **1893** *Ib.* April 666/2 'A people with a highly developed common-school system,' said he, 'is better than a dull, degraded, despairing peasantry.'

c. *Common-school district,* a limited portion of a county or state provided with, or supporting, a common school.

1849 CHAMBERLAIN *Ind. Gazetteer* 152 The common school districts are generally organized and support schools from three to ten months in the year. *Ib.* 337 Good schools are kept up in most of the common school districts into which the whole county is divided.

d. Misc. with *fund, house, instruction,* etc.

1866 *Fla. Acts 1865-6* 39 A tuition fee shall be collected . . . whic[h] shall be paid into the treasury of the State as a portion of the common school fund for freedmen. **1844** *Indiana Senate Jrnl.* 140 Resolved, That the committee on education enquire in to the propriety of adopting by law, common school houses as county seminaries. **1883** *Harper's Mag.* Sept. 636/2 Mr. Adams' interest in what is called the Quincy system of common-school instruction. **1881** *Ib.* April 640/2 Every reputable person . . . knows that the state [of Vermont] has the same . . . common-school intelligence as the rest of New England. **1856** STOWE *Dred* I. 107 He was as guiltless of all knowledge of common-school learning as Governor Berkeley. **1873** *Harper's Mag.* XLVI. 785 Mr. Stewart introduced a bill in the Senate, February 17, granting the State of Nevada 1,000,000 acres of the public lands for common-school purposes. **1844** *Indiana Senate Jrnl.* 292 A bill to authorize the school trustees of congressional townships to act as examiners of common school teachers.

Commonweal.* +The organized following of Jacob S. Coxey (1854–) which in 1894 marched on Washington in an effort to secure relief from a financial depression. Also attrib. — **1894 *Columbus* (O.) *Dispatch* 4 April, It begins to look as though the commonweal will go through to Washington. If the commonwealers under Frye . . . succeed in effecting a union with the Coxeyites the general army will be a formidable thing. **1894** *Chautauquan* XIX. 335/1 Carl Browne saw in this the spirit of the reincarnated Christ abroad in the army, but to mere mortals it appeared to be due to the military organization of the Commonweal and to the strict discipline enforced by the next in rank to Browne. **1900** *Ohio Archæol. & Hist. Publ.* IX. 163 The organizers . . . tempered their appeal with the hope that no one in ill health would join the Commonweal. *Ib.* 166 The day brought a number of recruits for the Commonweal Army.

+**Commonwealer.** A believer in the principles of J. S. Coxey (1854–). — **1894** *Lancaster* (Pa.) *Morning News* 16 May, A freedom from the wear and tear of manual labor—which will appeal strongly to the mind of the advanced Commonwealer. **1894** in D. L. McMurry *Coxey's Army* (1929) 52 But to say, as has been said, that the Commonwealers do not know what they want in Washington is nonsense.

***Commonwealth.**

+1. The organized community, or body politic, of any one of the American colonies. Now hist.

'They now [in 1634] retained the outward form of their charter, and changed a trading company into a government, which they called "Commonwealth." The word was not new; the government was' (Ernst in *Bostonian Soc. Proc. 1897* 23).

a1649 WINTHROP *Hist.* I. 132 They ought not to depart from us, being . . . bound by oath to seek the welfare of this commonwealth. **1677** *N.E. Hist. & Gen. Reg.* III. 43 The p[er]sons Whose names ar vnder wretten . . . Desire that they may be admited to the freedom of this Common welth.

+2. Any individual state of the United States.

But specifically, 'Massachusetts, Pennsylvania, Virginia, and Kentucky are officially styled commonwealths' (*Cent.*).

1779 *Penna. Gaz.* 24 March 4/3 All the best whigs in the commonwealth. **1788** in Marshall *Kentucky* (1812) 375 On the western waters the commonwealth of Virginia possessed a fertile but uninhabited wild. **1837** JACKSON in *Pres. Mess. & P.* III. 279 A letter addressed to me . . . by the governor of the State of New Hampshire, communicating several resolutions of the legislature of that Commonwealth. **1865** LOWELL in *N. Amer. Rev.* C. 161 The sturdy commonwealths which have sprung from the seed of the Mayflower. **1884** BLAINE *20 Years Congress* I. 460 Its [West Virginia's] organization and admission to the Union would complete the chain of loyal Commonwealths on the South side of Mason and Dixon's line. **1903** R. T. ELY *Evol. Industrial Soc.* 328 There may be some ground to apprehend that in the U.S. the cities and federal government are increasing in importance more rapidly than our commonwealths.

+**Commonwealth paper.** A bond or security issued by a state government. — **1845** SOL. SMITH *Theatr. Apprent.* 121, I asked him at what rate he took Commonwealth paper?

‖**Commote,** *v. tr.* To put into commotion, disturb. — **1852** HAWTHORNE *Blithedale Rom.* xvi. 165 An unfriendly state of feeling could not occur between any two members, without the whole society being more or less commoted and made uncomfortable thereby. **a1864** — *Dr. Grimshawe's Secret* 334 The Warden, greatly commoted for the nonce, complied with the maiden's fantasy.

***Commune,** *v. intr.* To participate in Holy Communion. {-1710, now archaic}

1787 CUTLER in *Life & Corr.* I. 237 The church which belongs to the two houses are but one corporate body, although they commune separately. **1823** FARMER & MOORE *New Hampshire Gaz.* 198 The first settlers had preaching before 1750—a church was gathered and occasionally communed. **1828** WEBSTER, *Commune,* . . . to partake of the sacrament or Lord's supper; to receive the communion; a common use of the word in America, as it is in the Welsh. *Ib.* s.v. *Communicate,* In America, at least in New England, commune is generally or always used. **1831** *Liberator* 26 Feb. 34/1 (Th.S.), Some of our citizens . . . were carrying on the slave trade, while with a smooth face they were praying in our religious societies, and communing at the Lord's table. **1846** WORCESTER 142/1 *Commune,* . . . to partake of the Lord's supper. U.S. **1856** STOWE *Dred* I. 322 For my part . . . I shouldn't *commune* with nobody that didn't believe in election, 'up to the hub.'

***Communicant.** One who receives the Holy Communion.

1671 J. ELIOT *Brief Narr. Progress* 25 We have betwixt forty and fifty Communicants at the Lord's Table. **1693** C. MATHER *Wond. Invis. World* 10 Churches, whose Communicants have been seriously examined about their Experiences of Regeneration. **1743** MACSPARRAN *Diary* 2, I . . . received a new Communicant. **1871** *Rep. Indian Affairs* (1872) 174 We had at the last report about twelve communicants among the Indians.

b. In a church which observes close communion, esp. the Baptist Church, a member of the congregation who has received baptism in accordance with the tenets of the church.

1747 *N.H. Hist. Soc. Coll.* IX. 7 They also informed us that a considerable Number of their Communicants & others of their Congregation had separated from them. **1831** PECK *Guide* 260 Churches 15, preachers 12, communicants 375. **1837** — *Gaz. Illinois* 73 The Baptist Denomination includes 22 Associations . . . and 7,350 communicants. **1849** CHAMBERLAIN *Ind. Gazetteer* 71 This denomination [=the Baptists] has, in this State, 42 Associations, 665 Churches, 275 Preachers, 95 Licentiates, and 27,200 communicants.

***Communication.**

1. A line or means of connection between places; a road or way. {1715-}

1787 CUTLER in *Life & Corr.* II. 395 Through the Sandusky and Scioto lies the most common pass from Canada to the Ohio and Mississippi, one of the most extensive and useful communications that are to be found in any country. **1811** *Boston Selectmen* 11 Dec., They find it to be an important object to them to lay open the communication. **1920** *3rd Nat. Country Life Conf. Proc.* 183 Country planning involves . . . the consideration of that sort of rural Communication which we denominate the road system.

b. *Mil.* The road or passage over which supplies and reinforcements are brought to an army.

1861 *Army Regulations* 106 In making an attack, the communications to the rear and for retreat must be secured. **1864** *Spectator* 31 Dec. 1478 Lee's communications through South-Western Virginia . . . have been cut by General Stoneman. **1881-5** MCCLELLAN *Own Story* 274 We would have found a new line of defence in front of us, completely covering the enemy's communications.

2. In Freemasonry, a conference or assembly of the lodge. {1723-}

1795 in H. M. Brooks *Gleanings* 77 The Officers and Members of the Grand Lodge . . . are hereby requested to attend a Quarterly Communication at Concert-Hall in Boston.

Communism. {1843-}

1. The theory favoring communal ownership of property, regarded unfavorably largely because it led to riots.

1854 SIMMS *Southward Ho.* 394 Until you reconcile this inequality, and exorcise this evil spirit, that now rages rampant through the Northern States—allied with all sorts of fanatical passions and principles—Agrarianism, Communism, Fourierism, Wrightism, Millerism, Mormonism, etc., . . . you will neither make peace nor secure union. **1870** BEADLE *Utah* 37 In March, 1832, Joe Smith and Sidney Rigdon . . . were tarred and feathered by a mob, 'for attempting to establish Communism, for forgery and dishonorable dealing,' according to their adversaries. **1877** *N.Y. Herald* 24 July 8/4 The project of holding a meeting in Tompkins square, which is sure to be dominated by the spirit of Communism, is deprecated by workingmen themselves. **1878** PINKERTON *Strikers* p. xi, The deadly spirit of Communism steals in and further embitters the workingman against that from which his very livelihood is secured, and gradually makes him an enemy to all law, order, and good society. **1883** *Harper's Mag.* Nov. 964/1 Socialism and Communism have engaged the interest and excited the apprehensions of the friends of law and order. **1884** LOWELL *Democracy,* Communism means barbarism, but Socialism means . . . co-operation and community of interests. **1921** *N.Y. Times* 21 Dec. 5/2, I [=F. A. Vanderlip] can say on the authority of its greatest leaders union labor has renounced its faith in communism.

2. In loose usage: Lawlessness, anarchy.

1874 *Chicago Times* 24 Feb. 7/4 Communism in Kentucky. Ku-Klux Attempts to Drive Labor Out of Franklin County. **1878** PINKERTON *Strikers* 387 Communism and Riot at Chicago.

Communist. {1841-}

1. One who believes in communism; also, loosely, an agitator.

1878 PINKERTON *Strikers* 365 The mobs . . . were composed, precisely as they were in Chicago, of the communists and the very scum of the place. **1887** *Courier-Journal* 5 Jan. 2/3 They never tire of telling you . . . how he 'bested,' as the pugilists say, 'the blatherskite Communist Arnold,' in joint debate at Jonesboro. **1891** *Congress. Rec.* 2 March 3777/1 If I had my say, I would stop the immigration of Mormons, communists, anarchists, nihilists, [etc.]. **1899** CHESNUTT *Wife of His Youth* 298 We expect to show that the defendent is a man of dangerous character, . . . in other words, a negro nihilist, a communist. **1923** LOVETT in *New Republic* XXXV. 198/1 The Workers' party . . . is the stage name of the Communists.

attrib. **1877** 'E. MARTIN' *Hist. Great Riots* 111 The desperate communist leaders and plunderers in the community saw their opportunity in the weakness of the citizens. **1922** *New Republic* XXXIII. 55/2 Members of the Communist Labor party [were] tried and convicted under the criminal syndicalist law in 1919. **1925** *N.Y. Times* 3 Sept. 1/2 The man in question is a Communist agitator.

2. A member of a colony or settlement conducted in accordance with communistic theory.

See also the earlier BIBLE COMMUNIST (1867–69).

1898 *Outing* XXXII. 29 Once we passed four stolid Dutch Communists plodding along the bank [of the Iowa R.]; with their clumsy oxen and lumbering wagon, out for a load of wood.

3. *attrib.* = COMMUNISTIC *a.*

1878 *N. Amer. Rev.* CXXVII. 56 When crossed in love they would prefer a nunnery to an Owen phalanstery or a communist settlement at Oneida.

Communistic, *a.* {1851–} Of, or characteristic of, the principles of communism.

1875 C. NORDHOFF (*title*), The Communistic Societies of the United States. **1878** *N. Amer. Rev.* CXXVII. 8 [Universal suffrage] gives power to the communistic attack on property. **1878** PINKERTON *Strikers* 161 From Martinsburg the communistic madness radiated in various directions. **1884** NYE *Baled Hay* 40 With a communistic laundress, it seems to me most anybody ought to be unhappy enough without a cat. **1889** *Century Mag.* XXXVII. 600/1 Thither Gerald was marshaled by a communistic-looking waiter. **1898** *Scribner's Mag.* XXIV. 100/1 Such Anarchists were of the 'Individualistic' type. Not all of those I met were so philosophical, however. The Communistic one, who was nodding at me in a friendly manner from a near table, notably was not.

‖**Communitarian.** {1841–} A member of a community in which are practiced communistic or socialistic theories. — **1852** HAWTHORNE *Blithedale Rom.* viii. 78 These mendacious rogues circulated a report that we communitarians were exterminated. **1880** *Scribner's Mo.* XIX. 487 When the 'communitarians,' as Hawthorne calls them in his 'Blithedale Romance,' came here, in 1841, there were only a farm-house and a barn on the place.

‖**Communitary,** *a.* Pertaining to community interest or welfare. Hence *Communitariness.* — **1895** *Advance* (Chicago) 14 March 846/1 The societies in which they [*sc.* Harvard and Yale] were placed were characterized by a communitariness of blood, belief, interest and character. *Ib.*, No communitary instinct pervades and unifies society [in the Western States].

***Community.** A communistic or socialistic society. {1874–} — **1844** EMERSON *New Eng. Ref.* Wks. I. 264 Following, or advancing beyond the ideas of St. Simon, of Fourier, and of Owen, three communities have already been formed in Massachusetts. **1879** J. H. NOYES in Estlake *Oneida Community* 36, I need hardly remind the Community that we have always claimed freedom of conscience to change our social practices. **1900** ESTLAKE *Ib.* 1 If John H. Noyes could harmonise his followers into a family of loving relations and happiness, it was not a fanatical proceeding . . . when he founded the Oneida Community and declared it to be the Kingdom of Heaven. — *attrib.* **1851** HAWTHORNE *House of 7 Gables* v, Community-men, and come-outers, as Hepzibah believed, who acknowledged no law, and ate no solid food.

***Commutation.** +In attrib. uses: Of or pertaining to the reduced rates for regular passengers between neighboring places.

1856 W. H. SWIFT *Mass. Railroads* 14 Commutation or season passengers, so called. **1887** GEORGE *40 Years on Rail* 89 You have had a great deal of experience in carrying commutation passengers in Boston. **1903** E. JOHNSON *Railway Transportation* 148 The 'resort' traffic and suburban traffic, or what is frequently called the commutation business, is zealously stimulated by reduction in fares and by offering an attractive service.

b. *Commutation ticket,* a passenger ticket good for several rides issued at a reduced rate; also a meal ticket issued at a reduced rate.

1849 *Pathfinder* Nov. 50 (Ernst). **1873** *Ill. Revised Statutes* (1883) 885 Nothing herein contained shall be so construed as to prevent railroad corporations from issuing commutation, excursion or thousand-mile tickets. **1885** *Good Words* July 450/1 A single 'Commutation' ticket is given, numbered and dated on the day on which it was issued. At each journey the conductor punches the ticket. **1899** F. NORRIS *McTeague* 290 Trina had lied again both as to the want of oil for the stove and the commutation ticket for the restaurant. **1903** E. JOHNSON *Railway Transportation* 295 Passenger fares in the United States range from about a cent a mile for some kinds of 'commutation' tickets up to 4 and 5 cents a mile in the sparsely settled and mountainous sections of the country.

Commute, *v.* {1633–} [Cf. COMMUTATION, COMMUTER.] +*intr.* To travel by use of a commutation ticket; esp. to ride back and forth between a city and a suburban residence.

1865 [implied in COMMUTER]. **1889** *Cent.* 1139 *Commuter,* one who commutes. **1893** *Stand.* 382 *Commute,* to . . . buy or use a commutation ticket. **1906** *Daily Chron.* (Lond.) 25 Feb. 4 There are many business men who practically divide their time between New York and Chicago, and 'commute' (the American term for taking season tickets). **1911** *N.Y. Ev. Post* Financial Suppl. 4 Feb. 3 A large number of Wall Street folk commute by the Erie. **1924** D. LAWRENCE *True Story W. Wilson* 88 Mr. Wilson continued to live in Princeton, commuting every morning the twelve miles between his home and his office.

+**Commuter.** [Back formation from COMMUTATION.] One who rides on a commutation ticket.

1865 *Atlantic Mo.* XV. 82 Two or three may be styled commuters' roads, running chiefly for the accommodation of city business-men with suburban residences. **1869** BARNUM *Struggles & Triumphs* 653, I urged that there was a tacit understanding between the railroad and these commuters and the public generally. **1898** *Harper's Weekly* 26 Feb. 205/3 Of all criminally good-natured individuals the New York commuter is the worst offender. **1907** 'O. HENRY' *Trimmed Lamp*, etc. 234 Miss Claribel Colby . . . belonged to that sad company of mariners known as Jersey commuters. **1908** A. RUHL *Other Americans* 47 Everybody seemed to know everybody else. It was like a commuter's train going out to Jersey at six o'clock. **1910** *N.Y. Ev. Post* 21 Feb. (Th.), The commuter, the man who has been lured from a Manhattan apartment to a suburban house and lot.

+**Compadre.** *S.W.* and *W.* [Sp. (f. *com* and *padre*) godfather.] An intimate male companion or associate, a friend; esp. used as a familiar term of address.

1834 A. PIKE *Sketches* 99 Nay, compadre, an American cannot steal. **1850** GARRARD *Wah-To-Yah* v. 72, I had apprehensions he would lie in wait with his compadres. **1852** R. H. WEIGHTMAN *Let.* 10 Sept. in *Manuel Alvarez Papers,* The efforts of Houghton and his compadres here (Reynolds etc.) to injure the people cannot now be misunderstood. **1869** BROWNE *Adv. Apache Country* 172 Every generation the population grows worse; and the Sonoranians may now be ranked with their natural compadres—Indians, burros, and coyotes. **1895** M. MCCLELLAND *St. John's Wooing* 136 Tell me, compadre, how many loves have you had! **1912** RAINE *Brand Blotters* 50 Not a single sweetheart in all this wide open country. Shall I go rope you one and bring him in, *compadre?* **1925** WHITE *Them Was the Days* 25 He come to the door and he look in and see hees big *compadre* drinking a bottle of beer.

+**Compañero, Companyero.** *S.W. & W. colloq.* [Sp.] A male companion; a 'pardner.'

1845 FRÉMONT *Exped.* 256 Four *compañeros* joined our guide at the pass. *a***1849** RUXTON *Life Far West* iii. 64 A trapper . . . has just recognized an old campanyero, with whom he hunted years before in the perilous country of the Blackfeet. **1850** GARRARD *Wah-To-Yah* xvii. 203 At the portal were several compañeros, discussing in a very light way the 'fun,' as they termed it, on hand. **1889** FARMER 161/2 *Companero,* . . . in the bucolic dialect of the plains, a companion or partner; equivalent to the mining slang Pard. [**1923** W. SMITH *Little Tigress* 209, I want to ride again with my companeros who sing with the hearts of children and die with the hearts of heroes.]

***Company.**

1. An association organized to colonize or carry on trade with America: **a.** *Virginia Company.* **b.** Any of the colonizing companies of New England.

(**a**) **1619** in Bradford *Hist.* 47 Thomas Smith, repining at his many offices & troubls, wished the Company of Virginia to ease him of his office in being Treasurer & Gover[no]r of the Virginia Company. **1622** J. SMITH *New Eng. Trials* (1884) 256 The Virginia Company, vpon this, sent 4 good ships. **1624** — *Virginia* 177 It came to be apprehended by some of the Virginia Company. *a***1656** BRADFORD *Hist.* 39 Other messengers were dispatched, to end with ye Virginia Company as well as they could.
(**b**) **1626** *Plymouth Laws* 28 A fine of twise the vallue for all so sold to be duly taken by the Governour for the use and benefit of the company. **1633** *Winthrop P.* II. 89, I have sent you this inclosed letter from our Company at London to that part of our Company which was then supposed to be here, the last yere. *a***1656** BRADFORD *Hist.* 384 Mr. Winslow was sente . . . into England, . . . partly to signifie unto ye partners in England, that the terme of their trade with ye company here was out.

***2.** An association for carrying on a commercial or industrial enterprise.

1796 *Essex Inst. Coll.* LIV. 105 [The co-partners] have agreed to form themselves into a Company, or, Co-partnership, for the purpose of erecting mills. **1827** DRAKE & MANSFIELD *Cincinnati* 80 [The] Ohio Insurance Company . . . was incorporated in January, 1826. **1854** BARTLETT *Personal Narr.* II. 67 The company possess a large tract of land here. **1878** PINKERTON *Strikers* 241 His thought, then, was that possibly by retiring within the machine-shop yards he might . . . offer a thorough protection to the company's property.

***3.** A body of soldiers or armed men.

1631 *Mass. Bay Rec.* I. 85 It is ordered, that euery Captaine shall traine his companie on Saturday in euerie weeke. **1707** *Boston News-Letter* 17 Nov. 2/2 Col. Winthrop Hilton with a Company of men marches to morrow to range the Woods of the Eastern Frontiers in quest of the Indian Enemy. **1790** *Ann. 1st Congress* II. 1815 Companies and battalions should be obliged to turn out only twice a year. **1864** EDWARDS *Shelby* 468 Official appeals had been in vain made to the inhabitants to organize military Companies. **1888** *Chicago Inter-Ocean* 23 Jan. (F.), The advice given to his company by a raw Yankee captain to advance backward.

b. A band of Indian (or Indian and French) warriors.
1704 *Boston News-Letter* 22 May 1/2 A Company of Indians and French, between day break and Sun-rising, about 60 Set upon a Garrison-house. **1775** ADAIR *Indians* 384 The common number of an Indian war company, is only from twenty to forty.

***4.** A person, or persons, visiting or living at the home of another; guests.
1869 TOURGEE *Toinette* i. 15 Your sisters have a good deal of company, and your aunt is a good housekeeper. **1904** T. WATSON *Bethany* 9 These new rooms were filled with costly furniture, and were dedicated to the use of 'company.'

5. *attrib.* **a.** In sense 2 with *bank*, etc. **b.** In sense 4 with *air, apron, cap*, etc.
(a) 1917 SINCLAIR *King Coal* 152 You'll find yourself facing a box with Jake Predovich as foreman, three company-clerks, two of Alf Raymond's saloon-keepers, a ranchman with a mortgage held by the company-bank, [etc.]. *Ib.* 34 Red-faced feller, Gus. Look out for him—company spotter. **1872** *Harper's Mag.* Nov. 841/1 This arrangement is a much better one than that of a 'company store,' which is so common elsewhere, especially with joint-stock companies. **1917** SINCLAIR *King Coal* 85 We've had laws passed, a whole raft of laws about coal-mining—the eight-hour law, the anti-scrip law, the company-store law, [etc.]. **1865** *Atlantic Mo.* XV. 69 Twenty-four hours have passed, and I hear them singing, . . . all down that company-street.
(b) 1886 *Harper's Mag.* Sept. 588/1 Large women, offensively dressed, sit about the veranda, and give a hearty and 'company' air to the drawing-rooms. **1891** WILKINS *New Eng. Nun* 3 Under that [apron] was still another; . . . that was Louisa's company apron. **1904** GLASGOW *Deliverance* 114 We . . . found old Mrs. Dudley just putting on her company cap. **1873** BAILEY *Life in Danbury* 116 Arriving at the school he stiffly returned the salutation of the polite teacher, and majestically settled into the 'company chair.' **1884** *Century Mag.* April 807/2 In early times this room was called the 'company dining-room,' to distinguish it from the family dining-room across the hall. **1844** *Knickerb.* XXIII. 192 An article we penned . . . many years ago, before we were hampered with the professorial 'we,' and could write out of our company dress. **1886** P. STAPLETON *Major's Christmas* 97 His wife . . . was kind and good to me, . . . making me sleep in her company room as I'd been the best leddy in the land. **1910** C. HARRIS *Eve's Husband* 109 He would come in the front gate, . . . creep upstairs to the 'company room,' undress and get in bed. **1881** *Harper's Mag.* Feb. 357/1 Our ancesters were content to dine from pewter plates and porringers, their . . . china being reserved for company use.

***Comparison.** +A game: (see quotation). — **1828** *Yankee* Sept. 288/1 Comparison is very amusing for a still play; in playing this, one of the company leaves the room; in his or her absence, some one names a subject; the absent person is then called in, who asks them all separately what it is like.

***Compass.**

***1.** An instrument used to determine the magnetic meridian, or the position of objects in reference to it.
See also *mariner's, pocket, surveying compass.*
a1649 WINTHROP *Hist.* I. 68 He always carried about him match and a compass. *Ib.* II. 225 D'Aulnay . . . denied them . . . any gun or compass, whereby it was justly conceived that he intended they should perish. **1787** *Md. Hist. Mag.* XIX. 265 The mother of the complainants wife sighted with a compass from the tree. **1805** LEWIS in *L. & Clark Exped.* (1904) II. 197 S[h]arbono lost his gun . . . and my wiping rod, Capt. Clark his Umbrella and compass or circumferenter. **1847** PARKMAN in *Knickerb.* XXX. 133, I had a little compass hung at my neck. **1877** W. WRIGHT *Big Bonanza* 37 It is the stuff they make compasses of—surveyors' compasses, mariners' compasses, and all them kind of compasses that pint to the North Pole.

b. *Compass line,* a line of direction used for reference and checking.
1799 ELLICOTT *Journal* App. 84 From the termination of the above mentioned 1080.15 perches, another guide, or compass line was continued east. *Ib.,* The termination of the compass line, not being in a proper place for a course of observations, the observatory was erected north of it.

2. Attrib. in the names of mechanical devices: *Compass board, c. joint, c. saw.*
1874 KNIGHT 599/2 *Compass-board,* the hole-board of the loom for fancy weaving. It is an upright board of the loom through which pass the neck-twines. **1871** *Rep. Comm. Patents* II. 98/1 Theodore Alteneder, Philadelphia, Pa. *China*—The halves *a* and *b* of a compass-joint . . . and the combination and arrangement thereof. **1874** KNIGHT 600/1 *Compass-joint,* a form of joint usual in compasses in which one leg has a circular disk or two, clamped between other disks belonging to the fellow leg. **1794** *Mass. Spy* 1 May 4/2 (*advt.*), Ready for Sale . . . Crosscut, Hand, Tenon, Sash, Dovetail, and Compass Saws [etc.].

+3. *Compass flower, c. plant,* the rosinweed, *Silphium laciniatum.*
[**1843** BOONE *Jrnl.* 191 The polar plant, a rosin weed. This plant is a tall plant, perhaps 7 feet high, with a few [*sic*] shaped leaf which ranges, generally north and south, affording a tolerable compass to the traveler over the prairies.] **1847** LONGFELLOW *Evangeline* 1219 This is the compass-flower, that the finger of God has planted. **1851** GLISAN *Jrnl. Army Life* 70 There is a very useful plant, called the compass-plant, because the edges of its leaves point due north and south. **1857** GRAY *Botany* 210 Lower leaves . . . on the wide open prairies, said to present their edges uniformly north and south, and hence called *Compass-Plant.* **1871** *Amer. Naturalist* V. 1 The first mention of the so-called 'polarity' of the Compass Plant, *Silphium laciniatum,* was made . . . in August, 1842. **1901** MOHR *Plant Life Ala.* 792.

***Compensation.** +A salary; payment for services rendered.
1787 *Constitution* i. § 6 The Senators and Representatives shall receive a compensation for their services to be ascertained by law, and paid out of the Treasury of the U.S. **1793** *Ann. 2nd Congress* 1431 From and after the third day of March . . . the compensation of the President of the United States shall be at the rate of twenty-five thousand dollars per annum. **1842** DICKENS *Amer. Notes* 48, The Presidential housemaids have high wages, or, to speak more genteelly, an ample amount of 'compensation:' which is the American word for salary, in the case of all public servants. **1852** GLISAN *Jrnl. Army Life* 101 Let our lawmakers who think the life of the officer so easy that he deserves but little compensation ponder over these things also. **1904** *Indian Laws & Tr.* III. 594 Who will prescribe suitable compensation for their services? **1907** C. C. ANDREWS *Recoll.* 198 Compensation must be such, as you and your employer can agree upon. **1924** C. A. BEARD *Amer. Govt.* 627 The salaries of judges are usually rather low in comparison with the compensation afforded to judicial officers in Europe.
attrib. **1816** *Niles' Reg.* X. 415/1 The 'compensation law' is doing wonders. **1817** *Ib.* XIII. 31/1 It is stated that not more than one of the old members of Congress will be returned by Tennessee, on account of the compensation law. **1852** *Harper's Mag.* V. 395/1 'Have I ever "flashed," ' continued Mr. Clay, 'except on the "Compensation bill?" '

+Comper. (See first quotation.) — **1836** *Yale Lit. Mag.* I. 26 (Th.), Any fracas or tumult, like the Calethump of Christmas eve memory, would be styled a 'comper.' *Ib.* 27 What pen can describe the 'comper' which this excited!

***Complain,** *v. intr.* Of a thing: To groan or creak from overstraining. {1722–, *naut.*} — **1711** SEWALL *Diary* II. 322 Our axel-tree, that complain'd before, and we mended it at Calef's, broke quite off by that time we got to Caperons.

‖**Complaint-book.** A book in which complaints may be written. — **1856** D. MACLEOD *F. Wood* 201 Two qualities suggested and produced the Complaint-Book. The public were notified through the press that such a book was opened at the Mayor's office, wherein might be registered complaints of dereliction from duty on the part of any corporation officers, of violated ordinances, of illegal incumbrances, of nuisances.

‖**Complainy,** *a.* Whiny; given to complaining because of illness. — **1887** *Harper's Mag.* March 547/2 News come to Cousin Cynthy only yisterday that her aunt was quite complainy.

+Complected, *ppl. a.* **a.** As the second element in compounds, as *black-, dark-, fair-, light-complected. colloq.*
For further illustration see DARK-, LIGHT-COMPLECTED.
1806 LEWIS in *L. & Clark Exped.* (1905) III. 315 They are generally low in stature, proportionably small, reather lighter complected and much more illy formed than the Indians of the Missouri. **1820** *Hillsborough* (N.C.) *Recorder* 3 May, Ran away . . . a Negro man, named Isaac . . . yellow complected, five feet six or eight inches high, two of his under fore teeth out. **1828** *Richmond Enquirer* 2 Feb. 4/3 (Th.), The said negro is . . . stout made; black complected. **1834** BRACKENRIDGE *Recoll.* 224 The next morning . . . poor Greaves's face . . . became as sallow complected and as spotted as a flounder. **c1847** WHITCHER *Bedott P.* 74 She was a dark complected woman. **1850** GARRARD *Wah-To-Yah* xi. 151 The universal accompaniment of this olive-complected race. **1886** *Harper's Mag.* Sept. 578/2 Olive, she's middlin' fair complected. **1907** 'O. HENRY' *Trimmed Lamp,* etc. 66 A heavy-sot man, sandy complected, about twenty-nine.

b. In predicative use.
1863 B. TAYLOR *H. Thurston* 52 He a'n't blacker 'n I'd be now, if I was complected like him. **1868** *Cincinnati Commercial* 9 June (De Vere), She was feeble and emaciated, and complected as I have never seen anyone out of malarious regions.

***Complete,** *a.* **1.** Thoroughly good; excellent; perfect. **2.** *It's complete,* it is just right, perfect. *colloq.* — **(1) 1835** H. C. TODD *Notes* 8 His more favored expressions are . . . Complete going, (good roads); get along, (how do you succeed). **1856** *Spirit of Times* 18 Oct. 106/2 We had a couple of the likeliest hound dogs round them regins—one ov 'em was the completest dog fer luggin' creeters I ever seed. **(2) 1895** A. BROWN *Meadow-Grass* 236 Our folks think it's complete to go over there and worship, and get up and down, and say their prayers out loud.

Compliment, *v.* {c1680–} *tr.* To present (one) with a ticket of admission, often in return for a favor. — **1887** I. ALDEN *Little Fishers* xiv, I wouldn't mind going myself [to the concert] if I could be complimented through. **1889** *Cent.* 1150/1 He complimented us with tickets for the exhibition.

Complimentary benefit. An entertainment or theatrical performance, the profits of which are used for a special purpose. — **1847** *Chicago Jrnl.* 6 Jan. (*advt.*), Complimentary benefit to Mrs. Anderson. **1860** E. COWELL *Diary* 109 Mr. Davie . . . will 'Stir the people' to get up a 'Complimentary Benefit' on Saturday. **1896** *N.Y. Dramatic News* 11 July 8/2 A complimentary benefit was given to Peter Maher and Frank Slavin at the Bijou theatre.

Complimentary ticket. A free ticket. Also ellipt. — **1874** 'MARK TWAIN' *Sk., Pleasure Excursion,* Complimentary round trip tickets have been tendered to General Butler, . . . and other eminent gentlemen. **1878** A. DALY in *Life* (1917) 254 No one threatened us with the vengeance of the White League unless we issued complimentaries to the city officials. **1879** B. F. TAYLOR *Summer-Savory* 27 The managers of the roads act wisely in issuing 'complimentaries' to the Indians. **1887** I. ALDEN *Little Fishers* xiv, 'They are complimentaries,' said Norm, . . . as though complimentary tickets to first-class concerts were every-day affairs with him.

* **Composition.** In various attrib. uses: *C. day,* a school day on which compositions are written or read; *c. roofer,* one who builds roofs of prepared roofing; *c. tea,* a beverage made from infusing various herbs in hot water; *c. work,* objects or parts of a structure made of a combination of metals or of mixed material.

1840 DANA *Two Years* 170 The brass and composition work about the capstan. **1851** CIST *Cincinnati* 49 Occupations [include] . . . Composition roofers, 14 [people]. **1884** J. C. HARRIS *Mingo* 215 In ten minutes you'll be snug in bed, and then you'll drink a cup of composition tea. **1887** PERRY *Flock of Girls* 243 It was a signal for her to begin reading the composition she held in her hand, for it was composition day.

* **Compositor.** One who sets type; a typesetter.

1771 FRANKLIN *Autobiog.* 302 Meredith was no compositor, a poor pressman, and seldom sober. **1810** *Columbian Centinel* 17 Jan. 4/1 Five Compositors, will meet with constant employ for five months, at the office of T. B. Watt and Co. **1833** *Niles' Reg.* XLIV. 375/2 The legislature of Georgia have passed a law, forbidding the employment of any slave or free person of color, as a compositor, (type setter) in any printing office in that state. **1871** *Harper's Mag.* Sept. 635 Either the reporter or the compositor who 'sets' the headings must be a member of some baseball club. **1893** [see COPY].

* **Compost,** *n.* A prepared mixture of fertilizing materials. Also attrib.

1660 *Watertown Rec.* 68 He shall not cary off the p[re]mises any compost. **1804** J. ROBERTS *Penna. Farmer* 15 The earth being mixed with the dung will make a good compost. **1840** in *Mich. Agric. Soc. Trans.* (1853) 302 The compost-heap affords the readiest process for effecting those chemical changes which are necessary to convert peat into nutriment for vegetation. **1868** G. CHANNING *Recoll. Newport* 153 Manhaden, a species of fish . . . which constituted the base of a powerful compost. **1880** *Harper's Mag.* March 527/2 The fields are strewn with compost.

* **Compost,** *v. tr.* To make into compost. {1778–(Marshall *Min. of Agric.*)}

1863 MITCHELL *My Farm* 237 But why don't you compost it; pack up your long manure with turf and muck? **1886** *Harper's Mag.* Sept. 530/1 Manure from the horse stable, therefore, is about doubled in value as well as bulk if composted with leaves, muck, or sods. **1896** *Vt. Agric. Rep.* XV. 62 Do you advise composting manure?

***Composting.** Forming or making into a compost; manuring. — **1837** COLMAN *Mass. Agric. Rep.* 91 The composting of manures . . . deserve[s] immediate and exact inquiry and experiment. **1883** SMITH *Geol. Survey Ala.* 112 Better results are reached by *composting,* as it is called.

+**Composuist.** A composer. — **1809** *Monthly Anthol.* 264 Of this base class of words some are forgotten, . . . such as . . . composuist. **1816** PICKERING 64 This extraordinary word has been much used at some of our colleges, but very seldom elsewhere. It is now rarely heard among us. **1851** HALL *College Words* 77 *Composuist,* a writer; composer. . . . The word is not found, I believe, in any dictionary of the English tongue.

Compotier. {1755–} A dish for fresh or stewed fruit. — **1776** *Penna. Ledger* 20 April, Joseph Stansbury . . . is selling off . . . his baking dishes, compotiers, pudding dishes [etc.]. **1885** *Harper's Mag.* April 740/2 Over the edge of a white compotier hung . . . grapes.

***Compound,** *a.* +**1.** *Compound basis;* the basis of being of the white race and possessed of property, used to determine the right of franchise. *S.* +**2.** *Compound interest note,* (see quotation.) — **(1) 1830** *Va. Lit. Museum* 477/2 By the compound basis, the West would have forty three, the east, seventy seven [delegates]. **(2) 1870** *Nation* Feb. 86 One of the means of raising money, adopted during the war pressure, was the issue of a large amount of what were called compound-interest notes, or legal-tender greenbacks bearing interest.

* **Compress.** +A machine for compressing cotton bales, etc.

1868 *Rep. Comm. Patents* II. 257/2 The table or platen of a compress is so constructed that with it cotton and other goods that have been . . . put up in bales, can be again compressed without removing the hoops. **1879** *Harper's Mag.* Oct. 717 Houston has two compresses at work. **1902** HARBEN *A. Daniel* 219 There was a cotton compress near by, with its vast sheds and platforms.

b. Attrib. in sense: Pertaining to the process of compressing with such a machine.

1879 *Harper's Mag.* Oct. 718 Compress rates are paid by transportation companies or ship captains, who charge freight by the bale, and are large gainers by the compress system. **1907** *Westm. Gaz.* 23 Sept. 6/3 The Gulf Compress Company.

+**Compressed burbot.** The eelpout, a fish (*Lota compressa*) characterized by its flattened form. — **1842** *Nat. Hist. N.Y., Zoology* IV. 285 Compressed Burbot. . . . Eel-pout. **1869** *Amer. Naturalist* III. 18 The Spotted Burbot (*Lota maculosa*) . . . and the Compressed Burbot (*Lota compressa*) which is very rare. **1870** *Ib.* IV. 251 The Compressed Burbot or Eel Pout. . . . My first acquaintance with this rare fish was early in the spring of 1859.

***Compressing,** *vbl. n.* +The process of compressing cotton bales. — **1879** *Harper's Mag.* Oct. 717 Considerably more than a million dollars is paid for the item of compressing.

* **Compromise.** +In U.S. history, applied esp. to various agreements which attempted settlement of sectional differences before the Civil War. Also attrib.

a. Of the Missouri Compromise (1820): An agreement in Congress prohibiting slavery north of 36°30′, north latitude, in the Louisiana Purchase, and admitting Maine and Missouri into the Union.

[**1820** *Niles' Reg.* XVII. 442 (*title*), Compromise on the 'Missouri Question.'] **1847** POLK *Diary* 183 He further expressed his willingness to extend the Missouri Compromise west to the Pacific. **1854** BENTON *30 Years' View* I. 5/1 This agitation . . . was quieted . . . by admitting the State without restriction. . . . This was called a 'compromise,' and was all clear gain to the antislavery side of the question. **1855** A. A. LAWRENCE in *Life* (1888) 90 Since the repeal of the 'Missouri Compromise' by the last Congress, this Territory has attracted the attention of distant not less than of the neighboring States. **1858** DOUGLAS in Logan *Great Conspiracy* 69 He says that if he is elected to the Senate he will introduce and pass a law just like the Missouri Compromise, prohibiting Slavery again in all the Territories. **1886** LOGAN *Ib.* 468 The strong effort to extend to the Pacific Ocean the Missouri-Compromise line of 36° 30′.

b. Of the tariff law of 1833: A law which by providing for gradual reduction of tariff rates induced South Carolina to repeal her nullification ordinance. Also attrib.

1833 *Congress. Deb.* 27 Feb. 1864 The olive branch, the compromise tariff bill, will probably allay the excited feelings of the South. **1840** *Niles' Nat. Reg.* 22 Aug. 393/2 Are you in favor of preserving entire the tariff compromise? **1841** TYLER in *Pres. Mess. & P.* IV. 82 Some of the provisions of the compromise act, which will go into effect on the 30th day of June next. **1842** *S. Lit. Messenger* VIII. 275/2 After the passage by Congress of the celebrated Compromise Act . . . which provided for the gradual reduction of all duties to 20 per cent.

c. Of the compromise of 1850: An agreement in Congress providing for admission of California into the Union, the creation of the territories of New Mexico and Utah, an extension of the fugitive slave law, etc.; esp. *Compromise measures.*

1848 POLK *Diary* IV. 31, I learned that . . . the vote on the compromise Bill establishing Territorial Governments in Oregon, California, & New Mexico would probably be taken to-night. **1851** *Harper's Mag.* II. 268/2 Resolutions expressive . . . of disapprobation of anti-slavery agitation, and of approval of Compromise measures, were adopted with much applause. **1852** *Ib.* V. 116/1 They [the Southern Whigs] can not sustain any candidate, except with the distinct avowal that he is in favor of the Compromise Measures. *Ib.* 544/2 General Scott . . . obstinately refused up to the time of his nomination, to give any public opinion in favor of the Compromise measures. **1853** PIERCE in *Pres. Mess. & P.* V. 202, I hold that the laws of 1850, commonly called the 'compromise measures,' are strictly constitutional and to be unhesitatingly carried into effect.

d. Of other specific compromises.

1858 BUCHANAN in *Pres. Mess. & P.* V. 500, I therefore cordially acquiesced in what has been called the English compromise and approved the 'act for the admission of the State of Kansas into the Union' upon the terms therein prescribed. **1886** LOGAN *Great Conspiracy* 45 In the House, however, a substitute offered by Mr. Montgomery (Douglas Democrat) known as the Crittenden-Montgomery Compromise, was adopted.

e. In general: A partial surrender of views on the slavery question in order to achieve agreement. Also attrib.

1820 *Niles' Reg.* XVIII. 113/2 The colonel is opposed either to compromise or restriction. **1846** CALHOUN in McCormac *Biog. Polk* (1922) 624 [Calhoun announced in the Senate that he was] against any compromise line. **1859** *Harper's Mag.* Dec. 137/2 Mr. Thomas . . . charged Polk with inconsistency. . . . 'Sir, in 1850–'51 you were a Compromise man; . . . then again you were "soft" on the "nigger question."' **1862** LOWELL *Biglow P.* II. v. 142 An' we wuzn't cherubs—wal, we found the buffer, For fear thet the Compromise System should suffer.

***Compromiser.** One who works out an agreement acceptable to contending parties; a conciliator. {–*a*1654} +Esp. applied to Henry Clay (1777–1852), who often reconciled Northern and Southern interests before the Civil War. Also *Great Compromiser.* — **1886** WILLEY *Hist. Antislavery Cause* 102 Henry Clay, the leader of the Whig party and aspirant for the presidency, the 'compromiser,' in 1839 offered a petition from people in the District [of Columbia]. **1913** BASSETT *Short Hist. U.S.* 454 It appealed to his [=Henry Clay's] imagination that 'the Great Compromiser,' as he was called, should finish his career with another compromise.

***Compromit,** *v.* +*tr.* To compromise by indiscreet action; to involve in difficulty, embarrassment, or loss of reputation; to imperil. (Becoming *Obs.*)

1787 JEFFERSON *Writings* VI. 136 The public reputation is, every moment, in danger of being compromitted with him. **1793** *Ib.* IX. 164 None but an enemy . . . would avail himself of the indiscretions of an individual to compromit two nations esteeming each other ardently. **1802** A. HAMILTON *Works* VII. 242 It has been often likely to compromit the interests of our country in favor of another. **1809** LEWIS in *L. & Clark Exped.* (1905) VII. 383 They may . . . vend ardent spirits, compromit the government, or the character of the whites, in the estimation of the Indians. **1843** *Amer. Pioneer* II. 209 Men of property and influence, who had become compromitted in the destruction of general Neville's house, exerted themselves to involve the whole country in open resistance to the laws. **1843** TYLER in *Pres. Mess. & P.* IV. 258 Nothing will be done to compromit the rights or honor of the United States. **1879** H. C. WOOD *Therapeutics* (ed. 3) 521 Mucus may so accumulate in the lungs . . . as seriously to embarrass, or even fatally compromit, respiration.

***Compting house.** A counting-house. *Obs.* {1777} — **1727** *New-Eng. W. Journal* 10 April, I have been frequently . . . represented as a Merchant . . . seated very conveniently in a Compting-House. **1752** *Boston Ev. Post* 6 Jan., Any person qualified for a Compting House. **1786** *Penna. Ev. Herald* 12 April 89/1 Stolen out of the Subscriber's compting house in Front-street.

Compting room. *Obs.* A room, or office, in which accounts are kept and business is transacted. (Cf. COUNTING ROOM.)

1800 *Columbian Centinel* 8 Feb. 3/2 Gentlemen . . . who are indebted to the Editor, are requested to apply at his Compting Room, for receipts. **1827** *Md. Hist. Mag.* XVII. 260 After breakfast went to Mr. Ladson's compting room and saw a number of friends who dropped in on business. **1845** *S. Lit. Messenger* XI. 66/2 Casting off the shackles which bound his genius to the compting-room . . . he visited many countries.

Comptonia. [See quot. 1857.] The sweet fern of the United States (*C. asplenifolia*), allied to *Myrica*.

1823 CRABB *Technol. Dict.* s.v., Fern-leaved Comptonia, a shrub, native of New England. **1850** S. F. COOPER *Rural Hours* 77 The Comptonia or sweet-fern is in flower, the brown, catkin-like blossoms are nearly as fragrant as the foliage. [**1857** GRAY 410 *Comptonia*, Solander. Sweet Fern. . . . Named after *Henry Compton*, Bishop of London, . . . a cultivator and patron of botany]. **1889** *Cent.* 1157/1 *Comptonia*. . . . The only species, *C. asplenifolia*, is the sweet-fern of the United States. . . . It is said to be tonic and astringent, and is a domestic remedy for diarrhea.

***Comptroller.** Also **controller.**

+1. An officer in the legislative court of the Massachusetts Bay Colony.

1644 *Mass. Rec.* III. 4 Capta[in] Cooke & Mr Tory are chosen comptrolers of ye howses for this Courte. **1650** *Ib.* 183 Capt. Willard is chosen Comptroulor for this session.

+2. An officer under the Articles of Confederation, serving as a check to the treasurer.

1778 *Jrnls. Cont. Congress* XI. 780 That it shall be the Duty of the Comptroller to keep the Seal of the Treasury. That he shall receive the Accounts transmitted to him [etc.].

+3. In reference to officers of the treasury department of the U.S. government: **a.** Formerly, an officer in charge of the accounting department, with the duty of approving disbursement of monies by the Secretary of the Treasury, of interpreting appropriation laws, etc. Esp. *C. of the Treasury.*

From 1789 to 1817, and again from 1894 to 1921, the powers and duties of the comptroller were vested in one person, called the Comptroller of the Treasury. From 1817 to 1894, this official's title was that of First Comptroller, a part of his duties being performed by the Second Comptroller. In 1921, the co-ordinating head of the whole department was officially named Comptroller General.

1789 *Ann. 1st Congress* I. 392 He hoped to see proper checks provided; a Comptroller, Auditors, Register, and Treasurer. *Ib.* App. 2174 There shall be a Department of Treasury, in which shall be the following officers, namely: A Secretary of the Treasury, . . . a Comptroller, [etc.]. **1792** *Ann. 2nd Congress* 59 A duplicate of every such contract . . . shall . . . be lodged in the office of the Comptroller of the Treasury of the United States. **1795** A. HAMILTON *Works* VII. 108 In this respect the Comptroller is a check upon the Secretary. **1816** *Ann. 14th Congress* 2 Sess. 29 Money will then be paid . . . upon the settlement of an auditor, only after it has been revised and approved by a comptroller. **1905** *Indian Laws & Tr.* III. 138 The disbursing clerk . . . is . . . directed to pay . . . such expenses . . . which remain unpaid by reason of a decision of the Comptroller of the Treasury. **1914** McLaughlin & Hart *Cycl. Amer. Govt.* I. 368 The duties of the Comptroller are twofold: (1) to him are referred all appeals from . . . the auditor; (2) he advises and aids the disbursing officers in determining the validity of payments, etc. **1924** E. KIMBALL *U.S. Govt.* 307 The Comptroller of the Treasury, although attached to the Treasury Department, . . . holds a semi-independent position of a quasi-judicial character.

b. *First Comptroller, Second Comptroller*, co-ordinate officers in charge of the Comptroller's office from 1817 to 1894.

1817 *Ann. 14th Congress* 1 Sess. 1305 It shall be the duty of the first comptroller to examine all accounts settled by the first and fifth auditors. . . . It shall be the duty of the second comptroller to examine all accounts settled by the second, third, and fourth auditors. **1825** *P.O. Laws & Reg.* (1843) 1. 22 The Postmaster General shall . . . transmit to the First Comptroller of the Treasury an account of such additional services, and the compensation to be allowed therefor. **1836** *Niles' Nat. Reg.* 24 Sept. 61/3 [Appropriations] for the first comptroller of the Treasury [$]3,500. **1842** *Ib.* 9 April 93 In this session . . . McCulloh . . . as first comptroller of the treasury, was concurred in by a large vote. **1861** *Army Regulations* 155 Two [contracts are] to be sent to the military bureau, one of which [is] for the office of the Second Comptroller of the Treasury. **1896** *Comptroller of Treasury Decisions* I. p. iii, The act of July 31, 1894, . . . abolished the offices of Commissioner of Customs and Second Comptroller, and made the First Comptroller the Comptroller of the Treasury.

c. *Comptroller of the Currency*, (see quots. 1914).

1875 *Scribner's Mo.* Dec. 228/1 It appears from the Report of the Comptroller of the Currency for 1872 that 69 per cent. of the entire paper circulation of the United States was in notes of less than 20 dollars. **1914** McLaughlin & Hart *Cycl. Amer. Govt.* I. 367/2 *Comptroller of the currency.* This officer is head of the Currency Bureau of the Treasury Department, and has special jurisdiction of the enforcement of the provisions of the National Bank Act. **1914** *New Internat. Encyl.* V. 696/2 The Comptroller of the Currency . . . is made a member of the Federal Reserve Board, having supervision over the reserve system erected by the law.

d. *Comptroller General*, the officer who succeeded to the duties of the Comptroller of the Treasury in 1921.

1922 *Decisions Comptroller-General* I. ii, Selected decisions of the Comptroller General and Assistant Comptroller General of the United States will be published in monthly pamphlets. *Ib.* 776 The Comptroller General shall make such rules and regulations as may be necessary for carrying on the work of the General Accounting Office.

4. An officer who controls, or checks, the disbursement of money; an auditor: **a.** In colonial, city, and state governments. **b.** In federal departments.

(a) 1703 SEWALL *Diary* II. 90 Harrison the Controller, and Mr. Wm. Pain are examined before the Govr and Council. **1840** *Niles' Nat. Reg.* 22 Aug. 400/3 The comptroller of the state of New York, has given notice that on the 25th instant he will cause to be sold . . . the following state stocks [etc.]. **1872** *Ill. Revised Statutes* 224 § 73 The city council may, in its discretion, . . . provide for the election . . . of a city . . . comptroller. **1873** *Mich. Gen. Statutes* (1882–3) I. 638 In cities electing a comptroller, he shall hold his office for the term of two years. **1884** *Century Mag.* April 869/2 The Comptroller and Street Commissioner moved in at the same time. **1903** *Chicago Chronicle* 11 April 1/5 E. V. Leow, former comptroller of New York.

(b) 1788 FRANKLIN *Autobiog.* 385 Having been for some time employed by the postmaster-general of America as his comptroller in regulating several offices, and bringing the officers to account, I was, upon his death in 1753, appointed . . . to succeed him. **1844** TYLER in *Pres. Mess. & P.* IV. 329 Payments under the authority of any Department shall be made upon its requisition, countersigned by the proper Auditor and Comptroller.

***Compulsory,** *a.* As applied to educational matters: **a.** Required or enforced by law; obligatory. **b.** Exercising or generating compulsion.

(a) 1867 *Nation* V. 192/1 Universal compulsory education is at first costly, but it is, in the long run, the truest economy. **1880** *Harper's Mag.* July 254/1 In the German Universities the studies are all elective and optional; in the colleges of the United States, compulsory. **1883** *Ill. Revised Statutes* 1054 Compulsory Attendance. An Act to secure to all children the benefit of an elementary education. **1918** *Outlook* CXVIII. 477/2 Compulsory education is not only justified, but demanded. — **(b) 1867** *Nation* V. 192/1 Laws exist in several of the United States imposing penalties for truancy . . . , but no State of the Union has yet adopted an effective compulsory system. **1880** *Harper's Mag.* LX. 222/2 One of the best results of the compulsory law has been the breaking up of many gangs of small boys. **1911** *Okla. Session Laws* 3 Legisl. 219 The children shall be governed by the regulations, rules and the compulsory school law of the district in which they have chosen to attend school.

‖**Computation man.** A computator; a calculator. — **1881** *Harper's Mag.* Jan. 318/1 The Rev. Joseph Capen . . . wrote in 1682 an elegy on the somewhat celebrated 'computation man' and printer, John Foster.

Computing, *ppl. a.* +As applied to a mechanism: Having such an arrangement of parts as to aid a person who computes. — **1868** *Rep. Comm. Patents* I. 621 *Computing Apparatus*. . . . The disk is turned by a pointer, and when the pointer is turned to a multiplicand . . . the product of that with another multiplicand . . . is shown. **1866** *Ib.* II. 1547 *Computing Machine*. . . . Nine disks, notched and numbered in their peripheries, are journaled on a shaft . . . , to compute numerically by the turning of the disks.

***Comrade.** +A member of the Grand Army of the Republic. — **1890** J. W. MORTON *Sparks from Camp Fire* 557 Prompt aid rendered by the Post has saved life and hope to a comrade otherwise broken down and discouraged. *Ib.*, If no comrade of the Post had ever been in needy circumstances . . . perhaps then the Post would never have needed the co-operation of women in its work.

||**Comstocker.** One associated with the famous Comstock lode mines at Virginia City, Nev. — **1877** WRIGHT *Big Bonanza* 356 A Comstocker who dropped in at a chop-house where about a dozen newcomers had just settled in a flock, at two or three adjoining tables. *Ib.* 362 The Comstocker first 'busted' his egg on the top of the Piocher's head, and the feat was loudly applauded by all present.

||**Conbobberation.** Disturbance. — **1835** KENNEDY *Horse Shoe Robinson* I. 65 What are you making such a conbobberation about! **1845** HOOPER *Daddy Biggs' Scrape* 194 There was somethin' a flouncin' and sloshin', and makin' a devil of a conbobberation at the end of the line.

+**Concageer.** 'A name applied to the small lizards and salamanders of the United States' (B. '59).

+**Concededly,** *adv.* Admittedly. — **1882** *N.Y. Tribune* 22 March, The present Executive Mansion . . . is concededly not what it ought to be. **1887** *Nation* 10 March 199/1 This offence is concededly so gross an outrage [etc.]. **1910** *N.Y. Ev. Post* 14 March (Th.), Manchuria is concededly a fruitful field for exploitation.

||**Concentral,** *a.* Having a common center; concentric. — **1754–5** in *Almon's Remembrancer* (1778) 490/1 The State House, Governor's House, Assembly, Courts, &c. were to have formed the centre, . . . with concentral streets going round the hill.

Concentrator. Also **concentrater.** {1853–} An apparatus for concentrating solutions and for separating ore from the associated rock.

1833 SILLIMAN *Man. Sugar Cane* 66 Without running any risk of burning the Sugar, the contents of the concentrator are emptied into the cooler. **1874** *Vt. Bd. Agric. Rep.* II. 757 The gold and black sand is steadily deposited in the upper end of a large, broad concentrator. **1882** C. KING *Rep. Prec. Metals* 586 Rankin, Brayton & Co., of San Francisco, Cal., manufacture a centrifugal concentrator adapted for the concentration of ores, sulphurets, &c. **1892** *Harper's Mag.* Sept. 600/2 The ores are being sent out, and concentraters are building.

* **Concern.** [Cf. CONSARN *v.*]

1. Religious anxiety; the feeling of a divine call. Originally among Quakers.

1707 *Penna. Hist. Soc. Mem.* X. 214 During their absence, I was under the greatest concern of mind that ever I knew in my life. **1772** in Fithian *Journal* I. 22 Our orations are put off lest they should do some harm to some under concern. **1838** COOPER *Home as Found* xvi, 'Have you heard that Grace is under concern?' . . . 'Not under the church parson's, I'll engage; no one ever heard of a real . . . conversion under his ministery.' **1875** STOWE *We & Neighbors* 172 If your friend Sibyl should have a 'concern' laid on her for your Mr. St. John, she would tell him some wholesome truths. **1879** *Scribner's Mo.* July 335/2 Thee will lay this concern before meeting to-morrow, father? **1886** *Amer. Missionary* Oct. 287 In a day or two Mrs. Tuttle [a Friend] 'had a concern' to visit the Modocs.

2. A business firm or commercial establishment. {1681–}

1815 *Niles' Reg.* IX. 108/2 The concern in which the writer was a partner was about to build a vessel of 40 tons. **1881** WHITMAN *Diary* 61, I had the . . . aid throughout of Henry H. Clark, principal proof-reader and book-superintendent of the concern. **1904** W. H. SMITH *Promoters* 252 The suite next to his was occupied by a leading school book concern. **1916** WILSON *Red Gap* 275 This here ranch you're on now is one of your going concerns.

fig. **1837** J. C. NEAL *Charcoal Sk.* (1838) 193, I belong to four people besides myself—the old woman and them three children. I'm a partnership concern.

* **Concert.** Also †**consort.**

1. The performance of a series of musical numbers. {consort, 1671–1774; concert 1689–} Also attrib.

1710 *Penna. Hist. Mag.* XL. 295 At night a Consort at Mr. Broughtons. **1732** *S.C. Gazette* 59/2 On Wednesday next, will be a Consort of Musick at the Council Chamber. **1767** E. Singleton *Social N.Y.* 297 The Subscription Concert [is] to be given this and every evening during the season exactly at Half Past Six o'clock. **1861** E. COWELL *Diary* 293 Sam intended to give a Concert here, . . . but the war news has so hurt theatres, concerts, saloons, etc., that he has given it up. **1898** *Kansas City Star* 24 Dec. 8 Fourth Concert by the Philharmonic Orchestra 35—Musicians—35. **1920** C. R. COOPER *Under Big Top* 203 In the preliminary 'concerts' which precede the main performance, half or more of the numbers are of the classical nature.

+**b.** The first part of a minstrel show.

1856 *Porter's Spirit of Times* I. 32/3 George Christy & Wood's Minstrels. . . . Concert commences at 8 o'clock. **1857** *Ib.* 344/3 Buckley's Serenaders. . . . The nightly concert which precedes the burlesque is also highly entertaining.

2. Attrib. and comb. with *bill*, a program; *clock*, a musical clock; *license;* etc.

1865 *Atlantic Mo.* XV. 718, I read over the concert-bill. First there was an overture. **1797** *Boston Chronicle* 19 Dec., Exhibition of Concert Clocks. *Ib.*, The above Concert Clocks have been exhibited in New-York. **1896** *N.Y. Dramatic News* 4 July 6/3 Owing to the misguided opposition of certain residents of the neighborhood a concert license has not yet been secured. **1850** NORTHALL *Yankee Hill* 92 The lecture and concert mania which prevailed for several years . . . tended to depress dramatic affairs. **1861** E. COWELL *Diary* 237, [I] gave him a statement of Concert matters. **1881** *Harper's Mag.* May 814/1 Their concert playing has been incidental only. **1855** W. B. WOOD *Recoll. Stage* 28 Mrs. Pownall . . . [was] long admired both as a stage vocalist and a concert singer. **1895** *N.Y. Dramatic News* 23 Nov. 3/1 James F. Roberts . . . sends a letter . . . telling of his own fruitless efforts to secure permission for a robust boy to sing ballads upon the concert stage. **1848** W. E. BURTON *Waggeries* 28 Billy always had play and concert tickets for the whole party.

Concert hall. {1746–} An auditorium in which concerts are given; a music hall.

1765 J. ROWE *Diary* 81 May 10. Went in the evening to Concert Hall. **1776** *Boston News-Letter* 22 Feb., On Monday, the 11th of March will be given at Concert-Hall, a Subscription Masked Ball. **1866** *Internal Revenue Guide* 76 Proprietors of theaters, museums, and concert halls, shall pay one hundred dollars. **1883** *Century Mag.* Nov. 41/1 American life is invading the thoroughfare,—uprearing concert-halls, with insufferably pompous names, multiplying flashy saloons and cheap restaurants, [etc.]. **1885** *Ib.* XXX. 678/2 If any person insists on obtruding himself upon this pair in the concert-hall, he can only succeed in getting himself put out.

||**Concertizer.** One who gives a concert. — **1863** S. C. MASSETT *Drifting About* 241 Stephen C. Massett, pioneer concertiser of Sacramento, poet, and by no means unknown to fame, . . . is to give a grand ballad concert this evening.

Concert room. {1799–} A room in which concerts are given.

1774 FITHIAN *Journal* I. 88 The Colonel . . . proposes to make the vacant End of our School-Room, where Dr. Frank lived a Concert-Room. **1842** *Knickerb.* XX. 490 It is arranged expressly for a concert-room and picture-gallery combined. **1867** EMERSON *Lett. & Soc. Aims* (1876) 107 Jenny Lind . . . complained of concert-rooms and town-halls, that they did not give her room enough to unroll her voice. **1881** *Harper's Mag.* May 814/1 Very few American pianists have adopted the concert-room as their field of labor, preferring . . . teaching as a profession. **1884** *Century Mag.* June 307/1 They introduce into the church the ideas and suggestions of the concert-room.

+**Concert saloon.** A place of amusement where music is played. Also attrib.

1867 A. DALY *Under Gaslight* II. 16 Nina, what's she, concert-saloon girl? **1869** J. H. BROWNE *Great Metropolis* 326 Concert-saloons, with pretty 'waiter-girl' attachments, . . . had their origin and earliest impetus here [=N.Y.]. **1880** *Harper's Mag.* Dec. 68 In the concert saloon, the billiard hall, the bowling alley or drinking saloon, are found these workers in iron and steel and glass. **1881** *Mich. Gen. Statutes* (1882–3) I. 539 No minor child under sixteen years of age shall be permitted to remain . . . in any place of amusement known as dance houses, concert saloons, variety theatres [etc.].

Concession. {1611–} +*pl.* The privileges, or charter, granted the inhabitants of New Jersey by the proprietors, Berkeley and Carteret, in 1664–5. — **1665** *N.J. Archives* 1 Ser. I. 28 The Concessions and Agreement of the Lords Propriators of the Province of . . . New Jersey to and with all and every the Adventurers and all such as shall settle or plant there. **1885** A. JOHNSTON *Hist. U.S.* 62 The proprietors [of New Jersey], in 1665, granted to the people certain 'concessions,' which were in fact a charter.

* **Conch.** [Cf. CONK.]

* **1.** The gastropod *Strombus gigas*, a large marine shellfish; also, a related species.

1737 BRICKELL *N. Carolina* 244 The Conchs, some of these are very large, but the lesser sort are the best Meat. **1869** *Amer. Naturalist* III. 286 We have here three species of univalve shells, called by the Floridians, Conchs (*Busycon*). **1881** INGERSOLL *Oyster Industry* 243 *Conch*, various large and univalved, and spiral mollusks, particularly *Fulgur carica.*

+**2.** One of the lower class of white inhabitants along the Florida keys.

1861 *N.Y. Tribune* 27 Nov., A Negro on this Key [Key West, Fla.] . . . is a more successful cultivator of the soil than all the rebel conchs together. **1875** *Hygiene U.S. Army* (Surgeon-Gen.'s Office) 144 White natives of the Bahamas and their descendants [are] classified here [=Key West] under the general title of 'Conchs.'

+**3.** A low class of inhabitants in parts of North Carolina.

1871 DE VERE 45 A corn cracker is looked upon as so low a person that he is simply called a cracker; he . . . appears as *Conch* or *Low Downer* in North Carolina.

+**Concha.** *S.W.* and *W.* [Sp. 'shell.'] A shell-like piece of metal used as a decoration, or washer, on the riding equipment of a cowboy. — **1887** *Scribner's Mag.* II. 512/1 And listen to the *conchas*, the silver ornaments outside the spur, as they jingle and ring to the broncho's tread! **1907** S. E. WHITE *Arizona Nights* 275 The leather chaps with the silver conchas hung behind the door. **1922** ROLLINS *Cowboy* (1926) 104 The belt, if of leather, commonly was studded with . . . 'conchas,' which were flat metal plates, usually circular, generally of silver, in rare instances of gold, in much rarer instances set with jewels.

+**Conchalagua.** Also **canchalagua.** *local.* [Sp.] A gentianlike plant of the genus *Erythræa*, used medicinally. — **1848** E. BRYANT *California* (1849) 452 There is another plant in high estimation with the Californians, called canchalagua, which is held by them as an antidote for all the diseases to which they are subject. **1889** *Cent.* 786 *Canchalagua*, . . . [a] species of . . . *Erythræa*, used as bitter tonics. **1894** *Amer. Folk-Lore* VII. 94 *Erythræa Muhlenbergii*, . . . conchalagua, Cal.

‖**Concher.** =CONCH 2. — *c*1873 DE VERE *MS. Notes* 45 *Conch* of Fla., conchers, mostly from Key West, fr[om] large shellfish (*Strombus gigans*) on which it is pretended they subsist. The common story is th[at] these islanders can dive to [the] bottom in 10 fathom water and crack a conch in the[ir] teeth.

+**Concho-grass.** *S.* [Cf. Sp. *concho* corn-husk.] Texas millet, *Panicum texanum.* — **1884** VASEY *Agric. Grasses* 36 It . . . has been called Concho grass in some parts. **1889** *Cent.* 1165/2 Concho-grass . . . is now cultivated in the southern United States and found to yield a large amount of valuable forage.

Conch shell. {1697–}

1. The shell of the conch.

1775 ADAIR *Indians* 83 [The shoes] are laid up in the beloved place, . . . [with] an heap of old broken earthen ware conch-shells. **1825** NEAL *Bro. Jonathan* III. 287 'With your what?'—'Our skunk shell; skunk's horn, they call it, in some parts.'—'O—a conch shell.' **1902** *Harper's Mag.* March 555/2 A hermit-crab, fitted into its conch-shell.

+**b.** *Conch-shell bead,* (see quotation).

1775 ADAIR *Indians* 170 Formerly, four deer-skins was the price of a large conch-shell bead, about the length and thickness of a man's forefinger; which they fixed to the crown of their head.

2. Such a shell used as a horn to be blown. {1697–} Also attrib.

1746 D. BRAINERD *Journal* (1902) 115 They [Indians] are easily and quickly called together with only the sound of a conch-shell. *a*1772 WOOLMAN *Journal* 200 After a while we heard a conch-shell blow several times. **1807** IRVING, etc. *Salmagundi* x, Ice passes New York—conch-shell sounds at a distance—ferry-man calls o-v-e-r. **1843** *Knickerb.* XXI. 225 My companion wound a stirring note from the conch-shell which hung by the post. **1845** COOPER *Chainbearer* xvii, The business of eating commenced simultaneously throughout the whole settlement, Prudence having blown a blast upon a conch-shell, as the signal. **1884** ROE *Nature's Story* 85 Hearing of Webb's expedition, the two neighbors who had recently joined them pushed on up the road, shouting and blowing the conch-shell as often as they deemed it necessary. **1887** *Century Mag.* April 904/1 It was a more common plan to blow a conch-shell dinner-horn in the streets [instead of a drum].

Conclude. *Obs.* A conclusion. — **1642** in Bradford *Hist.* 478 For peace sake, . . . and to pass by all Failings of all, the conclude is accepted of. **1643** in *Ib.* 485, I shall write this generall leter . . . hoping it will be a good conclude of a . . . costly and tedious bussines.

‖**Concoa.** *local.* (See quotation.) — *a*1870 CHIPMAN *Notes on Bartlett* 93 *Concoa,* the butter-nut. So called (or oftener pronounced as the word conquer), and thus written and printed in Essex County, Mass. The word may be of Indian origin (or que. Portuguese?). **1877** BARTLETT 136.

* **Concord.** [The name of a town in Massachusetts and of the capital of New Hampshire.]

+**1.** Ellipt. for CONCORD GRAPE (variety, vine, or berry).

1858 *Mich. Agric. Soc. Trans.* X. 217 Mr. Prince thought it a better grape than the Concord. **1860** *Ill. Agric. Soc. Trans.* IV. 474 The Clinton and Concord are hardy, and consequently better adapted to vineyard culture here. **1863** *Horticulturist* XVIII. 250 The Concord . . . is at present planted more extensively in the West than any other, and deservedly so. **1864** *Maine Bd. Agric. Rep.* IX. 35 Years after the introduction of the Isabella came the Diana, Concord, and some others. **1911** S. E. WHITE *Bobby Orde* x. 125 The satiny 'Concords' from the trellis, however, were better dipped in cool water. **1913** STRATTON-PORTER *Laddie* xi, The newly-opened bottles of grape juice filled the house with the tang of concord and muscadine.

+**2.** A variety of sweet corn.

1894 *Vt. Agric. Rep.* XIV. 379 (*caption*), Sweet Corn. Moore's Concord.

+**3.** Ellipt. for CONCORD COACH, WAGON.

1908 MULFORD *Orphan* 38 Bill Howland emerged from the . . . office of the . . . Stage Company and strolled down the street to where his Concord stood. **1925** — *Cottonwood Gulch* 172 Along the road came a dusty Concord, . . . drawn by six horses.

attrib. **1902** MCFAUL *Ike Glidden* 89 As they approached Squirmtown they saw numerous teams,—some of the two-seated 'Democrat' type, others of the Concord pattern.

+**Concord coach.** A type of stagecoach, lighter at the top than the ordinary coach, widely used in the early West. (Cf. CONCORD WAGON.)

This was first manufactured at Concord, New Hampshire, about 1827.

1855 F. S. MARRYAT *Mts. & Molehills* 249 The stage coach was of American manufacture, and of the class known as 'Concord' coaches. **1867** DIXON *New America* I. 35 The stage being an old and much worn Concord Coach; a vehicle of a kind unknown in Europe. **1870** RAE *Westward by Rail* 98 The coach which meets the train is what is styled a 'Concord Coach.' It has seats for nine persons inside and for at least five on the roof. **1880** G. INGHAM *Digging Gold* 407 We entered one of Barlow & Sanderson's Concord coaches, at Gunnison City, one morning at five o'clock. **1884** W. SHEPHERD *Prairie Exper.* 106 The concord coach is the sanctioned design for a mail-coach. It is slung high on leather straps, has three seats, which neither can hold nor accommodate three people each; but nine persons are shoved inside. **1909** C. H. STERNBERG *Life of Fossil Hunter* 144, I entered a Concord coach drawn by a team of eight horses, and continued my journey by stage.

b. *Concord stage(coach),* =CONCORD COACH.

1912 DAWSON *Pioneer Tales* 76 These were called Concord stages or coaches. *Ib.* 82 The Mortons of Nebraska City, possess an old Concord stagecoach . . . which was used . . . for many years between Atchison and Denver.

+**Concord grape.** A variety of grape, the fruit or vine.

'Developed at Concord, Mass., by Ephraim W. Bull in 1840 and put on the market in 1854' (J. L. Swayne *Story of Concord* 160).

1863 *Horticulturist* XVIII. 219, I have asked [50 people] what they thought of the Concord grape. **1871** R. SOMERS *Southern States since War* 128 (*note*), The 'Concord' grape is almost black, of rather thick skin, but juicy and sweet. **1898** E. C. HALL *Aunt Jane* 171 Concord and Catawba grapes loaded the vines on the rickety old arbor. **1906** *Ladies' Home Jrnl.* Feb. 65 It is simply the rich, pure, unfermented juice of the best Concord grapes.

+**Concord wagon.** =CONCORD COACH.

1860 HOLLAND *Miss Gilbert* 399 Strings of rustic lovers in Concord wagons make pilgrimages to the shrines of learning. **1870** F. H. LUDLOW *Heart of Continent* 10 (Th. S.), The Overland Mail vehicle is of that description known as the Concord wagon. **1871** RICHARDSON *Beyond Miss.* 159 Concord wagon . . . is covered with duck or canvas, the driver sitting in front at a slight elevation above the passengers. **1877** J. S. CAMPION *On Frontier* 3 The 'outfit' consisted of a light concord waggon, having a tilt or cover, four good Missouri mules, [etc.]. **1903** C. B. LOOMIS *Cheerful Americans* 3, I climbed into the Concord wagon, and had driven a mile on my way when [etc.].

* **Concourse.** +A place through which a large number of people pass, as a boulevard or the lobby of a large railway station.

'*Concourse* is a spec. term in the vocab. of Am. railways' (Horwill *Mod. Am. Usage* 79).

1862 *Harper's Mag.* Dec. 42/1 One Saturday afternoon in June a group of cavaliers had assembled on the 'Concourse' at the Central Park. **1871** *Scribner's Mo.* I. 226 It is not much more than a shaded 'concourse,' destitute of every attribute of a park. **1906** *N.Y. Ev. Post* 17 May 7 Connecting with the main waiting room is the concourse, a covered assembling place over 100 feet wide, extending the entire width of the station and under the adjoining streets. **1912** *Independent* LXXII. 553/1 Adjoining the waiting rooms on their different levels will be the concourses, enclosed and heated. **1925** *Chicago Tribune* 23 July 3/5 One of the features of the concourse is that the tracks are laid across it transversely, permitting trains from the east and west to enter and leave simultaneously.

Concrete, *v.* {1635–} *tr.* To lay, line, or cover with concrete. {1882} — **1875** *Boston Audit.* 129 Concreting side and cross-walks, \$2170. **1888** *Harper's Mag.* Nov. 870/1 The first proposition to concrete the side walks of this village. **1907** *Indian Laws & Tr.* III. 273 For concreting reservoir, three thousand dollars.

***Concur,** *v. tr.* To concur with; to assent to. {1818} — **1721** *Mass. Ho. Repr. Jrnls.* III. 52 As hath been the constant Usage and Practise of that Board by Concurring or Non-Concurring the Votes of this House. **1816** PICKERING 65 A peculiar use of this verb, which is not uncommon in some of the Northern States. *Ex.* 'The house of Representatives has passed a *Resolve* or *Bill;* it will not *be concurred* by the Senate.' **1829** *Va. Lit. Museum* 16 Dec. 419.

***Concurrence.** +**a.** Agreement by the Senate and House of Representatives on a measure. +**b.** Agreement by the Senate or House of Representatives with a resolution, bill, etc., passed by the other. +**c.** A document stating that the Senate or the House concurs in a measure. — (**a**) **1787** *Constitution* I. § 7 ¶ 3 Every order, resolution, or vote, to which the concurrence of the Senate and House of Representatives may be necessary, . . . shall be presented to the President of the United States. (**b**) **1809** *Ann. 10th Congress* 2 Sess. 323 The bill last brought up for concurrence was read, and passed to the second reading. **1896** *Boston Journal* 18 Feb. 3/4 The committee [of the House of Rep.] recommended concurrence in several amendments made by the Senate and non-concurrence in most of them. (**c**) **1789** *Ann. 1st Congress* I. 21 A letter from the Speaker of the House to the President was read, enclosing a concurrence of the House.

* **Concurrent,** *a.* +Embodying an agreement of the Senate and the House of Representatives.

1802 *Ann. 7th Congress* 1 Sess. 1285 Mr. Van Cortlandt moved that the House do now . . . take into consideration a motion referred to them on the nineteenth of February last, in the form of a concurrent resolution of the two Houses, [etc.]. **1813** *Niles' Reg.* III. 288 To make the choice requires a concurrent vote. **1843** TYLER in *Pres. Mess. & P.* IV. 256 The two Houses, by concurrent vote, had already agreed to terminate the session by adjournment at 2 o'clock on that day. **1886** ALTON *Among Law-Makers* 43 As . . . neither body can adjourn . . . without the consent of the other, it became necessary for both Houses to agree to this, which was done by means of a concurrent resolution.

* **Condemn,** *v.* +*tr.* To declare (property) to be seized for public use, under the right of eminent domain.

1833 *Niles' Reg.* XLIV. 192/2 All expenses to be incurred, in condemning, or purchasing ground . . . shall be . . . at the proper cost of the rail road company. *Ib.* 263 In the case of the Chesapeake and Ohio canal company *vs.* George Lefever, . . . being a proceeding to condemn land for the canal, the jury returned an inquisition of $6,500 damages. **1869** 'MARK TWAIN' *Innocents* 128 He [=Napoleon] condemns a whole street at a time, assesses the damages, pays them and rebuilds superbly. **1876** *Congress. Rec.* 2 Aug. 5079/1 The Government cannot of its own right condemn this property. **1909** *Indian Laws & Tr.* III. 385 To condemn any of said lands necessary for the purpose of reclamation.

***Condemnation.** +The seizure (of property) for public use, also for payment of debt.

1852 DUNLAP *Book Forms* (1857) 853 Schedule or Inquisition of Real Estate levied upon by Fi. Fa., for Condemnation. **1861** *Ill. Private Laws* 494 The act . . . approved June 22d, 1852, for the condemnation of lands by incorporated companies. **1876** *Congress. Rec.* 2 Aug. 5079/1 The amendment proposed by the Senator from Oregon confers by statute on the circuit court of the United States for that district jurisdiction to proceed for this condemnation. **1883** *Ill. Revised Statutes* 1202/2 Condemnation of Property. See 'Eminent Domain.' **1911** *Okla. Session Laws* 3 Legisl. 191 Any city or town, having acquired possession, by purchase, condemnation, gift, or otherwise, of a reservoir for public water supply [etc.].

+**b.** *Condemnation proceeding(s)*, a special court proceeding by means of which private property is taken for public use and suitable compensation awarded.

1903 *Mont. Supreme Ct.* XXIX. 155 Condemnation proceedings are special proceedings provided for by the statute. **1905** *Md. Court of Appeals* CI. 560 When in a condemnation proceeding by a municipality of mortgaged land [etc.].

***Condemned,** *ppl. a.* and *adv.* Confounded; confoundedly. Euphem. for 'damned.' *colloq.* — **1861** WINTHROP *Open Air* 249 'But I took a big cold,' the diver continued, 'and I'm condemned hoarse yit.' **1921** PAINE *Comr. Rolling Ocean* 140 Bless my soul, what sort of a condemned rumshop have I stumbled into?

Condemned pew. {1836} +(See quotation.) — **1846** *Knickerb.* XXVIII. 466 He was led . . . to the 'condemned pew,' where all bad boys were placed as in a criminal dock.

Condensed, *ppl. a.* {1606–}

+**1.** *Condensed milk*, milk concentrated by evaporation, usually with addition of sugar. {1871–} Also ellipt.

1863 NORTON *Army Lett.* 177 We buy condensed milk of the sutlers. **1869** W. MURRAY *Adventures* 62 All you need to carry in with you is . . . Pork, and Condensed Milk. **1875** KNIGHT 1438 There are a number of factories for preparation of condensed milk in and about New York, where it is sold from house to house fresh from the condensing-vats. **1887** *Mich. Agric. Rep.* 386 Condensed milk has been used more or less for the last thirty years. **1892** *Vt. Agric. Rep.* XII. 149 The manufacture of condensed milk . . . affords the means of diversifying . . . the uses of the product of Vermont dairies. **1909** WASON *Happy Hawkins* 254 Jabez wasn't the man to weep over upsettin' a can o' condensed, an' purty soon the theft was forgot.

attrib. **1888** *Cycl. Amer. Biog.* I. 321/1 [Gail Borden] in 1853 applied for a patent for 'producing concentrated sweet milk.' . . . Later the New York Condensed Milk Company was formed. **1892** *Vt. Agric. Rep.* XII. 150 There are only six condensed milk factories in this country, and none of them are in New England. **1904** E. ROBINS *Magnetic North* I. 233 Haven't you got a condensed milk can with some bacon grease in it, and a rag wick?

||**2.** *Condensed water*, distilled water.

1865 NORTON *Army Lett.* 264 Brazos has not much to recommend it as a pleasant place to garrison. . . . The worst feature is that we must use condensed water.

+**Condensing company.** A business firm engaged in manufacturing milk products, esp. butter and cheese. — **1878** *Ill. Dept. Agric. Trans. 1876* XIV. 293 The condensing company are particular in all respects; they take only good milk, and make only a good product.

+**Condescentious,** *a.* {1651} Confused form of 'conscientious.' — **1835** KENNEDY *Horse Shoe Robinson* I. 81 We have no condesentious scruples against a fair rap or two over the knowledge box.

***Condition,** *n. Educ.* +The requirement that a student do additional work in order to obtain 'credit' in a subject; the subject in which such a requirement is made.

1832 in *Atlantic Mo.* Oct. (1887) 434/1 She straightway got a tutor, and prodded Ralph night and day to make up the conditions. **1833** *Ib.* 443/2 Ralph is . . . actually gone back to Cambridge to make up his conditions. **1850** THAXTER *Poem before Iadma* 14 To assist a poor Sub Fresh at the dread Examination, And free from all 'conditions' to insure his first vacation. **1851** HALL *College Words* 78 The branches in which he [an entering student] is deficient are called conditions. **1871** BAGG *At Yale* 44 *Condition*, requirement to make up an unsatisfactory examination. **1894** 'MARK TWAIN' *P. Wilson* v, He went [to Yale] handsomely equipped with 'conditions,' but otherwise he was not an object of distinction there. **1903** K. WIGGIN *Rebecca* 226 She passed in only two subjects, but went cheerfully into the preparatory department with her five 'conditions.' **1907** *Scribner's Mag.* XLI. 506/1 At the end of sophomore year it became imperative for him to work off his accumulated conditions in the science he loathed.

***Condition,** *v.*

+**1.** *tr.* To require (a student) to do additional work to obtain 'credit' in a study not satisfactorily completed or done; to admit (a student) to a given status provided he make good the deficiencies in his preparation.

1832 in *Atlantic Mo.* Oct. (1887) 434/1 On his examination at Cambridge last Fall, he was heavily conditioned. **1849** in Hall *College Words* (1856) 124 A young man [from the country] . . . shall be examined and 'conditioned' in everything, and yet he shall come out far ahead of his city Latin-school classmate. **1856** HALL *Ib.* (ed. 2) 124 *Condition*, to admit a student as member of a college, who on being examined has been found deficient, . . . the provision of his admission being that he will make up the deficiency. **a1862** in *Harvard Mem. Biog.* (1866) II. 240, I was conditioned in Greek Grammar, and prose reading, but soon rubbed the conditions off. **1900** *Dialect Notes* II. 29 *Condition*, v.t. (Of an instructor) to mark a student deficient in a subject. **1923** *University of Okla. Bul.* No. 261, 58 D means that a student is conditioned because of poor quality of work.

2. To put into good condition. {1892–}

1849 *Rep. Comm. Patents: Agric.* 322 The next process in this troublesome but beautiful crop is to 'condition' it for 'packing.'

***Conditioning,** *vbl. n.* +The giving of a 'condition.' — **1897** *Educat. Rev.* XIII. 8 [Some students] get through by much coaching and conditioning.

Condolence. {1603–} +*Condolence council*, 'a tribal council of the Iroquois, held after the death of a sachem' (Th.S.). — **1890** *Smithsonian Rep.* 49 He . . . successfully made special effort to obtain the chants and speeches used in the condolence council of the league.

Condor. {1604–} A large bird of the vulture family (*Sarcorhamphus gryphus*), esp. of South America, but loosely applied to a vulture of either America.

1833 C. L. BONAPARTE *American Ornithology* IV. 17 The Condor is diffused over the continent of South America from the straits of Magellan, extending its range also to Mexico and California, and the western territory of the United States beyond the Rocky Mountains. **1883** *Harper's Mag.* Feb. 439/2 Longfellow's vultures, by-the-way, are condors.

+**b.** *California condor*, the California vulture: (see quot. 1889).

1889 *Cent.* 1176/2 *California condor*, the large vulture of California, *Cathartes* or *Pseudogryphus californianus*, resembling the Andean condor and fully as large. **1914** *New Internat. Encycl.* V. 716/2 The great vulture (*Sarcorhamphus gryphus*) of the Andes, one of the largest of known flying birds, . . . the California condor sometimes exceeding it. **1917** *Birds of Amer.* II. 54 The range of the California Condor is more restricted than that of any other bird of prey.

***Conduct,** *n.* **a.** Attrib. with *book*. In schools or, esp., the navy, a book in which the record of behavior is kept. **b.** With *roll*. A list of students in order of their standing. — **(a)** **1856** COZZENS *Sparrowgrass P.* xiii, 185 A conduct-book! There was G for good boy, and R. for reading, and S. for spelling and so on. **1889** *Cent.* 1177 *Conduct-book*, . . . a book kept on board of United States men-of-war, in which the conduct and ability of each man of the crew is noted. **(b)** **1862** STRONG *Cadet Life W. Point* 151 The aggregate of these [demerits] decides his standing on the conduct roll at the end of the year.

***Conduct,** *v.* +*intr.* To comport oneself; to behave. *Obs.* {with reflexive, 1706–}

'By a customary omission of the pronoun, to *conduct*, in an intransitive sense, is to behave; to direct personal actions' (W. '28). 'This offensive barbarism is happily confined to New England, where it is common both in speech and writing. Like many other expressions in the same predicament, it has received the tacit sanction of Dr. Webster, himself a New England man' (B. '48).

1754 EDWARDS *Works* (1843) II. 17 *n.*, I say not only doing, but conducting; because a voluntary forbearing to do, sitting still, keeping silence, &c., are instances of persons' conduct, about which Liberty is exercised. **1775** *Essex Inst. Coll.* XIII. 194 Nicolls conducted very oddly. **1802** J. COWLES *Diary* 74 His father does not conduct well but renders himself a grief to his children. **1809** E. A. KENDALL *Travels* I. 40 It has an 'effect to render permanent the seats of those who conduct well.' **a1843** A. BRADFORD *Wonders of Heavens* (De Vere), Castor and Pollux in their famous Argonautic expedition conducted with great gallantry. **1849** N. KINGSLEY *Diary* 68, I think that if he had cared for the interest of the company he would have conducted far different. **1871** *Binghamton Republ.* 17 Jan. (De Vere), Mr. Schutt said to him, How strangely you have conducted!

+**Conducta.** *S.W.* [Sp.] A caravan or escorted party. — **1836** HOLLEY *Texas* vi. 117 There are already heavy capitalists located there, and one conducta has arrived from Chihuahua with three hundred thousand dollars. **1844** KENDALL *Santa Fé Exped.* II. 404 A large conducta, or escort guarding nearly a million dollars in silver, was entering the city at the same time. **1871** DE VERE 105 The caravan is quite at home in New Mexico and Sonora, although frequently called there by its Spanish name, conducta.

||**Conductment.** The action of directing; command. — **1757** *Lett. to Washington* II. 128 A Return of Provisions &c for the Cherokee Indians commanded by the Young Warrior under my conductment from Winchester . . . to Wassers Fort.

* **Conductor.**

+**1.** One who has charge of mail, etc., in a stagecoach. *Obs.*
1790 *Independent Chron.* 4 March 4/2 A person to go through with the mail to take Care of it. . . . This conductor shall transact all . . . business committed to him. **1858** *N.Y. Tribune* 1 Dec. 3/4 The Santa Fé mail of the 8th ult. reached Independence on the 28th. The conductor reports snow a foot deep from the Arkansas River to Wilmot Creek. **1872** 'MARK TWAIN' *Roughing It* ii. 25 By the side of the driver sat the 'conductor,' the legitimate captain of the craft; for it was his business to take charge and care of the mails, baggage, express matter, and passengers.

+**2.** An official in charge of a railroad train, who is responsible for executing the orders of the train master, directing the movements of the train, collecting tickets, etc.
1839 *Eastern Argus* (Portland, Me.) 24 Sept. 2/4 (Th.), Mr. John C. Poole, one of the conductors of the Baltimore and Ohio railroad. **1858** *Texas Almanac 1859* 193 Railroad conductors, baggage masters, &c., are required to wear upon their hats some badge indicating their office. **1864** CUMMING *Hospital Life* (1866) 136/1 On our way down we met a gentleman, who informed us that the train would not be down, as the conductor was fearful of its being captured. **1873** *Newton Kansan* 24 April 3/2 The new time card . . . allows the conductors . . . to lay over here. **1873** BAILEY *Life in Danbury* 121 Conductor Phillips, of the eastern train, after giving the word to start, waited until the last car reached him. **1888** STOCKTON *Dusantes* iii, You kin send telegraphs all along the line to one station an' another for conductors to give to him in the cars. **1896** *Boston Ev. Rec.* 16 Dec. 1/4 Dunning was a conductor and on the day mentioned left the depot at Boston in charge of a train. **1903** BURNHAM *Jewel* 57, I'll tell the conductor to see that you get off at Bel-Air. **1925** BRYAN *Memoirs* 201, I have a delightful recollection of a conductor on one of the railroads running into Lincoln.

b. An official in charge of other conveyances. {(on an omnibus) 1837–}
1883 *Harper's Mag.* Sept. 648/1 Job Doolittle . . . walked into the [horse railway] office and asked if they wanted a conductor. **1891** S. M. WELCH *Recoll. 1830–40* 199 They [=omnibusses] were handsomely fitted out and richly upholstered, . . . with young men of sixteen to twenty, in uniform, for conductors. **1897** *Boston Herald* Sept., A conductor on one of the reservoir cars should be taught to say Park street. **1900** GOODLANDER *Fort Scott* 5 The drivers of these wagons [freight wagons in ox trains] were under the control or lead of what was called the wagon boss, or you might say, conductor, whose word was law.

3. A substance that permits the passage of electricity. {1737–}
1778 J. CARVER *Travels North-Amer.* 85 Apprehensive of the danger that might ensue from standing near anything which could serve for a conductor, . . . I took my stand as far as possible [etc.]. **1860** PRESCOTT *Telegraph* 260 The wire conductors . . . used . . . in this country [are] of No. 9 [wire].

+**4.** A rod attached to the top of a structure in order to conduct lightning away safely; a lightning rod (see also quot. 1789). {1770–}
1764 in N. F. Moore *Hist. Sk. Columbia Coll.* (1846) 49 Ordered, that a conductor be fixed to the cupola of the college, as a security against lightning. **1776** M'ROBERT *Tour* 52 Lightning . . . used to do frequent damage to their houses, but they have mostly all got conductors, which . . . are a spike of iron fixed upon the highest part of the building and carried down along the side of the wall till it enters the ground. **1789** *Ann. 1st Congress* I. 688 The petition of Andrew McPherson . . . praying that an exclusive privilege may be granted him . . . to make and vend lightning rods, . . . conductors and umbrellas [was presented to the House]. **1796** H. WANSEY *Excursion U.S.* 228 A conductor for lightning is fixed to almost every house [in New York]. **1823** *New Eng. Farmer* II. 77 A conductor constructed and put up agreeably to the above directions, will perfectly secure a building.

* **Cone.**

1. *Cone wheat*, a variety of wheat, named from its cone-like spike. {1677–}
1804 J. ROBERTS *Penna. Farmer* 43 The cone or bearded, is hardy, and will stand the inclemency of the weather better than either.

2. Comb. in the names of plants, as *cone-bearing willow, cone-fruit catchfly, cone-gall willow:* (see quotations).
1813 MUHLENBERG *Cat. Plants* 91 Cone-bearing Willow. **1817–8** EATON *Botany* (1822) 459 *Silene conica*, cone-fruit catchfly. . . . Flowers small. *Ib.* 442 *Salix conifera*, rose willow, cone-gall willow. . . . The scaly cones are mere excrescences or galls, caused by the stings of insects.

3. *Cone-crowned hat*, a hat with a cone-shaped crown.
1836 SIMMS *Mellichampe* iii, A cone-crowned hat . . . lay beside him, and formed another portion of his habiliments. **a1846** *Quarter Race Ky.*, etc. 155 A tall, thin man, . . . wearing an old cone-crowned, gray, woollen hat, walked hurriedly and agitatedly up to where a group of boarders was standing.

4. Attrib. with *frame* and *work:* Made with fir or pine cones.
1863 'M. HARLAND' *Husks* 18 You hate the very sight of shell-work, and cone-frames, and Grecian painting, and all such vanities. **1876** *Wide Awake* 78/2 On the walls were Mr. Brewer's certificate of good service done in the army, and a wood-cut of President Lincoln, both in curious cone-frames of the mother's contriving. **1864** *Maine Agric. Soc. Ret. 1863* 30 The exhibition of domestic manufactures . . . [including] cone-works, . . . was very large and fine.

5. A conelike formation of nature; a peak.
1850 *Western Journal* IV. 377 These are the Black Hills, the outer skirts of which are diminutive knobs and cones, which increase in magnitude. **1862** J. D. WHITNEY *Life & Lett.* 216 We saw the white snow-covered cone of Lassen's Butte, two hundred miles distant in an air line. **1866** 'F. KIRKLAND' *Bk. Anecdotes* 367 The man and his crew . . . proceeded to run the steamer to a point known as 'The Cone' on the Virginia shore.

+**Coneflower.** One or other plant of the genus *Rudbeckia.*
1817–8 EATON *Botany* (1822) 436 *Rudbeckia laciniata*, cone-flower, cone-disk sunflower. **1836** LINCOLN *Botany* App. 135. **1886** J. BURROUGHS in *Century Mag.* Sept. 787/1 There are several kinds of tall ones; the blossom has yellow leaves and brown velvety centers (cone-flower, or Rudbeckia, probably now common in the East). **1891** H. HERMAN *His Angel* 8 The trappers jumped down . . . among the reeds . . . and cone-flowers. **1901** MOHR *Plant Life Ala.* 797 *Rudbeckia triloba.* . . . Many-flowered Cone-Flower. . . . Carolinian and Louisianian areas. . . . *Rudbeckia hirta.* . . . Rough-stemmed Cone-Flower. *Ib.* 798 *Rudbeckia fulgida.* . . . Golden Cone-Flower.

+**b.** *Purple coneflower*, a closely allied plant (*Echinacea purpurea*), found on the western prairies.
1857 GRAY *Botany* 214. **1869** *Amer. Naturalist* III. 8 In contrast with these the purple cone-flower, *Echinacea*, displays its long drooping purple rays.

+**Conestoga.** Also **Coni-, Conostoga, Conestogoe, Cane-, Canastoga, Canastota.** [The name of a town in Lancaster county, Pa., from a local tribe of Iroquoian Indians that became extinct in 1763.]

1. *Conestoga wagon*, a covered wagon with broad wheels, suitable for travel in soft soil: (see quot. 1912.) *Obs.* except hist. (Evidently named before 1750; see sense b below.)
'The excellence of the wagons made in the Conestoga Valley of Lancaster County caused the name to become famous throughout the country, and the wagons were known as Conestogas. They were designed and built by local wheelwrights out of swamp oak, white oak, hickory, locust, gum and poplar, from the neighboring woodlands, and were ironed by the village blacksmiths' (1930 Omwake *Conestoga Six-Horse Bell Teams* 17).
1808 *Balance* (Hudson, N.Y.) 16 Feb. 28 (Th.), The throng of Pittsburg and Conestoga waggons. **1817** PAULDING *Lett. from South* I. 247 The caravan of poems, . . . which labour with electricity, and rumble along like a Canestoga wagon over the pavement, noisy in proportion as it is empty. **1843** 'CARLTON' *New Purchase* I. 137 The loads he had in his earlier days seen crammed into a Conestoga wagon. **1846** Emory *Military Reconn.* 496 There were forty large Conestoga wagons in this train and a due proportion of men. **1857** *Harper's Mag.* Oct. 641 A train of fourteen white-tilted Conostoga wagons . . . were slowly rumbling along the bank of the Arkansas toward the fort. **1867** *Atlantic Mo.* Feb. 155/2 A belated Conestoga wagon, coming through the forest, sunk into a rut below Kearns's place and remained there until morning. **1884** *Century Mag.* Jan. 440/1 By the middle of the eighteenth century, eight or nine thousand of the great white-topped Conestoga wagons, drawn each by four, six, or even eight horses, were required to bring to the busy little market city of Philadelphia the produce of the farms of the interior. **1891** S. M. WELCH *Recoll. 1830–40* 422 But it [=Erie Canal] did prove another long step forward; as a means of travel and transportation much in advance of stages and Canastota wagons. **1912** DAWSON *Pioneer Tales* 69 The wagons of early times were generally sixteen feet in length, six feet in depth, with the bottom swaying down in the middle, boat like in shape, with canvas top. They were called Conestoga wagons.
ellipt. **1901** CHURCHILL *Crisis* 11 After many years the streams began to move again, . . . by white conestogas threading flat forests and floating over wide prairies.

b. The name of a Philadelphia tavern.
1750 *Penna. Gazette* 26 Feb., Just imported and to be sold very cheap for ready money by Thomas White, at his house in Market Street, almost opposite the sign of the Conestoga Waggon. **1775** WASHINGTON *Diaries* II. 196 Went to the Commencement. at the College, and dind at Mr. Saml. Griffin's. After wch. attended a Comee at the Conistoga Waggon. **c1782** in W. Gordon *Hist. Amer. Revol.* (ed. 2) III. 329 A small dirty room in the Philadelphia tavern called the Canastoga-waggon.

c. *Conestoga wagoner*, a man whose business was to transport goods on a Conestoga wagon.
1788 FRENEAU *Misc. Works* 88 Plain Johan Shovelshoes, the Conestogoe waggoner, immagines the soul to be a thin airy substance. **1863** *Harper's Mag.* Feb. 425/1 The Conestoga wagoners, like the chimney-sweepers, have nearly faded from the remembrance of the oldest inhabitants.

2. *Conestoga horse*, a heavy breed of horse, suitable for drawing Conestoga wagons.
1839 E. HOOFER *Practical Farmer* 474 [The] Suffolk Punch . . . strongly resembles the famous Chester Balls and the Canestoga horses of Pennsylvania. **1844** *Congress. Globe* App. 748/2 Mr. Buchanan . . . could come upon the turf successfully with his celebrated breed of Conestoga dray

horses. **1857** H. W. HERBERT *Horse & Horsemanship* II. 59, I am inclined to suspect, the Conestoga-horse is descended from a mixture of the Flemish cart-horse with the English breed to which it bears so considerable a resemblance. **1868** BEECHER *Norwood* 516 It was the horses that gave to Pete his chief delight. . . . Two teams of huge gray Conestoga horses; a span of sorrels. **1884** *Century Mag.* Jan. 445/1 To the German farmers of Pennsylvania is due the credit of producing the great Conestoga horses, the finest draught animals on the continent in the colonial age.

b. *ellipt.* A horse of this breed.

1834 C. A. DAVIS *Lett. J. Downing* 144 The best kind of horses—rale Conestogas. **1860** R. JENNINGS *Horse* 61 The vast, white-topped wagons, drawn by superb teams of the stately Conestogas, were (once) a distinguishing feature in the landscape of that great agricultural State.

3. A stout, coarse shoe or boot. (Cf. STOGY.) Usu. *pl.*

1896 *Dialect Notes* I. 229 Kentucky Words: . . . *Conostogas,* . . . brogans.

+**Coney Island.** An island to the southwest of Long Island, noted as a pleasure resort. Attrib. with *clam chowder, maze.* — **1895** *Outing* XXVII. 238/2 Curried mussel . . . in aroma and taste is not unlike a Coney Island clam chowder. **1904** *N.Y. Ev. Post* 24 Oct. 7 Such a fort . . . is worse than a Coney Island maze.

* **Confectioner.** One whose business is to make candy, cake, pastry, etc.; one who conducts a confectionery (sense 1 and 1b).

'Used in this country much in the sense of the English *pastry-cook.* In England, a confectioner never sells cakes, ice-cream, &c.' (B. '77).

1679 *Boston Rec.* 65 Alexander Hamilton, confectioner, Shall not be Chargeable to the towne. **1807** IRVING, etc. *Salmagundi* viii, The Giblets . . . gave dinners, and they gave balls; they hired cooks, they hired confectioners. **1819** M'MURTRIE *Sk. Louisville* 137 There are at this moment, in Louisville, . . . one nail factory, twenty-eight groceries, two confectioners' shops. *c*1835 J. D. WHITNEY *Life & Lett.* 13 Never let me hear of your being once seen in an oyster shop, or eating or drinking house, or even Confectioners' Shops. **1850** S. F. COOPER *Rural Hours* 26 Formerly much of our sugar was sent to Albany and New York, and a portion is still sold there to the confectioners. **1870** 'M. HARLAND' *For Better, for Worse* 298 He had encountered her upon the threshold of the confectioner's saloon; they had eaten their ices together. **1903** BURNHAM *Jewel* 178 Mrs. Forbes recalled the confectioner's window.

* **Confectionery.** Also †**confectionary.**

+**1.** A store in which candy and pastry are sold; a confectioner's shop.

1803 E. S. BOWNE *Life* 156, I never go by a toy shop, or confectionery without longing to have them [children] here. **1820** FLINT *Lett. from Amer.* 212 The enumeration of houses, made in March, 1819, was as follows: . . . Groceries, 102; Druggists' stores, 11; Confectionaries, 4. **1847** *Knickerb.* XXX. 396 After dinner you could see them . . . lounging at the front window of a hotel or confectionary. **1870** R. TOMES *Decorum* 188 [The repast] should never be slurred over by any of the miserable pretexts of the bar-room, eating-house, or confectionery. **1878** C. COALE in *Ann. S.W. Va.* (1929) 1557 We have three large and well-kept hotels, nine variety stores, . . . half a dozen confectioneries, an agricultural warehouse, [etc.]. **1887** *Courier-Journal* 21 Jan. 6/4 Mrs. Jett started a confectionery at Lexington and afterward . . . she established millineries.

+**b.** A barroom or liquor store.

1836 *Quarter Race Ky.* (1846) 24, I went to town last night to the confectionary, (a whiskey shop in a log pen fourteen feet square). **1842** BUCKINGHAM *Slave States* I. 232 Dram-shops, under the name of confectionaries, exist in great numbers. *Ib.* 246 In the town [of Columbus, Ga.] itself, we observed a more than usual number of the places called 'Confectionaries,' where sweetmeats and fruits are sold; but the great staple supplies of which are peach-brandy, whiskey, rum, and other ardent spirits. **1859** BARTLETT 94 *Confectionary,* in the South-west and some parts of the West, a bar-room.

2. Attrib. with *business, shop, store.*

1891 O'BEIRNE *Leaders Ind. Territory* 40/1 In 1890 he opened a drug store and confectionery business in Caddo. **1825** J. NEAL *Bro. Jonathan* II. 342 She began with loving flowers; but such flowers, only, as were to be had in the confectionery shops, or the milliners. **1886** *Stand. Guide of Washington* 161 Velati's Confectionary Store . . . is noted for its famous Caramels, . . . also the finest fruits of the season, and exquisite Confections. **1887** *Courier-Journal* 11 Jan. 3/4 Annie Heinrich . . . clerked for . . . the proprietress of an ice-cream and confectionery store. **1899** NORRIS *McTeague* x, She could see the big market, a confectionery store, a bell-hanger's shop, and . . . the glass skylights and water tanks of the big public baths.

+**Confed,** *n.* and *a. colloq.* [Abbrev. of CONFEDERATE.]

1. *n.* = CONFEDERATE *n.* (sense 2).

1861 *N.Y. Tribune* 7 Feb., The Confeds seemed to like the liquors hugely. **1890** *Century Mag.* Nov. 100/1 You couldn't tell Yank from Confed. **1895** *N.Y. Dramatic News* 23 Nov. 3/3 What became of that comedy of yours which I produced under the title of Feds and Confeds?

2. *adj.* Designating the currency issued by the Confederate States. Also absol.

1865 BOUDRYE *Fifth N.Y. Cavalry* 259 For one dollar greenbacks, we can get from five to ten dollars Confed. **1865** G. SABRE *Prisoner of War* 60 Who's the lucky man to buy this last slice of bread for ten cents greenback or one dollar Confed? **1888** GRIGSBY *Smoked Yank* xxii. 193, I had nothing to offer as a bribe, except a few dollars in confed., as we called the rebel money.

* **Confederacy.** Used in abstract senses and in the following concrete applications:

+**1.** A league of Indian tribes.

1622 'MOURT' *Relation* 120 The Company assembled together, and resolued . . . to reuenge the supposed death of Tisquantum . . . and to retaine Nepeof, another Sachim or Governour, who was of this confederacy. **1764** HUTCHINSON *Hist. Mass.* I. 119 This confederacy had been in agitation for several years. *Ib.* 166 In 1653 information was given by the Indians . . . that the Dutch governor was privately soliciting them to a general confederacy, in order totally to extirpate the English. **1775** ADAIR *Indians* 329 The French having drawn off some towns from the national confederacy, and corrupted them, they . . . publicly offered rewards for our scalps. **1873** BEADLE *Undevel. West* 378 Traders penetrating their country from Pensacola named it, from the number of streams, the Creek Country, and gave the Muscokee Nation the title of Creek Confederacy. **1895** *Cent. Cycl. of Names* 532/1 *Iroquois,* . . . a well-known confederacy of North American Indians.

+**2.** The union of the American states under the Articles of Confederation.

1777 *Jrnls. Cont. Congress* IX. 907/1 The stile of this confederacy shall be, 'The United States of America.' **1781** HAMILTON *Works* (1886) VIII. 34 The accession of Maryland to the Confederacy will be a happy event if it does not make people believe that the Confederacy gives Congress power enough. **1785** in *S. Lit. Messenger* XXVIII. 39/1 As it will indirectly affect the whole confederacy, Congress ought clearly to be made a party to it. **1788** in Marshall *Kentucky* 334 Severing a part of the said state [of Virginia] from the other parts thereof, and admiting it into the confederacy formed by the articles of confederation and perpetual union, as an independent member thereof. *c*1798 WEBSTER in Benton *30 Years' View* I. 140 The people had had quite enough of that kind of government under the confederacy. **1837** VAN BUREN in *Pres. Mess. & P.* III. 338 There can be no doubt that those who framed and adopted the Constitution, having in immediate view the depreciated paper of the Confederacy, . . . intended to prevent the recurrence of similar evils. **1881–5** MCCLELLAN *Own Story* 31 The right of secession would virtually have carried us back to the old Confederacy.

+**3.** The United States regarded as a political unit.

1827 COOPER *Prairie* x, His body was enveloped in a hunting-shirt of dark green, trimmed with the yellow fringes and ornaments that were sometimes seen among the border-troops of the Confederacy. *Ib.* xiv, I summon ye all, in the name of the Confederacy of the United Sovereign States of North America, to submit yourselves to the laws. **1832** CLAY *Speeches* (1842) 242 The question how it shall be subsequently applied for the use and benefit of such of the United States as compose the confederacy, is one of modus only. **1836** *Diplom. Corr. Texas* I. 81 In my estimation it is all important to become a portion of this confederacy. **1841** HARRISON in *Pres. Mess. & P.* IV. 16 Our Confederacy, fellow-citizens, can only be preserved by the same forbearance. **1848** POLK *Ib.* 613 Already our Confederacy consists of twenty-nine States. **1856** HAMBLETON *H. A. Wise* 31 He is entitled to the confidence of the friends of Constitutional Liberty in every section of the Confederacy. **1858** DOUGLAS in Logan *Great Conspiracy* 72 This Republic . . . may yet expand . . . until it covers the whole Continent, and becomes one vast ocean-bound Confederacy.

+**4.** The Confederate States of America. Hist. since 1865.

1860 in Kettell *Hist. Rebellion* II. 44 In the opinion of South Carolina the constitution of the United States will form a suitable basis for the Confederacy of the Southern States withdrawing. **1860** ABBOTT *South & North* 307 Until the Southern confederacy shall again have its free North, and its slaveholding South, as now. **1862** JACKSON in M. A. Jackson *Life* 365, I would rather be stationed there . . . than anywhere else in the Confederacy. **1865** *Nation* I. 651 The Southern States he still called the Confederacy. **1867** EDWARDS *Shelby* 62 He was hung at Little Rock two weeks afterwards, for treason to the Confederacy. **1884** *Century Mag.* Nov. 107, I have heard him repeatedly express the wish that all the civil and general officers of the last Confederacy might be court-martialed and shot. **1885** *Ib.* April 923/1 These States could not only raise half a million soldiers, but could furnish the confederacy with provisions of all kinds, and cotton enough to supply the Rebel Government with the sinews of war. **1892** GUNTER *Miss Dividends* 8 During the War of the Confederacy, speculators, under the guise of Government contractors, had stolen great sums from Uncle Sam.

attrib. **1861** *Vanity Fair* 15 June 281/2 Floyd insulted me by offering to pay his bets, honestly lost, in Confederacy Bonds! **1861** *N.Y. Times* 12 April, On one side was the Confederacy flag.

+**Confederal,** *a.* Of or pertaining to the United States before the Constitution was adopted. — **1782** *Independent Ledger* 4 Feb. 3/2 May the confederal armies, be always mindful of the end for which they drew their swords. **1784** J. F. MERCER in Bancroft *Hist. Const.* (1882) I. 397 It is the disposition of the people of America to place their confederal government on the most respectable basis. **1866** H. PHILLIPS *Amer. Paper Curr.* II. 94 On the 15th of September [1778] a report . . . was communicated; . . . such portions as related to a confederal fund . . . were referred to . . . Messrs. Duer, Gerry and A. Adams.

***Confederate,** *n.*

+1. Of Indians: One of certain tribes leagued together.

The best known Indian confederation was that of Iroquois tribes—Mohawk, Oneida, Onondaga, Cayuga, Seneca, and (after 1726) Tuscarora. Cf. *Five Nations, Six Nations.* The league was formed about 1570 and was powerful in the eighteenth century.

1622 'MOURT' *Relation* 94 Masasoyt . . . should send to his neighbour Confederates, to certifie them of this, that they might not wrong vs. **1637** R. WILLIAMS in *Winthrop P.* 194, I hope the continuance of the number will be seasonable, if not for pursuit of Sasacous & the Pequots . . . yet for the quelling of their confederates. **1755** L. EVANS *Anal. Map Colonies* 11 The Confederates actual Settlements were bounded Northward [etc.]. *Ib.* 12 Tho' the Confederates lay no Claim to these Parts in Right of the Tuscaroras.

+2. A citizen of the Southern States while they were organized as the Confederate States of America. Usu. *pl.*, the forces of the South during the Civil War, 1861–65.

1861 *Boston Transcript* 14 May, The capture of the President by the doughty Confederates. **1862** in F. Moore *Rebellion Rec.* V. II. 228 An apparently interminable train, loaded, as was afterward learned, with nearly three thousand confederates, was just about departing south. **1864** H. GREELEY *American Conflict* I. 415 The joyous anticipations with which the struggle was commenced by the Confederates. **1865** *Nation* I. 109 Anybody might tell that you're no Unionist. I'm sure the child appears like he was a little Confederate. **1873** 'MARK TWAIN' & WARNER *Gilded Age* xxxviii. 347 My husband sometimes says that he doesn't see but Confederates are just as eager to get at the Treasury as Unionists. **1885** *Century Mag.* March 775/1 We saw emerging from the little ravine to the left of the fort a swarm of Confederates, who opened on us with a terrible and deadly fire. **1907** C. C. ANDREWS *Recoll.* 158 Twice, indeed, the Confederates were repulsed.

+3. (See quotation.)

1864 CUMMING *Hospital Life* (1866) 122/2 They have a very nice oil, distilled from pitch, called Confederate, which is a great improvement on the 'pine-knot' lights.

***Confederate,** *a.*

***1.** Allied, bound in a league. (Said of the colonies, Indian tribes, and, in loose usage, the states.)

1675 in Hubbard *Indian Wars* I. 78 The Confederate Colonies. **1682** *Mass. H. S. Coll.* 4 Ser. V. 69, My great disbursement in the year 1675, by General Winslow's order, for the preservation of the wounded men of the Confederate Army. **1687** SEWALL *Diary* I. 185 It seems . . . the French and the Confederat Indians make war upon the Mohawks and theirs. **1832** *Congress. Deb.* IX. 171/2 The political ties which connect us with our confederate States.

+2. Of, pertaining to, or belonging to, the Confederate States of America: **a.** The army and navy. **b.** The government and its period of existence. **c.** The currency and financial system. **d.** Concrete objects. **e.** Post-Civil War phenomena.

(a) 1907 C. C. ANDREWS *Recoll.* 12 After the surrender of the Confederate armies General Andrews was in command of districts in Alabama and Texas. **c1874** 'MARK TWAIN' *Sk., True Story,* My marster he was a Confedrit colonel, an' I was his family's cook. **1888** *Scribner's Mag.* Jan. 24/2 Uncle Obed . . . made himself very prominent by resisting a Confederate cruiser with harpoons and a couple of bomb-lance guns. **1885** *Century Mag.* April 934 The Confederate fleet mounted, all told, thirty-nine guns. *Ib.* 918/1 Every afternoon found us around in Coliseum Place, standing or lying on the grass watching the dress parade of the 'Confederate Guards.' *Ib.* 952/1 This shows how difficult it was for the Confederate gunners in the former work to fight while enduring the terrible pounding of the mortars. **1865** BOUDRYE *Fifth N.Y. Cavalry* 40 Having spent a night in chasing through the Confederate lines, all men returned to their own side of the Rapidan. **1865** S. COX *In Congress* 22 Mr. Mallory has been Secretary of the Confederate Navy. **1885** *Century Mag.* March 774/1 The officer in command had a force of Confederate prisoners at work removing them [torpedoes]. **1887** *Courier-Journal* 6 Feb. 13/7 Col. John S. Mosby, the famous Confederate raider, was at the Fifth Avenue Hotel today. **1861** *New Haven Palladium* 27 May, He and his brother were impressed into the Confederate service. **1862** S. COX *In Congress* (1865) 280 England . . . now permits a thousand hammers to rivet the iron mail upon a score of Confederate steamers. **1885** *Century Mag.* April 923/2 The only Confederate vessel then in commission was a small river-boat, the Ivy, mounting one four-pounder rifled gun.

(b) 1897 C. A. DANA *Recoll. Civil War* 280, I saw it was the key to the official Confederate cipher. **1867** J. M. CRAWFORD *Mosby* 31 The next day the Virginia delegates to the Confederate Congress arrived. **1861** *Chicago Tribune* 19 July 1/6 A Charleston paper, which asserts that he (May) said to the so-called 'Confederate Government,' that 30,000 men in Maryland were ready to arm against the Federal forces in that city. **1884** *Century Mag.* April 826/1 These newspapers . . . being conveyed all night by the Confederate mail-carriers, would be in the hands of the rebel Cabinet next morning. **1863** J. R. BALME *Amer. States* (1864) 185 Jefferson Davis, the Confederate President, whom Lincoln's soldiers intended to have hung. **1877** *Harper's Mag.* Feb. 377/2 The conversation turned upon their experiences in 'Confederate times.'

(c) 1899 CHESNUTT *Wife of His Youth* 271 Colonel Myrover . . . had invested most of his wealth in Confederate bonds, which were now only so much waste paper. **1907** C. C. ANDREWS *Recoll.* 163 An officer . . . came and gave me ten dollars in Confederate Currency. **1885** *Century Mag.* March 772 We found on attempting to pay it [=local scrip] out again that they were rather reluctant to receive it, even at that early stage in Confederate finance. **1875** *Chicago Tribune* 2 Nov. 4/5 The Confederate graybacks became valueless, simply because they will never be redeemed. **1862** *Picayune* 23 March, I could not pay you with anything else, . . . for I have nothing but Confederate money. **1865** CUMMING *Hospital Life* (1866) 190/2 The owner would take nothing but Confederate money as ferriage, and charged seventy dollars. **1863** L. BAKER *U.S. Secret Service* (1867) 169 The property found on the persons . . . consisted of . . . Confederate notes, . . . $4,586.00. **1867** J. M. CRAWFORD *Mosby* 169 As he was just from New York, he was pretty flush with greenbacks, which he was advised to exchange for Confederate notes, as he was going to Richmond. **1863** in F. Moore *Rebellion Rec.* V. I. 27 Hereafter the dealing in and passage of currency known as 'confederate scrip' or 'confederate notes' is positively prohibited. **1891** *Harper's Mag.* Dec. 46/1 This suit of clothes cost me twelve hundred dollars in Confederate scrip. **1889** 'MARK TWAIN' *Conn. Yankee* xxxi. 396 In the North a carpenter got three dollars; . . . in the South he got fifty—payable in Confederate shinplasters worth a dollar a bushel.

(d) 1911 HARRISON *Queed* 259 Some seated, . . . but all . . . wearing the Confederate colors. **1885** *Century Mag.* April 950/2 In less than ten minutes Confederate flags were hauled down. **1867** J. M. CRAWFORD *Mosby* 169 One of the men exchanging a Confederate hat (little worn) and home-spun woollen gloves for his elegant fur cap and mink-skin gloves. **1879** TOURGEE *Fool's Errand* xviii. 96 The other letter . . . written on the coarse, dingy paper known as 'Confederate paper.'

(e) 1898 *Kansas City Star* 18 Dec. 4/2 There are two cemeteries here, side by side, National and Confederate, separated only by a fence. **1911** *Okla. Session Laws* 3 Legisl. 25 Ten thousand dollars (10,000) for the purpose of completing, furnishing and equipping the Oklahoma Confederate Home for indigent and disabled confederate soldiers and sailors, is hereby appropriated. **1899** CHESNUTT *Wife of His Youth* 270 On the Confederate Memorial Day no other grave was so profusely decorated with flowers. **1896** *N.Y. Dramatic News* 4 July 16/2 Benefits of various kinds will be given for several of the Confederate veteran camps.

+3. *slang.* Emphatically correct; exactly or positively right.

1869 *Overland Mo.* III. 128 When a Texan wishes to express the strongest possible approval of some sentiment, he will exclaim 'You're mighty Confederate!'

+4. In plant names: *Confederate jasmine,* star jasmine. *S. Confederate pintree,* the honey locust.

1897 R. M. STUART *Simpkinsville* 49 He turned . . . to see the . . . edge of a woman's skirt as it disappeared behind the hedge of Confederate jasmine. — **1897** SUDWORTH *Arborescent Flora* 254 *Gleditsia triacanthos.* . . . Common names. . . . Confederate Pintree (Fla.).

+Confederate brigadier. A member of Congress who was formerly an officer in the Confederate army.

Further quotations are given in Thornton's *Suppl.* 189.

1879 *Congress. Rec.* 19 April 591/1 The 'confederate brigadiers,' who allied themselves with that party [Republican] are not only harmless, but the very quintessence of patriotism. *Ib.* 10 June 1901/2 When you see here confederate brigadiers and Union soldiers joining in the work of legislation—the 'era of good feeling' will very soon enter the jury-box at the South. **1881** *Ib.* 24 March 48/1 A great deal was said . . . during the last two years about confederate brigadiers having control of the democratic side of the House, the democratic side controlling the Senate, and therefore the Confederate brigadiers controlling the Senate. **1895** A. O. MYERS *Bosses & Boodle* 109 The 'Negro' and the 'Confederate Brigadier' became the scare-crows that the two great parties used to keep their wavering followers in line.

+Confederate candle. (See quotation.) — **1888** *Century Mag.* XXXVI. 770/2 Another light in great vogue was the 'Confederate,' or 'endless,' candle. It was constructed by dipping a wick in melted wax and resin and wrapping it around a stick, one end of the wick being passed through a wire loop fastened to the end of the stick.

Confederated, *ppl. a.* {1605–}

+1. Of Indian tribes: Joined in a league.

1789 MORSE *Amer. Geog.* 273 All the confederated tribes except the Oneidas and Tuscaroras sided with the British. **1793** in *Mass. H. S. Coll.* 3 Ser. V. 159 Lord Dorchester's speech to the chiefs and warriors deputed by the confederated Indian nations of the Ottawas, Chippeways, [etc.] **1855** PIERCE in *Pres. Mess. & P.* V. 306 The chiefs of certain confederated tribes of Indians residing in the Willamette Valley of Oregon.

+2. Made up or composed of associated states in the United States.

This word was used, esp. by certain statesmen and politicians before the Civil War, to imply the theory of state sovereignty under the Constitution.

1777 in Buckingham *Newspaper Lit.* I. 251 Which [interest with Britain] the Grand Council of these Confederated States, in their Wisdom, have seen fit for ever to dissolve. **1783** R. PUTNAM in *Memoirs* 216 This country is of sufficient extent . . . to form a distinct government (or colloney of the United States)—in time to be admitted, one of the Confedirated

States of America. **1819** E. DANA *Geogr. Sk.* 55 And a great experiment is about to be made, in a confederated republic, by the effects of slavery on the morals and manners of republican freemen. **1829** *Western Mo. Rev.* III. 56 Nothing gives us such magnificent conceptions of the real power and future resources of our great confederated republic, as such statements as this before us. **1834** JACKSON in *Pres. Mess. & P.* III. 65 States . . . magnanimously sacrificed domains which would have made them the rivals of empires, only stipulating that they should be disposed of for the common benefit of themselves and the other confederated States. **1839** CALHOUN *Works* III. 365 We hold the public domain as a common property or fund, belonging to the States of the Union in their confederated, and not in their individual character. **1844** TYLER in *Ib.* IV. 313 Our confederated Republic consisted originally of thirteen members. **1847** POLK in *Ib.* IV. 564 It is difficult to estimate the 'immense value' of our glorious Union of confederated States.

+3. *Confederated States*, the Confederate States of America.

1861 in Logan *Great Conspiracy* 143, I look for nothing else than that the Commissioners from the Confederated States will be received here and recognized by Abraham Lincoln.

+Confederate duck. (See quotation.) — **1888** *Century Mag.* XXXVI. 766/2 A rare and famous dish of those days [1861–5] was 'Confederate duck'. . . . This peculiarly named fowl was no fowl at all but a tender and juicy beefsteak rolled and pinioned around a stuffing of stale bread crumbs, [etc.].

+Confederate gray. The gray uniform worn by members of the Confederate army during the Civil War. — **1866** in Fleming *Hist. Reconstruction* I. 47 No armed foe being in the field, the great armies of the North waged active and honorable warfare against Confederate grey and its brass buttons. **1867** J. M. CRAWFORD *Mosby* 26 The gray-haired man of sixty years, as well as the boy of sixteen summers, hastened to don the Confederate gray.

fig. **1892** *Nation* 3 March 176/1 The book is handsomely uniformed in Confederate gray.

+Confederate States (of America). The southern states that seceded from the federal union as organized under a separate government, 1861–1865.

'The Confederate States of America were organized at a congress of delegates from the seceded states of South Carolina, Georgia, Florida, Alabama, Mississippi and Louisiana which met at Montgomery, February 4, 1861' (*Cycl. Amer. Govt.* I. 369/1).

1861 Kettell *Hist. Rebellion* I. 53 We, the delegates of the people of Virginia, . . . do, by this ordinance, adopt and ratify the Constitution of the Provisional Government of the Confederate States of America. **1861** in *Official Rec. Rebellion* 4 Ser. I. 426 The said Confederate States . . . and the Creek Nation . . . have agreed to the following articles. **1861** *Chicago Tribune* 19 July 1/2 To the true and loyal citizens of Virginia on all the Ohio border . . . if they will now return to their patriotic duty and acknowledge their allegiance to Virginia and her Confederate States [etc.]. **1885** *Century Mag.* March 684 They tried fur ter mek me fight fur the Confed'ret States an' they never done hit, an' 'en they tried ter conscrip' me. **1888** *Ib.* Sept. 763/2 The Register and the Treasurer of the Confederate States were reduced to the extremity of hiring men to sign the almost innumerable bills for them.

*** Confederation.**

+1. The leaguing together of certain New England colonies for common defence (1643–83); also, the league thus formed. (Cf. NEW ENGLAND CONFEDERATION.)

'To it were admitted the colonies of Massachussets, Plymouth, Connecticut. and New Haven' (J. S. Bassett *Short Hist. U.S.* 71).

1643 in Bradford *Hist.* 498 It is by these conffederats agreed, yt the charge of all just warrs . . . shall . . . be borne by all ye parts of this confederation. **1652** *Plymouth Colony Records* III. 13 Conserning the difference betwixt the jurisdictions of Massachusetts and Plymouth about the lands, . . . the Court have refered the determinacōn thereof unto the commissioners att theire next meeting, according to the articles of confederacōn. **1654** JOHNSON *Wonder-w. Prov.* 182 They concluded a firm confederation to assist each other in all just and lawful war. **1675** in Hubbard *Indian Wars* I. 56 As agreed in the Articles of Confederation.

+2. The leaguing together of American states during the Revolutionary War, esp. under the Articles of Confederation; also, the union established by this action.

1776 S. ADAMS in Wells *Life* II. 436 A plan of confederation has been brought into Congress. **1777** *Jrnls. Cont. Congress* IX. 924/2 Canada acceding to this confederation, and joining in the measures of the United States, shall be admitted into and entitled to all the advantages of this union. **1790** *Ann. 1st Congress* II. 1202 The States would never have entered into the Confederation, unless their property had been guarantied to them. **1836** *S. Lit. Messenger* II. 685 We are proceeding in the same manner that was done when the confederation was first formed. **1838** COOPER *Homeward B.* viii, He clearly demonstrated that the confederation itself had, in reality, no distinctive character of its own. **1855** PIERCE in *Pres. Mess. & P.* V. 345 When the ordinance which provided for the government of the territory northwest of the river Ohio . . . was adopted in the Congress of the Confederation. **1886** LOGAN *Great Conspiracy* 14 None knew better than they [the British], that the failure of the subsequent political Confederation of States was due mainly to its failure to encourage and protect the budding domestic manufactures of those States. **1902** E. C. MEYER *Nominating Systems* 5 The history of the caucus is found mainly in its extension to all the colonies, and in its rapid growth especially during the Revolution and under the Confederation.

b. The agreements upon which such union was based; the Articles of Confederation.

1784 in *S. Lit. Messenger* XXVIII. 35/1, I think it would be wise in Congress to recommend to the States the calling a Convention for the sole purpose of amending the Confederation. **1787** *Constitution* vi. 1 All debts contracted and engagements entered into, before the adoption of this Constitution, shall be as valid against the United States under this Constitution, as under the Confederation. **1789** *Ann. 1st Congress* I. 66 The States of North Carolina and Georgia protested against said treaties as infringing their legislative rights, and being contrary to the confederation. **1821** JEFFERSON *Autobiog.* Writings I. 77 A majority of the States, necessary by the Confederation to constitute a House even for minor business, did not assemble until the 13th of December.

+3. *Articles of Confederation*, a set of agreements providing for union among the original thirteen American states, framed in 1775, adopted by the Continental Congress in 1777, ratified by 1781, and in effect until 1789.

1775 *Jrnls. Cont. Congress* II. 195 Articles of Confederation and perpetual Union, entred into . . . by the Delegates of the several Colonies. **1777** *Ib.* IX. 923/1 Provided that no power be delegated to the said committee for the exercise of which by the articles of confederation the voice of nine states, in the Congress of the United States assembled is requisite. **1788** *Steele Papers* I. 21 The old Constitution or articles of Confederation. **1838** *Democratic Review* I. 226 The general dread of a return to the anarchy . . . of the old Articles of Confederation.

+4. Sometimes applied to the Union since 1789.

1845 POLK in *Pres. Mess. & P.* IV. 380 Our Union is a confederation of independent States, whose policy is peace with each other and all the world.

+Confederationist. {1865} A supporter of the Confederate States of America. — **1861** *Louisville Jrnl.*, The confederationists may be of one bone with their new President.

+Confederatism. The doctrine and practice of the supporters of the Confederate States of America. — **1870** E. MULFORD *Nation* xvii. 340 Confederatism, in its attack upon the nation, is in league with hell.

+Conferee. One who is chosen and deputed to confer on some particular question.

1771 J. BOUCHER *Causes Amer. Revol.* (1797) 238 By some logic of their own, their conferees have found out, that 'none of our parishes are so inconsiderable but that the worst is too good for the worst clergymen.' **1779** in W. B. Reed *Life Jos. Reed* II. 52 The Conferees of Congress gave this committee very ample assurances of the disposition of Congress to preserve the most perfect harmony. **1862** *Harper's Mag.* Feb. 375/1 Tom the Tinker declared in the Pittsburg Gazette, that the conferees had been bribed by the Government. **1884** *Science* IV. 47 Provision has been made for two additional conferees on the part of our government. **1903** *N.Y. Ev. Post* 11 Sept., Mr. Grout is still in Europe and has not communicated with the Fusion conferees.

b. A member of a committee of one house of Congress appointed to confer with a committee from the other house.

1794 *Ann. 4th Congress* 2 Sess. 2804 One of the conferees then inquired whether the President could not suspend the execution of the excise acts. **1809** *Ann. 10th Congress* 2 Sess. 328 Mr. Bradley, of the conferees from the Senate, on the disagreement between the two Houses, . . . made the following report. **1836** *Congress. Deb.* 8 Feb. 433 Whose fault was it that there was no time left for acting on the report of the conferees? **1871** *N.Y. Tribune* 27 Feb. (De Vere), The Conferees on the part of the House would not agree to the proposition of the Senate to raise the salaries of all the United States Judges. **1909** *Westminster Gaz.* 30 July 7/4 The Tariff conferees have accepted the President's demands and signed the report.

*** Conference.**

***1.** A consultation or meeting on political or other important matters.

1666 *Md. Archives* II. 11 They would be pleased to admitt the Lower House to be present at the Piscattoway Indians Conference. **1668** *Conn. Public Rec.* II. 102 This Court . . . formerly commissionated the Secretary . . . to treat in behalfe of this Colony, . . . which conferrance hath produced no sattisfaction. **1688** *Penna. Col. Rec.* I. 223 The Assembly Came with their Speaker, and was admitted: the Conferrance was Chiefly about their privileges. **1777** *Jrnls. Cont. Congress* IX. 911/1 No state . . . shall . . . enter into any conference, agreement, alliance or treaty with any king, prince, or state. **1791** *Ann. 2nd Congress* 95 The House of Representatives . . . desire a conference with the Senate on the subject-matter of the amendments. **1836** *Diplom. Corr. Texas* I. 117, I went to the State Department, to have a conference with the Present Acting Secretary of State. **1846** POLK *Diary* 106, [I] had a conference with the Secretary of War and General Wool today. **1882** *Nation* 16 Nov. 416/3 He could see nothing wrong there which could not be cured by a 'conference' or a 'new deal.'

b. *Committee of conference*, a group of persons appointed to consult on a matter; +esp. during the Amer. Revolution, a committee appointed by the Continental Congress to confer with General Washington.

1775 *Jrnls. Cont. Congress* III. 330 Resolved, That the farther consideration of the report of the Committee of conference be referred till to Morrow. **1776** *Ib.* IV. 410 The Congress then resolved itself into a committee of the whole, to take into their farther consideration, the report of the Committee of Conference. **1854** BENTON *30 Years' View* I. 712/1 Then a committee of 'conference' was appointed, and they 'disagreed.' **1859** *Harper's Mag.* April 687/2 A joint Committee of Conference was then appointed, who recommended the passage of a new Bill.

c. Attrib. with *chamber, committee, system.*

1753 *Md. Hist. Mag.* III. 365 A Conversation between Mr. Jennings & me, in the Conference Chamber at a Ball given by the Governor. **1789** *History of Congress* (1834) 21 If either house shall request a conference, and appoint a committee for that purpose, and the other house shall also appoint a committee to confer, such committees shall . . . meet in the conference chamber. **1871** *Harper's Mag.* XLIII. 150/2 The Senate amendments were non-concurred in by the House, and a conference committee was appointed. **1902** E. C. MEYER *Nominating Systems* 2 There also sprung up the conference and correspondence systems [of nominating candidates].

2. A legislative and judicial assembly of the ministers, officials, etc., of certain churches, esp. of the Methodist Church. {1744-}

1793 T. COKE *Journal* 113 On the 28th, we opened our last Conference in New York for that State. **1829** SHERWOOD *Gaz. Georgia* (ed. 2) 248 The first Conference held in the State was at a private house in Wilkes. **1849** E. A. HITCHCOCK *Journal* 43 He was converted by a Methodist itinerant from the conference. **1857** *Harper's Mag.* Feb. 424/2 Holston Conference was in session. It embraces East Tennessee, part of Western Virginia and North Carolina. **1883** *Dakota Mission Conf. of M.E. Ch.* 4 Session 35 The Bishop gave most interesting reminiscences of his first year in the ministry, and also of his adventures in the west in reaching Conferences. **1902** L. RICHARDS *Mrs. Tree* 46 It was one summer, and Conference was held here in Elmerton.

+b. Modified by certain adjectives to designate assemblies of the Methodist Church which have special powers and functions or are held at particular times.

1825 J. PICKERING *Inquiries Emigrant* (1831) 77 Only a few of the Wesleyan Methodists . . . are now subject to the American Conference. **1840** *Niles' Nat. Reg.* 18 April 112/2 In the United States the Methodist episcopal church has 28 annual conferences. **1844** Rupp *Relig. Denominations* 448 A quarterly meeting conference is composed of all the travelling and local preachers, exhorters, stewards, and leaders, belonging to any particular circuit or station, in which the presiding elder presides. **1845** in *Ind. Mag. Hist.* XXIII. 21 These persons, with a few others, met together and drew up and sent a memorial, or petition, to the Western conference. **1866** 'F. KIRKLAND' *Bk. Anecdotes* 81 The autumnal session of the Pittsburg Annual Conference of the Methodist Church, 1864, was characterized by an incident of patriotic and thrilling interest. **1896** FREDERIC *Theron Ware* 160 Every succeeding day brought closer to hand the ordeal of his first Quarterly Conference in Octavius. **1897** R. M. STUART *Simpkinsville* 17 Yes, I was stationed here at fall conference a year ago.

+c. A revival or meeting for prayer and exhortation.

1832 TROLLOPE *Domestic Manners* I. 298 We arrived at Baltimore at the season of the 'Conference.' . . . From what I could learn, it much resembles a Revival. **1856** GOODRICH *Recoll.* I. 217 Deacons and laymen, gifted in speech, were called upon to pray and exhort, and tell experiences in the private meetings, which were now called *conferences.*

+Conference meeting. A gathering for prayer and religious discussion.

1670 I. MATHER *Life R. Mather* 79 The last private Conference-Meeting which he was at in Dorchester, he had prepared to speak. **1676** SEWALL *Diary* I. 29 The first Conference meeting that ever I was at, was at our House. **1835** REED & MATHESON *Visit* II. 15 Conference or Inquiry Meetings.—These are instituted for those persons who have become anxiously concerned for their salvation. **1846** WHITCHER *Bedott P.* ii. 28 Parson Potter seldom went to confrence meetin'. **1850** *Knickerb.* XXXV. 22 They attempted a conference-meeting once, but Deacon —— . . . was so drunk that he could not articulate. **1861** *Chicago Tribune* 19 July 1/8 There will be Conference Meeting in the Hall at 2 o'clock P.M. the same day. **1881** *Harvard Coll. Ann. Rep.* 67 General Exercises [of the Divinity School include] conference meeting, conducted by students.

Conference room. {1867} (See quotation *a*1870.) — **a1870** CHIPMAN *Notes on Bartlett* 94 *Conference-Room,* a room for conference and prayer, and for the pastor's less formal address.—Conn. **1881** STODDARD *E. Hardery* 101 Some people called it the 'conference-room' and some by other names. . . . The Bible-class met there on Sundays, and the prayer-meetings were held there at all times.

Confessor. In the witchcraft trials, one who acknowledged herself to be a witch. — **1692** *Witchcraft Cases* 173 The confessours, (as they are improperly called,) or such as confesse themselves to be witches.

*** Confidence,** *n.*

Freq. in recent colloq. use (1909-) in clipped form: *con-game, con-man.*

+1. *Confidence man,* one who swindles others by taking advantage of the confidence reposed in him.

1849 *Knickerb.* XXXIV. 279 One of the good effects resulting from the arrest of the 'Confidence-Man' was an article in the '*Herald.*' **1856** *Chicago W. Times* 31 Jan. 4/2 A Shrewd 'Confidence' Man Arrested.—Benjamin Greer, one of the most shrewd and successful 'confidence' operators ever known in this country, was arrested in Broadway, New York, on Wednesday. **1873** *Congress. Globe* 18 Jan. 692/1 [He,] like a 'confidence-man' as he is, endeavoring to hoist himself into respectability by referring to Chief Justice Chase. **1875** *Chicago Tribune* 21 Nov. 13/1 These lottery-dealers are confidence-men of the most despicable description. **1884** *Lisbon* (Dak.) *Star* 30 May, A confidence-man swindled St. Paul business houses out of several thousand dollars' worth of goods by means of forged checks last week. **1922** PARRISH *Case & Girl* 271 He is a confidence man, with one charge of assault with attempt to kill against him.

+2. *Confidence game,* a method of swindling in which someone prevails upon another to invest in false securities, to accept a bogus check, etc. {=E. confidence trick.}

1867 in *Ill. Rev. Statutes* (1883) 388 Every person who shall obtain . . . any money or property, by means or by use of any false or bogus checks, or by any other means, instrument or device, commonly called the confidence game, shall be imprisoned in the penitentiary. **1868** CHADWICK *Base Ball* 104 The *Tribune* pronounced the whole proceeding as 'a regular confidence game.' **1887** *Detroit Free Press* 16 July 3 Horace knew not whether the old fellow was cracked or attempting to play some shrewd confidence game with them. **1887** *Courier-Journal* 20 Jan. 5/1 His mission [was] . . . to identify Charlie Henderson as the man who relieved him of $5,000 in a confidence game. **1911** *N.Y. Ev. Post* 12 Sept. 1 S. A. Potter was arrested to-day on a charge of operating a confidence game.

+3. Comb. with *line, operator, sharp, woman.*

1856 [see 1]. **1872** *Chicago Tribune* 19 Oct. 8/4 Robert H. Young, . . . a noted swindler and confidence operator. **1886** HOWELLS *Minister's Charge* 43 'Beats? I don't know what you mean,' said Barker. 'Confidence sharps, young feller. They're 'round everywhere, and don't you forget it.' **1887** *Harper's Mag.* March 514/1 Bertha Heymann, 'queen of the confidence women.' **1910** 'O. HENRY' *Strictly Business* 29 Jimmy Dunn . . . was an artist in the confidence line.

+Confidence, *v. tr.* To use the confidence game on (a person). — **1875** *Chicago Tribune* 1 Oct. 4 [In] a back room of some large building . . . they are 'confidenced' of what money they may have about them. **1888** *Missouri Republ.* 15 Feb. (F.), Detectives . . . arrested Lawrence Stanley . . . on a charge of confidencing Henry Mueller. **1888** *Chicago Inter-Ocean* 20 Feb. 1/4 The missing Hindsboro merchant has at last turned up alive and well. He had been on the trail of two sharpers who had confidenced him.

||**Confirmate,** *v.* [Back formation from *confirmation.*] *tr.* To confirm. — **1888** *Century Mag.* (F.), 'Sir, do I exaggerate?' 'Forty miles,' replied the planter; 'sometimes fifty.' 'Friends, —confirmated! more than twice-fold confirmated.'

*** Confirmation.** *+attrib. C. class:* A group of persons who, by a special rite after baptism, are strengthened or confirmed in their Christian faith. *C. grant:* A conveyance replacing a voidable one. *C. line:* A new boundary line extending the limits of an estate or land grant. — **1902** *Harper's Mag.* May 925 You remember your first confirmation class? **1902** G. M. MARTIN *Emmy Lou* 174 Rebecca and Gertie and Rachel must thereafter be excused on certain days at an early hour for attendance at Confirmation Class. — **1798** I. ALLEN *Hist. Vermont* 20 Some leading characters on the east side, by yielding up their New Hampshire Grants, had new or confirmation grants from New York in paying half fees. — **1755** *Huntington Rec.* II. 424 A certain piece of Land Lying Between ye old pattent Line and the confirmation Line.

+Confirmed claim. A piece of land or mining property taken up by claim under the mining laws or public-land laws, of which the ownership has been confirmed by deed. (Cf. CLAIM *n.* 2, 3.) — **1838** COLTON *Ind. Delineated 66 Fractions,* are parts of quarter sections intersected by streams, or confirmed claims.

*** Confiscate,** *v.* *+tr.* With spec. reference to the Revolutionary or the Civil War: To appropriate (the private property of persons supporting the British or the Southern cause).

1777 *Jrnls. Cont. Congress* IX. 971 Resolved, That it be earnestly recommended to the several states . . . to confiscate . . . the real and personal estate therein, of such of their inhabitants and other persons who have forfeited the same. **1779** *Vt. State P.* III. 53 Resolved that the Governor and Council be a court to confiscate the estates lying in this state of the enemies of this and the United States. **1861** *Statutes at Large* XII. 319 If, during the present or any future insurrection . . . , any person or persons . . . shall purchase or acquire, sell or give, any property . . . to be used or employed in . . . promoting such insurrection, . . . the same [is] to be seized, confiscated, and condemned. **1862** *Ib.* 589 An Act to suppress Insurrection, to punish Treason and Rebellion, to seize and confiscate the Property of Rebels.

*** Confiscation.**

+1. The appropriation of the property of British subjects and supporters by American governmental authorities during the Revolutionary War.

1776 *Jrnls. Cont. Congress* V. 572 A resolution for subjecting to confiscation the property of the subjects of the crown of Great Britain . . . taken on the high seas. **1779** *Vt. State P.* III. 56 It is hereby recommended to the hon[oura]ble Court of confiscation, to make confiscation and sale of the estates . . . formerly the property of persons who have joined the enemies of this and the United States. **1853** SIMMS *Sword & Distaff* 33

That you are a creditor of some of the rebels, and hold mortgages upon their estates, are only additional reasons for the confiscation of your property. **1894** *Harper's Mag.* LXXXVIII. 699 The Court of Confiscation . . . had the extraordinary power of ordering the confiscation and sale of the estates 'of the enemies of this State, living within the State.'

+**2.** The seizure and appropriation by the Northern government during the Civil War of property which was being used to support the Southern cause.

1861 *Congress. Globe* 22 July 219/1, I understand this amendment to be in the nature of a confiscation for treason. **1865** in Fleming *Hist. Reconstruction* I. 352 All land or other property . . . to which the United States have . . . acquired title by confiscation, or sale, or otherwise, during the late rebellion. **1868** *U.S. Reports* (Wallace) VII. 454 The act of August 6th, 1861, which subjects to confiscation . . . property whose owner used or consented to its use in aiding the Rebellion. **1870** *Ib.* XI. 295 The act of Congress does not require that proceedings in confiscation shall conform precisely to those in admiralty or revenue cases.

b. *Confiscation Acts*, the popular name applied to the acts of Congress which provided for the appropriation of property used to support the Southern cause. (See later quotations under CONFISCATE *v.*)

1863 in *U.S. Reports* (Wallace) XI. 274 You are hereby directed, under and by virtue of the acts . . . commonly called the Confiscation Acts, to seize all . . . common stock in the Michigan Southern. **c1862** GRANT in 'Penniman' *Tanner-Boy* 108 The interpreting of confiscation-acts by troops themselves has a demoralizing effect.

Confisticate, *v.* Erron. for CONFISCATE *v. colloq.*[2] — **1781** WITHERSPOON *Druid P.* No. 7, *Confisticate*, for *confiscate*. The most ignorant of the vulgar only use this phrase. **1795** B. DEARBORN *Columbian Grammar* 134 Improprieties, commonly called Vulgarisms, . . . [include] Confisticated for Confiscated. **1864** TROWBRIDGE *Cudjo's Cave* xxxiv. 334 The prop'ty of these yer durned Union-shriekers is all gwine to be confisticated.

+**Conflab.** [Colloq. variant of *confab.*] A talk or discussion. — **1873** *Winfield* (Kansas) *Courier* 7 Aug. 3/1 'Conflabs' lively among the lawyers. **1887** *Saginaw Ev. Jrnl.* 7 Dec., As Don has always come out ahead in his conflabs with the Michigan delegation, he will probably visit the big cage of congressmen frequently and prod them in the ribs.

||**Conflabber,** *v. colloq.*[2] [CONFLAB.] *intr.* To converse. — **1843** *Yale Lit. Mag.* IX. 76 Beg your pardon, Miss Orra, but I can't help it—conflabberin' away with a white man, never mind who that was.

Conflagrate, *v.* {1657–} *tr.* To burn up (a house, town, etc.) in a large or extensive fire. {1835–}

'On this, and some other words, an English friend remarks—"They are so obviously uncouth and ridiculous, that I think they will do little injury, and must be considered as peculiar to the quaintness or ignorance of the single writer that we first observe them in." This word is very rarely to be found in American publications' (Pickering 66).

1797 Priest *Travels* 39 From lake Champlain almost all has been conflagrated. **1814** *Ann. 13th Congress* II. 1693 Has he already forgot the speeches in which he and his friends portrayed the effects of the war? . . . Rebellion, civil war, prostrated liberty, and conflagrated towns, all mingled in one horrid group. **a1816** in Pickering 66 With the exception of conflagrating the navy-yard. **1817** *Ann. 14th Congress* 2 Sess. 427 If a house is conflagrated in a city, the spontaneous bounty of individuals is awakened. **1820** *Niles' Reg.* XVIII. 33/1 Many attempts . . . have been made to conflagrate the town of Petersburg, Va.

+**Conflictionist.** One whose alleged rights conflict with those of another, esp. with respect to land claims. — **1858** *N.Y. Tribune* 15 Nov. 6/2 Not so the 'Kansas Conflictionists.' They are jealous of every emigrant for fear he will 'jump their claim,' and howl around his cabin like so many famished wolves.

||**Conflutement.** A decoration with a complicated design. — **1896** J. C. HARRIS *Sister Jane* 168 Your Aunt Prue had saw some new-fangled bonnet . . . an' pictur'd out to your Aunt Sally ev'ry flower an' folderol an' all the conflutements that the consarn had on it.

***Confound,** *v.* +*tr.* To say 'confound' regarding (a thing). — **1879** STOCKTON *Rudder Grange* ii. 22 Again and again I confounded—as far as mental ejaculations could do it—his suggestions.

Congeree. *local.* =CONGER EEL 3. — **1884** in Goode *Fisheries* I. 629 This species [*Sidera mordax*] . . . is always known as 'Conger Eel' or 'Congeree.' . . . Its flesh . . . is very palatable when fried.

Conger eel. 1. The European sea eel, sometimes found on the east coast of the U.S. {1602–} +**2.** The mutton fish, a kind of eelpout, *Zoarces anguillaris*. +**3.** A kind of moray, *Gymnothorax mordax*. Calif. — **(1) 1814** MITCHILL *Fishes N.Y.* 360 Conger eel. *Anguilla conger*. . . . Flesh white, and very dainty eating. **1842** *Nat. Hist. N.Y., Zoology* IV. 314 The Conger Eel may be considered as rare on our coast. I have seen few in the markets; the flesh has a peculiar unsavory taste. **1855** BAIRD in *Smithsonian Rep.* 351 The Conger Eel, *Conger occidentalis*. . . . Only one specimen of this species was taken at Beesley's point. **(2) 1889** *Cent.* 1190. **(3) 1884** [see prec.].

Congestive, *a.* Characterized by congestion; usu. in phr. +*congestive chill, c. fever.* {1864–}

1834 in J. S. Bassett *Plantation Overseer* 76 Jim and enykey all have had the congestif fever. **1837** *Diplom. Corr. Texas* I. 262 The President . . . has had an attack of congestive fever. **1847** DEWEES *Lett. Texas* 303 The summer diseases are mostly bilious and congestive fevers, which readily yielded to proper care and attention. **1848** BRYANT *Calif.* (1849) 37 Of late years, in the winter season, the congestive fever prevails. **1871** EGGLESTON *Queer Stories* 108 His father died of a congestive chill.

Congo.[1] [A region in west central Africa.]

+**1.** In attrib. uses: From the Congo. {1866–}

1810 LAMBERT *Travels thro' U.S.* II. 443 All the papers are well stocked, with advertisements, among which, prime Congo, Gambia, and Angola slaves for sale at Gadsden's wharf, were very conspicuous. **1860** OLMSTED *Back Country* 439 If all the slaves in the United States were 'real Congo niggers,' which not one in one thousand is, [etc.]. **1880** CABLE *Grandissimes* 89 A dwarf Congo woman, as black as soot, had ushered her in.

+**2.** A Negro, orig. one from the Congo region in Africa.

1855 *Chicago Times* 5 July 1/2 A number of native Congoes—real Guinea negroes—arrived in Salem, Massachusetts, a few days ago. . . . Congo, showing his ivory, tumbled into the ship's boat. **1866** KEILEY *Prisoner of War* 47 An odorous Congo, with a claymore two-thirds his length, . . . was strutting up and down before me. **1886** — in *Century Mag.* Feb. 518 The negro was the most despised of human creatures and the Congo the plebeian among negroes.

attrib. **1855** *Putnam's Mo.* Jan. 79/2 Then Ethiopian Serenaders, and Congo Minstrels will draw crowded houses at three dollars a seat, and one dollar for a promenade ticket.

+**3.** A kind of dance performed originally by the Negroes, later by southern whites. Orig. attrib. with *dance, minuet.*

1803 J. DAVIS *Travels* 380 My young master himself could shake a desperate foot at the fiddle; there was nobody that could face him at a Congo Minuet. **1823** I. HOLMES *Account* 332 In Louisiana, and the state of Mississippi, . . . upon many plantations they dance for several hours during the afternoon of this day [=Sunday]. The general movement is in what they call the Congo dance. **1835** LONGSTREET *Ga. Scenes* 160 Except the minuet . . . and the Congo, which was only to chase away the solemnities of the minuet, it was all a jovial . . . amusement. **1860** S. MORDECAI *Virginia* iii. 47 Wheels, bands and pullies revolve where minuets, reels and congos were danced at a ball given in honor of General Washington. **1886** *Century Mag.* Feb. 527 The Congo . . . was a kind of Fandango, they say, in which the Madras kerchief held by its tip-ends played a graceful part.

+**4.** (See quotation.)

1888 CABLE *Bonaventure* 284 A large moccasin—not of the dusky kind described in books, but of that yet deadlier black sort, . . . which the swampers call the Congo.

Congo.[2] [f. Chinese *kung-fu.*] A kind of black tea. Attrib. with *tea.* {'congou,' 1725–} — **1774** Pattee *Cent. Readings* (1923) 73 Farewell . . . The pretty tea-chest, also, lately stor'd With Hyson, Congou and best double fine. **1787** FRENEAU *Misc. Works* 426 No Hyson or Congo to give a sick stranger. **1820** *Niles' Reg.* XVII. 400/2 It appears that a quantity of Congo tea was imported into New York. **1839** *Knickerb.* XIII. 231 How nicely is it [tea] adapted, by its delicately varying shades, to every especial palate! There is your . . . congo.

+**Congo eel.** =CONGER EEL 2. — **1884** Goode *Fisheries* I. 247 The Mutton-fish, . . . called Congo Eel and Ling, . . . is often seen near the shore north of Cape Cod, and in winter especially is frequently taken with hook and line from the wharves.

* **Congregation.** A body of persons who habitually gather in one place of worship.

In early New England the religious and civil governments had much in common, and 'congregation' in many cases referred to the people of a settlement as a whole.

'A *church*, as *a body of persons* . . . "is distinguished in New England from a *Congregation*, by the privileges which the former in general reserve to themselves of receiving exclusively in that church the sacrament and baptism. . . . Marriage, burial, and public worship, are open to the members of the congregation at large"' (Pickering 60).

1638 *Watertown Rec.* 4 Ordered that those Freemen of the Congregation shall build & dwell upon their Lotts at the Towne plott. **a1649** WINTHROP *Hist.* I. 55 Richard Garrett, a shoemaker of Boston, and one of the congregation there. *Ib.* 71 The congregation at Watertown . . . had chosen one Richard Brown for their elder. **1683** *Mass. H. S. Coll.* 4 Ser. V. 85 At Duxborough . . . where, the congregation being convened to give their answer to the letter they had received from the General Court, . . . the matter was put to vote. **1706** *Braintree Rec.* 64 Whether the south end shall be a congregation by themselves for the worship and service of God. **1724** *New-Eng. Courant* 7–14 Sept. 2/1 The Majority of each Town-Congregation should have the Choice of their own Teachers. **1782** CRÈVECŒUR *Lett. Farmer* iii, There, on a Sunday, he sees a congregation of respectable farmers and their wives, all clad in neat homespun. **1849** D. NASON *Journal* 21 The audience were . . . less care-worn than the congregations at the North. **1880** *Harper's Mag.* Dec. 158 Brother Bledso was pastor of a colored congregation in Texas. **1913** LONDON *Valley of Moon* III. vi, There was neither priest nor worshiper [in the Mission], yet they found all the evidences of use, by a congregation which Billy judged must be small.

Congregational, *n.* A member of the Congregational denomination. {1653 *Obs.*} — [**1692** C. MATHER *Blessed Unions* (*title-page*), A most happy union, has been lately made between those two eminent parties in England, which have now changed the names of Presbyterians, and Congregationals, for that of United Bretheren.] **1845** COOPER *Chainbearer* ix, My first decision, as moderator, was that the Congregationals have it by a majority of one.

Congregational, *a.* {1639–} Of or pertaining to the denomination of CONGREGATIONALISTS.

'After the 17th c. *Independent* was chiefly used in England, while *Congregational* was decidedly preferred in New England' (*O.E.D.*).

1654 JOHNSON *Wonder-w. Prov.* x. 118 In writing so many books to prove the Congregationall or Independant Churches to be the sluce, through which so many flouds of Error flow in. **1672** SEWALL *Letter-Book* I. 10 That something be allowed yearely to any Godly Congregational Minister whoe shall be willing to Settle in that place. **1747** *N.H. Hist. Soc. Coll.* IX. 4 We think it expedient that the Ministers of the Province of Congregational Principles who have been regularly ordained meet all together once a year. **1793** *Mass. H. S. Coll.* III. 10 The religious profession, or persuasion of the inhabitants, is of the Congregational kind. **1835** REED & MATHESON *Visit* II. 87 The principles which regulate the particular church whether Baptist, Presbyterian, or Congregational, have a strong resemblance. **1891** S. M. WELCH *Recoll. 1830–40* 62 [He] secured his adhesion to the Congregational Church.

Congregationalism. A system of organization of a religious body by which each local church has full control of its own affairs. (See also quot. 1861.) {1835}

'Also [in England] called Independency' (*O.E.D.*).

1716 I. MATHER *Disq. Eccl. Councils* 6 Mr. [Wm.] Bradshaw, an eminent Nonconformist Minister, ... was the Author of that Judicious Script [*English Puritanism*, 1605]. It is perfect Congregationalism. **1767** CHAUNCY *Lett.* (1768) 26 Zealous endeavours to make converts from Presbyterianism and Congregationalism to Episcopacy. **1870** BANCROFT *Hist. U.S.* (ed. 23) I. 359* The three great principles of congregationalism: a right faith attended by a true religious experience as the requisite qualifications for membership; the equality of all believers, including the officers of the church; the equality of the several. **1878** STOWE *Poganuc People* 25 Congregationalism—or, as it was then called by the common people, Presbyterianism—was the religion established by law in New England. **1892** *Advance* (Chicago) 25 Feb., We might infer that the overdose of Congregationalism, swallowed at the Auditorium last night, had resulted in an overdoze this morning with many of the habitues of 59 Dearborn St.

Congregationalist.

1. A member of a Congregational church. {1708–}

1712 I. MATHER in R. Mather *Answer* pref. 6 The renowned Dr. Owen was as famous a Congregationalist. **1793** CUTLER in *Life & Corr.* II. 277 In Massachusetts the Congregationalists were the favorites of Government, and every other denomination was considered as dissenters from them. **1828** SHERBURNE *Memoirs* 181, I was fully satisfied that there were Congregationalists who were as really pious, as were the Baptists. **1841** PARK *Pantology* 156 The Congregationalists, are so called because they believe each church or parish to be entirely independent of all others; its members having a right to select and ordain their own minister. **1875** STOWE *We & Neighbors* 140 Well, you know, dear, that Harry isn't of our church—he is a Congregationalist. **1896** *Home Missionary* (N.Y.) Oct. 323 The Congregationalists ... join leadingly in the Union Sunday-school.

2. Attrib. with *church:* A church of the Congregational denomination.

1864 BOWEN *Logic* xiii. 448 We go to the Episcopal, Presbyterian, or Congregationalist Church, simply because parents and friends ... did so, formerly.

Congregational way. The system of church polity practiced by the Congregationalists. *Obs.* {1647–}

1644 R. WILLIAMS *Cottons Let. Examined* (1866) 54 Might it please God to perswade the mother to permit the inhabitants of New England her daughter to enjoy their conscience to God, after a particular Congregationall way. **1670** I. MATHER *Life R. Mather* 52 God gave him in those dayes not onely to see, but also to Instruct others in the Substance of the Congregationall-Way. *Ib.* 82 Touching Worship and Discipline, he was for the true Congregational-Way. **1680** *Mass. H. S. Coll.* 4 Ser. V. 50 The order of the gospel; which order, according to the general profession here, is the Congregational way.

*** Congress.**

1. An assembly of delegates for the discussion of some problem. {1678–} **+a.** Applied to the formal meetings of the governors of the colonies in the eighteenth century.

1711 *Boston News-Letter* 2 July 2/1 Her Majesty by Her Royal Commands having ordered the Honourable Lieut-General Nicholson with the several Governours of the Massachusetts-Bay, New-Hampshire, Rhode Island, Connecticut, New-York and Jersey's to meet and consult about the present intended Expedition, a Congress was accordingly held at New-London in Connecticut Colony, on Thursday the 20th of June. *Ib.*, And on Saturday following ... each Governour returned to his own Government in order to forward the Affairs concerted in the said Congress. **1761** S. NILES *Indian Wars* II. 328 A congress was appointed at New London, being nearest the centre; where the several Governors met.

+b. A meeting at Augusta, Ga., in 1763, at which the governors of certain southern colonies conferred with the Indians to adjust differences between the Indians and the white settlers.

1763 *N.C. Col. Rec.* VI. 991, I before acknowledged the receipt of Your Lordship's letter about the Indian Congress which is appointed at Augusta on the 15th of October. **1764** *Ib.* 1020 The original not having come to hand until last month after my return from the Congress at Augusta. **1772** DE BRAHM *Hist. Georgia* (1849) 33 In the year 1763, the Governors from Virginia, North Carolina, South Carolina and Georgia, met in Congress at Augusta.

+c. One or other of the meetings of colonial delegates leading up to the Continental Congress.

1765 *Mass. Papers* 4 The late General Congress of the British Colonies at New York, having agreed to recommend [etc.]. **1773** S. ADAMS in Wells *Life S. Adams* II. 84 Should the correspondence from Virginia produce a Congress and then an assembly of States. **1773** in A. Bradford *Sp. Governors Mass.* 354 We should be unwilling to propose it, without their [=the other colonies'] consent in Congress. **1773** B. CHURCH *Oration* (ed. 3) 11 *n.*, Some future congress will be the glorious source of the salvation of America. **1774** *Jrnls. Cont. Congress* I. 15 Voted, That Major John Sullivan ... attend and assist in the General Congress of delegates from the other Colonies.

+2. Spec., the federal or national legislative body of the United States.

From 1774 to 1781 this referred to the Continental Congress, from 1781 to 1789 to the Congress under the Articles of Confederation, and after 1789 to that under the Constitution. It is here conceived as a continuing body.

a. With the definite article or *a* and *of*.

(*a*) **1774** *Journals Cont. Congress* I. 102 Ordered, That the Journal of the proceedings of the Congress, as now corrected, be sent to the press. **1774** *Carroll P.* in *Md. Hist. Mag.* XVI. 31, I arrived here [Philadelphia] yesterday about 12 o'clock. The Congress was sitting. **1779** E. PARKMAN *Diary* 171 Mr. Gale came up to ye Pulpit to desire me to read ye Congress's Circular Letter. **1787** *Constitution* I. §1 All legislative powers herein granted shall be vested in a Congress of the United States, which shall consist of a Senate and House of Representatives. **1836** *S. Lit. Messenger* II. 407 These great men ... thought Senators were amenable to their Legislatures for their acts and votes in the National Congress.

(*b*) *collective.* **1775** S. DEANE *Corr.* 289 The Post office is not yet completed. The Congress have now sat ... since the 10th of May. **1775** FITHIAN *Journal* II. 60 The hon: Congress are yet sitting, & have published to the world reasons for our taking up arms against Britain.

b. Without article.

'Congress ..., originally a common name, and still so used in England, has with us become a proper name. We, of course, use it without the article; but English writers, in speaking of American affairs, generally use it with the article' (Pickering 67).

(*a*) **1775** in *Amer. Hist. Rev.* I. 289, I attended at Congress for the first Time since the Adjornment. **1775** *Jrnls. Cont. Congress* II. 246 Sundry letters received during the recess of Congress. **1777** FRANKLIN *Writings* VII. 77, I see in a Vote of Congress shown to me by Captain Franval, that Mr. Dean is disown'd. **1784** T. HUTCHINSON *Diary & Lett.* II. 399 Congress is despised by all Governments. **1789** *Ann. 1st Congress* I. 18 A letter was received ... tendering to Congress the use of the City Hall [of New York City]. **1836** *Diplom. Corr. Texas* I. 93 Public Meetings are getting up in all directions petitioning Congress to recognise our Independence. **1846** POLK *Diary* 63, I called to their recollection that the Democratic party were in a decided majority in both houses of Congress. **1897** in Dale & Rader *Okla. Hist.* 645 Congress is memorialized to definitely fix the width of said rights of way.

(*b*) *collective.* **1780** *Heath Papers* 40 Congress have not yet done any thing. **1788** JEFFERSON *Writings* V. 16 Congress, by the Confederation, have no original and inherent power over the commerce of the States. **1789** *Ib.* VIII. 358 Congress have agreed to borrow a sum of money in Holland, to enable them to pay the individual demands in Europe. **1794** S. WILLIAMS *Hist. Vermont* 235 Congress have not been prevailed on to assist in dismembering a state.

c. As a proper name or appellative.

1776 *Jrnls. Cont. Congress* IV. 250 A petition from P. Moore, in behalf of the owners of the sloops *Congress* and *Chance*, privateers, for 400 lb. of powder ... was presented and read. **1807** J. R. SHAW *Life* (1930) 91 From Carlisle we were ordered to Lancaster, in order to relieve the Congress-regiment, and to do duty over the prisoners who were taken with Cornwallis. **1813** J. ADAMS *Works* X. 27 That immortal mortar, which was called the Congress, ... finally drove the British army out of Boston. **1819** *Niles' Reg.* XVII. 63/2 The Congress frigate, captain Henley, having on board Mr. Graham, our minister to the court of Brazil, has arrived at Rio Janerio [*sic*], all well.

+3. The national legislative body as reconstituted in membership every two years.

'The body of senators and representatives for each term of two years for which representatives are chosen is called *one Congress.* Each Congress expires at noon of the 4th of March next succeeding the beginning of its second regular session, when a *new Congress begins*' (1885 A. Johnston *Hist. U.S.* 417). According to the twentieth Constitutional Amendment (in effect since Oct. 15, 1933), 'The Congress shall assemble at least once in every year, and such meeting shall begin at noon on the 3rd day of January, unless they by law appoint a different day.'

[**1774** *Jrnls. Cont. Congress* I. 102 Resolved, as the Opinion of this Congress, that it will be necessary, that another Congress should be held on the tenth day of May next.] **1791** *Ann. 2nd Congress* 9 Monday, October 24, 1791. This being the day fixed by law for the annual meeting of Congress, at the first session of the second Congress, the following members of the Senate appeared. **1854** BENTON *30 Years' View* I. 91/2 The nineteenth Congress, commencing its legal existence, March the 4th, 1825. **1873** *Newton Kansan* 30 Jan. 1/6 There are from 5,000 to 6,000 bills per Congress.

+**4.** The House of Representatives, the lower house of Congress. (Cf. CONGRESSMAN and CONGRESSIONAL 3 note.)

1842 *Niles' Nat. Reg.* 28 May 208/2 Election for Congressman. The election for a member of congress . . . took place in Washington county. **1881** *Harper's Mag.* March 538/2 The 'old Patroon' was a member of the Congress that elected John Quincy Adams President. **1888** LOWELL *Independent in Politics*, Members of Congress must be residents of the district that elects them.

+**5.** The legislative body of other political units whose territory is now within the United States, such as the individual states, Texas, the Confederate States.

(*a*) **1774** CUTLER in *Life & Corr.* I. 47 Thanksgiving appointed by the Provincial Congress, and not by the Governor. **1775** in H. M. Brooks *Gleanings* 51 Measures that have been recommended by the Continental and Provincial Congresses. **1853** RAMSEY *Tennessee* 130 No vestige of the royal government was left, and a Whig Congress had assumed the control of North Carolina.

(*b*) **1836** in Sayles *Early Laws Texas* I. 217 An act authorizing the printing and publishing the laws of . . . the present congress. **1839** *4th Congress Texas Jrnls.* I. 6 The act of the last Congress directing the removal of the Public Archives from the city of Houston was an expression of legislative will too decisive to permit me one moment to falter in carrying it out. **1842** *Niles' Nat. Reg.* 13 Aug. 384/3 The Texian congress adjourned on the 23d July. **1848** POLK in *Pres. Mess. & P.* IV. 596 By an act of the Congress of Texas passed in December, 1836, her western boundary was declared to be the Rio Grande [etc.].

(*c*) **1861** *Constitution Confederate States* i. § 9 The importation of negroes of the African race, from any foreign country other than the slaveholding States or Territories of the United States of America, is hereby forbidden; and Congress is required to pass such laws as shall effectually prevent the same. **1867** [see CONFEDERATE *a.* 2(b)]. **1923** *Southern Hist. Soc. P.* XLIV. 4 The Provisional Congress had four sessions: February 4, 1861 . . . to February 17, 1862. . . . The regular Congress of the Confederate States was elected in November, 1861.

6. Comb. and attrib. with *bill, chamber, commissary*, etc.

1784 T. HUTCHINSON *Diary & Lett.* II. 399 France hath protested Congress Bills. **1787** CUTLER in *Life & Corr.* I. 237 Congress Chamber is an apartment in the second story of the City Hall [of New York City]. **1776** T. HUTCHINSON *Diary & Lett.* II. 39 He read me a letter from one of the Congress Commissaries at N. York. **1784** *Ib.* 399 The Congress Financier hath clipped all the English and foreign gold to pay their subsidies. **1776** *Battle of Brooklyn* I. 28 [Putnam] gives him a handfull of Congress notes. **1790** *Kentucky Petitions* 155 [He] being much reduced by the Depreciation of the Congress paper money could only purchas one hundred acres. **1774** *Carroll P.* in *Md. Hist. Mag.* XVI. 41, I shall bring up at all events a printed copy of the Congress Resolves. **1842** *Amer. Pioneer* I. 329 We came out also with a view of purchasing land at the congress sales, which were to take place in the ensuing May at Chillicothe. **1776** *N.C. Col. Rec.* X. 457 This being a day of humilation, fasting and prayer (or in vulgar language Congress Sunday), [etc.].

+**b.** *Congress caucus*, a congressional caucus.

1803 B. AUSTIN *Constitutional Republicanism* 87 If a Congress Caucus is to decide, we have only to inquire who the man is in whom they have agreed, and notify him of his appointment. **1854** BENTON *30 Years' View* I. 86/1 Congress caucuses for the nomination of presidential candidates fell under the ban of public opinion.

attrib. **1854** [see CAUCUS NOMINATION and C. SYSTEM].

+**Congress boot.** An elastic-sided shoe: (see quots. 1853, 1865).

Cf. CONGRESS GAITER, SHOE.

1851 CIST *Cincinnati* 178 Men's dress boots, congress boots, and fine shoes. **1853** FELT *Customs New Eng.* 90 Six years ago, Congress Boots, for both sexes, were introduced. They come up so as to cover the foot neatly and closely by means of India rubber cloth inserted in the leather, on each side, wide enough to cover the ankles. **1865** LEWIS & NEWHALL *Hist. Lynn* 417 The congress boot began to be manufactured at this time [1846]. Its peculiarity consisted mainly in the substitution of an elastic gore for the old lacing, thus rendering the boot easier about the ankle. **1923** K. D. WIGGIN *My Garden of Memory* 46 A Congress boot, with the triangle of elastic on the side which characterized that creation of the late sixties.

+**Congress gaiter.** =CONGRESS BOOT.

1862 NORTON *Army Lett.* 71 The paramatta cloak, the black satin Congress gaiters. **1892** *Harper's Mag.* Jan. 272/2 Her Congress gaiters were soaked above her overshoes. **1893** HOWELLS *Coast of Bohemia* 30 She gave the large, dangling congress gaiter of her husband a little push with the point of her slipper. **1901** ADE *40 Modern Fables* 23 If any one had to be Speared, they preferred that it should be some Dead Card who wore Congress Gaiters and Throat Warmers. **1910** 'O. HENRY' *Strictly Business* 103 Downstairs the usual horde of gibbering cave-dwellers were waiting with their hands full of old Congress gaiters and paper bags of hominy.

+**Congress Hall.** The room in which the House of Representatives (or the Senate) meets. — **1806** FESSENDEN *Orig. Poems* 57 *n.* This infamous s——? spat in a gentleman's face, on the floor of congress-hall. **1837** *S. Lit. Messenger* III. 277 Even the clapping in the gallery of Congress Hall was sudden and momentary.

+**Congressional,** *a.* [Irreg. f. CONGRESS.]

This word has been attacked for its irregular formation: 'Such barbarous terms as *Presidential* and *Congressional*, with some others, are equally unnecessary, and offensive to the ear' (1816 *N. Amer. Rev.* III. 359). Cf. also 1872 F. Hall *Recent Exemp. False Philology* 29, note.

1. Pertaining to the Congress of the United States.

1775 in *N.E. Hist. & Gen. Reg.* XI. 166, I hope . . . that ye next congressional appointment of a Relig[iou]s nature may be a day of thanksgiving. **1781** *English Chron.* 23–26 June 4/1 The above is the most accurate account of the annihilation of the Congressional currency. **1781** S. PETERS *Hist. Conn.* 419 This faithful disciple disregarded the congressional mandate [to pray for the Commonwealth]. **1783** JEFFERSON *Writings* IV. 443 My hopes of the success of the Congressional propositions here have lessened exceedingly. **1783** FRENEAU *Poems* (1786) 323 When your army I saw without . . . money . . . (Excepting your wretched Congressional paper, That stunk in my nose like the snuff of a taper). **1789** MACLAY *Deb. Senate* 67 The gentlemen of Congress have, it seems, called on Mrs. Washington and all the congressional ladies. **1816** *Nat. Intelligencer* 9 April 1/1 The Nomination of candidates for the Presidency and Vice Presidency by the Republican Congressional Meeting, appears to have received the approbation of a large majority of the Republican party. **1838** *N.Y. Advertiser & Exp.* 3 March 1/5 Felix Grundy [was] in the Chair as President of the Society—which, by the way, is the Congressional Temperance Society. **1847** LOWELL *Biglow P.* I. iv. 61 In reading Congressional debates, . . . I detected a slender residuum of valuable information. **1867** J. M. CRAWFORD *Mosby* 43 At Fairfax Court House a Congressional party and some ladies had come out to witness the carnage and celebrate their victory with a splendid banquet at Manassas. **1871** *Harper's Mag.* XLIII. 11/1 The machinery which successfully carries on such an important branch of the government was the result of Congressional legislation. **1883** *Harper's Mag.* Nov. 938/2 A . . . Congressional report . . . places it at 48,215,040 acres. **1886** A. DALY *Nancy & Co.* 19, I promise you I'll make the last days of your probation worse than a congressional investigation.

b. Esp. as pertaining to the House of Representatives.

1840 *Niles' Nat. Reg.* 29 Aug. 405/1 Congressional candidate, John B. Thompson, . . . is a candidate for Congress to fill the vacancy occasioned by the death of Mr. Anderson. **1851** *Harper's Mag.* IV. 120/1 The same division prevailed in the Congressional contest, the nominees being Unionists and Secessionists. **1862** *Fraser's Mag.* July 26 In their Congressional representation, for instance, which under the Federal constitution is based upon population merely, the South counts out of its census two fifths of its negroes.

2. Pertaining to a congress in general.

[*a* **1812** BARLOW (W. '28), The congressional institution of Amphictyons in Greece.]

3. *Congressional election*, an election every two years at which members of the House of Representatives are chosen.

Before the adoption (May 31, 1913) of the seventeenth amendment, which provided for the popular election of Senators, a congressional election was limited to the election of members of the House of Representatives. The expression, 'Congressional election,' therefore, took on a limited meaning.

1814 *Niles' Reg.* VI. 216/2 New-York congressional election.—The returns are all in. **1837** *Democratic Rev.* I. 21 Still further triumphs awaited the hero of the democracy in the congressional election in the Halifax district. **1840** *Niles' Nat. Reg.* 24 Oct. 116/3 Congressional election. First district. **1872** *Harper's Mag.* XLVI. 92 When this practice obtains in Congressional elections [etc.].

4. *Congressional Directory*, a directory containing information about members of Congress.

1842 F. WOOD in MacLeod *Biog.* 99 The honorable chairman (Mr. Saltonstall) has, in the two counties which he is set down in the Congressional Directory as representing, 19,567 persons engaged in manufactures and trades. **1867** LATHAM *Black & White* 51, I have bought the 'Congressional Directory of the Second Session of the Thirty-ninth Congress of the U.S. of America.'

5. *Congressional districting*, the action of dividing a state into Congressional districts (q.v.).

1889 *Voice* (N.Y.) 9 May, Congressional districting and gridironing, such as has been attempted in New Jersey, . . . is a great danger to our country.

6. *Congressional library*, the Library of Congress.

1801 *Ann. 7th Congress* 2 Sess. 1292 To place on each book some proper mark or marks, to designate it as belonging to the Congressional library. **1816** *Niles Register* IX. p. iv, Index . . . Congressional library 76. **1900** *Congress. Rec.* 4 Jan. 643/1, I move that the report . . . be printed and bound in paper for the use of the Congressional Library.

7. *Congressional convention.* **a.** =CONGRESSIONAL CAUCUS. (See also sense 1, quot. 1816.)

1824 *Nat. Intelligencer* 17 Feb. 1/3 Mr. Markley . . . felt that a Congressional Convention to nominate candidates, should be as numerously attended, as it was practicable that it would be.

b. A political meeting of party delegates within a congressional district for the purpose of selecting a candidate for the House of Representatives. (Cf. note, sense 3.)

1855 Hambleton *H. A. Wise* 204 That our delegates to the congressional convention be . . . instructed to act accordingly. **1872** *Newton Kansan* 22 Aug. 3/1 A Republican County Convention will be held . . . to select delegates to attend . . . the Republican Congressional Convention. **1883** *Harper's Mag.* June 162/2 Austin was crowded with strangers in attendance on the Democratic Congressional Convention.

+**Congressional caucus.** A meeting of those members of Congress who were of one party for the purpose of selecting presidential and vice-presidential candidates. Now hist., having been replaced by party conventions.

'The congressional caucus naturally divides into two periods: (1) the period of development, or mixed congressional caucuses, extending from 1788 to 1804; (2) the period of purely congressional caucuses or the reign of the caucus, 1804–1824' (McLaughlin & Hart *Cycl. Amer. Govt.* I. 233). Cf. CONVENTION 2b.

1803 B. AUSTIN *Const. Republicanism* xx. 88 If they [=the people] mean to be led by Congressional or Legislative Caucusses, it is best the business should be openly acknowledged. **1816** M. CAREY *Olive Branch* (1818) 445 The paramount influence of the congressional caucus overpowered all competition; and the votes of the presidential electors were . . . James Madison 122 C. C. Pinckney 48 George Clinton 6. **1824** *Nat. Intelligencer* 10 Feb. 3/1 The Republicans of the United States are generally opposed to a Congressional Caucus. *c*1830 CALHOUN in Benton *30 Years' View* (1854) I. 180/1, I was decidedly opposed to a congressional caucus. **1880** *Harper's Mag.* Aug. 470 In 1824, however, so few members attended the Congressional caucus that its action was repudiated. **1884** *Ib.* June 128/2 The Presidential candidates were . . . nominated by Congressional caucus.

+**Congressional district.** A division of a state, composed of contiguous territory, wherein the population is roughly equal to the population in like divisions throughout the United States, and wherein the voters elect one representative to the House of Representatives.

1812 *Ann. 12th Congress* 1 Sess. II. 1436 The proceedings of a public meeting of the Republican citizens of the First Congressional district of Pennsylvania. **1819** (*title*), To the Electors of the Third Congressional District of Kentucky. **1842** *Niles' Nat. Reg.* 27 Aug. 405/3 A wit communicated . . . the following description of the shape of some of the congressional districts as arranged by the majority. **1849** CHAMBERLAIN *Ind. Gazetteer* 66 The State is at present divided into ten Congressional Districts. **1864** PENNIMAN *Tanner-Boy* 39 The number of cadets entered at West Point is limited, and proportioned to the ratio of voters in every national congressional district. **1882** *Mich. Gen. Statutes* (1882–3) I. 106 This state shall be divided into eleven Congressional districts pursuant to a ratio of representation fixed by an act of Congress. **1892** M. A. JACKSON *Gen. Jackson* 30 A young man from the congressional district in which he lived had received an appointment to the Military Academy at West Point.

+**Congressional school.** *local.* A school supported by income derived from the townships that Congress set aside from public land for school purposes. — **1838** *Indiana Ho. Rep. Jrnl.* 126 Resolved, That the committee on education be instructed to inquire into the expediency of so amending the law regulating Congressional schools, as to repeal said act.

+**Congressional township.** A township set aside from the public lands by Congress to yield school funds. Also attrib. — **1838** *Indiana Ho. Rep. Jrnl.* 98 *Resolved*, that the committee on Education be instructed to inquire into the expediency of repealing the fifteenth section of an act entitled An act incorporating congressional townships. **1847** *Ind. Hist. Soc. Publ.* III. 439 Had we been as wise as our Peninsular sister [Michigan], we should have ultimately realized a common school fund of $3,164,800, instead of the present congressional township fund of $1,410,942. **1873** *Newton Kansan* 3 April 3/5 The question of consolidating the congressional townships of Harvey and Walton was presented.

+**Congress land.** Public land controlled by Congress.

1806 T. ASHE *Travels in A.* 89 The great part then of this land being obtained by Congress from the Indians by an imposition, called by the fallacious name of a legal purchase, is known by the name of 'Congress Lands.' **1817** S. BROWN *Western Gaz.* 68 Congress lands, after the auction sales are closed, sell invariably for $2 an acre. **1834** *Ind. Mag. Hist.* XXII. 431 This was an action brought by the plaintiffs for a sawmill built on Congress lands. **1837** PECK *Gaz. Illinois* III. 278 The land office for the sale of Congress lands . . . is at this place [=Quincy]. **1871** EGGLESTON *Hoosier Schoolm.* iii. 28 You see this ere bottom was all Congress land in them there days. **1886** *Century Mag.* Nov. 34/2 They cut the timber, with frontier innocence, from 'Congress land,' and soon had a serviceable craft afloat.

+**Congressman.**

1. A member of Congress, esp. of the House of Representatives.

Before 1789 Congress consisted of one chamber; but after that date the term *congressman* could apply to both senators and representatives. Yet it 'is commonly used to describe a member of the House of Representatives, though . . . it ought to include senators also' (Bryce *Amer. Commonwealth* I. 197 note). Cf. quot. 1897 and CONGRESSIONAL 3 note.

1780 *Amer. Times* iii. 28 Ye coxcomb Congressmen, declaimers keen, Brisk puppets of the Philadelphian scene. **1783** in *Boston Transcript* 13 May (1899) 18/4 On our arrival found one of our Congressmen and Capt. Green. **1789** S. LOW *Politician Outwitted* IV. ii, You can't tell a Congressman from a marchant's 'prentice, every body dresses so fine. **1795** in J. Jay *Corr. & Papers* IV. 172 *note*, By papers which came in this ship we learn . . . the more mortifying intelligence of the success of the Anti-federal party in the elections of Congress men. **1809** IRVING *Knickerb.* Account of author, My wife . . . learnt that he was . . . cousin-german to the Congress-man. **1840** *Niles' Nat. Reg.* 24 Oct. 128/1 Arkansas Election. . . . For the congressman we have returns from only 3 counties. **1871** *Echo* 15 Dec., Senators and Congressmen are rapidly arriving at the Capital. **1897** *Nation* LXV. 496/2 Allow me to enter a plea in behalf of the accurate use of the word Congressman. . . . The tendency to restrict its application to Representatives is to be regretted. **1902** *Harper's Mag.* April 695/2 The rural Congressman's wife, . . . who fondly imagines that election to the House of Representatives carries with it the golden key to unlock all doors.

attrib. **1909** WHITE *Rules of Game* I. i, This congressman game is all right, and I don't see how I can very well get out of it, even if I wanted to.

b. As a title, designating a member of the House of Representatives.

1894 P. L. FORD *P. Stirling* 313, I met Congressman Pell yesterday at the Tennis Tournament. **1895** *Voice* (N.Y.) 25 April 6/4 Congressman Ganson, of Buffalo, N.Y., a Democrat, who supported the president, was a very bald man. **1925** BRYAN *Memoirs* 101 He being favorable to Congressman Bland for President, [etc.].

2. *Congressman at large*, a member of the House of Representatives elected from a state as a whole rather than from a single congressional district.

1882 *Nation* 12 Oct. 298/1 On Tuesday the New York Republican State Committee nominated Mr. Howard Carroll for Congressman-at-large, to fill the vacancy. **1920** *Chicago Tribune* 3 Nov. 1/1 [Ill.] State officers elected: . . . Congressmen at large—William E. Mason, Chicago; Richard Yates, Springfield.

3. *Congressman-elect*, a man who has been elected to the House of Representatives, but whose term has not yet begun.

1847 *Whig Almanac* 1848 6 Henry Nicoll, the Congressman elect from the lower District, . . . [was] one of the Vice-Presidents [of a mass meeting]. **1871** *Harper's Mag.* XLIII. 151/2 Certificates were issued to Congressmen-elect Strong, Starkweather (Republicans), Barnum (Democrat), and Mr. Kellogg (Republican). **1883** *Boston Advertiser* 9 Nov., Congressman-elect Andrew, in his capacity as president of the Algonquin, stands in the centre of the large reception room on the second floor.

+**Congress money.** Paper money authorized esp. by the Continental Congress and the Congress during and after the Panic of 1837. — **1777** *N.J. Archives* 2 Ser. I. 442 The generality of people that have those articles to dispose of, are unwilling to take the Congress money, . . . looking upon country produce better than such cash. **1790** *Kentucky Petitions* 154 Your petitioner was obliged . . . to take Depreciated Congress money as pay for his land. **1841** *Knickerb.* XVII. 384 Some hay, oats for your horse, wheat, rye, wood, butter, and cider for yourselves, etc., to be paid for in congress money.

+**Congress price.** A price established by Congress, esp. for the sale of public lands.

1776 A. ADAMS in *Fam. Lett.* (1876) 183, I find you have licensed tea, but I am determined not to be a purchaser unless I can have it at Congress price. **1818** *Niles' Reg.* XV. 64/2 The persons who had laid the plan then appeared, and agreed to take the land at congress price! **1831** PECK *Guide* 256 Estimating the lands at Congress price, the aggregate value of this provision for education cannot be much less than $2,000,000! **1849** CHAMBERLAIN *Ind. Gazetteer* 281 Digby had bought the town site at the United States land sale, at a little more than Congress price.

+**Congress shoe.** =CONGRESS BOOT. — **1899** A. BROWN *Tiverton Tales* 109 Her shoes—congress, with world-weary elastics at the side—were her own, inherited from an aunt. **1902** LORIMER *Lett. Merchant* 173 No one in her house had ever owned a button-hook, because her old man wore jack-boots and she wore congress shoes, and little Johnny wore just plain feet.

+**Congress spring.** A mineral spring at Saratoga, N.Y., noted for its medicinal qualities. — **1818** J. M. DUNCAN *Travels U.S.* II. 234, I drank a tumbler of the water of 'Congress spring.' **1841** BUCKINGHAM *Amer., N. States* II. 430 In 1792 . . . the second spring was discovered by Mr. John Taylor Gilman, . . . at that time a member of Congress. It was this which caused it to be called the 'Congress Spring.' **1884** L. DE COLANGE *Nat. Gazetteer* 902/1 The most celebrated [springs at Saratoga] are the Congress, Empire, . . . [and five other] Springs.

+**Congress water.** A mineral water obtained from the Congress spring: (see prec.).

1833 J. STUART *Three Years N.A.* I. 192 The quantity of gas is such, that a very nice sort of breakfast bread is baked with Congress water, instead of yeast. **1838** H. MARTINEAU *Retrospect* III. 261 As soon as we had warmed ourselves, and ascertained the dinner hour, we set forth to view the place, and taste the Congress Water. **1841** BUCKINGHAM *America* II. 101 The Congress water, being the most acidulous and saline, is drank most copiously, and exported most largely from hence to every part of the Union in bottles. **1843** *Knickerb.* XXII. 447 All this had 'come and gone through my mind, unconsciously, like a glass of Congress-water elsewhere.' **1864** NICHOLS *Amer. Life* I. 399 Drink from six to twelve tumblers of Congress water—it tastes like Glauber salts, and produces a similar effect. **1866** W. REID *After the War* 236 To be waked up in the morning by a negro, . . . to have him presently return with a glass of iced Congress water, an orange, and the morning paper, [etc.]. **1894** ALDRICH *Two Bites*, etc. 190 Its place [*i.e.* of a mint julep, was] supplied by iced Congress water.

+**Coniacker.** (See quotation.) — **1848** BARTLETT 396 *Coniacker*, a counterfeiter of coin.

+**Conjeprezion, Conjeprezite.** ['From *Con*gregation of *Je*hovah's *Pre*sbytery of *Zion*' (*Annals of Iowa* 2 Ser. III. 17)]. (See quotation.) — **1858** *N.Y. Tribune* 2 Nov. 3/3 This town [Preparation, Iowa] is the Zion of a new body of religious enthusiasts, who call themselves 'Conjeprezites,' and their system of religion or religious organization 'the Conjeprezion.'

+**Conjure,** *n. comb.* With names of objects: Used in the practice of conjuration. With persons: That cures by conjuring.

1891 'THANET' *Otto the Knight*, etc. 83 One of us—no matter which—took a foreign coin out of her purse, saying, 'That is my own private conjure charm, Jerry.' — *Ib.* 64 Thanks to a gifted 'conjure doctor,' Uncle Rufe Lemew, no one had died, though to my knowledge one woman lay ill for months. **1898** J. C. HARRIS *Tales of Home Folks* 65 It seemed to be a bundle of rags. 'It's his conjure-bag,' the colonel said to himself. **1899** CHESNUTT (*title*), The Conjure Woman. **1900** H. ROBERTSON *Red Blood & Blue* 92 Wingate's Lane was a brier-grown byway that led through weeds and thickets to . . . the hut of old Dru Wingate, the conjure-worker, the sole human being who lived on the shores of the Dead Sea.

* **Conjure,** *v.* Also *dial.* **cunjer, kunjer, -ger.**

1. *tr.* To drive out (an evil spirit); to treat (a person) by means of magic; to make appear as by magic or supernatural power.

1846 L. M. CHILD *Fact & Fiction* 201, I hear an old conjuring woman say she could conjure de Divil out of anybody. **1891** 'THANET' *Otto the Knight*, etc. 68 A right smart of people ben conjured right in this settlement—say so theyseffs; reckon they had oughter know. **1896** J. C. HARRIS *Sister Jane* 84 If she can't cure him, she can conjure him. **1898** DUNBAR *Folks from Dixie* 91 Sis' Williams ain't gwine conju' nobidy. **1911** ROLT-WHEELER *Boy with Census* 35 Bein' able to put a cunjer on, so's the one yo' cunjer has got to do anythin' yo' want. **1921** C. GREER-PETRIE *Angeline at Seelbach* 17 'Peared like he kungered them beds out of space.

2. *intr.* To practice, or engage in, the art of influencing supernatural powers, as by incantation.

1866 in Fleming *Hist. Reconstruction* I. 92 The negroes here spend their time going to 'funerals,' religious howlings, . . . and 'conjuring.' **1902** L. BELL *Hope Loring* 125 Remember my heart will be with you, and Mammy will be 'kunjering' for you with all her might!

* **Conjurer.** Also **conjuror.** One who calls upon spirits or magical powers. Chiefly among Indians (the medicine man) and Negroes.

1624 SMITH *Virginia* II. 30 They seldome steale one from another, least their coniurers should reveale it. **1705** BEVERLEY *Virginia* III. 6 The Conjurer shaves all his Hair off, except the Crest on the Crown. **1757** *Lett. to Washington* II. 54 It was determin'd, that the King, with his Brother and Conjurer, shou'd go to W[illia]msburg. **1819** *Niles' Reg.* XVI. *Suppl.* 101/1 The [Cherokee] conjurer takes some of the grains of seven ears of corn and feeds the fire with them. **1827** COOPER *Prairie* xxi, 'Where is your conjurer?' demanded the chief, turning suddenly to the trapper. **1890** CHESNUTT *The Conjure Woman* 103 (*story title*), The Conjurer's Revenge.

* **Conjuring,** *vbl. n.* The art or practice of exerting a sinister or unnatural influence upon a person or thing. Freq. attrib.

1765 TIMBERLAKE *Mem.* 48 They [=Cherokees] have many beautiful stones of different colours; . . . but as they use them in their conjuring ceremonies, they believe their parting with them, . . . would prejudice their health or affairs. **1878** *Harper's Mag.* Feb. 336/1 Along the beach [at Atlantic City] . . . there are marionette theatres, conjuring booths. **1899** CHESNUTT *Conjure Woman* 11 Well, I dunno whe'r you b'lieves in cunj'in' er not. **1903** WHITE *Forest* 230 Had it been a question of Rupert's River Crees with their fierce blood-laws, their conjuring-lodges, . . . the affair might have been different. **1911** ROLT-WHEELER *Boy with Census* 37 He was carryin' a twisted thing in his hand, like a ram's horn, an' I knew it was his cunjerin' horn.

***Conjuring,** *ppl. a.* Using conjurations. — **1846** [see CONJURE *v.*].

Conk.[1] Also **conque.** [Respelling of CONCH according to pronunciation.]

1. =CONCH 1. Also attrib. with *shell.*

1705 BEVERLEY *Virginia* III. 6 The Ladies of Distinction wear deep Necklaces, Pendants and Bracelets, made of small Cylinders of the Conque Shell, which they call Peak. **1773** *Hist. British Dom. N.A.* III. 83 Peltry of all kinds is purchased with . . . blankets, strouds, and wampum or conque-shell beads. **1791** J. LONG *Voyages* 46 Wampum is of several colours, but the white and black are chiefly used; the former is made of the inside of the conque, or clam shell. **1827** A. SHERWOOD *Gaz. Georgia* 15 Conk and other shells are seen in abundance. **1842** E. A. HITCHCOCK *Journal* 128 Other towns have other articles used in celebrating the green corn dance; the Cowetas for instance have large Conk shells out of which they take the black drink. **1891** *Scribner's Mag.* X. 478/1 If any star-fish 'borers' or 'conks' are caught they are crushed to death.

+**2.** =CONCH 2.

1848 BARTLETT 198 *Conks*, wreckers are so called, familiarly, at Key West.

+**Conk.**[2] A fungus (*Trametes pini* and others) that grows on the pine and other trees; also, the decay caused by this fungus.

1851 SPRINGER *Forest Life* 99 There is a cancerous disease peculiar to the Pine-tree, to which lumbermen give the original name of 'Conk' or 'Konkus.' **1902** *Forestry Bureau Bul.* No. 33, 15 The conk or bracket seen on affected trees is the fruiting organ. *Ib.*, Conk spores never enter through the bark, but usually through the scars of broken branches. **1905** *Ib.* No. 61, 33 Conk . . . [is] the decay in the wood of trees caused by a fungus.

Conkus. (See KONKUS.)

* **Connect,** *v.*

+**1.** *intr.* Of a conveyance: To run on such a schedule that passengers at its destination may transfer without delay to another conveyance.

1856 OLMSTED *Slave States* 134 The train was advertised to connect here with a steamboat for Norfolk.

+**2.** Of persons: To reach a conveyance before the time of departure. *colloq.*

1874 B. F. TAYLOR *World on Wheels* I. 106 His chronic mania is to 'connect.' He didn't 'connect' yesterday. **1883** 'MARK TWAIN' *Life on Miss.* lvii, The stage still remained vacant—the distinguished stranger had failed to connect. *a***1925** THORNTON in *Dial. Notes* VI. 190 When the first conveyance is delayed, he [the traveler] may fail . . . to 'connect.'

‖ **Connecticotian.** An inhabitant of Connecticut. — **1702** C. MATHER *Magnalia* (1853) I. 82 The confusions then embarrassing the affairs of the English nation, hindred our Connecticotians from seeking any further settlement.

+**Connecticut.** Also †**Conetticot, Connecticot, Connectacut.**

1. A tribe or tribes of Indians of central New England.

1634 WOOD *New Eng. Prospect* II. i. 56 Those [Indians] who are seated West-ward be called Connectacuts, and Mowhacks. **1638** UNDERHILL *Newes from Amer.* 15 The Conetticot company having with them threescore Mohiggeners, whom the Pequeats had drove out of their lawful possessions, these Indians were earnest to join with the English.

2. The name of a New England colony or state, used attrib.: **a.** Living or being in Connecticut.

1638 R. WILLIAMS *Letters* (1874) 118 The Massachusetts English did but glean after the Connecticut men, &c., in the wars. **1671** J. ELIOT *Brief Narrative* 26 The people were well known to the English so long as Connecticot Road lay that way. **1843** *Knickerb.* XXII. 2 Its execution [*i.e.* of a thought] would have done honor to a Connecticut pedler.

b. Made or invented in Connecticut.

1660 R. WILLIAMS *Letters* (1874) 306 Your loving lines in this cold, dead season, were as a cup of your Connecticut cider. **1711** *Boston News-Letter* 1 Oct. 2/2 The same day arrived Her Majesty's Ship Hector and Shoram from Great Britain . . . and brought in a Connecticut Sloop. **1761** in H. M. Brooks *Gleanings* 42 To be sold . . . , choice Connecticut Pork, Hogs Fat, and Cheese. **1818** J. PALMER *Travels U.S.* 443 Cheese, Goshen, Connecticut, English. **1835–7** HALIBURTON *Clockm.* 1 Ser. xix, Go ahead, you old clinker built villain, said he, and show the gentleman how wonderful handsum you can travel. Give him the real Connecticut quick step. **1843** *Knickerb.* XXII. 5 [A planter asked] while pointing to a Connecticut wooden clock which stood upon a shelf. **1846** *Spirit of Times* 18 April 86/2 Drinking to La Chasse La Liberté—et la belle France, in bumpers of '*Connecticut Claret.*' **1856** GOODRICH *G. Go-Ahead* 223 Did you ever see a Connecticut clock?

c. Designating money issued by Connecticut before the adoption of the U.S. Constitution.

1751 HEMPSTEAD *Diary* 572, I Recd £100 Connecticut Bills of Deacon Green. **1775** *Deane Papers* 9 The Bearer comeing to Philadelphia is apprehensive that Connecticut Paper wont Pass. **1888** *Western Reserve Hist. Soc.* II. 71 These pieces, or Connecticut cents, . . . were to weigh forty to the pound, and it is known that during the first three years [1785–88] at least 28,944 pounds were coined.

d. Designating shad that abounds in Connecticut waters.

1824 *Shipping & Comm. List* 31 July (Pettigrew P.), Shad, Conn't Mess. **1880** 'MARK TWAIN' *Tramp Abroad* xlix. 574, I have selected a few dishes and made out a little bill of fare, which will go home in the steamer that precedes me, and be hot when I arrive—as follows: . . . Connecticut shad.

1907 *Springfield W. Republican* 21 March 13 Shad were formerly so plenty in this region as to be known as 'Connecticut river pork.'

+**Connecticut claimant.** One who holds a title to land on the basis of Connecticut's claims to western territory. — **1787** *Penna. Laws* (1803) III. 201 An Act for ascertaining and confirming to certain persons, called Connecticut claimants, the lands by them claimed in the county of Luzerne.

‖**Connecticutensian.** An inhabitant of Connecticut. — **1781** S. PETERS *Hist. Conn.* p. iv, Another reason for the obscurity in which the Connecticutensians have hitherto been involved, is to be found among their own sinister views and purposes.

+**Connecticut stone.** A kind of sandstone found in Connecticut. Also attrib. — **1771** in *Copley-Pelham Lett.* 153 Connecticut Stone hearths I think will be best. **1809** E. A. KENDALL *Travels* I. 90 A mile or two above the city . . . is a quarry of free-stone, of a coarse garnet-coloured grit, commonly called Connecticut-stone.

+**Connecticut warbler.** A ground warbler (*Aporornis agilis*), first discovered in Connecticut.

1812 WILSON *Ornithology* V. 64 [The] Connecticut Warbler . . . is a new species, first discovered in the state of Connecticut. **1828** BONAPARTE *Synopsis* 84 The Connecticut Warbler . . . [is] a spring visitant in Pennsylvania, New-York, and New-England: rare. **1868** *Amer. Naturalist* II. 174 The Connecticut Warbler (*Aporornis agilis*) . . . frequents low, bushy swamps . . . and utters, at times, a feeble chirp. **1892** TORREY *Foot-Path Way* 190 Almost the first specimen I saw was a Connecticut warbler perched in full view.

Connection. {1609–}

+**1.** The means or arrangement for continuing a journey by transferring to another train, stage, etc., at a junction point; esp. in *to miss* or *to make connections.*

Now also in Eng. use, which has had the antecedent phrases 'in connection with' and 'in connection' from 1841 onwards.

1858 W. P. SMITH *Railway Celebrations* 2 (*advt.*), Containing the Time Tables, Fares, Connections and Distances on all the Railways. **1862** TROLLOPE *N. Amer.* II. 99, I have missed every connection all through from Washington here. **1864** A. DALY in *Life* (1917) 62 No water, dim lights, filthy stations and long waits for 'connections' are a few of the evils. **1870** W. F. RAE *Westward by Rail* 229 The passengers by the train in which I journeyed across the continent of America 'missed connections' at Sacramento. This is the American way of stating that the train which arrived did not correspond with that which departed. **1873** *Ill. Dept. Agric. Trans.* X. 64 Owing to the extreme cold of Monday, trains were delayed, connections missed. *a***1925** THORNTON in *Dial. Notes* VI. 190 When the first conveyance is delayed, he [the traveler] may fail to make connections.

+**2.** *College slang.* (See quotation.)

1851 HALL *College Words* 297 Take up one's connections. In students' phrase, to leave college. Used in American institutions.

Conner. [Cf. CUNNER.] {1836–} +The bergall or sea perch (*Tautogolabrus adspersus*). *New Eng.*

1685 SEWALL *Diary* I. 93 Supped with a new sort of Fish called Conners, my wife had bought. **1839** STORER *Mass. Fishes* 16 The Greenland Sculpin . . . I have . . . often taken, while fishing from the rocks there [at Nahant, Mass.], for the Sea-perch or Conner. **1842** *Nat. Hist. N.Y., Zoology* IV. 173 The Bergall has various popular names: . . . among the eastern fishermen, Cunner, or Conner. **1859** BARTLETT 58 Other names for the same fish [the burgall] are Nibbler, . . . and in New England, those of Blue Perch and Conner.

+**Conniption fit.** Also **caniption, kniption.** A seizure of hysteria; a tantrum or loss of control of temper. *colloq.*

1833 S. SMITH *Major J. Downing* 209 Ant Keziah fell down in a conniption fit. **1843** STEPHENS *High Life N.Y.* II. 171 By Golly! it was enough to drive any human critter into a conniption-fit. **1872** EGGLESTON *End of World* 130 It's only one of the old woman's conniption fits. **1897** BRODHEAD *Bound in Shallows* 153, I can't ask Alexa to come and live over in Wayne, in the old place; she'd have a kniption-fit. **1911** QUICK *Yellowstone N.* 290 One of the lawyers . . . threw a conniption fit every block. **1917** FREEMAN in *Woman's Home Comp.* Nov. 60 It saves her from having conniption fits sometimes to scold about it.

b. Ellipt. (also *pl.*) in the same sense.

1848 J. MITCHELL *Nantucketisms* 40 *Conniption*, fainting fit. **1858** G. K. WILDER *MS. Diary* 19 July, I . . . had conniptions. **1872** *Harper's Mag.* April 663/1 'Conniptions,' said he, as if trying to remember his catechism—'conniptions are fits.' **1889** *N.Y. Tribune* 31 March 19/6 The first [ovation] was the silly conniption over Alvary. **1902** L. RICHARDS *Mrs. Tree* 52 He was in a complete caniption, screeching that he was possessed of a devil, and desired the prayers of the congregation. **1907** *Scribner's Mag.* May 522 Before she cleared the harbor she scared half the ships into conniptions.

Connubiate, *v.* {1814} +*intr.* 'To act in concert with; to unite with' (F.). — **1888** *San Francisco News Letter* 4 Feb. (F.), When the machine had nominated Blaine and connubiated with Tammany and waved the shirt, [etc.].

Conque. Variant of CONK.

+**Conquedle.** *New Eng.* The bobolink. — **1783** LATHAM *Synop. Birds* II. 189 This species is known in the country by the names of Bob-Lincoln and Conquedle. **1796** MORSE *Amer. Geog.* I. 210 *n.*, The rice bird and pied rice bird are . . . called in New-England Boblincoln; Conquedle. **1858** *Atlantic Mo.* Oct. 601 The Bobolink, or Conquedle, has unquestionably great talents as a musician.

***Conqueror.** +A name given to an early Spanish explorer of the Southwest. — **1873** S. W. COZZENS *Marvellous Country* (1876) 30 The Spanish Conqueror now busied himself in fitting out an expedition to visit this land of Cibola.

Consarn, *v.* [Var. *concern.*] *tr.* In the imperative, as a mild imprecation. *humorous* and *dial.* {1854–, *dial.*}

1825 J. NEAL *Bro. Jonathan* I. 177 Winslow, . . . placing himself behind the door, 'for a leetle bit o' fun,' as he said; 'con-sarn it all; there!' **1839** C. A. MURRAY *Travels* II. 122 Why, Fox, consarn your old skin! is that you? **1846** WHITCHER *Bedott P.* i. 24 He only said, says he, 'Consarn it.' **1898** WESTCOTT *D. Harum* 166 'Consarn it all!' exlaimed Mr. Harum. . . . '[The colt] don't seem to take no int'rist in his feed. . . . Consarn a hoss, anyhow!' **1912** RAINE *Brand Blotters* 314 Then why can't you come at a reasonable hour?—consarn it!

b. *Consarn his picture*, a phrase of imprecation.

1832 KENNEDY *Swallow Barn* II. 222 'Consarn his picter!' said Jeff. **1847** J. S. ROBB *Squatter Life* 85 Whar is *he?*—Which is *him?*—consarn his comic pictur, show him out—ha-ha-ha!

+**Consarned,** *ppl. a.* Deuced, confounded. *dial.*

1843 STEPHENS *High Life N.Y.* II. 208, I was a consarned sight more to blame than you was. I hadn't no bisness to aggevate you so. **1846** WHITCHER *Bedott P.* ii. 26 But that's the consarndest lie that ever was told. **1854** 'O. OPTIC' *In Doors & Out* (1876) 183, I tell you, neighbor Parker, they [=newspapers] are a consarned humbug! **1856** 'MARK TWAIN' in *Keokuk Sat. Post* Nov., Madam, beggin your pardon, them other fellers is a consarned sight meaner'n him. **1887** WILKINS *Humble Romance* 405, I've always heard tell that there was two kinds of old maids—old maids an' consarned old maids. **1903** WIGGIN *Rebecca* 79 If I could once ketch that consarned old thief . . . I'd make him dance.

+**Consarned,** *adv. dial.* Deucedly. — **1843** STEPHENS *High Life N.Y.* I. 200 It raly made me ketch my breath to look at her, she was so consarned harnsome. **1847** ROBB *Squatter Life* 43 Well, I'm consarned sorry you did any sich a thing. **1853** 'PAXTON' *Yankee in Texas* 51 Ye can keep your money. I'm consarned sorry for it, but I must take that ar yaller gal back with me.

+**Conscience Whig.** A member of the Whig party, *c*1850, who refused to agree to compromises with regard to slavery. — **1884** BLAINE *20 Yrs. Congress* I. 77 There was a considerable body of men in New England . . . known as 'Conscience Whigs,' who had deep convictions on the subject of slavery. *Ib.* 263 These are somewhat extraordinary words in 1861 from a man who in 1850 had, as a Conscience Whig, declined to support Mr. Webster.

Conscript, *n.* One who has been compulsorily recruited for military service. {1800–}

1862 MCCLELLAN *Own Story* 626 Several persons recently from Richmond say that there are no troops there except conscripts, and they few in number. **1867** EDWARDS *Shelby* 234 Seedy mountain conscripts . . . were met the second day's march from Huntsville. **1890** J. C. HARRIS in *Century Mag.* Dec. 285 Now what kind of a soldier will one of these conscripts make? **1899** *Mo. So. Dakotan* I. 183 Arthur . . . reported at the provost marshal's office as a substitute for his brother and served as a conscripted soldier to the end of the war and subjected to all the indignities which were the conscript's portion.

attrib. **1865** TROWBRIDGE *Three Scouts* 168 We have orders to send all such cases to the conscript camp at Murfreesborough. **1865** CUMMING *Hospital Life* (1866) 187/2 Have the conscript officers taken none for the army, that the surgeons had discharged some three or four times?

+**Conscript,** *v.* [Cf. CONSCRIPTION and CONSCRIPT *n.*] *tr.* To compel (one) to go into military service. {1887–}

1813 *Conn. Courant* 23 Nov. 3/5 State troops which had been remanded to their homes by the Governor [of Vermont] had been conscripted under the orders of the former Captain General. **1814** *Columbian Centinel* 21 Dec. 2/5 The bill for drafting, or Conscripting, the militia has passed both Houses of Congress, by very spare majorities. **1863** in *Century Mag.* XXX. 769 He could not leave his position and go also without being conscripted. **1865** TROWBRIDGE *Three Scouts* 40, I stuck to the Union, 'long with the old man, till I was conscripted. **1907** ANDREWS *Recoll.* 180 General Steele had made arrangement for a Union Citizen who had been conscripted into the confederate service to go north the next day.

***Conscription.** The compulsory enlistment of men in military service. {1813–}

'The word was introduced in connection with a law of the French Republic, 5 Sept. 1798. . . . Technically, as distinguished from universal military service, it implies the enrolment by lot of a fixed number of those liable to service, with the option given of procuring a substitute' (*O.E.D.*).

1809 WEEMS *Washington* (1867) xvi. 236 Our persons have been free from the impressments and conscriptions. **1863** SEWARD in *N. Amer. Rev.* CVII. 677 It was foreseen that some emigrants . . . might complain of surprise if they were immediately subjected to conscription. **1871** T. C. CLAFLIN *Constitutional Equality* 44 All we would ask is that when the conscription is made, none may be accepted [etc.]. **1917** *New Republic* X. 319 The object of all the three systems tried in the Civil war—volunteering, draft, conscription, each with several modifications—was the raising of a temporary army. **1917** *Outlook* CXV. 689/2 *Conscription* is as inevitable in this war, if there is no unexpected peace, as it has been in each of our other greatest wars.

attrib. **1814** *Portsmouth Oracle* 19 Nov. 4/1 Synopsis of the Conscription Bill. **1862** J. DAVIS in F. Moore *Rebellion Rec.* V. II. 336 The constitutional question discussed by you in relation to the conscription law, had been fully weighed. **1863** *Nat. Almanac* 586/1 [On] May 16 [1862] the Confederate Conscription Act went into operation.

Consequential. {*a*1734} +A person of importance or reputation. *colloq.* — **1817** ROYALL *Lett. from Ala.* 5, I suspect they must be some of the consequentials of the neighborhood.

+**Consequentiousness.** The quality of being 'consequential.' — **1862** *N.Y. Herald* 26 April, He rides at the State's expense upon steamboats and railroad cars, seeking in all places to impress upon beholders an idea of his consequentiousness.

* **Conservative,** *a.* and *n.*

1. *adj.* Characterized by the desire to maintain existing institutions in political and related matters. {In politics, 1830–; in a generalized sense, 1845–}

1832 *Congress. Deb.* 20 April 1308 These, sir, . . . are the true conservative principles of this republic. **1834** *Ib.* 25 Feb. 687, I had supposed . . . that the tendency of those principles [Jackson's] was conservative. **1853** *Harper's Mag.* VI. 269 The *conservative South* it has been called; and certainly in no part of our land is a true conservatism more demanded by considerations of domestic safety as well as of national dignity. **1875** E. KING *Southern States N. Amer.* 601 The negro in the Conservative States gains many more educational advantages by a separate school system than he could by mixed schools. **1898** *Kansas City Star* 18 Dec. 2/1 George L. Cake of Pittsburgh, the most conservative unionist in the convention, made his way into the center aisle.

b. Applied specifically to various minority parties or party factions, esp. to a group that supported Andrew Johnson in his struggle with Congress.

1867 in McPherson *Polit. Manual* 249 We, the Conservative men of Tennessee, adopt the following platform of principles. **1867** *N.Y. Herald* 19 April 3 A conservative meeting was held to-night [in Petersburg, Va.], and passed resolutions fully affirming equal rights for whites and blacks. *c***1868** GARFIELD in Stryker *A. Johnson* 677, I have a few words to whisper in your private ear, concerning what Conservative Republicans think. **1869** GRANT in Fleming *Hist. Reconstruction* II. 93 The success of the so-called Conservative Republican party of Mississippi would result in the defeat of what I believe to be the best interests of the State. **1875** *43rd Congress 2 Sess.* H. R. Rep. No. 265, 31 It became a well-recognized fact that every colored man who permitted his name to be put upon the ticket of what was called either the democratic or conservative party, was immediately ostracised by his own race.

2. Moderate; safe (with reference to estimates, predictions, etc.). {1900–}

This sense has been criticized in E. as a 'misuse' and a 'slipshod extension,' as Horwill, *Dict. Mod. Am. Usage* p. 80, points out; he says, 'Actually it is an importation from Am., where it became current long ago.' This view, however, is not borne out by the evidence.

1903 ELY *Evolution Industrial Soc.* 204 Lecky's History of European Morals gives a conservative statement of the ethical consequences of luxury. **1903** *N.Y. Tribune* 6 Sept. II. 7/6 The visitors were spending on the island the enormous total of $1,500,000 a day—and this is a conservative estimate. **1921** LANSING *Peace Negotiations* 155 It is conservative to say that between two and three months were spent in the drafting of a document which in the end was rejected by the Senate.

b. *Conservative-minded,* entertaining moderate expectations.

1904 *N.Y. Sun* 5 Sept. 3 This and the Fifteenth are the only two Congress districts which conservative minded Republicans think their party will be able to carry next November.

3. *n.* A person who believes in the principles of conservatism; one who is conservative. {in politics 1831–}

1847 *Amer. Whig Rev.* VI. 243/2 Conservatives in America also return continually to the original principles of their government; and they believe them to be the highest on which any state can rest. **1865** *Atlantic Mo.* XV. 252 We are utterly unable to understand what a recent reviewer means in commending this work [on philosophy] to conservatives as a noble text-book. **1913** LAFOLLETTE *Autobiog.* 479 In this way he sought to win approval, both from the radicals and the conservatives. **1913** BASSETT *Short Hist. U.S.* 845 Republican dissensions had much interest for the democrats, who had their own conservatives and progressives.

+**4.** *pl.* The name of certain political parties or factions: **a.** The branch of the Democratic party which opposed the Treasury Bill of 1837, and continued on, for a short time, as an independent force. **b.** The conservative wing of the New York Democratic Party opposed to the Barn-burners. (Cf. HUNKER.) **c.** (See quot. 1914.)

a. 1838 *Democratic Rev.* I. 2 No little uncertainty prevailed as to the course that would be pursued by . . . the friends of the Administration to whom the specific name of 'Conservatives' had been applied. **1842** BUCKINGHAM *Slave States* II. 354 A new party is rising up, however, called by themselves Conservatives, who will not ally themselves to either. By both the old parties, however, these Conservatives are called 'Impracticables.' **1914** McLaughlin & Hart *Cycl. Amer. Govt.* I. 566 A proposal to establish an independent, or subtreasury system [in 1837] . . . was passed by the Senate but twice rejected by the House, a Democratic faction known as Conservatives uniting with the Whigs to defeat it.

b. 1853 [see BARN-BURNER]. **1860** *De Bow's Rev.* XXVIII. 515 That he [=J. C. Frémont] was not triumphantly elected, was only because of the active exertions of the South, aided by the superhuman struggles of the Northern Conservatives. **1875** E. KING *S. States N. Amer.* 641 During this year [1865] the Conservatives attempted to inaugurate a practical serfdom of the freedmen, by means of vagrant laws. **1888** M. LANE in *America* 27 Sept. 16 *Conservatives,* a name self-given to that wing of the New York Democracy known as Hunkers. The name of Hunkers was accepted and the other was not.

c. 1867 *N.Y. Herald* 20 April 3/3 The Convention of the Conservatives of Tennessee met in Nashville on the 16th inst. **1914** McLaughlin & Hart *Cycl. Amer. Govt.* I. 402 The Conservatives or Johnson men were the adherents of President Johnson in his contest with Congress over the question of reconstruction. . . . The Conservatives played a rather important part in the South where for a time they took the old name of 'Constitutional Unionists,' and their opponents the term 'Radicals.'

Conservatively, *adv.* {1834–} **1.** In a conservative manner. **2.** According to a moderate estimate. — **(1) 1887** *Phila. Ledger* 30 Dec. (*Cent.*), It is very conservatively English to make concession at the eleventh hour and fifty-ninth minute; but the clock is fast in Ireland. (2) **1904** *San Francisco Chronicle* 12 July 7 Wearing a diamond pin, conservatively valued at $75.

+**Conservativeness.** Conservatism. {1928–} — **1838** H. WINSLOW *Boston Oration* 4 July 19 That the comparative silence of those who stand upon the side of conservativeness, implies a gradual concession.

* **Conservator.**

***1.** *Conservator of the peace,* an official whose duty is to preserve the peace; a constable. *Obs.*

1653 *Providence Rec.* II. 75 Two conservatours of the Peace inhabiting in th[e] Town. **1653** *Portsmouth* (R.I.) *Rec.* 59 Mr Sanford Mr Balstone and Mr John porter Conservators of the peace in this towne. **1681** *Providence Rec.* XV. 220 John Spenser Consurveter of the pece. **1753** *Ga. Col. Rec.* VI. 404 He had begun a Settlement (by Leave of Mr. James Fraser Conservator of the Peace at Augusta).

+**2.** A person who superintends the financial affairs of lunatics, idiots, etc.

1828 WEBSTER s.v., *Conservator,* in Connecticut, a person appointed to superintend idiots, lunatics, &c., manage their property, and preserve it from waste. **1874** in *Ill. Rev. Statutes* (1883) 735 Whenever any idiot, lunatic or distracted person has any estate . . . [etc.], it shall be the duty of the court to appoint some fit person to be the conservator of such person. **1903** *N.Y. Ev. Post* 9 Sept., Conservators are daily appointed over men who hold less crazy notions.

* **Conservatory.** An institution in which music is taught. {1846–}

This sense is 'frequent in U.S.; in England, the French form of the word is commonly used' (*O.E.D.*). 'In Eng. *conservatory* commonly denotes a *greenhouse.* The French form *conservatoire* is preferred in the sense of *school of music.* In Am. conservatory is ordinarily used in the latter sense' (Horwill *Mod. Am. Usage* 80).

1865 *Atlantic Mo.* XV. 575 There he directs . . . the phantom of a Conservatory for singing. **1877** *Harper's Mag.* Feb. 463/1 The foundation of Mr. Peabody is very simple and popular, including a library, a conservatory of music, and a course of popular and scientific lectures. **1879** GROVE *Dict. Mus.* I. 10 The chief public institution in New York for teaching music is the New York Conservatory of Music. **1879** HOWELLS *L. Aristook* 129 You are going to study at the conservatory in Milan? **1893** *Amer. Conservatory* (*Chicago*) *Summer Normal Session* [4] The Director of the Conservatory . . . will deliver a course of lectures. **1905** *Etude* XXIII. 36 A concert by the orchestra and chorus class of the Broad Street Conservatory of Music, Philadelphia, . . . was given December 14th.

‖**Conservatress.** A female conservator. — **1841** FOOTE *Texas* I. 17 That high moral grandeur . . . appertained to Rome as the genial mother and bounteous conservatress of Science and the Arts.

+**Conserve-slavery party.** [*conserve* v. and *slavery.*] A political party favoring the continuance of slavery. *colloq.* — **1862** *N.Y. Tribune* 13 May 6/1 Several of the members of the new Conserve Slavery Party [in the House] did not vote with their friends of the Caucus upon the bill excluding Slavery from the . . . Territories.

* **Considerable,** *a.*

1. Fairly numerous or abundant; of fairly large amount or extent. *colloq.*

The examples given differ from ordinary English usage by the adj. being applied to material or quasi-concrete things.

1677 W. HUBBARD *Indian Wars* (1865) I. 285 The Indians . . . lighted upon a considerable Party of the Enemy. **1711** SEWALL *Diary* II. 326 When came out found a Considerable Snow on the ground. **1847** ROBB *Squatter Life* 106 Thar wur considerable folks at Alic's, fur some of the families in them diggins [a region thirty miles in range] had about twenty in number. **1849** KINGSLEY *Diary* 62 There is considerable fruit here such as apples. **1855** MITCHELL *Fudge Doings* I. 69 Thus far it appears to me that the French are a tall people, and talk considerable English. **1876** 'MARK TWAIN' *Tom Sawyer* ii. 32 The privilege costs them considerable money. **1880** — *Tramp Abroad* xxvii. 276, I know considerable French. **1890** *Daily Times* (Troy, N.Y.) 15 Feb. 3/3 The . . . speculators are purchasing considerable lumber at Rutland, to use in erecting buildings.

+**2.** *absol.* In various colloquial uses: **a.** *Considerable of*, a fair or large number or amount of something.

1685 *Mass. H. S. Coll.* 4 Ser. V. 132 One more, of Long Island, [who hath] . . . lost considerable of wheat and Indian corn. **1716** CHURCH *Philip's War* II. 112 Spending that day in ranging to & fro, found considerable of their goods, and but few People. **1778** I. ANGELL *Diary* (1899) 8 There was a Considerable of firing between the sentries. **1832** FERRALL *Ramble* 216 The Mississippi woodcutters scrape together 'considerable of dollars.' **1842** M. CRAWFORD *Journal* 21 We find considerable of sage yet in places. **1878** BEADLE *Western Wilds* xix. 302 In two days' intercourse, we had learned considerable of each other's views and experiences. **1903** K. D. WIGGIN *Rebecca* 132 Rebecca took her scolding . . . like a soldier. There was considerable of it.

+**b.** *Considerable of a(n)*, something clearly perceptible or of considerable size, magnitude, etc.; of persons, important, worthy of recognition or consideration.

(1) **1766** CUTLER in *Life & Corr.* I. 10 This morning about 6 o'clock considerable of a shock of an earthquake was felt in Boston. **1779** D. LIVERMORE in *Coll. N. H. Hist. Soc.* VI. 326 This is considerable of a village, consisting of about twenty houses. **1779** *N.H. Hist. Soc. Coll.* VI. 311 The water is carried under ground down the hill and through the bottom of the river, to a considerable of an eminence on the opposite side. **1780** *Heath Papers* 5 A considerable of a trade carried on. **1805** *Lewis & Clark Exped.* (1905) VII. 89 This rapid had considerable of a fall, which gave us Some trouble. **1842** *Knickerb.* XX. 305, I had 'considerable of a day's work' before me. *c***1845** PAULDING *Noble Exile* 141, I shouldn't wonder if I could make a pretty considerable of a sharp guess. *a***1861** T. WINTHROP *Life in Open Air* (1863) 37 When you come to get seven or eight feet more of water atop of this in spring, it is considerable of a puddle. *c***1871** 'MARK TWAIN' *Sk., Journalism in Tenn.*, A brick came through the window with a splintering crash, and gave me a considerable of a jolt in the back. **1889** JEWETT *Betty Leicester* ii. 19, I was in considerable of a hurry to get home.

(2) **1781** WITHERSPOON *Druid P.* No. 7, He is considerable of a surveyor, considerable of it may be found in that country. This manner of speaking prevails in the northern parts. **1831** ROYALL *Southern Tour* II. 110 This snag (I mean a Vermonter) was pretty tolerable clever, and considerable of a merchant. **1852** BRISTED *Upper Ten Thous.* 142 He is really worth knowing and considerable of a man, as we say—no fool at all. **1909** A. C. RICE *Mr. Opp* 97, I was considerable of a performer at one time.

+**c.** Much, a good deal, esp. of money. {1847–}

(1) **1722** *Lancaster Rec.* 200 He promising to Leve the hiway there Wider by Considerable then five Rods. **1837** COLMAN *Mass. Agric. Rep.* (1838) 88 We have done considerable at underdraining our low and wet grounds to very great advantage. **1850** KINGSLEY *Diary* 110 They had been detained a considerable on the passage. **1886** *Leslie's Mo.* XXI. 219/1 The captain . . . is always the smartest man in the crowd, which is often saying considerable. **1903** *N.Y. Ev. Post* 6 Oct. 6 They will find considerable to interest them in certain figures recently published. **1911** LINCOLN *Cap'n Warren* 178 The Boston papers had considerable about it.

(2) **1837** MARTINEAU *Society* I. 340 She has a widowed mother to support, and she 'gets considerable' by sewing. **1848** W. ARMSTRONG *Stocks* 36 A. N. Gifford.—An old bachelor, worth considerable, and loves money next to his God. **1858** VIELÉ *Following the Drum* 30 'The bargain was closed'; . . . Noble Lovely . . . 'realized quite a little considerable' in consequence. **1882** THAYER *From Log-Cabin* x. 149 Each boy does more work, and where there's twenty of them, it's considerable in my pocket. **1900** E. A. DIX *Deacon Bradbury* 245 It's cost 'em consider'ble, an' they was so sure o' gittin' back half or more.

Consideration money. Money given as an equivalent for something undertaken or promised. — **1715** *N.C. Col. Rec.* II. 206 The owner of the said land for the consideration money by the said Appraisers appointed shall be bound. **1779** *N.J. Archives* 2 Ser. III. 234 Whereas the subscriber purchased a plantation . . . and paid the greater part of the consideration money. *a***1861** T. WINTHROP *Canoe & Saddle* x. 207 'Loolowkan,' said she, 'can take the consideration-money, and buy me "ikta," what not, at the Dalles.'

‖**Consigneeship.** The state of being a consignee. — **1876** BANCROFT *Hist. U.S.* (rev. ed.) VI. 503/1 [A Boston] town-meeting adopts the Philadelphia resolves, and invites the Hutchinsons to resign their consigneeship.

***Consociate,** *v.* +*tr.* With reference to Congregational polity in New England: To join together in an association. Esp. in *consociated churches. Obs.* Also absol.

1735 COLMAN in Turell *Life B. Colman* 108 The consociated Churches of every Neighbourhood must have their stated Meetings. **1756** M. Blake *Mendon Association* (1853) 49 Dispensed by a superior Number of Consociated Churches, the said offending church shall remain. **1757** *Ib.* 51 As the mutual Edification of these ch[urc]h[e]s (the End of Consociating) cannot be Expected. **1796** MORSE *Amer. Geog.* I. 270 There are few congregational churches that are consociated on the above principles. [**1844** Rupp *Relig. Denominations* 585 In the year 1766, a proposition was made in the Synod of New York and Philadelphia, for a correspondence with 'the Consociated Churches of Connecticut.']

***Consociation.**

1. An alliance for mutual defense, etc. *Obs.* {1603–1685}

1643 *Plymouth Laws* 308 Wee therefore doe conceive it our bounden Dutye without delay to enter into a present Consotiation amongst our selves for mutuall help and strength in all our future concernments. **1676** *Ib.* 180 Where the commission officers and Towne Councell of divers Townes are or shalbe in a consosiation or vicinety for their mutuall defence and preservation.

+**2.** A confederation of Congregational churches. *New England. Obs.*

1644 J. COTTON *Keyes* 57 Touching this great work of communion and consociation of churches. **1662** *Congregational Synod Boston* pref., If therefore the things here propounded concerning . . . the Consociation of Churches, be a part of the Will of God contained in the Scriptures, . . . that doth sufficiently bespeak their entertainment. **1711** *Essex Inst. Coll.* X. 91 The ministers discoursed: . . . that the consociation of churches might be strengthened. **1735** COLMAN in Turell *Life B. Colman* 107 The Consociation of Churches, is the very Soul and Life of the Congregational Scheme. **1757** M. Blake *Mendon Association* (1853) 51 That this Association in their Proposal to their sev[era]l ch[urc]hes of Forming into a Consociation, [etc.]. **1764** HUTCHINSON *Hist. Mass.* I. 223 There ought to be a consociation of churches.

+**3.** 'A convention of pastors and messengers of churches' (W. '06); a council of churchmen.

'It is usually composed of the pastors of the Congregational churches of the district represented and one lay delegate from each' (*Cent.*).

1781 PETERS *Conn.* (1829) 162 This quarrel continued till 1764, when it subsided in a grand continental consociation of ministers. **1844** Rupp *Relig. Denominations* 209 In Rhode Island, an evangelical association of ministers was formed in 1808. The next year the name was changed to that of the 'Evangelical Consociation,' by which it is now known. **1855** BARNUM *Life* 45 He overtook a brother clergyman . . . , who was wending his way to the Consociation. **1865** *Atlantic Mo.* XV. 304 From time to time there are meetings of the 'Consociation,' or other ministerial assemblages. **1869** STOWE *Oldtown Folks* 451 The Consociation was another meeting of the clergy, but embracing also with each minister a lay delegate.

+**Consociational,** *a.* Having to do with a consociation (esp. sense 3 above). — **1806** WEBSTER *Consociational*, pertaining to a consociation. *a***1817** T. DWIGHT *Travels* IV. 320 The Clergyman . . . attends every associational, and consociational, meeting within his district.

+**Consociationism.** The system of ecclesiastical organization in which independent churches co-operate by means of a confederation. — *a***1840** in E. A. Park *Memoir N. Emmons* (1861) 163 Associationism leads to Consociationism; Consociationism leads to Presbyterianism. **1884** *Advance* (Chicago) 11 Dec., They now sought a middle way between Presbyterianism and Congregationalism. That middle way was Consociationism.

‖**Consolidarian.** One who believes in consolidating. — **1788** *Mass. Spy* 16 April 2/2 The cause of the contest I found to be, that the people of Exeter were high Consolidarians, and lent every possible aid to those of their own party in convention.

Consolidated, *a.* (In special uses.)

+**1.** *Consolidated (state) note*, an interest-bearing treasury note issued to replace other bills of credit, esp. in the states or colonies before the Constitution.

'An earnest discussion, in 1777, of the proposal to call in all bills of credit and substitute therefore interest-bearing treasury notes, ended in the issue of seventy-five thousand pounds sterling in such notes' (1892 C. H. J. Douglas *Financial Hist. Mass.* 135).

1784 *Mass. Centinel* 10 July 1/1 Lost . . . a leather pocket-book, containing . . . five Consolidated State Notes. **1788** *Mass. Spy* 3 April 3/1 Empowering them to sell all the unappropriated lands . . . and to receive in payment either specie, or the consolidated State Notes. **1832** WILLIAMSON *Maine* II. 539 For which [land] they gave £3,000 in consolidated notes.

2. Created by the merging of two or more business companies into one.

1867 in *Ill. Revised Statutes* (1883) 301 In all cases when any company . . . shall consolidate its property, stock or franchises with any other company or companies, such consolidated company shall be liable for all debts or liabilities of each company included in said consolidated company. **1877** W. WRIGHT *Big Bonanza* 563 The Consolidated Virginia hoisting work's assay-office . . . and the stock of mining supplies on hand was a loss of $800,000. **1898** *Boston Herald* 22 April 7/1 There are . . . a number of new open cars for use on the electrical equipped branches of the Consolidated road.

+**3.** *Consolidated engine*, (see quotation and cf. CONSOLIDATION 2.).

1887 *Sci. Amer.* n.s. LVI. 3/2 The locomotive was one of the heaviest kind known as a consolidated engine, having four drive-wheels on a side, and weighing 106,000 pounds.

+**4.** *Consolidated school* as attrib. with *district, plan*, etc.: Of or pertaining to a school established by the merging of two or more schools into one.

1911 *Okla. Session Laws* 3 Legisl. 245 All the lands and funds that have heretofore been or may hereafter be derived from the sale thereof, . . . shall be set aside and credited to a fund which is hereby created to be known as the 'Union Graded or Consolidated School District Fund.' *Ib.*, There shall be set aside and credited to a fund . . . to be used only to assist in constructing or paying for school buildings or consolidated school districts. **1920** *3rd Nat. Country Life Conf. Proc.* 5 Practically no impression had been made thus far upon the farmers in getting them to adopt the consolidated-school plan.

+**5.** *Consolidated ticket office*, (see quotation).

'In Eng. such an office would be called a *joint booking office*' (Horwill 81). **1924** F. J. Haskin *Amer. Govt.* 393 Instead of a separate ticket office in cities for each railroad, consolidated ticket offices, where a ticket for any train on any road could be purchased, were established.

***Consolidation.**

1. The combining of two or more companies, businesses, or properties into one.

1850 *Daily Ev. Traveller* 22 July 2/5 The preliminary arrangements for the consolidation of the Auburn and Syracuse and Auburn and Rochester railway companies, have been perfected. **1870** *Ill. Constitution* xi. § 11 No railroad corporation shall consolidate its stock, property or franchises with any other railroad corporation owning a parallel or competing line; and in no case shall any consolidation take place, except upon public notice. **1871** Raymond [*3rd Rep.*] *Mines* 135 The contending parties . . . determined at last, very wisely, to compromise the suit by consolidation. **1882** *Nation* 9 Nov. 392/1 The decision of the Superior Court . . . is a severe blow to the business of consolidation, brought to its present pitch of perfection, if not invented, by Jay Gould. If consolidation were what its name implies—the mere union of the stock of different companies in one—there would not be any harm in it.

+**b.** The company formed by the merging of two or more companies.

1882 C. King *Rep. Prec. Metals* 74 The consolidation owns about 35 miles of ditches.

+**2.** A kind of locomotive that has very heavy driving wheels. (Cf. Consolidated *a.* 3.)

1884 Knight *Suppl., Consolidation* (Locomotive), a type of freight locomotive, the name of the engine, the first of its class, built in 1866, at the Baldwin locomotive works. **1898** *Engineering Mag.* XVI. 160/1 Consolidation Locomotive for the Chesapeake & Ohio.

+**3.** *Educ.* The combining or merging of two or more schools into one, esp. in rural areas.

1902 *Forum* XXXIII. 104 One town reports that prior to consolidation there had been a rapid diminution of the school population in the outlying districts.

+**Consolidationist.** One who advocates the strengthening of the federal government.

1833 Webster *Works* (1860) I. 295 For one, I repel all such imputations. I am no consolidationist. **1835** P. H. Nicklin *Virginia Springs* 29 From the east you have consolidationists, tariffites and philanthropists. **1838** *Democratic Rev.* I. 19 No ingenuity could make it an easy task for the strong consolidationist and the State-Rights man to work together effectively. **1883** *American* VI. 202 Would it not unite the consolidationist and the advocate of state rights?

Consort. Obs. variant of Concert.

***Constable.** Also †**cunstable.**

***1.** A local officer charged with keeping the peace and with certain minor legal duties; 'a town officer of the peace, with the powers of an under sheriff' (W. '06).

'The constable was formerly of much more consequence both in England and the colonies, being the chief executive officer of the parish or town' (*Cent.*).

1630 *Mass. Bay Court Assist. Rec.* II. 5 John Woodbury is chosen Constable of Salem & Thom[as] Stoughton Constable of Dorchester. **1683** *Providence Rec.* VI. 97 Wee . . . haue seene Cause . . . to Jshue forth warrant to our Cunstable . . . to remoove ye sd person. **1788** Franklin *Autobiog.* 352 The constable, for a little drink, often got such ragamuffins about him as a watch, that respectable housekeepers did not choose to mix with. **1852** Stowe *Uncle Tom* xvii, They said that there were two constables, in a town a little piece ahead, who would go in with 'em to get 'em taken up. **1880** Cable *Grandissimes* xli. 321 He saw Aurora and Clotilde . . . offering woman's pleadings to deaf constables.

attrib. **1711** Sewall *Diary* II. 304 About 150 £ received for Constable Fines. **1839** *Diplom. Corr. Texas* I. 382 One of my mules was levied upon by the constable and but for one of my neighbors would have been sold for the debt and constable costs.

2. *Constable('s) staff*, a staff carried by a constable. *Obs.*

1647 *Watertown Rec.* 17 Mending . . . the Constables staue. **1659** *Plymouth Laws* 123 It is enacted by the Court that every cunstable of this Jurisdiction shall have a Cunstable staffe wherby to distinguish them in theire office from others. **1687** *Groton Rec.* 96 To Purchis a Constabls Stafe.

3. *Constable's watch*, the watch kept by a constable. *Obs.*

1677 *Boston Rec.* 108 The Selectmen craue the . . . assistance of the . . . Milicia . . . for settinge of a Constables or other watch. **1681** *Watertown Rec.* II. 8 Ye select men . . . doe think it meet that the present melitary watches be turned into constables watches.

Constablerick. [After *bishopric*, etc.] The territory, usually part of a town(ship), under the jurisdiction of a constable. *Obs.* {constablewick, *a*1618–}

1633 *Plymouth Laws* 34 It is enacted by the court that every cunstablerick have a sufficient pound to impound cattle that shall transgresse any such orders. **1640** *Ib.* 46 Corn to be raysed of the constablerick or liberties. **1689** *Ib.* 222 All . . . persons . . . who live or reside out of the bounds of any of our Towns shall be under the Constablerick of the nearest of our Towns whereunto they so live or reside. **1703** in N. Mitchell *Hist. Bridgewater, Mass.* (1840) 68 Voted to divide the town into three constablericks.

***Constableship.**

***1.** The office of constable.

1638 *R.I. Col. Rec.* I. 65 Samuel Willbore by the consent of this Body is chosen Constable, and is invested with the authority aforesayed, and what else shall be found meet to concurr with that office of Constableship. **1659** *Watertown Rec.* 63 Noe Constable shall be free from his Constableship. **1788** Franklin *Autobiog.* 352 Those who chose never to attend, paid him six shillings a year to be excus'd, which . . . made the constableship a place of profit. **1842** C. M. Kirkland *Forest Life* II. 33 There was one tall fellow . . . , who was insisting on his own qualifications for a constableship.

2. = Constablerick. *Obs.*

1674 *Plymouth Laws* 171 That wheras Mannamoiett Paomitt and Satuckett have bin put under the Constableshipp of Eastham [etc.].

Constituency. *Politics.* A body of constituents; the citizens and voters in a voting district. {1831–} — **1837** *Democratic Rev.* I. 86 His constituency is to be found among the hardy and true-hearted pioneers of civilization. **1893** *Harper's Mag.* April 702/2 He presumed too far upon the toleration of a constituency which had honored him so long and forgiven him so much. **1902** E. C. Meyer *Nominating Systems* 6 The caucus system . . . was found entirely inadequate where the constituency was large or the district extensive.

Constituent. {1622–} One of a body that elects a certain person as their representative. {1714–}

1768 *N.E. Hist. & Gen. Reg.* XXIII. 454 The [Mass.] House [of Representatives] have some Thoughts of asking his Excellency for a Recess—that they may consult their Constituents upon this great Concern. **1789** *Ann. 1st Congress* I. 148 He called upon gentlemen to exercise liberality and moderation in what they proposed, if they wished to give satisfaction and do justice to their constituents. **1841** *Knickerb.* XVII. 375 A new election was ordered a few days afterward, at which his constituents of the first ward evinced their unabated confidence. **1885** *Century Mag.* April 820 A number of men . . . elected by constituents too ignorant to hold them to a proper accountability for their actions.

transf. **1899** S. Hale *Letters* 343 You can circulate the tale among the various constituents [*i.e.*, the family circle].

***Constitution.**

***1.** A regulation, ordinance, or by-law; +*Fundamental Constitutions*, the laws drawn up by John Locke (1632–1704) for the governance of the Carolinas.

'The Fundamental Constitutions never acquired any legal force. A committee of the Council reported, May 7, 1745, that the Proprietors at various times had made five different drafts, none of which was ever passed into law by the consent of the people'—(1934 D. D. Wallace *Hist. S.C.* I. 120).

1620 *'Mayflower' Compact*, We . . . doe . . . combine our selves together into a civill body politike, . . . to enact . . . such just and equal Lawes, Ordinances, acts, constitutions, offices from time to time, as shall be thought most meet. **1669** J. Locke *Fundamental Constitutions S.C.* (1680) cxx, These Fundamental Constitutions . . . shall be and remain the sacred and unalterable form and rule of government of Carolina for ever. Witness our hands and seals, the first day of March, 1669.

2. The body of principles by which a group of people are governed. {1735–}

1744 *N.J. Archives* 1 Ser. VI. 231 We are willing to impute their present conduct to . . . their want of a necessary knowledge of the true boundaries that divide the distinct parts of which our happy Constitution is composed, that is, the three branches of the Legislature. **1748** *Ib.* VII. 118 The Kings Governour . . . is to be confined to a single vote nor is he to call or adjourn a meeting but in conformity to the Constitution. **1776** *Declar. Independence*, He has combined with others to subject us to a jurisdiction foreign to our constitution, and unacknowledged by our laws. **1789** Morse *Amer. Geog.* 441 This constitution [of 1669, framed by Mr. Locke for the proprietors of S.C.] . . . was aristocratical.

+**b.** (See quotation and Confederation 3.)

1788 *Steele Papers* I. 21 The old Constitution or articles of Confederation.

+**3.** The body of law by which the government of the United States was established, framed in 1787 and adopted in 1789; usually, the written document embodying this.

[**1776** J. Adams *Works* IX. 402 When we . . . get an American constitution formed, something will be done.] **1787** *Constitution*, We the people of the United States, . . . do ordain and establish this Constitution for the United States of America. **1788** CUTLER in *Life & Corr.* I. 381 The ratification of the *Federal Constitution* has given them [shares] a sudden start. **1789** S. LOW *Politician Outwitted* I. i, I'm sure 'tis strange to hear so many people praise this same new Constitution, as it is call'd. **1789** MACLAY *Deb. Senate* 79 My mind revolts in many instances against the Constitution of the United States. **1792** MORRIS in Sparks *Life G. Morris* II. 205 The basis of our own constitution is the indefeasible right of the people to establish it. **1831** P. HONE *Diary* I. 39 They took the lead in paying a merited compliment to Mr. Webster for his manly and eloquent defence of the Constitution against the nullifying doctrines of the South. **1856** D. MACLEOD *F. Wood* 69 Hasty legislation, either in the enactment of laws or their repeal, is objectionable. . . . To guard against it, the framers of the Constitution devised many ways. **1884** *Century Mag.* Nov. 124 Our Constitution is, in its theory, the most nearly perfect system of free government that was ever devised. **1925** BRYAN *Memoirs* 245 We stand upon the Constitution.

+**4.** The body of fundamental law of an individual state within the United States.

1780 CUTLER in *Life & Corr.* I. 78 Attended town-meeting for receiving the Constitution. *c***1828** in Benton *30 Years' View* 95/1 There is but one American System, and that is delineated in the State and Federal constitutions. **1845** POLK *Diary* 12 Intelligence was received today that the convention of Texas had formed a State Constitution. **1877** JOHNSON *Anderson Co., Kansas* 68 The object of the meeting was to discuss the question of electing delegates to the Lecompton convention, to frame a State constitution.

+**5.** The body of fundamental law adopted by the states of the Southern Confederacy: **a.** The provisional constitution. **b.** The permanent constitution.

(**a**) **1861** Moore *Rebellion Rec.* I. II. 29 We the deputies of the sovereign and independent States of South Carolina, Georgia, Florida, Alabama, Mississippi and Louisiana, . . . do hereby . . . ordain and establish this Constitution for the provisional government of the same, to continue . . . until a permanent Constitution or confederation . . . be put in operation. *Ib.* 30 All the other portions of the Constitution are almost identical with the Constitution of the United States. **1861** *Commercial Advertiser* 8 Feb., The Congress at Montgomery this evening unanimously agreed to a constitution and provisional government.

(**b**) **1861** *Constitution of the Confederate States* vii. § 1 When five States shall have ratified this Constitution in the manner before specified, the Congress, under the provisional Constitution, shall prescribe the time for holding the election of President and Vice-president, etc. **1913** J. BASSETT *Short Hist. U.S.* 587 By autumn [1861] the permanent constitution was adopted, and elections were held for presidential electors and members of congress.

6. Comb. and attrib. with *breaking, monger, making,* etc.

1779 J. ADAMS *Works* IX. 507, I should not have left the first unanswered seven days, if it had not been for my new trade of a Constitution monger. **1820** *Ann. 16th Congress* 1 Sess. I. 945 Nineteen out of twenty of our agricultural citizens know better the art of constitution-making than the best methods of raising cabbages. **1827** G. MELLEN *Chronicle of '26* 15, I've heard of scriveners and ticket-venders, But keep me, above all, from Constitution-menders! **1844** 'UNCLE SAM' *Peculiarities* II. 178 'Ole ooman hab join de tumperance.' . . . 'Oh! that's the constitution-ticket, is it, Old Horse?' **1863** S. COX *In Congress* (1865) 283 These central and western states . . . do not intend to be ruled, however, by the Constitution-breaking, law-defying, negro-loving Phariseeism of New England! **1865** *Atlantic Mo.* XV. 194 There he wrote his 'Advice to the Privileged Classes,' . . . and became an active member of the Constitution Society.

Constitutional, *a.* {1682–}

1. In the colonial period: In harmony with the governmental principles of the country. {1765–}

1760 *N.J. Archives* XX. 458 Governor Bernard, whose mild and constitutional administration . . . has given universal Satisfaction. **1764** *Boston Rec.* XVI. 120 They have delegated to you the power of acting in their Publick Concerns in general as your own prudence shall direct you, always reserving to themselves the Constitutional Right of expressing their Mind. **1764** *R.I. Col. Rec.* VI. 426 Is not this the most easy . . . and most constitutional way of raising money in the colonies? **1766** in R. Roger *Journals* (1883) 219 The unconstitutional steps pursued to obtain constitutional redress, can hardly be parallelled. **1775** in F. Chase *Dartmouth Coll.* I. 349, I sent out and invited my neighbors to come and join our evening prayers, . . . and appealed to them that I had ever been from the first steadily and firmly attached to the constitutional rights and liberties of the Colonies.

+**b.** *Constitutional post,* the mail service of the revolting colonies as distinguished from that of the British government or 'ministerial post.'

1775 *Jrnls. Cont. Congress* III. 488 A constitutional post is now established from New Hampshire to Georgia. *Ib.*, Deane is for a recommendation to the people to write by the constitutional post.

+**2.** Formed by, based upon, in accord with, or pertaining to, the U.S. Constitution of 1787.

1787 CUTLER in *Life & Corr.* I. 197, [I] addressed them on the nature of our Constitutional Government. **1805** *Ann. 8th Congress* 2 Sess. 1037 Were the members of the Legislature of Georgia, in 1796, invested with the Constitutional power of rescinding the acts of their predecessors in relation to such sale? **1831** P. HONE *Diary* I. 38 [Men] should have protested and seceded from the convention when a proposition so monstrous as the denying to Congress the constitutional right to pass these laws was about to be adopted. **1835** C. P. BRADLEY *I. Hill* 36 Constitutional scruples were overcome, the courts were entirely remodelled. **1854** BENTON *30 Years' View* I. 118/2 The vote wanting one of the constitutional number of two thirds. **1860** in E. D. Fite *Pres. Campaign of 1860* (1911) 254 The conflict of constitutional construction is indeed a mere incident of the great struggle, a mere symptom of the crisis. **1872** *Atlantic Mo.* April 515 The 'constitutional' question has intruded itself at every step into politics. **1886** ALTON *Among Law-Makers* 92 The President of the Senate . . . [gives] the electoral envelopes the 'constitutional rip.' *Ib.* 182 Visitors to Washington . . . will sit for hours and listen to . . . black-letter lawyers discussing grave questions of constitutional law. **1892** M. A. JACKSON *Gen. Jackson* 143 It was for her constitutional rights that the South resisted the North.

+**b.** *Constitutional amendment,* a formal alteration or revision of the Constitution.

1854 BENTON *30 Years' View* I. 122/1 In the meantime, the friends of popular election should press the constitutional amendment. **1861** in Logan *Great Conspiracy* 155 It must be by Legislation; which is more ready, more certain, and more likely to be satisfactory, than Constitutional Amendment. **1865** WHITTIER *Laus Deo!* (*caption*), On hearing the bells ring on the passage of the constitutional amendment abolishing slavery. **1865** *Nation* I. 171 Is not the real solution of the question to be found in submitting it to the people in the form of a constitutional amendment? **1891** *Cycl. Temperance* 98/2 State and National Prohibition, secured by Constitutional Amendments, . . . would be but the logical outcome of the earliest and most limited Local Option victory.

+**3.** *Constitutional lawyer.* (1) A lawyer versed in matters pertaining to the Federal Constitution. (2) (See quot. 1910.)

(1) **1830** *Congress. Deb.* 75/2 The venerable Connecticut senator [James Hillhouse] is a constitutional lawyer, of sound principles, and enlarged knowledge. **1877** *Vermont Sup. Ct. Rep.* XLIX. 524 His [Isaac F. Redfield's] views upon these questions were those of the best constitutional lawyers of the country. **1898** *Kansas City Star* 20 Dec. 10/1, I would like for some of these constitutional lawyers to account for the fact that thereafter the states of North Carolina and Georgia ceded other territory. (2) **1910** *N.Y. Ev. Post* 26 Oct. 8 'Constitutional lawyer' . . . in Indiana, . . . signifies a member of the bar who was admitted to practice without any except the constitutional qualifications.

+**4.** Pertaining to the constitution of a state.

1842 *Niles' Nat. Reg.* 7 May 148 On May 4th, Wednesday, the old and regular constitutional legislature assembled at the state house at Newport. **1881** *Harper's Mag.* Jan. 316/1 The people of Kansas adopted a Constitutional amendment forbidding the manufacture and sale of intoxicating liquors except for medicinal, mechanical, or scientific purposes. **1891** *Cycl. Temperance* 98/1 In a still wider and more important sense Constitutional Prohibition is superior to Local Option.

+**5.** *Constitutional convention,* a body of delegates who meet to frame a constitution.

1843 (*title*), Journal of the Constitutional Convention of Vermont. **1865** S. ANDREWS *South since War* 188 One of the delegates to the Constitutional Convention chuckles over the fact that some of his constituents don't yet know that slavery is abolished. **1872** *Atlantic Mo.* Feb. 255 The duty of calling a constitutional convention devolves this winter on the Ohio Legislature. **1884** *Century Mag.* March 643/2 Many of the members of that Congress [in Philadelphia, 1783] were delegates to the Constitutional Convention four years later. **1910** *New Mex. Const. Convention Proc.* 3 The delegates-elect to the Constitutional Convention, to be held in accordance with the provisions of an Act of Congress. **1914** *Nation* XCVIII. 518/2 The farcical vote by which, at the special election of April 7, a Constitutional Convention for New York State next year was decreed has been the subject of much comment.

Constitutionalist. {1766–} +One who supports a constitution: **a.** In Pennsylvania politics from about 1780 to 1800, the opponents of change in the state constitution. **b.** The supporters of the U.S. Constitution against the nullifiers.

(**a**) **1782** J. ADAMS *Diary* 26 Dec. Wks. III. 353 Vaughan has a brother in Philadelphia, who has written him a long letter about the Constitutionalists and the Republicans. **1796** MORSE *Amer. Geog.* I. 564 This party was styled republicans; the other, constitutionalists [in Pennsylvania]. *a***1821** C. BIDDLE *Autobiog.* iii. 195, I found Council nearly divided between what were then called Republicans and Constitutionalists. **1890** W. G. SUMNER *Hamilton* 136 The constitutionalists—that is, supporters of the Constitution of Pennsylvania—were the opponents of the Federal Constitution. (**b**) **1802** CUTLER in *Life & Corr.* II. 100 It is most probable we may sit a week longer. The Constitutionalists say little; it only wastes time. **1833** *Niles' Reg.* XLIV. 1/1 State-rights men or constitutionalists—tariffites or anti-tariffites, &c. &c. have been so jostled that no party knows exactly where is its own present location. **1834** *U.S. Telegraph* 2 Jan., Whatever dispute remains between the Constitutionalists of the North and the quondan Nullifiers, may be settled when the common enemy [Jacksonism] is overthrown.

Constitutionality. {1801–} +The quality of being in harmony with the constitution: **a.** A state constitution. **b.** The Constitution of the U.S.

(a) 1787 A. HAMILTON *Works* VII. 9, I pass now to an examination of the constitutionality of the measure proposed by the bill. **1902** E. C. MEYER *Nominating Systems* 352 The question of the constitutionality of primary election laws has been raised in a large number of States.

(b) 1790 JEFFERSON *Writings* III. 65 The constitutionality of the bill now before the President. **1791** WASHINGTON *Writings* XII. 18 'An act to incorporate the subscribers to the Bank of the United States' is now before me for consideration. The constitutionality of it is objected to. **1802** CUTLER in *Life & Corr.* II. 77 Mr. Giles . . . took care to pass over without notice . . . every argument pertinent to the great point of Constitutionality. **1822** *Ann. 17th Congress* 1st Sess. I. 80 A duty is said to be created in them [judges] to decide upon the constitutionality of the laws of Congress. **1838** *Democratic Rev.* I. 408 As early as 1818, . . . [Kendall] called in question and thoroughly discussed the constitutionality and expediency of a bank of the United States. **1884** *Century Mag.* May 122/2 The passage of the Edmunds bill, in spite of the grave question as to its constitutionality, may have been a wise step. **1898** *Kansas City Star* 20 Dec. 10/1 (*caption*), The Constitutionality of It [=the acquisition of foreign territory].

Constitutionalize, *v.* {1831–} ‖*tr.* To make to agree or harmonize with the federal Constitution. — **1854** BENTON *30 Years' View* I. 185 It [a clause in an Act of 1812] is the language of a soldier's enlistment . . . ; and was a fiction invented to constitutionalize the act.

Constitutionally, *adv.* {1742–} +By virtue of the Constitution. — **1804** *12th Amend. Constitution* § 3 But no person constitutionally ineligible to the office of the president shall be eligible to that of vice president of the United States.

+**Constitutional Union.** Used attrib. to designate certain political groups or factions having conservative tendencies.

1. A party formed in 1850 by Georgians who opposed disunion.

1852 in A. C. Cole *Whig Party in South* 240 Let the Constitutional Union party be firm, and the South will be safe.

2. A party of southern Whigs and other conservative elements which ignored the slavery issue in the presidential campaign of 1860 and favored the continuance of the Union. Also absol.

1860 *Polit. Text-Book 1860* 29 As representatives of the Constitutional Union men of the country . . . we hereby pledge ourselves [etc.]. **1860** *Western Citizen* 11 May 3/2 Constitutional Union Convention. This body met at Baltimore on Wednesday. **1874** J. T. SCHARF *Chron. Baltimore* 576 The Constitutional Union Convention, composed almost wholly of the old Whig party and the warring organization known as the 'American' or 'Know-Nothing' party, assembled in the old Presbyterian church. **1884** BLAINE *20 Years of Congress* I. 163 The Constitutional-Union Party was in a position to make a strong canvass against Douglas. **1900** *Miss. Hist. Soc. Pub.* III. 77 A tabular view of the convention . . . shows that it was composed of 100 delegates [among which were] . . . 3 Reconstructionists, . . . 2 Constitutional Union, 2 Union Conservatives, . . . 2 Henry Clay Whigs, 4 Old Whigs.

Construct, *v.* {1610–} Quasi-passive use of the pr. ppl. *constructing:* Being constructed; being built.

This usage developed on the analogy of *building*, 'being built.'

1807 in Marshall *Kentucky* (1824) II. 425 Burr's plan of operations is, to move down . . . in light boats now constructing for that purpose. **1831** PECK *Guide* 293 The great National Road, now constructing through Ohio, Indiana, and Illinois, to the seat of government in Missouri. **1834** — *Gaz. Illinois* 199 A wharf is here [at Caledonia] constructing to secure a good landing for boats which is wanted at America. **1835** HOFFMAN *Winter in West* II. 130 The railroad, now constructing between Lexington and Frankfort, occasionally intersected our route.

* **Construction.**

***1.** The interpretation or explanation of a text, +spec. the U.S. Constitution; often modified by *liberal* or *strict.* Also attrib. and transf.

1791 *Ann. 1st Congress* II. 195 If we look at their [=Congress's] acts under the existing Constitution, we shall find they are generally the result of a liberal construction. *Ib.* 1958 The constructions of the Constitution . . . go to the subversion of every power whatever in the several States. **1792** HAMILTON *Works* VIII. 264 A disposition on my part towards a liberal construction of the powers of the national government. **1829** B. HALL *Travels in N.A.* II. 233 The framers of the Constitution took more than ordinary pains to leave nothing to implication, or to 'construction,' as it is called. **1848** POLK in *Pres. Mess. & P.* IV. 654 The enlargement of the powers of the Federal Government by construction, which obtained, was not warranted by any just interpretation of the Constitution. **1854** BENTON *30 Years' View* I. 24/1 It has been shown, after the most liberal construction of all the enumerated powers of the general government, that the territory within the limits of the respective States belonged to them. **1855** Hambleton *H. A. Wise* 205 His strict construction principles entitle him to exalted rank among the truest defenders of the constitution. **1904** *N.Y. Ev. Post* 22 Dec. 6 Tammany has never held to the theory of strict construction as to the purposes for which money may be spent at election time.

+**2.** *Construction train,* a railroad train which carries equipment for building railroad tracks. Also *construction car.*

1869 BRACE *New West* 184 Every stick of fuel, every railroad tie, and beam for trestle-work, must be carried on construction-trains from these mountains. **1873** BEADLE *Undevel. West* 397 We went over on the first locomotive which crossed: hitherto construction cars had been shoved across singly by hand. **1878** — *Western Wilds* 388 We carried our baggage a mile, across the bridge and through Fargo, Dakota, to the construction train. **1881** *Chicago Times* 18 June, The caboose of the construction train, containing workmen and several boys. **1887** C. B. GEORGE *40 Years on Rail* 193, I was in charge of a construction train, being engineer, conductor and gang-boss combined. **1888** *Harper's Mag.* March 565/2 The construction train contained box cars two and three stories high, in which workmen were boarded and lodged.

+**3.** *Construction camp,* the camplike living quarters of workmen engaged in building something.

1884 *Century Mag.* Oct. 843 Adventurers who had followed the construction camps on the Northern Pacific Railroad, and had been left stranded when that highway was completed, drifted into the new diggings. **1891** *Harper's Mag.* Nov. 887/1 It was Dunn's headquarters—the construction camp. **1925** TILGHMAN *Dugout* 3 They worked as teamsters and on the railroad construction camp.

+**4.** *Construction stock,* (see quotation).

1853 *Mich. Laws* 66 Any such [plank road] company may create and issue shares of guaranteed stock, to be denominated 'construction stock.'

+**Constructionist.** *Strict constructionist,* one who interprets the Federal Constitution strictly.

1838 *Democratic Rev.* I. 14 The attempt to maintain it [the unconstitutionality of raising money for the purpose of deposit] came with an ill grace from a strict-constructionist. **1841** *Congress. Globe* App. Jan. 260/3, I am, sir, a strict constructionist. **1845** POLK *Diary* 37, I resolved to appoint no man who was not an original Democrat and strict constructionist. **1854** BENTON 30 *Years' View* I. 3/1 Thus a great question of constitutional construction . . . three times decided by the events of war, and twice against the constitution and the strict constructionists, was decided the last time in their favor. **1903** W. F. JOHNSON *Century of Expansion* 101 He was a 'strict constructionist,' and as the Constitution did not say in so many words that the U.S. might acquire new territory, he denied the ability of the U.S. to do so.

b. In regard to various laws, the Bible, etc.

1848 S. A. ELIOT *Hist. Harvard Coll.* 58 That board, however, contained too many 'strict constructionists' of the act, to admit that clergymen of the Church of England could ever be technical teaching elders of the law. **1855** J. HOLBROOK *Among Mail Bags* 407, I am a strict constructionist, and the order says no person is allowed here except those connected with the Department. **1872** EGGLESTON *End of World* 104 Cynthy Ann was a 'strict constructionist.' **1880** WALLACE *Ben-Hur* 266 They were strict constructionists and rigorous observers of the Law. **1888** *Nation* XLVI. 245/1 He was a strict constructionist, and he was persuaded that the Bible did not forbid such marriages.

Constructive, *a.* {a1680–} Based upon the 'construction' of a document; resulting from the interpretation of the Constitution, a deed, etc.

1834 D. WEBSTER in *Congress. Deb.* 7 May 1665 The power of control and direction . . . is derived, by those who maintain it, from the right of removal: that is to say, it is a constructive power: it has an express warrant in the Constitution. **1883** *Ill. Revised Statutes* 767 Constructive mortgage. . . . Every deed conveying real estate, which shall appear to have been intended only as a security in the nature of a mortgage, though it be an absolute conveyance in terms, shall be considered as a mortgage.

+**b.** *Constructive blockade,* (see quotation).

1809 *Ann. 10th Congress* 2 Sess. 392 The second head of dispute regards the practice of constructive blockades. The complaint on this subject was, that blockades were formed by proclamations, and that neutrals were compelled to consider ports blockaded before which no force was stationed.

+**c.** *Constructive mileage,* an allowance made to members of Congress ostensibly for traveling expenses, even though they may not leave Washington.

1848 BARTLETT 224 Many of the Senators, in 1845, when Mr. Polk was inaugurated, refused to pocket their constructive mileage, holding it to be an imposition on the public. **1851** JOHNSTON *Notes N. Amer.* II. 325 Under the name of constructive mileage, members were allowed the same sum in the event of a special session being called, whether they had gone home or not. **1851** *Whig Almanac 1852* 5 In March, 1845, a new Senate was . . . convened, on Mr. Polk's accession; and, for the first time, a general allowance of Constructive Mileage was made. **1871** DE VERE 263 *Constructive mileage* is paid when the members [of Congress] are only supposed to have gone home, and to have returned to the seat of government, without having actually been absent. **1888** M. LANE in *America* 18 Oct. 15.

***Consul.**

***1.** An agent of a government, appointed to reside in a foreign city or port, to deal chiefly with commercial matters.

1778 *Jrnls. Cont. Congress* XI. 443 The two contracting parties grant, mutually, the liberty of having each in the ports of the other, consuls, vice-consuls [etc.]. **1787** *Constitution* ii. § 2 He shall nominate, and . . . appoint Ambassadors, other public Ministers and Consuls. **1841** *Diplom. Corr. Texas* I. 499, I also send you extracts of a letter from Cincinnati . . . pointing out the necessity of the recognition of a Consul for Texas, at that place. **1886** SCHUYLER *Amer. Diplomacy* 95 A consul is appointed . . . without preliminary examination, on the nomination of the President, and is confirmed by the Senate.

+2. *Consul's man,* (see quotation).

1824 W. N. BLANE *Excursion U.S.* 2 In addition to our crew, we had on board several 'Consul's men,' as they are called. An American seaman, if in distress in a foreign country, has only to inform his Consul that he wishes to return home; and is immediately sent on board some American vessel, returning to the United States. The government allows ten dollars for his passage; and at that price every vessel is obliged to take a certain number of these men.

***Consular,** *a.* Pertaining to a consul or the duties of consuls; composed of consuls. {1830– (*Parl. P., Acc. & P.* XXI. No. 684)}

1789 *Ann. 1st Congress* I. 51 *Ordered,* That the Secretary of Foreign Affairs attend the Senate to-morrow, and bring with him such papers as are requisite to give full information relative to the consular convention between France and the United States. **1790** *State P.* (1819) I. 19 The Consular Convention too with his Most Christian Majesty, has stipulated . . . the aid of the national authority to his consuls established here. **1839** *S. Lit. Messenger* V. 6/1 Of late years . . . the consular letter bag has been made up in the New York post office. **1877** *Harper's Mag.* March 627/1 The Consular and Diplomatic Appropriation Bill was passed by the House January 12. **1886** SCHUYLER *Amer. Diplomacy* 101 As consuls are in no sense political officers, there is no reason . . . why the principles of Civil Service Reform should not be applied to the consular system. **1896** CLEVELAND in *Pres. Mess. & P.* IX. 722 The scheme of examining applicants for certain consular positions to test their competency and fitness, adopted under an Executive order issued on the 20th of September, 1895, has fully demonstrated the usefulness of this innovation.

fig. **1910** O. JOHNSON *Varmint* I. 13 Consular Jimmy . . . glanced behind at the only other passenger, a man of consular mould, and they looked at Stover in sardonic amusement. *Ib.* 99 Directly in front of him . . . sat the big consular frame of his stage companion of the day before.

+b. *Consular seal,* a wine from abroad that has been sealed by a consul.

1870 R. TOMES *Decorum* 140 All smacking of the lips, even over your host's finest Tokay, Consular Seal, or Burgundy, is but a barbarous mode of expressing an appreciation of vinous excellence.

***Consulary.** ‖*Consulary men,* (?) men who had been councillors. — **1718** SEWALL *Diary* III. 196 Col. Pynchon and Mr. Cooke Consulary Men were there. **1720** *Ib.* 249 Gov[erno]r Dudley is buried. . . . Councillours and Ministers had Scarvs, and Consulary men.

***Consulate.** The office or jurisdiction of a consul {1702–}; also, the premises occupied by a consul. {1848–}

1791 *Ann. 2nd Congress* 34 The copies of the said acts, duly authenticated by the said consuls or vice consuls, under the seal of their consulates. **1800** J. ADAMS *Works* IX. 77, I received . . . the representation of three masters of vessels . . . relative to the consulate of Madeira. **1884** *Century Mag.* April 811/2 He is no more required to examine petitions and hear applications concerning all the post-offices, consulates, and collectorships, than he is to buckle on a saber, mount a horse, and maneuver the troops. **1916** DU PUY *Uncle Sam* 59 Billy Gard managed to get ashore and find his way to the American consulate.

Consul general. {1753–} A consul or head consul stationed at an important place.

'*Consuls general* are charged with the ordinary duties of a consul, but have supervisory powers over the consulates and consular agencies within their consular districts' (McLaughlin & Hart *Cycl. Amer. Govt.* I. 449).

1812 *Ann. 12th Congress* 2 Sess. 152 Another Message was received . . . transmitting copies of a letter from the Consul General of the United States to Algiers. **1836** *Diplom. Corr. Texas* I. 156 John Woodward Esqr. has been appointed by this Govt consul general of this republic for the ports of Boston. **1858** BUCHANAN in *Pres. Mess. & P.* V. 506 Through the energetic yet conciliatory efforts of our consul-general in Japan a new treaty has been concluded with that Empire. **1886** SCHUYLER *Amer. Diplomacy* 67 At Matamoras the Consul-General in addition to the ordinary consular duties, has to try to prevent smuggling along the line of the Rio Grande.

***Consumption.** A wasting disease that attacks the lungs and other organs; esp. tuberculosis of the lungs. {1651–}

1731 HEMPSTEAD *Diary* 232 Richd Morgan . . . died of a Consumption. **1775** FITHIAN *Journal* II. 121 His disorder was consumption. When I came in he was too far wasted to converse; his body, even his breast, was cold. **1783** CUTLER in *Life & Corr.* II. 211 Consumption, by which the Physicians intend a disorder of the lungs. *c***1820** HARMON *Journal* (1903) 271 The venereal complaint is common to all the tribes [of Indians] of the north; many die of a consumption. **1831** PECK *Guide* 233, I have not yet seen half a dozen cases of the genuine New England consumption in all my travels, and but few of asthma. **1835** HOFFMAN *Winter in West* I. 130 Consumption, for instance, which a reference to the bills of mortality will show destroys almost as many in New-York . . . as does the yellow-fever in New-Orleans—is here unknown. **1855** GLISAN *Jrnl. Army Life* 188 To be doomed by the insidious progress of the most fatal of all maladies, consumption. **1891** WILKINS *New Eng. Nun* 156 People said she had the old-fashioned consumption.

b. *Thirty years'* (etc.) *consumption,* slow tuberculosis.

1842 *Lowell Offering* II. 4 Did you ever hear of the 'thirty years' consumption'? a disease at present unknown in New England. **1881** MCLEAN *Cape Cod Folks* 214 It's pretty hard to have forty years' consumption and then go off with a fever.

c. *Quick* or *rapid consumption,* tuberculosis that runs a rapid course.

1865 *Atlantic Mo.* XV. 316 He had been forced . . . to abandon a snug abode, . . . and was now prostrate on his bed, dying of rapid consumption. **1875** *Chicago Tribune* 31 Oct. 3/6 If I notice one trying to put down the car window and it refuses to budge, I look the other way, and hope the cold stream of air will give her the quick consumption. **1896** FREDERIC *Damnation Theron Ware* 414 Michael . . . has been seized with quick consumption. He will hardly last till snow flies.

+Consumption root. A perennial herb (genus *Pyrola*) of the heath family. — **1784** CUTLER in *Mem. Academy* I. 444 *Pyrola*. . . . Consumption-Root. Blossoms white; in woodland. July. **1795** WINTERBOTHAM *Hist. View* III. 398 Among the native and uncultivated plants of New-England, the following have been employed for medical purposes: . . . Bistort, . . . Spice wood, or feverbush, . . . Consumption root.

+Consumptive's weed. The bear's weed or yerba santa (*Eriodictyon glutinosum*) of California. — **1889** *Cent.* 1221/1.

Contact. {1626–} +In mining, the plane of rock lying between layers of dissimilar rock. Also attrib. — **1871** RAYMOND *3rd Rep. Mines* 262 It is . . . a contact vein, porphyry forming the hanging and syenite the foot wall. **1899** NORRIS *McTeague* 404 Here's a 'contact' and here it is again, and there, and yonder. . . . That's grano-diorite on slate. **1923** BOWER *Parowan Bonanza* 13, I'm hoping it'll run into higher values when I hit the contact.

+Contador. *S.* [Sp.] An accountant or collector. — **1803** in *Ann. 8th Congress* 2 Sess. 1521 The Contador, Treasurer, and Interventor, are officers subordinate to the Intendant. The first . . . keeps all accounts and documents respecting the receipt and expenditure of the revenue; and is, therefore, a check upon the Intendant. **1809** F. CUMING *Western Tour* 312, I returned to my friend Egan's, who accompanied me to the house of Don Gilbert Leonard, the contador (or collector).

Contest. {1643–} +A legal, or quasi-legal, dispute over a land grant. — **1877** JOHNSON *Anderson Co., Kansas* 87 And the board then appointed James Y. Campbell as agent to represent the county in the contest for the lands. **1898** *Mo. So. Dakotan* I. 14 It is related of him that in the course of the contest for this land, he walked all the way from Yankton to Washington to argue his own case before the general land office.

Contestant. {1665; 1870–}

1. *Mil.* A member, or unit, of an army which is fighting the enemy for a particular position.

'Common during Civil War in U.S. and since' (*O.E.D.*).

*a***1860** SEWARD in Worcester. **1861** *N.Y. Tribune* 26 Oct. 8/3 A little after 6 o'clock the remaining contestants withdrew down the precipitous river bank, and endeavored to recross to the island.

+2. An unsuccessful candidate for office who challenges the validity of the election returns.

1870 *Congress. Globe* 16 Feb. 1342/2 Nor can [this House] . . . ever have presented to them a more unfounded and spurious pretension to a seat on this floor than that exhibited by the contestant, Charles H. Van Wyck. **1872** *Ill. Rev. Statutes* 515 The contestant shall . . . serve on the person whose election he will contest, a notice of his intention. **1896** *Congress. Rec.* 9 June 6335/2 In this manner there were 5 colored votes unlawfully refused which would have been cast for the contestant.

+3. A participator in a friendly contest or competition.

'Until recent years it [*contestant*] has been seldom used in Eng. In Am., on the other hand, it has long occupied the place of the Eng. *competitor*' (Horwill 82). Evidence earlier than 1900 has, however, not been found.

1902 J. CORBIN *Amer. at Oxford* 135 The friends of the various contestants make up a far larger audience than one finds at similar sports in America. **1903** WHARTON *Sanctuary* 89 The designs being submitted to a jury of architects who voted on them without knowing the names of the contestants.

Contested election. An election the result of which is disputed. Also attrib. {1771–}

This use, once current in England, is now confined to the U.S. 'In Eng. a *contested election* is one at which there is more than one candidate for a vacancy; i.e. where there is a contest, and not an unopposed return' (Horwill 82).

1794 *Ann. 3rd Congress* 42 *Resolved,* That the doors of the Senate be opened, and continue open, during the discussion upon the contested election of Albert Gallatin. **1797** *Ann. 5th Congress* I. 639 Mr. Harper said, he should lay upon the table some resolutions respecting the mode of taking evidence in contested elections. **1870** *Daily Morning Chron.*

21 Feb. 1/2 Since this Congress began there were 35 contested election cases. **1924** Beard *Amer. Govt.* 229 The House of Representatives and the Senate are the judges of the election, returns, and qualifications of their own members, and therefore contested elections are not determined by a judicial tribunal as in England.

+Contestee. One against whom a contesting claim is brought, esp. in a contested election. (Cf. Contestant 2.)

1870 *Congress. Globe* 16 Feb. 1340/2 In these three precincts the majority of the contestee is larger than his majority on the return. **1887** *Statutes at Large* XXIV. 445 Upon receipt of the contestee's brief the clerk shall forward two copies thereof to the contestant. **1888** *Troy Daily Times* 4 Feb. (F.), O'Ferral of Virginia spoke in support of the majority resolution, and contended that the contestee, James B. White, had failed utterly to make proof of his naturalization. **1896** *Congress. Rec.* 9 June 6333/1 Two hundred and twenty votes were found to be there for the contestee.

+Conthieveracy. An abusive name for the Southern Confederacy, coined to show indignation for the confiscation of U.S. property. — **1861** *N.Y. Tribune* 15 July, A boat . . . communicated to the officers of the Preble all the particulars of the depredations of the piratical craft, named after the President of the Southern 'Conthieveracy.' **1862** Browne *A. Ward His Book* 196 You're too small powder for me! sed the President of the conthieveracy. **1867** *Atlantic Mo.* March 278/1 Across the level marshes there came a nasal sound, as of the 'Conthieveracy' in its slumbers. It may have been a bull-frog, but it sounded like a human snore.

*** Continent.**

1. A main body of land. {1614–} In Amer. usage the reference, when not otherwise specified, is to the N.A. continent.

1648 Shepard *Clear Sunshine* 56 The beginnings and foundations of the Spaniards in the Southern parts of this vast continent . . . shall certainly therefore bee utterly rooted up. **1705** *Boston News-Letter* 9 April 2/2 Several Prints from England . . . are ordered to come by all Vessels coming to our Continent. **1760** *N.J. Archives* XX. 514 Now we the . . . Creditors of the said Myer Levy, do hereby request the Assistance of . . . every well disposed Person, either on the Continent, or in the West India Islands, to apprehend the said Myer Levy. **1784** Filson *Kentucke* 27 Serpents . . . are such as are to be found in other parts of the continent, except the bull, the horned and the mockason snakes. **1838** *Democratic Rev.* I. 207 It was objected that, by the separation, Upper Canada would be insulated in the interior of the continent. **1862** in F. Moore *Rebellion Rec.* V. II. 462 Thus ended one of the hardest battles ever fought on this continent. **1887** G. B. Thayer (*title*), Pedal and Path. Across the Continent Awheel and Afoot.

+b. The territory of the colonies. *Obs.*

The early American view that the whole North American continent was ultimately to be controlled by the English-speaking American serves to explain this usage. (Cf. sense 1, quots. 1648, 1705.)

1769 *Boston Rec.* 300 Resolved, That many of the Letters & Memorials aforesaid are false scandalous and infamous Libels upon the Inhabitants of this Town, Province and Continent. *Ib.* 324 Much less will it [=revised revenue act] remove the grounds of the discontent, which runs thro' the Continent, upon much higher principles. **1789** *Ann. 1st Congress* I. 161, I believe we have only to try the experiment [of taxing salt], to be convinced it would have a similar effect throughout the Continent.

+c. *fig.* The people living within this territory. *Obs.*

1774 Morris in Sparks *Life G. Morris* I. 27 Uniting the whole continent in one grand legislature. **1776** T. Hutchinson *Diary & Lett.* II. 64 He says ye Colonists are prepared for every Thing that can happen; the whole Continent in arms. **1798** Allen *Hist. Vermont* 56 The battle of Lexington, threw the whole continent into a ferment.

+2. A collective name for the general government over the colonies and states during the War of the Revolution, as distinct from the individual states and from the British authorities. *Obs.*

1775 J. Adams *Works* IX. 363, I am to inquire what number of seamen . . . would probably enlist in the service, either . . . in the pay of the continent or in the pay of the province. **1777** *Md. Hist. Mag.* V. 207, I have sent the Commissary to provide for us at Gloster, where I am inform'd there are Some provisions belonging to the Continent. **1777** *Jrnls. Cont. Congress* VII. 15 *Resolved,* That . . . Mr. Pennel be directed . . . not to bid upon others purchasing for the Continent. **1777** Hamilton *Works* VII. 481 He considered the Continent at all times bound to make good the number borrowed from your State. **1781** Jefferson *Writings* IV. 174 There are some collections of forage and provisions belonging to the Continent, and some to the State.

Continental, *n.* {1828–}

+1. A soldier or former soldier in the Continental army.

1777 *Md. Hist. Mag.* V. 210 Perhaps it would be in your Excellency's power to spare 3 or 400 Continentals. **1781** H. Clinton *Narrative* (1783) 97 General Washington's letter . . . intimates, that there will be opposed to his Lordship, above two thousand Continentals more than General Green had with him before. **1807** Irving, etc. *Salmagundi* xi. 268, A squabble . . . took place between two old continentals. **1823** J. Thacher *Journal* 93 Colonel Whitcomb with a party of continentals was ordered to pursue the Indians. **1845** *Yale Lit. Mag.* XI. 40 (Th.), The 'Old Continentals,' of which our grandfathers tell, would have been most arrant cowards in comparison with a regiment of our modern heroes. **1860** Whittier *Home Ballads* 49 Each war-scarred Continental, Leaving smithy, mill, and farm, Waved his rusted sword in welcome.

+b. A supporter of the American cause, opposed to the British or the loyalists.

1781 *Independent Ledger* 24 Dec., Come all Continentals, who Washington love, The pride of Columbia, the fav'rite of Jove.

+2. A flag borne by Continental troops.

1834 C. A. Davis *Lett. J. Downing* 24 The wind kinder shook 'em all together so you couldn't tell a checkered shirt from an old Continental.

+b. In *pl.* The uniform worn by a soldier in the Continental army.

1887 *Scribner's Mag.* (F.), The Englishman . . . will know one thing, the Yankee, who contemplates his grandfather in continentals above the chimney-piece, will know another.

+3. *ellipt.* Currency issued by the authority of the Continental Congress. Also pl.

1783 Freneau *Poems* (1786) 323 That damnable bubble the old Continental That took people in at this wonderful crisis. **1821** Cooper *Spy* xvi, If it's silver or goold . . . it's but little I have, though I've a trifling bit of the continental. **1825** J. Neal *Bro. Jonathan* I. 159, 'I outs with a handful o' the right stuff; old continental'—paper money issued by the colonies. **1835** Bird *Hawks of Hawk-H.* I. 246 Were I a rebel, you would have found naught but a roll of beggarly continentals. **1842** in Benton *30 Years' View* II. 392 Within you have a few continentals, or promises to pay in gold or silver, which may now be serviceable to the Treasury. **1845** Cooper *Chainbearer* ii, I had provided myself with a little silver . . . and some thirty or forty thousand dollars of 'continental,' to defray my traveling expenses.

+b. *Not to give* or *care a continental,* to have no regard. (Cf. the adj. 3.)

1872 'Mark Twain' *Roughing It* xlvii. 334 He didn't give a continental for anybody. **1874** B. F. Taylor *World on Wheels* II. 203 'Port' . . . said he did not care a 'Continental' for the whole business. **1888** *Missouri Republican* 16 Feb. (F.), I am not worrying about the nomination. . . . I don't care a continental if I don't receive it. **1898** Hamblen *Gen. Manager's Story* 70, I don't know nor care a continental who you are. **1904** W. H. Smith *Promoters* 170 They don't give a continental whether the stock of the Experimental Sky Bombarding Company ever pays a cent or not.

Continental, *a.* {1760–}

+1. Pertaining to, of, the N.A. continent.

1760 Franklin *Writings* IV. 47, I entirely agree . . . that we are in North America 'a far greater continental as well as naval power.' **1781** Peters *History Conn.* (1829) 162 This quarrel continued till 1764, when it subsided in a grand continental consociation of ministers. **1855** in Hambleton *H. A. Wise* 247 The stranger who consults the chart of our Continental Republic, hardly discovers our State amid her leviathan sisters. **1910** *Nation* XCI. 569 All this relates to 'Continental United States'—a term which seems to be coming into use for the continuous region we usually think of as the United States exclusive of Alaska.

+b. *Continental divide,* the divide which separates the watersheds of the Pacific from those of the Atlantic. *C. backbone,* (see Backbone 1).

1868 W. J. Palmer *Surveys Across Continent* 171 The great Continental Divide at Arkansas Pass. **1891** *Scribner's Mag.* X. 215 The road . . . re-crossed the main range, the highest ridge of the continental backbone. **1923** J. H. Cook *On Old Frontier* 4 In 1882 I am quite sure that I saw seven of them on the west side of the Continental divide, in Grant County, New Mexico.

+2. Of or pertaining to the colonies or states collectively during the War of the Revolution or to the general government formed by them.

1774 in J. Adams *Works* IX. 344 There is an opinion . . . that the Massachusetts gentlemen . . . do affect to dictate and take the lead in continental measures. **1775** in *Amer. Hist. Review* I. 304, I recd. from the Continental Treasury the 1000 Dollars lately advanced to our Com[mitt]ee of Safety. **1778** *Mass. H. S. Coll.* 2 Ser. II. 448 [We] drove off 90 head of Continental Fat Cattle. **1782** *Ann. S. W. Virginia* 774 Richard Trimbel produced satisfactory proof . . . that he ought to be paid the sum of £ 27 for drawing a Continental waggon twelve months. **1787** Cutler in *Life & Corr.* I. 254 Members of the Continental Convention, now convened in this city for the purpose of forming a Federal Constitution. **1893** 'Thanet' *Stories* 182 He recalled how, as a boy, he had gone to a fancy-dress ball in Continental smallclothes, so small that he had been strictly cautioned . . . not to bow.

+b. Esp. in reference to the army and navy.

1775 *Jrnls. Cont. Congress* II. 84 *Resolved:* That the Provincial Convention of New York be requested to convey . . . five thousand barrels of flour for the use of the Continental Army. **1775** *Mass. Spy* 20 Oct. 3/3 As the time for which the present army is raised will expire in 2 or 3 months, these gentlemen . . . are appointed to meet and confer with his Excellency General Washington on the subject of forming and establishing another Continental Army. **1776** in Johnston *N. Hale* 155, I proposed going with Dudley, who is appointed to Comm[a]n[d] a Twenty Gun Ship in the Continental Navy. **1778** *Md. Jrnl.* 24 March (Th.), Came to my house on the night of the 14th inst., a Continental soldier. **1796** *Ann. 4th Congress* 2 Sess. 1703 Captain Harris had eighteen months' pay due to him as an officer in the late Continental Army. **1823** J. THACHER *Journal* 66 The continental army consisted of ten thousand five hundred and fourteen effectives only. **1860** CLAIBORNE *Sam. Dale* i. 28 We raised a subscription and bought an old Continental uniform coat, the best in the fort, for the negro fellow.

+**c.** As applied to the currency and securities of the Confederation.

1776 *Jrnls. Cont. Congress* V. 432 Colonel Roberdeau, . . . having tendered to Congress the moiety belonging to them, in exchange for continental dollars [bills of credit]. **1784** *Mass. Centinel* 4 Sept. 3/2 Bought, Sold, and Negotiated, at the Land Office, . . . Continental Certificates, and every other kind of publick securities. **1790** *Steele Papers* I. 65, I am well informed that six millions of our Continental Securities are now in the hands of persons living in Holland. **1854** BENTON *30 Years' View* I. 440/1 Our own country filled up with Spanish milled dollars . . . at the conclusion of the Revolutionary War, and the suppression of the continental bills. **1862** S. BRECK *Let. to B. J. Lossing* (*Stand.*), I have seen a barber shop in Boston papered with Continental Money.

+**3.** As a term of disparagement, on account of the depreciation and repudiation of the 'Continental money.' *colloq.*

1841 SIMMS *Kinsmen* I. 98, I wouldn't give a continental copper for the safety of your skin. **1851** *Knickerb.* XXXVII. 554 That clock you sold me ain't worth a continental cuss. **1874** EGGLESTON *Circuit Rider* 148, I tole him as how I didn't keer three continental derns fer his whole band. **1879** TOURGEE *Fool's Errand* 259 These carpet-baggers don't care a continental cuss how many niggers your ancestors had. **1890** *Amer. Notes & Q.* V. 169 'A Tinker's Dam' is equivalent to the expression, 'A Continental Damn.'

+**Continental Congress.** The general assembly of delegates from the colonies and states during the War of the Revolution.

This term embraces both the first and second congresses of the Revolution. The first met on Sept. 5, 1774 at Philadelphia, and adjourned Oct. 26th. The second met in Philadelphia on May 10, 1775.

1774 in *Jrnls. Cont. Congress* II. 13 *Resolved*, that the proceedings of the American Continental Congress held at Philadelphia, on the fifth day of September last . . . have . . . been considered by us. **1775** FITHIAN *Journal* II. 4 We hear the Continental Congress began business yesterday. **1775** *Penna. Packet* 22 May, The Honorable Members of the Continental Congress were pleased to proceed in a body from the State-House to the College. **1776** *Battle of Brooklyn* II iv, It is one of the baits that the Continental Congress threw out, for the people of America to bite at. **1841** *Knickerb.* XVII. 373 When General Schuyler arrived at Albany in July, 1775, to take charge of the military command in the department of New-York, under his recent appointment from the Continental Congress, a public reception was given him. **1871** *Scribner's Mo.* I. 234 Charles Thompson, first and long the confidential secretary of the Continental Congress.

+**Continentaler. 1.** A soldier in the Continental army. **2.** A musket of the type used during the War of Independence. — (1) **1775** in *Harper's Mag.* LXII. 639/2 Come out ye Continentallers! We're going for to go To fight the red-coat enemy. **1850** H. C. WATSON *Camp-Fires Revol.* 41 The continentallers . . . were ordered to march to Bunker Hill. (2) **1857** *Mag. of Travel* I. 180 [An Iowa pioneer is speaking:] I don't want none of yer brass and German fixens round my old Continentaler.

+**Continental fast.** A fast recommended by Congress for the nation in dedication to the principles of the Revolutionary War. — **1775** FITHIAN *Journal* II. 47 A number of the town gentlemen proposed, if my appointments will allow me, to preach in this town on the day of the Continental Fast. **1780** CUTLER in *Life & Corr.* I. 77 Continental Fast and Annual for this State [Massachusetts]. Preached.

Continentalist. {1834-} +An advocate of a federal government for the revolted colonies after the Revolutionary War. — **1781** A. HAMILTON (*title*), The Continentalist.

+**Continentally,** *adv.* **1.** In reference to American interests, esp. those of the Continental Congress, as opposed to the British or loyalists. **2.** *fig.* With wide views or extensive sympathies. — (1) **1783** HAMILTON in Sparks *Corr. Revol.* IV. 22 They are the men who think Continentally. (2) **1883** *Amer. Home Missionary Soc. 57th Rep.* 100 If there ever was a time when Christians needed to accustom their minds to larger things, when they needed to think 'continentally,' it is now.

+**Continental money.** A currency of paper notes issued by the Continental Congress.

At first (June, 1775) continental money was issued in moderation but later it became so inflated that the government redeemed it at forty to one (March, 1780) and even a hundred to one (1790).

1775 *Jrnls. Cont. Congress* II. 207 That each gentleman who signs the continental money, be . . . paid out of the continental treasury, one Dollar and one third of a dollar for each and every thousand bills signed and numbered by him. **1776** *Wyllys Papers* 449, I can inform you of nothing more than of my good health: and that Continental Money will not pass in N. York. **1780** in W. B. Reed *Life Jos. Reed* II. 200 The Continental money has evidently appreciated and still goes on, though slowly. **1812** *Ann. 12th Congress* 1 Sess. II. 1498 The old Congress issued paper not bearing interest, called Continental money, which entitled the holder to the sum expressed on the face, without any pledge to reimburse at a given time. **1838** CLAY *Speeches* (1842) 349 Then we should have the days of continental money, and of assignats, restored! **1844** 'UNCLE SAM' *Peculiarities* II. 209 My old grandmother has a hundred thousand dollars of the revolutionary continental money, which Uncle Sam never paid.

Contingency fund. In accounting, a fund set aside to take care of unforeseen expenditures dependent upon future events. Also *Contingent fund.* — **1881** *Rep. Indian Affairs* p. xli, I consented to have the . . . expense paid from the contingency funds of the Indian Department. **1886** ALTON *Among Law-Makers* 275 Some of the members of the House endeavored to have similar refreshments [=iced tea and lemonade] ordered out of its contingent fund!

***Continuance.** The adjournment of a suit or trial to a later term of court.

'In England now *Obs.* in civil processes' (*O.E.D.*).

1730 *Md. Hist. Mag.* VIII. 159 (Lawyer's bill), To appearance & continuance in May. **1828** WEBSTER, *Continuance*, . . . in the United States, the deferring of a trial or suit from one stated term of the court to another. **1845** HOOPER *Simon Suggs' Adv.* xi. 135 The Captain whispered to his lawyer, and urged him to put him on the stand, and make a showing for a continuance. **1885** *Century Mag.* XXX. 331/2 It is on account of the long intervals between terms that continuances (which now constitute the chief means of the 'postponement swindle') are so eagerly sought. **1888** *Chicago Inter-Ocean* 14 March 2/3 Boylan and Needham insisted they were innocent and asked for a continuance. It was granted. **1902** MCFAUL *Ike Glidden* 285 Every time our lawyer pressed the case for a trial Burgess has secured a continuance on the ground of inability to have his witness present.

***Continuation.** *pl.* Orig., gaiters continuous with knee breeches; later, a playful euphemism for trousers. {1825-}

1833 E. T. COKE *Subaltern's Furlough* i, He came down stairs the very beau ideal of a dandy, . . . with his nether man cased in a pair of red striped 'continuations.' **1848** W. E. BURTON *Waggeries* 74 An orthodox Quaker, with an undeniable and buttonless shad-bellied coat and drab continuations. **1852** BRISTED *Upper Ten Th.* iii. 77 [He] regularly put himself into a dress coat and black continuations. **1859** *Harper's Mag.* Sept. 574/2 A tall, slim stranger, with white hat, . . . drab coat, and checkered continuations, was seen upon the track.

***Continue,** *v. Law. tr.* To adjourn; to keep (a case) on the calendar for further consideration. — **1797** DALLAS *Ct. Rep.* II. 44 The cause was continued on a rule for trial at the next term. **1890** *Boston Jrnl.* 23 May 1/6 He appeared before Judge Sanger of the District court in Cambridge this morning, and has his case continued until June 4. **1912** RAINE *Brand Blotters* 163 Her father returned with the news that the 'Monte Cristo' contest had been continued to another term of court.

+**Continued sixes.** 'Six per cent. bonds issued in 1861 and 1863, redeemable in 1881, and at that time continued at 3½ per cent' (*Cent.* 5662/2).

Continuous, *a.* {1673-} +Applied to performances of vaudeville: Proceeding without intermission from early afternoon to closing time. — **1895** *N.Y. Dramatic News* 6 July 17/4 Union Square Theatre Devoted to Mr. Keith's Original idea Continuous Performance. *Ib.* 16 Nov. 13/2 Another new departure in continuous vaudeville will be made November 18, at the Pleasure Palace. **1903** ADE *In Babel* 280 When these continuous shows started, so that she could go any afternoon and get a good seat for thirty cents, she got crazy on the theater.

+**Continuous-service certificate.** 'Continuous service certificate, a certificate issued to enlisted men in the United States navy who reënlist at the expiration of their term of service' (*Cent.*).

***Contraband.**

***1.** Articles or goods banned from commerce by some authority; smuggled goods; goods prohibited during war time (esp. as *contraband of war*). Freq. attrib. with *goods*, etc.

1775 *R.I. Commerce* II. 5 We have full information that the above Schooner was loaded with Contraband Goods. **1776** *Jrnls. Cont. Congress* V. 585 This Liberty of Navigation and Commerce shall extend to all Kinds of Merchandizes, excepting those only which are distinguished by the Name of Contraband: and under this Name of Contraband, or prohibited goods, shall be comprehended Arms, Great Guns [etc.]. **1793** *State P.* I. 39 It seemed . . . to be my duty, to admonish our citizens of the consequences of a contraband trade. **1842** *Diplom. Corr. Texas* I. 608 If articles Contraband of War should be found on board, they are still liable to seizure and detention for adjudication. **1857** E. STONE *Life Howland* 35 The Gaspee armed schooner . . . under pretence of searching for contraband goods chased a New York packet. **1869** BROWNE *Adv. Apache Country* 249, I am informed by merchants of Sonora that this harbor has been always used for landing contraband goods. **1911** *Okla. Session Laws* 3 Legisl. 162 The sworn complaint of affidavit . . . shall constitute *prima facie* evidence of the contraband character of the property and things seized.

+**2.** Spec., a Negro that escaped from slavery in the Confederacy to the Union lines. In full *Contraband of war.*

'The term was first employed by Gen. B. F. Butler, in the time of the Great Rebellion (1861)' (W. '64).

(1) **1861** in J. Parton *Butler in New Orleans* (1864) 127 These men are Contraband of War; set them at work. **1861** E. COWELL *Diary* 392 Fugitive slaves begin to flock into camps, since Gen. Butler pronounced them

'contraband of war.' **1862** KETTELL *Hist. Rebellion* I. 147 General Butler . . . issued an order declaring them 'contraband of war,' and ordered the able-bodied to be employed.

(2) **1861** NEWELL *Orpheus C. Kerr* I. 342 Just skin that horse and let me have his frame for a numble chaple, wherein to convert contrabands. **1862** NORTON *Army Lett.* 79 Contrabands are pouring in on us every day. Almost every officer has one or two along now. **1862** MCCLELLAN in *Own Story* 367 All the information obtained from balloons, deserters, prisoners, and contrabands agrees. **1863** in F. Moore *Rebellion Rec.* V. I. 1 The large number of persons known as 'contrabands' flocking to the protection of the United States flag. **1864** S. COX *In Congress* (1865) 357, I would beseech you to go into the camps of the contrabands . . . who are starving and pining for their old homes. **1906** *Springfield W. Republican* 15 Feb. 8 At one time he had under his charge 150,000 of 'contrabands'; many of these he placed on abandoned plantations, and 70,000 of these able-bodied men were enlisted as soldiers.

+**b.** Attrib. with *camp, hue, slave.*

1865 SCHURZ in *39th Congress 1 Sess.* Sen. Ex. Doc. No. 2, 15 The government was feeding the colored refugees, who could not be advantageously employed, in the so-called contraband camps. **1867** *Atlantic Mo.* Nov. 609/1 After the play, Rice, having shaded his own countenance to the 'contraband' hue, ordered Cuff to disrobe, and proceeded to invest himself in the cast-off apparel. **1886** LOGAN *Great Conspiracy* 381 The Contraband-Slave question, however, continued to agitate the public mind for many months.

Contrabandist. {1818-} A smuggler. — **1813** *Columbian Centinel* 28 Aug. 2/3 An expedition has been fitted out below to destroy the nest of French and creole Contrabandists and Pirates, who have so long . . . bid defiance to the law.

***Contract.**

***1.** An agreement, compact, or covenant.

1628 *Va. House Burgesses Jrnl.* App. 122 Those late contracts on our Tobacco [were] intended & made w[i]thout our consents. **1694** *N.C. Col. Rec.* I. 409 The s[ai]d Hassold unjustly detaineth certaine writing ac-c[oun]ts and bookes relating to contracts and copartnerships. **1775** *Jrnls. Cont. Congress* III. 367 Certain frauds have been attempted in executing contracts for the Continent. **1843** *Diplom. Corr. Texas* III. 1119 Touching the Colonization Contracts I will state [etc.]. **1898** PAGE *Red Rock* 38 Though Bolter had gone to Washington, he had not gone to war, but to see about contracts.

b. Spec., an agreement for building something; a construction contract. {1881}

1873 *Newton Kansan* 3 April 3/4 A new hotel . . . is now under contract. **1901** MERWIN & WEBSTER *Calumet 'K'* 1 The contract for the two million bushel grain elevator, Calumet K, had been let to McBride & Company, of Minneapolis. *Ib.* 329 He told me that we've got a contract for a new house at Indianapolis.

+**2.** *fig.* An enterprise; an undertaking. *colloq.*

1881 HAYES *New Colorado* 87 A person should carefully study his temperament and possible disabilities before he takes a contract to go into a deep shaft. *Ib.* 159 Here, too, was Armijo to have annihilated General Kearny, but for the unfortunate circumstance of his troops declining, as they say in the West, 'to take the contract.' **1891** E. S. ELLIS *Check No. 2134* 50 Any person might well shrink from the contract of corralling a couple [of such men].

3. *attrib.* Being subject to, conforming to, or requiring, a contract. {1665-}

1813 *Ann. 12th Congress* 2 Sess. 110 What is the contract price of the arms contracted for under authority of the act? **1866** *39th Congress 1 Sess.* Sen. Ex. Doc. No. 27, 60 In returning the labor contract bill, he [=the Governor of Alabama] states [etc.]. **1869** *Ill. Agric. Soc. Trans.* VII. 420 A large number of contract cattle were delivered this month. **1880** F. ROE *Army Lett.* 242 A young contract surgeon, who has been recently appointed, will go with us, and our Chinese cook will go also. **1881** *Rep. Indian Affairs* 3 The contract teacher arrived with his wife and babe. **1900** S. A. NELSON *A B C Wall St.* 135 *Contract grade*, the grade of wheat delivered in fulfillment of future contracts. *c***1900** R. L. HALE *Log of Forty-Niner* 141 The coolies were contract labourers, and were secured from China by agents. **1911** JENKS & LAUCK *Immigration Problem* 338 In some cases our government has emphasized too strongly our contract labor law, so that individuals whose service in special lines of employment would be distinctly beneficial to the country have been excluded.

4. *Contract system*, a system or practice of doing or letting work only under contract.

1860 *36th Congress 1 Sess.* H. R. Rep. No. 249, 65 Question. They [types used in printing] were used by whom? Answer. By Wendell & Van Benthuysen, under their contract system. **1866** *39th Congress 1 Sess.* Sen. Ex. Doc. No. 27, 60, I found the contract system established here [=Ala.], practically and in orders. The planters liked it, and so vigorously demanded contracts that there was danger they would not undertake to plant at all without them. **1883** *Century Mag.* July 397 Under the contract system the Ring had many thousand men in its pay.

b. A scheme that permits a private contractor to employ convicts. Also *contract-labor system.*

1884 *Century Mag.* Feb. 583/2 These [systems of prison management] are known as the Public Accounts System and the Contract System. **1885** *Ib.* April 828 He was speaking against the convict contract-labor system.

+**Contracting agent.** (See quot.) — **1859** *Harper's Mag.* Aug. 425 The freight lines represented in New York employ a small army of freight solicitors, or, as they delight to call themselves, 'contracting agents.'

***Contraction.** +The reduction of the volume of currency in circulation. — **1875** *Nation* XXI. 113/1 A decision in favor . . . of inflation that will be the same thing as contraction . . . will certainly bring about one of the most tremendous financial catastrophes ever witnessed. **1875** *Chicago Tribune* 8 Nov. 4/3 In this statement is substantially contained the whole objection of the great multitude of persons who . . . assert that resumption or 'contraction' would ruin the whole 'debtor class.' **1892** *Nation* LV. 19 The anxiety of the advocates of free coinage . . . is . . . due . . . to a fear that this would result in a contraction of the currency.

+**Contractionist.** One who supports the policy of reducing the volume of currency.

1875 *Nation* XXI. 112/2 As regards the Republican party, its own desire is to please everybody—both contractionist and inflationist, the solvent and insolvent, the creditor and the debtor. **1875** *Chicago Tribune* 14 Oct. 1/6 The schemes of the contractionists, bullionists, and resumptionists, had been interfered with. **1881** *Nation* XXXII. 160 Whether the new Secretary [of the Treasury] . . . would be an expansionist or a contractionist. **1890** *Congress. Rec.* 12 July 7208/1 This bold confession is made . . . by this distinguished Senator and contractionist. **1892** *Ib.* 30 June 5658/1 It was the duty of Senators to return here when a bill of this kind was pending; but they can defeat the will of the people and serve the gold-standard contractionists; they can serve Lombard and Wall streets by being absent.

***Contractor.** One who undertakes by contract to perform certain work. Often in reference to building trades, without a modifier: One who takes contracts to build structures. {1724-}

1750 *Ga. Col. Rec.* VI. 326 By the Vouchers which these Contractors have produced, it appears, that only a few of these Setlers remain to be satisfied. **1788** FRANKLIN *Autobiog.* 428 Beating down their price in favour of the contractors, in whose profits, it was said, perhaps from suspicion only, he had a share. **1792** *Ann. 2nd Congress* 1107 Mr. Smith, agent for the contractor, was actively engaged in furnishing supplies for the troops. **1860** GREELEY *Overland Journey* 52 [They] were delayed by a great contractor's train which had been all day crossing. **1873** *Winfield* (Kansas) *Courier* 11 Jan. 3/2 The worthy efforts of the mail contractors to supply us with mail through the prevailing epidemic among horses will be appreciated by every one. **1884** *Century Mag.* Feb. 497/1 His father was a contractor for the construction of various important roads at the West, and spent most of his time away from home. **1901** MERWIN & WEBSTER *Calumet 'K'* 329, I was working for a firm of contractors up on the North Side.

Contra-dance. [F. *contre-danse*, It. and Sp. *contra-danza*, alt. from E. *country dance.*] A dance of rural origin, in which partners stand opposite each other in lines. {1830-}

1803 FESSENDEN *Terrible Tractoration* 14 So fam'd Aldini, erst in France Led dead folks down a contradance. [**1807** IRVING, etc. *Salmagundi* vii, No pigeon-wing disturbs your *contre-danse.*] **1834** A. PIKE *Sketches* 143 Their dances are very graceful and considerably complicated, and as regular as our contra dances. **1841** BUCKINGHAM *America* II. 457 Country dances, called here, more accurately than with us in England, 'contra-dances.' **1845** GREEN *Texian Exped.* 134 Nothing can exceed the grace of their quadrilles and contra-dances. **1882** C. WAITE *Adv. Far West* 101 Cotillions, contra-dances and old fashioned reels are in high esteem. **1888** CABLE *Bonaventure* 10 At thirteen, of course, she began to move in society, which meant to join in the contra-dance.

Contraption. A device or contrivance. (Often derogatory in tone.) {1847- *dial.*}

Further quotations are given in Thornton.

1834 'J. DOWNING' *A. Jackson* iii. 24 The gineral oney intended tu see what he wou'd do, and then by a leetle contrapshion, have him secur'd. **1837** J. C. NEAL *Charcoal Sk.* (1838) 95 For my part, I can't say as how I see what's to be the end of all their new-fangled contraptions. **1857** OLMSTEAD *Journey thru Texas* 71 Our contraption should have at least a fair trial. *c***1870** BAGBY *Old Va. Gentleman* 9 These new-fangled 'contraptions' are to the old system what the little, dirty, black steam-tug is to the three-decker. **1897** *Outing* XXX. 469/1 Thomas Clapham, with his ugly watermelon 'contraption,' beat the smart and handsome cutters. **1900** ROBERTSON *Red Blood* 42 When he sold his crop he went off North and came back with a lot of 'new contraptions' in harrows and ploughs that set the countryside agog. **1903** *N.Y. Sun* 22 Nov., Some massive mahogany bookcases which were about to be replaced by the new steel contraptions.

***Contribution.** In various attrib. uses: **a.** Consisting of a contribution. **b.** Eliciting a contribution. **c.** Holding a contribution. (Cf. CONTRIBUTION BOX.) — **(a)** **1676** *Conn. Public Rec.* II. 454 The Councill doe recommend it to Mr. James Steele and Sarjt Standly to lade what contribution corn they haue gathered for the releife of those that are burnt and droue out of their habitations. **1692** SEWALL *Letter-Book* I. 5 An Account of Connecticut Contribution-Money which now send to Mr. Secretary Allen. **(b)** **1821** NUTTALL *Trav. Arkansa* 223 In the spring and autumn the Iuapaws have a custom of making a contribution dance, in which they visit also the whites, . . . and the chief alms which they crave is salt or articles of diet. (c) **1835** [see next]. **1883** *Harper's Mag.* Sept. 643/2 The late Governor Jewell took one of the contribution plates and passed it around.

+Contribution box. A box in which contributions are received, esp. a wooden box with a long handle passed among the pews of a church for the collection.

1666 *Cambridge Proprietors' Rec.* (1896) 211 Whether the Inhabitants, who are Assessed to pay the Ministers Salary, and put the Same into the contribution Box, Shall either put their money in papers . . . or Shall Mark their Money. **1835** INGRAHAM *South-West* I. 215 The contribution-box or bag makes its begging tour among the pews. *c***1849** PAIGE *Dow's Sermons* I. 50 You will entertain no fears of an awful Future—no more than I apprehend a ten sixpence being found in the contribution-box. *c***1865** 'MARK TWAIN' *Sk.*, 'Answers to Correspondents,' In church you are always down on your knees, with your eyes buried in the cushion, when the contribution-box comes around. **1882** THAYER *From Log-Cabin* xvi. 236 On the Sabbath after James' return to the seminary he was at public worship, when the contribution-box was passed through the audience. **1899** *Chicago Record* 2 Aug. 4/4 [The conductor] reaches out the box . . . just as a church deacon passes the contribution box.

***Contrive,** *v.*

+1. *tr.* To carry; to transport. *local,* now *Obs.*

'*Contrive.* . . . I doubt whether this strange expression is ever used at the present day. I never heard it myself, nor have I found any person that has heard it from any class of people in this country' (Pickering 70).

1781 WITHERSPOON *Druid P.* No. 5, I wish we could contrive it to Philadelphia. The words *to carry it, to have it carried,* or some such, are wanting. **1791** in Jillson *Dark & Bl. Ground* 74 When they had contrived the wounded within, they confined themselves to the defence of the fort.

+2. *intr.* To imagine or guess. *colloq.*

1893 *Nation* LVII. 67 We [in Amer.] have, too, a colloquial sense for *contrive,* which we do not find noticed [in the *O.E.D.*], but which must have occurred more than once in the great body of New England tales. 'I can't contrive how he did it'—*i.e.,* guess, imagine, divine.

Controller. (See COMPTROLLER.)

+Contwisted, *ppl. a. colloq.* A euphemistic exclamation to express annoyance; dratted, doggoned. — **1834** CARRUTHERS *Kentuckian* I. 23, I wish I may be contwisted. **1845** C. M. KIRKLAND *Western Clearings* 71 His father . . . tore his boot almost off with what he called 'a contwisted stub of the toe.'

‖**Contwistification.** (See quotation.) — **1835** KENNEDY *Horse Shoe Robinson* I. 77 We hold in despise all sorts of contwistifications—either by laying of tongue-traps, or listenings under eaves of houses.

‖**Conundered,** *pp.a.* [? Based on *conundrum.*] *colloq.* Perplexed, confounded. Hence *Conunderment.* — **1865** A. D. WHITNEY *Gayworthys* 320 Mrs. Hopeley avowed herself 'conundered' to tell. *Ib.* 325 'Well, if I ain't conundered, now!' she exclaimed.—*Ib.* 385 This solution of what 'had been, verily, her main conunderment.'

***Convene,** *v.*

***1.** *intr.* To meet together in a body.

'The verb *convene* is much more in vogue in Scotland and in the United States than in England' (*Nation* LVII. 67).

1692 *Mass. Acts* (1726) 1 Be it ordained and enacted by the Governour, Council and Representatives, Convened in General Court or Assembly, [etc.]. **1715** *Boston News-Letter* 17 Jan. 1/1 Writs were Issued for Summoning a Great and General Court or Assembly to Convene [etc.]. **1783** J. JONES *Letters* 105, I proceed immediately to Virginia in order to attend the Assembly now convening. **1798** ALLEN *Hist. Vermont* 207 When the Court convened on this subject, Colonel Allen went into the lobby, and began to write a memorial to the Legislature of New Hampshire. **1855** R. GLISAN *Jrnl. Army Life* 213 The City Council convened and passed an act fining the man five hundred dollars. **1907** T. ROOSEVELT in *Westminster Gazette* 19 Nov. 9/1 [The bill] will be passed at an early date after Congress convenes two weeks hence.

***2.** *tr.* To call together; to convoke a session of (a body).

1787 *Constitution* ii. § 3 He may, on extraordinary occasions, convene both Houses, or either of them. **1911** *Okla. Session Laws* 3 Legisl. 236 If the court be at the time adjourned, the Chief Justice shall immediately convene the same for such hearing.

+3. To suit; to be convenient or agreeable to.

1816 PICKERING 70 *Ex.* This road will convene the public. . . . Used only by the illiterate [in parts of New England]. **1835–7** HALIBURTON *Clockmaker* 1 Ser. xviii. 158 Father . . . never confined himself to water neither, when he could get anything convened him better. **1844** 'UNCLE SAM' *Peculiarities* I. 104 A murder, gentlemen, is where it convenes to one man's base passions to murderously kill another. *Ib.* 161 The temperance movement, as they call it, don't convene to a man like me.

***Convenient,** *a.* Near at hand; easily accessible. {1848–; chiefly Irish}

'This expression is not often to be found in American publications' (Pickering 70).

1804 MARSHALL *Life Washington* III. 120 At Morristown, the American army was more convenient to the highlands of New York. **1848** POLK *Pres. Mess. & P.* IV. 636 Situated on a safe harbor . . . convenient to excellent timber for ship-building, . . . it [=San Francisco] must become our great Western naval depot.

***Conventicle.** A meeting of some dissenting sect; also a meeting place or house of such a body. Often opprobrious in connotation. *Obs.*

1661 *Jamaica* (L.I.) *Rec.* I. 105 Iff any meetings or Conventicles of quakers shall be in this Town of Rustdorp that wee know, wee will give infformation to ye aughtority. **1704** S. KNIGHT *Journal* 54 There are also a Dutch and Divers Conventicles as they call them, viz. Baptist, Quakers, &c. **1705** BEVERLEY *Virginia* IV. 27 They have no more than five Conventicles amongst them, namely, three small Meetings of Quakers, and two of Presbyterians. **1712** *N.J. Archives* 1 Ser. IV. 156 The Quakers or other Dissenters, who have at their head one Coll: Morris . . . who has joyned in endeavours to settle a conventicle in the City of New York. **1797** WEEMS *Letters* II. 92 As to Religious books sent as you sent me before, you might as well send Fiddles to a Methodist conventicle.

***Convention,** *n.*

***1.** An assembly of persons gathered for a political or legislative purpose. **a.** For political action, usually in addition to the regularly constituted authorities.

On the background of this word, see J. F. Jameson 'The Early Political Uses of the Word Convention' in *Amer. Hist. Rev.* III. 477–87.

1689 *Plymouth Laws* 211 In refference to the motion made by the honorable Councill & Generall Convention of our friends & neighbours at Boston for our advice & assistance in repelling & suppressing the barbarous Heathen. **1705** *Suffield Doc. Hist.* 151 At a legall convention of the Inhabitants . . . Capt. Joseph Sheldin was chosen to serve as their Representative, at the next convention . . . in Boston; there to manage the Town's business, or case. **1768** *Annals of America* II. 158 The general court of Massachusetts having been dissolved by Governor Bernard . . . on the proposal of the selectmen of Boston to the several towns in the Colony, a Convention met in that town on the 22d of September. *Ib.*, The Convention disclaiming legislative authority, petitioned the governor [etc.]. **1778** *Jrnls. Cont. Congress* X. 172 A letter . . . from Thomas Cushing, Esq. president of a convention of committees from the New England states, which met at New Haven, 15 to 20 January, . . . was read. **1836** *Texas Declaration of Independence,* We, therefore, . . . in solemn Convention assembled, . . . do hereby resolve and declare that our political connexion with the Mexican nation has forever ended. **1863** (*title*), Missouri State Radical Emancipation Convention, held at Jefferson City September 1 to 2, 1863.

+b. For the purpose of forming, ratifying, or amending a state constitution or the Federal Constitution. **1.** A state-wide convention. **2.** A nation-wide convention.

For group (1), see also CONSTITUTIONAL *a.* 4.

(1) **1776** FITHIAN *Journal* II. 194 Towards evening we were also honoured with the company of Messrs. Hugg, & Leaming two delegates in the New-Jersey Convention. **1779** *Amherst Rec.* (1884) 75/2 Calling a State Convention for the sole purpose of forming a new Constitution. **1789** S. LOW *Politician Outwitted* I. i, Our convention will pass the federal government by a considerable majority. **1836** *Texas Constitution* VI. Schedule, It is declared by this Convention that all laws now in force in Texas . . . shall remain in full force until declared void, etc. **1862** *Jrnl. Constitutional Convention* 452 Be it ordained by the People of the State of Illinois, represented in the Constitutional Convention, That the following article, proposed as an amendment to the Constitution of the United States, [be passed]. **1870** *Nation* 10 Feb. 85/2 If Congress enable a Territorial Legislature to call a convention to form a State Constitution, can the Legislature first call the Convention, then repeal the law and disperse the Convention? **1910** *New Mex. Const. Convention Proc.* 10 Delegate Catron moved that this Convention extend its sympathy to the family of Mrs. Sargent.

(2) **1783** MORRIS in Sparks *Life G. Morris* (1832) I. 256 Have a convention of the states to form a better constitution. **1787** J. BARLOW *Oration 4 July* 11 Much is expected from the Federal Convention now sitting at Philadelphia. **1787** in Elliot *Debates* (1836) I. 134 Our General Assembly . . . did . . . elect Richard Caswell, Alexander Martin, [etc.] . . . deputies to attend a Convention of delegates from the several United States of America, . . . for the purpose of revising the Federal Constitution. **1788** in *Mem. Theo. Parsons* (1859) 462 The Governor . . . has come out, and tells us, that two very respectable States, Virginia and New York, propose a convention to consider amendments. **1836** *S. Lit. Messenger* II. 684 No body of men ever encountered successfully greater difficulties than the Federal Convention.

+c. A joint meeting of the two houses of a state legislature.

1800 CUTLER in *Life & Corr.* II. 41 This day 16 Electors of President and Vice-President of the U.S. were chosen in convention of the two Houses. **1887** *Courier-Journal* 11 Jan. 1/2 The Republican majority . . . seemed to think that there must be some pretense to a joint convention.

+d. Among the Southern States, a meeting of elected delegates for the purpose of formally seceding, or considering secession, from the Union. *Obs.*

1860 in W. R. Smith *Alabama Convention Hist. & Deb.* 34 The General Assembly at its last session passed . . . resolutions requiring the Governor, in the event of the election of a Black Republican [as president of the U.S.], to order elections to be held for the delegates to a Convention of the State. **1860** *S.C. Convention Jrnl.* 122 This Convention approves the conduct of the Governor in taking immediate possession of Castle Pinckney and Fort Moultrie. **1861** *Texas Secession Convention Jrnl.* (1912) 194 It is the sense of this Convention that the jurisdiction of the federal courts of the Confederate States shall be so defined and restricted by law as to avoid a repetition of such abuses. **1861** E. COWELL *Diary* 347 The Convention of Western Virginia met at Wheeling, yesterday.

+**e.** Special conventions: (1) the Albany Convention of 1754, the first concerted effort of the colonies for political unity; (2) the Hartford Convention of 1814, which protested U.S. participation in the War of 1812 by threatening a secession of New England states; (3) the Nashville Convention of 1850, which expressed the views of the South on the Compromise Measures.

Constitutional Union convention (see CONSTITUTIONAL UNION).

(1) **1754** FRANKLIN *Writings* III. 207 Plan of Union Adopted by the Convention at Albany; with the Reasons and Motives for Each Article of the Plan. — (2) **1814** *Niles' Reg.* VII. 155 Against the resolution proposing a convention of delegates from the New-England states [at Hartford], and the resolutions connected therewith, the undersigned feel bound ... most earnestly to remonstrate. *Ib.* 257 It is said, in Baltimore, by those disposed to put the most favorable construction on the intended proceedings of the convention at *Hartford*, that they will only propose some amendments to the constitution. **1831** *Ib.* XLI. 101/2 What happened in 'the days of the Hartford Convention' so immodest and outrageous as the preceding? — (3) **1849** CALHOUN in H. von Holst *J. C. Calhoun* (1899) 325 There is but one thing that holds out the promise of saving both ourselves and the Union, and that is a Southern convention. *c***1850** in H. von Holst *op. cit.* 323 Mississippi, in the incipient movement towards the Nashville Convention, ... was instigated by South Carolina. **1889** J. PHELAN *Hist. Tenn.* 434 The Southern Convention had met at Nashville in May, 1850, as the Whigs said, 'to inaugurate a Southern Confederacy.'

+**2.** An extralegal meeting of delegates, or members, of a political party, usually for the purpose of selecting candidates for public office, and for drawing up resolutions.

a. As applied to local or state conventions. (Cf. CONGRESSIONAL 7 b.)

1808 *Independent Chron.* (Bost.) 29 Feb. 2/3 A convention of republican delegates from the several towns in the county of Essex. **1812** *Boston Selectmen* 51 A committee from the Republican Convention of the County of Suffolk. **1817** *Niles' Reg.* XII. 96 At a convention of the republican members of the legislature of New-York, and of delegates from several counties represented therein by federalists, ... held for the purpose of nominating a suitable person ... for ... governor of the state. **1836** *Ib.* L. 1 The state convention which assembled at Columbus, Ohio, ... nominated Wm. H Harrison for president. **1840** *Niles' Nat. Reg.* 4 July 276/2 The whigs of Maine, through their delegates, assembled in convention at Augusta. **1847** EMERSON *Soc. & Solitude* (1870) 56 Our county conventions often exhibit a small-pot-soon-hot style of eloquence. **1852** *Harper's Mag.* V. 832/1 A number of State and general Conventions have been held, for the nomination of public officers. **1862** in F. Moore *Rebellion Rec.* V. 1. 8 A Convention of Unionists was held at Nashville, Tennessee, this day.

b. As applied to a congressional caucus.

1808 in M. Carey *Olive Branch* (1818) 441, I deem it expedient, for the purpose of nominating suitable characters for the president and vice-president of the United States, ... to call a convention of republican members, to meet at the senate Chamber. **1816** *Niles' Reg.* X. 59/2 *Resolved,* That the practice of nominating candidates for the offices of president and vice president of the United States, by a convention of senators and representatives in congress, is inexpedient and ought not to be continued. **1824** *Nat. Intelligencer* 17 Feb. 1 Heretofore conventions of the Republican Members of Congress, for the nomination of candidates for President and Vice President, have been held upon the presumed approbation of their constituents only.

c. As applied to national conventions.

'State nominating conventions arose about 1825, superseding legislative caucuses. The first national convention to select presidential candidates was held by the Antimasonic party in Baltimore in September, 1831, and all presidential nominations have since been made by such conventions' (*Cent.* 1241).

1831 *Niles' Reg.* 1 Oct. 74 The anti-masonic convention, to nominate a president and vice-president of the United States, met in this city [Baltimore] on Monday last. **1831** J. Q. ADAMS *Memoirs* VIII. 437 [Henry Clay] was nominated by the National Republican Convention at Baltimore yesterday for the Presidency. **1840** *Niles' Nat. Reg.* 9 May 147/1 The nomination of Martin Van Buren for the presidency, made by the national convention, was enthusiastically concurred in. **1867** J. N. EDWARDS *Shelby* 12 As early as May 10, 1860, the first meeting which ever assembled in a Slave State to consider the question of taking public position with the anti-slavery element of the North met in St. Louis and sent delegates to the Chicago Convention. **1881** *Nation* XXXIII. 4 The slipshod method in which the Vice-President is commonly chosen by party conventions. **1891** *Boston Journal* 25 Nov. 3/1 A National Republican Convention of delegated representatives of the Republican party will be held at the city of Minneapolis ... for the purpose of nominating candidates for President and Vice President. **1925** BRYAN *Memoirs* 97, I formed early the habit of attending national conventions.

3. A meeting for the consideration of religious matters, as of the ministers of a district; also, among several denominations, the assembly that meets at stated intervals to govern the affairs of the denomination.

*a***1720** in *Boston Mem. Hist.* II. 223 It was thought advisable that this gathering of the clergy should have a more formal character, and the 'Convention of Congregational Ministers' was organized. **1725** *New-Eng. Courant* 3–10 July 1/1 The Memorial of the General Convention of Ministers met at Boston. **1785** *Constitution of Oct.* in Perry *Hist. Amer. Episc. Church* II. 99 There shall be a general Convention of the Protestant Ep[iscopa]l church in ye Ud States of America; which shall be held in ye City of Philadelphia ... in ye year of our Lord 1786, & for ever after once in three years. **1823** *Amer. Baptist Mag.* IV. 137/1 On Wednesday, April 30, the Baptist General Convention commenced its fourth triennial session. **1886** *Church Rev.* XLVIII. 289 In every diocese, the mode of trying Presbyters and Deacons may be instituted by the Convention of the Diocese.

4. A meeting of delegates from, or members of, various branches of an organization to discuss social, commercial, professional or other matters.

'The extension of the last-named term [convention] has been vastly greater in the United States than in the mother country' (*Nation* LVII. 67).

1793 *Penna. Soc. for Abol. of Slavery Mem.* 41 The Society ... will appoint Delegates to the proposed Convention, provided a majority of the Abolition Societies in the United States do agree to the measure. **1831** P. HONE *Diary* I. 41, I attended the tariff convention this morning. **1844** in Rupp *Relig. Denominations* 56 In most states we have conventions for the purpose of promoting education, the Sunday-schools, and missionary labour. **1856** M. THOMPSON *Plu-ri-bus-tah* 30 In the style of Mrs. Bloomer, At the Woman's Rights Convention, Mister Jupiter sat smoking. **1865** *Nation* 14 Sept. 330 If the Englishman can initiate no public enterprise without a public dinner, the American is equally helpless until he has called a convention. ... There have been conventions of carpenters and of beer-brewers, of discharged soldiers and of discontented women, of farmers and of horse-dealers, of teetotallers and of anti-tobacconists, of Millerites, whose world is just ending, and of freedmen, whose world is just beginning. **1873–4** *Vt. Bd. Agric. Rep.* II. 200 When doctors meet in convention, they select persons from their own number to read papers. **1891** *Boston Journal* 13 Nov. 9/1 The great national convention of the Woman's Christian Temperance Union opened in Tremont Temple this morning.

+**5.** Attrib. with *regiment, soldier, troop* in sense: Pertaining to the British soldiers who surrendered according to the 'Convention of Saratoga' in 1777.

'Burgoyne ... at Saratoga, October 17, ... surrendered his army, the conditions being that the troops should march to Boston, whence they might return to England with the understanding that unless they were exchanged they were not to serve again in North America during the war' (Bassett *Short Hist. U.S.* 197–98).

1780 *Heath Papers* 136 Many Convention soldiers get to New York. **1781** WASHINGTON *Diaries* II. 222 The 46th and 86th Regim[en]ts—the first of them being a convention Regim[en]t and the other not in America. **1786** in Chalkley *Scotch-Irish Settlement Va.* I. 384 Defendants, ... stationed at the barracks, in the County of Albemerle, did, on 1st September, 1780, ... seize John Sowers, a yeoman, and one of said convention-troops. **1849** H. HOWE *Hist. Coll. Va.* 165 The British and German prisoners taken at Saratoga in the revolution and known as the 'Convention troops' were sent to Charlottesville in the beginning of the year 1779.

6. Attrib. and comb. with *ball, bonnet, business,* etc.

1889 MUNROE *Golden Days* 347 The great convention ball came to an end. **1830** ROYALL *Southern Tour* I. 36 These silly women, ... when the Convention was about to meet, fabricated these large umbrella bonnets, which they named Convention-bonnets. **1876** *Harper's Mag.* Dec. 158/1 Senator Jones, of Nevada, gave a little dinner to several of his brother Senators and a few members of the House who happened to be at Cincinnati on Convention business. **1887** C. B. GEORGE *40 Years on Rail* 92 Chicago ... is the greatest railroad center on the globe, [and] is the chief convention city in America. **1910** *New Mex. Const. Convention Proc.* 20 Delegate Mabry ... moved that the privileges of the floor be extended to the representatives of organized labor who were present in the Convention Hall. **1780** CUTLER in *Life & Corr.* I. 78 The Rev. Mr. McCarty ... [is] to preach the next Convention Sermon. **1880** *Harper's Mag.* Aug. 470 Meanwhile progress has been made in defining the convention system.

+**Convention,** *v. tr.* To establish religious conventions in (a region). — **1824** MARSHALL *Kentucky* I. 268 The mighty project, for conventioning the western country, ... exhibited but the fantasy of an abortion.

***Conventional,** *a.* Of or pertaining to a convention or assembly. (Cf. esp. CONVENTION *n.* 1e, 2.) {1812-} — **1820** JAY *Corr.* IV. 434 The Massachusetts Conventional account of the matter. **1850** in H. von Holst *J. C. Calhoun* (1899) 323 Intimating ... that this Conventional movement of ours was stimulated by South Carolina.

Conventionalist. {1801-} +A member or supporter of a constitutional (or similar) convention. — **1817** in Fearon *Sketches* (1818) 145 It is an unholy league between ... the monarchists, the aristocrats, the

Hartford conventionalists [etc.]. **1824** W. N. BLANE *Excursion* 171 Those who have been the cause of this convention [to adopt a state constitution], are the men who have come from the slave-holding States. On their success in getting the votes of two-thirds of the legislature, the Conventionalists assembled at two or three public dinners. **1901** JAMESON & BUEL *Dict. Amer. Hist.* I. 180 *Conventionalists*, in the Pennsylvania politics of 1804–1808, the name assumed by those extreme Democrats who desired to see a new convention called, to modify the Constitution of the State in a radically democratic sense.

Conventioner. {1691–1721} +**1.** A member of the 'Convention regiment' of the British army. +**2.** A member of the convention that framed the U.S. constitution, 1787. — **(1) 1786** in Chalkley *Scotch-Irish Settlement Va.* I. 384 Defendants, pretending to have . . . authority to take up and secure any of the . . . soldiers in the British service, commonly called conventioners [etc.]. **(2) 1842** *Supreme Court Rep.* XLI. 638 Let it be remembered, that the conventioners who formed the Constitution, were the representatives of equal sovereignties.

Conventionist. {1768–} One who supports the purposes of, or attends, a convention. {1823–} — **1815** *Niles' Reg.* VIII. 56/2 Hartford Conventionists. . . . Reports have reached us . . . that the state[s] of Massachusetts, Connecticut, New Hampshire, Rhode-Island, and Vermont, have absolved all ties by which they were bound to the former federal government. **1831** *Ib.* XLI. 101/2 Are they who most bawled at the 'Hartford Conventionists' made of so much better stuff that more extravagant acts in themselves are patriotic? **1886** *Harper's Mag.* June 116/1 The bathers were few—nursery-maids, fragments of a day-excursion, and some of the fair conventionists.

Convention room. A room in which a legislative body convenes. — **1784** *Mass. Centinel* 7 April 1/3 The House of Assembly of this state . . . have ordered it [a picture] to be placed in their Convention Room.

Conveyancer. {1623–} One who prepares documents for the transfer of property. {1650–}

1771 FRANKLIN *Autobiog.* 269 The two first were clerks to an eminent scrivener or conveyancer in the town, Charles Brogden. **1790** *Penna. Packet* 5 Jan. 4/2 Charles Jones, Notary-public and Conveyancer, . . . draws Deeds, Bonds, Mortgages, . . . and all other instruments in Writing. **1816** U. BROWN *Journal* I. 267, [I] was presently accompanied to the Springs by James W. Wheat, A Deputy Surveyor & a Conveyancer who was friendly with me. **1845** J. W. NORRIS *Chicago Directory* 84 Henry W. Clarke, . . . Conveyancer and General Land Agent. **1866** *Internal Revenue Guide* 73 Surveyors, who draft the deeds of lands surveyed by them, must take a conveyancer's license.

* **Conveyer, -or.** A mechanical contrivance for carrying material from one place to another.

1813 *Niles' Reg.* III. Add. 7/2 The machinery invented . . . consisted of an improved elevator, an improved conveyor, &c. **1849** *Rep. Comm. Patents* 444 If the screen be removed it will act like a common mill conveyor. **1886** *Century Mag.* May 43/2 From this bin 'conveyers'—long wooden boxes in which revolve large iron screws—carry it [=wheat] along to the cleaning-house. **1901** MERWIN & WEBSTER *Calumet 'K'* 114 Now there was to be no more delaying . . . until engines, conveyors, and scales should be working smoothly.

* **Convict.** In attrib. uses.

+**1.** *Convict servant (man)*, a convict serving his sentence as an indentured servant. *Obs.*

1751 *Virginia Gaz.* 1 Aug. 3/2 Ran away from the Subscriber, last night, a Convict Servant Man, Named Edward Sutton. **1759** *Boston Gazette* 15 Sept., Ran-Away from the Subscriber, . . . in June last, a Convict Servant Man, named Thomas Read. **1759** *Newport Mercury* 16 Oct. 2/3 Whoever takes up the said Convict Servant, and returns him to his Master, shall have Fifteen Pistoles Reward. **1761** *Penna. Gazette* 8 Oct. 4/3 Run away . . . an English Convict Servant Man.

2. *Convict labor*, the labor of convicts used by contractors, or for the market. {1843–} Also attrib.

1843 in Commons, etc., *Doc. Hist.* VIII. 225 Convict labor in our state prisons so far as it affects mechanical occupations. **1869** 'MARK TWAIN' *Innocents* xxxvii. 401 He says he has tried convict labor on his railroads, and with perfect success. **1887** *Courier-Journal* 18 Feb. 2/5 [A] resolution . . . to prevent the General Government from accepting bids for supplies, etc., from corporations and firms using convict labor. **1903** *Chicago Chronicle* 11 April, The convict labor bill has passed the house.

+**3.** *Convict camp*, a camplike prison for convicts working out on contract, or on roads, levees, etc.

1884 *Century Mag.* Feb. 593/2 One can turn again only to leased prisons elsewhere, to find numbers with which to compare the ghastly mortality of some of these Texas convict camps. **1891** 'THANET' *Otto the Knight*, etc. 71 His mother dead and his father in a convict camp somewhere, he had scrambled through a friendless youth. **1899** CHESNUTT *Wife of His Youth* 317 In the shifting life of the convict camp they [=letters] had long since ceased to reach him, if indeed they had been written.

***Convicted,** *ppl. a.* +Overcome by the consciousness of sinfulness. (Cf. CONVICTION.) — **1845** HOOPER *Simon Suggs' Adv.* x. 124 By this time it had come to be generally known that the 'convicted' old man was Captain Simon Suggs, the very 'chief of sinners' in all that region. **1885** 'CRADDOCK' *Prophet* 5 'The boys air convicted, then?' he asked. . . . 'The boys hev got thar religion, too,' she faltered.

* **Conviction** Phr. *Under conviction*, with a consciousness of sin. {1675–}

1845 JUDD *Margaret* II. 291, I was under conviction three months. **1871** DE VERE 231 In the Methodist church this open avowal is frequently made by persons who . . . have been struck under conviction. **1875** E. KING *Southern States* 781 If the brother or sister under conviction cannot say this phrase exactly, the preachers and deacons will . . . refuse to admit them to religious communion. **1885** 'CRADDOCK' *Prophet* 5 'Who air under conviction hyar?' he demanded. . . . 'Mebbe it air yer granny,' he suggested with a sneer. **1898** DUNBAR *Folks from Dixie* 9 Aunt Hannah remarked . . . she 'nevah knowed de gal was unner c'nviction.'

Conviction bill. A bill certifying that a convict servant has been convicted of a crime. — **1776** *Ann. S.W. Virginia* 252 The said Richard confessing that he had stole his conviction bill from his said Master.

+**Convict lease system.** The practice of placing convicts in charge of a contractor, who uses their labor, usu. in work gangs outdoors. — **1885** *Century Mag.* XXX. 687/1 The popular mind has been seduced by the glittering temptations of our Southern convict-lease system. **1889** *Cent.* 1245 *Convict-lease system*, a system employed in some of the southern United States. **1908** *Outlook* XC. 238/2 (*caption*), The End of the Convict Lease System in Georgia.

+**Convict lessee.** A contractor who leases convict labor. — **1887** *Courier-Journal* 19 Feb. 2/3 The Governor . . . ordered the convict lessee to depart his presence.

* **Convocation.** +A meeting or organization of the clergymen of part of a diocese.

'The analogue in England is a conference of the clergy of an archdeaconry or rural deanery' (*O.E.D.*).

1692 SEWALL *Diary* I. 367 A bill is sent in about calling a Fast, and Convocation of Ministers, that may be led in the right way as to the Witchcrafts. **1747** D. NEAL *Hist. New-Eng.* (ed. 2) I. 155 There was no such Thing as a Synod or Convocation in the Country [New England], till the Year 1637. **1747** *N.H. Hist. Soc. Coll.* IX. 1 A Record of the Transactions of the Annual Convocation of Ministers in the Province of N: Hampshire, Began July 28th, 1747. **1906** *Churchman* 20 Oct. 585 The thirty-second annual convocation of the missionary district of Sacramento was held in Trinity church, Sacramento.

***Convolvulus.** An erect, trailing, or climbing plant having showy trumpet-shaped flowers, belonging to the genus *Convolvulus;* bindweed. Also attrib. — **1784** CUTLER in *Mem. Academy* I. 416 Great Convolvulus. Common in hedges and by stone walls. . . . The roots of the Convolvulus is [*sic*] a very acrid purgative to the human race. **1847** DARLINGTON *Weeds & Plants* 247 Field Convolvulus. Bind-weed. . . . This foreigner has been introduced into some portions of our country,—and may give the farmers some trouble.

***Convoy. a.** A party conveying or guarding goods or supplies. +**b.** A consignment of goods under escort; a conducted party. — **1791** in *Ann. 2nd Congress* Appendix 1054 It was reported . . . that their design was to plunder the convoys which were upon the road. **1837** IRVING *Bonneville* I. 23 To this rendezvous the company sends annually a convoy of supplies from its establishment on the Atlantic frontier. *Ib.* 224 In company with Campbell's convoy, was a trapping party of the Rocky Mountain Company. **1864** LOWELL *Fireside Trav.* 152 M. had brought back his convoy without even seeing a moose.

+**Convulsion root.** *local.* Indian pipe, *Monotropa uniflora.* — **1891** *Amer. Folk-Lore* IV. 148 Grandmother called *Monotropa uniflora* Convulsion Root. (New Hampshire.)

* **Cony.** Also **coney.**

* **1.** A rabbit. Also attrib.

Formerly the usual name. '*Cony* . . . is wholly disused in the United States except in Scripture reading' (*Nation* LVII. 67).

1629 J. SMITH *Adv. Unexp. Planters* (1631) xi. 24, 150. head of cattell, . . . 41. goats, some conies, with all provision for houshold and apparel. **1789** MORSE *Amer. Geog.* 54 Beasts common to North America: Bahama coney. **1820** *Columbian Centinel* 5 Jan. 4/3 Richard D. Tucker & Co. Have for sale . . . 3 casks Cony Wool. **1821** NUTTALL *Trav. Arkansa* 259 La Vega enumerates conies (or hares), some of which were larger than those of Spain; these the natives caught by means of spring traps.

+**2.** The little chief hare or pika, *Lagomys princeps*, of the western mountains.

1878 H. H. JACKSON *Travel at Home* 319 But conies are said to be a fearless folk: and well they may be who dwell in impregnable homes in the walls of the Ute Pass. **1884** *Stand. Nat. Hist.* V. 81 The miners and hunters in the West know these oddities as 'conies' and 'starved rats.' **1890** *Cent.* 3331/2 The last [species] is known as the little chief hare, cony, and starved rat. It inhabits the mountains of the West as far south as New Mexico and Arizona.

+**3.** A hat made of rabbit fur, instead of beaver.

1855 BARNUM *Life* 99 If a 'peddler' wanted to trade with us for a box of beaver hats . . . he was sure to obtain a box of 'coneys.'

+**4.** The niggerfish (genus *Epinephelus*), found along the Florida coast.

1888 GOODE *Amer. Fishes* 51 The Coney of Key West, *Epinephelus apua*, the Hind of Bermuda, is an important food-fish. **1889** *Cent.* 3990 Nigger-fish . . . is found . . . along the coast of Florida. It is one of the groupers, and is also called . . . cony.

Cony fish. {1721–} The burbot or eelpout. *Obs.* — **1612** SMITH *Virginia* 15 Of fish we were best acquainted with . . . Conyfish, Rockfish,

Eeles, Lampreyes, Catfish, Shades. **1675** JOSSELYN *Two Voyages* 113 Fish . . . to be seen and catch'd in the Sea and fresh waters in New-England . . . [include] Cat-fish, Cony-fish, Cusk [etc.].

||**Coochee,** *v. tr.* 'To call (poultry) by an imitation of clucking' (*Cent.*). — **1868** BAKER *New Timothy* (1870) 92 The voice of Mrs. General Likens coocheeing the poultry to their morning meal, ordering the servants in their duties, [etc.].

+**Coody.** *Obs.* One of a political faction in New York about 1814, federalist in tendency, opposing De Witt Clinton. Named from Abimelech *Coody*, penname of Gulian C. Verplanck. — **1814** DE W. CLINTON in Hammond *Hist. Polit. Parties* I. 398 [Coody, alias Verplanck,] has become the head of a political sect called the Coodies, of hybrid nature, composed of the combined spawn of federalism and Jacobinism. **1829** in Mackenzie *Van Buren* (1846) 218 With all the adroitness peculiar to that family, [Hoffman] rakes up old prejudices, enlists Duer, who is attached to young Hoffman, with all the coodies, high minded, and Clintonians.

||**Coodyitism.** *Obs.* The doctrines of the Coodies. — **1815** *Columbian Centinel* 12 April 2/3 Ipswich. Our votes have fallen off; but there have been no converts to Coodyitism.

***Cook.**

***1.** One whose occupation is the preparing of food for eating.

1650 *Harvard Rec.* I. 32 Disbursements . . . have been issued out . . . to the Steward himselfe, Butler, Cook, or any other officers of the house. **1687** SEWALL *Diary* I. 182 This Same day Andrew Bordman, Steward and Cook of Harvard Colledge, is buried. **1720** *Wkly. Mercury* 28 July 2/1 Thirty four men and the Purser of the Man of War were saved and not one other Officer but the Cook who was blind. **1815** *Austin Papers* (1924) I. 248 You will see that the Cook in the negro Kitchen keeps it in proper order. **1872** 'MARK TWAIN' *Roughing It* liv. 392 The house servants, cooks, etc., in California and Nevada, were chiefly Chinamen. **1875** *Scribner's Mo.* Dec. 277/2 Considering the number of 'French cooks' we have in this country, it may seem surprising that so few of our domestic servants should have been born in France.

+**2.** Attrib. with *box, boy, kettle*, etc.

'In Am. *cook* takes the place of Eng. *cookery* or *cooking* in compound words' (Horwill 84).

1897 *Outing* XXX. 113/1 Under the forward seat [of a yawl] stood the oilstove boxes, with the cook-box sandwiched in between them. **1802** E. S. BOWNE *Life* 109 On her [a ship's] passage the cook boy dyed suddenly. **1863** 'E. KIRKE' *Southern Friends* 215 A large iron pot . . . serving for both washtub and cook-kettle. **1866** *Rep. Indian Affairs* 182 One cook stove, August 14, 1861. One cook range, August 21, 1861. **1909** WASON *Happy Hawkins* 38, I felt a sting in the left shoulder, spun around and fell, but jumped up just as Jabez changed directions for the cook shack. **1895** *Outing* XXVI. 393/1 It was a blazing bonfire of hemlock bark in a deep hole, which threw a flickering warm light on the side of the cook-shanty. **1898** WISTER *Lin McLean* 2 He returned . . . to camp, where they were just sitting at breakfast to the rear of the cook-shelf of the wagon.

Cookable. Something that may be cooked for food. {1858-} — **1843** 'CARLTON' *New Purchase* I. 47 Next came a resolution that the ladies should prepare the cookables—i.e. stuff the chicken with filling—beat eggs for puddings, and the like. **1853** SIMMS *Sword & Distaff* 52 Tom, 'light, old fellow, and get out your cookables.

+**Cook-all.** (See quotation.) — **1819** W. FAUX *Memorable Days* 311 Some three families cook and bake in one iron skillet, called the cook-all.

+**Cookania.** Molasses candy. *Obs.* — **1855** BARNUM *Life* 21 My stock in trade consisted of a gallon of molasses, boiled down and worked into molasses candy, called in those times [1820-25] 'cookania.'

+**Cookbook.** A book in which recipes for preparing food are given. {=E. *cookery-book*, 1810-}

1809 R. TYLER *Yankey in London* 179, I can send you an assortment of culinary reviews, vulgarly called cook-books. **1844** *Knickerb.* XXIV. 423 She found it quite a different thing now, when she had no one . . . whose advice to ask where the cook book says 'use your own judgment.' **1854** SHILLABER *Mrs. Partington* 254 [Anecdote of] Mrs. Partington *vs.* Cookbooks. **1875** STOWE *We & Neighbors* 299, I turned to my cook-book, and saw that so much time must be given to so many pounds. **1880** 'MARK TWAIN' *Tramp Abroad* xlix. 575, I have often furnished recipes for cookbooks. **1925** BRYAN *Memoirs* 265 Many churches and schools issued cookbooks.

attrib. **a1909** in Wesselhoeft *Effect of Coffee* 11, 4 ozs. of caffeine-free coffee of cook-book strength, with milk and sugar.

+**Cook camp.** In a logging camp, a building in which food is prepared and eaten. — **1893** *Scribner's Mag.* June 703/2 There is . . . a cook camp, which is a large dining-room and kitchen combined. **1895** *Outing* XXVI. 393/2 'Yer supper's ready,' said Payson, emerging from the cook-camp. **a1904** WHITE *Blazed Trail Stories* 44 The camp consisted . . . of three buildings, . . . a cook-camp, a sleeping-camp, and a stable.

+**Cookee.** Also **cookie, cookey.** [f. COOK and dim. ending *-ee*.] A cook; usu. an assistant to a cook in a camp.

1846 *Spirit of Times* 4 July 218/2 We embarked . . . in company with . . . a cookie who was lord and master of the culinary department. **1851** SPRINGER *Forest Life* 172 Arrangements are made, as usual, for the crew, by the cook and 'cookee,' as his assistant is called. **1888** BILLINGS *Hardtack* 287 Not at all daunted by this experience [being almost drowned], the cookey harnessed the mule again as before. **1891** *Harper's Mag.* Nov. 890/2 The rule is to have one cook and two 'cookees' to each sixty men. **1901** WHITE *Westerners* 250 The move necessitated a cook and 'cookee,' and the weekly purchase of provisions. **1911** — *Bobby Orde* i, Bobby could hear the cook and his helpers, called cookees.

+**Cook fire.** An open-air fire suitable for cooking.

1852 STANSBURY *Great Salt Lake* 148 Numbers of the latter tribe [Shoshonees] . . . hung around the camp, crowding the cook-fires, more like hungry dogs than human beings. **1862** NORTON *Army Lett.* 54 Last night the cook-fires on all the hills in sight were spluttering in the rain. **1867** in Custer *Tenting on Plains* 518, I could tell that Eliza had not been within several miles of my cook-fire. **1894** WISTER in *Harper's Mag.* LXXXIX. 518/1 Sergeant Keyser . . . had adopted the troop cook fire for his camp guard after the cooks had finished their work.

Cookhouse. A structure in which food is prepared, as the galley of a ship, or on southern plantations a small separate house, etc. {1795-}

1831 PECK *Guide* 126 Around it [a dwelling house] are usually put up a meat or smoke house, a kitchen or cook house, a stable and corn crib, and perhaps a spring house to keep milk cool in summer. **1852** *Knickerb.* XL. 154 The ice . . . raked the 'Fulton' aft and fore, and slung her cookhouse out on shore. **1865** S. ANDREWS *South since War* 307 The cookhouse, a building standing forty or fifty rods north of the northwestern corner of the stockade walls [of a Georgia military prison]. **a1870** CHIPMAN *Notes on Bartlett* 98 *Cook-house*, house for cook's use. Southern U.S. 2. On board of ships, the galley. **1885** *Rep. Indian Affairs* 6 During the year a new storehouse, a new barn and stables, and a new cook-house have been built.

+**Cookie.** Also **cooky, cookey.** [ad. Dutch *koekje*, a small cake. The use in Scotland is app. an independent borrowing.] A small flat sweet cake. Orig. local in N.Y., a confection eaten in celebration of New Year's day. {*Sc.* as a plain bun, cuckie 1701 (*D.O.S.T.*); cookie *c*1730-}

1786 (N. Y. newspaper), 20 March, Idle boys, who infest our markets and streets, with baskets of cookies. **1803** *Port Folio* (Phila.) III. 14 (Th.), When dears and sweets were as plenty as cookies on a new-year's day. **1808** IRVING, etc. *Salmagundi* xx. 522 Our respectable new-year-cookies, and cherry-bounce, [have been] elbowed aside by plum-cake and outlandish liqueurs. **1819** J. M. DUNCAN *Travels U.S.* II. 286 He did not remain long enough to eat his cookie, as the little round cake provided for the occasion is called. **1837** P. HONE *Diary* I. 241 One out of twenty taking a single glass of wine or cherry bounce, and a morsel of pound-cake or New Year's cookies. **1861** STOWE *Pearl Orr's Isl.* I. 151 Miss Emily had provided a plate of seed cake, otherwise called cookies, for the children. **1898** S. HALE *Letters* 338 Ma and Pa Sparrow . . . coming regularly to afternoon-tea for crumbs of cookie. **1910** *N.Y. Ev. Post* 19 Nov. suppl. 4 A great stone jar of ginger cookies and a barrel of sweet cider, with some winter russets, made a splendid feast. **1913** STRATTON-PORTER *Laddie* xi, She knew and acknowledged the great importance of trying cookies, pies, and cake while they were hot. **1921** M. L. MATTHEWS *Foods & Cookery* 154 Cookies are best for little children because they are drier and require more chewing.

attrib. **1888** BILLINGS *Hardtack* 131 Their culinary skill—or lack of it—was little appreciated by men within easy reach of home, friends, and cooky shops.

+**b.** Phr. *to bet* (or *wager*) *a cookie*, expressing assurance by pretending to wager a small amount.

1843 STEPHENS *High Life N.Y.* II. 37 But look a here, I'll bet a cookey you can't turn that into fust rate English as soon as I can. **c1850** WHITCHER *Bedott P.* xxiii. 251, I'll bet a cookey you'll wish you hadent a went afterward. **1870** HARTE *Notes by Flood & Field* II, Don't know whar he is! . . . He lost every hoof and hide, I'll bet a cookey! **1908** 'YESLAH' *Tenderfoot S. Calif.* 139, I bet a cookie whoever named it took their first trip over to the island [Catalina] on a rough day. — **1874** ALDRICH *P. Palfrey* vi, I'd wager a cookey, now, young Dent has ben settin' up to that Palfrey gal, an' there's ben trouble.

Cooking, *vbl. n.* {1645-} In various attrib. uses: **a.** With food names, as *apple, butter*, etc. **b.** With equipment, as *boiler, machine*, etc. **c.** With *circle, class*, etc. **d.** With *fire*. (Cf. COOKING RANGE, STOVE.)

(a) 1817 W. COXE *Fruit Trees* 108 The Hagloe is an uncommonly fine cooking apple. **1861** *Vanity Fair* 2 Feb. 50/1 The servants . . . were forever scanting the coffee, or taking the cooking butter for the table. **1872** *Florida Plant. Rec.* 199 Lillie requests you to get . . . some cooking cheese, 1 lb. black cooking pepper. **1872** *Harper's Mag.* XLVI. 28 This is genuine soda-water—cooking soda with nearly an equal amount of sulphate of soda [etc.]. **1879** A. D. WHITNEY *Just How* 275 Use the ordinary ground cooking-salt.

(b) 1815 *Gales's N.C. Almanack* 28 The ashes are sifted of impurities, the corn put in a pot, dutchoven, or other convenient cooking utensil. **1858** *Rep. Comm. Patents* I. 742 Improvement in Cooking Boilers for Ranges and Stoves. **1867** GOSS *Soldier's Story* 249 'Go into the prison and get your traps, and I will set you at work.' 'I have no traps,' said I. 'No cooking dishes?' 'No!' **1876** *Wide Awake* 24/2 Then she ran to the iron cooking-shelf with the pans, where the platter, the butter, and the salt were in waiting. **1906** F. LYNDE *Quickening* 75 The railway traffic

manager . . . suggested to the iron-master the taking of a partner with capital, . . . the installation of cooking ovens . . . and foundry plants.
(c) **1854** M. CUMMINS *Lamplighter* 104 Gerty was engaged in stirring up an Indian cake for tea—one of the few branches of the cooking department in which she had acquired some little skill. **1857** C. VAUX *Villas* 82 The left hand panel slides up easily, and discloses a large dumb waiter, or lift, communicating at once with the cooking kitchen. **1866** MOORE *Women of War* 157 Mrs. Lee stood by her little cooking tent, wiping dishes. **1881** *Harper's Mag.* April 667/1 The cooking class under a teacher who has had charge of the 'North End Mission' cooking school in Boston, is a favorite 'branch.' **1882** 'M. HARLAND' *Eve's Daughters* 321, I enjoy—nobody more—the fun of salad-clubs and cooking-circles.
(d) **1856** KANE *Arctic Explor.* II. 288 Two entire planks . . . were devoted to a grand cooking-fire, and we enjoyed a rare and savage feast. **1861** WINTHROP *Open Air* 77, I entered the circle about the cooking-fire of driftwood by the lake. **1901** WHITE *Westerners* 29 In front of it the cooking-fire is built.

+**Cooking range.** A large stove with several openings for cooking operations. {=E. *kitchen-range*}
1846 *Rep. Comm. Patents* 330 What I claim as my invention . . . is the combination of the additional boiling chambers with the front boilers and elevated oven of cooking ranges as described. **1853** FOWLER *Home for All* 100 See what a handy little basement kitchen—close by well and cooking-range—this plan furnishes. **1865** STOWE *House & Home P.* 7 Would our Revolutionary fathers have gone barefooted and bleeding over snows to defend air-tight stoves and cooking-ranges? **1881** STODDARD *E. Hardery* 78 The hot air from a well-devised cooking-range can be made to warm various rooms.

+**Cooking stove.** =COOKSTOVE.
1846 *Rep. Comm. Patents* 293 Having thus fully described the nature of my improvements in the cooking stove, [etc.]. **1861** STOWE *Pearl Orr's Isl.* I. 56 The advent of those sullen gnomes, the 'air-tights,' or . . . the cooking stoves. **1872** HOLMES *Poet* xii. 401 Cooking-stove doesn't burn so well as it does other days. **1885** E. B. CUSTER *Boots & Saddles* v. 52 The little sheet-iron cooking-stove . . . was placed in the kitchen-tent on stormy nights. **1894** P. L. FORD *P. Stirling* 55 Four bottles, with the corks partly drawn, were on the cold cooking stove.

Cookmaid. A female servant who assists in cooking. {1654-}
1676 *Conn. Public Rec.* II. 486 The Councill grants vnto Ninicraft's daughter, her cooke mayd and another old woman, that were promised to her by the committee. **1758** *Broadside Verse* (1930) 127/2 The women out with tongs did run, The cookmaids with their spits. **1806** FESSENDEN *Orig. Poems* 131 *n.*, [The dinner horn] is usually lodged with the cookmaid. **1819** A. PEIRCE *Rebelliad* 47 The Goodies hearing [the harp], cease to sweep And listen; while the Cook-maids weep. **1847** C. F. BRIGGS *Tom Pepper* I. 19 The Irish cook maid gave me some cold meat.

***Cookroom.** A kitchen; a room in which food is cooked. {-1818}
*a***1649** WINTHROP *Hist.* I. 25 A maid . . . fell down at the grating by the cook-room. *a***1656** BRADFORD *Hist.* 386 But Captaine Norton defended him selfe a long time against them all in the cooke-roome. **1776** J. LEACOCK *Fall Brit. Tyranny* IV. iii, I should never be able to keep them out of the cook room, or their noses out of the slush-tub. **1791** BARTRAM *Travels* 191 This house is divided equally, across, into two apartments, one of which is the cook room and common hall, and the other the lodging room. **1828** SHERBURNE *Memoirs* 84 South of this yard was the cook room on the ground floor. **1856** M. J. HOLMES *L. Rivers* vi. 69 A southern lady would almost as soon think of eating in the barn as in her cook room. **1874** *Vt. Bd. Agric. Rep.* II. 509 The cook room . . . should be one of great convenience, large enough to hold the flour, the meal, the rye, the graham, butter. **1882** *Maine Bd. Agric. Rep.* XXVI. 152 The practice of setting milk in the cook room cannot be recommended. **1896** J. C. HARRIS *Sister Jane* 54, I made haste to go to the cook-room, intending to start the fire, and in this way, help sister Jane as much as possible.

***Cookshop.** Also **cook's shop.** A place where food is prepared and sold.
1663 *Boston Rec.* 18 John Lewis is allowed to kepp a Cook shopp for the refreshing of Trauilers. **1698** in *Century Mag.* XXIX. 882/1 [In Philadelphia are] several cook-shops, both Roasting and Boyling, as in the city of London. **1834** H. BRACKENRIDGE *Recoll.* 201 The exterior is undoubtedly sublime; but with the exception of the handsome library room . . . and the cook-shops below, it is a melancholy failure. **1837** *S. Lit. Messenger* III. 389 Fortunately a sort of cook's-shop was at hand. **1845** M. M. NOAH *Gleanings* 30, I passed by a cellar in Broadway, which was lighted up, and from which a steam refreshing savoury issued. It was a cook-shop or refectory. **1870** 'F. FERN' *Ginger-Snaps* 24 Finally . . . let China, or Africa, or Professor Blot with his traveling cook-shop . . . come speedily to the rescue and find us a way of escape.

+**b.** (See quotation.)
1863 KEMBLE *Journal* 18 Immediately opposite to this building is a small shed, which they [people of Ga.] call the cook's shop, and where the daily allowance of rice and corn grits of the people is boiled and distributed to them [slaves].

+**Cookstove.** A stove upon which food may be cooked.
'The vulgar wash-tub, shoe-horn, brew-house, cook-stove, . . . which are merely slovenly and uncouth abbreviations of washing-tub, shoeing-horn, brewing-house, and cooking-stove' (**1871** R. G. White *Words and Uses* 232).
1837 COLMAN *Mass. Agric. Rep.* (1838) 80 The wood when cut fit for a cook stove is worth $4 a cord. **1852** STOWE *Uncle Tom* xviii, An arrangement which St. Clare had vainly tried to persuade Dinah to exchange for the convenience of a modern cook-stove. **1868** *Mich. Agric. Rep.* VII. 348 Sales & Pelgrim, Detroit, [exhibited a] cook stove for wood or coal. **1877** *Rep. Indian Affairs* 61 Fifty good cook-stoves have been given to those Indians actually living in houses. **1890** *Century Mag.* Dec. 303 It was the dream of her life to save money enough to freight a good Northern cook-stove over from Chattanooga. **1912** COBB *Back Home* 66 Aunt Dilsey was a master hand at a cookstove. *a***1918** G. STUART *On Frontier* I. 32 My father-in-law used to tell a story about an old couple who were the first to invest in a cook stove in his neighborhood.
attrib. **1889** *Anthony's Photogr. Bul.* II. 220 A kitchen with a cook-stove attachment.

Cook tent. A tent, as with armies, circuses, and other traveling parties, in which food is cooked.
1885 E. B. CUSTER *Boots & Saddles* 53 We looked out, to find the cook-tent blown flat to the ground. **1890** — *Following Guidon* 300 The servants perpetually travelled to and fro from the cook tent to ours. **1895** *N.Y. Dramatic News* 7 Dec. 14/2 The last day of the Barnum and Bailey season was fittingly celebrated in the cook tent. **1910** MCCUTCHEON *Rose in Ring* 81 Presently the food came in from the cook-tent.

+**Cook wagon.** A wagon equipped for the cooking of food (used chiefly on cattle ranges in the West). — **1900** GARLAND *Eagle's Heart* 162 On the ground, scattered among the tents, and in the shade of the cook wagon, were some twenty or thirty herders. *a***1904** WHITE *Blazed Trail Stories* x. 178 The ponies, and the cook-wagon, and the cook . . . had done the alkali for three days. **1907** MULFORD *Bar-20* 119 Two cook wagons were stalled a short distance from the corral.

***Cooler.**

1. A container in which materials are allowed to cool, as in sugar making, distilling, etc. {1616-}
1766 in Chalkley *Scotch-Irish Settlement Va.* I. 127 Attached—2 iron crooks, . . . 2 funnels, 1 washing tub, 1 cooler, 1 tin saucepan. **1779** W. FLEMING in *Travels Amer. Col.* 620 They put the brine into a Cooler and let it stand till cold or near it. **1790** *Penna. Packet* 6 Jan. 4/2 To be Sold on Moderate Terms, Two large copper coolers, and two Boilers for Sugar-Bakers. **1819** M'MURTRIE *Sk. Louisville* 128 It is let down into large fermenting vessels, that (immediately under the coolers) command the stills. **1849** *Rep. Comm. Patents* 303 Returning the flour to the 'cooler,' to be re-bolted with the superfine flour. **1877** *Vt. Dairymen's Ass. Rep.* VIII. 90 The exhibition of the cans and coolers . . . gave the spectators a better idea of the working of this new method than can well be given on paper.
attrib. **1853** *Harper's Mag.* VII. 763/1 The interior of a sugar house can be properly divided into the 'cooler room,' the 'purgery,' the place for the kettles, and the mill.

+**2.** A cooling, spirituous drink. *colloq.*
1840 *Picayune* 16 Sept. 2/2 Juleps are supposed, by most people, to be a modern invention . . . and others, perchance, imagine that the art of mingling these coolers beautifully, was brought from the climes of the sun. **1877** BARTLETT 144 *Cooler*, a drink of spirits.

+**3.** 'A coat of some kind. *Obs.*' (Th.).
1848 *Knickerb.* XXXII. 227 What if his waistcoat boasted but two . . . buttons, and his ill-fitted cooler came but half-way down to the bend of his knee in a spare 'swallow-tail' behind? **1880** N. BROOKS *Fairport Nine* 25 In summer time he [=Nosey] wore a parti-colored tunic, or cooler.

+**4.** A vessel containing cooled drinking water; a water cooler.
1888 *Century Mag.* XXXVI. 771/2 A car, that had . . . its painted tin cooler with the refreshing liquid ice-water. **1905** F. H. SMITH *At Close Range* 250, 'I'll go to the cooler and wash up what I can, . . . ' she said . . . as she . . . made her way to the wash-basin.

+**5.** A jail or prison. *slang.*
1884 *Milnor* (Dak.) *Teller* 8 Aug., Two Milnor bloods were . . . arrested on the charge of drunken[n]ess, lodged in the cooler over night and then fined $5 in the morning. **1885** *Lisbon* (Dak.) *Star* 18 Sept., Along comes an officer, and gives me the collar. He was taking me to the cooler. **1896** ADE *Artie* 181 Of course a man livin' in this Indian village may think he's on the square as long as he keeps out o' the cooler. **1900** DRANNAN *Plains & Mts.* 348 All surrendered at once, and the entire crowd, six in number, were escorted to the cooler. **1910** MCCUTCHEON *Rose in Ring* 262 'Sing Sing! The penitentiary?' 'The sure-enough cooler. He's been there for nearly three years.'
fig. **1906** *N.Y. Ev. Post* 30 Jan. 1 This is taken to indicate that, to use the legislative phrase, the resolution will be 'put in the cooler' for the time, and only released if public pressure gets too strong.

+**Cooley.** Also **coolie, cooly,** etc. *W.* [Var. of COULÉE.] A ravine or gullylike valley.
1839 C. A. MURRAY *Travels* II. 97 In the coolies, or little valleys [near Prairie du Chien], lying between the ridges of hill, by which the country is intersected, are springs of the purest and most delicious water. **1881** *Chicago Times* 14 May (*O.E.D.*), These 'coolies' are dry during the summer season, but are flooded in the spring of the year. **1881** *N.Y. Times* 18 Dec. 4/3 Every ravine short of an inhabitable valley is called a

'cooley.' **1882** *Uncle Rufus & Ma* 43 At intervals are marshy sink-holes, or 'coolies,' as they are called in this country. **1884** *Lisbon* (Dak.) *Clipper* 13 March, She [a cow] was discovered in a cooley. **1888** CABLE *Bonaventure* 66 He saw her squatting on a board at the edge of a coolée, . . . pounding her washing with a wooden paddle. **1890** *Harper's Mag.* Aug. 383/1 Reno came quickly to a shallow 'cooley' (frontierism for gully), that led down . . . to the stream.

* **Coolie, Cooly.** A cheap laborer of an Oriental race. {1638–}

1852 *Harper's Mag.* V. 257/1 A demand by the State of California for the prompt interposition of Congress, by the passage of an Act prohibiting 'Coolies,' shipped to California under contracts, from laboring in the mines of this State. **1860** ABBOTT *South & North* 47 But the object most revolting . . . was the aspect of the Coolies. **1865** SCHURZ in *39th Congress 1 Sess.* Sen. Ex. Doc. No. 2, 21 Wild speculations were indulged in, how to remove the colored population at once and to import white laborers to fill its place; how to obtain a sufficient supply of coolies, &c., &c. **1880** *Harper's Mag.* LXI. 650/2 We had to console ourselves, as our coolies assuredly did, with the consequent coolness of the weather. *c***1900** R. L. HALE *Log of Forty-Niner* 141 The coolies were contract labourers, and were secured from China by agents.

attrib. **1852** *Harper's Mag.* V. 119/1 The bill allowing long contracts to be made for Coolie labor from China, and for calling a Convention to revise the State Constitution, were still pending. **1871** *Scribner's Mo.* II. 67/1 It is thus . . . that we owe the immigration of Chinese into California to the coolie system. *Ib.* 67/2 The present coolie-trade is conducted under so many restrictions as to deprive it of many of its worst features.

+**Coolieism.** The system of importing cheap labor from the Orient, chiefly China. — **1870** *Congress. Globe* 21 Jan. 654/1 [To seek to produce manufactures] by reductions on labor alone, . . . is to depress labor, not to protect it. To seek it by Chinese immigration in the form of coolieism is still worse. **1879** *Calif. Constitution* Art. xix. § 4 Asiatic coolieism is a form of human slavery, and is forever prohibited in this State.

+**Cooling board.** A board on which a corpse is placed during preparation for burial. — **1853** SIMMS *Sword & Distaff* 224 He wouldn't care ef I was on my cooling board to-morrow. **1855** J. E. COOKE *Ellie* 284, I know my time's a-comin', fast, an' I'm a-goin. You won't b'lieve it till you see me on the coolin' board. **1859** BARTLETT 98 *Cooling-board*, the board on which a dead body is laid out. Pennsylvania and Maryland. **1896** J. C. HARRIS *Sister Jane* 19, I'm old and ugly, but I don't want to be put on my cooling-board on account of driving a new set of nails in the front palings.

Cooling room. a. A room in which things are cooled. +**b.** *fig.* A waiting room before an office. — **(a) 1869** BROWNE *Adv. Apache Country* 533 As soon as the ores are sufficiently roasted they are removed from the ovens to the cooling and screening-room. **1891** CHASE & CLOW *Industry* II. 112 When the meat is thoroughly cold the cars are run up near the cooling-room. **(b) 1889** 'THANET' in *Harper's Bazar* 4 May 330/2 She walked through the two 'cooling-rooms,' into the office, and so into the street.

+**Coolweed.** The clearweed or richweed, *Pilea pumila.* — **1843** TORREY *Flora N.Y.* II. 223 *Adike pumila*. . . . Richweed. Coolweed. . . . Moist shady places, particularly in cool ravines. **1889** *Cent.* 1250 *Coolweed*, . . . so called from its succulent pellucid stems and its habit of growing in cool places.

+**Coolwort. a.** The false miterwort, *Tiarella cordifolia.* **b.** The bishop's-cap or miterwort, genus *Mitella.* — **(a) 1848** BARTLETT 90 *Coolwort* (*Tiarella cordifolia*), the popular name of an herb, the properties of which are diuretic and tonic. It is prepared by the Shakers. **1850** S. F. COOPER *Rural Hours* 85 The white cool-wort is mingled in light and airy tufts with the blue and yellow violets. **1891** *Cent.* 6326 *Tiarella cordifolia*, native from Canada to Virginia, is called false miterwort and coolwort. **(b) 1891** *Amer. Folk-Lore* IV. 148 Our name for *Mitella diphylla* was Coolwort.

+**Coon,** *n.* Also **'coon.** [Aphetic form of RACCOON.]

1. The raccoon, *Procyon lotor.*

1742 HEMPSTEAD *Diary* 388 Josh . . . kiled another Coon to Day. **1834** CARRUTHERS *Kentuckian* I. 95 You see he has the rogues in the city like a coon when he's treed. **1836** CROCKETT *Exploits* 19 He knew that a coon was as good a legal tender for a quart in the west, as a New York shilling, any day in the year. **1847** in H. Howe *Hist. Coll. Ohio* 27 The squatter helps himself out by hunting deer and coons. **1855** SIMMS *Forayers* 455 The Santee country was the land . . . of molasses, corn in abundance, any number of pigs, and 'coon and 'possum beyond any computation. **1871** EGGLESTON *Hoosier Schoolm.* i. 16 They's a coon what's been a eatin' our chickens lately. **1875** *Chicago Tribune* 16 Oct. 6/6 'Coons' smoked in the big cabin chimney, were served up with pound-cake, puddings, chicken-pie, 'store tea' and locust and persimmon beer. **1903** *N.Y. Sun* 1 Nov. 4 He was shot while in a tree attempting to dislodge a coon.

2. A fellow, usually of a rustic, frontiersman type. *Old coon*, 'old timer': (see also quot. 1877).

1834 SIMMS *Guy Rivers* 155 Matter enough . . . to be robbed of our findings by a parcel of blasted 'coons that haven't soul enough to keep them from freezing. **1835** LONGSTREET *Ga. Scenes* 22 'Well, my old coon,' said he, 'do you want to swap hosses?' **1843** HALIBURTON *Attaché* II. 37 A knowin' old coon, bred and born to London, might, but you couldn't. *a***1846** *Quarter Race Ky.*, etc. 135 Then there commenced a series of jibes, jokes, and stories, that no one can hear, or witness, except on an Arkansas hunt with 'old coons.' **1850** GARRARD *Wah-To-Yah* xix. 226 The old coon invited me to take a cigar. **1855** *Harper's Mag.* X. 850/1 How are you, old fellow? mighty glad to see you, old horse; looking well, old coon. **1877** BARTLETT 436 'He's an old coon,' is said of one who is very shrewd; often applied to a political manager. **1897** 'THANET' *Missionary Sheriff* 13, I tell you the coons that say you never must hit a woman don't know anything about that sort of women.

3. *Pol.* A nickname for a member of the Whig party. Now hist.

'*Coons*, a nick-name for the Whig party during Henry Clay's time. In the campaigns of that day raccoons were painted on banners, and live specimens were frequently borne in processions' (*Mag. Amer. Hist.* XIII. 99/2).

1842 *Spirit of Times* (Phila.) 5 May (Th.), 'The old Tip coon' is pictured flat on his back, in consequence of the Virginia elections. **1846** CORCORAN *Pickings* 190 'Why are you not a locofoco?' said we. . . . 'I live too near the old coon (Harrison) for that.' **1848** BARTLETT 91 *Coon*, . . . a nickname applied to those who belong to the Whig party. **1848** LOWELL *Biglow P.* 1 Ser. ix, Fust place, I've ben consid'ble round in bar-rooms an' saloons Agethrin' public sentiment, 'mongst Demmercrats and Coons. *a***1859** *Boston Post* (B.), Democrats, freemen! keep your council-fires brightly burning. . . . Rout the coons, beat them, overwhelm them. **1892** W. S. WALSH *Literary Curiosities* 190 In American politics, coon was a nickname for a Whig, first applied during the Presidential campaign of 1836.

4. A Negro. Often contemptuous. *colloq.*

1887 *Detroit Free Press* 23 July (Hoppe), The flasks are filled from the same barrel, but labeled variously to please the palate of the 'coon' or 'crackers.' **1892** *Congress. Rec.* 4 Feb. 856/2 Instead of seating one colored Representative, they seated two—two coons in place of the elected Representatives of the people. **1895** *N.Y. Dramatic News* 7 Dec. 10/3 After the coons were paid off on Saturday, some of them started on a jamboree. **1897** ADE *Pink Marsh* 59 Ain't safe to call cullud man coon no mo' any mo' 'an it is to say niggeh. **1906** *Springfield W. Republican* 4 Oct. 15 There was an unusually large midway. There were five 'hit the coon' howlers, no less than a dozen gypsy fortune tellers, and many other side attractions.

5. Phrases: **a.** *To tree (the) coon*, to solve a problem, or to corner a sought-after person. **b.** In comparisons or fig. language, wherein the coon is looked upon as prompting special excitement, or characterized by cleverness, sharpness, etc. **c.** *To skin* (or *hunt*) *the same old coon*, to defeat the Whigs again (cf. sense 3); also fig., to do a thing again and again. **d.** *To go the whole coon*, (see quotation). Cf. GONE COON.

(a) 1840 *Kentucky Rifle* 31 Oct., They've treed the coon. **1852** STOWE *Uncle Tom* xvii, Well, Tom, yer coons are fairly treed. **(b) 1846** CORCORAN *Pickings* 47 To use his own words, 'he dropped on him like a catamount on a coon.' **1847** ROBB *Squatter Life* 106, I slid atween 'em [snags and sawyers], sarpentine fashion, and got over clar as a pet coon. **1855** WILLIS *Convalescent* 14 He was 'still full of fun and as sharp as a 'coon.' **1861** *Vanity Fair* 9 Feb. 70/1 Every youth south of Mason and Dixon's, who had an average coon's sense, devoted himself to Po-li-tics. **1910** Hodge *Indians* II. 348 To be 'as forlorn as an unmated coon' is to be extremely wretched. **(c) 1842** [see COONISM]. **1848** LOWELL *Biglow P.* 1 Ser. v, The perfection o' bliss Is in skinnin' thet same old coon,' sez he [=J. Davis]. **1879** —*Poetical Wks.* 384 Meanwhile I inly curse the bore of hunting still the same old coon. **(d) 1892** W. S. WALSH *Literary Curiosities* 190 *Coon, Go the whole*, an American equivalent for 'go the whole hog.'

6. In various attrib. and comb. uses: **a.** In sense 1 with *catcher, catching, fur*, etc. **b.** With *whelp*, as a term of insult. **c.** In sense 3 with *campaign* and *tavern*. **d.** In sense 4 with *baby, barber shop, driver*, etc.

(a) 1825 in *Murphey Papers* I. 315 Our Bear Hunter and Coon Catcher the . . . accomplished Colo. David Crocket. **1842** *S. Lit. Messenger* VIII. 146/2 With their . . . 'fire hunts,' and turkey shooting, and coon-catching, and what not, it would have taken a regiment of sentinels to check the stragglers. **1863** *Ladies' Repository* XXIII. 89 A large tree from each side is felled that enables us to place poles from one to the other. Upon these we crawl over in what is called the 'coon fashion.' **1861** *Harper's Mag.* Dec. 136/2 The hat was made of coon fur, and . . . it weighed six pounds and a quarter! **1893** M. A. OWEN *Voodoo Tales* 40 Yo' done fegit bake' possum an' sweet-taters wid coon gravy. **1852** E. F. ELLET *Pioneer Women* 260 Raccoons also were abundant . . . , and were much used by settlers, although in after years of plenty they lost all relish for 'coon meat.' **1871** *Atlantic Mo.* XXVIII. 565/2 The old woman was in the exciting *dénouement* of a coon-story. **1895** *Outing* XXVI. 434/2 It is 'roastin' yere an' coon-time now.' **1856** *Spirit of Times* 18 Oct. 106/2 Lishe Proper's hounds struck coon-tracks, an' tooned up their pipes like moosicianers.

(b) 1837 BIRD *Nick of Woods* I. 223 You half-niggurs! you 'coon-whelps! you snakes! you varmints!

(c) 1887 *Scribner's Mag.* May 621/1 The venerable Mr. Pratt . . . remained clean-shaven in pious memory of Henry Clay and the coon campaign. **1844** *Chambers's Jrnl.* I. 264/2 A loco-foco and a 'coon' tavern.

(d) 1905 N. DAVIS *Northerner* 153 'Is n't she a dream of a 'coon baby?' **1901** HARRIGAN *Mulligans* 110 That's fine stuff to read in a coon barber shop! **1912** Cobb *Back Home* 224 He's got every coon bellhop around the place fighting for a chance to wait on him. **1907** Lillibridge *Trail* 106 They'll be having a bevel plate hearse with carved wood tassels and a coon driver next! **1900** *Musical Courier* 30 May 20/2 The writer in the *Sun* further declares that Germans, Italians and French write the so-called 'coon-music.'

+**Coon,** *v.* [f. the noun.]

1. *tr.* To crawl or creep along (a log, etc.) in the manner of a raccoon.

1835 Simms *Partisan* 320 That curious sort of locomotion which, in the South and West, is happily styled 'cooning the log.' **1840** — *Border Beagles* 96 Without stopping like more wary adventurers to probe his footing with a pole, then drive his horse through the stream while he 'cooned a log' above it. **1854** *Oregonian* 28 Oct. (Th.), A deep chasm had, reaching across it, a small ancient looking cedar log, which had either to be walked or cooned. **1890** *Amer. Notes & Q.* IV. 280 To *'coon* a log, for instance, when it is off the ground or across water. The meaning is to go on all fours along the log.

b. *To coon it,* in the same sense.

1834 A. Pike *Sketches* 77 Irwin . . . was obliged to straddle the log, and as they quaintly call it in the west, 'Coon it across.' **1845** Hooper *Daddy Bigg* 193 He must a' . . . cooned it on the top o' the limb. **1883** Shields *S. S. Prentiss* 27 In time of freshets, Prentiss and his scholars had to coon it over Second Creek. **1887** 'Craddock' *Keedon Bluffs* 10, I' b'lieve I could . . . coon it roun' that thar ledge an' git the ball.

2. *intr.* To crawl along on hands and knees.

1886 *Century Mag.* Nov. 16/2 *note,* In trying to 'coon' across Knob Creek on a log, Lincoln fell in. **1912** Wason *Friar Tuck* 141 The Friar had him coon up on the ledge.

3. *tr.* To steal (an article). *slang.*

1901 *Dialect Notes* II. 138 *Coon,* v. tr. Steal; 'to go cooning melons.' N.Y. **1916** Wilson *Red Gap* 92 'I found 'em,' pleaded the bad man. . . . 'Cooned 'em, you mean!' thundered the judge. 'You cooned 'em from Buck or Sandy.'

‖**Coona.** A kind of dance. — **1846** Emory *Military Reconn.* 43 This cold and formal dance soon gave way to the more joyous dances of the country, the Coona, the Bolero, and the Italiana.

+**Cooncan.** *S.W.* [Sp. *conquian* < *con quien,* with whom.] A card game. — **1889** *Century Mag.* April 905/1 The men got out a pack of Mexican cards and gambled at a game called 'Coon-can' for a few nickels and dimes.

+**Coon dog.** A dog especially useful in hunting raccoons.

1833 J. Hall *Harpe's Head* 230 An old 'coon dog, has a face covered with scars. **1853** Simms *Sword & Distaff* 295 All coon dogs, on this place, Cappin, must be owned by a white man; by you, by me, or by the lieutenant. **1855** M. Reid *Hunters' Feast* 97 Uncle Abe's dog—a stout terrier —was esteemed the 'smartest' 'coon-dog in a circle of twenty miles. **1872** Eggleston *End of World* 77 Like the man who warranted his dog to be a good coon-dog, bekase he warn't good for nothin' else. **1876** Burroughs *Winter Sunshine* 85 But every such neighborhood has its coon-dog, and the boys and young men dearly love the sport. **1887** 'Craddock' *Keedon Bluffs* 99 The Sawyers had brought with them the dutiful clerk, who was also preeminent as a coon-dog. **1897** *Chicago Tribune* 22 Aug. 2/5 Coon dogs are usually supposed to be the most important factors at an orthodox badger pull.

b. *Coon-dog principle,* the principle that a person, etc., is suitable for a certain purpose only because he is not good for anything else. (Cf. quot. 1872 above.)

1878 Beadle *Western Wilds* 173 On the Hoosier's 'Coon-dog principle,' [the region] ought to be rich in mines.

‖**Coonee-lat(t)ee.** [?Amer. Indian.] The mockingbird, *Mimus polyglottos.* — **1835** Simms *Yemassee* I. 73 The Catawba . . . speaks with the trick-tongue of the Coonee-lattee. [Note] The mocking bird. *Ib.* 169 The Coonee-latee, or Trick-tongue of the Yemassees—together with the gleesome murmur of zephyr and brook, gave to the scene an aspect of wooing and seductive repose.

+**Cooner.** *S.* 'A common term . . . for a canoe' (B. '59). Cf. Cunner.

+**Coonery.** [f. Coon *n.* 3.] The doctrines of the Whig party, powerful in the 1840's. — **1843** *Missouri Republican* 21 March (Th.), The beggary which Whiggery (or, to adopt the latest alias, Coonery) has brought upon the Government. *a***1859** *Boston Post* (B.), Democrats, . . . we must achieve a victory— . . . coonery must fall with all its corruptions and abominations.

+**Cooneyite.** (See quotation.) — **1856** *Spirit of Times* 4 Oct. 70/3 Those dwellers of the old dominion [=Virginia] are here [in Washington, D.C.] nick-named 'Cooneyites,' and are the greatest drinkers of bad whiskey extant.

+**Coon hunt.** A hunt for the raccoon.

1835 Audubon *Ornith. Biog.* III. 235 With your leave, then, Reader, I will take you to a 'Coon Hunt.' **1851** *S. Lit. Messenger* XVII. 619/2 Has your imagination ever discerned in that nocturnal diversion called a 'coon-hunt' anything of the picturesque? **1853** 'P. Paxton' *Yankee in Texas* 114 All children are inclined to make companions of the negroes, . . . to accompany them upon their 'coon hunts,' &c. **1860** Claiborne *Sam. Dale* 27 Before day the same morning my brother and I slipped out for a 'coon hunt. **1884** Roe *Nature's Story* 306 A 'coon hunt usually takes place near midnight. Men, with dogs trained to the sport, will repair to a corn-field known to be infested. **1887** 'Craddock' *Keedon Bluffs* 98 All the boys of Tanglefoot Cove and the mountain slopes had gathered for a coon-hunt. **1895** *Outing* XXVI. 434/1 Long after I could down my quail and break my own dogs, I have sneaked away of an August night to join a crowd of 'brack niggers' for a good old-fashioned coon-hunt.

+**Coon-hunting.** The hunting of the raccoon.

1840 *S. Lit. Messenger* VI. 386/1 He is fond of possum, rabbit, and coon-hunting. **1845** C. M. Kirkland *Western Clearings* 83, I was out a 'coon-hunting, and see the light, but . . . they'd got it pretty well down before I got there. **1851** *Polly Peablossom* 94 Bill Sweeney and Tom Culpepper is the two greatest old coveys in our settlement for coon-huntin. **1855** M. Reid *Hunters' Feast* 96 'Coon-hunting is peculiarly a negro sport. **1887** 'Craddock' *Keedon Bluffs* 100 Any one who did not think respectfully of Bose was some one who did not care to go coon-hunting. **1895** *Outing* XXVI. 436/1 His red-hot fighting quality furnishes the real excitement of coon-hunting.

+**Cooning.** **1.** The hunting of raccoons. Also attrib. **2.** The act of creeping on all fours like a raccoon. — **(1)** *c***1845** *Big Bear Arkansas,* etc. 93 He went a Coonin' of it with his dogs. **1876** Burroughs *Winter Sunshine* 85 At this time, cooning in the remote interior is a favorite pastime. *Ib.* 86 Then follows a pell-mell rush of the cooning party up the hill. **(2)** **1883** Shields *S. S. Prentiss* 27 The crossing of such a [log] bridge, in Western parlance, is styled *cooning.*

‖**Coonish.** (See quotations and cf. Coon *n.* 5 b.) — **1840** Haliburton *Clockmaker* 3 Ser. ii, I thought I should a-died for shame one minit, and the next I felt so coonish I had half a mind to fly at the Speaker and knock him down. *Ib.* xiv, The old women began to whisper and look coonish, and, at last . . . I got a notice to make myself scarce from Judge Lynch.

+**Coonism.** **a.** The doctrines and practices of the Whigs. **b.** The Whig party. — **(a)** **1842** *Spirit of Times* 9 Oct. (Th.), Ohio has gone most unexpectedly for Democracy,—has skinned the coons, and repudiated Coonism, Federalism, Clayism, and every other species of Whiggism. **(b)** **1844** *Congress. Globe* App. 4 June 663 Such are the qualifications which constitute Mr. Clay a Simon Pure in the eyes of coonism.

+**Coon oyster.** A small oyster: (see quot. 1881). — **1870** *Amer. Naturalist* III. 460 The small oysters . . . are not generally eaten except by the raccoons, hence the common name for them of 'coon oysters.' **1881** E. Ingersoll *Oyster Industry* 243 *Coon Oyster,* small, shapeless, worthless stock, growing in heavy clusters along the salt marshes, or forming great bars. (Southern coast.) At Cape May the word is restricted to young oysters caught on the sedges.

+**Coonroot.** [Aphetic form of Puccoonroot.] The bloodroot, *Sanguinaria canadensis.* — **1893** *Amer. Folk-Lore* VI. 137 *Sanguinaria Canadensis,* . . . puccoon root. Anderson, Ind.; coon-root. West Va. [**1910** in Hodge *Indians* II. 315 In s.w. Virginia puccoon is locally abbreviated 'coon.']

+**Coon's age.** A considerable length of time. *colloq.*[2]

1845 Thompson *Chron. Pineville* 72 We won't hear the eend of this bis'-ness for a coon's age: you see if we do. *Ib.* 128 He can talk more sense in a minute than old Rogers can understand in a coon's age. **1845** Hooper *Taking Census* i. 155 We had not seen the amount of cash mentioned as lost, in a 'coon's age.' *a***1846** *Quarter Race Ky.,* etc. 85 Jim Clark has gone to the woods for fat pine, and Peggy Willet is along to take a lite for him—they've been gone a coon's age. **1851** *Polly Peablossom* 74 That's the best red eye I've swallered in er coon's age. **1896** J. C. Harris *Sister Jane* 186 Why, Janey, I ain't seen you in a coon's age. **1912** Raine *Brand Blotters* 189, I ain't see you long enough for a good talk in a coon's age.

‖**Coonship.** The state of being a coon (in the political sense of a supporter of the Whig party). — **1842** *Spirit of Times* (Phila.) 20 Oct. (Th.), 'Twas there his coonship sat in state, a-watching of the moon, O the instant you'd lay eyes on him, you'd know that same Old Coon.

+**Coonskin, Coon-skin.**

1. The skin of a raccoon.

1818 A. Royall *Lett. from Ala.* 103 He . . . axed Marchant if he didn't want to trade for some coonskins. **1836** Crockett *Exploits* 5, I threw down the coon skin upon the counter, and called for a quart. **1845** *Knickerb.* XXV. 320 The common currency of the country at that day, as now, in many places, was 'coon skins,' and other peltries. **1851** *Polly Peablossom* 50 That feller, Bonnel, sold me a pint of red-eye whiskey . . . for a coon-skin. **1871** *Atlantic Mo.* Nov. 569 No man could have Susan who couldn't show coon-skins enough of his own killing to make a bedquilt. **1873** 'Mark Twain' & Warner *Gilded Age* I. 22 [He] traded a quart of thick molasses for a coonskin and a cake of beeswax. **1895** *Century Mag.* Aug. 620/2 The darkies used to drag a coon-skin through the woods, and run mongrels after it.

b. With reference to its use as a political symbol of the Whig party, chiefly in the presidential campaign of 1840. Also attrib.

1840 *Niles' Nat. Reg.* 14 March 21/2 The delegation from Fairfield county . . . came, carriages, horsemen, music; . . . then the 'Mad river trappers' in their lodge, . . . 'coon skins' nailed on the sides. **1841** *Congress. Globe* App. Jan. 153/1 Ridiculous displays of log cabins, beset in coon skins, fox tails, [etc.]. *Ib.* 3 Feb. 147 The log cabins and coon skin banners, which you used so successfully in the late contest, will not avail you now. *Ib.* 26 Aug. 308/2 All the coon skins in America will not cover the deformity of the measures which they have brought forward this session. **1846** Corcoran *Pickings* 154 If I find they are locofocos, I damn coon skins, log cabins, and hard cider. **1885** *Harper's Mag.* Oct. 743/1

This law grew out of the 'log-cabin, hard-cider, and 'coon-skin' campaign of 1840.

2. Attrib. with *cape, robe.*

1851 *Polly Peablossom* 75 When I drops this koon-skin cape, then you pull! **1876** *Vt. Bd. Agric. Rep.* III. 120 The young farmer, in these days, must have . . . a two hundred dollar buggy, and a splendid set of coon skin or wolf skin robes.

b. *Coonskin cap,* a cap made of coonskin, which fits like a cylinder upon the head.

1836 SIMMS *Mellichampe* i, He gathered up his rifle, drew the 'coon-skin cap over his eyes, and at once fell in procession with the rest. **1838** DRAKE *Tales & Sk.* 64 The colonists presented, indeed, a curiously grotesque appearance, loitering about the 'station' in ruffle shirts and coon-skin caps. **1855** SIMMS *Forayers* 122 The costume . . . was of ordinary blue homespun, trowsers and hunting shirt, yellow fringed, a rough and ragged coon-skin cap. **1870** KEIM *Sheridan's Troopers* 130 His companions were arrayed in . . . coon-skin caps, buffalo leggins, blankets. **1893** *Atlantic Mo.* Feb. 151/2 They stood with . . . coonskin caps slouching over their brows. **1895** KING *New Orleans* 162 The tall, lanky Westerner, in coonskin cap and leathern hunting shirt. **1905** N. DAVIS *Northerner* 228 My father's 'coon-skin cap; he was a captain in the Raccoon Roughs.

+**Coonskin-capped,** *a.* Wearing a coonskin cap. — **1881** *Harper's Mag.* April 712/1 As for . . . plains-men and coon-skin-capped hunters . . . of the 'West,' . . . you see no more of them.

‖**Coonskinner.** *Obs.* A supporter of the Whig party, whose symbol was a coonskin. — **1842** *Congress. Globe* App. 9 July 650/1 What can be a more protective tariff? Why, there is not a tariff in the world half so dear to a coonskinner.

+**Coon song.** A popular song, common among Negroes, or about Negro life. Also attrib.

'So called because originally associated with coon-hunting' (*Cent.* 1909). 'Coon-song means to the Negro any popular song, not religious, composed by a white man about the Negro' (*Amer. Speech* IV. 213).

1896 *N.Y. Dramatic News* 18 July 11/4 Caroline Hull has met with success in singing Thomas LaMark's new coon song, 'Black Baby Mine.' **1899** *Chicago Record* 11 Jan. 4/4 The so-called 'coon song' . . . appeared in its present shape a little more than five years ago. *Ib.*, Syncopation . . . or else the steady use of a strong accent, . . . combined with a swinging melody, have given the 'coon-song' music much of its character. **1899** *Chicago Tribune* 17 April 7/2 The songs were introduced [into the play by May Irwin] at any and all times. . . . All were 'coon songs.' **1902** LORIMER *Lett. Merchant* 167 The Doctor was quite a hand at card tricks, played the banjo, sung coon songs [etc.]. **1902** WHITLOCK *13th District* 30 They . . . fled with relief to the banjo, the mandolin, and the coon songs that echoed . . . along the borders of Silver Lake. **1904** *N.Y. Sun* 7 Aug. 18 Time was when 'coon songs,' whether of the old plantation variety or the modern ragtime kind, were written by white men.

+**Coontie.** Also **coonta, coonte,** etc. [Seminole *kunti.*] The arrowroot (*Zamia integrifolia*) of southern Florida; also, the China or bull brier (q.v.). Also attrib. with *blossom, root.*

1800 B. HAWKINS *Sk. Creek Country* 21 This [China] briar is called *Coonte*, and the bread made of it . . . is an important article of food among the hunters. **1823** G. A. MCCALL *Lett. from Frontiers* (1868) 60 He was absent; but to-day I found him digging the coonta-root. **1836** *Ib.* 295 He stated . . . that the 'koonta,' a very good species of the arrow-root, grew plenteously everywhere. **1852** F. R. GOULDING *Young Marooners* 173 Harold discovered a fine patch of Coontah or arrowroot from which a beautiful flour can be manufactured. **1862** *Rep. Comm. Patents: Agric.* 403 [In tropical Florida] the earth produces the *Coonte* and the cabbage tree. **1899** M. GOING *Flowers* 295 What goes down through the pollen-tube of the coontie-blossom is not a mere globule of jelly.

b. The foodstuff obtained from its root. Also attrib.

1791 W. BARTRAM *Travels* 241 A very agreeable, cooling sort of jelly, which they [Indians in Florida] call conte, . . . is prepared from the root of the China briar. **1819** *Penna. Gazette* 22 June 2/3 [The Seminoles] use a root called coonty, as a substitute [for corn]. **1837** WILLIAMS *Florida* 33 The inhabitants living principally on fish, turtle, and coonti; the last, they bring from the main.

Co-op. *Co-op store,* a co-operative store. Also ellipt. {1884–, *dial.*}

1873 BEADLE *Undevel. West* 339 The co-op. store bought a thousand muskets at the Government sale. **1893** GUNTER *Miss Dividends* 187 This Mormon gentleman suddenly exclaims, . . . 'They would have cost in our co-op. up in Heber nigh onto five dollars a pair in farm produce.' **1904** STEEDMAN *Bucking the Sagebrush* 17 All trading was done at the 'co-op' stores. *Ib.* 18 These 'co-ops' had some system of exchange with the headquarters in Salt Lake City.

***Coop,** *n.*[1] +**1.** A place in which voters are held: (see the verb). +**2.** *To fly the coop,* to depart without notice. *colloq.* — **(1) 1889** *Pall Mall Gaz.* 18 Feb. 6/2 They were made to vote the ticket of the party that controlled the 'coop.' Our coop was in the rear of an engine-house on Calvert-street. **(2) 1907** WHITE *Arizona Nights* 138, I suppose you thought I'd flew the coop. **1909** WASON *Happy Hawkins* 75 Jabez had hunted over the place to find something to fuss about as soon as he discovered 'at Barbie an' me had flown the coop.

Coop, *n.*[2] {*a*1825–} *Coop-and-seek,* the game of hide-and-seek. (Cf. HIDE-AND-COOP.) — **1884** *Advance* (Chicago), And then we play at coop and seek.

***Coop,** *v.* +*tr.* (See quot. 1885.)

1844 *Lexington Observer* 16 Oct. 2/3 He is said to have been 'cooped' by the locofocos. **1859** BARTLETT 98 *Cooping of voters*, collecting and confining them, several days previous to an election, in a house or on a vessel hired for the purpose. **1885** *Mag. Amer. Hist.* XIII. 99/2 *Coop*, to 'coop voters' is to collect them as it were in a coop or cage, so as to be sure of their services on election day. **1889** *Pall Mall Gaz.* 18 Feb. 6/2 Four of us, including [E. A.] Poe, . . . were nabbed by a gang of men who were on the look out for voters to 'coop.'

+**Cooped voter.** (See quotation.) — **1888** M. LANE in *America* 27 Sept. 15 *Cooped voters*, a lot of voters, collected and kept under a kind of guard, so that the other side cannot get at them. They are usually well fed and liquored, and on election day are taken to the polls and voted, being carefully watched to see that no one tampers with them.

***Cooper,** *n.*[1] Also †**cowper.** One whose occupation is to make or repair wooden vessels such as barrels and tubs.

1637–8 *Mass. Bay Rec.* I. 223 The m[a]rshall, taking w[i]th him a cowper, shall . . . give notice to . . . all the inhabitants there to bring their measures & weights to a certain place. **1641** *Conn. Public Rec.* I. 65 Smithes and Coopers, shall not take aboue 20d for a dayes worke. **1714** *Boston News-Letter* 28 March 2/2 An Indian Lad aged about Eighteen years, a Cooper by Trade, to be Sold and seen at the Shop of Joseph Sevell Cooper in King-Street. **1755** in *Lett. to Washington* I. 106, I have spoke to all the Coopers . . . who ask Extravagant Rates for Casks to wit 4/ a bar[re]l. **1809** F. CUMING *Western Tour* 223 Pittsburgh [has] five coopers; thirteen weavers. **1839** TOWNSEND *Narrative* 318 Extensive preparations had been made to prosecute the salmon fishery, and the coopers have been engaged the whole winter in making barrels to accommodate them. **1883** 'MARK TWAIN' *Life on Miss.* liv, The coopers had sunk a pile of green hickory hoop-poles.

attrib. **1659** *Rowley Rec.* 104 Upon Consideration of the Decay of usefull timber for Cowper stuf . . . it is ordered [etc.]. **1824** DODDRIDGE *Notes* 145 Their cooper ware, which comprehended every thing for holding milk, and water, was generally pretty well executed.

+**Cooper,** *n.*[2] One who collects and holds voters, in order to have them vote on a certain side. — **1885** *Mag. Amer. Hist.* XIII. 99/2 Liquor dealers are the usual 'coopers,' for obvious reasons.

Cooper, *v.* {1746–}

1. *tr.* To secure (a barrel or cask) with hoops; to make or repair (barrels, etc.) Also fig.

1742 *Md. Hist. Mag.* XX. 166 Get the Barrells coopered. **1780** *N.H. Hist. Soc. Coll.* I. 235 All the Caskes Whether of Provisions or Water [are to be] Cooperd. **1856** *Florida Plant. Rec.* 451, 1 Carpentor coopering hogsheads. **1868** BEECHER *Norwood* 45 No work today. Tell old Brett, if he don't like it, to cooper his own barrels!

transf. **1867** G. W. HARRIS *Sut Lovingood* 256 When Daltin got his hed cooper'd up arter that cavin in. **1906** *Springfield W. Republican* 30 Aug. 8 There is a belief that the nomination will still be contested by the conservatives, and that Moran has by no means got the nomination all coopered up tight.

b. To put away in a cask.

1775 *Essex Inst. Coll.* XIII. 190, I have had it cooper'd and will watch it constantly.

+**2.** To understand. *slang.*

*a***1889** in Barrère & Leland I. 270 Why on earth nature made you in the shape she did is more than I can cooper.

Cooperage. The making or repairing of barrels, casks, etc. {1714–} Also attrib.

1705 *Va. State P.* I. 97 The Agent shall . . . only pay twenty pounds of tobacco for such cask, the other ten being allowed him for the trouble of Cooperage. **1735** *Essex Inst. Coll.* XLV. 220 To Cooperidge for Triming water cask [£]1. **1778** *Jrnls. Cont. Congress* XI. 459 To send . . . a person of diligence and skill to Virginia, there to . . . cause necessary cooperage, fresh brine, or smoaking, and other necessary precautions to be taken, for the preservation of the public provisions. **1852** J. REYNOLDS *Hist. Illinois* 87 The cooperage of the country amounted to very little more than making well-buckets. **1857** *Harper's Mag.* March 443/1 We might now take a walk through the extensive cooperage and packing-rooms [of the fisheries]. **1875** *Chicago Tribune* 11 Sept. 3/4 There was inevitable 'cooperage.' The average box was recoopered half a dozen times on the way.

b. The product made by a cooper.

1860 CURTIS *Woody Plants N.C.* 46 [The wood of the chestnut] is sometimes used for cooperage. **1884** SARGENT *Rep. Forests* 515 Manufacturers of cooperage and wheel stock.

Co-operationist. {1831–} +Political, in South Carolina: One who favored co-operating with other states in the matter of secession. — **1851** *Harper's Mag.* IV. 120/1 The following table shows the relative strength of each party in the State—those in favor of the Union as it is, of course, voting with the Co-operationists. *Ib.* III. 557/2 A letter . . . was also read, reflecting in severe terms upon the spirit manifested by the 'actionists' toward the 'co-operationists.' **1851** *Whig Almanac 1852* 43/2 The Co-Operationists . . . carried six districts; and the Secessionists . . . carried one.

Co-operative, *a.* {1603–} Pertaining to a system in which the profits of an enterprise are distributed among the participants or customers. {1821–}

1873 *Winfield* (Kansas) *Courier* 14 Aug. 1/6 The idea of establishing co-operative stores and shops was a great mistake, and a very foolish one. **1882** *Harper's Mag.* Nov. 920/2 The latest . . . attempt to secure moderate rents was made some three years ago by the promulgation of a plan to build co-operative apartment-houses. **1887** *Ib.* May 972/1 In a co-operative establishment it is, as a rule, understood that the workers are owners of the greater part or even all of the capital. **1892** *Vt. Agric. Rep.* XII. 115 There are good cheese factories at Dorset and co-operative creameries at Rupert.

absol. **1920** *3rd Nat. Country Life Conf. Proc.* 53 Farmers' co-operatives . . . are more analogous . . . to the workmen producers' co-operatives than they are to the consumers' co-operatives.

Coopering. {1746–} The act of making or repairing casks, barrels, etc. — **1720** SEWALL *Diary* III. 276, I . . . bid him [Thomas Wheeler] leave off working at his Trade of Set-Work Coopering. **1768** WASHINGTON *Diaries* I. 282, I agreed with Jonathan Palmer to come and Work with my Carpenters; either at their Trade—Coopering—or, in short at anything that he may be set about. **1874** KNIGHT 616/1 Dry coopering consists of making barrels for flour, etc.

attrib. **1874** *Index of Patents* I. 363 Coopering-machine [invented by] O. Barber [of] Hartford, Conn. [patented] Jan. 8, 1810.

+**Cooper's hawk.** [Wm. *Cooper*, fl. 1828.] A common kind of hawk, *Accipiter cooperi.*

1828 BONAPARTE *Synopsis* 433 The Cooper's Hawk, *Falco cooperii*, . . . inhabits North America: appearing in autumn and the beginning of winter in the middle states. **1839** PEABODY *Mass. Birds* 267 Cooper's Hawk, *Falco Cooperii*. . . . [These birds] are said [in the southern states] . . . to be troublesome in consequence of their depredations upon the poultry. **1844** *Nat. Hist. N.Y., Zoology* II. 18 Cooper's Hawk . . . is a bold and swift bird, attacking chiefly the smaller birds. **1868** *Amer. Naturalist* II. 377, I have full sets of Cooper's-hawks' eggs, without a blotch upon them, and others blotched with brown, and one set blotched with red. **1874** COUES *Birds N.W.* 337 Cooper's Hawk is . . . abundant in most parts of the United States; particularly so in New England, where it is perhaps the most numerous of all the birds of prey.

Cooper shop. The establishment in which a cooper carries on his business. {1632 *Obs.*}

1730 J. COMER *Diary* 112 A fire broke out at Capt. Malbone's wharf in a cooper shop. **1827** DRAKE & MANSFIELD *Cincinnati* 65 Eleven cooper shops 48 men. **1868** BEECHER *Norwood* 41 The ground floor was a cooper shop and general tinkering establishment. **1894** FREDERIC *Copperhead* 55 He had been a well-to-do man . . . with a big cooper-shop. **1901** DUNCAN & SCOTT *Allen & Woodson Co., Kansas* 595 At that time there was a small building two lots north of Dubinsky's store that was used as a cooper shop.

attrib. **1866** MOORE *Women of War* 343 A vote of thanks from the Cooper Shop committee to Miss Ross.

+**Cooper's reed.** The cattail, *Typha latifolia.* — **1847** DARLINGTON *Weeds & Plants* 347 Cooper's Reed. . . . The leaves of this plant are (or formerly were) much used, by the coopers, to secure the joints of casks, &c., from leaking.

+**Cooper's sandpiper.** (See quotation.) — **1874** COUES *Birds N.W.* 491 Cooper's sandpiper.—*Tringa cooperi*. . . . *Hab.*—Long Island. The type specimen remains unique.

***Coot.**

+**1.** Any of various web-footed birds, esp. the flusterer, *Fulica americana.*

'There are several sorts of sea-fowl on our coast . . . that are known by the general name of "coot" ' (1875 *Fur, Fin, & Feather* 119).

1709 LAWSON *Carolina* 149 Black Flusterers. . . . Some call these the great bald Coot. **1791** BARTRAM *Travels* 118 The laughing coots with wings half spread were tripping over the little coves. **1812** WILSON *Ornithology* VI. 27 The Rail, or as it is called in Virginia the Sora, and in South Carolina the Coot. **1813** *Ib.* IX. 62 Common Coot. . . . It is known in Pennsylvania by the name of Mud-hen. **1844** *Nat. Hist. N.Y., Zoology* II. 333 The Eider Duck . . . is known on Long island under the names of Black and White Coot. **1870** *Amer. Naturalist* III. 226 Myriads of sea-ducks from the Northern seas . . . which are so absurdly designated by fishermen and gunners as 'Coots.' **1882** GODFREY *Nantucket* 157 In the early spring, at Coatue and in the upper harbor, brant, sheldrakes, coots, and whistlers are to be found in considerable numbers. **1885** *Harper's Mag.* March 657/2 He killed a coot, a species of wild-duck proverbial for their toughness and their tenacity in holding on to life. **1891** *Boston Journal* 12 March 4/1 Twelve redheads, one bald pate and a coot were secured during the day. **1906** E. W. PRINGLE *Rice Planter* 382, I saw Green ahead of me carrying a pair of wild ducks and a string of coots.

b. Proverbial phrases: *Crazy* (or *silly*) *as a coot.*

1844 *Knickerb.* XXIII. 552 He's as crazy as a coot. **1874** LONG *Wild-Fowl* 63 Coot are uncommonly foolish ducks, so much so that 'silly as a coot' has become a frequent expression of the coast-gunners when speaking of a light-headed or tipsy person.

2. A silly person; a fellow. *colloq.*

(*a*) **1794** *Gazette of U.S.* (Phila.) 17 Jan. (Th.), But Satan was not such a coot To sell Judea for a goat. **1845** JUDD *Margaret* I. xv, Little coot! Don't you know the Bible is the best book in the world. **1857** *Harper's Mag.* Jan. 284/1 A poor coot of a fellow who had spent hundreds of dollars at a well-known grocery. **1886** HOWELLS *Minister's Charge* 155 Statira said she behaved like a perfect coot all the way through, and Lemuel said that he guessed he had been the coot, if there was any.

(*b*) **1843** STEPHENS *High Life N.Y.* I. 1 The lazy coot did nothing on arth but eat raw turnips and drink cider brandy. *c***1847** WHITCHER *Bedott P.* ix. 92 He's an amazin' ignorant old coot. **1860** HOLLAND *Miss Gilbert* 56 You remember old Bob Sampson—drunken old coot—he was my father. **1887** *Scribner's Mag.* (F.), He was debarred the rude heraldry of a nickname of achievement, and . . . was known vaguely as 'him,' Skeesicks, or that coot.

3. Attrib. and comb. with *fever, shooter, shooting.*

1874 LONG *Wild-Fowl* 62 [Flat decoys] seemed to work first-rate, especially in coot-shooting. **1875** *Fur, Fin, & Feather* 121 In coot-shooting on the New England coast we have not met with it [brant]. *Ib.* 124 The coot-shooter has to dare the combing breakers. **1905** E. W. PRINGLE *Rice Planter* 217 He is intoxicated with the rice bird and coot fever and spends every night out hunting.

+**Cooter.** [West African (Bambara, Malinké) *kuta;* Central African (Congo basin) *nkudu.*]

1. The Carolina box turtle, *Cistudo carolina. S.*

'It is never here pronounced "cooter" as spelled, but ku-duh, ku-tuh' (1936 J. Bennett [of Charleston, S.C.] *Let.* 5 April).

1832 T. COOPER *Memoirs of Nullifier* (1860) 24 It was a large cooter, that . . . rose to the surface, only a few feet distant. **1835** SIMMS *Partisan* 308 You're turned now . . . on the flat of your back like a yellow-belly cooter. **1859** *Knickerb.* LIII. 413 It turns out to be a large 'cooter,' (which we take to be a sort of snapping-turtle) that . . . rose to the surface. **1872** W. J. FLAGG *Good Investment* xx. 903/2 A live 'cooter' (terrapin) resting bottom upward. **1888** *Century Mag.* Dec. 296/2 Two years before his death Minc had caught and tamed a little cooter about twice the size of a silver dollar. **1903** E. W. PRINGLE *Rice Planter* 14 As I walked down the bank I found a 'cooter' (terrapin) which had come out of the river to lay eggs. **1918** *Dialect Notes* V. 18 *Cooter*, a turtle, especially a fresh-water turtle (N.C. dialect).

transf. **1853** *Turnover: a Tale of N.H.* 43 (Th.), What 'u'd these darned cooters think, if they could see us naow?

b. *Drunk as a cooter.*

1827 *Mass. Spy* 22 Aug. (Th.), A few jolly topers, who wallowed in the sand, 'as drunk as a cooter.' **1851** *Polly Peablossom* 45, I can manage to have him as drunk as a cooter by dark. **1908** *Dialect Notes* III. 307.

2. A turtle or tortoise, *Pseudemys concinna*, of Florida.

1884 GOODE *Fisheries* 155 *Pseudemys concinna*, the 'Florida Cooter,' is found in all the Southern States.

+**Cop,** *n.*[1] [Cf. COPPER. *n.*[2]] A policeman. *colloq.*[2]

1859 MATSELL *Vocabulum* 124 Oh! where will be . . . all the cops and beaks so knowin', A hundred stretches hence? **1870** *Mass. Reports* CVII. 200 The district attorney stated 'that it was a slang word not to be found in the ordinary dictionaries of the language.' . . . The witness answered that 'State Cop.' meant 'a deputy state constable—of the Commonwealth.' **1883** *Wheelman* I. 431 Keep your eyes out for cops. **1893** POST *Harvard Stories* 110 The 'super' captain was going to turn me over to the cop. **1907** 'O. HENRY' *Trimmed Lamp*, etc. 79 Now will you take me home, or will I have to call a cop? **1920** SANDBURG *Smoke & Steel* 19 And the traffic cop a spot of blue.

+**Cop,** *n.*[2] (See quotation.) — **1875** *Chambers's Jrnl.* 13 March 172/2 During the rebellion, the Peace party, being suspected of favouring the South, were nicknamed Copperheads or Cops.

Cop, *v. slang.* {1704–, *n. dial.* and *slang*}

1. *tr.* To arrest.

1875 G. P. BURNHAM *Three Years* p. v, Copped, arrested or secured by a 'Cop,' or Detective. **1899** HARTE *Jack Hamlin's Mediation*, etc. 87 Since you're here and expect the papers to-morrow, why don't you 'cop' him now?

+**2.** *To cop out*, to win (a girl or woman) as a sweetheart or wife.

1896 ADE *Artie* 91 There's no need of a man goin' nanny just because he's copped out a nice girl all for himself. **1909** 'O. HENRY' *Options* 254 'Why don't you cop the lady out?' asked Mack. **1910** MCCUTCHEON *Rose in Ring* 197 Oh, I'm not asking you to give her up, kid—not for a minute. Cop her out if you can.

b. = sense 1.

1901 FLYNT *World of Graft* 102, He hadn't been there more'n a day when he was copped out on suspicion.

+**Copalm.** The sweet gum tree, *Liquidambar styraciflua;* also, the gum derived from the tree.

1775 ROMANS *Florida* 336 Live oak abound here, intermixed with copalm and other timber. **1797** IMLAY *Western Territory* (ed. 3) 277 The liquidambar, copalm, or maple-leaved storax, is not only extremely common, but it affords a balm, the virtues of which are infinite. **1832** BROWNE *Sylva* 200 This tree is universally called Sweet Gum, and by the French of Louisiana, Copalm. **1889** *Cent.* 3474 In hot regions it [the tree] exudes a gum, sometimes called copalm . . . or copal-balsam, used in the preparation of chewing-gum, and to some extent in medicine as a substitute for storax.

Copenhagen, *n.* **1.** *attrib.* For the purpose of seizure. (Cf. verb.) +**2.** A kissing game played by children. — (1) **1813** *Boston Gaz.* 11 Feb. (Th.), Letters from Georgia say the 'Copenhagen' expedition against the Floridas goes on swimmingly, anything in the laws of the U.S. to the contrary notwithstanding. (2) **1873** BAILEY *Life in Danbury* 77 The only people saved are those who drink lemonade out of a dipper and play copenhagen with their aunts. *Ib.* 246 A guest at a River-Street party, Monday evening, lost one of his eyes while playing Copenhagen. **1889** *Cent.* 1253 *Copenhagen*, . . . a children's game in which the players form a circle with their hands on a rope, and one inside the circle tries to touch the hands of any other player and kiss that one before he or she can get inside the rope.

Copenhagen, *v.* [Capital of Denmark.] *tr.* To seize suddenly, 'as the English under Nelson did the Danish fleet' (Th.). — **1811** *Mass. Spy* 13 Feb. (Th.), Hints are given that a plan was organized to 'Copenhagen' Canada.

***Copper,** *n.*[1]

***1.** A well-known metal, with the chemical symbol Cu.

1602 BRERETON *Virginia* 9 They [the Indians] have also great store of Copper, some very redde, and some of a paler colour; none of them but have chaines, earrings or collars of this mettall. **1608** SMITH *Newes from Va.* Wks. 1884 I. 32 The King wee presented with a piece of Copper. **1674** *Cal. State P., Amer. & W.I.* VII. 581 [In] Maine . . . the bowels of the earth are enriched with plenty of iron ore, tin, copper, lead, coals, sulphur, and other minerals. **1733** BYRD *Journey to Eden* (1901) 291 There are so many appearances of Copper in these Parts, that the Inhabitants seem to be all Mine-mad, and neglect making of Corn for their present necessitys, in hopes of growing very rich hereafter. **1765** R. ROGERS *Acc. N. America* 70 The commodities exported from hence [New York] are . . . bar iron, and some copper. **1814** *Western Gleaner* (Pittsburgh) I. 130 In our western country large masses of copper exist on lake Superior. **1840** *Niles' Nat. Reg.* 16 May 176/2 Missouri copper. The Commercial Journal states that another parcel of pig copper . . . has been received by the agents in this city. **1877** H. C. HODGE *Arizona as It Is* 122 The whole of the eastern portion of Pinal County seems to be a mass of mineral, including gold, silver, copper, lead, and iron.

2. A vessel or container made of copper, used for cooking, brewing, and other purposes. {1667-}

1650 in *Mayflower Desc.* X. 173 It. 3 kettles one copper one bakeing pan. *c***1689** *Wyllys Papers* 313 Wee have bought Mr Samuell Willis . . . his wholl Intrest and estate . . . with all the Negroes, Cattle, Mills, Stills, Coppers, and other Appurt[enances]. **1774** F. MOORE *Voy. Georgia* 99 One of them stole away the machines for winding, broke the coppers and spoiled all the eggs which he could not steal. **1795** *Ann. 4th Congress* 2 Sess. 2577 The caboose with a forge, hearth, armorer's tools, spare coppers, boilers, &c are all complete. **1804** J. ROBERTS *Penna. Farmer* 40 Take half a bushel of the grain, . . . put it to five pailfuls of water, and boil it in a copper till the grain bursts. **1870** EMERSON *Soc. & Solitude* 148 Now it only needs a fireman, and a boy to know the coppers, to pull up the handles.

3. A copper coin.

In the colonial period copper coins of England Spain, Portugal, several colonies, and even private persons were current. Later, state governments and the Continental Congress issued copper coins. In 1792, Congress authorized one-cent and half-cent pieces of copper, but for many years the older coins were still in circulation.

'At Granby, Conn., about the year 1737, coppers circulated, called Highley's coppers' (1858 J. H. Hickcox *Amer. Coinage* 74).

1767 T. SMITH *Journal* (1849) 276 We had smelts to-day, two coppers a dozen. **1772** in F. Chase *Hist. Dartmouth Coll.* (1891) I. 262 *n.*, Let Mr. Ripley have a guinea, half a jo, and 9 coppers. **1782** *Broadside Verse* (1930) 107 Sold near Liberty-Stump and next the Swan-Tavern, . . . (Price 6 Coppers single). **1785** in J. H. Hickcox *Amer. Coinage* (1858) 102 All Coppers by him [=R. Harmon] coined, shall be in pieces of one third of an ounce. **1802** *Ann. 7th Congress* 488 Coppers were brought by the cask from Birmingham; after a short time circulating their baseness was discovered. **1816** PICKERING 70 The common name in New England for British half-pence. . . . We used to say a copper's worth of anything. . . . Nearly obsolete. **1825** NEAL *Bro. Jonathan* II. 137 It amounted to one dollar and a quarter, 'hard money'; or ten shillings 'York currency'— or two hundred and fifty half coppers. **1833** — *Down-Easters* I. 151 At so many coppers a week . . . every member is entitled to a cup of tea.

+**b.** Esp. applied to the half-cent and one-cent pieces of the U.S.

The minting of half-cent pieces ceased in 1857.

1835 H. C. TODD *Notes* 7 The word coppers designates cents. **1858** HOLMES *Autocrat* 13 People that make puns are like wanton boys that put coppers on the railroad tracks. **1873** HOWELLS *Chance Acquaintance* xiii, The colonel stuck a copper into the sand as he spoke, and a small shower of arrows hurtled around it. **1876** 'MARK TWAIN' *Tom Sawyer* i. 24 The new boy took two broad coppers out of his pocket and held them out. **1883** J. S. DYE *Coin Encycl.* 247 The Fugios were the first coinage made by authority of the United States. There is but little on record concerning this series of coppers. **1890** TOWNSEND *U.S. Index* 426 Have you any coppers?

c. A unit for measuring value in money; usu. with negative.

1788 JEFFERSON *Writings* VII. 40 Neither had a wish to lay up a copper. **1796** A. BARTON *Disappointment* III. i, If it hadn't been for her we shou'dn't have had a copper! **1832** KENNEDY *Swallow Barn* II. 91 The daughter . . . looking as innocent as if she wa'nt worth one copper. **1853** COZZENS *Prismatics* 176, I have been surprised lately to find persons whom I did not imagine worth a copper, freely acknowledging themselves to be wealthy. **1867** D. R. LOCKE *Swingin' Round* 45 When dead you ain't wuth a copper. **1878** B. F. TAYLOR *Between Gates* 114 Their board does not cost them a copper. **1904** GLASGOW *Deliverance* 40 The old gentleman hadn't a red copper to his name.

+**d.** Used in gaming and gambling; also the name of a game. (Cf. *v.* 1.)

1758 C. REA *Journal* 18 No officer nor Soldier shou'd play at Cards or Coppers. **1829** *Western Mo. Review* III. 18 Mike proposed to 'sky a copper' with Carpenter; that is, to throw up a copper. **1851** *Harper's Mag.* Feb. 417/1 It represents a genuine sable Long-Islander, whom a 'lucky throw' of the Coppers has made the owner of a fat goose. **1858** DOUGLAS in Logan *Great Conspiracy* 677 He [=Lincoln] could beat any of the boys wrestling, or running a foot-race, in pitching quoits or tossing a copper. **1876** H. TRIPP *Student-Life* 466 We can . . . pitch coppers, or play leapfrog. **1913** MULFORD *Coming of Cassidy* 51 If yo're bettin' on that card you wants to have a copper handy. . . . It's awful fatal when it's played to win.

+**e.** Used as a weight to close the eyes of a dead person.

1856 A. CARY *Married* 131 He is . . . the closest man I ever worked for— mean enough to steal the coppers off the eyes of a dead man. **1865** WHITMAN *Specimen Days* (1882) 77 The attendants had just straighten'd the limbs, put coppers on the eyes, and were laying it out.

+**4.** An American Indian. (Cf. COPPERSKIN.) *Obs.*

1772 in *Travels Amer. Col.* 523 He said there would be Copers and White people present at the meeting.

+**5.** *pl.* Shares or stocks in a company that mines copper.

1899 *Boston Globe* 28 April 9/5 The largest owners of 'coppers' know of no investment that will be as safe and give as large returns as 'coppers.' **1900** NELSON *A B C Wall St.* 135 *Coppers*, copper mine stocks.

6. *attrib.* **a.** In sense: Made of copper. **b.** In sense: Pertaining to copper ore or the mining of copper. (Cf. COPPER MINE, ORE, PLATE, etc.)

(**a**) **1622** 'MOURT' *Relation* 92 We sent to the King a payre of Kniues, and a Copper Chayne. **1742** *Md. Hist. Mag.* XX. 258 A Copper Still to contain about fifty Gallons with a Head and pewter Worm Suitable. **1820** *Niles' Reg.* XVIII. 256/2 The several acts establishing the mint show, that copper coin was not intended to be a legal tender. **1835** HOFFMAN *Winter in West* II. 176 Whimsically enough, the individual who gave the writer this information subsequently palmed a copper dollar upon him. **1863** [see COPPERHEAD 6].

(**b**) **1840** *Niles' Nat. Reg.* 13 June 229/2 The 'New Jersey Copper Mining and Smelting company' is making arrangements to go into immediate operation. **1853** *Harper's Mag.* VI. 441 This [a public house] being in the heart of the copper region, the particular object of my visit, I stop here for the present. **1865** *Atlantic Mo.* XV. 694/1 Another branch of the Lake trade . . . which promises to reach vast proportions . . . is the iron and copper trade of Lake Superior. **1869** BROWNE *Adv. Apache Country* 285 Mr. Hill d'Amit . . . considers it one of the best copper leads in the country—quite equal to the celebrated Maricopa lead on the Gila. **1871** RAYMOND *3rd Rep. Mines* 267 This copper district [in Arizona] contains perhaps the richest copper ores in the world. **1882** THAYER *From Log-Cabin* xii. 182 Copper mining was carried on extensively on Lake Superior, and the ore was brought down to Cleveland in schooners.

+**Copper,** *n.*[2] *slang.* [f. COP *v.*] A policeman. (Cf. COP *n.* 1.) {1864-}

1848 E. JUDSON *Mysteries N.Y.* I. 36 In Boston, the coppers there aint half so keen with their peepers as they are here! **1875** G. P. BURNHAM *Three Years* p. v, Cop, or Copper, a U.S. Detective, or Police officer. **1893** *Chicago Tribune* 23 April 42/5 Three 'coppers' constituted Chicago's police force until 1840, although the press frequently urged the Council to increase the number. **1901** FLYNT *World of Graft* 67 A 'copper' stood on a corner like a pillar of salt only a block away.

***Copper,** *v.*

+**1.** *tr.* To lay a bet against (a card, person, or thing); orig. from the game of faro: (see quot. 1864).

1864 W. B. DICK *Amer. Hoyle* (1866) 277 *Coppering a Bet.*—If a player wishes to bet that a card will lose (that is, win for the bank), he indicates his wish by placing a cent . . . upon the top of his stake. It is called 'coppering,' because coppers were first used to distinguish such bets. **1866** *Chicago Tribune* 25 Dec. 3/5 'To copper,' or to 'take one's pile,' belongs to the gambling epoch of our civilization [*i.e.*, in California]. **1878** BEADLE *Western Wilds* 46 He . . . scarcely ate or slept till the tail of his last mule was 'coppered on the jack.' **1883** 'MARK TWAIN' *Life on Miss.* xxviii. 304, I reckon the safe way, where a man can afford it, is to *copper* the operation, and at the same time buy enough property in Vicksburg to square you up in case they win. **1898** WESTCOTT *D. Harum* 284 If you ever find out how I'm bettin' on a race jest 'copper' me an' you c'n wear di'monds. **1905** BEACH *Pardners* 56 Boy, if I was backing your system, . . . I'd copper this move and play her to lose. **1908** LORIMER *J. Spurlock* 283 You can bet the market to win, or copper it, and the house gets its regular rake-off.

absol. **1887** *Courier-Journal* 6 Feb. 4/3 If I had to place my money on the turn of the card or be shot at sundown, I should copper. **1913** MULFORD *Coming of Cassidy* 108 He had played to win when he should have coppered, coppered when he should have played to win.

fig. **1885** *Century Mag.* XXXI. 67/1 'Problikely the colonel's got him coppered.' . . . 'What do you mean by coppered?' 'Bet'n he won't turn up,' several voices replied. **1904** *N.Y. Ev. Post* 6 May 2 For some time, local politicians have 'coppered' with success Platt's predictions. **1908** K. MCGAFFEY *Show-Girl* 109 A couple of tears will always copper any wrong play you make. **1909** WASON *Happy Hawkins* 310 When it came to what they called a publicity agent I had played every winnin' number open an' coppered all the ones that lost. **1924** MULFORD *Rustlers' Valley* 107 But Skinner . . . likewise told me to go east for a job; but . . . I coppered Bud an' come here.

+**2.** *tr.* To appropriate or embezzle. *To copper* (one's) *pocket*, to enrich (oneself). *slang.*

1832 T. HAMILTON *Men & Manners* II. 387 One member of Congress . . . was charged with selling franks at twopence apiece, and thus coppering his pocket at the expense of the public. **1884** (U.S. Newspaper) Aug., He's been in office for a long while an' never coppered a d——n cent.

*** Copperas.**

***1.** Sulphate of iron, copper, or zinc, but usu. crystallized ferrous sulphate, a salt of astringent taste, used as a disinfectant and medicine.

1634 in Winthrop *Hist.* (1853) I. 462 Yourself know what will be needful. . . . Remember copperas, white and green, and two or three pounds of Paracelsus's plaister. **1733** *S.C. Gazette* 172/1 By whom is also to be sold . . . Nux vomica, Allom, Copperas, Gauls. **1856** *Spirit of Times* 18 Oct. 115/3 When any stock is infested with lice, whether horses, cattle, sheep or hogs, I give copperas in their food every other day. **1879** *Diseases of Swine* 121 When confined in close pens, these pens should be cleaned daily, and disinfected when there is stench, by the use of copperas. **1883** *Century Mag.* July 431/2 Copperas, he tolerates; lime, the same; all odorless disinfectants, indeed; but carbolic acid—no!

b. Used esp. in making dyes.

1752 *Va. Gazette* 22 May (*advt.*), Just imported . . . by the subscriber in Williamsburg, a fresh assortment of drugs and medicines, oil of turpentine, copperas, Prussian Blue, [etc.]. **1759** *Newport Mercury* 26 June 4/1 Just Imported by John Tweedy . . . Copperas, Brimstone, . . . Dyers and Painters Wares, &c. **1800** *Columbian Centinel* 22 Jan. 4/4 Just received . . . Dye Stuffs and Paints, . . . Copperas, Madder, [etc.]. **1847** T. FORD *Hist. Illinois* (1854) 41 A little copperas and indigo, with the bark of trees, furnished dye stuffs for coloring.

2. Applied to the native hydrous sulphates: melanterite, goslarite, chalcanthite, etc.

1778 CARVER *Travels* 139, I observed that many of the small islands . . . were covered with copper ore. They appeared like beds of copperas, of which many tuns lay in a small space. **1784** FILSON *Kentucke* 32 Different places abounding with copperas . . . in its present impure state sufficient for the use of the inhabitants. **1786** *Mem. Academy* II. I. 148 Some of the vitriolick springs are very strongly impregnated with the taste of copperas. **1807** GASS *Journal* 29 We . . . passed bluffs on the south side, where there is copperas, allum and ore of some kind. **1812** *Emporium Arts & Sci.* (Phila.) May 73, I may mention too the abundance of copperas which West Tennessee and Vermont afford. **1831** PECK *Guide* 89 Copperas . . . may be found here [in Illinois]. **1838** C. NEWELL *Revol. Texas* 172 Lead, copper, copperas, and alum, are found in considerable quantities.

3. *attrib.* and *comb.* Denoting the color green. +Also ellipt: Green.

(**a**) **1850** H. C. LEWIS *La. Swamp Dr.* 84 Clothed in homespun of the copperas hue. *Ib.* 138 Copperas-coloured linsey pants occupy their proper position. **1861** in F. Moore *Rebellion Rec.* I. III. 113 Just give him his old copperas-colored trowsers, and his own rifle. **1879** EGGLESTON *Circuit Rider* 271 The girls, in short linsey dresses, with copperas-dyed cotton pantalettes. **1889** *Century Mag.* April 937/1 There she stood, in a copperas-dyed cotton riding-skirt. **1900** J. C. HARRIS *On the Wing* 65 He wore brogans of undressed leather, his copperas-colored breeches short enough to show his woolen socks.

(**b**) **1850** H. C. LEWIS *La. Swamp Dr.* 46, I'll never let on you cuddent tell copperas breeches from bar-skin. **1851** *Polly Peablossom* 14 'Hello, Floyd!' shouted old Captain Peablossom out of doors to his copperas-trowsered son. **1859** *Harper's Mag.* Oct. 712/2 In the crowd . . . there was a . . . country chap . . . clad in the plainest 'home-spun'-copperas pants and coarse cotton shirt. **1871** *Ku Klux Conspiracy Rep.* VII. 608 He had on copperas pants, and near the edge a slug had gone through.

‖**Copperas-coloreds.** Trousers dyed with copperas. (Cf. COPPERAS 3 a.) — **1851** *Polly Peablossom* 29 The first step upon arriving in the city was to lay aside their 'copperas-coloureds.'

+**Copper-bellied snake.** =COPPERHEAD I. — **1705** BEVERLEY *Virginia* IV. 64 The black Viper-Snake, and the Copper-bellied Snake, are said to be as venemous as the Rattle-Snake. **1789** MORSE *Amer. Geog.* 61 Of the Snakes which infest the United States, are the following, viz. . . . The Copper-bellied Snake.

+Copper-belly.

1. A red-bellied water snake, *Natrix erythrogaster*, common in the Carolinas. In full, *copper-belly snake.*

1736 CATESBY *Carolina* II. 46 *Anguis ventre cuprei coloris.* The Copper-belly Snake. . . . They are of a brown Colour, except their Bellies, which are of a muddy Red or Copper Colour. **1791** BARTRAM *Travels* 276 There are many other species of snakes in the regions of Florida and Carolina as the . . . copper belly, ring neck and two or three varieties of vipers. **1818** *Jrnl. Science* I. 258 The Copper-belly is a very distinct species. **1853** BAIRD & GIRARD *Cat. Serpents* 165 Copperbelly (*Ner[odia] erythr[ogaster]*). **1871** DE VERE 387 The true Copperbelly (*Nerodia erythrogaster*) is perfectly harmless and of aquatic habits.

2. =COPPERHEAD I.

1842 *Nat. Hist. N.Y., Zoology* III. 54 The Copper-head . . . has various popular names in different districts; the most common of these are, in this State [N.Y.], Copper-head, Red Adder, and Dumb Rattlesnake. In other districts, it is called Copper-belly, Red Viper, Deaf Adder and Chunk-head. **1871** DE VERE 387 The Copperhead (*Trigonocephalus contortrix*) . . . is known as Copperbelly and Chunkhead.

+**Copper captain.** 'One who calls himself a captain without any right to the title' (*Cent.*). {1865-} — **1809** IRVING *Knickerb.* V. vii, No sooner did this thrice valiant copper captain receive marching orders, [etc.].

Copper-colored, *a.* {1697-}

+**1.** Of the North Amer. Indians: Having a skin the color of copper.

1781 PETERS *Conn.* 324 The deist asks those divines, If Eve was not the common mother of the white, black, and copper-coloured women. **1837** *S. Lit. Messenger* III. 237, I found a half-breed Cherokee Indian who had with him a little daughter, copper-colored and shy. **1841** CATLIN *Indians* I. 6 The Indians of North America . . . are copper-coloured, with long black hair, black eyes, tall, straight, and elastic forms. **1847** [see COPPERHEADED *a.* I].

+**2.** Of Negroes: Light-brown mulatto.

1852 in Stowe *Key* 176 Runaway from my plantation, in Bolivar County, Miss., a negro man named May, . . . copper colored, and very straight. **1860** J. DOY *Narr.* 92 My cell doors were opened and in walked a colored man, such as they call a light copper-colored negro. *Ib.* 96 One day a fine-looking, copper-colored man was brought into the lock-up, terribly mangled.

+Copperhead.

1. A poisonous snake (*Agkistrodon mokasen*), related to the rattlesnake in being a pit viper, but without rattles. (Cf. COPPER-BELLY 2 and COPPERHEAD(ED) SNAKE.)

1775 FITHIAN *Journal* II. 54 The snake that wounded her they call a 'Copper-head.' **1782** J. H. ST. JOHN *Letters* 236 The most dangerous one is the pilot or copperhead. **1817** S. BROWN *Western Gaz.* 31 The only venomous serpents, are the common and prairie rattlesnakes, and copperheads. **1836** HOLLEY *Texas* V. 104 Land and water moccasin, coach whip, and copper heads are the only venomous snakes, besides the rattlers found in Texas. **1867** *Atlantic Mo.* April 406/2 A rattlesnake rattles, a viper hisses, an adder spits, a black snake whistles, a water-snake blows, but a copperhead just sneaks! **1871** *Scribner's Mo.* I. 283 Take that band of yaller paint off her; it looks like the ring about a copperhead's neck. **1891** *Boston Journal* Nov., The supposed bee-tree contained three copperheads, fifty-eight large rattlers, and nine other poisonous snakes. **1913** STRATTON-PORTER *Laddie* xiii, Through the rough puncheon floor a copperhead stuck up its gleam of bronzy gold, and shot its darting tongue within a foot of her bare leg.

b. *fig.* A hostile, vindictive person.

1853 SIMMS *Sword & Distaff* 446 'Come, copper-head! march!' and Millhouse, planting himself on one side of the captive, Frampton took his place on the other.

2. One of the Dutch inhabitants of New York; a descendant of the Dutch settlers.

1809 IRVING *Knickerb.* VI. iv, These were the men who vegetated in the mud along the shores of Pavonia, being of the race of genuine copperheads. **1828** PAULDING *New Mirr. Travellers* (1868) 108 Death . . . has sometimes had his match with some of these tough old copperheads. **1848** IRVING *Knickerb.* (rev. ed.) VII. i, The Yankees sneeringly spoke of the round-crowned burghers of the Manhattoes as the 'Copperheads.'

3. *S.* A Presbyterian. *Obs.*

1831 ROYALL *Southern Tour* II. 63 For his bold and manly stand against the copper-heads, as the Presbyterians are often called.

4. An American Indian.

1838 *S. Lit. Messenger* IV. 295/1 He said . . . it would be a sin to kill one, but if he was to go he should want to kill one of the damned copperheads. **1853** COZZENS *Prismatics* 103 Hosea sent a faithful copperhead, Squidko by name, to hunt up his wife. **1853** C. W. WEBBER *Shot in Eye*, etc. (1855) 132 He had a hatred for the 'yaller bellies,' and 'copper heads,' as he called the Mexicans and Indians, which was refreshingly orthodox. *a***1861** T. WINTHROP *Canoe & Saddle* X. 149 Meanwhile those five copperheads watched me, as I have seen a coterie of wolves . . . watch a wounded buffalo.

5. During the Civil War, a Northerner who sympathized with the South.

For further quotations and discussion, see Albert Matthews 'Origin of Butternut and Copperhead,' in *Mass. Col. Soc. Publ.* XX. 205-37.

1862 *Chicago Tribune* 24 Sept. 2/5 John Pettit has been nominated for Congress by the Copperheads of the 8th Indiana district. **1862** *Cincin-*

nati Commercial 14 Oct., It looks very much as if the Trinity of the Adoration . . . of the Copperheads of Ohio, Vallandigham, Pendleton and Cox, would be obliterated by the election of this day. **1863** J. L. MOTLEY *Corr.* II. 143 As to Massachusetts, of course I should as soon have thought of the sun's forgetting to rise as of her joining the pro-slavery Copperheads. **1863** WHITMAN *Nov. Boughs* (1888) 447 The Copperheads are getting furious, and want to recognize the Southern Confederacy. **1865** *Nation* I. 492 The doughface, the Copperhead, the theologian who finds Scripture authority for the existence and specific character of Southern negro slavery, will approve these words. **1879** TOURGEE *Fool's Errand* 99 'The party in the North who were opposed to the war—' 'Wasn't they called "Copperheads?"' interrupted Andy. **1917** B. MATTHEWS *These Many Years* 62, I was only twelve, but . . . I promptly responded, 'I won't be a copperhead anyhow!'

b. *transf.* A traitorous, disloyal person.

1917 *N.Y. Times* 7 Aug., Of course it is not agreeable to be called a cuckoo, but one who is so dubbed has the gratification of knowing that nobody can call him a copperhead or can accuse him of disloyalty. . . . Which would you rather be, a cuckoo or a copperhead?

6. A token or badge, consisting of a head cut from a cent piece or of a pin of similar design, used by the Copperheads (sense 5).

'The . . . Copperheads had been so called for nearly six months before there is any trace of their wearing a badge' (A. Matthews in *Mass. Col. Soc. Publ.* XX. 220).

1863 *New York World* 26 March 5/6 The copperhead, or Badge of Liberty. Now ready. **1863** *Crisis* III. 79/2 By 'Copperheads,' politicians must not be understood, but a sort of copper badge, representing the head of Washington for example. *Ib.* 93 The small boys here [Brimfield, Ohio] are making Copper-heads by taking old copper cents and cutting away all but the head, which leaves a copper head with the word Liberty stamped upon the forehead. **1917** *Amer. Jrnl. of Numismatics* 54 *Copperheads,* a name commonly applied to the tokens issued during the Civil War in the United States (1862–1865). In the latter part of the year 1862 the first of these copper tokens were issued in Cincinnati, Ohio, and other western cities. Many of them have on the obverse the Indian head copied from the United States cent, and this feature probably gave them their name.

7. Attrib. (in senses 5 and 6) with *badge, candidate, convention,* etc. (In sense 1 see COPPERHEAD SNAKE.)

1862 *Cincinnati Gazette* 30 July, The Copperhead Bright Convention meets in Indianapolis today. **1863** *Chicago Tribune* 7 Jan. 2/2 But we have yet to see the 'copperhead' journal that is not filled, day after day, with articles bitterly denunciatory of the President. **1863** *New York World* 31 March 5/2 The undersigned are the original and sole manufacturers of the true Copperhead Badge of Liberty, as worn by the great Copperhead Party of the United States. **1864** *Ohio Agric. Rep.* XVIII. 29, I would not locate the State Fair permanently in any Copperhead county. **1866** F. CARPENTER *At White House* 173, I knew it was a copperhead lie! . . . Why, they told me he [Lincoln] was an ugly looking man. **1867** L. BAKER *U.S. Secret Service* 590 So much has been said through the copperhead press . . . that I desire here to make a plain unvarnished statement. **1869** BARNUM *Struggles & Triumphs* 660 Fairfield County was entitled to the nomination of the copperhead candidate for Congress from the Fourth District. **1886** LOGAN *Great Conspiracy* 595 With a Copperhead platform, this Democratic Convention thought it politic to have a Union candidate for the Presidency. **1900** *Kansas Hist. Coll.* VI. 324 All the yellow journals, called during the war of the rebellion 'copperhead sheets,' held him up as an infamous destroyer of peaceable homes.

Copper-headed, *a.* **1.** *Copper-headed snake* = COPPERHEAD 1. **2.** Having the attributes of a COPPERHEAD (in senses 1, 4, and 5). — **(1) 1806** ASHE *Travels* II. 287 We called the following at least to our attention. Rattle Snake, Yellow Ditto, . . . Two Headed Ditto, Copper Headed Ditto. **1847** in Drake *Pioneer Life Ky.* 25 The copper-colored man, and the copper-headed snake [were] then extremely common. **(2) 1853** SIMMS *Sword & Distaff* 446 It is sich a little mean copper-headed son of a skunk, that has the impudence to come here and to seize the rightful property of a gentleman. **a1861** WINTHROP *Canoe & Saddle* 248 The copper-headed, snaky beguiler continued his solicitations. **1863** *Congress. Globe* 936/2 The seat of the rebellion . . . is among the copperheaded traitors of the North.

+**Copperheadism.** The beliefs and practices of the Copperheads (sense 5).

1863 *Harper's Weekly* 28 Feb., [Title of an editorial] Copperheadism. **1863** *N.Y. Tribune* 11 March, The celebrated People's Regiment—44th New York—has spoken out in the matter of Copperheadism. **1864** F. WOOD *Copperhead Catechism* 11 The chief aim of a Copperhead is . . . the uprooting of Abolitionism, the annihilation of Republicanism, the establishment of Copperheadism . . . and the general display of Universal Submission. **1867** D. R. LOCKE *Swingin' Round* 15 [People of] the North who have gone so far into copperheadism. **1870** *Nation* 6 Jan. 4/1 The foul-mouthed organs of Northern Copperheadism. **1882** *N.Y. Tribune* 15 March, How he [Jackson] would excoriate Tilden for his copperheadism. **1893** T. MORSE *Lincoln* II. 182 Many causes conspired to induce an obstreperous outbreak of 'Copperheadism' in the spring of 1863.

+**Copperhead snake.** = COPPERHEAD 1.

1788 J. MAY *Jrnl. & Lett.* (1873) 70 One of Colonel Stacey's men bit by a copperhead snake. **1822** *Mass. Spy* 31 July (Th.), A few days since a woman in Salisbury township, Bucks county, discovered a copperhead snake on her dresser. **1846** M'KENNEY *Memoirs* I. 178 He seized a bit of wood, and to my question—What's the matter? answered, 'A copperhead-snake!' **1866** GREGG *Life in Army* 18 There were also to be found great dens of the Copperhead Snake, and this species were considered the most poisonous, deceptive, dangerous and mean of all the snake family.

‖**Copper-Johnny.** = COPPERHEAD 5. — **1872** *Newton Kansan* 10 Oct. 2/3 Such a course reminds me of the inconsistency of the Democratic, late 'copper-Johnny' party in espousing the lost cause.

Copper mine. A mine that yields copper. Also attrib.

1637 MORTON *New Canaan* II. vi, Copper mines are there found likewise, that will enrich the inhabitants. **1713** *Wyllys Papers* 380 To dig or Cause to be dugg at the Copper Mines in Symsbury as much Copper Oar as will produce and make three Tunns and half of Copper. **1733** BYRD *Journey to Eden* (1901) 320 The Colo. had been surveying Lands . . . on which Mr. Stith's Copper Mine lys. **1814** *Western Gleaner* (Pittsburgh) I. 130 It is known how uncommonly rich is the Schuyler copper-mine in New-Jersey. **1821** *Jrnl. Science* III. 201, I enclose you a copy of my report on the Copper Mines of Lake Superior. **1840** *Niles' Nat. Reg.* 18 July 307/3 A copper mine. We were shown several specimens of copper ore this morning, taken from a newly discovered mine. **1909** 'O. HENRY' *Options* 289 The pickerel and trout are so ravenous that I believe they would swallow your hook with a Montana copper-mine prospectus fastened on it. **1913** *Nev. Hist. Soc. 3rd Rep.* 179 John T. Reid . . . is interested in carrying on large exploration works in copper mines at that point [*i.e.* Coppereid, Nev.].

Copper ore. Ore that contains copper.

1713 [see prec.] **1721** *N.J. Archives* 1 Ser. V. 7 The Copper Oare which now rises very rich . . . in a New-discover'd mine of one Mr. Schuyler in New-Jersey. **1789** MORSE *Amer. Geog.* 182 In Attleborough Gore, is some copper ore. **a1817** DWIGHT *Travels* I. 35 Copper ore abounds in the range of Mount Lane, in various places. **1852** MARCY *Expl. Red River* (1854) 7 In a gulley washed out by the rains, we found many pieces of copper ore, of a very rich quality. **1877** *Harper's Mag.* LIV. 626/2 A large and valuable deposit of copper ore is said to have been discovered in . . . Pennsylvania.

+**Copper-picker.** A petty thief that steals copper fixtures. — **1872** BRACE *Dangerous Classes N.Y.* 94 The Eleventh Ward and 'Corlear's Hook,' where the 'copper-pickers,' and young wood-stealers, and the thieves who beset the ship-yards congregated.

Copperplate. {1665–} Used attrib. in sense: A plate or sheet of copper.

1. In printing: Designating the machine or person that makes, or uses, an engraved copperplate.

1771 FRANKLIN *Autobiog.* 294 The New Jersey jobb was obtained, I contriv'd a copper-plate press for it, the first that had been seen in the country. **1777** *Jrnls. Cont. Congress* VIII. 578 There is due to William Smith, copper-plate printer, . . . the sum of 2359/90 dollars. **1820** FLINT *Lett. from Amer.* 239 [The Cincinnati Directory for 1819 lists a] Copperplate engraver, Gilder, [etc.].

b. Denoting objects printed from such a plate.

1799 WEEMS *Letters* II. 120 What say you to printing it for me and ordering a copper plate Frontispiece? **1809** FRENEAU *Poems* I. Adv. 4 The Author will only add, that to this Edition are prefixed two copper-plate engravings. **1873** 'MARK TWAIN' & WARNER *Gilded Age* xxviii. 250 That a copper-plate card with 'Engineer-in-Chief' on it should be received with such tranquillity as this, annoyed Mr. Brierly not a little.

+**c.** Denoting objects or materials having designs transferred or printed from a copperplate.

1774 *Copley-Pelham Lett.* 281, I designd to have given you money eno' to have bot. me 76 Coper plate Tiles for my Chambers. **1790** *Columbian Centinel* 29 Sept. 19 [For sale,] Mahogany Chairs, . . . dining and card Tables, one suit of purple and white copper-plate Bed Curtains. **1790** *Penna. Packet* 2 Jan. 1/4 A great variety of chintzes, calicoes, and copperplate furnitures and printed handkerchiefs. **1871** *Harper's Mag.* Dec. 116/1 Anna glanced in, and saw straw matting, painted pine, copperplate counterpane and curtains.

+**Copperskin.** An Indian; a redskin.

1840 HOFFMAN *Greyslaer* II. 26 'Go on, go on, Kit; d'ye say a dozen Injuns?' 'Yes, uncle, not a Copperskin less.' **1841** SIMMS *Kinsmen* (1854) xvi. 176 They tell strange stories of his nightly rambles after wolves and copper-skins. **a1861** WINTHROP *Canoe & Saddle* 172 All along the journey I had been quietly probing the nature of Loolowcan, my most intimate associate thus far among the unalloyed copper-skins. **1861** *N.Y. Tribune* 29 Nov., The same binding effect which that sublime force would have over Comanche Indians—were our troops to hunt them down, make each copper-skin kiss the book and turn him loose. **1904** WHITE *Silent Places* 72 What the hell do we care for a lot of copper-skins from Rupert's House!

+**Copper skipper.** (See quotation.) — **1867** *Amer. Naturalist* I. 221 The mature larva of another much smaller butterfly, the little Copper Skipper (*Chrysophanus Americanus*), so abundant at this time, may sometimes be found on the clover.

* **Coppersmith.** One whose occupation is working in copper.

1722 *New-Eng. Courant* 10–17 Sept. 1/2 A Copper-Smith (one of the Senate) Stood up and cry'd. **1790** *Penna. Packet* 3 April 3/4 Benjamin

Harbeson, Coppersmith & Tin-Plate Worker, Acquaints . . . the Public that he has removed his Work Shop from his late dwelling house. **1792** *Ann. 2nd Congress* 1021 Coppersmiths . . . are numerous in the United States. **1809** F. CUMING *Western Tour* 222 Pittsburgh [has] . . . seven coppersmiths, tinplate workers, and japanners. **1840** *Niles' Nat. Reg.* 11 April 96/2 Fire in Louisville. . . . Among the sufferers were the following: . . . Willace & Lithgow, tin and copper smiths.

+**Copper snake.** = COPPERHEAD 1.

1765 TIMBERLAKE *Mem.* 46 The copper-snake, whose bite is very difficult to cure. **1799** WELD *Travels* 115 Of the venomous kind, the most common are the rattle snake, and the copper or moccassin snake. **1858** *Harper's Mag.* Aug. 291/2 The arch-enemy of souls . . . had . . . crawled into his cabin like a copper-snake, and tried to bite him. **1891** RYAN *Pagan* 62 He rode on, . . . crossing the summit that divides the copper-snake's range on the west side from the domain of its more honest relative.

transf. **1849** J. B. JONES *Wild West Scenes* 86 It's that copper-snake, traitor, skunk, water-dog, lizard-hawk, horned frog.

+**Copper-toed,** *a.* Having the tips of (one's) shoes covered with copper. Hence *copper toes.* — **1872** HOLMES *Poet* 54 She was ashamed to let her little boy go out in his old shoes, and copper-toed shoes they was too. **1876** *Wide Awake* 241/1 The ceaseless clatter of his little copper-toed boots over all the bare places in the house . . . rendered it impossible for his mamma or the new baby to get any rest. **1896** E. HIGGINSON *Tales* 25 Esther forgot her buff calico dress and her copper-toed shoes. **1902** C. MORRIS *Stage Confidences* 292 [They swore] they would kick with their copper toes any one who tried to kiss them.

Coppery, *a.* {1791–} +**1.** *Coppery whip snake,* (see quot.). +**2.** Sympathetic to the Copperheads (sense 5). — **(1) 1870** *Amer. Naturalist* III. 187 A few of the former [reptiles] are not known northward, viz., . . . the Coppery Whipsnake (*Drymobius testaceus*). **(2) 1866** 'F. KIRKLAND' *Bk. Anecdotes* 63 In old Eastern Massachusetts . . . resides a certain Dr. —, whose loyalty was commonly reputed as rather 'coppery.' **1906** *Nation* LXXXII. 179/2 The Rev. Ambrose Converse . . . made his proslavery *Christian Observer* so 'coppery' during the civil war that Seward suppressed it and arrested him.

***Copy.** Used attrib. and comb. in sense: Manuscript (or typewritten) matter to be set up for printing.

1858 WILLIS *Convalescent* 383 The 'copy-drawer' is a sacred obligation! **1893** in M. M. Philips *Making of Newspaper* 8 The foreman of the composing-room is ready to feed, through the 'copy-cutter,' a mass of news in manuscript to the regiment of compositors. *Ib.* 267 What would the old-time 'typo' think of a composing-room with its walls of white enamel . . . , its electric calls connecting each case with the copy-box, its aerial railway? *Ib.* 274 Henry Watterson . . . was sending jingling letters from Washington to *The Press*, which I used to read in manuscript before they were snipped into copy-takes and given out to the printer. **1894** SHUMAN *Steps into Journalism* 21 Now we have reached the bottom of the list—unless we include the copy boy. **1899** J. L. WILLIAMS *Stolen Story* 232 He had already had a chance to be a copy-editor. **1903** SHUMAN *Prac. Journalism* 25 In the first ten years the young journalist masters reporting, copy-reading, and the rest of the routine work. **1907** FIELD *Six-Cylinder Courtship* 67 'Just a minute, Mr. Snowden,' said Bellows, reaching for his pencil and copy-paper.

+**Copycat.** *colloq.* A person who acts in the same way that another has already acted. — **1896** JEWETT *Pointed Firs* xiii. 102, 'I ain't heard of a copy-cat this great many years,' said Mrs. Fosdick, laughing; ''twas a favorite term o' my grandmother's.' **1907** FIELD *Six-Cylinder Courtship* 101 Good old Tom, with . . . his picture-gallery full of bogus Old Masters! How often have I called him a silly copy-cat.

Copyholder. +**a.** (See quotation.) +**b.** A person who assists a proof-reader by reading copy aloud. — **(a) 1874** KNIGHT 619/2 Copy-holder, a clasp to hold matter while being set up. **(b) 1888** *Congress. Rec.* 24 Jan. 666/1 Persons employed in the Printing Office under the names of proof-readers and copy-holders receive already . . . as much as or more than the 25 per cent. **1905** *N.Y. Ev. Post* 27 Sept. 4 The proofreader's copyholders are here [in an English book on printing] designated as reading-boys.

Copying press. An apparatus for taking an impression of a writing by pressure. {1820– (Abridgm. Spec. Patents)}

1785 JEFFERSON *Writings* V. 110 Have you a copying press? If you have not, you should get one. **1851** *Rep. Comm. Patents 1850* 278 Improvement in Dampening Paper for Copying Presses. **1855** *Chicago Times* 16 Jan. 1/6 The subscribers having made extensive arrangements for the sale of copying presses. **1873** *Newton Kansan* 15 May 1/5 These substances are said to produce a like effect . . . under the action of the dies in the copying-press. **1874** KNIGHT 619 *Copying-press.* . . . The usual system is to write with an ink having a somewhat viscid character, and to expose the written page to pressure in contact with a leaf of bibulous paper.

Copyist. One whose occupation is transcribing documents. {1699–} — **1810** *Columbian Centinel* 6 Jan. 1/2 C. Edwards, Scrivener and Copyist. . . . Draws or copies conveyances of every kind on paper or parchment. **1882** GODFREY *Nantucket* 262 Professions [include] Artists, . . . Bill Posters, . . . Book-keepers, . . . [and] Copyists. **1916** DU PUY *Uncle Sam* 199 He thought of Jane Gates, . . . the deaf copyist at headquarters.

+**Copy-reader.** One who edits copy for printing. — **1892** *Harper's Weekly* 9 Jan. 42/4 Upon the taste, the good judgment, and discretion of these copy-readers the character of the paper very greatly depends. **1894** SHUMAN *Steps into Journalism* 21 His [the city editor's] assistants—those who read over and edit the copy written by the reporters—are called copy-readers. **1902** E. BANKS *Newspaper Girl* 247 One of the copy-readers stood at her desk speaking.

Copyright.

1. A right granted by law to an author, composer, etc., (or his assignee), for the exclusive publishing or sale of his work. {1767–}

1788 in *Rep. Comm. Patents 1849* 558 Your petitioner made an entry of his said boiler with the prothonotary . . . , being told the copy-rights of books were there entered. **1789** *History of Congress* (1834) 707 The subject of copyrights was brought before the House of Representatives. **1800** WEEMS *Letters* II. 130 You gave a sum for the Copy Right. **1817** *Niles' Reg.* XII. 288/2 The report that Mr. Webster had sold the copy-right of his spelling book to the Messrs. Goodwins, of Hartford, . . . is not true. **1875** *Scribner's Mo.* Dec. 280/1 There is not a rational argument which sustains the laws of international patent right that does not apply perfectly to international copyright.

2. Attrib. (or adj.) with *act, bill, book,* etc.

1831 *Congress. Deb.* 6 Jan. 424 His colleague . . . had described the copyright act as simply a remedy for the abuse of that right. **1888** *Boston Journal* 30 July 2/3 The Copyright Bill Receives a Bad Set-back. **1870** *Statutes at Large* XVI. 213 [To] deposit in the mail two copies of such copyright book or other article. **1843** *Niles' Nat. Reg.* 16/2 A copyright club has been formed in New York. **1835** *Knickerb.* VI. 289 The passage of an international copy-right law betwixt America and Great Britain.

Copyrighted, *ppl. a.* {1860–} Made secure by copyright. — **1806** WEBSTER, *Copyrighted,* a., the sole right being secured. **1896** *Columbus (O.) Dispatch* 14 Dec., Governor-elect Rogers has issued a copyrighted pamphlet containing about 2,200 words.

+**Coquimbo owl.** [A province in Chile.] A burrowing owl (genus *Speotyto*), found in the Southwest. — **1844** GREGG *Commerce of Prairies* II. 230 This has been called the Coquimbo owl. Its note, whether natural or imitative, much resembles that of the prairie dog. **1867** J. MELINE *Santa Fé & Back* 276 The prairie owl found among them is the burrowing owl (*Strix cunicularia*), sometimes called the Coquimbo owl.

+**Coquina.** [Sp.] A soft stone consisting of marine shells bound together by calcareous cement, used as building material in Florida. Attrib. with *formation, house, stone, wall.*

1837 WILLIAMS *Florida* 44 The quarries of Coquina stone are extensive. *Ib.* 52 This river being choked up by the Coquina formation . . . , the waters were driven laterally into the St. Lucia. *Ib.* 118 [The court house] is built of coquina stone. **1877** PHELPS *Story of Avis* 404 They settled themselves in a yellow old coquina house. **1883** *Pall Mall Gaz.* 20 Oct. 5/1 St. Augustine, a still older settlement [with its] white coquina walls, quaint Peninsular houses, etc. **1890** JEWETT in *Harper's Mag.* Dec. 100/1 Their old coquina house . . . faced one of the narrow lanes that ran up from the water.

***Coral.**

***1.** A hard chalklike substance, usually of a beautiful red color. Also attrib.

1761 in H. M. Brooks *Gleanings* 26 Coral Beeds, Stick ditto for Whistles, Forgeing Anvils. **1775** in E. Singleton *Social N.Y.* 254 Charles Oliver Bruff . . . buys rough coral, handsome pebbles and black cornelian, fit for seal stones. **1843** N. BOONE *Journal* 193 The limestone of today contained innumerable minute shells somewhat of the shape and size of a barley grain, besides coral. **1863** 'M. HARLAND' *Husks* 164 The sleeves looped up with bands of coral and gold.

+**2.** In the names of various plants having scarlet berries.

1885 HAVARD *Flora W. & S. Texas* 500 *Sophora secundiflora*, Lag. Frijolillo; Coral Bean. Stout ornamental shrub, with deep green foliage, common from the Gulf Coast to the Pecos. **1892** *Amer. Folk-Lore* V. 96 *Begonia* sp. (similar to *B. maculata*, but not spotted), coral begonia. Bedford, Mass. *Ib.* 105 *Lycopodium clavatum*, coral evergreen. Stratham, N.H. **1884** SARGENT *Rep. Forests* 54 *Rhus Metopium*. . . . Poison Wood, Coral Sumach, [etc.]. **1791** MUHLENBERG *Index Florae* 174 *Dentaria enneaphylla*. Coralwort.

+**Coralberry.** A shrub (*Symphoricarpos orbiculatus*), related to the snowberry.

1859 BARTLETT 99 Coral Berry. (*Symphoricarpus vulgaris.*) The Indian Currant of Missouri. **1860** CURTIS *Woody Plants N.C.* 87 Coral Berry. . . . The flowers are of no beauty, but the compact clusters of dark red berries . . . which hang on through the Winter, have made it an object of attention among gardeners and florists. **1870** *Amer. Naturalist* IV. 216 The Snowberry . . . and the Coral-berry . . . are in general cultivation. **1901** MOHR *Plant Life Ala.* 85 Coral-berry and shrubby St. John's wort (*Hypericum prolificum*) [form] the bushy covering of the ground.

Coralroot. A plant of the genus *Corallorhiza*. {1828– (Smith *Eng. Flora* IV. 49)} — **1821** *Mass. H. S. Coll.* 2 Ser. IX. 149 Plants, which are indigenous in the township of Middlebury, [Vt., include] . . . *C. corallorhizum*, Coral-root. **1839** in *Mich. Agric. Soc. Trans.* VII. 405 *Corallorhiza verna*. Coral-root. **1901** MOHR *Plant Life Ala.* 458 *Corallorhiza odontorhiza*. . . . Small-flowered Coral-root. *Ib. Corallorhiza wisteriana*. . . . Wister's Coral-root.

Coral snake. {1760–} +Any one of various small venomous snakes of the genus *Elaps. S.* — **1883** *Harper's Mag.* Oct. 708/1 None of my venomous acquaintances, whether . . . black-snake, whip-snake, coral-snake, or viper, has ever . . . [sprung] off the ground at me. **1889** *Cent.* 1261/1 *Coral-snake,* . . . Elaps . . . fulvius, . . . E. corralina.

Coral tree. The scarlet-flowered *Erythrina corallodendron* of the West Indies. {1756-} — **1863** *Harper's Mag.* March 532/2 Here [in Florida], too, . . . I found the gay 'Coral-tree' (*Erythrina*), with its lance-like scarlet banners.

* **Cord,** *n.*

1. *ellipt.* = BEDCORD.

1648 in *Mayflower Desc.* X. 199 It[em], one trundle bedstead with a coard, [£]1. **1653** *Essex Probate Rec.* I. 157 One bedsteed and cord. **1775** *Ann. S.W. Virginia* 645 One walnut bedsted and cord. **1845** DRAKE *Pioneer Life Ky.* 238 In the course of the night the cords hurt him through the feathers, which were then a scarce article, and the cord (quite as scarce an article) broke in one place. **1922** A. BROWN *Old Crow* 483 How had she carried the heavy hardwood pieces [of the bed] down, fitted them together and corded them? He was curious enough to lift the tick to find out what she had used for cord.

2. A fabric having a cordlike or ribbed surface. {1776-}

1790 *Columbian Centinel* 2 Oct. 23/4 [For sale:] . . . Sheetings, Flannels, Elliots and fancy Cords. **1822** *Ann. 17th Congress* 1 Sess. I. 319 Quantities of goods, purchased at Georgetown, . . . and transmitted to the factories in the year 1820 . . . [include] 316 yards cords and velvets $210.14.

3. A cubic measure, as for the amount of cut wood in a pile eight feet long, four feet high and four feet wide. {1616-now chiefly *dial.*}

1666 *Groton Rec.* 17 There to Cord for him the aforesaid 30 cord of wood at fiue shilling per cord. **1726** *New-Eng. Courant* 19-26 Feb. 2/2 Allowing 3 Sled Load to one Cord, it comes out at 51 Shillings per Cord. **1781** *Va. State P.* I. 608 The Yard can Tann fifteen hundred Hides this year, which will require One hundred and fifty cords of good Bark. **1817** BIRKBECK *Notes* (1818) 33 Fire-wood [in w. Penna.] is two dollars per cord. **1831** PECK *Guide* 195 The furnace burns two cords of wood, and seven bushels of coal. **1887** *Harper's Mag.* March 610/2 The negroes would draw ashore with ease a quantity of logs, which they cut into cords, and sold to their master for a dollar per cord.

b. A measure of stone or rock. {1703-}

1871 RAYMOND *3rd Rep. Mines* 305 The number of cords or tons from which this product was obtained is not stated. **1874** *Congress. Rec.* 3 June 4500/2 We have taken out thousands upon thousands of cords of rock.

+**c.** A measure of barnyard manure.

1837 COLMAN *Mass. Agric. Rep.* 21 We use from four to ten cords of manure, average eight cords per acre. **1848** *Cultivator* n.s. V. 185 Before plowing I spread over one-third of the ground about ten cords of common barn-yard manure per acre. **1884** *Vt. Agric. Rep.* VIII. 14 [He] would not put on more than twelve loads, or four or five cords of manure, to the acre.

+**d.** Designating a boat's carrying capacity. *Obs.*

1758 *N.J. Archives* XX. 303 A convenient Wharf lately built, sufficient to stow 500 Cord of Wood, from which Place a ten Cord Boat at any common Tide, may go loaded. **1777** *Ib.* 2 Ser. I. 356 A wharf or landing place belonging to said place, where a 12 cord boat may load.

+**4.** A large number; a great amount. *colloq.*

1834 C. A. DAVIS *Lett. J. Downing* 167 Now jest see about the Bank. There it stands . . . with its hundred cord of specie, and its cart load of books. **a1846** *Quarter Race Ky.*, etc. 93 When I lived up on Deer Creek, thar was a perfect cord of all sorts [of snakes]. **1847** FIELD *Drama in Pokerville*, etc. 13 Manager Dust was just nat'rally bound to make 'a corde of money!' **1847** *Knickerb.* XXX. 394 From childhood we had been told that there were 'cords' of snakes in the southern country. **1861** NORTON *Army Lett.* 10, I counted two hundred and forty-four cannon lying round in the yard . . . and I should think twenty-five or thirty cords of cannon balls. **1902** LORIMER *Lett. Merchant* 108 It just naturally sold cords of papers.

* **Cord,** *v.*

***1.** *tr.* To provide or equip (a bed) with a bedcord.

1750 HEMPSTEAD *Diary* 548, I was att home . . . helping Ms [*sic*] Hobbs Cord up her bed. **1843** *Knickerb.* XXI. 224 Carpets are to be laid, curtains hung, . . . beds corded. **c1870** BAGBY *Old Va. Gentleman* 14 Beings who . . . do not so much as know the meaning of cording a bed. **1872** M. HOLLEY *My Opinions* (1891) 93 Where the wife has to . . . hang out clothes lines, cord beds, cut up pork, [etc.]. **1922** [see CORD *n.* 1].

2. To stack *up* or arrange (wood) in cords. {1640-; now *dial.*}

1666 *Groton Rec.* 17 To cutt and Car[t] to his house and there to Cord for him the aforesaid 30 cord of wood. **1677** [see CORDER 1]. **1728** *Boston Rec.* 223 There are Several Sorts of Wood not fit for Burning in famalys, Corded up and Exposed to Sale with and among Firewood. **1833** *Sketches D. Crockett* 13 Was [the timber] corded up like steamboat wood, and in that manner devoured? **1882** THAYER *From Log-Cabin* xi. 168 The German had cut and corded two cords a day,—just the amount he himself had cut.

transf. **1909** WASON *Happy Hawkins* 286 We had divided his wages, an' she had a nice little roll of her own corded away.

b. To put ore into cords.

1887 *Courier-Journal* 7 May 6/7 The company has about 10,000 tons of ore corded up.

3. To equip or provide (a shoe) with a cord or welt.

1887 WILKINS *Humble Romance* 28 The women had corded boots at home, while the man had worked in the shop.

***Corded,** *a.* Of fabrics: Having raised lines on the surface. {1760-} — **1744** *Md. Hist. Mag.* XXI. 245 One peice of Corded Dimity. **1754** *S.C. Gazette* 22-29 Jan. 3/1 William Taylor . . . has just imported . . . white and brown hollands, corded dimity. **1886** B. P. POORE *Reminisc.* II. 305 The eight brides-maids wore dresses of white corded silk, alike in every particular.

+**Cordelle,** *n.* [F.] A rope or line used in towing a boat.

1811 BRACKENBRIDGE *Louisiana* 214 Continued until eleven, with cordelle, or towing line—the banks being favorable. **1821** NUTTALL *Trav. Arkansa* 66 We proceeded chiefly by means of the cordelle, but at a very tedious and tiresome rate. **1826** FLINT *Recoll.* 91 You then have to apply, what is commonly called here a 'cordelle,' which is a long rope fastened at one end of the boat, thrown ashore and seized by sufficient . . . hands to drag or track the boat upstream. **1831** AUDUBON *Ornith. Biog.* I. 131 Both these kinds of vessels were provided with a mast, a square-sail, and coils of cordage, known by the name of *cordelles.* **1845** *Cincinnati Misc.* 125 Where the shore or beach permitted, the cordelle was also resorted to. This was a stout rope, which being fastened to the mast, was carried along the beach, on the shoulders of the whole boat's crew, stationed at regular distances. **1889** E. W. GOULD *Fifty Years on Mississippi* 193 Its propelling power was by oar, sail, setting poles, the cordelle.

+**Cordelle,** *v. tr.* To tow or work (a boat) forward by means of a cordelle. Also absol.

1826 T. FLINT *Recoll.* 96 In two instances the boatmen . . . when cordelling the boat directly at the base of these rocks, disengaged snakes from their retreats. **1832** S. A. FERRALL *Ramble* 228 The crew being obliged to poll or cordelle the whole distance. **1847** J. PALMER *Rocky Mts.* 226 We were compelled to cordelle our boat, and sometimes lift it over the rocks for several rods. **1853** *Harper's Mag.* VII. 751/1 Vessels of large size . . . floating and cordelling through innumerable bays and bayous, finally work their way into the 'interior.' **1883** EGGLESTON *Hoosier School-Boy* 108 They . . . started home, now rowing against the current and now cordelling along the river shore. **1890** *Harper's Mag.* Oct. 869/1 Sometimes they seemed sailing or being cordelled straight through the cemetery.

+**Cordelling.** The towing or working of a boat forward with a cordelle.

1832 PAULDING *Westward Ho!* 83 A rope was taken ashore, and fastened to a rock, or stump, or sapling, and by this the boat was dragged along. This process is called cordelleing. **1841** E. R. STEELE *Summer Journey* 208 The crew landed, and fastening ropes to the trees drew their bark along; this process was called cordelling. **1842** *Amer. Pioneer* I. 99 The men in the skiff carried forward another cord and fastened it in the same manner; keeping up the process of 'cordelling,' as it was called by the boatmen, till they had passed by the rapid water. **1845** *Cincinnati Misc.* 125 The shore . . . did not present the opportunity of cordelling. **1850** G. HINES *Voyage* 121 They are ascended by cordeling, and it is frequently necessary to work for hours in the water among the rocks. **1870** NOWLAND *Indianapolis* 27 The Wabash and White Rivers were ascended by what is called 'cord-elling.'

attrib. **1816** H. KER *Travels* 36 After getting above their cordaling ground, in swift water they make use of their warp. **1828** *Western Mo. Rev.* II. 324 A very moderate expense would form cordelling, or tow paths, along our rivers.

* **Corder.**

+**1.** A town official whose duty was to pile merchantable wood into standard cords. *Obs.*

1654-5 *Boston Rec.* 123 Att a meething this Day . . . was Chosen . . . for Corders of Wood, Tho. Leader, Rich. Tayler. **1671** *Ib.* 59 For preuentinge of Fraude & deceipte in Cordinge of wood It is ordered that the Select men shall haue powre to apoynt cordrs of wood for this towne. **1677** *N.Y. State Col. Hist.* XII. 568 The Go: proposed . . . That no sale wood be brought to the Towne but it shall bee corded; . . . ordered to that end one or more Corders to bee appointed. **1733** *Phila. Council Minutes* (1847) 326 The Question was Putt whether Peter Cahoun, one of the present Corders of Wood, should be Removed. **1811** MEASE *Philadelphia* 94 He [the mayor] appoints the city commissioners, the high constables, watchmen, the corders of wood at the public landings, etc.

2. One who provides shoes with cords or welts.

1885 *Harper's Mag.* Jan. 280/2 Lining and outside are stitched together on the wrong side, and to get them right side out, a 'corder' forms the top and button scallops over a round-pointed piece of steel securely fastened to a table.

Cord grass. A marsh grass of the genus *Spartina.* {1824- (J. E. Smith *Eng. Flora* I. 135)}

1857 GRAY *Botany* 551 Cord or Marsh Grass . . . [has] very smooth sheaths, and long and tough leaves. **1871** *Ill. Agric. Soc. Trans.* VIII. 145 A grass, the spartina, or cord grass, grows in this State in the rankest luxuriance, on the swampy bottoms on the Mississippi. **1889** VASEY *Agric. Grasses* 56 Cord grass . . . is frequently cut for hay, but is of inferior quality unless cut very early. **1895** *Dept. Agric. Yearbook* 436 The stouter fresh-water cord grass (fig. 110) grows . . . also along the margins of fresh-water lakes and rivers. **1901** MOHR *Plant Life Ala.* 49.

+**Cordies.** 'An American name for a kind of felt hat, covered with camel or goat hair' (1858 Simmonds *Dict. Trade*).

+Cordillera. [Sp.] A range of mountains. Freq. in pl. (See quot. 1890.)

1814 BRACKENRIDGE *Louisiana* 48 Red River takes its source in the Cordilleras, at no great distance north of Sta. Fé. **1857** E. STONE *Life of Howland* 285 Under easy sail she crossed the entrance to Mount Hope Bay, and doubling Popasquash point, the Tiverton cordillera was lost from sight. **1875** BOURKE *Journal* 12 May–22 June, The knolls . . . would afford sustenance to great herds of sheep, requiring no protection from the weather other than that afforded by the elevated cordillera a mile north of us. **1890** TOWNSEND *U.S. Index* 136 The western shore of mountains, lining the continent, are spoken of as *The Cordilleras*, divided into the Andes, the Rocky and Cordilleras of Mexico.

Corduroy, *n.*

1. A kind of heavy, ribbed cotton cloth. {1795–} Freq. attrib.

1792 *Ann. 2nd Congress* 1028 Manufactories of cotton goods . . . produce . . . corduroys. **1794** FRENEAU *Poems* (1795) 10 All that would suit man, woman, girl, or boy; Muslins and muslinets, jeans, grograms, corduroy. **1883** *Harper's Mag.* Sept. 534/2 A man . . . almost fantastically like old Rip, . . . his . . . dress half corduroy, half a sort of rough cloth.

attrib. **1805** CLARK in *Lewis & C. Exped.* (1904) I. 269 He . . . had received . . . from M. Chaboillez . . . the following articles 3 Brace of Cloth 1 Brace of Scarlet a par Corduroy overalls. **1807** IRVING, etc. *Salmagundi* xiv. 384 The noble County Paris had the misfortune to tear his corduroy breeches. **1837** *Crockett Almanac* 43 This upper garment . . . impended over a pair of full corduvor pantaloons. **1880** *Harper's Mag.* July 177/1 He had donned a flannel shirt and patched corduroy trousers. **1895** WILLIAMS *Princeton Stories* 91 Somehow Darnell could not make his corduroy coat hang in that way. **1902** *Harper's Mag.* March 618 Beside it sat a pretty girl in corduroy jacket and knickerbockers.

2. *pl.* Trousers made of corduroy. {1787–}

1857 D. H. STROTHER *Virginia* 60 At present, his wardrobe in active service consists of a double-frilled shirt, a sack of Weidenfeldt's cut, stained corduroys, and a pair of stringless shoes. **1867** RICHARDSON *Beyond Miss.* 24 A backwoods Missouri boy in white wool hat and corduroys . . . throws the dice. **1881** *Harper's Mag.* April 749/1 He is prouder of long tailed coat and boots and corduroys. **1889** *Century Mag.* March 749/2 The hero . . . appears in his riding-boots, corduroys, and sack coat. **1902** *Harper's Mag.* Jan. 219 He put on a flannel shirt and some corduroys, loaded a push-cart with cherries. **1907** LILLIBRIDGE *Trail* 191 Ranchers there were in corduroys and denims.

+3. A causeway made of small logs or tree trunks, usually laid transversely, and forming a road or part of a road.

1832 MCCALL *Lett. from Frontiers* 255 We passed over many miles of those execrable roads called 'corduroys';—they are roads through the Swamp, made by laying fence-rails round or angular, crooked or straight, perpendicularly across the way. **a1861** WINTHROP *Canoe & Saddle* 162 My friends the woodsmen had constructed an elaborate inclined plane of very knobby corduroy down the steepest steep. **1874** B. F. TAYLOR *World on Wheels* 241 Bounce over the 'Corduroy,' went the old road. **1915** E. ATKINSON *Johnny Appleseed* 185 These young pioneers knew . . . how to fell trees, and with them build blockhouses and log bridges, and lay the swamps with corduroy.

attrib. **1834** CARRUTHERS *Kentuckian* I. 111 Oh! The comforts and blessings of a corduroy turnpike. **1848** *Knickerb.* XVIII. 499 Oh the delights of travelling on a Georgia road! Those picturesque gulleys; those corduroy cross-ways! **1871** BURROUGHS *Wake-Robin* (1886) 117 [The road] was here a dilapidated corduroy structure that compelled the traveller to keep an eye on his feet. **1876** TASISTRO & COPPÉE trs. Comte de Paris *Civil War in Amer.* II. 9 The whole Federal army was at work, . . . constructing long solid corduroy causeways through the marshy forests.

transf. **1883** RILEY *Old Swimmin'-Hole* 46 My playin's only middlin'—tunes I picked up when a boy—The kindo'-sorto' fiddlin' that the folks calls 'cordaroy.'

Corduroy, *v.* +*tr.* To lay (soft, swampy, or muddy stretches of a road) with logs or poles placed transversely.

1861 *Md. Hist. Mag.* V. 313 We have mapped out the woods with new roads, and corduroyed the swamps for miles. **1862** *N.Y. Times* 12 May, We had perfectly impassable roads, (until corduroyed). **1865** BOUDRYE *Fifth N.Y. Cavalry* 49 In front of the tents is a street which has to be corduroyed, or it will become impassable for mud. **1875** BOURKE *Journal* 24 June, The progress being slow on account of the great number of ravines and gulches met with, which had to be spanned with wooden bridges or 'corduroyed.' **1890** CUSTER *Following Guidon* 3 Banks of stream miry—obliged to corduroy it. **1907** ANDREWS *Recoll.* 195 Meantime details were busy with axes cutting down small pines and corduroying the constantly occurring bad places.

+Corduroy bridge. A crude bridge made of small transverse logs or poles.

[**1822** J. WOODS *English Prairie* 71 Along a rough road with many log-bridges; but some of my fellow passengers . . . called them corderoy.] **1842** BUCKINGHAM *Slave States* I. 237 A corduroy bridge, composed of round trunks of trees with the bark on, laid side by side, sometimes close to each other, but often with spaces of two or three inches between them. **1847** *Knickerb.* XXX. 170 We reached a maximum speed of three miles an hour, notwithstanding the undulating character of the rail, which imparted the exercise of a corduroy bridge. **1852** *S. Lit. Messenger* XVIII. 693/2 The motion of a wheeled vehicle in one of these prairies awakens very touching reminiscences of the corduroy bridges. **1860** ABBOTT *South & North* 122 The land route is so exceedingly uncomfortable, leading through miry roads, or over corduroy bridges, that nearly all the travel is in boats. **1862** in Moore *Rebellion Rec.* V. II. 89 The First Minnesota had thrown a corduroy bridge, several thousand feet long, across the Chickahominy.

‖**Corduroying.** The material used in making a corduroy road. — **1876** BOURKE *Journal* 945 The road travelled had much 'corduroying' upon it, and heavy excavations and grading.

+Corduroy road. A road through a muddy or swampy area made of transverse tree trunks, logs, or poles.

1824 BLANE *Excursion* 147 A Corderoy Road consists of small trees, stripped of their boughs, and laid touching one another, without any covering of earth. **1837** *S. Lit. Messenger* III. 737 The road is always either a deep sand, or a corduroy road made necessary by swamps and marshes. **1858** *Harper's Mag.* June 46/1 We were blissfully ignorant of the character of a 'corduroy road.' **1880** *Scribner's Mo.* June 247/1 This is the time of logging and building 'bees,' and . . . of hard drinking and 'corduroy' roads. **1904** GLASGOW *Deliverance* 401 She turned from the lane into a strip of 'corduroy road.' **1923** J. B. COOK *On Old Frontier* 96 We cut clumps of these, tied them into bunches, and used them to make a sort of corduroy road to those of the cattle which were farthest from shore.

fig. **c1849** PAIGE *Dow's Sermons* I. 50 Time will take you smoothly and gently over the rough, corduroy road that leads to the grave.

***Cordwainer.** A shoemaker. Now archaic or hist.

1658 *Suffolk Deeds* III. 130 Jarvis Gold late of Boston aforesajd Cordwayner deceased. **1719** *N.H. Probate Rec.* II. 91 Bond of Samuel Adams, maltster, with John Vifen, rope maker, and Samuel Holbrook, cordwainer, as Sureties, all of Boston. **1784** *Mass. Centinel* 12 May 2/3 Daniel Parks, Cordwainer. **1834** PECK *Gaz. Illinois* 264 Jacksonville has . . . six tailors, two cordwainers, four blacksmiths, three chair makers, [etc.]. **1845** *Knickerb.* XXVI. 415 Of the cordwainer's shop itself, the paraphernalia is simple. **1914** *Essex Inst. Coll.* L. 339 Sylvanus Plumer . . . was a cordwainer by trade, and lived in Newbury [c1750].

Cordwaining. *Obs.* The occupation or profession of a cordwainer. — **1758** in Chalkley *Scotch-Irish Settlement Va.* I. 470 [He] binds himself . . . to learn cord waining. **1820** *Niles' Reg.* XVIII. 365/2, 254 males and 55 females, are at present confined in this establishment, variously employed in weaving, cordwaining, hatting, &c.

Cordwinder. *Obs.* Variant of CORDWAINER. {1682–; now *Obs.*}

1644 *Suffolk Deeds* I. 51, I Richard Cranniwell of Woodbridge in the County of Suffolk Cordwinder. **1658** *Ib.* III. 104 Richard Curtis of Dorchester in the Countie of Suffolke in New England Cordwinder. **1673** *East-Hampton Rec.* I. 363 This Towne of Easthampton have granted to mee James Looper four acres of land . . . : uppon this Condition that I shall follow my trade at all Convenient times, of a Cordwinder. **1758** *Southampton Rec.* III. 180 John Jennings sells to Bethnel Reeves cord winder a messuage and tract of land at North sea. **1790** in L. Summers *Ann. S.W. Virginia* (1929) 440 Thomas McGinnis bound to Philip Cole, (cord winder).

Cordwood. Wood for fuel cut in four foot lengths in order that it may be piled in cords. {1638–, now only *local* or *dial.*}

1679 *Manchester Town Rec.* 16 The current standing price of Coard wood at the landing place at Ketle Cove is & have beene from time to time four shillings 6d acoard in Currant money. **1713** *Braintree Rec.* 81 The Parents or Masters of all children or servants, that go to school shall forthwith . . . deliver in to the Present school master for the use of the school, at the schoolhouse, Three foot of cord wood. **1775** in *Boston Ev. Transcript* 26 April III. 12/7 We are not alowd to send up any Cordwood to Boston. **1811** MEASE *Philadelphia* 126 The stand for cord wood brought by land to the city, is the upper end of High street. **1845** C. MATHEWS *Writings* II. 168 (Th.), A customer on the banks of the Mississippi, who was sitting on a pile of cord wood. **1865** *Nation* I. 174 On the railroad the colored laborers when employed in cutting cord-wood are expected to cut what a white man usually cuts. **1881** *Rep. Indian Affairs* 173 A considerable quantity of cordwood is sold by the Indians to steamers at Tulalip and Swinomish Reservations. **1922** TITUS *Timber* 186 That night a settler drives in to talk to Paul 'bout some cord wood.

attrib. **1743** *Duxbury Rec.* 165 Begining at the country road . . . where a path called the cord wood path, comes into said country road. **1748** *N.H. Probate Rec.* III. 625, I give and bequeath unto Martha My dearly beloved Wife . . . seven cord of good firewood cordwood length. **1771** *Boston Gaz.* 11 Feb. (Th.), He was then armed with two cordwood sticks. **1884** ROE *Nature's Story* 53 They use for the substratum of the domicile quite respectable cord-wood sticks, thicker than one's wrist.

Coreopsis. An American genus of plants of the natural order *Compositæ*, several species of which are cultivated for their flowers. {1753–} — **1766** J. BARTRAM *Journal* 3 Jan. 21 Saw . . . many alligators, tho' so very cold that it had froze the great convolvolus and coreopsis. **1772** ROMANS in Phillips *Notes on B. Romans* (1924) 124 They also have a Species of Coreopsis of which they make a Sort of Sweet Bread, tho' in no great Quantity. **1857** GRAY *Botany* 220 *C. tripteris*, tall coreopsis. *Ib.* 221 *C. rosea*, rose-flowered coreopsis. **1868** —*Field Botany* 201 *C. tinctoria*, of Arkansas, &c., [is] the commonest Coreopsis or Calliopsis of all country gardens. **1878** WHITMAN *Specimen Days* (1882) 123 These perennial blossoms and friendly weeds [include] . . . Dandelions, yarrow, coreopsis, wild pea.

*** Coriander.**

***1.** A plant of the genus *Coriandrum* resembling parsley.

1676 GLOVER *Acc. Va.* in *Phil. Trans.* XI. 629 Such Herbs as grow wild in England, and do not grow there, they plant, as Wormwood, . . . Rue, Coriander, Enula, and the like. **1709** LAWSON *Carolina* 78 The more Physical [herbs] are . . . Dill, Carawa, Cummin, Anise, Coriander. **1865** A. D. WHITNEY *Gayworthys* ix. 86 Pinks and sweetwilliam, and southernwood, and ladies' delights, and bits of coriander.

***2.** *Coriander seed.* **a.** (See quotations.)

1845 *Knickerb.* XXVI. 509 Those smallest preparations of refined sugar, wherewith the confectioner delighteth the heart of our young Hope, under the name of Coriander-seed. **1863** GRAY *Botany* p. lv, *Coriandrum sativum*, Coriander, . . . [is] occasionally cultivated for its aromatic fruit, the Coriander-seed of the shops.

b. *slang.* Coin, money. {1737}

1841 H. PLAYFAIR *Papers* I. 121 Coriander seed, a Yankee term for money.

*** Corinthian,** *n.* +An amateur yachtsman.

1883–4 *Forest & Stream* XXI (*Cent.*), It is to canoeists . . . that the yachtsman may look for some of the most valuable additions to the ranks of Corinthians, as those who follow canoeing do so from pure love of sport.

***Corinthian,** *a. Sport.* +Amateur. — **1885** *Harper's Mag.* June 83/1 On the yacht of a friend who was fond of sailing Corinthian races.

*** Cork,** *n.*[1]

+1. (See quotation.) *Obs. slang.*

1851 HALL *College Words* 85 *Cork, calk.* In some of the Southern colleges, this word, with a derived meaning, signifies a *complete stopper.* Used in the sense of an entire failure in reciting.

+2. Burnt cork used by actors in making up as Negro minstrels. Also *cork opera.*

1867 *Atlantic Mo.* Nov. 611/1 Between acts the extravaganzaist in cork and wool would appear, and . . . command . . . full share of admiration in the arena. **1869** *Ib.* July 79/1 Mitchell, poor fellow, like Lynch and Sliter and so many of my old associates in the cork-opera, has passed away.

3. *attrib.* Made of the cortical tissue of the cork oak.

1769 in E. Singleton *Social N.Y.* 266 A cork-cutter . . . informed the public that he had 'cork jackets of different prices for swimming, which had saved many from drowning.' **1867** J. M. CRAWFORD *Mosby* 65 Dahlgren's body—minus his cork leg—was brought to Richmond for identification. **1857** R. GLISAN *Jrnl. Army Life* 391 They had been floating on a piece of the deck of the hurricane deck, with cork life-preservers to their persons. **1790** *Penna. Packet* 21 Dec. 3/4 Cork Socks [are] an effectual defence for the feet against damps and cold. **1847** ROBB *Squatter Life* 180 Earth shook beneath the tread of his patent cork soles.

Cork, *n.*[2] [Erroneous spelling of *calk, caulk.*]

1. =CALK *n.*[1] 2.

1806 WEBSTER, *Cork,* . . . a sharp point on a horse shoe. **1816** PICKERING 71 *Corks,* the steel points fixed under the shoes of horses, in the winter, to prevent them from falling, on the ice. *a***1846** *Quarter Race Ky.*, etc. 162, I then just took my old mare down to a blacksmith's shop, and had some shoes made with 'corks' about four inches long, and had 'em nailed on to her hind feet.

2. =CALK *n.*[1] 1.

1902 S. E. WHITE *Blazed Trail* xxvii. 187 His face and flesh were ripped and torn everywhere by the 'corks' on the boots. **1922** TITUS *Timber* 286 There'll never be a Michigan man who is lonesome for white pine who can't . . . feel the corks in his boots biting into the bark—if he wants to.

Cork, *v. tr.* =CALK *v.* — **1776** *N.J. Archives* 2 Ser. I. 168 A chestnut sorrel Mare, . . . shod before, shoes are steel corked. *a***1817** DWIGHT *Travels* II. 415 When the surface of well-made roads has become hard, a slight rain makes them so slippery, as to be impassable with safety, unless with horses corked in the same manner, as when they are to travel on ice. **1829** *Va. Lit. Museum* 16 Dec. 419 To *cork.* 'To shoe a horse with points —or with frost nails.'

***Cork-bark.** Used in names of trees whose bark resembles cork. {cork-barked 1866} — **1850** *New Eng. Farmer* II. 142 We have grafted the Slippery and the Cork-bark Elm on the White Elm. **1892** APGAR *Trees Northern U.S.* 87 *Acer campestre,* L. (English or Cork-Bark Maple.)

Cork-cutter. One who cuts cork into proper shape for stoppers. {1709-} — **1769** [see CORK *n.*[1] 3]. **1789** *Boston Directory* 188 Hunt, Abraham, wine-broker and cork-cutter. **1803** *Ann. 7th Congress* 2 Sess. 1288 The petitions . . . of the following manufactures of the United States, to wit . . . of combmakers, gunsmiths, cork cutters, calico printers.

Cork elm. +A variety of elm (*Ulmus racemosa*) having bark somewhat resembling cork.

1813 MUHLENBERG *Cat. Plants* 29. **1848** *Knickerb.* XXXI. 31 We add . . . the Northern Cork-Elm and the Heart-leaved Balsam-Poplar. **1849** EMMONS *Agric. N.Y.* II. 323 Cork Elm (*Ulmus racemosa*). . . . The structure of this wood is singular and beautiful. **1861** *Ill. Agric. Soc. Trans.* IV. 452 Mr. Freeman called attention to the White Cork Elm of Southern Illinois as an ornamental tree. **1892** APGAR *Trees Northern U.S.* 134 Cork or Rock Elm. . . . A large tree with fine-grained, heavy and very tough wood. Southwest Vermont, west and south, southwestward to Missouri, on river-banks.

Corker. {1723-} +Something decisive or difficult to counter; a 'settler'; anything fine or excellent that serves its purpose admirably. *colloq.*[2]

1835–7 HALIBURTON *Clockmaker* 1 Ser. xix. 174 Then I lets him have it, right, left, right, jist three corkers. **1887** *Nation* 14 April 307/3 'Consistency' sends us an enquiry which he evidently considers a 'corker.' **1889** 'MARK TWAIN' *Conn. Yankee in King Arthur's Court* xvi. 192 For just a modest little one-line ad., it's a corker. **1897** C. M. FLANDRAU *Harvard Episodes* 223 Then we [college students] raced the car until the horses—oh, they were corkers!—began to run away. **1903** ADE *In Babel* 353 He's a little corker; that's what he is. **1904** W. H. SMITH *Promoters* 73 He had a cough that was a corker. **1921** PAINE *Comr. Rolling Ocean* 145 If he wished to proclaim what a perfect corker of a fellow he was, he had to tell it to himself.

+b. (See quotation.)

1868 CHADWICK *Base Ball* 137 Smith then hit a 'corker'—a ball that flies from the bat like a cork from a champagne bottle.

Corking, *a.* and *adv.* Fine, excellent, first class. *colloq.* {*dial.*}

1895 *Outing* XXVII. 193/2 Corking great fences the Vale doubles are. **1897** FLANDRAU *Harvard Episodes* 192 He had a corking big oak table. **1904** STRATTON-PORTER *Freckles* 84 How the divil am I ever to learn them corkin' big words by meself? **1906** L. BELL *C. Lee* 270 She was dancing with a corking looking man. **1909** WASON *Happy Hawkins* 108, I ain't no tenderfoot when it comes to a book, but this one was sure the corkin'est I ever met up with. **1910** E. A. WALCOTT *Open Door* 188 It was a corking good story, Captain. **1919** *Detective Story Mag.* XXVIII. 17 We might have doped out a corking yarn.

+Corkonian. An Irishman from Cork. — *a***1837** R. J. BRECKINRIDGE *Memoranda* I. 29 This city [Cork] gives name to one of those bloody factions, which under the appellations of *Corkonians* and *Fardowns* divide the lowest classes of Irish Catholics in that distant land [U.S.]. **1905** VALENTINE *H. Sandwith* 180 The 'Corkonians' employed on the Dunkirk branch of the Pennsylvania and Erie Canal [in 1856] became more notorious.

+Cork pine. The common white pine, *Pinus strobus.* Also attrib. — **1873** *Michigan Atlas* pref. 20 The soft or cork-pine, so called from the resemblance in softness and texture of its wood to the cork of commerce. **1879** *Lumberman's Gaz.* 15 Oct., Valuable cork pine timber. **1902** WHITE *Blazed Trail* 119 Often in the hollows it shaded gradually into the rough-skinned cork pine.

Corkscrew, *n.* {1720-} **1.** A spirally twisted ringlet of hair; a curl. Also attrib. and comb. **+2.** (See quotation.) — **(1) 1815** *N. Amer. Rev.* I. 20 The innocent animated imitations of the Medicean Venus, with their thousand cork-screw ringlets. **1880** *Harper's Mag.* April 735/1 Bangs were at that time *out,* and corkscrews *in.* **1883** *Ib.* Feb. 402/1 No small mincing . . . 'corkscrews,' but a goodly sized tress. **1899** *Mo. So. Dakotan* I. 180 The women who lately plead for suffrage before the Iowa Legislature were much sweeter looking, more womanly, more matronly . . . than the cork-screw curled anties. **(2) 1905** *Forestry Bureau Bul.* No. 61, 33 *Corkscrew,* a geared logging locomotive (P[acific] C[oast] F[orest]).

Corkscrew, *v.* {1837-} ‖*intr.* To twist or arrange hair into a corkscrew. — **1876** MILLER *First Families* 152 Then she would . . . wind and wind with her two hands, and cork-screw at her back hair.

Corky, *a.* {1601-} Having corklike bark. — **1857** GRAY *Botany* 396 *Ulmus racemosa,* Corky White Elm. . . . River-banks, W. New England, New York, and Michigan. April.

+Corliss engine. [f. G. H. *Corliss,* Amer. engineer, 1817–88.] An engine having a distinctive type of trip valve gear. — **1874** KNIGHT 624/2 *Corliss-engine,* a form of steam-engine having a variable and automatic cut-off of peculiar character. **1881** *Harper's Mag.* April 665/2 A sixty-horsepower Corliss engine . . . supplies the power to these shops and to a saw-mill.

*** Cormorant.** One or other species of two genera of large, voracious sea birds, *Phalacrocorax* or *Nannopterum.*

1616 SMITH *New England* 16 Geese, Brants, Cormorants, Ducks, . . . and many other sorts, whose names I knowe not. **1637** MORTON *New Canaan* II. vii, In many places, I have seen the Cormorants in length 3. miles feedinge. **1806** in *Ann. 9th Congress* 2 Sess. 1108 They saw many cormorants, and the whooping crane. **1839** PEABODY *Mass. Birds* 397 The Double-crested Cormorant, *Phalacrocorax dilophus,* . . . spend the winter on the coast of the eastern states. . . . No fish comes amiss to their insatiable appetites. **1883** *Harper's Mag.* Oct. 714/1 Egg Island during the nesting season is the haunt of innumerable gulls, of flocks of pelicans, and some cormorants and cranes.

*** Corn,** *n.*

+1. Indian corn or maize, *Zea mays.*

This special sense arose naturally from the greater abundance and use of the native grain as compared with those kinds brought from England, which for some time were distinguished as *English corn* (q.v.).

1608 J. SMITH *Works* (1884) 9 Shortly after it pleased God (in our extremity) to moue the Indians to bring vs Corne, ere it was halfe ripe, to refresh vs. *c***1618** STRACHEY *Virginia* 37 Shewing them [*sc.* scalps] to such the English as came unto him at his appointment, to trade with him for corne. **1650** *Md. Archives* I. 349 Every Taxable person planting Tobacco shall plant and tend two acres of Corne, upon forfeiture of Every two acres not so planted. **1684** I. MATHER *Providences* (1856) x. 225 Several acres of corn . . . were . . . destroyed by the hail. **1705** BEVERLEY *Virginia* II. 40 None of the Toils of Husbandry were exercised by this happy People; except the bare planting a little Corn, and Melons. **1770** *Carroll P.* in *Md. Hist. Mag.* XIII. 72, I Have a great deal of soft Corn at all the Plantations where the Virginia Corn was Planted. **1776** CARVER *Travels* 263 Unripe corn . . . and beans in the same state, boiled together with bears flesh. . . . They call this food Succatosh. **1809** *Ann. 10th Congress* 2 Sess. 428 In the slave States the allowance for the subsistence of a negro, is one peck of corn per week. **1840** BIRD *Robin Day* 86 We sat down to an Indian dinner of corn, pumpkins, and sweet potatoes. **1845** KIRKLAND *Western Clearings* 10 An old grey-headed Indian was . . . shelling corn on the edge of a hoe. **1885** *Century Mag.* May 14/2 The new State of Nebraska . . . proclaims . . . that 'Corn is King.' **1916** *Dept. Agric. Yearbook* 469 Farmers . . . are at a loss to know what to do with the soft corn which early frost leaves on their hands.

+**b.** *ellipt.* Corn whisky; also the condition of drunkenness caused by corn whisky. *colloq.*

1845 HOOPER *Simon Suggs' Adv.* v. 54 Let me git one o' these booklarnt fellers over a bottle of 'old corn.' **1846** *Spirit of Times* 18 April 92/1 'Now, look this way, strangers!' cried he, 'you hain't none of you got any particular idee of what a bad corn is!

+**2.** In phrases: **a.** *To feed on soft corn,* to flatter, to 'soft-soap.' *slang.*

1836 *Quarter Race Ky.* (1846) 22 He replied that I need not try to feed him on soft corn that way.

+**b.** *To acknowledge (admit, confess, own) the corn,* to concede the truth about a matter. *colloq.*

1840 *Daily Pennant* (St. Louis) 14 July (Th.), David Johnson acknowledged the corn, and said that he was drunk. **1845** in *Tall Tales of S.W.* (1930) 26, I was frightened the first night I slept there. I own it; yes, sir, I acknowledge the corn. **1846** *Spirit of Times* 6 June 177/3 The Anglo-Saxon 'never can acknowledge the corn' to the cross of negro and Indian. **1850** *Congress. Globe* 7 March 488/1 Has he not 'confessed the corn'? **1861** *Harper's Mag.* July 280/2 Sure enough it was his own house. . . . He 'owned the corn,' flung Cæsar a dollar to pay for the information, and passed the remainder of the night at home with his guests. **1868** W. BAKER *New Timothy* (1870) 211 You just acknowledge the corn—hand over your hat! **1875** G. P. BURNHAM *Three Years* 99 Then the Colonel proceeded to an interview with his prisoner, who at once 'knuckled' to the Chief; . . . he 'acknowledged the corn.' **1882** *Tomahawk* (Buffalo) No. 2, 1/2 'The editor of the Clipper admits the corn,' says a correspondent in the Vigilant. **1892** FORD *Dr. Dodd's School* 88, I want you and all the rest of you who went off bounds that morning to march into the Doctor's study to-night and acknowledge the corn. **1911** R. D. SAUNDERS *Col. Todhunter* 109 'It's generally the other man's money that looks dirty, Bill.' . . . 'I got to acknowledge the corn myself.'

+**c.** *All for corn,* (see quotation).

1877 BARTLETT 147 *All for corn,* honest, well-meant, sincere. 'He took it all for corn'; *i.e.,* he believed it to be true. 'All for wheat' is also heard.

3. In various attrib. and comb. uses with *bottom, district, fair, feast,* etc.; *cleaner, crusher, gatherer, harvester, pounder; growing, hoeing, parching, raising, setting.*

(*a*) **1843** *Ind. Mag. Hist.* III. 193 We are gaining meadows, and corn bottoms, and green hillsides, and town plots, by an utter extermination of the forest. **1874** *Dept. Agric. Rep. 1873* 55 The average value per acre is in one case $41.70, and in the other $35.63, a difference of 17 per cent. in favor of the corn district. **1888** *Boston Journal* 24 Nov. 2/4 Portsmouth, Ohio, is to have a corn fair. **1826** COOPER *Mohicans* xxii, Had they held their corn-feast—or can you say anything of the totems of their tribe? **1904** *Brooklyn Eagle* 31 Aug. 4 Corn festivals in Kansas are public celebrations in recognition of good crops. **1854** *Penna. Agric. Rep.* 77 A double corn harrow, or plow, a very useful article. **1881** *Rep. Indian Affairs* p. ix, The spirits had notified him that the dead warriors could not return to the country until the whites had left it, and fixed the date of leaving at the time of the corn harvest. **1849** *Rep. Comm. Patents: Agric.* 335 So long as the weather remains hot the weevils do not quit the corn-heaps they have invaded. **1763** WASHINGTON *Diaries* I. 183, 190 Corn holes. **1788** *Ib.* III. 295, 16 Barls. [of corn were] . . . deposited in the Corn loft. **1869** BROWNE *Adv. Apache Country* 279 The water . . . has rather a strong flavor of alkali, corn-manure, dead coyotes, Indian sign, and decayed vegetable matter. **1691** *Mass. Bay Currency Tracts* 31 Do not our Brethren at Connecticut find, Corn-mony will do their business for them? **1677** *Braintree Rec.* 18 Twenty shillings a year out of the corne pay. **1685** *Springfield Rec.* II. 188 Said Persons as make the Corne Payment of ye money Rate. **1852** WATSON *Nights in Block-House* 215 Skyles immediately arose, took down his master's rifle, shot-bag, and corn-pouch, and . . . quickly gained the wood. *c***1849** PAIGE *Dow's Sermons* I. 35 You will . . . feel like a jaybird indulging unmolested at a corn-rack. **1654** *Springfield Rec.* I. 332 Benjamin Mun is to pay for Corne Roome 5 [shillings]. **1851** A. O. HALL *Manhattaner* 5 It was a modest commercial plain . . . with . . . corn sacks, in quantities. **1840** *Picayune* 3 Oct. 2/1 There is a man in the city whose hands are as large as a pair of corn shovels. **1846** *Spirit of Times* 11 July 235/2 A sea-voyage from Philadelphia to Accomac, Virginia, in a corn sloop. **1860** T. D. PRICE *MS. Diary* 15 Sept., Tied some corn stands [for putting up shocks]. **1853** RAMSEY *Tennessee* 718 This superiority still exists, and Tennessee, by the census of 1840, was *the* corn State. **1899** ADE *Doc' Horne* 292 The book-agent . . . was managing his wife's lecture tour throughout the corn states. **1835** MARTIN *Description Va.* 127 The mills . . . turn two pair of corn, and the same number of Burr stones. **1636** *Plymouth Laws* 56 Mr. John Jenney . . . shall have a pottle of Corne toule upon every bushell for grinding the same. **1868** G. BRACKETT *Farm Talk* 15 The year 1866 was a 'hard corn year' throughout all New England.

(*b*) **1825** *Austin Papers* (1924) II. 1028, I should suppose some of our patent corncleaners would be desirable. **1851** A. CARY *Clovernook* 32 The corn-gatherers, with their oxen and dogs, were all gone. **1858** *Rep. Comm. Patents* I. 410 Improvement in Corn-Harvesters. **1857** *Ill. Agric. Soc. Trans.* III. 62, I lay off my ground with a corn-marker . . . into checks of three feet three inches square. **1836** *Knickerb.* VII. 387 You say you have given us a hoe and a corn-pounder, and told us to plant and pound for you.

(*c*) **1851** CIST *Cincinnati* 278 Cincinnati, being the business centre of an immense corn-growing and hog-raising region, is, in fact, the principal pork market in the United States. **1898** CUSHMAN *Hist. Indians* 282 By the time the corn-hoeing moon came the forlorn wanderer entered once more his native village. **1854** THOREAU *Walden* 283 Might not the basket, stable-broom, mat-making, corn-parching, linen-spinning, and pottery business have thrived here? **1867** *Iowa Agric. Soc. Rep.* 92 Southern Iowa is distinctly a grazing if not a corn-raising state. **1631** in Hutchinson *Coll. Orig. P.* (1769) 52 Mens labour are precious heere in corne setting tyme.

b. In the names of various foods and drinks made from maize.

1839 *Jeffersonian* 26 Jan. 399 (Th.), Fellows whose richest loaf is corn ash-cake. **1884** OWENS *Cook-Book* 163 [Recipe for] Corn Batter Cakes. **1891** *Century Mag.* March 706, [I] carried with me some of the corn beer brewed in the camp. **1839** KEMBLE *Journal* 18 Immediately opposite to this building is a small shed, which they call the cook's shop, and where the daily allowance of rice and corn grits of the people is boiled. **1811–4** BRACKENRIDGE *Journal* 202 Their food consists of lied corn homony for breakfast. **1855** SIMMS *Forayers* 330 There were some fragments of chicken; a plate of corn johnny-cake. **1829** T. FLINT *George Mason* 11 The repast of smoking corn loaf, sweet potatoes, and fried bacon were arranged on it. **1920** R. L. ALSAKER *Eating for Health* 131 Corn mush: Cook corn meal in plain water until it is done, using moderate amount of salt. **1843** 'CARLTON' *New Purchase* II. 58 That emboldened us to trot on very fast, in the comfortable assurance of rapidly approaching a snug breakfast of chicken fixins, eggs, ham-doins, and corn slap-jacks. **1891** *Wide Awake* Xmas no., All the guests were invited to partake of the old-time national dish,—the corn soup, and its accompanying relish, the delicious hulled-corn boiled bread. **1764** J. INGERSOLL *Lett. relating to Stamp-Act* (1766) 7 They . . . have erected Works for the Distilling of Corn Spirits.

* **Corn,** *v.*

***1.** *tr.* To cure, season, or preserve with salt.

1794 M'DONALD & M'LEOD *Acc. Captivity* 6 We corned our meat. **1839** *S. Lit. Messenger* V. 377/1, Polly and me will have a plenty to do to-morrow to corn them [=mullet] down. **1850** S. F. COOPER *Rural Hours* 430 Some pork is to be corned; hams, and jowls, and bacon are to be looked after. **1871** STOWE *Sam Lawson* 188 We ken corn the meat.

+**2.** To make drunk. *colloq.*

*a***1848** in Northall *Yankee Hill* 118 Jedide said it wasn't eating the cherries, but swallowing the stones, that corned the hogs. **1864** WEBSTER 294/3 Ale strong enough to corn one.

+**3.** To plant or crop with Indian corn.

1886 *Consular Rep.* No. lx, 40 Those hundreds of thousands of acres of once valuable Southern lands, corned to death, and now lying to waste in worthless sage grass.

+**Corn ball.** **a.** A corn pone or corndodger. **b.** (See quot. 1889.) — (**a**) **1843** 'CARLTON' *New Purchase* I. 64 Nanny remained near the dutch oven to keep us supplied with red-hot pones, or corn-balls. (**b**) **1873** E. S. PHELPS *Trotty's Wedding* i, They were eating a corn-ball at recess. **1889** FARMER 170/1 *Corn-balls,* a sweetmeat made of pop-corn . . . and molasses, very similar to English hard bake and almond rock.

* **Corn barn.** +A barn in which Indian corn is stored.

1852 *Harper's Mag.* April 590/2 A corn-barn is a small square building standing upon high posts at the four corners. **1864** NICHOLS *Amer. Life* I. 22 At a little distance was . . . a corn-barn for storing Indian corn. **1867** 'LACKLAND' *Homespun* I. 75 The harsh clangor of the geese, getting ready to take up their late afternoon march for a night on the bare ground under the corn-barn. **1874** *Vt. Bd. Agric. Rep.* II. 513 In 1865 I built me a corn barn, at an expense of $150. **1877** HALE *G. T. T.* 65 The architecture of every thing, from a corn-barn up to a plantation house. **1888** BILLINGS *Hardtack* 237 [The task of foragers] was to go out with wagons in quest of the contents of smoke-houses or barns or corn-barns.

+**Corn basket.** A basket designed for holding Indian corn.

1648 *Conn. Public Rec.* I. 487 Inventory [includes] . . . 1 spade . . . a corne baskitt . . . a Howse at Hartford, with the homelott. **1792** *N.Y. State Soc. Arts* I. 69 It [clover] is then raked immediately into small heaps or cocks, of the quantity of about the bigness of a large corn basket. **1809** IRVING *Knickerb.* III. iv, The contents filled three corn baskets. **1852** *Knickerb.* XXXIX. 203 There is the big two-bushel corn-basket of chips. **1860** S. WARNER *Say & Seal* 264 In one corner of the hearth sat Mr. Skip, . . . a full corn basket beside him, and empty one in front. **1871** STOWE *Sam Lawson* 66 Hand me that corn-basket; we'll put that over him.

+**Corn bean.** A domesticated variety of edible bean. — **1806** *Lewis & Clark Exped.* (1905) VI. 87 [The wolves] hunt on the rivers Platt & Loup above their Village; they cultivate Corn Beens &c. **1821** FOWLER *Journal* 52 The Indeans ware frendly takeing us to the lodges of their great men and all ways seting some meat for us to eat tho some times boiled corn beens or mush . . . precured from the Spanyards.

+**Corn beef.** = CORNED BEEF.

1802 CUTLER in *Life & Corr.* II. 57 A table was elegantly spread with ham, cold corn-beef, cold fowl, red-herring, and cold mutton. **1853** SIMMS *Sword & Distaff* 353 Roast-beef for dinner;—a round of corn-beef—also! **1879** BURDETTE *Hawkeyes* 112, I'm just certain that cold corn beef will spoil. **1882** GODFREY *Nantucket* 24 Ther'll be a meat ox at half-a-past ten o'clock in front of Burgesses market. Corn beef! mut'n! 'n' lam'! **1884** NYE *Baled Hay* 197 Animals worked into . . . pressed corn beef. **1896** E. HIGGINSON *Tales* 44 Why, we've got corn beef to boil.

attrib. **1862** BROWNE *A. Ward His Book* 46 Just so soon as a man becums a . . . Sperret rapper he . . . is a cuss to society & a pirit on honest peple's corn beef barrils. **1870** 'MARK TWAIN' *Sk., Great Beef Contract*, The Third sent me to the First Comptroller of the Corn-Beef Division.

+**Corn belt.** The region in the central portion of the United States where Indian corn is extensively grown.

1882 *Nation* 13 July 24/3 Crop reports from the West still continue favorable, though there are some discouraging accounts of the prospects in the 'corn belt.' **1891** *Boston Financial Rec.* 7 Nov. 4/2 Sioux City (Iowa) is in the centre of the great corn-belt. **1902** LORIMER *Lett. Merchant* 203 It's from the weather man or some liar in the corn belt. **1922** TITUS *Timber* 12 Didn't Michigan Pine build th' corn belt? An' where'd this country be without its grain lands now?

+**Corn bird.** (See quotation.) — **1857** *Rep. Comm. Patents: Agric.* 140 The blue-jay or 'Corn Bird,' as it is called in some localities.

+**Corn biscuit.** (See quot. 1889.) — **1856** *Spirit of Times* 6 Sept. 2/3 If there be but corn biscuits in the place of white wheaten rolls [etc.]. **1889** *Amer. Notes & Q.* IV. 60 Johnny-cake . . . was a rough, coarse, corn cake. . . . A better quality, and among better people, was dignified by the name of 'corn biscuit.'

+**Corn blade.** *pl.* The blade or leaf of Indian corn, esp. as cured and used as forage. (Cf. BLADE *n.* 1.)

(1) [**1688** CLAYTON *Acc. Va.* in *Phil. Trans.* XVII. 947 Their Indian Corn-blades, which they gather for their Fodder.] **1775** *Essex Inst. Coll.* XIII. 160 [On] the Western shore their feed [*i.e.*, of horses] is Corn-Blades and Oats. **1831** PECK *Guide* 166 In autumn they [=oxen] were . . . fed with . . . corn blades, with water. **1848** *Rep. Comm. Patents 1847* 376 Large crops of clover hay, . . . together with our corn blades and tops, shucks and wheat straw, make ample supply of provender for our stock.

(2) **1775** ADAIR *Indians* 407 The women . . . knead both [chestnuts and corn] together, wrape them up in green corn-blades of various sizes, about an inch-thick, and boil them well. **1820** *Western Rev.* II. 373 He should hear a signal agreed on by a sound made with corn blades. **1829** *Va. Lit. Museum* 16 Dec. 420 Corn blades—the leaves of Indian corn. Southern States. **1865** A. D. WHITNEY *Gayworthys* vi. 59 Say skipped . . . between the whispering corn-blades. **1912** N. M. WOODROW *Sally Salt* 151 The corn blades gleamed a brighter and harder green than ever.

+**Corn boat.** A boat used for transporting corn. — **1872** W. J. FLAGG *Good Investment* 901/1 Bella and Hector . . . took passage in a corn-boat bound for Georgetown. **1874** R. H. COLLINS *Kentucky* I. 228 Many houses, coal and iron boats, corn boats, &c., [were] washed away.

+**Corn bread.** Bread made from the meal of Indian corn.

[**1796** I. WELD *Travels* (1800) I. 183 Indian corn bread . . . is a coarse, strong kind of bread, which has something of the taste of that made from oats.] **1817** E. P. FORDHAM *Narr.* 53 Corn bread, when new, is very palatable, and, I believe, wholesome. **1826** FLINT *Recoll.* 210 Corn bread, made of maize pounded in a mortar, was their whole bread. **1842** *S. Lit. Messenger* VIII. 63/1 The log cabin of a settler, where those great western commodities, corn-bread and corn, could be had for man, and beast. **1863** CUMMING *Hospital Life* (1866) 91/2 The fare is very good, but we had no wheat-bread for breakfast, and I am not southern enough to like corn-bread. **1898** HARRIS *Tales of Home Folks* 17 Miss Molly is eighteen, and if she can bake a pone of corn-bread as it ought to be baked, she's ready to get married. **1913** STRATTON-PORTER *Laddie* xii, There wasn't a crumb there except cornbread, and she didn't want that.

+**Corn broom.** A broom made from the panicles of broom corn.

*a*1817 DWIGHT *Travels* IV. 485 [Manufactures of Mass. include] Straw bonnets, Brushes, Corn Brooms. **1824** *N.H. Hist. Soc. Coll.* I. 239 Garden seeds, wooden ware, corn brooms, leather, &c. of their own manufacture, are some of the articles of their traffick. **1845** *Mass. Acts & Resolves* 499 The number of corn and other brooms manufactured during said year. **1854** *Penna. Agric. Rep.* 128 Corn Broom, to Charles Kitchen, of Solebury, the first premium of two dollars. **1856** GOODRICH *G. Go-Ahead* 10, I made a trip in one of their vessels, called Ben Beecher, having in my especial charge two thousand corn brooms.

‖**b.** = BROOMCORN.

1836 C. GILMAN *Recoll.* (1838) 225 My silk rustled like a patch of cornbroom in a breeze.

+**Corn cake.** Corn bread in the form of a cake; a hoecake or johnnycake.

1791 BARTRAM *Travels* 38 It is . . . an ingredient in most of their cookery, especially homony and corn cakes. **1818** E. P. FORDHAM *Narr.* 204, I like corn or hoe cakes. **1835** HOFFMAN *Winter in West* II. 199 But Venus's cestus itself could not more magically bring smiles and roses into faded cheeks, than did a cold corn-cake and piece of smoked venison. **1852** STOWE *Uncle Tom* iv, Her corn-cake, in all its varieties of hoe-cake, dodgers, muffins, and other species, . . . was a sublime mystery to all less practised compounders. **1863** B. TAYLOR *H. Thurston* 337 The old Melinda alone remained in the kitchen, to prepare her incomparable corn-cake. **1907** ANDREWS *Recoll.* 182 We found the Confederate kitchen fires still burning and their corn-cakes yet warm.

+**Corncob.**

1. The axis on which the grains of Indian corn grow.

1793 J. BARLOW *Hasty Pudding* III, The dry husks rustle, and the corn-cobs crack. **1808** PIKE *Sources Miss.* App. II. 175 [We] ascended the river, both sides of which were covered with old Indian camps, at which we found corn cobs. **1829** B. HALL *Travels in N.A.* III. 294 To the core of the maize, or to what is called in America a corn-cob. **1851** MELVILLE *Moby Dick* iii. 22 Whether that matteress was stuffed with corn-cobs or broken crockery, there is no telling. **1898** CUSHMAN *Hist. Indians* 388 The two boys got into a play in which they soon began to throw corn cobs at one another. **1909** J. BIGELOW *Retrospections* 13 Wood and corn-cobs were the only fuel which I had then ever seen used.

2. An entire ear of boiled or roasted green corn.

[**1813** J. LAMBERT *Travels* I. 132 They [=Canadians] are extravagantly fond of the corn cobs boiled or roasted, and rubbed over with a little butter and salt.] **1885** PHILLIPS-WOLLEY *Trottings of Tenderfoot* 5 (F.), We . . . gazed in terror at the pretty jewelled fingers and white teeth opposite making short work of a very buttery corn-cob.

3. Attrib. and comb. with *bowl*, *crusher*, etc.

1853 *Mich. Agric. Soc. Trans.* IV. 83 Best corn-cob crusher by horse power. **1856** *Yale Lit. Mag.* XXI. 145 (Th.), He was employed in whittling a corn cob bowl into a pipe. **1888** in Farmer 170/1 Soon after that disgrace, a party of the boys prepared a lot of grenades—corn-cob shells they called them—and determined to storm head quarters.

+**Corncob pipe.** A pipe the bowl of which is made of a piece of corncob.

1832 KENNEDY *Swallow Barn* II. 246 He stood in the group, with his corncob pipe, puffing the smoke from his bolster-lips. **1880** *Harper's Mag.* Aug. 363/2 There the men . . . sit smoking corn-cob pipes in dirt, poverty, and good-humored content inconceivable to Northerners. **1884** *Century Mag.* April 814/2 Presidents no longer smoke corn-cob pipes as Andrew Jackson did. **1887** *Outing* X. 119/1 Old John came out of the house smoking a corn-cob pipe. **1898** *Mo. So. Dakotan* I. 133 Charlie stared at the stove and chewed the stem of his corn-cob pipe. **1904** WALLER *Wood-Carver* 129 It came about in the silences of the night, when the smoke from our corn-cob pipes curled about the roof-timbers. **1917** MCCUTCHEON *Green Fancy* 16 He re-inserted the corn-cob pipe and took a couple of pulls at it.

+**Corncob stopper.** A stopper for a bottle, jug, etc., made of a corncob.

[**1801** *Spirit Farmer's Museum* 236 Jotham, get the great case bottle, Your teeth can pull its corn cob stopple.] *c*1866 BAGBY *Old Va. Gentleman* 49 He must now go to old-field school, and carry his snack in a tin bucket, with a little bottle of molasses, stopped with a corn-cob stopper. **1883** ZEIGLER & GROSSCUP *Alleghanies* 93, I felt a small jug placed in my hands, and heard the corn-cob stopper being drawn from it. **1884** *Century Mag.* Nov. 154 An occasional dance-party, where the fiddle and the jug of crooked whisky, with its corn-cob stopper, produce something faintly resembling gayety. **1888** 'CRADDOCK' *Despot* 53 An aroma lingered about its [a jug's] corn-cob stopper. **1898** CANFIELD *Maid of Frontier* 174 A beneficent jug, with a corn cob stopper stood stoutly on the hearth. **1902** HARBEN *Abner Daniel* 227 There were several one-gallon jugs with corn-cob stoppers. **1912** COBB *Back Home* 286 'Business pretty good, ain't it Squire?' 'It's good,' the Squire would say, licking off the corn-cob stopper of a molasses jug.

Corn cockle. A weed (*Agrostemma githago*), found esp. in fields of grain. {1713–}

1843 TORREY *Flora N.Y.* I. 102 *Lychnis Githago*, Lam. Cockle. Corn-cockle. Rose Campion. . . . Common in cultivated fields, particularly among wheat and rye. June. **1850** S. F. COOPER *Rural Hours* 108 Thus the corn-cockle bears a fine flower, not unlike the mullein-pink of the garden. **1872** *Vt. Bd. Agric. Rep.* I. 268 The wild mustard has been known to ripen eight thousand seeds, and the corn cockle twenty five hundred. **1899** M. GOING *Flowers* 225 The red campion or corn-cockle is already resolving itself into a nuisance.

+**Corn coffee.** A drink made of Indian corn parched and used as coffee. — **1844** FEATHERSTONHAUGH *Slave States* 114 The supper consisted of . . . coffee made of burnt acorns and maize. . . . He laughed at our fastidiousness, and advised us to drink some of the corn-coffee. **1894** ROBLEY *Bourbon Co., Kansas* 68 The menu consisted of cornbread, bacon, fried potatoes and corn coffee with 'long sweetnin'.'

***Corn country.** +A region where Indian corn is or may be grown successfully. — **1817** WEEMS *Letters* III. 201 This Department of Rural Economy is not thought of in this Tobacco & Corn Country. **1847** D. COYNER *Lost Trappers* 251 Now it is generally conceded that Oregon is not a corn country. **1882** *Uncle Rufus & Ma* 31 Minnesota is not at all a corn country.

+Corn-cracker.

1. A nickname given to the inhabitants of various southern states, esp. Kentucky. Also attrib.

1835 A. PARKER *Trip to Texas* 87 The inhabitants . . . of Kentucky [are called] *corn-crackers.* **1838** HALIBURTON *Clockmaker* 2 Ser. xix. 289 The corn-crackers of Virginia. **1848** DURIVAGE & BURNHAM *Stray Subjects* 79 There is a swarm of 'suckers,' 'hoosiers,' 'buckeyes,' 'corn-crackers,' and 'wolverines' eternally on the *qui vive* [in Wisconsin]. **1851** J. F. W. JOHNSTON *Notes N. Amer.* II. 326 They come with the peculiar manners and nicknames of their several regions . . . from Kentucky, Corn-crackers; from Tennessee, Red-horses. **1854** SIMMS *Southward Ho* 347 Strickland's quite too big a mouthful for a corn-cracker. **1862** 'E. KIRKE' *Among Pines* 187 He's a North Carolina 'corn-cracker,' one of the ugliest specimens of humanity extant. **1879** *Harper's Mag.* Dec. 42/1 No doubt I'm an utterly useless Corn-cracker—but, Sir, I am a Georgian! **1880** *Scribner's Mo.* Oct. 914/1 A medley of legends and anecdotes was then served up for us in Corn-cracker vernacular. **1887** *Courier-Journal* 25 Jan. 8/1 The title is 'Kentucky Politicians—Sketches of Representative Corn-crackers.'

2. A mill or similar apparatus for grinding or cracking corn.

1844 LEE & FROST *Oregon* 134 At the mission we had a small cast-iron corncracker, in which we ground wheat after a fashion. **1850** *New Eng. Farmer* II. 363 Beal's Patent Corn-Cracker and Cob-Crusher. This machine is used for cracking cobs and corn previous to passing through the millstones. **1873** *Newton Kansan* 16 Jan. 3/4 Besides the work of a few 'corn crackers,' all of our breadstuffs will have to be shipped here. **1883** ZEIGLER & GROSSCUP *Alleghanies* 104 A primitive 'corncracker' at one point is likely to produce a lasting impression. It is a tall, frail structure with gaps a foot wide between every two logs. **1900** SMITHWICK *Evolution of State* 76 There was a saw mill with a corn cracker attached.

3. (See quotation.)

1884 GOODE *Aquatic Animals* 666 Of the Eagle Ray family, *Myliobatidae,* . . . only one [species] seems to be found in Florida and the Gulf; this is the 'Whipparee' or 'Corn-cracker' of the South (*Rhinoptera quadriloba*).

***Corn crake.** The land rail, *Crex crex.* — **1853** 'P. PAXTON' *Yankee in Texas* 265 The monster grass-hopper of the country had ceased his shrill Italian note, the corn-cracke was mute. **1858** BAIRD *Birds Pacific R.R.* 751 The well known corn-crake of Europe has, on several occasions, been found on the eastern coast of the United States. **1877** BARTLETT 780 Corn-Crake. (*Crex pratensis.*) A bird of the rail species, which frequents corn-fields; the Land-rail. **1888** *Harper's Mag.* LXXVI. 202/1 A corn-crake, moving cautiously among the withered water-grasses.

+Corncrib. A crib or barn in which Indian corn is kept.

1687 *Brookhaven Rec.* 51, I, Hannah Huls, Through inadvertance and pasion, defamed Nathanell Norten, of this towne, by saying he had stollen Indian corn out of my fatther Daiton's his corn cribb. **1716** CHURCH *Philip's War* 15 About a dozen of them ran right over the Log into the Fort, and took into a sort of a Hovel that was build with Poles, after the manner of a corn crib. **1756** *Bristol* (Va.) *Vestry Bk.* 164 Ordered . . . a Corn Crib Eight Feet by Fourteen and the Church Wardens to agree with Workmen to perform the same. **1787** TYLER *Contrast* (1790) III. i, I saw a power of topping folks, all sitting around in little cabbins, 'just like father's corn-cribs.' **1809** *Mass. Spy* 6 Sept. (Th.), If they will establish a non-intercourse with my corn-crib, they will find their account in it. **1824** DODDRIDGE *Notes* 61, I well remember the labour of opening roads through those deep snows, which often fell in a single night, to the barn, spring, smoke house, and corn crib. **1862** in F. Moore *Rebellion Rec.* V. II. 22, I was amused to see the Count de Paris struggling through the mud to the corn-crib, bag in hand, to procure feed for his horse. **1888** STOCKTON *Dusantes* 142 Smoke-houses, corn-cribs, chicken-houses, and so on, down to pumps and hitching-posts, were painted. **1896** *Boston Globe* 18 July 3/1 A corncrib, I may tell the eastern reader, is a roughly constructed 'shack' of boards, in which the buyers of corn store it until such time as there is a demand for its use. **1904** T. WATSON *Bethany* 8 It did not, in the least, resemble a Grecian Temple which had been sent into exile, and which was striving . . . to look at ease among corn-cribs, cow-pens, [etc.]. **1908** *Dialect Notes* III. 301 The regular bulged corn-crib, common in the north and west, is rarely seen in the south.

Corn crop. {1834-} +The produce or yield of Indian corn in a season.

1856 *Rep. Comm. Patents: Agric.* p. xii, Estimating the present annual corn-crop of New England, New York, [etc.]. **1873** *Newton Kansan* 9 Jan. 2 The corn crop of Kansas for the year 1872 is estimated . . . at 30,000,000 bushels. **1883** WILDER *Sister Ridnour* 261 The fall in stocks—bad debts, limited salary, the failure of the corn crop, prospect of grasshoppers. **1894** *Vt. Agric. Rep.* XIV. 41 The corn crop as a whole is . . . more digestible than clover.

Corn crusher. {1865-} +A mill or machine for crushing or grinding Indian corn. — **1852** *Mich. Agric. Soc. Trans.* III. 29 Best corn and cob crusher, by horse power. **1857-8** *Ill. Agric. Soc. Trans.* III. 524 The coal [is] broken or ground coarsely in a corn crusher or other mill of some sort. **1862** *Rep. Comm. Patents: Agric.* 308 The granulating mill is simple, like a bark-mill or corn-crusher.

Corn cultivator. +A tool or implement for use in cultivating Indian corn. — **1840** *26 Congress 1 Sess.* Sen. Doc. No. 111, 3 Cultivator, corn. [Patented by] John B. Smith . . . [on] April 15 [1839]. **1852** *Mich. Agric. Soc. Trans.* III. 101 Best corn cultivator.

Corn-cutter. +A machine for cutting up the stalks of Indian corn; a knife or sickle for cutting down Indian corn. — **1877** BARTLETT 780 *Corn-Cutter,* a machine for cutting up the stalks of Indian corn for the food of cattle. **1897** ROBINSON *Uncle Lisha* 170 A work-bench stood at the other end, . . . and a corn-cutter made from a broken scythe.

+Corn dance. A ceremonial or religious dance or festival held by American Indians in connection with the planting or harvesting of maize.

1725 CHICKEN in *Travels Amer. Col.* 155 At Little Terriquo where was mett together at the Corn dance Several of the head men. **1837** *S. Lit. Messenger* III. 391 The celebrated corn dance of the Seminoles is said to be connected with their religion. **1878** *Rep. Indian Affairs* 8 Witnessed, by invitation, two of their important dances, the bean and the corn. **1887** *Century Mag.* XXXIV. 51/2 The 'corn-dance,' to make that plant productive, is also a monopoly of the medicine-men. **1903** WHITE *Forest* 128 Belts of beadwork, yellow and green, for the Corn Dance.

b. A dance indulged in by Negroes at the time of planting Indian corn.

1840 HOFFMAN *Greyslaer* III. 185 De boys . . . has gone to de village to hold corn-dance for seedtime.

Corn doctor. *colloq.* and often depreciative. A chiropodist. {1767-}

1839 'M. PENCIL' *White Sulphur P.* 40 There are several resident physicians here; . . . and a corn-doctor's card has been posted up for several days. **1886** *Harper's Mag.* Sept. 648/2 A tall seedy-looking individual came in, whom the doctor recognized as a 'corn-doctor,' a genuine quack. **1902** LORIMER *Lett. Merchant* 95 If a fellow needs a six or seven-syllable word to describe his profession, he's a corn doctor. **1923** WATTS *L. Nichols* 69 Mrs. Siefert's establishment . . . with the corn-doctor in the basement, and the I.W.W. agitator in the garret.

+Corndodger. Bread made of Indian corn meal baked hard in small cakes or pones; also, one of these pones. (Cf. DODGER.)

1834 in *Prophet* 15 March 1845 (Th.), We sometimes had to live mostly on johnny-cake and corn-dodgers. **1851** *Polly Peablossom* 183 Corn dodgers and milk were the best fixings the house afforded. **1863** *Ladies' Repository* XXIII. 479/1 They were grinding corn to make 'corn-dodger' for breakfast. **1872** *Newton Kansan* 19 Sept. 2/2 It may sound valiant to talk of living on 'corn-dodgers and hoe-cake.' **1881** H. W. PIERSON *In the Brush* 49 Followed to the door by their sable mother, with arms a-kimbo and hands fresh from mixing the pone or corn-dodger for the family supper. **1889** *Amer. Notes & Q.* IV. 60 Johnny-cake . . . was a rough, coarse, corn cake, popularly called corn dodger in the Western States, and perhaps equivalent to the 'Virginia hoe cake.' **1895** CHAMBLISS *Diary* 324 The menu at the meal stations along through Texas and Arizona consists of . . . overdue eggs, bad-smelling butter, corn dodgers, and 'boot-leg' coffee. **1903** *Dialect Notes* II. 310 *Corndodger,* a kind of cornbread baked in a skillet. It is not sweetened or shortened and is very hard, but quite palatable. **1909** A. C. RICE *Mr. Opp* 41 Aunt Tish had . . . set forth some cold corn dodger, a pitcher of foaming buttermilk, and a plate of cold corned beef.

+Corn drill. An implement used in planting Indian corn. — **1853** *Mich. Agric. Soc. Trans.* IV. 84 Corn drill, an excellent article. **1856** *Rep. Comm. Patents: Agric.* 172. **1874** KNIGHT 624/2.

+Corn dumpling. A dumpling made of Indian corn meal boiled with vegetables or soup. — **1880** *Harper's Mag.* Feb. 330/1 Here were they 'lustily entertained' . . . feasting on 'corn dumplings,' venison, and hominy.

+Corn-ear worm. A larva that feeds on Indian corn, cotton, etc. — **1889** *Secy. of Agric. Rep.* 360 The Corn Ear-worm (*Heliothis armigera*) has done considerable damage to the ears of field corn.

+Corn-eater. A corn weevil. — **1854** EMMONS *Agric. N.Y.* V. 265 Index, *Calandra,* or Corneater: . . . *Calandra granaria.*

Corned, *ppl. a.*

1. Of meat or fish: Salted or cured by salting. {1621-} Cf. CORNED BEEF.

1775 *Essex Inst. Coll.* LIII. 84 Went to Notomi to see John Farrington, and carried corned victuals to those who were taking care of him. **1828** SHERBURNE *Memoirs* 52 They procured a plenty of corned codfish, and boiled it. **1850** S. F. COOPER *Rural Hours* 162 The common piece of meat, day after day, was corned pork from their pork-barrel. **1891** CHASE & CLOW *Industry* II. 109 Salt is applied either dry or as a brine, when the meat is said to be 'cured' or 'corned.'

2. Drunk; intoxicated. *slang.* {1785-, *slang*}

1823 *Mass. Spy* 22 Dec. (Th.), 'Pretty well corned' and 'up to everything,' Drunk as a lord and happy as a king. **1834** CARRUTHERS *Kentuckian* II. 206 It's twisted strange, ain't it, when a feller gets half corned, everybody reels around. **1851** *Alta Californian* 8 Dec., A large party got corned while discussing the dainty morsels and cracking jokes over the principal adventure. **1880** *Harper's Mag.* March 636/2 Living near him were two farmers named Jervis and Dixon, who commonly got well 'corned' when they came to town. **1901** ADE 40 *Modern Fables* 65 By the time that he lands into his Happy Clothes of an Evening he is fairly well Corned.

Corned beef. Beef cured with salt or brine to which a small amount of saltpeter is often added to preserve the natural color of the meat; = CORN BEEF. {beef . . . corned 1621–}

1794 E. DRINKER *Journal* (1889) 232 A piece of nice corned beef which we intended for part of our dinner stolen out of the spring-house. **1813** J. LAMBERT *Travels* (1813) II. 142 Large supplies of corned beef and pork are brought from the northern states. **1845** KIRKLAND *Western Clearings* 184 She did not despair of the highest step—to induce Mrs. Larkins to boil corned beef instead of frying it. **1868** BEECHER *Norwood* 453 To dried beef was added cold chicken—small, but young and tender; and to this, cold corned-beef. **1902** LORIMER *Lett. Merchant* 94 We were piling up canned corned beef in stock faster than people would eat it.

+**b.** *Corned-beef hash*, a hash the principal ingredient of which is corned beef.

1902 LORIMER *Lett. Merchant* 94 After he had schemed out ten different combinations, the other ninety turned out to be corned-beef hash. **1905** PHILLIPS *Social Secretary* 68 It's pretty hard for any man to get indigestion, even from corned beef hash and hot cornbread and buckwheat cakes with maple syrup, if it's perfectly cooked. **1906** 'O. HENRY' *Four Million* 101 His theory was fixed around corned-beef hash with poached egg. **1917** C. MATHEWSON *Sec. Base Sloan* 61 That corned beef hash is pretty good tonight.

* **Cornel.** Any one of various trees or shrubs of the genus *Cornus.*

1784 CUTLER in *Mem. Academy* I. 411 *Cornus.* . . . Cornel. Dogberry. The stem is quadrangular . . . Blossoms white. In woodland. May–June. **1832** WILLIAMSON *Maine* I. 115 Dogwood, or Cornel. . . . Its wood is hard, bark rough, and has upon some people an effect like the Peruvian bark; to others it is deleterious. **1858** THOREAU *Maine Woods* 100 The bright red berries of the tree-cranberry, . . . mingled with the alders and cornel along the shore. **1901** MOHR *Plant Life Ala.* 650.

+**b.** *Dwarf cornel*, the bunchberry.

1821 *Jrnl. Science* III. 276 Floral . . . Calendar for Plainfield, Mass. . . . May 27. Dwarf cornel and hispid gaultheria in flower. **1882** *Century Mag.* May 153/2 Birthwort, Virginia creeper, dwarf cornel.

||**Cornellian.** A student at Cornell University. — **1897** *Outing* XXX. 475/1 It certainly is not going beyond the limits of veracity to say that most rowing men, except Cornellians, desired the success of Harvard.

+**Corn emperor moth.** (See quotation.) — **1854** EMMONS *Agric. N.Y.* V. 231 *Saturnia maia.* Corn Emperor moth. *Ib.* 232 *Saturnia io.* Corn Emperor Moth. . . . These caterpillars feed upon the leaves of the elm, poplar, dogwood and sassafras, and also upon clover and indian corn.

* **Corner,** *n.*

***1.** The point of junction of two boundary lines of land owned by an individual, or marked out by a survey.

1640 *New Haven Col. Rec.* I. 27 The way to them both to begin att Mr. Tenches corner. **1693** SEWALL *Diary* I. 377 The first stone is laid in the new building, being the great Stone that lay at Capt. Wyllys's Corner. **1738** W. STEPHENS *Proc. Georgia* 71 He had only marked out the two extream Corners of the Land which lay next the Road. **1743** *N.J. Archives* 1 Ser. VI. 158 [If] any person be with you who knows the corners of any patent or survey thro which your line runs especially those of West Jersey beg him to show you that corner thereof which will come nearest to your line. **1816** U. BROWN *Journal* I. 363 In Cases where the Corners Cannot be found the Land is lost to the Owner. **1898** C. C. POST *10 Yrs. Cowboy* 167 Phil and two others . . . started out . . . to find a corner post or mark of some kind which would locate a corner and give them a start [in homesteading].

+**2.** A small piece or parcel *of* land.

1650 *Warwick* (R.I.) *Rec.* 86 Henry Townsend shall have a corner of land in the front. **1682** *Providence Rec.* VIII. 122 That Corner of land being next the streete. **1685** *Charlestown Land Rec.* 204, I david ffisk then Layd out those Severall nookes & Corners of Land found within the former divident.

+**3.** A tree that designates the junction of two boundaries of a surveyed tract; a stake or marker set up at such a point or contemplated junction.

1699 *Derby* (Conn.) *Rec.* 202 The southered corner is an ash tree. **1721** *Mass. Ho. Repr. Jrnls.* III. 24 A Tree marked by the Indians for a corner of said Land. **1746** *N.H. Probate Rec.* III. 453 A tree spotted on four sides . . . is the North East Corner of the Lot. **1765** HABERSHAM *Letters* 29 Many of the Surveyors employed therein carried with them Stakes notched and crossed, and upon their coming to any piece of land on the River they liked, they put down one of them for a Corner. **1785** V. B. HOWARD *Heroes* (1932) 143 Begining at a poplar and a small ash corner to Bledsow land. **1816** U. BROWN *Journal* II. 221 If the old original white oak Corner Cannot be found Establish a Corner there in Lieu & in place of said White Oak. **1871** DE VERE 173 We have frequently heard the old surveyors along the Ohio say that they often met with his [Col. Crawford's] corners.

+**4. a.** *To turn the double corner,* (see quot. 1821). *Obs. slang.* **b.** *fig. To trim one's corners,* to take a chance or risk.

(a) 1821 in Kittredge *Old Farmer* (1904) 275 Bob Raikins and Jo Jakins, with 6 or 8 more, turning the double corner, as they call it; or, to use a military term, firing off sling and punch from right to left. **(b) 1904** STRATTON-PORTER *Freckles* 157 Freckles was trimming his corners as closely as he dared.

+**5.** A locality of limited extent: (see quotations).

1825 J. NEAL *Bro. Jonathan* II. 10 They continued watching him until he came to the 'corner,' the west end of every Yankee village, or settlement. **1841** *Knickerb.* XVII. 365 A stranger might notice a habit which has obtained here, as in most of the northern towns of the State [New-Hampshire], of designating every small cluster of buildings as a Corner. **1892** *Vt. Agric. Rep.* XII. 130 Each town has a small village or 'Corners,' where the Churches, post-office, store, and various shops are located.

+**6.** *Stock exchange.* A condition produced by operators who secure all or practically all of a stock or commodity.

1846 *Knickerb.* XXVIII. 119 Our conversation I found took a uniform turn to stocks . . . with some peculiarity of terms as to making a good 'corner' on this stock, [etc.]. **1870** MEDBERY *Men Wall St.* 13 In January the famous Morris Canal and Banking Company 'corner' culminated. **1883** *N.Y. Tribune* 9 Jan. 1 A 'corner' in corn is said to be developing. **1901** MERWIN & WEBSTER *Calumet 'K'* 125 They are fighting to break the corner in December wheat. **1902** NORRIS *Pit* i, Never should have tried to swing a corner. The short interest was too small and the visible supply was too great.

+**7.** In poker, the position of a player or the player himself.

1873 MILLER *Amongst Modocs* 155 They fell into an exciting game of poker, at ten dollars a corner. **1903** A. ADAMS *Log Cowboy* xvi. 102 We found Stallings and Honeyman entertaining our visitor in a little game of freeze out for a dollar a corner.

8. Attrib. (in sense 1) with *boundary, bounder, end,* etc.

1705 *Derby* (Conn.) *Rec.* 371 The butments or corner bounderyes at the east end are at each corner a white oake tree. **1668** *Warwick* (R.I.) *Rec.* 421 A great walnut Tree being ye Corner bounder. **1702** *Derby* (Conn.) *Rec.* 333 The land . . . on ye corner ende off Centinel Hill. **1786** *Baltimore Town Rec.* 59 Beginning at the Corner of Market Square at a Corner Stone known by the Name of Enloe's Corner. **1816** U. BROWN *Journal* II. 221 We Could not find the Corner White oak as represented by Jacob Beesons survey.

* **Corner,** *v.*

+**1.** *intr.* To meet or converge at a corner or angle.

1821 *Boston Selectmen* 189 A point where said fence and his other fence join cornering on said streets. **1858** D. K. BENNETT *Chronology N.C.* 94 On the Potato Top, one may stand in a moment in the counties of Burke, McDowell, Buncombe and Yancy, all of which corner there. **1891** F. CHASE *Hist. Dartmouth Coll.* I. 600 Landaff was bounded on the north by Gunthwaite (now Lisbon), on the west by Bath, and on the south by Coventry (now Benton), and cornered upon Haverhill. **1913** STRATTON-PORTER *Laddie* i, The Big Elm . . . stood where four fields cornered. *Ib.*, She was . . . one of those new English people who had moved on the land that cornered with ours on the north-west.

+**2.** *tr.* To force into a corner. {1866–} Also with *up.*

*c***1835** CATLIN *Indians* II. 67 Their enemy, who had cornered them up in such a way that there was no other possible mode for their escape. **1849** LANMAN *Alleghany Mts.* 77 When we came near the falls, one of the Hyatts and myself stopped fishing, and went to work to corner the buck. **1870** EMERSON *Soc. & Solitude*, etc. 229 Animal resistance, the instinct of the male animal when cornered, is no doubt common. **1888** *Amer. Humorist* 2 June 2/3 'He [the grizzly bear] attacks on sight,' hunters say, while the other species do not attack a man unless cornered.

fig. **1834** CROCKETT *Narr. Life* 28, I commenced a close courtship, having cornered her from her old beau.

+**3.** To get or place in an embarrassing or difficult position. Also with *up. colloq.*

1824 *Mass. Spy* 21 April (Th.), Cornered up so unexpectedly, she candidly confessed. **1871** *Scribner's Mo.* I. 381 The old doctor and the young parson were soon hurling at one another . . . arguments about woman's fitness and woman's unfitness for many things. At last, perhaps because he was a little cornered, Hubert said [etc.]. **1873** MILLER *Amongst Modocs* 87 When a man of that nature gets cornered, he is going to endure a great deal before he makes any sign. **1884** 'MARK TWAIN' *H. Finn* xi. 91, I felt sort of cornered, and was afeard I was looking it, too. **1894** — *P. Wilson* xv, Wilson detected it in his hand, by palmistry, and charged him with it, and cornered him up so close that he had to confess.

+**4.** *Stock exchange.* **a.** To subject (a person) to financial difficulties by manipulating the market. **b.** To secure control over (stocks or commodities); to form a corner in.

1836 *Knickerb.* VII. 42 He has been cornered by the brokers on the — stock, and has lost all his fortune. **1848** *Ib.* XXXII. 273 Something had gone wrong in Wall-street. Suspect he'd been 'cornered.' **1869** BRACE *New West* 248 To corral a stock is to get the stock into your hands—to 'corner' it, as we would say. **1887** *Courier-Journal* 21 June 4/4 The great American pork cornerer was asked the other day whether he had really cornered pork. **1902** NORRIS *Pit* viii, Somebody has got all the wheat there is. . . . I guess the visible supply of May wheat in the Chicago market is cornered. *Ib.* ix, Corner wheat! It's the wheat that has cornered me. It's like holding a wolf by the ears, bad to hold on, but worse to let go. **1910** 'O. HENRY' *Strictly Business* 95 Perceiving that the flour crop was short, and that the Stock Exchange was having no perceptible effect on the growing wheat, Mr. Kinsolving cornered the flour market.

1925 BOWER *Parowan Bonanza* 275, 'I suppose,' said Doris, 'you consider it a great achievement, buying up Parowan. Cornering a worn-out mine!'

+**Corner ball.** A ball game similar to cat. — **1848** in Drake *Pioneer Life Ky.* 149 This was the case with that admirable game, a favorite at all country schools, corner ball.

+**Corner board.** In a frame building, a board used in finishing off a corner. — **1845** KIRKLAND *Western Clearings* 40 The siding is plain white to be sure; but the frames of doors and windows, the cornices, the 'corner-boards' and the piazza railing are all bright green. **1857** C. VAUX *Villas* 60 One main thing that has to be attended to in wooden buildings is to make the corner-boards, the facias, the architraves, and base-boards broad and heavy.

+**Corner bound.** *Obs.* A tree or a marker standing or set up at the corner or angle of a tract or surveyed area.

1669 *Essex Inst. Coll.* VI. 175/2 The corner bound between Mr. Endecots & Mr. Reads land. **1675** *Providence Rec.* XIV. 25 Bounded at ye South East Corner with a walnutt tree, . . . & marked for ye sayd corner boundes thereof. **1695** *Conn. Hist. Soc. Coll.* VI. 241 Prouided they keep the east & west corner Bownds as it hath been stated for this many years. **1703** *Providence Rec.* V. 53 A chesnut Tree Marked, the which is a southerne Corner bound of said percell of land. **1723** *Ib.* XVI. 223 A heape of stones which is a Corner bound of a Lott of Land.

Corner cupboard. A cupboard designed for use in the corner of a room. {1851–}

1813 in O. A. Rothert *Muhlenberg Co.* 32, I give and bequeath . . . the corner cupboard and chest and my large Bible. **1848** IRVING *Knickerb.* (rev. ed.) II. vii, A fleet of boats . . . were piled up with all kinds of household articles: . . . quaint corner-cupboards; beds and bedsteads; [etc.]. **1880** *Harper's Mag.* Dec. 87 The corner cupboards were set open to display the old china and glass that filled them. **1889** R. T. COOKE *Steadfast* 13 A corner cupboard, with a smaller one in the wall above the shelf, completed the belonging of the dingy little room.

+**Cornerer.** [f. CORNER *v.* 4.] *Comm.* One who secures a corner on a particular stock or commodity.

1865 *Nation* I. 222 The supply in the open market could be fairly 'cornered' upon the importing merchants, and controlled by the 'cornerers.' **1887** [see CORNER *v.* 4]. **1902** *N.Y. Herald* 10 Oct. 8/3 Interest in such a great gamble in one of the standard products of the country is not confined to the cornerers and the cornered. **1904** 'O. HENRY' *Cabbages & Kings* (1916) 192 'My name is Pinkney Dawson,' said the cornerer of the cockleburr market.

+**Corner grocery. a.** A grocer's shop situated at a street corner. **b.** A saloon or barroom similarly located. Now rare.

1852 *Knickerb.* XXXIX. 106 What's the use-t of Sabbath, if our young men must frequent corner groceries and a bowling saloon? **1859** BARTLETT 101 *Corner-grocery*, a grocer's shop on the corner of two streets, a favorite location for such establishments in American towns. **1872** HOLMES *Poet* iv. 120 Nowadays the precious juice of a long-dead vintage is transferred carefully into a cut-glass decanter, and stands side by side with the sherry from a corner grocery. **1877** *Harper's Mag.* Jan. 292/2 His dad kep' a corner grocery. **1883** *Congress. Rec.* 5 Dec. 42/1 Paying a reckoning at a corner grocery. **1890** *Picayune* 13 Jan., The circulation of silver dollars in New Orleans has grown to serious proportions, and the back sections of the drawers of corner groceries and saloons are filled with spurious money.

attrib. **1862** *Congress. Globe* 7 July 3159/1 Men may well differ, without subjecting themselves to the charge of disloyalty by every corner-grocery politician in the land. **1869** 'MARK TWAIN' *Innocents* xxvi. 278 When the clothing-store merchant wished to consume the corner-grocery man with envy, he bought reserved seats in the front row and let the thing be known. **1870** 'F. FERN' *Ginger-Snaps* 106 Tea to the working-girl, taken in this way, is like the 'corner-grocery-drink' to the working-man.

Cornering. {1802–}

+**1.** The action of embarrassing or confronting with difficulties.

*a***1836** CROCKETT in Watterson *Oddities* (1883) 247 Pay to-day and trust to-morrow. Now, that idea . . . was a sort of cornering in which there was no back out, for ready money in the west, in those times, was the shyest thing in all natur.

+**2.** Making or securing a commercial corner on stocks, etc.

1841 *Week in Wall St.* 27 No cornering, I hope. **1845** *Cincinnati Misc.* 135 Had the lot of the individuals of whom I speak been cast in Wall street N. York, they would no doubt have reached a high standing in the practice of what is called cornering. **1870** MEDBERY *Men Wall St.* 82 When there are high stakes, it is 'cornering.' **1872** TALMADGE *Abominations Modern Soc.* 116 The broker guilty of 'cornering' as well knows that he is sinning against God and man.

attrib. **1848** W. ARMSTRONG *Stocks* 15 The first and principal move in a cornering operation is to create a demand for particular Stocks, and at the same time cause a scarcity of the articles. **1872** TALMADGE *Abominations Modern Soc.* 133 Satan will play upon him the 'cornering' game.

+**Corner lot.** A lot or division of a block in a city or proposed city having frontage on two streets.

1702 *Penn-Logan Corr.* (1870) I. 129, I have sold the corner lot next the Meeting-House for £115. **1764** J. HABERSHAM *Letters* 27, I have agreed for Bricks to build a range of stores of 60 feet long on my Corner Lott. **1805** *Raleigh* (N.C.) *Register* 28 Jan., The Lot marked No. 44, . . . being a corner lot situate on Bloodworth and Cabarras streets. **1837** A. WETMORE *Gaz. Missouri* 63 The best 'corner lots' are still encumbered with the native crab-tree. **1862** BROWNE *A. Ward His Book* 230 The advisin him to keep away from . . . proprietors of corner-lots of the West. **1871** W. M. GROSVENOR *Protection* 37 Much the greater part had no better security than government lands, paper cities projected thereon, and corner lots.

attrib. **1868** *Putnam's Mag.* I. 24 No corner-lot banditti, Or brokers from the city.

+**Corner mark.** A stake, post, or similar marker set up at the corner of a tract of land. — **1690** *Duxbury Rec.* 71 A stake & a heap of stones for the north east corner, where was the former corner mark of said land. **1710** *Ib.* 84 A stone set in the ground, which is his North West corner mark. **1868** *Comm. Agric. Rep.* 343 These fragile corner-marks are strictly respected by the neighbors, and a case of trespass rarely occurs. **1898** [see CORNER POST].

+**Corner-marked,** *a.* Of trees: Marked in such a way as to designate the corner of a surveyed tract of land. — **1676** *N.Y. State Col. Hist.* XII. 547 From the head of the branch to a corner mark't Spanish Oake. **1681** *New Castle Court Rec.* 503, 40 perches to a corner marked swamp oake.

Corner post. a. A post forming the corner of a house or fence. {1601–} +**b.** A post that designates the corner of a piece of land.

1649 *Charlestown Land Rec.* 110, I have sould . . . a parcell of land lying within and between the upper corner post of the house, and runing with a straight line to the Garden of . . . Abraham Jaquith. **1650** *Rowley Rec.* 67 [The fence belonging to] Thomas Dickinson begines at Cornerpost Twelue Lengths ends at XVI. **1657** *Suffolk Deeds* III. 388 All yt part of a Garden plott w[hi]ch runnes one a line from ye Corner post of Walter Merrys Garden west Southerly to a plumb tree [etc.]. **1678** *Boston Rec.* 119 The Highway . . . was layd out . . . in breadth from Mr John Pooles gate post to the cornr post of Mr. Theodore Atkisons fence. **1716** SEWALL *Diary* III. 87, I sat in the nearest Shop, and saw them raise the 3d post towards the Ferry from the Çorner-post. **1785** A. ELLICOTT in *Life & Lett.* 41 Joseph went with some Hands to enlarge the Pile of Stones about the Corner Post. **1881** *Mich. Gen. Statutes* (1882–3) I. 390 The distance from the point of intersection to the nearest section corner post. **1898** C. C. POST *10 Yrs. Cowboy* 167 Phil and two others shouldered their guns and started out with them to find a corner post or mark of some kind.

+**Corner stake.** A stake that marks the corner of a piece of land.

1678 *Oyster Bay Rec.* I. 114 A lott of Land, . . . rainging from ye corner stake [etc.]. **1739** *Southampton Rec.* III. 16 They both of them accepted of ye division where they set ye corner stakes. **1873** EGGLESTON *Myst. Metrop.* 97 They sought first to guess out the line of a railroad; they examined corner-stakes. **1891** *Scribner's Mag.* X. 471 At each corner of his ground, ranging in extent from twenty to twenty-five acres, every individual captain directed these stakes to be forced down as far as possible. Such were called 'corner-stakes.'

+**Corner store.** A store located at a corner. — **1817** *Cape-Fear Recorder* 5 April, Having removed from the red corner store at Mud Market. **1842** *Knickerb.* XX. 467 Corner-stores tear one flag into two pieces. **1876** *Wide Awake* 314/2 A certain subject was talked over at the hotel, the corner-store, the post-office, and in every private house.

+**Corner tree.** A tree that marks the corner of a surveyed tract of land.

1661 *Portsmouth Rec.* 108 That ye lotters are to run the line . . . from Corner tree to Corner tree. **1686** *Conn. Public Rec.* III. 220 This Court grants and orders Norwich Patent to joyne New London line from Mohegan river two miles to the corner tree at Robert Allyn's. **1786** WASHINGTON *Diaries* III. 55 Not having Hough's field Notes, and no Corner trees being noted in His Plat, I did not attempt to look for lines. **1818** E. P. FORDHAM *Narr.* 234 Not being able to make out the corner trees, and being besides too busy to leave home two days in succession. **1843** 'CARLTON' *New Purchase* I. 87 We began to look through the legal blazes to espy a corner tree cut and notched in a peculiar way. **1880** LAMPHERE *U.S. Govt.* 196/1 The Deputy Surveyors must . . . note carefully in their field-books the names of the corner-trees marked and the numbers so made.

‖**Cornerways,** *adv.* [Variant of **cornerwise.*] Diagonally. — **1851** *Polly Peablossom* 83, I'll tear you into doll-rags cornerways.

***Cornet.** *Mil.* An officer who carried the colors in a cavalry unit. *Obs.*

1672 *Plymouth Laws* 166 It is ordered . . . To the Captaine Leiftenant and Cornett to exercise each Squadron twise in the yeare. **1675** *Conn. Public Rec.* II. 258 Put the company upon a new choyse of a Cornett in whome they may better accord. **1707** *Braintree Rec.* 64 The same day Cornet Jos Allin was chosen Town Treasurer. **1792** *Ann. 2nd Congress* 81 Each troop shall [include] . . . one cornet.

+**Cornetist.** One who plays a cornet. — **1881** *Musical Standard* 29 Jan. 72/1 In the *Musical Record* (Boston, U.S.) mention is made of a young lady cornetist. **1890** *Lippincott's Mag.* June App. viii, What do you think of that young cornetist? **1916** WILSON *Red Gap* 233 Ed was known far and wide as the world's challenge cornetist.

* **Corn-fed,** *a.*

+**1.** Fed on Indian corn.

1793 BARLOW *Hasty Pudding* III, Brown, corn-fed nymphs and strong, hard-handed beaux, Alternate ranged, extend in circling rows. **1835** BIRD *Hawks of Hawk-H.* II. 223 While you was lying snorting here like a corn-fed pig, we was knocking the tories on the head at the yardgate. **1845** *Knickerb.* XXVI. 511 A pair of spring chickens, ... [which had] been corn-fed for some time. **1855** *Amer. Inst. N.Y. Trans.* 409 Beach nut fed pork differs from potato fed, or milk fed, or corn fed pork. **1865** *Atlantic Mo.* XV. 450 Mine, bein' corn-fed, ought to bring half a cent more.

+**2.** *colloq.* (See quot. 1877.)

1809 IRVING *Knickerb.* III. vi, They grew up a ... hardy race of ... strapping corn-fed wenches. **1862** BROWNE *A. Ward His Book* (1865) 154 The corn fed gals of Ohio and Injianny. **1877** BARTLETT 148 *Corn-fed*, stout, plump, spoken of a woman. **1902** WISTER *Virginian* 5 That corn-fed biscuit-shooter at Rawlins yu' gave the canary. **1916** WILSON *Red Gap* III There was a corn-fed hussy in a plush bonnet with forget-me-nots, two hundred and thirty or forty on the hoof.

* **Cornfield.**

+**1.** A field in which Indian corn is grown.

The earliest example may not refer to a maize field.

1608 SMITH *Newes from Va.* Wks. 1884 I. 32 His next course South, where within a quarter of a mile, the riuer diuideth in two, the neck a plaine high Corne field. **1634** *Md. Plantation Rel.* 13 Yet doe they daily relinquish their houses, lands, and Corne-fields, and leaue them to us. **1751** HEMPSTEAD *Diary* 569, I was out to the Cornfield dropping Corn &c. **1775** ADAIR *Indians* 140 The Muskohge men, if newly married, are obliged by ancient custom, to get their own relations to hoe out the corn-fields of each of their wives, that their marriages may be confirmed. **1788** J. MAY *Jrnl. & Lett.* 75, I put ... a gun in his hand, with a bottle of grog by his side, and told him to live in my corn-field, and keep off squirrels and crows. **1823** in *So. Dak. Hist. Coll.* I. 220 We were about to withdraw our troops from the upper village, that they might leave the Aricara corn fields in sufficient season, to save their struggles from the tomahawks of the Aricaras. **1851** W. K. NORTHALL *Curtain* 95 His duty was to sit in the cornfields with a rattle in his hands to scare away the birds, an animate scare-crow. **1899** *Mo. So. Dakotan* I. 175 In the corn field the dry blades beating, the crackling husks and creaking stalks made deafening confusion. **1904** *McClure's Mag.* Feb. 427 With the wood at my right, I closely skirted the corn-field.

+**2.** Attrib. in sense: **a.** Frequenting, growing, or situated in a cornfield.

1846 THORPE *Myst. Backwoods* 102 Then followed the Indian, and beside him 'Breeches,' so closely that you would have thought a dark Apollo on a mettled charger, by some necromancy casting the shadow of a cornfield scarecrow. **1878** *Nat. Museum Proc.* I. 170 *Dendrocygna fulva*. ... Like the Corn-field Duck, it is a summer visitant. **1895** 'CRADDOCK' *Myst. Witch-Face Mt.* 157, I wouldn't hev trested him with a handful o' cornfield peas.

b. Suitable for, or accustomed to, work in a cornfield; rural, rustic, unlearned.

1851 *Polly Peablossom* 117 We worked like a cornfield nigger. **1883** *Century Mag.* Nov. 132/1 Spencer was inefficient, unsightly, and unclean,—a black Caliban,—and had the manners of a cornfield darky. **1902** HARBEN *Abner Daniel* 197 He said a thief was a thief, ef you spelt it back'ards or for'ards, or ef he was akin to a king or a corn-fiel' nigger. **1906** *Springfield W. Republican* 29 March 2 Senator Tillman's phrase, 'cornfield lawyer' seems to hit the public fancy. The people may be impatient with an elaboration of legal subtleties; if so, they will applaud cornfield law. The people may not enjoy legal and constitutional obscurantism; if so the cornfield lawyer will delight their hearts.

c. *Cornfield school*, =OLD-FIELD SCHOOL.

1871 DE VERE 48 So-called self-made men are to this day fond of boasting that they never received any other education but in an old cornfield school.

***Corn flag.** An ornamental plant of the genus Gladiolus. — **1828** WEBSTER, *Cornflag*, a genus of plants, the Gladiolus, of several species, bearing red or white flowers. **1841** EMERSON *Essays* I. xi, You shall still see ... the tasselled grass, or the corn-flags. **1863** GRAY *Botany* p. lxxxiii, Gladiolus or Corn-flag. Familiar garden plants, raised from solid bulbs or corms.

+**Corn flour. a.** Meal made from maize. **b.** Cornstarch. {1860-} — **1674** *S.C. Hist. Soc.* V. 458 Two fatt turkeys to helpe out with our parcht corne flower broth. **1791** BARTRAM *Travels* 456 They fast seven or eight days, during which time they eat or drink nothing but a meagre gruel, made of a little corn-flour and water. **1876** *Wide Awake* 21 Yours, Effie, is the jelly-custard pie. Jane Graves, yours is a Marlborough. Mine is real custard, and yours, Caddy, is the lemon corn-flour.

***Cornflower.** The bluebottle or bachelor button, *Centaurea cyanus*. Also attrib. with reference to the color of this flower. — **1825** J. NEAL *Bro. Jonathan* I. 346 One would have thought ... the cruel storm had been spoiling bright birds of their plumage,—instead of the red poppy and blue corn flower. **1884** *Harper's Mag.* May 861/2 The Emperor ... is a great friend of the corn-flower (the bachelor's-button). **1911** VANCE *Cynthia* 255 Its colour an incredible, nitid blue like the blue of a cornflower sapphire.

+**Corn fodder.**

1. The blades or leaves of Indian corn cured and used as forage.

1772 *Carroll P.* in *Md. Hist. Mag.* XIV. 288 We shall get in all our Corn Fother by the middle of next week. **1790** *Penna. Packet* 29 March 1/1 To be Sold at Public Vendue ... a quantity of hay and corn fodder. **1837** COLMAN *Mass. Rep. Agric.* 24 Farmers ... estimate the corn fodder or stover upon an acre as equal to three fourths of a ton of English hay. **1856** OLMSTEAD *Slave States* 41 Maize leaves ('corn fodder'), 75 cents per cwt. **1888** GRIGSBY *Smoked Yank* xix. 161, I waited two days for the wagon, concealed in the daytime in a fodder house under the bundles of corn fodder.

2. (See quot. 1889.)

1863 MITCHELL *My Farm* 131 Made the experiment of growing corn-fodder with a flimsy dressing and no care. **1874** *Dept. Agric. Rep. 1873* 281 Mr. William Crozier ... cures his corn-fodder (sowed corn) by stacking it on pole platforms. **1884** *Comm. Agric. Rep.* 220 Pribbernow had fed his yearlings on millet, oats, and corn-fodder. **1889** FARMER 170/2 *Corn-fodder*, maize sown broadcast and left to take care of itself. Used as fodder for cattle, both in the dried and undried state. **1894** *Vt. Agric. Rep.* XIV. 36 A crop of green corn fodder grown from a later variety of western or southern red cob corn.

attrib. **1904** WALLER *Wood-Carver* 22, I can look ... up the slope of the mountain, across the stony corn-fodder patch.

+**Corn fritter.** (See quot. 1877.) — **1862** STOWE *Pearl Orr's Isl.* xxix, A very minute account which Mrs. Kittridge was giving of the way to make corn-fritters, which should taste exactly like oysters. **1877** BARTLETT 148 *Corn-fritter*, a fritter in the batter of which green Indian corn has, after being grated, been mingled. (U.S.) **1903** *N.Y. Ev. Post* 26 Sept., Corn is ... becoming somewhat hard and tough. Corn fritters may be made of this hard corn.

+**Corn-grinder.**

1. A mill or similar apparatus for grinding Indian corn.

1841 *Knickerb.* XVII. 234 Improved coffee-mills, ... corn-grinders, ... and a thousand other half-completed plans. **1849** *Rep. Comm. Patents: Agric.* 227 A machine called a corn-grinder has recently been invented by Mr. Whitney.

transf. **1843** STEPHENS *High Life N.Y.* II. 197, I ... grinned jest enough to show my corn-grinders.

2. *Archaeology.* (See quot. 1847.)

1846 EMORY *Military Reconn.* 82 Nothing was found except the corn-grinder, always met with among the ruins and on the plains. **1847** *Ib.* 133 The corn grinder is merely a large stone, well worn, slightly concave, and another of different shape, convex, intended to fit the first and crush the corn between by the pressure of the hand. **1854** BARTLETT *Personal Narr.* II. 245 Several broken metatees, or corn-grinders, lie about the pile.

* **Corn ground.** +Land upon which Indian corn is grown.

1622 'MOURT' *Relation* 17 We went and found more Corne ground, but not of this yeare. **1647** *Springfield Rec.* I. 188 All Swine that breake into any mans corne ground or meadows yt is sufficiently fenced agaynst yoked hogs [etc.]. *c***1669** *N.Y. State Doc. Hist.* (1849) I. 87 The Lots of Meadow or Corne Ground are peculiar to each Planter. **1740** *Ga. Col. Rec.* IV. 665 They have a great deal of Cattle and Corn-Ground. **1760** WASHINGTON *Diaries* I. 160, [I] find ... not half a Crop, especially of Corn Ground, prepared. **1786** *Ib.* III. 30 Nothing but the lateness of the Season could (if that will) justify my doing it whilst the ground is so wet, or beginning to inlist corn ground. **1820** *Hillsborough* (N.C.) *Recorder* 12 July, I break up and strike out my corn ground in the old usual way. **1886** Z. F. SMITH *Kentucky* 367 If Uncle Ben ... plowed the corn-ground, ... Mars Tom often bore a hand.

+**Corn-grower.** A farmer who grows Indian corn.

1831 PECK *Guide* 199 The farmers of Madison county [Illinois] produce large quantities of beans where they otherwise would raise corn; which they sell for cash and store goods, thus giving greater scope for market to the corn-growers. **1832** *Congress. Deb.* 9 Feb. 339/1 Other markets are presented to the corn grower, of considerable value. **1862** *Rep. Comm. Patents: Agric.* 428 Extensive corn-growers in Indiana say [etc.]. **1886** STAPLETON *Major's Christmas* 27 A cornerser [connoisseur] (the Major pronounced it as if he referred to some large corn grower).

‖**Corn-high,** *a.* Tall as a stalk of Indian corn. — **1892** GUNTER *Miss Dividends* (1893) 52, I was born in Chicago ... and railroaded ever since I was corn high.

+**Corn hill.** A portion of ground hilled up for planting one or more plants of Indian corn; a hillock or heap of earth raised about the roots of such plants.

1751 *Virginia Gaz.* 17 Oct., A new Tobacco-House being built, and about 35,000 Corn-Hills cleared. **1785** in Commons, etc. *Doc. Hist.* I. 131, I have one hundred and sixty thousand Corn hills that aught to be plowed. **1791** W. BARTRAM *Travels* 354 The Beans planted at the Corn-hills were above ground. **1818** *Jrnl. Science* I. 121 The Indians, it is to be presumed, never cultivated any other grain than maize, or Indian corn, and yet we see few or no corn-hills in any part of this country. **1850** S. F. COOPER *Rural Hours* 126, [I] saw an old neighbor of threescore and fifteen at work in his garden, hoeing his dozen corn-hills, and weeding his cucumber vines. **1873** *Newton Kansan* 1 May 1/5 Rhode Island farmers will plant miniature torpedoes in their corn-hills as a substitute for scare-crows.

+**Corn hoe.** A hoe suitable for use in cultivating maize.
1790 *Penna. Packet* 14 April 3/2 William Perkins, Blacksmith, Makes and sells . . . A Quantity of the best kind of corn or tobacco hoes. **1822** *Ann. 17th Congress* 1st Sess. I. 324 Mr. B. then read from the document an account of axes, spades, corn hoes . . . bought at Georgetown. **1854** *Penna. Agric. Rep.* 394 Best six Corn Hoes. **1869** BROWNE *Adv. Apache Country* 63 A third [Indian], one of the unbreeched multitude, wore a frying-pan in front by way of an apron, and a corn-hoe behind.

* **Corn house.** +A house in which maize is stored.
1699 J. DICKENSON *God's Protecting Providence* 82 The People had . . . large Cropps of Corn, as We could tell by their Corn-houses. **1725** CHICKEN in *Travels Amer. Col.* 109, I Expected they . . . would build a large house with a Corn house thereto. **1787** WASHINGTON *Diaries* III. 176 My Corn house . . . was burned down in the Night. **1815** *Austin Papers* (1924) I. 248 You will also take charge of the Keys of the Meat and Corn House, also, the Wagon Yard. **1857** *Harper's Mag.* Nov. 859/2, I feel like a corn house what's locked up and the key is done lost. **1891** WILKINS *New Eng. Nun* 422 One had the key of his corn-house.
attrib. **1772** TAITT in *Travels Amer. Col.* 555 Some other Chiefs were Smoking and talking with me on a Cornhouse Scaffold.

+**Corn husk.** The coarse axile leaves or bracts that enclose the ear of Indian corn.
1712 *N.H. Probate Rec.* I. 693 He shall give unto his mother in law Ellener the sixth part of the produce of the hole farm the Corn husks and the grain. **1808** *Medical Jrnl.* XIX. 122 They scrubbed him with corn-husks. **1834** A. PIKE *Sketches* 98 All of them, of both sexes, with their never-failing companion, a segar of punche (their country tobacco) rolled in a slip of corn-husk. **1884** *Century Mag.* Jan. 443/1 A few corn-husks and a little wheat-straw were sometimes fed to cows.
attrib. **1819** *Amer. Farmer* I. 55 Plough Gier. We have seen in use, in a particular neighborhood in this state, wooden hames or collar, as a substitute for the leathern or corn-husk collar. **1860** S. WARNER *Say & Seal* lxxviii. 695 A couple of corn husk mats. **1880** *Harper's Mag.* July 168/1 A corn-husk bed, or a mosquito in the woods, will overturn a whole summer's airy fabric of happiness. **1903** WIGGIN *Rebecca* 18 The packet landed exactly as it was intended on the corn-husk mat in front of the screen door.

+**Corn-husker.**

1. A machine, implement, or device for removing the husks from Indian corn.
1858 *Rep. Comm. Patents* I. 358, I claim an improved corn-husker. **1870** *Rep. Comm. Agric. 1869* 328 Considerable activity is noted in improvements in corn huskers and shellers. **1871** *Amer. Naturalist* V. 317 Several Indian stone implements . . . which are said to bear a striking resemblance to iron corn huskers now in use in the West. **1876** *Vt. Bd. Agric. Rep.* III. 609 The corn harvest may now be greatly accelerated by the use of the corn husker, driven by horse power.

2. One who husks corn.
1893– in dicts. **1898** *Decatur Rev.* 29 Oct. 2 An expert corn husker. **1924** *Wallace's Farmer* 5 Dec. 1 [The] champion cornhusker of the middle west.

+**Corn-husking.**

1. A social gathering of neighbors to husk the Indian corn belonging to the one at whose home they meet.
1821 NUTTALL *Trav. Arkansa* 29 We took up our lodging where there happened to be a corn-husking, and were kept awake with idle merriment and riot. **1843** *Amer. Pioneer* II. 451 The frequent necessity for united effort at house-raisings, log-rollings, corn-huskings, &c., produced in him habitual charity. **1858** T. WEED *Autobiog.* (1883) I. 18 Those [amusements] that I remember as most pleasant and exciting were corn huskings and coon-hunts. **1875** STOWE *Deacon Pitkin* iv. 56 She would go with him . . . over to a neighbor's, where was a corn-husking. **1897** BRODHEAD *Bound in Shallows* 169 And, law, the log-raisin's and corn-huskin's they used to have!
attrib. **1838** *N.Y. Advertiser & Exp.* 24 Jan. 2/4 This entertainment was the winding up of a corn husking frolic.

2. The husking and gathering of Indian corn. Also attrib.
1890 *Lordsburg Californian* 4 Sept. 5/3 Corn husking has begun. **1890** *Boston Journal* Dec., All Western Iowa has been excited over a big corn-husking match. **1897** C. F. LUMMIS *Land of Poco Tiempo* 49 The corn-husking is done thus with the aid of young men who go from house to house to strip the blue ears.

* **Cornice.** +*Cornice rock, cliff,* (see quotations.) — **1836** J. HALL *Statistics of West* iii. 49 The cornice rocks, are great curiosities. **1838** FLAGG *Far West* II. 219 The Mississippi now rolls through a broad, deep valley, bounded by an escarpment of cliffs upon either side; and wherever these present a bold façade to the stream, they are grooved, as at the cornice-rocks, by a series of parallel lines. *Ib.* 208 Beyond the stream [Mississippi], stretching away to the northwest, the range of heights you view are the celebrated cornice-cliffs above Herculeaneum.

+**Corn juice.** *colloq.* Whisky made from Indian corn; whisky of any kind.
a1846 *Quarter Race Ky.*, etc. 83 He . . . only axes a 'fip' for a reel, and two 'bits' fur what corn-juice you suck. **1862** 'P. V. NASBY' *Struggles* 74 Send me a eucher deck, a two-gallon jug uv corn joose. **1872** *Harper's Mag.* Nov. 951/2 A Republican and a Democrat of that city, standing together, saw approaching a man under the influence of corn juice. **1898** HARTE *Tales of Trail & Town* 335 Just you put two fingers o' that corn juice inside ye. **1907** MULFORD *Bar-20* 241 Tex swaggered over to the bar and tossed a quarter upon it: 'Corn-juice,' he laconically exclaimed.

+**Corn knife.** A knife used in cutting down Indian corn. — **1856** *Mich. Agric. Soc. Trans.* VII. 54 D. O. & W. S. Penfield . . . [exhibited] six corn knives. **1862** *Rep. Comm. Patents: Agric.* 287 The best mode of cutting is with a heavy corn-knife, and striking with the point down. **1873** *Winfield* (Kansas) *Courier* 20 Nov. 3/1 There is a man confined in the county jail for the offense of stealing a corn knife.

* **Cornland.** +Land upon which Indian corn is grown.
1654 JOHNSON *Wonder-w. Prov.* 41 Their Corne Land in Tillage in this Towne is about 1200. Acres. **1723** *Weekly Mercury* 12–19 Sept. 2/2 To be Sold . . . the Farm late of Thomas Stevenson, containing about 1300 Acres of very good Corn Land, with a Water Grist-Mill upon it. **1792** *Fayetteville* (N.C.) *Gaz.* 25 Sept., A considerable part of which is suitable for tobacco, and the whole excellent Corn land. **1834** BAIRD *Valley Miss.* 293 The bottoms are fine cotton, and corn-lands. **1894** *Vt. Agric. Rep.* XIV. 35 How much corn land will a man tend? **1896** READ *Jucklins* 15 Thus I worked until much of his corn-land was broken.

+**Corn leaf.** A leaf or blade of Indian corn.
1802 ELLICOTT *Journal* 4 A very heavy hoar frost, vines, potato tops and corn leaves killed in the vallies between the mountains. **1838** WHITTIER *Pentucket* 15 Many a rood of open land . . . With corn-leaves waving freshly green. **1856** OLMSTED *Slave States* 414 These carts would contain . . . some bundles of corn-leaves, to be fed to the horse. **a1868** in Brace *Dangerous Classes N.Y.* (1872) 251 Little Mag . . . brought in a 'nosegay,' . . . a mullen-stock and corn-leaf, twisted with grass! **1888** [see CORN SHOOK].

Corn meal. {1820} +Meal made from maize.
1821 NUTTALL *Trav. Arkansa* 38 Mills are much wanted, and, in order even to obtain corn-meal, every one has to invent something of the kind for himself. **1836** SIMMS *Mellichampe* ii. 20 He brought forth from the recess which had supplied him with his evening repast a small sack of corn-meal. **1844** *Congress. Globe* App. 21 March 631/3 At this dinner, a large ash-cake was baked, containing about three bushels of corn meal. **1874** *Dept. Agric. Rep. 1873* 93 The foreign exports are small, embracing, . . . 380 barrels of corn-meal [etc.]. **1894** *Vt. Agric. Rep.* XIV. 43 Two and one-half pounds of stalks contain as much actual food as one pound of clear corn meal.
attrib. **1818** E. P. FORDHAM *Narr. Travels* 230 My nurse, by constantly supplying me with corn meal gruel and chicken broth, prevented me from sinking under the violence of my disorder. **1863** CUMMING *Hospital Life* (1866) 82/2 On his explaining, we understood that he wished corn meal batter-cakes. **1881** *Harper's Mag.* Jan. 227/2 The villagers preferred their tartines to her corn-meal puddings. **1898** WESTCOTT *D. Harum* 173, I reckon it's a sight easier to have faith on meat an' potatoes 'n it is on corn meal mush. **1904** GLASGOW *Deliverance* 112 Cynthia . . . mixed the corn-meal dough in a wooden tray.

Corn-measurer. *Obs.* A town official having oversight of the measuring of corn. — **1646** *New Haven Rec.* I. 242 The order for a corne measurer in this towne was repealed.

* **Corn mill.** +A mill for grinding maize.
1637 *Dedham Rec.* 27 Abraham Sharve is Resolved to erect a Corne-mill in our towne of Dedham. **1674** *Braintree Rec.* 17 Being chosen a committee at a legall towne meeting to conferre . . . about the rebuilding of the Corne mill being demolished by fier. **1700** *N.H. Probate Rec.* I. 469, I doe, Give and bequeath . . . my corn mill & saw mill. **1798** I. ALLEN *History Vermont* 41 The agents of Colonel Reed found means (by hooping) to repair the stones of the corn-mill. **1835** *S. Lit. Messenger* I. 260 In the city and its vicinity there are five corn or grist mills. **1862** in F. Moore *Rebellion Rec.* V. II. 199 The Yankees on their arrival, destroyed his loom and put him to work in his master's corn and flour-mill. **1882** *Rep. Indian Affairs* 31 Aug. 4 Nearly every family has a corn mill.

b. = CORN-GRINDER 2.
1846 EMORY *Military Reconn.* 80 These could be nothing else than the corn-mills of long extinct races.

+**Corn moth.** The grain moth *Tinea granella.* — **1868** *Comm. Agric. Rep.* 315 The clothes-moth and corn-moth are representatives of the family [*Tineidae*]. **1889** *Cent.* 1271/3 Corn-moth . . . [is] exceedingly destructive to grain-sheaves in the field, and to stored grain.

+**Corn muller.** *Archaeology.* (See quotation.) — **1881** *Smithsonian Rep.* 612 The stone, with a hole in the center, which is called a corn-muller, I found about 80 yards from the grand mound.

+**Corn oyster.** (See quot. 1877.) — **1862** STOWE *Pearl Orr's Isl.* xxx, In this secret direction about the mace lay the whole mystery of corn-oysters. **1877** BARTLETT 148 *Corn-oyster,* a fritter to which the combined effects of grated Indian corn (not quite ripe) and heated butter impart a taste like that of oysters.

+**Corn patch.** A small field or patch of maize.
1784 W. WALTON *Captivity B. Gilbert* 53 His Employ was to fence and secure the Corn-patch. **1788** E. DENNY *Journal* 122 A corn patch adjoining the necessary. **1850** H. C. LEWIS *La. Swamp Dr.* 175 They swore they would hav thought, 'stead of a bar-fight, that I had been cuttin' cane and deadenin' timber for a corn-patch, the sile war so worked up. **1879** *Scribner's Mo.* June 334/1 My Luke, he ran the furrers in her corn-patch last May. **1904** WALLER *Wood-Carver* 111 Makin' scarecrows fer the corn-patch. **1920** HUNTER *Trail Drivers Texas* I. 202, I found them grazing on one of those high-priced corn patches.